REFERENCE
DOES NOT CIRCULATE

R 920.077 Whos
2003

Who's who in the
Midwest.
c1949-

OCT 28 2002

Who'sWho in the Midwest®

Who's Who in the Midwest®

2003

Including Illinois, Indiana, Iowa, Kansas, Michigan, Minnesota, Missouri, Nebraska, North Dakota, Ohio, South Dakota, and Wisconsin, and in Canada, Manitoba and western Ontario

29th Edition

121 Chanlon Road
New Providence, NJ 07974 U.S.A.
www.marquiswhoswho.com

EVANSTON PUBLIC LIBRARY
1703 ORRINGTON AVENUE
EVANSTON, ILLINOIS 60201

Who'sWho in the Midwest®

Marquis Who's Who®

General Manager Sandra S. Barnes

Senior Managing Director Fred Marks

Senior Managing Research Editor Lisa Weissbard

Senior Managing Editor Robert Docherty

Editorial

Senior Editor Danielle Netta
Associate Editor Kate Spirito
Assistant Editors Ryan Karwell, Jeffrey Ramesar, Deanna Richmond, Michael Roukas

Editorial Services

Director Debby Nowicki
Production Manager Paul Zema
Freelance Manager Mary San Giovanni
Special Projects Supervisor Sola Osofisan
Mail Processing Manager Kara A. Seitz
Mail Processing Staff Betty Gray, Hattie Walker

Production Editor Matthew J. Heintz
Editorial Services Assistant Ann Chavis

Creative Services

Creative Services Director Michael Noerr
Creative Services Coordinator Rose Butkiewicz
Production Manager Jeanne Danzig

Research

Managing Editor Kerry Nugent Morrison
Senior Research Editors Musa Muromets, Jennifer Podolsky

Associate Research Editors Maria L. Izzo, Adam P. Ingrassia

Assistant Research Editor Todd Kineavy

Editorial Systems

Director Jack Zimmerman
Programmers/Analysts Ben Loh, Tom Haggerty

Published by Marquis Who's Who, a member of the Lexis-Nexis Group.

President and Chief Executive Officer John Lawler
Chief Information Officer John Roney

Copyright ©2002 by Reed Elsevier Inc. All rights reserved.

No part of this publication may be reproduced, stored in a retrieval system, or transmitted, in any form or by any means—including, but not limited to, electronic, mechanical, photocopying, recording, or otherwise—or used for any commercial purpose whatsoever without the prior written permission of the publisher and, if publisher deems necessary, execution of a formal license agreement with publisher.

For information, contact:
Marquis Who's Who
121 Chanlon Road
New Providence, New Jersey 07974
1-908-673-1000
www.marquiswhoswho.com

WHO'S WHO IN THE MIDWEST is a registered trademark of Reed Publishing used under license.

Library of Congress Catalog Card Number 50-289
International Standard Book Number 0-8379-0732-2
International Standard Serial Number 0083-9787

No payment is either solicited or accepted for the inclusion of entries in this publication. Marquis Who's Who has used its best efforts in collecting and preparing material for inclusion in this publication, but does not warrant that the information herein is complete or accurate, and does not assume, and hereby disclaims, any liability to any person for any loss or damage caused by errors or omissions in this publication, whether such errors or omissions result from negligence, accident, or any other cause.

Manufactured in the United States of America.

Table of Contents

Preface

The 29th Edition of *Who's Who in the Midwest* provides the latest biographical information on men and women who are shaping the development and growth of midwestern North America. Such individuals are of decided reference value locally and, to an increasing degree, nationally.

The volume contains approximately 15,000 biographies of people working in Illinois, Indiana, Iowa, Kansas, Michigan, Minnesota, Missouri, Nebraska, North Dakota, Ohio, South Dakota, and Wisconsin in the United States, and from Manitoba and western Ontario in Canada. Some individuals listed are not residents of this region; however, the professional activities of these listees have been widely influential in the midwest.

The persons sketched in this volume represent virtually every important field of endeavor. Included are executives and officials in government, business, education, religion, the press, law, civic activities, and many other fields. Also included are leaders in the fields of science, healthcare, engineering, and notable people involved in the arts and cultural affairs.

Most Biographees have furnished their own data, thus assuring a high degree of accuracy. As in previous editions, Biographees were given the opportunity to review prepublication proofs of their sketches. In some cases where individuals of distinct reference value failed to supply information, Marquis staff members compiled the data through independent research. Such sketches are noted with an asterisk.

Also included in this 29th Edition of *Who's Who in the Midwest* is a Professional Index, which groups Biographees professionally, and within profession, geographically. This reference tool makes it easy for interested readers to find Biographees in any given field or locality.

The question is often asked, "How do people get into a Marquis Who's Who volume?" Name selection is based on one fundamental principle: reference value. Biographees of *Who's Who in the Midwest* can be classified in two basic categories: persons who are of regional reference importance to colleagues, librarians, researchers, scholars, the press, participants in business and civic affairs, and others with specific or general inquiry needs; and individuals of national interest who are also of such regional or local importance that their inclusion in the book is essential. Only those individuals deemed reference-worthy have sketches presented in a Marquis publication.

Marquis Who's Who editors exercise the utmost care in preparing each biographical sketch for publication. Occasionally, however, errors do occur. Users of this directory are requested to draw the attention of the publisher to any errors so that corrections can be made in a subsequent edition.

Board of Advisors

Marquis Who's Who gratefully acknowledges the following distinguished individuals who have made themselves available for review, evaluation, and general comment with regard to the publication of the 29th Edition of *Who's Who in the Midwest.* The advisors have enhanced the reference value of this edition by the nomination of outstanding individuals for inclusion. However, the Board of Advisors, either collectively or individually, is in no way responsible for the final selection of names, or for the accuracy or comprehensiveness of the biographical information or other material contained herein.

Mindy Aloff
Freelance Writer

William C. Anderson
Executive Director
American Academy of Environmental Engineers
Annapolis, Maryland

Steven C. Beering
President Emeritus
Purdue University
West Lafayette, Indiana

Willard L. Boyd
President Emeritus
Field Museum of Natural History

Dr. Thomas C. Dolan
President and CEO
American College of Healthcare Executives

Charles C. Eldredge
Hall Distinguished Professor of American Art
University of Kansas
Lawrence, Kansas

Barbara Haskell
Curator
Whitney Museum of American Art

Thomas R. Horton
Former Chairman
American Management Association

Jill Krementz
Author and Photographer

Charles F. Larson
President
Industrial Research Institute, Inc.

Andrew Leckey
Syndicated Investment Columnist
The Chicago Tribune

Judith P. Lotas
Founding Partner
Lotas Minard Patton McIver, Inc.

Martin E. Marty
Professor Emeritus
University of Chicago Divinity School

Robert G. McKinnell
Former President
International Society of Differentiation, Inc.
University of Minnesota
St. Paul, Minnesota

Jeremiah P. Ostriker
Provost
Princeton University
Princeton, New Jersey

Louis Rukeyser
Economic Commentator
Host, Louis Rukeyser's Wall Street

James B. Sales
Former Senior Partner
Fulbright & Jaworski
Houston, Texas

Catharine R. Stimpson
University Professor
New York University

John Fox Sullivan
President and Publisher
National Journal

Elie Wiesel
Author
Professor of Philosophy
Boston University

Standards of Admission

The foremost consideration in selecting Biographees for *Who's Who in the Midwest* is the extent of an individual's reference interest. Such reference interest is judged on either of two factors: (1) the position of responsibility held, or (2) the level of achievement attained by the individual.

Admissions based on the factor of position include:

Members of the U.S. Congress

Federal judges

Governors of states covered by this volume

Premiers of Canadian provinces covered by this volume

State attorneys general

Judges of state and territorial courts of highest appellate jurisdiction

Mayors of major cities

Heads of major universities and colleges

Heads of leading philanthropic, educational, cultural, and scientific institutions and associations

Chief ecclesiastics of the principal religious denominations

Principal officers of national and international business

Admission for individual achievement is based on objective qualitative criteria. To be selected, a person must have attained conspicuous achievement.

Key to Information

[1] **WATTS, BENJAMIN GREENE,** [2] lawyer; [3] b. May 21, 1935; [4] s. George and Sarah (Carson) W.; [5] m. Ellen Spencer, Sept. 12, 1960; [6] children: John Allen, Lucy Anne. [7] BS, Northwestern U., 1956; JD, U. Chgo, 1965. [8] Bar: Ill. 1965, U.S. Supreme Ct. 1980. [9] Mem. legal dept. Standard Publs. Corp., Chgo., 1965-73, asst. counsel, 1973-81, cousel, 1981-83; ptnr. Watts, Clayborn, Johnson & Miller, Oak Brook, Ill., 1983-85, sr. ptnr., 1985—; [10] lectr. Coll. of DuPage, 1983-98. [11] Author: Legal Aspects of Edn. Pub., 1975, Copyright Legalities, 1990, Issues of Intellectual Property Law, 1997. [12] Chmn. Downers Grove (Ill.) chpt. ARC, 1982-83; active DuPage coun. Boy Scouts Am.; trustee Elmhurst (Ill.) Hist. Mus., 1980—; bd. dirs. Big Bros./Big Sisters DuPage County, 1994—. [13] Served to lt. USAF, 1956-61. [14] Recipient Outstanding Alumnus award Northwestern U., 1971. [15] Mem. ABA, Ill. Bar Assn., Chgo. Bar Assn., Am. Mgmt. Assn., Phi Delta Phi, Caxton Club, Tavern Club (Chgo.), Masons. [16] Democrat. [17] Lutheran. [18] Home: 543 Farwell Ave Elmhurst IL 60126 [19] Office: Watts Clayborn Johnson & Miller 1428 Industrial Ct Oak Brook IL 60521

KEY

[1] Name
[2] Occupation
[3] Vital statistics
[4] Parents
[5] Marriage
[6] Children
[7] Education
[8] Professional certifications
[9] Career
[10] Career-related
[11] Writings and creative works
[12] Civic and political activities
[13] Military
[14] Awards and fellowships
[15] Professional and association memberships, clubs and lodges
[16] Political affiliation
[17] Religion
[18] Home address
[19] Office address

Table of Abbreviations

The following abbreviations and symbols are frequently used in this book.

*An asterisk following a sketch indicates that it was researched by the Marquis Who's Who editorial staff and has not been verified by the Biographee.
A Associate (used with academic degrees only)
AA, A.A. Associate in Arts, Associate of Arts
AAAL American Academy of Arts and Letters
AAAS American Association for the Advancement of Science
AACD American Association for Counseling and Development
AACN American Association of Critical Care Nurses
AAHA American Academy of Health Administrators
AAHP American Association of Hospital Planners
AAHPERD American Alliance for Health, Physical Education, Recreation, and Dance
AAS Associate of Applied Science
AASL American Association of School Librarians
AASPA American Association of School Personnel Administrators
AAU Amateur Athletic Union
AAUP American Association of University Professors
AAUW American Association of University Women
AB, A.B. Arts, Bachelor of
AB Alberta
ABA American Bar Association
ABC American Broadcasting Company
AC Air Corps
acad. academy, academic
acct. accountant
acctg. accounting
ACDA Arms Control and Disarmament Agency
ACHA American College of Hospital Administrators
ACLS Advanced Cardiac Life Support
ACLU American Civil Liberties Union
ACOG American College of Ob-Gyn
ACP American College of Physicians
ACS American College of Surgeons
ADA American Dental Association
a.d.c. aide-de-camp
adj. adjunct, adjutant
adj. gen. adjutant general
adm. admiral
adminstr. administrator
adminstrn. administration
adminstrv. administrative
ADN Associate's Degree in Nursing
ADP Automatic Data Processing
adv. advocate, advisory
advt. advertising
AE, A.E. Agricultural Engineer
A.E. and P. Ambassador Extraordinary and Plenipotentiary
AEC Atomic Energy Commission
aero. aeronautical, aeronautic
aerodyn. aerodynamic
AFB Air Force Base
AFL-CIO American Federation of Labor and Congress of Industrial Organizations
AFTRA American Federation of TV and Radio Artists
AFSCME American Federation of State, County and Municipal Employees
agr. agriculture
agrl. agricultural
agt. agent
AGVA American Guild of Variety Artists
agy. agency
A&I Agricultural and Industrial
AIA American Institute of Architects
AIAA American Institute of Aeronautics and Astronautics
AIChE American Institute of Chemical Engineers
AICPA American Institute of Certified Public Accountants
AID Agency for International Development
AIDS Acquired Immune Deficiency Syndrome
AIEE American Institute of Electrical Engineers
AIM American Institute of Management
AIME American Institute of Mining, Metallurgy, and Petroleum Engineers
AK Alaska
AL Alabama
ALA American Library Association
Ala. Alabama
alt. alternate
Alta. Alberta
A&M Agricultural and Mechanical
AM, A.M. Arts, Master of
Am. American, America
AMA American Medical Association
amb. ambassador
A.M.E. African Methodist Episcopal
Amtrak National Railroad Passenger Corporation
AMVETS American Veterans of World War II, Korea, Vietnam
ANA American Nurses Association
anat. anatomical
ANCC American Nurses Credentialing Center
ann. annual
ANTA American National Theatre and Academy
anthrop. anthropological
AP Associated Press
APA American Psychological Association
APGA American Personnel Guidance Association
APHA American Public Health Association
APO Army Post Office
apptd. appointed
Apr. April
apt. apartment
AR Arkansas
ARC American Red Cross
arch. architect
archeol. archeological
archtl. architectural
Ariz. Arizona
Ark. Arkansas
ArtsD, ArtsD. Arts, Doctor of
arty. artillery
AS American Samoa
AS Associate in Science
ASCAP American Society of Composers, Authors and Publishers
ASCD Association for Supervision and Curriculum Development
ASCE American Society of Civil Engineers
ASHRAE American Society of Heating, Refrigeration, and Air Conditioning Engineers
ASME American Society of Mechanical Engineers
ASNSA American Society for Nursing Service Administrators
ASPA American Society for Public Administration
ASPCA American Society for the Prevention of Cruelty to Animals
assn. association
assoc. associate
asst. assistant
ASTD American Society for Training and Development
ASTM American Society for Testing and Materials
astron. astronomical
astrophys. astrophysical
ATLA Association of Trial Lawyers of America
ATSC Air Technical Service Command
AT&T American Telephone & Telegraph Company
atty. attorney
Aug. August
AUS Army of the United States
aux. auxiliary
Ave. Avenue
AVMA American Veterinary Medical Association
AZ Arizona
AWHONN Association of Women's Health Obstetric and Neonatal Nurses

B. Bachelor
b. born
BA, B.A. Bachelor of Arts
BAgr, B.Agr. Bachelor of Agriculture
Balt. Baltimore
Bapt. Baptist
BArch, B.Arch. Bachelor of Architecture
BAS, B.A.S. Bachelor of Agricultural Science
BBA, B.B.A. Bachelor of Business Administration
BBB Better Business Bureau
BBC British Broadcasting Corporation

BC, B.C. British Columbia
BCE, B.C.E. Bachelor of Civil Engineering
BChir. B.Chir. Bachelor of Surgery
BCL, B.C.L. Bachelor of Civil Law
BCLS Basic Cardiac Life Support
BCS, B.C.S. Bachelor of Commercial Science
BD, B.D. Bachelor of Divinity
bd. board
BE, B.E. Bachelor of Education
BEE, B.E.E. Bachelor of Electrical Engineering
BFA, B.F.A. Bachelor of Fine Arts
bibl. biblical
bibliog. bibliographical
biog. biographical
biol. biological
BJ, B.J. Bachelor of Journalism
Bklyn. Brooklyn
BL, B.L. Bachelor of Letters
bldg. building
BLS, B.L.S. Bachelor of Library Science
BLS Basic Life Support
Blvd. Boulevard
BMI Broadcast Music, Inc.
BMW Bavarian Motor Works (Bayerische Motoren Werke)
bn. battalion
B.&O.R.R. Baltimore & Ohio Railroad
bot. botanical
BPE, B.P.E. Bachelor of Physical Education
BPhil, B.Phil. Bachelor of Philosophy
br. branch
BRE, B.R.E. Bachelor of Religious Education
brig. gen. brigadier general
Brit. British, Brittanica
Bros. Brothers
BS, B.S. Bachelor of Science
BSA, B.S.A. Bachelor of Agricultural Science
BSBA Bachelor of Science in Business Administration
BSChemE Bachelor of Science in Chemical Engineering
BSD, B.S.D. Bachelor of Didactic Science
BSEE Bachelor of Science in Electrical Engineering
BSN Bachelor of Science in Nursing
BST, B.S.T. Bachelor of Sacred Theology
BTh, B.Th. Bachelor of Theology
bull. bulletin
bur. bureau
bus. business
B.W.I. British West Indies

CA California
CAA Civil Aeronautics Administration
CAB Civil Aeronautics Board
CAD-CAM Computer Aided Design–Computer Aided Model
Calif. California
C.Am. Central America
Can. Canada, Canadian
CAP Civil Air Patrol
capt. captain
cardiol. cardiological
cardiovasc. cardiovascular
CARE Cooperative American Relief Everywhere
Cath. Catholic
cav. cavalry
CBC Canadian Broadcasting Company
CBI China, Burma, India Theatre of Operations
CBS Columbia Broadcasting Company
C.C. Community College
CCC Commodity Credit Corporation
CCNY City College of New York
CCRN Critical Care Registered Nurse
CCU Cardiac Care Unit
CD Civil Defense
CE, C.E. Corps of Engineers, Civil Engineer
CEN Certified Emergency Nurse
CENTO Central Treaty Organization
CEO chief executive officer
CERN European Organization of Nuclear Research
cert. certificate, certification, certified
CETA Comprehensive Employment Training Act
CFA Chartered Financial Analyst
CFL Canadian Football League
CFO chief financial officer
CFP Certified Financial Planner
ch. church
ChD, Ch.D. Doctor of Chemistry
chem. chemical
ChemE, Chem.E. Chemical Engineer
ChFC Chartered Financial Consultant
Chgo. Chicago
chirurg. chirurgical
chmn. chairman
chpt. chapter
CIA Central Intelligence Agency
Cin. Cincinnati
cir. circle, circuit
CLE Continuing Legal Education
Cleve. Cleveland
climatol. climatological
clin. clinical
clk. clerk
C.L.U. Chartered Life Underwriter
CM, C.M. Master in Surgery
CM Northern Mariana Islands
CMA Certified Medical Assistant
cmty. community
CNA Certified Nurse's Aide
CNOR Certified Nurse (Operating Room)
C.&N.W.Ry. Chicago & North Western Railway
CO Colorado
Co. Company
COF Catholic Order of Foresters
C. of C. Chamber of Commerce
col. colonel
coll. college
Colo. Colorado
com. committee
comd. commanded
comdg. commanding
comdr. commander
comdt. commandant
comm. communications
commd. commissioned
comml. commercial
commn. commission
commr. commissioner
compt. comptroller
condr. conductor
Conf. Conference
Congl. Congregational. Congressional
Conglist. Congregationalist
Conn. Connecticut
cons. consultant, consulting
consol. consolidated
constl. constitutional
constn. constitution
constrn. construction
contbd. contributed
contbg. contributing
contbn. contribution
contbr. contributor
contr. controller
Conv. Convention
COO chief operating officer
coop. cooperative
coord. coordinator
CORDS Civil Operations and Revolutionary Development Support
CORE Congress of Racial Equality
corp. corporation, corporate
corr. correspondent, corresponding, correspondence
C.&O.Ry. Chesapeake & Ohio Railway
coun. council
CPA Certified Public Accountant
CPCU Chartered Property and Casualty Underwriter
CPH, C.P.H. Certificate of Public Health
cpl. corporal
CPR Cardio-Pulmonary Resuscitation
C.P.Ry. Canadian Pacific Railway
CRT Cathode Ray Terminal
C.S. Christian Science
CSB, C.S.B. Bachelor of Christian Science
C.S.C. Civil Service Commission
CT Connecticut
ct. court
ctr. center
ctrl. central
CWS Chemical Warfare Service
C.Z. Canal Zone

D. Doctor
d. daughter
DAgr, D.Agr. Doctor of Agriculture
DAR Daughters of the American Revolution
dau. daughter
DAV Disabled American Veterans
DC, D.C. District of Columbia
DCL, D.C.L. Doctor of Civil Law
DCS, D.C.S. Doctor of Commercial Science
DD, D.D. Doctor of Divinity
DDS, D.D.S. Doctor of Dental Surgery
DE Delaware
Dec. December
dec. deceased
def. defense
Del. Delaware
del. delegate, delegation
Dem. Democrat, Democratic
DEng, D.Eng. Doctor of Engineering
denom. denomination, denominational
dep. deputy
dept. department
dermatol. dermatological
desc. descendant
devel. development, developmental
DFA, D.F.A. Doctor of Fine Arts
D.F.C. Distinguished Flying Cross
DHL, D.H.L. Doctor of Hebrew Literature
dir. director
dist. district
distbg. distributing
distbn. distribution
distbr. distributor
disting. distinguished
div. division, divinity, divorce
divsn. division
DLitt, D.Litt. Doctor of Literature
DMD, D.M.D. Doctor of Dental Medicine
DMS, D.M.S. Doctor of Medical Science
DO, D.O. Doctor of Osteopathy
docs. documents
DON Director of Nursing
DPH, D.P.H. Diploma in Public Health
DPhil, D.Phil. Doctor of Philosophy
D.R. Daughters of the Revolution
Dr. Drive, Doctor
DRE, D.R.E. Doctor of Religious Education
DrPH, Dr.P.H. Doctor of Public Health, Doctor of Public Hygiene
D.S.C. Distinguished Service Cross

DSc, D.Sc. Doctor of Science
DSChemE Doctor of Science in Chemical Engineering
D.S.M. Distinguished Service Medal
DST, D.S.T. Doctor of Sacred Theology
DTM, D.T.M. Doctor of Tropical Medicine
DVM, D.V.M. Doctor of Veterinary Medicine
DVS, D.V.S. Doctor of Veterinary Surgery

E, E. East
ea. eastern
E. and P. Extraordinary and Plenipotentiary
Eccles. Ecclesiastical
ecol. ecological
econ. economic
ECOSOC Economic and Social Council (of the UN)
ED, E.D. Doctor of Engineering
ed. educated
EdB, Ed.B. Bachelor of Education
EdD, Ed.D. Doctor of Education
edit. edition
editl. editorial
EdM, Ed.M. Master of Education
edn. education
ednl. educational
EDP Electronic Data Processing
EdS, Ed.S. Specialist in Education
EE, E.E. Electrical Engineer
E.E. and M.P. Envoy Extraordinary and Minister Plenipotentiary
EEC European Economic Community
EEG Electroencephalogram
EEO Equal Employment Opportunity
EEOC Equal Employment Opportunity Commission
E.Ger. German Democratic Republic
EKG Electrocardiogram
elec. electrical
electrochem. electrochemical
electrophys. electrophysical
elem. elementary
EM, E.M. Engineer of Mines
EMT Emergency Medical Technician
ency. encyclopedia
Eng. England
engr. engineer
engring. engineering
entomol. entomological
environ. environmental
EPA Environmental Protection Agency
epidemiol. epidemiological
Episc. Episcopalian
ERA Equal Rights Amendment
ERDA Energy Research and Development Administration
ESEA Elementary and Secondary Education Act
ESL English as Second Language
ESPN Entertainment and Sports Programming Network
ESSA Environmental Science Services Administration
ethnol. ethnological
ETO European Theatre of Operations
Evang. Evangelical
exam. examination, examining
Exch. Exchange
exec. executive
exhbn. exhibition
expdn. expedition
expn. exposition
expt. experiment
exptl. experimental
Expy. Expressway
Ext. Extension
F.A. Field Artillery
FAA Federal Aviation Administration
FAO Food and Agriculture Organization (of the UN)
FBA Federal Bar Association
FBI Federal Bureau of Investigation
FCA Farm Credit Administration
FCC Federal Communications Commission
FCDA Federal Civil Defense Administration
FDA Food and Drug Administration
FDIA Federal Deposit Insurance Administration
FDIC Federal Deposit Insurance Corporation
FE, F.E. Forest Engineer
FEA Federal Energy Administration
Feb. February
fed. federal
fedn. federation
FERC Federal Energy Regulatory Commission
fgn. foreign
FHA Federal Housing Administration
fin. financial, finance
FL Florida
Fl. Floor
Fla. Florida
FMC Federal Maritime Commission
FNP Family Nurse Practitioner
FOA Foreign Operations Administration
found. foundation
FPC Federal Power Commission
FPO Fleet Post Office
frat. fraternity
FRS Federal Reserve System
FSA Federal Security Agency
Ft. Fort
FTC Federal Trade Commission
Fwy. Freeway

G-1 (or other number) Division of General Staff
GA, Ga. Georgia
GAO General Accounting Office
gastroent. gastroenterological
GATE Gifted and Talented Educators
GATT General Agreement on Tariffs and Trade
GE General Electric Company
gen. general
geneal. genealogical
geod. geodetic
geog. geographic, geographical
geol. geological
geophys. geophysical
geriat. geriatrics
gerontol. gerontological
G.H.Q. General Headquarters
GM General Motors Corporation
GMAC General Motors Acceptance Corporation
G.N.Ry. Great Northern Railway
gov. governor
govt. government
govtl. governmental
GPO Government Printing Office
grad. graduate, graduated
GSA General Services Administration
Gt. Great
GTE General Telephone and ElectricCompany
GU Guam
gynecol. gynecological

HBO Home Box Office
hdqs. headquarters
HEW Department of Health, Education and Welfare
HHD, H.H.D. Doctor of Humanities
HHFA Housing and Home Finance Agency
HHS Department of Health and Human Services
HI Hawaii
hist. historical, historic
HM, H.M. Master of Humanities
HMO Health Maintenance Organization
homeo. homeopathic
hon. honorary, honorable
Ho. of Dels. House of Delegates
Ho. of Reps. House of Representatives
hort. horticultural
hosp. hospital
H.S. High School
HUD Department of Housing and Urban Development
Hwy. Highway
hydrog. hydrographic

IA Iowa
IAEA International Atomic Energy Agency
IATSE International Alliance of Theatrical and Stage Employees and Moving Picture Operators of the United States and Canada
IBM International Business Machines Corporation
IBRD International Bank for Reconstruction and Development
ICA International Cooperation Administration
ICC Interstate Commerce Commission
ICCE International Council for Computers in Education
ICU Intensive Care Unit
ID Idaho
IEEE Institute of Electrical and Electronics Engineers
IFC International Finance Corporation
IGY International Geophysical Year
IL Illinois
Ill. Illinois
illus. illustrated
ILO International Labor Organization
IMF International Monetary Fund
IN Indiana
Inc. Incorporated
Ind. Indiana
ind. independent
Indpls. Indianapolis
indsl. industrial
inf. infantry
info. information
ins. insurance
insp. inspector
insp. gen. inspector general
inst. institute
instl. institutional
instn. institution
instr. instructor
instrn. instruction
instrnl. instructional
internat. international
intro. introduction
IRE Institute of Radio Engineers
IRS Internal Revenue Service
ITT International Telephone & Telegraph Corporation

JAG Judge Advocate General
JAGC Judge Advocate General Corps
Jan. January
Jaycees Junior Chamber of Commerce
JB, J.B. Jurum Baccalaureus
JCB, J.C.B. Juris Canoni Baccalaureus
JCD, J.C.D. Juris Canonici Doctor, Juris Civilis Doctor

JCL, J.C.L. Juris Canonici Licentiatus
JD, J.D. Juris Doctor
jg. junior grade
jour. journal
jr. junior
JSD, J.S.D. Juris Scientiae Doctor
JUD, J.U.D. Juris Utriusque Doctor
jud. judicial

Kans. Kansas
K.C. Knights of Columbus
K.P. Knights of Pythias
KS Kansas
K.T. Knight Templar
KY, Ky. Kentucky

LA, La. Louisiana
L.A. Los Angeles
lab. laboratory
L.Am. Latin America
lang. language
laryngol. laryngological
LB Labrador
LDS Latter Day Saints
LDS Church Church of Jesus Christ of Latter Day Saints
lectr. lecturer
legis. legislation, legislative
LHD, L.H.D. Doctor of Humane Letters
L.I. Long Island
libr. librarian, library
lic. licensed, license
L.I.R.R. Long Island Railroad
lit. literature
litig. litigation
LittB, Litt.B. Bachelor of Letters
LittD, Litt.D. Doctor of Letters
LLB, LL.B. Bachelor of Laws
LLD, L.L.D. Doctor of Laws
LLM, L.L.M. Master of Laws
Ln. Lane
L.&N.R.R. Louisville & Nashville Railroad
LPGA Ladies Professional Golf Association
LPN Licensed Practical Nurse
LS, L.S. Library Science (in degree)
lt. lieutenant
Ltd. Limited
Luth. Lutheran
LWV League of Women Voters

M. Master
m. married
MA, M.A. Master of Arts
MA Massachusetts
MADD Mothers Against Drunk Driving
mag. magazine
MAgr, M.Agr. Master of Agriculture
maj. major
Man. Manitoba
Mar. March
MArch, M.Arch. Master in Architecture
Mass. Massachusetts
math. mathematics, mathematical
MATS Military Air Transport Service
MB, M.B. Bachelor of Medicine
MB Manitoba
MBA, M.B.A. Master of Business Administration
MBS Mutual Broadcasting System
M.C. Medical Corps
MCE, M.C.E. Master of Civil Engineering
mcht. merchant
mcpl. municipal
MCS, M.C.S. Master of Commercial Science
MD, M.D. Doctor of Medicine
MD, Md. Maryland
MDiv Master of Divinity
MDip, M.Dip. Master in Diplomacy
mdse. merchandise
MDV, M.D.V. Doctor of Veterinary Medicine
ME, M.E. Mechanical Engineer
ME Maine
M.E.Ch. Methodist Episcopal Church
mech. mechanical
MEd., M.Ed. Master of Education
med. medical
MEE, M.E.E. Master of Electrical Engineering
mem. member
meml. memorial
merc. mercantile
met. metropolitan
metall. metallurgical
MetE, Met.E. Metallurgical Engineer
meteorol. meteorological
Meth. Methodist
Mex. Mexico
MF, M.F. Master of Forestry
MFA, M.F.A. Master of Fine Arts
mfg. manufacturing
mfr. manufacturer
mgmt. management
mgr. manager
MHA, M.H.A. Master of Hospital Administration
M.I. Military Intelligence
MI Michigan
Mich. Michigan
micros. microscopic, microscopical
mid. middle
mil. military
Milw. Milwaukee
Min. Minister
mineral. mineralogical
Minn. Minnesota
MIS Management Information Systems
Miss. Mississippi
MIT Massachusetts Institute of Technology
mktg. marketing
ML, M.L. Master of Laws
MLA Modern Language Association
M.L.D. Magister Legnum Diplomatic
MLitt, M.Litt. Master of Literature, Master of Letters
MLS, M.L.S. Master of Library Science
MME, M.M.E. Master of Mechanical Engineering
MN Minnesota
mng. managing
MO, Mo. Missouri
moblzn. mobilization
Mont. Montana
MP Northern Mariana Islands
M.P. Member of Parliament
MPA Master of Public Administration
MPE, M.P.E. Master of Physical Education
MPH, M.P.H. Master of Public Health
MPhil, M.Phil. Master of Philosophy
MPL, M.P.L. Master of Patent Law
Mpls. Minneapolis
MRE, M.R.E. Master of Religious Education
MRI Magnetic Resonance Imaging
MS, M.S. Master of Science
MS, Ms. Mississippi
MSc, M.Sc. Master of Science
MSChemE Master of Science in Chemical Engineering
MSEE Master of Science in Electrical Engineering
MSF, M.S.F. Master of Science of Forestry
MSN Master of Science in Nursing
MST, M.S.T. Master of Sacred Theology
MSW, M.S.W. Master of Social Work
MT Montana
Mt. Mount
MTO Mediterranean Theatre of Operation
MTV Music Television
mus. museum, musical
MusB, Mus.B. Bachelor of Music
MusD, Mus.D. Doctor of Music
MusM, Mus.M. Master of Music
mut. mutual
MVP Most Valuable Player
mycol. mycological

N. North
NAACOG Nurses Association of the American College of Obstetricians and Gynecologists
NAACP National Association for the Advancement of Colored People
NACA National Advisory Committee for Aeronautics
NACDL National Association of Criminal Defense Lawyers
NACU National Association of Colleges and Universities
NAD National Academy of Design
NAE National Academy of Engineering, National Association of Educators
NAESP National Association of Elementary School Principals
NAFE National Association of Female Executives
N.Am. North America
NAM National Association of Manufacturers
NAMH National Association for Mental Health
NAPA National Association of Performing Artists
NARAS National Academy of Recording Arts and Sciences
NAREB National Association of Real Estate Boards
NARS National Archives and Record Service
NAS National Academy of Sciences
NASA National Aeronautics and Space Administration
NASP National Association of School Psychologists
NASW National Association of Social Workers
nat. national
NATAS National Academy of Television Arts and Sciences
NATO North Atlantic Treaty Organization
NATOUSA North African Theatre of Operations, United States Army
nav. navigation
NB, N.B. New Brunswick
NBA National Basketball Association
NBC National Broadcasting Company
NC, N.C. North Carolina
NCAA National College Athletic Association
NCCJ National Conference of Christians and Jews
ND, N.D. North Dakota
NDEA National Defense Education Act
NE Nebraska
NE, N.E. Northeast
NEA National Education Association
Nebr. Nebraska
NEH National Endowment for Humanities
neurol. neurological
Nev. Nevada
NF Newfoundland

NFL National Football League
Nfld. Newfoundland
NG National Guard
NH, N.H. New Hampshire
NHL National Hockey League
NIH National Institutes of Health
NIMH National Institute of Mental Health
NJ, N.J. New Jersey
NLRB National Labor Relations Board
NM New Mexico
N.Mex. New Mexico
No. Northern
NOAA National Oceanographic and Atmospheric Administration
NORAD North America Air Defense
Nov. November
NOW National Organization for Women
N.P.Ry. Northern Pacific Railway
nr. near
NRA National Rifle Association
NRC National Research Council
NS, N.S. Nova Scotia
NSC National Security Council
NSF National Science Foundation
NSTA National Science Teachers Association
NSW New South Wales
N.T. New Testament
NT Northwest Territories
nuc. nuclear
numis. numismatic
NV Nevada
NW, N.W. Northwest
N.W.T. Northwest Territories
NY, N.Y. New York
N.Y.C. New York City
NYU New York University
N.Z. New Zealand

OAS Organization of American States
ob-gyn obstetrics-gynecology
obs. observatory
obstet. obstetrical
occupl. occupational
oceanog. oceanographic
Oct. October
OD, O.D. Doctor of Optometry
OECD Organization for Economic Cooperation and Development
OEEC Organization of European Economic Cooperation
OEO Office of Economic Opportunity
ofcl. official
OH Ohio
OK Oklahoma
Okla. Oklahoma
ON Ontario
Ont. Ontario
oper. operating
ophthal. ophthalmological
ops. operations
OR Oregon
orch. orchestra
Oreg. Oregon
orgn. organization
orgnl. organizational
ornithol. ornithological
orthop. orthopedic
OSHA Occupational Safety and Health Administration
OSRD Office of Scientific Research and Development
OSS Office of Strategic Services
osteo. osteopathic
otol. otological
otolaryn. otolaryngological

PA, Pa. Pennsylvania
P.A. Professional Association
paleontol. paleontological
path. pathological
PBS Public Broadcasting System
P.C. Professional Corporation
PE Prince Edward Island
pediat. pediatrics
P.E.I. Prince Edward Island
PEN Poets, Playwrights, Editors, Essayists and Novelists (international association)
penol. penological
P.E.O. women's organization (full name not disclosed)
pers. personnel
pfc. private first class
PGA Professional Golfers' Association of America
PHA Public Housing Administration
pharm. pharmaceutical
PharmD, Pharm.D. Doctor of Pharmacy
PharmM, Pharm.M. Master of Pharmacy
PhB, Ph.B. Bachelor of Philosophy
PhD, Ph.D. Doctor of Philosophy
PhDChemE Doctor of Science in Chemical Engineering
PhM, Ph.M. Master of Philosophy
Phila. Philadelphia
philharm. philharmonic
philol. philological
philos. philosophical
photog. photographic
phys. physical
physiol. physiological
Pitts. Pittsburgh
Pk. Park
Pky. Parkway
Pl. Place
P.&L.E.R.R. Pittsburgh & Lake Erie Railroad
Plz. Plaza
PNP Pediatric Nurse Practitioner
P.O. Post Office
PO Box Post Office Box
polit. political
poly. polytechnic, polytechnical
PQ Province of Quebec
PR, P.R. Puerto Rico
prep. preparatory
pres. president
Presbyn. Presbyterian
presdl. presidential
prin. principal
procs. proceedings
prod. produced (play production)
prodn. production
prodr. producer
prof. professor
profl. professional
prog. progressive
propr. proprietor
pros. atty. prosecuting attorney
pro tem. pro tempore
PSRO Professional Services Review Organization
psychiat. psychiatric
psychol. psychological
PTA Parent-Teachers Association
ptnr. partner
PTO Pacific Theatre of Operations, Parent Teacher Organization
pub. publisher, publishing, published
pub. public
publ. publication
pvt. private

quar. quarterly
qm. quartermaster
Q.M.C. Quartermaster Corps
Que. Quebec

radiol. radiological
RAF Royal Air Force
RCA Radio Corporation of America
RCAF Royal Canadian Air Force
RD Rural Delivery
Rd. Road
R&D Research & Development
REA Rural Electrification Administration
rec. recording
ref. reformed
regt. regiment
regtl. regimental
rehab. rehabilitation
rels. relations
Rep. Republican
rep. representative
Res. Reserve
ret. retired
Rev. Reverend
rev. review, revised
RFC Reconstruction Finance Corporation
RFD Rural Free Delivery
rhinol. rhinological
RI, R.I. Rhode Island
RISD Rhode Island School of Design
Rlwy. Railway
Rm. Room
RN, R.N. Registered Nurse
roentgenol. roentgenological
ROTC Reserve Officers Training Corps
RR Rural Route
R.R. Railroad
rsch. research
rschr. researcher
Rt. Route

S. South
s. son
SAC Strategic Air Command
SAG Screen Actors Guild
SALT Strategic Arms Limitation Talks
S.Am. South America
san. sanitary
SAR Sons of the American Revolution
Sask. Saskatchewan
savs. savings
SB, S.B. Bachelor of Science
SBA Small Business Administration
SC, S.C. South Carolina
SCAP Supreme Command Allies Pacific
ScB, Sc.B. Bachelor of Science
SCD, S.C.D. Doctor of Commercial Science
ScD, Sc.D. Doctor of Science
sch. school
sci. science, scientific
SCLC Southern Christian Leadership Conference
SCV Sons of Confederate Veterans
SD, S.D. South Dakota
SE, S.E. Southeast
SEATO Southeast Asia Treaty Organization
SEC Securities and Exchange Commission
sec. secretary
sect. section
seismol. seismological
sem. seminary
Sept. September
s.g. senior grade
sgt. sergeant
SHAEF Supreme Headquarters Allied Expeditionary Forces
SHAPE Supreme Headquarters Allied Powers in Europe
S.I. Staten Island
S.J. Society of Jesus (Jesuit)

SJD Scientiae Juridicae Doctor
SK Saskatchewan
SM, S.M. Master of Science
SNP Society of Nursing Professionals
So. Southern
soc. society
sociol. sociological
S.P.Co. Southern Pacific Company
spkr. speaker
spl. special
splty. specialty
Sq. Square
S.R. Sons of the Revolution
sr. senior
SS Steamship
SSS Selective Service System
St. Saint, Street
sta. station
stats. statistics
statis. statistical
STB, S.T.B. Bachelor of Sacred Theology
stblzn. stabilization
STD, S.T.D. Doctor of Sacred Theology
std. standard
Ste. Suite
subs. subsidiary
SUNY State University of New York
supr. supervisor
supt. superintendent
surg. surgical
svc. service
SW, S.W. Southwest
sys. system

TAPPI Technical Association of the Pulp and Paper Industry
tb. tuberculosis
tchg. teaching
tchr. teacher
tech. technical, technology
technol. technological
tel. telephone
Tel. & Tel. Telephone & Telegraph
telecom. telecommunications
temp. temporary
Tenn. Tennessee
Ter. Territory
Ter. Terrace
TESOL Teachers of English to Speakers of Other Languages
Tex. Texas
ThD, Th.D. Doctor of Theology
theol. theological
ThM, Th.M. Master of Theology
TN Tennessee
tng. training
topog. topographical
trans. transaction, transferred
transl. translation, translated
transp. transportation
treas. treasurer
TT Trust Territory
TV television
TVA Tennessee Valley Authority
TWA Trans World Airlines
twp. township
TX Texas
typog. typographical

U. University
UAW United Auto Workers
UCLA University of California at Los Angeles
UDC United Daughters of the Confederacy
U.K. United Kingdom
UN United Nations
UNESCO United Nations Educational, Scientific and Cultural Organization
UNICEF United Nations International Children's Emergency Fund
univ. university
UNRRA United Nations Relief and Rehabilitation Administration
UPI United Press International
U.P.R.R. United Pacific Railroad
urol. urological
U.S. United States
U.S.A. United States of America
USAAF United States Army Air Force
USAF United States Air Force
USAFR United States Air Force Reserve
USAR United States Army Reserve
USCG United States Coast Guard
USCGR United States Coast Guard Reserve
USES United States Employment Service
USIA United States Information Agency
USMC United States Marine Corps
USMCR United States Marine Corps Reserve
USN United States Navy
USNG United States National Guard
USNR United States Naval Reserve
USO United Service Organizations
USPHS United States Public Health Service
USS United States Ship
USSR Union of the Soviet Socialist Republics
USTA United States Tennis Association
USV United States Volunteers
UT Utah
VA Veterans Administration
VA, Va. Virginia
vet. veteran, veterinary
VFW Veterans of Foreign Wars
VI, V.I. Virgin Islands
vice pres. vice president
vis. visiting
VISTA Volunteers in Service to America
VITA Volunteers in Technical Assistance
vocat. vocational
vol. volunteer, volume
v.p. vice president
vs. versus
VT, Vt. Vermont

W, W. West
WA Washington (state)
WAC Women's Army Corps
Wash. Washington (state)
WATS Wide Area Telecommunications Service
WAVES Women's Reserve, US Naval Reserve
WCTU Women's Christian Temperance Union
we. western
W. Ger. Germany, Federal Republic of
WHO World Health Organization
WI Wisconsin
W.I. West Indies
Wis. Wisconsin
WSB Wage Stabilization Board
WV West Virginia
W.Va. West Virginia
WWI World War I
WWII World War II
WY Wyoming
Wyo. Wyoming

YK Yukon Territory
YMCA Young Men's Christian Association
YMHA Young Men's Hebrew Association
YM & YWHA Young Men's and Young Women's Hebrew Association
yr. year
YT, Y.T. Yukon Territory
YWCA Young Women's Christian Association

zool. zoological

Alphabetical Practices

Names are arranged alphabetically according to the surnames, and under identical surnames according to the first given name. If both surname and first given name are identical, names are arranged alphabetically according to the second given name.

Surnames beginning with De, Des, Du, however capitalized or spaced, are recorded with the prefix preceding the surname and arranged alphabetically under the letter D.

Surnames beginning with Mac and Mc are arranged alphabetically under M.

Surnames beginning with Saint or St. appear after names that begin Sains, and are arranged according to the second part of the name, e.g. St. Clair before Saint Dennis.

Surnames beginning with Van, Von, or von are arranged alphabetically under the letter V.

Compound surnames are arranged according to the first member of the compound.

Many hyphenated Arabic names begin Al-, El-, or al-. These names are alphabetized according to each Biographee's designation of last name. Thus Al-Bahar, Neta may be listed either under Al- or under Bahar, depending on the preference of the listee.

Also, Arabic names have a variety of possible spellings when transposed to English. Spelling of these names is always based on the practice of the Biographee. Some Biographees use a Western form of word order, while others prefer the Arabic word sequence.

Similarly, Asian names may have no comma between family and given names, but some Biographees have chosen to add the comma. In each case, punctuation follows the preference of the Biographee.

Parentheses used in connection with a name indicate which part of the full name is usually deleted in common usage. Hence Chambers, E(lizabeth) Anne indicates that the usual form of the given name is E. Anne. In such a case, the parentheses are ignored in alphabetizing and the name would be arranged as Chambers, Elizabeth Anne. However, if the name is recorded Chambers, (Elizabeth) Anne, signifying that the entire name Elizabeth is not commonly used, the alphabetizing would be arranged as though the name were Chambers, Anne. If an entire middle or last name is enclosed in parentheses, that portion of the name is used in the alphabetical arrangement. Hence Chambers, Elizabeth (Anne) would be arranged as Chambers, Elizabeth Anne.

Where more than one spelling, word order, or name of an individual is frequently encountered, the sketch has been entered under the form preferred by the Biographee, with cross-references under alternate forms.

Who'sWho in the Midwest®

Biographies

AARSVOLD, OLE, state legislator; m. Marilyn Haugen; 3 children. BS, Mayville State U., 1963; MS, U. ND, 1969. Tchr., prin. secondary sch.; instr. Univ.; farmer; mem. N.D. Ho. of Reps. from 20th dist., 1989—. Appt. com. budget sect. Edn. Svcs. Com.; bd. dirs. Farmers Union Oil Co., Clifco Energy. Bd. dirs. Traill County Econ. Devel. Commn.; clerk-treas. Greenfield (N.D.) Twp.; commr., v.p. N.D. Tchrs. Practices Commn.; field dir. No. Plains Indian Tchr. Corps. Recipient Outstanding Young Educator award, Outstanding Agriculturist award, Disting. Alumni award Mayville State U. Mem. Traill County Crop Improvement Assn. (past bd. dirs., past pres.), Traill County Farmers Union (bd. dirs.). Democrat. Address: RR 2 Box 12 Blanchard ND 58009-9513

ABBETT, WILLIAM S. former dean; Dean Mich. State U. Coll. Human Medicine, East Lansing, 2000—00. Office: Mich State U Office Dean A110 E Fee Hall East Lansing MI 48824

ABBEY, G(EORGE) MARSHALL, lawyer, former health care company executive, general counsel; b. Dunkirk, N.Y., July 24, 1933; s. Ralph Ambrose and Grace A. (Fisher) A.; m. Sue Carroll, July 13, 1974; children: Mark, Steven, Michael, Lincoln BA with high distinction, U. Rochester, 1954; JD with distinction, Cornell U., 1957. Bar: N.H. 1957, Ill. 1965. Atty. McLane, Carleton, Graf, Greene & Brown, Manchester, N.H., 1957-65, Baxter Internat. Inc., Deerfield, Ill., 1965-69, gen. counsel, 1969-72, sec., gen. counsel, 1972-75, v.p., sec., gen. counsel, 1975-82, sr. v.p., gen. counsel, 1985-90, sr. v.p., sec., gen. counsel, 1990-93; pvt. practice, 1993-97; of counsel Bell Boyd & Lloyd, Chgo., 1997—. Editor Cornell Law Rev., 1956-57. Mem. vis. com. Law Sch., U. Chgo., 1978-81; dir. Coun. Puerto Rico-U.S. Affairs, 1988-92; mem. indsl. adv. coun. U. P.R.; dir. P.R.-USA Found., 1975-93, B.U.I.L.D., Chgo., 1980-84, bus. adv. com. B.U.I.L.D. Inc.; bd. dirs. Hundred Club of Lake County, Ill., 1976-86; dir. Food and Drug Law Inst., 1975-93; bd. dirs. Evanston Inventure, 1986-88; former trustee Winnetka Congl. Ch.; dir. Nat. Com. for Quality Health Care, 1988-93; mem. Northwestern U. Corp. Coun. adv. bd., 1976-93; dir. P.R. Cmty. Found., 1986-94; bd. dirs. Better Bus. Bur. Chgo. and No. Ill., 1991-93; mem. Chgo. Bd's. Coun. Chief Legal Officers and Legal Quality Coun., 1991-93. Mem. ABA, Ill. Bar Assn., Lake County Bar Assn., Chgo. Bar Assn., Health Industry Mfrs. Assn. (chmn. legal/regulatory affairs 1976-78, bd. dirs. 1978-80, chmn. govt. affairs com. 1980-81), Univ. Club, Exmoor Country Club, Bankers Club (P.R.), Order of the Coif, Phi Beta Kappa. Office: 836 Skokie Blvd Northbrook IL 60062-4001

ABBOTT, BILL, radio personality; b. Kansas City, Jan. 12; children: Brett, Suzette, Tony. Radio host WDAF, Westwood, Kans., 1977—. Office: WDAF 4935 Belinder Rd Westwood KS 66205*

ABBOTT, BOB, state supreme court justice; b. Kans., Nov. 1, 1932; BS, Emporia State U.; JD, Washburn U.; LLM, U. Va. Bar: Kans. 1960. Pvt. practice, Junction City, Kans., from 1960; former chief judge Kans. Ct. Appeals; justice Kans. Supreme Ct., 1990—. Office: Kansas Supreme Court 314 Kansas Judicial Ctr 301 SW 10th St Topeka KS 66612-1507

ABBOTT, DAVID HENRY, manufacturing company executive; b. Milton, Ky., July 6, 1936; s. Carl and Rachael (Miles) A.; m. Joan Shefchik, Aug. 14, 1976; children— Kristine, Gina, Beth, Linsey B.S., U. Ky., 1960, M.B.A., 1961. With Ford Motor Co., Louisville, Mpls. and Dearborn, Mich., 1961-69; div. controller J I Case Co., Racine, Wis., 1970-73, gen. mgr. service parts supply div., 1973-75, v.p., 1975, v.p. and gen. mgr. constrn. equipment div., 1975-77, v.p., gen. mgr. Drott div. Wausau, 1977-79, exec. v.p. worldwide constrn. equipment, 1979-81; pres., chief operating officer Portec, Inc., Oak Brook, Ill., 1981-87, also dir.; pres., chief exec. officer, dir. E.D. Etnyre & Co., Oregon, 1988—. Dir. Oak Brook Bank, 1982-88. Served with U.S. Army, 1958 Mem. Constrn. Industry Mfrs. Assn. (bd. dirs. 1979-81, 82—, chmn. 1992), Am. Rd. and Transpn. Builders Assn. (dir. 1988—). Republican Home: 2690 W Pines Rd Oregon IL 61061-9068 Office: E D Etnyre & Co 1333 S Daysville Rd Oregon IL 61061-9778

ABBOTT, DAVID L. agricultural products executive; CEO Purina Mills, St. Louis; pres., CEO E-markets Inc., Ames, Iowa. Office: E-markets Inc Ste 108 1606 Golden Aspen Dr Ames IA 50010-8011

ABBOUD, ALFRED ROBERT, banker, consultant, investor; b. Boston, May 29, 1929; s. Alfred and Victoria (Karam) A.; m. Joan Grover, June 11, 1955; children: Robert G., Jeanne Frances, Katherine Jane. B.S. cum laude, Harvard U., 1951, LL.B., 1956, M.B.A., 1958. Bar: Mass. 1957, Ill. 1959. Asst. cashier First Nat. Bank of Chgo., 1960-62, asst. v.p., 1962-64, v.p., 1964-69, sr. v.p., 1969-72, exec. v.p., 1972-73, vice chmn. bd., 1973-74, dep. chmn. bd., 1974-75, chmn. bd., CEO, 1975-80; pres., COO Occidental Petroleum Corp., L.A., 1980-84; pres. A. Robert Abboud & Co., Fox River Grove, Ill., 1984—; chmn., CEO First City Bancorp. of Tex. Inc., Houston, 1988-91. Bd. dirs. AAR Corp., Elk Grove Village, Alberto-Culver Co., Melrose Park, Ill. Author: Money in the Bank: How Safe Is It?, 1988. Capt. USMC, 1951-53. Decorated Purple Heart, Bronze Star; Baker scholar, 1958. Mem. Econ. Comml. Club, The Chgo. Club, Harvard Club Chgo., Harvard Club N.Y.C., Barrington Hills Country Club. Home: 209 Braeburn Rd Barrington IL 60010-9637 Office: PO Box 33 212 Stone Hill Ctr Fox River Grove IL 60021-0033

ABBOUD, FRANCOIS MITRY, physician, educator; b. Cairo, Egypt, Jan. 5, 1931; arrived in U.S., 1955, naturalized, 1963; s. Mitry Y. and Asma (Habac) Abboud; m. Doris Evelyn Khal, June 5, 1955; children: Mary Agnese, Susan Marie, Nancy Louise, Anthony Lawrence. Student, U. Cairo, 1948—52; MBBCh, Ein Chams U., 1955; D (hon.) , U. Lyon, France, 1991; DSc (hon.) , Med. Coll. Wis., 1994. Diplomate Am. Bd. Internal Medicine, Am. Bd. Cardiovasc. Disease (bd. govs. 1987-93). Intern Demerdash Govt. Hosp., Cairo, 1955; resident Milw. County Hosp., 1955—58; Am. Heart Assn. rsch. fellow cardiovasc. labs. Marquette U., 1958—60; Am. Heart Assn. advanced rsch. fellow U. Iowa, 1960—62, asst. prof., 1961—65, assoc. prof. medicine, 1965—68, prof. medicine, 1968—, prof. physiology and biophysics, 1975—, Edith King Pearson prof. cardiovascular rsch., 1988—, dir. cardiovasc. divsn., 1970—76, chmn. dept. internal medicine, 1976—, dir. cardiovasc. rsch. ctr., 1974—. Attending physician U. Iowa Hosps., 1961—, VA Hosp., Iowa City, 1963—; chmn. rsch. rev. com. Nat. Heart, Lung and Blood Inst., 1978—80, adv. coun., 1995—99. Editor Circulation Rsch., 1981—86, Procs. Assn. Am. Physicians, 1995—, assoc. editor Advances in Internal Medicine, 1991—96, editl. bd. Medicine, 1992—. Recipient European Traveling fellowship, French govt., 1948, NIH Career Devel. award, 1962—71. Master: ACP; mem.: AMA, Assn. Patient Oriented Rsch. (founding mem.), Am. Acad. Arts and Scis., Internat. Soc. Hypertension (Merck Sharp & Dohme Internat. award for rsch. in hypertension 1994), Am. Soc. Pharmacology and Exptl. Therapeutics (award exptl. therapeutics 1972), Am. Clin. and Climatol. Assn. (councillor 1992), Am. Physiol. Soc. (chmn. circulation group 1979—80, chmn. clin. physiology sect. 1979—83, publ. com. 1987—90, Wiggers award 1988), Assn. Am. Physicians (treas. 1979—84, councillor 1984—89, pres.-elect 1989—90, councillor 1989—, pres. 1990—91), Assn. Profs. Medicine (bd. dirs. 1993—97, Robert H. Williams Disting. Chmn. of Medicine award 1993), Assn. Univ. Cardiologists, Am. Fedn. Clin. Rsch. (pres. 1971—72), Am. Heart Assn. (bd. dirs. 1977—80, pres.-elect 1989—90, pres. 1990—91, past chmn. rsch. coms., award of merit 1982, Disting. Achievement award 1988, CIBA award for hypertension rsch. 1990, Gold Heart award 1995, Rsch. Achievement award 1999), Soc. Exptl. Biology and Medicine, Ctrl. Soc. for Clin. Rsch. (pres. elect 1984—85, pres. 1985—86), Am. Soc. Clin. Investigation, Inst. Medicine NAS, Alpha Omega Alpha (bd. dirs. 1989—), Sigma Xi. Achievements include research and publications in cardiovascular physiology on neurohumoral control of circulation and mechanisms of baroreceptor activation. Home: 24 Kennedy Pky Iowa City IA 52246-2780 Office: U Iowa Coll Medicine SE 308 General Hosp Dept Internal Medicine Iowa City IA 52242

ABCARIAN, HERAND, surgeon; b. Ahvaz, Iran, Jan. 23, 1941; arrived in U.S., 1966; s. Joseph and Stella (Banki) A.; m. Karen Jane Berger, May 10, 1969; children: Gregory, Ariane, Margot. MD, Teheran U., 1965. Intern Cook County Hosp., Chgo., 1966—67, resident in gen. surgery, 1967—71, resident in colon and rectal surgery, 1971—72, chmn. colon and rectal surgery, 1972—93; head dept. surgery, Turi Josefson prof. U. Ill. Coll. Med., 1989—; exec. dir. Am. Bd. Colon & Rectal Surgery, Taylor, Mich. Assoc. editor: Diseases of Colon and Rectum, 1981—95. Fellow ACS (various coms. and offices), Am. Soc. Colon and Rectal Surgeons (sec. 1985-87, pres. 1988-89); mem. Am. Surg. Assn., Soc. Am. Gastroendoscopic Surgeons (founder), Sydney Soc. Colon and Rectal Surgeons (hon.), Assn. Coloprotology of Gt. Britain (hon. fellow). Republican. Roman Catholic. Avocations: visual arts, music, philately. Office: U Ill 840 S Wood St # 518 Chicago IL 60612-7317 Also: Am Bd Colon & Rectal Surgery 20600 Eureka Rd Ste 713 Taylor MI 48180-5376

ABDOO, RICHARD A. utilities company executive; b. Port Huron, Mich., 1944; BSEE, U. Dayton, 1965; MA, U. Detroit, 1969. With Wis. Energy Corp., 1975—, chmn., pres., chief exec. officer, 1991—. Bd. dir. ARI Network Svcs., M & I Marshall & Ilsley Bank, Blue Cross Blue Shield United of Wis. Office: Wis Energy Corp PO Box 2046 231 W Michigan St Milwaukee WI 53203-2918

ABDOU, NABIH I. physician, educator; b. Cairo, Oct. 11, 1934; came to U.S., 1962, naturalized, 1972; m. Nancy L. Layle, Aug. 26, 1939; children— Mark L., Marie L. MD, Cairo U., 1958; PhD, McGill U., 1969. Intern then resident Cairo Univ. Hosp., 1959-62; resident, fellow in allergy and immunology Hosp. U. Pa., 1963-65, Mayo Clinic, 1965-67, Royal Victoria Hosp., Montreal, Que., Can., 1967-69; asst., assoc. prof. U. Pa., 1969-75; assoc. prof. medicine U. Kans. Med. Ctr., Kansas City, 1975-78, prof. medicine, 1978-89; pvt. practice Ctr. for Rheumatic Disease and Ctr. for Allergy Immunology, 1989—. Clin. prof. medicine U. Mo., 1989—. Fulbright scholar, 1962-65 Fellow ACP, Am. Acad. Allergy, Am. Coll. Rheumatology; mem. Am. Assn. Immunologists, Cen. Soc. Clin. Rsch., Clin. Immunology Soc. Office: Ctr for Rheumatic Disease and Ctr Allergy Immunology 4330 Wornall Rd Ste 40 Kansas City MO 64111-3217

ABDUL-JABBAR, KARIM, professional football player; b. L.A., June 28, 1974; m. Sabria; 1 child, Ibarhim Abdullah. BS in Econs., UCLA, 1997. Running back Miami Dolphins, 1996-98, Cleve. Browns, 1998-99, Indianapolis Colts, 2000—. Holder club rookie rushing record; voted to all-rookie teams Football News Pro Football Writers Am. and Coll. and Pro Football Newsweekly; named AFC Offensive Player of the Week. Office: Indianapolis Colts RCA Dome PO Box 535000 Indianapolis IN 46253-5000

ABEL, GREGORY E. utility company executive; Degree, U. Alta., Can. Chartered acct., Can. With Price Waterhouse, San Francisco, Calif. Energy Co., Inc., 1992, sr. v.p.; pres., COO MidAm. Energy Holdings Co., Des Moines, 1997—. Office: Mid Am Energy Holdings Co 666 Grand Ave Des Moines IA 50309

ABEL, HAROLD, psychologist, educator, academic administrator; b. N.Y.C., July 31, 1926; s. Felix N. and Jennie (Schaefer) A.; m. Iris Tash, Jan. 30, 1949; children: Lawrence William, Matthew Robert. AB, Syracuse U., 1949, MA, 1951, PhD, 1958; DLitt (hon.), Hanyang U., Republic of Korea, 1979. Tchr. mentally retarded, Syracuse and Rochester, N.Y., 1950-52; asst. instr. Syracuse U., 1952-56; assoc. prof. to prof. depts. psychology and home econs. and dir. child devel. lab. U. Nebr., 1956-65, chmn. dept. human devel., 1963-65; dir. divsn. psycho-ednl. studies, prof. edn. U. Oreg., 1965-68, assoc. dean, prof. ednl. psychology Coll. Edn., 1968-70; pres. Castleton State Coll., 1970-75, Cen. Mich. U., 1975-85, prof. psychology and ednl. adminstrn., 1985-93; pres. Walden U., Mpls., 1988-91, Grad. Sch. Am., Mpls., 1993-95; chancellor Grad. Sch. Am. (now Capella U.), 1995-98; chair bd. dirs. Capella, 1998—. With AUS, 1945-46. Mem. AAAS, Am. Psychol. Assn., Soc. Rsch. in Child Devel., Sigma Xi, Phi Delta Kappa. E-mail: habel@capella.edu.

ABEL, MARK ROGERS, federal judge; b. 1944; BA, Ohio U., 1966; JD, Ohio State U., 1969. Bar: Ohio 1969, U.S. Dist. Ct. (so. dist.) Ohio 1971. Law clk. to Hon. Judge Joseph Kinneary U.S. Dist. Ct. (so. dist.) Ohio, 1969-71, magistrate judge, 1971—. Mem. FBA, Ohio Bar Assn., Columbus Bar Assn. Office: US Dist Ct So Dist Ohio 208 US Courthouse 85 Marconi Blvd Columbus OH 43215-2823 Fax: (614) 469-5666.

ABELES, NORMAN, psychologist, educator; b. Vienna, Austria, Apr. 15, 1928; came to U.S., 1939, naturalized, 1944; s. Felix and Bertha (Gronich) A.; m. Jeanette Bueller, Apr. 14, 1957; children: Linda, Mark. BA, NYU, 1949; MA, U. Tex., 1952, PhD, 1958. Diplomate: Am. Bd. Profl. Psychology (Midwest regional bd. 1972-78, chmn. regional bd. 1975-77; nat. trustee 1975-77). Fellow in counseling U. Tex., Austin, 1956-57; instr. Mich. State U., East Lansing, 1957-59, asst. prof., 1959-64, asso. prof., 1964-67, prof. psychology, 1968—, dir. psychol. clinic, 1978—, co-dir. clin. tng., 1981-96, asst. dir. counseling center, 1965-71. U.S. State Dept. ednl. exch. prof. U. Utrecht, Netherlands, 1969, vis. prof., 1975; cons. Peace Corps, 1965-69; vocat. cons. Social Security Office of Hearings and Appeals, 1962—; med. advisor Social Security Office of Hearings and Appeals, 1986—; mem. Mich. Commn. Cert. of Psychologists, 1962-77, chmn., 1966-68; mem. coun. Nat. Register Health Svc. Providers in Psychology, 1974—, vice chmn., 1975-80; del. White House Conf. on Aging, 1995. Editor: Acad. Psychology bull., 1978-82; cons. editor Jour. Personality Assessment, 1988—, Clin. Psychology: Sci. and Practice, 1994—, Clin. Psychology Rev., 1995-98, Profl. Psychology: Rsch. and Practice, 1979-81, 89—, editor, 1983-88; contbr. articles to profl. jours. Served with U.S. Army, 1954-56. Fulbright-Hays grantee, 1969; recipient Disting. Psychologist award Mich. Soc. Clin. Psychologists, 1984; Disting. Practitioner, Nat. Acad. Practice, 1982; Arthur Furst Ethics Lectureship medal Pacific Grad. Sch. Psychology, 1996; Dept. Vets. Affairs Spl. Contbns. award, Battle Creek Mich., 1997. Fellow APA (coun. reps. 1972-75, 77-79, 89-91, 93-95, 99—, policy and planning bd. 1975-79, chmn. 1976, rec. sec. 1980-86, chmn. edn. and tng. bd. 1988, bd. ednl. affairs 1999-2001, com. on internat. rels. in psychology 2002--, pres.-elect divsn. clin. psychology 1989, pres. divsn. psychotherapy and divsn. clin. psychology 1990, publs. and comm. bd. 1990-96, chmn. 1995, pres.-elect 1996, pres. 1997, past pres. 1998, Disting. Prof. divsn. psychotherapy 1996), Coun. Sci. Socs. Pres.; mem. Midwestern Psychol. Assn., Mich. Psychol. Assn. (legis. chmn. 1964-72, pres. 1971-72, Disting. Psychologist 1974), Internat. Union Psychol. Scis. (U.S. com. 1999—), Sigma Xi. Home: 953 Rosewood Ave East Lansing MI 48823-3126 Office: Mich State U Dept Psychology 129 Psychology Research East Lansing MI 48824-1117 E-mail: abeles@msu.edu.

ABELL, DAVID ROBERT, lawyer; b. Raleigh, N.C., Nov. 24, 1934; s. De Witt Sterling and Edna Renilde (Doughty) A.; children: David Charles, Elizabeth A. Harrington, Kimberly A. Creasman, Hilary Ayres, Glenn Bryan; m. Ellen Penrod Hackmann, July 27, 1985. BA, Denison U., 1956; JD (Internat. fellow), Columbia U., 1963. Bar: Pa. 1963, Ill. 1973. Assoc. Ballard, Spahr, Andrews & Ingersoll, Phila., 1963-68; sec., counsel Hurst Performance, Inc., Warminster, Pa., 1969-70; sec., gen. counsel STP Corp., Des Plaines, Ill., 1970-72; ptnr. David R. Abell Ltd., Winnetka, 1974-96, Rooks, Pitts & Poust, Chgo., 1996-2000, Schuyler, Roche & Zwirner, Chgo. and Evanston, Ill., 2000—. Author: Residential Real Estate System, 1977, 2d edit., 1990. Trustee Music Inst. Chgo., 1988-96; bd. govs. Winnetka Cmty. House, 1993-96. Aviator USMCR, 1956-60. Mem. ABA, Ill. Bar Assn., Chgo. Bar Assn., Rotary (pres. Winnetka 1977-78). Episcopalian. Home: 740 Oak St Winnetka IL 60093-2521 Office: Schuyler Roche & Zwirner One Prudential Plz Ste 3800 130 E Randolph St Chicago IL 60601 Office Fax: 312-565-8300. Business E-Mail: dabell@srzlaw.com.

ABELMAN, STEVE, automotive company executive; CEO, pres., COO Oxford Automotive, Troy, Mich. Office: Oxford Automotive 1250 Stephenson Hwy Troy MI 48083-1115

ABELOV, STEPHEN LAWRENCE, uniform clothing company executive, consultant; b. N.Y.C., Apr. 1, 1923; s. Saul S. and Ethel (Esterman) Abelov; m. Phyllis S. Lichtenson, Nov. 18, 1945; children: Patricia C., Gary M. B.S., NYU, 1945, M.B.A., 1950. Asst. divsn. mgr. Nat. Silver Co., NY, 1945; sales rep. Angelica Uniform Co., 1945—50, asst. sales mgr., 1950—56, western regional mgr., 1956—66; v.p. Angelica Uniform Co. of Calif., 1958—66, nat. v.p. sales, 1966—72; v.p. Angelica Corp., 1958—88, cons., 1988—92, group v.p. mktg., 1972—80; exec. v.p., chief mktg. officer Angelica Uniform Group, 1980—88. Vis. lectr. mktg. NYU Grad. Sch. Bus. Adminstrn. Contbr. articles to profl. jours. Vice comdr. Am. Legion; mem. vocational adv. bd. VA; adv. bd. Woodcraft Rangers; bd. dirs. Univ. Temple. Served with USAF, 1942—44. Mem.: various trade assns., Inst. Environ. Scis., Health Industries Assn. Am. (dir.), Am. Mktg. Assn., Am. Soc. for Advancement Mgmt. (chpt. pres.), Am. Assn. Contamination Control (dir.), Coast Guard Aux. (Flotilla comdr.), B'nai B'rith (past pres.), NYU Alumni Assn., St. Louis Coun. on World Affairs, Lake of the Ozarks Yachting Assn., Moorings Yacht Club (v.p.), Sales Execs. Club (bd. dirs.), Aqua Sierra Sportsmen Club, NYU Club, Men's Club (exec. v.p.), Town Hall Club, Phi Epsilon Pi (treas.). Home: 9821 Log Cabin Ct Saint Louis MO 63124-1133

ABELSON, HERBERT TRAUB, pediatrician, educator; b. St. Louis, Feb. 19, 1941; s. Benjamin J. and Ann (Traub) Abelson; m. Constance Faye Caldwell, May 17, 1968; children: Matthew, Rebecca, Jonathan, Daniel. AB with high honors, U. Ill., 1962; MD, Washington U., St. Louis, 1966. Diplomate Diplomate Am. Bd. Pediat. (examiner 1988—, bd. dirs. 1992-97, sec.-treas. 1995, chmn.-elect 1995-96, chmn. 1996-97), Am. Bd. Pediatric Hematology-Oncology. Intern pediat. U Colo. Med. Ctr., Denver, 1966—67; resident Boston Children's Hosp., 1969—71; staff assoc. Nat. Cancer Inst. NIH, Bethesda, Md., 1967—69; Jane Childs Meml. Fund for Med. Rsch. fellow NIH, 1971, spl. postdoctoral fellow, 1972; teaching fellow Med. Sch. Harvard Coll., Boston, 1970—71, instr. pediat., 1973—74, asst. prof., 1974—79; tutor in med. scis., 1977—79; assoc. prof. Harvard Coll., Boston, 1979—83; vis. prof., Ctr. for Cancer Rsch. MIT, Cambridge, 1982—83; prof., chmn. dept. pediat. Med. Sch. U. Wash., Seattle, 1983—95; prof., chmn., physician-in-chief dept. pediat. U. Chgo., 1995—. Rsch. fellow in hematology Children's Hosp. Med. Ctr., Boston, 1971—73; rsch. assoc. in biology MIT, 1971—73; mem. pediatric residency rev. com. Accreditation Coun. for Grad. Med. Edn.; mem. exec. com. Am. Med. Sch. Pediatric Dept. Chairmen. Contbr. articles to profl. jours. Recipient Rsch. Career Devel. award, NIH, 1975—80. Fellow: Am. Acad. Pediat.; mem.: Am. Bd. Med. Spltys. (fin. com.), Am. Pediatric Soc., Soc. Pediatric Rsch., Am. Soc. Clin. Oncology, Am. Assn. Cancer Rsch., Am. Soc. Hematology (mem. sci. subcom. on pediatric hematology 1987—91). Office: Univ Chgo Dept Pediatrics 5841 S Maryland Ave # Mc1051 Chicago IL 60637-1463

ABERLE, ELTON DAVID, dean; b. Sabetha, Kans., Aug. 30, 1940; s. Alphia Henry and Irene Judith A.; n. Carrie Rae Campbell, Sept. 11, 1965; children; Krista Kaye, Barbara Ann. BS, Kans. State U., 1962; MS, Mich. State U., 1965, DPhil, 1967. Asst. prof. Purdue U., West Lafayette, Ind., 1967-71, assoc. prof., 1971-76, prof., 1976-83; prof., dept. head U. Nebr., Lincoln, 1983-98; dean, dir., prof. U. Wis., Madison, 1998—. Author: Principles of Meat Science, 1975, 3d edit., 1994; contbr. articles to profl. jours. Fellow Am. Soc. Animal Sci. (pres. 1994-95, Meat Rsch. award 1982, Signal Svc. award 1998); mem. Am. Meat Sci. Assn. (dir. 1979-80, pres. 1985-86, Disting. Teaching award 1983, Disting. Rsch. award 1986), Inst. Food Tech., Coun. Agrl. Sci. & Tech. (dir. 1996-99), Kiwanis. Avocations: golf, fishing, hunting. Home: 5810 Windsona Cir Madison WI 53711-5853 Office: U Wis Office of Dean 1450 Linden Dr Madison WI 53706-1522

ABHYANKAR, SHREERAM S. mathematics and industrial engineering educator; b. Ujjain, India, July 22, 1930; came to U.S., 1951, naturalized, 1989; s. Shankar Keshav and Uma (Tamhankar) A.; m. Yvonne Margit Kraft, June 5, 1958; children: Hari Shreeram, Kashi Shreeram. BSc, Bombay U., 1951; AM, Harvard U., 1952, PhD, 1955; DHD (hon.), U. Angers, 1998. Rsch. instr. Columbia U., N.Y.C., 1955-56, vis. asst. prof., 1956-57; asst. prof. Cornell U., Ithaca, N.Y., 1957-58; vis. asst. prof. Princeton (N.J.) U., 1958-59; assoc. prof. Johns Hopkins U., Balt., 1959-63; pres. math. Purdue U., West Lafayette, Ind., 1963-67, Marshall disting. prof. math., 1967—, prof. indsl. engring., 1987—, prof. computer scis., 1988—. Vis. lectr. Harvard U., 1960-61; vis. prof. Munster U., Erlangen U., summer 1963, Matsci., Madras, India, fall 1963, Tata Inst., Bombay, 1969-70, 75-76, spring 1974, Kyoto U., fall 1976, U. Ky., fall 1978, U. Paris, spring 1980, ENS St. Cloud, France, spring 1982, U. Nice, spring 1983, U. Sydney, spring 1986, U. Strasbourg, spring 1991, Ohio State U., spring 1995; vis. assoc. prof. Yale U., spring 1963; spkr. numerous profl. meetings, univ., insts., symposia, confs., and congresses, 1960—. Author: Ramification Theoretic Methods in Algebraic Geometry, 1959, Local Analytic Geometry, 1964, Resolution of Singularities of Embedded

Algebraic Surfaces, 1966, 2d enlarged edit. 1998, A Glimpse of Algebraic Geometry, 1971, Algebraic Space Curves, 1971, Lectures on Expansion Techniques in Algebraic Geometry, 1977, Weighted Expansions for Canonical Desingularization, 1982, Enumerative Combinatorics of Young Tableaux, 1988, Algebraic Geometry for Scientists and Engineers, 1990; also over 150 articles. Recipient Herbert Newby McCoy award Purdue U., 1973, Medal of Honor, U. Valliadolid, Spain, 1990; grantee NSF, 1960-87, 89-91, 89-2002, Office Naval Rsch., 1986-90, Army Rsch. Office, 1988-90, Nat. Security Agy., 1992-99; rsch. fellow Alfred P. Sloan Found., 1958-60. Fellow Indian Nat. Sci. Acad., Indian Acad. Scis.; mem. Am. Math. Soc., Math. Assn. Am. (Lester R. Ford prize 1977, Chauvenet award 1978), Phi Beta Kappa. Achievements include research in algebraic geometry, commutative and local algebra, theory of functions of several complex variables, quantum electrodynamics, circuit and invariant theory, combinatorics, computer aided design, and robotics. Home: 111 Waldron St West Lafayette IN 47906-2836 Office: Purdue U Div Math Sci West Lafayette IN 47907

ABID, ANN B. art librarian; b. St. Louis, Mar. 17, 1942; d. Clarence Frederick and Luella (Niehaus) Bartelsmeyer; m. Amor Abid (div. 1969); children: Rod, Kady; m. Cleon R. Yohe, Aug. 10, 1974 (div.); m. Roldo S. Bartimole, Feb. 1, 1991. Cert. in Librarianship, Washington U., St. Louis, 1976. Asst. to libr. St. Louis Art Mus., 1963-68, libr., 1968-85; head libr. Cleve. Mus. Art, 1985—. Vis. com. univ. librs. Case We. Res.U., 1987-90, co-chairperson, 1990. Co-author: Documents of Surrealism, 1918-1942, 1981, Planning for Automation of the Slide and Photograph Collections at the Cleveland Museum of Art: A Draft Marc Visual Materials Record, 1998; contbr. articles to profl. jours. Grantee Mo. Coun. Arts, 1978, Mo. Com. Humanities, 1980, Nat. Hist. Pubs. and Records Commn., 1981, Reinberger Found., 1987, Japan Found., 1996. Mem. ALA, Art Librs. Soc. N.Am. (chmn. mus.-type-of-libr. group nat. chpt. 1979-81, chmn. New Orleans 1980, nominating com. 1980, 84, Wittenborn awards com. 1981, 90, v.p., pres.-elect 1987-88, pres. 1988-89, past pres. 1989-90, chmn. N.Am. art libr. resources com. 1991-93, search com. new exec. dir. 1993-94. chmn. fin. com. 1996-98, presenter numerous papers, chmn. nominating com. 1999-2000, co-chair conf. program com. 1999-2000), Soc. Am. Archivists, Midwest Mus. Conf. (co-chmn. program com. ann. meeting 1982), Spl. Librs. Assn., Rsch. Librs. Group (shares exec. group 1996-98, shares participation com. 1997-99). Office: Cleve Mus of Art 11150 East Blvd Cleveland OH 44106-1711 E-mail: abid@cma-oh.org.

ABITZ, JAMES H. religious organization executive; BSBA, U. Wis., 1967. Dir. bond investments Aid Assn. Lutherans, Appleton, Wis., 1967-81, asst. v.p. bond investments, 1981-82, 2d v.p. bond investments, 1982, 2d v.p. securities, 1983-87, v.p. securities, 1987-97, sr. v.p. capital mgmt. corp. investment dept., 1997-99, chief investment officer, 1999—. Vol. Fox Vly. Luth. H.S. Found.; bd. dirs. Luther Haven Retirement Cmty. Office: Aid Assn Lutherans 4321 N Ballard Rd Appleton WI 54919-0001

ABLE, WARREN WALTER, natural resource company executive, physician; b. Seymour, Ind., Mar. 3, 1932; s. Walter Cudwith and Edith (Harmon) A.; m. Joan Graham, May 6, 1956; children: Susan, Nancy, Cynthia, Wally. AB, Ind. U., 1953, MD, 1956, JD, 1968. Bar: Ind. 1968. Intern Indpls. Gen. Hosp., 1956-57; surgeon USPHS, 1957-59; pres. Able Ventures, Inc., Columbus, Ind., 1968—. Bd. dirs. Salin Bank & Trust. Editor: Lawyer's Medical Cyclopedia, 1967-68. Bd. dirs. Bartholomew Consol. Sch. Corp., Columbus, 1970-74; trustee Christian Theol. Sem., 1991—. Mem. AMA, Ind. Med. Soc., ABA, Ind. Bar Soc., Nat. Benevolent Assn. (bd. dirs. 1983-90). Democrat. Mem. Disciples of Christ Ch. Avocations: aviation, farming. Home and Office: 4253 E Windsor Ln Columbus IN 47201-9681

ABNEE, A. VICTOR, trade association executive; b. Lexington, Ky., June 12, 1923; s. A. Victor and Irene Sarah (Brogle) A.; m. Doris Heuck, Dec. 28, 1946 (deceased); children: Janice Lee Abnee Williams, A. Victor III. BA, U. Cin., 1948. With U.S. Gypsum Co., Chgo., 1948-63, dir. advt. and promotion, 1961-64; with Gypsum Assn., Evanston, Ill., 1964—, exec. v.p., 1964-83, pres., 1983-88; cons., 1988—. Served to capt. C.E., AUS, 1943-46, PTO. Named Alumna of Yr., U. Cin., 1967, Constrn. Industry Man of Yr. Wall and Ceiling Industries Assn., 1980. Mem. Nat. Assn. Mfrs. (councilman 1983—), Am. Soc. Assn. Execs., Ariz. Econ. Soc. Assn. Execs., Exec. Svc. Corps, Internat. Exec. Svc. Corps., Economic, Ariz., Chgo. Soc. Assn. Execs. (hon. life), Les Cheneaux Islands Assn. (pres. 1986-87), Bohemian Club, Sigma Chi (Significant Sig award 1986). Clubs: Les Cheneaux Yacht (bd. dirs. 1982-85), Foundation (Chgo.) (pres. 1985), University (Chgo.) (pres. 1981-83), Adventurers (Chgo.), University (Evanston) (pres. 1984-85), Skokie Country (Glencoe, Ill.), Skyline Country (Tucson), Gyro Internat. Lodge: Shriners, Masons. Office: Gypsum Assn 1603 Orrington Ave Evanston IL 60201-3841

ABOLINS, MARIS ARVIDS, physics researcher and educator; b. Liepaja, Latvia, Feb. 5, 1938; came to U.S., 1949, naturalized, 1956; s. Arvids Gustavs and Olga Elizabete (Grintals) A.; m. Frances Delano, Dec. 19, 1959 B.S. magna cum laude, U. Wash., 1960; M.S., U. Calif.-San Diego, 1962, Ph.D., 1965. Research asst. U. Calif.-San Diego, 1960-65; physicist Lawrence Berkeley Lab., 1965-68; assoc. prof. physics Mich. State U., East Lansing, 1968-73, prof. physics, 1973—. Cons. U.S. Dept. Energy; sci. assoc. CERN, Geneva, 1976-77; vis. research scientist, Saclay, France, 1977, Fermi Nat. Accelerator Lab., 1990-92, Saclay, France, 1997; mem. tech. adv. com. Argonne Nat. Lab., 1971-72; mem. prep. com. Fermilab, 1978-79; chmn. Fermilab Users' Exec. Com., 1982-83; mem. SSC Users Exec. Com., 1988-91; chmn. bd. dirs. ATLAS Trigger/DAQ Instnl., 1997-99. NSF research grantee, 1971—; Disting. Faculty award 1998. Fellow Am. Phys. Soc. (exec. com. div. particles and fields 1984-86); mem. AAAS, Patria, Phi Beta Kappa, Sigma Xi. Home: 1430 Fairoaks Ct East Lansing MI 48823-1812 Office: Mich State U Dept Physics And Astro East Lansing MI 48824 E-mail: abolins@pa.msu.edu.

ABRAHAM, SPENCER, federal official, former senator; b. Lansing, Mich., June 12, 1952; BA in Social Sci.and Polit. Sci., Mich. State U., 1974; JD, Harvard U., 1979. Asst. prof. law Thomas M. Cooley Law Sch., 1981-83; chmn. Mich. Republican Party, 1983-90; dep. chief of staff to Vice President Dan Quayle, 1990-91; co-chair Nat. Republican Congressional Com., 1991-93; of counsel Canfield, Paddock & Stone, 1993-94; U.S. senator from Mich., 1995-2001; sec. U.S. Dept. Energy, 2001—. Office: US Dept Energy 1000 Independence Ave SW Washington DC 20585*

ABRAHAM, WILLIAM JOHN , JR. lawyer; b. Jan. 17, 1948; s. William John and Constance (Dudley) A.; m. Linda Omeis, Aug. 31, 1968; children: Richard S., Heidi K. BA with honors, U. Ill., 1969; JD magna cum laude, U. Mich., Ann Arbor, 1972. Bar: Wis. 1973, U.S. Supreme Ct. 1975. Jud. clk. U.S. Ct. Appeals (D.C. cir.), Washington, 1972-73; ptnr. Foley & Lardner, Milw., 1973—. Former mem. mgmt. com., former chmn. bus. law dept; bd. dirs. The Vollrath Co., Windway Capital Corp., Phillips Plastics Corp., Sirco, Inc., Park Bank, TransPro, Inc.; lectr. MBA program U. Wis. Mem. Greater Milw. Com. Greater Milw. Open, Children's Hosp. of Milw.; mem. adv. bd. Wis. Policy Rsch. Inst.; past bd. dirs. United Way of Greater Milw., Family Svc. of Milw., Milw. Zool. Soc.; bd. dirs., former chmn. Children's Hosp. Found. Named All-Am. Big 10 Fencing Champion, 1968—69. Mem. ABA, State Bar of Wis. (chmn. legis. com.), Milw. Bar Assn., Barristers, Tripoli Country Club (bd. dirs., pres.), Milw. Athletic Club, Univ. Club, Desert Mountain Country Club. Office: Foley & Lardner 777 E Wisconsin Ave Ste 3800 Milwaukee WI 53202-5367

ABRAHAMSON, SHIRLEY SCHLANGER, state supreme court chief justice; b. N.Y.C., Dec. 17, 1933; d. Leo and Ceil (Sauerteig) Schlanger; m. Seymour Abrahamson, Aug. 26, 1953; 1 son, Daniel Nathan. AB, NYU, 1953; JD, Ind. U., 1956; SJD, U. Wis., 1962. Bar: Ind. 1956, N.Y. 1961, Wis. 1962. Asst. dir. Legis. Drafting Research Fund, Columbia U. Law Sch., 1957-60; since practiced in Madison, Wis., 1962-76; mem. firm LaFollette, Sinykin, Anderson & Abrahamson, 1962-76; justice Supreme Ct. Wis., Madison, 1976-96, chief justice, 1996—; prof. U. Wis. Sch. Law, 1966-92. Bd. visitors Ind. U. Sch. Law, 1972—, U. Miami Sch. Law, 1982-97, U. Chgo. Law Sch., 1988-92, Brigham Young U., Sch. Law, 1986-88, Northwestern U. Law Sch., 1989-94; chmn. Wis. Rhodes Scholarship Com., 1992-95; chmn. nat. adv. com. on ct.-adjudicated and ct.-ordered health care George Washington U. Ctr. Health Policy, Washington, 1993-95; mem. DNA adv. bd. FBI, U.S. Dept. Justice, 1995—; bd. dirs. Inst. Jud. Adminstrn., Inc., NYU Sch. Law; chair Nat. Inst. Justice's Commn. Future DNA Evidence, 1997—. Editor: Constitutions of the United States (National and State) 2 vols, 1962. Mem. study group program of rsch., mental health and the law John D. and Catherine T. MacArthur Found., 1988-96; mem. coun. fund for rsch. on dispute resolution Ford Found., 1987-91; bd. dirs. Wis. Civil Liberties Union, 1968-72; mem. ct. reform adv. panel Internat. Human Rights Law Group Cambodia Project, 1995-97. Mem. ABA (coun., sect. legal edn. and admissions to bar 1976-86, mem. commn. on undergrad. edn. in law and the humanities 1978-79, standing com. on pub. edn. 1991-95, mem. commn. on access to justice/2000 1993—, mem. adv. bd. Ctrl. and East European law initiative 1994—, mem. consortium on legal svcs. and the public 1995—, vice-chair ABA Coalition for Justice 1997—), Wis. Bar Assn., Dane County Bar Assn., 7th Cir. Bar Assn., Nat. Assn. Women Judges, Am. Law Inst. (mem. coun. 1985—). Office: Wis Supreme Ct PO Box 1688 Madison WI 53702-1688*

ABRAMS, GERALD DAVID, physician, educator; b. Detroit, Apr. 27, 1932; s. Arthur and Esther (Kushner) A.; m. Gloria Sandra Turner, June 6, 1954; children— Kathryn, Nancy A.B., Wayne U., 1951; M.D., U. Mich., 1955. Diplomate Am. Bd. Pathology. House officer pathology U. Mich., Ann Arbor, 1955-59, instr. pathology, 1959-60, asst. prof. pathology, 1963-66, assoc. prof., 1966-69, prof., 1969—, dir. anatomic pathology, 1985-89; asst. chief dept. exptl. pathology Walter Reed Army Inst. Research, 1961-62. Dep. med. examiner, Washtenaw County, Mich., 1963— ; cons. physician Ann Arbor VA Hosp., 1970— Served to capt. M.C., U.S. Army, 1961-62 Markle scholar John and Mary Markle Found., 1963-68; recipient Elizabeth Crosby Teaching award U. Mich., 1969, 87, 96, Kaiser-Permanente Teaching award U. Mich., 1978. Mem. AAAS, U.S.-Can. Acad. Pathology, Mich. Soc. Pathologists Office: U Mich Dept Pathology Ann Arbor MI 48109 E-mail: gabrams@umich.edu.

ABRAMS, LEE NORMAN, lawyer; b. Chgo., Feb. 28, 1935; s. Saul E. and Evelyn (Cohen) A.; m. Myrna Parker, Dec. 26, 1965; 1 dau., Elana Shira. AB, U. Mich., 1955, JD, 1957. Bar: Ill. 1957, U.S. Supreme Ct. 1961, U.S. Tax Ct. 1972. Assoc. firm Mayer, Brown, Rowe & Maw and predecessors, Chgo., 1957-66, ptnr., 1966—. Mem. visitors com. U. Mich. Law Sch., 1970—; bd. assocs. Nat. Coll. Edn., Chgo., 1973-80. Recipient Gold medal AICPA, 1958. Mem. ABA (coun. antitrust sect. 1975-77, fin. officer 1977-81, program chair antitrust sect. 1988-91, vice chair antitrust sect. 1991-92, chmn. forum on franchising 1982-85, chmn. antitrust com. sect. bus. law 1995-99), Chgo. Bar Assn. (antitrust law com. 1970-85), Ill. State Bar Assn. (antitrust section coun. 1994-2001), U.S. C. of C. (antitrust and trade regulation com. 1974-80), Briarwood Country Club, Royal and Ancient Golf Club of St. Andrews (Scotland). Office: Mayer Brown Rowe & Maw 190 S La Salle St Ste 3100 Chicago IL 60603-3441

ABRAMS, RONALD LAWRENCE, state legislator; b. Apr. 1952; m. Joanne Abrams; two children. BA, U. Minn.; JD, Harvard U. State rep. Dist. 45A Minn. Ho. of Reps., 1998—, asst. minority leader, 1992-99; atty., 1985—. Mem. Fin. Instn. & Ins. Com., Gen. Legislation Com., Vet. Affairs & Elections Com., Rules & Legis. Adminstrn. Com., Ways & Means & Taxes Coms.; chair tax com. 1999—; spkr. pro tem Minn. Ho. of Reps., 1999—. Address: 100 Constitution Ave Saint Paul MN 55155-1232

ABRAMS, SYLVIA FLECK, religious studies educator; b. Buffalo, Apr. 5, 1942; d. Abraham and Ann (Hanf) Fleck; m. Ronald M. Abrams, June 30, 1963; children: Ruth, Sharon. BA magna cum laude, Western Res. U., 1963, MA, 1964, PhD, 1988; BHL, Cleve. Coll. Jewish Studies, 1976, MHL, 1983; postgrad., U. Haifa, 1975, Yad Va Shem Summer Inst., Hebrew U., 1983. Hebrew tchr. The Temple, 1959-77, Hebrew coord., 1973-77; tchr. Beachwood H.S., 1964-66; tchr. Hebrew and social studies Agnon Sch., Cleve., 1975-77, social studies resource tchr., 1976-77; ednl. dir. Temple Emanu El, 1977-85; asst. dir. Cleve. Bur. Jewish Edn., 1985-92, acting exec. v.p., 1993-94; exec. dir. ednl. svcs. Jewish Edn. Ctr. Cleve., 1994-99; dean Cleve. Coll. Jewish Studies, 1999—. Chmn. ednl. dirs. coun. Cleve. Bd. Jewish Edn., 1982-85. Editor: You and Your Schools, 1972. Appointed to Ohio Coun. Holocaust Edn., 1986; co-chair Cmty. Holocaust Remembrance Com., 1999-2001, bd. dirs. 2001. Recipient Elbert J. Benton award Western Res. U., 1963; Fred and Rose Rosenwasser Bible award Coll. Jewish Studies, 1974; Emmanuel Gamoran Meml. Curriculum award Nat. Assn. Temple Educator, 1978; Samuel Lipson Meml. award Coll. Jewish Studies, 1981, Bingham fellow Case Western Res. U., 1984-86. Mem. ASCD, Nat. Assn. Temple Educators (bd. dirs. 1984-88), Coun. Jewish Edn. (bd. dirs. 1991—, v.p. 1995), Assn. Dirs. Ctrl. Agys. (sec.-treas. 1995-98), Coalition for Advancement of Jewish Edn. (bd. mem. at large 1989-93, chair 1996-2000, bd. dirs. 2000—), Union Am. Hebrew Congregations (Israel curriculum task force), Cleve. Bur. Jewish Edn. (chmn. ednl. dirs. coun. 1982-85), Nat. Coun. Jewish Women (life), Hadassah (life), Phi Beta Kappa. Jewish. Office: Cleve Coll Jewish Studies 26500 Shaker Blvd Cleveland OH 44122-7197

ABRAMSON, EDWARD J. magazine publisher; Publisher Home Mag., N.Y.C., 1989—, Car and Driver, Ann Arbor. Office: Hachette Filipacchi Magazines Inc 1633 Broadway New York NY 10019-6708

ABRAMSON, HANLEY NORMAN, pharmacy educator; b. Detroit, June 10, 1940; s. Frederick Jacob and Lillian (Kampner) A.; m. Young Hee Kim, Aug. 4, 1967; children: Nathaniel, Deborah, Stephen. BS in Pharmacy, Wayne State U., 1962; MS in Pharm. Chemistry, U. Mich., 1963, PhD in Pharm. Chemistry, 1966. Registered pharmacist. Rsch. assoc. The Hebrew U., Jerusalem, 1966-67; asst. prof. Wayne State U., Detroit, 1967-73, assoc. prof., 1973-78, prof., 1978—, chmn. dept. pharm. sci., 1986-95, interim dean Eugene Applebaum Coll. of Pharmacy and Health Scis., 1987—88, assoc. provost, 1991-95, assoc. dean, 1996-99, dep. dean pharmacy, 2000—02. Author numerous published articles in field of medicinal chemistry. Bd. trustees 1st Bapt. Ch. of Oak Park, Mich., 1974-78; deacon Bloomfield Hills (Mich.) Bapt. Ch., 1986-89; dir. Met. Detroit Alliance for Minority Participation, 1994-2000. Recipient rsch. grants Mich. Heart Assn., Detroit, 1967-76, Nat. Cancer Inst., Bethesda, Md., 1982-91. Mem. AAAS, Am. Chem. Soc., Am. Pharm. Assn., Am. Assn. Colls. Pharmacy. Baptist. Avocations: astronomy, numismatics, baseball history, classical music. Home: 5530 Hammersmith Dr West Bloomfield MI 48322-1452 Office: Wayne State U 3607 Applebaum Bldg Detroit MI 48201

ABRAMSON, PAUL ROBERT, political scientist, educator; b. St. Louis, Nov. 28, 1937; s. Harry Benjamin and Hattie Abramson; m. Janet Carolyn Schwartz, Sept. 11, 1966; children— Lee Jacob, Heather Lyn B.A., Washington U., St. Louis, 1959; M.A., U. Calif.-Berkeley, 1961, Ph.D., 1967. Asst. prof. polit. sci. Mich. State U., East Lansing, 1967-71, assoc. prof. polit. sci., 1971-77, prof. polit. sci., 1977—. Lady Davis vis. prof. Hebrew U. Jerusalem, 1994. Author: Generational Change in American Politics, 1975, The Political Socialization of Black Americans, 1977, Political Attitudes in America, 1983; co-author: Change and Continuity in the 1980 Elections, 1982, rev. edit., 1983, Change and Continuity in the 1984 Elections, 1986, rev. edit., 1987, Change and Continuity in the 1988 Elections, 1990, rev. edit., 1991, Change and Continuity in the 1992 Elections, 1994, rev. edit., 1995, Value Change in Global Perspective, 1995, Change and Continuity in the 1996 Elections, 1998, Change and Continuity in the 1996 and 1998 Elections, 1999, Change and Continuity in the 2000 Elections, 2001; contbr. articles to profl. jours. Served to lt. U.S. Army, 1960—62. Woodrow Wilson fellow, 1959-60; Ford Found. faculty research fellow, 1972-73; Fulbright grantee sr. lectr. Hebrew U. of Jerusalem, 1987-88. Mem. Am. Polit. Sci. Assn., Midwest Polit. Sci. Assn., So. Polit. Sci. Assn., Am. Sociol. Assn., Internat. Polit. Sci. Assn., Phi Beta Kappa Home: 2830 Turtlecreek Dr East Lansing MI 48823-6333 Office: Mich State U Dept Polit Sci East Lansing MI 48824-1032 E-mail: abramson@pilot.msu.edu.

ABROMOWITZ, HERMAN I. family physician, occupational medicine physician; m. Joyce Abromowitz; children: Leslie M., David M. MD, Ohio State U., 1958. Clin. prof. Wright State U. Sch. of Medicine. Past pres., v.p. Montgomery County Combined Health Dist. Fellow Am. Acad. of Family Physicians; mem. AMA (bd. trustees 1997, coun. med. svc. 1990-96, exec. com., chair, mem. couns. subcom. on health care rev., svc. and chaimanship reference coms., forum for med. affairs, 1989—), Am. Med. Polit. Action Com., AMA Found. (sec.-treas. 1998-99), Am. Coll. Occupl. and Environtl. Medicine, Ohio State Med. Assn. (county del.), Orgn. of State Med. Assn. Pres. (past pres. 1991). Office: AMA 515 N State St Chicago IL 60610-4325

ABT, JEFFREY, art and art history educator, artist, writer; b. Kansas City, Mo., Feb. 27, 1949; s. Arthur and Lottie (Weinman) A.; m. Mary Kathleen Paquette, July 16, 1972; children: Uriel, Danya. BFA, Drake U., 1971, MFA, 1977. Curator collections Wichita (Kans.) Art Mus., 1977-78; gen. mgr. Billy Hork Galleries, Ltd., Chgo., 1978-80; exhbns. coordinator U. Chgo. Libr., 1980-86; asst. dir. Smart Mus. of Art, U. Chgo., 1986—87, acting dir., 1987—89; assoc. prof. dept. art and art history Wayne State U., Detroit, 1989—, dept. chair, 1989-94, mem. adv. bd. Humanities Ctr., 1993-95. Author: (book) A Museum on the Verge: A Socioeconomic History of the Detroit Institute of Arts, 1882-2000, 2001; exhbn. catalogues The Printer's Craft, 1982, The Book Made Art, 1986; one-man shows include Cliff Dwellers, 1997, Cary Gallery, 1998, Wayne State U., 1999, Worthington Arts Coun. Gallery, 2000; editor ann. Book and Paper Group Am. Inst. for Conservation, 1985-86; editor exhbn. catalogue Up From the Streets: Detroit Art from the Duffy Warhehouse Collection, 2001; mem. editl. bd. Wayne State U. Press, 1990-96, chmn. editl. bd., 1996—; illustrator: Water: Sheba's Story, 1997; contbr. articles and book revs. to profl. jours., chpts. to books and encys. Bd. dirs. Hyde Pk. Jewish Cmty. Ctr., Chgo., 1988-89, Detroit Artists Market, 1994—, sec., 1996-99, pres. and chmn. bd. dirs., 1999-2001; trustee Ragdale Found., Lake Forest, Ill., 1985-96, mem. nat. adv. coun., 1996—; mem. intercultural programs com., 1990-92, libr. adv. com., 1990-96, mem. edn. adv. com., 1992-95, Detroit Inst. Arts; mem. visual arts com. Detroit Festival of the Arts, 1989-92; juror numerous art exhbns., 1986—. Recipient numerous purchase prizes, awards and commns. for artistic work, 1974—; Hebrew Union Coll.-Jewish Inst. Religion fellow, Jerusalem, 1971-72; grantee IMS, NEA, NEH, Rockefeller Archive Ctr., Rockefeller U., Logan Found., Wayne State U. Humanities Ctr., Kaufman Meml. Trust, Woodrow Wilson Nat. Fellowship Found. Mem. Am. Assn. Mus., Coll. Art Assn., Assn. Mus. History (co-founder). Office: Wayne State U Dept Art and Art History 150 Art Bldg Detroit MI 48202 E-mail: j_abt@wayne.edu.

ACHELPOHL, STEVEN EDWARD, lawyer; b. Wichita, Kans., July 15, 1950; s. Ray Edward and Juanita J. (Barnes) A.; m. Shelley R. Kiel (div. Sept. 1987); m. Sara K. Nabity, Nov. 24, 1989; children: Joseph E., Samuel B., Raechel A., Ryan Sullivan, Peter Sullivan, Rebecca Sullivan. BA, U. Nebr., 1972, JD with distinction, 1975. Bar: Nebr. 1975, U.S. Dist. Ct. Nebr. 1975, U.S. Ct. Appeals (8th cir.) 1981. Law clk. hon. Donald R. Ross U.S. Ct. Appeals, Omaha, 1975-77; atty. McGrath, North, O'Mally, Kratz, 1977-80, Dwyer, O'Leary & Martin, Omaha, 1980-83; assoc. Schumacher & Achelpohl, 1983-92, Smith Peterson, Omaha, 1992-93; pvt. practice, 1994—. Dir. Vis. Nurses Assn., Omaha, 1993—, fin. com., 1994—. Democrat. Avocations: golf, baseball. Home: 6420 Underwood Ave Omaha NE 68132-1812 Office: 1823 Harney St Ste 1010 Omaha NE 68102-1900 E-mail: achelpohl@usa.net.*

ACHENBACH, JAN DREWES, engineering educator, scientist; b. Leeuwarden, Netherlands, Aug. 20, 1935; came to U.S., 1959, naturalized, 1978; s. Johannes and Elizabeth (Schipper) A.; m. Marcia Graham Fee, July 15, 1961. Candidate engr., Tech. U. Delft, 1959; PhD, Stanford U., 1962. Preceptor Columbia U., 1962-63; asst. prof. Northwestern U., Evanston, Ill., 1963, assoc. prof., 1966-69, prof. dept. civil engring., 1969—, Walter P. Murphy prof. civil engring., mech. engring. and applied math., 1981—, dir. Ctr. for Quality Engring. and Failure Prevention, 1986—; vis. assoc. prof. U. Calif., San Diego, 1969; vis. prof. Tech. U. Delft, 1970-71; prof. Huazhong Inst. Sci. and Tech., 1981. Mem. at large U.S. Nat. Com. Theoretical and Applied Mechanics, 1972-78, 86—. Author: Wave Propagation in Elastic Solids, 1973, A Theory of Elasticity with Microstructure for Directionally Reinforced Composites, 1975, (with A.K. Gautesen and H. McMaken) Ray Methods for Waves in Elastic Solids, 1982, (with Y. Rajapakse) Solid Mechanics Research for Quantitative Non-Destructive Evaluation, 1987; editor: (with J. Miklowitz) Modern Problems in Elastic Wave Propagation, 1978 (with S.K. Datta and Y.S. Rajapakse) Elastic Waves and Ultrasonic Nondestructive Testing, 1990; editor-in-chief: Wave Motion, 1979—. Recipient award C. Gelderman Found., 1970, C.W. McGraw Rsch. award Am. Soc. Engring. Edn., 1975, Tempo All-Professor Team, Sciences, Chicago Tribune, 1993, Model of Excellence award McDonnell-Douglas, 1996, Disting. Svc. medal Am. Acad. Mechanics, 1997, Prager medal Soc. Engring. Sci., 2001. Fellow AAAS, Am. Acad. Arts Scis., ASME (Timoshenko medal 1992), Acoustical Soc. Am.; mem. IEEE, Royal Dutch Acad. Scis., U.S. Nat. Acad. Scis., U.S. Nat. Acad. Engring., Am. Soc. Nondestructive Testing. Home: 711 Roslyn Ter Evanston IL 60201-1721 Office: Northwestern U Room 324 2137 N Sheridan Catalysis Bldg Evanston IL 60208 E-mail: achenbach@northwestern.edu.

ACHGILL, RALPH KENNETH, retired research scientist; b. Indpls., June 17, 1938; s. Kenneth and Lois Ann (Philips) A.; m. Virginia Ann Swisher, July 21, 1956 (dec. Nov. 1992); children: Kenneth Edward, Douglas Alan, Kerry Wayne, Bridget Marie; m. Diane K. McCauley, Dec. 26, 1993. Student, Purdue U., 1956-60. Rsch. scientist Eli Lilly & Co., Indpls., 1956-93, internat. tech. coord., 1974-93; ret., 1993. Patentee in field. Mem. Masons (past master), Optimist Club (charter pres.). Republican. Avocation: philatelic dealer and auctioneer. Home: PO Box 6508 Lafayette IN 47903-6508 E-mail: rka@rkacovers.com.

ACKER, ANN, lawyer; b. Chgo., July 21, 1948; BA, St. Mary's Coll.; JD, Loyola U. Bar: Ill. 1973. Mem. Chapman and Cutler, Chgo. Office: Chapman and Cutler 111 W Monroe St Ste 1700 Chicago IL 60603-4006

ACKER, FREDERICK GEORGE, lawyer; b. Defiance, Ohio, May 7, 1934; s. Julius William and Orah Louise (Dowler) A.; m. Cynthia Ann Wayne, Dec. 1, 1962; children: Frederick Wayne, Mary Katherine, Richard Hoghton, Jennifer Ruth. Student, Ind. U., 1952-54; BA, Valparaiso U., 1956; MA, Harvard U., 1957, JD, 1961; postgrad., U. Manchester (Eng.), 1957-58. Bar: Ill. 1961, Ind. 1961. Ptnr. Winston & Strawn, Chgo.,

1961-88, McDermott, Will & Emery, Chgo., 1988—. Co-chmn. Joint Prin. and Income Act. com., Chgo., 1976-81. Co-author: (portfolio) Generation-Skipping Tax, 1991; contbr. articles to profl. jours. Bd. dirs. Max McGraw Wildlife Found., Dundee, Ill., 1984—, chmn., pres. 1997-2001; trustee L.S. Wood Ednl. Trust, Chgo., 1975—; trustee Ill. chpt. The Nature Conservancy, Chgo., 1981-90, chmn., 1986-90. Danforth Found. fellow, 1956; Fulbright scholar, 1957. Fellow Am. Coll. Trust and Estate Counsel; mem. ABA, Ill. Bar Assn., Trout Unlimited, Fulbright Assn. (bd. dirs. 1994-2000, pres. 2000), Met. Chgo. Club, Anglers Club, Chgo. Farmers Club. Lutheran. Avocations: hunting, fishing. Home: 543 N Madison St Hinsdale IL 60521-3213 Office: McDermott Will & Emery 227 W Monroe St Ste 3100 Chicago IL 60606-5096

ACKERMAN, EUGENE, biophysics educator; b. Bklyn., July 8, 1920; s. Saul Benton and Dorothy (Salwen) A.; m. Dorothy Hopkirk, June 5, 1943; children— Francis H., Emmanuel T., Amy R. Ackerman de Canésie. B.A., Swarthmore Coll., 1941; Sc.M., Brown U., 1943; Ph.D., U. Wis., 1949; postgrad., U. Pa., 1949-51, fellow, 1957-58. Instr. Brown U., 1943; from asst. prof. to prof. biophysics Pa. State U., 1951-60; mem. faculty U. Minn. Mayo Grad. Sch. Medicine, 1960-67, prof. biophysics, 1965-91, Hill Family Found. prof. biomed. computing, prof. biometry also computer scis. Mpls., 1967-79, prof. dept. lab. medicine and pathology, 1969-91, prof. emeritus, 1991—, dir. div. health computer sci., 1969-79; staff cons. biophysics Mayo Found. and Mayo Clinic, 1960-67; dir. computer facility Mayo Found., 1964-65. Cons. bioacoustics USAF, 1957-62; mem. epidemiology and biometry tng. com. NIH, 1963-67, spl. study sect. ultrasonic applications, 1965-67, spl. study sect. lab. med. scis., 1967-69, computer and biomath. sci. study sect., 1969-73; dir. nat. resource for simulation of stochastic micropopulation models, 1983-90 Author: Biophysical Science, 1962, (with L. Ellis and L. Williams), 2d edit., 1979; (with L. Gatewood) Math Models in the Health Sciences, 1979, (with L. Elveback and J. Fox) Infectious Disease: Simulation of Epidemics and Vaccination Strategies, 1984; editor Biophys. Jour., 1983-87; also articles, tech. reports, chpts. in books. Rsch. grantee Am. Cancer Soc., 1953-56, NSF, 1958-64, NIH, 1954-90 Mem. Biophys. Soc., Am. Physiol. Soc., Assn. Computing Machinery, IEEE, Phi Beta Kappa, Sigma Xi, Gamma Alpha. Mem. Soc. of Friends. Home: 11301 Park Ridge Dr W Minnetonka MN 55305-2551 Office: U Minn Health Ctr Box 511 MMC 420 Delaware St SE Minneapolis MN 55455-0374 E-mail: acker004@tc.vmn.edu.

ACKERMAN, F. KENNETH, JR. health facility administrator; b. Mansfield, Ohio, Apr. 2, 1939; m. Patricia Ackerman, Dec. 17, 1960; children: Franklin Kenneth III, Robert Christian, Peter Jonathan. BS in Biology, Denison U., 1961; MHA, U. Mich., 1963. Adminstrv. resident Henry Ford Hosp., Detroit, 1963-64; from asst. adminstrv. dir. to pres. Geisinger Med. Ctr., Danville, Pa., 1964-94; sr. v.p. adminstrv. affairs Geisinger Found., 1981-94; prin. assoc. McManis Assocs., Washington, 1994-97, v.p., 1997-2001; ptnr., sr. cons. Clark/Bardes Consulting-Healthcare Group, Mpls., 2001—02, pres., 2002—. Bd. dirs. Pa. Millers Mut. Ins. Co., Wilkes-Barre. Mem. Nat. Adv. Com. on Rural Health, Washington, 1988—94; bd. trustees Suburban Hosp. and Health Sys., Bethesda, Md., 1995—2000; Bd. dirs. Nat. Com. for Quality Healthcare, Washington, 1985—, Pa. Chamber of Bus. and Industry, Harrisburg, 1977—90, Healthcare R&D Inst., Pensacola, Fla., 1990—95. Recipient Adminstr. Yr. award Am. Group Practice Assn., 1988, Polit. Action Com. award Hosp. Assn. Pa., 1982, 85, 86, 88, 90, 91, Nat. Merit award Duke U. Hosp. and Health Adminstrn. Alumni Assn., 1991, Harry Harwick award for Excellence, 1994, Article of Yr. award Am. Coll. Med. Practice Execs., 1994. Mem. Am. Coll. Healthcare Execs. (regents adv. coun. 1989—, Hudgens' Meml. Award 1975). Office: Clark/Bardes Consulting-Healthcare Group Ste 370 608 2d Ave S Minneapolis MN 55402 Fax: (612) 339-2569. E-mail: ken.ackerman@clarkbardes.com.

ACKERMAN, JOHN HENRY, health services consultant, physician; b. Fond du Lac, Wis., Feb. 27, 1925; s. Henry Theodore and Clara Frances (Voss) A.; m. Eugenia Ellen Mulligan, May 22, 1948 (dec. 1996); children: H. John, Mary, Lisa, Paul. Student, Cornell U., 1943-44, Ind. U., 1944; M.D., Marquette U., 1948; M.P.H., Johns Hopkins U., 1955. Intern St. Agnes Hosp., Fond du Lac, 1948-49; family practice medicine Clarksville, Iowa, 1949-51; commd. officer USPHS, 1951-70; dep. chief tng. program Center Disease Control, Atlanta, 1970, ret. as capt., 1970; dep. dir. Ohio Dept. Health, Columbus, 1970-75, dir., 1975-83; utilization rev. cons. Grant Med. Ctr., Columbus, Ohio, 1985-88; med. dir. Ohio Health Choice Plan, 1985-88; dir. med. affairs CRT, Inc., 1988-92; med. dir. Co. Rehab. Svcs.; med. cons. EBMC, 1991-95. Clin. prof. preventive medicine Ohio State U.; cons. WHO; med. cons. EBMC, Inc., ACMS, Inc., 1989-95. Served with AUS, 1943-46. Fellow APHA, Am. Coll. Preventive Medicine, Royal Soc. Health; mem. Commd. Officers Assn., N.Y. Acad. Sci., Ohio Med. Assn., Columbus Acad. Medicine, Alpha Kappa Kappa. Roman Catholic. Home: 4183 Reedbury Ln Columbus OH 43220-3946 E-mail: RDMassie@aol.com.

ACKERS, GARY KEITH, biophysical chemistry educator, researcher; b. Dodge City, Kans., Oct. 25, 1939; s. Leo Finley and Mabel Ida (Hostetler) A.; children: Lisa, Sandra, Keith. BS in Chemistry and Math., Harding Coll., Searcy, Ark., 1961; PhD in Physiol. Chemistry, Johns Hopkins U., 1964. Instr. physiol. chemistry Johns Hopkins U. Sch. Medicine, Balt., 1965-66, prof. biology and biophysics, 1977-89, dir. Inst. Biophys. Rsch., 1987-89; asst. prof. biochemistry U. Va. Sch. Medicine, Charlottesville, 1966-67, assoc. prof., 1967-72, prof. biochemistry and biophysics, 1972-77; prof. biochemistry and molecular biophysics Washington U., St. Louis, 1989—, head dept. biochemistry and molecular biophysics, 1989-96. Instr. physiology Marine Biol. Labs., Woods Hole, Mass., 1974-76; chmn. Gordon Conf. on Proteins, 1985; disting. lectr. Red Cell Club, 1997—. Mem. editorial bd. Analytical Biochemistry, 1970-79, Biophys. Chemistry, 1973-78, Proteins, Structures, Functional Genetics, 1991—; contbr. over 150 articles to sci. jours. Guggenheim fellow, 1972-73; recipient NIH Merit award, 1987. Fellow Biophys. Soc. (coun. 1972-74, 80-83, pres. 1984-85, Cole rsch. award 1994); mem. Am. Chem. Soc. (program chair biol. chem. divsn. 1994), Am. Soc. Biochem. Molecular Biology. Office: Washington U Med Sch Dept Biochem and Molecular Biophysics 660 S Euclid Ave Saint Louis MO 63110-1010

ACKLIE, DUANE WILLIAM, transportation company executive; s. William R. and Irene (Bove) A.; m. Phyllis Ann Osborn, Dec. 19, 1933; children: Dodie Acklie Nakajima, Laura Acklie Schumacher, Holly Acklie Ostergard. BS, U. Nebr., 1953, LLB, 1955, JD, 1959; cert., Army Intelligence Ctr., Balt., 1956; LLD (hon.), Nebr. Wesleyan U., 1988. Lt., spl. agt. Counter Intelligence Corps—Investigations, Europe, 1955-57; pvt. practice Acklie & Peterson, 1958-71; pres., chief exec. officer Crete Carrier Corp., Lincoln, Nebr., 1971-92, chmn., 1992—. Mem. Nebr. State Highway Commn., 1981—, State of Nebr. Econ. Devel. Commn., 1986-88; bd. dirs. Exec. Com. Interstate Carriers Conf., Alexandria, Va.; bd. dirs., Nebr. State v.p. Am. Trucking Assns.; Nebr. adv. bd. Peoples Natural Gas, Omaha. Mem. exec. com. Nebr. State Rep. Party, 1963—, nat. committeeman, 1984—; chmn. bd., chmn. exec. com. Lincoln Found. Inc., 1986-90; vice chair RNC, 1989—; adv. coun. U. Nebr.-Lincoln Food Processing Ctr., 1988-90; world bd. govs. USO, 1987—. Recipient Disting. Alumnus award U. Nebr., Lincoln, 1985, Outstanding Bus. Leader award U. Nebr. Coll. Bus., 1986, Outstanding Alumnus award Norfolk (Nebr.) Jr. Coll., 1987; named Entrepreneur of the Yr. U. Nebr. Coll. Bus. Adminstrn. Mem. ABA, Nebr. Bar Assn., Lincoln Bar Assn., Transp. Lawyers Assn., Chief Execs. Orgn., World Bus. Council Inc. Republican. Methodist. Office: Crete Carrier Corp PO Box 81228 Lincoln NE 68501-1228

ADAIR, WENDELL HINTON, JR. lawyer; b. Ft. Benning, Ga., Mar. 17, 1944; s. Wendell H. Sr. and Jacqueline (Moore) A.; children: Elizabeth Carroll, John Michael, Benjamin David. BA, Emory U., 1966, postgrad., 1966-67; JD, U. Chgo., 1969. Bar: Ill. 1969. Assoc. Ross, Hardies, O'Keefe, Babcock & Parsons, Chgo., 1969-72; ptnr. Mayer, Brown & Platt, 1972-89, McDermott, Will & Emery, Chgo., 1989—. Bd. dirs. ARC Mid-Am. chpt. 1991—, Chgo. Opera Theatre, 1993—; mem. Evanston Zoning Amendment Com., 1980-83. Mem. ABA (bus. sect., natural resources sect., pub. utilities sect.), Ill. Bar Assn., Fed. Energy Bar Assn. (bd. dirs. 1985-87, program chmn. 1990-91), Am. Gas Assn. (bd. dirs. legal sect. 1986-89), Turnaround Mgmt. Assn. (program and publs. coms.). Republican. Club: Econ. (Chgo.), Chicago. Home: 5682 Sawyer Rd Sawyer MI 49125-9249 Office: McDermott Will & Emery 227 W Monroe St Ste 3100 Chicago IL 60606-5096

ADAM, PATRICIA ANN, legislative aide; b. Mobridge, S.D., May 22, 1936; d. George T. and Madge Mickelson; m. Thomas C. Adam, Aug. 28, 1959; children: Kathleen Bykowski, Paula Adam-Burchill, Karlton Adam, Sarah Adam Axtman. BA in Speech Pathology, U. S.D., 1958, MA in Speech Pathology, 1961. Dir. 1st Nat. Bank, Selby, S.D.; sec. S.D. State Senate. Bd. dirs. Cmty. 1st Bancshares. Bd. dirs. AAUW Nursery Sch., 1965—, YMCA, Children's Care Hosp. and Sch., Sioux Falls, S.D., U. S.D. Found., Vermillion, Oahe Found., S.D., Pierre Sch. Found.; pres. Pierre Sch. Bd., 1977-86; bd. dirs. Sch. Bd. Assn., pres.; mem. City of Pierre Pk. and Recreation Bd.; pres. bd. trustees S.D. State Hist. Soc. Office: State Capitol Pierre SD 57501

ADAMAK, M. JEANELLE, broadcast executive; b. Odessa, Tex., Aug. 18, 1952; d. E.W. and Jo Martin; m. Russell J. Adamak, July 19, 1973; children: Aaron, Ashley. BS in Mgmt./Telecom., Ind. Wesleyan U., 1995. Dir. devel. Odessa Coll., 1986-90; exec. v.p. WFYI TelePlex, Indpls., 1990—. Chair Exec. Women's Leadership Program, Indpls., 1994-96, Vol. Action Ctr. Com., Indpls., 1996—. Mem. Vol. Action Ctr., United Way, 1996-98; bd. dirs. YWCA, Indpls., 1995-99, Cmty. Svc. Coun.-United Way, Indpls., 1996—, Prevent Blindness, Ind., 1996-2000. Recipient Devel. award So. Ednl. Comm. Assn., 1988. Office: WFYI TelePlex 1401 N Meridian St Indianapolis IN 46202-2304 E-mail: jadamak@wfyi.org.

ADAMLE, MIKE, sports commentator; b. Oct. 4, 1949; Grad., Northwestern U., 1971. Fullback Kansas City Chiefs, 1971-72, N.Y. Jets, 1973-74, Chgo. Bears, 1975-77; host SportsWorld, reporter NBC Sports, 1977-83; sports anchor WLS TV, Chgo., 1983-89; host Am. Gladiators, 1989-95; studio host ESPN, 1996-98; sports edit. WMAQ TV, Chgo., 1998—. Office: WMAQ 454 N Columbus Dr Fl 1 Chicago IL 60611-5555*

ADAMO, KENNETH R. lawyer; b. Staten Island, N.Y., Sept. 27, 1950; BS, ChE, Rensselaer Polytech. Inst., 1972; JD, Union U., Albany, 1975; LLM, John Marshall Law Sch., 1989. Bar: Ill. 1975, N.Y. 1976, Ohio 1984, Tex. 1988, U.S. Patent and Trademark Office. Ptnr. Jones, Day, Reavis & Pogue, Cleve. Mem. Internat. Bar Assn. Office: Jones Day Reavis & Pogue N Point 901 Lakeside Ave Cleveland OH 44114

ADAMS, ALBERT WILLIE, JR. lubrication company executive; b. Detroit, Nov. 22, 1948; s. Albert Willie and Goldie Inez (Davis) A.; m. Linda Maureen North, Sept. 2, 1972; children— Nichole Leahna, Albert Willie III, Melanie Rachel, Kimberly Monet. BA in Elem. Edn., Harris Tchrs. Coll., St. Louis, 1970; MBA, So. Ill. U., Edwardsville, 1974. Recreation leader City of St. Louis, 1967-69; recreation supr. Mo. Hills Home for Boys, 1969-70; tchr. spl. edn. St. Louis Bd. Edn., 1968-71; personnel asst. Equal Opportunity Adminstrn., Seven-Up Co., St. Louis, 1971-75, corporate equal opportunity adminstr., 1975-80, sr. employee relations adminstr., 1980-81, personnel mgr., 1981-82, mgr. indsl. relations, 1982-83, mgr. personnel programs and services, 1983-85, mgr. personnel ops., 1985-87; regional mgr. A. L. Williams, St. Louis, 1987-89; staff v.p. human resources Citicorp Mortgage Inc., 1989-91; v.p. human resources and quality Lincoln Indsl., Pentair Co., 1991—. Residence counselor Magdala Found., halfway house, 1971-77 Community-at-large mem. Affirmative Action Commn. Minorities St. Louis U., 1974-76; chmn. St. Louis corp. solicitation United Negro Coll. Fund, 1972; mem. adv. com. Statewide Job Placement Svc., 1979-84, Project Search, 1980-85; mem. Family and Children's Svc. N.W. Community Adv. Coun., 1982-85; mem. allocations com. United Way, 1985-90, bd. dirs., 1989-93; apptd. commr. St. Louis Civil Rights Enforcement Agy., 1988; bd. dirs. Vanderschmidt Sch., 1989-98, Habitat for Humanity, St. Louis, 1996-98, Pentair Found., 1998-01, Gateway Eagles of Mo., 2000--; statewide adv. bd. Internat. Student Internship, 2001--. U.S. Naval Acad. nominee, 1965; St. Louis Post-Dispatch scholar, 1971; Parsons-Blewett Meml. scholar tchrs., 1971; recipient Jr. Achievement scholarship award, 1966, St. Louis Sales and Mktg. Execs. award, 1966, St. Louis Sentinel achiever award, 1980 Mem.: AAIM (bd. dirs. 1998—2001), Assn. MBA Execs., St. Louis Indsl. Rels. Assn., Kappa Alpha Psi. Baptist. Home: 2331 Albion Pl Saint Louis MO 63104-2524

ADAMS, CHARLES FRANCIS, advertising and real estate executive; b. Detroit, Sept. 26, 1927; s. James R. and Bertha C. (DeChant) A.; m. Helen R. Harrell, Nov. 12, 1949; children: Charles Francis, Amy Ann, James Randolph, Patricia Duncan. BA, U. Mich., 1948; postgrad., U. Calif., Berkeley, 1949. With D'Arcy-MacManus & Masius, Inc., 1947-80, exec. v.p., dir., 1970-76, pres., chief operating officer, 1976-80; pres. Adams Enterprises, 1971—; exec. v.p., dir. Washington Office, Am. Assn. Advt. Agys., 1980-84. Chmn., chief exec. officer Wajim Corp., Detroit; past mem. steering com. Nat. Advt. Rev. Bd.; mem. mktg. com. U.S. Info. Agy.; pres. Internat. Visitors Ctr. of the Bay Area, 1988-89. Author: Common Sense in Advertising, 1965, Heroes of the Golden Gate, 1987, California of the Year 2000, 1992, The Magnificent Rogues, 1999. Past chmn. exec. com. Oakland U. Mem. Am. Assn. Advt. Agys. (dir., mem. govt. relations com.), Advt. Fedn. Am. (past dir.), Nat. Outdoor Advt. Bur. (past chmn.), Carmel Valley Ranch Club (Calif.), Nat. Golf Links Am. Club (Southampton, L.I.), Olympic Club, The Family Club, Theta Chi, Alpha Delta Sigma (hon.) Republican. Roman Catholic. Home: 2240 Hyde St # 5 San Francisco CA 94109-1509 Office: 10 W Long Lake Rd Bloomfield Hills MI 48304-2707

ADAMS, CHARLES GILCHRIST, pastor; b. Detroit, Dec. 13, 1936; Student, Fisk U., 1954-56; BA with honors, U. Mich., 1958; MDiv. with honors, Harvard U., 1964; DD (hon.), Birmingham Bapt. Coll., 1976, Shaw Coll., Detroit, 1980, Morris Coll., 1980, Morehouse Coll., 1984; LHD (hon.), Marygrove Coll., 1985; LLD (hon.), Dillard U., 1985; D Hum (hon.), U. Mich., 1986; DD (hon.), Edward Waters Coll., 1987; LHD (hon.), Kalamazoo Coll., 1994. Pastor Concord Bapt. Ch., Boston, 1962-69, Hartford Meml. Bapt. Ch., Detroit, 1970—. Instr. theology Boston U., Andover Newton Sch. Theology, Ctrl. Bapt. Sem., Kansas City, Iliff Sch. Theology, Denver; invited speaker UN, 1989, World Congress of Bapt. World Alliance, Seoul, Korea, 1990, 7th Gen. assembly of World Coun. Chs., Canberra, Australia, 1991, Evian, France, 1992; conf. preacher Hampton (Va.) U. Ministers Conf., 1993-94. Doctoral fellow Union Theol. Sem., N.Y.C.; named One of Ebony's Top 100 Influential Black Ams., 1990-94, One of 15 Greatest Black Preachers, 1993-94. Office: Hartford Memorial Baptist Church 18700 James Couzens Hwy Detroit MI 48235-2573

ADAMS, EDMUND JOHN, lawyer; b. Lansing, Mich., June 6, 1938; s. John Edmund and Helen Kathryn (Pavlick) A.; m. Mary Louise Riegler, Aug. 11, 1962. BA, Xavier U., 1960; LLB, U. Notre Dame, 1963. Bar: Ohio 1963. Assoc. Paxton & Seasongood, Cin., 1965-70, Frost & Jacobs (now Frost Brown Todd), 1970-71, ptnr., 1971-2000, mem. exec. com., 1985-88, 90-96, mng. ptnr., 1994-96, chmn., 1996-2000, of counsel, 2000—. Author: Catholic Trails West, The Founding Catholic Families of Pennsylvania, Vol. 1, 1988, Vol. 2, 1989. Mem. Ohio Bd. Regents, 1999—, sec., 2002-; trustee Jewish Hosp., 1995-2001, Cin. Internat. Visitors Ctr., 1989-91, Japan Am. Soc. Greater Cin., 1988-96, Ursuline Acad., 1992-94; trustee S.W. Ohio Regional Transit Authority, 1980-91, pres., 1983, 88; trustee Sister Cities Assn. Greater Cin., 1984-91, chmn., 1984-90; trustee Greater Cin. Ctr. for Econ. Edn., 1996—, mem. exec. com., 1999-, vice chmn., 2002-; chmn. USTA Nat. Father and Son Clay Ct. Tennis Championships, 1990-92; mem. Hamilton County Rep. Exec. Com., 1982—; mem. Hamilton County Rep. Fin. Com., 1990—, chmn., 1992-94; mem. Hamilton County Rep. Ctrl. Com., 2000—. 1st lt. U.S. Army, 1963-65. Fellow Am. Coll. Bankruptcy; mem. ABA, Ohio Bar Assn., Cin. Bar Assn., Cin. Tennis Club (trustee 1990-98, treas. 1992-93, sec. 1994-95, pres. 1996-98, historian 2001—), Queen City Club, Met. Club. (bd. dirs. 1996-2001). Roman Catholic. Home: 3210 Columbia Pky Cincinnati OH 45226-1042 Office: Frost Brown Todd 2500 PNC Ctr 201 E 5th St Cincinnati OH 45202-4182 E-mail: adamschoice@fuse.net., eadams@fbtlaw.com.

ADAMS, JAMES S. accountant, treasurer, finance executive; b. Aug. 19, 1959; BS in Gen. Mgmt., Purdue U. CPA, Ind.; registered fin. prin.; gen. securities registered rep. Various fin. mgmt. positions Firstmark Corp.; v.p., controller Conseco, Inc., 1986-97, chief acctg. officer, 1997—. Fellow Life Mgmt. Inst.; mem. Ind. CPA Soc., Fin. Exec. Inst. Office: Conseco Inc 11825 N Pennsylvania St Carmel IN 46032-4604

ADAMS, JOHN MARSHALL, lawyer; b. Columbus, Ohio, Dec. 6, 1930; s. H.F. and Ada Margaret (Gregg) A.; m. Janet Hawk, June 28, 1952; children: John Marshall, Susan Lynn, William Alfred. B.A., Ohio State U., 1952; J.D. summa cum laude, 1954. Bar: Ohio 1954. Mem. Cowan & Adams, Columbus, 1954-55; asst. city atty. City of Columbus, 1955-56; mem. Knepper, White, Richards & Miller, 1956-63; practiced in Columbus, 1963-74; ptnr. Porter, Wright, Morris & Arthur, 1975-91, of counsel, 1992—. Vice chmn. Ohio Bar Liability Ins. Co., 1990-93, chmn., 1994-2002, chair emeritus, 2002-; trustee Ohio Legal Ctr. Inst., 1976-81, Ohio Lawpac, 1980-89. Fellow Am. Coll. Trial Lawyers, Am. Bar Found., Ohio Bar Found. (trustee 1975-84); mem. ABA, Ohio State Bar Assn. (exec. com. 1975-80, pres. 1978-79), Columbus Bar Assn. (bd. govs. 1970-76, pres. 1974-75), Lawyers Club (pres. 1968-69, 6th cir. jud. conf. life mem., Ohio Bar medal 1994), Order of Coif, Grey Oaks Country Club (Naples, Fla.), Scioto Country Club, Masons, Delta Upsilon, Phi Delta Phi. Republican. Home: 2535 Canterbury Rd Columbus OH 43221-3081 Office: 41 S High St Columbus OH 43215-6101

ADAMS, JOHN STEPHEN, geography educator; b. Mpls., Sept. 7, 1938; s. Edward Francis and Ellen Cecilia (Cullen) A.; m. Judith Estelle Nielsen, Sept. 1, 1962; children: John D., Ellen Anastasia, Martin Francis, David Joseph Cullen. BA, U. St. Thomas, 1960; MA, U. Minn., 1962, PhD, 1966. Rsch. asst., rsch. fellow Upper Midwest Econ. Study, Mpls., 1960-64; teaching asst. dept. geography U. Minn., 1964-66, assoc. prof., then prof. geography, 1970—, now prof. geography, planning and pub. affairs, dir. Sch. Pub. Affairs and H.H. Humphrey Inst. Pub. Affairs, 1976-79, chmn. dept. geography, 1981-84, 92-93, 99—, Fesler-Lampert prof. Urban and Regional Affairs; asst. prof. geography Pa. State U., State College, 1966-70. Rsch. asst. N. Star Rsch. and Devel., Inc., Mpls., 1964; Fulbright prof. geog. Econ. U. Vienna, Austria, 1975-76; vis. prof. geography U. Wash., Seattle, 1979; vis. prof. geography and environ. engring. U.S. Mil. Acad., West Point, N.Y., 1990-91; vis. prof. geography and earth scis. Marie Curie-Sklodowska U., Lublin, Poland, 1997; mem. nat. adv. com. H.H. Humphrey N.-S. Fellowship Program, Inst. Internat. Edn., N.Y.C., 1979-81, coord. at U. Minn., 1981-87, 89-90; econ. geographer in residence Bank of Am., San Francisco, 1980-81; mem. exec. com. Nat. Com. Rsch. on 1980 census Social Sci. Rsch. Coun., N.Y.C., 1981-88; bd. dirs. Consortium of Social Sci. Assns., Washington, 1983-85, FVB Energy Inc.; mem. geography panel Coun. for Internat. Exchange of Scholars, Washington, 1983-85, chair, 1986, mem. Soviet-Eastern European panel, 1990-93; mem. geography div. adv. com. U.S. Bur. Census, Washington, 1985; Bush sabbatical fellow, 1987-88, Fulbright prof. geography Moscow State U., 1988. Author: (with R. Abler and P. Gould) Spatial Organization, 1971, (with Abler and K. Lee) A Comparative Atlas of America's Great Cities, 1976 (Geog. Soc. Chgo. award 1977), Housing America in the 1980s, 1987); editor: Contemporary Metropolitan America, 4 vols., 1976, Urban Policy Making and Metropolitan Dynamics, 1976, (with B. Van Drasek) Minneapolis-St. Paul People, Place and Public Life, 1993; mem. editl. bd. Geographia Polonica, Govt. and Policy, Urban Geography, Post-Soviet Geography and Economics. Bd. dirs. Newman Ctr., Mpls., 1983—88, 1994—2002. Sr. Scientist Rsch. fellow NSF, Berkeley, Calif., 1980-81. Mem. Assn. Am. Geographers (nat. sec. 1975-78, v.p. 1981-82, pres. 1982-83, honors award 1988, editorial bd. Annals), Nat. Coun. Geog. Edn., Mpls. Com. Fgn. Rels. Democrat. Roman Catholic. Avocations: photography, numismatics, gardening. Home: 2611 W 49th St Minneapolis MN 55410-1902 Office: U Minn Dept Geography 267 19th Ave S Minneapolis MN 55455-0499 E-mail: adams004@umn.edu.

ADAMS, KENT J. state legislator; b. Bremen, Ind., Aug. 6, 1936; m. Nancy Adams. BS, Manchester Coll.; MA, Ball State U.; EdD, Walden U. Trustee German Twp. Marshall County, 1978-88; spl. agt. FBI; state rep. Dist. 22, 1988-92; mem. pub. health, urban affairs and ways and means coms. Ind. Ho. Reps.; mem. Ind. Senate from dist. 9, 1992—; mem. agrl. and small bus. edn. Ind. Senate; environ. affairs coms. Ind. State Senate; mem. Ind. state pension mgmt. oversight commn. Ind. Senate, gov.'s state adv. com. on child mental health; dir. fin. Warsaw Cmty. Sch.; state police trooper; pub. sch. adminstr. Pvt. cons. Dalton Foundries Inc.; mem. Warsaw Cmty. Develop Corp. Mem. Ind. Twp. Trustees Assn., Ind. Assn. Pub. Sch. Supts., Ins. Assn. Sch. Bus. Offcls., Bashor Home Bd. Home: 1303 Lakewood Hills Dr Warsaw IN 46580-2163

ADAMS, MILLIE B. judge; b. Atok, Tenn., Aug. 30, 1947; 1 child. BS, U. Mo., 1976; MA, Webster U., 1984. Acctg. clk. City of St. Louis, 1971-75; asst. Mo. Ct. Appeals, St. Louis, 1976-81, asst. cir. exec., 1981—, judge, 1997—. Office: US Court & Custom House 1114 Market St Rm 611 Saint Louis MO 63101-2042

ADAMS, WILLIAM JOHNSTON, financial and tax consultant; b. Detroit, Nov. 24, 1934; s. William Montgomery and Sara Emogene (Johnston) A.; m. Lynn Laviolette, Aug. 24, 1957 (div. Sept. 1976); 1 child, William David; m. Donna Wolcott, Apr. 24, 1977. BBA, U. Mich., 1957, MBA, 1958. CPA, Mich. Staff acct. Arthur Andersen & Co., Detroit, 1958-62, tax mgr., 1962-70, tax ptnr., 1970-90, corp. dir., fin. and tax cons., 1990—. Bd. dirs. Detroit Exec. Svc. Corps., chmn., 2001—. Trustee, sec., treas., pres. Grosse Pointe (Mich.) Pub. Sch., 1969-72; chmn. Greater Detroit Fgn. Trade Zone, Inc., 1983—; mem. adv. bd. Paton Fund, 1988-96; bd. dirs. Civic Searchlight, Detroit, 1985—, 2d v.p., 1989-92, pres., 1992—; chmn. bd. for advancement of acctg. edn. U. Mich. Bus. Sch., 1996—. Named Outstanding Young Man of Yr. Grosse Pointe Jaycees, 1970; named to Pres.' Club U. Mich., Ann Arbor, 1975. Mem. AICPA, Mich. Assn. CPAs (bd. dirs. 1997-2000, Disting. Svc. award 1992), Tappan Soc., Detroit Regional Yachting Assn. (exec. com. 1993—, commodore 1996-97), Detroit Club (bd. dirs. 1998-2001), Detroit Boat Club (bd. dirs., treas. 1985-87, com. 1986), Detroit Yacht Club. Congregationalist. Home: 1453 Iroquois St Detroit MI 48214-2715

ADAMSON, JAMES B. business executive; b. 1948; Various positions The Gap, 1975-84; exec. v.p. mktg. Revco Inc., 1984-91; various positions, CEO Burger King Corp., 1991-95; chmn., pres., CEO Advantica Restaurant Group, Spartanburg, S.C., 1995—. Office: Advantica Restaurant Group 203 E Main St Spartanburg SC 29319-0002

ADAMSON, JOHN WILLIAM, hematologist; b. Oakland, Calif., Dec. 28, 1936; s. John William and Florence Jean Adamson; m. Susan Elizabeth Wood, June 16, 1960; children: Cairn Elizabeth, Loch Rachael; m. Christine Fenyvest, Sept. 1, 1989. BA, U. Calif., Berkeley, 1958; MD, UCLA, 1962. Intern, resident in medicine U. Wash. Med. Ctr., Seattle, 1962-64, clin. and rsch. fellow hematology, 1964-67, faculty, 1969-90, prof. hematology, 1978-90, head divsn. hematology, 1981-89; pres. N.Y. Blood Ctr., N.Y.C., 1989-97; dir. Lindsley F. Kimball Rsch. Inst., 1989-98; exec. v.p. rsch., dir. Blood Rsch. Inst. Blood Ctr./Southeastern Wis., Milw., 1998—. Josiah Macy Jr. Found. scholar, vis. scientist Nuffield dept. clin. medicine, U. Oxford, Eng., faculty medicine, 1976-77. Author papers in field, chpts. in books. With USPHS, 1967-69. Recipient Rsch. Career Devel. award NIH, 1972-77, Rsch. grant, 1976-95. Fellow AAAS; mem. Am. Soc. Hematology (pres. 1995-96), Assn. Am. Physicians, Am. Soc. Clin. Investigation, Western Assn. Physicians.

ADAMSON, THOMAS CHARLES, JR. aerospace engineering educator, consultant; b. Cicero, Ill., Mar. 24, 1924; s. Thomas Charles and Helen Emily (Koubek) A.; m. Susan Elizabeth Huncilman, Sept. 16, 1949; children: Thomas Charles III, William Andros, Laura Elizabeth BS, Purdue U., 1949; MS, Calif. Inst. Tech., 1950, PhD, 1954. Rsch. engr. Jet Propulsion Lab., Pasadena, Calif., 1952-54; assoc. research engr. U. Mich., Ann Arbor, 1954-56, asst. prof., 1956-57, assoc. prof., 1957-61, prof., 1961-93; prof. emeritus, 1993—; chmn. dept. aerospace engring. U. Mich., Ann Arbor, 1983-92. Mem. François-Xavier Bagnoud Aerospace Prize Bd., 1992—, chmn., 1992-2000. Editor: (with M.F. Platzer) Transonic Flow Problems in Turbo Machinery, 1977; contbr. articles to profl. jours. Bd. trustees Mich. Aviation Hall of Fame, 1987—. With U.S. Army, 1943-46, ETO. Guggenheim fellow, 1950-52; recipient Disting. Faculty Achievement award U. Mich., 1980. Fellow AIAA; mem. Combustion Inst., Am. Phys. Soc., Francois-Xavier Bagnoud U.S. Found., Sigma Xi. Episcopalian Home: 667 Worthington Pl Ann Arbor MI 48103-6138 Office: U Mich Dept Aerospace Engring 1320 Beal Ave Ann Arbor MI 48109-2140 E-mail: tcajr@engin.umich.edu.

ADAWI, IBRAHIM HASAN, physics educator; b. Palestine, Apr. 18, 1930; came to U.S., 1951, naturalized, 1961; s. Hasan and Dabella (Miari) A.; children: Omar, Nadia, Yasmin, Rhonda, Tariq. B.S. in Engring. Physics, Washington U., St. Louis, 1953; Ph.D. in Engring. Physics, Cornell U., 1957. Mem. tech. staff RCA Labs., Princeton, N.J., 1956-60; research cons. Battelle Meml. Inst., Columbus, Ohio, 1960-68; adj. prof. elec. engring. Ohio State U., 1965-68; prof. physics U. Mo., Rolla, 1968-97, emeritus prof. physics, 1997—. Vis. prof. U. Hamburg, W.Ger., winter 1977, Sch. Math. and Physics, U. East Anglia, Norwich, Eng., fall 1982; Fulbright lectr. Rabat, Morocco, 1982; sr. scientist Motorola, Phoenix, summer 1979; rsch. leader Internat. Ctr. Theoretical Physics, Trieste, Italy, summers 1982, 83, 85. Jr. fellow Cornell U., 1953-54; J. McMullen scholar, 1954-55; Sigma Xi fellow, 1955-56 Mem. Am. Phys. Soc. Home: 10540 County Road 3010 Rolla MO 65401-7754 Office: U Mo-Rolla Dept Physics Rolla MO 65401 E-mail: adawi@umr.edu.

ADDERLEY, TERENCE E. corporate executive; b. 1933; married. BBA, U. Mich., 1951, BMA, 1956. Fin. analyst Standard Oil Co. of N.J., 1956-57; with Kelly Services, Inc., Troy, Mich., 1957-61, v.p., 1961-65, exec. v.p., 1965-67, pres., COO, 1967—, also dir., chmn., pres., CEO, 1998—. Office: Kelly Svcs Inc 999 W Big Beaver Rd Troy MI 48084-4716

ADDIS, LAIRD CLARK, JR. philosopher, educator, musician; b. Bath, N.Y., Mar. 25, 1937; s. Laird Clark and Dora Ersel (Webber) A.; m. Patricia Karen Peterson, Dec. 20, 1962; children— Kristin, Karin. B.A., U. Iowa, 1959, Ph.D., 1964; M.A. (Woodrow Wilson fellow), Brown U., 1960. Instr. U. Iowa, Iowa City, 1963-64, asst. prof., 1964-68, asso. prof., 1968-74, prof. philosophy, 1974—, also chmn. dept. philosophy., 1977-85. Sr. Fulbright lectr. State U. Groningen, Netherlands, 1970-71 Author: (with Douglas Lewis) Moore and Ryle: Two Ontologists, 1965, The Logic of Society, 1975, Natural Signs, 1989, Of Mind and Music, 1999; contbr. articles to profl. jours. Mem. Am. Philos. Assn., Philosophy of Sci. Assn., Am. Soc. for Aesthetics, Am. Fedn. Musicians, Quad City Symphony Orch. (ret.). Home: 20 W Park Rd Iowa City IA 52246-2304 Office: U Iowa Dept Philosophy Iowa City IA 52242 E-mail: laird-addis@uiowa.edu.

ADDIS, PAUL D. utilities executive; Pres. Am. Electric Power Co., Inc., Columbus, Ohio, 1999—. Office: Am Electric Power Co Inc 1 Riverside Plz Columbus OH 43215-2355

ADDUCCI, JOSEPH EDWARD, obstetrician, gynecologist; b. Chgo., Dec. 1, 1934; s. Dominee Edward and Harriet Evelyn (Kneppreth) A.; m. Mary Ann Tiertje, 1958; children— Christopher, Gregory, Steven, Jessica, Tobias B.S., U. Ill., 1955; M.D., Loyola U., Chgo., 1959. Diplomate Am. Bd. Ob-Gyn., Nat. Bd. Med. Examiners. Intern Cook County Hosp, Chgo., 1959-60; resident in ob-gyn Mt. Carmel Hosp., Detroit, 1960-64; practice medicine specializing in obstetrics and gynecology Williston, N.D., 1966—. Chief staff, chmn. obstetrics dept. Mercy Hosp., Williston, mem. governing bd., 1996; clin. prof. U. N.D. Med. Sch., 1973—; mem. gov. bd. Mercy Hosp. Cath. Health Corp.; mem. coun. Accreditation Coun. for Gynecologic Endoscopy, 1999—. Mem. N.D. Bd. Med. Examiners, 1974—, past chmn.; project dir. Tri County Family Planning Svc.; past pres. Tri County Health Planning Coun.; mem. governing bd. Mercy Hosp., Williston, N.D. With Med. Corps, AUS, 1964-66. Fellow Am. Soc. Abdominal Surgeons, ACS (regent N.D. 1990—), Am. Coll. Obstetrics and Gynecologists (sect. chmn. N.D.), Internat. Coll. Surgeons (regent 1972-74, 88-89), Am. Fertility Soc., Am. Assn. Internat. Lazar Soc., Gynecol. Lataropists, N.D. Obstetricians and Gynecologists Soc. (pres. 1966, 76); mem. Am. Soc. for Colposcopy and Colpomicroscopy, Am. Soc. Cryosurgery, Am. Soc. Contemporary Medicine and Surgery, Am. Assn. Profl. Ob-Gyn., Pan Am. Med. Assn., Am. Coll. Surgeons (regent 1989— N.D.). Lodge: Elks Home: 1717 Main St Williston ND 58801-4244 Office: Medical Ctr OB GYN Williston ND 58801

ADDY, ALVA LEROY, mechanical engineer; b. Dallas, Mar. 29, 1936; s. Alva Isaac and Nellie Amelia (Brumbaugh) A.; m. Sandra Ruth Turney, June 8, 1958 BS, S.D. Sch. Mines and Tech., 1958; MS, U. Cin., 1960; PhD, U. Ill., 1963. Engr. Gen. Electric Co., Cin., also Lancaster, Calif., 1958-60; prof. mech. engring. U. Ill., Urbana, 1963-98, prof. emeritus, 1998—, dir. mech. engring. lab., 1965-97, assoc. head mech. engring. dept., 1980-87, head, 1987-98. Aerodynamics cons. U.S. Army Missile Command, Redstone Arsenal, Ala., summers 1965-98; cons. U.S. Army Research Office, 1964— ; cons. in high-speed fluid dynamics to indsl. firms, 1963— ; vis. research prof. U.S. Army, 1976; lectr. Von Karman Inst. Fluid Dynamics, Brussels, 1968, 75, 76 Fellow ASME, AIAA (assoc.), Am. Soc. for Engring. Edn. (Ralph Coates Roe award 1990); mem. Sigma Xi, Pi Tau Sigma, Sigma Tau. Home: 726 Elk Run Rd Spearfish SD 57783 Office: U Ill 1206 W Green St Urbana IL 61801-2906

ADELBERG, ARNOLD MELVIN, mathematics educator, researcher; b. Bklyn., Mar. 17, 1936; s. David and Evelyn (Brass) A.; m. Harriet Diamond, June 30, 1962; children: Danielle Hamill, Erica. BA, Columbia U., 1956; MA, Princeton U., 1959, PhD, 1996. Instr. Columbia U., N.Y.C., 1959-62; instr., asst. prof., assoc. prof., prof. Grinnell (Iowa) Coll., 1962—, Myra Steele prof. math., 1991—. Chair math. dept., sci. div. several times, chmn. faculty Grinnell Coll., 1974-76, dir. Noyce vis. prof. program, 1997—. Contbr. articles to profl. jours. Mem. Math. Assn. Am., Am. Math. Soc. Avocations: bridge, chess. Home: 1930 Manor Cir Grinnell IA 50112-1136 Office: Grinnell Coll Math Dept PO Box 805 Grinnell IA 50112-0805 E-mail: adelbe@grinnell.edu.

ADELMAN, LYNN, federal judge; b. Milw., Oct. 1, 1939; s. Albert B. and Edith Margoles Adelman; m. Elizabeth Halmbacher, 1976; children: Lisa, Mia. AB, Princeton U., 1961; LLB, Columbia U., 1965. State senator dist. 28 State of Wis., Milw., 1977-97; judge U.S. Dist. Ct. (Ea. Dist.) Wis., 1997—. Chmn. judiciary and consumer affairs com. Wis. State Senate; pvt. practice as atty. Democrat. also: U.S.Courthouse & Fed Bldg 517 E Wisconsin Ave Milwaukee WI 53202-4500

ADELMAN, RICHARD CHARLES, gerontologist, educator; b. Newark, Mar. 10, 1940; s. Morris and Elanor (Wachman) A.; m. Lynn Betty Richman, Aug. 18, 1963; children— Mindy Robin, Nicole Ann A.B., Kenyon Coll., 1962; M.A., Temple U., 1965, Ph.D., 1967. Postdoctoral fellow Albert Einstein Coll. Medicine, Bronx, N.Y., 1967-69; from asst. prof. to prof. Temple U., Phila., 1969-82, dir. inst. aging, 1978-82; prof. biol. chemistry U. Mich., Ann Arbor, 1982-2000, dir. inst. gerontology, 1982-97, prof. emeritus, 2001—. Mem. study sect. NIH, 1975-78; adv. coun. VA, 1981-85; chmn. Gordon Rsch. Conf. Biol. Aging, 1976; adv. com. VA, 1981-91; chmn. VA Geriatrics and Gerontology Adv. Com., 1987-91; dir. univ. rels. Univ. Living, Inc., 2001—. Mem. various editorial bds. biomed. research jours., 1972—. Bd. dirs. Botsford Continuing Care Ctrs., Inc., Farmington Hills, Mich., 1984-88. Recipient Medalist award Intrasci. Research Found., 1977; grantee NIH, 1970—; established investigator Am. Heart Assn., 1975-78 Fellow Gerontol. Soc. Am. (v.p. 1976-77, pres. elect 1986-87, Kent award 1990); mem. Am. Soc. Biol. Chemists, Gerontol. Soc. Am. (pres. 1986-87), Am. Chem. Soc., AAAS, Phila. Biochemists (pres.), Practictioners in Aging. Jewish

ADELMAN, STANLEY JOSEPH, lawyer; b. Devils Lake, N.D., May 20, 1942; s. Isadore Russell Adelman and Eva Claire (Robins) Stoller; m. Mary Beth Petchaft, Jan. 30, 1972; children: Laura E., Sarah A. BS, U. Wis., 1964, JD, 1967. Bar: Ill. 1967, U.S. Dist. Ct. (no. dist.) Ill. 1967, Wis. 1968, U.S. Ct. Appeals (7th cir.), U.S. Dist. Ct. (ea. dist.) Wis. 1979, U.S. Supreme Ct. 1982, U.S. Ct. Appeals (10th cir.) 1984, U.S. Ct. Appeals (fed. cir.) 1987. Assoc. Sonnenchein, Carlin, Nath & Rosenthal, Chgo., 1967-75, ptnr., 1975-85; co-chmn. litigation dept. Rudnick & Wolfe, 1985-91, 96-97, ptnr., 1985—, profl. responsibility ptnr., 1992-94, mem. mgmt. policy com., 1985-97, co-chmn. complex litigation practice group, 1997-98. Bd. dirs. Legal Assistance Found., Chgo., 1982-83. Fellow Nat. Inst. Trial Advocacy; mem. Chgo. Bar Assn., Chgo. Coun. Lawyers, Am. Inns of Ct. (pres. Markey/Wigmore chpt. 1998-99), Lawyers Club Chgo., Order of Coif. Jewish. Home: 115 Crescent Dr Glencoe IL 60022-1303 Office: Piper Marbury Rudnick & Wolfe 203 N La Salle St Ste 1800 Chicago IL 60601-1210 E-mail: stanley.adelman@piperrudnick.com.

ADELMAN, STEVEN ALLEN, theoretical physical chemist, chemistry educator; b. Chgo., July 4, 1945; s. Hyman and Sarah Adelman; m. Barbara Stolberg, May 13, 1974 BS, Ill. Inst. Tech., 1967; Ph.D., Harvard U., 1972. Postdoctoral fellow MIT, Cambridge, 1972-73; postdoctoral fellow U. Chgo., 1973-74; asst. prof. chemistry Purdue U., West Lafayette, Ind., 1975-77, assoc. prof., 1977-82, prof., 1982—. Cons. Exxon Rsch. Co., Los Alamos Nat. Lab.; vis. prof. U. Paris, 1985; nominator 1994 Nobel Prize in Chemistry, Royal Swedish Acad. Scis. Contbr. articles to profl. jours. Vol. U.S. Peace Corp., Ankara, Turkey, 1969-70. Fellow Alfred P. Sloan Found., 1976-78, Guggenheim Found., 1982-83; NSF grantee, 1976—; named Outstanding Sr. in Chemistry, Am. Inst. Chemistry, 1967. Fellow Am. Phys. Soc.; mem. AAAS, Am. Chem. Soc., Am. Statis. Assn., Math. Assn. Am., Sigma Xi. Avocations: long-distance running, strength training, Turkish language and literature. Home: 3037 Courthouse Dr W Apt 2C West Lafayette IN 47906-1035 Office: Purdue U Dept Chemistry West Lafayette IN 47907 E-mail: saa@purdue.edu.

ADELMAN, STEVEN HERBERT, lawyer; b. Dec. 21, 1945; s. Irving and Sylvia (Cohen) A.; m. Pamela Bernice Kozoll, June 30, 1968; children: David, Robert. BS, U. Wis., Madison, 1967; JD, DePaul U., 1970. Bar: Ill. 1970, U.S. Dist. Ct. (no. dist.) Ill. 1970, U.S. Ct. Appeals (7th cir.) 1975. Ptnr. Keck, Mahin & Cate, Chgo., 1970-93, Lord, Bissell & Brook, Chgo., 1993—. Bd. dirs. Bur. Jewish Employment Problems, Chgo., 1983—, pres. 1991, 92; employment relations com. Chgo. Assn. Commerce and Industry, 1982-90. Contbr. chpts. to books, articles to profl. jours. Fellow Coll. Labor and Employment Lawyers; mem. ABA (Silver key award 1969), Chgo. Bar Assn. (chmn. labor and employment law com. 1988-89), Ill. State Bar Assn., Chgo. Coun. Lawyers, Decalogue Soc. Office: Lord Bissell & Brook 115 S La Salle St Ste 3200 Chicago IL 60603-3902 E-mail: sadelman@lordbissell.com.

ADELMAN, SUSAN HERSHBERG, surgeon; b. Rochester, N.Y., Oct. 8, 1941; m. Martin Adelman. BA in Geology, U. Mich.; MD, Wayne State U., 1967. Diplomate Am. Bd. Surgery, Am. Bd. Pediatric Surgery. Intern Henry Ford Hosp., Detroit, 1967-68, resident in surgery, 1968-72; resident in pediatric surgery Childrens Hosp., 1972-74; clin. assoc. prof. surgery U. Mich.; med. dir. Coordinated Health Care Inc. Hosp. staff Riverview Hosp., Detroit, Children's Hosp., Detroit, Oakwood Hosp., Dearborn, Mich., Mott Children's Hosp.-U. Mich.; rep. AMA, White House Health Profls. Rev. Group, 1993. Editor Detroit Med. News, 1981—. Fellow ACS (mem. profl. liability com., Cert. of Spl. Competence in Pediatric Surgery); mem. AMA (del. 1991—, coun. on med. svcs., intracoun. taskforce on Medicaid, chair surg. caucus, pres. OSMAP, adv. com. women in medicine, consortium on study of the fedn. and health policy agenda), Am. Soc. of Gen. Surgeons (bd. dirs.), Mich. State Med. Soc. (1st woman pres.), Wayne County Med. Soc. (1st woman pres.). Office: AMA 515 N State St Chicago IL 60610-4325

ADELMAN, WILLIAM JOHN, university labor and industrial relations educator; b. Chgo., July 26, 1932; s. William Sidney and Annie Teresa (Goan) A.; m. Nora Jill Walters, June 26, 1952; children: Michelle, Marguerite, Marc, Michael, Jessica. Student, Lafayette Coll., 1952; BA, Elmhurst Coll., 1956; MA, U. Chgo., 1964. Tchr. Whitecross Sch., Hereford, Eng., 1956-57, Jefferson Sch., Berwyn, Ill., 1957-60, Morton High Sch., Berwyn, 1960-66; mem. faculty dept. labor and indsl. relations U. Ill., Chgo., 1966-91, prof., 1978-91, prof. emeritus, 1991—; coordinator Chgo. Labor Edn. Program, 1981-87. Lectr. Road Scholar Program, Ill. Humanities Coun., 1997. Author: Touring Pullman, 1972, Haymarket Revisited, 1976, Pilsen and the West Side, 1981; writer: film Packingtown U.S.A., 1968; narrator: Palace Cars and Paradise: Pullman's Model Town, 1983. Bd. dirs. Chgo. Regional Blood Program, 1977-80; mem. Ill. State Employment Security Adv. Bd., 1974-75; Democratic candidate U.S. Ho. of Reps. from 14th dist. Ill., 1970; organizer Haymarket Centennial Events, 1986; chmn. Jane Addams' Hull House Adv. Bd., 1991—. Ill. Humanities Council grantee, 1977; German Marshall Fund U.S. grantee, 1977; recipient Tradition of Excellence award Oak Park/River Forest H.S., 1993, Eugene V. Debs award Midwest Labor Press assn., 1995. Mem. Ill. Labor History Soc. (founding mem., v.p., Union Hall of Honor 1993), Am. Fedn. Tchrs., Doris Humphrey Soc. (v.p. 1990—). Unitarian. Home and Office: 613 S Highland Ave Oak Park IL 60304-1524 E-mail: www.Dooper@aol.com.

ADKINS, GREGORY D. higher education administrator; b. Charleston, W.Va., May 20, 1941; s. Wondel Lafayette and Corda Christenia (Carnes) A.; m. Dolores June Lowe, Sept. 9, 1961; children: Christenia Lea, Angela Dawn BS, U. Charleston, 1962; MEd, Fla. Atlantic U., 1966; M.C.S., U. Miss., 1968, EdD, 1970. Assoc. prof. edn. Palm Beach Atlantic Coll., West Palm Beach, Fla., 1972-74, chair dept. edn., 1972-73, chair div. profl. studies, dir. tchr. edn., 1973-74; assoc. dean career edn. W.Va. No. Community Coll., Wheeling, 1974-75, dean acad. affairs, 1975-79; coordinator instrn. and planning Colo. State Bd. C.C.s. and Occupational Edn., Denver, 1979-81; pres. So. W.Va. Community Coll., Logan, 1981-88, Bluefield (W.Va.) State Coll., 1988-93, Franklin County Schs., Frankfort, Ky., 1993-94, Jefferson Coll., Hillsboro, Mo., 1994—. Vice chmn. adv. coun. of pres. W.Va. Bd. Regents, 1986-87; chair legis. affairs com., 1986-87; bd. dirs. Missourians for Higher Edn., Mo. Coordinating Bd. for Higher Edn. Com. on Transfer and Articulation, 1997—, Jefferson Coll. Found. Inc. Mem. Gov.'s Labor/Mgmt. Coun., Charleston, 1986-93, W.Va. Enterprise Zone Authority, Charleston, 1987-93, Mercer County Econ. Devel. Authority, 1989-93; bd. dirs. Bluefield Regional Med. Ctr., 1988-89, W.Va. Joint Commn. for Vocat. and Occupational Edn., 1989-93, Missourians for Higher Edn., 1996—; mem. coms. on transfer and articulation Mo. Coordinating Bd. for Higher Edn., 1996—. Recipient Alumnus of Yr. award U. Charleston, 1984, award VFW, Chapmanville, 1987; NSF grad. fellow 1967-68, Richard Weaver fellow Intercollegiate Studies Inst., 1969-70. Mem. W.Va. Assn. Coll. and Univ. Pres. (pres. 1984-85), W.Va. C.C. Assn. (pres. 1985-86), Mo. C.C. Assn. (bd. dirs. 1995-97, adv. coun. of pres. 1994—), North Ctrl. Assn. (cons., evaluator 1984—, commr.-at-large 1984-90), Kiwanis, Rotary Internat., Chi Beta Phi (pres.). Mem. Ch. of Christ. Avocations: outdoor sports, gardening. Office: Jefferson Coll 1000 Viking Dr Hillsboro MO 63050-2440

ADKINS, SUSAN, health services administrator; Grad., U. Kans. Dir. Menninger Ctr. Family Solutions, Topeka. Office: Menninger Ctr Family Solutions PO Box 829 Topeka KS 66601-0829

ADLER, JULIUS, biochemist, biologist, educator; b. Edelfingen, Germany, Apr. 30, 1930; came to U.S., 1938, naturalized, 1943; s. Adolf and Irma (Stern) A.; m. Hildegard Wohl, Oct. 15, 1963; children: David Paul, Jean Susan. AB, Harvard U., 1952; MS, U. Wis., 1954, PhD, 1957; postdoctoral fellow, Washington U., St. Louis, 1957-59, Stanford U., 1959-60; hon. doctorate, U. Tübingen, Germany, 1987, U. Regensburg, 1995. Asst. prof. biochemistry and genetics U. Wis., Madison, 1960-63, assoc. prof., 1963-66, prof., 1966-96; prof. emeritus U.Wis., 1996—; Edwin Bret Hart prof. biochemistry and genetics U. Wis., 1972, Steenbock prof. microbiol. scis., 1982-92. Recipient hon. symposium on behavior and signaling in microorganisms, 1995. Research, publs. in field. Recipient Otto-Warburg medal German Soc. Biol. Chemistry, 1986, R.H. Wright award Simon Fraser U., 1988, Hilldale award U. Wis., 1988, Abbott-Am. Soc. Microbiology Lifetime Achievment award, 1995, William C. Rose award Am. Soc. Biochemistry and Molecular Biology, 1996. Mem. NAS (Selman A. Waksman Microbiology award 1980), Am. Acad. Arts and Scis., Am. Philos. Soc., Wis. Acad. Scis., Arts and Letters. Home: 1234 Wellesley Rd Madison WI 53705-2232 Office: U Wis Dept Biochemistry Madison WI 53706 E-mail: adler@biochem.wisc.edu.

ADOLPH, ROBERT J. physician, medical educator; b. Chgo., May 12, 1927; s. Abe and Ina Adolph; m. Ivadean Lair, July 12, 1986. PhB, U. Chgo., 1947; BS, U. Ill., 1950, MD, 1952. Diplomate Am. Bd. Internal Medicine (chmn. com. cardiovascular diseases 1979-81). Instr., then asst. prof. medicine U. Ill. Med. Sch., 1958-60, asst. dir. med. clinics, Rsch. and Edn. Hosps., 1958-60; spl. rsch. fellow NIH U. Wash. Med. Sch., Seattle, 1960-62; mem. faculty U. Cin. Med. Sch., 1962—, now prof. medicine, 1970—, dir. div. cardiology, 1986-90. Cons. VA, U. Cin. hosps.; dir. cardiac clinic, U.cin. Hosp. Author papers, abstracts in field; mem. editorial bds. profl. jours. Mem. ACP, AAAS, Am. Heart Assn. (adv. bds., sects. and couns., trustee Southwest Ohio chpt.), Assn. Univ. Cardiologists, Am. Coll. Cardiology (gov. Ohio chpt. 1982-85, chmn. bd. govs. 1984-85, mem. various coms.), Cin. Soc. Internal Medicine (pres. 1982-83), Laennec Soc. (pres. 1978-79), Am. Coll. Cardiology (trustee 1986-91), Sigma Xi, Alpha Omega Alpha, Pi Kappa Epsilon. Office: 231 Bethesda Ave Cincinnati OH 45229-2827

ADRAY, DEBORAH, retail executive; Pres. Adray Appliance & Photo Ctr., Dearborn, Mich. Office: Adray Appliance/Photo Ctr 20219 Carlysle St Dearborn MI 48124-3898 Fax: 313-274-6874.

AFIFI, ADEL KASSIM, physician; b. Akka, Palestine, Oct. 19, 1930; came to U.S., 1984; naturalized, 1988; s. Kassim and Zeinnab (Akki) A.; m. Larryanna Patten, June 17, 1960; children: Rema, Walid. MD, Am. U., Beirut, 1957; MS, U. Iowa, 1965. Intern Am. U. of Beirut, 1956-57, resident in internal medicine, 1959-61; resident in neurology U. Iowa, 1962-64, fellow in neuroanatomy, 1961-62; fellow in neurology N.Y. Neurol. Inst., 1964-65; fellow in electron microscopy Johns Hopkins U., Balt., 1967-68; asst. prof. Am. U., Beirut, 1965-69, assoc. prof., 1969-74, prof., 1974-84, asst. dean Coll. Medicine, 1969-78, chmn. Dept. Human Morphology, 1969-84; prof. U. Iowa, Iowa City, 1984—. Author: Atlas of Microscopic Anatomy, 1974, 89, Basic Neuroscience, 1980, 86, Compendium of Anatomical Variation, 1988, Atlas of Human Anatomy, 1991; contbr. articles to jours. in field. Trustee Diana Tamari Sabbagh Found., Beirut, 1979—, Med. Welfare Fund, Switzerland, 1991—; mem. King Faisal Internat. Prize in Medicine, Riyadh, Saudi Arabia, 1981-85. Fulbright scholar U. Iowa, 1980-81. Mem. Am. Neurol. Assn., Am. Acad. Neurology, Child Neurology Soc., Soc. for Neurosci., Alpha Omega Alpha. Home: 1147 Penkridge Dr Iowa City IA 52246-4933 Office: U Iowa Coll Medicine Dept Anatomy Iowa City IA 52242

AGARWAL, GYAN CHAND, engineering educator; b. Bhagwanpur, India, Apr. 22, 1940; came to U.S., 1960; s. Hari Chand and Ramrati (Jindal) A.; m. Sadhna Garg, July 7, 1965; children: Monika, Mudita. BS, Agra U., India, 1957; BE with honors, U. Roorkee, India, 1960; MSEE, Purdue U., Ind., 1962, PhD, 1965. Lic. profl. engr. Ill., Wis. Asst. prof. engring. U. Ill., Chgo., 1965-69, assoc. prof. engring., 1969-73, prof. engring., 1973-99, prof. emeritus, 1999—, dir. grad. studies, 1975-79, 82-85, 91-99; vis. prof. Rush Med. Coll., 1976—. Vis. prof. Indian Inst. Sci., Bangalore, 1971, Indian Inst. Tech., Kanpur, 1972, Rush Med. Coll., Chgo., 1976—; cons. FDA, Washington, 1979—; mem. study sect. NIH, 1990-94. Co-editor: Biomaterials, 1969; cons. editor Jour. Motor Behavior, 1981-93; assoc. editor IEEE Transactions on Biomed. Engring., 1988-96, Jour. Electromyography and Kinesiology, 1994—; contbr. articles to profl. jours. U. Roorkee merit scholar, 1958-60; NSF, NIH, NASA, VA, Wright-Patterson AFB rsch. grantee. Fellow AAAS, IEEE, Am. Inst. for Med. and Biol. Engring. (founding); mem. Soc. Neurosci., Sigma Xi, Phi Kappa Phi, Eta Kappa Nu. Home: 947 Lathrop Ave River Forest IL 60305-1448 Office: U Ill Coll Engring Dept Elec Engring 851 S Morgan St Rm 1120 SEO Chicago IL 60607-7042

AGARWAL, RAMESH KUMAR, aeronautical scientist, researcher, educator; b. Mainpuri, India, Jan. 4, 1947; came to U.S., 1968; s. Radhakishan and Parkashvati (Goel) A.; m. Sugita Goel, Oct. 26, 1976; children: Vivek, Gautam. BS, U. Allahabad, 1965; BTech, Indian Inst. Tech., 1968; MS, U. Minn., 1969; PhD, Stanford U., 1975. Rsch. assoc. NASA Ames Rsch. Ctr., Moffett Field, Calif., 1976-78; McDonnell Douglas fellow, program dir. McDonnell Douglas Aerospace, St. Louis, 1978-94; Bloomfield disting. prof., chair aerospace engring. Wichita (Kans.) State U., 1994-96, Bloomfield disting prof., exec. dir. Nat. Inst. Aviatn Rsch., 1997—2001; William Palm prof. engring., dir. Aerospace Rsch. and Edn. Ctr. Washington U., St. Louis, 2001—. Affiliate prof. Washington U., St. Louis, 1986-95. Contbr. more than 200 articles to profl. jours. Fellow AIAA, AAAS, ASME, SME, Soc. Automotive Engring., Royal Aero. Soc.; mem. IEEE (sr.), Am. Phys. Soc., Am. Helicopter Soc., Tau Beta Pi, Sigma Gamma Tau, Pi Tau Sigma. Office: Washington U Dept Mech Engring Saint Louis MO 63130 E-mail: rka@me.wustl.edu.

AGARWAL, SUMAN KUMAR, editor; b. Bolpur, India, Jan. 21, 1945; came to U.S., 1980; s. Hari Prasad and Rukmini (Modi) A.; children: Tripti, Samantha Rani. BSc with honors, Visva-Bharati, Santiniketan, India, 1966; MSc, Delhi U., India, 1971; PhD, U. Paris, 1975, DSc, 1979. Rsch. scholar Atomic Energy Commn. of France, Saclay, 1976-80; rsch. assoc. Purdue U., West Lafayette, Ind., 1980-82; sr. sci. info. analyst Chem. Abstracts Svc., Columbus, Ohio, 1982—; pres. Commodities Internat. Ltd. Inc., 1992—2002. Contbr. articles to profl. jours. Vol. Columbus Schs., 1984-85, Ohio State U. TV, Columbus, 1986-88. Scholar Govt. of France, 1973-76. Mem. Am. Chem. Soc. Avocations: bridge, photography, tennis. E-mail: suman@netwalk.com., suman@commod.com.

AGEMA, GERALD WALTON, broadcasting company executive; b. Rockford, Ill., Sept. 9, 1947; s. Samuel W. and Lillian (Walton) A.; m. Marcia L. Vander Meer, June 14, 1969; children: Jerry, Matt and Mike (twins). BS in Acctg., No. Ill. U., 1970; MBA, U. Chgo., 1984. CPA, Ill. Staff/sr. auditor Price Waterhouse, Chgo., 1971-76, audit mgr., 1976-79, Tribune Co., Chgo., 1979-80, asst. contr., 1980-85; dir., CFO Tribune Broadcasting Co., 1985-86, v.p., CFO, 1986-88, v.p. ops., CFO, 1988-97, v.p. adminstrn., CFO, 1997—, Tribune Pub. Co., Chgo., 2001—. Bd. dirs. Mus. of Broadcast Comms., Chgo., 1986—, treas., 1986-97. Mem. AICPA, Ill. Soc. CPAs, Internat. Newspapers Fin. Exec. Assn. Avocations: reading, boating, fishing, travel. Office: Tribune Pub Co 435 N Michigan Ave Ste 1900 Chicago IL 60611-4066

AGLER, BRIAN, professional basketball coach; m. Robin Agler; children: Bryce, Taylor. BA, Wittenberg U.; MEd, Pittsburg (Kans.) State U. Profl. basketball player, Blackpool, Eng., 1980-81; coach Northeastern Okla. A&M U., U. Mo., Kansas City; head women's basketball coach Kans. State U.; head coach Columbus Quest; head coach, gen. mgr. Minn. Lynx, Mpls., 1998—. Inductee Wittenberg U. Athletic Hall of Honor, 1995; named ABL Ea. Conf. All-Star head coach, 1997, 98, ABL Coach of the Yr., 1996-97. Mem. Women's Basketball Coaches Assn. Office: Minnesota Lynx Target Ctr 600 1st Ave N Minneapolis MN 55403-1400

AGNELLO, GINO J. federal court administrator; BS, U. Ill.; JD, Ill. Inst. Tech. Pvt. practice; with U.S. Bankruptcy Ct. (no. dist.) Ill., Chgo.; dep. cir. exec.; clk. of ct. U.S. Ct. Appeals (7th cir.), Chgo., 1997—. Office: US Ct Appeals (7th cir) 219 S Dearborn St Ste 2710A Chicago IL 60604-1803

AGNO, JOHN G. management consultant; b. Gloversville, N.Y., Dec. 8, 1940; s. John G. and Margretta (Luff) Anagnostopulos; m. Lynn Airey Mar. 30, 1968 (div. Oct. 1979); children; J. Robert, Constance Blythe, Randy R.; m. Karen Clark Mikus, June 29, 1985; 1 stepchild, Luke Ravlin. BBA, U. Fla., 1962. Mktg. specialist Eastman Kodak Co., Rochester, N.Y., 1965-73; gen. mgr. sanitation appliance divsn. Thetford Corp., Ann Arbor, Mich., 1973-80; v.p. mktg. and adminstrn. Stirling Power Systems Corp. divsn. McDonnell Douglas Corp., 1980-87; pres. Signature, Inc., 1983—. Deacon First Presbyn. Ch., Ann Arbor; bd. dirs. Washtenaw United Way, 1991-95; bd. dirs. YMCA, 1995-2000. 1st lt. U.S. Army, 1963-65. Mem. Recreational Vehicle Industry Assn. (chmn. mktg. commn. 1978-82, bd. dirs. 1981-83), Turnaround Mgmt. Assn., Ann Arbor Country Club, Rotary. Republican. Home: 4701 Midway Dr Ann Arbor MI 48103-9427 Office: Signature Inc PO Box 2086 Ann Arbor MI 48106-2086 E-mail: johnagno@signatureseries.com.

AGOOS, JEFF, professional soccer player; b. Geneva, May 2, 1968; Student, U. Va. Defender DC United, Herndon, Va. Mem. U.S. Under-15, Under-17, Under-20, World Univ. and Indoor Nat. Teams; competitor 13 internat. matches in 1996, scoring winning goal in 2d internat. appearance, Guatemala, mem. silver-medal U.S. Futsai Nat. Team, Hong Kong, 1992; helped lead DC United to inaugural MLS Cup title and 1996 U.S. Open Cup championship. Vol. asst. coach, Bruce Arena, U. Va., 1995. Named one of Soccer Am.'s 11 most valuable players, 1989, Soccer Am.'s co-freshman of yr., 1986. Office: US Soccer Fedn 1801-1811 S Prairie Ave Chicago IL 60616 and: DC United 13832 Redstein Dr Herndon VA 20171

AGOSTINI, GIULIO, manufacturing company executive; b. Genoa, Italy, Mar. 6, 1935; Grad. in econ. scis., U. Perugia, Italy, 1960. Divsn. contr. 3M Italy, 1966-69, contbr., 1970-72, dir. fin. and adminstrn., 1972-91; contr. Ferrania, 1969-70; sr. v.p. fin. 3 M Co., St. Paul, 1991-93, sr. v.p. fin. and adminstrv. svcs., 1993—. Trustee Minn. Mut. Life Ins. Co.; mem. coun. fin. execs. Conf. Bd.; mem. fin. coun. I, MAPI. Bd. dirs. Minn. Orchl. Assn. Mem. Fin. Execs. Inst. Office: 3 M Ctr Saint Paul MN 55144-0001

AGRANOFF, BERNARD WILLIAM, biochemist, educator; b. Detroit, June 26, 1926; s. William and Phyllis (Pelavin) A.; m. Raquel Betty Schwartz, Sept. 1, 1957; children: William, Adam. MD, Wayne State U., 1950; BS, U. Mich., 1954. Intern Robert Packer Hosp., Sayre, Pa., 1950-51; commd. surgeon USPHS, 1954-60; biochemist Nat. Inst. Neurol. Diseases and Blindness, NIH, Bethesda, Md., 1954-60; mem. faculty U. Mich., Ann Arbor, 1960—, prof. biochemistry, 1965—; R.W. Gerard prof. of neurosci. in psychiatry, 1991. Rsch. biochemist Mental Health Rsch. Inst., 1960—, assoc. dir., 1977-83, dir. 1983-95, dir. neurosci. lab., 1983-2000; vis. scientist Max Planck Inst. Zellchemie, Munich, 1957-58, Nat. Inst. Med. Rsch., Mill Hill, Eng., 1974-75; Henry Russel lectr. U. Mich., 1987; cons. pharm. industry, govt. Contbr. articles to profl. jours. Fogarty scholar-in-residence NIH, Bethesda, Md., 1989-95; named Mich. Scientist of Yr. Mus. of Sci., Lansing, 1992. Fellow Am. Assn. Adv. Sci., N.Y. Acad. Sci., Am. Coll. Neuropsychopharmacology; mem. AAAS, Am. Soc. Biochemistry and Molecular Biology, Am. Chem. Soc., Inst. Medicine of NAS, Internat. Soc. Neurochemistry (treas. 1985-89, chmn. 1989-91), Am. Soc. Neurochemistry (pres. 1973-75). Achievements include research in brain lipids, biochem. basis of learning, memory and regeneration in the nervous system, human brain imaging. Office: MHRI U of M C 560 MSRB II 1150 W Medical Center Dr Ann Arbor MI 48109-0669 E-mail: agranoff@umich.edu.

AGRAWAL, DHARMA PRAKASH, engineering educator; b. Balod, India, Apr. 12, 1945; came to U.S., 1976; s. Saryoo Prasad and Chandra K. Agrawal; m. Purnima Agrawal, June 7, 1971; children: Sonali, Braj. BE, Ravishankar U., Raipur, India, 1966; ME with honors, Roorkee (India) U., 1968; DSc in Tech., Fed. Inst. Tech., Lausanne, Switzerland, 1975. Lectr. M.N.R. Engring. Coll., Allahabad, India, 1968-72, Roorkee U., 1972-73; asst. Fed. Inst. Tech., Lausanne, 1973-75; instr., postdoctoral work So. Meth. U., Dallas, 1976-77; asst. prof., then assoc. prof. Wayne State U., Detroit, 1977-82; assoc. prof. N.C. State U., Raleigh, 1982-84, prof., 1984-98; OBR Disting. prof. U. Cin., 1998—. Gen. co-chair Advamced Computing Conf., 1997—2000; keynote spkr. Internat. Conf. on Parallel and Distributed Sys., 1997. Book editor: Advanced Computer Architecture, 1986, Advances in Distributed System Reliability, 1990, Distributed Computing Network Reliability, 1990; editor: Jour. Parallel and Distg. Computing, 1984, Computer mag., 1986-91, Internat. Jour. High Speed Computing, IEEE Transactions on Computers, 1992-96, IEEE Computer Soc. Press Tutorials, 1992-94. Fellow IEEE (chair tech. com. on computer architecture, IEEE Computer Soc. 1991-94, chair McDowell Award and Harry Grode Award coms. 1991-99, chair Eckerdt Mauchley award in computer architecture, program chair internat. conf. on parallel processing 1994, workshop chair internat. conf. on parallel processing 1995, gen. chair fourth internat. workshop on modeling analysis and simulation of computer and telecom. sys. 1996, 2001), Assn. for Computing Machinery; mem. Soc. for Indsl. and Applied Math. E-mial. Office: U Cin ECE&CS PO Box 210030 Cincinnati OH 45221-0030 E-mail: dpa@ececs.uc.edu.

AGRAWAL, HARISH CHANDRA, neurobiologist, researcher, educator; b. Allahabad, Uttar Pradesh, India; came to U.S., 1964, naturalized, 1982; s. Shambhu and Rajmani Devi A.; m. Daya Kumari Bhushan, Feb. 6, 1960; children— Sanjay, Sanjeev B.Sc., Allahabad U., 1957, M.Sc., 1959, Ph.D., 1964. Med. research assoc. Thudichum Psychiat. Lab., Galesburg, Ill., 1964-68; lectr. dept. biochemistry Charing Cross Hosp., London, 1968-70; prof. neurology Washington U. Sch. Medicine, St. Louis, 1970—. Mem. neurology study sect. NIH, 1979-82 Author: Handbook of Neurochemistry, 1969, Developmental Neurobiology, 1970, Biochemistry of Developing Brain, 1971, Membranes and Receptors, 1974, Proteins of the Nervous System, 1980, Biochemistry of Brain, 1980, Handbook of Neurochemistry, 1984; contbr. numerous papers on various aspects of myelin proteins and their role in demyelinating disrders. Jr. research fellow Council Sci. and Indsl. Research, New Delhi, 1960-62, sr. research fellow, 1963-64; Research Career Devel. award Nat. Inst. Neurol. and Communicative Disorders, 1974-79 Mem. Internat. Soc. Neurochemistry, Internat. Brain Rsch. Orgn., Am. Soc. Neurochemistry, Am. Soc. Biol. Chemists and Molecular Biologists, Am. Soc. Physiology. Home: 11 Morwood Ln Saint Louis MO 63141-7620 Office: Washington U Dept Neurology 660 S Euclid Ave Dept Saint Louis MO 63110-1093

AGRE, JAMES COURTLAND, physical medicine and rehabilitation; b. Northfield, Minn., May 2, 1950; s. Courtland Leverne and Ellen Violet (Swedberg) A.; m. Patti Dee Soderberg, Aug. 6, 1982. MD, U. Minn., 1976, PhD, 1985. Diplomate Nat. Bd. Med. Examiners; bd. cert. Am. Acad. Phys. Medicine and Rehab. Rsch. fellow dept. phys. medicine and rehab. U. Minn., Mpls., 1979-80, instr. dept. phys. medicine and rehab., 1980-84; asst. prof. dept. phys. medicine and rehab. U. Wis., Madison, 1984-90, assoc. prof. dept. rehab. medicine, 1990-93, chmn. dept. rehab. medicine, 1991-97, prof. dept. rehab. medicine, 1993-97; practitioner in svc. Ministry Health Care, Woodruff, Rhinelander, Eagle River, Wis., 1997—. Mem. editorial bd. and contbr. articles to Archives of Phys. Medicine and Rehab., 1988-2000. Ski coord. Wis. Ski for Light, Madison, 1985-95. Fellow Am. Acad. Phys. Medicine and Rehab. (Elizabeth and Sidney Licht award 1989, Excellence in Sci. Writing award 1990), Am. Coll. Sports Medicine (New Investigator award 1991). Office: Ministry Health Care PO Box 470 Woodruff WI 54568-0470

AGRUSS, NEIL STUART, cardiologist; b. Chgo., June 2, 1939; s. Meyer and Frances (Spector) A.; m. Janyce Zucker; children: David, Lauren, Michael, Joshua, Susan, Robyn, Bryan. BS, U. Ill., 1960; MD, 1963. Diplomate Am. Bd. Internal Medicine. Resident in internal medicine, 1964-65, 67-68; fellow in cardiology Cin. Gen. Hosp., 1968-70; dir. coronary care unit, 1971-74; dir. echocardiography lab., 1972-74; dir. cardiac diagnostic labs. Ctr. DuPage Hosp., Winfield, Ill., 1974—; asst. prof. medicine U. Cin., 1970-74, Rush Med. Coll., 1976—. Chmn. coronary care com. Heart Assn. DuPage County, 1974-76. Author: coauthor publs. in field. Active Congregation Beth Shalom, Naperville, Ill. Capt. M.C. U.S. Army, 1965-67. Fellow ACP, Am. Coll. Cardiology, Am. Coll. Chest Physicians, Coun. Clin. Cardiology, Am. Heart Assn.; mem. AMA, DuPage County Med. Soc., Ill. Med. Soc., Am. Fend. Clin. Rsch., Chgo. Heart Assn. Office: 454 Pennsylvania Ave Glen Ellyn IL 60137-4418

AGUILAR, RAYMOND M. state legislator; b. Grand Island, Nebr., Oct. 24, 1947; m. Susan Ann, Dec. 14, 1973; chldren: Toni, Polly, Scott, Dean, T.C., Ali, Shelly, Audra, Jason. Undergrad., Central Cmty. Coll. Bldg., grounds dir. Grand Island Ctrl.; constrn. Chief Industries; prodn. mgr. Merrick Machine Co.; mem. Nebr. Legislature from 35th dist., Lincoln, 1999—. Mem. Grand Island City Coun., Lincoln Sch. PTA (pres.), Mayor's Youth Coun., Mayor's Cmty. Crime Commn., Am. Red Cross, lectr., eucharistic min., religious edn. com. St. Mary's Cath. Ch. Mem. Hall Cty. Leadership Tomorrow, Grand Island Little Theatre; minority adv. mem. Nebr. Coordinating Commn. for Postsecondary Edn. Roman Catholic Office: State Capitol (Dist 35) Room 1115 PO Box 94604 Lincoln NE 68509-4604

AGUILERA, RICHARD WARREN (RICK AGUILERA), baseball player; b. San Gabriel, Calif., Dec. 31, 1961; Student, Brigham Young U. Pitcher N.Y. Mets, 1985-89, Minn. Twins, 1989-95, 96-99, Boston Red Sox, 1995; relief pitcher Chgo. Cubs, 1999—. Player Am. League All-Star Game, 1991-93. Achievements include ranked 2nd in Am. League in saves, 1992. Office: Chgo Cubs Wrigley Field 1060 W Addison St Chicago IL 60613-4383

AGUIRRE, PAMELA ANN, manufacturing executive; b. Dearborn, Mich., Dec. 12, 1958; d. Hank Aguirre; 3 children. Doctorate (hon.), Lawrence Technol. U., 1998. CEO, chmn. bd. Mexican Industries, Detroit, 1994—. Bd. dirs. SBA, 1996; bd. dirs. Mich. Minority Bus. Devel. Coun., Hank Aguirre Cancer Awareness Found., The Children's Ctr. Recipient Hispanic Bus. Alliance award, 1996 Mem. Econ. Club of Detroit, (bd. dirs.), others. Office: Mexican Industries Aguirre Plaza 1801 Howard St Detroit MI 48216-1920 Fax: 313-963-6217.

AHERN, MARY ANN, reporter; m. Thomas Ahern; 3 children. BA, John Carroll U., 1976; MEd, Northeastern Ill. U., 1979; M Journalism, Northwestern U., 1982. Tchr. 2 Chgo. area H.S., 1976—79; reporter, weekend anchor Sta. WEEK-TV, Peoria, Ill., 1982—85; polit. reporter Sta. WXIA-TV, Atlanta, 1985—89; gen. assignment reporter NBC 5, Chgo., 1989—. Office: NBC 454 N Columbus Dr Chicago IL 60611*

AHLERICH, STAN, farmer, farm association administrator; m. Molly Ahlerich; children: Alexis, Nicholas. Degree in agrl. econs., Kans. State U. Farmer, Cowley County, Kans.; pres. Kans. Farm Bur., Manhattan, 1999—. Pres. bd. Cowley County Farm Bur., v.p.; chmn. Young Farmers and Ranchers; polit. edn. chmn., policy chmn., info. chmn., voting del. state conv. Young Farmers and Ranchers ; chmn. Young Farmers and Ranchers state com. Kans. Farm Bur., 1983—84, chmn., 1984; bd. dirs. Am. Farm Bur., Commerce Bank of Wichita, Kans. Charter mem. state bd., chmn. Kans. Agr. and Rural Leadership, 1992—93; mem. Kans. Inc., Walnut River Basin Adv. Bd.; mem. farm and ranch adv. bd. Sen. Bob Dole, 1986. Office: Kans Farm Bur 2627 KFB Plz Manhattan KS 66503

AHLERS, LINDA L. retail executive; BA in Retailing, U. Wisc. Buyer, Target Stores Dayton Hudson Corp., 1977-83, divsn. mdse. mgr., Target Stores, 1983-85, dir. mdse. planning and control, 1985-88, v.p. mdse. planning and control, 1988, sr. v.p. Target Stores, 1988-95, exec. v.p. merchandising, dept. store divsn., 1995-96, pres., dept. store divsn., 1996—, bd. dirs., 1997—. Dir. Guthrie Theatre; mem. Com. of 200, Detroit Renaissance Bd., Minn. Women's Econ. Roundtable. Office: Target Corp 1000 Nicollet Mall Minneapolis MN 55403-2467

AHLQUIST, PAUL GERALD, molecular biology researcher, educator; b. Des Moines, Jan. 9, 1954; s. Irving Elmer and Sigrun Evelyn (Eidbo) A. BS in Physics, Iowa State U., 1976; PhD in Biophysics, U. Wis., 1981. Asst. sci. in biophysics U. Wis., Madison, 1981-84, asst. prof. biophysics and plant pathology, 1984-87, assoc. prof. molecular virology and plant pathology, 1987-91, prof., 1991—, prof. molecular virology, oncology and plant pathology, 1997—, chmn. molecular virology, 1996-97, Paul J. Kaesberg prof., 2000—; investigator Howard Hughes Med. Inst., 1997—. Mem. exec. com. Internat. Commn. Taxonomy of Viruses, 1987-93; van Arkel hon. faculty chair in biochemistry Leiden (The Netherlands) U., 1995. Editor: RNA Genetics, vols. I, II, III, 1988, Molecular Biology of Plant-Microbe Interactions, 1989; assoc. editor Virology, 1988-93, Molecular Plant-Microbe Interactions, 1988-95, Plant Molecular Biology, 1987-90; contbr. articles to profl. jours. Recipient Presdl. Young Investigator award NSF, 1985-90, Romnes Faculty Fellowship award, 1988, Shaw Faculty Scholar award Milw. Found., 1985-90, Allen Rsch. award Am. Phytopathology Soc., 1988, Pound Rsch. award, 1987, WARF Mid-Career Rsch. award, 1995, NIH Merit award, 1995—. Mem. NAS, Am. Soc. Virology (mem. exec. coun. 1993-96), Internat. Soc. Plant Molecular Biology (bd. dirs. 1989-93), Am. Soc. for Microbiology, Genetics Soc. Am.

AHMANN, JOHN STANLEY, psychologist, educator; b. Struble, Iowa, Oct. 17, 1921; s. Henry Frank and Philomane (Wictor) Ahmann; children: Sandi Ann, Sheri Kay, Gregory Steven, Shelly Joan. BA, Trinity Coll., 1943; BS, Iowa State U., 1947, MS, 1949, PhD, 1951. Instr. profl. studies Iowa State U., 1949-51, prof. edn. and psychology, 1975—, disting. prof. edn., 1981—, chmn. dept. profl. studies, 1975-84; asst. prof. div. ednl. psychology and psychol. measurement Cornell U., 1951-54, asso. prof., 1954-58, prof., 1958-60; prof. psychology Colo. State U., 1960-75; assoc. dir. Human Factors Rsch. Lab., 1969-71, asst. to pres., 1961-64, head dept. psychology, 1962-64, acad. v.p., 1964-69. Adj. prof. psychology and edn. U. Denver, 1971—76; vis. prof. Colo. State U., 1951, Wash. State U., 1960, Western Wash. U., 1970; cons. rsch. programs U.S. Dept. Edn.; cons. evaluation ednl. programs, Colo., NY, La., Tex., Ark., Hawaii, Ga., Ariz., Ohio, Minn., Iowa; project dir. Nat. Assessment Ednl. Progress, 1971—75; dir. various fed. and state sponsored rsch. projects; hon. lectr. Mid-Am. State U. Assn., 1976—77. Author: (book) Statistical Methods in Educational and Psychological Research, 1954, Evaluating Student Progress, 6th edit., 1981, Evaluating Elementary School Pupils, 1960, Testing Student Achievement and Aptitudes, 1962, Measuring and Evaluating Educational Achievement, 2d edit., 1975, How Much Are Our Young People Learning?, 1976, Needs Assessment for Program Planning in Vocational Education, 1979, Academic Achievements of Young Americans, 1983; assoc. editor: Ednl. Studies, 1975—79. With USNR, 1943—46, PTO. Recipient Laureate award, Iowa State U., 1975. Fellow: APA, AAAS; mem.: Nat. Coun. Measurement Edn., Am. Ednl. Rsch. Assn., Psi Chi, Alpha Chi Sigma, Phi Lambda Upsilon, Phi Delta Kappa, Phi Kappa Phi, Sigma Xi. Home: 3738 Franklin Ave Loveland CO 80538-2204 Office: Iowa State Univ N243 Quadrangle Ames IA 50011-0001

AHRENS, FRANKLIN ALFRED, veterinary pharmacology educator; b. Leigh, Nebr., Apr. 27, 1936; s. Alfred Henry and Agnes Elizabeth (Higgins) A.; m. Katherine Aldene Henning, May 8, 1960; children— Jeffrey, Gregory, Matthew, Kristin D.V.M., Kans. State U., 1959; M.S., Cornell U., 1965, Ph.D., 1968. Instr. U. Minn.-St. Paul, 1959-60; asst. prof. pharmacology Coll. Vet. Medicine, Iowa State U., Ames, 1968-70, assoc. prof. pharmacology, 1970-75, prof. pharmacology, 1975—2001, chmn. dept. vet. physiology and pharmacology, 1982-90; prof. emeritus Coll. Vet. Medicine Iowa State U., 2001—. Served as capt. USAF, 1960-63, lt. col. Air N.G., 1971-91. Recipient Norden Disting. Tchr. award Iowa State U., 1981; NIH spl. research fellow Cornell U., 1967-68 Mem. AVMA, N.Y. Acad. Scis., Assn. Mil. Surgeons U.S., Sigma Xi Democrat. Lutheran.

AHRENS, KENT, museum director, art historian; b. Martinsburg, W.Va. s. Fred E. and Mary C. (Routzahn) A. A.B., Dartmouth Coll., 1961; M.A., U. Md., 1966; Ph.D., U. Del., 1972. Mem. faculty Fla. State U., Tallahassee, 1971-74, Randolph-Macon Woman's Coll., Lynchburg, Va., 1974-77; mem. curatorial staff Wadsworth Atheneum, Hartford, Conn., 1977-78; mem. faculty Georgetown U., Washington, 1979-82; dir. Everhart Mus., Scranton, Pa., 1982-90, Rockwell Mus., Corning, N.Y., 1990-95, Civic Fine Arts Ctr., Sioux Falls, S.D., 1996-97, Kennedy Mus. of Art, Ohio U., Athens, 1997—. Mem. task force on art activities Lynchburg Bicentennial Commn., 1975-76; project evaluator Md. Com. Humanities, 1980-82; mem. adv. panel The Lucan Ctr., Scranton, Pa., 1983-84; mem. mus. adv. com. Pa. Hist. and Mus. Commn., 1984-86; trustee Williamstown (Mass.) Regional Art Conservation Lab., Inc., 1984-92; mem. art mus. adv. panel Pa. Coun. on Arts, 1984-87; mem. adv. panel Pa. Fedn. Mus. and Hist. Orgns., 1989-90; mem. adv. com. on exhbns. at Pa. Gov.'s residence, 1987-90; juror Regional Art '89, Marywood Coll. Art Galleries, Scranton, 1989, Regional 1991, Arnot Art Mus., Elmira, 1991, Cmty. Cultural Ctr,. Brookings, S.D., 1996; bd. dirs. Mus. West, 1990-95; juror Fiber and Textile Exhibn. Civic Fine Arts Ctr., Sioux Falls, S.D., 1996, Wilbur Stilwell Student Awards Exhibn., U. S.D., Vermillion, 1997, Zanesville (Ohio) Art Ctr., 2000; adj. prof. Sch. Art, Ohio U., Athens, 1997—, mem. percent for art com., 1997-99. Author: (with others) Rembrandt in the National Gallery of Art, 1969; contbg. author: American Paintings and Sculpture: Illustrated Catalogue, Nat. Gallery of Art, 1970, Wadsworth Atheneum Paintings: The Netherlands and German-speaking Countries, 1978, Dictionary of Women Artists, 1997; author: The Drawings and Watercolors by Truman Seymour (1824-1891), Everhart Mus. 1986; co-author: Frederic C. Knight (1898-1979), Everhart Mus., 1987; author: The Oils and Watercolors by Edward D. Boit (1840-1915), Everhart Mus., 1990, Cyrus E. Dallin: His Small Bronzes and Plasters, Rockwell Mus., 1995; contbg. author: Allgemeines Künsterlexikon, 1999—, Currier & Ives: Selection from the Nationwide Collection, Kennedy Mus. Art, 2000. Vol. Bosnia-Herzegovina Heritage Rescue, London, 1995—. Served as 1st lt. U.S. Army, 1962-64. Recipient grant-in-aid Am. Philos. Soc., 1975; Samuel H. Kress fellow Nat. Gallery of Art, 1968-69; Chester Dale fellow Nat. Gallery Art, 1970-71; NEH fellow, 1973-74, Mus. Mgmt. Inst., J. Paul Getty Trust, 1991, award for superior vol. svc. Am. Assn. Mus., 1999. Mem. Coll. Art Assn., Am. Assn. Mus. (on-site surveyor mus. assessment program 1984-89, 92—, accreditation com. 1986, 90—), Mus. Assn. Pa. (chmn. 1984-90), Mid-Atlantic Assn. Mus., Rotary.

AIKEN, MICHAEL THOMAS, academic administrator; b. El Dorado, Ark., Aug. 20, 1932; s. William Floyd and Mary (Gibbs) A.; m. Catherine Comet, Mar. 28, 1969; 1 child, Caroline R. BA, U. Miss., 1954; MA, U. Mich., 1955, PhD, 1964. Asst. prof. U. Wis., Madison, 1963-67, assoc. prof., 1967-70, prof., 1970-84, assoc. dean coll. arts and scis., 1980-82; prof. U. Pa., Phila., 1984-93, dean sch. arts and scis., 1985-87, provost, 1987-93; chancellor U. Ill., Urbana, 1993-2001, Champaign/Urbana, 1993-2001. Author: (with others) The Dynamics of Idealism, 1971, Economic Failure, Alienation, and Extremism, 1968; editor: (with others) Complex Organizations: Critical Perspectives, 1981, The Structures of Community Power, 1970. Mem. Am. Sociol. Assn. (sec. 1986-89). Office: 3413 N Highcross Rd Urbana IL 61802 E-mail: aiken@uiuc.edu.

AINSWORTH, JOHN HENRY, state legislator; b. Sept. 21, 1940; Grad. high sch. State assemblyman dist. 4 State of Wis., 1990-92, state assemblyman dist. 6, 1993—. Mem. agrl. adv. com. Wis. State Assmebly; dairy farmer. Mem. Shawano County Rep. Com. Mem. Shawano County Farm Bur. (former pres.). Republican. Office: W6382 Waukechon Rd Shawano WI 54166-7042

AITAY, VICTOR, concert violinist, music educator; b. Budapest, Hungary; came to U.S., 1946, naturalized, 1952; s. Sigmund and Irma (Fazekas) A.; m. Eva Vera Kellner; 1 child, Ava Georgianna. Pvt. studies with father; entered, Royal Acad. Music at age 7; studies with Bela Bartok, studies with Ernest von Dohnanyi, studies with Leo Weiner, studies with Zoltan Kodaly; artist diploma, Franz Liszt Royal Acad. Music, Budapest, 1939; DFA, Lake Forest Coll., 1986. Prof. 1st Internat. String Congress; prof. violin DePaul U., Chgo., 1962—. Organizer, leader Aitay String Quartet, European tour, recitals; also solo symphony orchs.; concertmaster Met. Opera Assn., N.Y.C., 948-54, Chgo. Symphony Orch., 1954—; leader Chgo. Symphony String Quartet; condr., music dir. Lake Forest (Ill.) Symphony Orch.; numerous performances Casals Festival by invitation of Pablo Casals. Office: Chgo Symphony Assn 220 S Michigan Ave Chicago IL 60604-2596

AKCASU, AHMET ZIYAEDDIN, nuclear engineer, educator; b. Aydin, Turkey, Aug. 26, 1924; s. Osman Nuri and Faika (Egel) A.; m. Melahat Turksal, July 16, 1954; children: Nur, Feza, Aydin. B.S., M.S., Tech. U. Istanbul, 1948; Ph.D., U. Mich., 1963. Asst. prof., then asso. prof. Tech. U. Istanbul, 1948-58; resident research asso. Argonne (Ill.) Nat. Lab., 1959-61; mem. faculty U. Mich., Ann Arbor, 1963—, prof. nuclear engring., 1968-95, emeritus, 1995—. Leading author: Mathematical Methods in Nuclear Reactor Dynamics, 1971; contbr. over 100 articles on statis. physics, reactor dynamics, plasma physics and polymer solution dynamic to profl. jours. Recipient Glenn Murphy award Am. Soc. Engring. Edn., 1986, Alexander von Humboldt rsch. award for sr. U.S. scientist, 1991, sci. award Turkish Sci. and Tech. Rsch. Coun., 1992, Excellence in Rsch. award U. Mich. Coll. Engring., 1995. Fellow Am. Nuclear Soc., Am. Phys. Soc.; mem. Turkish Phys. Soc., N.Y. Acad. Scis., Sigma Xi. Home: 2820 Pebble Creek Dr Ann Arbor MI 48108-1728 Office: U Mich Dept Nuclear Engring and Radiol Scis Ann Arbor MI 48109-2104 E-mail: ziya@engin.umich.edu.

AKEEL, HADI ABU, robotics executive; b. Cairo, Egypt, Apr. 9, 1938; came to U.S., 1961; s. Kobaisi Aly Abu-Akeel and Zeinab Makhlouf; children: Shereef, Nezar; m. Naglaa Mostafa. BS in Mech. Engring., Cairo U., 1959; MS in Applied Mechanics, UCLA, 1963; PhD in Mech. Engring., U. Calif., Berkeley, 1966. Cert. mfg. engr. Acting instr. U. Calif., Berkeley, 1963-66; analytical specialist Bendix Corp., South Bend, Ind., 1966-69; assoc. prof. Ain Shams U., Cairo, 1969-74; sr. staff engr. GM Mfg., Warren, Mich., 1974-76; program mgr. GM Corp., 1976-78; dept. head mfg. staff GM, 1978-80, chief engr. flexible automation systems, 1980-82; v.p., chief engr. GMFanuc Robotics Corp., Auburn Hills, Mich., 1982-92; sr. v.p. Fanuc U.S.A., 1992-96, also bd. dirs., vice chmn., 1992-98; gen. mgr. Berkeley Lab. Fanuc Am. Corp., Union City, Calif., 1992—; sr. v.p. Fanuc Robotics N.A., Inc., 1996-98. Tech. advisor FANUC Ltd., Japan, 1992—; advisor Mgmt. of Tech. Program U. Calif., Berkeley, 1988-92; chmn. bd. dirs. Robotics Internat. of SME, Dearborn, Mich., 1992-93 Author: Machine Design, 1972; contbr. articles to profl. jours.; holds over 60 U.S. and fgn. patents. Soccer coach Am. Youth Soccer Orgn.; mem. bd. advisors Sch. Engring., U. Mich., Dearborn, 1991—; chmn. bd. visitors Sch. Engring., Oakland U., 1991-92. Recipient Joseph F. Engleberger award Robotic Industries Assn., 1989, Mich. Sci. Trailblazer award State Mich., 1989. Fellow ASME, Soc. Mfg. Engrs. (internat. dir. 1998—); mem. IEEE, Nat. Acad. Engring. Republican. Muslim. Avocations: tennis, swimming, camping, travel, machine shop. Office: Fanuc Robotics Corp 3900 W Hamlin Rd Rochester Hills MI 48309-3253 E-mail: akeel@frc.com.

AKEMANN, DAVID ROY, lawyer; b. Elgin, Ill., Oct. 31, 1951; s. Theodore H. and Lois (Marr) A.; m. Vickie C. Skala, Aug. 5, 1978; children— Carrie, Julie. B.S., Brigham Young U., 1972; J.D., Lewis U., 1978. Bar: Ill. 1978, U.S. Dist. Ct. (no. dist.) Ill. 1978, U.S. Ct. Appeals (7th cir.) 1979, U.S. Supreme Ct. 1981. Clk. States Atty. Office, Kane County, Geneva, Ill., 1977-78; asst. states atty., 1978-79, chief civil div., 1979— ; sole practice, Elgin, 1978— ; ptnr. Gov. Services Enterprises, Elgin, 1985— ; labor cons. Ill. States Attys. Appellate Prosecutor Commn. Author booklet in field. Precinct committeeman Elgin Twp. Republican Central Com., 1980, 82, 84. Recipient Am. Jurisprudence Constn. Law award Lawyers Coop. Pub. Co., 1978. Mem. ABA, Ill. Bar Assn., Kane County Bar Assn., Ill. Pub. Employers Labor Relations Assn. (prin.). Methodist. Home: 420 Hoxie Ave Elgin IL 60123-3220

AKER, ALAN D. state legislator; Logging contractor, Rapid City, S.D.; senator Senate of S.D., Pierre, 1995-99; pres., homebuilder Aker Woods Co., Piedmont, S.D., 1999—. Mem. agr. and natural resources com., edn. and local govt. coms. S.D. State Senate.

AKERLOF, CARL WILLIAM, physics educator; b. New Haven, Mar. 5, 1938; s. Gosta Carl and Rosalie Clara (Hirschfelder) A.; m. Carol Irene Ruska, Sept. 4, 1965; children— Karen Louise, William Gustav B.A., Yale U., 1960; Ph.D., Cornell U., 1967. Research assoc. U. Mich., Ann Arbor, 1966-68, asst. prof., 1968-72, assoc. prof., 1972-78, prof. physics, 1978—. Contbr. articles to profl. jours. Incorporator Ann Arbor Hands-On Mus. Fellow Am. Phys. Soc.; mem. Am. Astron. Soc. Office: U Mich Randall Lab Physics Dept Physics Ann Arbor MI 48109

AKERS, MICHELLE ANNE, soccer player; b. Santa Clara, Calif., Feb. 1, 1966; BS in Liberal Studies and Health, U. Ctrl. Fla., 1989. Forward Tyreso Football Club, Sweden, 1990, 92, 94, Orlando (Fla.) Calibre Soccer Club, 1993, U.S. Women's Nat. Soccer Team, Chgo., 1985—. Author: Face to Face with Michelle Akers: Standing Fast; columnist Soccer Jr. mag., 1995—, Sidekicks mag., 1994, 95. Recipient Hermann Trophy, Golden Boot award FIFA Women's World Championship, 1991, Silver Ball award, 1991, Gold medal Atlanta Olympics, 1996; named All-Am., Ctrl. Fla. Athlete of Yr., 1988-89, MVP CONCACAF Qualifying Championship, 1994, U.S. Soccer Female Athlete of Yr., 1990, 91; named ESPN Athlete of Yr., 1985. Mem. Soccer Outreach Internat. (founder 1998), U.S. Soccer Fedn. (nat. bd. dirs. 1990-95), Women's Sports Found. (adv. bd. 1992—). Office: US Soccer Fedn US Soccer House 1801 S Prairie Ave Chicago IL 60616-1319

AKIL, HUDA, neuroscientist, educator, researcher; b. Damascus, Syria, May 19, 1945; came to U.S., 1968; d. Fakher and Widad (Al-Imam) A.; m. Stanley Jack Watson Jr., Dec. 21, 1972; children: Brendon Omar, Kathleen Tamara. BA, Am. U., Beirut, Lebanon, 1966, MA, 1968; PhD, UCLA, 1972. Postdoctoral fellow Stanford U., Palo Alto, Calif., 1974-78; from asst. prof. to prof. psychiatry and neuroscience U. Mich., Ann Arbor, 1979—. Mem. adv. bd. Neurex Corp., Menlo Park, Calif., 1986—, Neurobiol. Techs., Inc., 1994-97; sec. Internat. Narcotics Rsch. Conf., 1990-94. Editor: (jour.) Pain and Headache: Neurochemistry of Pain, 1990; contbr. articles over 300 articles to profl. jours. Recipient Pacesetter award Nat. Inst. Drug Abuse, 1993, Pasarow award Pasarow Found., 1994, Bristol-Myers Squibb award, 1998, Edward Sachar award Columbia U., 1998; Rockefeller scholar, Beirut, 1963-66; Alfred P. Sloan fellow, Stanford, Calif., 1974-78; grantee Nat. Inst. Drug Abuse, Washington, 1978—, NIMH, Washington, 1980—, Markey Found., U. Mich., 1988-97. Fellow Am. Coll. Neuropsychopharmacology (pres. 1997-98), U. Mich. Soc. Fellows; mem. Inst. Medicine/NAS. Achievements include first to produce physiological evidence for existence of naturally occurring opiate-like substances (endorphins) in brain; described phenomenon of stress-induced analgesia; described functions and regulation of endorphins in brain and pituitary gland; contributed to understanding of biological mechanisms of morphine tolerance and physical dependence; (with colleagues) cloned two main types of opiate receptors, described critical brain circuits relevant to stress and depression. Office: Mental Health Rsch Inst 205 Zina Pitcher Ann Arbor MI 48109-2214

AKIN, W. TODD, congressman, state legislator; b. N.Y.C., July 5, 1947; m. Lulli Boe, 1971; six children. BS, Worchester Polytechnic Inst.; MDiv, Covenant Theol. Sem. Mo. State rep. Dist. 86, 1988-2000; corp. mgmt. Laclede Steel Co.; bus. mgr., educator; former mktg. profl. IBM Computer Systems; mem. U.S. Congress from 2d Mo. dist., 2000—. Mem. energy and environ. com., judiciary com., higher edn. com. and edn. appropriations com. Officer Army Engrs. Office: 501 Cannon Ho Office Bldg Washington DC 20515-2502*

AKINS, CINDY S. human resources professional; BS, U. Ill.; MS in Labor and Indsl. Rels., Loyola U., Chgo. Various supervisory positions pub. sector; mgr. human resources Zurich Life Ins., Schaumburg, Ill.; dir. human resources Morningstar Inc., Chgo., from 1996, v.p. human resources. Mem. Am. Compensation Assn. (cert. compensation profl.). Office: Morningstar Inc 225 W Wacker Dr Chicago IL 60606-1224 Fax: 312-696-6001.

AKOS, FRANCIS, violinist, conductor; b. Budapest, Hungary, Mar. 30, 1922; came to U.S., 1954; s. Karoly and Rose (Reti) Weinberg; m. Phyllis Malvin Sommers, June 7, 1981; children from previous marriage— Katherine Elizabeth, Judith Margaret. Baccalaureate, Budapest, 1941; M.A., Franz Liszt Acad. Music, Budapest, 1940, Ph.D., 1941. Concertmaster, Budapest Symphony Orch., 1945-46, Royal Opera and Philharmonic Soc., Budapest, 1947-48, Gothenburg (Sweden) Symphony Orch., 1948-50, Municipal Opera, West Berlin, Ger., 1950-54, Mpls. Symphony Orch., 1954, asst. concertmaster, Chgo. Symphony Orch., 1955—, concertmaster emeritus, 1997—, also performed as soloist; performed at Salzburg Festival, 1948, Scandinavian Festival, Helsinki, Finland, 1950, Berlin Festival, 1951, Prades Festival, 1953, Bergen Festival, 1962, Vienna Festival, 1962, founder, condr., Chgo. Strings, chamber orch., 1961, condr., Fox River Valley Symphony, Aurora, Ill., 1965-73, Chicago Heights (Ill.) Symphony, 1975-79, Highland Park Strings, 1979—. Prizewinner Hubay competition, Budapest, 1939, Remenyi competition, Budapest, 1939 Home: 1310 Maple Ave Evanston IL 60201-4325 Office: 220 S Michigan Ave Chicago IL 60604-2596

AKRE, DONALD J. school system administrator; Supt. Selby (S.D.) Area Sch. Dist. State finalist Nat. Supt. Yr., 1992. Office: PO Box 222 Selby SD 57472-0222

ALBERS, SHERYL KAY, state legislator; b. Sauk County, Wis., Sept. 9, 1954; d. Marcus J. and Norma Anderson Gumz; 1 child, Joel Albert. BA, Ripon Coll., 1976; student, WW Law Sch. Publicity chmn. Sauk County Rep. Party, 1978-80, vice chmn., 1980-82, chmn., 1982-83, mem. exec. com.; assembly Rep. Caucus Wis., 1987-91; state assemblyman dist. 50 State of Wis., 1991—92, mem. govt. export strategy com., chair assembly ins., securities and corp. policy com., mem. environ. resources com., mem. rural affairs com., mem. natural resources com., mem. colls. and univs. com., mem. state bldg. commn.; mem. Local Emergency Planning Com. Juneau County; mem. Joint Com. on Fin., 1997- Recipient Campbell award Sauk County Rep. Com., 1981, 90, Top 10 County award Wis. State Rep. Party, 1982, Pacesetter award Wis. Forage Coun., 1983, Bovay award Rep. Party Wis., 1990; named one of Outstanding Farmers Sauk County Farm Bur., 1982. Mem. Sauk County Farm Bur. (dir., treas. 1977-82), Agrl. Bus. Coun. Wis., Kiwanis. Republican.

ALBERT, DANIEL MYRON, ophthalmologist, educator; b. Newark, Dec. 19, 1936; s. Maurice I. and Flora Albert; m. Eleanor Kagle, June 26, 1960; children: B. Steven, Michael. BS, Franklin and Marshall Coll., 1958; MD, U. Pa., 1962; MA (hon.), Harvard U., 1976; D honoris causa, Louis Pasteur U., Strasbourg, 1992; MS, U. Wis., Madison, 1997. Diplomate: Am. Bd. Ophthalmology. Intern Hosp. U. Pa., 1962-63, resident, 1963-66; surgeon USPHS, 1966-68; NIH spl. fellow in ophthalmic pathology Armed Forces Inst. Pathology, 1968-69; asst. prof. ophthalmology Yale U. Sch. Medicine, 1969-70, assoc. prof., 1970-75, prof., 1975-76; practice medicine specializing in ophthalmology; assoc. surgeon Mass. Eye and Ear Infirmary, 1976-86, surgeon, 1986-92, dir. David G. Cogan eye pathology lab., 1979-92; prof. ophthalmic pathology Harvard U. Med. Sch., 1976-84, David G. Cogan prof. ophthalmology, 1984-92; Frederick Allison Davis prof., chmn. dept. ophthalmology U. Wis., Madison, 1992—. Author: (with Scheie) A History of Ophthalmology at the University of Pennsylvania, 1965, Textbook of Ophthalmology, 8th edit. 1969, 9th edit. 1977; co-author: Jaeger's Atlas of Ophthalmology, 1972, (with Puliafito) Foundations of Ophthalmology, 1979, Men of Vision, 1993, (with Jakobiec) Atlas of Clinical Ophthalmology, 1996; (with Edwards) History of Ophthalmology, 1996; editor: (with Edwards) The History of Ophthalmology, 1996, John Jeffres' Lectures on the Diseases of the Eye, 1998, Ophthalmic Surgery: Principles and Techniques, 1998, A Physician's Guide to Health Care Management, 2002; co-editor Principles and Practice of Ophthalmology, 1994, 2d edit., 1999, A Physician's Guide to Healthcare Management, 2002, Dates in Ophthalmology, 2002; editor Archives of Ophthalmology, 1994—; contbr. articles to profl. jours. Recipient Oliver Meml. medal, U. Pa., 1962, Friedenwald award, 1981, Von Sallmann award in vision and ophthalmology, INternat. Conf. for Eye Rsch., 1988, award, Humboldt Found., 1991, MacKenzie medal, Scottish Ophthal. Soc., 1992, Lighthouse Pisart Vision award, The Lighthouse Inc., 1997, Lorenz E. Zimmerman (WARF) professorship, 1999, Disting. Alumni award, U. Pa. Sch. Medicine, 2001; scholar William and Mary Greve scholar, 1978—79, Alcon Rsch. Inst., 1984—85. Fellow ACS; mem. Am. Assn. Ophthalmic Pathology (Zimmerman medal 1993), Am. Acad. Ophthalmology (Jackson Meml. lectr. 1996), Am. Bd. Ophthalmology (dir. 1997—). Jewish. Home: 1106 Wellesley Rd Madison WI 53705-2230 Office: U Wis Hosp and Clinics Dept Ophthalmology F4/334 600 Highland Ave Madison WI 53792-0001

ALBERTY, WILLIAM EDWIN, lawyer; b. Quincy, Ill., Jan. 3, 1944; s. Edwin Harry and Elizabeth May (Barth) A.; m. Carol Ellen Pinion, June 27, 1970; children: Wade Dixson, Anne Elizabeth. BA, Culver-Stockton Coll., Canton, Mo.; JD, U. Mo., 1969. Bar: Mo. 1969. Asst. prosecutor Buchanan County Prosecutor's Office, St. Joseph, Mo., 1969-70; asst. city atty. City of St. Joseph, 1970-71; pvt. practice Edina, Mo., 1971-82; ptnr. Alberty & Deveny, 1982—. Avocation: golf. Home: 112 W Marion St Edina MO 63537-1006 Office: Alberty & Deveny 215 N Main St Edina MO 63537-1350

ALBRECHT, RONALD FRANK, anesthesiologist; b. Chgo., Apr. 17, 1937; s. Frank William and Mabel Dorothy (Cassens) A.; children: Ronald Frank II, Mark Burchfield, Meredith Ann. A.B., U. Ill., 1958, B.S., 1959, M.D., 1961. Diplomate Am. Bd. Anesthesiology. Intern U. Cin. Hosp., 1961-62; resident in anesthesiology U. Ill. Hosp., Chgo., 1962-64, attending physician, 1966-73, 89—; clin. assoc. NIH, Bethesda, Md., 1964-66; practice medicine specializing in anesthesiology Chgo., 1966—; asst. prof. anesthesiology U. Ill., 1966-70, clin. assoc. prof., 1970-73, prof. anesthesiology, head dept. Coll. Medicine, 1989—; chief dept. anesthesiology U. Ill. Hosp., 1989—, pres. med. staff, 1999-2001. Chmn. dept. anesthesiology Michael Reese Med. Ctr., Chgo., 1971—; prof. anesthesiology U. Chgo., 1973-89. Contbr. articles to profl. jours. Served to lt. comdr. USPHS, 1964-66. Fellow Am. Coll. Anesthesiologists; mem. AMA, Internat. Anesthesia Rsch. Soc., Am. Soc. Anesthesiologists, Assn. Anesthesists Gt. Britain and Ireland, Am. Physiol. Soc., Soc. Acad. Anesthesiology Chairs, Assn. Anesthesiology Program Dirs. (pres. 1991-93), Ill. Soc. Anesthesiologists (pres. 1980-81), Ill. State Med. Soc., Chgo. Med. Soc., Chgo. Soc. Anesthesiologists (pres. 1986-90), Assn. Univ. Anesthesiologists. Presbyterian. Home: 1020 Chestnut Ave Wilmette IL 60091-1732 Office: U Ill Chgo Coll Medicine Dept Anesthesiology MC/515 1740 W Taylor St Ste 3200 Chicago IL 60612-7239 E-mail: ralbrech@uic.edu.

ALBRECHT, WILLIAM PRICE, economist, educator, government official; b. Pitts., Jan. 7, 1935; s. William Price and Jane Lanier (Moses) A.; m. Alice Annette Cooper, June 14, 1956 (div. Nov. 1975); children— William, Alison, Jonathan, Jeffrey; m. Fran Jaecques, July 4, 1976 AB, Princeton U., 1956; MA, U. S.C., 1962, Yale U., 1963, PhD, 1965. Asst. prof. U. Iowa, Iowa City, 1965-70, assoc. prof., 1970-82, prof. econs., 1982-88, assoc. dean Coll. Bus. Adminstrn., 1984-88; self-employed antitrust cons., 1978-88; commr. Commodity Futures Trading Commn., Washington, 1988-93; prof. econs. U. Iowa, Iowa City, 1993—, dir. Inst. for Internat. Bus., 1998—, Justice prof. Internat. Bus., 2000—. TV fin. advisor. Author: Economics, 1974, 4th edit., 1986, Black Employment, 1970, Microeconomic Principles, 1979, Macroeconomic Principles, 1979 Candidate U.S. Ho. of Reps., 1970; legis. asst. U.S. Senator Dick Clark, 1974. Served to lt. USN, 1956-61 Mem. Am. Econ. Assn., Midwest Econ. Assn. (v.p. 1981-82). Avocations: tennis; farming. Home: 5770 NE Morse Rd Solon IA 52333-8806 Office: U Iowa Dept Econs Iowa City IA 52242

ALBRIGHT, JACK LAWRENCE, animal science and veterinary educator; b. San Francisco, Mar. 14, 1930; s. George Clarence and Elizabeth Ann (Murphy) A.; m. Lorraine Aylmer Hughes, Aug. 17, 1957; children: Maryann A. Williams, Amy Elizabeth. BS with honors, Calif. State Poly. U., 1952; MS, Wash. State U., 1954, PhD, 1957. Rsch. asst. Wash. State U., 1952-54, 55-57, acting instr., 1954-55; instr. Calif. State Poly. U., 1955, 57-59; asst. prof. U. Ill., Urbana, 1959-63; assoc. prof. Purdue U., West Lafayette, Ind., 1963-66, prof. animal sci. Sch. Agr., 1966-96, prof. animal mgmt. and behavior Sch. Vet. Medicine, 1974-96, prof. emeritus animal sci. and vet. medicine, 1996—. Mem. Ctr. Applied Ethology and Human-Animal Interactions Human/Animal Bond Purdue U., 1982-96, Purdue Interdisciplinary Undergrad. Program in Animal Welfare and Societal Concerns, 1992-96, Purdue Animal Care and Use com., 1989-92, Ctr. for Rsch. on Well-Being in Food Animals, 1992-96; vis. prof. U. Ariz., Tucson, 1995, N.Mex. State U., Las Cruces, 1995, U. Ill., Urbana, 1988-89; vis. prof. pure and applied zoology U. Reading, Eng., 1977-78; vis. scientist N.Z. Dept. Agr., Ruakura, Hamilton, 1971-72, Dairy Shrine, Ft. Atkinson, Wis., 1958—; cons., lectr. in field, animal mgmt., behavior, care and welfare; mem. Ind. Commn. Farm Animal Care, 1981-99; numerous invited lectures worldwide. Author more than 900 papers, revs., chpts., guidelines, and books; reviewer sci. jours. Vestryman St. John's Episcopal Ch., Lafayette, Ind., 1979-82; bellringer Salvation Army, 1964—; mem. judging teams Cal Poly Dairy Cattle, Dairy Products and Livestock; vol. Ind. Livestock Care Assistance Project Helpline, 1999—. Fulbright scholar, N.Z., 1971-72; NSF Animal Behavior grantee, summer 1964; USDA/FAS/ICD Sci. and Tech. Exch. Program awardee to Rep. of Ireland, 1994; recipient Guardian award Ind. Vet. Med. Assn., 1995, Sci., Edn. and Tech. award dept. animal scis. Washington State U., 1996; one of 7 named to inaugural Renaissance Acad. Hall of Fame, Paso Robles H.S., 1998. Fellow AAAS, Am. Dairy Sci. Assn., Ind. Acad. Sci.; mem. Am. Dairy Sci. Assn. (sec. 1972-73, chmn. profl. coun. 1973-74, Dairy Mgmt. Rsch. award 1986, invited lectrs. ann. meeting, 1982, 86-87, 92, 94, found. charter 1992), Animal Behavior Soc. (charter), Am. Soc. Animal Sci. (chmn. animal behavior com. 1970, 76, 85, Animal Mgmt. Rsch. award 1988, Found. charter 1993, animal care com. 1994-96), Am. Registry Profl. Animal Sci. (dairy and animal behavior 1993—), Humane Slaughter Assn., Am. Coll. Animal Behavior Sci. (cert., charter, diplomate 1995), Am. Soc. Vet. Ethology (charter), Internat. Soc. Applied Ethology, Chillingham Wild Cattle Assn. (life), Soc. Study Ethics and Animals, Scientist's Ctr. Animal Welfare (corr.), Univs. Fedn. for Animal Welfare, Hooved Animal Humane Soc., Los Lecheros Dairy Club Calif. State Poly. U. (hon.), Kiwanis (pres. Lafayette club 1969-70, sec. found. 1976-77, Tablet of Honor Internat. Kiwanis Found. 2000), Blue Key, Delta Soc., Sigma Xi, Alpha Zeta, Gamma Sigma Delta, Farm House. Republican. Home: 188 Blueberry Ln West Lafayette IN 47906-4810 Office: Purdue Univ Poul Bldg Dept Animal Scis West Lafayette IN 47907-1026 E-mail: jla9@juno.com.

ALBRIGHT, JUSTIN W. retired lawyer; b. Lisbon, Iowa, Oct. 14, 1908; m. Mildred Carlton, 1935; 1 child, Carlton J. B.S.C., U. Iowa, 1931, J.D., 1933. Bar: Iowa 1933. Former counsel firm Simmons, Perrine, Albright & Ellwood, P.L.C., Cedar Rapids, Iowa; ret. Editor: Iowa Law Rev, 1932-33. Past trustee, bd. trustees YMCA of Met. Cedar Rapids; bd. dirs. Cedar Rapids Symphony Orch.; founding mem., past pres. St. Paul's United Meth. Ch. Found., Cedar Rapids. Served with AUS, World War II. Mem. ABA, Iowa Bar Assn., Linn County Bar Assn. (life), Am. Judicature Soc., Hoover Presdl. Libr. Assn., Cedar Rapids C. of C., Phi Delta Phi. Clubs: Cedar Rapids Country, Pickwick (Cedar Rapids) (past pres.). Lodges: Masons (32 deg.), Shriners, Rotary (Paul Harris fellow). Office: Simmons Perrine Albright & Ellwo 115 3rd St SE Ste 1200 Cedar Rapids IA 52401-1266

ALBRIGHT, LYLE FREDERICK, chemical engineering educator; b. Bay City, Mich., May 3, 1921; s. William Edward and Isabella (Sidebotham) A.; m. Jeanette Van Belle, Mar. 4, 1950; children: Christine, Diane. B.S. in Chem. Engring, U. Mich., 1943, M.S. in Chem. Engring, 1944, Ph.D. in Chem. Engring, 1950. Lab. technician Dow Chem. Co., Midland, Mich., 1939-41; chem. engr. E.I. duPont de Nemours & Co., Hanford, Wash., 1944-46; research chem. engr. Colgate-Palmolive Co., Jersey City, 1950-51; asst. prof. U. Okla., Norman, 1951-54, assoc. prof., 1954-55, Purdue U., West Layette, Ind., 1955-58, prof. chem. engring., 1958—. Cons. to numerous chem. petroleum cos., 1960— Author: Industrial and Laboratory Pyrolyses, 1976, Industrial and Laboratory Alkylations, 1977, Coke Formation on Metals, 1982, Pyrolysis: Theory and Industrial Practice, 1983, Processes for Major Addition Type Plastics and Their Monomers, 2d edit., 1985, Novel Production Methods for Ethylene, Light Hydrocarbons, and Aromatics, 1992, Nitrations: Recent Laboratory and Industrial Developments, 1996. Recipient Shreve prize Purdue U., 1960, 70, 88, Potter award for best instr. Schs. of Engring. Purdue U., 1988. Fellow Am. Inst. Chem. Engrs. (dir. 1982-84); mem. Am. Chem. Soc., Internat. Brotherhood Magicians, Sigma Xi, Tau Beta Pi. Methodist. Home: 4750N N 250 W West Lafayette IN 47906-5525 Office: Purdue Univ Sch Chem Engring West Lafayette IN 47907

ALBRIGHT, TERRILL D. lawyer; b. Lebanon, Ind., June 23, 1938; s. David Henry and Georgia Pauline (Doty) A.; m. Judith Ann Stoelting, June 2, 1962; children: Robert T., Elizabeth A. AB, Ind. U., 1960, JD, 1965. Bar: Ind. 1965, U.S. Dist. Ct. (so. dist.) Ind. 1965, U.S. Dist. Ct. (no. dist.) Ind. 1980, U.S. Ct. Appeals (7th cir.) 1981, U.S. Ct. Appeals (3d and D.C. cirs.) 1982, U.S. Supreme Ct. 1972; cert. arbitrator for large complex cse program constrn. and internat. commercial cases Am. Arbitration Assn., cert. mediator. Assoc. Baker and Daniels Law Firm, Indpls., 1965-72, ptnr., 1972—. Mem. panel of disting. neutrals. nat. panel for constrn. and regional comml. panel CPR Inst. for Dispute Resolution, N.Y.C. Pres. Christamore House, Indpls., 1979-86; bd. dirs. Greater Indpls. YMCA, 1980-82; chmn. Jordan YMCA, Indpls., 1982; pres. Community Ctrs. Indpls., 1987-90. 1st lt. U.S. Army, 1960—62. Fellow: Acad. Law Alumni, Ind. U. Sch. of Law (bd. dirs. 1974—80, pres. 1979—80), Am. Coll. Trial Lawyers, Indpls. Bar Found., Ind. Bar Found, Am. Bar Found.; mem.: Ind. State Bar Assn. (chmn. young lawyers sect. 1971—72, rep. 11th dist. 1983—85, bd. dirs., v.p. 1991—92, pres.-elect 1992—93, pres. 1993—94), Nat. Conf. Bar. Pres. (exec. coun. 1995—96). Democrat. Office: Baker & Daniels 300 N Meridian St Ste 2700 Indianapolis IN 46204-1782 E-mail: tdalbright@bakerd.com.

ALDAG, RAMON JOHN, management and organization educator; b. Beccles, Suffolk, Eng., Feb. 11, 1945; came to U.S., 1947; s. Melvin Frederick and Joyce Evelyn (Butcher) A.; m. Hollis Maura Jellinek, June 11, 1977; children— Elizabeth, Katherine B.S., Mich. State U., 1966, M.B.A., 1968, Ph.D., 1974. Thermal engr. Bendix Aerospace div., Ann Arbor, Mich., 1966-70; teaching asst., instr. Mich. State U., East Lansing, 1966-73; asst. prof. mgmt. U. Wis., Madison, 1973-78, assoc. prof., 1978-82, prof. mgmt. and orgn., 1982—, chmn. dept. mgmt., 1986-88, assoc. dir. Indsl. Rels. Rsch. Inst., 1977-83, co-dir. Ctr. for Study of Orgnl. Performance, 1982—, faculty senator, 1980-84, Pyle Bascom prof. leadership, 1992—, student advisor, 1979—, Glen A. Skillrud Family chair in bus., 2001—, chmn. dept. mgmt. and human resources Sch. Bus., 1995—, co-dir. Weinert Ctr. for Entrepreneurship, 2000—. Mgmt. cons. various businesses and industries, 1973— Author: Task Design and Employee Motivation, 1979, Managing Organizational Behavior, 1981, Introduction to Business, 1984, (now titled Business in a Changing World), 3d edit., 1993, 4th edit., 1996, Management, 1987, 2d edit., 1991, Leadership and

Vision, 2000, Organizational Behavior and Management, 2002; contbr. articles to profl. jours.; cons. editor for mgmt. South-Western Pub. Co., 1987—; assoc. editor Jour. Bus. Rsch., 1988—; essays co-editor Jour. Mgmt. Inquiry. Bd. dirs. Family Enhancement Program, Madison, 1981— Grantee U. Wis., HEW, 1975-85; recipient Adminstrv. Rsch. Inst. award, 1976, Jerred Disting. Svc. award, 1993; U. Wis. faculty rsch. fellow, 1985-88 Fellow. Acad. of Mgmt. (div. chmn. 1971—, bd. govs. 1986—, v.p. and program chair 1989—, pres. elect 1990, pres. 1991, past pres. 1992—, recipient Disting Svc. award, 1995); mem. Midwest Acad. Mgmt. (pres. 1973—), Decision Scis. Inst. (track chmn. 1975—), Indsl. Rels. Rsch. Assn. (elections commn. 1980—), Found. Administrn. Rsch. (pres. 1992—), Pi Tau Sigma, Tau Beta Pi, Sigma Iota Epsilon, Beta Gamma Sigma, Alpha Iota Delta. Avocations: gardening, fishing. Home: 2818 Van Hise Ave Madison WI 53705-3620 Office: U Wis 3112 Grainger Hall 975 University Ave Madison WI 53706-1324 E-mail: raldag@bus.wisc.edu.

ALDERMAN, ROBERT K. state legislator; b. Nov. 14, 1942; m. Susan M. Toycen. Student, Ind. U. Ind. state rep. Dist. 19, 1976-91, Dist. 83, 1991—; chmn. housing aged and aging com. Ind. Ho. Reps., Vet. Affairs com., pub. safety com., human affairs and interstate coop. coms., ranking minority mem., pub. policy com., ethics com., rules and legis. procedures com., local govt. com. Capt. Allen County Police Dept., Ft. Wayne. With U.S. Army Nat. Guard. Recipient Acad. Achievement award Ind. Law Enforcement Acad., 1971; named Top 10 Legislators Am. Nat. Assembly Govt. Employee, 1983. Republican. Home: 5715 Kroemer Rd Fort Wayne IN 46818-9328

ALDINGER, WILLIAM F., III, diversified financial services company executive; b. 1947; BA, CUNY, 1969. With U.S. Trust Co., N.Y.C., 1969-75, Citibank Corp., N.Y.C., 1975-76; exec. v.p. Wells Fargo Bank NA, San Francisco, 1986-98; CEO Household Internat., Inc., Prospect Heights, Ill., 1994—, chmn. bd. dirs., 1996-97, chmn., CEO. Office: Household Internat 2700 Sanders Rd Prospect Heights IL 60070-2701

ALDRICH, ANN, federal judge; b. Providence, June 28, 1927; d. Allie C. and Ethel M. (Carrier) A.; m. Chester Aldrich, 1960 (dec.); children: Martin, William; children by previous marriage: James, Allen; m. John H. McAllister III, 1986. BA cum laude, Columbia U., 1948; LLB cum laude, NYU, 1950, LLM, 1964, JSD, 1967. Bar: D.C. bar, N.Y. bar 1952, Conn. bar 1966, Ohio bar 1973, Supreme Ct. bar 1956. Research asst. to mem. faculty N.Y. U. Sch. Law; atty. IBRD, 1952; atty., rsch. asst. Samuel Nakasian, Esq., Washington, 1952-53; mem. gen. counsel's staff FCC, 1953-60; U.S. del. to Internat. Radio Conf., Geneva, 1959; practicing atty. Darien, Conn., 1961-68; asso. prof. law Cleve. State U., 1968-71, prof., 1971-80; judge U.S. Dist. Ct. (no. dist.) Ohio, Cleveland, 1980—. Bd. govs. Citizens' Communications Center, Inc., Washington; mem. litigation com.; guest lectr. Calif. Inst. Tech., Pasadena, summer 1971 Mem. Fed. Bar Assn., Nat. Assn. of Women Judges, Fed. Communications Bar Assn., Fed. Judge Assn. Episcopalian. Office: US Dist Ct 201 Superior Ave E Cleveland OH 44114-1201

ALDRIDGE, ALFRED OWEN, English language educator; b. Buffalo, Dec. 16, 1915; s. Albert and Jane (Ette) A.; m. Mary Hennen Dellinger, May 18, 1941 (div. 1956); 1 dau., Cecily (Mrs. John Ward); m. Adriana García Davila, June 7, 1963 (div. 1988). B.S. in Edn, Ind. U., 1937; M.A., U. Ga., 1938; Ph.D., Duke U., 1942; D.U.P., U. Paris, France, 1955. Prof. comparative lit. U. Buffalo, 1942-47, U. Md., 1947-67, U. Ill., 1967-86, prof. emeritus, 1986—; Will and Ariel Durant chair St. Peter's Coll., Jersey City, 1986-87; prof. comp. lit. Pa. State U., 1987-88. Fulbright prof., France, 1953, Korea, 1988; Smith-Mundt prof., Brazil, 1957; vis. prof. Nihon U., Japan, 1976, 82, Kuwait U., 1983, Nat. Cheng Chi U., Taiwan, 1989-90, Nat. Tsing Hua U., Taiwan, 1991. Author: Franklin and His French Contemporaries, 1957, Man of Reason: Life of Thomas Paine, 1959, Jonathan Edwards, 1964, Benjamin Franklin: Philosopher and Man, 1965, Benjamin Franklin and Nature's God, 1967, Comparative Literature: Matter and Method, 1969, The Ibero-American Enlightenment, 1971, Voltaire and the Century of Light, 1975, Hikaku Bungaku: Comparative Literature East and West, 1979, Early American Literature: A Comparatist Approach, 1982, Thomas Paine's American Ideology, 1984, Fiction in Japan and the West, 1985, The Reemergence of World Literature, 1986, The Dragon and the Eagle: China in the American Enlightenment, 1993; editor Jour. Comparative Lit. Studies, 1963—; adv. editor: 18th Century: Theory and Interpretation, Modern Age. NEH fellow 1973-74 Mem. Am. Comparative Lit. Assn. (adv. bd. 1965-71, 74-77, v.p. 1977-80, pres. 1980-83), Internat. Comparative Lit. Assn. (adv. bd. 1970-78), Am. Soc. 18th Century Studies (adv. bd. 1968-75) Home: 101 E Chalmers St Champaign IL 61820-6001 Office: U Ill Modern Lang Bldg Urbana IL 61801

ALDRIDGE, DONALD O'NEAL, military officer; b. Solo., Mo., July 22, 1932; BA in History, U. Nebr., Omaha, 1974; postgrad., Creighton U., 1975. Commd. 2d lt. USAF, 1958, advanced through grades to lt. gen., 1988, asst. dir. plans, 1978-79; spl. asst. to dir. Joinr Chiefs of Staff, 1979-80; dep. dir. Def. Mapping Agy., 1980-81; dep. U.S. rep. NATO Mil. Com., Brussels, 1981-83; rep. Joint Chiefs of Staff, Geneva, 1983-86; comdr. 1st Strat. Aerospace Divsn. USAF, Vanderberg AFB, Calif., 1986-88, vice-CINC Strategic Air Command Offutt AFB, Nebr., 1988—91; mgmt. cons. Sacramento, 1991—. Chmn. bd. dir. Octus, Inc., 1995—98, Ceracon, Inc., 1996—, BAE Sys. Office: BAE Sys 1620 Wilshire Dr Bellevue NE 68005-6600 E-mail: donald.aldridge@baesystems.com.

ALDRIDGE, SANDRA, civic volunteer; b. Iowa, Apr. 22, 1939; d. Maurice D. and Maureen M. (Bennett) Anderson; m. Guy E. Seymour, Jan. 8, 1960 (div. Oct. 1966); m. Victor E. Aldridge, Jr., Nov. 11, 1970 (dec. May 1995); 1 child, Victor E. III. Student, Millikin U., Decatur, Ill., 1957-58. Pres. Crawford Sch. PTA, 1976-78, Terre Haute Lawyers Aux., 1979; pres., dir. Wabash Valley Assn. for Gifted and Talented Children, 1981-83, Vigo County Task Force for Alcohol and Drug Abuse, 1983-84; treas., dir. Union Hosp. Svc. League; bd. dirs. YWCA of Terre Haute, Inc., 1987-89; v.p., fin. chair, mem. exec. coun. Wabash Valley coun. Boy Scouts Am., Inc.; mem. Vigo County Tax Adjustment Bd., 1986-88; mem. Class IX Leadership Terre Haute, 1985; bd. trustees Vigo County Sch. Corp., Terre Haute, 1985-97, v.p., 1992-93, 96; sec. Ernie Pyle Chapter, The Ret. Officers Assn., 1998-; active Children's Theatre, United Way of Wabash Valley. Mem. Ind. Assn. Gifted Children, Swope Art Gallery, Vigo County Hist. Soc., Women's Dept. Club, Arts Illiana, Elks Women's Golf League. Democrat. Episcopalian. Home: 2929 Winthrop Rd Terre Haute IN 47802-3443

ALESIA, JAMES H(ENRY), judge; b. Chgo., July 16, 1934; m. Kathryn P. Gibbons, July 8, 1961; children: Brian J., Daniel J. BS, Loyola U., Chgo., 1956; JD, Ill. Inst. Tech., Chgo., 1960; grad. Nat. Jud. Coll., U. Nev., 1976. Bar: Ill. 1960, Minn. 1970. Police officer City of Chgo., 1957-61; assoc. Law Office Anthony Scariano, Chicago Heights, Ill., 1960-61, Pretzel & Stouffer, Chgo., 1961-63; asst. gen. counsel Chgo. & North Western Transp. Co., 1963-70; assoc. Rerat Law, Mpls., 1970-71; asst. U.S. atty. No. Dist. Ill., Chgo., 1971-73; trial counsel Chessie Sys., 1973; U.S. adminstrv. law judge, 1973-82; ptnr. Reuben & Proctor (merged with Isham, Lincoln & Beale), 1982-87; judge U.S. Dist. Ct. for No. Dist. Ill., 1987—. Mem. faculty Nat. Jud. Coll., U. Nev., Reno, 1979-80. Mem. FBA, Justinian Soc. Lawyers, Celtic Legal Soc. Republican. Roman Catholic. Office: US Dist Ct 219 S Dearborn St Ste 2050 Chicago IL 60604-1800

ALEXA, WILLIAM E. state legislator; b. June 20, 1941; m. Joyce Ann Alexa. JD, Valparaiso U. Atty. Valparaiso Planning Commn. and Bd. Zoning Appeals, 1974; dep. and chief prosecuting atty. Porter County, 1975-79; pres. Valparaiso Park Bd.; mem. Ind. Senate from 5th dist., 1988—; mem. labor, govt. and regulatory affairs, corrections; criminal and civil procedures and fin. coms.; ranking minority mem., judiciary and pub. policy coms.; atty. Douglas, Alexa, Koeppen & Hurley. Bd. dirs. Porter county Assn. for Retarded Citizens, 1975-76; past pres. Valparaiso Park Bd.; mem. Thunderhouse Campus Ministry Ctr.; mem. United Way Budget and Allocation Com. Mem. Valparaiso Univ. Law Alumnae Assn., Porter County and Ind. State Bar Assn., Valparaiso C. of C. Democrat. Home: 337 Deerfield Rd Valparaiso IN 46383-6954

ALEXANDER, ANTHONY J. electric power industry executive; BS, U. Akron, 1972, JD, 1975. Bar: Ohio 1976. Sr. tax acct. Ohio Edison Co., Akron, 1972-76, atty., 1976-83, sr. atty., 1984-87, assoc. gen. counsel, 1987-89, v.p., gen. counsel, 1898-91, sr. v.p., gen. counsel, 1991—; now pres. 1st Energy Corp. Office: 1st Energy Corp 76 S Main St 18th Fl Akron OH 44308-1812

ALEXANDER, JAMES WESLEY, surgeon, educator; b. El Dorado, Kans., May 23, 1934; s. Rossiter Wells and Merle Lydia Alexander; m. Maureen L. Strohofer; children: Joseph, Judith, Elizabeth, Randolph, John Charles, Lori, Molly. Student, Tex. Technol. Coll., 1951-53; MD, U. Tex., 1957; ScD, U. Cin., 1958-64; postgrad., U. Minn., 1966-67. Diplomate Am. Bd. Surgery, Am. Bd. Thoracic Surgery, lic. physician Ohio. Intern Cin. Gen. Hosp., 1957-58; resident U. Cin.-Cin. Gen. Hosp., 1958-64; mem. faculty Coll. Medicine, U. Cin., 1962-64, 66—, prof. surgery, 1975—, dir. transplantation div., dept. surgery, 1967-99, dir. surg. immunology lab., 1967—2000; dir. research Shriners Burns Inst., 1979-90; practice medicine and surgery Cin., 1966—; dir. Ctr. for Surg. Weight Loss, 2001—. Mem. staff U. Cin. Hosp., Bethesda Hosp., Cin. Children's Hosp., Christ Hosp., Good Samaritan Hosp., Jewish Hosp.; mem. study sect. NIH, 1983—87, 1989—93, chmn, , 1990—93, mem. ad hoc com., 1990—99. Author (with R.A. Good): Fundamentals of Clinical Immunology, 1977; contbr. more than 650 articles to sci. jours. Capt. M.C.1966 U.S. Army, 1964. Mem.: ACS, AAAS, Am. Soc. Bariatric Surgeons, Mont Reid Surg. Soc., Shock Soc., Transplantation Soc., Surg. Infection Soc. (sec. 1981—84, pres.-elect 1985—86, pres. 1986—87), Soc. Univ. Surgeons, Ohio Med. Assn., St. Paul Surg. Soc. (hon.), Peruvian Acad. Surgery, Colombian Coll. Surgeons, Internat. Soc. Surgery, Halsted Soc., Am. Surg. Assn., Am. Soc. Parenteral and Enteral Nutrition, Am. Soc. Transplant Surgeons (sec. 1985—87, pres.-elect 1987—88, pres. 1988—89), Am. Burn Assn. 1984—85, Am. Assn. Immunologists, Am. Assn. for Surgery of Trauma, Surg. Biology Club, Phi Eta Sigma, Alpha Epsilon Delta, Alpha Chi, Alpha Omega Alpha. Home: 757 Riverwatch Dr Crescent Springs KY 41017-4480 Office: U Cin Coll Medicine 231 Albert Sabin Way Cincinnati OH 45267-0558 E-mail: JWesley.Alexander@uc.edu.

ALEXANDER, JEFFREY, performing company executive; Grad., New Eng. Conservatory of Music, Boston. Gen. mgr. Grapa Concerts, U.S.A., New York, 1980-82, Laredo Philharm. Orch., Laredo, Tex., 1982-84; dir. Cin. Symphony Orch., 1984-88, mgr., 1988-93, gen. mgr., 1993—; also gen. mgr. Cin. May Festival. Office: Cincinnati Symphony Orch 1241 Elm St Cincinnati OH 45210-2231

ALEXANDER, JOHN J. chemistry educator; b. Indpls., Apr. 13, 1940; s. John Gregory and Inez Helene (Snedaker) A. A.B. summa cum laude, Columbia U., 1962, M.A., 1963, Ph.D., 1967. Postdoctoral fellow Ohio State U., Columbus, 1967-69, research assoc., 1977-78; asst. prof. chemistry U. Cin., 1969-73, assoc. prof., 1973-79, prof., 1979—, dir. undergrad. studies in chemistry, 1998—, faculty fellow, 1972-74. Vis. prof. Ohio State U., 1985-86, 94. Author: (with M.J. Steffel) Chemistry in the Laboratory, 1976, 2d edit., 1988, (with B.E. Douglas, D.H. McDaniel) Concepts and Models of Inorganic Chemistry, 3d edit., 1994, Problems for Inorganic Chemistry, 1994; column editor: Jour. Chem. Edn., 1976—; mem. editl. adv. team for chemistry Ency. Britannica, 1999-2001; contbr. chpts. to books, articles to profl. jours. Vestryman Calvary Episcopal Ch., 1999—. Woodrow Wilson fellow; NSF fellow Columbia U., 1963-65, faculty fellow, 1966; grantee NSF, Petroleum Rsch. Fund. Mem. Am. Chem. Soc. (past chmn., trustee), Phi Beta Kappa, Sigma Xi, Phi Lambda Upsilon. Democrat. Episcopalian. Home: 3446 Whitfield Ave Cincinnati OH 45220-1537 Office: U Cin Dept Chemistry Cincinnati OH 45221-0001

ALEXANDER, JOHN THORNDIKE, historian, educator; b. Cooperstown, N.Y., Jan. 18, 1940; s. Edward Porter and Alice Wagner (Bolton) A.; m. Maria Kovalak Hreha, June 13, 1964; children— Michal Porter, Darya Ann B.A., Wesleyan U., Middletown, Conn., 1961; cert. regional specialization Russian Inst., M.A., Ind. U., 1963, Ph.D., 1966. Asst. prof. U. Kans., Lawrence, 1966-70, assoc. prof., 1970-74, prof. history, 1974—. Fellow Inter-Univ. Com. on Travel Grants, 1964-65, Internat. Research and Exchanges Bd., 1971, 75, 96. Author: Autocratic Politics, 1969, Emperor of the Cossacks, 1973, Bubonic Plague in Russia, 1980, Catherine the Great, 1989 (Byron Caldwell Smith award for best book by a Kans. author pub. in 1987-88), reissued luxury edit., 1999; translator, editor: Platonov, Time of Troubles, 1970, Anisimov, Reforms of Peter the Great, 1993, Anisimov, Empress Elisabeth, 1995. Recipient Balfour Jeffrey Higuchi Endowment Rsch. Achievement award, 1992. Mem. Am. Assn. for Advancement Slavic Studies, Brit. Study Group on 18th Century Russia, So. Conf. on Slavic Studies (ann. sr. scholar award 2001). Democrat. Roman Catholic Avocation: sports. Home: 2216 Orchard Ln Lawrence KS 66049-2706 Office: U Kans Dept History Wescoe Hall Rm 3001 1445 Jayhawk Blvd Lawrence KS 66045-7590 E-mail: jatalex@ku.edu.

ALEXANDER, MARTHA SUE, librarian; b. Washington, June 8, 1945; d. Lyle Thomas and Helen (Goodwin) Alexander; m. David Henry Bowman, June 11, 1965 (div. 1982); 1 child, Elaine B.A., U. Md., 1967; M.S. in Library Sci., Cath. U. Am., 1969. Librarian U. Md., College Park, 1969-72, head acquisitions, 1973-75; asst. univ. librarian George Washington U., Washington, 1975-78, assoc. univ. librarian, 1978-82; univ. librarian U. Louisville, 1983-90; dir. libraries U. Mo., Columbia, 1990—. Chmn. bd. dirs. SOLINET (Southeastern Library Network), 1987-88. Coord. U. Louisville United Way, 1987; bd. dirs. Mo. Libr. Network Corp., 1990-96. Mem. ALA (chmn. poster sessions 1983-85, co-chmn. nat. conf. in Cin. 1989), Am. Assn. Higher Edn., Athletic Assn. U. Louisville (vice chmn., bd. dirs. 1989-90), D.C. Library Assn. (pres. 1981-82), Women Acad. Libr. Dirs. Exch. Network. Episcopalian Home: 100 Mumford Dr Columbia MO 65203-0226 Office: Univ Mo Columbia Ellis Libr Columbia MO 65201

ALEXANDER, RALPH WILLIAM, JR. physics educator; b. Phila., May 17, 1941; s. Ralph William and Gladys (Robin) A.; m. Janet Erdien Bradley, Sept. 4, 1965; children: Ralph III, Margaret. BA, Wesleyan U., Middletown, Conn., 1963; PhD, Cornell U., Ithaca, N.Y., 1968; postdoctoral study, U. of Freiburg, Fed. Republic Germany, 1968-70. From asst. to assoc. prof. physics U. Mo., Rolla, 1970-80, prof., 1980—, chmn. dept., 1983-92. Contbr. articles to profl. jours. Mem. Am. Phys. Soc., Assn. Am. Physics Tchrs. Office: U Mo Dept Physics Rolla MO 65409-0001 E-mail: ralexand@umr.edu.

ALEXANDER, RICHARD DALE, zoology educator; b. White Heath, Ill., Nov. 18, 1929; m. 1950; two children. BSc, Ill. State U., 1950; MSc, The Ohio State U., 1951, PhD in Entomology, 1956; LHD, Ill. State U. Rsch. assoc. Rockefeller Found., N.Y.C., 1956-57; from instr. to assoc. prof. U. Mich., Ann Arbor, 1957-69; curator Insects U. Mich. Mus. Zoology, 1957—, prof. Zoology, 1969—, Hubbell Dist. U. Prof. Evolutionary Biol., 1990—. Recipient Daniel Giraud Elliot medal, 1971; Newcomb Cleveland prize, AAAS, 1961. Mem. Fellow AAAS, Animal Behavior Soc., mem. Nat. Acad. Scis. Office: Mus Zool U Mich 1109 Geddes Ave Ann Arbor MI 48109-1079 E-mail: rdalex@umich.edu.

ALEXANDER, THOMAS BENJAMIN, history educator; b. Nashville, July 23, 1918; s. Thomas Benjamin and Mary Christine (Sanders) A.; m. Elise Hadley Pritchett, June 16, 1941; children: Wynne Hadley Alexander Guy, Elaine Elliston Alexander Gates, Carol Pope Alexander Gajek. BA, Vanderbilt U., 1939, MA, 1940, PhD, 1947. From asst. prof. to assoc. prof. history Clemson U., S.C., 1946-49; prof., chmn. div. social scis. Ga. So. U., Statesboro, 1949-57; from assoc. prof. to prof. history U. Ala., Tuscaloosa, 1957-69; prof. history U. Mo., Columbia, 1969-88, Middlebush prof. history, 1979-82, prof. emeritus, 1988—, Sesquicentennial prof., 1990. Author: Political Reconstruction in Tennessee, 1950, Thomas A.R. Nelson of East Tennessee, 1956, Sectional Stress and Party Strength, 1836-1860, 1967, The Anatomy of the Confederate Congress, 1972 (Sydnor award 1973, Jefferson Davis award 1972). Served to lt. USNR, 1943-46, ETO. Fellow Guggenheim Found., 1955-56; grantee Social Sci. Research Council, 1947, 67-68; fellow Inst. So. History, 1968-69 Mem. AAUP, So. Hist. Assn. (pres. 1980), Am. Hist. Assn., Orgn. Am. Historians, Social Sci. History Assn. (pres. 1986), S.C. Hist. Assn. (pres. 1958). Home: 2606 Summit Rd Columbia MO 65203-1336 Office: U Mo Dept History Columbia MO 65211-0001

ALFINI, JAMES JOSEPH, dean, educator, lawyer; b. Yonkers, N.Y., Oct. 12, 1943; s. James Joseph and Olga (Genish) A.; m. Carol Miller, Dec. 23, 1966; children: David James, Michael Steven. AB, Columbia U., 1965; JD, Northwestern U., 1972. Bar: N.Y. 1973, Ill. 1976, U.S. Dist. Ct. (no. dist.) Ill. 1976, U.S. Ct. Appeals (7th cir.) 1982, U.S. Supreme Ct. 1977. Reginald Heber Smith cmty. lawyer Monroe County Legal Assistance Corp., Rochester, N.Y., 1972-73; asst. dir. research Am. Judicature Soc., Chgo., 1973-77, dir. rsch., 1977-80, asst. exec. dir. programs, 1980-85; adj. prof. law IIT Chgo.-Kent Sch. Law, 1978-85; assoc. prof. of law Fla. State U., Tallahassee, 1985-90, prof. law, 1990-91; dean, prof. No. Ill. U. Coll. Law, 1991-97, prof., 1997—. Co-author: (books) Making Jury Instructions Understandable, 1982, Judicial Conduct and Ethics, 1990, 95, 2000, Mediation Theory and Practice, 2000; mem. Christian Ch. Bd. Editors Ohio State Jour. Dispute Resolution, 1994-98. Mem. governing bd. Cook County Legal Assistance Found., 1981-83; arbitration and mediation rules com. Fla. Supreme Ct., 1988-91; mem. Ill. Jud. Ethics com., 1993-97; chmn. coord. coun. Nat. Ct. Orgns., 1982-83; bd. govs. Chgo. Coun. Lawyers. 1st lt. U.S. Army, 1965-69. Decorated Army Commendation medal. Mem. ABA (sect. dispute resolution, chair), ACLU, Am. Law Inst., Law and Soc. Assn. Democrat. E-mail: jalfini@niu.edu. Home: 525 Wing Ln Saint Charles IL 60174-2339

ALFORD, STEVE, college basketball coach; b. New Castle, Ind., Nov. 23, 1964; m. Tanya Frost: children: Kory, Bryce, Kayla. B in Bus., Ind. U. Mem. gold-medal U.S. basketball team Olympic Games, L.A., 1984; professional basketball player Dallas Mavericks, Golden St. Warriors; head coach Manchester (Ind.) Coll., 1992-95; conf. title champions, 1994, 95, S.W. Mo. State U. Bears, 1995-99, reached NCAA Sweet 16, 1999; headcoach U. Ia. Hawkeyes, 1999—. Named Ind. Collegiate Conf. Coach of Yr., 1993, 94, 95. Office: c/o U Ia Athletic Dept 240 Carver Hawkeye Arena Iowa City IA 52242-1020

ALGEO, JOHN THOMAS, retired educator, association executive; b. St. Louis, Nov. 12, 1930; s. Thomas George and Julia Winifred (Wathen) A.; m. Adele Marie Silbereisen, Sept. 6, 1958; children: Thomas John, Catherine Marie. EdB cum laude, U. Miami, 1955; MA, U. Fla., 1957, PhD, 1960. Instr. Fla. State U., Tallahassee, 1959-61; from asst. to full prof. U. Fla., Gainesville, 1961-71, asst. dean grad. sch., 1969-71, dir. program in linguistics, 1969-71; prof. U. Ga., Athens, 1971-88, dir. program in linguistics, 1974-79, head dept. English, 1975-79, alumni found. disting. prof., 1988-94; nat. pres. Theosophical Soc. in Am., Wheaton, Ill., 1993—94; internat. v.p. Theosophical Soc., Adyar, India, 2002—. Mem. gen. coun. Theosophical Soc., Adyar, India, 1993—94; dir. Manor Found. Ltd., Sydney, Australia, 1995—; accreditation cons. So. Assn. Colls. and Schs., Atlanta, 1967-90; cons. NEH, Washington, 1974-94; dir. Commn. on the English Lang., Nat. Coun. Tchrs. of English, Urbana, Ill., 1976-82; del. Am. Coun. Learned Socs., N.Y.C., 1984-87; cons. in lang. and lexicography Cambridge Univ. Press, N.Y.C., 1987-93; cons. in Am. usage Kenkyusha Ltd., Tokyo, 1991-99; cons. Webster's New World Dictionary, 4th edit., Cleve., 1993-95. Author: Problems in the Origins and Development of the English Language, 1966, 4th edit., 1993, On Defining the Proper Name, 1973, Exercises in Contemporary English, 1974, Reincarnation Explored, 1987, Fifty Years "Among the New Words": A Dictionary of Neologisms, 1941-91, 1991, Eigo no kigen to hatatsu, 1991; co-author: English: An Introduction to Language, 1970, Spelling: Sound to Letter, 1971, The Origins and Development of the English Language, 1982, 4th edit., 1993, Elements of Literature, Sixth Course: Literature of Britain, 1989, The Power of Thought, 2001; editor: American Speech 1972-81, Thomas Pyles: Selected Essays on English Usage, 1979, Among the New Words, American Speech, 1987-97, Cambridge History of the English Language, vol. 6, English in North America, 2001; assoc. editor: The Oxford Companion to the English Language, 1992; mem. editl. bd. Jour. of English Linguistics, 1970—, Internat. Jour. Lexicography, 1990—, World Englishes, 1996—, Names, 1997—, Language Problems Language Planning, 1997-99. Sgt. U.S. Army, 1951-54, Korea. Fellow Guggenheim Found., London, 1986-87; Fulbright scholar U. Coll. London, Eng., 1986-87. Mem. Am. Dialect Soc. (pres. 1979), Am. Name Soc. (pres. 1984), Internat. Assn. Univ. Profs. English, Internat. Linguistic Assn., Ea. Order Internat./Co-Freemasonry, Internat. Phonetic Assn., Internat. Soc. Anglo-Saxonists, Linguistic Assn. of the U.S. and Can., Linguistic Soc. Am., Modern Lang. Assn. Am., Philological Soc., Southeastern Conf. on Linguistics (pres. 1970-71), Dictionary Soc. N.Am. (pres. 1995-97), Theosophical Soc. (nat. pres. 1993-2002, internat. v.p. 2002-), Ea. Order Internat. Co-Freemasonry. Democrat. Home: PO Box 80206 Athens GA 30608-0206 Office: Theosophical Soc Am PO Box 270 Wheaton IL 60189-0270 E-mail: johnalgeo@aol.com.

ALGER, CHADWICK FAIRFAX, political scientist, educator; b. Chambersburg, Pa., Oct. 9, 1924; s. Herbert and Thelma (Drawbaugh) A.; m. Elinor Reynolds, Aug. 28, 1948; children: Mark, Scott, Laura, Craig. BA, Ursinus Coll., 1949, LLD, 1979; MA, Johns Hopkins U., 1950; PhD, Princeton, 1958. Internat. relations specialist Dept. Navy, 1950-54; instr. Swarthmore Coll., 1957; faculty Northwestern U., Evanston, Ill., 1958-71, prof. polit. sci., 1966-71, dir. internat. relations program, 1967-71; Mershon prof. polit. sci. and pub. policy Ohio State U., 1971-95, emeritus prof., 1995—, dir. transnat. intellectual cooperation program, 1971-80, dir. world affairs program, Mershon Ctr., 1980-88, coord. working group on global rels. and peace studies, 1988-95, acting dir. univ. ctr. for internat. studies, 1990-91. Vis. prof. UN affairs N.Y.U., 1962-63 Author: Internationalization from Local Areas: Beyond Interstate Relations, 1987, Perceiving, Understanding and Coping with World Relations in Everyday Life, 1993, The United Nations System: Potential for the Twenty-First Century, 1998; co-author: Simulation in International Relations, 1963, You and Your Community in the World, 1978, Conflicts and Crisis of International Order: New Tasks for Peace Research, 1985, A Just Peace Through Transformation: Cultural, Economic and Political Foundations for Change, 1988, The United Nations System: The Policies of Member States, 1995; contbr. articles to profl. jours. Mem. Trade Coun., State of Ohio, 1984-87. Served with USNR, 1943-46. Recipient Disting. Scholar award Internat. Soc. for Ednl., Cultural and Sci. Interchanges, 1980, Golden Apple award Am. Forum for Global Edn., 1993. Mem. Am. Polit. Sci. Assn. (coun. 1970-72),

Internat. Polit. Sci. Assn., Internat. Studies Assn. (pres. 1978-79), Internat. Studies Assn. Midwest (Quincy Wright disting. scholar award 2000), Internat. Peace Rsch. Assn. (coun. 1971-77, sec.-gen. 1983-87), Midwest Conf. Polit. Scis. (recipient prize 1966), Consortium on Peace Rsch., Edn. and Devel. (exec. com. 1971-77, chmn. 1976-77), Hunger and Devel. Coalition of Cen. Ohio (bd. dirs. 1983-90), Columbus Coun. on World Affairs (bd. dirs. 1974-88), UN Assn. (pres. Columbus chpt. 1991-93). Home: 2674 Westmont Blvd Columbus OH 43221-3354 Office: Ohio State U Mershon Ctr 1501 Neil Ave Columbus OH 43201-2602

ALIBER, ROBERT Z. economist, educator; b. Keene, N.H., Sept. 19, 1930; s. Norman H. and Sophie (Becker) A.; m. Deborah Baltzly, Sept. 9, 1955; children: Jennifer, Rachel, Michael. BA, Williams Coll., 1952, Cambridge U., 1954, MA, 1957; PhD, Yale U., 1962. Staff economist Commn. Money and Credit, N.Y.C., 1959-61; staff economist Com. on Econ. Devel., Washington, 1961-64; sr. econ. advisor AID, Dept. State, 1964-65; assoc. prof., then prof. internat. econs. and fin. U. Chgo., 1965—. Vis. prof. Brandeis U., 1987-93; vis. Bundesbank prof. Free U. Berlin, 1999; Houblon-Norman fellow, Bank of Eng., 1996. Author: The International Money Game, 1973, 76, 79, 83, 87, 2001, Exchange Risk and Corporate International Finance, 1978, Your Money and Your Life, 1982; co-author: Money, Banking, and the Economy, 1981, 84, 87, 90, 93, The Multinational Paradigm, 1993; editor: National Monetary Policies and the International Financial System, 1974, The Political Economy of Monetary Reform, 1976, The Reconstruction of International Monetary Arrangements, 1987, The Handbook of International Financial Management, 1989; co-editor Global Portfolios, 1991, Readings in International Business: A Decision Approach, 1993. With U.S. Army, 1954—56. Fulbright fellow, 1952-54. Mem. Am. Econs. Assn., Acad. Internat. Bus., Quadrangle Club, Williams Club of N.Y., Post Mills Soaring Club, Chgo. Gliding Club. Home: 5638 S Dorchester Ave Chicago IL 60637-1722 Office: 1101 E 58th St Chicago IL 60637-1511 E-mail: rza@gsb.uchicago.edu.

ALIEV, ELDAR, artistic director, choreographer, educator; Grad. with honors, Baku Choreographic Acad. Artistic dir. Ballet Internationale, Indpls., 1994—. Former prin. ballet dancer with the Kirov Ballet, appearing in more than 30 countries; guest star with Bolshoi Ballet and the Australian Ballet; choreographer ballets 1001 Nights, 1995, The Nutcracker, 1996, The Firebird, Eugene, Oreg., 1999. Office: Ballet Internationale USA 502 N Capitol Ave Ste B Indianapolis IN 46204-1204

ALIG, FRANK DOUGLAS STALNAKER, retired construction company executive; b. Indpls., Oct. 10, 1921; s. Clarence Schirmer and Marjory (Stalnaker) A.; m. Ann Bobbs, Oct. 22, 1949; children: Douglas, Helen, Barbara. Student, U. Mich., 1939-41; BS, Purdue U., 1948. Registered profl. engr., Ind. Project engr. Ind. State Hwy. Commn., Indpls., 1948; pres. Alig-Stark Constrn. Co., Inc., 1949-57, Frank S. Alig, Inc., 1957-97—; ret. V.p., bd. dirs. Bo-Wit Products Corp., Edinburg, Ind.; pres., bd. dirs. Home Stone Realty, Inc. With AUS, 1943-46. Mem. Dramatic Club, Lambs Club. Republican. Presbyterian.

ALJETS, CURTIS J. federal agency administrator; b. Carrington, N.D., May 21, 1946; m. Catherine Seil, Nov. 18, 1967; 3 children. BS in Math. Edn., N.D. State U., 1968. Tchr. sci. Dunseith (N.D.) Pub. Schs., 1970-72; immigration inspector, port dir. U.S. Immigration & Naturalization, Dept. Justice, 1972-87, asst. regional commr. examination & adjudication, 1987-92, staff asst. field ops. No. Regional Office, 1992-95, assoc. regional dir. Ctrl. Regional Office, 1995-97, dist. dir. Minn., 1997—. 2d lt. U.S. Army, 1968-70. Mem. Hennepin County (Minn.) Chiefs of Police Assn., Minn. State Sheriffs Assn. Evangelical. Avocations: reading, jogging, computers, photography. Office: US Dept Immigration & Naturalization Dept Justice 2901 Metro Dr Ste 100 Bloomington MN 55425-1555

ALKIRE, BETTY JO, artist, commercial real estate broker, marketing consultant; b. Kansas City, Mo., June 20, 1942; d. Robert Emmitt and Gladys Faye (Craigg) Sharp; m. Daniel Wayne Hedrick, Nov. 15, 1968 (div.); children: Diane Laurie, Lisa Kay, Brett, Darin, Julie; m. William Edgar Alkire, Sept. 23, 1975 (dec. Dec. 7, 2001). Tchr. art Independence (Mo.) Art Edn., 1967—; portait artist Silver Dollar City Nat. Crafts Festival, 1971—; owner, operator artist's concession Kansas City Worlds of Fun, 1972-96; tchr. pvt. art classes, 1970—; tchr., lectr. mktg. art U. Mo. Extension Program, 1982—. Cons. mktg. and life-planning for artists; broker and cons. comml. investment real estate. Contbr. articles to mags. Mem. Bur. of Tourism; mem. edn. com. Tri-Lakes Bd. Realtors; mem. Rockaway Beach Bd. Planning and Zoning; chmn. Rockaway Beach Park and Mus. Bd. Mem. Mo. Arts Coun., Table Rock Art Guild, Ind. Profl. Artists Assn. (pres. 1980—), Branson (Mo.) C. of C. (mem. leadership program), Rockaway Beach Ladies Club, Rockaway Beach Booster Club. Methodist. Avocations: local art and history, antiques, real estate. Home: Historic Taneywood Rockaway Beach MO 65740 Address: PO Box 655 Rockaway Beach MO 65740 E-mail: BettyJoAlkire@realtor.com.

ALLDREDGE, WILLIAM T. metal products executive; CFO, v.p. fin. Newell Co., Freeport, Ill. Office: Newell Co 29 E Stephenson St Freeport IL 61032-4251

ALLDRITT, RICHARD, state legislator; m. Carmen Alldritt. Mem. from dist. 105 Kans. Ho. of Reps., Topeka. Mem. calendar and printing com., utilities com., info. tech. com., Kans. 2000 select com., legis. post audit com. Kans. Ho. of Reps., also minority whip. Democrat. Home: 613 W 15th St Harper KS 67058-1514 E-mail: alldritt@house.state.ks.us., alldritt@attica.net.

ALLEGRUCCI, DONALD LEE, state supreme court justice; b. Pittsburg, Kans., Sept. 19, 1936; s. Nello and Josephine Marie (Funaro) A.; m. Joyce Ann Thompson, Nov. 30, 1963; children: Scott David, Bowen Jay. AB, Pittsburg State U., 1959; JD, Washburn U., 1963. Bar: Kans. 1963. Asst. county atty. Butler County, El Dorado, Kans., 1963-67; state senator Kans. Legislature, Topeka, 1976-80; mem. Kans. Pub. Relations Bd., 1981-82; dist. judge Kans. 11th Jud. Dist., Pittsburg, 1982-87, adminstrv. judge, 1983-87; justice Kans. Supreme Ct., Topeka, 1987—. Instr. Pittsburg State U., 1969-72; exec. dir. Mid-Kans. Community Action Program, Inc. Mem. Dem. State Com., 1974-80; candidate 5th Congl. Dist., 1978; past pres. Heart Assn.; bd. dirs. YMCA. Served with USAF, 1959-60. Mem. Kans. Bar Assn. Democrat. Office: Kansas Supreme Court 374 Kansas Judicial Ctr 301 SW 10th Ave Fl 3 Topeka KS 66612-1507*

ALLEN, BARBARA, state legislator; Atty.; mem. Kans. Ho. of Reps. from 21st dist., 1987-2000, Kans. Senate from 8th dist., Topeka, 2001—. Mem. appropriations com., fiscal oversight com., social svcs. budget com., chairperson tourism com. Kans. Ho. of Reps. Republican. Office: Kansas Senate State Capitol Topeka KS 66612 Home: 7427 Walmer St Overland Park KS 66204-2056 Home Fax: 913 384 5400; Office Fax: 913 498 8488. E-mail: allen@house.state.ks.us.

ALLEN, BELLE, management consulting firm executive, communications company executive; b. Chgo. d. Isaac and Clara (Friedman) Allen. , U. Chgo. Cert. conf. mgr. Internat. Inst. Conf. Planning and Mgmt., 1989. Report, spl. correspondent The Leader Newspapers, Chgo., Washington, 1960-64; cons., v.p., treas., dir. William Karp Cons. Co. Inc., Chgo., 1961-79, chmn. bd., pres., treas., 1979—; pres. Belle Allen Comms., 1961—; nat. corr. CCA Press, 1990—. Apptd. pub. mem., com. on judicial evaluation Chgo. Bar Assn., 1998—; v.p., treas., bd. dirs. Cultural Arts Survey Inc., Chgo., 1965-79; cons., bd. dirs. Am. Diversified Rsch. Corp., Chgo., 1967-70; v.p., sec., bd. dirs. Mgmt. Performance Systems Inc., 1976-77; cons. City Club Chgo., 1962-65, Ill. Commn. on Tech. Progress, 1965-67; hearing mem. Ill. Gov.'s Grievance Panel for State Employees, 1979—; hearing mem. grievance panel Ill. Dept. Transp., 1985—; mem. adv. governing bd. Ill. Coalition on Employment of Women, 1980-88; spl. program advisor President's Project Partnership, 1980-88; mem. consumer adv. coun. FRS, 1979-82; reporter CCA Press Svc., 1990—; panel mem. Free Press vs. Fair Trial Nat. Ctr. Freedom of Info. Studies Loyola U. Law Sch., 1993, mem. planning com. Freedom of Info. awards, 1993; conf. chair The Swedish Inst. Press Ethics: How to Handle, 1993. Editor: Operations Research and the Management of Mental Health Systems, 1968; contbr. articles to profl. jours. Mem. campaign staff Adlai E. Stevenson II, 1952, 56, John F. Kennedy, 1960; founding mem. women's bd. United Cerebral Palsy Assn., Chgo., 1954, bd. dirs., 1954-58; pres. Dem. Fedn. Ill., 1958-61; pres. conf. staff Eleanor Roosevelt, 1960; mem. Welfare Pub. Rels. Forum, 1960-61; bd. dirs., mem. exec. com., chmn. pub. rels. com. Regional Ballet Ensemble, Chgo., 1961-63; bd. dirs. Soc. Chgo. Strings, 1963-64; mem. Ind. Dem. Coalition, 1968-69; bd. dirs. Citizens for Polit. Change, 1969; campaign mgr. aldermanic election 42d ward Chgo. City Coun., 1969; mem. selection com. Robert Aragon Scholarship, 1991; mem. planning com. mem. Hutchins Era reunion U. Chgo., 1995, 2000. Recipient Outstanding Svc. award United Cerebral Palsy Assn., Chgo., 1954, 55, Chgo. Lighthouse for Blind, 1986, Spl. Comms. award The White House, 1961, cert. of appreciation Ill. Dept. Human Rights, 1985, Internat. Assn. Ofcl. Human Rights Agys., 1985; selected as reference source Am. Bicentennial Rsch. Inst. Libr. Human Resources, 1973; named Hon. Citizen, City of Alexandria, Va., 1985; selected to be photographed by Bachrach nat. exhibit for Faces of Chicago, 1990. Mem. AAAS, NOW, AAAU, Affirmative Action Assn. (bd. dirs. 1981-85, chmn. mem. and programs com. 1981-85, pres. 1983—), Fashion Group (bd. dirs. 1981-83, chmn. Restrospective View of an Hist. Decade 1960-70, editor The Bull. 1981), Indsl. Rels. Rsch. Assn. (bd. dirs., chmn. pers. placement com. 1960-61), Sarah Siddons Soc., Soc. Pers. Adminstrs., Women's Equity Action League, Nat. Assn. Inter-Group Rels. Ofcls. (nat. conf. program 1959), Publicity Club Chgo. (chmn. inter-city rels. com. 1960-61, Disting. Svc. award 1968), Ill. C. of C. (cmty. rels. com., alt. mem. labor rels. com. 1971-74), Chgo. C. of C. and Industry (merit employment com. 1961-63), Internat. Press Club Chgo. (charter 1992—, bd. dirs. 1992—), Chgo. Press Club (chmn. women's activities 1969-71), U. Chgo. Club of Met. Chgo. (program com. 1993—, chair summer quarter programs 1994), Soc. Profl. Journalists (Chgo. Headline Club 1992—, regional conf. planning com. 1993, co-chair Peter Lisagor awards 1993, program com. 1992—), Assn. Women Journalists, Nat. Trust for Historic Preservation. Office: 111 E Chestnut St Ste 15F Chicago IL 60611-6013

ALLEN, BRUCE TEMPLETON, economics educator; b. Oak Park, Ill., Jan. 27, 1938; s. William Hendry and Harriet (Iverson) A.; m. Virginia Elizabeth Peterson, June 16, 1962; children: Elizabeth Rachel, Catherine Grace. AB, De Pauw U., 1960; MBA, U. Chgo., 1961; PhD, Cornell U., 1965. Asst. prof. econs. Mich. State U., East Lansing, 1965-75, assoc. prof., 1975-80, prof., 1980—. Mem. Am. Econ. Assn. Avocations: railroads. Office: Mich State U Dept Econs East Lansing MI 48824

ALLEN, CHARLES EUGENE, university administrator, agriculturist, educator; b. Burley, Idaho, Jan. 25, 1939; s. Charles W. and Elsie P. (Fowler) A.; m. Connie J. Block, June 19, 1960; children: Kerry J., Tamara S. BS, U. Idaho, 1961; MS, U. Wis., 1963, PhD, 1966. NSF postdoctoral fellow, Sydney, Australia, 1966-67; asst. prof. agr. U. Minn., St. Paul, 1967-69, assoc. prof., 1969-72, prof., 1972—, dean Coll. Agr., assoc. dir. Agrl. Expt. Sta., 1984-88, acting v.p., 1988-90, v.p. agriculture, forestry and home econs., dir. Minn. Agr. Expt. Sta., 1990-95, provost profl. studies, dir. Minn. Agr. Expt. Sta., 1995-97, dir. global outreach, 1997-98, exec. dir. internat. programs, 1998—. Vis. prof. Pa. State U., 1978; cons. to industry; C. Glen King lectr. Wash. State U., 1981; Univ. lectr. U. Wyo., Laramie, 1984; adj. prof. Hassan II U., Rabat, Morocco, 1984 Contbr. numerous chpts. to books, articles to sci. jours. on growth and metabolism of muscle and adipose tissue, meat quality Recipient Horace T. Morse-Amoco Found. award in undergrad. edn. U. Minn., 1984, Disting. Tchr. award U. Minn. Coll. Agr., 1984, Disting. Alumni award U. Idaho, 1989. Fellow AAAS, Inst. Food Tech.; mem. Am. Meat Sci. Assn. (dir. 1970-72; Research award 1980, Signal Service award, 1985), Am. Soc. Animal Sci. (Exceptional Research Achievement award 1972, Research award 1977), Sigma Xi. Avocations: photography, reading, outdoor sports, golf.

ALLEN, DAVID JAMES, lawyer; b. East Chicago, Ind. BS, Ind. U., 1957, MA, 1959, JD, 1965. Bar: Ind. 1965, U.S. Dist. Ct. (so. dist.) Ind. 1965, U.S. Ct. Appeals 1965, U.S. Ct. Appeals (fed. and 7th cirs.) 1983, U.S. Tax Ct. 1965, U.S. Supreme Ct. 1965. Of counsel Hagemier, Allen and Smith, Indpls., 1975—. Adminstrv. asst. Gov. of Ind. Mathew E. Welsh, 1961—65; counsel Ind. Gov. Roger D. Branigin, 1965—69; asst. to Gov. Edgar D. Whitcomb, 1969—70; legis. counsel Ind. Gov. Evan Bayh, 1989—90; spl. counsel Gov. Frank O'Bannon State of Ind., 1999—; mem. Spl. Commn. on Ind. Exec. Reorgn., 1967—69; commr. Ind. Utility Regulatory Commn., 1970—75; mem. Ind. Law Enforcement Acad. Bd. and Adv. Coun., 1968—85, Ind. State Police Bd., 1968—; commr. for revision Ind. Commn. to REcommend Changes in Ind. Legis. Process, 1990—; commr. Ind. Criminal Code Revision Study Commn., 1998—; nat. judge adv. Acacia Frat., 1980—86, 1992—; chief counsel Ind. Ho. Reps., 1976—76, spl. counsel, 1979—89, Ind. Senate, 1990—97; adj. prof. pub. law Sch. Pub. and Environ. Affairs, Ind. U., Bloomington, 1976—. Author: New Governor In Indiana: Transition of Executive Power, 1965. Mem. ABA, Ind. State Bar Assn. (mem. adminstrv. law com. 1968-77, chmn. adminstrv. law com. 1973-76, mem. law sch. liaison com. 1977-78, criminal justice law exec. com. 1966-72), Indpls. Bar Assn. Office: Hagemier Allen & Smith 1170 Market Tower 10 W Market St Ste 1170 Indianapolis IN 46204-5924 Office Fax: 317-464-8146. E-mail: allendindy@worldnet.att.net.

ALLEN, DENSIL E., JR. agricultural studies educator; Prof. agriculture Ctrl. Mo. State U., Warrensburg. Fellow Nat. Assn. Colls. Tchrs. Agriculture, 1992. Office: Central Missouri State U Dept Agriculture Warrensburg MO 64093

ALLEN, GARLAND EDWARD, biology educator, science historian; b. Louisville, Feb. 13, 1936; s. Garland Edward and Virginia (Blandford) A.; children: Tania Leigh, Carin Tove. AB, U. Louisville, 1957; AMT, Harvard U., 1958, AM, 1963, PhD, 1966. Programmer, announcer WFPL-WFPK, Louisville, 1956-58; tchr. Mt. Hermon (Mass.) Sch., 1958-61; Allston-Burr sr. tutor, instr. history of sci. Harvard, 1965-67; asst. prof. biology Washington U., St. Louis, 1967-72, assoc. prof., 1972-80, prof., 1980—. Cons. Ednl. Rsch. Corp., Cleve., 1967-85; commr. Commn. Undergrad. Edn. in Biol. Scis., 1967-70; mem. NSF Panel for Social Scis., 1968-71; trustee Marine Biol. Lab., Woods Hole, Mass., 1985-93; Sigma Xi nat. lectr., 1973-74, bicentennial lectr., 1974-77; Watkins vis. prof. Wichita State U., 1984; vis. prof. dept. history of sci. Harvard U., 1989-91, Sarton Award Lecture, AAAS, 1998. Author: Life Sciences in the Twentieth Century, 1975, 1978, T.H. Morgan: The Man and His Science, 1978; author: (with J.J.W. Baker) Matter, Energy and Life, 1965, 1970, 1975, 1981; author: The Study of Biology, 1967, The Study of Biology, 4th edit., 1982, Hypnothesis, Prediction and Implication, 1969, The Process of Biology, 1970, Biology: Scientific Process and Social Issues, 2001; co-editor: Mendel Newsletter, 1989—92, Jour. History of Biology, 1996—; mem. editl. bd.: San Josè Studies, —, mem. editl. bd.: Jour. History of Biology, 1968—91, mem. editl. bd.: , 1998—, mem. editl. bd.: Folia Medeliana. Fellow Charles Warren Ctr. for Studies in Am. History, Harvard U., 1981-82; sr. fellow Dibner Inst. for the History of Sci. and Tech., MIT, 2002. Mem. AAAS (coun., sect. L exec. com. 1975, Sarton award lectr. 1998), History Sci. Soc. (chmn. Schumann Prize com. 1972, Pfizer prize com. 1977, 80, 91-94, HSS coun. 1994-96, vis. lectr. program 1985-87), Sigma Xi. Home: 1526 Mississippi Ave Saint Louis MO 63104-2512 Office: Washington U Biology Dept Saint Louis MO 63130

ALLEN, GARY, radio personality; m. Laurie Allen; children: Michael, Patrick. With WTIQ-AM, Manistique, Mich., WTOC-AF/FM, Savannah, Ga., WBIA-AM, Augusta, KBZB-AM, Odessa/Midland, Tex., WCUZ-AM, Grand Rapids, Mich., WOOD 1300, Grand Rapids, 1981—, co-host Grand Rapids First News. Active Heal the Children-Mich., Mich.; vol. pub. TV auction WGVU-TV; active West Mich. coun. Boy Scouts Am., Mich. Office: Newsradio WOOD 1300 777 Monroe Center Ste 100 Grand Rapids MI 49503

ALLEN, JON G. psychologist; BS, U. Conn.; D in Clin. Psychology, U. Rochester. Clin. psychology fellowship Karl Menninger Sch. of Psychiatry and Mental Health Scis., faculty, Washburn U., U. Kans., Kans. State U. Author: Coping With Trauma: A Guide to Self-Understanding; editor: (with others) Diagnosis and Treatment of Dissociative Disorders, Contemporary Treatment of Psychosis: Healing Relationships in the Decade of the Brain; co-author: Borderline Personality Disorder: Tailoring the Therapy to the Patient; past editor Bull. of the Menninger Clinic; cons. editor Psychiatry; contbr. chpts. to books and numerous articles to profl. publs. Recipient I. Arthur Marshall Disting. Alumnus award Menninger Alumni Assn. Office: Menninger PO Box 829 Topeka KS 66601-0829

ALLEN, JULIE O'DONNELL, lawyer; BA, Stanford U., 1980; JD, U. Iowa, 1983. Bar: Iowa 1983, Ill. 1985, U.S. Dist. Ct. (no. dist.) Ill., U.S. Ct. Appeals (8th and 7th cirs.). Jud. clk. to Chief Judge Donald P. Lay, U.S. Ct. Appeals for 8th Circuit, 1983-84; assoc. Sidley & Austin, Chgo., 1985—, ptnr. Contbr. articles to law publs. Office: Sidley & Austin 1 S First National Plz Chicago IL 60603-2000 Fax: 323-853-7036. E-mail: jallen@sidley.com.

ALLEN, LAYMAN EDWARD, law educator, research scientist; b. Turtle Creek, Pa., June 9, 1927; s. Layman Grant and Viola Iris (Williams) A.; m. Christine R. Patmore, Mar. 29, 1950 (dec.); children: Layman G., Patricia R.; m. Emily C. Hall, Oct. 3, 1981 (div. 1992); children: Phyllip A. Hall, Kelly C. Hall; m. Leslie A. Olsen, June 10, 1995. Student, Washington and Jefferson Coll., 1945-46; AB, Princeton U., 1951; MPub. Admnstrn., Harvard U., 1952; LLB, Yale U., 1956. Bar: Conn. 1956. Fellow Ctr. for Advanced Study in Behavioral Scis., 1961-62; sr. fellow Yale Law Sch., 1956-57, lectr., 1957-58, instr., 1958-59, asst. prof., 1959-63, assoc. prof., 1963-66; assoc. prof. law U. Mich. Law Sch., Ann Arbor, 1966-71, prof., 1971—. Chmn. bd. trustees Accelerated Learning Found., 1998—; sr. rsch. scientist Mental Health Rsch. Inst., U. Mich., 1966-99; cons. legal drafting Nat. Life Ins. Co., Mich. Blue Cross & Blue Shield (various law firms); mem. electronic data retrieval com. Am. Bar Assn.; ops. rsch. analyst McKinsey & Co.; orgn. and methods analyst Office of Sec. Air Force.; trustee Ctr. for Study of Responsive Law. Editor: Games and Simulations, Artificial Intelligence and Law Jour.; author: WFF 'N Proof: The Game of Modern Logic, 1961, latest rev. edit., 1990, (with Robin B.S. Brooks, Patricia A. James) Automatic Retrieval of Legal Literature: Why and How, 1962, WFF: The Beginner's Game of Modern Logic, 1962, latest rev. edit., 1973, Equations: The Game of Creative Mathematics, 1963, latest rev. edit., 1994, (with Mary E. Caldwell) Reflections of the Communications Sciences and Law: The Jurimetrics Conference, 1965, (with J. Ross and P. Kugel) Queries 'N Theories: The Game of Science and Language, 1970, latest rev. edit., 1973, (with F. Goodman, D. Humphrey and J. Ross), On-Words: The Game of Word Structures, 1971, rev. edit., 1973; contbr. articles to profl. jours.; co-author/designer: (with J. Ross and C. Stratton) DIG (Diagnostic Instrnl. Gaming) Math; (with C. Saxon) Normalizer Clear Legal Drafting Program, 1986, MINT System for Generating Dynamically Multiple-Interpretation Legal Decision-Assistance Systems, 1991, The Legal Argument Game of Legal Relations, 1997. With USNR, 1945-46. Mem. ABA (coun. sect. sci. and tech.), AAAS, ACLU, Assn. Symbolic Logic, Nat. Coun. Tchrs. Math. Democrat. Unitarian. Home: 2114 Vinewood Blvd Ann Arbor MI 48104-2762 Office: U Mich Sch Law 625 S State St Ann Arbor MI 48109-1215 E-mail: laymanal@umich.edu.

ALLEN, LEATRICE DELORICE, psychologist; b. Chgo., July 15, 1948; d. Burt and Mildred Floy (Taylor) Hawkins; m. Allen Moore, Jr., July 30, 1965 (div. Oct. 1975); children: Chandra, Valarie, Allen; m. Armstead Allen, May 11, 1978 (div. May 1987). AA in Bus. Edn., Olive Harvey Coll., Chgo., 1975; BA in Psychology cum laude, Chgo. State U., 1977; M.Clin. Psychology, Roosevelt U., 1980; MA in Health Care Adminstrn., Coll. St. Francis, Joliet, Ill., 1993. Lic. clin. profl. counselor. Clk., U.S. Post Office, Chgo., 1967-72; clin. therapist Bobby Wright Mental Health Ctr., Chgo., 1979-80; clin. therapist Community Mental Health Council, Chgo., 1980-83, assoc. dir., 1983—; cons. Edgewater Mental Health, Chgo., 1984—, Project Pride, Chgo., 1985—; victim services coordinator Community Mental Health Council, Chgo., 1986-87; mgr. youth family services Mile Square Health Ctr., Chgo., 1987-88; coord. Evang. Health Systems, Oakbrook, Ill., 1988-93; adminstr. Human Enrichment Devel. Assn., Hazel Crest, Ill., 1993-96; dir. Ada S. McKinley, Chgo., 1996—. Scholar Chgo. State U., 1976, Roosevelt U., 1978; fellow Menninger Found., 1985. Mem. Am. Profl. Soc. on Abuse of Children, Nat. Orgn. for Victim Assistance, Ill. Coalition Against Sexual Assault (del. 1985—), Soc. Traumatic Stress Studies (treatment innovations task force), Chgo. Sexual Assault Svcs. Network (vice-chair, bd. dirs.), Chgo. Coun. Fgn. Rels. Avocations: aerobics, reading, theatre, dining, making and collecting dolls.

ALLEN, LEE HARRISON, industrial consultant, wholesale company executive; b. Cleve., Oct. 12, 1924; s. Horace Joseph and Eleanor Quayle (Malone) A.; m. Marieke Sellenraad, Sept. 18, 1954; children: Horace, Jan, Adrian, Carel, Eleanor. BEngring. in Metallurgy, Yale U., 1948. With Hickman, Williams & Co., Detroit, 1948—, metallurgist, 1951-70, divsn. mgr., 1970—, v.p., dir., 1971-76, pres., 1976-84, chmn. bd., chief exec. officer, 1984-89, Hickman, Williams Can., Inc., 1980-89; owner L.H. Allen & Sons, Frankenmuth, Mich., 1969—. Chmn. bd. dirs. Mich. Shelf Distbrs. Inc., 1985—. Trustee Grosse Pinte Bd. Edn., 1968-76. Mem. Am. Arbitration Assn. (arbitrator), Country Club Detroit. Home and Office: 84 Hall Pl Grosse Pointe Farms MI 48236-3805 Fax: 313-888-5321. E-mail: Squeedunk@aya.yale.edu.

ALLEN, LYLE WALLACE, lawyer; b. Chillicothe, Ill., June 17, 1924; s. Donald M. and Mary Ellen (McEvoy) A.; m. Helen Kolar, Aug. 16, 1947; children: Mary Elizabeth Watkins, Bryan James. Student, N.C. State Coll., 1943-44; B.S., Northwestern U., 1947; postgrad., Columbia Law Sch., 1947-48; J.D., U. Wis., 1950. Bar: Ill. 1950, Wis. 1950. Of counsel Heyl Royster Voelker & Allen, Peoria, Ill., 1951—. Served with 87th Inf. Div. U.S. Army, World War II. Decorated Purple Heart, Bronze star. Mem. ABA, Ill. State Bar Assn. (pres. 1972-73), Assn. of Ins. Attys. (pres. 1965-66), Illinois Valley Yacht Club, Wig and Pen Club (London). Democrat. Presbyterian. Office: 124 SW Adams St Ste 600 Peoria IL 61602-1392

ALLEN, MARC KEVIN, emergency physician, educator; b. Bedford, Ind., Sept. 2, 1956; s. Robert Edward and Edna Ruth (Little) A.; m. Marita Ann Volk, May 13, 1995. AB, Washington U., St. Louis, 1978; MD, Wright State U., 1982. Diplomate Am. Bd. Emergency Medicine. Intern Mt. Sinai Med. Ctr., Cleve., 1982-83, chief resident in emergency medicine, 1984-85, rsch. dir. emergency med. residency, 1986-96; attending physician Worcester (Mass.) City Hosp., 1985-86; flight physician Metro Lifeflight, Cleve., 1984—; attending physician Summa Health Sys., Akron, Ohio, 1999—.

Co-author: A Practical Approach Emergency Medicine, 1987. Co-chmn. Washington U. YWCA-YMCA, 1977—78; med. dir. Aurora Fire Dept., Six Flags Worlds of Adventure. Fellow Am. Coll. Emergency Medicine (councillor 1996-98); mem. Assn. Air Med. Svcs., Assn. Air Med. Physicians, N.E. Soc. Emergency Med. (bd. dirs. 1992-99), Phi Rho Sigma. Avocations: skiing, golf, cooking. Home: 485 Club Dr Aurora OH 44202-8564 Office: Summa Health Sys Akron City Hosp 525 E Market St Akron OH 44304-1619 E-mail: ermarc@aol.com.

ALLEN, MARCUS, retired professional football player; b. San Diego, Mar. 26, 1960; Student, U. So. Calif. Running back with Los Angeles Raiders, NFL, El Segundo, Calif., 1982-92; with Kansas City Chiefs, NFL, 1993-97; nat. analyst, broadcaster CBS Sports, N.Y.C., 1998; co-host Marcus Allen Show KCTV 5, Kansas City, Mo., 1997-98; features/sideline reporter CBS Sports, 1999—. Co-owner Pro Ball Beverage Corp.; v.p. Marcus Allen's Broadway Ford, Kansas City, Mo. Author: (with Carlton Stowers) Marcus: The Autobiography of Marcus Allen, 1997. Recipient Heisman Trophy Downtown Athletic Club of N.Y.C., 1981; named Coll. Football Player of Yr., Sporting News, 1981, The Sporting News NFL Rookie of Yr., 1982, Player of Yr., 1985; named to Sporting News Coll. All-Am. Team, 1981. Achievements include playing in NFL championship game, 1984, Pro Bowl, 1983, 85, 86, 88; establishing NFL season record for most combined yards, 1985; holds NFL record for most consecutive games with 100 or more yards rushing (11), 1986. Office: Marcus Allen's Ford 3401 Broadway St Kansas City MO 64111-2403

ALLEN, MAURICE BARTELLE, JR. architect; b. Lansing, Mich., Mar. 20, 1926; s. Maurice Bartelle and Marguerite Rae (Stahl) A.; m. Nancy Elizabeth Huff, June 29, 1951; children— Robert (dec.), Katherine, David. Student, Western Mich. U., 1944, Notre Dame U., 1944-46; BArch, U. Mich., 1950. Registered profl. architect, Mich. Draftsman, designer Smith, Hinchman & Grylls (architects), Detroit, 1950-51; designer, asso. Eero Saarinen & Assos., Bloomfield Hills, Mich., 1951-61; v.p. design and planning TMP Assos. (architects, engrs. and planners), 1961-92; emeritus, 1993; design critic, lectr. Coll. Architecture and Urban Planning, U. Mich., 1958—. Cons. arch. Camelback Bible Ch., Paradise Valley, Ariz. Prin. archtl. works include Gen. Motors Inst. campus devel. and bldgs, Flint, Mich., Mackinac and Manitou halls, Grand Valley State Coll, O'Dowd Hall, Oakland U, Prototype Regional Correctional Facilities, Mich. Dept. Corrections, Fine Arts Ctr. and Theater, Allied Scis. Bldg., Macomb Community Coll., Scheide Music Ctr., Coll. of Wooster, Towsley Ctr. Sch. of Music, U. Mich., Performing Arts Ctr. and Student Ctr., Lake Superior State U., Art Music Humanities Ctr., Wabash Coll., Univ. Community Ctr., U. Western Ont., Drama Theater and Arts Bldg., Concordia Coll., St. Paul. Active Detroit Area council Boy Scouts Am., 1969—, Detroit Inst. Arts, Detroit Symphony; mem. environmental arts com. Mich. Council for Arts, 1970; vice chmn. Mich. Gov.'s Spl. Commn. on Architecture, 1971. Served with USNR, 1944-47. Recipient honor awards Detroit chpt. AIA, 1970-71, Gold medal, 1994, citation for design high rise structures Am. Iron and Steel Inst., 1971, citation of excellence Architecture for Justice Exhbn., 1982. Mem. Coll. of Fellows AIA (co-chair urban priorities Detroit chpt. 1995—), Mich. Soc. Architects (honor awards 1970-71), Sr. Men's Club Birmingham, Masons, Alpha Tau Omega. Republican. Episcopalian. Home and Office: 4325 Derry Rd Bloomfield Hills MI 48302-1835

ALLEN, RENEE, principal; Prin. Villa Duchesne Sch., St. Louis, 1988—. Recipient Blue Ribbon Sch. award U.S. Dept. Edn., 1990-91. Office: Villa Duchesne Oakhill Sch 801 S Spoede Rd Saint Louis MO 63131-2606

ALLEN, RICHARD BLOSE, legal editor, lawyer; b. Aledo, Ill., May 10, 1919; s. James Albert and Claire (Smith) A.; m. Marion Treloar, Aug. 27, 1949; children: Penelope, Jennifer, Leslie Jean. BS, U. Ill., 1941, JD, 1947; LLD, Seton Hall U., 1977. Bar: Ill. 1947. Staff editor ABA Jour., 1947-48, 63-66, exec. editor, 1966-70, editor, 1970-83, editor, pub., 1983-86; pvt. practice Aledo, 1949-57; gen. counsel Ill. Bar Assn., 1957-63; mng. editor Def. Counsel Jour., Chgo., 1987—. Editor Sr. Lawyer, 1986-90, 94-2000. Maj. Q.M.C., AUS, 1941-46. Mem. ABA (mem. ho. of dels. 1996-99, chair sr. lawyers divsn. 2000-01), Ill. Bar Assn. (mem. assembly 1972-74), Chgo. Bar Assn., Am. Law Inst., Selden Soc., Scribes, Mich. Shores Club, Sigma Delta Chi, Kappa Tau Alpha, Phi Delta Phi, Alpha Tau Omega. Office: Def Counsel Jour 1 N Franklin St Ste 2400 Chicago IL 60606-2401 E-mail: dickall2@aol.com., rallen@iadclaw.org.

ALLEN, RONALD JAY, law educator; b. Chgo., July 14, 1948; s. J. Matteson and Carolyn L. (Latchum) A.; m. Debra Jane Livingston, May 25, 1974 (div. 1982); children: Sarah, Adrienne; m. Julie O'Donnell, Sept. 2, 1984; children: Michael, Conor. BS, Marshall U., 1970; JD, U. Mich., 1973. Bar: Nebr. 1974, Iowa 1979, U.S. Ct. Appeals (8th cir.) 1980, U.S. Supreme Ct. 1981, Ill. 1986. Prof. law SUNY, Buffalo, 1974-79, U. Iowa, Iowa City, 1979-82, 83-84, Duke U., Durham, N.C., 1982-83, Northwestern U., Chgo., 1984—, John Henry Wigmore prof., 1992—. Pres. faculty senate U. Iowa, 1980-81. Author: Constitutional Criminal Procedure, 1985, 91, 95, An Analytical Approach to Evidence, 1989, Evidence: Text, Cases and Problems, 1997, Arthritis of the Hip and Knee: The Active Person's Guide to Taking Charge, 1998, Comprehensive Criminal Procedure, 2001, Evidence: Text, Problems, Cases, 2002; contbr. articles to profl. jours. Mem. ABA (rules com. criminal justice sect.), Am. Law Inst. Office: Northwestern U Sch Law 357 E Chicago Ave Chicago IL 60611-3059 E-mail: rjallen@northwestern.edu.

ALLEN, SALLY LYMAN, biologist; b. N.Y.C., Aug. 3, 1926; d. Alexander Victor and Dorothy (Rogers) Lyman; 1 dau., Susan L. AB, Vassar Coll., 1946, PhD (John M. Prather fellow); PhD (USPHS fellow), U. Chgo., 1954. Research assoc. dept. zoology U. Mich., Ann Arbor, 1955-73, assoc. prof. botany, 1967-71, prof., 1971-75, prof. zoology, 1973-75, prof. biol. scis., 1975—, assoc. dean Coll. Lit., Sci. and the Arts, 1988-91. Chmn. dept. cellular and molecular biology, div. biol. scis., 1975-77; vis. prof. genetics Ind. U., 1967; cons. Am. Type Culture Collection, 1975-80. Co-author: (with Ewen Harrison) Instructor's Resource Manual for An Introduction to Genetic Analysis, 2000, Instructors Resource Manual for Modern Genetic Analysis, 1999; mem. editorial bd. Jour. Protozoology, 1974-78, Devel. Genetics, 1990-92; assoc. editor: Genetics, 1973—; co-editor spl. issues Devel. Genetics, 1992; contbr. articles to profl. jours. Fellow AAAS; mem. Am. Inst. Biol. Sci., Genetics Soc. Am., Soc. Protozoologists, Am. Naturalists Soc. (v.p. 1978), Am. Soc. for Cell Biology (mem. council 1973-75), Phi Beta Kappa, Sigma Xi, Golden Key (hon.). Office: U Mich Dept Biology Ann Arbor MI 48109 E-mail: slallen@umich.edu.

ALLEN, STEPHEN D(EAN), pathologist, microbiologist; b. Linton, Ind., Sept. 8, 1943; s. Wilburn and Betty Allen; m. Vally C. Autrey, June 17, 1964; children: Christopher D., Amy C. BA, Ind. U., 1965, MA, 1967; MD, Ind. U., Indpls., 1970. Diplomate Am. Bd. Pathology. Intern in pathology Vanderbilt U. Hosp., Nashville, 1970-71, resident in pathology, 1971-74; clin. asst. prof. pathology Emory U., Atlanta, 1974-77; asst. prof. clin. pathology Ind. U., Indpls., 1977-79, asst. prof. pathology, 1979-81, assoc. prof. pathology, 1981-86, prof. pathology, 1986-92, prof. pathology and lab. medicine, 1992—; assoc. dir. div. clin. microbiology, dept. pathology, 1977-92, dir. grad. progam pathology, 1986—, sr. assoc. chmn. dept. pathology, 1990-91, dir. divsn. clin. microbiology dept. pathology/lab. medicine, 1992-98, assoc. chair dept. pathology and lab. medicine & dir. labs., 1996-99; dir. disease control lab. divsn. Ind. State Dept. Health, 1994—; dir. divsn. clin. microbiology dept. pathology/lab. medicine Clarian-Meth.-Ind U.-Riley Hosps., 1998—. Mem. residency rev. com. for pathology Accreditation Coun. for Grad. Med. Edn., 1996—, mem. residency rev. com. for molecular genetic pathology, 1999—, mem. molecular genetic pathology policy com., 1999—. Co-author: Color Atlas of Diagnostic Microbiology, 5th edit., 1997, Introduction to Diagnostic Microbiology, 1994, (CD-ROM) Direct Smear Atlas, 1998; contbr. Fellow: Binford-Dammin Soc. Infectious Disease Pathologists, Infectious Diseases Soc. Am., Am. Acad. Microbiology, Coll. Am. Pathologists, Sigma Xi; mem.: Am. Bd. Pathology (anatomic and clin. pathology and med. microbiology com., trustee 1995—, chmn. microbiology test com. 1995—, sec. bd. 2000—01, v.p. 2002—), Am. Soc. Clin. Pathologists (coun. microbiology 1983—89), Shriners, Masons (32d deg.). Avocation: Avocations: music, electric bass and trumpet, fly-fishing. Office: Ind U Hosp Rm 4430 550 University Blvd Indianapolis IN 46202-5149 E-mail: sallen@iupui.edu.

ALLEN, THOMAS DRAPER, lawyer; b. Detroit, June 25, 1926; s. Draper and Florence (Jones) A.; m. Joyce M. Johnson, July 18, 1953; children— Nancy A. Bowser, Robert D., Rebecca A. Hubbard. BS, Northwestern U., 1949; JD, U. Mich., 1952. Bar: Ill. 1952, U.S. Supreme Ct. 1971. Assoc. Kirkland & Ellis, Chgo., 1952-60, ptnr., 1961-67, Wildman, Harrold, Allen & Dixon, Chgo., 1967-96, of counsel, 1997—. Chmn. Community Caucus, Hinsdale, Ill., 1960-61; mem. Hinsdale Bd. Edn., 1965-71, pres., 1970-71; pres. West Suburban coun. Boy Scouts Am., 1980-82, mem. nat. exec. bd., 1986—, chmn. internat. com., 1995-99, mem. world program com., 1983-93; moderator Union Ch., Hinsdale, 1983-84; trustee Chgo. Theol. Sem., 1988-97, chair, 1990-96, life trustee, 1997—. With USN, 1944-46. Recipient Silver Beaver award Boy Scouts Am., 1964, Silver Buffalo award, 1997, Bronze Wolf award World Scout Orgn., 1993. Fellow Am. Coll. Trial Lawyers (state chair 1984-85, chair internat. com. 1997-99); mem. ABA, Ill. Bar Assn., Chgo. Bar Assn. (bd. of mgrs 1989-91), Law Club of Chgo., Legal Club of Chgo., Jaycees Internat. (senator, 1965), Internat. Bar Assn., Hinsdale Golf Club. Mem. United Ch. of Christ. Home: 505 N Lake Shore Dr Chicago IL 60611-3427 Office: Wildman Harrold Allen & Dixon 225 W Wacker Dr Chicago IL 60606-1224

ALLEN, WILLIAM CECIL, physician, educator; b. LaBelle, Mo., Sept. 8, 1919; s. William H. and Viola O. (Holt) A.; m. Madge Marie Gehardt, Dec. 25, 1943; children: William Walter, Linda Diane Allen Deardeuff, Robert Lee, Leah Denise Rogers. A.B., U. Nebr., 1947, M.D., 1951; M.P.H., Johns Hopkins U., 1960. Diplomate Am. Bd. Preventive Medicine. Intern Bishop Clarkson Meml. Hosp., Omaha, 1952; practice medicine specializing in family practice Glasgow, Mo., 1952-59; specializing in preventive medicine Columbia, 1960—; dir. sect. chronic diseases Mo. Div. Health, Jefferson City, 1960-65; asst. med. dir. U. Mo. Med. Ctr., 1965-75; assoc. coordinator Mo. Regional Med. Program, 1968-73, coordinator health programs, 1969—, clin. asst. prof. community health and med. practice, 1962-65, asst. prof. community health and med. practice, 1965-69, assoc. prof., 1969-75, prof., 1975-76, prof. dept. family and community medicine, 1976-87, prof. emeritus, 1987—. Cons. Mo. Regional Med. Program, 1966-67, Norfolk Area Med. Sch. Authority, Va., 1965-66; governing body Area II Health Systems Agy., 1977-79, mem. coordinating com., 1977-79; founding dir. Mid-Mo. PSRO Corp., 1974-79, dir., 1976-84. Contbr. articles to profl. jours. Mem. Gov.'s Adv Council for Comprehensive Health Planning, 1970-73; trustee U. Mo. Med. Sch. Found., 1976— . Served with USMC, 1943-46. Fellow Am. Coll. Preventive Medicine, Am. Acad. Family Physicians (sci. program com. 1972-75, commn. on edn. 1975-80), Royal Soc. Health; mem. Mo. Acad. Family Physicians (dir. 1956-59, 76-82, alt. del. 1982-87, pres. 1985-86, chmn. bd. 1986-87), Mo. Med. Assn., Howard County Med. Soc. (pres. 1958-59), Boone County Med. Soc. (pres. 1974-75), Am. Diabetes Assn. (pres. 1978, dir. 1974-77), Mo. Diabetes Assn. (pres. 1972-73), Soc. Tchrs. Family Medicine, AMA, Mo. Public Health Assn., Am. Heart Assn. (program com. 1979-82), Am. Heart Assn. of Mo. (sec. 1980-81), Mo. Heart Assn. (sec. 1979-82, pres.-elect 1982-84, pres. 1984-86). Methodist. Office: U Mo M218 Medical Ctr Columbia MO 65203

ALLER, HUGH DUNCAN, astronomer, educator; Prof. astronomy, dir. obs., chmn. dept. astronomy U. Mich., Ann Arbor. Office: 810 Dennison 500 Church St Ann Arbor MI 48104-2514

ALLINGTON, ROBERT WILLIAM, instrument company executive; b. Madison, Wis., Sept. 18, 1935; s. William B. and Norma Evelyn (Peterson) A.; m. Mary Lynn Kaylor, Sept. 4, 1976. BS, U. Nebr., 1959, MS, 1961, ScD (hon.), 1985. CEO, chmn. Isco, Inc., Lincoln, Nebr., 1961—. Inventor in field; contbr. numerous articles to profl. jours. Bd. dirs. League Human Dignity, Lincoln, 1981—, Nebr. Rsch. and Devel. Authority Lincoln, 1986-94, chmn., 1990-94; mem. Gov.'s Com. on Employment of the Handicapped, Lincoln, 1983; mem. Indsl. Adv. Bd., Dept. Chemistry, U. Nebr., 1988—; bd. dirs. Lincoln Cmty. Found. Inc., 1989-96; chmn. Nebr. EPSCOR Com., 1991—. Named Handicapped Nebraskan of the Yr., Gov. of Nebr., 1972, Outstanding Engring. Achievement Profl. Engrs., 1975, Nat. Small Bus. Person of the Yr., SBA, 1985, Exec. of the Yr., R&D Mag., 1991, U. of Nebr. Outstanding Alumnus, 1993, Entrepreneur of Yr. Nebr. Ctr. Entrepreneurship Lincoln Coll. Bus. Adminstrn. U. Nebr., 1998; recipient Disting. Svc. award Kiwanis, 1978, Support of Rsch. award Sigma Xi, 1986. Mem. Am. Chem. Soc., Am. Inst. Chemists, IEEE, Instrument Soc. Am., Nat. Soc. Profl. Engrs., Analytical and Life Sci. Sys. Assn. (bd. dirs. 1992-95), Nebr. Club, The Club. Episcopalian. Avocation: sci. and tech. history. Office: Isco Inc 4700 Superior St Lincoln NE 68504-1398

ALLISON, DIANNE J. HALL, retired insurance company official; b. Wadsworth, Ohio, June 9, 1936; d. Glenn Mackey and Dorothy Laverne (Broomall) Hall; widowed; children: Christine M. Gardner Fiocca, Jon R. Gardner; m. David L. Allison, May 8, 1998. BA in Speech, Heidelberg Coll., Tiffin, Ohio, 1958. Receptionist Buckeye Union Ins. Co., Akron, Ohio, 1966-67; adjuster Liberty Mut. Ins. Co., 1967-69; claims liaison Ostrov Agy., 1969-70; underwriter Clark Agy., Wadsworth, 1971-72; adjuster Celina Group, 1972-73, Nationwide, Canton, Ohio, 1973-77; asst. claim mgr. Motorist Mut. Ins. Co., Akron, 1977-87; claim rep. Ohio Casualty Ins. Co., San Diego, 1987-88; claims adminstr. Riser Foods, Inc. Risk Mgmt., Bedford Heights, Ohio, 1989-97; claims specialist Motorists Ins. Co., Uniontown, 1998-2000; ret. Mem. Ohio Hist. Soc., Friends of Gettysburg. Mem.: Akron Claims Assn. (pres. 1985), Ohio State Claims Assn., Civil War Preservation Trust. Avocations: Civil War history, genealogical research, reading, painting.

ALLISON, JOHN ROBERT, lawyer; b. San Antonio, Feb. 9, 1945; s. Lyle (stepfather) and Beatrice (Kaliner) Forehand; m. Rebecca M. Picard; 1 child, Katharine. BS, Stanford U., 1966; JD, U. Wash., 1969. Bar: Wash. 1969, D.C. 1973, Minn. 1994, U.S. Supreme Ct. 1973. Assoc. Garvey, Schubert & Barer, Seattle, 1969-73; ptnr., 1973-86; prin. Betts, Patterson & Mines, P.S., 1986-94; sr. counsel Minn. Mining & Mfg. Co., 1994-2000, asst. gen. counsel, 2000—. Lectr. bus. law Seattle U., 1970, U. Wash., 1970-73; judge pro tem, King County Superior Ct., 1983-94. Mem. ABA (vice chmn. toxic and hazardous substances and environ. law com. 1986-91, chair elect 1991-92, chair 1992-93), Minn. Bar Assn., Seattle-King County Bar Assn. (chmn. jud. evaln. polling com. 1982-83), Wash. State Bar Assn. (bd. bar examiners 1984-94), D.C. Bar Assn., Nat. Inst. Pollution Liability (co-chmn. 1988), Order of the Coif. Office: Minn Mining & Mfg Co 3 M Ctr Saint Paul MN 55144-1000 E-mail: jrallison@mmm.com.

ALLISON, MARK S. trust company executive; BSBA, U. Kans.; MBA, U. Tex. Exec. v.p., chief investment officer Midwest Trust Co., Overland Park, Kans. Office: The Midwest Trust Co 10740 Nall Ave Ste 100 Overland Park KS 66211*

ALLISON, SANDY, genealogist, appraiser, political consultant; b. Newburg, Mo., June 30, 1950; d. Jimmy James and A. Colleen (Bricker) Arthur; m. Lynn Leonard Allison, Oct. 3, 1969 (div., 1998); children: Eric Lynn, Jason Wayne. AA, Columbia Coll., Rolla, Mo., 1995, BA, 1996, postgrad., 1996—; student, U. Mo., Rolla. Sec./bookkeeper Biederman Furniture Store, Rolla, 1969-72; bookkeeper/clk. Rolla Auction Co.; degree State Farm Ins., Rolla, 1995; demonstrator, salesperson Roth Distbn., St. Louis; home inspector Allison Assn., Rolla; owner/designer Allison Residential Contr.; owner/acct. Flowers Unltd. Inc.; appraiser Stoltz Appraisal Co., 1985-91; med. placement cons. Assoc. Svcs., 1991-92; pub. adminstr. Phelps County, 1992—, dir. econ. devel., 1996—; field dir. Carnahan for Gov. Campaign, St. Louis, 1991-92; with Sumner County Econ. Devel., Wellington, Kans., 1998-99; dir. Higginsville (Mo.) Econ. Devel., 1999—. Bus. devel. specialist St. Louis Econ. Devel. Coun. Author/editor: Allison Book, 1995; editor, chmn. com.: The Phelps County Missouri Heritage, 1991. Dem. Nat. committeewoman for State of Mo., 1992—; 8th Dist. pres. Dem. Party, 1990-95; bd. dirs. Connect Mo., 1993-94; v.p., pres., bd. dirs. PHelps County Univ. Ext., 1989-95; chairwoman Phelps County Dem. Party; v.p., membership chair Jeffersonian Women's Group; mem. solid waste commn. Meramec Regional Planning Commn.; mem. Mothers Against Drunk Drivers; dir. Sumner Cty. Econ. Devel., 1997-98; bd. mem. Sumner Cty. Geneology Soc. Named Dem. Outstanding Woman. Mem. Geneal. Soc. Mo. (pres., v.p., bd. dirs., State award 1992), Nat. Assn. Counties for Cmty. and Econ. Devel. (bd. dirs. 1992-93), Bus. and Profl. Women's Club (pres., legis. state chair 1991-94), Rolla Area C. of C., Phelps County Geneal. Soc. (founder, pres.), Toastmasters Internat., Nat. Assn. Real Estate Appraisers, Ind. Fee Appraisers Assn., Internat. Platform Assn., Alpha Sigma Alpha. Avocations: horseback riding, golf, gardening, reading, computers. Address: 218 Hickory Cir Higginsville MO 64037 E-mail: sandydallison@hotmail.com.

ALLMAN, MARGARET ANN LOWRANCE, counselor, academic advisor; b. Carmel, Calif., June 2, 1938; d. Edward Walton and Rhoda Elizabeth (Patton) Lowrance; m. Jackie Howard Hamilton, Dec. 21, 1959 (div. May 1976); children: John Scott, David Lee, Dennis Lynn; m. Jack Fredrick Allman, Dec. 22, 1977; stepchildren: John Frederick, James Paul, Jeffrey Lee. AA, Christian Coll., 1958; BA in Spanish, U. Mo., 1960, MEd, 1971, EdD, 1994. Tchr. Spanish Neosho (Mo.) H.S., 1961-62, asst. prin., 1974-77; florist Wallflower Shop and Greenhouse, Joplin, Mo., 1962-69; dean girls Joplin Sr. H.S., 1967-69; florist, bookkeeper Mueller's Garden Ctr., Columbia, Mo., 1969-71; instr. edn., asst. dean of students Columbia (Mo.) Coll., 1971-74; dir. guidance Am. Cmty. Sch., Buenos Aires, 1978-81; tchr. Spanish, psychology Ava (Mo.) H.S., 1982-84; tchr. Spanish, social studies McDonald County H.S., Anderson, Mo., 1984-88; counselor, acad. advisor Mo. So. State Coll., Joplin, 1988—. Mem. adv. bd. Adult Basic Edn., Joplin, 1992—; cons. Mo. So. State Coll., 1990—, mem. internat. task force, 1994-96; presenter Ctr. for Applications of Psychol. Type Internat. Conf., 1996. Recipient William D. Phillips Music award 1st Christian Ch., Columbia, 1956; named to Outstanding Young Women of Am., 1972. Mem.: Southwest Mo. Sch. Counselor Assn. (sec. 1994—97, v.p. 1992—94, 1999—2001, mem. governing bd., chmn. publs. and rsch. com. 1997—99), Mo. Sch. Counselor Assn., Phi Theta Kappa, Sigma Delta Pi, Phi Sigma Iota (romance lang., pres. 1959—60), Delta Eta Chi, Sigma Phi Gamma, Kappa Delta Pi. Avocations: music, photographer, sketch artist, needlecrafts, jewelry crafts. Home: 1214 Circle Dr Neosho MO 64850-1301 Office: Mo So State Coll 3950 Newman Rd Joplin MO 64801-1512

ALMEIDA, RICHARD JOSEPH, finance company administrator; b. N.Y.C., Apr. 29, 1942; s. Caetano Escudero and Grace (Maya) A.; m. Jill Farris, Mar. 17, 1979; 1 child, Alexis Farris. BA in Internat. Affairs, George Washington U., 1963; MA in Internat. Adminstrn., Maxwell Sch. Syracuse U., 1965. Comml. and internat. banker Citibank, N.Y. and South Am., 1966; area head comml. and internat. banking Citicorp/Citibank, Chgo., 1976, L.A., 1978-84, dep. strategic planning N.Y.C., 1984; head fin. inst. and investment banking origination Citicorp Investment Bank, 1985-87; CFO Heller Fin., Inc., Chgo., 1987—, also bd. dirs., chmn., CEO, 1995—. Bd. dirs. Fuji Bank and Trust, N.Y. Trustee The Latin Sch. of Chgo.; chmn. bd. dirs. High Jump; bd. dirs. Chgo. Youth Programs, Execs. Club Chgo.; mem. Chgo. Coun. Fgn. Rels. With USCG, 1966-72. Mem. Chgo. Club, The Casino, Chgo. C. of C., The Racquet Club, Econ. Club Chgo., Mid Am. Club. Roman Catholic. Office: Heller Fin Inc 500 W Monroe St Chicago IL 60661-3630

ALMEN, LOWELL GORDON, church official; b. Grafton, N.D., Sept. 25, 1941; s. Paul Orville and Helen Eunice (Johnson) A.; m. Sally Arlyn Clark, Aug. 14, 1965; children: Paul Simon, Cassandra Gabrielle. BA, Concordia Coll., Moorhead, Minn., 1963; MDiv, Luther Theol. Sem., St. Paul, 1967; LittD (hon.), Capital U., 1981; DD (hon.), Carthage Coll., 1989, Concordia Coll., 1994. Ordained to ministry Luth. Ch., 1967. Pastor St. Peter's Luth. Ch., Dresser, Wis., 1967-69; asso. campus pastor, dir. communications Concordia Coll., Moorhead, Minn., 1969-74; mng. editor Luth. Standard ofcl. publ. Am. Luth. Ch., Mpls., 1974-78; editor Luth. Standard, 1979-87; sec., officer Evangelical Luth. Ch. Am., Chgo., 1987—. Author: Old Songs for a New Journey, 1990, One Great Cloud of Witnesses, 1997; author, co-editor: The Many Faces of Pastoral Ministry, 1989; editor: World Religions and Christian Mission, 1967, Our Neighbor's Faith, 1968. Recipient Disting. Alumnus award Concordia Coll., 1982; Bush Found. grantee, 1972 Office: Evang Luth Ch 8765 W Higgins Rd Chicago IL 60631-4101

ALMONY, ROBERT ALLEN, JR. librarian, businessman; b. Charleston, W.Va., Oct. 14, 1945; s. Robert Allen and Margaret Elizabeth A.; m. Carol A. Krzeminski, May 6, 1972; children— Rob, Michael, Chandra, Rachel. A.A., Grossmont Coll., 1965; B.A., San Diego State U., 1968; M.L.S., U. Calif.-Berkeley, 1977. Sr. div. clk. San Diego State U. Library, 1965-68; acct. Calif. Tchrs. Fin. Services, Orange County, 1968-70, v.p., gen. mgr., 1971-76; research asst. library sch. U. Calif.-Berkeley, 1976-77; reference librarian Oberlin Coll. Library, Ohio, 1977-79; asst. dir. libraries U. Mo., Columbia, 1980—; owner Almony & Assocs. Tax and Fin. Planning, 1980—; distbr. USA Today, 1984-88. Guest lectr. libr. budgeting, personal fin. planning; cons. libr. copy svcs.; faculty coun. exec. bd., 1994-2000, recorder Mo. U., 1994-98, chair fiscal affairs, 1998-2000, learning strategies tchr., 1986—, adj. faculty Libr. Sch., 1997—. Contbr. articles to profl. jours. Treas. Bahai's of Columbia, 1982-86, 95-97, sec., 1987-89, 93-95, 1998-2001, 2001—, chmn., 1989-93; coach Columbia Youth Soccer League, 1981-92; cubmaster Boy Scouts Am., Columbia, 1983-85; asst. scoutmaster, 1985-91; hon. warrior Mic-O-Say, 1986—, treas. Mo. U. Soccer Boosters, 1996—; mem. Daniel Boone Regional Libr. Devel. Bd., 1999-2000; treas. MV Kickens, 1998—. Mem. ALA, Mo. Libr. Assn. (treas. 1996-97, 98-99), Assn. Coll. and Rsch. Libr. (exec. com. 1983-86), Libr. Adminstrn. and Mgmt. Assn. (chmn. mem. 1991-93, 2000-01, Outstanding Svc. award 1994, B & F Officers Group Libr. Adminstrn. and Mgmt. (chmn. 1987-91), Nat. Commn. on Ednl. Stats. Integrated Post-Secondary Edn. Data Sys. Acad. Librs. (coord. for Mo. 1992—), Mo. Assn. Coll. and Rsch. Librs. (vice chmn., chmn. 1982-84), Hickman Athletic Boosters (pres. 1991-94), Maplewood Barn Theater (bd. dirs. 1993-2000, sec., treas. 1998-2000), COE Coll. Parents (bd. dirs. 1993-95). Home: 301 Rothwell Dr Columbia MO 65203-0257 Office: U Mo 104 Ellis Libr Columbia MO 65201-5149 E-mail: almonyr@missouri.edu.

ALOMAR, ROBERTO VELAZQUEZ, professional baseball player; b. Ponce, P.R., Feb. 5, 1968; With San Diego Padres, 1988-90, Toronto Blue Jays, 1990-95, Balt. Orioles, 1996-98, Cleve. Indians, 1998—. Recipient Am. League Gold Glove award, 1991-94; named to All-Star team,

1990-96, Sporting News Am. League Silver Slugger Team, 1992, 96, All-Star Team, 1992. Office: New York Mets Shea Stadium 123-01 Roosevelt Avenue Flushing NY 11368*

ALOMAR, SANDY, JR. (SANTOS VELAZQUEZ ALOMAR), professional baseball player; b. Salinas, P.R., June 18, 1966; With San Diego Padres, 1988-89, Cleve. Indians, 1990—2000, Chicago White Sox, 2001—02, Colorado Rockies, 2002—. Named Rookie of Yr. Baseball Writers' Assn. Am., 1990, Sporting News, 1990, named to Am. League All-Star team, 1990, 91; recipient Am. League Gold Glove award, 1990. Office: Colorado Rockies Coors Field 2001 Blake Street Denver CO 80205-2000*

ALPERS, DAVID HERSHEL, physician, educator; b. Phila., May 9, 1935; s. Bernard Jacob and Lillian (Sher) A.; m. Melanie Goldman, Aug. 12, 1977; children: Ann, Ruth, Barbara. BA, Harvard U., 1956, MD, 1960. Intern Mass. Gen. Hosp., Boston, 1960-61, resident in internal medicine, 1961-62; instr. medicine Harvard U., 1965-67, assoc. in medicine, 1967-68, asst. prof., 1968-69; asst. prof. medicine Washington U., St. Louis, 1969-72, assoc. prof., 1972-73, prof., 1973—, William B. Kountz prof., 1997—, dir. gastrointestinal divsn., 1969-97, asst. dir. clin. nutrition rsch. unit, 1999—; sr. cons. R&D GlaxoSmithKline, 2002—. Author: (with others) Manual of Nutritional Therapeutics, 4th edit., 1998; assoc. editor: Textbook of Gastroenterology, 3d edit., 1999, Physiology of the Gastrointestinal Tract, 4th edit., 2001; assoc. editor Jour. Clin. Investigation, 1977-82; editor Am. Jour. Physiology, Gastrointestinal and Liver Physiology, 1991-97; contbr. articles and revs. to profl. jours., chpts. to books. With USPHS, 1962-64. Mem. Am. Soc. Clin. Investigation, Assn. Am. Physicians, Am. Gastroent. Assn. (pres. 1990-91, Friedenwald medal 1997), Am. Soc. Biochem. Molecular Biology (editl. bd. 1998—), Am. Fedn. Clin. Rsch., Am. Soc. Clin. Nutrition. Office: Washington U Med Sch Dept Internal Medicine PO Box 8031 Saint Louis MO 63156-8124 E-mail: DAlpers@im.wustl.edu.

ALPERT, DANIEL, television executive; b. Chgo., June 20, 1952; s. Herbert and Miriam Florence (Nemiroff) A.; m. Doreen Marie Podolski, Apr. 30, 1976; children: Hilary Marie, Neil Andrew. BA, Mich. State U., 1973, postgrad., 1974-76. News reporter, disk jockey Sta. WITL-AM-FM, Lansing, Mich., 1973; audio producer Instructional Media Ctr. Mich. State U., East Lansing, 1973-74; dir. pub. info. Sta. WKAR-TV, 1974-76; v.p., dir. pub. info. Sta. WTVS, Detroit, 1976-82, sr. v.p., acting gen. mgr., 1983, sr. v.p., asst. gen. mgr., 1983-96, sr. v.p. sta. mgr., 1996-2000, COO, Sta. mgr., 2000—. Contbr. articles on travel and sci. local newspapers. Trustee Karmanos Cancer Inst., Detroit, 1984—. Recipient Devel. award Corp. for Pub. Broadcasting, 1976, Promotion award Broadcast Promotion Assn., 1978, Pub. Broadcasting Svc., 1981, Govt. Rels. awards Nat. Assn. Pub. TV Stas., 1989, 96, ACE award Mich. Assn. Broadcasters, 1991. Mem. Nat. Acad. TV Arts and Scis. (gov. Detroit chpt. 1980-97, Silver Circle award Mich. chpt. 2000), Mich. Assn. Broadcasters, Mich. Pub. Broadcasters (exec. com. 1995—). Office: Sta WTVS 7441 2nd Ave Detroit MI 48202-2796 E-mail: alpert@dptv.org.

ALSOP, DONALD DOUGLAS, federal judge; b. Duluth, Minn., Aug. 28, 1927; s. Robert Alvin and Mathilda (Aaseng) A.; m. Jean Lois Tweeten, Aug. 16, 1952; children: David, Marcia, Robert. BS, U. Minn., 1950, LLB, 1952. Bar: Minn. 1952. Pvt. practice, New Ulm, Minn.; ptnr. Gislason, Alsop, Dosland & Hunter, 1954-75; judge U.S. Dist. Ct. Minn., St. Paul, 1975—, chief dist. judge, 1985-92, sr. dist. judge, 1992—. Mem. 8th cir. jud. coun., 1987-92, Jud. Conf. Com. to Implement Criminal Justice Act, 1979-87; mem. exec. com. Nat. Conf. Fed. Trial Judges, 1990-94. Chmn. Brown County (Minn.) Republican Com., 1960-64, 2d Congl. Dist. Rep. Com., 1968-72, Brown County chpt. ARC, 1968-74. Served with AUS, 1945-46. Mem. 8th Cir. Dist. Judges Assn. (pres. 1982-84), New Ulm C. of C. (pres. 1974-75), Order of Coif. Office: US Dist Ct 754 Fed Bldg 316 Robert St N Saint Paul MN 55101-1495

ALSPAUGH, DALE WILLIAM, university administrator, aeronautics and astronautics educator; b. Dayton, Ohio, May 25, 1932; m. Marlowe Anne Alspaugh; 4 children. ME, U. Cin., 1955; MS in Engring. Scis., Purdue U., 1958, PhD in Engring. Scis., 1965. Profl. engr., Ohio. Project engr. GMC Frigidaire div., 1955-56, 59; instr. sch. aeronautics and astronautics & engring. Purdue U., West Lafayette, Ind., 1957-58, 59-64, asst. prof., 1964-68, assoc. prof., 1968-81; vice chancellor for acad. svcs., prof. Purdue U. North Cen. campus, Westville, 1981-82, acting chancellor, prof., 1982-84, chancellor, prof. aeronautics and astronautics, 1984-99, chancellor emeritus, prof. aeronautics and astronautics, 2000—. Mem. numerous coms. Purdue U.; cons. Midwest Applied Sci. Corp., West Lafayette, 1959-66, Ruper Corp., West Lafayette, 1972-73, Switzer div. Wallace Murray Corp., Indpls., 1972-73, Los Alamos (N.Mex.) Scientific Lab., 1977, U.S. Army MICOM, Huntsville, Ala., 1978-82, Campbell & Pryor Cons. Corp., Michigan City, Ind., 1984-86, Colsa, Inc., Huntsville, 1988; reviewer Applied Mechs. Rev., J. Franklin Inst., ASME Jour. Heat Transfer, Internat. Jour. Engring. Sci., also NSF rsch. proposals, various books; bd. dirs. Meml. Hosp. Michigan City, 1st Citizens Bank of Michigan City, Horizon Bancorp. Contbr. articles to profl. jours.; also numerous reports, papers, seminars. Mem. West Lafayette Bd. Sch. trustees, 1976-81, sec., 1976-77, v.p. 1977-78, pres. 1978-79; mem. West Lafayette Park & Recreation Bd., 1976-81, treas. 1979-80; mem. West Lafayette Sch. Bd. Negotiating Team, 1977-78, chief negotiator, 1978; mem. West Lafeyett Sch. Supt. screening Com., 1980-81; mem. West Lafayette Community Sch. Coun., 1970-73, pres., 1973; pres. Burtsfield PTA, 1970-71; supt. Covenant Presbyn. Ch. Sch., 1969-74; mem. West Lafayette Little League Bd., 1969-72; bd. dirs. N.W. Ind. Forum, 1983—, mem. subcom. on strategic planning, 1983-85, N.W. Ind. ednl. pub. TV consortium, 1984, subcom. on legis. affairs, 1985—, subcom. on hazardous materials, 1986-87, ednl. consortium, 1988—; mem. Barker Commn., 1986—; bd. dirs. Friends of Barker; mem. City of Valparaiso Ethics Commn., 1995—. Recipient grants NASA, Purdue Rsch. Found., Fund for Instructional Devel. & Innovative Teaching, Fund for Alternatives in Engring. Edn., U.S. Army MICOM. Mem. AIAA (coun. Cen. Ind. sect. 1969-71), Am. Soc. Engring. Edn. (space engring. com. 1970-78), Greater Valparaiso C. of C. (bd. dirs. 1985-90, chmn. div. on local & govtl. affairs 1987-88), Rotary. Office: Purdue U N Cen Campus Office of the Chancellor 1401 S Us Highway 421 Westville IN 46391-9542

ALTAN, TAYLAN, engineering educator, mechanical engineer, consultant; b. Trabzon, Turkey, Feb. 12, 1938; came to U.S., 1962; s. Seref and Sadife (Baysal) Kadioglu; m. Susan Borah, July 18, 1964; children: Peri Michele, Aylin Elisabeth Diploma in engring., Tech. U., Hannover, Fed. Republic Germany, 1962; M.S. in Mech. Engring., U. Calif.-Berkeley, 1964, Ph.D. in Mech. Engring., 1966. Research engr. DuPont Co., Wilmington, Del., 1966-68; research scientist Battelle Columbus Labs, Ohio, 1968-72, research fellow, 1972-75, sr. research leader, 1975-86; prof. mech. engring., dir. engring. rsch. ctr. Ohio State U., Columbus, 1985—. Chmn. sci. com. N.Am. Mfg. Rsch. Inst. Soc. Mfg. Engrs., Detroit, 1982-86, pres., 1987; dir. Ctr. for Net Shape Mfg. Co-author: Forging Equipment, 1973, Metal Forming, 1983, Metal Forming and the Finite Element Method, 1989; assoc. editor Jour. Materials Processing Tech., Eng., 1978-99; contbr. over 400 tech. articles to profl. jours. Fellow Am. Soc. Metals (chmn. forging com. 1978-87), Soc. Mfg. Engrs. (Gold medal 1985), ASME. Avocations: languages, travel. Office: Ohio State U 210 Baker Bldg 1971 Neil Ave Columbus OH 43210-1210 E-mail: altan1@osu.edu.

ALTER, WILLIAM, state legislator; b. Iowa City, May 15, 1944; m. Merijo Robinson, 1963; children: Angela, William Brett (dec.). Student, Jefferson Coll. Law, Enforcement Tng. Ctr., 1982-84. mem. consumer protection com., elections com., criminal law com. Mo. State rep. Dist. 90, 1988-2000; owner, mgr. sml. bus.; sales v.p. Nat. Co.; police officer small municipality, Mo.; pres. Alter Mgmt., 1977—. Founder N. Jefferson C. of C., Mo; treas. High Ridge Ch. of Christ. Mem. NRA (life), Hist. Soc. and Rep. Club, Rotary (past pres.). Home: 1800 Gravois Rd High Ridge MO 63049-2610

ALTERMAN, IRWIN MICHAEL, lawyer; b. Vineland, N.J., Mar. 4, 1941; s. Joseph and Rose A.; m. Susan Simon, Aug. 6, 1972 (dec. Apr. 1997); 1 son, Owen. AB, Princeton U., 1962; LLB, Columbia U., 1965. Bar: N.Y. 1966, Mich. 1967. Law clk. to chief judge Theodore Levin U.S. Dist. Ct. (ea. dist.) Mich., 1965-67; assoc. Kaye, Scholer, Fierman, Hays & Handler, N.Y.C., 1967-70, Hyman, Gurwin, Nachman, Friedman & Winkelman, Southfield, Mich., 1970-74, ptnr., 1974-88, Kaufman and Payton, Farmington Hills, Mich., 1988-89, Kemp, Klein, Umphrey & Endelman, Troy, 1989—. Author: Plain and Accurate Style in Court Papers, 1987; founding editor: Mich. Antitrust, 1975—92; editor: Mich. Antitrust Digest, 3d edit., 2001; contbr. Bd. gov. Jewish Fedn. Detroit, 1990—; mem. nat. young leadership cabinet United Jewish Appeal, 1978-79, mem. nat. exec. com., 1980; past pres. Adat Shalom Synagogue, Farmington Hills, Mich. Mem. ABA, Am. Law Inst., State Bar Mich. (past chmn. com. on plain English, past. chmn. antitrust sect.), Princeton Club (past pres. Mich.). Office: Kemp Klein Umphrey & Endelman 201 W Big Beaver Rd Ste 600 Troy MI 48084-4136 E-mail: irwin.alterman@kkue.com.

ALTHAVER, LAMBERT EWING, manufacturing company executive; b. Kansas City, Mo., May 18, 1931; s. Edward William and Dorothy Lambert (Ewing) A.; m. Holly Elizabeth Walpole, Feb. 28, 1953; children: Brian, Lauren BA, Principia Coll, 1952. Account exec. Walbro Corp., Cass City, Mich., 1954-58, asst. to pres., 1958-65, v.p. fin., 1965-70, exec. v.p., 1970-77, pres., chief ops. officer, 1977-82, pres., CEO, 1982-87, chmn., pres., CEO, 1987-96, also bd. dirs., chmn., CEO, 1996-98, chmn. emeritus, 1998-2000. Councilman Village of Cass City, 1963-65, pres., 1965-84, 87-2000; mem. Tuscola County Planning Commn., Caro, Mich., 1966-94; chmn. Cass City Econ. Devel. Corp., 1983-96, Tuscola area Airport Authority, 1994—; bd. dirs. Tuscola County Econ. Devel. Corp.; vice-chmn., sec., dir. Artrain, Inc., 1975-96, chmn., 1996—; v.p., bd. dirs. Lake Huron area Boy Scouts Am., 1988-94; co-founder, v.p. Village Bach Festival, 1979—; trustee Jordan Coll., 1990-95, Northwood U., 2000—; mem. Mich Jobs Commn., 1996-99; trustee Hills & Dales Hosp., Cass City, 1998—; dir. Am. Bus. Conf. Found., Washington, 1998—; dir. Mich. Mcpl. League Found., Ann Arbor, 1999-2002. With U.S. Army, 1952-54. Recipient Silver Beaver award Boy Scouts Am., 1995, Disting. Eagle Scout award, 1989; named Citizen of Yr. Cass City C. of C., 1978; Paul Harris fellow Rotary Internat., Evanston, Ill., 1979, 94, 99; named Outstanding Bus. Leader, Northwood U., 1997. Mem. Mich. C. of C. (bd. dirs. 1986-92), Cass City C. of C. (bd. dirs. 1985—), Detroit Athletic Club, Rotary. Avocation: golf. Office: PO Box 27 Cass City MI 48726-0027 E-mail: althaver@avci.net.

ALTHOFF, J(AMES) L. construction company executive; b. McHenry, Ill., June 9, 1928; s. William H. and Eleanor M. (Smith) A.; m. Joan E. Andreen, June 18, 1949; children: Tim, Betsy, Kate, Tod, Patti, Jim Jr., Karyn. Grad., McHenry (Ill.) High Sch., 1947. Owner, pres. Althoff Gas Svc., McHenry, 1949-60, Fox Valley Propane, 1952-60, No. Equip. Corp., McHenry, 1958-72; CEO Althoff Industries, Crystal Lake, Ill., 1961—, Althoff & Assocs., McHenry, 1962—, Brookside Indsl., McHenry, 1991—. Trustee Plumbers Welfare Fund, Chgo., 1972—; dir. McHenry Bank. Pres. McHenry High Sch. Bd. Edn., 1967-79, Fire Protection Dist., McHenry, 1964-92; chmn. bd. govs. Ill. Univs., 1980-91; commr. Ill. State Lottery, 1991—. Recipient award for outstanding leadership Chgo. State U., 1986, Leadership award No. Med. Ctr., McHenry, 1984, Ea. Ill. U., 1987. Mem. Contrs. Assn. No. Ill. (pres. 1969-72), Bradley Dads' Assn., Kiwanis. Home: 508 N Green St Mchenry IL 60050-5684 Office: Althoff Industries 8001 S State Route 31 Crystal Lake IL 60014-8184

ALTING, RONNIE JOE, state legislator, restaurateur; b. Lafayette, Ind., Mar. 15, 1956; s. Frank and Estell (Buschong) A., m. Elizabeth; two children, Ronnie Jr., Ashley. BS, Purdue U., 1977. Program dir. Lafayette YMCA, 1977-80; pres. Price Properties, Inc., Lafayette, 1980-83; v.p. Shook Mgmt., Inc., 1983-84; property mgr. U.S. region R.W.B. Realty, New Orleans, 1984-86; co-owner, gen. mgr. Patout's Restaurant, 1986—; mem. Ind. Senate, 1998—. Pub. relations chmn., bd. dirs. Big Bros., New Orleans, 1987—; bd. dirs. New Orleans YMCA, 1987—. Named One of Outstanding Young Men of Am., 1985. Mem. Sons of Am. Legion. Republican. Methodist. Avocations: running, assisting youth charities, racquetball. Home: 3600 Cedar Ln Lafayette IN 47905-3914

ALTMAN, ARNOLD DAVID, business executive; b. South Bend, Ind., Dec. 10, 1917; s. David and Goldie (Mooren) A.; children: Daniel Blair, Jonathan Estes. BSEE, U. Notre Dame, 1941. With Newman and Altman, Inc., South Bend, 1946-64; pres. Avanti Motor Corp., 1976-82, Nat. Inventory Res., Inc., South Bend, 1980—; pres., CEO Rosenstein & Co., 1985—. Lt. USN, 1942-46. Democrat. Jewish. Home: 1527 E Colfax Ave South Bend IN 46617-2601 Office: PO Box 603 Mishawaka IN 46546

ALTOSE, MURRAY DAVID, physician, educator; b. Winnipeg, Man., Can., Oct. 1, 1941; came to U.S., 1969; m. Connie Jean Tesmer, Jan. 14, 1973; children: Michael Dov, Aaron Judah, Benjamin Isaac. BSc, MD, U. Man., 1965. Diplomate Am. Bd. Internal medicine, Am. Bd. Pulmonary Disease. Rotating intern Winnipeg Gen. Hosp., 1965-66, asst. resident in medicine, 1966-67, resident in critical care medicine, 1968-69; asst. resident medicine Cleve. Met. Gen. Hosp., 1969-70, resident-in-charge pulmonary disease sect., 1970-71, chief pulmonary divsn. dept. medicine, 1977-88, assoc. dir. dept. medicine, 1981-88; fellow pulmonary disease sect. Hosp. U. Pa., Phila., 1971-73, co-dir. respiratory ICU, 1973-74, dir. diagnostic svcs., 1973-77; assoc. in medicine U. Pa. Sch. Medicine, Phila., 1973, asst. prof. medicine, 1973-77; assoc. prof. medicine Case Western Res. U. Sch. Medicine, Cleve., 1977-84, prof. medicine, 1984—; chief of staff Dept. Vets. Affairs Med. Ctr., 1988—. Assoc. dean Vets. Hosp. Affairs, 1988—; attending physician pulmonary in-patient svc. med. ICU and Pulmonary Cons. Svc. Cleve. Met. Gen. Hosp., 1977-78, med. dir. respiratory therapy dept., 1977-88, dir. respiratory ICU, 1977-81, attending physician med. ICU Univ. Hosps., Cleve., 1978—; mem. med. rsch. svc. rev. bd. for respiration VA, 1986-89; spl. reviewer NIH Clin. Sci., 1985, 88; cons. spl. emphasis panel NIH Nat. Heart, Lung and Blood Inst., 1996; temp. mem. NIH Respiratory and Applied Physiology Study Sect., 1996; attending physician respiratory ICU VA Med. Ctr., Cleve., 1988—, attending physician med. svc., 1988; lectr. in field. Mem. editl. bd. Jour. Applied Physiology, 1984-93, editl. referee, 1980—; contbr. articles to profl. publs., chpts. to books, abstracts. Trustee Northeast Ohio affiliate Am. Heart Assn., 1993-98, mem. rsch. allocation com., 1989-93. Mem. Am. Fedn. Clin. Rsch. (mem. program 1982, steering com. sect. on respiratory pathophysiology 1981-82, chmn. sect. 1982-84, mem. program and awards coms. ann. sci. assembly 1985), Am. Thoracic Soc. (program com. sci. assembly on respiratory structure and function 1989-90), Ohio Thoracic Soc., Am. Coll. Chest Physicians (program com., awards com. ann. sci. assembly 1985), Am. Physiol. Soc., Am. Coll. Physician Execs., Am. Heart Assn., Nat. Assn. VA Chiefs of Staff (pres. elect 1996, pres. 1997-98). Office: Cleve VA Med Ctr 10701 East Blvd Cleveland OH 44106-1702

ALTSCHAEFFL, ADOLPH GEORGE, civil engineering educator, retired; b. Passaic, N.J., July 20, 1930; s. Ludwig and Crescenz (Liebl) A.; m. Martha Anne Filiatreau, Aug. 6, 1966. B.S.C.E., Purdue U., 1952, M.S.C.E., 1955, Ph.D., 1960. Instr. civil engring. Purdue U., West Lafayette, Ind., 1952-60, asst. prof. civil engring., 1960-64, assoc. prof., 1964-74, prof., 1974-2000, asst. head dept., 1983-91, head geotech. engring., 1994-2000; with Waterways Expt. Sta., C.E., Vicksburg, Miss., 1955, U.S. Geol. Survey, Indpls., 1956. Cons. civil engring. with various architect and contractor firms. Contbr. articles to profl. jours. Served with USAR, 1950-61. Mem. Am. Soc. Engring. Edn., ASCE, Nat. Soc. Profl. Engrs. Office: Purdue U Civil Engring Bldg West Lafayette IN 47907 E-mail: altsch@ecn.purdue.edu.

ALUMBAUGH, JOANN MCCALLA, magazine editor; b. Ann Arbor, Mich., Sept. 16, 1952; d. William Samuel and Jean Arliss (Guy) McCalla; m. Lyle Ray Alumbaugh, Apr. 27, 1974; children: Brent William, Brandon Jess, Brooke Louise. BA, Ea. Mich. U., 1974. Cert. elem. tch., Mich. Assoc. editor Chester White Swine Record Assn., Rochester, Ind., 1974-77; prodn. editor United Duroc Swine Registry, Peoria, Ill., 1977-79; dir., pres. Nat. Assn. Swine Records, Macomb, 1979-82; free-lance writer, artist Ill. and Nat. Specific Pathogen Free Assn., Ind. producers, Good Hope, Emden, 1982-85; editor The Hog Producer Farm Progress Publs., Urbandale, Iowa, 1985-99; exec. editor Nebr. Farmer, Kans. Farmer, Mo. Ruralist, We. Beef Prodr., Beef Prodr., Farm & Fireside, 1999—. Family Living Program, Farm Progress Show, 1985-, Master Farm Homemaker Program, 1989-99; mem. U.S. Agrl. Export Devel. Coun., Washington, 1979-82, apptd. mem. Blue Ribbon Com. on Agr., 1980-81. Contbr. numerous articles to profl. jours. Precinct chmn. Rep. Party, Linden, Iowa, 1988; mem. Keep Improving Dist. Schs., Panora, Iowa, 1990-91; v.p. Sunday sch. com. Sunset Circle, United Meth. Ch., Linden, 1990-91; pres. PTA, Panorama Schs., Panora, 1993-94; coach Odyssey of Mind Program World Competition, 1994—. Mem.: Iowa Master Farm Homemakers, Guthrie County Prok Prodrs., McDonough County and Ill. Porkettes (county pres. 1978—79, Bellerimger award 1979), Nat. Pork Prodrs. Coun., Iowa Pork Prodrs. Assn. (legis. com. 1990—95, hon. master pork prodr.), U.S. Animal Health Assn., Am. Agrl. Editors Assn. (chmn. dist. svc. com. 1991, master writer 1997, pres.-elect 1998, pres. 1999, co-chmn. comm. clinic, chmn. comms. clinic, chmn. adv. coun. 1999—, World of Difference award 1995, Oscar in Agr. 1999), Internat. Platform Assn. Avocations: reading, painting, flower gardening. Home: 2644 Amarillo Ave Linden IA 50146-8029 Office: Farm Progress Publs/Wallaces Farmer 6200 Aurora Ave Ste 609E Urbandale IA 50322-2863

ALUTTO, JOSEPH ANTHONY, university dean, management educator; b. Bronx, N.Y., June 3, 1941; s. Anthony and Concetta (Del Prete) Alutto; m. Laral Newcomb, Sept. 9, 1948; children: Patricia, Christina, Kerrie, Heather. BBA, Manhattan Coll., Riverdale, N.Y., 1962; MA, U. Ill., 1965; PhD, Cornell U., 1968. Asst. prof. orgnl. behavior SUNY, Buffalo, 1966-72, assoc. prof., 1972-75, prof., 1975-91, dean Sch. Mgmt., 1976-91, Clarence S. Marsh chair mgmt., 1990; dean Fisher Coll. of Bus. Ohio State U., Columbus, 1991—. Bd. dirs. United Retail Group, Inc., Comptek, Inc., Bank One Columbus, INROADS/Columbus; prs. Am. Assembly Collegiate Schs. of Bus., 1996—98. Author: (with others) Theory Testing in Organizational Behavior: The Varient Approach, 1983; contbr. 60 articles to profl. jours. United Way, Buffalo, 1982—91; pres. Amherst Cen. Sch. Bd., 1982—86. Mem. APA, AAAS, Acad. Mgmt. (pres. Ea. divsn. 1980-81), Am. Sociol. Assn., Capital Club, Athletic Club. Home: 810 Curleys Ct Columbus OH 43235-2161 Office: Ohio State U Main Campus Office Dean of Bus 201 Fisher Hall 2100 Neil Ave Columbus OH 43210-1309

ALVERSON, WILLIAM H. lawyer; b. Rockford, Ill., July 23, 1933; A.B., Princeton U., 1955; LL.B., U. Wis., 1960. Bar: Wis. 1960. Mem. firm Godfrey & Kahn. Pres. Milw. Profl. Sports and Services, 1972-76; chmn. Houston Rockets basketball team, 1977-79; chmn. bd. govs. Nat. Basketball Assn., 1975-76. Mem. Milw., Am. bar assns., State Bar Wis., Phi Delta Phi. Office: 780 N Water St Milwaukee WI 53202-3512

AMACK, REX, state agency administrator; Dir. Nebr. Games and Pks. Commn., Lincoln, 1998—. Office: Nebr Games & Pks Commn 2200 N 33rd St Lincoln NE 68503-1417

AMAN, ALFRED CHARLES, JR. dean; b. Rochester, N.Y., July 7, 1945; s. Alfred Charles Sr. and Jeannette Mary (Czebatul) Aman; m. Carol Jane Greenhouse, Sept. 23, 1976. AB, U. Rochester, 1967; JD, U. Chgo., 1970. Bar: (D.C.) 1971, Ga. 1972, N.Y. 1980. Law clk. U.S. Ct. Appeals, Atlanta, 1970—72; assoc. Sutherland, Asbill & Brennan, 1972—75, Washington, 1975—77; assoc. prof. Sch. Law, Cornell U., Ithaca, NY, 1977—82, prof. law, 1983—91, exec. dir. Internat. Legal Studies Program, 1988—90; prof. law, dean Sch. Law, Ind. U., Bloomington, 1991—99, dean, Roscoe C. O'Byrne chair in law, 1999—, disting. Fulbright chair in comparative constitutional law, 1998; vis. prof. law U. Paris II, 1998. Cons. U.S. Adminstrv. Conf., Washington, 1978—80, Washington, 1986—; trustee U. Rochester, 1980—; vis. fellow Wolfson Coll., Cambridge U., 1983—84, 1990—91. Author: Energy and Natural Resources, 1983, Administrative Law in a Global Era, 1992, Administrative Law Treatise, 1992, 2d edit., 2001. Chmn. Ithaca Bd. Zoning Appeals, 1980—82. Mem.: ABA, N.Y. State Bar Assn., Ga. Bar Assn., D.C. Bar Assn., Am. Assn. Law Schs., Phi Beta Kappa. Avocations: music, jazz drumming, piano, composition and arranging. Office: Ind U Sch Law 211 S Indiana Ave Bloomington IN 47405-7001

AMAN, MOHAMMED MOHAMMED, university dean, library and information science educator; b. Alexandria, Egypt, Jan. 3, 1940; came to U.S., 1963, naturalized, 1975; s. Mohammed Aman and Fathia Ali (al-Maghrabi) Mohammed; m. Mary Jo Parker, Sept. 15, 1972; 1 son, David. BA, Cairo U., 1961; MS, Columbia U., 1965; PhD, U. Pitts., 1968. Librarian Egyptian Nat. Libr., 1961-63, Duquesne U., Pitts., 1966-68; asst. prof. libr. sci. Pratt Inst., N.Y.C., 1968-69; from asst. prof. to assoc. prof. St. John's U., Jamaica, N.Y., 1969-73, prof., dir. divsn. libr. and info. sci., 1973-76; prof. libr. sci., dean Palmer Grad. Libr. Sch., C.W. Post Ctr., L.I. U., 1976-79; prof., dean, interim dean Sch. Edn. U. Wis., Milw., 2000—, dean Sch. Info. Studies, 1979—. Cons. UNESCO, U.S., AID and UNIDO; USIA acad. specialist, Germany, 1989; Fulbright lectr. Cairo U., 1990-91; USIA-sponsored lectr. Mohamed V. Univ., Rabat, Morocco, 1997. Author: Librarianship and the Third World, 1976, Cataloging and Classifications of Non-Western Library Material: Issues, Trends and Practices, 1980, Arab Serials and Periodicals: A Subject Bibliography, 1979, Online Access to Databases, 1983, On Developing Computer-Based Library Systems (Arabic), 1984, Information Services (Arabic), 1985, Trends in Urban Library Management, 1989, The Bibliotheca Alexandrina: A Link in the Chain of Cultural Continuity, 1991, Information Technology Use in Libraries (Arabic), 1998, Internet Use in Libraries, 2000, The Gulf War in World Literature, 2002; editor: Digest of Middle East Studies. Chmn. Black Faculty Coun., U. Wis., Milw.; mktg. com. Milw. Art Mus.; bd. dirs. Clara Mohammed Sch. Recipient Outstanding Achievement award Egyptian Libr. Assn., 1997. Mem. NAACP, ALA (chmn. internat. rels. com. 1984-86, John Ames Humphry/Forest Press Outstanding Contbn. award 1989, standing com. on libr. edn., internat. subcom. 1990-91, chmn. 1991-93, internat. rels. Round Table 1993-94, leadership award black caucus 1994, excelence award black caucus 1995), Assn. Libr. and Sci. (Svc. award 1988), Am. Soc. for Info. Sci. (chmn. spl. interest group in internat. info. issues, internat. rels. com.), Egyptian Libr. Assn. (life, Outstanding Achievement award 1997), Arab/Jewish Dialogue, Egyptian-Am. Scholars Assn., Assn. for Libr. and Info. Sci. Edn. (chmn. internat. rels. com. 1983-85), Wis. Libr. Assn. (Svc. award 1992, P.N. Kaula Internat. award and medal 1996, Wis. Libr. of Yr. 1998), Libr. Svcs. and Constrn. Act. (adv. com. 1986-89), Internat. Archtl. Jury for Bibliotheca Alexandrina, Internat. Fedn. Libr. Assns. and Insts. (sec. on edn. and tng. 1983-92), Coun. on Egyptian Am. Rels., The Gamaliel Chair (bd. dirs. 1995-97), Leaders

Forum (bd. dirs. 1995—), America's Black Holocaust Mus. (bd. dirs. 1999—), Islamic Social Family Svcs. (bd. dirs. 1999—), Milw. Tchr.'s Edn. Ctr. (bd. dirs.). Democrat. Moslem. Office: U Wis-Milw Sch Libr & Info Sci PO Box 413 Milwaukee WI 53201-0413 E-mail: aman@uwn.edu.

AMANN, CHARLES ALBERT, mechanical engineer, researcher; b. Thief River Falls, Minn., Apr. 21, 1926; s. Charles Alois and Bertha Ann (Oetting) Amann; m. Marilynn Ann Reis, Aug. 26, 1950; children: Richard, Barbara, Nancy, Julie. BS, U. Minn., 1946, MSME, 1948. Instr. U. Minn., Mpls., 1946-49; rsch. engr. GM Rsch. Labs., Detroit, 1949-54, supervisory rsch. engr. Warren, 1954-71, asst. dept. head, 1971-73, dept. head, 1973-89, rsch. fellow, 1989-91; prin. engr. KAB Engring., 1991—. Spl. instr. Wayne State U., Detroit, 1952—55; guest lectr. Mich. State U., 1980—; outside prof. U. Ariz., 1983; mem. adv. com. Gas Rsch. Inst., 1992—98, Oak Ridge Nat. Lab., 1996—98; invited lectr. Inst. Advanced Engring., Seoul, Republic of Korea, 1994. Author (with others): (book) Automotive Engine Alternatives, 1986, Advanced Diesel Engineering and Operations, 1988; co-editor: Combustion Modeling in Reciprocating Engines, 1980. Lt. (j.g.) USNR, 1944—46. Recipient James Clayton prize, Inst. Mech. Engrs., 1975, Oustanding Achievement award, U. Minn., 1991. Fellow: Soc. Automotive Engrs. (Arch T. Colwell merit award 1972, 1984, Disting. Spkr. award 1981, 1991, Forest R. McFarland award 2001); mem.: ASME (Richard S. Woodbury award 1989, Soichiro Honda lectr. 1992, Spkr. award Internal Combustion Engine Divsn. 1997, Internal Combusion Engine award 2000), NAE, Tau Beta Pi, Tau Omega, Sigma Xi. Presbyterian. Achievements include patents in field.

AMATO, ISABELLA ANTONIA, real estate executive; b. Noto, Italy, July 17, 1942; d. Raimondo and Giuseppa (Pinna) Sesta; m. Vincent Amato; children: Alice, Claudine. Acctg. diploma, Inst. Tech. and Commerce, 1962. Cert. Comml. Investment Mgr., Comml. Investment Inst., Specialist Real Estate Securities, Real Estate Securities and Syndication Inst. V.p., dir. Thomas F. Seay & Assocs., Chgo., 1977-81; treas. Seay & Thomas Inc., 1979-81; CFO Group One Investments, 1981—; exec. v.p., registered prin. First Group Securities, Ltd., 1983-95, pres., 1995—. Vol. translator Altrusa Lang. Bank, Chgo., 1980-86; v.p. Jr. Woman Club, Elk Grove Village, Ill., 1977; chairperson Atty. Exec. Forum, Chgo., 1985. Mem. Nat. Assn. Securities Dealers (prin.), Nat. Assn. Realtors, Chgo. Real Estate Bd., Real Estate Fin. Forum, Altrusa Profl. Woman (treas. Chgo. club 1984-85), YWCA Circle of Friends. Office: Group One Investments 77 W Washington St Ste 1005 Chicago IL 60602-2805

AMBERG, THOMAS L. public relations executive; b. Glen Cove, N.Y., Apr. 13, 1948; s. Richard Hiller Amberg and Janet Law Volkman; m. Tauna Urban, June 19, 1971 (div. Jan. 1980); children: Edward, Robert; m. Kathy Stewart, Oct. 9, 1982; 1 child, Thomas Jr. BA, Colgate U., 1971; MBA, U. Mo., St. Louis, 1980. Reporter, editor St. Louis Globe-Democrat, 1971-83; pres., coo Aaron D. Cushman and Assocs., Chgo., 1991—; pres. Cushman Amberg Comms. Mem. adv. bd. Salvation Army, St. Louis, 1986-91, Chgo., 1992—; bd. dirs. Wishing Well Found., St. Louis, 1985-91, Hope Ctr., St. Louis, 1985-91; bd. trustees St. Patrick's Sch., Chgo., 1994—. Recipient Disting. Achievement award Inland Daily Press Assn., 1978, 82, Frank Kelly Meml. award, 1980, Gavel award ABA, 1983, Unity awards in Media Lincoln U., 1984. Mem. Mental Health Assn. St. Louis (pres. 1987-88), Pub. Relations Soc. Am., Press. Club Met. St. Louis (pres. 1981-83), Internat. Assn. Bus. Communicators, Soc. Am. Writers. Presbyterian. Home: 1783 Bowling Green Dr Lake Forest IL 60045-3559 Office: Cushman Amberg Comms 180 N Michigan Ave Ste 1600 Chicago IL 60601-7478

AMDAHL, BYRDELLE JOHN, business consulting executive; b. Ossian, Iowa, June 5, 1934; s. John G. and Mae (Vikse) A.; m. Agnes Nestegard, June 17, 1955 (div. May 1981); children: Gary, Mark; m. Gwen Nelson Clark, June 11, 1983. Student, Luther Coll., Decorah, Iowa, 1952-54; BBA, U. Minn., 1958, postgrad., 1971. CPA, Minn. Auditor Dept. Agr., Mpls., 1958, Ernst & Ernst, 1958-64; exec. Cornelius Co., Mpls., 1964-74, v.p. fin., 1969-72, v.p. finance and adminstrn., 1972-73, exec. v.p., 1973-74, dir., 1971-74; exec. v.p. fin. and adminstrn., chief fin. officer Medtronic Inc., 1974-77, exec. v.p. diversified ops., 1977-81; chmn., chief exec. officer, dir. Bionexus, Inc., 1981-87; v.p. Glaxo Latin Am. Inc., 1987-90, exec. v.p., regional dir., 1988-90; pres., chief oper. officer Orthomet, Inc., Mpls., 1990-92; pres., CEO AAMDAC Inc., 1992-95; pres., prin. Global Bus. Ptnrs., Inc., 1995—; pres., CEO InterAct Security Corp., St. Paul, 1995-98; CEO S.F. Found., 2000—. Bd. dirs. Luth. Youth Encounter, 1968-75, Luth. Youth Encounter Found., 1990-96, Coun. for Entreprenurial Devel. of N.C. Served with AUS, 1954-56. Mem. Decathlon Club, Alpha Kappa Psi. E-mail: bert@globalgrace.net., bert@SF.org.

AMDURSKY, SAUL JACK, library director; b. Rochester, N.Y., Aug. 11, 1945; s. Harry S. and Eva (Forman) A.; m. Marion Susan Arndt, May 30, 1969; 1 child, Jacob Arthur. BA, St. John Fisher Coll., 1969; MSLS, U. Ky., 1971. Asst. mgr. Lincoln First Banks, Rochester, 1966-70; supervising libr. Prince William County Pub. Libr., Manassas, Va., 1971-75; dir. Albion (Mich.) Pub. Libr., 1975-79; adminstr. Racine (Wis.) County Libr. Sys., 1979-82; libr. dir. Bloomington (Ill.) Pub. Libr., 1982-87, Kalamazoo (Mich.) Pub. Libr., 1987—. Interim part-time adminstr. Woodlands Libr. Coop., Albion, 1978-79; instr. Ill. State U., Normal, 1984. Contbr. articles to Libr. Jour., Ill. Librs., Va. Libr., book revs. to Libr. Jour., Sch. Libr. Jour., Am. Reference Books Ann. Mem. ALA, Mich. Libr. Assn. (pub. policy com.), Ill. Libr. Assn. (legis. com.), Pi Gamma Mu (lifetime). Office: Kalamazoo Pub Libr 315 S Rose St Kalamazoo MI 49007-5201

AMELIO, WILLIAM J. computer hardware products; BSChemE, Lehigh U.; MS in Mgmt., Stanford U. With IBM; pres., CEO transp. and power systems divsn. Honeywell; COO retail and fin. group NCR. Patentee in field. Office: NCR Corp 1700 S Pableson Blvd Dayton OH 45479

AMES, DONALD PAUL, retired aerospace company executive, researcher; b. Brandon, Manitoba, Can., Sept. 13, 1922; came to U.S., 1932; s. Paul and Della Johanna (Hebel) A.; m. Doris Elizabeth Ubbelohde, Dec. 30, 1949; children: Elizabeth Carol Ames Herbert, Barbara Louise Ames Jones. BS in Chemistry, U. Wis., 1944, PhD in Phys. Chemistry, 1949; LLD (hon.), U. Mo., St. Louis, 1978. AEC postdoctoral fellow, 1949-50; staff chemist Los Alamos Sci. Lab., 1950-52; asst. prof. physical chemistry U. Ky., Lexington, 1952-54; staff chemist DuPont Co., Aiken, S.C., 1954-56; sr. rsch. chemist, scientist/fellow Monsanto, St. Louis, 1956-61; from scientist to sr. scientist rsch. div. McDonnell Aircraft Co., 1961-68; from dep. dir. rsch. to dir. rsch. McDonnell Douglas Rsch. Labs., 1968-71, dir., 1971-76, staff v.p., 1976-86, staff v.p., gen. mgr., disting. fellow, 1986-89, cons., 1989—; pres. Fluotech Inc., 1991—. Adj. prof. physics U. Mo., St. Louis, 1989—, Washington U., St. Louis, 1989-99; mem. vis. com. dept. mech. engring. Lehigh U., 1984-90; mem. adv. bd. Coll. Engring., U. Ill., Urbana, 1986-89; mem. spl. com. U. Chgo. 7 GeV Synchrotron Light Source, 1984-89; adv. com. U. Mo. Rsch. Reactor, Columbia, 1985-92; mem. indsl. adv. coun. dept. chemistry U. Mo., St. Louis, 1985-95; mem. subcom. on materials sci. and engring. needs and opportunities in aerospace industry NAS, 1985-86; bd. dirs. St. Louis Tech. Ctr., 1983-95; participant Manhattan Project U.S. Army, 1944-46. Contbr. articles to profl. jours.; patentee in field. With U.S. Army, 1944-46. Recipient Civic award St. Louis sect. AIAA, 1985; Wis. Alumni Rsch. fellow, 1946-48, AEC fellow, 1948-49, Monsanto fellow, 1959-61, McDonnell Douglas Disting. fellow, 1986-89. Mem. Am. Phys. Soc., Am. Chem. Soc., Soc. Engring Sci., Combustion Inst., Mo. Acad. Sci., Phi Beta Kappa, Sigma Xi, Phi Eta Sigma, Phi Kappa Phi, Phi Lambda Upsilon, Gamma Alpha, Alpha Chi Sigma. E-mail: dpa922@cs.com.

AMIDON, PAUL CHARLES, publishing executive; b. St. Paul, July 23, 1932; s. Paul Samuel and Eleanor Ruth (Simons) A.; m. Patricia Jean Winjum, May 7, 1960; children: Karen, Michael, Susan. BA, U. Minn., 1954. Bus. mgr. Paul S. Amidon & Assocs., Inc., St. Paul, 1956-66, pres., 1966—. Served with AUS, 1954-56. Home: 1582 Hillcrest Ave Saint Paul MN 55116-2147 Office: 1966 Benson Ave Saint Paul MN 55116-3214 E-mail: paul@amidongraphics.com.

AMIRIKIA, HASSAN, obstetrician, gynecologist; b. Tehran, Iran, Dec. 10, 1937; came to U.S., 1966; d. Ahmad and Showkat (Asgari) Cheftsaz; m. Mino Vassigh Amirikia, Apr. 4, 1964; children: Arezo, Omid. MD, Tehran U., 1964. Cert. Am. Bd. Ob-Gyn. Intern Cook County Hosp., Chgo., 1966-67; resident Wayne State U., Detroit, 1967-71, fellow, 1971-72; practice reproductive endocrine specializing in infertility, 1972—; asst. prof. Wayne State U., 1972—, dir. ob-gyn. tng. dept. family medicine, 1979—; dir. infertility and reproductive endocrinology St. Joseph's Hosp., Pontiac, 1990-93; chief staff Detroit Med. Ctr., 1993—, pres. med. staff, 1997—; chief staff Hutzel Hosp., 1996—. Researcher effects of androgens on the ovary; pres. med. staff Detroit Med. Ctr., 1998—; del. to AMA, 1996.. Contbr. articles to profl. jours. Fellow ACS, Am. Coll. Ob-Gyn (Mich. sect.), Royal Coll. Physicians and Surgeons, Wayne County Med. Soc. (pres. 1995-96), Mich. State Med. Soc. (bd. dirs. 1996—); mem. Mich. State Med. Soc. (bd. dirs. 1996—). Home: 1435 Lone Pine Rd Bloomfield Hills MI 48302-2632 Office: 4727 Saint Antoine St Detroit MI 48201-1461 also: 29877 Telegraph Rd Southfield MI 48034-1332 E-mail: hamirikia@.com.

AMLADI, PRASAD GANESH, management consulting executive, health care consultant, researcher; b. Mudhol, India, Sept. 12, 1941; came to U.S., 1967, naturalized, 1968; s. Ganesh L. and Sundari G. Amladi; m. Chitra G. Panje, Dec. 2, 1970; children: Amita, Amol. B in Engring. with honors, Indian Inst. Tech., Bombay, 1963; MS in Indsl. Engring., Ops. Rsch., Stanford U., 1968; MBA with high distinction, U. Mich., 1975. Sr. rsch. engr. Ford Motor Co., Dearborn, Mich., 1968-75; mgr. strategic planning Mich. Consol. Gas Co., Detroit, 1975-78; mgr. planning svcs. The Resources Group, Bloomfield Hills, Mich., 1978-80; project mgr., sr. cons. Mediflex Systems Corp., 1980-85; mgr. strategic planning svcs. Mersco Corp., 1985-86; mgr. corp. planning and rsch. Diversified Techs., Inc., New Hudson, Mich., 1986-87; mgr. planning and rsch. Blue Cross & Blue Shield of Mich., Detroit, 1987—. Contbr. papers to profl. publs. Recipient Kodama Meml. Gold medal, 1957; India Merit scholar Govt. of India, 1959-63, K.C. Mahindra scholar, 1967, R.D. Sethna Grad. scholar, 1968. Mem. Inst. Indsl. Engrs. (sr.), N.Am. Soc. Corp. Planning, Econ. Club Detroit, Beta Gamma Sigma. Office: Blue Cross Blue Shield Mich 27000 W Eleven Mile Rd B528 Southfield MI 48034-2200

AMMAR, RAYMOND GEORGE, physicist, educator; b. Kingston, Jamaica, July 15, 1932; came to U.S., 1961, naturalized, 1965; s. Elias George and Nellie (Khaleel) A.; m. Carroll Ikerd, June 17, 1961; children: Elizabeth, Robert (dec.), David. AB, Harvard U., 1953; PhD, U. Chgo., 1959. Research assoc. Enrico Fermi Inst., U. Chgo., 1959-60; asst. prof. physics Northwestern U., Evanston, Ill., 1960-64, assoc. prof., 1964-69; prof. physics U. Kans., Lawrence, 1969—, chmn. dept. physics and astronomy, 1989—; (on sabbatical leave Fermilab and Deutsches Elektronen Synchrotron, 1984-85). Cons. Argonne (Ill.) Nat. Lab., 1965-69, vis. scientist, 1971-72; vis. scientist Fermilab, Batavia, Ill., summers 1976-81, Deutsches Elektronen Synchroton, Hamburg, Germany, summers 1982-88, lab. of nuclear studies Cornell U., summers 1989-98; project dir. NSF grant for rsch. in high energy physics, 1962-2001. Contbr. articles to sci. jours. Fellow Am. Phys. Soc.; mem. AAUP. Home: 1651 Hillcrest Rd Lawrence KS 66044-4525 Office: U Kans Dept Physics And Astronomy Lawrence KS 66045-0001 E-mail: ammar@ku.edu.

AMMER, WILLIAM, retired judge; b. Circleville, Ohio, May 21, 1919; s. Moses S. and Mary (Schallas) A. BS in Bus. Adminstrn., Ohio State U., 1941, JD, 1946. Bar: Ohio 1947. Atty., examiner Ohio Indsl. Commn., Columbus, 1947-51; assty. atty. gen. State of Ohio, 1951-52; pvt. practice Circleville, 1953-57; pros. atty. Picaway County, 1953-57, common pleas judge, 1957-95; ret., 1995. Judge by assignment Supreme Ct. Ohio, 1995—; asst. city solicitor Circleville, 1955-57. Past. pres. Pickaway County ARC, Am. Cancer Soc. Served with inf., AUS, 1942-46. Mem. ABA, Ohio Bar Assn. (chmn. criminal law com. 1964-67), Pickaway County Bar Assn. (pres. 1955-56), Ohio Common Pleas Judges Assn. (pres. 1968), Masons, K.T., Shriners, Kiwanis (Ohio dist. chmn., past lt. gov.). Methodist. Home: PO Box 87 Circleville OH 43113-0087 Office: 113 1/2 South Court St PO Box 87 Circleville OH 43113-0087

AMMON, HARRY, history educator; b. Waterbury, Conn., Sept. 4, 1917; s. Grover and Lena Mary (Pyne) Amman. B.S., Georgetown U., 1939, M.A., 1940; Ph.D., U. Va., 1948. Editor Md. Hist. Mag., Balt., 1948-50; asst. prof. So. Ill. U., Carbondale, 1950-57, assoc. prof., 1957-66, prof. history, 1967—, prof. emeritus, 1984—, chmn. dept., 1977-1983. Fulbright lectr. U. Vienna, Austria, 1954-55, Seoul Nat. U., Korea, 1984-85; vis. prof. U. Va., Charlottesville, 1968-69; guest lectr. Northeast Normal and Liaoning Univs., People's Republic of China, 1986, 88. Author: James Monroe: The Quest for National Identity, 1971, new edit. 1990, The Genet Mission, 1973, James Monroe A Bibliography, 1991. Mem.: Phi Beta Kappa. Home: 401 S Orchard Dr Carbondale IL 62901-2340 Office: So Ill U History Dept Carbondale IL 62901 E-mail: harryam@siu.edu.

AMONTE, ANTHONY LEWIS, professional hockey player; b. Weymouth, Mass., Aug. 2, 1970; Student, Boston U. Profl. hockey player N.Y. Rangers, 1988-94, Chgo. Blackhawks, 1994—. Named to Hockey East All-Rookie Team, 1989-90, NCAA All-Tournament Team, 1990-91, Hockey East All-Star 2d Team, 1990-91, NHL All-Star Rookie Team, 1991-92, NHL Rookie of the Yr., 1991-92. Office: Chgo Blackhawks 1901 W Madison St Chicago IL 60612-2459

AMSDEN, TED THOMAS, lawyer; b. Cleve., Dec. 11, 1950; s. Richard Thomas and Mary Agnes (Hendricks) A.; m. Ruth Anna Rydstedt, May 1, 1982; children: Jennifer Rydstedt, Matthew Lars, Alexis Linnea. BA, Wayne State U., 1972; JD, Harvard U., 1975. Bar: Mich. 1975, U.S. Dist. Ct. (ea. dist.) Mich. 1975, U.S. Ct. Appeals (6th cir.) 1975, U.S. Supreme Ct. 1979. From assoc. to ptnr. Dykema Gossett PLLC and predecessor firm, Detroit, 1975—. Chmn. Baha'i Justice Soc., 1986-88, corr. sec., 1988-92, bd. dirs., 1986-93, 95—; bd. dirs. Internat. Inst., Detroit, 1989-97, 99—, v.p. legal affairs, 1991-94, v.p., 1994-95, pres.-elect 1995-96, pres., 1996-97, co-chair Ethnic Summit '96; bd. dirs. Racial Justice Ctr., Grosse Pointe, Mich., 1992-94, Greater Detroit Interfaith Roundtable, 1994—, bd. dirs. Model of Racial Unity, Inc., 1995-97, treas., 1997—, chmn., 1998—, vice chmn.; mem. Mich. Bar Rep. Assembly, 1988-94. Recipient Detroit Principles award of Race Relations Coun. of Metropolitan Detroit, 1993, Spirit of Detroit award City of Detroit Common Coun., 1996, 97. Mem. ABA, Mich. Bar Assn., Wolverine Bar Assn., Detroit Bar Assn., Detroit Bar Assn. Found. (bd. dirs. 1992-98, sec., 1993-95, pres. 1995-97), Macomb County Bar Assn., Assn. Def. Counsel, Civic Searchlight (Macomb County steering com., jud. com. 1990-91, Wayne County jud. com. 1992-95). Home: 987 Lake Shore Rd Grosse Pointe Shores MI 48236-1171 Office: Dykema Gossett 400 Renaissance Ctr Ste 3800 Detroit MI 48243-1603

AMSLER, JANA, chef; Grad., CHIC; student, Las Belles Artes, Elmhurst, Ill. Pastry, soup and salad chef Salbute, Hinsdale, Ill., 1997—. Office: Salbute 20 E 1st St Hinsdale IL 60521

AMSTADTER, LAURENCE, retired architect; b. Chgo., Apr. 9, 1922; s. Frank J. and Irene B. (Black) A.; m. Erma Jacqueline Kallen, Mar. 8, 1948; children: John Kallen, Marc Robert. BA in Architecture, Chgo. Tech. Coll., 1948; postgrad., Northwestern U., Evanston, Ill., 1948-49. Registered architect, Ill., 20 other states. Architect Ford Bacon & Davis Inc., Chgo., 1949-50, Skidmore Owings & Merrill, Chgo., 1950-51, Sidney Morris & Assocs., Chgo., 1951-52, Chgo. Housing Authority, 1952-53; sr. v.p. A. Epstein and Sons Inc., Chgo., 1953-87; cons., 1987—. Mem. Exec. Svc. Corps of Chgo. With Air Corps, U.S. Army, 1941-45, ETO. Mem. AIA (corp.), Svc. Corps Ret. Execs., Soc. Am. Registered Architects, Chgo. Com. on High Rise Bldgs. Democrat. Home: 1633 Cambridge Ave Flossmoor IL 60422-2127 Office: Amstadter Architects 200 W Superior St Chicago IL 60610-3553 E-mail: lekamstadter@aol.com.

AMSTUTZ, HAROLD EMERSON, veterinarian, educator; b. Barrs Mill, Ohio, June 21, 1919; s. Nelson David and Viola Emma (Schnitzer) A.; m. Mabelle Josephine Bower, June 26, 1949; children: Suzanne Marie, Cynthia Lou, Patricia Lynn, David Bruce. BS in Agr, Ohio State U., 1942, DVM, 1945. Diplomate Am. Coll. Vet. Internal Medicine (pres. 1972-73, chmn. bd. regents 1973-74); hon. diplomate Am. Coll. Theriogenology. Pvt. practice vet. medicine, Orrville, Ohio, 1946-47; instr. vet. medicine Ohio State U., 1947-52, asst. prof., 1952-54, asso. prof., 1954-56, prof., 1957-61, prof., head dept. vet. medicine, 1956-61; head dept. vet. clinics Purdue U., West Lafayette, Ind., 1961-75, prof. large animal clinics, 1975-89, prof. emeritus, 1989—. Editor: Bovine Medicine and Surgery Book, 1979; contbg. editor: Modern Veterinary Practice, 1979-84; mem. editorial bd. The Merck Vet. Manual, 6th, 7th and 8th edits.; contbr. to books on diseases of large domestic animals. Mem. exec. bd. Ind.-Ky. synod Luth. Ch. Am., 1986-88; pres. World Assn. for Buiatrics, 1972-84. Served with U.S. Army, 1945-46. Recipient Borden award for outstanding research in diseases of dairy cattle, 1978; named Disting. Alumnus Ohio State U. Coll. Vet. Medicine, 1974; recipient Alumni Faculty award Sch. Vet. Medicine, Purdue U., 1989, Sagamore of the Wabash Ind. Gov., 1990, Ark. Traveler award Ark. Gov., 1969, Gustav Rosenberger Meml. award Dutch Veterinary Assn., 1992, Alumni Recognition award Vet. Medicine Alumni Soc. Ohio State U., 1998. Mem. AVMA (12th Internat. Congress prize for contributing to internat. understanding of vet. medicine 1995), Am. Assn. Vet. Clinicians (pres. 1972), Am. Assn. Bovine Practitioners (exec. sec. 1971-89, exec. v.p. 1989-93, hon. mem. 1993), World Assn. Buiatrics (pres. 1972-84), Am. Coll. of Theriogenologists (hon. diplomate 1993), Sigma Xi, Phi Zeta, Gamma Sigma Delta (award of merit), Omega Tau Sigma (nat. Gamma award). Republican. Office: Purdue Univ Dept Veterinary Sci West Lafayette IN 47907 E-mail: amstutzh@purdue.edu.

AMSTUTZ, RONALD, state legislator; b. Wooster, Ohio, June 2, 1961; m. Joanne Amstutz; children: Julianne, Jefferson. BA, Capitol U.; postgrad., Kent State U.; BA, Malone Coll.; postgrad., Goshen Coll. Mem. Ohio Ho. of Reps., Columbus, 1981-2000; vice chmn. policy com.; mem. Ohio Senate from 22nd dist, Columbus, 2001—. Chair tech. and elections com., fin. and appropriations com., primary and secondary edn. subcom., ethics and stds. com., ways and means com. Ohio Ho. of Reps. Mem. Orrville (Ohio) City Charter Commn., 1974-75; mayor City of Orrville, 1976-80; mem. Wayne County Rep. Exec. Com., past pres. and chmn.; bd. dirs. United Conservatives Ohio. Mem. Farm Bur., Am. Legis. Exch. Coun., Nat. Tax Payers Union Ohio, Orrville Jaycees (past pres. and chmn.), Rotary. Office: 4456 Wood Lake Trl Wooster OH 44691-8582

AMUNDSON, JOY A. pharmaceutical and health products executive; V.p. corp. hosp. mktg. Abbott Labs., Abbott Park, Ill., 1993-94, v.p. Abbott HealthSys., 1994-95, sr. v.p. chem. and agrl. products, 1995-98, sr. v.p. Ross Products, 1998—; corp. officer, 1990. Office: Abbott Labs 100 Abbott Park Rd Abbott Park IL 60064-6400

AMUNDSON, ROBERT A. state supreme court justice; m. Katherine Amundson; children: Robert, Beth, Amy. BBA, Augustana Coll., 1961; JD, U. S.D., 1964. Asst. atty. gen. Atty. Gen's. Office, 1965-69; mem. firm Belle Fourche and Lead, 1970-89; cir. judge 2d Jud. Cir., 1989-91; justice Supreme Ct. of S.D., Vermillion, 1991—. Office: Supreme Court of South Dakota State Capitol Bldg 500 E Capitol Ave Pierre SD 57501-5070*

AMY, JONATHAN WEEKES, scientist, educator; b. Delaware, Ohio, Mar. 3, 1923; s. Ernest Francis and Theresa Louise (Say) A.; m. Ruthanna Borden, Dec. 20, 1947 (dec. Apr. 1999); m. Betty Joy Flood, July 2, 2000; children— Joseph Wilbur, James Borden, Theresa B.A., Ohio Wesleyan U., 1948; M.S., Purdue U., 1950, Ph.D., 1955. Rsch. assoc. dept. chemistry Purdue U., West Lafayette, Ind., 1954-60, assoc. prof., 1960-70, prof., 1970—, assoc. dir. labs., 1960—, dir. instrumentation, 1970-84, emeritus, 1988. Cons. chem. instrumentation; sec.-treas. Technometrics, Inc., 1968-2001; mem. adv. panels AAAS, Assn. Am. Univs., NSF, Am. Chem. Soc.; vis. scholar Stanford U., 1992. Assoc. editor Ind. Chem. News; patentee elec. measuring equipment and chem. instrumentation Pres. Wabash Twp. Vol. Fire Dept., 1970-86. Served with U.S. Maritime Service, 1943-46. Recipient George award Lafayette Jour. and Courier, 1978, Sagamore of the Wabash award State of Ind., 1999. Mem. AAAS, Am. Chem. Soc. (Chem. Instrumentation award), Sigma Xi, Sigma Chi. Episcopalian. Home: 357 Overlook Dr West Lafayette IN 47906-1249 Office: Purdue U Dept Chemistry West Lafayette IN 47907

ANAPLE, ELSIE MAE, medical, surgical and geriatrics nurse; b. Urbana, Ohio, Apr. 22, 1932; d. Marion N. and Mae Irene (Newell) Bodey; div.; children: Glenn, Gretchen, Gloria, Giselle, Gregory, Gordon, Gary. BSN, Ohio State U., 1955. Cert. med.-surg. nurse. Night supr. Shriner's Burn Inst., Cin., 1971-73; clin. instr. med.-surg. Deaconess Hosp. Sch. Nursing, 1973-75; staff nurse Good Samaritan Hosp., 1960-92; clin. nurse, staff nurse Univ. Hosp.-U. Cin., 1984-95, asst. head nurse med. unit, 1992; ret., 1995. Part-time nurse Mercy Hosp., Fairfield, Ohio, 1980-2000, Drake Rehab. Ctr., Cin., 1995-97; part-time home nursing, 1996—; clin. instr. Scarlet Oans Sch. of Lic. Practical Nurses, Hamilton County, Cin., 2000. Active Cin. chpt. ARC, Our Lady of Rosary Ch. Mem. ANA, Ohio Nurses Assn., S.W. Ohio Dist. Nurses Assn., Ohio State U. Alumni Assn.

ANDERHALTER, OLIVER FRANK, educational organization executive; b. Trenton, Ill., Feb. 14, 1922; s. Oliver Valentine and Catherine (Vollet) A.; m. Elizabeth Fritz, Apr. 30, 1945; children: Sharon, Stephen, Dennis. B.Ed., Eastern Ill. State Tchrs. Coll., 1943, Ped.D. (hon.), 1956; A.M., St. Louis U., 1947, Ph.D., 1949. Mem. faculty St. Louis U., 1947—, prof. edn., 1957—; dir. Bur. Instl. Research, 1949-65, 1949-65, Univ. Computer Center, 1961-69, chmn. research methodology dept., 1968-76; v.p. Scholastic Testing Service, Chgo., 1951-89; pres. Scholastic Testing Svc., Chgo. and St. Louis, 1989—. Chmn. finance com. Greater St. Louis Campfire Girls Orgn., 1958-59 Author, editor standardized tests. Served as pilot USNR, 1943-46. Mem. Am. Ednl. Research Assn., Nat. Council Measurement, Am. Statis. Assn., N.E.A. Home: 12756 Whispering Hills Ln Saint Louis MO 63146-4449 Office: Scholastic Testing Svc 4320 Green Ash Dr Earth City MO 63045-1208 E-mail: ststesting@email.com.

ANDERS, KIMBLE, football player; b. Galveston, Tex., Sept. 10, 1966; Football player Pittsburgh Steelers, 1990-91, Kans. City Chiefs, 1991—. Bd. dirs. Kans. City Boys and Girls Club; founder Helping Hands Found., 1995—. Achievements include 3 time Pro Bowl player. Office: Kans City Chiefs One Arrowhead Stadium Kansas City MO 64129

ANDERSEN, BURTON ROBERT, physician, educator; b. Chgo., Aug. 27, 1932; s. Burton R. and Alice C. (Mara) A.; m. Susan Berg; children: Ellen C., Julia A., Brian E., Jennifer Berg. Student, Northwestern U.,

1950-51; BS, U. Ill., Urbana, 1953; MS, U. Ill., Chgo., 1957; MD, U. Ill., 1957. Intern Mpls. Gen. Hosp., 1957-58; resident and fellow U. Ill. Hosp., 1958-61; clin. assoc. NIH, Bethesda, Md., 1961-64; asst. prof. U. Rochester, N.Y., 1964-67; assoc. prof. Northwestern U., 1967-70; prof. medicine and microbiology U. Ill., Chgo., 1970—, chief infectious diseases, 1986-99, West Side VA Med. Ctr., 1970-90. Contbr. sci. research articles to profl. jours. Served as sr. surgeon USPHS, 1961-63. Fellow ACP; mem. Am. Assn. Immunologists, Am. Soc. for Clin. Investigation, Central Soc. for Clin. Research. Office: U Ill Sect Infectious Diseases 808 S Wood St Chicago IL 60612-7300

ANDERSEN, HAROLD WAYNE, contributing editor, newspaper executive; b. Omaha, July 30, 1923; s. Andrew B. and Grace (Russell) A.; m. Marian Louise Battey, Apr. 19, 1952; children: David, Nancy. BS in Edn., U. Nebr., Lincoln, 1945; DHL (hon.), U. Nebr., Omaha, 1975; LHD (hon.), Dana Coll., 1983, Doane Coll., 1984; LLD (hon.), Creighton U., 1986; D of Internat. Communications, Bellevue Coll., 1986. Reporter Lincoln (Nebr.) Star, 1945-46; with Omaha World-Herald, 1946—, dir., 1964-95, pres., 1966-85, also bd. dirs., chmn. bd. dirs., pub., 1985-89, dir., 1964-95, Raleigh (N.C.) News & Observer, 1976-94, Newspaper Advt. Bur., 1974-90; chmn. World Press Freedom Com., 1980-96; past chmn. Fed. Res. Bank, Kansas City (Mo.), 1977-79. Bd. dirs. infoUSA Inc., 1993—; dir. Williams Cos., 1988-96. Past pres. United Arts/Omaha; past bd. govs. Ak-Sar-Ben; past chmn. U. Nebr. Found., past pres. Jr. Achievement Omaha; chmn. Nebr. Game and Pks. Found.; past sr. v.p. North Ctrl. Flyway, Ducks Unltd.; past bd. dirs. Bellevue Coll. Found.; past bd. dirs. Creighton U.; past trustee Nebr. Nature Conservancy. Recipient Disting. Journalist award U. Nebr. chpt. Kappa Tau Alpha, 1972, Americanism citation Henry Monsky lodge B'nai B'rith, 1972, Nebr. Builder award U. Nebr., Lincoln, 1976, Nat. Soc. Pks. Resources award, 1984, Comm. award Nat. Assn. Resource Dists., 1987, Casey award Inland Press Assn., 1989, Disting. Nebraskan award Nebr. Soc. Washington, 1989, Philanthropy Leadership award Heartland chpt. ARC, 1992, Humanitarian award NCCJ, 1993; named Omaha Health Citizen of Yr., 1986, Citizen of Yr., United Way of Midlands, 1987, Air Force Assn., 1990; named to Nebr. Newspaper Hall of Fame, 1988; inductee Omaha Bus. Hall of Fame, 1997. Mem. Newspaper Assn. Am. (past chmn., dir.), Internat. Fedn. Newspapers Pubs. (past pres.), Nebr. Press Assn. (Master Editor-Pub. award 1979), Coun. Fgn. Rels., Omaha C. of C. (bd. dirs., chmn. 1987-88), U. Nebr. Coll. Bus. Adminstrn. Alumni Assn. (hon. life), Phi Beta Kappa, Phi Gamma Delta. Republican. Presbyterian. Home: 6545 Prairie Ave Omaha NE 68132-2747 Office: infoUSA 5711 S 86th Cir Omaha NE 68127-4146

ANDERSEN, WAYNE R. federal judge; b. Chgo., July 30, 1945; m. Sheila M. O'Brien, Jan. 5, 1991. BA with honors, Harvard Coll., 1967; JD, U. Ill., 1970. Adminstrv. asst. Henry J. Hyde, majority leader Ill. House Reps., 1970-72; assoc. Burditt & Calkins, Chgo., 1972-76, ptnr., 1977-80; dep. sec. state Ill., 1981-84; judge Cir. Ct. Cook County, 1984-91; supr. judge traffic divsn. First Municipal Dist., 1989-91; dist. judge No. U.S. Courthouse, Ill., 1991—. Dir. Rehab. Inst. Chgo.; interviewer schs. com. Harvard Club Chgo. Contbr. articles to profl. jours. Pres., dir., precinct capt. Maine Township Regular Rep. Orgn.; alt. del. Rep. Nat. Conv., Sixth Congrl. Dist. Ill., 1984; Rep. candidate for treas. Cook County, 1974. Mem. Ill. Judges Assn., Chgo. Bar Assn., Fed. Judges Assn. Office: US Courthouse 1486 Dirksen Bldg 219 S Dearborn St Chicago IL 60604-1702

ANDERSLAND, ORLANDO BALDWIN, civil engineering educator; b. Albert Lea, Minn., Aug. 15, 1929; s. Ole Larsen and Brita Kristine (Okland) A.; m. Phyllis Elaine Burgess, Aug. 15, 1958; children: Mark, John, Ruth BCE, U. Minn., 1952; MSCE, Purdue U., 1956, PhD, 1960. Registered profl. engr., Minn., Mich. Staff engr. NAS, Am. Assn. State Hwy. Ofcls. Road Test, Ottawa, Ill., 1956-57; rsch. engr. Purdue U., West Lafayette, Ind., 1957-59; mem. faculty Mich. State U., East Lansing, 1960—, prof. civil engring., 1968—, prof. emeritus, 1994—. Co-author: Geotechnical Software for the IBM, PC, 1987, Geotechnical Engineering and Soil Testing, 1992, An Introduction to Frozen Ground Engineering, 1994, 2d edit., 2002; co-editor: Geotechnical Engineering for Cold Regions, 1978; contbr. chpt. Ground Engineer's Handbook, 1987; contbr. articles to profl. jours.; patentee in field. 1st lt. C.E., U.S. Army, 1952-55 Decorated Nat. Def. Svc. medal; UN Svc. medal; Korean Svc. medal; recipient Best Paper award Assn. Asphalt Paving Technologists, 1956; postdoctoral fellow Norwegian Geotech. Inst., 1966; grantee NSF, EPA, Dept. of Energy. Fellow ASCE (best paper award Cold Regions Engring. Jour. 1991); mem. ASTM (sr.), Internat. Soc. Soil Mechanics and Found. Engring., Am. Soc. Engring. Edn. (life), Sigma Xi, Chi Epsilon, Tau Beta Pi. Lutheran. Home: 901 Woodingham Dr East Lansing MI 48823-1855 Office: Mich State U Dept Civil/Environ Engring East Lansing MI 48824

ANDERSON, AUSTIN GOTHARD, lawyer, university administrator; b. Calumet, Minn., June 30, 1931; s. Hugo Gothard and Turna Marie (Johnson) A.; m. Catherine Antoinette Spellacy, Jan. 2. 1954; children: Todd, Susan, Timothy, Linda, Mark. BA, U. Minn., 1954, JD, 1958. Bar: Minn. 1958, Ill. 1962, Mich. 1974. Assoc. Spellacy, Spellacy, Lano & Anderson, Marble, Minn, 1958-62; dir. Ill. Inst. Continuing Legal Edn., Springfield, 1962-64; dir. dept. continuing legal edn. U. Minn., Mpls., 1964-70, assoc. dean gen. extension divsn., 1968-70; ptnr. Dorsey, Marquart, Windhorst, West & Halladay, 1970-73; assoc. dir. Nat. Ctr. State Cts., St. Paul, 1973-74; dir. Inst. Continuing Legal Edn. U. Mich., Ann Arbor, 1973-92; dir. Inst. on Law Firm Mgmt., 1992-95; prin. AndersonBoyer Group, Ann Arbor, 1995—; pres. Network of Leading Law Firms, 1995—. Adj. faculty U. Minn., 1974, Wayne State U., 1974-75; mem. adv. bd. Ctr. for Law Firm Mgmt. Nottingham Trent U., Eng.; draftsman ABA Guidelines for Approval of Legal Asst. Programs, 1973, Model Guidelines for Minimum Continuing Legal Edn., 1988; chair law practice mgmt. sect. State Bar Mich., 2000-2001; mem. Task Force on Court Filing, State Bar of Mich., 2000-2001; mem. com. on quality of life, 2000-2001; cons. in field. Co-editor, contbg. author: Lawyer's Handbook, 1975, co-editor 3d edit., 1992; author: A Plan for Lawyer Development, 1986, Marketing Your Practice: A Practical Guide to Client Development, 1986; cons. editor, contbg. author: Webster's Legal Secretaries Handbook, 1981; cons. editor Merriam Webster's Legal Secretarial Handbook, 2d edit., 1996; co-author: The Effective Associate Training Program-Improving Firm Performance, Profits and Prospective Partners, Associate Retention: Keeping Our Best and Brightest, 2002; contbr. chpt. to book and articles to profl. jours. Chmn. City of Bloomington Park and Recreation Adv. Commn., Minn., 1970-72; chmn. Ann Arbor Citizens Recreation Adv. Com., 1981-89, Ann Arbor Parks Adv. Com., 1983-92, chair, 1991-92; rep. Class of '58 U. Minn. Law Sch., 1996—. Recipient Excellence award CLE sect. Assn. of Am. Law Schs., 1992. Fellow Am. Bar Found. (Mich. chmn. 2002-), State Bar Mich. Found.; mem. ABA (vice chmn. continuing legal edn. com. sect. legal edn. and admission to bar 1988-93, standing com. continuing edn. of bar 1984-90, 2000-, chmn. law practice mgmt. sect. 1981-82, ALI-ABA com. on continuing profl. edn. 1993-96, ALI-ABA com. on continuing profl. edn. 1999—2002, spl. com. on rsch. on future of legal profession 1998-2000, sec. Coll. of Law Practice Mgmt. 1993-97, house of dels. 1993-99, commn. on lawyer advt. 1994-97, futures com.), Internat. Bar Assn., Mich. Bar Assn., State Bar of Mich. (chair law practice mgmt. sect., 2000-2001), Ill. Bar Assn., Minn. Bar Assn., Assn. Continuing Legal Edn. Adminstrs.(pres. 1969-70), Ann Arbor Golf and Outing Club. Home: 4660 Bayberry Cir Ann Arbor MI 48105-9762 Office: AndersonBoyer Group 3840 Packard St # 110 Ann Arbor MI 48108-2280 E-mail: aga@andersonboyer.com.

ANDERSON, BOB, state legislator, business executive; b. Wadena, Minn., Jan. 16, 1932; s. Alfred Emmanuel and Frances Agnes (Hassler) A.; m. Janet Lynn Hemquist, Aug. 3, 1967 BBA, U. Miami, 1959; student, U.S. Army War Coll., 1996. Owner small business, Minn., 1954-96; mem. Minn. Ho. of Reps., 1976-96; mem. steering com. House DFL Caucus, 1993-94. Mem. ways and means com., 1993-96, chair human svcs. fin. divsn., 1985-86, chair health and housing fin. divsn., 1993-94, chair health and human svcs. com., 1995-96; chair NCSL com. Agrl., 1985; vice chair, sec., mem. exec. com. Legis. Commn. on Waste Mgmt., 1980-96; dir. NCSL Found. for State Legislatures, 1987-93; legis. cons., 1997—; past pres. Viking-Land USA; bd. dirs. West Ctrl. Minn. Emergency Med. Svcs., Inc., 1999—, mem. exec. com., 2000--; mem. Minn. Emergency Med. Svcs. Regulatory Bd., 2001-2002. Past pres. Otter Tail Lake Property Owners Assn.; mem. Fergus Falls N.G. Citizens Com.; bd. dirs. Friends of History Mus. of East Otter Tail County, 2002--. With U.S. Army, 1952-54. Decorated D.S.M. Named Hon. Citizen, City of Winnipeg, Chief Author Glendalough State Pk., Fergus Falls Vets. Home, Prairie Wetlands Environ. Learning Ctr.; recipient Highroad Explorer award, Hon. Viking award, Svc. award Minn. Assn. Rehab. Facilities, West Cen. Emergency Med. Corp, Minn. Ambulance Assn., Nat. Fedn. Ind. Bus., Minn. Head Start Assn., Econ. Justice award MNCAP, Ctrs. For Ind. Living, Minn. Community Action award, Pub. Ofcl. Yr. award Minn. Nurses Assn., 1994, Food First Coalition award, 1995. Mem. NRA (life), Nat. Conf. State Legislatures (exec. com. 1986-88, commerce, labor and regulation com. 1991-94), Nat. Parks Conservations Assn., Nat. Wild Turkey Fedn., Minn. Meat Processors Assn. (past pres.), Rocky Mountain Elk Fedn., Pioneer Heritage Conservation Trust, Nature Conservancy, Friends of Prairie Wetlands Learing Ctr., Otter Tail County Hist. Soc. (life), Am. Legion, VFW (Ladies Aux. Vet. of Yr. award 1994), Minn. Outdoor Heritage Caucus, Fergus Falls Fish and Game Club, Millerville Sportsmen Club, Evansville Sportsmen Club, Ottertail Rod and Gun Club, Knob Hill Sportsmen, Sons of Norway, Elks, Masons, Shriners, Theta Chi, Alpha Kappa Psi. Democrat. Home: PO Box 28 Ottertail MN 56571-0028

ANDERSON, BRADBURY H. retail executive; Pres., COO Best Buy Co., Inc., Eden Prairie, Minn., 1993—. Office: 7075 Flying Cloud Dr Eden Prairie MN 55344-3532

ANDERSON, BRUCE JOHN, foundation administrator; b. Waterbury, Conn., Mar. 9, 1943; s. George E. and Mary M. (Taylor) A.; m. Ann Marie Heath, July 8, 1967; children: Christopher, Carrie, Mark. BS, Ctrl. Conn. State, 1965, MS, 1967; CAGS, Fairfield U., 1969; EdD, U. Va., 1971. Tchr. Southington (Conn.) Sch., 1965-68; instr. Ctrl. Conn. State U., New Britain, Conn., 1968-69; jr. instr. U. Va., Charlottesville, 1969-71; assoc. prof. Old Dominion U., Norfolk, Va., 1971-80, prof., chair dept., 1981-83; v.p. Danforth Found., St. Louis, 1983-91, pres., 1991—. Bd. dirs. St. Louis Regional Edn. Partnership; mem. adv. bd. Mo. Gov. Edn. Panel, Jefferson City, Mo. Co-editor: Democratic Leadership: Changing Context of Administrative Preparation, 1993. Bd. dirs. Met. Assn. Philanthropy, St. Louis, 1990—; mem. adv. bd. St. Louis Zoo, 1989—; mem. parish coun. St. Clares Roman Cath. Ch., St. Louis, 1991—. Office: Danforth Foundation 211 N Broadway # 2390 Saint Louis MO 63102-2733

ANDERSON, CAROLE ANN, nursing educator, academic administrator; b. Chgo., Feb. 21, 1938; d. Robert and Marian (Harrity) Irving; m. Clark Anderson, Feb. 14, 1973; 1 child, Julie. Diploma, St. Francis Hosp., 1958; BS, U. Colo., 1962, MS, 1963, PhD, 1977. Group psychotherapist Dept. Vocat. Rehab., Denver, 1963-72; psychotherapist Prof. Psychiatry and Guidance Clinic, 1970-71; asst. prof., chmn. nursing sch. U. Colo., 1971-75; therapist, coordinator The Genessee Mental Health, Rochester, N.Y., 1977-78; assoc. dean U. Rochester, 1978-86; dean, prof. Coll. Nursing Ohio State U., Columbus, 1986-2001, prof., 2001—, vice provost acad. adminstrn., 2001—. Lectr. nursing sch. U. Colo., Denver, 1970-71; prin. investigator biomed. rsch. support grant, 1986-93, clin. rsch. facilitation grant, 1981-82; program dir. profl. nurse traineeship, 1978-86, advanced nurse tng. grant, 1982-85. Author: (with others) Women as Victims, 1986, Violence Toward Women, 1982, Substance Abuse of Women, 1982; editor Nursing Outlook, 1993—. Pres., bd. dirs. Health Assn., Rochester, 1984-86; mem. north sub area council Finger Lakes Health Systems Agy., 1983-86, longrange planning com., 1981-82; mem. Columbus Bd. Health; dir. Netcare Mental Health Ctr. Am. Acad. Nursing fellow. Mem. ANA, Ohio Nurses Assn., Am. Assn. Colls. Nursing (bd. dirs. 1992-94, pres.-elect 1994-96, pres. 1996-98), Sigma Theta Tau. Home: 406 W 6th Ave Columbus OH 43201-3137 Office: The Ohio State U Office Acad Affairs 203 Bricker Hall 190 N Oval Mall Columbus OH 43210-1358 E-mail: anderson.32@osu.edu.

ANDERSON, CHRISTOPHER, astronomy educator; b. Las Cruces, N.Mex., Feb. 21, 1941; m. Dorothy Nemec, Mar. 7, 1970; twins. BS in Astronomy, U. Ariz., 1963; PhD in Astronomy, Calif. Inst. Tech., 1968. Asst. prof. astronomy dept. U. Wis., Madison, 1968-74, assoc. prof. astronomy dept., 1974-79, prof. astronomy dept., 1979—. Mem. facility definition team STARLAB, 1975-85; STARLAB rep. Instrument Control and Data Handling Working Group for Spacelab Facilities, 1976-78; co-investigator Wis. Ultraviolet Photo-Polarimeter Experiment, 1978—; mem. observers com. Kitt Peak Nat. Obs., 1977-78; prin. investigator for devel. Midwestern Astron. Data Reduction and Analysis Facility, NSF, 1978-80. Contbr. articles to profl. jours. Mem. Internat. Astron. Union, Am. Astron. Soc., Phi Beta Kappa. Office: U Wis Madison Dept Astronomy 475 N Charter St Madison WI 53706

ANDERSON, CHRISTOPHER JAMES, lawyer; b. Chgo., Nov. 26, 1950; s. James M. and Margaret E. (Anderson) A.; m. Lyn R. Buckley, Jan. 3, 1976; children: Vaughn Buckley, Weston Buckley. BA, Grinnell Coll., 1972; JD with highest distinction, U. Iowa, 1975. Bar: Mo. 1975. From assoc. to ptnr. Armstrong Teasdale LLP, Kansas City, Mo., 1975—. Mem. ABA, Mo. Bar Assn., Kans. City Bar Assn., Lawyers Assn. Kansas City, Estate Planning Soc. Office: Armstrong Teasdale Et Al 2345 Grand Blvd Ste 2000 Kansas City MO 64108-2617 E-mail: canderso@armstrongteasdale.com.

ANDERSON, DAVID GASKILL, JR. Spanish language educator; b. Tarboro, N.C., Feb. 21, 1945; s. David G. Sr. and Lucile (Gammon) A.; m. Jonetta Gentemann, Jan. 29, 1968; children: Allene Q., David III, James H., John G. AB, U. N.C., 1967; MA, Vanderbilt U., 1974, PhD, 1985. Instr. of langs. Union U., Tenn., 1975-76; from instr. Spanish to asst. prof. Ouachita Bapt. U., Ark., 1976-85; asst. prof. fgn. langs. N.E. La. U., 1985-87; asst. prof. Spanish, John Carroll U., Cleve., 1987-93, assoc. prof., 1993—, acting chmn. dept. classical and modern langs., 1996, chmn., 1997—, George Grauel faculty fellow rsch. sabbatical, spring 1997. Tchg. fellow Vanderbilt U., 1983-84, NEH summer seminar on poetry, 1990; presenter in field. Author: On Elevating the Commonplace: A Structuralist Analysis of The Odas of Pablo Neruda, 1987; contbr. articles to profl. jours. Vol. ESL Peace Corps, Colombia, 1968-70. Named Outstanding Young Men of Am., 1979. Mem. Am. Assn. U. Suprs. and Coords. Fgn. Lang. Programs, Am. Assn. Tchrs. Spanish and Portuguese, Modern Lang. Assn., Cleve. Diocesan Fgn. Lang. Assn. (bd. mem. 1988-93), Cleve. Assn., Phi Beta Kappa. Democrat. Home: 2573 Dysart Rd Cleveland OH 44118-4446 Office: John Carroll Univ Spanish Dept Cleveland OH 44118 E-mail: unc67@msn.com.

ANDERSON, DAVID R. insurance company executive; m. Mary Anderson; 5 children. B, M, U. Wis. Budget dir. Am. Family Mut. Ins. Co., Madison, Wis., 1975, fin. planning dir., acctg. dir., v.p. info. svcs., 1996-98, pres., COO, 1998—. Office: Am Family Ins Group 6000 American Pky Madison WI 53783

ANDERSON, DAVID TREVOR, law educator; b. Winnipeg, Man., Can., Oct. 25, 1938; s. David and Mary (Irwin) A. BA, U. Man., 1959; BA in Jurisprudence, U. Oxford (Eng.), 1961, B in Civil Law, 1962. Asst. prof. law U. Alta., Edmonton, Can., 1962-66, assoc. prof. Can., 1966-69, prof. Can., 1969-71; prof. law U. Man., Winnipeg, 1971—, assoc. dean faculty of law, 1972-77, dean, 1984-89. Bd. dirs. Alta. Inst. Law Rsch. and Reform, Edmonton, 1968-71; mem. Man. Law Reform Commn., Winnipeg, 1981-84, Man. Pub. Utilities Bd., 1988-2000. Named Queen's Counsel, Province of Man., 1985; Rhodes scholar, 1959. Mem. Law Soc. Man. (dir. edn. 1977-80, bencher 1984-89), Can. Bar Assn. Conservative. Presbyterian. Office: U Man Faculty of Law Robson Hall Winnipeg MB Canada R3T 2N2

ANDERSON, DAVIN CHARLES, business representative, labor consultant; b. Mpls., July 26, 1955; s. Roland Lawrence Anderson and Merlyne (Aldrich) Bissell; m. Diane Elmshauser, Aug. 14, 1982; children: Kiersten Janel, Matilda Rae. Student, St. Cloud State U., Minn., 1973-76; BS, U. Minn., 1979. Technician Northwest Cinema, Mpls., 1976-78, Mann Cinemas, Mpls., 1978-81, Gen. Cinema Corp., Mpls., 1981-99, Tacora Theatre, 1999—; account exec. Van Clemens & Co., Mpls., 1987—. Sec. Assn. Entertainment Industries Unions, St. Paul, 1987—. Mem. AFL-CIO (del.), Internat Alliance Theatrical and Stage Employees (bus. rep. Local 219 1986—), Nat. Assn. Investors Clubs, Trades and Labor Council (del.), Cen. Labor Union Council (del.), Toastmasters. Lutheran. Avocations: fishing, boating, skiing, hiking, flying. Home: 201 3d Ave S PO Box 626 Biwabik MN 55708-0626

ANDERSON, DONALD KENNEDY, JR. English educator; b. Evanston, Ill., Mar. 18, 1922; s. Donald Kennedy and Kathryn Marie (Shields) A.; m. Kathleen Elizabeth Hughes, Sept. 11, 1949; children: David J., Lawrence W. A.B., Yale U., 1943; M.A., Northwestern U., 1947; Ph.D., Duke U., 1957. Instr. Geneva Coll., Beaver Falls, Pa., 1947-49; from instr. to asst. prof. Rose Poly. Inst., Terre Haute, Ind., 1952-58; asst. prof., assoc. prof. Butler U., Indpls., 1958-65; assoc. prof. U. Mo., Columbia, 1965-67, prof. dept. English Columbia, 1967-92, prof. emeritus, 1992—, assoc. dean Grad. Sch. Columbia, 1970-74. Author: John Ford, 1972; editor: John Ford's Perkin Warbeck, 1965, John Ford's The Broken Heart, 1968, Concord in Discord, The Plays of John Ford, 1586-1986, 1987. Served to lt. (j.g.) USNR, 1943-46. Folger fellow, 1965; U. Mo. Summer Research fellow, 1966, 68, 76, 79, 84 Mem. MLA (midwest regional del. 1972-75), AAUP (sec.-treas. 1962-63) Democrat. Methodist. Home: 1309 Ridge Rd Columbia MO 65203-2323 Office: U Mo Dept English Columbia MO 65211-0001

ANDERSON, DYKE A. medical association administrator; Dir. Nat. Assn. Bds. Pharmacy, Park Ridge, Ill. Office: Nat Assn Bds Pharmacy 700 Busse Hwy Park Ridge IL 60068-2402

ANDERSON, EDGAR RATCLIFFE, JR. career officer, hospital administrator, physician; b. Baton Rouge, Mar. 13, 1940; m. Sandra Caston; children: Melisa, Edward, Mark. MD, La. State U., 1964; grad., Industrial Coll. Armed Forces, 1972, Air War Coll., 1982. Diplomate Am. Bd. Family Practice, Am. Bd. Dermatology, Am. Bd. Aerospace Medicine. Commd. 2d lt. USAF, 1965, advanced through grades to lt. gen., 1994, flight surgeon 464th Troop Carrier Wing N.C., 1965-68, chief aerospace medicine 33d Tactical Fighter Wing Eglin AFB, Fla., 1968-69, undergrad. pilot tng. Williams AFB, Ariz., 1969-71, completed F-4 combat crew tng. MacDill AFB, Fla., 1971, aircraft comdr. 336th Tactical Fighter Squadron Seymour Johnson AFB, N.C., 1971, asst. ops. officer Ubon Royal Thai AFB, chief aeromed. svcs. USAF Regional Hosp. MacDill AFB, 1973-75, comdr. USAF Hosp. Seymour Johnson AFB, 1975-77, staff dermatologist USAF Med. Ctr. Keesler AFB, Miss., 1980-81, chief flight test ops. USAF-RAF exchange program Royal Air Force Station, Farnborough, Eng., 1981-83, comdr. USAF Regional Hosp. Langley AFB, Va., 1983-84, dir. profl. svcs. Office of Command Surgeon Tactical Air Command, 1984, command surgeon HQ Pacific Air Forces Hickam AFB, Hawaii, 1984-86, command surgeon SAC Offutt AFB, Nebr., 1986-90, comdr. Wilford Hall USAF Med. Ctr. Lackland AFB, Tex., 1990, surgeon general Washington, ret., 1996; CEO Truman Health Sys., Kansas City, Mo., 1996-98. Dean, prof. Sch. Med. U. Mo., Kansas City, 1996-97; exec. v.p., CEO AMA, Chgo., 1998—. Decorated D.S.M. with oak leaf cluster, Legion of Merit with oak leaf cluster, D.F.C. with oak leaf cluster, Meritorious Svc. Medal with two oak leaf clusters, Air medal with nine oak leaf clusters, Air Force Commendation Medal. Office: AMA 515 N State St Fl 16 Chicago IL 60610-4325

ANDERSON, ELLEN RUTH, state legislator; b. Gary, Ind., Nov. 25, 1959; d. John Ernest Anderson and Marion Jane (Reeves) Martin; m. Andrew J. Dawkins. BA in History, Carleton Coll., 1982; JD, U. Minn., 1986. Bar: Minn., 1987, U.S. Dist. Ct. Minn. 1988. Jud. law clk. Minn. Ct. Appeals, St. Paul, 1987-88; atty. Hennepin County Pub. Defender, Mpls., 1988-91; staff atty. Minn. Edn. Assn., St. Paul, 1991-92; mem. Minn. Senate from 66th dist., 1993—. Democrat. Office: State of Minn G-24 Capitol 75 Constitution Ave Saint Paul MN 55155-1601

ANDERSON, ERIC ANTHONY, city manager; b. New Orleans, June 2, 1946; s. Eric Albert and Edna (Barrie) A.; m. Linda Jane Briefstein, June 22, 1967; children: Eric Scott, Stacy Alissa. BA, Syracuse U., 1967; MPA, SUNY, Albany, 1968; MA, Maxwell Sch., Syracuse U., 1970, Harvard U., 1994. Adminstrv. intern City of Phoenix, 1970-71; asst. dir. Rsch. and Devel. Ctr., Internat. City Mgmt. Assn., Washington, 1971-73; asst. town mgr. Town of Windsor (Conn.), 1973-78; town mgr. Munster (Ind.), 1978-83; city mgr. Eau Claire (Wis.), 1984-91, Evanston, Ill., 1991-95, Des Moines, 1995—. Bd. mgrs. Windsor-Bloomfield YMCA, 1976-78; adv. coun. Urban League N.W. Ind., 1979. NEH fellow, Princeton Univ., 1977. Fellow Nat. Acad. Pub. Adminstrn.; mem. Ind. Mcpl. Mgmt. Assn. (pres. 1979-80), Conn. City Mgmt. Assn. (treas. 1977-78), Internat. City Mgmt. Assn. (v.p. midwest 1987-89, trustee retirement corp. 1989-92), Nat. League of Cities (community and econ. devel. policy com. 1984-91), League of Wis. Municipalities (com. on fin. and taxation 1984-90, bd. dirs. 1991), N.W. Mcpl. Conf. (exec. bd. 1991-92); mapping sci. com., Nat. Resource Coun., 2000—; fed. graphic data com., U.S. Dept. Interior, 1998—; mem local leaders for GIS, 1998—; trustee Geodata Alliance, 2001—. Home: 3309 Wolcott Ave Des Moines IA 50321-1949 Office: Office of the City Manager City Hall 400 E 1st St Des Moines IA 50309-1809

ANDERSON, ERIC SCOTT, lawyer; b. Grand Forks, N.D., Aug. 26, 1949; s. Lyle William and Norma Sylvia (Lundeby) A.; children: Peter Scott, Nathan William. BSChE, U. Wis., 1971, JD, 1977. Bar: Wis. 1977, Minn. 1977, U.S. Dist. Ct. (we. dist.) Wis. 1977, U.S. Dist. Ct. Minn. 1978. Assoc. Fredrikson & Byron, P.A., Mpls., 1977-83, shareholder, 1983—. Mem. Wis. Bar Assn., Minn. Bar Assn., Hennepin County Bar Assn., Phi Eta Sigma, Tau Beta Pi, Phi Kappa Phi, Order of Coif. Avocations: golf, running, music. Office: Fredrikson & Byron PA 200 S 6th St Ste 4000 Minneapolis MN 55402-1425 E-mail: eanderson@fredlaw.com.

ANDERSON, G. BARRY, judge; b. Oct. 24, 1954; m. Louise Helleoid, June 30, 1884; 3 children. BA magna cum laude, Gustavus Adolphus Coll., 1976; JD, U. Minn., 1979. Bar: Minn. 1979, U.S. Dist. Ct. Minn. 1979, U.S. Ct. Appeals (8th cir.) 1980; cert. civil trial specialist. City atty. City of Hutchinson, Minn., 1987-88; gen. counsel Minn. Rep. Party, 1987-97; chair Minn. Ethical Practices Bd., 1997-98; judge Minn. Ct. Appeals, St.

Paul, 1998—. Bd. dirs. Hutchinson Cmty. Video Network, pres., 1984-98. Mem. Alpha Kappa Psi, Rotary (pres. Hutchinson chpt. 1997-98). Lutheran. Avocations: golf, historical and biographical works. E-mail: gba@hutchtel.net.

ANDERSON, GARY ALLAN, professional football player; b. Parys, South Africa, July 16, 1959; naturalized, 1985; married; 2 children. BS, Syracuse U., 1982. Mem. Buffalo Bills Football Team, 1982; placekicker Pitts. Steelers Football Team, 1982-94, Phila. Eagles, 1995-96, San Francisco 49ers, 1997-98, Minn. Vikings, 1998—. Named to NFL All Rookey Team, 1982, NFL Pro Bowl, 1983, 85, 93, Offensive rookei of Yr., Dapper Dan Club, 1983, Placekicker of Yr., NFL Alumni, 1983, Leading Scorer, Am. Football League, 1983, 84, 85; recipient MacKey Leading Scorer award, 1985, 86. Avocations: fly fishing, golf. Office: Minn Vikings 9520 Viking Dr Eden Prairie MN 55344-3898

ANDERSON, GERARD M. energy company executive; Cons. McKinsey & Co.; v.p. DTE Energy Co., Detroit, 1993-98, pres., chief operating officer, 1998—. Office: DTE Energy Co 2000 2d Ave Detroit MI 48226-1279

ANDERSON, HALVOR, corporate officer; CEO Siegal-Robert, St. Louis. Office: Siegel-Robert 12837 Flushing Meadows Dr Saint Louis MO 63131-1830

ANDERSON, HAROLD E. trucking company executive; married Jeanette Anderson. Pres., founder Anderson Trucking Svc., St. Cloud, Minn., 1955—. Served to capt. USAF, WWII. Decorated Air medal, Disting. Flying Cross. Office: Anderson Trucking Svc 203 Cooper Ave N Saint Cloud MN 56303-4446

ANDERSON, HARRISON CLARKE, pathologist, educator, biomedical researcher; b. Louisville, Sept. 2, 1932; married, 1961. BA in Zoology, U. Louisville, 1954, MD, 1958. Diplomate Am. Bd. Pathology. Pathology intern Mass. Gen. Hosp., Boston, 1958-59; NIH rsch. trainee U. Louisville, Ky., 1959-60; resident in pathology Sloan Kettering Meml. Hosp, N.Y.C., 1960-62; postdoctoral fellow Sloan Kettering Inst., Rye, N.Y., 1962-63; from asst. prof., assoc. prof. to prof. pathology SUNY Downstate Med. Ctr., Bklyn., 1963-78; prof. pathology, chmn. dept. U. Kans. Med. Ctr., Kansas City, 1978-90, Harrington prof. orthopedic rsch., 1990—. Mem. study sect. NIH, Bethesda, Md., 1977-81, 99-; chmn. Gordon Research Conf. on Bone, Meriden, N.H., 1981. Edit. bd. Am. Jour. Pathology, others, 1981—; contbr. articles to profl. jours. Recipient Biol. Mineralization Research award Internat. Assn. Dental Research, 1985, Sr. Faulty Research award U. Kans. Med. Ctr., 1986, Kappa Delta Orthopedic Rsch. award Orthopedic Rsch. Soc., 1982, Higuchi Biomed. Rsch. award U. Kansas, 1991; NIH rsch. fellow Strangeways Lab., Cambridge, Eng., 1971-72, NIH sr. rsch. fellow in cell biology Yale U., New Haven, , 1984-85; grantee NIH, 1967—. Mem. Am. Soc. Investigative Pathologists, Assn. Pathology Chmn. (pres. 1988-90), Am. Soc. Cell Biology, Am. Soc. Bone and Mineral Research, Orthopaedic Research Soc. Clubs: Am. Yacht (Rye); Carriage (Kansas City). Avocations: tennis, skiing, sailing. Office: U of Kansas Dept of Pathology 39th & Rainbow Kansas City KS 66160-0001

ANDERSON, HARRY FREDERICK, JR. architect; b. Chgo., Feb. 4, 1927; s. Harry Frederick and Sarah Matilda (Anderson) A.; m. Frances Annette Zeilstra, Jan. 27, 1951 (div. Jan. 1979); children: Scott H., Mark S., Robert R., Grant Alan; m. Elizabeth Jane Elden, Jan. 17, 1979 (dec. Apr. 1982); m. Joanell Vivian Mangan, Mar. 22, 1983. B.Arch., Ill. Inst. Tech., 1953. Chief draftsman Stade & Cooley, Chgo., 1953-55; ptnr. Stade, Dolan & Anderson, 1955-65; project architect Perkins & Will Partnership, 1965-67, ptnr., v.p., 1967-85, sr. v.p., 1973-74, exec. v.p., 1974-75, pres., chief exec. officer, 1975-85, chmn. bd., 1982-85; chmn., chief exec. officer Anderson, Mikos Architects Ltd., Oak Brook, Ill., 1985—. Bd. dirs. Chgo. Bldg. Congress. Prin. works include Rockford (Ill.) Coll. Library, 1967, Sci. Bldg, 1968, Arts Complex, 1970, Women's Dormitory, 1969, Silver Cross Hosp, Joliet, Ill., 1971, Westlake Hosp, Melrose Park, Ill., 1970, Am. Soc. Clin. Pathologists bldg., Chgo., 1971, Ingalls Hosp, 1974, St. Mary of Nazareth Hosp, 1975, Childrens Meml. Hosp., Chgo., 1980, U. Chgo. Hosp, 1980, Northwestern Meml. Hosp., Chgo., 1987, Michael Reese Hosp., Chgo., 1987, Ctrl. Dupage Hosp., Winfield, Ill., 1998, Advocate Health Care Sys., Chgo., 1998. Chmn. adv. council Booth Meml. Hosp., Chgo., 1969-81; adv. bd. Chgo. Salvation Army, 1969-81. Served with USN, 1944-47. Fellow AIA; Mem. Internat. Hosp. Fedn., Am. Pub. Health Assn., Soc. Hosp. Planning and Mktg., Hinsdale Golf Club. Home: 721 W Walnut St Hinsdale IL 60521-3062 Office: Anderson Mikos Architects Ltd 1420 Kensington Rd Ste 306 Hinsdale IL 60523-2147

ANDERSON, HUGH GEORGE, bishop; b. Los Angeles, Mar. 10, 1932; s. Reuben Leroy and Frances Sophia (Nielsen) A.; m. Synnøve Anna Hella, Nov. 3, 1956 (dec. Apr. 1982); children: Erik, Kristi; m. Jutta Ilse Fischer, July 2, 1983; children: Lars, Niels. AB, Yale U., 1953; BD, Luth. Theol. Sem., Phila., 1956, STM, 1958; MA, U. Pa., 1957, PhD, 1962; LittD, Lenoir Rhyne Coll., 1971; DD, Roanoke Coll., 1971, Wagner Coll., 1987, Gen. Theol. Sem., N.Y.C., 1996, Luther Coll., Decorah, Iowa, 1996; LHD, Newberry Coll., 1979, Columbia (S.C.) Coll., 1981. Ordained Lutheran minister. Tchg. fellow Luth. Theol. Sem., Phila., 1956-58; prof. ch. history Luth. Theol. So. Sem., Columbia, S.C., 1958-70, dir. grad. studies, pres., until 1982, Luther Coll., Decorah, Iowa, 1982-95; presiding bishop Evang. Luth. Ch. Am., 1995—. Chair Pub. House of the Evang. Luth. Ch. Am., 1987-93; co-chmn. U.S. Luth.-Roman Cath. Dialogue, 1979-90; mem. Commn. for a New Luth. Ch., 1982-86; v.p. Luth. World Fedn., 1996—. Author: Lutheranism in the Southeastern States, 1969, A Good Time to be the Church, 1997; co-author: Lutherans in North America, 1975; translator: I Believe (H. Thielicke), 1968, Historical Commentary on the Augsburg Confession (W. Maurer), 1986. Bd. dirs. Minn. Pub. Radio, St. Paul, 1983-91. Mem. Luth. World Fedn. (commn. on studies 1984-90). Avocations: astronomy, sailing. Home: PO Box 719 Prospect Heights IL 60070-0719 Office: Office of the Bishop ELCA 8765 W Higgins Rd Chicago IL 60631-4101

ANDERSON, J. TRENT, lawyer; b. Indpls., July 22, 1939; s. Robert C. and Charlotte M. (Pfeifer) A.; m. Judith J. Zimmerman, Sept. 8, 1962; children: Evan M., Molly K. BS, Purdue U., 1961; LLB, U. Va., 1964. Bar: Ill. 1965, Ind. 1965. Teaching asst. U. Cal. Law Sch., Berkeley, 1964-65; assoc. Mayer, Brown & Platt, Chgo., 1965-72; ptnr. Mayer, Brown, Rowe & Maw, 1972—. Instr. Loyola U. Law Sch., Chgo., 1985. Mem. Law Club, Union League Club, Mich. Shores Club. Home: 3037 Iroquois Rd Wilmette IL 60091-1106 Office: Mayer Brown Rowe & Maw 190 S La Salle St Ste 3100 Chicago IL 60603-3441 E-mail: janderson@mayerbrown.com.

ANDERSON, JAMES GEORGE, sociologist, educator; b. Balt., July 24, 1936; s. Clair Sherrill and Kathryn Ann (Plovanich) A.; m. Marilyn Anderson, 1984; children: Robin Marie, James Brian, Melissa Lee, Derek Clair. B in Engring. Scis. in Chem. Engring, Johns Hopkins U., 1957, MSE in Ops. Rsch. and Indsl. Engring., 1959, MAT in Chemistry and Math., 1960, PhD in Edn. and Sociology, 1964. Adminstrv. asst. to dean Eve. Coll., Johns Hopkins U., 1964-65, dir. divsn. engring., 1965-66; rsch. prof. ednl. adminstrn. N.Mex. State U., 1966-70; mem. faculty Purdue U., Lafayette, Ind., 1970—, prof. sociology, 1974—; asst. dean for analytical studies Sch. Humanities, Social Sci. and Edn., 1975-78. Assoc. dir. AIDS Rsch. Ctr., Purdue U., 1991—, co-dir. Rural Ctr. for AIDS/STD Prevention, 1993—; adj. prof. med. sociology grad. med. edn. program Meth. Hosp. Ind., 1991—; dir. Social Rsch. Inst., Purdue U., 1995-98; cons. in field. Author: Bureaucracy in Education, 1968; co-author: Use and Impact of Computers in Clinical Medicine, 1987, Simulation in Emergency Management and Engineering and Simulation in Health Care, 1991, Simulation in Health Care and Social Services, 1992, Simulation in the Health Sciences and Services, 1993, Simulation in the Health Sciences, 1994, Evaluating Health Care Information Systems: Methods and Applications, 1994, Health Sciences Physiological and Pharmacological Simulation Studies, 1995, Simulation in the Medical Sciences, 1996, 1997, Medical Scis. simulation Conf. Preceedings, 1998, Health Scis. Simulation, 1999, 2000, Ethics and Information Technology: A Case-Based Approach to a Health Care System in Transition, 2002, Simulation in the Health and Medical Sciences, 2001, Health Sciences Simulation, 2002; guest editor spl. issue on siumlation in health sci.: Simulation, Apr. , 1996, spl. issues on modeling episemics: ; contbr. Mem. Am. Assn. for Med. Systems and Informatics Del. to the Peoples Republic of China, 1985; mem., citizens amb. People to People Med. Informatics Del. to Hungary and Russia, 1993. USPHS grantee; recipient award for outstanding paper Am. Assn. Med. Sys. and Informatics, 1983, Gov.'s award for Outstanding Contbns. to State of Ind., 1987, T. Hale New Investigators award Assn. Am. Med. Colls., 1988, Wyeth-Ayerst/William Campbell Felch, M.D. award Alliance for Continuing Med. Edn., 1995. Mem.: APHA, AAAS (rep. soc. for computer simulation biol. scis. sect. 1992—99), AAUP, Social Sci. Computing Assn. (chair life scis. 1991—), Internat. Sociol. Assn. (chair sect. sociology and computers 2000—01), Internat. Soc. Sys. Sci. in Health Care, Internat. Network for Social Network Analysis (chair life scis. 1997—), Soc. Computer Simulation (assoc. v.p. simulation in health care 1992—), Am. Med. Informatics Assn. (internat. affairs com. 1993—96, chmn. sect. ethical, legal and social issues 1997—2000, sci. program com. ann. conf. 1999, mem. editl. bd. for jour. 2000—, chair-elect sect. on quality improvement 2001—, best theoretical paper award 1997), Am. Ednl. Rsch. Assn. (treas. spl. interest group 1969—71), Am. Sociol. Assn., Assn. for Computing Machinery.

ANDERSON, JAMES MILTON, lawyer; b. Chgo., Dec. 29, 1941; s. Milton H. and Eunice (Carlson) A.; m. Marjorie Henry Caldwell, Jan. 22, 1966; children: James Milton, Joseph H., Hilding F., Marjorie II. BA, Yale U., 1963; JD, Vanderbilt U., 1966. Bar: Ohio 1967. Assoc. rifm Taft, Stettinius & Hollister, Cin., 1968-75, ptnr., 1975-77, 82-96, mem. exec. com., 1975-77, 91-96; pres. U.S. ops., dir. Xomox Corp., 1977-81; sec. Access Corp., 1984-96; asst. sec. Carlisle Cos., 1985-90; bd. dirs. Cin. Stock Exch., 1978—, chmn., 1980-89. Bd. dirs. Command Sys. Inc.; trustee, chmn. Monarch Found., 1988—. Mem. Indian Hill Coun., 1981-89, vice-mayor, 1985-87, mayor, 1987-89; mem. Hamilton County Airport Authority, 1980-85; trustee Children's Hosp. Med. Ctr., 1977—, chmn. bd. trustees, 1991-96, pres., CEO, 1996—; trustee The Children's Hosp. Found., 1990—, chmn. bd. trustees, 1990-93; trustee Cin. Ctr. for Devel. Disorders, 1969—, pres., 1974-80; trustee Dan Beard coun. Boy Scouts Am., 1982—, chmn., 1984-87, area pres. Ea. Ctrl. Region, 1989-91; trustee Cin. Mus. Natural History, 1984-87, Coll. Mt. St. Joseph, 1990-98; trustee Joy Outdoor Edn. Ctr., 1984-2000, pres., 1991-93, chmn., 1993-95. Capt. AUS, 1966-68. Decorated Bronze Star with two oak leaf clusters, Air medal. Mem. ABA, Ohio Bar Assn., Cin. Bar Assn., Valve Mfrs. Assn., Young Pres. Orgn., Camargo Club, Queen City Club, Commonwealth Club, Yale Club of N.Y., Cin. Yale Club, Order of Coif. Avocation: sailing. Office: 1800 Star Bank Ctr 3333 Burnet Ave Cincinnati OH 45229-3026

ANDERSON, JERRY WILLIAM, JR. technical and business consulting executive, educator; b. Stow, Mass., Jan. 14, 1926; s. Jerry William and Heda Charlotte (Petersen) A. ; m. Joan Hukill Balyeat, Sept. 13, 1947; children: Katheleen, Diane. BS in Physics, U. Cin., 1949, PhD in Econs., 1976; MBA, Xavier U., 1959. Rsch. and test project engr. Wright-Patterson AFB, Ohio, 1949-53; project engr., electronics div. AVCO Corp., Cin., 1953-70, program mgr., 1970-73; program dir. Cin. Electronics Corp., 1973-78; pres. Anderson Industries Unltd., 1978—. Chmn. dept. mgmt. and mgmt. info. svcs. Xavier U., 1980-89, prof. mgmt., 1989-94, prof. emeritus, 1994—; lectr. No. Ky. U., 1977-78; tech. adviser Cin. Tech. Coll., 1971-80; co-founder, exec. v.p. Loving God "Complete Bible" Christian Ministries, 1988—. Contbr. articles on radars, lasers, infrared detection equipment, air pollution to govt. pubs. and prof. jours.; author: 3 books in field; reviewer, referee: Internat. Jour. Energy Sys., 1985—86. Mem. Madeira (Ohio) City Planning Commn., 1962-80; founder, pres. Grassroots, Inc., 1964; active United Appeal, Heart Fund, Multiple Sclerosis Fund. With USNR, 1943-46 Named Man of Year, City of Madeira, 1964 Mem. MADD, VFW (life), Am. Mgmt. Assn., Assn. Energy Engrs. (charter), Internat. Acad. Mgmt. and Mktg., Nat. Right to Life, Assn. Cogeneration Engrs. (charter), Assn. Environ. Engrs. (charter), Am. Legion (past comdr.), Acad. Mgmt., Madeira Civic Assn. (past v.p.), Cin. Art Mus., Cin. Zoo, Colonial Williamsburg Found., Omicron Delta Epsilon. Republican Home and Office: 7208 Sycamorehill Ln Cincinnati OH 45243-2101

ANDERSON, JOHN ROBERT, retired mathematics educator; b. Stromsburg, Nebr., Aug. 1, 1928; s. Norris Merton and Violet Charlotte (Stromberg) A.; m. Bertha Margery Nore, Aug. 27, 1950; children: Eric Jon, Mary Lynn. Student, Midland Coll., 1945-46; A.A., Luther Jr. Coll., 1949; B.S. (Regents scholar), U. Nebr., Lincoln, 1951, M.A. in Math, 1954; Ph.D., Purdue U., 1970. Tchr. math., coach Bloomfield (Nebr.) High Sch., 1951-52; control systems analyst, Allison div. Gen. Motors Corp., Indpls., 1954-60; prof. math. Depauw U., Greencastle, 1960, asst. dean, dir. grad. studies, 1973-76, dir. grad. studies, 1976-84, chmn. math. dept., 1984-90, prof. math., 1990-92, ret., 1992; adj. prof. math. IVTC, 1996—; resident dir. W. European studies program Depauw U., Germany, 1975, resident dir. Mediterrenean Studies program, 1982, 90; dir. NSF Coop. Coll. Sch., Sci. Inst., 1969-70; instr. NSF summer inst., 1972; instr. Challenge sci. and math. program U.S. Students in Europe, 1976, 77, 78, 80, 82. Bd. dirs. Law Focused Edn., Indpls., 1975-77, Ind. Regional Math. Consortium, 1977-92; adj. prof. math. IVTC Coll., Greencastle, 1997—. Bd. dirs. Luth. Brotherhood br. 8746, United Way Of Greencastle, Ind., 1992-98, treas., Putnam Co. Food Pantry, 1993-98; officer Peace Evangel. Luth. Ch., 1960—. Served with U.S. Army, 1946-48. Danforth Tchr. fellow, 1963-64; NSF sci. faculty fellow, 1964-65; Lilly Found. edn. grantee, summers 1961-63 Mem. Math. Assn. Am., Nat. Council Tchrs. Math., North Central Assn. (commr. 1974-78), Sigma Xi, Pi Mu Epsilon, Kappa Delta Pi, Beta Sigma Psi. Club: Rotary Internat. (sec. 1976-77, v.p. 1977-78, pres. 1978-79, 1998-99). Home: 1560 S Bloomington St Greencastle IN 46135-2212

ANDERSON, JON MAC, lawyer, educator; b. Rio Grande, Ohio, Jan. 10, 1937; s. Harry Rudolph and Carrie Viola (Magee) A.; m. Deborah Melton, June 1, 1961; children— Jon Gordon, Greta. AB, Ohio U., 1958; JD, Harvard Law Sch., 1961. Bar: Ohio 1961. Law clk. Hon. Kingsley A. Taft Ohio Supreme Ct., Columbus, 1961-62; assoc. Wright, Harlor, Morris & Arnold, 1962-67, ptnr., 1968-76, Porter, Wright, Morris & Arthur, Columbus, 1977—. Adj. prof. law Ohio State U. Law Sch., Columbus, 1975-83; bar examiner State of Ohio, 1971-76, chmn., 1975-76; lectr. tax and estate planning insts.; bd. dirs. White Castle System, Inc., Columbus. Trustee Berea Coll, Ky., 1976-2000, Pro Musica Chamber Orch., Columbus, 1980-98, Opera Columbus, 1985-88, 1st Congl. Ch., Columbus, 1979-83, Greater Columbus Arts Coun., 1989-99; chmn., 1996-98; mem. adv. council The Textile Mus. Mem. ABA, Ohio State Bar Assn., Columbus Bar Assn., The Columbus Club, Rocky Fork Hunt and Country Club. Democrat. Avocations: music, art, textiles, literature, antique collections. Office: Porter Wright Morris & Arthur 41 S High St Ste 2800 Columbus OH 43215-6194 E-mail: janderson@porterwright.com.

ANDERSON, JON STEPHEN, newswriter; b. Montreal, Que., Can., Mar. 13, 1936; came to U.S., 1963; s. William Howard and Dorothy Beatrice (Ryan) A.; m. Gail Rutherford, Feb. 20, 1960 (div. 1966); 1 child Jon Gregory (dec.) ; m. Pamela Sherrod, Sept. 23, 2001; m. Abra Prentice, Sept. 14, 1968 (div. 1976); children: Ashley Prentice, Abra Cantrill. BA, Mt. Allison U., Sackville, Can., 1955; BCL, McGill U., Montreal, 1959; MAW, U. Iowa, 1991. Reporter Montreal Gazette, 1957-60; chief bur. Time Mag., Montreal, 1960-63, staff corr. Chgo., 1963-66; staff writer Chgo. Sun-Times, 1967-69; columnist Chgo. Daily News, 1969-72; pub. Chicagoan Mag., 1972-74; staff writer Chgo. Tribune, 1978—; writing instr. U. Iowa, 1989—. Author: City Watch: Discovering the Uncommon Chicago, 2000; contbr. articles to Readers Digest, 1977—, Chgo. Mag., 1977, Clothesline Rev., 1986. Gen. mgr. Second City Ctr. Pub. Arts, 1966-67; bd. dirs. Chgo. Internat. Film Festival, 1975-78 Recipient Stick o' Type award Newspaper Guild Am., 1969, Studs Turkel Journalism award, 1999. Mem. TV Critics Assn., Order Ky. Cols. Roman Catholic. Home: 30 j 6007 N Sheridan Rd Chicago IL 60660 Office: Chgo Tribune 435 N Michigan Ave Chicago IL 60611-4066

ANDERSON, JUDITH HELENA, English language educator; b. Worcester, Mass., Apr. 21, 1940; d. Oscar William and Beatrice Marguerite (Beaudry) A.; m. E. Talbot Donaldson, May 18, 1971 (dec. Apr. 1987). AB magna cum laude, Radcliffe Coll., 1961; MA, Yale U., 1962, PhD, 1965. Instr. English Cornell U., Ithaca, N.Y., 1964-66, asst. prof. English, 1966-72; vis. lectr. Coll. Seminar Program, Yale U., New Haven, 1973; vis. asst. prof. English U. Mich., Ann Arbor, 1973-74; assoc. prof. Ind. U., Bloomington, 1974-79, prof., 1979—, Chancellors' prof., 1999—, dir. grad. studies, 1986-90, 93, mem. governing bd. univ. Inst. for Advanced Study, 1983-85, 86-88. Morris W. Croll lectr. Gettysburg Coll., 1988, Kathleen Williams lectr., 1989, 95; dir. Folger Inst. Seminar, 1991. Author: The Growth of a Personal Voice, 1976, Biographical Truth, 1984, Words that Matter, 1996; editor: (with Elizabeth D. Kirk) Piers Plowman, 1990, (with Donald Cheney and David A. Richardson) Spenser's Life and the Subject of Biography, 1996; mem. editl. bd. Spenser Ency., 1979-90, Duquesne Studies in Lang. and Lit., 1976—, Spenser Studies, 1986—; mem. adv. bd. Textbase of Women Writers, Brown U., 1989-2000; contbr. articles on Renaissance lit. to profl. jours. Woodrow Wilson fellow, 1961-62, 63-64, NEH summer fellow and sr. rsch. fellow, 1979, 81-82, Dulin fellow Folger Libr., 1991; Huntington Libr. rsch. grantee, 1978, 97, fellow, 1985-86, Mayers Found. fellow, 1990-91, Nat. Humanities Ctr. fellow, 1995-96, Newberry-NEH fellow, 2002–; recipient Outstanding Scholar award Office of Women's Affairs Ind. U., 1996. Mem. MLA (mem. exec. com. Renaissance divsn. 1973-78, 86-90, del. to assembly 1991-93, publs. com. 1999-2002), AAUP, Spenser Soc. (pres. 1980, 88), Renaissance Soc. Am. (rep. for English to coun. 1991-93), Milton Soc., Donne Soc., Shakespeare Assn., Chaucer Soc., Phi Beta Kappa. Home: 2525 E 8th St Bloomington IN 47408-4214 Office: Ind U Dept English Bloomington IN 47405

ANDERSON, KARL STEPHEN, editor; b. Chgo., Nov. 10, 1933; s. Karl William and Eleanor (Grell) a.; m. Saralee Hegland, Nov. 5, 1977; children by previous marriage: Matthew, Douglas, Eric. BS in Editl. Journalism, U. Ill., 1955. Asst. to pub., plant mgr. Pioneer Press, Oak Park, St. Charles, Ill., 1955-71; successively advt. mgr., asst. to pub., then pub. Crescent Newspapers, Downers Grove, 1971-73; assoc. pub., editor Chronicle Pub. Co., St. Charles, 1973-80; assoc. pub. Chgo. Daily Law Bull., 1981-88; dir. comms., editor Ill. State Bar Assn., 1988—. Past pres. Chgo. Pub. Rels. Forum. Trustee emeritus Chi Psi Ednl. Trust; trustee Leo Sowerby Found.; bd. dirs. Ill. Press Found., Chgo. Legal Svcs. Found., Swedish Am. Hist. Soc., Copley First Amendment Ctr. Recipient C.V. Amenoff award No. Ill. U. Dept. Journalism, 1976, Bd. Govs. award Ill. State Bar, 1987, Print Media Humanitarian award Coalition Sub Bar Assns., 1987, Robert C. Preble, Jr. award Chi Psi, 1991, Asian-Am. Bar Media Sensitivity award, 1991, Liberty Bell award DuPage County Bar Assn., 1993, Glass Ceiling Busters award Assn. Women Lawyers, 1993, Disting. Svc. award Chgo. Vol. Legal Svcs. Found., 1993, Gratitude award Lawyers Assistance Program, 1993, Outstanding Achievement in Comm. award Justinian Soc., 1994, Communicator of Yr. award, 1999, 3rd prize Nat. Libr. Poetry, 1995, Svc. award Women's Bar Assn. Ill., 1998, Peoria County Bar Assn., 1998. Mem. Am. Judicature Soc. (sec. Ill. chpt.), Nat. Assn. Bar Execs., Baltic Bar Assn., Chgo. Legal Sec. Assn., Chgo. Press Vets. Assn. (bd. sec.), Ill. Press assn. (Will Loomis award 1977, 80), Kane County Bar Assn., DuPage Women Lawyers Assn., West Suburban Bar Assn., N. Suburban Bar Assn. (Pub. Svc. award 1997), Bohemian Lawyers Assn. (Liberty award 1999), No. Ill. Newspaper Assn. (past pres.), Pub. Rels. Soc. Ctrl. Ill. (Master Communicator award of achievement 1997), Soc. Profl. Journalists, Headline Club (past pres.), Nordic Law Club, Nellie Fox Soc., Union League Club of Chgo., Chi Psi. Home: 3180 N Lake Shore Dr Apt 14D Chicago IL 60657-4851 Office: Ill State Bar Assn 20 S Clark St Ste 900 Chicago IL 60603-1885

ANDERSON, KERRII B. construction company executive; b. 1957; BS, Elon Coll., 1978; MBA, Duke U., 1987. With Peat, Marwick, Mitchell & Co., Greensboro, N.C., 1978-84, RJ Reynolds Corp., Winston-Salem, 1984-85, Key Co., Greensboro, 1985-87; sr. v.p., CFO, chmn. bd. M/I Schottenstein Homes Inc., Columbus, 1987—. Address: MI Schottenstein Homes 3 Easton Oval Columbus OH 43219-6030

ANDERSON, KIMBALL RICHARD, lawyer; b. San Antonio, Aug. 20, 1952; s. Richard John and Martha (Bishop) A.; m. Karen Gatsis, Aug. 18, 1974; children: Alexis Katrina, Melissa Martha, Sophia Diane. BA, U. Ill., 1974, JD, 1977. Bar: Ill. 1977, U.S. Ct. Appeals (7th cir.) 1979, U.S. Supreme Ct. 1987; CPA, Ill. Assoc. Winston & Strawn, Chgo., 1977-84, ptnr., 1984—, mem. exec. com., 1994—, gen. counsel. Bd. dirs. Pub. Interest Law Initiative; Disting. Neutral, CPR Inst. for Dispute Resolution. Named Person of Yr. 1996 Chgo. Lawyer. Fellow Am. Coll. Trial Lawyers; mem. ABA, Ill. Bar Assn., Chgo. Bar Assn. (bd. mgrs. 1990-92), Ill. CPA Soc., Chgo. Bar Found. Home: 2045 N Seminary Ave Chicago IL 60614-4109 Office: Winston & Strawn 35 W Wacker Dr Ste 4200 Chicago IL 60601-1695 E-mail: kanders@winston.com.

ANDERSON, LAURENCE ALEXIS, lawyer; b. Willmar, Minn., July 20, 1940; s. Laurence Alexis and Ann Victoria (Carlson) A.; m. Elaine Mae Sather, Aug. 19, 1961; children: Jeanne Louise, Ross Laurence; m. Elizabeth J. McKie, Dec. 30, 1989; 1 child, Rachael McKie. BA in Polit. Sci. and Econs., Macalester Coll., 1962; JD, U. Minn., 1965; LLM in Taxation, William Mitchell Coll. of Law, 1994. Bar: Minn. 1965, U.S. Dist. Ct. Minn. 1965, U.S. Tax Ct. 1994. Assoc., Olson, Kief & Kalar, Bemidji, Minn., 1965-67; spl. asst. atty. gen. State of Minn., St. Paul, 1967-69; ptnr., dir., Crawford & Anderson, West St. Paul, Minn., 1969-84; mem., bd. dir. Bowman and London Ltd., 1984-89; mem., officer, bd. dirs. Jacobsen, Stromme & Harwood P.A., 1989-92, London, Anderson, Antolak & Hoeft, Ltd., Mpls., 1992—; bd. dirs., officer Legal Assistance of Dakota County (Minn.). Active Greater St. Paul United Way. Mem. ABA, Minn. State Bar Assn., Dakota County Bar Assn., Ramsey County Bar Assn., Hennepin County Bar Assn., West St. Paul C. of C., Southview Country Club, Optimists Club (West St. Paul). Republican. Office: 2250 One Financial Plz 120 S 6th St Minneapolis MN 55402-1803

ANDERSON, LLOYD LEE, animal science educator; b. Nevada, Iowa, Nov. 18, 1933; s. Clarence and Carrie G. (Sampson) A.; m. Janice G. Peterson, Sept. 7, 1958 (dec. Dec. 1966); m. JaNelle R. Hall, June 15, 1970; children: Marc C., James R. Student, Simpson Coll., 1951-52, Iowa State U., 1952-53, BS in Animal Husbandry, 1957, PhD in Animal Reproduction, 1961. NIH postdoctoral fellow Iowa State U., Ames, 1961-62, asst. prof., 1961-65, assoc. prof., 1965-71, prof. animal sci., 1971—, Charles F. Curtiss Disting. prof. agr., 1992—. Lalor Found. fellow Sta. Recherches Physiologie Animale, Inst. Nat. Recherche Agronomique, Jouy-en-Josas, France, 1963-64; rschr. physiology of reprodn. and cen. nervous sys.-pituitary regulation of growth for increased prodn. efficiency of farm animals; mem. reproductive biology study sect. NIH, 1984-88,

NIH Reviewers Res. (NRR), 1988-92; mem. peer rev. panel animal health spl. rsch. grants on beef and dairy cattle reproductive diseases USDA, 1986-88; Honor lectr. representing Iowa State U., Mid-Am. State Univs. Assn., 1989-90; mem. sustainable agrl. panel U.S. Dept. Agr., Agrl. Rsch. Svc., Nat. Program Staff to rev. rsch. projects, 1993; mem. referees panel for sponsored rsch. Kuwait U., 1998—; mem. Janice Peterson Anderson Excellence award and scholarship Coll. of Design, Iowa State U. Mem. editl. bd. Biology Reprodn., 1968-70, 86-90, Jour. Animal Sci., 1982-87, 98—, Animal Reprodn. Sci., 1978—, Inst. for Sci. Info. Atlas of Sci., 1987-90, Domestic Animal Endocrinology, 1992-95, Endocrinology, 1993-97; contbr. articles to profl. jours. Mem. 4-H Club. With Constrn. Engrs., U.S. Army, 1953-55, Germany, Signal Corps USAR, 1955-61. Grantee USDA, 1978—. Fellow AAAS, Am. Soc. Animal Sci. (hon. Animal Physiology and Endocrinology award 1988, Nat Pork Prodrs. Coun. Innovation award in basic rsch. 1993, Outstanding Achievement in Rsch. award 2001); mem. ACLU, NRA, VFW, Endocrine Soc., Am. Physiol. Soc., Iowa Physiol. Soc., Am. Assn. Anatomists, Soc. for Study of Reprodn., Soc. for Exptl. Biology and Medicine (mem. coun. 1980-83), Brit. Soc. for Study of Fertility, Soc. for Neurosci., Iowa Acad. Sci., Pituitary Soc., Am. Legion, Nat. Block and Bridle Club, Osborn Rsch. Club (chair 1994), Sigma Xi, Gamma Sigma Delta. Methodist Home: 2812 Valley View Rd Ames IA 50014-4506 Office: Iowa State U Dept Animal Sci 2356 Kildee Hl Ames IA 50011-0001

ANDERSON, LOUIS WILMER, JR. physicist, educator; b. Houston, Dec. 24, 1933; s. Louis Wilmer and Margaret Quarles (Brockett) A.; m. Marguerite Gillespie, Aug. 30; children— Margaret Mary, Louis Charles, Elizabeth Brockett B.A., Rice U., 1956; A.M., Harvard U., 1957, Ph.D., 1960. Asst. prof. U. Wis.-Madison, 1960-63, assoc. prof., 1963-68, prof. physics, 1968-94, Julian E. Mack prof. physics, 1994—. Cons. U. Calif.-Berkeley Lawrence Lab. Author 2 textbooks. Contbr. articles to profl. jours. Patentee type of N2 laser , collisional pumping ion source. Fellow U. Wis. Tchg. Acad.; co-recipient IEEE Particle Accelerator Conf. Tech. award for invention and devel. of optically pumped polarized H-Ion source, 1993. Fellow Am. Phys. Soc.; mem. Sigma Xi Home: 1818 Chadbourne Ave Madison WI 53726 Office: U Wis Dept Physics Madison WI 53706 E-mail: lwanders@facstaff.wisc.edu.

ANDERSON, LYLE ARTHUR, retired manufacturing company executive; b. Jewell, Kans., Dec. 29, 1931; s. Arvid Herman and Clara Vera (Herman) A.; m. Harriet Virginia Robson, June 12, 1953; children— Brian, Karen, Eric. BS, U. Kans., 1953; MS, Butler U., 1961. C.P.A., Mo., Kans. Mgmt. trainee, internal auditor RCA, Camden, N.J. and Indpls., 1955-59; auditor Ernst & Ernst (C.P.A.'s), Kansas City, Mo., 1959-63; v.p. fin. and adminstrn., treas., dir. Affiliated Hosp. Products, Inc., St. Louis, 1963-71; sr. v.p. Sara Lee Corp., Deerfield, Ill., 1971-74; exec. v.p. fin. Consol. Foods Corp., Chgo., 1974-76. Pres. Autotrol Corp., Crystal Lake, Ill. Bd. dirs. Crystal Lake Civic Ctr. Authority, Raue Ctr. for the Arts. With U.S. Army, 1953-55. Mem. Omicron Delta Kappa. Republican. Methodist. Home: 9804 Partridge Ln Crystal Lake IL 60014-6627

ANDERSON, MARY JANE, public library consultant; b. Des Moines, Jan. 23, 1935; d. William Kenneth and Margaret Louise (Snider) McPherson; m. Charles Robert Anderson, Oct. 21, 1965 (div. Oct. 24, 1989); 1 child, Mary Margaret. BA in Edn., U. Fla., 1957; MLS, Fla. State U., 1963. Elem. sch. librarian Dade County Schs., Miami, Fla., 1957-61; children's/young adult librarian Santa Fe Regional Library, Gainesville, 1961-63; br. librarian Jacksonville (Fla.) Pub. Library, 1963-64, chief of children's services, 1964-66, head of circulation, 1966-67; pub. library cons. Fla. State Library, Tallahassee, 1967-70; dir. tech. processing St. Mary's Coll. of Md., St. Mary's City, 1970-72; coordinator children's services Balt. County Pub. Library, Towson, Md., 1972-73; exec. dir. young adult services div. ALA, Chgo., 1973-75, exec. dir. assn. for library service to children, 1973-82; pres. Answers Unltd., Inc., Deerfield, Ill., 1982-92; dir. Wilmington (Ill.) Pub. Libr., 1993-97; dir. media svcs. Newark (Ill.) County Sch. Dist., 1997-98; dir. Maud P. Palenske Pub. Libr., St. Joseph, Mich., 1998-2000; coord. Sr. Net Learning Ctr., Ariea IV Agy. Aging, 2000—; libr. cons., 2000—. Instr. and cons. in field; part-time faculty No. Ill. U., 1985-86, Nat. Coll. Edn., Evanston, Ill., 1989; head youth svcs. Waukegan (Ill.) Pub. Libr., 1988-93; mem. exec. com. U.S. sect. Internat. Bd. on Books for Young People, 1973-82; mem. adv. bd. Reading Rainbow, TV series, 1981-84; mem. sch. bd. Avoca Sch. Dist. 37, 1985-87; mem. ALSC Newbery Medal Com., 1991. Editor: Top of the News, 1971-73, Fla. State Library Newsletter, 1967-70, Nor'Easter (North Suburban Library System Newsletter), 1984-88; contbr. articles to profl. jours. Bd. dirs. Child Devel. Assocs. Consortium, 1975—83, Coalition for Children and Youth, 1978—80; mem. Episcopal Diocese Chgo. Diocesan Coun., 1988—94, standing com., 1994—97, dep. to gen. conv., 1997; mem. Bishop's search com., 1997—98; province V rep., 1998—99; mem. vestry St. Thomas' Episcopal Ch., Morris, Ill., 1996—98; mem. Episcopal Diocese West, Mich., 1999—; deanery rep. St. Paul's Episc. Ch., St. Joseph, 2000—01, lay eucharistic min., 1999—; mem. City of Wilmington Downtown Redevel. Commn., 1996—98, Diocesan cons. team, 1999—, adl. dep. to gen. conv., 2001—. Mem. ALA (coun. 1992-2000, com. on orgn. 1999-01), Rotary (sec.-treas. 1994-96, pres. 1996-97), Wilmington C. of C. (bd. dirs. 1996-97, sec. 1997), Caxton Club (Chgo.), Beta Phi Mu, Sigma Kappa. Episcopalian. Office: Senior Net Learning Ctr 211 Hilltop Rd Saint Joseph MI 49085

ANDERSON, MAX ELLIOT, television and film production company executive; b. Nov. 3, 1946; s. Kenneth O. and Doris I. (Jones) A.; m. Claudia Lynd, Aug. 17, 1978; children: James Brightman, Sarah Lynd. BA in Psychology, Grace Coll., 1973. Advt. rep., cameraman Ken Anderson Films, Warsaw, 1969-78; prodr. Q Media Group, Rockford, Ill., 1978-83; pres. Philip Lasz Gallery, Warsaw, 1973—. Pres., owner The Market Place, Rockford, 1986—; prodr., dir. Eagle Video, Rockford, 1986—; regional product distbr. Laney Honey, 1994—; founder MVP Prodns., 1998—; prodr., writer, dir. Tracy's Choices, 1997; prodr. promotional video W.A. Whitney (German, French, Italian, Mandarin transl.), 1996; prodr. corp. video programs W.A. Whitney, Roper Whitney, Barber Colman, Longview Fibre, 1995, 96, patient video promotion and orientation Swedish Am. Hosp., 1995-96, puppet video programs Woodward Gov.; nat. distbr. home video cassettes, 1985—; mktg. dir. Alley Oop Bowling Alley Ramp for People with Disabilities. Prodr.: (videos) Tracy's Choices, 1997 (Telly award 1998, Dove Found.'s seal of approval, 1999, Best Christian documentary, 1999), Youth Haven, A Safe Place for Kids (Telly award 1999), Celebrating Our Past...Creating Our Future, 2000, The Shenandoah North Fork Project, 2000, Angels Among Us, 2000; prodr. nat. TV spots for True Value Hardware, 1985-96, 40th anniversary TV spots for Rockford Clin. (Raddy award 1992); assoc. prodr.: Gospel at the Symphony, 1979; cinematographer: (film) Pilgrims Progress (Best Cinematographer award Christian Film Distbrs. Assn. 1978) With U.S. Army, 1967-69. Recipient 1st pl. award Video Internat. Tech. Video Assn., 1989, award for Sunstrand sales video, 1991, award for Woodward Gov. corp. video, 1991, Raddy Award of Excellence, No. Ill. Advt. Coun., 1989-90, 1st pl. video award Hosp. Satellite Network, 1990, award Ill. Soc. for Healthcare Mktg. and Pub. Rels., 1998. Mem. Internat. Christian Video Assn., Am. Beekeeping Assn., Christian Booksellers Assn. Republican. Mem. Evang. Free Ch. Home and Office: 4112 Marsh Ave Rockford IL 61114-6142

ANDERSON, MIKE, newscaster; Student, La. State U., Career Acad. Journalism and Broadcasting Sch. Radio journalist, Birmingham, Ala.; with Sta. WISN TV, Milw., 1981—, anchorman 12 News This Morning and 12 News at Noon. Avocations: exercising, writing songs. Office: WISN PO Box 402 Milwaukee WI 53201-0402*

ANDERSON, MILTON ANDREW, chemical executive; b. Fond du Lac, Wis., Oct. 22, 1927; s. Andrew Andreas and Bertha Victoria (Almquist) A.; m. Dorothy Mae Verke, Nov. 27, 1954; children: Edward, Victoria. BS, U. Wis., Madison, 1954; MS in Mgmt., Lake Forest Grad. Sch. Mgmt., 1980. Registered profl. engr., Calif. Specification engr. Johns-Manville, Waukegan, Ill., 1955-59, supr., 1959-64, chemist, 1964-70, devel. engr., 1970-73; supr. Abbott Labs., North Chicago, 1973-74, quality engr., 1974-77, cons., auditing., 1977-81, mgr. rsch. auditing good lab. practices/good clin. practices, 1981-92; pres. Rsch. Compliance Svcs. Ltd., Lake Villa, Ill., 1992—. Author: GLP Quality Audit Manual, 1987, 3rd edit., 2000, GLP Essentials, 1995, 2d edit., 2002. Pres. Millburn Elem. Sch. Bd., 1971-73. Lt. naval aviator, 1948-52. Mem. Soc. Quality Assurance, Am. Soc.. for Quality Control (chmn. Northea. Ill. sect. 1980-82, sect. bd. dirs. 1982—). Republican. Home and Office: Rsch Compliance Svcs Ltd 19176 W Grass Lake Rd Lake Villa IL 60046-9242 E-mail: milton@aol.com.

ANDERSON, PAUL HOLDEN, state supreme court justice; b. May 14, 1943; m. Janice M. Anderson; 2 children. BA cum laude, Macalester Coll., 1965; JD, U. Minn., 1968. Atty. Vols. in Svc. to Am., 1968—69; spl. asst. atty. gen. criminal divsn. dept. pub. safety Office Minn. Atty. Gen., 1970—71; from assoc. to ptnr. LeVander, Gillen & Miller, South St. Paul, 1971—92; chief judge Minn. Ct. Appeals, 1992—94; assoc. justice Minn. Supreme Ct., 1994—. Mem. PER coms. Ind. Sch. Dist. 199, 1982—84, chmn. cmty. svcs. adv. com., bd. dirs., chmn. bd.; deacon, ruling elder, clk. of session House of Hope Presbyn. Ch., St. Paul. Mem.: Dakota County Bar Assn. (bd. dirs., pres.), South St. Paul/Inver Grove Heights C. of C. (bd. dirs., exec. com.). Avocations: tennis, gourmet cooking, bike riding. Office: Minn Supreme Court 425 Minnesota Judicial Ctr Saint Paul MN 55155-0001 Fax: 651-282-5115. E-mail: paul.anderson@courts.state.mn.us.

ANDERSON, RICHARD CHARLES, geology educator; b. Moline, Ill., Apr. 22, 1930; s. Edgar Oscar and Sarah Albertina (Olson) A.; m. Ethel Irene Cada, June 27, 1953; children: Eileen Ruth, Elizabeth Sarah, Penelope Cada. AB, Augustana Coll., Rock Island, Ill., 1952; SM, U. Chgo., 1953, PhD, 1955. Geologist Geophoto Svcs., Denver, 1955-57; from asst. prof. to prof. geology Augustana Coll., Rock Island, 1957-96; prof. emeritus, 1996—. Rsch. affiliate Ill. State Geol. Survey, Champaign, 1959—. Editor: Earth Interpreters, 1992; author reports. Recipient Neil Miner award Nat. Assn. Geology Tchrs., 1992. Fellow Geol. Soc. Am. (sect. co-chair 1990). Lutheran. Home: 2012 24th St Rock Island IL 61201-4533 Office: Augustana Coll Dept Geology 639 38th St Rock Island IL 61201-2210 E-mail: glanderson@augustana.edu.

ANDERSON, RICHARD H. air transportation executive; Various positions Harris County Dist. Atty.'s office, Houston; staff v.p., dep. gen. cousel Continental Airlines; v.p., dep. gen. counsel Northwest Airlines Corp, 1990, exec. v.p., COO, 1998—, CEO. Office: Northwest Airline Corp 5101 Northwest Dr Mailstop 110 Saint Paul MN 55111-3034

ANDERSON, RICHARD TODD, college president; BSc in Indsl. Edn., U. Wis., Stout, 1957; MEd, Marquette U., 1963, PhD in Edn., 1975. Tchr. Waukesha Vocat. Sch., Pewaukee, Wis., 1957-62; various adminstrv. positions Waukesha County Tech. Coll., 1962-68, asst. dist. dir., 1968-73, pres., 1973—. Co-chair Waukesha County VTAE/DPI Articulation Com. (chair certification hearing bd. 1978-79), Waukesha County Tech Prep Advisory Council; mem. Wis. Hispanic Council Higher Edn.; bd. dirs. Public Policy Com., Special Transportation Com. Recipient Eagle award Wisc. Instructional Svcs. Assn., 1984, Distinguished Svc. award Am. Assn. Women Cmty. Jr. Colls., 1985, Outstanding Corp. Leadership award Waukesha YWCA, 1991; Fulbright scholar India, 1986. Mem. Nat. Assn. Pub. Sch. Adult Edn., Am. Mgmt. Assn., Am. Tech. Edn. Assn., Am. Vocat. Assn., USAF Assn., U.S. Apprenticeship Assn., Cmty. Colls. Internat. Dev. (bd. dirs.), Council Occupl. Edn., Wis. Assn. Vocat. Adult Edn., U. Wis. Alumni Assn., Kiwanis Early Risers, Phi Delta Kappa, Phi Sigma Epsilon. Office: Waukesha County Technical College Office of the President 800 Main St Pewaukee WI 53072-4601

ANDERSON, RICHARD VERNON, ecology educator, researcher; b. Julesburg, Colo., Sept. 9, 1946; s. Vernon Franklin and Charolett Iona (Jeppesen) A.; m. Arline June Rosentreter, Jan. 23, 1971; children: Rustle R., Michael C., Theodore F. Student, Chadron State Coll., 1964-66, Western State Coll., 1970; BS, No. Ill. U., 1974, MS, 1975; PhD, Colo. State U., 1978. Grad. teaching asst. No. Ill. U., DeKalb, 1974-75; grad. rsch. asst. Colo. State U., 1975-78, postdoctoral fellow Nat. Resource Ecology Lab., 1978-79; asst. prof. Western Ill. U., Macomb, 1979-82, assoc. prof., 1982-87, prof., dir. Kibbe Life Scis. Field Sta., 1987-2001, chmn. dept. biol. scis., 1987-2001. Vis. asst. prof. inst. for. environ. studies Water Resources Ctr., U. Ill., 1980; mem. assoc. faculty Argonne Nat. Lab., 1985—; assoc. supportive scientist Ill. Natural History Survey, 1985—; proposal reviewer ecology, ecosystem studies, regulatory biology, divsn. internat. programs NSF, 1981—, mem. proposal panel for equipment and facilities grants, 1987; proposal reviewer U.S./Israel Binational Sci. Found., 1981-82, Natural Environ. Rsch. Coun., Eng., 1983-84; environ. cons. aquatic sect. Environ. Cons. and Planners, DeKalb, 1974; program chmn. Internat. Conf. on Ecological Integrity of Large Floodplain Rivers, 1994. Reviewer Natural Resource Ecology Lab., 1977-81, Jour. Nematology, 1977-81, Archives Environ. Contamination and Toxicology, 1978-81, Ecology, 1978-85, Argonne Nat. Lab., 1980—, Pedobiologia, 1982-87, Jour. Freshwater Ecology, 1982—, Freshwater Invertebrate Ecology, 1982—; contbr. over 250 sci. articles, reports, papers and abstracts; presenter papers in field. Grantee NSF, 1972, 73, 82, 83, 84, 85, (two grants), 86, (two grants), 87, 88, 99, Western Ill. U., 1980, (two grants), 81, Upper Miss. River Basin Comm./U. Ill., 1980, Abbott Labs., 1981, Ill. Dept. Transp., 1981, 85, Ctrl. Ill. Light Co., 1981, 82, 83, 84, Nat. Fish and Wildlife Svc., 1983, Ill. Dept. Conservation, 1985, 87, 88, 89, 91, U.S. Fish and Wildlife Svc./Ill. Dept. Conservation, 1988, 89, 90, 91, Environ. Cons. and Planners, Inc., 1988, 89, 91, Booker Assocs., Inc., 1989, (two grants), Ill. Natural History Survey, 1989, Wetlands Rsch., Inc., 1989, 90, 91, 92, 95, 98, USDA, U. Ill., 1991, 92, Hey and Assocs., Inc. Biotic Surveys, 1992, 83, 94, 95, 96, 97, 98, 99. Mem. Entomol. Soc. Am., N.Am. Benthological Soc. (program com. 1982-83, reviewer jour. 1990—), Ecol. Soc., Soc. Nematologists (ecology com. 1981-82, systematic resources com. 1981-82), Internat. Congress Ecologists, Ill. State Acad. Sci., Miss. River Rsch. Consortium (mem. exec. bd. 1981-82, v.p. bd. dirs. 1991-92, pres. bd. dirs. 1992-93, 99-2000), Internat. Conf. on Integrity of Large Floodplain River (program chmn. 1994), Xerces Soc., Sigma Xi (Rsch. of Yr. award 1984), Phi Kappa Phi. Achievements include research in invertebrate ecology, aquatic biology with an emphasis on large river ecosystems, aquatic invertebrates and freeliving nematodes, the effects of invertebrates on nutrient cycling. Home: 704 S Randolph St Macomb IL 61455-2966 Office: Western Ill U Dept Biol Scis Macomb IL 61455

ANDERSON, ROBERT MORRIS, JR. electrical engineer; b. Crookston, Minn., Feb. 15, 1939; s. Robert Morris and Eleanor Elaine (Huotte) A.; m. Janice Ilene Pendell, Sept. 3, 1960; children— Erik Martin, Kristi Lynn. B.E.E., U. Mich., 1961, M.E.E., 1963, M.S. in Physics, 1965, Ph.D. in Elec. Engring, 1967. Asst. research engr. U. Mich., Ann Arbor, 1963-67; research engr. Conductron Corp., summer 1967; asst. prof. elec. engring. Purdue U., West Lafayette, Ind., 1967-71, assoc. prof., 1971-79, prof., 1979, engring. coordinator for continuing edn., 1973-79, Ball Bros. prof., 1976-79; mgr. engring. edn. and tng., corp. cons. services GE, Bridgeport, Conn., 1979-82, mgr. tech. edn. operation, corp. engring. and mfg., 1982-88; mgr. tech. edn., corp. mgmt. devel. Gen. Electric Co., 1988-90; vice provost, dir. coop. extension Iowa State U., Ames, 1990-95, prof. elec. engring., 1990-2000, prof. emeritus, elec. engring., 2000—. Author: multi-media learning package Fundamentals of Vacuum Technology, 1973, (with others) Divided Loyalties, 1980; contbr. (with others) articles to profl. jours. Named Best Tchr. Elec. Engring. Purdue U., 1974; recipient Dow Outstanding Young Faculty award, 1974 Fellow Am. Soc. Engring. Edn. (cert. of merit 1977, Joseph M. Biedenbach Disting. Svc. award 1986), IEEE (Meritorious Achievement award in continuing edn. activities 1987). Lutheran. Home: 3321 Kingman Rd Ames IA 50014-3942 Office: Iowa State U 303 Coover Hl Ames IA 50011-0001

ANDERSON, ROGER GORDON, minister; b. Milw., Feb. 1, 1937; s. Arthur Gordon and Dorothy K. (Junger) A.; m. Margery V. Burleson; children: Jonathan P., Nancy L., Leslie J., Kristi A. BA, Grace Bible Coll., Grand Rapids, Mich., 1958; postgrad., Purdue U., U. Minn. Ordained to ministry Grace Gospel Fellowship, 1960. Pastor Grace Bible Ch., Lafayette, Ind., 1958-60, Preakness Bible Ch., Wayne, N.J., 1960-69, Bethesda Free Ch., Mpls., 1969-86, Grace Community Ch., Salinas, Calif., 1986-91; pres. Grace Gospel Fellowship, Grand Rapids, Mich., 1991—. Pres. Evang. Ministers' Fellowship, Mpls., 1972-85; trainer Evangelism Explosion, Mpls., 1980-89. Bd. dirs. Goodwill Home and Rescue Mission, Newark, 1962-69; bd. dirs. Grace Bible Coll., Grand Rapids, 1975—, chmn. bd., 1984-91; bd. dirs. Grace Missions Inc., Grand Rapids, 1966-75; chaplain Police Dept., Mpls., 1975-80. Recipient Meritorious Svc. award City of Mpls., 1977. Mem. Grace Gospel Fellowship (bd. dirs. 1966-68). Republican. Office: Grace Gospel Fellowship 2125 Martindale Ave SW Grand Rapids MI 49509-1837

ANDERSON, RON, advertising executive; Formerly exec. v.p., midwest creative dir., then pres. midwest Bozell & Jacobs (now Bozell Inc.), Mpls., until 1988; assoc. chief creative officer N.Y.C., 1987-88; vice-chmn., chief creative officer Bozell Inc., 1988—; now vice chmn, exec creative dir Bozell, Kamstra, Minneapolis, MN. Office: Bozell Kamstra 100 N 6th St Ste 800A Minneapolis MN 55403-1523

ANDERSON, RONALD GORDON, insurance company executive; b. Rice Lake, Wis., Oct. 2, 1948; s. Gordon Robert and Jean Beverly (Randall) A.; m. Patricia Jo Scheide, Aug. 23, 1973; children: Erik, Ian. BS, U. Wis., 1971, MS, 1972, U. Mich., 1975. Rsch. analyst Vector Rsch., Ann Arbor, Mich., 1974-76, St. Paul Cos., Minn., 1976-78, rsch. officer, 1978-81, corp. devel. officer, 1981, v.p. corp. devel., 1981-84; v.p. Gen. Reins. Corp., Stamford, Conn., 1984-99; pres. AAL Capital Mgmt., Appleton, Wis., 1999—. Mem. Citizen's League, St. Paul, 1978-82. Mem. Assn. for Corp. Growth, Planning Execs. Inst., Inst. Mgmt. Sci. Office: Aid Association for Lutherans 4321 N Ballard Rd Appleton WI 54919-0001

ANDERSON, RUSSELL A. state supreme court justice; b. Bemidji, Minn., May 28, 1942; m. Kristin Anderson; children: Rebecca, John, Sarah. BA, St. Olaf Coll., 1964; JD, U. Minn., 1968; LLM, George Washington U., 1977. Pvt. practice, 1976-82; atty. Beltrami County, 1978-82; dist. ct. judge 9th Jud. Dist., 1982-98; assoc. justice Minn. Supreme Ct., 1998—. Mem. Jud. Edn. Adv. Com., Sentencing Guidelines Commn., Supreme Ct. Adv. Com. on Rules of Criminal Procedure, Supreme Ct. Gender Fairness Implementation com., Connect U.S.-Russian Domestic Violence Delegation to Russia, 1995, 97. Lt. comdr. USN, 1968—76. Mem.: 14th Dist. Bar Assn., Minn. State Bar Assn. Office: Minn Supreme Ct 25 Constitution Ave Saint Paul MN 55155-1500

ANDERSON, SCOTT ROBBINS, hospital administrator; b. Fargo, N.D., Mar. 25, 1940; BA, U. N.D., 1962; M Health Adminstrn., U. Iowa, 1964. Adminstrn. res. St. Luke's Methodist Hosp., Veteran's Adminstrn. Med. Ctr., Cedar Rapids, Iowa City, 1963-64; adminstrv. asst. North Meml. Med. Ctr., Robbinsdale, Minn., 1964-65, asst. dir., 1965-69, adminstr., 1969-76, v.p., 1976-81, pres., 1981—; pres., ceo North Meml. Med. Ctr. (now North Meml. Health Care), 1981—. Adj. prof. in field. Office: N Meml Health Care 3300 Oakdale Ave N Robbinsdale MN 55422-2926

ANDERSON, STEFAN STOLEN, banker; b. Madison, Wis., Apr. 15, 1934; s. Theodore M. and Siri (Stolen) A.; m. Joan Timmermann, Sept. 19, 1959; children: Sharon Jill, Theodore Peter. AB magna cum laude, Harvard, 1956; MBA, U. Chgo., 1960; PhD (hon.), Ball State U., 1993. With Am. Nat. Bank & Trust Co. of Chgo., 1960-74, exec. v.p., 1969-74, 1st Mchts. Bank, Muncie, Ind., 1974, pres., 1979-98, chmn. bd. dirs., 1987—; pres., dir. First Mchts. Corp., 1983-98, chmn. bd. dirs., 1987—; dir. Fed. Res. Bank of Chgo., 1991-97. Past pres., dir. Del. Advancement Corp., 1991-95; bd. dirs. Maxon Corp., Ind. Tech. Partnership, Pub. Radio Capital Fund. Past pres. Delaware County United Way, Muncie Symphony Orch.; trustee Roosevelt U., 1970-74, George Francis Ball Found., BMH Found., Ziegler Found.; past chair Ind. Nature Conservancy; past pres. Cmty. Found. of Muncie and Delaware County. Mem. Ind. Acad., Minnetrista Cultural Found., Skyline Club (Indpls.), Rotary (past pres.), Phi Beta Kappa, Beta Gamma Sigma. Home: 2705 W Twickingham Dr Muncie IN 47304-1050 Office: 1st Mchts Bank 200 E Jackson St Muncie IN 47305-2800

ANDERSON, TIM, airport terminal executive; Dir. of airports Mpls. St. Paul Internat. Airport, 1996, dep. exec. dir. of ops., 1998—. Office: Mpls-St Paul Internat Airport 6040 28th Ave S Minneapolis MN 55450-2701

ANDERSON, WARREN, distribution company executive; BA in Polit. Sci., U. Mich., 1974, M in Journalism, 1977. CEO Anderson-DuBose Co., Cleve. Office: Anderson-DuBose Co 6575 Davis Industrial Pkwy Cleveland OH 44139-3549 Fax: (440) 248-6208.

ANDERSON, WILLIAM CORNELIUS, III, lawyer; b. Haddonfield, N.J., Dec. 1, 1947; s. William Cornelius Jr. and Madelyn Anna (Penny) A.; m. Christine Joan Keck, June 20, 1970; children: William C. IV, Teresa, Stephen, Geoffrey, Thomas, Matthew. BA, Georgetown U., 1969; JD, Villanova U., 1975. Bar: Del. 1975, Ill. 1979. Atty. Morris, Nichols, Arsht & Tunnell, Wilmington, Del., 1975-77, Biggs & Battaglia, Wilmington, 1978, Lord, Bissell & Brook, Chgo., 1979-85, ptnr., 1985-2000; founding ptnr. Anderson, Bennett & Ptnrs., 2000—. Contbr. chpt. to book, articles to law jours. Capt. USAR, 1969-72. Fellow Am. Coll. Trial Lawyers; mem. ABA, Internat. Assn. Def. Counsel, Am. Acad. Healthcare Attys., Soc. Trial Attys., Union League Club of Chgo., North Shore Country Club, Kenilworth Club. Home: 717 Kent Rd Kenilworth IL 60043-1031 Office: Anderson Bennett & Ptnrs 55 E Monroe St Ste 3650 Chicago IL 60603-5713 E-mail: w.anderson@abandpartners.com.

ANDERSON, WILLIAM HOPPLE, lawyer; b. Cin., Feb. 28, 1926; s. Robert Waters and Anna (Hopple) A.; m. Jean Koop, Feb. 3, 1951; children: Susan Hopple, Nancy, Barbara, William Hopple Jr., Francie. Student, Carleton Coll., 1946; LL.B., U. Cin., 1952. Bar: Ohio bar 1952, U.S. Supreme Ct 1964. Mem. firm Becker, Loeb, & Becker, Cin., 1952-54; asst. pros. atty. Hamilton County, Ohio, 1953-57; ptnr. Graydon, Head & Ritchey, Cin., 1957—; judge Wyoming (Ohio) Mcpl. Ct., 1960-67. Mem. Ohio Ho. of Reps., 1967-69. With USMC, 1944-46. Mem. Cin. Bar Assn. Republican. Presbyterian. Home: 297 Mount Pleasant Ave Cincinnati OH 45215-4212 Office: 511 Walnut St Cincinnati OH 45202-3115

ANDERSON, WILLIAM R. botanist, educator, curator; BS Botany, Duke U., 1964; MS Systematic Botany, U. Mich., 1965, PhD, 1971. Assoc. curator N.Y. Botanical Garden, 1971-74; from asst. prof. to prof., dept. Biology U. Mich., 1974—, also assoc. curator, 1974-86, curator, 1986—, dir. Herbarium, 1986-99. Field work in Jamaica, 1963, 66, Hawaii, 1964, Mexico, 1965, 66, 68, 70, 81, 83, 88, 94, 95, 98, Costa Rica, 1969, 90,

Brazil, 1972-76, 78, 82, 90, Argentina, 1982, 90, Venezuela, 1984, 96. Gen. editor numerous vols., chpts. in field; contbr. articles in field to profl. jours. Office: U of Mich Herbarium N University Building Ann Arbor MI 48109-1057

ANDERTON, JAMES FRANKLIN, IV, real estate development executive; b. Lansing, Mich., Aug. 2, 1943; s. James Franklin III and Florence Ethel (Bear) A.; m. Deborah Anne Garlock, Apr. 2, 1966 (div.); 1 child, James Franklin, V.; m. Denise Marie Thelen, July 6, 1985; 1 child, Sarah Elizabeth. BA, Hobart Coll., Geneva, N.Y., 1965; MBA, Cornell U, 1967; PhD, Mich. State U., 1997. Controller Summit Steel Processing Corp., Lansing, 1967-69, exec. v.p., 1970, pres., 1971-90, Processed Plastics Co., Ionia, Mich., 1986-90, Universal Steel Co. of Mich., Lansing, 1988-90; chmn., pres., CEO, Summit Holdings Corp., East Lansing, Mich., 1986—; pres. Lansing C.C., 1999-2000; mng. gen. ptnr. Summit Holdings Ltd. Partnership, 1996—. Pres. Inst. of Scrap Recycling Industries, Washington, 1982-83, bd. dirs.; v.p. Bur. Internat. de la Recuperation, Brussels, 1984-85; bd. dirs. Alpena (Mich.) Power Co., Fed. Forge Inc., Lansing, Auto-Owners Ins. Co., Lansing; mem. Mich. Resource Recovery Com., 1975-77, Mich. Job Devel. Authority, 1977-79, nat. adv. coun. Mich. State U. Coll. of Edn., 1998—; mem. Mich. com. on financing postsecondary edn., 1999—; mem. Tchr. Edn. Accreditation Coun., 2001—. Pres. Lansing Met. Devel. Authority, 1971-72, Delta Twp. Econ. Devel. Authority, 1975-76; campaign chmn. Capital Area United Way, Lansing, 1976; chmn. Lansing Regional C. of C., 1977; chmn. Montessori Children's House, Lansing, 1982-85, St. Lawrence Hosp., Lansing, 1985-86, Capital Region Cmty. Found., Lansing, 1992-93; trustee Hobart and William Smith Colls., Geneva, N.Y., 1993-98. Sgt. USNG, 1968-74. Episcopalian. Avocations: reading, hiking, piano, tennis, golf, skiing. Home: 1618 Stanlake Dr East Lansing MI 48823-2018

ANDORFER, DONALD JOSEPH, university president; b. Ft. Wayne, Ind., Dec. 31, 1937; s. Joseph and Cecil J. (Minich) A.; married Dec. 26, 1960; children: Susan, Joseph, Barbara. BS in Edn., Ball State U., 1960, MA in Edn., 1965; LLD (hon.), Tiffin U., 1989. Instr. Internat. Jr. Coll. Bus., Ft. Wayne, 1960-70, dean, dir., 1971-77; controller Ind. Inst. Tech., 1978-81, v.p. fin., 1982-85, pres., 1985—. Mem. acad. com. Luth. Hosp. Bd., 1989-93; bd. dirs. Robert Morris Coll., Chgo., 1985—; bd. dirs. Ind. Pub. Broadcasting. Mem. Ind. Colls. Ind. (bd. dirs., chmn. 1994), Nat. Assn. Ind. Colls. and Univs., Nat. Assn. Ind. Athletics (nat. coun. pres. 1991-94), Ft. Wayne C. of C., Ind. Bus. Edn. Assn. (pres. 1980-81), Future Bus. Leaders Am. (bd. dirs. Outstanding Bus. Person for Ind. award 1981), Rotary (bd. dirs., v.p. 1994, pres.-elect 1995, pres. 1996, Paul Harris fellow 1998), Summit Club (bd. dirs. 2000—), Delta Pi Epsilon. Roman Catholic. Avocations: golf, fishing, spectator sports. Home: 15423 Connors Rd Fort Wayne IN 46819-9720 Office: Ind Inst of Tech Office of the President 1600 E Washington Blvd Fort Wayne IN 46803-1228

ANDORKA, FRANK HENRY, lawyer; b. Lorain, Ohio, July 25, 1946; s. Frank Henry and Sue (Parham) A.; m. M. Jean Deliman, Aug. 10, 1968; children: Frank Henry Jr., Claire E. AB, Ohio U., 1968; postgrad., Ind. U., 1968-69; JD, Cornell U., 1975. Bar: Ohio 1975, U.S. Dist. Ct. (no. dist.) Ohio 1975. From assoc. to ptnr. Baker & Hostetler, Cleve., 1975—. Author: A Practical Guide to Copyrights and Trademarks, 1989, What is a Copyright?, 1992. Served to 1st lt. U.S. Army, 1969-72. Mem. ABA (chmn. internat. copyright laws and treaties com. 1984-86, chmn. govt. rels. to copyright com. 1986-88, chmn. broadcasting, sound rec. and performing artists com. 1988-90, chmn. divsn. III copyrights 1990-92, chmn. divsn. IX publs. 1992-93), Ohio Bar Assn., Greater Cleve. Bar Assn. Avocations: bowling, tennis. Home: 31000 Clinton Dr Cleveland OH 44140-1500 Office: Baker & Hostetler 3200 Nat City Ctr 1900 E 9th St Ste 3200 Cleveland OH 44114-3475 E-mail: fandorka@bakerlaw.com.

ANDRASSY, TIMOTHY FRANCIS, trade association executive; b. Cleve., Feb. 13, 1948; s. Robert Steven and Matilda A.; m. Grace Elizabeth Wills, Jan. 3, 1970; children— Timothy Francis, Courtney, Alyson. BS, John Carroll U., Cleve., 1970. Assoc. producer, prodn. asst. Sta. WKBF-TV, Cleve., 1968-69; asst. dir. public rels. Thistledown Racing Club, North Randall, 1969-70, dir. promotions and community rels., 1976-77; asst. to pres. Gaffney Advt., Mentor, Ohio, 1970-71; stadium mgr., dir. broadcast ops. Cleve. Indians Profl. Baseball Club, 1971-74; mgr. communications Am. Soc. Metals, Metals Park, Ohio, 1974-76; exec. dir. Assn. Steel Distbrs., Cleve., 1977-81; v.p. Steel Svc. Ctr. Inst., 1981-92; exec. dir. Steel Tube Inst. N.Am., 1992—2002; exec. v.p. Precision Machined Products Assn., Brecksville, 2002—. Mem. adv. coun. Cleve. Conv. Ctr. Dir. community rels. Geauga County Bi-Centennial Organizing Com., 1975-76. Mem. Am. Soc. Assn. Execs., Meeting Planners Internat., Greater Cleve. Growth Assn. (v.p. bd. dirs.), Greater Cleve. Soc. Assn. Execs., Downtown Euclid Assn., Walt Disney World Council of Advisors. Home: 8341 Twin Creek Ct Mentor OH 44060-8617 Office: Precision Machined Producst Assn 6700 W Snowville Rd Brecksville OH 44141-3292 Office Fax: 440-526-5803. Business E-Mail: andrassy@pmpa.org.

ANDRE, L. AUMUND, management consultant; b. Marquette, Kans., Dec. 21, 1916; s. Anders and Lillian Amanda (Johnson) A.; m. Elsie Viola (Nelson), June 1, 1941 (dec. Feb. 1986); children: Carolyn Aleda, Denise Ardis; m. Phyllis Jean Richter-Russo, Sept. 17, 1988. BS, CUNY, 1939; postgrad., Columbia U., 1940-41, George Williams Coll., 1947. Youth program dir. various YMCAs, N.Y.C., Syracuse, Chgo., 1939-51; exec. dir. YMCA Met. Chgo., 1951-65; sr. v.p. Cen. YMCA Coll., Chgo., 1965-80; pvt. practice cons., 1980-96; ret., 1997. Instr. Sch. Edn. Syracuse (N.Y.) U., 1941-44; adj. prof. George William Coll., Chgo., 1948-55; lectr. Northwestern U., Evanston, Ill., 1978-80. Author: So Now You Are a Fund Raiser, 1977, Boys and Dogs Have Right of Way, 1987; author poetry; contbr. articles to profl. jours. Mem. county com. Am. Labor Party, Syracuse, 1943; chmn. Northwest Community Coun., 1954-56, Citizens Com. to Establish Triton Coll., River Grove, Ill., 1962-64; advisor Ill. Atty. Gen. Commn. to Study Fund Raising Laws and Enforcement., 1980. Named Father of Year Chgo. Area Father's Day Coun., 1962; recipient Svc. to Youth award, Lincolnland Assn. Profl Dirs. (YMCA), 1977. Mem. Nat. Soc. Fund Raising Execs. (officer , dir. 1968-79, Founder's award 1980). Democrat. Lutheran. Avocations: reading, music, traveling, writing poetry. Home and Office: 224 N Kenilworth Ave Oak Park IL 60302-2079

ANDREAS, DAVID LOWELL, banker; b. St. Paul, Mar. 1, 1949; s. Lowell Willard and Nadine B. (Hamilton) A.; m. Debra Kelley, June 20, 1985; 2 children. BA, U. Denver, 1971; MA, Mankato State U., 1976. Credit mgmt. trainee United Calif. Bank, Los Angeles, 1976-77; comml. loan officer Nat. City Bank of Mpls., 1977-80; from v.p., sr. vp., to chmn., chief exec. officer Nat. City Bancorp., Mpls., 1980—. Chmn. ADAPA, Inc., Mpls., 1986-93; chmn. bd. Nat. City Bank, Mpls., 1991-94; pres., CEO Nat. City Bank, Mpls., 1994-2001. Bd. mem. Minn. Ctr. Victims of Torture; mem. exec. com., dir. Children's Heart Link, 1988—, Ctr. Ethical Bus. Cultures, Mankato U. Coll. Bus. Adv. Coun.; mem. Minn. State U. Mankato Coll. bus. adv. coun.; mem. Coll. of Social and Behavioral Scis. adv. bd.; trustee Breck Sch., Golden Valley, Minn., 1997, Mpls. Coll. Art and Design. With U.S. Army, 1971-73. Mem. Mpls. Club. Avocations: skiing, swimming. Office: M & I Marshall and Isely Bank 651 Nicollet Mall Minneapolis MN 55402-1611 E-mail: dandreas@nationalcitybank.com.

ANDREAS, DWAYNE ORVILLE, business executive; b. Worthington, Minn., Mar. 4, 1918; s. Reuben P. and Lydia (Stoltz) A.; m. Bertha Benedict, 1938 (div.); 1 dau., Sandra Ann Andreas McMurtie; m. Dorothy Inez Snyder, Dec. 21, 1947; children: TerryLynn, Michael D. Student, Wheaton (Ill.) Coll., 1935-36; hon. degree, Barry U. V.p., dir. Honeymead Products Co., Cedar Rapids, Iowa, 1936-46; chmn. bd., chief exec. officer Honeymead Products Co. (now Nat. City Bancorp.), Mankato, Minn., 1952-72; v.p. Cargill, Inc., Mpls., 1946-52; exec. v.p. Farmers Union Grain Terminal Assn., St. Paul, 1960-66; chmn. bd., chief exec. officer Archer-Daniels-Midland Co., Decatur, Ill., 1970-97, chmn. bd., 1997-98, chmn. emeritus, 1999—. Mem. Pres.'s Gen. Adv. Commn. of Fgn. Assistance Programs, 1965-68, Pres.'s Adv. Coun. on Mgmt. Improvement, 1969-73; chmn. Pres.'s Task Force on Internat. Pvt. Enterprise. Nat. bd. dirs. Boys' Club Am.; former chmn. U.S.-USSR Trade and Econ. Coun.; former chmn. Exec. Coun. on Fgn. Diplomats; former trustee Hoover Inst. on War, Revolution and Peace; former vice chmn. Woodrow Wilson Internat. Ctr. for Scholars; former mem. Trilateral Commn.; chmn. Found. for Commemoration of the U.S. Constitution, 1986. Mem. Fgn. Policy Assn. N.Y. (dir.), Indian Creek Country Club (Miami Beach, Fla.), Blind Brook Country Club (Purchase, N.Y.), Links, Knickerbocker, Friars (N.Y.C.).

ANDREAS, GLENN ALLEN, JR. agricultural company executive; b. Cedar Rapids, Iowa, June 22, 1943; s. Glenn Allen and Vera Irene (Yates) A.; m. Toni Kay Hibma, June 19, 1964; children: Bronwyn Denise, Glenn Allen III, Shannon Tori. BA, Valparaiso U., 1965, JD, 1968. Bar: Colo. 1969. Atty. U.S. Treas. Dept., Denver, 1969-73, Archer Daniels Midland Co., Decatur, Ill., 1973-75, asst. treas., 1975-86, treas., 1986—, v.p., chief fin. officer Europe, 1986-94, v.p., counsel to chief exec., 1994-96, mem. office of chief exec., 1996-97, pres., CEO, 1997-99, chmn., CEO, 1999—. Bd. dirs. Nat. City Bancorp., Mpls., Oelmühle Hamburg A.G, Hamburg, Federal Republic of Germany. Mem. ABA, Colo. State Bar Assn., Decatur Bar Assn. Democrat. Clubs: Country of Decatur, Decatur. Avocation: golf. Office: Archer Daniels Midland Co 4666 E Faries Pkwy Decatur IL 62526-5666

ANDREASEN, JAMES HALLIS, retired state supreme court judge; b. Mpls., May 16, 1931; s. John A. and Alice M. Andreasen; m. Janet Andreasen, June 25, 1961 (dec. July 1985); children: Jon A., Amy E., Steven J.; m. Marilyn McGuire, May 17, 1987. BS in Commerce, U. Iowa, 1953, JD, 1958. Bar: Iowa 1958. Pvt. practice law, Algona, Iowa, 1958-75; with Algona City Coun., 1961-68; judge 3d Jud. Dist. Ct., 1975-87, Supreme Ct. Iowa, Des Moines, 1987-98, ret., sr. judge, 1998—. Lt. col. USAFR, 1954-75. Mem. ABA, Iowa State Bar Assn., Kossuth County Bar Assn. Methodist. Office: Kossuth County Courthouse Algona IA 50511

ANDREASEN, NANCY COOVER, psychiatrist, educator, neuroscientist; d. John A. Sr. and Pauline G. Coover; children: Robin, Susan. BA summa cum laude, U. Nebr., 1958, PhD, 1963; MA, Radcliffe Coll., 1959; MD, U. Iowa, 1970. Instr. English Nebr. Wesleyan Coll., 1960-61, U. Nebr., Lincoln, 1962-63; asst. prof. English U. Iowa, Iowa City, 1963-66, resident, 1970-73, asst. prof. psychiatry, 1973-77, assoc. prof., 1977-81, prof. psychiatry, 1981-92, Andrew H. Woods prof. psychiatry, 1992-97, Andrew H. Woods chair psychiatry, 1997—. Dir. Mental Health Clin. Rsch. Ctr., 1987—; sr. cons. Northwick Pk. Hosp., London, 1983; acad. visitor Maudsley Hosp., London, 1986. Author: The Broken Brain, 1984, Introductory Psychiatry Testbook, 1991; editor: Can Schizophrenia be Localized to the Brain?, 1986, Brain Imaging: Applications in Psychiatry, 1988, Brave New Brain: Conquering Mental Illness in the Era of the Genome , 2001; : book forum editor Am. Jour. Psychiat., 1988—, : dep. editor, 1989—93, : editor-in-chief, 1993—; contbr. articles to profl. jours. Recipient Rhonda and Bernard Sarnat award NAS, 1999, C. Charles Burlingame award, 1999, Arthur P. Noyes award in schizophrenia, 1999, Lieber prize Nat. Alliance for Rsch. on Schizophrenia and Depression, 2000, Pres.'s Nat. Medal Sci., 2000; Woodrow Wilson fellow, 1958-59, Fulbright fellow Oxford U., London, 1959-60. Fellow Royal Coll. Physicians Surgeons Can. (hon.), Am. Psychiat. Assn. (Adolf Meyer award 1999), Am. Coll. Neuropharmacologists, Royal Soc. Medicine; mem. Am. Acad. Arts and Scis., Am. Psychopathol. Assn. (pres. 1989-90), Inst. Medicine of NAS (coun. 1996—). Office: U Iowa Hosps and Clinics 200 Hawkins Dr Iowa City IA 52242-1009

ANDREASEN, NIELS-ERIK ALBINUS, religious educator; b. Asminderod, Denmark, May 14, 1941; came to U.S., 1963; s. Caleb A. and Erna E. (Pedersen) A.; m. Demetra Lougani, Sept. 5, 1965; 1 child, Michael. BA, Newbold Coll., England, 1963; MA, Andrews U., Mich., 1965, BD, 1966; PhD, Vanderbilt U., 1971. From asst. to assoc. prof. Pacific Union Coll., Calif., 1970-75; vis. lectr. Avondale Coll., Australia, 1975-77; prof., dean of religion Loma Linda (Calif.) U., 1977-90; pres. Walla Walla (Wash.) Coll., 1990-94, Andrews (Mich.) U., 1994—. Author: The Old Testament Sabbath, 1972, Rest and Redemption, 1978, The Christian Use of Time, 1978. Mem. Soc. Bibl. Lit. Seventh Day Adventist. Office: Andrews University Office Of The President Berrien Springs MI 49104-0001 E-mail: NEAA@Andrews.edu.

ANDREOFF, CHRISTOPHER ANDON, lawyer; b. Detroit, July 15, 1947; s. Andon Anastas and Mildred Dimitry (Kolinoff) A.; m. Nancy Anne Krochmal, Jan. 12, 1980; children: Alison Brianne, Lauren Kathleen. BA, Wayne State U., 1969; postgrad. in law, Washington U., St. Louis, 1969-70; JD, U. Detroit, 1972. Bar: Mich. 1972, U.S. Dist. Ct. (ea. dist.) Mich. 1972, U.S. Ct. Appeals (6th cir.) 1974, Fla. 1978, U.S. Supreme Ct. 1980. Legal intern Wayne County Prosecutor's Office, Detroit, 1970-72; law clk. Wayne County Cir. Ct., 1972-73; asst. U.S. atty. U.S. Dept. Justice, 1973-80; asst. chief criminal divsn. U.S. Atty.'s Office, 1977-80; spl. atty. organized crime and racketeering sect. U.S. Dept. Justice, 1980-84, dep. chief Detroit Organized Crime Strike Force, 1982-85, mem. narcotics adv. com., 1979-80; ptnr. Evans & Luptak, Detroit, 1985-93, Jaffe, Raitt, Heuer & Weiss, Detroit, 1995—. Lectr. U.S. Atty. Gen. Advocacy Inst., 1984. Recipient numerous spl. commendations FBI, U.S. Drug Enforcement Adminstrn., U.S. Dept. Justice, U.S. ATty. Gen. Mem. ABA, FBA (spkr. trial adv. and criminal law sect. Detroit 1983—, bd. dirs. 1989-91, chmn. criminal law sect. 1990-91), Mich. Bar Assn., Fla. Bar Assn., Nat. Assn. Criminal Def. Lawyers, Detroit Bar Assn. Greek Orthodox. Home: 4661 Rivers Edge Dr Troy MI 48098-4161 Office: Jaffe Raitt Heuer & Weiss One Woodward Ave Ste 2400 Detroit MI 48226

ANDREOLI, KATHLEEN GAINOR, dean, nurse; b. Albany, N.Y., Sept. 22, 1935; d. John Edward and Edmunda Elizabeth (Ringlemann) Gainor; children: Paula Kathleen, Thomas Anthony, Karen Marie. BSN, Georgetown U., 1957; MSN, Vanderbilt U., 1959; DSN, U. Ala., Birmingham, 1979. Staff nurse Albany Hosp. Med. Ctr., 1957; instr. St. Thomas Hosp. Sch. Nursing, Nashville, 1958—59, Georgetown U. Sch., Nursing, 1959—60, Duke U. Sch. Nursing, 1960—61, Bon Secours Hosp. Sch. Nursing, Balt., 1962—64; ednl. coordinator, physician asst. program, instr. coronary care unit nursing inservice edn. Duke U. Med. Ctr., Durham, NC, 1965—70; ednl. dir. physician asst. program dept. medicine U. Ala. Med. Ctr., Birmingham, 1970—75, clin. assoc. prof. cardiovascular nursing Sch. Nursing, 1970—77, asst. prof. nursing dept. medicine, 1971, assoc. prof., 1972—, assoc. prof. nursing Sch. Pub. and Allied Health, 1973—; assoc. dir. Family Nurse Practitioner Program, 1976, assoc. prof. community health nursing Grad. Program, 1977—79, assoc. prof. dept. pub. health, 1978—79; prof. nursing, spl. asst. to pres. for ednl. affairs U. Tex. Health Sci. Ctr., Houston, 1979—82, acting dean Sch. Allied Health Scis., 1981, v.p. for ednl. services, interdisciplinary edn., internat. programs, 1983—87; v.p. nursing affairs Rush-Presbyn.-St. Lukes's Med. Ctr., Chgo., 1987—; dean Rush U. Coll. Nursing, 1987—. Mem. nat. adv. nursing coun. VHA, 1992; cons. in field. Author, editor, with others: Comprehensive Cardiac Care, 1983; editor: Heart and Lung, Jour. of Total Care, 1971; contbr. articles to profl. jours. Active Internat. Nursing Coalition for Mass Casualty Edn., 2002—; mem. adv. bd. Robert Wood Johnson Clin. Nurse Sch. Program; mem. vis. com. Vanderbilt U. Sch. Nursing; mem. Leadership Ill., 1991; mem. nat. nursing asdv. com. Voluntary Hosp. Am., 1991; mem. governing coun. Inst. for Hosp. Clin. Nursing Edn., Am. Hosp. Assn., 1993; bd. dirs. Ill. League for Nursing, 1994. Recipient Founder's award, N.C. Heart Assn., 1970, Disting. Alumni award, Vanderbilt U. Sch. Nursing, 1985, Leadership Tex. award, 1985, Disting. Alumni award, U. Ala. Sch. Nursing, 1991. Fellow: Am. Acad. Nursing; mem.: ACNA, ANA, Nat. Nursing Adv. Coun. Hosps. Am., Am. Heart Assn. Coun. Cardiovasc. Nursing, Coun. Family Nurse Practitioners and Clinicians, Ala. Heart Assn., Nat. League Nursing, Inst. Medicine, Am. Assn. Colls. Nursing, Rotary One Club Chgo., Phi Kappa Phi, Alpha Eta, Sigma Theta Tau. Roman Catholic. Home: 1212 S Lake Shore Dr Chicago IL 60605-2402 Office: Rush Presbyn-St Luke's Med Ctr 600 S Paulina St Ste 1080 Chicago IL 60612-3806 Business E-Mail: kandreoli@rushu.rush.edu.

ANDREOZZI, LOUIS JOSEPH, lawyer; b. N.J., 1959; m. Lisa Marie Clark, Apr. 12, 1987. BS in Bus. Adminstrn. with hons., Rutgers U., 1981; JD, Seton Hall U., 1984. Bar: N.J. 1984. Asst. gen. counsel Gordon Pub., Inc., Randolph, NJ, 1984—93; dep. gen. counsel Elsevier U.S. Holdings, Morris Plains, 1985—93; v.p., sec., gen. counsel Reed Elsevier Med. Pub., Belle Mead, 1994—95; v.p., gen. counsel, sec., head ops. support and svcs., purchasing, sales force homeworking project, customer svc. integration project Lexis-Nexis, Miamisburg, Ohio, 1994—97; pub. Martindale-Hubbell, 1996; chief legal counsel Lexis-Nexis, 1997—98; COO Martindale-Hubbell, New Providence, NJ, 1997—99, Marquis, NRP, New Providence, 1998—99; vice-chmn. Reed Tech. and Info. Svcs., Inc., 1999—2000; pres., CEO Martindale-Hubbell, Marquis, NRP, New Providence, 1999—2000, Lexis, 2000—. Mem. legal adv. bd. Lexis-Nexis, 1994—, exec. bd., 1994—; mem. Friends of the Law Libr. of Congress; bd. dirs. Am. Assn. of Pub. Named to Dept. Distinction in Bus., Rutgers U., 1981, Nat. Honor Soc. in Econs. and Bus., 1981. Mem.: ABA, N.J. Employment Law Assn., Am. Corp. Counsel Assn., Internat. Bar Assn., N.J. Bar Assn. Roman Catholic. Office: Lexis Nexis Group 9443 Springboro Pike Miamisburg OH 45342-4425

ANDRES, RONALD PAUL, chemical engineer, educator; b. Chgo., Jan. 9, 1938; s. Harold William and Amanda Ann (Breuhaus) A.; m. Jean Mills Elwood, July 15, 1961; children: Douglas, Jennifer, Mark. BS, Northwestern U., 1959; PhD, Princeton U., 1962. Asst. prof. Princeton U., 1962-68, assoc. prof., 1968-76, prof. chem. engring., 1976-81, Purdue U., West Lafayette, Ind., 1981—, head Sch. Chem. Engring., 1981-87, Engring. Research prof., 1987—. Mem. AAAS, Am. Chem. Soc., Am. Inst. Chem. Engrs., Am. Phys. Soc., Materials Rsch. Soc., Sigma Xi, Tau Beta Pi, Pi Mu Epsilon, Phi Lambda Upsilon, Phi Eta Sigma. Office: Purdue U Sch Chem Engring West Lafayette IN 47907-1283 E-mail: ronald@ecn.purdue.edu.

ANDREWS, FRANK LEWIS, lawyer; b. Rhinebeck, N.Y., June 8, 1950; s. William Fisher and Merna Louise (Lewis) A.; m. Barbara Della Chapman, Aug. 30, 1980; children: William Chapman, S. Ross Chapman. Student, U. Vienna, Austria, 1971; BS magna cum laude, Mich. State U., 1973; JD cum laude, Harvard U., 1976. Bar: Mich. 1976. Sr. prin. Miller, Canfield, Paddock & Stone PLC, Detroit, Bloomfield Hills, Mich., 1983—, co-chmn. environ. law group, 1987—. Speaker on corp. law, environ., hazardous materials, and corp. compliance to various bus. and bar assns.; course dir. and speaker on multiple environ. law programs Nat. Assn. Corp. Real Estate Execs., Inst. for Continuing Legal Edn., Continuing Legal Edn. Internat., Cambridge Inst., 1982—. Mem. legal subocm. Alexander Graham Bell Assn. for Deaf, Washington, 1989—; gen. counsel Mich. Host Com. for World Cup Soccer, 1994, 92-94. Mem. ABA (chmn. environ. legis. subcom. bus. law sect. 1993—). Avocations: skiing, sailing. Office: Miller Canfield Paddock & Stone 1400 N Woodward Ave Bloomfield Hills MI 48304-2854

ANDREWS, OAKLEY V. lawyer; b. Cleve., Apr. 15, 1940; BA, Yale U., 1962; JD, Western Reserve U., 1965. Bar: Ohio 1965, U.S. Tax Ct. 1968, U.S. Dist. Ct. (no. dist.) Ohio 1968, U.S. Ct. Appeals (6th cir.) 1968. Ptnr. Baker & Hostetler, LLP, Cleve. Fellow Am. Coll. Trust and Estate Coun.; mem. Ohio State Bar Assn., Estate Planning Coun. Cleve. (pres. 1982-83), Cleve. Bar Assn. (chmn. Estate Planning, Probate and Trust law sect. 1984-85), Phi Delta Phi Office: Baker & Hostetler LLP 3200 Nat City Ctr 1900 E 9th St Ste 3200 Cleveland OH 44114-3475 E-mail: oandrews@baker-hostetler.com.

ANDREWS, RICHARD VINCENT, physiologist, educator; b. Arapahoe, Nebr., Jan. 9, 1932; s. Wilber Vincent and Fern (Clawson) A.; m. Elizabeth Williams, June 1, 1954 (dec. Dec. 1994); children: Thomas, William, Robert, Catherine, James, John; m. Wyoma Upward, Oct. 18, 1997. BS, Creighton U., 1958, MS, 1959; PhD, U. Iowa, 1963. Instr. biology Creighton U., Omaha, 1958-60; instr. physiology U. Iowa, 1960-63; asst. prof. Creighton U., Omaha, 1963-65, assoc. prof., 1965-68, prof. physiology, 1968-97, asst. med. dean, 1972-75, dean grad. studies, 1975-85, dean emeritus, 1995—, prof. emeritus, 1997—. Vis. prof. Naval Arctic Rsch. Lab., 1963-72, U. B.C., 1985-86, U. Tasmania, 1993-94; cons. VA, NSF, NRC, ARS; plenary speaker USSR Symposium on Environment, 1970, Internat. Soc. Biomet., 1972. Contbr. articles to profl. jours. Served with M.C. U.S. Army, 1951-54. NSF fellow, 1962-63; NSF-NIH-ONR-AINA grantee, 1963— Fellow Explorers Club, Arctic Inst. N.Am.; mem. Am. Physiol. Soc., Am. Mammal Soc., Endocrine Soc., Soc. Exptl. Biology and Medicine, Internat. Soc. for Biometeorology, Sigma Xi.

ANDRIST, JOHN M. senator; b. Crosby, N.D., Aug. 1, 1931; s. Calvin L. and Lela G. (Revis) A.; m. Elaine G. Thvedt, June 17, 1951; children: Pamela, Paula, Steve, Stan, Penny. Pub. Crosby (N.D.) Jour., 1958-91; mem. ND Senate from 2nd dist., 1993—; mem. legis. coun. and appropriations com. ND Senate, 1997—99. Mem. N.D. Newspaper Assn. (past pres.), Nat. Newspaper Assn. (N.D. state chmn. 1970-82, bd. dirs., representing Iowa, N.D., S.D., Minn. 1982-87, treas. 1988, v.p. 1989, pres. 1990), Crosby Bus. Builders (pres.), Crosby Jaycees (past pres.), N.D. Jaycees (state sec.), N.D. Profl. chpt. Soc. Profl. Journalists (past pres.). Presbyterian. Lodges: Kiwanis, Moose. Avocations: golf, running, cycling. Office: PO Box E Crosby ND 58730-0660

ANGEL, AUBIE, physician, academic administrator; b. Winnipeg, Man., Can., Aug. 28, 1935; s. Benjamin and Minnie (Kaplan) A.; m. Esther-Rose Newhouse; children: Jennifer, Jonathan, Suzanne, Steven, Michael. BSc in Medicine, MD, U. Man., 1959; MSc, McGill U., 1963. Speciality resident in diabetes and endocrinology Montreal Gen. Hosp., 1961-62; postgrad. dept. exptl. medicine McGill U., 1962-63; asst. resident in medicine Royal Victoria Hosp., Montreal, 1963-64; asst. prof. pathology McGill U., Que., Can., 1965-68; staff physician Royal Victoria Hosp., 1965-68; sr. physician and staff endocrinologist Toronto Gen. Hosp., 1968-90; asst. prof. medicine U. Toronto, Ont., Can., 1968-72, assoc. prof. Can., 1972-81, prof. medicine Can., 1981-90, dir. Inst. Med. Sci. and clin. scis. divsn. Canada, 1983-90; prof., head dept. medicine U. Man., 1991-95; physician in chief Health Sci. Ctr., Winnipeg, Man., 1991-95. Vis. scientist U. Calif., San Diego, 1977—78, Hammersmith Hosp., London, 1978; founding pres. Diabetes Rsch. and Treatment Ctr., Winnipeg, 1991—; foundinf pres., chmn. bd. dirs. Friends of CIHR, 1994—; scholar-in-residence MRC, Canada, 1996; pres. 7th Internat. Congress on Obesity, 1994; co-chair Internat. Conf. Diabetes and Cardiovascular Disease, 1999. Editor (with C.H. Hollenberg and D.A.K. Roncari): (novels) The Adipocyte and Obesity: Cellular and Molecular Mechanisms, 1983; editor: (with J. Frohlich) Lipoprotein Deficiency Syndromes: Advances in Experimental Medicine and Biology, 1986; editor: (with N. Sakamoto and N. Hotta) New Directions in Research and Clinical Works for Obesity and Diabetes Mellitus, 1991; editor: (with H. Anderson, C. Bouchard, D. Lau, L. Leiter, R. Mendels) Progress in Obesity Research, 1996; editor: (with N. Dhalla, G. Grant, P. Singal)

Diabetes and Cardiovascular Disease, 2001. Project dir. Can. Internat. Devel. Agy., Toronto and Costa Rica, 1987-94. Recipient Outstanding Svc. award Heart and Stroke Found. Ont., 1985; U. Toronto Med. Rsch. Coun. scholar, 1965-71; Trinity Coll., Toronto, fellow, 1989— Fellow Royal Coll. Physicians and Surgeons Costa Rica (hon.), N.Am. Assn. Study Obesity (pres. 1986-87), Can. Soc. Clin. Investigation (councillor 1977-80), Am. Soc. Clin. Investigation, Can. Inst. Acad. Medicine (founding pres. 1990-92), Internat. Assn. Study Obesity (bd. govs. 1986—), Juvenile Diabetes Found. Internat. (hon. bd. dirs. 1987-90), Obesity Canada (founding bd. dirs. 1999-2001). Office: U Man Dept Internal Med 820 Sherbrook St Rm GB-409 Winnipeg MB Canada R3A 1R9 E-mail: aangel@hsc.mb.ca.

ANGELO, JEFF M. state legislator; b. St. Louis, Dec. 5, 1964; m. Debbie. Chair Union County Rep. Ctrl. Com.; mem. Iowa Senate from 44th dist., 1996—. Mem. Univ. Ext. Coun.; stewardship, fin. chair First Congl. Ch., Creston, Iowa. Republican. Home: 808 W Jefferson St Creston IA 50801-3132 Office: State Capitol Dist 44 3 9th And Grand Des Moines IA 50319-0001 E-mail: jeff_angelo@legis.state.ia.us.

ANGELO, JERRY, professional sports team executive; m. Bernie Angelo; children: Leisa Rice, Sutton. Part-time defensive line coach Colo. State U., 1972; defensive line coach, recruiting coord. U. Tampa, Tampa, Fla., 1973—74; defensive line coach Syracuse, 1975—79; dir. player personnel Tampa Bay Buccaneers, Fla.; gen. mgr. Chgo. Bears. Office: 1000 Football Drive Lake Forest IL 60045

ANGINO, ERNEST EDWARD, retired geology educator; b. Winsted, Conn., Feb. 16, 1932; s. Alfred and Filomena Mabel (Serluco) A.; m. Margaret Mary Lachat, June 26, 1954; children— Cheryl Ann, Kimberly Ann B.S. in Mining Engring., Lehigh U., Bethlehem, Pa., 1954; M.S. in Geology, U. Kans., 1958, Ph.D. in Geology, 1961. Instr. geology U. Kans., Lawrence, 1961-62, prof. civil engring., 1971-99, prof. geology, 1972-99, prof. emeritus, 1999—, chmn. dept. geology, 1972-86, dir. water resources ctr., 1990-99; asst. prof. Tex. A&M U., College Station, 1962-65; chief geochemist Kans. Geol. Survey, Lawrence, 1965-70, assoc. state geologist, 1970-72. Cons. on water chemistry and pollution to various cos. and govt. agys. including Dow Chem. Co., Ocean Mining Inc., Envicon, Oak Ridge Lab., Fisheries Research Bd. Can., Midwest Research Inst., Coast and Geodetic Survey, U.S. Geol. Survey Author: (with G.K. Billings) Atomic Absorption Spectrometry in Geology, 1967; author, editor: (with D.T. Long) Geochemistry of Bismuth, 1979; editor: (with R.K. Hardy) Proc. 3d Forum Geol. Industrial Minerals, 1967, (with G.K. Billings) Geochemistry Subsurface Brines, 1969; contbr. more than 125 articles to sci. and profl. jours. Mem. Lawrence City Police Rels. Commn., 1970-76, Lawrence City Commn., 1983-87, mayor, 1984-85; mem. Lawrence 2020 Planning Commn., 1992-94, Police Adv. Coun., 1994—, Crimestoppers Bd., 1994—, Lawrence Tax Abatement Commn., 2001-02. With U.S. Army, 1955-57. NSF fellow Oak Ridge Lab., 1963; recipient Antarctic Service medal Dept. Def., 1969; Angino Buttress named in his honor, 1967 Mem. Geochem. Soc. (sec. 1970-76), Soc. Environ. Geochemistry and Health (pres. 1978-79), Internat. Assn. Geochemistry and Cosmochemistry (treas. 1980-94), Am. Polar Soc., Am. Philatelist Soc., Am. Soc. Polar Philatelists, Meter Stamp Soc., Forum Club (Factotum 1978-79), Rotary (pres. 1993-95). Republican. Roman Catholic. Avocations: philately, Western history, Indian lore. Home: 4605 Grove Dr Lawrence KS 66049-3777 Office: U Kans Dept Geology Lindley 120 Lawrence KS 66045-0001 E-mail: rockdoc@cjnetworks.com.

ANGST, GERALD L. lawyer; b. Chgo., Dec. 29, 1950; s. Gerald L. Sr. and Audrey M. (Hides) A.; m. Candace Simning, Jan. 29, 1983. BA magna cum laude, Loyola U., Chgo., 1972, JD cum laude, 1975. Assoc. Sidley Austin Brown & Wood, Chgo., 1975-82, ptnr., 1982—. Mem. ABA (constrn. litigation com. litigation sect.), Chgo. Bar Assn. (civil practice com.). Office: Sidley Austin Brown & Wood Bank One Plz 47th Fl 10 So Dearborn St Chicago IL 60603-2000 E-mail: gangst@sidley.com.

ANGSTADT, DAVID W. business executive; Exec. v.p., chief mktg. officer Luth. Brotherhood, Mpls., 1998—. Office: Luth Brotherhood 625 4th Ave S Minneapolis MN 55415-1665

ANGUS, JOHN COTTON, chemical engineering educator; b. Grand Haven, Mich., Feb. 22, 1934; s. Francis Clark and Margaret (Cotton) A.; m. Caroline Helen Gezon, June 25, 1960; children: Lorraine Margaret, Charles Thomas. BSChemE, U. Mich., 1956, MS, 1958, PhD in Engring, 1960; DSc (hon.), Ohio U., 1998. Registered profl. engr., Ohio. Research engr. Minn. Mining & Mfg. Co., St. Paul, 1960-63; prof. Case Inst. Tech. (now Case Western Res. U.), Cleve., 1963-67, prof. chem. engring., 1967—, chmn. dept., 1974-80, interim dean engring., 1986-87. Vis. lectr. U. Edinburgh, Scotland, 1972-73; vis. prof. Northwestern U., 1980-81; pres. Angus Engring., Inc. Trustee Ohio Scottish Games. NSF fellow, 1956-57; NATO sr. fellow, 1972-73 Fellow AIChE, Electrochem. Soc. (Pioneer award); mem. NAE, Am. Chem. Soc., Materials Rsch. Soc., Sigma Xi, Tau Beta Pi, Phi Lambda Upsilon. Achievements include research in fields of crystal growth, diamond synthesis, conducting diamond laser applications, electrochemical devices, thermodynamics. Office: Case Western Res U Dept Chem Engring Cleveland OH 44106-7217

ANSBACHER, RUDI, physician; b. Sidney, N.Y., Oct. 11, 1934; s. Stefan and Beatrice (Michel) A.; m. Elisabeth Cornelia Vellenga, Nov. 19, 1965; children— R. Todd, Jeffrey N. Grad., Harvard Coll., 1951; B.A., Va. Mil. Inst., 1955; M.D., U. Va., 1959; M.S., U. Mich., 1970. Diplomate Am. Bd. Ob-Gyn. Staff ob-gyn, chief clin. investigation Brooke Med. Ctr., San Antonio, 1971-75, asst. chief ob-gyn, 1975-77; chief dept. ob-gyn Letterman Army Med. Ctr., San Francisco, 1977-80; from prof. ob-gyn to prof. emeritus U. Mich., Ann Arbor, 1980—2002, prof. emeritus, 2002—. Cons. Biomed. Adv. Com. Population Resource Ctr., 1978-81; bd. dirs. Health Policy Internat. Contbr. articles to profl. jours., chpts to books; mem. editorial bds., reviewer jours. Served to col. U.S. Army, 1960-80. Named Disting. Mil. Grad. Va. Mil. Inst., Lexington, Va., 1955; NIH grantee, 1973-78 Fellow ACOG (Chmn.'s award 1970), AAAS; mem. Am. Fertility Soc. (dir. 1979-82), Am. Soc. Andrology (sec. 1978-80, pres. 1984-85), Central Assn. Ob-Gyn, Assn. Mil. Surgeons U.S., Soc. for Study Reprodn., Mich. Med. Soc. (bd. dirs. 1995—). Republican. Presbyterian Avocations: tennis; softball; gardening; skiing. Home: 3755 Tremont Ln Ann Arbor MI 48105-3022 Fax: 739-647-9727. E-mail: ansbache@med.umich.edu.

ANTHONISEN, NICHOLAS R. respiratory physiologist; b. Boston, Oct. 12, 1933; AB, Dartmouth Coll., 1955; MD, Harvard U., 1958; PhD in Exptl. Medicine, McGill U., 1969. Intern medicine N.C. Meml. Hosp., 1958-59, jr. asst. resident, 1959-60; sr. asst. resident respiratory dept. Royal Victoria Hosp., 1963-64; demonstrator medicine McGill U., 1964-66, from asst. to assoc. prof. exptl. medicine, 1969-73, prof., 1973-75; prof. medicine U. Man., Winnipeg, 1975—; dean fac. of med. U. Man. Winnipeg, 1989—. Scholar Med. Rsch. Coun. Can., 1969-71. Mem. Can. Soc. Clin. Investigation, Can. Thoracic Soc., Am. Physiol. Soc., Am. Soc. Clin. Investigation, Am. Thoracic Soc. Achievements include research in chest disease, pulmonary physiology, physiologic aspects of respiratory disease. Office: U Man Fac Med 753 McDermot Ave Rm A101 Winnipeg MB Canada R3E 0W3

ANTHONY, DONALD BARRETT, engineering executive; b. Kansas City, Kans., Jan. 28, 1948; s. Donald W. and Marjorie (Lifsey) A.; m. Darla S. Donovan, Dec. 16, 1972; children: Jennifer L., Danielle S. BSChemE, U. Toledo, 1970; MS, MIT, 1971, DSc, 1974. Asst. prof., practice sch. dir. dept. chem. engring. MIT, Cambridge, Mass., 1974-75; group supr. coal R&D Std. Oil Co. Ohio, Cleve., 1976-77, mgr. marine planning, 1978-79, mgr. synthetic fuels devel., 1980-83, v.p., gen. mgr. Pfaudler Divsn. Rochester, N.Y., 1983-85; v.p. R&D Std. Oil Co., Cleve., 1985-87, BP Am., Inc., Cleve., 1987-88, BP Exploration, Inc., Cleve., 1989-90; v.p. tech. Bechtel, Inc., Houston, 1990-94, v.p. ops., 1994-95, v.p. ref., 1995-96; pres. Bailey Controls Co., 1996-98, Process Ind. Group, ABB Automation, 1999—2000; pres., CEO NineSigma, Inc., Cleve., 2001—. Contbr. articles to profl. jours.; patentee in field. Capt. AUS, 1970-78. MIT Esso fellow, 1970-71, Little rsch.-devel. fellow, 1971-72, Procter & Gamble fellow, 1972-73, Bechtel fellow, 1992. Mem. AIChE, Am. Chem. Soc., Sigma Xi, Phi Kappa Phi, Tau Beta Pi, Pi Mu Epsilon, Phi Eta Sigma. Lutheran. Home: 6336 Canterbury Dr Hudson OH 44236-3488 Office: NineSigma Inc 29145 Chagrin Blvd Cleveland OH 44122

ANTHONY, MICHAEL FRANCIS, lawyer; b. Chgo., Dec. 19, 1950; s. Rudolph A. and Margaret M. (Shea) A.; m. Megan P. O'Connell; children: Erin Christine, Ian O'Connell, Connor Cullerton, Madeline Shea, McKenzie Galligan. BS cum laude, Xavier U., Cin., 1972, MHA, 1974; JD, U. Balt., 1978. Bar: Md. 1978, Fla. 1979, Ill. 1980, D.C. 1989. Adminstrv. positions Johns Hopkins Hosp., Balt., 1973-78; assoc. Ober Kaler Grimes & Shriver, 1978-80; from assoc. to ptnr. McDermott, Will & Emery, Chgo., 1980-87, nat. head health law dept., 1989-2001; sr. v.p. for legal affairs Am. Hosp. Assn., 1987-89. Contbr. articles to profl. jours. Mem. adv. bd. De Paul Inst. for Health Law. Fellow Am. Coll. Healthcare Execs. (various coms.), Am. Health Lawyers Assn. (past pres.). Office: McDermott Will & Emery 227 W Monroe St Ste 3100 Chicago IL 60606-5096

ANTHONY, THOMAS DALE, lawyer; b. Cleve., July 23, 1952; m. Susan Shelly; children: Lara, Elizabeth. BS, Miami U., Oxford, Ohio, 1974; JD, Case Western Res. U., 1977. Bar: Ohio 1977. Tax specialist Ernst & Young, Cleve., 1977-79; ptnr. Benesch, Friedlander, Coplan and Aronoff, Cin., 1979-89, Frost and Jacobs, Cin., 1989-98; exec. v.p., chief legal officer, sec. Choice Care, 1996-98; pres., CEO PacifiCare of Ohio, 1998—2002; counsel Frost Brown Todd LLC, 2001—. Speaker various orgns. Mem. Cin. Coun. on World Affairs, 1980-82; vol. fundraising drive Sta. WVIZ, 1978-79, Sta. WCET, 1980-82; legal counsel Children's Internat. Summer Villages, 1979—; account capt. United Way of Hamilton County, 1986-88, cabinet mem., 1993; pres. State Libr. Bd., Ohio, 1987-89; mem. bus. adv. coun., subcom. ednl. legis. Mariemont City Schs. and Bd. of Edn.; bd. dirs. Greater Cin. Ctr. for Econ. Edn., Am. Heart Assn. (Cin. chpt.), Juvenile Diabetes Found. Mem. ABA (taxation sect., tax acctg. problems com., tax shelter subcom., small bus. com., mem. health law forum), Ohio State Bar Assn. (health law com., ins. sect.), Cin. Bar Assn. (chmn. tax. inst. com. 1990, adminstrn. and fin. com. 1991-93, chmn. tax sect. 1993, health law com.), Cin. C. of C., Miami U. Alumni Assn. (bd. dirs., treas. 1989-91, v.p. 1991-92), Nat. Health Lawyers Assn., Rotary (co-chair youth in city govt. program), Omicron Delta Kappa, Sigma Phi Epsilon. Home: 4337 Ashley Oaks Dr Cincinnati OH 45227-3947 Office: PacifiCare 11260 Chester Rd Ste 800 Cincinnati OH 45246-4096

ANTICH, ROSE ANN, state legislator; b. Apr. 11, 1938; widow; 1 son, Marc. Grad., Hammond Bus. Coll.; postgrad., Ind. U. N.W. Radio and TV personality, lectr. positive mental attitude and stress control, astrologist; mem. Ind. Senate from 4th dist., 1991—; asst. minority whip, 1996—. Mem. town coun., 1983-87. Democrat. Roman Catholic. Home: 5401 Lincoln St Merrillville IN 46410-1926 Office: Ind State House 200 W Washington St Indianapolis IN 46204-2728

ANTONINI, RICHARD LEE, insurance executive; b. Grand Rapids, Mich., May 5, 1942; s. Ned and Mabel Antonini; m. Linda Sue Caldwell; children: Richard Lee, Robert Alan, Ross William, Rachel Lynn. BA in Acctg., Ferris State U., Big Rapids, Mich., 1964. Audit mgr. Seidman & Seidman, Grand Rapids, 1964-69; exec. v.p., chief fin. officer Foremost Corp. Am., 1969-86, pres., chief exec. officer, 1986—. Bd. dirs. Old Kent Bank & Trust Co., Grand Rapids. Chmn. Kent County United Way Campaign, Grand Rapids, 1989. Recipient Disting. Alumni award Ferris State U., 1986. Mem. Am. Inst. CPAs, Cascade Hills Country Club, Penn Club. Avocation: hockey. Office: Foremost Corp of America po Box 2450 5600 Beech Tree Ln Caledonia MI 49316

ANTONSEN, ELMER HAROLD, Germanic languages and linguistics educator; b. Glens Falls, N.Y., Nov. 17, 1929; s. Haakon and Astrid Caroline Emilie (Sommer) A.; m. Hannelore Gertrude Adam, Mar. 24, 1956; children: Ingrid Carol, Christopher Walter. B.A., Union Coll., Schenectady, N.Y., 1951; postgrad., U. Vienna, 1951-52, U. Goettingen, 1956; M.A., U. Ill., 1957, Ph.D., 1961. Instr. German, Northwestern U., Evanston, Ill., 1959-61; asst. prof. U. Iowa, Iowa City, 1961-64, assoc. prof., 1964-67, U. Ill., Urbana, 1967-70, prof. Germanic langs. and linguistics, 1970—, head dept. Germanic langs., 1973-82, head dept. linguistics, 1990-96, assoc. Ctr. for Advanced Studies, 1984. Vis. prof. U. N.C., Chapel Hill, 1972-73, U. Goettingen, 1988. Author: A Concise Grammar of the Older Runic Inscriptions, 1975, Runes and Germanic Linguistics, 2002; editor: The Grimm Brothers and the Germanic Past, 1989, Studies in the Linguistic Sciences, 1995—; co-editor: Staefcraeft: Studies in Germanic Linguistics, 1991, Runes and Germanic Linguistics, 2002; contbr. articles to profl. jours. Served with AUS, 1953-56. Fulbright scholar, 1951-52 Mem. Linguistic Soc. Am., Royal Norwegian Soc. Scis. and Letters, Soc. Advancement of Scandinavian Study, Institut für Deutsche Sprache (corr. mem.), Selskab for nordisk filologi, Soc. for Germanic Philology, Phi Beta Kappa. Home: 2210 Plymouth Dr Champaign IL 61821-6542 Office: Univ Ill 4088 Flb Urbana IL 61801 E-mail: antonsen@uiuc.edu.

ANVARIPOUR, M. A. lawyer; b. Tehran, Iran, Jan. 23, 1935; arrived in U.S., 1957; s. Ahmed and Monir (Georgi) A.; m. Patricia Matson Lynch (div. 1971); 1 dau., Sandra M.; m. Guilda Eshtehardi, Mar. 31, 1978 (div. 1984); 1 son, Cyrus Ramsey; m. Tess Temel, May 15, 1995. LLB, U. Tehran, 1956; BS, U. San Francisco, 1959; student, U. Calif. Hastings Coll. Law, San Francisco, JD, 1973. Bar: Ill. 1973, Fed. cts. Asst. field dir. Am. Friends of Middle East, Inc., Iran, 1962-64, field dir., 1964-66; asst. dean students, dean internat. students and faculty affairs Ill. Inst. Tech., Chgo., 1966-81; practiced in, 1973—, in San Francisco, 1985—; ednl. and legal adviser Consulate Gen. Iran, Chgo., 1973-79; aux. lawyer NAACP, 1973-74. Lectr. immigration and law seminar Ill. Inst. Tech.-Chgo.-Kent Coll. Law Sch., 1974 Mem. Am., Iran-Am. (sec.-gen. 1964-66), Chgo. Bar Assn. (chmn. immigration com. 1982-83), Iran Am. Alumni Assn. (sec. 1964-66), Nat. Assn. Fgn. Student Affairs (Ill. chmn. 1968-69), U. Tehran, U. San Francisco, Idaho State U. (hon.), Ill. Inst. Tech., Chgo.-Kent Coll. Law alumni assns., Am. Immigration Lawyers Assn. (sec.-treas. Chgo. chpt. 1976-78, v.p. 1978-80, pres. 1980-81), Armour Faculty Club (pres. 1977-78), Phi Delta Phi. Home: 512 N McClurg Ct Chicago IL 60611-3051 Office: 180 N La Salle St Chicago IL 60601-2501

APICELLA, MICHAEL ALLEN, physician, educator; b. Bklyn., Apr. 4, 1938; s. Anthony D. and Fay (Kahn) A.; m. Agnes Dengler, Aug. 19, 1961; children: Michael P., Christopher A., Peter N. AB, Holy Cross Coll., 1959; MD, SUNY, Bklyn., 1963. Diplomate Am. Bd. Internal Medicine, Am. Bd. Infectious Disease. Postdoctoral fellow Johns Hopkins Hosp., Balt., 1966-68; asst. prof. microbiology SUNY, Buffalo, 1970-74, assoc. prof., 1974-78, prof., 1981-92; prof., chmn. dept. microbiology Coll. Medicine U. Iowa, Iowa City, 1993—. Contbr. over 100 articles to profl. jours. Maj. USAF, 1968-70. Office: U Iowa Coll Medicine Dept Microbiology Coll Medicine 3-403 Science Bldg Iowa City IA 52242

APPEL, JOHN C. investment company executive; Pres., COO Dain Bosworth Inc., Mpls., 1992-98; vice chmn., CFO Dain Rauscher (formerly Dain Bosworth Inc.), 1998-99, pres., CFO, vice-chmn., 2000—, pres. fixed incopme capital markets. Office: Dain Rouscher Inc 60 S 6th St Mail Stop 18C9 PO Box 1160 Minneapolis MN 55440-4422

APPEL, NINA SCHICK, law educator, dean; b. Feb. 17, 1936; d. Leo and Nora Schick; m. Alfred Appel Jr.; children: Karen Oshman, Richard. Student, Cornell U.; JD, Columbia U., 1959. Instr. Columbia Law Sch., 1959-60; adminstr. Stanford U., mem. faculty, prof. law, 1973—, assoc. dean, 1976-83; dean Sch. Law Loyola U., 1983—. Mem. Am. Bar Found., Ill. Bar Found., Chgo. Bar Found., Chgo. Legal Club, Chgo. Network. Jewish. Office: Loyola U Sch Law 1 E Pearson St Chicago IL 60611-2055

APPEL, WILLIAM FRANK, pharmacist; b. Mpls., Oct. 8, 1924; s. William Ignatius and Elna Antonia (Mulzahn) A.; m. Louise D. Altman, Sept. 24, 1949; children— Nancy, Peggy, James, Elizabeth. B.S. in Pharmacy, U. Minn., 1949; D.Sc. (hon.), Phila. Coll. Pharmacy and Sci., 1978. Intern in pharmacy Northwestern Hosp., Mpls.; pres., pharmacist, mgr. Appel Com-Pharm, Inc., 1949—; pres. Pharm. Cons. Services, P.A., St. Paul, 1960—. Mem. Minn. Bd. Pharmacy, 1960-65, pres., 1965; preceptor internship requirement program; chmn. Minn. Gov.'s. Commn. on Drug Abuse, 1971-73; mem. Mpls. Health Dept. Task Force on Pub. Health Approaches to Chem. Dependency; clin. instr. U. Minn. Coll. Pharmacy, 1970— ; cons. HEW; long term care facilities; rep. Nat. Pharmacy/Industry Com. on Nat. Health Ins.; mem. revision com. U.S. Pharmacopeial Conv., 1980— Served with USN, 1942-46. Recipient Good Neighbor award, Sta. WCCO, Mpls., 1973. Mem. Twin City Met. Drug Assn., Minn. Pharm. Assn. (v.p., Harold R. Popp award 1974, mem. continuing edn. faculty 1970—), Am. Pharm. Assn. (pres. N.W. br., nat. pres. 1976-77, Daniel B. Smith award 1970, treas. 1979—) pharm. assns), Minn. Gerontol. Soc., U. Minn. Coll. Pharmacy Alumni Assn. (v.p., Distinguished Pharmacist award 1971) Home: 7204 Trillium Ln Minneapolis MN 55435-4020

APPELSON, MARILYN IRENE, director of college development; b. Bklyn., 1933; d. Abraham and Sophie (Porosoff) Backinoff; m. Wallace B. Appelson; children: Teri, Bruce, Andrew, CJ. BA, Bklyn. Coll., 1953; MA, Coll. of N.J., 1967; postgrad., Hunter Coll. Tchr. elem. Newport News (Va.) Pub. Sch., 1953-54; tchr. English, ESL White Plains (N.Y.) Pub. Sch., 1954-57; tchr. ESL Ewing Adult Schs., Ewing Twp., N.J., 1964-76; tchr. English, ESL Mercer County C.C., Trenton, 1974-76; coord. ESL Chgo. Urban Skills Inst., 1977-79; dir. vols. in tchg. adults Oakton C.C., Des Plaines, Ill., 1979-84, dir. coll. devel., 1984—, exec. dir. ednl. found. Chair Fed. Funding Task Force, Washington, 1989-90. Author: (handbook) Handbook for Teachers of English & Citizenship, 1971; editor: (ann. report) NCRD: Federal Funding for Two Year Colleges, 1989-90, (news mag.) NCRD: Dispatch, 1993-94. Mem., v.p. LWV, Trenton, N.J., 1970, 72; mem. Nat. Libr. Literacy Coun., Cook County, Ill., 1997—. Mem. Coun. for Resource Devel. (pres. 1997-98, v.p. programs 1991, Life Time Svc. award 1995), Ill. Resource Devel. Commn. (pres. 1986-87), Skokie Ill. Rotary (treas. 1997-98). Avocations: tennis, skiing. Office: Oakton C C 1600 E Golf Rd Des Plaines IL 60016-1234 E-mail: marilyna@oakton.edu.

APPLEBAUM, EDWARD LEON, otolaryngologist, educator; b. Detroit, Jan. 14, 1940; s. M. Lawrence and Frieda (Millman) A.; m. Amelia J. Applebaum; children: Daniel Ira, Rachel Anne. A.B., Wayne State U., 1961, M.D., 1964. Diplomate: Am. Bd. Otolaryngology. Intern Univ. Hosp., Ann Arbor, Mich., 1964-65; resident Mass. Eye and Ear Infirmary Harvard Med. Sch., Boston, 1966-69; practice medicine specializing in otolaryngology Chgo., 1972—; assoc. prof. Northwestern U. Med. Sch., 1972-79; prof., head dept. otolaryngology, head and neck surgery Coll. Medicine, U. Ill., 1979-2000; acting chmn. dept. otolaryngolgoy Northwestern U. Med. Sch., Chgo., 2000—. Mem. staff Northwestern Meml. Hosp. Author: Tracheal Intubation, 1976; mem. editorial bd. Am. Jour. Otolaryngology, Laryngoscope. Served as maj. U.S. Army, 1969-71. Recipient Anna Albert Keller Rsch. award Wayne State U. Coll. Medicine, 1964, Disting. Alumni award, 1989, William Beaumont Soc. Original Rsch. award, 1964. Fellow ACS, Am. Soc. for Head and Neck Surgery, Am. Acad. Facial Plastic and Reconstructive Surgery, Am. Acad. Otolaryngology, Head and Neck Surgery, Am. Laryngol., Rhinol. and Otol. Soc. (v.p. 1993, pres. 2000), Am. Laryngol. Assn., Am. Otol. Soc., Soc. Univ. Otolaryngologists, Head and Neck Surgeons (pres. 1988), Assn. Acad. Depts. Otolaryngology-Head and Neck Surgery (pres. 1995-96). Home: 161 E Chicago Ave Apt 42B Chicago IL 60611-6677

APPLETON, R. O., JR. lawyer; b. San Francisco, Aug. 17, 1945; s. Robert Oser and Leslie Jeanne (Roth) A.; m. Susan Frelich, June 3, 1971; children: Jesse David, Seth Daniel. AB, Stanford U., 1967; JD, U. Calif., San Francisco, 1970; postgrad., NYU, 1971. Bar: Calif. 1971, U.S. Dist. Calif. (no. dist.) Calif. 1971, Mo. 1973, U.S. Dist. Ct. (ea. dist.) Mo. 1974, U.S. Ct. Appeals (8th cir.) 1975, U.S. Ct. Internat. Trade, 1980. Assoc. Dinkelspiel & Dinkelspiel, San Francisco, 1971-73, Schramm & Morganstern, St. Louis, 1973-75; pvt. practice, 1975-77; ptnr. Braun, Newman, Stewart & Appleton, St. Louis, 1977-82, Appleton, Newman & Kretmar, St. Louis, 1982-84, Appleton, Newman & Gerson, St. Louis, 1984-89, Appleton & Kretmar, St. Louis, 1989—, Appleton, Kretmar & Beatty. Adj. prof. pre-trial litigation Washington U. Sch. Law, St. Louis, 1985-88. Arbitrator, vol. Better Bus. Bur. of St. Louis, 1980—; St. Louis Gymnastic Centre, 1984—; bd. dirs. St. Louis Friends of Tibet, 1991-94. Mem. ABA, Calif. Bar Assn., Met. Bar Assn. of St. Louis, St. Louis County Bar Assn., Am. Arbitration Assn. (arbitrator comml. panel, arbitrator mass claims appeals com. 1999), Stanford Club (pres. 1991—). Democrat. Jewish. Avocations: jogging, swimming, cooking, model trains, reading. Home: 8317 Cornell Ave Saint Louis MO 63132-5025 Office: Appleton Kretmar Beatty & Stolze 8000 Maryland Ave Ste 900 Saint Louis MO 63105-3911 E-mail: roajratty1@aol.com.

APPLEYARD, DAVID FRANK, mathematics and computer science educator; b. South Haven, Mich., July 13, 1939; s. Edwin Ray and Hortense Ruth (Guilford) A.; m. Joey Hierlmeier, Aug. 5, 1967; children: David Wayne, Gregory Jay, Robert James. B.A., Carleton Coll., 1961; M.S., U. Wis., 1963, Ph.D., 1970. Teaching asst. in math. U. Wis., Madison, 1961-66; prof. math. and computer science Carleton Coll., Northfield, Minn., 1966—, Lloyd P. Johnson Norwest Found. prof. liberal arts, 1993—, dean students Minn., 1977-83, faculty pres., 1988-91. Carleton Coll. faculty athletic rep. to Midwest Collegiate Athletic Conf., 1975-83, pres., 1982-83 Trustee United Ch. Christ, Northfield, 1969-72 NSF fellow, 1964, grantee prin. investigator, 1993—; NASA traineeship, 1965-66; Sloan Found. grantee, 1969, 73, 84. Mem. Math. Assn. Am., Nat. Coun. Tchrs. Math., Sigma Xi. Avocations: long-distance running; canoeing. Home: 6450 134th St E Northfield MN 55057-4611 Office: Carleton Coll 1 N College St Northfield MN 55057-4021

APRISON, MORRIS HERMAN, biochemist, experimental and theoretical neurobiologist, emeritus educator; b. Milw., Oct. 6, 1923; s. Henry and Ethel Aprison; m. Shirley Reder, Aug. 21, 1949; children— Barry, Robert. BS in Chemistry, U. Wis., 1945, tchrs. cert., 1947, MS in Physics, 1949, PhD in Biochemistry, 1952. Grad. teaching asst. in physics U. Wis., Madison, 1947-49; grad. research asst. in pathology Sch. Medicine, 1950-51, grad. research asst. in biochemistry, 1951-52; tech. asst. in physics Inst. Paper Chemistry, Appleton, Wis., 1949-50; biochemist, prin. investigator, head biophysics sect. Galesburg (Ill.) State Research Hosp., 1952-56; prin. research investigator in biochemistry Inst. Psychiat. Research; asst. prof. depts. biochemistry and psychiatry Ind. U. Med. Sch., Indpls., 1956-60, asso. prof., 1960-64, prof. biochemistry, 1964-78, distinguished prof. neurobiology and biochemistry, 1978-93, disting. prof. emeritus, 1993—, chief neurobiology sect., 1969-74. Mem. exec. com. dept. psychiatry, exec. adminstr. Inst. Psychiat. Research, 1973-74, dir. inst., 1974-78, chief sect. applied and theoretical neurobiology, 1978-93; co-chmn. session on neurotransmitters 23d Internat. Physiol. Congress, 1965; chmn. session neurochemistry and neuropharmacology 25th Congress, 1971; ad hoc mem. study sect. psychopharmacology NIMH, 1967-71, mem. neuropsychology study sect., 1970-74; mem. molecular and cellular neurobiology program adv. panel NSF, 1984-86; mem. com. recommendations U.S. Army scientific research Nat. Research Council Bd. Physics and Astronomy, 1987-89; mem. gov. bd. Inst. for Advanced Study Ind. U., Bloomington, 1989-92; vis. prof. 4th ASPET Workshop, Vanderbilt U., 1972; guest scholar Grad. Sch., Kans. State U., 1973. Adv. editor Neurosci. Rsch., 1968-73, Jour. Biol. Psychiatry, 1968-83, Neuropharmacology, 1969-93, Jour. Neurochemistry, 1972-75, Pharmacology, Biochemistry and Behavior, 1973-89 , Jour. Comparative and General Pharmacology, 1974-75, Jour. Gen. Pharmacology, 1975-93, Jour. Developmental Psychobiology, 1974-77; regional editor Life Scis., 1970-73; co-editor Advances in Neurochemistry, 1973-92; mem. editorial bd. Jour. Neurochemistry, 1975-79, dep. chief editor, 1980-83; mem. editorial bd. Neurochem. Rsch., 1975-82, Jour. Neurosci. Rsch., 1984-92; co-editor 10 books; contbr. more than 355 rsch. articles and abstracts to profl. jours., chpts. to books, including History of Neuroscience in Autobiography, vol. 3, 2001. Mem. Ind. regional adv. bd. Anti-Defamation League, 1973-76; bd. overseers St. Meinrad Sem., 1974-77. Served with USNR, 1944-46. Prof. M.H. Aprison awards for best rsch. toward PhD in med. neurobiology at dept. psychiatry Ind. U. Sch. Medicine created in his honor, 1999. Mem. Am. Physiol. Soc., Biophys. Soc., Soc. Biol. Psychiatry (program com. 1974-75, co-chmn. 1975-76, gold medal 1975), Internat. Brain Rsch. Orgn., Internat. Soc. Neurochemistry (co-chmn. session 1st internat. meeting Strasbourg, France 1967, 4th meeting Tokyo 1973, 7th meeting Jerusalem 1979, coun. 1973-75, sec. 1975-79, chmn. 1979-81, publicity com. 1975-83, nominating com. 1983-87, policy adv. com. 1985--, ad hoc and founding rules com. 1998—), Am. Soc. Neurochemistry (co-chmn. sci. program com. 1972, mem. 1973), Soc. for Neurosci. (pres. Indpls. chpt. 1970-71), Sigma Xi. Home: 9268 Spring Forest Dr Indianapolis IN 46260-1266 E-mail: maprison@iupui.edu.

ARBIT, BRUCE, direct marketing executive, consultant; b. Milw., Nov. 16, 1954; s. Saul B. and Naomi (Chase) A.; m. Tanya Arbit; children: Oren, Carmiel, Eugene. Student, U. Haifa, Israel, U. Wis. Founder, co-mgr., dir. A B Data, Ltd., Milw., 1977—. Chmn., bd. dirs. Integrated Mail Industries Ltd.; bd. dirs. State Fin. Bank, Asset Devel. Group, Inc., Integrated Mail Industries Israel, Ltd. Gen. campaign chmn., bd. dirs. Milw. Jewish Fedn. Keshet, Milw. Jewish Day Sch., Habonim Dror Found.; mem. United Jewish Appeal Young Leadership Cabinet; mem. Wexner Heritage Found., United Israel Appeal., Non-profit Mailers Fedn., Campaign Cabinet Devel. Corp. for Israel; trustee United Israel Appeal; bd. govs. Jewish Agy. for Israel. Recipient Benjamin E. Nickoll Young Leadership award Milw. Jewish Fedn., 1989. Mem. Direct Mktg. Assn., Israel Direct Mktg., Wis. Direct Mktg. Assn. (Direct Marketer of Yr. award 1997), Am. Assn. Polit. Cons. Office: AB Data Ltd 8050 N Port Washington Rd Milwaukee WI 53217-2600

ARBUCKLE, JOSEPH W. military officer; b. Lincoln, Ill., Feb. 28, 1946; married; 2 children. BA in Psychology, Western State Coll., Colo.; MS in Sys. Mgmt., U. So. Calif.; grad., Command and Gen. Staff Coll., Army War Coll. Commd. 2d lt. U.S. Army, 1970, advanced through grades to maj. gen., various assignments; dep. chief of staff for ammunition U.S. Army Material Command, Alexandria, Va.; comdr. armament rsch., devel. and engring. ctr. U.S. Army Tank-automotive and Armament Command, Rock Island; commdg. gen. U.S. Army Indsl. Ops. Command, Ill., 1998—. Decorated Legion of Merit with 5 oak leaf clusters, Bronze Star with 2 oak leaf clusters, Meritorious Svc. medal with 3 oak leaf clusters, Vietnamese Cross of Gallantry with 2 Silver stars, Vietnamese Svc. medal.

ARCHABAL, NINA M(ARCHETTI), historical society director; b. Long Branch, N.J., Apr. 11, 1940; d. John William and Santina Matilda (Giuffre) Marchetti; m. John William Archabal, Aug. 8, 1964; 1 child, John Fidel. BA in Music History cum laude, Radcliffe Coll., 1962; MAT in Music History, Harvard U., 1963; PhD in Music History, U. Minn., 1979. Asst. dir. humanities art mus. U. Minn., Mpls., 1975-77; asst. supr. edn. divsn. Minn. Hist. Soc., St. Paul, 1977-78, dep. dir. for program mgmt., 1978-86, acting dir., 1986-87, dir., 1987—. Bd. dirs. U.S. nat. com. Internat. Coun. Mus. Trustee, bd. dirs. Am. Folklife Ctr., Libr. of Congress, 1989-98; bd. dirs. N.W. Area Found., 1989-98, St. Paul Acad. and Summit Sch., 1993—; v.p. Friends of St. Paul Pub. Libr., 1983-93; bd. regents St. John's U., Collegeville, Minn., 1997—; overseer Harvard Coll., Cambridge, Mass., 1997—. NDEA fellow U. Minn., 1969-72, U. Minn. grad. fellow, 1974-75; recipient Nat. Humanities medal The White House, 1997. Mem. Am. Assn. State and Local History (sec. 1986-88), Am. Assn. Mus. (v.p. 1991-94, chair bd. dirs. 1994-96). Office: Minn Hist Soc 345 Kellogg Blvd W Saint Paul MN 55102-1906

ARCHER, DENNIS WAYNE, mayor, lawyer; b. Detroit, Jan. 1, 1942; s. Ernest James and Frances (Carroll) A.; m. Trudy Ann DunCombe, June 17, 1967; children: Dennis Wayne, Vincent DunCombe BS, Western Mich. U., 1965; JD, Detroit Coll. Law, 1970; LLD (hon.), Western Mich. U., 1987, Detroit Coll. Law, 1988, U. Detroit, 1988, John Marshall Law Sch., 1991, Gonzaga U., 1991, U. Mich., 1994; D in Pub. Svc. (hon.), Ea. Mich. U., 1994. Bar: Mich. 1970. Tchr. spl. edn. Detroit Bd. Edn., 1965-70; assoc. Gragg & Gardner, 1970-71; ptnr. Hall, Stone, Allen, Archer & Glenn, P.C., 1971-73, Charfoos, Christensen & Archer, P.C., 1973-85; assoc. justice Mich. Supreme Ct., 1986-90; ptnr. Dickinson, Wright, Moon, Van Dusen & Freeman, Detroit, 1991-93; mayor City of Detroit, 1994—. Assoc. prof. Detroit Coll. Law, 1972-78; adj. prof. Wayne State U. Law Sch., Detroit, 1984-85; mem. Mich. Bd. Ethics, 1979-83; mem. adv. bd. U.S. Conf. Mayors, 1994—; bd. dirs. Nat. Conf. Black Mayors, 1994—; mem. intergovtl. policy adv. com. U.S. Trade Rep. Contbr. articles to legal jours. Bd. dirs. Legal Aid and Defenders Assn., Detroit, 1980-82, Nat. Conf. Black Mayors, 1994; co-chmn. Met. Detroit Cmty. Coalition for Dems., 1979-80; bd. trustees Olivet Coll., 1991-93; active numerous local Dem. campaigns, 1970-85; host local pub. svc. radio programs; co-chair platform com. Dem. Conv., 1996; pres. Nat. Conf. Dem. Mayors, 1996; mem. Nat. Com. on Crime Control and Prevention, 1995. Named Most Respected Judge in Mich. Mich. Lawyers Weekly Jour., 1990. Mem. ABA (ho. dels. 1979-93, chmn. drafting com. 1986-88, com. on scope and correlation of work sect. officers liaison 1987-90, chmn. gen. practice sect. 1987-88, chair commn. on opportunities for minorities in the profession 1987-91, sect. legal edn. and admissions to the bar, coun. mem. 1989-95, task force on profl. skills instrn. 1989-91, task force on law schs. and the profession, Narrowing The Gap, 1989-91, chmn. spl. com. prepaid legal svcs. 1981-83, chmn. sect. officers conf. 1988-90, resource devel. coun. 1988-91, bd. editors ABA Jour. 1988-94, bd. editors The Practical Litigator 1989-94, chmn. rules and calendar com. 1990-92, state del. 1990-96), ATLA, Nat. Bar Assn. (pres. 1983-84), Am. Judicature Soc. (bd. dirs 1977-81), State Bar Mich. (pres. 1984-85), Wolverine Bar Assn. (pres. 1979-80), Detroit Bar Assn. (bd. dirs. 1973-75), Mich. Trial Lawyers Assn. (exec. bd. 1973-74), Econ. Club, Alpha Phi Alpha. Roman Catholic. Office: City of Detroit 2 Woodward Ave Rm 1126 Detroit MI 48226-3443

ARCHER, J(OHN) BARRY, municipal official; b. Ft. Jackson, S.C., Mar. 21, 1946; BS in Civil Engring., Va. Mil. Inst., 1968; MA in Engring. Adminstrn., George Washington U., 1979; student, JFK Ctr. Spl. Warfare. Registered profl. engr.; cert. bldg. ofcl.; cert. profl. codes adminstr. Engr. trainee Va. Dept. of Transp.; project mgr. George Hyman Constrn. Co.; asst. city engr. Fairfax City, Va.; structural engr. Fairfax County, 1974-78; county bldg. ofcl., dep. dir. devel. adminstrn./pub. works Prince William County, Va., 1978-94; dir. dept. codes adminstrn. City of Kansas City, 1994—. Chmn. Manufactured Homes Constrn. and Safety Stds. Code Change Com.; mem. manufactured home adv. com. U.S. Dept. HUD. Mem. rev. bd. Va. State Tech. Maj. U.S. Army Green Berets, 1969-70, Vietnam. Decorated Bronze Star with 1 oak leaf cluster, Combat Infantrymans Badge, Master Parachutist Wings, Vietnamese Spl. Forces Parachutist Wings; named Local Ofcl. of Yr. Northeastern Region Nat. Assn. Home Builders, 1992, Codes Adminstr. of Yr. Gtr. Kansas City Automatic Sprinkler Contractors Assn., 1997; recipient Meritorius Svc. award Va. Bldg. and Code Ofcls. Assn., 1994. Mem. NSPE, Am. Concrete Inst. Internat., Mo. Assn. Code Adminstrs., Internat. Conf. Bldg. Ofcls., Mo. Assn. Bldg. Ofcls. and Insps. Spl. Forces Assn. (life), Spl. Ops. Assn., Vietnam Vets. Assn. Am., VFW. E-mail: barry. Office: City of Kansas City Codes Adminstrn Dept City Hall 18th Fl 414 E 12th St Kansas City MO 64106-2702 E-mail: archer@kcmo.org.

ARDINGER, ROBERT HALL, JR. physician, educator; b. Corona, Calif., Dec. 4, 1956; s. Robert Hall Sr. and Alice Marie (Schaal) A.; m. Holly Hutchison, Nov. 6, 1982; children: Andrew, Patrick. BS, Calif. State Polytech. U., 1979; MD, U. Calif., San Diego, 1983. Diplomate Am. Bd. Pediats. Intern U. Iowa, Iowa City, 1983-84, resident, 1984-86, fellow, 1986-89; instr. U. Rochester, N.Y., 1989-90; asst. prof. U. Kans., Kansas City, 1990-96, assoc. prof., 1996-2001, U. Mo., Kansas City, 2001—. Fellow Am. Acad. Pediats., Am. Coll. Cardiology. Office: Chlidren's Mercy Hosp Cardiology 2401 Gillham Rd Kansas City MO 64108

ARDISANA, BETH, communications company executive; BS in Math./Computer Sci., U. Tex.; MBA, U. Detroit; M in Mech. Engring., U. Mich. Various mgmt. positions in vehicle design/devel., product planning and mktg. Ford Motor Co.; prin. owner ASG Renaissance, Detroit. Active Pres.'s Task Force for Implementation of Alternative Fuel Vehicles; bd. dirs. Heidelberg Project. Mem. Nat. Assn. Women Bus. Owners (named top 25 women bus. owners of distinction in Mich. by Detroit chpt. 1996, 97), Nat. Tech. Svc. Assn., Mich. Minority Bus. Devel. Coun., Mich. Hispanic C. of C. (bd. dirs.). Office: ASG Renaissance Fairlane Plaza N 290 Town Center Dr Ste 624 Dearborn MI 48126-2754 Fax: 248-358-4499.

AREF, HASSAN, fluid mechanics educator; b. Alexandria, Egypt, Sept. 28, 1950; s. Moustapha and Jytte (Adolphsen) A.; m. Susanne Eriksen, Aug. 3, 1974; children: Michael, Thomas. Cand.Sci., U. Copenhagen, Denmark, 1975; PhD, Cornell U., 1980. Asst. prof. Brown U., Providence, 1980-85, assoc. prof., 1985; assoc. prof. fluid mechanics U. Calif., San Diego, 1985-88, prof. fluid mechanics, 1988-92; chief scientist San Diego Supercomputer Ctr., 1989-92; prof., head dept. theoretical and applied mechanics U. Ill., Urbana-Champaign, 1992—. Corrsin lectr. Johns Hopkins U., Baltimore, 1988; Westinghouse disting. lectr. U. Mich., Ann Arbor, 1991; lectr. Midwest Mechanics, 1991. Editor Cambridge Texts in Applied Math., 1987-94, Advances in Applied Mechanics, 2001—; assoc. editor Jour. Fluid Mechanics, 1984-93; contbr. articles to profl. jours. Recipient Presdl. Young Investigator award, NSF 1985, Otto Laporte award, Am. Physical Soc., 2000. Fellow: World Innovation Found., Am. Acad. Mechanics, Am. Phys. Soc. (Otto Laporte award 2000); mem.: Soc. Indsl. and Applied Math. Office: U Ill Dept Theoretical and Applied Mechanics 104 S Wright St Urbana IL 61801-2935 E-mail: h-aref@uiuc.edu.

ARENA, BRUCE, professional soccer coach; b. Brooklyn, N.Y., Sept. 21, 1951; m. Phyllis Arena; 1 child, Kenny. Student, Nassau (N.Y.) C.C., 1969-71; BS in Bus., Cornell U., 1971-73. Asst. lacrosse coach, asst. soccer coach Cornell U., Ithaca, N.Y., 1973-76; head soccer coach U. Puget Sound, Tacoma, 1976-78; head soccer coach, asst. men's lacrosse coach U. Va., Charlottesville, 1978-95; head coach DC United, Washington, 1995-98, U.S. Nat. Soccer Team, Chgo., 1998—. Mem. U.S. nat. teams in both soccer and lacrosse and competed professionally in both sports; past chmn. ACC soccer coaches, ISAA Divsn. I nat. poll; "A" coaching lic. from U.S. Soccer Fedn.; mem. NCAA Divsn. I soccer com., 1989-95. Named ACC Coach of Yr., 1979, 84, 86, 88, 89, 91, South Atlantic Region Coach of Yr., 1982, 83, 87, nat. Coach of Yr. by Lanzera, 1993. Inducted into Cornell Athletic Field Hall of Fame, 1986, Long Island Lacrosse Hall of Fame, 1990. Head coach U.S. under-23 nat. team which will compete in 1996 Olympics. Achievements include career record of 295-58-32 (.808) in 18 yrs. at U. Va., leading U. Va. to NCAA titles in 1989, 91, 92, 93, 94, taking U. Va. to 6 or the last 7 NCAA semi-finals and 8 straight quarter finals, directing U. Va. to 15 straight NCAA tournament appearances (longest active streak in U.S.), Major League Soccer Cup Championships, 1996, 97, U.S. Open Cup Championship, 1996. Office: US Soccer 1801 S Prairie Ave Chicago IL 60616-1319

ARENDS, HERMAN JOSEPH, insurance company executive; b. 1945; M of Math., Mich. State U., 1967. Tchr. Laningsburg (Mich.) H.S., 1967-72; chmn., CEO Auto Owners Ins. Co., Lansing, Mich., 1972—. Office: Auto Owners Insurance Co 6101 Anacapri Dr Lansing MI 48917-3994

ARENS, ALVIN ARMOND, accountant, educator; b. Marshall, Minn., Nov. 24, 1935; married, 3 children. BBA, U. Minn., 1960, M, 1967, PhD, 1970. CPA, Minn., 1963. Staff auditor Boulay, Anderson, Waldo & Co., Mpls., 1960-63, Ernst & Ernst, Mpls., 1963-64; lectr. U. Minn., 1962-66; instr. Augsburg Coll., 1966-67; asst. prof. Mich. State U., East Lansing, Mich., 1968-72, assoc. prof., 1972-77, acting dept. chmn. acctg., 1976-77, prof., 1977—, dir. acad. initiatives for Ctr. for Internat: Bus. Edn., 1990-91, Price Waterhouse Auditing prof., 1978—, chmn. dept. acctg., 1994—. Tchr. auditing to local grain officials in China, June, 1986; lectr. at Univs. in Beijing, Shanghai, Wuhan, Chengdu, China; Jackarta, Jojakarta, Indonesia; Singapore; Bangkok, Thailand; Kuala Lumpur, Malaysia, 1988; guest spkr. Young Accts. Meeting, Kolding, Denmark, 1989, Copenhagen, Denmark, 1991, U. Denmark, Aarhus and Kolding, 1989, Oslo Sch. of Bus., 1989; tchr. Norwegian Sch. of Econs. and Bus. Adminstrn., Bergen, Norway, 1989; guest spkr. Conv. of Nat. Changchi U. and Fedn. of CPAs in Republic of China, Tapei, Taiwan, June, 1991, at Erasmus U., Rotterdam, the Netherlands, 1992; mem. evaluation team bus. sch. United Arab Emirates U., Al Ain, 1989, 90, 92; mem. vis. team to Bus. Sch. DeLaSalle U., Manila, 1993; co-chair Price Waterhouse Auditing Conf., 1988, Auditing Symposium, San Francisco, 1993; seminar leader Arthur Anderson's Symposium, St. Charles, Ill., 1992, 94; mem. Nat. Assn. State Bds. of Accountancy, 1988-89, Auditing Standards Bd. Attestation Compliance Guidance Task Force, 1991-94, Going Concern Task Force, 1992-94, Agreed Upon Procedures Task Force, 1994; mem. acad. adv. bd. Deloitte & Touche, 1991-97. Author: Auditing (CPA Rev. Manual), 1972, Statistical Sampling for Small Audit Clients, 1974, Statistical Sampling: Attributes for Small Audit Clients, 1976, CPA Review Manual, 1979, The Use of Attributes Sampling for Small Audit Clients, 1982; co-author: (with James K. Loebbecke) Auditing: An Integrated Approach, 1976, 6th rev. edit., 1994 (also Canadian, French-Canadian, Singaporean, Australian and Russian versions), Applications of Statistical Sampling to Auditing, 1981; (with D. Dewey Ward) Systems Understanding Aids for Auditing and Financial Accounting, 4th edit., 1995, Systems Understanding Aid-Microcomputer Version, 1985, 3d edit. 1989, (with David S. Kerr) Integrated Audit Practice Case, 1993; contbr. articles to profl. jours and chpts. to books. With U.S. Army, 1955-57. Named Price Waterhouse Auditing Prof., 1978—, Alumnus of Yr., 1993, Beta Alpha Psi, U. Minn., 1993; fellow Arthur Young & Co., 1965, Price Waterhouse & Co, 1966, Ernst & Whinney Dissertation 1967-68; grantee: Ford Found., 1967. Mem. AICPA (mem. statistical sampling in auditing com. 1974-76, sole acad. mem. auditing standards bd. 1992-94, founding ptnr., mng. ptnr. AHI Assocs., 1975—, joint venture with AICPA, 1990—, Educator of Yr. 1993), Am. Acctg Assn. (numerous coms. and offices including pres. auditing sect. 1977-78, mem. exec. com. and sec.-treas. 1983-85, pres. elect 1989-90, pres. 1990-91, Disting. Internat. Visiting Lectr. 1987-88), Mich. Assn. Cert. Pub. Accts. (mem. com. on profl. edn. 1971-74, mandatory continuing edn. com. 1974-75, accounting and auditing com., and industry govt. edn. com. 1975-76, Outstanding Acctg. Educator award 1992, 93), Mich. Soc. Cert. Pub. Accts., Beta Alpha Psi (acct. of yr. award 1995). Office: Mich State U Eli Broad Coll Bus Dept Acctg East Lansing MI 48824-1121

ARIS, RUTHERFORD, applied mathematician, educator; b. Bournemouth, Eng., Sept. 15, 1929; came to U.S., 1955, naturalized, 1962; s. Algernon Pollock and Janet (Elford) A.; m. Claire Mercedes Holman, Jan. 1, 1958. B.Sc. (spl.) with 1st class honours in Math, London (Eng.) U., 1948, Ph.D., 1960, D.Sc., 1964; student, Edinburgh (Scotland) U., 1948-50; D.Sc. (hon.), U. Exeter, 1984, Clarkson U., 1985; DEng honoris causa, U. Notre Dame, 1990; Ch.M., fellow, Inst. Math. Appications, 1992; D Engring. honoris causa, Tech. U., Athens, Greece. Tech. officer Billingham div. I.C.I. Ltd., 1950-55; research fellow U. Minn., 1955-56; lectr. tech. math. Edinburgh U., 1956-58; mem. faculty U. Minn., 1958—, prof. chem. engring., 1963—, Regents' prof., 1978-96, Regents prof. emeritus, 1996—. O.A. Hougen vis. prof. U. Wis., 1979; Sherman Fairchild Disting. scholar Calif. Inst. Tech., 1980-81; cons. to industry, lectr., 1961—; IXth Centennial lectr. in chem. engring. U. Bologna, 1988; mem. Inst. for Advanced Study, Princeton, 1994. Author: Optimal Design of Chemical Reactors, 1961, Vectors, Tensors and the Basic Equations of Fluid Mechanics, 1962, reprint edit., 1989, Discrete Dynamic Programming, 1964, Introduction to the Analysis of Chemical Reactors, 1965, Elementary Chemical Reactor Analysis, 1969, reprint edit., 1990, (with N.R. Amundson) First-Order Partial Differential Equations with Applications, 1973, reprint 1999, (with W. Strieder) Variational Methods Applied to Problems of Diffusion and Reaction, 1973, The Mathematical Theory of Diffusion and Reaction in Permeable Catalysts, 1975, Mathematical Modelling Techniques, 1978, 2d edit., 1994, Chemical Engineering in the University Context, 1982; co-editor: Springs of Scientific Creativity, 1982, An Index of Scripts for E.A. Lowe's Codices Latini Antiquiores, 1982, (with Amundson and Rhee) First-order Partial Differential Equations, Vol. I Theory and Applications of Single Equations, 1986, Vol. II Theory and Applications of Systems of Quasilinear Hyperbolic Equations, 1986, 2d edit., 2002, Explicatio Formarum Litterarum*The Unfolding of Letterforms, 1990, (with K. Alhumaizi) Surveying A Dynamical System: The Gray/Scott Reaction In A Two-Phase Reactor, 1995, Mathematical Modeling--A Chemical Engineer's Perspective, 1999. Recipient E. Harris Harbison award for disting. teaching, 1969, Alpha Chi Sigma award Am. Inst. Chem. Engrs., 1969, Chem. Engring. lectr. award Am. Soc. Engring. Edn., 1973, Damköhler medal Deutsche Vereinigung fur Chemie und Verfahrenstechnik, 1991, Richard E. Bellman Control Heritage award Am. Automatic Control Coun., 1992, N.R. Amundson award Internat. Symposium on Chem. Reaction Engring., 1998; sr. rsch. fellow NSF, 1964-65, Guggenheim fellow, 1971-72. Fellow Am. Acad. Arts and Scis., Inst. Math. and Applications, Instn. of Chem. Engring. (hon.); mem. NAE, Soc. Nat. Philosophy, Soc. Indsl. and Applied Math., AIChE (R.H. Wilhelm award 1975, Inst. lectr. 1997, Founders award 1999), Mediaeval Acad. Lutheran. Office: Univ Minn Dept Chem Engring & Materials Sci Minneapolis MN 55455 E-mail: raris@umn.edu.

ARMBRUSTER, BOB, radio personality; b. Louisiana, Mo. m. Trila Fugman. BA, Principia Coll.; MA, Lindenwood U. Announcer, traffic manager Classic 99, St. Louis. Avocation: kite flying. Office: Classic 99 85 Founders Ln Saint Louis MO 63105

ARMBRUSTER, JEFFRY J. state legislator; b. Normal, OH, Aug. 30, 1947; BS, Milliken U., 1969. Mayor North Ridgeville (OH); pres. Pinzone-Armbruster, Inc.; mem. Ohio Senate from 13th dist., Columbus, 1999—, North Ridgeville City Coun. Mem. Westlake C. of C., North Ridgeville C. of C., Greater Cleveland Growth Assn. (COSE). Recipient Shell Inner Cir. of Success. Mem. OH Assn. Retail Mchts., Loraine County Farm Bur. Office: Senate Bldg 13th Dist State House Room 142 1st Fl Columbus OH 43215

ARMITAGE, JAMES O. medical educator; b. L.A., Dec. 19, 1946; m. Nancy Elaine Roker, Aug. 12, 1967; children: Amy Jolane, Gregory Olen, Anne Marie, Joel Donald. BS, U. Nebr., Lincoln, 1969; MD, U. Nebr., Omaha, 1973. Diplomate in internal medicine, med. oncology and hematology Am. Bd. Internal Medicine. Med. intern U. Nebr. Med. Ctr., Omaha, 1973-74, resident in internal medicine, 1974-75; fellow hematology/oncology U. Iowa Hosps. and Clinics, Iowa City, 1975-77; clin. asst. prof. medicine U. Nebr. Coll. Medicine, Omaha, 1977-79, assoc. prof., 1982-87, vice chmn. dept. internal medicine, 1982-90; from assoc. prof. to prof. internal medicine Epley Inst. for Rsch. in Cancer and Allied Diseases, 1985—; chief sect. oncology/hematology U. Nebr. Coll. Medicine, 1986-89, prof. internal medicine, 1987—, chmn. dept. internal medicine, 1990-99, dean, 2000—; pvt. practice hematology/oncology, 1977-79. Contbr. articles to profl. jours. Recipient Sir William Osler Teaching award, 1988, Arnold Ungerman-Robert Lubin Cancer Rsch. award, 1993, Richard and Hinda Rosenthal Found. award, 1996, numerous others. Fellow ACP, Am. Assn. Cancer Rsch., Am. Soc. Blood and Marrow Transplantation, Am. Soc. Clin. Oncology, Am. Soc. Hematology, Am. Fedn. for Clin. Rsch., Assn. Profs. Medicine, Ctrl. Soc. for Clin. Rsch., European Soc. Med. Oncology, Internat. Soc. Exptl. Hematology, Nebr. Med. Assn., Met. Omaha Med. Soc., Midwest Blood Club, Royal Coll. Physicians Edinburgh, Internat. Soc. for Hematotherapy and Graft Engring., European Hematology Soc., Phi Beta Kappa, Sigma Xi, Alpha Omega Alpha, others. Office: U Nebr Med Ctr Dept Internal Medicine 986545 Nebr Med Ctr Omaha NE 68198-0001

ARMITAGE, KENNETH BARCLAY, biology educator, ecologist; b. Steubenville, Ohio, Apr. 18, 1925; s. Albert Kenneth and Virginia Ethel (Barclay) A.; m. Katie Lou Hart, June 5, 1953; children: Karole, Keith, Kevin BS summa cum laude, Bethany Coll., W.Va., 1949; MS, U. Wis.-Madison, 1951, PhD, 1954. Instr. U. Wis.-Green Bay, 1954-55; instr. U. Wis.-Wausau, 1955-56; asst. prof. biology U. Kans., Lawrence, 1956-62, assoc. prof., 1962-66, prof., 1966-96, William J. Baumgartner disting. prof., 1987-96, chmn. dept. systematics & ecology, 1982-88, dir. environ. studies program, 1976-82, dir. exptl. and applied ecology program, 1974-94, prof. emeritus, 1996—. Vis. prof. U. Modena, Italy, 1989; mem. com. examiners Grad. Record Exam. Biology Test, 1986-92, chmn., 1988-92; sr. investigator Rocky Mountain Biol. Lab., Gothic, Colo., 1962—, trustee, 1969-86, pres. bd. trustees, 1985-86; cons. Vancouver Island Marmot Recovery Program. Author: (lab. manual) Investigations in General Biology, (with others) Principles of Modern Biology; contbr. articles to profl. jours.; co-editor 3d Internat. Marmot Conf. proceedings; mem. editl. bd.: Ethology, Ecology and Evolution, 1989—, Ibex Jour. Mountain Ecology, 1994—, Oecologia Montana, 1996—; sci. editor: Die Mummeltiere der Welt. Pres. Douglas County chpt. Zero Population Growth, 1969-71; bd. dirs. Children's Hour, Inc., Lawrence, 1969-70; v.p. Mt. Oread Fund, Lawrence, 1998—. Recipient Antarctic medal NSF, 1968, Edn. Service award U. Kans., 1979, Alumni Achievement award Bethany Coll., 1989. Fellow AAAS, Animal Behavior Soc.; mem. Am. Soc. Naturalists (treas. 1984-86), Am. Inst. Biol. Scis. (mem. task force for 90s), Ecol. Soc. Am., Am. Soc. Zoologists, Am. Soc. Mammalogists (C. Hart Merriam award 1997), Orgn. Biol. Field Stations (v.p. 1986-87, pres. 1988-89), Sigma Xi, Phi Beta Kappa, Beta Beta Beta, Gamma Sigma

Kappa. Avocations: stamp collecting, gardening, natural history, western history. Home: 505 Ohio St Lawrence KS 66044-2245 Office: U Kans Dept Ecology & Evolutionary Biology Lawrence KS 66045-7534 E-mail: marmots@ukans.edu.

ARMITAGE, THOMAS EDWARD, library director; b. Torrington, Wyo., Dec. 11, 1946; s. Ross Eugene Armitage and Mary Kathleen (Donley) Wieland; m. Linda Lou Theisen, May 23, 1987; children: Anne, Nicholas, Rachel. AA in History, Santa Barbara (Calif.) C.C., 1971; BA in History, Kans. State U., Pittsburg, 1973; MLS, U. Mo., 1974. Asst. dir. Ottumwa (Iowa) Pub. Libr., 1975-77; libr. dir. Ft. Dodge (Iowa) Pub. Libr., 1977-86, Cedar Rapids (Iowa) Pub. Libr., 1987—. With USN, 1967-69. Mem. ALA, Iowa Libr. Assn., Iowa Urban Pub. Libr. Assn. (pres. 1999—, sec. 1995-98), Linn County Libr. Assn. (v.p. 1993—), Linn County Libr. Consortium (sec. 1995—), Rotary, Greater Cedar Rapids C. of C. Office: Cedar Rapids Pub Libr 500 1st St SE Cedar Rapids IA 52401-2002

ARMSTRONG, DANIEL WAYNE, chemist, educator; b. Ft. Wayne, Ind., Nov. 2, 1949; s. Robert Eugene and Nila Louise (Koeneman) A.; m. Linda Marilyn Todd, June 11, 1972; children: Lincoln Thomas, Ross Alexander, Colleen Victoria. BS, Washington and Lee U., 1972; MS in Chem. Oceanography, Tex. A&M U., 1974, PhD in Chemistry, 1977. Prof. Bowdoin Coll., Brunswick, Maine, 1978-79, Georgetown U., Washington, 1980-83, Tex. Tech. U., Lubbock, 1983-87; Curators' disting. prof., head ctr. environ. sci. and tech.; head dept. analytical chemistry U. Mo., Rolla, 1987-2000; Caldwell prof. chemistry, dept. chair Iowa State U., 2000—. Bd dirs. Advanced Separations Techs., Whippany, N.J.; Moreton lectr. Millsaps Coll., 2001. Host Univ. Forum Radio Show, Washington, 1981-83; writer, host weekly radio show We're Sci. Nat. Pub. Radio, 1993—; author film, radio shows; contbr. articles to profl. publs.; patentee in field. Recipient Tchg. Excellence award U. Mo., 1985, 88, 89, 92, 94, Faculty Excellence award U. Mo., 1988, 89, Martin medal, 1991, EAS Chromatography award, 1990, Isco award, 1992, Presdl. award for rsch. and creativity, 1993, Perkin Elmer award for CE, 1994, R&D 100 award R&D Mag., 1995, Benedetti-Pichler award Am. Microchem. Soc. 1996, Helen M. Free award for pub. outreach, 1998, CLDG merit award for separations, 2001, Moreton lectureship, Millsaps Coll., 2001, Weber medal for contbns. to pharm. sci., 2001; grantee Rsch. Corp., 1979, Petroleum Rsch. Fund, 1979, 91, NSF, 1981; Rsch. grantee Whatman Corp., 1981, Dept. Energy, 1984, 87, 91, 94, Dow Chem., 1985-90, NIH, 1986, 91, 95, 2000, EPA, 1995, Shell Co., 1989, 90-92. Fellow Am. Assn. Pharm. Scientists; mem. Am. Chem. Soc. (49th Midwest award for chemistry 1993, award in chromatography 1999), Slovak Pharm. Soc. (hon.), Sigma Xi, Phi Lambda Upsilon. Office: Iowa State U Dept Chemistry Gilman Hall Ames IA 50011 E-mail: sec4dwa@iastate.edu.

ARMSTRONG, DOUGLAS DEAN, journalist; b. Wichita, Kans., Mar. 12, 1945; s. H. Glenn and Emma F. (Starkey) A.; m. Paige Prillaman, Jan. 3, 1967 (div. Sept. 1982); children: David Douglas, Christine Elizabeth; m. Mary Alyce Dooley, Mar. 8, 1987; children: Patrick Glenn, Gillian Marie. BA, U. Minn., 1967. Entertainment writer Milw. Jour. Sentinel, 1967-72, editl. writer, 1972-74, consumer writer, 1974-81, movie critic, 1981-95, bus. writer, 1995-2000, personal fin. columnist, 1995-2000. Guest lectr. U. Wis., Milw., 1982-89; movie reviewer WISN-TV, Milw., 1984-85; movie critic WKTI-FM, Milw., 1989-97; pres. Lexington Software Corp., 1996—. Contbr. short fiction to Ellery Queen's Mystery Mag., Alfred Hitchcock's Mystery Mag., Boys' Life. Recipient Pub. Interest award Ctr. for Pub. Representation, 1978. Mem. Mystery Writrs Am., Milw. Press Club. Avocations: video, piano, golf. Office: PO Box 170374 Milwaukee WI 53217-8031

ARMSTRONG, EDWIN RICHARD, lawyer, publisher, editor; b. Chgo., Sept. 25, 1921; BA, Knox Coll., 1942; JD, Northwestern U., 1948. Ptnr. Reimers & Armstrong, 1949-55; assoc. Friedman & Friedman, 1957-62; ptnr. Friedman, Armstrong & Donnelly, 1962-78, Armstrong & Donnelly, Chgo., 1978—. Home: 860 N Lake Shore Dr Apt 17M Chicago IL 60611-1788 Office: 77 W Washington St Ste 515 Chicago IL 60602-2802

ARMSTRONG, J. HORD, III, pharmaceutical company executive; Chmn. bd., CEO D&K Healthcare Resources, Inc., Saint Louis, 1993—. Office: D&K Healthcare Resources Inc 8000 Maryland Ste 920 Saint Louis MO 63105

ARMSTRONG, NEIL A. former astronaut; b. Wapakoneta, Ohio, Aug. 5, 1930; s. Stephen A.; children: Eric, Mark. B.S. In Aero. Engring., Purdue U., 1955; M.S. in Aero. Engring., U. So. Calif. With Lewis Flight Propulsion Lab., NACA, 1955; then aero. research pilot for NACA (later NASA, High Speed Flight Sta.), Edwards, Calif.; astronaut Manned Spacecraft Center, NASA, Houston, 1962-70; command pilot Gemini 8; comdr. Apollo 11; dep. assoc. adminstr. for aeros. Office Advanced Research and Tech., Hdqrs. NASA, Washington, 1970-71; prof. aerospace engring. U. Cin., 1971-79; chmn. AIL Sys., Inc., 1989-2000, EDO Corp., 2000—. Mem. Pres.'s Commn. on Space Shuttle, 1986, Nat. Commn. on Space, 1985-86. Served as naval aviator USN, 1949-52, Korea. Recipient numerous awards, including Octave Chanute award Inst. Aero. Scis., 1962, Presdl. Medal for Freedom, 1969, Exceptional Service medal NASA, Hubbard Gold medal Nat. Geog. Soc., 1970, Kitty Hawk Meml. award, 1969, Pere Marquette medal, 1969, Arthur S. Fleming award, 1970, Congl. Space Medal of Honor, Explorers Club medal. Fellow AIAA (hon., Astronautics award 1966), Internat. Astronautical Fedn. (hon.), Soc. Exptl. Test Pilots; mem. Nat. Acad. Engring. Office: EDO CORPORATION 60 EAST 42nd St Ste 5010 New York NY 10165

ARMSTRONG, THEODORE MORELOCK, financial executive; b. St. Louis, July 22, 1939; s. Theodore Roosevelt and Vassar Fambrough (Morelock) A.; m. Carol Mercer Robert, Sept. 7, 1963; children: Evelyn Anne, Robert Theodore. BA, Yale U., 1961; LLB, Duke U., 1964. Bar: Mo. 1964. With Miss. River Transmission Corp. and affiliated cos., 1964-85; corp. sec. Mo. Pacific Corp., 1971-75, River Cement Co., 1968-75; asst. v.p. Miss. River Transmission Corp., 1974-75, v.p. gas supply, 1975-79, exec. v.p., 1979-83, pres., chief exec. officer, 1983-85; exec. v.p. Natural Gas Pipeline of Am., 1985; sr. v.p. fin. and adminstrn., chief fin. officer Angelica Corp., St. Louis, 1986—. Bd. dir. UMB Bank of St. Louis, Gen. Am. Capital Co. Bd. dirs., pres. Boys and Girls Town Mo.; past pres. Tenn. Soc. St. Louis; mem. St. Louis County Boundary Commn.; former alderman City of Frontenac; past pres. Ctrl. Inst. for Deaf. Mem. ABA, Mo. Bar Assn., St. Louis Bar Assn., Bellerive Country Club, Saint Louis Club (bd. dirs.), Yale Club (St. Louis, N.Y.C.), Phi Alpha Delta. Republican. Presbyterian. Home: 43 Countryside Ln Saint Louis MO 63131-3310 Office: Angelica Corp 424 S Woods Mill Rd Chesterfield MO 63017-3406 E-mail: tarmstrong@angelica.com.

ARNESON, GEORGE STEPHEN, manufacturing company executive, management consultant; b. St. Paul, Apr. 3, 1925; s. Oscar and Louvia Irene (Clare) A.; children: George Stephen, Deborah Clare, Diane Elizabeth, Frederick Oscar. BS in Marine Transp., U.S. Mcht. Marine Acad., 1945; BEE, U. Minn., 1949. Certified mgmt. cons. Sales engr. Hubbard & Co., Chgo., 1949-54; cons. Booz, Allen & Hamilton, 1954-57; mgr. mktg. cons. services, dir. mktg., plant mgr. Borg-Warner Corp., 1957-60; asst. gen. mgr., then v.p., gen. mgr. Delta-Star Electric div. H.K. Porter Co., Inc., Pitts., 1960-63, v.p., gen. mgr. elec. divs., 1963-65; v.p. mktg. Wheeling Steel Corp., 1965-66; pres., chief exec. officer Vendo Co., Kansas City, Mo., 1966-72, also dir., chmn. exec. com.; pres., chmn. Dun-Lap Mfg. Co., Newton, Iowa, 1973-77; pres. Arneson & Co., Overland Park, Kans., 1974—. Contbr. articles on mgmt. cons., bus. valuation and appraisal of mgmt. to profl. jours. Chmn. adv. bd. Kans. Dept. Corrections, Topeka, 1980-92. Lt. (j.g.) USNR, 1943-46. Recipient Outstanding Alumnus award U.S. Mcht. Marine Acad., 1968, Past Dir. award Automatic Merchandising Assn. Mem. Phi Gamma Delta (life), Alpha Phi Omega (life). Presbyterian. Clubs: Masons, KT, Shriners. Home: 3031 Shrine Park Rd Leavenworth KS 66048-4806 E-mail: georgearneson@yahoo.com.

ARNEY, RANDALL, artistic director; Artistic dir. Steppenwolf Theatre Co., Chgo., now ensemble mem. Office: 1650 N Halsted St Chicago IL 60614-5518

ARNOLD, A. JOEL, pharmaceuticals company executive; Grad., Ohio State U. Registered pharmacist. Various positions in retail drug industry; dir. merchandising and ops. Drug Emporium, Inc., 1993-95, sr. v.p., 1995—. Office: 155 Hidden Ravines Dr Powell OH 43065-8739

ARNOLD, ALLEN D. academic administrator; b. Lebanon, Pa., Apr. 4, 1943; s. Henry J. and Mary (Heisey) A.; m. Judith Moreland, Aug. 1, 1970; children: Caroline, David. BA in English and Philosophy, U. Scranton, 1965; MA in English, Vanderbilt U., 1971; EdD, Va. Poly. Inst. and State U., 1980. Instr. English Lebanon Valley Coll., Annville, Pa., 1967-68, Cath. U. Puerto Rico, Ponce, 1969-71; assoc. prof. English Dabney Lancaster Community Coll., Clifton Forge, Va., 1973-77, asst. chmn. devel. studies, dir. spl. svcs., 1977-79, div. chair humanities and sponsored programs, 1979-83; dir. humanities div. Lakeland Community Coll., Mentor, Ohio, 1983-85, dean, 1986-87; v.p. acad. affairs Triton Coll., River Grove, Ill., 1987-88, exec. v.p., 1988-95; pres., dean Charles S. Mott C.C., Flint, Mich., 1995—. Editor: New Directions for Community Colleges: Alternative Funding Sources, 1989, (newsletter) Fusions, 1989-90. Bd. dirs. Oak Park (Ill.) Housing Ctr., 1989-90. Mem. Rotary. Office: Charles S Mott CC 1401 E Court St Flint MI 48503-6208

ARNOLD, GARY L. retail executive; b. Ft. Wayne, Ind. married; 5 children. Mgr. mktg. svcs. firm; various positions Hollywood Records, Trans World Music Corp., Disc Records; merchandise mgr. music Best Buy Co., 1994-96, v.p. mktg., 1996—2001; pres. Redline Entertainment, 2001—. Avocations: cooking, gardening. Office: 7075 Flying Cloud Dr Eden Prairie MN 55344-3532 E-mail: info@redline-entertainment.com.

ARNOLD, JEROME GILBERT, lawyer; s. Edward F. and Annastacia (Thielen) A.; m. Judith Lindor, Dec. 18, 1971; children: Thomas, Mark, John, Jason, Maria. BS, U. Minn., 1964; LLB, U. N.D., 1967. Bar: Minn. 1967, S.D. 1967, U.S. Dist. Ct. S.D. 1967, U.S. Dist. Ct. Minn. 1973, U.S. Ct. Appeals (8th cir.) 1986. Law clk. U.S. Dist. Ct., Aberdeen, S.D., 1967-68; asst. city atty. City of Duluth, Minn., 1968-69; asst. county atty. St. Louis County, Duluth, 1969-70, chief criminal prosecutor, 1970-71; spl. asst. to county atty. County of Carlton, Minn., 1971; ptnr. Hunt & Arnold, Duluth, 1971-86; U.S. atty. U.S. Dist. Ct. Minn., Mpls., 1986-91; ptnr. Larson, Husby. Brodin & Arnold, Duluth, Md., 1992-93; compensation judge State of Minn., 1993—. Mem. adv. com. Supreme Ct. Appointments, St. Paul, 1980; chmn. selection com. 6th Jud. Dist., Duluth, 1978-83. Chmn. St. Louis City (Minn.) Bd. Adjustment, 1978-82; Rep. nominee 8th Congl. Dist, Minn., 1974; mem. state steering com. Reagan for Pres., 1976, 80, 84. Mem. Fed. Bar Assn. (bd. dirs. 1986-91), Minn. Bar Assn. Roman Catholic. Avocations: fishing, hunting.

ARNOLD, JOHN FOX, lawyer; b. St. Louis, Sept. 17, 1937; s. John Anderson and Mildred Chapin (Fox) A.; m. Martha Ann Freeman, June 29, 1963 (div. Oct. 1993); children: Lisa A. Galena, Laura Wray, Lynne A. Binder, Lesli Johnston. AB, U. Mo., 1959, LLB, 1961. Bar: Mo. 1961, U.S. Dist. Ct. (ea. dist.) Mo. 1961, U.S. Ct. Appeals (8th cir.) 1961, U.S. Supreme Ct. 1971. Ptnr. Green, Hennings, Henry & Arnold, St. Louis, 1963-70; mem. Lashly & Baer, P.C., 1970—, chmn., 1987—. Mem. St. Louis County (Mo.) Charter Revision Com., 1968; chmn. St. Louis County Bd. Election Commrs., 1981—86; chmn. bd. dirs. Downtown St. Louis Inc., 1996—98, Downtown St. Louis Partnership, Inc., 1997—99; chmn. bd. overseers Lindenwood U., 1992—93, bd. dirs., 1993—95. Lt. USAR, 1961—63. Recipient citation of merit U. Mo. Law Sch., Columbia, 1984. Fellow Am. Bar Found.; mem. ABA (mem. house of dels. 1986-90), Bar Assn. Met. St. Louis (pres. 1975-76), Mo. Bar (pres. 1984-85), Nat. Conf. Commrs. on Uniform State Laws (drafting com. Securities Act, Partnership Act, article 2 sales, 2A leases and 8 investment securities of Uniform Comml. Code), Am. Law Inst. Republican. Office: Lashly & Baer 714 Locust St Saint Louis MO 63101-1699 E-mail: jfarnold@lashlybaer.com.

ARNOLD, PERI ETHAN, political scientist; b. Chgo., Sept. 21, 1942; s. Joseph Evon and Eve (Jacobs) A.; m. Beverly Ann Kessler, Aug. 22, 1965; children: Emma, Rachel. BA, Roosevelt U., Chgo., 1964; MA, U. Chgo., 1967, PhD, 1972. Lectr. Roosevelt U., Chgo., 1966-68; instr. polit. sci. Western Mich. U., Kalamazoo, 1970-71; asst. prof. polit. sci. U. Notre Dame, Ind., 1971-76, assoc. prof. govt., 1976-86, prof. of govt. and internat. studies, 1986; chair dept. govt., 1986-92. Compton vis. prof. of world politics Miller Ctr., U. Va., 1993-94; dir. Hesburgh Program in Pub. Svc., 1995-2001; dir. Notre Dame Semester in Washington, 1997-2001. Author: Making the Managerial Presidency, 1986 (Louis Brownlow Book award 1987), 2nd rev. ed., 1998; mem. editl. bd. Am. Jour. Polit. Sci., 1991-94, Polity, 1995—, Presdl. Studies Quar., 1997—; co-editor Jour. of Policy History, 1987-88; contbr. articles to profl. jours. and edited vols. Bd. dirs. South Bend Hebrew Day Sch., Mishawaka, Ind., 1985-88; chair Comty. Rels. Coun. of Jewish Fedn. of St. Joseph Valley, South Bend, Ind., 1990-94; bd. trustees Congregation Beth El, South Bend, 1994-2000, sec. and exec. com., 2000-2002; mem. acquisitions com. Snite Mus. Art, Notre Dame, Ind., 1994-99; bd. dirs. Jewish Fedn. of St. Joseph Valley, 1999—, v.p., 2001—. Recipient Spl. Presdl. award U. Notre Dame, 1993, Marshall Dimock award Am. Soc. Pub. Adminstrn., 1996; grantee Am. Coun. Learned Socs., 1974; rsch. grantee Herbert Hoover Libr. Assn., 1993-94; Ford Found. fellow, 1978-81. Mem. Am. Polit. Sci. Assn. (program chmn., exec. com. presidency sect.), Midwest Polit. Sci. Assn., The Cliff Dwellers Club (Chgo.). Democrat. Jewish. Avocations: literature, music, drama. Home: 1419 E Colfax Ave South Bend IN 46617-3307 Office: U Notre Dame Dept Govt Internat Studies Notre Dame IN 46556 E-mail: peri.e.arnold.1@nd.edu.

ARNOULD, RICHARD JULIUS, economist, educator, consultant; b. Rochelle, Ill., Nov. 18, 1941; s. Elliott and Blanch (Colwell) A.; m. Carol Foster, Aug. 27, 1960; children: Debra, Laura. BS, Iowa State U., 1963, MS, 1965, PhD, 1968. Instr. Iowa State U., Ames, 1963-65; asst. prof. econs. and bus. adminstrn. U. Ill., Champaign, 1967-72, assoc. prof., 1973-82, prof., 1982—, dir. Coll. Rsch. Office, 1995-96, assoc. dean for acad. affairs, Coll. Commerce and Bus. Adminstrn., 1979-87, prof. econs., Coll. Medicine, 1984—, adj. prof. Inst. of Govt. and Pub. Affairs, 1987—, head dept. econs., 1996—, dir. Program in Health Econs., Mgmt. & Policy, 1989—. Acting dir. Exec. Devel. Ctr., part-time 1982, 84, mem. Med. Scholars Steering Com., active numerous other univ., coll. and dept. coms.; rsch. economist pricing and competition grp., USDA, 1965-67; vice chmn. Dept. Econs., U. Ill., 1970-73; vis. economist Econ. Policy Office, U.S. Justice Dept., 1973-74; regional economist U.S. Comptroller of Currency, 1976-79; vis. rsch. prof. Duke U., 1977-78; vis. rsch. scholar York (Eng.) U.; cons. Carle Found., chmn. bd., 1989-91; mem. Gov's Task Force on Health Care Reform, 1992-95; cons. Auditor Gen. State of Ill., GAO, Health Care Financing Adminstrn., Anti-trust div. U.S. Justice Dept., ABA, AMA, Prepaid Legal Svcs. Inst., others; bd. dirs. First Busey Trust & Investment Co.; expert witness numerous law firms; speaker profl. meetings. Author: Extra Territorial Application and Effects of Certain U.S. and Canadian Laws, 1978, (monograph) Blue Shield Fee Setting in the Physicians' Service Market: A Theoretical and Empirical Analysis, (pamphlets) Diversification and Profitability Among Large Food Processing Firms, USDA, 1970, (with R. Resek) A Comparative Cost Study of Staff Panel and Participating Attorney Panel Prepaid Legal Servcie Plans, ABA, 1982; editor spl. issue Quar. Rev. of Econs. and Bus., 1990, also book chpts. and revs.; co-editor: (with R. Rich and W. White) Competitive Approaches to Health Care Reform, 1993; contbr. numerous articles to profl. jours. Bd. dirs. City Bank Champaign, First Basey Trust and Investment Co.; trustee Carle Found., 1981-93, chmn. fin. com., 1982-86, chmn. bd., 1989-91; elder 1st Presbyn. Ch., Champaign; mem. Gov.'s Task Force on Health Care Reform; mem. U.S. Govt. Study of Econ. Underpinning of Vaccine Markets. Brookings Inst. Econ. Policy fellow, 1973; recipient Outstanding Service award, U.S. Justice Dept., 1974; grantee Internat. Bur. Edn., 1979, Carle Found., 1982-83, Grad. Research Bd., 1983-86; named Outstanding Tchr. U. Ill. various yrs. Mem. Am. Econ. Assn., So. Econ. Assn., Internat. Health Econs. Assn., Midwest Econ. Assn. Avocation: golf. Office: U Ill 1206 S 6th St Champaign IL 61820-6978 E-mail: rarnould@uiuc.edu.

ARNOVE, ROBERT FREDERICK, education educator; b. Chgo. s. Isadore and Julie (Zeplowitz) A.; m. Toby Strout; 1 child, Anthony Keats BA, U. Mich., 1969; MA, Tufts U., 1961; PhD, Stanford U., 1969. Vol. tchr. Peace Corps, Venezuela, 1962-64; Ford Found. edn. advisor Bogota, Colombia, 1969-71; prof. comparative edn. Ind. U., Bloomington, 1969—, Ind. U.-Hangzhou, People's Rep. China, 1983; vis. prof. Stanford U., McGill U. Edn. cons. to Latin Am. ministries and agys.; dir. Overseas Study Program of Ind., Purdue, and Wis. univs. in Madrid, 1989—; USIA Exch. scholar, Ryazan, Russia, 1996, Yaounde, Cameroon, 1997, Salamanca, Spain, 2001; UNESCO-chair vis. scholar U. Palermo, Buenos Aires, 1997-2001. Author, editor, co-editor: Student Alienation, Educational Television, Education and American Culture Comparative Education, Philanthropy and Cultural Imperialism, Education and Revolution in Nicaragua, National Literacy Campaign: Historical and Comparative Perspectives, Emergent Issues in Education: Comparative Perspectives, Education as Contested Terrain: Nicaragua 1979-93, 1994, Comparative education: The Dialectic of the Global and the Local, 1999; prodr. documentary film Alternative Public Schools, 1978, Asi Fue: Election Time Nicaragua, 1984; also articles. Citizens Party candidate for U.S. Congress, 8th dist. Ind., 1982 Fulbright grantee, India, 1982; Fulbright lectr. Fed. U. Bahai, Brazil, 1995. Mem. Comparative and Internat. Edn. Soc. (pres., 2001), Latin Am. Studies Assn., Am. Ednl. Rsch. Assn. Phi Delta Kappa. Office: Ind U Sch Edn Bloomington IN 47405 E-mail: arnove@indiana.edu.

ARNSTEIN, WALTER LEONARD, historian, educator; b. Stuttgart, Germany, May 14, 1930; arrived in U.S., 1939, naturalized, 1944; s. Richard and Charlotte (Heymann) A.; m. Charlotte Culver Sutphen, June 8, 1952; children: Sylvia, Peter. B.S.S., CCNY, 1951; M.A., Columbia U., 1954; Ph.D., Northwestern U., 1961; postgrad., U. London, Eng., 1956-57. Asst. prof. history Roosevelt U., Chgo., 1957-62, assoc. prof., 1962-66, prof., acting dean grad. div., 1966-67; prof. history U. Ill., Urbana, 1968-98, LAS Jubilee prof. history, 1989-98, prof. history and LAS Jubilee prof. history emeritus, 1998—, chmn. dept., 1974-78, assoc. Ctr. for Advanced Study, 1972-73. Vis. assoc. prof. history Northwestern U., 1963—64; vis. fellow Clare Hall, Cambridge U., 1982; hon. fellow U. Edinburgh, 1989. Author: The Bradlaugh Case: A Study in Late Victorian Opinion and Politics, 1965, 2d edit., 1984, Britain Yesterday and Today, 1966, 8th edit., 2001, Protestant Versus Catholic in Mid-Victorian England, 1982, (with the late William B. Willcox) The Age of Aristocracy, 3d edit., 1976, 8th edit., 2001, Queen Victoria, 2002; editor: The Past Speaks: Sources and Problems in British History Since 1688, 1981, 2d edit. 1993; editor: Recent Historians of Great Britain, 1990; bd. editors The Historian, 1976-2000, Am. Hist. Rev., 1982-85, Albion, 1988-93; mem. bd. advisers: Victorian Studies, 1966-75; contbr. articles profl. jours. Vice chmn. Ill. Humanities Council, 1983-84. Served with AUS, 1951-53, Korea. Fulbright scholar, 1956-57; Fellow Am. Council Learned Socs., 1967-68 Fellow Royal Hist. Soc.; mem. Am. Hist. Assn., Brit. Hist. Assn., N.Am. Conf. Brit. Studies (exec. com. 1971-76, v.p. 1993-95, pres. 1995-97), Midwest Conf. on Brit. Studies (pres. 1980-82), Midwest Victorian Studies Assn. (pres. 1977-80), Phi Beta Kappa, Phi Alpha Theta. Home: 804 W Green St Champaign IL 61820-5017 Office: U Ill Dept History 309 N Gregory Hall 810 S Wright St Urbana IL 61801-3644 E-mail: warnstei@uiuc.edu.

ARONSON, HOWARD ISAAC, linguist, educator; b. Chgo., Mar. 5, 1936; s. Abe and Jean A. B.A., U. Ill., 1956; M.A., Ind. U., 1958, Ph.D., 1961. Asst. prof. Slavic langs. and lit. U. Wis., Madison, 1961-62; asst. prof. Slavic linguistics U. Chgo., 1962-65, assoc. prof. depts. slavic langs. and lit. and linguistics, 1965-73, prof., 1973—2002, chmn. dept. linguistics, 1972-80, prof. emeritus, 2002—, chmn. dept. Slavic langs. and lits., 1983-91, 2000-01. Editor: Annual of the Society for the Study of Caucasia, 1989—. Mem. Am. Assn. Advancement Slavic Studies, Am. Assn. Tchrs. Slavic and East European Langs. Jewish. E-mail;. Home: 415 W Aldine Ave Apt 7B Chicago IL 60657-3601 Office: U Chgo Dept Slavic Langs and Lit Chicago IL 60637 E-mail: hia5@midway.uchicago.edu.

ARONSON, VIRGINIA L. lawyer; b. Bremerton, Wash., June 4, 1947; BA, U. Chgo., 1969, MA, 1973, JD, 1975. Bar: Ill. 1975. Ptnr. Sidley Austin Brown & Wood, Chgo. Staff mem. U. Chgo. Law Review, 1974—75; mem. exec. & mgmt. com. Sidley Austin Brown & Wood. Contbr. articles to profl. jours. Mem. Am. Coll. Real Estate Lawyers, Chgo. Mortgage Atty.'s Assn., Chgo. Fin. Exchange, The Chgo. Network (dir. Chgo. ctrl. area com., Chgo. Pub. Edn. Fund). Office: Sidley Austin Brown & Wood Bank One Plz 10 South Dearborn St Chicago IL 60603

ARORA, JASBIR SINGH, engineering educator; b. Tarn-Taran, India, Apr. 13, 1943; came to U.S., 1965; naturalized 1977; m. Rita Arora, June 21, 1972. BS in Engring. with honors, Punjab U., India, 1964; MS, Kans. State U., 1967; PhD, U. Iowa, 1971. Asst. prof. G.N. Engring Coll., Ludhiana, India, 1964-65; from asst. prof. to prof. U. Iowa, Iowa City, 1972—2002, F. Wendell Miller disting. prof. engring., 2002—. Author: Introduction to Optimum Design, 1989; co-author: Applied Optimal Design, 1979; contbr. articles to profl. jours. Fellow: ASCE, ASME; mem.: AIAA (sr.). Home: 2980 Dubuque St NE Iowa City IA 52240-7915 Office: U Iowa # 4106 SC Iowa City IA 52242 E-mail: jasbir-arora@uiowa.edu.

ARPINO, GERALD PETER, performing company executive; b. Staten Island, N.Y., Jan. 14, 1928; s. Luigi and Anna (Santanastasio) A. Student, Wagner Coll., PhD (hon.), 1980; student ballet under Mary Ann Wells, student modern dance under May O'Donnell and Gertrude Shurr. Dancer Ballet Russe, 1951-52; co-founder Joffrey Ballet, 1956, dancer, to 1962, former assoc. artistic dir., now artistic dir., resident choreographer, until 1990; with faculty Joffrey Ballet Sch. N.Y.C., from 1953, now artistic dir., assoc. dir., to 1988, prin. choreographer, to 1988. Bd. dirs. Dance Notation Bur., Dancers in Transition; mem. adv. coun. to dept. dance Calif. State U., Long Beach, also mem. Disting. Artists Forum. Choreographer ballets including Incubus, 1962, Viva Vivaldi!, 1965, Olympics, Nightwings, both 1966, Cello Concerto, Arcs and Angels, Elegy, all 1967, Secret Places, The Clowns, Fanfarita, A Light Fantastic, 1968, Animus, The Poppet, 1969, Confetti, Solarwind, Trinity, all 1970, Reflections, Valentine, Kettentanz, all 1971, Chabriesque, Sacred Grove on Mount Talmalpais, both 1972, Jackpot, 1973, The Relativity of Icarus, 1974, Drums, Dreams on Banjos, 1975, Orpheus Times Light 2, 1976, Touch Me, 1977, Choura, L'Air d 'Esprit, Suite Saint-Saens, all 1978, Epode, 1979, Celebration, 1980, Ropes, Partita for Four, Sea Shadow, Diverdissement, 1980, Light Rain, 1981, Round of Angels, 1982, Italian Suite, Quarter-Tones, 1983, Jamboree (commd. by City of San Antonio) Adv. Sportsmedicine Edn. & Rsch. Found., L.A.; mem. adv. com. N.Y. Internat. Festival of the Arts; mem. nat. adv. coun. ITI/USA Internat. Ballet Competition; mem. hon. com. The Yard Benefit-Vineyard Celebration, 1989; mng. dir., bd. dirs. Found. for Joffrey Balllet, Inc. Served with USCG, 1945-48. Recipient Dancemagazine award, 1974, Bravo award San Antonio Performing Arts Assn., 1984, Disting. Achievement award Nat. Orgn. Italian-Am. Women, 1987, Tiffany award Internat. Soc. Performing Arts Adminstrs., 1989, Outstanding Artistic Achievement award Staten Island Coun. on Arts, 1990, Ammy award Am. Express Corp. Office: Joffrey Ballet Chgo 70 E Lake St Fl 1300 Chicago IL 60601-5917

ARRINGTON, MICHAEL BROWNE, company executive; b. Chgo., Mar. 24, 1943; s. W. Russell and Ruth Marian (Browne) A.; m. DeEtta Jane Watson, Dec. 15, 1966 (div. 1969); m. Trudi Jeanne Robertson, Dec. 4, 1971 (div. 1992); children: Jennifer Lorraine, Patrick Browne. AA, Kendall Coll., Evanston, Ill.; BA in Polit. Sci., U. Ill. Adminstrv. asst. to Senate Majority Leader State of Ill., Springfield, 1966-67; dir. pub. affairs Union League Club of Chgo., 1967-68; exec. dir. South Loop Improvement Orgn., Chgo., 1968-69; pres., chief exec. officer The Arrington Found., 1979—, Arrington Travel Ctr., Inc., Chgo., 1969-99, Recon Mgmt Svcs., Evanston, Ill., 1999—. Mem. Nat. White House Conf. Travel and Tourism, Disting. Entrepreneurship Bd., U. Ill., Chgo. Bd. dirs. Robert R. McCormick Chgo. Boys & Girls Club, 1982—, Friends of Prentice Hosp., Chgo., 1986—; mem. chancellor's adv. bd. U. Ill., Chgo. Cpl. USMC, 1962-64. Named finalist Entrepreneur of Yr., 1989, 1990, Man of Yr., Ill. Vietnam Vets Leadership Program, 1993; named to Hall of Fame, Nat. Assn. Trade and Tech. Schs., 1988, Entrepreneurship Hall of Fame, 1994; recipient Excellence in Phys. Fitness award, USMC, 1962, Significant Contbn.. to Dental Health award, Ill. Dental Health Soc., 1967. Mem. World Pres.'s Orgn., Econ. Club of Chgo., Chgo. Club, Union League, Westmoreland Country Club, 100 Club Cook County, Chgo. Pres.'s Orgn., Chief Execs. Orgn. Republican. Episcopalian. Avocations: golf, boating, skiing, scuba diving. Office: Recon Mgmt Svcs Inc 929 Edgemere Ct Evanston IL 60202-1428 E-mail: arringtonusa@ameritech.net.

ARTEST, RON, professional basketball player; Profl. basketball player Chicago Bulls, 1999—. Office: Indiana Pacers Market St Arena 300 E Market St Fl 1 Indianapolis IN 46204-2603*

ARTH, LAWRENCE JOSEPH, insurance executive; b. Lincoln, Nebr., July 8, 1943; s. William John and Josephine Marie (Willie) A.; children: Laura, Susan, William. BBA, U. Nebr., 1965, MA in Bus. Adminstrn., 1969. Asst. v.p. securities Bankers Life Ins. Co. Nebr., Lincoln, 1973-78, 2nd v.p. fin., 1978-83, v.p. fin., 1983, v.p. fin. treas., 1983-85, sr. v.p. investents, treas., 1985-88; chmn. Ameritas Investment Advisors, Inc., 1986—; pres., COO Ameritas Life Ins. Corp., 1988-94, chmn., CEO, 1995—, Ameritas Acacia Mutual Holding Co., Lincoln, 1999—. Fellow Fin. Analysts Fedn.; mem. Omaha/Lincoln Soc. Fin. Analysts (bd. dirs. 1978-84, pres. 1983-84), Lincoln C. of C. (chmn. 1997), Lincoln Country Club (bd. dirs. 1984-87). Republican. Roman Catholic. Avocations: hunting, fishing, golf, tennis. Office: Ameritas Life Ins Corp PO Box 81889 Lincoln NE 68501-1889

ARTNER, ALAN GUSTAV, art critic, journalist; b. Chgo., May 14, 1947; s. Gustav and Katherine Rose (Lucas) A. B.A., Northwestern U., 1968, M.A., 1969. Apprentice music critic Chgo. Tribune, 1972-73, art critic, 1973—; contbg. editor The Art Gallery Mag., 1975-76; corr. Artnews Mag., 1977-80. Contbr. to Playbill, 1994—. Decorated Chevalier de l'ordre des Arts et des Lettres; Rockefeller Found. grantee, 1971-72 Office: Chgo Tribune Co 435 N Michigan Ave Chicago IL 60611-4066

ARTZT, EDWIN LEWIS, consumer products company executive; b. N.Y.C., Apr. 15, 1930; s. William and Ida A.; m. Ruth Nadine Martin, May 12, 1950; children: Wendy Anne, Karen Susan, William M., Laura Grace, Elizabeth Louise. BS, U. Oreg., 1951. Account exec. Glasser Gailey Advt. Agy., L.A., 1952-53; with Procter & Gamble Co., Cin., 1953-95, brand mgr. advt. dept., 1955-58, assoc. brand promotion mgr., 1958-60, brand promotion mgr., 1960, 62-65, copy mgr., 1960-62, mgr. advt. dept. paper products div., 1965-68, mgr. food products divsn., 1968-69, v.p. food products divsn., 1969-70, v.p., acting mgr. coffee div., 1970, v.p., group exec., 1970-75, bd. dirs., 1972-75, 80-95, exec. v.p. then vice chmn. internat. ops., 1980-89, group v.p. European ops. Europe, Belgium, 1975-80; pres. Procter & Gamble Internat., 1984-89, chmn., chief exec. officer, 1995-99. Bd. dir. GTE Corp., Delta Air Lines, Am. Express Co., Spalding Holdings Corp., Barilla G.e R.F.lli S.p.A., Italy, Am. Inst. for Contemporary German Studies, Am. Enterprise Inst. for Public Policy Rsch. Bd.; mem. Internat. Adv. Bd. Babson Coll. Internat. councilor Ctr. for Strategic and Internat. Studies, Washington; mem. Coun. on Fgn. Rels., The Jackson Hole Land Trust; bd. trustees Cin. Inst. of Fine Arts; mem. exec. com. The Business Coun.; past chmn. residential div. United Appeal; past chmn. Public Library Capital Funds campaign; past dist. chmn. Capital Fund Raising dr. Boy Scouts Am., past leadership tng. chmn.; past chmn. advt. com. Sch. Tax Levy, County Govt. Issue; past trustee Kansas City Philharmonic, Nutrition Found., Boys' Clubs Greater Cin.; past bd. dirs. Kansas City Lyric Theater; past bd. govs. Kansas City Art Inst. Recipient Martin Luther King, Jr. Salute to Greatness award, 1995, Leadership Conf. on Civil Rights Private Sector Leadership award, 1995; inducted to Nat. Sales Hall of Fame, 1995, Advt. Hall of Fame, 1996. Mem. Am. C. of C. Belgium (v.p.), Conf. Bd. Europe (adv. council), Internat. C. of C. (exec. com. U.S. council), Nat. Fgn. Trade Council, Queen City Club, Commercial Club, Camargo Club, Teton Pines Club. Clubs: Queen City (Cin.), Cin. Country (Cin.), Comml. (Cin.). Office: Procter & Gamble Co 1 Procter And Gamble Plz Cincinnati OH 45202-3393

ARZBAECHER, ROBERT C(HARLES), research institute executive, electrical engineer, researcher; b. Chgo., Oct. 28, 1931; s. Hugo L. and Caroline G. A.; m. Joan Collins, June 16, 1956; children: Carolyn, Robert, Mary Beth, Jean, Thomas. B.S., Fournier Inst., 1953; M.S., U. Ill., 1958; Ph.D., 1960. Asst. prof. elec. engring. Christian Bros. Coll., Memphis, 1960-63, assoc. prof., 1963-67; assoc. prof. elec. engring. U. Ill.-Chgo., 1967-70, prof., 1970-76; chmn. dept. elec. engring. U. Iowa, Iowa City, 1976-81; dir. Pritzker Inst. Med. Engring., Ill. Inst. Tech., Chgo., 1981—; v.p. U. Iowa Research Found., 1978-81; pres. Arzco. Inc., Chgo., 1980-87. Contbr. articles to profl. jours.; inventor Arzco pill electrode. Trustee Ill. Cancer Coun., Chgo., 1981-92. Fellow IEEE, Am. Coll. Cardiology, Am. Inst. Med. Biol. Engring. Home: 5757 N Sheridan Rd Chicago IL 60660-4746 Office: Ill Inst Tech Pritzker Inst Med Engr 10 E 32nd St Chicago IL 60616-3813

ASCH, SUSAN MCCLELLAN, pediatrician; b. Cleve., Dec. 31, 1945; d. William Alton and Alice Lonore (Heide) McClellan; m. Marc Asch, Sept. 10, 1966; children: Marc William, Sarah Susan, Rebecca Janney. AB, Oberlin (Ohio) Coll., 1967; MA, Mich. State U., 1968, PhD, 1975; MD, Case Western Res., 1977. Diplomate Nat. Bd. Med. Examiners, Am. Bd. Pediatrics, Am. Bd. Emergency Pediatrics. Instr. sociology Mich. State U., East Lansing, 1971-73; resident in pediatrics Children's Nat. Med. Ctr., Washington, 1977-80, chief resident in ambulatory and emergency pediatrics, 1979-80; asst. to dir. Office for Med. Applications of Rsch. NIH, Bethesda, 1980-81; pvt. practice in pediatrics Millinocket (Maine) Regional Hosp., 1981-84; assoc. dir. emergency Akron (Ohio) Children's Hosp., 1984-87; asst. prof. pediatrics Northeastern Ohio U. Coll. Medicine, 1984-87; dir. emergency St. Paul Children's Hosp., 1987-91; asst. prof. pediatrics U. Minn., 1987-93, clin. asst. prof., 1993—; pvt. practice pediatrics Stillwater, Minn., 1992—. Nat. faculty PALS Am. Heart Assn., Mpls., Dallas, 1987-94; mem. task force, sub-bd. emergency pediatrics Am. Bd. Pediatrics, 1987-93. Assoc. editor Pediatric Emergency Medicine, 1992, contbr., 1992, 96. State bd. dirs., nat. and affiliate faculty PALS Minn. affiliate Am. Heart Assn., 1988—; chmn. SIDS task force, Minn. Dept. Maternal and Child Health, St. Paul, 1990-92. Mem. Am. Acad. Pediatrics (nat. faculty advanced pediatric life support 1989—, exec. com. sect. on emergency pediatrics 1988-90, chair Minn. emergency pediatric com. 1989-91, nat. svc. commendation 1991), Minn. Med. Assn. (emergency svcs. com. 1990, ho. of dels. 1994), Alpha Omega Alpha. Democrat. Quaker. Avocations: travel, quarter horses. Home: 34 N Oaks Rd North Oaks MN 55127-6325 Office: Stillwater Med Group 921 Greeley St S Stillwater MN 55082-5935

ASCHAUER, CHARLES JOSEPH, JR. corporate director, former company executive; b. Decatur, Ill., July 23, 1928; s. Charles Joseph and Beulah Diehl (Kniple) A.; m. Elizabeth Claire Meagher, Apr. 28, 1962; children: Karen A. Vorwald, Thomas Arthur, Susan A. Baisley, Karl Andrew. B.B.A., Northwestern U., 1950; certificate internat. bus. adminstr., Centre d'Etudes Industrielles, Geneva, Switzerland, 1951. Prin. McKinsey & Co., Chgo., 1955-62; v.p. mktg. Mead Johnson Labs. div. Mead Johnson & Co., Evansville, Ind., 1962-67; v.p., pres. automotive group Maremont Corp., Chgo., 1967-70; v.p., group exec. Whittaker Corp., Los Angeles, 1970-71; v.p., pres. hosp. products div. Abbott Labs., North Chicago, Ill., 1971-76, v.p., group exec., 1976-79, exec. v.p., dir., 1979-89, ret., 1989. Bd. dirs. Collateral Therapeutics, Inc., San Diego, Solar Comm., Naperville, Ill. Lt. Supply Corps, USNR, 1951-55. Mem.: Shadow Wood Country Club, Sunset Ridge Country Club, Econs. Club Chgo., Univ. Club Chgo.

ASH, J. MARSHALL, mathematician, educator; b. N.Y.C., Feb. 18, 1940; s. Barney and Rosalyn (Hain) A.; m. Alison Igo, Nov. 24, 1977; children: Michael A., Garrett A., Andrew A. SB, U. Chgo., 1961, SM, 1963, PhD, 1966. Joseph Fels Ritt instr. Columbia U., N.Y.C., 1966-69; asst. prof. math. DePaul U., Chgo., 1970-72, assoc. prof., 1972-74, prof., 1975—. Vis. prof. Stanford U., 1977. Author: Studies in Harmonic Analysis, 1976; contbr. articles to profl. jours. George Westinghouse fellow, 1961, NSF fellow, 1962-66. Mem. AAUP, Am. Math. Soc., Math. Assn. Am., Sigma Xi. Home: 662 Maple St Winnetka IL 60093-2312 Office: De Paul U Math Dept Chicago IL 60614 E-mail: mash@math.depaul.edu.

ASH, MAJOR MCKINLEY, JR. dentist, educator; b. Bellaire, Mich., Apr. 7, 1921; s. Major McKinley Sr. and Helen Marguerite (Early) A.; m. Fayola Foltz, Sept. 2, 1947; children: George McKinley, Carolyn Marguerite, Jeffrey LeRoy, Thomas Edward. BS, Mich. State U., 1947; DDS, Emory U., 1951; MS, U. Mich., 1954; Doctoris Medicine Honoris Causa, U. Bern, 1975. Instr. sch. dentistry Emory U., Atlanta, 1952-53; instr. U. Mich., Ann Arbor, 1953-56, asst. prof., 1956-59, assoc. prof., 1959-62, prof., 1962—, chmn. dept. occlusion, sch. dentistry, 1962-89, dir. stomatognathic physiology lab., sch. dentistry, 1969-89, dir. TMJ/oral facial pain clinic, sch. dentistry, 1983-89, Marcus L. Ward prof. dentistry, 1984-89, prof. emeritus, rsch. scientist emeritus, 1989—; cons. N.E. Regional Dental Bd., 1988-92. Vis. prof. U. Bern, 1989, U. Tex., San Antonio, 1990-98; pres. Basic Sci. Bd., State of Mich., 1962-74; cons. over the counter drugs FDA, Washington, 1985-89. Author, co-author 69 textbooks, 1958—; editor 4 books; contbr. over 186 articles to profl. jours. Served to tech. sgt. Signal Corps, U.S. Army, 1942-45, ETO. Nat. Inst. Dental Research grantee, 1962-85. Fellow Am. Coll. Dentists, Internat. Coll. Dentists, European Soc. Craniomandibular Disorders, European Soc. Oral Physiology; mem. AAAS, Am. Dental Assn. (cons. coun. on dental therapeutics 1982—, cons. coun. sci. affairs 1995—), N.Y. Acad. Scis., Washtenaw Dist. Dental Soc. (pres. 1963-64), Phi Kappa Phi. Presbyterian. Avocations: photography, bird watching. Office: U of Mich Sch of Dentistry Ann Arbor MI 48109 E-mail: mmash@umich.edu.

ASHCROFT, JOHN DAVID, attorney general; b. Chgo., May 9, 1942; m. Janet Elise; children: Martha, Jay, Andrew. B cum laude, Yale U., 1964; JD, U. Chgo., 1967. Bar: Mo., U.S. Supreme Ct. Assoc. prof. S.W. Mo. State U., Springfield, 1967-72; pvt. practice, 1967-73; state auditor State of Mo., 1973-75, asst. atty. gen., 1975-77, atty. gen., 1977-84, gov., 1985-92; atty. Suelthaus and Kaplan P.C., 1993-94; U.S. senator from Mo., 1995-2001; U.S. atty. gen. U.S. Dept. Justice, 2001—. Mem. commerce, sci. and transp. coms., aviation subcom., comm. subcom., chmn. consumer affairs, fgn. commerce & tourism subcom., mfg. and competitiveness subcom., mem. fgn. rels. com., European affairs subcom., Near Ea. & South Asian affairs subcom., Western Hemisphere Peace Corps subcom., mem. jud. com., chmn. constitution, fedn. and property rights subcom.; mem. Presdl. Adv. Coun. Intergovtl. Affairs, The Pres.'s Export Coun.; nat. chmn. Edn. Commn. States, 1987-88, Jud. Com., Subcom., chmn. constn.; chmn. Nat. Govs. Assn. Task Force on Coll. Quality, 1985, Nat. Govs. Assn. Task Force on Adult Literacy; co-chair Renewal Alliance. Gospel singer: records include In the Spirit of Life and Liberty, The Gospel According to John; author: Lessons from a Father to a Son, 1998, (with wife) College Law for Business, 7th, 8th, 9th, 10, 11th edits., It's the Law, 1979-91; contbr. articles to profl. jours. Chmn. Task Force on Adult Literacy, Task Force on College Quality Nat. Gov.'s Assn., 1991; chmn. Rep. Gov.'s Assn., 1990; co-chmn. Rep. Platform Com., 1992. Recipient Nat. Sheriffs Assn. award, 1996; named Christian Statesman of Yr., 1996. Mem. ABA (ho. of dels.), Mo. Bar Assn., Cole County Bar Assn., Nat. Assn. Attys. Gen. (pres. 1980-81, chmn. budget com., exec. com., Wyman award 1983), Nat. Govs. Assn. (vice chmn. 1990, chmn. 1991-92, chmn. Pres.'s Commn. on Urban Families 1992). Republican. Mem. Assembly of God Ch. Office: US Dept Justice 950 Pennsylvania Ave NW Washington DC 20530

ASHE, ARTHUR JAMES, III, chemistry educator; b. N.Y.C., Aug. 5, 1940; s. Arthur James and Helen Louise (Hawelka) A.; m. Penelope Guerard Vaughan, Aug. 25, 1962; children: Arthur J., Christopher V. B.A., Yale U., 1962, M.S., 1965, Ph.D., 1966; postgrad., Cambridge U., 1962-63. Asst. prof. chemistry U. Mich., Ann Arbor, 1966-71, assoc. prof., 1971-76, prof., 1976—, chmn. dept., 1983-86, prof. macromolecular sci. and engring., 2000—. Vis. scientist Phys. Chemistry Inst., U. Basle, Switzerland, 1974 Mem. editorial avd. bds. profl. jours, 1984—. Alfred P. Sloan fellow, 1972-76 Mem. Am. Chem. Soc. Office: U Mich Dept Chemistry Ann Arbor MI 48109 E-mail: ajashe@umich.edu.

ASHENFELTER, DAVID LOUIS, reporter; b. Toledo, Oct. 20, 1948; s. Duaine Louis and Betty Jean A.; m. Barbara Ann Dinwieddie, Feb. 22, 1974. B.S. in Edn., Ind. U., 1971. Reporter Kokomo Morning Times, Ind., 1966-67, Bloomington Daily Herald-Telephone, 1968-69, Bloomington Courier-Tribune, 1970-71, Detroit News, 1971-82, Detroit Free Press, 1982—. Recipient Disting. Svc. award Soc. Profl. Journalists, 1981, 83, 85, Pulitzer prize for meritorious pub. service Columbia U., 1982, Silver Gavel award ABA, 1986, Worth Bingham Prize, 1986, and more than 40 local, state and nat. newswriting awards; named to Mich. Journalism Hall of Fame. Mem. Sigma Chi. Office: Detroit Free Press 600 W Fort St Detroit MI 48226-2706 E-mail: ashenf@freepress.com.

ASHER, FREDERICK M. art educator, art historian; Pref., chmn. dept art history U. Minn., Mpls. Mem.: Am. Inst. Indian Studies (pres.), Coll. Art Assn. (mem. program com.). Office: U Minn Dept Art History 340 Heller Hall 271 19th Ave S Minneapolis MN 55455

ASHLEY, RENEE, creative writing educator, consultant; b. Palo Alto, Calif., Aug. 10, 1949; BA in English with honors, BA in French, BA in World and Comparative Lit., San Francisco State U., 1979, MA, 1981. Instr. creative writing West Milford (N.J.) Cmty. Sch., 1983-85; creative writing instructor, cons. artist residencies Rockland Ctr. for Arts, West Nyack, N.Y., 1985—; mem. MFA in Creative Writing faculty Fairleigh Dickinson U., 2001—. Author: Salt, 1991 (Brittingham prize in Poetry 1991), The Various Reasons of Light, 1998, The Revisionist's Dream, 2001; contbr. to anthologies including Touching Fire: Erotic Writings by Women, 1989, What's a Nice Girl Like You?, 1992, Breaking Up Is Hard to Do, 1994, Dog Music, 1996, (textbook) Writing Poems, 1995; contbr. to American Voice, Antioch Rev., Harvard Rev., Kenyon Rev., Poetry. Fellow N.J. State Coun. Arts, 1985, 89, 94, Yaddo, Saratoga Springs, N.Y., 1990, McDowell Colony, Peterborogh, N.H., 1993-94, NEA, 1997-98; grantee Poets and Writers, Inc., 1986, N.Y. State Coun. Arts, 1986; recipient Washington prize in poetry Word Works, Inc., 1986, Lit. Excellence award, Kenyon Review, 1990, 92, Pushcart prize, 2000. Mem. MLA, Acad. Am. Poets, Poetry Soc. Am. (Ruth Lake Meml. award 1987, Robert H. Winner award 1989). Office: care Publicity Dir U Wis U Wis Press 2537 Daniels St Madison WI 53718-6772 E-mail: reneea@bellatlantic.net.

ASHMAN, CHARLES H. retired minister; b. Johnstown, Pa., June 1, 1924; s. Charles H. Sr. and Flora A.; m. Frances Marie Bradley, July 12, 1946; children: Kenneth W., Judy Ashman Fairman, Karl W. BA cum laude, Westmont Coll., 1947; MDiv magna cum laude, Grace Theol. Seminary, Winona Lake, Ind., 1950. Ordained to ministry Grace Brethren Ch., 1950. Sr. pastor Grace Brethren Ch., Rittman, Ohio, 1950-55, Phoenix, 1955-62, Winona Lake, Ind., 1962-89, pastor emeritus, 1989—; asst. coord. Fellowship of Grace Brethren Chs., 1979—. Prof. Grace Theol. Sem., 1969-89. Mem. Nat. Fellowship Grace Brethren Ministers (pres. 1984, Pastor of Yr. 1989, moderator nat. conf. 1973-74), Kiwanis (pres. 1991-92). Home: 1531 S Cherry Creek Ln Warsaw IN 46580-7691 Office: Fellowship Grace Brethren PO Box 386 Winona Lake IN 46590-0386 E-mail: charlesashman@fgbc.org.

ASHMAN, MARTIN C. federal judge; b. 1931; m. Betty Ashman; two children. JD, DePaul U., 1953. Bar: Ill. 1953, U.S. Supreme Ct. 1959. Atty. Ashman & Jaffe, 1954-70, Martin C. Ashman, Ltd., 1970-87; commr. Ill. Ct. Claims, 1974-87; corp. counsel Village of Morton Grove, Ill., 1977-87; cir. judge domestic rels. divsn., law divsn. State of Ill., 1987-95; magistrate judge U.S. Dist. Ct. (no. dist.) Ill., 1995—. Vol. Legal Svcs. Found., Chgo. Recipient Spl. Tribute award Ill. Coun. Against Handgun Violence; Outstanding Svc. to Legal Profession award, DePaul U. Law Sch., 2001. Mem. ABA, Fed. Bar Assn., Fed. Magistrate Judges Assn., Ill. State Bar Assn., Decalogue Soc. Lawyers, Chgo. Bar Assn. (Cert. of Appreciation). Office: US Dist Ct 1366 Dirksen Bldg 219 S Dearborn St Chicago IL 60604-1800

ASHMUS, KEITH ALLEN, lawyer; b. Cleve., Aug. 19, 1949; s. Richard A. and Rita (Petti) A.; m. Marie Sachiko Matsuoka, Dec. 15, 1973; children: Emmy Marie, Christopher Todd. BA in Policy Sci., Mich. State U., 1971, MA in Econs., 1972; JD, Yale U., 1974. Bar: Ohio 1974, Calif. 1991, U.S. Dist. Ct. (no. dist.) Ohio 1975, U.S. Dist. Ct. (no., so. and cen. dists.) Calif. 1991, U.S. Dist. Ct. (so. dist.) Ohio 2000, U.S. Ct. Appeals (6th cir.) 1975, U.S. Supreme Ct. 1980. Assoc. Thompson Hine & Flory LLP, Cleve., 1974-82, ptnr., 1982—, ptnr.-in-chg. Cleve. office, 1996-99, dept. chmn., 1999-2000; founding ptnr. Frantz Ward LLP, 2000—. Mediator/arbitrator Am. Arbitration Assn. Comml. Employment Panels, 1995—. Co-author: Public Sector Collective Bargaining: The Ohio System, 1984. Trustee community arts Baycrafters, Bay Village, Ohio, 1981-84, Hospice Council No. Ohio, 1982-84, Inst. for Personal Health Skills, Cleve. 1985-90; trustee Coun. Smaller Enterprises, 1990-96, 98—, 1st vice chmn., 2000-2001, chmn., 2001--; trustee Village Found., 1997—, Vocat. Guidance Svcs. 1999-2002. Youth Opportunities Unltd., 2000—, Cleve. Saves, 2001—; sec. George W. Codrington Charitable Found., 1994-2000; chmn. job placement for older persons Skills Available, Cleve., 1980-87; gov.'s appointee to Health Care Quality Adv. Coun., 1996; mem. adv. bd. Greater Cleve. Salvation Army, 1997—, treas., 2000-01, vice chmn., 2001—. Named one of Outstanding Vols. award Nat. Hospice Orgn., 1982, Vol. of Yr. Vocat. Guidance and Rehab. Services, 1985, 86. Mem. ABA, State Bar Calif., Ohio Bar Assn. (coun. dels. 1995—, bd. govs. 1998-2001, pres.-elect 2002), Cleve. Bar Assn. (trustee 1985-88, 98—, chmn. labor law sect. 1983-84), Def. Rsch. Inst., Pub. Sector Labor Rels. Assn. (exec. com. 1989-93). Avocations: golf, fishing. Office: Frantz Ward LLP 55 Public Sq 19th Fl Cleveland OH 44113-1999 E-mail: kashmus@frantzward.com.

ASHWORTH, JULIE, elementary education educator; Tchr. Hawthorne Elem. Sch., Sioux Falls, S.D., 1990—. Participant Internat. Space Camp, Huntsville, Ala., 1993; S.D. tchr. participant Goals 2000 Forum, U.S. Dept. Edn., Washington, 1993; mem. S.D. Gov.'s Adv. Coun. on Cert. for Tchrs., 1994—; mem. exceptional needs standards com. Nat. Bd. for Profl. Tchg. Stds., Washington, 1994—; initiator, organizer S.D. Tchrs. Forum, 1994. Named S.D. Tchr. of Yr., Sioux Falls Sch. Dist., 1992, S.D. Elem. Tchr. of Yr., 1993. Home: 2015 Pendar Ln Sioux Falls SD 57105-3022 Office: Hawthorne Elem Sch 601 N Spring Ave Sioux Falls SD 57104-2721

ASKEY, RICHARD ALLEN, mathematician, educator; b. St. Louis, June 4, 1933; s. Philip Edwin and Bessie May (Yates) Askey; m. Elizabeth Ann Hill, June 14, 1958; children: James, Suzanne. BA, Washington U., St. Louis, 1955; MA, Harvard U., 1956; PhD, Princeton U., 1961. Instr. in math. Washington U., St. Louis, 1958-61; instr. U. Chgo., Chgo., 1961-63; asst. prof. U. Wis., Madison, 1963-65, assoc. prof., 1965-68, prof., 1968-86, Gabor Szego prof., 1986-95, John Bascom prof., 1995—. Author: (book) Orthogonal Polynomials and Special Functions, 1975; author: (with G. E. Andrews and R. Roy) Special Functions, 1999; editor: Theory and Application of Special Functions, 1975, Collected Papers of Gabor Szego, 1982. Fellow Guggenheim, 1969—70. Fellow: AAAS, Am. Acad. Arts and Scis., Indian Acad. Sci. (hon.); mem.: Soc. Indsl. and Applied Math., Math. Assn. Am., Nat. Acad. Sci., Am. Math. Soc. Home: 2105 Regent St Madison WI 53726-3941 Office: U Wis Van Vleck Hall Madison WI 53706 E-mail: askey@math.wisc.edu.

ASP, WILLIAM GEORGE, librarian; b. Hutchinson, Minn., July 4, 1943; s. George William and Blanche Irene (Mattson) A. BA, U. Minn., 1966, MA, 1970; postgrad., U. Iowa, 1972-75. Dir. East Cen. Regional Libr., Cambridge, Minn., 1967-70; asst. prof. Sch. Libr. Sci. U. Iowa, 1970-75; dir. Minn. Office Libr. Devel. and Svcs., St. Paul, 1975-96, Dakota County Libr., Eagan, Minn., 1996—. Mem. Nat. Coun. Quality Continuing Edn. for Info., Libr. and Media Pers., 1979-85; bd. dirs. Bakken Libr. Electricity and Life, Mpls.; vice chmn. White House Conf. on Libr. and Info. Svcs. Task Force, 1980-81, chmn., 1982, mem. adv. com., 1989-91; pres. Continuing Libr. Edn. Network and Exch., 1986-87. Mem. Minn. Regional Network Bd., 1992-96. Mem. ALA (mem. coun. 1985-88, 00-02), Minn. Libr. Assn., Chief Officers State Libr. Agys. (chmn. 1979-80), Minn. Ednl. Media Orgn., Minn. Assn. Continuing and Adult Edn., Assn. Specialized and Coop. Libr. Agys. (pres. 1989-90), Am. Field Svc. Home: 4137 42nd Ave S Minneapolis MN 55406-3530

ASPEN, MARVIN EDWARD, federal judge; b. Chgo., July 11, 1934; s. George Abraham and Helen (Adelson) A.; m. Susan Alona Tubbs, Dec. 18, 1966; children: Jennifer Marion, Jessica Maile, Andrew Joseph. BS in Sociology, Loyola Univ., 1956; JD, Northwestern U., 1958. Bar: Ill. 1958. Individual practice, Chgo., 1958-59; draftsman joint com. to draft new Ill. criminal code Chgo. Bar Assn.-Ill. Bar Assn., 1959-60; asst. state's atty. Cook County, Ill., 1960-63; asst. corp. counsel City of Chgo., 1963-71; pvt. practice law, 1971; judge Cir. Ct. Cook County, Ill., 1971-79; judge ea. divsn. U.S. Dist. Ct. (no. dist.) Ill., Chgo., 1979-95, chief judge, 1995—. Edward Avery Harriman adj. prof. law Northwestern U. Law Sch.; past chmn. new judges, recent devels. in criminal law, and evidence coms. Ill. Judicial Conf., past chmn., adv. bd. Inst. Criminal Justice, John Marshall Sch. Law; past mem. Ill. Law Enforcement Commn., Gov. Ill. Adv. Commn. Criminal Justice, Cook County Bd. Corrections; past chmn. assoc.

rules com. Ill. Supreme Ct., com. on ordinance violation problems; past vice chmn. com. on pattern jury instrns. in criminal cases; lectr. at judicial confs. and trial advocacy programs nationally and internationally; planner, participant in legal seminars at numerous schools including Harvard U., Emory U., U. Fla., Oxford U. (Eng.), U. Bologna, Nuremberg (Germany) U., U. Cairo, Egypt, U. Zimbabwe, U. Malta, U. The Philippines, U. Madrid; past mem. Georgetown U. Law Ctr. Project on Plea Bargaining in U.S., spl. faculty NITA advanced Trial Advocacy Program introducing Brit. trial techniques to experienced Am. litigators, spl. faculty of ABA designed to acquaint Scottish lawyers with modern litigation and tech.; frequent faculty mem. Nat. Judiciary Coll., Fed. Judicial Ctr., U. Nev. (Reno), Nat. Inst. for Trial Advocacy, Colo.; bd. dir. Fed. Judicial Ctr., past chair dir. search com.; past mem. Judicial Conf. Com. on Adminstrn. of the Bankruptcy System, Trial Bar Implementation Com. on Civility of the 7th Fed. Cir.; mem. Northwestern U. Law Bd. Co-author Criminal Law for the Layman-A Citizen's Guide, 2d edit., 1977, Criminal Evidence for the Police, 1972, Protective Security Law, 1983; contbr. over two dozen articles to legal publs. Past mem. vis. com. Northwestern U. Sch. Law, chmn. adv. com. for short courses (post law sch. ednl. program), mem. law bd.; past mem. vis. com. U. Chgo. Law Sch.; mem. vis. com. No. Ill. U. Sch. Law; organizer, past pres. Northwestern Univ. Sch. of Law chpt. Amincourt Program U.S. Judicial Conf; past mem. Cook County Bd. Corrections, John Howard Assn.; active CEELI programs in Bulgaria and Yugoslavia Ford Found. Jud. Tng. Program in China. With USAF, 1958-59; trustee Am. Inns Ct. Recipient Nat. Ctr. Freedom of Info. Studies award, Ctr. for Pub. Resources award, Merit award Northwestern U. Alumni Assn., Herbert Harley award Am. Judicature Soc.; named Person of Yr. Chgo. Lawyer, 1995. Mem. Am. Bar Found. (bd. dirs.), Judicature Soc. Ill. (past chmn. coms.), Chgo. Bar Assn. (bd. mgrs. 1978-79, past chmn. criminal law com., past bd. editors Chgo. Bar Record, mem. commn. on criminal justice. coms. on cont. legal edn., devel. of law, civil disorder and others), Ill. State Bar Assn. (past chmn. pub. rels., corrections, fair trial/free press, criminal law coms., mem. others), Northwestern U. Law Alumni Assn. (past pres., Merit award), ABA (co-chair, sec. of litigation Inst. for Trial practical task force, mem. standing com. on fed. jud. improvements, pres. ABA mus., mem. bd. Am. Bar Fedn., past mem. ABA bd. govs., mem. house dels., past chmn. exec com., mem. bd. editors ABA Jour.), Nat. Conf. Fed. Trial Judges (past mem. coun. sect., past chmn. exec. com. litigation, past chmn., coun. sect. criminal justice, mem. edn. bd. sect. criminal justice mag., past co-chmn. liason jud. com. sect. litigation, mem. jury comprehension study com., ho. dels., standing com. fed. jud. improvements, co-chmn. sect. litigation Inst. Trial Practice Task Force), Am. Inns Ct. Office: US Dist Ct 2548 US Courthouse 219 S Dearborn St Ste 2050 Chicago IL 60604-1800 E-mail: aspen@ilnd.uscourts.gov.

ASPLIN, EDWARD WILLIAM, retired packaging company executive; b. Mpls., June 25, 1922; s. John E. and Alma (Carlbom) A.; m. Eleanor Young Rodgers, Oct. 20, 1951; children— Sarah L., William R., Lynn E. B.B.A., U. Minn., 1943; postgrad., U. Mich., 1947-48, Wayne State, 1949-50, Rutgers U. Sch. Banking, 1957-59. Cost accountant Nat. Bank Detroit, 1947-50; asst. v.p. adminstrn. Northwest Bancorp., Mpls., 1950-59; v.p. mktg. Northwestern Nat. Bank, 1959-67; chmn. Bemis Co., Inc., 1967-88. Advisor Opportunity Ptnrs., Inc.; hon. bd. dirs. Mpls. YMCA, Minn. Hist. Soc.; adv. bd. dirs. U. Minn. Cancer Adv. Bd. Mem. Woodhill County Club, Mpls. Club.

ASTRACHAN, BORIS MORTON, psychiatry educator, consultant; b. N.Y.C., Dec. 1, 1931; s. Isaac and Ethel (Kahn) A.; m. Batja Sanders, June 17, 1956; children: David Isaac, Joseph Henry, Michael Sanders, Ellen Beth Astrachan-Fletcher. BA cum laude, Alfred (N.Y.) U., 1952; MD, Albany Med. Coll., 1956. Lic. Ill.; bd. cert. in psychiatry. Intern, resident USN Hosp., St. Albans and Phila., N.Y., 1956-57, 57-58; asst. depot psychiatrist recruitment tng. depot USMC, Parris Island, S.C., 1958-61; resident in psychiatry dept. psychiatry Yale U., New Haven, 1961-63, from asst. prof. to assoc. prof. dept. psychiatry, 1963-71; dir. Conn. Mental Health Ctr., 1971-87; prof. dept. psychiatry Yale U., 1971-90; prof., head dept. psychiatry U. Ill., Chgo., 1990-98, disting. prof. psychiatry, 1998—2001, disting. prof. emeritus psychiatry, 2001—. Mem. NIMH Initial Rev. Group, Rockville, Md., 1987-90, chmn., 1989-91; mem. IBM Mental Health Adv. Bd., White Plains, N.Y., 1990—; mem. adv. bd. Alcohol, Drug Addiction, Mental Health Adminstrn., Washington, 1985-86; mem. rsch. task force Pres. Commn. on Mental Health and Illness, Washington, 1977-78; vis. prof. U. Rotterdam, Amsterdam, 1986, Boston U., 1996. Co-author: (with Tischler) Quality Assurance in Mental Health, 1983; contbr. articles to profl. jours. (Citation classic 1986). Mem. State Health Clin. Coordinating Com., Hartford, Conn., 1980s; mem. clin. adv. com. Ill. Dept. Mental Health and Devel. Disabilities, Chgo., 1995-97; chair mental health task force Ill. Dept. Children and Family Svcs., Chgo., 1993-97; chair Mental Health Svc. Sys. Adv. Coun., Springfield and Chgo., Ill., 1992-95. Lt. comdr. USN, 1955-61. Recipient Disting. Faculty award U. Ill., Chgo., 1997; named Alumnus of Yr., Albany Med. Coll., 1999. Fellow Am. Coll. Psychiatrists, Am. Psychiat. Assn. (life, trustee-at-large, Adminstrv. Psychiatry award 1995), Am. Assn. Psychiat. Adminstrs. (Past. Pres. award 1992); mem. AMA. Jewish. Avocations: time with family, listening to music, reading. Home: 333 E Ontario St Apt 2902B Chicago IL 60611-4882 Office: Dept Psychiatry M/C 913 912 S Wood St Chicago IL 60612-7325

ATCHISON, CHRISTOPHER GEORGE, public health director; AB in Pol. Sci., Loyola U., Chgo., 1971; MPA, U. Ill., Springfield, 1990; student, Harvard U., 1996. Chief staff Office Lt. Gov., Springfield, Ill., 1978-81; exec. dir. Ill. Rep. State Com., 1981-85; spl. asst. to dir. Ill. Dept. Pub. Health, 1985-87, acting chief epidemiological studies, 1987, asst. dir., 1987-91; dir. Iowa Dept. Pub. Health, Des Moines, 1991-99, Ctr. Pub. Health Practice, U. Iowa, Iowa City, 1999—. Chair One Gift Campaign, Iowa, 1993, Health Data Commn., Iowa, 1993-96, Health Regulation Task Force, Iowa, 1996—; sec. Prospective Minor Parent Program Adv. Commn., Iowa, 1996—; vice chair Long Term Care Coord. Unit, Iowa, 1993—; mem. Iowa Leadership Consortium, 1991-92, Govs. Health Care Reform Council, Iowa, 1993-94. Pub. Health scholar Pub. Health Leadership Inst., 1992-93. Mem. AMA, Am. Pub. Health Assn. (pres. Iowa chpt. 1994-95, Ill. chpt., pub. health medicine steering com. 1995—), Assn. State Territorial Health Ofcls. (pres. 1994-95, chair nominations com. 1995—, exec. com. 1992—, chair primary care com. 1992-93, chair joint council official pub. health agys. 1994-95), N.Y. Acad. Med. (medicine pub. health panel 1996—), Milbank Found. (reforming states group 1995—), Pub. Health Leadership Inst., Am. Soc. Pub. Adminstrn. (Iowa chpt., pres. ctrl. Ill. chpt. 1990-91, exec. council Ill. 1987-91). Office: U Iowa College of Public Health 2700 Steinsler Building Iowa City IA 52242-1008

ATHAS, GUS JAMES, lawyer; b. Chgo., Aug. 6, 1936; s. James G. and Pauline (Parhas) A.; m. Marilyn Carres, July 12, 1964; children: Paula C. Vlahakos, James G., Christopher G. BS, U. Ill., 1958; JD cum laude, Loyola U., Chgo., 1965. Bar: Ill. 1965, U.S. Dist. Ct. (no. dist.) Ill. 1965, U.S. Ct. Appeals (7th cir.) 1970. With Isham, Lincoln & Beale, Chgo., 1965-69; group gen. counsel, asst. sec. ITT, Skokie, Ill., 1969-87; assoc. gen. counsel Itel Corp., Chgo., 1987; sr. v.p., gen. counsel, sec. Eagle Industries, Inc., 1987-97; exec. v.p. adminstrn., gen. counsel, sec. Falcon Bldg. Products, Inc., 1994-99; sr. v.p., gen. counsel Great Am. Mgmt. and Investment, Inc., 1995-97; ptnr. Stamos & Trucco, 2000—. Contbr. articles to profl. jours. 1st lt. U.S. Army, 1958-62. Mem. ABA, Am. Corp. Counsel Assn., Ill. Bar Assn., Chgo. Bar Assn. Greek Orthodox. Home: 1240 Hawthorne Ln Downers Grove IL 60515-4503 Office: Stamos & Trucco Ten North Dearborn 5th Fl Chicago IL 60602

ATKINS, STEVEN, construction executive, contractor; CFO Hunt Constrn. Group, Indpls. Office: Hunt Construction Group PO Box 128 Indianapolis IN 46206 Office Fax: (317) 227-7810.

ATKINSON, RICHARD LEE, JR. internal medicine educator; b. Petersburg, Va., May 15, 1942; s. Richard Lee and Ruth (Scarborough) A.; m. Susan Stayner Hume, Aug. 13, 1966; children: Catherine Crane, Barbara Hill, Deborah Gildea. BA, VA Mil. Inst., 1964; MD, Med. Coll. Va., 1968. Liaison endocrinologist Vanderbilt U., Nashville, 1973-74; adj. asst. prof. UCLA, 1975-77; asst. prof. internal medicine U. Va. Sch. Medicine, Charlottesville, 1977-83; assoc. prof. internal medicine U. Calif., Davis, 1983-87; prof. internal medicine Ea. Va. Med. Sch., Norfolk, 1987-93; assoc. chief staff for rsch. VA Med. Ctr., Hampton, Va., 1987-93; prof. medicine and nutritional scis., dir. Beers-Murphy Clin. Nutrition Ctr. U. Wis., Madison, 1993—. Mem. nutrition study sect. NIH, 1991-95, chair, 1993-95. Contbr. articles to profl. jours. Maj. U.S. Army, 1970—74. Mem. N.Am. Assn. Study Obesity (pres. 1990-91), Am. Soc. Clin. Nutrition (pub. info. com. 1988-91, membership com. 1986-90, pres. 1994-95), Am. Obesity Assn. (pres.). Home: 2132 Vintage Dr Fitchburg WI 53575-1928 Office: U Wis Nutritional Scis Bldg 1415 Linden Dr Madison WI 53706-1527 E-mail: rla@medicine.wisc.edu.

ATKINSON, THOMAS P. environmental engineer; Commd. 2d lt. USAF. Named Fed. Engrs. of Yr., 1998. Mem. NSPE. Office: Minot AFB 5th Svcs Squad 5 SVS/SVtl 201 Summit Dr Minot AFB ND 58705

ATREYA, SUSHIL KUMAR, planetary-space science educator, astrophysicist; b. Apr. 15, 1946; came to U.S., 1966, naturalized, 1975; s. Harvansh Lal and Kailash Vati (Sharma) A.; 1 child Chloè E. ScB, U. Rajasthan, India, 1963, MSc, 1965; MS, Yale U., 1968; PhD, U. Mich., 1973. Rsch. assoc. physics U. Pitts., 1973-74; asst., then assoc. rsch. scientist U. Mich., Ann Arbor, 1974-78, ast. prof., 1978-81, assoc. prof. atmospheric sci., 1981-87, prof. atmospheric and space sci., 1987—, dir. planetary sci. lab. Assoc. prof. U. Paris, 1984-85, vis. prof., 2000-01; vis. sr. rsch. scientist Imperial Coll., London, 1984; mem. sci. and exptl. team Cassini-Huygens Probe to Saturn-Titan, Galileo Jupiter Probe, Nozomi Japanese Mars Mission, Mars Express Mission, Russian Mars '96 and Soviet Phobos projects, Voyager spacecraft missions to the giant planets, Comet Rendezvous/Asteroid Flyby, 1986-92, and SpaceLab I; guest observer/investigator on Hubble Space Telescope, Internat. Ultraviolet Spectrometer and Copernicus Orbiting Astron. Obs.; mem. sci. working groups NASA, Jet Propulsion Lab., European Space Agy. Author: Atmospheres and Ionospheres of the Outer Planets and their Satellites, 1986; editor: Planetary Aeronomy and Astronomy, 1981, Outer Planets, 1989, Cometary Environments, 1989, Origin and Evolution of Planetary and Satellite Atmospheres, 1989; contbr. numerous articles to books and profl. jours. Recipient NASA award for exceptional sci. contbns. Voyager Project, 1981, NASA Group Achievement award for Voyager Ultraviolet Spectrometer Investigations, 1981, 86, 90, NASA Group Achievement awards for Galileo Probe Mass Spectrometer experiment, and for Significant Outstanding Contbns. to the Galileo Probe and Orbiter to Jupiter, Excellence in Rsch. award U. Mich. Coll. Engring., 1995. Mem. AAAS, Internat. Assn. Meteorology and Atmospheric Scis. (pres. commn. planetary atmospheres and their evolution 1987-95, sec. 1983-87), Am. Geophys. Union (assoc. editor Geophys. Rsch. Letters jour. 1986-89), Internat. Astron. Union, Am. Astron. Soc., Internat. Acad. Astronautics (academician 1993—). Office: U Mich Dept Atmospheric Oceanic and Space Sci 2455 Hayward St Ann Arbor MI 48109-2143

ATTERBURY, ROBERT RENNIE, III, lawyer; b. Englewood, N.J., July 11, 1937; s. Robert Rennie Jr. and Beatrice May (Tether) A.; m. Lynda Duer Smith, Sept. 14, 1963; children: Stockton Ward, Kendall C. B. BA, U. Pa., 1960, LLB, 1963. Bar: N.Y. 1963, Ill. 1966. Assoc. Donovan, Leisure, Newton & Irvine, N.Y.C., 1963-66; atty. Caterpillar Tractor Co., Peoria, Ill., 1966-73; sr. atty. Caterpillar Overseas S.A., Geneva, 1973-78; gen. atty. Caterpillar Tractor Co., Peoria, 1978-83; assoc. gen. counsel Caterpillar Inc., 1983-91, v.p., sec., gen. counsel, 1991—. Mem. planning com. Ray Garrett Jr. Corp. and Securities Law Inst., Chgo., 1991—; mem. steering com. Civil Justice Reform Group; mem. adv. bd. Southwestern Legal Found., Internat. and Comparative Law Ctr., 1991—; mem. adv. coun. Asia/Pacific Ctr. for Resolution of Internat. Bus. Disputes, San Francisco, 1991—, corp. exec. bd., gen. counsel roundtable, 1999—; mem. Mfrs. Alliance Law Coun. I., Arlington, Va., 1992-98, vice chair, 1998-99, chair, 1999—; mem. The Forum for U.S.-European Union Legal-Econ. Affairs, Boston, 1995—, large law dept. coun., 1996—; mem. corp. counsel com. Nat. Ctr. for State Cts., 1998—; mem. adv. bd. Georgetown U. Law Ctr. Corp. Cousel Inst., 1999—; dir. Ill Equal Justice Found., 1999—; trustee Eureka Coll., 1999—. Pres. AMC Found., 1991—; bd. dirs. Lakeview Mus. Arts and Scis., 1995—98, vice chmn., 1998—99, chmn., 1999—2001; bd. dirs., sec. Lakeview Mus. Found., 1998—; bd. dirs. Prairie State Legal Svcs., 1998—. Mem. SAR, Am. Judicature Soc. (dir. 1998—), Am. Corp. Counsel Assn., Am. Soc. Corp. Secs., Assn. Gen. Counsel, Country Club Peoria (dir.), Rotary. Home: 315 W Crestwood Dr Peoria IL 61614-7328 Office: Caterpillar Inc 100 NE Adams St Peoria IL 61629-7310

ATWATER, HORACE BREWSTER, JR. retired food company executive; b. Mpls., Apr. 19, 1931; s. Horace Brewster and Eleanor (Cook) A.; m. Martha Joan Clark, May 8, 1955; children: Elizabeth C., Mary M., John C., Joan P. AB, Princeton U., 1952; MBA, Stanford U., 1954. Divisional v.p., dir. mktg. Gen. Mills. Inc., Mpls., 1958-65, mktg. v.p., 1965-70, exec. v.p., 1970-76, chief operating officer, 1976-81, pres., 1977-82, chief exec. officer, 1981-95, chmn. bd., also dir., 1982-95, ret. exec., 1995. Bd. dirs. Amax Mutual Funds. Trustee Mayo Found. Office: 4900 IDS Ctr 80 S 8th St Minneapolis MN 55402-2100

ATWATER, JOHN, news correspondent; b. Chgo. Grad. Journalism and Econs., Northwestern U. Internship Sta. WUWM-FM, Milw., Sta. WISN-TV, Milw.; with pub. rels. dept. Hadley Sch. for the Blind; gen. assignment reporter Sta. WKYT-TV, Lexington, Ky., Sta. WISN-TV, Milw., 2001—. Avocations: being outdoors, biking in summer, snowboarding. Office: Sta WISN PO Box 420 Milwaukee WI 53201-0402*

ATWOOD, HOLLYE STOLZ, lawyer; b. St. Louis, Dec. 25, 1945; d. Robert George and Elise (Sauselle) Stolz; m. Frederick Howard Atwood III, Aug. 12, 1978; children: Katherine Stolz, Jonathan Robert. BA, Washington U., St. Louis, 1968; JD, Washington U., 1973. Bar: Mo. 1973. Jr. ptnr. Bryan Cave, St. Louis, 1973-82, ptnr., 1983—2001, mem. exec. com., 1995-2000, of counsel, 2002—. Bd. dirs. St. Louis coun. Girl Scouts U.S., 1976-86; trustee John Burroughs Sch., St. Louis, 1983-86. Mem. ABA, Met. St. Louis Bar Assn., Washington U. Law Sch. Alumni Assn. (pres. 1983-84). Club: Noonday (St. Louis) (bd. govs. 1983-86). Office: Bryan Cave One Metropolitan Sq 211 N Broadway Saint Louis MO 63102-2733 E-mail: hsatwood@bryancave.com.

AUBRIOT, ERIC, chef; m. Stephanie Aubriot. Chef Trio, Evanston, Ill., Carlos' , Highland Park; owner, chef Aubriot, Chgo. Named One of Six Hot Chgo. Chefs, Chgo. Social, 1998, Best New Restaurant, Esquire mag., 1998, Chgo. mag., 1998. Office: Restaurant Aubriot 1962 N Halsted Chicago IL 60614

AUBURN, NORMAN PAUL, university president; b. Cin., May 22, 1905; s. Joseph and Huldah A.; m. Kathleen Montgomery, June 28, 1930 (dec. 1974); children: Ames Auburn Latta, Richard, Mark, David Bruce; m. Virginia Kirk, Jan. 4, 1977. AB, U. Cin., 1927, postgrad., 1927-28, 34-35, LLD, 1952, Parsons Coll., 1945, U. Liberia, 1959, U. Akron, 1971; DSc, U. Tulsa, 1957; LittD, Washburn U., 1961; LHD, Coll. of Wooster, 1963; DCL, Union Coll., 1979. Editor Cin. Constructor, 1928-33; asst. mgr. Asso. Gen. Contractors of Am., 1928-33; publicity mgr. Allied Constrn. Industries, 1930-33; exec. sec. U. Cin. Alumni Assn., 1933-36; editor Cin. Alumnus, 1929-36; asst. dir., asst. prof. Evening Coll., U. Cin., 1936-38; assoc. prof. U. Cin., 1938-40, acting dean, 1940-41, dean and prof., 1941-43, dean of univ. adminstrn., clk. bd. dirs., 1943-51, v.p., 1943-51, acting pres., 1949; exec. dir. U. Cin. Research Found., 1943-51; pres. U. Akron, 1951-71, pres. emeritus, cons., 1971—. Acting pres. Council Fin. Aid to Edn., N.Y.C., 1957-58, bd. dirs., 1957-71; spl. asst. univ. relations AID, U.S. State Dept., 1965-66, cons., 1966— ; cons. Acad. Ednl. Devel., Inc., N.Y.C., 1965-70, sr. v.p., dir. institutional ops., 1971-89, sr. v.p., emeritus, 1989—; acting pres. Poly. Inst., Bklyn., 1973, Stephens Coll., Columbia, Mo., 1974-75, Cedar Crest Coll., Allentown, Pa., 1977-78, Union Coll., Schenectady, N.Y., 1978-79; acting chancellor Union U., Albany, N.Y., 1978-79; sr. v.p., provost Widener U., Chester, Pa., 1979-82; acting pres. Salem Coll., W.Va., 1982-83, Lincoln U., Jefferson City, Mo., 1987-88; spl. asst. to pres. for planning W.Va. U., Morgantown, 1983-86; chmn. Univ. Council on Edn. for Pub. Responsibility, 1965-66; dir. Great Lakes Megalopolis Research Project, 1968-74; vice chmn. Am. Council Edn., 1963-64, dir., 1969-72; bd. dirs. First Fed. Savs. and Loan Assn., Akron, 1963, chmn., 1973—; bd. dirs. Charter One Fin., Cleve., 1988—, Charter One Bank, 1988—, 1st Nat. Bank Akron, emeritus; hon. pres. Lane Theol. Sem., Cin., 1990—. Contbr. articles to ednl. jours. Bd. dirs. Akron Gen. Hosp., U. Akron Devel. Found., 1967—; trustee Greater Akron Musical Assn., 1967—; trustee, sec. Lane Theol. Sem., Cin., 1945—, hon. pres., 1990—; trustee Ohio Coll. Assn., pres., 1960-61; mem. Air Force ROTC Adv. Panel to Dept. USAF, 1960-64; mem. exec. com. Ohio Research and Devel. Bd., 1962-65; pres. Herman Muehlstein Found., 1965—; mem. U. Cin. Endowment Fund Assn. Recipient Bert A. Polsky Humanitarian award Akron Cmty. Found., 1997, Judge Harold K. Stubbs Emeriti award for lifetime of disting. svc. African Meth. Episcopal Ch., 2000. Fellow AAAS; mem. Assn. Am. Colls. (vice chmn. commn. coll. adminstrn. 1965-68), Am. Soc. Engring. Edn., Am. Assn. State Colls. and Univs. (chmn. com. on internat. programs 1970-71), Assn. Univ. Evening Colls. (pres. 1944), Assn. Urban Univs. (pres. 1955-56, sec.-treas. 1956-65), Newcomen Soc., Cincinnatus Soc., Summit County Hist. Soc. (trustee 1975-80), Queen City Assn., Alpha Kappa Psi, Phi Alpha Delta, Lambda Chi Alpha, Omicron Delta Kappa, Scabbard and Blade. Presbyterian. Clubs: Rotary (pres. Cin. 1950-51, Akron 1958-59), Commonwealth (Cin.), Univ. (N.Y.C., Columbus, Ohio), City, Portage Country (Akron), Lago Mar Beach (Ft. Lauderdale, Fla.). Home: 2385 Covington Rd Akron OH 44313-4335 Office: U Akron Office Of Pres Emeritus Akron OH 44325-3002

AUER, JAMES MATTHEW, art critic, journalist; b. Neenah, Wis., Dec. 2, 1928; s. Matthew George and Charlotte Agnes (Friedland) A.; m. Marilyn Mills, Feb. 1, 1964; 1 son, Charles William. B.A., Lawrence Coll., Appleton, Wis., 1950. With accounting dept. George Banta Co., 1950-51; reporter Twin City News-Record, 1953-56, asst. to editor, 1957-60, news editor, 1960-61; asst. Sunday editor Appleton Post-Crescent, 1960-65, Sunday editor, 1965-72; art critic Milw. Jour., 1972—. Author: The Spirit is Willing, 1960; plays: The City of Light, 1961, Tell It to Angela, 1971; motion pictures: The Magic World of Patrick Farrell, 1978, The Bohrod Touch, 1984, An Artist's Vision: Born on the Stone, 1986, Olgivanna Lloyd Wright: A Partner to Genius, 1993, In Your Face: The Distorted World of John Kascht, 1994, Etched in Acid: Warrington Colescott, 1998. Presiding officer Attic Theatre, Inc., 1959-62; pres. Friends of Bergstrom Art Center, 1967-68; mem. Neenah Municipal Mus. Found., Inc. Recipient Pres.'s award Wis. Heart Assn., 1969 Mem. Am. Assn. Sunday and Feature Editors (pres. 1972-73), State Hist. Soc. Wis. (award of merit 1962), Soc. Profl. Journalists, Milw. Press Club, Phi Kappa Tau. Congregationalist. Home: 1849 N 72nd St Wauwatosa WI 53213-2353 Office: Milw Jour Sentinel 333 W State St Milwaukee WI 53203-1305 E-mail: jauer@onwis.com.

AUER, RON, state legislator; b. St. Louis, Jan. 24, 1950; s. Lawrence J. and Loretta B. Goettler A.; m. Ann Marie Hoelscher, 1980; children: Amanda Marie, Lindsey Marie, Neal Collins, Tracy Collins. BS, S.E. Mo. State U., 1972. Mo. State rep. Dist. 59, 1977—; educator, 1972-77; real estate and ins. agt., 1979-83; mktg. acct. rep. Health Maintenance Orgn. HMO, 1983—. Office: 3120 S Compton Ave Saint Louis MO 63118-2110

AUFDERHEIDE, ARTHUR CARL, pathologist; b. New Ulm, Minn., Sept. 9, 1922; s. Herman John and Esther (Sannwald) A.; m. Mary Lillian Buryk, Jan. 26, 1946; children: Patricia Ann, Tom Paul, Walter Herman. MD, U. Minn., 1946; DSc (hon.), Coll. of St. Scholastica, 1983. Chief dept. pathology Mpls. VA Hosp., 1952-53, St. Mary's Hosp., Duluth, Minn., 1953-57; chief dept. pathology Sch. Medicine U. Minn., 1970-87, dean Sch. Medicine, 1974-75, dir. paleobiology lab. Sch. Medicine, 1977—. Mem. Plaisted Polar Expdn., 1968; rsch. cons. anthropology lab. U. Colombia, Bogota, 1989—, Pigorini Mus., Rome, 1988, Archeol. Mus. of Tenerife, Canary Islands, 1989-90; chmn. sci. com. Cronos Rsch Project, Santa Cruz, Tenerife, 1991—. Author: Cambridge Ency. Author: Scientific Story of Mummies 2002 Human Paleopathology, 1998; co-editor: Paleopathology, 1991; author: (documentary film) Copper Eskimo, 1970; contbr. numerous articles to profl. publs. Chmn. civil com. to devel. a degree-granting med. sch., Duluth, 1988. Capt. U.S. Army, 1947-49. Fellow AAAS; mem. Paleopathology Assn., N.Y. Acad. Scis. Democrat. Lutheran. Achievements include research in soft tissue paleopathology. Home: 4711 Colorado St Duluth MN 55804-1512 Office: U Minn 10 University Dr Duluth MN 55812-2403

AUGELLI, JOHN PAT, geographer, educator , writer, consulant, rancher; b. Celenza, Italy, Jan. 30, 1921; s. Pat John and M. Antoinette (Iacaruso) A.; divorced; children: John, Robert. BA, Clark U., 1943; MA, Harvard U., 1949, PhD, 1951. Teaching fellow Harvard U., Cambridge, Mass., 1948—49; from asst. to assoc. prof. geography U. P.R., Rio Piedras, 1949—51; assoc. prof. U. Md., College Park, 1952—61; prof. U. Kans., Lawrence, 1961—70, 1971—91; prof. geography, dir. Ctr. Latin Am. Studies U. Ill., Champaign-Urbana, 1970—71. Lectr., travel cons. Mediterranean and Latin Am. cruises, 1991-95; mem. Bd. Fgn. Scholarships, Washington, 1967-70; cons. Nat. Geographic Soc., Washington, 1984-87; del. U.S. Acad. Scis., New Delhi, 1968; sec. Coun. of Inter-Am. Affairs, Washington, 1959-60. Author: Carribean Lands, 1965, Puerto Rico, 1973, Middle America, 3d edit., 1989; cons.: (atlas) World & North America, 1984; contbr. 76 articles to profl. jours. Served to lst lt. U.S. Army, 1943-46, PTO, Res., 1949-51. Recipient Fulbright research grant, 1982. Fellow Am. Geog. Soc.; mem. Assn. Am. Geographers (sec. 1966-69), Latin Am. Studies Assn. (pres. 1969), Nat. Council Geographic Edn. (master tchr. 1979), Conf. of Latin Americanist Geographers (outstanding contbn. to research and teaching award 1982). Democrat. Roman Catholic. Avocations: travel, fishing. Address: 35 Mediterranean Blvd E Port Saint Lucie FL 34952-8557

AULT, JOHN L. paint manufacturing company executive, accountant; b. Findlay, Ohio, Mar. 5, 1946; s. Herman Cedric and Janice J. (Steegman) A.; m. Sean J. Locklear, Dec. 17, 1979; children: John Scott, Jamie Fawn, Wendy Dawn Rogers, Edward H. Rogers III. BS, Miami U., Oxford, Ohio, 1968. CPA, Ohio. Audit supr. Ernst & Whinney, Cleve., 1968-76; fin. analyst Sherwin-Williams Co., 1976-78, dir. acctg., 1978-81, asst. contr., 1981-87, v.p., corp. contr., 1987—. Mem. AICPA, Ohio Soc. CPA's, Nat. Assn. Accts., Fin. Execs. Inst. Methodist. Home: 1491 Adelaide St Cleveland OH 44145-2469 Office: Sherwin-Williams Co 101 Prospect Ave NW Cleveland OH 44115

AUNE, DEBRA BJURQUIST, lawyer; b. Rochester, Minn., June 13, 1956; d. Alton Herbert and Violet Lucille (Dutcher) Bjurquist; m. Gary ReMine, June 6, 1981 (div. June 1993); children: Jessica Bjurquist ReMine, Melissa Bjurquist ReMine; m. David Aune, Jan. 1, 1995. BA, Augsburg Coll., 1978; JD, Hamline U., 1981. Bar: Minn. 1981. Assoc. Hvistendahl & Moersch, Northfield, Minn., 1981-82; adjuster Federated Ins. Cos., Owatonna, 1982-84; advanced life markets advisor Federated Life Ins. Co., 1984-87; mktg. svcs. advisor Federated Ins. Cos., 1987-89, 2d v.p., corp. legal counsel, 1989-92, v.p. gen. counsel, 1992-95, 1st v.p., gen. counsel, 1996-99; ind. cons., 1999—. Mem. Hamline Law Rev., 1979-80. Pres. Owatonna Ins. Women, 1983-84; charter commr. City of Owatonna, 1992—. Mem. ABA, Minn. State Bar Assn., 5th Dist. Bar Assn., Steele County Bar Assn. (sec. 1986-87, v.p. 1987-88, pres. 1988-89), Assn. Life Ins. Counsel, Alliance Am. Insurers (legal com. 1989—). Lutheran. Office: Federated Ins Cos 121 E Park Sq Owatonna MN 55060-3046

AUPPERLE, ERIC MAX, data network center administrator, research scientist, engineering educator; b. Batavia, N.Y., Apr. 14, 1935; s. Max Karl and Hedwig Elise (Haas) A.; m. Nancy Ann Jach, June 21, 1958; children: Bryan, Lisa. BSEE, BSE in Math, U. Mich., 1957, MSE in Nuclear Engring., 1958, Instm.E., 1964. Registered profl. engr., Mich. Lectr. dept. electrical engring. U. Mich., 1972, lectr. dept. indsl. & ops. engring., 1973-74, 1963—, from asst. rsch. engr. to rsch. engr. Cooley Electronics Lab., 1957-69, rsch. engr. Inst. Sci. & Tech., 1969-74, rsch. scientist Inst. Sci. & Tech., 1974—; project leader Merit Computer Network of Inst. Sci. & Tech., U. Mich., 1969-73, assoc. dir., 1973-74, dir., 1974-78; assoc. dir. comm. Computing Ctr. U. Mich., 1981-89, interim dir. Info. Tech. Divsn. Network Systems, 1990-92, pres. Merit Network, Inc. Info. Tech. Divsn. Network Systems, 1988—. Alt. mem. senate assembly U. Mich., 1975, coll. engring. rep. senate assembly, 1976-79, mem. univ. hierarchical computing study com., 1978-79, mem. univ. com. computer policy and utilization, 1979-80, chmn., 1980-84; guest lectr. computer sci. sect. dept. math. Wayne State U., 1975; cons. Cholette, Perkins & Buchanan, Computer Tech. Mgmt. Svcs., Reliance Electric Co., Votrax, Prentice Hall, IMB, Owens-Ill., Donnelly Mirror, Inc., others; panelist instructional sci. equipment program NSF, 1978; mem. program com. Nat. Electronic Conf., 1962-65, 70-73, chmn. student activities com., 1966, chmn. intensive refresher seminar com. 1967, faculty mem. profl. growth seminar series, 1969-74. Editorial bd. Spectrum, 1975-80. Mem. IEEE (sr., dir. Southeastern Mich. sect. 1963-64, 65-67, mem. aid to Apelscor com. 1967-76, mem. Jackson ednl. com. 1967—, Southeastern Mich. sect. treas., 1972, Southeastern Mich. sect. sec. 1973, Southeastern Mich. sect vice chmn. 1974, Southeastern Mich. sect. chmn. 1975, jr. past chmn. 1976, sr. past chmn. 1977), U. Mich. Sci. Rsch. Club, Phi Eta Sigma, Eta Kappa Nu, Tau Beta Pi, Sigma Xi, Pi Kappa Phi. Office: Merit Network Inc U Mich 4251 Plymouth Rd Ann Arbor MI 48105-2789

AURAND, CLAY, state legislator; m. Gina Aurand. Mem. Dist. 109 Kans. Ho. of Reps., 1995—; farmer, rancher. Mem. agriculture com., environment com., Kans. 2000 select com., vice chairperson taxation com. Kans. Ho. of Reps. E-mail: aurand@house.state.ks.us.

AURIN, ROBERT JAMES, entrepreneur; b. St. Louis; m. Kathryn L. Engel, 1998. B in Journalism, U. Mo., 1965. Copywriter Leo Burnett Co., Chgo., 1971-72, Young & Rubicam, Inc., Chgo., 1972-73; from copywriter to v.p., creative dir. Foote, Cone & Belding, Inc., 1973-79; exec. v.p., dir. creative services Grey-North Inc., 1979-82; pres. Robert Aurin Assocs., 1982—; owner ROMAR Investments Co., 1984-99. Exec. creative dir. DraftWorldwide, Inc., 1996-99. Served to lt. USN, 1965-70, Vietnam.

AUSMAN, ROBERT K. surgeon, research executive; b. Milw., Jan. 31, 1933; s. Donald Charles and Mildred (Shafrin) A.; m. Christine McCann, 1992. Ed., Kenyon Coll., 1953; M.D., Marquette U., 1957. Damon Runyon cancer fellow U. Minn., 1958-61; dir. Health Research Inc. Roswell Park Meml. Inst., 1961-69; dep. dir. Fla. Regional Med. Assn., 1969-70; v.p. clin. research Baxter Travenol Labs., 1970-82, pres. advanced devel. group, 1982-90; pres. Mildon Corp., 1985—, Citation Pub. Co., 1991—. Clin. prof. surgery Med. Coll. Wis., 1972—. Named Outstanding Young Man in N.Y. Buffalo Evening News, 1966, Citizen of Year, 1967 Mem.: Am. Assn. Cancer Rsch., Am. Soc. Clin. Oncology, Masons. Home: PO Box 3538 Long Grove IL 60047 Office: Willow Valley Rd Long Grove IL 60047

AUSTIN, ARTHUR DONALD, II, lawyer, educator; b. Staunton, Va., Dec. 2, 1932; s. George Milnes and Mae (Eichner) A.; m. Irene Clara Wittenberg, June 12, 1960; 1 son, Brian Carl. B.S. in Commerce, U. Va., 1958; J.D., Tulane U., 1963. Bar: Va. 1964, D.C. 1970. Asst. prof. Coll. of William and Mary, Williamsburg, Va., 1963-64, Bowling Green State U., Ohio, 1964-66; asst. prof. law Cleve. State U., 1966-68; prof. law Case Western Res. U., Cleve., 1968-70, 72-78, Edgar A. Hahn prof. jurisprudence, 1978—. Atty. Dept. Justice, Washington, 1970-71 Author: Antitrust: Law, Economics, Policy, 1976, Complex Litigation Confronts the Jury System, 1984, The Empire Strikes Back: Outsiders and the Struggle Over Legal Education, 1998; contbr. articles to law revs. Served with U.S. Army, 1952-54. Decorated Bronze Star medal with V, Purple Heart. Home: 1174 Stony Hill Rd Hinckley OH 44233-9538 Office: 11075 East Blvd Cleveland OH 44106-5409

AUSTIN, JAMES H(OWARD), JR. healthcare executive; b. Durham, N.C., June 6, 1951; s. James Howard and Constance E. (Shaw) A.; m. Susan Conger, Sept. 6, 1986; children: James Tanner, Samuel Conger. BA, Yale U., 1976; M.Pub. Policy, M. Urban & Regional Plan., Princeton U., 1982. Economist Govt. of Botswana, 1976-80; cons. Arthur D. Little, Inc., Cambridge, Mass., 1982-86; dir. strategy Anchor HMO, Chgo., 1986-88; cons. Baxter Healthcare, Deerfield, Ill., 1988-90; dir. strategy devel. Renal div. Baxter Healthcare, 1990—. Mem. Planning Forum (internat. bd. dirs. 1991—), Univ. Club of Chgo. (bd. dirs. 1991-93).

AUSTIN, SAM M. physics educator; b. Columbus, Wis., June 6, 1933; s. A. Wright and Mildred G. (Reinhard) A.; m. Mary E. Herb, Aug. 15, 1959; children: Laura Gail, Sara Kay. BS in Physics, U. Wis., 1955, MS, 1957, PhD, 1960. Rsch. assoc. U. Wis., Madison, 1960; NSF postdoctoral fellow Oxford U., Eng., 1960-61; asst. prof. Stanford U., Calif., 1961-65; assoc. prof. physics Mich. State U., East Lansing, 1965-69, prof., 1969-90, univ. disting. prof., 1990-2000, univ. disting. prof. emeritus, 2000—, chmn. dept., 1980-83, acting dean Coll. Natural Sci., 1994, assoc. dir. Cyclotron Lab., 1976-79, rsch. dir., 1983-85, co-dir., 1985-89, dir., 1989-92. Guest Niels Bohr Inst., 1970; guest prof. U. Munich, 1972-73; sci. collaborator Saclay and Lab. Rene Bernas, 1979-80; vis. scientist Triumf-U. B.C., 1993-94; invited prof. U. Paris, Orsay, 1996; mem. grant selection com. for sub-atomic physics, NSERC (Can.), 1996-99; mem. com. on nuc. physics Nat. Rsch. Coun., 1996-99; mem. steering com. Nuc. Physics Summer Sch. Author, editor: The Two Body Force in Nuclei, 1972, The (p,n) Reaction and Nucleon-Nucleon Force, 1980; editor Phys. Rev. C, 1988-2002; assoc. editor Atomic Data and Nuc. Data Tables, 1990—. Fellow NSF, 1960-61, Alfred P. Sloan Found., 1963-66; recipient Mich. Assn. of Governing Bds. Disting. Prof., 1992. Fellow AAAS (chair nominating com.), Am. Phys. Soc. (vice chmn. nuc. physics divsn. 1981-82, chmn. 1982-83, exec. com. 1983-84, 86-89, coun. 1986-89, coun. exec. com. 1987-88, panel on pub. affairs 1996-98); mem. APS, Sigma Xi (Sr. rsch. award 1977). Achievements include research in nuclear physics, nuclear astrophysics and nitrogen fixation. Home: 1201 Woodwind Trl Haslett MI 48840-8994 Office: Mich State U Nat Supercondr Cyclotron Lab East Lansing MI 48824 E-mail: austin@nscl.msu.edu.

AUSTON, DAVID HENRY, university administrator, educator; b. Toronto, Ont., Can., Nov. 14, 1940; came to U.S., 1963; BS, U. Toronto, 1962, MS, 1963; PhD, U. Calif. at Berkeley, 1969. Rsch. physicist GM, Santa Barbara, Calif., 1963-66; tech. staff AT&T Bell Labs., Murray Hill, N.J., 1969-82, head dept., 1982-87; former prof. Columbia U., N.Y.C., chmn. elec. engring. dept., 1990, dean sch. engring. and applied sci., 1991-94; provost Rice U., Houston, 1994-99; pres. Case Western Res. U., Cleve., 1999—. Author: 1 book; also numerous sci. papers; holder 7 patents. Fellow IEEE (Quantum Electronics award 1990, Morris E. Leeds award 1991), Optical Soc. Am. (R.W. Wood prize 1985), Am. Acad. Arts and Scis., Am. Phys. Soc.; mem. Nat. Acad. Scis., NAE. Office: Case Western Res U Office of Pres 10900 Euclid Ave Cleveland OH 44106-1712

AUSTRIA, STEVE, state legislator; BA in Polit. Sci., Marquette U. Mem. Ohio Ho. Reps. from 76th dist., Columbus, 1998-2000, Ohio Senate from 10th dist., Columbus, 2001—. Recipient Great Am. Family of the Yr. award Reagan Adminstrn. Mem. KC (Family of the Yr. award), Miami Valley Mil. Affairs Assn., Ohio Twp. Assn., Beavercreek C. of C., Fairborn C. of C., Xenia C. of C., Rotary. Office: Rm # 034 Senate Bldg Columbus OH 43215

AUWERS, STANLEY JOHN, motor carrier executive; b. Grand Rapids, Mich., Mar. 22, 1923; s. Joseph T. and Cornelia (Moelhoek) A.; m. Elizabeth Kruis, Apr. 6, 1946; children— Ellen (Mrs. William Northway), Stanley John, Thomas. Student, Calvin Coll., 1940-41; B.B.A., U. Mich., 1943. C.P.A., Mich. With Ernst & Ernst, Detroit, 1943-51; controller Interstate Motor Freight System, Grand Rapids, Mich., 1951-61, v.p., controller, 1961-65, v.p. finance, 1965-69, exec. v.p., 1969-72; also dir.; pres. Transam. Freight Lines, Detroit, 1973—. Chmn. cost com. Mich. Trucking Adv. Bd. to Mich. Pub. Service Commn., 1958-63; mem. citizens com. to study Mich. tax structure advisory Mich. Ho. Reps., 1958 Mem. Am. Motor Carriers Central Freight Assn. (gov. regular common carrier conf.), Mich. Motor Carriers Central Freight Assn. (v.p., gov.), Tax Execs. Inst., Am. Inst. C.P.A.s, Trucking Employers. Presbyn. Home: 3099 Lakeshore Dr Douglas MI 49406 Office: 3684 28th St SE Grand Rapids MI 49512-1606

AVANT, GRADY, JR. lawyer; b. New Orleans, Mar. 1, 1932; s. Grady and Sarah (Rutherford) A.; m. Katherine Willis Yancey, Feb. 23, 1963; children: Grady M., Mary Willis Yancey. B.A. magna cum laude, Princeton U., 1954; J.D., Harvard U., 1960. Bar: N.Y. 1961, Ala. 1962, Mich. 1972. Assoc. Bradley, Arant, Rose & White, Birmingham, Ala., 1961-63; assoc., ptnr. Long, Preston, Kinnaird & Avant, Detroit, 1972-87; ptnr. Dickinson, Wright, Moon, Van Dusen & Freeman, 1988-94; sr. v.p. investment banking North Am. Capital Advisors, Inc., Bloomfield Hills, 1995-96; pvt. practice Grosse Pointe, 1996—2001, Birmingham, Ala., 2001—. Contbr. articles to legal jours. Served to lt. USMC, 1954-57. Mem. ABA (bus. law sect., fed. regulation of securities com.), State Bar of Mich. (coun. sect. antitrust law 1978-85, chmn. sect. 1983-84, bus. law sect.), Detroit Com. on Fgn. Rels. (exec. com. 1979—2001, chmn. 1986-88), Mountain Brook Club, Knickerbocker Club, Princeton Club of Mich. (pres. 1976-77, 94-95). Episcopalian. Home and Office: 13 Cross Creek Dr Birmingham AL 35213 Fax: 313-868-6556.

AVELLA, JOSEPH RALPH, university executive; b. N.Y.C., Nov. 13, 1942; s. Salvatore Ralph and Bianca (Artoni) A.; m. Elizabeth Theresa Eberhardt, Aug. 12, 1967 (div. May 1991); children: Edward Jay, James Joseph. BS in Chemistry, Rensselaer Poly. Inst., 1964; MA, Cath. U. Am., 1992, PhD, 1995. Mgr. Md. ops. The Great Atlantic and Pacific Tea Co., Inc., 1978-83; program mgr. Honeywell Fed. Sys., Inc., McLean, Va., 1984-86, mgr. integration svcs., 1987-89; dep. dir. mobilization Office of Sec. Def., Washington, 1990-92, dir. internat. programs, 1992-93; sr. fellow global strategy program Potomac Found., McLean, 1995-98; prof. and acad. dean Am. Mil. U., Manassas, Va., 1995-98. Cons. Masi Rsch. Cons., Inc., Washington, 1995-97; exec. sec. NATO Forces Com., Brussels, Belgium, 1992-94; seminar moderator U.S. Naval War Coll., Newport, R.I., 1989-91; pres. Delphic Consulting Inc., 1998; exec. v.p. Capella U., 1998—. Contbr. articles to profl. jours. With USNR, 1970-95. Recipient Achievement award No. Va. Navy League, 1989, Cert. of Appreciation Sec. of Navy, 1986, 88, Award of Appreciation U.S. Naval Sea Cadet Corps, 1986. Mem. Am. Polit. Sci. Assn., Ctr. for Study of Presidency (contbg. author), U.S. Strategic Inst., Assn. Naval Aviation (past chpt. sec.), Navy League of U.S. (former mem. bd. dirs.), U.S. Naval Inst. (contbg. author), Pi Sigma Alpha. Home: 608 Edwards Rd Annapolis MD 21401 Office: Capella Univ 222 S 9th St 20th Fl Minneapolis MN 55402 E-mail: javella@aol.com.

AVENT, SHARON L. HOFFMAN, consumer products company executive; Former sr. exec. v.p. Smead Mfg. Co., Hastings, Minn., pres., CEO, 1999—. Office: Smead Mfg Co 600 E Smead Blvd Hastings MN 55033-2219

AVERY, DENNIS THEODORE, state legislator; b. Evansville, Ind., Sept. 28, 1946; 1 child, Jessica. BS, U. Evansville, 1969. Ind. state rep. Dist. 75, 1974—; mem. environ. affairs, cts. and criminal code com. Ind. Ho. Reps.; ways and means com. Coord. adult mktg. U. So. Ind. Mem. adv. com. Evansville State Hosp.; active Vanderburgh County Arts Coun., Beacon Group, Vanderburgh County Soil Water Conservation Dist. Mem. Med. Sch. Adv. Coun. Address: 11400 Big Cynthiana Rd Evansville IN 47720-7303 E-mail: davery@usi.edu., hts@ai.org.

AVERY, ROBERT DEAN, lawyer; b. Youngstown, Ohio, Apr. 23, 1944; s. Donald Carson and Alta Belle (Simon) A.; m. Ann Mitchell Lashen, May 16, 1993; 1 child from previous marriage: Benjamin Robert. BA, Northwestern U., 1966; JD, Columbia U., 1969. Bar: Ohio 1971, Calif. 1973, Ill. 2001. Law clk. to Hon. Robert P. Anderson U.S. Ct. Appeals 2d Cir., N.Y.C., 1969-70; assoc. lawyer Jones, Day, Reavis & Pogue, Cleve., 1970-74, L.A., 1974-76, ptnr., 1977-98, adminstrv. ptnr., 1990-92, ptnr. Chgo., 1999—. Editor: Columbia Law Rev., 1968-69. Dir. Wilshire YMCA, L.A., 1981-88. Harlan Fiske Stone Scholar. Home: 45 E Division St Chicago IL 60610-2316 Office: Jones Day Reavis & Pogue 77 W Wacker Dr Chicago IL 60601-1662 E-mail: rdavery@jonesday.com.

AVIS, ROBERT GRIER, investment company executive, civil engineer; b. St. Louis, June 23, 1931; s. Clarence W. Avis and Mary (Grier) Edwards; m. Ann Y. Freedman, June 12, 1954; children— Lisa Avis Savage, Mary L. Avis Bolin, Stephen G. B.S.C.E., U. Mo., Columbia, 1958. Dept. mgr. Proctor & Gamble Co., Cin., 1958-65; various positions A. G. Edwards, St. Louis, 1965-89; vice chmn. A.G. Edwards, 1989—; chmn. A.G. Edwards Trust Co., 1989—. Bd. govs. Am. Stock Exchange, 1992—. Served to lt. USN, 1952-56 Mem. Securities Industry Assn. (bd. dirs. 1989-92), Chi Epsilon, Tau Beta Pi. Presbyterian. Clubs: Old Warson Country (St. Louis); Royal Poinciana Country (Naples, Fla.); Port Royal (Naples, Fla.). Avocations: all sports. Office: A G Edwards & Sons Inc 1 N Jefferson Ave Saint Louis MO 63103-2205

AWAIS, GEORGE MUSA, obstetrician, gynecologist; b. Ajloun, Jordan, Dec. 15, 1929; arrived in U.S., 1951; s. Musa and Meha (Koury) A.; m. Nabila Rizk, June 24, 1970 AB, Hope Coll., 1955; MD, U. Toronto, 1960. Diplomate Am. Bd. Obstetrics and Gynecology. Intern U. Toronto Hosps., Ont., Can., 1960-61, resident in obstetrics and gynecology Can., 1961-64, chief resident Can., 1965, Harlem Hosp., Columbia U., N.Y.C., 1966; asst. obstetrician and gynecologist Cleve. Met. Gen. Hosp., 1967, assoc. obstetrician and gynecologist, 1969; instr. obstetrics and gynecology Case Western Res. U., Cleve., 1967-70, asst. obstetrician and gynecologist MacDonald House, 1970, asst. prof., 1970, asst. clin. prof. dept. reproductive biology, 1971, asst. obstetrician and gynecologist Univ. Hosps., 1971; mem. staff, dept. gynecology Cleve. Clinic Found., 1971-91. Chmn. dept. ob-gyn. King Faisal Specialist Hosp. and Rsch. Ctr., Riyadh, 1975-76; cons. panel mem. Internat. Corr. Soc. Obstetricians and Gynecologists, 1971; emeritus staff Cleve. Clinic Found., 1991; pres. Task Force on Humanitarian Aid and Relief Inc., 1997. Contbr. articles to pubs. in field, papers, reports to confs., TV appearances, Saudi Arabia Named Grand Officer of Order of Independence His Majesty King Hussein of Jordan, 1992. Fellow ACS, Am. Coll. Obstetricians and Gynecologists, Royal Coll. Surgeons Can.; mem. AMA, AAAS, Am. Infertility Soc., Arab Am. Med. Assn. (pres. 1991—, chmn. humanities relief 1996), Acad. Medicine of Cleve. Office: Cleve Clinic Found Emeritus Office EE/40 9500 Euclid Ave Cleveland OH 44195-0001 E-mail: emeritus@ccf.org.

AXE, JOHN RANDOLPH, lawyer, financial executive; b. Grand Rapids, Mich., Apr. 30, 1938; s. John Jacob and Elizabeth Katherine (Lynott) A.; m. Linda Sadlier Stroh, June 1, 1989; children from previous marriage: Catherine, Peter, Meredith, Sara, Jay, stepchildren: Suzanne Stroh, Greg Stroh. AB, U. Mich., 1960; LLB, Harvard U., 1963. Bar: Mich. 1964. Ptnr. Dickinson, Wright, McKean, Cudlip, Detroit, 1972-80, Martin, Axe, Buhl & Schwartz, Bloomfield Hills, Mich., 1981-82, Axe & Schwartz, Bloomfield Hills, 1983-85, Dykema, Gossett, Spencer, Goodnow, Detroit, 1985-89; prin. John R. Axe and Assocs., 1989—. Pres. Mcpl. Fin. Cons., Inc., Detroit, 1982—; adj. prof. Wayne State U. Law Sch., 1992—. Mem. Mich. Higher Edn. Assistance Authority, Lansing, Mich., 1977-83. Served to lt. USNR, 1965-69. Mem. Nat. Assn. Bond Lawyers (steering com. 1981-83, 86, bd. dirs. 1987-90), Mich. Assn. County Treas. (gen. counsel 1977-88), Downtown Assn. Club (N.Y.C.), Doubles Club (N.Y.C.), Mill Reef Club (Antigua). Office: Axe & Ecklund PC 21 Kercheval Ave Ste 360 Grosse Pointe Farms MI 48236-3633

AXELROD, LEONARD, court administrator; b. Oct. 27, 1950; s. Morris and Doris S. A. BA, Ind. U., 1972; MPA, U. So. Calif., 1974; JD, Hamline U., 1982. Asst. dir. Ind. Jud. Ctr. Ind. U. Sch. Law, Indpls., 1974-76; cons. Booz, Allen & Hamilton, Washington, 1976-77; staff assoc. Nat. Ctr. State Cts., St. Paul, 1977-82; ptnr. Ct. Mgmt. Cons., Mpls., 1982-87, Friedman, Farrar & Axelrod, Mpls., 1984-86; prin. Ct. Mgmt. Cons., 1987-94; sec., treas. CMC Justice Svcs., Inc., 1994—95; project mgr. Legal Rsch. Ctr., 1996-97; ct. adminstr. U.S. Bankruptcy Ct., 1997—. Cons. Ctr. Jury Studies, Vienna, Va., 1979-82, Calif. Atty. Gen., 1972-73, Control Data Bus. Advisers, Mpls., 1982-88. Author: North Dakota Bench Book, 1982; contbr. articles to profl. jours.; assoc. editor Law Rev. Digest, 1982. Mem. presdl. search com. Hamline U., 1980-81; reporter Minn. Citizen Conf. on Cts., 1980; appointed to The Petrofund Bd., 1994. Samuel Miller scholar, 1981. Mem. ABA, ASPA, So. Calif. Soc. Pub. Adminstrn., Booz, Allen & Hamilton Alumni (pres. Minn. 1980), The Brandeis Soc. (exec. dir. Mpls. 1980), U. so. Calif. Midwest Alumni (exec. bd. Chgo. 1974), Phi Alpha Alpha, Phi Alpha Delta. Office: US Bankruptcy Ct Minn Rm 200 316 Robert St N Ste 200 Saint Paul MN 55101-1241 E-mail: LAxelrod@juno.com.

AXFORD, ROY ARTHUR, nuclear engineering educator; b. Detroit, Aug. 26, 1928; s. Morgan and Charlotte (Donaldson) A.; m. Anne-Sofie Langfeldt Rasmussen, Apr. 1, 1954; children: Roy Arthur, Elizabeth Carole, Trevor Craig Charles. B.A., Williams Coll., 1952; B.S., Mass. Inst. Tech., 1952, M.S., 1955, Sc.D., 1958. Supr. theoretical physics group Atomics Internat., Canoga Park, Calif., 1958-60; assoc. prof. nuclear engring. Tex. A&M, 1960-62, prof., 1962-63; assoc. prof. nuclear engring. Northwestern U., 1963-66; assoc. prof. U. Ill., Urbana, 1966-68, prof., 1968—. Cons. Los Alamos Nat. Lab., 1963— Vice-chmn. Mass. Inst. Tech. Alumni Fund Drive, 1970-72, chmn., 1973-75; sustaining fellow MIT, 1984. Recipient cert. of recognition for excellence in undergrad. teaching U. Ill., 1979, 81; Everitt award for teaching excellence, 1985. Mem. ASME, Am. Nuclear Soc. (Excellence in Undergrad. Teaching award 1990, 95, 97, 99, 2002, Disting. faculty Alpha Nu Sigma 1991), SAR (sec.-treas. Piankeshaw chpt. 1975-81, v.p. chpt. 1982-3, pres. chpt. 1984-86), Kiwanis (charter life patron fellow 1992), Sigma Xi, Tau Beta Pi, Phi Kappa Phi. Home: 2017 S Cottage Grove Ave Urbana IL 61801-6353

AXINN, GEORGE HAROLD, rural sociology educator; b. Jamaica, N.Y., Feb. 1, 1926; s. Hyman and Celia (Schneider) A.; m. Nancy Kathryn Wigsten, Feb. 17, 1945; children: Catherine, Paul, Martha, William. B.S., Cornell U., 1947; M.S., U. Wis., 1952, Ph.D., 1958. Editorial asst. Cornell U. Geneva, N.Y., 1947; bull. editor U. Md., College Park, 1949; chmn. dept. rural communication U. Del., Newark, 1950; mem. faculty Mich. State U., East Lansing, 1953—, assoc. dir. coop. extension service, 1955-60; coordinator U. Nigeria program, 1961-65, prof. agrl. econs., 1970-85, prof. resource devel., 1985-95, prof. emeritus, 1996—, asst. dean internat. studies and programs, 1964-85; pres., exec. dir. Midwest Univs. Consortium for Internat. Activities, Inc., 1969-76, 1969-76. FAO rep. to Nepal, 1983-85, India and Bhutan, 1989-91; cons. World Bank, 1973-74, Ford Found., 1968, UNICEF, 1978, FAO, 1974, 87, 89, Govt. of India, 1988; vis. prof. Cornell U., Ithaca, N.Y., 1958-60, U. Ill., Urbana, 1969-70 Author: Modernizing World Agriculture: A Comparative Study of Agricultural Extension Education Systems, 1972, New Strategies for Rural Development, Rural Life Associates, 1978, FAO Guide Alternative Approaches to Agricultural Extension, 1988, Collaboration in International Rural Development - A Practitioner's Handbook (with Nancy W. Axinn), 1997; contbr. articles to various publs. Served with USNR, 1944-46. Recipient Outstanding Alumni award Cornell U. Coll. Agrl. and Life Sci., 1993; W.K. Kellogg Found. fellow, 1956-57. Mem.: AAAS, Assn. Farming Sys. Rsch. and Extension, Indian Soc. Extension Edn., Soc. Applied Anthropology, Soc. Internat. Devel., Rural Sociol. Soc., Phi Kappa Phi. Clubs: Lansing Tennis, Michigan State U. Office: Mich State U 313 Natural Resources East Lansing MI 48824-1222 Home: 280 E Morning Sun Ct Tucson AZ 85704-6945 E-mail: axinn@msu.edu.

AXLEY, DIXIE L. insurance company executive; B in Social Welfare, Ill. Wesleyan U. Chartered property casualty underwriter. Pers. devel. specialist State Farm Mutual Automobile Ins. Co., Bloomington, Ill., 1987-88, supt., 1988-91, dir. mgmt. planning and info., 1991-93, mgr. pub. affairs, 1993-94, asst. divsn. mgr., 1994-95, asst. dir.- pub. affairs, then dir.- pub. affairs, 1995-96, asst. v.p.- pub. affairs, 1996-97, v.p. pub. affairs, 1997—. Office: State Farm Ins Cos Pub Affairs Dept 1 State Farm Plz Bloomington IL 61710-0001

AXLEY, FREDERICK WILLIAM, lawyer; b. Chgo., June 23, 1941; s. Frederick R. and Elena (Hoffman-Pinther) A.; m. Cinda Jane Russell, Mar. 29, 1969; children: Sarah Elizabeth, Elizabeth Jane. BA, Holy Cross Coll., 1963; MA, U. Wis., 1966; JD, U. Chgo., 1969. Bar: Ill. 1969, U.S. Dist. Ct. (no. dist.) Ill. 1969, U.S. Ct. Appeals (7th cir.) 1970. Assoc. McDermott, Will & Emery, Chgo., 1969-74, jr. ptnr., 1974-80, sr. ptnr., 1980—. Trustee Wilmette Elem. Sch. Dist. #39, Ill., 1976-81, Ill. chpt. Nature Conservancy, 1983-91; bd. dirs. Bus. and Profl. People for the Pub. Interest, Chgo., 1984—; bd. dirs. Friends of the Chgo. River, 1994—, pres., 1998—; bd. dirs. Shore Line Place, 1994—, pres. 2001—, Interfaith Housing Devel. Corp., 1997—, 1st. v.p., 2000—. Served to lt. USN, 1963-65. Mem. Mich. Shores Club (Wilmette). Democrat. Roman Catholic. Office: McDermott Will & Emery 227 W Monroe St Ste 3100 Chicago IL 60606-5096 E-mail: faxley@msn.com.

AXTELL, JOHN DAVID, genetics educator, researcher; b. Mpls., Feb. 5, 1934; s. Maynard J. and Caroline (Kolstad) A.; m. Susan Dee Kent, Aug. 17, 1957; children— Catherine Dee, John D. Jr., Laura Jean B.S., U. Minn., St. Paul, 1957, M.S., 1965; Ph.D., U. Wis., Madison, 1967. Research asst.

U. Minn., St. Paul, 1957-59; research assoc. U. Wis., Madison, 1959-67; prof. agronomy Purdue U., West Lafayette, Ind., 1967-84, Lynn Disting. prof., 1984—. Mem. Research Adv. com. AID, Washington, 1983— , sci. liaison officer, 1984— Contbr. chpts. to books, articles to profl. jours. Recipient Cert. of Appreciation award U.S. AID, 1975; Alexander Von Humboldt award, 1976; Rsch. award Crop Sci. Soc. Am., 1977; Internat. award Disting. Svc. to Agr., 1984; Sigma Xi Purdue Faculty Rsch. award, 1975; Nat. Inst. Gen. Med. Scis. fellow. Fellow AAAS, Am. Soc. Agronomy; mem. NAS, Am. Soc. Agronomy, Crop Sci. Soc. Agronomy, Sigma Xi, Gamma Sigma Delta, Alpha Zeta Home: 1824 Sheridan Rd West Lafayette IN 47906-2226 Office: Purdue U Agronomy Dept Life Sci Bldg West Lafayette IN 47907

AXTELL, ROGER E. writer, retired marketing professional; m. Mitzi Axtell. Degree, U. Wis., 1953. With Parker Pen Co., v.p.; ret. Author: Do's & Taboos Around the World: A Guide to International Behavior, Do's & Taboos of International Trade: A Small Business Primer, Do's & Taboos of Hosting International Visitors, Do's & Taboos of Preparing for Your Trip Aborad, Gestures: Do's & Taboos of Body Language Around the World, LINDO: The Do's & Taboos of Using American/English. Mem. bd. regents U. Wis., 1999—; vice chmn. Gov.'s Task Force on Internat. Edn.; mem. Gov.'s Commn. on U. Wis. Sys. Compensation, Wis., 1992. Named one of 25 most influential people in internat. trade, World Mag., 1998. Office: One Parker Pl Ste 360 Janesville WI 53545

AYERS, JEFFREY DAVID, lawyer; b. Grant, Nebr., Nov. 30, 1960; s. William D. and Lela R. (Gilmore) A.; m. Shelly Jo Dodds, June 11, 1988; children: Sydney Elizabeth, Bailey Anne. BS, Graceland U., 1982; MBA, JD, U. Iowa, 1985. Bar: Mo. 1985. Assoc. Stinson, Mag & Fizzell, Kansas City, Mo., 1985-88, Bryan, Cave, McPheeters & McRoberts, Kansas City, 1989-92; ptnr. Blackwell Sanders Peper Martin LLP, Mo., 1992-95, mng. ptnr. London, 1996-99; sr. v.p., gen. counsel and corp. sec. Aquila Mcht. Svcs., Inc., Kansas City, 1999—. Mayor City of Lake Tapawingo, Mo., 1993-96. Trustee Little Blue Valley Sewer Dist., 1994-95. Democrat. Mem. Cmtys. of Christ. Office: Aquila IMcht Svcs nc 1100 Walnut St Ste 3300 Kansas City MO 64106-2109 E-mail: jeff.ayers@aquila.com.

AYLWARD, RONALD LEE, lawyer; b. St. Louis, May 30, 1930; s. John Thomas and Edna (Ketcherside) A.; m. Margaret Cecilia Hellweg, Aug. 10, 1963; children: Susan Marie, Stephen Ronald, Carolyn Ann. AB, Washington U., St. Louis, 1952, JD, 1954; student, U. Va., 1955. Bar: Mo. 1954, Ill. 1961, U.S. Supreme Ct. 1968. Assoc. Heneghan, Roberts & Cole, St. Louis, 1958-59; asst. counsel Olin Corp., East Alton, Ill., 1960-64; asst. gen. counsel INTERCO, Inc., St. Louis, 1964-66, asso. gen. counsel, mgr. law dept., 1966-69, asst. sec., 1966-74, gen. counsel, 1969-81, mem. operating bd., 1970-92, v.p., 1971-81, mem. exec. com., dir., 1975-92, exec. v.p., 1981-85, vice chmn. bd. dirs., 1985-92; chmn., pres. Aylward & Assocs., Inc., St. Louis, 1992—. Mem. dist. export coun. U.S. Dept. Commerce, 1974-77; dir., mem. exec. com. Boatmen's Nat. Bank St. Louis, 1982-91, trust estates com., 1982-85, chmn. audit com., 1986-91; bd. dirs. Boatmen's Bancshares, Inc., mem. audit com., 1984-91, mem. compensation com., 1986-91; trustee Maryville U., 1989-92, chmn. bd., 1991-92. Trustee St. Louis Coun. World Affairs, sec., 1977—84; chmn. lay bd. DePaul Health Ctr., 1979—81; mem. exec. com. lay bd., 1981—89; mem. lay adv. bd. Chaminade Coll. Prep. Sch., 1980—84, chmn. bd. trustees, 1981—84; mem. lay bd. Acad. of the Visitation, 1981—85; bd. dirs. Cath. Charities of St. Louis, 1994—2001, vice chmn., 1995—97, chmn., 1997—99; mem. coun. Archdiocesan Devel. Appeal, 1994—97, chmn., 1996—97, vice chmn., 1995—97, mem. exec. com., 1995—97, chmn. rev./planning com., 1995—96, chmn., 1996—, hon. life mem.; mem. fin. coun. Archdiocese of St. Louis, 1995—98, mem. investment com., 1995—97; bd. dirs. St. Louis chpt. Nat. Found. March of Dimes, 1974—84, sec., 1976—78, chmn., 1979—82; bd. dirs. Cardinal Ritter Inst., 1975—90, chmn. pers. com., 1986—90; bd. dirs. St. Louis chpt. ARC, 1977—82, Linda Vista Montessori Sch., 1975—77, BBB Greater St. Louis, 1978—81, YMCA Greater St. Louis, 1981—2001, adv. dir., 2001—, NCCJ, 1992—93; bd. dirs. Carindal Glennon Children's Hosp., 1991—96, mem. exec. com., 1992—96, bd. dirs. Found., 1996—2001, dir.emeritus, 2001—; bd. dirs., fin. United Way Greater St. Louis, 1986—2001; mem. investment com. St. Louis Cmty. Found., 1993—95. With U.S. Army, 1955—58. Recipient of Order of St. Louis's King, Archdiocese of St. Louis. Mem.: NAM (taxation com. 1970—76, pub. affairs com. 1973—76, govt. ops./expenditures com. 1973—78), St. Louis Bar Assn., Mo. Bar Assn., Am. Soc. Corp. Secs. (pres. St. Louis regional group 1972—73), Am. Footwear Industries Assn. (nat. affairs vice chmn. 1970, chmn. 1971—75), Am. Apparel Mfrs. Assn. (bd. dirs. 1983—85), Assoc. Industries Mo. 1973—80, (exec. com. 1974—80, 2d v.p. 1974—76, pres. 1976—78), St. Louis C. of C. (legis. and tax com. 1966—74, vice-chmn. 1970—71), Bellerive Country Club, Mo. Athletic Club, Rotary (bd. dirs. St. Louis Club 1976—79), Bellerive Country Club (bd. dirs. 1981—84), Order of St. Louis King, Knights of Holy Sepulcher, Knights of Malta, Delta Theta Phi (dist. chancellor Mo. 1970—79, pres. St. Louis Alumni 1963). Home: 55 Muirfield Saint Louis MO 63141-7372 Office: Aylward and Assoc Inc One City Place Dr Saint Louis MO 63141 Fax: 314-434-6528.

AYRES, RALPH DONALD, state legislator; b. Sept. 12, 1948; BS, Ind. U., 1970, MS, 1975. Coun. mem., Porter County, Ind., 1978-80; state rep. dist. 4 Ind. Ho. of Reps., Indpls., 1980—, mem. cts. and criminal code com., mem. ways and means com.; educator Duneland Sch. Corp., Chesterton, Ind. Named Outstanding Young Hoosier; recipient Elvis J. Stahr Outstanding Tchr. award. Mem. NEA, Ind. Tchrs. Assn., Phi Delta Kappa. Republican. Home: 520 Park Ave Chesterton IN 46304-2929 E-mail: R4@ai.org.

AYRES, TED DEAN, lawyer, academic counsel; b. Hamilton, Mo., July 14, 1947; m. Marcia Sue Busselle; children: John Corbett, Jackson Frazer, Joseph Dean. BSBA, Ctrl. Mo. State Coll., 1969; JD, U. Mo., 1972. Bar: Mo. 1972, U.S. Dist. Ct. (we. dist.) Mo. 1972, U.S. Ct. Appeals (8th cir.) 1977, U.S. Supreme Ct. 1977, Colo. 1984, U.S. Dist. Ct. Colo. 1984, U.S. Ct. Appeals (10th cir.) 1984, Kans. 1987. Law clk. to presiding justice Mo. Supreme Ct., Jefferson City, 1972-73; ptnr. Stubbs & Ayres, Chillicothe, Mo., 1973-74; atty. Southwestern Bell Tel. Co., St. Louis, 1974-76; counsel U. Mo., Columbia, 1976-84, U. Colo., Boulder, 1984-86; gen. counsel Kans. Bd. Regents, Topeka, 1986-92, gen. counsel, dir. govtl. rels., 1992-96; acting pres. Pitts. State U., 1995; gen. counsel, assoc. to pres. Wichita (Kans.) State U., 1996—, interim dir. Edwin A. Ulrich Mus. Art, 1999-2000. Adj. asst. prof. coll. bus. adminstrn. U. Colo., Denver, 1984-85, adj. assoc. prof., 1985-86; spl. asst. atty. gen. State of Colo., 1984-86, State of Kans., 1987—; presenter region II conf. Assn. Coll. Unions Internat., U. Mo., Rolla, 1983; spkr. Soc. Colo. Archivists, U. Colo., Boulder, 1985; adj. prof. Washburn U., Topeka, 1989; adj. prof. kinesiology and sport studies Wichita State U., 1999—. Contbr. articles to profl. jours. Active adv. com. Boone County (Mo.) Cmty. Svcs.; mem. com. social concerns Mo. United Meth. Ch., 1979-81, supervisory com. Mothers' Morning Out program, 1980-84; adminstv. bd., com. on fin. and stewardship 1st United Meth. Ch., Topeka, 1989-91, family life coun., 1994-95; trustee Mid-Mo. chpt. Nat. Multiple Sclerosis Soc., 1981-84; mem. bd. mgrs. Topeka YMCA-Downtown Br., 1991-96, fedn. coun. Indian Guides program, 1988-91; treas. pack 175 Cub Scouts, 1990-95; bd. dirs. Innovative Tech. Enterprise Corp., 1991-94, S.W. Youth Athletic Assn., Inc., 1994-96, Friends of Topeka Zoo, 1995-2000, Wichita Tech. Corp., 1997—, Wichita State U. Hist. Preservation Commn., 1998—, parents coun. Truman State U., 1997-99. Curator scholar, 1969-70, Omar E. Robinson scholar, 1970-71, John M. Dalton Ednl. Trust scholar 1971-72. Mem. Mo. Bar Assn., Nat. Assn. Coll. and Univ. Attys. (chairperson Southwestern region 1979-81, bd. dirs. 1985-88, com. mem. 1979—, del. and presenter numerous CLE workshops), Friends of Topeka Zoo, U. Mo. Alumni Assn. (life). Home: 2214 SW Brookfield St Topeka KS 66614-4236 Office: Wichita State Univ 201 Morrison Hall Wichita KS 67260-0001 E-mail: ted.ayres@wichita.edu.

AZZI, JENNIFER L. basketball player; b. Oak Ridge, Tenn., Aug. 31, 1968; d. James and Donna Azzi. Diploma, Stanford U., 1990. Basketball player Arvika Basket, Sweden, 1995-96, Viterbo, Italy, Orchies, France. Mem. Nat. Women's Basketball Team. Recipient gold medal Goodwill Games, 1994, World Championship Qualifying team, 1993, U.S. Olympic Festival West Team, 1987; 2 gold medals World Championship and Goodwill Games, 1990, bronze medal Pan Am. Games, 1991, World Championship team, 1994, Wade Trophy, 1990; named Al-Pac 10 1st team, 1988, 89, 90, MVP NCAA Final Four, 1990, NCAA West Region, 1990, Naismith Nat. Player Yr., 1990, Kodak All-Am. 1st team, 1989, 90. Office: Detroit Shock Palace at Auburn Hills 2 Championship Dr Auburn Hills MI 48326-1753

BABA, MARIETTA LYNN, business anthropologist, university administrator; b. Flint, Mich., Nov. 9, 1949; d. David and Lillian (Joseph) Baba; m. David Smokler, Feb. 14, 1977 (div. 1982); 1 child, Alexia Nicole Baba Smokler. BA with highest distinction, Wayne State U., 1971, MA in Anthropology, 1973, PhD in Phys. Anthropology, 1975; MBA, Mich. State U., 1994. Asst. prof. sci. and tech. Wayne State U., Detroit, 1975-80, assoc. prof. anthropology, 1980-88, prof., 1988—, spl. asst. to pres., 1980-82, econ. devel. officer, 1982-83, asst. provost, 1983-85, assoc. provost, 1985-89, dir. internat. programs, interim assoc. dean Grad. Sch., 1988-89, assoc. dean Grad. Sch., 1989-90, acting chair dept. anthropology, 1990-92, chair dept. anthropology, 1996-2001; dean Coll. Social Sci. Mich. State U., 2001—. Program dir. transformations to quality orgns., dir. social, behav., and econ. scis. NSF, 1994—96; evolution rschr. Wayne State U., 1975—82; cons. GM Rsch. Labs., 1988—92, Electronic Data Sys., 1990—93, McKinsey Global Inst., 1991; rsch. contractor GM/EDS, 1990—94; lectr. nat. and internat. symposia, profl. confs. Adv. for editor orgnl. anthropology: American Anthropologist, 1990-93; issued letters patent for method to map joint ventures and maps produced thereby; contbr. numerous papers and abstracts to tech. jours.; patentee in field. Mem. State Rsch. Fund Feasibility Rev. Panel, 1982—84; mem. adv. panel on tech. innovation and U.S. trade U.S. Congl. Office Tech. Assessment, 1990—91, mem. panel on electronic enterprise, 1993—94; active Leadership Detroit Class IV, 1982—83; dir. Mich. Tech. Coun. (S.E. divsn.), 1984—85. With USAF, 1992—94. Job Partnership Tng. Act grantee, 1981-90, NSF grantee, 1982, 84-85, 99-01. Fellow Am. Anthrop. Assn. (bd. dirs. 1986-88, exec. com. 1986-88, del. to Internat. Union Anthrop. and Ethnol. Sci. 1990-94, chair global commn. anthropology 1993-98), Nat. Assn. Practice Anthropology (pres. 1986-88), Soc. Applied Anthropology, Phi Beta Kappa, Sigma Xi (Morton Fried award 1991), Beta Gamma Sigma.

BABB, RALPH W., JR. banker; b. Sherman, Tex., Feb. 4, 1949; s. Ralph Wheeler and Billie Margaret (Odneal) B.; m. Barbara Louise Alexander, Aug. 30, 1970; children: Dana P., Derek R. BS in Acctg., U. Mo., Columbia, 1971. CPA, Mo. Audit mgr. Peat, Marwick, Mitchell & Co., CPA's, St. Louis, 1971-78; constr., sr. v.p. Mercantile Bancorp. Inc., 1978-83, treas., sr. v.p., 1979-83, CFO, exec. v.p., 1983-94, vice chmn., 1987-95; vice-chmn., CFO Comerica, Inc., Detroit, 1995—2002, pres., CEO, dir., 2002—, Comerica Bank, Detroit, 2002—. Mem. Fin. Execs. Inst. (pres. St. Louis chpt. 1986-87). Methodist. Office: Comerica Inc PO Box 75000 Detroit MI 48275-0001

BABBITT, GEORGE T. career officer; b. Wash. m. Louise Babbitt; children: Ian, Megan. BSME, U. Wash., 1965; MS in Logistics Mgmt., Air Force Inst. Tech., 1970. Commd. 2d lt. USAF, 1965, advanced through grades to lt. gen., 1995; maintenance officer Royal Air Force Sta. Alconbury, Eng., 1966-69; squadron maintenance officer 12th Tactical Reconnaissance Squadron, Tan Son Nhut Air Base, South Vietnam, 1970-71; maintenance planner B-1A Sys Program Office Rockwell Internat., L.A., 1971-73; support equipment and spares mgr. B-1A Sys. Program Office, Wright-Patterson AFB, Ohio, 1973-76; dep. program mgr. logistics Precision Location Strike Sys. Program Office, 1976-78; from maintenance officer to comdr. 1st Aircraft Generation Squadron, Langley AFB, Va., 1978-80; comdr. 36th Aircraft Generation Squadron, Bitburg Air Base, West Germany, 1980-81; from asst. dep. comdr. maintenance to dep. comdr. maintenance 36th Tactical Fighter Wing, West Germany, 1981-85; from divsn. chief to dep. dir. logistics plans and programs Hdqs. USAF, Washington, 1986-90, dir. supply, 1993-94, dep. chief staff logistics, 1995-96; dir. logistics Hdqs. Air Tng. Command, Randolph AFB, Tex., 1990-92, Hdqs. USAF Europe, Ramstein Air Base, Germany, 1992-93; dep. dir. material mgmt. Def. Logistics Agy., Alexandria, Va., 1994-95, dir. Ft. Belvoir, 1996-97; comdr. Air Force Material Command, Wright Patterson AFB, Ohio, 1997—. Decorated Legion of Merit, Bronze Star medal.

BABCOCK, CHARLES LUTHER, classics educator; b. Whittier, Calif., May 26, 1924; s. Robert Louis and Margarette Estelle (Fuller) B.; m. Mary Ayer Taylor, Aug. 6, 1955; children: Robert Sherburne, Jennie Rownd Chapman, Jonathan Taylor. AB in Latin, U. Calif., Berkeley, 1948, MA in Latin, 1949, PhD in Classics, 1953. Asst. in classics U. Utah, Salt Lake City, 1949-50; instr. classics Cornell U., Ithaca, N.Y., 1955-57; acting. instr. Stanford U., Calif., summer 1956; asst. prof. classical studies U. Pa., Phila., 1957-62, assoc. prof., 1962-66, asst. dean, vice dean of coll., 1960-62, 62-64, acting dean, spring 1964; prof. classics Ohio State U., Columbus, 1966-92, prof. emeritus, 1992—, chmn. dept., 1966-68, 80-88, dean Coll. of Humanities, 1968-70. Prof.-in-charge summer sch. Am. Acad. in Rome, 1966, resident in classical studies, 1986, acting Mellon prof.-in-charge sch. classical studies, 1988-89, chmn. adv. coun. sch. classical studies, 1992-94; mem. Latin exam. com. Advanced Placement Program, 1967-74, chmn., 1972-74; prof.-in-charge Intercollegiate Ctr. Classical Studies, Rome, 1974, chair mng. com., 1975-82; scholar in residence Hope Coll., 1993. Co-author: Aspects of Roman Civilization, 1980; contbr. articles on Latin lit. (especially Horace), Latin epigraphy, Roman civilization. Served to capt. inf. U.S. Army, 1943-47, ETO. Recipient Alumni Disting. Teaching award Ohio State U., 1982, Exemplary Faculty award Coll. Humanities, Ohio State U., 1989, Disting. Svc. award, 1996; Univ. fellow in classics U. Calif., Berkeley, 1951-53; fellow Am. Acad. in Rome, Fulbright scholar in classics, Rome, 1953-55. Fellow Am. Acad. in Rome (trustee 1981-83, trustee emeritus 1994); mem. Am. Philol. Assn. (bd. dirs. 1968-72), Classical Assn. of Mid. West and South (Ovatio award 1982, pres. 1977-78), Vergilian Soc. Am. (pres. 1975-76), Assn. Depts. Fgn. Langs. (pres. 1986), Phi Beta Kappa (pres. Epsilon of Ohio 1969-70), Phi Kappa Phi, Phi Sigma Kappa (former pres. U. Calif., regional dep. 1949-51). Clubs: Scabbard and Blade (U. Pa.) (hon.), Philomathean Soc. (hon.). Home: 973 Lynbrook Rd Columbus OH 43235-3307 Office: Ohio State U Dept Greek & Latin 230 N Oval Mall Columbus OH 43210-1319 E-mail: babcock.2@osu.edu.

BABCOCK, LYNDON ROSS, JR. environmental engineer, educator; b. Detroit, Apr. 8, 1934; s. Lyndon Ross and Lucille Kathryn (Miller) B.; m. Betty Irene Immonen, June 21, 1957; children— Lyndon Ross III, Sheron Lucille Babcock Fruehauf, Susan Elizabeth Babcock Williams, Andrew Dag BSChemE, Mich. Tech. U., 1956; MSChemE, U. Washington, 1958, PhD in Environ. Engring., 1970. Registered profl. engr., Ill. Chem. engr. polymers Shell Chem. Co., Calif., N.J., N.Y., 1958-67; assoc. prof. environ. engring., geography, pub. health U. Ill., Chgo., 1970-75, prof. environ. engring., geography, pub. health, 1975-90, prof. emeritus, 1990—, dir. environ. health scis. program Sch. Pub. Health, 1978-79, dir. environ. and occupational health scis. program Sch. Pub. Health, 1979-84, assoc. dean Sch. Pub. Health, 1984-85. Cons. WHO, 1985, Interam. Devel. Bank, 1990-91, Environ. Secretariat Fed. Dist., Mexico City, 1995-97; USA coord. air quality project for Gestión de la Calidad del Aire, Mexico City, 1986-92; environ. cons./lectr. Tech. Instns., Mexican Secretariat of Pub. Edn., 1993-95; vis. prof. El Colegio de Mexico, Mexico City, 1996—. Mem. editorial bd. The Environ. Profl., 1979-90; contbr. environ. articles to profl jours.; patentee plastics composition and processing. Bd. dirs. Chgo. Lung Assn., 1981-92. Fulbright lectr., Turkey and India, 1975-76, Mexico, 1986-87, 1992-93; fed. and state environ. research and ednl. grantee Mem. Air and Waste Mgmt. Assn. (chmn. Lake Michigan sect. 1977-78), League Am. Bicyclists, Chicagoland Bicycle Fedn. (v.p. 1985-86). Office: U Ill Sch Pub Health EOHS MC922 2121 W Taylor St Chicago IL 60612-7260 E-mail: lyndonrb@aol.com.

BABINGTON, CHARLES MARTIN, III, lawyer; b. St. Louis, Mar. 15, 1944; s. Charles Martin Jr. and Sarah Elizabeth (Karraker) B.; m. Ann Baker, July 6, 1974; children: Martin, Anthony, Liza. AB, Dartmouth Coll., 1965; JD, U. Mich., 1968; LLM in Tax, Washington U., St. Louis, 1975. Bar: Mo. 1968, U.S. Dist. Ct. (ea. dist.) Mo. 1968, U.S. Ct. Appeals (8th cir.) 1973, U.S. Ct. Claims 1974, U.S. Tax Ct. 1975. Judge adv. USAF, Beale AFB, Calif., 1968-72; assoc. Thompson & Mitchell, St. Louis, 1972-77, ptnr., 1978-95; of counsel Thompson Coburn, 1996-98; ret., 1999. Dir., sec. St. Louis Steam Tain Assn., 1986—; dir. Ecumenical Housing Prodn. Corp., 1992-97, U. Club. St. Louis, 1994-98. Capt. USAF, 1968-72. Mem. Mo. Bar Assn. (mem. staff benefits com. 1979-96). Republican. Episcopalian. Avocations: steam locomotive restoration, photography. Home: 25 Warson Ter Saint Louis MO 63124-1680 E-mail: cbabing3@swbell.net.

BABLER, JAMES CARL, lawyer; b. Antigo, Wis. Oct. 13, 1955; s. Carl Leo and Barbara Ruth (Hoppe) B. B.A., U. Wis., 1976, J.D., 1979. Bar: Wis. 1979, U.S. Dist. Ct. (we. dist.) Wis. 1979. Asst. dist. atty Barron County, Barron, Wis., 1979-80; asst. dist. atty. Polk County, Balsam Lake, Wis., 1980-83; dist. atty. Barron County, 1983— ; instr. Wis. Indianhead Tech. Inst., Rice Lake, Wis., 1981— . Mem. Wis. Dist. Attys. Assn., Wis. Law Enforcement Officers Assn. Democrat. United Methodist. Home: 266 W Monroe Ave Barron WI 54812-1327 Office: Barron County Dist Attys Office 237 Courthouse Barron WI 54812

BABLER, WAYNE E., JR. lawyer; b. Detroit, Apr. 29, 1942; s. Wayne E. and Mary E. (Blome) B.; m. Patricia A. Ward, Feb. 5, 1972; children: Dean W., Anne E. BA, Wittenberg U., 1964; JD, U. Wis., 1967. Bar: Wis. 1967, U.S. Ct. Appeals (7th cir.) 1971, U.S. Supreme Ct. 1980, U.S. Dist. Ct. (ea. and we. dists.) Wis., 1967, U.S. Dist. Ct. (ctrl. and no. dists.) Ill. 1987, U.S. Dist. Ct. (ea. and we. dists.) Mich. 1990; U.S. Ct. Appeals (9th and 10th cirs.) 1981, U.S. Ct. Appeals (D.C. cir.), 1983. Assoc. Quarles, Herriott, Clemons, Teschner & Noelke, Milw., 1971-74, Quarles & Brady, Milw., 1974-76, ptnr., 1976—. Rep. of chief justice Wis. Supreme Ct. to Wis. Jud. Compensation Com., 1983-84. Author: (with others) Business and Commercial Litigation in Federal Court, 1998; Rsch. editor Wis. Law Rev., 1966-67, Antitrust, Federal Civil Litigation, State Civil Litigation. Mem. U. Wis. Benchers Soc.; campaign cabinet United Performing Arts Fund, Inc., Milw., 1977-78; bd. dirs. Milw. Bar Found., 1976-79, treas., 1977-78; bd. dirs. Wis. Bar Found., 1983—, pres., 1985-87; bd. dirs. Legal Aid Soc. Milw., 1997—. With JAGC, USN, 1967-71. Fellow: Wis. Law Found., Am. Coll. Trial Lawyers, Am. Bar Found.; mem.: ABA (ho. of dels. 1984—96), Bar Assn. 7th Fed. Cir., Nat. Inst. Trial Advocacy Advocates, Nat. Conf. Bar Pres., State Bar Wis. (bd. govs. 1983—87), Milw. Bar Assn. (bd. dirs. 1976—83, pres. 1981—82), Tripoli Country Club, Univ. Club, Order of Coif. Home: 1475 E Fairy Chasm Rd Milwaukee WI 53217-1433 Office: Quarles & Brady 411 E Wisconsin Ave Milwaukee WI 53202-4497 E-mail: web@quarles.com.

BABLITCH, WILLIAM A. state supreme court justice; b. Stevens Point, Wis., Mar. 1, 1941; B.S., U. Wis., Madison, 1963, J.D., 1968. Bar: Wis. 1968. Pvt. practice law, Stevens Point, Wis.; mem. Wis. Senate, 1972-85, senate majority leader, 1976-82; justice Wis. Supreme Ct., Madison, 1985—; dist. atty. Portage County, Wis., 1969-72. Mem. Nat. Conf. State Legislators (exec. com. 1979) Office: Wis Supreme Ct PO Box 1688 Madison WI 53702-1688*

BABROWSKI, CLAIRE HARBECK, fast food chain executive; b. Ottawa, Ill., July 25, 1957; d. John Clayton Harbeck and Corrine Ann (Lavender) French; m. David Lee Babrowski, July 3, 1982. Student, U. Ill., 1975-77. Dental asst., Ottawa, 1975-76; crew person McDonald's Corp., 1974-76, mem. restaurant mgmt. Champaign, Ill., 1976-80, ops. and tng. cons. St. Louis, 1980-84, ops. mgr., 1984-86, dir. nat. ops. Oak Brook, Ill., 1986-88, dir. ops. Phila., 1988-89, sr. regional mgr. Raleigh, N.C., 1989-98, exec. v.p., 1998—. Chmn. N.C. Ronald McDonald's Children's Charities, Raleigh, 1989—. Author: (manual) Training Consultants Development Program, 1987. Mem. N.C. Restaurant Assn. (bd. dirs. 1992—). Republican. Roman Catholic. Avocations: tennis, gardening. Office: McDonald's Corp One Kroc Dr Oak Brook IL 60523

BACH, JAN MORRIS, composer, educator; b. Forrest, Ill., Dec. 11, 1937; s. John Nicholas and Anne (Morris) B.; m. Dalia Zakaras; children: Dawn, Eva. MusB, U. Ill., 1959, MusM, 1961, MusD, 1971; postgrad., U. Va., Arlington, 1963-65, Yale U., summer 1960, Berkshire Music Ctr., summer 1961. Instr. music U. Tampa, Fla., 1965-66; prof. music No. Ill. U., DeKalb, 1966—, Presdl. Rsch. prof. Dekalb, 1982-86, Disting. Rsch. prof., 1986—; composer-in-residence Institut de Hautes Etudes Musicales, Montreux, Switzerland, 1976; editor for brass compositions M.M. Cole, Chgo., 1969-72. Mem. Ill. Arts Coun., 1986-89, Ind. Arts Coun., 1992. Composer: Skizzen, 1967, Woodwork, 1970, Eisteddfod, 1972, Turkish Music, 1968, Four Two-Bit Contraptions, 1971, The System, 1973, Dirge for a Minstrel, 1974, Three Choral Dances, 1975, Laudes, 1975, Piano Concerto, 1975, Three Bagatelles, 1978, Hair Today, 1978, The Happy Prince, 1978, My Wilderness, 1979, Student from Salamanca, 1979, Rounds and Dances, 1980, Horn Concerto, 1982, Helix, 1984, Escapade, 1984, Dompes & Jompes, 1986, Harp Concerto, 1986, Trumpet Concerto, 1987, A Solemn Music, 1987, Triptych, 1989, Euphonium Concerto, 1990, With Trumpet and Drum, 1991, Anachronisms String Quartet, 1991, People of Note, 1993, Concerto for Steelpan and Orchestra, 1994, The Last Flower, 1995, Foliations, 1995, Bassoon Concertino, 1996, Pilgrimage, 1997, Variations on a Theme of Brahms, 1997, Kimberly's Song, 1998, Dear God, 1998, NIU MIUSIC, 1999, In the Hands of the Tongue, 1999, The Duel, 1999, Songs of the Streetwise, 2000, Music for a Low Budget Epic, 2001, If Music be the Food of Love, 2001. Served with U.S. Army, 1962—65. Recipient BMI student composers 1st prize, 1957, Koussevitsky composition award, 1961, Harvey Gaul composition award, 1973, Mannes Opera award, 1973, Pulitzer prize nomination, 1973, 81, 82, 84, 92, SAI composition award, 1974, Excellence in Tchg. award No. Ill. U., 1978, choral composition award Brown U., 1978, Nebr. Sinfonia Chamber Orch. contest, 1979, N.Y.C. Opera contest, 1980; commns. include Tuba Brotherhood, 1977, Internat. Trumpet Guild, 1978, 86, Internat. Brass Congress, 1980, Greenwich Philharmonia, 1981, Orch. of Ill., 1982, NACWPI, 1982, Minot Symphony, 1984, Am. Brass Quintet-Chamber Music Am., 1988, Sacramento Symphony-N.C. Symphony, 1989, Camarata Singers, 1991, WFMT-Vermeer Quartet, 1991, Woodstock Chimes Fund, 1994, Ronen Chamber Ensemble, 1994, Stockholm Chamber Brass, 1994, Eileen Gress-N.C. Symphony, 1995, Elmhurst Symphony, 1996, Ramon Parcells, 1996, Palos Park Cmty. Chorale, 1997, Cantori of Hobart and William Smith Colls., 1998, Northern Ill. Children's Chorus, 1999, So. Bend Chamber Singers, 1999, Robert Sims, 1999, Regina H. Helcher, 2000, Jeff

Nesseth, 2001, Jay Hunsberger, 2002. Mem. Coll. Mus. Soc., Broadcast Music, Phi Eta Sigma, Phi Mu Alpha, Phi Kappa Phi, Pi Kappa Lambda., Omicron Delta Kappa E-mail: janbach@janbach.com.

BACH, STEVE CRAWFORD, lawyer; b. Jackson, Ky., Jan. 31, 1921; s. Bruce Grannis and Evelyn (Crawford) B.; m. Rosemary Husted, Sept. 6, 1947; children— John Crittenden, Greta Christine AB, Ind. U., 1943, JD, 1948; postgrad. Eastern studies, U. Mich., 1944, Nat. Trial Judges Coll., 1966, U. Minn. Juvenile Inst., 1967. Bar: Ky. 1948, Ind. 1948. Atty. Bach & Bach, Jackson, Ky., 1948-51; investigator U.S. CSC, Indpls., 1951-54; sole practice Mt. Vernon, Ind., 1954-65, 83—; judge 11th Jud. Circuit, 1965-82; pres. Internat. Inst. for Youth, Inc., 1985-90; sr. judge State of Ind., 1997—. Spl. overseas rep. Nat. Council Juvenile and Family Ct. Judges, 1983-86, bd. trustees, 1979-83; moderator Ind. Conf. Crime and Delinquency, Indpls., 1968; tchr. seminar on juvenile delinquency, Ind. Trial Judges Assn., 1969, del. Internat. Youth Magistrates Conf., Geneva, 1970, Oxford, Eng., 1974, Can., 1977; faculty adviser Criminal Law Inst., Nat. Trial Judges Coll., 1973; treas. Ind. Council Juvenile Ct. Judges, 1975, v.p., 1976, pres., 1978-79; bd. dirs. Jud. Conf., Ind. Jud. Ctr., 1978-79; faculty adviser Nat. Jud. Coll., 1978; mem. faculty Seminar for Inst. for New Judges, State of Ind., 1979. Pres. Greater Mt. Vernon Assn., 1958-59; past mem. Juvenile Justice divsn. Ind. Jud. Study Commn.; mem. Ind. Gov.'s Juvenile Justice Delinquency Prevention Adv. Bd., 1976-78, community adv. coun. Ind. U. Sch. Medicine, 1986-96. With intelligence Signal Corps, AUS, 1943-46. Mem. Nat. Coun. Juvenile Ct. Judges, Am. Legion, Ind. Bar Assn. (del.), Ind. Judges Assn. (mem. bd. mgrs. 1966-71), Masons, Elks, Kiwanis, Sigma Delta Kappa, Delta Tau Delta. Democrat. Methodist. Home and Office: 512 Walnut St Mount Vernon IN 47620-1862

BACHE, ROBERT JAMES, physician, medical educator; MD, Harvard U. Diplomate Am. Bd. Internal Medicine, Am. Bd. Cardiovasc. Disease. Resident in internal medicine Duke U., Durham, N.C., assoc. prof. medicine; prof. medicine U. Minn., Mpls. Contbr. articles to profl. jours. Fellow Am. Coll. Cardiology; mem. Am. Soc. for Clin. Investigation, Assn. of Am. Physicians, Assn. Univ. Cardiologists, Am. Heart Assn. Office: U Minn Med Sch Med Box 508 Mayo 420 Delaware St SE Minneapolis MN 55455-0374

BACHELDER, CHERYL ANNE, marketing professional; b. Columbus, Ohio, May 4, 1956; d. Max Edwin and Margaret Anne Stanton; m. Christopher Frank Bachelder, June 13, 1981; 2 children. BS, Ind. U., 1977, MBA, 1978. Asst. product mgr. Procter & Gamble Co., Cin., 1978-81; product mgr. The Gillette Co., Boston, 1981-84; sr. product mgr. R.J.R. Nabisco, Planters Life Savers Co., Parsippany, N.J., 1984, group product mgr., 1985-87; dir. mktg. Winston-Salem, N.C., 1987; v.p. mktg. R.J.R. Nabisco, Planters Life Savers Co., 1988-91; v.p., gen. mgr. Life Savers Div., Nabisco Foods Group, 1991-92; pres. Bachelder & Assoc., 1992-95; v.p. mktg. and product devel. Domino's Pizza Inc., Ann Arbor, MI, 1995—. Named one of 100 best and brightest women in advt. Advt. Age mag., Chgo., 1988; featured in Fortune Mag. People to Watch column, 1990. Office: Domino's Pizza Inc 30 Frank Lloyd Wright Dr Ann Arbor MI 48105-9759

BACHER, ROBERT NEWELL, church official; b. Houston; m. Shirley Ann Good; children: Carol Lynn March, Laurie Ann Andrews, Joy Marie. BA in English, BS in Indsl. Engring., Tex. A&M U., 1957; MDiv, Luth. Sch. Theology, Chgo., 1961; MEd in Edn. Psychology, Temple U., 1970; MPA, DPA, U. So. Calif., 1981. ordained, 1961. Pastor St. Mark Luth. Ch., Lakewood, Colo., 1961-66; assoc. youth dir. Commn. Youth Ministry Luth. Ch. in Am., Phila., 1966-72; project mgr. action rsch., dept. rsch. and planning Divsn. for Parish Svcs., Luth. Ch. in Am., 1972-75, asst. dir. dept. rsch. and planning, 1975-77, asst. exec. dir. planning and budgeting, 1977-85, exec. dir., 1985-87; exec. for adminstrn., asst. to bishop Evang. Luth. Ch. in Am., 1987—. Contbr. articles to profl. jours. Office: Evang Luthern Church in Am 8765 W Higgins Rd Chicago IL 60631-4101

BACHMAN, SISTER JANICE, healthcare executive; b. Coshocton, Ohio, Oct. 25, 1945; d. Edward Michael and Kathryn Elizabeth (Norris) B. Student, Ohio Dominican Coll., 1963-67; BS in Pharmacy, Ohio State U., 1971; MBA in Mgmt., Xavier U., 1976; MA in Christian Spirituality, Creighton U., 1989. Joined Dominican Sisters, 1963. Staff pharmacist St. George Hosp., Cin., 1971-73, dir. pharmacy svcs., 1973-76; instr. pharmacology and related courses Coll. Mt. St. Joseph, 1973-74; instr. pharmacology Sch. Nursing Bethesda Hosp., 1975; adminstrv. resident St. Joseph Hosp., Mt. Clemens, Mich., 1976-77, adminstrv. asst., 1977-78, asst. adminstr., 1978-79; corp. dir. religious programs St. Francis-St. George Hosp., Inc., Cin., 1979-80, asst. v.p. hosp. support svcs., 1980-82, v.p. therapeutic and diagnostic svcs., 1983-89; dir. exec. affairs Benedictine Health Sys., Inc., Duluth, Minn., 1989-90; vicaress Dominican Sisters St. Mary of the Springs, Columbus, Ohio, 1990-96. Editor: Guidelines for Developing an IV Admixture, 1976. Trustee Ohio Dominican Coll., 1980-96, mem. devel. com., 1984-94, physical facilities com., 1994-96; mem. radiologic tech. adv. bd. Xavier U., Cin., 1983-89; mem. MLT adv. bd. Coll. Mt. St. Joseph, 1983-85; trustee Program for Medically Underserved dba Health Moms and Babes, 1986-91, co-founder, chair, 1986-89; bd. dirs. Franciscan Health Sys. Cin., 1990-92; chmn. bd. dirs. Nazareth Towers, Columbus, 1990-94; bd. dirs. Dominican Acad., N.Y.C., 1990-95; trustee St. Mary of the Springs Montessori Sch., Columbus, 1990-95; trustee Milford (Ohio) Spiritual Ctr., 1993-99, vice chair, 1993-94, chair, 1994-98; mem. fin. com. Dominican Leadership Conf., 1994-96; bd. dirs. Westwood Civic Assn., Cin., 1979-86, past sec., past 1st v.p., past pres.; mem. steering com. Cong. Neighborhood Groups, Cin., treas., 1981-84; mem. planning divsn. bd. Cmty. Chest and Coun., Cin., 1981-88, chair single parent task force study, 1983-85; mem. rev. bd. City of Cin. Commercial/Indsl. Revolving Loan Fund, 1982-84; bd. dirs. Cin. Area Chpt. ARC, 1982-89, chair nursing and health com., 1983-87, bd. exec. com., 1987-89; bd. dirs. SW Ohio Residences, Cin., 1983-89, vice chair, 1984-87, chair, 1987-89; trustee Providence Fund, Franciscan Sisters of Stella, Niagara, N.Y., 1996—, C.G. Jung Assn. Ctrl. Ohio, co-chair program com., 1996-99; trustee Las Casas (Ministry to Cheyenne and Arapaho Native Ams.), Canton, Okla., 1996, treas., 1997—. Recipient Cmty. Leadership award United Appeal and Cmty. Chest, 1985, 9th Ann. Living Faith award Columbus Met. Area Ch. Coun., 2000. Fellow Am. Coll. Healthcare Execs.; mem. Spiritual Dirs. Internat. Avocations: swimming, cross-country skiing, biking. Office: St Mary of the Springs 2320 Airport Dr Columbus OH 43219-2098 E-mail: janbachman@aol.com.

BACHMANN, JOHN WILLIAM, securities firm executive; b. Centralia, Ill., Nov. 16, 1938; s. George Adam and Helen (Johnston) B.; m. Katharine I. Butler; children: John C., Kristene Ellen Bachmann Wright. AB, Wabash Coll., 1960; MBA, Northwestern U., 1962; LLD (hon.), Wabash Coll., 1990. Researcher Edward Jones, St. Louis, 1962-63, investment rep., 1963-70, gen. ptnr., 1970-80, mng. ptnr., 1980—. Bd. dirs. Am. Airlines, Inc. Trustee Wabash Coll., Crawfordsville, Ind., 1980—; chmn. bd. visitors Drucker Ctr. Claremont (Calif.) Grad. Sch., 1987—; past chmn., bd. dirs. Arts and Edn. Coun. Greater St. Louis; commr. St. Louis Art Mus.; past chmn. St. Louis Symphony Soc.; chmn. St. Louis Regional Chamber and Growth Assn. Mem. Nat. Assn. Securities Dealers (past dist. chmn.), Securities Industry Assn. (bd. dirs., chmn. 1976-79), Securities Industry Found. for Econ. Edn. (chmn. trustees 1988-92), Civic Progress, U.S. C. of C. (dir.), St. Louis Club, Bogey Club. Office: Edward Jones 12555 Manchester Rd Saint Louis MO 63131

BACHMANN, MICHELE, state legislator; m. Marcus Bachmann; 5 children. JD, Coburn Law; LLM, Coll. William and Mary. Mem. Minn. State Senate, 2000—, mem. capital investment com., edn. com., taxes com., E-12 edn. budget divsn. com., jobs, housing and cmty. devel. com., property tax budget divsn. com. Republican. Home: 1801 Johnson Dr Stillwater MN 55082 Office: 125 State Office Bldg 100 Constitution Ave Saint Paul MN 55155-1206 E-mail: sen.michele.bachmann@senate.leg.state.mn.us.

BACKER, GRACIA YANCEY, state legislator; b. Jefferson City, Mo., Jan. 25, 1950; m. F. Mike Backer; 1 child, Justin. Student, S.W. Mo. State Coll. Mem. from dist. 20 Mo. Ho. of Reps., 1983—; majority floor leader, 1996-98. Active NAACP. Democrat. Baptist. Home: 2885 State Road Tt New Bloomfield MO 65063-1643 Office: Mo Ho of Reps State Capitol Building Jefferson City MO 65101-1556

BACON, BRETT KERMIT, lawyer; b. Perry, Iowa, Aug. 8, 1947; s. Royden S. and Aldeen A. (Zuker) B.; m. Bonnie Jeanne Hall; children: Jeffrey Brett, Scott Michael. BA, U. Dubuque, 1969; JD, Northwestern U., 1972. Bar: Ohio 1972, U.S. Ct. Appeals (6th cir.) 1972, U.S. Supreme Ct. 1980. Assoc. Thompson, Hine & Flory, Cleve., 1972-80, ptnr., 1980-2000; founding ptnr. Frantz Ward, 2000—. Spkr. in field. Author: Computer Law, 1982, 84. V.p. profl. sect. United Way, Cleve., 1982-86; pres. Shaker Heights Youth Ctr., Inc., Ohio, 1984-86; elder Ch. of Western Res., 1996—. Mem. Fedn. Ins. and Corp. Counsel, Bar Assn. Greater Cleve., Cleve. Play House Club (officer 1986-94, pres. 1991-93, pres. men's com. 1993-96), Pepper Pike Civic League (trustee and treas. 1994-97). Home: 33076 Woodleigh Rd Cleveland OH 44124-5257 Office: Frantz Ward LLP Ste 1900 55 Public Sq Bldg Cleveland OH 44114

BACON, BRUCE RAYMOND, physician; b. Amherst, Ohio, Nov. 7, 1949; s. Raymond Clifford and Cathryn E. (Fowell) B.; children: Jeffrey Dale, Laurie Katherine. BA in chem., Coll. Wooster, 1971; MD, Case Western Reserve U., 1975. Diplomate Am. Bd. Internal Medicine and Gastroenterology. Asst. prof. medicine Case Western Reserve U., Cleve., 1982-87, assoc. prof. medicine, 1987-88; assoc. prof. medicine, chief gastroenterology sect. La. State U., Shreveport, 1988-90; prof. internal medicine, dir. gastroenterology divsn. St. Louis U. Sch. Medicine, St.Louis, 1990—. Chair subspecialty bd. gasteroenterology Am. Bd. Internal Medicine, 1999—. Co-author: Essentials of Clinical Hepatology, 1993; co-editor: Liver Disease: Diagnosis and Management, 2000; contbr. numerous articles to profl. jours. Fellow ACP, Am. Coll. Gastroenterology, Am. Soc. Clin. Investigation; mem. Am. Assn. Study Liver Disease (councilor 2000—). Presbyterian. Avocation: photography. Office: St Louis U Health Sci Ctr 3635 Vista Ave PO Box 15250 Saint Louis MO 63110-0250

BACON, GEORGE EDGAR, pediatrician, educator; b. N.Y.C., Apr. 13, 1932; s. Edgar and Margaret Priscilla (Anderson) B.; m. Grace Elizabeth Graham, June 30, 1956; children: Nancy, George, John BA, Wesleyan U., 1953; MD, Duke U., 1957; MS in Pharmacology, U. Mich., 1967. Diplomate Am. Bd. Pediatrics, subsplty. Bd. Pediatric Endocrinology. Intern in pediatrics Duke Hosp., Durham, N.C., 1957-58; resident in pediatrics Columbia-Presbyn. Med. Ctr., N.Y.C., 1961-63; from instr. to prof. emeritus U. Mich., Ann Arbor, 1963—86, prof. emeritus, 1986—, chief pediatric endocrinology svc., dept. pediatrics, 1970-83, dir. house officer programs, dept. pediatrics, 1981-86, assoc. chmn. dept. pediatrics, 1983-86, mem. senate assembly, 1978-80; vice chmn. dir.'s adv. coun. Univ. Hosp., 1981-82; prof. pediatrics Tex. Tech U., Lubbock, 1986-89, chmn. dept., 1986-89, chmn. med. practice income plan, 1989; chief staff pediatrics Lubbock Gen. Hosp., 1986-89; dir. med. edn. and rsch. Butterworth Hosp., Grand Rapids, Mich., 1990-91, med. dir. dept. pediatrics, 1991-94; prof. pediatrics Mich. State U., East Lansing, 1990-94; pediatric endocrinologist Univ. Mich. Hosp., Ann Arbor, 1995—, Detroit Medical Ctr., Southfield, Mich., 1996—2001. Coord. profl. svc. C.S. Mott Children's Hosp., 1973-83, mem. exec. com. for clin. affairs, 1975-76, 77-79, assoc. vice chmn. med. staff, 1978-79; chmn. exec. com. Women's Hosp., Holden Hosp., Ann Arbor, 1973-82. Author: A Practical Approach to Pediatric Endocrinology, 1975, 3d edit., 1990; contbr. articles to profl. jours. Capt. U.S. Army, 1958-61. Fellow Am. Acad. Pediatrics (treas. Mich. chpt. 1983-86, alt.-at-large 1995-2001, coun. Tex. chpt. 1986-89); mem. Am. Pediatric Soc., Pediatric Endocrine Soc. Home: 3911 Waldenwood Dr Ann Arbor MI 48105-3008 Office: PO Box 718 Ann Arbor MI 48106-0718

BACON, JENNIFER GILLE, lawyer; b. Kansas City, Kansas, Dec. 26, 1949; BA with honors, U. Kansas, 1971, JD, 1976; MA, Ohio State U., 1973. Bar: Mo. Ptnr. Shughart, Thompson & Kilroy, Kansas City, Mo. Contbr. articles to profl. jours. Mem. ABA, Mo. Bar (pres.), Kansas City Metro. Bar Assn., Lawyers Assn. Kansas City. Office: Shughart Thompson & Kilroy 12 Wyandotte Plz 120 W 12th St Ste 1600 Kansas City MO 64105-1924

BADAL, DANIEL WALTER, psychiatrist, educator; b. Lowellville, Ohio, Aug. 22, 1912; s. Samuel S. and Angelina (Jessen) Badal; m. Julia Lovina Cover, June 1939 (dec. May 1968); children: Petrina Badal Gardner, Julia Badal Graf, Peter C.; m. Eleanor Bosworth Spitler, Sept. 5, 1969 (dec. Feb. 1994). AB, Case Western Res. U., 1934, MD, 1937. Resident in medicine, neurology and psychiatry Peter Bent Brigham Hosp., Mass. Gen. Hosp., Boston City Hosp., 1937-41; fellow in psychiatry and neurology Harvard U., Boston, 1941-45; asst. prof. psychiatry Washington U., St. Louis, 1945; mem. faculty Sch. Medicine Case Western Res. U., Cleve., 1946—, assoc. clin. prof. emeritus psychiatry, 1983—; practice medicine specializing in psychiatry and psychoanalysis, 1955—. Mem. faculty Cleve. Psychoanalytic Inst., 1975—. Author: (book) Treatment of Depression and Related Moods, 1968; contbr. articles to profl. jours. Fellow NRC Office Sci. R&D, 1941—45. Fellow: Am. Psychiat. Assn. (cert. Excellence Tchg. 1999), Internat. Psychoanlytic Assn. (life); mem.: AMA, Cleve. Psychoanalytic Soc. (pres. 1963), Phila. Assn. Psychoanalysis, Am. Psychoanalytic Soc., Acad. Medicine Cleve., Cleve. Psychiat. Soc., Ohio Med. Assn. Home: Judson Pk Apt 312 2181 Ambleside Rd Cleveland OH 44106

BADALAMENT, ROBERT ANTHONY, urologic oncologist; b. Detroit, Mar. 20, 1954; s. Louis F. and Grace D. (Costello) B.; m. Providence F. Vitale, Nov. 9, 1980; children: Louis F., Peter P., Grace F. BS in Biology, So. Meth. U., 1976; MD, Emory U., 1980. Diplomate Am. Bd. Urology. Surg. intern Henry Ford Hosp., Detroit, 1980-81, surg. resident, 1981-82, urologic resident, 1982-85; fellow in urologic oncology Meml. Sloan Kettering Cancer Ctr., N.Y.C., 1985-87; asst. prof. Ohio State U., Columbus, 1987-92, assoc. prof., 1992-95, prof. Sch. Pub. Health, 1995—; mem. attending staff Arthur James Cancer Ctr., 1990-95, Crittenton Hosp., Rochester Hills, Mich., 1995—. Contbr. chpt. to book, articles to profl. jours. Fellow ACS; mem. AMA, Soc. Urologic Oncology, Soc. for Basic Urologic Rsch., Am. Cancer Soc. (bd. trustees Mich. divsn.). Office: Rochester Urology PC 1135 W University Dr Ste 420 Rochester Hills MI 48307-1893

BADALAMENTI, ANTHONY, financial planner; b. St. Louis, Apr. 1, 1940; s. Sebastino and Grace (Orlando) B.; 1 child, Annette Marie. BS in Acctg., Washington U., 1970. CPA, Mo.; registered investment advisor. Staff acct. Fischer & Fischer, CPAs, St. Louis, 1959-63; acct. McDonnell Aircraft Corp., 1963-65; asst. chief acct. Dempsey Tegler, Inc., 1965-66; contr. Cummins Mo. Diesel, Inc., 1966-67; sr. acct. Elmer Fox & Co., CPAs, 1967-71; pvt. practice, 1972-94; fin. planner Asset Builders Fin. Planners, 1995—. Tchr. Meramec C.C., St. Louis, 1973-75. Mem. Mo. Soc. CPAs, Crestwood-Sunset Hills C. of C. (pres. 1980-81, Bus. Profl. Month award 1986, 91), Rotary (pres. Crestwood-Sunset Hills chpt. 1982-83). Republican. Roman Catholic. Avocations: basketball, softball, dancing. Home: 1865 Locks Mill Dr Fenton MO 63026-2662 Office: 4400 S Lindbergh Blvd Ste 3 Saint Louis MO 63127-1603

BADEER, HENRY SARKIS, physiology educator; b. Mersine, Turkey, Jan. 31, 1915; came to U.S., 1965, naturalized, 1971; s. Sarkis and Persape Hagop (Koundakjian) B.; m. Mariam Mihran Kassarjian, July 12, 1948; children: Gilbert H., Daniel H. M.D., Am. U., Beirut, Lebanon, 1938. Gen. practice medicine, Beirut, 1940-51; asst. instr. Am. U. Sch. Medicine, 1938-45, adj. prof., 1945-51, asso. prof., 1951-62, prof. physiology, 1962-65, acting chmn. dept., 1951-56, chmn., 1956-65; research fellow Harvard U. Med. Sch., Boston, 1948-49; prof. physiology Creighton U. Med. Sch., Omaha, 1967-91, emeritus prof., 1991—, acting chmn. dept., 1971-72. Vis. prof. U. Iowa, Iowa City, 1957-58, Downstate Med. Center, Bklyn., 1965-67; mem. med. com. Azounieh Sanatorium, Beirut, 1961-65; mem. research com. Nebr. Heart Assn., 1967-70, 85-88. Author textbook Spanish translation; contbr. chpts. to books, articles to profl. jours. Recipient Golden Apple award Students of AMA, 1975, Disting. Prof. award, 1992; Rockefeller fellow., 1948-49; grantee med. research com. Am. U. Beirut, 1956-65 Mem. Internat. Soc. Heart Rsch., Am. Physiol. Soc., Internat. Soc. for Adaptive Medicine (founding mem.). Home: 2808 S 99th Ave Omaha NE 68124-2603 Office: Creighton U Med Sch 2500 California Plz Omaha NE 68178-0001

BADEL, JULIE, lawyer; b. Chgo., Sept. 14, 1946; d. Charles and Saima (Hrykas) Badel. Student, Knox Coll., 1963-65; BA, Columbia Coll., Chgo., 1967; JD, DePaul U., 1977. Bar: Ill. 1977, U.S. Dist. Ct. (no. dist.) Ill. 1977, U.S. Ct. Appeals (7th and D.C. cirs.) 1981, U.S. Supreme Ct. 1985, U.S. Dist. Ct. (ea. dist.) Mich. 1989. Hearings referee State of Ill., Chgo., 1974-78; assoc. Cohn, Lambert, Ryan & Schneider, 1978-80, McDermott, Will & Emery, Chgo., 1980-84, ptnr., 1985-2001, Epstein, Becker & Green, PC , Chgo., 2001—. Legal counsel, mem. adv. bd. Health Evaluation Referral Svc. Chgo., 1980-89; bd. dirs. Alternatives, Inc., Chgo. chpt. Asthma and Allergy Found., 1993-94, Glenwood Sch. Author: Hospital Restructuring: Employment Law Pitfalls, 1985; editor DePaul U. Law Rev., 1976-77. Mem. ABA, Chgo. Bar Assn., Labor & Employment Alliance for Women, Columbia Coll. Alumni Assn. (1st v.p., bd. dirs. 1981-86), Pi Gamma Mu. Office: Epstein Becker & Green 150 N Michigan Ave Ste 420 Chicago IL 60601-7553

BADEN, MARK, meteorologist; m. Heather Baden; 1 child Grace Marie. BS in Meteorology, Western Ill. U. Meteorologist KMOV-TV, St. Louis, KCAU-TV, Sioux City, Iowa, KMIZ-TV, Columbia, Mo.; chief meteorologist WOI-TV, Des Moines, WISN, Milw., 1997—. Recipient Seal of Approval, Am. Meteorol. Soc., 1993. Office: WISN PO Box 402 Milwaukee WI 53201-0402

BADER, ALFRED ROBERT, chemist; b. Vienna, Austria, Apr. 28, 1924; came to U.S., 1947, naturalized, 1964; s. Alfred and Elizabeth Maria (Serenyi) B.; m. Isabel Overton, Jan. 26, 1982; children from previous marriage: David, Daniel. BS in Engring. Chemistry, Queens U., Can., 1945, BA in History, 1946, MS in Organic Chemistry, 1947, LLD (hon.), 1986; MA, Harvard U., 1949, PhD, 1950; DS (hon.), U. Wis.-Milw., 1980, Purdue U., 1984, U. Wis.-Madison, 1984, Northwestern U., 1990; D.Univ. (hon.), U. Sussex, Eng., 1989; DSc, U. Edinburgh, 1998, Glasgow U., 1999, Masaryk U., 2000. Rsch. chemist PPG Co., Milw., 1950-53, group leader, 1953-54; chief chemist Aldrich Chem. Co., 1954-55, pres., 1955-81, chmn., 1981-91; pres. Sigma-Aldrich Corp., 1975-80, chmn., 1980-91, chmn. emeritus, 1991-92; pres. Alfred Bader Fine Arts, Milw., 1991—. Author: Adventures of a Chemist Collector, 1995; patentee in field. Guest curator Milw. Art Mus., 1976, 89. Recipient Winthrop-Sears medal Chem. Industry Assn., 1980, J.E. Purkyne medal Acad. Scis., Czech Republic, 1994, Gold medal Am. Inst. Chemists, 1997, Boron USA award, 1997; named Entrepreneur of Year Research Dirs. Assn., 1980, Hon. Citizen, U. Vienna, 1995, Comdr. of the Brit. Empire, 1998. Fellow: Royal Soc. Arts, Royal Soc. Chemistry (hon.); mem.: Appraisers Assn. Am., Am. Chem. Soc. (award Milw. sect. 1971, Parsons' award 1995, named one of the top 75 disting. contbrs. to the chem. enterprise in the last 75 years 1998). Jewish. Club: University (Milw.). Office: Alfred Bader Fine Arts 924 E Juneau Ave Ste 622 Milwaukee WI 53202-2748 Fax: 414-277-0709. E-mail: baderfa@execpc.com.

BADER, RONALD L. advertising executive; b. 1931; With Amana (Iowa) Refrigeration, 1949-55, Gittens Co., Milw., 1955-60, Brady Co., Milw., 1961-70, Hoffman, York, Baker & Johnson, Milw., 1971-74, Bader Rutter & Assocs., Inc., Brookfield, Wis., 1975—, now pres., sec., treas., CEO. Office: Bader Rutter & Assoc Inc Bishop's Wood Ctr 13555 Bishops Ct Ste 300 Brookfield WI 53005-6231

BADGER, DAVID HARRY, lawyer; b. Indpls., June 16, 1931; s. David Henry and Mayme Pearl (Wright) B.; m. Donna Lee Bailey, June 24, 1954; children: David Mark, Lee Ann, Steven Michael. BEE, Rose Poly. Inst., 1953; JD, Ind. U., 1964. Bar: Ind. 1964, U.S. Dist. Ct. (so and no. dists.) Ind. 1964, U.S. Patent Office 1964, U.S. Ct. Customs and Patent Appeals 1971, U.S. Ct. Appeals (fed. cir.) 1982. Engr. GE, 1953-56, Ransburg Corp., Indpls., 1956-62; chief elec. engr. Rex Metal Craft, Inc., 1963-64; patent counsel, corp. sec. Ransburg Corp., 1974-76; legal counsel Ball Corp., Muncie, Ind., 1976-77; ptnr. Jenkins, Coffey, Hyland, Badger & Conard, Indpls., 1977-82; mng. ptnr. Brinks, Hofer, Gilson & Lione, 1982-98. Contbr. articles to profl. jours.; patentee in U.S. and fgn. countries. With USN, 1953-55, lt. comdr. USNR. Named Hon. Alumnus Rose Hulman Inst. Tech., 1987. Mem. ABA (various coms.), IEEE, Ind. Bar Assn. (various coms.), Am. Intellectual Property Law Assn. (various coms.), Licensing Execs. Soc. (various coms.), Indpls. Bar Assn., Internat. Assn. Intellectual Property Law, Indpls. Jazz Club (bd. dirs. 1983-85, 95-97), Junto of Indpls. (bd. dirs. 1997-99). Home: 3524 Inverness Blvd Carmel IN 46032-9379 Office: Brinks Hofer Gilson & Lione 1 Indiana Sq Ste 2425 Indianapolis IN 46204-2045 E-mail: badger938@aol.com.

BADGEROW, JOHN NICHOLAS, lawyer; b. Macon, Mo., Apr. 7, 1951; s. Harry Leroy Badgerow and Barbara Raines (Buell) Novaria; m. Teresa Ann Zvolanek, Aug. 7, 1976; children: Anthony Thornton, Andrew Cameron, James Terrill. BA in Bus. and English with honors, Principia Coll., 1972; JD, U. Mo., Kansas City, 1975. Bar: Kans. 1976, U.S. Dist. Ct. Kans. 1976, U.S. Ct. Appeals (10th cir.) 1977, U.S. Ct. Appeals (4th cir.) 1979, U.S. Supreme Ct. 1982, U.S. Ct. Appeals (fed. cir.) 1985, U.S. Ct. Appeals (8th cir.) 1986, Mo. 1986, U.S. Dist. Ct. (we. dist.) Mo. 1986. Ptnr. McAnany, VanCleave & Phillips, P.A., Kansas City, Kans., 1975-85; ptnr.-in-charge Spencer, Fane, Britt & Browne, Kansas City, Mo. and Overland Park, Kans., 1986—. Co-author, co-editor: Kansas Lawyer Ethics, 1996; chmn. ethics grievance com. Johnson County, 1988—; mem. Kans. Jud. Coun., 1995—, Kans. Bd. Discipline for Attys., 2000—. Co-author: Kansas Employment Law, 1992, 2d edit., 2001. Co-chmn. Civil Justice Reform Act Commn., Dist. of Kans., 1995-96. Mem. ABA, Kans. Jud. Coun., Kans. Bar Assn. (employment seminars, bd. editors 1982-88, CLE com. 1989-95, Outstanding Svc. award 1995, mem. ethics adv. opinion com. 1997—), Kans. Met. Bar Assn. (chmn. civil rights com.), Lawyers' Assn. Kansas City, Kans. Assn. Def. Counsel (age discrimination seminar), Mission Valley Hunt Club (Stilwell, Kans.), Kans. Bd. of Discipline for Attys. Republican. Christian Scientist. Avocations: horseback riding, carpentry, reading. Office: Spencer Fane Britt & Browne 9401 Indian Creek Pkwy Ste 700 Shawnee Mission KS 66210-2038

BADO, KENNETH STEVE, automotive company administrator; b. Amherst, Ohio, Mar. 13, 1941; s. Steve and Hildegarde Paulene (Gutosky) B.; m. Linda Bonita Crabtree, May 30, 1962 (div. Oct. 1989); children: Bradley Steve, Cheryl Lynn Smith, John Robert; m. Polly Ann Steele, Nov. 28, 1989. Student, Ohio U., 1958-60, Lorain County Community Coll., 1960-62. Mfg. planning specialist Ford Motor Co., Lorain, Ohio, 1961-97; farmer Henrietta, 1972—; owner, mgr. The Galleon, Lorain, 1986—. Leader Sub-System Group (Group Tng.), Lorain, 1987-92. Advisor Lorain County Steer Club (4-H), Lorain County, 1977-93, Henrietta Hazers Club (4-H), Lorain County, 1976-88. Mem. Am. Quarter Horse Assn., Ohio Quarter Horse Assn., Moose, Masons (32 degree), Scottish Rite Soc. Republican. Lutheran. Avocations: boating, fishing, horseback riding, computer work. Home: 12359 Baird Rd # 2 Oberlin OH 44074-9632 Office: The Galleon 4875 W Erie Ave Lorain OH 44053-1331 E-mail: Galleon@aol.com.

BADRA, ROBERT GEORGE, philosophy, religion and humanities educator; b. Lansing, Mich., Dec. 8, 1933; s. Razouk Anthony and Anna (Paul) B.; m. Maria Teresa Beer, Oct. 25, 1968 (div. 1973); m. Kristen Lillie Stuckey, Dec. 30, 1977 (div. 2001); children: Rachal Jennifer, Danielle Elizabeth Jane. BA, Sacred Heart Sem., 1957; MA, Western Mich. U., 1968; MDiv, St. John's Provincial Sem., 1985. Ordained priest Roman Cath. Ch., 1961. Mem. faculty Kalamazoo Valley C.C., 1968—, prof. philosophy, religion and humanities, 1968—. Adj. prof. Nazareth Coll., 1985-91, Siena Heights Univ., 1993—; mem. faculty ministry formation, Cath. Diocese of Kalamazoo, 1999—. Author: Meditations for Spiritual Misfits, 1983; columnist Western Mich. Cath., Grand Rapids, 1983-88. Bd. dirs. Kalamazoo Coun. for Humanities, 1983-86, Van Buren Youth Camp, 1993-95. Recipient Edn. award Exxon, 1996; NEH grantee 1991—. Mem. Assn. Religion and Intellectual Life. Office: Kalamazoo Valley CC PO Box 4070 Kalamazoo MI 49003-4070

BAER, ERIC, engineering and science educator; b. Nieder-Weisel, Germany, July 18, 1932; came to U.S., 1947, naturalized, 1952; s. Arthur and Erna (Kraemer) B.; m. Ana Golender, Aug. 5, 1956; children: Lisa, Michelle. M.A., Johns Hopkins, 1953, D. of Engring., 1957. Research engr., polychems. dept. E.I. du Pont de Nemours & Co., Inc., 1957-60; asst. prof. chemistry and chem. engring. U. Ill., 1960-62; assoc. prof. engring. Case Inst. Tech., 1962- 66; prof., head dept. polymer sci. Case Western Res. U., 1966-78; dean Case Inst. Tech., 1978-83, Leonard Case prof. macromolecular sci., 1984-89, Herbert Henry Dow prof. sci. and engring., 1989—. Cons. to industry, 1961—, Edison Polymer Innovations Corp. Author articles in field.; Editor: Engineering Design for Plastics, 1963, Polymer Engineering and Science, 1967-90, Journal of Applied Polymer Science, 1988—. Recipient Curtis W. McGraw award ASEE, 1968 Mem. Am. Chem. Soc. (Borden award 1981), Am. Phys. Soc., Am. Inst. Chem. Engring., Soc. Plastics Engring. (internat. award 1980), Plastics Inst. Am. (trustee) Home: 2 Mornington Ln Cleveland Heights OH 44106 Office: Case Western Reserve Univ Engring Dept Cleveland OH 44106

BAER, JOHN RICHARD FREDERICK, lawyer; b. Melrose Park, Ill., Jan. 9, 1941; s. John Richard and Zena Edith (Ostreyko) B.; m. Linda Gail Chapman, Aug. 31, 1963; children: Brett Scott, Deborah Jill. BA, U. Ill., Champaign, 1963, JD, 1966. Bar: Ill. 1966, U.S. Dist. Ct. (no. dist.) Ill. 1967, U.S. Ct. Appeals (7th cir.) 1969, U.S. Ct. Appeals (D.C. cir.) 1975, U.S. Ct. Appeals (9th cir.) 1979, U.S. Supreme Ct. 1975. Assoc. Keck, Mahin & Cate, Chgo., 1966-73, ptnr., 1974-97; of counsel Sonnenschein Nath & Rosenthal, 1997-99, ptnr., 2000—. Mem. Ill. Atty. Gen.'s Franchise adv. bd., 1992-94, 96—, chair 1996—. Editor Commerce Clearing House Sales Representative Law Guide, 1998—; mem editl. bd. U. Ill. Law Forum, 1964-65, asst. editor, 1965-66; contbg. editor: Commercial Liability Risk Management and Insurance, 1978. Mem. Plan Commn., Village of Deerfield (Ill.), 1976-79, chmn., 1978-79, mem. Home Rule Study Commn., 1974-75, mem. home rule implementation com., 1975-76. Mem. ABA (topics and articles editor Franchise Law jour. 1995-96, assoc. editor 1996-99, editor-in-chief The Franchise Lawyer 1999—), Internat. Franchise Assn. (legal/legis. com. 1990—), Inter-Pacific Bar Assn., Ill. Bar Assn. (competition dir. region 8 nat. moot ct. 1974, profl. ethics com. 1977-84, chmn. 1982-83, spl. com. on individual lawyers advt. 1981-83, profl. responsibility com. 1983-84, standing com. on liaison with atty. registration and disciplinary commn. 1989-93, spl. com. on ethics 2000 1999—), Internat. Bar Assn. Office: Sonnenschein Nath & Rosenthal 8000 Sears Tower 233 S Wacker Dr Chicago IL 60606-6491 E-mail: jbaer@sonnenschein.com.

BAER, ROBERT J. transportation company executive; b. St. Louis, Oct. 25, 1937; s. Charles A. and Angeline Baer; m. Jo Baer, Aug. 27, 1960; children: Bob Jr., Angie, Tim, Cathy. BA, So. Ill. U., 1962, MS, 1964. Regional supr. div. recreation City of St. Louis, 1957-64; dep. dir. Human Devel. Corp., St. Louis, 1964-70; chief to staff to co. exec. St. Louis County Govt., 1970-74; exec. dir. Bi-State Devel. Agy., St. Louis, 1974-77; v.p., gen. mgr. United Van Lines Inc. and subs., Fenton, Mo., 1977-80, exec. v.p., 1980-82; pres. COO, 1982-95; CEO United Van Lines, Fenton, 1995—, Vanliner Ins. Co., Fenton, Total Transp. Svcs. Inc., Mayflower Transit, Fenton, 1995—, UniGroup Worldwide, Inc., Fenton, 1998—; pres., COO UniGroup Inc., Mo., 1987—. Bd. dirs. Firstar-St. Louis. Pres. St. Louis Bd. Police Commn., 1984-89; chmn. St. Louis Regional Conv. and Sports Conv. and Sports Complex Authority, 1990-96; mem. Civic Progress, Inc., 1996—. Office: UniGroup 1 Premier Dr Fenton MO 63026-2989

BAER, WERNER, economist, educator; b. Offenbach, Germany, Dec. 14, 1931; came to U.S., 1945, naturalized, 1952; s. Richard and Grete (Herz) B. 58776, CUNY, N.Y.C., 1953; MA, Harvard U., 1955, PhD, 1958; D honoris causa, Fed. U. Pernambuco, Brazil, 1988, New U. Lisbon, Portugal, 2000, Fed. U. Ceara, Brazil, 1993. Instr. Harvard U., 1958-61; asst. prof. Yale U., New Haven, 1961-65; asso. prof. Vanderbilt U., Nashville, 1965-69, prof., 1969-74; prof. econs. U. Ill., Urbana, 1974—. Vis. prof. U. São Paulo, Brazil, 1966-68, Vargas Found., Brazil, 1966-68; Rhodes fellow St. Antony's Coll., Oxford (Eng.) U., 1975 Author: The Brazilian Economy: Growth and Development, 5th edit., 2001, Privatization in Latin America, vol. 17, 1994, The Changing Role of International Capital in Latin America, 1998; co-author: (with P.Elosegui and A. Gallo) The Achievements and Failures of Argentina's Neo-Liberal Policies, 2002; co-editor: Paying the Costs of Austerity in Latin America, 1989, U.S. Policies and the Latin American Economies, 1990, Latin America-Privatization, Property Rights and Deregulation, 1993, (with W. Maloney) Neo-Liberalism and Income Distribution in Latin America, 1997, (with W. Miles, A. Moran) The End of the Asian Myth, 1999, The State and Industry in the Development Process, 1999. Decorated Order So. Cross (Brazil) Mem. Am. Econ. Assn., Latin Am. Studies Assn. Home: 1703 Devonshire Dr Champaign IL 61821-5901 Office: U Ill 1407 W Gregory Dr Urbana IL 61801-3606

BAERENKLAU, ALAN H. hotel executive; b. N.Y.C. Grad., Cornell U. V.p. ops. Howard Johnson Co.; pres., COO MOA Hospitality; also bd. dirs. Founder, pres. Fla. Hospitality Group; lectr. Cornell U., Hillsborough Cmty. Coll; mem. Howard Johnson Internat. Operators Coun. Mem. Walt Disney Hotel Assn Office: MOA Hospitality Inc 701 Lee St Ste 1000 Des Plaines IL 60016-4555

BAERNSTEIN, ALBERT, II, mathematician, educator; b. Birmingham, Ala., Apr. 25, 1941; s. Albert and Kathryn (Wiesel) B.; m. Judith Haynes, June 14, 1962; children— P. Renée, Amy. Student, U. Ala., 1958-59; A.B., Cornell U., 1962; M.A., U. Wis., 1964, Ph.D., 1968. Instr. math. U. Wis., Whitewater, 1966-68; asst. prof. math. Syracuse U., N.Y., 1968-72; assoc. prof. math. Washington U., St. Louis, 1972-74, prof. math., 1974—. Fulbright sr. research scholar Imperial Coll., London, 1976-77 Mem. Am. Math. Soc., Math. Assn. Am. Office: Washington U Dept Math Saint Louis MO 63130

BAETZ, W. TIMOTHY, lawyer; b. Cin., Aug. 5, 1944; s. William G. and Virginia (Fauntleroy) Baetz. BA, Harvard U., 1966; JD, U. Mich., 1969. Bar: Ill. 1969, D.C. 1980. Assoc. McDermott, Will & Emery, Chgo., 1969-74, income ptnr., 1975-78, capital ptnr., 1979—. Mem. mgmt. com. McDermott, Will & Emery, 1987-92, 95-2001. With U.S. Army, 1969-75. Fellow Am. Coll. Trust and Estate Counsel; mem. ABA, Ill. Bar Assn., Chgo. Bar Assn., Chgo. Coun. Lawyers, D.C. Bar Assn. Republican. Episcopalian. Home: 940 Golfview Rd Glenview IL 60025-3116 Office: McDermott Will & Emery 227 W Monroe St Ste 3100 Chicago IL 60606-5096

BAGLEY, BRIAN G. materials science educator, researcher; b. Racine, Wis., Nov. 20, 1934; s. Wesley John and Ethel (Rasmussen) B.; m. Dorothy Elizabeth Olson, Nov. 20, 1959 (div. Aug. 1993); children: Brian John, James David, Kristin Marie. BS, U. Wis., 1958, MS, 1959; AM, Harvard U. , 1964, PhD, 1968. Mem. tech. staff Bell Telephone Labs., Inc., Murray Hill, N.J., 1967-83, Bell Communications Rsch. Inc., Red Bank, N.J., 1984-91; NEG endowed chair, dir. Eitel Inst., prof. physics U. Toledo, 1991—. Served to 1st lt. AUS, 1960-61. Xerox predoctoral fellow Harvard U., 1964-66, Robert J. Painter predoctoral fellow Harvard U., 1966-67. Mem. Am. Phys. Soc., Am. Vacuum Soc. (chpt. chmn. 1991), Materials Rsch. Soc., Sigma Xi, Sigma Pi Sigma. Home: 16474 W River Rd Bowling Green OH 43402-9469 Office: U Toledo Eitel Inst for Silicate Rsch McMaster Hall Rm 4004 Toledo OH 43606-3328

BAHADUR, BIRENDRA, display specialist, liquid crystal researcher; b. Gorakhpur, India, July 1, 1949; came to Can., 1981; s. Bijai Bahadur and Shakuntala Srivastva; m. Urmila Bahadur, May 29, 1970; children: Shivendra, Shachindra. BS in Physics, Chemistry and Math., Gorakhpur U., 1967, MS in Physics, 1969, PhD, 1976. Rsch. scholar physics dept. Gorakhpur U., 1969-76, asst. prof. physics dept., 1976-77; sr. sci. officer Nat. Phys. Lab. India, New Delhi, 1977-81; v.p. R&D Data Images, Ottawa, Ont., Can., 1981-85; mgr. R&D Litton Data Images, 1985-91; engr. mgr. liquid crystal display material and process Litton Systems, Can., Toronto, 1988-97; prin. engr. Display Ctr. Rockwell Collins Inc., 1997—. Adj. prof. dept. computers and elec. engring. Waterloo (Can.) U., 1995; active various Internat. Confs. on Liquid Crystals; participant numerous profl. meetings; mem. liquid crystal tech. com. SID, 1993—. Author: Liquid Crystal Displays, 1984; editor: Liquid Crystals--Applications and Uses, vol. I, 1990, vol. II, 1991, vol. III, 1992; mem. editoral bd. Displays, 1993—, Liquid Crystal Today, 1995—; mem. abstracting panel Liquid Crystal Abstracts, 1978-80; author more than 75 articles. V.p. nat. capitol region India Can. Assn., 1989-90, pres., 1990-91. Grantee Indsl. Rsch. Assistance Program, NRC Can., 1982-85, 84-87, 88-91, Wright Patterson AFB, 1991-94. Mem. Internat. Liquid Crystal Soc., Soc. Info. Displays (Spl. Recognition award 1993, LC tech. com. 1993-96, chmn. 1997), Inst. Physics, Soc. de Chimie Physique. Achievements include patent for Process for Production of Printed Electrode Pattern for Use in Electro-Optical Display Devices (India); co-development of technology of various liquid crystal displays; patent for wide viewing angle dye doped TN LCDs with retardation sheets. Home: 935 71st St NE Cedar Rapids IA 52402-7295 Office: Rockwell Collins Inc Mail Sta 106-191 400 Collins Rd Cedar Rapids IA 52498-0001 E-mail: bbahadur@rockwellcollins.com.

BAHAR, EZEKIEL, electrical engineering educator; U.S. citizen; s. Silas and Hannah Bahar; m. Ophira Rodoff; children: Zillah, Ruth Iris, Ron Jonathan. BS, Technion IIT, Haifa, Israel, 1958, MS, 1960; PhD, U. Colo., 1964. Instr. Technion, Haifa, Israel, 1960-62; rsch. assoc. U. Colo., Boulder, 1962-64, asst. prof., 1964-67; assoc. prof. U. Nebr., Lincoln, 1967-71, prof., 1971-80, Durham prof., 1981-89, George Holmes Disting. prof., 1989—, Univ. prof., 1999—, dir. program revs., 1981-83. Vis. prof. NOAA, Boulder, 1979 Prin. investigator radio wave propagation rsch., 1964—. Pres. faculty senate U. Nebr., Lincoln, 1980. Recipient Outstanding Rsch. and Creative Activities award U. Nebr., Lincoln, 1980, Scholarship citation U. Colo., Boulder, 1964 Fellow IEEE (life); mem. Internat. Union Radio Sci. (rep. 1978, 81, 84, 87, 90, 93, 96, 99). Avocation: swimming. Home: 2431 Bretigne Dr Lincoln NE 68512-1913 Office: U Nebr WSEC 218 N Lincoln NE 68588-0511 E-mail: ebahar1@unl.edu.

BAHLMAN, WILLIAM THORNE, JR. retired lawyer; b. Cin., Jan. 9, 1920; s. William Thorne and Janet (Rhodes) B.; m. Nancy W. DeCamp, Mar. 21, 1953; children: Charles R., William Ward, Baker D. B.A., Yale U., 1941, LL.B., 1947. Bar: Ohio 1947. Prin. Paxton & Seasongood, L.P.A., Cin., 1947-67, 73-88; ptnr. Paxton & Seasongood, 1954-67, Thompson Hine, LLP, Cin., 1989-94; prof. law U. Cin. Coll. Law, 1967-73, lectr., 1965-67, 73-77; ret., 1994. Served with USAAF, 1942-46. Mem. Am. Law Inst., ABA, Ohio State Bar Assn., Cin. Bar Assn. Office: Thompson Hine LLP 312 Walnut St Fl 14 Cincinnati OH 45202-4024

BAHLS, STEVEN CARL, law educator, dean; b. Des Moines, Sept. 4, 1954; s. Carl Robert and Dorothy Rose (Jensen) B.; m. Jane Emily Easter, June 18, 1977; children: Daniel David, Timothy Carl, Angela Emily. BBA, U. Iowa, 1976; JD, Northwestern U., Chgo., 1979. Bar: Wis. 1979, Mont. 1989, Ohio 1994; CPA, Iowa. Assoc. Frisch, Dudek & Slattery, Milw., 1979-84, dir., 1985; assoc. dean and prof. U. Mont. Sch. of Law, Missoula, 1985-94; dean., prof. law sch. Capital U. Law Sch., Columbus, Ohio, 1994—. Coordinating exec. editor Northwestern U. Law Rev., 1979. Vice chair Columbus Works. Mem. ABA, Am. Agrl. Law Assn. (pres.), Wis. Bar Assn., Mont. Bar Assn., Ohio Bar Assn., Ohio State Bar Found. (bd. govs.), Order of Coif. Republican. Methodist. Avocations: photography, travel, hiking. Home: 499 N Columbia Ave Bexley OH 43209-1003 Office: Capital U Law Sch 303 E Broad St Columbus OH 43215-3200

BAHNIUK, EUGENE, mechanical engineering educator; b. Weirton, W.Va., Mar. 10, 1926; s. Michael and Mary (Sikora) B.; m. Margaret J. Hilton, June 11, 1977; children— Douglas Eugene, Joy Ruth, Barbara Jane, Becky Lynn, David Robert BS, Case Inst. Tech., 1950, MS, 1961; PhD, Case Western Res. U., 1970. Registered profl. engr., Ohio. Devel. engr. Air Brake, Watertown, N.Y., 1950-54; project engr. Lear Corp., Elyria, Ohio, 1954-56; supr. Borg Warner Corp., Bedford Heights, 1956-61; mgr. research and devel. Weatherhead Corp., Cleve., 1961-68; faculty Case Western Res. U., 1970—, prof. mech. engring., 1972—. Contbr. articles to profl. jours.; patentee in field Served to 1st lt., inf. U.S. Army, 1944-46 NIH fellow, 1969-70, NSF fellow, 1968-69, NASA fellow, 1982 Fellow ASTM (award of merit 1988); mem. Am. Soc. Biomechanics, Internat. Soc. Ski Safety, Sigma Xi Home: 7629 Cairn Ln Gates Mills OH 44040-9738 Office: Case Western Reserve Univ Engring Dept Cleveland OH 44106

BAHR, CHRISTINE MARIE, special education educator; b. Rolla, Mo., July 4, 1958; m. Michael Welton Bahr, June 16, 1984. BA, Fontbonne Coll., 1980; MS, So. Ill. U., 1984; PhD, Ind. U., 1988. Project coord. Vanderbilt U., Nashville, 1986-88; assoc. prof. Western Mich. U., Kalamazoo, 1988—. Mem. Coun. for Exceptional Children, Am. Ednl. Rsch. Assn.

BAILAR, BARBARA ANN, statistician, researcher; b. Monroe, Mich., Nov. 24, 1935; d. Malcolm Laurie and Clara Florence (Parent) Dezendorf; m. John Francis Powell (div. 1966); 1 child, Pamela; m. John Christian Bailar; 1 child, Melissa. BA, SUNY, 1956; MS, Va. Poly. Inst., 1965; PhD, Am. U., 1972. With Bur. of Census, Washington, 1958-88, chief Ctr. Rsch. Measurement Methods, 1973-79, assoc. dir. for statis. standards and methodology, 1979-88; exec. dir. Am. Statis. Assn., Alexandria, Va., 1988-95; 01v.p. for survey rsch. Nat. Opinion Rsch. Ctr., Chgo., 1995. Instr. George Washington U., 1984-85; head dept. math. and stats. USDA Grad. Sch., Washington, 1972-87. Contbr. articles, book chpts. to profl. publs. Pres. bd. dirs. Harbour Sq. Coop., Washington, 1988-89. Recipient Silver medal U.S. Dept. Commerce, 1980. Fellow Am. Statis. Assn. (pres. 1987); mem. AAAS (chair sect. stats. 1984-85), Internat. Assn. Survey Statisticians (pres. 1989-91), Internat. Statis. Inst. (Pres.'s invited speaker 1983, v.p. 1993-95), Cosmos Club. E-mail: bbailar@health.bsd.uchicago.edu.

BAILAR, JOHN CHRISTIAN, III, public health educator, physician, statistician; b. Urbana, Ill., Oct. 9, 1932; married; 4 children. BA, U. Colo., 1953; MD, Yale U., 1955; PhD in Stats., Am. U., 1973. Intern U. Colo. Med. Ctr., Denver, 1955-56; field investigator, biometry br. Nat Cancer Inst., NIH, Bethesda, Md., 1956-62, head demography sect., 1962-70, dir. 3d nat. cancer survey, 1967-70, dep. assoc. dir. for cancer control, 1972-74; editor-in-chief JNCI, 1974-80; dir. research service VA, Washington, 1970-72; lectr. in biostats. Harvard U., Cambridge, Mass., 1980-87; prof. McGill U., Montreal, 1987-95, chair dept. epidemiology and biostats. Can., 1993-95; sr. scientist Office Disease Prevention and Health Promotion, Dept. HHS, Washington, 1983-92; prof. dept. health studies U. Chgo., 1995-99, chair dept. health studies, 1995-98, assoc. faculty Harris Sch. Pub. Policy, 1999-2000, prof. emeritus, 2000—. Sr. scientist health and environ. rev. divsn. EPA, 1980-83; lectr. epidemiology and pub. health Yale U., New Haven, Conn., 1958-83; mem. faculty math. and stats. USDA Grad. Sch., Washington, 1966-76; vis. prof. stats. SUNY, Buffalo, 1974-80; professorial lectr. George Washington U., Washington, 1975-80; cons. in biostats. and epidemiology Dana-Farber Cancer Inst., Boston, 1977-83; vis. prof. Harvard U., 1977-79; spl. appointment grad. faculty U. Colo. Med. Ctr., Denver, 1979-81; scholar in residence NAS, 1992-96. Mem. editorial adv. bd. Cancer Rsch., 1968-72; statis. cons. New Eng. Jour. Medicine, 1980-91; mem. bd. editors New England Jour. Medicine, 1992—; contbr. numerous articles to profl. jours.; editor JNCI, 1974-80. John D. and Catherine T. MacArthur Found. fellow, 1990-95. Fellow AAAS (chair sect. U 2000—), Am. Coll. Epidemiology, Am. Statis. Assn. (chair-elect and chair biometric sect. 1979-81, founding chair sect. stats. and environment 1990); mem. Am. Med. Women's Assn. (hon.), Inst. of Medicine, Internat. Statis. Inst., Coun. Biology Editors (chair publishing policy com. 1983-89, pres.-elect, pres., past pres. 1986-89), Soc. Risk Analysis (founding chair Boston chpt. 1985-86). Office: U Chgo Divsn Biol Scis MC-2007 5841 S Maryland Ave Chicago IL 60637-1463 E-mail: jcbailar@midway.uchicago.edu.

BAILEY, DANIEL ALLEN, lawyer; b. Pitts., Aug. 31, 1953; s. Richard A. and Virginia (Henry) B.; m. Janice Abraham, Oct. 10, 1981; children: Jeffrey, Megan. BBA, Bowling Green State U., 1975; JD, Ohio State U., 1978. Bar: Ohio 1978, U.S. Dist. Ct. (so. dist.) Ohio 1978, U.S. Tax Ct. 1979. Ptnr. Arter & Hadden, Columbus, Ohio, 1978—, chair exec. com., 2000—. Co-author: Handbook for Corporate Directors, 1985, Liability of Corporate Officers and Directors, 6th edit., 1998. Bd. dirs. Columbus Met. Community Action Orgn., 1979-80, Franklin County Head Start, Columbus, 1979-80, Faith Luth. Ch., Whitehall, Ohio, 1985-90, Luth. Social Svcs. Cen. Ohio, 1991-2000, Concorde Counseling Svcs., 2000—. Mem. ABA, Ohio Bar Assn., Columbus Bar Assn., Phi Kappa Phi, Beta Gamma Sigma, Omicron Delta Kappa. Office: Arter & Hadden 10 W Broad St Ste 2100 Columbus OH 43215-3422

BAILEY, DARLYNE, social worker, educator; b. N.Y.C., July 21, 1952; d. Arthur and Iris B. AB in Pyschology and Secondary Edn., Lafayette Coll., 1974; MSc in Pychiatric Social Work, Columbia U., N.Y.C., 1976; PhD Orgn. Behavior, Case Western Reserve U., 1988. Lic. ind. social worker, Ohio. Coord. specialized treatment Essex County Guidance Ctr., East Orange, N.J., 1976-82; dir. emergency access svcs. Cmty. Mental Health Orgn., Englewood, 1980-83; field instr. NYU Sch. of Social Work, 1981-82; instr. Case Western Reserve U. Weathered, Cleve., 1986-87; program faculty Case Western Reserve U. Mandel Ctr., 1988-94; asst. prof. Case Western Reserve U. Mandel Sch., 1988-94; rsch. faculty assoc. prof. Case Western Reserve U. Mandel Sch. Ctr. for Urban Poverty, 1991—, dean and assoc. prof., 1994-99, dean, prof. applied social scis., 1999—. Cons. to numerous profl. groups; orgnl. devel. specialist Mid-Atlantic Regional Med. Edn. Ctr. VA, Brecksville, Ohio, 1985-88, Shaker Heights (Ohio) Sch. Dist., 1988-90, Cuyahoga Plan, Cleve., 1989-90; trainer 9-to-5 Nat. Assn. Working Women, Cleve., Family Children and Adult Svcs., Columbus, 1988, Exec. Tng. Inst., 1988-90, The Free Med. Clinic of Greater Cleve., Cuyhoga County Dept. Human Svcs., Sr. and Adult Svcs., Luth. Chaplaincy Svc., Cleve., 1993, KPMG Peat Marwick project, Chgo., 1990-91, Ghana Assn. Pvt. Vol. Orgns. in Devel., Accra, 1992-94, Old Stone Ch. Project, Cleve., 1994, Cleve. Rape Crisis Ctr. Project, 1995; chair secretariat Mandel Ctr., 1994—. Contbr. articles to profl. jours., also book reviews and chpts. to books. Mem. exec. com. bd. trustees Heights Youth Ctr., Inc., Cleveland Heights, Ohio, 1983-95; mem. Human Resources Devel. Com., Neighborhood Ctrs. Assn., Cleve., chair mgmt. and governance task force, 1988-90; bd. trustees Neighborhood Ctrs., Cleve., 1991-94, Tiffin U., 1992-95, Fedn. for Cmty. Planning, Cleve., 1995—, Nat. Coun., Cleve., 1995—; mem. book rev. com. NASW Press, Washington, 1992-95; cons. editor Social Work, 1996—; mem. philantropy and volunteerism adv. com. Kellogg Found., Battle Creek, Mich., 1992—, and many others. Named Nat. Fellow W.K. Kellogg Found., Battle Creek, Mich., 1993-94; recipient George Washington Kidd award Lafayette Coll., Easton, Pa., 1994. Fellow Am. Othopysciatric Assn., Nat. Assn. Social Workers; mem. Nat. Bd. Organizational Behavior Tchg. Soc. (co-chair). Home: 23850 S Woodland Rd Cleveland OH 44122-3310 Office: Case Western Res U Ctr Urban Poverty and Social Change 10900 Euclid Ave Cleveland OH 44106-1712

BAILEY, GLENN E. wholesale distribution executive; b. Scranton, Pa., July 17, 1954; s. Harry E. and Naomi K. (Lee) B.; m. Karan Clover Thomasson, July 16, 1982; children: Virginia, Lee. BSBA, Oral Roberts, 1976; MBA, Harvard U., 1978. Chief fin. officer Spring Arbor Distributors, Belleville, Mich., 1986-87, chief exec. officer, 1987—, also bd. dirs. V.p. planning Word, Inc., Waco, Tex., 1978-82, chief fin. officer, Waco, 1982-86; bd. advisors M Bank, Waco, 1984-86. Founding bd. mem. Habitat for Humanity of Waco, 1985-86. Mem. Am. Wholesale Booksellers Assn. (bd. trustees 1990—). Office: Spring Arbor Distbrs 10885 Textile Rd Belleville MI 48111-2315

BAILEY, JUDITH IRENE, university official, consultant; b. Winston-Salem, N.C., Aug. 24, 1946; d. William Edward Hege Jr. and Julia (Hedrick) Hege; m. Brendon Stinson Bailey, Jr, June 8, 1968. BA, Coker Coll., 1968; MEd, Va. Tech., 1973, EdD, 1976; postgrad., Harvard U., 1994, , 1994—95. Tchr. Chariho Regional H.S., Wood River Junction, RI, 1969—70, Prince William County Pub. Schs., Woodbridge, Va., 1968—72; asst. prin. Osbourn H.S., Manassas, 1973; secondary sch. coord. Stafford (Va.) County Schs., 1973—74; middle sch. coord. Stafford County Schs., 1975—76; human rels. coord. Coop. Extension Svc. U. Md., College Park, 1976—79; dep. dir. Coop. Extension Svc. U. D.C., Washington, 1980-88; asst. v.p., dir. Coop. Extension U. Maine, Orono, 1988—92, interim v.p. for rsch. and pub. svc., 1992—93, v.p. rsch. and pub. svc., 1993—95, v.p. acad. affairs, provost Mich., 1995—97; pres. No. Mich. U., Marquette, 1997—. Adj. prof. George Mason U., Fairfax, Va., 1978; grad. student adv. U. Md., 1979—80; spkr. and cons. in field. Co-author: Contingency Planning for a Unitary School System; contbr. articles to profl. jours. Co-v.chmn. Lake Superior Cmty. Partnership, 1997—; bd. trustees Marquette (Mich.) Gen. Health Sys., 1998—; active Mich. Humanities Coun., 1999—, sec., treas., 2002—; bd. dirs. Pine Tree State 4-H Found., 1988—97, Maine Toxicology

Inst., 1992—95, Bangor (Maine) Symphony Orch, 1991—97, Shorebank, 1997—. Recipient Disting. Alumni Achievement award, Coker Coll., 1998, Northwoods Woman Educator of Yr. award, 1999; fellow Susan Coker Watson fellow, 1967. Mem.: AAUW, Econ. Club Marquette County (bd. dirs. 1997—), Rotary, Epsilon Sigma Phi (sec. Mu chpt. 1987, v.p. 1988, State Disting. Svc. award), Phi Kappa Phi, Phi Delta Kappa. Republican. Avocations: cooking, hiking. Home: 1440 Center St Marquette MI 49855-1625 Office: Northern Mich U Office of the President 1401 Presque Isle Ave Marquette MI 49855-5305 E-mail: jbailey@nmu.edu.

BAILEY, MICHAEL J. manufacturing executive; CFO SC Johnson Commercial Mkts., Sturtevant, Wis. Office: SC Johnson Commercial Mkts 8310 16th St Sturtevant WI 53177 Office Fax: (262) 260-4282.

BAILEY, REEVE MACLAREN, museum curator; b. Fairmont, W.Va., May 2, 1911; s. Joseph Randall and Elizabeth Weston (Maclaren) B.; m. Marian Alvinette Kregel, Aug. 13, 1939; children— Douglas M., David R., Thomas G., Susan Helen. Student, Toledo U., 1929-30; A.B., U. Mich., 1933, Ph.D., 1938. Instr. zoology Iowa State Coll. (now univ.), 1938-42, asst. prof., 1942-44; asst. prof. zoology U. Mich., 1944-50, asso. prof., 1950-59, prof., 1959-81, prof. emeritus, 1981—. Assoc. curator Mus. Zoology, 1944-48, curator, 1948—; rsch. assoc. Am. Mus. Nat. History, 1964—. Contbr. over 150 articles, bulls., revs. to profl. jours. on ichthyology and herpetology. Fellow Iowa Acad. Sci.; mem. Am. Soc. Ichthyologists and Herpetologists (editl. bd., v.p. 1954, pres. 1959, Robert H. Gibbs Jr. Meml. award 1995), Am. Fisheries Soc. (pres. 1974, hon. mem. 1979—, recipient Award of Excellence 1980, Meritorious Svc. award 1989, Justin W. Leonard award of excellence Mich. chpt. 1985), Am. Inst. Fisheries Rsch. Biologists (Outstanding Achievement award 1996), AAAS (coun. 1968-72), Ecol. Soc. Am., Soc. Study Evolution, Soc. Systematic Biologists, Soc. Limnology and Oceanography, Mich. Acad. Sci., Arts and Letters. Avocation: ichthyol. expdns. in U.S., Bermuda, Bolivia, Guatemala, Paraguay, Zambia. Home: 2730 Whitmore Lake Rd Ann Arbor MI 48105-9226 Office: Univ Mich Museum Zoology Ann Arbor MI 48109 E-mail: reevemarian@ameritech.net.

BAILEY, RICHARD, food company executive; Exec. v.p. ops. Kraft Foods N.Am., 1988-96; exec. v.p. worldwide food ops. Phillip Morris Cos. Inc., 1996-98; pres., COO Dean Foods Co., Franklin Park, Ill., 1998—. Office: 3600 River Rd Franklin Park IL 60131-2152

BAILEY, ROBERT, JR. advertising executive; b. Kans. City, Apr. 27, 1945; s. Robert and Sarah (Morgan) B.; m. Rita Carol Burdinie, June 26, 1971; children: Rebecca, Sarah. AB, U. Kans., 1967; MA, Northwestern U., Ill., 1968; PhD, Northwestern U., 1972, MBA, 1979. Research supr. BBDO Chgo., 1973-78, v.p. research dir., 1978-82, sr. v.p., mktg. services dir., 1982-85, exec. v.p., rsch. and planning dir. Author: Radicals In Urban Politics, 1974; contbr. articles to profl. jours. Am. Mktg. Assn.. Office: BBDO Chgo 410 N Michigan Ave Ste 8 Chicago IL 60611-4273 E-mail: bob.bailey@chicago.bbdo.com.

BAILEY, ROBERT L. finance company executive; CEO State Auto Fin. Corp., 1989—, pres., 1991-96, also chmn. bd. dirs. Office: State Auto Fin Corp 518 E Broad St Columbus OH 43215-3901

BAILEY, ROBERT SHORT, lawyer; b. Bklyn., Oct. 17, 1931; s. Cecil Graham and Mildred (Short) B.; m. Doris Furlow, Aug. 29, 1953; children: Elizabeh Jane Goldentyer, Robert F., Barbara A. Jongbloed. AB, Wesleyan U., Middletown, Conn., 1953; JD, U. Chgo., 1956. Bar: Ill. 1965, U.S. Dist. Ct. D.C. 1956, U.S. Supreme Ct. 1960. Atty. criminal divsn. U.S. Dept. Justice, 1956-61, asst. U.S. atty. No. dist. Ill., 1961-65; ptnr. LeFevour & Bailey, Oak Park, Ill., 1965-68; pvt. practice, Chgo., 1968—. Panel atty. Fed. Defender Program, 1965—. Mem. NACDL (faculty 1976-78, legis. chmn. 1976-78). Home: 17 Timber Trail Streamwood IL 60107-1353 Office: 53 W Jackson Blvd Ste 918 Chicago IL 60604-3607

BAILEY, WILLIAM L. communications executive; b. Bay City, Mich., Mar. 23, 1952; s. Benjamin E. and Kathryn Ann (Kehoe) B.; m. Penny Kay Weber, Feb. 28, 1988; children: Mike, Ryan. BS, Western Mich. U., 1975; postgrad., Saginaw Valley State U., 1976-78. Journalist Booth Newspaper, TV, Radio, Mich., 1978-82; publisher Glovebox Guidebooks Am., Saginaw, 1988—; dir. comm. City of Saginaw, Mich., 1997—. Comm., pub. rels. cons. Bailey & Assoc., Saginaw, 1985—. Prodr., host: Dateline Radio and TV Talk Show, 1995—; contbr. articles to profl. jours. Mem. Outdoor Writer Am. Avocations: reading, writing. Home and Office: Glovebox Guidebooks Am 1112 Washburn Pl E Saginaw MI 48602-2977

BAILEY, WILLIAM W. state legislator, realtor; b. Mayfield, Ky., Aug. 1, 1948; m. Donna R. Bailey. BS, Murray State U., 1970; postgrad., Ind. U. City councilman, Seymour, Ind., 1976-80; mayor, 1983-90; Ind. state rep. Dist. 66, 1990—; mem. com. rules and legis. procedures and human affairs com. Ind. Ho. Reps., ranking minority mem., local govt. com., chmn. cities and towns. Mem. Ind. Job Tng. Coord. Coun.; chief offcl. So. Ctrl. Ind. Pvt. Industry Coun. Democrat. Home: 1137 Ernest Dr Seymour IN 47274-3100

BAILIS, DAVID PAUL, lawyer; b. Dec. 19, 1955; B in Commerce, McGill U., 1977; JD, Washington U., 1981; LLM in Taxation, NYU, 1985. Bar: Mo. 1981, N.C. 1990, Nebr. 1991. Atty. Peper, Martin, Jensen, Maichel and Hetlage, St. Louis, 1981-89; gen. counsel Health Sys. Group First Data Corp., Omaha, 1989-91, gen. counsel First Data Resources, 1991-92, gen. counsel, 1992—. Contbr. articles to profl. jours. Office: First Data Corp 212 N 117th Ave # 30 Omaha NE 68154-2211

BAILLIE, JAMES LEONARD, lawyer; b. Mpls., Aug. 27, 1942; s. Leonard Thompson and Sylvia Alfreda (Fundberg) B.; m. Constance Samson, June 19, 1965; children: Jennifer, Craig, John. AB in History, 1964; JD, U. Chgo., 1967. Bar: Minn. 1967, U.S. Dist. Ct. Minn. 1968, U.S. Ct. Appeals (8th cir.) 1969, U.S. Ct. Appeals (5th cir.) 1980. Law clk. to presiding justice U.S. Dist. Ct., Mpls., 1967-68; assoc. Fredrikson & Byron, P.A., 1968-73, shareholder, 1973—. Mem. ABA (litigation sect. co-editor Bankruptcy Litigation 1998, bus. law sect. editl. bd. Bus. Law Today 1993-98, bus. sect. chair pro bono com. 1999—, standing com. on lawyer pub. svc. responsibility 1991-96, chmn. 1993-96, nat. pro bono award 1984, John Minor Wisdom award 1999), Minn. State Bar Assn. (chmn. bankruptcy sect. 1985-88, sec. 2000-01, treas. 2001-02) Hennepin County Bar Assn. (sec. 1992-93, treas. 1993-95, pres.-elect 1995-96, pres. 1996-97). Home: 2851 E Lake Of The Isles Pky Minneapolis MN 55408-1055 Office: Fredrikson & Byron PA 1100 Internat Ctr 900 2nd Ave S Minneapolis MN 55402-3314 E-mail: jbaillie@fredlaw.com.

BAINES, DON A. company executive; BBA in Acctg., St. Edward's U., Austin. CPA. Various positions including contr. process/transport divsn. Trade Co. (predecessor ALTEC), 1976-85; v.p., mgr. of fin. ALTEC, 1986-89; CFO HIS, 1989—; CFO, treas. Chart Industries, 1992—. Office: 5885 Landerbrook Dr Ste 150 Mayfield Hts OH 44124-4031

BAIR, GERALD D. state government official; BS in Bus. Adminstrn., Morningside Coll., 1965. From corp. auditor to dir. revenue and finance Department of Revenue, Des Moines, 1965-75, dir. revenue and finance, 1975—. Mem. Fedn. Tax Adminstrs. (exec. bd.), Legislative Interstate Coop. com., Ankeny Rotary (internat. bd.), Drake U. adv. council. Office: Iowa Revenue and Finance Dept Hoover State Office Bldg Des Moines IA 50319-0001

BAIRD, DOUGLAS GORDON, law educator, dean; b. Phila., July 10, 1953; s. Henry Welles and Eleanora (Gordon) B. BA, Yale U., 1975; JD, Stanford U., 1979; LLD, U. Rochester, 1994. Law clk. U.S. Ct. Appeals (9th cir.), 1979, 80; asst. prof. law U. Chgo., 1980-83, prof. law, 1984—, assoc. dean, 1984-87, Bigelow prof. law, 1988—, dean, 1994-99. Author: (with others) Security Interests in Personal Property, 1984, 2d edit., 1987, Bankruptcy, 1985, 3d edit., 2000, Elements of Bankruptcy, 1992, 3d edit., 2001; (D. Baird, R. Gertner, R. Picker) Game Theory and the Law, 1994. Mem. AAAS, Order of Coif. Office: U Chgo Sch Law 1111 E 60th St Chicago IL 60637-2776 E-mail: Douglas_Baird@law.uchicago.edu.

BAIRD, ROBERT DAHLEN, religious educator; b. Phila., June 29, 1933; s. Jesse Dahlen and Clara (Sonntag) B.; m. Patty Jo Lutz, Dec. 18, 1954; children: Linda Sue, Stephen Robert, David Bryan, Janna Ann. BA, Houghton Coll., 1954; BD, Fuller Theol. Sem., 1957; STM, So. Meth. U., 1959; PhD, U. Iowa, 1964. Instr. philosophy and religion U. Omaha, 1962-65; fellow Asian religions Soc. for Religion in Higher Edn., 1965-66; asst. prof. religion U. Iowa, Iowa City, 1966-69, assoc. prof., 1969-74, prof., 1974-2001, acting dir. Sch. Religion, 1985; Leonard S. Florsheim Sr. Eminent Scholar's chair New Coll., U. South Fla., Sarasota, 1988-89; dir., Sch. of Religion U. Iowa, Iowa City, 1995—2000, prof. emeritus, 2001—. Faculty fellow Am. Inst. Indian Studies, India, 1972, sr. fellow, 1992; vis. prof. Grinnell Coll., 1983; Goodwin-Philpot Eminent chair in religion, Auburn U., 2001—. Author: Category Formation and the History of Religions, 1971, 2d paperback edit., 1991, (with W.R. Comstock et al) Religion and Man: An Introduction, 1971, Indian and Far Eastern Religious Traditions, 1972; editor, contbr.: Methodological Issues in Religious Studies, 1975, Religion in Modern India, 1981, 2d edit., 1988, 3rd rev. edit., 1995, 4th edit., 2001, Essays in the History of Religion, 1991; editor, contbr. Religion and Law in Independent India, 1993; book rev. editor: Jour. Am. Acad. Religion, 1979-84; contbr. articles to profl. jours. Ford Found. fellow, 1965-66; U. Iowa Faculty Devel. grantee, 1979, 86, 92; Am. Inst. Indian studies sr. fellow, 1972, 92. Mem. Am. Acad. Religion, Assn. Asian Studies, N.Am. Assn. for the Study Religion. Democrat. Presbyterian. Office: U Iowa Sch of Religion Iowa City IA 52242

BAIRD, SAMUEL P. state finance director; Dir. Nebr. Fin. & Banking Dept., Lincoln. Office: Nebr Fin & Banking Dept PO Box 95006 Lincoln NE 68509-5006

BAISLEY, JAMES MAHONEY, retired lawyer; b. Dec. 21, 1932; s. Charles Thomas and Katherine (Mahoney) B.; m. Barbara Brosnan, Sept. 7, 1960; children— Mary Elizabeth, Katherine, Barbara, Paul, Genevieve, Charles, James BS, Fordham U., 1954, LLB, 1961. Bar: N.Y. 1961, Ill. 1969. Assoc. Naylon, Aronson, Huber & Magill, N.Y.C., 1961-66; asst. counsel GTE Corp, 1966-69; v.p., gen. counsel GTE Automatic Electric Inc., Northlake, Ill., 1969-81; gen. counsel, v.p. W. W. Grainger Inc., Skokie, 1981-92, corp. sec., 1991-2000, ret., 2000. Bd. dirs. EAC, Inc. Served with USMC, 1954-57 Mem. ABA, Chgo. Bar Assn., Union League Club Chgo., North Shore Country Club. Republican. Roman Catholic. Home: 530 Longwood Ave Glencoe IL 60022-1737 Office: W W Grainger Inc 100 Grainger Pkwy Lake Forest IL 60045-5201

BAKER, BERNARD ROBERT , II, lawyer; b. Toledo, Nov. 19, 1915; s. Joseph Lee and Grace (Baker) O'Neil; m. Elinor Shutts, Oct. 16, 1943; children: Bernard Robert III, Lynn Agnes. AB, Kenyon Coll., 1936; JD, Harvard U., 1941. Bar: Ohio 1946. Practice in, Toledo, 1947—; ptnr. Brown, Baker, Schlageter & Craig and predecessor firm, 1950-91, ret. Pres. B.R. Baker Co., 1946-60; dir. emeritus First Nat. Bank Toledo, First Ohio Bankshares (now Fifth Third Bank); ret. sec., dir. Toledo Blade Co., Blade Comm., Inc. Regional vice chmn. U.S. Com. for UN, 1955-62; past pres. St. Vincent Hosp. Found., Toledo United Appeal, Toledo C. of C.; past trustee Med. Coll. Ohio at Toledo, Salvation Army, Toledo, Goodwill Industries, Toledo; trustee emeritus Rutherford B. Hayes Presdl. Ctr., Fremont, Ohio; past trustee Boys Clubs Toledo; past pres., trustee Med. Coll. Ohio Found., Toledo. Lt. comdr. USNR, 1940-45. Recipient Boys Club Bronze Keystone award, 1965, Disting. Citizen award Med. Coll. Ohio, 1986; named Toledo Outstanding Man of Year, 1948. Mem. ABA, English Speaking Union, Young Pres. Orgn., Harvard Club (N.Y.C.), Belmont Country Club, Carranor Hunt and Polo Club (Toledo), Bath and Tennis Club, Beach Club, Chevaliers du Tastevin (Palm Beach), Psi Upsilon, Old Guard Soc. Roman Catholic. Home: Apt 905 311 S Flagler Dr West Palm Beach FL 33401-5628

BAKER, CARL LEROY, lawyer; b. Woodland, Calif., Nov. 9, 1943; s. Elmer L. and Lucea G. (Tickner) B.; m. Suzon L. Lockhart, June 13, 1966; children: Michele S., Eric L. BA, Sacramento State Coll., 1965; JD, Ind. U., 1968. Bar: Ind. 1968, U.S. Dist. Ct. (no. and so. dists.) Ind. 1968, U.S. Supreme Ct. 1978. Atty. Lincoln Nat. Corp., Ft. Wayne, Ind., 1968-74, asst. gen. counsel, 1974-77, assoc. gen. counsel, 1977-81, 2d v.p., 1979-85, v.p., 1985—, v.p., deputy gen. counsel, 1992—. Mem. assoc. faculty Ind.-Purdue U. at Ft. Wayne, 1976—. Mem. staff Law Jour. Ind. U. Sch. Law, 1966-67. Bd. dirs., v.p. Garrett (Ind.) Pub. Libr., Ch. Builders, Inc., Ft. Wayne, 1986—, pres., 1994; pro bono atty. indigent clients, Ft. Wayne, 1968—; mem. adv. bd. Lincoln Mus. Mem. Ind. Bar Assn. (conf. speaker 1988), Am. Coun. Life Ins. (legal sect. 1972—), Assn. Life Ins. Counsel, Am. Judicature Soc., Ind. Trial Lawyers Assn., Am. Corp. Counsel Assn., Nat. Lawyers Club (Washington), Delta Theta Phi, Sigma Phi Epsilon. Avocations: trout fishing, splitting firewood, hiking, Indiana U. basketball. Office: Lincoln Nat Corp 1300 S Clinton St Fort Wayne IN 46802-3506

BAKER, DAVID HIRAM, nutritionist, nutrition educator; b. DeKalb, Ill., Feb. 26, 1939; s. Vernon T. and Lucille M. (Severson) B.; m. Norraine A. Baker; children: Barbara G., Michael D., Susan G., Debora A., Luann C., Beth A. BS, U. Ill., 1961, MS, 1963, PhD, 1965. Sr. scientist Eli Lilly & Co., Greenfield, Ind., 1965-67; mem. faculty U. Ill., Champaign-Urbana, 1967—, prof. nutrition, dept. animal sci., nutritional biochemist, 1974—, dept. head, 1988-90. Author: Sulfur in Nonruminant Nutrition, 1977, Bioavailability of Nutrients for Animals, 1995; mem. editorial bd. Jour. Animal Sci., 1969-73, Jour. Nutrition, 1975-79, 89-99, Poultry Sci., 1978-84, Nutrition Revs., 1983-92; contbr. numerous articles to sci. jours. Chmn. bd. Champaign-Urbana Teen Challenge Drug Rehab. Program, 1977-80. Recipient Disting. Svc. award USDA, 1987; Univ. Scholar award, 1986; Nutrition Rsch. award, 1986; Am. Feed Mfrs., 1973; Merck award, 1977; Paul A. Funk award, 1977; H. H. Mitchell teaching award, 1979, 85; Broiler Rsch. award, 1983. Mem. Am. Soc. Animal Sci. (Young Scientist award 1971, Gustaf Bohstedt award 1985, Hoffman LaRoche award 1985, Morrison award 1994), Poultry Sci. Assn., Am. Soc. Nutritional Sci. (Borden award 1986), Fedn. Am. Socs. Exptl. Biology, Sigma Xi, Phi Kappa Phi, Alpha Zeta, Gamma Sigma Delta. Home: 2609 Wadsworth Ln Urbana IL 61802-9403 Office: U Ill Nutrition Dept Urbana IL 61801 E-mail: d-baker1@uiuc.edu.

BAKER, DOUGLAS FINLEY, library director; b. Highland, Ill., July 21, 1950; s. Elmer Eugene and Winifred Ilona (Timmons) B.; children: Gretchen, Richard, Charles. BA with distinction, U. Iowa, 1972, MA in Libr. Sci., 1973. Libr. West Side Br., Des Moines Libr., 1974; I-LITE coord. State Libr. of Iowa, 1974-77, dir. office in interlibr. cooperation, 1977-78; dir. N.W. Wis. Libr. System (now No. Waters Libr. Svc.), Ashland, 1978-86, Kenosha (Wis.) Pub. Libr., 1986—. Mem. ALA, System and Resource Libr. Adminstrs. Assn. of Wis., Wis. Libr. Assn., Wis. Assn. of Pub. Librs. Office: Kenosha Pub Libr PO Box 1414 812 56th St Kenosha WI 53140-3735

BAKER, EDWARD MARTIN, engineering and industrial psychologist; b. Bklyn., Mar. 13, 1941; s. Harold H. and Paula B.; m. Shige Jajiki; 1 son, Evan Keith. B.A., CCNY, 1962, M.B.A., 1964; Ph.D. (Research fellow), Bowling Green State U., 1972. Human factors research engr. environ. and safety engring. staff Ford Motor Co., Dearborn, Mich., 1972-77, tech. tng. assoc. mgmt. and tech. tng. dept. Detroit, 1977-79, orgn. devel. cons., personnel and orgn. staff, 1979-81, statis. assoc., ops. support product quality office, 1981-83, statis methods mgr. Asia-Pacific and Latin-Am. automotive ops., 1983-87, dir. total quality planning, cons. and statis. methods corp. quality office, 1987—, dir. quality strategy and ops. support, 1990-92; sr. fellow Aspen Inst., Wye, Md., 1992-95. Mgmt. cons., 1993—. Author: Scoring a Whole in One, 1999; contbr. articles to profl. jours.; editorial referee: Jour. Quality Tech, 1974-75, 77-81. Trustee The W. Edwards Deming Inst., Washington, 1993—. Fellow Am. Soc. Quality (Brumbaugh award 1975, Craig award 1976, 79, 86, 88, Ishikawa medal 1995, Deming medal 1997).

BAKER, ELAINE R. radio station executive; V.p., gen. mgr. WOMC-FM, Detroit. Office: WOMC-FM 2201 Woodward Hts Ferndale MI 48220-1511

BAKER, FRANK C. (BUZZ BAKER), advertising executive; m. Terry Baker; 1 child, Scott. BA in History and Econs., postgrad., Harvard U. With Fletcher/Mayo Assocs., St. Joseph, Mo., 1976-81; pres. & mng. dir. Cedar Rapids unit, dir. acct. mgmt. Creswel Munsell Fultz & Zirbel, Cedar Rapids, Iowa, 1981-90, pres., CEO, 1990—. Bd. dirs. United Way, Hugh O'Brien Found., March of Dimes, Young Parent's Network. Named to Ad Fed Hall of Fame, 1991. Mem. Nat. AgriMktg. Assn., Cedar Rapids Advt. Fedn. Avocation: sports. Office: Creswell Munsell Fultz & Zirbel 4211 Signal Rdg NE Cedar Rapids IA 52402-2524

BAKER, FREDERICK MILTON, JR. lawyer; b. Flint, Mich., Nov. 2, 1949; s. Frederick Milton Baker and Mary Jean (Hallitt) Rarig; m. Irene Taylor; children: Jessica, Jordan. BA, U. Mich., 1971; JD, Washington U., St. Louis, 1975. Bar: Mich. 1975, U.S. Dist. Ct. (we. dist.) Mich. 1980, U.S. Dist. Ct. (ea. dist.) Mich. 1981, U.S. Ct. Appeals (6th cir.) 1983, U.S. Supreme Ct. 1986. Instr. law Wayne State U., Detroit, 1975-76; research atty. Mich. Ct. Appeals, Lansing, 1976-77, law clk. to chief judge, 1977; asst. prof. T.M. Cooley Law Sch., Mich., 1978-80; ptnr. Willingham & Cote, 1980-86, Honigman, Miller, Schwartz & Cohn, Lansing, 1986—. Adj. prof. Detroit Coll. Law Mich. State U., East Lansing, 2001—. Author: Michigan Bar Appeal Manual, 1982; editor Mich. Bar Jour., 1984—; contbr. articles to profl. jours. Founder, pres. Sixty Plus Law Ctr., Lansing, 1978-87, bd. dirs., 1987—; mem. community adv. bd. Lansing Jr. League, 1983-90; co-founder, dir., sec.-treas. John D. Voelker Found., 1989—; bd. dirs. Lansing chpt. ACLU, 1997—, bd. dirs. Greater Lansing chpt., 1997-99; treas. Kehillat Israel, 1996-98; trustee Thoman Found., 2000—. Recipient Disting. Brief award T.M. Cooley Law Rev., 1988, 99. Fellow Mich. State Bar Found.; mem. ABA (Outstanding Single Project award 1980), Mich. Bar Assn. (vice chmn. jour. adv. bd. 1984-87, chmn. jour. adv. bd. 1987—, young lawyers sect. coun. 1980-84, grievance com. 1982-84, John W. Cummiskey award 1984), Ingham County Bar Assn. (Disting. Vol. award 2000). Unitarian. Club: Big Oak (Baldwin, Mich.). Avocations: photography, fishing, running, frisbee, squash. Home: 5127 Barton Rd Williamston MI 48895-9304 Office: Honigman Miller Schwartz & Cohn 222 N Washington Sq Ste 400 Lansing MI 48933-1800 E-mail: fmb@honigman.com.

BAKER, HAROLD ALBERT, federal judge; b. Mt. Kisco, N.Y., Oct. 4, 1929; s. John Shirley and Ruth (Sarmiento) B.; m. Dorothy Ida Armstrong, June 24, 1951; children: Emily, Nancy, Peter. A.B., U. Ill., 1951, J.D., 1956. Bar: Ill. 1956. Practiced in, Champaign, Ill., 1956-78; partner firm Hatch & Baker, 1960-78; chief judge U.S. Dist. Ct. (cen. dist.) Ill., Danville, 1978-94, sr. judge, 1994—. Adj. mem. faculty Coll. Law, U. Ill., 1972-78; sr. counsel Presdl. Commn. on CIA Activities within U.S., 1975 Pres. Champaign Bd. Edn., 1967-76, pres., 1967-76. Served to lt. j.g. USN, 1951-53. Mem. ABA, Ill. Bar Assn. Democrat. Episcopalian. Office: US Dist Ct 201 S Vine St Rm 338 Urbana IL 61802-3369

BAKER, HOLLIS MACLURE, furniture manufacturing company executive; b. Allegan, Mich., Apr. 27, 1916; s. Hollis Siebe and Ruth (MacClure) B.; m. Betty Jane Brown, Aug. 2, 1947; children: Tomelyn Ann, Susan MacClure. Student, U. Va., 1935-37. With Baker Furniture, Inc., Holland, Mich., 1938-40, 45-73, v.p., treas., 1959-61, pres., 1961-70, chmn. bd., 1970-73; v.p., gen. mgr. Grand Rapids Chair Co., Mich., 1959-61, pres., 1961-70. V.p., dir. Manor House, Inc., N.Y.C., 1958-70; pres. Boyne City R.R. Co., Mich., 400 Bldg. Corp., Palm Beach, Fla.; dir. Mich. Nat. Bank, Lansing, 1968-83, Am. Seating Co., Grand Rapids, 1973-83, Mich. Nat. Bank, Grand Rapids, 1959-84, Norton Gallery, Palm Beach, 1984-91. Author: A Brief History of Schloss Branzoll, 1975, A History of the Chateau de Caussade, 1980, A History of the Chateau de la Roque, 1985, Five Castles Are Enough, 1989. Bd. dirs. USCG Found., 1981-91. Lt. (s.g.) USNR, 1941-45. Mem. Nat. Assn. Furniture Mfrs. (dir.), Furniture Mfrs. Assn. Grand Rapids (dir., past pres 1970-84), Zeta Psi. Episcopalian. Clubs: Brook (N.Y.C.), River (N.Y.C.), New York Yacht (N.Y.C.), Leash (N.Y.C.); Kent Country (Grand Rapids), University (Grand Rapids), Indian (Grand Rapids), Peninsular (Grand Rapids); Everglades (Palm Beach), Bath and Tennis (Palm Beach); Buck's (London). Home: 301 Chapel Hill Rd Palm Beach FL 33480-4124 Office: 2220 Wealthy St Grand Rapids MI 49506

BAKER, JACK SHERMAN, architect, designer, educator; b. Champaign, Ill., Aug. 8, 1920; s. Clyde Lee and Jane Cecilia (Walker) B. BA with honors, U Ill., 1943, MS, 1949; cert., N.Y. Beaux Art Inst. Design, 1943. Aero engr., designer Boeing Aircraft, Seattle, 1943-44; assoc. Atkins, Barrow & Lasswith, Urbana, 1947-50; pvt. practice architecture Champaign, 1947—; mem. faculty U. Ill., Urbana, 1947—, prof. architecture, 1950-90, acting prof. emeritus, 1990—. Former mem. exec. com. Sch. Architecture, U. Ill.; hon. bd. dirs. Gerhart Music Festival, Guntersville, Ala., Stravinsky awards, Champaign, Conservatory of Cen. Ill.; hon. bd. dirs. Ruth Hindman Found., Huntsville, Ala.; dir., performer personal performance loft space for Interaction of the Arts and Architecture, 1960—; participant U. Ill. Exploring the Arts course (Act-NCEA award), 1970—, campus honors program, 1995—; former mem. Chancellor's com. on graphic design and art acquisition and installation, former mem. adv. bd., designer of exhbn., Krannert Mus., U. Ill., engr. basic, Ft. Leonard Wood, Mo., topog. engr., Ft. Blevoir, Va. Contbr. ;exhibitions include Monograph and Retrospective Arch. Exhibit: "I" Space Gallery, Chgo., 1997, U. Ill. Temple Buell Arch. Gallery, 1998, Temple Buell Hall Gallery, 2000, Japanese House Drawings Exhibit, Krannert Art Mus., U. Ill., 1998. Mem. U. Ill. Pres.'s Coun., U. Ill. Bronze Cir., 1986; mem. mus. bd. and affiliate World Heritage Mus.; former mem. adv. bd. Krannert Ctr. for Performing Arts, Assembly Hall U. Ill.; exhbn. designer World Heritage Mus., U. Ill. Served with U.S. Army, AFH, 1945-46, Caserta, Italy, ETO. Recipient Excellence in Tchg. awards, U. Ill., "prix d'Emulation Societe des Architectes Diplomes par le Gouvernment" Beaux-Arts medal, 1942, cert. for dedicated and disting. svc., Nat. AIA Com. on Environ. and Design, 1955, Decade of Achievement award, World Heritage Mus., 1992, Art and Humanities award, 1981, 1982, Honor award for advancing profession architecture, CIC/AIA, 1983, Excellence in Edn. award, IC/AIA, 1989, Heritage award, PACA, 1997, numerous other honors and design excellence awards in field. Fellow: AIA (medal 1977), Nat. Coun. Archtl. Registration Bds. (cert.); mem.: Soc. Archtl. Historians, Ill. Coun./AIA, The Nature Conservancy, Nat. Resources Def. Coun., Gargoyle, Scarab, Cliff Dwellers Club (Chgo.), Alpha Rho Chi. Home: 71 1/2 E Chester St Champaign IL 61820-4149 Office: U Ill 117 Temple Hoyne Buell Hall 611 Taft Dr MC-621 Champaign IL 61820-6922

BAKER, JAMES EDWARD SPROUL, retired lawyer; b. Evanston, Ill., May 23, 1912; s. John Clark and Hester (Sproul) B.; m. Eleanor Lee Dodgson, Oct. 2, 1937 (dec. Sept. 1972); children: John Lee, Edward Graham (dec. Aug. 1988). A.B., Northwestern U., 1933, J.D., 1936. Bar: Ill. 1936, U.S. Supreme Ct. 1957. Practice in, Chgo., 1936—; assoc. Sidley & Austin, and predecessors, 1936-48, ptnr., 1948-81; of counsel Sidley & Austin, 1981-93. Lectr. Northwestern U. Law Sch., 1951-52; nat. chmn. Stanford U. Parents Com., 1970-75; mem. vis. com. Stanford Law Sch., 1976-79, 82-84, Northwestern U. Law Sch., 1980-89, DePaul U. Law Sch., 1982-87. Served to comdr. USNR, 1941-46. Fellow: Am. Coll. Trial Lawyers (regent 1974—81, sec. 1977—79, pres. 1979—80); mem.: ABA, Soc. Trial Lawyers Ill., Chgo. Bar Assn., Ill. State Bar Assn., Bar Assn. 7th Fed. Cir., Northwestern U. Law Alumni Assn. (past pres.), Pauma Valley Country Club (Calif.), Legal Club (Chgo.), Univ. Club, John Evans Club (Northwestern U., chmn. 1982—85), John Henry Wigmore Club (past pres.), Law Club (Chgo., pres. 1983—85), Westmoreland Country Club (Wilmette, Ill.), Sigma Nu, Phi Lambda Upsilon, Order of Coif. Republican. Methodist. Home: 1300 N Lake Shore Dr Chicago IL 60610-2167 Office: Sidley & Austin Bank One Plz 10 S Dearborn St Chicago IL 60603

BAKER, JOHN, electronics executive; Pres. Micro Electronics, Columbus, Ohio. Office: Micro Electronics Inc PO Box 1143 Hilliard OH 43026-6143

BAKER, JOHN RUSSELL, utilities executive; b. Lexington, Mo., July 21, 1926; s. William Frederick and Flora Anne (Dunford) B.; m. Elizabeth Jane Torrence, June 16, 1948; children— John Russell, Burton T. BS, U. Mo., 1948, MBA, 1962. With Mo. Public Service Co., Kansas City, 1948—, treas., 1966-68, v.p. fin., 1968-71, sr. v.p., 1971-73, exec. v.p., 1973—, also dir. Lectr. fin. U. Mo.; vice-chmn. Aquila Inc., 1991—. Vice-pres. Mid-Continent coun. Girl Scouts U.S., 1981; mem. adv. coun. Sch. Acctg., U. Mo., Columbia. Recipient Outstanding alumnus award Sch. Adminstrn. U. Mo., Kansas City, 1965; citation of merit U. Mo., 1995. Mem. Tax Execs. Inst. (pres. Kansas City 1968), U. Mo. Sch. Adminstrn. Alumni Assn. (pres. 1965). Republican. Methodist. Clubs: Kansas City, Blue Hills Country. Home: 205 NW Oxford Ln Lees Summit MO 64063-2118 Office: Aquila Inc 20 W 9th St Kansas City MO 64105-1704

BAKER, KENDALL L. academic administrator; b. Clearwater, Fla., Nov. 1, 1942; s. Robert B. and Anne E. Baker; m. Tobin Ratliff McGough, Apr. 12, 1981; children: Kraig, Kris, John, Shannon, Brian. BA with honors, U. Md., 1963; MA, Georgetown U., 1967, PhD, 1969. Instr., Dept. Polit. Sci. U. Wyo., Laramie, 1967-69, asst. prof., 1969-73, assoc. prof., 1973-77, prof., 1977-82, chmn., 1979-82, asst. v.p. for Acad. Affairs, 1976-77; dean, Coll. Arts & Scis., Bowling Green State U., Ohio, 1982-87; v.p., provost No. Ill. U., DeKalb, 1987-92; pres. U. N. D., 1992-99, Ohio Northern U, 1999—. Cons. on survey research to various agys. and polit. candidates, 1967—; panel chmn. Rocky Mt. Social Sci. Conv. 1973, We. Social Sci. Conv., 1975, Council Colls. Arts and Scis., 1983, 86; guest participant study trip to Fed. Republic of Germany, 1977; election observer Fed. Republic of Germany, 1980. Author: The Wyoming Legislature: Lawmakers, the Public, and the Press, 1973; (with R. Dalton and K. Hildebrandt) Germany Transformed: Political Culture and the New Politics, 1981; contbr. articles on polit. sci. to profl. jours. Coach Laramie Soccer Assn., 1978-81. Mem. Am. Polit. Sci. Assn. (chmn. panel ann. conv. 1983), Midwest Polit. Sci. Assn. (chmn. panel ann. conv. 1985, 86), Conf. Group on German Politcs (exec. com. 1984-87, co-editor newsletter 1985-91), Phi Kappa Phi, Omicron Delta Kappa, Pi Sigma Alpha. Home: 920 West Lima Ada OH 45810 Office: President's Office 525 S Main St Ada OH 45810-1599 E-mail: k-baker@onu.edu.

BAKER, KENNETH R. energy company executive; Various mgmt. positions GM Corp., 1969-99; former vice-chmn., chief operating officer Energy Conversion Devices, Inc., 1999; pres., CEO Environmental Rsch. Inst. of Mich., Ann Arbor, 1999—. Bd. dirs. Energy Conversion Devices. Recipient award for outstanding engring. contbn. to environment, City of Los angeles, 1996; named to World's Top 25 R&D Mgrs., A.D. Little, 1997. Office: Energy Conversion Devices 1675 W Maple Rd Troy MI 48084

BAKER, LAURENCE HOWARD, oncology educator; b. Bklyn., Jan. 14, 1943; s. Jacob and Sylvia (Tannenbaum) B.; m. Maxine V. Friedman, July 25, 1964; children: Mindy, Jennifer. BA, Bklyn. Coll. of CUNY, 1962; DO, U. Osteo. Medicine and Surgery, Des Moines, 1966. Diplomate Am. Bd. Internal Medicine. Rotating intern Flint Osteo. Hosp., Flint, Mich., 1966-67; med. resident Detroit Osteo. Hosp., 1967-69; fellow in oncology Wayne State U., Detroit, 1970-72; asst. prof. medicine, dept. oncology Wayne State U. Sch. Medicine, 1972-76, assoc. prof. medicine, dept. oncology, 1976-79, prof. medicine, dept. oncology, 1979-82, assoc. chmn., dept. oncology, 1980-82, prof. medicine, dir. div. med. oncology, dept. internal medicine, 1982-86, prof. medicine, dir. div. hematology and oncology, dept. internal medicine, 1986-93, asst. dean for cancer programs, 1988-94; dir. Meyer L. Prentis Comprehensive Ctr. Met. Detroit; now prof. internal med. U. Mich. Sch. Medicine, Ann Arbor, dep., dir. clin. rsch. Comprehensive Cancer Ctr., 1994—. Bd. dirs. Mich. Cancer Consortium, Dept. Pub. Health, Mich. Cancer Found., U.S. Bioscis. Sci. Bd.; assoc. chmn. S.W. Oncology Group; presenter in field. Author or co-author over 150 articles, 28 books, 15 case reports, over 90 abstracts in field; mem. editl. adv. bd. Primary Care and Cancer; assoc. editor New Agents and Pharmacology; reviewer Cancer Rsch., Cancer Treatment Reports, Cancer, Am. Jour. Clin. Oncology, JAMA, Investigational New Drugs. Major U.S. Army, 1968-70, Vietnam; USAR, 1970-74. Recipient Faculty Ednl. Devel. award bur. Health Manpower NIH, 1973; grantee S.W. Oncology Group, 1974—, Intergroup Sarcoma Contract, 1986-89, Cancer Ctr., 1989-90, Clin. Therapeutics, Kasle Trust, 1988-89, Marilyn J. Smith Breast Cancer Rsch. Fund, 1986—, Program Project, New Drug Devel., 1989-94. Mem. Am. Soc. Cancer Rsch., Am. Soc. Clin. Oncology, Am. Soc. for Clin. Pharmacology and Therapeutics, Am. Assn. Clin. Rsch., Am. Assn. Cancer Edn., Am. Coll. Osteo. Internists, Cen. Soc. Clin. Rsch. Office: U Mich 1904 Taubman Ctr Box 0312 1500 E Medical Center Dr Ann Arbor MI 48109-0005

BAKER, MARK, television newscaster; b. Hannibal, Mo., Feb. 21, 1959; m. Jacqueline Christine Baker; 2 children. BA, U. Mo., 1981. Rep. candidate 17th dist. Ill. U.S. House of Reps., 1996. Methodist. Office: 46 Lincoln Hl SW Quincy IL 62301-9730

BAKER, MARK, food service executive; Chef Seasons Restaurant, Four Seasons Hotel, Chgo. Recipient award, James Beard Found., 2001. Office: Seasons Restaurant Four Seasons Hotel 120 Delaware Pl Chicago IL 60611

BAKER, NANNETTE A. lawyer, city official; b. Tuscaloosa, Ala., Oct. 3, 1957; BS, U. Tenn., 1978; JD, St. Louis U., 1994. Bar: Mo., Ill. TV journalist, St. Louis, Memphis, Knoxville; law clk. to Odell Horton U.S. Dist. Judge, Memphis, 1994-95; with firm Lashley & Baer, P.C., 1995-96; assoc. firm Schlichter, Bogard & Denton, St. Louis, 1996-99; chair Bd. Election Commrs. for City of St. Louis, 1997-99; judge State of Mo. (22d jud. cir.), 1999—. Bd. dirs. St. Patrick's Ctr., Nat. Mus. Transport, Coll. for Living; mem. adv. bd. SSM Rehab. Inst. Mem. ABA, ATLA, Mo. Trial Lawyer Orgn., Ill. Trial Lawyer Orgn., Nat. Bar Assn., Mound City Bar Assn. Office: 100 S 4th St Ste 900 Saint Louis MO 63102-1823

BAKER, PAMELA, lawyer; b. Detroit, Apr. 6, 1951; d. William D. and Lois (Tukey) Baker; m. Jay R. Franke, June 10, 1972; children: Baker Eugene, Alexandra Britell. AB, Smith Coll., 1972; JD, U. Wis. Madison, 1976. Bar: Ill. 1976, Wis. 1976. Ptnr. Sonnenschein, Nath & Rosenthal, Chgo. Contbr. articles to profl. jours. Fellow Am. Coll. Employee Benefits Counsel (charter), Am. Bar Found.; mem. ABA (mem. employee benefits com. 1984—, chair-elect 1998-99, chair 1999-2000, mem. plan mergers and acquisitions com. 1985— mem. fed. regulation of securities com. 1989—, chair 1989-95), Ill. State Bar Assn. (sec. employee benefits sect. coun. 1989-90, vice chair 1990-91, chair 1991-92), Chgo. Bar Assn. (employee benefits com. 1978—, sec. 1984-85, vice chair 1985-86, chair 1986-87, fed. taxation com. 1980—, exec. coun. 1982-85). Office: Sonnenschein Nath & Rosenthal Sears Tower 233 S Wacker Dr Ste 8000 Chicago IL 60606-6491

BAKER, RICHARD GRAVES, geology educator, palynologist; b. Merrill, Wis., June 12, 1938; s. Dillon James and Miriam Baker; m. Debby J.Z. Baker; children: Kristina Kae, James Dillon, Charity Ann. BA, U. Wis., 1960; MS, U. Minn., 1964; PhD, U. Colo., 1969. Asst. prof. geology U. Iowa, Iowa City, 1970-75, assoc. prof., 1975-81, prof., 1981—, chmn. dept., 1992-95, prof. botany, 1988-92, prof. biol. scis., 1992-2000, prof. emeritus, 2000—. Contbr. articles and chpts. to profl. publs. Chmn. Iowa chpt. Nature Conservancy, Des Moines, 1981-82. Grantee NSF, 1984-86, 88-90, 94-97, NOAA, 1992-93; recipient Disting. Scientist award Iowa Acad. Sci., 2001. Fellow Geol. Soc. Am., Iowa Acad. Sci.; mem. Am. Assn. Stratigraphic Palynologists, Am. Quaternary Assn., Ecol. Soc. Am. Office: Univ Iowa 121 Trowbridge Hall Dept Geology Iowa City IA 52242-1319 E-mail: dick-baker@uiowa.edu.

BAKER, RICHARD LEE, book publishing company executive; b. Grand Rapids, Mich., July 27, 1935; s. Herman and Angeline (Sterkenberg) B.; m. Frances Leona Gesink, June 10, 1957; children: Dawn, Dwight, David, Daniel. Student, Calvin Coll., Grand Rapids, 1954-56. Pres. Baker Book House, Grand Rapids, 1957-97, chmn. bd. dirs., 1997—. Bd. dirs. Christian Schs. Internat., 1981-86; pres. bd. dirs. Christian Schs. Internat. Found., 1988—. Mem. Christian Booksellers Assn. (bd. dirs. 1985-93), Evang. Christian Pubs. Assn. (bd. dirs. 1981-84). Republican. Mem. Christian Reformed Ch. Avocations: golf, skiing, racquetball. Home: 2240 Shawnee Dr SE Grand Rapids MI 49506-5335 Office: Baker Book House PO Box 6287 Grand Rapids MI 49516-6287

BAKER, RICHARD SOUTHWORTH, lawyer; b. Lansing, Mich., Dec. 18, 1929; s. Paul Julius and Florence (Schmid) B.; m. Kathleen E. Yull, 1956 (dec. 1964); m. Marina J. Vidoli, 1965 (div. 1989); children: Garrick Richard, Lydia Joy; m. Barbara J. Walker, 1997. Student, DePauw U., 1947-49; AB cum laude, Harvard, 1951; JD, U. Mich., 1954. Bar: Ohio 1957, U.S. Dist. Ct. (no. dist.) Ohio 1958, U.S. Tax Ct. 1960, U.S. Supreme Ct. 1971, U.S. Ct. Appeals (6th cir.) 1972. Mem. firm Fuller & Henry, and predecessors, 1956-91; pvt. practice Toledo, 1991—. Chmn. nat. com. region IV Mich. Law Sch. Fund, 1967-69, mem.-at-large, 1970-85. Bd. dirs. Asso. Harvard Alumni, 1970-73. Served with AUS, 1954-56. Fellow Am. Coll. Trial Lawyers; mem. ABA, Ohio Bar Assn., Toledo Bar Assn., Toledo Club, Harvard Club (pres. Toledo chpt. 1968-77), Capital Club, Phi Delta Theta, Phi Delta Phi. Office: 2819 Falmouth Rd Toledo OH 43615-2215

BAKER, ROBERT I. business executive; b. Bridgeport, Conn., Sept. 28, 1940; s. Irwin Henry and Anna (Keane) B.; m. Patricia Turoczi, Nov. 28, 1968; children: Scott Allen, Christopher Keane. BA, U. Conn., 1962; postgrad., Syracuse U., 1975, U. Pa., 1978. With U.S. Electric Motors div. Emerson, Milford, Conn., 1963-66; with Henry G. Thompson div. Vt. Am., Branford, 1966-75, pres., gen. mgr. Magna div. Elizabethtown, Ky., 1977-84, corp. v.p., 1982-84, pres., CEO, Louisville, 1984-91; pres., owner Distbrs. Source, Portsmouth, N.H., 1991-92; CEO The Chamberlain Group, Inc., Elmhurst, Ill., 1992-96, The Chamberlain Group, Elmhurst, 1996—. Mem. President's Roundtable, Martinsville, Ind., 1993—. Mem. Medinah Country Club, Abenaqui Country Club. Avocations: snow skiing, golf, woodworking. Home: 845 N Larch Ave Elmhurst IL 60126-1114 Office: The Chamberlain Group Inc 845 N Larch Ave Elmhurst IL 60126-1114

BAKER, ROBERT J(OHN), hospital administrator; b. Detroit, Feb. 2, 1944; s. Wesley Ries and Irma Louise (Richards) B.; m. Priscilla Horschak, Sept. 10, 1966; children: Scott, Katherine. B.A., Kalamazoo Coll., 1966; M.B.A., U. Chgo., 1968. Adminstr. Indian Hosp., Sells, Ariz., 1968-70; asst. dir. U. Minn. Hosp., Mpls., 1970-73, assoc. dir., 1973-74, assoc. dir. ops., 1974-77, sr. assoc. dir., 1977; dir. U. Nebr. Hosp. and Clinic, Omaha, 1977-86; pres., chief exec. officer U. Health Sys. Consortium, Oak Brook, Ill., 1986—. Served with USPHS, 1968-70. Recipient Mary H. Bachmeyer award U. Chgo., 1968; Carl A. Erickson fellow, 1966 Mem. Council Teaching Hosps., Omaha-Council Bluffs Hosp. Assn. (pres. 1983) Office: U Health Systems Consortium 2001 Spring Rd Ste 700 Oak Brook IL 60523-1890

BAKER, ROBERT THOMAS, interior designer; b. Kansas City, Mo., Mar. 23, 1932; s. Robert Blume and Justina (Early) B. B.A. in Art, U. Mo., Columbia, 1954, M.A. in Interior Design, 1962; cert., Parsons Sch. Design, N.Y.C., 1958. Interior designer Edward Keith, Inc., Kansas City, Mo., 1958-60, 63-71, Nereoux Interiors, New Iberia, La., 1960-61, Bloomingdales, N.Y.C., 1962-63, Thomas Price Interiors, Kansas City, Mo., 1971-78; owner Robert Baker Interiors Inc., 1978-89; chmn. interior design dept. Au Marché, Inc., 1989; pres. Baker Design, Inc., 1989—. Mem. guidance com. Found. Interior Designer Edn. Research, 1972-82 Bd. visitors Found. Interior Design Edn. Research, 1984-90. Mem. adv. bd. Toy & Miniature Mus. Kansas City, 1985—; bd. govs., chmn. adv. bd. Hand-in-Hand, 1995—. With USAAF, 1954-57. Award of merit Mo.W./Kans. chpt., 1971 Fellow Am. Soc. Interior Designers (pres. Mo.W./Kans. chpt. 1966-72, 73-74, regional v.p. 1969-71, nat. gov. 1969-74) Presbyterian. Home and Office: 12801 Cherry St Kansas City MO 64145-1308

BAKER, RONALD LEE, English educator; b. Indpls., June 30, 1937; m. Catherine Anne Neal, Oct. 21, 1960; children: Susannah Jill, Jonathan Kemp. B.S., Ind. State U., Terre Haute, 1960; M.A., Ind. State U., 1961; postgrad., U. Ill., 1963-65; Ph.D., Ind U., 1969. Instr. English U. Ill., Urbana, 1963-65; teaching assoc. Ind. U., Ft. Wayne, 1965-66; prof. English Ind State U., Terre Haute, 1966—, chmn. dept., 1980—; vis. lectr. U. Ill., 1972-73; vis. assoc. prof. Ind. U., Bloomington, 1975, vis. prof., 1978, 84. Author: Folklore in the Writings of Rowland E. Robinson, 1973, Hoosier Folk Legends, 1982, Jokelore, 1986, French Folklife in Old Vincennes, 1989, The Study of Place Names, 1991, From Needmore to Prosperity: Hoosier Place Names in Folklore and History, 1995, Homeless, Friendless, and Penniless: The WPA Interviews with Former Slaves Living in Indiana, 2000; (with others) Indiana Place Names, 1975. Fellow Am. Folklore Soc.; mem. MLA, Am. Name Soc. (v.p. 1981-82), Hoosier Folklore Soc. (pres. 1970-79, exec. sec.-treas. 1988—). Home: 3688 N Randall St Terre Haute IN 47805-9736 Office: Indiana State University Terre Haute IN 47809-9989 E-mail: ronbaker@indstate.edu.

BAKER, SAUL PHILLIP, geriatrician, cardiologist, internist; b. Cleve., Dec. 7, 1924; s. Barnet and Florence (Kleinman) B. B.S. in Physics, Case Inst. Tech., 1945; postgrad., Western Res. U., 1946-47; M.Sc. in Physiology, Ohio State U., 1949, M.D., 1953, Ph.D. in Physiology, 1957; J.D., Case Western Res. U., 1981. Intern Cleve. Met. Gen. Hosp., 1953-54; sr. asst. surgeon Gerontology Br. Nat. Heart Inst, NIH, now Gerontology Research Ctr., Nat. Inst. Aging, 1954-56; asst. vis. staff physician dept. medicine Balt. City Hosps. (now Francis Scott Key Hosp.) and Johns Hopkins Hosp., 1954-56; sr. asst. resident in internal medicine U. Chgo. Hosps., 1956-57; asst. prof. internal medicine Chgo. Med. Sch., 1957-62; assoc. prof. internal medicine Cook County Hosp. Grad. Sch. Medicine, Chgo., 1958-62; assoc. attending physician Cook County Hosp., 1957-62; practice medicine specializing in geriatrics, cardiology, internal medicine Cleve., 1962-70, 72-93; cons., 1993—. Head dept. geriatrics St. Vincent Charity Hosp., Cleve., 1964-67; cons. internal medicine and cardiology Bur. Disability Determination, Old-Age and Survivors Ins., Social Security Adminstrn., 1963—; cons. internal medicine City of Cleve., 1964—; medicare med. cons. Gen. Am. Life Ins. Co., St. Louis, 1970-71; cons. internal medicine and cardiology Ohio Bur. Worker's Compensation, 1964—; cons. cardiovascular disease FAA, 1973—; cons. internal medicine and cardiology State of Ohio, 1974—. Contbr. articles to profl. and sci. jours. Mem. sci. coun. Northeastern Ohio affiliate Am. Heart Assn.; former mem. adv. com. Sr. Adult div. Jewish Community Ctr. Cleve.; mem. vis. com. colls. Case Western Res. U.; former mem. com. older people Fedn. Community Planning Cleve. Fellow AAAS, Am. Coll. Cardiology, Gerontol. Soc. Am. (former Ohio regent), Am. Geriatrics Soc., Cleve. Med. Library Assn. (life); mem. Am. Physiol. Soc., AMA, Ohio Med. Assn., N.Y. Acad. Scis., Chgo. Soc. Internal Medicine, Am. Fedn. Clin. Research, Soc. Exptl. Biology and Medicine, Am. Diabetes Assn., Diabetes Assn. Greater Cleve. (profl. sect.), Am. Heart Assn. (fellow council arteriosclerosis), Nat. Assn. Disability Examiners, Nat. Rehab. Assn., Am. Pub. Health Assn., Acad. Medicine Cleve., Internat. Soc. Cardiology (council epidemiology and prevention), Am. Soc. Law and Medicine, Sigma Xi, Phi Delta Epsilon, Sigma Alpha Mu (past pres. Cleve. alumni club). Club: Cleve. Clinical (past sec.). Lodges: Masons (32 degree), Shriners Home: PO Box 24246 Cleveland OH 44124-0246

BAKER, SHIRLEY KISTLER, university administrator; b. Lehighton, Pa., Mar. 16, 1943; d. Harvey Daniel and Miriam Grace (Osenbach) Kistler; m. Richard Christopher Baker, Oct. 22, 1966; children: Nicholas Christopher, India Jane. BA, Muhlenberg Coll., 1965; MA, MALS, U. Chgo., 1974. Undergrad. libr. Northwestern U., Evanston, Ill., 1974-76; access libr. Johns Hopkins U., Balt., 1976-82; assoc. dir. librs. MIT, Cambridge, 1982-89; dean univ. librs. Washington U., St. Louis, 1989-95, vice chancellor for info. tech., dean univ. librs., 1995—. Contbr. articles to profl. jours. Mem. ALA, Nat. Info. Standards Orgn. (bd. dirs. 1990-94), Assn. Rsch. Librs. (bd. dirs. 1996-2002, pres. 2000-01), Coalition for Networked Info. (steering com. 1999—), Mo. Libr. Network Corp. (bd. dirs. 1990-2000). Democrat. Avocations: reading, travel. Home: 6310 Alexander Dr Saint Louis MO 63105-2223 Office: Washington U Campus Box 1061 1 Brookings Dr Saint Louis MO 63130-4899 E-mail: baker@wustl.edu.

BAKER, THOMAS C. state legislator; b. McCook, Nebr., Aug. 24, 1948; m. Patricia L. Anderson, Aug. 30, 1969; children: Kimberly Peterson, Jeff Baker, Mike Baker. BS in Agronomy, U. Nebr., 1971. Cert. secondary sci. edn. Owner Trails West Convenience Store and Truck Stop; mem. Nebr. Legislature from 44th dist., Lincoln, 1998—. Treas. B and A Enterprises Inc. Mem. Trenton Rural Fire Bd.; bd. trustees St. James Cath. Ch., Nebr. Farm Bur., Nebr. Cattlemen; former mem. Nebr. Oil and Gas Commn., Trenton Sch. Bd., Hitchcock County Ext. Bd.; bd. dirs. Trenton Ambulance Svc.; former bd. dirs. Nebr. Leadership Coun. Mem. Elks Club, KC. Home: HC 2 Box 140 Trenton NE 69044-9754 Office: State Capitol Dist 44 PO Box 94604 Rm 1528 Lincoln NE 68509

BAKER, VERNON G. lawyer; JD, Am. U., Wash. Coll. Law; BA, Dartmouth Coll. Assoc. Schnader, Harrison, Segal & Lewis; counsel Scott Paper Co.; assoc. gen. counsel Advanced Materiel Group; v.p., gen. counsel, Corp. Rsch. Tech. Hoechst Celanese Corp; sr. v.p., gen. counsel, sect. Meritor, 1999—. Office: Meritor Auto Inc 2135 W Maple Inc Troy MI 48084

BAKER, W. RANDOLPH, brewery executive; V.p., CFO Anheuser-Busch Cos. Inc., St. Louis. Office: Anheuser-Busch Cos Inc One Busch Pl Saint Louis MO 63118

BAKK, THOMAS, state legislator; b. June 8, 1954; 2 children. BBA in Labor Mgmt. Rels., U. Minn., Duluth. Labor rep.; rep. Dist. 6A Minn. Ho. of Reps., 1994—. Mem. commerce com., environment and natura resources policy com., environment and natural resources finance com. Minn. Ho. of Reps. Office: 345 State Office Bldg Saint Paul MN 55155 also: 307 1st St N Virginia MN 55792 E-mail: rep.Thomas.Bakk@house.leg.state.mn.us.

BAKKEN, DOUGLAS ADAIR, foundation executive; b. Breckenridge, Minn., Mar. 12, 1939; s. John and Marie (Folstad) B.; m. Jacquelyn Ann Nielsen, July 8, 1962; children: Amy Michelle, Wendy Kay. BS, N.D. State U., 1961; cert. archives adminstrn., Am. U., 1966; MA in History, U. Nebr., 1967. Archivist Nebr. State Hist. Soc., Lincoln, 1966-67; assoc. archivist Cornell U., Ithaca, N.Y., 1967-71; archivist adminstr. Anheuser Busch Cos., St. Louis, 1971-77; dir. archives and library Henry Ford Mus., Dearborn, Mich., 1977-83; exec. dir. Ball Bros. Found., Muncie, Ind., 1983—. Pres. Ind. Donors Alliance Found., 1993—; mem. Minn. Cultural Found., 1989—. Served to 1st lt. Intelligence Corps U.S. Army, 1962-64. Sagamore of the Wabash, 1992. Fellow Soc. Am. Archivists; mem. Muncie Rotary Club, Ind. Colls. of Ind., Sports and Hobby Devel. Group Inc., Ind. Donors Alliance (founding mem.) Republican. Lutheran. Home: 4801 N Everett Rd Muncie IN 47304-1092 Office: Ball Bros Found 222 S Mulberry St Muncie IN 47305-2802

BAKKEN, EARL ELMER, electrical engineer, bioengineering company executive; b. Mpls., Jan. 10, 1924; s. Osval Elmer and Florence (Hendricks) B.; m. Constance L. Olson, Sept. 11, 1948 (div. May 1979); children: Wendy, Jeff, Brad, Pam; m. Doris Jane Marshall, Oct. 21, 1982. BEE, U. Minn., 1948, postgrad. in elec. engring., DSc (hon.), 1988, Tulane U., 1988. Ptnr. Medtronic, Inc., Mpls., 1949-57, pres., 1957-74, chmn., CEO, 1974-76, founder, sr. chmn., 1976-85, sr. chmn., 1985-89, dir., 1989-94, founder, dir. emeritus, 1994—. Contbr. articles to profl. jours.; developer first wearable, external, battery-powered heart pacemaker. Pres., bd. dirs. Bakken Libr. and Mus. Electricity in Life, Mpls., 1975-94, v.p., 1994—; pres. North Hawaii Cmty. Hosp., 1990-2000, Five Mtn. Med. Cmty., Waimea, Hawaii, 1997—; vice chmn. Pavek Mus. Broadcasting, Mpls., 1989—; chmn. bd. dirs. Archaeus Project, Waimea, Hawaii, 1985—. Staff sgt. USAAF, 1942-46. Decorated royal officer Order of Orange-Nassau (Netherlands); recipient Minn. Bus. Hall of Fame award, 1978, Outstanding Achievement award U. Minn., Mpls., 1981, Med.-Tech. Outstanding Achievement award Wale Securities, 1984, Engring. for Gold award NASPE, 1984, Achievement award Sci. Mus. Minn., 1988, Govs. award Minn. Med. Alley Assn., 1988, Centennial medal Coll. St. Thomas, 1986; named Outstanding Minnesotan of Yr. Minn. Broadcasters Assn., 1988, Lifetime Achievement award Entrepreneur of the Yr. program, 1991, Entrepreneur of Yr. award Minn. Entrepreneur's Club, 1993, Spl. Svc. award Richard Smart Big Island Cmty. Achievement, Waimea, Hawaii, 1995, Am. Creativity Assn. Lifetime Creative Achievement award, 1996, Lifetime Achievement award Minn. High Tech. Coun., 1996, Am. Heart Assn. Heart Ball honoree, Hawaii, 1996, Found. Laufman-Greatbatch prize, 1998, Spl. award Cardiostim 98 XX Anniversary for Engrs. and Industry Founders, 1998, Honpa Hongwanji Mission of Hawaii Living Treasure of Hawaii award, 1998, Heart Inst. Innovator award, 1998; named to Minn. Inventors Hall of Fame, 1995, Am. Heart Assn. West Hawaii Hall of Fame, 1998. Fellow IEEE (Centennial medal 1984, Eli Lilly award in med. and biol. engring. 1994), Bakken Soc., Instrument soc. Am., Am. Coll. Cardiology (hon.), Internat. Coll. Surgeons (hon.); mem. N.Am. Soc. Pacing and Electrophysiology (assoc., Disting. Svc. award 1985), Assn. Advancement Med. Instrumentation (Tex. Heart Inst. Innovator award

1998), Am. Antiquarian Soc., Minn. Med. Alley Assn. (bd. dirs. 1985-94), NAE, 1990—. Lutheran. Avocations: history of medical electrical technology, future studies, ballroom dancing. Office: Medtronic Inc MS LC110 710 Medtronic Pkwy Minneapolis MN 55432-5604

BAKWIN, EDWARD MORRIS, banker; b. N.Y.C., May 13, 1928; s. Harry and Ruth (Morris) B. BA, Hamilton Coll., 1950; MBA, U. Chgo., 1961. With Nat. Stock Yards Nat. Bank, National City, Ill., 1953-55; with Mid-City Nat. Bank Chgo., 1955—2001, pres., 1962-72, chmn. bd., CEO, 1967—2001, Mid-City Fin. Corp., 1982—2001, Darling-Del. Corp., Chgo., 1972-86, Nat. Stock Yards Co., 1985-93; chmn. bd. MBFI, Chgo., 2001—. Mem. Chgo. Crime Commn. Adv. bd. U. Chgo., 1967—; bd. dirs. Duncan-Med. YMCA, 1963-72, Northwestern Meml. Hosp., 1980-88; bd. dirs. West Ctrl. Assn., 1962-67, pres., 1962-65; trustee Am. Mus. Fly Fishing, 1990—. With AUS, 1951-52. Mem. Am. Bankers Assn., Ill. Bankers Assn. (bd. govs. 1966-69), Explorers Club, Adventurers Club (Chgo.), Chgo. Yacht Club, Mid-Am. Club, N.Y. Yacht Club. Home: 175 E Delaware Pl Chicago IL 60611-1756 Office: MBFI Ste 612 801 W Madison St Chicago IL 60607

BALANOFF, CLEM, county official; b. Chgo., Apr. 14, 1953; m. Virginia Balanoff; 2 children. Student, Ripon Coll., 1971-73. Mem. Ill. House, 1989-95; Dem. candidate U.S. House, 1994, 96. Home: 5606 S Blackstone #3 Chicago IL 60637 Office: Balanoff Realty 10100 S Ewing Ave Chicago IL 60617-6021

BALASI, MARK GEOFFREY, architect; b. Chgo., Feb. 29, 1952; s. Alfred Victor and Betty Lou (Biggs) B.; m. Barbara Jane Ritt, May 25, 1985; children: Geoffrey Adam, Maria Elizabeth. Student, Ecole-des-Beaux-Arts, Versailles, France, 1974-75; BS in Archtl. Studies, U. Ill., 1975; postgrad., U. Wis., 1986, 89, 92. Lic. architect, Ill., Mich., Ohio. Architect Davy McKee, Chgo., 1976-80, Perkins & Will, Chgo., 1980-82; prin. Hansen Lind Meyer Inc., 1982-95; v.p. Phillips Swager Assocs., Naperville, Ill., 1995—. Lectr. Italian Nat. Ctr. Hosp. Bldg. and Technique. Editor: Balasi Archives, U. Iowa Librs. Spl. Collections: Austro-Hungarian Army, 1996, Sgt. Balasic WWI Album-Austro-Hungarian Army, 1996; author: Balasic Family Vaudeville Album, 1994; contbr.: (with Paul F. Stevens) Low Level Liberators in World War II, 1998; contbr. articles to profl. jours.; prin. works include Villa Schaefer, Mattoon, Ill., Nunamaker House, Mattoon, Mary Brown Stephenson Radiation Oncology Ctr., Zion, Ill. Active Hist. Preservation Commn., McHenry County, Ill. Mem. AIA (Nat. Coun. Archel. Registration Bds. cert.), Am. Soc. Hosp. Engring., Acad. Architecture for Health, Health Facility Inst., PB4Y Assn., U. Ill. Alumni Assn. Avocations: genealogy, entomology, travel. Office: Phillips Swager Assocs 343 S Dearborn St Ste 203 Chicago IL 60604 E-mail: balasi.m@psa-ae.com.

BALBACH, STANLEY BYRON, lawyer; b. Normal, Ill., Dec. 26, 1919; s. Nyle Jacob and Gertrude (Cory) B.; m. Sarah Troutt Witherspoon, May 22, 1944; children: Stanley Byron Jr., Nancy Ann Fehr, Barbara Haines, Edith. BS, U. Ill., 1940, LLD, 1942. Bar: Ill. 1942, Fla. 1980, U.S. Ct. Appeals (7th cir.) 1961, U.S. Supreme Ct. 1950. Ptnr. Couchman & Balbach, Hoopeston, Ill., 1945-48, Webber & Balbach, Urbana, 1948-81, Balbach & Fehr, Urbana, 1981—. Nat. chmn. Jr. Bar Conf., 1955; bd. dirs. Atty.'s Title Guaranty Fund, Champaign, Ill. Author: Reverse Mortgages, 1997, The Lawyers Guide to Retirement: Serving a New Clientele in a Second Career in Real Estate, 1998. Capt. USAAF, 1942-45. Mem. ABA (ho. of dels. 1956, lawyer title guaranty fund com., past mem. coun. law office practice and real property, probate and trust law sects.), LWV, Ill. State Bar Assn. (elder law com.), Am. Judicature Soc., Masons, Rotary, Phi Delta Phi, Alpha Kappa Lambda. Home: 1009 S Douglas Ave Urbana IL 61801-4933 Office: Balbach & Fehr Box 217 102 N Broadway Ave Urbana IL 61801-2705

BALCERZAK, STANLEY PAUL, physician, educator; b. Pitts., Apr. 27, 1930; B.S., U. Pitts., 1953; M.D., U. Md., 1955. Diplomate Am. Bd. Internal Medicine, Am. Bd. Hematology, Am. Bd. Oncology. Instr. medicine U Chgo., 1959-60, U. Pitts., 1962-64, asst. prof., 1964-67; assoc. prof. medicine Ohio State U., Columbus, 1967-71, prof., 1971-99, prof. emeritus, 1999—, dir. div. hematology and oncology, 1969-94, dep. dir. Ohio State U. Comprehensive Cancer Ctr., 1984-97, assoc. chmn. dept. medicine, 1984-98, dir. Hemophilia Ctr., 1975-79, 1981-99. Mem. clin. rev. com. Am. Cancer Soc., N.Y.C., 1976-82 Contbr. chpts. to books, numerous articles to profl. jours. Served to capt. U.S. Army, 1960-62 Recipient numerous grants Fellow ACP; mem. Central Soc. for Clin. Research (chmn. subsplty. council in hematology 1980-81, councillor 1980-83), Am. Soc. for Clin. Oncology, Am. Assn. for Cancer Research, Am. Soc. Hematology, Phi Beta Kappa, Alpha Omega Alpha Home: 3113 N 3 Bs And K Rd Sunbury OH 43074-9582 Office: Ohio State U Divsn Hematology Oncology 300 W 10th Ave Columbus OH 43210-1240 E-mail: balcerzak.1@osu.edu.

BALDUS, ALVIN J. state legislator; b. Apr. 26, 1926; married; 5 children. AA, Austin Jr. Coll. Former rep. dist. 3 State of Wis., state assemblyman, 1966-72; mem. U.S. House Reps. Washington, 1974-80; state assemblyman dist. 29 State of Wis., 1988-96. Pub. rels. cons. Decorated Bronze star. Mem. VFW. Democrat. Address: 631 Grandview Ct Menomonie WI 54751-1753

BALDWIN, DEWITT CLAIR, JR. physician, educator; b. Bangor, Maine, July 19, 1922; s. DeWitt Clair and Edna Frances (Aikin) B.; m. Michele Albre, Dec. 27, 1957; children: Lisa Anne, Mireille Diane. BA, Swarthmore Coll., 1943; postgrad. Div. Sch., Yale U., 1943-45, MD, 1949. Diplomate Am. Bd. Med. Examiners, Am. Bd. Pediatrics, Am. Bd. Family Practice. Intern, then resident in pediatrics U. Minn. Hosps., Mpls., 1949-51; rsch. fellow Yale Child Study Ctr., New Haven, 1951-52; instr., asst. prof. pediatrics U. Washington Sch. Medicine, Seattle, 1952-57; resident in psychiatry Met. State Hosp., Waltham, Mass., 1957-58; chief resident in psychiatry Mass. Meml. Hosps., Boston, 1958-59; fellow in child psychiatry Boston City Hosp., 1959-61; asst. prof. pediatrics Harvard Med. Sch., Boston, 1961-67; prof., chmn. behavioral scis. and community health U. Conn. Health Ctr., Farmington, 1967-71; prof., chmn. behavioral scis. U. Nev. Sch. Medicine, Reno, 1971-73, dir. health scis. program, 1971-81, prof. psychiatry and behavioral scis., 1971-83, asst. dean rural health, 1977-83, prof. emeritus psychiatry and behavioral scis., 1983—; pres. Earlham Coll. and Earlham Sch. Religion, Richmond, Ind., 1983-84, Connor Prairie Pioneer Settlement Mus., Noblesville, 1983-84; dir. office edn. research Am. Med. Assn., Chgo., 1985-88, dir. divsn. med. edn., rsch., info., 1988-91, scholar-in-residence, 1991—; adj. prof. psychiatry and behavioral scis. Northwestern U. Med. Sch., 1986—, 1986—, sr. assoc. Inst. Ethics, 1991—; adj. prof. med. edn. U. Ill. Coll. Medicine, 1988-93; pres. Med. Edn. and Rsch. Assocs., Inc., 1992—. Trustee Friends World Coll., Huntington, N.Y., 1980-83; bd. dirs. Nat. League Nursing, N.Y.C., 1981-83, Gt. Lakes Colls. Assn., 1983-84, Am. Rural Health Assn., 1985-87; mem. Nat. Bd. Med. Examiners, 1979-88, Nat. Adv. Coun. Nursing Tng., 1978-82; mem. coun. acad. socs. AAMC, Washington, 1987-94. Author: (with others) Behavioral Sciences and Medical Education, 1983, other books; author, editor: (with others) Interdisciplinary Health Care Teams in Teaching and Practice, 1981, Interdisciplinary Health Team Training, 1978; contbr. over 150 articles to scholarly publs. Recipient Rsch. Career Devel. award USPHS, 1961-67, Louis Gorin award in rural health, 1991, John P. McGovern award Health Scis., 1997; Commonwealth Fund fellow, 1951-52, Milbank Fund fellow, 1968, Rural Health fellow WHO, 1976. Mem. Assn. Behavioral Scis. and Med. Edn. (pres. 1978-79, 90-91), Nev. Bd. Oriental Medicine (pres. 1976-83). Democrat. Mem. Soc. of Friends.

BALDWIN, EDWIN STEEDMAN, lawyer; b. St. Louis, May 5, 1932; s. Richard and Almira (Steedman) B.; m. Margaret Kirkham, July 1, 1958; children: Margaret B. Dozler, Edwin S. Jr., Harold K. AB, Princeton U., 1954; LLM, Harvard U., 1957. Bar: Mo. 1957, U.S. Dist. Ct. (ea. dist.) Mo. 1957. Assoc. Teasdale, Kramer & Vaughan, St. Louis, 1957-64; ptnr. Armstrong Teasdale, LLP, 1965-97, of counsel, 1998—. Fellow Am. Coll. Trust and Estate Counsel, St. Louis Country Club, Noonday Club. Republican. Episcopalian. Avocations: golf, hunting, sailing. Office: Armstrong Teasdale LLP 1 Metropolitan Sq Ste 2600 Saint Louis MO 63102-2740 E-mail: tbaldwin@armstrongteasdale.com.

BALDWIN, PATRICIA ANN, lawyer; b. Detroit, May 3, 1955; d. Frank Thomas and Margaret Elyne (Velghe) Mathews; m. Jeffrey Kenton Baldwin, Aug. 23, 1975; children: Matthew, Katherine, Timothy, Philip. BA summa cum laude, Ball State U., 1976; JD, Ind. U., 1979. Bar: Ind. 1979, U.S. Dist. Ct. (so. dist.) Ind. 1979. Ptnr. Baldwin & Baldwin, Danville, Ind., 1979-94; dep. pros. atty. Hendricks County, 1980-90, Boone County, Ind., 1990-94; pros. atty. Hendricks County, 1995—. Sec.-treas., dir. T.F.W., Inc., Danville, 1983—. Bd. dirs. Cummins Mental Health Ctr., 1982-86; mem. Hendricks County Rep. Women, 1976—; Rep. vice precinct com.; mem. parish coun. Mary Queen of Peace Cath. Ch., 1976-80, 81-83; ; bd. dirs. Cath. Social Svcs., Archdiocese of Indpls., sec. bd., 1986—; active Girl Scouts U.S.A., 1964-2000; Cub Scout leader, 1986-99; nominating chmn. Boy Scouts Am. Mon Koda dist., 1998—. Mem. Nat. Dist. Attys. Assn., Ind. Pros. Attys. Assn., Hendricks County Bar Assn., Danville Conservation Club. Office: One Courthouse Sq #105 Danville IN 46122

BALDWIN, SHAUN MCPARLAND, lawyer; b. Chgo., Oct. 19, 1954; BS, No. Ill. U., 1976; JD with distinction, John Marshall Law Sch., 1980. Bar: Ill. 1980, U.S. Dist. Ct. (no. dist.) Ill. 1980, U.S. Ct. Appeals (7th cir.) 1981. Assoc. McKenna, Storer, Rowe, While & Farrug, Chgo., 1980-86, Tressler, Soderstrom, Maloney & Priess, Chgo., 1986-87, ptnr., 1987—. Mem. ABA, Ill. Bar Assn., Def. Rsch. Inst. (chair ins. law com. 1996-98), Ill. Assn. Def. Trial Counsel (bd. dirs. 1996, amicus com. chair 1992—), Ill. Appellate Lawyers Assn. (bd. dirs. 1987-89), John Marshall Alumni Assn. (bd. dirs. 1982-86), Internat. Assn. Def. Trial Counsel (chair membership com. 1996-97, chair casualty ins. com. 1995-96), Profl. Liability Underwriting Soc. Office: Tressler Soderstrom Maloney & Priess 233 S Wacker Dr Ste 2200 Chicago IL 60606-6399 E-mail: sbaldwin@mail.tsmp.com.

BALDWIN, TAMMY, congresswoman; b. Madison, Wis., Feb. 11, 1962; AB, Smith Coll.; JD, U. Wis. Pvt. practice as atty., 1989-92; Dane Country supr. Board of Supervisors, 1986-1994; mem. 78th dist. Wis. State Assembly, 1993-99; mem. U.S. Congress from 2d Wis. dist., Washington, 1999—; mem. budget com., judiciary com. Mem. NOW, ACLU, Wis. State Bar Assn., Internat. Network Lesbian and Gay Ofcls., Nat. Women's Polit. Caucus. Democrat. Office: 1022 Longworth Ho Office Bldg Washington DC 20515 also: 10 E Doty St Ste 405 Madison WI 53703-5103*

BALES, KENT ROSLYN, English language educator; b. Anthony, Kans., June 19, 1936; s. Roslyn Francis and Irene E. (Brinkman) B.; m. Maria Gyorei, Aug. 25, 1958; children— Thomas Imre, Elizabeth Irene B.A., Yale U., 1958; M.A., San Jose State U., 1963; Ph.D., U. Calif., Berkeley, 1967. Instr. Menlo Sch., Menlo Park, Calif., 1958-63; acting instr. U. Calif., Berkeley, 1967; asst. prof. English U. Minn., Mpls., 1967-71, assoc. prof. English, 1971-82, prof. English, 1982—, chmn. dept. English, 1983-88, 2000—. Vis. fellow Literary Studies Inst., Budapest, Hungary, 1973-74, 80-81, 88-89. Contbr. chpts. to books and articles to profl. jours. Fulbright lectr., Budapest, 1980, Fulbright Research fellow, Budapest, 1988-89. Mem. MLA, Midwest Modern Lang. Assn. Home: 2700 Irving Ave S Minneapolis MN 55408-1049 Office: Univ Minn Dept English 207 Church St SE Minneapolis MN 55455-0134 E-mail: bales@umn.edu.

BALGEMAN, RICHARD VERNON, radiology administrator, alcoholism counselor; b. Berwyn, Ill., Dec. 25, 1929; s. Vernon Ernest and Regina Marie (Fitzgerald) B.; m. Wauneta Frances Laird, Nov. 15, 1952; children: Marcia, Kathleen, Barbara, Daniel. Radiology technician, Cook County Grad. Sch. of Med., 1951; BA in Health Svc., Governor State U., 1976, MA in Sci., 1978. Cert. technologist; ordained Deacon Roman Cath. Ch., 1997. Radiology adminstr. Manteno (Ill.) Mental Health Ctr., 1951-84; adminstrv. asst. bus. office Shapiro Devel. Ctr., Kankakee, Ill., 1984-88; with St. James Hosp., Chicago Heights, 1990-99. Inventor DuPont Cronex Tech. Aid, 1965. Village trustee Village of Manteno, 1969-72, chmn. planning commn., 1985-93; pres. Village View TV, Channel 10. With USNG, 1948-56. Gov.'s award Ill. Dept. Mental Health, Manteno, 1971; named Citizen of Yr. Manteno Hist. Soc., 1996. Mem. Am. Legion, Rotary. Roman Catholic. Avocations: camping, making miniature furniture, writing short stories. Home: 555 Park St Manteno IL 60950-1045 E-mail: mvvtv10@iwon.com.

BALISTRERI, WILLIAM FRANCIS, physician, pediatric gastroenterologist; b. Geneva, June 24, 1944; s. Francis William and Mary (Yannotti) B.; m. Rebecca Ann McLeod, May 31, 1969; children: Anthony, Jennifer, William Phillip. Student, St. Bonaventure U., 1962; BA, SUNY, Buffalo, 1966; MD, U. Buffalo, 1970. Diplomate Am. Bd. Pediat., Sub. Bd. of Gastroenterology. Intern Children's Hosp. Med. Ctr., Cin., 1970-71, resident, 1971-72, postdoctoral fellow, 1972-74; rsch. fellow Mayo Clinic, Rochester, Minn., 1974; pediat. instr. Sch. Medicine U. Cin., 1972-74; staff pediatrician U.S. Naval Hosp., Phila., 1974-76; asst. prof. pediat. U. Pa. Sch. Medicine, 1976-78; from assoc. prof. pediat. to prof. medicine U. Cin. Sch. Medicine, 1978-91, prof. pediat., 1983—; prof. medicine U. Cin., 1991—. Bd. dirs. Am. Bd. Pediat., 1991-97, chmn. sub-bd. of pediatric gastroenterology, 1991-93; mem. ednl. coun. Nat. Hepatology Detection and Treatment Prevention Program, 1993-98. Author, editor: Pediatric Hepatology, 1990, Pediatric Gastroenterology and Nutrition, 1990, Jour. Pediatrics, 1995—. Lt. comdr. USN, 1974-76. Recipient Disting. Alumnus award U. Buffalo, 1993. Mem. Am. Assn. for Study of Liver Disease (pres. 1999-2000), N.Am. Soc. for Pediat. Gastroenterology and Nutrition (editor-in-chief Western Hemisphere Jour. 1991-95, pres. 1985-86), Am. Gastroenterol. Assn. Roman Catholic. Avocations: skiing, hiking. Office: Children's Hosp Med Ctr 3333 Burnet Ave Cincinnati OH 45229-3026

BALK, ROBERT A. medical educator; BA, U. Mo., Kansas City, 1976, MD, 1978. Resident internal medicine U. Mo., Kansas City, 1978-81; fellow pulmonary and critical care medicine U. Ark., Little Rock, 1981-83, instr. medicine, 1981-83, asst. prof. medicine, 1983-85; staff physician Little Rock VA Med. Ctr., 1983-85; asst. prof. medicine Rush-Presbyn.-St. Luke's Med. Ctr., Chgo., 1985-88, assoc. prof., 1988-95, prof. medicine, 1995—, asst. dir. sect. pulmonary medicine, 1985-90, med. dir. respiratory care svcs., 1985-93, med. dir. noninvasive respiratory care unit, 1985-87, co-dir. med. intensive care unit, 1986-88, dir. med. intensive care unit, 1988-95, assoc. dir. sect. pulmonary & crit. care medicine, 1993-97, assoc. dir. sect. critical care medicine, 1995—; dir. pulmonary & critical care medicine fellowship tng. program Rush-Presbyn.-St. Luke's Med. Ctr., dir. sect. Pulmonay CCC, 1994-97, 97—. Contbr. articles to profl. jours. Recipient Dedicated Svc. & Superior Individual Effort in Patient Care Alice Sachs Meml. award, 1991, Alfred Soffer Rsch. award Am. Coll. Chest Physicians, 1995, Take Wing award U. Mo.-Kansas City Sch. Medicine, 1998. Office: Rush-Presbyn St Luke's Med Ctr 1653 W Congress Pkwy Chicago IL 60612-3833 E-mail: rbalk@rush.edu.

BALL, KENNETH LEON, manufacturing company executive, organizational development consultant; b. N.Y.C., Aug. 11, 1932; s. Oscar and Elvira (Klein) B.; m. Patricia Ann Whitley; children: David B., Dana K. BA, Antioch Coll., Yellow Springs, Ohio, 1954; PhD, Washington U., St. Louis, 1958. Lic. psychologist, Mo. Gen. mgr. Pacific Coast div. Orchard Corp. Am., 1960-62, indsl. rels. dir., 1963-64, v.p. indsl. rels., 1965-66, v.p., dir., 1967-72, exec. v.p., dir., 1972-75, pres., dir., 1976-88; pres. Orchard Decorative Products div. Borden, Inc., St. Louis, 1988-92, Ken Ball Mgmt. Resources, St. Louis, 1993—. Adj. prof. Washington U., 1978—79. Contbg. author: Humanizing Organizational Behavior, 1976, Making Organizatios Humane and Productive, 1981; contbr. articles to publs. Trust Antioch U., 1980-85, 89-2000; dir. Met. Employment and Rehab. Svc., St. Louis, 1975-2001, chair, 1985-86; dir. St. Louis chpt. Young Audiences, 1990, Narcotic Svc. Coun., 1976, MERS/Goodwill, 2001—. Human Rels. Rsch. Found. fellow, 1955-58. Mem.: APA, Soc. Psychologists in Mgmt. (dir. 1989—, pres. 1992—93). Home: 9875 Northbridge Rd Saint Louis MO 63124-1025 Office: Ken Ball Mgmt Resources 165 N Meramec Ave Ste 400 Clayton MO 63105-3772 E-mail: kenlball@aol.com.

BALL, PATRICIA ANN, physician; b. Lockport, N.Y., Mar. 30, 1941; d. John Joseph and Katherine Elizabeth (Hoffmaster) Ball; m. Robert E. Lee, May 18, 1973; children: Heather Lee, Samantha Lee. BS, U. Mich., 1963; MD, Wayne State U., 1969. Diplomate Am. Bd. Internal Medicine, Am. Bd. Hematology, Am. bd. Med. Oncology. Intern, resident Detroit Gen. Hosp., 1969-71; resident Jackson Meml. Hosp., Miami, Fla., 1971-72; fellow Henry Ford Hosp., Detroit, 1972-74; staff physician VA Hosp., Allen Park, Mich., 1974-77; pvt. practice in hematology and oncology Bloomfield Hills, 1977—. Faculty dept. medicine Wayne State U. Sch. Medicine, Detroit, 1974—. Mem.: AMA, ACP, Mich. Soc. Hematology and Oncology, Oakland County Med. Soc., Mich. Med. Soc., Detroit Inst. Arts, Founders Soc., Alpha Omega Alpha. Avocations: photography, skiing. Office: 44038 Woodward Ave Ste 101 Bloomfield Hills MI 48302-5036

BALLAL, DILIP RAMCHANDRA, mechanical engineering educator; b. Nagpur, India, Jan. 16, 1946; came to U.S., 1979; s. Ramchandra Govind Ballal and Padma (Balwant) Zadkar; m. Shubhangi Sadashiv Ayachit, Dec. 17, 1975; children: Rahul, Deepti. BSME, Coll. Engring., Bhopal, India, 1967; PhD, Cranfield (U.K.) Inst. Tech., 1972, DSc in Engring. (hon.), 1983. Registered profl. engr., Ohio. Lectr. mech. engring. Cranfield Inst. Tech., 1972-79; sr. staff engr. GM Rsch. Labs., Warren, Mich., 1979-83; prof. mech. engring. U. Dayton (Ohio), 1983—. Cons. GMR Labs. and GE Aircraft, Warren, Cin., 1987—. Author: (with others) Combustion Measurements and Modern Development in Combustion, 1990, 91; contbr. about 130 articles on combustion, turbulence, heat transfer and pollution to profl. jours. Project leader Engrs. Club Dayton, 1986, 88, 90; judge, organizer "Odyssey of Mind" Sch. Contest, Dayton, 1985, 87, 88; vice chmn. edn. com. Miami Valley Sch., Dayton, 1988, 90. Named Outstanding Engr., Engrs. Club, Dayton, 1988. Fellow ASME (chmn. combustion and fuels com. 1995—, Best Rsch. award 1986, 92), AIAA (Energy Systems award 1993). Achievements include patents on Ignitor Plug for Jet Engine Combustor. Home: 950 Olde Sterling Way Dayton OH 45459-3100 Office: U Dayton KL 465 300 College Park Ave Dayton OH 45469-0001

BALLARD, BARBARA W. state legislator; m. Albert L. Ballard. B in Music Edn., Webster Coll., 1967; MS, Kans. State U., 1976, PhD, 1980. Rep. dist. 44 State of Kansas, 1993—; adminstr., dir. U. Kans., 1980—, asst. vice-chancellor, 1998—. Democrat. Home: 1532 Alvamar Dr Lawrence KS 66047-1605

BALLARD, CHARLIE, state legislator; Mem. Mo. Ho. of Reps., Jefferson City, 1994—. Republican.

BALLBACH, PHILIP THORNTON, political consultant, investor; b. Lansing, Mich., May 22, 1939; s. Nathan Anthony and Thelma Frances (Bowes) B. BA, Mich. State U., 1960; student, U. Mich., 1960-61; MA, Mich. State U., 1967. Social worker State of Mich., Corunna, 1961-64; legis. aide State Rep. H. James Starr, Lansing, Mich., 1964-67; exec. asst. State Atty. Gen.'s Dept., 1967-81; county commr. Ingham County, Mason, 1980-93. Pub., Lansing This Weekend, 1963-64, The Gooseneck Tidings, 1977. Coord. Greater Lansing Assn. for Cmty. Edn., 1961-66; mem. Lansing Bd. Election Canvassers, 1965-69; dir. Cmty. Mental Health Bd., Lansing, 1977-99; treas. Zolton Ferency for Gov. Com., 1977-83; county liaison Eastside Neighborhood Orgn., Lansing, 1980-93; commr. Tri-County Regional Planning Com., Lansing, 1981-84; chairperson Ingham County Emergency Planning Com., Mason, Mich., 1988-93; campaign dir. Citizens for Pub. Recycling, Lansing, 1990; treas. People Achieving Legis. Power, 1992-95; campaign coord. Citizens for a Better Lansing, 1993-2002; bd. dirs. Peace Edn. Ctr., 1999-2002. Recipient Achievement award Nat. Assn. Counties, 1986, Dem. Party Ferency Activist Achievement award, 1998. Mem. Mich. Assn. Community Mental Health Bds. Democrat. Avocations: writing poetry, history studies, skiing, softball. Home: 312 Leslie St Lansing MI 48912-2723

BALLOU, JOHN DENNIS, state legislator; Grad., Shawnee Mission North H.S., Kans., 1975. Plasterer, 1979-83; owner Ballou Plastering Inc., 1984-95; mem. Kans. State Ho. of Reps. Dist. 43, 1995—; owner, ptnr. Kleier Plastering, Inc., 1997—.

BALSAM, THEODORE, physician; b. N.Y.C., Apr. 11, 1931; s. Abraham and Esther (Golden) B.; m. Barbara Korn, Dec. 25, 1952; children: Hugh, Adrienne, Lisbeth. BA, NYU, 1952; MD, Chgo. Med. Sch., 1957; MPH, Johns Hopkins U., 1959. Diplomate Am. Bd. Internal Medicine. Intern Charity Hosp., New Orleans, 1957-58; fellow Johns Hopkins U., Balt., 1958-59; resident in medicine Bklyn. Hosp., 1959-61, fellow in gastroenterology, 1961-62; physician USPHS, S.I., 1964-97; pvt. practice Founders Med. Group, Chgo., 1997—. Pres. med. staff Louis A. Weiss Meml. Hosp., Chgo., 1976-78, 93-95, dir. patient hosp. orgn., 1996—. Mem. Sch. Bd., Lincolnwood, Ill., 1970-72. Fellow Am. Coll. Gastroenterology; mem. AMA, Ill. State Med. Soc., Chgo. Med. Soc. Avocation: travel. Office: Weiss Meml Hosp 4640 N Marine Dr Chicago IL 60640-5719

BALTAZZI, EVAN SERGE, engineering research consulting company executive; b. Izmir, Turkey, Apr. 11, 1921; came to U.S., 1959, naturalized, 1964; s. Phocion George and Agnes Zoe (Varda) B.; m. Nellie Despina (Biorlaro), July 17, 1945; children— Agnes, James, Maria D.Phys. Scis., Sorbonne U., Paris, 1949; D.Phil. in Chemistry, Oxford (Eng.) U., 1954. Rsch. dir., prof. rsch. French Nat. Rsch. Ctr., Paris, 1947-59; group leader organic chemistry rsch. Nat. Aluminate Corp., Chgo., 1959-61; mgr. organic chemistry sect. IIT Rsch. Inst., 1961-63; dir. rsch. lab. Addressograph-Multigraph Corp., Chgo. and Cleve., 1963-77; pres. Evanel Assocs., Sagamore Hills, Ohio, 1977—. Mem. com. on U.S. currency NRC, 1985-86. Author: Basic American Self-Protection, 1972, Kickboxing, 1976, Stickfighting, 1977, Self-Protection at Close Quarters, 1981, Self-Protection Complete: The A.S.P. System, 1992, Dog Gone West: A Western for Dog Lovers, 1994, Plato and Socrates Trial, 1995; patentee in field; originator Am. Self-Protection System. Mem. judo com. U.S. Olympic Com., 1967-74 Recipient Citizen of Yr. award Citizenship Coun. Met. Chgo., 1964; Outstanding Achievement award in sci. Immigrants Service League, 1965, citation, 1965; Outstanding Program award YMCA, 1967; recognition award Gordon Rsch. Confs., 1976; Ohio Spl. Olympics Gold medal volunteering award, 1999; named Outstanding Scientists of XXth Century Internat. Biog. Ctr., 2000; NRC Can. fellow, 1955, Brit. Coun. fellow, 1952-54 Fellow Am. Inst. Chemists (vice chmn. Chgo. chpt. 1970), Am. Chem. Soc. (sr.), Royal Chem. Soc. U.K., Am. Inst. Chem.,

Soc. Photog. Scientists and Engrs. (pres., bd. dirs. Cleve. chpt. 1975-82), Am. Self-Protection Assn. (pres. 1965—), N.Y. Acad. Scis. Avocations: fencing, judo, aikido, Am. self-protection originator. E-mail: ebaltazzi@aol.com.

BALZEKAS, STANLEY, JR. museum director; b. Chgo., Oct. 8, 1924; s. Stanley and Emily B.; widowed; children— Stanley, III, Robert, Carole Rene. B.S., DePaul U., Chgo., 1950, M.A., 1951. Pres. Balzekas Mus. Lithuanian Culture, Chgo., 1966—, Balzekas Motor Sales, Chgo., 1952—; hon. consul Consulate of the Republic of Lithuania, Palm Beach, Fla. Hon. consul for Republic of Lithuania, Palm Beach, Fla. Trustee Lincoln Acad., Cath. Charities, Am.-Lithuanian Coun.; chmn. Sister Cities/Chgo.-Vilnius Friendship Com., Trade & Cultural Ctr.; mem. adv. bd. Chgo. Cultural Affairs; hon. consul Rep. of Lithuania, Palm Beach, Fla. Served with AUS, 1942-45, ETO. Decorated Bronze Star; decorated 3d degree order Grand Duke Gediminas, Pres. Lithuania; recipient Wigilia medal Polish Geneal. Soc. Am., medal DAR, Disting. Alumni award DePaul U., 1991. Mem. Am. Assn. Mus., Ethnic Cultural Preservation Coun. (pres. 1977—), Press Club (Chgo.), Literary Club (Chgo.), City Club (Chgo., ethnic chmn.), Exec. Club (Chgo.), Am. Legion Office: 4030 S Archer Ave Chicago IL 60632-1140

BAMBERGER, DAVID, opera company executive; b. Albany, N.Y., Oct. 14, 1940; s. Bernard J. and Ethel K. Bamberger; m. Carola Beral, June 8, 1965; 1 son, Steven B. Student, U. Paris, 1961; BA, Swarthmore Coll., 1962; postgrad., Yale U., 1963; DHL (hon.), Swarthmore Coll., 1994. Mem. directing staff N.Y.C. Opera, 1966-70; guest dir. Nat. Opera Chile, 1970, Cin. Opera, 1968, Augusta Opera (Ga.), 1970, Pitts. Opera, 1971, 76, 81, Columbus Opera (Ohio); gen. dir. Cleve. Opera, 1976—. Artistic dir. Toledo Opera Assn., 1983-85. Bd. dirs. Opera Am., Nat. Alliance Musical Theatre Prodrs. Author: Jewish history textbooks; contbr. articles to Opera News. Office: Cleveland Opera 1422 Euclid Ave Ste 1052 Cleveland OH 44115-2063

BAMBERGER, RICHARD H. lawyer; b. Cleve., Sept. 18, 1945; BA, Bowdoin Coll., 1967; JD, Case Western Res. U., 1972. Bar: Ohio 1972. Law clk. to Hon. William K. Thomas U.S. Dist. Ct. (no. dist.), Ohio, 1972-74; ptnr. Baker & Hostetler, Cleve. Adj. prof. law Case Western Res. U., 1996—. Mem. ABA (mem. employee benefits com.), Ohio State, Cleve. Bar Assn. Office: Baker & Hostetler LLP 3200 Nat City Ctr 1900 E 9th St Ste 3200 Cleveland OH 44114-3475

BAMBRICK, JAMES JOSEPH, labor economist, labor relations executive; b. N.Y.C., Apr. 26, 1917; s. James Joseph and Mae (Murphy) B.; m. Margaret Mary Donlan, June 26, 1948; children: Patricia Bambrick Benek (dec.), Thomas G., Mary Alice Bambrick Schneider, Kathleen Bambrick Guzaukas, James Joseph Jr. BS, NYU, 1940, MBA, 1942; BS, U.S. Mcht. Marine Acad., 1946. Exec. dir. Labor Bur., N.Y.C., 1940-42; personnel dir. Allegheny Airlines, Wilmington, Del., 1942-44; mgr. labor relations research The Conf. Bd., N.Y.C., 1947-58; corp. labor economist Standard Oil Co., Cleve., 1958-81; exec. dir. Labor Econ. Inst., Cleveland Heights, Ohio, 1981—. Mem. bus. adv. council U.S. Bur. Labor Stats., Washington, 1971—, chmn. wages and indsl. relations com., 1980-85; instr. NYU, 1946-53, John Carroll U., University Heights, Ohio, 1968-71; lectr. Cleve. State U., 1963-68. Author: Preparing for Collective Bargaining, 1959, Handbook of Modern Personnel Administration, 1972; contbr. chpts. to The Foreman/Supervisor's Handbook, 1984; contbr. articles to profl. jours. Chmn. Ohio Rep. Fin. Com., Cuyahoga County, Cleve., 1963—; pres. Cath. Interracial Council, Cleve., 1965-68, bd. dirs. 1969—; v.p. Navy League of U.S., Cleve., 1984—. Served to lt. USNR, 1944-46. Named Hibernian Man of the Yr. Ancient Order of Hibernians, 1974. Fellow Soc. for Advancement of Mgmt. (pres. 1955-58); mem. Am. Econ. Assn., Indsl. Relations Research Assn., U.S. Mcht. Marine Acad. Alumni Assn. (pres., bd. dirs. N.E. Ohio, 1965-70). Republican. Clubs: City (Cleve.) (trustee 1972-75, v.p. Forum Found. 1981-88). Lodge: K.C. Avocations: fencing, sailing, golf.

BAN, STEPHEN DENNIS, natural gas industry research institute executive; b. Hammond, Ind., Dec. 16, 1940; s. Stephen and Mary Veronica (Holecsko) B.; m. Margie Cahill, Aug. 17, 1963; children: Stephen, Mary Beth, Brian. BSME, Rose Hulman Inst. Tech., 1962; MS in Engring. Sci., Case Inst. Tech., 1964, PhD in Engring., 1967. Chief div. fluid and chem. processes Battelle Columbus (Ohio) Labs., 1970-72, chief div. emission systems, 1972-76, corp. coord. engring. scis. program, 1972-76; v.p. R & D, Bituminous Materials, Inc., Terre Haute, Ind., 1976-81, Gas Rsch. Inst., Chgo., 1981-83, sr. v.p. R & D ops., 1983-86, exec. v.p., chief oper. officer, 1986-87, pres., chief exec. officer, 1987-2000. Bd. dirs. UGI Corp., Valley Forge, Pa., Energen Corp., Birmingham, Ala.; mem. indsl. adv. bd. U. Ill., Chgo., 1983-93; mem. energy rsch. adv. bd. U.S. Dept. Energy, Washington, 1987-90, mem. adv. com. on renewable energy and energy efficiency joint ventures, 1992-95; mem. Coun. Energy Engring. Rsch., Washington, 1983-87; mem. bd. on energy and environ. sys. NRC, 1993-96; mem. Natural Gas Coun., 1993-97. Fellow NDEA, 1962-65, NSF, 1965-67. Mem. U.S. Energy Assn. (bd. dirs. 1992-2000), Chgo. Econs. Club, Sigma Xi, Tau Beta Pi.

BANACH, ART JOHN, graphic artist; b. Chgo., May 22, 1931; s. Vincent and Anna (Zajac) B. Grad. Art. Inst. of Chgo., 1955; pupil painting studies Mrs. Melin, Chgo.; m. Loretta A. Nolan, Oct. 15, 1966; children: Heather Anne, Lynnea Joan. Owner, dir. Art J. Banach Studios, 1949—, cartoon syndicate for newspapers, house organs and advt. functions, 1954—, owner and operater advt. agy., 1954-56, feature news and picture syndicate, distbn. U.S. and fgn. countries. Dir. Speculators S Fund. Recipient award 1st Easter Seal contest Ill. Assn. Crippled, Inc., 1949. Chgo. Pub. Sch. Art Soc. Scholar. Mem. Artist's Guild Chgo., Am Mgmt. Assn., Chgo. Assn. of Commerce and Industry, Chgo. Federated Advt. Club, Am. Mktg. Assn., Internat. Platform Assn., Chgo. Advt. Club, Chgo. Soc. Communicating Arts, Am. Ctr. For Design, Chgo. Calligraphy Collective, Columbia Yacht Club, Advt. Execs. Club, Art Dirs. Club (Chgo.). Home: 1076 Leahy Cir East Des Plaines IL 60016-6050

BANAS, C(HRISTINE) LESLIE, lawyer; b. Swindon, Wiltshire, Eng., Oct. 29, 1951; arrived in U.S., 1957; d. Stanley M. and Helena Ann (Boryn) Banas; m. Dale J. Buras, May 1, 1976; children: Eric Buras, Andrea Buras. BA magna cum laude, U. Detroit, 1973; JD cum laude, Wayne State U., 1975. Bar: Mich. 1976, U.S. Supreme Ct. 1980. Atty. Hyman & Rice, Southfield, Mich., 1976-77, Hyman, Gurwin, Nachman, Friedman & Winkelman, Southfield, 1977-82, ptnr., 1982-87, Honigman Miller Schwartz and Cohn LLP, Detroit, 1987—. Contbr. articles to profl. jours. Mem.: ABA, Fed. Bar Assn., Oakland County Bar, State Bar Mich. (bd. dirs. real property sect. coun.), Brimingham Athletic Club, Women's Econ. Club (bd. dirs., past pres.). Roman Catholic. Avocations: gardening, photography, skiing. Office: Honigman Miller Schwartz and Cohn LLP 32270 Telegraph Rd Ste 225 Bingham Farms MI 48025-2457 E-mail: lbanas@honigman.com.

BANASZYNSKI, CAROL JEAN, educator; b. Hawkins, Wis., Jan. 3, 1951; BS in Biology, U. Wis., LaCrosse, 1973; MS in Profl. Devel., U. Wis., Whitewater, 1987. Tchr. Deerfield Cmty. Schs., 1973—. Coach Youth T-ball/softball; co-chairperson Adopt-A-Highway; group leader 4-H Club; counselor Boy Scout Environtl. Merit Badge program Recipient Wis. H.S. Tchr. of Yr., 1997-98, Wis. Tchr. of Yr. 1998, Award of Excellence Wis. Assn. of Sch. Bds., 1997, Wis. Dept. of Instrn., 1997, Wis. Edn. Assn. Coun., 1997, Wis. Legis. Citation for Tchg. Excellence, 1997-98; named Educator of Yr. Nat. H.S. Assn., 1998, Outstanding Tchr. Radioshack/Tandy, 1999; Kohl fellowship, 1997, Monsanto fellowship, 2000. Mem. Nat. Biology Tchrs. Assn., Nat. Sci. Tchrs. Assn., Nat. Parks and Conservation Assn., Wis. Secondary Sci. Tchrs. (state conf. presenter), Wis. Elem. Sci. Tchrs., BioNet, DEA (scholarship com. chairperson), Wis. Edn. Assn. Coun., Dane County Talented and Gifted Coords. Assn. (vision com., dist. math meet coord.), Wis. Ctr. for Academically Talented Youth.

BANCHET, JEAN, chef; Head chef, owner Le Francais, Wheeling, Ill. Office: Le Francais 269 S Milwaukee Ave Wheeling IL 60090-5097

BANCROFT, ANN E. polar explorer; b. 1955; d. Dick and Debbie B. Former tchr., coach, wilderness instr., St. Paul. Mem. Steger Internat. Polar Expedition, 1986 (first woman to reach the North Pole by dogsled); leader Am. Women's Antarctic Expedition, 1993 (first women's team to reach the South Pole on skis); mem. The Bancroft Arnesen Expdn. (first all women's crossing of Antarctica), 2000. Subject (corp. video) Vision of Teams, 1998, (documentary) Poles Apart, 1999; featured in Remarkable Women of the 20th Century, 1998. Founder Ann Bancroft Found. Named Ms. Mag. Woman of Yr., 1987; inductee Girls and Women in Sport Hall of Fame, 1992, Nat. Women's Hall of Fame, 1995; recipient Women First award YWCA, 1993; first woman in world to travel across the ice to North and South poles. Office: yourexpedition 119 N 4th St Ste 406 Minneapolis MN 55401-1790 Fax: 612-333-1325. E-mail: susan@yourexpedition.com.

BANDES, SUSAN JANE, museum director, educator; b. N.Y.C., Oct. 18, 1951; d. Ralph and Bessie (Gordon) B. BA, NYU, 1971; MA, Bryn Mawr Coll., 1973, PhD, 1978; postgrad., Mus. Mgmt. Inst., Berkeley, Calif., 1990. Asst. prof. Sweet Briar (Va.) Coll., 1978-83; project dir. Am. Assn. Mus., Washington, 1983-84; program officer J. Paul Getty Trust Grant Program, L.A., 1984-86; prof., dir. Kresge Art Mus. Mich. State U., East Lansing, 1986—. Author, editor: Caring for Collections, 1984, Affordable Dreams: The Goetsch-Winckler House and Frank Lloyd Wright, 1991; author: Abraham Rattner, The Tampa Museum of Art Collection, 1997; editor: The Prints of John S. de Martelly, 1903-1979. Recipient award Am. Philos. Soc., 1981, publ. award AIA, 1990; Samuel H. Kress fellow, 1972-73, 75-76, Whiting fellow, 1976-77; Fulbright-Hayes grant, 1974-75. Mem. Nat. Inst. for Conservation (treas. 1986-90), Mich. Alliance for Conservation (treas. 1994-95, sec. 1996-97, treas. 1997-98, pres. 1998-2000), Mich. Mus. Assn. (bd. dirs. 1987-92), Mich. Coun. for Humanities (coun. 1988-92), Midwest Art History Soc. (bd. dirs. 1997-2000). Avocations: sailing, collecting oriental rugs. Office: Mich State U Kresge Art Mus East Lansing MI 48824

BANDYOPADHYAY, BISWANATH PRASAD, manufacturing engineer, educator, consultant; b. Bankura, West Bengal, India, Aug. 24, 1945; came to U.S, 1985; s. Amarnath and Bibha (Mukherjee) B.; m. Irina T. Tunik, Aug. 21, 1989; children: Anjeli, Sharmila. BSc in Physics (hons.), Burdwan U., India, 1964; MSME (hons.), People's Friendship U., Moscow, 1969, PhD in Mech. Engring., 1979; postgrad., U. Wis., St. Augustine, 1984. Asst. engr. (design) Mining Machinery Corp., Durgapur, India, 1969-70; asst. engr. Ctrl. Workshop, Korba, India, 1970-72; rsch. scientist Mech. Engring. Rsch. and Devel. Orgn., Poona, India, 1972-75; asst. prof. Indian Inst. Tech., Bombay, 1980-82; lectr. dept mech. engring. U. West Indies, Trinidad, 1982-85; asst. prof. dept. mech. engring. U. N.D., Grand Forks, 1985-89, assoc. prof., 1989—. Vis. lectr. Govt. Polytechnic, Poona, India, 1971-75; vis. lectr. U. Nederland Antilles, Curacao, 1983-84; mem. faculty Concordia U., Ottawa, Can., 1982; postdoctoral fellow Mich. Tech. U., 1984; postdoctoral rsch. fellow Auburn U., Ala., 1985; rsch. cons. Argonne Nat. Lab., Chgo., 1989, Oak Ridge (Tenn.) Nat. Lab., 1991—; cons. Lucas Western, N.D., 1990; attended numerous confs. and workshops. Contbr. articles to profl. jours. including: Jour. of Materials, Processing Tech., Jour. Mfg. Systems, others. Fellow Japan Ministry Edn., Toyohash, Japan, 1992, Riken Rsch. Ctr., Tokyo, 1994. Mem. ASME, Soc. Mfg. Engrs. (sr.). Achievements include: collaboration with Japanese scientist in area of mirror surface grinding of structural ceramics. Avocations: travel, badminton, tennis. Office: U ND Dept Engring. Univ Sta Grand Forks ND 58202-8359

BANERJEE, PRASHANT, industrial engineering educator; b. Calcutta, West Bengal, India, Apr. 15, 1962; came to U.S., 1986; s. Prabhat K. and Bani Banerjee; m. Madhumita Banerjee, Dec. 11, 1987; children: Jay, Ann. BSME, Indian Inst. Tech., Kanpur, India, 1984; MS in Indsl. Engring., Purdue U., 1987, PhD, 1990. Indsl. engr. Tata Steel Co., Jamshedpur, India, 1984-85; asst. prof. U. Ill., Chgo., 1990-96, assoc. prof., 1996—. Cons. Caterpillar Inc., Peoria, Ill., 1992, Motorola Inc., 1994-97, Monsanto, Inc., 1996—. Author: Automation and Control of Manufacturing Systems, 1991, Object-oriented Technology in Manufacturing, 1992; contbr. articles to profl. jours. NSF rsch. grantee, 1992, 95, Nat. Inst. Standards and Tech. rsch. grantee, 1995. Mem. ASME, Inst. Indsl. Engrs., Inst. Mgmt. Scis., Soc. Mfg. Engrs. Avocations: sports, current events, religious discussions. Home: 11 Foxcroft Rd Naperville IL 60565 Office: Univ Ill Engring Dept Chicago IL 60607-7022

BANFIELD, JILLIAN, mineralogist, geomicrobiologist, educator; b. Armidale, NSW, Australia, Aug. 18, 1959; BSc, Australian Nat. U., Canberra City, 1981, MSc; MA, PhD, Johns Hopkins U., 1990. Assoc. prof. geology and geophysics U. Wis., Madison, 1995-99, affiliate faculty mem. dept. chemistry, 1998—, prof., 1999—. Prof. Mineral. Inst. U. Tokyo, 1996-98; vis. rsch. fellow ANU, 1998-2000. Recipient Geol. Soc. of Australia prize 1979, W.B. Clark prize in geology, 1979, Ampol prize, 1980, Dept. Energy's award for outstanding rsch., 1995, D.A. Brown medal Australin Nat. U., 1999; Mineraological Soc. of Am. grantee, 1989; Owen Fellowship award, 1986-89, Eby fellow, 1986-90, Gilman Tuition fellow, 1986-90, H.I. Romnes Faculty fellow, 1998, John D. and Catherine T. MacArthur Found. fellow, 1999—, John Simon Guggenheim Found. fellow, 2000; Australian Nat. U. MSc scholar, 1983-84, Fulbright scholar, 1986, JFOL scholar Ariz. State U., 1988; Gast lectr. Geochem. Soc., 2000; NSF Earth Sci. Wk. lectr., 2000. Fellow Mineralological Soc. Am. (Disting. lectr. 1994-95, mem. coun. 1996, award 1997); mem. Clay Minerals Soc. (mem. coun, Marion L. and Christie M. Jackson Mid-Career Clay Scientist award 2000). Office: U Wis Dept Geology and Geophysics 1215 W Dayton St Dept And Madison WI 53706-1600

BANGERT, BILL, radio personality; Radio host WEBN, Cin. Office: WEBN 1111 St Gregory St Hamilton OH 45020

BANIAK, SHEILA MARY, accountant, educator; b. Chgo., Feb. 26, 1953; d. DeLoy N. and Ann (Pasko) Slade; m. Mark A. Baniak, Oct. 7, 1972 (div. Feb. 1994); 1 child, Heather Ann. Assocs. in Acctg., Oakton Community Coll., 1986; student, Roosevelt U., 1986—; MBA, North Park Coll., Chgo., 1995; Cert. in Human Resources, North Park U. , Chgo., 2001. Cert. enrolled agt. IRS; accredited tax adviser Accreditation Coun. Accountancy and Taxation. Owner, mgr. Baniak and Assocs., Chgo., 1984—; acct. Otto & Snyder, Park Ridge, 1984-87; spl. projects coordinator, supplemental instr. Oakton Community Coll., Des Plaines, Ill., 1986—, acctg. computer instr., 1987—; acctg. and credit mgr. Fragomen, Delrey, Bernsen & Loewy P.C., 1996—, fin. and human resources mgr., 1999—. Adm. mem. acctg. Oakton C.C., Des Plaines, 1986—, cons., mem. Edn. Found., 1986—; instr. Ray Coll. Design, 1987—, dir. evening sch., 1994, fin. aid officer, Chgo. and Woodfield, 1994; mem. rsch. bd. advisors Am. Biog. Inst., Inc., 1988; tchr. fin. mgmt., retail math., bus. math., bus. computers, strategic retail mgmt. and econs.; part-time coll. instr. commerce dept. Northwestern Bus. Coll., 1995—; asst. to interim fin. dir. Art Inst. Ill., 1995-96. Author: A Small Business Collection Cycle Primer for Accountants, 1985, The Mathematics of Business, 1989. Ill. CPA Soc. scholar, 1984, Roosevelt U. scholar, 1986, Nat. Assn. Accts. scholar, 1985. Mem. Nat. Assn. Accts. (dir. community responsibility suburban Chgo. chpt. 1986—, speaker 1988, dir. profl. devel. seminars 1988, dir. communications 1989—), Nat. Assn. Tax Practitioners, Nat. Assn. Enrolled Agts., Ill. Soc. Enrolled Agts. (pres.; pres. N.W. Chgo. chpt. 1992, chmn. edn. 1990—). Home: 5718 W Cullom Ave Chicago IL 60634-1718

BANKER, GILBERT STEPHEN, industrial and physical pharmacy educator, administrator; b. Tuxedo Park, N.Y., Sept. 12, 1931; s. Gilbert Miller and Mary Edna (Gladstone) B.; m. Gwenivere May Hughes, Mar. 31, 1956; children: Stephen, Susan, David, William. BS in Pharmacy, Union Coll., Albany, N.Y., 1953; MS, Purdue U., 1955, PhD, 1957. Research found. fellow Purdue U., West Lafayette, Ind., 1955-57, asst. prof. pharmacy, 1957-61, assoc. prof., 1961-64, prof., 1964-67, head indsl. and phys. pharmacy dept., from 1967; dean, prof. pharmacy U. Minn., Mpls., 1985-92; dean emeritus, disting. prof. drug delivery U. Iowa, Iowa City, 1992. In coop. tng. program Upjohn Co., Kalamazoo, 1958. Editor: Modern Pharmaceutics, 1970, 90, Pharmaceuticals and Pharmacy Practice, 1980, Pharmaceutical Dosage Forms: Dispense Systems, 1988, 2d edit., 1994; contbr. articles to profl. jours.; patentee in field. Recipient Outstanding Alumnus of Yr. award Albany Coll. Pharmacy-Union U., 1977, Disting. Alumni award Sch. Pharmacy and Pharmacal Scis. Purdue U., 1989. Fellow Acad. Pharm. Scis. (v.p. 1971-72), Am. Pharm. Assn. (Indsl. Pharmacy award 1971, ho. dels. 1977-80), Am. Assn. Advancement of Scis., Am. Assn. Pharm. Scis. (chair 1993-94); mem. Sigma Xi (pres. Purdue chpt. 1971-72), Rho Chi. Office: Univ of Iowa Coll of Pharmacy Iowa City IA 52242 E-mail: gilgwenb@aol.com., gilbert-banker@uiowa.edu.

BANKOFF, SEYMOUR GEORGE, chemical engineer, educator; b. N.Y.C., Oct. 7, 1921; s. Jacob and Sarah (Rashkin) B.; m. Elaine K. Forgash; children: Joseph, Elizabeth, Laura, Jay. BS, Columbia U., 1940, MS, 1941; PhD in Chem. Engring., Purdue U., 1952. Research engr. Sinclair Refining Co., East Chicago, Ind., 1941-42; process engr. du Pont Manhattan project U. Chgo., Richland, Wash., Arlington, N.J., 1942-48; asst. prof. dept. chem. engring. Rose Poly. Inst., Terre Haute, Ind., 1948-52, assoc. prof., 1952-54, prof., chmn. dept. chem. engring., 1954-58; NSF sci. faculty fellow Calif. Inst. Tech., Pasadena, 1958-59; prof. chem. engring. Northwestern U., Evanston, Ill., 1959—, Walter P. Murphy prof. chem., mech. and nuclear engring., 1971-92; prof. emeritus, 1992—; chmn. energy engring. council Northwestern U., 1975-80, chmn. Ctr. for Multiphase Flow and Transport, 1988—. Vis. scientist Centre d'Etudes Nucléaires, Commissariat d'Energie Atomique, Grenoble, France, 1980; vis. prof. Imperial Coll. Sci. and Tech., London, 1985; cons. to U.S. Nuclear Regulatory Commn., 1974-87, Los Alamos Sci. Lab., 1974-89, Electric Power Research Inst., 1984-86, Westinghouse, 1984—, Savannah River Lab., duPont, 1987—, Korea Atomic Energy Research Inst., 1988; mem. adv. council Ams. for Energy Independence, Washington, 1978—; chmn. vis. com. Brookhaven Nat. Lab., 1984, engring. tech. div. Oak Ridge Nat. Lab., 1986; pres. SGB Assocs. Inc., 1986—. Mem. editl. adv. bd.: Internat. Jour. Multiphase Flow, 1975—, Nuc. Engring. and Design, 1984—; editor 6 vols. on heat transfer; contbr. 200 articles on rsch. in heat transfer and control theory to profl. jours. Recipient Max Jakob Meml. award AICE and ASME, 1987, Donald Q. Kern award AIChE, 1996, Outstanding Chem. Engr. award Purdue U., 1994; named Disting. Engring. Alumnus, 1971; Guggenheim fellow, 1966, Fulbright fellow, 1967, Internat. Ctr. Health and Mass Transfer, Yugoslavia. Fellow AICE (chmn. edn. com. 1968-71, chmn. heat transfer and energy conversion divsn. 1987, Robert E. Wilson Nuc. Chem. Engring. award 1994, Heat Transfer and Energy Conversion Divsn. award 1995), ASME; mem. Am. Nuclear Soc. (co-chmn. U.S. Sci. com., 9th Internat. Heat Transfer Conf., U.S. del. Internat. Heat Transfer Assembly), Nat. Acad. Engring. Achievements include co-invention of resistivity probe for void fraction measurement in gas-liquid flows; contbn. to theory of boiling heat transfer, vapor explosions, stratified condensing flows, stability of thin liquid films. Office: Northwestern Univ Chem Engring Dept Evanston IL 60208-0001

BANKS, DONNA JO, food products executive; b. Ft. McClellan, Ala., Sept. 6, 1956; d. Walter Dow and Joanne (Phelps) Cox; m. Bobby Dennis Banks, Dec. 27, 1983; children: Cynthia Marie, Elizabeth Anne, Sarah Diane. BS, U. Tenn., 1979, MS, 1980; PhD, Mich. State U., 1984. Assoc. statistician Kellogg Co., Battle Creek, Mich., 1983-84, mgr. product evaluation and stats., 1984-87, dir. cereal product devel., 1987-91, v.p. rsch. and devel., 1991-97, sr. v.p. rsch. and devel., 1998—. Mem. Am. Statis. Assn., Sigma Xi. Democrat. Baptist. Avocations: racquetball, tennis, needlework, sewing. Home: 2027 Birch Bluff Dr Okemos MI 48864-5965 Office: 2 Hamblin Ave E Battle Creek MI 49017-3547

BANKS, ROBERT J. bishop; b. Winthrop, Mass., Feb. 26, 1928; s. Robert Joseph and Rita Katherine (Sullivan) B. AB, St. John's Sem., Brighton, Mass., 1949; STL, Gregorian U., Rome, 1953; JCD, Lateran U., Rome, 1957. Ordained priest Roman Cath. Ch., 1952, ordained titular bishop of Taraqua, 1985. Prof. canon law St. John Sem., Brighton, Mass., 1959-71, acad. dean, 1967-71; rector St. John's Sem., 1971-81; vicar gen. Boston Archdiocese, 1984; aux. bishop Boston, 1985-90; bishop Diocese of Green Bay, Wis., 1990—. Office: Diocese of Green Bay PO Box 23825 Green Bay WI 54305-3825

BANNEN, JOHN THOMAS, lawyer; b. LaCrosse, Wis., Oct. 29, 1951; s. James J. and Ruth J. (Frisch) B.; m. Carol A. Swanson, Aug. 16, 1975; children: Ryan M., Kelly A., Erin C. BA summa cum laude, Coll. of St. Thomas, 1973; JD, Marquette U., 1976; LLM in Taxation, DePaul U., 1989. Bar: Wis. 1976, U.S. Dist. Ct. (ea. and we. dists.) Wis. 1976, U.S. Tax Ct. 1979, U.S. Claims Ct. 1983, U.S. Supreme Ct. 1984. Shareholder Charne, Clancy & Taitelman, S.C., Milw., 1976-91; ptnr. Quarles & Brady, 1991—. Mem. coun. Christ the King Parish, Wauwatosa, Wis., 1989-93, trustee, 1996-98; bd. dirs. Guardianship Svcs. for Indigents, Milw., 1983-87; mem. adv. bd. Sch. Sisters of Notre Dame, 1993-98, pres., 1995-98. Fellow Am. Coll. Trust and Estate Counsel (state law coord. for Wis. 1990-95, chmn. com. on employee benefits); mem. ABA, Assn. Advanced Life Underwriters (assoc.), Wis. Bar Assn. (bd. dirs. probate sect.). Avocations: reading, gardening, Spanish language, cooking. Office: Quarles & Brady LLP Ste 2040 411 E Wisconsin Ave Milwaukee WI 53202-4497 E-mail: jtb@quarles.com.

BANNISTER, GEOFFREY, university president, geographer; b. Manchester, Eng., Sept. 19, 1945; came to U.S., 1973; s. Leslie and Doris (Shankland) B.; m. Margaret Janet Sheridan, Jan. 28, 1968; children: Katherine, Janet. BA, U. Otago, New Zealand, 1967, MA with honors, 1969; PhD, U. Toronto, Can., 1974. Asst. prof. Boston U., 1973-77, acting chmn. geography, 1977-78, dean liberal arts, grad. sch., 1978-87; exec. v.p. Butler U., Indpls., 1987-89, pres., 1989—. Cons. Urban Affairs Ministry of State, Can., 1973; legal cons. U.S. Dept. of State 1982-84; bd. dirs. Somerset Group, Ind. Nat. Bank. Co-author atlas Spatial Dynamics of Postwar County Economic Change, 1977; contbr. articles to profl. jours. Chmn. bd. trustees Cambridge (Mass.) Montessori Sch., 1979-80; mem. corp. Sea Edn. Assn., Woods Hole, Mass., 1979-87; bd. dirs. United Way of Cen. Ind., 1990—, chmn. 1992 Premeire Campaign, edn. chmn.; bd. dirs. Greater Indpls. Progress Com., 1988—; pres. Midwest Collegiate Cons; chmn. World Rowing Championship, 1994. Fellow U. Toronto, 1970-71, Can. Council, 1972. Mem. Nat. Labor/Higher Edn. Coun., Nat. Assn. Scholars, Indpls. Bus. Jour. Blue Ribbon Panel, Indpls. Commn. on African-Am. Males, C. of C., Econ. Club, English Speaking Union U.S. (Indpls. br.), Coun. Urban Coll. of Arts, Letter and Scis., Kiwanis, Phi Beta Kappa. Avocations: bicycling, golf, skiing.

BANOFF, SHELDON IRWIN, lawyer; b. Chgo., July 10, 1949; BSBA in Acctg., U. Ill., 1971; JD, U. Chgo., 1974. Bar: Ill. 1974, U.S. Tax Ct. 1974. Ptnr. Katten Muchin Zavis, Chgo., 1974—. Chmn. tax conf. planning com. U. Chgo. Law Sch., 1993-94. Co-editor Jour. of Taxation, 1984—; contbr. articles to profl. jours. Mem. ABA, Chgo. Bar Assn. (fed. taxation com., mem. exec. coun. 1980—, chmn. large law firm com., 1999-2000), Chgo. Fed. Tax Forum, Am. Coll. Tax Counsel. E-mial. Office: Katten Muchin Zavis 525 W Monroe St Ste 1600 Chicago IL 60661-3693 E-mail: sheldon.banoff@kmzr.com.

BANSTETTER, ROBERT J. lawyer; b. 1940; BS, St Louis U., 1963; JD, U. Ill., 1966. Bar: Mo. 1967, Ill. 1966. Atty. Labor Rels. Internat. Shoe, 1966-70; v.p., gen. coun. & sec. Gen. Am. Life Ins. Co., 1992—. Office: Gen Am Life Ins Co PH#2: (314) 444-0634 700 Market St Saint Louis MO 63101-1829

BANTON, STEPHEN CHANDLER, lawyer; b. St. Louis; s. William Conwell and Ruth (Chandler) B. AB, Bowdoin Coll., 1969; JD, Washington U., St. Louis, 1973, MBA, 1974. Bar: Mo. 1973, U.S. Dist. Ct. (ea. and we. dists.) Mo. 1973. Asst. pros. atty. St. Louis County, 1973-75; sole practice Clayton, Mo., 1975-83; ptnr. Quinn, Ground & Banton, Manchester, 1983—. Pres. Coll. for Living, 1997-98. Exploring chmn. St. Louis council Midland Dist. Scouts, 1975-77; pres. Am. Youth Hostels Ozarks area, 1976-80; bd. trustees St. Louis Art Mus., 1985-94. Served with USMC. Recipient Leadership award Lafayette Community Assn., 1983, Service award The Meramec Palisades Community Assn., 1985, Service award Profl. Remodeling Assn., 1985, Service award St. Louis Symphony Orch., 1985. Mem. ABA, Mo. Bar Assn., St. Louis County Bar Assn., Bar Assn. Met. St. Louis, Assn. Trial Lawyers Am., St. Louis County League of C. of C. (pres. 1978), West Port C. of C. (bd. dirs. 1978-81, Service award 1983), Rotary (pres. Ballwin club 1997-98). Republican. Club: Toastmasters (Clayton) (adminstrv. v.p.). Lodge: Lions (pres. 1977). Office: Quinn Ground & Banton 14611 Manchester Rd Ballwin MO 63011-3700 Home: 929 Saint Paul Rd Ballwin MO 63021-6061

BANWART, WAYNE LEE, agronomy, environmental science educator; b. West Bend, Iowa, Jan. 9, 1948; s. Albert R. and Betty R. (Zaugg) B.; m. Charlen Ann Schrock, Mar. 22, 1970; children: Krista, Kara, Neil. MS, Iowa State U., 1972, PhD, 1975. Asst. prof. U. Ill., Urbana, 1975-79, assoc. prof., 1979-84, prof., 1984-89, prof., assoc. head dept. agronomy, 1989-94, asst. dean, 1994—. Vis. scientist Constrn. Engrng. Lab., Champaign, 1985-86; chmn. Nat. Atmospheric Deposition Program, 1986. Co-author: (textbook) Soils and Their Environment, 1992. Mem. patient satisfaction com. HMO, Champaign, 1987-93; pres. citizen's adv. com. Mahomet-Seymour Schs., 1981. Nat. Coll. Tchrs. of Agr. fellow, 1987. Fellow Am. Soc. Agronomy (George D. Scarseth award 1973), Soil Sci. Soc. Am.; mem. Internat. Soil Sci. Soc., Gamma Sigma Delta (pres.). Achievements include discovery that agricultural crops subject to acid rain will suffer little or no yield reduction or physiological damage; discovery that plant uptake and translocation of TNT is very limited while RDX is readily taken up and concentrated in plant tissues; that organic amendments offer promise for bioremediation of soils contaminated with these explosives. Home: 3201 Sandhill Lnt Champaign IL 61822 Office: U Ill 1301 W Gregory Dr Urbana IL 61801-9015 E-mail: wanwart@uiuc.edu.

BAPTIST, ALLWYN J. healthcare consultant; b. India, July 10, 1943; came to U.S., 1971; s. Peter L.G. and Trescilla (Lobo) B.; m. Anita Lobo, Sept. 8, 1973; children: Alan, Andrew, Annabel, Arthur. BCS, U. Calcutta, India, 1962; cert. mgmt., U. Chgo., 1978. CPA, Ill; chartered acct., India. Divisional acct. Rallis India Ltd., Bombay, 1967-71; mgr. Chgo. Blue Cross, 1972-79; sr. mgr. Price Waterhouse, Chgo., 1979-84; v.p., dir. Truman Esmond and Assocs., Barrington, Ill., 1984-86; ptnr. Laventhol and Horwath, Chgo., 1986-90, BDO Seidman, Chgo., 1991-2000; pres. Baptist Cons. Inc., 2000—. Mem. adv. bd. St. Mary of Nazareth Hosp., 1989—, mem. gov. bd., 1992-94, 96-98, lifetime trustee. Contbr. articles to profl. jours. Mem. fin. com. St. James Ch., Arlington Heights, Ill., 1987; mem. AICPA Health Care Com., 1991-94. Mem. Healthcare Fin. Mgmt. Assn. (dir., sec. 1983—, pres. 1988-89, recipient William J. Follmer award 1984, Reeves award 1989, Muncie Gold award 1992, founders medal of honor 1998), India Cath. Assn. Am. (treas. 1980, 87, pres. 1988). Avocations: travel, reading, tennis, golf. Office: BDO Seidman 205 N Michigan Ave Chicago IL 60601-5927

BAR, ROBERT S. endocrinologist, educator; b. Gainesville, Tex., Dec. 2, 1943; s. Samuel and Emma (Kaplan) B.; m. Laurel Ellen Burns, June 23, 1970; children: Katharine June, Matthew Thomas. BS, Tufts Univ., 1964; MS in Biochemistry, MD, Ohio State U., 1970. Medicine intern Pa. Hosp., Phila., 1970-71; medicine resident Ohio State Univ., Columbus, 1971-72; asst. prof., dept. medicine Univ. Iowa, Iowa City, 1977-82, assoc. prof., dept. medicine, 1982-86, prof., dept. medicine, 1986—. Acting dir. divsn. of endocrinology and metabolism, U. Iowa, 1985-90; dir. diabetes-endocrinology rsch ctr., U. Iowa, 1986—, rsch. svc. award in endocrinology, 1984—, endocrinology fellowship program, 1979—, divsn. of endocrinology and metabolism, 1990—; mem. ad hoc study sect. NIH, 1985, dir. diabetes-endocrinology rsch. ctr. 1986; mem. editorial bd. Jour. of Clin. Endocrinology and Metabolism, 1984-87; mem study sect. Nat. Veterans Adminstrn., 1984-87; v.p. rsch. Nat. Am. Diabetes Assn., 1987-88; mem. orgn. com. Endothelium and Diabetes Symposium, Melbourne, 1988; dir. VA/JDF Diabetes Rsch. Ctr., 1997; mem. study sect. numerous assns. and coms.; guest reviewer numerous jours. Editor Endocrinology, 1987-89, Advances in Endocrinology and Metabolism, 1989—. Mem. Am. Diabetes Assn., Am. Soc. for Clin. Investigation, Assn. Am. Physicians, Endocrine Soc., Ctrl. Soc. for Clin. Rsch., Sigma Xi. Office: U Iowa Hwy 6 West 3E19 VA Iowa City IA 52246

BARANOVA, ELENA, basketball player; b. Russia, Jan. 28, 1972; came to U.S., 1997; Ctr., Israel, 1992-94, CKSK, Russia, 1994-97, WNBA - Utah Starzz, Salt Lake City, 1997-99, Cleve. Rockers, 1999—. Recipient Gold medal European Championship, Soviet Nat. Team, 1991, Barcelona Olympics, 1992, Bronze medal, European Championship, 1995. Avocations: shopping, housekeeping, electric piano. Office: Cleveland Rockers Gund Arena 1 Center Ct Cleveland OH 44115-4001

BARBARIN, OSCAR ANTHONY, psychologist; b. New Orleans, July 25, 1945; s. Oscar Anthony and Inez M. (Molison) B. AB, St. Joseph's Sem., Washington, 1968; MA, NYU, 1971; PhD in Psychology, Rutgers U., 1975. Dir. community field sta. U. Md., College Park, 1974-79; assoc. prof. U. Mich., Ann Arbor, 1979-2000, dir. family devel. project, 1981-96, prof. psychology and social work, 1990-2000, dir. ctr. for the child and the family, 1992-94, exec. dir. South Africa Initiative, 1996-2000; Preyer disting. prof. social work, fellow Porter Graham Child Devel. Ctr., U. N.C., Chapel Hill, 2000—. Author: Childhood Cancer and the Family, 1987, Mandela's Children, 2000. Fellow APA, Am. Orthopsychiat. Assn. (bd. dirs., pres. 2001—); mem. Assn. of Black Psychologists (life). Office: Frank Porter Granan Child Devel Ctr Bank of America Bldg 127 E Franklin St Chapel Hill NC 27599-8040

BARBER, EARL EUGENE, consulting firm executive; b. Dayton, Ohio, Dec. 8, 1939; s. Earl Garnet and Mary Helen (Brown) B.; m. Sandra Kay Reese, Mar. 11, 1960; children: Steven, Amy, Dana. BS, Ball State U., 1963; MDiv., Asbury Theol. Sem., Wilmore, Ky., 1977. Tchr. Muncie (Ind.) Community Schs, 1963-65; exec. mem. Gen. Motors, Muncie, 1965-73; pres. Barber Electric, Wilmore, 1973-77; sr. pastor Calvary Temple, Plainview, Tex., 1977-79; exec. Borg Warner Corp., Muncie, 1979-84; chief ops. officer Barber Cons. Resources, 1984—. Author: Statistical Process Control for the Worker, 1985, Statistical Process Control: The Basic Tools, 1986, Team Leader Training, 1989, Problem Solving, 1992, 96, Understanding SPC for Short Production Runs, 1990, Total Quality Management, 1991, Team Building, 1992, Problem Solving, 1994, Time Management, 1995. Mem Mayor's Task Force, Muncie 1980. Mem. Am. Soc. Quality Control (Ptnrs. award for quality 1989, sustaining mem.), Delaware County Ministerial Assn., Epsilon Pi Tau. Republican. Methodist. Avocations: writing, music, boating. Office: Barber Cons Resources Inc 4501 N Wheeling Ave #2-209 Muncie IN 47304-6028

BARBER, JOHN W. insurance company executive; V.p. Gen. Am. Life Ins. Co., St. Louis; ret. Office: Gen Am Life Ins Co 700 Market St Saint Louis MO 63101

BARBOSA, MANUEL, judge; b. Mex., Oct. 28, 1947; m. Linda Kupfer, Oct. 26, 1974; 3 children. BA, Ill. Benedictine Coll., 1969; JD, John Marshall Law Sch., 1969. Bar: Ill. 1977, U.S. Dist. Ct. (no. dist.) Ill. 1993. Chair Ill. Human Rights Commn., 1990-98; judge U.S. Bankruptcy Ct., Rockford, Ill., 1998—. Bd. dirs. Grand Victoria Found., 1977, YMCA, 1985, Rotary, 1992. Recipient Social Svc. award Quad County Urban League, 1992. Mem. ABA, Ill. Bar Assn., Kane County Bar Assn., Winnebago County Bar Assn. Roman Catholic. Avocations: sports, guitar, history.

BARCIA, JAMES A. congressman; b. Bay City, Mich., Feb. 25, 1952; Grad., Saginaw Valley State U., 1974. Staff asst. to U.S. Senator Philip Hart, 1971; cmty. svc. coord. Mich. Cmty. Blood Ctr., Bay City, 1974-75; mem. Ho. of Reps. from 101st Mich. Dist., 1977-82, mem. edn. com., 1977-82, chmn. pub. works com., 1979-82, majority whip, 1979-82; mem. Mich. Senate, 1983-92, U.S. Congress from 5th Mich. dist., 1993—; mem. sci. and transp. and infrastructure coms. Mem. UAW Local 688, 1970-71, Saginaw Valley Univ. Bd. Control, 1973-74. Recipient disting. svc. award Saginaw Valley State U. Alumni Assn., 1977, Golden Eagle award Am. Fedn. Police; named Fed. Legislator of Yr., Mich. Credit Union League, Legislator of Yr., Satari Club Internat.; elected to Bay City Ctrl. Hall of Fame, 1981. Mem. NRA, Bay Area C. of C., Mich. Assn. Osteopathic Physicians and Surgeons (hon. lay mem.), Bay City Jaycees (Disting. Svc. award 1982), United Conservation clubs, Elks, Bay City Lions. Home: 3190 Hidden Rd Bay City MI 48706-1203 Office: US Ho of Reps 2419 Rayburn House Ofc Bldg Washington DC 20515-0001*

BARD, JOHN FRANKLIN, consumer products executive; b. Owatonna, Minn., Mar. 1, 1941; s. Franklin Spencer and Nina Carolyn (Geyer) B.; m. Barbara Ann Bowers, Aug. 1, 1964; children: Steven George, Kristin Elizabeth Taylor. BS in Bus., Northwestern U., 1963; MBA, U. Cin., 1972. Internat. contr. Procter & Gamble Co., Cin., 1963-78; group v.p. Clorox Co., Oakland, Calif., k1978-84, dir., 1979-84; exec. v.p., pres., chief oper. officer Tambrands Inc., Lake Success, N.Y., 1985-90, dir., 1986-89; sr. v.p., exec. v.p. Wm. Wrigley Jr. Co., Chgo., 1990—, dir., 1999—. Bd. dirs. Alameda County YMCA, Oakland, 1979-87, L.I. United Way, 1989-90, Greater N. Mich. Ave. Assn., Chgo., 1991—; dir., vice-chmn. Keep Am. Beautiful, Inc. Mem. Tax Found. (policy com.), 410 Club, Econ. Club Chgo., Fin. Execs. Inst., Sea Pines Country Club (S.C.), Office: Wm Wrigley Jr Co 410 N Michigan Ave Chicago IL 60611-4213

BARDEEN, WILLIAM ALLAN, research physicist; b. Washington, Sept. 15, 1941; s. John and F. Jane (Maxwell) B.; m. Marjorie Ann Gaylord; children: Charles Gaylord, Karen Gail. AB in Physics, Cornell U., 1962; PhD in Physics, U. Minn., 1968, DSc (hon.) , 2002. Rsch. assoc. SUNY, Stony Brook, 1966-68; mem. Inst. for Advanced Study, Princeton, N.J., 1968-69; asst. prof. Stanford (Calif.) U., 1969-72, assoc. prof., 1972-75; scientist Fermilab, Batavia, Ill., 1975-93, head theoretical physics, 1987-93, scientist, 1994—; head theoretical physics SSC Lab., Dallas, 1993-94. Vis. scientist CERN, Geneva, Switzerland, 1971-72, Max Planck Inst. for Physics, Munich, 1977, 86. Author: Barden-Bardeen Genealogy, 1993; editor: Symp. on Anomalies, Geometry, Topology, 1985; mem. editl. bd. Phys. Rev., 1981-84, 92-94, Jour. Math. Physics, 1986-90, European Physics Jour. C, 1997-2000; contbr. numerous articles to profl. jours. Trustee Aspen Ctr. for Physics, 1987-91. Fellowship Alfred P. Sloan Found., 1971-74, John Simon Guggenheim Found., 1985-86; recipient sr. scientist award Alexander von Humboldt Found., 1977 Fellow Am. Phys. Soc. (exec. com. divsn. of particles and fields 1988-90, J. J. Sajurai prize for theoretical particle physics 1996); mem. Am. Acad. Arts and Scis., NAS. Avocations: genealogy, basketball. Office: Fermilab MS 106 PO Box 500 Batavia IL 60510-0500

BARDEN, DON H. communications executive; b. Detroit, Dec. 20, 1943; s. Milton Sr. and Hortense (Hamilton) B; m. Bella Marshall, May 14, 1988; 1 child, Keenan. Student, Ctrl. State U., 1963-64. Councilman City of Lorain, 1972-75; owner, pres. Don H. Barden Co., 1976-81; talk show host WKYC-TV NBC, Cleve., 1977-80; chmn., pres. Barden Comm., Inc., Detroit, 1981—. Pres. Urban Action Inc.; del. White House Conf. on Small Bus.; pres. Lorain City Com. Action Agy.; bd. dirs. Nat. Cable TV Assn. IOB, MI Cable TV Assn., 1st Independence Nat. Bank, Met. Detroit Conv. Bur. Mem. exec. com. Dem. Party; mem. Edn. Task Force; dir. Detroit Symphony Orch., 1986—. Office: Barden Cos Inc 400 Renaissance Ctr Ste 2400 Detroit MI 48243-1676

BARDEN, ROLAND EUGENE, university administrator; b. Powers Lake, N.D., Sept. 11, 1942; s. Harry S. and Sena (Furness) B.; m. Carolyn Jane, Nov. 25, 1967; children: Carl, Janine, Ann. BS, U. N.D., 1964; MS, U. Wis., 1966, PhD, 1969. Postdoctoral fellow Case Western Res. U., Cleve., 1969-71; prof. U. Wyo., Laramie, 1971-89, dept. head, 1980-83, assoc. dean, 1983-84, assoc. provost, 1984-89; v.p. acad. affairs Minn. State U., Moorhead, 1989-94, pres., 1994—. Cons./evaluator North Ctrl. Assn. Schs. and Colls., Chgo., 1988—; commr. Tri Coll. U., 1989-94, dir. 1994—. Contbr. articles to profl. jours. Recipient Rsch. Career Devel. award NIH, 1976-80. Mem. Am. Chem. Soc., Am. Soc. Biochem. Molecular Biology. Avocations: hiking, reading, fishing. Office: Minn State U Moorhead Office Of President Moorhead MN 56563-0001

BAREISS, ERWIN HANS, computer scientist, mathematician, nuclear engineer, educator; b. Schaffhausen, Switzerland, May 10, 1922; came to U.S., 1951, naturalized, 1957; s. Karl Johann and Helene Fredericke (Kraft) B.; m. Doris Lilly Wicky, June 4, 1960; children: John Frederick, Peter Andrew. Diploma in Math., Physics and Chemistry, U. Zurich, 1949, Ph.D. in Math, 1951; M.S. in Applied Mechanics, Lehigh U., 1952. Mathematician U.S. Navy Taylor Research and Devel. Ctr., Washington, 1952-56, cons., 1956-57; analyst Argonne Nat. Lab., Ill., 1957-63, sr. mathematician, 1963-76; sci. lectr. Harvard U., 1964; prof. computer sci. Northwestern U., Evanston, Ill., 1970-71, prof. computer sci. and engrng. sci., 1971-76, prof. elec. engrng. and computer sci., engrng. sci. and applied math. and nuclear engrng., 1976-92, prof. emeritus Ill., 1992—, chmn. computer sci. program, 1978-88, dir. tech. computing. Bd. dirs. Swiss Benevolent Soc., Chgo., pres., 1969-77, hon. mem., 1980— Contbr. articles on sci. computation to profl. publs. Janggen-Poehn fellow, 1950-51; K.C. Baldwin research fellow, 1951-52 Mem. Am. Math. Soc., Soc. Indsl. and Applied Maths., Swiss Math. Soc., Swiss Soc. Natural History, Sigma Xi. Home: 3400 Lake Knoll Dr Northbrook IL 60062-6318 Office: Northwestern U Robert R McCormick Sch Engrng & Applied Sci Evanston IL 60208-0001

BARENBOIM, DANIEL, conductor, pianist; b. Buenos Aires, Argentina, Nov. 15, 1942; s. Enrique and Aida (Schuster) B.; m. Jacqueline DuPre, June 15, 1967 (dec.); m. Elena Bashkirova, Nov. 28, 1988; 2 children. Student, Mozarteum, Salzburg, Austria, Accademia Chigiana, Siena, Italy; grad., Santa Cecilia Acad., Rome, 1956. Music dir. Chgo. Symphony Orch., 1991—. Debut with Israel Philharm. Orch., 1953, Royal Philharm. Orch., Eng., 1953, debut as pianist, Carnegie Hall, N.Y.C., 1957, Berlin Philharm. Orch., 1963, N.Y. Philharm. Orch., 1964, 1st U.S. solo recital, N.Y.C., 1958, as pianist performed in N.Am., South Am., Europe, Soviet Union, Australia, New Zealand, Near East; condr., 1962—, conducted English Chamber Orch., London Symphony Orch., Israel Philharm. Orch., N.Y. Philharm. Orch., Phila. Symphony, Boston Symphony, Chgo. Symphony Orch., others; mus. dir., Orchestre de Paris, 1975-89, Chgo. Symphony Orch., 1991—, Staatsoper Berlin, 1992—; artistic adviser, Israel Festival, 1971-74, over 100 recordings as pianist and condr.; debut as pianist at age 7, Buenos Aires. Recipient Beethoven medal, 1958; Harriet Cohen Paderewski Centenary prize, 1963, Legion of Honor, France, 1987. Office: 29 rue de la Coulouvreniere 1204 Geneva Switzerland also: Chgo Symphony Orch c/o Synneve Carlino 220 S Michigan Ave Chicago IL 60604-2596

BARFIELD, JON E. employment company executive; b. 1951; BA, Princeton U.; JD, Harvard U., 1977. Assoc. Sidley & Austin; pres. Barfield Mfg. Co.; chmn., CEO Bartech Group, Livonia, Mich. Bd. dirs. Granite Broadcasting Corp. Office: Baretech Group Inc 17199 N Laurel Park Dr Ste 224 Livonia MI 48152-7903

BARGER, VERNON DUANE, physicist, educator; b. Curllsville, Pa., June 5, 1938; s. Joseph F. and Olive (McCall) Barger; m. Annetta McLeod, 1967; children: Victor A., Amy J., Andrew V. BS, Pa. State U., 1960, PhD, 1963. Rsch. assoc. U. Wis., Madison, 1963-65, from asst. prof. to assoc. prof., 1965-68, prof. physics, 1968—, J.H. Van Vleck prof., 1983—, dir. Inst. Elem. Particle Physics Rsch., 1984—, Hilldale prof., 1987-91, Vilas prof., 1991—. Vis. prof. U. Hawaii, 1970, 79, 82, U. Durham, 1983, 84; vis. scientist CERN, 1972, Rutherford Lab., 1972, SLAC, 1975. Co-author: (book) Phenomenological Theories of High Energy Scattering, Classical Mechanics, Classical Electricity and Magnetism, Collider Physics. Recipient Alumni Fellow award, Pa. State U., 1974; fellow Guggenheim, 1972, Fermilab Frontier, 1999. Fellow: Am. Phys. Soc. Methodist. Achievements include research in in elementary particle theory and phenomenology;classification of hadrons as Regge recurrences;analyses of neutrino scattering and oscillations;research in weak boson, Higgs boson and heavy quark production;research in electroweak modesl;research in supersymmetry and grand unification;research in future collider physics. Office: U Wis Dept Physics 1150 University Ave Madison WI 53706-1302

BARIFF, MARTIN LOUIS, information systems educator, consultant; b. Chgo., Jan. 26, 1944; s. George and Mae (Goldberg) B. BS in Acctg., U. Ill., 1966, MA in Acctg., 1967, PhD in Acctg., 1973. CPA, Chgo. Asst. prof. acctg. and decision scis. Wharton Sch., Phila., 1973-78; vis. asst. prof. acctg. U. Chgo., 1978-79; assoc. prof. acctg. and mgmt. info. decision systems Case Western Res. U., Cleve., 1979-83; Coleman Found. assoc. prof. info. mgmt., dir. Ctr. for Rsch. on Impacts of Info. Systems, Ill. Inst. Tech., Chgo., 1983—, acad. dir. MS e-commerce program, 2000—, dir. e-bus. certificate program, 2001—. Cons. in field, N.Y.C., Phila., Washington, 1976—; exec. v.p. EDP Auditors Found., 1979-80; program chmn. Internat. Conf. Info. Systems, Phila., 1980; co-founder Info. Integrity Coalition, 2001--. Contbr. articles to profl. jours. Bd. dirs. Community Accts. Inc. of Phila., 1974-75. Mem. AICPA, INFORMS, Am. Acctg. Assn. (chmn. acctg., behavior and orgns. sect. 1987-88), Assn. Computing Machinery (sec. spl. interest group on security, auditing and control 1981-85), Soc. Info. Mgmt. (treas. Chgo. chpt. 1988-90, 95-96), Internat. Engrng. Consortium (bd. dirs. ednl. overseers 1991-96). Jewish. Avocations: running, flying, photography. Office: Ill Inst Tech 565 W Adams St Ste 422 Chicago IL 60661-3613 E-mail: bariff@stuart.iit.edu.

BARISH, LAWRENCE STEPHEN, nonpartisan legislative staff administrator; b. Bklyn., Nov. 30, 1945; s. Louis C. and Anna (Sanders) B.; m. Sharon Lee Shapiro, July 2, 1967; 1 child, Lauren. BS in Polit. sci., U. Wis.-Madison, Wis., 1967; MA in Govt., U. Ariz., 1970. Legis. analyst Legis. Reference Bur., Madison, Wis., 1971-87, dir. of reference and info. svcs., 1987—. Chmn. rsch., comm. staff sec. Nat. Conf. State Legislatures, Denver, 1995-97; redistricting cons. Wis. Legis. and Local Govt. units, 1980—. Editor State Almanac, 1987—; contbr. articles to profl. jours. Home: 1429 W Skyline Dr Madison WI 53705-1134 Office: Wis Legis Reference Bur 100 N Hamilton St Madison WI 53703-4118 E-mail: larry.barish@legis.state.wi.us.

BARKAN, JOEL DAVID, political science educator, consultant; b. Toledo, Apr. 28, 1941; s. Manuel and Toby (Wolfe) B.; m. Sandra Lynn Hackman, Sept. 9, 1962; children: Bronwyn Michelle, Joshua Manuel. AB, Cornell U., 1963; MA, UCLA, 1965, PhD, 1970. Asst. prof. polit. sci. U. Calif., Irvine, 1969-72; asst. prof. polit. sci. U. Iowa, Iowa City, 1972-76, assoc. prof., 1976-81, prof., 1981—, chmn. dept. polit. sci., 1985-87, dir. ctr. internat. and comparative studies, 1981-83. Vis. rsch. fellow Makerere U., Uganda, 1966—67, U. Dar es Salaam, Tanzania, 1973—74, Fondation Nat. des Scis. Politiques, Paris, 1978—79, U. Nairobi, Kenya, 1979, 80, Ctr. Study of Developing Socs., New Delhi, 1984, Cornell U., 1990, U.S. Inst. Peace, 1997—98, Nat. Endowment for Democracy, 2000, Woodrow Wilson Internat. Ctr., 2001—02; regional governance advisor for Ea. and So. Africa U.S. AID, 1992—94; cons. World Bank, 2000—. Co-author, editor: Politics and Public Policy in Kenya and Tanzania, 1979, rev. edit., 1984, Beyond Capitalism Versus Socialism in Kenya and Tanzania, 1994; co-author: The Legislative Connection, 1984; author: An African Dilemma, 1975; contbr. articles to profl. jours. Pres. Iowa City Fgn. Rels. Coun., 1989—90. Fellow, Social Sci. Rsch. Coun., 1966—68, Fulbright fellow, 1978—79, Indo-Am. fellow, 1984, Randolph fellow, 1997—98, Woodrow Wilson fellow, 2001—02; grantee, Rockefeller Found., 1973—74, U.S. AID, 1978—81, Ford Found., 1992—99. Mem. Am. Polit. Sci. Assn., African Studies Assn. (bd. dirs. 1990-93), Coun. Fgn. Rels. Office: U Iowa Dept Polit Sci Iowa City IA 52242 E-mail: joel-barkan@uiowa.edu.

BARKEN, BERNARD ALLEN, lawyer; b. St. Louis, July 20, 1924; s. Gottlieb and Hattie E. (Rubin) B.; m. Jocelyn Moss Kopman, Sept. 1, 1948; children: Thomas L., Dale Susan. JD, Washington U., 1947. Bar: Mo. 1947, U.S. Dist. Ct. (ea. dist.) Mo. 1947, U.S. Ct. Appeals (8th cir.) 1954, U.S. Tax Ct. 1966, U.S. Ct. Appeals 2nd cir.) 1985, U.S. Supreme Ct. 1984. Sole practice, St. Louis, 1947-80; ptnr. Shifrin & Treiman, 1980-88; pres. Bernard A. Barken, 1988-91; ptnr. Barken & Bakewell L.L.P., 1991—. With USAAF, 1943-44. Mem. ABA, Bar Assn. Met. St. Louis (v.p. 1958, chmn. young lawyers 1953). Jewish. Avocations: piano, tennis, gardening. Home: 30 Vouga Ln Saint Louis MO 63131-2628 Office: Barken & Bakewell LLP 500 N Broadway Ste 2000 Saint Louis MO 63102-2130 Fax: 314-444-7892. E-mail: babarken@hotmail.com.

BARKER, KEITH RENE, investment banker; b. Elkhart, Ind., July 28, 1928; s. Clifford C. and Edith (Hausmna) B.; children by previous marriage: Bruce C., Lynn K.; m. Elizabeth S. Arrington, Nov. 24, 1965; 1 child, Jennifer Scott. AB, Wabash Coll., 1950; MBA, Ind. U., 1952. Sales rep. Fulton, Reid & Co., Inc., Ft. Wayne, Ind., 1951-55, office, 1955-59, asst. v.p. then v.p., 1960, dir., 1961, asst. sales mgr., 1963, sales mgr., 1964, dir. Ind. ops.; sr. v.p. Fulton, Reid & Co., 1966-75; pres., CEO Fulton, Reid & Staples, Inc., 1975-77; ptnr. William C. Roney & Co., 1977-79; exec. com. Cascade Industries, Inc.; assoc. A.G. Edwards & Sons, Inc., 1984-89, v.p. investments, 1989—. Dir. Fulton, Reid & Staples, Inc., Craft House Corp., Nobility Homes, Inc. Pres. Historic Ft. Wayne, Inc.; cons. to Mus. Historic Ft. Wayne; nominee, trustee Ohio Hist. Soc.; mem. Smithsonian Assocs.; mem. fin. com. E. Tenn. Hist. Soc., dir., treas. collections com.; v.p. Ft. Wayne Hist. Soc.; bd. dirs. Ft. Wayne YMCA, 1963-64. Recipient

Achievement cert. Inst. Investment Banking, U. Pa., 1959. Mem. Alliance Française, VFW (past comdr.), Co. Mil. Historians, Cleve. Grays, Am. Soc. Arms Collectors, 1st Cleve. Cavalry Assn., Nat. Assn. Securities Dealers (bus. conduct com.), Beaver Creek Hunt Club, Cleve. Athletic Club, Rockwell Springs Club, Hill and Dale Club, Masons, Phi Beta Kappa. Episcopalian. Home: 170 Cheeskogili Way Loudon TN 37774-7811 Office: AG Edwards & Sons Inc 8848 Cedar Springs Ln Knoxville TN 37923-5408

BARKER, LINDA K. state legislator; Rep. S.D. State Ho. Reps. Dist. 13, 1993-98, mem. commerce and taxation coms.; v.p. Bus. Aviation Svcs., Sioux Falls, S.D. Mem. nat. civil aviation review commn. Mem. Nat. Air Transport Assn. (chmn.). Home: 2016 S Pendar Ln Sioux Falls SD 57105-3023 Office: Bus. Aviation Svcs Joe Foss Field 3501 Aviation Ave Hanger 1 Sioux Falls SD 57104

BARKER, LLYLE JAMES, JR. management consultant, jounalism educator; b. Columbus, Ohio, July 28, 1932; s. Llyle James and Mabel Lucile (Johnson) B.; m. Maxine Ruth Metcalf, Jan. 15, 1956; children: Llyle J., Daryl Alan. BS, Ohio State U., 1954; postgrad., U. Wis., 1961; MS in Mass. Comm., Shippensburg State Coll., 1975. Commd. officer U.S. Army, advanced through grades to maj. gen.; served in Korea, Vietnam, Thailand and Germany; pub. affairs officer Hawaii, 1957-59, NORAD, 1961-63, Dept. Army, 1966-69, 7th Army, 1969-71, Joint Casualty Resolution Ctr., 1974, European Command, 1975-77, U.S. Army Europe, 1979-80; dep. chief info. Dept. Army, 1980-81, chief pub. affairs, 1981-84; prof. Sch. Journalism Ohio State U., Columbus, 1984-98. Cons. mgmt. comm.; assoc. Gannett Ctr. Media Studies (now Freedom Forum Media Studies Ctr.), Columbia U. Contbr. articles to profl. jours. Decorated D.S.M., Legion of Merit, others. Mem. World Future Soc., Pub. Rels. Soc. Am., Assn. Edn. Journalism and Mass Comm. Home: 6844 Chateau Chase Dr Columbus OH 43235-3942 Office: Ohio State U Sch Journalism 242 W 18th Ave Columbus OH 43210-1107 E-mail: llylejb@cs.com.

BARKER, SARAH EVANS, judge; b. Mishawaka, Ind., June 10, 1943; d. James McCall and Sarah (Yarbrough) Evans; m. Kenneth R. Barker, Nov. 25, 1972. BS, Ind. U., 1965, LLD (hon.), 1999; JD, Am. U., 1969; LLD (hon.), U. Indpls., 1984; D in Pub. Svc. (hon.), Butler U., 1987; LLD (hon.), Marian Coll., 1991; LHD, U. Evansville, 1993; LLD (hon.), Wabash Coll., 1999, Hanover Coll., 2001. Bar: Ind. 1969, U.S. Dist. Ct. (so. dist.) Ind., 1969, U.S. Ct. Appeals (7th cir.) 1973, U.S. Supreme Ct., 1978. Legal asst. to senator U.S. Senate, 1969-71; spl. counsel to minority, govt. ops. com. permanent investigations subcom., 1971-72; dir. rsch. scheduling and advance Senator Percy Re-election Campaign, 1972; asst. U.S. atty. So. Dist. Ind., 1972-76, 1st asst. U.S. atty., 1976-77, U.S. atty., 1981-84; judge U.S. Dist. Ct. (so. dist.) Ind., 1984-94, chief judge, 1994—2000. Assoc., then ptnr. Bose, McKinney & Evans, Indpls., 1977-81; mem. long range planning com. Jud. Conf. U.S., 1991-96, exec. com., 1989-91, standing com. fed. rules of practice and procedure, 1987-91, dist. judge rep., 1988-91; mem. jud. coun. 7th cir. Ct. Appeals, 1988-2000, jud. fellows commn. U.S. Supreme Ct., 1993-98; jud. adv. com., sentencing commn., 1995-97, bd. advisors, Ind. U., Purdue U., Indpls., 1989—; mem. pres.'s cabinet Ind. U., 1995—; bd. visitors Ind. U. Sch. of Law, Bloomington, 1984—; bd. dirs. Clarian Health Ptnrs., 1996—, Christian Theol. Sem., 1999-2001; bd. dirs. Einstein Inst. for Sci., Health and the Cts., 2001—; mem. spl. redaction rev. panel U.S. Jud. Conf., 2000—. Recipient Peck award Wabash Coll., 1989, Touchstone award Girls Club of Greater Indpls., 1989, Leach Centennial 1st Woman award Valparaiso Law Sch., 1993, Most Influential Women award Indpls. Bus. Jour., 1996, Paul Buchanan award of excellence Indpls. Bar Found., 1998, Thomas J. Hennessy award Ind. U., 1995, Disting. Citizen fellow Ind. U., 1999-2001; named Ind. Woman of Yr., Women in Comm., 1986, Ind. Univ. Disting. Alumni, 1996, Disting. Citizen fellow Ind. U., 1999-2001, Singing Hoosiers Disting. Alumni award Ind. U., 2000, Man for All Seasons award St. Thomas More Soc., 2000. Mem. ABA, Ind. Bar Assn., Indpls. Bar Assn. (Antoinette Dakin Leach award 1993), Fed. Judges Assn. (exec. com., bd. dirs. 2001—), Com. on Budget (judicial conf. 2001-), Einstein Inst. Sci., Health and Cts. (bd. dirs. 2001-), U.S. Judicial Conf. (spl. redaction rev. panel 2000-), Christian Theol. Sem. (bd. trustees 1999-), Lawyers Club, Kiwanis. Republican. Methodist. Office: US Dist Ct 210 US Courthouse 46 E Ohio St Indianapolis IN 46204-1903

BARKER, WILLIAM THOMAS, lawyer; b. Feb. 28, 1947; s. V. Wayne and Cordelia (Whitten) B.; m. June K. Robinson, Jan. 30, 1981. BS, MS, Mich. State U., 1969; JD, U. Calif., Berkeley, 1974. Bar: Calif. 1975, Ill. 1976. Assoc. programmer-analyst Control Data Corp., Sunnyvale, Calif., 1969-71; law clk. Pa. Supreme Ct., Erie, 1974-75; assoc. Sonnenschein Carlin Nath & Rosenthal, Chgo., 1975-82, ptnr., 1982—. Moderator Ill. Ins. Law Forum, Counsel Connect, 1994-98; co-moderator Nat. Ins. Law gen. forum, 1996-98; moderator Ins. Law Forum, Lexis One, 2001. Bd. editors: Def. Counsel Jour., 1987—; editor Bad Faith Law Report, 1999-2001, contbg. editor 1990-99; mem. editl. bd. Ins. Litigation Reporter, 1987—. editl. dir. and sr. contbg. editor, 2001—; editor Covered Events, 1995-96, editor emeritus, 1996—; ins. law publs. bd. Def. Rsch. Inst., 1992-97; contbr. articles to profl. jours. Fellow Am. Bar Found.; mem. ABA (chair-elect com. on appellate advocacy, tort and ins. practice sect. 1994-95, chair 1995-96, chair gen. comm. bd. 1996-97), Internat. Assn. Def. Counsel (Yancey Meml. award for best article 1995, chair spl. com. on Amicus Curia 1996-97, chair ad hoc com. on interstate practice 2000—), Chgo. Coun. Lawyers (sec. 1987-88, bd. govs. 1989-91, chair com. profl. responsibility 1990-95), Chgo. Bar Assn. (chmn. com. constl. law 1984-85), Def. Rsch. Inst., Am. Law Inst., Ill. Assn. Def. Trial Coun. Home: 132 E Delaware Pl Apt 5806 Chicago IL 60611-4951 Office: Sonnenschein Nath Et Al 8000 Sears Tower 233 S Wacker Dr Ste 8000 Chicago IL 60606-6491

BARKSDALE, CLARENCE CAULFIELD, banker; b. St. Louis, June 4, 1932; s. Clarence M. and Elizabeth (Caulfield) B.; m. Emily Catlin Keyes, Apr. 4, 1959; children: John Keyes, Emily Shepley. AB, Brown U., 1954; postgrad., Washington U. Law Sch., St. Louis, 1957-58, Stonier Grad. Sch. Banking, Rutgers U., 1964, Columbia U. Grad. Sch. Bus., 1968; LLD (hon.), Maryville Coll., St. Louis, 1976, Westminster Coll., Fulton, Mo., 1982, St. Louis U., 1989. From asst. cashier to chmn. bd. , CEO Centerre Bank NA (formerly 1st Nat. Bank), St. Louis, 1960—76, chmn. bd., chief exec. officer, 1976-88; vice chmn. Bank of Am. (formerly Boatmen's Bancshares, Inc.), 1988-89; vice chmn. bd. dirs. Washington U., 1989—. Bd. dirs. SBC Comms., Inc., Thomas Lawrence & Assocs., Inc. Bd. dirs. Mo. Bot. Gardens, Alzheimers Assn., Grand Ctr. Inc., Wash. U. Mus. Contemporary Art, St. Louis Boy Scouts, and Girls, Inc. With M.I., U.S. Army, 1954-57. Mem. St. Louis Club, St. Louis Country Club, Noonday Club, Bogey Club of St. Louis, Harbor Point Golf Club, Little Harbor Club), Wequetosing Golf Club (Harbor Springs, Mich.), Ocean Club, Gulfstream Golf Club, Gulf Stream Bath & Tennis Club (Delray Beach, Fla.), Alpha Delta Phi. E-mail: clarence. Office: Washington U 7425 Forsyth Blvd Saint Louis MO 63105-2161 E-mail: clarence_barksdale@aismail.wustl.edu.

BARLETT, JAMES EDWARD, data processing executive; b. Akron, Ohio, Jan. 1, 1944; s. Willard Paul and Pauline (Candlish) B.; m. Sue Patterson, June 20, 1964; 1 child, Jamie Catherine B.A., U. Akron, 1967, M.B.A., 1971. Systems analyst B.F. Goodrich, Akron, Ohio, 1962-69; ptnr. Touche Ross & Co., Detroit, 1971-79; 1st. v.p., then sr. v.p. Nat. Bank Detroit, 1979-84; exec. v.p. ops. NBD Bancorp and Nat. Bank Detroit; exec. v.p. worldwide ops. and syss. MasterCard Internat. Corp.; pres., CEO Galileo Internat., Rosemont, Ill., 1994—, chmn., 1997—. Bd. dirs. TeleTech Holdings, Inc., Korn/Ferry Internat., Computer Communications Am., Detroit, Cirrus System, Inc., also vice chmn. Trustee Sta. WTVS-TV, Detroit, 1984—, Detroit Country Day Sch., 1984—. Served to 1st lt. U.S. Army, 1967-69, Vietnam Decorated Bronze Star, Army Commendation medal Mem. Am. Bankers Assn., Mich. Bankers Assn., Detroit Athletic Club, Econ. Club, Bloomfield Hills Country Club, Detroit Club, Bloomfield Open Hunt Club. Republican. Episcopalian. Avocations: jogging; reading. Office: Galileo Internat 9700 W Higgins Rd Rosemont IL 60018

BARLIANT, RONALD, federal judge; b. Chgo., Aug. 25, 1945; s. Lois I. Barliant; children: Claire, Anne. BA in History, Roosevelt U., Chgo., 1966; postgrad., Northwestern U., Chgo., 1966-67; JD, Stanford U., 1969. Bar: Ill. 1969, U.S. Dist. Ct. (no. dist.) Ill., U.S. Ct. Appeals (7th cir.). VISTA vol., staff atty. Cook County Legal Assistance Found., Chgo., 1969-72; assoc. Miller, Shakman, Hamilton and Kurtzon, 1972-76, ptnr., 1976-88; judge U.S. Bankruptcy Ct. (no. dist.) Ill., 1988—. Adj. prof. debtor-creditor rels. John Marshall Law Sch., 1991-92; bd. dirs. Cook County Legal Assistance Found., 1975-82; gen. counsel Chgo. Coun. Lawyers, 1983-86. Mem. Fed. Bar Assn. (bd. dirs. 1992-94), Nat. Conf. Bankruptcy Judges (bd. govs. 1997—). Avocations: opera, theatre, golf, Cubs baseball. Office: US Bankruptcy Ct 219 S Dearborn St Rm 738 Chicago IL 60604-1702

BARLOW, JOHN F. automotive glass products company executive; BS in Bus. Mgmt., Fla. So. U. Pres., CEO Western Auto Stores divsn. Western Auto Supply Co.; pres, COO Safelite Glass Corp. and Safelite AutoGlass, 1991, pres., CEO, 1997.

BARMANN, LAWRENCE FRANCIS, history educator, retired; b. Maryville, Mo., June 9, 1932; s. Francis Lawrence and Clary Weber (LaMar) B. B.A., St. Louis U., 1956, Ph.L., 1957, S.T.L., 1964; M.A., Fordham U., 1960; postgrad., Princeton, 1965-66; Ph.D., Cambridge U., Eng., 1970. Tchr. history St. Louis U. High Sch., 1957-59; asst. prof. history St. Louis U., 1970-73, asso. prof., 1973-78, prof., 1978—, asst. dir. Am. Studies Program, 1981-83, prof. Am. studies, 1981-01; dir. Am. Studies Program, 1983-88; prof. theol. studies St. Louis U., 1996-01, ret., 2001, prof. emeritus, 2002—. Author: Newman at St. Mary's, 1962, Baron Friedrich von Hügel and the Modernist Crisis in England, 1972, The Letters of Baron Friedrich von Hügel and Professor Norman Kemp Smith, 1982; editor Sanctity and Secularity, 1999; contbr. articles profl. jours. Recipient award Mellon Faculty Devel. Fund, 1987, 92, 94, Emerson Electric Outstanding Tchr. award, 1999; rsch. grantee Am. Philos. Soc. PHila., 1971, Beaumont Fund, 1977, 82; Danforth assoc., 1978—. Mem. Am. Acad. Religion, Cambridge Soc. (founding 1977), Am. Cath. Hist. Assn., Phi Beta Kappa. Home: The Lindell Ter 12-A 4501 Lindell Blvd Saint Louis MO 63108-2038 Office: 221 N Grand Blvd Saint Louis MO 63103-2006 E-mail: barmann@slu.edu.

BARNABY, ALAN, retail executive; BS in Bus. Adminstrn. and Econs., Emporia State U., 1972. Asst. mgr. Home Depot, Inc., Fla., 1983, store mgr., 1984, regional mgr. South Fla., 1985-88, regional mgr. Atlanta region, 1988-90, dir. store system, 1990-92, labor mgmt., 1992-94, sr. v.p. store ops., 1994-99, pres. Ea. Great Lakes region Mich., 1999—. Office: The Home Depot Inc # 300 12100 Inkster Rd Redford MI 48239-2585

BARNARD, ROBERT N. lawyer; b. Madison, Wis., Dec. 15, 1947; s. Robert Julian and Dorothy Jane (Nichol) B.; m. Katherine Elaine Chott, Mar. 1, 1980; children: Suzanna Katherine, Sarah Elizabeth. AB, Harvard U., 1969; JD, Stanford U., 1975. Bar: Ill. 1975, U.S. Dist. Ct. (no. dist.) Ill. 1975. Assoc. Mayer, Brown & Platt, Chgo., 1975-81, ptnr. London, Eng., 1982-88, Chgo., 1988—. Trustee U. Notre Dame, London, 1986-88. Lt. U.S. Army, 1969-72. Office: Mayer Brown Rowe & Maw 1675 Broadway New York NY 10019-5820

BARNES, A. JAMES, academic dean; b. Napoleon, Ohio, Aug. 30, 1942; s. Albert James and Mary Elizabeth (Morey) Barnes; m. Sarah Jane Hughes, June 19, 1976; children: Morey Elizabeth, Laura LeHardy, Catherine Farrell. BA with high honors, Mich. State U., 1964; JD cum laude, Harvard U., 1967. Asst. prof. bus. adminstrn. Ind. U., 1967—69; trial atty. Dept. Justice, 1969—70, asst. to dep. atty. gen., 1973; asst. to adminstr. EPA, 1970—73; campaign mgr. for Gov. Milliken of Mich., 1974; ptnr. Beveridge, Fairbanks & Diamond, Washington, 1975—81; gen. counsel Dept. Agr., 1981—83; adj. prof. Georgetown U. Sch. Bus. Adminstrn., Washington, 1978—80; gen. counsel EPA, 1983—85, dep. adminstr., 1985—88; dean Sch. Pub. Environ. Adminstrn., prof. pub. and environ. affairs Ind. U., 1988—. Spl. counsel Beveridge, Fairbanks & Diamond, Washington, 1988—97; cons., mediator, expert witness Nat. Acad. Pub. Adminstrn., 1988—; adj. prof. law Ind. U., 2001—. Co-author: Essentials of Business Law, 1994, Law of Commercial Transactions and Business Associations, 1995, Law for Business, 8th edit., 2002, Business Law and the Regulatory Environment, 11th edit., 2000. Del. Ind. Rep. Conv., 1968, Mich. Rep. Conv., 1974. Named Sagamore of Wabash, 2000; recipient Outstanding Tchg. award, Ind. U., 1969. Fellow: Nat. Acad. Pub. Adminstrn.; mem.: Sagamore of Wabash, Vineyard Haven Yacht Club (Mass.), Edgartown (Mass.) Yacht Club, Skyline Club (Indpls.), Met. Club (Washington). Office: Ind U SPEA 418 Bloomington IN 47405 E-mail: barnesaj@indiana.edu.

BARNES, GALEN R. insurance company executive; b. Vevay, Ind. m. June Ann Ladd; two children. Degree in maths., Ind. U. Actuarial officer Nationwide Mut. Ins. Co., Columbus, Ohio, 1975-81, vice pres. actuary, 1981—83; pres., COO Colonial Ins. Co., Calif., 1983-87; v.p. personal and comml. ins. svcs. Nationwide Ins. Co., Columbus, Ohio, 1987-89, sr. v.p. nationwide personal and comml. ins. svcs., 1989-93; pres., COO Wausau Ins. Co., 1993-96; pres. Nationwide Ins. Enterprise, 1996-99; pres., COO Nationwide Ins., 1999—. Bd. dirs. Ohio Dominican Coll., Franklin County United Way, Arthur C. James Cancer Hosp. Fellow Casualty Actuarial Soc., Am. Acad. Actuaries. Office: Nationwide Mut Ins Co 1 Nationwide Plz Columbus OH 43215-2220

BARNES, HARPER HENDERSON, movie critic, editor, writer; b. Greensboro, N.C., July 2, 1937; s. Bennett Harper and Cora Emmaline Barnes; m. Janice Stauffacher, May 10, 1961 (div. 1985); m. Roseann Marie Weiss, May 31, 1986. Critic, reporter St. Louis Post-Dispatch, 1965-70, editor, critic, 1973-97; editor The Phoenix, Boston, 1970-72, St. Louis mag., 1997-99. Instr. Washington U., St. Louis, 1990, 94. Author: Blue Monday, 1991, Standing on a Volcano, 2001. With U.S. Army, 1959-62. Avocations: bicycling, fishing. Office: St Louis Mag 6358 Delmar Blvd Saint Louis MO 63130-4719 E-mail: hbarnesl@mindspring.com.

BARNES, JAMES BYRON, university president; b. Akron, Ohio, Apr. 4, 1942; s. Roy and Kathleen (Elrod) B.; m. Tommie Schade, Aug. 14, 1965. AB in Social Sci., Ind. Wesleyan U., 1965; MEd in History, Kent State U., 1969; Ed.S. in History and Social Sci., Vanderbilt U., 1972; EdD in Social Sci. Edn., U. Ga., 1976. Assoc. prof. Cen. (S.C.) Wesleyan Coll., 1970-76, Ind. Wesleyan U., Marion, 1976-81, dean of coll., 1981-84; asst. gen sec. Dept. Edn. and Ministry Wesleyan Ch., 1984-85; v.p. acad. affairs Houghton (N.Y.) Coll., 1985-87; pres. Ind. Wesleyan U., Marion, 1987—. Mem. Grant Co. Community Found., Marion, 1987—; mem. adv. bd. Salvation Army, 1989—. Grantee NEH, 1987. Mem. Rotary, Marion/Grant County C. of C. Mem. Wesleyan Ch. Office: Ind Wesleyan U 4201 S Washington St Rm 4990 Marion IN 46953-4990

BARNES, JAMES GARLAND, JR. lawyer; b. Ga., Mar. 3, 1940; s. James Garland Sr. and Carolyn L. (Stewart) B.; m. Lucy Curtis Ferguson, Nov. 1976; children: Susan Whitney, David Lawrence, Matthew Martin. BA, Yale U., 1961; LLB, U. Mich., 1966. Bar: Ill. 1967. With firm Baker & McKenzie, Chgo., 1966—, ptnr., 1973—. Co-author: The ABCs of the UCC Article 5: Letters of Credit. Mem. adv. com. Ill. Sec. of State's Corp. Acts, 1981-95; U.S. del. to UN Commn. on Internat. Trade Law, Internat. C. of C., 1994-2000. Mem. ABA (chmn. letter of credit subcom. 1991-96), Ill. Bar Assn. (chmn. corp. and security law sect. 1977-78), Chgo. Bar Assn. (chmn. corp. law com. 1982-83, chmn. profl. responsibility com. 1983-84), Legal Club Chgo. Office: Baker & McKenzie 1 Prudential Pla 130 E Randolph St Ste 3700 Chicago IL 60601-6342 E-mail: james.g.barnes@bakernet.com.

BARNES, JAMES JOHN, history educator; b. St. Paul, Nov. 16, 1931; s. Harry George and Bertha (Blaul) B.; m. Patience Rogers Plummer, July 9, 1955; children— Jennifer Chase, Geoffrey Prescott BA, Amherst Coll., 1954; B.A., New Coll., Oxford, 1956, MA, 1961; PhD, Harvard U., 1960; DHL, Coll. of Wooster, 1976, Amherst Coll., 1999. Instr. history Amherst Coll., 1959-62; asst. prof. history Wabash Coll., Crawfordsville, Ind., 1962-67, assoc. prof. history, 1967-76, prof. history, 1976—, chmn. dept. history, Hadley prof., 1979-97. Author: Free Trade in Books: A Study of the London Book Trade since 1800, 1964, Authors, Publishers and Politicians: The Quest for an Anglo-American Copyright Agreement 1815-54, 1974, (with Patience P. Barnes) Hitler's Mein Kampf in Britain and America 1930-39, 1980, (with Patience P. Barnes) James Vincent Murphy: Translator and Interpreter of Fascist Europe, 1880-1946, 1987, (with Patience P. Barnes) Private and Confidential Letters from British Ministers in Washington to the Foreign Secretaries in London, 1849-67, 1993, (with Patience P. Barnes) Nazi Refugee turned Gestapo Spy: The Life of Hans Wesemann, 1895-1971, 2001; contbr. articles to profl. jours. Mem. Rhodes Scholar Selection Com. for Ind., 1965-89, Crawfordsville Community Action Coun., 1966-69, Crawfordsville Community Day Care Com., 1966-67; mem. vestry St. John's Episcopal Ch., 1966-69; mem. Ind. Adv. Com. State Rehab. Svcs. for Blind, 1979-81; trustee Ind. Hist. Soc., 1982—. Recipient Disting. Alumni award St. Paul Acad. and Summit Sch., 1989; Rhodes scholar, 1954-56, Fulbright scholar, 1978; Woodrow Wilson fellow, 1956-57, Kent fellow, 1958, Great Lakes Colls. Assn. Teaching fellow, 1958, Great Lakes Colls. Assn. Teaching fellow, 1975; rsch. grantee Amherst Coll., 1960-61, Social Sci. Rsch. Coun., 1962, 70, Wabash Coll., 1962—, Am. Coun. Learned Socs., 1964-65, 80, Am. Philos. Soc., 1964, 68, 76, 91; named Hon. Alumnus, Wabash Coll., 1994. Mem. Am. Hist. Assn., Ouiatenon Literary Soc., Conf. Brit. Studies, Rsch. Soc. Victorian Periodicals, Am. Rhodes Scholars, Soc. Historians Am. Fgn. Rels., Ind. Hist. Soc., Montgomery County Hist. Soc., Midwest Victorian Studies Assn. (pres. 1989-91), Ind. Assn. Historians, N.E. Victorian Studies Assn., Soc. for History of Authorship, Reading and Pub., Am. Coun. of Blind, United Oxford and Cambridge Club of London, Phi Beta Kappa. Home: 7 Locust Hl Crawfordsville IN 47933-3347 Office: Wabash Coll History Dept Crawfordsville IN 47933 E-mail: barnesj@wabash.edu.

BARNES, JAMES MILTON, physics and astronomy educator; b. Ypsilanti, Mich., July 5, 1923; s. J. Milton and Elsie (Fischer) B.; m. Marjorie Ruth Petersen, Dec. 17, 1949. BS, Eastern Mich. U., 1948; MS, Mich. State U., 1950, PhD, 1955. Asst. prof. Eastern Mich. U., Ypsilanti, 1955-58, asso. prof., 1958-61, prof., 1961-88, prof. emeritus, 1988—, head dept. physics and astronomy, 1961-74. Served with AUS, 1942-46. Mem. A.A.A.S. (life), Nat. Sci. Tchrs. Assn. (life), Am. Assn. Physics Tchrs., Sigma Xi, Sigma Pi Sigma, Pi Mu Epsilon. Club: Ann Arbor (Mich.) Country. Home: 4872 N Whitman Cir Ann Arbor MI 48103-9774 Office: Eastern Mich U Physics Dept Ypsilanti MI 48197

BARNES, KAREN KAY, lawyer; b. June 22, 1950; d. Walter William and Vashti (Greenlee) Sessler; m. James Alan Barnes, Feb. 12, 1972; children: Timothy Matthew, Christopher Michael. BA, Valparaiso U., 1971; JD, DePaul U., 1978, LLM in Taxation, 1980. Bar: Ill. 1978, U.S. Dist. Ct. (no. dist.) Ill. 1978. Ptnr. McDermott, Will & Emory, Chgo., 1978-88; prin. William M. Mercer, Inc. and predecessor firm, 1989-93; staff dir. legal dept. McDonald's Corp., Oak Brook, Ill., 1993-95, home office dir. legal dept., 1995-97, regulatory practice group leader and mng. counsel, 1998—. Instr. John Marshall Grad. Sch. Law, Chgo., 1986-87; mem. adv. bd. John Marshall Sch. Law, 1996—; bd. dirs. Flutes Unlimited; mem. adv. bd. dirs. Plan Sponsor Mag., 2000—. Contbr. case note to DePaul Law Rev., 1976, note and comment editor DePaul Law Rev., 1976-77, editor Taxation For Lawyers, 1986-88. Mem. Am. Coll. Employee Benefit Attys., Chgo. Bar Assn. (chair employee benefits com. 1991-92, co-chair symphony orchestra 1999—), Midwest Pension Conf. (name chged to Midwest Benefits Coun.), WEB (pres. Chgo. chpt. 1986-88, v.p. nat. bd. 1988, pres. 1989-90), Profit Sharing Coun. Am. (legal and legis. com. 1994—, bd. dirs. 1997—, 2d vice chair 1997-98, 1st vice chair 1998-2000, chair 2000—). Lutheran. Home: 3 S 102 Black Cherry Ln Glen Ellyn IL 60137 Office: McDonald's Corp McDonald's Plz Oak Brook IL 60523-1900 E-mail: karen.barnes@mcd.com.

BARNES, KAY, mayor; BS in Secondary Edn., U. Kans.; MS in Secondary Edn. and Pub. Adminstrn., U. Mo., Kansas City. Staff mem. Westport area Cross-Lines Coop. Coun.; pres. Kay Waldo, Inc., human resources devel. co., Kansas City, Mo.; mayor City of Kansas City, 1999—. Condr. over 400 pub. seminars Nat. Seminars, Inc.; cons., keynote spkr. 14 reginal confs. through U.S., Am. Bus. Women's Assn.; former co-host, prodr. cable TV show Let's Talk; former instr. U. Mo., Kansas City, U. Kans., Ctrl. Mich. U. Author: About Time! A Woman's Guide to Time Management. Co-founder Ctrl. Exch.; vol. Cross-Lines Coop. Coun.; a founder women's resource svc. U. Mo., Kansas City; developer multicultural women's speaking panels through western U.S.; mem. Jackson County (Mo.) Legislature, from 1974; mem. Kansas City City Coun., from 1979; chmn. Tax Increment Financing Commn., 1993-97; pres. bd. dirs. Women's Employment Network; mem. or dir. numerous other orgns., including Women's Found. Greater Kansas City, Greater Kansas City Sports Commn.; mem. chancellor's adv. bd. of Women's Ctr., U. Mo., Kansas City. Named One of 7 Outstanding Women in Kansas City, 1977. Mem. Greater Kansas City C. of C. (com.). Office: Mayor's Office City Hall 29th Fl 414 E 12th St Ste 2902 Kansas City MO 64106-2778*

BARNES, MICHAEL PHILLIP, prosecutor; b. Bradford, Ill., Dec. 2, 1947; s. Lee and Alice Barnes; m. Alberta Barnes; children: Timothy, John. BA in History, St. Ambrose Coll., Davenport, Iowa, 1970; JD, U. Notre Dame, 1973. Dep. prosecutor St. Joseph County, South Bend, Ind., 1973-78, prosecuting atty., 1978—. Chmn. Ind. State Correction Adv. Com., 1989. Bd. dirs. Am. Cancer Soc., 1981-83, Alcoholism Coun. of St. Joseph County, 1983, Corvilla Inc., 1984; adv. bd. Community Based Corrections Project, 1983, Ind. U. at South Bend Paralegal Studies Prog., 1985; co-chmn. Nat. Child Abuse Prevention Wk., 1982; steering com. Community Edn. Roundtable Prog., Ind. U., 1986; adv. bd. Dismas House, 1989-90. Named Citizen of the Yr., Nat. Assn. Social Workers, 1990, Pacesetter award, Ind. Coalition Against Domestic Violence, 1989, Spl. Advocate award, Ind. Victim Assistance network, 1989, Domestic Violence Coalition Inc. award for outstanding svc., 1989, Community Svc. award, Better Bus. Bur., 1988, DAR Law Enforcement medal, 1987, Gov.'s award for exemplary project, Pretrial Diversion Prog., 1987, Community Svc. award, Planned Parenthood of North Ctrl. Ind., 1986, many others. Mem. Ind. Prosecuting Attys. Coun. (pres. 1982-83, ethics com. 1985), Ind. Bar Assn. (ethics com. 1986), Nat. Dist. Attys. Assn. (bd. dirs. 1987, pres. 1995-96), Ind. Criminal Justice Inst. (bd. dirs. 1989), St. Joseph County Bar assn., Ind. Bar Assn., Ill. Bar Assn., Nat. Dist. Attys. Assn. (pres. 1995-96). Office: Saint Joseph County County-City Bldg 10th Fl 227 W Jefferson Blvd South Bend IN 46601-1830

BARNES, PAUL MCCLUNG, lawyer; b. Phila., June 27, 1914; s. Andrew Wallace and Luella Hope (Andrew) B.; m. Elizabeth McClenahan, Dec. 28, 1940 (dec.); children: Andrew M., Margaret L. Lenart, James D., John R. (dec.). B.A., Monmouth (Ill.) Coll., 1936; J.D., U. Chgo., 1939. Bar: Colo. bar 1939. Assoc. Bannister & Bannister, Denver, 1939-40, Foley & Lardner, Milw., 1940-47, ptnr., 1948-88, of counsel, 1988—. Dir. Wis. Public Service Corp., 1974-77, Kickhaefer Mfg. Co., 1965-85, Attys. Liability Assurance Soc., Ltd., 1979-87; sec. Sta-Rite Industries, Inc., 1965-73 Mem. adv. bd. Milw. Protestant Home, 1975-87. Served with USNR, 1942-45. Mem. ABA, Wis. Bar Assn., Order of Coif. Office: Foley & Lardner 777 E Wisconsin Ave Ste 3800 Milwaukee WI 53202-5367 E-mail: pbarnes@webtv.net.

BARNES, RICHARD GEORGE, physicist, educator; b. Milw., Dec. 19, 1922; s. George Richard and Irma (Ott) B.; m. Mildred A. Jachens, Sept. 9, 1950; children: Jeffrey R., David G., Christina E., Douglas A. B.A., U. Wis., 1948; M.A., Dartmouth Coll., 1949; Ph.D., Harvard U., 1952. Teaching fellow Harvard, 1950-52; asst. prof. U. Del., 1952-55, asso. prof., 1955-56, Iowa State U., 1956-60, prof., 1960-88, chmn. dept. physics, 1971-75, prof. emeritus, 1988—; sr. physicist Ames Lab., U.S. Dept. Energy, 1960-88; chief physics div. Ames Lab., AEC, 1971-75. Vis. rsch. prof. Calif. Inst. Tech., 1962-63; guest prof. Tech. U. Darmstadt, Germany, 1975-76; vis. prof. Cornell U., 1982-83; program dir. solid state physics NSF, 1988-89, condensed matter physics NSF, 1995; chmn. Metal Hydrides Gordon Rsch. Conf., 1987. Served with USAAF, 1942-43; C.E. AUS, 1944-46 (Manhattan Project). Recipient U.S. Sr. Scientist award Alexander von Humboldt Found., 1975-76 Fellow Am. Phys. Soc. Home: 3238 Aspen Rd Ames IA 50014 Office: Iowa State U Physics Dept Ames IA 50011-0001

BARNES, ROBERT F, agronomist; b. Estherville, Iowa, Feb. 6, 1933; s. Chester Arthur and Pearl Adella (Stoelting) B.; m. Bettye Jeanne Burrell, June 25, 1955; children: Bradley R., Rebecca L. Reinalda, Roberta K. Nixon, Brian L. AA, Estherville Jr. Coll., 1953; BS, Iowa State U., 1957; MS, Rutgers U., 1959; PhD, Purdue U., 1963. Rsch. agronomist USDA-Agrl. Rsch. Svc., West Lafayette, Ind., 1959-70, lab. dir. University Park, Pa., 1970-75, staff scientist nat. program staff Beltsville, Md., 1975-79, assoc. dep. adminstr. So. region New Orleans, 1979-84, dep. adminstr. So. region, 1984-86; exec. v.p. Am. Soc. Agronomy, Madison, Wis., 1986-99; exec. dir. Agronomic Sci. Found., exec. dir. emeritus, 1999—; also fellow Am. Soc. of Agronomy, Madison, Wis. Asst. prof. Purdue U., West Lafayette, 1963-66; assoc. prof., 1966-70; adj. prof. Pa. State U., University Park, 1966-70; adj. prof. agronomy U. Wis., Madison, 1986-99; pres. Internat. Grassland Congress, Lexington, Ky., 1981; cons. Agronomic Sci. Found., Am. Soc. Agronomy. Editor: Forages, 1995; contbr. articles to profl. jours. With U.S. Army, 1953-55, Germany. Recipient H.S. Stubbs Meml. Lecture award Tropical Grassland Soc., Brisbane, Australia, 1984, Henry A. Wallace award Iowa State U., 1991. Fellow AAAS, Crop Sci. Soc. Am. (pres. 1984-85); mem. Am. Forage and Grassland Coun. (medallion 1981, Disting. Grasslander award 2001), Grazing Lands Forum (pres. 1986-87), Forage and Grassland Found. (pres. 1993-97). Avocations: walking, reading. Office: Am Soc of Agronomy 677 S Segoe Rd Madison WI 53711-1048 E-mail: rbarnes@agronomy.org.

BARNES, ROSEMARY LOIS, minister; b. Grand Rapids, Mich., Sept. 17, 1946; d. Floyd Herman and Cora Agnes (Beukema) Herms; m. Louis Herbert Adams, Feb. 22, 1969 (div. Oct. 1976); 1 child, Louis Herbert Jr.; m. Robert Jearold Barnes, Oct. 8, 1976. BA, Calvin Coll., 1968; postgrad., Wagner Leadership Inst., 1999—. Ordained to ministry Home Ministry Fellowship, 1980; cert. social worker. Group worker Kent County Juvenile Ct., Grand Rapids, Mich., 1966-68; tchr. Sheldon Elem. Sch., 1968-69; social worker Kent Dept. Social Services, 1969-75, 75-84; tchr., mission worker Emmanuel House, San Diego, 1975; co-pastor, founder River of Life Ministries, Grand Rapids, 1980—; instr. Gt. Lakes Inst. Bible Studies, 1988. Tchr., founder River of Life Sch. Christian Leadership, Grand Rapids, 1981—; v.p. Aglow, Grand Rapids, 1982-83; sec., treas. Western Mich. Full Gospel Ministers Fellowship, Grand Rapids, 1984-85; mem. bd. chaplains Dunes Correctional Facility, Saugatuck, Mich., 1986-91; coord. 1988 Washington for Jesus March, One Nation Under God, Inc.; co-pastor Gun Lake River of Life, 1988; prof. Great Lakes Inst., 1988; county coord. Grand Rapids Full Gospel Ministers Fellowship, 1990-92; co-pastor Defiance, Ohio River of Life, 1992-93; founder St. Joseph Sch. Christian Leadership. Participant TV show Ask the Pastor, 1993—; dir., producer TV show River Reflections, 1994—; Mich. women's coord. Let The Redeemed of the Lord Say So, 1994; sponsor Grand Rapids cable TV Jewish Jewels, 1995—. Bd. dirs. Alcohol Incentive Ladder, Grand Rapids, 1979; overseer River City Outreach Ch., 1994—. Mem. Women in Leadership. Republican. Mem. Ind. Charismatic Ch. Avocation: playing the trumpet. Address: PO Box 140735 Grand Rapids MI 49514-0735 Fax: (616) 454-6525. E-mail: RBarnesROL@aol.com.

BARNES, SANDRA HENLEY, publishing company executive; b. Seymour, Ind., Jan. 15, 1943; d. Ray C. and Barbara (Cockerham) Henley; m. Ronald D. Barnes, Sept. 3, 1961; children: Laura Winkler, Barrett and Garrett (twins). Student, Ind. State U., 1962-63. Asst. sales mgr. Marquis Who's Who, Indpls., 1973-79, sales, svc. mgr., 1979-82, mktg. ops. mgr., 1982-84, mktg. mgr. Chgo., 1984-86, dir. mktg. Wilmette, 1986-87; v.p. mktg. Macmillan Directory Div., 1987-88; group v.p. product mgmt. Marquis Who's Who, 1988-89, pres., 1989-92; v.p. Reed Reference Pub., New Providence, N.J., 1992-96; v.p., fulfillment Reed Elsevier-New Providence, 1996-97, LEXIS-NEXIS, Dayton, Ohio, 1997-98, Lexis Law Pub., Charlottesville, Va., 1997-98, Congrl. Info. Svc., Bethesda, Md., 1997-98; sr. v.p. Ednl. Comms., Inc., Lake Forest, Ill., 1998—2001; gen. mgr. Marquis Who's Who, New Providence, NJ, 2002—. Republican. Avocation: reading. Office: 121 Chanlon Rd New Providence NJ 07974

BARNES, STEVEN W. diagnostic equipment company executive; Various exec. level positions Executone Bus. Solutions; dir. Miltex Instruments; pres., COO, dir. Holson Burnes Group Inc.; exec. v.p. Bain Capital; COO Dade Behring, Deerfield, Ill., CEO, 1999—.

BARNES, THOMAS JOHN, lawyer; b. Grand Rapids, Mich., Apr. 1, 1943; s. James and Adeline (Molenda) B.; m. Lynn Marie Owens, Aug. 19, 1967; children: Nicolle, Cynthia. BA in Acctg., Mich. State U., 1965, BA in Polit. Sci., 1966; JD, Wayne State U., 1972. Bar: Mich. 1972, U.S. Dsit. Ct. (ea. and we. dists.) Mich. 1972, U.S. Ct. Appeals (6th cir.) 1974, U.S. Dist. Ct. (no. dist.) Ind. 1994, U.S. Ct. Appeals (7th cir.) 1995. Ptnr. Varnum, Riddering, Schmidt & Howlett, Grand Rapids, 1972—. Arbitrator Mich. Employment Rels. Commn.; spkr. in field. Editor-in-chief Wayne Law Rev.; contbr. articles to profl. jours. Fellow Coll. Labor and Employment Lawyers; mem. ABA (nat. labor rels. bd. practice and procedures com.), Am. Employment Law Coun., Mich. Bar Assn. (labor coun., sec., treas. 1987-88, chmn. 1989-90). Roman Catholic. Avocations: reading, horse racing, sports. Office: 333 Bridge St NW Grand Rapids MI 49504-5356

BARNES, VIRGIL EVERETT, II, physics educator; b. Galveston, Tex., Nov. 2, 1935; s. Virgil Everett and Mildred Louise (Adlof) B.; m. Barbara Ann Green, 1957 (dec. 1964); 1 son, Virgil Everett III; m. Linda Dwight Taylor, 1970; children— Christopher Richard Dwight, Charles Jeffrey, Daniel Woodbridge. AB magna cum laude with highest honors, Harvard U., 1957; PhD, Cambridge (Eng.) U., 1962. Rsch. assoc. Brookhaven Nat. Lab., Upton, N.Y., 1962-64, asst. physicist, 1964-66, assoc. physicist, 1966-69; mem. faculty Purdue U., 1969—, prof. physics, 1979—; asst. dean Purdue U. (Sch. Sci.), 1974-78. Cons. in field. Author papers on exptl. high energy particle physics. NSF predoctoral fellow Gonville and Caius Coll., Cambridge U., 1959-62; Marshall scholar Cambridge U., 1957-59; recipient Perkin Elmer prize Harvard U., 1956. Mem. AAAS, AAUP, Am. Phys. Soc., N.Y. Acad. Scis., Phi Beta Kappa, Sigma Xi. Home: 801 N Salisbury St West Lafayette IN 47906-2715 Office: Purdue U Dept Physics West Lafayette IN 47907

BARNES, W. MICHAEL, electronics executive; B in Indsl. Engring., M in Indsl. Engring., Tex. A&M U., PhD in Ops. Rsch., 1968. Expert cons. Asst. Postmaster Gen., Washington; corp. ops. rsch. staff Collins Radio Co. now Rockwell Internat., 1968-72; dir. fin. MOS/Components Divsn. Rockwell Internat., Newport Beach, Calif., 1972-73; contr. Rockwell's Collins Comm. Switching Sys. Divsn., 1973-74, Rockwell Electronic Sys. Group, Dallas, 1974-77; v.p., gen. mgr. Rockwell's Collins Comm. Switching Sys. Divsn., 1977-82; v.p. fin. Rockwell's Telecom. Group, 1982-85, v.p. mktg. and bus. devel., 1985-89; corp. v.p. bus. devel. and planning Rockwell Internat. Corp., 1989-91, sr. v.p. fin. and planning, CFO, 1991—. Vis. prof. computer scis. So. Meth. U.; instr. maintainability engring. U.S. Army Logistics Tng. Ctr., Red River Depot. Named Disting. Alumni, Tex. A&M U. Coll. Engring., 1992 Mem. Coun. Fin. Execs. (chmn. conf. bd. 1996). Office: Rockwell Internat Corp 777 E Wisconsin Ave Ste 1400 Milwaukee WI 53202

BARNETT, GENE HENRY, neurosurgeon; b. Phila., Feb. 2, 1955; s. Edgar Tryon and Anne Shirley (Wenner) B.; m. Kathleen Marie Seng, May 9, 1984 (div. Sept. 1989); 1 child, Alexander; m. Cathy Ann Sila, Dec. 9, 1990; children: Austin, Addison. BA summa cum laude, Case Western Res. U., 1976, MD, 1980. Intern Cleve. Clinic Found., 1980-81, neurosurgery resident, 1981-86, staff neurosurgery, 1987—, co-dir. residency program, 1992-95, vice chmn. dept. neurosurgery, 1993—2002, program dir. dept. neurosurgery, 1995—, dir. Brain Tumor Ctr., 1995—2001, chmn. Brain Tumor Inst., 2001—, dir. Gamma Knife Ctr., 1997—. Hon. registrar U. Edinburgh, Scotland, 1985; fellow Harvard Med. Sch., Mass. Gen. Hosp., 1986-87; cons. in field. Editor: Image Guided Neurosurgery: Clinical Applications of Surgical Navigation Systems, 1998; contbr. over 120 articles to profl. jours., 27 chpts. to books. Grantee Epilesy Found. Am., 1979, NINDS, 1995; clin. and rsch. fellow Harvard Med. Sch., Mass. Gen. Hosp., Boston, 1986-87. Office: Cleve Clinic Found 9500 Euclid Ave Cleveland OH 44195-0001

BARNETT, JAMES A. state legislator; m. Yvonne Barnett. Mem. Kans. State Senate, 2001—, vice chair pub. health and welfare com., mem. fed. and state affairs com., mem. fin. instns. and ins. com., mem. health care reform legis. oversight com. Home: 1400 Lincoln Emporia KS 66801 Office: Ste 202 1301 W 12th Emporia KS 55801 Fax: 316-342-6520. E-mail: jbarnett@cadvantage.com., barnett@senate.state.ks.us.

BARNETT, MARILYN, advertising agency executive; b. Detroit; d. Henry and Kate (Boesky) Schiff; children: Rhona, Ken. BA, Wayne State U. Founder, part-owner, pres. Mars Advt. Co., Southfield, Mich. Bd. dirs. Mich. Strategic Fund; apptd. to Mich. bi-lateral trade team with Germany. Named Outstanding Retail Woman of Yr., Outstanding Retail Mktg. Exec., Bd. Dirs. Oakland U., Entrepreneur of Yr., Oakland Exec. of Yr.; named to Mich.'s Top 25 Women Bus. Owner's List. Mem. AFTRA (dir.), SAG, Exec. Women Am., Am. Women in Radio & TV (Top Agy. Mgmt. award, Outstanding Woman of Yr.), Internat. Women Forum, Com. of 200, Women's Econ. Club (Ad Woman of Yr.), Adcraft. Office: MARS Advt 23999 Northwestern Hwy Southfield MI 48075-2528 also: MARS Advt Co 6671 W Sunset Blvd Ste 1591 Los Angeles CA 90028-7170

BARNETT, MARK WILLIAM, state attorney general; b. Sioux Falls, S.D., Sept. 6, 1954; s. Thomas C. and Dorothy Ann (Lievrance) Barnett; m. Deborah Ann Barnett, July 14, 1979. BS in Govt., U. S.D., 1976, JD, 1978. Bar: S.D. Pvt. practice, Sioux Falls, 1978—80; asst. atty. gen. State of S.D., Pierre, 1980—83, spl. prosecutor, 1984—90, atty. gen., 1990—; ptnr. Schmidt, Schroyer, Colwill and Barnett, 1984—90. Mem. S.D. Bar Commn., 1986—92, S.D. Law Enforcement Tng. Commn., 1987—, S.D. Corrections Commn., 1987. Bd. dirs. D.A.R.E., 1987—. Mem.: State's Atty. Assn. (bd. dirs. 1987—90), Am. Judicature Soc. (nat. bd. dirs. 1984—88), S.D. Bar Assn. (pres. young lawyers' sect. 1985). Republican. Avocations: golf, weight lifting, snowmobiling. Office: Office Atty Gen 500 E Capitol Ave Pierre SD 57501-5070*

BARNETT, REX, state legislator; Mem. from dist. 4 Mo. State Ho. of Reps., 1995—. Home: 708 W Lincoln St Maryville MO 64468-2748 Office: State Capitol House Post Office House Post Office Rm 116-a2 Jefferson City MO 65101-1556

BARNETT, WILLIAM ARNOLD, economics educator; b. Boston, Oct. 30, 1941; s. Marcus Jack and Elizabeth Leah (Forman) B.; m. Melinda Gentry, Sept. 1, 1991. BS, MIT, 1963; MBA, U. Calif., Berkeley, 1965; MS, Carnegie Mellon U., 1972, PhD, 1974. System devel. engr., Apollo Project, Rocketdyne div. Rockwell Internat. Corp., Canoga Park, Calif., 1963-67; research econometrician Bd. Govs., Fed. Reserve System, Washington, 1973-81; Stuart Centennial prof. econs. U. Tex., Austin, 1981-90; prof. econs. Washington U., St. Louis, 1990—. Vis. prof. econs. U. Aix-Marseille, Aix-en-Provence, France, 1979, Duke U., Durham, N.C., 1987-88; organizer ann. symposia in econ. theory and econometrics; assoc. dir. Ctr. for Econ. Rsch., U. Tex., Austin, 1981-90. Author: Consumer Demand and Labor Supply, 1981; editor three spl. edits. Jour. of Econometrics, 1979, 80, 85, Cambrige U. Press Monograph series, 1985—, Cambridge U. Press Jour. Macroeconomic Dynamics, 1997—; assoc. editor Jour. of Bus. and Econ. Stats., 1982-97; contbr. approx. 75 articles to profl. jours. Contract selection panel mem. NIH, Washington, 1983; cons. World Bank, Washington, 1985. R.K. Mellon Found. fellow, 1971-73; rsch. grantee NSF, Washington, 1977-89, Hogg Found., Houston, 1983. Fellow ICC Inst. (sr., editor 1983—), Am. Statis. Assn. (assoc. editor 1982—, fellow 1989—, program chair 1992—), Jour. Econometrics (charter fellow 1989—); mem. Inst. Math. Stats., Econometric Soc. (contbr. to jour.), Am. Econ. Assn., MIT Club (St. Louis). Home: 11030 Wellsley Ct Saint Louis MO 63146-5529 Office: Washington U Dept Econs Saint Louis MO 63130

BARNETTE, JOSEPH D., JR. bank holding company executive; b. 1939; BA, Wabash Coll., 1961; MBA, Ind. U., 1968; postgrad., Rutgers U., 1972. With Am. Fletcher Nat. Bank & Trust, Indpls., 1962-69, 82—; pres., chief operating officer Am. Fletcher Nat. Bank & Trust, now Banc One, Indpls., NA subs. Banc One Corp., 1982—; pres., chief operating officer, chmn., CEO Banc One Ind. Corp. subs. Banc One Corp., 1987—; sr. v.p., then pres., chief exec. officer First Nat. Bank, Evanston, Ill., 1969-76; pres., chief exec. officer Lakeview Trust and Savs. Bank, Chgo., 1976-81. Office: Banc One Ind Corp 101 Monument Cir Indianapolis IN 46204-2903 also: Lake View Trust & Savs Bank 3201 N Ashland Ave Chicago IL 60657-2138 also: 100 E Broad St Columbus OH 43215-3607

BARNEY, CAROL ROSS, architect; b. Chgo., Apr. 12, 1949; d. Chester Albert and Dorothy Valeria (Dusiewicz) Ross; m. Alan Fredrick Barney, Mar. 22, 1970; children: Ross Fredrick, Adam Shafer, John Ross. BArch, U. Ill., 1971. Registered architect, Ill. Assoc. architect Holabird & Root, Chgo., 1972-79; prin. architect Orput Assoc., Inc., Wilmette, Ill., 1979-81; prin. architect, pres. Ross Barney & Jankowski, Inc., Chgo., 1981—, also bd. dirs. Studio prof. Ill. Inst. Tech., Chgo., 1993-94; asst. prof. U. Ill., Chgo., 1976-78. Prin. works include Cesar Chavez Elem. Sch., Chgo., Glendale Heights (Ill.) Post Office (Inst. Honor award for interior architecture 1999, for architecture 2002), Little Village Acad. Pub. Sch. (Inst. Honor award AIA 1999), Fed. Campus, Oklahoma City, 1999. Plan commn. Village of Wilmette, 1986-88, mem. Econ. Devel. Commn., 1988-90, chmn. Appearance Rev. Commn., 1990-2000; trustee Children's Home and Aid Soc. Ill., Chgo., 1986—; mem. adv. bd. Small Bus. Ctr. for Women, Chgo., 1985—. Recipient Fed. Design Achievement award, 1992, Firm award AIA Chgo., 1995; Francis J. Plym travelling fellow, 1983. Fellow AIA (bd. dirs. Chgo. chpt. 1978-80, v.p. 1981-82, Disting. Svc. award Chgo. chpt. 1978, Ill. Coun. 1978, Honor award 1991, 94, 99, 2002); mem. Nat. Coun. Archtl. Registration Bds. (cert.), Chgo. Women in Architecture (founding pres. 1978-79), Chgo. Network, Cliff Dwellers Club (bd. dirs. 1995). E-mail: cross. Home: 601 Linden Ave Wilmette IL 60091-2819 Office: Ross Barney & Jankowski Inc 10 Hubbard St Chicago IL 60610 E-mail: crossbarney@rbjarchitects.com.

BARNEY, CHARLES RICHARD, transportation executive; b. Battle Creek, Mich., June 7, 1935; s. Charles Ross and Helena Ruth (Croose) Barney; m. Grace Leone Nightingale, Aug. 16, 1958; children: Richard Nolan, Patricia Lynn. BA, Mich. State U., 1957; MBA, Wayne State U., 1961. Fin. analyst Ford Motor Co., Dearborn, Mich., 1958-65; gen. mgr. RentCo div. Fruehauf Corp., Detroit, 1965-72; pres. Evans Trailer Leasing, Des Plaines, Ill., 1973-77; v.p., gen. mgr. U.S. Rlwy. Equipment Co., 1972-77; pres. Evans Railcar div. Evans Trans. Co., 1978-84; pres. W.H. Miner div. Miner Enterprises, Geneva, 1985-2000. Mem. exec. com. Rlwy. Progress Inst., 1984—2000, chmn., 1990—. Served to 1st lt. inf. U.S. Army, 1958. Mem.: Rlwy. Supply Assn. (dir. 1977—80), Wildcat Run Country Club. Congregationalist. Home: 20411 Wildcat Run Dr Estero FL 33928-2014

BARNHILL, CHARLES JOSEPH, JR. lawyer; b. Indpls., May 22, 1943; s. Charles J. and Phyllis (Landis) Barnhill; m. Elizabeth Louise Hayek, Aug. 14, 1971; children: Eric Charles, Colin Landis. BS in Econs., U. Pa., 1965; JD, U. Mich., 1968. Bar: Ill. 1968, U.S. Dist. Ct. (no. dist.) Ill. 1968, U.S. Ct. Appeals (7th cir.) 1969, U.S. Supreme Ct. 1972. Assoc. Kirkland & Ellis, Chgo., 1968; Reginald Heber Smith fellow Chgo. Legal Aid, 1968-69; assoc. Katz & Friedman, 1969-72; ptnr. Davis, Miner, Barnhill & Galland, P.C. (now Miner, Barnhill & Galland), Madison, Wis., 1972—. Spl. master Fed. Dist. Ct. (no. dist.) Ill. Asst. editor: Mich. Law Rev., 1968. Chmn. Wis. Ctr. Tobacco Rsch. and Intervention, 1996; bd. dirs. Combined Health Appeal, Legal Assistance Found., Chgo., 1972—74, Old Town Triangle Assn., Chgo., 1972—75. Fellow: ABA (chmn. employment litig. litig. section 1975—78), Am. Coll. Trial Lawers; mem.: Order of Coif, Barristers Soc., Chgo. Coun. Lawyers (bd. dirs. 1974—76). Office: Miner Barnhill & Galland 44 E Mifflin St Ste 803 Madison WI 53703-2800

BARNHOLT, BRANDON K. gas station/convenience store executive; COO, exec. v.p. mktg. Clark USA Inc. (now Clark Retail Group Inc.); CEO, pres. Clark Retail Group, Inc., Glen Ellyn, Ill., 1999—. Office: Clark Retail Group Inc 3003 Butterfield Rd Oak Brook IL 60523

BARNICK, HELEN, retired judicial clerk; b. Max, N.D., Mar. 24, 1925; d. John K. and Stacy (Kankovsky) B. BS in Music cum laude, Minot State Coll., 1954; postgrad., Am. Conservatory of Music, Chgo., 1975-76. With Epton, Bohling & Druth, Chgo., 1968-69; sec. Wildman, Harrold, Allen & Dixon, 1969-75; part-time assignments for temporary agy., 1975-77; sec. Friedman & Koven, 1977-78; with Lawrence, Lawrence, Kamin & Saunders, 1978-81; sec. Hinshaw, Culbertson et al., 1982; sec. to magistrate judge U.S. Dist. Ct. (we. dist.) Wis., Madison, 1985-91; dep. clk., case adminstr. U.S. Bankruptcy Ct. (we. dist.) Wis., 1992-94; ret., 1994. Mem. chancel choir 1st Bapt. Ch., Mpls.; mem. choir, dir. sr. high choir Moody Ch., Chgo.; mem. chancel choir Fourth Presbyn. Ch., Chgo., Covenant Presbyn. Ch., Madison; dir. chancel choir 1st Bapt. Ch., Minot, N.D.; bd. dirs., sec.-treas. Peppertree at Tamarack Owners Assn., Inc., Wisconsin Dells, Wis.; mem. Festival Choir, Madison. Mem. Christian Bus. and Profl. Women (chmn.), Bus. and Profl. Women Assn., Participatory Learning and Tchg. Orgn., Madison Civics Club, Sigma Sigma Sigma. Home: 7364 Old Sauk Rd Madison WI 53717-1213

BARNWELL, FRANKLIN HERSHEL, zoology educator; b. Chattanooga, Oct. 4, 1937; s. Columbus Hershel and Esther Bernice (Ireland) B.; m. Adrienne Kay Knox, June 13, 1959; 1 child, Elizabeth Brooks. BA, Northwestern U., 1959, PhD, 1965. Instr. biol. sci. Northwestern U., Evanston, Ill., 1964, research assoc., 1965-67; asst. prof. U. Chgo., 1967-70; from asst. prof. to prof. zoology, ecology and behavioral biology U. Minn., Mpls., 1970—, head dept. ecology, evolution and behavior, 1986-93. Mem. adv. panel NASA, 1963-67, NSF, Washington, 1980; faculty Orgn. for Tropical Studies, San Jose, Costa Rica, 1966-85, bd. dirs.; Nat. Confs. on Underground Rsch., bd. dirs., treas., 1990-96; investigator rsch. R/V Alpha Helix, various locations, 1979, vis. scientist. Contbr. articles on zoology to profl. jours. NSF fellow, 1965; named Minn. Coll. Sci. Tchr. of Yr., Minn. Acad. Sci. and Minn. Sci. Tchrs. Assn., 1997. Fellow Linnean Soc. London, AAAS; mem. Soc. Intergrative and Comparative Biology, Internat. Soc. for Chronobiology, Assocs. Orgn. for Tropical Studies, Crustacean Soc. (founding and sustaining mem., bd. dirs., sec. 1991-98), Phi Beta Kappa, Sigma Xi. Office: U Minn Dept Ecology Evol & Behav 1987 Upper Buford Cir Saint Paul MN 55108-1051 E-mail: fhb@umn.edu.

BARON, JEFFREY, retired pharmacologist; b. Bklyn., July 10, 1942; s. Harry Leo and Terry (Goldstein) Baron; m. Judith Carol Rothberg, June 27, 1965; children: Stephanie Ann, Leslie Beth, Melissa Leigh. BS in Pharmacy, U. Conn., 1965; PhD in Pharmacology, U. Mich., 1969. Rsch. fellow in biochemistry U. Tex. Southwestern Med. Sch., Dallas, 1969-71, rsch. asst. prof. biochemistry and pharmacology, 1971-72; asst. prof. pharmacology U. Iowa, Iowa City, 1972-75, assoc. prof., 1975-80, prof., 1980—2002; ret., 2002. Mem. chem. pathology study sect. NIH, Bethesda, Md., 1983—87, mem. environ. health scis. rev. com., Md., Nat. Inst. Environ. Health Scis., Research Triangle Park, NC, 1990—94. Contbr. chapters to books, articles to profl. jours. Recipient Rsch. Career Devel. award, NIH, 1975—80. Mem.: Internat. Soc. Study Xenobiotics, Soc. Toxicology, Am. Assn. Cancer Rsch., Am. Soc. Biochem. and Molecular Biology, Am. Soc. Pharmacology and Exptl. Therapeutics. Achievements include discovery of of the role of heme synthesis in regulating the induction of cytochrome P450 in liver;participation in the discovery of oxygenated cytochrome P450;research in immunohistochemical localization of cytochromes P450 and other xenobiotic-metabolizing enzymes in liver and extrahepatic tissues.

BARONE, JAMES L. state legislator; b. Chgo., May 20, 1941; m. Donita Barone. BSBA, Pitts. State U., 1962. With Bell Sys.-S.W. Bell Telephone, 1962-91; mem. Kans. Senate from 13th dist., Topeka, 1996—; ranking minority mem. commerce com.; mem. fin. instns. and ins. com.; ranking minority mem. utilities com.; mem. joint com. on econ. devel.; mem. joint com. on pensions, investments and benefits com. Named to Order Ky. Cols. Mem. Pittsburg State Alumni Assn. (bd. dirs.), Pittsburg C. of C., Eagles, Rotary, KC. Democrat. Office: 300 SW 10th Ave Rm 504-n Topeka KS 66612-1504

BARR, DAVID JOHN, civil, geological engineering educator; b. Evansville, Ind., Mar. 5, 1939; s. Ralph Emerson and Selma Louise (Sander) B.; m. Kay Arlene Porter, Jan. 23, 1965; 1 child, John Matthew. C.E., U. Cin., 1962; MSCE, Purdue U., 1964, PhD, 1968. Registered prof. engr., Ohio. Asst. prof. civil engring. U. Cin., 1968-72; prof. geol. engring. U. Mo., Rolla, 1972—, chmn. dept. geol. and petroleum engring., 1987-92, dir. Mo. Mining and Mineral Resources Rsch. Inst., 1980-87, asst. to vice chancellor for acad. computing, 1986-87. Cons. in field. Author: (with others) Remote Sensing for Resource Managemnt, 1983; contbr. Ency. Applied

Geology, 1984. Bd. dirs., fireman Rolla Rural Fire Protection Assn., 1975-88. Recipient New Tech. award NASA, 1973-74; NASA rsch. fellow Manned Spacecraft Ctr., Houston, 1969, 70. Mem. NSPE, ASCE (chmn. aerospace div. 1977), Mo. Soc. Profl. Engrs. (Rolla chpt. pres. 1992-93), Am. Soc. Photogrammetry (pres. Rolla region 1975), Soc. Mining Engrs., Assn. Engring. Geologists, Am. Soc. for Engring. Edn., Nat. Assn. Mineral Inst. Dirs. (nat. chmn. 1987-88). Avocations: hunting, fishing. Office: U Mo-Rolla Dept Geol and Petroleum Engring 129 McNutt Rolla MO 65401-0249

BARR, EMILY, television station executive; BA in Film Studies, Carleton Coll., 1980; MBA in Mktg., George Washington U., 1986. News editor KSTP-TV, St. Paul, 1980-81, news promotion specialist, 1981-82; writer, prodr. WJLA-TV, Washington, 1983-85; advtg. & promotion mgr. KHOU-TV, Houston, 1985-87, dir. creative svcs., 1987-88; dir. broadcast ops. WMAR-TV, Balt., 1988-93, acting gen. mgr., 1993, asst. gen. mgr., 1993-94; pres., gen. mgr. Sta. WTVD, Raleigh, N.C., 1994-97, Sta. WLS-TV, Chgo., 1997—. Grad. leadership program Greater Balt. Com., 1990; active NAPTE, 1988—, BPME, 1983-93, CBS Promotion Caucus, 1987-88. Vol. Mus. Broadcast Comms.; bd. dirs. United Cerebral Palsy-Chgo., Children's Meml. Hosp. Found.; commr. Chgo. State St. Commn. Recipient Dante award Joint Civic com. for Italian Americans, 1998. Mem. Ill. Broadcast Assn., Chgo./Midwest TV Acad., Chgo. C. of C. (bd. dirs.), Chgo. Cen. Area Com. (bd. dirs.). Office: 190 N State St Chicago IL 60601-3302

BARR, JAMES, III, telecommunications company executive; b. Oak Park, Ill., Mar. 2, 1940; s. James Jr. and Florence Marie (Erichsen) B.; m. Joan Benning, Aug. 12, 1961; children: James IV, Brett Christopher, Heather Kathryn, Stephanie Alexandra. BS in Engring., Iowa State U., 1962; MBA, U. Chgo., 1967. Engr. Ill. Bell Tel. Co., Chgo., 1962-66, staff mgr. for regulatory affairs, 1966-69; dist. mgr. for planning AT&T, N.Y.C., 1969-72, dir. regulatory affairs, 1975-80, dir. product mgmt. Basking Ridge, N.J., 1980-85, sales v.p. N.Y.C., 1985-90; gen. mktg. mgr. Bell Can., Ottawa, Ont., 1972-75; pres., CEO, TDS TELECOM, Madison, Wis., 1990—. Exec. vp., bd. dirs. NY Bd. Trade, 1985—90; bd. dirs. Tel. and Data Sys., Chgo., Ctr. for Telecom. Mgmt., L.A., TDS Telecom, Madison, Wis. Mem. dean's adv. coun. Bus. Sch. U. Wis., 1997— Republican. Roman Catholic. Office: TDS TELECOM 301 S Westfield Rd Madison WI 53717-1799

BARR, JOHN ROBERT, retired lawyer; b. Gary, Ind., Apr. 10, 1936; s. John Andrew and Louise (Stentz) B.; m. Patricia A. Ferris, July 30, 1988; children: Mary Louise, John Mills, Jennifer Susan. BA, Grinnell Coll., 1957; LL.B. cum laude, Harvard U., 1960. Bar: Ill. 1960. Assoc. Sidley Austin Brown & Wood, Chgo., 1960—69, ptnr., 1970—99, sr. counsel, 2000—02; ret., 2002. Mem. Ill. Ho. of Reps., 1981-83, Commn. on Presdl. Scholars, Washington, 1975-77; mem. Ill. Electric Utility Property Assessment Task Force, 1998-99. Chmn. Ill. Bd. Regents, 1971-77; mem. Ill. Bd. Higher Edn., 1971-77, 87—; chmn. Ill. Student Assistance Commn., 1985—; chmn. Rep. Ctrl. Com. of Cook County, Chgo., 1978-85; mem. Rep. state ctrl. com. 9th Congl. Dist. Ill., 1986-93; trustee Grinnell Coll., 1996—, Evanston Hist. Soc., 2001—; bd. dirs. Steppenwolf Theatre Co., Chgo., 1992—. Mem. ABA (chmn. task force on utility deregulation of state and local tax coms.), Ill. State Bar Assn. (chmn. state tax sect. coun. 1986-87), Chgo. Bar Assn. (chmn. com. on state and mcpl. taxation 1974-75), Taxpayers' Fedn. Ill. (treas. 1990-92, vice chmn. 1992-95, chmn. 1995-97), The Civic Fedn. (bd. dirs. 1993-97), Selden Soc., Nat. Assn. State Bar Tax Sects. (sec.-treas. 1989-90, vice chmn. 1990-91, chmn. 1991-92), Emil Verban Soc., Lawyer's Club Chgo., Chgo. Club, Phi Beta Kappa. Episcopalian. Home: 1144 Asbury Ave Evanston IL 60202-1137 Office: Sidley Austin Brown & Wood Bank One Plz 10 S Dearborn Chicago IL 60603 E-mail: jrbarr@sidley.com.

BARR, SANFORD LEE, dentist; b. Chgo., Jan. 18, 1952; s. Mike and Bernice (Kaplan) B.; m. Randy Joyce Briskman, Dec. 24, 1973; children: Shelby Paige, Blake Jared, Taylor Ashley. BS, U. Ill., 1972; DDS, Northwestern U., 1976. Resident gen. practice VA Hosp., Chgo., 1976-77; gen. practice dentistry, 1977—. Attending dentist Rush Med. Coll., Chgo., 1977—; asst. prof. Presbyn.-St. Luke's Hosp., Chgo., 1977—, Northwestern U. Sch. Dentistry, Chgo., 1977-83; cons. VA Hosp., Chgo., 1978—. Mem. adv. bd. Homehealth of Ill. Chgo., 1984—. Fellow Acad. Gen. Dentistry, Acad. Facial Aesthetics; mem. ADA, Acad. Hosp. Dentistry, Chgo. Dental Soc., Alpha Omega (treas. 1984, pres. elect 1988), Tau Delta Phi. Jewish. Lodge: B'nai B'rith (v.p. Chgo. chpt. 1984—). Avocations: computers, photography, golf, baseball. Home: 632 Dauphine Ct Northbrook IL 60062-2256 Office: 25 E Washington St Chicago IL 60602-1708

BARRETT, FRANK JOSEPH, lawyer, former insurance company executive; b. Greeley, Nebr., Mar. 2, 1932; s. Patrick J. and Irene L. (Printy) B.; m. Ruth Ann Nealon, Aug. 20, 1956; children: Patrick, Mary, Anne, Karen, Thomas. BS in Law, U. Nebr., 1957; LLB, Nebr. Coll. Law, 1959. Bar: Nebr. 1959, U.S. Supreme Ct. 1976. Asst. gen. counsel, asst. sec. Nebr. Nat. Life Co., 1957-61; dir. ins. State of Nebr., Lincoln, 1961-67; exec. v.p., sec., gen. counsel Ctrl. Nat. Ins. Group of Omaha, 1967-75; exec. v.p., chief counsel Mut. of Omaha (and Affiliates), 1975-81; pres., CEO Ctrl. Nat. Ins. Co. of Omaha, 1981-89, Ins. Rsch. Svc. Co., Omaha, 1989—; of counsel Lamson, Dugan & Murray, 1990—. Bd. dir. Am. Family Life Assurance Co. State organizational chmn. 3 Nebr. gubernatorial campaigns. Served in U.S. Army, 1953-55, Korea. Recipient service citation Am. Nat. Red Cross, 1964, 65 Mem. Nebr. Bar Assn., Omaha Bar Assn., Am. Arbitration Assn., Fedn. Ins. Counsels, Consumer Credit Ins. Assn. (past pres. and dir.), Nat. Assn. Ind. Insurers (gov., past chmn.), Nat. Assn. Ins. Commrs. (past pres.), Am. Legion, Irish-Am. Cultural Soc., KC., ARIAS-U.S. (cert.). Democrat. Roman Catholic. Home: 516 S 119th St Omaha NE 68154-3115 Fax: 402-333-2341. E-mail: fbarrett@ldmlaw.com.

BARRETT, JANET TIDD, academic administrator; b. Crystal City, Mo., Nov. 29, 1939; d. Lewis Samuel and Mamie Lou (Hulvey) Tidd; m. David Clark Barrett, June 3, 1961; children: Barbara, Pam. Diploma in nursing, St. Lukes Hosp. Sch. Nursing, 1960; BSN with honors, Washington U., St. Louis, 1964, MSN, 1979; PhD, St. Louis U., 1987. Assoc. prof. Maryville Coll., St. Louis, 1979-89; acad. dean Barnes Coll., 1989-91; dir. BSN program Deaconess Coll. Nursing, 1991-2000, acad. dean, 2000—. Contbn. author to Beare and Meyers: Principles of Medical-Surgical Nursing. St. Lukes Hosp. scholar; recipient Sister Agnita Claire Day Rsch. award St. Louis U. Mem.: Mo. League Nursing, Nat. League Nursing, St. Luke's Alumni Assn., Phi Delta Kappa, Pi Lambda Theta, Sigma Theta Tau. E-mail: barretjan@hotmail.com.

BARRETT, ROGER WATSON, lawyer; b. Chgo., June 26, 1915; s. Oliver R. and Pauline S. B.; m. Nancy N. Braun, June 20, 1940; children—Victoria Barrett Bell, Holly, Oliver. A.B., Princeton U., 1937; J.D., Northwestern U., 1940. Bar: Ill. 1940. Mem. firm Poppenhusen, Johnson, Thompson & Raymond, Chgo., 1940-43; 45-50; charge documentary evidence Nuremberg Trial, 1944-45; regional counsel Econ. Stablzn. Agy., Chgo., 1951-52; ptnr. Mayer, Brown & Platt, 1952-91, of counsel, 1991—. Life trustee Mus. Contemporary Art, Chgo. With AUS, 1943-45. Mem. ABA, Ill. Bar Assn., Chgo. Bar Assn., Am. Coll. Trial Lawyers, Indian Hill Club (Winnetka), Old Elm Club, Commonwealth Club (Chgo.), Caxton Club (Chgo.). Home: 84 Indian Hill Rd Winnetka IL 60093-3934 Office: Mayer Brown Rowe & Maw 190 S La Salle St Chicago IL 60603-3410

BARRETT, THOMAS M. congressman; b. Milwaukee, Wis., Dec. 8, 1953; m. Kristine Barrett; children: Thomas John, Anne Elizabeth. BA in Economics, U. Wis., 1976, JD with honors, 1980. Atty. Smith & O'Neill, Milw., 1982-84; mem. Wis. State Assembly, 1984-89, Wis. State Senate from 5th Dist., 1989-92, U.S. Congress from 5th Wis. dist., Washington, 1993—; mem. energy and commerce com. Bd. dirs. Sojourner Truth House, Shalom High Sch., Transcenter Home for Youth. Recipient Circle of Friends award Milw. Advocates for Retarded Citizens, 1989, Health Leadership award State Med. Soc., Govt. Leadership award Rehab. for Wis.; named to Clean Sixteen list for environ. voting record by Wis. Environ. Decade, 1987, 89, 90. Mem. Wis. Bar Assn., Phi Beta Kappa. Office: US Ho Reps 1214 Longworth Office Bldg Washington DC 20515-4905*

BARRETT, WILLIAM E. former congressman; b. Lexington, Nebr., Feb. 9, 1929; s. Harold O. and Helen Stuckey B.; m. Elsie L. Carlson, 1952; children: William C., Elizabeth A., David H., Jane M. AB, Hastings (Nebr.) Coll., 1951; grad., Nebr. Realtors Inst. Cert. real estate broker, Nebr. Admissions counselor Hastings Coll., 1952-54, asst. dir. admissions, 1954-56; ptnr. Barrett Agy., Lexington, 1956-59; pres. Barrett-Housel & Assocs., Inc., 1970-90; former pres. Dawson County Young Rep.; del. Rep. Co. Conv., from 1958; mem. Nebr. Rep. State Exec. Com., 1964-66; chmn., formerly mem. Rep. Nat. Com., state coord. Mobilization of Rep. Enterprise Programs, 1965-66; del. Rep. Nat. Conv., 1968; mem. Nebr. Legislature, 1979-90, speaker, 1987-90; mem. 102nd-106th Congresses from 3rd Nebr. Dist., 1991-2001. Work in campaigns for various rep. candidate, 1960; officer Barrett-Housel & Assocs., Inc., 1969—; dir. Farmers State Bank; chmn. Agr. subcom. on Gen. Farm Commodities, mem. forestry, resource conservation & rsch. coms.; mem. oversight & investigations, worker protections, agr., edn. and workplace coms.; mem. Econ. & Ednl. Opportunity Com. Trustee, co-founder Nebr. Real Estate Polit. Edn. Com.; elder First Presbyn. Ch., Lexington; moderator Presbytery of Platte, 1972-73, chmn. gen. coun., 1973, mem. staff nominating com. Synod of Lakes and Prairies, from 1973. With USN, 1951-52. Named Legislator of Yr. Nat. Rep. Legislators Assn., 1990. Mem. Nebr. Assn. Ins. Agts., Nat. Assn. Ins. Agts., Dawson Co. Bd. Realtors, Nebr. Assn. Realtors, Nat. Assn. Realtors, Nebr. Jaycees (named one of three outstanding young men of Nebr. 1962), Rotary (Lexington).*

BARRON, HOWARD ROBERT, lawyer; b. Chgo., Feb. 17, 1930; s. Irwin P. and Ada (Astrahan) B.; m. Marjorie Shapira, Aug. 12, 1953; children: Ellen Barron Feldman, Laurie A. PhB, U. Chgo., 1948; BA, Stanford U., 1950; LLB, Yale U., 1953. Bar: Ill. 1953. Assoc. Jenner & Block, Chgo., 1957-63, ptnr., 1964-97; assoc. Schiff Hardin & Waite, 1953, of counsel, 1997—. Contbr. articles to profl. jours. and books. Mem., then pres. Lake County Sch. Dist. 107 Bd. Edn., Highland Park, 1964-71; pres. Lake County Sch. Bd. Assn., 1970-71; mem. Lake County High Sch. Dist. 113 Bd. Edn., Highland Park, 1973-77; mem. Highland Park Zoning Bd. Appeals, 1984-89. Lt. (j.g.) USNR, 1953-57. Mem. ABA (co-chmn. subcom. labor and employment law, com. corp. counsel litigation sect. 1983-2002), Ill. State Bar Assn. (chmn. antitrust sect. 1968-69), Fed. Bar Assn., Chgo. Bar Assn., Yale Law Sch. Assn. (v.p. 1978-81), Yale Law Sch. Assn. Ill. (pres. 1962), Internat. Bar Assn., Standard Club, Metro. Club, Yale Club (N.Y.C.). Democrat. Home: 1366 Sheridan Rd Highland Park IL 60035-3407 Office: Schiff Hardin & Waite 6600 Sears Tower Chicago IL 60606 E-mail: hbarron@schiffhardin.com.

BARRON, MILLARD E. retail executive; With Hill Dept. Stores Inc., 1974-94, sr. v.p. store ops., 1990-94, sr. v.p., COO, 1994-96; pres., CEO Zellers Stores Hudson's Bay Co., Toronto, Can., 1996-98; pres., CEO Payless Cashways, Inc., Lee's Summit, Mo., 1998—. Office: Payless Cashway Inc Ste 700 127 W 10th St Kansas City MO 64105-1716

BARRY, ANNE M. public health officer; BA in Occupl. Therapy, Coll. St. Catherine; JD, William Mitchell Coll. Law; MPH, U. Minn. Dep. commr. health Minn. Dept. Health, Mpls., commr. health, 1995—. Office: Minn Dept Health 121 7th Pl E Ste 450 Saint Paul MN 55101-2117

BARRY, JAMES PATRICK, lawyer; b. Muscatine, Iowa, July 17, 1960; s. Richard Paul and Janet Lynn (Hahn) B.; m. Cheryl Jo Mewhirter, Sept. 22, 1990. BS, Drury Coll., 1983; JD, Wash. U., 1986. Bar: U.S. Dist. Ct. (no. and so. dists.) Iowa, U.S. Dist. Ct. (we. dist.) Mo. Assoc. Otto and Lorence Law Firm, Atlantic, 1986-90; asst. county atty. Cass County, Iowa, 1987-90, county atty., 1991—; ptnr. Otto, Lorence & Barry, 1990—. Bd. dirs. ARC, Cass County chpt., Atlantic, 1987-90, YMCA, Atlantic, 1989-90; pres. and sec. Am., Heart Assn., Atlantic, 1988-89, bd. dirs., 1988-90; adv. fund dir. chmn. United Way, Atlantic, 1988. Mem. ABA, Mo. Bar Assn., Iowa State Bar Assn., Southwest Iowa Bar Assn., Cass County Bar Assn. (treas. 1988-89, sec. 1989-90, v.p. 1990-91), Elks, Atlantic Golf and County Club (bd. dirs. 1990-91). Republican. Methodist. Avocations: fishing, hunting, golfing, jogging, water skiing. Office: Otto Lorence & Barry 522 Chestnut St Atlantic IA 50022-1248

BARRY, JONATHAN B. chemicals executive, communications executive; Degree, U. Wis. Exec. v.p. WYG Corp.; pres. Gammex-RMI Corp.; pres., owner W.T. Rogers Co.; pres., chmn. Good Bugs, Inc.; pres., owner J.B. Barry Co., Tyrol Basin Ski Resort, Mt. Horeb, Wis. Mem. bd. regents U. Wis., Wis.; mem. Dane County Bd. Suprs.; exec. Dane County; pres. bd. Wis. Tech. Coll. Sys.; mem. Wis. State Assembly, Madison. Home: 9286 Ness Rd RR 1 Mount Horeb WI 53572

BARRY, NORMAN J., JR. lawyer; b. Chgo., Apr. 1, 1950; BA, U. Notre Dame, 1972, JD, 1975. Bar: Ill. 1975. Ptnr. Donohue, Brown, Mathewson, & Smyth, Chgo. Office: Donohue Brown Mathewson & Smyth 140 S Dearborn St Ste 700 Chicago IL 60603-5201

BARRY, RICHARD A. public relations executive; b. Chgo., Nov. 11, 1934; BS in Polit. Sci., Loyola U., 1956; cert. in publ. and graphics, U. Chgo., 1958. Asst. editor No. Ind. Pub. Svc. Co., Hammond, 1956-58; dir. pub. rels. Loyola U., Chgo., 1958-66; dir. devel. and pub. rels. St. Xavier Coll., 1966-68; sr. v.p. Daniel J. Edelman, Inc., 1968-70; exec. v.p. PCI, 1970-72; pres. Pub. Comms., Inc., 1972—. Office: Public Communications Inc 35 E Wacker Dr Ste 1254 Chicago IL 60601-2109

BARTA, JAMES JOSEPH, judge; b. St. Louis, Nov. 5, 1940; BA, St. Mary's U., 1963; JD, St. Louis U., 1966. Bar: Mo. 1966, U.S. Supreme Ct. 1969. Spl. agt. FBI, Washington, Cleve., and N.Y.C, 1966-70; chief trial atty. St. Louis Cir. Atty., 1970-76; assoc. Guilfoil, Symington & Petzall, St. Louis, 1976-77; asst. U.S. atty. U.S. Dist. Ct. (ea. dist.) Mo., 1977-78, judge bankruptcy ct., 1978—, chief judge bankruptcy ct., 1986-89, 95-99. Lectr. Greater St. Louis Police Acad., 1970-76; mem. U.S. Supreme Ct. Adv. Com. on Bankruptcy Rules, 1987-94, chmn. tech. subcom., 1990-94, style subcom., 1992-94; mem. tech. adv. com. St. Louis Coun. on Criminal Justice, 1972-74; dir. Organized Crime Task Force, St. Louis, 1972-74; project dir. St. Louis Crime Commn., 1975-77. Fellow Am. Coll. Bankruptcy (cir. chmn. 1990-94, bd. dirs. 1994-97, sec. bd. dirs. 1995-97); mem. ABA, Am. Bankruptcy Inst. (bd. dirs. 1989-94), Am. Judicature Soc., Mo. Bar Assn., St. Louis Bar Assn., St. Louis Bar Assn. CLE Inst. (at-large 1989-93), Former Spl. Agts. FBI. Office: US Bankruptcy Ct US Courthouse 111 S 10th St 7th Fl S Saint Louis MO 63102

BARTA, JAMES OMER, priest, psychology educator, church administrator; b. Fairfax, Iowa, Oct. 22, 1931; s. Omer J. and Bertha (Brecht) B. BA, Loras Coll., 1952; Sacrae Theologiae Licentiatus, Gregorian U., Rome, 1956; PhD, Fordham U., 1962. Ordained priest Roman Cath. Ch., 1955. Prof. psychology Loras Coll., Dubuque, Iowa, 1957-94, v.p. acad. affairs, 1977-87, pres., 1987-94; archbishop's vicar Cedar Rapids (Iowa) region, 1994-99; vicar Gen. Archdiocese of Dubuque, 1999—. Office: Archdiocesan Chancery 1229 Mount Loretta Ave Dubuque IA 52003-7826

BARTCH, FLOYD O. police chief; b. St. Joseph, Mo., Mar. 2, 1941; BA, MA, Ctrl. Miss. State U. Patrolman St. Joseph Police Dept., 1965-67, North Kansas City Police Dept., 1967-68; patrolman through ranks to asst. chief of police Kansas City (Mo.) Police Dept., 1968-95, chief of police, 1996—. Recipient Meritorious Svc. award Urban League, 1981, 94, Difference Maker award, 1996. Office: Kansas City Police Dept 1125 Locust St Kansas City MO 64106-2687

BARTEL, FRED FRANK, consulting engineer executive; b. Milw., Nov. 4, 1917; s. Fred F. and Alma O. (Koppelmeyer) B.; m. Ann E. Staudacher, Oct. 23, 1943; children— Betty Jo, Susan, Mary Jo, Robert B.S. in Civil Engring., U. Wis., 1940; M.S., U. Md., 1942. Engring. aide Wis. Hwy. Dept., 1936-40; asst. dir. engring. Nat. Ready Mixed Concrete Assn., Silver Spring, Md., 1942-49; chief engr., sales mgr. Tews Lime and Cement Co., Milw., 1949-75, pres., chief exec. officer, 1975-83; cons. engr. on concrete and concrete aggregates, 1983-89; ret., 1989. Trustee in bankruptcy, 4X Corp., Neenah, Wis., 1985. Contbr. to books and other tech. publs. Served to capt. USAAF, 1942-46 Stanton Walker research fellow U. Md., 1942 Fellow ASCE; mem. ASTM, Am. Concrete Inst., Nat. Ready Mixed Concrete Assn. (chmn. bd. dirs. 1979), Wis. Ready Mixed Concrete Assn. (pres. 1969), Builders Exchange Milw. (pres. 1966-67) Republican. Roman Catholic. Lodge: Rotary. Home and Office: 5421 N Shoreland Ave Milwaukee WI 53217-5132

BARTELL, ERNEST, economist, educator, priest; b. Chgo., Jan. 22, 1932; PhB, U. Notre Dame, 1953; AM, U. Chgo., 1954; MA, Coll. Holy Cross, 1961; PhD, Princeton U., 1966; LLD (hon.), China Acad., Taipei, Taiwan, 1975, St. Joseph's Coll., 1983, King's Coll., 1984, Stonehill Coll., 1992. Ordained priest Roman Cath. Ch., 1961. Instr. econs. Princeton (N.J.) U., 1965-66; asst. prof. econs. U. Notre Dame, Ind., 1966-68, assoc. prof., 1968-71, chmn. dept. econs., 1968-71, dir. Ctr. Study of Man in Contemporary Soc., 1969-71, prof. econs., 1981—, exec. dir. Helen Kellogg Inst. Internat. Studies, 1981-97; pres. Stonehill Coll., North Easton, Mass., 1971-77; dir. Fund for Improvement Post Secondary Edn. U.S. Dept. Health, Edn. and Welfare, Washington, 1977-79; dir. Project 80 Assn. Cath. Colls. and Univs., 1979-80; overseas mission coord. Priests of Holy Cross, Ind. Province, 1980-84, assoc. dir. Holy Cross Mission Ctr., 1984-95; asst. to pastor St. Anthony Ch., Ft. Lauderdale, Fla., 1993—. Active Inst. East-West Securities Studies Working Group on Sources in Instability, 1989-90, Internat. Ctr. Devel. Policy Commn. on U.S.-Soviet Rels., 1988-89, Overseas Devel. Coun., 1988-2000, The Bretton Woods Com., 1992-2002; mem. policy planning commn. Nat. Inst. Ind. Colls. and Univs., 1982-85; bd. dirs. Ctr. for Health Promotion, Internat. Life Scis. Inst.; trustee emeritus Stonehill Coll., 2002-. Author; Costs and Benefits of Catholic Elementary and Secondary schools, 1969; co-editor: Business and Democracy in Latin America, 1995, The Child in Latin America, 2000; contbr. articles to profl. jours. Bd. regents U. Portland, Oreg., 1984—; bd. dirs. Missionary Vehicle Assn. Am., 1981-88, Big Bros. and Big Sisters Am., 1978-80, Brockton Community Housing Corp., 1974-77, The Brighter Day, 1974-77, Brockton Hosp., 1973-77, King's Coll., Wilkes-Barre, Pa., 1969-82; bd. trustees Emmanuel Coll., 1977-78, U. Notre Dame, 1974-2002, bd. fellows, 1974-2002; bd. trustees Regis Coll., 2002--; mem. adv. bd. Brockton Art Ctr., 1974-77; mem. exec. com. Opera New Eng., 1977; parochial vicar St. Anthony's Ch., Ft. Lauderdale, 1993—. Recipient Fenwick Alumni Recognition award, 1974; named Fenwick Hall of Fame, 1990. Fellow Soc. Values in Higher Edn.; mem. Am. Econ. Assn., Am. Assn. Higher Edn., Nat. Cath. Ednl. Assn. (chmn. govtl. rels. com. 1976-77, vice chmn. exec. com. 1976-77, chmn. mgmt. and planning com. 1974-76), Assn. Soc. Econs., Latin Am. Studies Assn., Young Pres. Orgn. (sec. 1974-77), Delta Mu Delta (hon.). Home: 227 Corby Hall Notre Dame IN 46556-5680 Office: U Notre Dame Kellogg Inst 211 Hesburgh Ctr Notre Dame IN 46556-5677 E-mail: ebartell@nd.edu.

BARTELL, LAWRENCE SIMS, chemist, educator; b. Ann Arbor, Mich., Feb. 23, 1923; s. Floyd Earl and Lawrence (Sims) B.; m. Joy Hilda Keer, Aug. 16, 1952; 1 son, Michael Keer. B.S., U. Mich., 1944, M.S., 1947, Ph.D., 1951. Research asst. Manhattan project U. Chgo., 1944-45; mem. faculty Iowa State U., 1953-65, prof. chemistry, 1959-65, U. Mich., 1965—, Philip J. Elving prof. chemistry, 1987-94, prof. emeritus, 1994—. Vis. prof. Moscow (USSR) State U., 1972, U. Paris XI, Orsay, France, 1973, U. Tex., 1978, 86; cons. Gillette Co., Chgo., 1956-62, Mobil Oil Corp., Paulsboro, N.J., 1960-84; mem. commn. on electron diffraction Internat. Union Crystallography, 1966-75 Assoc. editor: Jour. Chem. Physics, 1963-66; mem. editorial bd.: Jour. Computational Chemistry, 1979-90, Chem. Physics Letters, 1981-84. Served with USNR, 1945. Recipient Disting. Faculty Achievement award U. Mich., 1981, Disting. Faculty award Mich. Assn. Governing Bds., 1982, Creativity award NSF, 1982. Mem. Am. Chem. Soc. (petroleum research fund adv. bd. 1970-73), Am. Phys. Soc. (chmn. div. chem. physics 1977-78), Am. Crystallographic Assn., AAAS, Phi Beta Kappa, Sigma Xi, Phi Kappa Phi, Phi Lambda Upsilon, Alpha Chi Sigma. Home: 381 Riverview Dr Ann Arbor MI 48104-1847 E-mail: lbart@umich.edu.

BARTELSMEYER, LINDA, state legislator; Mem. from dist. 132 Mo. Ho. of Reps., Jefferson City, 1985—. Mem. appropriations for econ. devel. natural resources com., elem. and secondary edn. com., transp. com., commerce com., elections com. Vice chair Mo. Film Commn. Republican. Office: Mo Ho of Reps State Capitol Building Jefferson City MO 65101-1556

BARTH, DAVID KECK, distribution industry consultant; b. Springfield, Ill., Dec. 7, 1943; s. David Klenk and Edna Margaret (Keck) B.; m. Dian Oldemeyer, Nov. 21, 1970; children— David, Michael, John. B.A. cum laude, Knox Coll., Galesburg, Ill., 1965; M.B.A., U. Calif., Berkeley, 1971. With data processing div. IBM Corp., Chgo., 1966; with No. Trust Co., 1971-72; mgr. treasury ops., then treas. fin. services group Borg-Warner Corp., 1972-79; treas. W.W. Grainger, Inc., Skokie, 1979-83, v.p., 1984-90; pres. Barth Smith Co., 1991—2001. Mem. faculty Lake Forest (Ill.) Grad. Sch. Mgmt., 1994—; bd. dirs. Indsl. Distbn. Group Inc., Atlanta, Gen. Roofing Svcs., Inc., Ft. Lauderdale, Fla. Served to lt. USNR, 1966-69. Mem. Econ. Club Chgo., Univ. Club of Chgo., Beta Gamma Sigma, Phi Delta Theta. Lutheran.

BARTH, JOHN M. manufacturing executive; Pres., COO Johnson Control, Inc., Plymouth, Mich., 1998—. Office: Johnson Control Inc 49200 Halyard Dr Plymouth MI 48170-2481

BARTH, ROLF FREDERICK, pathologist, educator; b. N.Y.C., Apr. 4, 1937; s. Rolf L. and Josephine Barth; m. Christine Ferguson, Oct. 30, 1965; children: Suzanna, Alison, Rolf, Christofer. AB, Cornell U., 1959; MD, Columbia U., 1964. Diplomate Am. Bd. Pathology. Surg. intern Columbia-Presbyn. Med. Ctr., N.Y.C., 1964-65; postdoctoral fellow Karolinska Inst., Stockholm, 1965-66; rsch. assoc. Nat. Inst. Allergy and Infectious Diseases, NIH, Bethesda, Md., 1966-68; resident pathology br. Nat. Cancer Inst., 1966-68, Nat. Inst. Health, 1968-70; Prof. dept. pathology and oncology U. Kans. Med. Ctr., Kansas City, 1970-77; clin. prof. dept. pathology Med. Coll. Wis. and U. Wis., Madison, 1977-79; prof. dept. pathology Ohio State U., Columbus, 1979—. Contbr. articles to profl. jours. Sr. asst. surgeon USPHS, 1966-70, inactive Res., 1970—. Grantee Dept. Energy, NIH. Mem. Am. Assn. Exptl. Pathology, Am. Assn.

Immunologists, Am. Assn. Cancer Rsch., Internat. Soc. for Neutron Capture Therapy, Sigma Xi, Phi Kappa Phi. Office: Ohio State U Dept Pathology 165 Hamilton Hall 1645 Neil Ave Columbus OH 43210-1218

BARTHELMAS, NED KELTON, investment and commercial real estate developer; b. Circleville, Ohio, Oct. 22, 1927; s. Arthur and Mary Bernice (Riffel) B.; m. Marjorie Jane Livezey, May 23, 1953; children: Brooke Ann, Richard Thomas. B.S. in Bus. Adminstrn., Ohio State U., 1950. Stockbroker Ohio Co., Columbus, 1953-58; pres. First Columbus Securities Corp., 1958—; pres., dir. Ohio Fin. Corp., Columbus, 1960—; pres. Thwirs, Inc., 1986—. Trustee, chmn. Am. Guardian Fin., Republic Fin.; bd. dirs. Nat. Foods, Midwest Capital Corp., Capital Equity Corp., Midwest Nat. Corp., 1st Columbus Realty Corp., Dublin Nat. Corp. (all Columbus). Served with Adj. Gen.'s Dept., AUS, 1944-47. Recipient Merit award, State of Ohio, 2001. Mem. Nat. Assn. Securities Dealers (past vice chmn. dist. bd. govs.), Investment Bankers Assn. (exec. com. 1973), Investment Dealers Ohio (sec., treas. 1956-72, pres. 1973), Nat. Stock Traders Assn., Young Pres.'s Orgn. (pres. 1971), World Bus. Coun., Columbus Pres.'s Assn., Nat. Investment Bankers (pres. 1973), Internat. Real Estate Inst., Columbus Jr. C. of C. (pres. 1956), Ohio C. of C. (trustee 1957-58), World's Pres.'s Assn. (Exec. Hall of Fame award 1993), Columbus Area C. of C. (dir. 1956, named an Outstanding Young Man of Columbus 1962), Newcomen Soc., Coun. for Ethics in Econs., Coun. of Orgn. of Am. States, Wisdom Hall of Fame, Internat. Soc. Financiers, Oxford Club, Execs. Club, Pres.' Club (Ohio State U.), Internat. Platform Assn., Stock and Bond Club (past pres.), named top 25 corp. Dirs. (1984-90), Columbus Club, Scioto Country Club, Crystal Downs Country Club, Ohio State U. Faculty Club, Kiwanis (legion of honor 1992), Am. Legion, Columbus Admirals Club, Alpha Kappa Psi, Phi Delta Theta (Golden Legion award). Office: 1241 Dublin Rd Columbus OH 43215-7000

BARTHOLOMAY, WILLIAM C. insurance brokerage company executive, professional baseball team executive; b. Evanston, Ill., Aug. 11, 1928; s. Henry C. and Virginia (Graves) B.; m. Sara Taylor, 1950, (div. 1964); children: Virginia, William T., Jamie, Elizabeth, Sara; m. Gail Dillingham, May 1968 (div. Apr. 1980). Student, Oberlin Coll., 1946-49, Northwestern U., 1949-50; BA, Lake Forest Coll., 1955. Ptnr. Bartholomay & Clarkson, Chgo., 1951-63; v.p. Alexander & Alexander, 1963-65; pres. Olson & Bartholomay, Chgo. and Atlanta, 1965-69; sr. v.p. Frank B. Hall & Co. Inc., N.Y.C. and Chgo., 1969-72, exec. v.p., 1972-73, pres., 1973-74, vice chmn., 1974-90; chmn. bd., dir. Atlanta Braves, 1966—; pvt. practice cons. Chgo., 1990-91; pres. Near North Nat. Group, 1991-2001, vice chmn., chmn. exec. com., 2001—, Turner Broadcasting Sys., Inc., Atlanta, 2001—. Bd. dirs. WMS Industries Inc., Chgo., Midway Games, Inc., Exec. Coun. Maj. League Baseball, Maj. League Baseball Players Pension Plan. Commr. Chgo. Park Dist., 1980—, Chgo. Pub. Bldg. Commn., 1989—; bd. dirs. Chgo. Maternity Ctr., Lincoln Park Zool. Soc.; trustee Adler Planetarium, Mus. Sci. and Industry, Roosevelt U., Chgo., Ill. Inst. of Tech.; former trustee Lake Forest (Ill.) Coll., Ogelthorpe Coll., Atlanta, Marymount Manhattan Coll., N.Y. With USNR, 1951-54. Mem. Chief Execs. Orgn., World Pres.'s Orgn., Chgo. Pres.'s Orgn., Nat. Assn. CLU, Chgo. Assn. CLU, Chgo. Club, Racquet Club, Saddle and Cycle Club, Econ. Club, Onwentsia Club, Shoreacres Club (Lake Forest), Brook Club, Links Club, Racquet & Tennis Club, Doubles Club (N.Y.C.), Piedmont Driving Club, Atlanta Country Club, Peachtree Golf Club, Commerce Club. Episcopalian. Home: 180 E Pearson St Chicago IL 60611-2130 Office: Near North Nat Group 875 N Michigan Ave Ste 2000 Chicago IL 60611-1954 also: Atlanta Braves PO Box 4064 Atlanta GA 30302-4064 E-mail: wbarthol@nnng.com.

BARTHOLOMEW, LLOYD GIBSON, physician; b. Whitehall, N.Y., Sept. 15, 1921; s. Emerson F. and Minnie (Swinton) B.; m. Elisabeth Thrall, Dec. 27, 1943; children: Suzanne, Lynne, Lloyd Gibson, Deborah, Douglass Thrall. AA, Green Mountain Jr. Coll., 1939; BA, Union Coll., Schenectady, 1941; MD, U. Vt., 1944; MS in Internal Medicine (fellow), U. Minn., 1952; LHD (hon.), Green Mountain Coll., 1984. Diplomate Am. Bd. Internal Medicine, subsplty. bd. gastroenterology. Intern Mary Hitchcock Meml. Hosp., Hanover, N.H., 1944-45, resident, 1945-46, 48-49; asst. internal medicine Dartmouth, 1948-49; 1st asst. div. internal medicine Mayo Clinic, Rochester, Minn., 1949-52, asst. to staff div. internal medicine, 1952-53; practice medicine, specializing in gastroenterology Rochester, 1952—; instr. internal medicine Mayo Found., U. Minn., 1952-58, asst. prof., 1958-63, assoc. prof. internal medicine, 1963-67, prof. medicine, 1967—, Mayo Med. Sch., 1973—. Attending physician St. Mary's, Meth. hosps., Rochester, 1952; mem. adv. bd. to surgeons gen. of armed forces and asst. sec. def., 1978-86; mem. policy bd. Bush Found., 1978-87. Contbr. articles profl. publs. Trustee Green Mountain Coll. Poultney, Vt., 1991—, chmn. bd. trustees, 1997—. Capt. M.C. AUS, 1946-47; col. M.C., 1960-86, ret. Recipient Woodbury prize in medicine, 1944, Carbee prize in obstetrics, 1994, disting. svc. award U. Vt. Coll. Medicine, 1977, Henry J. Plummer disting. clinician award Mayo Found. Internal Medicine, 1992, disting. svc. award Green Mtn. Coll. Alumni Assn., 1995. Mem. AMA (sec. gastroenterology sect. 1962-68, vice chmn. gastroenterlogy sect. 1968-69, chmn. 1969-70, mem. council sci. assembly 1969, chmn. program planning com. 1971-75, chmn. council sci. assembly 1974-76, chmn. council continuing physician edn. 1976-77), Minn. Med. Assn. (del. ho. dels. 1964—, chmn. scholarship and loan com. 1967—, alt. del. to AMA 1974-77, 85—, del. to AMA 1978-83, Pres.'s award 1983, Disting. Service award 1987), So. Minn. Med. Assn. (pres. 1963-64), Zumbro Valley Med. Soc. (sec.-treas. 1969-70, v.p. 1970-71, pres. 1971-72), Soc. Med. Cons. to Armed Forces (mem. governing council 1980-86, pres. 1984, del. to AMA 1984-92), Am. Gastroent. Assn. (com. on procedures 1970-72, presdl. commn. on future of assn. 1973-74, com. on constn. and by-laws 1980-85), Minn. Soc. Internal Medicine, Sigma Xi. also: 1201 6th St SW Rochester MN 55902-1918 Office: Mayo Med Sch 200 1st St SW Rochester MN 55902 Home: 1201 6th St SW Rochester MN 55902-1918

BARTLETT, ALEX, lawyer; b. Warrensburg, Mo., Aug. 7, 1937; s. George Vest and May (Woolery) B.; m. Sue Gloyd, June 5, 1961 (div. June 1978); children: Ashley R., Nathan G.; m. Eleanor M. Veltrop, Oct. 27, 1978. BA, Cen. Mo. State U., 1959; LLB, U. Mo., 1961. Bar: Mo. 1962, U.S. Ct. Mil. Appeals 1963, U.S. Supreme Ct. 1965, U.S. Dist. Ct. (we. dist.) Mo. 1966, U.S. Ct. Appeals (8th cir.) 1968. From assoc. to ptnr. Hendren & Andrae, Jefferson City, Mo., 1965-79; mem. Bartlett, Venters, Pletz & Toppins, P.C., 1980-87; pvt. practice, 1987-90; mem. Husch & Eppenberger, LLC, 1990—. With Transit Casualty Co. Receivership, 1986-90, commr. claims, 1986-87, spl. claims counsel, 1987-89, dir. legal affairs dept., 1989-90; lectr. law U. Mo., Columbia, 1965-66. Contbr. editor Mo. Law Rev., 1960-61. Served to capt. JAGC, U.S. Army, 1962-65. Mem. ABA, FBA, Mo. Bar Assn. (chmn. young lawyers sect. 1972-73, ct. modernization com. 1972-74, jud. reform com. 1974-76, chmn. cts. and jud. com. 1978-79, legis. com. 1981-84, President's award 1976, Smithson award 1976), Cole County Bar Assn., Am. Coll. Trial Lawyers (chmn. Mo. 1994-96), Order of Coif. Democrat. Office: Husch and Eppenberger PO Box 1251 235 E High St Jefferson City MO 65102-3236

BARTLETT, PAUL DANA, JR. agribusiness executive; b. Kansas City, Mo., Sept. 16, 1919; s. Paul D. and Alice May (Hiestand) B.; m. Joan Jenkins, May 14, 1949; children— J. Alison Bartlett Jager, Marilyn Bartlett Hebenstreit, Paul Dana III, Frederick Jenkins BA, Yale U., 1941. Chmn. Bartlett and Co., Kansas City, Mo., 1961-77; pres., chmn. bd. Bartlett and Co. (formerly Bartlett Agri Enterprises, Inc.), 1977—, chmn., dir. Bd. dir. United Mo. Bank, United Mo. Bancshares. Lt. USN, 1942-46 Office: Bartlett and Company 4800 Main St Ste 600 Kansas City MO 64112-2509

BARTLETT, ROBERT JAMES, principal; Prin. Robinwood Elem. sch., Florissant, Mo., 1985-98; dir. staff devel. Furguson Florissant (Mo.) Sch. Dist., 1998—. Recipient Elem. Sch. Recognition award U.S. Dept. Edn., 1989-90, St. Louis Prin. of Yr., 1994. Mem. St. Louis Suburban Prins. Assn. Office: Furguson Florissant Sch Dist 1005 Waterford Dr Florissant MO 63033-3649

BARTLETT, SHERIE, printing company executive; m. Tom Bartlett. CEO, pres. Data Source, Kansas City, Mo. Office: Data Source Inc 1400 Universal Ave Kansas City MO 64120-2140 Fax: 816-483-3284. E-mail: info@data-source.com.

BARTLO, SAM D. lawyer; b. Cleve., Oct. 5, 1919; BBA, Case Western Res. U., 1941; JD, Cleve.-Marshall Law Sch., 1950. Bar: Ohio, 1950, U.S. Supreme Ct., 1958. Mem. firm Buckingham, Doolittle & Burroughs, Akron, Ohio, 1971-90. Capt. U.S. Army, 1942-46. Fellow Am. Bar Found. (life), Ohio Bar Found. (life, pres. 1981-82, trustee 1976-81); mem. ABA (bd. govs. 1989-92, ho. of dels. 1977-94, state del. 1981-89, exec. com. 1990-92, chair ops. com. 1991-92, trustee FJE resource coun. 1992-94), Akron Bar Assn. (pres. 1967-68, exec. com. 1968-7), Ohio State Bar Assn. (coun. dels. 1970-86, pres. 1977-78, exec. com. 1973-79), Am. Judicature Soc., Nat. Conf. Bar Presidents (trustee 1979-82), Ohio Legal Ctr. Inst. (pres. 1979-81, trustee 1977-81). Office: Buckingham Doolittle Burroughs PO Box 1500 Akron OH 44309-1500

BARTMAN, ROBERT E. state education official; Commdr. of edn., elem. and secondary edn. State of Mo. Office: State Dept Edn PO Box 480 Jefferson City MO 65102-0480

BARTMANN, WILLIAM R. financial services company executive; Law degree, Drake U. Self-employed entrepreneur; founder, chmn. Comml. Fin. Svcs. Inc., Tulsa, 1986-98; co-founder, CEO, pres. Neighborhood Fin. Ctr., Clayton, Mo., 2000—. Recipient Blue Chip Enterprise award U.S. C. of C., So. Gov.'s Cup award, 1996; named Nat. Entrepreneur of Yr., Nasdaq, 1997, Ernst & Young, 1997, USA Today, 1997. Office: Neighborhood Fin Ctr 120 S Central Ave Clayton MO 63105

BARTON, GLEN A. manufacturing company executive; b. Alton, Mo. BS in Civil Engring., U. Mo., Columbia, 1961; grad. Exec. Program, Stanford U., 1977. With Caterpillar Inc., Peoria, Ill., 1961—, mgr. merchandising divsn. gen. offices, 1983-84, mgr. products control, 1984-86, v.p., 1987-89, exec. v.p., 1989-90, group pres., 1990-98, vice chmn., CEO, bd. dirs., 1998—. Mem. adv. bd. Bank One, Peoria, Bradley U., Peoria, INCO Ltd. Mem. Nat. Mining Assn. (bd. dirs., chmn. mfrs. divsn. bd. govs.), Mineral Info. Inst.

BARTON, JANICE SWEENY, chemistry educator; b. Trenton, N.J., Mar. 22, 1939; d. Laurence U. and Lillian Mae (Fletcher) S.; m. Keith M. Barton, Dec. 20, 1967. BS, Butler U., 1962; PhD, Fla. State U., 1970. Postdoctoral fellow Johns Hopkins U., Balt., 1970-72; asst. prof. chemistry East Tex. State U., Commerce, 1972-78, Tex. Woman's U., Denton, 1978-81; assoc. prof. Washburn U., Topeka, 1982-88, prof., 1988—, chair chemistry dept., 1992—. Mem. undergrad. faculty enhancement panel NSF, Washington, 1990; mem. NSF instr. lab. improvement panel, 1992, 96, 99; mem. NSF-AIRE site visit team, 2000. Contbr. articles to profl. jours. Active Household Hazardous Waste Collection, Topeka, 1991, Solid Waste Task Force, Shawnee County, Kans., 1990; mem. vol. com. YWCA, Topeka, 1984-87. Rsch. grantee Petroleum Rsch. Fund, Topeka, 1984-86, NIH, Topeka, 1985-88; instrument grantee NSF, Topeka, 1986, 95. Mem. Am. Chem. Soc. (sec. Dallas-Ft. Worth sect. 1981-82), Kans. Acad. Sci. (pres.-elect 1991, pres. 1992, treas. 1995—), Biophys. Soc., Sigma Xi (pres. TWU club 1980-81), Iota Sigma Pi (mem.-at-large coord. 1987-93). Home: 3401 SW Oak Pky Topeka KS 66614-3218 Office: Washburn U Dept Chemistry Topeka KS 66621 E-mail: zzbart@washburn.edu.

BARTON, JOHN JOSEPH, obstetrician, gynecologist, educator, researcher; b. Rockford, Ill., Mar. 19, 1933; s. L. David and Helen M. (Fox) B.; m. Lois Maltby, 1959 (div. 1965); children: Mary Katherine, Karen Ann. BA in History, U. Ill., 1957; BS in Medicine, U. Ill., Chgo., 1959, MD, 1961; student Law, Loyola U., Chgo., 1966-69. Diplomate Am. Bd. Ob.-Gyn.; cert. Advanced Cardiac Life Support. Rotating intern Cook County Hosp., Chgo., 1961-62, resident in ob.-gyn., 1962-65; fellow gynecologic pathology Northwestern U., 1963, clin. asst. ob.-gyn., 1963-64, clin. instr. ob.-gyn., 1964-65, assoc. in ob.-gyn., 1965-71; prof. ob.-gyn. Cook County Grad. Sch. of Medicine, 1965—; dir. ob.-gyn. rsch. and edn. Cook County Hosp., 1965-69; chmn. ob.-gyn. Ill. Masonic Med. Ctr., 1970—2001; assoc. prof. ob.-gyn. U. Ill. Coll. Medicine, 1971-83, prof., 1983-93, lectr. in ob.-gyn., 1993—; prof. ob.-gyn. Rush Med. Coll., 1993—; chmn. emeritus ob-gyn Ill. Masonic Med. Ctr., 2002—. Clin. clerkship subcom. U. Ill. Coll. Medicine, 1974-90, acad. senate 1977-91, 85-87, perinatal steering com., 1977-92, admissions com. 1985-91, screening subcom. 1988-89; ad hoc com. on rules for governance, Rush Med. Coll., Chgo., 1993—, curriculum com. 1993, com. on student evaluation and promotions, 1994—, core ckerkship subcom. of curriculum com. 1995—; editl. bd. Jour. Obstetrics and Gynecology, Am. Jour. Obstetrics and Gynecology, Internat. Jour. Obstetrics and Gynecology Contbr. numerous articles to profl. jours., chpts. to books. including Laparoscopy in Gynecologic Practice, 1972, Guidelines for Perinatal Care, 1983, Antepartum HIV Screenings: A Comparison of Methodologies, 1990. Vol. cons. Ob.-Gyn. Claremore (Okla.) Indian Hosp., 1979-80, 86, Fort Defiance (Ariz.) Indian Hosp., 1981, Red Crescent Soc., Heliopolis, Cairo, Egypt, 1987; vol. surgeon Internat. Red Cross and Red Crescent Soc. Vols., West Beirut, Lebanon, 1982; mem. Ill. Gov.'s AIDS adv. coun.; advisor, expert witness Atty. Gen. State of Ill. on Standards of Practice in Ob.-Gyn.; mem. com. formation of outcome-oriented surveillance systems for Ill. Dept. of Pub. Health, adv. com. to Health Planning Com. for Chgo., perinatal adv. com. Ill. Dept. Health, steering com. Mayor Washington's Infant Mortality Reduction Initiative and others. Sgt. USMC, 1950-55, Korea. Fellow Am. Coll. Obstetricians and Gynecologists (adv. coun. 1977-81, adv. coun. dist. VI 1977-81, chmn. Ill. sect. 1977-78, com. on profl. liability 1989-92, Jr. Fellow Rsch. prize award 1991), Ctrl. Assn. Obstetricians nd Gynecologists (ctrl. travel club, sci. awards com. 1985-89. chmn. 1987-89, Ann. prize award 1988), Chgo. Gynecol. Soc. (exec. com. 1994—, pres. 1995-96), Am. Coll. Surgeons, Soc. Contemporary Medicine and Surgery, Am. Soc. Clin. Hypnosis, Chgo. Inst. Medicine, Royal Soc. Medicine (London); mem. Ill. Assn. Maternal and Child Health, Assn. Profs. Gynecology and Obstetrics, Am. Pub. Health Assn., Phi Kappa Phi, Nu Sigma Nu. Avocations: rancher quarter horses, exotic animals, hounds, harleys. Home: Bar T Ranch 20516 Bunker Hill Rd Marengo IL 60152-8003 Office: Ill Masonic Med Ctr 836 W Wellington Ave Chicago IL 60657-9224

BARTON, ROBERT H., III, automotive executive; CEO Meridian Automotive Sys., Dearborn, Mich. Office: Meridian Automotive Systems 550 Town Center Dr Dearborn MI 48126 Office Fax: (313) 336-4184.

BARTON, THOMAS JACKSON, chemistry educator; b. Dallas, Nov. 5, 1940; s. Ralph and Florence (Whitfield) Barton; m. Elizabeth Burton, Oct. 1, 1966; children: Ralph, Brett. BS, Lamar U., 1962; PhD (hon.) , U. Fla., 1967. NIH fellow Ohio State U., 1967; mem. faculty Iowa State U., Ames, 1967—, prof. chemistry, 1978—, disting. prof., 1984—, program dir. Ames Lab., 1986—88, dir. Ames Lab, 1988—, dir. Inst. for Phys. Rsch. and Tech., 1998—. NAS exch. scientist, Former Soviet Union, 1975; assoc. prof. U. Montpellier, France; mem. coun. on materials scis. Dept. Energy, 1992—97. Contbr. rsch. papers to profl. publs. Recipient Fredric Stanley Kipping award in organosilicon chemistry, 1982, Gov.'s medal for sci. tchg., 1983, Excellence in Tchg. faculty achievement award, Burlington No. Found., 1988, Outstanding Sci. Accomplishment in Materials Chem. award, Dept. Energy, Materials Sci. Divsn., 1989. Fellow: Japan Soc. Promotion of Sci.; mem.: Am. Chem. Soc. (Midwest award 1995). Methodist. Home: 815 Onyx Cir Ames IA 50010-8429 Office: Iowa State Univ Dept Chemistry Ames IA 50011-0001

BARTREM, DUANE HARVEY, retired military officer, designer, building consultant; b. Lansing, Mich., June 4, 1928; s. Harvey Theodore and Ruby Leola (Thomas) B.; m. Frances Lillie Bushee, Sept. 12, 1948 (dec. Jan. 2000); children: Lawrence Duane, Jeffrey Earl. BA in Bus. Adminstrn., Columbia Coll., Mo., 1976. Enlisted U.S. Army N.G., Lansing, 1948, commd. 2d lt., 1951, advanced through grades to col., 1951-76, comdr. battery, 1956-60; facilities engr. Mich. Nat. Guard, 1960-69, chief engr. Mich., 1969-76, comdr. 119 FA Bn., 1971-75, comdr. 46th Brigade, 1975-76, comptr., 1976-83, ret., 1983; prin. residential design office, 1955-60, Grand Ledge, Mich., 1967—. Chmn. congregation Bretton Woods Covenant Ch., 1986-89, vice chmn., 1995-97; scout leader local and regional levels Boy Scouts Am. With USNR, 1946-48. Decorated Army Commendation with 3 clusters, Meritorious Svc. medal with 2 clusters, Legion of Merit. Mem. Retired Officers Assn., Assn. of the U.S. Army (mem. resolutions com. 1973, 74, chair resolutions com. 1975, area v.p. 1976—, mem. adv. bd. 1978—, chair by-laws com. 1978—, past state pres., past region pres. 1988-92, coun. of trustees 1992-96, Pres.'s medal 1998), Grand Lodge Rotary (pres. 1989-90, Paul Harris award 1992), Boy Scouts Am. (pres. 1973-79, exec. bd. 1970—; disting. Eagle Scout 1989, Silver Beaver award 1969, Silver Antelope 1983, God and Svc. award 1992, James E. West fellow, 1910 Soc., Ernest Thompson Seton Mem. 1999). Protestant. Avocation: golf.

BARTTER, BRIT JEFFREY, investment banker; b. Berea, Ohio, Dec. 27, 1949; s. Lynn Martin Bartter and Scharlie Ellen (Watson) Handlan; m. Marilyn McCullough, Aug. 25, 1973; children: Bryndl Lynn and Blake McCullough (twins). AB in Econs., Duke U., 1972; MS in Fin., Cornell U., 1976, PhD in Fin., 1977. Asst. prof. computer sci. Grad. Sch. Bus. Cornell U., Ithaca, N.Y., 1976; asst. prof. fin. Grad. Sch. Mgmt. Kellogg Grad. Sch. Mgmt., Northwestern U., Evanston, Ill., 1977-79; assoc., then v.p. Merrill Lynch Capital Markets, Chgo., 1979-83; v.p. The First Boston Corp., 1983-87, dir., 1988-89, mng. dir., 1989-94, Merrill, Lynch Investment Banking, Chgo., 1995—. Bd. dirs. Coun. for Young Profls., Chgo., 1985-87. Contbr. articles to Jour. of Fin., Fin. Mgmt. Bd. dirs. Cornell Coun. Chgo., 1987-88, Duke Campaign Chgo., 1987-88; mem. governing bd. Chgo. Symphony Orch. Mem. Econ. Club Chgo., Northwestern U. Assocs., Glen View Golf Club, Chgo. Club. Home: 221 Apple Tree Rd Winnetka IL 60093-3703 Office: Merrill Lynch Investment Bkng 5500 Sears Tower Chicago IL 60606

BARTZ, MERLIN E. state legislator; b. Mason City, Iowa, Mar. 16, 1961; BA in Polit. Sci. and Music cum laude, Luther Coll., 1983. Livestock and grain farmer and laborer; with Grafton Industries, David Mfg. Co.; mem. Iowa Ho. of Reps., 1991-92, Iowa Senate from 10th dist., 1992—. Mem. Worth County Hist. Soc.; dir. ch. choir. Mem. Worth County Pork Prodrs., Farm Bur., N. Iowa Pheasants Forever, Ducks Unltd., Rotary Internat. Republican. Home: 2081 410th St Grafton IA 50440-7510 Office: State Capitol Dist 10 3 9th And Grand Des Moines IA 50319-0001 E-mail: merlin_bartz@legis.state.ia.us.

BARUCH, HURD, lawyer; b. N.Y.C., Nov. 29, 1937; s. Eduard and Dorothy (Hurd) B.; m. Mary Ellen Kinney, July 8, 1964; children: Edward, Michael, Amy. BA, Hamilton Coll., 1957; LLB, Yale U., 1960; MBA, Columbia U., 1961. Bar: Conn. 1960, N.Y. 1966, D.C. 1971, Pa. 1972, Ill. 1988, U.S. Supreme Ct. 1964. Ptnr. Winston & Strawn, Chgo. Spl. counsel divsn. trading and markets, SEC, 1969-72. Author: Wall Street Security Risk, 1971. Capt. USAFR, 1961-64. Mem. Ill. State Bar Assn., KM, Order of Coif, Phi Beta Kappa, Beta Gamma Sigma. Office: Winston & Strawn 35 W Wacker Dr Ste 4200 Chicago IL 60601-1695

BASAR, TAMER, electrical engineering educator; b. Istanbul, Turkey, Jan. 19, 1946; came to U.S., 1969; s. Munir and Seniye (Pirilsu) B.; m. Tangul Unerdem, Dec. 27, 1975; children: Gozen, Elif. B.S. in Elec. Engring., Robert Coll., Istanbul, 1969; M.S., Yale U., 1970, M.Phil., 1971, Ph.D., 1972. Research fellow Harvard U., Cambridge, Mass., 1972-73; sr. researcher scientist Marmara Research Inst., Gebze, Kocaeli, Turkey, 1973-80; adj. assoc. prof. Bogazici U., Istanbul, 1974-80; assoc. prof. elec. engring. U. Ill., Urbana, 1980-83, prof., 1983—, disting. prof., 1998—. Co-author: Dynamic Noncooperative Game Theory, 1982, 2d edit., 1995, H-infinity Optimal Control and Related Minimax Design Problems, 1991, 3rd edit., 1999; editor: Dynamic Games and Applications in Econs., 1986; co-editor: Differential Games and Applications, 1989, Advances in Dynamic Games and Applications, 1994; contbr. articles to profl. jours.; editor 2 jours. in control theory; assoc. editor 1 jour. in econs. and 1 in control. Recipient Young Scientist award in Applied Math., Turkish Nat. Rsch. Coun., 1976, Sedat Simavi Found. award, 1979, Medal of Sci., Turkey, 1993. Fellow IEEE (v.p. Control Sys. Soc. 1997-98, pres.-elect 1999, pres. 2000, Disting. Mem. award 1993, Best Paper award 1995); mem. Soc. for Indsl. Applied Math., Internat. Soc. Dynamic Games (pres. 1990-94), Game Theory Soc., Am. Math. Soc., Nat. Acad. of Engring., Sigma Xi. Home: 2810 Valley Brook Dr Champaign IL 61822-7621 Office: U Ill 1308 W Main St Urbana IL 61801-2307 E-mail: tbasar@control.csl.uiuc.edu.

BASART, JOHN PHILIP, electrical engineering and remote sensing researcher; b. Des Moines, Feb. 26, 1938; s. Philip Edwin and Hildreth Pauline (Belden) B.; m. Luann Kay Stow, Mar. 2, 1960; children— Jill Eileen Urban, Ann Marie B.S., Iowa State U., 1962, M.S., 1963, Ph.D. in Elec. Engring., 1967. Rsch. assoc. Nat. Radio Astronomy Obs., Charlottesville, Va., 1967-69; system scientist Very Large Array, Socorro, N.Mex., 1979-81; asst. prof. elec. engring. Iowa State U., Ames, 1969-73, assoc. prof., 1973-80, prof., 1980-2000, prof. emeritus, 2000—. Rschr. in radio astronomy, image processing, wave propagation, remote sensing; campus coord. Iowa Space Grant Consortium. Contbr. articles to profl. jours. Served with USAF, 1955-59 Recipient student award IRE, 1962 Mem. IEEE (sr. mem.), AIAA, Am. Geophys. Union, Am. Astron. Soc., Royal Astron. Soc., Internat. Astron. Union, Internat. Soc. for Optical Engring., Sigma Xi, Eta Kappa Nu, Tau Beta Pi, Phi Kappa Phi. Office: Iowa State U 2271 Howe Hl Rm 2348 Ames IA 50011-0001 E-mail: jpbasart@iastate.edu.

BASCOM, C. PERRY, retired foundation administrator; b. Boston, July 30, 1936; s. William Richardson and Jean Ames (Hall) B.; m. Sally Cissel Greenwood, July 18, 1995; children: Elisabeth Brooke, Heather Ames, Sarah Duff Greenwood, Amy Greenwood Dunaway. BA, Yale U., 1958; LLB, Harvard U., 1961. Assoc. Bryan Cave, St. Louis, 1962-72, ptnr., 1972-95; adminstr. Gateway Found., 1995—2001, ret., 2001. Judge St. Louis Night Housing Ct., 1970-72; lectr. on various topics, including Truth in Lending, Real Estate Settlement Procedures Act, techniques in comml. bank lending, devels. in Mo. banking law, electronic funds transfers. Sr. warden Trinity Ch., St. Louis, 1974-78. Served with USAR, 1961-68. Mem. Mo. Bar Assn. Home: 4650 Pershing Pl Saint Louis MO 63108-1908

BASH, PHILIP EDWIN, publishing executive; b. Huntington, Ind., Aug. 13, 1921; s. Philip Purviance and Nell (Johnson) B.; m. Flora Wiley Oberg, Mar. 11, 1944; children: Barbara, Kingsley, Roger, Amy. B.A., DePauw U., 1943. Account exec. Leo Burnett Co., Inc., Chgo., 1947-54; account supr., v.p., sr. v.p. mktg. services Clinton E. Frank Inc., 1954-64, pres., 1964-72,

Barrington (Ill.) Press, Inc., 1972-86, also bd. dirs. Chmn. bd. trustees Shimer Coll., 1989—; trustee Garrett Theol. Sem., 1976—, chmn. bd., 1989-95. Served to lt. (j.g.) USNR, 1943-46, PTO. Mem. Am. Assn. Advt. Agys. (bd. govs. Chgo. council), Am. Mktg. Assn., Sigma Chi. Methodist (trustee). Clubs: University (Chgo.), Economics (Chgo.); Barrington Hills Country. Office: 200 James St Barrington IL 60010-3328

BASHOOK, PHILIP G. medical association executive, educator; b. Bklyn., Mar. 10, 1943; children: Jeremy, Amy, Jeffrey, Gregory, Richard. BS in Zoology, U. Calif., Santa Barbara, 1965; MSc in Biology, Calif. State U., Northridge, 1968; EdD, U. B.C., Can., 1971. From asst. to assoc. prof, Ctr. Ednl. Devel. Health Sci. Ctr. U. Ill., Chgo., 1971-74; assoc. dir. Michael Reese Hosp. and Med. Ctr., 1975-80, dir., 1980-87; dir. Office Edn. Am. Psychiatric Assn., Washington, 1987-90; dir. evaluation and edn. Am. Bd. Med. Specialities, Evanston, Ill., 1991—. Adj. assoc. prof. dept. med. edn. U. Ill. Coll. Medicine, Chgo., 1975-87, 91—; adj. assoc. prof. dept. psychiatry and behavior scis. George Washington, 1988-91; adj. assoc. prof. Northwestern U. Med. Sch., 1999—; mem. accreditation rev. com. Accreditation Coun. Continuing Med. Edn., 1980-87, vice chmn., 1982-87, mem. monitoring com., 1996—, vice-chair, 1999—. Co-author: Construction and Use of Written Simulations, 1976; author 17 books; contbr. chpts. to books and articles to profl. jours. Bd. dirs. Pub. Sch. Dist. # 69 Cook County, Ill., 1980-87, bd. sec., 1985-87. Office: Am Bd of Med Specialties 1007 Church St Ste 404 Evanston IL 60201-5913 E-mail: p6b@abms.org.

BASHWINER, STEVEN LACELLE, lawyer; b. Cin., Aug. 3, 1941; s. Carl Thomas and Ruth Marie (Burlis) B.; m. Arden J. Lang, Apr. 24, 1966 (div. 1978); children: Heather, David; m. Donna Lee Gerber, Sept. 13, 1981; children: Margaret, Matthew. AB, Holy Cross Coll., 1963; JD, U. Chgo., 1966. Bar: Ill. 1966, U.S. Dist. Ct. (no. dist.) Ill. 1967, U.S. Ct. Appeals (7th cir.) 1968, U.S. Supreme Ct. 1970, U.S. Dist. Ct. (ea. dist.) Wis. 1988, U.S. Ct. Appeals (4th cir.) 1990. Assoc. Kirkland & Ellis, Chgo., 1966-72, ptnr., 1972-76, Friedman & Koven, Chgo., 1976-86, Katten Muchin Zavis, Chgo., 1986—. Served to sgt. USAFR, 1966-72. Mem. ABA, 7th Cir. Bar Assn., Chgo. Bar Assn., Chgo. Inn of Ct., Lawyers Club Chgo. Home: 834 Green Bay Rd Highland Park IL 60035-4630 Office: Katten Muchin Zavis 525 W Monroe St Ste 1600 Chicago IL 60661-3693

BASIL, BRAD L. technology education educator; Middle sch. tchr. Mt. Logan Middle Sch., Chillicothe, Ohio, asst. prin.; middle sch. tchr. Smith Middle Sch., 1988—. Recipient Tchr. Excellence for Ohio award Internat. Tech. Edn. Assn., 1992. Office: Smith Middle Sch 345 Arch St Chillicothe OH 45601-1519 also: Mt Logan Middle Sch 841 E Main St Chillicothe OH 45601-3509

BASKA, JAMES LOUIS, wholesale grocery company executive; b. Kansas City, Kans., Apr. 3, 1927; s. John James and Stella Marie (Wilson) B.; m. Juanita Louise Carlson, Oct. 14, 1950; children: Steven James, Scott David. BSBA, U. Kans., 1949; JD, U. Mo., 1960. Bar: Kans. 1960. Pres., chief exec. officer Baska Laundry Co., Kansas City, 1951-62; ptnr. Rice & Baska, 1962-76; corporate sec., gen. counsel Assoc. Wholesale Grocers Inc., 1976-77, v.p., sec., gen. counsel, 1977-79, exec. v.p., chief fin. officer, sec., gen. counsel, 1979-84, pres., chief exec. officer, 1984-92; pres. emeritus, 1992. Mem. SDC com. Wakefern Food Corp., 1998—; bd. dirs. Raley's. Served as staff sgt. U.S. Army, 1944-46. Mem. Nat. Grocers Assn. (bd. dirs. 1987-89, chmn. 1987-88), Food Mktg. Inst. (bd. dirs. 1988-93). Republican. Roman Catholic. Avocations: hunting, golf. Office: Assoc Wholesale Grocers Inc PO Box 2932 5000 Kansas Ave Kansas City KS 66106-1135

BASOLO, FRED, chemistry educator; b. Coello, Ill., Feb. 11, 1920; s. John and Catherine (Marino) Basolo; m. Mary P. Nutley, June 14, 1947; children: Mary Catherine, Freddie, Margaret-Ann, Elizabeth Rose. BE, So. Ill. U., 1940, DSc (hon.) , 1984; MS, U. Ill., 1942, PhD in Inorganic Chemistry, 1943; LLD (hon.) , U. Turin, 1988; Laurea Honoris Causa (hon.) , U. Palermo, Italy, 1997. Rsch. chemist Rohm & Haas Chem. Co., Phila., 1943—46; mem. faculty Northwestern U., Evanston, Ill., 1946—, prof. chemistry, 1958—, Morrison prof. chemistry, 1980—90, chmn. dept. chemistry, 1969—72; Charles E. and Emma H. Morrison prof. emeritus Nortwestern U., 1990—. Guest lectr. NSF summer insts.; chmn. bd. trustees Gordon Rsch. Conf., 1976; pres. Inorganic Syntheses, Inc., 1977—81; mem. bd. chem. scis. and tech. NRC-NAS; adv. bd. Who's Who in Am., 1983; cons. in field. Recipient Ballar medal, 1972, So. Ill. U. Alumni Achievement award, 1974, Dwyer medal, 1976, James Flack Norris award for Outstanding Achievement in Tchg. of Chemistry, 1981, Oesper Meml. award, 1983, IX Century medal, Bologna U., 1988, Mosher award, 1990, Padova U. medal, 1991, Chinese Chem. Soc. medal, 1991, G.C. Pimental award, 1992, Chem. Pioneer award, 1992, Gold medal, Am. Inst. Chemists, 1993, Joseph Chatt medal, Royal Soc. Chemistry, 1996, Inauguration mem. Hall of Fame, Chem. Dept. So. Ill. U., 1996; fellow Guggenheim, 1954—55, NSF, 1961—62, NATO sr. scientist, Italy, 1981, Sr. Humboldt, 1992. Fellow: AAAS (chmn. chemistry sect. 1979), NAS, Am. Acad. Arts and Scis.; mem.: Nat. Acad. Lincei (Italy), Royal Soc. Chemistry (Joseph Chatt medal 1996), Italian Chem. Soc. (hon.), Am. Chem. Soc. (assoc. editor jour. 1961—64, chmn. divsn. inorganic chemistry 1970, pres. 1983, bd. dirs. 1982—84, award for rsch. in inorganic chemistry 1964, Disting. Svc. award in inorganic chemistry 1975, N.E. regional award 1971, award in chem. edn. 1992, Chem. Pioneer award 1992, Gold medal 1993, Willard Gibbs medal 1996), Sigma Xi (Monie A. Ferst medal 1992), Kappa Delta Phi, Phi Kappa Phi, Alpha Chi Sigma, Phi Lambda Upsilon, Phi Lambda Theta (hon.). Office: Northwestern U Chemistry Dept Rm GG40 2145 Sheridan Rd Evanston IL 60208-0834

BASS, LEE MARSHALL, food products company executive; b. 1950; With Bass Enterprises Prodn. Co., Ft. Worth, 1970—; chmn. bd. Nat. Farms, Inc., Kansas City, Mo., 1992—, also bd. dirs.; pres. Lee M. Bass Inc., Ft. Worth. Office: Nat Farms Inc 4800 Main St Kansas City MO 64112-2510 also: Modern Art Mus 1309 Montgomery St Fort Worth TX 76107-3015 also: Bass Bros Enterprises 201 Main St Fort Worth TX 76102-3105 also: Lee M Bass Inc 201 Main St Fort Worth TX 76102-3105

BASS, PAUL, pharmacology educator; b. Winnipeg, Man., Can., Aug. 12, 1928; came to U.S., 1958; s. Benjamin and Sarah B.; m. Ruth Zipursky, May 31, 1953; children: Stuart, Susan. B.S. in Pharmacy, U. B.C., 1953, M.A. in Pharmacology, 1955; Ph.D. in Pharmacology, McGill U., 1957, fellow in Biochemistry, 1957-58; fellow in Physiology, Mayo Found., 1958-60. Research asst. Ayerst, McKenna & Harrison, Can., 1956; assoc. lab. dir. Parke, Davis & Co., 1960-70; prof. pharmacology Sch. Pharmacy and Sch. Medicine, U. Wis., Madison, 1970-2000, prof. emeritus, 2001—. Mem. editorial bd.: Am. Jour. Physiology, 1976-79, 81-92, Jour. Pharmacology and Exptl. Therapeutics, 1980-99 ; contbr. chpts. to books, articles to profl. jours. Mem. Am. Soc. Pharmacology and Exptl. Therapeutics, Am. Gastroent. Assn. Home: 777 Highland Ave Madison WI 53705-2222

BASS, STEVEN CRAIG, computer science educator; b. Indpls., July 29, 1943; s. Leland Ellsworth and Isabelle Frances (Ross) B.; m. Sara Ann Hiday, Sept. 4, 1965 (div. Apr. 1988); children: Leland Kai, Marshall Lynn; m. Kevyn Anne Salsburg, Jan. 2, 1989. BSEE, Purdue U., 1966, MSEE, 1968, PhD in Elec. Engring., 1971. Prof. elec. engring. Purdue U., Lafayette, Ind., 1971-88; prof. elec. and computer engring. George Mason U., Fairfax, Va., 1988-91; prin. engr. Mitre Corp., McLean, 1988-91; prof. computer sci. and engring., chmn. dept. U. Notre Dame, Notre Dame, Ind., 1991-2000. Cons. Magnovox Co., Ft. Wayne, Ind., 1971-73, Admiral Corp., Chgo., 1973-76, Kimball Internat., Jasper, Ind., 1978-84, Tektronix Corp., Wilsonville, Oreg., 1987-88. Contbr. over 25 articles to profl. jours., delievered over 35 papers at sci. confs. Rescue officer Stockwell (Ind.) Vol. Fire Dept., 1985-88. Recipient numerous grants from NSF, USAF, IBM, Mitre Corp., others. Fellow IEEE (v.p. circuits and sys. soc. 1981, 91-93, mem. audio engring. soc.); mem. Tau Beta Pi. Roman Catholic. Achievements include 3 U.S. and 6 fgn. patents in the field of digital signal processing. Office: U Notre Dame Dept Computer Sci & Engring 384 Fitzpatrick Hl Engrng Notre Dame IN 46556-5637 E-mail: bass@cse.nd.edu.

BASSETT, JOHN E. academic administrator, dean, English educator; b. Washington, May 12, 1942; s. J. Earl and Frances E. (Walker) B.; m. Kay E. Hobart, Sept. 5, 1964; children: Laura, Gregory. BA in History, Ohio Wesleyan U., 1963, MA in English, 1966; PhD in English, U. Rochester, 1970. Instr. U. Rochester, N.Y., 1969-70; asst. prof. Wayne State U., Detroit, 1970-75, assoc. prof., 1975-84; prof., head dept. English No. Carolina State U., Raleigh, 1984-93; dean Coll. Arts and Scis., prof. English Case Western Res. U., Cleve., 1993-2000; pres. Clark U., Worcester, 2000—. Author: William Faulkner: An Annotated Checklist of Criticism, 1972, Faulkner: The Critical Heritage, 1975, Faulkner: A Checklist of Recent Criticism, 1983, Vision and Revisions: Essays on Faulkner, 1989, Faulkner in the Nineties: A Bibliography of Criticism, 1991, A Heart of Ideality in My Realism and Other Essays on Howells and Twain, 1991, Harlem in Review: Critical Reactions to Black American Writers 1917-1939, 1992, Defining Southern Literature, 1997, Thomas Wolfe: An Annotated Bibliography of Criticism, 1996; contbr. articles to profl. jours. Mem. MLA, Mark Twain Soc., Thomas Wolfe Soc., Soc. for Study of So. Lit., Assn. Depts. of English (pres. 1990-91), Phi Beta Kappa, Phi Kappa Phi, Phi Alpha Theta. Office: Clark U 950 Main St Worcester MA 01610-1477 E-mail: jbassett@clarku.edu.

BASSETT, LESLIE RAYMOND, composer, educator; b. Hanford, Calif., Jan. 22, 1923; s. Archibald Leslie and Vera (Starr) B.; m. Anita Elizabeth Denniston, Aug. 21, 1949; children— Wendy Lynn (Mrs. Lee Bratton), Noel Leslie, Ralph (dec.). B.A. in Music, Fresno State Coll., 1947; M.Music in Composition, U. Mich., 1949, A.Mus.D., 1956; student, Ecole Normale de Musique, Paris, France, 1950-51. Tchr. music pub. schs., Fresno, 1951-52; mem. faculty U. Mich., 1952—, prof. music, 1965—, Albert A. Stanley disting univ. prof., 1977—, chmn. composition dept., 1970, Henry Russel lectr., 1984, emeritus, 1992. Guest composer Berkshire Music Center, Tanglewood, Mass., 1973 Served with AUS, 1942- 46. Fulbright fellow, 1950-51; recipient Rome prize Am. Acad. in Rome, 1961-63; grantee Soc. Pub. Am. Music, 1960, Nat. Inst. Arts and Letters, 1964, Nat. Council Arts, 1966; Guggenheim fellow, 1973-74, 80-81; recipient Pulitzer prize in music for Variations for Orch., 1966; citation U. Mich. regents, 1966; Walter Naumburg Found. rec. award for Sextet, 1974; Disting. Alumnus award Calif. State U., Fresno, 1978; Disting. Artist award Mich. Council Arts, 1981; Citation of Merit, U. Mich. Sch. Music Alumni, 1980 Mem. Am. Composers Alliance, Mich. Soc. Fellows, Am. Acad. of Arts and Letters, Pi Kappa Lambda, Phi Kappa Phi, Phi Mu Alpha. Methodist.

BASSETT, TINA, communications executive; b. Detroit; m. Leland Kinsey Bassett; children: Joshua, Robert. Student, U. Mich., 1974, 76-78, 81, Wayne State U., 1979-80. Advt. dir. Greenfield's Restaurant, Mich. and Ohio, 1972-73; dir. advt. and pub. rels. Kresco, Inc., Detroit, 1973-74; pub's. rep. The Detroiter mag., 1974-75; pub. rels. dir. Detroit Bicentennial Commn., 1975-77; prin. Leland K. Bassett & Assocs., Detroit, 1976-86; intermediate job devel. specialist Detroit Coun. of the Arts, 1977; project dir. Detroit image campaign dept. pub. info. City of Detroit, 1975, spl. events dir., 1978, dep. dir. dept. pub. info., 1978-83, dir. dept. pub. info., 1983-86; pres., prin. Bassett & Bassett, Inc., Detroit, 1986—. Bd. dirs. Diverse Steel Corp. Publicity chmn. Under the Stars IV, V, VI, VII, VIII, IX and X, Benefit Balls, Detroit Inst. of Arts Founders Soc., 1983-88, Detroit Inst. of Arts Founders Centennial Ball, 1985, publicity chmn. Mich. Opera Theater, Opera Ball, 1987; program lectr. Wayne County Close-Up Program, 1984; mem. ctrl. planning com. Am. Assn. Mus.; mem. Founders Soc., Detroit Inst. Arts, 1988—; mem., publicity chair Grand Prix Ball, 1989; co-chair, prodr. Mus. Hall Ctr. for Performing Arts; bd. dirs. arts coun. Detroit Inst. Arts, 1996, bd. dirs. cinema arts coun., 1996—; bd. dirs. Weizman Inst. Sci., 1996-97. Named Outstanding Woman in Agy. Top Mgmt., Detroit chpt. Am. Women in Radio and TV, 1989. Mem. AIA (hon., pub. dir. 1990-91, Richard Upjohn fellowship 1991), Detroit Hist. Soc., , Internat. Women's Forum, Music Hall Assn., Pub. Rels. Soc. Am. (Advt. Woman of Yr. 1989), Woman's Advt. Club Detroit, Cinematic Arts Coun., DIA Board of Dirs., 1996—. Home: 30751 Cedar Creek Dr Farmington Hills MI 48336-4989 Address: Bassett & Bassett 1502 Randolph St Ste 200 Detroit MI 48226-2295

BASSIOUNY, HISHAM SALLAH, surgeon, educator; b. Cairo, Mar. 30, 1954; m. Sandra Bassiouny; children: Deenah, Faith-Iman. Mb. Bch. Diploma with honors, Cairo U., 1977. Diplomate Am. Bd. Surgery; lic. surgeon, Ill., Mich., Md. Intern Cairo U. Hosps., 1977-78; surg. externship Linz (Austria) Gen. Hosp., 1980-81; intern Md. Gen. Hosp., Balt., 1981-82; resident Henry Ford Hosp., Detroit, 1982-86, clin. vascular fellow, 1986-87; postdoctoral rsch. fellow, instr. surgery U. Chgo., 1987-89, asst. prof. surgery, 1989-96, assoc. prof. surgery, 1996—, dir. non-invasive vascular lab., 1988—, Weiss Meml. Hosp., 1989—, dir. Chgo Ctr. for Minimally Invasive Vascular Therapy, 1998—. Mem. staff U. Chgo. Med. Ctr., Little Co. Mary Hosp., Weiss Meml. Hosp., dir. non-invasive vascular lab. Contbr. chpts. to books and numerous articles to profl. jours. Recipient Louis Block award, 1989; grantee W.L. Gore, 1987-89, NIH, 1988—, Mellon Found., 1990, U. Chgo., 1992-93, Washington Sqare Found., 1992, Am. Heart Assn., 1995—. Fellow ACS; mem. AAAS, AAS, Am. Heart Assn. (sci. coun. 1992—, coun. atherosclerosis, coun. cardiothoracic and vascular surgery), Am. Venous Forum, Midwestern Vascular Soc., North Am. Vascular Biology Orgn., Internat. Soc. Cardiovascular Surgery, Chgo. Surg. Soc., Peripheral Vascular Surg. Soc., Soc. Vascular Surgery. Office: U Chgo 5841 S Maryland Ave # Mc5028 Chicago IL 60637-1463

BASTIAN, GARY WARREN, judge; b. St. Paul, Nov. 7, 1948; s. Warren John and Virginia (Brower) Bastian; children: Alexander, Christopher. BS, Wis. State U., 1970; JD, William Mitchell Co., 1974. Bar: Minn. 1975. Rschr. Minn. Taxpayers Assn., 1970-73; dir. IR rsch. staff Minn. Senate, 1974-85; project dir. labor mgmt. com. Minn. Sch., 1985-87; pvt. practice, 1987-91; asst. commr. Dept. Labor and Industry, 1991, dep. commr., 1991-95, commr., 1995-97; judge 2d Jud. Dist. Ramsey County, 1997—. Mem. Maplewood City council, Minn., 1980-90. mayor 1990-97; bd. dirs. East Communities Family Ctr., 1986-90, Minn. League of Cities, 1988-92, Nat. Assn. Govt. Labor Officials, 1995-97, sec.-treas., 1996-97, Ramsey-Washington Counties Suburban Cable Commn., 1991-97, State Fund Mut. Ins. Co., 1995-97, Minn. Safety Coun., 1996-97; chmn. Minn. Workers' Compensation Adv. Coun., 1995-97. Mem. Criminal Def. Svcs. Bd., 1998—; bd. dirs. U. Wis.-River Falls Found., 1997—; mem. Ramsey County Violence Coord. Coun., 1999—. Recipient award of merit Local 320, Pub. and Law Enforcement Teamsters Mpls., 1979. Mem. Assn. Met. Municipalities (bd. dirs. 1981-89, pres. 1987-88), Suburban C. of C. (bd. dirs. 1979-84), Polar Wrestling Club. Roman Catholic. Home: 2042 Holloway Ave Maplewood MN 55109 Office: Ramsey County Courthouse 15 W Kellog Blvd Saint Paul MN 55102

BASU, ASIT PRAKAS, statistician; b. India, Mar. 17, 1937; arrived in U.S., 1962, naturalized, 1979; m. Sandra Bergquist; children: Amit K., Shumit K. BS with honors, Calcutta U., 1956, MS, 1958; PhD, U. Minn., 1966. Asst. prof. stats. U. Wis., Madison, 1966-68; mem. research staff IBM Research Center, Yorktown Heights, N.Y., 1968-70; asst. prof. indsl. engring. and mgmt. sci. Northwestern U., Evanston, Ill., 1970-71; asso. prof. math. U. Pitts., 1971-74; prof. stats. U. Mo., Columbia, 1974—, chmn. dept., 1976-83. Co-author: Statistical Methods for the Reliability of Repairable Systems, 2000; co-editor: Reliability and Quality Control, 1986, Advances in Reliability, 1993, The Exponential Distribution: Theory, Methods and Application, 1995, Frontiers in Reliability, 1997; contbr. articles to profl. jours. Fellow AAAS, Royal Statis. Soc., Am. Statis. Assn., Inst. Math. Stats.; mem. Calcutta Statis. Assn., Internat. Statis. Inst., Am. Soc. Quality Control, Biometric Soc. Office: Univ Mo Dept Stats Columbia MO 65211-0001

BATAILLON, JOSEPH FRANCIS, federal judge, lawyer; b. Omaha, Oct. 3, 1949; s. Joseph Franklin and Norma Jean (Lock) B.; m. Pamela Dawn Nelson, Aug. 17, 1971; children: Aimee, Jared, Margery, Patrick, Kathryn. BA, Creighton U., 1971, JD, 1974. Bar: Nebr. 1974, U.S. Dist. Nebr. 1974, U.S. Ct. Appeals (8th cir.) 1982. Dep. pub. defender Pub. Defender's Office County of Douglas, Omaha, 1971-80; assoc. Sodoro, Daly & Sodoro, 1980—. Def. counsel USAR, Omaha, 1976-86; commr. Nebr. Jud. Resources Commn., Lincoln, Nebr., 1986—; lector U. Nebr. Med. Ctr., Omaha, 1988—. Congl. chair Nebr. Dems., Lincoln, 1985—; mem. parish coun. St. Pius X Ch., Omaha, 1988—; commr. Nebr. Jud. Resources Commn., Lincoln, 1986. Recipient chair's award Douglas County Dems., 1990. Mem. ABA, Nebr. Bar Assn. (del. Omaha chpt. 1981—), Omaha Bar Assn., Nebr. Assn. Trial Attys., Nebr. Criminal Def. Atty.'s Assn., Optimists (pres. 1984-85). Roman Catholic. Home: 2017 N 55th St Omaha NE 68104-4237 Office: Federal Judge US Dist Ct 215 N 17th St PO Box 277 Omaha NE 68101-0277

BATCH, CHARLIE, professional football player; b. Homestead, Pa., Dec. 5, 1974; Student, U. Ea. Mich. Football player Detroit Lions, 1998—. Office: Detroit Lions 1200 Featherstone Rd Pontiac MI 48342

BATCHELDER, ALICE M. federal judge; b. Aug. 15, 1944; m. William G. Batchelder III; children: William G. IV, Elisabeth. BA, Ohio Wesleyan U., 1964; JD, Akron U., 1971; LLM, U. Va., 1988. Tchr. Plain Local Sch. Dist., Franklin County, Ohio, 1965-66, Jones Jr. High Sch., 1966-67, Buckeye High Sch., Medina County, 1967-68; assoc. Williams & Batchelder, Medina, Ohio, 1971-83; judge U.S. Bankruptcy Ct., 1983-85, U.S. Dist. Ct. (no. dist.) Ohio, Cleve., 1985-91, U.S. Ct. of Appeals (6th cir.), Cleveland, 1991—. Mem. ABA, Fed. Judge's Assn., Fed. Bar Assn., Medina County Bar Assn. Office: US Ct of Appeals (6th cir) 143 W Liberty St Medina OH 44256-2215

BATEMAN, C. BARRY, airport terminal executive; Airport dir. Gen. Mitchell Internat. Airport, Milw. Office: Gen Mitchell Internat Airport 5300 S Howell Ave Milwaukee WI 53207-6156

BATEMAN, JOHN JAY, classics educator; b. Elmira, N.Y., Feb. 17, 1931; s. Joseph Earl and Etha M. (Edwards) B.; m. Patricia Ann Hageman, July 5, 1952; children: Kristine M., Kathleen A., John Eric. BA, U. Toronto, 1953; MA, Cornell U., 1954, PhD, 1958. Lectr. Univ. Coll., U. Toronto, 1956-57; lectr., then asst. prof. U. Ottawa, 1957-60; mem. faculty U. Ill., Urbana, 1960—, prof. classics and speech, 1968-93; prof. emeritus, 1993—; head dept. classics U. Ill., 1966-73, chmn., 1988-92, acting dir. Sch. Humanities, 1973-74. Author, editor books and articles. Dem. precinct committeeman, 1964-68; sec. Champaign Dem. Central Com., 1965-66. Mem. Am. Philol. Assn. (sec.-treas. 1968-73), Soc. Bibl. Lit., Renaissance Soc. Am. Home: 5508 41st Ave E Bradenton FL 34208-6835 E-mail: jjbateman@aol.com.

BATEMAN, LEONARD A. engineering executive; Pres., CEO Bateman & Assocs., Winnipeg, Man., Can. Recipient Gold Medal award CCPE, 1994. Office: Bateman & Assocs 231 Brock St Winnipeg MB Canada R3N OY7 E-mail: lenmary@shaw.ca.

BATEMAN, SHARON LOUISE, public relations executive; b. St. Louis, Oct. 18, 1949; d. Frank Hamilton and Charlotte Elizabeth (Hogan) B. Student, Drury Coll., 1967-69; BJ, U. Mo., 1971. Asst. dir. pub. relations Cardinal Glennon Hosp. for Children, St. Louis, 1971-76; staff asst. pub. relations Ozark Air Lines, 1976-80; mgr. corp. relations Kellwood Co., 1980-83; mgr. corp. communications May Dept. Stores Co., 1983-86, dir. corp. communications, 1986-94; mgr. comm. Arthur Andersen, 1995-96; mgr. editl. and adminstrv. svcs. The Falk Design Group, 1996—2001; v.p. corp. comms. May Dept. Stores Co., 2000—. Bd. dirs. St. Michael's Houses, 1996-97, Gateway Greening, 1999—. Recipient Best Regional Airline Employee Publ. award Editor's Assn. Am. Transp. Assn., 1978. Mem.: Pub. Rels. Soc. Am. (sec.St. Louis chpt. 1983, bd. dirs. 1988—90, v.p. 1991), Internat. Assn. Bus. Comms. (pres. St. Louis chpt. 1977). Office: May Dept Stores Co 611 Olive St Saint Louis MO 63101-1721

BATES, WALTER ALAN, former lawyer; b. Wadsworth, Ohio, Oct. 27, 1925; s. Edwin Clinton and Gertrude (Connor) B.; m. Aloise Grasselli O'Brien, Feb. 9, 1957; children: Charles, Aloise, Walter Alan Jr., Thomas, David BS cum laude, Harvard U., 1945, LLB, 1950. Bar: Ohio 1950, U.S. Dist. Ct. (no. dist.) Ohio 1954, U.S. Ct. Appeals (6th cir.) 1965, U.S. Ct. Appeals (7th cir.) 1966, U.S. Dist. Ct. Conn. 1976, U.S. Ct. Appeals (2nd cir.) 1977, U.S. Dist. Ct. Minn. 1978, U.S. Ct. Appeals (8th cir.) 1980, U.S. Ct. Appeals (5th cir.) 1984, U.S. Dist. Ct. (no. dist.) Tex. 1988, U.S. Supreme Ct. 1989. Assoc. McKeehan, Merrick, Arter & Stewart, Cleve., 1950-60; ptnr. Arter & Hadden, 1960-94; ret., 1994. Chmn. bd. trustees Cleve. Inst. Music, 1980-85, hon. trustee, 1985—; assoc. v.p., chmn. new programs com. United Way Svcs., Cleve., 1982-85, trustee, 1985-88; mem. Cleve. panel Ctr. for Pub. Resources; trustee Apollo's Fire, 1998—. Lt. USN, 1945-46, 51-53. Mem. ABA (antitrust sect.), Ohio State Bar Assn. (chmn. bd. govs. antitrust sect. 1987-91), Cleve. Bar Assn. (joint com. on bar admissions 1990-97, cert. grievance com. 1992-95). Republican. Roman Catholic. Clubs: Kirtland Country (sec., bd. dirs. 1981-86), Mentor Harbor Yachting (bd. dirs. 1980-89, commodore 1988), Tavern, Harvard (Cleve. pres. 1968-69). Avocations: sailing; traveling. Home: 18235 Shaker Blvd Cleveland OH 44120-1754 Office: Arter & Hadden 1100 Huntington Bldg Cleveland OH 44115 E-mail: sailor74@prodigy.net.

BATES, WILLIAM HUBERT, lawyer; b. Lexington, Mo., Apr. 14, 1926; s. George Hubert and E. Norma (Comer) B.; m. Joy LoRue Godbehere, Oct. 20, 1956; children: William Brand, Joy Ann. BA, U. Mo., 1949; JD, U. Mich., 1952. Bar: Mo. 1952. With Lathrop & Gage L.C., Kansas City, Mo., 1952—, chmn., 1988-95. L Mem., pres. bd. curators U. Mo. Multi-Campus U., 1983-89. Sgt. U.S. Army, 1943-46, ETO. Recipient Brotherhood award NCCJ, 1984; Disting. Alumni award U. Mo., 1989, Geyer award for pub. svc., 1991. Fellow Am. Bar Found. (state chmn. 1990-97); mem. ABA (ho. of dels. 1990-93), Mo. Bar Assn. (bd. dirs. 1982-91, v.p., pres. 1988-91), Kansas City Bar Assn. (pres. Found. 1985-87), Lawyers Assn. Kansas City (Charles Evans Whittaker award 1990), Mo. C. of C. (chmn., bd. dirs. 1983-85), Greater Kansas City C. of C. (bd. dirs., chmn. 1975-92), Van Guard Club, Mercury Club, Beta Theta Pi (Man of Yr. award Kansas City 1985, Oxford Cup 1996). Democrat. Methodist. Avocations: golf, swimming, music. Home: 310 W 49th St Apt 1002 Kansas City MO 64112-3400 Office: Lathrop & Gage L C 2345 Grand Blvd Ste 2600 Kansas City MO 64108-2617

BATIUK, THOMAS MARTIN, cartoonist; b. Akron, Ohio, Mar. 14, 1947; s. Martin and Verna (Greskovics) B.; m. Catherine L. Wesemeyer, June 26, 1971; 1 child, Brian. B.F.A., cert. edn., Kent (Ohio) State U.,

1969. Tchr. art Eastern Heights Jr. High Sch., 1969-72; syndicated cartoonist, 1972—. Cartoonist: comic strip Funky Winkerbean, 1972—, John Darling, 1979—, Crankshaft, 1987—; collections include Funky Winkerbean, 1973, Funky Winkerbean, Play It Again Funky, 1975, Funky Winkerbean, Closed Out, 1977, Yearbook, 1979, You Know You've Got Trouble When Your Mascot is a Scpaegoat, 1984, Football Fields are for Band Practice, 1986, Sunday Concert, 1987, Henry C. Dinkle-Live at Carnegie Hall, 1988, A Pizza Pilgrim's Progress, 1990, Funky Winkerbean: Gone with the Woodwinds, 1992, Would the Ushers Please Lock the Doors, 1994, Crankshaft: I've Still Got It, 1995; co-author: And One Slice With Anchovies!, 1993, Crankshaft, 1992; forward: A PArent's Guide to Band and ORchestra, 1991, Attack of the Band Moms, 1996. Recipient 46th Annual Ohio Gov.'s award-Journalism, 1995. Mem. Nat. Cartoonists Soc., Newspaper Features Coun. Office: care Universal Press Syndicate 4520 Main St Ste 700 Kansas City MO 64111-1816

BATSAKIS, JOHN GEORGE, pathology educator; b. Petoskey, Mich., Aug. 14, 1929; s. George John and Stella (Vlahkis) B.; m. Mary Janet Savage, Dec. 28, 1957; children: Laura, Sharon, George. Student, Va. Mil. Inst., 1947, Albion Coll., Mich., 1948-50; M.D., U. Mich., 1954. Diplomate Am. Bd. Pathology. Intern George Washington Univ. Hosp., Washington, 1954-55; resident in pathology U. Mich. Hosp., Ann Arbor, 1955-59; prof. pathology U. Mich., 1969-79; chmn. dept. pathology M.D. Anderson Hosp. U. Tex., Houston, 1981-96, chm. and prof. emeritus dept pathology, 1996—. Ruth Legett Jones prof. U. Tex., Austin, 1982-96; adj. prof. oral pathology U. Tex. Dental Br., Houston; cons. Armed Forces Inst. Pathology, 1972—, VA Hosp., Ann Arbor, 1968-79; Hayes Martin lectr. Am. Soc. for Head and Neck Surgery, 1994; Gunnar Holmgren lectr. Swedish Nat. Ear, Nose, Throat Meeting, 1994; William Christopherson lectr. U. Louisville Dept. of Pathology, 1995; external examiner U. Hong Kong Dental Sch., 1995—; Francis A. Sooy lectr. dept. otolaryngology, head and neck surgery U. Calif., San Francisco, 1997; 2d Matthews lectr. dept. pathology Emory U., 1997; spkr. in field. Author: Tumors of the Head and Neck, 2d edit., 1979; editor: Clin. Lab. Ann., 1981—86; co-editor: Advances in Anatomic Pathology, 1994—; contbr. articles. Bd. trustees, v.p. Mike Hogg Found., Houston, 1991—; trustee George C. Marshall Found., Lexington, Va., 1995-00, emeritus trustee, 2000—. Capt. U.S. Army, 1959-61. Recipient William H. Rorer award Am. Coll. Gastroenterology, 1972, Disting. Alumnus award Albion Coll., 1987, Reviewer of the Decade award AMA Archives Orolaryngology Head Neck Surgery, 1990, Presdl. award Am. Soc. Head and Neck Surgery, 1991, Harlan Spjut award Houston Soc. Clin. Pathologists, 1992, Honor award Am. Laryngologic Assn., 1995; Spl. Honored Guest of Am. Soc. for Head and Neck Surgery, 1993. Fellow ACP, Am. Soc. Clin. Pathologists, Am. Acad. Otolaryngology (assoc., honor award 1994), Coll. Am. Pathologists (chmn. commn. anatomic pathology), Royal Soc. Medicine. Republican. Episcopalian. Home: 1701 Hermann Dr Unit 3304 Houston TX 77004-7373 Office: 1452 W Bear Lake Rd NE Kalkaska MI 49646-9051

BATT, NICK, property and investment executive; b. Defiance, Ohio, May 6, 1952; s. Dan and Zenith (Dreher) B. BS, Purdue U., 1972; JD, U. Toledo, 1976. Asst. prosecutor Lucas County, Toledo, 1976-80, civil divsn. chief, 1980-83; village atty. Village of Holland, Ohio, 1980-91; law dir. City of Oregon, 1984-91; spl. counsel State of Ohio, 1983-93; pres. Property & Mgmt. Connection, Inc., Toledo, 1993—. Mem. Maumee Valley Girl Scout Coun., Toledo, 1977-80; bd. mem. Bd. Cmty. Rels., Toledo, 1975-76; mem. Lucas County Dem. Exec. Com., 1981-83. Named One of Toledo's Outstanding Young Men, Toledo Jaycees, 1979. Mem. KC, Elks. Democrat. Roman Catholic. Office: Property & Mgmt Connection Inc 1732 Arlington Ave Toledo OH 43609-3050 E-mail: battnick@aol.com.

BATTENBERG, J. T., III, automotive company executive; With GM, 1986, mng. dir. GM Continental divsn. Belgium, gen. mgr. overseas truck ops. Eng., v.p. Buick-Oldsmobile-Cadillac group, 1986, v.p., group exec. Buick-Oldsmobile-Cadillac, v.p., group exec. automotive components group, 1992, sr. v.p., pres. group, 1992-95, exec. v.p., 1995; pres., CEO, chmn. bd. Delphi Automotive Systems (formerly ACG Worldwide), Troy, Mich., 1995—. Mem. GM's Pres. Coun.; nat. adv. bd. Chase Manhattan Corp. Bd. trustees Kettering U.; bd. overseers Columbia U. Bus. Sch.; exec. bd. Detroit area Coun. of Boy Scouts Am.; exec. bd. Oakland County Automation Alley; bd. dirs. For Inspiration and Recognition of Sci. and Tech.; mem. Coun. on Competitiveness; adv. bd. Covisint; mem. Bus. Roundtable and Bus. Coun. Named Internat. Bus. Coun. World Trader of the Yr. Detroit Regional Chamber, 1998. Mem. Soc. of Automotive Engrs., Soc. of Body Engrs., Engring. Soc. of Detroit, Exec. Leadership Coun., Automobile Nat. Heritage Area, Econ. Club of Detroit. Office: Delphi Automotive Systems Corp 5725 Delphi Dr Troy MI 48098-2815

BATTERSBY, JAMES LYONS, JR. English language educator; b. Pawtucket, R.I., Aug. 24, 1936; s. James Lyons and Hazel Irene (Deuel) B.; m. Lisa J. Kiser, Aug. 6, 1990; 1 child, Julie Ann. BS magna cum laude, U. Vt., 1961; MA, Cornell U., 1962, Ph.D., 1965. Asst. prof. U. Calif., Berkeley, 1965-70; assoc. prof. English Ohio State U., Columbus, 1970-82, prof., 1982—. Cons. Ohio State U. Press, U. Ky. Press, U. Calif. Press, Prentice-Hall, McGraw Hill, Fairleigh Dickinson U. Press, U. Mich. Press, U. Ala. Press. Author: Typical Folly: Evaluating Student Performance in Higher Education, 1973, Rational Praise and Natural Lamentation: Johnson, Lycidas and Priciples of Criticism, 1980, Elder Olson: An Annotated Bibliography, 1983, Paradigms Regained: Pluralism and the Practice of Criticism, 1991, Reason and the Nature of Texts, 1996, Unorthodox Views: Reflections on Reality, Truth, and Meaning in Current Social, Cultural, and Critical Discourse, 2002; contbg. author: Domestick Privacies: Samuel Johnson and the Art of Biography, 1987, contbg. author: Fresh Reflections on Samuel Johnson: Essays in Criticism, 1987, contbg. author: Criticism, History and Intertextuality, 1988, Beyond Poststructuralism: The Speculations of Theory and the Experience of Reading, 1996; contbr. articles to profl. jours. With U.S. Army, 1954—57. Woodrow Wilson fellow, 1961-62, 64-65, Samuel S. Fels fellow, 1964-65, U. Calif. Summer Faculty fellow, 1966, Humanities Research fellow, 1969; recipient Kidder Medal U. Vt., 1961. Mem. MLA, Am. Soc. 18th Century Studies, Midwest Soc. 18th Century Studies, Royal Oak Found., Phi Beta Kappa, Phi Kappa Phi, Kappa Delta Pi. Home: 472 Clinton Heights Ave Columbus OH 43202-1277 E-mail: batterjay@msn.com.

BATTEY, RICHARD HOWARD, judge; b. Aberdeen, S.D., Oct. 16, 1929; m. Shirley Ann Battey; children: David, Russell, Dianne. BA, U. S.D., 1950, JD, 1953. Bar: S.D. 1953. Atty. City of Redfield, S.D., 1956-63; state's atty. Spink County, 1959-65, 81-84; chief judge U.S. Dist. Ct. S.D., Rapid City, 1994—, sr. judge, 1999—. Practicing atty., Redfield, 1956-85; mem. criminal laaw com. Jud. Conf. U.S., 1993-99; adj. prof. U. S.D., 1973-75. Served with AUS, 1953-55. Mem. Dist. Judges Assn. 8th Cir. Ct. Appeals (past pres.). Office: US Dist Ct 318 Fed Bldg 515 9th St Rapid City SD 57701-2626

BATTINO, RUBIN, chemistry educator, retired; b. N.Y.C., June 22, 1931; s. Sadik and Anna (Decastro) B.; m. Charlotte Alice Ridinger, Jan. 30, 1960; children— David Rubin, Benjamin Sadik B.A., CCNY, 1953; M.A., Duke U., 1954, Ph.D., 1957; M.S., Wright State U., 1978. Lic. profl. clin. counselor, Ohio. Research chemist Leeds & Northrup Co., Phila., 1956-57; asst. prof. Ill. Inst. Tech., Chgo., 1957-66; prof. Wright State U., Dayton, Ohio, 1966-95, ret., 1995, prof. emeritus, 1995—. Vis. prof. U. Vienna, Austria, Oxford U., Eng., Hebrew U. Jerusalem, Ben Gurion U., U. New Eng., Australia, U. Canterbury, N.Z., Okayama U. Sci., Japan, Rhodes U., U. Turku, Finland. Author: (with S.E. Wood) Thermodynamics-An Introduction, 1968; Oxygen and Ozone, 1981, Nitrogen and Air, 1982, (with S.E. Wood) The Thermodynamics of Chemical Systems, 1990, (with T.L. South) Ericksonian Approaches, A Comprehensive Manual, 1999, Guided Imagery and other Approaches to Healing, 2000, Coping: A Practical Guide for People Who Have Life-Challenging Diseases and Their Caregivers, 2001; mem. editorial bd. Solubility Data Series, Jour. Chem. and Engring. Data; contbr. tech. papers to profl. jours. Fulbright fellow, 1979; recipient Outstanding Tchr. award Wright State U., 1979, 93, Outstanding Engr. award Engring. and Sci. Found., Dayton, 1985, Bd. Trustees award Wright State U., 1985. Mem. AAAS, Am. Chem. Soc., Internat. Union Pure and Applied Chemistry (commn.), Sigma Xi, Phi Lambda Upsilon Democrat. Jewish Office: Wright State U Chemistry Dept Dayton OH 45435 E-mail: rubin.battino@wright.edu.

BATTLES, JOHN MARTIN, lawyer; b. Pitts., May 10, 1957; s. John and Rosemarie B.; m. Mary Ann Battles; children: John David, Katherine Rose. BA, U. Pitts., 1978; BA in Bus. Adminstrn., U. Cin., 1980, JD, 1990. Asst. corp. counsel Cincom Systems, Cin.; now corp. counsel Lexis-Nexis Group, divsn. Reed Elsevier Inc., Dayton, Ohio. Home: 7 Crescent Ct Fort Thomas KY 41075-2113 Office: Lexis Nexis Group Div Reed Elsevier Inc 9443 Springboro Pike Miamisburg OH 45342-4425

BATZLI, GEORGE OLIVER, ecology educator; b. Mpls., Sept. 23, 1936; s. Oscar H. and Bertha M. B.; m. Sandra Lou Scharf, Jan. 2, 1959; children— Jeffrey, Samuel B.S. in Psychology, U. Minn., 1959; M.A. in Biology, San Francisco State U., 1965; Ph.D. in Zoology (Ecology), U. Calif., Berkeley, 1969. Research assoc. U. Calif., Davis, 1969-71, lectr. biology Santa Cruz, 1971; asst. prof. zoology U. Ill., Urbana, 1971-76, assoc. prof. ecology, 1976-80, prof. ecology, 1980—, head dept. ecology, ethology and evolution, 1983-88, 95-97. Sr. scientist research in arctic environs., 1976-78, mem. ecology program adv. panel NSF, 1984-87; research scientist DSIR, N.Z., 1979; chmn. ecology program U. Ill., 1976-82. Contbr. articles on ecology to profl. jours.; spl. issue editor Arctic and Alpine Research, 1980, Oikos, 1983; mem. editorial bd. Ecology, Ecol. Monographs, 1981-84. Fellow NSF, 1962-63, NIH, 1967-69, 69-71, Zool. Inst. U. Oslo, Norway, 1982. Fellow AAAS; mem. Am. Inst. Biol. Scis., Am. Soc. Mammalogy, Ecol. Soc. Am., Brit. Ecol. Soc., Intecol, Am. Soc. Naturalists, Comp. Nutrition Soc. Office: U Ill Shelford Vivarium 606 E Healey St Champaign IL 61820-5502 E-mail: g-batzli@life.uiuc.edu.

BAUER, ALAN R. internet company executive; Internet distbn. leader The Progressive Corp., Mayfield Village, OH. Office: The Progressive Corp 6300 Wilson Mills Rd Cleveland OH 44143-2109

BAUER, BURNETT PATRICK, state legislator; b. LaPorte, Ind., May 25, 1944; s. Burnett Calix and Helen (Cryan) B.; m. Karen Bella, 1980; children: Bartholomew, Meagan, Maureen. BA, U. Notre Dame, 1966; postgrad., Miami U., 1966-68; MS, Ind. U. Ind. state rep. Dist. 7, 1970-91, Dist. 6, 1991—; asst. minority leader, 1977, 83; ranking minority leader Ind. Ho. Reps., 1984-89, chmn., ways and means, 1989, ranking minority mem., state budget com., 1989. Tchr. Muessel Jr. H.S., South Bend, Ind., 1968-74, Madison Jr. H.S., 1974-75, Dickinson Jr. H.S., 1976-78, Washington H.S.; asst. to supt. South Bend Cmty. Sch. Corp. Recipient Legis. award EPA Region V, 1976. Mem. K.C., Am. Fedn. Tchrs., Ind. State Tchrs. Assn. Home: 1307 Sunnymede Ave South Bend IN 46615-1017

BAUER, CHRIS MICHAEL, banker; b. Milw., Sept. 2, 1948; s. Heinz Gerald and Maria (Weber) B.; m. Susan Marie Branton, June 28, 1969. BBA, U. Wis., 1970; MBA, Marquette U., 1976. Mgmt. trainee 1st Wis. Nat. Bank, Milw., 1970-72, spl. enterprise officer, 1972-74, asst. mgr., 1974-75; v.p. 1st Wis.-Racine, 1976-78; pres. 1st Wis.-Brookfield, 1978-84; 1st v.p. Firstar Corp. (formerly 1st Wis. Corp.), Milw., 1984-86, sr. v.p., 1986-89; pres., COO Firstar Bank Milw. (formerly 1st Wis. Nat. Bank), 1989-91, chmn., CEO, 1991-99, 1999—; chmn, CEO Business Banc Group Ltd.; also bd. dirs. Firstar Bank Milw. (formerly 1st Wis. Nat. Bank). Bd. dirs. Aurora Health Care Metro Region, Milw. Pub. Libr. Found., J.A. of Wisconsin, Inc., Next Door Found., Siebert Lutheran Found., The Auto Club Group Inc., AAA Wisconsin; mem. Greater Milw. Com. Mem. Milw. Country Club, Univ. Club, Westmoor Country Club. Lutheran. Office: Bus Banc Group Ltd 18500 W Corporate Dr Ste 170 Brookfield WI 53045-6309

BAUER, DIETRICH CHARLES, retired medical educator; b. Elgin, Ill., July 1, 1931; s. Karl. E. and Martha (Dietrich) B.; m. Lois L. Reed, Nov. 13, 1954. Student, Lake Forest (Ill.) Coll., 1949-51; BS, U. Ill., 1954; MS, Mich. State U., 1957, PhD, 1959; postgrad., Case Western Res. U., Cleve., 1959-61. Rsch. asst. dept. microbiology Mich. State U., East Lansing, 1957-59; asst. prof. dept. microbiology and immunology Ind. U. Sch. Medicine, Indpls., 1961-65, acting chmn. dept., 1964-65, 81, assoc. prof., 1965-68, prof., 1968-96, chmn. dept. microbiology/immunology, 1981-96, prof. emeritus. Cons. Chas. Pfizer Co., 1968-71, John Wiley, Pub., 1979-80. Recipient Disting. Teaching award Ind. U., 1978, Faculty Colloquium on Excellence in Teaching award FACET, 1992. Mem. AAAS, Am. Soc. Microbiology, Am. Assn. Immunologists, Assn. Med. Sch. Microbiology and Immunology Chmn., Sigma Xi. Office: Indiana Univ Sch Medicine 635 Barnhill Dr Indianapolis IN 46202-5126

BAUER, FRED T. technology products executive; b. 1943; married. Degree in electrical engring. cum laude, Mich. State U. Founder Simicon Co., late 1960s-72; divsn. mgr., corp. officer, v.p. Robertshaw; founder Gentex Corp., Zeeland, Mich., 1974, chmn., CEO; bd. dirs. Photobit Corp. Former dir. Jr. Achievment in Holland/Zeeland; former adv. bd. dirs. Underwriters Labs. Industry Coun. Recipient Master Entrepreneur of Yr. award Ernst & Young, 1988. Office: Gentex Corp 600 N Centennial St Zeeland MI 49464-1318

BAUER, OTTO FRANK, university official, communication educator; b. Elgin, Ill., Dec. 1, 1931; s. Otto Leland and Cora Dorothy (Berlin) B.; m. Jeanette L. Erickson, May 27, 1956; children: Steven Mark, Eric Paul. B.S., Northwestern U., 1953, M.A., 1955, Ph.D., 1959; D of Humanitarian Svcs. (hon.), Clarkson Coll., 1999. Instr., then asst. prof. English USAF Acad., Colo., 1959-61, dir. debate, 1959-61; instr. to prof. Bowling Green State U., Ohio, 1961-71, dir. grad. admissions and fellowships, 1965-69, asst. dean Grad. Sch., 1967-69, asst. v.p., 1970-71; ACE fellow U. Calif.-Berkeley, 1969-70; prof. communication U. Wis.-Parkside, Kenosha, 1971-79; vice chancellor U. Wis. -Parkside, 1971-76; acting chancellor U. Wis.-Parkside, 1974-75; vis. prof. communication, spl. asst. to chancellor U. Wis., Madison, 1976-77; vice chancellor for acad. affairs U. Nebr., Omaha, 1979-94, prof. communication, 1979—, vice chancellor emeritus, 1995. Cons. Bishop Clarkson Coll. Nursing, Omaha, also 4 others, 1981—; mem. Commn. on Instns. Higher Edn., North Ctrl. Assn. Colls. and Schs., 1975-77, 84-88, cons., evaluator, 1976—, bd. dirs. 1989-94. Author: Fundamentals of Debate, 1966, rev. edit., 1999, Lower Moments in Higher Education, 1997; co-author: Guidebook for Student Speakers, 1966; editor: Introduction to Speech Communication, 1968. Bd. dirs. United Way Kenosha County, Wis., 1973-79, Kenosha County coun. Girl Scouts U.S., 1977-79; chmn. spkrs. bur. United Way Midlands, Omaha, 1983, mem. allocations coms., 1985-93, steering com., 1989-93; bd. dirs. Fontenelle Forest Assn., 1987-94, v.p., 1990-92; bd. dirs. Clarkson Coll., 1992—, vice-chair, 1995-97, chair, 1997—. Recipient Faculty Disting. Svc. award U. Wis., Parkside, 1978, Chancellor's medal U. Nebr., Omaha, 1994, Disting. Svc. award U. Nebr. Aviation Inst., Omaha, 1994; named Faculty Man of Yr., Bowling Green State U., 1967, Exec. of Yr., Nat. Secs. Assn., Omaha, 1980; Clarion DeWitt Hardy scholar, 1949-53; humanitarian svc. award named in his honor Clarkson Coll., 1999. Mem. Am. Coun. on Edn. (exec. com. coun. of fellows 1982-85), Nat. Comm. Assn., Rotary. Office: U Nebr 6001 Dodge St Omaha NE 68182-0001

BAUER, WILLIAM JOSEPH, judge; b. Chgo., Sept. 15, 1926; s. William Francis and Lucille (Gleason) Bauer; m. Mary Nicol, Jan. 28, 1950; children: Patricia, Linda. AB, Elmhurst Coll., 1949, LLD, 1969; JD, DePaul U., 1952, LLD (hon.) , 1993; , John Marshall Law Sch., 1987; LLD (hon.) , Roosevelt U., 1994. Bar: Ill. 1951. Ptnr. Erlenborn, Bauer & Hotte, Elmhurst, Ill., 1953—64; asst. state's atty. Du Page County, 1952—56; 1st asst. state's atty., 1956—58; state's atty., 1959—64; judge 18th Jud. Cir. Ct., 1964—70; U.S. dist. atty. No. Ill. Chgo., 1970—71; judge U.S. Dist. Ct. (no. dist.), 1971—75, U.S. Ct. Appeals (7th cir.), 1975—86, chief judge, 1986—93, senior judge, 1994—. Instr. bus law. Elmhurst Coll., 1952—59; adj. prof. law DePaul U., 1978—91; former mem. Ill. Supreme Ct. Com. on Pattern Criminal Jury Instrns.; chmn. Fed. Criminal Jury Instrn. Com. 7th Cir. Trustee Elmhurst Coll., 1979—, DePaul U., 1984—, DuPage Meml. Hosp.; bd. advisors Mercy Hosp. With U.S. Army, 1945—47. Mem.: FBA (former bd. dirs.), ABA, Chgo. Bar Assn., DuPage County Bar Assn. (past pres.), Ill. Bar Assn., Legal Club (Chgo.), Law Club, Union League Club. Roman Catholic. Office: US Ct Appeals 219 S Dearborn St Ste 2754 Chicago IL 60604-1803

BAUERLY, RONALD JOHN, marketing educator; b. Monroe, Wis., Oct. 31, 1953; s. Jack Leroy and Josephine (Wiegel) B.; m. Robin Rochelle Kramer, Aug. 8, 1981; children: Shannon Marie, Thomas Joseph. BBA, U. Iowa, 1975, MBA, 1977; DBA, Southern Ill. U., Carbondale, 1989. Asst. mgr. K-Mart Corp., Racine, Wis., 1977-78; instr. Metropolitan Tech. Community Coll., Omaha, 1978, Loras Coll., Dubuque, Iowa, 1979-81, Northwest Mo. State U., Maryville, 1981-82; asst. prof. Brescia Coll., Owensboro, Ky., 1983-86; asst. prof. mktg. Western Ill. U., Macomb, 1987-91, assoc. prof., 1991-96, prof., 1996—. Editor Jour. of Contemporary Business Issues; contbr. articles to jours. Mem. Am. Acad. Advt., Am. Mktg. Assn., Assn. for Consumer Rsch., Acad. Mktg. Sci., Mktg. Mgmt. Assn., Phi Kappa Phi, Beta Gamma Sigma. Office: Western Ill U 424 Stipes Macomb IL 61455 E-mail: moviefan@macomb.com.

BAUGHER, PETER V. lawyer; b. Chgo., Oct. 2, 1948; s. William and Marilyn (Sill) B.; m. Robin Stickney, Nov. 25, 1978; children: Julia Allison, Britton William Herbert. AB, Princeton U., 1970; JD, Yale U., 1973. Bar: Ill. 1974, U.S. Dist. Ct. (no. dist.) Ill. 1974, U.S. Ct. Appeals (7th cir.) 1974, U.S. Supreme Ct. 1987. Law clk. to judge U.S. Ct. Appeals (7th cir.), Chgo., 1973-74; from assoc. to ptnr. Schiff Hardin & Waite, 1974-85; ptnr. Adams, Fox, Adelstein & Rosen, 1985-89, Schopf & Weiss, Chgo., 1989—. Pres. Chgo. Internat. Dispute Resolution Assn.; trustee Sta. WTTW Channel 11, Chgo., 1976-81, Kendall Coll., Evanston, Ill., 1980-92, WBEZ, Chgo. Pub. Radio, 1992-98, Ill. Humanities Coun., 1997—. Mem. adv. com. Rep. Nat. Com., Washington, 1976-81; alt. del. Rep. Nat. Conv., Detroit, 1980; pres. Chgo. Lincoln Inn of Ct., 1994-96; mem. adv. com. Northwestern U. Sch. Law Ctr. for Internat. Human Rights. Mem. ABA, Chgo. Bar Assn. (chair internat. and fgn. law com., chair fed. civil procedure com.), Am. Law Inst., Chgo. Coun. Fgn. Rels., Am. Coun. Germany, Ripon Soc. (chmn. 1975-76), Univ. Club, Econ. Club Chgo., Michigan Shores Club. Republican. Home: 1310 Sheridan Rd Wilmette IL 60091-1834 Office: Schopf & Weiss 312 W Randolph St Chicago IL 60606-1721 E-mail: baugher@sw.com.

BAUGHMAN, R(OBERT) PATRICK, lawyer; b. Zanesville, Ohio, Nov. 18, 1938; s. Robert G. and Kathryn E. B.; m. Joyce Hall, June 17, 1959; 1 dau., Patricia. B.S., Ohio State U., 1960, J.D., 1963. Bar: Ohio 1963. Assoc. firm Sindell & Sindell, Cleve., 1964-71, Jones, Day, Reavis & Pogue, Cleve., 1972-73; asst. atty. gen. State of Ohio, Columbus, 1971-72; pres., prin. firm Baughman & Assocs., Cleve., 1973—. Mem. ABA, Ohio Bar Assn., Cuyahoga County Bar Assn., Nat. Council Self-Insurers, Internat. Assn. Indsl. Accident Bds. and Commns., Internat. Platform Assn. Episcopalian. Club: Columbia Hills Country. Office: Baughman & Assocs 55 Public Sq Ste 2215 Cleveland OH 44113-1996

BAUKOL, RONALD OLIVER, company executive; b. Chgo., Aug. 11, 1937; s. Oliver Peter and Clara Marie (Haugstad) B.; m. Gay Lynn Gollan, Aug. 29, 1959; children: David, Andrew, Kathlyn. BSChemE, Iowa State U., 1959; MSChemE, MIT, 1960. Engr., group leader Procter & Gamble, Cin., 1960-66; lab. supr. 3M Co., 1966-70; White House fellow Washington, 1970-71; dept. mgr. dental, new enterprises, diagnostic depts. Minn. Mining & Mfg. Co., St. Paul, 1972-82; v.p., gen. mgr. 3M/Riker Labs., 1982-86; mng. dir., CEO 3M U.K. PLC, 1986-89; mng. dir. 3M Ireland, 1988-89; group v.p. Pharms. and Dental Products Group, 3M Co., St. Paul, 1989-90, Med. Products Group, 1990-91; v.p. Asia Pacific, 1991-94, Asia Pacific Can. and L.Am., 1994-95, exec. v.p. internat. ops., 1995—2002. Bd. dirs. Graco, Inc., Mpls., 3M, The Toro Co.; mem. exec. bd. Internat. C.of C., 2001-. Chmn. bd. ARC St. Paul, 1979-81, dir. regional blood com., 1972-86; mem. alumni assn. bd. dirs. Iowa State U., 1974-76, gov. found., 1990—; trustee Minn. Med. Found., 1990-93, Children's Hosp., St. Paul, 1993-95; trustee U.S. Coun. Internat. Bus., 1994—, vice-chmn., 2000—; mem. adv. coun. U. St. Thomas Ctr. Health and Med. Affairs, Minn., 1990-97, internat. programs adv. coun. Carlson Sch. Mgmt., U. Minn., 1998—; bd. dirs. Children's Health Care Found., St. Paul, 1995-97. Named Outstanding Young Alumnus, Iowa State U., 1969. Mem. Brit. Inst. Mgmt. (companion 1988-89), Internat. C. of C. (exec. bd. 2001—). Methodist. Avocation: tennis. Home: 70 Spruce St Saint Paul MN 55115-1947 Office: 3050 Minn World Trade Ctr 30 Seventh St East Saint Paul MN 55101

BAUM, BERNARD HELMUT, sociologist, educator; b. Giessen, Germany, Apr. 18, 1926; arrived in U.S., 1933, naturalized, 1934; s. Theodor and Beatrice (Klee) Baum; m. Barbara B. Eisendrath, June 13, 1953; children: David Michael, Jonathan Klee, Victoria, Lisa Baum Kritz. PhB, U. Chgo., 1948, MA, 1953, PhD, 1959. Qualifications rating examiner, bd. adviser U.S. CSC, Chgo., 1952-54; instr. human relations, psychology Chgo. Police Officers' Coll. Edn. Program, 1955-59; dir. orgnl. analysis CNA Ins., 1960-66; assoc. prof. mgmt. and sociology U. Ill., 1966-69, assoc. dean Coll. Bus. Adminstrn., 1967-68, prof. mgmt. and sociology, 1969—, prof. health policy and adminstrn. Sch. Pub. Health, 1973—, dir. health policy and adminstrn. Sch. Pub. Health, 1977-92. Lectr. Roosevelt U., 1955—66, U. Chgo., 1961—68, Northwestern U., 1968—70, U. Colo., 1971—76; mem. spkr.'s bur. Adult Edn. Coun. Greater Chgo., 1963—76; team leader joint evaluation mission UN devel. program WHO primary health care and health mgmt. devel. projects in South Pacific, 1985; vis. scholar Chiang Mai U., Thailand, 1988. Author: (book) Decentralization of Authority in a Bureaucracy, 1961; author: (with others) Basic for Business, 1968; contbr. articles to profl. jours.; editor (with others): (book) Intervention: the Management Use of Organizational Research, 1975. Bd. dirs. Selfhelp Home for Aged, Chgo. Decorated Legion of Merit, Bronze Star; recipient Bus. Adminstrn. and Social Sci. Doctoral Dissertaion award, Ford Found., 1960. Mem.: APHA, AAAS, Acad. Mgmt., Am. Acad. Polit. and Social Sci., Am. Sociol. Assn., Sigma Xi. Office: U Ill Sch Pub Health M/C 923 Chicago IL 60680 Home: Apt 3B 2610 Central St Evanston IL 60201-1354 E-mail: bhbaum@uic.edu.

BAUMAN, JOHN DUANE, lawyer; b. Kaskaskia, Ill., Aug. 22, 1930; s. Louis Wells and Veronica Genevieve (Schmerbauch) B.; m. Avis Crysella Moore, Sept. 15, 1956; children: Mark Duane, Thomas Jon, Jeffery Paul. BA, S.E. Mo. U., 1952; JD, Washington U., St. Louis, 1957. Bar: Mo. 1957, Ill. 1957. Assoc. Baker, Kagy & Wagner, East Saint Louis, Ill., 1957-62; ptnr. Wagner, Bertrand, Bauman & Schmieder, Belleville, 1962-86, Hinshaw & Culbertson, Chgo. and Belleville, 1986—. Bd. dirs. Breeders Cup/Nat. Thoroughbred Racing Assn. Pres. Ill. Thorooughbred Breeders & Owners Found., 2001—02; gen. counsel Okaw Valley coun. Boy Scouts Am., 1980—90; bd. dir. Breeders Cup/Nat. Thoroughbred Racing Assn. With U.S. Army, 1952—54. Mem. ABA, Ill. Bar Assn., Internat. Assn. Ins. Counsel (state membership chmn.), Assn. of Def. Trial

Counsel (pres. 1975-76), St. Clair County Bar Assn. (pres. 1972-73), Horsemen's Benevolent and Protective Assn. (v.p. 1989-98), Ill. Thoroughbred Breeders and Owners Found. (bd. dirs. 1999-2002, v.p. 1996-99, sec.-treas. 1999-2000, pres. 2000—), Bradenton Country Club, St. Clair Country Club (pres. 1972-74), Paducah Country Club, Elks, Mo. Athletic Club (pres. emeritus 1998). Roman Catholic. Avocations: horse racing, golf. Office: Hinshaw & Culbertson PO Box 509 521 W Main St Belleville IL 62220-1533 E-mail: jb222555@aol.com.

BAUMAN, JOHN E., JR. chemistry educator; b. Kalamazoo, Jan. 18, 1933; s. John E. and Teresa A. (Wauchek) B.; m. Barbara Curry, June 6, 1964; children— John, Catherine, Amy B.S., U. Mich., 1955, M.S., 1960, Ph.D., 1962. Chemist Midwest Research Inst., Kansas City, Mo., 1955-58; research assoc. U. Mich., Ann Arbor, 1958-61; prof. chemistry U. Mo., Columbia, 1961-97, prof. emeritus, 1997—. Active Mo. Symphony Soc. Recipient Faculty Alumni award, 1969, Amoco Teaching award, 1975, Purple Chalk award, 1980, all U. Mo. Mem. Am. Chem. Soc. (nat. lectr.), Mo. Acad. Sci., U. Mo. Retirees Assn. (pres. 2000—), Kiwanis, Sigma Xi, Alpha Chi Sigma. Roman Catholic Home: 3703 S Woods Edge Rd Columbia MO 65203-6607 Office: Univ Mo 125 Chemistry Building Columbia MO 65211-7600 E-mail: baumanj@missouri.edu.

BAUMAN, SUSAN JOAN MAYER, mayor, lawyer; b. N.Y.C., Mar. 2, 1945; d. Curt H. J. and Carola (Rosenau) Mayer; m. Ellis A. Bauman, Dec. 29, 1968. BS, U. Wis., 1965, JD, MS, 1981; MS, U. Chgo., 1966. Bar: Wis. 1981, U.S. Dist. Ct. (we. dist.) Wis. 1981, U.S. Ct. Appeals (7th cir.) 1983, U.S. Dist. Ct. (ea. dist.) Wis. 1985. Tchr. Madison (Wis.) Pub. Sch., 1970-78; research asst. U. Wis. Law Sch., Madison, 1981; ptnr. Thomas, Parsons, Schaefer & Bauman, 1981-84; sole practice, 1984-85; ptnr. Bauman & Massing, 1985-87; pvt. practice, 1987-97; mayor City of Madison, 1997—. Alderman Madison Common Coun., 1985-97, coun. pres., 1989-90; commr. equal opportunities com. City of Madison, 1985-89; mem. Econ. Devel. Commn., 1986-87, chmn. human resources com., 1987-90, mem. affirmative action com., 1988-93; mem. Cmty. Action Commn., 1988-97, pres., 1991-96; mem. Pub. Health Commn., 1991-97, Monona Terr. Conv. and Cmty. Ctr. Bd., 1993-97; pres. South Madison Health and Family Ctr., Inc., 1993-97; bd. visitors U. Wis. Coll. Letters and Scis., Madison, 1997—; mem. exec. com. Wis. Alliance Cities, 1996—; mem. adv. bd. U.S. Conf. Mayors, 1999—. Mem. Wis. Bar Assn., Dane County Bar Assn., Wis. Indsl. Rels. Alumni Assn. (pres. 1985-86), Madison Civics Club. Democrat. Avocations: knitting, reading, backpacking, cross-country skiing. Home: 430 W Main St #309 Madison WI 53703 Office: Office of the Mayor 210 Martin Luther King Blvd Madison WI 53709-0001 E-mail: sjmbauman@aol.com.

BAUMAN-BORK, MARCEIL, health services administrator; Grad., Midland Luth. Coll., U. Nebr. Bd. cert. Am. Bd. Psychiatry & Neurology. Resident Menninger Sch. Psychiatry & Mental Health; dir. gen. residency program Menninger. Presenter in field. Office: Menninger PO Box 829 Topeka KS 66601-0829

BAUMANN, DANIEL E. newspaper executive; b. Milw., Apr. 10, 1937; s. Herbert F. and Agnes V. (Byrne) B.; m. Karen R. Weinkauf, Apr, 29, 1961; children: James W., Jennifer R., Colin D. BJ, U. Wis., 1958, MA in Polit. Sci., Cert. in Russian Area Studies, U. Wis., 1962. Reporter South Milwaukee (Wis.) Voice Jour., 1958-59, East St. Louis (Ill.) Jour., 1959-60; pub. relations rep. Credit Union Nat. Assn., Washington, 1962-64; reporter Paddock Publs., Inc., Arlington Heights, Ill., 1964-66, mng. editor, 1966-68, exec. editor, 1968-70, editor and pub. Paddock Circle newspapers, 1970-75, v.p., editor, 1975-83, sr. v.p., gen. mgr., editor, 1983-86, pres., editor, 1986-90, dir., 1986—, pres., chief operating officer, 1990-98, publ., CEO, 1998—. Mem. High Tech. Corridors Coun., Palatine, Ill., 1986—; bd. dirs. Greater Woodfield Conv. and Visitors Bur., Schaumburg, Ill., 1985-93. With USNR. Recipient William Alan White award U. Kans., 1976. Mem. Newspaper Assn. Am., Am. Soc. Newspaper Editors, Internat. Newspaper Advt. and Mktg. Execs., Soc. Profl. Journalists, Chgo. Headline Club (Peter Lisagor award 1983), Chgo. Assn. Dir. Mktg., Sigma Delta Chi. Avocations: photography, travel. scuba diving. Office: Paddock Publs Daily Herald 155 E Algonquin Rd Arlington Heights IL 60005-4617

BAUMANN, EDWARD ROBERT, environmental engineering educator; b. Rochester, N.Y., May 12, 1921; s. John Carl and Lillie Minnie (Roth) B.; m. Mary A. Massey, June 15, 1946; children: Betsy Louise, Philip Robert. BSCE, U. Mich., 1944; BS in San. Engring, U. Ill., 1945, MS, 1947, PhD, 1954; NSF faculty fellow, U. Durham, Eng., 1959-60. Research assoc. U. Ill., 1947-53; assoc. prof. civil engring. Iowa State U., 1953-56, prof., 1956-91, Anson Marston Disting. prof. engring., 1972-91, emeritus Disting. prof., 1991—. Cons. Water Quality Office of EPA, Culligan Internat., Lakeside Engring. Co., Bolton & Menk, many cities and industries. Author: Sewerage and Sewage Treatment, 1958; mem. editorial bd.: Internat. Jour. Air and Water Pollution, London, 1960-67; asst. editor: San. Engr. Newsletter of ASCE, 1962-74; contbr. articles to profl. jours. V.p., treas. Water Found., Inc., 1978-83; mem. Iowa Bd. Health, 1975-76, Iowa State U. Rsch. Found., 1975-78, 83-91. With C.E., AUS, 1944-46. Recipient George B. Gascoigne medal Water Pollution Control Fedn., 1962, 80, Publs. award, 1963, Purification divsn. award Am. Water Works Assn., 1965, Anson Marston medal Iowa Engring. Soc., 1966, Disting. Svc. award, 1968, Gold medal Filtration Soc. Eng., 1970, Bedell award, 1977, Rsch. award, 1978, Philip F. Morgan award Water Pollution Control Fedn., 1986; named Water Works Man of Yr., 1972, Disting. Alumni award U. Ill. Alumni Assn., 1992. Fellow ASCE (life), Iowa Acad. Scis. (disting. sci. 1990), Am. Filtration Separations Soc. (F.M. Tiller award 1994); mem. NSPE (nat. bd. dirs.), AAUP, Am. Water Works Assn. (hon., life, internat. bd. dirs. 1978-80), Assn. Environ. Engring. Profs. (pres. 1967-70, 86-87, Nalco award, Founders award 1991), Am. Soc. Engring. Edn., Am. Inst. Chem. Engrs., Am. Acad. Environ. Engring. (diplomate), Filtration Soc. (Eng., bd. dirs., tech. editor, vice chmn. 1993, chmn. 1994, Fluid/Particle Separation Jour.), Rotary, Sigma Xi, Phi Kappa Phi (Centennial medal 1997), Chi Epsilon. Home: 1627 Crestwood Cir Ames IA 50010-5520

BAUMER, MARTHA ANN, minister; b. Cleve., Sept. 12, 1938; d. Harry William and Olga Erna (Zenk) B. BA, Lakeland Coll., 1960; MA, U. Wyo., 1963; MDiv, United Theol. Sem., 1973; D Ministry, Eden Theol. Sem., 1990. Parish minister Congl. United Ch. of Christ, Amery, Wis., 1973-79; organizing minister United Ch. of Santa Fe (N.Mex.), 1979-85; conf. minister Ill. South Conf. United Ch. of Christ, Highland, Ill., 1985-93; pastor Windsor (Wis.) United Ch. of Christ, 1993-99; vis. prof. pastoral studies Eden Theol. Sem., St. Louis, 1999—. Trustee pension bds. United Ch. of Christ, N.Y.C., 1983—, mem., chair exec. coun., 1977-83; del. World Coun. Chs., 1961, 83; trustee Eden Theol. Sem., St. Louis, 1990-99. Contbr. articles to profl. publs. Mem. Coun. of Conf. Ministers United Ch. of Christ (sec.-treas. 1989-93). Home: 814 Amherst Dr East Alton IL 62024 Office: Eden Theol Sem 475 E Lockwood Ave Saint Louis MO 63119-3124 E-mail: mbaumer@eden.edu.

BAUMGARDNER, EDWARD, financial company executive; CEO, pres. Potters Fin. Corp., East Liverpool, Ohio, 1994—. Office: Potters Fin Corp 519 Broadway St East Liverpool OH 43920-3137 Fax: 330-385-3508.

BAUMGARDNER, JOHN DWANE, manufacturing company executive; b. Minburn, Iowa, Aug. 21, 1940; s. John Henry and Oda Lee Baumgardner; m. Shirley Ann Hoene, Sept. 4, 1965 (dec. Oct. 1985); children: Kenneth Mark, Sandra Lynn; m. Kathy Lynn Ende, May 2, 1987. BS in Physics, U. Mo., 1963; PhD in Optics, U. Rochester, 1969. Research asst. McDonnell Douglas, St. Louis, 1963-65; mgr. research and devel. Donnelly Corp., Holland, Mich., 1969-75, mgr. advanced devel., 1975-78, v.p. tech., 1978-80, chmn., chief exec. officer, pres., 1980—. Bd. dirs. Scanlon Plan Assocs., Nat. Bank of Detroit-Grand Rapids, Holland Econ. Devel. Corp. Bd. dirs. Econ. Alliance for Mich. Mem. Am. Mgmt. Assn. Republican. Club: Econ. Grand Rapids. Office: Donnelly Corp 49 W THIRD St Holland MI 49423

BAUMGARDNER, MICHAEL H. marketing professional; BA, MS, PhD in Social Psychology, Ohio State U. Consumer sci. specialist FDA, Washington; with Burke, Inc., Cin., 1979—, pres. Lectr. quantitative methods and psychology, Ohio State U., Ohio Dominican Coll., Columbus; spkr. in field. Contbr. articles to profl. publs., including Jour. Personality and Social Psychology, Psychol. Rev., others. Office: Burke Inc 805 Central Ave Fl 5 Cincinnati OH 45202-5747

BAUMGARDT, BILLY RAY, association executive, agriculturist; b. Lafayette, Ind., Jan. 17, 1933; s. Raymond P. and Mildred L. (Cordray) B.; m. D. Elaine Blain, June 8, 1952; children: Pamela K. Baumgardt Farley, Teresa Jo Baumgardt Adolfsen, Donald Ray. B.S. in Agr., Purdue U., 1955, M.S., 1956; Ph.D., Rutgers U., 1959. From asst. to assoc. prof. U. Wis., Madison, 1959-67; prof. animal nutrition Pa. State U., University Park, 1967-70, head dept. dairy and animal sci., 1970-79, assoc. dir. agrl. expt. sta., 1979-80; dir. agrl. research, assoc. dean Purdue U., West Lafayette, Ind., 1980-98; exec. v.p. Am. Registry Profl. Animal Scientists, Savoy, Ill., 1998—. Contbr. chpts. to books, articles to sci. jours. Recipient Wilkinson award Pa. State U., 1979. Fellow AAAS, Am. Dairy Sci. Assn. (Nutrition Rsch. award 1966, pres. 1984-85, award of Honor 1993); mem. Am. Inst. Nutrition, Am. Soc. Animal Sci., Nat. Agrl. Biotech. Coun. (chair 1993-94), Rotary, Sigma Xi. Home and Office: 2614 Trace 26 West Lafayette IN 47906-1888

BAUMGARDT, JUSTI MICHELLE, former soccer player; b. Federal Way, Wash., July 22, 1975; Student in sociology, U. Portland. Mem. U.S. Women's Nat. Soccer Team, 1993—, playing in Nike Victory Tour, St. Charles (Ill.), 1997, Nordic Cup, Denmark, 1993, Germany, 1994. Named Athlete of Yr. Seattle Times 1993, also Player of Yr. state of Wash.; 2-time H.S. All-Am.; named Most Valuable Player, U. Portland, 1994; voted WCC Player of Yr., 1996. Office: US Soccer Fedn 1801-1811 S Prairie Ave Chicago IL 60616

BAUMGART, JAMES RAYMOND, state legislator; b. Dec. 22, 1938; 1 child. BA, U. Wis., Stevens Point. State assemblyman dist. 26 State of Wis., 1990-99; mem. Wis. Senate from 9th dist., Madison, 1999—. Outdoor writer. Mem. Sheboygan County Izaak Walton League (pres.). Democrat. Address: 722 N 26th St Sheboygan WI 53081-3727

BAUMGARTNER, JOHN H. refining and petroleum products company executive; b. 1936; married. With Clark Oil & Refining Corp., Milw., 1956-82, retail sales rep., 1960-65, dist. mgr., 1965-72, regional mgr., 1972-74, v.p. retail mktg., asst. gen. sales mgr., 1974-75, sr. v.p. mktg., 1975-78, exec. v.p., 1978-82; pres. J.H. Baumgartner Enterprises, Brookfield, Wis., 1982—; v.p., owner Robert Kidd & Assocs. Inc., 1990—. Served with USMC, 1954-56.

BAUMGARTNER, REUBEN ALBERT, retired school administrator; b. Pearl City, Ill., Dec. 30, 1912; s. Albert Centennial and Laura Anna (Hummermeir) B.; m. Arleigh Camille Mears, June 27, 1942 (dec. Aug. 1969); 1 child, Richard. BA, U. Ill., 1934, MA, 1935; postgrad., U. Iowa, 1938, 41, 55. Math. instr. Polo (Ill.) High Sch., 1935-38, N.D. State U., Fargo, 1938-40; dept. head, math. instr. Freeport (Ill.) High Sch., 1940-56; dir. adult edn. Freeport Pub. Schs., 1949-55; prin. Freeport High Sch., 1956-72; curriculum dir. Freeport Pub. Schs., 1972-77. Contbr. articles to profl. jours. State coord. 55 Alive/Mature Driving, Ill., 1985-88; pres. Stephenson County Sr. Ctr., Freeport, 1975-77; mem. Sec. of State Sr. Adv. Com., Ill., 1985-88. Lt. USN, 1942-46. Mem. Kiwanis (pres. 1954-55, lt. gov. 1975-76). Presbyterian. Avocations: reading, swimming, walking. Home: 1729 W Parkview Dr Freeport IL 61032-4661

BAUMHART, RAYMOND CHARLES, Roman Catholic church administrator; b. Chgo., Dec. 22, 1923; s. Emil and Florence (Weidner) B. BS, Northwestern U., 1945; PhL, Loyola U., 1952, STL, 1958; MBA, Harvard U., 1953; DBA, Harvard, 1963; LLD (hon.), Ill. Coll., 1977; DHL (hon.), Scholl Coll. Podiatric Medicine, 1983, Rush U., Chgo., 1987, Northwestern U., 1993, Xavier U., Cin., 1994, Ill. Benedictine Coll., 1994. Joined Jesuit Order, 1946; ordained priest Roman Cath. Ch., 1957. Asst. prof. mgmt. Loyola U., Chgo., 1962-64, dean Sch. Bus. Adminstrn., 1964-66, exec. v.p., acting v.p. Med. Ctr., 1968-70, pres., 1970-93; cons. to Cardinal George, Cath. Archdiocese of Chgo., 2000—. Alfred Ring lectr. U. Fla., 1988; John and Mildred Wright lectr. Fairfield U., 1992; D. B. Reinhart lectr. Viterbo Coll., 2000; bd. dirs. Ceres Food Group, Inc. Author: An Honest Profit, 1968, (with Thomas Garrett) Cases in Business Ethics, 1968, (with Thomas McMahon) The Brewer-Wholesaler Relationship, 1969; corr. editor: America, 1965-70. Trustee St. Louis U., 1967-72, Boston Coll., 1968-71, Cristo Rey Prep. Sch.; bd. dirs. Coun. Better Bus. Burs., 1971-77, Cath. Health Alliance Met. Chgo., 1986-93; mem. U.S. Bishops and Pres.'s Com. on Higher Edn., 1980-84, Jobs for Met. Chgo., 1984-85, Chgo. Health Care Industry, 1990-94. Decorated cavalier Order of Merit, Italy, 1971, commendatore, 1994; recipient Rale medallion Boston Coll., 1976, Daniel Lord S.J. award Loyola Acad., Wilmette, Ill., 1992, Mary Potter Humanitarian award Little Company of Mary Hosp., Ill., 1993, Sword of Loyola Loyola U., Chgo., 1993, Theodore Hesburgh award Assn. Cath. Colls. and Univs., 1995; John W. Hill fellow Harvard U., 1961-62, Cambridge Ctr. for Social Studies Rsch. fellow, 1966-68. Mem. Comml. Club, Mid-Am. Club, Tavern Club. Home: 6525 N Sheridan Rd Chicago IL 60626-5344 E-mail: rbaumhart@archdiocese-chgo.org.

BAUNER, RUTH ELIZABETH, library administrator, reference librarian; b. Quincy, Ill. d. John Carl and M. Irene (Nutt) B. BS in Edn., Western Ill. U., 1950; MS, U. Ill., 1956; postgrad., So. Ill. U., 1974, PhD, 1978. Asst. res. libr. Western Ill. U., Macomb, 1950; tchr., libr. Sandwich (Ill.) Twp. High Sch., 1950-54; circulation dept. asst. U. Ill. Libr., Urbana, 1955; asst. edn. libr. So. Ill. U., Carbondale, 1956-63, acting edn. libr., 1963-64, edn. and psychology libr., 1965-93, assoc. prof. curriculum and instrn. dept., 1971-93; coord. freshman yr. experience program, vis. assoc. prof. Coll. of Liberal Arts, 1994-96. Dir. Grad. Residence Ctr. Librs., So. Ill. U., 1973-79; subject matter expert Learning Resources Svc. Interactive Video, Carbondale, 1990-91, also scriptwriter. Co-author: The Teacher's Library, 1966; contbr. articles to profl. jours. Pres. alumni constituency bd. Coll. Edn., Carbondale, 1988—89; mem. Carbondale Bd. Ethics, 1989—2001; tchr. I Can Read Program, 2001—; mem. Carbondale Citizens Adv. Commn., 1999—2001; bd. dirs. So. Ill. U. chpt. UN, 1985—86, 1994—97, So. Ill. Learning in Retirement, So. Ill. U. Emeritus Assn., Jackson County AARP, 1997—99. Recipient Luck Has Nothing To Do With It award Oryx Press, 1993. Mem. ALA, AAUP (v.p. So. Ill. U. chpt. 1972-73), AAUW (univ. rep. Carbondale br. 1988-89), Assn. Coll. and Rsch. Librs. (chmn. edn. and behavioral scis. sect. 1976-77, Most Active Mem. award 1968-93), Ill. Libr. Assn., Phi Delta Kappa, Phi Kappa Phi, Delta Kappa Gamma. Office: 1206 W Freeman St Carbondale IL 62901-2351 E-mail: rbauner@siu.edu.

BAXTER, ELAINE, retired state official; b. Chgo., Jan. 16, 1933; d. Clarence Arthur and Margaret (Clark) Bland; m. Harry Youngs Baxter, Oct. 2, 1954; children: Katherine, Harry, John. BA, U. Ill., 1954; teaching cert., Iowa Wesleyan Coll., 1970; MS, U. Iowa, 1978. Tchr. history Burlington (Iowa) H.S., 1971-72; mem. Burlington City Coun., 1973-75; sr. liaison officer HUD, Washington, 1979-81; mem. Iowa Ho. of Reps., Des Moines, 1982-86; sec. state State of Iowa, 1987-94; ret., 1994. Nat. co-chmn. Dukakis-Bentsen campaign, 1988; del. Dem. Nat. Conv., Atlanta, 1988, mem. at large Dem. Nat. Com.; mem. Exec. Coun. and Voter Registration Commn.; chmn. State Records Commn., State Ins. Commn., Iowa; internat. del. Nat. Dem. Inst. for Internat. Affairs to Paraguay, 1989; hon. res. chmn. Iowa chpt. Am. Heart Assn., 1989; pres. Heritage Truste, 1997-99, Hist. Burlington; bd. dirs. Iowa Alliance for Hist. Preservation,1998— Humanities Iowa, Gov.'s Mansion Soc. Found.; pres. Terrace Hill Soc. 2000—; candidate U.S. Ho. of Reps. from 3d dist. Iowa, 1992, 94. RJR Nabisco fellow to Sr. Execs. in State and Local Govt., J.F. Kennedy Sch. Govt., Harvard U., 1988. Avocations: gardening, historic preservation. Home: 1016 N 4th St Burlington IA 52601-4803 E-mail: elainbax@interlinklc.net.

BAXTER, RANDOLPH, judge; b. Columbia, Tenn., Aug. 15, 1946; s. Lenon Pillow and Willie Alexine (Hood) B.; m. Yvonne Marie Williams, Nov. 26, 1980; children: Mark, Melissa, Scott; m. Rebecca Terrell, Oct. 10, 1968; (div. Apr. 1976); 1 child, Kimberly Lynn. BS, Tuskegee Inst., 1967; JD, U. Akron, 1974. Bar: Ohio 1976, U.S. Dist. Ct. (no. dist.) Ohio 1978, U.S. Ct. Appeals (6th cir.) 1978, U.S. Supreme Ct. 1980. Salary analyst B.F. Goodrich Co., Akron, 1971-73; courts planner Criminal Justice Commn., Akron, 1973-76; dep. dir., pub. service dept. City Akron, 1976-78; asst. U.S. atty. U.S. Dept. Justice, Cleve., 1978-85, chief appellate litigation, 1982-85; judge U.S. Bankruptcy Court (no. dist.) Ohio, 1985-96, judge bankruptcy appellate panel U.S. Ct. Appeals for 6th Cir., 1996—; instr. real estate law Kent State U., 1974-78; adj. prof. U. Akron Coll. Law; v.p., dir. Alpha Phi Alpha Homes, Inc., Akron, 1971-85. Bd. dirs. Western Res. Hist. Soc., 1988-92, Christian Radio Fellowship, Tuskegee U., 1989—, Akron Auto Assn., 1990—, Children's Svcs. Inc., 1993—, Salvation Army, Akron, 1993—, Emmanuel Christian Acad., 1994—, Stan Hywet Found., 1995—, trustee, 1995—. Served to capt. AUS, 1968- 71, Vietnam. Named Man of Yr., Akron Jaycees, 1977; recipient Disting. Service award City Akron, 1978, Spl. Achievement award U.S. Dept. Justice, 1981, 82, Disting. Vets. award Fed. Exec. Bd. Cleve., 1982. Mem. ABA, Akron Barristers Club (pres. 1978-79), Fed. Bar Assn., Nat. Bar Assn., Akron Bar Assn., Nat. Conf. Bankruptcy Judges, Am. Bankruptcy Inst., Comml. Law League Am., Akron City Club, Alpha Phi Alpha. Office: US Bankruptcy Ct Key Tower 127 Public Sq Ste 3205 Cleveland OH 44114-1216

BAXTER, TIMOTHY C. prosecutor; b. Prairie du Chien, Wis., Sept. 2, 1964; s. Gary Lee and Shirley Esther (Volenec) B.; m. Margaret J. Baxter, May 23, 1992. BS, U. Wis., River Falls, 1987; JD, William Mitchell Coll. Law, St. Paul, 1990. Bar: Wis. 1990. Dist. atty. Crawford County, Praire du Chien, 1991—. Mem. ABA, Wis. Bar Assn., Jaycees (Prairie du Chien chpt., sec. 1992, pres. 1994). Avocations: outdoor activities, reading, wood-working. Office: Crawford County Dist Atty Office 220 N Beaumont Rd Prairie Du Chien WI 53821-1405

BAYER, GARY RICHARD, advertising executive; b. St. Louis, Mar. 15, 1941; s. Kenneth Joseph and Ruth Margarite (Johnson) B.; m. Jeanette Marie Stis, July 13, 1963; children: Gregory Scott, Keith Russell, Kristen Holly. BA, Washington U., 1963. Copywriter Adult Edn. Council of Greater St. Louis, St. Louis, 1962, D'Arcy Advt. Co., St. Louis, 1963-67; from v.p. creative dir. to sr. v.p. exec. creative dir. D'Arcy MacManus & Masius, 1968-80; pres. Adcom. div. Quaker Oats Co., Chgo., 1980-85; pres., chief ops. officer Backer & Spielvogel Chgo., Inc., 1985-87; chmn., CEO, chief creative officer Bayer Bess Vanderwarker Advt., 1987-96; exec. v.p. devel. True North Comm., 1996—. Chmn. Vols. Am., Ill. Mem. Am. Assn. Advt. Agys. (gov.-at-large 1988-95, sec.-treas. bd. dirs. 1991-92, bd. dirs. 1993-95, vice chair Ill. bd. govs.), Chgo. Advt. Fedn. (pres. 1990-93), Am. Advt. Fedn. (Hall of Fame judge 1994-95), Univ. Club, Met. Club, Phi Beta Kappa, Omicron Delta Kappa. Republican. Avocations: music, writing, travel, tennis, certified scuba diver. Home: 1010 E Illinois Rd Lake Forest IL 60045-2410 Office: True North Comms 101 E Erie St Chicago IL 60611-2812

BAYH, EVAN, senator, former governor; b. Terre Haute, Ind., Dec. 26, 1955; s. Birch Evans Jr. and Marvella (Hern) B.; married. BS in Bus. Econs., Ind. U., 1978; JD, U. Va., 1981. Atty. Bingham, Summers, Welsh & Spilman; sec. of state State of Ind., Indpls., 1987-89, gov., 1989-96; ptnr. Baker & Daniel Assocs., 1997-98; U.S. senator from Ind., 1999—. Chmn. State Recount Commn. & Corp. Law com.; mem. Nat. Edn. Goals Panel & Nat. Assessment Edn. Panel; chmn. Edn. Commn. States; vice chmn. Nat. Govs. Assn. Task Force Workforce Devel. Democrat. Office: US Senate 463 Russell Senate Office Bldg Washington DC 20510-0001 also: 10 W Market St Ste 1650 Indianapolis IN 46204-2934

BAYLESS, CHARLES T. business executive; Wtih Archer Daniels Midland Co., Decatur, Ill., 1957—, exec. v.p., 1998—, spl. asst. to CEO, 1999—. Office: Archer Daniels Midland Co 4666 E Faries Pkwy Decatur IL 62526-5666

BAYLESS, RICK, chef; b. Oklahoma City, 1953; m. Deann Bayless. Host PBS TV series Cooking Mexican, 1978—79; owner, chef Frontera Grill, Chgo., 1987—, Topolombampo, Chgo., 1989—; host PBS series Mexico One Plate at a Time With Rick Bayless, 2000—. N. Cheffs Collaborative 2000; ptnr. Frontera Foods, 1995. Author: Authentic Mexican, 1987, Rick Bayless's Mexican Kitchen, 1996, Salsas That Cook, 1999; (appeared on TV programs): Today, Good Morning Am., This Morning, Martha Stewart Living, Cooking Live, In Julia's Kitchen with Master Chefs, Great Chefs of Am., others; contbr. to numerous food and cooking publs.; contbg. editor: Saveur. Named Best New Chef of 1988, Food and Wine mag., Best Am. Chef: Midwest, James Beard Found., 1991; recipient Nat. Chef of Yr. award, 1995, Chef of Yr. award, Internat. Assn. Clinary Profls., 1995, Humanitarian of Yr., James Beard Found., 1998. Office: Frontera Grill 445 N Clark St Chicago IL 60610

BAYLOR, DON EDWARD, professional baseball manager; b. Austin, Tex., June 28, 1949; s. George Edward and Lillian Joyce B.; m. Rebecca Giles, Dec. 12, 1987; 1 child by previous marriage, Don Edward. Student, Miami-Dade Jr. Coll., Miami, Fla., Blinn Jr. Coll., Brenham, Tex. With Balt. Orioles, 1970-76, Oakland Athletics, 1976, 88, California Angels, 1976-82, N.Y. Yankees, 1983-86, Boston Red Sox, 1986-87, Minnesota Twins, 1987; mem. World Series Championship Team, 1987; mgr. Colorado Rockies, Denver, 1992-98; hitting/batting coach Atlanta Braves, 1999; mgr., coach Chgo. Cubs, 1999—. Set new career record for hit by pitches; hit safely in 12 consecutive Am. League Championship Series games. Author: (with Claire Smith) Don Baylor, Nothing But the Truth: A Baseball Life, 1989. Chmn. nat. sports Cystic Fibrosis Found. Recipient Designated Hitter of Yr. award, 1985, 86, Roberto Clemente award, 1985; named Am. League's Most Valuable Player, 1979, Sporting News Player of Yr., 1979; player All-Star Game, 1979; named Nat. League Mgr. of Yr. Sporting News, 1995, Baseball Writers Assn. Am., 1995. Achievements include being a holder of Am. League playoff record most RBI (10), 1982, Am. League single season record most times hit by pitch (35), 1986. Office: Chicago Cubs 1060 W Addison St Chicago IL 60613-4397 also: Major League Baseball Players Assn 805 3d Ave New York NY 10022-7513*

BAYLOR, RICHARD C. financial company executive; m. Maura Baylor; 3 children. BS in Indsl. Edn., Bowling Green State U. With State Savs. Bank, Columbus, Ohio, 1989-98; exec. v.p., COO Camco Fin. Corp., Cambridge, 1998-2000, pres., COO, 2000—. Mem. Ohio Mortgage Bankers Assn. (v.p. residential lending 1997). Office: Camco Fin Corp 6901 Glenn Hwy Cambridge OH 43725-8685

BAYLY, GEORGE V. manufacturing executive; CEO Ivex Packaging, Lincolnshire, Ill. Office: Ivex Packaging 100 Tri State Dr Lincolnshire IL 60069-4403

BAYM, GORDON ALAN, physicist, educator; b. N.Y.C., July 1, 1935; s. Louis and Lillian B.; children— Nancy, Geoffrey, Michael, Carol. A.B., Cornell U., 1956; A.M., Harvard U., 1957, Ph.D., 1960. Fellow Universitetets Institut for Teoretisk Fysik, Copenhagen, Denmark, 1960-62; lectr. U. Calif., Berkeley, 1962-63; prof. physics U. Ill., Urbana, 1963—. Vis. prof. U. Tokyo and U. Kyoto, 1968, Nordita, Copenhagen, 1970, 76, Niels Bohr Inst., Copenhagen, 1976, U. Nagoya, 1979; vis. scientist Academia Sinica, China, 1979; mem. adv. bd. Inst. Theoretical Physics, Santa Barbara, Calif., 1978-83; mem. subcom. theoretical physics, physics adv. com. NSF, 1980-81, mem. phys. adv. com., 1982-85; mem. nuclear sci. adv. com. Dept. of Energy/NSF, 1982-86, subcom. on theoretical physics; mem. adv. com. physics Los Alamos Nat. Lab., 1988; mem. nat. adv. com. Inst. Nuclear Theory. Author: Lectures on Quantum Mechanics, 1969, Neutron Stars, 1970, Neutron Stars and the Properties of Matter at High Density, 1977, (with L.P. Kadanoff) Quantum Statistical Mechanics, 1962, (with C.J. Pethick) Landau Fermi Liquid Theory: Concepts and Applications, 1991; assoc. editor Nuclear Physics; mem. editorial bd. Procs. Nat. Acad. Scis., 1986-92. Trustee Assoc. U. Inc., 1986-90. Recipient Alexander von Humboldt Found. Sr. U.S. Scientist award, 1983; fellow Am. Acad. Arts and Scis.; Alfred P. Sloan Found. research fellow, 1965-68; NSF postdoctoral fellow, 1960-62 Fellow AAAS, Am. Phys.Soc. (exec. com. div. history of physics 1986-88, 96-97, chair forum history of physics 1994-95, chair-elect 1995-96; mem. NAS (chair physics sect. 1995-98), Am. Astron. Soc., Internat. Astron. Union.

BAYM, NINA, English educator; b. Princeton, N.J., June 14, 1936; d. Leo and Frances (Levinson) Zippin; m. Gordon Baym, June 1, 1958; children— Nancy, Geoffrey; m. Jack Stillinger, May 21, 1971 B.A., Cornell U., 1957; M.A., Harvard U., 1958, Ph.D., 1963. Asst. U. Calif.-Berkeley, 1962-63; instr. U. Ill., Urbana, 1963-67, asst. prof. English, 1967-69, assoc. prof., 1969-72, prof., 1972—, Jubilee prof. liberal arts and scis., 1989—, dir. Sch. Humanities, 1976-87, sr. Univ. scholar, 1985, assoc. Ctr. Advanced Study, 1989-90, permanent prof. Ctr. Advanced Study, 1997—, Swanlund Endowed chair, 1997—. Author: The Shape of Hawthorne's Career, 1976, Woman's Fiction: A Guide to Novels By and About Women in America, 1978, 2d rev. edit., 1993, Novels, Readers and Reviewers: Responses to Fiction in Antebellum America, 1984, The Scarlet Letter: A Reading, 1986, Feminism and American Literary History, 1992, American Women Writers and the Work of History, 1790-1860, 1995, American Women of Letters and the 19th Century Sciences, 2001; gen. editor: Norton Anthology of American Literature; sr. editor Am. Nat. Biography; also author essays, edits., revs.; mem. editl. bd. Am. Quar., New Eng. Quar., Legacy, A Jour. of 19th Century Am. Women Writers, Jour. Aesthetic Edn. Am. Lit., Tulsa Studies in Women's Lit., Am. Studies, Studies Am. Fiction, Am. Periodicals, Hemingway Rev., Resources for Am. Lit. Study, Am. Lit. History, Cambridge U.P. Studies in Am. Lit. and Culture; mem. editl. adv. bd. PMLA. Guggenheim fellow, 1975-76, AAUW hon. fellow, 1975-76, NEH fellow, 1982-83; rec pient Arnold O. Beckman award U. Ill., 1992-93, Hubbell Lifetime Achievement medal, Am. Let. Sect., 2000. Mem. MLA (exec. com. 19th century Am. Lit. divsn., chmn. 1984, chmn. Am. Lit. sect. 1984, Hubbell Lifetime Achievement medal 2000), Am. Studies Assn. (exec. com. 1982-84, nominating com. 1991-93), Am. Lit. Assn., Am. Antiquarian Soc., Mass. Hist. Soc., Nathaniel Hawthorne Soc. (adv. bd.), Mortar Bd., Phi Kappa Phi, Phi Beta Kappa. Office: U Ill Dept English 608 S Wright St Urbana IL 61801-3630 E-mail: Baymnina@uiuc.edu.

BAYMAN, JAMES L. electronics executive; Gen. mgr. Pioneer-Std. Electronics, Inc., Dayton, Ohio, 1969-83, v.p., COO, 1983-84, pres., COO, 1984-95, CeO, 1995—. Office: Pioneer Std Electronics Inc 4800 E 31st St Cleveland OH 44105

BAYNE, DAVID COWAN, priest, legal scholar, law educator; b. Detroit, Jan. 11, 1918; s. David Cowan and Myrtle (Murray) B. AB, U. Detroit, 1939; LLB, Georgetown U., 1947, LLM, 1948; MA, Loyola U., Chgo., 1946, STL, 1953; SJD (grad. fellow), Yale, 1949; LLD (hon.), Creighton U., 1980. Bar: Fed. and D.C. 1948, Mich. 1960, Mo. 1963. Joined Soc. of Jesus, 1941; ordained priest Roman Catholic Ch., 1952; asst. prof. law U. Detroit, 1954-60; acting dean U. Detroit (Law Sch.), 1955-59, dean, 1959-60; research assoc. Nat. Jesuit Research Orgn., Inst. Social Order, St. Louis, 1960-63; vis. lectr. St. Louis U. Law Sch., 1960-63, prof. law, 1963-67; vis. prof. Mich. Law Sch., 1967, Inst. fur Auslandisches und Internationales Wirtschaftrecht, Frankfurt, 1967; prof. U. Iowa Coll. Law, Iowa City, 1967-88, prof. emeritus, 1988—. Vis. prof. U. Koln, Germany, 1970, 74 Author: Conscience, Obligation and the Law, 1966, 2d edit., 1988; The Philosophy of Corporate Control, 1986; editor legal materials; contbr. articles to profl. jours. Achievements include research in corp. law. E-mail: dcbsj@netzero.net., dcbsj@buckeye-express.com.

BAZANT, ZDENEK PAVEL, structural engineering educator, scientist, consultant; b. Prague, Czechoslovakia, Dec. 10, 1937; came to U.S., 1968, naturalized, 1976; s. Zdenek and Stepanka (Curikova) B.; m. Iva Marie Krasna, Sept. 27, 1967; children: Martin Zdenek, Eva Stephanie. Civil Engr., Tech. U., Prague, 1960; PhD in Mechanics, Czechoslovak Acad. Sci., 1963; postgrad. diploma in theoretical physics, Charles U., Prague, 1966; hon. doctorate, Czech Tech. U., Prague, 1991, Karlsruhe (Germany) U., 1998; D honoris causa, U. Colo., 2000, Poly. Milan, 2001. Registered structural engr., Ill. Scientist, adj. prof. Bldg. Research Inst., Tech. U., Prague, 1963-67; docent habilitation Tech. U., Czechoslovakia, 1967; vis. research engr. Centre d'Étude et de Recherche du Bâtiment et des Travaux Publics, Paris, 1967, U. Toronto, 1967-68, U. Calif., Berkeley, 1969; assoc. prof. civil engring. Northwestern U., Evanston, Ill., 1969-73, prof., 1973-90, Walter P. Murphy prof., 1990—, coordinator structural engring. program, 1974-78, 92—; founding dir. Ctr. for Concrete and Geomaterials, 1981-86. Cons. Argonne Nat. Lab., many other orgns. Author: Creep of Concrete in Structural Analysis, 1966, Stability of Structures: Elastic, Inelastic, Fracture and Damage Theories, 1991, Concrete at High Temperatures, 1996, Fracture and Size Effect, 1997, Scaling of Structural Strength, 20001, Inelastic Analysis of Structures, 2001; editor 13 books; editor in chief Jour. Engring. Mechanics, 1989-94; regional editor Internat. Jour. Fracture, 1991—; assoc. editor Applied Mechanics Rev., 1987—, Cement and Concrete Research Internat. Jour, 1970—, Materials and Structures, 1979— Solid Mechanics Archives, 1980-91, Materials and Structures, 1981—; mem. editl. bds. of 16 hours.; contbr. (with others) over 350 articles to profl. jours.; patentee in field. Recipient Best Engring. Book of Yr. award Soc. Am. Pubs., 1992, Outstanding New Citizen award Chgo. Citizenship Coun., 1976, IR100 award, 1982, A. von Humboldt award, 1990, Šolín medal Czech Tech. U., Prague, 1998, Stodola gold medal Slovak Acad. Scis., 1999; grantee NSF, 1970—, Air Force Office Scientific Rsch., 1975—, Los Alamos Sci. Lab., 1978-80, European Power Rsch. Inst., 1980—, Office Naval Rsch., 1990—. Dept. Energy, 1984—; Ford Found. fellow, 1967-68, Guggenheim fellow, 1978-79, Kajima Found. fellow U. Tokyo, 1987, NATO fellow, Paris, 1988, Japan Soc. Promotion of Sci. fellow U. Tokyo, 1995-96. Fellow ASME (Worcester Reed Warner medal 1997), Am. Acad. Mechanics, ASCE (chmn. com. properties of materials 1976-78, 82-84, editor in chief Jour. Engring. Mechanics 1988-94, Walter L. Huber rsch. prize 1976, T.Y. Lin Prestressed Concrete award 1977, Newmark medal 1996, Croes medal 1997), Am. Concrete Inst. (chmn. fracture mechanics com. 1985-92), Internat. Assn. for Fracture Mechanics of Concrete Structures (pres. 1991-93), Internat. Union Testing and Rsch. Labs. Materials Structures (chmn. com. on creep, L'Hermite gold medal 1975), Soc. Engring. Sci. (pres. 1993, Prager medal 1996); mem. NAE, Nat. Acad. Sci., Wash., Austrian Acad. Scis., Internat. Assn. Structural Mechanics Reactor Tech. (coord. concrete structures divsn.), ASTM (mem. concrete com., skiing com.), Prestressed Concrete Inst., Am. Ceramic Soc. (D.M. Roy award 2001), Internat. Assn. Soil Mech. Found. Engring., Internat. Assn. Bridge and Structural Engring., Soc. Exptl. Mechanics, Am. Soc. Engring. Edn., Bldg. Rsch. Inst. Spain (hon., Torroja Gold medal 1990), Czech Soc. Civil Engring. (hon.), Czech Soc. Mechanics (award of merit 1993), Structural Engrs. Assn. Ill. (Meritorious Paper award 1992), Engring. Acad. Czech Republic (fgn. mem.). Home: 707 Roslyn Ter Evanston IL 60201-1721 Office: Northwestern Univ Dept Civil Engring Evanston IL 60208-0001

BEACHLEY, NORMAN HENRY, mechanical engineer, educator; b. Washington, Jan. 13, 1933; s. Albert Henry and Anna Garnet (Eiring) B.; m. Marion Ruth Iglehart, July 18, 1959; children: Brenda Ruth, Rebecca Sue, Barbara Joan. B.M.E., Cornell U., 1956, Ph.D., 1966. Mem. tech. staff Hughes Aircraft Co., Culver City, Calif., 1956-57; mem. tech. staff Space Tech. Labs., Redondo Beach, 1959-63; mem. faculty U. Wis., Madison, 1966—, prof. mech. engring., 1978-94, prof. emeritus, 1994—. Cons. numerous orgns., 1967— Co-author: Introduction to Dynamic System Analysis, 1978. Served with USAF, 1957-59. Sci. and Engring. Research Council Gt. Britain fellow, 1981-82 Fellow Soc. Automotive Engrs.; mem. ASME, Sigma Xi. Achievements include research in field of energy storage powerplants for motor vehicles, 1970—. Home: 2332 Fitchburg Rd Verona WI 53593-9278 Office: U Wis 1513 University Ave Madison WI 53706-1539 E-mail: beachley@facstaff.wisc.edu.

BEACHY, ROGER, biologist, plant pathology researcher; b. Plain City, Ohio, Oct. 4, 1944; divorced; children: Kathryn C., Kyle A. BA, Goshen Coll., 1966; PhD in Plant Pathology, Mich. State U., 1973. Rsch. assoc. Cornell U., Ithaca, N.Y., 1973-76, U.S. Plant, Soil & Nutrition Lab., Ithaca, 1976-78; from asst. prof. to prof. dept. biology Washington U., St. Louis, 1976—; mem., head divsn. plant biology, Scripps Family chair Scripps Rsch. Inst., La Jolla, Calif. Plant Virology fellow NIH, 1973-76. Fellow AAAS; mem. Am. Phytopath Soc. (Ruth Allen award 1990), Am. Soc. Plant Physiologists, Am. Soc. Virologists, Am. Soc. Biol. Chemists, Internat. Soc. Plant Molecular Biology. Achievements include research in control of synthesis of soybean seed proteins, plant viral messenger RNAs, effects of virus gene products on infected host cells, gentetic transformation of plants for virus resistance. Office: Wash U Ctr Plant Sci and Biotech Dept Biology Saint Louis MO 63130 also: Scripps Rsch Inst Dept Cell Biology La Jolla CA 92037

BEAHRS, OLIVER HOWARD, surgeon, educator; b. Eufaula, Ala., Sept. 19, 1914; s. Elmer Charles and Elsa Katherine (Smith) B.; 1 child, Gean Beahrs Landy; m. Helen Edith Taylor, July 27, 1947; children: John Randolf, David Howard, Nancy Ann Beahrs Oster. BA, U. Calif., Berkeley, 1937; MD, Northwestern U., 1942; MS in Surgery, Mayo Grad. Sch. Medicine, 1949; D of Mil. Medicine honoris causa, Uniform Svcs. U. Health Sci., 1999. Diplomate Am. Bd. Surgery. Fellow surgery Mayo Grad. Sch. Medicine, Rochester, Minn., 1942, 46-49, prof. surgery, 1966-79; Joel and Ruth Roberts prof. surgery Mayo Med. Sch., 1978-79; prof. emeritus Mayo Grad. Sch. Medicine, Rochester, Minn., 1979—; asst. surgeon Mayo Clinic, 1949-50, head sect. gen. surgery, 1950-79, vice-chmn. bd. govs., 1964-75. Bd. dirs. Rochester Meth. Hosp.; trustee Mayo Found.; mem. cancer control and rehab. adv. com. Nat. Cancer Inst., 1975-84; mem. Am. Joint Com. on Cancer, 1975-78, exec. dir., 1980-92. Editor: Surgical Consultations; editorial bd.: Surgery, Surg. Techniques Illustrated; contbr. over 400 articles to profl. jours. Hon. life, bd. dirs. Am. Cancer Soc., 1975—; trustee Rochester Meth. Hosp.; adv. bd. Uniform Svcs. Univ. Health Scis.; med. cons. Pres. and Mrs. Reagan. Capt. USNR, 1942-64, ret. Recipient Leadership and Humanitarian awards Am. Cancer Soc. Fellow Royal Coll. Surgery in Ireland (hon.), Royal Australasian Coll. Surgery (hon.); mem. AMA, ACS (mem. exec. com., bd. govs., chmn. cen. jud. com., long-range planning com., chmn. bd. govs., chmn. bd. regents, pres. 1988-89), Am. Group Practice Assn. (sec.-treas. 1974-75), Minn. Surg. Soc. (pres. 1960-61), Am. Thyroid Assn., James IV Assn. Surgeons, Am. Surg. Assn. (pres. 1979-80, chmn. com. on issues 1980-83), So. Surg. Assn., Cen. Surg. Assn., Western Surg. Assn., Soc. Head and Neck Surgeons (pres. 1966-67), Am. Assn. Endocrine Surgeons (pres. 1986-87), Am. Assn. Clin. Anatomists (pres. 1986-87), Soc. Surgery Alimentary Tract, Soc. Pelvic Surgeons (pres. 1983-84), Soc. Surg. Oncology, Am. Assn. Clin. Anatomists (pres.), Philippine Coll. Surgeons (hon.), Hellenic Coll. Surgery (hon.), Assn. Française de Chirurgie Française, Northwestern U. Alumni Assn. (Merit award), Sigma Xi, Phi Kappa Epsilon, Phi Beta Pi, Theta Delta Chi. Republican. Methodist. Home: 2253 Baihly Ln SW Rochester MN 55902-1023 Office: 200 1st St SW Rochester MN 55905-0001 E-mail: beahrs.oliver@mayo.edu.

BEAK, PETER ANDREW, chemistry educator; b. Syracuse, N.Y., Jan. 12, 1936; s. Ralph E. and Belva (Edinger) B.; m. Sandra J. Burns, July 25, 1959; children: Bryan A., Stacia W. B.A., Harvard U., 1957; Ph.D., Iowa State U., 1961. From instr. to prof. chemistry U. Ill., Urbana, 1961—, Roger Adams prof. chemistry, 1997—, Jubille prof. liberal arts and sci., 1997—. Cons. Abbott Labs., North Chicago, Ill., 1964—, Monsanto Co., St. Louis, 1969-99; G.D. Searle Co., Ill., 1987-2001, Pharmacia, 2001—. Contbr. articles to profl. jours. A.P. Sloan Found. fellow, 1967-69; Guggenheim fellow, 1968-69 Fellow AAAS (chmn. chemistry sect. 1999); mem. Am. Chem. Soc. (editl. and adv. bds., sec. and divsn. officer, A.C. Cope scholar 1993, Mosher award 1994, Gilman award 1997, Gassman award 2000). Home: 304 E Sherwin Ave Urbana IL 61802 E-mail: beak@scs.uloc.edu.

BEAL, GRAHAM WILLIAM JOHN, museum director; b. Stratford-on-Avon, Eng., Apr. 22, 1947; came to U.S., 1973; s. Cecil John Beal and Annie Gladys (Barton) Tunbridge; m. Nancy Jane Andrews, Apr. 21, 1973: children: Priscilla Jane, Julian William John. BA, Manchester U., Eng., 1969; MA, U. London, 1972. Acad. asst. to dir. Sheffield City (Eng.) Art Galleries, 1972-73; gallery dir. U. S.D., Vermillion, 1973-74, Washington U., St. Louis, 1974-77; chief curator Walker Art Ctr., Mpls., 1977-83; dir. Sainsbury Ctr. for Visual Arts, Norwich, Eng., 1983-84; chief curator San Francisco Mus. Modern Art, 1984-89; dir. Joslyn Art Mus., Omaha, 1989-96, Los Angeles County Mus. Art, 1996-99, Detroit Inst. Arts, 1999—. Mem. Fed. Adv. Com. on Internat. Exhbns., 1991-94. Author: (book, exhbn. catalog) Jime Dine: Five Themes, 1984; co-author: (book, exhbn. catalog) A Quiet Revolution, 1987, David Nash: Voyages and Vessels, 1994, Sainsbury Collection Catalogue, vol. I, 1997, Joslyn Air Museum: Fifty Favorities, Joslyn Art Museum: A Building History, 1998, American Beauty: American Paintings and Sculpture from the Detroit Institute of Arts, 2002; contbg. to Apollo Mag., London, 1989-91. Trustee Djerassi Found., Woodside, Calif., 1987-89. Mem.: Assn. Art Mus. Dir. (bd. trustees), Century Club. Avocations: history, cooking, music. Office: Detroit Inst Arts 5200 Woodward Ave Detroit MI 48202

BEALE, SUSAN M. electric power industry executive; Atty. Consumer Power and So. Calif. Edison; with Detroit Edison, 1982-95, v.p., corp. sec., 1995—. Office: Detroit Edison Co 2002 2d Ave Detroit MI 48226

BEALKE, LINN HEMINGWAY, banker; b. St. Louis, Nov. 14, 1944; s. Charles Francis and Miriam Frances (Hemingway) B.; m. Jean Long Wells, Sept. 6, 1969; children: David Q.W., Emily R., Linn H. BA, U. Ark., 1966; MBA, Washington U., 1969. Fin. analyst Edison Brothers Stores, St. Louis, 1969-74; sr. v.p. Commerce Bank of St. Louis, 1975-78; v.p. fin. and adminstrn. Curlee Clothing Co., Lexington, Ky., 1978-80; vice chmn. County Bank of St. Louis, 1980-84, Southwest Bank of St. Louis, 1984—. Bd. dirs. Zoltek Cos., Inc.; bd. dirs. Miss. Valley Bancshares, pres., 1984—. Treas. Forsyth Sch., St. Louis, 1980-87; pres. Edgewood Childrens Ctr., Webster Groves, Mo., 1986-88; dir. Mo. Colls. Fund, Jefferson City, Mo., 1990-93. Mem. Mo. Bankers Assn. (dir. 1988-90, 99—), Fin. Execs. Inst. (pres. St. Louis chpt. 1989-90, dir. 1991-94), Am. Bankers Assn. Leadership Conf. (del. 1990-92), Racquet Club (v.p. 1987-89), Bellerive Country Club, Boone Valley Golf Club. Office: SW Bank St Louis PO Box 790178 Saint Louis MO 63179-0178

BEALL, CYNTHIA, anthropologist, educator; b. Urbana, Ill., Aug. 21, 1949; d. John Wood and J. Alene (Beachler) Beall. BA in Biology, U. Pa., 1970; MA in Anthropology, Pa. State U., 1972, PhD in Anthropology, 1976. Asst. prof. Case Western Res. U., Cleve., 1976—82, assoc. prof. of anthropology, 1982—87, prof. anthropology, 1987—. Co-editor: Jour. of Cross-Cultural Gerontology, 1986—95; contbr. articles to profl. jours. Active Internat. Rsch. Exch. Program, 1990, 1991. Fellow Nat. Program for Advanced Study and Rsch. in China, NAS, 1986—87, 1997; grantee rsch., NSF, 1981, 1983, 1986, 1987, 1993, 1994, 1995, 1997, 2000, Am. Fedn. for Aging Rsch., 1983, 1986, Nat. Geog. Soc., 1983, 1986—87, 1993, 1995. Fellow: AAAS; mem.: NAS, Assn. for Anthropology and Gerontology, Soc. for Study Human Biology, Human Biology Coun. (exec. com. 1989—92, pres. 1992—94), Am. Assn. Phys. Antrhopology (exec. com. 1989—92), Am. Anthrop. Assn., Am. Philo. Soc. Achievements include research in in Peru, Bolivia, Nepal, Tibet, Mongolia and Ethiopia. Office: Case Western Res U Dept Anthropology 238 Mather Memorial Bldg Cleveland OH 44106-7125 E-mail: cmb2@po.cwru.edu.

BEALS, ROBERT J. ceramic engineer; Dir Hall China Co. Recipient Albert Victor Bleininger award Am. Ceramic Soc., 1994. Office: Hall China Co 438 Smithfield St East Liverpool OH 43920-1723

BEALS, VAUGHN LE ROY , JR. retired motorcycle manufacturing executive; b. Cambridge, Mass., Jan. 2, 1928; s. Vaughn Le Roy and Pearl Uela (Wilmarth) B.; m. Eleanore May Woods, July 15, 1951; children: Susan Lynn, Laurie Jean. BS, M.I.T., 1948, MS, 1954. Research engr. Cornell Aero. Lab., Buffalo, 1948-52, MIT Aero Elastic and Structures Research Lab., 1952-55; dir. research and tech. N.Am. Aviation, Inc., Columbus, Ohio, 1955-65; exec. v.p. Cummins Engine Co., Ind., 1965-70, also dir.; chmn. bd., chief exec. officer Formac Internat., Inc., Seattle, 1970-75; dep. group exec. Motorcycle Products Group, AMF Inc., Milw., 1975-77, v.p. and group exec. Stamford, Conn., 1977-81; chief exec. officer Harley-Davidson, Inc., Milw., 1981-89, chmn., 1981-96, chmn. emeritus, 1996—. Mem. Desert Mountain Club, Desert Forest Golf Club, Forest Highlands Golf Club. Home: PO Box 3260 Carefree AZ 85377-3260 Office: Harley-Davidson Inc Box 653 3700 W Juneau Ave Milwaukee WI 53208-2865

BEAM, CLARENCE ARLEN, judge; b. Stapleton, Nebr., Jan. 14, 1930; s. Clarence Wilson and Cecile Mary (Harvey) Beam; m. Betty Lou Fletcher, July 22, 1951; children: Randal, James, Thomas, Bradley, Gregory. BS, U. Nebr., 1951, JD, 1965. Feature writer Nebr. Farmer Mag., Lincoln, 1951; with sales dept. Steckley Seed Co., Mount Sterling, 1954—58, advt. mgr. Ill., 1958—63; from assoc. to ptnr. Chambers, Holland, Dudgeon & Knudsen, Berkheimer, Beam, et al, Lincoln, 1965—82; judge U.S. Dist. Ct. Nebr., Omaha, 1982—87, chief judge, 1986—87; cir. judge U.S. Ct. Appeals (8th cir.), 1987—. Mem. com. on lawyer discipline Nebr. Supreme Ct., 1974—82; mem. Conf. Commrs. on Uniform State Laws, 1979—, chmn. Nebr. sect., 1980—82; mem. jud. conf. com. on ct. and jud. security, 1989—93; chmn., 1992—93. Contbr. articles to profl. jours. Mem. Nebr. Rep. Ctrl. Com., 1970—78. Capt. U.S. Army, 1951—53, Korea. Scholar Regents, U. Nebr., Lincoln, 1947, Roscoe Pound scholar, 1964. Mem.: Nebr. State Bar Assn. Office: US Ct Appeals 8th Cir 435 Federal Bldg 100 Centennial Mall N Lincoln NE 68508-3859

BEAN, JERRY JOE, lawyer; b. Lebanon, Ind., Apr. 19, 1954; s. Russell Lowell and Mary Ethel (Jett) B.; m. Cheryl Lynn Smith, May 29, 1976; 1 child, Angela. B.A., Wabash Coll., 1976; D. Jurisprudence, Ind. U., 1979; Bars: U.S. Dist. Ct. (so. and no. dists.) Ind. 1979, 81. Exec. dir. Legal Aid Corp., Lafayette, Ind., 1979-80; dep. prosecuting atty. IV-D, Tippecanoe County Prosecutors Office, Lafayette, 1980-81, county ct., 1981-83, felony intake, 1983-84, chief dep. prosecutor, 1984— . Mem. ABA, Assn. Trial Lawyers Am., Ind. State Bar Assn., Tippecanoe County Bar Assn. Republican. Methodist. Lodge: Arman, Fraternal Order of Police (hon.). Office: Tippecanoe County Prosecutor's Office Court House Lafayette IN 47901

BEANE, MARJORIE NOTERMAN, academic administrator; b. Adams, Minn., Oct. 3, 1946; d. Matthias Hubert and Anna Helen (Boegeman) Noterman. BA, Marillac Coll., St. Louis, 1969; MEd, U. Ariz., 1979; PhD, Loyola U., Chgo., 1988. Tchr. St. Alphonsus Sch., Prospect Heights, Ill., 1969-73; tchr., asst. prin. St. Raphael Sch., Chgo., 1973-75; prin. St. Theresa Sch., Palatine, Ill., 1975-84; pres. Mallinckrodt Coll. of the North Shore, Wilmette, 1986-90; sr. v.p. for adminstn. Loyola U., Chgo., 1991—. Trustee Mallinckrodt Coll. of the North Shore, 1980-90; cons. Jospehinum High Sch., Chgo., 1976, St. Viator High Sch., Arlington Heights, Ill., 1986. Mem. History of Women Religious, Fedn. Ind. Ill. Colls. and Univs. (exec. com. 1989), Wilmette C. of C., Sisters of Christian Charity (councilor 1980-88). Rotary. Roman Catholic. Avocations: sewing, bicycling, swimming, travel. Office: Loyola U 820 N Michigan Ave Fl 1 Chicago IL 60611-2196

BEARDMORE, DOROTHY, state education official; b. Chgo. m. William Beardmore; 2 children. BA, Cornell U. Cert. due process spl. edn. hearing officer Mich. Dept. Edn. Mem. bd. edn. Rochester Cmty. Schs., 1967-75; mem. Bd. Edn. Oakland County Schs., Oakland County Intermediate Sch. Dist., 1974-84; mem. State Bd. Edn., Lansing, Mich., 1984—, pres., 1990-92, 99—. Chair study Nat. Assn. State Bds. Edn., 1988, chair study group on edn. governance, 1995-96, chair study on social issues and the role for schs., 1999, bd. dirs. representing 12 midwestern states, chair by-laws com.; apptd. by gov. Midwestern Higher Edn. Com.; at-large del. Southeast Mich. Coun. Govts.; chmn. Health Schs. Network. Mem. Rep. Women's Forum. Recipient Disting. Svc. award Mich. Assn. Career Edn., 1989, Svc. award Phi Delta Kappa, 1989, Can Doer award Sci. and Tech. Quest Honor Roll, 1991, Spirit of Independence award Oakland-Macomb Counties Ctr. for Ind. Living, 1991, Paul Harris fellow Rotary Internat., 1989, Edn. Leadership award Mich. Elem. and Mid. Sch. Prins. Assn., 1995; inducted into Mich. Edn. Hall of Fame, 1996. Mem. Delta Kappa Gamma (hon.). Office: Edn Bd PO Box 30008 Lansing MI 48909-7508

BEARDSLEY, JOHN RAY, public relations firm executive; b. Mpls., Jan. 10, 1937; s. Ray Homer Beardsley and Dorothy Louise (Refsell) Ripley; m. Sharon Ruth Olson, Aug. 24, 1960; children— Elizabeth Ruth, Alison Leigh, Leslie Anne B.A., Augustana Coll., 1961. News editor Sioux Falls (S.D.) Argus Leader, 1961-64; city editor Worthington (Minn.) Daily Globe, 1964; Corr. AP, Fargo, N.D. and Mpls., 1965-68; comms. mgr. Pillsbury Co., Mpls., 1968-69; pub. rels. mgr. Dayton Hudson Corp., 1969-70; successively account exec., v.p., sr. v.p. Padilla and Speer, Inc., 1970-83, CEO, 1983-86; chmn., CEO Padilla Speer Beardsley Inc., 1987—, nat. dir. at large, 1991-92, treas., 1993, pres.-elect, 1994, pres., 1995. Mem. Pub. Rels. Soc. Am. (pres. Minn. chpt. 1981), Nat. Investor Rels. Inst. (v.p., dir. Minn. chpt. 1981-84), Mpls. Athletic Club Home: 3904 Williston Rd Minnetonka MN 55345-2054 Office: Padilla Speer Beardsley Inc Ste 400 1101 W River Pkwy Minneapolis MN 55415-1241

BEARMAN, DAVID, finance company executive; Sr. v.p., CFO NCR, Dayton, Ohio, 1998—. Office: NCR 1700 S Patterson Blvd Dayton OH 45479-0002

BEARMON, LEE, lawyer; BBA, JD, U. Minn. Bar: Minn. 1956. Sr. v.p., exec. cons. Carlson Cos., Inc, Mpls.; of counsel Briggs & Morgan, 2000—. Office: Carlson Cos Inc PO Box 59159 Minneapolis MN 55459-8200 also: Briggs and Morgan 2400 IDS Ctr 80 S 8th St Minneapolis MN 55402-2100

BEARY, JOHN FRANCIS, III, physician, researcher, pharmaceutical executive; b. Melrose, Iowa, Dec. 14, 1946; s. John F. and Dorothy (McGrath) B.; m. Bianca E. Mason, May 6, 1972; children: John Daniel, Vanessa, Webster, Nina. BS summa cum laude, U. Notre Dame, 1969; MD, Harvard U., 1973; MBA, Georgetown U., 1988. Diplomate Am Bd. Internal Medicine, Am. Bd. Rheumatology and Geriatric Medicine, Am. Bd. Clin. Pharmacology. Flight surgeon 89th Mil. Airlift Wing (Air Force One), 1974—77; Osler medicine resident Johns Hopkins Hosp., Balt., 1977—78; rsch. fellow Cornell Med. Coll., N.Y.C., 1978—80; from asst. prof. to clin. prof. Georgetown U. Sch. Medicine, Washington, 1980—2000; prin. dept. asst. sec. health affairs Dept. Def., 1981—83; assoc. dean strategic planning Georgetown U. Sch. Medicine, 1984—87; sr. v.p. regulatory and sci. affairs Pharm. Rsch. and Mfg. Assn., 1988—97; med. dir. arthritis rsch. Procter and Gamble Pharms., Cin., 1997—. Steering com. Internat. Conf. on Harmonization of Pharm. Stds., 1990-97; clin. prof. rheumatology and immunology U. Cin., 1997—. Editor: Manual of Rheumatology, 1981, 4th edit., 2000; mem. editorial bd. Jour. Pharm. Medicine, 1990—, Drug Devel. Rsch., 1992-2000. Bd. dirs. Scleroderma Found., Washington, 1982-92. Served to capt. USNR, 1984— Recipient disting. pub. service medal Dept. Def., 1983, Navy and Marine Corps Commendation medal, 1997. Fellow ACP, Am. Coll. Rheumatology, Am. Coll. Clin. Pharmacology; mem. AMA, Am. Geriatrics Soc., Am. Soc. Clin. Pharmacology and Therapeutics, Osteoarthritis Rsch. Soc., Res. Officers Assn., U.S. Naval Inst., Johns Hopkins Med. and Surg. Assn., Chevy Chase Club, Notre Dame Club, Cinn., Harvard Club. Office: Procter & Gamble Pharms 8700 Mason Montgomery Rd Mason OH 45040-8006

BEASLEY, JIM SANDERS See LEE, JACK

BEATTIE, TED ARTHUR, zoological gardens and aquarium administrator; b. Salem, Ohio, Jan. 13, 1945; s. Don Earl and Frances (Webster) B.; children: Lauralyn, Sean, Kimberly; m. Penelope Johnson, July 13, 1985. BA in Journalism, Ohio State U., 1971, MA in Pub. Rels., 1972. Advt./pub. rels. dir. Shaw-Barton Co., Coshocton, Ohio, 1972-78; mktg. dir. Cin. Zoo, 1978-81; assoc. dir. Brookfield Zoo, Chgo., 1981-87; exec. dir. Knoxville (Tenn.) Zool. Gardens, 1987-92; dir., CEO Ft. Worth Zool. Pk., 1992-94; pres., CEO John G. Shedd Aquarium, Chgo., 1994—. Cons. Zoo Plan Assn., Wichita, Kans., 1981-88. Vice chmn. and chmn. United Way campaign, Coshocton, 1977-78; mem. Leadership Knoxville, 1988. With U.S. Army, 1967-69, Vietnam. Fellow: Am. Assn. Zool. Pks. and Aquariums (bd. dirs. 1989—91, 1994—2002); mem.: Am. Zoo & Aquarium Assn. (v.p. 1998—99, pres. 2000—01, mem. pres.'s commn. on oceans 2001—), Sawgrass Country Club, Onwentsia Club, Arts Club, Chgo. Econ. Club. Avocations: golf, boating. Home: 260 E Chestnut St Apt 2802 Chicago IL 60611 Office: John G Shedd Aqarium 1200 S Lake Shore Dr Chicago IL 60605-2402

BEATTY, OTTO, JR. former state legislator, lawyer; m. Joyce Beatty; children: Otto III, Laural. BA, Howard U.; JD with honors, Ohio State U. Bar: Ohio. Ptnr. Beatty & Roseboro, Columbus; mem. Ohio Ho. of Reps., 1980-99. Mem. pub. utilities com., vice chmn. civil and comml. law com., mem. judiciary and criminal justice com., state govt. com., fin. instns. com., set-aside rev. bd., ct. reorgn. com., state penitentiary devel. commn.; pres. Otto Beatty Jr. LPA Co., Otto Beaty Jr. & Assocs., real estate developers. Recipient Cmty. Svc. award Ohio Minority Bus. Assn., Outstanding Svc. award Franklin County Children's Svcs., award Black C. of C., Ea. Union Missionary Bapt. Assn., Ohio Assn. Real Estate Brokers, Pioneer award Ohio Equal Opportunities Ctr., 1992. Mem. ABA, Ohio Bar Assn. (lectr., Leadership award 1992), Columbus Bar Assn., Franklin County Trial Lawyers Assn. (past pres.), Nat. Conf. Black Lawyers, Nat. Inst. Justice, Black Elected Dems. Ohio, Robert B. Elliott Law Club (past pres.), Home: 233 N High St Columbus OH 43215-2405

BEAUBIEN, ANNE KATHLEEN, librarian; b. Detroit, Sept. 15, 1947; d. Richard Parker and Edith Mildred Beaubien. Student, Western Mich. U., 1965-67; BA, Mich. State U., 1969; AM in Libr. Sci., U. Mich., 1970. Reference libr., bibliographic instr. U. Mich. Libr., Ann Arbor, 1971-80, dir. MITS, 1980-85, head coop. access svcs., 1985—. Head Business & Cooperative Access Svcs., 1995-99, Cooperative Access Svcs. and Grants, 2000—. Author: (booklet) Psychology Bibliography, 1980; co-author: Learning the Library, 1982; contbr. articles to profl. jours., editor, conf. proc., 1987. Pres. Ann Arbor Ski Club, 1978—79; mem. vestry St. Clare's Episcopal Ch., 1986—89, 2002—. Recipient Woman of Yr. award Ann Arbor Bus. and Profl. Women's Club, 1982, Disting. Alumnus award Sch. Info. and Libr. Studies, U. Mich., 1987. Mem. ALA, Assn. Coll. and Rsch. Librs. (pres. 1991-92). Avocations: skiing, bicycling, ballroom dancing. Office: U Mich Libr 106 Hatcher Grad Libr Ann Arbor MI 48109

BEAUCHAMP, ROY E. career officer; b. July 1, 1945; Commd. U.S. Army, advanced through grades to maj. gen., 1997; with U.S. Army Tank--Automotive and Armaments Command, Warren, Mich. Office: US Army Automotive TACOM/AMSTA-CG Warren MI 48397-5000

BEAVER, FRANK EUGENE, communication educator, film critic and historian; b. Cleve., July 26, 1938; s. John Whitfield and Mary Louise (Shell) B.; m. Gail Frances Place, June 30, 1962; children: Julia Clare, John Francis, Johanna Louise. BA, U. N.C., 1960, MA, 1966; PhD, U. Mich., 1970. Instr. speech Memphis State U., 1965-66; instr. radio-TV-motion pictures U. N.C., Chapel Hill, 1966-68; asst. prof. speech comm. U. Mich., Ann Arbor, 1969-74, assoc. prof., 1974-79, assoc. prof. comm., 1979-84, prof., chmn. dept. comm., 1987-91, Arthur F. Thurnau prof., 1989-92, dir. grad. program in telecom. arts and film, 1991-96. Advisor Muskegon (Mich.) Film Festival, 2001. Film critic radio Stas. WUOM, WVGR, WFUM, Ann Arbor, Grand Rapids, Mich., 1975-97; author: Bosley Crowther, 1974, On Film, 1983, Dictionary of Film Terms, 1983, 94 (Mandarin-Chinese translation 1993), Oliver Stone: Wakeup Cinema, 1994; writer, dir. documentary film Under One Roof, 1967; editor (book series) Framing Film, 98-, gen. editor Twayne Pubs., N.Y., 1987—; editor-in-chief: 100 Years of Cinema, 2000. Bd. dirs. Mich. Theater Found., Ann Arbor, 1977-79, 86—; alumni adv. bd. Lambda Chi Alpha, Ann Arbor, 1989-94; advisor Ann Arbor Film Festival, 1975—, Muskegon Film Fesstival, 2000-. With M.I. Corps, U.S. Army, 1962-65, Vietnam. Recipient Playwriting award Carolina Playmakers, 1962, Major Hopwood writing awards for drama and essays U. Mich., 1969, Outstanding Teaching award Amoco Found., Ann Arbor, 1985; fellow NEH, 1975. Mem.: Speech Comm. Assn., Soc. Cinema Scholars, Racquet Club, Azazels Club, Phi Kappa Phi, Kappa Tau Alpha. Democrat. Roman Catholic. Home: 1835 Vinewood Blvd Ann Arbor MI 48104-3609 Office: U Mich Film and Studios 2512 Frieze Bldg Ann Arbor MI 48109-1285 E-mail: fbeaver@umich.edu.

BEBAN, GARY JOSEPH, real estate corporation officer; b. San Francisco, Aug. 5, 1946; s. Frank and Anna (Consani) B.; m. Kathleen Hanson, June 14, 1968; children: Paul, Mark. BA in History, UCLA, 1968. Real estate specialist, sales and mgr. positions CB Comml., Calif. and Ill., 1970-87, pres., 1987-89; sr. exec., mng. dir. CB Richard Ellis, Chgo., 1984—. Mem. IDRC, 1986—, UCLA Assocs., 1980—; bd. trustee New Hampton Sch. Recipient Heisman Trophy award N.Y. Downtown Athletic Club, 1967; NCAA Scholar Athlete, 1968, Football Hall of Fame, 1988. Mem. Urban Land Inst., Nat. Realty Commn., UCLA Ctr. Fion. and Real Estate. Office: CB Richard Ellis 233 N Michigan Ave Ste 2200 Chicago IL 60601-5806

BECHER, WILLIAM DON, electrical engineer, engineering educator, writer; b. Bolivar, Ohio, Nov. 26, 1929; s. William and Eva Vernette (Richardson) Becher; m. Helen Norma Hager, Aug. 31, 1950; children: Eric Alan, Patricia Lynn. BS in Radio Engring., Tri-State U., 1950; MSEE, U. Mich., 1961, PhD, 1968. Registered profl. engr., Mich., N.J. Project engr. Bogue Electric, Paterson, NJ, 1950-53; sr. devel. engr. Goodyear Aircraft Corp., Akron, Ohio, 1953-57; sr. systems engr. Beckman Instruments, Fullerton, Calif., 1957-58; engring. supr. Bendix Aerospace Systems, Ann Arbor, Mich., 1958-63; research engr. U. Mich., 1963-68, adj. prof. elec. engring., 1978-79, 81-94, lectr. elec. engring. Dearborn, 1964-68, prof. elec. engring., 1968-78, chmn., 1971-76; engring. dept. mgr. Environ. Rsch. Inst. Mich., Ann Arbor, 1977-79, assoc. dir., 1981-87, tech. cons., 1988-90, engr. emeritus, 1990—; prof. elec. engring., dean Coll. Engring. N.J. Inst. Tech., Newark, 1979-81; cons. Widbec Engr, Ann Arbor, 1978—. Pres. Mich. Computers & Instrumentation, Inc., Ann Arbor, 1983—87; prof., chmn. elec. engring. Calif. State U., Fresno, 1988. Author: (book) Courses in Continuing Education for Electronics Engineers, 1975, 1976, Logical Design Using Integrated Circuits, 1977, An Ocean Between, 2000. With U.S. Army, 1953—55. Fellow GE, 1962—63. Mem.: IEEE (life), Order of Engrs., Am. Soc. Engring. Edn., Tau Beta Pi, Sigma Xi. Achievements include patents in field. Home and Office: Widbec Engring 691 Spring Valley Rd Ann Arbor MI 48105-1060

BECHERER, HANS WALTER, retired agricultural equipment executive; b. Detroit, Apr. 19, 1935; s. Max and Mariele (Specht) B.; m. Michele Beigbeder, Nov. 28, 1959; children: Maxime (dec.), Vanessa. BA, Trinity Coll., Hartford, Conn., 1957; postgrad., Munich U., 1958; MBA, Harvard U., 1962. Exec. asst. office of chmn. Deere & Co., Moline, Ill., 1966-69; gen. mgr. John Deere Export, Mannheim, Germany, 1969-73; dir. export mktg. Deere & Co., Moline, 1973-77, v.p., 1977-83, sr. v.p., 1983-86, exec. v.p., 1986-87, pres., 1987-90, COO, 1987-89, CEO, 1989-2000, chmn., 1990-2000, also bd. dirs. Bd. dirs. Schering-Plough Corp., Honeywell Internat. Inc., Chase Manhattan Corp. and Chase Manhattan Bank; mem. industry sector adv. com. U.S. Dept. Commerce, 1975-81; mem. Bus. Roundtable, 1989—; mem. adv. com. Chase Manhattan Bank Internat., 1990-98; trustee Com. for Econ. Devel., 1990—. Trustee St. Katherine's/St. Mark's Sch., Bettendorf, Iowa, 1983—. 1st lt. USAF, 1958-60. Mem. Coun. on Fgn. Rels., Conf. Bd., Equipment Mfgs. Inst. (bd. dirs. 1987-90), Rock Island (Ill.) Arsenal Golf Club. Republican. Roman Catholic. Office: Deere & Co One John Deere Pl Moline IL 61265-8098

BECHTEL, STEPHEN E. mechanical engineer, educator; BS in Engring. summa cum laude, U. Mich., 1979; PhD in Engring., U. Calif., Berkeley, 1983. Prof. dept. mech. engring. Ohio State U., Columbus, 1983—. Reviewer design, mfg. and computer-integrated engring. divsn., fluid dynamics and hydraulics directorate, thermal transport and thermal processing directorate NSF, 1985—, USDA food characterization, process, product rsch. program; cons. Hoechst Celanese Corp., Los Alamos Nat. Lab., Battelle Meml. Inst., Corning, Inc., Proctor & Gamble. Referee Jour. Rheology, Jour. Applied Mechanics, Jour. Non-Newtonian Fluid Mechanics, others. James B. Angell scholar U. Mich., 1976-79. Mem. ASME (mem. fluid mechanics com. applied mechanics divsn. 1989—, rec. sec. gen. com. 1991-92, rec. sec. exec. com. 1992-93, Henry Hess award 1990), Am. Acad. Mechanics, Soc. Rheology, Tau Beta Pi. Achievements include research in modeling of industrial polymer processing and fiber manufacturing, viscoelastic fluid flows, free surface flows and instability mechanisms, fundamental modeling of thermal expansion, material characterization, transducer characterization in non-destructive evaluation. Office: Ohio State U Mech Engring 206 W 18th Ave Columbus OH 43210-1189 E-mail: bechtel.3@osu.edu.

BECK, ANATOLE, mathematician, educator; b. Bronx, N.Y., Mar. 19, 1930; s. Morris and Minnie (Rosenblum) B.; m. Evelyn Torton, Apr. 10, 1954 (div.); children— Nina Rachel, Micah Daniel B.A., Bklyn. Coll., 1951; M.S., Yale U., 1953, Ph.D., 1956. Instr. math. Williams Coll., Williamstown, Mass., 1955-56; Office Naval Rsch. rsch. assoc. Tulane U., New Orleans, 1956-57; traveling fellow Yale U., 1957-58; from asst. to assoc. prof. U. Wis., Madison, 1958-66, prof. math., 1966—; chair of math. London Sch. Econ./U. London, England, 1973-75. Vis. prof. Cornell U., 1960, Hebrew U., Jerusalem, 1964-65, U. Göttingen, Fed. Republic Germany, 1965, U. Warwick, 1968, Imperial Coll., U. London, 1969, U. Erlangen, Fed. Republic Germany, 1969, U. Md., 1971, Tech. U. Munich, Fed. Republic Germany, 1973, London Sch. Econs. and Univ. Coll., U. London, 1985, 91-92, 94-97, 99—; v.p. Wis. Fedn. Tchrs., 1975-83; co-founder Wis. U. Union, 1984, pres., 1988-91. Author: Continuous Flows in the Plane, 1974, (with M.N. Bleicher and D.W. Crowe) Excursions into Mathematics, 1969, 2d edit., 2000, The Knowledge Business, 1997; contbr. articles to profl. jours. Recipient Disting. Alumnus award Bklyn. Coll., 1976 Mem. Am. Math. Soc. (council 1973-75), Math. Assn. Am., AAUP, Sigma Xi, Phi Beta Kappa, Pi Mu Epsilon. Democrat. Address: 480 Lincoln Dr Madison WI 53706-1325 Office: U Wis 480 Lincoln Dr 721 Van Vleck Hall Madison WI 53706-1329 E-mail: beck@math.wisc.edu., a.beck@lse.ac.uk.

BECK, JAMES V. mechanical engineering educator; b. Cambridge, Mass., May 18, 1930; BS in Mech. Engring., Tufts U., 1956; SM in Mech. Engring., MIT, 1957; PhD in Mech. Engring., Mich. State U., 1964. Prof. mech. engring. Mich. State U., East Lansing, 1964-98, dir. heat transfer property measurement, prof. emeritus; pres. Beck Engring. Cons. Co., Okemos, Mich. Do-organizer Joint Am.-Russian Workshop on Inverse Problems in Heat Transfer, 1992. Contbr. articles to profl. publs. Achievements include research on inverse problem solutions for selected composite materials, development of a user-friendly three-dimensional transfer heat conduction program and measurement of temperature fields of electronic components using infrared thermography, multidimensional thermal and sensing properties of high terperature structures consisting of composites and CVD diamond films. Office: Mich State U Dept Mech Engring 2328E Engring Bldg East Lansing MI 48824 E-mail: beck@egr.msu.edu., jvb@BeckEng.com.

BECK, LOIS GRANT, anthropologist, educator; b. Bogota, Colombia, Nov. 5, 1944; d. Martin Lawrence and Dorothy (Sweet) Grant; m. Henry Huang; 1 dau., Julia. BA, Portland State U., 1967; MA, U. Chgo., 1969, PhD, 1977. Asst. prof. Amherst (Mass.) Coll., 1973-76, Univ. Utah, Salt Lake City, 1976-80; from asst. to assoc. prof. Washington U., St. Louis, 1980-92, prof., 1992—. Author: Qashqa'i of Iran, 1986, Nomad, 1991; co-editor Women in the Muslim World, 1978. Grantee Social Scis. Rsch. Coun., 1990, NEH, 1990-92, 98, Am. Philos. Soc., 1998. Mem. Middle East Studies Assn. (bd. dirs. 1981-84), Soc. Iranian Studies (exec. sec. 1979-82, edit. bd. 1982-91, coun. mem. 1996-98). Office: Washington U Dept Anthropology 1 Brookings Dr Saint Louis MO 63130-4899

BECK, PAUL ALLEN, political science educator; b. Logansport, Ind., Mar. 15, 1944; s. Frank Paul and Mary Elizabeth (Flanegin) B.; m. Maria Teresa Marcano, June 10, 1967; children: Daniel Lee, David Andrew. A.B., Ind. U., 1966; M.A., U. Mich., 1968, Ph.D., 1971. Asst. prof. U. Pitts., 1970-75, assoc. prof., 1976-79; prof. Fla. State U., Tallahassee, 1979-87, chmn. dept., 1981-87; prof. Ohio State U., Columbus, 1987—, chmn. dept., 1991—. Co-author: Political Socialization Across the Generations, 1975, Individual Energy Conservation Behaviors, 1980, Electoral Change in Advanced Industrial Democracies, 1984, Party Politics in America, 9th edit., 2001. Chmn. council Inter-Univ. Consortium for Polit. and Social Research, 1982-83, mem., 1980-83; mem. NSF polit. sci. panel, 1988-89. Recipient Disting. Svc. award Ohio State U., 2000. Mem. Am. Polit. Sci. Assn. (exec. coun. 1981-82, 93-94, book rev. editor 1976-79, program chair 1994, chair strategic planning com. 1999-2000), Midwest Polit. Sci. Assn. (exec. coun. 1987-90, mem. editl. bd. 1988-90, program chair 1991, v.p. 1996-98), So. Polit. Sci. Assn. (mem. editl. bd. 1982-87). Democrat. Home: 7003 Perry Dr Columbus OH 43085-2815 Office: Ohio State U Dept Polit Sci Columbus OH 43210-1373 E-mail: beck.9@osu.edu.

BECK, PHILIP S. lawyer; b. Chgo., Apr. 30, 1951; BA, U. Wis., 1973; JD, Boston U., 1976. Bar: Ill. 1977. Clerk U.S. Ct. Appeals DC Cir., 1976-77; ptnr. Bartlit Beck Herman Palenchar & Scott, Chgo. Office: Bartlit Beck Herman et al 54 W Hubbard St Chicago IL 60610-4645 E-mail: philip.beck@bartlit-beck.com.

BECK, ROBERT N. nuclear medicine educator; b. San Angelo, Tex., Mar. 26, 1928; married, 1958. AB, U. Chgo., 1954, BS, 1955. Chief scientist Argonne Cancer Rsch. Hosp., 1957-67, assoc. prof., 1967-76; prof. radiological sci. U. Chgo., 1976; dir. Franklin McLean Inst., 1977-94, dir. Ctr. Imaging Sci., 1986-98; prof. emeritus U. Chgo., 1998—. Cons. Internat. Atomic Energy Agency, 1966-68; mem. Internat. Com. on Radiation Units, 1968—, Nat. Coun. on Radiation, Protection & Measurements, 1970—. Recipient Aebersold award FDR, 1991. Mem. IEEE (Med. Imaging Sci. award 1996), Soc. Nuclear Med., Am. Assn. Physicists in Medicine, Soc. Magnetic Resonance. Achievements include research in development of a theory of the process by which images can be formed of the distribution of radioactive material in a patient in order to diagnose his disease. Office: U Chgo (MC 2026) Franklin McLean Meml Rsch Inst 5841 S Maryland Ave Chicago IL 60637-1463

BECK, VAUGHN PETER, lawyer; b. Eureka, S.D., Nov. 13, 1966; s. Floyd and Gladys M. (Zimmerman) B.; m. Julie I. Meier, Jan. 2, 1993; children: Emily I., Philip F. BS, U. S.D., 1989, JD, 1992. Bar: S.D. 1992, U.S. Dist. Ct. S.D. 1993. Legal intern Governmental Rsch. Bureau, Vermillion, S.D., 1990, S.D. Pub. Utilities, Pierre, 1991, Freiberg, Rudolf & Peterson, Beresford, 1992; staff atty. Pub. Defenders Office, Deadwood, 1992; atty. Beck Law Office, Ipswich, 1993—. Bd. dirs. Ipswich Devel. Corp., 1993—, Ipswich Comml. Club, 1993—; com. mem. Consumer Protection S.D., 1994—. Mem. Ipswich Vol. Fire Dept., 1993—; trustee, officer United Church of Christ, 1993—. Republican. Office: Beck Law Office P O Box 326 509 Bloemendaal Dr Ipswich SD 57451

BECK, WILLIAM G. lawyer; b. Kansas City, Mo., Mar. 4, 1954; s. Raymond W. Beck and Wanda Williams; 1 child, Collin M. BA in Econs., U. Mo., Kansas City, 1974, JD, 1978. Bar: Mo. 1978, U.S. Dist. Ct. (we. dist.) Mo. 1978, U.S. Ct. Appeals (5th cir.) 1988, U.S. Dist. Ct. (ea. dist.) Mich. 1991, U.S. Dist. Ct. (no. dist.) Ill. 1992, U.S. Ct. Appeals (6th cir.) 1992, U.S. Dist. Ct. (ea. dist.) Wis. 1997, U.S. Ct. Appeals (2d cir.) 1997, U.S. Ct. Appeals (10th cir.) 1997, U.S. Supreme Ct. 1997, U.S. Ct. Appeals (1st cir.) 1998, U.S. Ct. Appeals (7th cir.) 1999, U.S. Dist. Ct. Colo. 2000. Shareholder Field, Gentry, Benjamin & Robertson, P.C., Kansas City, 1978-89; ptnr. Lathrop & Norquist, 1989-95, Lathrop & Gage, L.C., Kansas City, 1996—. Commr. Human Rels. Commn., Jackson County, Mo., 1985-89; chmn. Citizens Assn., Kansas City, 1991-92, 95—; mem. Pub. Improvement Adv. Com., Kansas City, 1991—, vice chmn., 1995-98, chmn. 1998—, fin. chmn. cmty. infrastructure com., 1996—; mem. Waste Minimization Com., Kansas City, 1990-91. Office: Lathrop & Gage LC 2345 Grand Blvd Ste 2800 Kansas City MO 64108-2684

BECKER, DAVID, artist, educator; b. Milw., Aug. 16, 1937; s. Walter Gustav and Fern Bertha (Raddatz) B.; m. Catherine Claytor, Aug. 27, 1960 (div. 1981); children: Sarah Lynne, Amelia Elisabeth; m. Patricia Ann Fennell, Nov. 13, 1988; 1 child, Sloane Fennell. Student, Layton Sch. Art, 1956-58; BS, U. Wis., Milw., 1961; MFA, U. Ill., 1965. Asst. prof. Wayne State U., Detroit, 1965-71, assoc. prof., 1971-80, prof., 1980-85; assoc. prof. U. Wis., Madison, 1985-87, prof., 1987—. Vis. prof. U. Wis., Madison, 1978-79; vis. artist Utah State U., Logan, 1981; art lectr. in field. Exhbns. include Mus. Fine Arts, Boston, 1965, 75, Butler Inst. Am. Art, Youngstown, Ohio, 1967, 68, 72, Lawrence Stevens Gallery, Detroit, 1968, Detroit Inst. Arts, 1971, 77, 86, 91, Richard Nash Gallery, Seattle, 1974, Franz Bader Gallery, Washington, 1974, 77, 80, Madison (Wis.) Art Ctr., 1975, 79, Libr. of Congress, Washington, 1975, Honolulu Acad. Arts, 1975, 83, ADI Gallery, San Francisco, 1975, London Arts Gallery, Detroit, 1976, Boston Ctr. Arts, 1976, 78, Museo de Arte Moderno, Cali, Colombia, 1976, 77, 81, Bawag Found., Vienna, Austria, 1976, Bklyn. Mus., 1976, 84, Met. Mus., Miami, Fla., 1977, 80, Habatat Galleries, Dearborn, Mich., 1977, Visual Arts Ctr. Alaska, Anchorage, 1978, 86, Cranbrook Acad. Art, Bloomfield Hills, Mich., 1980, Associated Am. Artists Gallery, Phila., 1980, Phila. Art Alliance/Phila. Print Club, 1980, Kalamazoo (Mich.) Inst. Arts, 1980, 86, Nat. Mus. Am. Art, Washington, 1982, DeCordova Mus., Lincoln, Mass., 1982, 86, USIA, 1983, Saginaw (Mich.) Mus. Art, 1984, Brockton (Mass.) Mus. Art, 1984, Mich. Gallery, Detroit, 1986, Neville-Sargent Gallery, Chgo., 1986, Intergrafic, East Berlin, 1984, 87, 9th Brit. Internat. Print Biennale, Bradford, 1986, Jane Haslem Gallery, Washington, 1987, 90, 92, 93, John Szoke Graphics, N.Y.C., 1988, Silvermine Gallery, Stamford, Conn., 1988, Elvehjem Mus. Art, Madison, 1989, Boston Printmaker's 42d and 43d Nat. Print Exhbn., 1993, Fitchburg (Mass.) Mus. Art, 1990, New Orleans Mus. Art, 1990, NAD, N.Y.C., 1986, 87, 90, 91, 92, 93, 94, The Hoyt Inst. Fine Arts, New Castle, Pa., 1992, Sodarco Gallery, Montreal, 1993, Davidson Galleries, Seattle, 1993, Galleria Mesa, Mesa, Ariz., 1993, Intergrafia, Katowice, Poland, 1994, Sapporo Internat. Print Biennale, Japan, 1993, Maastricht Internat. Print Biennale, The Netherlands, 1993; permanent collections include: Libr. of Congress, Washington, Art Inst. Chgo., Rose Art Mus., Waltham, Mass., Elvehjem Mus. Art, Madison, Wis., Butler Inst. Am. Art, Minot (N.D.) Art Assn., Silvermine Guild Arts, New Canaan, Conn., Honolulu Acad. Arts, N.Y. Pub. Libr., Detroit Inst. Art, Museo de Arte Moderno, Bklyn. Mus., Met. Mus., Miami, Nat. Mus. Am. Art, Washington, Portland (Oreg.) Art Mus., Art Ctr., South Bend, Ind., USIA, Prague, Czech Republic, and numerous colls. and univs. 1st lt. U.S. Army, 1961-63. Creative Artist grantee Mich. Coun. Arts, 1982; NEA Visual Arts fellow, 1993-94. Fellow The MacDowell Colony; mem. NAD (nat. academician). Home: 2512 Lunde Ln Mount Horeb WI 53572-2440 Office: U Wis Art Dept 6241 Humanities Bldg Madison WI 53706 E-mail: dhbecker@facstaff.wisc.edu.

BECKER, DAVID MANDEL, law educator, author, consultant; b. Chgo., Dec. 31, 1935; m. Sandra Kaplan, June 30, 1957; children: Laura, Andrew, Scott. AB, Harvard Coll., 1957; JD, U. Chgo., 1960. Bar: Ill. 1960. Assoc. Becker and Savin, Chgo., 1960-62; instr. law U. Mich., Ann Arbor, 1962-63; from asst. prof. law to prof. Washington U., St. Louis, 1963—93, Joseph H. Zumbalen prof. law, 1993—, assoc. dean external rels., 1998—. Author: (with David Gibberman) Legal Checklists, 1968, and ann. supplements; Legal Checklists-Specially Selected Forms, 1977, and ann. supplements; Perpetuities and Estate Planning: Potential Problems and Effective Solutions, 1993; contbr. numerous articles to profl. jours. Recipient Founders Day award Washington U. Alumni Assn., 1973, Tchr. of Yr. award Washington U., 1980, 89, Disting. Tchr. award Washington U. Sch. Law Alumni, 1988. Home: 843 Woodmoor Dr Saint Louis MO 63132-3518 Office: Washington U Sch Law Saint Louis MO 63130

BECKER, DWIGHT LOWELL, physician; b. Mercer County, Ohio, July 21, 1918; s. George and Maude R. (Purdyzz) B.; m. Mary Lauer, Sept. 6, 1942; children— Lawrence, Judith, George Edward. B.A., Ohio State U., 1940, M.D., 1943. Intern Christ Hosp., Cin., 1943-44; gen. practice medicine Lima, Ohio, 1946-65; emergency room practice, 1965-87; mem.

staff Lima Meml. Hosp.; med. dir. Blue Cross of Lima, 1970-87; past student health dir. Ohio No. U.; med. dir. Auglaize County Health Dept., Wapakoneta, Ohio, 1994—; ret., 1999. Past chmn. bd. Ohio Med. Indemnity, Inc., Worthington; field med. cons. Ohio Vocat. Rehab.; past bd. dir. Met. Bank, Lima. Mem. Allen County Bd. Health, 1952-55; past v.p. bd. dirs. Allen County Coun. on Aging; past med. advisor Lima and Allen County Vis. Nurses Assn.; past bd. dirs. Sta WIMA, Lima. Served to capt. M.C. AUS, 1944-46. Mem. Am. Coll. Emergency Physicians, AMA, Ohio Med. Assn., Phi Beta Kappa. Republican. Clubs: Masons, Shawnee Country, Elks. Home and Office: 1 Galvin Ln Lima OH 45805-3870 E-mail: dlbmkl@wcoil.com.

BECKER, GARY STANLEY, economist, educator; b. Pottsville, Pa., Dec. 2, 1930; s. Louis William and Anna (Sisking) Becker; m. Doria Slote, Sept. 19, 1954 (dec.); children: Judith Sarah, Catherine Jean; m. Guity Nashat, Oct. 31, 1979; children: Michael Claffey, Cyrus Claffey. AB summa cum laude, Princeton U., 1951, PhD (hon.) , 1991; AM, U. Chgo., 1953, PhD, 1955, Hebrew U., Jerusalem, 1985, Knox Coll., 1985, U. Ill., Chgo., 1988, SUNY, 1990, U. Palermo, Buenos Aires, 1993, Columbia U., 1993, Warsaw (Poland) Sch. Econs., 1995, U. Econs., Prague, Czech Republic, 1995, U. Miami, 1995, U. Rochester, 1995, Hofstra U., 1997, U. d'Aix-Marselles, 1999, U. Athens, 2002. Asst. prof. U. Chgo., 1954—57; from asst. prof. to assoc. prof. Columbia U., N.Y.C., 1957—60, prof. econs., 1960—68, Arthur Lehman prof. econs., 1968—70; prof. econs. U. Chgo., 1970—83, Univ. prof. econs. and sociology, 1983—, chmn. dept. econs., 1984—85. Ford Found. vis. prof. econs. U. Chgo., 1969—70; assoc. Econs. Rsch. Ctr. Nat. Opinion Rsch. Ctr., Chgo., 1980—; mem. domestiv adv. bd. Hoover Instn., Stanford, Calif., 1973—91, sr. fellow, Calif., 1990—; mem. acad. adv. bd. Am. Enterprise Inst., 1987—91; rsch. policy advisor Ctr. for Econ. Analysis Human Behavior Nat. Bur. Econ. Rsch., 1972—78; mem. and sr. rsch. assoc. Monetary Policy, Min. Fin., Japan, 1988—; bd. dirs. Unext.com, 1999—; affiliate Lexecon Corp., 1990—. Author: The Economics of Discrimination, 1957, (2d edit.) , 1971, Human Capital, 1964, (3d edit.) , 1993, (Japanese transl.) , 1975, (Spanish transl.) , 1984, (Chinese transl.) , 1987, (Romanian transl.) , 1997, Human Capital and the Personal Distribution of Income: An Analytical Approach, 1967, Economic Theory, 1971, (Japanese transl.) , 1976; author: (with Gilbert Ghez) The Allocation of Time and Goods Over the Life Cycle, 1975; author: The Economic Approach to Human Behavior, 1976, (German transl.) , 1982, (Polish transl.) , 1990, (Chinese transl.) , 1993, (Romanian transl.) , 1994, (Italian transl.) , 1998, A Treatise on the Family, 1981, (expanded edit.) , 1991, (Spanish transl.) , 1987, (Chinese transl.) , 1988, 2000, Accounting for Tastes, 1996, (Czech transl.) , 1998, (Chinese transl.) , 1999, (Italian transl.) , 2000; author: (with Guity Nashat Becker) The Economics of Life, 1996, (Chinese transl.) , 1997, with Guity Nashat Becker: The Economics of Life, 1998, (Spanish transl.) , 2001; author: (in German) Family, Society and State, 1996; author: (in Italian) L'approccio Economico al Comportamento Umano, 1998; author: (with Kevin M. Murphy) Social Economics, 2000; editor: Essays in Labor Economics in Honor of H. Gregg Lewis, 1976; co-editor (with William M. Landes): Essays in the Economics of Crime and Punishment, 1974; columnist: Bus. Week, 1985—; contbr. articles to profl. jours. Recipient W.S. Woytinsky award, U. Mich., 1964, Profl. Achievement award, U. Chgo. Alumni Assn., 1968, Frank E. Seidman Disting. award in Polit. Economy, 1985, merit award, NIH, 1986, John R. Commons award, Omicron Delta Epsilon, 1987, Nobel prize in Econ. Sci., 1992, award, Lord Found., 1995, Irene Taeuber award, 1997, Nat. medal Sci., 2000, Phoenix award, U. Chgo., 2000, award, Am. Acad. Achievement, 2001. Fellow: Am. Econ. Assn. (Disting., v.p. 1974, pres. 1987, John Bates Clark medal 1967), Am. Acad. Arts and Scis., Nat. Assn. Bus. Economists, Econometic Soc., Am. Statis. Assn.; mem.: NAE, NAS, Nat. Assn. Bus. Economists, Econ. History Assn., Pontifical Acad. Scis., Western Econ. Assn. (v.p. 1995—96, pres. 1996—97), Mont Pelerin Soc. (exec. bd. dirs. 1985—96, v.p. 1989—90, pres. 1990—92), Internat. Union for Sci. Study Population, Am. Philos. Soc., Nat. Assn. Bus. Economists, Phi Beta Kappa. Office: U Chgo Dept Econs 1126 E 59th St Chicago IL 60637-1580

BECKER, JOANN ELIZABETH, insurance company executive; b. Chester, Pa., Oct. 29, 1948; d. James Thomas and Elizabeth Theresa (Barnett) Clark; m. David Norbert Becker, June 7, 1969. BA, Washington U., St. Louis, 1970, MA, 1971. CLU, ChFC, FLMI/M, CFA. Tchr. Kirkwood (Mo.) Sch. Dist., 1971-73; devel. and sr. devel. analyst Lincoln Nat. Life Ins. Co., Ft. Wayne, Ind., 1973-77, systems programming specialist, 1977-79, sr. project mgr., 1979-81, asst. v.p., 1981-85, 2d v.p., 1985-88, v.p., 1988-91; pres., CEO The Richard Leahy Corp., 1991-93; pres. Lincoln Nat. Corp. Equity Sales Corp, 1993-94; v.p. portfolio mgmt. group Lincoln Nat. Investment Mgmt. Co., 1994-97; dir. investment mgmt. SVP, 1997—. Contbr. articles to profl. jours. Bd. dirs. Ind. Humanities Coun., Indpls., 1991-96, treas., mem. exec. com., 1994-95, mem. devel. com., 1995-96; bd. dirs. Auburn (Ind.) Cord Duesenberg Mus., 1995—, mem. devel. and exec. com., 1997—. Named Women of Achievement, YWCA, Ft. Wayne, 1986, Sagamore of Wabash, Gov. State of Ind., 1990. Fellow Life Mgmt. Inst. Soc. Ft. Wayne (pres. 1983-84, honors designation 1980); mem. Life Ins. Mktg. Rsch. Assn. (Leadership Inst. fellow, mem. exec. com. 1993-94, mem. fin. svcs. com. 1993-94), Am. Mgmt. Assn., Ft. Wayne C. of C. (mem., chmn. audit-fin. com. 1989—).

BECKER, JOHN ALPHONSIS, retired banker; b. Kenosha, Wis., Jan. 26, 1942; s. Paul Joseph and Hedwig (Hammacke) B.; m. Bonny J. Anderson, July 4, 1963; children: Danial, Todd, Kathryn, Erik B.S., Marquette U., 1963, M.B.A., 1965. Asst. v.p. 1st Wis. Nat. Bank of Milw., 1970-73, v.p., 1973-76, 1st v.p., 1976-79; pres. 1st Wis. Nat. Bank of Madison, 1979-86; exec. v.p. 1st Wis. Nat. Bank of Milw., 1986-87, pres., chief oper. officer, 1987-89, also chief exec. officer, 1988-89, chmn., chief exec. officer, 1989-91; pres. Firstar Corp., Milw., 1990-99; ret., 1999. Div. chmn. United Way, Madison, 1984; trustee Edgewood Coll., Madison, 1980—; mem. fin. com. Madison Republican Com. Served to 1st lt. U.S. Army, 1965-67. Mem. Wis. Bankers Assn. (exec. com.), Greater Madison C. of C. (chmn. bd. 1983). Roman Catholic. Clubs: Madison, Maple Bluff Country. Office: Firstar Corp 777 E Wisconsin Ave Milwaukee WI 53202-5300

BECKER, MARVIN BURTON, historian, educator; b. Phila., July 20, 1922; s. Benjamin and Florence (Wachs) B.; m. Beatrice Lapayowker, Jan. 16, 1944; children: Wendy, Dana. BS, U. Pa., 1946, MA, 1947, PhD, 1950. Asst. prof. history U. Ark., 1950-52, Baldwin-Wallace Coll., Berea, Ohio, 1952-56; asso. prof. Western Res. U., 1957-63; prof. U. Rochester, N.Y., 1964-73; from prof. history to prof. emeritus U. Mich., Ann Arbor, Mich., 1973—95, prof. emeritus, 1995—. Seminar presenter Spelman Villa of Johns Hopkins U., Florence, Italy, 1995. Author: Florence in Transition, 2 vols., 1967-68, Medieval Italy: Constraints and Creativity, 1981, transl. into Italian, 1986, Civility and Society in Western Europe, 1300-1600, 1988, The Emergence of Civil Society in the 18th Century: A Privileged Moment in the History of England, Scotland, and France, 1994, An. Essay on the Vicissitudes of Civil Society in Scotland, 18th Century, Indiana Law Jour., vol. 72, 1997; series gen. editor Studies in Medieval and Early Modern Civilization for U. Mich. Press, 17 vols., 1990—. Served with AUS, 1944. Fulbright fellow, 1953-55; fellow Guggenheim Found., 1956-57; fellow Am. Council Learned Socs., 1963-64; fellow Inst. Advanced Study, Princeton, N.J., 1968-69; Harvard fellow I Tatti, 1963-64; sr. fellow Humanities Inst., Johns Hopkins U., 1966-67; hon. mem. Deputazione di Storia Patria per la Toscana, 1976. Mem. Medieval Acad., Renaissance Soc. Am., Am. Hist. Assn., Nat. Humanities Faculty, Soc. Scholars (Johns Hopkins U. 1992). Jewish. Home: 2335 Hill St Ann Arbor MI 48104-2651 Office: 4609 Haven Hall Ann Arbor MI 48109

BECKER, MICHAEL ALLEN, physician, educator; b. N.Y.C., Oct. 3, 1940; s. David S. and Sylvia M. (Salomon) B.; m. Mary E. Baim; children: David, Jonathan, Abigail, Arielle, Daniel. BA, U. Pa., Phila., 1961, MD, 1965. Diplomate Am. Bd. Internal Medicine, Am. Bd. Rheumatology. Intern Barnes Hosp., Washington U., St. Louis, 1965-66, resident, 1969-70; asst. prof. U. Calif., San Diego, 1972-77, assoc. prof., 1977-80; prof. medicine U. Chgo. Pritzker Sch. Medicine, 1980—. Mem. biochemistry study sect. NIH, Bethesda, Md., 1991-95. Contbr. numerous rsch. articles to med. publs. Sr. asst. surgeon USPHS, 1966-69. Fellow John Simon Guggenheim Meml. Found.; mem. Am. Soc. Clin. Investigation, Assn. Am. Physicians, Am. Coll. Rheumatology. Office: U Chgo Med Ctr MC0930 Chicago IL 60637 E-mail: mbecker@medicine.bsd.uchicago.edu.

BECKER, RICH, state legislator; b. St. Louis, Apr. 16, 1931; m. Nancy Becker; 2 children. BA, Ottawa U., 1992. Ret. sales exec. Sta. KSHB-TV, Kansas City; mem. Kans. Senate, Topeka, 1996—, mem. fin. instns. and ins. com., mem. pub. health and welfare com., mem. fed. and state affairs com. Mem. Humane Soc. Greater Kansas City, past bd. dirs.; bd. dirs. Johnson County C.C.; mem. Lenexa Hist. Soc.; mem. del. Rep. Nat. Conv., 1992; mayor Lenexa, Kans., 1983-95, mem. Lenexa City Coun., 1979-83. Mem. Kans. Mayors Assn. (past pres.) Office: 300 SW 10th Ave Rm 136-n Topeka KS 66612-1504

BECKER, ROBERT JEROME, allergist, health care consultant; b. Milw., May 29, 1922; s. Jacob and Sarah (Saxe) B.; m. June Granof, June 25, 1950; children: Scott M., Jill Becker Wilson, Jon G. BS, U. Wis., Milw., 1943; MD, Med. Coll. Wis., 1949. Intern Michael Reese Hosp., Chgo., 1949-50; resident in internal medicine VA Hosp., Wood, Wis., 1950-53; resident in allergy Roosevelt Hosp., N.Y.C., 1955-56; pvt. practice specializing in allergy Joliet, Ill., 1956-82; founder, chmn. bd. dirs. HealthCare COMPARE, 1982-90, chmn. bd. dirs. emeritus, 1990—; cons. health care utilization co., 1982-90; founder, pres. Becker Cons. Corp., 1990—; founder, chmn. bd. dirs. Healthcare Comm. Mgmt. Corp., 1990-93. Med. dir. Quad river Found. Med. Care, 1976-84; pres. Am. Assn. Profl. Stds. Rev. Orgns., 1980-82; exec. v.p. Joint Coll. Allergy and Immunology, 1978-86; mem. adv. coun. Nat. Inst. Environ. Health Scis., 1984-88; bd. dirs. Impac Corp., Am. Psych Sys.; vice chmn, bd. dirs. Madison Info. Technologies, Inc.; bd. dirs. CPR Corp., 2001; chmn. Utilization Rev. Accreditation Commn., 1991-94, bd. dirs., 1994-96. Author articles in field. Pres. bd. edn. Joliet Twp. H.S. Dist. 204, 1969-70, 75-76; mem. bus. adv. com. U. Ill. Sch. Bus., Chgo., 1987—. Recipient Clemens von Pirquet award Georgetown U. Internat. Interdisciplinary Ctr. Immunology, 1978; named Entrepreneur of Yr. Arthur Young/Venture Mag., 1988. Fellow ACP, Am. Acad. Allergy, Am. Coll. Allergists (pres. 1987), Am. Coll. Chest Physicians; mem. Ill. Soc. Internal Medicine (pres. 1984-86), Asthma and Allergy Assn. Am. (bd. dirs. 1987—), Asthma and Allergy Found. Am. (bd. dirs. 1990-94), Am. Managed Care and Rev. Assn. (bd. dirs. 1989-95), Am. Assn. Preferred Providers Assn. (bd. dirs. 1989—), Utilization Rev. Accreditation Commn. (chair 1991-94, bd. dirs. 1991-96), Am. Assn. Preferred Provider Orgns. (bd. dirs. 1988-93), Am. Psychiat. Sys. (bd. dirs. 1994—), Alpha Omega Alpha, Alpha Sigma Nu. Office: 1S 045 Spring Rd Oakbrook Terrace IL 60181 E-mail: wsimed@aol.com.

BECKER, THOMAS BAIN, lawyer; b. St. Charles, Mo., Sept. 3, 1944; s. John Bruere and Marie Louise (Denker) B.; m. Linda Ann Flynn, May 25, 1974; children: Thomas Bain Jr., Shannon Flynn. BSBA, Georgetown U., 1966; MBA, U. Mo., Columbia, 1968, JD, 1976. Bar: Mo. 1976. Acct. Kerber, Eck & Braeckel, St. Louis, 1966, Rothaus, Bartels & Earley, St. Louis, 1968; acctg. analyst U.S. Dept. Commerce, Washington, 1971-73; shareholder Stinson, Mag & Fizzell, Kansas City, 1976-98, Gilmore & Bell, P.C., Kansas City, 1998—. Bd. dirs., v.p., pres. Westport Citizens Action Coalition, Kansas City, 1987—; bd. dirs. Hist. Kansas City Found., 1981-89, Kansas City Union Sta., Inc., 1988-97; bd. commrs., vice chair Mo. Housing Devel. Commn., 1995-98; mem. task force Mayor's Odyssey 2000, Kansas City, 1993; bd. dirs., vice chmn. Citizens Assn. Kansas City, 1996—. Recipient Community Svc. award Westport Coop. Svcs., 1991. Mem. ABA, Nat. Assn. Bond Lawyers, Rockhill Tennis Club (pres., bd. govs., treas. 1999—). Democrat. Roman Catholic. Avocations: sports, politics, reading, travel. Home: 816 Gleed Ter Kansas City MO 64109-2617 Office: Gilmore & Bell PC 2405 Grand Blvd Ste 1100 Kansas City MO 64108-2521

BECKER, VANETA G. state representative; b. Alton, Ill., Oct. 7, 1949; m. Andrew C. Guarino. Attended, U. Evansville. Rep. dist. 75 State of Ind., 1981-91, rep. dist. 78, 1991—, ranking minority leader, 1991—; mem. pub. health & cities & towns coms.; mem. asst. minority caucus State of Ind.; realtor Don Cox & Assoc. Mem. bd. dirs. Albion Fellows Bacon Ctr., Patchwork Cent. Recipient Legis. Excellence award United Mine Workers, 1989; named Legislator of the Yr. Ind. Primary Health Care Assn., 1990. Mem. Nat. Assn. Realtors, Ind. Primary Health Care Assn., Evansville Zool. Soc., A Network of Evansville Women, Leadership Evansville, Crisis Prevention Nursery. Republican. Methodist. Home: 420 E Buena Vista Rd Evansville IN 47711-2720 Office: Ind Ho of Reps State Capitol Indianapolis IN 46204

BECKER, WALTER HEINRICH, vocational educator, planner; b. St. Louis, Mar. 20, 1939; s. Anthon and Maria (Fleischman) B.; m. Ayse Nur Alpyoruk, Aug. 3, 1971; children: Volkan P., Kristal S. BS, S.E. Mo. State U., 1963; MS, U. Mo., Columbia, 1969; PhD, St. Louis U., 1978; MS, Fontbonne Coll., 1989. Cert. tchr. Secondary tchr. Sch. Dist. of Hancock Pl., Lemay, Mo., 1963-64, Mascoutah (Ill.) Sch. Dist., 1964-65, U.S. Dept. of Def., Japan, Turkey, Philippines, 1965-70; vocat. edn. supr. Mo. Divsn. of Mental Health, Farmington, Mo., 1971-79; program analyst Arabian Am. Oil Co., Dhahran, Saudi Arabia, 1979-80, planning and programs analyst Saudi Arabia, 1981-85; vocat. edn. supr. Mo. Dept. of Corrections, Jefferson City, 1990-93.

BECKETT, THEODORE CHARLES, lawyer; b. Boonville, Mo., May 6, 1929; s. Theodore Cooper and Gladys (Watson) B.; m. Daysie Margaret Cornwall, 1950; children: Elizabeth Gayle, Theodore Cornwall, Margaret Lynn, William Harrison, Anne Marie. BS, U. Mo., Columbia, 1950, JD, 1957. Bar: Mo. 1957. Of counsel Baker, Sterchi, Cowden & Rice, LLC; instr. polit. sci. U. Mo., Columbia, 1956-57; asst. atty. gen. State of Mo., 1961-64. Mem. City Plan Commn., Kansas City, 1976-80; bd. curators U. Mo., 1995-2001, pres. 1998. 1st lt. U.S. Army, 1950-53. Mem. Am., Mo., Kansas City bar assns., Lawyers Assn. Kansas City, Newcomen Soc. N.Am., SAR, Order of Coif, Sigma Nu, Phi Alpha Delta. Presbyterian. Clubs: Kansas City (Kansas City, Mo.), Blue Hills Country (Kansas City, Mo.). Office: 2400 Pershing Rd Ste 500 Kansas City MO 64108

BECKETT, VICTORIA LING, physician; m. Peter G.S. Beckett, 1954 (dec. 1974); 1 child, Paul T. (dec.); m. Joseph C. Sharp, 1996. BA, Mt. Holyoke Coll., 1945; MD, U. Mich., 1949; MA, St. Mary's U., 1995. Intern Mpls. Gen. Hosp., 1949-50; fellow Mayo Grad. Sch., 1951-55; clin. instr. Wayne State U. Sch. Medicine, Detroit, 1956-67; staff cons. internal medicine oncology svc. Henry Ford Hosp., 1957-60; rsch. physician Darling Meml. Ctr., 1965-69; rsch. assoc. rheumatology Wayne State U. Sch. Medicine, 1970-72, postgrad. tutor, 1972-73, dir., 1973-76; med. dir. Rochester (Minn.) Health Care Ctr., 1985—90; cons. physician in rheumatology Federated Dublin Vol. Hosps., 1973-76; staff cons. rheumatology Mayo Clinic, 1976-90, emeritus staff, 1990—; asst. prof. medicine Mayo Med. Sch., 1976-90. Fellow ACP; mem. Mayo Med. Alumni Assn., Am. Coll. Rheumatology (ret. mem.), Minn. State Med. Assn., Zumbro Valley Med. Soc., Phi Beta Kappa, Sigma Xi. Methodist. Avocations: teaching exercise class, creative writing. Office: Mayo Clinic 200 1st St SW Rochester MN 55905-0002

BECKHOLT, ALICE, clinical nurse specialist; b. N.Y.C., Aug. 7, 1941; d. Julius and Mary (Katz) Kalkow; m. Richard H. Polakoff, Aug. 12, 1962 (div. 1984); children: Katherine, Michael, Matthew; m. Kenneth Eugene Beckholt, Feb. 3, 1990. BA, Syracuse U., 1962; ADN, El Centro Coll., 1977; BSN, U. Tex., Arlington, 1980; MS, Tex. Women's U., 1988. RN, Tex., Ohio. Staff nurse, outpatient mgr. Irving (Tex.) Cmty. Hosp., 1977-86; staff nurse Meth. Hosp., Dallas, 1986-89, U. Tex. S.W. Med. Ctr., Dallas, 1989-90; pediat. home care nurse various agys., Columbus, Ohio, 1990-94; advanced practice nurse, pub. speaking, preceptor Columbus Health Dept., 1994—. Sec., 2nd v.p., 1st v.p., pres. Am. Cancer Soc., 1971-76, bd. dirs. Irving, Tex., 1971-90, BSE instr., nurse's com., 1990-97, triple touch coord., 1991-97, BSE faculty, 1986-90; vol., auction subchair Sta. KERA-TV, Dallas, 1972-84; CPR instr. Am. Heart Assn., 1984-98. Recipient Outstanding Svc. award Am. Cancer Soc. Columbus chpt., 1992-93; named Outstanding Vol., Am. Cancer Soc., Irving, Tex., 1973, 74, 76. Mem. APHA, Ohio Pub. Health Assn., Sigma Theta Tau. Avocations: gourmet cooking, classical music, travel. Home: 2605 Brookwood Rd Columbus OH 43209-2904 Office: Columbus Dept Health 181 Washington Blvd Columbus OH 43215-4022

BECKLEY, ROBERT MARK, architect, educator; b. Cleve., Dec. 24, 1934; s. Mark Ezra and Marie Elizabeth (Kuhl) Beckley; m. Jean Dorothy Love, Feb. 26, 1956 (div. May 1988); children: Jeffery, Thomas, James; m. Jytte Dinesen, Oct. 24, 1992. BArch, U. Cin., 1959; MArch, Harvard U., 1961. Registered architect, Mich., Ohio, Ill., Wis. From asst. to assoc. prof. U. Mich., Ann Arbor, 1963—69, dean, prof., 1987—97, prof., 1997—2002, prof., dean emeritus, 2002—; from assoc. prof. to prof. U. Wis., Milw., 1969—86. Prin. Beckley-Myers, Architects, Milw., 1980—91. Prin. works include Theater Facilities, 1980—81 (award, 1983), Theater Dist., 1981—82 (award, 1984), Bellevue Downtown Park, 1985 (1st place award, 1985). Recipient Distinction award, Milw. Art Mus., 1986. Fellow: Graham Found., Inst. Urban Design, Am. Inst. Architects (Mich. Pres.'s award 1994). Home: 1016 Scott Pl Ann Arbor MI 48105-2585 Office: U Mich Coll Arch 2000 Bonisteel Dr Ann Arbor MI 48109-2069

BECKMAN, DAVID, lawyer; b. Burlington, Iowa, 1950; BSIE, Iowa State U., 1973; MBA, JD, U. Iowa, 1976. Bar: Iowa 1976; CPA, Iowa. Ptnr. Beckman and Hirsch, Burlington, Iowa. Mem. Iowa Supreme Ct. Commn. on Cts. in the 21st Century, team co-chair, mem. steering com. Fellow Iowa State Bar Found.; mem. ABA (chair lotus notse interest group 1994-98), AICPA, Iowa Soc. CPAs (bd. dirs., sec., exec. com. 1985-88, ethics com. 1988—, chair by laws com. 1987-89, continuing profl. edn. com. 1983-86), Iowa State Bar Assn. (bd. govs. 1990-96, pres. 1998-99), Des Moines County Bar Assn. (pres. 1994-95), Gamma Epsilon Sigma. Office: Beckman and Hirsch 314 N 4th St Burlington IA 52601-5314 E-mail: ddb@iowalaw.com.

BECKMAN, TRACY, state legislator; b. Jan. 7, 1945; m. Janel Beckman; five children. Senator Dist. 26, Minn. State Senate, 1986—; mgr., Owatonna Canning Co., 1996—; cons., 1996—. vice-chmn. Econ. Devel. & Housing com., edn. com.; mem. Agrl. & Rural Devel. Com., Crime Prevention Com., Edn. Com., Edn. Funding Divsn., Fin. Com. & Govt. Ops. & Reform Com.; chmn. Crime Prevention Fin. Divsn., Joing Claims Divsn. State senator Dist. 26 Minn. State Senate, 1986-99; mgr. Owatonna Canning Co.; cons., 1996-99; state exec. dir. Farm Svc. Agy. USDA, St. Paul, 1999—. Vice-chmn. Econ. Devel. & Housing com., edn. com.; mem. Agrl. & Rural Devel. Com., Crime Prevention Com., Edn., Com., Edn. Funding Divsn., Fin. Com. & Govt. Ops. & Reform Com.; chmn. Crime Prevention Fin. Divsn., Joing Claims Divsn. Address: 361 Summit Ave Apt 3 Saint Paul MN 55102-2168 Office: USDA Farm Svc Agy 375 Jackson St Ste 400 Saint Paul MN 55101-1828

BECKMEYER, HENRY ERNEST, anesthesiologist, medical educator, pain management specialist; b. Cape Girardeau, Mo., Apr. 13, 1939; s. Henry Ernest Jr. and Margaret Gertrude (Link) B.; m. Virginia Hobson; children: Henry, James, Martha, Leigh, Hillary, Nicole. BA, Mich. State U., 1961; DO, Des Moines U., 1965. Diplomate Am. Bd. Med. Examiners, Am. Acad. Pain Mgmt.; cert. Am. Osteo. Bd. Anesthesiology. Chief physician migrant worker program and op. head start Sheridan (Mich.) Community Hosp., 1967-69; resident in anesthesia Bi-County Community Hosp./DOH Corp., Detroit, 1969-71, chief resident, 1968-69; staff anesthesiologist Detroit Osteo. Hosp./BCCH, 1971-75; founding chmn. dept. anesthesia Humana Hosp. of the Palm Beaches, West Palm Beach, Fla., 1975-79; assoc. prof. Mich. State U., East Lansing, 1979-88, prof. anesthesia, 1988—, chmn. dept. osteo. medicine, 1985-96; chmn. dept. osteo. surg. specialities, 1996-97; chief staff Mich. State U. Health Facilities, 1988-90, chmn. med. staff exec. and steering coms., 1988-90; chmn. of anesthesia St. Lawrence Hosp., Lansing, Mich., 1984-90, adminstrv. dir. dept. anesthesia and pain mgmt., 1994-98. Chief of staff Sheridan Community Hosp., 1968-69; mem. adminstrv. coun. Mich. State U., 1988-97, mem. acad. coun., 1992-96, mem. faculty coun., 1992-96, mem. clin. practice bd., bd. dirs. sports medicine; mem. internal mgmt. com. Mich. Ctr. for Rural Health; cons. Ministry Health, Belize C.A., 1993-97; amb. Midwestern Univ. Consortium Internat. Activities, 1993; mem. Coll. Hearing Com. 1999-20001, Coll. Admission Com. 1999-2002, Coll. Bylaws Com. 1999-2001, adv. com. on pain mgmt. State of Mich., 1999-2001; program chmn. Am. Russian Med. Exch., 1993-97; bd. dirs. Belize Med. Partnership. Speaker Sta. WKAR, Mich. State U.; bd. dirs. Boy Scouts Am., W. Bloomfield, Mich., 1973-74, Palm Beach Mental Health, 1977-79, Care Choices HMO, Lansing, 1987-88; mem. adv. com. pain and symptom mgmt. State of Mich., 1999—. Fellow Am. Coll. Osteo. Anesthesiologists; mem. AMA, Am. Osteo. Coll. Anesthesiology (chmn. commn. on colls. 1988-89), Soc. Critical Care Medicine, Internat. Anesthesiology Rsch. Soc., Am. Coll. Physician Execs., Am. Osteo. Assn. (spkr.), Am. Acad. Pain Mgmt., Am. Arbitration Assn., Mich. State Med. Soc., Mich. Pain Soc., Mich. Peer Rev. Orgn., Mich. Osteo. Assn. (edn. com.), Ingham County Med. Soc. (edn. com.), Am. Soc. Regional Anesthesia, Soc. Security Disability Evaluation, Soc. Internat. Scholars, Phi Beta Delta. Office: Mich State U West Fee Hall East Lansing MI 48824

BECKWITH, BARBARA JEAN, journalist; b. Chgo., Dec. 11, 1948; d. Charles Barnes (dec.) and Elizabeth Ann (Nolan) Beckwith. BA in Journalism, Marquette U., 1970. News editor Lake Geneva (Wis.) Regional News, 1972-74; asst. editor St. Anthony Messenger, Cin., 1974-82, mng. editor, 1982—. Mem. Cath. Conf. Comm. Com., 1990—92. Mem.: Cath. Journalism Scholarship Fund (bd. dirs. 1993—, v.p. 1995—96, pres. 1996—99, 2001—), Nat. Cath. Assn. for Broadcasters and Communicators (bd. dirs. 1989—96, 1997—98), Fedn. Ch. Press Assns. of Internat. Cath. Union of the Press (3d v.p. 1989—92, pres. 1992—), Cin. Editors Assn., Women in Comms., Cath. Press Assn. (bd. dirs. 1986—96, v.p. 1988—90, pres. 1990—92, best interview 1982, best photo story 1985, St. Francis de Sales award for outstanding contbn. to CAth. journalism 1994, best poetry 1997). Office: St Anthony Messenger 28 W Liberty St Cincinnati OH 45202

BECKWITH, DAVID E. lawyer; b. Madison, Wis., Mar. 5, 1928; m. Natalie Biart, Nov. 19, 1948; children: Steven V.W., John B., David T. BS, U. Wis., 1950, LLB, 1952. From assoc. to ptnr. Foley & Lardner, Milw., 1952-98; ret., 1998. Bd. editors Fed. Litigation Guide Reporter, 1985—. Mem. bd. regents U. Wis., Madison, 1977-84, pres., 1982-84; dir., chmn. U. Wis. Madison Found. With USN, 1945-46. Fellow Am. Bar Found., Am. Coll. Trial Lawyers; mem. Order of Coif, Phi Beta Kappa. Unitarian. Avocations: golf, skiing, fishing. Office: Foley & Lardner Firstar Ctr 777 E Wisconsin Ave Ste 3800 Milwaukee WI 53202-5367

BECKWITH, LEWIS DANIEL, lawyer; b. Indpls., Jan. 30, 1948; s. William Frederick and Helen Lorena (Smith) B.; m. Marcia Ellen Ride, June 27, 1970; children: Laura, Gregory. BA, Wabash Coll., 1970; JD, Vanderbilt U., 1973. Bar: Ind. 1973, U.S. Dist. Ct. (so. dist.) Ind. 1973. Assoc. Baker & Daniels, Indpls., 1973-80, ptnr., 1981—. Articles editor Vanderbilt Law Rev., 1972-73. Mem. ABA, Ind. Bar Assn., Indpls. Bar Assn., Ind. C. of C. (com. occupational safety and health law 1982—), Associated Gen. Contractors of Ind. (com. occupational safety and health 1988—, safety and health counsel), Indpls. Athletic Club, ORder of Coif, Eta Sigma Phi, Beta Theta Pi. Republican. Lutheran. Avocation: sports. Office: Baker & Daniels 300 N Meridian St Ste 2700 Indianapolis IN 46204-1782 E-mail: ldbeckwi@bakerd.com.

BECKWITH, SANDRA SHANK, judge; b. Norfolk, Va., Dec. 4, 1943; d. Charles Langdale and Loraine (Sterneberg) Shank; m. James Beckwith, Mar. 31, 1965 (div. June 1978); m. Thomas R. Ammann, Mar. 3, 1979. BA, U. Cin., 1965, JD, 1968. Bar: Ohio 1969, Ind. 1976, Fla. 1979, U.S. Dist. Ct. (so. dist.) Ohio 1971, U.S. Dist. Ct. Ind. 1976, U.S. Supreme Ct. 1977. Sole practice, Harrison, Ohio, 1969-77, 79-81; judge Hamilton County Mcpl. Ct., Cin., 1977-79, 81-86, commr., 1989-91; judge Ct. Common Pleas, Hamilton County Divsn. Domestic Rels., 1987-89; assoc. Graydon, Head and Ritchey, 1989-91; judge U.S. Dist. Ct. (so. dist.) Ohio, 1992—. Mem. Ohio Chief Justice's Code of Profl. Responsibility Commn., 1984, Ohio Gov.'s Com. on Prison Crowding, 1984-90, State Fed. Com. on Death Penalty Habeas Corpus, 1995—; pres. 6th Cir. Dist. Judges Assn., 1998-99; chair So. Dist. Ohio Automation Com., 1997—. Bd. dirs. Cin. chpt. ARC, 1996—, Tender Mercies. Mem. Fed. Judges Assn., Am. Judges Assn., Am. Judicature Soc., Fed. Bar Assn. (exec. com.), Fed. Cir. Bar Assn. Office: Potter Stewart US Courthouse Ste 810 Cincinnati OH 45202

BEDARD, PATRICK JOSEPH, editor, writer, consultant; b. Waterloo, Iowa, Aug. 20, 1941; s. Gerald Joseph and Pearl Leona (Brown) B. B.S. in Mech. Engring, Iowa State U., 1963; M.Automotive Engring., Chrysler Inst. Engring., 1965. Product engr. Chrysler Corp., Highland Park, Mich., 1963-67; tech. editor Car and Driver mag., N.Y.C., 1967-69, exec. editor, 1969-78, editor-at-large, 1978—. Race driver, cons. in field; freelance writer mags. and TV films. Author: Expert Driving, 1987. Mem. Soc. Automotive Engrs., U.S. Ultralight Assn., Aero Sports Connection, Sports Car Club Am., Pi Tau Sigma. Roman Catholic. Achievements include first driver to win profl. road race in N.Am. in Wankel-powered car, 1973; raced at Indpls. 500, 1983-84; 1st driver to go 200 miles per hour at Indpls. in Stockblock-powered car, 1984. Home: Rt 1 Box 779 Port Saint Joe FL 32456 Office: Car and Driver 2002 Hogback Rd Ann Arbor MI 48105-9795

BEDELL, GEORGE NOBLE, physician, educator; b. Harrisburg, Pa., May 1, 1922; s. George Harold and Elsie Clair (Noble) B.; m. Betty Jane Goldzier, Nov. 4, 1950 (dec. Mar. 1970); children: David, Mark, Barbara, Bruce; m. Mirriel Shields Hummel, Oct. 17, 1970; step-children: Judy, Jeffrey, Eric, Deborah, Andrew. B.A., DePauw U., 1944; M.D., U. Cin., 1946. Intern U. Iowa, 1946-47, resident in pathology, 1947-48, resident in internal medicine, 1950-52, research fellow in internal medicine, specializing in cardiology, 1952-54; research fellow physiology Postgrad. Sch. Medicine, U. Pa., 1954-55; asst. prof. dept. medicine Coll. Medicine, U. Iowa, 1955-59, asso. prof. dept. medicine, 1959-68, prof., 1968—; dir. Pulmonary Disease div. Dept. Medicine, 1968-81. Cons. VA Hosp., Iowa City, 1954— ; mem. staff U. Hosps., Iowa City Contbr. articles to profl. jours. Mem. Johnson County Democratic Central Com., 1956-69, treas., 1958-64. Served with AUS, 1948-50. NIH Spl. fellow, 1954-55; recipient Career Devel. award, 1960-70, Walter L. Bierring award Am. Lung Assn. Iowa, 1973 Mem. ACP, Am. Lung Assn. (dir. 1972-80), Am. Lung Assn. Iowa (dir. 1971-81), Am. Fedn. Clin. Research, Am. Thoracic Soc., Iowa Thoracic Soc. (v.p. 1960-61, pres. 1962-63), Iowa Tb and Health Assn. (dir. 1961-65, 67-71), AMA (vice chmn. sect. council on diseases of chest 1971-73, chmn. sec. council diseases of chest 1974-76, Am. Thoracic Soc. del. to AMA 1979-85), Iowa, Johnson County med. socs., Soc. Exptl. Biology and Medicine, Iowa Clin. Soc. Internal Medicine, Central Soc. Clin. Research, Am. Coll. Chest Physicians, Am. Physiol. Soc., Am. Soc. Clin. Investigation, A.C.P., Central Clin. Research Club. Democrat. Unitarian. Home: 903 Highwood St Iowa City IA 52246-3807 E-mail: george-bedell@uiowa.edu.

BEDFORD, NORTON MOORE, accounting educator; b. Mercer, Mo., Nov. 11, 1916; s. Cornelius David and Mary (Moore) B.; m. Helen Grace Horn, Mar. 19, 1943; children— Norton Mark, Martha Ann. B.B.A., Tulane U., 1940, M.B.A., 1947; Ph.D., Ohio State U., 1950. CPA 1947. Faculty Ohio State U., 1947-50, Washington U., St. Louis, 1950-53; prof. U. Ill., Urbana, 1954-90, prof. emeritus, 1987—, Arthur Young prof., 1974-87; prof. Harvard U., 1981-82, U. Calif., Santa Barbara, 1987-92, Claremont Coll., 1993-95, Calif. Inst. Tech., 1996—. Mgmt. cons. Author: Income Determination Theory, 1965, Advanced Accounting, 1961, 2d edit., 1967, 3d edit., 1973, 4th edit., 1979, Introduction to Modern Accounting, 1968, Future of Accounting in a Changing Society, 1970, Extensions in Accounting Disclosures, 1973; Contbr. articles to profl. jours. Served with AUS, 1942-46. Named Sch. Bus. Outstanding Alumnus, Tulane U., 1963, Acct. of Yr., Beta Alpha Psi, 1976; inducted into Acctg. Hall of Fame, 1988; Weldon Powell prof., 1969; Fulbright scholar, 1972 Mem. AICPA (bd. dirs., Outstanding Educator 1988), Am. Acctg. Assn. (pres., named Outstanding Educator 1980), Nat. Assn. Accts. (v.p., bd. dirs.), Rotary. Home: 101 W Windsor Rd Urbana IL 61802-6663 Office: U Ill 302 Commerce W Urbana IL 61801

BEDNAROWSKI, KEITH, construction, design and real estate executive; BS, Marquette U. Joined Opus Corp., Minnetonka, Minn., 1969, advanced through mgmt. and sr. mgmt. positions, pres., CEO; chmn., CEO Opus Corp. and Opus LLC, 1999—.

BEEBY, THOMAS H. architect; Architect C.F. Murphy, Chgo., 1965-71; ptnr. Hammond, Beeby, Rubert, Ainge Inc., 1971—; mem. faculty dept. architecture Ill. Inst. Tech., 1973-80; dir. Sch. Architecture U. Ill.-Chgo., 1980-85; dean, prof. archtl. design Yale U. Sch. Architecture, 1985-91. Adj. prof. Archtl., Yale U., 1992—; mem. adv. bd. dept. arch. Ill. Inst. Tech., 1993—, trustee, 1997—. Designs exhibited: Art Inst. Chgo., Mus. Contemporary Art, Chgo., Cooper-Hewitt Mus., N.Y.C., Walker Art Ctr., Mpls., Venice Biennale; contbr. articles to profl. jours. Recipient Progressive Architecture citation, 1976, 87, 89, Louis Sullivan award, 1989. Fellow AIA (mem. nat. com. on design, nat. honor award 1984, 87, 89, 91, 93); mem. Soc. Archtl. Historians (bd. dirs. 1996-2000), U.S. State, Office Fgn. Bldg., Archtl. adv. bd., 1989-93, Graham Found. (bd. dirs. 1992—). Office: Hammond Beeby Rupert Ainge Inc 440 N Wells St Ste 630 Chicago IL 60610-4546

BEEDLES, WILLIAM LEROY, finance educator, financial consultant; b. Independence, Kans., Apr. 9, 1948; s. Roy William Beedles and Opal Irene (Connor) Hunter; m. Margaret Ann Vanderlip, Dec. 21, 1974; children: Margaret Micaela, Patricia Opal, Cyrus Dean. BS, Kans. State U., 1970, MS, 1971; PhD, U. Tex., 1975. Asst. prof. Ind. U., Bloomington, 1975-78; vis. prof. Monash U., Melbourne, Victoria, Australia, 1984, U. NSW, Sydney, Australia, 1985; assoc. prof. to prof., dir. Masters program U. Kans., Lawrence, 1978—. Vis. rsch. fellow Pub. Utilities Commn., Austin, Tex., 1981 Contbr. articles to profl. jours. Capt. U.S. Army, 1970-78 Mem. Am. Fin. Assn., Western Fin. Assn., So. Fin. Assn. (assoc. editor jour. 1979-84), Fin. Mgmt. Assn. Congregational. Avocation: raquetball. Office: U Kans Summerfield Hall Lawrence KS 66045-7585 E-mail: wbeedles@ku.edu.

BEELER, VIRGIL L. lawyer; b. Inpls., June 6, 1931; s. Elmer L. and Margaret Gwendolyn (Turney) B.; m. Patricia McAtee Walker; children: Stephen L., Philip E. AB in Econs., Ind. U., 1953, JD, 1959. Bar: Ind. 1959, U.S. Dist. Ct. Ind., U.S. Ct. Appeals (7th cir.), U.S. Supreme Ct., U.S. Tax Ct. Assoc. Baker & Daniels, Indpls., 1959-65, ptnr., 1966-95, of counsel, 1995—. Contbr. articles to profl. jours. 1st lt. U.S. Army, 1954—56. Fellow Am. Coll. Trial Lawyers, Ind. Bar Found.; mem. Indpls. Bar Assn., Ind. State Bar Assn., 7th Cir. Bar Assn., Order of Coif, Phi Beta Kappa. Office: Baker & Daniels 300 N Meridian St Ste 2700 Indianapolis IN 46204-1782

BEEM, JACK DARREL, lawyer; b. Chgo., Nov. 17, 1931; AB, U. Chgo., 1952, JD, 1955. Bar: Ill. 1955. Assoc. firm Wilson & McIlvaine, Chgo., 1958-63; ptnr. firm Baker & McKenzie, 1963—. Mem. vis. com. Ctr. for East Asian Studies U. Chgo. Decorated Order of the Sacred Treasure gold rays with rosette Japan. Mem. ABA, Chgo. Bar Assn., Japan-Am. Soc. Chgo. (pres. 1988-92), Am. Fgn. Law Assn. (chmn. Chgo. br.), Univ. Club of Chgo., Tokyo Club, Tokyo Am. Club, Phi Beta Kappa, Alpha Phi. Home: 175 E Delaware Pl Apt 8104 Chicago IL 60611-7746 Office: Baker & McKenzie 1 Prudential Plz 130 E Randolph St Ste 3700 Chicago IL 60601-6342

BEER, BARRETT LYNN, historian; b. Goshen, Ind., July 4, 1936; s. Peter J. and Mabel M. Beer; m. Jill Parker, 1965. B.A., DePauw U., 1958; M.A., U. Cin., 1959; Ph.D., Northwestern U., 1965. Instr. history Kent State U., Ohio, 1962-65, assoc. prof., 1968-76, prof., 1976—; asst. prof. U. N.Mex., Albuquerque, 1965-68, asst. dean Coll. Arts and Scis., 1966-68; Fulbright prof. U. Tromso, Norway, 1983. Author: Northumberland: The Political Career of John Dudley, Earl of Warwick and Duke of Northumberland, 1973, Rebellion and Riot: Popular Disorder in England during the Reign of Edward VI, 1982, (with others) Recent Historians of Great Britain, 1990, Tudor England Observed: The World of John Stow, 1998; editor: (with S.M. Jack) The Letters of William, Lord Paget of Beaudesert, 1547-1563, 1974, The Life and Raigne of King Edward the Sixth (John Hayward), 1993. Am. Philos. Soc. grantee, 1966; Am. Council Learned Socs. grantee, 1973; fellow Newberry Libr., 1991, Folger Shakespeare Libr., 1997. Fellow Royal Hist. Soc.; mem. Conf. on Brit. Studies, Ohio Acad. History, Phi Beta Kappa Episcopalian. Home: 445 Dansel St Kent OH 44240-2626 Office: Kent State U Dept History Kent OH 44242-0001 E-mail: bbeer@kent.edu.

BEER, WILLIAM L. appliance company executive; From market analyst asst. to corp. strategy rsch. dir. Maytag Corp., Newton, Iowa, 1974-91, v.p. mktg., 1991-96, v.p. strategic mktg., 1996, sr. v.p. product supply, 1997, pres. major appliance divsn. Iowa, 1998—. Office: Maytag Corp 403 W 4th St N Newton IA 50208-3026

BEERING, STEVEN CLAUS, academic administrator, medical educator; b. Berlin, Germany, Aug. 20, 1932; arrived in U.S., 1948, naturalized, 1953; s. Steven and Alice (Friedrichs) Beering; m. Catherine Jane Pickering, Dec. 27, 1956; children: Peter, David, John. BS summa cum laude, U. Pitts., 1954; DSc (hon.), Ind. Cen. U., 1983; MD, U. Pitts., 1958; DSc (hon.), U. Evansville (Ind.), 1984; ScD (hon.), U. Pitts., 1998; DSc (hon.), Ramapo Coll., 1986, Anderson Coll., 1987; ScD (hon.), Ind. U., 1988; LLD (hon.), Hanover Coll., 1986; DsC (hon.), Purdue U., 2000; LLD (hon.) , Tex. Wesleyan, 2001. Intern Walter Reed Gen. Hosp., Washington, 1958—59; resident Wilford Hall Med. Center, San Antonio, 1959—62, chief internal medicine, edn. coordinator, 1967—69; prof. medicine Ind. U. Sch. Medicine, Indpls., 1969—, asst. dean, 1969—70, assoc. dean, dir. postgrad. edn., 1970—74, dir. statewide med. edn. system, 1970-83, dean, 1974—83; chief exec. officer Ind. U. Med. Center, 1974—83; pres. Purdue U. and Purdue U. Rsch. Found., West Lafayette, 1983—2000, pres. emeritus, 2000—; chmn. Purdue Rsch. Found., 2000—. Prof. pharmacology and toxicology Purdue U.; bd. dirs. Arvin Industries, Eli Lilly Co., NISource, Inc., Am. United Life, Veridian Corp.; cons. Indpls. VA Hosp., St. Vincent Hosp.; chmn. Ind. Commn. Med. Edn., 1978—83, Med. Edn. Bd. Ind., 1974—83, Liaison Com. on Med. Edn., 1976—81. Contbr. articles to sci. jours. Sec. Ind. Atty. Gen.'s Trust, 1974—83; regent Nat. Libr. Medicine, 1987—91; mem. Lafayette Cmty. Coun.; trustee U. Pitts. Lt. col. M.C. USAF, 1957—69. Fellow: ACP, Royal Soc. Medicine; mem.: Ind. Acad., Nat. Acad. Sci. Inst. of Medicine, Assn. Am. Univs. (chair 1995—96), Coun. Med. Deans (chmn. 1980—81), Assn. Am. Med. Colls. 1982—83, Endocrine Soc., Am. Diabetes Assn., Am. Fedn. Med. Rsch., Meridian Hills Club, Columbia Club, Skyline Club, Phi Rho Sigma (U.S. v.p. 1976—85), Alpha Omega Alpha, Sigma Xi, Phi Beta Kappa. Presbyterian. Home: 3746 Westlake Ct West Lafayette IN 47906-8612 Office: Purdue U Office of Pres Emeritus Rm 218 Memorial Union West Lafayette IN 47906-3584 Fax: 765-496-7561. E-mail: scb@purdue.edu.

BEERMANN, ALLEN J. former state official; b. Sioux City, Iowa, Jan. 14, 1940; B.A., Midland Lutheran Coll., Fremont, Nebr., 1962; J.D., Creighton U., Omaha, 1965; LLD (hon.), Midland Luth. Coll., 1995. Bar: Nebr. 1965. Legal counsel, adminstrv. asst. to sec. state, State of Nebr., 1965-67; dep. sec. state, 1967-71; sec. of state, 1971-95. Mem. Fed. Election Commn. adv. panel. Bd. dirs. NebraskaLand Found.; exec. bd. Cornhusker coun. Boy Scouts Am.; state chair N.E. Commn. Employer Support for Guard and Res., 1997-2000. Lt. col. U.S. Army, ret. Recipient Disting. Svc. plaque Omaha Legal Aid Soc., 1964, Silver Beaver award Boy Scouts Am., 1979, Fgn. Svc. Medallion Rep. of China, 2001, Homeland Def. Ribbon Rep. of China, 2001; named Outstanding Young Man Lincoln Jaycees, 1975, Outstanding Young Man Nebr. Jaycees, 1975 Mem. ABA, Nat. Assn. Secs. State (pres. 1976-77), Nebr. Bar Assn. (exec. dir. 1995—), Nebr. Press Assn., Am. Legion (fed. election commn. adv. panel, Cert. Appreciation). Lutheran. Office: Nebr Press Assn 845 S St Lincoln NE 68508-1226 E-mail: nebpress@nebpress.com.

BEERS, ANNE, protective services official; BA in Edn., Hamline U., 1975. Trooper trainee Minn. State Patrol, 1975-76, trooper East Metro dist. 2400, 1976-80, trooper 1, 1981-83, lt., 1984-88, capt., 1988-92, comdr. East Metro dist. 2400, 1993-95, maj., 1995-97, chief, 1997—. Named Woman of Yr. Women's Transp. Sem. of Minn., 1998. Mem. Minn. Chiefs of Police Assn., Internat. Assn. of Women Police, Internat. Assn. of Chiefs of Police, Law Enforcement Opportunities, Minn. Assn. of Women Police (Carolen Bailey Mentoring award 1992), Minn. Police and Peace Officers Assn. Office: Minn State Patrol 444 Cedar St Ste 130 Saint Paul MN 55101-2142

BEERS, V(ICTOR) GILBERT, publishing executive; b. Sidell, Ill., May 6, 1928; s. Ernest S. and Jean (Bloomer) B.; m. Arlisle Felten, Aug. 26, 1950; children: Kathleen, Douglas, Ronald, Janice, Cynthia. A.B., Wheaton Coll., 1950; M.R.E., No. Baptist Sem., 1953, M.Div., 1954, Th.M., 1955, Th.D., 1960; Ph.D., Northwestern U., 1963. Prof. No. Baptist Sem., Chgo., 1954-57; editor Sr. High Publs., David C. Cook Pub. Co., Elgin, Ill., 1957-59, exec. editor, 1959-61, editorial dir., 1961-67; pres. Books for Living Inc., 1967—; editor Christianity Today, 1982-85, sr. editor, 1985-87; pres. Scripture Press Publs. Inc., Wheaton, Ill., 1990-96, Scripture Press Ministries, 1990—. V.p. ministry devel. Cook Cmty. Ministries, 1996—2000. Author: more than 150 books, including: Family Bible Libr., 10 vols., 1971, The Book of Life, 23 vols., 1980. Bd. dirs. Christian Camps Inc., N.Y., Wheaton (Ill.) Youth Symphony, 1961-63, pres. 1962-63; trustee Wheaton Coll., 1975-92, adv. life trustee, 1992—; trustee Scripture Press Ministries, 1973—. Office: Scripture Press Ministries 250 Pennsylvania Ave Glen Ellyn IL 60137-4327 E-mail: gil3319@aol.com.

BEGGS, CAROL EDWARD, state legislator; m. Betty Beggs. Retailer; mem. Kans. State Ho. of Reps. Dist. 71, 1995—.

BEGGS, DONALD LEE, academic administrator; b. Harrisburg, Ill., Sept. 16, 1941; s. C. J. and Mary (Fitzgerald) Beggs; m. Shirley Malone, Mar. 19, 1963; children: Brent A., Pamela A. BS in Edn., So. Ill. U., 1963, MS in Edn., 1964; PhD, U. Iowa, 1966. Prof. So. Ill. U., Carbondale, 1966—98, assoc. dean grad. sch., 1970—71, asst. dean edn., 1973—75, acting asst. v.p. acad. affairs, 1975—76, assoc. dean edn., 1975—81, dean Coll. Edn., 1981—96, chancellor, 1996—98; pres. Wichita (Kans.) State U., 1998—, prof., 1999—. Cons. Ill. State Bd. Edn., 1966—, Quincy (Ill.) Pub. Schs., 1974—79, Chgo. Pub. Schs., 1977—80, Nat. Inst. Edn., Washington, 1983. Author: Measurement and Evaluation in the Schools, Evaluation and Decision Making in the Schools, 1971, Research Design in the Behavioral Sciences, 1969, Nat. Standardized Tests, 1980. Active United Way Campaign, 1978, Carbondale Schs. PTA, 1972—83; bd. dirs. NCAA, 2001—. Named Outstanding Tchr. in Edn., Coll. Edn., 1969; grantee, Ill. State Bd. Edn., 1979, Ill. Supt. Pub. Instrn., 1968, U.S. Office Edn., 1969. Mem.: Rsch. and Evaluation Adv. Council Ill. Office Edn. (chmn. 1982—83), Ill. Pub. Sch. Deans of Edn. 1982—83, Am. Edn. Rsch. Assn. (sec. div. D. 1976—79), Phi Delta Kappa (one of 75 Young Leaders 1981). Office: Wichita State Univ Office of Pres 1845 Fairmount St Wichita KS 67260-0001

BEGGS, PATRICIA KIRK, performing company executive; BA, Stephens Coll., 1970; MBA, U. Cin., 1984. Mktg. dir. Provident Bank, Cin.; with pub. rels. dept. Ctrl. Trust Co. (now PNC Bank); dir. mktg. Cin. Opera, 1984-91, asst. mng. dir., 1991-97, mng. dir., 1997—. Office: Cin Opera Assn Music Hall 1241 Elm St Cincinnati OH 45210-2231

BEGLEITER, MARTIN DAVID, law educator, consultant; b. Middletown, Conn., Oct. 31, 1945; s. Walter and Anne Begleiter; m. Ronni Ann Frankel, Aug. 17, 1969; children: Wendy Cara, Hilary Ann. BA, U. Rochester, 1967; JD, Cornell U., 1970. Bar: N.Y. 1970, U.S. Dist. Ct. (ea. dist.) N.Y. 1971, U.S. Ct. Appeals (2d cir.) 1975. Assoc. Kelley Drye & Warren, N.Y.C., 1970-77; assoc. prof. Law Sch., Drake U., Des Moines, 1977-80, prof., 1980-87, 93—, Richard M. and Anita Calkins disting. prof. law, 1987-93. Contbr. articles to legal jours. Mem. ABA (com. on estate and gift taxes, taxation sect. 1980—, com. on tax legislation and regulations, lifetime transfers, real property, probate and trust law sect. 1980—, study com. law reform 1996—, chmn. task force on spl. use valuation 1988-93, advisor Nat. Conf. Commns. on Uniform State Laws 1988-93), Iowa Bar Assn. (adviser, resource person, probate, trust sect. 1983-89, 93—), Am. Law Inst. (adviser restatement 3d trusts 1994—). Jewish. Avocations: science fiction, golf. Office: Drake U Sch Law 2707 University Ave Des Moines IA 50311 E-mail: martin.begleiter@drake.edu.

BEHBEHANI, ABBAS M. clinical virologist, educator; b. Iran, July 27, 1925; came to U.S., 1946, naturalized, 1964; s. Ahmad M. and Roguia B. (Tasougi) B.; married; children— Ray, Allen, Bita B.A., Ind. U., 1949; M.S., U. Chgo., 1951; Ph.D., Southwestern Med. Sch., U. Tex., 1955. Asst. prof. Baylor U. Coll. Medicine, Houston, 1960-64; assoc. prof. pathology U. Kans. Sch. Medicine, Kansas City, 1967-72, prof., 1972-90, prof. emeritus, 1990—. Author three books, 5 chpts. in books, more than 70 articles. Fellow Am. Acad. Microbiology; mem. AAAS, Am. Soc. Microbiology, Soc. Exptl. Biology and Medicine Moslem Achievements include current research on history of smallpox, history of yellow fever and Persian founders of Islamic medicine during middle ages. Home: 5415 Hazen Ave Kansas City KS 66106-3229 Office: U Kans Med Ctr Dept Pathology & Lab Med Kansas City KS 66160-0001 E-mail: kulgener@kumc.edu.

BEHLING, CHARLES FREDERICK, psychology educator; b. St. George, S.C., Sept. 8, 1940; s. John Henry and Floy (Owings) B.; m. Jennifer Crocker; children: John Charles, Andrew Crocker. BA, U. S.C., 1962, MA, 1964, Vanderbilt U., 1966, PhD, 1969. Asst. dean of students U. S.C., Columbia, 1962-63; asst. state news editor The State Newspaper, 1963-64; asst. prof. psychology Lake Forest (Ill.) Coll., 1968-74; assoc. prof. Lake Forest Coll., 1974-88, chmn. dept., 1977-84; pvt. practice psychotherapy Lake Bluff, Ill., 1970-88, Buffalo, 1988-95; clin. assoc. prof. SUNY, 1988-95; dir. of undergraduate studies, 1989-95; adj. prof. U. Mich., Ann Arbor, 1995—; dir. intergroup rels., conflict and cmty., 1995—. Contbr. articles to profl. jours. Bd. dirs. Nat. Abortion Rights Action League, Planned Parenthood; mem. long-range planning com. Lake Bluff Bd. Edn. Named Outstanding Prof., Underground Guide to Colls., 1971, Birnbaum Guide, 1992, Outstanding Tchr., Lake Forest Coll., 1981, SUNY, Buffalo, 1991; NASA fellow. Mem. Am. Psychol. Assn., Soc. Psychol. Study of Social Issues, Assn. Humanistic Psychology, AAUP, Univ. S.C. Alumni Assn., Psi Chi, Sigma Delta Chi. Democrat. Office: U Mich Dept Psychology Ann Arbor MI 48109 Address: 1325 Wynnstone Dr Ann Arbor MI 48105-2894

BEHM, R. JAMES, protective services official; b. St. Louis, Jan. 10, 1942; m. Mary Ann Gotway, Dec. 20, 1968; 3 children. B, St. Louis U., 1966; MSW, U. Denver, 1970. Chief probation officer U.S. Dist. Ct., St. Louis. Office: US Ct & Custom House 1114 Market St Saint Louis MO 63101-2043

BEHN, JERRY, state legislator; b. Boone County, Iowa, 1955; m. Dennise. Student, United Cmty. Schs., Boone. Farmer; county supr.; mem. Iowa Senate from 40th dist., 1996—. Mem. Iowa Assn. Bus. and Industry, Iowa Farm Bur. Republican. Home: 1313 Quill Ave Boone IA 50036-7575 Office: State Capitol 40th Dist 3 9th And Grand Des Moines IA 50319-0001 E-mail: jerry_behn@legis.state.ia.us.

BEHNING, ROBERT W. state legislator; b. Indpls., Jan. 18, 1954; m. Rosalie Dix; children: Nathan, Grant. BS, Ind. U., 1976. Vice ward chmn. Wayne Twp., Ind.; vol. Crane for Congrl. campaign; precinct committeeman Decatur; registered and polling coord. Decatur Twp., 1991; mem. Eagle Creek GOP, Wayne Twp. GOP; 2nd v.p. Decatur Twp. GOP; Ind. state rep. Dist. 91, 1992—; mem. com. and econ. devel., labor and employment, 1993—; govt. affairs com., 1993—; chmn. elections and apprortionment com. Ind. Ho. Reps. With L.S. Ayres & Co., Indpls., 1971-73, Great A&P Tea Co., 1973-84; co-owner Plants, Posies and Accents, Inpls., 1977-81; owner Berkshire Florist, Indpls., 1981—; bd. dirs. Multi Svc. Ctr. Mem. Decatur Twp. Civic Coun.; past pres. Luth. Laymen's League No 6. Mem. Nat. Fedn. Ind. Bus., Teleflora Golden Dove Club, Allied Florist Assn. (past dir.). Republican. Home: 3315 S Tibbs Ave Indianapolis IN 46221-2270

BEHNKE, WILLIAM ALFRED, landscape architect, planner; b. Cleve., Jan. 7, 1924; s. Walter William and Constance Helen (Ireson) B.; m. Virginia E. Woolever, Sept. 18, 1948; children: Lee, Deborah, Mitchel, Mark. B.Landscape Architecture, Ohio State U., 1951. Designer Grier Riemer Assos., Cleve., 1951-55; prin. William A. Behnke, 1955-57; asso. Charles L. Knight, 1957-58; partner Behnke, Szynyog & Ness, 1958-61, Behnke, Ness & Litten, Cleve., 1961-70; mng. partner William A. Behnke Assoc., 1970-89; ret. Assoc. prof. Kent State U., 1973-74; pres. Ohio State Bd. Landscape Archtl. Examiners, 1973; vice-chmn. Ohio Bd. Unreclaimed Strip Mined Lands, 1973-74; bd. dirs. Landscape Architecture Found., 1981-85, pres., 1983; mem. adv. bd. Trust for Pub. Lands, 1988—. Mem. Ohio Arts Coun., 1983-84; pres. metro bd. Lake County YMCA, 1989-90. Served with USNR, 1943-46. Named Distinguished Alumnus Ohio State U., 1978; inductee Willoughby-Eastlake Sch. Dist. Hall of Fame, 1999. Fellow Am. Soc. Landscape Architects (v.p. 1977-79, pres.

1980-81). Home: 37334 Harlow Dr Willoughby OH 44094-5758 Office: William Behnke Assocs Inc 700 St Clair Ave W # 416 Cleveland OH 44113-1230 E-mail: wbehnke@rn.com.

BEHRENDT, DAVID FROGNER, retired journalist; b. Stevens Point, Wis., May 25, 1935; s. Allen Charles and Vivian (Frogner) B.; m. Mary Ann Weber, Feb. 4, 1961; children: Lynne, Liza, Sarah. BS, U. Wis., 1957, MS, 1960. Reporter Decatur (Ill.) Review, 1957-58; reporter Milw. Jour., 1960-70, copy editor, 1970-71, editorial writer, 1971-84, editorial page editor, 1984-95; Crossroads sect. editor Milw. Jour. Sentinel, 1995-98. Home: 1110 E Ogden Ave Apt 305 Milwaukee WI 53202-2939

BEHRENDT, RICHARD LOUIS, academic administrator; BA in Secondary Edn., U. Pitts., 1964, MEd in Secondary Edn., 1965; PhD in Higher Edn., U. Mich., 1980. Tchr. Mt. Lebanon (Pa.) High Sch., 1963, Hempfield Area High Sch., Greensburg, Pa., 1965; departmental asst. U. Mich., Ann Arbor, 1965-66; dir. instnl. rsch. Washtenaw Community Coll., Ypsilanti, Mich., 1967; asst. to pres. Ind. State U., Terre Haute, 1967-68, dir. student rsch., 1968-69; dir. instnl. rsch. Hagerstown (Md.) Jr. Coll., 1969-74, dir. instl. rsch. and dir. personnel svcs., 1974-76, dean of supportive svcs., 1976-81; dean of coll. svcs. Clark County Community Coll., North Las Vegas, Nev., 1982-84; pres. Lincoln Trail Coll., Robinson, Ill., 1984-86, Sauk Valley Community Coll., Dixon, 1986—. Instr. bus. and speech U. Pitts., 1964; assoc. prof. mgmt. Frostburg (Md.) State Coll., 1971-74; mem. master planning com. Clark County Sch. Dist.; chmn. Washington County (Md.) Bd. Edn. Open versus Traditional Schs. Study Commn.; mem. Employment and Tng. Coun., Clark County, Nev., Pvt. Industry Coun., Nev., steering com. Correctional Ctr. Location, Ill. Contbr. articles to profl. jours. Bd. dirs. Community Theatre of Terre Haute, Family Svc. Agy. of Washington County (Md.), Big Bros. of Washington County, Crawford County (Ill.) Opportunities; v.p. bd. Potomac Playmakers, Md.; gen. vice chmn. United Way of Sterling-Rock Falls, 1988-89, chmn., 1989-90. Mem. Am. Assn. Higher Edn., Coll. and Univ. Pers. Assn., Assn. Instl. Rsch., Nat. Coun. on Community Svcs. and Continuing Edn., Md. Community Coll. Rsch. Group, Md. Community Coll. and Bus. Pers. Officers Assn., Nev. Assn. for Community Edn., Ill. Coun. Pub. Community Colls., Ill. Pres.'s Coun. (chmn. profl. devel. com.), Coun. North Cen. Community Jr. Colls. (sec., treas. 1987-88, 2d v.p. 1988-89, pres. 1989-90), Jaycees (Sterling, Ill. chpt.), Rotary (bd. dirs., pres.), Greater Sterling Area C. of C. (bd. dirs., v.p., pres.), Phi Delta Kappa. Home: 805 E 19th St Sterling IL 61081-1334 Office: Sauk Valley Community Coll 173 Ill Route 2 Dixon IL 61021 E-mail: behrenr@svcc.edu.

BEHRMAN, EDWARD JOSEPH, biochemistry educator; b. N.Y.C., Dec. 13, 1930; s. Morris Harry and Janet Cahn (Solomons) B.; m. Cynthia Fansler, Aug. 29, 1953; children: David Murray, Elizabeth Colden, Victoria Anne. B.S., Yale, 1952; Ph.D., U. Calif. at Berkeley, 1957. Research asso. biochemistry Cancer Research Inst., Boston, 1960-64; bd. tutors biochem. scis. Harvard, 1961-64; asst. prof. chemistry Brown U., Providence, 1964-65; mem. faculty Ohio State U., Columbus, 1965—, asso. prof. biochemistry, 1967-69, prof., 1969—. Rschr. in peroxydisulfate and nucleotide chemistry. Contbr. articles to profl. jours. USPHS fellow, 1955-56, 57-60; NSF grantee, 1966-73; NIH grantee, 1973-81 Mem. Am. Chem. Soc., Royal Soc. Chemistry, Phi Beta Kappa, Sigma Xi. Home: 6533 Hayden Run Rd Hilliard OH 43026-9642 Office: Ohio State U Dept Biochemistry Columbus OH 43210 E-mail: behrman.1@osu.edu.

BEHROUZ, ELIZABETH JEAN, service director; b. New London, Conn., May 6, 1957; d. Dale and Jane (Senne) Daggett; m. Homayoun Behrouz, Jan. 1983; twins: Darmaan, Shaheen. BS in English, Mt. Scenario Coll., Ladysmith, Wis., 1982. Exec. asst. to dean grad. studies Lincoln U., Jefferson City, Mo., 1983-85, prison ednl. program coord., 1983-85; exec. asst. to sales tax divsn. mgr. Mo. Dept. Revenue, 1985-87; staff asst. Office of Senator Christopher S. Bond, 1989-91, dir. Office Constituent Svcs., 1992—.

BEIERWALTES, WILLIAM HOWARD, physiologist, educator; b. Ann Arbor, Mich., Oct. 6, 1947; s. William Henry and Mary-Martha (Nichols) B.; m. Patricia Sue Olson, July 11, 1982; children: William N., Peter L., Nora R. BA, Kalamazoo Coll., 1969; PhD, U. N.C., 1978. Instr. Mayo Med. Sch., Rochester, Minn., 1979-81; sr. staff scientist Henry Ford Hosp., Detroit, 1981—. Prof. Case Western Res. Sch. Medicine, Detroit, 1994—. Contbr. articles to profl. jours. Pres. Grosse Point Soccer Assn. With U.S. Army, 1971—72. Mem. Am. Physiol. Soc., Am. Heart Assn. (fellow coun. on high blood pressure 1992, honor roll coun. on kidney 1988, chair rsch. fellowship com. Mich. chpt. 1987-90, 92-94, established investigator 1983-88), Am. Soc. Nephrology, Inter-Am. Soc. Hypertension, Mich. Soc. Med. Rsch. (bd. dirs. 1988-94, pres. 1992-94), Nat. Kidney Found. Mich. (rsch. rev. com. 1984-85, 88). Presbyterian. Avocation: collecting antique toy soldiers. Home: 750 Lakepointe St Grosse Pointe Park MI 48230-1706 Office: Henry Ford Hosp 2799 W Grand Blvd Detroit MI 48202-2689

BEIHL, FREDERICK, lawyer; b. St. Joseph, Mo., Jan. 26, 1932; s. Ernst F. and Evelyn E. (Kline) B.; m. Lillis Prater, Mar. 3, 1962. AB, U. Mo., 1953, LLB, 1955. Bar: Mo. 1955, U.S. Supreme Ct. 1968. With Shook Hardy & Bacon, Kansas City, 1955-99, ptnr., 1961-99, shareholder, 1992-99. Chmn. bd. dirs. UMKC Conservatory of Music, Kansas City, 1988-91, Visiting Nurses Assn., Kansas City, 1977-79; pres. Heart of Am. Family and Children Svcs., Kansas City, 1982-84, Friends of Art Nelson Mus., Kansas City, 1979-81. Avocations: tennis, skiing, art collecting. Office: Shook Hardy & Bacon 1200 Main St Ste 3000 Kansas City MO 64105-2122 E-mail: fbeihl@shb.com.

BEINEKE, LOWELL WAYNE, mathematics educator; b. Decatur, Ind., Nov. 20, 1939; s. Elmer Henry and Lillie Agnes (Snell) B.; m. Judith Rowena Wooldridge, Dec. 23, 1967; children: Jennifer Elaine, Philip Lennox. BS, Purdue U., 1961; MA, U. Mich., 1962, PhD, 1965. Asst. prof. Purdue U., Ft. Wayne, Ind., 1965-68, assoc. prof., 1968-71, prof., 1971-86, Jack W. Schrey prof., 1986—. Tutor Oxford (Eng.) U., 1974, The Open U., Milton Keynes, Eng., 1974, 75; vis. lectr. Poly. N. London, Eng., 1980-81; vis. scholar Wolfson Coll., Oxford U., 1993-94, mem. SCR, Keble Coll., 2000-01. Co-author, co-editor: Selected Topics in Graph Theory, 3 vols., 1978, 83, 88, Applications of Graph Theory, 1979, Graph Connections, 1997; mem. editl. bd., assoc. editor Jour. Graph Theory, 1977-80, editl. bd., 1977—; mem. editl. bd. Internat. Jour. Graph Theory, 1991-95, co-editor: Congressus Numerantium, Vols., 1963-64, 1988; contbr. numerous articles to profl. jours. Corp. mem. Bd. for Homeland Ministries, United Ch. of Christ, N.Y., 1988-91, del. Gen. Synod, 1989, 91. Recipient Outstanding Tchr. award AMOCO Found., 1978, Friends of the Univ., 1992, Outstanding Rsch. award Ind. U.-Purdue U. Ft. Wayne, 1999; Fulbright Found. grantee London, 1980-81, rsch. grantee Office Naval Rsch., Washington, 1986-89; fellow Inst. Combinatorics and its Applications, 1990—. Mem. AAUP, Math. Assn. Am. (chairperson Ind. sect. 1987-88, bd. govs. 1990-93, Disting. Tchg. award Ind. Sect. 1997, Disting. Svc. award Ind. sect. 1998), Am. Math. Soc., London Math. Soc., Common Cause, Amnesty Internat., Summit Book Club, Internat. Affairs Forum, Sigma Xi (club pres. 1984-86, chpt. pres. 1997-98), Phi Kappa Phi (chpt. pres. 1993), Pi Mu Epsilon. Achievements include characterization of line graphs and thickness of complete graphs; enumeration of multidimensional trees. Avocations: British culture, reading, gardening, stamp collecting, jogging. Home: 4529 Bradwood Ter Fort Wayne IN 46815-6028 Office: Ind U-Purdue U Dept of Math Scis 2101 E Coliseum Blvd Fort Wayne IN 46805-1445 E-mail: beineke@ipfw.edu.

BEINERT, HELMUT, biochemist; b. Lahr, Germany, Nov. 17, 1913; came to U.S., 1947; m. Elisabeth Meyhoefer, 1955; 4 children. Dr rer nat, U. Leipzig, 1943; DSc, U. Wis., Milw., 1987, U. Konstanz, Germany, 1994. Rsch. assoc. Kaiser Wilhelm Inst. Med. Rsch., Germany, 1943-45; biochemist Air Force Aeromed Ctr., Germany, 1946, USAF, Sch. Aviation Medicine, 1947-50; postdoctoral rschr. U. Wis., Inst. Enzyme Rsch., Madison, 1950, rsch. assoc., 1951-52, asst. prof. to prof. enzyme chemistry, 1952-84, chmn. section III, 1958-84, prof. biochemistry, 1967-84, emeritus prof. enzyme chemistry and biochemistry, 1984—. Prof. biochemistry, dist. scholar resident Med. Coll. Wis., 1985-94; permanent guest prof. U. Konstanz, Germany, 1967. Recipient Rsch. Career award NIH, 1963, Sr. Scientist award Alexander von Humboldt Found., 1981, Keilin medal Biochem. Soc. London, 1985, Krebs medal Fed. European Biochem. Soc., 1989, Warburg medal German Soc. Biochem. and Molecular Biology, 1994, Lipmann plaque Am. Soc. Biol. Chem. Molecular Biology, 1993. Fellow Am. Acad. Arts and Sci., Wis. Acad. Scis. Arts and Letters; mem. NAS, Internat. EPR Soc., Am. Chemical Soc., Am. Soc. Biol., Chemistry and Molecular Biology, Soc. Biol. Inorganic Chemistry. Office: Univ Wis Inst Enzyme Rsch 1710 University Ave Madison WI 53705-4098

BEJA, MORRIS, English literature educator; b. N.Y.C., July 18, 1935; s. Joseph and Eleanor (Cohen) B.; children: Andrew Lloyd, Eleni Rachel; m. Ellen Carol Jones, 1990. BA, CCNY, 1957; MA, Columbia U., 1958; PhD, Cornell U., 1963. From instr. to prof. English Ohio State U., Columbus, 1961-2000, prof. emeritus, 2000—. Vis. prof. U. Thessaloniki, Greece, 1965-66, Univ. Coll. Dublin, 1972-73. Author: Epiphany in the Modern Novel, 1971, Film and Literature, 1979, Joyce the Artist Manqué and Indeterminacy, 1989, James Joyce: A Literary Life, 1992; editor: Virginia Woolf's Mrs. Dalloway, 1996, Joyce in the Hibernian Metropolis, 1996, Perspectives on Orson Welles, 1995, Samuel Beckett: Humanistic Perspectives, 1983, James Joyce Newestlatter, 1977—, James Joyce's Dubliners and Portrait of the Artist, 1973, 5 other books. Pres. Internat. James Joyce Found., 1982-90, sec. 1990—; dir. Internat. James Joyce Symposia, 1982, 86, 92. With USAR, 1958-63. Guggenheim fellow, 1972-73; Fulbright lectr., 1965-66, 72-73. Mem. MLA, Virginia Woolf Soc. (trustee 1976-84), Am. Conf. Irish Studies. Jewish. Avocations: photography, travel, cycling. Home: 1135 Middleport Dr Columbus OH 43235-4060 Office: Ohio State U Dept of English 164 W 17th Ave Columbus OH 43210-1326 E-mail: beja.1@osu.edu.

BELANGER, WILLIAM V., JR. state legislator; b. Mpls., Oct. 18, 1928; m. Lois Jean Winistorfer, 1953; seven children. , St. Thomas Coll., 1948-50. With Honeywell Def. Sys., 1951-90, ret., 1990; mem. Minn. Senate, St. Paul, 1980—. Mem. Commerce and Consumer Protection Com., Rules and Adminstrn. Com., Taxes and Tax Laws Com., Transp. and Pub. Transit Com. Mem. exec. com. Nat. Conf. State. Legislators, Midwestern Leadership Conf., Coun. State Govts. Cpl. inf. U.S. Army, 1946-51. Office: 10716 Beard Ave S Bloomington MN 55431-3616 also: State Senate 113 State Office Bldg Saint Paul MN 55155-0001

BELATTI, RICHARD G. state legislator; m. Marilyn Belatti; four children. Student, Coll. St. Thomas, U. S.D., Creighton U., Mayo Grad. Sch. Senator S.D. State Senate Dist. 13, 1989-92, former vice chmn. health and human svc. com., former mem. taxation com., transp. com.; rep. S.D. State Ho. Reps. Dist. 8, 1995-98, mem. health and human svc. and judiciary coms. Rep. cand. for S.D. State Senate, 2000. Home: 940 N Division Ave Madison SD 57042-3703

BELAY, STEPHEN JOSEPH, lawyer; b. Joliet, Ill., May 30, 1958; s. Donald L. and Miriam A. (Madden) B.; m. Trudy L. Patterson, Nov. 7, 1987; children: Jacob, Katherine. BA, U. Iowa, 1980, JD, 1983. Bar: Iowa 1983, U.S. Dist. Ct. (no. dist.) Iowa 1985. Pvt. practice, Cedar Rapids, Iowa, 1983-88; asst. county atty. State of Iowa, Burlington, 1988-89, Decorah, 1989-92, 95—; assoc. Anderson, Wilmarth & Van Der Maaten, 1993-96; ptnr. Anderson, Wilmarth, Van Der Maaten & Belay, 1997—. Chair Winneshiek County Rep. Party, Decorah, 1992-94. Mem. ABA (chair juvenile justice com. young lawyers divsn. 1992-93), Iowa State Bar Assn. (chair juvenile law com. young lawyers divsn. 1992-94), Lions (bd. dirs. 1991-93). Roman Catholic. Avocations: trout fishing, bicycling, camping. Home: 903 Pine Ridge Ct Decorah IA 52101-1135 Office: Anderson Wilmarth Van Der Maaten & Belay PO Box 450 Decorah IA 52101-0450

BELCASTRO, PATRICK FRANK, pharmaceutical scientist; b. Italy, June 3, 1920; came to U.S., 1927, naturalized, 1943; s. Samuel and Sarah (Mosca) B.; m. Hanna Vilhelmina Jensen, July 6, 1963; children— Helen Maria, Paul Anthony. B.S., Duquesne U., 1942; M.S. (Am. Found. Pharm. Edn. fellow), Purdue U., 1951, Ph.D. in Pharmacy and Pharm. Chemistry (Am. Found . for Pharm. Edn. fellow), 1953. Instr. pharmacy Duquesne U., 1946-49; asst. prof. pharmacy Ohio State U., 1953-54; prof. indsl. pharmacy Purdue U., 1954-90, prof. emeritus, 1990—. Author: Physical and Technical Pharmacy, 1963; contbg. editor: (with others) Internat. Phar. Abstracts, 1970— , Pharm. Tech, 1977— ; contbr. to: (with others) Jour. Pharm. Scis. Served with U.S. Army, 1942-46. Mem. AAUP, Am. Pharm. Assn., Rho Chi, Phi Lambda Upsilon. Roman Catholic. Home: 327 Meridian St West Lafayette IN 47906-2603 Office: Purdue U Sch Pharmacy and Pharm Scis West Lafayette IN 47907 E-mail: pbelcas1@purdue.edu.

BELCHAK, FRANK ROBERT, computer technologist; b. Chgo., June 21, 1943; s. Paul and Marion (Vrba) B. BS, Roosevelt U., 1969; MBA, Ill. Inst. Tech., 1990. Computer tech. capacity planner, systems developer, dealer support analyst Navistar Internat. Corp., Oakbrook Terrace, Ill., 1969—, also mgr., sales mktg. tng., mem. council future employee recognition program. Chief fin. officer, systems. cons. Innovative Software Solutions, Inc., Lombard, Ill. Mem. keystone council John G. Shedd Aquarium. Recipient Gen. Robert E. Wood Citizenship award, 1965. Mem. Computer Measurement Group, Assn. Individual Investors, Art Inst. Chgo., Chgo. Zool. Soc., Edward J. Sparling Soc., Keystone Coun., Internat. Platform Assn., Ill. High Sch. Athletic Assn. Roman Catholic. Office: Navistar Internat Corp 4201 Winfield Rd Warrenville IL 60555

BELCHER, LOUIS DAVID, marketing and operations executive, former mayor; b. Battle Creek, Mich., June 25, 1939; s. Louis George and Josephine (Johnson) B.; children: Debora Louise, Sheri Lynn, Stacy Elizabeth; m. Jane Elisabeth Dillon, May 8, 1987. Student, Kellogg Community Coll., 1959; B.S., Eastern Mich. U., 1962. With Gen. Motors Corp., Livonia, Mich., 1962; adminstr. U. Mich., Ann Arbor, 1962-63; with NCR, Lansing, Mich., 1963-69, Veda, Inc., Ann Arbor, 1969-72; owner, v.p., treas. First Ann Arbor Corp., 1972-83; owner, chief fin. officer Third Party Services, Inc. and Data Scan, Inc., Ann Arbor, Mich., 1983-84; pres., chief exec. officer Data Scan, Inc., 1984-86, Ann Arbor Rod & Gun Co., 1986-88; ptnr. Shipman, Corey, Belcher, Ann Arbor, 1984-86; sr. asst. to pres. and dir. tech. svcs. Environ. Rsch. Inst. Mich., 1988-93; owner, prin. L. D. Belcher and Assocs. Mgmt. Cons., 1993—; v.p. Cybernet Syss. Corp., 1996-97; v.p., owner, dir. Innovative Rsch. Corp., 1999—. Bd. dirs. The Geosat Com., Inc., Washington; corp. dir. M.W. Microwave, Inc., Ann Arbor, Environment Tech. Corp., Ann Arbor, Innovative Rsch. & Svcs., Inc.; adv. bd. dirs. Mich. Consol. Gas Co.; mem. exec. com. Ann. Conf. Earth Observations and Decision Making - A National Partnership, Washington, 1988—, Ann. Internat. Symposium on Remote Sensing of Environment, 1990—, Thematic Conf. Geol. Remote Sensing, 1990, Ann. Thematic Conf. Coastal and Marine Environment, 1992—; co-founder, dir. Ann Arbor IT Zone, 1999. Mem. City Coun., Ann Arbor, 1974-78, mayor pro tem, Ann Arbor, 1976-78, mayor, 1978-85; mem. adv. coun. region 5 SBA, Detroit, 1982-86; pres. bd. dirs. U. Mich. Theatre, 1983-85; bd. dirs. Marcel Marceau World Ctr. for Mime, Inc., Ann Arbor, 1986-89, Mich. Theatre Found., Ann Arbor, 1986-92; mem. nat. Rep. campaign team, 1980. Served to capt. Air N.G., 1956-70. Recipient Outstanding Alumni awards Kellogg C.C., Outstanding Alumni awards Ea. Mich. U. Coll. Bus., Silver Elephant award Rep. Party, Commendation Adminstr. Vets. Affairs, Commendation Ann Arbor Vets. Hosp.; Bügermedaille, City of Tübingen, Fed. Republic Germany; elected Mayor's Hall of Fame, 1995. Mem. Air Force Assn., U.S. Conf. Mayors (past pres.), Mich. Conf. Mayors (past pres.), Am. Soc. for Photogrammertry and Remote Sensing, Ann Arbor Club. Republican. Mem. Ch. of Christ. Home: 1352 Cobblestone Ct Ann Arbor MI 48108-9553 Office: IRIS Corp 1350 Highland Dr Ste E Ann Arbor MI 48108-2263

BELCK, NANCY GARRISON, dean, educator; b. Montgomery, Ala., Aug. 1, 1943; d. Lester Moffett and Stella Mae (Whaley) Garrison; m. Jack Belck, May 27, 1976; 1 child, Scott Brian. BS, La. Tech. U., 1964; MS, U. Tenn., 1965; PhD, Mich. State U., 1972. Cert. tchr., La. State textile specialist coop. extension svc. U. Ga., Athens, 1965-67, chair, dir. Tucson, 1976-79; asst. prof./instr. Mich. State U., East Lansing, 1967-73; family econ. researcher USDA Agrl. Res. Svcs., Hyatsville, Md., 1973-75, nat. extension evaluation coord. Washington, 1978-79; dean, prof. Coll. Human Ecology U. Tenn., Knoxville, 1979-87; dean, prof. Coll. Edn. Cen. Mich. U., Mt. Pleasant, 1987—, interim provost, v.p. acad. affairs, 1988-89. Author: Development of Egyptian Universities Linkages, 1985, Mid-Career Administrators, 1986, Textiles for Consumers, 1990. Mem. exec. com. Mich. Milescular Inst., Midland, strategic planning team Pub. Schs., Mt. Pleasant, 1989—; chair Women's Networking Group, Mt. Pleasant, 1990—. Mem. Am. Home Econs. Assn., Am. Assn. for Higher Edn., Am. Assn. for Colls. Tchr. Edn., Am. Home Econs. Assn., Rotary, Sigma Iota Epsilon, Omicron Nu, Phi Delta, Kappa, Omicron Delta Kappa, Phi Kappa Phi. Avocations: gardening, walking, internat. food tasting, traveling. Office: U of Nebraska at Omaha Office of the Chancellor Omaha NE 68182

BELEW, ADRIAN, guitarist, singer, songwriter, producer; Lead singer, co-guitarist King Crimson; v-drummer Projekct Two; former pop band The Bears. Performed on record and on tour with numerous entertainers and bands including Frank Zappa, David Bowie, Talking Heads, Laurie Anderson, David Byrne, Herbie Hancock, Paul Simon, Nine Inch Nails, Crash Test Dummies, others; albums: (with King Crimson) Discipline, 1981, Beat, 1982, Three of a Perfect Pair, 1984, The Compact King Crimson, 1987, Vrooom, 1994, Thrak, 1995, Thrakattak, 1996, (solo) Lone Rhino, 1982, Twang Bar King, 1983, Desire Caught by the Tail, 1986, Mr. Music Head, 1989, Young Lions, 1990, Desire of the Rhino King, 1991, Inner Revolution, 1992, Here, 1993, The Acoustic Adrian Belew, 1994, The Guitar as Orchestra, 1995, Op Zop Too Wah, 1996, Belewprints, 1998, Project Two/Space Groove, 1998, Salad Days, 1999, Coming Attractions, 2000, (with The Bears) The Bears, 1987, Rise and Shine, 1988; writer: Fantasy (by Mariah Carey); appeared in films Baby Snakes, Home of the Brave, Return Engagement; prodr. Caifanes/BMG, Santa Sabina/BMG, Jars of Clay/Essential-Silvertone, Sara Hickman/Shanachie, Rick Altizer/KMG, Irresponsibles/ABP. Office: Umbrella PO Box 8385 Cincinnati OH 45208-0385

BELL, ALBERT JEROME, lawyer; b. Columbus, Ohio, Apr. 24, 1960; s. Albert Leo and Jean Marie (DeFino) B.; m. Carla Jean Hudak, June 7, 1986; 2 children, Brian Albert, Kristin Elizabeth. BA, Ohio State U., 1982; JD, Capital U., 1985. Bar: Ohio 1985. Writer Battelle Meml. Inst., Columbus, 1982-84; pvt. practice law, 1985-86; vice chmn., chief adminstrv. officer Big Lots Inc., 1987—. Mem. devel. coun. St. Anthony's Hosp., 1990. Mem. ABA, Ohio Bar Assn., Columbus Bar Assn., Assn. Trial Lawyers Am., Internat. Assn. Corp. Real Estate Execs., Ohio State U. Alumni Assn. Roman Catholic. Avocations: golf, skiing, exercising, basketball. Office: Big Lots Inc 300 Phillipi Rd # 924dp Columbus OH 43228-1310

BELL, BAILLIS F. airport terminal executive; Budget analyst City of Wichita, Kans., 1970-75; dir. Wichita Airport Authority, 1975—. Office: Witchita Airport Authority 2173 Air Cargo Rd Wichita KS 67209-1958

BELL, CHARLES EUGENE, JR. industrial engineer; b. N.Y.C., Dec. 13, 1932; s. Charles Edward and Constance Elizabeth (Verbelia) B.; B. Engring., Johns Hopkins U., 1954, M.S. in Engring., 1959; m. Doris R. Clifton, Jan. 14, 1967; 1 son, Scott Charles Bell. Indsl. engr. Signode Corp., Balt., 1957-61, asst. to plant mgr., 1961-63, plant engr., 1963-64, div. indsl. engr., Glenview, Ill., 1964-69, asst. to div. mgr., 1969-76, engring. mgr., 1976-93; cons., 1993—; host committeeman Internat. Indsl. Engring. Conf., Chgo., 1984, 92. Served with U.S. Army, 1955-57. Registered profl. engr., Calif. Mem. Am. Inst. Indsl. Engrs. (pres. 1981), Indsl. Mgmt. Club Central Md. (pres. 1964), Nat. Soc. Profl. Engrs., Ill. Soc. Profl. Engrs., Soc. Plastics Engrs. Republican. Roman Catholic. Home: 1021 W Old Mill Rd Lake Forest IL 60045-3749

BELL, CLARK WAYNE, business editor, educator; b. Casper, Wyo., Feb. 7, 1951; s. Homer James and Jeanette (Hoban) B.; m. Victoria Anne Boucher, Jan. 2, 1971 (divorced); 1 child, Heidi Elizabeth; m. Suzanne Cerny, Mar. 6, 1989; 1 child, Natalie Taylor. BS, Drake U., 1973; MA, Loyola U., Chgo., 1978. Copy editor Chgo. Daily News, 1973-74, reporter, 1974-79; bus. columnist Chgo. Sun-Times, Chgo., 1979-84; exec. bus. editor Dallas Times Herald, 1984-86; editor, assoc. pub. Modern Healthcare Mag., Chgo., 1986—. Lectr. Northwestern U., Evanston, Ill., 1980-83; cons. editor Sales & Mktg. Mgmt. mag., N.Y.C., 1982-84. Bd. dirs. Youth Comm., Chgo., 1981-84, Next Theatre Co., Evanston, 1982-84, Heartland Alliance, 1994—, Chgo. Health Outreach, 1995—, Health Insights, 1996-99. Sloan fellow Princeton U., 1975-76. Mem. United Ch. Christ. Office: Modern Healthcare Crain Comm 360 N Michigan Ave Chicago IL 60601-3806

BELL, C(LYDE) R(OBERTS) (BOB BELL), foundation administrator; b. Balt., Apr. 12, 1931; s. William and Rachel (Roberts) B.; m. Carol Ann Murphy, June 14, 1980 (dec. Aug. 1997); children: Diane, Nancy, Mary Lynn, Catherine, Robert, Brian, Douglas, Jeffrey, Lawrence, Laura; m. Jean Creighton Chapman, Feb. 13, 1999. BS with distinction, U.S. Naval Acad., 1953. Registered profl. nuclear engr. Commd. ensign USN, 1953, advanced through grades to vice adm., 1987, ret., 1988; pres. Greater Omaha C. of C., 1989—. Bd. dirs. Ctr. for Human Nutrition, Omaha, WELCOM, Omaha. Trustee Boy Scouts Am., Omaha, 1990—; bd. dirs. NCCJ, Omaha, 1991—. Mem. Omaha Country Club, Omaha Club (Man of Yr. 1991), Omaha Plaza Club, Omaha Press Club. Avocations: golf, reading, the arts, family. Office: Greater Omaha C of C 1301 Harney St Omaha NE 68102-1832 E-mail: gocc@accessomaha.com.

BELL, DAVID ARTHUR, advertising agency executive; b. Mpls. , May 29, 1943; s. Arthur E. and Frances (Tripp) B.; m. Gail G. Galvani; children: Jennifer L., Jenny L., Jeffrey D., Ashley Tripp, Andrew Joseph. BA in Polit. Sci., Macalester Coll., 1965. Account exec. Leo Burnett, Chgo., 1965-67; pres. Knox Reeves, Mpls., 1967-74; pres. Atlantic div. Bozell & Jacobs, 1974-85; pres. Bozell, Jacobs, Kenyon & Eckhardt, 1986-92; chmn., CEO Bozell Worldwide Inc., 1992-96, True North Comm., Inc., 1996—2001; vice chmn. Interpublic Group of Cos., N.Y.C., 2001—. Bd. dirs. Bus. Publs. Audit, Primedia, Inc.; chmn. Am. Advt. Fedn. Nat. com. coord. United Way Am., Minn., 1975—; trustee Macalester Coll., 1986—88, 1998—, Pitts. Theol. Sem., New Sch. Social Rsch., 1995—, Sacred Heart Acad., NY; bd. dirs. True North, 1998—; chmn. Advt. Ednl. Found.; chmn. Ad Coun. Recipient charter centennial medallion Macalester Coll., 1974; named disting. alumnus Macalester Coll., 1978; recipient Minn. Airman of

Yr. award, 1967 Mem. Am. Advt. Fedn. (chmn. nat. bd. dirs. 1988-91), Am. Assn. Advt. Agys. (chmn. 1996-97. Republican. Presbyterian. Office: Interpublic Group of Cos Inc 1271 Avenue of the Americas New York NY 10020

BELL, DELORIS WILEY, physician; b. Solomon, Kans., Sept. 30, 1942; d. Harry A. and Mildren H. (Watt) Wiley; children: Leslie, John. BA, Kans. Wesleyan U., 1964; MD, U. Kans., 1968. Diplomate Am. Bd. Ophthalmology. Intern St. Luke's Hosp., Kansas City, Mo., 1968-69; resident U. Kans. Med. Ctr., 1969-72; practice medicine specializing in ophthalmology Overland Park, Kans., 1973—. Mem. AMA, Kans. Med. Soc. (pres. sect. ophthalmology 1985-86, spkr. house 1994-97), Am. Acad. Ophthalmology (councillor 1988-93, chmn. state govtl. affairs 1993-97, bd. trustees 2000—), Kans. Soc. Ophthalmology (pres. 1985-86), Kansas City Soc. Ophthalmology and Otolaryngology (sec. 1984-86, pres.-elect 1988, pres. 1989). Avocations: photography, travel. Office: 7000 W 121st St Ste 100 Shawnee Mission KS 66209-2010 E-mail: cd2c@aol.com.

BELL, GRAEME I. biochemistry and molecular biology educator; BSc in Zoology, U. Calgary, 1968, MSc in Biology, 1971; PhD in Biochemistry, U. Calif., San Francisco, 1977. Sr. scientist Chiron Corp.; prof. dept. biochemistry and molecular biology U. Chgo. Contbr. articles to profl. jours. Recipient Outstanding Sci. Achievement award Am. Diabetes Assn., Rolf Luft award Swedish Med. Soc., Gerold and Kayla Grodsky Basic Rsch. Scientist award Juvenile Diabetes Found. Internat. Office: U Chgo Howard Hughes Inst 5841 S Maryland Ave Rm Ambn237 Chicago IL 60637-1463 E-mail: g-bell@uchicago.edu.

BELL, JEANETTE LOIS, former state legislator; b. Milw., Sept. 2, 1941; d. Harold Arthur and Luella Ruth (Block) Jeske; m. Chester Robert Bell Jr., 1962; children: Chester R. III, Colleen M., Edith L. BA, U. Wis., Milw., 1988. State assemblywoman dist. 22 State of Wis., 1982-92, state assemblywoman dist. 15, 1993-96; mayor City of West Allis, Wis., 1996—. Chairwoman ways and means com. Wis. State Assembly. Active child abuse prevention program. Recipient Clean 16 Environment award, Child Abuse Prevention award. Mem. LWV. Home: 1415 S 60th St West Allis WI 53214-5159

BELL, JOHN WILLIAM, lawyer; b. Chgo., May 3, 1946; s. John and Barbara Bell; m. Deborah Bell, Aug. 25, 1974; children: Jason, Alicia. Student, U. So. Calif., 1964-65; BA, Northwestern U., 1968; JD cum laude, Loyola U., Chgo., 1971. Bar: Ill. 1971. Assoc. Kirkland & Ellis, Chgo., 1972-75; ptnr. Johnson & Bell, Ltd. (formerly Johnson, Cusack & Bell, Ltd.), 1975—. Mem. ABA (vice chmn. products, gen. liability and consumer law com. sect. tort and ins. practice 1986-87, 88—, com. on torts and ins. practice sect.), Ill. Bar Assn., Chgo. Bar Assn. (tort liability sect., aviation com. 1982—, chmn. med.-legal rels. com. 1994-95), Internat. Assn. Ins. Def. Counsel, Ill. Def. Coun. (faculty mem. trial acad. 1994), Soc. Trial Lawyers Am., Ill. Trial Lawyers Assn., Am. Coll. Trial Lawyers, Fed. Trial Bar.

BELL, KEVIN J. zoological park administrator; b. N.Y., Aug. 14, 1952; s. Joseph L. and Muriel E. (Beck) B.; m. Catharine Kleiman, Sept. 8, 1991. BS in Biology, Syracuse U., 1974; MS Zoology, SUNY, Brockport, 1976. Rsch. asst. Nat. Audubon Soc., Ea. Egg Rock, Maine, 1975; curator of birds Lincoln Park Zoological Gardens, Chgo., 1975-92, dir., 1993—; pres., CEO Lincoln Park Zool. Soc., 1995—. Leader Zoo Soc. Tours to Africa, India, Nepal and Thailand. Contbr. articles to jours. in field. Office: Lincoln Pk Zool Gardens 2001 N Clark St Chicago IL 60614-4712 also: PO Box 14903 Chicago IL 60614-0903

BELL, MARVIN HARTLEY, poet, English language educator; b. N.Y.C., Aug. 3, 1937; s. Saul and Belle (Spector) B.; m. Mary Mammosser, 1958 (div.); m. Dorothy Murphy; children: Nathan Saul, Jason Aaron. BA, Alfred U., 1958, LHD (hon.), 1986; MA, U. Chgo., 1961; MFA, U. Iowa, 1963. Mem. faculty, Writers' Workshop U. Iowa, Iowa City, 1965—, Flannery O'Connor prof. of letters, 1986—. Vis. lectr. Goddard Coll., 1970; disting. vis. prof. U. Hawaii, 1981; vis. prof. U. Wash., 1982; Lila Wallace-Reader's Digest Writing fellow U. Redlands, 1991-92, 92-93; Woodrow Wilson vis. fellow St. Mary's Coll. of Calif., 1994-95, Nebr. Wesleyan U., 1996-97, Pacific U., 1996-97, Hampden-Sydney Coll., 1998-99, W.Va. Wesleyan Coll., 2000-2001, Birmingham So. U., 2000-2001; judge Lamont Award-Acad. Am. Poets, 1989-91, Pushcart Prizes, 1991, 97, Western Book Awards-Western States Arts Fedn., 1991, Nat. Poetry Series, NEA, N.C. Arts Coun., Coordinating Coun. Lit. Mags., Discovery Contest-Poetry Ctr. of 92nd St Y, N.Y.C., Poetry Soc. Am., Hopwood Awards, Tulsa Arts Coun., Anhinga Poetry Prize-Fla. State U. Press, numerous others. Author: (poems) Things We Dreamt We Died For, 1966, A Probable Volume of Dreams, 1969 (Lamont award Acad. Am. Poets 1969), The Escape into You, 1971, 94, Residue of Song, 1974, Stars Which See, Stars Which Do Not See, 1977 (Nat. Book award finalist 1977), 92, These Green-Going-To-Yellow, 1981, Drawn by Stones, by Earth, by Things That Have Been in the Fire, 1984, New and Selected Poems, 1987, Iris of Creation, 1990, The Book of the Dead Man, 1994, Ardor: The Book of the Dead Man, vol. 2, 1997, Wednesday: Selected Poems, 1998, Poetry for a Midsummer's Night, 1998, Nightworks: Poems 1962-2000, 2000, Ashes Poetica, 2002; (essays) Old Snow Just Melting: Essays and Interviews, 1983; (anthology) A Marvin Bell Reader, 1994; co-author: Segues: A Correspondence in Poetry, 1983, Annie-Over, 1988, editor, pub. Statements, 1959-64; poetry editor The Iowa Rev., 1969-71, guest poetry editor, 1980; poetry editor The Pushcart Prize, vol. XXI, 1996-97, editor-at-large vol. series, 1994-96, series editor, poetry, 1997—; columnist The Am. Poetry Rev., 1975-78, 90-92; contbr. and commd. poetry to numerous mags. and anthologies. Fellow Guggenheim Found., 1977, NEA, 1978, 84; Sr. Fulbright scholar to Yugoslavia, 1983, Sr. Fulbright scholar to Australia, 1986; recipient Bess Hokin award Poetry, 1969, Emily Clark Balch prize Va. Quar. Rev., 1970, Am. Poetry Rev. prize, 1982, Lit. award Am. Acad. Arts and Letters, 1994; named Poet Laureate of Iowa, 2000. Home: 1416 E College St Iowa City IA 52245-4409 also: PO Box 1759 Port Townsend WA 98368-0180 Office: U Iowa Writer's Workshop Dey House Iowa City IA 52242

BELL, ROBERT, orchestra executive; Ops. & pers. mgr. Toledo Symphony Orch., mng. dir., pres., CEO, 1984—. Office: Toledo Symphony Orch 1838 Parkwood Ave Ste 310 Toledo OH 43624-2502

BELL, ROBERT HOLMES, county judge; b. Lansing, Mich., Apr. 19, 1944; s. Preston C. and Eileen (Holmes) B.; m. Helen Mortensen, June 28, 1968; children: Robert Holmes Jr., Ruth Eileen, Jonathan Neil. BA, Wheaton Coll., 1966; JD, Wayne State U., 1969. Bar: Mich. 1970, U.S. Dist. Ct. (we. dist.) Mich. 1970. Asst. prosecutor Ingham County Prosecutor's Office, Lansing, Mich., 1969-72; state dist. judge Mich. State Cts., 1973-78, state cir. judge, 1979-87; judge U.S. Dist. Ct. Mich., Grand Rapids, Mich., 1987-2001, chief judge, 2001—. Office: US Dist Ct 402 Fed Bldg 110 Michigan St NW Grand Rapids MI 49503-2363 E-mail: kim@miwd.uscourts.gov.

BELL, SAMUEL H. federal judge, educator; b. Rochester, N.Y., Dec. 31, 1925; s. Samuel H. and Marie C. (Williams) B.; m. Joyce Elaine Shaw, 1948 (dec.): children: Henry W., Steven D.; m. Jennie Lee McCall, 1983 BA, Coll. Wooster, 1947; JD, U. Akron, 1952. Pvt. practice, Cuyahoga Falls, Ohio, 1956-68; asst. pros. atty. Summit County, 1956-58; judge Cuyahoga Falls Mcpl. Ct., 1968-73, Ct. of Common Pleas, Akron, 1973-77, Ohio Ct. Appeals, 9th Jud. Dist., Akron, 1977-82, U.S. Dist. Ct. (no. dist.) Ohio, Akron, 1982-2000, sr. status, 1996; sr. judge. Adj. prof. Coll. Wooster, 1987—; adj. prof., adv. bd. U. Akron Sch. Law, past trustee Dean's club; bd. dirs. Jos. R. Miller Found. Co-author: Federal Practice Guide 6th Cir., 1996. Recipient Disting. Alumni award U. Akron, 1988, St. Thomas More award, 1987. Fellow Akron Bar Found. (trustee 1989-94, pres. 1993-94); mem. Fed. Bar Assn., Akron Bar Assn., Akron U. Sch. Law Alumni Assn. (Disting. Alumni award 1983), Charles F. Scanlon Akron Inn Ct. (pres. 1990-92), Akron City Club, Masons, Phi Alpha Delta. Republican. Presbyterian. Office: US Dist Ct 526 Fed Bldg & US Courthouse 2 S Main St Akron OH 44308-1813

BELL, STEPHEN SCOTT (STEVE BELL), journalist, educator; b. Oskaloosa, Iowa, Dec. 9, 1935; s. Howard Arthur and Florance (Scott) B.; m. Joyce Dillavou, June 16, 1957; children: Allison Kay, Hilary Ann. B.A., Central Coll., Pella, Iowa, 1959, Ph.D. (hon.), 1969; M.S. in Journalism, Northwestern U., 1963. Announcer Radio Sta. KBOE, Oskaloosa, 1955-59; reporter WOI-TV, Ames, Iowa, 1959-60; news writer WGN Radio-TV, Chgo., 1960-61; reporter, anchorman WOW-TV, Omaha, 1962-65; anchorman Radio Sta. WNEW, N.Y.C., 1965-66; corr. ABC News, 1967-86, assignments include corr. Vietnam, 1970-71, polit. corr., 1968, 72, chief Asia corr., 1972-73, White House corr., 1974-75; news anchorman World News This Morning and Good Morning Am., 1975-86; news anchor KYW-TV, Phila., 1987-91, USA Network Updates, 1989-92; prof. telecomm. Ball State U., Muncie, Ind., 1992—. Recipient Emmy nominations, 1965, 73, Overseas Press Club award, 1969, Headliner award, 1975 Mem. AFTRA, Council Fgn. Relations. Presbyterian (elder). Office: Ball State U Dept Telecommunications Muncie IN 47306-0001

BELL, WILLIAM VERNON, utility executive; b. Council Bluffs, Iowa, July 30, 1919; s. William Henry and Lillian May (Roper) B.; m. Virginia Nelson, Nov. 15, 1942; children— Patricia Jane, Stephen William. B.S. in Chem. Engring., U. Iowa, 1942. Registered profl. engr., Ind. Sales dir. Met. Utilities Dist., Omaha, 1946-62; sales mgr. Ind. Gas Co. Inc., Indpls., 1962-64, v.p., 1964-74, sr. v.p. gas supply and consumer services, 1974-85; bus. counselor SCORE, Carmel, IN, 1991—. Bd. mem., OH Valley Gas Co., bd. mem., Meals on Wheels. Served to capt. C.E., U.S. Army, 1942-46. Named Energy Man of Yr.-Ind., Ind. State Dept. Commerce, 1981, Ind. State Energy Service Award, 1984. Mem. Nat. Soc. Profl. Engrs., Am. Gas Assn. (chmn. mktg. sect.), Blue Flame Gas Assn.-Nebr. (chmn.), Midwest Gas Assn. Episcopalian. Club: Kiwanis. Office: Indiana Gas Co Inc 1630 N Meridian St Indianapolis IN 46202-1402

BELLE, GERALD, pharmaceutical executive; BSBA Mktg., cum laude, Xavier U., Cin., 1968; MBA, Northwestern U., 1969. Mem. staff Merrell-Nat. Labs., Cin., 1969-77, mem. sales and mktg. staff U.S. and Philippines Manila, 1978-82; East Asia regional mgr. pharms. Dow Chem. Pacific Ltd., Hong Kong, 1982-83; product group dir. Merrell-Nat. Labs., Cin., 1983-85; dir. product planning and promotion Lakeside Pharms., 1985-87; dir. mktg. Merrell Dow Pharms. KK, Tokyo, 1987-90; v.p. mktg. and sales Marion Merrell Dow Europe AG, Zurich, Switzerland, 1990-95; pres. Hoechst Marion Roussel Can., Montreal, Que., 1995-97; pres., N.Am., CEO Hoechst Marion Roussel, Inc. Hoechst Marion Roussel, Kansas City, Mo., 1998—. Bd. dirs. Nat. Pharm. Coun., Mid-Am. Coalition on Health Care. Mem. Civic Coun. Greater Kansas City. Office: Hoechst Marion Roussel PO Box 9627 10236 Marion Park Dr Kansas City MO 64137-1405 Home Fax: 913-663-2562; Office Fax: 816-966-3152.

BELLER, STEPHEN MARK, university administrator; b. Chgo., Aug. 14, 1948; s. I.E. and De Vera (Jameson) B.; m. Luanne Evelyn Heyl, June 28, 1970; children: Clancy Dee, Corby Lu. BS, U. Ill., 1970; MS, Western Ill. U., 1972; PhD, Oregon State U., 1977. Asst. head ed. Awards of Rotary Found., Evanston, Ill., 1972-73; asst. dean of students SUNY, Geneseo, N.Y., 1977-81; dean of student svcs. Tenn. Wesleyan Coll., Athens, 1981-83, MacMurray Coll., Jacksonville, Ill., 1984-88, Capital U., Columbus, Ohio, 1988-99, vice pres., dean of student svcs., 1999—. Mem. Nat. Assn. Student Pers. Adminstrs., Am. Coll. Personnel Assn., Assn. of Student Jud. Affairs, Ohio Coll. Pers. Assn., Phi Kappa Phi, Phi Delta Kappa. Methodist. Avocations: railroading, photography. Home: 2474 Seneca Park Pl Bexley OH 43209-1750 Office: Capital U 2199 E Main St Columbus OH 43209-2394 E-mail: sbeller@capital.edu.

BELLET, PAUL SANDERS, pediatrician, educator; b. Phila., June 28, 1945; BA, Johns Hopkins U., 1967; MD, U. Rochester, 1971. Diplomate Am. Bd. Pediatrics. Intern in pediat. Cleve. Met. Gen. Hosp., 1971-72; resident in pediat. Case Western Res., Cleve., 1972-73, fellow in pediat. cardiology, 1973-75; pediatrician USAF/Maxwell AFB Regional Hosp., Montgomery, Ala., 1975-77; asst. prof. pediat. U. Ala., Tuscaloosa, 1977-81, assoc. prof. of pediat., 1981-83; assoc. prof. pediat. Children's Hosp. Med. Ctr./U. Cinn. Coll. Medicine, Cin., 1983-94, prof. pediat., 1994—. Author: The Diagnostic Approach to Symptoms and Signs in Pediatrics, 2d edit., 2002. Fellow Am. Acad. Pediat. (steering com. provisional sect. on hosp. care); mem. Ambulatory Pediat. Assn., Cin. Pediat. Soc., Nat. Assn. of Inpatient Physicians. Office: Cin Children's Hosp Med Ctr 3333 Burnet Ave Cincinnati OH 45229-3026

BELLING, MARK, radio personality; b. Fox Valley, Wis. Grad., U. Wis., LaCrosse. News and program dir. WTDY-AM, Madison, Wis.; news dir. Springfield, Ill., St. Joseph-Benton Harbor, Mich., Oshkosh, Wis.; radio host 1130 WISN, Milw., 1989—. Recipient Best Radio Editorial, Milw. Press Club, Best Investigative Reporting in Midwest, Radio-Television News Dirs. Assn. Office: WISN 759 N 19th St Milwaukee WI 52233

BELLOCK, PATRICIA RIGNEY, state legislator; b. Chgo., Oct. 14, 1946; d. John Dungan and Dorothy (Comiskey) Rigney; m. Charles Joseph Bellock, Nov. 8, 1969; children: Colleen, Dorothy. BA, St. Norbert Coll., 1968. With customer rels. 3M Corp., Chgo., 1968-69; tchr. jr. h.s. Milw. and Fairbanks, Alaska, 1970-72; v.p. sports corps. Dor-Mor-Pat Corp., River Forest, Ill., 1976-84; mem. DuPage County Bd. from Dist. 3, Wheaton, 1992-98, Ill. Ho. of Reps., Springfield, 1999—. Asst. treas. DuPage County Forest Preserve Dist. Mem. sch. bd. St. Isaac Jogues Sch., Hinsdale, Ill., 1989-91; bd. dirs. Hinsdale Cmty. House, 1987-89, U. Ill. Gerontology Rsch., 1988-91, Hinsdale Youth Ctr., 1987-90, DuPage County Bd. Health, Wheaton, 1990—, Care and Counseling Ctr., Downers Grove, 1977—, pres., 1986-89. Recipient award Ill. Health Dept., 1992, Woman of Yr. award Serenity House, Addison, Ill. Roman Catholic. Office: 6301 S Cass Ave Westmont IL 60559-3277 Home: 431 Canterbury Ct Hinsdale IL 60521-2825

BELLOW, ALEXANDRA, mathematician, educator; b. Bucharest, Romania, Aug. 30, 1935; d. Dumitru and Florica Bagdasar; m. Cassius Ionescu Tulcea, Apr. 1956 (div. 1969); m. Saul G. Bellow, Oct. 1974 (div. 1986); m. Alberto P. Calderon, Sept., 1989 (dec. 1998). M.S. in Math, U. Bucharest, 1957; Ph.D. in Math., Yale U., 1959. Research assoc. Yale U., New Haven, 1959-61, U. Pa., Phila., 1961-62, asst. prof., 1962-64; assoc. prof. U. Ill., 1964-67; prof. Northwestern U., Evanston, Ill., 1967-96, prof. emeritus, 1996—. Emmy Noether lectr., 1991. Author: (with C. Ionescu Tulcea) Topics in the Theory of Lifting, 1969; assoc. editor: Annals of Probability, 1979-83, Advances in Math., 1979— . Recipient Sr. Disting. Scientist award Alexander von Humboldt Found., 1987; Fairchild Disting. scholar Calif. Inst. Tech., 1980; NSF grantee Mem. Sigma Xi. Office: Northwestern U Dept of Math 2033 Sheridan Rd Evanston IL 60208-2730 E-mail: a_bellow@math.northwestern.edu.

BELLUSCHI, ANTHONY C. architect; b. Portland, Oreg., Aug. 2, 1941; s. Pietro and Helen (Hemila) B.; m. Helen Risom, June 25, 1966 (div. 1975); children: Pietro Antonio, Catharine Camilla; m. Martha Mull Page, July 17, 1992. BArch, R.I. Sch. Design, 1966. Lic. arch. 28 states including N.Y., Mass., R.I., Calif., N.J., Oreg., Ill., Fla., Ga. Draftsman Ernest Kump Assocs., San Francisco, 1964; designer Zimmer-Gunsel-Frasca, Portland, 1965; assoc. Jung/Brannen Assocs., Boston, 1968-73; prin., treas. Belluschi/Daskalakis Inc., 1973-77; sr. v.p. Charles Kober Assocs., L.A., 1977-84; mng. ptnr. Kober/Belluschi Assocs., Chgo., 1984-87; pres. Anthony Belluschi Assocs. Inc., 1984-87; founder Anthony Belluschi Archs., Ltd., Chgo., 1988-2000; pres. Belluschi-OWP&P Arch. INc., 2000—. Archtl. cons. U.S. Peace Corps, El Salvador, 1966-68; trustee R.I. Sch. Design, 1986—, vice chmn., 1995-2000, chair bd., 2000—. Bd. adv. Inland Arch. Mag., 1992-95. Bd. dirs. Friends of the Park, Chgo., 1993—. Recipient First prize sculpture contest RKO & Redevel. Agy., Boston, 1973, award of merit Mass. Commn. Housing, 1975, Alumni of Yr. award RISD, 1982-83. Mem. AIA (award of excellence 1997), Urban Land Inst. (award of excellence 1997), Internat. Coun. Shopping Ctrs. (design awards for Erieview Galleria, Clevel., Bridgewater Commons, N.J., 1989, Sportsgirl Office/Retail Hirise Bldg., Melbourne, Australia, 1991, Park Meadows Retail Resort, Denver, Univ. Retail Ctr., Tampa, Fla., 1996, The Falls, Miami, 1996, Northwood Cafe, Appleton, Wis., 1999), RISD Alumni Assn. (founder Chgo. chpt.). Avocation: collecting stamps and coins, automobiles, skiing, hunting.. Home: The Coach House 119 W Chestnut St Chicago IL 60610-3254 Office: Belluschi-OWP&P Arch Inc 111 W Washington St Ste 2100 Chicago IL 60602-2783

BELOT, MONTI L., III, federal judge; b. Kansas City, Mar. 4, 1943; m. Karen Ann Neeley. BA, U. Kansas, 1965, JD, 1968. Law clk. to Hon. Wesley E. Brown U.S. Dist. Ct., Kans., 1971-73; asst. U.S. atty. Topeka, 1973-76; atty. Weeks, Thomas & Lysaught, Kansas City, 1976-83, Hall, Levy, Lively, DeVore, Belot & Bell, Coffeyville, 1983-91; U.S. dist. judge, 1991—. Spl. asst. to U.S. Atty., Topeka, 1976-78; mem. adv. com. Civil Justice Reform Act. Trustee Coffeyville Regional Med. Ctr., Kans. U. Alumni Assn. With USN, 1968-71. Mem. Kansas Bar Assn., Southeast Kansas Bar Assn., Montgomery County Bar Assn. (pres. 1991), Kansas Bd. Law Examiners, Assn. Defense Trial Attys., U.S. Dist. Ct. Kansas, Coffeyville Rotary Club, Sigma Chi. Office: 111 US Courthouse 401 N Market St Wichita KS 67202-2089

BELTER, WESLEY R. state legislator; b. Fargo, N.D., Apr. 18, 1945; s. Wesley R. and Rachel (Dimmer) B.; m. Judy Grauman; children: Michael, Matthew, Mark. BS, MS, N.D. State U., 1970. Farmer; mem. N.D. Ho. of Reps. from 22d dist., 1985—. Mem. Fin. and Taxation Com. N.D. Ho. of Reps., chmn. Transp. Com. Mem. drug adv. bd. Leonard Sch. Major N.D. Air Nat. Guard. Mem. Am. Legion, N.D. Stockmen's Assn., Lions (pres.), Farm Bur. Republican. Address: 15287 47th St SE Leonard ND 58052-9763

BELTON, Y. MARC, food products executive; Bachelor's in Econ. and Environ. Studies, Dartmouth Coll., 1981; MBA in Mktg. and Fin., U. Pa., 1983. Various positions General Mills, 1983-91, v.p., 1991-99, pres. Snack Products div., 1999—. Office: General Mills Inc PO Box 1113 One General Mills Blvd Minneapolis MN 55440-1113

BELYTSCHKO, TED, civil and mechanical engineering educator; b. Proskurov, Ukraine, Jan. 13, 1943; came to U.S., 1950; s. Stephan and Maria (Harpinak) B.; m. Gail Eisenhart, Aug. 1967; children: Peter, Nicole, Justine. BS in Engring. Sci., Ill. Inst. Tech., 1965, PhD in Mechanics, 1968; PhD (hon.), U. Liege, 1997. Asst. prof. structural mechanics U. Ill., Chgo., 1968-73, assoc. prof., 1973-76, prof., 1976-77; Walter P. Murphy prof. civil and mech. engring. Northwestern U., Evanston, Ill., 1977—, chair mech. engring., 1998—. Editor (assoc.): (journals) Computer Methods in Applied Mech. and Engring., 1977—83, Jour. Applied Mechanics, 1979—85; editor: Nuclear Engring. and Design, 1980—88, Engring. with Computers, 1984—98, Internat. Jour. Numerical Methods in Engring., 1998—. NDEA fellow, 1965-68; recipient Thomas Jaeger prize Internat. Assn. Structural Mechanics in Reactor Tech., 1983, Japanese Soc. Mech. Engrs. Computational Mechanics award, 1993, Gold medal Internat. Conf. on Computational Engring. and Scis., 1996, Computational Mechanics award Internat. Assn. for Computational Mechanics, 1998. Fellow: Am. Acad. Mechanics (Walter Huber Rsch. prize 1977, Structural Dynamics and Materials award 1990, Theodore von Karman medal 1999), ASME (chmn. applied mechanics divsn. 1991, Pi Tau Sigma Gold medal 1975, Timoshenko medal 2001); mem.: NAE, Shock and Vibration Inst. (Baron medal 1999), U.S. Assn. for Computational Mechanics (pres. 1992—94, Computational Structural Mechanics award 1997, von Neumann medal 2001), ASCE (chmn. engring. mechanics divsn. 1982). Office: Northwestern Univ Mech Engring Dept 2145 Sheridan Rd Evanston IL 60208-3111 E-mail: t_belytschko@northwestern.edu.

BELZ, MARK, lawyer; b. Marshalltown, Iowa, July 19, 1943; s. Max Victor and Jean (Franzenburg) B.; m. Linda Cole, July 24, 1965; children: Aaron Sanderson, Jane Evangelyn. BA, Covenant Coll., Lookout Mountain, Ga., 1965; JD, U. Iowa, Iowa City, 1970; MDiv, Covenant Theol. Sem., St. Louis, 1981. Bar: Iowa 1970, Mo. 1976. Ptnr. Rosenberger, Peterson, Conway & Belz, Muscatine, Iowa, 1970-72, Keyes & Crawford, Cedar Rapids, 1972-78, Belz & Belz, St. Louis, 1983-87; prin. Belz & Beckemeier, P.C., 1987-94, Belz & Jones, P.C., Clayton, Mo., 1995—. Author: Suffer the Little Children, 1989. Bd. dirs. Westminster Acad., 1977-85, Covenant Coll., 1972-81, Cono Christian Sch., 1993—; moderator Presbyn. Ch. Am., Atlanta, 1991-92, mem. standing jud. com., 1989—. Named Alumnus of Yr., Covenant Coll., 1989. Republican. Office: Belz & Jones PC 7777 Bonhomme Ave Ste 1710 Clayton MO 63105-1911

BELZ, RAYMOND T. manufacturing company executive; b. Chgo., 1941; BS, St. Vincent Coll., 1962; MBA, Ind. U., 1964. Sr. mgmt. USG Corp., Chgo., 1964-94, v.p., controller, 1994-96, v.p. fin. ops. N.Am. Gypsum & Worldwide Ceilings 1996-99, sr. v.p., controller, 1999—. Office: USG Corp 125 S Franklin St Fl 2 Chicago IL 60606-4678

BEMENT, ARDEN LEE, JR. engineering educator; b. Pitts., May 22, 1932; s. Arden Lee and Edith Ardelia (Bigelow) B.; m. Mary Ann Baroch, Aug. 24, 1952 (dec.); children: Kristine, Kenneth, Vincent, Cynthia, Mark, David, Paul, Mary; m. Louise Coquestrain, June 15, 2001. Degree of Engr. in Metallurgy, Colo. Sch. Mines, 1954; MSMetE, U. Idaho, 1959; PhD, U. Mich., 1963; PhD honoris causa, Cleve. State U., 1997, Case Western Res. U., 2002. Rsch. metallurgist Hanford Labs., GE, Richland, Wash., 1954-65; sr. rsch. mgr. Pacific N.W. Lab., Battelle Meml. Inst., 1965-70; prof. nuclear materials MIT, 1970-76; dir. Def. Advanced Rsch. Projects Agy. Office Materials Sci., DARPA, DOD, Washington, 1976-79, dep. undersec. rsch. and advanced tech., 1979-80; v.p. tech. resources TRW, Lyndhurst, Ohio, 1980-89, v.p. sci. and tech., 1990-92; Basil S. Turner disting. prof. engring. Purdue U., West Lafayette, Ind., 1992-98, head sch. nuclear engring., 1998—2001; dir. Nat. Inst. Standards & Tech., Dept. Commerce, Gaithersburg, Md., 2001—. Tech. assistance expert to Mexico UNIAEA, 1974-76; cons. NRC, Taiwan, 1975; mem. Nat. Sci. Bd., 1988-94; mem. sci. adv. com. Electric Power Rsch. Inst., 1987—, Advanced Tech. Inc., 1993—. Author publs. in field; editor: Biomaterials: Structural and Biomedical Bases for Hard Tissue and Soft Tissue Substitutes, 1971; co-editor: Dislocation Dynamics, 1968, Creep of Zirconium Alloys in Nuclear Reactors, 1983; mem. edit. bd. Jour. Nuclear Materials, 1970-77, Materials Tech., 1987-99; contbr. articles to profl. jours. Chmn. bd. health Mental Health/Mental Retardation, Benton-Franklin Counties, Wash., 1968-70; mem. Richland, Wash. city coun., 1968-70; pres. Arts Coun., Richland, Pasco and Kennewick, Wash., 1968-70; bd. dirs. Cleve. Opera Bd., treas., 1982-86, v.p., 1986-91, nat./internat. bd. mem., 1992—; bd. dirs. LaFayette Symphony, 1998—; bd. overseers Fermi Nat. Accelerator Lab., 1999—. Lt. col. USAR, 1954-79. Recipient Outstanding Achievement award Colo.

Sch. Mines, 1984, Melville F. Coolbaugh award, 1991, Disting. Engr. award UCLA, 1987, Honor Roll award U. Idaho Alumni Assn., 1991, Engring. Alumnus of Yr. award U. Mich. Alumni Assn. (Cleve. br.), 1992, Merit award U. Mich. Alumni Assn., 1993, Nat. Mats. Adv. award Fedn. of Mats. Socs., 1997. Fellow Am. Nuclear Soc., Am. Soc. Metals (Disting. Life mem. 1998), Am. Inst. Chemists; mem. Nat. Acad. Engrs., ASTM, AIME, Metals Soc. of AIME (Leadership award 1988, life mem. 2000), Sigma Xi, Tau Beta Pi, Sigma Gamma Epsilon. Republican. Roman Catholic. Home: 4027 Falconswalk Ct Stow OH 44224 E-mail: arden.bement@nist.gov.

BENDER, BOB, advertising executive; Grad., Columbus Coll. Art & Design. With Lord, Sullivan & Yoder Inc., Worthington, Ohio, 1965—, mem. exec. com., bd. dirs., 1984—, pres., CEO, 1997—. Work included in publs. N.Y. Illustrators Ann., Creativity Ann., Advt. Age, Print, Graphis, Comm. Arts. Recipient N.Y. Art Dir.'s Gold award, 3 Silver awards. Office: Lord Sullivan & Yoder Inc 250 Old Wilson Bridge Rd Worthington OH 43085

BENDER, BRIAN, consumer products executive; Sr. v.p., CFO Sibley's and May D&F Divsn.; corp. v.p. capital planning and analysis May Dept. Stores Co.; sr. v.p., contr. Younkers, Des Moines; sr. v.p., CFO Proffitt's, Jackson, Miss., Egghead.com, ShopKo Stores, Green Bay, Wis., 2000—. Office: Shopko Stores Inc 700 Pilgrim Way Green Bay WI 54304

BENDER, CARL MARTIN, physics educator, consultant; b. Bklyn., Jan. 18, 1943; s. Alfred and Rose (Suberman) B.; m. Jessica Dee Waldbaum, June 18, 1966; children— Michael Anthony, Daniel Eric AB summa cum laude with distinction, Cornell U., 1964; AM, Harvard U., 1965, PhD, 1969. Mem. Inst. for Advanced Study, Princeton, N.J., 1969-70; asst. prof. math. MIT, Cambridge, 1970-73, assoc. prof., 1973-77; prof. physics Washington U., St. Louis, 1977—; research assoc. Imperial Coll., London, 1974. Cons. Los Alamos Nat. Lab., 1979—; vis. prof. Imperial Coll., London, 1986-87, 95-96, Technion Israel Inst. of Technology, Haifa, Israel, 1995. Author: Advanced Mathematical Methods for Scientists and Engineers, 1978; editor: Am. Inst. Physic series on math. and computational physics; mem. editl. bds. Jour Math. Physics, 1980-83, Advances in Applied Math., 1980-85, Jour. Physics A, 1999—; contbr. more than 200 articles to sci. jours. Trustee Ctr. for Theoretical Study of Phys. Sys., Clark Atlanta U. Recipient Burlington No. Found. Faculty Achievement award, 1985, Fellows award Acad. Sci. St. Louis, 2002; Telluride scholar, 1960-63, NSF fellow, 1964-69, Woodrow Wilson fellow, 1964-65, Sloan Found. fellow, 1973-77, Fulbright fellowship to U.K., 1995-96, Lady Davis fellowship to Israel, 1995, Rockefeller Found. grantee to visit Bellagio Study and Conf. Ctr., 1999. Fellow: St. Louis Acad. Sci., Am. Phys. Soc.; mem.: Phi Kappa Phi, Phi Beta Kappa. Home: 509 Warren Ave Saint Louis MO 63130-4155 Office: Washington U Dept Physics Saint Louis MO 63130

BENDER, DARRELL G. former state legislator; Former mayor; senator S.D. State Senate Dist. 23, mem. appropriations and legis. procedure coms. Home: 1509 Kennedy Memorial Dr Mobridge SD 57601-1020

BENDER, JOHN R. retired state legislator; b. Pitts., Dec. 14, 1938; s. John R. and Ruth (Brown) B.; m. Cookie Bender, 1963 (dec. Dec. 12, 1993); children: Jay, Jennifer. BS, U. Pitts., 1960, MA, 1962, PhD in Higher Edn., 1969. Dir. residence halls, 1960-61, 63-65; admissions asst. Pa. State U., 1961-62, 65-70, counselor, 1993-2000; ret.; dir. student activities Lorain County C. C., 1970-87; mem. Ohio Ho. of Reps. Columbus, 1993—. Mem. Elyria (Ohio) City Coun., 1984-89, 91-92, Elyria Planning Commn., 1984, Health Svc. Agy., 1991-92; bd. dirs. Lorain Internat. Assn.; mem. Lorain County Sr. Citizens Bd. Named Treas. of Yr., Nat. Assn. Campus Activities, 1984, 87, Nat. Environ. award Izaak Walton League, 1988. Mem. Western Res. Civil War Round Table, Urban League, Lorain County C. of C., KC, Phi Delta Kappa (Pitt Hall of Fame award 1960), Omicron Delta Kappa, Sigma Chi. Democrat. Home: 2346 Roxbury Rd Avon OH 44011

BENEDICT, BARRY ARDEN, university administrator; b. Wauchula, Fla., Feb. 7, 1942; s. Clifford Allen and Caroline Mae (Watzke) B.; m. Sharon Gail Parker; children: Erin, Beau, Brooke, Mark. BCE, U. Fla., 1965, MS in Engring., 1967, PhD in Civil Engring., 1968. Rsch. assoc. U. Fla., Gainesville, 1968-69, prof., 1980-86; asst. prof. Vanderbilt U., Nashville, 1969-72, assoc. prof., program dir., 1972-75; assoc. prof. Tulane U., New Orleans, 1975-77, U. S.C., Columbia, 1978-80; prof., dept. head La. Tech. U., Ruston, 1986-88, dean., Jack Thigpen prof., 1988-98; v.p. acad. affairs Rose-Hulman Inst. Tech., Terre Haute, Ind., 1998—. Project dir. La. NSF-EPSCoR, 1989-94; cons. to numerous industries; dir. Inst. Micromanufacturing, 1997-98. Contbr. articles to profl. jours. and chpts. to books. Mem. NSPE (gov.-at-large profl. engrs. in edn. divsn.), La. Dept. Econ. Devel., La. Transp. Rsch. Ctr. (vice chair 1993-98). Methodist. Avocation: jogging. Office: Rose-Hulman Inst Tech 5500 Wabash Ave Terre Haute IN 47803-3999 Home: 75 Cedar St Port Orange FL 32127-6412 E-mail: barry.a.benedict@rose-hulmon.edu.

BENEDICT, ELISE, moving company executive; div.; 1 child, Steve; m. Marvin Howard; children: Kris, Kim Howard Parks. Grad. in journalism and mktg./acctg. Dispatcher, commn. saleswoman, claims mgr., sales mgr. Univ. Moving & Storage Co., Farmington Hills, Mich., gen. mgr., v.p., pres., CEO, 1986—; co-owner Univ. Bus. Interiors, 1996—. Office: Univ Moving & Storage Co 23305 Commerce Dr Farmington Hills MI 48335-2727 Fax: 810-615-4715.

BENES, ANDREW CHARLES, professional baseball player; b. Evansville, Ind., Aug. 20, 1967; Student, U. Evansville. With San Diego Padres, 1988-95, Seattle Mariners, 1995, St. Louis Cardinals, 1996-98, Ariz. Diamondbacks, 1998-99; pitcher St. Louis Cardinals, 1999—. Mem. U.S. Olympic Baseball Team, 1988, Nat. League All-Star Team, 1993. Named Sporting News Rookie Pitcher of Yr., 1989. Office: St Louis Cardinals 250 Stadium Plz Saint Louis MO 63102-1722

BENFORD, HARRY BELL, naval architect; b. Schenectady, Aug. 7, 1917; s. Frank Albert and Georgia (Rattray) B.; m. Edith Elizabeth Smallman, Apr. 26, 1941; children— Howard Lee, Frank Alfred, Robert James. B.S.E. in Naval Architecture and Marine Engring, U. Mich., 1940. With Newport News Shipbldg. Co., Va., 1940-48; mem. faculty U. Mich., Ann Arbor, 1948-59, 60-83, prof. naval architecture, 1959-83, prof. emeritus, 1983—, chmn. dept. naval architecture and marine engring., 1967-72. Exec. dir. maritime rsch. adv. com. NRC, 1959-60 Author 4 books, 150 tech. papers. Fellow Soc. Naval Architects and Marine Engrs. (hon. mem., pres.'s award 1957, Linnard prize 1962, Taylor medal 1976), Royal Instn. Naval Architects; mem Tau Beta Pi, Phi Kappa Phi. Home: 6 Westbury Ct Ann Arbor MI 48105-1411 Office: U Mich Dept Naval Architecture Ann Arbor MI 48109-2145 E-mail: harben@engin.umich.edu.

BENJAMIN, ANN WOMER, state legislator; m. to David M. Benjamin; children: Katherine, Johanna. BA magna cum laude, Vanderbilt U., 1975; JD, Case Western Reserve U., 1978. Bar: Ohio. Counsel Arter & Hadden, Cleve., 1984—; mem. Ohio Ho. Reps., Columbus, 1995—. Adj. prof. law Case Western Reserve U., Cleve. Producer: Aurora (Ohio) Comty. Theatre; contbr. articles to Estate Planning. Trustee, advocate Broadway Sch. Music and Arts; former chmn. Aurora (Ohio) Civil Svc. Commn. Mem. Ohio Bar Assn., Cleve. Bar Assn., Portage County Bar Assn., Phi Beta Kappa. Office: 77 S High St Fl 13 Columbus OH 43266-0001 also: Arter & Hadden 925 Euclid Ave Ste 1100 Cleveland OH 44115-1486

BENJAMIN, BEZALEEL SOLOMON, architecture and architectural engineering educator; b. Anand, India, Feb. 21, 1938; came to U.S., 1971; s. Solomon and Penninah (Ellis) B.; m. Nora Jacob David, Feb. 25, 1962; children— Ashley Bezaleel, Jennifer Elana B.E. in Civil Engring., Bombay U., India, 1957; D.I.C., Imperial Coll., London, 1958; M.S. in Engring., London U., 1959, Ph.D., 1965. Design engr. M.N. Dastur & Co., Bombay, 1961-63; postdoctoral fellow U. Surrey, Eng., 1965-66; prin. lectr. Hatfield Poly., Eng., 1966-71; asst. prof. archtl. engring. U. Kans., Lawrence, 1971-72, assoc. prof., 1972-76, prof., 1976—. Vis. Fulbright prof. Technion, Haifa, Israel, 1987-88. Author: The Analysis of Braced Domes, 1963, Structural Design with Plastics, 1969, Structures for Architects, 1975, Building Construction for Architects and Engineers, 1978, Structural Evolution: An Illustrated History, 1990, Statics, Strengths and Structures for Architects, 1992; children's book) Susan Altencroft, 1976; (novels) Rampaging Lovers, 1988, A Nazi Among Jews, 1990, Bene Israel Tales, 1991, The Jewish Amendment, 1992, David Rahabi, 1993. Jewish Avocation: writing. Office: U Kans Sch Architecture Lawrence KS 66045-0001 E-mail: benj@ukans.edu.

BENJAMIN, JANICE YUKON, development executive; b. Kansas City, Mo., Aug. 12, 1951; d. Stanley and Frances (Weneck) Yukon; m. Bert Lyon Benjamin, June 14, 1975; children: Brett David, Blair Yukon. AS, Bradford Coll., 1971; BA, Newcomb Coll., 1973; MA, U. Mo., 1978. Tchr. secondary, dept. chmn. Shawnee Mission (Kans.) Sch. Dist., 1973-80; career counselor Career Mgmt. Ctr., Kansas City, 1980-82, pres., owner, 1982-97; v.p., chief devel. officer Menorah Med. Ctr. Found., 1997—2001; develop. dir. Kans. U. Endowment Assn. for U. Kans. Hosp., 2001—. Ptnr. Career Mgmt. Press, Kansas City, 1983-97, The MBL Human Resources Cons. Group, 1989-91. Co-author: How to Be Happily Employed, 1983, 2d edit., 1995; contbr. articles to profl. jours. Bd. dirs. Cmty. Jr. League, Kansas City, 1988-89, v.p., 1989-90, pres.-elect, 1990-91, pres., 1991-92; bd. dirs. Menorah Med. Ctr., Overland Park, Kans., 1995-97, gen. chair grand hosp. opening, 1996; bd. dirs. Menorah Med. Ctr. Aux., 1984-97, auditor, 1990-92, v.p., 1994-96; bd. dirs. Health Partnership Clinic of Johnson County, 1997-2001, sec., 2000-01; bd. dirs. Women's Found. Greater Kansas City, 1991-96, chair bd. devel., 1993-95; bd. dirs. Kansas City Friends of Alvin Ailey, 1992-94, co-chair planning com.; bd. dirs. Ctrl. Exch., Kansas City, 1988-90, 2000—, vice-chair comms., 2000-01, co-chair capital campaign, 1999-2000, chair-elect, 2001-; adv. bd. women's coun. U. Mo. Kansas City, 1988-89; initiator, sponsor Kansas City Youth Vol. Svc. awards United Way, 1989-90, adv. com. Heart of Am. United Way, 1994-97; mem. Promise Project steering com. Kansas City Consensus, 1994-96; co-chmn. Youth Declaration; adv. com. Vol. Connection, 1998; bd. dirs. The New Reform Temple, 1999—; active Kans. Pub. Employee Rels. Bd., 2000—; adv. bd. Health Partnership Clinic, 2001-. Recipient Miss T.E.E.N. Encouraging Excellence award, 1990; named one of 25 Up and Comers award Jr. Achievement of Mid. Am., 1994, a woman to watch in 2002, Kansas City Star. Mem. Greater K.C. Coun. Philanthropy. Republican. Jewish. Office: Kans U Med HEO 1215 3901 Rainbow Blvd Kansas City KS 66160 Address: 4000 W 101 Terrace Overland Park KS 66207

BENJAMIN, LAWRENCE, food service executive; Pres., CEO Specialty Foods Corp., Deerfield, Ill., 1997—. Office: Specialty Foods Corp PO Box 3400 Saint Charles IL 60174-9093

BENLON, LISA L. state legislator; b. July 9, 1953; m. Randal, July 9, 1953; 2 children. Student, Johnson County C.C. Councilman City of Shawnee, 1988-91; rep. dist. 17 State of Kans., 1991—; mgr. acctg. office, 1975-88. Mem. edn., fed and state affairs coms.; chmn. govtl. orgn. and elections com. Home: 7303 Earnshaw St Shawnee KS 66216-3505 Office: Kans Ho of Reps State Capitol Topeka KS 66612

BENNANE, MICHAEL J. former state legislator; b. Detroit, Jan. 27, 1945; s. John M. and Harriet (Fortner) B. BA, Wayne State U., 1970, JD, 1997. Mem. Mich. State Ho. of Reps., 1977-97; pres. Bennane and Assocs., Detroit, 1997—. Assoc. spkr. pro tem, 1985-88; tchr. Christ the King Sch., Detroit, 1968-69; tchr., footbal lcoach St. Agatha H.S., 1969-74; ins. estate planner N.Am. Life Assurance Co., 1975-76. Transp. coord. Kennedy for Pres., 1972; state press. coord. McGovern for Pres., 1972; field coord. Reuther for Cong., 1974; mem. Emerson Cmty Homwowners Orgn., 17th Dist. Dems., Northwest Cmty. Orgn. Recipient Coach of Yr. award, Detroit News, 1969. Home: 9355 W Outer Dr Detroit MI 48219-4059

BENNER, RICHARD EDWARD, JR. community service volunteer, investor; b. Jersey City, Dec. 7, 1932; s. Richard E. and Dorothy (Linstead) B.; m. Virginia Hart; children: Linda, Richard III, Christopher. BS, Lehigh U., 1954; postgrad., NYU, 1959-63. Sales exec. IBM Corp, Norwalk, Conn., 1955-58; with Avon Products, Inc., N.Y.C., 1959-78, group v.p. mktg. and internat., 1972-78; exec. v.p. The Fuller Brush Co., Kansas City, Mo., 1979-86; mktg. cons., 1987—. Bd. dirs. Game Hill, Inc., Weston, Mo., exec. com., chmn. Exec. Svc. Corp., 1993-97, bd. dirs.; LINC, Local Investment commn., 21st Century Initiative; mentor Helzberg Entrepreneurial Mentoring Program, 1998—. Bd. dirs., pres. Northland Homes Partnership for the Homeless, 1988-94; active Eccumedia, 1987-89; maj. corp. com. chmn. United Way, N.Y.C., 1976; Rep. committeeman, Bergan County, 1973; mem. SCORE, 1990—, vice chmn., 1991-92; vice chair cmty. rels. SCORE, 1990—; trustee Shepherd Ctr. North, 2000—; Stephen minister, 1998—. Mem. Direct Selling Assn. Edn. Found. (bd. dirs. 1982-84). Lutheran. Club: Beaverkill Trout (Livingston Manor, N.Y.) (bd. dirs. 1975-78); Old Pike Country (bd. dirs. 1987-90). Lodge: Rotary (bd. dirs., Polio Plus area coord., pres.). Avocations: fly fishing, investing, gardening. Home and Office: 4404 NW Normandy Ln Kansas City MO 64116-1553

BENNET, RICHARD W., III, retail executive; With May Dept. Stores Co., 1976—, pres., Famous-Barr, pres., CEO Kaufmann's Pitts., vice chmn. St. Louis, 2000—. Office: May Dept Stores Co 611 Olive St Saint Louis MO 63101

BENNETT, BRUCE W. construction company executive, civil engineer; b. St. Joseph, Mo., Dec. 24, 1930; s. Bruce W. and Laura Louella (Clark) B.; m. Barbara Gail Haase, July 26, 1957; children: Stacy Suzanne, Bruce W. B.S. in Civil Engring., U. So. Calif., 1954. Project mgr. George A. Fuller & Co., Chgo., 1956-61; contract mgr. Huber, Hunt & Nichols, Indpls., 1961-70, v.p., 1970-82, exec. v.p., 1982-84, pres., 1984-95, ret., 1995. Pres. Hunt Corp., 1988-95, bd. dirs. Served to capt. USAF, 1954-57 Mem. Archimedes Circle, David Wilson Assocs., Newcomen Soc. Republican. Clubs: Indpls. Athletic, Skyline (Indpls.) Avocations: tennis; golf. Home: 437 Seville Ave Newport Beach CA 92661-1528

BENNETT, CORNELIUS, professional football player; b. Birmingham, Ala., Aug. 25, 1965; m. Tracey Bennett. Student, U. Ala. With Buffalo Bills, 1987-96, Atlanta Falcons, 1996-98; linebacker Indianapolis Colts, 1999—. Named to Pro Bowl team, 1988, 90-93, Sporting News All-Pro team, 1988, Sporting News Coll. All-Am. team, 1984-86; recipient Lombardi award, 1986. Office: Indianapolis Colts Atlanta Falcons Complex PO Box 535000 Indianapolis IN 46253-5000

BENNETT, DICK, college basketball coach; b. Pitts., Apr. 20, 1943; m. Anne; children: Kathi, Amy, Tony. BS in phys. edn., Ripon Coll., 1965; MEd, UW-Stevens Point. Basketball coach West Bend (Wis.) H.S., 1965-66; coach various Wis. H.S. teams, 1966-76, UW-Stevens Point, 1976-85, UW-Green Bay, 1985-95, U. Wis., Madison, 1995—. 1st team at U. Wis. (17-15) appeared in 1996 N.I.T.; 2d team (18-10) made 2d U. Wis. appearance in N.C.A.A. tournament in 50 yrs., put together sch.'s 1st 6-game winning streak since 1951. Named WSUC Coach of Yr., 1982, 1985, NAIA Coach of Yr., 1984, NAIA Area IV Coach of Yr., 1985, Mid-Continent Coach of Yr., 1990, 1992, NABC Dist. 11 Coach of Yr., 1992, 1994, Basketball Times Midwest Coach of Yr., 1994. Achievements include 21-yr. collegiate coaching record, 395-214 (.649). Office: U Wis 1440 Monroe St Madison WI 53711-2051

BENNETT, DOUGLAS CARLETON, academic administrator; b. Rochester, N.Y., June 25, 1946; s. Frank Clinton Jr. and Roberta Lincoln (Evans) B.; m. Dulany Young Ogden, June 20, 1981 (div. 1993); 1 child, Thomas Baldrige; m. Ellen Trout, 1997. BA magna cum laude, Haverford Coll., 1968; M of Philosophy, Yale U., 1971, PhD, 1976. Asst. prof. dept. polit. sci. Temple U., Phila., 1976-80, assoc. prof., 1980-88, prof., assoc. dean Coll. Arts and Scis., 1988-89; provost Reed Coll., Portland, Oreg., 1989-93; exec. dir. Portland Area Libr. Sys., 1993-94; v.p. Am. Coun. Learned Socs., N.Y.C., 1994-97; pres. Earlham Coll., Richmond, Ind., 1997—. Author: Transnational Corporations v.s. the State, 1985; contbr. numerous articles and book revs. to polit. sci. jours. Mem. nat. community rels. com. Am. Friends Svc. Commn., Phila., 1982-86, mem. Latin Am. panel internat. div., 1985-89, clk. Latin Am. panel, 1988-89; bd. trustees Germantown Friends Sch., 1985-89, Friends Sem., N.Y.C., 1996-97; trustee Germantown monthly meeting Soc. of Friends Ch., 1984-89. Recipient Alumni award Haverford Coll., 1988; fellow Woodrow Wilson Internat. Ctr. for Scholars, 1980-81; fellowship grantee Am. Coun. Learned Socs./Social Sci. Rsch. Coun., 1976-77, Carnegie Endowment for Internat. Peace, 1976-77. Mem. Ctr. for Rsch. Librs. (bd. dirs. 1997—). Democrat. Avocations: reading, films. Office: Earlham Coll 801 National Rd W Richmond IN 47374-4021 E-mail: dougb@earlham.edu.

BENNETT, GEORGE H., JR. lawyer, healthcare company executive; b. 1952; BS, U. Miami, 1975; JD, Ohio State U., 1978. Bar: Ohio 1978. Assoc. Mortiz McClure Hughes & Kerscher, 1978-80, Baker & Hostetler, 1980-83; gen. counsel Cardinal Distbn. Inc., 1984-86, v.p., 1986-91, v.p., chief adminstrv. officer, 1991-94; exec. v.p., gen. counsel Cardinal Health Inc., Dublin, 1994-99. Office: Cardinal Health Inc 7000 Cardinal Pl Dublin OH 43017-1092

BENNETT, GRACE, publishing executive; Adminstrv. mgr. Detroit Free Press. Office: Detroit Free Press 600 W Fort St Detroit MI 48226-2706

BENNETT, JAMES E. finance company executive; m. Leigh Bennett; three children. BS, Cornell U., 1965; JD, Harvard U., 1968. Various dir. positions McKinsey's Co., Cleve. and Pitts., 1982-93; sr. exec. v.p., strategic and operational svcs. Key Corp, Cleve., 1998—. Past chmn. Cleve./San Jose Ballet; past chmn. Vis. Com., Weatherhead Sch. Mgmt., Case Western Res. U.; bd. dirs. The Cleve. Found., Cleve. Initiative for Edn., United Way Svcs. in Cleve.; chmn. Greater Cleveland Media Devel. Corp. Office: Key Corp 127 Public Sq Cleveland OH 44114-1216

BENNETT, JON, state legislator; Mem. Ho. of Reps., Jefferson City, 1995—; mem. transp., labor, mcpl. corp. and higher edn. coms.; mem. appropriations com. for end. and public safety; mem. Ho. of Reps., Jefferson City. Republican.

BENNETT, LOREN, state legislator; b. Jan. 17, 1951; Grad., Schoolcraft Coll. Clk. Canton Twp., Mich.; mem. Mich. Senate from 8th dist., Lansing, 1995—. Chmn. natural resources and environ. affairs com. Mich. State Senate, vice chair fin. svc. com., local, urban & state affairs com. Address: PO Box 30036 Lansing MI 48909-7536

BENNETT, MARGARET AIROLA, lawyer; b. San Francisco; AB cum laude, U. Calif., Berkeley, 1972; JD, U. San Francisco and Loyola U., 1976. Bar: Ill.1976, U.S. Dist. Ct. (no. dist.) Ill. 1977, U.S. Ct. Appeals (7th cir.) 1983. Intern Cook County State's Atty.'s Office, Chgo., 1975-76; assoc. Dunlap, Thompson & Boyd, Ltd., Libertyville, Ill., 1977-79; ptnr. Bennett & Bennett, Ltd., Oak Brook, 1980-96; pvt. practice The Law Offices of Margaret A. Bennett, 1996—. Atty. rep. McDonald's Corp., Oak Brook, 1982—, County of DuPage, Wheaton, Ill., 1990-95. Counsel fo DuPage Ill. Fair and Exposition Authority, County of DuPage, 1991-95, co-chmn. next generation com.; mem. devel. coun. Good Samaritan Hosp., 1988-92. Mem. DuPage County Bar Assn. (chmn. real estate law com. 1994-95, Cert. of Appreciation 1989, Bd. Dirs. award 1998, chmn. profl. responsibility com. 1996-97, chmn. family law com. 1997-98), Ill. State Bar Assn. (assembly mem., 1996-2000, Cert. of Appreciation 1990, real estate sect. counsel 1996—, jud evaluation com. 1998—), Womens Bar Assn. DuPage County, Evang. Health Found. (bd. sponsors 1988-92). Republican. Episcopalian. Avocations: golf, reading, skiing, travel. Office: Ste 718 1200 Hanger Rd Oak Brook IL 60523-1908

BENNETT, MARK WARREN, judge, lawyer, educator; b. Milw., June 4, 1950; BA in Polit. Sci., Gustavus Adolphus Coll., 1972; JD, Drake U., 1975. Bar: Iowa 1975, U.S. Dist. Ct. (so. dist.) Iowa 1975, U.S. Dist. Ct. (no. dist.) Iowa 1978, U.S. Ct. Appeals (7th cir.) 1981, U.S. Supreme Ct. 1978. Ptnr. Babich, Bennett and Nickerson, Des Moines, 1975—; judge U.S. Dist. Ct., Sioux City. Vis. prof. polit. sci. and sociology U. S.D., Vermillion, 1975-76; asst. prof. law enforcement adminstrn. Western Ill. U., Macomb, 1976-77; adj. prof. law Drake U., Des Moines, 1981—; lectr. law U. Iowa, summers 1984-85; guest lectr. on civil rights, employment discrimination and constl. litigation, 1981—. Del. Dem. Nat. Conv., 1972; trustee Legal Aid Soc. Polk County, 1978-83, pres. 1980-81; bd. dirs. ACLU, 1987—. Named Civil Libertarian of Yr. Iowa Civil Liberties Union, 1986. Fellow Iowa Acad. Trial Lawyers; mem. Iowa Bar Assn. (com. legal aid 1985—, study com. women and minorities involvement in bar assn. and jud. system Iowa 1987—, com. labor law 1988-89), Polk County Bar Assn. (pro bono com. 1985—), Iowa Assn. Trial Lawyers (co-chmn. amicus curiae com. 1986—, co-chmn. constl. law com. 1987—). Avocations: making brass mobiles, gardening, golf. Office: US Dist Ct Federal Bldg 320 6th St Ste 311 Sioux City IA 51101-1262

BENNETT, PATRICIA ANN, radio executive; 1 child, Jessica. BA in Communications, Sangamon State U., 1978, MA in Communications, 1981. Vol. coord. Sta. WSSR-FM, Springfield, Ill., 1977-79; sta. mgr. Stas. WRRS, KMUW, Wichita, Kans., 1979-85; gen. mgr. Sta. KGOU, Norman, Okla., 1985-87; mgr. sta. grant programs Corp. for Pub. Broadcasting, Washington, 1987-89; dir., gen. mgr. Sta. KWMU-FM, St. Louis, 1989—. Bd. dirs. NPR, 1992-94, 95-97; participant NPR Pub. Radio Conf., 1979-90, Pub. Broadcasting Svc. Conf., 1987-89, Corp. for Pub. Broadcasting Conf., 1977-80, Rocky Mountain Pub. Radio Meetings, 1987-89, SECA Meetings, 1987-89; bd. dirs. Pub. Radio in Mid-Am. Conf., 1986-88; mem. gerontology faculty Wichita State U., 1983-84; promotion and pub. svc. announcer Sta. KPTS-TV, Wichita, 1979-80; judge coord. Ohio State Awards, 1986-87. Mem. adv. com. for handicapped svcs. Wichita State U., 1980-82. Mem. Pub. Telecommunication Fin. Mgmt. Assn. (bd. dirs. 1990—), Alpha Epsilon Rho (pres. 1979-84, advisor 1990). Office: Sta KWMU-FM U Mo-St Louis 8001 Natural Bridge Rd Saint Louis MO 63121-4401

BENNETT, ROBERT THOMAS, lawyer, accountant; b. Columbus, Ohio, Feb. 8, 1939; s. Francis Edmund and Mary Catherine (Weiland) B.; B.S., Ohio State U., 1960; J.D., Cleve. Marshall Law Sch., 1967; m. Ruth Ann Dooley, May 30, 1959; children— Robert Thomas, Rose Marie. Admitted to Ohio bar, 1967; C.P.A., Ernst and Ernst, Cleve., 1960-63; with tax assessing dept. Cuyahoga County (Ohio) Auditor's Office, Cleve., 1963-70; mem. firm Bartunek, Bennett, Garofoli and Hill, Cleve., 1975-79;

mem. firm Bennett & Klonowski, Cleve., 1979-83; mem. firm Bennett & Harbarger, Cleve., 1983-88. Exec. vice chmn. Cuyahoga County Rep. Orgn., 1974-88; state chmn. Ohio Rep. Orgn., 1988—; mem. Rep. Nat. Com., 1988—; bd. dirs. Univ. Hosp. of Cleve. and S.W. Gen. Health Ctr. Republican. Roman Catholic. Mem. Citizens League Club, Capitol Hill Club (Washington). Contbr. articles to profl. publs. Home: 4800 Valley Pky Cleveland OH 44126-2847 Office: Ohio Rep Party 211 S 5th St Columbus OH 43215-5203

BENNETT, ROBERT WILLIAM, law educator; b. Chgo., Mar. 30, 1941; s. Lewis and Henrietta (Schneider) B.; m. Harriet Trop, Aug. 19, 1979. B.A., Harvard U., 1962, LL.B., 1965. Bar: Ill. bar 1966. Legal asst. FCC commr. Nicholas Johnson, 1966-67; atty. Chgo. Legal Aid Bur., 1967-68; asso. firm Mayer, Brown & Platt, Chgo., 1968-69; faculty Northwestern U. Sch. Law, 1969—, prof. law, 1974—, dean, 1985-95. Author: (with LaFrance, Schroeder and Boyd) Hornbook on Law of the Poor, 1973. Knox Meml. fellow London Sch. Econs., 1965-66 Fellow Am. Bar Found. (pres., bd. dirs.); mem. ABA, Chgo. Coun. Lawyers (pres. 1971-72), Am. Law Inst. Home: 2130 N Racine Ave Chicago IL 60614-4002 Office: Northwestern U Sch Law 357 E Chicago Ave Chicago IL 60611-3059

BENNETT, STEVEN ALAN, lawyer; b. Rock Island, Ill., Jan. 15, 1953; s. Ralph O. and Anne E. B.; m. Jeanne Aring; children: Preston, Spencer, Hunter, Whitney. BA in Art History, U. Notre Dame, 1975; JD, U. Kans., 1982. Bar: Tex. 1983, Ohio 1995, U.S. Dist. Ct. (no. dist.) Tex. 1983, U.S. Ct. Appeals (5th cir.) 1983, U.S. Supreme Ct. 1995. Atty. Freytag, Marshall et al, Dallas, 1982-84, Baker, Mills & Glast, Dallas, 1984-87; ptnr. Shank, Irwin, Conant et al, 1987-89; gen. counsel Bank One, Tex., N.A., 1989-94; sr. v.p., gen. counsel, sec. Banc One Corp., Columbus, Ohio, 1994-99; exec. v.p., chief legal officer, sec. Cardinal Health, Inc., Dublin, 1999-2001; pvt. practice Columbus, 2001—. City councilman, Mesquite, Tex., 1984-86, mayor pro tem, 1995; trustee Meadowview Sch., Mesquite, 1985-92; chair fin. com. St. Brendan Ch., Hilliard, Ohio, 1998—; pres., bd. dirs. Dallas Dem. Forum, 1993-94; bd. dirs. Ohio Hunger Task Force, Columbus; trustee Woodrow Wilson Internat. Ctr. for Scholars, Washington, 1996—, vice-chmn., 1999—; bd. dirs. Capital U. Law Sch., Columbus, Ctr. for Thomas More Studies, Dallas. Fellow, Ohio State Bar Found.; mem. ABA, Dallas Bar Assn., Ohio State Bar Assn., Columbus Bar Assn., St. Thomas More Soc. (Dallas bd. dirs. 1990-94), Am. Corp. Counsel Assn. (sec. 1999—, bd. dirs. 1996—, chair policy com. 1997-99), Phi Beta Kappa. Avocation: landscape photography. E-mail: sbennett@columbus.rr.com.

BENNETT, THOMAS, orchestra executive; Exec. dir. S.D. Symphony Orch., Sioux Falls, 1996—. Office: SD Symphony Orch Ste 112 300 N Dakota Ave Sioux Falls SD 57104

BENNING, JOSEPH RAYMOND, principal; b. Streator, Ill., May 23, 1956; s. Joseph Charles and Shirley Ann (Smith) B.; m. Katherine Marie Turner, Apr. 24, 1976; children: Jennifer Nichole, Joseph Donald. BA, Augustana Coll, 1978; MS in Edn., No. Ill. U., 1988. Cert. state supr., teaching, Ill. Tchr., coach Fulton (Ill.) High Sch., 1978-79; recreation dir. Fulton Recreation Corp., 1979; tchr., coach Streator (Ill.) High Sch., 1979-80, Woodland High Sch., Streator, 1980-83; program dir. Ill. State Bd. Edn., Ottawa, 1983-85; prin. St. Mary Grade Sch., Streator, 1985-89; assoc. supt. schs. Cath. Diocese Peoria, Ill., 1989-91, supt. schs., 1991-94; prin. St. Bede Acad., Peru, 1994-99, St. Columba Sch., Ottawa, 1999—. Pres. Streator Youth Football League, 1984-90; adv. bd. Streator High Sch., 1985-89; prins. adv. bd. Cath. Diocese Peoria, 1987-89. Recipient CJ McDonald award Streator Youth Football League, 1989. Mem. ASCD, Nat. Cath. Edn. Assn., Nat. Assn. Secondary Sch. Prin., Nat. Assn. Elem. Sch. Prin., Ill. Elem. Sch. Assn., Cath. Conf. Ill., KC. Roman Catholic. Avocations: sports, music. Office: St Columba Schd 1110 Lasalle Ottawa IL 61350 E-mail: benningjr@hotmail.com.

BENNINGTON, RONALD KENT, lawyer; b. Circleville, Ohio, July 16, 1936; s. Ralph P. and Delorice (Dudley) B.; m. Barbara Schumm, June 19, 1959; children; Scott C., Amy E. BA magna cum laude, Kenyon Coll., 1958; JD summa cum laude, Ohio State U., 1961. Assoc. Black, McCuskey, Souers & Arbaugh, Canton, Ohio, 1961-65, ptnr., 1965—. Sec. Hoover Worldwide Corp., 1969-86; bd. dirs. United Hard Chrome, Inc. Bd. trustees Plain Twp., Canton, 1972-78, Malone Coll., Canton, 1982—, chmn. 1984-86, Timken Mercy Med. Ctr., Canton; adv. com. Kenyon Coll., Gambier, Ohio; mem. Leadership Canton; bd. dirs. ARC, Canton; fund-raising United Way Fund Drive; trust com. Hoover Found.; ambassador Ohio Found. Ind. Colls.; steering com. Pro Football Hall of Fame, 1985—; Big Ten football ofcl., 1984—; trustee The Hoover Found., Canton, Greater Canton C. of C.; bd. assocs. Union Coll., Alliance, Ohio. Fellow Am. Bar Found., Ohio State Bar Found.; mem. ABA, Ohio Bar Assn., Stark County Bar Assn., Greater Canton C. of C. (bd. trustees), Ea. Ohio Football Ofcls. Assn. (pres. 1986—), Stark County Law Libr. Assn. (pres.). Republican. Presbyterian. Home: 3528 Darlington Rd NW Canton OH 44708-1714 Office: Black McCuskey Souers & Arbaugh 1000 United Bank Plz Canton OH 44702

BENSELER, DAVID PRICE, foreign language educator; b. Balt., Jan. 10, 1940; s. Ernest Parr and Ellen Hood Escar (Turnbaugh) B.; m. Suzanne Shelton, May 25, 1985; children: James Declan, Derek Justin. BA, West Wash. U., 1964; MA, U. Oreg., 1966, PhD, 1971. Prof. german, dept. chair Ohio State U., 1977-85; chair dept. modern langs and lits. Case Western Reserve U., 1991-98, Louis D. Beaumont U. Prof. Humanities, 1991-98, Emile B. de Sauzé prof. modern lang. and lit., 1998—. Disting. vis. prof. fgn. langs. U.S. Mil. Acad., West Point, N.Y., 1987-88, N.Mex. State U., Las Cruces, 1989; founding dir. German Studies program Case Western Reserve U. and Max Kade Ctr. for German Studies; mem. numerous coms. Case Western Res. U., U.S. Military Acad., U.S. Naval Acad., U. Akron, Ohio State U., Wash. State U., Ind. U., Emory U., U. Md., U. Cin., U. Wis., Pa. State U., U. Va., U. Mich., various others; lectr., panel mem., workshop condr., cons. in field. Compiler, editor: (with Suzanne S. Moore) Comprehensive Index to the Modern Language Journal, 1916-1996, MLJ Electron Index, 1997—; editor 50 books, bibliographies, jours.; contbr. chpts. to books and articles to profl. jours. With USN, 1958-60. Recipient Bundesverdienstkreuz I. Klasse, Pres. Fed. Republic Germany, 1985, Army Commendation medal for disting. civilian svc. U.S. Mil. Acad., 1988; Lilly Found. Faculty Renewal fellow, Stanford U., 1975, Fullbright Graduate fellow, 1967-68, NDEA fellow, U. Oreg., 1964-67; various other grants, fellowships, scholarships. Mem. MLA, TESOL, Am. Assn. Applied Linguistics, Am. Assn. Tchrs. of German, Am. Assn. Univ. Profs., Am. Goethe Soc., Am. Soc. for 18th Century Studies, German Studies Assn., Lessing Soc., Soc. German-Am. Studies, Phi Sigma Iota, Sigma Kappa Phi, Delta Phi Alpha. Office: Case Western Res U Dept Modern Langs and Lits Cleveland OH 44106-7118 E-mail: dpb5@po.cwru.edu.

BENSINGER, PETER BENJAMIN, consulting firm executive; b. Chgo., Mar. 24, 1936; s. Benjamin Edward and Linda Elkus (Galston) B.; m. Judith S. Bensinger; children: Peter Benjamin, Jennifer Anne, Elizabeth Brooke, Virginia Brette. Grad., Phillips Exeter Acad., 1954; BA, Yale, 1958; hon. degree, San Marcos U., Peru, 1978; LLD (hon.), Dan Kook U., Seoul, Republic of Korea, 1980. Various mktg. positions Brunswick Corp., Chgo., 1958-65, new products mgr., 1966-68; gen. sales mgr. Brunswick Internat., Europe, 1965-66, spl. products mgr. Europe, 1966-68; chmn. Ill. Youth Commn., 1969-70; dir. Ill. Dept. Corrections, Chgo., 1970-73; exec. dir. Chgo. Crime Commn., 1973; adminstr. Drug Enforcement Adminstrn., Washington, 1976-81; pres. Bensinger, DuPont & Assocs., Chicago, 1982—. Chmn. Ill. Criminal Justice Info. Authority, 1991—; cons. various orgns.; del. White House Conf. on Corrections, 1971, Drug Abuse, 1988, U.S. Del. to Interpol, 1978. Pres. Lincoln Park Zool. Soc., Chgo., 1962-63; governing life mem., also mem. men's council Chgo. Art Inst.; mem. Ill. Alcoholism Adv. Council, Ill. Law Enforcement Commn., Ill. Council on Diagnosis and Evaluation Criminal Defendants, Ill. Narcotics Adv. Council; adv. com. Center for Studies in Criminal Justice, So. Ill. U., Center for Studies in Criminal Justice, U. Chgo.; vice chmn. ad hoc adv. com. U.S. Dept. Justice Nat. Inst. Corrections; mem. exec. com. Am. Bar Assn. Nat. Commn. Corrections; chmn. Ill. Task Force on Corrections, 1969; mem. bd. Fed. Prison Industries, Inc., 1973-85; bd. dirs. Jewish Fedn. Met. Chgo., Council Community Services Met. Chgo., Ill. Commn. on Children, Children's Meml. Hosp., Chgo., 1988—; bd. dirs., mem. exec. council Anti-Defamation League; regional bd. dirs. NCCJ; trustee Phillips Exeter Acad.; chmn. nat. law enforcement explorers conf. Boy Scouts Am., 1981, U.S. del. to, Interpol, 1978. Recipient Young Leadership award Jewish Fedn.-Welfare Bds. Met. Chgo., 1969, award for excellence John Howard Assn., 1972, Disting. Svc. award Govt. of Peru, 1978, U.S. Dept. of Justice award, EEO award, 1979, Disting. Svc. medal USCG, 1981, John Phillips award Phillips Exeter Acad., 1990, Lincoln medal Lincoln Acad., 1998. Mem. Am. Correctional Assn. (bd. dirs.), Assn. State Correctional Adminstrs. (sec. 1971-72, pres. 1972-73), Internat. Assn. Chiefs of Police (mem. exec. com.), Nat. Sheriffs Assn. (life), Chgo. City Club (bd. dirs.), Arts Club, Comml. Club Chgo., Yale Club (N.Y.C.), Shoreacres Club (Lake Bluff), Casino Club (Chgo.). Office: 20 N Wacker Dr Chicago IL 60606-2806

BENSON, DONALD ERICK, holding company executive; b. Mpls., June 1, 1930; s. Fritz and Annie (Nordstrom) B.; children: Linda K., Nancy A., Stephen D.; m. Roberta Mann, 1992. BBA in Acctg., U. Minn., 1955. CPA, Minn. From staff to partnership Arthur Andersen & Co., Mpls., 1955-68; pres. MEI Corp., 1968-86, MEI Diversified Inc., Mpls., 1986-94; exec. v.p. Marquette financial companies, 1992—; also bd. dirs. Bd. dirs. Mesaba Holdings, Inc., Champion Air, Minn. Twins Baseball Club, Mass. Mut. Corp. Investors, Mass. Mut. Participation Investors, Capital Cargo Holdings, Inc., Delta Beverage Group, Inc., Nat. Merc. Bancorp.; dir. Swedish Coun. Am. and its Royal Round Table. Chmn. Bethel Coll. Found., St. Paul, Park Nicollet Health Svcs.; past chmn. Health Sys. Minn., Mpls.; past pres. Boys and Girls Clubs Mpls. Served with U.S. Army, 1951-53. Mem. AICPA, Minn. CPA Soc., Mpls. Club, Interlachen Country Club. Office: Marquette Bancshares Inc 3900 Dain Rauscher Plz Minneapolis MN 55480-1000

BENSON, JACK DUANE, mechanical engineer, research scientist; b. Mich. BSME, U. Mich., 1963, MSME, 1964. Mech. engr. Rsch. and Design Ctr. GM, 1964-98; pres. AFE Cons. Svcs., Commerce Twp., Mich., 1998—. Recipient Soichiro Honda medal ASME, 1997. Fellow Soc. Automotive Engrs. Achievements include research in fuels and their effect on vehicle performance. Office: AFE Cons Svcs 5900 Ford Rd Commerce Township MI 48382-1025

BENSON, JOANNE E. former lieutenant governor; b. Jan. 4, 1943; m. Robert Benson; 2 children. BS, St. Cloud State U. Mem. Minn. Senate, St. Paul, 1991-94; lt. gov. State of Minn., 1994-98.

BENSON, KEITH A. retail executive; Pres. mall div. Sam Goody and Suncoast Motion Picture Co. Musicland Stores Corp., Minnetonka, Minn., vice-chmn., CFO, 1997—. Office: Musicland Stores 10400 Yellow Cir Dr Minnetonka MN 55343

BENTLEY, CHARLES RAYMOND, geophysics educator; b. Rochester, N.Y., Dec. 23, 1929; s. Raymond and Janet Cornelia (Everest) B.; m. Marybelle Goode, July 3, 1964; children: Molly Clare, Raymond Alexander. BS, Yale U., 1950; PhD, Columbia U., 1959. Rsch. geophysicist Columbia U., 1952-56; Antarctic traverse leader and seismologist Arctic Inst. N.Am., 1956-59; project assoc. U. Wis., 1959-61, asst. prof., 1961-63, assoc. prof., 1963-68, prof. geophysics, 1968-98, A.P. Crary prof. geophysics, 1987-98, prof. emeritus, 1998—. Recipient Bellingshausen-Lazarev medal for Antarctic rsch. Acad. Scis. USSR, 1971; NSF sr. postdoctoral fellow, 1968-69; NAS-USSR Acad. Sci. exch. fellow, 1977, 90 Fellow AAAS, Am. Geophys. Union, Arctic Inst. N.Am., Am. Polar Soc. (hon., bd. dirs.); mem. AAUP, Soc. Exploration Geophysicists, Internat. Glaciological Soc. (Seligman Crystal award 1990), Am. Quarternary Assn., Oceanography Soc., Am. Geol. Inst., Geol. Soc. Am., Phi Beta Kappa, Sigma Xi. Achievements include research on Antarctic glaciology and geophysics, satellite studies of geomagnetic anomalies, magnetotelluric exploration of Earth structure, satellite radar and laser altimetry, ice coring and drilling services. Home: 5618 Lake Mendota Dr Madison WI 53705-1036 Office: U Wis Geophys & Polar Rsch Ctr Weeks Hall 1215 Dayton St Madison WI 53706 E-mail: bentley@geology.wisc.edu.

BENTLEY, JEFFREY, performing company executive; Grad., U. Wash. Ballet dancer, N.Y.C.; from asst. to producing dir. to adminstrv. dir. Seattle Repertory Theatre, 1973-81; exec. dir. Northlight Theatre Co., Evanston, Ill.; mng. dir. dance ctr. Columbia Coll., Chgo., 1983-85; exec. dir. Eugene Ballet Co., Oreg.; dir. DanceAspen Festival and Sch., Aspen, Colo.; exec. dir. Royal Winnipeg Ballet, 1993-96, State Ballet of Mo. (now Kansas City Ballet), Kansas City, Mo. Panelist, site visitor NEA, Colo. Coun. Arts, Ill. Arts Coun.; cons. Western States Art Fedn., Santa Fe, Found. Ext. and Devel. Am. Profl. Theatre. NEA fellow Wash. State Arts Commn. Office: Kansas City Ballet 380 Graham Ave Kansas City MO 64108

BENTLEY, ORVILLE GEORGE, retired agricultural educator, dean emeritus; b. Midland, S.D., Mar. 6, 1918; s. Thomas O. and Ida Marie (Sandal) B.; m. Enolia J. Anderson, Sept. 19, 1942; children: Peter T., Craig E. B.S., S.D. State Coll., 1942; M.S. in Biochemistry, U. Wis., 1947, Ph.D., 1950, hon. degree, 1984, S.D. State U., 1974. Asst. prof. animal sci. Ohio Agrl. Expt. Sta.; also mem. dept. animal sci. and dept. agrl. biochemistry Ohio State U., 1950-58; dean Coll. of Agr. and Biol. Scis., S.D. State U., 1958-65, Coll. Agr., U. Ill. at Urbana, 1965-82; asst. sec. agr. for sci. and edn. USDA, Washington, 1982-89; dean emeritus, coll. agr. U. Ill., Urbana, 1986—. Mem. com. animal nutrition NRC-Nat. Acad. Scis., 1958-67; mem. Coun. U.S. Univs. for Rural Devel. in India, 1967-74; mem. ad hoc adv. com. Ill. Inst. for Environ. Quality, 1971; mem. tech. adv. com. on food and agr. U.S. Dept. Agr., Vietn Nam, 1966; mem. panel NAS to meet mems. Indonesian Acad. Scis., 1968; co-chmn. Agrl. Rsch. Policy Adv. Com., 1973-77; mem. Bd. for Internat. Food and Agrl. Devel., 1976-80; co-chmn. U.S. Dept. Agr. Joint Coun. for Food and Agrl. Scis., 1982-89; mem. NAS Govt.-Univ. Industry Rsch. Roundtable, 1985-89; mem. com. of earth sci., com. on life scis., biotech. sci. coordinating com. Fed. Coordinating Coun., Soc., Engring., and Tech.; head U.S. del. U.S./Indo Subcommn. on Agr., 1986-88, Ohio Coun. Rsch. and Econ. devel., 1989-90, U.S.-Japan high level adv. panel Sci. and tech. agreement, 1989-92; co-chair USDA Joint Venezuela-U.S. Agrl. Commn., 1990-95. Mem. editorial bd. Jour. Animal Sci., 1956-59; contbr. articles to profl. jours. Bd. trustees Am. U. Beirut, Midwest Univs., 1973-92, Consortium for Internat. Activities, 1966-76; chmn. bd. dirs. Farm Found., 1971-78. Served to maj., chem warfare svc. AUS, 1942-45. Named Young Man of Year Wooster Jr. C. of C., 1953; recipient Distinguished Alumnus award S.D. State U., 1967, U. Ill., 1985. Fellow Am. Soc. Animal Sci. (pres. midwestern sect. 1963, Am. feed mfrs. award 1958); mem. Am. Inst. Nutrition, Am. Soc. Animal Sci., Am. Dairy Sci. Assn., Internat. Union of Nutritional Scis., Farm House (hon.), AAAS (committeeman-at-large 1971-82), Sigma Xi, Phi Kappa Phi. Club: Rotary Home and Office: 2030 Bentbrook Dr Champaign IL 61822-9201

BENTLEY, ROSEANN, state legislator, educational consultant; b. Joplin, Mo., Apr. 22, 1936; d. Lincoln John and Marcella (Donahue) Knauer; m. John D. Bentley, Apr. 12, 1958; children: Jeffrey, Christopher, Melissa, Jonathan. BS in Edn., U. Mo., 1958. Tchr. U.S. Army Schs., Okinawa, Japan, 1959-60, West Phila. (Pa.) Schs., 1961-63, Madison (Wis.) Pre-sch., 1966-67; mem. local sch. bd. Springfield (Mo.) Pub. Schs., 1974-83; mem. state sch. bd. Mo. Dept. Edn., Jefferson City, 1983-92; mem. Mo. Senate from 30th dist., 1995—. Mem. edn. com., pub. health and welfare com., gubernatorial appointment com., aging family and mental health com., fin. and govt. ops. com., civil and criminal jurisprudence com. Mo. State Senate; bd. mem. Lit. Investment for Tomorrow, St. Louis, Nat. Parents as Tchrs. Bd., St. Louis, Nat. Coun. for Accreditation on Tchr. Edn.; task force mem. Right From the Start, 1989. Pres. Springfield Sch. Bd., 1981, 82, Community Found., 1986-87, Mo. State Bd. Edn., 1988, 89, Nat. Assn. State Bds. Edn., Washington, 1990, United Way of Ozarks, 1992; co-chmn. Code Blue: Uniting for Healthier Youth, 1990. Named Mo. Gifted Educator of Yr., Gifted Assn. Mo., Jefferson City, 1990; recipient Mary Harriman award Assn. of Jr. Leagues Internat., N.Y.C., 1992. Mem. Springfield C. of C., Jr. League of Springfield (pres. 1976), Pi Beta Phi. Office: Senate PO Capitol Bldg Jefferson City MO 65101

BENTON, W. DUANE, judge; b. Springfield, Mo., Sept. 8, 1950; s. William Max and Patricia F. (Nicholson) B.; m. Sandra Snyder, Nov. 15, 1980; children: Megan Blair, William Grant. BA in Polit. Sci. summa cum laude, Northwestern U., 1972; JD, Yale U., 1975; MBA in Accounting, Memphis State U., 1979; student Inst. Jud. Adminstrn., NYU, 1992; LLD (hon.), Ctrl. Mo. State U., 1994; LLM, U. Va., 1995; LLD (hon.), Westminster Coll., 1999. Bar: Mo. 1975; CPA, Mo. Ensign USN, 1972; advanced through grades to capt., 1993; judge advocate USN, Memphis, 1975-79; chief of staff for Congressman Wendell Bailey, Washington, 1980-82; pvt. practice Jefferson City, Mo., 1983-89; dir. revenue Mo. Dept. of Revenue, 1989-91; judge Mo. Supreme Ct., 1991—, chief justice, 1997-99. Adj. prof. Westminster Coll., U. Mo.-Columbia Sch. Law. Contbr. articles to profl. jours.; mng. editor Yale Law Jour., 1974-75 Chmn. Multistate Tax Commn. Washington, 1990-91; chmn. Mo. State Employees Retirement System, Jefferson City, 1989-93; regent Ctrl. Mo. State U., 1987-89; dir. Coun. for Drug Free Youth, Jefferson City, 1989-97; mem. Mo. Mil. Adv. Com., 1989-91; mem. Mo. Commn. Intergovernmental Coop., Jefferson City, 1989-91; trustee, deacon 1st Bapt. Ch., Jefferson City. Danforth fellow JFK Sch. Govt. Harvard U., 1990. Mem. AICPA (tax com. 1983—), Mo. Bar Assn. (tax com. 1975—), Mo. Soc. CPA's (tax com. 1983—), Navy League, Mil. Order of World Wars, Vietnam Vets of Am., VFW, Am. Legion, Phi Beta Kappa, Beta Gamma Sigma, Rotary. Baptist. Lt. USN, 1975-80. Capt. JAGC USNR. Office: Supreme Court PO Box 150 Jefferson City MO 65102-0150 E-mail: dbenton@osca.state.mo.us.

BENTZ, DALE MONROE, librarian; b. York County, Pa., Jan. 3, 1919; s. Solomon Earl and Mary Rebecca (Wonders) B.; m. Mary Gail Menius, June 13, 1942; children: Dale Flynn, Thomas Earl, Mary Carolyn. A.B., Gettysburg Coll., 1939; B.S.L.S., U. N.C. Chapel Hill, 1940; M.S., U. Ill., 1951. With Periodicals dept. U. N.C. Library, Chapel Hill, 1940-41, Serials Dept., Duke U. Library, Durham, N.C., 1941-42; asst. librarian E. Carolina Tchrs. Coll., Greenville, 1946-48; head processing dept. U. Tenn. Library, Knoxville, 1948-53; assoc. dir. libraries U. Iowa, Iowa City, 1953-70, univ. librarian, 1970-86, univ. librarian emeritus, 1986—. Editor U. Tenn. Library Lectures, 1952; contbr. articles to profl. jours. Pres. Iowa City Bd. Edn., 1962-63 Mem. Iowa Library Assn. (pres., 1959-60), ALA (pres. resources and tech. services div. 1975-76), AAUP, Assn. Coll. and Research Libraries, Beta Phi Mu (pres. 1966-67) Lutheran. Clubs: Triangle (pres. 1958-59), Univ. Athletic (sec. 1979-80). Home: 701 Oaknoll Dr # 430 Iowa City IA 52246-5168 E-mail: dalembentz@hotmail.com.

BEPKO, GERALD LEWIS, university administrator, law educator, lecturer, consultant, lawyer; b. Chgo., Apr. 21, 1940; s. Lewis V. and Geraldine S. (Bernath) B.; m. Jean B. Cougnenc, Feb. 24, 1968; children: Gerald Lewis Jr., Arminda B. BS, No. Ill. U., 1962; JD, Ill. Inst. Tech.-Chgo. Kent Coll. Law, 1965; LLM, Yale U., 1972. Bar: Ill. 1965, U.S. Supreme Ct. 1968, Ind. 1973. Assoc. Ehrlich, Bundesen, Friedman & Ross, Chgo., 1965; spl. agt. FBI, 1965-69; asst. prof. law Ill. Inst. Tech.-Chgo. Kent Coll. Law, 1969-71; prof. Ind. U., Indpls., 1972-86, assoc. dean acad. affairs, 1979-81, dean, 1981-86, v.p., 1986—. Vis. prof. Ind. U.-Bloomington, summers, 1976, 77, 78, 80, U. Ill., 1976—77, Ohio State U., 1978—79; cons. and reporter Fed. Jud. Ctr.; bd. dirs. First Ind. Bank/Corp., Ind. Energy Inc. & Ind. Gas Co., Inc., 1989—97, Lumina Found. for Edn., Indpls. Life Ins. Co.; mem. Conf. Commrs. on Uniform State Laws, 1982, Permanent Editl. Bd. for the Uniform Comml. Code, 1993—; mem. Ind. Lobby Registration Commn., 1992—, vice chair, 1992—96, chair, 1996—2000. Author: (with Boshkoff) Sum and Substance of Secured Transactions, 1981; contbr. articles on comml. law to profl. jours. Indpls. Chgo. Title and Trust Co. Found. scholar 1962-65; Ford Urban law fellow, 1971-72. Fellow Am. Bar Found., Ind. State Bar, Indpls. Bar Found.; mem. ABA, Ind. State Bar Assn., Indpls. Bar Assn., Country Club Indpls., Rotary. Methodist. Office: Ind U 355 Lansing St Indianapolis IN 46202-2815

BERACHA, BARRY HARRIS, food company executive; b. Bronx, N.Y., Feb. 28, 1942; s. Nissim Macy and Celia Grace (Sides) B.; m. Barbara Marie Capobianco, Dec. 23, 1967; children: Brian, Bradley, Bonnie. BChE, Pratt Inst., 1963; MBA, U. Pa., 1965. Ops. researcher Celanese Corp., 1965-67; tech. economist Sun Oil Co., 1964-65; with Anheuser-Busch Cos., Inc., 1967-96, v.p. corp. planning, 1974-76, v.p., group exec., 1976-96; chmn., CEO Earthgrains Co., Clayton, Mo., 1996—2001; exec. v.p. Sara Lee Corp., 2001—; CEO Sara Lee Bakery Group , 2001—. Office: Sara Lee Bakery Group 8400 Maryland Ave Clayton MO 63105

BERAN, GEORGE WESLEY, veterinary microbiology educator; b. Riceville, Iowa, May 22, 1928; s. John and Elizabeth (Buresh) B.; m. Janice Ann Van Zomeren, Dec. 21, 1954; children: Bruce, Anne, George. DVM, Iowa State U., 1954; PhD, Kans. U., 1959; LHD, Silliman U., Philippines, 1973. Diplomate Am. Coll. Vet. Preventive Medicine, Am. Coll. Epidemiology. Epidemic intelligence officer USPHS, 1954-56; asst. prof. biology Silliman U., Dumaguete City, Philippines, 1960-63, chmn. dept. agr. Philippines, 1962-71, assoc. prof. microbiology Philippines, 1963-67, prof. microbiology Philippines, 1967-73; prof. vet. microbiology and preventive medicine Iowa State U., Ames, 1973-93, disting. prof. vet. microbiology, immunology-preventive med., 1993—; dir. WHO Collaborating Ctr. in Food Safety, 1994—. Cons. WHO, Belize, Ecuador, Mex., India, Laos, Malaysia, Philippines, Jamaica, Surinam, Barbados; rsch. del. USSR/Iowa State U. exch. program, Moscow, 1989-90, Latvia, 1993; rsch. cons., Taiwan, 1983, 96, 98, Hungary, 1988, 90, U. Yucatan, 1989-90, 97, 98, Ukraine, 1996, Japan, 1998; vis. lectr. Nat. Inst. Vet. Bioproducts and Pharms., Beijing, Faculty Vet. Medicine, Huazhong Agrl. U. Wuhan, Peoples Republic of China, 1988; cons. Pan Am. Health Orgn., 1979, 85, 93, 95, 96, 98, 99, 2000; cons., mem. WHO Expert Panel on Zoonoses, 1980-99; mem. expert panel on risk assessment WHO-FAO; Fulbright prof. Ahmadu Bello U., Zaria, Nigeria, 1980; mem. subcom. on drug use in animals NRC, 1993-98, mem. nat. adv. com. on microbiol. criteria for foods, 1997-99; adv. com. Wellcome Trust, 1998-99; mem. Food Safety and Inspection Svc. Task Force for Veterinarians, 1999-2000; mem. HACCP Based Inspection Models Project, 1999-2000 Editor, co-editor books on zoonoses; contbr. articles to profl. jours., chpts. to books. Active Ames Humane League, Ames chpt. Ptnrs. of Ams., UN Assn.; election supr. OSCE, Bosnia, 1998, Kosovo, 2000; mem. adv. com. Nat. Cath. Rural Life Ctr., 2001—. Recipient James H. Steele award World Vet. Epidemiology Soc., 1979, Nat. Meritorious Svc. award Livestock Conservation

Inst., 1989, Gold Head Cane award Am. Vet. Epidemiology Soc., 1993. Mem. AVMA (mem. coun. pub. health and regulatory vet. medicine, Internat. Svc. award 1996, Pub. Svc. award 1999), Am. Coll. Vet. Preventive Medicine (pres.), Conf. Pub. Health Veterinarians (pres.), Am. Assn. Food Hygiene Veterinarians (Outstanding Tchr. award 1978), Assn. Tchrs. Vet. Pub. Health and Preventive Medicine, Iowa Vet. Med. Assn. (chair pub. health com.), Iowa Pork Producers Assn. (pseudorables com.), U.S. Animal Health Assn. (com. on pseudorables, pub. health, food safety, feed safety, chair com. on feral swine), Cardinal Key, Sigma Xi, Phi Beta Delta, Phi Kappa Phi (pres.), Gamma Sigma Delta (Svc. to Agr. Merit award 1995), Phi Zeta, Alpha Zeta, Phi Eta Sigma. Home: 304 24th St Ames IA 50010-4834 Office: Coll Vet Medicine Iowa State U Rm 2134 Ames IA 50011-0001 E-mail: gberan@iastate.edu.

BERAN, JOHN R. banker; Pres., CEO Money Access Svc.; exec. v.p., chief info. officer Comerica Inc., Detroit, 1995—. Bd. dirs. Channel 56, U. Dayton. Office: Comerica Tower 500 Woodward Ave Detroit MI 48226-3416

BERARDI, JOHN FRANCIS, agricultural products company executive; b. Waterbury, Conn., Mar. 9, 1943; s. John August and Coletta (Gannon) B.; m. Karen Anne Fahey, Sept. 4, 1967; children: Maura, John, Meghan. BBA, Cleve. State U., 1970. CPA, Ohio. Audit sr. Ernst & Whinney, Cleve., 1970-76; controller staff AM Internat., Shaker Heights, Ohio, 1976-78; v.p. controller Harvest Cos. (subs. Harcourt Brace Jovanovich), Cleve., 1978-82, exec. v.p., 1982-84; controller Harcourt Brace Jovanovich Inc., Orlando, Fla., 1984-85, v.p., controller, 1985-86, sr. v.p., treas., 1986-89, also bd. dirs., 1988-90; exec. v.p., CFO Farmland Industries, Inc., Kansas City, Mo., 1992—. Advisor Jr. Achievement, Cleve., 1972-76; group leader Cath. Charities, Cleve., 1979-84; council mem. St. Brendan Ch., North Olmsted, Ohio, 1982; bd. dirs. Bishop Moore High Sch., Orlando, 1986. Served with USN, 1961-66. Mem. Fin. Execs. Inst., Sabal Point Country Club (Longwood, Fla.), Am. Royal Club (dir. 1995—). Republican. Office: Farmland Industries Inc 3315 N Oak Trfy Kansas City MO 64116-2798

BERCIER, DENNIS, state legislator; m. 2 children. Undergrad., Turtle Mountain; BA, U. N.D. Mem. N.D. Senate from 9th dist., Bismark, 1999—. Mem. Standing: Judiciary, transp.; Interim: Budget Com. on Human Svcs, Judiciary. Mem. Turtle Mountain Pow-Wow Com.; bd. dirs. Turtle Mountain Pow-Wow Com., Turtle Mountain Heritage Ctr., Miss Indian Am.; dir. FIPSE Drug and Alcohol Prog. with U.S. Army, Vietnam. Recipient N.D. DOT Minority Businessman of the Year, Turtle Mountain Cmty. Svc. award. Life mem. VFW. Democrat. Office: Dist 9 PO Box 1209 Belcourt ND 58316-1209 E-mail: dbercier@state.nd.us.

BERENBAUM, MAY ROBERTA, entomology educator; b. Trenton, N.J., July 22, 1953; BS, Yale U., 1975; PhD, Cornell U., 1980. Asst. prof. entomology U. Ill., Urbana-Champaign, 1980-85, assoc. prof. entomology, 1985-90, prof. entomology, 1990-95, head dept., 1992—, Swanlund prof. entomology, 1996—. Assoc. editor Am. Midland Naturalist, 1982-85; mem. editl. bd. Jour. Chem. Ecology, Chemoecology, Proceedings of the Nat. Acad. Scis. USA. Recipient Presdl. Young Investigator award NSF, 1984, Founder's award Entomol. Soc. Am., 1994; U. Ill. scholar, 1985-88. Mem. AAAS, NAS, Am. Philos. Soc., Am. Assn. Arts and Scis., Entomol. Soc. Am., Ecol. Soc. Am., Phytochem Soc. Am., Internat. Soc. Chem. Ecology, Sigma Xi. Achievements include research in chemical aspects of insect-plant interaction, evolutionary ecology of insects, phototoxicity of plant products, host-plant resistance. Office: U Ill Dept Entomology 320 Morrill Hall 505 S Goodwin Ave Urbana IL 61801-3707

BERENDT, ROBERT TRYON, lawyer; b. Chgo., Mar. 8, 1939; s. Alex E. and Ethel L. (Tryon) B.; m. Sara Probert, June 15, 1963; children: David, Elizabeth, Katherine. BA, Monmouth Coll., 1961; JD with distinction, U. Iowa, 1965. Bar: Iowa 1965, Ill. 1968, U.S. Dist. Ct. (no. dist.) Ill. 1968, U.S. Ct. Appeals (7th cir.) 1968, Mo. 1979, U.S. Dist. Ct. (ea. dist.) Mo. 1979. Assoc. Schiff Hardin & Waite, Chgo., 1968-73, ptnr., 1973-78; litigation counsel Monsanto Co., St. Louis, 1978-83, asst. gen. counsel, 1983-85, assoc. gen. counsel, 1986-96; of counsel Thompson Coburn, 1996—. Disting. Neutral, Ctr. for Pub. Resources; editl. adv. bd. Alternatives, Inside Litigation, Product Safety and Liability Reporter-Bur. Nat. Affairs. Contbr. articles to profl. jours. Lt. USNR, 1965-68. Mem. ABA (litigation sect., coun. mem. 1993-96), Mo. Bar Assn., Ill. Bar Assn., Iowa Bar Assn., Bar Assn. Met. St. Louis, Product Liability Adv. Coun. (bd. dirs., exec. com., Inst. for the Judiciary, pres.-trustee Found. 1992-98). Avocations: golf, tennis, reading. Office: Thompson Coburn 1 Mercantile Ctr Ste 3400 Saint Louis MO 63101-1643

BERENS, MARK HARRY, lawyer; b. St. Paul, Aug. 4, 1928; s. Harry C. and Gertrude M. (Scherkenbach) B.; m. Barbara Jean Steichen, Nov. 20, 1954; children: Paul J., Joseph F. (dec.), John M., Stephen M., Thomas M., Michael M., Lisa M., James M., Daniel M. BS in Commerce (Acctg.) magna cum laude, U. Notre Dame, 1950, JD magna cum laude, 1951; postgrad. U. Chgo., 1951-53. Bar: Ill. 1951, D.C. 1955, U.S. Supreme Ct. 1971; CPA, Ill. Assoc. Mayer, Brown and predecessors, Chgo., 1956-61, ptnr., 1961-96; chmn., CEO Attys.' Liability Assurance Soc., Inc., Chgo., 1987-95; ptnr. Altheimer & Gray, 1996—. Chmn. bd. dirs. Attys.' Liability Assurance Soc. (Bermuda) Ltd., 1979-95; bd. dirs. Accts. Liability Assurance Co.; nat. chmn. Nat. Assn. Law Rev. Editors, 1950-51. Editor-in-chief Notre Dame Law Rev., 1950-51; contbr. articles to profl. jours. 1st lt. JAGC U.S. Army, 1953-56. Mem. ABA, D.C. Bar Assn., Chgo. Bar Assn., Am. Law Inst., The Comml. Bar Assn. (London), Am. Assn. Atty.-CPAs, Union League Club, Lawyers Club of Chgo., Met. Club, Sunset Ridge Country Club (Northbrook). Republican. Roman Catholic. Home: 1660 North Ln Northbrook IL 60062-4708 Office: Altheimer & Gray 10 S Wacker Dr Chicago IL 60606-7482

BERENS, WILLIAM JOSEPH, lawyer; b. New Ulm, Minn., Dec. 12, 1952; s. Robert J. and Lorraine M. (O'Brien) B.; m. Janet Christiansen, June 13, 1975; children: Margaret, Elizabeth, Catherine. BA, Coll. St. Thomas, 1975; JD, U. Minn., 1978. Bar: Minn. 1978. Assoc. Dorsey & Whitney, LLP, Mpls., 1978-83, ptnr., 1984—. Adj. prof. William Mitchell Coll. of Law, St. Paul, 1981-84. Fellow: Am. Coll. Trust and Estate Counsel. Home: 1601 Beechwood Ave Saint Paul MN 55116-2409 Office: Dorsey & Whitney LLP 50 S 6th St Minneapolis MN 55402-1498

BERENZWEIG, JACK CHARLES, lawyer; b. Bklyn., Sept. 29, 1942; s. Sidney A. and Anne R. (Dubowe) B.; m. Susan J. Berenzweig, Aug. 8, 1968; children: Mindy, Andrew. B.E.E., Cornell U., 1964; J.D., Am. U., 1968. Bar: Va. 1968, Ill. 1969. Examiner U.S. Pat. Off., Washington, 1964-66; pat. adviser U.S. Naval Air Systems Command, 1966-68; ptnr. Brinks, Hofer, Gilson & Lione and predecessor firm, Chgo., 1968—. Editorial staff Am. U. Law Rev., 1966-68; contbr. articles to profl. jours. Mem. ABA, Chgo. Bar Assn., Ill. State Bar Assn., Bar Assn. 7th Fed. Cir., Va. State Bar, Internat. Trademark Assn. (bd. dirs. 1983-85), Brand Names Edn. Found. (bd. dirs. 1993-2000), Meadow Club (Rolling Meadows, Ill.), Miramar Club (Naples, Fla.), Delta Theta Phi. Home: 127 W Oak St Apt A Chicago IL 60610-5422 Office: Brinks Hofer Gilson & Lione Ltd Ste 3600 455 N Cityfront Plaza Dr Chicago IL 60611-5599 E-mail: jcb@brinkshofer.com.

BEREUTER, DOUGLAS KENT, congressman; b. York, Nebr., Oct. 6, 1939; s. Rupert Wesley and Evelyn Gladys (Tonn) B.; m. Louise Meyer, June 1, 1962; children: Eric David, Kirk Daniel. BA, U. Nebr., 1961; M in City Planning, Harvard U., 1966, MPA, 1973. Urban planner HUD, San Francisco, 1965-66; dir. div. state and urban affairs Nebr. Dept. Econ. Devel., 1967-68, state planning dir., 1968-70; coord. fed.-state relations Nebr. State Govt., 1967-70, urban planning cons., 1971-78; assoc. prof. U. Nebr., Kans. State U., 1971-78; mem. Nebr. Legislature, 1974-78, U.S. Congress from 1st Nebr. Dist., 1979—; mem. fin. svcs. com., vice chmn. internat. rels. com., mem. intelligence com., mem. transp. and infrastructure com. Mem. Nebr. State Crime Commn., 1969-71; chmn. standing com. on urban devel. Nat. Conf. State Legislatures, 1977-78; mem. Nat. Agrl. Export Commn., 1985-86. Served as officer U.S. Army, 1963-65. Mem. Am. Planning Assn., Phi Beta Kappa, Sigma Xi. Republican. Lutheran. Office: Ho of Reps 2184 Rayburn Ofc Bldg Washington DC 20515-0001*

BERG, CHARLES A. state legislator; b. Oct. 15, 1927; m. Carol Berg; seven children. , Ctrl. Sch. Agriculture. Mem. Minn. Senate from 13th dist., 1973-74, 81—; farmer, 1996—. Chmn. Gaming Regulation Com.; mem. Agrl. & Rural Devel., Environ. & Natural Resources Com., Rules & Adminstrn. Com. Office: RR 1 Box 29 Chokio MN 56221-9706 also: State Senate State Capital Building Saint Paul MN 55155-0001

BERG, JOHN A. banker; b. Lemmon, S.D., Sept. 18, 1945; s. Carl A. and Helen L. (Fields) B.; m. Nancy Blair, Mar. 23, 1974; children— Cinthia, Megan, Kristen. B.S., U. N.D., 1967, B.A., 1968; M.B.A., U. Mo., 1972; postgrad. Stonier Sch. Banking, Rutgers U., 1979. Teller, proof clk. First Mchts. & Farmers Bank, Cavalier, N.D., 1962-65; internal auditor Red River Nat. Bank, Grand Forks, N.D., 1965-68; installment loan officer, 1968; asst. cashier No. City Nat. Bank, Duluth, Minn., 1972-74; liason credit officer First Bank System, Mpls., 1974-76; pres., chief exec. officer Wayzata Bank & Trust (Minn.), 1976— ; v.p., sec. Northstar Bancorp., Wayzata, 1979— ; chmn., dir. Wayzata Mortgage Co., 1983— ; dir. Minn. State Bank. Chmn., bd. dirs. Ridgedale YMCA, Minnetonka, Minn., 1983-84; bd. dirs. Wayzata Area Pub. Sch. Found., 1983-84. Served with U.S. Army, 1968-71. Decorated Bronze Star. Mem. Minn. Bankers Assn. (dir. 1981-84), Wayzata C. of C. (chmn., dir. 1981-82). Republican. Presbyterian. Clubs: Wayzata. Lodge: Rotary. Office: Wayzata Bank & Trust Company 900 Wayzata Blvd E Wayzata MN 55391-1863

BERG, LEONARD, retired neurologist, educator, researcher; b. St. Louis, July 17, 1927; s. Jacob and Sara (Kessler) B.; m. Gerry Saltzman, Mar. 25, 1948; children: Kathleen, John, Nancy. A.B. cum laude, Washington U., St. Louis, 1945, M.D. cum laude, 1949. Diplomate: Am. Bd. Psychiatry and Neurology (dir. 1978-85, pres. 1985). Intern Barnes Hosp., St. Louis, 1949-50, resident, 1950-51, Neurol. Inst., N.Y.C., 1951-53; clin. assoc. Nat. Inst. Neurol. Diseases and Blindness, NIH, 1953-55; mem. faculty Washington U. Med. Sch., 1955—, prof. clin. neurology, 1972-89, prof. neurology, 1989-98, prof. emeritus neurology, 1998—; ret., 1998. Attending neurologist Barnes Hosp., Jewish Hosp., St. Louis; dir. Alzheimer's Disease Rsch. Ctr., Washington U., 1985-97; expert U.S. FDA, 1992-96; mem. U.S. Congress Adv. Panel on Alzheimer's Disease, 1993-96, Leonard Berg Annual Symposiums Nat. Spkrs. Co-author: Atlas of Muscle Pathology in Neuromuscular Diseases, 1956. Bd. dirs. Temple Israel, St. Louis, 1972-74, Jewish Center for Aged, 1981-98, hon. dir., 1999—. With USPHS, 1953-55. Recipient Lifetime Disting. Rsch. on Alzheimer's Disease and Related Disorders award, 7th World Alzheimer's Congress, 2000, Robert E. Schlueter Leadership award, St. Louis Met. Med. Soc., 2001. Mem. AMA, Am. Acad. Neurology, Am. Neurol. Assn. (1st v.p. 1988-89), Soc. for Neurosci., Alzheimer's Assn. (Chgo.) (bd. dirs. 1989-95, 96-98, chair med. and sci. adv. bd. 1991-95), Phi Beta Kappa, Sigma Xi, Alpha Omega Alpha. Home: 816 S Hanley Rd Apt 7D Saint Louis MO 63105-2678 Office: Washington U Alzheimer's Disease Rsch Ctr 4488 Forest Park Ave Ste 130 Saint Louis MO 63108-2212

BERG, MICHELE, health services administrator; Degree in psychology, U. Kans.; degree in edn., Washburn U; degree learning disabilities, degree in spl. edn., Kans. State U. Jack Aaron prof. Karl Menninger Sch. Psychiatry & Mental Health Scis., 1995; dir. Menninger Ctr. Learning Disabilities, Topeka. Mem. Nat. Assn. Learning Disabilities, Coun. Learning Disabilities, Internat. Dyslexia Assn. (v.p. Kans./Western Mo. br.). Office: Menninger PO Box 829 Topeka KS 66601-0829

BERG, RICK ALAN, state legislator, real estate investor; b. Maddock, N.D., Aug. 16, 1959; s. Bert R. and Francie (Brink) B.; m. Tracy Jane Martin, Sept. 19, 1987. BS in Agrl. Econ., N.D. State U., 1981. Cert. comml. investment mem. Mem. N.D. Ho. of Reps., Fargo, 1985—, Rep. caucus chmn., 1990-92, speaker, 1992-94, chmn. Industry, Bus. and Labor com.; owner, broker Goldmark Comml. Corp. Mem. Farmhouse Frat. (bd. dirs., pres. 1990-94). Lutheran. Home: 6437 13th St N Fargo ND 58102-6012

BERG, STANTON ONEAL, firearms and ballistics consultant; b. Barron, Wis., June 14, 1928; s. Thomas C. and Ellen Florence (Nedland) Silbaugh; m. June K. Rolstad, Aug. 16, 1952; children: David M., Daniel L., Susan E., Julie L. Student, U. Wis., 1949-50; LLB, LaSalle Ext. U., 1951; postgrad., U. Minn., 1960-69. Claim rep. State Farm Ins. Co., Mpls., Hibbing and Duluth, Minn., 1952-57, claim supt., 1957-70; regional mgr. State Farm Fire and Casualty Co., St. Paul, 1970-84; firearms cons. Mpls., 1961—. Bd. dirs. Am. Bd. Forensic Firearm and Tool Mark Examiners; instr. home firearms safety, Mpls., 1975—; cons. to Sporting Arms and Ammunition Mfrs. Inst., 1974-84; internat. lectr. on forensic ballistics Adv. Bd. Milton Helpern Internat. Ctr. for Forensic Scis., 1975—; mem. bd. cons. Inst. Applied Sci., Chgo., 1974—; cons. for re-exam. of ballistics evidence in Robert Kennedy assassination/Sirhan case Superior Ct. L.A., 1975; ct. expert witness in most state cts., Mil. Gen. Ct. Martial Territorial Ct. at V.I. and U.S. Dist. Cts., Supreme Ct. of Ont., Can.; mem. Nat. Forensic Ctr., 1979-98, internat. study group in forensic scis., 1985—; chmn. internat. symposiums on forensic ballistics, Edinburgh, Scotland, 1972, Zurich, 1975, Bergen, Norway, 1981, Dusseldorf, Germany, 1993. Contbg. editor: Am. Rifleman mag., 1973—84, mem. editl. bd.: Internat. Microform Jour. Legal Medicine and Forensic Scis., 1979—, mem. editl. bd.: Am. Jour. Forensic Medicine and Pathology, 1979—91; contbr. articles to profl. jours.; (presenter): Forensic Firsts, History Channel, 2001. With U.S. Army Counter Intelligence Corp., 1948-52. Fellow Am. Acad. Forensic Sci., Am. Coll. Forensic Examiners (life, bd. cert. forensic examiner and diplomate); mem. ASTM (criminalistics subcom. 1989—, non powder guns subcom. 1990—, paintball guns and sys. subcom. 1994—), NRA, Assn. Firearms and Tool Mark Examiners (life, charter mem., exec. coun. 1970-71, editl. com. AFTE jour., 1989-92, Disting. Mem. and Key Man award 1972, exam. and standards com. 1975-76, Spl. Honors award 1976, nat. peer group on cert. of firearms examiners 1978—), Forensic Sci. Soc., Internat. Assn. forensic Scis., Internat. Assn. for Identification (life, disting. mem., firearms subcom. of sci. and practice com. 1961-74, 86-2000, chmn. firearm subcom. 1964-66, 69-70, 91-95, lab. rsch. and techniques subcom. 1980-81, life charter mem. Minn. divsn.), Internat. Wound Ballistics Assn., Western. Conf. Criminal and Civil Problems (sci. adv. com.), Am. Gunsmithing Assn. (life), Am. Legion (life), Army Counter-Intelligence Corp. Vets. Assn. (life), Browning Arms Collectors Assn. (life), Am. Ordnance Assn. (life), Minn. Weapons Collectors, Internat. Cartridge Collectors Assns. (life), Internat. Reference Orgn. Forensic Medicine and Scis., Internat. Assn. Bloodstain Pattern Analysts. Address: 6025 Gardena Ln NE Minneapolis MN 55432-5840 E-mail: foressicb@msn.com., forensicb@aol.com.

BERG, THOMAS KENNETH, lawyer; b. Willmar, Minn., Feb. 10, 1940; s. Kenneth Q. and Esther V. (Westlund) B.; m. Margit Kathryn Larson, July 31, 1965; children: Erik, Jeffrey. BA, U. Minn., 1962, LLB, 1965. Bar: Minn. 1965, U.S. Dist. Ct. Minn. 1968, U.S. Ct. Appeals (8th cir.) 1974, U.S. Supreme Ct. 1980. Atty. Dept. Navy, Washington, 1965-67; assoc. Carlsen, Greiner & Law, Mpls., 1967-79; state rep. Minn. Ho. of Reps., St. Paul, 1970-78; U.S. atty. Dept. of Justice, Mpls., 1979-81; ptnr. Popham, Haik, Schnobrich & Kaufman, 1981-97, Hinshaw & Culbertson, Mpls., 1997—. Chair Gov.'s Re-election Com., St. Paul, 1984-86, Gov.'s Commn. for Drug Abuse, Mpls., 1989; U.S. Senate candidate for endorsement Dem. Farmer Labor Party, Mpls., 1994; chmn. bd. dirs. St. Paul Rehab. Ctr., 1995-97. Recipient Outstanding Narcotics Prosecution award U.S. Drug Enforcement Adminstrn., 1981. Mem. Am. Health Lawyers Assn. Office: Hinshaw & Culbertson 3100 Piper Jaffray Tower 222 S 9th St Minneapolis MN 55402-3389

BERG, WILLIAM JAMES, French language educator, writer, translator; b. Dunkirk, N.Y., Oct. 26, 1942; s. Francis John and Adalyn Huldah (Goodwin) B.; m. Verity Anne Fry, July 2, 1966 (div. 1985); children—Jennifer Anne, Jessica Lyn; m. Laurey Kramer Martin, Feb. 1, 1986; stepchildren: Stirling Brooke Martin, Hunter Kirk Martin. Cert. pratique, Sorbonne, Paris, 1962-63; B.A., Hamilton Coll., 1964; M.A., Princeton U., 1966, Ph.D., 1969. NDEA inst. asst. Hamilton Coll., Clinton, N.Y., 1964; teaching asst. Princeton (N.J.) U., 1966; instr. French U. Wis., 1967-68, asst. prof., 1968-73, assoc. prof., 1973-79, prof., 1979—, assoc. chmn. French dept., 1974-75, 78-79, 79-80, 90-92, 99-2000, chmn. dept. French and Italian, 1982-85; dir. Acad. Yr. Abroad, Paris and N.Y.C., 1973-74. Outside examiner Swarthmore Coll., 1978, No. Ill. U., 1985, 86; outside program evaluator U. Mich., 1979; tenure reviewer Swarthmore Coll., 1982, Tulane U., 1985, Marquette U., 1992, 2000; invited lectr. Rice U., 1985, U. Tenn., 1993; full prof. reviewer Georgetown U., 1984, Swarthmore Coll., 1992, U. Mich., 1994, Northwestern U., 1996, U. Colo., 1997, Va. Tech., 1999, U. Mich., 2001, NYU, 2002; editl. bd. Summa Publs., Birmingham, Ala., 1983—; reviewer panel for travel and collections NEH, 1989. Author: (with P. Schofer and D. Rice) Poèmes, Pièces, Prose, 1973, (with G. Moskos and M. Grimaud) Saint/Oedipus. Psychocritical Approaches to Flaubert's Art, 1982, (with L. Martin) Images, 1989, The Visual Novel, 1992, (with L. Martin) Emile Zola Revisited, 1992, Gustave Flaubert, 1997, (with S. Magnan, Y. Ozzello and L. Martin-Berg) Paroles, 1999, 2d edit., 2002; author study guides on Twain's Huckleberry Finn, 1986, Tom Sawyer, 1987, (with L. Martin) Flaubert's Madame Bovary, 1989, Zola's Germinal, 1989, Maupassant's Short Stories, 1992; translator: (with P. Scott) Graphics and Graphic Information-Processing, 1981; Semiology of Graphics (design award Midwest Books Competition 1983), 1983-84; mem. editl. bd. Substance, 1971-79; contbr. articles to profl. jours. Travel grantee Am. Philos. Soc., 1969, rsch. grantee U. Wis., 1969, 75, 81-82, 86, 87; Vilas assoc., 1991-93, honors fellow, 1994—; Halverson-Bascom professorship, 1995-2000; recipient U. Wis. Chancellor's award for excellence in tchg., 1995. Mem. MLA, Am. Coun. Tchrs. of Fgn. Langs., Phi Beta Kappa. Avocations: tennis, guitar. Home: 5201 Pepin Pl Madison WI 53705-4724 Office: U Wis Dept French and Italian Madison WI 53706 E-mail: wjberg@facstaff.wisc.edu.

BERGER, CHARLES MARTIN, lawn and garden company executive; b. Wilkes-Barre, Pa., May 2, 1936; s. Edward and Sadie (Zwass) B.; m. Jane Elrod Purdy, June 5, 1960; children: Cary John Aaron, Elizabeth Anne, Valerie Ann. A.B., Princeton U., 1958; M.B.A., Harvard U., 1960. Mktg. mgmt. Procter and Gamble Co., Cin., 1960-64; with H.J. Heinz Co., 1964-96, gen. mgr. mktg. U.S.A. div., 1964-69, dir. corp. planning world hdqrs., 1969-70; mktg. dir. Heinz-London, 1970-72; mng. dir. Plasmon SpA, Milan, 1972-78; pres., CEO, chmn. Weight Watchers Internat. Inc., Jericho, N.Y., 1978-94; chmn., CEO Heinz India Pvt. Ltd., Bombay, 1994-96; chmn., pres. and CEO The Scotts Co., Columbus, Ohio, 1996—2001, chmn., 2001—. Bd. dirs. The Scotts Co., Inc.; lectr. Carnegie-Mellon Grad. Sch. Indsl. Adminstrn., 1968-69 Chmn. bd. dirs. Am. Sch. Milan, 1975-78; bd. dirs. Buckley Country Day Sch., Manhasset, N.Y., 1983-89, Columbus Symphony Orch.; exec.-in-residence Ohio Wesleyan U., Delaware, Ohio. Mem. World Pres'. Orgn. (bd. dirs.), Princeton Club, Village Club of Sands Point (N.Y.), Columbus Club, Capital Club (bd. gov.'s), Port Royal Club. Republican. Jewish. Office: Scotts World Hdqrs 14111 Scottslawn Rd Marysville OH 43041

BERGER, JERRY ALLEN, museum director; b. Buffalo, Oct. 8, 1943; BA in Psychology, U. Wyo., 1965, BA in Art, 1971, MA in Art History, 1972. Curator collections U. Wyo. Art Mus., Laramie, 1972-88, asst. dir., 1980-83, 87-88, acting dir., 1984-86; dir. Springfield (Mo.) Art Mus., 1988—. Office: Springfield Art Mus 1111 E Brookside Dr Springfield MO 65807-1829 E-mail: jerry_berger@ci.springfield.mo.us.

BERGER, JOHN TORREY, JR. lawyer; b. St. Louis, Apr. 14, 1938; s. John Torrey Sr. and Maud Alice (Beattie) B.; m. Helen Lee Thompson, Aug. 26, 1961; children: John Torrey III, Helen E. JD, Washington U., 1963. Bar: Mo. 1963. Assoc. Lewis, Rice & Fingersh, L.C., St. Louis, 1963-70; mem. Lewis & Rice, 1971—, chmn. real estate sect. Bd. dirs. Carr Lane Mfg. Co., St. Louis, St. Louis Audubon Soc., Logos Sch., St. Louis; adv. bd. dirs. St. Louis Screw & Bolt Co. Deacon, elder, trustee Presbyn. Ch., St. Louis, 1970-75, 75—. Mem. ABA (corp. sect., real estate sect.), Mo. Bar Assn. (real estate sect., banking and securities com.), Bar Assn. Met. St. Louis, Internat. Conf. Shopping Ctrs., SAR, Phi Delta Phi. Avocations: fishing, birding, photography. Home: 1257 Takara Ct Saint Louis MO 63131-1013 Office: Lewis Rice & Fingersh 500 N Broadway Ste 2000 Saint Louis MO 63102-2147 E-mail: jberger@lewisrice.com.

BERGER, MELVIN, allergist, immunologist; b. Phila., Mar. 7, 1950; MD, PhD in Biochemistry, Case Western Res. U., 1976. Internship, resident pediatrics Children's Hosp. Med. Ctr., Boston, 1976-78; fellow allergy & immunology Nat. Inst. Allergy & Infectious Diseases, Bethesda, Md., 1978-81; pediatrician, chief Immunology-Allergy Divsn. Rainbow Babies and Children's Hosp., Cleve., 1984—. Prof. peds. & pathology Case Western Res. U. USPHS, 1978-81, col. U.S. Army Res., 1981—. Fellow Am. Acad. Pediatrics. Office: Rainbow Babies Hosp Div Pediatrics/Immunology Cleveland OH 44106 E-mail: mxb12@po.cwru.edu.

BERGER, MILES LEE, land economist; b. Chgo., Aug. 9, 1930; s. Albert E. and Dorothy (Ginsberg) B.; m. Sally Eileen Diamond, Aug. 27, 1955; children: Albert E., Elizabeth Ann. Student, Brown U., 1948-50. Engaged in real estate and fin. svc. fields, 1950—; mng. chmn. bd. Berger Fin. Svcs. Corp., Chgo., 1950—. Chmn. bd. Mid-Am. Appraisal & Rsch. Corp., Chgo., 1959-80, also dir.; chmn. bd. Real Estate Svcs. Corp., 1969—; vice chmn. bd., trustee Heitman Fin. Ltd., 1970-98; chmn. bd. Mid Town Bank Chgo., 1974—; vice chmn. bd., prin. econ. cons. Columbia Nat. Bank, Chgo., 1965-96; bd. dirs. Franklin Corp., Evans Inc., Franklin Capital Corp., Innkeepers USA Trust, Universal Health Svcs., Inc.; trustee Heitman Mortgage Investors, Innkeepers Am. Mem., chmn. Chgo. Plan Commn., 1980-84; cons. city Chgo. on Ill. Ctrl. Air Rights, 1967—; trustee Latin Sch. Chgo., 1967-73, treas., 1953-55, bd. dirs. Latin Sch. Found.; bd. govs. Met. Planning Coun.; bd. mgrs. James Jordan Boys Club. Mem. Am. Inst. Real Estate Appraisers, Soc. Real Estate Appraisers, Soc. Real Estate Counselors, Am. Right-of-Way Assn., Nat. Assn. Housing and Redevel. Ofcls., Nat. Tax Assn., Internat. Assn. Assessing Officers, Lambda Alpha. Jewish (trustee synagogue). Office: Berger Mgmt Svcs LLC 900 N Michigan Ave Ste 2010 Chicago IL 60611-6519

BERGER, NATHAN ALLEN, dean, university administrator; b. Phila., July 8, 1940; s. Meyer and Lillian (Salko) B.; m. Sosamma John, June 23, 1968; children: Joshua S., Ravi B., Sarina H. AB, Temple U., 1962; MD, Hahneman U., 1966. Intern Michael Reese Med. Ctr., Chgo., 1967-68; rsch. assoc. NIH, Balt., 1968-71; assoc. prof. Washington U. Sch. Medicine, St. Louis, 1971-82; prof. medicine, biochemistry, and oncology Case Western Res. U., Cleve., 1983-95, dir. cancer ctr., 1985-95, interim dean, v.p. med. affairs, 1995-96, dean, v.p. med. affairs, 1996—. Bd. trustees Edison Biotech. Am. Cancer Soc., U. Hosp. Cleve., Henry Ford Health System, Menorah Park, Ohio Biomed. Rsch. and Tech. Task Force. Contbr. articles to profl. jours.; mem. editl. bd. Jour. Clin. Investigation, Jour. Biol. Chemistry, Cancer Rsch.; others. Lt. comdr. USPHS, 1968-71. Fellow Washington U. Sch. Medicine, 1971-82; Leukemia Soc. Am. scholar. Mem. Am. Soc. Hematology, Am. Soc. Biol. Chemists, Am. Soc. Clin. Oncology, Am. Soc. Cancer Rsch., Am. Soc. Clin. Investigation, Am. Assn. Physicians. Office: Case Western Res U 10900 Euclid Ave Cleveland OH 44106-1712 E-mail: nab@po.cwru.edu.

BERGER, P(HILIP) JEFFREY, animal science educator, quantitative geneticist; b. Newark, June 28, 1943; s. Philip Graham and Jean Bar (Weller) B.; m. Frances Ann Williams, June 25, 1965; children— Sarah Katherine, Philip Calvin B.S., Delaware Valley Coll., 1965; M.S., Ohio State U., 1967, Ph.D., 1970. Research and teaching asst. Ohio State U., Columbus, 1965-70; mem. faculty Iowa State U., Ames, 1972—, prof. animal sci., 1982—. Cons. computer applications, animal prodn. div. FAO, Rome, 1979; vis. coop. scientist Bet Dagan, Israel, 1980; participant 1st Animal prodn. Conf., San Jose, Costa Rica, 1981; developer mixed model animal prediction programs, 1972—; participant tech. transfer project to develop genetic evaluation program for dairy cattle in tunisia, 1988, Sabbatical Wageningen Agrl. U., The Netherlands, 1994. Contbr. articles to profl. jours. Mem. Am. Dairy Sci. Assn., Am. Soc. Animal Sci., Sigma Xi, Delta Tau Alpha Republican. Methodist Home: 2518 Kellogg Ave Ames IA 50010-4863 Office: Ia State U Dept Animal Sci 225 Kildee Hl Ames IA 50011-0001

BERGER, ROBERT MICHAEL, lawyer; b. Chgo., Jan. 29, 1942; s. David B. and Sophia (Mizock) B.; m. Joan B. Israel, Aug. 16, 1964; children: Aliza, Benjamin, David. AB, U. Mich., 1963; JD, U. Chgo., 1966. Bar: Ill. 1966, U.S. Supreme Ct. 1975. Law clk. to cir, judge Henry J. Friendly U.S. Ct. Appeals, 2d Circuit, N.Y.C., 1966-67; atty. Chgo. Legal Aid Bur. Law Reform Unit, 1967-68; mem. firm Mayer, Brown & Platt, Chgo., 1968-72, ptnr., 1972-2001; adjunct prof. Northwestern U. Law Sch., 1997—; exec. v.p., gen. counsel, sec. Capri Capital LP, 2001—; sr. counsel Krasnow, Sanberg, Cornblath & Hobbs, 2001—. Lectr. Northwestern U. Law Sch., 1973; adj. prof. grad. program in real estate law John Marshall Law Sch., 1995-97; summer inst. faculty mem. Nat. Inst. Law-Focused Edn., Chgo., 1969-74; mem. hearing bd. Ill. Supreme Ct. Atty. Disciplinary Sys., 1973-79; mem. Ill. Sec. State Adv. Com. on Revised Uniform Ltd. Partnership Act, 1984-88, mem. spl. tax adv. commn. to Ill. Dept. Ins., 1972; bd. dirs., legal counsel Consumer Fedn. Ill., 1967-71; mem. regional consumer adv. coun. coun. FTC, 1969; bd. dirs., chmn. program com. Legal Assistance Found., Chgo., 1975-78; mem. Highland Park (Ill.) Zoning Bd. Appeals, 1984-86; chmn. blue ribbon com. Cook County Recorder, 1989-92; mem. real estate adv. bd. Dai-Ichi Kangyo Bank, Chgo., 1988-93; lectr. continuing legal edn. seminars. Comment editor: U. Chgo. Law Rev, 1965-66; author: Law and the Consumer, 1969, 74; author 500 page chpt. Lending, Finance and Banking, Construction Law, 1986, 92, ann. supplements; reporter Revised Uniform Ltd. Partnership Act, 1984-88; contb r. articles to law jours. Sec. Chgo. area Anti-Defamation League; trustee Am. Friends of Hebrew U., bd. dirs. Mem. ABA (chmn. subcom. on rev. uniform ltd. partnership act 1981-85, chmn. com. on partnerships and unincorporated bus. orgns. 1985-88), Am. Law Inst. (consultative group), Am. Coll. Real Estate Lawyers (bd. govs. 1995-98, nominating com., vice chmn. program com.), Chgo. Bar Assn. (bd. mgrs. 1970-72, chmn. com. on real estate fin. 1984-86, chmn. real property law com. 1987-88), Chgo. Coun. Lawyers (founder, bd. govs. 1969-71), Am.-Israel C. of C. (1st vice-chmn.), Order of Coif, Phi Beta Kappa, Phi Kappa Phi. Office: Capri Capital LP Ste 3430 875 N Michigan Ave Chicago IL 60611 E-mail: rberger@capricap.com.

BERGER, SANFORD JASON, lawyer, securities dealer, real estate broker; b. Cleve., June 29, 1926; s. Sam and Ida (Solomon) B.; m. Bertine Mae Benjamin, Aug. 6, 1950 (div. Dec. 1977); children: Bradley Alan, Bonnie Jean. B.A., Case Western Res. U., 1950, J.D., 1952. Bar: Ohio 1952, U.S. Supreme Ct. 1979, U.S. Ct. Appeals, 1981. Field examiner Ohio Dept. Taxation, Cleve., 1952; pvt. practice law, Cleve., 1952—; real estate cons., Cleve., 1960—; investment cons., Cleve., 1970—. Contbr. author: Family Evaluation in Child Custody Litigation, 1982, Child Custody Litigation, 1986, The Parental Alienation Syndrome and the Differentiation Between Fabricated and Genuine Child Sex Abuse, 1987, Family Evaluation in Child Custody Mediation, Arbitration and Litigation, 1989; Copyright 10 songs, 1977. Candidate police judge, East Cleve., 1955, Bd. Edn., Beachwood, Ohio, 1963, mayor, Beachwood, 1967, judge ct. common pleas, Cuyahoga County, Ohio, 1984, 1986, Ct. Appeals, 1988, 90, 92, 94. Successful lawyer in U.S. Supreme Ct. Case of Cleveland Bd. of Edn. vs. Loudermill, 1985. With USMC, 1944-45, PTO. Recipient Cert. Appreciation Phi Alpha Delta, 1969, U.S. Supreme Ct. Chief Justice Warren E. Burger Healer Award, 1987, Outstanding Ohio Citizen award Ohio Gen. Assembly, 1987. Republican. Jewish. Lodge: B'nai B'rith (editor 1968-70). Avocations: poet, lyricist, legal writer, drag racer, scuba diving. Home: 1032 Som Center Rd Cleveland OH 44143-3527 Office: Sanford J Berger 1836 Euclid Ave # 305 Cleveland OH 44115-2234

BERGERE, CARLETON MALLORY, contractor; b. Brookline, Mass., Apr. 4, 1919; s. Jason J. and Anna Lillian B.; m. Jean J. Pach, Oct. 1, 1950. Student, Burdett Bus. Coll., 1938, Babsons Sch. Bus., 1940. Self-employed contractor, Chgo., 1949-57; pres. Permanent Bldg. Supply Co., Inc., 1957-62, Gt. No. Bldg. Products, Inc., Chgo., 1962-67, C.M. Bergere Co., Inc., Cgho., 1967-96, Carleton M. Bergere & Assocs., 1996—. Served with USN, 1944. Named Man of Yr., Profl. Remodelers Assn. Greater Chgo., 1978. Mem. Nat. Assn. Remodeling Industry (pres. Greater Chicagoland chpt., exec. dir., reg. v.p. 1991-95, Pres.'s award 1990, Profl. award 1992), Chgo. Assn. Commerce and Industry (indsl. devel. com.), Better Bus. Bur. Met. Chgo., Industry Trade Practice Com. on Home Improvment (chmn., bd. dirs. 1992—), Nat. Panel Consumer Arbitrators, Exec. Club (Chgo.). Address: 175 E Delaware Pl Chicago IL 60611-1756

BERGERON, CLIFTON GEORGE, ceramic engineer, educator; b. Los Angeles, Jan. 5, 1925; s. Lewis G. and Rose C. (Dengel) B.; m. Laura H. Kaario, June 9, 1950; children— Ann Leija, Louis Kaario. B.S., U. Ill., 1950, M.S., 1959, Ph.D., 1961. Sr. ceramic engr. A. O. Smith Corp., Milw., 1950-55; staff engr. Whirlpool Corp., St. Joseph, Mich., 1955-57; research asso. U. Ill., Champaign-Urbana, 1957-61, asst. prof., 1961-63, asso. prof., 1963-67, prof., 1967-78, head dept. ceramic engring., 1978-86, prof. emeritus, 1988—. Cons. A. O. Smith Corp., Whirlpool Corp., Ingraham Richardson, U.S. Steel Corp., Pfaudler Corp., Ferro Corp. Editor, Ann. Conf. on Glass Problems. Served in U.S. Army, 1943-46, ETO. NSF grantee, 1961-82. Fellow Am. Ceramic Soc.; mem. AAAS, Nat. Inst. Ceramic Engrs., AAUP, KERAMOS, Am. Soc. Engring. Edn., Sigma Xi. Achievements include research in crystallization kinetics in glass; high temperature reactions. Home: 208 W Michigan Ave Urbana IL 61801-4944 Office: 105 S Goodwin Ave Urbana IL 61801-2901 E-mail: clifcraft@aol.com.

BERGERSON, DAVID RAYMOND, lawyer; b. Mpls., Nov. 23, 1939; s. Raymond Kenneth and Katherine Cecille (Langworthy) Bergerson; m. Nancy Anne Heeter, Dec. 22, 1962; children: W. Thomas C., Kirsten Finch, David Raymond. BA, Yale U., 1961; JD, U. Minn., 1964. Bar: Minn. 1964. Assoc. Fredrikson Law Firm, Mpls., 1964-67; atty. Honeywell Inc., 1967-74, asst. gen. counsel, 1974-82, v.p., asst. gen. counsel, 1983-84, v.p., gen. counsel, 1984-92; pvt. practice law, 1992-94; v.p., sec. Telcom Sys. Svcs., Inc., Plymouth, 1994-96, dir., cons., 1996-97; v.p. bd. dirs. Hogan Bergerson, Inc., Mpls., 1997—. Bd. dirs. Pillsbury Neighborhood Svcs., Inc., Mpls., 1983—92. Mem.: Mpls. Club. Republican. Avocations: scuba diving, bird-hunting. Home: 2303 Huntington Point Rd E Wayzata MN 55391-9740 Office: Hogan Bergerson Inc 4040 IDS Ctr Minneapolis MN 55402 E-mail: dbergerson1@mchsi.com.

BERGES, JAMES G. electric and electronic products executive; BSEE, U. Notre Dame. Various engring. and mgmt. positions GE; various positions in mfg. Emerson Electric Co., St. Louis, 1976, pres. Emerson Specialty Motors, group v.p., 1988-89, exec. v.p., 1989-97, vice chmn., dir., 1997-99, pres., 1999—. Office: Emerson Electric Co 8000 W Florissant Ave PO Box 4100 MS2269 Saint Louis MO 63136-8506

BERGESON, JAMES, advertising executive; Pres., COO, CEO Colle and McVoy Inc., Mpls. Mem. Internat. Comms. Agy. Network (pres. 1999—). Office: Colle & McVoy Inc Ste 2400 8500 Normandale Lake Blvd Minneapolis MN 55437-3809

BERGGREN, RONALD BERNARD, surgeon, emeritus educator; b. S.I., N.Y., June 13, 1931; s. Bernard and Florence (Schmidt) B.; m. Mary Beth Griffith, Nov. 25, 1954; children: Karen Berggren Murray, Eric Griffith. BA, Johns Hopkins U., 1953; MD, U. Pa., 1957. Diplomate Am. Bd. Surgery, Nat. Bd. Med. Examiners, Am. Bd. Plastic Surgery (bd. dirs. 1982-88, chmn. 1987-88). Asst. instr. surgery U. Pa., 1958-62, instr., 1962-65; gen. surg. resident Hosp. U. Pa., 1958-62, resident plastic surgery, 1963-64, chief resident plastic surgery, 1964-65; sr. resident surgery Phila. Gen. Hosp., 1962-63; asst. prof. surgery Ohio State U. Sch. Medicine, 1965-68, dir. div. plastic surgery, 1965-85, assoc. prof. surgery, 1968-73, prof. surgery, 1973-86, emeritus prof. surgery, 1986—; attending staff Ohio State U. Hosps., chief of staff, 1983-85, hon. staff, 1986—. Attending staff, dir. div. plastic surgery Children's Hosp., Columbus, Ohio, 1965-90; v.p. Plastic Surgery Ednl. Found., 1984-85, pres., 1986-87; sec. Plastic Surgery Tng. Program Dirs., 1981-83, chmn., 1983-85; mem. med. adv. bd. Ohio Bur. for Children with Med. Handicaps, 1974—. Trustee Mid Ohio Health Planning Fedn., 1979-82, 84, PSRO, 1980-84, Scioto Valley Health Systems Agy., 1985-87; del. Coun. Med. Splty. Socs., 1982-90, dir., 1988-90. Recipient Disting. Svc. award Plastic Surgery Edn. Foun., 1990. Fellow: ACS (gov. 1996—2001, chair gov.'s com. on ambulatory surg. care); mem.: AMA, Coun. Plastic Surgical Orgn. (convenor 1996—2000), Coun. Med. Specialty Socs. (dir. 1989—90, sec. 1991—92, pres.-elect 1993, pres. 1994), Accreditation Coun. for Grad. Med. Edn. (rev. com. for plastic surgery 1983—90, mem. exec. com. 1987—90, designate chmn. 1988, chmn. 1989, mem. exec. com. 1994, chmn. 1994, institutional rev. com. 1996—, co-chair 2001—), Am. Soc. Maxillofacial Surgery, Am. Soc. Aesthetic Plastic Surgery (parliamentarian 1992—93), Am. Trauma Soc., Am. Burn Assn., Assn. Acad. Surgery, Am. Assn. Surgery Trauma, N.Y. Acad. Scis., Plastic Surg. Rsch. Coun. (chair 1975—76), Franklin County Med. Soc. (pres.-elect 1982—83, pres. 1983—84), Am. Assn. Plastic Surgeons (treas. 1982—85, v.p. 1988—89, pres.-elect 1989—90, pres. 1990—91), Am. Cleft Palate Assn., Ohio Valley Plastic Surg. Soc., Am. Soc. Plastic and Reconstructive Surgeons (spl. hon. citation 1995, Trustees award for spl. achievement in plastic surgery 2000), Columbus Surg. Soc., Ctrl. Surg. Soc., Alpha Kappa Kappa, Phi Kappa Psi, Sigma Xi. Office: 9787 Windale Farms Cir Galena OH 43021-9609

BERGHOLZ, DAVID, foundation administrator; b. Chgo., Jan. 2, 1938; s. Arthur C. and Sarah (Tarler) B.; 1 child from previous marriage, Jonathan; m. Eleanor Jean Mallet, Sept. 17, 1970; children: Louis Daniel, Max Arthur. Student, U. Chgo., 1955-57; AB in Anthropology, U. Pitts., 1962. Asst. dir. com. on human resources Office of Mayor, City of Pitts., 1966-67; asst. to exec. dir. Allegheny Council to Improve Our Neighborhoods-Housing, Inc., Pitts., 1967-72; asst. to pres. Mallet & Co., Inc., Carnegie, Pa., 1972-73; assoc. planning Comprehensive Health Planning Assn. of Western Pa., Pitts., 1973-75; assoc. dir. cancer ctr. planning project Allegheny Gen. Hosp., 1976-77; asst. exec. dir. Allegheny Conf. on Community Devel., 1977-88; pres. Pub. Edn. Fund, 1983-88; exec. dir. George Gund Found., Cleve., 1989—. Adj. assoc. prof. cmty. devel. Carnegie Mellon U., Pitts., 1985-88; mem. adv. com. Health Policy Inst.; mem. steering com. Robert Wood Johnson Affordable Health Care Project. Recipient Recognition award Boys and Girls Club of Western Pa., 1984, Pitts. Bd. Edn. award, 1986. Mem. Coun. on Founds., Coun. on Basic Edn., Ind. Sector, Phi Delta Kappa (Lay Leader award 1985). Office: George Gund Found 1845 Guildhall Bldg 45 W Prospect Ave Cleveland OH 44115-1039

BERGLIN, LINDA, state legislator; b. Oakland, Calif., Oct. 19, 1944; d. Freeman and Norma (Lund) Waterman; m. Glenn Sampson; 1 child, Maria. BFA, Mpls. Coll. Art and Design. Mem. Minn. Ho. of Reps., St. Paul, 1972-80, Minn. Senate, St. Paul, 1980—. Chmn. Health and Human Svcs. Com.; mem. senate judiciary com., family svcs. com., tax and tax laws com., others; mem. various legis. commns. including Econ. Status of Women, Healthcare Oversight Commn.; U.S. rep. U.S.-Japan Legis. Exch. Program; seminar participant health care reform U.S.-Sweden, also Austria, 1981; studied health care reform Great Britain, 1992; rep. Nat. Coun. State Legislatures Women's Network Del., Korea, 1989. Bd. dirs. Freedom House, Better Jobs for Women, founding mem., Cornerhouse, Whittier Alliance, founding, St. Stephen's Guild Hall, Orgnl. Industrialization Ctrs., Children's Theater; mem. scattered site housing com. Powderhorn Cmty. Coun., Food and Land Resource Ctr., Joint Urban Mission Project, Phillips Neighborhood Improvement Assn., numerous others; trustee Inst. Arts. Recipient Pub. Citizen of Yr. award Nat. Assn. Social Workers, 1980, Nursing Home Residents Adv. Coun. award, 1983, NAACP Cert. Appreciation, 1984, Common Space Mutual Housing award, 1984, Award of Excellence Minn. Dept. Human Svcs., 1986, Leadership award Mpls. Conv. Ctr. Greater Mpls. C. of C., 1986, Children's Champion award Children's Defense Fund, 1987, March of Dimes award, 1988, Child Health Care citation Am. Acad. Pediatrics and Children's Defense Fund, 1988, Health Span Coalition award, 1989, Outstanding Achievement award Med. Alley, 1989, Minn. Psychol. Assn. award, 1990, Disting. Svc. award Minn. Assn. Edn. Young Children, 1991, Cert. of Merit Minn. Women's Consortium, 1992, Minn. Assn. Cmty. Mental Health Programs, Inc., 1993, others; named Outstanding Woman of Yr. YWCA, 1980, Legislator of Yr. ARC, 1989, Pub. Official of Yr. Minn. Homes for the Aging, 1991, many other honors. Mem. Dem.-Farmer-Labor Party. Office: Minn Senate 309 State Capitol 75 Constitution Ave Saint Paul MN 55155-1606

BERGMAN, BRADLEY ANTHONY, trust company executive; b. Portsmouth, Va., Sept. 23, 1953; s. Willis Anthony and Suzanne (Florey) B.; m. Elizabeth Robertson, June 17, 1983; children: Alexander Nicholas, Katherine Suzanne. BS, Ill. State U., 1974; JD, Washburn Law Sch., 1978. Bar: Kans. 1978, Mo. 1981, Okla. 1987. Exec. v.p. United Mo. City Bank, Kansas City, 1980-85; sr. v.p. Bank Okla. Trust, Oklahoma City, 1986-87; exec. v.p. Johnson County Bank, Prarie Village, Kans., 1988; pres., chief exec. officer Kans. Trust Co., 1988—. Mem. Kans. Bar Assn., Mo. Bar Assn., Okla. Bar Assn., Estate Planning Soc., Hallbrook Country Club. Home: 11804 Fairway Ave Shawnee Mission KS 66211-3040 Office: Midwest Trust Co 10740 Nall Ave., Suite 100 Overland Park KS 66211

BERGMAN, BRUCE E. municipal official; m.; 2 children. BA, Simpson Coll., 1970; JD, U. Houston, 1972. Clk. to Hon. M.E. Rawlings Iowa Supreme Ct., 1973-74; assoc. Williams, Hart, Lavorato & Kirtley, West Des Moines, Iowa, 1974-78, ptnr., 1978-79, Davis, Baker & Bergman, Des Moines, 1980-85, Isaacson, Clarke & Bergman, P.C., Des Moines, 1985-89; asst. city atty. City of Des Moines Legal Dept., 1989-90, solicitor, 1990-91, chief solicitor, 1991-96, corp. counsel, 1996—. Mem.: ABA, Iowa Mcpl. Attys. Assn. (bd. dir. 1996—99, 2002—), Polk County Bar Assn., Iowa State Bar Assn. Home: 4508 49th St Des Moines IA 50310-2970 Office: Office of the Corp Counsel City of Des Moines City Hall 400 E 1st St Des Moines IA 50309 E-mail: bebergman@ci.des-moines.ia.us.

BERGONIA, RAYMOND DAVID, venture capitalist; b. Spring Valley, Ill., May 21, 1951; s. Raymond A. and Elva M. (Bernadini) B.; m. Linda Goble, Dec. 31, 1988; children: Alexandra, Andrew, Caroline, Margot. BBA, U. Notre Dame, 1973; JD, Harvard U., 1976. Bar: Ill. 1976, U.S. Dist. Ct. (no. dist.) Ill. 1976, U.S. Tax Ct. 1977; C.P.A., Ill. Assoc. Winston & Strawn, Chgo., 1976-79; legal counsel, v.p. adminstrn. Heizer Corp., 1979-86; v.p. corp. fin. Chgo. Corp., 1986-89; exec. v.p., prin. N.Am. Bus. Devel. Co. L.L.C., Chgo., 1989—. Bd. dirs. numerous pvt. cos. Recipient Elijah Watts Sells award Am. Inst. C.P.A.s, 1973 Mem. ABA, Chgo. Bar Assn. Home: 605 Essex Rd Kenilworth IL 60043-1129 Office: NAM Bus Devel Co LLC 135 S La Salle St Chicago IL 60603-4159 E-mail: dbergonia@northamericanfund.com.

BERGQUIST, GENE ALFRED, farmer, rancher, county commissioner; b. Paynesville, Minn., Aug. 5, 1927; s. Albin and Viola (Heinrich) B.; m. Ann Dorothy Corwin, Aug. 2, 1958; children: Wayne A., Viola M. Grad. high sch., Rhame, N.D. Self-employed farmer-rancher, Rhame, 1948—; Slope County commr. Amidon, N.D., 1982—. Bd. dirs. Rhame, N.D. Cenex, 1970-82; bd. dirs. Harper Twp. Rhame; com. mem. Slope County Agrl. Stabilization and Conservation Svc.-USDA Commn., Amidon, 1968-84. Bd. dirs. Rhame Rural Fire Dept., 1976—, Bowman-Slope Social Svc. Bd., Bowman, N.D., 1991—, Deep Creek Twp., 1958-64, Richland Center Twp. Bd., 1952-57; elder Lyle Presbyn. Ch.; youth leader 4-H Slope County, 1950-57; mem. Bowman-Slope Revolving Loan Fund Com., 1998—; mem. job devel. bd. Slope and Bowman Counties, 1999—. Mem. Nat. Assn. Counties, N.D. Assn. Counties. Presbyterian. Avocations: reading, painting, fishing, riding, gardening. Office: Courthouse Amidon ND 58620

BERGSMARK, EDWIN MARTIN, mortgage bank executive; b. July 14, 1941; married; 2 children BBA, U. Cin., 1964; postgrad. in mgmt., U. Colo.; JD, U. Toledo, 1972; postgrad. in banking, U. Wis. Bar: Ohio 1972, U.S. Dist. Ct. Ohio, U.S. Tax Ct., Ct. Customs and Patent Appeals, U.S. Supreme Ct. 1975. Indsl. rels. pers. dir. Textileather div. Gen. Tire and Rubber, 1967-70; exec. v.p., gen. counsel TrustCorp, Inc., Toledo, 1970-89. Chmn., CEO Cavista Corp.; chmn. Vista Capital Group Inc., Cavalear Corp., Cavalear Realty Co., Cavalear Ins.; bd. dirs. Unimast Corp., Vista Devel. Inc., Gen. Aluminum and Chem. Corp., N.Am. Travel Corp. Past chmn. Sta. WGTE-TV (PBS); past pres., trustee Toledo Zool. Soc.; trustee Lourdes Coll.; chmn., trustee Toledo Mud Hens Baseball Club; pres. bd. trustees Lucas County Recreation Ctr.; past pres. Kidney Found. Northwestern Ohio, Toledo Neighborhood Housing Svcs.; vice chmn., treas., commr. Ohio Turnpike Commn. Served to capt. U.S. Army, Vietnam. Named Toledo's Outstanding Young Man of Yr., 1972 Mem. ABA, Toledo Bar Assn., Fed. Bar Assn. (trustee), Legal Inst. of Gt. Lakes, Am. Econ. Coun., Burning Tree Golf Club, Inverness Country Club. Office: Vista Capital Group Inc 6444 Monroe St Ste C Sylvania OH 43560-1430

BERGSTEIN, JERRY MICHAEL, pediatric nephrologist; b. Cleve., June 26, 1939; s. Sol R. and Hilda (Nittscoff) B.; m. Renee M. Hillman, July 7, 1963; children: Stephanie, Michael, Jeffrey. BA, UCLA, 1961; MD, U. Minn., 1965. Diplomate Nat. Bd. Med. Examiners, Am. Bd. Pediat., Am. Bd. Pediat. Nephrology; lic. physician, Ind. Intern in pediat. U. Minn., Mpls., 1965-66, jr. pediat. resident, 1966-67, chief pediat. resident, 1969-70, postdoctoral fellow in pediat. nephrology, 1970-73; asst. prof., head pediat. nephrology UCLA, 1973-77; assoc. prof. Ind. U. Sch. Medicine, Indpls., 1977-82, head pediat. nephrology, 1977—, prof., 1982—. Mem. adv. bd. Nat. Kidney Found. Ind., 1980—; mem. adv. coun. Am. Heart Assn., 1988—. Mem. editl. bd. Child Nephrology and Urology, 1980-90, Pediat. Nephrology, 1995—; contbr. chpts. to books. Lt. comdr. USN, 1967-69. Recipient Fellowship USPHS, Washington, 1970; grantee Thrasher Fund, 1980, Amgen, 1990. Mem. Am. Soc. Nephrology, Am. Soc. Pediat. Nephrology, Am. Soc. Investigative Pathology, Soc. Exptl. Biology and Medicine. Achievements include research on the role of the fibrinolytic inhibitor plasminogen activator inhibitor-1 in the pathogenesis and outcome of the hemolytic-uremic syndrome; development of anti-tubular basement membrane antibody disease; development of radiation nephritis in bone marrow transplant patients. Avocations: fishing, gardening, reading, racquetball. Office: James Whitcomb Riley Hosp for Children 702 Barnhill Dr Indianapolis IN 46202-5128 E-mail: jbergste@iupui.edu.

BERGSTROM, STIG MAGNUS, geology educator; b. Skovde, Sweden, June 12, 1935; s. Axel Magnus and Karin Margareta (Engberg) B.; m. Disa Birgitta Kullgren Fil. lic., Lund U., Sweden, 1961, hon. doctorate, 1987. Amanuensis Lund U., 1958-62, asst. lectr., 1962-68; asst. prof. geology Ohio State U., Columbus, 1968-70, assoc. prof., 1970-72, prof., 1972—; dir. Orton Geol. Mus., 1968—. Contbr. numerous articles to profl. jours. Recipient Assar Hadding prize 1995, Raymond C. Moore medal, 1999, Golden medal Faculty of Sci., Charles U., Czech Rep., 1999, Pander Soc. medal, 2001; Am.-Scandinavian Found. fellow, 1964; Fulbright scholar, 1960; grantee numerous orgns., 1958—. Fellow Geol. Soc. Am., Ohio Acad. Sci.; mem. Royal Physiographic Soc. Office: Ohio State U Orton Geol Mus 155 S Oval Mall Columbus OH 43210-1308

BERICK, JAMES HERSCHEL, lawyer, director; b. Cleve., Mar. 30, 1933; s. Morris and Rebecca Alice (Gerdy) B.; children: Michael, Daniel, Robert, Joshua. AB, Columbia U., 1955; JD, Case Western Res. U., 1958. Assoc. Burke, Haber & Berick, Cleve., 1958-60, ptnr., 1960-86, mng. ptnr., 1968-83; chmn. Berick, Pearlman & Mills Co. L.P.A., 1986-99; ptnr. Squire, Sanders & Dempsey, LLP, 2000—. Bd. dirs. MBNA Corp., MBNA Am. Bank, N.A., MBNA Internat. Bank, Ltd., The Town and Country Trust, The Town and Country Funding Corp.; sec. A. Schulman, Inc., 1973—; lectr. law Case Western Res. U., 1969—78; sec. Cleve. Browns Football Co. LLC; bd. vis. Case Western Res. U. Sch. Law, 1998—. Founding trustee, treas., chmn. fin. com., mem. exec. com. Rock and Roll Hall of Fame and Mus.; mem. Shaker Heights (Ohio) Bd. Edn., 1980-83; bd. visitors Columbia Coll., 1981-87, 90-96, emeritus, 2000—; bd. dirs. Univ. Circle Inc., 1994—; mem. univ. coun. Case We. Res. U., 1994-99, chmn., 1996—, presidl. adv. coun., 2000—. Mem.: Cleve. 50 Club, Soc. of Benchers, Ct. of Nisi Prius, Shoreby Club, Hermit Club, Union Club (Cleve.), Order of Coif. Home: 14 W Mather Ln Bratenahl OH 44108-1158 Office: Squire Sanders & Dempsey LLP 4900 Key Tower 127 Public Sq Cleveland OH 44114-1216

BERKE, AMY TURNER, health science association administrator; b. Cleve., Oct. 27, 1942; d. Elliott L. and Evelyn (Silverman) Glicksberg; m. Donald Alan Turner, Dec. 16, 1962 (div. 1979); children: Matthew, Kelli; m. Joseph Jerold Berke, June 21, 1981; children: Richard, Rachel, Jason. Student, Ohio State U., 1960-63; BS, Wayne State U., 1965, MA, 1966. Tchr. Waterford (Mich.) Sch. System, 1965-67; v.p. Apt. Referral Service, Oak Park, Mich., 1970-73; instr. Detroit Coll. Bus., Dearborn, 1975-79; exec. dir. Detroit Neurosurgical Found., 1979—. Past bd. dirs. Internat. Mus. Surg. Sci., Friends of Belle Isle; bd. dirs. Goodwill Industries Found., Alliance for Safer Greater Detroit; mem. Citizens Adv. Wayne County Youth; commr., vice chair Detroit Recreation Adv. Commn.; commr. Youth Sports and Recreation Commn. Mem. Coun. Mich. Founds., Project Pride Detroit C. of C., Wayne State U. Alumni Club, Ohio State U. Alumni Club, Coun. of Mich. Founds., Detroit Area Grantmakers. Avocations: reading, hiking, aerobics, traveling. Office: Detroit Neurosurg Found 3333 E Jefferson Ave Detroit MI 48207

BERKLEY, EUGENE BERTRAM (BERT BERKLEY), envelope company executive; b. Kansas City, Mo., May 8, 1923; s. Eugene Bertram (Bert) Berkowitz and Caroline Newman (Newburger) B.; m. Joan Meinrath, Sept. 1, 1948; children: Janet Lynn Berkley Dubrava, William (Bill) Spencer, Jane Ellen Berkley Levitt. BA, Duke U., 1948; MBA, Harvard U., 1950. Pres., CEO Tension Envelope Corp., Kansas City, Mo., 1962-88, chmn. bd., 1967—. Patentee in field. Bd. dirs. The Inst. for Ednl. Leadership Inc., Washington; trustee, chmn. U. Kansas City, 1983-85, vice chmn., 1981-83, North Campus Devel. Com., policy bd., charter mem. Univ. Assocs.; chmn. bd. dirs. Minority Supplier Coun., 1986-88, bd. dirs. Ewing Marion Kauffman Found., Ctr. for Entrepreneurial Leadership, 1991—; chmn. Ctr. for Bus. Innovation, 1987-89; bd. dirs. Nat. Youth Info. Network, 1997—; mem. adv. bd. Nat. Coun. Econ. Edn., 1993-95, human resources com. Heart of Am. United Way, 1983, chmn. Comprehensive Needs and Svc. Survey Com., 1971; pres. Civic Coun. of Greater Kansas City, 1967-68, charter mem., bd. dirs. 1982-83; pres. C. of C. of Greater Kansas City, 1968-69; bd. dirs. Menorah Med. Ctr. Bd., 1980-94; mem. Kitchen Cabinet, Kansas City, Mo. Sch. Dist., 1990-92; chmn. adv. com., bd. dirs. Ctr. for Workplace Preparation, U.S. C. of C., 1989-91; trustee Midwest Rsch. Inst., exec. com., 1969-72; bd. dirs. Kansas City Area Health Planning Coun., Inc., 1982-83, Nat. Minority Supplier Devel. Coun., 1989-98; chmn. bd. dirs. Human Svcs. Testing and Retng. Coun., 1983-90; active Bus. Roundtable Dept. Social Svcs. State of Mo., 1989—; adv. bd. U. Kans. Natural History Mus., 1994-2000, Nat. Parks and Conservation Assn., 1986—; bd. dirs. Can. Cellulose Co., Vancouver, BC, 1973-80, founder, LINC, 1992; chmn. local investment commn. LINC Mo. Dept. Social Svcs., 1992-95, exec. comm., 1992—; mem. exec. com. Ctr. for Mgmt. Assistance, 1980-83; mem. Mayor's Prayer Breakfast Com., 1964-84; mem. exec. com., met. chmn. Nat. Alliance of Businessmen of Met. Kansas City, 1973; chmn. bd. dirs. Decorated Bronze Star; recipient Brotherhood award NCCJ, 1968, numerous other awards, including Mr. Kansas City award C. of C. of Greater Kansas City, 1972, Disting. Svc. award Johnson County Friends of the Libr. (Johnson County, Kans.), 1982, Chancellor's medal U. Mo.-Kansas City, 1989. Mem. Envelope Mfrs. Assn. (exec. com. 1960-63, 67-70, 76-79, vice chmn. exec. com. 1981-83, v.p. 1981-83, pres. 1983-85), Flexographic Tech. Assn. (bd. dirs. 1993-97), Oakwood Country Club, Homestead Country Club. Avocations: flyfishing, race walking, camping, white water rafting, backpacking. Office: Tension Envelope Corp 819 E 19th St Kansas City MO 64108-1781 E-mail: BertBerkley@tension.com.

BERKLEY, GARY LEE, newspaper publisher; b. Omaha, Jan. 14, 1943; s. Dale Kenneth and Mildred Fern (Little) B.; m. M. Allison Brown, Dec. 28, 1960; children: Todd, Susan Berkley Markle, Jennifer. BA, U. Nebr., Omaha, 1968. Omaha br. mgr. computer sales and svc. Mohawk Data Scis., 1968-70; Chgo. br. mgr. Data Action Corp., 1970-72; v.p. mktg. Suburban Newspaper and Directory Group Sun Newspapers, Mpls., 1972-77; v.p. mktg. Belleville (Ill.) News-Democrat, 1978-87, pres., pub., 1987—. Bd. dirs. St. Louis Regional Commerce and Growth Assn., United Way of Greater St. Louis, Leadership Coun. Southwestern Ill.; mem. exec. com. Belleville Econ. Progress; bd. trustees McKendree Coll.; mem. adv. bd. Okaw Valley coun. Boy Scouts Am.; mem. adv. bd. Big Bros./Big Sisters; bd. dirs. So. Ill. U.-Edwardsville Found., Southwestern Ill. Devel. Authority; mem. Belle-Scott Com. Recipient award of merit St. Louis Urban League, 1991, Disting. Citizen award Mil. Airlift Command USAF, Human Dignity award YWCA, 1993, Disting. Svc. awrd So. Ill. U., 1995, Outstanding Svc. award Belleville Area Coll., 1995. Mem. Nat. Newspaper Assn., Ill. Press Assn., Inland Press Assn., St. Clair Country Club, Rotary. Avocations: family, photography, fiction, politics, golf. Office: Belleville News-Democrat 120 S Illinois St Belleville IL 62220-2130

BERKMAN, MICHAEL G. lawyer, chemical consultant; b. Poland, Apr. 4, 1917; came to U.S., 1921; s. Harry and Bertha (Jay) B.; m. Marjorie Edelstein, Nov. 28, 1941; children— Laurel, William BS, U. Chgo., 1937, PhD, 1941; JD, DePaul U., 1958; LLM in Intellectual Property, John Marshall Law Sch., 1962; spl. courses, Harvard U., 1943, MIT, 1943. Bar: U.S. Patent Office 1960. Research chemist Argonne Nat. Lab., 1946-51; assoc. dir., chief chemist Colburn Labs., Chgo., 1951-59; instr. chemistry Roosevelt U., 1946-49; patent lawyer Mann, Brown & McWilliams, 1959-63; ptnr. Kegan, Kegan & Berkman, 1963-84, Trexler, Bushnell, Giangiorgi & Blackstone, Chgo., 1984-91; pvt. practice law Glenview, Ill., 1991—. Chem. cons.; expert witness in patent law. Contbr. articles to profl. jours. Served to 1st lt. Signal Corps, U.S. Army, 1942-46. Mem. Am. Chem. Soc., ABA, Patent Law Assn., Chgo., Sigma Xi. Home and Office: 939 Glenview Rd Glenview IL 60025-3172

BERKOFF, MARSHALL RICHARD, lawyer; b. Milw., Apr. 10, 1937; s. Louis S. and Edith E. (Cohen) B.; m. Bebe R. Brandwein, June 19, 1960; children: Mark Andrew, Jonathan Hale, Adam Todd. BA, U. Wis., 1959; LLB, Harvard U., 1962. Bar: Wis. 1962, U.S. Dist. Ct. (we. and ea. dists.) Wis. 1962. Ptnr. Michael, Best & Friedrich, Milw., 1962—. Co-author: Employment Law Challenges of 1987, 1987, Labor Relations: The New Rules of the Game, 1984, The Legal Issues of Managing Difficult Employees, 1987; author/editor Currier and Ives "The New Best 50", 1991. Chmn. Charles Allis and Villa Terrace Art Mus., Milw., 1983-96; chmn. Milw. County War Meml. Corp., 1989-94, bd. dirs., 1983; chmn. bd. dirs. St. Michael Hosp., Milw., 1988-89; bd. dirs. Covenant Health Care, 1993-95. Mem. ABA (labor and employment sect., hosp. and health care law sect.), Wis. Bar Assn., (chmn. labor law sect. 1977-78), Milw. Bar Assn., Am. Hist. Print Collector Soc. (pres. 1987-90). Avocations: collecting, speaking, writing, restoring and cataloguing antique Am. lithographs, fishing. Office: Michael Best & Friedrich 100 E Wisconsin Ave Ste 3300 Milwaukee WI 53202-4108

BERKOWITZ, LAWRENCE M. lawyer; b. Leavenworth, Kans., Nov. 29, 1941; s. Barney and Sarah (Kramer) B.; m. Ursula Lustenberger, Sept. 2, 1969; children: Lizbeth Berkowitz, Leslie Berkowitz. BA Polit. Sci., U. Mich., 1963, JD, 1966. Bar: Mo. 1966. Law clerk U.S. Dist. Ct., Kansas City, Mo., 1966-68; assoc., ptnr. Stinson, Mag & Fizzell, P.C., 1968-97; ptnr. Berkowitz, Feldmiller, Stanton, et al, 1997—. Mng. ptnr. Stinson, Mag & Fizzell, Kansas City, 1991-92. Bd. dirs. Nelson Gallery Bus. Coun., Kansas City, 1989—, Downtown coun., Kansas City, 1992-93; trustee Kansas City Art Inst., 1994—. Fellow Am. Coll. Trial Lawyers, Am. Bar Found.; mem. ABA, Am. Judicature Soc., Kansas City Met. Bar Assn., Lawyers Assn. Kansas City, Mo. Bar Assn., Am. Coll. Trial Lawyers (state bd. 1989—). Avocations: tennis, hiking, skiing, history, reading. Office: Berkowitz Feldmiller Stanton et al Ste 550419251 Two Brush Creek Blvd Kansas City MO 64112

BERLAND, ABEL EDWARD, lawyer, realtor; b. Cin., Aug. 27, 1915; s. Samuel and Anne (Brod) B.; m. Meredith E. Tausig, Aug. 31, 1940; children: Michael Gardner, Richard Bruce, James Robert. JD, DePaul U., 1938, LHD, 1975. Bar: Ill. 1938. Vice chmn. Rubloff, Inc., Chgo. Real estate cons. Contbr. articles on real estate to profl. scholarly and trade jours. Life trustee, mem. acad. affairs com. DePaul U.; chmn. Civic Fedn. Chgo., 1989-90; bd. dirs. Crime Commn. Chgo.; mem. adv. bd. Salvation Army; mem. Newberry Libr. pres.'s coun. Fellow Brandeis U., 1958— ; recipient Nat. Community Service award Jewish Theol. Sem. Am. Mem. Am. Chgo. Bar Assns., Nat. Assn. Realtors, Realtors Nat. Mktg. Inst. (C.C.I.M.), Am. Soc. Real Estate Counselors (pres. 1970), Pvt. Libraries Assn., Manuscript Soc., Am. Arbitration Assn. (nat. panel arbitrators), Shakespeare Soc. Am., Lex Legio, Assn. Internat. de Bibliophile, The Realty Club of Chgo. (pres. 1988), Gamma Mu, Pi Kappa Delta, Lambda Alpha, Omega Tau Rau. Clubs: Book of California; Caxton, Mid-Day, Economic, Brandeis University (founder 1949, pres. 1954), Standard (Chgo.); Grolier (N.Y.C.); Roxburghe of San Francisco; Philobiblon (Phila.). Home: 251 Sylvan Rd Glencoe IL 60022-1225 Office: 233 N Michigan Ave Ste 2200 Chicago IL 60601-5806

BERLAND, DAVID I. psychiatrist, educator; b. St. Louis, Aug. 1, 1947; s. Harry I. and Mildred (Cornblath) B.; m. Elaine Prostak, May 22, 1977; children: Katharine J., Rachel P. BA, U. Pa., 1969; MD, U. Mo., 1973. Diplomate Am. Bd. Psychiatry and Neurology. Resident psychiatry Menninger Found., Topeka, 1973-78, staff child and adolescent psychiatrist, 1978-83; dir. div. child and adolescent psychiatry St. Louis U. Med. Sch., 1983-93; with dept. adolescent psychiatry St. Luke's Hosp., Chesterfield, Mo., 1993-97; pvt. practice St. Louis, 1997—. Contbr. articles to profl. jours. Fellow Am. Acad. of Child and Adolescent Psychiatry; mem. AMA (rotating seat relative value update com. 1996-99), Soc. of Profs. of Child and Adolescent Psychiatry,. Jewish. Office: 7700 Clayton Rd Ste 103 Saint Louis MO 63117

BERLINE, JAMES H. advertising executive, public relations executive; b. Youngstown, Ohio, Aug. 6, 1946; s. James Howard and Eloise Blanche (Smith) Berline; children: Erin Michele, Jess Brandon, Quincy Blaine. BA in Econs., U. Mich., 1968; MS in Advt., U. Ill., 1971. V.p. Campbell-Ewald Co., Detroit, 1971-76; sr. v.p. Batten Barton Durstine & Osborn Inc., Troy, 1976-78, exec. v.p. Southfield, 1984-85; pres. Yaffe Berline Inc., 1980-82; pres., CEO Berline Group, Birmingham, 1982—. Bd. dirs. Leadership Detroit Alumni. Program chmn. United Found., Detroit, 1984; mem. adv. bd. Jr. League; founder Winning Futures; trustee Detroit Sci. Ctr., 1985—, Juvenile Diabetes Found., 1994; chmn. comm. com. Leadership Detroit, 1993; bd. dirs. Make-A-Wish Found.; trustee CATCH, mem. exec. com. Mem.: Young Pres. Orgn. (trustee, chair office commn. 1994, com. chmn. Ea. Mich. chpt.), World Pres. orgn., Detroit C. of C. (mktg. com. 1987—88), Greater Detroit Alliance Bus. (bd. dirs. 1984—86), U. Mich. Grad. M Club 1986, U. Mich. Club Detroit (past bd. govs.), Adcraft Club (bd. dirs. 1980—99, pres. 1988). Avocations: squash, travel, golf. Office: The Berline Group 6001 N Adams Rd Bloomfield Hills MI 48304-1566

BERLOW, ROBERT ALAN, lawyer; b. Detroit, Feb. 11, 1947; s. Henry and Shirley (Solovich) B.; m. Elizabeth Ann Goldin, Sept. 20, 1972; children: Stuart, Lisa. BA, U. Mich., 1968; JD, Wayne State U., 1971. Bar: Mich. 1971, U.S. Supreme Ct. 1978. Asst. to dean, instr. law sch. Wayne State U., Detroit, 1971-72; mem. Radner, Radner, Shefman, Bayer and Berlow, P.C., Southfield, Mich., 1972-78; gen. counsel Perry Drug Stores, Inc., Pontiac, 1978-80, gen. counsel, sec., 1980-82, v.p., gen. counsel, sec., 1982-88, sr. v.p., gen. counsel, sec., 1988-93, sr. v.p., chief adminstrn. officer, gen. counsel, sec., 1993-94, exec. v.p., gen. counsel, sec., 1994-95; sr. mem. Dykema Gossett, PLLC, Bloomfield Hills, 1995—, also chmn. retail practice group. Pres. Agy. for Jewish Edn., Metro Detroit, 1993-95, v.p., 1987-93; bd. dirs. Jewish Cmty. Ctr. Met. Detroit, 1989-2001, v.p., 1992-93, treas., 1996-97, sec., 1997-98. Mem. ABA, Mich. Bar Assn. (chair comml. leasing and mgmt. com. of real estate com. of real property law sect. 1993-98, chmn. real property law sect. 2001—, frequent spkr. continuing legal edn. programs), Internat. Coun. Shopping Ctrs. (roundtable leader nat. law conf.). Avocations: sports, photography. Office: Dykema Gossett PLLC 39577 N Woodward Ave Bloomfield Hills MI 48304-2837 E-mail: r.berlow@dykema.com.

BERMAN, ARTHUR LEONARD, retired state senator; b. Chgo., May 4, 1935; s. Morris and Jean (Glast) B.; m. Barbara Dombeck; children: Adam, Marcy Padorr. BS in Commerce & Law, U. Ill., 1956; JD, Northwestern U., 1958. Bar: Ill. 1958. Atty. pvt. practice, Chgo.; ptnr. White, White & Berman, 1958-74, Chatz, Berman, Maragos, Haber & Fagel, Chgo., 1981-82, Berman, Fagel, Haber, Maragos & Abrams, Chgo., 1982-86, Karlin & FLeisher, Chgo., 1986-99; dir. labor mediations svcs. Chgo. Bd. Edn., 2000—. Spl. atty. Bur. Liquidations, Ill. Dept. Ins., 1962-67; spl. asst. atty. gen. Ill., 1967-68; mem. Ill. Ho. of Reps., 1969-76, Ill. Senate, 1977-99. Pres. 50th Ward Young Dems., 1956-60; v.p. Cook County Young Dems., 1956-60, 50th Ward Regular Dem. Orgn., 1955-99; active 48th Ward Regular Dem. Orgn., 1967-99; exec. bd. Dem. Party, Evanston, Ill., 1973-99; bd. govs. State of Israel Bonds. Mem. ABA, Ill. Bar Assn., Chgo. Bar Assn. (bd. mgrs. 1988-89), Nat. Assn. Jewish Legislators (pres. 1987-89), Am. Trial Lawyers Assn., U. Ill. Alumni Assn., Phi Epsilon Pi, Tau Epsilon Rho. Office: 6007 N Sheridan Rd Chicago IL 60660-3039

BERMAN, CHERYL R. advertising company executive; b. Chgo. BA in Journalism, U. Ill., Urbana. Copywriter, various positions Leo Burnett Co., Chgo., 1974-99, chief creative officer, chmn. U.S. bd. dirs., 1999—. Composer advt. music for McDonald's, Hallmark, Kraft, Walt Disney World. Named Ad Woman of Yr. Women's Advt. Club Chgo., 1997. Office: Leo Burnett Co 35 W Wacker Dr Ste 3710 Chicago IL 60601-1648 E-mail: cheryl.berman@chi.leoburnett.com.

BERMAN, LAURA, journalist, writer; b. Detroit, Dec. 8, 1953; d. Seymour Donald and Rose (Mendelson) B. AB, U. Mich., 1975. Writer, reporter Detroit Free Press, 1976-86; columnist The Detroit News, 1986-93; freelance writer, 1994—; sr. writer The Detroit News, 1995-98; columnist Detroit News, 1998—. Mem. Soc. Profl. Journalists. Office: The Detroit News 999 Haynes St Ste 260 Birmingham MI 48009 E-mail: lberman@detnews.com.

BERMAN, LYLE, recreational facility executive; m. Janis Berman; 4 children. BA, U. Minn., 1964. With Berman Bucksin, 1964-79, pres., CEO, 1979-87, Wilsons, 1987-96; co-founder Grand Casino, 1990-98; chmn., CEO Rainforest Cafe, Inc., 1994—, Lakes Gaming Inc., 1998—. Dir. G-III Apperal Group, Ltd., Innovative Gaming Corp. Am., New Horizon Kids Quest Inc., Pk. Pl. Entertainment Corp., Wilsons. Recipient Gt. Traditions award B'nai B'rith, 1995, Gaming Exec. award, 1996. Office: 130 Cheshire Ln Minnetonka MN 55305-1053

BERMAN, MITCHELL A. orchestra executive; Gen. mgr. Wichita (Kans.) Symphony Orch. Office: Wichita Symphony Orch 225 W Douglas Ste 207 Wichita KS 67202

BERNABEI, MARC P. lawyer; b. Spring Valley, Ill., Apr. 1, 1954; m. Linda S. Bernabei; children: Jason, Cara, Liza. BA, Lewis U.; JD, No. Ill. U. Police officer, Spring Valley, 1975-81; pvt. practice Bernabei Assocs., 1981-84; state's atty. Bureau County, Princeton, Ill., 1984—. Recipient Kahla Lansing Meml. award Kahla Lansing Meml. Com., 1992. Home: PO Box 91 Spring Valley IL 61362-0091 Office: Bureau County State's Atty's Office 700 S Main St Princeton IL 61356-2037

BERNARDINI, CHARLES, lawyer, former alderman; BS, U. Ill., 1968, JD, 1972; LLM, John Marshall Law Sch. Legis. asst. to Spkr. Ill. Ho. of Reps., 1972-73; sr. counsel Am. Hosp. Supply Corp., 1974-81; alternate del. Dem. Nat. Conv., 1980; spl. prosecutor for election fraud Cook County, Ill., 1981-83; commr., 1986-92; mem. Gov.'s Election Reform Commn., 1985; del. Dems. Abroad Dem. Conv., 1992; alderman City of Chgo., 1993-99; ptnr. Dykema Gossett Law Firm, Chgo., 1999—. Instr. internat. law Loyoa U. Chgo., Rome campus, 1981; counsel Allstate Ins. Co., 1983-91. Mem. Chgo.-Milan Sister City Com., 1988—. Mem. Am. C. of C. in Italy (mng. dir.). Office: Dykema Gossett Law Firm 55 E Monroe St Ste 3050 Chicago IL 60603-5709 E-mail: crb43@aol.com.

BERNATOWICZ, FRANK ALLEN, management consultant, expert witness; b. Chgo., Nov. 3, 1954; s. Chester and Pauline (Maciula) B.; m. Kathleen Ann Carlson, Apr. 29, 1978; children: Amy Elizabeth, Laura Ann. BSEE, U. Ill., 1976; MBA in Fin., Loyola U., Chgo., 1981, postgrad. in acctg., 1982-84. Registered profl. engr., Ill.; CPA, Ill. Engr. Commonwealth Edison Co., Chgo., 1976-79, gen. engr., 1979-82, prin. engr., 1982-84; sr. cons. Brenner Group, 1984-85; supr. Ernst & Young (formerly Ernst & Whinney), 1985, mgr., 1985-86; sr. mgr. Ernst & Young, 1986-88, ptnr., 1989-96; prin. J. Alix & Assoc., 1996-99; ptnr. PricewaterhouseCoopers, 1999-2001, BDO Seidman, Chgo., 2001—. Spkr. in field. Mem. bd. regents Mercy Boys Home, 1990—. Mem. ABA (assoc.), AICPA, Am. Bankruptcy Inst., Ill. Soc. CPAs, Nat. Soc. Profl. Engrs., Turnaround Mgmt. Assn., Comml. Law League, Am. Bankruptcy Inst., Chgo. Soc. Clubs (Met.). Avocations: golf, racquetball, computers, investments. Home: 6543 Hillcrest Dr Hinsdale IL 60527 Office: BDO Seidman 233 N Michigan Ave Chicago IL 60601 E-mail: fbernatowicz@bdo.com.

BERNAUER, DAVID W. retail company executive; married; three children. Grad., N.D. State U., 1967. Pharmacist Walgreen Co., 1967-79, dist. mgr., 1979-87, regional v.p., 1987-90, v.p., treas., 1990-92, v.p. pres. purchasing, chief info. officer, 1992-94, sr. v.p., chief info. officer, 1996-99, pres., COO Ill., 1999—. Office: Walgreen Co 200 Wilmot Rd Deerfield IL 60015

BERNDT, ELLEN GERMAN, company executive; b. N.Y.C., 1953; BS, Denison U., 1975; JD, Capital U., 1984. Bar: Ohio 1984. Legal asst. Borden Inc., Columbus, Ohio, 1978-84, corp. atty., 1984-90, asst. sec., corp. atty., 1990-96, corp. sec., asst. gen. counsel, 1996—. Mem. Am. Corp. Counsel Assn., Ctrl. Ohio Corp. Counsel Assn. (pres. 1997). Office: Borden Inc 180 E Broad St Columbus OH 43215-3799 E-mail: eberndt@bordencapital.com.

BERNER, ROBERT LEE, JR. lawyer; b. Chgo., Dec. 9, 1931; s. Robert Lee and Mary Louise (Kenney) B.; m. Sheila Marie Reynolds, Jan. 12,. 1957; children: Mary, Louise, Robert, Sheila, John. A.B., U. Notre Dame, 1953; LL.B., Harvard U., 1956. Bar: Ill. 1956, NY 1989. With Petit, Olin, Overmyer & Fazio, Chgo., 1956-63, Baker & McKenzie, Chgo., 1963—; ptnr., 1964—. Mem. vis. com. Northwestern U. Law Sch., 1981-85; mem. legal adv. com. N.Y. Stock Exch., 1995-98. Mem. vis. com. U. Chgo. Div. Sch., 1972—, chmn., 2001—; mem. legal aid com. United Charities, Chgo., 1971—, chmn., 1983—85; pres. Link Unltd., 1991—93; mem. adv. bd. Cath. Charities, 1971—, Loyola U., 1972—; mem. coun. Coll. Arts and Letters, U. Notre Dame, 2001—; trustee Cath. Theol. Union, Chgo., 1999—; bd. dirs., chmn. United Charities, 1983—85; bd. dirs. Link Unltd., 1969—, World Trade Ctr. of Chgo. Mem. ABA (chmn. bus. law sect. 1987-88), Ill. State Bar Assn., Chgo. Bar Assn., Legal Club Chgo. (pres. 1974-75), Law Club Chgo. (pres. 1991-92). Home: 932 Euclid Ave Winnetka IL 60093-1418 Office: Baker & McKenzie One Prudential Plz 130 E Randolph St Ste 3500 Chicago IL 60601-6342 E-mail: robert.l.berner@bakernet.com.

BERNHARD, ROBERT JAMES, mechanical engineer, educator; b. Algona, Iowa, July 28, 1952; s. David Louis and Darlene Justine (Kohlhaas) B.; m. Deborah S. Kell; children: Jay David, Jacqueline Elizabeth, Jonathan Christian, Justin Brian. BS in Mech. Engring., Iowa State U., 1973, PhD, 1982; MS, U. Md., 1976. Engr. Westinghouse Electric, Inc., Balt., 1973-77; asst. prof. Iowa State U., Ames, 1977-82; asst. prof. dept. mech. engring. Purdue U., West Lafayette, Ind., 1982-87, assoc. prof., 1987-91, prof., 1991—. Dir. Ray W. Herrick Labs Purdue U., 1994—, Inst. for Safe, Quiet, and Durable Hwys, 1998—; cons. to GM, Electricite de France, Automated Analysis; prin. investigator many firms; lectr. CETIM, U. Wis., U. Mich. Assoc. editor: Noise Control Engring. Jour., 1984-85, 90—. Fellow ASME (co-editor procs. 1989), Acoustical Soc. Am.; mem. AIAA, Soc. Automotive Engrs., Inst. Noise Control Engrs. (bd. dirs. 1988-97, pres. 1994), Am. Soc. Engring. Educators. Office: Purdue U 1077 Ray W Herrick Labs Lafayette IN 47907

BERNHARDSON, IVY SCHUTZ, lawyer; b. Fargo, N.D., Aug. 22, 1951; d. James Newell and Phyllis Harriet (Iverson) Schutz; m. Mark Elvin Bernhardson, Sept. 1, 1973; children: Andrew Schutz, Jenna Clare. BA, Gustavus Adolphus Coll., 1973; JD, U. Minn., 1978. Bar: Minn. 1978, U.S. Dist. Ct. Minn. 1978. Staff atty. Gen. Mills, Inc., Mpls., 1978-83, asst. sec. to bd. dirs., 1982-96, assoc. counsel, 1983-85, sr. assoc. counsel, 1985-96, v.p., 1988-2000; assoc. gen. counsel, sec., 1996-2000; shareholder Leonard, Street and Deinard, 2000—. Trustee Gustavus Adolphus Coll., 1989-98, Fairview Southdale Hosp., 1993—, chair, 1999—; dir. Fairview Healthcare Svcs., 1996—, vice chair, 1999—; bd. dirs. The Bush Found., 1997—. Mem. ABA, Am. Soc. Corp. Secs., Minn. Bar Assn., Hennepin County Bar Assn. Lutheran. Office: Gen Mills Inc 1 General Mills Blvd Minneapolis MN 55426-1348

BERNICK, CAROL LAVIN, corporate executive; m. Howard Bernick; three children. BA, Tulane U., 1974. Mem. mktg. staff Alberto-Culver Co., Melrose Park, Ill., 1974-79, dir. new products, 1979-81, dir. new bus. devel. group, 1981-84, v.p., 1984-88; co-dir., 1984; group v.p. Alberto-Culver Co., Melrose Park, Ill., 1988-90, exec. v.p. worldwide mktg., 1990-92, exec. v.p., 1992—94; pres. Alberto-Culver USA, 1994—98; vice chmn., pres. N.Am. Alberto-Culver Co., 1998—. Founder Friends of Prentice; mem. women's bd. Ptnrs. Home Care; active Boys and Girls Clubs of Chgo.; regent Lincoln Acad. Ill.; mem. adv. bd. Kellogg Sch., Northwestern U.; bd. dirs. Northwestern Meml. Healthcare. Recipient Leadership in Bus. award YWCA Met. Chgo., 1992. Mem. Young Pres. Orgn., Econ. Club Chgo., Exec. Club Chgo. Office: Alberto-Culver Co 2525 Armitage Ave Melrose Park IL 60160-1163

BERNICK, HOWARD BARRY, manufacturing company executive; b. Midland, Ont., Can., Apr. 10, 1952; came to U.S., 1974, naturalized, 1976; s. Henry and Esther (Starkman) B.; m. Carol Lavin, May 30, 1976; children: Craig, Peter, Elizabeth. B.A., U. Toronto, Ont., 1973. Investment banker Wood Gundy Ltd., Toronto, 1973-74, First Boston Corp., Chgo., 1974-77; dir. of profit planning Alberto Culver Co., Melrose Park, Ill., 1977-79, v.p. corp. devel., 1979-81, group v.p., chief fin. officer, 1981-85, exec. v.p., 1985-88, pres., COO, 1988-94, also bd. dirs.; pres., CEO, 1994—. Bd. dirs. AAR Corp. Mem. Cosmetic, Toiletry & Fragrance Assn., Econ. Club Chgo. Office: Alberto-Culver Co 2525 Armitage Ave Melrose Park IL 60160-1163

BERNING, LARRY D. lawyer; b. Kendallville, Ind., Oct. 21, 1940; s. Melvin and Dolores (Sorge) B.; m. Phyllis Low Cameron, Oct. 24, 1987; children: Emily Lyn, Scott Michael. AB, Ind. U., 1963, JD, 1968. Bar: Ill. 1968, Ind. 1968. Assoc. Sidley Austin Brown & Wood, Chgo., 1968-74, ptnr., 1974—. Trustee Old People's Home of Chgo., 1999—2001; pres. William H. Miner Found. With U.S. Army, 1963—65. Mem. ABA, Ill. Bar Assn., Chgo. Bar Assn., Ind. Bar Assn., Am. Coll. Truste and Estate Counsel, Chgo. Estate Planning Coun., Mid-Day Cub. Law Club, Legal Club, Skokie Country Club. Office: Sidley Austin Brown & Wood Apt 605 425 W Surf St Chicago IL 60657-6139 E-mail: lberning@sidley.com.

BERNSTEIN, DONALD CHESTER, brokerage company executive, lawyer; b. St. Louis, July 29, 1942; s. Michael Charles and Laura (Schmidt) B.; m. Estelle Marla Cohen, Jan. 17, 1946; children: Kimberleigh, Chad, Aaron. BSBA, Washington U., 1964, JD, 1967; LLM, U. London, 1968. Bar: Mo. 1967. V.p., counsel A.G. Edwards & Sons, Inc., St. Louis, 1969—. Mem. Mo. Bar Assn., Bar Assn. Met. St. Louis. Republican. Jewish. Home: 22 Twin Springs Ln Saint Louis MO 63124-1138 Office: A G Edwards & Sons Inc 1 N Jefferson Ave Saint Louis MO 63103-2205

BERNSTEIN, H. BRUCE, lawyer; b. Omaha, Dec. 9, 1943; s. David and Muriel (Krasne) B.; m. Janice Ostroff, Aug. 27, 1967; children: Daniel J., Jill M. AB, Cornell U., 1965; JD, Harvard U., 1968. Bar: Ill. 1968. Ptnr. Sidley & Austin, Chgo., 1974—. Gen. counsel Comml. Fin. Assn. Bd. dirs. Jewish Family and Community Svc. Agy. Mem. ABA, Ill. Bar Assn., Chgo. Bar Assn., Am. Coll. Comml. Fin. Lawyers, Am. Coll. Bankruptcy, Nat. Bankruptcy Conf., Standard Club, Mid-Day Club, Northmoor Country Club, Harvard Club. Avocation: golf. Home: 1740 W Summit Ct Deerfield IL 60015-1817 Office: Sidley & Austin Bank One Plaza 425 W Surf St Apt 605 Chicago IL 60657-6139

BERNSTEIN, JAY, pathologist, researcher, educator; b. N.Y.C., May 14, 1927; s. Michael Kenneth and Frances (Kaufman) B.; m. Carol Irene Kritchman, Aug. 11, 1957; children: John Abel, Michael Kenneth. BA, Columbia U., 1948; MD, SUNY, Bklyn., 1952. Diplomate Am. Bd. Pathology. Asst. pathologist Children's Hosp. Mich., Detroit, 1956-58, assoc. pathologist, 1959, attending pathologist, 1960-62, cons. in lab. medicine, 1977—93, cons. emeritus, 1993—; attending pathologist Bronx Mcpl. Hosp. Ctr., N.Y.C., 1962-68; asst. prof. pathology Albert Einstein Coll. Medicine, Bronx, N.Y., 1962-64, assoc. prof. pathology, 1964-68; dir. dept. anatomic pathology William Beaumont Hosp., Royal Oak, Mich., 1969-90, dir. Rsch. Inst., 1983-98, assoc. med. dir., 1990-98, hon. consulting pathologist, 1999—; clin. prof. pathology Wayne State U. Sch. Medicine, Detroit, 1977—79. Chmn. sci. adv. bd. Nat. Kidney Found. Mich., 1986-88, nat. sci. adv. bd., 1976-82; sci. advisor Nat. Inst. Child Health, USPHS, 1976-81; profl. adv. bd. Nat. Tuberous Sclerosis Assn., 1990-93; clin. prof. health sci. Oakland U., Rochester, Mich., 1980-90; vis. prof. pathology Albert Einstein Coll. Medicine, Bronx, 1974-2001; com. on renal disease WHO; cons. pathologist Internat. Study of Kidney Diseases in Children, Lupus Study Group. Co-editor: Perspectives in Pediatric Pathology; past contbg. editor Jour. Pediatrics; past mem. editl. bd. Pediatric Nephrology; mem. editl. bd. Jour. Urologic Pathology; contbr. articles to profl. jours. With USN, 1945-46. Recipient Henry L. Barnett award Am. Acad. Pediats., 1997. Mem. AMA, Am. Soc. Investigative Pathology, Internat. Acad. Pathology (U.S.-Can. divsn.), Am. Soc. Clin. Pathologists, Soc. Pediatric Pathology (co-founder, past pres., Farber lectr. 1982, Spl. Disting. Colleague award 1987, 97), Am. Pediatric Soc., Am. Soc. Nephrology, Internat. Pediat. Nephrology Assn., Renal Pathology Soc. (past pres., Renal Pathology Founder award 1997), Am. Soc. Pediatric Nephrology (Founder's award 1999). Office: William Beaumont Rsch Inst 3601 W 13 Mile Rd Royal Oak MI 48073-6712 E-mail: bernstein@beaumont.edu.

BERNSTEIN, LEROY G. state legislator; m. Kathleen Bernstein; 4 children. Pres., owner Valley Movers, Inc.; mem. N.D. Ho. of Reps. from 45th dist., 1989—. Vice chmn. Transp. Com. N.D. Ho. of Reps., mem. Indsl. Appropriations Com, Govt. Ops., Bus. and Labor Com. Mem. DAV, KC, U.S. C. of C., Am. Legion, Eagles. Republican. Address: 3949 10th St N Fargo ND 58102-1048

BERNSTEIN, MARK D. theater director; Grad., U. Pa. Gen. mgr. Phila. Drama Guild; instr. financial mgmt. Nonprofit Arts Inst., Drexel U.; instr. Nonprofit Mgmt. Ctr., Wash. U.; mng. dir. The Repertory Theatre of St. Louis. Mem. nat. negotiating com. League of Resident Theatres; mem. citizens adv. panel Mo. Regional Arts Commission. Mem. membership com. Greater Phila. Cultural Alliance. Office: Repertory Theatre St Louis PO Box 191730 Saint Louis MO 63119-7730

BERNSTEIN, MERTON CLAY, law educator, lawyer, arbitrator; b. N.Y.C., Mar. 26, 1923; s. Benjamin and Ruth (Frederica (Kleeblatt)) B.; m. Joan Barbara Brodshaug, Dec. 17, 1955; children: Johanna Karin, Inga Saterlie, Matthew Curtis, Rachel Libby. B.A., Oberlin Coll., 1943; LL.B., Columbia U., 1948. Bar: N.Y. 1948, U.S. Supreme Ct. 1952. Assoc. Schlesinger & Schlesinger, 1948; atty. NLRB, 1949-50, 50-51, Office of Solicitor, U.S. Dept. Labor, 1950; counsel Nat. Enforcement Commn., 1951, U.S. Senate Subcom. on Labor, 1952; legis. asst. to U.S. Sen. Wayne L. Morse, 1953-56; counsel U.S. Senate Com. on R.R. Retirement, 1957-58; spl. counsel U.S. Senate Subcom. on Labor, 1958; assoc. prof. law U. Nebr., 1958-59; lectr., sr. fellow Yale U. Law Sch., 1960-65; prof. law Ohio State U., 1965-75; Walter D. Coles prof. law Washington U., St. Louis, 1975-96, Walter D. Coles prof. emeritus, 1997—; mem. adv. com. to Sec. of Treas. on Coordination of Social Security and pvt. pension plans, 1967-68. Prin. cons. Nat. Commn. on Social Security Reform, 1982-83; vis. prof. Columbia U. Law Sch., 1967-68, Leiden U., 1975-76; mem. adv. com. rsch. U.S. Social Security Adminstrn., 1967-68, chmn., 1969-70; cons. Adminstrv. Conf. of the U.S., 1989, Dept. Labor, 1966-67, Russell Sage Found., 1967-68, NSF, 1970-71, Ctr. for the Study of Contemporary Problems, 1968-71. Author: The Future of Private Pensions, 1964, Private Dispute Settlement, 1969, (with Joan B. Bernstein) Social Security: The System That Works, 1988; contbr. articles to profl. jours. Mem. Bethany (Conn.) Planning and Zoning Commn., 1962-65, Ohio Retirement Study Commn., 1967-68; co-chmn. transition team for St. Louis Mayor Freeman Bosley Jr., 1993; mem. Bd. of Health, City of St. Louis, 1993-2000; bd. dirs. St. Louis Theatre Project, 1981-84; pres. bd. Met. Sch. Columbus, Ohio, 1974-75; del. White House Conf. Aging, 1995. With AUS, 1943-45. Fulbright fellow, 1975-76, Elizur Wright award, 1965. Mem. ABA (sec. sect. labor rels. law 1968-69), Internat. Assn. for Labor Law and Social Security (bd. dirs. U.S. chpt. 1973-83, 88-91), Fulbright Alumni Assn. (bd. dirs. 1976-78), Indsl. Rels. Rsch. Assn., Am. Arbitration Assn. (mem. adv. com. St. Louis region 1987—), Nat. Acad. Social Ins. (founding mem., bd. dirs. 1986-91). Democrat. Jewish. E-mail: bernstein@wulaw.wustl.edu.

BERNSTEIN, ROBERT, advertising executive; m. Phyliss Bernstein; children: Steven, David, Susan. Grad., U. Okla., 1960. With Potts Woodbury Advt., 1962-64; founder Bernstein-Rein, Kansas City, Mo., 1964—, pres, CEO. Bd. dirs., chmn. Mark Twain Bank Kansas City. Active Youth Vol. Corps, Epilepsy Found., Heart Am. Shakespeare Festival, Met. Luth. Ministry, STOP Violence Coalition, Children's Pl., Children's Mercy Hosp., Genesis Sch., Ronald McDonald Houses, Variety Club Kansas City; pres. Starlight Theatre Assn.; bd. dirs. Kansas City Art Inst. Recipient Spirit of Kansas City award, 1991, Hy Vile Cmty. Svc. award, 1995, Advt. Profl. of Yr. award Am. Advt. Fedn., 1995, Manking award Cystic Fibrosis award, 1995. Mem. Am. Assn. Advt. Agys., Nat. Assn. Broadcasters. Office: Bernstein-Rein Advt Inc 4600 Madison Ave Ste 1500 Kansas City MO 64112-3016

BERNTHAL, DAVID GARY, judge; b. Danville, Ill., Apr. 18, 1950; s. Albert F. and Mary Lou (Ackelmire) B. B, U. Ill., 1972, JD, 1976. Bar: U.S. Dist. Ct. (cen. dist.) Ill. Assoc. Brittingham, Sadler & Meeker, Danville, 1976-78; ptnr. Brittingham, Sadler, Meeker & Bernthal, 1979-80, Meeker & Bernthal, Danville, 1980-84, Snyder Meeker & Bernthal, Danville, Ill., 1984-86; assoc. judge 5th Jud. Cir. Ct., 1986—. Bd. dirs. Vermilion County chpt. ARC, 1982-87, Lakeview Meml. Found., 1984-87, Danville Area Community Coll. Found., 1985-87; mem. Danville Zoning Com., 1982-86. Mem. Vermillion County Bar Assn., Assn. Trial Lawyers Am., Ill. Judges Assn., Jaycees (Dist. Svc. award 1984). Mem. Vermillion County Bar Assn., Assn. Trial Lawyers Am., Am. Judges Assn., Ill. Judges Assn., Jaycees (Dist. Svc. award 1984), Rotary (pres., bd. dirs. Danville club 1980-84). Republican. Avocations: golf, traveling. Office: US Dist Ct 201 S Vine St Urbana IL 61802-3369

BERNTHAL, HAROLD GEORGE, healthcare company executive; b. Frankenmuth, Mich., June 11, 1928; s. Wilfred Michael and Olga Bertha (Stern) B.; m. Margaret Hrebek, Jan. 25, 1958; children: Barbara Anne, Karen Elizabeth, James Willard. B.S. in Chemistry, Mich. State U., 1950. Pres. Am. Hosp. Supply Corp., Evanston, Ill., 1974-85; chmn. Cobern Inc., Lake Forest, 1986—. Trustee Northwestern Meml. Hosp., Chgo., Valparaiso (Ind.) U., Wheat Ridge Found; former governing mem. Chgo. Symphony Orch. Served with AUS, 1950-52. Recipient Lumen Christi medal Valparaiso U., 1988. Mem. Health Industries Assn. (past pres.), Health Industry Mfr.'s Assn. (past mem. exec. com.), Pharm. Mfrs. Assn. (past chmn. med. device com., Knollwood Club, Old Elm Club, The Reserve, Bigfoot Country Club.

BERNTSON, GARY GLEN, psychiatry, psychology and pediatrics educator; b. Mpls., June 16, 1945; s. Edward Mathias and Meryle (Nelson) B.; m. Sarah Till Boysen, Mar. 5, 1984. BA, U. Minn., 1968, PhD, 1971. Postdoctoral fellow Rockefeller U., N.Y.C., 1971-73; asst. prof. dept. psychology Ohio State U., Columbus, 1973-77, assoc. prof., 1977-81, prof., 1981—, prof. dept. pediatrics, 1983—, prof. of psychiatry, 1988—. Affiliate scientist Yerkes Regional Primate Rsch. Ctr., Emory U., Atlanta, 1984-95; mem. initial rev. group ADAMHA, Washington, 1989-91, NIMH, Washington, 1991-93; mem. fellowship rev. panel NSF, Washington, 1991-95. Contbr. over 100 articles to profl. jours., 12 chpts. to books. Fellow NSF, 1969, USPHS, 1972. Mem. Soc. for Neurosci., Soc. for Psychophysiol. Rsch.; fellow AAAS. Achievements include novel concepts of control of the autonomic nervous system and psychosomatic relations. Office: Ohio State U Dept Psychology 1885 Neil Ave Columbus OH 43210-1222

BEROLZHEIMER, KARL, lawyer; b. Chgo., Mar. 31, 1932; s. Leon J. and Rae Gloss (Lowenthal) B.; m. Diane Glick, July 10, 1954; children: Alan, Eric, Paul, Lisa. BA, U. Ill., 1953; JD, Harvard U., 1958. Bar: Ill. 1958, U.S. Ct. Appeals (7th cir.) 1964, U.S. Ct. Appeals (9th cir.) 1969, U.S. Supreme Ct. 1976. Assoc. Ross & Hardies, Chgo., 1958-66, ptnr., 1966-76, of counsel, 1993—; v.p. legal Centel Corp., 1976-77, v.p., gen. counsel, 1977-82, sr. v.p., gen. counsel, 1982-88, sr. v.p., gen. counsel, sec., 1988-93. Nat. adv. bd. Ctr. for Informatics Law, John Marshall Law Sch., Chgo., 1988-93; mem. Corp. Counsel Ctr., Northwestern U. Law Sch., 1987-93, mem. emeritus, 1993—; mem. adv. bd. Litigation Risk Mgmt. Inst., 1989-95; bd. dirs. Milton Industries, Chgo., Devon Bank, Chgo.; cons. Mt. Pulaski Tel. and Elec. Co., Lincoln, Ill., 1981-86; sec., gen. counsel Consol. Water Co., Chgo., 1968-72; mem. human rels. task force Chgo. Cmty. Trust, 1988-90. Bd. dirs. The Nat. Conf. Commn. and Justice, Chgo., presiding co-chmn., 1987-90, mem. nat. exec. bd. dirs., 1988-98, chair investment com., 1991-94, nat. co-chair, 1992-95, pres., 1993-94, chair, 1995-98; exec. bd. Internat. Coun. Christians and Jews, 1996-2000, v.p., 1998-2000; bd. dirs. Evanston (Ill.) Mental Health, 1975-82, chair, 1978-80; dir. Evanston Comty. Found., 1996—, vice chair, chair grants com., 1996-98, chair, 1999-2001; bd. dirs. Beth Emet Found., 1997; trustee Northlight Theatre, Evanston, 1992—, vice-chair, 1993-99; mem. coun. The Communitarian Network, 1993-96; trustee Beth Emet Synagogue, Evanston, 1985-87, 89, sec., 1985-89; chair Capital Campaign Plan com., 1994-97; discrimination priority com. United Way, 1990-97, vice-chair, 1993; mem. assembly Parliament of the World's Religions, 1993; mem. Ill. atty. gen.'s ad hoc com. for creation of justice commn., 1994; adv. com. Ill. Justice Commn., 1995-96; adv. bd. Nat. Underground R.R. Freedom Ctr., 1997—. 1st lt. U.S. Army, 1953-55. Fellow Am. Bar Found.; mem. ABA (chair telcom. com. bus. law sect. 1982-86, dispute resolution com. 1986-90, office com. 1991-95, mem. Coalition for Justice 1993-97, bd. editors Bus. Law Today 1995-97, co-chair conflicts of interest com. 1997-2001), Chgo. Bar Assn. (devel. of law com. 1963-77, chair 1971-73), Chgo. Coun. Lawyers. Democrat. Home: 414 Ashland Ave Evanston IL 60202-3208 Office: Ross & Hardies 150 N Michigan Ave Ste 2500 Chicago IL 60601-7567 E-mail: dkberolz@aol.com.

BERRA, P. BRUCE, computer educator; b. Smiths Creek, Mich., Apr. 14, 1935; s. Mike John and Dorothy (Nelson) B.; 1 son, Marshall R. B.S., U. Mich., 1958, M.S., 1962; Ph.D., Purdue U., 1968. Sr. engr. Hughes Aircraft Corp., Culver City, Calif., 1958-60; engr., tech. advisor Bendix Corp., Ann Arbor, Mich., 1960-63; instr. U. Mich.-Dearborn, 1964-65; asst. prof. info. engring. Boston U., 1965-66; assoc. prof. Syracuse U. (N.Y.), 1968-74, 74—, prof., chmn. indsl. engring. and ops. research, 1978-82, prof. elec. and computer engring., 1982-96; dir. N.Y. State Ctr. for Advanced Tech./Software Engring., 1991-96; dir. Info. Tech. Rsch. Inst., disting. prof. info. tech. Wright State U., Dayton, Ohio, 1997-2000. Cons. IBM Corp., Bell No. Rsch., IITRI, PAR Tech., SCEEE, Singer Link, TRW, KAMAN, Opticomp. Gen. chmn., organizer Workshop on Database Machines, 1980-89. USAF Office of Sci. Research univ. resident research fellow, 1982-83 Fellow IEEE; mem. IEEE Computer Soc. (editor-in-chief CS Press 1981-83, vice chmn. publs. bd. 1984-85, governing bd. 1985-86, 89-91, disting. visitors program 1986-88, 89-91, gen. chmn. internat. conf. on data engring. 1986). E-mail: bberra@worldnet.att.net.

BERRA, ROBERT LOUIS, human resources consultant; b. St. Louis, June 24, 1924; s. Angelo John and Clara Catherine B.; m. Vivian Lorene Miles, Nov. 11, 1944; children— Kathleen Patricia Berra Schrage, Patricia Susan Berra Babcock. B.S. in Econs, St. Louis U., 1947; M.B.A., Harvard U., 1947. Faculty mem. St. Louis U., 1947-51; with Monsanto Co., 1951-70, 74-89, v.p. personnel, 1974-80; sr. v.p. adminstrn. St. Louis, 1980-89. V.p. pers. and pub. rels. Foremost-McKesson, Inc., San Francisco, 1970-74; adj. faculty Washington U., U. Ill., Urbana-Champaign. Bd. trustees St. John's Mercy Med. Center, St. Louis; trustee Maryville Coll. Recipient Alumni Merit award St. Louis, U., 1977, Tchr. Yr. award Washington U. Olin Sch. Business, 1994. Fellow Nat. Acad. Human Resources; mem. Soc. Human Resource Mgmt., Indsl. Rels. Assn. St. Louis (past pres.), Bellerive Country Club, Isla Del Sol Country Club, Vinoy Renaissance Country Club. Roman Catholic.

BERRY, CHUCK (CHARLES EDWARD ANDERSON BERRY), singer, composer; b. St. Louis, Oct. 18, 1926; s. Henry William, Sr., and Martha Banks Berry; m. Themetta Suggs, Oct. 1948; 4 children: Darlen Ingrid, Melody Exes, Aloha Isa Lei, Charles Edward Anderson, Jr. Popular artist in rock and roll music, plays guitar, saxophone, piano; concert, TV appearances, 1955—; rec. artist Chess Records; appeared in film Go, Johnny Go, Rock, Rock, Rock, 1956, Jazz on a Summer's Day, 1960, Let the Good Times Roll, 1973; composer: Rock 'n' Roll Music; albums include: After School Sessions, 1958, One Dozen Berry's, 1958, Rockin' At The Hops, 1959-60, New Juke Box Hits, 1960, Chuck Berry, 1960, More Chuck Berry, 1960, On Stage, 1960, Twist, 1960, You Can Never Tell, 1964, Greatest Hits, 1964, 2 Great Guitars, 1964, Chuck Berry in London, 1965, Fresh Berrys, 1965, St. Louis to Liverpool, 1966, Golden Hits, 1967, At the Fillmore, 1967, Medley, 1967, In Memphis, 1967, Concerto in B Goods, 1969, Home Again, 1971, The London Sessions, 1972, Golden Decade, 1972, St. Louis to Frisco to Memphis, 1972, Let the Good Times Roll, 1973, Golden Decade, Vol. 2, 1973, Bio, 1973, Back in the U.S.A., 1973, Golden Decade, Vol. 5, 1974, I'm a Rocker, 1975, Chuck Berry 75, 1975, Motorvatin', 1976, Rockit, 1979, Chess Masters, 1983, The Chess Box, 1989, Missing Berries: Rarities, 1990, On the Blues Side, 1993, others; soundtrack Hail! Hail! Rock n' Roll, 1987; author: autobiography Chuck Berry, 1987. Recipient Grammy award for Lifetime Achievement, 1984; named to Rock and Rock Hall of Fame, 1986. Office: Berry Park 691 Buckner Rd Wentzville MO 63385-5442

BERRY, DAVID J. former financial services company executive; b. Columbus, Ohio, Apr. 14, 1944; s. Maurice Glenn Berry and Janice (Eshelman) Read; m. Janet Lynn Tewksbury, Mar. 24, 1977; children: Jeffrey James, Jennifer Jean, Jon Andrew, Amy Jo. Student, Miami U., Oxford, Ohio, 1963-64, Ohio State U., 1965-66. Registered prin. SEC. Ind. fin. svc. salesman, 1966-74; gen. agt. Sun Life Assurance Co. Can., Columbus, 1975-85; pres. Strategic Info. Svcs., 1986-87; v.p. IDS Life Ins. Co., Mpls., 1990—; assoc. mgr. IDS Fin. Svcs. Inc., Columbus, 1988, region dir., 1989; v.p. IDS Life Ins. Co., Mpls., 1991-2000; ret., 2000. Chmn. Agy. Mgmt. Tng. Coun., Columbus, 1982-83. Bell ringer Salvation Army, Columbus, 1975-85; vol. instr. Learning Disabled Children, Columbus, 1980-83; pres. PTA, Worthington, Ohio, 1983. Fellow Life Underwriting Tng. Coun., Columbus, 1981. Mem. Nat. Assn. Securities Dealers, Gen. Agts. and Mgrs. Assn. (pres. 1979-82), Mpls. Life Underwriters Assn. Avocations: travel, various sport participation, writing poetry. Office: IDS Life Ins Co IDS Tower # 10 Minneapolis MN 55402-2100

BERRY, DEAN LESTER, lawyer; b. Chgo., Jan. 20, 1935; s. Ruben W. and Leonore C. (Nelson) B.; m. Donna J. Zack, Nov. 16, 1962; children: Megan, Thomas. BA with distinction, DePauw U., 1955; JD with distinction, U. Mich., 1960. Bar: Ohio 1961, U.S. Dist. Ct. (no. dist.) Ohio 1962. Assoc. Squire, Sanders & Dempsey L.L.P., Cleve., 1960-70, ptnr., 1970—2002, counsel, 2002—. Lectr. various programs, Order of Coif. Author: Local Government in Michigan, 1960; contbr. articles to profl. jours.; participant in Quiz Kids radio program, 1945-47. Mem. council City of Rocky River, Ohio, 1967-71; mem. cen. com. Cuyahoga County Rep. Orgn., Ohio, 1963-75, mem. exec. com., 1969-2001. Served to 1st lt. USAF, 1955-57. Mem. ABA, Ohio Bar Assn., Greater Cleve. Bar Assn. (com. chmn. 1978) Soc. Profl. Journalists, Sigma Delta Chi. Methodist. Avocations: traveling, crossword puzzles. Home: 478 Ravine Dr Aurora OH 44202-8236 Office: Squire Sanders & Dempsey LLP 4900 Key Tower 127 Public Sq Cleveland OH 44114-1216

BERRY, WILLIAM LEE, business administration educator; b. Indpls., Dec. 24, 1935; s. George Lee and Anna Marie (Hansert) B.; children: Ann Kathleen, Lee Michael, Lynn Colleen. BS, Purdue U., 1957; MS, Va. Poly. Inst., 1964; DBA, Harvard U., 1969. Mfg. trainee GE, various locations, 1957-60, supr. mfg. Salem, Va., 1960-64; from asst. prof. to assoc. prof. indsl. mgmt. Purdue U., West Lafayette, Ind., 1968-76; prof. prodn. mgmt. Ind. U., Bloomington, 1976-82; C. Maxwell Stanley prof. prodn. mgmt. U. Iowa, Iowa City, 1982-87, sr. assoc. dean Coll. Bus. Adminstrn., 1983-87, dir. Mfg. and Productivity Ctr., 1986-87; Belk prof. bus. adminstrn., chmn. ops. mgmt. area U. N.C., Chapel Hill, 1988-92; prof. bus. adminstrn. Ohio State U., 1992—, Richard Ross chair in mgmt., dir. Ctr. Excellence in Mgmt., 1995—. Vis. prof. IMD, Lausanne, Switzerland, 1987-88; cons. in field. Co-author: Operations and Logistics Management, 1972, Production Planning, Scheduling and Inventory Control: Concepts, Techniques and Systems, 1974, Master Production Scheduling: Principles and Practice, 1979, Manufacturing Planning and Control Systems, 1984, 2d edit., 1988, 3rd edit., 1992, 4th edit., 1997, ITEC: Manufacturing Planning and Control/Manufacturing Strategy Simulation, 1992, Production and Inventory Control Integrated, 1992; contbr. articles to profl. jours. 1st Enterprise fellow Kenan Inst., 1988-90. Fellow Decision Scis. Inst. (v.p. 1983-84, sec. 1985-86, pres.-elect 1987, pres. 1988); mem. Inst. Indsl. Engrs. (v.p. 1979-81, dir., Disting. Service award 1979), Ops. Mgmt. Assn. (v.p. 1981-85, pres.-elect 1985-86, pres. 1986-87, dir., Disting. Leadership award 1987), Am. Prodn. and Inventory Control Soc., Inst. Mgmt. Sci., Ops. Research Soc. Office: Fisher Coll of Bus Ohio State U Columbus OH 43210

BERRYMAN, DIANA, radio personality; b. Gary, Ind., Oct. 10; m. Patrick Berryman; 1 stepchild Shannon. Radio host, morning program announcer, asst. program dir. Sta. WMBI, Chgo. Office: WMBI 820 N LaSalle Blvd Chicago IL 60610*

BERRYMAN, JAMES, state legislator; b. Feb. 17, 1947; m. Susan; children: Steve, Eric, Julie. Student, Adrian Coll., 1965-69. State senator Mich. State Senate, Dist. 17, 1990-98. Asst. minority whip, 1993, majority floor leader, 1995—, mem. tech. & energy, fin. svc., agrl. & forestry coms., Mich. State Senate. Mem. Adrian (Mich.) City Planning Commn., 1978-81; mem. Adrian City Commn., 1979-85; mayor City of Adrian, 1985; mem. Govs. Health Occupations Coun., 1989—; Dem. cand. for Congress, 1998. Mem. Mich. Assn. Mayors (pres. 1987—). Address: 380 S Scott St Adrian MI 49221

BERRYMAN, ROBERT GLEN, accounting educator, consultant; b. Freeport, Ill., Nov. 22, 1928; s. Loyd Vernon and Gladys Leone (Hicks) B.; m. Ruth Madelyn Bjorngjeld, Aug. 25, 1955; children: Peter, David, Kathryn. BSBA, Northwestern U., 1950, MBA, 1951; PhD, U. Ill., 1958. CPA, Ill., Minn. Staff auditor Deloitte & Touche, Chgo., 1951-54, mgr. Mpls., 1969-70; instr. U. Ill., Champaign, 1954-58; asst. prof. acctg. U. Minn., Mpls., 1958-61, assoc. prof., 1961-65, prof., 1965-95, dir. grad. studies in acctg., 1980-83, chmn. dept. acctg., 1963-65, 70-73, 1990-95; exec. dir. fin. Cedar Riverside Assocs., 1974-75. Cons. in field. Mem. editl. bd. Issues in Acctg. Edn., 1995-98; contbr. articles to profl. publs. Adviser to audit com. Minn. State Colls. and Univs. Recipient Horace T. Morse-Amoco All Univ. Tchg. award U. Minn., 1976, Outstanding Tchr. award Carlson Sch. Mgmt., U. Minn., Green Eyeshade award Minn. Acctg. Assn., Tchg. award U. Minn. Alumni Assn., Mpls., 1978, Leon Radde Outstanding Educator award Inst. Internal Auditors, 1988. Mem. AICPA (chmn. acctg. theory subcom. 1979-83, continuing profl. edn. exec. com. 1979-82, bd. examiners 1980-83, Disting. Achievement in Acctg. Edn. award 1999), Inst. Internal Auditors (bd. regents 1979-83, bd. govs. Twin City chpt. 1981-91, cert. internal auditor), Minn. Soc. CPA (bd. dirs. 1965-69, 78-83, first recipient and honoree R. Glen Berryman award 1976), Minn. Acctg. Aid Soc. (pres. and bd. dirs.), Am. Acctg. Assn. (Outstanding Acctg. Educator 1994, Auditing Educator 1992). Home: 1462 Brenner Ave Saint Paul MN 55113-1671 Office: Univ MN Carlson Sch of Mgmt 321 19th Ave S Minneapolis MN 55455-0438 E-mail: gberryman@csom.umn.edu.

BERS, DONALD MARTIN, physiology educator; b. N.Y.C., Dec. 13, 1953; s. Harold Theodore and Penny (Wall) B.; m. Kathryn Eileen Hammond, July 17, 1976; children: Brian Alexander, Rebecca Ann. BA, U. Colo., 1974; PhD, UCLA, 1978. Postdoctoral research fellow UCLA, 1978-79, asst. research physiologist, 1980-82, adj. asst. prof., 1981-87; postdoctoral research fellow Edinburgh (Scotland) U., 1979-80; asst. prof. U. Calif., Riverside, 1982-86, assoc. prof., 1986-89, prof., 1989-92, divisional dean, dir. biomed. scis. program, 1991-92; prof., chmn. dept. physiology Loyola U., Chgo., 1992—. Author: Excitation-Contraction Coupling and Cardiac Contractile Force, 1991, 2001; assoc. editor News in Physiol. Sci.; mem. editl. bd. Am. Jour. Physiology, Circulation Rsch., Jour. Pharm. and Exptl. Therapeutics, Jour. Molecular Cell Cardiology; contbr. articles to profl. jours. Bd. dirs. Am. Heart Assn., Riverside, 1985-92, pres., 1989-91. Fellow Am. Heart Assn., L.A., 1978-80, Brit.-Am., Am. Heart Assn., 1980-81; recipient New Investigator Rsch. award NIH, 1982-85, Rsch. Career Devel. award NIH, 1985-90. Fellow: Internat. Soc. Heart Rsch. (mem. coun.), Am. Heart Assn.; mem.: AAAS, Biophys. Soc. (mem. coun., mem. exec. bd.), Am. Physiol. Soc., Soc. Gen. Physiology.

BERSCHEID, ELLEN S. psychology educator, author, researcher; b. Colfax, Wis., Oct. 11, 1936; d. Sylvan L. and Alvilde (Running) Saumer; m. Dewey Mathias Berscheid, Nov. 21, 1959. BA, U. Nev., 1959, MA, 1960; PhD, U. Minn., 1965. Market rsch. analyst Pillsbury Co., Mpls., 1960-62; asst. prof. psychology and mktg. U. Minn., 1965-66, asst. prof. psychology, 1967-68, assoc. prof., 1969-71, prof., 1971-88, Regents' prof. psychology, 1988—. Mem. NRC Assembly Behavioral and Social Scis., 1973-77. Co-author: Interpersonal Attraction, 1969, 78, Equity: Theory and Research, 1978, Close Relationships, 1983, also numerous articles; mem. numerous editorial bds., past editorships. Recipient Disting. Scientist award Soc. Exptl. Social Psychology, 1993. Fellow APA (Donald T. Campbell award 1984, editor Contemporary Psychology Jour. 1985-91, Disting. Sci. Contbn. award 1997), Soc. Personality and Social Psychology (pres. 1985), Soc. for Psychol. Study Social Issues, Am. Acad. Arts and Scis.; mem. Internat. Soc. for the Study Personal Relationships (pres.

1990-92), Soc. Exptl. Social Psychology (exec. bd. 1971-74, 77-80, 85-89, Disting. Scientist award 1993), Gown-in-Town Club. Presbyterian. Avocation: interior design. Home: 506 Grand Hl Saint Paul MN 55102-2613 Office: U Minn Dept Psychology N309 Elliott Hall Minneapolis MN 55455

BERTAGNOLLI, LESLIE A. lawyer; b. Bloomington, Ill., Nov. 11, 1948; BA, Ill. State U., 1970, MA, 1971; PhD, U. Ill., 1975, JD, 1979. Bar: Ill. 1979. Ptnr. Baker & McKenzie, Chgo. Office: Baker & McKenzie 130 E Randolph Dr Ste 3700 Chicago IL 60601-6342

BERTENTHAL, BENNETT IRA, psychologist, educator; b. N.Y.C., Mar. 22, 1949; married; 2 children. BA in Psychology, Brandeis U., 1971; MA in Devel. Psychology, U. Denver, 1976, PhD, 1978. Postdoctoral fellow Brain Rsch. Inst. and dept. pediats. UCLA Sch. Medicine, 1978-79; asst. prof. dept. psychology U. Va., 1979-85, assoc. prof., 1985, prof., 1991—, dir. devel. tng. program, 1989-96; asst. dir. NSF, Arlington, Va., 1997-99; prof. dept. psychology U. Chicago, 1999—. Mem. human devel. and aging study sect, Nat. Inst. Child Health and Human Devel., 1987, 91-96, chair, 1994-96; extramural reviewer NSF, Nat. Inst. Neurol. Diseases & Communicative Disorders, NIMH; cons. NINCDS; mem. performance and safety monitoring com. NINCDS, 1981-88; program com. Internat. Conf. Infant Studies, 1984, 88, 96, Southeastern Conf. Human Devel., 1988; mem. MacArthur Network on Transition From Infancy to Childhood, 1987-92; mem. MacArthur Network Task Force-Devel. of Computer Workstas. for Psychol. Rsch., 1988-92. Assoc. editor Devel. Psychology, 1988-90, mem. editl. bd., 1988-90; mem. editl. bd. Jour. Exptl. Child Psychology, 1985-88, Child Devel., 1980-83; reviewer Psychophysiology, infant Behavior and Devel., Perception and Psychophysics, Devel. Psychology, Child Devel., SRCD Monographys, Internat. Jour. Behavioural Devel., Jour. Exptl. Psychology, Human Perception and Performance. Recipient Boyd R. McCandless Young Scientist award, 1985, rsch. career devel. awarrd NIH, 1985-90, Cattell Sabbatical award, 1990, MHTP postdoctoral fellowship, 1978-79; grantee U. Va. Rsch. Policy Coun., 1979-80, 87-90, 89—, NIMH, 1979-80, 85-90, 91—, NINCDS, 1980-81, NIH, 1982-84, 85-88, 89—, John D. and Catherine T. MacArthur Found., 1984-85, 89—, Va. Ctr. Innovative Tech., 1985-86, NATO, 1989—, United Cerebral Palsey Rsch. and Edn. Found., 1989-90, McDonnell-Pew Program Cognitive Neuroscis., 1991-93 Fellow APA (program com. 1987, 88, nominations com. 1988, mem.-at-large divsn. 7 exec. com. 1995-98, mem. com. on sci. awards, 1991-94, chair, 1994), Am. Psychol. Soc.; mem. AAAS, Soc. Rsch. in Child Devel. (co-chair program com. 1995-97), Assn. Rsch. in Vision and Ophthalmology, Internat. Soc. Infant Studies, Internat. Soc. Study Behavioural Devel., Internat. Soc. Study of Posture and Gait, Psychonomic Soc. Office: U of Chicago Dept Psychology 5848 S University Ave Chicago IL 60637-1515

BERTHOUEX, PAUL MAC, civil and environmental engineer, educator; b. Oelwein, Iowa, Aug. 15, 1940; s. George Albert and LaVadia Fay (McBride) B.; m. Susan Jean Powell, Sept. 8, 1962; 1 child, Stephanie Fay. BSCE, U. Iowa, 1963, MSCE, 1964; PhD, U. Wis., 1969. Registered profl. engr., Iowa. Instr. U. Iowa, Iowa City, 1964-65; asst. prof. civil engring. U. Conn., Storrs, 1965-67; chief rsch. engr. GKW Cons., Mannheim, Fed. Republic of Germany, 1969-71; prof. civil engring. U. Wis., Madison, 1971-99, emeritus prof., 1999—. Author: Strategy of Pollution Control, 1978, Statistics for Environmental Engineers, 1994, 2d edit., 2002; contbr. numerous articles to profl. jours. Recipient Radebaugh Prize, CSWPCA, 1989, 91. Mem. ASCE (Rudolf Herring medal 1974, 92), Water Environment Fedn. (Eddy medal 1971), Internat. Assn. Water Quality, Assn. Environ. Engring. Profs. Office: U Wis 1415 Johnson Dr Madison WI 53706-1607

BERTOLET, RODNEY JAY, philosophy educator; b. Allentown, Pa., Mar. 22, 1949; s. Frank and Helen (Johnson) B. BA, Franklin & Marshall Coll., 1971; PhD, U. Wis., 1977. Asst. prof. philosophy Purdue U., West Lafayette, Ind., 1977-82, assoc. prof. philosophy, 1982-90, prof. philosophy, 1990—, dept. head, 1991—. Author: What Is Said, 1990. Mem. Am. Philos. Assn., Ind. Philos. Assn. (pres. 1983-84). Office: Dept Philosophy BRNG/Purdue Univ West Lafayette IN 47907 E-mail: bertolet@purdue.edu.

BERTRAM, MICHAEL WAYNE, secondary education educator; b. Princeton, Ind., Jan. 24, 1945; s. Leroy Victor and Lela Mae (Redman) B.; m. Bonnie Lee Holmes, Aug. 21, 1985; 1 child, John. BS, U. Indpls., 1967; MS, U. Wyo., 1972; MA, U. Evansville, 1975. Cert. secondary math. and physics tchr., Ind. Tchr. math. and physics South Gibson Sch. Corp., Ft. Branch, Ind., 1967—, chmn. math. dept., 1974—. Athletic dir. Gibson So. High Sch., 1977-79. Recipient cert. of merit Ind. Acad. Competitions for Excellence, 1988, 95, 96; grantee NSF, 1971. Mem. Nat. Coun. Tchrs. Math., Math. Assn. Am., Am. Assn. Physics Tchrs. Methodist. Avocation: farming. Home: RR 1 Box 197 Fort Branch IN 47648-9717 Office: Gibson So High Sch RR 1 Box 496 Fort Branch IN 47648-9776

BERTSCHY, TIMOTHY L. lawyer; b. Pekin, Ill., Nov. 12, 1952; AB magna cum laude, U. Ill., 1974; JD, George Washington U., 1977. Bar: Ill. 1977, U.S. Dist. Ct. (cen. dist.) Ill., U.S. Ct. Appeals (7th cir.) 1982, U.S. Supreme Ct. Ptnr. Heyl, Royster, Voelker & Allen, Peoria, Ill., 1977—. Editor Bus. Torts Newsletter. Fellow Ill. State Bar Found., Am. Bar Found.; mem. ABA (ho. dels. 1995—), Ill. State Bar Assn. (pres. 1998-99), Peoria County Bar Assn. Office: Heyl Royster Voelker & Allen PC 124 SW Adams St Ste 600 Peoria IL 61602-1352 E-mail: tbertschy@hrva.com.

BE SANT, CRAIG, company executive; Pres. TMP Worldwide, Chgo.; dir. mktg. Monster.com, Indpls., 1998—; mgr. recruiting adv. Chgo. Tribune. Office: Chgo Tribune 435 N Michigan Ave Chicago IL 60611-4066

BESCH, HENRY ROLAND, JR. pharmacologist, educator; b. San Antonio, Sept. 12, 1942; s. Henry Roland and Monette Helen (Kasten) B.; m. Frankie R. Drejer; 1 child, Kurt Theodore. B.Sc. in Physiology, Ohio State U., 1964, Ph.D. in Pharmacology (USPHS predoctoral trainee 1964-67), 1967; USPHS postdoctoral trainee, Baylor U. Coll. Medicine, Houston, 1968-70. Instr. ob-gyn. Ohio State U. Med. Sch., Columbus, 1967-68; asst. prof. Ind. U. Sch. Medicine, Indpls., 1971-73, assoc. prof., 1973-77, prof., 1977, chmn. pharmacology and toxicology, 1977—, Showalter prof., 1980—; dir. Ind. State Dept. Toxicology, 1991-96, dir. emeritus, 1996—. Can. Med. Rsch. Coun. vis. prof., 1979, Swiss Fed. Tech. Inst. vis. prof., 1995; investigator fed. grants, mem. nat. panels and coms.; cons. in field. Contbr. numerous articles pharm. and med. jours.; mem. editorial bds. profl. jours. Fellow Brit. Med. Research Council, 1970-71; Grantee Showalter Trust, 1975— Fellow Am. Coll. Cardiology, Am. Coll. Forensic Examiners; mem. AAAS, Am. Assn. Clin. Chemistry, Am. Physiol. Soc., Am. Soc. Biochem. Molecular Biology, Am. Soc. Pharmacology and Exptl. Therpeutics, Assn. Med. Sch. Pharmacologists (exec. com. 1985-96, pres. 1994-96), Biochem. Soc., Cardiac Muscle Soc., Internat. Soc. Heart Rsch. (exec. com. Am. sect. 1986-92), Nat. Acad. Clin. Biochemistry, N.Y. Acad. Scis., Sigma Xi. Office: Ind U Sch Medicine 635 Barnhill Dr Indianapolis IN 46202-5126 E-mail: besch@indiana.edu.

BESHARSE, JOSEPH CULP, cell biologist, researcher; b. Hickman, Ky., Jan. 21, 1944; s. Herschell and June Elizabeth (Bush) B.; m. Janie Iris Robinson, Aug. 21, 1966; children: Joseph Galen, Kari Elizabeth. BA, Hendrix Coll., 1966; MA, So. Ill. U., 1969, PhD, 1973. Asst. prof. Old Dominion U., Norfolk, Va., 1972-75; postdoctoral fellow Columbia U., N.Y.C., 1975-77; asst. prof. Emory U. Sch. Medicine, Atlanta, 1977-80, assoc. prof., 1980-84, prof., 1984-89; prof., chmn. dept. anatomy & cell biology U. Kans. Sch. Medicine, Kansas City, 1989-97; prof., chmn. dept. cell biology, neurobiology and anatomy Med. Coll. Wis., Milw., 1997—. Mem. study sect. NIH, Bethesda, Md., 1981-86, 92-96. Mem. editl. bd. Exptl. Eye Rsch., 1985-98, editor retina sect., 1997-2000; mem. editl. bd. Investigative Ophthalmology, 1987-92, Visual Neurosci., 1990-92; contbr. more than 100 articles to sci. jours. Rsch. grantee NIH, 1976-2001; recipient Rsch. Career Devel. award, 1979-84, Alcon Rsch. award, 1993. M Democrat. Achievements include advances in understanding the cell biology of photoreceptors in the retina, in the regulation of retinal metabolism and the 24-hour photoreceptor clock (i.e. Circadian clock). Office: Med Coll Wis Dept Cellular Biology and Anatomy Milwaukee WI 53226

BEST, WILLIAM ROBERT, physician, educator, university official; b. Chgo., July 14, 1922; s. Gordon and Marian Burton (Shapland) B.; m. Ruth Joanna Stuchlik, Sept. 2, 1944; children: Barbara Ann Best Mulch, Patricia Marian Best Williams. BS, U. Ill., 1945; MD, U. Ill., Chgo., 1947, MS, 1951; postgrad. math. biology, U. Chgo., 1964-65. Diplomate Am. Bd. Internal Medicine, Am. Bd. Hematology. From intern to fellow in hematology then to resident U. Ill. Hosp., 1947-51; asst. prof., assoc. prof. medicine U. Ill. Coll. Medicine, Chgo., 1953-67, prof., assoc. dean, 1972-81; chief Midwest Rsch. Support Ctr., VA Hosp., Hines, Ill., 1967-72, chief staff, 1981-92, sr. health svcs. rschr., 1992—; prof. medicine, assoc. dean for VA affairs Loyola U. Stritch Sch. Medicine, Maywood, 1981-92; chief staff U. Ill. Hosp., Chgo., 1976-81. Contbr. numerous articles to sci. jours. 1st lt. U.S. Army, 1951—53. Named Alumnus of Yr., U. Ill. Med. Alumni Assn., 1980. Fellow ACP; mem. AMA (br. pres. 1985), Internat. Soc. Hematology, Am. Statis. Assn., AAAS. Episcopalian. Avocations: sailing, computing, radio-controlled model airplanes. Home: 1712 Waverly Cir Saint Charles IL 60174-5869 Office: Midwest Ctr Health Svcs and Policy Rsch Edward Hines Jr VA Hosp Hines IL 60141 E-mail: best@research.hines.med.va.gov., wmrbest@aol.com.

BETTERMANN, HILDA, state legislator; b. Oct. 22, 1942; m. William; two children. , U. Minn., St. Cloud U., Moorhead U., Hamline U. Rep. Dist. 10B Minn. State Ho. of Reps., 1991-98, asst. minority leader, 1993-98; instr. Alexandria Tech. Coll., 1982—. Mem. Commerce Com., Econ. Devel. Com., Labor Mgmt. Rels., Agrl. & Higher Edn. Fin. Divsn. Coms.; mem. Minn. Bd. Med. Practice, 1998—; bd. dirs. Douglas County Hosp. Mem. NEA, Minn. Edn. Assn., Am. Vocat. Assn., Minn. Vocat. Assn., Minn. Sec. Assn., Nat. Sec. Assn. Office: 8435 Sara Rd NW Brandon MN 56315-8351

BETTIGA, MICHAEL J. retail executive; Various positions including pharmacy mgr., sr. v.p. retail health svcs. ShopKo Stores, Inc., Green Bay, Wis., 1977-99, sr. v.p. store ops., 1999—. Office: ShopKo Stores Inc 700 Pilgrim Way Green Bay WI 54304-5276

BETTS, GENE M. telecommunications industry executive; BBA, MBA, U. Kans. CPA. Various positions in audit and tax depts. Arthur Young, 1975; ptnr. Arthur Young & Co.; asst. v.p. tax dept. Sprint Corp., 1987-88, v.p., 1988-90, sr. v.p. fin. svcs. and taxes, 1990-98, sr. v.p., treas., 1998—. Office: Sprint Corp 2330 Shawnee Mission Pkwy Westwood KS 66205-2090

BETTS, HENRY BROGNARD, physician, health facility administrator, educator; b. New Rochelle, N.Y., May 25, 1928; s. Henry Brognard and Marguerite Meredith (Denise) B.; m. Monika Christine Paul, Apr. 25, 1970. AB, Princeton U., 1950; MD, U. Va., 1954; DSc (hon.), Hamilton Coll., 1992; D in Pub. Svc. (hon.), Ohio State U., 2001. Diplomate: Am. Bd. Phys. Medicine and Rehab. Intern Cin. Gen. Hosp., 1954-55; resident, teaching fellow NYU Med. Center Inst. Rehab. Medicine (Rusk Inst.), N.Y.C., 1958-63; practice medicine, specializing in phys. medicine and rehab. Chgo., 1963—; staff physiatrist Rehab. Inst. Chgo., 1963-64, assoc. med. dir., 1964-65, med. dir., 1965-86, med. dir., CEO, 1986-94, pres., CEO, 1994-97, past med. dir., pres., CEO, 1997—; chmn. Rehab. Inst. Found., 1997. Chmn. dept. phys. medicine and rehab. Northwestern U. Med. Sch., 1967-94, prof., 1967—, Magnuson prof., 1994-97, assoc. mem. Robert H. Lurie Cancer Ctr., 1993—; cons. Northwestern Meml. Hosp., Chgo.; mem. adv. bd. Commn. on Future Structure of Vets. Health Care, Dept. Vets. Affairs, 1990-92, Vets. Adv. Com. on Rehab., 1990-96; med. adv. com. Spl. Olympics Internat., 1991—. Contbr. articles to profl. jours. Bd. dirs. Very Spl. Arts, 1981—, The Hastings Ctr., Nat. Orgn. on Disabilities, Old Masters Soc., Art Inst. Chgo.; chmn. Physicians Against Land Mines, Access Living, Am. Assn. People with Disabilities, The Admiral, Chgo. Botanic Garden, Crossroads Ctr./Antigua, Legal Clinic for the Disabled, World Com. Disability, World Rehab. Fund, Pres. Com. Employment of People with Disabilities, VSArts, 2001. Recipient Disting. Svc. award Ill. Congress Orgns. Physically Handicapped, 1982, Disting. Svc. award Marine Scholarship Found., Chgo., 1993, Individual Leadership award Infinitec-United Cerebral Palsy, 1994, Disting. Pub. Svc. award Am. Acad. Phys. Medicine and Rehab., 1994, John W. Goldschmidt award for excellence in rehab. Nat. Rehab. Hosp., Washington, 1996, James Brady award Ill. Head Injury Assn., 1989, Disting. Svc. award Nat. Orgn. on Disabilities, 1989, Milton Cohen Disting. Career award Nat. Assn. Rehab. Facilities, 1990, Henry H. Kessler Human Dignity award Kessler Inst. Rehab. Inc., 1992, The Scopus award Am. Friends of the Hebrew U., 1995, The August W. Christmann award for Tech. and Info., City of Chgo. Mayor's Office for People with Disabilities and MOPD Adv. Council, 1995, Hon. diploma for humanitarian svcs. Archeworks, Chgo., 1997, Achievement award Rusk Inst., 1997, Disting. Mem. award Am. Acad. Phys. Medicine and Rehab., 1998, Disting. Svc. award Am. Hosp. Assn., 1998, Madonna Spirit award Madonna Rehab. Hosp., 1999, Order of Lincoln award Lincoln Acad. Ill., 2001, 2001 Henry Russe Citation Exemplary Compassion in Healthcare, Lifetime Achievement award Am. Spinal Injury Assn., 2001, Order of Lincoln award Lincoln Acad. Ill., 2001; named Physician of Yr., Ill. Gov.'s Com., 1964, Exec. of Yr., Ill. Assn. Rehab. Facilities, 1989—, Disting. Svc. award Am. Hosp. Assn., 1998, Achievement award Rusk Inst., 1997, Hon. Diploma for Diplomatic Svcs. Archeworks, 1997, Pub. Svc. award Assn. Acad. Physiatrists, 1998, Disting. Alumnus award Dept. Rehab. Medicine Rusk Inst., NYU Med. Sch., 1998, Paul J. Corcoran Disting. lectr. Harvard Med. Sch. PM&R Grad., 1999; commended by Ill. Gen. Assembly, 1967; cited for meritorious svc. Pres.'s Com. on Employment of Handicapped, 1965. Mem. Ill. Med. Soc., Assn. Acad. Physiatrists (pres. 1968-69, bd. dirs. 1990-95, Pub. Svc. award 1998), Am. Congress Rehab. Med. (med. adv. com., pres. 1976-77, Gold Key 1984), Mid-Am. Soc. Phys. Med. and Rehab. (pres. 1969), Brain Trauma Found. (bd. dirs. 1990-93). Home: 1727 N Orleans St Chicago IL 60614-5719 Office: Rehabilitation Inst 345 E Superior St Chicago IL 60611-4805

BETZ, EUGENE WILLIAM, architect; b. Dayton, Ohio, Jan. 12, 1921; s. Jesse Earl and Elizabeth Freda (Meyer) B.; m. Marjorie Lois Frank, Oct. 30, 1948; children: Douglas William, Gregory Vincent. BS, U. Cin., 1944. Pres. Eugene W. Betz, Architects, Inc., Dayton, 1956—; Chmn. Bd. Building Standards and Appeals, 1960-63, Kettering Planning Commn., 1957-61. Served with AUS. Recipient Honor award Architects Soc. Ohio, 1967, 71; Award of Merit, 1968, 77, 78; Nation's Sch. Month award Nat. Council Schoolhouse Constrn., 1967; Nat. Citation Am. Assn. Sch. Adminstrs., 1967, 71; Masonry award of excellence, 1976, 78; Outstanding Health Care Facility award UCLA/Columbia U./Archtl. Record, 1980 Mem. AIA (nat. com. architecture for health, 25 Yr. Bldg. award, Dayton Lifetime Excellence in Arch. award), Masons (32nd degree), Rotary. Home and Office: 820 Greenspire Ct Dayton OH 45459-1500 E-mail: betzarcht@cs.com., betzEbetz@cs.com.

BETZ, HANS DIETER, theology educator; b. Lemgo, Lippe, Germany, May 21, 1931; came to U.S., 1963, naturalized, 1973; s. Ludwig and Gertrude (Vietor) B.; m. Christel Hella Wagner, Nov. 10, 1958; children: Martin, Ludwig, Arnold. Student, Kirchliche Hochschule, Bethel, Fed. Republic Germany, 1951-52, U. Mainz, Fed. Republic Germany, 1952-55, 56-58, Westminster Coll, Cambridge, Eng., 1955-56; Doctor Theologiae, U. Mainz, Fed. Republic Germany, 1957; Habilitation, U. Mainz, 1966. Pastor Evangelical Ch., Rhineland, Fed. Republic Germany, 1961-63; from asst. prof. to prof. Sch. Theology, Claremont Grad. Sch., Calif., 1963-78; prof. N.T. and early Christian lit. U. Chgo., 1978-2000, Shailer Mathews prof., 1989—; prof. emeritus; chmn. dept. N.T. and early Christian lit. U. Chgo., 1985-94. Rsch. fellow Inst. Advanced Study, Hebrew U., Jerusalem, 1999. Author, editor numerous books and articles in German and English, 1959— Recipient Humboldt Rsch. prize, 1986; Lady Davis fellow Hebrew U., Jerusalem, Israel, 1990, Sackler scholar Tel Aviv U., 1995; NEH rsch. grantee, 1970-83, Am. Assn. Theol. Schs. grantee, 1977, 84. Mem. Soc. Bibl. Lit. (pres. 1997), Studiorum Novi Testamenti Societas (pres. 1999-2000), Chgo. Soc. Bibl. Rsch. (pres. 1983-84). Office: U Chgo 1025 E 58th St Chicago IL 60637-1509 E-mail: hansbetz@midway.uchicago.edu.

BETZ, RONALD PHILIP, pharmacist; b. Chgo., Nov. 26, 1933; s. David Robert and Olga Marie (Martinson) B.; m. Rose Marie Marella, May 18, 1963; children: David Christian, Christopher Peter. BS, U. Ill., 1955; MPA, Roosevelt U., 1987. Asst. dir. pharmacy U. Ill., Chgo., 1959-62; dir. pharmacy Mt. Sinai Hosp., 1962-2001; pres. Pharmacy Systems, Inc., 1982-89; teaching assoc. Coll. Pharmacy, U. Ill., Chgo., 1977-88. Adj. clin. asst. prof. pharmacy, U. Ill., 1988-2001; pres. Pharmacy Svc. and Systems, 1972-81; dir. Ill. Coop. Health Data Systems, 1976-80. Contbr. articles to profl. jours. Bd. dirs. Howard/Paulina Redevel. Corp., 1983-92. With U.S. Army, 1956-58. Mem. Am. Soc. Health Sys. Pharmacists, Ill. Pharm. Assn. (pres. 1975), Ill. Acad. Proceptirs in Pharmacy (pres. 1972), No. Ill. Soc. Hosp. Pharmacists (pres. 1966), Kappa Psi. Democrat. Lutheran. Home: 1021 Sussex Dr Northbrook IL 60062-3328 E-mail: rbetznb@aol.com.

BETZOLD, DONALD RICHARD, state legislator; b. Mpls., Aug. 27, 1950; s. Donald A. and Georgiana (Beauchamp) B.; m. Leesa Marie Simonson, Aug. 11, 1989; 1 child, Ben Anthony. BA, U. Minn., 1972; JD, Hamline U., 1979. Bar: Minn. 1979. Atty., Brooklyn Center, Minn., 1980—; mem. Minn. Senate, St. Paul, 1993—. Col. JAGC, USAR, ret. Mem. Minn. State Bar Assn. (chair bar media com. 1987-90). Roman Catholic. Avocation: black and white photography. Home: 6150 Briardale Ct NE Fridley MN 55432-5210 Office: Minn State Senate G-9 Capitol Saint Paul MN 55155-0001

BEUGEN, JOAN BETH, communications company executive; b. Mar. 9, 1943; d. Leslie and Janet (Glick) Caplan; m. Sheldon Howard Beugen, July 16, 1967. BS in Speech, Northwestern U., 1965. Founder, prin., pres. The Creative Establishment, Inc., Chgo., N.Y.C., San Francisco and L.A., 1969—87; founder, pres. Cresta Comms. Inc., Chgo., 1988—. Spkr. on entrepreneurship for women. Contbr. articles to profl. jours. Trustee Mt. Sinai Hosp. Med. Ctr.; del. White House Conf. on Small Bus., 1979; bd. dirs. Chgo. Network, Chgoland Enterprise Ctr., Girl Scouts Chgo. Named Entrepreneur of Yr., Women in Bus.; recipient YWCA Leadership award, 1985. Mem.: Overseas Edn. Fund Women in Bus. Com., Nat. Women's Forum, Com. of 200, Women in Film, Chgo. Film Coun., Chgo. Audio-Visual Producers Assn., Midwest Soc. Profl. Cons., Chgo. Assn. Commerce and Industry, Ill. Women's Agenda, Nat. Assn. Women Bus. Owners (pres. Chgo. bhpt. 1979), Econ. Club Chgo. Office: The Cresta Group 1050 N State St Chicago IL 60610-7829

BEUKEMA, JOHN FREDERICK, lawyer; b. Alpena, Mich., Jan. 30, 1947; s. Christian F. and Margaret Elizabeth (Robertson) B.; m. Cynthia Ann Parke, May 25, 1974; children: Frederick Parke, David Christian. BA, Carleton Coll., 1968; JD, U. Minn., 1971. Bar: Minn. 1971, U.S. Ct. Mil. Appeals 1974, U.S. Dist. Ct. Minn. 1975, U.S. Ct. Appeals (8th cir.) 1981, U.S. Ct. Appeals (fed. cir.) 1984, U.S. Supreme Ct. 1988, U.S. Dist. Ct. (we. dist.) Wis. 1997, U.S. Ct. Appeals (9th cir.) 1999. Assoc. Faegre & Benson, Mpls., 1971, 75-79, ptnr., 1980—. Vestryman Cathedral Ch. St. Mark, Mpls., 1983-86; bd. dirs. Neighborhood Involvement Program, Mpls., 1986-90, pres., 1989-90; bd. dirs. Ronald McDonald House of Twin Cities, 1991-97, sec., 1995-97. Lt. JAGC, USNR, 1972-75. Mem. ABA, Minn. State Bar Assn., Hennepin County Bar Assn. Republican. Episcopalian. E-mail: jbeukema@faegre.com.

BEUMER, RICHARD EUGENE, engineer, architect, construction firm executive; b. St. Louis, Feb. 26, 1938; s. Eugene Henry and C. Florence (Braun) Beumer; m. Judith Louise Rockett, June 25, 1960; children: Kathryn, Karen, Mark. BSEE, Valparaiso U., 1959. Registered profl. engr., Mo., Ill., Ariz., Md., Okla., Ohio, Ga., Va., Mich., D.C., Mass., N.Y., N.C. With Sverdrup Corp. Cos., 1959—; v.p. Sverdrup & Parcel and Assocs., St. Louis, 1974—78; sr. v.p., exec. v.p., dir. Sverdrup & Parcel Assocs., 1979—81; pres. Sverdrup & Parcel Assos., 1982—85; sr. v.p. Sverdrup Corp., 1986—88, exec. v.p., 1989—92, pres., 1993; pres., CEO Sverdrup Corp., 1994—95; chmn., CEO Sverdrup Corp., 1996. Dir. Sverdrup Ltd., St. Louis, 1979; vice-chmn. Jacobs Engring. Group, Inc., 1999, Jacobs Engring. Co., 2002—, Aid Assn. for Luths., Valparaiso U. Chmn. St. Louis Regional Chamber and Growth Assn., 1998—99; divsn. chmn. United Way St. Louis, 1980; bd. dirs. Downtown St. Louis, Inc., 1982—91, Jr. Achievement, St. Louis Sci. Ctr.; past chmn. Luth. Med. Ctr., St. Louis; trustee, chmn. St. Louis Luth. High Schs. Recipient Disting. Alumni award, Valparaiso U., 1983. Mem.: NSPE, Mo. Soc. Profl. Engrs., Constrn. Industry Pres. Forum, Design Profls. Coalition, Cons. Engrs. Coun. Mo. (pres. 1980), Am. Cons. Engrs. Coun. (nat. bd. dirs. 1979—82), St. Louis Elec. Bd. (pres. 1983), The Bogey Club, Old Warson Club, Univ. Club, The Moles. Lutheran. Office: Jacobs Engring Group Inc 501 N Broadway Saint Louis MO 63102

BEUTLER, CHRISTOPHER JOHN, state legislator; b. Omaha, Nov. 14, 1944; s. John E. and Dorothy M. (Lanning) B.; m. Patty Hershey, 1967; children: Alexa, Erica, Mikahla, Samuel. BA, Yale U., 1966; JD, U. Nebr., 1973. Tchr. Peace Corps, Turkey, 1966-67; rschr. Nebr. Crime Commn., 1972-73; assoc. Cline, Williams, Wright, Johnson & Oldfather, Lincoln, 1973-78; pvt. practice, 1978—; mem. Nebr. Legislature from 28th dist., Lincoln, 1978-86, 90—; chmn. judiciary com. Nebr. Legislature, 1983-84, mem. natural resources com., mem. rules com., com. on coms., edn. com.; owner Beutler Svc. Inc., 2000—. Named to Benson H.S. Hall of Fame, 1984. Mem. Nebr. Bar Assn., Lincoln Bar Assn., Nebr. Art Assn., Kiwanis (mem. exec. com. 1976), Beta Theta Phi. Office: State Capitol Rm 1124 Lincoln NE 68509-4604

BEUTLER, FREDERICK JOSEPH, information scientist; b. Berlin, Oct. 3, 1926; came to U.S., 1936, naturalized, 1943; s. Alfred David and Kaethe (Italiener) B.; m. Suzanne Armstrong, Jan. 5, 1969; children— Arthur David, Kathryn Ruth, Michael Ernest. SB, MIT, 1949, SM, 1951; PhD, Calif. Inst. Tech., 1957. Faculty U. Mich., Ann Arbor, 1957—, prof. info. and control engring., 1963-90, prof. emeritus, 1990—, chmn. computer info. and control engring., 1970-71, 77-90, chmn. grad. elect. engring. systems program, 1985-90. Vis. prof. Calif. Inst. Tech., 1967-68; vis. scholar U. Calif. at Berkeley, 1964-65 Editorial cons. Math. Rev., 1965-67, 75-88; contbr. articles to profl. jours. and books. Bd. dirs. Ann Arbor Civic Theatre, 1976-78, 91-94. With AUS, 1945-46. NSF rsch. grantee, 1971-75, 76-81, 92-94, Air Force Office Sci. Rsch. grantee, 1970-74, 75-80; NASA grantee, 1959-69. Fellow IEEE (life); mem. Soc. Indsl. and Applied Math. (coun. 1969-74, mng. editor Jour. Applied Math. 1970-75, editor 1984-90, editor Rev. 1967-70), Am. Math. Soc., U. Mich. Retirees Assn. (bd. dirs., sec.-treas. 1994—), Barton Boat Club, Racquet

Club of Ann Arbor. Office: Elec Engr and Comp Sci Bldg Univ Michigan Ann Arbor MI 48109-2122 E-mail: fjb@umich.edu.

BEVAN, ROBERT LEWIS, lawyer; b. Springfield, Mo., Mar. 23, 1928; s. Gene Walter and Blanche Omega (Woods) B.; m. Ronice Diane Gartin, Jan 25, 1977; children: Matthew Gene, Lisa Ann. AB, U. Mo., 1950; LLB, U. Kansas City, 1957. Bar: Mo. 1957, D.C. 1969. Adminstrv. asst. U.S. Senator T. Hennings Jr., Washington, 1957-60; legis. asst. U.S. Senator E.V. Long, 1960-69; sr. govt. relations counsel Am. Bankers Assn., 1970-84; ptnr. Hopkins & Sutter, 1984-95; of counsel Stinson, Mag and Fizzell, Kansas City, Mo., 1995-2001. Ghost author: The Intruders, 1967; contbg. editor U.S. Banker, 1985-88. Fieldman Dem. Nat. Com., 1968. Served with U.S. Army, 1946-47, 1951-53. Mem. ABA (bus. law sect., chmn. banking law com. 1988-92, commn. on IOLTA 1997-2000, co-chmn. joint banking com. 1999-2000), Echequer Club. Avocations: art and antiques. Office: 4545 Wornall Rd Ste 805 Kansas City MO 64111

BEVERLINE, JERRY, state agency administrator; Dir. land mgmt. Ill. Dept. Conservation, Springfield, 1994—. Office: Ill Dept Conservation 600 N Grand Ave W Springfield IL 62706-0001 Fax: 217-524-5612.

BE VIER, WILLIAM A. religious studies educator; b. Springfield, Mo., July 31, 1927; s. Charles and Erma G. (Ritter) Be V.; m Jo Ann King, Aug. 11, 1949; children: Cynthia, Shirley. BA, Drury Coll., 1950; ThM, Dallas Theol. Sem., 1955, ThD, 1958; MA, So. Meth. U., 1960; EdD, ABD, Wayne State U., 1968. With Frisco Rlwy., 1943-45, 46-51, John E. Mitchell Co., Dallas, 1952-60; instr. Dallas Theol. Sem., 1958-59; prof. Detroit Bible Coll., 1960-74, registrar, 1962-66, dean, 1964-73, exec. v.p., 1967-74, acting pres., 1967-68; prof., dean edn., v.p. for acad. affairs Northwestern Coll., Roseville, Minn., 1974-81, prof., 1981-95, prof. emeritus, 1995—. Editor The Discerner. Bd. dirs. Religion Analysis Svc., Mpls., 1979—, pres., 1989—. With USMC, 1945-46, 50-51; ret. col. Army Res. Mem. Res. Officers Assn., Ind. Fund Chs. of Am. (nat. exec. com. 1991-94, v.p. 1993-94), Huguenot Hist. Soc., Bevier-Elting Family Assn., Phi Alpha Theta. Office: Religion Analysis Svc 5693 Geneva Ave N Oakdale MN 55128-1018 E-mail: wabjab41@juno.com.

BEVINGTON, DAVID MARTIN, English literature educator; b. N.Y.C., May 13, 1931; s. Merle Mowbray and Helen (Smith) B.; m. Margaret Bronson Brown, June 4, 1953; children: Stephen, Philip, Katharine, Sarah. B.A., Harvard U., 1952, M.A., 1957, Ph.D., 1959. Instr. English Harvard U., 1959-61; asst. prof. U. Va., 1961-65, asso. prof., 1965-66, prof., 1966-67; vis. prof. U. Chgo., 1967-68, prof., 1968—, Phyllis Fay Horton disting. svc. prof. in the humanities, 1985—. Vis. prof. N.Y. U. Summer Sch., 1963, Harvard U. Summer Sch., 1967, U. Hawaii Summer Sch., 1970, Northwestern U., 1974 Author: From Mankind to Marlowe, 1962, Tudor Drama and Politics, 1968, Action is Eloquence, Shakespeare's Language of Gesture, 1984; editor: Medieval Drama, 1975, The Complete Works of Shakespeare, 4th edit., 1997, The Bantam Shakespeare, 1988. Served with USN, 1952-55. Guggenheim fellow, 1964-65, 81-82; sr. fellow Southeastern Inst. Medieval and Renaissance Studies, summer 1975; sr. cons. and seminar leader Folger Inst. Renaissance and Eighteenth-Century Studies, 1976-77 Mem. MLA, AAUP, Renaissance Soc. Am., Shakespeare Assn. Am. (pres. 1976-77, 95-96), Am. Acad. Arts and Scis., Am. Philos. Soc. Home: 5747 S Blackstone Ave Chicago IL 60637-1823 Office: Univ Chgo English Dept 5801 S Ellis Ave Chicago IL 60637-5418

BEZNER, JODY, agricultural products company executive; m. Kay Bezner. BS, Tex. Tech. U. Vice chmn. bd. dirs. Farmland Industries, Kansas City, Mo., 1991—; pres., gen. mgr. Benzer Cattle & Grain, Texline, Tex., 1997—. Pres. Texline Ind. Sch. Dist. Bd., 1989—, Dalhart Consumers Fule Assn.; active 4-H. Mem. Dallam-Hartley C. of C. (past bd. dirs.), XIT Rodeo and Reunion Assn. Office: Farmland Industries Inc 3315 N Oak Trfy Kansas City MO 64116-2798

BHATTACHARYA, PALLAB KUMAR, electrical engineering educator, researcher; b. Calcutta, West Bengal, India, Dec. 6, 1949; came to U.S., 1978; s. Promode Ranjan and Sipra (Chatterjee) B.; m. Meena Mukerji, Aug. 11, 1975, children: Ramona, Monica. BSc with honors, U. Calcutta, 1968, B of Tech., 1970, M of Tech., 1971; M of Engring., U. Sheffield, Eng., 1976, PhD, 1978. Sr. rsch. asst. Radar and Communication Ctr., Kharagpur, India, 1972-73; asst. stores officer Hindustan Steel Ltd., Rourkela, India, 1973-75; asst., then assoc. prof. dept. elec. engring. Oreg. State U., Corvallis, 1978-83; assoc. prof. dept. elec. engring. and computer sci. U. Mich., Ann Arbor, 1984-87, prof., 1987—, dir. Solid State Electronics Lab., 1991—. Invited prof. Swiss Fed. Inst. Tech., Lausanne, 1981-82. Contbr. articles to profl. jours. Fellow IEEE; mem. Am. Phys. Soc. Avocations: photography, music. Office: U Mich Dept Elec Engring & Comp Sci 2228 EECS Bldg Ann Arbor MI 48109-2122

BHUSHAN, BHARAT, mechanical engineer; b. Jhinjhana, India, Sept. 30, 1949; came to U.S., 1970, naturalized, 1977; s. Narain Dass and Devi (Vati) B.; m. Sudha Bhushan, June 14, 1975; children: Ankur, Noopur. B Mech. Engring. with honors, Birla Inst. Tech. and Sci., 1970; MSME, MIT, 1971; MS in Mechanics, U. Colo., 1973, PhD in Mech. Engring., 1976; MBA, Rensselaer Poly. Inst., 1980; DSc, U. Trondheim, Norway, 1990; D of Tech. Scis., Warsaw (Poland) U. Tech., 1996; D honoris causa, Metal Polymer Rsch. Inst., Nat. Acad. Scis. at Gomel, Belarus, 2000. Mem. rsch. staff dept. mech. engring. MIT, Cambridge, 1971-72; rsch. asst., instr. dept. mech. engring. U. Colo., Boulder, 1973-76; program mgr. R&D divsn. Mech. Tech. Inc., Latham, N.Y., 1976-80; rsch. scientist SKF Industries, Inc., King of Prussia, Pa., 1980-81; adv. engr. IBM, Tucson, 1981-85, devel. engr., mgr., 1985-86; sr. engr., mgr. head-disk interface Almaden Rsch. Ctr. IBM, San Jose, Calif., 1986-91; Ohio eminent scholar, Howard Winbigler prof. mech. engring. Ohio State U., Columbus, 1991—, dir. Computer Microtribology and Contamination Lab., 1991—. Expert investigator Automotive Specialists, Denver, 1973-76; vis. sr. scientist Royal Norwegian Coun. for Sci. and Indsl. Rsch., U. Trondheim, 1987, USSR Acad. Sci., Moscow, 1989; vis. scholar dept. mech. engring., chemistry and materials sci. and mineral engring. U. Calif., Berkeley, 1989; Sony sabbatical chair prof. Sony Corp. Rsch. Ctr., Fujitsuka, Japan, 1997; invited presenter worldwide; spkr. internat. confs. Author: Tribology and Mechanics of Magnetic Storage Devices, 1990, Handbook of Tribology, 1991, Mechanics and Reliability of Flexible Magnetic Media, 1992, Handbook of Micro/Natrotribiology, 1995, 2d edit., 1999, Principles and Applications of Tribology, 1999, Modern Tribology Handbook, Vol. 1 Principles of Tribology, 2001, Vol. 2 Materials, Coatings and Industrial Applications, 2001; editor 25 books; editor-in-chief, founding editor ASME series Advances in Info. Storage Sys., 1991—; editor-in-chief CRC Mechanics and Materials Sci. series; contbr. handbook chpts., tech. papers, over4005 articles to profl. jours. Recipient Alfred Noble prize ASCE, IEEE, ASME, AIME, Western Soc. Engrs., 1981, Tech. Excellence award Am. Soc. Engrs. India, 1989, Cert. Appreciation award NASA, 1987, Alexander von Humboldt Rsch. prize for sr. scientists U. Ulm, 1998-99, U. Karlsruhe, 1998-99, Fulbright Sr. Scholar award and guest prof. Tech. U. Vienna, 1999; Ford Found. fellow MIT, 1971; grantee USN, NASA, Dept. Energy, USAF, Franco-Am. Commn. for Ednl. Exch. Interfound. grantee Ecole Cen. Lyon, 1999. Fellow ASME (cert. of recognition Design Engring. Conf., Henry Hess award 1980, Burt L. Newkirk award 1983, Gustus L. Larson Meml. award 1986, tribology divsn. Best Paper award 1989, Melville medal for best current original paper 1992, Bd. Govs. award 1997, 98, Charles Russ Richards Meml. award 2000), N.Y. Acad. Scis.; mem. NSPE, IEEE (sr.), Soc. Tribologists and Lubrication Engrs., Am. Soc. Lubrication Engrs., Am. Acad. Mechanics, Internat. Humanists Soc., Tri-City India Assn., Internat. Acad. Engring. Russia (fgn.), Byelorussian Acad. of Engring. and Tech. (fgn.), Acad. of Triboengring. of Ukraine (fgn.), Soc. of Tribologists of Belarus (hon. mem.), Rotary, Sigma Xi, Tau Beta Pi. Hindu. Achievements include 8 patents in field; pioneer in tribology and mechanics of magnetic storage devices; leading researcher in field of micro/nanotribology using single probe microscopy. Avocations: music, photography, hiking, traveling. Home: 10235 Widdington Close Powell OH 43065-9059 Office: Ohio State U 206 W 18th Ave Columbus OH 43210-1189 E-mail: bhushan.2@osu.edu.

BIBART, RICHARD L. lawyer; b. Apr. 10, 1942; m. Lois Ann Rey, Sept. 8, 1963; children: Laurie, Jennifer, Kristen, Ted. BA in Econs., Harvard U., 1964; JD, U. Mich., 1966. Bar: Ohio 1967, U.S. Tax Ct. 1967, U.S. Dist. Ct. (so. dist.) Ohio 1969. Assoc. Porter, Wright, Morris & Arthur, Columbus, Ohio, 1967-72, ptnr., 1972-84; v.p. corp. planning Red Roof Inns., Inc., Hilliard, 1984-86; mgmt. co. pres. Red Roof Inns, Inc., 1986-89, pres., CEO, 1989-91; ptnr. Baker & Hostetler LLP, Columbus, 1991—. Mem. ABA, Ohio Bar Assn., Columbus Bar Assn., Columbus Country Club. Office: Baker & Hostetler LLP 65 E State St Ste 2100 Columbus OH 43215-4215

BICHA, KAREL DENIS, historian, educator; b. LaCrosse, Wis., Jan. 7, 1937; s. Stephen John and Lauretta Katherine (Horan) B.; m. Roberta Gail Gobar; children: Paul Edwin, Anne Marie. BA, U. Wis., 1958; PhD, U. Minn., 1963. Asst. prof. Colo. State U., Ft. Collins, 1963-64, U. Man., Winnipeg, Can., 1964-66, U. Minn., Morris, 1966-67; assoc. prof. Carleton U., Ottawa, Ont., Can., 1967-69, Marquette U., Milw., 1969-77, prof., 1977—. Author: American Farmer and the Canadian West, 1968, Western Populism, 1976, Czechs in Oklahoma, 1980, C.C. Washburn and the Upper Mississippi Valley, 1995. Am. Philos. Soc. grantee, 1964, 68, Can. Council grantee, 1966-68, NEH grantee, 1978-80, Bradley Inst. for Democracy and Pub. Values grantee, 1991, 97. Mem. Orgn. Am. Historians, Immigration History Soc. Office: Marquette U PO Box 1881 Coughlin Hall Dept Of Histo Milwaukee WI 53201-1881

BICKNELL, BRIAN KEITH, dentist; b. Orlando, Fla., Mar. 8, 1957; s. Keith Arthur and Mary Lou (Papish) B.; m. Gina Rose Smajo; children: Michael Brian, Daniel Keith. BS, U. Notre Dame, 1979, U. Ill., Chgo., 1981, DDS, 1983. Practice gen. dentistry, Batavia, Ill., 1984—. Fellow Acad. Gen. Dentistry; mem. ADA, Ill. State Dental Soc., Fox River Valley Dental Soc. Roman Catholic. Home: 594 N Van Nortwick St Batavia IL 60510-1119 Office: 109 E Wilson St Batavia IL 60510-2658

BICKNELL, O. GENE, financial executive; Chmn., CEO, founder NPC Internat. Office: NPC International Inc PO Box 643 Pittsburg KS 66762-0643

BICKNER, BRUCE, food products executive; b. 1943; BBA, De Pauw U., 1965; JD, U. Mich., 1968. Law clk. U.S. Dist. Ct., 1968-70; ptnr. Sidley & Austin, Chgo., 1970-75; with DeKalb (Ill.) Corp., 1975—, v.p., 1976, group v.p., 1980, exec. v.p., dir., 1980, pres., 1986-90, CEO, chmn. bd., 1988-98, DeKalb Energy Co., 1988-98, DeKalb Swine Breekers Inc.; co-pres. Monsanto Global Seed Group, Monsanto, Inc., DeKalb, 1998—, exec. v.p. agrl. sector. Office: Monsanto Global Seed Group 3100 Sycamore Rd Dekalb IL 60115-9600

BIDDLE, BRUCE JESSE, social psychologist, educator; b. Ossining, N.Y., Dec. 30, 1928; s. William Wishart and Loureide Jeanette (Cobb) B.; m. Ellen Catherine Horgan; children: David Charles, William Jesse, Jennifer Loureide; m. Barbara Julianne Bank, June 19, 1976. A.B. in Math., Antioch Coll., Yellow Springs, Ohio, 1950; postgrad., U. N.C., 1950-51; Ph.D. in Social Psychology, U. Mich., 1957. Asst. prof. sociology U. Ky., 1957-58; assoc. prof. edn. U. Kansas City, 1958-60; assoc. prof. psychology and sociology U. Mo., Columbia, 1960-66, prof., 1966-2000, prof. emeritus, 2000—, dir. Ctr. Rsch. in Social Behavior, 1966-96. Vis. assoc. prof. U. Queensland, Australia, 1965; vis. prof. Monash U., Australia, 1969, vis. fellow Australian Nat. U., 1977, 85, 93. Author: (with R.S. Adams) Realities of Teaching: Explorations with Videotape, 1970, (with M.J. Dunkin) The Study of Teaching, 1974, (with T.L. Good and J. Brophy) Teachers Make a Difference, 1975, Role Theory: Expectations, Identities and Behaviors, 1979, (with D.C. Berliner) The Manufactured Crisis: Myths, Fraud, and the Attack on America's Public Schools, 1995; editor: (with W.J. Ellena) contemporary Research on Teacher Effectiveness, 1964, (with E.J. Thomas) Role Theory: Concepts and Research, 1966, (with P.H. Rossi) The New Media: Their Impact on Education, 1966, (with D.S. Anderson) Knowledge for Policy: Improving Education Through Research, 1991, (with T.L. Good and I.F. Goodson) International Handbook of Teachers and Teaching, 1997, Social Class, Poverty, and Education, 2001. Served with U.S. Army, 1954-56. Fellow APA, Am. Psychol. Soc., Australian Psychol. Soc.; mem. Am. Ednl. Research Assn., Australian Assn. Rsch. Edn., Am. Sociol. Assn., Midwest Sociol. Soc. Home: 924 Yale Columbia MO 65203-1874 Office: U Mo Dept Psychology McAlester Hall Rm 210 Columbia MO 65211-0001 E-mail: BiddleB@missouri.edu.

BIDELMAN, WILLIAM PENDRY, astronomer, educator; b. L.A., Sept. 25, 1918; s. William Pendry and Dolores (De Remer) B.; m. Verna Pearl Shirk, June 19, 1940; children: Lana Louise Stone (dec. Mar. 2000), Linda Elizabeth McKinley, Billie Jean Little, Barbara Jo Talley. Student, U. N.D., 1936-37; SB, Harvard, 1940; PhD, U. Chgo., 1943. Physicist, Aberdeen Proving Ground, Md., 1943-45; instr., then asst. prof. astronomy Yerkes Obs., U. Chgo., 1945-53; asst. astronomer, then. assoc. astronomer Lick Obs., U. Calif., 1953-62; prof. U. Mich., 1962-69, U. Tex. at Austin, 1969-70, Case Western Res. U., Cleve., 1970-86, prof. emeritus, 1986—. Chmn. dept., dir. Warner and Swasey Obs., 1970-75; mem. adv. panel on astronomy NSF, 1959-62; mem. NRC adv. com. on astronomy Office Naval Rsch., 1964-67. Contbr. articles to profl. jours. Mem. Am. Astron. Soc. (councilor 1959-62, participant vis. prof. program 1961-65), Astron. Soc. Pacific (editor Publs. 1956-61), Internat. Astron. Union (commns. 29, 45, pres. 1964-67), Phi Beta Kappa. Presbyterian. Achievements include discovery of lines of mercury, krypton and xenon in stellar spectra; discovery of phosphorus stars; co-discovery of barium stars; research in spectral classification, astronomical data and observational astrophysics. Home: 3171 Chelsea Dr Cleveland OH 44118-1256 Office: Case Western Res U Dept Astronomy 10900 Euclid Ave Cleveland OH 44106-7215 E-mail: wsobs@grendel.astr.cwru.edu.

BIDWELL, CHARLES EDWARD, sociologist, educator; b. Chgo., Jan. 24, 1932; s. Charles Leslie and Eugenia (Campbell) B.; m. Helen Claxton Lewis, Jan. 24, 1959; 1 son, Charles Lewis. AB, U. Chgo., 1950, AM, 1953, PhD, 1956. Lectr. on sociology Harvard U., 1959-61; asst. prof. edn. U. Chgo., 1961-65, assoc. prof., 1965-70, prof. edn. and sociology, 1970-85, Reavis prof. edn. and sociology, 1985-2001, Reavis prof. emeritus edn. and sociology, 2001—, chmn. dept. edn., 1978-88, chmn. dept. sociology, 1988-94, dir. Ogburn-Stouffer Ctr., 1988-94. Author books in field; contbr. numerous articles to profl. jours.; editor Sociology of Edn., 1969-72, Am. Jour. Sociology, 1973-78, Am. Jour. Edn., 1983-88. With U.S. Army, 1957-59. Guggenheim fellow, 1971-72 Fellow AAAS; mem. Sociol. Rsch. Assn., Nat. Acad. Edn. (sec.), Phi Beta Kappa. Office: Dept Sociology 5848 S University Ave Chicago IL 60637-1515 E-mail: cbidwell@uchicago.edu.

BIEBEL, PAUL PHILIP, JR. lawyer; b. Chgo., Mar. 24, 1942; s. Paul Philip Sr. and Eleanor Mary (Sweeney) B.; divorced; children: Christine M., Brian E., Jennifer A., Susan E. AB, Marquette U., 1964; JD, Georgetown U., 1967. Bar: Ill. 1967, U.S. Dist. Ct. (no. dist.) Ill. 1967, U.S. Ct. Appeals (6th cir.) 1985, U.S. Supreme Ct. 1972. Asst. dean of men Loyola U., Chgo., 1967-69; asst. state's atty. Cook County State's Atty., 1969-75, dep. state's atty., 1975-81; 1st asst. atty. gen. Ill. Atty. Gen., 1981-85; pub. defender Cook County Pub. Defender, 1986-88; ptnr. Winston & Strawn, 1985-86, 88-94, Altheimer & Gray, Chgo., 1994-96; judge Cir. Ct. Cook County, Ill., 1996—. Contbr. articles to profl. publs. Mem. Fed. Bar Assn. (bd. dirs., pres. 1994-95), Cath. Lawyers Guild (bd. dirs., Cath. Lawyer of Yr. 1988), Ill. Judges Assn., Ill. Appellate Lawyers, 7th Cir. Bar Assn., Chgo. Bar Assn. (chmn. com. 1991-93), Georgetown Law Alumni Assn. (bd. dirs. 1991-96). Roman Catholic. Avocations: reading, golf. Home: 5415 N Forest Glen Ave Chicago IL 60630-1523 Office: Presiding Judge Criminal Divsn RM 101 2600 S California Ave Chicago IL 60608

BIEBER, OWEN F. labor union official; b. North Dorr, Mich., Dec. 28, 1929; s. Albert F. and Minnie (Schwartz) B.; m. Shirley M. Van Woerkom, Nov. 25, 1950; children: Kenneth, Linda, Michael, Ronald, Joan. H.H.D., Grand Valley Coll., 1983; hon., Ferris State Coll., 1986. Rep. Internat. Union UAW, Grand Rapids, Mich., 1961-72, asst. regional dir. Region ID, 1972-74, regional dir Region ID, 1974-80; v.p. Internat. Union UAW, Detroit, 1980-83, pres., 1983-96; ret., 1995. Chmn. Kent County Dem. Com., Wyoming, Mich., 1964-66, mem. exec. bd., 1966-80; del. Nat. Dem. Convs., 1968, 76, 80. Named Labor Man of Yr., Kent County AFL-CIO, 1965 Mem. NAACP (life), Grand Rapids Urban League Roman Catholic. Club: Economic of Detroit.

BIEDERMAN, JERRY H. lawyer; b. Chgo., July 2, 1946; BA, Stanford U., 1968; JD, U. Chgo., 1971. Bar: Ill. 1971. Mng. ptnr. Neal, Gerber & Eisenberg, Chgo. Mem. ABA (law practice mgmt. sec.) Chgo. Bar Assn. Office: Neal Gerber & Eisenberg 2 N La Salle St Ste 2200 Chicago IL 60602-3801

BIEDRON, THEODORE JOHN, newspaper advertising executive; b. Evergreen Park, Ill., Nov. 30, 1946; s. Theodore John and Ione Margaret B.; m. Gloria Anne DeAngelo, Nov. 7, 1970; children: Jessica Ann, Lauren. BA in Polit. Sci., U. Ill., 1968. Recruitment advt. mgr. Chgo. Sun-Times, 1968-74; classified advt. mgr. Pioneer press, Wilmette, Ill., 1974-76, v.p. advt. and promotion, 1993-94, sr. v.p. sales and mktg., 1994-97, exec. v.p., 1997-2000. Pub. North Shore mag., 1997-2000; classified mgr., v.p. Lerner Newspapers, Chgo., 1976-79, assoc. pub., 1980-82, advt. dir., 1982-87; v.p., classified advt. mgr. Chgo. Sun-Times, 1987-92; pres. Chicagoland Pub. Co. divsn. Chgo. Tribune, 2000—. Pres. Northeastern Ill. U. Found., 1998-2002; trustee Northlight Theater, 1993-98. Home: 1130 Lake Ave Wilmette IL 60091-1661 Office: Chicagoland Pub Co 2000 S York Rd Oak Brook IL 60523 E-mail: tbiedron@earthlink.net.

BIEGEL, DAVID ELI, social worker, educator; b. N.Y.C., July 3, 1946; s. Jack and Estelle (Lentin) B.; m. Margaret S. Smoot, Jan. 31, 1976 (div.); 1 child, Geoffrey S. BA, CCNY, 1967; MSW, U. Md., 1970, PhD, 1982. Field coord. United Farm Workers, AFL-CIO, Balt., 1971; exec. dir. Junction, Inc., Westminster, Md., 1971-72; dir. office planning and program devel. Cath. Charities, Balt., 1973-76; ctr. assoc., dir. neighborhood and family svcs. project U. So. Calif., Washington Pub. Affairs Ctr., 1976-80; asst. prof. social work U. Pitts., 1980-85, assoc. prof., 1985-86; Henry L. Zucker prof. social work practice Mandel Sch. Applied Social Scis., Case Western Res. U., 1987—, prof. psychiatry and sociology, 1987—, co-dir. Ctr. for Practice Innovations, 1991-97, chair doctoral program, 1998—. Co-dir. Cuyahoga County Cmty. Mental Health Rsch. Inst., 1994—2002; pres. Inst. for the Advancement of Social Work Rsch., 1999—; dir. rsch. and evaluation Ohio Substance Abuse and Mental Illness Coord. Ctr. of Excellence. Co-editor: Innovations in Practice and Service Delivery with Vulnerable Populations Series, Family Caregiving Applications Series; contbr. articles to profl. jours., books; co-author: Neighborhood Networks for Humane Mental Health Care, 1982, Community Support Systems and Mental Health: Practice, Policy and Research, 1982, Building Support Networks for the Elderly: Theory and Applications, 1984, Social Networks and Mental Health: An Annotated Bibliography, 1985, Social Support Networks: A Bibliography 1983-1987, 1989, Aging and Caregiving: Theory, Research and Policy, 1990, Family Preservation Programs: Research and Evaluation, 1991, Family Caregiving in Chronic Illness: Alzheimer's Dsiease, Cancer, Heart Disease, Mental Illness, and Stroke, 1991, Family Caregiving: A Lifespan Perspective, 1994, The Jewish Aged in the U.S. and Israel: Diversity, Programs and Services, 1994, Innovations in Practice and Service Delivery with Vulnerable Populations Across the Lifespan, 1999. Cons. Vol. VISTA, Raton, N.Mex., and Balt., 1967-70; active Big Bros. Am., Balt., 1974-77. N.Y. State Incentive scholar, 1963-64; VISTA Fellows Program fellow, 1968-70. Fellow Gerontol. Soc. Am.; mem. APHA, NASW, Acad. Cert. Social Workers, Soc. Social Work Rsch. Democrat. Jewish. E-mail: deb@po.cwru.edu.

BIEHL, MICHAEL MELVIN, lawyer; b. Milw., Feb. 24, 1951; s. Michael Melvin Biehl and Frieda Margaret (Krieg) Davis. AB, Harvard U., 1973, JD, 1976. Bar: Wis. 1976, U.S. Dist. Ct. (ea. dist.) Wis. 1976. Assoc. Foley & Lardner, Milw., 1976-84, ptnr., 1984—. Author: Medical Staff Legal Issues, 1990, Doctoral Evidence, 2002; editor: Physician Organizations and Medical Staff, 1996. Mem. Mt. Sinai Med. Ctr. Clin. Investigations Com., Hastings Ctr.; election monitor first multi-party elections in Rep. Ga., 1990; dir. Colorlines Found. for Arts and Culture, Inc., chmn., bd. dirs. Milw. Psychiat. Hosp. and Aurora Behavioral Health Svcs. Mem. ABA, Am. Health Lawyers Assn., Am. Coll. of Med. Quality, Am. Soc. Law and Medicine. Mem. Unitarian Ch. Home: 10315 N Versailles Ct Mequon WI 53092-5231 Office: Foley & Lardner 777 E Wisconsin Ave Ste 3800 Milwaukee WI 53202-5367

BIELIAUSKAS, VYTAUTAS JOSEPH, clinical psychologist, educator; b. Plackojai, Lithuania, Nov. 1, 1920; came to U.S., 1949, naturalized, 1955; s. Antanas and Anele (Kasparaite) B.; m. Danute G. Sirvydaite, Mar. 12, 1947; children— Linas A., Diana B., Aldona O., Cornelius V. PhD in Psychology, U. Tuebingen, Germany, 1943. Diplomate Clin. Psychology, Marital Family Therapy, Am. Bd. Family Psychology, Am. Bd. Profl. Psychology. Asst. prof. U. Munich, Germany, 1944-48; instr. King's Coll., Wilkes-Barre, Pa., 1949-50; mem. faculty Sch. Clin. and Applied Psychology, Coll. William and Mary, 1950-58, prof. psychology, 1953-58, head dept. psychology, 1951-57; assoc. prof. Xavier U., Cin., 1958-60, chmn. dept. psychology, 1959-78, prof., 1960-78, Riley prof. psychology, 1978-88, disting. prof. psychology emeritus, 1988—. Author: zmogus siu dienu problematikoje, 1945, Community Relations Training for Police Supervisors, 1969; H-T-P Research Rev., 1980, CSSS for the H-T-P Drawings, 1981; contbr. articles to profl. jours. Pres., exec. officer Lithuanian World Cmty., 1988-92; exec. v.p. Lithuanian-Am. Cmty., Inc., 1994-2000; adviser on spl. programs Pres. of Republic of Lithuania, 1995-96. Lt. col. M.S.C., USAR, 1958-65. Recipient Ellis Island medal of honor, 1990. Fellow APA (pres. divsn. 13, 1986, Dist. Svc. award divsn. 36 1998); mem. Ohio Psychol. Assn. (pres. 1978-79, Disting. Svc. award 1980), Soc. Personality Assessment, Internat. Assn. for Study Med. Psychology and Religion (pres. 1972-75), Cin. Acad. Profl. Psychology, Psychologists Interested in Religious Issues (pres. 1971, exec. sec. 1973-75), Cath. Acad. Scis. in the U.S.A. (academician 1987—). Office: Xavier U Dept Psychology Cincinnati OH 45207 E-mail: bieliaus@xavier.xu.edu

BIELINSKI, DONALD EDWARD, financial executive; b. Chgo., June 27, 1949; s. Edward and Helen (Smialek) B.; m. Laura Ann Bicego, Mar. 10, 1984; children: Natalie, Michael, Rebecca, David. BS in Acctg., U. Ill., Chgo., 1971; postgrad., Stanford U., 1987. CPA, Ill. Jr. div. acct. W.W. Grainger, Inc., Niles, Ill., 1972-73, acctg. supr., 1973-74, acctg. mgr., 1974-79, dir. acctg., 1979-81, asst. contr., 1981-83, div. contr., 1983-85, v.p., corp. contr. Skokie, 1985-89, v.p. fin., 1989-90, v.p., chief fin. officer, 1990-96, s.r. v.p., 1996—. Mem. Orchard Village Bd., Niles, 1982-92; bd.

dirs. U. Ill., 1989-92. Fellow Fin. Execs. Inst., Econ. Club Chgo. Office: WW Grainger Inc 100 Grainger Pkwy Lake Forest IL 60045-5201

BIELKE, PATRICIA ANN, psychologist; b. Bay Shore, N.Y., May 11, 1949; d. Lawrence Curtis and Marcella Elizabeth (Maize) Widdoes; m. Stephen Roy Bielke, July 10, 1971; children: Eric, Christine. BA, Carleton Coll., 1971; PhD, U. Minn., 1979. Lic. psychologist, Wis.; cert. marriage and family therapist. Rsch. asst. Nat. Inst. Mental Health, Washington, 1972-74; sch. psychologist Roseville Pub. Schs., St. Paul, 1978-79; psychologist Southeastern Wis. Med. and Social Svcs., Milw., 1979-93; staff psychologist Elmbrook Meml. Hosp., 1986-2000; pvt. practice Brookfield, Wis., 1991-2000; sch. psychologist Cedarburg (Wis.) Pub. Schs., 1999—. Bd. dirs. LWV, Brookfield, 1984-88, Elmbrook Sch. Bd., 1989-99. Mem. Nat. Sch. Psychologist Assn., Wis. Sch. Psychol. Assn. Home: 17455 Bedford Dr Brookfield WI 53045-1301 Office: Cedarburg Sch Dist W68n611 Evergreen Blvd Cedarburg WI 53012-1847 E-mail: bielke@execpc.com.

BIEN, JOSEPH JULIUS, philosophy educator; b. Cin., May 22, 1936; s. Joseph Julius and Mary Elizabeth (Adams) B.; m. Françoise Neve, Apr. 8, 1965. BS, Xavier U., MA, 1958; DTC, U. Paris, 1968; postgrad., Laval Univ., 1958, Emory U., 1961-62, U. Edinburgh, 1962; D (hon.), Lucian Blaga U., 1999. Asst. prof. philosophy Univ. Tex., Austin, 1968-73; asso. prof. philosophy Univ. Mo., Columbia, 1973-79, prof. philosophy, 1979—, chmn. dept. philosophy, 1976-80, 81-83, 1993—; vis. prof. Tex. A&M U., 1980, Dubrovnik Inst. Postgrad. Studies, Yugoslavia, 1983, 84, 85, 89, co-dir. Yugoslavia, 1990—; Mid-Am. States Univs. Assn. hon. lectr. in philosophy, 1985-86. Rsch. assoc. Russian and Slavic Rsch. Ctr., 1989-91; vis. prof. Lucian Blaga U., 1996, Hubei U., 1997, Wichita State U., 1998, Univ. of the Western Cape, 2000. Author: History, Revolution and Human Natue: Marx's Philosophical Anthropology, 1984; transl.: (M. Merleau-Ponty) Adventures of the Dialectic, 1973; editor: Phenomenology and the Social Sciences, A Dialogue, 1978, Political and Social Essays by Paul Ricoeur, 1974, Leviathan, 1986, Contemporary Social Thought, 1989, Ethics and Politics, 1992, Philosophical Issues and Problems, 1998. Am. Council Learned Socs. grantee, 1973; Dubrovnik Inst. Postgrad. Studies grantee, 1984; recipient U. Mo. faculty alumni award, 1998. Mem. Soc. Social and Polit. Philosophy (pres. 1979-80, 86-87, 93-94, 97-98), Ctrl. States Philos. Assn. (pres. 1978-79), Ctrl. Slavic Conf. (sec.-tres. 1977, 84), Southwestern Philosophy Soc. (pres. 1997-98). Democrat. Home: 100 W Brandon Rd Columbia MO 65203-3508 Office: Univ Mo Dept Philosophy Columbia MO 65211-0001

BIENEN, HENRY SAMUEL, political science educator, university executive; b. N.Y.C., May 5, 1939; s. Mitchell Richard and Pearl (Witty) Bienen; m. Leigh Buchanan, Apr. 28, 1961; children: Laura, Claire, Leslie. BA with honors, Cornell U., 1960; MA, U. Chgo., 1961, PhD, 1966. Asst. prof. politics U. Chgo., 1965—66; asst. prof. politics & internat. affairs Princeton U., NJ, 1966—69, assoc. prof., 1969—72, prof., 1972—95, William Stewart Tod prof. politics and internat. affairs, 1981—85, James S. McDonnell Disting. Univ. prof., 1985, dir. Ctr. Internat. Studies, 1985—92, chair dept. politics, 1973—76, dir. African studies progrm, 1977—78, 1983—84, dir. rsch. Woodrow Wilson Sch. Pub. & Internat. Affairs, 1979—82, dean; pres. Northwestern U., Evanston, Ill., 1995—. Mem. exec. com. Inter-Univ. Seminar on Armed Forces and Soc., 1968—78; cons. U.S. State Dept., 1972—88, Nat. Security Coun., 1978—79, World Bank, 1981—89, CIA, 1982—88, Hambrecht & Quist Investment Co., Boeing Corp., Econ Corp., Enserch Corp., Ford Found., Rockefeller Found., John D. an dCatherine T. MacArthur Found.; nat. co. dir. Movement for A New Congress, 1970—71; mem. Inst. Advanced Study, 1984—85, Ctr. Advanced Study in the Behavioral Scis., 1976—77; vis. prof. Makerer Coll., Kampala, Uganda, 1963—65, U. Coll., Nairobi, Kenya, 1968—69, U. Ibadan, 1972—73. Editor: World Politics, 1970—74, 1978—; author: Tanzania: Party Transformatin and Economic Development, 1967, 1970, Kenya: The Politics of Participation and Control, 1974, Violence and Social Change, 1968, Armies and Parties in Africa, 1978, Political Conflict and Economic Change in Nigeria, 1985. Fellow Seeger fellow, 1989; grantee, Rockefeller Found., 1968—69, 1972—73. Mem.: Am. Acad., Coun. Fgn. Rels., Am. Polit. Sci. Assn. Office: Northwestern U Office of Pres Z-130 Crown Evanston IL 60208-0001

BIER, DENNIS M. medical educator; b. Hoboken, N.J., July 24, 1941; MD, 1966. Diplomate Am. Bd. Pediat. Intern U. Calif., San Francisco, 1966—67, resident in pediat., 1967—68, fellow in endometab, 1968—69, Wash. U., St. Louis, 1971—73; attending physician Tex. Childrens Hosp., Houston, 1993—; prof. pediat. Baylor Coll. Medicine, 1993—, dir. children's nutrition rsch. Contbr. articles to profl. jours. Mem.: NAS (mem. Inst. Medicine), Am. Acad. Pediat. Office: Baylor Coll Medicine 1100 Bates St Houston TX 77030

BIERIG, JACK R. lawyer, educator; b. Chgo., Apr. 10, 1947; s. Henry J. and Helga (Rothschild) B.; m. Barbara A. Winokur; children: Robert, Sarah. BA, Brandeis U., 1968; JD, Harvard U., 1972. Bar: Ill. 1972, U.S. Dist. Ct. (no. dist.) Ill. 1972, U.S. Ct. Appeals (1st-3d, 5th-11th and D.C. cirs.) 1974, U.S. Supreme Ct. 1980. Ptnr. Sidley Austin Brown & Wood, Chgo., 1972—; prof. Ill. Inst. Tech.-Chgo. Kent Coll. Law, 1974-95; lectr. law. U. Chgo. Law Sch. and Harris Sch. Pub. Policy , 2000—. Chmn. legal sect. Am. Soc. Assn. Execs., 1994-95. Contbr. articles to profl. jours. Pres. Neighborhood Justice Chgo., 1983-87; pres. Jewish Vocat. Svc., 1997-99. Mem. Ill. Assn. of Hosp. Attys. (pres. 1991), Chgo. Bar Assn. (bd. govs., 1982-84). Jewish. Club: Standard (Chgo.). Office: 1 Bank One Plz Chicago IL 60670-0001 E-mail: jbierig@sidley.com.

BIERLEY, PAUL EDMUND, musician, author, publisher; b. Portsmouth, Ohio, Feb. 3, 1926; s. William Frederick and Minnie Genieve (Atkin) B.; m. Pauline Jeanette Allison, Sept. 17, 1948; children: Lois Elaine Bierley Walker, John Emerson. B of Aero. Engring., Ohio State U., 1953, DMusic (hon.) , 2001. Aero. engr. N.Am. Aviation, Columbus, Ohio, 1953-73; engr., data mgr. Ellanef Mfg. Corp., 1973-88; tubist Columbus Symphony Orch., 1965-81, Detroit Concert Band, 1973-92. Lectr. in field. Author: John Philip Sousa, A Descriptive Catalog of His Works, 1973, John Philip Sousa, American Phenomenon, 1973, rev. edit., 1986 (Deems Taylor award 1986), Office Fun!, 1976, Hallelujah Trombone!, 1982, The Music of Henry Fillmore and Will Huff, 1982, The Works of John Philip Sousa, 1984, Sousa Band Fraternal Society News Index, 1997, (with Kozo Suzuki) All About Sousa Marches, 2001; co-author: (with K. Suzuki) All About Sousa Marches, 2001, also numerous articles, radio and TV copy, concert programs and record jackets; asst. condr., Rockwell Internat. Concert Band, 1961-76; tubist World Symphony Orch., N.Y.C., 1971, Hallelujah Brass Quintet, 1983-92, Brass Band of Columbus, 1984-97, Village Brass, 1993—; editor: Integrity Press, Columbus, 1982—, The Heritage Ency. of Band Music, 1991, supplement, 1996, El Capitan (John Philip Sousa), 1994, Marching Along (John Philip Sousa), 1994. Bd. trustees. Robert Hoe Found., Poughkeepsie, N.Y., 1984—, dir. rsch. Integrity Rsch. Found., 1999—. Recipient Deems Taylor award ASCAP, 1986, God and Country award Salvation Army, 1995, Ohioana Libr. Assn. Citation, 1996; inductee Wall of Fame, Portsmouth, Ohi, 1994, Columbus Sr. Musicians Hall of Fame, 1997. Mem. Am. Bandmasters Assn. (hon., Edwin Franko Goldman citation 1974), Am. Sch. Band Dirs. Assn. (assoc., A. Austin Harding award 1990), Am. Fedn. Musicians, Sonneck Soc. for Am. Music, Nat. Band Assn., Assn. Concert Bands, Tubists Universal Brotherhood Assn., Windjammers Unltd., John Philip Sousa Found. (Sudler medal 1986, Sudler Order of Merit 2001), Ohio Hist. Soc., Am. Aviation Hist. Soc., Westerville Hist. Soc., Masons, Phi Beta Mu (Outstanding Contbr. to Bands award 1983). Methodist.

BIERMAN, JANE, wood products company executive; Pres., founder Lincoln Wood Products, Inc., 1947—. Office: 701 N State St Merrill WI 54452-1355

BIGELOW, CHARLES CROSS, retired biochemist, retired university administrator; b. Edmonton, Alta., Can., Apr. 25, 1928; s. Sherburne Tupper and Helen Beatrice (Cross) B.; m. Elizabeth Rosemary Sellick, Aug. 22, 1977; children: Ann K. Bigelow Siess, David C. B.A.Sc., U. Toronto, 1953; M.Sc., McMaster U., 1955, Ph.D., 1957. Postdoctoral fellow Carlsberg Lab., Copenhagen, 1957-59; assoc. Sloan-Kettering Inst. Cancer Research, N.Y.C., 1959-62; asst. prof. chemistry U. Alta., Can., 1962-64, assoc. prof., 1964-65; vis. prof. Fla. State U., Tallahassee, 1965; assoc. prof. biochemistry U. Western Ont., London, Can., 1965-69, prof. Can., 1969-74; prof., head biochemistry Meml. U. Nfld., St. John's, Can., 1974-76; dean of sci., prof. chemistry St. Mary's U., Halifax, N.S., Can., 1977-79; dean of sci. U. Man., Winnipeg, Can., 1979-89, dean emeritus, 1990—, prof. chemistry Can., 1979-2000, ret., 2000. Fellow Univ. Coll., 1989, sr. adminstrv. fellow, 1993-94, Univ. Coll. provost 1995-97, sr. scholar, 1997-2000; vis. prof. U. Toronto, 1973-74; vis. scientist Nat. Inst. for Med. Rsch., London, 1984-85; chmn. Ont. Confedn. Univ. Faculty Assns., 1970-71; pres. Can. Assn. Univs. Tchrs., 1972-73. Contbr. articles on protein structure and denaturation to sci. jours. Bd. govs. U. Western Ont., 1972-73, U. Man., 1982-84, Man. Mus. of Man and Nature, 1986-91; bd. mgmt. TRIUMF, Vancouver, 1987-89; pres. N.S. New Democratic party, 1978-79; pres. Man. New Dem. party, 1982-84. Grantee NRC Can., Med. Research Council, Natural Scis. and Engring. Research Council Can. Fellow Chem. Inst. Can.; mem. Can. Biochem. Soc., Am. Chem. Soc., Am. Soc. Biol. Chemists, AAAS, Sigma Xi Home: 10 Eberts St Victoria BC Canada V85 5L6

BIGELOW, DANIEL JAMES, aerospace executive; b. Harrisville, Pa., Mar. 26, 1935; s. Raymond James and Hilda Irene (Graham) B.; m. Elizabeth Jane Allison, Sept. 10, 1955; 1 child, Allison Jane. BFA in Art Advt., Kent (Ohio) State U., 1957; MA in Edn., La. Tech. U., 1974; MS in Polit. Sci., Auburn U., 1986; MS, Air U., 1987; postgrad., Ohio State U., 1989—. Commd. 2d lt. USAF, 1957, advanced through grades to col., 1979, ret., 1987; command pilot 167 combat missions Vietnam; air attaché to Soviet Union, 1983-85; dir. Soviet program Air War Coll. Air U., Ala., 1985-87; gen. mgr. aerospace divsn. Modern Techs. Corp., Dayton, Ohio, 1988-98, dir. programs corp. hdqrs., 1998—2001, dir. bus. svcs. corp. hdqrs., 2002—. Contbr. articles to profl. jours.; author, editor: Soviet Studies, 1968—88. Decorated Legion of Merit with one oak leaf cluster, DFC, 14 Air medals, Def. Superior medal; recipient U.S. Am. Nat. award CIA Dir., William J. Casey, 1985. Mem. Acad. Polit. Sci., Air Rescue Assn. (nat. bd. dirs., historian), Air Force Assn. (v.p. state legis. affairs 2001-), Am. Def. Preparedness Assn., Discussion Club Dayton (v.p. 1999-2000), Internat. Platform Assn., F-86 Sabre Pilots' Assn., B-52 Stratofortress Assn., The Ret. Officers' Assn., Order Daedalians (flight capt., pres. 2001-02), Shriners, Airlift/Tanker Assn., Dayton Area Def. Contractors Assn. (pres. 1999-2000, bd. dirs.), Armed Forces Comms. and Electronics Assn., Def. Planning and Analysis Soc., Miami Valley Mil. Affairs Assn., Inst. of Navigation, Pararescue Assn., Internat. Test & Evaluation Assn., Pedro Helicopter Assn., Royal Air Force Club, Electronic Engring. and Mfg. Group, Air Force Mus. Found., Nat. Def. Indsl. Assn., Dayton Art Inst., Assn. Old Crows, Air Force Assn. of Cmty. Ptnrs., Dayton Area C. of C. (mil. affairs com.), Disting. Flying Cross Soc., Grand Lodge of Ancient Free Masons, Scottish Rite Bodies. Presbyterian. Avocations: art, photography, jogging. Home: 2537 Indian Wells Trl Xenia OH 45385-9373 E-mail: dbigelow@modtechcorp.com.

BIGGERT, JUDITH BORG, congresswoman, lawyer; b. Aug. 15, 1937; d. Alvin Andrew and Marjorie Virginia (Mailler) Borg; m. Rody Patterson Biggert, Sept. 21, 1963; children: Courtney Ray, Alison Mailler, Rody Patterson, Adrienne Taylor. BA, Stanford U., 1959; JD, Northwestern U., 1963. Bar: Ill. 1963. Law clk. to presiding justice U.S. Ct. Appeals (7th cir.), Chgo., 1963-64; sole practice Hinsdale, Ill., 1964—. Rep. Ill. Gen. Assembly, 1993-98, asst. Rep. leader, 1995-98; mem. U.S. Congress from 13th Ill. dist., 1999—, mem. fin. svcs. com., edn. and workforce com. stds. ofcl. conduct, sci. com., mem. bipartisan working group on youth violence, co-chair womens caucus, speakers task force for drug free Am. Mem. bd. editors Law Rev., Northwestern U. Sch. Law, 1961-63. Pres. Hinsdale Twp. High Sch. Dist. 86 Bd. Edn., 1983-85; pres. Jr. League Chgo., 1976-78, treas., bd. mgrs., 1966—; chmn. Hinsdale Antiques Show, 1980; pres. Oak Sch. PTA, Hinsdale, 1976-78; pres.-treas. Chgo. jr. bd. Travelers Aid Soc., 1965-70; Sunday sch. tchr. Grace Episcopal Ch., Hinsdale, 1978-80, 82-85; chair, treas., 2d v.p. bd. dirs. Vis. Nurses Assn. Chgo., 1978; bd. dirs. Salt Creek Ballet, 1990—98. Recipient Servian award Jr. aux. U. Chgo. Cancer Rsch. Foun., Woman of Yr. in Govt., Politics, and Civic Affairs DuPage YWCA, 1995, Spirit of Enterprise award U.S. C. of C.; named on of 100 Women Making a Difference; inductee to Hinsdale Ctrl. H.S. Hall of Fame, 1997. Mem. ABA, Ill. Bar Assn., DuPage Bar Assn., Coalition Women Legislatures. Republican. Office: US Ho of Reps 1213 Longworth House Off Bl Washington DC 20515-0001 also: 13th Dist of Ill 115 W 55th St Ste 100 Clarendon Hills IL 60514-1593*

BIGGINS, ROBERT A. state legislator; b. Oak Park, Ill., Oct. 20, 1946; m. Judy Biggins; children: Jennifer, Kevin. BA, Northeastern Ill. U., 1969. Assessor Addison Twp., Ill., 1973-77; Ill. state rep. Dist. 78, 1992—. Mem. Gen. Svcs., Consumer Protection, Fin. Insts. and Revenue Coms.; tchr. Mannheim Jr. H.S., Northlake, Ill., 1969, Daniel Webster Elem. Sch., Chgo., 1970-73; property tax cons., Chgo., 1977-81; ptnr. Property Assessment Advisors, Inc., 1981—, exec. v.p. Bd. dirs. Suburban Bank Elmhurst, 1975—, chmn., 1983-84; chmn. Bank of Bellwood, 1981-85; mem. Elmhurst Gardens Homeowners Assn. (past pres.), Edison Sch. PTA (past pres.). Recipient award Internat. Assn. Assessing Officers, 1990. Mem. DuPage County Assessors Assn. (legis. liaison 1975-76, pres. 1976), Inst. Property Taxation (cert.). Address: 114 W Park Ave Elmhurst IL 60126-3399

BIGGS, DONALD, state legislator; b. Kingman, Kans., Feb. 19, 1930; m. Alleta Biggs. BS, Kans. State U., 1952. With Home Savs. Assn., 1954-64; pres. Mut. Savs. Assn., 1964-95; mem. Kans. Senate, Topeka, 1996—, mem. agr. com., mem. fed. and state affairs com., ranking minority energy and natural resources com., mem. fin. instns. and ins. com., mem. joint com. on arts coun. and cultural resources. Mem. Leavenworth Coun. St. Mary Coll.; mem. Leavenworth (Kans.) Sch. Bd., 1977-85. With U.S. Army, 1952-54. Mem. Am. Legion, Sierra Club (Kansas City), Rotary (Leavenworth), KC. Democrat. Office: 300 SW 10th Ave Rm 140-n Topeka KS 66612-1504

BIGGS, J. O. lawyer, general industry company executive; b. Kansas City, Mo., Feb. 17, 1925; s. John Olin and Parilee Catherine (Story) B.; m. Marilyn Frances Sweeney, Dec. 27, 1947; children— Melissa Anne, John Kevin, Brian Sweeney. AB, U. Kans., 1947, LLB, 1949. Bar: Kan. bar 1949, Mo. bar 1950, Ia. bar 1953. With legal dept. Kansas City Life Ins. Co., 1950-51; exec. asst. to industry members Regional Wage Stblzn. Bd., 1951-52; dir. labor relations Meredith Pub. Co., 1952-58; with Gustin-Bacon Mfg. Co. (merger into Certain-teed Products Corp. 1966), 1958—, v.p., asst. to pres., 1962-63, pres., chief exec. officer, 1963-66; exec. v.p. Ardmore, Pa., 1966-69; pres. Thermo-Kinetic Corp., 1969-76; mem. firm Wagner, Leek & Mullins, 1976—. Cons. in field; sr. v.p., gen. counsel Exec. Hills, Inc., Shawnee Mission, Kans., 1979—. Active Big Bros. of Tucson. Mem. Am., Mo., Kans., Johnson County bar assns., Kansas City Met. Bar Assn., Am. Mgmt. Assn., Sigma Alpha Epsilon, Phi Alpha Phi. Republican. Presbyn. Clubs: Skyline (Tucson), Country (Tucson); Carriage (Kansas City). Home: 8743 Riggs Ln Shawnee Mission KS 66212-1281 Office: 7101 College Blvd Ste 1100 Shawnee Mission KS 66210-2078

BIGGS, ROBERT DALE, Near Eastern studies educator; b. Pasco, Wash., June 13, 1934; s. Robert Lee and Elenora Christina (Jensen) B. B.A. in Edn, Eastern Wash. Coll. Edn., 1956; Ph.D., Johns Hopkins U., 1962. Research asso. Oriental Inst., Univ. Chgo., 1963-64; asst. prof. Assyriology, 1964-67, asso. prof., 1967-72, prof., 1972—. Author: ŠÀ.ZI.GA: Ancient Mesopotamian Potency Incantations, 1967, Inscriptions from Tell Abu Salabikh, 1974, Inscriptions from al-Hiba-Lagash: The First and Second Seasons, 1976; co-author: Cuneiform Texts from Nippur, 1969, Nippur II: The North Temple and Sounding E, 1978; editor: Discoveries from Kurdish Looms, 1983; assoc. editor: Assyrian Dictionary, 1964-87; editor Jour. Near Ea. Studies, 1972—; mem. editorial bd. Assyrian Dictionary, 1995—. Fulbright scholar Univ. Toulouse, France, 1956-57; fellow Baghdad Sch., Am. Schs. Oriental Rsch., 1962-63, Am. Rsch. Inst. in Turkey, 1972, Danforth fellow, 1956-62. Mem. Am. Oriental Soc. (pres. Mid. Western br. 1978-79), Archaeol. Inst. Am. (pres. Chgo. soc. 1985-92), Brit. Sch. Archaeology Iraq. Office: U Chgo 1155 E 58th St Chicago IL 60637-1540

BILCHIK, GARY B. lawyer; b. Cleve., Dec. 7, 1945; s. Hyman M. and Leah (Gitleson) B.; m. Janice Rossen, Dec. 26, 1971; children: Susan, Steven. BBA, Ohio U., 1967; JD cum laude, Ohio State U., 1971. Bar: Ohio 1971, Fla. 1981. Atty., ptnr. Benesch, Friedlander, Coplan & Aronoff LLP, Cleve., 1981—. V.p. Jewish Family Svc., Cleve.; treas. Council Gardens, Cleve. Recipient Danzig Leadership award Jewish Family Svc., 1992. Mem. ABA, Ohio State Bar Assn., Cleve. Bar Assn. Democrat. Home: 25415 Letchworth Rd Cleveland OH 44122-4187

BILELLO, JOHN CHARLES, materials science and engineering educator; b. Bklyn., Oct. 15, 1938; s. Charles and Catherine (Buonadonna) B.; m. Mary Josephine Gloria, Aug. 1, 1959; children: Andrew Charles, Peter Angelo, Matthew Jonathan. B.E., NYU, 1960, M.S., 1962; Ph.D., U. Ill., 1965. Sr. rsch. engr. Gen. Telephone & Electronics Lab., Bayside, N.Y., 1965-67; mem. faculty SUNY, Stony Brook, 1967-87, asst. prof., 1967-71, assoc. prof., 1971-75, prof. engring., 1975-87, dean, 1977-81; dean Sch. Engring and Computer Sci., prof. mech. engring. Calif. State U., Fullerton, 1986-89; prof. materials sci. and engring., prof. applied physics U. Mich., Ann Arbor, 1989—, dir. Ctr. for Nanomaterials Scis., 1995—. Vis. prof. Poly. of Milan, 1973-74; vis. scholar King's Coll., London U., 1983; vis. fellow NATO exchange scholar Oxford U., 1986; project dir. synchroton topography project Univ. Consortium, 1981-86; NATO vis. fellow Oxford (Eng.) U., 1998—. NATO sr. faculty fellow Enrico Fermi Center, Milan, Italy, 1973 Fellow Am. Soc. for Metals; mem. AIME, Am. Phys. Soc., Materials Rsch. Soc. Office: U Mich Dept Material Sci Engring Ann Arbor MI 48109

BILEYDI, SUMER, advertising agency executive; b. Antalya, Turkey, Feb. 7, 1936; came to U.S., 1957; s. Abdurrahman M. and Neriman (Akman) B.; m. Lois E. Goode, Dec. 30, 1961; children: Can M., Sera N. BA, Mich. State U., 1961, MA, 1962. Mktg. cons. Export Promotion Ctr., Ankara, 1962; planner Gardner Advt. Agy., St. Louis, 1963-65; planning supr. Batten, Barton, Durstine & Osborn, N.Y.C., 1965-69; assoc. dir. Ketchum, Macleod & Grove, Pitts., 1969-73; sr. ptnr., dir. Carmichael Lynch, Inc., Mpls., 1974-91, sr. ptnr., 1992-98; CEO, pres. Manajans/Thompson AS, Istanbul, Turkey, 1999-2001, ret. Turkey, 2001. Cons. Carmichael-Lynch, Mpls., 1999—; cons. Leading Ind. Advt. Agy. Network, 1987-89, chmn., pres., 1989-91. Contbr. articles to profl. jours. Pres. Turkish Am. Assn., 1974-75. Mem. Am. Mktg. Assn., Advt. Rsch. Found., Advt. Fedn. Minn., Min. Turkish Am. Club. Home: 16670 Baywood Terr Eden Prairie MN 55346 E-mail: sumer.bileydi@jwt.com.

BILLER, JOEL WILSON, lawyer, former foreign service officer; b. Milw., Jan. 17, 1929; s. Saul Earl and Mildred (Wilson) B.; m. Geraldine Pollack, May 1, 1955; children— Sydney, Andrew, Charles. B.A., U. Wis., 1950; J.D., U. Mich., 1953; M.A., Northwestern U., 1959. Bar: Wis. 1953. Atty., Milw., 1953-55; vice consul Am. consulate, Le Havre, France, 1956-58; econ. officer Am. Embassy, The Hague, Netherlands, 1959-62; internat. relations officer State Dept., Washington, 1962-66; econ. officer, asst. dir. AID mission, Quito, Ecuador, 1966-69; econ. counselor Am. embassy, Buenos Aires, Argentina, 1969-71; dir. AID mission, Santiago, Chile, 1971-73; spl. asst. to undersec. state for econ. affairs Washington, 1973-74; spl. asst. to dep. sec. state, 1974; dep. asst. sec. state for comml. and spl. bilateral affairs, 1974-76; dep. asst. sec. state for transp., telecommunications and comml. affairs, after, 1976; sr. v.p. Manpower Inc., Milw., 1979-97, sr. v.p., gen. counsel, 1997-98; pvt. practice bus. cons., 1999—. Mem. Am. Fgn. Service Assn., Wis. Bar Assn. Office: Manpower Inc 5301 N Ironwood Rd PO Box 2053 Milwaukee WI 53201-2053

BILLER, JOSE, neurologist; b. Montevideo, Uruguay, Jan. 18, 1948; B in Medicine, A.V. Acevedo Inst., Montevideo, Uruguay, 1965; MD, U. de la Republica, Montevideo, Uruguay, 1974. Diplomate Am. Bd. Psychiatry and Neurology (bd. dirs. 1994—). Intern Columbus Hosp., Chgo., 1976-77; resident in neurology Henry Ford Hosp., Detroit, 1977-78, Loyola U. Hosp., Maywood, Ill., 1978-80; fellow cerebral vascular diseases Bowman Gray Sch. Med., Winston Salem, N.C., 1980-81; asst. prof. neurology Loyola U., Chgo., 1982-84, U. Iowa Coll. Medicine, Iowa City, 1984-87, assoc. prof. neurology, 1987-90, prof. neurology, 1990-91; prof. Northwestern Sch. Medicine, Chgo., 1991-94; dir. stroke program, dir. acute stroke care unit Northwestern Meml. Hosp., 1991-94; prof., chmn. dept. neurology Ind. U., 1994—. Prof. ad-honorem U. of the Republic Sch. of Medicine, Uruguay, 1997—; mem. editl. bd. Stroke, Stroke-Clin. Update, Journal of Stroke and Cerebrovascular Disease, Neurol. Rsch.; Internat. bd. editors: CNS Drugs; cons. physician neurology svc. VA Hosp., Iowa City, 1984-91, staff physician Northwestern Meml. Hosp., Chgo., 1991-94; neurology cons. Rehab. Inst. Chgo., 1991-94; active med. staff Ind. U. Hosps., 1994—, cons. Roudebush VA Med. Ctr., 1994—. Author, co-author of more than 350 articles, book chpts., abstracts; 6 edited books. Fellow ACP, Am. Acad. Neurology, Stroke Coun. Am. Heart Assn.; mem. AMA, N.Y. Acad. Sci., Am. Soc. for Neurology Investigation, Internat. Stroke Soc., Inter-Am. Coll. Physicians and Surgeons, Am. Neurolog. Assn., Am. Heart Assn., Argentinian Neurol. Soc. (hon.), Uruguayan Neurol. Soc. (hon.). Office: Ind U Sch of Medicine Dept Neurology Emerson Hall 545 Barnhill Dr # 125 Indianapolis IN 46202-5112

BILLER, LESLIE STUART, banker; b. N.Y.C., Mar. 16, 1948; s. Max David and Sylvia (Gottesman) B.; m. Sheri Jean Wolfson, Aug. 7, 1969; 1 child, Kimberly. BS in Chem. Engring., CCNY, 1969; MBA in Mgmt., Xavier U., 1973. Engr. Proctor & Gamble, Cin., 1969-73; prodn. analyst Citicorp., N.Y.C., 1973-76, bus. mgr. Italy, 1976-82, regional bus. mgr. Eng., 1982-85; exec. v.p. consumer markets Bank Am., San Francisco, 1985-87; pres., COO, vice chmn. Norwest Corp., Mpls., 1987—. Avocations: golf, skiing. Office: Norwest Corp 420 Montgomery St San Francisco CA 94104

BILLIG, ETEL JEWEL, theater director, actress; b. N.Y.C., Dec. 16, 1932; d. Anthony and Martha Rebecca (Klebansky) Papa; m. Steven S. Billig, Dec. 23, 1956 (dec. Aug. 1996); children: Curt Adam, Jonathan Roark. BS, NYU, 1953, MA, 1955; student, Herbert Berghof Studio, N.Y.C., 1955-56. Cert. elem. and high sch. tchr. Actress Washington Square Players, N.Y.C., 1950-55, Dukes Oak Theatre, Cooperstown, N.Y., 1955, Triple Cities Playhouse, Binghampton, 1956, Candlelight Dinner Playhouse, Summit, Ill., 1970, 73, 77, 79, 90; mng. dir. Theatre 31, Park Forest, 1971-73; asst. mgr. Westroads Dinner Theatre, Omaha, 1973-76; mng. dir., actress Forum Theatre, 1973, 94; mng. dir., actress, producing dir. Ill. Theatre Ctr., Park Forest, 1976—; mng. dir., actress Goodman Theatre, Chgo., 1987, 95, Ct. Theatre, 1990, Wisdom Bridge Theatre, 1991; dir. drama Rich Ctrl. H.S., Olympia Fields, Ill., 1978-86. Del. League of Chgo. Theatres Russian Exchange to Soviet Union, 1989; actress Drury Lane, Oak Brook, Ill., 1989; cons. and lectr. in field. Appeared in films including the Dollmaker, Running Scared, Straight Talk, Stolen Summer; (TV series) Hawaiian Heat, Missing Persons, Untouchables. V.p. Nat. Coun. Jewish Women, Park Forest, 1968-70; sec. Community Arts Coun., Park Forest, 1984-86; pres. Southland Regional Arts Coun., 1986-92. Recipient Risk Taking award NOW, 1982; grantee Nebr. Arts Coun., 1975, Ill. Arts Coun., 1995, 96, 2000, Athena award Matteson Area C. of C., 1997, Abby Found. award, 1997; named to Park Forest Hall of Fame, 2000. Mem. AFTRA, SAG, Actors' Equity Assn., League Chgo. Theatres, Ill. Arts Coun. Theatre Panel, Prodrs. Assn. Chgo. Area Theatre (sec. 1988-89), Bus. in the Arts Coun. of C. of C. (charter), Rotary (bd. dirs. Park Forest chpt. 1988-97, sec. 2000, hall of fame 2000). Avocations: travel, antiques. Office: Ill Theatre Ctr PO Box 397 Park Forest IL 60466-0397 E-mail: ilthctr@bigplanet.com.

BILLIG, THOMAS CLIFFORD, publishing and marketing executive; b. Pitts., Aug. 20, 1930; s. Thomas Clifford and Melba Helen S. B.; m. Helen Page Hine, May 14, 1951; children: Thomas Clifford, James Frederick. BSBA summa cum laude, Northwestern U., 1956. Ins. mgr., asst. dir. pers., asst. to chmn. Butler Bros. (now City Products Corp.), Chgo., 1954-59; market rsch. mgr. R.R. Donnelley & Sons, 1959-61; pres., dir. Indsl. Fiber Glass Products Corp., Scottville and Ludington, Mich., 1962-69; cons. mass mktg. mgr. Mpls., 1969-71; v.p. Mail Mktg. Systems and Services, St. Paul and Bloomington, Minn., 1971-74; pres., chmn., chief exec. officer Billig Communications (formerly Billig & Assocs.), Duluth, 1974—; pres. NIARS Corp., 1974-85, 95—, also bd. dirs.; pres. Fins and Feathers Pub. Co., Mpls., 1977-89; also bd. dirs. Fins. and Feathers Pub. Co.; pres., dir. North Coast Mktg. Corp., St. Paul, 1992—; chmn., CEO Sportsman's Mktg. Inc., Superior, Wis., Lake Elmo, Minn., 1998—, also bd. dirs. Author Nat. Ins. Advt. Regulation Svc., 1972—. Author, pub. NAIC Model Laws, Regulations and Guidelines, 1976-83. Served with USNR, 1948-56. Recipient Samuel Dresner Plotkin award Northwestern U., 1956 Mem. Delta Mu Delta, Beta Gamma Sigma. Office: 1423 N 8th St Superior WI 54880-6664 also: 3390 Lake Elmo Ave N Lake Elmo MN 55042-9799 E-mail: niarsi@aol.com.

BILLINGS, CHARLES EDGAR, physician; b. Boston, June 15, 1929; s. Charles Edgar and Elizabeth (Sanborn) B.; m. Lillian Elizabeth Wilson, Apr. 16, 1955; 1 dau., Lee Ellen Billings Kreinbihl. Student, Wesleyan U., 1947-49; M.D., N.Y. U., 1953; M.Sc. (Link Found. fellow), Ohio State U., 1960. Diplomate: Am. Bd. Preventive Medicine. Instr. to prof. depts. preventive medicine and aviation Sch. Medicine Ohio State U., 1960-73, dir. div. environ. health Sch. Medicine, 1970-73, clin. prof. Sch. Medicine, 1973-83, prof. emeritus, 1983—; rsch. scientist indsl. and systems engring., 1992—. Med. officer NASA Ames Rsch. Ctr., Moffett Field, Calif., 1973-76; chief Aviation Safety Rsch. Office, 1976-80, asst. chief for rsch. Man-Vehicle Systems rsch. divsn., 1980-83, sr. scientist, 1983-91; chief scientist Ames Rsch. Ctr., 1991-92; cons. Beckett Aviation Corp., 1962-73; surgeon gen. U.S. Army, 1965-77, FAA, 1967-70, 75, 83; mem. NATO-AGARD Aerospace Med. Panel, 1980-86; assoc. advisor USAF Sci. Adv. Bd., 1978-90; mem. human factors adv. panel U.K. Civil Aviation Authority, 1999-2001; mem. aviation adv. bd. Ohio U., 2000-01. Contbr. chpts. to books, numerous articles in field to med. jours. Served to maj. USAF, 1955-57. Recipient Air Traffic Svc. award FAA, 1969, Walter M. Boothby rsch. award, 1972, PATCO Air Safety award, 1979, Disting. Svc. award Flight Safety Found., 1979, John A. Tamisea award, 1980, Laura Taber Barbour Air Safety medal, 1981, Outstanding Leadership medal NASA, 1981, 90, Jeffries Aerospace Med. Rsch. medal AIAA, 1986, Lovelace award NASA Soc. Flight Surgeons, 1996, Forrest and Pamela Bird award Civil Aviation Med. Assn., 2001, Henry L. Taylor Founders award Aerospace Human Factors Assn, 2002; Ames Rsch. Ctr. fellow, 1989. Fellow AIAA (assoc.), Royal Aero. Soc., Aerospace Med. Assn. (pres. 1979-80); mem. AMA, Internat. Acad. Aviation and Space Medicine, Am. Whippet Club, Midland Whippet Club, RAF Club (Gt. Britain). Home: 1372 Hickory Ridge Ln Columbus OH 43235-1131 Office: 265 Baker ISE Bldg 1971 Neil Ave Columbus OH 43210-1210

BILLION, JOHN JOSEPH, orthopedic surgeon, former state representative; b. Sioux Falls, S.D., Mar. 4, 1939; s. Henry Alphonse and Evelyn Margaret (Heinz) B.; div.; children: Matthew, Suzanne, John, James, Jane; m. Deborah Wagner, Mar. 22, 1980; children: Timothy, Allyson. BA, Loras Coll., 1960; MD, Stritch-Loyola U., 1964. Diplomate Am. Bd. Orthopedic Surgery. Resident orthopedics St. Francis Hosp., Peoria, Ill., 1964-69; orthopedic surgeon Sioux Falls, 1971-96; state rep. State of S.D., 1992-96. Vice chair S.D. Dem. party, 1997-98. Maj. USAF, 1969-71. Fellow Am. Acad. Orthopedic Surgeons. Democrat.

BILLUPS, CHAUNCEY, professional basketball player; b. Sept. 25, 1976; Student, U. Colo., 1997. Guard Boston Celtics, 1996-97, Toronto Raptors, 1997-98, Denver Nuggets, 1998-00, Minnesota Timberwolves, Minneapolis, 2000—. Named Second Team All-Am. AP. Avocation: music. Office: Minn Timberwolves 600 1st Ave North Minneapolis MN 55403-9801

BILLUPS, NORMAN FREDRICK, college dean, pharmacist, educator; b. Portland, Oreg., Oct. 15, 1934; s. John Alexander and Myrtle I. (Morris) B.; m. Shirley Mae Brooks, July 7, 1956; children: Tamra Mae, Timothy Fredrick. Student, Portland State U., 1952-55; BS in Pharmacy, Oreg. State U., 1958, MS in Pharmacy, 1961, PhD (Am. Found. Pharm. Edn. fellow), 1963. Instr. Oreg. State U., 1958-60, grad. asst., 1960-63; asso. prof. pharmacy U. Ky., 1963-73, prof., 1974-77; dean, prof. pharmacy Coll. Pharmacy, U. Toledo, 1977-00; pharmacist Ohio, Oreg., Ky., 1961—. Dir. internat. adv. com. Pharm@Sea. Author: American Drug Index, ann, 1977— . Lay leader, chmn. pastor-parish com. local Meth. Ch. Recipient Rsch. Achievement award Am. Soc. Hosp. Pharmacists, 1975, Outstanding Svc. award Ky. Pharm. Assn., 1977; NIH rsch. fellow, 1962-63; Dr. Norman F. Billups Disting. Svc. award established by U. Toledo Pharmacy Alumni Assn., 1992. Mem. Am. Assn. Colls. Pharmacy (Lyman award 1971), Am. Pharm. Assn., Ohio Pharm. Assn. (bd.dirs. Beal award 2001), Ohio Soc. Hosp. Pharmacists, Toledo Acad. Pharmacy (bd. dirs., Pharmacist of Yr. 1997), Coun. Ohio Colls. Pharmacy (chmn. bd. trustees, chmn. coun.), Sigma Xi, Phi Kappa Phi (pres. U. Toledo chpt.), Rho Chi (chpt. advisor, nat. exec. com.). Phi Lambda Sigma (chpt. adv.), Kappa Psi (grand coun. dep., nat. officer), Lambda Kappa Sigma (hon. mem., nat. patron). Office: Univ Toledo Coll Pharmacy 2801 W Bancroft St Toledo OH 43606-3328 E-mail: snbillups@aol.com.

BILYEU, GARY EDWARD, government official; b. Forest City, Iowa, Nov. 9, 1954; s. Roy Marcellus and Norma Jean (Hillesland) B.; m. Lonnie Jo Ann Bartel, Apr. 6, 1974; children: Rachel, Rebekah, Abraham, Deborah. AA, North Iowa Area Cmty. Coll., 1975. Cert. gen. real property appraiser, Iowa. Field appraiser Mason City (Iowa) Assessor, 1976-77, deputy assessor, 1977-80, Cerro Gordo County, Mason City, 1980-82; assessor Story County, Nevada, Iowa, 1982—; assessment adminstrn. specialist IAAO, 1998—. Author: Reference Handbook for Iowa's Property Tax System, 1999; contbr. articles to profl. jours. Apptd. pub. mem. Legis. Task Force to study Iowa's Sys. of State and Local Taxation, 1997. Mem. Internat. Assn. of Assessing Officers (assessment adminstrn. specialist designation 1998, sect. chair 1995-96). Mem. Assembly of God. Avocations: sports, basketball. Office: Story County 900 6th St Nevada IA 50201-2004

BINDER, CHARLES E. magistrate judge; b. Kalamazoo, Apr. 23, 1949; married; two children. BA, Western Mich. U., 1971; JD, Duke U., 1974. Law clk. to Hon. Wendell Miles, 1974-76; pvt. practice, 1976-84; magistrate judge U.S. Dist. Ct. (ea. dist.) Mich., Bay City, 1984—. Mem. Fed. Magistrate Judges Assn., State Bar Mich., Bay County Bar Assn. Office: US Dist Ct Ea Dist Mich 1000 Washington Ave Rm 323 Bay City MI 48708-5749 Fax: (517) 894-8819.

BINDLEY, WILLIAM EDWARD, pharmaceutical executive; b. Terre Haute, Ind., Oct. 6, 1940; s. William F. and Gertrude (Lynch) B.; children: William Franklin, Blair Scott, Sally Ann. BS, Purdue U., 1961; grad. wholesale mgmt. program, Stanford U., 1966. Asst. treas. Controls Co. Am., Melrose Park, Ill., 1962-65; vice-chmn. E.H. Bindley & Co., Terre Haute, 1965-68; pres., chmn. bd., CEO Bindley Western Industries, Inc., Indpls., 1968—. Scholl scholarship guest lectr. Loyola U., Chgo., 1982; guest lectr. Young Pres. Orgn., Palm Springs, Calif. and Dallas, 1981, 82, 84, Ctr. for Entrepreneurs, Indpls., 1983, Purdue U., West Lafayette, Inc., De Pauw U., Greencastle, Ind., disting. lectr. Georgetown U., Washington, 1989—, mem. adv. bd.; bd. dirs. Key Bank NA, Cleve., Shoe Carnival, Inc.; former owner basketball team Ind. Pacers. State dir. Bus. for Reagan-Bush, Washington and Indpls., 1980; trustee Marian Coll., Indpls., Indpls. United Way, St. Vincent Hosp., Indpls.; bd. dirs. Indpls. Entrepreneurship Acad., Nat. Entrepreneurship Found., U.S. Ski Team, chmn. fin., exec. com. mem.; mem. adv. bd. Rose Hulman Inst. Tech.; mem. pres.'s coun. Purdue U., dean's adv. bd. Named Hon. Ky. Col., 1980, Sagamore of the Wabash, Gov. Orr, State of Ind., 1989, Entrepreneur of Yr., State of Ind., 1992. Mem. Young Pres. Orgn. (area dir., chmn. 1982, award 1983), Nat. Wholesale Druggists Assn. (dir. 1981-84, Svc. award 1984), Purdue U. Alumni Assn. (life), Woodstock Club, Meridian Hills Countryn Club. Republican. Roman Catholic. Avocations: skiing; tennis; golf; boating. Address: Bindley Western Ind 8909 Purdue Rd Indianapolis IN 46268-3146 Office: Bindley Western Industries Inc Ste 300 8909 Purdue Rd Indianapolis IN 46268-3146

BINFORD, GREGORY GLENN, lawyer; b. Canton, Ohio, Oct. 8, 1948; s. Edwin and Helen Marie B. BA, Case Western Res. U., 1970, JD, 1973. Bar: Ohio 1973. Ptnr. Guren, Merritt, Cleve., 1973-84, Benesch, Friedlander, Cleve., 1984—. Mem. men's com. Cleve. Playhouse, 1980—. Mem. ABA, Nat. Health Lawyers Assn., Cleve. Bar Assn. (chair health law sect.), Ohio State Bar Assn. Office: Benesch Friedlander America Bldg 200 Public Sq Ste 2300 Cleveland OH 44114-2378

BING, DAVID, retired basketball player, metal products executive; b. Washington, Nov. 29, 1943; children: Cassaundra, Bridgett, Aleisha. BA in Econ., Syracuse U., 1966. With Detroit Pistons, 1966-74, Wash. Bullets, 1975-77, Boston Celtics, 1977-78; owner, chmn., CEO, The Bing Group, Detroit, 1980—. Named Rookie of Yr., 1967, Basketball Hall of Fame, 1989, Most Valuable Player, NBA All-Star Game, 1976, Nat. Small Bus. Person of Yr., 1984, Nat. Minority Suppplier of Yr., 1984; recipient Schick Achievement award, 1990. Achievements include named to First Team NBA All Star, 1968, 71, Second Team, 1974, All Rookie Team, 1967; leading scorer in Syracuse U. history; All-Star 7 times. Office: The Bing Group 11500 Oakland St Detroit MI 48211-1073

BINGAY, JAMES S. banking executive; b. Seattle; m. Jean Bingay. BS in Econs., Brown U., 1965; MS in Fin., U. Pa., 1967. Regional exec. Citibank, Cleve., 1970-90; group exec. v.p. Key Corp, 1990—. Trustee Cleve. Play House, Cleve. Coun. on World Affairs; bd. dirs. Nat. Corp. Theatre Fund, Cleve. Inst. of Music. Lt. USN, 1967-70. Office: Key Corp 127 Public Sq Cleveland OH 44114-1216

BINGHAM, CHRISTOPHER, statistics educator; b. N.Y.C., Apr. 16, 1937; s. Alfred Mitchell and Sylvia (Knox) B.; m. Carolyn Higinbotham, Sept. 23, 1967 A.B., Yale U., 1958, M.A., 1960, Ph.D., 1964. Research fellow Conn. Agrl. Expt. Sta., New Haven, 1958-64; research assoc. in math. and biology Princeton U., N.J., 1964-66; asst. prof. stats. U. Chgo., 1967-72; assoc. prof. applied stats. U. Minn., Mpls., 1972-79, prof., 1979—. Contbr. articles to profl. jours. Fellow Am. Statis. Assn., Inst. Math. Stats.; mem. Royal Statis. Soc., Biometric Soc., Soc. Indsl. and Applied Math. Unitarian. Home: 605 Winston Ct Mendota Heights MN 55118-1039 Office: U Minn Sch Stats 313 Ford Hall 224 Church St SE Minneapolis MN 55455-0493 E-mail: kb@stat.umn.edu.

BINSFELD, CONNIE BERUBE, former state official; b. Munising, Mich., Apr. 18, 1924; d. Omer J. and Elsie (Constance) Berube; m. John E. Binsfeld, July 19, 1947; children: John T., Gregory, Susan, Paul, Michael. BS, Siena Heights Coll., 1945, DHL (hon.), 1977; LLD (hon.), Mich. State U., 1998; DHL (hon.), Mich. State Univ., 1998, Thomas Cooley Sch. of Law, 1999; LLD (hon.), Grand Valley State U., 2000, Lake Superior State U., 2000; DHL (hon.), U. Notre Dame, 2000, Grand Valley State U., 2000. County commr. Leelanau County, Mich., 1970-74; mem. Mich. Ho. of Reps., 1974-82, asst. rep. leader, 1979-81; del. Nav. Conv., 1980, 88, 92; mem. Mich. Senate, 1982-90, asst. rep. leader, 1979, 81; lt. gov. State of Mich., 1990-98. Mem. adv. bd. Nat. Park Sys. Named Mich. Mother of Yr., Mich. Mothers Com., 1977; Northwestern Mich. Coll. fellow. Mem. Nat. Coun. State Legislators, LWV, Siena Heights Coll. Alumnae Assn. Republican. Roman Catholic.

BINSTOCK, ROBERT HENRY, public policy educator, writer, lecturer; b. New Orleans, Dec. 6, 1935; s. Louis and Ruth (Atlas) B.; m. Martha Burns, July 27, 1979; 1 dau., Jennifer. AB, Harvard U., 1956, PhD, 1965. Lectr. Brandeis U., Waltham, Mass., 1963-65, asst. prof., 1965-69, assoc. prof., 1969-72, Stulberg Prof. law and politics, 1972-84, dir. Policy Ctr. Aging, 1979-84; prof. aging, health and soc. Case Western Res. U., Cleve., 1985—. Mem. com. on an Aging Soc. Nat. Acad. Scis., Washington, 1982-86. Author: America's Political System, 1972, 5th edit., 1991, America's Political System: Urban, State and Local, 1972, 3d edit., 1979, Feasible Planning for Social Change, 1966; editor: The Politics of the Powerless, 1971, Too Old for Health Care?, 1991, Dementia and Aging, 1992, International Perspectives on Aging: Population and Policy Changes, 1982, Handbook of Aging and the Social Sciences, 1976, 5th edit., 2001, The Future of Long Term Care, 1996, Home Care Advances: Essential Research and Policy Issues, 2000, The Lost Art of Caring: A Challenge to Health Professionals, Families, Communities and Society, 2001. Bd. dirs. White House Task Force on Older Ams., 1967-68; chmn. adv. panel Office Tech. Assessment, U.S. Congress, 1982-84 ; tech. adviser, del. White House Conf. on Aging, 1971, 81; trustee Boston Biomed. Research Inst., 1971-84; mem. gov.'s adv. com. Dept. of Elder Affairs Mass., 1974-84; chair, adv. bd. Nat. Acad. on Aging, 1991-95. Recipient Haak-Lilliefors award Mich. State U., 1979, Arthur S. Flemming award Nat. Assn. State Units on Aging, 1988, Key award APHA, 1992, Am. Soc. Aging award, 1994; fellow Ford Found., 1959-69; rsch. grantee NIH, 1968-73. Fellow Gerontol. Soc. Am. (pres. 1976, Donald P. Kent award 1981, Brookdale Prize award 1983), Assn. Gerontol. in Higher Edn.; mem. APHA (chair gerontol. health sect. 1996-97). Office: Case Western Res Univ 2040 Adelbert Rd Cleveland OH 44106-4901

BIONDI, LAWRENCE, university administrator, priest; b. Chgo., Dec. 15, 1938; s. Hugo and Albertina (Marchetti) B. B.A., Loyola U., Chgo., 1962, Ph.L., 1964, M.Div., S.T.L., Loyola U., 1971; M.S., Georgetown U., 1966, Ph.D. in Socioloinguistics, 1975. Ordained priest Roman Cath. Ch., 1970. Joined Soc. Jesus; asst. prof. sociolinguistics Loyola U., Chgo., 1974-79, assoc. prof., 1979-81, prof., 1982-87, dean Coll. Arts and Scis., 1980-87; pres. St. Louis U., 1987—. Mem. Joint Commn. on Accreditation of Health Care Orgs., 1998—. Author: The Italian-American Child: His Sociolinguistic Acculturation, 1975, Poland's Solidarity Movement, 1984; editor: Poland's Church-State Relations in the 1980s, 1980, Spain's Church-State Relations, 1982. Trustee Xavier U., 1981-87, Loyola Coll., Balt., 1988-94, Santa Clara U., 1988-98, Kenrick-Glennon Sem., 1988-94, St. Louis U., 1982—, Loyola U., Chgo., 1988-97; bd. dirs. Epilepsy Found. Am., 1985-95, Civic Progress, St. Louis, 1987—, Regional Commerce and Growth Assn., 1987—, Mo. Bot. Gardens, 1987—, St. Louis Zoo, 1994, St. Louis Symphony, 1994, Harry S. Truman Inst. for Nat. and Internat. Affairs, 1987—, Tenet Health Care Sys., 1998—, St. Louis Sci. Ctr., 2000—, Boys Hope Girls Hope, 1996—, St. Louis Art Mus., 1997—, Grand Ctr., St. Louis, 1987—. Mellon grantee, 1974, 75, 76, 82 Mem. Linguistic Soc. Am., MLA, Am. Anthrop. Assn. Office: St Louis U 221 N Grand Blvd Saint Louis MO 63103-2006

BIRCK, MICHAEL JOHN, manufacturing company executive, electrical engineer; b. Missoula, Mont., Jan. 25, 1938; s. Raymond Michael and Mildred (Johnson) B.; m. Katherine Royer, Sept. 3, 1960; children: Kevin, Joni Birck Stevenson, Christopher. BSEE, Purdue U., 1960, PhD in Engring. (hon.), 1995; MSEE, NYU, 1962. Mem. tech. staff Bell Tel. Labs., Murray Hill, N.J., 1960-66; dir. engring. Communication Apparatus Corp., Melrose Park, Ill., 1967-68, Wescom, Inc., Downers Grove, 1968-75; pres. Tellabs, Inc., Lisle, 1975—, pres., CEO. Mem. engring. adv. coun. U. Notre Dame, 1983-91; bd. dirs. Profl. Tng. Ctrs., Inc., Hinsdale, Ill., ITW, Glenview, Ill., USF&G, Balt., Molex Inc., Lisle, Ill. Patentee in field. Dir. Purdue Rsch. Found., West Lafayette, 1989—; mem. bus. adv. com. to Rep. Harris Fawell, Washington, 1986—; trustee Benedictine Univ., 1988—; mem. pres.'s coun. Purdue U., 1984—; bd. dirs. Hinsdale Hosp., 1995. Recipient High Tech Entrepreneur award Crain's Ill. Bus., Chgo., 1984, Outstanding Engring. Alumni award Purdue U., 1991, Outstanding Master Entrepreneur award Inc. Mag./Ernst & Young, 1995; named Outstanding Elec. Engring. Alumnus Purdue U., 1995. Mem. Telecommunications Industry Assn. (chmn. pub. rels. 1989-90, bd. dirs., vice-chmn. 1984-91, chmn. 1991), Hinsdale Golf Club, Salt Creek Tennis Club (pres. 1986). Republican. Roman Catholic. Avocations: running, tennis, golf. Office: Tellabs Inc 4951 Indiana Ave Lisle IL 60532-1698

BIRD, FORREST M. retired medical inventor; b. Stoughton, Mass., June 9, 1921; Technical air trng. officer Army Air Corps. Inventor Bird Universal Medical Respirator for acute or chronic cardiopulmonary care, 1958, "Babybird" respirator, 1970. Inductee Nat. Inventors Hall of Fame, 1995. Office: Nat Inventors Hall of Fame 221 S Broadway St Akron OH 44308-1505

BIRD, LARRY JOE, former professional basketball player, coach; b. West Baden, Ind., Dec. 7, 1956; s. Joe and Georgia B; m. Dinah Mattingly Oct. 1, 1989. Student, Ind. U., 1974, Northwood Inst., West Baden, Ind., 1974; BS, Ind. State U., 1979. Player Boston Celtics, 1979-92, spl. asst. to exec. v.p., 1992-97; head coach Ind. Pacers, 1997—. Mem. U.S. Olympic Basketball Team, 1992. Author: (with Bob Ryan) Drive, 1989; actor (film) Blue Chips, 1994. Mem. U.S. Gold Medal team World Univ. Games, Sophia, Bulgaria, 1977, Nat. Basketball Assn. championship team, 1981, 84, 86, Nat. Basketball Assn. All-Star Team, 1980-92; named Collegiate Player of Yr. AP, UPI and Nat. Assn. Coaches, 1978-79; Rookie of Yr. Nat. Basketball Assn., 1980; Most Valuable Player Nat. Basketball Assn. All-Star Game, 1982, Nat. Basketball Assn., 1984-86, Nat. Basketball Assn. Playoffs, 1984, 86. Office: Ind Pacers 300 E Market St Indianapolis IN 46204-2603

BIRD, ROBERT BYRON, chemical engineering educator, author; b. Bryan, Tex., Feb. 5, 1924; s. Byron and Ethel (Antrim) Bird. Student, U. Md., 1941—43; B.S. in Chem. Engring., U. Ill., 1947; Ph.D. in Chemistry, U. Wis., 1950; postdoctoral fellow, U. Amsterdam, 1950—51; DEng (hon.) , Lehigh U., 1972, Washington U., 1973, Tech. U. Delft, Holland, 1977, Colo. Sch. Mines, 1986; ScD (hon.) , Clarkson U., 1980, The Technion U., Israel, 1993, Tex. A&M U., 1999; D in engring. sci. (hon.) , Eidgenössische Tech. Hochschule, Zürich, Switzerland, 1994; DrEngring (hon.) , Kyoto (Japan) U., 1996. Asst. prof. chemistry Cornell U., 1952—53, Debye lectr., 1973, Julian C. Smith lectr., 1988; rsch. chemist DuPont Exptl. Sta., 1953; mem. faculty U. Wis., 1951—52, 1953—57, prof. chem. engring., 1957—92, C.F. Burgess distinguished prof. chem. engring., 1968—72, John D. MacArthur prof., 1982—92, Vilas research prof., 1972—92, chmn. dept., 1964—68, emeritus prof., 1992—; Burgers prof. Technische Univ. Delft, The Netherlands, 1994. Vis. prof. U. Calif., Berkeley, Calif., 1977, Univ. Catholique de Louvain, Belgium, 1994; D. L. Katz lectr. U. Mich., 1971; W. N. Lacey lectr. Calif. Inst. Tech., 1974; K. Wohl Meml. lectr. U. Del., 1977; W. K. Lewis lectr. MIT, 1982; R. H. Wilhelm lectr. Princeton U., 1991; G. N. Lewis lectr. U. Calif., Berkeley, 1993; Ascher Shapiro lectr. MIT, 1997; lectr. Lectures in Sci. Humble Oil Co., 1959, 61, 64, 66; lecture tour Am. Chem. Soc., 1958, 75, Canadian Inst. Chemistry, 1961, 65; cons. to industry, 1965—90; mem. adv. panel engring. sci. divsn. NSF, 1961—64. Author (with others): Molecular Theory of Gases and Liquids, 2d printing, 1964; author: Transport Phenomena, 62d printing, 2001, Spanish edit., 1965, Czech edit., 1966, Italian edit., 1970, Russian edit., 1974, Chinese edit., 1990, 2d English edit., 2002, Een Goed Begin: A Contemporary Dutch Reader, 1963, 2d edit., 1971, Comprehending Technical Japanese, 1975, Chinese edit., 1985, Dynamics of Polymeric Liquids, Vol. 1, Fluid Mechanics, Vol. 2, Kinetic Theory, 1977, 2d edit., 1987, Japanese transl., 1999, Reading Dutch: Fifteen Annotated Stories from the Low Countries, 1985, Basic Technical Japanese, 1990, Technical Japanese Supplements: Polymer Science and Engineering, 1995, also numerous rsch. publs.; Am. editor (with others) Applied Sci. Rsch., 1969—86, 1989—98; mem. adv. bd. : Indsl. and Engring. Chemistry, 1970—72, mem. editl. bd.: Jour. Non-Newtonian Fluid Mechanics, 1975—; contbr. Decorated Bronze Star; named Fulbright fellow, Holland, 1950, Guggenheim fellow, 1958, Fulbright lectr., 1958, Japan, 1962—63, Sarajevo, Yugoslavia, 1972; recipient Curtis McGraw award, Am. Assn. Engring. Edn., 1959, Westinghouse award, 1960, Corcoran award, 1987, Centennial Medallion, 1993, Nat. Medal Sci., 1987. Fellow: AIChE (William H. Walker award 1962, Profl. Progress award 1965, Warren K. Lewis award 1974, Founders award 1989, Inst. Lect. award 1992 1992), Am. Acad. Arts and Scis., Am. Phys. Soc.; mem.: NAE, NAS, Royal Flemish Acad. Belgium for Scis and Arts (fgn.), Royal Dutch Acad. Scis., Soc. Rheology, Soc. Chem. Engrs. Japan (hon.), Am. Chem. Soc. (chmn. Wis. sect. 1966, unrestricted rsch. grant Petroleum Rsch. Fund 1963), Am. Assn. Netherlandic Studies, Wis. Acad. Scis., Am. Acad. Mechanics, Arts and Letters, Sigma Tau, Omicron Delta Kappa, Phi Kappa Phi, Alpha Chi Sigma, Tau Beta Pi, Sigma Xi (v.p. Wis. sect. 1959—60), Phi Beta Kappa. Office: U Wis Dept Chem Engring 3004 Engring Hall 1415 Engineering Dr Madison WI 53706-1607 E-mail: bird@engr.wisc.edu.

BIRDSALL, DOUG, airline company executive; Chmn., CEO, pres. Travelmatin Corp.; sr. v.p., mktg., planning Continental Airlines; planning systems Ea. Airlines; v.p., mktg. alliances, strategic planning Northwest Airlines Corp, sr. v.p., alliances, 1999—. Office: Northwest Airline Corp 5101 Northwest Dr Saint Paul MN 55111-3075

BIRKETT, JOSEPH E. lawyer; b. Chgo. m. Patti Hill; 2 children. BA Polit. Sci. and English with honors, North Ctrl. Coll., Naperville, Ill., 1977; JD, John Marshall Law Sch., 1981. Bar: Ill. 1981. Asst. state's atty. DuPage County Office of the State's Atty., 1981-85, chief of maj. crimes unit, 1985-86, dep. chief criminal divsn., 1986-91, chief criminal divsn.,

1991-96, DuPage County State's Atty., 1996—. Adj. faculty Nat. Louis U., Wheaton, Ill.; lectr. in field. Vol. coach DuPage County Crime Commn. Boxing Club. Mem. Assn. Govt. Attys. in Capital Litigation (pres. 2001), DuPage County Bar Assn., Delta Theta Phi. Roman Catholic. Address: 505 N County Farm Rd Wheaton IL 60187-3907

BIRKHOLZ, RAYMOND JAMES, metal products manufacturing company executive; b. Chgo., Nov. 11, 1936; s. Raymond I. and Mary (Padian) B.; m. Judy Ann Richards, Apr. 23, 1966; children: Raymond J. Jr., Scott C., Matthew R. BSME, Purdue U., 1958; MBA, U. Chgo., 1963. Registered prof. engr., Ill. V.p. apparatus divsn. Gen. Cable Corp., Westminster, Colo., 1973-77; v.p. ops. metals divsn. Ogden Corp., Cleve., 1977-80, v.p. mfg. and engring. N.Y.C., 1980-81, pres. indsl. products, 1981-84, v.p., 1984-86; pres., COO Amcast Indsl. Corp., Dayton, Ohio, 1986-90; CEO Hollander Industries Corp., 1993-94; pres., CEO Republic Storage Systems Co., Inc., Canton, 1994—. Home: 2268 Brookelake Dr Atlanta GA 30338-7015 Office: Republic Storage Systems Co 1038 Belden Ave NE Canton OH 44705-1454

BIRMINGHAM, WILLIAM JOSEPH, lawyer; b. Lynbrook, N.Y., Aug. 7, 1923; s. Daniel Joseph and Mary Elizabeth (Tighe) B.; m. Helen Elizabeth Roche, July 23, 1955; children: Deirdre, Patrick, Maureen, Kathleen, Brian. ME, Stevens Inst. Tech., 1944; MBA, Harvard U., 1948; JD, DePaul U., Chgo., 1953. Bar: Ill. 1953, U.S. Patent and Trademark Office, 1955, U.S. Dist. Ct. (no. dist.) Ill. 1960, U.S. Supreme Ct. 1961, U.S. Ct. Appeals (7th cir.) 1962, U.S. Ct. Appeals (3rd cir.) 1968, U.S. Ct. Mil. Appeals 1973, U.S. Ct. Appeals (Fed. cir.) 1982, U.S. Ct. Claims 1986; registered profl. engr., Ill., Ind. Chem. engr. Standard Oil Co. Ind., Chgo., 1948-53; patent atty., 1953-59; assoc. Neuman, Williams, Anderson & Olson, Chgo., 1959-60; ptnr., 1961-91, Leydig, Voit & Mayer, Ltd., Chgo., 1991-93; of counsel, 1994-96. Served to capt. USNR, 1942-75, ret. Mem. ABA, ASME, Fed. Cir. Bar Assn., Am. Intellectual Property Law Assn., Intellectual Property Law Assn. Chgo. Home: 233 Pine St Deerfield IL 60015-4853

BIRNBAUM, HOWARD KENT, materials science educator; b. N.Y.C., Oct. 18, 1932; s. Jack and Ida (Kornblau) B.; m. Freda Silber, Dec. 25, 1954; children: Elisa, Scott, Shari. BS, Columbia U., 1953, MS, 1955; PhD, U. Ill., 1958. Asst. prof. U. Chgo., 1958-61; assoc. prof. U. Ill., Urbana, 1961-64, prof., 1964-99, dir. Materials Rsch. lab., 1987—, prof. emeritus, 1999—. Contbr. numerous articles to profl. jours. Fellow AAAS, Am. Phys. soc., Am. Soc. Metals, Materials Soc., Japanese Inst. of Metals (hon.); mem. AIME (Inst. Metals lectr. 1984, Mehl Gold medal 1984), NAE, Am. Acad. Arts and Scis. Jewish. Office: U Ill Materials Rsch Lab 104 S Goodwin Ave Urbana IL 61801-2902

BIRNEY, WALTER LEROY, religious administrator; b. Garden City, Kans., Apr. 25, 1934; s. Claude David and Mildred Elizabeth (Ferris) B.; m. Iva Lou Mosher, June 18, 1954; children: Mickey, Scotty, Gary, Lorrie, Lindie. BA, Dallas Christian Coll., 1956. Min. First Christian Ch., Benjamin, Tex., 1954-57, Bellaire Christian Ch., San Antonio, 1957-58, Copeland (Kans.) Christian Ch., 1958-84; coord. Nat. Missionary Conv., Copeland, 1966—. Dean, promoter Ashland (Kans.) Christian Camp, 1961-84; promoter S.W. Sch. Missions, Copeland, 1973-84. Named Outstanding Alumnus Dallas Christian Coll., 1988. Avocation: long distance running. Office: Nat Missionary Conv PO Box 11 Copeland KS 67837-0011 E-mail: wbirney11@aol.com.

BIRNKRANT, SHERWIN MAURICE, lawyer; b. Pontiac, Mich., Dec. 20, 1927; BBA, U. Mich., 1949, MBA, 1951; JD with distinction, Wayne State U., 1954. Bar: Mich. 1955, U.S. Dist. Ct. (ea. dist.) Mich. 1960, U.S. Supreme Ct. 1960, U.S. Ct. Appeals (6th cir.) 1966. Mem. Oakland County Bd. Suprs., 1967-68; asst. atty. City of Pontiac, Mich., 1956-67, city atty., 1967-83; of counsel Schlussel, Lifton, Simon, Rands, Galvin & Jackier, Southfield, 1983-90, Sommers, Schwartz, Silver & Schwartz, Southfield, 1990-95; shareholder Birnkrant & Birnkrant P.C., Bloomfield Hills, 1995—. Mem.: ABA (Mich. chmn. pub. contract law sect. 1979—97, chmn. urban, state and local govt. law sect. 1987—88, ho. dels. 1990—93, alt. del. to ho. dels. 1993—96, vice chmn. coordinating com. model procurement code state and local 1974—), Mich. Assn. Mcpl. Attys. (pres. 1975, coun. pres. 1992—), Am. Judicature Soc., Oakland County Bar Assn. (chmn. ethics and unauthorized practices com. 1961—62), State Bar Mich. (chmn. pub. corp. law sect. 1973—74, coun. adminstrv. law sect. 1975—76). Office: Birnkrant & Birnkrant PC 7 W Square Lake Rd Bloomfield Hills MI 48302

BISGARD, GERALD EDWIN, biosciences educator, researcher; b. Denver, Aug. 4, 1937; s. Harry Herman and Lucille Margaret (Matson) B.; m. Sharon Kay Cummings, Sept. 9, 1961; children— Jennifer, Kristine, Bradley B.S., Colo. State U., 1959, D.V.M., 1962; M.S., Purdue U., 1967; Ph.D., U. Wis., 1971. Instr., then asst. prof. Purdue U., West Lafayette, Ind., 1962-69; asst. prof., then assoc. prof. bioscis. U. Wis., Madison, 1971-77, prof., 1977-2001, emeritus prof., 2001—, dept. chmn. bioscis., 1980-97. Vis. prof. U. Calif.-San Francisco, 1977-78; mem. respiratory and applied physiol. study sect. NIH, 1988-92. Recipient Merit award NIH, 1987; named NIH fellow, 1969-71, Fogarty NIH Sr. Internat. fellow Oxford U., 1993; grantee NIH, 1973—. Mem. Am. Soc. Vet. Physiologists and Pharmacologists (pres. 1982-84), Am. Physiol. Soc., AVMA, Wis. Assn. Biomed. Res. Edn. (pres. 1998-2000). Avocations: sailing; skiing; gardening; hiking. Office: U Wis Sch Vet Medicine 2015 Linden Dr W Madison WI 53706-1100

BISHARA, SAMIR EDWARD, orthodontist; b. Cairo, Oct. 31, 1935; s. Edward Constantin and Georgette Ibrahim (Kelela) B.; children: Dina Marie, Dorine Gabrielle, Cherine Noelle. B. Dental Surgery, Alexandria U., Egypt, 1957; diploma in orthodontics, 1967; M.S., cert. in orthodontics, U. Iowa, 1970, D.D.S., 1972. Diplomate Am. Bd. Orthodontics (pres. Coll. Diplomates 1992). Practice gen. dentistry, Alexandria, 1957-68; specializing in orthodontics Iowa City, 1970—; fellow in clin. pedontics Guggenheim Dental Clinic, N.Y.C., 1959-60; resident in oral surgery Moassat Hosp., Alexandria, 1960-61, mem. staff, 1961-68; asst. prof. dentistry U. Iowa, 1970-73, asso. prof., 1973-76, prof., 1976—. Vis. prof. Alexandria U., 1974. Contbr. articles profl. jours., chpts. in books. Fellow Am. Coll. Dentists, Internat. Coll. Dentists; mem. ADA, AAAS, Am. Assn. Orthodontics, Internat. Dental Fedn., Internat. Assn. Dental Research, Am. Cleft Palate Assn., Assn. Egyptian Am. Scholars, Egyptian Orthodontic Soc. (hon.), Columbian Orthodontic Soc. (hon.), Greek Orthodontic Soc. (hon.), Mexican Bd. Orthodontists (hon.), Omicron Kappa Upsilon, Sigma Xi. Home: 1014 Penkridge Dr Iowa City IA 52246-4930 Office: U Iowa Coll Dentistry Orthodontic Dept Iowa City IA 52242

BISHOP, CAROLYN BENKERT, public relations counselor; b. Monroe, Wis., Aug. 28, 1939; d. Arthur C. and Delphine (Heston) Benkert; m. Lloyd F. Bishop, June 15, 1963. BS, U. Wis., 1961; grad., Tobe-Coburn Sch., N.Y.C., 1962. Merchandising editor Co-Ed Mag., N.Y.C., 1962-63; advt. copywriter Woodward & Lothrop, Washington, 1963-65; home furnishings editor Co-Ed Mag., N.Y.C., 1965-68; editor Budget Decorating Mag., 1968-69; home furnishings editor Family Cir. Mag., 1969-75; v.p., pub., editorial dir. Scholastic, Inc., 1975-80; owner Mesa Store Home Furnishings Co., Aspen, Colo., 1980-83; dir. pub. rels. Snowmass Resort Assn., Snowmass Village, 1983-86; pres. Bishop & Bishop Mktg. Comm., Aspen, 1986-93, Monroe, 1993-99; acct. supr. Hiebing Group, 1999—. Mem. media rels. com. Colo. Tourism Bd., Denver, 1987-90. Author: 25 Decorating Ideas Under $100, 1969; editor: Family Circle Special Home Decorating Guide, 1973. Bd. dirs. Aspen Camp Sch. for the Deaf, 1987-90. Recipient Dallas Market Editorial award Dallas Market Ctr., 1973, Dorothy Dawe award Chgo. Furniture Market, 1973, Guardian of Freedom award, Anti-Defamation League Appeal, 1974. Mem. Rocky Mountain Pub. Rels. Group (chmn. 1991-93), Pub. Rels. Soc. Am. (accredited, small firms co-chair counselors acad. 1992-93), Aspen Writers' Found. (bd. dirs. 1991-93), Tobe-Coburn Alumni Assn., U. Wis. Alumni Assn. Democrat. Office: The Hiebing Group 315 Wisconsin Ave Madison WI 53703-4102

BISHOP, CHARLES JOSEPH, manufacturing company executive; b. Gary, Ind., June 22, 1941; s. Charles K. and Angela (Marich) Yelusich; m. Yvonne M. Stazinski, June 8, 1963; children: Stephen, Scott. BS, Purdue U., 1963; PhD, U. Wash., 1969. Mgr. advanced energy systems Boeing Co., Seattle, 1969-77; mgr. systems devel. Solar Energy Research Inst., Denver, 1977-81; v.p. tech. A.O. Smith Corp., Milw., 1981—. Mem. adv. bd. S.W. Wis. Rsch. Ctr., Milw., 1987; bd. dirs. Indsl. Rsch. Inst., 1989-92, v.p., 1993, pres. 1995-96. Contbr. articles to profl. jours. Treas. Cedarburg Comty. Scholarship Com., Wis., 1985-91; mem. indsl. liaison coun. U. Wis., Milw., 1985—, U. Wis. Coll. Engring., Madison, 1990-95; mem. Gov.'s Coun. on Sci. and Tech., 1992-94; mem. nat. coun. Alverno Coll. Recipient Cert. Recognition NASA, 1975. Mem.: Milw. Athletic Club. Republican. Roman Catholic. Avocations: fishing, travel, golf. Office: A O Smith Corp-Corp Tech 12100 W Park Pl Milwaukee WI 53224-3029

BISHOP, DAVID FULTON, library administrator; b. N.Y.C., Nov. 23, 1937; s. Donald McLean and Clara (Zelley) B.; m. Nancy Driscoll, May 15, 1959; children: Karen McLean, Michael David. MusB, U. Rochester, 1959, postgrad., 1959-60; MS in Library Sci., Cath. U. Am., 1964; postgrad., U. Md., 1967-73. Head serials dept. U. Md. Libraries, College Park, 1967-69, coordinator tech. services, 1969-70, head systems, 1970-73; head cataloger U. Chgo. Libraries, 1973-75, asst. dir. tech. services, 1975-79; dir. libraries U. Ga., Athens, 1979-87; prof., univ. librarian U. Ill., Urbana, 1987-92; univ. libr. Northwestern U., Evanston, Ill., 1992—. Trustee Ednl. Comms. (EDUCOM), Washington, 1988-94; bd. dirs. Ctr. for Rsch. Librs., 1992-99; vice-chmn. bd. dirs. Ctr. for Rsch. Librs., 1996-97; chmn. bd. dirs. Ctr. for Rsch. Librs., 1997-98. Mem. ALA, INFORMA (steering com. 1989-93), Assn. Coll. and Rsch. Librs., Coun. on Libr. Resources (proposal rev. com. 1991-95), Coalition for Networked Info. (steering com. 1992-98). Home: 2518 Indian Ridge Dr Glenview IL 60025-1032 Office: Northwestern U Librs Evanston IL 60201

BISHOP, DAVID T. state legislator; b. Mar. 29; m. Bea Bishop; 5 children. JD, Cornell U.; MPA, Harvard U. Pvt. practice law, 1954-76; rep. Dist. 30B Minn. Ho. of reps., 1982—, mem. ethics and judiciary coms., chmn. ways and means com., mem. capitol investment com. Office: 453 State Office Bldg Saint Paul MN 55155-0001

BISHOP, ELIZABETH SHREVE, psychologist; b. Ann Arbor, Mich., Nov. 18, 1951; d. William Warner Jr. and Mary Fairfax (Shreve) B. AB, U. Mich., 1972; MA, Ohio State U., 1973, PhD, 1976. Lic. psychologist, Mich. Psychologist Franklin County Program for the Mentally Retarded, Columbus, Ohio, 1974, WC Mental Health, Willmar, Minn., 1977-83; chief psychologist Battle Creek (Mich.) Child Guidance Ctr., 1981; dir. psychometrics Meridian Profl. Psychol. Cons., East Lansing, Mich., 1983-92; pres. Arbor Psychol. Cons., Ann Arbor, 1991—. Troop leader Girl Scouts U.S.A., Minn., 1971—87, Mich., 1971—87, Ohio, 1971—87, trainer, 1993—; assoc. Univ. London Inst. Edn., 1976; deacon 1st Congl. Ch., 1996—2000, 2002—. Assoc. Univ. London Inst. Edn., 1976. Fellow Am. Orthopsychiat. Assn.; mem. APA, AAUW, Mich. Psychol. Assn., Mich. Women Psychologists, Coun. for Exceptional Children (local pres. 1977-78), Internat. Coun. Psychologists (bd. dirs. 1999—), Internat. Sch. Psychology Assn., LWV (Willmar v.p. 1989-91). Avocations: reading, traveling, birdwatching, photography, music. Home: 1612 Morton Ave Ann Arbor MI 48104-4441 Office: Arbor Psychol Cons 1565 Eastover Pl Ann Arbor MI 48104-6316 E-mail: apc1565@msn.com.

BISHOP, GEORGE FRANKLIN, political scientist, educator; b. New Haven, July 26, 1942; s. George Elwood and Mary Bridget (Trant) B.; m. Pama Mitchell, July 15, 1995; 1 child, Kristina. BS in Psychology, Mich. State U., 1966, MA, 1969, PhD, 1973. Instr. multidisciplinary social sci. program Mich. State U., East Lansing, 1972-73; asst. prof. dept. sociology and anthropology U. Notre Dame, Ind., 1973-75; dir. Greater Cin. Survey, 1981-95; rsch. assoc. behavioral sci. lab U. Cin., 1975-77, sr. rsch. assoc. Inst. for Policy Rsch., 1981-93, dir. behavioral scis. lab., 1994-95, assoc. prof. polit. sci., 1982-87, prof., 1987—, dir. grad. cert. program in pub. opinion and survey rsch., 1999—; dir. Internet Pub. Opinion Lab. Univ. Cin., 2000—. Assoc. dir. Ohio Poll, 1981-95; guest prof. Zentrum für Umfragen, Methoden und Analysen, Mannheim, Germany, 1985, 90, 92; fellow Ctr. for Study of Dem. Citizenship, Dept. Polit. Sci., U. Cin., 1992-99, fellow Inst. for Data Scis., 1996-98; summer inst. faculty Survey Rsch. Ctr., Inst. for Social Rsch., U. Mich., summer 1993; sr. cons. Burke Mktg. Rsch., Inc., Cin., 1996-98. Sr. editor The Presdl. Debates: Media, Electoral and Policy Perspectives, 1978; sr. author various articles in profl. jours.; mem. editl. bd. Pub. Opinion Quar., 1987-90, Free Inquiry, 1999—; mem. editl. adv. bd. Public Perspective, 2000—. Served with U.S. Army N.G., 1960-63. NSF grantee, 1977-84. Mem. AAUP (Maita Levine Svc. award 2002), Midwest Assn. Pub. Opinion Rsch. (pres. 1977-78, Mapor fellow Disting. Scholarship in pub. opinion rsch. 1994), Am. Assn. Pub. Opinion Rsch., Am. Polit. Sci. Assn., World Assn. Pub. Opinion Rsch. (treas. 1983-85). Home: 825 Dunore Rd Cincinnati OH 45220-1416 Office: U Cin Cincinnati OH 45221-0001

BISHOP, MARK, radio personality; Radio host WLVQ, Columbus, Ohio, 1979—98, WMMS, Cleve., 1990—94, WHK, 1994—96, WMJI, 1994—96, WTVN, Columbus, 1994—96, WMJI, 1998—. Office: WMJI 6200 Oaktree Blvd 4th Fl Cleveland OH 44131

BISHOP, MARY OLTMAN, advertising executive; With Leo Burnett Co., Chgo., pres., chief mktg. officer. Office: 35 W Wacker Dr Chicago IL 60601-1614 E-mail: mary_bishop@chi.leoburnett.com.

BISHOP, MICHAEL D. emergency physician; b. Anna, Ill., Feb. 10, 1945; m. Mary Susan Wilkens, Dec. 28, 1965; children: Amy Elizabeth, Amanda Marie. AB, GreenvilleColl., 1967; MD, U. Ill., 1971. Diplomate Am. Bd. Emergency Medicine (oral examiner 1980—, dir. 1988-96, mem. exec. com. 1990-95, mem. several bd. coms., sec.-treas. 1991-92, pres.-elect 1992-93, pres. 1993-94). Intern Meth. Hosp. Dallas, 1971-72; emergency physician Bloomington (Ind.) Hosp., 1972—, Morgan County Meml. Hosp., Martinsville, Ind., 1978—, Fayette Meml. Hosp., Connersville, 1989—, Jackson County Meml. Hosp., Seymour, 1989—; gen. dir. Immediate Care Ctrs. in Ind., various cities, 1981—; clin. assoc. prof. med. scis. Ind. U., Bloomington, 1980—; pres., CEO Unity Physician Group P.C., Ind., 1971—. Bd. trustee, Sunday sch. tchr. Ellettsville (Ind.) Christian Ch.; bd. dirs. Peoples State Bank, Ellettsville; bd. dirs., sec. Ellettsville Bancshares, Ellettsville Elem. Sch. Bldg. Corp. Fellow Am. Coll. Emergency Physicians (charter, pres. Ind. chpt. 1979-80, nat. councillor 1976-81, 83, mem. nat. multi-hosp./multi-state blue ribbon task force 1981, mem. nat. ins. com. 1976-77, mem. coun. long-range planning com. 1981-82, mem. coun. steering com. 1983-85, chmn. medicare task force 1984-86, chmn. task force on physician payment reform 1986-88, mem. govt. affairs com. 1983-88, 89-93, chmn. 1984-87, 89-93, mem. nat. emergency medicine polit. action com. bd. trustees 1984-88, 89-93, chmn. 1987, 89-93, mem. fin. com. 1987-93, James D. Mills Outstanding Contbn. to Emergency Medicine award 1990, mem. awards com. 1991-93, mem. reimbursement com. 1992—, dir. 1995—, lectr. in field), AHA (mem. Ind. affil. faculty, ACLS), Am. Coll. Physician Execs., Soc. Acad. Emergency Medicine, Christian Med. Dental Soc., Ind. State Med. Assn., Med. Group Mgmt. Assn., Owen Monroe County Med. Soc. Office: Unity Physician Group PC 1155 W 3rd St Bloomington IN 47404-5016

BISHOP, STEPHEN GRAY, physicist; b. York, Pa., Jan. 26, 1939; s. John Schwartz and Carrie (Gray) B.; m. Helene Barbara Evenson, July 6, 1963; children: Hans Stephen, Lars Michael. BA in Physics with honors, Gettysburg Coll., 1960; PhD in Physics, Brown U., 1965. Postdoctoral rsch. assoc. physics Brown U., 1965-66; NAS-NRC postdoctoral rsch. assoc. Naval Rsch. Lab., Washington, 1966-68, rsch. physicist, supr., 1968-80, head semiconductor br., 1980-89; dir. Engring. Rsch. Ctr. Compound Semiconductor Electronics and Microelectronics Lab. U. Ill., Urbana-Champaign, 1989-2000, prof. elec. and computer engring., 1989—; dir. Ctr. Optoelectronics Sci. and Techs., 1994-98. With Max Planck Inst. fur Festkorperforschung, Stuttgart, West Germany, 1973-74; mem. navy com. Amorphous Semiconductor Tech. Rev., 1974, navy inter-lab. com. on pers. adminstrn., 1985; rsch. scientist Royal Signals and Radar Establishment, Great Malvern, U.K., 1978-79; adj. prof. physics SUNY, Buffalo, 1984—, U. Utah, 1986—; mem. tech. rev. com. Joint Svcs. Electronics program, 1980-89, tech. adv. com. Ctr. for Compound Semiconductor Microelectronics, U. Ill., Urbana-Champaign; mem. ONR Univ. Rsch. Initiative Rev. Panel, 1986, external rev. panel Ctr. for Electronic and Electro-Optic Materials, SUNY, Buffalo, 1988; mem. NSF Site Visit Rev. Panel for materials rsch. lab., U. Ill., NSF panel on light wave technology, 1988, NSF panel on interface of optical devices and systems, 1989; vis. com. Sherman Fairchild Ctr. for Solid State Studies, Lehigh U., 1991—; mem. Nat. Adv. Com., URI-ARO Ctr. for High-Frequency Microelectronics, U. Mich., 1993; edit. bd. Semiconductor Sci. and Tech., Inst. of Physics, 1992. Editor: (with others) Optical Effects in Amorphous Semiconductors, 1984, Proceedings of the MRS Symposium on the Microscopic Identification of Electronic Defects in Semiconductors, 1985; author: (with others) Deep Centers in Semiconductors, 1985, Gallium Arsenide Technology, 1990; contbr. more than 200 articles to profl. jours. Patentee in field. Trustee Gettysburg Coll., 1992—. Recipient Disting. Alumni award Gettysburg Coll., 1990. Felow Am. Phys. Soc., AAAS, Optical Soc. Am.; mem. IEEE, Lasers and Electronics Soc., Materials Rsch. Soc., Phi Beta Kappa, Sigma Pi Sigma, Sigma Xi (Pure Sci. award 1977), Tau Beta Pi (UIUC Chapt., Eminent Engr. award 1993). Office: Coordinated Scis Lab 1308 W Main St Urbana IL 61801-2307 E-mail: sgbishop@uiuc.edu.

BISPING, BRUCE HENRY, photojournalist; b. St. Louis, Apr. 27, 1953; s. Harry and Marian B.; m. Joan M. Berg, Sept. 29, 1984; children: Erin Elizabeth Giovanna, Trevor Thomas. B.J., U. Mo., Columbia, 1975. Summer intern Cleve. Press, 1974, The Virginian/Pilot-Ledger Star, Norfolk, 1975; staff photojournalist Mpls. Tribune, 1975-82, Mpls. Star and Tribune, 1982—. Freelance photographer Black Star Pub. Co., N.Y.C., 1975— , Sporting News, St. Louis, Underwater USA, Business Week, Time, U.S. News World Report, Newsweek, Am. Illustrated, N.Y. Times, Los Angeles Times, other nat. and local publs.; past mem. faculty Mo. Photojournalism Workshop. Mem. Nat. Press Photographers Assn. (assoc. dir. Region 5 1981-82, dir. Region 5 1983-86, rep. to exec. com. 1984, Nat. Newspaper Photographer of Year award 1976, Regional Newspaper Photographer of Year award 1977, citation for dedication to profession 1985), Twin Cities News Photographers Assn. (pres. 1979-80), Profl. Assn. Diving Instrs. (open water instr. rating), Oldsmobile Club of Am. (bd. dirs. Minn. Club, news editor). Office: Mpls Tribune 6020 View Ln Edina MN 55436-1827 E-mail: bruceb65@citilink.com.

BISSELL, JOHN HOWARD, marketing executive; b. Bklyn., July 8, 1935; s. Donald Henry and Lillian (Eckberg) B.; m. Joan Becker, Sept. 7, 1963; children: John Edward, Mary Katherine. BA in Polit. Sci., Yale U., 1956. Brand mgr. Procter and Gamble, Inc., Cin., 1960-71; v.p., new products mktg. Frito-Lay, Inc., Dallas, 1971-80; v.p. mktg. The Stroh Brewery Co., Detroit, 1980-85, sr. v.p., spl. products div., 1985-91; pres. Stroh Foods, Inc. subs. The Stroh Brewery Co., 1985-91; mng. ptnr. cons. div. Gundersen Ptnrs., L.L.C., Bloomfield Hills, Mich., 1991—. Chmn. corp. funds campaign Sta. WTVS, Detroit, 1986. Served as 1st lt. USAF, 1957-59. Mem. Adcrafters, Birmingham Athletic Club, Yale Club (N.Y.C.). Republican. Presbyterian. Home: 3310 Morningview Ter Bloomfield Hills MI 48301-2472

BITNER, JOHN HOWARD, lawyer; b. Indpls., Feb. 27, 1940; s. Harry M. Jr. and Jeanne B. (Eshelman) B.; m. Vicki Ann D'Ianni, 1961; children: Kerry, Holly, Robin. AB in English and History, Northwestern U., 1961; JD cum laude, Columbia U., 1964. Bar: Ill. 1964. Assoc. Bell, Boyd & Lloyd LLC, Chgo., 1964-71, ptnr., 1972-99, chair corp. and secs. dept., 1988-99, vice chmn. firm, 1992-99, mem., 2000—. Contbr. articles to profl. jours.; editor Columbia Law Rev. Mem. St. Gregory Episcopal Sch. Bd.; mem. bd. visitors Columbia Law Sch. Mem. ABA, Ill. Bar Assn., Chgo. Bar Assn., Union League, Mid-Day Club, Glen View Club, Lawyers Club, Delta Upsilon, Phi Delta Phi. Episcopalian. Avocations: tennis, reading, scuba. Home: 2329 Lincolnwood Dr Evanston IL 60201-2048 Office: Bell Boyd & Lloyd 70 W Madison St Chicago IL 60602 Fax: (312) 827-8048. E-mail: jbitner@bellboyd.com.

BITONDO, DOMENIC, engineering executive; b. Welland, Ont., Can., June 7, 1925; came to U.S., 1950, naturalized, 1956; s. Vito Leonard and Vita Maria (Gallipoli) B.; m. Delphine May Dicola, June 11, 1949; children— Michael, Annamarie, David, Marisa. BS, U. Toronto, 1947, MS, 1948, PhD, 1950. Aerodynamist, Aerophysics div. N.Am. Aviation Co., Downey, Calif., 1950-51; project engr. to chief of aerodynamics Aerophysics Devel. Corp., Santa Barbara, 1951-59; staff engr. Northrup Corp., Hawthorne, Calif., 1959-60; head test planning and analysis TRW Systems, Inc., El Segundo, 1960-61; dept. head aeromechanics dept. Systems Research and Planning div., founder, dir. Advanced Ballistic Reentry Systems Program (ABRES) Aerospace Corp., 1961-63; dir. engring. Aerospace Systems div. Bendix Corp., Ann Arbor, Mich., 1963-69; engring. mgr. Apollo lunar sci. expts., 1966; dir., gen. mgr. Bendix Research Labs., Southfield, Mich., 1969-79; exec. dir. research and devel. Bendix Corp., 1979-80; pres. Bitondo Assocs. Inc., Ann Arbor, 1980—. Gordon N. Patterson lectr. U. Toronto, 1976; trustee Central Solar Energy and Research Corp., Detroit, 1978-80; dir. Continental Controls Corp., San Diego.; Def. Research Bd. Can. asst., 1948, NRC asst., 1947 Contbr. tech. articles to profl. jours. Mem. AIAA, NRC (mem. com. on mgmt. tech.), NAS (mem. task force to Indonesia in methodology of tech. planning), Mich. Energy Resource Rsch. Assn. (trustee 1978), Nat. Mgmt. Assn. (Gold Knight award), Indsl. Rsch. Inst. (emeritus). Office: 5 Manchester Ct Ann Arbor MI 48104-6562 E-mail: deldom@mymailstation.com.

BIXBY, FRANK LYMAN, lawyer; b. New Richmond, Wis., May 25, 1928; s. Frank H. and Esther (Otteson) B.; m. Katharine Spence, July 7, 1951; children— Paul, Thomas, Edward, Janet. AB, Harvard U., 1950; LLB, U. Wis., 1953. Bar: Ill. 1953, Wis. 1953, Fla. 1974. Ptnr. firm Sidley Austin Brown & Wood, Chgo., 1963—97, sr. counsel, 1998—. Editor-in-chief Wis. Law Rev, 1952-53; mem. editorial bd. Chgo. Reporter, 1973-89. Trustee MacMurray Coll., Jacksonville, Ill., 1973-85; bd. dirs. Chgo. Urban League, 1962—, v.p., 1972-86, gen. counsel, 1972—, chmn. 1986-89; bd. dirs. Community Renewal Soc., 1973-86, Voices for Ill. Children, 1987-90; chmn. trustees Unitarian Ch., Evanston, Ill., 1962-63; bd. dirs. Spencer Found., 1967-2001, chmn. 1975-90; mem. dist. 202 bd. edn. Evanston Twp. High Sch., 1975-81, pres., 1977-79. Recipient Man of Year award Chgo. Urban League, 1974 Mem. ABA, Ill. Bar Assn., Chgo. Bar Assn., Chgo. Coun. Lawyers, Chgo. Coun. Fgn. Rels., Order of Coif, Harvard Club (pres. 1964-65), Mid-Day Club., Phi Beta Kappa. Bus.

Home: 505 N Lake Shore Dr Apt 4607 Chicago IL 60611-3409 Office: Sidley Austin Brown & Wood 10 S Dearborn St Chicago IL 60603-2000 E-mail: fbixby@sidley.com., kfbixby@yahoo.com.

BIXBY, HAROLD GLENN, manufacturing company executive; b. Lamotte, Mich., July 14, 1903; s. Charles Samuel and Laura (Schenk) B.; m. Pauline Elizabeth Summy, July 3, 1928; children: Mary Louise and Richard Glenn (twins). A.B., U. Mich., 1927, LL.D. (hon.), 1972. Began in accounting dept. Ex-Cell-O Corp., Detroit, 1928, asst. sec., 1929, controller, 1933, sec., treas. and dir., 1937, became v.p., treas., dir., 1947, pres., gen. mgr., 1951-70, chmn. bd., chief exec. officer, 1970-72, chmn. bd., 1972—, chmn. exec. com., 1973-79. Bd. dirs., hon. trustee Kalamazoo Coll. Mem. Greater Detroit C. of C., Tau Kappa Epsilon. Clubs: Economic, Detroit Athletic, Detroit Golf. Home and Office: 16351 Rotunda Dr Ste 357 Dearborn MI 48120-1159

BIXENSTINE, KIM FENTON, lawyer; b. Providence, Feb. 26, 1958; d. Barry Jay and Gail Louise (Traverse) Weinstein; m. Barton Aaron Bixenstine, June 25, 1983; children: Paul Jay, Nathan Alexis. BA, Middlebury Coll., 1979; JD, U. Chgo., 1982. Bar: Ohio 1982, U.S. Dist. Ct. (no. and so. dists.) Ohio 1983, U.S. Ct. Appeals (6th cir.) 1983. Law clk. to presiding judge U.S. Dist. Ct. (so. dist.) Ohio, Cin., 1982-83; assoc. Jones, Day, Reavis & Pogue, Cleve., 1983-90, ptnr., 1991-99; sr. counsel TRW, Inc., 1999—2001, v.p., chief litig. counsel, 2002—. Vice chair comml. adv. coun. N.E. Ohio chpt. Am. Arbitration Assn. Bd. dirs. Planned Parenthood Greater Cleve., 1991—99, sec., 1992—93, v.p., 1994—96, pres., 1996—98; chair corp. giving subcom. Cleve. Bar Found. Campaign, 2001—; bd. dirs. Boys and Girls Club Cleve., 2001—. Mem.: Cleve. Bar Assn. (commn. women in the law 1988—2001, bd. dirs. 1993—96, minority outreach com. 1993—99, chair standing com. lawyer professionalism 1994—96, bd. liaison to jud. selection com. 1996, nominating com. 1997—99, chair nominating com. 1998—99), Ohio Women's Bar Assn. (chair legis. com. 1994—95, trustee). Avocation: jogging. Office: TRW Inc 1900 Richmond Rd Cleveland OH 44124-3760

BJELLAND, ROLF F. business executive; Exec. v.p., chief investment officer Luth. Brotherhood, Mpls., 1986—. Office: Luth Brotherhood 625 4th Ave S Minneapolis MN 55415-1665

BJORNDAL, ARNE MAGNE, endodontist; b. Ulstein, Norway, Aug. 19, 1916; s. Martin I. and Anne Bjorndal; m. Katharine G. Benson, Jan. 12, 1952; children: Katharine, Kari, Lee. BS, State Coll., Volda, 1939; DDS, U. Oslo, 1947, U. Iowa, 1954, MS, 1956. Diplomate Am. Bd. Endodontics. Instr. Coll. Dentistry U. Oslo, 1948-50, 51-53; intern Forsyth Dental Infirmary, Boston, 1950-51, NIDR, 1960; mem. faculty U. Iowa, Iowa City, 1954—, prof., 1964—, founder, head dept. endodontics, 1956-80. Vis. prof. U. Alexandria, Egypt, 1978. Author: Anatomy and Morphology of Human Teeth, 1983. Maj. USNG, 1963-70. Decorated King Haakon VII medal (Norway); Fulbright scholar, 1950-51. Fellow Am. Coll. Dentists; mem. ADA (Svc. Fgn. Countries award 1979), Iowa Dental Assn. (life), Am. Assn. Endodontics, N.Y. Acad. Sci., Optimists, Elks, Omicron Kappa Upsilon. Republican. Lutheran. Home: 2510 Bluffwood Cir Iowa City IA 52245-3543 E-mail: bjorndal@blue.weeg.uiowa.edu.

BLACK, DALE R. casino executive; m. Sheila Dawn Hilliard, Dec. 26, 1981; 2 children. BS in Acctg., So. Ill. U., 1984. V.p., contr. Argosy Gaming Co., Alton, Ill., 1993—98, sr. v.p., CFO, 1998—; crew leader Bonanza restaurant, Mt. Vernon, 1979—84; staff acct. Arthur Andersen, 1984—91; contr. Creative Data Svcs., 1991—93. Office: Argosy Gaming Co 219 Plaza St Alton IL 62002-6232

BLACK, DAVID DELAINE, retired investment consultant; b. Cin., Mar. 3, 1926; s. Robert L. Black and Anna (McNaughton) Smith; m. Maralyn Anderson (dec.); children: Robert, Dorothy, James; m. Polly P. Black, Oct. 7, 1967 (dec. Apr. 1996); children: Evelyn; m. Nancy Kohnen, Jan. 16, 2000. BS in Engring. with honors, Princeton U., 1949; MBA, Harvard U., 1951. Mgr. co. planning Cin. Millacron, Cin., 1952-77; owner Planning Counsel, 1977-84; sr. v.p. Gradison divsn. McDonald & Co., 1984—. Vice-chmn. bd. The Children's Hosp., Cin., 1985-97; chmn. bd. WCET-TV 48, Cin., 1980-83; pres. Cincinnatus Assn., 1966-67; chmn. Agnes and Murray Seasongord Good Govt. Found., 1993-95; chmn. Children's Hosp. Found., 1993-97; treas. Planned Parenthood Assn. Cin., 1986; vestry Indian Hill Ch., 1997-99; sec. bd. stewards, 2000—. Mem. Rotary (bd dirs. 1992-95, treas. Cin. Rotary Found. 1993-94).

BLACK, DENNIS H. state legislator; b. Randolph, Nebr., Dec. 18, 1939; m. Faun Stewart. BS, Utah State U., 1963, MS, 1965. Mem. Iowa Ho. of Reps., 1982-94, Iowa Senate from 29th dist., 1994—. Dir. Jasper County Conservation Bd.; bd. dirs. Iowa Sister State: Newton Cmty. Sch.; mem. Taiwan Com.; dist. commr. Jasper County Soil Conservation. Mem. Terrace Hill Soc. (bd. dirs.), Iowa Peace Inst. (bd. dirs.), Jasper County Farm Bur., Izaak Walton League. Democrat. Home: 5239 E 156th St S Grinnell IA 50112-7511 Office: State Capitol Dist 29 3 9th And Grand Des Moines IA 50319-0001 E-mail: dennis_black@legis.state.ia.us.

BLACK, LARRY DAVID, library director; b. Section, Ala., Mar. 3, 1949; s. Haskin Byron and Mima Jean (Holcomb) B.; m. Mary Frances Patterson, Aug. 29, 1971; 1 child, Amy Susan. BA in History & Polit. Sci., U. Ala., 1971, MLS, 1972; M in Pub. Adminstrn., Ohio State U., 1981. Asst. dir. Bedsole Library Mobile (Ala.) Coll., 1972-73; dir. Baldwin County Libr. System, Summerdale, Ala., 1973-76; dir. libr. svc. Troy State U., Bay Minette, 1976-77; dir. main libr. Columbus Met. Libr., Ohio, 1977-83, asst. exec. dir., 1983-84, exec. dir., 1984—. Mem. Ohio Libr. Assn., Am. Soc. Pub. Adminstrs. Democrat. Club: Cen. Ohio Corvette (Columbus). Avocations: woodworking, gardening, restoration of old Corvette automobiles and Harley-Davidson motorcycles. Home: 7381 Seeds Rd Orient OH 43146-9608 Office: Columbus Met Libr 96 S Grant Ave Columbus OH 43215-4702

BLACK, NATALIE A. lawyer; b. 1949; AB, Stanford U., 1972; JD, Marquette U., 1978. Bar: Wisc. Group pres., gen. coun. Kohler Co., Kohler, Wisc. Mem. ABA. Office: Kohler Co Legal Dept 444 Highland Dr Kohler WI 53044-1515 Fax: 920-459-1583.

BLACK, RICHARD A. former community college president; b. Mar. 29, 1944; m. Jo Ann Black, 1974; 2 children. BS in Math., S.E. Mo. State U., 1966; MEd, U. Mo., Columbia, 1967, postgrad., 1971-73, Harvard U., 1995. Instr. math. Ritenour Sr. H.s., Overland, Mo., 1966-69; adminstrv. assoc., asst. dean for continuing edn. St. Louis C.C. at Meramec, 1973-79, asst. and assoc. dean for continuing edn., 1979-86, dean of instrn., 1986-91, pres., 1992-99; ret., 1999. Bd. dirs. Higher Edn. Ctr. St. Louis. Served with U.S. Army. Mem. Mo. C.C. Assn. (trustee 1989-92, pres. adminstrv. sect.), St. Louis Conf. on Edn., St. Louis Symphony Soc., Kirkwood Area C. of C., St. Loius Art Mus., Mo. Hist. Soc., Kirkwood Rotary. Avocations: music, golf, photography, microcomputers, travel. Home: 148 Saylesville Dr Chesterfield MO 63017-3456 Office: Saint Louis Community College at Meramec 11333 Big Bend Rd Kirkwood MO 63122-5799

BLACK, RONNIE DELANE, religious organization administrator, mayor; b. Poplar Bluff, Mo., Oct. 26, 1947; s. Clyde Olen and Leona Christine Black; m. Sandra Elaine Hulett, Aug. 27, 1966; 1 child, Stephanie. BA, Oakland City (Ind.) Coll., 1969; M Div, So. Bapt. Theol. Sem., 1972. Ordained to ministry Gen. Assn. of Gen. Bapts., 1967. Pastor Gen. Bapt. Ch., Fort Branch, Ind., 1972-78; stewardship dir. Gen. Bapt. Hdqrs., Poplar Bluff, Mo., 1978-97, exec. dir., 1997—; councilman City of Poplar Bluff, 1985-97, mayor, 1990-92, 95-96. Office: Gen Bapts 100 Stinson Dr Poplar Bluff MO 63901-8736

BLACK, SPENCER, state legislator; b. N.Y.C., May 25, 1950; married. BA, SUNY, Stony Brook, 1972; MS, U. Wis., 1980, MA, 1981. State assemblyman dist. 77 State of Wis., 1984—. Edn. curator Wis. State Hist. Soc. Democrat. Address: 5742 Elder Pl Madison WI 53705-2516

BLACK, STEPHEN L. lawyer; b. Cin., Dec. 3, 1948; AB magna cum laude, Harvard U., 1971, JD, 1974. Bar: Ohio 1974, U.S. Ct. Appeals (6th cir.). Law clerk to Hon. George Edwards U.S. Ct. Appeals (6th cir.), 1974-75; mayor City of Indian Hill, Ohio, 1995-99; ptnr. Graydon, Head & Ritchey, Cin., 1980—. Mem. Ohio State Bar Assn., Cin. Bar Assn. Office: Graydon Head & Ritchey 1900 5th Third Ctr 511 Walnut St Cincinnati OH 45202-3157

BLACK, WILLIAM B. state legislator; b. Danville, Ill., Nov. 11, 1941; m. Sharon Black; 2 children. BA, William Jewel Coll.; MA, Ea. Ill. U.; postgrad., Ill. State U. Ill. state rep. Dist. 105, 1986—. Spokesman Econ. Devel. Com., mem. Edn. Com., Transp. and Motor Vehicles Com., Urban Redevel. Com., Elem. and Secondary Com., Human Svc. Com.; educator and adminstr. Address: 119 1/2 S Gilbert St Danville IL 61832-6229 Office: 634 State House Springfield IL 62706-0001

BLACKBURN, HENRY WEBSTER, JR. retired physician; b. Miami, Fla., Mar. 22, 1925; s. Henry Webster and Mary Frances (Smith) B.; m. Nelly Paula Trocme, Jan. 10, 1951 (div. 1984); children: John Keith, Katherine Ann, Heidi Elizabeth; m. Stacy Richardson, Sept. 1, 1991. Student, Fla. So. Coll., Lakeland, 1942-43; BS, U. Miami, 1947; MD, Tulane U., 1948; MS, U. Minn., 1957; Dr honoris causa, U. Kuopio, Finland, 1988; DSc (hon.), Tulane U., 1999. Intern Chgo. Wesley Meml. Hosp., 1948-49; resident in medicine Am. Hosp. Paris, 1949-50; med. officer in charge USPHS, Austria, Fed. Republic Germany, 1950-53; med. fellow U. Minn., Mpls., 1953-56; retired Divsn. Epidemiology, 1996; med. dir. Mut. Svc. Ins. Co., St. Paul, 1956; asst. prof. physiol. hygiene U. Minn., 1958-61, assoc. prof., 1961-68, prof., 1968—, lectr. medicine, 1956—, dir. lab. physiol. hygiene Sch. Pub. Health, 1972—, prof. medicine, 1972—, chmn. div. epidemiology, 1983-90, Mayo prof. pub. health, 1990-96. Vis. prof. U. Geneva, 1970; mem. adv. coun. Nat. Heart, Lung and Blood Inst., 1989-93; mem. com. on diet and health NRC, 1986-89; Ancel Keys lectr., 1991; mem. food adv. com. FDA, 1995-2000. Author: Cardiovascular Survey Methods, 1968, On the Trail of Heart Attacks in Seven Countries, 1995, "P.K." Irreverent Memoirs of a Preacher's Kid, 1999, If It Isn't Fun...Memoir of a Different Sort of Medical Life, Vol. I, 2001; mem. editl. bd. numerous jours.; contbr. articles to profl. jours. Lt. (j.g.) USNR, 1942-50, capt. USPHS inactive res. Recipient Thomas Francis award in epidemiology, 1975, Naylor Dana award in preventive medicine, 1976, Louis Bishop award in cardiology, 1979, Gold Heart award Am. Heart Assn., 1990, Rsch. Achievement award Am. Heart Assn., 1992; Mayo chair in pub. health, 1988. Fellow APHA, Am. Coll. Cardiology, Am. Epidemiol. Soc.; mem. AAAS (chmn. med. sect.), Belgian Royal Acad. Medicine, Am. Heart Assn. (dir. 1971-74), Internat. Soc. Cardiology (coun. epidemiology 1971-74, chmn. 1986-91), Internat. Epidemiol. Soc., Alpha Omega Alpha, Phi Kappa Phi, Delta Omega. Home: 1525 Kaltern Ln Minneapolis MN 55416-3507 Office: U Minn Div Epidemiology 1300 S 2d St Minneapolis MN 55454-1075 E-mail: blackburn@epi.umn.edu.

BLACKIE, SPENCER DAVID, physical therapist, administrator; b. Endicott, N.Y., Sept. 27, 1946; s. Norman and June (Spencer) B.; m. Bonnie Jean Randall Moulton, June 11, 1967 (div. Apr. 1985); children: Rhonda, Randy, Brenda; m. Sharon Joan Clingman, May 10, 1986; children: Kristen, Sean, Alex. BS, Loma Linda U., 1968; MA, U. So. Calif., 1973; MS, Boston U., 1980. Cert. in manual therapy, clin. specialist in orthop. phys. therapy, quantum medicine; bd. cert. naturopathic physician; bd. cert in iridology. Clin. dir. Loma Linda (Calif.) U. Med. Ctr., 1972-74; dir. rehab. svcs. New Eng. Meml. Hosp., Stoneham, Mass., 1974-84, Mt. Carmel Hosp., Colville, Wash., 1984-92, Regina Med. Ctr., Hastings, Minn., 1992—. Mem. Pool Com., Hastings, 1994; chmn. Parks and Recreation Bd., Colville, 1991-92. Capt. U.S. Army, 1969-71. Cmty. Fitness grantee Perrier Mineral Waters, Stoneham, 1978; decorated U.S. Army commendation medal. Mem. Am. Naturopathic Med. Assn., Am. Phys. Therapy Assn., Am. Occupl. Therapy Assn., Am. Acad. Orthop. Manual Phys. Therapy, Am. Soc. Hand Therapists, Am. Acad. Quantum Medicine, Internat. Iridology Practitioners Assn., Minn. and Wis. Occupl. Therapy Assn., Rotary. Seventh-Day Adventist. Avocations: bicycling, classical guitar, karate, hiking/backpacking. Office: Regina Med Ctr 1175 Nininger Rd Hastings MN 55033-1056 E-mail: blackied@reginamedical.com.

BLACKLOW, ROBERT STANLEY, physician, medical college administrator; b. Cambridge, Mass., June 24, 1934; s. Leo Alfred and Clara Edna (Cumenes) B.; m. Winifred Young, Dec. 7, 1958; children: Stephen Charles, Kenneth Lawrence, David Alan. A.B. summa cum laude, Harvard U., 1955, M.D. cum laude, 1959; DSc (hon.), Kent State U., 1998; DMed. (hon.) , U. Pecs, Hungary, 2001. Intern Peter Bent Brigham Hosp., Boston, 1959-60, resident, 1960-61, 63-64, 67-68; instr. Harvard U., 1967-70, asst. prof. medicine, 1970-76, asso. prof., 1976-78, asst. to dean faculty of medicine, 1969-73, asso. dean, 1973-78; prof., internal medicine Rush Med. Coll., 1978-85, dean, 1978-81; v.p. for med. affairs Rush-Presbyn.-St. Luke's Med. Center, Chgo., 1978-81; prof. medicine Jefferson Med. Coll., Phila., 1985-92, sr. assoc. dean, 1985-92; pres., dean Northeastern Ohio Univs. Coll. Medicine, 1992—, prof. community medicine, prof. medicine, 1992—. Mem. sci. adv. com. Nat. Fund for Med. Edn., 1981-84, Nat. Cancer Inst., 1986-95; bd. dirs. Nat. Resident Matching Program, 1993—, pres.-elect, 1994-95, 99—, pres. 1995-96, treas., 1998-99, pres.-elect, 1999-2000, pres., 2000-01. Editor: Signs and Symptoms, 1971, 6th edit., 1983; mem. editl. bd. Jour. Med. Humanities, 1997—. Trustee Chestnut Hill Sch., Newton, Mass., 1970-79, Belmont (Mass.) Hill Sch., 1973-79, Chgo. chpt. ARC, 1979, Greater Akron (Ohio) Musical Assn., 1993—, mem. exec. com., 1998—; dir. Akron Regional Devel. Bd., 1998—; mem. Ill. Health Svc. Corps Task Force, Ill. Dept. Pub. Health, 1980; corporator Belmont Hill Sch., 1978—. Served with USPHS, 1961-63. Fellow: ACP, Chgo. Soc. Internal Medicine, Inst. medicine Chgo.; mem.: AAAS, Assn. Acad. Health Ctrs., Assn. Am. Med. Colls., NY Acad. Sci., Twin Lakes Country Club, Cliff Dwellers Club (Chgo.), Badminton & Tennis Club (Boston), Portage Country Club (Akron), Harvard Musical Assn., Longwood Cricket Club (Boston), Harvard Club (Boston, NYC, Chgo) (Chgo. bd. dir.), Literary Club (Chgo.), Franklin Inn (Phila.), Alpha Omega Alpha, Sigma Xi, Phi Beta Kappa. Home: 1150 Pin Oak Dr Kent OH 44240-6254 Office: Northeastern Ohio Univs Coll Medicine PO Box 95 Rootstown OH 44272-0095

BLACKMAN, EDWIN JACKSON, software engineer; b. Pulaski, Tenn., Nov. 19, 1947; s. Alley J. and Martha (Williams) B.; m. Nancy Kamin, Mar. 11, 1982 (div. Mar., 1990); m. Michelle Fautz, May 25, 1990. AA, Martin Coll., Pulaski, Tenn., 1972; BS, Tenn. Tech. U., 1974. State auditor State of Tenn., Nashville, 1974-76; internal auditor Firestone Tire & Rubber Co., Akron, Ohio, 1976-79; mgr. internal audit Leewards Creative Crafts, Elgin, Ill., 1979-81; acct. mgr. Mgmt. Sci. Am., Oakbrook, 1981-85, sales cons., 1985-88, sr. mktg. rep., 1988-90; customer svc. mgr. Dun & Bradstreet Software, Columbus, Ohio, 1990-92, acct. exec., 1993-94; sr. application sales rep. Oracle Corp., 1994-96; acct. exec. Gt. Plains Software, 1996—. With U.S. Navy, 1966-70, Vietnam. Mem. Moose, Young Ams. for Freedom, Elks, Exchange Club. Methodist. Avocations: sailing, golf. Home: 13824 Bainwick Dr Pickerington OH 43147-8722 Office: Great Plains Software 13824 Bainwick Dr NW Pickerington OH 43147-8722

BLACKWELL, JOHN, science educator; b. Oughtibridge, Sheffield, Eng., Jan. 15, 1942; came to U.S., 1967; s. Leonard and Vera (Brook) B.; m. Susan Margaret Crawshaw, Aug. 5, 1965; children: Martin Jonathan, Helen Elizabeth. BSc in Chemistry, U. Leeds, Eng., 1963, PhD in Biophysics, 1967. Postdoctoral fellow SUNY-Syracuse Coll. Forestry, 1967-69; vis. asst. prof. Case Western Res. U., Cleve., 1969-70, asst. prof., 1970-74, assoc. prof., 1974-77, prof. macromolecular sci., 1977—; chmn. dept., 1985-95; F. Alex Nason prof., 1991-2000; Leonard Case Jr. prof., 2001—. Vis. prof. Kennedy Inst. Rheumatology, London, 1975, Centre National de Recherche Scientifique, Grenoble, France, 1977, U. Frieburg, Fed. Republic Germany, 1982; chmn. Gordon Conf. on Liquid Crystalline Polymers, 1992; cons. in field. Author: (with A.G. Walton) Biopolymers, 1973; mem. editorial bd. Macromolecules, 1989-92; adv. bd. Jour. Macromolecular Sci.-Physics, 1986—; internat. adv. bd. Acta Polymerica, 1992—; contbr. articles to profl. jours. Recipient award for disting. achievement Fiber Soc., 1981, Sr. Scientist award Alexander von Humboldt Found., Max Planck Inst. for Polymer Rsch., Mainz, Fed. Republic Germany, 1991, Rsch. Career Devel. award, 1973-77. Fellow Am. Phys. Soc. (exec. com. divsn. high polymer physics 1986-90, vice chmn. 1987-88, chmn. 1988-89); mem. Am. Chem. Soc. (chmn. cellulose divsn. 1999, Anselm Payen award 1999, divsn. councillor 2000—), Am. Crystallography Soc. (chmn. fiber diffraction spl. interest group 1993-94), Biophys. Soc. (chmn. biopolymer subgroup 1975-76), Fiber Soc. Episcopalian. Home: 2951 Attleboro Rd Shaker Heights OH 44120-1815 Office: Case Western Res U Dept Macromolecular Sci Cleveland OH 44106-7202 E-mail: jxb6@po.cwru.edu.

BLACKWELL, J(OHN) KENNETH, state official; b. Feb. 28, 1948; m. Rosa Blackwell; children: Kimberly, Rahshann, Kristin. BS, Xavier U., Cin., 1970, MEd, 1971. Cert. govt. fin. mgr. Treas. State of Ohio, Columbus, 1994-98, sec. of state, 1999—. Mem. city coun., City of Cin., 1977-89, vice mayor, 1977-78, 85-86, mayor, 1979-80; vice-chmn. Cin. Employees Retirement Sys. Fund., 1988; dep. undersec. U.S. Dept. HUD, 1989-90; mem. Nat. Commn. Econ. Growth and Tax Reform, 1995; participant Nat. Summit on Retirement Income Savings, 1998; ptnr. Bituminex Co., 1978-82; coord. urban affairs, Xavier U., 1971-74, asst. prof. edn., 1974-77, assoc. prof., 1977-91, dir. cmty. rels., 1975-79, assoc. v.p., 1979-91; assoc. prof. U. cin., 1993; chmn. bd. adv. trustees Govt. Investment Found., Inc., 1999; ambassador U.N. Human Rights Commn., 1992-93; adv. bd. John M. Ashbrook Ctr. Pub. Affairs Ashland U., 1997; Children's Ednl. Opportunity Am. Found., 1999; bd. dirs. Black Alliance for Edn. Options; pres. Nat. Electronic Commerce Coord. Coun., 2002; bd.dir. Nat. Coun. UN, Internat. League Human Rights, nat. Coun. Lawyer's Com. for Human Rights; mem. Fed. Election Commn. adv. panel, 1999; bd. trustees Am. Coun. Young Polit. Leaders, 1995' treas. State of Ohio, 1994-99; sec. State of Ohio, 1999-. Contbr. articles to profl. jours. Mem. The Jerusalem com., 1981; co-chmn. Hamilton County Reagan-Bush campaign, Ohi, 1984; mem. exec. com. Nat. Conf. Rep. Mayors; co-chmn. Blacks for Bush campaign, Ohio, 1988; mem. adv. coun. Ohio victims of Crime, 1989; bd. dirs. Internat. Rep. Inst., 1993; nat. chmn. Steve Forbes for Pres. campaign, 1999; bd. dirs. Wilberforce U., 1989; chmn. Cin. Riverfront Classic and Jamboree, 2000-01; mem. exec. bd. Youth Voter Corps, 2001; mem. nat. bd. visitors Mazza Collection, U. Findlay, 1999; hon. co-chair Meml. to Our Lost Children, 1995; trustee Grant/Riverside Hosps., 1996, Wilmington Coll., 1996; v.p. Nat. Electronic Commerce Coordinating Coun., 2001; mem. bd. advisors John M. Ashbrook Ctr. Pub. Affairs, Ashland U., 1997; exec. bd. Youth Voter Corps., 2001. Harvard U. fellow, 1987, The Aspen Inst., 1984, Salzburg Seminar, Austria, 1988, Heritage Found., 1992, The Ditchley Found., 1993; scholar-in-residence Urban Morgan Inst. Human Rights, 1993; recipient Disting. Alumnus award Xavier U., 1992, Superior Honor award U.S. Dept. State, 1993, Peace of City award Cin. Jewish Cmty. Rels. Coun., 1994, Family of Yr. award Nat. Coun. Negro Women, 1994, Advocacy award U.S. Small Bus. Adminstrn., 1995, Martin Luther King Dream Keeper award, 1996, Veritas award Albertus Magnus Coll., 1998, Thomas A. Van Meter scholar award Ashbrook Ctr., 1997, Pub. Svc. award NAACP, 1996, numerous others. Mem. Nat. Govt. Fin. Officers Assn. (excellence award 1999), Nat. Assn. State Treasurers, Nat. Assn. State Auditors, Comptrs. and Treasurers (exec. com. 1995-99, Pres. award, 1996), Nat. Taxpayers Union, Nat. Assn. of Secs. of State (v.p. midwest region 2001), Nat. Assn. Securities Profls., Internat. City Mgmt. Assn. (bd. dirs. 1999), Federalist Soc., Econ. club of Columbus. Office: State of Ohio Sec of State 180 E Broad St Fl 16 Columbus OH 43215 E-mail: blackwell@sos.state.oh.us.

BLACKWELL, THOMAS FRANCIS, lawyer; b. Detroit, Nov. 25, 1942; m. Sandra L. Kroczek; children: Robert T., Katherine M. BA, U. Notre Dame, Ind., 1964; JD, U. Mich., 1967. Bar: Mich and U.S. Dist. Ct. (we. and ea. dists.) Mich. 1968, U.S. Ct. Appeals (6th cir.) 1969. Assoc. Smith, Haughey, Rice & Roegge, Grand Rapids, Mich., 1967-71, ptnr., 1971—, treas., 1979-85, 89—, exec. com., 1985-89. Spl. asst. atty. gen. State of Mich., 1972-82. Fellow Mich. State Bar Found.; mem. ABA, State Bar Mich., Grand Rapids Bar Assn., FBA, Products Liability Adv. Coun., Mich. Def. Trial Attys., Peninsular, Kent Country Club. Office: Smith Haughey Rice & Roegge 250 Monroe Ave NW Ste 200 Grand Rapids MI 49503-2251 E-mail: tblackwell@shrr.com.

BLAD, BLAINE L. agricultural meteorology educator, consultant; b. Cedar City, Utah, Apr. 2, 1939; s. Carl Hamblin and Loueda (Allan) B.; m. Virginia Jean Blackham, Feb. 14, 1964; children: Dean, Sheryl Kay, Colleen, Kenneth L., Stephen L., Kirk L., Kerry Kim. BS, Brigham Young U., 1964; MS, U. Minn., 1968, PhD, 1970. NDEA fellow U. Minn., St. Paul, 1964-67, technician, 1966-70, rsch. asst., 1967-70; asst. prof. U. Nebr., Lincoln, 1970-76, assoc. prof., 1976-82, prof., 1982—, head dept. agrl. meteorology, 1987-97, dir. Sch. Natural Resource Scis., 1997-2000; assoc. dir. Gt. Plains Regional Ctr. for Global Environ. Change, 1992—. Cons. NASA, Houston, 1978-80, Standard Oil Co. Ohio, Cleve., 1983-86. Author: Microclimate: Biological Environment, 1983; sect. editor: International Crop Science, 1992; assoc. editor Agronomy Jour., 1981-87. Scoutmaster Cornhusker coun. Boy Scouts Am., 1976-94. Fellow Am. Soc. Agronomy (chair div. 1976-77); mem. Crop Sci. Soc. Am., Gamma Sigma Delta (chair membership com. 1992). Mem. LDS Ch. Avocations: sports, reading, camping, fishing, hunting. Office: U Nebr Sch Natural Resource Scis 243 LW Chase Hall Lincoln NE 68583-0728 Home: PO Box 376 Kanosh UT 84637-0376

BLADE, MARK J. state legislator; b. Terre Haute, Ind., Dec. 16, 1953; m. Vickie Blade; children: Marcus, Stephanie, Yolanda, Mark Jr. BS, Ind. State U., 1976. Cmty. devel. planner West Ctrl. Ind. Econ. Devel. Dist., 1976-80; asst. dir. for cmty. and econ. devel. Terre Haute (Ind.) Dept. Redevel., 1980-86; dir. purchasing and warehousing Vigo County Sch. Corp., 1986—; mem. Ind. Senate from 38th dist., Indpls., 1997—; mem. fin. com., mem. govt. and regulatory affairs com.; mem. planning and econ. devel. com., ranking mem.; mem. pub. policy com. Mem. Vigo County Coun., 1992—, pres. pro tempore, 1994, pres. 1995, 96, pres., 1997; sec. Vigo County Dem. Ctrl. Com., 1993-96, treas., 1997—; trustee Ind. State U., 1996; v.p., pres. Ind. State U. Alumni Coun., 1991-96; bd. dirs. Family Svc. Assn. Bd., 1992-96, 1st v.p., 1995, 96; mem. adv. bd. Cmty. Corrections, 1990-94, pres., 1994; bd. dirs. United Way of the Wabash Valley, 1985-90, v.p. for allocations, pres.; bd. dirs. Trees, Inc., 1993-96. Democrat. Avocations: reading, travel. Office: 200 W Washington St Indianapolis IN 46204-2728

BLAGG, JOE W. retail executive; Chmn. bd. TruServ Corp., Chgo. Office: TruServ Corp 8600 W Bryn Mawr Ave Chicago IL 60631-3505

BLAGOJEVICH, ROD R. congressman; b. Chgo. s. Rade and Millie (Govedarica) B.; m. Patti Blagojevich; 1 child, Amy. BA in History, Northwestern U., 1979; JD, Pepperdine U., 1983. Past pvt. practice law, Chgo.; past asst. state atty. Cook County, Ill.; mem. Ill. Ho. of Reps., 1992-96, U.S. Congress from 5th Ill. dist., 1997—; mem. govt. reform and armed svcs. coms. Pvt. practice atty. Office: US Ho of Reps 331 Cannon House Off Bldg Washington DC 20515-0001 also: 4064 N Lincoln Ave Chicago IL 60618-3038 also: 11 W Conti Pkwy Fl 3D Elmwood Park IL 60707-4505*

BLAHUT, RICHARD EDWARD, electrical and computer engineering educator; b. Orange, N.J., June 9, 1937; s. Edward John and Julia Anna (Chamer) B.; m. Barbara Ann Krachenfels, Aug. 30, 1958; children: Gregory, Kenneth, Janice, Jeffrey. B.S. in Elec. Engring., MIT, 1960; M.S. in Physics, Stevens Inst. Tech., Hoboken, N.J., 1964; Ph.D. in Elec. Engring., Cornell U., 1972. Engr. Kearfott (GPI), Little Falls, N.J., 1960-64, IBM, Owego, N.Y., 1964-94; courtesy prof. elec. engring. Cornell U., 1974-94; Henry Magnuski prof. elec. and computer engring. U. Ill., Urbana, 1994—, adj. prof. elec. engring., 1986-94. Sys. cons. Ioptics Corp., Bellview, Wash., 1994-99. Author: Theory and Practice of Error Control Codes, 1983, Fast Algorithms for Digital Signal Processing, 1985, Principles and Practice of Information Theory, 1987, Digital Transmission of Information, 1990. IBM fellow, 1980. Fellow IEEE (pres. info. theory group 1982, editor Transactions on Info. theory, Alexander Graham Bell award 1998), NAE. Republican. Roman Catholic. Home: 1502 Bridge Point Ln Champaign IL 61822-9272 Office: U Ill Coordinated Sci Lab Urbana IL 61801 E-mail: blahut@ribeye.csl.uiuc.edu.

BLAIN, CHARLOTTE MARIE, physician, educator; b. Meadeville, Pa., July 18, 1941; d. Frank Andrew and Valerie Marie (Serafin) B.; m. John G. Hamby, June 12, 1971 (dec. May 1976); 1 child, Charles J. Hamby. Student, Coll. of St. Francis, 1958-60, DePaul U., 1960-61; MD, U. Ill., Chgo., 1965. Diplomate Am. Bd. Family Practice, Am. Bd. Internal Medicine. Intern, resident U. Ill. Hosps., 1967-70; fellow in infectious diseases U. Ill., 1968-69; practice medicine specializing in internal medicine, Elmhurst, Ill., 1969—. Instr. medicine U. Ill. Hosp., 1969-70; asst. prof. medicine Loyola U., 1970-71; mem. staff Elmhurst Meml. Hosp., 1970—; clin. asst. prof. Chgo. Med. Sch., 1978-95, U. Ill. Med. Sch., 1995—, Rush Med. Coll., 1997—. Contbr. articles to med. jours., chpts. to texts. Bd. dirs. Classical Symphony. Fellow ACP, Am. Acad. Family Practice; mem. AMA, AAAS, Am. Soc. Internal Medicine, Am. Profl. Practice Assn., Royal Soc. Medicine, DuPage Med. Soc., Univ. Club (Chgo.). Roman Ctholic. Avocation: Hapki Do. Home: 320 Cottage Hill Ave Elmhurst IL 60126-3302 Office: 135 Cottage Hill Ave Elmhurst IL 60126-3330

BLAINE, EDWARD H. health science administrator, educator; b. Farmington, Mo., Jan. 30, 1940; s. Theodore Warren and Tessa Ella (McClanahan) B.; m. Susan Irene Cring (div. 1992); children Jennifer, Marquis Edward. AB, U. Mo., 1962, MA, 1967, PhD, 1970, DSc (hon.), 1989. Player Green Bay Packers, Green Bay, Wisc., 1962-63, Phila. Eagles, Phila., 1963-67; asst. prof. physiology U. Pitts., 1973-77; dir. renal Pharmacology Merk Inst., West Point, Pa., 1977-86; sr. dir. G.D. Searle Rsch. & Devel., St. Louis, 1986-92; dir. Dalton Cardio-Vascular Rsch. Ctr., U. Mo., Columbia, Mo., 1992—. Adv. com. NIH, Bethesda, Md., 1974-86; adv. bd. Global Interaction, Phoenix, Ariz., 1991-93. Contbr. to profl. jours. Deans adv. bd. grad. divsn. U. Mo., Columbia, 1988-92; chmn. Searle-St. Louis United Way, 1990; exec. com. U. Mo. Development Coun., 1993-94; bd. dirs. Mo. Found. for Med. Rsch., Columbia, Mo., 1993—; pres. Varsity M Assn. U. Mo., 1993-94. Named All Am. UPI/Look Mag., 1961; recipient Rsch. Career Development award NIH, 1975. Mem. Am. Soc. Hypertension (v.p. 1992-94), Am. Physiological Soc., Am. Soc. Pharm. Exptl. Therapeutics, Endocrine Soc. Avocations: canoeing, scuba, hiking, skiing. Home: 4 E Clarkson Rd Columbia MO 65203-3520 Office: Univ of Missouri Dalton Cardiovascular Rsch Ctr Columbia MO 65211-0001 E-mail: blainee@missouri.edu.

BLAIR, BEN, real estate company executive; JD, Washburn U., 1965. Chmn. Coldwell Banker Griffith & Blair Realtors, Topeka. Mem. bd. regents Washburn U., Kirkville, Mo.; trustee Washburn Endowment Assn., 1993—, past chmn. endowment bd. Office: Coldwell Banker Griffith & Blair 2222 SW 29th St Topeka KS 66611

BLAIR, CARY, insurance company executive; b. Hartford City, Ind. BS, Butler U. Joined Westfield Cos., 1961, from mgmt. trainee to exec. v.p., 1961-83; chmn., CEO Westfield Cos., Westfield Mgmt. and Westfield Fin., Westfield Ctr., Ohio.

BLAIR, EDWARD MCCORMICK, investment banker; b. Chgo., July 18, 1915; s. William McCormick and Helen Haddock (Bowen) B.; m. Elizabeth Graham Iglehart, June 28, 1941; children: Edward McCormick, Francis Iglehart. Grad., Groton Sch., 1934; B.A., Yale U., 1938; M.B.A., Harvard U., 1940. With William Blair & Co., Chgo., 1946—, ptnr., 1950-61, mng. ptnr., 1961-77, sr. ptnr., 1977—. Bd. dirs. George M. Pullman Ednl. Found.; trustee Coll. of Atlantic, Bar Harbor, Maine; life trustee U. Chgo., Rush-Presbyn.-St. Luke's Med. Ctr., Chgo., Art Inst. Chgo. Lt. comdr. USNR, 1941-46. Home: PO Box 186 Sheridan Rd Lake Bluff IL 60044 Office: William Blair & Co 222 W Adams St Chicago IL 60606-5307

BLAIR, REBECCA SUE, English educator, lay minister; b. Terre Haute, Ind., Mar. 26, 1958; d. Albert Eldon and Genevieve Virginia (Smith) B.; m. Richard Volle Van Rheeden, May 27, 1989. BA in English magna cum laud, U. Indpls., 1980; MA in Medieval Lit. with honors, U. Ill., Springfield, 1982; MA, Ind. U., 1986, PhD, 1988. Grad. asst. U. Ill., Springfield, 1980-82; dir. English language tng. Ind. U., Bloomington, 1982-83, assoc. instr., 1982-88; assoc. prof., chmn. dept. English Westminster Coll., Fulton, Mo., 1989-99, dir. writing assessment, 1989-99; assoc. prof. Univ. Indpls., Ind., 1999—. Vis. prof. Webster U., St. Louis, Mo., 1988-89; writing assessment cons. Pepperdine U., Malibu, Calif., 1995, numerous colleges and univs., 1989—; mem. exec. com. of the faculty Westminster Coll.; mem. Assessment Com., College-Wide Budget Com., Profl. Stds. Com., Pers. Com., Dean's Cabinet Coun. of Chairs and Dirs., Edn. Task Force, Task Force to Reorganize the Acad. Area, Enrollment Svcs. Task Force; women's studies rep. Mid-Mo. Am. Coun. of Univs.; faculty sponsor Alpha Chi Scholastic Hon. Soc.; faculty organizer awareness of rape/domestic violence Take Back the Night Rally. Author: The Other Woman: Women Authors and Cultural Stereotypes in American Literature, 1988; author conf. papers, articles; presenter workshops, seminars; spkr. in field. Bd. dirs. Am. Cancer Soc., Callaway County, Mo., 1989-92; mem. pastor nominating com. First Presbyterian Ch., Fulton, Mo., 1990-91, elder, 1990—, session mem., elected mem., 1990-93, 97-2000, chmn. nominating com., 1993-94, chmn. music search com., 1994-95; pulpit supply Mo. Union Presbytery, 1995—, mem. com. on ministry, 1997-2000, stated clk., 1997—; mem. Greater Mo. Focus on Leadership, 1992; vol. Habitat for Humanity, Fulton, 1993—; bd. dirs., founding mem. Coalition Against Rape and Domestic Violence, Fulton, 1995-97; bd. dirs. Friends of the Libr., Fulton, 1995-98, pres., 1997-98; sec. Fulton Art League, 1996—. Named Outstanding Faculty Mem., Westminster Coll., Fulton, 1991-92, Panhellenic Faculty Mem. of Year, Westminster Coll., 1996-97. Mem. Nat. Coun. for Rsch. on Women, Nat. Coun. Tchrs. of English, Am. Studies Assn., Midwest Modern Lang. Assn., Modern Lang. Assn., Writing Prog. Adminstrs., Coll. Composition and Comm., Fulton C. of C. (vol. 1992-96), Kiwanis (bd. dirs. 1990—, founder Circle K Club 1994, v.p. 1995-96, pres.-elect 1996-97, pres. 1997-98). Presbyterian. Avocations: gourmet cooking, reading, trains, writing. Home: 11332 Arborview Dr #1506 Indianapolis IN 46236 Office: Univ Indianapolis 1400 East Hanna Ave Indianapolis IN 46227-3697 E-mail: rblair@windy.edu.

BLAIR, ROBERT CARY, insurance company executive; BS, Butler U., Indpls., 1961. From mgmt. chmn. and trainee to dir., CEO Westfield Cos., 1961—. Office: Westfield Cos 1 Park Cir Westfield Center OH 44251

BLAIR, VIRGINIA ANN, public relations executive; b. Kansas City, Mo., Dec. 20, 1925; d. Paul Lowe and Lou Etta (Cooley) Smith; m. James Leon Grant, Sept. 3, 1943 (dec. July 1944); m. Warden Tannahill Blair, Jr., Nov. 7, 1947; children: Janet, Warden Tannahill III. BS in Speech, Northwestern U., 1948. Free-lance writer, Chgo., 1959-69; writer, editor Smith, Bucklin & Assocs., Inc., 1969-72, account mgr., 1972-79, account supr., 1979-80, dir. pub. rels., 1980-85; pres. GB Pub. Rels., 1985—. Judge U.S. Indsl. Film Festival, 1974, 75; instr. Writer's Workshop, Evanston, Ill., 1978; dir. Northwestern U. Libr. Coun., 1978-91, dir. alumnae bd., 1986—, John Evans Club bd., 1990-98. Author dramas (produced on CBS): Jeanne D'Arc: The Trial, 1961, Cordon of Fear, 1961, Reflection, 1961, If I Should Die, 1963; 3-act children's play: Children of Courage, 1967. Emmy nominee Nat. Acad. TV Arts and Scis., 1963; recipient Svc. award Northwestern U., 1978, Creative Excellence award U.S. Indsl. Film Festival, 1976, Gold Leaf merit cert. Family Cir. mag. and Food Coun. Am., 1977, cert. Excellence superior achievement in media rels. N.Am. Percis Sundicate, 1997. Mem. Pub. Rels. Soc. Am. (counselors acad.), Am. Advt. Fedn. (lt. gov. Ill. 6th dist.), Women's Advt. Club Chgo. (pres.), Publicity Club Chgo., Nat. Acad. TV Arts and Scis., John Evans Club (bd. dirs.), Woman's Club Evanston (pres.), Zeta Phi Eta (Svc. award 1978, 93), Alpha Gamma Delta, Philanthropic and Ednl. Orgn. (Ill. chpt. pres. dist. pres.). Home and Office: Unit 206 2601 Central St Evanston IL 60201-1395

BLAKE, DARCIE KAY, radio news director, anchor; b. Worland, Wyo., Aug. 29, 1958; d. Jerry Haley and Helen Ileen (Kerbel) Bloom; m. Paul Henry Reifschneider, Aug. 30, 1980; children: Sara Jayne, Mathew James. BS in Journalism, U. N.D., 1979. Anchor, reporter Sta. KFYR Radio, Bismarck, N.D., 1979, Sta. WHB Radio, Kansas City, Mo., 1980-82; news dir. Sta. KUDL Radio/Sta. WHB Radio, 1982—. Bd. dirs. Harvestors-Food Bank, Kansas City, 1990, Girl Scouts U.S., Kansas City, 1990; vol. Arthritis Assn (citation 1989), United Minority Media Assn. (citation 1989). Mem. Kansas City Press Club (bd. dirs. 1984-85), Radio/TV News Dirs., Kansas City Media Profls., Kans. Assn. Broadcasters, Soc. Profl. Journalists. Episcopalian. Avocations: golf, tennis. Office: Sta KUDL/WHB 3101 Broadway St Ste 460 Kansas City MO 64111-2478

BLAKE, NORMAN PERKINS, JR. information technology company executive; b. N.Y.C., Nov. 8, 1941; s. Norman Perkins and Eleanor (Adams) B.; m. Karen Cromwell, Sept. 12, 1965; children: Kellie, Kimberly, Adam. BA, Purdue U., 1966, MA, 1967. With GE, 1967-74, 76-84, mgr. strategic planning ops., plastics bus. div. Mass., 1976-78, mgr. bus. devel. consumer products and services sector, 1978-79, staff exec. Fairfield, Conn., 1979; v.p., gen. mgr. comml. and indsl. fin. div. GE Credit Corp., Stamford, 1979-81, exec. v.p. financing ops., 1981-84; chmn. and chief exec. officer Heller Internat. Corp., Chgo., 1984-90, pres., 1984-90; chmn., chief exec. officer Heller Fin., Inc., until 1990, Heller Overseas Corp., Chgo., 1984-90; now chmn., CEO, pres. U.S. Fidelity & Guaranty Co., Baltimore, 1990-98; chmn., pres. Fidelity & Guaranty Ins. Underwriters., Balt., 1990-98; vice chmn. St. Paul Cos., Marco Island, Fla., 1990-98; chmn., pres., CEO Promus Hotel Corp., Memphis, 1998-99; CEO, chmn., pres. Comdisco Inc., Rosemont, Ill., 2001—. With Top, Inc., Troy, Mich., 1974-76, pres., 1976; bd. dirs. Owens/Corning Fiberglas. Office: Comdisco Inc 6111 N River Rd Rosemont IL 60018

BLAKE, WILLIAM HENRY, credit and public relations consultant; b. Jasonville, Ind., Feb. 18, 1913; s. Straude and Cora (Pope) B.; m. Helen Elizabeth Platt, Jan. 2, 1937 (dec. Feb. 1990); children: William Henry, Allen Howard. Student, Knox Coll., 1932-35; BS, U. Ill., 1936, MS, 1941, postgrad., 1946; student, NYU, 1950-51, Am. U., 1955-56, 1958; grad., Columbia U. Grad. Sch. Consumer Credit, 1956, Northeastern Inst., Yale U., 1957. Cert. assn. exec. Tchr. Champaign (Ill.) Pub. Schs., 1936-41; exec. sec. Ill. Soc. CPAs, Chgo., 1941-44; dean men, assoc. prof. bus. adminstrn. Catawba Coll., 1947-51; dir. rsch. Nat. Consumer Fin. Assn., Washington, 1954-59; exec. v.p. Internat. Consumer Credit Assn., St. Louis, 1959-78; pres. Consumer Trends Inc., also Blake Enterprises, cons., 1978—. Cons. Decatur Consumer Credit Assn., 1979-88; adminstr. Soc. Cert. Consumer Credit Execs., 1961-78 Author: Good Things of Life on Credit, 1960, rev., 1975, How to Use Consumer Credit Wisely, 1963, rev., 1975, Home Study Courses in Credit and Collections, 1968, Human Relations, 1969, Communications, 1970, Retail Credit and Collections, rev., 1974, Adminstrative Office Management, 1972, Consumer Credit Management, 1974; pub.: Consumer Trends Newsletter, The Credit World mag. Mem. pres.'s adv. cabinet Southeastern U.; adviser Office Edn. Assn.; chmn. public relations com. Ill. Heart Assn., 1979-85; bd. dirs. Salvation Army, Decatur, 1979— ; mem. fund raising com. Sch. Edn., U. Ill., 1979-84; chmn. bd. trustees Alta Deana div. University City, 1970-73, congressional liaison, 1959-78; trustee Internat. Consumer Credit Assn. Ins. Trust and Retirement Program, 1960-78; mem. Session Westminster Presbyn. Ch., Decatur, 1971-84, fin. con., 1981-84, 89-92. trustee. 1981-84 ; apptd. by mayor to Decatur Aging Adv. Commn., 1991-94. Served to lt. USNR, 1944-47; lt. comdr. 1951-54, ret. Named Man of Yr., Mo. Consumer Credit Assn., 1977; recipient Knox Coll. Scroll of Honor, Knox-Lombard 50 Yr. Club, Galesburg, 1991, Alumni Achievement award Knox Coll., 1994, Class Agt. award, 1995. Mem. Credit Grantors Assn. Can. (bd. dirs. 1959-72), U.S. C. of C. (mem. banking and currency com. 1968-71, mem. trade assn. com. 1964-67), Am. Soc. Assn. Execs. (bd. dirs. 1965-66), Pub. Rels. Soc. Am. (chpt. sec.-treas. 1979-85), Internat. Platform Assn., Washington Trade Assn. Execs., Am. Pub. Rels. Assn. (nat. treas. 1960-61, chpt. pres. 1958-59), U. Ill. Alumni Assn., Press Club St. Louis, Capitol Hill Club (Washington), Exchequer Club (Washington), Rotary (pres. Decatur chpt. 1985-86, Paul Harris fellow 1984, Svc. Above Self award 1996), Phi Sigma Kappa. Republican. Home: 5 Edgewood Ct Decatur IL 62522-1860

BLAKLEY, DERRICK, newscaster; b. Chgo. B Journalism, Northwestern U., 1975; M Comms., U. Ill., 1976. Reporter Chgo. Tribune Newspaper, 1976—78, Sta. WBNS-TV, Columbus, Ohio, 1978—80; midwest reporter CBS News, Chgo., 1980—83, European, African, and Middle Eastern reporter London, 1984—87, Bonn, Germany, 1984—87; gen. assignment reporter NBC 5, Chgo., 1987—, weekend morning newscast anchor, weekend evening anchor, 1998—. Recipient award, Ohio AP, local emmy award. Mem.: Chgo. Assn. Black Journalists, Nat. Assn. Black Journalists. Office: NBC 454 N Columbus Dr Chicago IL 60611*

BLANC, CARYN, retail executive; Sr. v.p. distbr. and store adminstrn. Kohl's Corp., Menomonee Falls, Wis. Office: Kohl's Corp 1700 Ridgewood Drive Menomonee Falls WI 53051-7026

BLANCHARD, ERIC ALAN, lawyer; b. 1956; BBA, U. Mich., 1978; JD, Harvard U., 1981. Bar: Ill. 1981. Atty. Schiff, Hardin & Waite, 1981-86; corp. atty. Dean Foods Co., Franklin Park, Ill., 1986-88, gen. coun., sec., v.p., pres. dairy divsn., 1988—. Office: Dean Foods Co 3600 N River Rd Franklin Park IL 60131-2185

BLANCHARD, J. A., III, publishing executive; CEO Deluxe Corp., St. Paul. Office: Deluxe Corp 3680 Victoria St N Saint Paul MN 55126-2906

BLAND, MARY GROVES, state legislator; b. Kansas City, Mo., Jan. 24, 1936; Student, Ottawa U., Penn Valley Coll., Pioneer C.C., Weaver Sch. Real Estate. Mem. Mo. Ho. of Reps. from 43rd dist., Jefferson City, 1980-98; cmty. specialist Lan Clearance for Redevel., Kansas City, 1971-79; mem. Mo. Senate from 9th dist., Jefferson City, 1999—. Vice-chmn. human rights and resources com., chair labor and indsl. rels. com., mem. aging families and mental health com., civil and criminal jurisprudence com., elections, vet. affairs and corrections com., pub. health and welfare com., health rev. com., cert. of need program com., joint com. on wetlands; free-lance cmty. cons., 1979—; exec. bd. Freedom, Inc. Active Mayor's Neighborhood Coun. on Crime Prevention; mem. S.E. Neighborhood Coalition, U.S. Commn. on Civil Rights; active Niles Home for Children. Home: 1632 Bushman Dr Kansas City MO 64110-3512 Office: Mo State Senate Rm 334 State Capitol Building Jefferson City MO 65101

BLANDER, MILTON, chemist; b. Bklyn., Nov. 1, 1927; s. Benjamin and Yetta (Schwartzman) B.; children: Benjamin, Alice, Kathryn, Daniel, Joshua. BS, CUNY, 1950; PhD, Yale U., 1953. Rsch. assoc. Cornell U., Ithaca, N.Y., 1953-55; chemist Oak Ridge (Tenn.) Nat. Lab., 1955-62; chemist, group leader Rockwell Internat. Sci. Ctr., Thousand Oaks, Calif., 1962-71; sr. chemist, group leader Argonne (Ill.) Nat. Lab., 1971-97; founder Quest Rsch., South Holland, Ill., 1995—. Recipient Materials Rsch. award U.S. Dept. Energy, 1984, Alexander von Humboldt award. Fellow AAAS, Meteoritical Soc.; mem. Metall. Soc., Am. Chem. Soc., Electrochem. Soc. (Max Bredig award 1987), Norwegian Acad. Tech. Scis. E-mail: mblander2@aol.com.

BLANDFORD, DICK, electrical engineering and communications educator; Chmn. dept. elec. engring. and computer sci. U. Evansville, Ind., 1994—. Office: U Evansville Dept Elec Engring/Computers 1800 Lincoln Ave Evansville IN 47722-0001

BLANFORD, LAWRENCE J. appliance company executive; With Johns Manville Corp., PPG Industries, Procter & Gamble Co., until 1997; v.p. strategic mktg. Maytag Corp., Newton, Iowa, 1997-99, pres. Maytag Internat., 1999—. Office: Maytag Corp 403 W 4th St N Newton IA 50208-3026

BLANK, DON SARGENT, dentist; b. Franklin, Nebr., Nov. 25, 1935; s. Thomas Wayne and Lila Louise (Sargent) B.; m. Janice Marie Halverson, June 10, 1962; children: Jeffrey, Steven, Randal. DDS, U. Nebr., 1960. Pvt. practice, McCook, Nebr., 1962--. Office: 411 W 5th St Mc Cook NE 69001-3635 Mailing: 811 Norris Ave. Mc Cook NE 69001

BLANK, REBECCA MARGARET, economist; b. Columbia, Mo., Sept. 19, 1955; d. Oscar Uel and Vernie (Backhaus) B.; m. Johannes Kuttner, 1994; 1 child, Emily. BS, U. Minn., 1976; PhD, MIT, 1983. Cons. Data Resources, Inc., Chgo., 1976-79; asst. prof. econs. Princeton U., 1983-89; assoc. prof. econs. Northwestern U., Chgo., 1989-94, prof. econs., 1994-99; sr. staff economist Coun. of Econ. Advisors, Washington, 1989-90, mem., 1998-99; dean, Henry Carter Adams prof. Gerald R. Ford Sch. Pub. Policy, U. Mich., Ann Arbor, 1999—. Author: It Takes A Nation: A New Agenda for Fighting Poverty, 1997; contbr. articles to profl. jours. Vis. Professorships for Women grantee, 1988-89; Sloan Found. fellow, 1982-83; recipient Jr. Faculty Teaching award Princeton U., 1985, David Kershaw award Assn. Pub. Policy Analysis and Mgmt., 1993, Richard Lester award for best book on labor econs., 1997. Mem. Nat. Bur. Econ. Rsch., Am. Econs. Assn., Assn. of Pub. Policy Analysis and Mgmt., Indsl. Rels. Rsch. Assn. United Ch. of Christ.

BLANKENSHIP, EDWARD G. architect; b. Martin, Tenn., Mar. 22, 1943; BArch, Columbia U., 1966, MSc in Arch., 1967; MLitt in Arch., Cambridge (Eng.) U., 1971. Sr. v.p. Landrum & Brown, Inc., Chgo. Home: 379 Woodland Rd Highland Park IL 60035 Office: 1021 W Adams St Chicago IL 60607-2911

BLANTON, LEWIS M. federal judge; b. Cape Girardeau, Mo., Mar. 5, 1934; AB, St. Louis U., 1958, MA, 1962; JD, U. Mo., 1965. Bar: Mo. Atty. Thompson, Walther & Shewmaker, St. Louis, 1965-69, Blanton, Rice & Sickal, Sikeston, Mo., 1969-71, Robison & Blanton, Sikeston, 1971-78; assoc. judge Cir. Ct. of Scott County, Mo., 1979-91; magistrate judge U.S. Dist. Ct. (ea. dist.) Mo., Cape Girardeau, 1991—. Contbr. articles to profl. jours. Mem. ABA, Mo. Bar, Scott County Bar Assn., Cape Girardeau County Bar Assn., Bar Assn. Met. St. Louis, Fed. Magistrate Judges Assn. Office: 111 US Courthouse 339 Broadway St Cape Girardeau MO 63701-7330

BLANTON, W. C. lawyer; b. LaRue County, Ky., Apr. 13, 1946; s. Crawford and Lillian (Phelps) B. BS in Math., BA in Social Sci., Mich. State U., 1968; MEd, U. Vt., 1970; JD, U. Mich., 1975. Bar: Ind. 1975, U.S. Dist. Ct. (no. and so. dists.) Ind. 1975, U.S. Ct. Appeals (7th cir.) 1977, (8th cir.) 1996, Minn. 1996, U.S. Dist. Ct. Minn. 1996, U.S. Dist. Ct. Wisc. (we. dist.) 1996. Residence hall dir. U. Wis., Madison, 1970-72; assoc. Ice Miller Donadio & Ryan, Indpls., 1975-81, ptnr., 1982-94, Popham, Haik, Schnobrich & Kaufman, Ltd., 1995-97, Oppenheimer Wolff & Donnelly LLP, Mpls., 1997—. Mem. ABA. Democrat. Avocations: skiing, travel, bridge. Office: Oppenheimer Wolff & Donnelly LLP 3300 Plaza VII 45 S 7th St Ste 3400 Minneapolis MN 55402-1609 E-mail: wblanton@oppenheimer.com.

BLATT, HAROLD GELLER, lawyer; b. Detroit, Apr. 8, 1934; s. Henry H. and Berdye (Geller) B.; m. Elaine K. Greenberg, July 9, 1960; children— Lisa K., James G., Andrew N. B.S., Washington U., St. Louis, 1955, LL.B., 1960; LL.M., NYU, 1961. Bar: Mo. 1960. Ptnr. Bryan Cave, St. Louis, 1961—. Dir. Artex Internat., Highland, Ill. Trustee Webster U., St. Louis, 1982-97, Washington U. Med. Ctr., St. Louis, 1983-96, Barnes-Jewish, Inc., 1993—; chmn. Jewish Hosp., St. Louis, 1983-88. 1st lt. U.S. Army, 1955-57. Mem. ABA, Mo. Bar Assn., Noonday Club (St. Louis), St. Louis Club.

BLATT, RICHARD LEE, lawyer; b. Oak Park, Ill., May 24, 1940; s. B. Lee Gray and Madelyn Gertrude (Bentley) B.; m. Carol Milner Jenkinson, May 21, 1965 (div. Dec. 1984); children: Christopher Andrew Lee, Katherine Lee, Susannah Lee; m. Carolyn Elizabeth LeBlanc, Jan. 31, 1987; 1 child, Jennifer Lee DeNux Blatt. BA, U. Ill., 1962; JD, U. Mich., 1965. Bar: Ill. 1968, U.S. Dist. Ct. (no. dist.) Ill. 1968, U.S. Ct. Appeals (7th cir.) 1968, U.S. Supreme Ct. 1974, U.S. Dist. Ct. (so. dist.) Ill. 1977, U.S. Ct. Appeals (4th cir.) 1987, N.Y. 1989, U.S. Ct. Appeals (3rd cir.) 1990, U.S. Dist. Ct. (ea. and so. dists.) N.Y. 1998. Assoc. Peterson, Lowry, Rall, Barber & Ross, Chgo., 1968-75; ptnr. Peterson, Ross, Schloeb & Seidel, 1975-91, Peterson & Ross, Chgo., 1991-94; sr. ptnr. Blatt, Hammesfahr & Eaton, 1994-2000; sr. mem. Cozen & O'Connor, 2000—. Rep. Disting. Neutral Ctr. Pub. Resources Inst. for Dispute Resolution; regulation bd. arbitrators NASD. Author: (with Robert G. Schloerb, Robert W. Hammesfahr, Lori S. Nugent) Punitive Damages: A Guide to the Insurability of Punitive Damages in the United States and Its Territories, 1988; (with Robert W. Hammesfahr and Lori S. Nugent) Punitive Damges: A State-by-State Guide to Law and Practice, 1991, 2002 (in Japanese 1995); (with Robert W. Hammesfahr and others) At Risk-Internet and E-Commerce Insurance and Reinsurance Legal Issues, 2000, 2002. Steering com. founders' coun. The Field Mus., Chgo. Capt. inf. USAR, 1965-67, Korea. Fellow Chartered Inst. Arbitrators; mem. ABA (litigation sect., dispute resolution sect.), NSSAR (Ft. Dearborn chpt.), Ill. State Bar Assn., Chgo. Internat. Dispute Resolution Assn. (planning com.), Soc. Mayflower Desc. State Ill., N.Y. State Bar Assn., Chgo. Bar Assn. (alternative dispute resolution com.), Chgo. Club, Pi Kappa Alpha Ednl. Found. (trustee), Phi Beta Kappa, Phi Kappa Phi. Home: 1415 N Dearborn Pkwy Chicago IL 60610-1559 Office: Cozen & O'Connor 222 S Riverside Plz Ste 1500 Chicago IL 60606-6000 Fax: 312-382-8910. E-mail: rblatt@earthlink.net., rblatt@cozen.com.

BLATTNER, ROBERT A. lawyer; b. Lima, Ohio, July 9, 1934; s. Simon James and Estelle Leila (Aarons) B.; m. Judith Reinfeld, Feb. 5, 1964 (div. July 1980); children: Wendy Lynn, Lauren Jill; m. Eileen Savransky, Dec. 18, 1983 BA, Northwestern U., 1956; LLB, Case Western Reserve U., 1959. Bar: Ohio 1959, Ill. 1965, U.S. Supreme Ct. 1984. Assoc. Hribar & Conway, Euclid, Ohio, 1960-62, Ulmer & Berne, Cleve., 1962-65; exec. dir. Ohio State Legal Svcs., Columbus, Ohio, 1965-67; gen. counsel, dir. real estate Sawyer Bus. Colls., Evanston, 1967-72; assoc. Guren Merritt Feibel Sogg & Cohen, Cleve., 1972-75, ptnr., 1975-84, Benesch, Friedlander, Coplan & Aronoff, Cleve., 1984-93; shareholder Kaufman & Cumberland Co., L.P.A., 1994—. Author: Consumer Affairs, 1973, The Construction Loan Process, 1979, Real Estate Financing, 1978, Acquisition, Development and Financing of a Commercial Complex-A Case Study, 1982; contbr. articles to profl. jours. Pres. Am. Jewish Com., Cleve., 1980-82, officer, 1976-80, chmn. adv. com., 1998—; v.p. Criminal Justice Coord. Com., Cleve., 1980-84, Cleve. Play House, 1988-92, bd. dirs., 1978—, pres., 1992-94, chmn., 1994-96, v.p., 1996—. Recipient Max Freedman Young Leadership award, Cleve., 1974. Mem. ABA, Nat. Assn. Bond Lawyers, Ohio State Bar Assn., Cleve. Bar Assn. (chmn. real estate com. 1978-79, chmn. real estate law insts. 1979, 82, 87). Jewish. Avocations: tennis, golf, classical music, reading. Office: 25 S Franklin St Chagrin Falls OH 44022-3212

BLATZ, KATHLEEN ANNE, state supreme court chief justice, state legislator; BA summa cum laude, U. Notre Dame, 1976; MSW, U. Minn., 1978, JD cum laude, 1984. Psychiat. social worker, 1979—81; mem. Minn. Ho. of Reps., St. Paul, 1979—93, chmn. crime and family law, fin. instns. and ins. coms., 1985—86; justice Minn. Supreme Ct., 1996—98, chief justice, 1998—. Office: Minn Judicial Ctr 25 Constitution Ave Rm 424 Saint Paul MN 55155-1500

BLAUSER, JEFFREY MICHAEL, professional baseball player; b. Los Gatos, Calif., Nov. 8, 1965; Student, Sacramento City Coll. With Atlanta Braves, 1984-97, Chgo. Cubs, 1997—. Mem. Nat. League All-Star Team, 1993. Recipient Silver Slugger award, 1997; named to N.L. All Star Team, 1997. Achievements include played in World Series, 1991, 92. Office: care Chgo Cubs Wrigley field 1060 W Addison St Chicago IL 60613-4383

BLEEKER, LAURIE, state legislator; b. Lincoln, Nebr., Nov. 30, 1952; m. Harry Bleeker; 2 children. BA, Bethel Coll. Homemaker, Great Bend, Kans.; mem. Kans. Senate, Topeka, 1996—, mem. edn. com., mem. pub. health and welfare com., mem. fed. and state affairs com., mem. arts and cultural resources com. Republican. Office: 300 SW 10th Ave Rm 460-e Topeka KS 66612-1504

BLEIBERG, EFRAIN, medical clinic executive; MD, Autonomous U. of Nuevo Leon. Diplomate Am. Bd. Psychiatry and Neurology. Staff psychiatrist Menninger Clinic, pres.; instr., tng. analyst Topeka Inst. for Psychoanlysis; faculty Karl Menninger Sch. Psychiatry and Mental Health Scis. Editl. bd. Bull. of the Menninger Clinic.; contbr. numerous articles to profl. publs. Named One of Nation's Top Mental Health Profls. Good Housekeeping mag. Fellow Am. Psychiat. Assn., Am. Acad. of Child and Adolescent Psychiatry; mem. Am. Psychoanlytic Assn. Office: Menninger PO Box 829 Topeka KS 66601-0829 Fax: 785-271-9723.

BLENKINSOPP, JOSEPH, biblical studies educator; b. Bishop Auckland, Durham, Eng., Apr. 3, 1927; came to U.S., 1968; s. Joseph William and Mary (Lyons) B.; m. Irene H. Blenkinsopp, Mar. 30, 1968 (div. 1991); children: David, Martin; m. Jean Porter, July 10, 1993. BA with honors in History, U. London, 1948; STL, Internat. Theologate, Turin, Italy, 1956; Licentiate in Sacred Scripture in Bibl. Studies, Bibl. Inst., Rome, 1958; DPhil in Bibl Studies, Oxford (Eng.) U., 1967. Lectr. Internat. Theologate, Romsey, Eng., 1958-62, Heythrop Coll., Oxford U., 1965; vis. asst. prof. Vanderbilt U., Nashville, 1968, Chgo. Theol. Sem., 1968-69; assoc. prof. Hartford (Conn.) Sem. Found., 1969-70; assoc. prof. bibl. studies U. Notre Dame, Ind., 1970-75, prof., 1975-85, John A. O'Brien prof., 1985—. Rector Ecumenical Inst., Tantur, Israel, 1978; coord. excavation Capernaum (Israel) Excavation, 1980-87. Author: Prophecy and Canon, 1977 (nat. religious book award 1977), History of Prophecy in Israel, 1983, 2d edit., 1996, Wisdom and Law in the Old Testament, 1983, 2d edit., 1995, The Pentateuch, 1992, Sage, Priest, Prophet: The Intellectual Tradition in Ancient Israel, 1995. Grantee NEH, Oxford U., 1982-83. Mem. Am. Acad. Religion, Soc. Bibl. Lit. (editl. bd. 1987-90), Cath. Bibl. Assn. (pres. 1990), Soc. O.T. Studies, Assn. Jewish Studies. Roman Catholic. Office: U Notre Dame 181 Decio Hall Notre Dame IN 46556-5644

BLESSING, LOUIS W., JR. state legislator, lawyer; b. Cin., Oct. 9, 1948; s. Louis W. and Rita (Roberts) B.; m. Linda Lameier, 1973; children: Billy, Alex. BBA, U. Cin., 1970; JD, No. Ky. U., 1976. Bar: Ohio. Practice law, Cin.; mem. Ohio Ho. of Reps., Columbus, 1983-97, Ohio Senate from 8th dist., 1997—. Common pleas referee Hamilton County, Cin., 1980-82. Trustee Colerain Twp., 1979-82. Named Legislator of Yr., Hamilton County Twp. Assn., 1983, Watchdog of Treasury, 1988, 90. Mem. Cin. Bar Assn., Hamilton County Trustees and Clks. Assn., Phi Kappa Theta. Republican. Home: 3153 Mcgill Ln Cincinnati OH 45251-3111

BLEUSTEIN, JEFFREY L. automotive executive; b. 1939; B in Mech. Engring., Cornell U.; MS in Engring. Mechanics, PhD in Engring. Mechanics, Columbia U. Tchr. engring. and applied scis. Yale U.; with AMF, Inc., 1971; v.p. parts and accessories Harley-Davidson Motor Co., v.p. motor co., pres., COO, 1993—, also bd. dirs. Office: Harley Davidson Inc 3700 W Juneau Ave Milwaukee WI 53208

BLEVEANS, JOHN, lawyer; b. Danville, Ill., Mar. 29, 1938; s. Edward Harold and Angelita (Robinson) B.; m. Luanna Harrison Burdick, Aug. 17, 1962; children: Lincoln Edward, Melanie Catherine. BA, Trinity U., 1960; LLB, U. Tex., 1965. Bar: Tex. 1965, D.C. 1967, U.S. Supreme Ct. 1969, Ill. 1971. Mem. gen. counsel's office Acacia Mut. Life Ins. Co., Washington, 1967-68; trial and appellate atty., civil rights div. U.S. Dept. Justice, 1966-67, 69-70; exec. dir. Washington Lawyers' Com., Civil Rights Under Law, 1970-71; chief counsel Lawyers' Com., Civil Rights Under Law, Cairo, 1971-72; assoc. Mayer, Brown & Platt, Chgo., 1972-74, ptnr., 1974-83, 91-92; sr. v.p., assoc., gen. counsel Continental Ill. Nat. Bank and Trust Co. of Chgo., 1983-89; dep. gen. counsel Continental Bank N.A., Chgo., 1989-91; ptnr. Mayer, Brown & Platt, 1991-92; of counsel Arthur Andersen & Co., 1992-95, Hong Kong, 1996-97, Sydney, Australia, 1995-96. Pres. Hanover Ambulance, Inc., 2000. Alderman City of Evanston, Ill., 1981-89; chmn. Evanston Zoning Bd. Appeals, 1991-92; vol. Hanover Ambulance, 1999—. Capt. USNR ret. Mem. Tex. Bar Assn., D.C. Bar Assn., Nat. Ski Patrol, Law Club Chgo.

BLEVINS, DALE GLENN, agronomy educator; b. Ozark, Mo., Aug. 29, 1943; s. Vernon Henry and Edna Gertrude (Payne) B.; m. Brenda Jo Graves, Aug. 27, 1967; 1 child, Jeremy. BS in Chemistry, S.W. Mo. State U., 1965; MS in Soils, U. Mo., 1967; PhD in Plant Physiology, U. Ky., 1972. Postdoctoral fellow botany dept. Oreg. State U., Corvallis, Oreg., 1972-74; asst. prof. botany U. Md., College Park, 1974-78; assoc. prof. agronomy dept. U. Mo., Columbia, 1978-86, prof., 1986—. Mem. Am. Soc. Plant Physiology, Am. Soc. Agronomy, Crop Sci. Soc. Am. Office: Univ Mo Dept Agronomy 1-87 Agriculture Building Columbia MO 65211-7140

BLEVINS, WILLIAM EDWARD, management consultant; b. Boissevan, Va., Oct. 18, 1927; s. Howard Muncey and Elsie Jane (Wire) B.; m. Mary Hester Jenkins, Aug. 25, 1951; children— Jeffrey Alexander, Jennifer Lynn, Bradley Edward AB, Marshall Coll., 1951; MPA, CCNY, 1960. Personnel mgr. Equitable Life, N.Y.C., 1951-66; asst. v.p., dir. mgmt. devel. Nat. Bank Detroit, 1966-69, v.p., dir. personnel, 1969-74, sr. v.p., dir. personnel, 1974-91; exec. v.p., dir. human resources NBD Bancorp, Inc., Detroit, 1980-92; pres. WEB Communications Co., 1993—. Bd. dirs. Blue Cross & Blue Shield Mich., Detroit, 1980—92, Human Resources Coun. AMA, 1979—84, 1987—92, Detroit Exec. Svc. Corps, 1996, Health Plan of Mich., 1997—2002. Trustee Bon Secour Hosp., Grosse Pointe, Mich., 1975-84, St. John Sr. Cmty., 1989—, chmn., 1995—, chmn. St. John Health Sys. Sr. Svcs., 2000—; bd. dirs. Oxford Inst., 1987-89, bd. dirs. Holy Cross Hosp., 1996-98; mem. corp. adv. bd. Am. Heart Assn., 1995-98; bd. trustees Frances Rhodes, M.D. Meml. Found., 1999—; bd. dirs. Mich. Diabetes Assn., 1982-86, Mich. Soc. for Mental Health, 1984-87. Recipient Outstanding Alumnus award Marshall U., 1976, Hall of Fame award Lambda Chi Alpha, 1996. Mem. Am. Bankers Assn. (bd. dirs. 1974-75), Am. Inst. Banking (bd. dirs., bd. regents, chmn. 1983-90), Am. Soc. Employers (bd. dirs. 1970-94, treas. 1970-90, vice chmn. 1991-92, chmn. 1992-94), Alpha Bank Pers Group (founder, chmn. 1972-74, 86), Mich. Pers. Indsl. Rels. Group (chmn. 1980-92), Bank Adminstr. Inst. (human resources commn. 1983-88), Detroit Athletic Club, Country Club Detroit. Republican. Office: WEB Comms Co 551 Fisher Rd Grosse Pointe Park MI 48230-1214 E-mail: webmjb@comcast.net.

BLEZNICK, DONALD WILLIAM, Romance languages educator; b. N.Y.C., Dec. 24, 1924; s. Louis and Gertrude (Kleinman) B.; m. Rozlyn Burakoff, June 15, 1952; children— Jordan, Susan BA, CCNY, 1946; MA, U. Nacional de Mex., 1948; PhD, Columbia U., 1954. Instr. romance langs. Ohio State U., 1949-55; prof. Pa. State U., 1955-67, U. Cin., 1967—, head dept., 1967-72; instr. Romance langs. Vis. prof. Hebrew U., Jerusalem, 1974. Bibliographer, MLA Internat. Bibliography, 1966-81; rev. editor Hispania, 1965-73, editor, 1974-83, editor's adv. coun., 1984—, El Ensayo Espanol del Siglo Veinte, 1964, Historia del Ensayo Espanol, 1964, Duelo en el Paraiso (Goytisolo), 1967, Madrugada (Buero Vallejo), 1969, (with W.T. Pattison) Representative Spanish Authors, 1971, Quevedo, 1972, Variaciones interpretativas en torno a la nueva narrativa hispanoamericana, 1972, Directions of Literary Criticism in the Seventies, 1972, Sourcebook for Hispanic Literature and Language, 1974, 3d expanded edit., 1995, Homenaje a Luis Leal, 1978, Studies on Don Quixote and other Cervantine Works, 1984, Critical Edition of La Diana (Jorge Montemayor), 1990, The Thought of Contemporary Spanish Essayists, 1993, Studies in Honor of Donald W. Bleznick, 1995; founder, exec. editor Cin. Romance Rev., 1982-88; field editor: Twayne Spanish Literature Series, 1981—; contbr. articles to profl. jours., Ency. Americana. With CIC, 1946-47. Decorated Knight's Cross Order Civil Merit (Spain); Am. Philos. Soc. rsch. grantee, 1964; Downer fellow CCNY, 1947-48; U. Cin. Taft rsch. and publ. grantee, 1972, 75, 78, 83, 88, 89, 92; named 1 of 15 outstanding scholars in Spanish lit. in Cuadernos Salmantinos de Filosofia, Salamanca, Spain, 1977; recipient Rieveschl award for excellence in rsch. U. Cin., 1980, award Hispania, U. So. Calif., 1983; fellow U. Cin. Grad. Sch., 1984. Mem. AAUP, Am. Assn. Tchrs. Spanish and Portuguese (exec. com. 1975—, award 1984, v.p. 1992, pres. 1993, Honored for Outstanding Career 1995, disting. svc. award 1997), MLA, Los Ensayistas (adv. bd. 1976—), Comediantes, Midwest Modern Lang. Assn., Conf. Editors of Learned Jours. (exec. com. 1978-79), Celestinesca, Cervantes Soc. Am., Phi Beta Kappa (pres. Delta chpt. of Ohio 1971-72, 86-87), Sigma Delta Pi (state dir. Ohio 1968-74, Order of Don Quijote 1970, v.p. Midwest 1975-83, Jose Martel award 1980, hon. pres. 1998), Phi Sigma Iota, Kappa Delta Pi. Home: 2444 Madison Rd Apt 1806 Cincinnati OH 45208-1255 Office: U Cin Dept Romance Langs Cincinnati OH 45221-0001 E-mail: donald.bleznick@uc.edu.

BLOCH, HENRY WOLLMAN, tax preparation company executive; b. Kansas City, Mo., July 30, 1922; s. Leon Edwin and Hortense Bienenstok; m. Marion Ruth Helzberg, June 16, 1951; children: Robert, Thomas M., Mary Jo, Elizabeth Ann. BS, U. Mich., 1944; D of Bus. Adminstrn. (hon.), Avila Coll., Kansas City, Mo., 1977, U. Mo., Kansas City, 1989; LLD (hon.), N.H. Coll., 1983, William Jewell Coll., Liberty, Mo., 1990, Kansas City Art Inst., 1999. Ptnr. United Bus. Co., 1946-55; hon. chmn., past CEO H & R Block, Inc., Kansas City, 1955—, also dir. Bd. dirs. Commerce Bancshares, Inc., Kansas City, CompuServe, Inc., Valentine Radford Advt.; past chmn. Midwest Rsch. Inst. Past bd. dirs. Menorah Med. Ctr.; bd. dirs., past pres. Menorah Med. Ctr. Found.; former mem. pres.'s adv. coun. Kansas City Philharmonic Assn.; chmn., dir. H & R Block Found.; past pres. of trustees U. Kansas City, Nelson-Atkins Mus. Art, trustee, dir., past chmn. bus. coun.; past bd. dirs. Jewish Fedn. and Coun. Greater Kansas City; dir., past pres. Civic Coun. Greater Kansas City; gen. chmn. United Negro Colls. Fund, 1986; bd. dirs. St. Luke's Hosp. Found., Internat. Rels. Coun., Kansas City Cmty. Found.; former mem. bd. dirs. Coun. of Fellows of Nelson Gallery Found., Am. Jewish Com.; former mem. bd. govs. Kansas City Mus. History and Sci.; bd. dirs. Midwest Rsch. Inst., vice chmn.; bd. dirs. Kansas City Symphony, past dir.; bd. dirs. Greater Kansas City Community Found.; gen. chmn. Heart of Am. United Way Exec. Com., 1978; past met. chmn. Nat. Alliance Businessmen; former mem. bd. regents Rockhurst Coll.; former mem. bd. chancellor's assocs. U. Kans. at Lawrence; former mem. bd. dirs. Harry S. Truman Good Neighbor Award Found.; bd. dirs. Internat. Rels. Coun.; bd. dirs., v.p. Kansas City Area Health Planning Coun.; past pres. Found. for a Greater Kansas City; dir. Mid-Am. Coalition on Health Care, St; Luke's Found.; trustee Jr. Achievement of Mid-Am.; vice chmn. corp. fund Kennedy Ctr. 1st lt. USAAF, 1943-45. Decorated Air medal with 3 oak leaf clusters; named Mktg. Man of Yr. Sales and Mktg. Execs. Club, 1971, Chief Exec. Officer of Yr. for svc. industry Fin. World, 1976, Mainstreeter of Decade, 1988, Entrepreneur of Yr., 1986; recipient Disting. Exec. award Boy Scouts Am., 1977, Salesman of Yr. Kansas City Advt. Club, 1978, Civic Svc. award Hyman Brand Hebrew Acad., 1980, Golden Plate award Am. Acad. Achievement, 1980, Chancellor's medal U. Mo.-Kansas City, 1980, Pres.'s trophy Kansas City Jaycees, 1980, W.F. Yates medal for disting. svc. in civic affairs William Jewell Coll., 1981, bronze award for svc. industry Wall Street Transcript, 1981, Disting. Missourian award NCCJ, 1982, Lester A. Milgram Humanitarian award, 1983, Hall of Fame award Internat. Franchise Assn., 1983; named to Bus. Leader Hall of Fame Jr. Achievement, 1980; honoree Sales and Mktg. Execs. Internat. Acad. of Achievement, 1991. Mem. Greater Kansas City C. of C. (past pres.), C. of C. Greater Kansas City (Mr. Kansas City award 1978), Acad. Squires, Golden Key Nat. Honor Soc. (hon.), Oakwood Country Club, River Club, Carriage Club, Kansas City Country Club. Jewish. Office: H&R Block Inc 4400 Main St Kansas City MO 64111-1812

BLOCH, RALPH JAY, professional association executive, marketing consultant; b. N.Y.C., Sept. 21, 1942; s. Alexander and Catherine (La Bue) B.; m. Patricia Ann Cassone, Aug. 18, 1963 (div.); 1 child, Marci Suzanne; m. Helen Lightstone, June 19, 1988. BS, UCLA, 1965. Sales rep. Lowell Wood Co., L.A., 1967-68; mgr. Home Furniture, 1968-72, co-owner, gen. mgr., 1972-78; pres. Concepts III, Inc., Greenville, S.C., 1978-79; from western exec. v.p. to mktg. v.p. Nat. Home Furnishings Assn., 1979-83; pres., owner The Access Group, Inc., Chgo., 1984-99, Ralph J. Bloch & Assocs., Inc., Chgo., 1999—. Mem. Chgo. Soc. Assn. Execs., Am. Soc. Assn. Execs. Avocations: backpacking, hiking, sailing, cooking. Office: Ralph J Bloch & Assocs Inc Apt 7A 1430 N Astor St Chicago IL 60610-5717

BLOCK, ALLAN JAMES, communications executive; b. Oct. 1, 1954; s. Paul Jr. and Marjorie (McNab) B. BA, U. Pa., 1977. Coord. electronic tech. planning Toledo Blade Co., 1981-83, dir. electronic planning, 1984-85; dir. mktg. Buckeye Cablevision Inc., Toledo, 1985-87; v.p. cablevision and TV Blade Communications, Inc., 1987-88, exec. v.p., 1989, mem., chief exec. com., co-CEO, 1989—; vice-chmn. bd. Block Comm. (formerly known as Blade Communications, Inc.), 1990—2001, pres., 1987—, 1987—; dir. Block Comms. Inc. Bd. dirs. Toledo Blade Co., Blade Comms., Inc., P.G. Pub. Co. Bd. dirs. C-SPAN, Nat. Cable TV Coop., Inc., Am. Cable Assn.; trustee Med. Coll. Ohio, 1991-2000. Mem. Toledo Club, Met. Club (N.Y.C.), Penn Club (N.Y.C.), Duquesne Club (Pitts.). Home: 235 14th St Toledo OH 43624-1401 Office: Block Communications Inc 541 N Superior St Toledo OH 43660-1000 E-mail: ABlock@cablesystem.com.

BLOCK, NEAL JAY, lawyer; b. Chgo., Oct. 4, 1942; s. William Emanual and Dorothy (Harrison) B.; m. Frances Keer Block, Apr. 19, 1970; children: Jessica, Andrew. BS, U. Ill., 1964; JD, U. Chgo., 1967. Bar: Ill. 1967, U.S. dist. Ct. (no. dist.) Ill. 1967, U.S. Ct. Appeals (3d and 6th cirs.) 1968, U.S. Claims Ct. 1990, U.S. Ct. Appeals (Fed. cir.) 1991. Atty., advisor U.S. Tax Ct., Washington, 1967-69; assoc. Baker & McKenzie, Chgo., 1969-74, ptnr., 1974—, client credit dir., 1989—. Adj. prof. law Kent Law Sch., Ill. Inst. Tech., Chgo., 1986-90. Mem. ABA, Chgo. Bar Assn. (chmn. fed. tax com. 1983-84), Ill. State Bar Assn., AICPA (honorable mention award 1964), Ill. Soc. CPA's. (silver medal 1964, Leading Ill. Atty. 1997). Office: Baker & McKenzie 1 Prudential Pla 130 E Randolph St Ste 3500 Chicago IL 60601-6342

BLOCK, PHILIP DEE, III, investment counselor; b. Chgo., Feb. 14, 1937; married; 2 children. BS in Indsl. Adminstrn. with high honors, Yale U., 1958. Trainee and engr. Inland Steel Co., Chgo., 1958-60, raw materials coordinator, 1961-65, gen. mgr. purchases, 1966-72, gen. mgr. corp. planning, 1973-76; v.p. materials and services Inland Steel Container, 1977-79, v.p. purchases, 1980-85; sr. v.p. Capital Guardian Trust Co., 1986—. Bd. dirs. Children's Meml. Hosp.; trustee Chgo. Hist. Soc., Shedd Aquarium Soc. With USAFR, 1959-64. Home: 1430 N Lake Shore Dr Chicago IL 60610-6682 Office: Capital Guardian Trust Co 21 S Clark St Chicago IL 60603-2000

BLOCK, WILLIAM K., JR. newspaper executive; b. New Haven, Nov. 28, 1944; s. William and Maxine (Horton) B.; m. Carol Pauline Zurheide, Aug. 1, 1970; children: Diana, Nancy, Katherine. BA, Trinity Coll., Hartford, Conn., 1967; JD, Washington and Lee U., 1972. Bar: Pa., U.S. Supreme Ct. Staff mem. Red Bank (N.J.) Register and Toledo Blade, 1972-77; advtg. mgr. Red Bank (N.J.) Register, Shrewsbury, N.J., 1977-79, sales mgr., 1979-80, pub., 1980-82; dir. ops. Toledo Blade Co., 1983-84, v.p. ops., 1984-86, v.p., gen. mgr., 1986-87, pres., 1987—, co-pub., 1990—, Pitts. Post Gazette, 1990—; v.p. Blade Communications, Inc., Toledo, 1987-88, pres., 1989—. V.p. Toledo Sesquicentennial Commn., 1986-87; pres. Inland Press Assn., 1998-99; bd. dirs. Toledo Symphony; pres. Read for Literacy, Inc. With U.S. Army, 1968-70, Vietnam. Mem. Toledo Country Club, Toledo Club. Avocations: reading, tennis, travel, fishing. Office: Block Communications Inc 541 N Superior St Toledo OH 43660-0001

BLOMQUIST, DAVID WELS, journalist; b. Detroit, June 16, 1956; s. August Wels and Sally Lou (Ball) B. AB, U. Mich., 1976; AM, Harvard U., 1978. Tchg. fellow Harvard U., Cambridge, 1978-82, asst. sr. tutor, 1981-82; supervising sect. editor CBS Inc., N.Y.C., 1982-84; staff writer The Record of Hackensack, N.J., 1984-86, state polit. corr., 1986-89, chief polit. writer, 1990-92, chief Trenton bur., 1992-94; dir. The Record Poll, Hackensack, 1992-99, dir. online devel., 1998-99; dir. new media Detroit Free Press, 1999—2001, sr. editor tech. and rsch., 2002—. Author: Elections and the Mass Media, 1982; contbr. articles to profl. jours. Mem. Am. Polit. Sci. Assn. (edn. com. 1984-86), N.J. Legis. Corrs. Club (pres. 1992), Harvard Club of N.Y., Nat. Press Club Washington. Avocations: music, ballet. Office: Detroit Free Press 600 W Fort St Detroit MI 48226-2706 E-mail: blomquist@freepress.com.

BLOOM, BENJAMIN S. education educator; b. Lansford, Pa., Feb. 21, 1913; married; 2 children. BA, MS, Pa. State U., 1935; PhD, U. Chgo., 1942; LHD (hon.), Rutgers U., 1970, Ohio State U., 1983, U. San Diego, 1990; Docteur Honoris Causa, U. Liege, Belgium, 1992. Rsch. worker Pa. State Relief Orgn., 1935-36, Am. Youth Commn., 1936-38; rsch. asst. Coop. Study in Gen. Edn., 1939-40; rsch. asst. bd. examinations U. Chgo., 1943-59, coll.-univ. examiner, 1943-59, from instr. to disting. svc. prof., 1943-70, Charles Swift Disting. Svc. prof. emeritus, 1970—; prof. edn. Northwestern U., Evanston, Ill., 1983-89. Vis. prof. edn. UCLA, summer 1968; Jacks disting. vis. prof. edn. Stanford U., 1969-70; edn. advisor Govt. of India, 1957-59, Govt. of Israel, 1963, 68, others; chmn. R & D com. Coll. Entrance Examinations Bd., Nat. Labs. Early Childhood Edn.; mem. adv. com. R & D ctrs. U. Ga., UCLA, U. Pitts., Sci. Rsch. Assocs., evaluation Rsch. Ctr. U. Va.; mem. panel to select edn. R & D ctrs. U.S. Office Edn., mem. adv. com. on R & D ctrs. and regional labs.; chmn. Invitational Conf. on Testing Problems, 1967; vice chmn. Meeting of Experts on Curriculum of Gen. Edn., UNESCO, Moscow, 1968; dir. Internat. Seminar Advanced Tng. in Curriculum Devel., Sweden, summer 1971. Author: Evaluation in Secondary Schools, 1958, Evaluation in Higher Education, 1961, Stability and Change in Human Characteristics, 1964, Human Characteristics and School Learning, 1976, All Our Children Learning: A Primer for Parents, Teachers and other Educators, 1980, Developing Talent in Young People, 1985; (with J. Axelrod et al.) Teaching by Discussion, 1948, (with G.G. Stern and M.I. Stein) Methods in Personality Assessment, 1956, (with D. Krathwohl and others) Taxonomy of Educational Objectives: Handbook I, Cognitive Domain, 1956, vol. II, The Affective Domain, 1964, (with L. Broder) Problem-solving Processes of College Students, 1958, (with F. Peters) Use of Academic Prediction Scales for Counseling and Selecting College Entrants, 1961, (with A. Davis and R. Hess) Compensatory Education for Cultural Deprivation, 1965, (with others) Handbook on Formative and Summative Evaluation of Student Learning, 1971, (with MESA student group) The State of Research on Selected Alterable Variables in Education, 1980, (with G.F. Madaus and J.T. Hastings) Evaluation to Improve Learning, 1981, (with Soshlak and others) Developing Talent in Young People, 1985; assoc. editor: International Study of Achievement in Mathematics, A Comparison of Twelve Countries, vols. I and II, 1966; editorial cons. Irish Jour. Edn., Internat. Jour. Eductional Scis., Jour. Applied Social Psychology, Sch. Rev., Jour. Educational Psychology; contbr. numerous chpts. to books and articles to profl jours. Recipient John Dewey award John Dewey Soc., 1968, Tchrs. Coll. medal for disting. svc. Columbia U., 1970, award for disting. contbns. to edn. Am. Educational Rsch. Assn. and Phi Delta Kappa, 1970, special medals and awards from govts. of Belgium, Israel and Finland; named Disting. Alumni fellow Pa. State U., 1973; fellow Ctr. Advanced Study in the Behavioral Scis., 1959-60. Fellow APA (Thorndike Meml. award

1972); mem. Internat. Assn. Evaluation of Educational Achievement (founding mem., mem. coun. 1959—), Internat. Curriculum Assn. (founding mem., mem. coun. 1972—), U.S. Nat. Acad. Edn., Am. Educational Rsch. Assn. (pres. 1965-66), Phi Delta Kappa, Psi Chi. Office: U Chgo Sch Edn Judd Hall 5835 S Kimbark Ave Chicago IL 60637-1635

BLOOM, JANE MAGINNIS, emergency physician; b. Ithaca, N.Y., June 22, 1924; d. Ernest Victor and Miriam Rebecca (Mansfield) M.; m. William Lee Bloom, Mar. 31, 1944; children: David Lee, Jan Christopher, Carolyn Wells, Eric Paul, Joseph William, Robert Carl, Mary Catherine, Thomas Mark, Patrick Martin (dec.), Arthur Emerson. BS, U. Mich., 1968, MD, 1974. Diplomate Am. Bd. Internal Medicine, Am. Bd. Emergency Medicine. Rotating intern Wayne County Gen. Hosp., Eloise, Mich., 1974-75; resident in internal medicine St. Mary's Hosp., Rochester, NY, 1975-77; emergency physician Emergency Physicians Med. Group, Ann Arbor, 1986—. Fellow Am. Coll. Emergency Physicians (life); mem. AMA, Mich. State Med. Soc., Am. Coll. Physicians, Am. Med. Womens Assn., Am. Assn. Women Emergency Physicians, Washtenaw County Med. Soc., Am. Coll. Emergency Physicians. Avocations: bird watching, planting trees, classical music, walking. Home and Office: 537 Elm St Ann Arbor MI 48104-2515

BLOOM, STEPHEN JOEL, distribution company executive; b. Chgo., Feb. 27, 1936; s. Max Samuel and Carolyn (Gumbiner) B.; m. Nancy Lee Gillan, Aug. 24, 1957; children: Anne, Bradley, Thomas, Carolyn. BBA, U. Mich., 1958. From salesman to gen. mgr. Cigarette Svc. Co., Countryside, Ill., 1957-65, pres., CEO, 1965—; exec. v.p., CEO S. Bloom, Inc.; v.p., then sr. v.p. Philip Morris USA, now ret. Bd. dirs. Amerimark Fin. Corp. Active Chgo. Crime Commn. Named Man of Yr. Chgo. Tobacco Table, 1972; named to Tobacco Industry Hall of Fame, 1985. Mem. Nat. Automatic Mdsg. Assn. (Minuteman award 1974), Nat. Assn. Tobacco Distbrs. (chmn. nat. legis. com. Young Exec. of Yr. award, dir. 1978), Ill. Assn. Tobacco Distbrs., Young Pres. Orgn., Chgo. Pres. Orgn., Morningside Rancho Mirage Club (pres. 1996-97), Rotary. Lodge: Rotary. Home: 3 Hamill Ln Clarendon Hills IL 60514-1462 Office: 120 Park Ave New York NY 10017

BLOSSER, HENRY GABRIEL, physicist; b. Harrisonburg, Va., Mar. 16, 1928; s. Emanuel and Leona (Branum) B.; m. Priscilla May Beard, June 30, 1951 (div. Oct. 1972); children: William Henry, Stephan Emanuel, Gabe Fawley, Mary Margaret; m. Mary Margaret Gray, Mar. 16, 1973 (dec. Jan. 1995); m. Amy June Conley, May 11, 1995 (div. Feb. 1997); m. Lois Pearlena Lynch, Oct. 17, 1998. BS, U. Va., 1951, MS, 1952, PhD, 1954. Physicist Oak Ridge (Tenn.) Nat. Lab., 1954-56, group leader, 1956-68; assoc. prof. physics Mich. State U., East Lansing, 1958-61, prof., 1961-90, Univ. Disting. prof., 1990—, dir. Cyclotron Lab., 1961-89. Cons. Harper Hosp., Detroit, 1983—, Ion Beam Applications, Belgium, 1996—, others; adj. prof. radiation oncology Wayne State U., Detroit, 1996—. Bd. dirs. Midwest Univs. Rsch. Assocs., 1960-63. With USNR, 1946-48. Predoctoral fellow NSF, 1953-54, sr. postdoctoral fellow, 1966-67; Guggenheim fellow, 1973-74. Fellow Am. Phys. Soc. (Bonner prize 1992); mem. Sigma Xi, Phi Beta Kappa, Kappa Alpha. Home: 2350 Emerald Forest Cir East Lansing MI 48823-7200 Office: Mich State U Nat Cyclotron East Lansing MI 48824-1321

BLOUIN, FRANCIS XAVIER, JR. history educator; b. Belmont, Mass., July 29, 1946; s. Francis X. and Margaret (Cronin) B.; m. Joy Alexander; children: Benjamin, Tiffany. AB, U. Notre Dame, 1967; MA, U. Minn., 1969, PhD, 1978. Asst. dir. Bentley Library U. Mich., Ann Arbor, 1974-75, assoc. archivist Bentley Library, 1975-81, dir. Bentley Library, 1981—, asst. prof. history and library sci., 1979-83, assoc. prof., 1983-89, prof., 1989—. Author: The Boston Region..., 1980, Vatican Archives: An Inventory and Guide to Historical Documentation of the Holy See, 1998; editor Intellectual Life on Michigan Frontier, 1985, Archival Implications Machine..., 1980. Trustee Much. Student Found., 1986-91; dir. Am. Friends of Vatican Libr., 1981—, Coun. on Libr. and Info. Resources, 2001—. Fellow Soc. Am. Archivist (mem. governing council 1985-88); mem. Am. Hist. Assn., Hist. Soc. Mich. (trustee 1982-88, pres. 1987-88), Assn. Records Mgrs. and Adminstrs., Internat. Council on Archives. Office: U Mich Bentley Hist Libr 1150 Beal Ave Ann Arbor MI 48109-2113

BLOUNT, MICHAEL EUGENE, lawyer; b. Camden, N.J., July 9, 1949; s. Floyd Eugene and Dorothy Alice (Geyer) Durham; m. Janice Lynn Brown, Aug. 22, 1969; children: Kirsten Marie, Gretchen Elizabeth. BA, U. Tex., 1971; JD, U. Houston, 1974. Bar: Tex. 1974, Ill. 1980, D.C. 1981, U.S. Ct. Appeals (D.C. cir.) 1978, U.S. Ct. Mil. Appeals 1975, U.S. Supreme Ct. 1977. Atty. advisor Office of Gen. Counsel SEC, Washington, 1977-78, legal asst. to chmn., 1978-79; assoc. Gardner, Carton & Douglas, Chgo., 1980-84; ptnr. Arnstein, Gluck, Lehr, Barron & Milligan, 1984-86, Seyfarth Shaw, Chgo., 1987—. Lt. JAGC USN, 1974—77. Mem.: ABA (fed. regulation of securities com.), Chgo. Bar Assn., Order of Barons, Assn. SEC Alumni, Univ. Club (Chgo.), Phi Alpha Delta (chpt. treas. 1973). Home: 1711 Galloway Dr Barrington IL 60010-5737 Office: Seyfarth Shaw 55 E Monroe St Ste 4200 Chicago IL 60603-5863 E-mail: mblount@seyfarth.com.

BLUESTEIN, PAUL HAROLD, management engineer; b. Cin., June 14, 1923; s. Norman and Eunice D. (Schullman) B.; m. Joan Ruth Straus, May 17, 1943; children: Alice Sue Bluestein Greenbaum, Judith Ann. B.S., B.Engring. in Mgmt. Engring., Carnegie Inst. Tech., 1946; M.B.A., Xavier U., 1973, MA in Humanities, 1992. Registered profl. engr., Ohio. Time study engr. Lodge & Shipley Co., 1946-47; adminstrv. engr. Randall Co., 1947-52; partner Paul H. Bluestein & Co. (mgmt. cons.), 1952—, Seinsheimer-Bluestein Mgmt. Services, 1964-70; gen. mgr. Baker Refrigeration Co., 1953-56; pres., dir. Tabor Mfg. Co., 1953-54, Bluejay Corp., 1954—, Blatt & Ludwig Corp., 1954-57, Jason Industries, Inc., 1954-57, Hamilton-York Corp., 1954-57, Earle Hardware Mfg. Co., 1955-57, Hermas Machine Co., 1956—, Panel Machine Co., Ermet Products Corp., 1957-86, Tyco Labs., Inc., 1968-69, All-Tech Industries, 1968. Gen. mgr. Hafleigh & Co., 1959-60; sr. v.p., gen. mgr. McCauley Ind. Corp., 1959-60; gen. mgr. Am. Art Works div. Rapid-Am. Corp., 1960-63; sec.-treas., dir. Liberty Baking Co., 1964-65; pres. Duguesne Baking Co., 1964-65, Goddard Bakers, Inc., 1964-65; pub. Merger and Acquisition Digest, 1962-69; partner Companhia Engenheiros Indsl. Bluestein Do Brasil, 1970-84; v.p., gen. mgr. Famco Machine div. Worden-Allen Co., 1974-75; exec. v.p., gen. mgr. Peck, Stow & Wilcox Co., Inc., 1976-77; mem. Joint Engring. Mgmt. Conf. Com., 1971-78 Com. mem. Cin. Art Mus. With AUS, 1943-46. Mem. ASME, Internat. Inst. Indsl. Engrs., Am. Soc. Engring. Mgmt., C.I.O.S.-World Council Mgmt. (dir., 1982-87). Home and Office: 3420 Section Rd Amberley Village Cincinnati OH 45237

BLUESTEIN, VENUS WELLER, retired psychologist, educator; b. Milw., July 16, 1933; d. Richard T. and Hazel (Beard) Weller; m. Marvin Bluestein, Mar. 7, 1954. BS, U. Cin., 1956, MEd, 1959, EdD, 1966. Diplomate Am. Bd. Profl. Psychology. Psychologist-in-tng. Longview State Hosp., Cin., 1956-58; sch. psychologist Cin. Pub. Schs., 1958-65; asst. prof. psychology U. Cin., 1965-70, assoc. prof., 1970-79, prof., 1979-93, prof. emerita, 1993—, dir. sch. psychology program, 1965-70, co-dir. sch. psychology program, 1970-75, dir. undergrad. studies, 1976-91, dir. undergrad. advising, 1991-93. Cons. child psychologist. Sec., U.S. exec. com. rsch. Children's Internat. Summer Villages, 1964-68; chmn. Ohio Interuniv. Coun. Sch. Psychology, 1967-68 Editor Ohio Psychologist, 1961-68, co-editor, 1972-79; contbr. articles to profl. publs. Vol. Hmilton County Parks, 1982—, vol. naturalist, 1995—; vol. educator Cin. Zoo, 1983—. Recipient George B. Barbour award, 1985 Fellow Am. Acad. Sch. Psychology; mem. AAUP, APA, Ohio Psychol. Assn. (citation 1972, Disting. Svc. award 1968), Cin. Psychol. Assn. (sec. 1961-62), Sch. Psychologists Ohio, Forum for Death Edn. and Counseling, Kappa Delta Pi, Sigma Delta Pi, Psi Chi (award for outstanding mentor 1985, award for outstanding contbns. to undergrad. psychology students 1994). Avocations: horseback riding, wildlife photography. Office: U Cin Dept Psychology Ml 376 Cincinnati OH 45221-0001

BLUFORD, GUION STEWART, JR. engineering company executive; b. Phila., Nov. 22, 1942; s. Guion Stewart and Lolita Harriet (Brice) B.; m. Linda M. Tull, Apr. 7, 1964; children: Guion Stewart, James Trevor. B.S. in Aerospace Engring., Pa. State U., 1964; grad., Squadron Officers Sch., 1971; M.S. in Aerospace Engring., Air Force Inst. Tech., 1974, Ph.D. in Aerospace Engring., 1978; D.Sc. hon., Fla. A&M U., 1983; MBA, U. Houston, 1987; DSc (hon.), Tex. So. U., Va. State U., Morgan State U., Stevens Inst. Tech., Tuskegee U., Bowie (Md.) State Coll., Thomas Jefferson U., Chgo. State U., Georgian Ct. Coll., Drexel U., Kent State U., Ctrl State U. Commd. 2d lt. U.S. Air Force, 1965, advanced through grades to col., 1983, F-4C fighter pilot 12 Tactical Fighter Wing Vietnam, 1966-67, T-38 instr. pilot 3630 Flying Tng. Wing Sheppard AFB, Wichita Falls, Tex., 1967-72; chief aerodynamics and airframe br. Air Force Flight Dynamics Lab., Wright-Patterson AFB, Dayton, Ohio, 1975-78; NASA astronaut Johnson Space Ctr., Houston, 1978-93; ret., 1993; v.p., gen. mgr. div. engring. svcs. NYMA Inc., Greenbelt, Md., 1993-97; v.p., gen. mgr. aerospace sector Fed. Data Corp., Bethesda, 1997—2000; v.p. micrograv-ity R&D ops. Northrup Grumman Info. Tech., Herndon, Va., 2000—. Decorated USAF Command Pilot Astronaut Wings, Air Force Commendation medal, Air Force Commendation medal, Air Force Meritorious Svc. award , Air medal with 9 oak leaf clusters, Def. Superior Svc. medal, Legion of Merit ; named Black Engr. of Yr., 1991; named to Internat. Space Hall of Fame, 1997; recipient Mervin E. Gross award Air Force Inst. Tech., 1974, Disting. Nat. Scientist award Nat. Soc. Black Engrs., 1979, Group Achievement award NASA, 1980, Disting. Alumni award Pa. State U. Alumni Assn., 1983, 85, 91, 92, Space Flight medal NASA, 1983, Pa. Disting. Svc. medal, 1984, NASA Exceptional Svc. medal, 1992, NASA Disting. Svc. medal, 1994, Def. Meritorious Svc. medal, Nat. Intelligence medal of achievement . Fellow: AIAA (bd. dirs.); mem.: U.S. Space Found., Aerospace Corp. (trustee), Nat. Rsch. Coun. Aeronautics and Space Engring. Bd., Tau Beta Pi. Christian Scientist. Office: Northrop Grumman 2001 Aerospace Pky Brookpark OH 44142-1003 E-mail: gbluford@cleveland.feddata.com.

BLUHM, NEIL GARY, real estate company executive; b. 1938; married B.S., U. Ill.; J.D., Northwestern U. Bar: Ill. Ptnr. firm Mayer, Brown & Platt, Chgo., 1962-70; pres. JMB Realty Corp., from 1970; pres., trustee JMB Realty Trust, 1972—. Office: Urban Shopping Ctrs Inc 132 E Delaware Ste Ste 6501 Chicago IL 60611 also: JMB Realty Corporation 900 N Michigan Ave Fl 19 Chicago IL 60611-1542

BLUM, ARTHUR, social work educator; b. Cleve., May 25, 1926; s. Rebecca (Pivowar) Blum; m. Lenore Sharrie Secord, Dec. 26, 1954; children: Alex, Joel. AB, Western Res. U., 1950, MS in Social Adminstrn., 1952, DSW, 1960. Group worker Cleve. Jewish Community Ctr., 1952, Cleve. Child Guidance Ctr., 1954-58; project dir. Case Western Res. U., Cleve., 1958-60, prof. social work, 1960—, Grace Longwell Coyle chair, 1987—; prof. Smith Coll., Northampton, Mass., 1961-63. Cons. Bellefaire Regional Treatment Ctr., Cleve., 1962-85, City of East Cleve., 1967-70, Jewish Welfare Fedn., Cleve., 1968-72, Fedn. Community Plannning, Cleve., 1976-78, 20 other human svcs. agys., 1960—; vis. prof. Tel Aviv U., 1971-72, 79-80. Editor: Healing Through Living, 1971, Aging and Care Giving, 1990, Innovations in Practice and Service Delivery, 1999; contbr. numerous articles to profl. jours. Sgt. U.S. Army, 1945-46, with Med. Svcs. Corp, 1952-54. Recipient Outstanding Alumnus award Case Western Res. U., 1968. Mem. AAUP, Nat. Assn. Social Workers, Coun. Social Work Edn., Assn. Group Workers. Democrat. Jewish. Avocations: camping, sailing, racquetball, gardening. Office: Case Western Res U Sch Applied Social Scis Univ Circle Cleveland OH 44106

BLUM, JON H. dermatologist; b. Detroit, Aug. 9, 1944; s. David and Hedwig B.; m. Rosie Jacobs, June 25, 1967; children: Michael, Steven, Suzanne. BS, Wayne State U., 1965, MD, 1969. Diplomate Am. Bd. Dermatology. Intern Beaumont Hosp., Royal Oak, Mich., 1969-70; med. resident Henry Ford Hosp., Detroit, 1970-71, dermatology resident, 1971-74; dermatologist Farmington Hills, Mich., 1974—. Staff physician, William Beaumont Hosp.; cons., Internat. Hair Route, Mississauga, Ontario, Can., 1980—; clin. asst. prof. dermatology, Wayne State U., Detroit, 1976—. Author: (with others) Electrolysis, 1984. Mem. Am. Acad. Dermatology, Mich. Dermatology Soc., Mich. State Med. Soc., Oakland County Med. Soc. Avocation: computers. Office: 32905 W 12 Mile Rd Ste 330 Farmington Hills MI 48334-3345

BLUME, PAUL CHIAPPE, lawyer; b. Omaha, Oct. 11, 1929; s. Herman Alexander and Marie (Simoni) B.; m. Mary Lou Higgins, June 28, 1958; children: Nancy, Julie, Paul II, William. BS in Commerce, Loyola U., Chgo.; JD. Bar: Ill. 1957. Legal sect. mgr. Aldens Inc., 1957-58; assoc. Lord, Bissell & Brook, 1959-63, of counsel, 1983—; v.p., gen. counsel Nat. Assn. Ind. Insurers, Des Plaines, Ill., 1963-83, Ill. Ins. Info. Svc., 1987-96; pres. Ins. Briefs, Inc., 1984—. Capt. U.S. Army, 1951-53. Mem. Chgo. Bar Assn., Fedn. Ins. Counsel. Office: 115 S La Salle St Chicago IL 60603-3801

BLUNT, ROY D. congressman; b. Niangua, Mo., Jan. 10, 1950; s. Leroy and Neva (Letterman) B.; m. E. Roseann Ray; children: Matthew Roy, Amy Roseann, Andrew Benjamin BA, S.W. Bapt. U., 1970; MA, S.W. Mo. State U., 1972. Tchr. Marshfield (Mo.) High Sch., 1970-73; instr. Drury Coll., Springfield, Mo., 1973-82; clk. Greene County, 1973-85; sec. of state State of Mo., Jefferson City, 1985-93; pres. Southwest Bapt. U., 1993-96; mem. 105th-107th Congresses from 7th Mo. dist., 1997—; apptd. chief dep. majority whip 106th-107th Congress. Mem. Fed. Election Commn. Adv. Panel; del. Atlantic Treaty Assn. Conf., 1987; mem. Congressional Com. on Commerce, 1999—, Internat. Rels., 1997-98, Ho. Reps. Steering Com., 1997; del. Nat. Hist. Publs. and Records Commn., 1997—; mem. ho. appropriations com., 1999. Author: (with others) Missouri Election Procedures: A Layman's Guide, 1977; Voting Rights Guide for the Handicapped Bd. dirs. Ctr. for Democracy; mem. Mo. Mental Health Advocacy Coun., 1998-99; mem. exec. bd. Am. Coun. of Young Polit. Leaders, 1998-99; chmn. Mo. Housing Devel. Commn., Kansas City, 1981, Rep. State Conv., Springfield, 1980; chmn. Gov.'s Adv. Coun. on Literacy; co-chmn. Mo. Opportunity 2000 Commn., 1985-87; Rep. candidate for lt. gov. of Mo., 1980; active local ARC, Muscular Dystrophy Assn., others. Named One of 10 Outstanding Young Americans U.S. Jaycees, 1986, Springfield's Outstanding Young Man Jaycees, 1980, Mo.'s Outstanding Young Civic Leader, 1981 Mem. Nat. Assn. Secs. of State (chmn. voter registration and edn. com., sec., v.p. 1990). Am. Coun. Young Polit. Leaders. Baptist. Lodges: Kiwanis, Masons Office: US Ho of Reps 217 Cannon Ho Office Bldg Washington DC 20515-0001 E-mail: blunt@mail.house.gov.*

BLUST, LARRY D. lawyer; b. Bushnell, Ill., Feb. 16, 1943; BS with high honors, U. Ill., 1965, JD with high honors, 1968. Bar: Ill. 1968; CPA, Ill. Mem. Jenner & Block, Chgo. Mem. Ill. Bd. CPA Examiners, 1978-81. Contbr. articles to profl. jours. Mem. ABA (tax sect., partnerships com. 1975-80, 1982-85), Ill. State Bar Assn., Order of the Coif. Office: Jenner & Block 1 E Ibm Plz Fl 4000 Chicago IL 60611-7603

BLYSTONE, JOHN B. manufacturing executive; Degree in Math and Econs., U. Pitts., car. With GE, 1978, with aircraft engine divsn.; v.p. J.I. Case divsn. Tenneco, Inc., 1988-91; v.p., gen. mgr. GE superabrasives GE, 1991; pres., CEO Nuovo Pignone, Florence, Italy, 1994, Europe Plus Pole of GE Power Sys., 1995; chmn., pres., CEO SPX, 1995—. Office: SPX Corp 700 Terrance Point Dr Muskegon MI 49440

BLYTH, ANN MARIE, secondary education educator; b. Sharon, Pa., June 18, 1949; d. Chester Stanley and Mary Clara (Romian) Kacerski; m. Lynn Allan Blyth, June 26, 1976 (dec. June 1983); 1 stepchild, Breton Alan Blyth; 1 child, Amanda Lynn. BS in Edn., Kent (Ohio) State U., 1971; postgrad., Loyola U., New Orleans, 1973-74; MS in Teaching, John Carroll U., 1978. Cert. comprehensive sci., maths. and physics tchr., Ohio. Jr. high math. tchr. New Philadelphia (Ohio) Bd. of Edn., 1971-72; high sch. sci. and math. tchr. Hubbard (Ohio) Exempted Village Bd. of Edn., 1972-76, Painesville (Ohio) City Local Bd. Edn., 1976—; head dept. sci. Harvey H.S., 2001—. Instr. math. Morton Salt, Painesville, 1979-80; part-time faculty Lake Erie Coll., 1992. Mem. Adv. Bd. Western Res. br. Am. Lung Assn. of Ohio, Painesville, 1986-89, sec, 1988-89, Northeastern br., Youngstown, Ohio, 1989-99; judge state level Nat. Pre-teen and Pre-Teen Petite Pageants, 1990. Martha Holden Jennings Found. scholar, 1984-85; named Tchr. of the Yr., Harvey High Sch. Key Club, 1981-82. Mem. NEA, Ohio Edn. Assn., Northeastern Ohio Edn. Assn., Painesville City Tchrs. Assn., Am. Assn. Physics Tchrs. (Ohio sect.), Nat. Sci. Tchrs. Assn., Cleve. Regional Coun. of Sci. Tchrs. Democrat. Episcopalian. Avocations: travel, gourmet cooking, baking, gardening, music. Home: 7243 Scottsdale Cir Mentor OH 44060-6408 Office: Thomas W Harvey High Sch 167 W Washington St Painesville OH 44077-3328

BOAL, MARCIA ANNE RILEY, clinical social worker, administrator; b. Carthage, Mo., Sept. 29, 1944; d. William Joseph and Thelma P. (Simpson) Riley; m. David W. Boal, Aug. 12, 1967; children: Adam J. W., Aaron D. Boal. BA, U. Kans., 1966, MSW, 1981. Lic. clin. social worker. Child therapist Gillis Home for Children, Kansas City, Mo., 1981; social worker Leavenworth (Kans.) County Spl. Edn. Cooperative, 1981-84; sch. social worker, dir. health and social svcs. Kans. State Sch. for the Blind, Kansas City, Kans., 1984—. Pvt. practice adoption counseling and workshops, 1981—; field instr. Sch. of Social Welfare, Kans. U., 1986—. Author: Surviving Kids, 1983, Teaching Social Skills to Blind and Visually Impaired Children, 1987. Nat. networking chmn. Jr. League Kansas City, 1977-81; bd. dirs. Wyandotte House Inc., 1973-81, Kans. Action For Children, Topeka, 1981, Gov.'s Commn. on Parent Edn., Topeka, 1984—, Lake of the Forest, 1994— (sec.). Named Kans. Sch. Social Worker of Yr., 1989. Mem. Council Exceptional Children, Nat. Assn. Social Workers, Kans. Assn. Sch. Social Workers, Am. Orthopsychiat. Assn., Kans. Conf. Social Welfare, R.P. Found., Phi Kappa Phi. Home: Lake Of The Forest Bonner Springs KS 66012Germany Office: Kans St Sch for Blind 1100 State Ave Kansas City KS 66102-4411 E-mail: mboal@kssb.net.

BOARDMAN, EUNICE, retired music educator; b. Cordova, Ill., Jan. 27, 1926; d. George Hollister and Anna Bryson (Feaster) Boardman. B. Mus. Edn., Cornell Coll., 1947; M. Mus. Edn., Columbia U., 1951; Ed.D., U. Ill., 1963; DFA (hon.), Cornell Coll., 1995. Tchr. music pub. schs., Iowa, 1947-55; prof. music edn. Wichita State U., Kans., 1955-72; vis. prof. mus. edn. Normal State U., Ill., 1972-74, Roosevelt U., Chgo., 1974-75; prof. mus. edn. U. Wis., Madison, 1975-89, dir. Sch. Music, 1980-89; prof. music, dir. grad. program in music edn. U. Ill., Urbana, 1989-98; ret. Author: Musical Growth in Elementary School, 1963, 6th rev. edit., 1996, Exploring Music, 1966, 3d rev. edit., 1975, The Music Book, 1980, 2d rev. edit., 1984, Holt Music, 1987; editor: Dimensions of Musical Thinking, 1989, Dimensions of Musical Thinking: A Different Kind of Music, 2002. Mem. Soc. Music Tchr. Edn. (chmn. 1984-86), Music Educators Nat. Conf. Avocations: reading, handwork. E-mail: EunBoardman@aol.com.

BOARDMAN, ROBERT A. lawyer; b. 1947; BA, Muskingum Coll., 1969; JD, Case Western Reserve U., 1972. Bar: Ohio 1972, Colo. 1976. Assoc. atty. Roetzel & Andress, 1972-75, atty., 1975-83; asst. gen. coun., sec. Manville Corp., Denver, 1983-87, v.p., sec., 1988-90; sr. v.p., gen. coun. Navistar Internat. Corp., Chgo., 1990—. Office: Navistar Internat Corp 4201 Winfield Rd Warrenville IL 60555 E-mail: robert.boardman@nav-international.com.

BOAT, THOMAS FREDERICK, physician, educator, researcher; b. Pella, Iowa, Sept. 7, 1939; s. Bert Reuben and Anne Marie (Schoenbohm) B.; m. Barbara Mary Walling, June. 9, 1962; children: Sarah Elizabeth, Mary Barbara, Anne Christine. BA, Cen. Coll., Pella, 1961; MS, U. Iowa, 1965, MD, 1966. Diplomate Am. Bd. Pediat., Am. Bd. Pediat. Pulmonology. Resident in pediat. U. Minn., Mpls., 1966-68; clin. assoc. NIH, Bethesda, Md., 1968-70; fellow in pediat. pulmonology Case Western Res. U., Cleve., 1970-72, instr. pediat., 1972-73, asst. prof., 1973-76, assoc. prof., 1976-81, prof., 1981-82; prof., chmn. dept. pediat. U. N.C., Chapel Hill, 1982-93; chmn. dept. pediat. U. Cin. Sch. Medicine, 1993—; dir. Cin. Children's Hosp. Rsch. Found., 1993—. Prin. investigator Pediat. Pulmonary Specialized Ctr. Rsch., NIH, 1991-93; chmn. Am. Bd. Pediat., 1994. Editor Current Opinions in Pediat., 1990-93; mem. editl. bd. Lung Rsch. jour. Bd. dirs. Ronald McDonald House, Chapel Hill, 1985-88, Cystic Fibrosis Found., chmn. rsch. devel. program, 1983—. Lt. comdr. USPHS, 1968-70. Fellow: Am. Acad. Pediat.; mem.: Inst. of Medicine, Assn. Med. Sch. Dept. Chairs (pres.-elect 1994—97, pres. 1997—99), Am. Thoracic Soc. (chmn. pediat. assembly 1983—84), Am. Pediat. Soc. (pres. 2000—01). Office: Children's Hosp Med Ctr 3333 Burnet Ave SEC D6 Cincinnati OH 45229-3039

BOATRIGHT, MATT, state legislator; Mem. Mo. Ho. of Reps., Jefferson City, 1994—. Republican. Office: Capitol Office Rm 105-H Jefferson City MO 65102

BOBCO, WILLIAM DAVID, JR. consulting engineering company executive; b. Chgo., Aug. 11, 1946; s. William David and Eleanor Josephine (Dvojack) B.; m. Donna Domenica DiFrancesca, Sept. 13, 1969; 1 child, Christina Marie. BS in Engring., U. Ill., Chgo., 1969; MBA in Prodn. Mgmt., U. Chgo., 1983. Prodn. mgr. Am. Can Co., Maywood, Ill., 1972-73; with Footlik & Assocs., Evanston, 1973—, exec. v.p., 1986—. Mem. indsl. adv. bd. U. Ill. Coll. Engring., Chgo., 1992—, chmn. alumni devel. com., 1991-95, mem. dean selection com., 1994. Vol. Art Inst. Chgo., 1983—84, Animal Care League, Oak Park, Ill., 2000—; mem. facilities and grounds com. St. Giles Parish, 1995—, co-chair, 1997—2001, chair, 2001—, treas. golf com., 2000—, chmn. golf scholarship com., 1999—, mem. lions leap com., 1998—2001. Mem. ASME (bd. dirs. Chgo. sect. 1984-2001, newsletter editor 1987-98, vice chmn. 1991, chmn. Chgo. sect. 1992-94, region VI rep. to A World in Motion K-12 tng. program, SAE (co-sponsor 1993), Engring. Alumni Assn. U. Ill. Chgo. (pres. 1984-88, bd. dirs. 1975-99), U. Ill. Alumni Assn. (bd. dirs. 1985-91, nominating com. 1991, Loyalty award 1988, Constituent Leadership award 1991, Disting. Svc. award 1994). Roman Catholic. Avocations: travel, art, music. Office: Footlik & Assocs 2521 Gross Point Rd Evanston IL 60201-4993

BOBINS, NORMAN R. banker; Vice chmn. Exch. Nat. Bank Chgo., 1969-90; formerly vice chmn. LaSalle Nat. Bank, Chgo.; now pres., ceo LaSalle Nat Bank (now LaSalle Bank, N.A.), 1990—. Office: LaSalle Bank NA 135 S La Salle St Fl 3 Chicago IL 60603-4404

BOBRICK, EDWARD A. federal judge; b. 1935; JD, DePaul U., 1964. Magistrate judge U.S. Dist. Ct. (no. dist.) Ill., 1990—. Office: US Dist Ct 1822 Dirksen Bldg 219 Dearborn St Ste 2050 Chicago IL 60604-1800

BOCHERT, LINDA H. lawyer; b. East Orange, N.J., May 13, 1949; BA, U. Wis., 1971, MS, 1973, JD, 1974. Bar: Wis. 1974. Dir. environ. protection unit Wis. Atty. Gen. Office, 1978-80; exec. asst. to the secy. Wis. Dept. Natural Resources, 1980-91; ptnr. Michael, Best & Friedrich, Madison, Wis., 1991—. Mem. ABA, Wis. State Bar Assn. Office: Michael Best & Friedrich PO Box 1806 Firstar Plaza 1 S Pinckney St Madison WI 53701-1806 E-mail: lhbochert@mbf-law.com.

BOCK, EDWARD JOHN, retired chemical manufacturing company executive; b. Ft. Dodge, Iowa, Sept. 1, 1916; s. Edward J. and Maude (Juday) B.; m. Ruth Kunerth, Aug. 9, 1941; children: Barbara, Edward, Nancy, Roger. M.S. in Mech. Engring, Iowa State U., 1940. With Monsanto Co., St. Louis, 1941—, asst. gen. mgr. inorganic chems. div., 1958-60, v.p., gen. mgr., 1960-65, v.p. adminstrn., mem. exec. com., dir., 1965-68, pres., CEO, chmn. corp. mgmt. and exec. coms., dir., 1968-72; chmn. bd., CEO, Cupples Co., 1975-85; cons. Bd. dirs. Harbour Group Ltd. Past chmn. bd. trustees Deaconess Hosp.; past trustee Ladue Chapel; bd. govs. Iowa State U. Found. Recipient Silver Anniversary All-Am. Football award Sports Illustrated, 1963; Anston Marston award Iowa State U., 1972; Significant Sig award, 1971; named to All Am. Football Team, 1938; elected to Nat. Football Found. Hall of Fame, 1970, 1st elected to Iowa State U. Athletic Hall of Fame, 1997. Mem. ASME, Sigma Chi, Tau Beta Pi. Clubs: St. Louis, Old Warson Country (pres. 1972), Bogey, Arnold Palmer's Bay Hill. Home and Office: 2232 Clifton Forge Dr Saint Louis MO 63131-3107

BOCK, PETER ERNEST, state legislator; b. Milw., Dec. 12, 1948; s. Peter R. and Thelma J. (Miron) B. BA, U. Wis., Milw., 1977. Former parcel delivery worker; state assemblyman dist. 7 Wis. State Assembly, 1987—. Chmn. environ. resources com. Wis. State Assembly, 1993—, mem. health, natural resources, labor and job tng., state affairs, urban and local affairs coms. Chmn. Milw. County Dem. Com., 1985-86. Office: 4710 W Bluemound Rd Milwaukee WI 53208-3648

BOCKSERMAN, ROBERT JULIAN, chemist; b. St. Louis, Dec. 20, 1929; s. Max Louis and Bertha Anna (Kremen) B.; m. Clarice K. Kreisman, June 9, 1957; children: Michael Jay, Joyce Ellen, Carol Beth. BSc, U. Mo., 1952; postgrad., Far East Intelligence Sch, Tokyo, 1954; MSc, U. Mo., 1955. Chemist Sealtest Corp., Peoria, Ill., 1955-56; prodn. mgr. Allan Drug Co., St. Louis, 1957-59; rsch. chemist Monsanto Co., 1960-65, purchasing agt. Sauget, Ill., 1966-67; founder, pres. Pharma-Tech Industries, Inc., Union, Mo., 1967-84; tech. dir. Overlock-Howe Consulting Group, St. Louis, 1984-85; founder, pres. Conatech Consulting Group, Chesterfield, Mo., 1985—. Sec., mem. industry packaging adv. com. Sch. of Engring. U. Mo., Rolla, 1979—, adj. prof. dept. food sci./nutrition, Columbia, adj. prof. dept. engring. mgmt., Rolla, vis. lectr., Clayton, Northwestern U., Evanston, Ill.; vol. tutor Ladue Sch. Dist.; tutor Parkway Sch. Dist., St. Louis, Clayton (Mo.) Sch. Dist. Tech. reviewer Jour. Inst. of Packaging Profls., Jour. Packaging Tech., Mo. Waste Control Scholarship Grants and Research, Medical Device and Diagnostic Industry Jour., Medical Plastics and Biomaterials Publication.; mem. editl. adv. bd. The Forensic Examiner; panelist (Help Desk column) Medical Device and Diagnostic Industry mag., The Forensic Examiner; contbg. author: Packaging Forensics - Package Failure in the Courts. Mem. Mo. Waste Control Coalition; mem. stormwater engring. com. City of Creve Coeur, Mo., also mem. recycling and environ. com.; nat. mem. Libr. Congress, Mo. Hist. Soc. With U.S. Army, 1952-54, Korea. Small Bus. Innovation rsch. grantee. Mem. ASTM, Am. Coll. Forensic Examiners, Cons. Packaging Engring. Coun., Inst. Packaging Profls. (cert. packaging profl.), Am. Technion Soc., Inst. Food Technologists Arrangements (St. Louis), Nat. Forensic Ctr., Teltech Resource Network, Am. Chem. Soc., Am. Plastics Coun., Mo. Acad. Scis., N.Y. Acad. Sci., Acad. Sci. St. Louis, Assn. Cons. Chemists and Chem. Engrs., Am. Nutraceutical Assn., Nat. Dir. Expert Witnessess, Rotary Internat. (Clayton, Mo.), Sigma Xi. Achievements include research on toxicological effects of additives from packaging materials upon foodstuffs, on biological and photo degradation of polymers, on technology of form/fill/seal packaging engineering, new sterilization technologies for medical devices and pharmaceuticals, barrier properties of polymer films, toxicology of chemical dusts and fumes, and food irradiation effects on humans. Home: 54 Morwood Ln Creve Coeur MO 63141-7621 Office: Conatech Cons Group 287 N Lindbergh Blvd Creve Coeur MO 63141-7849 E-mail: rjbockserman@conatech.com.

BODEM, BEVERLY A. state legislator; b. Wis., Feb. 22, 1940; m. Denise Bodem; 3 children. Student, U. Wis. State rep. Mich. Ho. Reps., Dist. 106, 1991-98; constituent svcs. dir. Sen. Mike Goschka. Mem. tourism & recreation com., co-chair econ. devel. com., conservation, environ. & great lakes com. & pub. health com., chair task force tourism, mem. task force sr. policy, Mich. Ho. Reps. Bd. dirs. Boys and Girls Club of Alpena. Mem. Club Alpena, Lions.

BODENHAMER, DAVID JACKSON, historian, educator; b. Macon, Ga., May 4, 1947; s. David Jackson and Mary Elizabeth (Cox) B.; m. Penny Jo McClelland, Dec. 27, 1988. BA, Carson-Newman Coll., 1969; MA, U. Ala., 1970; PhD, Ind. U., 1976. Asst. prof., then assoc. prof. U. So. Miss., Hattiesburg, 1976-84, prof., asst. v.p. acad. affairs, 1985-88; dir. Polis Ctr. Ind. U., Indpls., 1989—. Head N.Am. team Electronic Cultural Atlas Initiative, 1997—. Author: Pursuit of Justice, 1986, Fair Trial, 1991; editor: Encyclopedia of Indianapolis, 1994; co-editor: Ambivalent Legacy, 1984, Bill of Rights in Modern America, 1992. Chmn. bd. dirs. South Miss. Community Action Agy., Hattiesburg, 1978-82; bd. dirs. Pine Belt Family YMCA, Hattiesburg, 1982-86; steering com. Regional Ctr. Plan, Indpls, 1989-92, New Ind. State Mus. Task Force, 1998—. With U.S. Army, 1970-72. Mem. Am. Soc. Legal History, Orgn. Am. Historians. Office: Polis Ctr Ste 100 1200 Waterway Blvd Indianapolis IN 46202-5140 E-mail: intu100@iupui.edu.

BODENSTEINER, CAROL A. public relations executive; b. Maqouketa, Iowa, Oct. 11, 1948; BA in Speech and English, U. No. Iowa, 1972. Tchr. Waterloo Cmty. Sch., 1972-73; editor Am. Soybean Assn., 1973-77; acct. exec. Freiberg-Frederick & Assoc., 1977-79, CMF&Z, 1979-81, acct. supr., 1982-83, acct. group mgr., 1983-87, v.p., assoc. mng. dir., 1987-88, sr. v.p., assoc. mng. fir., 1988-89, exec. v.p. gen. mgr., 1989-90, pres., pub. rels., 1990—. Mem. Pub. Rels. Soc. Am. (nat. mem. com., 1991, Cedar Valley devel. chair., 1981), Counselors Acad., Nat. Agrl. Mktg. Assn. Office: CMF&Z Pub Rels 600 E Court Ave Des Moines IA 50309-2021

BODIKER, RICHARD WILLIAM, SR. state legislator; b. Richmond, Ind., Aug. 17, 1936; m. Nancy Bodiker; 7 children. Student, Ball State U., Ind U. East. Mem. Richmond Common Coun., 1983-86; Ind. state rep. Dist. 56, 1986—; mem. commerce com., utility regulatory flexibility com.; interstate coop com. and econ. devel. and govt. affairs com.; mem. Ind. Ho. of Reps., Richmond Power and Light, 1983-86. With Dana Engine Products. Mem. Richmond Evening Optimist, Richmond/Wayne County C. of C., Cambridge City C. of C. Office: State House Rm 336 Indianapolis IN 46204-2728 Home: 4286 S C Ct Richmond IN 47374-6030

BODINE, LAURENCE, marketing consultant; b. Kissimmee, Fla., Nov. 4, 1950; s. Cornelius and Tatiana (Krupenin) B.; 1 child, Theodore Laurence. Student, Universitat Munchen, Munich, Germany, 1970-71; BA, Amherst Coll., 1972; JD, Seton Hall U., 1981. Bar: Wis. 1981, U.S. Dist. Ct. (we. dist.) Wis. 1981. Reporter The Star-Ledger, Newark, 1973-76, N.Y. Daily News, N.Y.C., 1976-78; reporter, asst. editor Nat. Law Jour., 1978-81; assoc. Stafford, Rieser, Rosenbaum & Hansen, Madison, Wis., 1982; assoc. editor ABA Jour., Chgo., 1982-85, editor, pub., 1986-89; pub. Lawyers Alert, 1989-91; dir. comm. Sidley & Austin, Chgo., 1991—2001; webmaster LawMarketing Portal, www.LawMarketing.com, 2001—, Legal Mktg. Assn., www.legalmarketing.org. Mktg. columnist: Law Practice Mgmt. Mag.; editor: LawMktg. Newsletter. Mem.: ABA, Legal Mktg. Assn. (bd. dirs. Chgo. chpt. 1995, 1997—98, 2000).

BODMER, ROLF A. medical educator; MS in Natural Scis., U. Basel, Switzerland, 1980, PhD in Biochemistry and Neurobiology, 1983. Post-doctoral fellow Friedrich Miescher-Institut, Basel, 1983-84, Albert Einstein Coll. Medicine, Bronx, N.Y., 1984; rsch. assoc. Dept. Physiology and Biochemistry U. Calif., San Francisco, 1984-90; asst. prof. biology U. Mich., Ann Arbor, 1990—. Contbr. over 20 rsch. articles to profl. jours. Grantee NIH, Am. Heart Assn., Muscular Dystrophy Assn. Achievements include research in cellular and molecular analysis of neural and mesodermal development; identification and characterization of genes involved in pattern formation and specifying cellular identities during neurogenesis and mesoderm/heart differentiation. Office: U Mich Dept Biology 3013 Natural Sci Bldg 1048 Ann Arbor MI 48109-1048

BODOH, WILLIAM T. federal judge; b. Newark, Sept. 5, 1938; m. Janet Beth Neibusch; three children. BS, Ohio U., 1961; JD, Ohio State U., 1964. Bar: Ohio 1964, U.S. Supreme Ct. 1970, U.S. Dist. Ct. (no. dist.) Ohio 1972, U.S. Dist. Ct. (6th cir.) 1980. Asst. atty. gen. U.S. Atty. Gen.'s office, Columbus, 1964-65, 66-67; atty. Capital Fin. Corp., 1965-66, East Ohio Gas Co., Cleve., 1967-72; assoc. Manchester, Bennett, Powers & Ullman, Youngstown, 1972-85; bankruptcy judge U.S. Dist. Ct. (no. dist.) Ohio, 1985—, chief judge, 2001—. Author: A Local Rules Guide for Ohio Northern District Bankruptcy Court, 1988, A Few Useful Provisions — The Adoption of the Bill of Rights, 1991, The Parameters of the Non-Plan Liquidating Chapter 11: Refining the "Lionel" Standard, 1992, On Judging Judges, 1994, Inequality Among Creditors: The Unconstitutional Use of Successor Liability to Create a New Class of Priority Claimants, 1996, Protective Orders in the Bankruptcy Court: The Congressional Mandate of Bankruptcy Code Section 107 and Its Constitutional Implications, 1996; contbr. articles to legal jours. Recipient Steel Baton award Youngstown Symphony Soc., 1975. Fellow Am. Coll. Bankruptcy; mem. Nat. Conf. Bankruptcy Judges, Am. Bankruptcy Inst., John H. Clarke Am. Inn of Ct., Phi Delta Phi, Pi Kappa Alpha. Office: US Bankruptcy Ct No Dist Ohio 125 Market St Rm 218 Youngstown OH 44503-1780 Fax: 330-746-0480.

BOE, DAVID STEPHEN, musician, educator, dean; b. Duluth, Minn., Mar. 11, 1936; s. Egbert Thomas and Beatrice Ella (Steen) Boe; m. Sigrid North, July 23, 1961; children: Stephen, Eric. B.A. magna cum laude, St. Olaf Coll., Northfield, Minn., 1958; M.Mus., Syracuse U., 1960. Asst. prof. music U. Ga., 1961-62; mem. faculty Oberlin (Ohio) Coll. Conservatory Music, 1962—2002, prof. organ and harpsichord, 1976—, dean, 1976-90; organ recitalist U.S. and Europe, 1962—. Mem. advanced placement music com. Coll. Entrance Exam. Bd., 1980—83; vis. prof. Fla. State U., 1991, U. Notre Dame, 1991—92. Dir. music, organist First Luth. Ch., Lorain, Ohio, 1962—. Scholar Fulbright, Germany, 1960—61. Mem.: Nat. Assn. Schs. Music (trustee, sec. 1981—87), Phi Beta Kappa, Pi Kappa Lambda (nat. pres. 1986—90). E-mail: david.boe@oberlin.edu.

BOE, GERARD PATRICK, health science association administrator, educator; b. Washington, Jan. 20, 1936; s. Harold David and Bernice Virginia (Lemon) Boe; m. Irene Margaret Dazevedo, Oct. 24, 1959 (div. Jan. 1988); children: Steven Alan, Christine Ann; m. Charlotte Greene Hudson, Dec. 30, 1989. BS in Biology, W.Va. Wesleyan Coll., 1958; MS in Clin. Pathology, Ohio State U., 1969; PhD in Edn. and Mgmt., Tex. A&M U., 1976. Commd. 2d lt. U.S. Army, 1963, advanced through grades to lt. col.; health care adminstr., 1963—81; ret., 1981; adminstrv. dir. Ga. Radiation Therapy Ctr., Augusta, 1981—83; pres. Profl. Mgmt. Cons., 1983—89; exec. dir. Am. Med. Technologists, Park Ridge, Ill., 1989—. Faculty Webster U., So. Ill. U., 1980—. Contbr. articles to profl. jours. Recipient cert. of appreciation, ARC, 1976, Pres.'s award, Augusta chpt. Internat. Mgmt. Coun., 1989. Mem.: Am. Soc. Clin. Pathologists (cert.), Inst. Cert. Profl. Mgrs. (bd. regents 1990—), Clin. Lab. Mgmt. Assn., Nat. Clearing House for Licensure, Enforcement and Regulation, Soc. Armed Forces Med. Lab. Scientists (Pres.'s award 1982). Republican. Methodist. Avocations: coins, stamps, racquetball, sports. Office: Am Med Technologists 710 Higgins Rd Park Ridge IL 60068-5737

BOEHM, JAMES, state legislator; m. Pat Boehm. Mem. N.D. Ho. of Reps. from 31st dist., 1991—. Vice chmn. Edn. Com. N.D. Ho. of Reps., mem. Transp. Com. Mem. Sch. Bd. Mem. KC, Future Farmers Am. (hon. state farmer), Elks, Moose, Eagles. Republican. Address: 3477 34th St Mandan ND 58554-8113

BOEHM, PEGGY, state agency administrator; BA, Mount Holyoke Coll. Dir. Ind. Budget Agy., Indpls., 1997—2000; exec. dir. White River State Pk., 2000—. Office: White River State Pk 801 W Washington St Indianapolis IN 46204

BOEHM, THEODORE REED, judge; b. Evanston, Ill., Sept. 12, 1938; s. Hans George and Frances (Reed) B.; children from previous marriage: Elisabeth, Jennifer, Sarah, Macy; m. Margaret Stitt Harris, Jan. 27, 1985. AB summa cum laude, Brown U., 1960; JD magna cum laude, Harvard U., 1963. Bar: D.C. 1964, Ind. 1964, U.S. Supreme Ct. 1975. Law clk. to Chief Justices Warren, Reed and Burton, U.S. Supreme Ct., Washington, 1963-64; assoc. Baker & Daniels, Indpls., 1965-70, ptnr., 1970-88, 95-96, mng. ptnr., 1980-87; gen. counsel major appliances GE, Louisville, 1988-89; v.p., gen. counsel GE Aircraft Engines, Cin., 1989-91; dep. gen. counsel Eli Lilly & Co., 1991-95; justice Ind. Supreme Ct., Indpls., 1996—. Pres. Ind. Sports Corp., 1980-88; chmn. organizing com. 1987 Pan Am. Games, Indp.s. Mem. ABA, Am. Law Inst., Ind. Bar Assn. Office: Ind Supreme Ct State House Rm 324 Indianapolis IN 46204-2728 E-mail: thoehm@courts.state.in.us.

BOEHNE, RICHARD, newspaper company executive; m. Lisa Graybeal; children: Luke, Jacob. BS, No. Ky. U., 1981. Bus. reporter, editor Cin. Post; mgr. corp. comms. E. W. Scripps Co., Cin., 1988-89, dir. corp. comms. and investor rels., 1989-99, v.p. corp. comms. and investor rels., 1999—. Mem. mgmt. com. YMCA Camp Ernst; trustee Bapt. Convalescent Ctrs. of No. Ky.; Sunday sch. tchr. Highland Hills Bapt. Ch., Highland Hills, Ohio. Mem. Nat. Investor Rels. Inst. Office: E W Scripps Co 312 Walnut St Ste 2800 Cincinnati OH 45202-4067

BOEHNEN, DAVID LEO, grocery company executive, lawyer; b. Mitchell, S.D., Dec. 3, 1946; s. Lloyd L. Boehnen and Mary Elizabeth (Buche) Roby; m. Shari A. Bauhs, Aug. 9, 1969; children: Lesley, Michelle, Heather. AB, U. Notre Dame, 1968; JD with honors, Cornell U., 1971. Bar: Minn. 1971. Assoc. Dorsey & Whitney, Mpls., 1971-76, ptnr., 1977-89; sr. v.p. law and external rels. Supervalu Inc., Mpls., 1991-97, exec. v.p., 1997—; vis. prof. law Cornell U. Law Sch., Ithaca, N.Y., fall 1982; bd. dirs. ATM Med. Inc.. Mem. adv. coun. on arts and letters U. Notre Dame, 1993—; mem. adv. Coun. Cornell U. Law Sch., 1983-92, chmn. coun. 1986-90. Mem. Minn. Bar Assn. (chmn. bus. law sect., 1986), Greater Mpls. C. of C. (bd. dirs. 1988-90), Minikahda Club (Mpls.), Spring Hill Golf Club. Roman Catholic. Home: 71 Otis Ln Saint Paul MN 55104-5645 E-mail: david.boehnen@supervalu.com.

BOEHNER, JOHN A. congressman; b. Reading, Ohio, Nov. 17, 1949; m. Deborah Gunlack, 1973; children: Lindsay M., Tricia A. BS, Xavier U., 1977. Pres. Nucite Sales, Inc.; mem. Ohio Ho. of Reps., 1984-90, U.S. Congress from 8th Ohio dist., Washington, 1991—; chmn. edn. and workforce com., mem. agr. com., oversight com. Exec. mem. Nat. Rep. Congl. Com.; chmn. Ho. Rep. Conf. Com. Active Ohio Farm Bur. Mem. KC, Cin., Dayton, Middletown C. of C. Roman Catholic. Republican. Office: US Ho of Reps 1011 Longworth Bldg Washington DC 20515-3508 also: District Office 8200 Beckett Park Drive, #202 Hamilton OH 45011*

BOELTER, PHILIP FLOYD, lawyer; b. Independence, Iowa, Mar. 25, 1943; s. Floyd Joseph and Eileen R. (Wilson) B.; m. Linda Lee Franck, June 7, 1964; children: Carrie Lynn, John Philip. BS in Indsl. Engring., Iowa State U., 1965; JD, U. Iowa, 1968. Ptnr. Dorsey & Whitney, Mpls., 1968—. Trustee Gustavus Adolphus Coll., 1996—. Mem. Mpls. Athletic Club (treas. 1992, sec. 1993, v.p. 1994, pres. 1995). Lutheran. Avocations: landscape gardening, skiing, golfing, reading, volleyball. Office: Dorsey & Whitney LLP 50 S 6th St Ste 1500 Minneapolis MN 55402 E-mail: boelter.phil@dorseylaw.com.

BOERNER, RALPH E. J. forest soil ecologist, plant biology educator; b. Bklyn., Oct. 2, 1948; s. Kurt Heinz and Erika Annalisa (Tappe) B.; m. Elizabeth Ann Wrobel, May 29, 1982; 1 child, Annalisa Marie. BS in Biology, SUNY, Cortland, 1970; MS in Biology and Marine Sci., Adelphi U., 1972; MPh in Botany, Rutgers U., 1974, PhD, 1980. Grad. tchg. asst. Adelphi U., Garden City, N.Y., 1970-72; environ. sci. N.Y. Dept. Environ. Protection, Huntington, 1972; grad. tchg. asst., rsch. fellow Rutgers U., New Brunswick, N.J., 1972-74, 78-80; asst. prof. Burlington County Coll., Pemberton, 1974-78, Ohio State U., Columbus, 1980-86, assoc. prof., 1986-93, prof., 1993—, chair dept. evolution, ecology and Organismal Biology, 1990—. Vis. prof. U. de Concepcion, Chile, 1987; cons. Columbus-Franklin County Met. Parks Commn., 1982—, Ohio Dept. Natural Resources, 1983—, The Nature Conservancy, 1988—, Denison U., 1991; contbr. papers to various profl. meetings. Mem. editl. bd. Mycorrhiza; contbr. articles and revs. to profl. jours. Bd. trustees The Nature Conservancy, 1987-95, also chair sci./land protection com., mem. strategic planning com. Predoctoral fellow NSF, 1972; grantee Columbia Gas Corp., 1982-85, Ohio Dept. Natural Resources, 1982-83, 85-86, 86-87, 88, 89-90, 91-92, 92-93, 93-94, Columbia-Franklin County Met. Parks Dist., 1984-89, NSF, 1986-89, 87-88, 89-90, 90-92, Tinker Found., 1987, USDA Forest Svc., 1993; recipient Alumni award for disting. tchg. Ohio State U., 1989, Oak Leaf award The Nature Conservancy, 1992. Fellow AAAS; mem. Am. Inst. Biol. Scis., Acad. Tchg., Ecol. Soc. Am. (mem. Buell Award com. 1981-86, chmn. 1982-85, mem. program com. 198-688, mem. awards com. 1983-86, chmn. local arrangements ann. meeting 1987, mem. profl. ethics com. 1994—), Internat. Assn. Ecology, Internat. Assn. Landscape Ecology, Natural Areas Assn., So. Appalachian Bot. Club, Soil Ecology Soc. Am., Torrey Bot. Club (mem. Hervey Award com. 1980), Sigma Xi. Office: Ohio State U Dept Evolution Ecology and Organismal Biol 1735 Neil Ave Columbus OH 43210-1220

BOERS, TERRY JOHN, sportswriter, radio and television personality; b. Harvey, Ill., Sept. 13, 1950; s. John and Ruth (Rubottom) B.; m. Carolyn Grace Imgruet, Feb. 20, 1971; children: John, Joseph, Cary, Chris. BJ, No. Ill. U., 1972. Sports editor Sun-Jour. Newspapers, Lansing, Ill., 1972-73; asst. sports editor Star Publs., Chicago Heights, 1973-78; sports copy editor Detroit Free Press, 1978-80, Chgo. Sun-Times, 1980-82, beat reporter, 1982-88, 90-92, columnist, 1988-90. Panelist program The Sportswriters, Sta. WGN-Radio, Chgo., 1988-92; panelist cable TV program Sportsfire, 1990-91, 94-97, co-host, 1990-91; co-host afternoon program Sta. WSCR, Chgo., 1992-99; co-host morning program Sta. WSCR, Chgo., 1999—; sports columnist Arlington Heights Daily Herald, 1994-98. Author articles for sports mags. Recipient 1st Pl. award for column Ill. AP Sports Editors, 1988, Peter Lisagor award, 1989. Office: Sta WSCR-AM 4949 W Belmont Ave Chicago IL 60641-4384

BOESE, GIL KARYLE, cultural organization executive; b. Chgo., June 24, 1937; s. Carl H. and Winifred A. Boese; m. Lillian R. Boese; children: Ann Carroll, Peter Austin, Sara Elisabeth. B.A., Carthage (Ill.) Coll., 1959; M.S., No. Ill. U., 1965; Ph.D.; NIMH trainee 1970, Johns Hopkins U., 1973. Instr. biology Thornton Community Coll., Harvey, Ill., 1965-67; asst. prof. biology Elmhurst (Ill.) Coll., 1967-69; dep. dir. Chgo. Zool. Park, Brookfield, Ill., 1971-80; dir. Milw. County Zool. Gardens, Milw., 1980-89; pres. Zool. Soc. Milw. County, 1989—, Found. for Wildlife Conservation, 1993—. Tech. cons. Belize Zoo and Tropical Edn. Ctr. ; founder Birds without Borders Aves Sin Frontera internat. program; dir. Miller Brewery Friends of the Field. Chmn., bd. dirs. Dian Fossey Gorilla Found., mem. internat. coordinating com., pres., 1997—; bd. dirs. Lewa Conservancy Kenya; mem. wetlands acquisition com. Pewaukee Lake, Wis. Fellow Royal Geog. Soc., Am. Assn. Zool. Parks and Aquariums (bd. dirs.); mem. Hemmingway Soc., Adventurers Club. Office: Zool Soc Milw County 10005 W Bluemound Rd Milwaukee WI 53226-4346 E-mail: boese@zoosociety.org.

BOESE, TED C. retired furniture designer; b. Oshkosh, Wis., Aug. 14, 1931; s. Walter Paul and Bertha Alma (Meyer) B.; m. Paula C. Schriefer, July 19, 1958; children: Tania, Eric, Lori. Grad. high sch., Detroit, 1949. Apprentice woodworker Splty. Cab, Detroit, 1950-52; ptnr. Boese Wood Products, 1954-76; owner, pres. Penta Assoc., Petoskey, Mich., 1976-96, retired, 1996. Inventor needle guard for syringe, 1989. Sgt. U.S. Army, 1952-54, Korea. Avocations: computer programs, CADD layouts of furniture and furniture design. Home and Office: 7920 10 Mile Rd NE Rockford MI 49341-8304

BOESEL, MILTON CHARLES, JR. lawyer, business executive; b. Toledo, July 12, 1928; s. Milton Charles and Florence (Fitzgerald) B.; m. Lucy Laughlin Mather, Mar. 25, 1961; children: Elizabeth Boesel Sagges, Charles Mather, Andrew Fitzgerald. BA, Yale U., 1950; LLB, Harvard U., 1953. Bar: Ohio 1953, Mich. 1953. Chmn., bd. dirs. Michabo, Inc. Lt. USNR, 1953-56. Episcopalian. Clubs: Toledo Country; Leland Country (Mich.). Sawgrass Country (Fla.). Home: Apt 101S 4243 W Bancroft St Toledo OH 43615-3953

BOETTGER, NANCY J. state legislator; b. Chgo., May 1, 1943; m. H. David Boettger; 4 children. BS, Iowa State U., 1965; BA, Buena Vista Coll., 1982. Owner farm, 1965—; spl. edn. tchr., 1965-66; tchr. jr. H.S., 1982-86; dir. edn. Myrtie Meml. Hosp., 1986-99; mem. Iowa Senate from 41st dist., 1994—; asst. majority leader, 1996-2000. Mem. Midwest Legis. Coun., 1996-2000. Mem. First Bapt. Ch., People Who Care; former bd. dirs. Harlan Cmty. Libr.; former mem. dean's adv. bd. Iowa State U. Ext. Mem. PEO, Am. Legis. Exchange Coun., Midwest Coun. State Govts. (chair health and human svcs. 1997-99), Coun. State Govts. (mem. drug task force 1998), Iowa Coun. Internat. Understanding Bd., Shelby County Found. for Edn. (former exec. dir.), Farm Bur., Pork Prodrs. Republican. Home: 926 Ironwood Rd Harlan IA 51537-5308 Office: State Capitol Dist 41 3 9th And Grand Des Moines IA 50319-0001 E-mail: nancy_boettger@legis.state.ia.us.

BOFF, KENNETH RICHARD, engineering research psychologist; b. N.Y.C., Aug. 17, 1947; s. Victor and Ann (Yunko) B.; m. Judith Marion Schoer, Aug. 2, 1969 (dec. Apr. 1997); children: Cory Asher, Kyra Melissa; m. Jacque Aelanda Coppler, Aug. 20, 1999. BA, CUNY, 1969, MA, 1972; MPhil, Columbia U., 1975, PhD, 1978. Research scientist Human Resources Lab., Wright Patterson AFB, Ohio, 1977-80; sr. scientist Armstrong Aerospace Med. Rsch. Lab. (now Armstrong Lab.), 1980—, dir. design tech., 1980-91, dir. human engring. div., 1991-97; chief scientist, human effectiveness directorate Air Force Rsch. Lab., 1997—. Project custodian Internat. Air. Standard Coordination Com., Washington, 1984; chmn. com. Tri-Service Human Factors Tech. Adv. Group, Washington, 1984—; chair human factors com. NATO Adv. Group Aerospace R&D, Paris, 1992—; chair human sys. tech. panel Dept. Def., 1994-97; U.S. coord. NATO Rsch. and Tech. Orgn. Human Factors, 1997—. Editor: Handbook of Perception and Human Performance, 1986, Human Engineering Data Compendium, 1988, System Design: Behavioral Perspectives on designers, Tools and Organizations, 1987; contbr. articles to profl. jours. Travel grantee Rank Prize Found., Cambridge, Eng., 1984; named Air Force Scientist of the Quarter, 1989; recipient Patent award for rap-com display tech., 1989, Human Factors Soc. award for best publ., 1989. Mem. IEEE, Human Factors Soc., Am. Psychol. Assn. (div. 21 engring. psychology). Avocations: computers, photography. Home: 6510 Shadow Wynd Cir Dayton OH 45459 Office: Armstrong Lab Human Engring Divsn Wright Patterson AFB OH 45433

BOGGS, ROBERT J. former state senator; m. Judie Sylak; children: Larissa, Kelly, Kristin. BS, Am. U., 1969; postgrad., Youngstown State U.; MPA, Kent State U. Mem. Ohio Ho. of Reps., Columbus, 1973-83, former chmn. edn. com. and edn. rev. com.; mem. Ohio Senate, 1983-96; commr. Ashtabula County, 1996—. Ranking minority mem. energy and natural resources com., mem. state and local govt. com., hwys. and transp. com., minority leader; mem. adj. faculty U. San Francisco, McLaren Coll. Bus. Co-chmn. Ohio Lake Erie Shore Area Redevel. Task Force; chmn. Ohio High Speed Rail Authority; mem. transp. and comm. com., mem. econ. devel. com. Nat. Conf. State Legislators. Recipient Disting. Svc. award Gt. Lakes Commn., Ohio Sea Grant Program, Ohio Environ. Coun., Western Res. Conservation Club, Ohio County Treas. Assn., Lake County Trustees and Clks. Assn., Elem. Adminstrs. Assn., Ohio Assn. Secondary Adminstrs. Mem. Ohio Trustees and Clks. Assn. (assoc.), Am. High Speed Rail Assn. (bd. dirs.), Farm Bur., Sierra Club, Omicron Delta Kappa. Democrat. Home: 2281 Morning Pt Rock Creek OH 44084-9654 Office: 25 W Jefferson St Jefferson OH 44047

BOGGS, ROBERT WAYNE, human services administrator, consultant; b. St. Helena, Calif., Sept. 17, 1941; s. Wayne Cress Boggs and Ann Isham Stevenson; m. Donna F. Ferguson, Nov. 24, 1967; children: Jacquelin, Ryan. BS, Fresno State U., 1964; PhD, U. Calif., Davis, 1970. Bd. cert. nutritionist. Staff mem. Procter & Gamble, Cin., 1970-73, sect. head, 1973-76, assoc. dir., 1976-83, dir., 1983-99; cons. RWB Mgmt. Sys., 1999—. Author: (book) Transforming Clinical Development Performance Through Benchmarking and Metrics, 2001. Exec. sec. Procter Found., 1982—; mem. pharm. sci. bd. U. Cin., 1987—, mem. adv. bd., 1991—94; pres. Glendale Youth Sports, 1989; mem. athletic bd. St. Xavier H.S., 1991—93; mem. adv. bd. Cin. Classics, 1995; sr. warden Christ Ch. Glendale, 1988; bd. dirs. Cin. Riverhawks, 1997—. Mem.: Drug Info. Assn., Nutrition Today Soc., Am. Inst. Nutrition (mem. adv. bd. 1988—91). Avocations: soccer, equestrian events, auto restoration. E-mail: boggrw@aol.com.

BOGGS, ROSS A., JR. former state legislator, dairy farmer; m. Eleanor Boggs; children: Robin, Leslie, Suzanne, Shelley. Student, Kent State U. Dairy farmer, Andover, Ohio; mem. Ohio Ho. of Reps., Columbus, 1983-99. Vice chmn. elecric and township com., mem. agr. and natural resources com., fin. and appropriations com., pub. utilities com., ways and means com., high speed rail task force and Ohio Rail Authority com., chmn. select com. to study effects of fed. cutbacks on local govt. and select com. on child abuse and juvenile justice, commerce and labor com. Named Legislator of Yr., Airplane Owners and Pilots Assn., 1987, Conservation Legislator of Yr., League Ohio Sportsmen, 1988, Outstanding Legislator, Pub. Children's Svc., 1988; recipient President's award Ohio Youth Svc. Assn., 1990. Mem. Ashtabula Clks. and Trustees Assn., Farm Bur., Ohio Farmers Union, Elks. Democrat. Home: 4779 State Route 7 Andover OH 44003-9621

BOGINA, AUGUST, JR. former state official; b. Girard, Kans., Sept. 13, 1927; s. August and Mary (Blazic) B.; m. Nancy L. Pock, 1988; children: Kathleen A., August III, Michael E., Mark A., Kathleen R., Korey A. B.S. Engring., Kans. State U., 1950. Registered profl. engr., Kans., Mo., Colo., Okla.; registered land surveyor Kans., Mo. Owner Bogina & Assocs., Lenexa, Kans., 1962-70; pres. Bogina Cons. Engrs., 1970-95; partner Bogina Petroleum Engineers, 1983-95; mem. Kans. Ho. of Reps., 1974-80, Kans. Senate, 1980-95; chair Kans. State Bd. Tax Appeals; ret., 1999. Precinct committeeman Kans. Republican party, 1970-74, chmn. city com., 1972-74. Served with U.S. Army, 1946-48. Mem. Nat. Soc. Profl. Engrs., Mo. Soc. Profl. Engrs., Kans. Engring. Soc., Kans. Soc. Land Surveyors, Mo. Registered Land Surveyors. Roman Catholic.

BOGUE, ALLAN GEORGE, history educator; b. London, Can., May 12, 1921; married; 3 children. B.A., U. Western Ont., 1943, M.A., 1946; Ph.D., Cornell U., 1951; LL.D., U. Western Ont., 1973; D.Fil (hon.), U. Uppsala, 1977. Lectr. econs. and history, asst. librarian U. Western Ont., 1949-52; from asst. prof. to prof. history U. Iowa, 1952-64, chmn. dept., 1959-63; prof. history U. Wis.-Madison, 1964-68, chmn. dept., 1972-73, Frederick Jackson Turner prof. history, 1968-91. Mem. hist. adv. com. Math. Soc. Sci. Bd., 1965-71; Scandinavian-Am. Found. Thord-Gray lectr., 1968; mem. Council Inter-Univ. Consortium Polit. Research, 1971-73, 89-91; vis. prof. history Harvard U., 1972; dir. Social Sci. Research Council, 1973-76 Author: Money at Interest, 1955, From Prairie to Corn Belt, 1963; co-author, editor: The West of the American People, 1970; co-author, contbr.: The Dimensions of Quantitative Research in History, 1972; co-editor, contbr.: American Political Behavior: Historical Essays and Readings, 1974; co-editor: The University of Wisconsin: One Hundred and Twenty Five Years, 1975; author: The Earnest Men, 1981, Clio and the Bitch Goddess, Quantification in American Political History, 1983, The Congressman's Civil War, 1989; co-editor: The Jeffersonian Dream: Studies in the History of American Law Land Policy and Development, 1996, Frederick Jackson Turner: Strange Roads Going Down, 1998, The Farm on the North Talbot Road. Lt. Can. Army, 1943-45. Social Sci. Rsch. Coun. fellow, 1955, 66, Guggenheim fellow, 1970, H.E. Huntington Libr. fellow, 1991, 93, Sherman Fairchild Disting. fellow Calif. Inst. Tech., 1975, Ctr. for Advanced Study in the Behavioral Scis. fellow, 1985, NEH fellow, 1985. Fellow Agr. Hist. Soc. (pres. 1963-64); mem. Orgn. Am. Historians (pres. 1982-83), Am. Hist. Assn., Econ. Hist. Assn. (pres. 1981-82), Social Sci. Hist. Assn. (pres. 1977-78), Nat. Acad. Scis., Western Hist. Assn. (hon. life). Office: 1914 Vilas Ave Madison WI 53711 E-mail: bogueag@mhub.history.wisc.edu.

BOGUE, ANDREW WENDELL, federal judge; b. Yankton, S.D., May 23, 1919; s. Andrew S. and Genevieve Bogue; m. Florence Elizabeth Williams, Aug. 5, 1945; children— Andrew Stevenson, Laurie Beth, Scott MacFarlane. B.S., S.D. State U., 1941; LL.B., U. S.D., 1947. Bar: S.D. 1947. States atty. Turner County, S.D., 1952-67; judge 2d Jud. Cir., 1967-70, U.S. Dist. Ct. S.D., Rapid City, 1970—, chief judge, from 1980, sr. judge, 1985—. Mem. S.D. Bar Assn., Fed. Judges Assn. Episcopalian. Office: US Courthouse Fed Bldg Rm 244 515 9th St Rapid City SD 57701-2626

BOGUE, ERIC H. state legislator, lawyer; b. Oct. 4, 1964; Bar: S.D. Lawyer pvt. practice, Dupree, S.D.; mem. S.D. Ho. of Reps., Pierre, 1995-96, S.D. Senate from 28th dist., Pierre, 1999—. Mem. judiciary and tax coms., appropriations com., vice chair govt. ops. and audit com. S.D. Ho. of Reps. Republican. E-mail: boguelaw@gwtc.net.

BOH, IVAN, philosophy educator; b. Dolenji Lazi, Yugoslavia, Dec. 13, 1930; s. France and Marija (Mihelic) B.; m. Magda Kosnik, Aug. 30, 1957; children: Boris, Marko. B.A., Ohio U., 1954; M.A., Fordham U., 1956; Ph.D., U. Ottawa, Ont., Can., 1958. Instr. Clarke Coll., Dubuque, Iowa, 1957-59, asst. prof., 1959-62; vis. asst. prof. U. Iowa, 1962-63; Fulbright research fellow U. Munich, Germany, 1964-65; asso. prof. Mich. State U., 1966-69; prof. philosophy Ohio State U., Columbus, 1969-95, prof. emeritus, 1995—. Rsch. in Spanish librs., 1972-73; MUCIA exch. prof. Moscow State U., 1979-80; Fulbright sr. rsch. fellow U. Ljubljana (Yugoslavia), 1982-83; Irex and Fulbright sr. rsch. fellow U. Halle-Wittenberg, German Dem. Republic, and Jagiellonsky U. (Poland), 1986-87 Author: Epistemic Logic in the Later Middle Ages, 1993; contbr. articles to profl. jours. Recipient Evans Latin prize Ohio U., 1954. Mem. Am. Philos. Assn., Am. Catholic Philos. Assn., Medieval Acad. Am. Home: 6171 Middlebury Dr E Columbus OH 43085-3374 Office: Ohio State U Dept Philosophy Columbus OH 43210

BOHLKE, ARDYCE, state legislator; b. Omaha, Nov. 2, 1943; m. Jan Bohlke, 1967; children: Jon Jr., Jason. BS, U. Nebr., 1965. Mem. from dist. 33 Nebr. State Senate, Lincoln, 1992—, mem. com. on coms., natural resources and rules coms., vice chair edn. com. Past pres. Hastings Bd. Edn., Hastings YWCA. Mem. LWV (past pres.), Bus. and Profl. Women, Rotary. Office: 7 Village Dr Hastings NE 68901-2436

BOHM, FRIEDRICH (FRIEDL) K.M. architectural firm executive; Degree in architecture, U. Vienna; M in City and Regional Planning, Ohio State U. With NBBJ, Columbus, Ohio, 1975—, mng. ptnr., 1987-97, pres., chmn., 1997—. Hon. consul to Austria; advisor internat. policy Prime Min. Austria; bd. dirs. Huntington Nat. Bank, M/I Homes. Recipient Disting. Alumnus award Ohio State U., numerous design awards and recognitions; named Entrepreneur of Yr., INC. mag., 1992; Fulbright scholar. Fellow AIA. Office: NBBJ 1555 Lake Shore Dr Columbus OH 43204-3825

BOHM, GEORG G. A. physicist; b. Brünn, Czechoslovakia, Oct. 7, 1935; came to U.S., 1966; s. Gustav Anton and Olga B.; m. Marga L. Girak; children: Astrid, Alexander. BSEE, U. Vienna, Austria, 1957, PhD in Physics, 1962, postgrad., 1962-64. Scientist Max-Planck Inst. Physikalische Chemie, Göttingen, Germany, 1972-75; group leader, mgr. Firestone Tire & Rubber Corp., Westbury, N.Y., 1967-72, asst. dir. rsch. lab. Akron, Ohio, 1973-93; dir. rsch. Bridgestone/Firestone, 1993—. Bd. dirs. Bridgestone Firestone Rsch. Inc.; vis. prof. IAEA, Vienna, 1964-66; adv. panel Nat. Acad. Sci., Washington, 1994-95; adv. bd. Ctr. Molecular & Microstructure Composits Case Western U./Akron U., 1990-94. Mem. editl. bd. Jour. Rubber Chemistry & Tech., 1982-85; contbr. articles to profl. jours.; patentee in field. Mem. Am. Chem. Soc. Avocations: chess, tennis, golf. Office: Bridgestone/Firestone Rsch 1200 Firestone Pkwy Akron OH 44317-0002

BOHM, HENRY VICTOR, physicist; b. Vienna, Austria, July 16, 1929; came to U.S., 1941, naturalized, 1946; s. Victor Charles and Gertrude (Rie) B.; m. Lucy Margaret Coons, Sept. 2, 1950; children: Victoria Rie, Jeffrey Ernst Thompson. AB, Harvard U., 1950; MS, U. Ill., 1951; PhD, Brown U., 1958. Jr. physicist GE, 1951, 53-54; teaching, research asst. Brown U., 1954-58, research assoc., summer 1958; staff mem. Arthur D. Little, Inc., Cambridge, Mass., 1958-59; asso. prof. physics dept. Wayne State U., Detroit, 1959-64, acting chmn. physics dept., 1962-63, prof., 1964-93, prof. emeritus, 1993—, v.p. for grad. studies and research, 1968-71, v.p. for spl. projects, 1971-72, provost, 1972-75, on leave, 1978-83, interim dean Coll. Liberal Arts, 1984-86; pres. Argonne Univs. Assn., 1978-83. Vis. prof. Cornell U., 1966-67, U. Lancaster, Eng., summer 1967, Purdue U., winter, 1977, Rensselaer Poly. Inst., winter 1992; cons.-examiner commn. on instns. higher edn. N. Central Assn. Colls. and Schs., 1971-80, mem. commn., 1974-78 Bd. dirs. Center for Research Libraries, Chgo, 1970-75, chmn., 1973; bd. overseers Lewis Coll., Ill. Inst. Tech., 1980-83. Lt. USNR, 1951-53. Fellow Am. Phys. Soc. Office: Wayne State U Dept Physics Detroit MI 48202

BOHN, ROBERT G. transportation company executive; Dir. ops. European automotive group Johnson Controls; with Oshkosh (Wis.) Truck Corp., 1992—, pres., COO, 1994-97, pres., CEO, 1997, chmn. bd., 2000—. Office: Oshkosh Truck Corp 2307 Oregon St Oshkosh WI 54902

BOHNHOFF, DAVID ROY, agricultural engineer, educator; b. Plymouth, Wis., June 10, 1956; s. Roy Arthur and Jean Audrey (Manneck) B.; m. Rhonda Kay Johanning, July 2, 1982; children: Benjamin, Christian, Aaron. BS in Agrl. Engring., U. Wis., Platteville, 1978; MS in Agrl. Engring., U. Wis., Madison, 1985, PhD in Agrl. Engring., 1988. Registered profl. engr., Wis. Design engr. Gehl Co., West Bend, Wis., 1979-80; dairy farmer Calmset Farms, Plymouth, 1981-82; rsch. asst. agrl. engring. dept. U. Wis., Madison, 1982-87, lectr. agrl. engring., 1987-88, asst. prof. agrl. engring., 1988-93, assoc. prof. agrl. engring., 1993-95; divsn. rsch. and product devel. mgr. Lester Bldg. Systems, Lester Prairie, Minn., 1995-96; assoc. prof. biological sys. engring. U. Wis., Madison, 1996-2000, prof. biological sys. engring., 2000—. Mem. Midwest Plan Svc., Ames, Iowa, 1988-95, chmn., 1993-94, mem. constrn. sect. com. 1993-95, chmn. task force, 1990, mem. design and constrn. com., 1988-94. Contbr. articles, reports to profl. jours. Youth soccer coach Regent Soccer Club, Madison, 1989-94, Madison 56ers Soccer Club, 1994-95, youth basketball coach YMCA, Madison, 1994; youth softball coach Madison Area Sch.-Cmty. Recreation League, Madison, 1994; Cub Scout den leader Boy Scouts Am., Madison, 1991-92; project leader 4-H Club, Madison, 1992-95, Glencoe Cmty. Recreational Soccer coach, 1996. Named Outstanding Recent Alumnus U. Wis.-Platteville, 1993, Young Engr. of Yr. ASAE Wis. Sect., 1994; named to Nat. Rural Builder Hall of Fame Rural Builder, 1996. Mem. Am. Soc. Agrl. Engring. (chmn. structures com. 1994-96, post and pole design com. 1991-97; mem. various coms., chmn. Wis. sect. 1991-92, program chair 1990-91, sec.-treas. 1989-90, 97-98, nominating com. 1988-89, career devel. com. 1998—, awards chair, 2000—, tech. reviewer trans. and Jour. Applied Engring. in Agr., Outstanding Paper award 1992, Superior Paper award 1997, Henry Giese Structures and Environ. award 2000), Nat. Frame Builders Assn. (mem. rsch. & edn. com., mem. editl. rev. com., Bernon C. Perkins award 1996, 2000), Alpha Gamma Rho (alumni sec. Beta Gamma chpt. 1980, pres. 1980-81), Alpha Zeta, Gamma Sigma Delta. Lutheran. Avocations: all sports, woodworking, playing cards. Home: 5931 Schroeder Rd Madison WI 53711-2573 Office: U Wis Biol Systems Engring 460 Henry Mall Madison WI 53706-1533

BOHO, DAN L. lawyer; b. Chgo., Sept. 18, 1952; s. Lawrence M. and Genevieve A. (Zurek) Boho; m. Sheri L. Krisco, Sept. 10, 1977; children: Courtney, Ashley. BA, Loyola U., Chgo., 1974, JD, 1977. Bar: Ill. 1977, Fed. Trial Bar 1977. Sr. ptnr., group leader litigation group Hinshaw & Culbertson, Chgo., 1977—. Mem. Fedn. Ins. and Corp. Counsel, Ill. Soc. Trial Lawyers (past bd. dirs.), Def. Rsch. Inst., Assn. Def. Trial Attys., Ill. Def. Coun., Advs. Soc., Ill. Bar Assn. (past del. assembly), Polish Am. Assn. (past chmn. bd. dirs.), Japan Am. Soc. (bd. dirs.), Heartland Alliance (bd. dirs.), Chgo. Trial Lawyers Club (past pres.), Phi Alpha Delta (past pres. Webster chpt.). Avocations: travel, tennis, skiing.

BOHR, NICK, reporter; BS in Broadcast Journalism, Marquette U. With WXRO Radio, Beaver Dam, WYKY, Beaver Dam, WBEV, Beaver Dam, WISN-AM Radio, Beaver Dam; reporter WISN 12, Milwaukee, Wis., 1994—. Office: WISN PO Box 402 Milwaukee WI 53201-3331

BOIES, WILBER H. lawyer; b. Bloomington, Ill., Mar. 15, 1944; s. W. H. and Martha Jane (Hutchison) B.; m. Victoria Joan Steinitz, Sept. 17, 1966; children: Andrew Charles, Carolyn Ursula. AB, Brown U., 1965; JD, U. Chgo., 1968. Bar: Ill. 1968, U.S. Dist. Ct. (no. dist.) Ill. 1968, U.S. Dist. Ct. (ea. dist.) Wis. 1973, U.S. Ct. Appeals (7th cir.) 1974, U.S. Ct. Appeals (5th cir.) 1975, U.S. Ct. Appeals (3d cir.) 1977, U.S. Supreme Ct. 1978, U.S. Ct. Appeals (8th cir.) 1994, U.S. Ct. Appeals (9th cir.) 1995. Assoc. Altheimer & Gray, Chgo., 1968-71; ptnr. McDermott, Will & Emery, 1971—. Contbr. articles to profl. jours. Active CPR Inst. for Dispute Resolution. Mem. ABA, Bar Assn. 7th Fed. Cir., Chgo. Bar Assn. (chmn. class litigation com. 1991-92), Chgo. Coun. Lawyers, Lawyers Club Chgo., Met. Club, Chgo. Bar Found.(dir.). Office: McDermott Will & Emery 227 W Monroe St Ste 4400 Chicago IL 60606-5096 E-mail: bboies@mwe.com.

BOLAND, JAMES C. sports association executive; Vice chmn. ctr. region Ernst & Young LLP, N.Y.C., 1988-96; pres., CEO Cavs/Gund Arena Co., Cleve. Office: Cavs/Gund Arena Co 1 Center Ct Cleveland OH 44115

BOLAND, MICHAEL JOSEPH, state legislator; b. Davenport, Iowa, Aug. 20, 1942; s. Francis Charles and Opal (Waites) B.; m. Mary Rose Lavorato, 1967; children: Susan, Barbara Ann. BA, Upper Iowa U., Fayette, 1967; MSE, Henderson State U., Arkadelphia, 1972. Del. County and Iowa State Conv., 1970; East Moline chmn. and 36th legis. dist. chmn. Polit. Action Coms. for Edn., 1974-75; mem. Bicentennial Com.; del. Ill. State Dem. Conv., 1978; alt. del. Dem. Nat. Mid-Term Conf., 1978; del. Dem. Nat. Conv., 1980; mem. from dist. 71 Ill. Ho. of Reps., 1994—. Coord. West Ill. Coalition for Polit. Honesty's Legis. Cutback Amendment; mem. United Twp. H.S. Bd. Edn., 1984-85; v.p. Citizens Utility Bd., Ill.civ Nat. bd. dirs. UN Reform Campaign Com.; libr. bd. trustees, East Moline, Ill., 1975-79. Named one of 11 Who Made a Difference in Ill., Chgo. Tribune Sunday Mag. Mem. LWV (mem. govt. com. 1980-81), Ill. Coalition Polit. Honesty (bd. dirs. 1987), Consumers and Taxpayers Together (founding mem.). Address: 2041-J Stratton Bldg Springfield IL 62706-0001 also: 4416 River Dr Moline IL 61265-1734

BOLAND, RAYMOND JAMES, bishop; b. Tipperary, Ireland, Feb. 8, 1932; came to U.S., 1957; Ed., Nat. U. Ireland and All Hallows Sem., Dublin. Ordained priest Roman Cath. Ch., Dublin, 1957. Vicar gen., chancellor of Washington archdiocese; ordained bishop Birmingham, Ala., 1988-93; transferred as bishop Kansas City, St. Joseph, Mo., 1993—. Address: PO Box 419037 Kansas City MO 64141-6037

BOLANDER, WILLIAM J. mechanical engineer; b. Rolla, Mich., 1960; m. Beth Bolander; 2 children. BA in Mechanical and Electrical Engring., 1983; MME, Purdue U., 1984. With Saturn; algorithm technical resource leader (automotive engr.) General Motors Powertrain, Pontiac, Mich., 1994. Recipient Jerome H. Lemelson prize for Excellence in Invention and Innovation MIT, 1995, 4 Boss Kettering awards. Achievements include patents for vehicle engine ignition timing system with adaptive knock retard, coast-sync-coast downshift control methods for clutch-to-clutch transmission shifting, valve position sensor diagnostic, throttle position sensor error recovery control method, vehicle ignition system having adaptive knock retard with starting temperature correction, method for adjusting engine output power to compensate forloading due to a variable capacity air conditioning compressor, fuel control system for engine during coolant failure. Office: General Motors Corp/GM Tech Ctr 30200 Mound Rd Warren MI 48092-2025

BOLCHAZY, LADISLAUS JOSEPH, publishing company executive; b. Michalovce, Slovakia, June 7, 1937; AA in Classics, Divine Word Coll. and Sem., Conesus, N.Y., 1960; BA in Philosophy, St. Joseph's Coll. and Sem., Yonkers, N.Y., 1963; MA in Classics, NYU, 1967; PhD in Classics, SUNY, Albany, 1973. Permanent cert. Latin tchr., N.Y. Tchr. Latin and English, Sacred Heart High Sch., Yonkers, 1962-65; instr. Siena Coll., Loudonville, N.Y., 1966-67; asst. prof. La Salette Coll. and Sem., Altamont, 1971-75; vis. asst. prof. Millersville (Pa.) State Coll., 1975-76, Loyola U., Chgo., 1976-77, adj. prof., 1979—; owner, mgr. U.S. Graphics, Chgo.-Scan Typographers, Inc., 1985—; pres. Bolchazy-Carducci Pubs., Inc., Wauconda, Ill., 1978—. Organizer seminar APA, 1975; condr. NEH summer inst. on Sophocles and Thucydides, Cornell U., 1976, on ancient history U. Mich., Ann Arbor, 1977; host Myth Is Truth, Sta. WLUC, Loyola U., 1977, Sta. WRRG, Triton Coll., 1978. Author: Hospitality in Early Rome, 1977, reprinted as Hospitality in Antiquity, 1994, A Concordance to the "Utopia" of St. Thomas More, 1978, The Coin-Inscriptions and Epigraphical Abbreviations of Imperial Rome, 1978, (with others) A Concordance to Ausonius, 1982; co-editor: The Ancient World, 1978—, The Classical Bulletin, 1988—; contbr. articles to profl. jours. Pres. Slovak-Am. Internat. Cultural Found., Inc., 1998. Teaching fellow SUNY, 1967-71; rsch. grantee Loyola U., 1977. Home: 698 Golf Ln Barrington IL 60010-7329 Office: Bolchazy Carducci Pub Inc 1000 Brown St Ste 101 Wauconda IL 60084-3120

BOLCOM, WILLIAM ELDEN, musician, composer, educator, pianist; b. Seattle, May 26, 1938; s. Robert Samuel and Virginia (Lauermann) B.; m. Fay Levine, Dec. 23, 1963 (div. 1967); m. Katherine Agee Ling, June 8, 1968 (div. 1969); m. Joan Clair Morris, Nov. 28, 1975. BA, U. Wash., 1958; MA, Mills Coll., 1961; postgrad., Paris Conservatoire de Musique, 1959-61, 64-65; D of Mus. Art, Stanford U., 1964; D of Music (hon.), San Francisco Conservatory, 1994, Albion Coll., 1995; studied with, Berthe Poncy Jacobson, 1949-58, John Verrall, 1951-58, Leland Smith, 1961-64, Darius Milhaud, 1957-61; George Rochberg, 1966. Acting asst. prof. music dept. U. Wash., Seattle, 1965-66; lectr., asst. prof. music Queens Coll., CUNY, Flushing, 1966-68; vis. critic music theater Drama Sch., Yale U., 1968-69; composer in residence Theater Arts Program, NYU, N.Y.C., 1969-71; asst. prof. U. Mich. Sch. Music, Ann Arbor, 1973-77, assoc. prof., 1973-83, prof., 1983-94, Ross Lee Finney disting. prof. composition, 1994—. Mem. jury Nat. Endowment for Arts, 1976-77, 84, 85. Composer: 6 symphonies, 1957, 64, 79, 86, 89, 97, String Quartets 1-8, 1950-65, String Quartet #9 (Novella), 1972, String Quartet #10, 1988, Décalage for cello and piano, 1961-62, Fantasy-Sonata for piano, 1960-62, Concertante for Flute, Oboe, Violin, and Orch, 1960, cabaret opera Dynamite Tonite, 1960-63, rev., 1966, Octet, 1962, Concerto-Serenade for Violin and Strings, 1964, 12 Etudes for Piano, 1959-66, Fives, Double Concerto for Violin, Piano and Strings, 1966, Morning and Evening Poems (Cantata), 1966, Session I for Chamber Ensemble, 1965, Session II for violin and viola, 1966, Session III for clarinet, violin, cello, piano, percussion, 1966, Session IV for chamber ensemble, 1967, Black Host for organ, percussion and taped sounds, 1967, Piano Rags, 1967-74, cabaret opera Greatshot, 1967-69, Praeludium for vibraphone and organ, 1969, Dark Music for timpani and cello, 1970, Duets for Quintet, 1970, Unpopular Songs, 1969-71, Hydraulis for organ, 1971, Commedia for chamber orch, 1971, Whisper Moon (chamber ensemble), 1971, Frescoes for two pianists, 1971, Seasons for solo guitar, 1974, Open House, song cycle on poems by Roethke, 1975, Piano Concerto, 1975-76, Piano Quartet, 1976, Revelation Studies for Carillon, 1976, Mysteries for Organ, 1976, score for stage works Puntila (Brecht), 1976, Man is Man (Brecht), 1977, Beggar's Opera (posthumous collaboration with Darius Milhaud), 1978, Violin Sonatas, 1956, 78, 92, 94, 12 Gospel Preludes for Organ, 1979, 81, 84, Humoresk for organ and orch., 1969, Brass Quintet, 1979, 24 Cabaret Songs, 1963-96, Aubade for Oboe and Piano, 1982, Songs of Innocence and of Experience (Blake), 1956-82, Violin Concerto in D, 1983, Lilith (saxophone, piano), 1984, Abendmusik, 1977, Little Suite of Dances in E flat for clarinet and piano, 1984, Orphée-Sérénade, 1984, Fantasia Concertante for viola, cello and orch., 1985, Capriccio for Violoncello and Piano, 1985, orchestral dance suite Seattle Slew, 1986, 12 New Etudes for Piano, 1977-86 (recipient Pulitzer Prize, 1988), Spring Concertino for Oboe and Chamber

Orch., 1986-87, Five Fold Five for woodwind quintet and piano, 1985-87, Clarinet Concerto, 1990, (musical) Casino Paradise (libretto Arnold Weinstein), 1986-90, Fairy Tales for viola, cello, bass, 1987-88, Sonata for Violoncello and Piano, 1989, (song cycle on Am. women poets) I Will Breathe a Mountain, 1989-90, The Mask (chorus and piano), 1990, Recuerdos for two pianos, 1991, opera McTeague (libretto A. Weinstein and R. Altman), 1990-92, Lyric Concerto for flute and orch., 1993, Trio for clarinet, violin and piano, 1993, Sonata for 2 pianos in one movement, 1993, Suite for play Broken Glass by Arthur Miller, 1994, Let Evening Come (soprano, viola, piano), 1994, A Whitman Triptych, (mezzo-soprano and orchestra), 1995, GAEA Concertos 1-3 for Left Hand and Orch., 1996, Second Piano Quartet, 1995, Briefly It Enters, 1996 (voice and piano), Fanfare for the Detroit Opera House, 1996 (brass), Cabaret Songs, Vol. 3&4 (voice and piano), 1996, Nine Bagatelles, 1996 (piano), Spring Trio, 1996 (piano trio), Turbulence-A Romance, 1996 (2 voices and piano), Sixth Sym., 1997, Collusions (piano written with Curtis Curtis-Smith), 1998, Illuminata (film score written with Arnold Black), 1998, A View From the Bridge (opera), 1998, The Digital Wonder Watch (voice and piano), 1999, The Miracle (male chorus, woodwind quintet, percussion), 1999, Bird Spirits (piano), 2000, Concerto Grosso for Saxophone Quartet and Orch., 1999-2000, From the Diary of Sally Hemings (medium voice and piano), 2000, Piano Quintet (string quartet and piano), 2000, Song (for band), 2001, Naumburg Cycle (baritone and piano), 2001, Borborygm (organ), 2001; pianist in recs: (with Gerard Schwarz) Cornet Favorites, (with Clifford Jackson, baritone) An Evening with Henry Russell, (with mezzo-soprano Joan Morris) Other Songs of Leiber and Stoller, (with Joan Morris and Max Morath) These Charming People, (with Joan Morris) The Girl on the Magazine Cover, (with Joan Morris) Songs of Ira and George Gershwin, (with Joan Morris and Lucy Simon) The Rodgers and Hart Album, (with Joan Morris and Max Morath) More Rodgers and Hart, (with Joan Morris) Silver Linings (anthology of Jerome Kern), (with Joan Morris) Blue Skies (anthology of Irving Berlin), (with Joan Morris) Black Max (Bolcom cabaret songs with A. Weinstein poetry), (with Joan Morris) Lime Jello: An American Cabaret, (with Joan Morris) Night & Day (anthology of Cole Porter), (with Joan Morris) Let's Do It, (with Sergiu Luca) Works for Violin and Piano (by Bolcom), (with Joan Morris) After the Ball, Vaudeville, Songs of the Great Ladies of the Musical Stage, Wild About Eubie, (with Joan Morris and Clifford Jackson and chorus) Who Shall Rule This American Nation: Songs of Henry Clay Work, (with Joan Morris and Robert White) Orchids in the Moonlight and The Carioca (songs of Vincent Youmans), (with Joan Morris) Moonlight Bay-Songs As Is and Songs As Was; recs. Bolcom's 4th Symphony (Grammy nominee 1987), Violin Concerto, 5th Symphony, Fantasia Concertante (Am. Composers Orch.), 10th String Quartet (Stanford String Quartet), 1st and 3rd Symphonies, Seattle Slew Suite (Louisville Orch.), Orphée-Sérénade (Grammy nominee 1994), others; solo recordings include Heliotrope Bouquet, Pastimes and Piano Rags, Bolcom Plays His Own Rags, Piano Music of George Gershwin, Piano Music of Darius Milhaud, Bolcom: 12 Etudes, Euphonic Sounds (Scott Joplin anthology); author: (with Robert Kimball) Reminiscing with Sissle and Blake, 1973, Trouble in the Music World, 1988; editor book of essays: The Aesthetics of Survival by George Rochberg, 1982; contbr. to Grove's Dictionary, 6th edit; contbg. editor: Annals of Scholarship. Recipient Kurt Weill award, 1963, William and Noma Copley award, 1960, Marc Blitzstein Award for Excellence Am. Acad. Arts and Letters, 1965, N.Y. State Coun. award, 1971, Nat. Endowment for Arts award, 1974, 79, 82-84, Koussevitzky Found. award, 1974, 93, Henry Russel award, U. Mich., 1977, Mich. Arts Coun. award, 1986, Gov.'s Arts award, 1987, Pulitzer Prize in Music, 1988, Citation of Merit U. Mich. Sch. Music Alumni Assn., 1989, Disting. Achievement award U. Wash., 1993, Alfred I. Du Pont award Del. Symphony Assn., 1994, Henry Russel lectr., U. Mich., 1997; named composer of yr. Am. Guild Organists, 1998; Guggenheim Found. fellow, 1964, 68; Rockefeller Found. grantee, 1965, 69, 72. Mem. Am. Acad. Arts and Letters, Am. Music Ctr., Am. Composer Alliance, Am. Repertory Theatre (bd. dirs.), Charles Ives Soc. (bd. dirs.), Delta Omicron (nat. patron), Azazels. Home: 3080 Whitmore Lake Rd Ann Arbor MI 48105-9649 Office: U Mich Sch Music 2243 Moore Bldg Ann Arbor MI 48109 E-mail: wbolcom@umich.edu.

BOLDT, MICHAEL HERBERT, lawyer; b. Detroit, Oct. 11, 1950; s. Herbert M. and Mary Therese (Fitzgerald) B.; m. Margaret E. Clarke, May 25, 1974; children: Timothy (dec.), Matthew. Student, U. Detroit, 1968-70; BA, Wayne State U., 1972; JD, U. Mich., 1975. Bar: Ind. 1975, U.S. Dist. Ct. (so. dist.) Ind. 1975, U.S. Ct. Appeals (7th cir.) 1979, U.S. Supreme Ct. 1980, U.S. Ct. Appeals (D.C. cir.) 1983. Assoc. Ice Miller, Indpls., 1975-81, ptnr., 1982—. Bd. dirs. Star Alliance, Inc. Contbr. articles to profl. jours. Mem. Ind. State Bar Assn., Indpls. Bar Assn., Highland Golf and Country Club. Office: Ice Miller Box 82001 1 American Sq Indianapolis IN 46282-0002 E-mail: Michael.Boldt@icemiller.com.

BOLDT, OSCAR CHARLES, construction company executive; b. Appleton, Wis., Apr. 20, 1924; s. Oscar John and Dorothy A. (Bartmann) B.; m. Patricia Hamar, July 9, 1949; children: Charles, Thomas, Margaret. BSCE, U. Wis., 1948. Pres. O.J. Boldt Constrn. Co., Appleton, 1950-79, CEO, chmn. bd. dirs., 1979-84; chmn. bd. dirs. The Boldt Group Inc., 1984—; sec. W.S. Patterson Co., 1963-89. Trustee Lawrence U., 1981—; emeritus bd. dirs. M&I Bank, L.A., 2002 Chmn. bd. dirs. Cmty. Found. for Fox Valley Region, 1991-93; pres. Appleton YMCA, 1955-57, Appleton Meml. Hosp., 1975-76; bd. dirs. United Health Wis., 1990-99; co-chmn. fund drive Fox Cities United Way, 1994. 2d lt. USAAF, 1943-45. Recipient Disting. Svc. award Appleton Jaycees, 1960, Disting. Engr. award U. Wis., 1985, Walter Rugland Cmty. Svc. award, 1988, Master Entrepreneur award Ernst and Young, 1991, Renaissance award, 1991, Regent's award St. Olaf's Coll., 1993, N.E. Wis.'s Sales amd Mktg. Mag. Exec. of Yr. award, 1994, Disting. Alumni award U. Wis. Alumni Assn., 1999, Disting. Contractor award ASCE, 2000; Paul Harris fellow, 1979; named to Paper Industry Internat. Hall of Fame, 2000. Mem. Appleton Area C. of C. (pres. 1967), Appleton Rotary (pres. 1975-76, Vocat. Svc. award 1977, Paul Harris fellow), Riverview Country Club (pres. 1968-69). Republican. Presbyterian. Home: 1715 W Reid Dr Appleton WI 54914-5175 Office: The Boldt Group Inc PO Box 373 2525 N Roemer Rd Appleton WI 54911-8623 Office Fax: 920-739-5329. Business E-Mail: oscarboldt@boldt.com.

BOLE, GILES G. physician, researcher, medical educator; b. Battle Creek, Mich., July 28, 1928; s. Giles Gerald, Sr. and Kittie Belle B.; m. Elizabeth J. Dooley, May 11, 1985; children: David Giles, Elizabeth Ann. BS, U. Mich., Ann Arbor, 1949, MD, 1953. Diplomate Am. Bd. Internal Medicine. Resident in internal medicine U. Mich., Ann Arbor, 1953-56, fellow rheumatology Rackham arthritis research unit, 1958-61, asst. prof. internal medicine, 1961-64, assoc. prof. internal medicine, 1964-70, prof. internal medicine, 1970—; physician-in-charge Rackham Arthritis Research Unit, 1971-86, chief rheumatology div., 1976-86; assoc. dean clin. affairs, sr. assoc. dean Med. Sch. U. Mich., 1986-88, exec. assoc. dean Med. Sch., 1988-90, interim dean Med. Sch., 1990-91, dean Med. Sch., 1991-96, dean emeritus Med. Sch., 1996—. Dir. U. Mich. Arthritis Ctr., Ann Arbor, 1977-86; bd. govs. Am. Bd. Internal Medicine, 1979-83, chmn. rheumatology com., 1979-83. Capt. M.C., USAF, 1956-58. Recipient Borden Academic Achievement award U. Mich., 1953; Postdoctoral Research fellow Arthritis Found., 1961-63 Mem. Am. Fed. Clin. Rsch. (chmn. Midwest sect. 1967-68), Cen. Soc. Clin. Rsch. (pres. 1976-77), Am. Rheumatism Assn. (pres. 1980-81). Office: U Mich Med Sch M 7300 Med Sci I 4101 Med Sci Bldg 1 C-wing Ann Arbor MI 48109-0600

BOLENDER, TODD, choreographer; b. Canton, Ohio, 1914; Student, Hanya Holm, N.Y.C.; enrolled, Sch. American Ballet, N.Y.C., 1936. Joined Lincoln Kirstein's Ballet Caravan, 1937; formed Am. Concert Ballet; choreographed 1st ballet, 1943; also danced with Ballet Theatre, 1944 and Ballet Russe de Monte Carlo, 1945, joined Ballet Soc., 1946; prin. dancer N.Y.C. Ballet, 1948-61; dir. ballet cos. of opera houses of Cologne and Frankfurt; numerous nat. and internat. freelance choreography assignments, 1952-80; artistic dir. State Ballet of Mo., Kansas City, 1981-96, artistic dir. emeritus, 1996. Recipient Mo. Arts Coun. awrd, 1987, W.F. Yates for disting. svc. William Jewell Coll., 1995. Office: Kansas City Ballet 1601 Broadway Kansas City MO 64108-1207

BOLER, JOHN, manufacturing executive; b. 1934; CEO, owner Boler Co., Itasca, Ill., 1978—. Office: Boler Co 500 Park Blvd Ste 1010 Itasca IL 60143-1285

BOLGER, DAVID P. bank executive; b. Aug. 23, 1957; BS in Acctg./Fin., Marquette U., 1979; MM in Fin., Northwestern U., 1980. Credit analyst Am. Nat. Bank & Trust Co., Chgo., 1980-82, comml. banking officer, 1982-89, sr. v.p., CFO, 1989-92, exec. v.p., 1992-93, exec. v.p., treas., 1993-94, pres., 1996-98; exec. dir. Banc One, 1998—. Bd. dirs. Mercy Hosp. & Med. Ctr., Impulse Theatre Co., Fist Non-Profit Ins. Co.; active United Way/Crusade of Mercy. Mem. Chgo. Hist. Soc., Execs. Club Chgo., Robert Morris Asscos. Office: Banc One 1 Banc One Plz Chicago IL 60670-0001

BOLIN, STEVEN ROBERT, veterinarian researcher; b. Tokyo, July 12, 1950; s. Robert Cornwall and Irene Fay (Temple) B.; m. Carole Ann Sawyer, May 23, 1981; children: Christopher, Matthew, Sarah, Kelsey. DVM, Purdue U., 1974, MS, 1979, PhD, 1982. Lic. veterinarian, Ind. Veterinarian pvt. practice, Ottawa, Ill., 1974-77; rsch. scientist Nat. Animal Disease Ctr., Ames, Iowa, 1982-84, lead scientist, 1984—, rsch. leader, 1992—. Contbr. over 80 sci. articles on viral disease of cattle and swine to profl. jours. and chpts. to books. Cubmaster Pack 196, Ames, 1994-96. Recipient Salmon award Nat. Assn. Fed. Veterinarians, 1987, Pestivirus Rsch. medal European Vet. Virology Soc., 1992. Mem. Am. Vet. Med. Assn., U.S. Animal Health Assn., Nat. Assn. Fed. Veterinarians, Conf. Rsch. Workers in Animal Disease. Achievements include rsch. accomplishments in the discovery of pathogenic mechanisms associated with mucosal disease of cattle; definition of factors of virulence for bovine viral diarrhea virus; definition of methods for identifying separate groups of bovine viral diarrhea virus. Office: USDA Nat Animal Disease Ctr Ames IA 50010-0070

BOLINDER, SCOTT W. publishing company executive; b. 1951; m. Jill Bolinder; children: Jamie, Jesse, Anna. BA in Literature, Wheaton Coll., 1973; MSW, U. Ill., 1975. Adv. sales Huebner Pub. Co., 1979-80; pub. dir. Campus Life Mag., 1980-81, exec. v.p., 1981-82; sr. v.p. Christianity Today Inc., Carol Stream, Ill., 1982-89; v.p., pub. Zondervan Pub. House, Grand Rapids, Mich., 1989—. Bd. dirs. Eden Assistance Ltd.; active Thornapple Evang. Covenant Ch., Grand Rapids. Capt. US Army, 1975-79. Mem. Acad. Cert. Social Workers. Avocations: music, reading, tennis, biking, Moroccan cooking. Office: Zondervan Pub House 5300 Patterson Ave SE Grand Rapids MI 49512-9512

BOLKCOM, JOE L. state legislator; b. Bloomington, Minn., July 29, 1956; m. Karen Kubby. BA in Sociology, St. Ambrose U., 1983; MA in Pub. Affairs, U. Iowa, 1988. Dir. Sr. Edn., Inc., 1981-86, Sr. Advs., Inc., 1986-88; with Johnson County Health Dept., 1988-92; supr. Johnson County, 1993—; mem. Iowa Senate from 23rd dist., 1998—. Mem. Iowa Ground Water Assn., Am. Fedn. Tchrs. (local 716), Iowa Civil Liberties Union, Sierra Club. Democrat. Roman Catholic. Home: 728 2d Ave Iowa City IA 52245 Office: State Capitol Dist 23 3 9th And Grand Des Moines IA 50319-0001 E-mail: joe@joebolkcom.org.

BOLLENBACHER, HERBERT KENNETH, steel company official; b. Wilkinsburg, Pa., Apr. 16, 1933; s. Curtis W. and Ebba M. (Frendberg) B.; m. Nancy Jane Cercena, June 29, 1957; children: Mary E., Kenneth E. AB, U. Pitts., 1960, MEd, 1963. Cert. safety profl. Staff asst. tng. J & L Steel Co., Pitts., 1963-66; mgr. tng., devel. and accident prevention Textron Corp., Pitts., 1966-72; supr. safety Copperweld Steel Co., Warren, Ohio, 1972-75, mgr. safety, security, 1975-78, mgr. human resources conservation, 1978-94; exec. v.p. Charles Mgmt., Inc., 1994—; mem. adj. faculty Pa. State U. mem. Eastminster Presbytery Com. on Ministry; bd. dirs. Trumbull County Prison Ministry. Served with U.S. Army, 1954-56. Mem. Am. Soc. Safety Engrs. (past pres. Ohio-Pa. chpt., Ohio Safety Profl. of Yr. 1983-84, 92-93), Ohio Soc. Safety Engrs. (state chaplain), Am. Iron and Steel Inst. (chmn. safety task force), Mfrs. Assn. Eastern Ohio and Western Pa. (safety chmn. 12 yrs.; safety profl. of yr. award 1984, coordinator Ohio seat belt coalition 1986, Gov.'s spl. recognition award), Gov.'s Traffic Safety Coun., 1989, Trumbull Camp Gideons Internat. (past pres.), Ohio Gideons (area coordinator, membership cabinet), Rotary (Paul Harris fellow, pres., benefactor, Ideal of Svc. in Workplace award), Boy Scouts Am. (western reserve coun., loss prevention com.). Presbyterian (elder). Author suprs. monthly discussion guide, article for tech. publ. Avocations: softball; volleyball; reading. Office: Charles Mgmt Inc 24850 Aurora Rd Cleveland OH 44146-1747

BOLLINGER, DON MILLS, retired grocery company executive; b. Seymour, Ind., Mar. 7, 1914; s. Don Albert and Hannah (Mills) B.; m. EmmyLou Groub, Nov. 5, 1938; children: Linda Bollinger McCoy, Thomas R., Barbara Bollinger Flaherty. AB, DePauw U., 1936; MBA, U. Pa., 1938. With Seymour Woolen Mills, Ind., 1938-51, pers. mgr., 1945-51; with John C. Groub Co. Inc., Seymour, 1951-99, chmn., sr. exec. officer, 1980-84, chmn., chief exec. officer, 1984-91, chmn., 1991-99, also bd. dirs.; chmn. bd. Fidelity Fed. Savs. & Loan (merged with Home Fed. Savs. Bank 1990), Seymour, until 1987; pres., bd. dir. Dotto Inc., 1984—. Pres. Jackson County United Fund, Seymour, 1961-64; officer ARC Jackson County, 1941-43, 72-77, chmn. 75-76, 76-77; bd. dirs. Jackson County Juvenile Home, Brownstown, Ind., 1978-92, pres., 1983-84. Recipient Man and Boy award Boys' Clubs Am., 1963, Svc. to Mankind award, La Sertoma, 1977; named Boss of Yr., Seymour Jaycees, 1964; inducted into DePauw U. Athletic Hall of Fame, 1991. Mem. Ind. Retail Coun. (bd. dirs. exec. com. 1977-94), Seymour C. of C. (pres. 1968, Citizen of Yr. award 1987), Ind. State C. of C. (bd. dirs. 1984-92), Washington C. DePauw Soc. Republican. Methodist. Club: Seymour Country. Lodges: Elks, Rotary (pres. 1962-63). Home: 660 Braewick Rd Seymour IN 47274-1430 Office: John C Groub Co Inc Freeman Field Ave A & D St Seymour IN 47274

BOLLINGER, LEE CARROLL, academic administrator, law educator; b. 1946; BS, U. Oreg., 1968; JD, Columbia U., 1971. Law clk. to Judge Wilfred Feinberg U.S. Ct. Appeals (2nd cir.), 1971—72; law clk. to Chief Justice Warren Burger U.S. Supreme Ct., 1972—73; asst. prof. law U. Mich., 1973—76, assoc. prof., 1976—78, prof., 1978—94, dean, 1987—94, pres., prof. law, 1997—; provost, prof. govt. Dartmouth Coll., 1994—96. Rsch. assoc. Clare Hall, Cambridge U., 1983. Co-author (with Jackson): (novels) Contract Law in Modern Society, 1980, The Tolerant Soc., 1986, Images of a Free Press, 1991. Bd. dirs. Gerald R. Ford Found., Royal Shakespeare Co. Fellow Am. Rockefeller Humanities. Fellow: Am. Acad. Arts and Scis. Office: Columbia University 2960 Broadway New York NY 10027-6902

BOLLINGER, MICHAEL, artistic director; b. St. Louis, July 1, 1954; s. Rollie Bollinger and Blanche (Bush) Easley; m. Stephanie McClain-Bollinger; children: Tanner Michael, Allison Jeanette. Student, Webster U., 1972-73, U. Mo., 1973-74, U. Mo., St. Louis, 1974-75; BFA, Webster U., 1978. Producing dir., founder Mainstage Theatre, Lake of the Ozarks, Mo., 1978-84; artistic producing dir. Arrow Rock (Mo.) Lyceum Theatre, 1980—. Dir. Lyceum Airwaves Theatre, 1985-88; guest instr. acting Mo. Baptist Coll., St. Louis, Stephens Coll., Columbia, Mo. Valley Coll., Marshall, mem. theatre adv. panel Mo. Arts Coun., St. Louis, 1987-90; co-prodr. Mo. State Theatre Conf., St. Louis; mem. citizens adv. bd. KBIA-PBS Radio; adv. com. InterAct; Teen to Teen Theatre, Columbia, 1992-93; adjudicator Am. Coll. Theatre Fest, Ruston, La., 1992, Tenn. Arts Commn. Artist Fellowship, Nashville, 1994, Am. Coll. Theatre, 1997. (prodr., dir., actor): (plays) almost 200 plays and musicals, including 6 world premieres. Facilities chmn. cultural planning com. Columbia Com. on the Arts, 1993-95; adjudicator Prelude awards, Indpls., 1993, 96, Am. Assn. Cmty. Theatre Festival Adjudication, Ill., 1997. Recipient Mo. Arts award Mo. Arts Coun., 1983, 94, Outstanding Young Men of Am. award U.S. Jaycees, 1983. Mem. Actors Equity Assn. Liberal. Baptist. Avocations: raising children, photography, outdoor activities, feminine appreciation, history. Office: Arrow Rock Lyceum Theatre High St Arrow Rock MO 65320 E-mail: rollie1954@aol.com.

BOLLS, IMOGENE LAMB, English language educator, poet; b. Manhattan, Kans., Sept. 25, 1938; d. Don Q. and Helen Letson (Keithley) Lamb; m. Nathan J. Bolls, Jr., Nov. 24, 1962; 1 child Laurel Helen. BA, Kans. State U., 1960; MA, U. Utah, 1962. Instr. French Kans. State U., Manhattan, 1959-60; instr. English U. Utah, Salt Lake City, 1960-62; instr. to prof. Wittenberg U., Springfield, Ohio, 1963—. Poet-in-residence, dir. journalism program Wittenberg U.; tchg. poet Antioch Writers' Workshop Antioch Coll., summers, 1992—93; intensive seminar poet Antioch Writers' Workshop Antioch Coll., summer, 1994; poetry tchr. Ohio Poet-in-the-Schs. program, 1972—82; poetry instr. acad. camp; state and nat. poetry judge. Author: (poetry) Glass Walker, 1983, Earthbound, 1989, Advice for the Climb, 1999, works represented in anthologies; contbr. more than 600 poems to mags. Recipient Individual Artist award Ohio Arts Coun., 1982, 90, Poetry prize S.D. Rev., 1983, Poetry award Kans. Quarterly, 1985, Ohioana Poetry award Ohioana Libr. Assn., 1995; finalist Vassar Miller Prize in Poetry, 1994; grantee Ireland, 1986, France, 1990, Am. Southwest. Mem. Acad. Am. Poets (assoc.), Poetry Soc. Am., Women in Comm. Avocations: hiking, backpacking, photography, music, travel. Address: 1466 Monterey Dr Taos NM 87571

BOLTON, WILLIAM J. food products executive; b. 1946; Pres. Jewel Food Stores, Melrose Park, Ill., 1991-95; corp. COO markets Am. Food Stores, 1995; chmn., CEO Bruno's Inc., Birmingham, Ala., 1995-97; exec. vice-pres.; pres. & COO Retail Food Cos. SUPERVALU Inc., Eden Prairie, MN, 1997—. Office: SUPERVALU Inc 11840 Valley View Rd Eden Prairie MN 55344-3691

BOMBA, STEVEN J. controls company executive; BS in Phyics, MS in Physics, PhD in Physics, U. Wis. Positions with Collins Group Rockwell Internat., v.p. advanced mfg. techs., 1987-90; positions with Tex. Instuments, Mobil R & D; dir. corp. tech. devel. Allen-Bradley, 1978-85, v.p. corp. tech., 1985-87, Johnson Controls, Inc., Milw., 1990—. Office: Johnson Controls Inc 5757 N Green Bay Ave Milwaukee WI 53209-4408

BOMKE, LARRY K. state legislator; b. Springfield, Ill., June 6, 1950; m. Sally Jo; 2 children. Student, Lincoln Land C.C. Ptnr. Ins. Agy.; mem. Ill. Senate, Springfield, 1995—, mem. exec. appts. com., local govt. & elections com. Republican. Office: State Capitol 111 Capitol Bldg Springfield IL 62706-0001

BONACORSI, MARY CATHERINE, lawyer; b. Henderson, Ky., Apr. 24, 1949; d. Harry E. and Johanna M. (Kelly) Mack; m. Louis F. Bonacorsi, Apr. 23, 1971; children: Anna, Kathryn, Louis. BA in Math., Washington U., St. Louis, 1971; JD, Washington U., 1977. Bar: Mo. 1977, Ill. 1981, U.S. Dist. Ct. (ea. dist.) Mo., U.S. Dist. Ct. (so. dist.) Ill., U.S. Ct. Appeals (8th cir.), U.S. Supreme Ct. 1995. Ptnr. Thompson Coburn, St. Louis, 1977—. Chairperson fed. practice com. eastern dist., St. Louis, 1987—, eight cir. jud. conf. com., St. Louis, 1987—. Mem. ABA, Assn. Trial Lawyers of Am., Mo. Bar Assn., Met. St. Louis Bar Assn., Order of Coif. Office: Thompson Coburn Firstar Plz Ste 3100 Saint Louis MO 63101 E-mail: mbonacorsi@thompsoncoburn.com.

BONAVENTURA, LEO MARK, gynecologist, educator; b. East Chicago, Ill., Aug. 1, 1945; s. Angelo Peter and Wanda D. (Kelleher) B.; student Marquette U., 1963-66; M.D., Ind. U., 1970; married; children—Leo Mark, Dena Anne, Angela Lorena, Nicole Palmira, Leah Michelle, Adam Xavier. Intern in surgery, Cook County Hosp., Chgo., 1970-71; resident in ob-gyn., Ind. U. Hosps., 1973-76, fellow in reproductive endocrinology and infertility, 1976-78; asst. prof. ob-gyn., Ind. U., 1976—, asst. head sect. reproductive endocrinology and infertility, 1978-80, head sect., 1980-81. Served with USN attached to USMC, 1971-73. Named Intern of Yr., Cook County Hosp., 1971. Diplomate Am. Bd. Obstetrics and Gynecology, Am. Bd. Reproductive Endocrinology and Infertility. Mem. Central Assn. Ob-Gyn., Am. Coll. Obstetricians and Gynecologists, Am. Fertility Soc., Can. Fertility Soc., Soc. Reproductive Endocrinologists, Soc. Reproductive Surgeons. Roman Catholic. Contbr. articles to profl. jours. Office: 8091 Township Line Rd Indianapolis IN 46260-2494

BOND, CHRISTOPHER SAMUEL (KIT BOND), senator, lawyer; b. St. Louis, Mar. 6, 1939; s. Arthur D. and Elizabeth (Green) B.; 1 child, Samuel Reid. BA with honors, Princeton U., 1960; LLB, U. Va., 1963. Bar: Mo. 1963, U.S. Supreme Ct. 1967. Law clk. to presiding chief justice U.S. Ct. of Appeals (5th cir.), Atlanta, 1963-64; assoc. Covington & Burling, Washington, 1965-67; pvt. practice law Mexico, Mo., 1968; asst. atty. gen., chief counsel consumer protection div. State of Mo., 1969-70, gov., 1973-77, 81-85; auditor, 1971-73; ptnr. Gage & Tucker, Kansas City, 1985-87; U.S. senator from Mo., 1987—; chmn. small bus. com. 104th Congress. Mem. appropriations com., 1991—, chmn. subcom. on VA, HUD and ind. appropriations agys., 1991—, subcom. on def., 1993—, subcom. on fgn. ops., 1999—, subcom. on transp., 1995—; budget com., 1989—, environment and pub. works com., 1995—, subcom. on drinking water, fisheries and wildlife, 1995—; chmn. small bus. com., senate Rep. policy com.; pres. Gt. Plains Legal Found., Kansas City, Mo., 1977-80; chmn. Rep. Gov.'s Assn., Midwestern Gov.'s Conf., chmn. con. on econ. and community devel., 1981-83, chmn. con. on energy and environment, 1983-84. Republican. Presbyterian. Office: US Senate 274 Russell Senate Bldg Washington DC 20510-0001*

BOND, RICHARD L. food products executive; Pres., COO IBP, Inc., Dakota Dunes, S.D.; also bd. dirs. Office: IBP Inc 800 Stevens Port Dr Ste 836 Dakota Dunes SD 57049-5005

BOND, RICHARD LEE, lawyer, state senator; b. Kansas City, Kans., Sept. 18, 1935; s. Clarence Ivy and Florine (Hardison) B.; m. Sue S. Sedgwick, Aug. 23, 1958; children: Mark, Amy. BA, U. Kans., 1957, JD, 1960. City atty., Overland Park, Kans., 1960-62; adminstrv. asst. to Congressman Robert Ellsworth, Washington, 1961-66, Congressman Larry Winn, Washington, 1967-85, Congressman Jan Meyers, Washington, 1986; chmn. bd. dirs. Home State Bank, Kansas City, 1983-94; ptnr. Bennett, Lytle, Wetzler et al, Prairie Village, Kans., 1986-89; senator State of Kans., Topeka, 1985-2001, senate pres., 1997-2001. Vice chmn. Guaranty Bank and Bancshares, Kansas City, Kans., 1995—. Named State Legislator of Yr. Governing Mag. Republican. Presbyterian. Avocations: gardening, tennis, hunting, fishing. Home: 9823 Nall Ave Shawnee Mission KS 66207-2915

BONDER, SETH, mechanical engineer; BS in Mech. Engring., U. Md.; PhD in Indsl. Engring., Ohio State U. Prof. dept. indsl. engring. U. Mich., dir. sys. rsch. lab.; founder, CEO Vector Rsch. Inc., Ann Arbor, Mich. Capt. USAF. Mem. NAE. Office: Vector Rsch Inc PO Box 1506 Ann Arbor MI 48106

BONFIELD, ARTHUR EARL, lawyer, educator; b. N.Y.C., May 12, 1936; s. Louis and Rose (Lesser) B.; m. Doris Harfenist, June 10, 1958 (dec. 1995); 1 child, Lauren; m. Eva Tsalikian, Apr. 8, 2000. BA, Bklyn. Coll., 1956; JD, Yale U., 1960, LLM, 1961, postgrad. (sr. fellow), 1961-62; DHL (hon.), Cornell Coll., 1999. Bar: Conn. 1961, Iowa 1966. Asst. prof. U. Iowa Law Sch., 1962-65, assoc. prof., 1965-66, prof., 1966-69, Law Sch. Found. disting. prof., 1969-72, John Murray disting. prof., 1972—, assoc. dean for research, 1985—; summer vis. prof. law U. Mich., 1970, U. Tenn., 1972, U. N.C., 1974, Hofstra U., 1977, Lewis and Clark U., 1984. Gen. counsel spl. joint com. state adminstrv. procedure act Iowa Gen. Assembly, 1974-75; spl. counsel adminstrv. procedure exec. br. State of Iowa, 1975; chmn. com. constl. law Nat. Conf. Bar Examiners Multi-State Bar Exam, 1977—; reporter 1981 Model State Adminstrv. Procedure Act, Nat. Conf. Commrs. Uniform State Laws, 1979-81; cons. Ark. State Constl. Conv., 1980; chmn. Iowa Gov.'s Com. State Pub. Records Law, 1983; Iowa commr. Nat. Conf. Commrs. on Uniform State Laws, 1984-2000; chmn. Iowa Gov.'s Task Force on Uniform Adminstrv. Rules, 1985-92; chmn. Iowa Gov.'s Task Force Team on Regulatory Process, Rule Making, and Rules Rev., 1999-2000. Prin. draftsman Iowa Civil Rights Act, 1965, Iowa Fair Housing Act, 1967, Iowa Adminstrv. Procedure Act, 1974, Iowa Open Meetings Act, 1978, Iowa Civil Rights Act, 1978, Amendments to Iowa Public Records Law, 1984, Amendments to Iowa Administrative Procedure Act, 1998; author: State Administrative Rule Making, 1986, State and Federal Administrative Law, 1989; contbr. numerous articles to law jours. Recipient Outstanding Service to Civil Liberties award Iowa Civil Liberties Union, 1974, Hancher Finkbine Outstanding Faculty Mem. award U. Iowa, 1980, Faculty Excellence award Iowa Bd. Regents, 1995, Outstanding Law Sch. Tchg. award U. Iowa, 1996; Frederick Klocksiem fellow Aspen Inst. Humanistic Studies, summer 1978. Mem. ABA (chmn. divsn. state adminstrv. law 1976-80, coun. 1980-84, chmn. sect. 1987-88, sect. adminstrv. law and regulatory practice), Am. Law Inst. (life mem.), Iowa State Bar Assn. (chmn. com. adminstrv. law 1971-85, coun. sect. adminstr. law 1990-93, 94-97, 98-99, 2000—, reporter and mem., task force on state adminstrv. law reform 1994-96, Pres. award Outstanding Svc. to Bar and Public 1996), Am. Coun. Learned Soc. (del. from Assn. Am. Law Schs. 1984-94). Home: 206 Mahaska Dr Iowa City IA 52246-1606 Office: U Iowa Sch Law Iowa City IA 52242

BONFIELD, GORDON BRADLEY, III, paper company executive; b. Grand Rapids, Mich., Aug. 1, 1951; s. Gordon Bradley Jr. and Ardella (Cowan) B.; m. Pamela Anne Grisham, July 23, 1953; children: Christopher, Michael. BBA, U. Iowa, 1973; MBA, Ohio State U., 1975. Sales rep. Packaging Corp. Am., Denver, 1976-78, sales mgr. Grand Rapids, 1978-81, gen. mgr., 1981-87, v.p., 1987-88, James River Corp., Kalamazoo, 1988-90, v.p., group exec. Cin., 1990—, sr. v.p. ops., 1995—. Dir. Paperboard Packaging Coun., Washington, 1990—. Mem. Ivy Hills Country Club. Office: Ivex Packaging Corp 100 Tri-State Dr Ste 200 Lincolnshire IL 60069

BONGIOVI, ROBERT P. career officer; BSc in Aerospace Engring., U. Notre Dame, 1969; MSc in Aerospace Engring., MIT, 1970. Commd. 2d. lt. USAF, 1970, advanced through grades to major gen., 1999; program mgr. Norton AFB, Calif., 1970-75; various assignments Wright-Patterson AFB, Ohio, 1975-82, 92-98; dir. requirements, 1998—; various assignments The Pentagon, Washington, 1983-87, 88-92, Indsl. Coll. Armed Forces, Washington, 1987-88. Decorated Legion of Merit with oak leaf cluster, Defense Meritorious Svc. medal with oak leaf cluster.

BONHAM, RUSSELL AUBREY, chemistry educator; b. San Jose, Calif., Dec. 10, 1931; s. Russell Aubrey and Margaret Florence (Wallace) B.; m. Miriam Anne Dye, Mar. 23, 1957; children: Frances, Margaret, Anne. BA, Whittier Coll., 1954; PhD, Iowa State U., 1958. Instr. Ind. U., Bloomington, 1958-60; postdoctoral fellow Naval Rsch. Lab., 1960; asst. prof. math. U. Md., 1960; asst. prof. chemistry Ind. U., Bloomington, 1960-63, assoc. prof., 1963-65, prof. chemistry, 1965-95, prof. emeritus, 1996—; rsch. prof. chemistry Ill. Inst. Tech., Chgo., 1995—. Co-author: High Energy Electron Scattering, 1974; mem. editorial bd.: The Jour. of the Brazilian Chem. Soc., 1989-2000; contbr. over 175 articles and papers to profl. jours. Recipient Fulbright fellowship U. Tokyo, 1964-65, Guggenheim fellowship, 1964-65, Humboldt prize, 1977, 81. Fellow Am. Phys. Soc., AAAS; mem. Am. Phys. Soc., Am. Crystallographic Assn., Am. Chem. Soc., Sigma Xi. Achievements include research on electron impact cross section measurements of molecular species of interest to low pressure processing plasmas and X-Ray scattering from gases. Office: Ill Inst Tech Dept Biol Chem Phys Scis 3101 S Dearborn Chicago IL 60616

BONINI, JAMES, federal court official; BA in Criminal Justice, Indiana U. of Pa., 1986; MPA, U. So. Calif., 1988. Administrv. asst. South Bay Mcpl. Ct. Los Angeles County, Calif., 1987—88, sr. adminstrv. asst., 1988—89, divsn. head budget and mgmt. svcs., 1989; chief dep. ct. adminstr. Ct. Common Pleas, Montgomery County, Pa., 1990—91, dist. ct. adminstr. Berks County, 1991—96; clk. of ct. U.S. Bankruptcy Ct. No. Dist. Ind., South Bend, 1996—. Mem. Nat. Assn. Ct. Mgmt., Nat. Conf. Bankruptcy Clks. Office: US Bankruptcy Ct 401 S. Michigan St PO Box 7003 South Bend IN 46634-7003

BONIOR, DAVID EDWARD, congressman; b. Detroit, June 6, 1945; s. Edward John and Irene (Gaverluk) B.; children: Julie, Andy BA, U. Iowa, 1967; MA in History, Chapman Coll., Calif., 1972. Mem. Mich. Ho. of Reps., 1973-77, U.S. Congress from 10th Mich. dist., 1977—; mem. com. on rules; Dem. whip, 1991—2002. Mem. VA, passport svs. and social security coms. U.S. Congress, 1999—. Author: The Vietnam Veteran: A History of Neglect, 1984 Served in USAF, 1968-72. Democrat. Roman Catholic. Office: US Ho of Reps 2207 Rayburn Bldg Washington DC 20515-2210*

BONNER, BRIGID ANN, marketing professional; b. Mpls., Apr. 27, 1960; d. John Patrick and R. Jeanne (Crahan) B. BS in Journalism and Indsl. Adminstrn., Iowa State U., Ames, 1982; MBA, Harvard U., 1988. Mktg. statistician Fingerhut, Minnetonka, Minn., 1982-83; mktg. rep. IBM Corp., Mpls., 1983-88, exec. cons., 1988-90, mktg. mgr., 1990-92, sector mgr., 1992—. Mem. com. United Way of Minn., Mpls., 1989—. Mem. Harvard Bus. Sch. Club Minn. (bd. dirs. Mpls. chpt. 1989, pres. 1992—, mgmt. assistance program cons. 1990—). Republican. Roman Catholic. Avocations: travel, running, tennis, bicycling. Home: 25 Willow Woods Dr Excelsior MN 55331-8426 Office: IBM Corp 650 3rd Ave S Ste 500 Minneapolis MN 55402-4300

BONNER, DENNIS, state legislator; b. Springfield, Mo., Mar. 14, 1964; BA, U. Mo., 1992, MA, 1994, student. Mem. Mo. Ho. of Reps., Jefferson City. Mem. appropriations com., commerce com. (vice chmn), labor com., local govt. and related matters com., joint com. on pub. employee retirement (chmn.), joint com. on econ. devel., policy & planning. Founding bd. mem. Northwest Cmtys. Devel. Corp.; citizen adv. bd. Cmty. Svc. League. Mem. Jackson County Hist. Soc., Am. Legion. Democrat.

BONOW, ROBERT OGDEN, medical educator; b. Camden, N.J., Mar. 11, 1947; m. Patricia Jeanne Hitchens, Sept. 12, 1982; children: Robert Hitchens, Samuel Crawford. BS in Chem. Engring. magna cum laude, Lehigh U., Bethelehem, Pa., 1969; MD, U. Pa., Phila., 1973. Diplomate Am. Bd. Internal Medicine, subspecialty bd. on cardiovascular disease. Intern in medicine Hosp. U. Pa., Phila., 1973-74, resident, 1974-76; clin. assoc. cardiology br. Nat. Heart, Lung and Blood Inst., Bethesda, Md., 1976-79, sr. investigator, attending physician cardiology br., 1979-92, chief nuclear cardiology sect., 1980-92, dep. chief, 1989-92; Goldberg prof. medicine Northwestern U. Med. Sch., Chgo., 1992—; chief divsn. cardiology Northwestern Meml. Hosp., 1992—; attending physician dept. medicine VA Lakeside Med. Ctr., 1993—, Evanston (Ill.) Hosp., 1994—. Pfizer vis. prof. cardiovascular medicine Yale U., 1992, U. Mass., 1998; AHA/ACC Task Force on Practice Guidelines Com. on Cardiac Radlonuclide Imaging, 1993-95; chair com. on mgmt. of patents with valvular heart disease, 1996—; vis. prof. various univs., 1982-99; working group on methods/technologies Nat. Heart Attack Alert Program, 1994—; invited presenter at sci. sessions, symposia and acad. med. ctrs. Mem. editl. bd. Am. Jour. Cardiology, 1983—, Jour. Am. Coll. Cardiology, 1983-87, 91-95, Circulation, 1986—, Cardiovascular Imaging, 1988—, Am. Jour. Cardiac Imaging, 1990-95, Internat. Jour. Cardiac Imaging, 1990—, Jour. Heart Valve Disease, 1982—, Jour. Nuclear Cardiology, 1993—, Jour. Nuclear Medicine, 1994—, Cardiologia, 1995—, Am. Heart Jour., 1998—; contbr. over 300 publs. in med. jours. and textbooks. Recipient NIH Director's award, 1986, USPHS Commendation medal, 1990, USPHS outstanding svc. medal, 1991. Fellow ACP, Am. Coll. Cardiology (exhibits com. 1986-92, 1999-2000, program com. 1991-92, chair extramural edn. com., 1998—, bd. trustees 1999—, Disting. fellow 2000), Am. Heart Assn. (chmn. sci. session program com. 1998-2000, bd. dirs. 1999—, chmn. Coun. on Clin. Cardiology, 1999-2001, pres.-elect 2002-); mem. AAAS, Am. Bd. Internal Medicine (subspecialty bd. cardiovasc. disease 1996-2001), Am. Soc. Clin. Investigation, Assn. Am. Physicians, Am. Heart Assn. Met. Chgo. (bd. govs. 1992-98, rsch. coun. 1992-98, pres. 2001-), Am. Soc. Nuclear Cardiology (bd. dirs. 1994-98, chmn. edn. com. 1994-2000, nominating com. 1994-96), Assn. Profs. Cardiology (nominating com. 1993—, councillor 1994—, sec., treas. 1996-99, v.p. 1999-2000, pres. 2000-2001), Chgo. Cardiology Group (pres. 1994-96), Soc. Nuclear Medicine (chmn. Cardiovascular Coun. 1990-91, publs. com. 1994-2000), Am. Fedn. Clin. Rsch., Assn. Am. Physicians, Assn. Univ. Cardiologists, Ctrl. Soc. Clin. Rsch., Alpha Omega Alpha. Office: Northwestern U Med Sch Cardiology Divsn 250 E Superior St Ste 524 Chicago IL 60611-2958

BOOKER, JOSEPH W., JR. warden; b. Bradford, Tenn., Sept. 25, 1954; m. Jackie Booker, Dec. 30, 1989; 5 children. Postgrad., Calif. Coast U. Capt. Fed. Correctional Instn., Tucson, 1987-89, Met. Correctional Ctr., San Diego, 1989-91, assoc. warden Chgo., 1991-92, U.S. Penitentiary, Marion, Ill., 1992-95; warden Fed. Correctional Instn., Florence, S.C., 1995-97, U.S. Penitentiary, Bur. of Prisons, Dept. of Justice, Leavenworth, Kans. Bd. dirs. N.Am. Wardens Assn. Sgt. USMC, 1972-76. Mem. Law Enforcement Correctional Adminstrs., Strategic Threat Intelligent Network Group, Am. Correctional Assn. Methodist. Avocations: golf, basketball, fishing.

BOOKER, W. WAYNE, automotive executive; b. Sullivan, Ind., Aug. 28, 1934; BS in Econs., Purdue U. With Ford Motor Co., 1959—, various fin. positions automotive assembly divsn., fin. dir. L.Am. ops., 1974-77, contr. engine divsn., 1977, contr. N.Am. automotive ops., 1978-81, asst. contr. intenrat. automotive ops., 1981-86, dir.-pres. Ford of Brazil, 1986-87, dir., exec. v.p. Autolatina, 1987-99, exec. dir. L.Am. automotive ops., 1999—, CFO, vice chmn. Bd. dirs. Hertz Corp., Park Ridge, N.J. Office: Ford Motor Co 1 American Rd Dearborn MI 48126-2798

BOOKOUT, JOHN G. insurance company executive; Chmn. bd. dirs. Woodmen of World Life Ins. Soc., Omaha. Office: Woodmen of the World Life 1700 Farnam St Omaha NE 68102-2007

BOOKSTEIN, ABRAHAM, information science educator; b. N.Y.C., Mar. 22, 1940; s. Alex and Doris (Cohen) B.; m. Marguerite Vickers, June 20, 1968. BS, CCNY, 1961; MS, U. Calif., Berkeley, 1966; PhD, Yeshiva U., 1969; MA, U. Chgo., 1970. Asst. prof. U. Chgo., 1971-75, assoc. prof. info. sci., 1975-82, prof. info. sci., 1982—. Vis. prof. Royal Inst. Tech., Stockholm, 1982, UCLA, 1985; vis. disting. scholar OCLC, Columbus, Ohio, 1988; bd. dirs. Religion Index, Evanston, Ill., 1984-96; adv. bd. Info. Sci. Rsch. Inst., U. Nev., 1995—. Bd. editors Info. Processing and Mgmt., Scientometrics, Information Retrieval, 1997—; editor Prospect for Change in Bibliographic Control, 1977, Operations Research: Implications for Librarians, 1970; contbr. articles to profl. jours. NSF grantee, 1981, 85, 93, U.S./Israel Binational Sci. Found. grantee, 1993-94; Fulbright fellow, India, 1992. Mem. IEEE Computer Soc., Am. Soc. Info. Scis. (Rsch. award 1991), Internat. Soc. Scientometrics and Informetrics (founding mem., chmn. conf. program com. 1995, keynote spkr., 1991, 97), Assn. Computing Machinery/SIGIR (gen. chmn. ann. internat. conf. 1991), Phi Beta Kappa. Avocations: personal computing, music, literature. Office: U Chgo/CILS 1010 E 59th St Chicago IL 60637-1512

BOONE, MORELL DOUGLAS, information and communications technology educator, director; b. Londonderry, Northern Ireland, Dec. 15, 1942; arrived in U.S., 1946; s. Paul J. and Margaret (Hill) B.; m. Carolyn June Gallagher, July 6, 1968; children— Ian Charles, Megan Elizabeth B.S., Kutztown State Coll., Pa., 1964; M.S., Syracuse U., 1968, Ph.D., 1980. Librarian Pennridge Schs., Perkasie, Pa., 1964-66; reference librarian Hobart and William Smith Colls., Geneva, 1968-70; lectr. Syracuse U., 1970-72; dean learning resources U. Bridgeport, Conn., 1973-80; prof. interdisciplinary tech. Eastern Mich. U., Ypsilanti, 1998—, dean learning resources and techs., 1980-2001. Cons. for internet ednl. devel. Iran, Switzerland, Yemen, others. Presenter at profl meetings; , co-author book; contbr. articles to profl. jours.; mem. editl. bd. The Tech. Source. Chmn. Community Cablecasting Commn., Ypsilanti, 1981-84, Ypsilanti Ednl. Found., 1988-94; pres. bd. dirs. Meals on Wheels, Ypsilanti, 1998—. Named to Pennridge HS Wall of Honor, 2001. Mem. ALA, EDUCAUSE, SCUP, Kiwanis. Democrat. Presbyterian (elder). Avocations: gardening, reading, travel. Home: 5774 Pineview Dr Ypsilanti MI 48197-8983 Office: Eastern Mich U Bruce T Halle Library Ypsilanti MI 48197 E-mail: morell.boone@emich.edu.

BOONE, ROBERT RAYMOND, professional baseball coach; b. San Diego, Nov. 19, 1947; 1 child, Bret. BA in Psychology, Stanford U., 1969. Baseball player Phila. Phillies, 1969-81, Calif. Angels, 1981-88, Kansas City Royals, 1988-93, Oakland Athletics, 1993; minor league mgr. Pacific Coast, Tacoma, 1992-93; major league baseball mgr. Cin. Reds, 1994, Kansas City Royals, 1995—. Player Nat. League All-Star Game, 1976, 78, 79, Am. League All-Star Game, 1983, World Series, 1980. Recipient Nat. League Gold glove, 1978-79, Am. League Gold glove, 1986-89; named Catcher, Sporting News Nat. League All-Star Team, 1976. Office: Cincinnati Reds 100 Cinergy Field Cincinnati OH 45202*

BOOR, MYRON VERNON, psychologist, educator; b. Wadena, Minn., Dec. 21, 1942; s. Vernon LeRoy and Rosella Katharine (Eckhoff) B. BS, U. Iowa, 1965; MA, So. Ill. U., 1967, PhD, 1970; MS, U. Pitts., 1981. Lic. psychologist, Mo. Research psychologist Milw. County Mental Health Ctr., 1970-72; asst. prof. clin. psychologist Ft. Hays State U., Hays, Kans., 1972-76, assoc. prof., 1976-79; NIMH postdoctoral fellow in psychiat. epidemiology U. Pitts., Western Psychiat. Inst. and Clinic, 1979-81; research psychologist R.I. Hosp. and Butler Hosp., Providence, 1981-84; clin. psychologist Newman Meml. County Hosp., Emporia, Kans., 1985-93, Heartland Health Sys., St. Joseph, Mo., 1994—. Clin. psychologist Ft. Hays State U., 1972-79; asst. prof. psychiatry and human behavior Brown U., Providence, 1981-84; adj. faculty Emporia State U., 1985-94. Contbr. articles to profl. jours. U.S. Pub. Health Service fellow, 1965-67, NIMH fellow 1979-81. Home: 3018 Cambridge St Saint Joseph MO 64506-1164 E-mail: mboor@ccp.com.

BOOTH, PAUL WAYNE, retired minister; b. Caraway, Ark., July 30, 1929; s. Arthur Irvin and Martha Belle (Wood) B.; m. Lavanda Joan Colbert, Dec. 29, 1949; children: Dennis Paul, Donald Wayne, Karen Sue. BS in Sociology and Bus. with honors, Ark. State U., 1963; MA in Sociology, U. Louisville, 1968; postgrad., Sch. of Restoration, Independence, Mo., 1974; MDiv, St. Paul Sch. Theology, 1975. Ordained to ministry Reorganized LDS Ch., 1953. Pastor, Caraway, 1953-60; dist. pres. Reorganized LDS Ch., Louisville, 1963-66, adminstr. Colo., Wyo., Kans. and Nebr. region, 1966-68, adminstr. Mo., Ill., Ind., Ky. region, 1969-70, coord. ch. relationship to Instn. Higher Edn. Independence, Mo., 1976—; ret., 1994. Chmn. Gen. Ch. Commn. on Theology, Evangelism and Zionic Cmty., 1970-76; min.-in-charge Ch. in Europe and Africa region, 1984-88; pres. Coun. of Twelve Apostles; owner Booth Properties. Author: The Church and Its Mission, 1971; contbr. articles to profl. jours. Chmn. Indsl. Devel. Com., Caraway, 1958-60; pres. Outreach Internat. Found. for Third World Comprehensive Cmty. Devel., 1980—, Restoration Trail Found.; bd. dirs. Graceland Coll., Lamoni, Iowa, Independence Symphony Orch., Ctr. for Profl. Devel. and Life Long Learning; chmn. corp. bds. Home: 3837 S Willis Ct Independence MO 64055-3195 Office: PO Box 1122 Independence MO 64051-0622

BOOTHBY, WILLIAM MUNGER, mathematics educator; b. Detroit, Apr. 1, 1918; s. Thomas Franklin and Florence (Munger) B.; m. Ruth Robin, June 8, 1947; children— Daniel, Thomas, Mark. A.B., U. Mich., 1941, M.A., 1942, Ph.D., 1949. Mem. faculty Northwestern U., Evanston, Ill., 1948-59; fellow Am.-Swiss Found. for Sci. Exchange, Swiss Fed. Inst. Tech., Zurich, 1950-51; assoc. prof. Washington U., St. Louis, 1959-62, prof. math., 1962-88, ret., 1988—. NSF sr. postdoctoral fellow Inst. for Advanced Study, Princeton, N.J., 1961-62, U. Geneva, Switzerland, 1965-66; professeur associe U. Strasbourg, France, 1971, 77 Author: Introduction to Differentiable Manifolds and Riemannian Geometry; co-editor: Symmetric Spaces; contbr. articles to profl. jours. Served with USAAF, 1942-46. Mem. Am., London math. Socs., Math. Assn. Am., Soc. Indsl. and Applied Math., Sigma Xi. Home: 6954 Cornell Ave Saint Louis MO 63130-3128 Office: Washington U Dept Math Saint Louis MO 63130-4899

BOOZELL, MARK ELDON, state official; b. Mason City, Iowa, Mar. 4, 1955; s. Eldon Dwayne Boozell and Betty Jean (Gordon) Kruger; m. Susan Elizabeth Abelt, Nov. 26, 1977; children: Kari Elizabeth, Lindsay Patricia. BA, Augustana Coll., 1977. Budget analyst rep. staff Ill. Ho. of Reps., Springfield, 1977-78, dep. dir. rep. staff, 1978-80; legis. liaison Ill. Dept. Transp., 1980-83; dir. legis. affairs Ill. Sec. State, 1983-95; chief of staff Office of Gov., State of Ill., 1998-99; exec. v.p. Aon Corp., Chgo., 1999—. Named one of Outstanding Young Men Am., 1980. Republican. Lutheran. Home: 24706 Royal Lytham Dr Naperville IL 60564-8100 Office: State of Ill Office of Gov Capitol Bldg Rm 207 Springfield IL 62706-0001

BOPP, JAMES, JR. lawyer; b. Terre Haute, Ind., Feb. 8, 1948; s. James and Helen Marguerite (Hope) B.; m. Cheryl Hahn, Aug. 8, 1970 (div.); m. Christine Marie Stanton, July 3, 1982; children: Kathleen Grace, Lydia Grace, Marguerite Grace. BA, Ind. U., 1970; JD, U. Fla., 1973. Bar: Ind. 1973, U.S. Supreme Ct. 1977. Dep. atty. gen. State of Ind., Indpls., 1973-75; ptnr. Bopp & Fife, 1975-79, Brames, Bopp, Abel & Oldham, Terre Haute, Ind., 1979-92, Bopp, Coleson & Bostrom, Terre Haute, 1992—; of counsel Webster, Chamberlain and Bean, Washington, 1997—. Dep. prosecutor Vigo County, Terre Haute, 1979-86; gen. counsel Nat. Right to Life Com., Washington, 1978—; pres. Nat. Legal Ctr. for Medically Dependent and Disabled, 1984—; gen. counsel James Madison Ctr. Free Speech, 1997—; instr. law Ind. U., 1977-78. Editor: Human Life and Health Care Ethics, 1985, Restoring the Right to Life: The Human Life Amendment, 1984; editor-in-chief Issues in Law and Medicine, 1985—. Mem. Pres.'s Com. on Mental Retardation, 1984-87, mem. congl. biomed. ethics adv. com., 1987-89; Vigo County Election Bd., 1991-93; vice chmn. Early for Gov., 1995-96; del. Rep. State Conv., Indpls., 1980, 82, 84, 86, 90, 92, 94, 96, 98, 2000, 2002; alt. del. Rep. Nat. Conv., 1992, 96, del., 2000; chmn. Vigo County Rep. Ctrl. Com., 1993-97, White House Conf. on Families, Washington, 1980, White House Conf. on Aging, Mpls., 1981; bd. dirs. Leadership Terre Haute, 1986-89, Nat. Rep. Pro-Life Com., Washington, 1983-91, Alliance for Growth and Progress, Terre Haute, 1993-97; chmn. bd. dirs. Hospice of Wabash Valley, Terre Haute, 1982-88; mem. The Federalist Soc., Free Speech & Election Law Practice Group, chmn. election law subcom., 1996—. Mem. Ind. State Bar Assn., Terre Haute Bar Assn., Terre Haute Rotary (bd. dirs. 1984-86). Roman Catholic. Home: 1124 S Center St Terre Haute IN 47802-1116 Office: Bopp Coleson & Bostrom 1 S 6th St Terre Haute IN 47807-3510

BORCH, RICHARD FREDERIC, pharmacology and chemistry educator; b. Cleve., May 22, 1941; s. Fred J. and Martha (Kananen) B.; m. Anne Wright Wilson, Sept. 8, 1962; children: Karen, Eric. BS, Stanford U., 1962; MA, PhD, Columbia U., 1965; MD, U. Minn., 1975. NIH postdoctoral fellow Harvard U., Cambridge, Mass., 1965-66; prof. chemistry U. Minn., Mpls., 1966-82, med. resident, 1975-76; dean's prof. pharmacology, prof. chemistry U. Rochester, N.Y., 1982-96; dir. U. Rochester Cancer Ctr., 1992-96; now dept. head medicinal chemistry & molecular pharmacology Purdue U., Lafayette, Ind., dir. Cancer Ctr., Lilly disting. prof., 1992-96. Dir. U. Rochester Cancer Ctr., 1993—; mem. cancer rsch. manpower com. Nat. Cancer Inst., 1982-86, chmn. cancer rsch. manpower rev. com. 1984-86; cons. 3M Pharms., St. Paul, 1972—. Contbr. over 70 articles to profl. jours.; patentee in field. Recipient Coll. Chemistry Tchr. award Minn. sect. Am. Chem. Soc., 1982, Louis P. Hammett award Columbia U., 1965, James P. Wilmot Disting. Professorship, U. Rochester, 1983-86; Alfred P. Sloan Found. fellow, 1970-72. Mem. AAAS, Am. Chem. Soc., Am. Assn. Cancer Resch., Am. Soc. Pharmacology and Exptl. Therapeutics. Office: Purdue U Cancer Ctr Hansen Life Scis Rsch Bldg S University St West Lafayette IN 47907-1524

BORCHERT, DONALD MARVIN, philosopher, educator; b. Edmonton, Alta., Can., May 23, 1934; s. Leo Ferdinand and Lillian Violet (Bucholz) B.; m. Mary Ellen Cockrell, Dec. 27, 1960; children: Carol Ellen, John Witherspoon. AB, U. Alta., Edmonton, 1955; BD, Princeton Theol. Sem., 1958, PhD, 1966; ThM, Ea. Bapt. Theol. Sem., 1959. Teaching fellow Princeton (N.J.) Theol. Sem., 1960-61; asst. prof. Juniata Coll., Huntingdon, Pa., 1966-67, Ohio U., Athens, 1967-71, assoc. prof., 1971-75, prof. philosophy, 1975—, assoc. dean Coll. Arts and Scis., 1980-86, chmn. dept. philosophy, 1987—. Author: Being Human in a Technological Age, 1979, Introduction to Modern Philosophy, 1981, 7th edit., 2001, Exploring Ethics, 1986, Medical Ethics, 1992, Philosophy of Sex and Love, 1997; editor in chief: Encyclopedia of Philosophy Supplement, 1996, Compendium of Philosophy and Ethics, 1999; contbr. articles to profl. jours. Assoc. Danforth Found. Nat. Humanities Inst. fellow, 1976-77; NEH Implementation grantee, 1981. Mem. Ohio Philos. Assn. (v.p. 1983-85, pres. 1985-90), Ohio Humanities Council (vice chmn. 1981-83, chmn. 1983-85). Presbyterian. Home: 9 Coventry Ln Athens OH 45701-3717 Office: Ohio U Dept Philosophy Ellis Hall Athens OH 45701 E-mail: borchert@ohio.edu.

BORCOVER, ALFRED SEYMOUR, journalist; b. Bellaire, Ohio, May 1, 1931; s. Joseph and Kate (Florman) B.; m. Doris E. Wellner, Sept. 13, 1958 (div. 1966); m. Linda A. Gredig, Oct. 11, 1989. B.Sc. in Journalism, Ohio State U., 1953; M.S.J., Northwestern U., 1957. Writer Northwestern

U., Evanston, Ill., 1957-58; reporter, copy editor Chgo. Tribune, 1959-63, asst. travel editor, 1963-73, assoc. travel editor, 1973-79, editor travel sect., 1979-81, travel editor, columnist, 1981-93; ret., 1994. Freelance travel columnist/writer, 1994—. Author: Dollarwise Guide to Chicago, 1967; contbg. editor Fodor's Chicago, 1985-88; contbr. to Around the World with the Experts, 1970, WGN Travel Show, 1986-93; travel columnist Prodigy On-line Svc., 1990-96. Served to 1st lt. USAF, 1953-55 Recipient spl. citation George Hedmon Awards, 1965, Outstanding Achievement in Travel Writing award N.Y. Travel Writers Assn., 1976, Econ. Impact Writing award Travel Industry Assn. Am., 1983, Lowell Thomas Writing award, 1986; Gold Medal Writing award Pacific Asia Travel Assn., 1987, Cen. States Consumerism Reporting award, 1987, Alumni Svc. award Northwestern U., 1991, Cen. States Best Fgn. Series award, Cen. States Henry E. Bradshaw Sweepstakes Writing award, 1991, Cen. States Fgn. Series and U.S. Article awards, 1992, Earl R. Lind Consumer Edn. award Better Bus. Bur. of Chgo., 1993. Mem. Soc. Am. Travel Writers (pres. 1973-74), Chgo. Headline Club (pres. 1983-84), Medill Sch. Journalism Alumni Assn. (bd. dirs. 1984-89, pres. 1989-91), Northwestern U. Alumni Assn. (bd. dirs. 1986-90), Soc. Profl. Journalists. Democrat. Jewish. Avocations: tennis, music, photography. Home and Office: 1022 Michigan Ave Evanston IL 60202-1436 E-mail: aborcover@aol.com.

BORDEN, ERNEST CARLETON, physician, educator; b. Norwalk, Conn., July 12, 1939; s. Joseph Carleton and Violet Ernette (Lanneau) B.; m. Louise Dise, June 24, 1967; children: Kristin Louise, Sandra Lanneau. AB, Harvard U., 1961; MD, Duke U., 1966. Diplomate Am. Bd. Internal Medicine, Am. Bd. Med. Oncology. Intern Duke U. Med. Ctr., 1966-67; asst. resident in internal medicine Hosp. of U. Pa., 1967-68; med. officer Viropathology Lab., Nat. Communicable Disease Ctr., USPHS/Atlanta, 1968-70; clin. instr. dept. medicine Emory U. Sch. Medicine also Grady Meml. Hosp., 1968-70; postdoctoral fellow oncology div. dept. medicine Johns Hopkins U. Sch. Medicine, Balt., 1970-73; asst. prof. div. clin. oncology and depts. human oncology and medicine Wis. Clin. Cancer Ctr., Univ. Hosps. and Sch. Medicine, U. Wis.-Madison, 1973-79, assoc. prof., 1979-83, assoc. dir., 1981-90, prof., 1983-90, Am. Cancer Soc. prof. clin. oncology, from 1984; prof. depts. medicine and microbiology Med. Coll. Wis., Milw., 1990-94; also dir. Med. Coll. Wis. Cancer Ctr.; prof. oncology, medicine, microbiology, pharmacology U. Md. Sch. Medicine, Balt., 1994-98; dir. U. Md. Cancer Ctr., 1994-98; dir. ctr. cancer drug discovery and devel. Cleve. Clinic Found., 1998—. Chief divsn. clin. oncology William S. Middleton VA Hosp., 1977-81; cons. staff Madison Gen. Hosp., 1974-90. Assoc. editor Jour. Interferon Rsch., 1980—, Jour. Biologic Response Modifiers, 1982-90; mem. editorial bd. Cancer Immunology and Immunotherapy, 1981-89, Investigational New Drugs, 1982—, Jour. Nat. Cancer Inst., 1987-91, Jour. Cancer Rsch., 1993-98, Jour. Bioactive and Compatible Polymers, Jour. Biol. Regulators and Homeostatic Agents, 1986; contbr. 300 articles to profl jours. Recipient Disting. Svc. award Am. Cancer Soc., 1994. Fellow ACP; mem. AAAS, Am. Soc. Microbiology, Am. Assn. Cancer Research, Eastern Coop. Oncology Group, Am. Soc. Clin. Oncology, Am. Assn. Immunologists, Am. Fedn. Clin. Research, Soc. Biol. Therapy (pres. 1986-88), Internat. Soc. Interferon Research (pres. 1987-89). Unitarian

BOREN, CLARK HENRY, JR. general and vascular surgeon; b. Marinette, Wis., Nov. 23, 1947; s. Clark Henry and Maryon Lillian (Peterson) Boren; children: Jenna Marie, Matthew William, Nathan Clark. BMS, Northwestern U., 1971, MD with distinction, 1973. Diplomate Am. Bd. Surgery. Resident in gen. surgery U. Calif.-H.C. Moffitt Hosp., San Francisco, 1973-79; rsch. fellow in vascular surgery Ft. Miley VA Hosp., 1976-77; vascular fellow Med. Coll. Wis./Milwaukee County Med. Complex, Milw., 1979-80; mem. staff Fox Valley Surg. Assocs., Ltd., Appleton, 1980—, pres., 1997—. Chmn. bd. United Health Wis., 1995—99. Contbr. articles to profl. jours. Mem.: AMA, ACS, Am. Assn. Vascular Surgery, Wis. Surg. Soc., Midwest Vascular Soc., Peripheral Vascular Surgery Soc., Wis. State Med. Soc., Phi Kappa Psi, Phi Eta Sigma, Phi Beta Pi, Alpha Omega Alpha. Democrat. Home: 519 E Timberline Dr Appleton WI 54913-7102 Office: Fox Valley Surg Assocs 1818 N Meade St Appleton WI 54911-3454

BORG, FRANK, hotel executive; CFO H Group Holding, Chgo. Office: H Group Holding 200 W Madison St 39th Flr Chicago IL 60606

BORG, RUTH I. home nursing care provider; b. Chgo., Mar. 29, 1934; d. Axel Gunner and Charlotte (Benston) B. Diploma, West Suburban Sch. Nursing, 1956; tchr.'s degree, Chgo. Conservatory, 1958; BSN, Alverno Coll., 1981. Staff nurse Boath Meml. Hosp., Chgo.; head nurse psychiatry, head nurse long-term medicine VA North Chgo. Med. Ctr.; staff nurse, night supr. intermediate care VA Clement Zabiocki Med. Ctr., Milw.; pool nurse, in-home nursing care provider Milw. County Mental Health Complex; home nurse care provider Dr. Ghonsham Sooknandan, Kenosha, Wis., 1994—99. In-home nursing care provider. Contbr. 2 articles to profl. jours. Recipient Mary D. Bradford Disting. Alumni award, 1998. Avocation: teaching and performing music.

BORGDORFF, PETER, church administrator; Exec. dir. of ministries Christian Ref. Ch. in N. Am., 1990. Office: Christian Ref Ch in N Am 2850 Kalamazoo Ave SE Grand Rapids MI 49560-0001

BORGENS, RICHARD, biologist; b. Little Rock, May 7, 1946; BS, N. Tex. State U., 1970, MS, 1973; PhD in Biology, Purdue U., 1977. Rsch. assoc. biology Purdue U., 1977-78, Yale U., 1978-80; assoc. staff scientist Jackson Lab., Bar Harbor, Maine, 1980-81; staff scientist Inst. Med. Rsch., 1981-98; fellow Nat. Paraplegia Found., 1978-80; Dir., prof. devel. anatomy Purdue U. Ctr. Paralysis Rsch., 1998—. Mem. Am. Soc. Zoologists, Soc. Devel. Biology. Office: Purdue Univ Dept Anatomy 1244 VCPR West Lafayette IN 47907-1244

BORGER, JOHN PHILIP, lawyer; b. Wilmington, Del., Apr. 19, 1951; s. Philip E. and Jane (Smyth) B.; m. Judith Marie Yates, May 24, 1974; children: Jennifer, Christopher, Nicholas. BA in Journalism with high honors, Mich. State U., 1973; JD, Yale U., 1976. Bar: Minn. 1976, U.S. Dist. Ct. Minn. 1976, U.S. Ct. Appeals (8th cir.) 1979, U.S. Supreme Ct. 1983, N.D. 1988, U.S. Dist. Ct. N.D. 1988, Wis. 1993. Editor-in-chief Mich. State News, East Lansing, 1972-73; assoc. Faegre & Benson, LLP, Mpls., 1976-83, ptnr., 1984—. Bd. dirs. Milkweed Edits., 1995-01; adj. prof. U. Minn. Sch. Journalism and Mass Comm., 1999. Contbr. articles to profl. jours. Recipient Freedom of Info., Soc. Profl. Journalist, 2002, First Amendment Award, St. Cloud State U. Dept. Mass. Comms., 2001. Mem. ABA (chmn. media law and defamation torts com. torts and ins. practice sect. 1996-97), Minn. Bar Assn., State Bar Assn. N.D., Wis. Bar Assn., Hennepin County Bar Assn. Office: Faegre & Benson LLP 2200 Wells Fargo Ctr 90 S 7th St Ste 2200 Minneapolis MN 55402-3901 E-mail: jborger@faegre.com.

BORGMAN, JAMES MARK, editorial cartoonist; b. Cin., Feb. 24, 1954; s. James Robert and Florence Marian (Maly) B.; m. Lynn Goodwin, Aug. 20, 1977 (dec. 1999). B.A., Kenyon Coll., 1976. Editorial cartoonist Cin. Enquirer, 1976—, King Features Syndicate, 1980—; contbr. to Newsweek Broadcasting's Cartoon-A-Torial (animated editorial cartoon feature), 1978-81. Author: (collection of editorial cartoons) Smorgasborgman, 1982, The Great Communicator, 1985, The Mood of America, 1986, Jim Borgman's Cincinnati, 1992, Disturbing the Peace, 1995; co-creator comic strip Zits, 1997. Recipient Sigma Delta Chi award, 1978, 95, Thomas Nast prize, 1980, 2d prize for editorial cartooning Internat. Salon Cartoons of Montreal, 1981, Ohio's Gov.'s award, 1990, Pulitzer Prize for editorial cartooning, 1991, Nat. Headliner award, 1991, Reuben award for outstanding cartooning of yr., 1993. Mem. Nat. Cartoonists Soc. (Best Editorial Cartoonist award 1987, 88, 89, 94, Best Comic Strip award 1998, 99). Office: 312 Elm St Cincinnati OH 45202-2739

BORIN, GERALD W. zoological park administrator; CEO, dir. Columbus (Ohio) Zool. Park Assn., Inc., 1994—. Office: Columbus Zool Gardens PO Box 400 Powell OH 43065-0400

BORIS, JAMES R. investment company executive; Chmn. bd., CEO Everen Securities Inc., Chgo., until 2000; chmn. JB Capitol Mgmt., 2000; bd. dirs. Corp, Inc., Irvine, Calif., 2000—. Office: Core Inc Ste 1750 18881 Von Karman Ave Irvine CA 92612

BORISY, GARY G. molecular biology educator; b. Chgo., Aug. 18, 1942; s. Philip and Mae Borisy; children: Felice, Pippa, Alexis. BS, U. Chgo., 1962, PhD, 1966. Postdoctoral fellow NSF, Cambridge, Eng., 1966-67, NATO, Cambridge, 1967-68; asst. prof. U. Wis., Madison, 1968-72, assoc. prof., 1972-75, prof., 1975-80, Perlman-Bascom prof. life scis., 1980—, chmn. lab. molecular biology, 1981—. Mem. numerous panels NIH and other govt. agys., ACS, HHMI; mem. Marine Biol. Lab. Editor Jour. Biol. Chemistry, 1978-80, Jour. Cell Biology, 1980-82, Internat. Rev. Cytology, 1971-91, Cell Motility and the Cytoskeleton, 1986-94, Jour. Cell Sci., 1988—; contbr. over 100 articles to profl. jours. Recipient Romnes award U. Wis., 1975-80, NIH Merit award, 1989; grantee NIH, NSF, ACS. Fellow AAAS; mem. Am. Soc. Cell Biology, Am. Soc. Biochemistry and Molecular Biology, Sigma Xi. Office: Univ Wis Lab Molecular Biology 1525 Linden Dr Madison WI 53706-1534 Home: Apt 14M 860 N Lake Shore Dr Chicago IL 60611-1785

BORLING, JOHN LORIN, military officer; b. Chgo., Mar. 24, 1940; s. Edward Gustav and Vivian K. (Strietelmeir) B.; m. Myrna Lee Holmstedt, June 22, 1963; children: Lauren, Megan. BS, U.S. Airforce Acad., 1963; grad., Armed Forces Staff Coll., 1975, Nat. War Coll., 1980, Harvard U., 1991, White House fellow, 1998. Commd. 2d lt. USAF, 1963, advanced through grades to maj. gen., 1989, prisoner of war North Vietnam, 1966-73, fighter pilot, comdr., 1974-80, asst. dir. ops. HQ Pentagon, 1981-82, comdr. 86th Combat Support Group Ramstein, Ger., 1982-83, comdr. 86th Fighter Group Ger., 1983-84, exec. officer to COS NATO Mons, Belgium, 1984-86, dep. plans/analysis HQ/SAC Jt. Stategic Target Planning Staff Omaha, 1986-87, comdr. HQ 57th Air Divsn. Minot, N.D., 1987-88, dep. ops. HQ SAC Omaha, 1988-91; dir. operational reg(s) HQ Pentagon, 1991-92; dep. chief of staff NATO, Norway, 1992-94, chief of staff, sr. U.S. mil. officer in Scandinavia Norway, 1994-96; pres., CEO United Way, Chgo., 1997-98; dir. The 5th Media, 1999—. Bd. dirs. Hyperfeed Tech., 1999—; chmn. Performance Cons. Group, 2000—; pres., CEO, SOS Am., 2000—; mem. Armed Forces Policy Coun., Chgo., Coun. Fgn. Rels., Chgo., Chgo. Com.; mem. adv. com. Ill. Fatherhood Initiative, Chgo. Founder, charter mem. Ramstein Coun. Internat. Rels., 1983; v.p., dir. Opera Omaha, 1988-91; treas., dir. White House Fellow Found., 1991—; mem. adv. com. Kellogg Sch., Northwestern U.; mentor Harris Sch., U. Chgo.; adv. bd. Stanton Chase Int., Maritime Trust Co.; bd. govs., Chgo. Mil. Acad.; adv. com. Maritime Trust Co.; bd. dirs. Nat. Jazz Mus., 2000; vice-chmn. Chgo. Meml. Day Parade Com., 2000; dir. Stars & Stripes Relief Fund, 2001 . Decorated Def. Disting. Svc. medal with oak leaf cluster, Air Force Disting. Svc. medal, Silver Star, Def. Superior Svc. medal, Legion of Merit with oak leaf cluster, D.F.C. with oak leaf cluster, Bronze Star medal with V device and 2 oak leaf clusters, Air medal with 5 oak leaf clusters, Purple Heart with one cluster; White House fellow, 1974; recipient George Washington medal Freedom Found., Valley Forge, Va., 1975, Good Scout award Boy Scouts Am., Chgo., 1974, Eagle Am. Hero award Benedictine U., 2001, Patriot's award GLMV C. of C., 2001. Mem. Assn. Grads. USAF Acad., VFW, Daedalians, Air Force Assn., Comml. Club Chgo., Execs. Club Chgo. Avocations: music, sports, reading. Office: SOS America Box 1543 Rockford IL 61110-1543 E-mail: jlbviking@yahoo.com.

BORMAN, PAUL DAVID, judge; BA, U. Mich., 1959, JD, 1962; LLM, Yale U., 1964. Staff atty. U.S. Commn. on Civil Rights, 1962-63; asst. U.S. atty. U.S. Atty. Office, 1964-65; spl. counsel Mayor's Devel. Team, 1967-68; asst. prosecuting atty. Wayne County Prosecutor's Office, 1974-75; dist. judge U.S. Dist. Ct. (ea. dist.) Mich., Detroit, 1994—. Mem. ABA, Fed. Bar Assn., State Bar Mich., Oakland County Bar Assn. Office: US Courthouse 740 231 W Lafayette Blvd Detroit MI 48226-2700

BORN, JAMES E. art educator, sculptor; b. Toledo, Nov. 16, 1934; s. Elmer Arthur and Dorthy (Halstead) B.; m. Donna Jones; children: Karl, Anna Born Ross, Thomas, Christopher, Tanya. BA, Toledo U., 1959; MFA, U. Iowa, 1962. Grad. teaching asst. U. Iowa, Iowa City, 1964-65; asst. prof. Calif. State U., Arcata, 1962-65, Calif. Western U., San Diego, 1965-67, Calif. State U., Turlock, 1967-69; prof. art Ctrl. Mich. U., Mt. Pleasant, 1969—. Bronze sculptures exhibited in group and one-man shows; represented in permanent collections Outdoor Sculpture Exhibit, Southfield, Mich., 1991; exhibited in one-man show Gallery Abbott Kinney, Venice, Calif., 1992, Mich. Competition, Birmingham, Bloomfield Art Ctr., 1992, Commn. Trans World Airlines, L.A. Airport, Watercolor Paintings, All Calif., San Diego Mus. of Art, 1995, Mich. Exhibition, Mt. Clemens, Mich., Art Mus., 1993-95, Mich. Art Exhibition, Saginaw Art Mus., 1993-94. Recipient honor award Battle Creek Art Mus., 1982, 1st award sculpture Ball State U., 1982, grand award S.W. Ark. Art Mus., 1982, 1st award sculpture Mt. Clemens Art Mus., 1989, sculpture award Saginaw Art Mus., 1992. Home: 2716 Greenfield Ave Los Angeles CA 90064-4032 Office: Ctrl Mich U Art Dept Mount Pleasant MI 48859-0001

BORN, SAMUEL ROYDON , II, lawyer; b. Atwood, Ill., Apr. 19, 1945; s. Samuel Roydon and Mary Elizabeth (Derr) B.; m. Brenda Alice Anderson, June 18, 1988; children: Samuel R. III, Holly Jean; 1 stepchild, Julie Chamberlain Sipe. Student, Northwestern U., 1963-64, Am. U., fall 1966; BA, Simpson Coll., 1967; JD, Ind. U., 1970. Bar: Ind. 1970, U.S. Dist. Ct. (so. dist.) Ind. 1970, U.S. Ct. Appeals (7th crct.) 1975, U.S. Dist. Ct. (no. dist.) Ind. 1990. Ptnr. Ice Miller, Indpls., 1970—. Mem. safety com. Associated Gen. Contractors Ind., 1988—. Co-author: Safety and Health Guide for Indiana Business, 1999, 4th edit., 2002; mem. bd. editors: Ind. Law Jour., 1969—70; contbr. articles to profl. jours. Mem. bd. visitors Ind. U. Sch. Law, 1988-89, 95-98; chmn. ch. cmty. athletics First Bapt. Ch., Indpls., 1975-78, trustee, 1978-80. Mem. ABA (mem. nat. conf. bar pres. 1987-99, ho. of dels. 1988-98, labor and employment law sect.), Am. Bar Found., Ind. State Bar Assn. (bd. govs. 1990-99, pres. 1997-98, labor law sect.), Ind. Bar Found., Indpls. Bar Assn. (bd. mgrs. 1987-95, pres. 1988), U.S. C. of C. (occupl. safety and health adminstrv. coun. 1981-86, 2000—), Ind. C. of C. (past chmn. occupl. safety health com.), Ind. Mfrs. Assn. (pers. labor rels. com. 1982-99), Highland Golf and Country Club, Crooked Stick Golf Club, Univ. Club, Indpls. Lawyers Club, Masons, Shriners, Kiwanis, Phi Eta Sigma, Sigma Alpha Epsilon. Presbyterian. Avocations: downhill skiing, golf, fly fishing, public speaking. Home: 5202 Grandview Dr Indianapolis IN 46228-1938 Office: Ice Miller 1 American Sq Indianapolis IN 46282-0020 E-mail: born@icemiller.com.

BORNSTEIN, GEORGE JAY, literary educator; b. St. Louis, Aug. 25, 1941; s. Harry and Celia (Price) B.; m. Jane Elizabeth York, June 22, 1982; children— Benjamin, Rebecca, Joshua. A.B., Harvard U., 1963; Ph.D., Princeton U., 1966. Asst. prof. MIT, Cambridge, 1966-69, Rutgers U., 1969-70; assoc. prof. U. Mich., Ann Arbor, 1970-75, prof. English, 1975—, C.A. Patrides prof. lit., 1995—. Cons. various univ. presses, scholastic jours., funding agys., 1970—; mem. adv. bd. Yeats: An Annual, 1982—, South Atlantic Rev., 1985-88, Rev., 1991—, Text, 1993—. Author: Yeats and Shelley, 1970, Transformations of Romanticism, 1976, Postromantic Consciousness of Ezra Pound, 1977, Poetic Remaking, 1988, Material Modernism: The Politics of the Page, 2001; editor: Romantic and Modern, 1977, Ezra Pound Among the Poets, 1985, W.B. Yeats: The Early Poetry, vol. 1, 1987, vol. 2, 1994, W.B. Yeats: Letters to the New Island, 1990, Representing Modernist Texts, 1991, Palimpsest: Editorial Theory in the Humanities, 1993, W.B. Yeats: Under the Moon, the Unpublished Early Poetry, 1995, Contemporary German Editorial Theory, 1995, The Iconic Page in Manuscript, Print, and Digital Culture, 1998. Cubmaster Wolverine council Boy Scouts Am., 1977-79. Recipient good teaching award Amoco Found., 1983, Warner Rice prize for rsch. in humanities, 1988, Rosenthal award for Yeats studies W.B. Yeats Soc., 2000; fellow Am. Coun. Learned Soc., 1972-73, NEH fellow, 1982-83, fellow Old Dominion Found., 1968, fellow Guggenheim Found., 1986-87. Mem. MLA (exec. com. Anglo-Irish 1976-80, exec. com. 20th Century English 1980-85, exec. com. Poetry 1987-92, exec. com. bibliography and textual studies 1993-98, exec. com. methods of rsch. 1998—), Soc. for Textual Scholarship (program chair 1997), Am. Conf. on Irish Studies (book prize judge 1991), Racquet Club, Princeton Club (N.Y.C.), Phi Beta Kappa. Home: 2020 Vinewood Blvd Ann Arbor MI 48104-3614 Office: U Mich Dept English Ann Arbor MI 48109-1003 E-mail: georgeb@umich.edu.

BORNSTEIN, MORRIS, economist, educator; b. Detroit, Sept. 4, 1927; m. Reva Rice, Apr. 7, 1962; children— Susan, Jane. A.B., U. Mich., 1947, A.M., 1948, Ph.D., 1952. Economist U.S. Govt., 1951-52, 55-58; mem. faculty U. Mich., Ann Arbor, 1958—, prof. econs., 1964—, dir. Center Russian and E. European Studies, 1966-69. Assoc. Harvard U. Russian Rsch. Ctr., 1962-63; vis. rsch. fellow Hoover Instn., Stanford, 1969-70; cons. in field, 1959—; mem. joint com. on Eastern Europe Am. Coun. Learned Socs.-Social Sci. Rsch. Coun., 1977-80. Author: Soviet National Accounts for 1955, 1961, The Soviet Economy, 1962, 4th edit., 1974, Comparative Economic Systems, 1965, 7th edit., 1994, Economia di Mercato ed Economia Pianificata, 1973, Sistemas economicos comparados, 1973, Plan and Market, 1975, Chinese transl., 1980, The Soviet Economy: Continuity and Change, 1981, East-West Relations and the Future of Eastern Europe, 1981, The Transfer of Western Technology to the USSR, 1985, French transl., 1985, contbr. articles to profl. jours.; mem. editorial bd. Jour. Comparative Econs., 1986-88, Problems of Economic Transition, 1987-97, Soviet Economy and Post Soviet Affairs, 1988—, Economic Policy in Transitional Economies, 1994—, Communist Economies and Econ. Transformation, 1997-98, Post-Soviet Geography and Econs., 1997-98, Post-Communist Economies, 1999—. With U.S. Army, 1953-55. Ford Found. faculty fellow, 1962-63, Sr. Fgn. Rsch. fellow French Ministry Rsch. and Tech., 1991. Mem. Am. Econ. Assn., Am. Assn. Advancement Slavic Studies, Assn. Comparative Econ. Studies (exec. com. 1965-67, 73-75). Office: U Mich Dept Econs Ann Arbor MI 48109-1220

BOROWITZ, JOSEPH LEO, pharmacologist, educator; b. Columbus, Ohio, Dec. 19, 1932; s. Joseph Peter and Anna Louise (Grundei) B.; divorced, 1985; children: Jon Joseph, Peter Joseph, Lynn Anne. BS in Pharmacy, Ohio State U., 1955; MS in Pharmacology, Purdue U., 1957; PhD in Pharmacology (NIH fellow), Northwestern U., 1960. Postdoctoral fellow dept. pharmacology Harvard U. Med. Sch., Boston, 1963—64; instr., then asst. prof. pharmacology Bowman Gray Sch. Medicine, 1964—69; assoc. prof. pharmacology and toxicology Purdue U., 1969—74, prof., 1974—; sabbatical leave to Cambridge, England, 1976, to Basel, Switzerland, 1984; vis. prof. sch. pharmacy U. P.R., 2001. Contbr. articles to profl. jours. Treas. Tippecanoe County (Ind.) Comprehensive Health Planning Coun., 1971-76. Capt. USAR, 1960. Recipient award for excellence in teaching Bowman Gray Sch. Medicine, 1969, Henry Heine award for excellence in teaching Purdue U. Coll. Pharmacy, 1983; named NIH postdoctoral fellow, 1962-64; grantee NSF, 1965-68, NIH, 1971-74, 86-89, 89-94, 94-98, 99—, U.S. Army Med. Rsch., 1989-96, 97-2000. Mem.: Rho Chi. Roman Catholic. Office: Purdue U Dept Med Chem and Molec Pharmacology West Lafayette IN 47907 E-mail: borowitz@pharmacy.purdue.edu.

BORROR, DAVID S. lawyer; BA, Ohio State U.; JD, Ohio State U. Coll. Law. Pvt. practice Porter, Wright, Morris & Aurthur, Columbus, Ohio, 1982-87; bd. dirs. Dominion Homes, Inc., 1985—, v.p., 1985-88, gen. counsel, 1988-93, exec. v.p., 1988—. Office: Dominion Homes Inc 5501 Frantz Rd Dublin OH 43017-7502

BORROR, DONALD A. construction company executive; b. 1929; Grad., Ohio State Univ., Columbus, Ohio State Univ. Sch. of Law. With Summer & Co. Inc., Columbus, Ohio, 1956-71, The Borror Corp. (now Borror Realty Co.), Dublin, 1971—, pres., 1976-82, chmn., 1977—, chmn. bd. dirs., 1994-97, Dominion Homes Inc. (formerly The Borror Corp.), Dublin, 1997—. With USAF. Office: Dominion Homes Inc PO Box 7166 5501 Frantz Rd Dublin OH 43017-7502

BORROR, DOUGLAS G. construction company executive; b. 1955; Grad., Ohio State U., 1977. With Huntington Nat. Bank, Columbus, 1977-79, Borror Corp. (now Borror Realty Co. Inc.), Dublin, 1979—; pres., CEO, COO Borror Corp. (now Dominion Homes, Inc.), 1994—; pres., CEO, chmn. bd. Office: Dominion Homes Inc 5501 Frantz Rd Dublin OH 43017-7502

BORST, LAWRENCE MARION, state legislator; b. Champaign County, Ohio, July 16, 1927; s. Lawrence M. and Mary (Waldeck) B.; m. Eldoris Borst; children: Philip, Elizabeth, David. DVM, Ohio State U. Mem. Ind. Ho. of Reps., 1966-68; del. Rep. Nat. Conv., 1968—; mem. state tax and financing policy com.; mem. funds mgmt. oversight com.; mem. Ind. Senate from dist. 36; chmn. fin. taxation com. Ind. Senate Dist. 36, 1968—, ranking mem. pensions and labor com., ethics com. ins., fin. inst. and transp. coms., interstate coop coms.; chmn. Ind. budget com. Home: 681 Foxmere Ter Greenwood IN 46142-4812 Office: 4994 Hayes St Gary IN 46408-4354

BORST, PHILIP CRAIG, veterinarian, councilman; b. Columbus, Ohio, May 19, 1950; s. Lawrence M. and Eldoris B.; m. Jill Patrice Alexander, Sept. 12, 1980; children: Alex, Eric. BS, Purdue U., 1972, DVM, 1975. Vet. Shelby St. Animal Clinic, Indpls., 1975—. Bd. dirs. Ind. Sports Corp., Indpls. Mem. Indpls. City-County Coun., 1980—, v.p., majority leader; del. Ind. State Rep. Convention, 1982; bd. dirs. Indpls. Conv. and Visitors Assn.; mem. Marion County Capital Improvement Bd.; mem. exec. com. 2000 NCAA Final Four. Named Best City-County Councilman Indpls. Mag., 1986; recipient Svc. to Mankind award Southside Indpl. Sertoma Club, 1987. Mem. Cen. Ind. Vet. Med. Assn. (pres. 1990), Purdue Vet. Med. Alumni Assn. (pres. 1988). Republican. Methodist. Avocations: golf, basketball, Purdue athletics. Home: 6554 Robin Hood Dr Indianapolis IN 46227-7309 also: City-County Coun Office 200 E Washington St Ste 241 Indianapolis IN 46204-3310

BOSCIA, JON ANDREW, insurance company executive; b. Pitts., Apr. 15, 1952; s. Louis C. and Stella (Weryha) B.; m. Donna M. Lowar, Aug. 18, 1973; children: Nicole Marie, Brandon Jon. BA, Point Park Coll., 1973; MBA, Duquesne U., 1979. Corp. planner Consolidated Nat. Gas, Pitts., 1974-79; fin. sales rep. Westinghouse, 1979-80; asst. v.p. Mellon Bank, 1980-83; sr. v.p. Lincoln Nat. Pension, Ft. Wayne, Ind., 1983—; ceo, pres., Lincoln Nat. Corp., Phila., 1998—. Sr. v.p. Lincoln Nat. Life, Ft. Wayne, 1984—; bd. dirs. Lincoln Nat. Investment Mgmt. Co., Ft. Wayne, 1985—. Contbr. articles to profl. jours. Mem. coms. Pitts. Bd. Edn., 1974-79; chmn. coms. Arlington Park, Ft. Wayne, 1983-86; mem. START program Ft.

Wayne Community Schs., 1985. PPC Found. scholar, 1973. Mem. Nat. Assn. Bus. Economists, Planning Forum. Democrat. Methodist. Avocations: jogging, racquetball, playing drums, swimming, reading. Office: Lincoln Nat Corp 1500 Market St Ste 3900 Philadelphia PA 19102-2100

BOSMA, BRIAN CHARLES, state legislator; b. Indpls., Oct. 31, 1957; s. Charles Edward and Margaret Hagge Bosma; m. Cheryl Lyn Hollingsworth, 1982. BSE, Purdue U., 1981; JD, Ind. U., 1984. Environ. engr. Ind. State Bd. Health, 1981-83; precinct committeeman Marian County Rep. Ctrl. Com., Ind., 1983-86; atty. Bingham, Summers, Welch & Spilman, Indpls., 1984-85, Kroger, Gardis & Regas, 1986—; ward vice chmn. Marian County Rep. Ctrl. Com., Ind., 1987—; legis. and congrl. liaison Ind. State Dept. Edn., 1985-86; Ind. state rep. Dist. 50, 1986-91, Dist. 88, 1991—; ranking mem. com., mem. ways and means com. Ind. Ho. Reps., mem. elections and apportionment, environ. affairs and natural resources coms. Recipient Commencement Spkr. award Ind. U. Law Sch., 1984, Lacy Exec. Leadership award Indpls. C. of C., 1986; named Outstanding Freshman Legislator Ind. Broadcasters Assn. Mem. ABA, Ind. Bar Assn., Indpls. Bar Assn. (Pres. Spl. award 1984), Ind. Environ. Policy Commn., Assn. Retarded Citizens Trust (adv. bd.), Nat. Rep. Lawyers Assn., Lawrence C. of C., Beta Sigma Psi, Phi Delta Phi. Republican. Home: 8971 Bay Breeze Ln Indianapolis IN 46236-8568

BOSNICH, BRICE, chemistry educator; b. Queensland, Australia, 1936; BS, U. Sydney, Australia, 1958; PhD, Australian NAt. U., 1962. Lectr. U. Coll., London, 1966-69; assoc. prof. U. Toronto, Can., 1970-75, prof. Can., 1975-87, U. Chgo., 1987—. Contbr. articles to profl. jours. Office: U Chgo Dept Chem 5735 S Ellis Ave Chicago IL 60637-1403

BOSSMANN, LAURIE, controller, hardware company executive; m. Jeff Bossmann; two children. BS, No. Ill. U. CPA, Ill. With KPMG Peat Marwick; gen. acctg. mgr. Ace Hardware Corp., 1986-90, asst. contr., 1990-94, contr., 1994—, v.p., 1997—, v.p. mdse., 2000—. Mem. AICPA, Ill. CPA Soc. Office: 2200 Kensington Ct Oak Brook IL 60523-2103

BOST, MIKE, state legislator; Ill. state rep., 1995—. Office: 300 E Main St Carbondale IL 62901-3029

BOSWELL, LEONARD L. congressman; b. Harrison County, Mo., Jan. 10, 1934; s. Melvin and Margaret B.; m. Dody Boswell; 3 children. BA in Bus. Adminstrn., Graceland Coll. Commd. 2d lt. U.S. Army, 1956, advanced through grades to lt. col. Vietnam, Germany, Portugal, resigned, 1976; mem. Iowa Senate, 1984-96, pres., 1993-97; mem. U.S. Congress from 3d Iowa dist., 1997—; mem. transp. and infrastucture com., agr. com., select copm. on intelligence, 1999—. Grain and livestock farmer Decatur County, 1976—. Past pres., bd. dirs. local Coop. Elevator, Lamoni. Decorated DFC (2), Bronze Star (2). Mem. VFW, Am. Legion, Cattleman's Assn., Lamoni Lions Club. Office: US Ho of Reps 1039 Longworth HOB Washington DC 20515-0001*

BOSWORTH, DOUGLAS LEROY, international company executive, educator; b. Goldfield, Iowa, Oct. 15, 1939; s. Clifford Leroy and Clara (Lonning) Bosworth; m. Patricia Lee Knock, May 28, 1961; children: Douglas, Dawn. BS in Agrl. Engring, Iowa State U., 1962; MS in Agrl. Engring, U. Ill., 1964. With Deere & Co., Moline, Ill., 1959-94; pres. WorkSpan, Inc., Mahomet, 1994—2001, Ill. Tech. Ctr., Savoy, 1995-97; div. engr. disk harrows Deere & Co., Moline, 1971-76, mgr. mfg. engring., 1976-80, works mgr., 1980-85, mgr. mfg., 1985-89, engring. test mgr., 1989-94. Mem. Engring. Accreditation Commn., 1985—90; v.p. Skills, Inc.; mem. Assoc. Employers Bd., 1989—91; adj. engring. prof. U. Ill., Champaign-Urbana, 1996—. Active Am. Cancer Soc., Rock Island Unit; bd. dirs. United Med. Ctr., 1984—95; exec. com. Quad-City United Way, 1984—89. Mem.: Am. Soc. Agrl. Engrs. (chmn. Ill.-Wis. 1973—74, nat. bd. dirs. 1974—76, 1979—82, v.p. 1979—82, pres. elect 1991—92, pres. 1992—93, Engring. Achievement Young Designer award 1973), Rotary, Gamma Sigma Delta, Alpha Epsilon, Sigma Xi. Lutheran. Home and Office: WorkSpan Inc 1111 E Briarcliff Dr Mahomet IL 61853-9558 E-mail: dlbos@aol.com.

BOTEZ, DAN, physicist; b. Bucharest, Romania, May 22, 1948; s. Emil and Ecaterina (Iacob) B.; m. Lynda Diane Arnold, Sept. 25, 1976; children: Anca, Adrian. BSEE with highest honors, U. Calif., Berkeley, 1971, MSEE, 1972, PhD, 1976; PhD (hon.), U. Politechnica, Bucharest, Romania, 1995. Fellow IBM Thomas J. Watson Rsch. Ctr., Yorktown Heights, N.Y., 1976-77; tech. staff RCA David Sarnoff Rsch. Ctr., Princeton, N.J., 1977-82, rsch. leader, 1982-84; dir. device devel. Lytel Inc., Somerville, 1984-86; chief scientist TRW Electro-Optic Rsch. Ctr., Redondo Beach, Calif., 1986, lab dir., 1986-87; sr. staff scientist TRW Rsch. Ctr., 1987-93, TRW tech. fellow, 1990-93; Philip Dunham Reed prof. elec. engring. U. Wis., Madison, 1993—; founder, bd. dirs. AlfaLight Inc., 2000—. Author: Electro-Optical Communications Dictionary, 1983, Diode-Laser Arrays, 1994; contbr. over 220 articles to profl. jours.; patentee in field. Named Outstanding Young Engr., IEEE Lasers and Electro-Optics Soc., San Jose, 1984, recipient Key to Future award, 1984. Fellow IEEE (chmn. tech. com. on semiconductor lasers 1989-90), Optical Soc. Am.; mem. Phi Beta Kappa. Republican. Mem. Ea. Orthodox Ch. Avocations: racquetball, travel, photography, skiing. E-mail: botez@engr.wisc.edu. Home: 200 N Prospect Ave Madison WI 53705-4027 Office: U Wis Dept Elec Engring 1415 Engineering Dr Madison WI 53706-1607

BOTT, HAROLD SHELDON, accountant, management consultant; b. Chgo., Dec. 12, 1933; s. Harold S. and Mary (Moseley) B.; m. Audrey Anne Connor, May 15, 1964; children: Susan, Lynda. AB, Princeton U., 1955; MBA, Harvard U., 1959; postgrad., U. Chgo., 1960-62. Adminstrv. asst. to exec v.p. Champion Paper, Hamilton, Ohio, 1959-61; mgmt. cons. Arthur Andersen & Co., Chgo., 1961-65, mgr., 1965-71, ptnr., 1971-89. Mng. dir. mgmt. info. cons., ptnr. Andersen Cons., 1988-91; ptnr. Strategic Tng. and Recruiting Svcs. Ctr.; vice-chmn. The Assn. Mgmt. Cons., 1982-84; bd. dirs. Harvard Bus. Sch. Assocs.; faculty Grad. Sch. Bus., U. Chgo., 1994-2000; of counsel Omnitech Cons., 1994-96; pres. H.S. Bott Co., 1994-2000. Officer, pres., dir. Urban Gateways, 1965—90; treas., dir. sch. bd., pres. Kenilworth Caucus, 1990; dir. The Cradle, 2000—, Kenilworth United Fund, 1983—89; bd. dirs. Orch. of Ill., 1988—89, The Joseph Sears Found., 2000—, co-pres., 2001—. With USN, 1955—56. Mem. AICPA, Ill. Soc. CPA's, Harvard Bus. Sch. Club. Chgo. (officer 1967-98, bd. dirs.), Am. Mktg. Assn., French-Am. C. of C. (bd. dirs.), Alliance Francaise (bd. dirs.), Kenilworth Sailing Club (commodore 1970-88), Kenilworth Club (treas., bd. dirs. 1975-79), Kenilworth Hist. Soc. (bd. dirs. 1995—), Indian Hill Club, Chgo. Club. Republican. Congregationalist. Home: 305 Kenilworth Ave Kenilworth IL 60043-1132 Office: U Chgo 6030 S Ellis Ave Chicago IL 60637-2608 E-mail: pete.bott@gsb.uchicago.edu.

BOTTI, ALDO E. lawyer; b. Bklyn., Dec. 27, 1936; s. Ettore and Filomena (DeLucio) B.; m. Sheila Higgins, Aug. 4, 1967; children: Michael, Joseph, Mark, Sarah, Elizabeth, John. BA, Rockhurst Coll., 1962; JD, St. Louis U., 1965. Bar: Ill. 1966, U.S. Dist. Ct. (no. and so. dists.) Ill. 1967, U.S. Supreme Ct. 1973, U.S. Ct. Appeals (7th cir.) 1979. Assoc. Frank Glazer & William O'Brien, Chgo., 1966-69; asst. state's atty. DuPage County, Wheaton, Ill., 1969-71, pub. defender, 1971-72; sr. ptnr. Botti, Marinaccio & DeLongis, Ltd., Oak Brook, 1972—. Atty. Village of Villa Park, 1985-88; gen. counsel Ill. State Crime Commn. Mem. Opera Theatre Ill., 1981-84; bd. dirs. Cmty. House, Hinsdale, Ill., 1988-91, mid-Am. chpt. ARC, 1991-94; chmn. bd. dirs. Hinsdale Cmty. Svcs., 1972-73; elected chmn. DuPage County, 1990-94; pres. Metro. Counties Coun., 1991-93. Served in U.S. Army, 1955-58. Mem. ABA, Ill. Bar Assn., Chgo. Bar Assn., DuPage County Bar Assn. (chmn. speakers bur. 1975-78, chmn. pub. relations 1973-75, gen. counsel 1988-89), Am. Judicature Soc., Assn. Trial Lawyers Am. Republican. Roman Catholic. Club: Butterfield Country (Oak Brook). Avocations: reading, painting. Office: Botti Marinaccio & DeLongis 720 Enterprise Dr Hinsdale IL 60523-1908

BOTTOM, DALE COYLE, management consultant; b. Columbus, Ind., June 25, 1932; s. James Robert and Sarah Lou (Coyle) B.; m. Frances Audrey Wilson, June 6, 1954 (div.); children: Jane Ellen, Steven Dale, Sharon Lynn, Carol Ann; m. Elaine McAuliffe, Aug. 20, 1988. BS, Ball State U., Muncie, Ind., 1954. Admissions counselor Stephens Coll., Columbia, Mo., 1958-61; exec. asst., then staff v.p. Inst. Fin. Edn., Chgo., 1961-67, pres., 1967-92; exec. v.p., chief fin. officer U.S. League Savs. Instns., 1985-89; chmn., dir. SAF-Systems & Forms Co.; sec.-gen. Internat. Union Fin. Instns., Chgo., 1989-95; cons. Resource Strategies Internat., Hinsdale, Ill., 1995—. Bd. dirs. Savs. Instn. Ins. Group, Ltd., v.p., chief fin. officer. Chmn. bd. Barrington (Ill.) United Meth. Ch., 1981. Served as officer USAF, 1955-58; comdr. USNR (ret.), 1967-78. Mem. Fin. Mgrs. Soc. (dir.), Savs. Instns. Mktg. Soc. Am., Navy League, Ind. Soc. Chgo., Tavern Club (v.p. 1993), Medinah. Republican. Home and Office: 606 Burr Ridge Clb Burr Ridge IL 60527-5209 E-mail: dalebottom@aol.com.

BOTTOMS, ROBERT GARVIN, academic administrator; b. Birmingham, Ala., June 28, 1944; s. Dalton Garvin and Mary Inez (Cruce) Bottoms; m. Gwendolynn Jean Vickers, June 14, 1968; children: David Timothy, Leslie Clair. BA, Birmingham So. U., 1966; BD, Emory U., 1969; D of Ministry, Vanderbilt U., 1972. Chaplain Birmingham (Ala.) So. Coll., 1973—74, asst. to pres., 1974—75; asst. dean, asst. prof. church and ministry Vanderbilt U., Nashville, 1975—78; v.p. for univ. rels. DePauw U., Greencastle, Ind., 1978—79, exec. v.p. external rels., 1979—83, exec. v.p., 1983—86, acting pres., 1985, pres., 1986—. Am. ctr. for internat. leadership organizer Edn. Policy Commn. U.S.-USSR Emerging Leaders Summit, Phila., 1988; chmn. audit com. Centel Cable TV Co., Oak Brook, Ill., 1987—89. Author: Lessons in Financial Development, 1982. Chmn. com. on ch. and coll. Episcopal Diocese Ind., 1979—84, chmn. com. on ch. and coll., 1979—84; bd. advisors Vanderbilt Div. Sch., 1980—93; bd. trustees Seabury-Western Theol. Sem., 2001—; bd. dirs. Joyce Found., 1994—, G.M. Constrn. Inc., Indpls., 1998—, Women in Govt., Washington, 2001—; bd. advisors Vanderbilt Div. Sch., 1980—93; bd. trustees Seabury-Western Theol. Sem., 2001—; bd. dirs. Joyce Found., 1994—, G.M. Constrn., Inc., Indpls., 1998—, Women in Govt., Washington, 2001—, The Posse Found., 2001—. Recipient CASE V Chief Exec. Leadership award, 2000. Mem.: NCAA, Great Lakes Colls. Assn., Ind. Colls. of Ind. Found., Ind. Colls. of Ind., Am. Coun. Edn., Assn. Governing Bds. Univs. and Colls., Nat. Assn. Schs. and Colls. United Meth. Ch., Nat. Assn. Ind. Colls. and Univs., Nat. Coun. Chs., Chgo. Club., Cosmos Club, Univ. Club of N.Y.C., Columbia Club. Avocation: boating. Home: 125 Wood St Greencastle IN 46135 Office: DePauw Univ Office of Pres 313 S Locust St Greencastle IN 46135-0037

BOTTORFF, JAMES, state legislator; b. Jeffersonville, Ind., July 28, 1944; m. Carlene Bottorff; children: Christopher, Robert. Student, Ind. U. Treas. Clark County, 1979-86, assessor, 1987-90; mem. Ind. State Rep. Dist. 71, 1990—; chmn. commerce com., mem. local govt., fin. instns. Ind. Ho. of Reps., county and twp. fin. inst. and natural resource coms.; former chmn. Clark County Dem. Ctrl. Com.; real estate appraiser. Charter chmn. Clark County Dem. Men's Club; mem. First Christian Ch. Mem. Elks, Moose, Eagles, Farm Bur. Home: 2413 E Highway 62 Jeffersonville IN 47130-6003

BOUBELIK, HENRY FREDRICK, JR. retired travel company executive; b. Chgo., Aug. 16, 1936; s. Henry Fredrick and Anna Mabel (Short) B.; m. Jane V. Boubelik, Oct. 27, 1978; children— Debra Ann, Henry Fredrick III, Steven W., Catherine Earle. Student, U. Ill., 1954-55, Trinity U., 1957-59. Asst. mgr. Avis Rent-A-Car, San Antonio, 1957-60; city mgr. Hertz Rent-a-Car, Corpus Christi, Tex., 1960-67; regional mgr. Nat. Car Rental System, Inc., Mpls., 1967-69, sr. v.p., 1969-92; chmn. Meyer-Boubelik and Assocs., Mpls., 1992-95; pres. Leisure divsns. Northwestern Travel Svc., Minnetonka, Minn., 1995-98; v.p. industry rels. TransGlobal Tours, Inc., Mpls., 1998-2001; ret., 2001. Mem. adv. bd. Corpus Christi Bayfront, 1963-66. Served with AUS, 1955-57. Mem. Car and Truck Rental and Leasing Assn. (v.p. 1973, dir. 1974-77), Am. Car Rental Assn. (pres. 1980-81) Club: Civitan (dir., pres.-elect 1963-66). Home: 9400 Woodbridge Dr Minneapolis MN 55438

BOUCHARD, MICHAEL J. state legislator; b. Flint, Mich., Apr. 12, 1956; s, Donald A. and Doris (Sams) B.; m. Pamela Johnson, 1988; 1 child, Makayla Kathryn. BA, Mich. State U., 1979; grad., Mich. Law Enforcement Ctr. Police officer Bloomfield Twp. (Mich.), 1977-78; pub. safety officer Beverly Hills (Mich.), 1978-88; pres. TACT, Inc., 1986-91; pres, founder Beverly Hills Gourmet Yogurt & Ice Cream, 1989-91; state rep. Mich. Ho. Reps.; state senator Mich. State Senate, Dist. 13. Chair fin. svc., vice chair families, mental & health & human svcs., mem. tech. & energy, asst. majority leader, Mich. State Senate. Del. Mich. State Rep. Conv., 1984-91; coun. mem. Village of Beverly Hills, 1986-90, pres., 1989-90; treas. 18th Dist. Rep. Com., 1989-91; chmn. Oakland County Rep. Campaign Com., 1990; mem. Oakland County Young Reps.; bd. dirs. Birmingham/Bloomfield Cultural Com. Recipient Leadership award Am. Cancer Humanitarian Com., Outstanding Svc. award March of Dimes, Legis. of Yr. award Police Officers Assn. Mich., Humanitarian award Arab-Am. & Chaldcan Coun., Birmingham Bro. Rice Disting. Alumnus award. Mem. Birmingham/Bloomfield C. of C. (bd. dirs.). Address: PO Box 30036 Lansing MI 48909-7536

BOUCHARD, THOMAS JOSEPH, JR. psychology educator, researcher; b. Manchester, N.H., Oct. 3, 1937; s. Thomas and Florence (Charest) B.; m. Pauline Marina Proulx, Aug. 13, 1960; children: Elizabeth, Mark. BA, U. Calif., Berkeley, 1963, PhD, 1966. Asst. prof. U. Calif., Santa Barbara, 1966-69, U. Minn., Mpls., 1969-70, assoc. prof., 1970-73, prof., 1973—, chmn. dept. psychology, 1985-91. Dir. Minn. Ctr. Twin and Adoption Rsch., U. Minn., 1980—. Editor (assoc.): (jour.) Jour. Applied Psychology, 1977—80, Behavior Genetics, 1982—86; contbr. articles jours. With USAF, 1955-58. Fellow AAAS, APA, Am. Psychol. Soc.; mem. Phi Beta Kappa, Sigma Xi. Home: 1860 Shoreline Dr Wayzata MN 55391-9771 Office: Univ of Minn Dept Psychology 75 E River Rd Minneapolis MN 55455-0280 E-mail: bouch001@tc.umn.edu.

BOUCHER, BILL, state legislator; Mo. State rep. dist. 48. Home: 11320 Sunnyslope Dr Kansas City MO 64134-3148

BOUCHER, MERLE, state legislator; m. Susan Boucher; 4 children. AA, N.D. State U.; BS, Mayville (N.D.) State U. Mem. N.D. Ho. of Reps. from 9th dist., 1991—; farmer. Mem. Human Svcs. and Agr. Coms. N.D. Ho. of Reps. Mem. Rolette Cmty. Improvement Inc., Rolette Jobs Auth. Mem. N.D. Edn. Assns. Democrat. Office: ND Ho of Reps State Capitol Bismarck ND 58505

BOUDOULAS, HARISIOS, physician, educator, researcher; b. Velvendo-Kozani, Greece, Nov. 3, 1935; married; 2 children. MD, U. Salonica, Greece, 1959. Resident in internal medicine Red Cross Hosp., Athens, Greece, 1960-61, U. Salonica First Med. Clinic, 1962-66, resident in internal medicine and cardiology, 1962-66, lectr., 1969-70; postgrad. fellow, instr. div. cardiology Ohio State U. Coll. Medicine, Columbus, 1970-73, asst. prof. medicine, 1975-78, assoc. prof., 1978-80, dir. cardiac non-invasive lab., 1978-80, prof. medicine div. cardiology, 1980—, prof. pharmacy, 1984—, dir. cardiovascular rsch. div., 1983-86, dir. cardiovascular teaching and rsch. lab., 1992—; prof. medicine div. cardiology Wayne State U., Detroit, 1980-82, chief clin. cardiovascular rsch., 1980-82, acting dir. div. cardiology, 1982; chief cardiovascular diagnostic and tng. center VA Med. Ctr., Allen Park, Mich., 1980-82; chief sect. cardiology Harper-Grace Hosps., Detroit, 1982. Mem. antepistelon Athens Acad., 1998—. Editor in chief Hellenic Jour. Cardiology; mem. editl. rev. bd. jours. cardiology; contbr. numerous articles to med. jours. Named Disting. Research Investigator, Cen. Ohio chpt. Am. Heart Assn., Columbus, 1983. Fellow ACP, Am. Coll. Angiology, Am. Coll. Clin. Pharmacology, Am. Coll. Cardiology (trustee Ohio chpt. 1993-97), Am. Heart Assn. (coun. clin. cardiology 1989-93, coun. exec. com. 1991-93, sci. com. 1991-93), European Soc. Cardiology (sci. com. 1991-93, valvular heart disease working group 1993—), Greek Heart Assn., Am. Fedn. Clin. Rsch., Laeneck Soc. (chmn. 1991-93). Office: Ohio State U Div Cardiology 1655 Upham Dr Columbus OH 43210-1251

BOUDREAU, LYNDA, state legislator; b. Mar. 9, 1952; m. Jim Boudreau; 3 children. Rep. Minn. Ho. of Reps., 1994—.

BOUDREAU, ROBERT JAMES, nuclear medicine physician, researcher; b. Lethbridge, Alta., Can., Dec. 27, 1950; came to U.S., 1983; s. George Joseph Boudreau and Eleanor Joyce (Dalzell) Hamilton; m. Francine Suzanne Archambault, Jan. 16, 1982. BSc with highest honors, U. Sask., Saskatoon, Can., 1972; PhD, U. B.C., Vancouver, Can., 1975; MD, U. Calgary (Alta.), 1978. Diplomate Am. Bd. Nuclear Medicine. Resident in diagnostic radiology and nuclear medicine McGill U., Montreal, Que., Can., 1978-82; asst. prof. U. Minn., Mpls., 1983-87, assoc. prof., 1987-93, prof., 1993-99, prof. emeritus, 2000—, dir. grad. studies dept. radiology, 1987-91, dir. nuclear medicine divsn., 1987-2000. Author book chpts.; contbr. articles to profl. jours. Recipient Gold Key award Soc. Chem. Industry, 1972, Soc. Clin. Investigation Young Investigator award, 1978; Can. Heart Found. Med. Scientist fellow, 1976-78. Fellow Royal Coll. Physicians; mem. Am. Heart Assn., Soc. Chiefs of Acad. Nuclear Medicine Sects. (treas. 1989-93), Soc. Nuclear Medicine (edn. and tng. com. 1983-91, trustee 1994-95, bd. govs. ctrl. chpt. 1989—, treas. 1992-94, pres. 1994-95), Radiol. Soc. N.Am. Avocations: skiing, boating, travel, computers. Office: U Minn FUMC 500 Harvard St SE Minneapolis MN 55455-0363

BOULANGER, RODNEY EDMUND, energy company executive; b. Detroit, Apr. 4, 1940; m. Nancy Ann Ewigleben, Dec. 29, 1962; children: Brent, Karla, Melissa. BS, Ferris State Coll., Big Rapids, Mich., 1963; MBA, U. Detroit, 1967. Various fin. planning and econ. positions Am. Nat. Resources Co., 1963-78; v.p. system econs. and diversification Am. Natural Service Co., Detroit, 1978-80; v.p. fin. adminstrn ANG Coal Gasification Co., 1980-82, v.p., fin. sec., 1983-84; treas., chief fin. officer Gt. Plains Gasification Assocs., 1982-84; exec. v.p., chief fin. and adminstrv. officer ANR Pipeline Co., 1984-86; pres., CEO ANG Coal Gasification Co., Bismarck, N.D., 1986-87, Midland Congeneration Venture, 1987-95; with CMS Generation Co., Dearborn, Mich., 1995—. Bd. dirs. Chem. Bank. Mem. Tournament Players Club, Detroit Athletic Club, Duck Lake County Club (Albion, Mich.), Caloosa Country Club (Fla.), Beta Gamma Sigma. Office: CMS Generation Co 330 Town Center Dr Dearborn MI 48126-2738

BOULEZ, PIERRE, composer, conductor; b. Montbrison, nr. Clermont-Ferrand, France, Mar. 26, 1925; s. Leon and Marcelle (Calabre) B. Student, recipient 1st prize, Olivier Messiaen at Paris Conservatory. Apptd. dir. music Jean-Louis Barrault's Theater Co., 1948; tchr., lectr., condr.; musical adviser, prin. guest condr. Cleve. Symphony Orch., 1970-71; chief condr. BBC Symphony Orch., 1970-75; musical dir. N.Y. Philharmonic Orch., 1971-77; prof. Coll. de France, 1976-95; dir. Inst. de Recherche et de Coord. Acoustique/Musique, 1976-91; apptd. prin. guest condr. Chgo. Symphony Orch., 1995. Pres. The Ensemble Intercontemporain, 1976-97. Composer; conducting appearances include: Edinburgh Festival, 1965, conducting appearances include: Bayreuth Festival, 1966, conducting appearances include: , 1976—80; composer: Sonatina for flute and piano, 1946, Three Piano Sonatas, 1946, 1950, 1957, Le Soleil des eaux for voice and orchestra, 1947, Structures, 1952, Le Marteau sans maître, 1955, Deux improvisations sur Mallarmé, 1957, Tombeau (on text of Mallarmé), 1959, Pli selon pli, 1960, Structures II, 1962, Eclat, 1964, Domaines, 1968, Eclat/Multiples, 1970, cummings ist der dichter, 1970, explosante-fixe, 1973, Rituel, 1975, Messagesquisse, 1976, Notations I-IV, 1980, Répons, 1981, Dialogue de l'ombre double, 1986, Mémoriale, 1985, Visage nuptial, 1989, Dérive I, 1985, Anthèmes pour violin solo, 1992, explosante-fixe for large ensemble and electronics, 1993, Anthèmes for Violin Solo and Electronics, 1997, sur Incises, 1998, Notations VII, 1999; author: Relevés d'apprenti, 1966, Points de Repère, 1981, le pays fertile-Paule Klee, 1989, Jalon-10 ans d'enseignement au Collège de France, 1989; musical criticism and analysis including: Penser la musique aujourd'hui, 1963. Recipient Praemium Imperiale of Japan Art Assn., 1989, Grosses Verdienstkreuz RFA, 1990, Polar Music prize, Sweden, 1996. Office: Ensemble Intercontemporain 223 Av. Jean-Jaures, Cite de la Musique F-75019 Paris France

BOUNSALL, PHILLIP A. electronics company executive; Sr. mgr. Ernst & Young LLP; CFO Walker Info., Inc., 1994-96; exec. v.p., CFO, treas. Brightpoint, Inc., Indpls., 1996—. Office: Bright Point Inc # 575 600 E 96th St Indianapolis IN 46240-3788

BOUQUIN, BERTRAND, chef; b. Nevers, France; m. Tanya Bouquin. Mem. staff restaurants in Lyons, Avignon, France and Switzerland; sous-chef Restaurant Bruneau, Brussels; chef Cafe Boulud, NY, Club XIX, Calif., Maisonette, Cin. Office: Maisonette 114 E 6th St Cincinnati OH 45202-3404

BOURDON, CATHLEEN JANE, professional society administrator; b. Sparta, Wis., July 13, 1948; d. Cletus John and Josephine Marie (Bourdon) Scheurich; children: Jill Krzyminski, Jeff Krzyminski. BA in Polit. Sci., U. Wis., 1973, MLS, 1974. Tchr. Peace Corps, Arba Minch, Ethiopia, 1969-72; asst. prof., dir. Alverno Coll. Libr., Milw., 1974-83; dep. exec. dir. Assn. Coll. and Rsch. Librs., Chgo., 1983-93; exec. dir. Ref. and User Svcs. Assn. divsn. ALA Assn. Specialized and Coop. Libr. Agys., 1993—. Mem. ALA (pres. Staff Assn. 1987-88). Avocations: reading mystery fiction, 1940s movies, building model doll house furniture. Office: Assn Specialized & Coop Libr Agys 50 E Huron St Chicago IL 60611-5295 E-mail: cbourdon@ala.org.

BOURGUIGNON, ERIKA EICHHORN, anthropologist, educator; b. Vienna, Austria, Feb. 18, 1924; d. Leopold H. and Charlotte (Rosenbaum) Eichhorn; m. Paul H. Bourguignon, Sept. 29, 1950. BA, Queens Coll., 1945; grad. study, U. Conn., 1945; PhD, Northwestern U., 1951; DHL, CUNY, 2000. Field work Chippewa Indians, Wis., summer 1946; field work Haiti; anthropologist Northwestern U., 1947-48; instr. Ohio State U., 1949-56, asst. prof., 1956-60, asso. prof., 1960-66, prof., 1966-90, acting chmn. dept. anthropology, 1971-72, chmn. dept., 1972-76, prof. emeritus, 1990—; dir. Cross-Cultural Study of Dissociational States, 1963-68. Bd. dirs. Human Relations Area Files, Inc., 1976-79 Author: Possession, 1976, rev. edit., 1991, Psychological Anthropology, 1979, Italian transl., 1983; editor, co-author: Religion, Altered States of Consciousness and Social Change, 1973, A World of Women, 1980; co-author: Diversity and Homogeneity in World Societies, 1973; adv. editor: Behavior Sci. Rsch., 1976-79; assoc. editor Jour. Psychoanalytic Anthropology, 1977-87; mem. editl. bd. Ethos, 1979-89, 97—, Jour. Haitian Studies, 2000—; editor: Margaret Mead: The Anthropologist in America—Occasional Papers in

Anthropology, No. 2, Ohio State U. Dept. Anthropology, 1986; (with Barbara Rigney) Exile: A Memoir of 1939 by Bronka Schneider, 1998; contbr. articles to profl. jours. Fellow Am. Anthrop. Assn.; mem. Ctrl. State Anthrop. Soc. (treas. 1953-56, exec. com. 1995-98), Ohio Acad Sci., World Psychiat. Assn. (transcultural psychiatry sect.), Am. Ethnol. Soc., Current Anthropology (assoc.), Soc. for Psychol. Anthropology (nominations com. 1981-82, bd. dirs. 1991-93, lifetime achievement award 1999), Soc. for the Anthropology of Religion, Phi Beta Kappa, Sigma Xi. Office: Ohio State U Dept of Anthropology 124 W 17th Ave Columbus OH 43210-1316 E-mail: bourguignon.1@osu.edu.

BOURNE, PATRICK J. state legislator; b. Omaha, Apr. 11, 1964; m. Cindy Bourne, May 18, 1985 (dec.); 1 child, Jack. A, S.E. C.C., 1984; BSBA, U. Nebr., Omaha, 1994; JD, Creighton U., 1997. Bar: Nebr. Atty.; mem. Nebr. Legislature from 8th dist., Lincoln, 1998—. Mem. ABA, Nebr. State Bar Assn., Omaha Bar Assn. Home: 5121 Erskine St Omaha NE 68104-4352 Office: State Capitol Dist 8 PO Box 94604 Rm 1101 Lincoln NE 68509

BOUTIETTE, VICKIE LYNN, educator, reading specialist; b. Valley City, N.D., Mar. 13, 1950; BS in Elem. Edn., Valley City State U., 1972; MS in Reading, Moorhead State U., 1997; postgrad., U. S.D., 1998—. 4th-5th grade tchr. Pillsbury Pub. Sch., 1973-74; 3rd grade tchr. West Fargo Pub. Schs., 1984-90, remedial reading tchr., elem. tchr., 1993-98, Reading Recovery tchr. leader, 1998—. Sunday sch. tchr., 1975—, ch. newsletter editor, 1993—; vol. U. Minn. Hosps. and Clinics, 1991-93. Recipient Nat. Educator Award Milken Family Found., 1998, Courage award N.D. Edn. Assn., 1994; Christa McAuliffe fellowship, 2000; named N.D. Tchr. of Yr., 1998, West Fargo Tchr. of Yr. 1997-98. Mem. NEA, West Fargo Edn. Assn. (exec. bd. 1989-90, elem. chairperson 1988-89, pub. rels. chairperson 1988-90), N.D. Edn. Assn., Valley Reading Assn. (rec. sec. 1997—), N.D. Reading Assn., Phi Delta Kappa, Alpha Mu Gamma (pres. 1972). Home: 7103 64th Ave S Fargo ND 58104-5715 Office: Westside Elem Sch 945 7th Ave W West Fargo ND 58078-1429 Fax: 701-356-2119.

BOUTWELL, ROSWELL KNIGHT, oncology educator; b. Madison, Wis., Nov. 24, 1917; s. Paul Winslow and Clara Gertrude (Brinkhoff) B.; m. Luella Mae Fairchild, Sept. 25, 1943; children— Paul F., Philip H., David K. B.S. in Chemistry, Beloit Coll., 1939; M.S. in Biochemistry, U. Wis., 1941, Ph.D., 1944; DSc, Beloit Coll., 1980. Instr. U. Wis., 1945-49, asst. prof., 1949-54, assoc. prof., 1954-67, prof. oncology med. ctr., 1967—. Vis. lectr. Inst. for Environ. Medicine, NYU, summer 1966; mem. cancer study group Wis. Regional Med. Program, 1967-70; mem. adv. com. on inst. research grants Am. Cancer Soc., 1967-74, chmn., 1972-74; mem. food protection com. NRC, 1971-75; mem. lung cancer segment Nat. Cancer Inst., 1971-75; mem. adv. com. on pathogenesis of cancer Am. Cancer Soc., 1960-63; mem. Nat. Cancer Adv. Bd., 1983-90; chief research Radiation Effects Research Found., Hiroshima, Japan, 1984-86; prof. emeritus, 1988—. Mem. editorial adv. bd. Cancer Research, 1959-64, assoc. editor, 1973-83; mem. editorial bd. Jpn. J. Cancer Res., 1985—; assoc. editor: Nutrition and Cancer, 1988—; mem. sci. adv. bd. Internat. Coun. for Coordinating Cancer Rsch., 1989-92, Dermigen, 1990—. Mem. Monona Grove Sch. Bd., 1952-54; bd. dirs. Madison Gen. Hosp. Found. Recipient Kenneth P. DuBois award Soc. Toxicology, 1998, medal of honor Am. Cancer Soc., 1998. Fellow AAAS, Am. Assn. Cancer Research (dir.), Am. Soc. Biol. Chemists (Clowes award). Office: U Wis Dept Oncology McArdle Lab 1400 University Ave Rm 1125 Madison WI 53706-1526

BOWDEN, JIM, professional sports team executive; b. May 18, 1961; m. Amy Bowden; children: J.B., Tyler, Chad. BBA, Rollins Coll., 1983. Asst. dir. player devel. and scouting Pitts. Pirates, 1985-88; asst. to sr. v.p. baseball ops. N.Y. Yankees, 1989-90; adminstrv. asst. scouting and player devel. Cin. Reds, 1982-92, gen. mgr., 1992—. Office: Cincinnati Reds 100 Cinergy Fld Cincinnati OH 45202-3543

BOWE, WILLIAM JOHN, lawyer; b. Chgo., June 23, 1942; s. William John Sr. and Mary (Gwinn) B.; m. Catherine Louise Vanselow, Nov. 10, 1979; children: Andrew M., Patrick D. BA, Yale U., 1964; JD, U. Chgo., 1967. Bar: Ill. 1967, Tenn. 1984. Assoc. Ross, Hardies, O'Keefe, Babcock, McDougall & Parsons, Chgo., 1967-68; assoc., then ptnr. Roan & Grossman, 1971-78; v.p., gen. counsel, sec. The Bradford Exchange Ltd., Niles, Ill., 1979-83; asst. gen. counsel, v.p., gen. counsel United Press Internat. Inc., Nashville, 1984-85; v.p. to exec. v.p., gen. counsel, sec. Ency. Britannica, Inc., Chgo., 1986—; sec. William Benton Found., 1987-96; pres. Merriam-Webster, Inc., Springfield, Mass., 1995-96, Ency. Britannica Ednl. Corp., Chgo., 1995-99. Co-chmn. managing the smaller law dept. Corp. Legal Inst., 1995. Mem. bd. editors Intellectual Property Studies, Chinese Acad. Social Studies, Beijing, 1996-99; contbr. articles to legal jours. Gen. counsel Gov.'s Task Force on Sch. Fin., Chgo., 1975-76; trustee Hull House Assn., Chgo., 1977-79; pres., bd. dirs. Clarence Darrow Comty. Ctr., Chgo., 1975-84; mem. bd. overseers Ill. Inst. Tech.-Kent Coll. Law, 1982-86; mem. The Annenberg Washington Program Anti-Piracy Project, Washington, 1988-89; bd. dirs. Internat. Anticounterfeiting Coalition, Washington, 1993—, chmn., 1994-96; mem. Gov.'s Task Force on Work-force Preparation, 1991-93, Gov.'s Work Group on Early Childhood Care and Edn., 1994-95. With U.S. Army, 1968-71. Mem.: ABA, Software and Info. Industry Assn. (govt. affairs coun. 1999—, gov.'s edn. summit 2000—02), Software Publs. Assn. (govt. affairs com. 1997—99), Intellectual Property Assn. Chgo., Chgo. Bar Assn., Ill. Bar Assn., Ill. State C. of C. (mem. edn. com. 1989—99, bd. dirs. 1989—96). Office: Ency Britannica Inc 310 S Michigan Ave Ste 900 Chicago IL 60604-4216 E-mail: wbowe@eb.com.

BOWEN, GARY ROGER, architect; b. Page, Nebr., Apr. 24, 1942; s. Roger David and Eugenia (Luben) B.; m. Elizabeth Ann Humphrey, Aug. 4, 1962; children— Ann, Leslie. Student Wayne State Coll., 1958-59; B.Arch., U. Nebr., 1964, M. Arch., 1974. Registered architect, Nebr., Iowa; cert. Nat. Council Archtl. Registration Bds. With Howell, Killick, Partridge, Amis, London, 1963, F.W. Horn Assocs., Quincy, Ill., 1964-66; design architect Leo A. Daly Co., Omaha, 1966-72; ptnr. Hartman Morford Bowen, Omaha, 1972-74, Bahr Vermeer Haecker, Omaha, 1974—, pres., 1996—; vis. critic Coll. Architecture, U. Nebr.; vis. lectr. Coll. Architecture, Kansas State U.; dir. Landmarks Inc., Omaha. Bd. dirs. Western Heritage Soc., Joslyn Castle Inst., Archtl. Found. Nebr., Omaha. Am. Collegiate Schs. of Architecture Fgn. Work Exchange scholar, 1963; recipient Housing Mag. Homes for Better Living Nat. Design award, 1981, 2 Ctrl. States Honor awards. Mem. AIA (nat. bd. dirs. 1994-96, Coll. of Fellows 1996, Richard Upjohn fellow 1996, S.D. award), Nebr. Soc. Architects (20 honor awards), Nebr. Coll. Architecture Alumni Assn. (bd. dirs.). Republican. Methodist. Club: Field of Omaha. Home: 6044 Country Club Oaks Pl Omaha NE 68152-2009 Office: Bahr Vermeer & Haecker Arch LTD 1209 Harney St Ste 400 Omaha NE 68102-1801

BOWEN, GEORGE HAMILTON, JR. astrophysicist, educator; b. Tulsa, June 20, 1925; s. George H. and Dorothy (Huntington) B.; m. Marjorie Evelyn Brown, June 19, 1948; children— Paul Huntington, Margaret Irene, Carol Ann, Dorothy Elizabeth, Kevin Leigh. B.S. with honor, Calif. Inst. Tech., 1949, Ph.D., 1952. Asso. biologist Oak Ridge Nat. Lab., 1952-54; asst. prof. physics Ia. State Coll., 1954-57; asso. prof. physics Iowa State U., 1957-65, prof., 1965-92, emeritus prof. astrophysics, 1993—. Served with USNR, 1944-46. Recipient Iowa State U. Outstanding Tchr. award, 1970, Faculty citation Iowa State U. Alumni Assn., 1971 Mem. Am. Astron. Soc., Astron. Soc. Pacific, Am. Assn. Physics Tchrs. (chmn. Iowa sect. 1966-67), Internat. Astron. Union, Sigma Xi, Tau Beta Pi. Home: 1919 Burnett Ave Ames IA 50010-4970 Office: Iowa State U Dept Physics & Astronomy Ames IA 50011-0001

BOWEN, MICHAEL ANTHONY, lawyer, writer; b. Ft. Monroe, Va., July 16, 1951; s. Harold James and Judith Ann (Carter-Waller) B.; m. Sara Armbruster, Aug. 30, 1975; children: Rebecca Elizabeth, Christopher Andrew, John Armbruster, Marguerite Judith, James Harold. AB summa cum laude, Rockhurst Coll., 1973; JD cum laude, Harvard U., 1976. Bar: Wis. 1976, U.S. Dist. Ct. (ea. and we. dists.) Wis., U.S. Ct. Appeals (4th, 5th, 7th, 8th and 10th cirs.), Wis. Supreme Ct. Assoc. Foley & Lardner, Milw., 1976-84, ptnr., 1984—. Author: Can't Miss, 1987, Badger Game, 1989, Washington Deceased, 1990, Fielder's Choice, 1991, Faithfully Executed, 1992, Act of Faith, 1993, Corruptly Procured, 1994, Worst Case Scenario, 1996, Collateral Damage, 1999, The Fourth Glorious Mystery, 2000; co-author: The Wisconsin Fair Dealership Law, 1988. Mem. ABA, Wis. Bar Assn., Milw. Bar Assn., St. Thomas More Lawyers' Soc. (pres. 1983), Milw. Young Lawyers' Assn. (pro bono legal services 1982). Roman Catholic. Avocations: photography, running, cross-country skiing. Office: Foley & Lardner 777 E Wisconsin Ave Ste 3800 Milwaukee WI 53202-5367

BOWEN, STEPHEN STEWART, lawyer; b. Peoria, Ill., Aug. 23, 1946; s. Gerald Raymond and Frances Arlene (Stewart) B.; m. Ellen Claire Newcomer, Sept. 23, 1972; children: David, Claire. BA cum laude, Wabash Coll., 1968; JD cum laude, U. Chgo., 1972. Bar: Ill. 1972, U.S. Dist. Ct. (no. dist.) Ill. 1972, U.S. Tax Ct. 1977. Assoc. Kirkland & Ellis, Chgo., 1972-78, ptnr., 1978-84, Latham & Watkins, Chgo., 1985—. Adj. prof. DePaul U. Masters in Taxation Program, Chgo., 1976-80; lectr. Practicing Law Inst., N.Y.C., Chgo., L.A., 1978-84, N.Y.C., 1986—. Mem. vis. com. U. Chgo. Div. Sch., 1984—, mem. vis. com. Sch. Law, 1991-93; mem. planning com. U. Chgo. Tax Conf., 1985—, chair, 1995-98; trustee Wabash Coll., 1996—. Fellow Am. Coll. Tax Counsel; mem. ABA, Ill. State Bar Assn., Order of Coif, Met. Club (Chgo.), Econ. Club Chgo., Phi Beta Kappa. Office: Latham & Watkins Sears Tower Ste 5800 Chicago IL 60606-6306

BOWEN, WILLIAM JOSEPH, management consultant; b. N.Y.C., May 13, 1934; s. Edward F. and Mary Alice (Drooney) B.; children: William J., Timothy M., Priscilla A., Robert B.; m. Betsy Bass, Oct. 31, 1983. BS, Fordham U., 1956; MBA, NYU, 1963. Trainee Smith, Barney, N.Y.C., 1959-61; asst. v.p. Citicorp, 1961-67; v.p. Hayden, Stone, 1967-69; 1st v.p. Shearson Hammill, 1969-73; assoc. Heidrick & Struggles, 1973-77, ptnr., 1977—, mgr., 1978-81, pres., CEO, 1981-83, vice chmn. N.Y.C., Chgo., 1983—. Capt. USAF, 1956-59. Mem. Chgo. Club, Onwentsia Club, N.Y. Club, Marco Polo, Union League (N.Y.C.). Republican. Office: Heidrick & Struggles Inc Sears Tower 233 S Wacker Dr Ste 7000 Chicago IL 60606-6350

BOWER, GLEN LANDIS, state agency administrator, lawyer; b. Highland, Ill., Jan. 16, 1949; s. Ray Landis and Evelyn Ferne (Ragland) Bower. BA, So. Ill. U., 1971; JD with honors, Ill. Inst. Tech., 1974. Bar: Ill. 1974, U.S. Ct. Mil. Appeals 1975, U.S. Ct. Appeals (7th cir.) 1976, U.S. Dist Ct. (so. dist.) Ill. 1977, U.S. Dist. Ct. (cen. dist.) Ill. 1992, U.S. Supreme Ct. 1978, U.S. Tax Ct. 1984, U.S. Ct. Claims 1986, U.S. Dist. Ct. (no. dist.) Ill. 1994, U.S. Ct. Veterans Appeals 1995. Sole practice, Effingham, Ill., 1974-83; prosecutor Effingham County, 1976-79; mem. Ill. House of Reps., Springfield, 1979-83; asst. dir., gen. counsel Ill. Dept. Revenue, Ill., 1983-90; Presdl. appointed chmn. U.S. Railroad Retirement Bd., Chgo., 1990-97; asst. to Ill. Sec. of State, 1998-99; apptd. dir. revenue State of Ill., 1999—. Mil. aide to Gov. of Ill.; liaison mem. Adminstrv. Conf. of U.S., 1991-95; mem. Nat. Adv. Com. for Juvenile Justice and Delinquency Prevention, Washington, 1976-80, U.S. Econ. Adv. Bd. of U.S. Dept. Commerce, Washington, 1981-85, Ill. Gen. Assembly State Adv. Com. on Cir. Ct. Fin., Springfield, 1984; mem. Revenue Bd. Appeals, Chgo., 1985-87, chmn., 1986-87; mem. Com. of 50 on Ill. Constn., 1987-88; adv. com. on electronic tax adminstrn. IRS, 2000, So. Ill. U. Pub. Policy Inst., 2000. Co-editor: Handbook on State Taxation, 1991; contbr. articles to profl. jours. Alt. del. Rep. Nat. Conv., Miami Beach, Fla., 1972, Rep. Nat. Conv., New Orleans, 1988, Rep. Nat. Conv. Houston, 1992, Phila., 2000; vice chmn. Effingham County Rep. Ctrl. Com., Ill., 1976-90; bd. dirs. Dana-Thomas House Found., Springfield, Ill., 1989-90, So. Ill. U. at Carbondale Found., 1993-2002, pres.'s coun.; trustee McKendree Coll., Lebanon, Ill., 1978-81; chmn. State of Ill. Organ and Tissue Donors Adv. Bd., 1993-98. Lt. col. USAFR, 1974-99, ret. Recipient The Univ. Disting. Svc. award, 1971, Recognition citation Am. Legion, 1980, Outstanding Svc. cert. to tchg. profession Ill. Edn. Assn., 1981, Disting. Svc. award Am. Vets., 1980, 82, Presdl. citation Navy League U.S., 1981, Constitution award Mus. of Our Nat. Heritage, 1988, Silver Good Citizenship medal Ill. Soc. SAR, 1990, Profl. Achievement award Ill. Inst. Tech., 1993, Friend of History award Ill. State Hist. Soc., 1994, Alumni Achievement award So. Ill. U., 1994, Disting. Alumnus award So. Ill. U. Coll. Liberal Arts, 2000; named Outstanding Freshman Legislator, Ill. Edn. Assn., 1980, Legislator of Yr., Ill. Assn. Rehab. Socs., 1981, 82, One of 10 Dels. to China, Am. Coun. Young Polit. Leaders, 1988. Fellow: Am. Bar Found. (life), Ill. Bar Found. (life); mem.: ABA (employment taxes com. 1990, adminstrv. practice com. of taxation sect., ct. procedure com., mem. exec. com. nat. assn. state tax bar sects.), Air Force Assn., Judge Advs. Assn., Am. Coun. Young Political Leaders, U.S. Capitol Hist. Soc. (charter), Effingham County Mental Health Assn. (pub. affairs com. 1977—78), SBA Adv. Coun., Effingham Regional Hist. Soc. (bd. dirs. 1973—77), Ill. State Hist. Soc. (v.o, 1979—81, Ralph C. Francis award 1967), Nat. Assn. Tax Adminstrs. (vice chmn. attys. sect. 1985—86, chmn. 1986—88, vice chmn. attys. sect. 1988—89, trustee 2001), Chgo. Bar Assn., Effingham County Bar Assn. (sec. 1976—77, pres. 1983—84), Ill. State Bar Assn. (labor law sect. coun. 1976—77, sec. state taxation sect. coun. 1987—88, vice-chair 1988—89, 1988—89, chair 1989—90, sect. coun. on employee benefits 1991—98, 1991—98, sect. coun. on adminstrv. law 2000, Bd. Gov.'s award 1999), Rep. Nat. Lawyers Assn., Fed. Tax Adminstrs. (bd. trustees 2001—), Fed. Cir. Bar Assn., Fed. Bar Assn., Sons of Am. Revolution, So. Ill. Univ. Alumni Assn. (life), Effingham County Old Settlers Assn. (pres., bd. dirs. 1983—86), Abraham Lincoln Assn., U.S. Supreme Ct. Hist. Soc., The Nat. Sojourners, Art Inst. of Chgo., Smithsonian Assocs., So. Ill. U. Carbondale Found. (bd. dirs. 1993—), Res. Officers Assn., Field Mus. of Natural History, Am. Legion, Army and Navy Club Washington D.C., Capitol Hill Club, Kiwanis (pres. 1977—78), Phi Alpha Delta. Methodist. Home: 1 E Scott St Ste 709 Chicago IL 60610-5244 Office: Ill Dept Revenue 100 W Randolph St Ste 7-100 Chicago IL 60601-3253

BOWER, ROBERT HEWITT, surgeon, educator, researcher; b. Omaha, Aug. 20, 1949; s. John Walter and Dorothy May (Sibert) B.; m. Debra Lea Goettsche, July 4, 1980; children: Timothy Conrad, Michael Harvey, Emily Frances. BA, Grinnell Coll., 1971; MD, U. Nebr., 1975. Diplomate Nat. Bd. Med. Examiners, Am. Bd. Surgery (dir. 1995-2001, sr. examiner 2001—). Intern U. Nebr., 1975-76, resident surgery, 1976-80, chief resident, 1979-80; clin. and rsch. fellow U. Cin., 1980-81, asst. prof. surgery, 1981-85; dir. dept. parenteral and enteral nutrition U. Hosp., 1981—, assoc. prof. surgery, 1985-95, prof. surgery, 1995—, dir. surg. residency, 1986—, vice chmn. edn., 1995—. Chief surgical svc. Cin. VA Med. Ctr., 1994—. Contbr. chpts. to books and articles to profl. jours. Pres., trustee, chmn. bd. trustees Vocal Arts Ensemble of Cin.; elder, trustee Knox Presbyn. Ch. Fellow ACS, Am. Surg. Assn.; mem. Ctrl. Surg. Assn., Am. Coll. Nutrition, Soc. Am. Gastrointestinal Endoscopic Surgeons, Assn. Acad. Surgery, Am. Soc. Parenteral and Enteral Nutrition, Ohio Med. Assn., Surg. Infection Soc., Acad. Medicine Cin., Soc. Univ. Surgeons, Soc. Surgery of Alimentary Tract, Cin. Surg. Soc., Halsted Soc. Office: U Cincinnati Dept Surgery PO Box 670558 231 Albert Sabin Way Cincinnati OH 45267-0558

BOWERS, BEGE K. English educator; b. Nashville, Aug. 19, 1949; d. John and Yvonne (Howell) B. BA in English cum laude, Vanderbilt U., 1971; student, U. Mich., 1985; MACT, U. Tenn., 1973, PhD, 1984. Asst. loan officer Ctr. for Fin. Aid and Placement, Baylor U., Waco, Tex., 1975-76; editorial asst. Wassily Leontief, NYU, N.Y.C., 1976-78; instr. bus. English Florence-Darlington Tech. Coll., Florence, S.C., 1979-80; tchr. English and French St. John's High Sch., Darlington, 1980-82; teaching asst. dept English U. Tenn., Knoxville, 1982-84; asst. prof. English Youngstown (Ohio) State U., 1984-88, assoc. prof., 1988-92, prof., 1992—, composition coord. dept. English, 1985-94, acting chmn. dept., 1989, asst. to dean Coll. Arts and Scis., 1992-93, dir. profl. writing and editing, 1996-2000, assoc. to the dean Coll. Arts and Scis., 2001—02, asst. provost acad. programs and planning, 2002—. Part-time freelance editor MLA, N.Y.C., 1978-80; cons. Project Arete, Youngstown and Mahoning County Pub. Schs., 1984-87, Youngstown Pub. Schs., 1986, 87-88, 90-91, Macmillan Pub. Co., 1986, Trumbull (Ohio) County Schs., 1988, Akron Beacon Jour., 1994-95, Ohio Dept. Edn., 1998-2001. Co-editor: CEA Critic, 1998-2002, CEA Forum 1988—, (with Barbara Brothers) Reading and Writing Women's Lives: A Study of the Novel of Manners, 1991, (with Chuck Nelson) Internships in Technical Communication, 1991; editorial bd. South Atlantic Review, 1987-89; editor: of more than 40 pamphlets, 7 children's books, and 1 videoscript. Alumni Found. Rsch. fellow U. Tenn., 1978, dissertation fellow U. Tenn., 1983, Davis editl. fellow U. Tenn., 1984; Grad. Rsch. Coun. grantee Youngstown State U. Mem.: MLA, Gould Soc. (pres. faculty com. 1991—93), No. Ohio Soc. for Tech. Comm., Soc. for Tech. Comm. (Jay R. Gould award for excellence in tchg. tech. comm. 1999, Disting. Chpt. Svc. award 2001, Assoc. fellow award 2002), Assn. Tchrs. Tech. Writing, New Chaucer Soc. (asst. bibliographer 1986—), Coll. English Assn. Ohio, Coun. Editors of Learned Jours., Coll. English Assn. (exec. bd., Disting. Svc. award 1996), Phi Beta Kappa, Phi Kappa Phi (pres. 1991—92, sec. 1994—98). Office: Youngstown State U Office of the Provost Youngstown OH 44555-0001 E-mail: bkbowers@ysu.edu.

BOWERS, CURTIS RAY, JR. chaplain; b. Lancaster, Pa., Feb. 6, 1933; s. Curtis Ray and Oleita (Geisler) B.; m. Doris Jean, June 18, 1955; children: Sharon, William, Stephen. BA, Asbury Coll., 1958; MDiv, Asbury Theol. Sem., 1960. Pastor Methodist Ch., Cynthiana, Ky., 1956-60, Ch. of the Nazarene, Cape May, N.J., 1960-61; chaplain U.S. Army, 1961-84; dir. chaplaincy ministries Ch. of the Nazarene, Kansas City, Mo., 1984-2000. Author: Forward Edge of the Battle Area: A Chaplain's Story. Col. U.S. Army, 1961-84. Decorated Silver Star; named Srs. Double Inter-Svc. Tennis Champion, 1982; named to 327th Infantry Regimental Hall of Fame, 1998; recipient Outstanding Chaplain of Yr. award, Ch. of the Nazarene, 2000. Avocation: tennis. Home: 3523 Portland Ave Nampa ID 83686-7993 E-mail: crbowers11@juno.com.

BOWIE, E(DWARD) J(OHN) WALTER, hematologist, researcher; b. Church Stretton, Shropshire, Eng., Mar. 10, 1925; came to U.S., 1958; s. Edgar Ormond and Ann Brown (Lorrimer) B.; m. Gertrud Susi Ulrich, Dec. 22, 1948; children— Katherine Ann, Christopher John, John Walter, James Ulrich MA, Oxford (Eng.) U., 1950, BM, BCh, 1952, DM, 1981; MS, U. Minn., 1961. House physician Univ. Coll. Hosp., London, 1953; sr. house officer Bethlem Royal and Maudsley Hosps., 1953-54; pvt. practice medicine Treherne, Man., Can., 1954; fellow in medicine Mayo Clinic, Rochester, Minn., 1958-60, cons. in internal medicine and hematology, 1961-90, head sect. hematology research, 1971-89; prof. medicine and lab. medicine Mayo Med. Sch., 1974-90, prof. emeritus, 1990-96, ret., 1996. Invited spkr. Gordon Confs., 1973, 76, 78, Royal Soc., London, 1980; chmn. thrombosis coun. Internat. Soc. and Fedn. Cardiology, 1991; internat. dir. Thrombosis Vascular Tng. Ctrs. Co-author 6 books; assoc. editor Jour. Lab. and Clin. Medicine, 1976-80; contbr. chpts. to books, numerous articles to profl. jours. Recipient Judson Daland travel award Mayo Found., 1963, named Disting. Investigator, 1988, Disting. Alumnus Mayo Found., 1996. Fellow ACP, AMA, Royal Coll. Pathology; mem. AAAS, Am. Heart Assn. Internat. Soc. on Thrombosis and Haemostasis (v.p. 1980-81, Disting. Career award 1991), Am. Soc. Hematology, Internat. Com. on Thrombosis and Haemostasis (chmn. 1989-90), Ctrl. Soc. for Clin. Rsch., Am. Fedn. for Clin. Rsch., World Fedn. Haemophilia. Office: Emeritus Section Mayo Clinic Rochester MN 55905

BOWIE, NORMAN ERNEST, university official, educator; b. Biddeford, Maine, June 6, 1942; s. Lawrence Walker and Helen Elizabeth (Jacobsen) B.; m. Bonnie Jean Bankert, June 11, 1966 (div. 1980); children: Brian Paul, Peter Mark; m. Maureen Burns, Sept. 19, 1987. AB, Bates Coll., 1964; PhD, U. Rochester, 1968. Mem. faculty Lycoming Coll., Williamsport, Pa., 1968-69; asst. prof. philosophy Hamilton Coll., Clinton, N.Y., 1969-74, assoc. prof., 1974-75, U. Del., Newark, 1975-80, prof., 1980-89, dir. Ctr. for Study of Values, 1977-89; Elmer L. Andersen chairperson corp. responsibility U. Minn., Mpls., 1989—, chair dept. strategic mgmt. and orgn., 1992-95; fellow in ethics and professions Harvard U., 1996-97; Dixons prof. bus. ethics and social responsibility London Bus. Sch., 1999-2000. Lynette S. Autrey vis. prof. bus. ethics Rice U., spring 1986; vis. prof. Sch. Mgmt. U. Scranton, 1986-87, Sch. Bus. Adminstrn., Georgetown U., 1988-89; exec. v.p. seminars The Aspen Inst., 1998-99. Author: Towards a New Theory of Distributive Justice, 1971, Business Ethics, 1982, (with Ronald Duska) 2nd edit., 1990, Making Ethical Decisions, 1985, University Business Partnerships: An Assessment, 1994, Business Ethics: A Kantian Perspective, 1999; co-author: The Individual and the Political Order, 1977, 3d edit., 1998; editor: Ethical Issues in Government, 1981, Ethical Theory in the Last Quarter of the Twentieth Century, 1983, Equal Opportunity, 1988; co-editor: Ethical Theory and Business, 1979, 6th edit., 2001, Ethics, Public Policy and Criminal Justice, 1982, The Tradition of Philosophy, 1986, Ethics and Agency Theory, 1992, Guide to Business Ethics, 2001; co-editor Bus. and Profl. Ethics Jour., 1981-88. Mem. N.Y. Coun. for Humanities, 1974-75. NDEA fellow, 1965-68 Mem. AAUP, Acad. Mgmt., Am. Philos. Assn. (nat. exec. sec. 1972-77), Am. Soc. for Value Inquiry (pres. 1980-81), Am. Soc. Polit. and Legal Philosophy, Soc. Bus. Ethics (pres. 1988), Phi Beta Kappa. Home: PO Box 508 Trappe MD 21673-0508 Office: Carlson Sch Mgmt 321 19th Ave S Minneapolis MN 55455-0438

BOWLES, BARBARA LANDERS, investment company executive; b. Nashville, Sept. 17, 1947; d. Corris Raemone Landers and Rebecca (Bonham) Jennings; m. Earl Stanley Bowles, Nov. 27, 1971; 1 son, Terrence Earl. BA, Fisk U., 1968; MBA, U. Chgo., 1971. Chartered fin. analyst. From bank official to v.p. First Nat. Bank of Chgo., 1968-81; asst. v.p. Beatrice Cos., Chgo., 1981-84; v.p. investor rels. Kraft Inc., 1984-86; pres., founder The Kenwood Group Inc., 1989—. Bd. dirs. Black & Decker Corp., Hyde Pk. Bank. Bd. dirs. Children's Meml. Hosp., Ga. Pacific Corp. and Dollar Gen. Corp. The Chgo. Urban League. Scholar United Negro College Fund, 1989. Mem. NAACP (life), Assn. for Investment Mgmt. and Rsch., Chgo. Fisk trustee(1998-), University (Chgo.). Mem. United Ch. of Christ. Avocations: tennis, bridge. E-mail: kenwoodg@aol.com.

BOWLES, EVELYN MARGARET, state legislator; b. Worden, Ill., Apr. 22, 1921; d. Ira Milton and Anna (Augustine) B. AA, Ill. State U., 1941; student, Greenville Coll., 1947, Southwest Photo Arts Inst., Dallas, 1945—46, Lewis & Clark C.C., 1984. Tchr. Livingston Elem. Sch., Edwardsville Elem. Sch., 1941—43, 1946—50; chief dep. County Clks. Office, Edwardsville, Ill., 1951-74; county clk. Madison County, 1974—94; state senator Ill. Senate, Springfield, 1974—. Mem. Madison County Welfare Com., 1980—; meml. chmn. Cancer Soc., Edwardsville, Ill., 1980—; bd. dirs. Madison County Hospice, Granite City, sec., 1983-84; pres. adv. bd. Rape and Sexual Abuse Care Ctr., 1984-86; mem. voting systems som. Ill. Bd. Elections; pres. parish council St. Mary's Ch., mem. lector soc. Served with USMC, 1943-45, USCG. Recipient Alice

Paul award Metro-East NOW, 1979. Mem. Ill. Assn. Clks., Recorders, Election Officials and Treas., Ill. Assn. County Officials, Ill. Fedn. Bus. and Profl. Women (Outstanding Working Women of Ill. 1986), Collinsville Bus. and Profl. Women (Boss of Yr. 1976), Edwardsville Bus. Profl. Women (pres. 1957-58, Woman of Achievement award 1978), Metro-East Women's Assn., Am. Legion. Avocations: reading, yard work, fishing. Address: M-103F Capitol Bldg Springfield IL 62706-0001 Also: 4 Club Centre Ct Edwardsville IL 62025-3518

BOWLING, JOHN C. academic administrator; Pres. Olivet Nazarene U., 1991—. Office: Olivet Nazarene Univ Office of Pres 1 Univ Ave PO Box 592 Kankakee IL 60901-0592

BOWLSBY, BOB, athletic director; b. Jan. 10, 1952; m. Candice Bowlsby; children: Lisa, Matt, Rachel, Kyle. BS, Moorhead State U., 1975; MS, U. Iowa, 1978. Asst. athletic dir. Northern Iowa Univ.; athletic dir. Univ. Northern Iowa, 1984-91, Univ. Iowa, 1991—. Chair NCAA Divsn. I Mgmt. Coun., 1997-99; mem. NCAA Divsn. I Basketball com., 2000—. Chmn. Big Ten Championships and awards com.; chair NCAA Olympic Sports Liaison Com., NCAA/USOC liaison com., Olympics com. mem; bd. dirs. Iowa Games. Mem. Nat. Assn. Collegiate Dir. of Athletics (exec. com.). Office: U Iowa Dir Athletics 338 Carver Hawkeye Arena Iowa City IA 52242-1020 E-mail: robert-bowlsby@uiowa.edu.

BOWMAN, BARBARA TAYLOR, institute president; b. Chgo., Oct. 30, 1928; d. Robert Rochon and Dorothy Vaugn (Jennings) Taylor; m. James E. Bowman, June 17, 1950; 1 child, Valerie Bowman Jarrett. BA, Sarah Lawrence Coll., 1950; MA, U. Chgo., 1952; DHL, Bankstreet Coll., 1988, Roosevelt U., 1998, Dominican U., 2002. Tchr. U. Chgo. Nursery Sch., 1950-52, Colo. Women's Coll. Nursery Sch., Denver, 1953-55; mem. sci. faculty Shiraz (Iran) U. Nemazee Sch. Nursing, 1955-61; spl. edn. tchr. Chgo. Child Care Soc., 1965—67; mem. faculty Erikson Inst., Chgo., 1967—, dir. grad. studies, 1978—94, pres., 1994—2002, prof. early edn., 2002. Mem. early childhood com. Nat. Bd. Profl. Tchg. Stds., 1992—; cons. early childhood edn., parent edn.; chair com. on early childhood pedagogy NRC, 1998-99. Contbr. articles to profl. jours. Bd. dirs. Ill. Health Edn. Com., 1969-71, Inst. Psychoanalysis, 1970-73, Ill. Adv. Coun. Dept. Children and Family Svcs., 1974-79, Child Devel. Assoc. Consortium, 1979-81, Chgo. Bd. Edn. Desegregation Commn., 1981-84, Bus. People in Pub. Inst., 1980—, High Scope Ednl. Rsch. Found., 1986-93, Gt. Books Found., 1988—, Cmty.-Corp. Sch., 1988-90; with Family Resource Coalition, 1992-96, nat. bd. profl. tchr. stds., 1996—. Mem. Ill. Assn. Edn. Young Children, Nat. Assn. Edn. Young Children (pres. 1980-82), Chgo. Assns. Edn. Young Children (pres. 1973-77), Black Child Devel. Assn., Am. Ednl. Rsch. Assn. Achievements include research on math. teaching and school improvement. Office: Erikson Inst 420 N Wabash Ave Chicago IL 60611-3568

BOWMAN, BILL, state legislator; b. Baker, Mont., May 26, 1946; m. Karen Bowman; 3 children. BS, Dickinson State U. Auctioneer, owner farm implement dealership, Bowman; mem. N.D. Senate from 39th dist., Bismark, 1991—. Mem. human svcs. com.; chmn. agr. com. N.D. State Senate. Recipient Bronze award Vigortone Premix Sales. Mem. N.D. Stockmen's Assn., N.D. Wheat Growers Assn., N.D. Implement Dealers Assn., Rotary. Republican. Home: RR 2 Box 227 Bowman ND 58623-9802

BOWMAN, GEORGE ARTHUR, JR. retired judge; b. Milw., Dec. 1, 1917; s. George Arthur and Edna Oral (Hunter) B.; m. Rose Mary Thorpe, Aug. 8, 1947 (dec. 1980); children: George A. III, Daniel Andrew. Student, U. Wis., 1936-39; JD, Marquette U., 1943. Bar: Wis. 1943, U.S. Supreme Ct. 1943. Asst. dist. atty. Milw. County, 1947-48, children's ct. judge, 1967-72; asst. city atty. City of Milw., 1948-67; adminstrv. law judge Office of Hearing and Appeals Social Security Adminstrn. Dept. HHS, Chgo., 1973-97, adminstrv. law judge emeritus, 1997; pvt. practice, 1997—. Appointed Pres.'s Task Force, Law Enforcement Assistance Adminstrn., 1972; former counsel Milw. Police Dept.; advisor Nat. Council of Juvenile Ct. Judges, Nat. Conv., Atlanta; chmn. conv. com. Nat. Council of Juvenile Ct. Judges, Milw., 1972; chmn. State Task Force on Juvenile Delinquency, 1970-71; legis. com. Wis. Bd. Juvenile Ct. Judges, 1970-71; former mem. numerous legis. coms., Milw.; pioneered Legal Defender System in Children's Ct.; lecturer, Marquette U. Co-author: LEAA Uniform Standards for Police Departments, 1973 (Pres.'s citation). Bd. dirs. Am. Indian Info. and Action Group, Inc. "Project Phoenix", Juneau Acad.; chmn. Milw. County Rep. Party, 1961-62; active supporter numerous community juvenile programs, including Milw. Boys' Club, St. Joseph's Home for Children, Mt. Mary Coll. Proglram for Truant and Delinquent Girls, Operation Outreach, others; Social Security judge. With USN, 1943-46. Recipient Continious Svc. award Office of Hearings and Appeals Soc. Security Adminstr., 1991. Mem. Fed. Assn. Adminstrv. Law Judges, Assn. Office of Hearing and Appeals Adminstrv. Law Judges, Wis. State Bar Assn., Milw. Bar. Assn., Nat. Council Juvenile Ct. Judges, Am. Judicature Soc., Nat. Council of Sr. Citizens, Inc., Internat. Juvenile Officers Assn., Am. Legion (former post comdr.), Nat. Probate Judges Assn., New Trier Rep. Orgn., Committeeman's Club, Hawthorne Turf Club, Sigma Alpha Epsilon. Roman Catholic. Home: 2824 Orchard Ln Wilmette IL 60091-2144

BOWMAN, JAMES EDWARD, physician, educator; b. Washington, Feb. 5, 1923; s. James Edward and Dorothy (Peterson) B.; m. Barbara Taylor, June 17, 1950; 1 child, Valerie June. BS, Howard U., 1943, MD, 1946. Intern Freedmen's Hosp., Washington, 1946-47; resident pathology St. Lukes Hosp., Chgo., 1947-50; chmn. dept. pathology Provident Hosp., 1950-53, Shiraz (Iran) Med. Ctr. Nemazee Hosp., 1955-61; vis. prof., chmn. dept. pathology faculty of medicine U. Shiraz, 1959-61; dir. labs. U. Chgo., 1971-80, prof. dept. pathology, medicine, com. on genetics , biol. scis., collegiate div., 1972-93, dir., 1973-93, prof. emeritus, 1993—. Cons. pathology, div. hosp. and med. facilities HEW, USPHS, 1968; mem. Health and Hosps. Governing Commn., Cook County, 1969-72; mem. exec. com. hemalytic anemia study group NHLI, NIH, Bethesda, Md., 1973-75, Sabbatical fellow Ctr. for Advanced Study in Behavioral Scis., Stanford U., 1981-82, Ethical, Legal & Social Issues, Nat. Human Genome Program NIH/DOE. Contbr. to books and articles to profl. jours. Capt. M.C., AUS, 1953-55. Spl. rsch. fellow NIH Galton Lab., Univ. Coll., London, 1961-62. Mem. Coll. Am. Pathologists, Am. Soc. Clin. Pathologists, Am. Soc. Human Genetics, Cen. Soc. Clin. Rsch., Am. Soc. Hematology, Am. Assn. Phys. Anthropologists, Acad. Clin. Lab. Physicians and Scientists. Home: 4929 S Greenwood Ave Chicago IL 60615-2815 Office: U Chgo Dept Pathology 5841 S Maryland Ave Chicago IL 60637-1463 Fax: 773 285-1549. E-mail: jbowman@midway.uchicago.edu.

BOWMAN, JOHN J. judge; b. Oak Park, Ill., Jan. 13, 1930; 5 children. BS, U. Ill., 1952; JD, John Marshall Law Sch., 1959. Pvt. practice law, 1959-72; state's atty. DuPage County, Ill., 1972-76, circuit judge, 1976-90; presiding judge 2d dist. Ill. Ct. Appeals, Oak Brook Terrace, 1998—2000. With U.S. Army, 1952—54, Japan. Mem.: Alpha Tau Omega.

BOWMAN, LEAH, fashion designer, consultant, photographer, educator; b. Chgo., Apr. 21, 1935; d. John George and Alexandra (Colovos) Murges; m. Veron George Broe, Aug. 31, 1954; 1 child, Michelle; m. John Ronald Bowman, Feb. 28, 1959 Diploma, Sch. of Art Inst., Chgo., 1962. Designer Korach Bros. Inc., Chgo., 1962-65; costume designer Hull House South Theatre, 1966-67, Wellington Theatre, Chgo., 1966-67; from instr. to prof. emeritus Sch. of Art Inst., 1967—2001, prof. emeritus, 2001—. Prodr. fashion performances and style exhbns.; vis. prof., cons. SNDT Women's U., Bombay, 1980, 85, 92, Ctrl. Acad. Arts and Design, Beijing, People's Republic of China, 1987; faculty sabbatical exhbn. Sch. of Art Inst., 1986, 93. Recipient Fulbright award Council for Internat. Exchange for Scholars, India, 1980, Pres. award Art Inst. Chgo., 1991, Honoror's award Sch. of Art Inst. Chgo., 1998. Office: Sch of Art Inst Chgo 37 S Wabash Ave Chicago IL 60603-3002

BOWMAN, LOUIS L. emergency physician; b. Toledo, Nov. 1, 1953; s. Louis J. and Jacquelyn (Perkins) B.; m. Deborah Lynn Hayden, Sept. 30, 1977; children: Heather, Kara, Jason, Benjamin, Michelle. BA in Chemistry, U. Toledo, 1976; DO, Kirksville Coll. Osteo. Med., 1980. Intern Doctor's Hosp., Columbus, Ohio; emergency physician Scioto Emergency Physicians, 1981—; med. dir. emergency medicine Columbis Cmty. Hosp., 1987-92; med. dir. Mid-Ohio Sports Car Course, Lexington, 1988—; med. dir., chmn. dept. medicine Med. Ctr. Hosp., Chillicothe, Ohio, 1995. Fellow Am. Coll. Emergency Physicians; Am. Osteo. Assn., Ohio Osteo. Assn., Columbus Acad. Osteo Medicine, Internat. Coun. Motor Sports Scis. Republican. Methodist. Avocations: golf, photography, travel, weight lifting. Office: Ambulatory Care Affiliates PO Box 292642 Columbus OH 43229-8642

BOWMAN, PASCO MIDDLETON, II, judge; b. Timberville, Va., Dec. 20, 1933; s. Pasco Middleton and Katherine (Lohr) Bowman; m. Ruth Elaine Bowman, July 12, 1958; children: Ann Katherine, Helen Middleton, Benjamin Garber. BA, Bridgewater Coll., 1955; JD, NYU, 1958; LLM, U. Va., 1986; LLD (hon.) , Bridgewater Coll., 1988. Bar: N.Y. 1958, Ga. 1965, Mo. 1980. Assoc. firm Cravath, Swaine & Moore, N.Y.C., 1958—61, 1962—64; asst. prof. law U. Ga., 1964—65, assoc. prof., 1965—69, prof., 1969—70, Wake Forest U., 1970—78, dean, 1970—78; vis. prof. U. Va., 1978—79; prof., dean U. Mo., Kansas City, 1979—83; judge U.S. Ct. Appeals (8th cir.), Mo., 1983—98, 1999—, chief judge, 1998—99. Mng. editor: NYU Law Rev., 1957—58, reporter, chief draftsman: Georgia Corporation Code, 1965—68. Col. USAR, 1959—84. Scholar Fulbright scholar, London Sch. Econs. and Polit. Sci., 1961—62, Root-Tilden scholar, 1955—58. Mem.: Mo. Bar, N.Y. Bar. Office: US Ct Appeals 8th Circuit 10-50 US Courthouse 400 E 9th St Kansas City MO 64106-2607

BOWMAN, ROGER MANWARING, real estate executive; b. Duluth, Minn., Dec. 3, 1916; s. Lawrence Fredrick and Gladys (Manwaring) B.; m. Judith Claypool, Apr. 10, 1942 (dec. 1993); Ann, David, Mary Bowman Johnson, Lawrence II. Attended, U. Mich., 1934-36; student, Wayne State U., 1937. Pres. N. Star Airways, Duluth, 1946-50, North Star Engring. Co., Duluth, 1946-50, Superior (Wis.) Aero, 1946-50, Lawrence F. Bowman Co., Duluth, 1950-70, Gen. Cleaning Corp., Duluth, 1954-92, Bowman Corp., Duluth, 1970-83, Bowman Properties, Duluth, 1983-92; chmn. Deltona Corp., Miami, Fla., 1985-89. Cons. Topeka Group, Duluth, 1985-89; bd. dirs. Parish Corp., Minn. Power, Norwest Bank; chmn. Bowman Properties, 1988-96, Gen. Cleaning Corp., 1985—; mng. gen. ptnr. 6 ltd. partnerships, 1990—. Chmn. St. Louis County Welfare, Duluth, 1964-69, chmn. Govs. Real Estate Adv. Commn., 1968-70; pres. Duluth Devel. Corp., 1960-68; trustee Ordean Found., 1968-92; bd. dirs. Duluth Bd. Realtors, 1958-62; pres. Duluth Bldg. Owners and Mgrs. Assn. Internat., 1963-65. Lt. col. USMCR, 1940-45. Recipient Silver Beaver award Boy Scouts Am., 1959, Mayor's Commendation, City of Duluth, 1976. Mem. Duluth Steam Coop. (bd. dirs. 1970-86), Duluth Bldg. Owners and Mgrs. Internat., Duluth Bd. Realtors, Real Property Adminstrs. Republican. Episcopalian. Clubs: Kitchi Gammi (dir. 1974-78), Northland Country, Boca Raton Resort and Club, Delray Beach Yacht Club. Avocation: cooking. Office: 575 Wells Fargo Ctr Duluth MN 55802 E-mail: rbowman16@aol.com.

BOWMAN, SCOTTY, professional hockey coach; Dir. player devel. Pitts. Penguins, 1991; head coach Detroit Red Wings, 1994—. Achievements include winningest coach in NHL history; 8 Stanley Cup championships. Office: Joe Louis Arena 600 Civic Ctr Dr Detroit MI 48226

BOWMAN, WILLIAM SCOTT (SCOTTY BOWMAN), professional hockey coach; b. Montreal, Sept. 18, 1933; s. John and Jane Thomson (Scott) B.; m. Suella Belle Chitty, Aug. 16, 1969; children— Alicia Jean, David Scott, Stanley Glen, Nancy Elizabeth and Robert Gordon (twins). Student, Sir George Williams Bus. Sch., 1954. Scout exec. Club de Hockey Canadien, Montreal, 1956-66, coach, 1971-79; coach, gen. mgr. St. Louis Blues Hockey Club, 1966-71; coach, gen. mgr., dir. hockey ops. Buffalo Sabres Hockey Club, 1979-86; TV analyst Hockey Night in Can., 1987-90; dir. player devel. Pitts. Penguins Hockey Club, 1990-91, interim head coach, 1991-92, head coach, 1992-93, Detroit Red Wings Hockey Club, 1993—, dir. player pers., 1993—. Recipient Jack Adams award, 1977, 96, Victor award for NHL Coach of Yr., 1993, 96, Stanley Cup Championship, 1997, Lester Patrick award, 2001, Can. Soc. N.Y. award, 2001; named NHL Exec. of Yr. Sporting News, 1979-80, NHL Coach of the Yr. Sporting News, 1995-96, NHL Coach of the Yr. Hockey News, 1976, 77, 93-97, NHL Exec. of the Yr. Hockey News, 1996-97, NHL Coach of the Yr., 1967-68, Hockey News Coach of Yr., 1968, 76, 95-96, Exec. of Yr., 1997; inducted into Hockey Hall of Fame, 1991, Mich. Sports Hall of Fame, 1999, Buffalo Sports Hall of Fame, 2000; holder NHL career regular season records for wins (1,243) and winning percentage (.670); holder NHL career playoffs records for wins (215) and games (341); recipient Stanley Cup as head coach Montreal Canadiens, 1973, 76, 77, 78, 79, Pitts. Penguins, 1992, Detroit Red Wings, 1997, 98; only coach in NHL history to win Stanley Cup with 3 different teams. Office: Detroit Red Wings Joe Louis Arena 600 Civic Center Dr Detroit MI 48226-4419

BOWSER, ANITA OLGA, state legislator, education educator; b. Canton, Ohio, Aug. 18, 1920; d. Nicholas B. Alby and Emile Stobbe. AB, Kent State U., 1945; LLB, William McKinley U., 1949; MS, Purdue U., 1967; MA, U. Notre Dame, 1972, PhD, 1976. Instr. Kent (Ohio) State U., 1945-46; prof. Purdue U. North Cen. Campus, Michigan City, Ind., 1950—; mem. Ind. Ho. Reps., 1980-92, Ind. Senate from 8th dist, 1992—. Mem. Delta Kappa Gamma. Office: Ind State Senate 200 W Washington St Indianapolis IN 46204-2728

BOYCE, DAVID EDWARD, transportation and regional science educator; b. Newark, June 24, 1938; s. Francis Henry and Martha Ann (Neutzel) B.; m. Nani Kulish, 1992; children: Lynn, Susan, Michael, Anna, Gregory. BSCE, Northwestern U., 1961; M in City Planning, U. Pa., 1963, PhD in Regional Sci., 1965. Registered profl. engr., Ohio. Rsch. economist Battelle Meml. Inst., Columbus, Ohio, 1964-66; asst. prof. U. Pa., Phila., 1966-70, assoc. prof., 1970-74, prof., 1974-77; prof. transp. and regional sci. U. Ill., Urbana, 1977-88, Chgo., 1988—. Sr. vis. fellow Brit. Sci. Rsch. Coun., Leeds, Eng., 1972-73; vis. prof. optimization U. Linkoping and Royal Inst. Tech., Sweden, 1983, 96. Co-author: Metropolitan Plan Making, 1970, Optimal Subset Selection, 1974, Regional Science, Retospect and Prospect, 1991, Modeling Dynamic Transportation Networks, 1996; co-editor Environment and Planning, 1979-88; assoc. editor Transp. Sci., 1978-94. Mem. Regional Sci. Assn. (sec. 1969-78, internat. conf. coord. 1978-86, pres. 1987), Informs (transp. sci. coun. 1978-80). Office: U Ill Civil Materials Engring Dep 842 W Taylor St Chicago IL 60607-7021

BOYD, ARTHUR BERNETTE, JR. surgeon, clergyman, beverage company executive; b. Durham, N.C., June 29, 1947; s. Arthur Bernette and Mammie Lee (Chalmers) B.; m. Delphine Victoria Huffman, Mar. 14, 1981; children: Arthur III, Vicki. BA, Fla. A&M Univ., 1969; postgrad., NYU, 1970; MD, Meharry Med. Coll., 1978; postgrad., U. N.C., Chapel Hill, 1998. Cert. ATLS instr., PALS. Intern in surgery Howard Univ. Hosp., Washington, 1978-80; resident and chief resident in surgery St. Luke's Hosp., Cleve., 1981-84; fellow in liver transplant U. Pitts., 1984-85; chief adminstrv. fellow trauma/surg. critical care R.A. Cowley Shock Trauma Ctr., U. Md. Med. Sys., Cali, Colombia, 1993-94, clin. instr. surgery, sr. fellow, traumatologist Baltimore County, 1994—; co-traumatologist Prince George Cmty. Hosp., Cheverly, Md., 1994-95; chief surgeon, pres. Phoenix Med. Surgical Svc., Inc., Cleve., Carribean, 1986—; clin. instr. surgery, sr. trauma fellow Shock Trauma Ctr. U. Md. Med. Ctr., Balt., 1995-96; pres., CEO Motown Beverage Co. of Ohio, Cleve., 1988—, Towne Club Internat. of Ohio, Inc., Cleve., 1988—; pres., CEO, vice chmn. Star Beverage Corp., Shaker Heights, Ohio, 1997; chief adminstrv. fellow in trauma/crit. care R.A. Cowley Shock Trauma Ctr./U. Md. Med. Systems, 1993-94, clin. instr., sr. trauma rsch. fellow, 1994-95; sr. trauma fellow, clin. instr. Shock Trauma Ctr./U. Md., 1995; CEO, pres. Nat. Fin. Group, Inc., Cleve., 1997—; vice chair Star Beverage Corp., 1997. Adj. prof. anatomy and physiology Cuyhoga C.C., Cleve., 1988—; cons. surgeon other hosps. and physicians, Cleve., 1988—; continuing med. educator dept. surgery Case Western Res. U. Sch. Medicine, Cleve., 1997-98; faculty med. bd. profl. preparation course U. Mo., Kansas City, 1997. Inventor: wheelchair with mechanism to raise or lower left or right buttocks of person, hemostat that carries two sutures, synthetic covering with zipper to cover bowel when abdomen unable to be closed after surgery. Vol. Cleve. Community Action Against Addiction, 1987-88; mentor Case Western U. Inner City Program, Cleve., 1988—; judge honors sci. projects Shaker Heights Middle Sch., 1998. Fellow ACS (assoc.), Internat. Coll. Surgeons; mem. AAAS, AMA, N.Y. Acad. Scis., Nat. Med. Assn. (mentor 1990—), Assn. of Black Cardiologists, Ohio State Med. Soc., Cleve. Surg. Soc., Nat. Assn. Small Bus. Owners, Internat. Assn. Small Bus. Owners, Assn. Black Cardiologists, Greater Cleve. Ministers Alliance, Masons, Omega Psi Phi, Alpha Phi Omega. Democrat. Methodist. Avocations: reading, sports, golf. Home and Office: Motown Beverage Co 3277 Lee Rd Cleveland OH 44120-3451 also: Star Beverage Corp Ste 107 20475 Farnsleigh Rd Shaker Heights OH 44122-3850 Fax: 216-283-6143.

BOYD, BARBARA, state legislator; m. Robert Boyd; 1 child, Janine. BS, St. Paul's Coll., 1965. Mem. Ohio Ho. of Reps., Columbus, 1992—. Named Officer of Yr. No. Ohio Police Benevolent Assn., 1989; recipient Black Women's History award, 1992. Mem. LWV, Delta Sigma Theta.

BOYD, BELVEL JAMES, newspaper editor; b. Winnemucca, Nev., May 15, 1946; s. James Connolly and Alice La Ferne (Elliott) B.; m. Carolyn Marie Friesen, Aug. 10, 1968 (div. July 1992); children: David, Christopher, Phillip; m. Jeanette St. John, Oct. 21, 2000. BS in Secondary Edn., Oreg. Coll. Edn., 1968; MA in Journalism, U. Mo., 1974; postgrad., Harvard U., 1979-80. Copy editor, reporter Idaho Statesman, Boise, 1974-76, state editor, 1976-77, editor editl. page, 1977-80; editl. writer Mpls. Tribune, 1980-82; dep. editor editl. page Star Tribune, Mpls., 1982—. Vestryman St. Mark's Cathedral, Mpls., 1983-90. Sgt. U.S. Army, 1968-72, Vietnam. Nieman fellow in journalism Harvard U., 1979-80. Mem. Nat. Conf. Editl. Writers. (chmn. for aff. com. 1997—). Home: 3305 46th Ave S Minneapolis MN 55406-2342 Office: Star Tribune 425 Portland Ave Minneapolis MN 55488-0002 E-mail: boyd@startribune.com.

BOYD, FRANCIS VIRGIL, retired accounting educator; b. Livermore, Iowa, Feb. 1, 1922; s. Ernest and Gertrude (Marley) B.; m. Mary Celeste Cranny, Nov. 6, 1943 (dec. Sept. 11, 1981); children: Kevin, Therese.; m. Elizabeth Haynes Mauer, Oct. 8, 1983. B.A., Iowa State Tchrs. Coll., 1943; M.B.A., Northwestern U., 1948, Ph.D., 1956; LLD honoris causa, Loyola U., Chgo., 1990. C.P.A., Ill. Tchr. accounting Northwestern U., 1946-63; asso. dean Northwestern U. (Sch. Bus.), 1963-66; dean Sch. Bus., Loyola U., 1966-77, prof. acctg., 1977-87, ret., 1987; dir., acad. dean Ctr. Liberal Arts, Loyola U., Rome, 1988-89. Cons., tchr. exec. programs, 1956— ; cons.-evaluator North Central Assn. Colls. and Univs. Author: (with others) Quantitative Controls in Business. Past bd. dirs. Chgo. Crime Commn.; vice chmn. Bd. dirs. Lake Forest Sch. Mgmt.; past mem. faculty adv. bd. Pepsi Cola Mgmt. Inst. Served to lt. (j.g.) USNR, 1943-46. Mem. Am. Inst. C.P.A.'s (past), Econ. Club Chgo., Am. Accounting Assn. (past), Am. Econ. Assn. (past), Beta Gamma Sigma.

BOYD, JOSEPH DON, financial services executive; b. Muncie, Ind., Jan. 22, 1926; s. Joseph Corneluis and Waneta May (Barrett) B.; m. Cynthia Reiley, Dec. 28, 1957; children— Jane Elizabeth, Craig A., Michael J. A.B. (Rector scholar), DePauw U., 1948; M.A., Northwestern U., 1950, Ed.D., 1955. Ednl. asst. First Meth. Ch., Anderson, Ind., 1948-49; residence hall counselor Northwestern U., Evanston, Ill., 1949-50, univ. examiner, instr. edn., guidance lab. asst., 1952-54, dean men, asst. prof. edn., 1955-61; exec. dir. Ill. Scholarship Commn., 1961-80; dir. instnl. relations and research Nat. Coll. Edn., Evanston, 1981-84; pres. Joseph D. Boyd & Assocs., Deerfield, Ill., 1984—. Residence hall dir., head tennis coach, asst. basketball coach Albion Coll., 1950-52 Mem. Nat. Assn. Adminstrs. State Scholarship Programs, Phi Delta Kappa, Delta Tau Delta, Phi Eta Sigma. Methodist. Club: Rotarian. Home: 1232 Warrington Rd Deerfield IL 60015-3145 Office: 600 Deerfield Rd Deerfield IL 60015-3229

BOYD, ROZELLE, retired university administrator, educator; b. Indpls., Apr. 24, 1934; s. William Calvin Sr. and Ardelia Louise (Leavell) B. BA, Butler U., 1957; MA, Ind. U., 1965. Welfare dept. worker Marion County DPW, Indpls., 1956-57; tchr. Crispus Attucks High Sch., 1957-68, adult edn. counselor, 1958-68; asst. dean U. Div., Ind. U., Bloomington, 1968-78, assoc. dean, 1978-82, dir., 1982-98; ret., 1998. Minority leader Indpls. City County Coun.; Dem. nat. committeeman, Dem. Party; mem. coms. Nat. League of Cities. Mem. Alpha Phi Alpha. Presbyterian. Office: Office City-County Council 241 City-County Bldg 200 E Washington St Indianapolis IN 46204-3307

BOYD, WILLARD LEE, academic administrator, educator, museum administrator, lawyer; b. St. Paul, Mar. 29, 1927; s. Willard Lee and Frances L. (Collins) B.; m. Susan Kuehn, Aug. 28, 1954; children: Elizabeth Kuehn, Willard Lee, Thomas Henry. BS in Law, U. Minn., 1949, LLB, 1951; LLM, U. Mich., 1952, SJD, 1962. Bar: Minn. 1951, Iowa 1958. Assoc. Dorsey & Whitney, Mpls., 1952—54; from instr. to prof. law U. Iowa, Iowa City, 1954—64, assoc. dean Law Sch., 1964, v.p. acad. affairs, 1964—69, pres., 1969—81, pres. emeritus, 1981—; pres. The Field Mus., Chgo., 1981—96, pres. emeritus, 1996—. Chmn. Nat. Mus. Scis. Bd., 1988-96. Mem. Nat. Coun. on Arts, Ill. Arts Alliance; past mem. adv. com. Getty Ctr. for Edn. in Arts.; chair bd. dirs. Harry S Truman Libr. Ints., 1997—2001; past adv. bd. Met. Opera; with Ill. Humanities Coun.; adv. com. Ill. Arts. Coun., Chgo. Cultural Affairs Bd. Recipient Charles Frankel prize Nat. Endowment for Humanities, 1989. Mem.: ABA (com. social labor and indsl. legislations 1963—65, chmn. 1965—66, coun. mem. 1975—82, mem. sect. legal edn. and admission to bar chmn. 1980—81, chmn. coun. of sect. on legal edn. and admission), Am. Law Inst., Iowa Bar Assn., Nat. Commn. Accrediting (past pres.), Am. Assn. Univs. (past chmn.). Home: 620 River St Iowa City IA 52246-2433 Office: Univ Iowa Law Sch Iowa City IA 52242-1113

BOYDA, DEBORA, advertising executive; Sr. ptnr., acct. mgr. Tatham Euro RSCG, Chgo., mng. ptnr., 1997-99; v.p., acct. dir. Leo Burnett, 1999-2000, sr. v.p., 2000—. Office: Leo Burnett 35 W Wacker Dr Ste 3710 Chicago IL 60601-1648

BOYE, ROGER CARL, academic administrator, journalism educator, writer; b. Lincoln, Nebr., Feb. 8, 1948; s. Arthur J. and Matilda J. (Danca) B. BA with distinction, U. Nebr., 1970; MS in Journalism with highest distinction, Northwestern U., 1971. News editor The Quill, Chgo., 1971-73; instr. Medill sch. journalism Northwestern U., Evanston, Ill., 1973-76;

vis. prof. journalism Niagara U., Niagara Falls, N.Y., 1976-78; gen. mgr. The Quill, 1980-84, bus. mgr., 1984-86; asst. dean, asst. prof. Medill sch. journalism Northwestern U., 1986-92, asst. dean, assoc. prof., 1992—. Judge various journalism awards and contests, 1970s; master comm. residential coll. Northwestern U., 1989—96. Weekly columnist Chgo. Tribune, 1974-93; contbr. Ency. Britannica Book of the Yr. and the Compton Yearbook, 1982-99; contbg. editor The Numismatist, 2001--. Recipient Maurice M. Gould award Numismatic Lit. Guild, 1981, 92. Mem. Phi Beta Kappa, Kappa Tau Alpha. Office: Northwestern Univ Medill Sch Journalism 1845 Sheridan Rd Evanston IL 60208-0815

BOYER, JEFFREY N. retail executive; BS in Fin. (hons.), U. Ill., 1980. cert. CPA., 1980. Sr. fin. mgmt. Pillsbury Co.; v.p. fin., v.p. fin. planning Kraft Foods, 1989-95; v.p. bus. devel. Diageo PLC, 1995-96; v.p. fin. Sears, 1996-98, v.p., controller, 1998-99, CFO, 1999—. Office: Sears Roebuck & Co 3333 Beverly Rd Hoffman Estates IL 60179

BOYER, JOHN WILLIAM, history educator, dean; b. Chgo., Oct. 17, 1946; s. William Dana and Mary Frances (Corbley) B.; m. Barbara Alice Juskevich, Aug. 24, 1968; children: Dominic, Alexandra, Victoria. BA, Loyola U., 1968; MA, U. Chgo., 1969, PhD, 1975. From asst. prof. to assoc. prof. U. Chgo., 1975-85, prof., 1985—, Martin A. Ryerson Disting. Svc. prof., 1996—, acting dean divsn. social scis., 1992-93, dean of the coll., 1992—. Author: Political Radicalism in Late Imperial Vienna, 1981, Culture and Political Crisis in Vienna, 1995, Three Views of Continuity and Change at the University of Chicago, 1999; editor: Jour. of Modern History. Capt. USAR, 1968-80. Recipient Theodor Körner prize Theodor Körner Found., 1978, John Gilmary Shea prize Am. Cath. Hist. Assn., 1982, Ludwig Jedlicka Meml. prize Kuratorium des Ludwig-Jedlicka-Gedächtnispreises, 1996; Alexander von Humboldt fellow, 1980-81. Mem. Am. Hist. Assn. Roman Catholic. Avocation: cooking. Home: 1428 E 57th St Chicago IL 60637-1838 Office: U Chgo 1126 E 59th St Chicago IL 60637-1580 also: U Chgo Press Jour Divsn 5720 S Woodlawn Ave Chicago IL 60637-1603 E-mail: jwboyer@midway.uchicago.edu.

BOYLAN, ARTHUR J. judge; Judge 8th jud. dist. Minn. Dist. Ct.; magistrate judge U.S. Dist. Ct., Minn., 1996—.

BOYLAN, JOHN LESTER, financial executive, accountant; b. Columbus, Ohio, Aug. 23, 1955; s. James Robert and Ruth Isabella (Capes) B.; m. Susan Marie Stakes, May 21, 1983; children: David, Laura. BBA, Ohio State U., 1977. CPA, Ohio. Staff acct. Deloitte, Haskins & Sells, Columbus, 1977-80, sr. acct., 1980-83, mgr., 1983-86; dir. fin. planning Lancaster Colony Corp., 1986-90, asst. treas., 1987-90, treas., 1990—, CFO, 1997—, dir., 1998—. Mem. Ohio Mfrs. Assn. (dir., treas. 1992—). Office: Lancaster Colony Corp 37 W Broad St Ste 500 Columbus OH 43215-4177

BOYLE, ANNE C. state commissioner; b. Omaha, Dec. 22, 1942; m. Make Boyle; children: Maureen, Michael, James, Patrick, Margaret. Chmn., co-chmn. various polit. campaigns, Omaha, 1974-78; office coord. for U.S. Senator James Exon., 1979-81; corp. and public fundraiser, 1983-85, 88; campaign mgr. pub. rels. firm, 1990-91; pres. Universal Rev. Svcs., 1992—; mem. Nebr. Pub. Svc. Commn., Lincoln, 1996—. Active Clinton for Pres. Campaign, organizer fund raisers, host open house, Omaha, 1992; cons., lobbyist, 1994-95. Former nat. committeewoman Nebr. Young Dems.; chmn. Douglas County Dem. Ctrl. Com.; mem. jud. nominating com. for Douglas County Juvenile Ct.; chmn. inaugural ball invitation com. for gov. of Nebr., 1982; co-chmn. Midwestern Govs. Conf., 1984, Jefferson-Jackson Day Dinner, 1976, 82; del. Dem. Nat. Conv., 1988, 92, 96; mem. Nebr. Rev. com. for Fed. Appts. to U.S. Atty., U.S. Marshall and 8th Dist. Ct. Appeals Fed. Judgeship, 1993-95; mem. Nebr. Dem. Ctrl. Com.; mem. Fin. Com. to Reelect Gov. Ben Nelson; mem. Nebr. Interagy. Coun. on Homeless, President's Adv. Com. on Arts, 1995; Nebr. authorized rep. '96 Clinton-Gore Campaign; Bd. dirs. Bemis Ctr. for Contemporary Arts, Omaha; chmn. Nebr. Dem. Party. Mem. Nat. Assn. Regulatory Utility Commrs. and Mid-Am. Regulatory Commrs. Office: PO Box 94927 Lincoln NE 68509-4927

BOYLE, FRANK JAMES, state legislator; b. Phillips, Wis., Feb. 20, 1945; s. Frank and Mary Boyle; m. Kate Boyle; children: Annie, Patrick. BA, U. Wis., 1967. Former bldg. contractor and constrn. worker. Mgmt. commr. Douling Lake, Wis., 1976—; former county supr. Douglas County Bd.; state assemblyman dist. 73 State of Wis., 1986—; sec. Douglas County Dem. Com.; pres. Tri-Lake Civic Club; v.p. Summit Vol. Fire Dept. Mem. Am. Legion. Home: 4900 E Tri Lakes Rd Superior WI 54880-8637

BOYLE, KAMMER, estate planner; b. New Orleans, June 17, 1946; d. Benjamin Franklin and Ethel Clair (Kammer) B.; m. Edward Turner Barfield, July 23, 1966 (div. 1975); children: Darren Barfield, Meloe Barfield. BS in Mgmt. magna cum laude, U. West Fla., 1976; PhD in Indsl./Organizational Psychology, U. Tenn., 1982. Lic. psychologist, Ohio, Tenn.; reg. securities rep. InterSecurities, Inc., Nat Assn. Securities Dealers. Pvt. practice mgmt. psychology, Knoxville, 1978-81; tchg. and rsch. asst. U. Tenn., 1977-81; mgmt. trainer U.S. State Dept., Washington, 1978; cons. PRADCO, Cleve., 1982-83; pres., cons. Mgmt. and Assessment Svcs., Inc., 1983-90; pres. Kammer Investment Co., 1989-96; fin. advisor O'Donnell Securities Corp., 1997-98. Registered securities prin., investment advisor rep. and retirement specialist Wealth Charter, Inc. of InterSecurities, Inc., 1998--. Mem. editl. rev. bd. Jour. of Managerial Issues, 1987; author and presenter ann. Conf. APA, 1980, Southeastern Psychol. Conf., 1979, ann. Conf. Soc. Indsl./Orgnl. Psychologists, 1987, ann. conf. Am. Soc. Tng. and Devel., 1988. Mem. Jr. League Am., Pensacola, Fla., 1970-75; treas. Bar Aux., Pensacola, 1971. Recipient Capital Gifts Stipend U. Tenn., 1976-80; Walter Bonham fellow, 1980-81. Mem. APA, Cleve. Psychol. Assn., Orgn. Devel. Inst., Acad. of Mgmt., Soc. Advancement Mgmt. (pres. 1974-75), Am. Soc. Tng. and Devel. (chpt. rep. career devel. 1984-86), Cleve. Psychol. Assn. (bd. dirs. 1987-88), Real Estate Investor's Assn. (Cleve., trustee/sec. 1992-94), Mensa. Office: Wealth Charter Co Ste 100 Corp Plz 1 6450 Rockside Woods Blvd S Independence OH 44131

BOYLE, PATRICIA JEAN, retired state supreme court justice; b. Detroit, Mar. 31, 1937; Student, U. Mich., 1955-57; B.A., J.D., Wayne State U., 1963. Bar: Mich. Practice law with Kenneth Davies, Detroit, 1963; law clk. to U.S. Dist. judge, 1963-64; asst. U.S. atty., Detroit, 1964-68; asst. pros. atty. Wayne County, dir. research, tng. and appeals, 1969-74; Recorders Ct. judge City of Detroit, 1976-78; U.S. dist. judge Eastern Dist. Mich., Detroit, 1978-83; assoc. justice Mich. Supreme Ct., 1983-98, ret., 1999. Active Women's Rape Crisis Task Force, Vols. of Am. Named Feminist of Year Detroit chpt. NOW, 1978; recipient Outstanding Achievement award Pros. Attys. Assn. Mich., 1978, 98, Mich. Women's Hall of Fame award, 1986, Law Day award ABA, 1998, Champion of Justice award State Bar Mich., 1998. Mem. Women Lawyers Assn. Mich., Fed. Bar Assn., Mich. Bar Assn., Detroit Bar Assn., Wayne State U. Law Alumni Assn. (Disting. Alumni award 1979) Avocation: reading. Address: 10765 Oxbow Lake Shore Dr White Lake MI 48386

BOYLE, WILLIAM CHARLES, civil engineering educator; b. Mpls., Apr. 9, 1936; s. Robert William and Daphne Jennette (Connell) B.; m. Nancy Lee Hahn, Apr. 11, 1959; children— Elizabeth Lynn, Michele Jenette, Jane Lynette, Robert William CE, U. Cin., 1959, MS in Sanitary Engring., 1960; PhD in Environ. Engring., Calif. Inst. Tech., 1963. Registered profl. engr., Wis., Ohio. With Milw. Sewerage Commn., 1955-56; civil engr. O. G. Loomis & Sons, Covington, Ky., 1956-59; asst. engr. Ohio River Valley Water Sanitation Commn., summer 1959; asst. prof. dept. engring. U. Wis., Madison, 1963-66, assoc. prof., 1966-70, prof. dept. civil and environ. engring., 1970-96, chmn. dept. civil and environ. engring., 1984-86, assoc. chair, 1988-96, emeritus prof., 1996—. Vis. prof. Rogaland Distriktshogskole, Stavanger, Norway, 1975-76; vis. prin. engr. Montgomery Engrs. Inc., Pasadena, Calif., 1988-89; cons. Procter & Gamble Co., Monsanto Co., S.B. Foot Tanning Co., Wis. Canners & Freezers Assn., Wis. Concrete Pipe Assn., Oscar Mayer & Co., Bartlett-Snow, Hide Service Corp., W.R. Grace & Co., Lake to Lake Dairies, Milw. Tallow, Wausau Paper Co., Packerland Packing Co., Ray-O-Vac, U.S. Army CERL, Owen Ayres & Assocs., Donohue Engrs., Davy Engrs., Carl C. Crane, Green Engring., RSE div. Ayres & Assocs., Schreiber Corp. Inc., Sanitaire, J.M. Montgomery, Engrs., Polkowski, Boyle, & Assocs., Rust E&I; mem. peer rev. panel on environ. engring. EPA; accreditation visitor Accreditation Bd. for Engring. and Tech., 1990—. Contbr. articles to profl. jours. Sr. warden St. Andrews Episcopal Ch., Madison, 1972-74, treas., 1979-85 Recipient Engring. Disting. Alumnus award U. Cin., 1986, Founders award U.S.A. nat. com. Internat. Assn. Water Pollution Rsch. & Control, 1988, commendation EPA, 1989; Mills Found. scholar U. Cin., 1954-59; USPHS trainee, U. Cin., 1959-60; fellow Ford Found., Calif. Inst. Tech., 1960-61, USPHS, Calif. Inst. Tech., 1961-63 Mem. ASCE (life, Wis. chpt., advisor U. Wis. student chpt. 1968-71, chmn. student affairs com. 1970-72, chmn. profl. activities com. 1972-74, nat., control mem. tech. council on codes and standards-environ. standards 1999—, chmn. environ. stds. devel. coun. 1998—, chair oxygen transfer standards com., 1975—, com. mem., reviewer EED Jour., Rudolf Hering medal 1975, Engring. Achievement award from Wis. chpt. 1986, Engr. of Yr. award Wis. sect. 1998), Water Environment Fedn. (life, research com., joint task force-pretreatment of wastewater, tech. practice com.-energy in treatment plant design, author chpt. Manual of Practice Design Wastewater Treatment Plants, author chpt. Ops. Manual on Activated Sludge, chmn. program com., bd. control, 1996-98, jour. reviewer, chmn. tech. practice com. task force on aeration, Radebaugh award 1978, Eddy award com. 1992-98, Harrison Prescot Eddy Rsch. medal 1989, chmn. rsch. symposia, Gordon Maskew Fair medal for environ. engring. edn., 1992, Arthur Bedell award 2001), Am. Water Works Assn. (life, chmn. task group on oxygen transfer, editorial bd., Sydney Bedall award for extraordinary svc.), Am. Acad. Environ. Engrs. (diplomate, life, accreditation vis. for Accreditation Bd. Engring and Tech., chmn. edn. com. 1993, trustee 1994-97, pres.-elect 1998, pres. 1999-2000, rep. bd. dirs. ABET, 1994-2000, commr. Engr. Accreditation comm. 2001-, Stanley E. Kappe award 2002), Am. Foundrymen's Soc. (com. on waste disposal, Outstanding Rsch. Paper award environ. cen. div. 1989), Sigma Xi, Theta Tau, Phi Eta Sigma, Chi Epsilon, Tau Beta Pi (advisor U. Wis. student chpt. 1994-96). Episcopalian. Avocations: photography, travel. Home: 105 Carillon Dr Madison WI 53705-4614 Office: Univ Wis 3206 Engineering Hall 1415 Engineering Dr Madison WI 53706-1607 E-mail: boyle@engr.wisc.edu.

BOYNTON, IRVIN PARKER, retired educational administrator; b. Chgo., Mar. 27, 1937; s. Ben Lynn and Elizabeth (Katterjohn) B.; m. Alyce Jane Coyle, Sept. 3, 1964; children: Gregory Allen, Cathy Lynn, Julie Marie, Michael Irvin, Jonathan David. BA, Ohio Wesleyan U., 1959; BS, U. Akron, 1964; MEd, Wayne State U., 1968; counseling endorsement, Siena Heights Coll., 1988. Cert. tchr., Ohio, Mich. Spl. edn. tchr., acting prin. Sagamore Hills Children's Psychiat. Hosp., Cleve., 1961-64; spl. edn. tchr. Fairlawn Ctr., Pontiac, Mich., 1964-68, Walled Lake (Mich.) High Sch., 1968-71; asst. prin. Oakland Tech. Ctr./Southwest Campus, Wixom, Mich., 1971-98; ret., 1998. Mem. spl. needs guideline com. Mich. Dept. Edn., Lansing, 1973-78; keynote speaker Utah Secondary Conf., Salt Lake City, 1978; evaluator North Cen. Accreditation Assn., Waterford, Mich., 1971-73; adv. com. State Tech.Instn. and Rehab. Ctr., Plainwell, Mich., 1978-85. Pres. Roger Campbell Ministries, Waterford, 1987—. Cited as exemplary spl. needs program U. Wis. Mem. ASCD, Am. Vocat. Assn., Mich. Occupational Edn. Assn., Mich. Occupational Spl. Needs Assn. (Outstanding Spl. Needs Educator), Nat. Assn. Vocat. Spl. Needs Personnel (Outstanding Spl. Needs Program 1975), Phi Delta Kappa. Republican. Home: 4901 Juniper Dr Commerce Township MI 48382-1545 E-mail: aiboynton@earthlink.net.

BOYSE, PETER DENT, academic administrator; b. Saginaw, Mich., Mar. 24, 1945; s. John Wesley and Ellen Elizabeth (Dent) B.; m. Barbra Ann Meehan, Sept. 2, 1972; children: Heather, Cassandra. BA, Albion Coll., 1967; MS, U. Mich., 1969, Oreg. State U., 1973, PhD, 1987. Nuclear scientist Westinghouse, Pitts., 1969-71; dir. student activities Calif. State U., Northridge, 1973-74, epic dir., 1974-76; dir. student devel. Linn-Benton Community Coll., Albany, Oreg., 1976-79, ctr. dir., 1979-82, asst. to pres., 1982-88; exec. v.p. Delta Coll., University Center, Mich., 1988—, pres., 1993—. Facilitator Emerging Leaders Inst., Ann Arbor, Mich., 1990. Contbr. articles to profl. jours. Unit chmn. Bay County United Way, Bay City, Mich., 1990; com. mem. South Willamette Rsch. Corridor, Albany, 1988. Mem. Am. Assn. Community and Jr. Colls. (NCSPOD 1990, NCRD 1988, NCRP 1988, NCCR 1988), Partnerships in Edn., Midland C. of C. Leadership (com. mem. 1990), Bus., Union, Govt., Torch Club, Rotary, Phi Kappa Phi, Sigma Pi Sigma, Kappa Mu Epsilon. Avocations: fishing, golf, travel. Office: Delta Coll 1961 Delta Dr University Center MI 48710-0001

BOZIC, MICHAEL C. retail company executive; Formerly pres., COO Sears Canada; chmn., CEO Sears Merchandising Group, Chgo., 1987-91; pres., CEO Hills Stores, 1991-95; vice chmn., chief adminstrv. officer Kmart Corp., 1998—. Office: Sears Roebuck & Co Sears Tower Chicago IL 60606-6306

BOZZOLA, JOHN JOSEPH, botany educator, researcher; b. Herrinn, Ill., Oct. 22, 1946; PhD, So. Ill. U., 1977. Instr. Med. Coll. Pa., Phila., 1976-79, asst. prof. microbiology, 1979-83; dir. Electron Microscopy Ctr./So. Ill. U., Carbondale, 1983—, assoc. prof. botany dept., 1985-93, prof., 1993—. Contbr. rsch. articles on electron microscopy to profl. jours. Recipient Young Investigator award Nat. Inst. Dental Rsch., Washington, 1978. Mem. Microscopy Soc. Am., Am. Soc. Microbiology, Ill. State Acad. Sci., Sigma Xi, Phi Kappa Phi, Kappa Delta Pi. Avocations: photography, bicycling, gardening, painting, computers. Office: So Ill U Ctr for Electron Microscopy Carbondale IL 62901 E-mail: bozzola@siv.edu.

BRACHMAN, RICHARD JOHN, II, financial services consultant, banking educator; b. Madison, Wis., Oct. 30, 1951; s. Richard John and Joan Katherine (Harrington) B.; m. Connie Beth Ten Haken, May 14, 1977; children: Samantha Joan, Richard John. BS, U. Wis., 1974. With The Rural Cos., Madison, 1975-83; v.p. CBI Ins. Svcs., Inc., Middleton, Wis., 1983-84, exec. v.p., 1984-85, pres., 1985-87; sr. v.p. Valley Bank Ins., Madison, 1987-94; pres. Cmty. Life Ins. Co., divsn. Valley Bancorporation, 1987-94; owner, v.p., dir. Lexlawn, Inc., Lexington, Ky., 1993-98; pres., CEO, The Brachman Group, Ltd., Madison, 1994—; owner Midwest Lawn Care, Inc., 2000—. Mem. faculty Iowa Sch. Banking, U. Iowa, 1998—; bd. dirs. Ins. Svcs. Inc., Cmty. Life Ins. Co., Madison, Career Mgmt. Group. Mem. parish coun. Our Lady Queen of Peace Ch., Madison, 1989—; bd. dirs. U. Wis. Meml. Union. Mem. U. Wis. Alumni Assn. (bd. dirs. 1988-94, Spark Plug award 1987), Mendota Gridiron Club (bd. dirs.), KC. Roman Catholic. Avocations: photography, reading, golf. Home and Office: 1217 Tramore Trail Madison WI 53717-1054

BRACKER, CHARLES E. plant pathology educator and researcher; b. Portchester, N.Y., Feb. 3, 1938; married, 1963; 2 children. BS, U. Calif., Davis, 1960, PhD in Plant Pathology, 1964. Rsch. asst. plant pathology U. Calif., Davis, 1960-64; from asst. prof. to assoc. prof., 1964-73; prof. botany and plant pathology dept. Purdue U., West Lafayette, Ind., 1973—, George B. Cummins Disting. prof. mycology. Annual lectr. Mycological Soc. Am., 1991. Recipient Ruth Allen award Am. Phytopathological Soc., 1983. Fellow AAAS; mem. Mycological Soc. Am. (disting. mycologist award 1993), Brit. Mycological Soc., Electronic Micros Soc., Am. Soc. Cell Biology. Achievements include research in fungal ultrastructure and development; developmental cytology; cell wall formation; endomembrane system and organelles; cell growth and reproduction; morphogensis cell ultrastructure. Office: Purdue University Rm 1155 Dept of Botany & Plant Pathology West Lafayette IN 47907

BRADBURY, DANIEL JOSEPH, library administrator; b. Kansas City, Kans., Dec. 7, 1945; m. Mary F. Callaghan, May 10, 1967 (div. 1987); children— Patricia, Tracy, Amanda, Anthony, Sean, m. Jobeth Baile Cannady, Nov. 23, 1988. B.A. in English, U. Mo., Kansas City, 1971; M.L.S., Emporia State U., 1972; LittD, Baker U., 1992. Assoc. dir. extension service Waco-McLennan Library, Tex., 1972-74; library dir. Rolling Hills Consol. Library, St. Joseph, Mo., 1974-77, Janesville Pub. Library, Wis., 1977-83; dir. leisure services City of Janesville, 1982-83; library dir. Kansas City Pub. Library, Mo., 1983—; interim exec. dir. Kansas City Sch. Dist., 1985. Faculty Baylor U., Waco, 1973-74; participant Gov.'s Conf. on Library and Info. Sci., Wis., 1979; mem. council Kansas City Metro Library Network, 1984—, pres., 1987, mem. coordinating bd. for higher edn. library adv. com., 1984—, chmn., 1986-87, pres. 1991—; bd. dirs. Greater Kansas City Coun. Philantrophy. Bd. dirs. Arrowhead Library System, Janesville, 1978-83, Mid-Town Troost Assn., Kansas City, St. John's Sch., Janesville, 1980-83, Pub. Sch. Retirement Fund, Kansas City, 1995—, treas., 1996—; bd. dirs. Jackson County Hist. Soc., 1998—, treas., 1999-2000, v.p.-elect, 2000—. Named Libr. of Yr. Libr. Jour., N.Y.C., 1991; recipient Disting. Grad. award Emporia State U., 1985, Cornerstone award Kansas City Econ. Devel. Corp., 1988, Achievement award U. Mo. Alumni Assn., 2000; Hon. Doctorate, Baker U., 1991. Mem. ALA (various offices 1972—), Am. Soc. Pub. Adminstrs. (bd. dirs. Kansas City chpt. 1994—), Mo. Libr. Assn. (legis. chmn. 1984-85), Libr. Adminstrn. and Mgmt. Assn. (sec. 1983-85), Wis. Libr. Assn. (pres. 1982). Roman Catholic. Lodge: Rotary Home: 3318 Karnes Blvd Kansas City MO 64111-3628 Office: Kansas City Pub Libr 311 E 12th St Kansas City MO 64106-2412

BRADBURY, DOUG, construction company executive; CFO Peter Kiewit Sons, Inc., Omaha. Office: Peter Kiewit Sons Inc 1000 Kiewit Plz Omaha NE 68131

BRADDOM, RANDALL LEE, physician, medical educator; b. Monarch, Va., Oct. 29, 1942; s. Audy Lee and Ruth Janet Braddom; m. Carolyn Lentz (div.); children: Eric C., Steven R., Karen L. BA, DePauw U., 1964; MD, Ohio State U., 1968, MS, 1971. Diplomate Am. Bd. Electrodiagnostic Medicine, Am. Bd. Phys. Medicine and Rehab. Rotating intern Mt. Carmel Hosp., Columbus, Ohio, 1968-69; resident in phys. medicine and rehab. Ohio State Univ. Hosps., 1969-72; physiatrist, electromyographer Rancocas Valley Hosp., Willingboro, N.J., 1972-74, Phila. Naval Med. Ctr., 1972-74; asst. prof. phys. medicine and rehab. U. Cin., 1974-75, assoc. prof., dir. phys. medicine and rehab., 1975-81; med. dir. phys. med. and rehab. St. Francis-St. George Hosp., Cin., 1987-89, Providence Hosp., Cin., 1982-89; assoc. prof., dep. chmn. rehab. medicine Temple U., Phila., 1989-91; chmn. rehab. medicine Albert Einstein Hosp., 1989-91; v.p. med. affairs Moss Rehab. Hosp., 1989-91; practitioner Rehab. Assocs., Indpls., 1991-96; med. dir. Hook Rehab. Ctr., 1991-98; prof., chmn. phys. medicine and rehab. Ind. U. Sch. Medicine, 1991-98; CEO, med. dir. Wishard Health Svcs, 1998-2000. Cons. physiatrist Albert Einstein Med. Ctr. N., Phila., 1973; clin. instr. rehab. medicine Thomas Jefferson Coll. Med., Phila., 1972-74; assoc. in medicine Jewish Hosp., Cin., 1974-89; cons. phys. medicine and rehab. VA Hosp., Cin., 1975-81; dir. phys. med. and rehab. U. Hosps., U. Cin., 1975-81; assoc. clin. prof. phys. med. Ohio State U., Columbus, 1984—; clin. assoc. prof. phys. medicine and rehab. U. Cin., Coll. Medicine, 1982-89; cons. St. Francis Hosp., Indpls., 1991-97; phys. med. and rehab. svc. chief Wishard Meml. Hosp., Indpls., 1991-2000; dir. phys. medicine and rehab. svc. Richard Roudebush VA Hosp., Indpls., 1991-97; presenter Internat. Rehab. Fedn., Montreal, 1968, U. Wash., Seattle, 1972, Thomas Jefferson U. Med. Coll., Phila., 1974, 75, 76, Santa Clara Valley Med. Ctr., San Jose, Calif., 1976, Ohio State U., 1976, Nat. Paraplegia Found., 1977, Am. Acad. Orthopaedic Surgery, New Orleans, 1977, Jewish Hosp., Cin., 1977, Rehab. Inst. Chgo., 1982, 84, Am. Assn. Electromyography and Electrodiagnosis, Toronto, 1984, Las Vegas, 1985, Pitts., 1985, Ky. Family Practice Assn. Symposium, Covington, 1984, Am. Heart Assn., Cin., 1984, Ohio State U. Coll. Medicine, Salt Fork, 1985, Am. Acad. Phys. Medicine and Rehab., Kansas City, 1985, Nat. Spinal Cord Injury Assn., Cin., 1985, Am. Rehab. Edn. Network, Pitts., 1985; presenter in field; vis. prof. Dept. Phys. Medicine and Rehab. U. Ark., 1992, U. Ky. Dept Phys. Medicine and Rehab., 1992, Dept. Internal Medicine Dvsn. Phys. Medicine & Rehab. La. State U. Sch. Medicine, New Orleans, La., 1994, Baylor Coll. Medicine Dept. Physical Medicine & Rehab., 1994, N.J. Sch. Medicine and Dentistry Dept. P.M. & R., lectr. in field; Licht lectr. Dept. Phys. Medicine & Rehab. U. Minn., 1993. Author: (with others) Physical Medicine & Rehabilitation Review, 1980; editor: Sports Medicine and Rehabilitation: A Sport-Scientific Approach, 1994, Physical Medicine and rehabilitation, 1996; contbr. articles to profl. jours. Founder, med. dir. ECCO Family Health Ctr., Inc., Columbus, 1970-72; bd. dirs. Nat. Paraplegia Found., 1975-80; med. adviser Easter Seals Soc. Southwestern Ohio, 1980-82; asst. scoutmaster Troop 291, Boy Scouts Am., 1982-84; chmn. Citizens for Our Schs. Tax Levy Campaign, Forest Hills Sch. Dist., Cin., 1985; trustee Total Living Concepts, Inc., Cin., 1977-85, Disability Svcs. Group, Inc., Cin., 1985-89; bd. examiners The Henry B. Betts award, 1991-94. Lt. comdr. USNR, 1972-74. Recipient Kiwanis Club Citizenship award, Dayton, 1960, Rsch. award Am. Paralyzed Vets. Assn., 1968, Am. Therapeutic Soc., 1968, Landacre Soc. award Ohio State U., 1978, Sidney Licht Lectureship Ohio State U., 1985, Alumni Achievement award Ohio State U., 1993, Sidney Licht Lectureship U. Minn., 1993, Randy Braddom award U. Cin. Coll. Medicine, 1989; named Man of Yr. Columbus Citizen-Jour., 1970, Landwerlen award Muscular Dystrophy Found. Ind., 1994. Mem. Indpls. Med. Soc., Ind. Soc. Phys. Med. and Rehab., Nat. Stroke Assn., Am. Kinesiotherapy Assn. (mem. adv. bd. 1993—), Am. Acad. Phys. Med. and Rehab. (med. edn. com. 1983-86, membership recruitment group 1987, career brochure devel. group 1987, joint annual meeting planning subcom. 1987-88, chairperson continuing med. edn. subcom. 1982-86, sci. program com. 1982-86, mktg. and comms. com. 1987-89, chairperson med. edn. com. 1986-88, sec. bd. govs. 1988-90, third-mem.-at-large 1990-91, 2nd mem.-at-large 1991-92, 1st mem.-at-large 1992-93, chair awards com. 1992-93, v.p. 1994-95, fin. com. 1994-95, chair annual meeting task force 1994-95, pres. elect 1994-95, pres. 1995-96, past pres. 1996-97, Disting. Clinician award 1997), Am. Assn. Electrodiagnostic Medicine (com. on edn. 1974-76, exam. com. 1975-76, liaision to assn. of acad. physiatrists 1988, chairperson courses com. 1986-89, pres.-elect 1989-90, bd. dirs. 1989-92, pres. 1990-91, immediate past pres.-chairperson long-range planning com. 1991-92, chmn. long range planning com. 1991-92, alt. del. AMA House of Dels. 1993-95, nominating com. 1993-94, chmn. 1994-95), Am. Assn. Electrodiagnostic Medicine, Assn. Acad. Physiatrists, Ohio State Med. Alumni Assn., AMA, Am. Bd. Electrodiagnostic Medicine (bd. dirs. 1994, long-range planning com. 1994, treas. 1995-98), Cin. Soc. of Phys. Medicine and Rehab. (pres., founder 1987-88), Internat. Med. Med. Assn. (U.S. counselor 1986-95). Office: IU Sch Medicine Dept PM&R Clin Bldg Rm 368 541 Clinical Dr Indianapolis IN 46202-5233 Fax: 317-278-0206. E-mail: rbraddom@earthlink.net.

BRADEN, BERWYN BARTOW, lawyer; b. Pana, Ill., Jan. 10, 1928; s. George Clark and Florence Lucille (Bartow) B.; m. Betty J.; children— Scott, Mark, Mathew, Sue, Ralph, Ladd, Brad Student, Carthage Coll., 1946-48, U. Wis., 1948-49, J.D., 1959. Bar: Wis. 1959, U.S. Supreme Ct.

1965. Ptnr. Genoar & Braden, Lake Geneva, Wis., 1959-63; individual practice law, 1963-68, 72-74; ptnr. Braden & English, 1968-72, Braden & Olson, Lake Geneva, 1974—. City atty. City of Lake Geneva, 1962-64; tchr. Law Sch., U. Wis., 1977 Bd. dirs. Lake Geneva YMCA. Mem. ABA, Walworth County Bar Assn. (pres. 1962-63), State Bar Wis. (chmn. conv. and entertainment com. 1979-81, chmn. adminstrn. Justice and Judiciary com., 1986-87, bench bar rels. com., 1987-90, mem. exec. com. Wis. Bicentennial Com. on Constn.), Wis. Acad. Trial Lawyers (sec. 1975, treas. 1976, dir. 1977-79), Assn. Trial Lawyers Am. Home: 1031 W Main St Lake Geneva WI 53147-1700 Office: 716 Wisconsin St Lake Geneva WI 53147-1826 also: PO Box 940 Lake Geneva WI 53147-0940 E-mail: bando@genevaonline.com.

BRADEN, JAMES DALE, former state legislator; b. Wakefield, Kans., Aug. 2, 1934; s. James Wesley and Olive (Reed) B.; m. Naomi Carlson, July 3, 1952 (div. Jan. 1982); children: Gregory, Michael, Ladd, Amy; m. Margie Clark Tidwell, Sept. 17, 1983; stepchildren: Richard, Lon, Dale. Grad. high sch., Wakefield. CLU, The Am. Coll. Meat cutter, Wakefield, 1952-64; ins. agt., securities broker Braden Fin. Svcs., Clay Ctr., Kans., 1964—; state rep. Kans. Ho. of Reps., Topeka, 1974-91, house majority leader, 1985-87, speaker of the house, 1987-91. Past chmn. econ. devel. com. Nat. Conf. State Legislatures, legis. coordinating council, calendar and printing com.; past chmn. assessment and taxation com.; mem. Council of State Govts. intergovtl. affairs com.; past chmn. taxation task force of Midwestern Conf. of Council State Govts.; chmn. Interstate Cooperation Commn.; former mem. State Fin. Council, Kans. Inc.; past chmn. Legis. Commn. on Kans. Econ. Devel.; past mem. Kans. Pub. Agenda Commn. Active St. Paul's Episcopal Ch., Clay Ctr.; mem. Rep. Party Exec. Com. Mem. NALU, Kans. Assn Life Underwriters (past pres.), Million Dollar Round Table (life), Rotary, Masons, Shriners, Elks. Episcopalian. Avocations: hunting, fishing, flying, sailing. Home: PO Box 58 Clay Center KS 67432-0058 Office: Braden Fin Svcs 1101 5th St # 58 Clay Center KS 67432-2021 E-mail: jbraden@kansas.net.

BRADING, CHARLES RICHARD, state representative; b. Lima, Ohio, Feb. 19, 1935; s. Richard H. Brading; m. Sandra Berry, June 26, 1963; children: William, Sarah, Amanda. BS in Pharmacy, Ohio No. U., 1957. From employee to owner Rhine and Brading Pharmacy, Wapakoneta, Ohio, 1958-92; state rep. State of Ohio, Columbus, 1991—. Bd. dirs. Wapakoneta Indsl. Devel. Inc.; mem. Wapakoneta City Coun., 1964-66, pres. 1974-75, 86-88; mayor of Wapakoneta, 1988-91. With U.S. Army, 1958-59, 61-62. Recipient Disting. Svc. award Wapakoneta Area Jaycee, 1965, Bowl of Hygeia award 1973, Retailer of Yr. 1978, Outstanding Achievement in Profession of Pharmacy award Merck, Sharp & Dohme 1991, Significant Contbn. to Profession of Pharmacy Beal award 1992, Alumni award Ohio No. U., 1993. Mem. Am. Pharm. Assn., Nat. Assn. Retail Druggists, Nat. Assn. Bds. of Pharmacy, Ohio State Pharm. Assn. (chmn. legis. com. 1971, chmn. bd. Pharmacy Replacement com. 1985), No. Ohio Pharm. Assn. (pres. 1969), Ohio State Bd. Pharmacy (apptd. 1976-84, pres. 1979-80), Wapakoneta C. of C., Auglaize County Hist. Soc., Elks, Eagles, Am. Legion, Masons, Shriners, Rotary Club (pres. 1971, Paul Harris fellow). Republican. Home: 1216 Oakridge Ct Wapakoneta OH 45895-9464

BRADLEY, ANN WALSH, state supreme court justice; married; 4 children. BA, Webster Coll., 1972; JD, U. Wis., 1976. Tchr. HS; pvt. law practice; former judge Marathon County Circuit Ct., Wausau, Wis.; justice Wis. Supreme Ct., Madison, 1995—. Office: Wis Ct Sys PO Box 1688 Madison WI 53701-1688*

BRADLEY, BOB, professional soccer coach; b. Montclair, N.J., Mar. 3, 1958; B.History, Princeton U.; M.Sports Adminstrn., Ohio U. Head coach soccer Ohio U., Athens, 1980-81; asst. coach U. Va., 1982-83; head coach Princeton U., 1984-95; asst. coach D.C. United, 1995-97; head coach Chgo. Fire, 1997—. Named Major League Soccer's 1998 All Sport Coach of the Yr., NCAA Divsn. I Men's Coach of the Yr., 1993. Office: Chicago Fire # 1998 980 N Michigan Ave Chicago IL 60611-4501

BRADLEY, FRAN, state legislator; b. June 13, 1942; m. Mary Knofczynski, Aug. 31, 1963; 4 children. BSME, S.D. State U.; postgrad., U. Minn. Engr., mgr. IBM; rep. Dist. 30A Minn. Ho. of Reps., 1994—. Office: 100 Constitution Ave Saint Paul MN 55155-1232

BRADLEY, KIM ALEXANDRA, sales and marketing specialist; b. Glen Cove, N.Y., Aug. 27, 1955; d. Harold William and Helen Doris (Rosenthal) Shepard; m. Gary Morgan Bradley, Oct. 2, 1982; children: Hunter Morgan, Parker Davis, Preston Carter. BS, U. Ill., 1977. Media estimator Lee King & Ptnrs., Chgo., 1977-78; asst. buyer Grey North Advt., 1978; broadcast negotiator J. Walter Thompson, 1978-80; acct. exec. Katz Communications, Inc., 1980-84, sales mgr., 1984-88, v.p. sales mgr., 1988-93; prin., pres. The Encore Group, Inc., 1993; pres., owner Bradley Mktg. Group, Northbrook, Ill., 1993—. Mem. mktg. com., bd. dirs. Child Abuse Prevention Svcs.; alliance mem. Art Inst. of Chgo.; vol. Infant Welfare Soc.; aux. bd. dirs. Juvenile Protection Assn. Mem.: Nat. Bur. Profl. Mgmt. Cons. (cert. profl. cons. to mgmtl.), Nat. Assn. Women Bus. Owners, Am. Mktg. Assn., Inst. Mgmt. Cons., Am. Mgmt. Assn., Broadcast Advt. Club (bd. dirs., v.p., exec. v.p., pres., chair for Child Abuse Prevention Svcs. charity com.). Home: 30 Barnswallow Ln Lake Forest IL 60045-2984 Fax: 847-412-9401. E-mail: kbradley@bradleymarketing.com.

BRADLEY, SISTER MYRA JAMES, health science facility executive; b. Cin., Feb. 1, 1924; d. John Joseph and Mary (McMannus) B. BS in Edn., Atheneum Ohio, 1950; BS in Nursing, Mt. St. Joseph Hosp., 1954; MHA, St. Louis U., 1959; LHD (hon.), Coll. Mt. St. Joseph, Cin., 1993; HHD (hon.), Xavier U., 1993. RN, Ohio. Mem. faculty U. Dayton, Ohio, 1955-57, Good Samaritan Hosp., Dayton, 1955-57; asst. adminstr. St. Mary-Corwin Hosp., Pueblo, Colo., 1960; adminstr. St. Joseph Hosp., Mt. Clemens, Mich., 1960-65; pres., chief exec. officer Penrose Hosp., Colorado Springs, Colo., 1965-90, Penrose-St. Francis Cath. Healthcare, Colorado Springs, 1987-91; pres., CEO Good Samaritan Hosp., Cin., 1991—. Recipient Bus. Citizen of Yr. award Colo. Springs C. of C., 1990, Disting. Svc. award U. Colo., 1983, Civic Princeps award Regis Coll., Colorado Springs, 1984, Elizabeth Ann Seton nursing award for excellence dept. nursing Penrose Hosp. and Penrose Community Hosp., 1987, Sword of Hope Am. Cancer Soc., 1988; named woman of Distinction Soroptimist Internat., 1988. Mem. Cath. Hosp. Assn., Am. Hosp. Assn., Colo. Hosp. Assn. (trustee), Nat. Coun. Community Hosps. (trustee), Am. Coll. Hosp. Adminstrs., Healthcare Forum (trustee), Downtown Rotary Club. Office: Good Samaritan Hosp 375 Dixmyth Ave Cincinnati OH 45220-2489

BRADLEY, RICHARD EDWIN, retired college president; b. Omaha, Mar. 9, 1926; s. Louis J. and Betsy (Winterton) B.; m. Doris I. McGowan, June 8, 1946; children— Diane, Karen, David. Student, Creighton U., 1946-48; B.S.D., U. Nebr., 1950, D.D.S., 1952; M.S., State U. Iowa, 1958. Instr. State U. Iowa, 1957-58; asst. prof. Creighton U., 1958-59; asst. prof., chmn. dept. periodontics U. Nebr., 1959-62, assoc. prof., 1962-65, prof., 1965-67; assoc. dean Coll. Dentistry, 1967-68, dean, 1968-80; pres. Baylor Coll. Dentistry, 1980-90, pres., dean emeritus, 1990—; clin. prof. Coll. Dentistry U. Nebr. Med. Coll., Lincoln, 1990—; cons. dental edn., 199-93. Mem. Commn. A, Coun. on Dental Edn., 1986-93; pres. Am. Assn. Dental Schs., 1977-78; mem. nat. adv. com. on health professions edn. Dept. Health and Human Resources, 1982-86; pres. Am. Fund for Dental Health, 1986-87. Editor: The New Dentist, 1992-94; contbg. editor Orban's Textbook of Periodontics, 1963; contbr. Clark's Clin., 1980. Mem. bd. visitors Temple U. Sch.Dentistry, 2001--. Served with USNR, 1944-46. Fellow AAAS, Internat. Coll. Dentists; mem. ADA, Am. Acad. Periodontology Found. (bd. dirs., pres. 1994-96), Am. Coll. Dentists (regent 1992-96, v.p. 1997-98, pres. Found. 2000-01), Sigma Xi, Omicron Kappa Upsilon. Home: 6831 Northridge Rd Lincoln NE 68516-2955 Office: U Nebraska Coll Dentistry Lincoln NE 68583-0740

BRADLEY, THOMAS A. insurance company executive; With St. Paul Cos., Inc., St. Paul, sr. v.p. fin., CFO, 2001—. Office: Saint Paul Companies Inc 385 Washington St Saint Paul MN 55102 Office Fax: (651) 310-8294.

BRADLEY, WALTER A., III, utilities company executive; Chief info. officer, v.p. Northwestern Corp., Sioux Falls, S.D. Office: Northwestern Corp 125 S Dakota Ave Sioux Falls SD 57104

BRADLEY, WALTER JAMES, emergency physician; b. Chgo., July 6, 1956; s. Walter James and Anna L. (Barbee) B. BS, Augsburg Coll., 1978; MD, U. Ill., 1984; MBA, U. South Fla., 1995. Diplomate Am. Bd. Emergency Medicine. Flight physician Flight for Life Milw. County Regional Med. Ctr., 1985-90; med. dir. PALS program Trinity Med. Ctr., Moline, Ill., 1990—. Edn. dir. Sinai-Samaritan Med. Ctr., 1988-90, EMS dir., 1987-90; paramedic base sta. physician Milw. County Regional Med. Ctr., 1985-90; pres. Emergency Medicine Mgmt. & Diagnostics, Trinity Med. Ctr., 1990—, dir. EMS svcs., 1990—, dir. regional trauma ctr., 1995—; state med. dir. Basic Traum Life Support, 1994—; pres., COO Trinity Ambulance, Inc.; pres., CEO Emergency Medicine Mgmt. and diagnostics, 1995—. Fellow Am. Coll. Emergency Physicians; mem. AMA, Am. Coll. Emergency Physicians, Am. Coll. Physician Execs., Nat. Assn. Managed Care Physicians, Nat. Assn. Emergency Med. Svcs. Physicians. Office: Trinity Med Ctr 2701 17th St Rock Island IL 61201-5351 E-mail: bradleyw@trinityqc.com.

BRADLEY, WILLIAM STEVEN, art museum director; b. Salina, Kans., Aug. 20, 1949; s. William Bernard and Jane Ray (Gebhart) B; m. Kathryn Mann, Mar. 18, 1972; children: Kate, Christina, Megan, Emma, Drew. BA, U. Colo., 1971; MA, Northwestern U., 1974, PhD, 1981. Instr. Wells Coll., Aurora, N.Y., 1979-81; curator, asst. prof. Tex. Tech. U. and Mus., Lubbock, Tex., 1982-85; chief curator San Antonio Mus. Art, 1985-86; dir. Alexandria (La.) Mus. Art, 1987-92, Davenport (Iowa) Mus. Art, 1992—. Vis. lectr. Cornell U., Ithaca, N.Y., 1980-81; cons. Am. Assn. Mus., Washington, 1989—. Author: Emil Nolde, 1986; editor: (catalog) Elemore Morgan, 1992, Emery Clark, 1989; reviewer Inst. Mus. Svcs., 1985-90. V.p. La. Assn. Mus., Baton Rouge, 1988, 90. Office: Davenport Mus Art 1737 W 12th St Davenport IA 52804-3596 E-mail: Wm549@aol.com.

BRADSHAW, BILLY DEAN, retired retail executive; b. Decatur, Ill., June 25, 1940; s. Lester H. and Gertrude (Davis) B.; children: Deborah, Amanda. Grad., Lakeview High Sch., Decatur, Ill., 1959. Retail div. supr. Schnepps Assocs., Decatur, 1964-74; store mgr. Firestone Tire & Rubber Co., 1975—, ret., 2001. Coach Decatur's Boys Baseball, 1965-69. With USAF, 1960-64. Mem. Am. Motorcyclist Assn., Tennessee-Squire, Am. Legion. Avocations: boating, golf. Home: 24 Lake Grove Clb Decatur IL 62521-2321 Office: Firestone Store 2605 N 22nd St Decatur IL 62526-4745

BRADSHAW, CONRAD ALLAN, lawyer; b. Campbell, Mo., Dec. 22, 1922; s. Clarence Andrew and Stella (Cashdollar) B.; m. Margaret Crassous Sanderson, Dec. 31, 1959; children— Dorothy A., Lucy E., Charlotte L. A.B., U. Mich., 1943, J.D., 1948. Bar: Mich. bar 1948. Since practiced in Grand Rapids with firm Warner, Norcross & Judd. Served to lt. USNR, 1943-46. Mem. Am. Bar Assn., State Bar Mich. (chmn. corp., fin. and bus. law sect. 1976), Grand Rapids Bar Assn. (pres. 1970) Home: 3261 Lake Dr SE Grand Rapids MI 49506-4320 Office: 900 Fifth Third Ctr 111 Lyon St NW Grand Rapids MI 49503

BRADSHAW, JEAN PAUL, II, lawyer; b. May 12, 1956; married; children: Andrew, Stephanie. BJ, JD, U. Mo., 1981. Bar: Mo. 1981, U.S. Dist. Ct. (we. dist.) Mo. 1982, U.S. Dist. Ct. (so. dist.) Ill. 1988, U.S. Ct. Appeals (8th cir.) 1986, U.S. Supreme Ct. 1987. Assoc. Neale, Newman, Bradshaw & Freeman, Springfield, Mo., 1981-87, ptnr., 1987-89; U.S. atty. we. dist. Mo. U.S. Dept. Justice, Kansas City, 1989-93; of counsel Lathrop & Gage, 1993-99, mem., 2000—. Named Spl. Asst. Atty. Gen. State of Mo., 1985-89; mem., chmn. elect U.S. Atty. Gen.'s adv. com., office mgmt. and budget subcom., sentencing guidelines subcom. Chmn. Greene County Rep. cen. com., 1988-89; pres. Mo. Assn. Reps., 1986-87; bd. dirs. Greene County TARGET, 1984-89; mem. com. on resolutions, family and community issues and del. 1988 Rep. Nat. Conv.; mem. platform com. Mo. Reps., 1988; chmn. Greene County campaign McNary for Gov., 1984, co-chmn. congl. dist. Dole for Pres., 1988, regional chmn. Danforth for Senate, 1988, co-chmn. 7th congl. dist. Webster for Atty. Gen., 1988; county chmn. U. Mo.-Columbia Alumni Assn., 1985-87; bd. dirs. Springfield Profl. Baseball Assn., Inc.; past mem. Mo. Adv. Coun. for Comprehensive Psychiat. Svcs., former bd. dirs. Ozarks Coun. Boy Scouts Am.; pres. bd. trustees St. Paul's Episcopal Day Sch., 1997—. Named Outstanding Recent Grad. U. Mo.-Columbia Sch. Law, 1991. Mem. ABA, Mo. Bar Assn., Kansas City Met. Bar Assn., U. Mo.-Columbia Law Sch. Alumni Assn. (v.p. 1988-89, pres. 1990-91), Law Soc. U. Mo.-Columbia Law Sch. Office: 2345 Grand Blvd Ste 2800 Kansas City MO 64108-2612 E-mail: jpbradshaw@rathropgage.com.

BRADTKE, PHILIP JOSEPH, architect; b. Chgo., Aug. 13, 1934; s. Felix Anthony and Frances Agnes (Mach) B.; m. Diane Gloria Westol, Oct. 19, 1963 (div. July 1987); children: Michael, Christine; m. Catherine Adler, Nov. 25, 1989. BArch cum laude, U. Notre Dame, 1957. Registered architect, Ill. Project architect Belli & Belli, Chgo., 1957-64; project mgr., v.p. A.M. Kinney Assoc., Inc., Evanston, Ill., 1964-80, v.p., pres., 1987-96; v.p., sr. assoc. Kober/Belluschi Assoc., Chgo., 1980-87; archtl. divsn. mgr., v.p. Patrick Engring. Inc., Glen Ellyn, Ill., 1996—. Lectr. U. Notre Dame, 1975. Commr. bldg. dept. Village of Glenview, Ill., 1980-83, commr. appearance commn., 1983—. Recipient Hon. Mention award Beaux Arts Inst. Design, 1955, 1st prize award Ch. Property and Adminstrn. Mag., 1956, 1st Mention award Indpls. Home Show Archtl. Competition, 1956, Hon. Mention award, 1959, Modernization Excellence award Bldgs. Mag., 1985. Mem. AIA (corp., housing com. 1968, chmn. honor awards com., 1973, treas., 1975-76), Notre Dame Club, Glenview Shoreline Tennis Team (capt. 1976—). Roman Catholic. Avocations: tennis, golf, basketball. Home: 1441 Canterbury Ln Glenview IL 60025-2252

BRADY, DANIEL R. state legislator; b. Oct. 7, 1953; m. one child. BA, OH U. Mem. Cleveland City Coun., 1986-96, Ohio Ho. of Reps., Columbus, 1995-98, Ohio Senate from 23rd dist., Columbus, 1999—. Democrat. Office: State House 23rd Dist Senate Bldg Columbus OH 43215

BRADY, EDMUND MATTHEW, JR. lawyer; b. Apr. 24, 1941; s. Edmund Matthew and Thelma (McDonald) B.; m. Marie Pierre Wayne, May 14, 1966; children: Edmund Matthew III, Meghan, Timothy BSS, John Carroll U., 1963; JD, U. Detroit, 1966; postgrad., Wayne State U., 1966-69; DHL (hon.), U. Detroit, 1998. Bar: Mich. 1966, U.S. Dist. Ct. (ea. dist.) Mich. 1966, U.S. Ct. Appeals (6th cir.) 1973, U.S. Supreme Ct. 1974. Sr. ptnr. Vandeveer & Garzia, 1973-90, Plunkett & Cooney, P.C., 1990—. Village clk. Grosse Pointe Shores, Mich., 1975-80; trustee St. John Hosp. and Med. Ctr., Detroit, 1992-2000, chmn., 1994-2000, Grosse Pointe Acad., Mich., 1977-83, adv. trustee, 1983-89; vice chmn. St. John Physicians Hosp. Orgn., 1994-95; supr. Grosse Pointe Twp., 1994-2000, trustee, 1989-2000; pres., dir. Grosse Pointe Hockey Assn., 1969-70; bd. dirs., chmn. maj. gifts divsn. 1st Fund, St. John Hosp. Guild; bd. dirs., pres. Friends of Bon Secours Hosp.; trustee, mem. exec. com., mem. fin. com. St. John Health Sys., 1998-2000. Recipient award of distinction U. Detroit Law Alumni, 1981, Michael Franck award State Bar of Mich. Rep. Assembly, 1998, Respected Advocate award Mich. Trial Lawyers Assn., 1998. Fellow Am. Bar Found, Mich. State Bar Found. (life); mem. ABA, Am. Coll. Trial Lawyers, Inter. Soc. Barristers, Am. Bd. Trial Advocates, Internat. Assn. Def. Counsel, Assn. Def. Trial Counsel (dir. 1975-80, pres. 1980-81), Mich. Def. Trial Counsel (dir. 1980-81), Def. Rsch. Inst. (Exceptional Performance citation 1981), Cath. Lawyers Soc., Soc. Irish-Am. Lawyers (founding dir. 1979-81), Mich. Soc. Health Law Attys., Mediation Tribunal Assn. (mem. panel Wayne County, Macomb County mediator 1989-98), Detroit Bar Assn. (dir. 1986-91, sec.-treas. 1988, pres.-elect 1989-90, pres. 1990-91), State Bar Mich. (commr. 1991-98, treas. 1994, v.p. 1995, pres.-elect 1996, pres. 1997-98), Country Club of Detroit, Detroit Athletic Club, Delta Theta Phi. Republican. Roman Catholic. Office: Plunkett & Cooney 535 Griswold St Ste 2400 Detroit MI 48226 E-mail: ebrady@plunkettcooney.com.

BRADY, JAMES S. lawyer; b. Grand Rapids, Mich., Sept. 17, 1944; s. George Joseph and Emily Mae (Sherman) B.; m. Catherine Ann Yared, Aug. 6, 1966; children: Monica Rose, Michael George, Paul Samuel. B.S., Western Mich. U., 1966; J.D., U. Notre Dame, 1969. Bar: Mich. 1969. Asso. Roach, Twohey, Maggini & Brady (and predecessors), 1969-77, partner, 1972-77; U.S. atty. Western Dist. Mich., Grand Rapids, 1977-81; mem. firm Miller, Johnson, Snell & Cummiskey, 1981—, chmn. litigation sect., 1992-99. Mem. teaching faculty Nat. Inst. Trial Advocacy, 1979-80, Inst. Continuing Legal Edn., 1980, trial skills U. Mich.; adj. prof. Cooley Law Sch., Lansing, Mich.; chmn. bd. trustees Western Mich. U. Pres. Grand Rapids Jaycees, 1975-76; legal counsel Mich. Jaycees, 1976-77; pres. Villa Elizabeth Adv. Bd., 1977-79; bd. dirs. Legal Aid and Defender Soc., 1970-77; mem. planning council Grand Rapids United Way, 1976-80, chmn. standing com., 1975-77; mem. adv. com. Kent County Sheriff's Dept., 1975-77; bd. dirs. Cath. Social Services; chmn. bd. Jr. Achievement. Recipient Disting. Service award Grand Rapids Jaycees, 1978 Mem. ABA, Fed. Bar Assn., Mich. Bar Assn., Grand Rapids Bar Assn. (dir. 1973-74, found. com., pres.), State Bar Mich. (criminal jurisprudence com., spl. com. law and media), Am. Trial Lawyers Assn. Roman Catholic. Clubs: Peninsular, Blythefield, Grand Rapids Press. Office: 800 Calder Plaza Bldg Grand Rapids MI 49503

BRADY, TERRENCE JOSEPH, judge; b. Chgo., Dec. 24, 1940; s. Harry J. and Othele R. Brady; m. Debra René, Dec. 6, 1969; children: Tara René, Dana Rose. BA cum laude, Coll. St. Thomas, 1963; JD, U. Ill., 1968. Bar: Ill. 1969, U.S. Dist. Ct. (no. dist.) Ill. 1970, U.S. Ct. Appeals (7th cir.) 1971. Pvt. practice, Crystal Lake, Ill., 1969-70, Waukegan, 1970-77; assoc. judge 19th Jud. Cir., Ill. Cir. Ct., 1977—. Lectr. Ann. Ill. Assoc. Judge Seminars, Statewide Ill. Traffic Conf., 1982, Lake County Bar Assn. Seminar, 1983, 88, others; invited participant Law and Econs. Seminar, U. Kans., 2000; mem. vis. jud. faculty Nat. Jud. Coll., U. Nev. Reno, 1997, condr. seminar civil mediation, 1999; presenter, lectr. in field; materials author, lectr. Pretrials and Negotiations Statewide Jud. Seminar, 1997; mem. long range planning com. 19th Jud. Circuit, Lake County, Ill., 1999; author, lectr. seminars in field. Author: Settle It, 1998; mem. editl. bd. The Docket; contbr. articles to profl. jours. Served with U.S. Army, 1963-64, 68-69. Mem. ISBA (bench and bar sect. coun., adv. polls com.), LCBA (civil trial, med., legal coms.), Ill. Bar Assn. (com. on jud. adv. polls 1994—, vice-chair adv. polls 1998, task force on domestic violence 1998—, chair jud. adv. polls, 1999, sec. com. on jud. adv. polls 1997-99, bench and bar coms., judicial polls), Ill. Judges Assn. (bd. govs.), Ill. Bar Found., Lake County Bar Assn. (seminar materials author and lectr. 1997, 98, 99, 2000), Libertyville Racquet Club, Am. Inns of Ct. Avocations: tennis, golf, writing, reading. Office: Lake County Courthouse 18 N County St Waukegan IL 60085-4304 E-mail: tbrady@co.lake.il.us.

BRADY, WILLIAM E. state legislator; m. Nancy Brady; children: Katie, William, Duncan. Grad., Ill. Wesleyan U., 1983. Founder, pres., oper. officer Brady Weaver Realtors/Better Homes & Gardens, 1984—, Brady Property Mgmt., 1984—; co-founder, sec. Brady & Assocs. Constrn. & Devel., 1986—; pres. Decade 200 Mortgage Svcs., Inc., 1991—; mem. from 88th dist. Ill. Ho. of Reps. Bd. dirs. YMCA, 1990—; v.p. bd. dirs. Ctrl. Cath. H.S. Found., 1980-94; mem. Rep. Ctrl. Com., 1986—; active in polit. campaigns of Ed Madigan and Jim Edgar. Mem. Bloomington/Normal Assn. Realtors (bd. dirs. 1990—), Bloomington/Normal Homebuilders Assn., McLean County Young Reps. (bd. dirs. 1986—), McLean County C. ofC. (bd. dirs. 1987-90, sec. 1990-91). Office: 2203 Eastland Dr Ste 3 Bloomington IL 61704-7924 Home: 1202 Elmwood Rd Bloomington IL 61701-3319

BRADY, WILLIAM ROBERT, former United States senator; b. Parsons, Kans., May 25, 1956; s. William Frances and Mary (Hemmer) B.; m. Nancy Brady. AA, Labette Cmty. Coll., 1975; BA, Pitts. State U., 1977, MS, 1981. Former atty. Maloney, Hedman & Assocs.; mem. Kans. Ho. of Reps., Topeka, 1981-90, mem. edn. com., agenda chmn., house leader; mem. U.S. Senate from Kans., Washington, 1991-97. Owner, floral and greenhouse. Active Patrick's Parish Coun.; bd. dirs. Youth Coun. Shelter. Mem. Parsons C. of C., Lions, Rotary (citizenship scholar Parsons 1974). Democrat. Address: 4513 W Trail Rd Lawrence KS 66049-2157

BRAEUTIGAM, RONALD RAY, economics educator; b. Tulsa, Apr. 30, 1947; s. Raymond Louis Braeutigam and Loys Ann (Johnson) Henneberger; m. Janette Gail Carlyon, July 27, 1975; children: Eric Zachary, Justin Michael, Julie Ann. BS, U. Tulsa, 1969; MSc, Stanford U., 1971, PhD, 1976. Petroleum engr. Standard Oil Ind., Tulsa, 1966-70; staff economist Office of Telecom. Policy, Exec. Office of Pres., Washington, 1972-73; from asst. to prof. econs. Northwestern U., Evanston, Ill., 1975—; dir. bus. instns. program, 1995—; Harvey Kapnick prof. Bus. Instns. dept. econs. Northwestern U., Evanston, Ill., 1990—, Charles Deering McCormick prof. tchg. excellence, 1997. Vis. prof. Calif. Inst. Tech., Pasadena, 1978-79. Co-author: The Regulation Game, 1978, Price Level Regulation for Diversified Public Utilities, 1989; assoc. editor Jour. Indsl. Econs., Cambridge, Mass., 1987-90; mem. editorial bd. MIT Press Series on Regulation, Cambridge, 1980-90, Jour. Econ. Lit., 1987-91, Rev. Indsl. Orgn., 1991—. Coach Skokie (Ill.) Indians Little League, 1985-91, Evanston Youth Baseball Assn., 1991-96. Grantee, Dept. Transp., NSF, Ameritech, Sloan Found., Mellon Found., others; sr. rsch. fellow Internat. Inst. Mgmt., Berlin, 1982-83, 91. Mem. Am. Econ. Assn., Econometric Soc., Internat. Telecommunications Soc. (bd. dirs. 1990-97), European Econ. Assn., European Assn. for Rsch. in Indsl. Econs. (exec. com. 1992—, pres. 1997-99), Soc. Petroleum Engrs. Avocations: travel, music, German lang., French lang. Home: 731 Monticello St Evanston IL 60201-1745 Office: Northwestern U Dept Econs Evanston IL 60208-0001

BRAGG, MICHAEL ELLIS, lawyer, insurance company executive; b. Holdrege, Nebr., Oct. 6, 1947; s. Lionel C and Frances E (Klinginsmith) Bragg; m. Nancy Jo Aabel, Jan. 19, 1980; children: Brian Michael, Kyle Christopher, Jeffrey Douglas. BA, U. Nebr., 1971, JD, 1975. CLU; bar: Alaska 1976, Nebr 1976; cert. ChFC, CPCU. Assoc. White & Jones, Anchorage, 1976-77; field rep. State Farm Ins., 1977-79, atty. corp. law dept. Bloomington, Ill., 1979-81, sr. atty., 1981-84, asst. counsel, 1984-86, counsel, 1986-88; asst. v.p., counsel gen. claims dept. State Farm Fire and Casualty Co., 1988-94; v.p., counsel, gen. claims dept. State Farm Ins. Cos., Ill., 1994-97, assoc. gen. counsel corp. law dept., 1997—. Lectr, contbr legal seminars. Contbr, ed: articles to legal and ins jours. Pres McLean County Crime Detection Network, 1988—95. Recipient Disting Legal Serv Award, Corp Legal Times, 1998. Fellow: Am. Bar Found.; mem.: ABA (vice chmn property ins law comt 1986—91, chmn ins coverage litigation comt 1991—92, various offices tort and ins practices sect including coun 2000—, chair task force on ins staff counsel 2000—, mem standing comt on ethics and profl responsibility 2001—), Internat. Assn. Def. Counsel, Fedn. Def. and Corp. Counsel (chair industry coop sect 1995—97), Def. Rsch. Inst., Am. Corp. Counsel Assn. Republican. Avocations: golf, tennis. Office: State Farm Ins Cos Assoc Gen Counsel One State Farm Plz A-3 Bloomington IL 61710 E-mail: buck.bragg.achk@statefarm.com.

BRAGG, MICHAEL B. engineering educator; BS in Aero. & Astronautical Engring., U. Ill., 1976, MS in Aero. & Astronautical Engring., 1977; PhD in Aero. & Astronautical Engring., Ohio State U., 1981. Prof. aerospace engring. U. Ill., Urbana. Invited lectr. First Bombardier Internat. Workshop, Montreal, 1991; cons. U.S. cos.; mem. FAA and other adv. panels. Contbr. numerous articles to profl. jours. Fellow AIAA (assoc., mem. 4 nat. tech. coms., Losey Atmospheric Scis. award 1998, chair applied aerodynamics tech. com., presenter); mem. Soc. Automotive Engrs. (past chmn. aircraft icing tech. com.). Achievements include research on reduction of maximum lift capability, increasing of drag leading to reduction of aircraft controllability due to ice accretion; unsteady aerodynamics. Office: U Ill 306 Talbot Lab 104 S Wright St Urbana IL 61801-2935 E-mail: mbragg@uiuc.edu.

BRAKE, CECIL CLIFFORD, retired diversified manufacturing executive; b. Ystrad, Mynach, Wales, Nov. 14, 1932; came to U.S., 1967; s. Leonard James and Ivy Gertrude (Berry) B.; m. Vera Morris, Aug. 14, 1954; children— Stephen John, Richard Colin, Vanessa Elaine Chartered engr.; B.Sc. in Engring., U. Wales, 1954; M.Sc., Cranfield Inst., Bedford, Eng., 1957; grad. A.M.P., Harvard U. Sch. Bus., 1985. Mgr. research and devel. Schrader Fluid Power, Wake Forest, N.C., 1968-70, engring. mgr., 1970-75; mng. dir. Schrader U.K. Fluid Power, 1975-77; v.p., gen. mgr. Schrader Internat., 1977-78; group v.p. Schrader Bellows, Fluid Power, Akron, Ohio, 1978-82; exec. v.p. Scovill, Inc., Waterbury, Conn., 1982-86; pres. Yale Security, Inc. subs. Scovill, Inc.; group exec. Eagle Industries, Inc., Chgo., 1986—; retired, 1997. Chief oper. officer Mansfield (Ohio) Plumbing Products Inc., Hart and Cooley Inc., Holland, Mich., Caron Internat., Inc., Rochelle, Ill., Caron Internat., Inc., Rochelle, Ill., Chemineer Inc., Dayton, Ohio, Pulsafeeder Inc., Rochester, N.Y., Clevaflex Inc., Cleve., Equality Specialties Inc., N.Y.C., De Vilbiss Co., Toledo, Hill Refrigeration, Trenton, N.J., Air-Maze Corp., Bedford Heights, Ohio, Burns Aerospace Corp., Winston Salem, N.C., Atlantic Industries, Inc., Nutley, N.J., Stimsonite Products, Niles, Ill.; ptnr., owner Prince of Wales Inc.; bd. dirs. CFI Industries. Avocations: sailing; golf. Office: Eagle Industries Inc 2 N Riverside Plz Chicago IL 60606-2600 also: 17 Harborview Rd Westport CT 06880-5061

BRAMNIK, ROBERT PAUL, lawyer; b. N.Y.C., Nov. 17, 1949; s. Abe and Ruth (Richman) B.; m. Sheryl Ann Kalus, Aug. 12, 1973; children: Michael Lawrence, Andrew Martin. BA, CCNY, 1970; JD, Bklyn. Law Sch., 1973. Bar: N.Y. 1974, Ill. 1980, U.S. Dist. Ct. (so. and ea. dists.) N.Y. 1974, U.S. Dist. Ct. (no. dist.) Ill. 1980, U.S. Dist. Ct. (ctrl. dist.) Ill. 1982, U.S. Ct. Appeals (2d cir.) 1974, U.S. Ct. Appeals (4th cir.) 1987, U.S. Ct. Appeals (3d and 7th cirs.) 1992, U.S. Ct. Fed. Claims 1994, U.S. Supreme Ct. 1977. Sr. trial atty. NYSE, Inc., N.Y.C., 1973-75; asst. gen. counsel E.F. Hutton & Co., Inc., 1975-77, Nat. Securities Clearing Corp., N.Y.C., 1977-79; with Arvey, Hodes, Costello and Burman, Chgo., 1979-86, ptnr., 1982-86, Wood, Lucksinger & Epstein, Chgo., 1987-88, Altheimer & Gray, Chgo., 1988-97, Wildman, Harrold, Allen & Dixon, Chgo., 1997—. Lectr. Securities Industry Assn. Compliance and Legal div., N.Y.C., 1980-91, 95-2001. Vice chmn. Ill. Adv. Com. on Commodity Regulation, Chgo., 1985-89, chmn., 1989-95. Fellow: Ill. Bar Found.; mem.: ABA (coms. on futures and derivatives regulation, co-chmn. subcom. on futures commn. merchants), Nat. Futures Assn. (hearing com. 2001—), Nat. Assn. Sec. Dealers, Assn. of Bar of City of N.Y. Jewish. Office: Wildman Harrold Allen & Dixon 225 W Wacker Dr Ste 3000 Chicago IL 60606-1224 E-mail: bramnik@wildmanharrold.com.

BRANAGAN, JAMES JOSEPH, lawyer; b. Johnstown, Pa., Mar. 5, 1943; s. James Francis and Caroline Bertha (Schreier) B.; m. Barbara Jeanne Miller, June 19, 1965; children: Sean Patrick, Erin MacKay, David Michael. B.A. in English Lit. with honors magna cum laude (Woodrow Wilson fellow), Kenyon Coll., Gambier, Ohio, 1965; LL.B. cum laude, Columbia U., 1968. Bar: Ohio 1968. Assoc. Jones, Day, Reavis & Pogue, Cleve., 1968-72; with Leaseway Transp. Corp., 1972-81, gen. counsel, 1975-80, sec., 1979-81, v.p. corp. affairs, 1980-81; also officer, dir. Leaseway Transp. Corp. (subsidiaries); v.p. Premier Indsl. Corp., Cleve., 1981-82; sr. counsel TRW Inc., 1982-88; pvt. practice Cleve., 1988—; treas., gen. counsel, sec. Biomec Inc., 1998—. Mem. ABA, Ohio Bar Assn., Cleve. Bar Assn., Phi Beta Kappa. E-mail: bizlaw@stratos.net.

BRANCEL, BEN, state agency administrator; m. Gail Brancel; children: Micheleen, Tod, Brandon. Degree, U. Wis., Platteville. Mem. State Assembly, 1986-97, assembly spkr., 1997; sec. Wis. Dept. Agr., Trade and Consumer Protection, 1997—. Mem. joint fin. com., gov.'s coun. on tourism, legis. coun., legis. audit com., joint com. on employment rels., state claims bd. Former mem. Portage Sch. Bd.; former chmn. Town of Douglas. Mem. Wis. Dairies Coop., Marquette County Farm Bur., Marquette Holstein Assn., World Dairy Authority. Office: PO Box 8911 Madison WI 53708-8911

BRAND, GEORGE EDWARD, JR. lawyer; b. Detroit, Oct. 25, 1918; s. George Edward and Elsie Bertie (Jones) B.; m. Patricia Jean Gould, June 7, 1947; children— Martha Christine, Carol Elsie, George Edward. B.A., Dartmouth Coll., 1941; postgrad., U. Minn., Harvard U., 1941; J.D., U. Mich., 1948. Bar: Mich. 1948, U.S. Supreme Ct. 1958. Mem. firm George E. Brand, Detroit, 1948-63, Butzel, Long, Gust, Klein & Van Zile, P.C., Detroit, 1963—; ptnr., dir., pres. Butzel, Long, Gust, Klein & Van Zile, 1974-89. Served with USNR, 1942-46. Fellow Am. Bar Found., Am. Coll. Trial Lawyers; mem. ABA, Am. Judicature Soc., Detroit Bar Assn., VFW. Club: N.S.S.C. Home: 1233 Kensington Ave Grosse Pointe Park MI 48230-1101 Office: 150 W Jefferson Ave Ste 900 Detroit MI 48226-4416

BRAND, GROVER JUNIOR, retired state agricultural official; b. Stark City, Mo., July 5, 1930; s. Grover Cleveland and Ada Neomi (Evans) B.; m. Juanita Sue Warden, Aug. 30, 1952 (div. Oct. 1968); children: Ellen E., Teresa L., Lisa S. B Liberal Studies, U. Okla., 1970. Cert. profl. purchasing agent. Mgr. Crest Drive-In Commonwealth Theatres, Joplin, Mo., 1952-58; buyer Eagle-Picher Ind., 1958-65, purchasing mgr., 1965-73; project coord. Atlas Industries, Oswego, Kans., 1973-78; warehouse examiner Kans. State Grain Inspection, Topeka, 1979-92. Recipient 6th pl. award Nat. Amateur Typing Contest, 1948. Mem. Nat. Assn. Purchasing Mgrs. (chmn. value techniques com. 1972-73). Avocation: stock investing. Home: 1990 NW 120th St Columbus KS 66725-3077

BRAND, MYLES, academic administrator; b. N.Y.C., May 17, 1942; s. Irving Philip and Shirley (Berger) B.; m. Wendy Hoffman (div. 1976); 1 child: Joshua; m. Margaret Zeglin, 1978. BS, Rensselaer Poly. Inst., 1964, PhD (hon.), 1991; PhD, U. Rochester, 1967. Asst. prof. philosophy U. Pitts., 1967-72; from assoc. prof. to prof., dept. chmn. U. Ill., Chgo., 1972-81; prof., dept. head U. Ariz., Tucson, 1981-83, dir. cognitive sci. program, 1982-85, dean, social & behavioral scis., 1983-86; provost, v.p. acad. affairs Ohio State U., Columbus, 1986-89; pres. U. Oreg., Eugene, 1989-94, Ind. U., Bloomington, 1994—. Author: Intending and Acting, 1984; editor: The Nature of Human Action, 1970, The Nature of Causation, 1976, Action Theory, 1976. Bd. dirs. Ariz. Humanities Coun., 1984-85, Am. Coun. on Edn., Washington, 1992-97. Recipient research award NEH, 1974, 79. Mem. Clarion Hosps. Assn. of Am. Phi, Assn. Am. Univs. (pres. 1999). Office: Ind Univ Bryan Hall 200 Bloomington IN 47405

BRAND, STEVE AARON, lawyer; b. St. Paul, Sept. 5, 1948; s. Allen A. and Shirley Mae (Mintz) B.; m. Gail Idele Greenspoon, Oct. 9, 1977. BA, U. Minn., 1970; JD, U. Chgo., 1973. Bar: Minn. 1973, U.S. Dist. Ct. Minn. 1974, U.S. Supreme Ct. 1977. Assoc. Briggs & Morgan, St. Paul, 1973-78, ptnr., 1978-91, Robins, Kaplan, Miller & Ciresi, LLP, 1991—. Pres. Jewish Vocat. Svc., 1981—84, Sholom Found., 1996—99; bd. dirs. Friends of the St. Paul Libr., 1997—; pres. Mt. Zion Hebrew Congregation, 1985—87. Mem. ABA, Minn. Bar Assn. (chmn. probate and trust law sect. 1984-85), Hebrew Union Coll.-Jewish Inst. Religion (bd. overseers 1987—, vice-chmn. 1996—), Am. Coll. Trust and Estate Counsel (Minn. chair 1991-96, regent 1998—), Ramsey County Bar Found. (pres. 1995-2000), Phi Beta Kappa, B'nai Brith. Democrat. Home: 1907 Hampshire Ave Saint Paul MN 55116-2401 Office: Robins Kaplan Miller & Ciresi LLP 2800 LaSalle Plz 800 Lasalle Ave Minneapolis MN 55402-2015 E-mail: sabrand@rkmc.com.

BRANDEMUEHL, DAVID A. state legislator; b. Dec. 7, 1931; Student, U. Wis. State assemblyman dist. 49 State of Wis., 1986—. Mem. transp. project com. and legis. coun. farm safety com.; farmer. Former mem. local sch. bd.; pres. Regional CESA. Office: 13081 Pine Rd Fennimore WI 53809-9619

BRANDES, JO ANNE, lawyer; BS, U. Wis., Eau Claire; JD, Willamette U. Assoc. Herz, Levin, Teper, Chernof & Sumner, SC, 1978—81; gen. counsel S.C. Johnson Comml. Markets, Sturtevant, Wis. Mem. bd. regents U. Wis., Wis., 1996—; mem. Gov.'s Commn. on Glass Ceiling; chmn. Wis. Child Care Coun.; past president Racine (Wis.) Area United Found. Office: SC Johnson Comml markets 8310 16th St PO Box 902 Sturtevant WI 53177-0902

BRANDL, JOHN EDWARD, public affairs educator; b. Aug. 19, 1937; m. Rochelle Jankovich; children: Christopher, Mary Katherine, Amy. BA in Econs. with honors, St. John's U., Collegeville, Minn., 1959; MA in Econs., Harvard U., 1962, PhD in Econs., 1963. Lectr. econs. Boston Coll., 1961-62; systems analyst Office of Sec. Def., Washington, 1963-65; asst. prof. econs. St. John's U., Collegeville, 1965-67; asst. prof., rsch. assoc. Inst. for Rsch. on Poverty, dir. Systematic Analysis Program U. Wis., Madison, 1967-68; dep. asst. sec. HEW, Washington, 1968-69; from assoc. prof. to prof. pub. affairs U. Minn., Mpls., 1969—, dir. sch. pub. affairs, 1969-76, dean Hubert H. Humphrey Inst. Pub. Affairs, 1998—; rep. State of Minn., 1977-78, 81-86, senator, 1987-90. Exec. bd. Ctr. for Policy Rsch. in Edn., 1986-96; vis. lectr. dept. econs. U. Philippines, 1968; vis. prof. pub. adminstrn. and pub. policy U. Sydney, Australia, 1973; teaching fellow dept. econs. Warsaw Sch. Econs., 1992-95. Author: Money and Good Intentions are Not Enough, 1998; (with A. Naftalin) Twin Cities Regional Strategy, 1981; co-editor: Public Policy and Educating Handicapped Persons, 1982; mem. editl. bd. Urban Affairs Quarterly, 1971-74, Sage Profl. Papers Adminstrv. Scis., 1972-76, Jour. Policy Analysis and Mgmt., 1981—; cons. editor Improving College and University Teaching, 1979-82; contbr. articles to pprofl. jours. Bd. dirs. Tri-Cap Community Action Agy. Inc., Mpls., 1966-67; trustee Mpls. Soc. Fine Arts, 1983-86; pres. Twin Cities Citizens' League, 1993; nat. adv. coun. St. John's U., Minn., 1975-91; chmn. Twin Cities Met. Coun. Cable TV Adv. Com., 1972-73, mem. FCC Cable Adv. Coun., 1972-73, Minn. State Planning Adv. Com., 1971-73, Gov.'s Adv. Com. on Mgmt. and Personnel Devel., 1971-76, Gov.'s Coun. of Econ. Advisors, 1971-76; Mem. study group Nat. Assessment of Student Achievement., 1986, Nat. Tchrs. Coun. Edn. Testing Svc., 1986-92, Nat. Commn. Indsl. Innovation, 1984-86; bd. dirs. policy studies orgns., 1985-90; asst. majority leader Minn. Ho. of Rep., 1983-84, minority caucus steering com., 1985-86; bd. regents St. John's U., Minn, 1991—. Recipient Presdl. prize Am. Evaluation Assn., 1988, Disting. Svc. award Nat. Govs. Assn., 1996. Fellow Nat. Acad. Pub. Adminstrn.; mem. NIMH (rsch. edn. adv. com. 1980-84), Assn. for Pub. Policy Analysis and Mgmt. (v.p. 1983-84, pres. 1986-87), Am. Soc. Pub. Adminstrn. (bd. dirs. Minn. chpt. 1975-76), Cath. Econ. Assn. (coun. dirs. 1968), Harvard Grad. Soc. (coun. 1988-91), Delta Epsilon Sigma.

BRANDON, DAVID A. food service executive/restaurant manager; b. 1952; With Procter & Gamble Distbg. Co., 1974-79, GFV Comm., Inc., 1979-83, COO, exec. v.p., dir., 1983-86; COO, exec. v.p., now pres., dir. Valassis Inserts, Inc., Livonia, Mich., 1986—; now pres., CEO Valassis Communications; chmn. & CEO Domino's Pizza, Inc., Ann Arbour, MI, 1999—. Office: 30 Frank Lloyd Wright Dr Ann Arbor MI 48105-9757

BRANDT, DONALD EDWARD, utilities company executive; b. St. Louis, July 22, 1954; s. Edward H. and Margaret E. (Hertling) b.; m. Jeanine M. Pulay, Nov. 1, 1986; 1 child, Matthew. BSBA, St. Louis U., 1975. CPA, Mo. Audit mgr. Price Waterhouse, St. Louis, 1975-83; sr. v.p. fin. and corp. svc. Union Electric Co., 1983—. Mem. Fin. Execs. Inst., Am. Inst. CPA's, Mo. Soc. CPA's. Roman Catholic. Club: Mo. Athletic (St. Louis). Office: Ameren Corporation 1901 Chouteau Ave Saint Louis MO 63103-3003

BRANDT, IRA KIVE, pediatrician, medical geneticist; b. N.Y.C. s. Charles Zachary and Hilda Eleanor B.; m. Dorothy Godfrey; children— Elizabeth, Laura, William, Rena. A.B., NYU, 1942; M.D., Columbia U., 1945. Diplomate Am. Bd. Pediatrics, Am. Bd. Med. Genetics. Intern Morrisania City Hosp., N.Y.C., 1945-46; resident Lincoln Hosp., 1948-50; fellow pediatrics Yale U., New Haven, 1955-57, asst. prof., 1957-61, assoc. prof., 1961-68; chmn. dept. pediatrics Children's Hosp., San Francisco, 1968-70; clin. prof. pediatrics U. Calif., 1970; prof. pediatrics and med. genetics Ind. U. Sch. Medicine, Indpls., 1970-89, prof. emeritus, 1989—. Served to capt. U.S. Army, 1946-47, 52 Mem. Am. Pediatric Soc., Am. Acad. Pediatrics, Soc. Pediatric Rsch., Soc. Inherited Metabolic Disorders, Am. Soc. Human Genetics, Am. Coll. Med. Genetics. Office: Ind U Sch Medicine Dept Pediatrics 702 Barnhill Dr # 0907 Indianapolis IN 46202-5128 E-mail: ibrandt@iupui.edu.

BRANDT, JOHN ASHWORTH, fuel company executive; b. Chgo., Oct. 3, 1950; s. William W. and Joan V. (Ashworth) B.; m. Debbie M. Fico, June 2, 1984; children: Briana Ashley, Bryan Ashworth. Student, U. Colo., 1969-72. Mgr. co. accounts Lincoln Wood Commodities, Chgo., 1972-74; pres. Lafayette Coal Co., Burr Ridge, Ill., 1974—, Hoosier King Coal Co., 1993—, Ind. Farms, Inc., 1996—. Pres. Chgo. Coal Shippers, 1984—; pres. Hoosier King Coal Co.; dir. Muliganeers Non-Profit Orgn. Office: Lafayette Coal Co 200 S Frontage Rd Ste 310 Hinsdale IL 60521-6953

BRANDT, JOHN REYNOLD, editor, journalist; b. Amarillo, Tex., Aug. 25, 1959; s. Reynold Francis Jr. and Patricia Levonne (Wallace) B.; m. Svetlana Stevovich, May 28, 1989; children: Emma Evangeline Stevovich Brandt, Aidan Reynold Stevovich Brandt. BA, Case Western Reserve U., Cleve., 1981. Sales rep. Merrell Dow Pharmaceuticals, Cleve., 1982-84, Miles Pharmaceuticals, Cleve., 1984-88, Tokos Perinatal Nursing Svcs., Cleve., 1988-89; sr. assoc. M. Zunt Assocs., 1989-90; dir. mgmt. devel. CSA Health System, 1990-91; assoc. editor Corp. Cleve. Mag., 1991-94; from exec. editor to pub. IndustryWeek Mag., Cleve., 1994—2000; chief editl. dir. Exec. Mag., 2000—, pres., pub., 2001—; pres. John R. Brandt, Inc., 2000—. V.p. Inst. Environ. Edn., Cleve., 1990-91. Bd. dirs. Work in N.E. Ohio Coun., 1997—; judge Workforce Excellence Awards of Nat. Assn. Mfrs., 1997—, Am. Bus. Media Neal awards, 2000. Recipient numerous awards in field from Am. Bus. Press, Assn. of Area Bus. Publs., The Press Club of Cleve., March of Dimes, Am. Soc. Bus. Press Editors. Mem. Press Club of Cleve. (dir. 1994-2001, v.p. 1996-98, pres. 1998-99). Office: 2835 Sedgewick Rd Cleveland OH 44120-1837

BRANDT, WILLIAM ARTHUR, JR. consulting executive; b. Chgo., Sept. 5, 1949; s. William Arthur and Joan Virginia (Ashworth) B.; m. Patrice Bugelas, Jan. 19, 1980; children: Katherine Ashworth, William George, Joan Patrice, John Peter. BA with honors, St. Louis U., 1971; MA, U. Chgo., 1972, postgrad., 1972-74. Asst. to pres. Pyro Mining Co., Chgo., 1972-74; commentator Sta. WBBM-AM, 1977; with Melaniphy & Assocs., Inc., 1975-76; pres., cons. Devel. Specialists, Inc., 1976—. Mem. adv. bd. Sociol. Abstracts, Inc., San Diego, 1979-83. Contbr. articles to profl. jours. Trustee Fenwick H.S., 1991-2000, Comml. Law League of Am., Internat. Coun. Shopping Ctrs., Nat. Assn. Bankruptcy Trustees, Ill. Sociol. Assn., Midwest Sociol. Soc., Urban Land Inst.; mem. Fla. del. to Dem. Nat. Conv., 1996, also mem. Dem. Party Platform Com., 2000. LaVerne Noyes scholar, 1971-74. Mem. Am. Bankruptcy Inst., Am. Sociol. Assn., Amelia Island Plantation Club, Union League Club Chgo., City Club of Miami, gov. mem. Chicago Symphony, Clinton/Gore '96 Natl. Finance Bd., mnging. trustee Democratic Natl. Comm., maj. trust mem. Democratic Senatorial Campaign Comm., life mem. Zoological Soc. of the Miami Metro Zoo. Democrat. Roman Catholic. Home: 2000 S Bayshore Dr Apt 39 Coconut Grove FL 33133-3251 Office: 3 First Nat Plz Ste 2300 Chicago IL 60602 also: Wells Fargo Ctr 333 S Grand Ave Ste 2010 Los Angeles CA 90071-1524

BRANNON-PEPPAS, LISA, chemical engineer, researcher; b. Houston, Sept. 19, 1962; d. James Graham and Patricia Ann (Hightower) Brannon; m. Nicholas A. Peppas, Aug. 10, 1988. BS, Rice U., 1984; MS, Purdue U., 1986, PhD, 1988. Sr. formulations chemist Eli Lilly & Co., Indpls., 1988-91; pres., founder Biogel Tech., 1991—. Author, editor: Absorbent Polymer Technology, 1990; mem. editl. bd.: Jour. Applied Polymer Sci., 1995—2001, mem. editl. bd.: Jour. Controlled Release, 1997—2001, mem. editl. bd.: Jour. Nanoparticle Rsch., 1998—, mem. editl. bd.: Biomaterials, 1999—. Vol. Indpls. Mus. Art, 1990—98, Humane Soc. Indpls., 1990—98, Indpls. Zoo, 1994—2000; trustee Chem. Engring. Found., 1999—2000. Recipient Harold B. Lamport award Biomed. Engring. Soc., 1989; named Outstanding Young Alumna, Kinkaid Sch., 1998-2000. Fellow Am. Inst. of Med. and Biol. Engring.; mem. AIChE (dir. 1998-2000, exec. bd. programming coun., dir. materials divsn., chmn. subcom. biomaterials divsn. 1990-93, dir.-at-large food, pharm. and bioengring. divsn. 1992-94, 2d vice chair materials divsn. 1994-95, 1st vice chmn. materials divsn. 1995-96, chmn. 1996-97, bd. dirs. 1998-2000), Am. Chem. Soc. (membership com. 1990—), Controlled Release Soc. (treas. 1995-98, internat. planning com. 1991, bd. govs. 1992-95), Jr. League Indpls. (bd. dirs. 1992-94). Avocations: fine art, dance, travel. Office: Biogel Tech PO Box 681513 Indianapolis IN 46268-7513

BRANSCOMB, LEWIS CAPERS, JR. librarian, educator; b. Birmingham, Ala., Aug. 5, 1911; s. Lewis Capers and Minnie Vaughn (McGehee) Branscomb; m. Marjorie Berry Stafford, Jan. 15, 1938 (dec. 1999); children: Lewis Capers III(dec.) , Ralph Stafford(dec.) , Carol Jean, Lawrence McGehee. Student, Birmingham-So. Coll., 1929-30; AB, Duke U., 1933; AB in Libr. Sci., U. Mich., 1939, AM in Libr. Sci., 1941; postgrad., U. Ga., 1940; PhD, U. Chgo., 1954. Clk. Young & Vann Supply Co., Birmingham, 1933-38; order libr. U. Ga., 1939-41; libr. Mercer U., 1941-42; libr., prof. libr. sci. U. S.C., 1942-44; asst. dir. pub. svc. depts., assoc. prof. libr. sci. U. Ill., 1944-48; assoc. dir. librs., prof., 1948-52; dir. librs., prof. Ohio State U., Columbus, 1952-71, prof. Thurber studies, 1971-81, prof. emeritus, 1981—. Mem. faculty compensation and benefits com. Ohio State U., 1981-90; chmn. Adv. Coun. on Libr. Svcs. and Constrn. Act, Ohio, 1967-70; cons. Punjab Agrl. U., India, 1967, Mansfield (Ohio) Pub. Libr., 1977; mem. adv. coun. Hitachi Found., 1985-88. Author: Ernest Cushing Richardson Research Librarian, Scholar, Theologian, 1993; editor: The Case for Faculty Status for Academic Librarians, 1970; contbr. articles to profl. jours. Mem. Ohio Commn. to Abolish Capital Punishment, 1960-69; bd. dirs. Ctr. for Rsch. Librs., 1953-64, mem. exec. com., 1954-56, chmn. bd. dirs., 1961-62, mem. coun., 1965-71; chmn. bd. trustees Ohio Coll. Libr. Ctr., 1968-70, vice chmn., 1970-72. Mem. AAUP (sec.-treas. U. Ill. chpt. 1947-48; sec.-treas. Ohio State U. chpt. 1948-52, pres. 1953-54; nat. council 1952-55, co-author History of the Ohio Conf. 1949-74, chmn. com. E 1979-91, mem. exec. com. 1981-91), ALA (chmn. nominating com. 1954-55), Assn. Coll. and Research Libraries (dir. 1953-55, v.p. 1957-58, pres. 1958-59), Ohio Library Assn. (chmn. coll. and univ. sect. 1952-53, chmn. library adminstrn. sect. 1969-70, chmn. local conf. com. 1970, chmn. awards and honors com. 1974-75, chmn. notable Ohio librarians com. 1978-79, award of merit 1971, Hall of Fame 1982), Franklin County Library Assn., Acad. Library Assn. Ohio, ACLU (exec. com. Central Ohio chpt. 1958-60, 64-66), Common Cause, Thurber Circle, Thurber House (bd. trustees emeritus 1985—), Friends of Ohio State U. Libraries, Ohio State U. Retirees Assn. (exec. bd. 1983-92), Beta Phi Mu (exec. council 1955-58), Sigma Alpha Epsilon. Democrat. Home: 3790 Overdale Dr Columbus OH 43220-4749 Office: Ohio State Univ Main Libr Columbus OH 43210

BRANSDORFER, STEPHEN CHRISTIE, lawyer; b. Lansing, Mich., Sept. 18, 1929; s. Henry and Sadie (Kohane) B.; m. Peggy Ruth Deisig, May 24, 1952; children: Mark, David, Amy, Jill. AB with honors, Mich. State U., 1951; JD with distinction, U. Mich., 1956; LLM, Georgetown U., 1958. Bar: Mich. 1956, U.S. Supreme Ct. 1959. Trial atty. Dept. Justice, Washington, 1956-58; atty., editor Office of Public Info., Office of Atty. Gen., 1958-59; spl. asst. U.S. Atty. for D.C., 1958-59; assoc. Miller, Johnson, Snell & Cummiskey, Grand Rapids, Mich., 1959-63, ptnr., 1963-89; dep. asst. atty. gen. civil div. U.S. Dept. Justice, Washington, 1989-92; pres. Bransdorfer & Bransdorfer, P.C., Grand Rapids, Mich., 1993-2000; ptnr. Bransdorfer & Russell, LLP, 2000—. Pres. State Bar of Mich., 1974-75, commr., 1968-75, chmn. sr. lawyers sect., 1994-95; pres. Grand Rapids chpt. Am. Inns of Ct., 1995-96; trustee Am. Inns of Ct. Found., 1997-2001; chmn. Mich. Civil Svc. Commn., 1977-78, mem., 1975-78; adv. com. 6th Cir. Jud. Conf., 1984-89; co-chair Mich. polit. leadership program Mich. State U., 1992-94; mem. comml. panel Am. Arbitration Assn., 1998-2001. Asst. editor: U. Mich. Law Rev, 1956. Pres. Grand Rapids Child Guidance Clinic, 1969-71; chmn. Kent County Coms., Griffin for Senator, 1972, Lenore Romney for Senator, 1966; mem. council legal advisers Rep. Nat. Com., 1981-89; Rep. candidate for atty. gen., Mich., 1978; trustee, v.p., Mich. State Bar Found., 1985-87, chmn., fellows, 1987-89; chmn. Mich. State Bd. Canvassers, 1985-87, Commn. on Future Directions in Health Care, West Mich., 1987-89. With U.S. Army, 1951-53. Recipient Spl. award for Superior Performance Civil Divsn. U.S. Dept. Justice, 1990. Fellow Am. Bar Found.; mem. ABA, 6th Cir. Jud. Conf. (life), Grand Rapids Bar Assn., FBA (pres. West Mich. chpt. 1984, Disting. Life Svc. award 1989), Rep. Nat. Lawyers Assn. (bd. govs. 1985-89), Mich. Rep. Party (Svc. award 1989), Rotary, Cascade Hills Country Club, Phi Kappa Phi. Presbyterian. Home: 7250 Bradfield Ave SE Ada MI 49301-9130 Office: Bransdorfer & Russell LLP Ste 411-S Waters Bldg 161 Ottawa Ave NW Grand Rapids MI 49503-2705 Fax: 616-458-4422. E-mail: sbrans@iserv.net.

BRANSFIELD, JOAN, principal; Prin. Sch. St. Mary, Lake Forest, Ill. Recipient Elem. Sch. Recognition award U.S. Dept. Edn., 1989-90, Nat. Disting. Prin. award, 1998. Office: Sch of St Mary 185 E Illinois Rd Lake Forest IL 60045-1915

BRANSTAD, TERRY EDWARD, former governor, lawyer; b. Leland, Iowa, Nov. 17, 1946; s. Edward Arnold and Rita (Garl) B.; m. Christine Ann Johnson, June 17, 1972; children: Eric, Allison, Marcus. BA, U. Iowa,

1969; JD, Drake U., 1974. Bar: Iowa. Sr. ptnr. firm Branstad-Schwarm, Lake Mills, Iowa, until 1982; farmer; mem. Iowa Ho. of Reps., 1973-78; lt. gov. State of Iowa, 1979-82, gov., 1983-99. Bd. dirs. Am. Legion of Iowa Found. With U.S. Army, 1969. Mem. Nat. Govs. Assn. (past chmn.), Rep. Govs. Assn. (task chair), Midwestern Govs. Assn., Am. Legion, Farm Bur. Republican. Roman Catholic. Lodges: Lions, KC. Office: Regency West 2 1401 50th St Ste 325 West Des Moines IA 50266-5924

BRASHEAR, KERMIT ALLEN, state legislator, lawyer; b. Crawford, Nebr., Mar. 16, 1944; s. Kermit A. and Marguerite (Pokorny) B.; m. Susan Wolf (div.); 1 child, Kermit A. III; m. Kathleen K. Wellman, Aug. 9, 1971; children: Kurth A., Kord A. BA, U. Nebr., 1966, JD, 1969. Bar: Nebr. 1969, Tex. 1994, Colo. 1996, U.S. Dist. Ct. Nebr. 1969, U.S. Ct. Appeals (8th cir.) 1976, U.S. Supreme Ct. 1976, U.S. Ct. Appeals (10th cir.) 1982, U.S. Tax Ct. 1987, U.S. Dist. Ct. (ea. dist.) Mich. 1987, U.S. Dist. Ct. Ariz. 1995. Ptnr. Nelson & Harding, Omaha, 1969-88, Heron, Burchette et al., Omaha, 1989, Brashear & Ginn, Omaha, 1990—; mem. Nebr. Legislature from 4th dist., Lincoln, 1995—. Spl. asst. atty. gen. State of Nebr., 1977-90. Mem. Republican Nat. Com., 1983-85; chmn. Nebr. Republican Party, 1983-85; candidate Republican Gubernatorial Nomination, Nebr., 1986. Lutheran. Office: Brashear & Ginn 1623 Farnam 800 Farnam St Omaha NE 68102-5097

BRASHEARS, DONALD ROBERT, advertising agency executive; b. Mexico, Mo., May 23, 1947; s. Robert Vaughn and Gail Curtis (Dollins) B.; m. Deborah Jane Williams, Dec. 20, 1969; children: Michelle, Matthew, Joshua, Katherine, Emily. BA in Psychology, Ctrl. Meth. Coll., Fayette, Mo., 1969; BJ in Advt., U. Mo., 1971. Acct. exec. J.B. Neiser & Co., San Diego, 1971-76; v.p., acct. supr., mgmt. supr. Marsteller Inc., L.A., 1976-79, group v.p. Chgo., 1979-86; sr. v.p. Cramer-Krasselt, 1986-93, exec. v.p., gen. mgr., 1993—, bd. dirs. Milw., 1993—. Recipient Clio award, 1987, Effie award, 1994. Republican. Baptist. Avocations: golf, tennis, running. Office: Cramer-Krasselt 225 N Michigan Ave Ste 800 Chicago IL 60601-7690 E-mail: dbrashea@c-k.com.

BRASITUS, THOMAS ALBERT, gastroenterologist, educator; b. Bridgeport, Conn., Aug. 2, 1945; s. Albert Joseph and Mary Frances (Gazdowskas) B.; m. Christine Ann Legace, Aug. 19, 1967; children: Kristie, Thomas Jr. BA, U. Conn., 1963; MD, Jefferson Med. Sch., Phila., 1967. Asst. prof. Columbia U., N.Y.C., 1977-83; assoc. prof. U. Chgo., 1983-86, prof., 1986—, Walter Lincoln Palmer disting. sci. prof. of medicine, 1987—. Dir. sect. of gastroenterology U. Chgo., 1985—. Contbr. numerous articles to profl. and sci. jours., 1973—. Bd. dirs. Gastrointestinal Rsch. Found., Chgo., 1985—. Maj. USAF, 1975-77. Recipient Merit award Nat. Cancer Inst./NIH, 1986—. Mem. Am. Assn. Physicians, Am. Soc. for Clin. Investigation, Am. Soc. for Biochemistry and Molecular Biology, Chgo. Soc. Gastrointestinal Endoscopy (pres. 1989-90), Chgo. Soc. Gastroenterology (pres. 1990-91). Avocations: sports, travel, bridge. Office: U Chgo Kirsner Ctr Study Digestive Diseases 5841 S Maryland Ave Chicago IL 60637-1463

BRASS, ALAN W. healthcare executive; MS in Hosp. and Health Svc. Adminstrn., Ohio State U., 1973. Pres., CEO Pro Medica Health Sys., 1998—. Recipient Pub. Health Svc. Traineeship award, 1973. Fellow Am. Coll. Healthcare Execs. Office: 2121 Hughes Dr Toledo OH 43606-3845

BRASUNAS, ANTON DE SALES, retired metallurgical engineering educator; b. Elizabeth, N.J., Mar. 11, 1919; s. Anthony J. and Stefana (Žekus) B.; m. Ellen Lydia Wirth, Nov. 16, 1946; children: James Anton, Kay Ellen, Anne Elizabeth. B.S., Antioch Coll., Yellow Springs, Ohio, 1943; M.S., Ohio State U., 1946; Sc.D., M.I.T., 1950. Cert. advanced metric specialist. Research engr. Battelle Meml. Inst., Columbus, Ohio, 1943-46; research metallurgist Oak Ridge Nat. Lab., 1950-53; ret. Assoc. prof. metallurgy U. Tenn., Knoxville, 1953-55; dir. edn. ASM Internat. (formerly Am. Soc. Metals), Metals Park, Ohio, 1955-64; mem. faculty U. Mo., Rolla, St. Louis, 1964-84, assoc. dean engr., prof. metall. engring., 1964-84, prof. emeritus, 1984-2001; cons. in field; guest lectr. U. Antioquia, Colombia, 1986. Author, editor in field. Recipient Alumni award U. Mo., Rolla, 1971, Fullbright award, 1986. Fellow Am. Soc. Metals, U.S. Metric Assn. (nat. sec. 1988-92, chmn. Cert. Metrication Specialist Bd. 1992-96); mem. Alpha Sigma Mu (pres. 1968-69). Avocations: sports, tennis. Home: 8030 Daytona Dr Saint Louis MO 63105-2510

BRATER, ELIZABETH, state legislator; b. Boston, Apr. 12, 1951; BA, MA, U. Pa. City councilwoman City of Ann Arbor, 1988-91, mayor, 1991-93; state rep. Mich. Ho. Reps., Dist. 53, 1995—. Mem. conservations, environ. & great lakes, higher edn. & mental health coms., Mich. Ho. Reps. Office: 480 Roosevelt Bldg Lansing MI 48909

BRAUCH, WILLIAM LELAND, lawyer; Bachelor's degree, U. Wis., Milw., 1980; JD, U. Iowa, 1987. Asst. atty. gen. Consumer Protection Divsn., Des Moines, 1987-95, spl. asst. atty. gen., dir., 1995—. Pres. Beaver Dale Neighborhood Assn. Recipient Consumer Advocate award Nat. Assn. Consumer Advocates. Mem. ABA (vice-chmn. consumer protection commn.), Polk County Bar Assn. Office: Consumer Protection Divsn Hoover State Office Bldg Fl 2 Des Moines IA 50319-0001

BRAUDE, MICHAEL, commodity exchange executive; b. Chgo., Mar. 6, 1936; s. Sheldon and Nan B.; m. Linda Rae Miller, Aug. 20, 1961; children— Peter, Adam B.S., U. Mo., 1957; M.S., Columbia U., 1958. Vice pres. Commerce Bank, Kansas City, Mo., 1960-73; vice pres. Mercantile Bank, 1966-73; exec. v.p. Am. Bank, 1973-84; pres., CEO Kansas City Bd. Trade, 1984—. Bd. dirs. Country Club Bank, Kansas City, Mo., Midwest Grain Products, Inc., Atchison, Kans. Author: Managing Your Money, 1975, also 12 childrens books Pres. Metr. Community Coll. Found., Kansas City, Mo., 1982-84; mayor City of Mission Woods, Kans., 1982-84 Mem. Futures Industry Assn., Nat. Futures Assn. (bd. dirs.), Nat. Grain Trade Coun. (bd. dirs., immediate past chmn.), U. Mo. Alumni Assn. (bd. dirs. 1985-87). Jewish. Avocations: running; public speaking. Home: 5319 Mission Woods Ter Shawnee Mission KS 66205-2013 Office: Kansas City Board of Trade 4800 Main St Ste 303 Kansas City MO 64112-2519

BRAUN, ROBERT CLARE, retired association and advertising executive; b. Indpls., July 18, 1928; s. Ewald Elsworth and Lila (Inman) B. BS in journalism-advtg., Butler U., 1950; postgrad., Ind. Univ., 1957, 66. Reporter Northside Topics Newspaper, Indpls., 1949; advt. mgr., 1950; asst. mgr. Clarence E. Crippen Painting Co., Indpls., 1951; corp. sec. Auto-Imports, Ltd., 1952-53; pres. O.R. Brown Paper Co., 1953-69; pres., chief exec. ofcr. Robert C. Braun Advt. Agy., 1959-70; with Zimmer Engraving Inc., Indpls, IN, 1964-69; former chmn. bd. O.R. Brown Paper, Inc. Advtg. cons. Rolls Royce Motor Cars, 1957-59, exec. dir., chief exec. ofcr. Historic Landmarks Found., Ind., 1969-73, exec. v.p. Purchasing Mgmt. Assn., Indpls., 1974-85, Midwest Office Systems abd Equipment Show, 1974-85, Grand Valley Indsl. Show, 1974-85; Evansville Indsl. Show, 1982-85, Ind. Bus. Opportunity Fair, 1985-88. Author: The Mr. Eli Lilly That I Knew, 1977. Editor: Historic Landmarks News, 1969-74; Hoosier Purchaser mag., 1974-85, I.R.M.S.D.C. News, 1985-88. Contbr. articles to profl. jours. Chmn. Citizens' Adv. Com. to Marion County Met. Planning Dept., 1963; pres. museum com. Indpls. Fire Dept., 1966-76; mem. adv. com. Historic Preservation Commn. Marion County, 1967-73; Midwestern artifacts cons. to curator of White House, Wash., 1971-73; mem. chmn. Mayor's Contract Compliance Adv. Bd., 1977-91; mem. Mayor's subcom. for Indpls. Stadium, 1981-83; adv. bd., exec. com. Indpls. Office Equal Opportunity 1982—; mem. Ind. Minority Bus. Opportunity Counc., 1985-88; mem. Met. Mus. Art, Indpls. Mus. of Art bd. dirs. Historic Landmarks Found. Ind., 1960-69; dir., sec. Ind. Arthritis and Rheumatism Found., 1960-67, pres., 1969, dir., 1970-90, hon. lifetime dir., 1992—, dir. Assoc. Patient Svcs., 1976-91, dir. emeritus, 1992; pres. Amanda Wasson Meml. Trust, 1961-72. Recipient Meritorious Svc. awd. St. Jude's Police League, 1961; citation for meritorious svc. Am. Legion Police Post 56, 1962; Tafflinger-Holiday Park appreciation awd., 1973; Nat. Vol. Svc. Citation, Arthritis Found., 1979; Margaret Egan Meml. awd. Ind. Arthritis Found., 1980; Indpls. Profl. Fire Fighters meritorious svc. awd., 1982. Mem. Marion County Hist. Soc. (dir. 1964—, pres. 1965-69, 74-76, 1st v.p. 1979), Am. Guild Organists (mem. Indpls. chpt., charter mem. Franklin Coll. br.), Indpls. Humane Soc., Ind. Mus. Soc. (treas., dir. 1967-74), Internat. Fire Buff Assocs., Indpls. Second Alarm Fire Buffs (sec.-treas. 1967, pres. 1969), Ind. Hist. Soc., Nat. Hist. Soc., Nat. Trust Historic Preservation, Smithsonian Assn., Friends of Cast Iron Architecture, Soc. Archtl. Historians, Am. Heritage Soc., N.A.P.M. Editors Grp. (nat. sec. 1979-81, nat. chmn./pres. 1981-84), Am. Assn. State and Local History, Decorative Arts Soc. Indpls., Ind. Soc. Assn. Execs., Nat. Assn. Purchasing Mgmt. (W.L. Beckham internat. pub. rels. awd. 1983), purchasing Mgmt. Assn. Indpls. (dir. 1974—), Victorian Soc. Am. (nat. sec. 1971-74), Lambda Chi Alpha, Alpha Delta Sigma, Sigma Delta Chi, Tau Kappa Alpha. Club: Indpls. Press, Rolls-Royce Owners. Home: 1415 W 52nd St Indianapolis IN 46228-2316

BRAUN, WILLIAM JOSEPH, life insurance underwriter; b. Belleville, Ill., May 21, 1925; s. Walter Charles and Florence (Lauer) B.; m. Elizabeth Ann Braun, July 7, 1951; children: Brian William (dec.), Roger Edward, Christopher Burnes, Thomas Barrett, Maura Tracey. B.S. in Mktg, U. Ill., 1949; grad., Inst. Life Ins. Mktg., So. Methodist U., 1950. CLU; chartered fin. cons.; accredited estate planner Nat. Assn. Estate Planners. Life underwriter Mass. Mut. Life Ins. Co., Decatur, Ill., 1949—. Pres. Am. Soc. C.L.U.s, 1976-77; bd. dirs. Am. Coll. C.L.U.s, Bryn Mawr, Pa., 1975-78 Served with USNR, 1943-46. Decorated Navy Air medal. Life mem. Million Dollar Round Table; Nat. Assn. Life Underwriters, Nat. Assn. Estate Planning Couns. (pres. 1985-86), KC, Decatur Club, Country Club Decatur, Decatur Athletic Club. Roman Catholic. Home: 4606 E Powers Blvd Decatur IL 62521-2549 Office: Mass Mutual Decatur Club Bldg 158 W Prairie Decatur IL 62523-1230

BRAUNSDORF, JAMES ALLEN, physics educator; b. South Bend, Ind., Apr. 13, 1938; s. Walter Louis and Ruth Harriet (Tuttle) B.; m. Donna Lou Munson, June 10, 1960; children: Kevin Scott, Allen Keith, Walter James. AB in Physics, De Pauw U., 1960; MS in Math., Purdue U., 1965. Cert. secondary tchr., Ind. Tchr. physics Greencastle Schs., 1960-62, Mishawaka (Ind.) Sch., 1962—. Tax preparer, Mishawaka, 1967—; adj. lectr. Ind. U., South Bend, 1981-89. Pres. Beiger Heritage Corp., Mishawaka, 1981-86; active Youth for Understanding, 1990—. Mem. NEA, Ind. State Tchrs. Assn., Am. Assn. Physics Tchrs. (Ind. Disting. Physics Tchr. 1984), Nat. Sci. Tchrs. Assn., Mishawaka Edn. Assn. (pres. 1970-74), Phi Beta Kappa. Methodist. Avocations: computing, genealogy. Home: 449 Edgewater Dr Mishawaka IN 46545-6909 E-mail: jbraunsdorf@msn.com.

BRAUNSTEIN, MARY, energy consulting company executive; AD in Elec. Engring., U. Cin., 1966. Project mgr. elec. & gas metering, customer billing; with Elec. distbn. & Engring.; mgr. info. tech. Cadence Networks, Cin. Trainer, mentor Rehab. Program Data Processing, U. Cin. Recipient J.H. Randolph award, 1993. Mem. Assns. Systems Mgmt. (past pres.). Office: Cadence Networks 105 E 4th St Ste 250 Cincinnati OH 45202-4006

BRAVERMAN, HERBERT LESLIE, lawyer; b. Buffalo, Apr. 24, 1947; s. David and Miriam P. (Cohen) B.; m. Janet Marx, June 11, 1972; children: Becca Danielle, Benjamin Howard. BS in Econs., U. Pa., 1969; JD, Harvard U., 1972. Bar: Ohio 1972, U.S. Dist. Ct. Ohio 1972, U.S. Supreme Ct. 1975, U.S. Ct. Appeals (6th cir.) 1980, U.S. Ct. Claims 1980. Assoc. Hahn, Loeser, Freedheim, Dean & Wellman, Cleve., 1972-75; sole practice, 1975-87; ptnr. Porter, Wright, Morris & Arthur, 1987-95, Walter & Haverfield LLP, Cleve., 1996—. Councilman Orange Village, Ohio, 1988—, pres., 1998-2001. Capt. USAR, 1970-82. Fellow Am. Coll. Trust and Estate Counsel; mem. ABA, Ohio Bar Assn., Bar Assn. Greater Cleve. (former chmn. estate planning trust and probate sect.), Suburban East Bar Assn. (pres. 1978-80), Rotary (Cleveland Heights pres. 1980), B'nai Brith (local pres. 1978-84), Wharton Club Cleve. (pres. 1991—), Am. Jewish Congress (Ohio pres. 1992—). Avocations: golf, symphony, reading. Home: 3950 Orangewood Dr Cleveland OH 44122-7406 Office: Walter & Haverfield LLP 1300 Terminal Tower 50 Public Sq Ste 1300 Cleveland OH 44113-2253 also: 23240 Chagrin Blvd Ste 600 Beachwood OH 44122-5402 E-mail: hbraverman@walterhav.com., hlblaw@aol.com.

BRAVO, KENNETH ALLAN, lawyer; b. Cleve., July 27, 1942; BS, Rutgers U., 1964; JD cum laude, Ohio State U., 1967. Bar: Ohio 1967, D.C. 1967. Trial atty. Criminal Divsn., U.S. Dept. Justice, 1967-69, spl. atty., 1969-79; ptnr. Benesch, Friedlander, Coplan & Aronoff, Cleve., 1979-94; of counsel Ulmer & Berne LLP, 1994-96, ptnr., 1997—. Mem. ABA, Ohio State Bar Assn. (coun. of dels. 1992-2001, bd. govs. 2001—), Cleve. Bar Assn. (chmn. fed. ct. com. 1984-85, bd. trustees 2001—), Cuyahoga County Bar Assn. (chmn. fed. ct. com. 1980-82, chmn. cert. grievance com. 1986-88), Nat. Assn. Criminal Def. Lawyers, Lawyer-Pilots Bar Assn., Jud. Conf. 8th Dist. Ohio (life). Office: Ulmer & Berne LLP 1300 E 9th St Ste 900 Cleveland OH 44114-1583 E-mail: kbravo@ulmer.com.

BRAY, DONALD LAWRENCE, religious organization executive, minister; b. Olwein, Iowa, Oct. 14, 1942; s. Arthur L. and Rachel C. (Archer) B.; m. Joy F. Failing, Aug. 15, 1964; children: Juli, Steven, Jeffrey. BA in Religion, Ind. Wesleyan U., 1964, DD (hon.), 1993; MA in Religion, Olivet Nazarene U., 1965. Ordained to ministry Wesleyan Ch., 1967. Pastor Mich. Dist. Wesleyan Ch., Grand Rapids, Mich., 1965-68; missionary Wesleyan World Missions, Indpls., 1968-77, dir. personnel, 1977-84, asst. gen. sec., 1984-88; dist. supt. Delta dist. Wesleyan Ch., Jackson, Miss., 1988-92; gen. dir. Wesleyan World Missions, Indpls., 1992—. Adj. prof. Wesley Bibl. Sem., Jackson, 1989-92. Author: (tng. manual) Christian Witness, 1985; contbr. articles to profl. jours. Trustee So. Wesleyan U., Central, S.C., 1989-99. Mem. Evang. Fellowship of Mission Agys. (bd. dirs. 1994—), U.S.-World Evang. Fellowship (bd. dirs.), Ind. Wesleyan U. Alumni Assn. (bd. dirs. 1984-86). Office: PO Box 50434 Indianapolis IN 46250-0434

BRAY, JOAN, state legislator; b. Lubbock, Tex., Sept. 16, 1945; m. Carl Hoagland; 2 children. BA, Southwestern U., 1967; MEd, U. Mass., 1971. Former tchr., journalist; former dist. dir. for Congresswoman Joan Kelly Horn; mem. dist. 84 Mo. Ho. of Reps., St. Louis, 1992—. Bd. dirs. Citizens for Modern Transit. Flemming fellow, 1995. Mem. PTO, Nat. Womens Polit. Caucus. Democrat. Home: 7120 Washington Ave Saint Louis MO 63130-4312 Office: Mo Ho of Reps Rm 412 State Capitol Building Jefferson City MO 65101-1556

BRAY, PIERCE, business consultant; b. Chgo., Jan. 16, 1924; s. Harold A. and Margaret (Maclennan) B.; m. Maud Dorothy Minto, May 14, 1955; children— Margaret Dorothy, William Harold, Andrew Pierce. BA, U. Chgo., 1948, MBA, 1949. Fin. analyst Ford Motor Co., Dearborn, Mich., 1949-55; cons. Booz, Allen & Hamilton, Chgo. and Manila, Philippines, 1955-58; mgr. pricing, then corp. controller Cummins Engine Co., Columbus, Ind., 1958-66; v.p. fin. Weatherhead Co., Cleve., 1966-67; from v.p. to dir. Mid-Continent Tel. Corp. (now ALLTEL Corp.), Hudson, 1967—76, dir., 1976—85; chmn. various subs. Mid-Continent Telephone Corp. (now ALLTEL Corp.). Instr. fin. and econs. U. Detroit, 1952-54; chmn. investor relations com. U.S. Telephone Assn., 1974-85; chmn. exec. com. Inst. Public Utilities, 1981-83. Trustee Beech Brook, Cleve., Ohio, 1972-96, life trustee, 1996—, treas., 1976-79, pres., 1979-81; bd. dirs. Breckenridge Village Retirement Cmty., 1991-2001, chmn. fin. com. 1995-2001; trustee Ohio Presbyn. Retirement Svcs., 1996-2001; chmn. fin. com., 1999-2001; chmn. safety com. Walloon Lake Assn., 1995-2000. With AUS, 1943-46. Mem. Fin. Execs. Inst. (bd. dirs. 1993-96), Cleve. Treasurers Club, Union Club Cleve., Walloon (Mich.) Yacht Club (chmn. bd. 1980-81, 85-86, 93—, commodore 1981-82, 87-88, bd. dirs., sec. 1988—), Ohio Masters Swim Club (hon., trustee 1985-92, 96-98, 2001-, sec. 1989-93), Lake Erie Local Masters Swim Com. (chmn. 1992-96), Delta Upsilon. Presbyterian. Avocations: competitive swimming, sailing, volunteer and church activities. Home and Office: 1847 Ridgebrook Cir Cleveland OH 44122-1077

BRAY, RICHARD D. state legislator; b. Martinsville, Ind., Mar. 1, 1931; m. Maurine Bray; 3 children. AB, JD, Ind. U. Precinct committeeman; prosecuting atty. Morgan County, 1959-70; chmn. state wages adjustment bd., 1973-74; mem. Ind. Ho. of Reps from 47th dist., 1974-90; mem. county and twp. com. Ind. Ho. of Reps., mem. govt. affairs com., co-chmn. cts. com.; criminal and civil procedures com., elections com.; elections com., agrl. and small bus. com.; ranking mem. judiciary com. Ind. Ho. Reps.; mem. Ind. Senate from dist. 37, 1992—; mem. corrections com. Ind. Senate dist. 37, 1992—. Pres. Sheriff Merit Bd., 1971-74. Mem. Masons, Scottish Rite, Shriners, Elks, Moose. Home: 289 E Morgan St Martinsville IN 46151-1546

BRAZELTON, WILLIAM THOMAS, chemical engineering educator; b. Danville, Ill., Jan. 22, 1921; s. Edwin Thomas and Gertrude Ann (Carson) B.; m. Marilyn Dorothy Brown, Sept. 23, 1943; children— William Thomas, Nancy Ann. Student, Ill. Inst. Tech., 1939-41; B.S. in Chem. Engring, Northwestern U., 1943, M.S., 1948, Ph.D., 1952. Chem. engr. Central Process Corp., 1942-43; instr. chem. engring. Northwestern U., 1947-51, asst. prof., 1951-53, asso. prof., 1953-63, prof., 1963-91, prof. emeritus, 1991—, chmn. dept., 1955-56, asst. dean Technol. Inst., 1960-61, assoc. dean, 1961-94, acting asst. dean, 1994-96, ret., 1996. Engring. and ednl. cons., 1949— Mem. Prospect Heights (Ill.) Bd. Edn., 1957-61; bd. dirs., exec. com. Chgo. Area Pre-Coll. Program. Recipient Vincent Bendix Minorities in Engring. award ASEE, 1986. Mem. Am. Inst. Chem. Engrs. (chmn. Chgo. sect. 1966-67), Am. Chem. Soc., Am. Soc. Engring. Edn. (chmn. Ill.-Ind. sect. 1963-64, 73-74, Vincent Bendix Minorities in Engring. award, 1986), Soc. for History of Tech., Soc. for Indsl. Archeology, Sigma Xi, Tau Beta Pi, Phi Lambda Epsilon, Alpha Chi Sigma, Triangle. Home: 10 E Willow Rd Prospect Heights IL 60070-1332 Office: Northwestern U Technol Institute Evanston IL 60208-0001 E-mail: wtb@northwestern.edu.

BREAUX, BILLIE J. state legislator; b. June 23, 1936; BS, W.Va. State U.; MS, Ind. U. Tchr. Indpl. Pub. Sch.; mem. Ind. Senate from 34th dist., 1990—; mem. legis. appropriations and elections; mem. natural resources, pensions and labor coms.; mem. corrections, cime and civil program com.; mem. health and environ. affairs com. and pub. policy com. Ind. State Senate Dist. 34. Mem. Indpls. Edn. Assn. (past pres.), Friends of Urban League (pres.), Indpls. Urban League, State Tchrs. Assn. Office: State House 200 W Washington St Indianapolis IN 46204-2728

BRECHT, ROBERT P. bank executive; Mgr. comml. loan dept. Peoples Savs. Bank, 1986-88, sr. v.p., then exec. v.p., 1988; exec. v.p. Firstbancorp. Ohio, Akron, exec. v.p. corp. retail Ohio; pres., CEO FirstMerit Peoples Bank, Ashtabula. Office: 3 Cascade Plz Ste 7 Akron OH 44308-1124

BRECKENRIDGE, JOANNE, political organization administrator; Attended, Ctrl. Meth. Coll., Fla. U. Mem. Nat. Fedn. Rep. Women, 1975—, mem.-at-large, 1996-97, regent, 4th v.p., dir. region 6, 1988-99, 3d v.p. dir. region 3, 2000-01, regent, 1984-2002. Pres. Mo. Fedn. Rep. Women; club pres. St. Louis Rep. Women Com. Spkr. in field. Co-chair fundraisers for U.S. Congress, State Senate and House candidates; active Bush Campaign, 1996, Dole/Kemp Advance Team, 1996; alternate del. Rep. Nat. Conv., 1976, 84, 92; Mo. Rep. chmn. of youth for Reagan, 1980; pres. Mo. Fedn. Rep. Women, 1992-96, Rep. Women's Club S., 2000; active Kirkwood Bapt. Ch., mem. mission team to St. Lucia. Joanne Breckenridge Legis. Day scholarships named in her honor by Mo. Fedn. Rep. Women. Office: 5838 Five Oaks Pkwy Saint Louis MO 63128-1403 Fax: 314-416-1954.

BREE, MARLIN DUANE, publisher, author; b. Norfolk, Nebr., May 16, 1933; s. George F. and Luile Bree; m. Loris Bree; 1 child, William Marlin. BA, cert. in journalism, U. Nebr., 1955. Mng. editor Davidson Pub. Co., 1958-61; editor Greater Mpls. mag., 1962-63; pub. rels. specialist Blue Shield, 1964-67; editor Sunday Mag., Star and Tribune, Mpls., 1968-72; columnist Corp. Report, 1973-77; publs. cons., 1978-83; co-founder, ptnr., editorial dir. Marlor Press, Inc., St. Paul, 1983-91, co-owner, pub., 1992—. Chmn. Midwest Book Awards, St. Paul, 1992. Author: In the Teeth of the Northeaster: A Solo Voyage on Lake Superior, 1988, Call of the North Wind: Voyages and Adventures on Lake Superior, 1996, Wake of the Green Storm: A Survivor's Tale, 2001; co-author: Alone Against the Atlantic, 1981. Dir. comm. Mpls. Bicentennial Celebration, 1976. With U.S. Army, 1955-57. Named Pub. of Yr., Midwest Ind. Pubs. Assn., 1994; honored as one of Best Ind. Pubs. in U.S., Top 101 Ind. Book Pubs., 1997. Avocation: sailing. Office: Marlor Press Inc 4304 Brigadoon Dr Saint Paul MN 55126-3100 E-mail: marlin.marlor@minn.net.

BREECE, ROBERT WILLIAM, JR. lawyer; b. Blackwell, Okla., Feb. 5, 1942; s. Robert William Breece Sr. and Helen Elaine (Maddox) Breece Robinson; m. Elaine Marie Keller, Sept. 7, 1968; children: Bryan, Justin, Lauren BSBA, Northwestern U., 1964; JD, U. Okla., 1967; LLM, Washington U., St. Louis, 1970. Bar: Oklahoma 1967, Mo. 1970. Pvt. practice, St. Louis, 1968—. Pres., chmn. bd. dirs. Crown Capital Corp., St. Louis. Mem. ABA, Internat. Bar Assn., Mo. Bar Assn., Okla. Bar Assn., Phi Alpha Delta, Beta Theta Pi, Melrose Club, Univ. Club, Forest Hills Country Club (pres. 1978). Home: 35 Crown Manor Dr Chesterfield MO 63005-6805 Office: 540 Maryville Centre Dr Ste 12 Saint Louis MO 63141-5828

BREEN, JOHN GERALD, manufacturing company executive; b. Cleve., July 21, 1934; s. Hugh Gerald and Margaret Cecelia (Bonner) B.; m. Mary Jane Brubach, Apr. 12, 1958; children: Kathleen Anne, John Patrick, James Phillip, David Hugh, Anne Margaret. B.S., John Carroll U., 1956; M.B.A., Case Western Res. U., 1961. With Clevite Corp., Cleve., 1957-73, gen. mgr. foil div., 1969-73, gen. mgr. engine parts div., 1973-74; group v.p. indsl. group Gould Inc., Rolling Meadows, Ill., 1974-77, exec. v.p., 1977-79; pres. Sherwin Williams Co., Cleve., 1979-86, CEO, 1979-99, chmn., 1980-2000, also dir., 1979—. Dir. Parker Hannifin Corp., Cleve., Nat. City Bank, Cleve., Mead Corp., Dayton, Ohio. With U.S. Army, 1956-57. Clubs: Pepper Pike, Union, Cleve. Skating. Home: 18800 N Park Blvd Cleveland OH 44122-1809 Office: Sherwin-Williams Co 101 Prospect Ave NW Cleveland OH 44115-1075

BREHL, JAMES WILLIAM, lawyer; BS engring., U. Notre Dame, 1956; JD, U. Mich., 1959. Bar: Wis. 1959; Minn. and various fed. cts. Lawyer Maun & Simon, St. Paul, 1963-2000; law practice and mediation/arbitration Nuetral Svcs., 2000—. Contbr. articles to law jours. Chmn. Minn. builder's adv. coun. Minn. Dept. Commerce, 1991-95; mem. planning commn. City of Afton, 1975-93; dir. Granville House Inc., 1985-95. Recipient Good Neighbor award WCCO, 1968. Mem. Minn. Bar Assn. (exec. com. 1996-97), Ramsey County Bar Assn. (exec. coun. 1977-80, 87-90, pres. 1993-94), Washington County Bar Assn. Fax: 651-436-5679.

BREHM, SHARON STEPHENS, psychology educator, university administrator; b. Roanoke, Va., Apr. 18, 1945; d. John Wallis and Jane Chappel (Phenix) Stephens; m. Jack W. Brehm, Oct. 25, 1968 (div. Dec. 1979) B.A., Duke U., 1967, Ph.D., 1973; M.A., Harvard U., 1968. Clin. psychology intern U. Wash. Med. Ctr., Seattle, 1973-74; asst. prof. Va. Poly. Inst. and State U., Blacksburg, 1974-75, U. Kans., Lawrence, 1975-78, assoc. prof., 1978-83, prof. psychology, 1983-90, assoc. dean Coll. Liberal Arts and Scis., 1987-90; prof. psychology, dean Harpur Coll. of Arts and Scis. SUNY, Binghamton, 1990-96; prof. psychology and interpersonal comm., provost Ohio U., Athens, 1996—. Vis. prof. U. Mannheim, 1978, Istituto di Psicologia, Rome, 1989; Fulbright sr. rsch. scholar Ecole des Hautes Etudes en Sciences Sociales, Paris, 1981-82; Soc. for Personality and Social Psychology rep. APA's Coun. of Reps., 1995-2000, finance com., 1999—; chair governing bd. Ohio Learning Network, 1998-99. Author: The Application of Social Psychology to Clinical Practice, 1976, (with others) Psychological Reactance: A Theory of Freedom and Control, 1981, Intimate Relationships, 1985, 2d edit., 1992, (with others) Social Psychology, 1990, 4th edit., 1999, also numerous articles, and chpts. Mem. APA (fin. com. 1999—). Office: Ohio U Office of Provost Cutler Hall Athens OH 45701-2979

BREILLATT, JULIAN PAUL, JR. biochemist, biomedical engineer; b. Pensacola, Fla., Mar. 2, 1938; s. Julian Paul and Ruth (Walser) B.; m. Gaye Sorensen, Apr. 9, 1962; children: Elise, Adrienne, Alain, Andre. BA in Biochem., U. Calif., Berkeley, 1959; PhD in Biochem., U. Utah, 1967. Rsch. assoc. Oak Ridge (Tenn.) Nat. Lab., 1967-69, rsch. scientist, 1967-74, acting dir. molecular anatomy program, 1974-77; rsch. supr. E I DuPont, Wilmington, Del., 1977-78, sr. rsch. chemist, 1978-85; Baxter rsch. scientist Baxter Healthcare Corp., Round Lake, Ill., 1986-90, rsch. dir., 1990-94, sr. rsch. dir., 1994—. Contbr. articles to scientific jours.; patentee in field. Active Boy Scouts Am., 1949—. Recipient IR-100 Indsl. Rsch. award, 1977. Mem. LDS Ch. Office: Baxter Healthcare Corp Baxter Tech Pk Round Lake IL 60073-0490

BREIMAYER, JOSEPH FREDERICK, patent lawyer; b. Belding, Mich., May 4, 1942; s. Ronald and Crystal Helen (Reeves) B.; m. Margaret Anne Murphy, Aug. 26, 1967; children: Kathleen A., Deborah L., Elizabeth L. BEE, U. Detroit, 1965; JD, George Washington U., 1969. Bar: D.C. 1970, N.Y. 1973, Minn. 1975. Cooperative engr. Honeywell Inc, Mpls., 1962-65; patent examiner U.S. Patent and Trademark Office, Washington, 1965-70; patent atty. Eastman Kodak Co., Rochester, N.Y., 1970-73; sr. patent counsel Medtronic Inc., Mpls., 1973-90; assoc. Fredrikson & Byron, 1990-93. Pres. Good Shepherd Home and Sch. Assn., 1984; precinct chmn. Dem. Farmer Labor Party, 1980-82. Mem. Minn. Intellectual Property Law Assn. (treas. 1986). Avocations: boating, skiing, travel. Home: 4700 Circle Down Minneapolis MN 55416-1101 Office: Breimayer Law Office 1221 Nicollet Mall Ste 206 Minneapolis MN 55403-2472

BREISACH, ERNST A. historian, educator; b. Schwanberg, Austria, Oct. 8, 1923; came to U.S., 1953; s. Otto and Maria (Eder) B.; m. Herma E. Pirker, Aug. 2, 1945; children: Nora Sylvia, Eric Ernst. PhD in History, U. Vienna, Austria, 1946; D in Econs., Wirtschafts U., 1950. Prof. Realgymnasium Vienna XIV, Austria, 1946-52; assoc. prof. Olivet (Mich.) Coll., 1953-57; prof. Western Mich. U., Kalamazoo, 1957-96. Author: Introduction to Modern Existentialism, 1962, Caterina Sforza: A Renaissance Virago, 1967, Renaissance Europe, 1300-1517, 1973, Historiography: Ancient, Medieval, and Modern, 1983, 2d edit., 1994, American Progressive History, 1993; editor: Classical Rhetoric and Medieval Historiography, 1985. Recipient fellowship, Nat. Found. for the Humanities, Washington, 1989-90. Mem. Am. Hist. Assn. Home: 228 W Ridge Cir Kalamazoo MI 49009-9108 Office: Western Mich U Dept History Kalamazoo MI 49008 E-mail: breisach@wmich.edu.

BREITENBECK, JOSEPH M. retired bishop; b. Detroit, Aug. 3, 1914; s. Matthew J. and Mary A. (Quinlan) B. Student, U. Detroit, 1932-35; B.A., Sacred Heart Sem., Detroit, 1938; postgrad., Gregorian U., Rome, Italy, 1938-40; S.T.L., Catholic U., Washington; J.C.L., Lateran U., Rome, 1949. Ordained priest Roman Catholic Ch., 1942; asst. at St. Margaret Mary Parish, Detroit, 1942-44; sec. to Cardinal Mooney, 1944-58, Cardinal Dearden, 1959; pastor Assumption Grotto, 1959-67; consecrated bishop, 1965; ordained titular bishop of Tepelta and aux. bishop of Detroit, 1965-69; bishop of Grand Rapids, Mich., 1969-90. Episcopal adviser Nat. Cath. Laymens Retreat Conf. Mem. Nat. Conf. Cath. Bishops (com. chmn.) Home and Office: Chancery Office 660 Burton St SE Grand Rapids MI 49507-3202

BREMER, CELESTE F. judge; b. San Francisco, 1953; BA, St. Ambrose Coll., 1974; JD, Univ. of Iowa Coll. of Law, 1977. Asst. county atty. Scott County, 1977-79; asst. atty. gen. Area Prosecutors Div., Iowa, 1979; with Carlin, Liebbe, Pitton & Bremer, 1979-81, Rabin, Liebbe, Shinkle & Bremer, 1981-82; with legal dept. Deere and Co., 1982-84; corp. counsel Economy Forms Corp., 1985-89; magistrate judge U.S. Dist. Ct. (Iowa so. dist.), 8th cir., Des Moines, 1984—. Instr. Drake Univ. Coll. of Law, 1985-96. Mem. ABA, Fed. Magistrate Judge Assn., Nat. Assn. Women Judges, Am. Judicature Soc., Iowa State Bar Assn. (bd. govs., 1987-90), Iowa Judges Assn., Iowa Supreme Ct. Coun. on Jud. Selection (chmn. 1986-90), Iowa Orgn Women Attys., Polk County Bar Assn., Polk County Women Attys. Office: US Courthouse Ste 435 123 E Walnut St Des Moines IA 50309-2036

BREMER, JOHN M. lawyer; b. 1947; BA, Fordham U., 1969; JD, Duke U., 1974. Bar: Wis. 1974. Atty. law dept. Northwestern Mutual Life Ins., Milw., 1974-78, asst. gen. counsel, 1978-90, v.p., gen. counsel and sec., 1990-94, sr. v.p., gen. counsel, sec., 1995-98, exec. v.p., gen. counsel, sec., 1998-2000, sr. exec. v.p., sec., 2000, exec. v.p., COO, 2001—. Office: Northwestern Mutual Life Ins Co 720 E Wisconsin Ave Milwaukee WI 53202-4703

BRENDTRO, LARRY KAY, psychologist, organization administrator; b. Sioux Falls, S.D., July 26, 1940; s. A. Kenneth and Bernice (Matz) B.; m. Janna Agena, July 14, 1973; children: Daniel Kenneth, Steven Lincoln, Nola Kristine. BA, Augustana Coll., 1961; MS, S.D. State U., 1962; PhD, U. Mich., 1965. Prin. Crippled Children's Hosp. and Sch., Sioux Falls, 1962-63; psychology intern Hawthorn Ctr., Northville, Mich., 1964-65; instr. U. Mich., 1965; asst. prof. U. Ill., Urbana, 1966-67; pres., CEO Starr Commonwealth, Albion, Mich., 1967-81; prof. Augustana Coll., Sioux Falls, S.D., 1981-99; pres. Reclaiming Youth Internat., Lennox, 1997—. Mem. U.S. Coordinating Coun. on Juvenile Justice and Delinquency Prevention, 1997—. Co-author: The Other 23 Hours, 1969, Positive Peer Culture, 1974, 1985, Re-educating Troubled Youth, 1983, Reclaiming Youth at Risk, 1990, No Disposable Kids, 2001, Kids Who Outwit Adults, 2002; co-editor: Reclaiming Children and Youth, 1992—, Reclaiming Our Prodigal Sons and Daughters, 2000. Lutheran. Home: PO Box 57 Lennox SD 57039-0057 Office: Reclaiming Youth Internat PO Box 57 Lennox SD 57039-0057 E-mail: courage@reclaiming.com.

BRENNAN, CHARLES MARTIN, III, construction company executive; b. New Haven, Jan. 30, 1942; s. Charles Martin Jr. and Margaret Mary (Gleeson) B.; m. Mary Day Ely, June 22, 1966; children: Elizabeth Brennan Lekberg, Cynthia Brennan Annibali. BA, Yale U., 1964; MBA, Columbia U., 1969. Gen. mgr. New Haven Malleable Iron co., 1966-68; fin. analyst Scovill Mfg. co., 1969-71; treas. Cerro Corp., N.Y.C., 1971-74, Gould Inc., Chgo., 1974-76; mng. dir. Imperial Trans Europe N.V. (46 percent subs. of Gould Inc.), London, 1976-79; v.p. Latin Am. Gould, Inc., Sao Paulo, Brazil, 1979-80, sr. v.p., chief. fin. officer Chgo., 1980-88, also bd. dirs.; chmn., chief exec. officer MYR Group Inc., Rolling Meadows, Ill., 1988—. Bd. dirs. ROHN Industries, Inc., Control Devices Inc., Northwestern Meml. Hosp., Mettawa Open Lands Assn., Lake County Rep. Fedn.; trustee Village of Mettawa, Ill. Mem. Chgo. Club, Comml. Club Chgo., Econ. Club Chgo. Republican. Episcopalian. Avocations: skiing, golf, fly fishing, shooting. Office: The MYR Group Inc 1701 Golf Rd Ste 1012 Rolling Meadows IL 60008-4227

BRENNAN, JAMES JOSEPH, lawyer, banking and financial services executive; b. Chgo., July 14, 1950; s. John Michael and Rosemary (Rickard) B.; m. Donna Jean Blessing, June 2, 1973; children: Michael James, Laura Jessica. BS, Purdue U., 1972; JD, Indiana U., 1975. Bar: Ind. 1975, U.S. Dist. Ct. (so. dist.) Ind. 1975, U.S. Tax Ct. 1975, U.S. Ct. Appeals (6th cir.) 1976 U. S. Ct. Appeals (4th cir.) 1977, Ill., 1978, U.S. Dist. Ct. (no. dist.) Ill. 1978, U.S. Ct. Appeals (7th cir.) 1978, U.S. Supreme Ct. 1981. Law clk. to judge U.S. Dist. Ct. (ea. dist.), Tenn., 1975-77; from assoc. to ptnr. Pope, Ballard, Shepard & Fowle, Ltd., Chgo., 1977-87; ptnr. Hopkins & Sutter, 1987-91; ptnr., co-chmn. fin. svcs. group Barack, Ferrazzano, Kirschbaum & Perlman, 1991-99; exec. v.p. corp. affairs, gen. counsel BankFinancial Corp., 2000—. Chmn. legal affairs com. Ill. Bankers Assn., Chgo., 1986, chmn. bank counsel sect., 1987, mem., 1988—; lectr. programs for bankers, bank examiners, accts. and bank counsel; participant drafting of various Ill. banking laws; adj. prof. grad. sch. bank law Ill. Inst. Tech. Kent Coll. Law, 1992—. Articles editor Ind. Law Rev., 1974-75; editor: Ill. Bankers Assn. Law Watch, 1988-94; contbr. articles to profl. jours. 1st recipient Disting. Bank Counsel award Ill. Bankers Assn., 1989. Mem. ABA (subcom. bank regulation YLD bus. com.), Ill. Bar Assn., Chgo. Bar Assn. (com. fin. instns.), Riverside Golf Club (bd. dirs. 1992-2000, sec.-treas. 1995-98), Western Golf Assn. (bd. dirs. 1998—, Evans Scholars (Purdue chpt. 1968-72, pres. 1970-71). Office: 1200 Internationale Pkwy Ste 101 Woodridge IL 60517-4976

BRENNAN, MAUREEN, lawyer; b. Morristown, N.J., Aug. 7, 1949; BA magna cum laude, Bryn Mawr Coll., 1971; JD cum laude, Boston Coll., 1977. Bar: Pa. 1977, U.S. Dist. Ct. (ea. dist.) Pa. 1978, Ohio 1989. Atty. U.S. EPA, Washington, 1977-80; asst. dist. atty. Phila. Trial and Appellate Divs., 1980-84; in-house environ. counsel TRW, Inc., 1985-87; assoc. Baker & Hostetler, Cleve., 1987-91, ptnr., 1991—. Adj. prof. Case Western Res. U., Cleve., 1990-92, 2000-01. Active Cleve. Tree Commn., 1991-96, co-chair, 1993-95; trustee Clean-Land Ohio, 1990-2000; rep. Canal Heritage Corridor Com., 2000—; mem. Cuyahoga County Greenspace Working Group, 1999—; bd. dirs. Crown Point Ecology Ctr., 2001--. Recipient Bronze Medal for Achievement, U.S. EPA, 1980. Mem. ABA (natural resources and environ. sect., standing com. environ law 1996-98), Pa. Bar Assn. (environ. law com.), Ohio State Bar Assn. (environ. law com.), Cleve. Bar Assn. (environ. law sect., chair wetlands com. 1991-92, sect. chair 1996-97, mem. steering com. adv. OEPA on Brownfield regulations 1995-97). Office: Baker & Hostetler LLP 3200 Nat City Center 1900 E 9th St Ste 3200 Cleveland OH 44114-3475 E-mail: mbrennan@bakerlaw.com.

BRENNAN, ROBERT LAWRENCE, educational director, psychometrician; b. Hartford, Conn., May 31, 1944; s. Robert and Irene Veronica (Connors) B. BA, Salem State Coll., 1967; M of Art in Tchg., Harvard U., 1968, EdD, 1970. Rsch. assoc., lectr. Grad. Sch. Edn., Harvard U., Cambridge, Mass., 1970-71; asst. prof. edn. SUNY, Stony Brook, 1971-76; sr. rsch. psychologist Am. Coll. Testing Program, Iowa City, 1976-79, dir. measurement rsch. dept., 1979-84, asst. v.p. for measurement rsch., 1984-92, disting. rsch. scientist, 1990-94. Adj. faculty Sch. Edn. U. Iowa, 1979-94, E.F. Lindquist prof. edn. measurement, dir. Iowa testing programs, 1994—. Author: Elements of Generalizability Theory, 1983, Test Equating Methods and Practices, 1995, Generalizability Theory, 2001; editor: Methodology Used in Scaling the Act Assessment and P-ACT, 1989, Cognitively Diagnostic Assessment, 1995; assoc. editor Applied Psychological Measurement, 1982—, Jour. Ednl. Measurement, 1978-83, 96—; contbr. articles to profl. jours. Harvard U. prize fellow, 1967. Fellow: APA; mem.: Iowa Acad. Edn. (pres. 1996—99), Psychometric Soc., Nat. Coun. Measurement Edn. (bd. dirs. 1987—90, v.p. 1995, pres. 1997—98, Tech. Contbn. award 1997, Career Contbn. award 2000), Am. Statis. Assn., Midwestern Ednl. Rsch. Assn. 1987—88, Am. Ednl. Rsch. Assn. (v.p. 1994—96, Divsn. D award 1980). Home: 1925 Liberty Ln Coralville IA 52241-1071 Office: U Iowa 334 Lindquist Ctr S Iowa City IA 52242-1533 E-mail: robert-brennan@uiowa.edu.

BRENNAN, ROBERT WALTER, association executive; s. Walter R. and Grace A. (Mason) B.; m. Mary J. Engler, June 15, 1962; children: Barbara, Susan (twins). BS, U. Wis., 1957. Tchr., coach Waukesha (Wis.) High Sch., 1960-63; track coach U. Wis., Madison, 1963-71; exec. asst. to mayor City of Madison, 1971-73; pres. Greater Madison C. of C., Madison, 1973—. Mem. adv. council U. Wis.-Madison Sch. Edn., 1984—; mem. Madison Urban League, 1971—; bd. dirs. Cherokee Park, Inc., Wis. Nordic Sports Found., Very Spl. Arts, Wis. Named Madison's Favorite Son, 1971. Mem. Wis. Alumni Assn. (pres. 1985-86, chmn. bd. 1986-87), "W" Club (life, cert. of merit), Theta Delta Chi. Home: 5514 Comanche Way Madison WI 53704-1026 Office: Greater Madison C of C 615 E Washington Ave Madison WI 53703-2952

BRENNAN, THOMAS EMMETT, law school president; b. Detroit, May 27, 1929; s. Joseph Terence and Jeannette Frances (Sullivan) B.; m. Pauline Mary Weinberger, Apr. 28, 1951; children: Thomas Emmett, Margaret Ann and John Seamus (twins), William Joseph, Marybeth, Ellen Mary. LL.B., U. Detroit, 1952; LL.D., Thomas M. Cooley Law Sch., 1976. Bar: Mich. 1953. Assoc. Kenny, Radom, Rockwell & Mountain, Detroit, 1952-53; ptnr. Waldron, Brennan & Maher, 1953-61; judge Detroit Ct. Common Pleas, 1962-63, Wayne County Circuit Ct., 1963-66; justice Mich. Supreme Ct., 1967-73, chief justice, 1969-70; adj. prof. polit. sci. U. Detroit, 1970-72; founder, pres., dean emeritus Thomas M. Cooley Law Sch., Lansing, 1972—. Mem. Mich. Commn. Law Enforcement and Criminal Justice, 1969-70; bd. dirs. Motor Wheel Corp., 1987-89. Author: Judging the Law Schools, 1997, The Bench, 2000. Founder, commr. Am. Golf League, 2000; bd. dir. Cath. League for Religious & Civil Rights, 1993—. Fellow Am. Bar Found., Mich Bar Found.; mem. ABA, Ingham County Bar Assn., State Bar Mich. (bd. commrs. 1979-83), Mich. Assn. of Professions (Disting. Citizens award 1982), Assn. of Ind. Colls. and Univs. Mich. (bd. dirs., exec. com., sec. 1990, chmn. 1991), Cath. Lawyers Soc. (Thomas More award 1987), Am. Jurisprudence Soc., Inc. Soc., Irish Am. Lawyers, Cooley Legal Author's Soc. (charter), v.p.-treas. 1990—), Mich. State C. of C. (bd. dirs. 1988-94), Walnut Hills Country Club (bd. dirs. 1992-95), Detroit Athletic Club, KC, Delta Theta Phi. Roman Catholic. Office: Thomas M Cooley Law Sch 217 S Capitol Ave Lansing MI 48933-1503 Home: American Golf League 14150 6th Street Dade City FL 33525

BRENNECKE, ALLEN EUGENE, lawyer; b. Marshalltown, Iowa, Jan. 8, 1937; s. Arthur Lynn and Julia Alice (Allen) B; m. Billie Jean Johnstone, June 12, 1958; children: Scott, Stephen, Beth, Gregory, Kristen BBA, U. Iowa, 1959, JD, 1961. Bar: Iowa 1961. Law clk. U.S. Dist. Judge, Des Moines, 1961-62; assoc. Mote, Wilson & Welp, Marshalltown, Iowa, 1962-66; ptnr. Harrison, Brennecke, Moore, Smaha & McKibben, 1966—. Contr. articles to profl. jours. Bd. dirs. Marshalltown YMCA, 1966-71; mem. bd. trustees Iowa Law Sch. Found., 1973-86, United Meth. Ch., Marshalltown, 1978-81, 87-89; fin. chmn. Rep. party 4th Congl. Dist., Iowa, 1970-73, Marshall County Rep. Party, Iowa, 1967-70. Fellow ABA (chmn. ho. of dels. 1984-86, bd. govs. 1982-86), Nat. Jud. Coll. (bd. dirs. 1982-88), Am. Coll. Trusts and Estates Counsel, Am. Coll. Tax Counsel, Am. Bar Found., Iowa Bar Assn. (pres. 1990-91, award of merit 1987); mem. Masons, Shriners, Promise Keepers. Republican. Methodist. Avocations: golf; travel; sports. Home: 703 Circle Dr Marshalltown IA 50158-3809 Office: Harrison Brennecke Moore Smaha & McKibben 302 Masonic Temple Marshalltown IA 50158

BRENNEMAN, HUGH WARREN, JR. judge; b. Lansing, Mich., July 4, 1945; s. Hugh Warren and Irma June Brenneman; m. Catherine Brenneman; 2 children. BA, Alma Coll., 1967; JD, U. Mich., 1970. Bar: Mich. 1970, D.C. 1975, U.S. Dist. Ct. (we. dist.) Mich. 1974, U.S. Dist. Ct. Md. 1973, U.S. Ct. Mil. Appeals 1971, U.S. Ct. Appeals (6th cir.) 1976, U.S. Ct. Appeals (D.C. cir.) 1981, U.S. Supreme Ct. 1980. Law clk. Mich. 30th Jud. Cir., Lansing, 1970-71; asst. U.S. atty. Dept. Justice, Grand Rapids, Mich., 1974-77; assoc. Bergstrom, Slykhouse & Shaw, P.C., 1977-80; U.S. magistrate judge U.S. Dist. Ct. (we. dist.) Mich., 1980—. Instr. Western Mich. U., Grand Valley State U., 1989-92. Mem. exec. bd. and adv. coun. Gerald R Ford coun. Boy Scouts Am., 1984—, v.p., 1988-92; mem. Grand Rapids Hist. Commn., 1991-97, pres., 1995-97; dir. Cmty. Reconciliation Ctr., 1991. Capt. JAGC, U.S. Army, 1971-74. Recipient Disting. Alumnus award Alma Coll., 1998. Fellow Mich. State Bar Found.; mem. FBA (pres. Western Mich. chpt. 1979-80, nat. del. 1980-84), State Bar Mich. (rep. assembly 1984-90), D.C. Bar Assn., Grand Rapids Bar Assn. (chmn. U.S. Constn. Bicentennial com., co-chmn. Law Day 1991), Fed. Magistrate Judges Assn., Am. Inns of Ct. (master of bench Grand Rapids chpt., pres.), Phi Delta Phi, Omicron Delta Kappa, Peninsular Club, Rotary (past pres., Charities Found. of Grand Rapids v.p., Paul Harris fellow), Econ. Club of Grand Rapids (past bd. dirs.). Congregationalist. Office: US Dist Ct West Mich 110 Michigan St NW Rm 580 Grand Rapids MI 49503-2313

BRENNER, DAVID H. marketing executive; m. Denise Brenner; 3 children. BBA in Mktg. summa cum laude, U. Notre Dame, 1973. With dept. gen. advt. Procter & Gamble, Cinn., 1973-76; sales promotion mgr. divsn. health care Johnson & Johnson, 1976-78, brand mgr. first aid products, 1978-80; new product devel. mgr. Kellogg's, 1980-82, past new product devel mgr. Europe, past mng. dir. bus. ops. England, Ireland, Belgium and The Netherlands, pres. U.S. subs., 1988-91; sr. v.p. new bus. ventures Amway, Ada, Mich., 1991—. Regent Edison New Products Yr.; guest lectr. Yale U., Notre Dame U., Aquinas Coll., Grand Valley State U. Bd. trustees Grand Rapids Art Mus., Cath. Soc. Svcs., Grand Rapids, Killgoar Found. Immaculate Heart Mary Sch.; chmn. ann. fund GRAM, 1995-97. Mem. Am. Mktg. Assn., Cascade Hills Country Club, Beta Gamma Sigma. Office: Amway Corp 7575 Fulton St E Ada MI 49355-0001

BRENT, HELEN TERESSA, school nurse; b. Grand Rapids, Mich., Oct. 4, 1946; d. William Henry and Anita Broyles Burress; m. Robert Lee Brent, June 10, 1967. AS, Grand Rapids C.C., 1966; diploma, Butterworth Hosp. Sch. Nursing, 1968; BSN summa cum laude, U. Mich., 1981; MPA, Western Mich. U., 1992. RN, Mich. Staff nurse Butterworth Hosp., Grand Rapids, Mich., 1968-69, head nurse psychiat. unit, 1969-72; DON Forest View Psychiat. Hosp., 1972-75; asst. DON, staff devel. coord. Kent Oaks Psychiat. Unit Kent Community Hosp., 1975-80; DON Kent Community Hosp. Complex, 1980-94; psychiat. nurse Pine Rest Christian Mental Health Svcs., 1994—; health planner Kent County Pub. Health Dept., 1996-97; sch. nurse Grand Rapids Pub. Schs., 1997—. Adj. faculty nursing divsn. Grand Rapids C.C., 1999—. Mem. adv. coun. Mich. Family Planning Mich. Dept. Cmty. Health, 1991-99, Family Outreach Ctr., Grand Rapids, 1980-95; mem. hospice care study panel United Way Kent County, 1984; vol. nursing health svcs. Kent County chpt. ARC, Grand Rapids, 1974—; vol. mediator West Mich. Dispute Resolution Ctr., 1995—. Recipient Outstanding Svc. award Family Outreach Ctr. Kent County Cmty. Mental Health, 1988, Helen Barnes award for outstanding vol. contbns. in nursing svcs. Kent County chpt. ARC, 1994, Eugene Browning Med. Svc. award Giants Orgn., Grand Rapids, 1995. Mem. Vis. Nurses Assn. (bd. dirs. local chpt. 1991-2000), Nat. Black Nurses Assn. (local chpt. 1999—), Harambe Black Nurses Assn. Grand Rapids, Alpha Kappa Mu (Mu Omicron chpt.). Democrat. Avocations: reading, traveling, volunteer and various ch. related activities. Home: 3834 Old Elm Dr SE Kentwood MI 49512-9523 Office: Grand Rapids Pub Schs KEC Mayfield 225 Mayfield Ave NE Grand Rapids MI 49503-3768 E-mail: hbrent5558@webtv.net., BrentH@grps.k12.mi.us.

BRENTLINGER, PAUL SMITH, venture capital executive; b. Dayton, Ohio, Apr. 3, 1927; s. Arthur and Welthy Otello (Smith) B.; m. Marilyn E. Hunt, June 23, 1951; children: Paula, David, Sara. BA, U. Mich., 1950, MBA, 1951. With Harris Corp., Melbourne, Fla., 1951-84, v.p. corp. devel., 1969-75, v.p. fin., 1975-82, sr. v.p. fin., 1982-84; ptnr. Morgenthaler Ventures, Cleve., 1984—. Bd. dirs. Allegheny Techs., Inc., Pitts., Hypres, Inc., Elmsford, N.Y.; mem. adv. bd. Wolverine Venture Fund. Trustee Cleve. Inst. Art. Mem. Union Club, Phi Beta Kappa. Home: 2755 Eaton Rd Cleveland OH 44122-1800 Office: Morgenthaler 50 Public Sq Ste 2700 Cleveland OH 44113-2236

BRESKE, ROGER M. state legislator; b. Nov. 8, 1938; Grad. high sch. Former tavern owner; mem. Wis. Senate from 12th dist., Madison, 1990—. Mem. Tavern League Wis. (former pres.), Nat. Lic. Beverage Assn. (v.p.). Home: 8800 State Highway 29 Eland WI 54427-9409 Office: PO Box 7882 Madison WI 53707-7882

BRESLIN, PEG M. judge; b. Ottawa, Ill., July 11, 1946; m. John X. Breslin, May 18, 1974. BA, Loyola U., Chgo., 1967, JD, 1970. Bar: Ill. 1971, U.S. Dist. Ct. (no. dist.) Ill. 1973. Mem. Chgo. Com. on Criminal Justice, 1970-71; atty. Allen and Narko, 1971-74, Ill. State Bd. Edn., 1974-76; mem. Ill. Ho. of Reps., 1976-90; pvt. practice, 1990-92; judge 3d Dist., Ill. Ct. Appeals, Ottawa, 1992—. Bd. dirs. Nat. Safe Workplace Inst. Recipient award Women's Bar of Ill., 1993; named Best Legis. 1990, Ill. Environ. Coun., Chgo. Tribune mag. Mem. Ill. State Bar Assn. (mem. coun. bench and bar sect. 1998), Ill. Cts. Commn. Roman Catholic. Avocations: art, gardening.

BRESTEL, MARY BETH, librarian; b. Cin., Feb. 5, 1952; d. John Wesley and Laura Alice (Knoop) Seay; m. Michael Charles Brestel, Aug. 3, 1974; 1 child, Rebecca Michelle. BS, U. Cin., 1974; MLS, U. Ky., 1984. Libr. asst. history and lit. dept. Pub. Libr. Cin. and Hamilton County, 1974-78, children's asst. Pleasant Ridge br., 1978-81, children's asst. Westwood br., 1981-84, reference libr. sci. and tech. dept., 1984-90, 1st asst. sci. and tech. dept., 1990-92, mgr. dept., 1992—. Mem. Ohio Libr. Coun. Mem. United Methodist Ch. Office: Pub Libr Cin and Hamilton County Sci and Tech Dept 800 Vine St Cincinnati OH 45202-2071

BRETHERTON, FRANCIS P. atmospheric and oceanic sciences educator; Prof. atmospheric and oceanic scis., dir. Space Sci. and Engring. Ctr., U. Wis., Madison, Wis., 1988-94, prof. atmospheric and oceanic scis., 1994—. Recipient Cleveland Abbe Award for Distinguished Service to Atmospheric Sciences, Am. Meteorological Assn., 1994 Office: U Wis Space Sci & Engring Ctr 1225 W Dayton St Madison WI 53706-1612

BRETT, GEORGE HOWARD, baseball executive, former professional baseball player; b. Glen Dale, W.Va., May 15, 1953; s. Jack Francis and Ethel (Hansen) B. Student, Longview C.C., Mo., El Camino Coll., Torrance, Calif. Former third baseman Kansas City (Mo.) Royals Profl. Baseball Team, v.p. baseball ops. Named Am. League batting champion, 1976, 80, 90, Am. League Most Valuable Player, 1980; player Am. League All-Star Game, 1976-88; Inductee Baseball Hall of Fame, Cooperstown, N.Y., 1999. Address: care Kansas City Royals attn: vp ops PO Box 419969 Kansas City MO 64141-6969

BRETZ, WILLIAM FRANKLIN, retired elementary and secondary education educator; b. Urbana, Ill., May 30, 1937; s. William Franklin and Lois Evelyn (Scheffler) B. AA, Springfield (Ill.) Coll., 1957; BA, Ill. Coll., 1959; MA, Georgetown U., 1972. Cert. tchr., Ill. Chief page Ill. Senate, Springfield, 1957-63; tchr. history Lanphier High Sch., 1964-78, Benjamin Franklin Sch., Springfield, 1979—, chmn. social sci. dept., 1989-94; ret., 1994. Staff mem. U.S. Ho. of Reps., Washington, 1975; site interpreter Lincoln's Tomb, Springfield, 1988—. Mem. Animal Protective League, Springfield. Univ. scholar Georgetown U., 1959-60. Mem. NEA, Ill. Edn. Assn., Springfield Edn. Assn., Ctr. for French Colonial Studies in Ill., Nat. Trust for Hist. Preservation, U.S. Capitol Hist. Soc. Home: 2325 S Park Ave Springfield IL 62704-4354

BREU, GEORGE, accountant; b. Milw., May 8, 1954; s. George and Grace (Rossmaier) B.; m. Nancy Lee Roblee, June 6, 1987; children: Michael G., Lisa A. BBA in Acctg. cum laude, U. Wis., Milw., 1976. CPA, Wis. Audit staff Reilly, Penner & Benton, Milw., 1976-78; tax mgr. Radke, Schlesner & Wernecke, S.C., 1978-88; contr. Megal Devel. and Constrn. Corp., 1988-2000; pres. George Breu CPA, S.C., Brookfield, Wis., 2000—. Treas. Elmbrook Hist. Soc., Brookfield, Wis., 1981-83. Mem. Am. Inst. CPA's (tax div.), Wis. Inst. CPA's, U. Wis. Milw. Tax Assn., Germany Philatelic Soc. (treas. Milw. chpt. 1978—), U. Wis. Milw. Philatelic Soc. (founder, treas. 1972-81), Milw. Philatelic Soc. Inc. (corp. registered agt. 1986—), U. Wis. Milw. Alumni Assn., Beta Gamma Sigma, Phi Eta Sigma. Republican. Roman Catholic. Avocations: stamp collecting, reading history, traveling. Home: 15840 Fieldbrook Dr Brookfield WI 53005-1419 Office: George Breu CPA SC 15840 Fieldbrook Dr Brookfield WI 53005-1419

BREWER, LINGG, state legislator; b. Oct. 13, 1944; BA, Mich. State U.; postgrad., Calif. State U., L.A. Rep. Mich. State Dist. 68, 1995—. Edn. com. Mich. Ho. Reps., higher edn. com., local govt. com. Address: South Tower Rm 1087 124 N Capitol Ave Lansing MI 48933

BREWER, MARK COURTLAND, lawyer; b. Hammond, Ind., Apr. 1, 1955; s. Harold Russell and Carol Joan (Odell) B. BA, Harvard U., 1977; JD, Stanford U., 1981. Bar: U.S. Dist. Ct. (ea. and we. dist.) Mich. 1983, U.S. Ct. Appeals (6th cir.) 1983. Law clk. U.S. Ct. Appeals (5th cir.), Austin, 1981-82; law clk. to justice Mich. Supreme Ct., Lansing, 1982-83; assoc. Sachs, Waldman, O'Hare, P.C., Detroit, 1983-89; mem. Sachs, Waldman & O'Hare, 1989-95; Chm. Mich Dem Party. Pres. Stanford Pub. Interest Law Found. Palo Alto, Calif., 1980-81; bd. dirs. Interfaith Ctr. for Racial Justice, Warren, Mich., Mich. Protection and Adv. Svc., Lansing, Mich. Contbr. articles on AIDS discrimination, drug testing, and employee privacy to profl. publs. Mem. Macomb County Dem. Com., Mich., 1982—, 12th Congl. Dist. Dem. Com. Macomb County, 1983-93, 10th Congl. Dist. Dem. Com. Macomb County, 1993—. Mem. ABA, FBA (pres. ea. dist. Mich., bd. dirs. 1999-2000), State Bar Mich. (Outstanding Young Lawyer 1988), Sierra Club (Detroit chpt. 1987—). Democrat. Lutheran. Office: Mich Democratic Party 606 Townsend St Lansing MI 48933-2313

BREWER, ROBERT ALLEN, physician; b. Inpls., Jan. 29, 1927; s. Robert Dewayne and Viola Mae (Grant) B.; m. Mildred Noreen Barnett, Jan. 1, 1950 (dec. May 1997); children: Robert A. Jr., Raymond, Richard, Brian, Andrew. AA, St. Petersburg Jr. Coll., Fla., 1949; AB, Ind. U., 1952; MD, Ind U., Inpls., 1955. Emergency dept. staff physician Mound Park Hosp., St. Petersburg, Fla., 1960; staff physician Pinellas Hosp., Largo, 1961-68; pvt. practice Logansport, Ind., 1969—. Mem. Cass County Republican Com., Logansport, Ind., candidate for city coun., 1995. Capt. U.S. Army, 1957-59. Mem. AMA, Am. Acad. Family Practitioner (bd. cert. diplomate), Ind. Med. Assn., Cass County Med. Assn. Republican. Avocations: stamp collecting, coin collecting. Office: PO Box 119 831 E Broadway Logansport IN 46947-3161

BREWSTER, JAMES HENRY, retired chemistry educator; b. Ft. Collins, Colo., Aug. 21, 1922; s. Oswald Cammann and Elizabeth (Booraem) B.; m. Christine Barbara Germain, Jan. 23, 1954; children— Christine Carolyn, Mary Elizabeth, Barbara Anne. A.B., Cornell U., 1942; Ph.D., U. Ill., 1948. Chemist Atlantic Refining Co., Phila., 1942-43; postdoctoral fellow U. Chgo., 1948-49; instr. Purdue U., 1949-50, asst. prof., 1950-55, assoc. prof., 1955-60, prof., 1960-91, prof. emeritus, 1991—. With Am. Field Service, 1943-45. Fellow AAAS; mem. Am. Chem. Soc., Chem. Soc. (London), Phi Beta Kappa, Sigma Xi, Phi Lambda Upsilon. Achievements include research in bond molecular orbitals, relation optical rotation and constitution, and origins of life. E-mail: Brewst. Home: 334 Hollowood Dr West Lafayette IN 47906-2146 Office: Purdue U Dept Chemistry Lafayette IN 47907 E-mail: jbrewst2@Purdue.edu.

BREYER, NORMAN NATHAN, metallurgical engineering educator, consultant; b. Detroit, June 21, 1921; s. Max and Fannie (Landesman) B.; m. Dorothy Atlas, Feb. 10, 1952 (dec. Sept. 1987); children: Matthew, Richard, Marjorie; m. Claire Shore, Mar. 16, 1989. B.S., Mich. Tech. U., Houghton, 1943; M.S., U. Mich., 1948; Ph.D., Ill. Inst. Tech., 1963. Aero. research scientist NACA, Cleve., 1948; chief armor sect. Detroit Tank Arsenal, Warren, Mich., 1948-52; dir. research cast steels and irons Nat. Roll & Foundry, Avonmore, Pa., 1952-54; metallurgist-in-charge armor Continental Foundry & Machine div. Blaw-Knox Co., East Chicago, Ind., 1955-57; mgr. tech. projects LaSalle Steel Co., Hammond, 1957-64; assoc. prof. metall. engring. Ill. Inst. Tech., Chgo., 1964-69, prof., 1969-91, prof. emeritus, 1991—, chmn. dept., 1976-85. Capt. U.S. Army, 1943-46, ETO. Mem. AIME, Am. Soc. Metals Home: 858 Timber Hill Rd Highland Park IL 60035-5121 Office: Ill Inst Tech Dept Metall & Materials Engring 10 W 33rd St Chicago IL 60616-3730

BRIAND, MICHAEL, chef; Mem. staff various pastry shops, Brittany, Paris and Bern, Switzerland; chef Froggy's French Cafe, Highwood, Ill.; exec. chef Little Dix Resort, Virgin Gorda; pastry chef Ambria, Chgo., 1994—, Mon Ami Gabi. Office: Ambria 2300 N Lincoln Park W Chicago IL 60614

BRICCETTI, JOAN THERESE, theater manager, arts management consultant; b. Mt. Kisco, N.Y., Sept. 29, 1948; d. Thomas Bernard and Joan (Filardi) B. AB in Am. History, Bryn Mawr Coll., 1970. Adminstrv. asst., program guide editor Sta. WIAN-FM, Indpls., 1970-72; adminstrv. asst. T. Briccetti, condr., 1970-72; dir. pub. rels. The Richmond (Va.) Symphony, 1972-73, mgr., 1973-80, St. Louis Symphony Orch., 1980-84, gen. mgr., 1984-86, chief oper. officer, 1986-92; ind. cons. for arts Arts & Edn., 1993—; mng. dir. Metro Theater Co., St. Louis, 1996—. Cons., panelist Arts Couns. Ohio, Va., Ky. Active orch. and planning sects., music programs Nat. Endowment fot the Arts, 1974-78, chmn. orch. panel, 1975-78, cons., evaluator, panelist, 1974—, mem. first challenge grant rev. panel, 1977, co-chmn. recording panel, 1983-84; mem. grant rev. panel Va. Commn. for the Arts, 1976-78; adv. bd. Eastern Music Festival, 1977-83, Richmond Friends Opera, 1979-80; adv. coun. Va. Alliance for Arts Edn., 1978, Federated Arts Coun. Richmond, 1979-80; steering com. BRAVO Arts, 1978-79 (gov.'s award); cons. Tenn. Arts Commn., 1979-80; bd. dirs. Theatre IV, Richmond, 1974-80, Am. Music Ctr, N.Y.C., 1980-84, St. Louis Forum, 1983—, New City Sch., St. Louis, 1987—, Metro Theatre Co., 1994—; mem. challenge grant evaluation panel Ky. Arts Commn., 1983; participant Leadership St. Louis, 1983-84, bd. dirs., 1987-89; commr. subdistrict Mo. History Mus., 1987—, sec., 1993; speaker, panelist, cons. numerous arts orgns. Mem. Am. Symphony Orch. League (chmn. orch. library info. svc. adv. com., recruiter, mem. final interview com., advisor mgmt. fellowship program), Regional Orch. Mgrs. Assn. (v.p. 1976, policy com. 1977-79), Women's Forum Mo. Office: Metro Theatre Co 8308 Olive Blvd Saint Louis MO 63132-2814

BRICE, ROGER THOMAS, lawyer; b. Chgo., May 7, 1948; s. William H. and Mary Loretta (Ryan) B.; m. Carol Coleman, Aug. 15, 1970; children: Caitlin, Coleman, Emily. AB, DePaul U., 1970; JD, U. Chgo., 1973. Bar: Ill. 1973, Iowa 1973, U.S. Ct. Appeals (10th, 4th, 6th and 7th cirs.) 1975, U.S. Dist. Ct. (no. and ctrl. dists.) Ill. 1977, 1995, U.S. Trial Bar (no. dist.) 1982, U.S. Supreme Ct. 1978. Staff atty. Office of Gen. Counsel NLRB, Washington, 1974-76; assoc. Kirkland & Ellis, Chgo., 1976-79, Reuben & Proctor, Chgo., 1979-80, ptnr., 1980-86, Isham, Lincoln & Beale, Chgo., 1986-88, Sonnenschein, Nath & Rosenthal, Chgo., 1988—, head of labor and employment group, 2000—. Legal counsel, bd. dirs. Boys and Girls Clubs Chgo., 1991—. Fellow Coll. Labor and Employment Lawyers. Roman Catholic. Home: 3727 N Harding Ave Chicago IL 60618-4026 Office: Sonnenschein Nath & Rosenthal 233 S Wacker Dr Ste 8000 Chicago IL 60606-6491 E-mail: rbrice@sonnenschein.com.

BRICHFORD, MAYNARD JAY, archivist; b. Madison, Ohio, Aug. 6, 1926; s. Merton Jay and Evelyn Louise (Graves) B.; m. Jane Adair Hamilton, Sept. 15, 1951; children— Charles Hamilton, Ann Adair Brichford Martin, Matthew Jay, Sarah Lourena. B.A., Hiram Coll., 1950; M.S., U. Wis., 1951. Asst. archivist State Hist. Soc. Wis., 1952-56; methods and procedures analyst Ill. State Archives, 1956-59; records and space mgmt. supr. Dept. Adminstrn. State of Wis., Madison, 1959-63; archivist U. Ill., Urbana, 1963-95, asso. prof., 1963-70, prof., 1970—. Contbr. articles in field. Mem. gen. commn. on archives and history United Meth. Ch., 1988-96; bd. chmn. U. Ill. YMCA, 1987-89. With U.S. Navy, 1944-46. Council on Library Resources grantee, 1966-69, 70-71; Nat. Endowment for the Humanities grantee, 1976-79; Fulbright grantee, 1985; Am. Phil. Soc. grantee, 1992. Fellow Soc. Am. Archivists (pres. 1979-80); mem. Ill. Archives Adv. Bd. (chmn. 1979-84) Republican. Methodist. Home: 409 Eliot Dr Urbana IL 61801-6725 Office: 19 Library 1408 W Gregory Dr Urbana IL 61801-3607

BRICKEY, KATHLEEN FITZGERALD, law educator; b. Austin, Tex., Sept. 16, 1944; d. Robert Bernard and Ina Marie (Daw) Fitzgerald; m. James Nelson Brickey, Aug. 22, 1969. BA, U. Ky., 1965, JD, 1968. Criminal law specialist/cons. Ky. Crime Commn., Frankfort, Cin., 1968-71; exec. dir. Ky. Judicial Conf. and Coun., Frankfort, 1971-72; adj. prof. law U. Ky., Lexington, 1972; asst. to assoc. prof. law U. Louisville, 1972-76; assoc. prof. to prof. law Washington U., St. Louis, 1976-89, George Alexander Madill prof. law, 1989-93, James Carr prof. of criminal jurisprudence, 1993—. Cons. U.S. Sentencing Commn., 1988, 91; witness U.S. Senate Com. on Judiciary, Washington, 1986. Author: Kentucky Criminal Law, 1974, Corporate Criminal Liability, 1984, 2d edit., 1992-94, Corporate and White Collar Crime, 1990, 3d edit., 2002; contbr. articles to profl. jours. Mem. Am. Law Inst., Soc. for Reform of Criminal Law, Assn. Am. Law Schs. (sect. on criminal justice chair 1989, exec. com. 1985-91, 94-95). Office: PO Box 1120 Saint Louis MO 63188-1120

BRICKEY, SUZANNE M. editor; b. Grand Rapids, Mich., Apr. 4, 1951; d. Robert Michael and Elizabeth (Rogers) Stankey; m. Homer Brickey, Jr. B.A., Ohio U., Athens, 1973; B.J., U. Mo., Columbia, 1977. Editor Living Today, The Blade, Toledo, 1980-82, Toledo Mag., The Blade, 1982-92, Living Today, Toledo, 1992—. Mem. Toledo Press Club, Toledo Rowing Club. Home: 2510 Kenwood Blvd Toledo OH 43606-3601 Office: The Blade 541 N Superior St Toledo OH 43660-0001

BRICKLER, JOHN WEISE, lawyer; b. Dayton, Ohio, Dec. 29, 1944; s. John Benjamin and Shirley Hilda (Weise) B.; m. Marilyn Louise Kuhlmann, July 2, 1966; children: John, James, Peter, Andrew, Matthew. AB, Washington U., St. Louis, 1966; JD, Washington U., 1968. Bar: Mo. 1968, U.S. Supreme Ct. 1972, U.S. Dist. Ct. (ea. dist.) Mo. 1974, U.S. Ct. Appeals (8th cir.) 1974. Assoc. Peper, Martin, Jensen, Maichel and Hetlage, St. Louis, 1973-77, ptnr., 1978-98, Blackwell Sanders Peper Martin LLP, St. Louis, 1998—. Bd. dirs. Concordia Pub. House, St. Louis, 1993-, chmn. 1998-2001. Bd. dirs. Luth. Family and Children's Svcs. Mo., St. Louis, 1988-93, vice chmn., 1988-89. Capt. JAGC, U.S. Army, 1969-73. Mem. ABA, Nat. Assn. Bond Lawyers, Bar Assn. Met. St. Louis. Office: Blackwell Sanders Peper Martin LLP 720 Olive St Fl 24 Saint Louis MO 63101-2338 E-mail: jbrickler@blackwellsanders.com.

BRICKMAN, KENNETH ALAN, state lottery executive; b. Hannibal, Mo., Sept. 10, 1940; s. Roy Frederick and Nita Wilma (Swearingen) B.; m. Mildred Darlene Myers, Aug. 10, 1963; children: Heather Katherine, Erik Alan. BS in Bus. and Econs., Culver-Stockton Coll., Canton, Mo., 1963; JD, U. Mo., 1970. Bar: Ill. 1970, Mo. 1970, U.S. Supreme Ct. Ptnr. firm Scholz, Staff & Brickman, Quincy, Ill., 1970-78; pres. real estate brokerage Landmark of Quincy, Inc./Better Homes & Gardens, 1978-79; counsel, chief counsel Ill. Dept. Commerce and Cmty. Affairs, Springfield, 1980—85; gen. counsel, dep. dir. Ill. State Lottery, 1986-91; sec.-treas., exec. v.p. La. Lottery Corp., Baton Rouge, 1991-95; exec. v.p. Iowa Lottery, Des Moines, 1995—. Served as capt. USAF, 1963-67. Mem. Culver Stockton Coll. Alumni Assn. (pres. 1979). Office: Iowa Lottery 2015 Grand Ave Des Moines IA 50312-4999

BRICKSON, RICHARD ALAN, lawyer; b. Madison, Wis., Feb. 10, 1948; s. William Louis and Nancy May (Gay) B.; m. Marilyn Joan Serenco, June 20, 1971; children: Jennifer Lynne, Katherine Anne, Evan Leigh. BA, Wabash Coll., 1970; JD, Georgetown U., 1973. Bar: Mo. 1973. Staff atty. The May Dept. Stores Co., St. Louis, 1973-77, assoc. gen. counsel, 1977-79, asst. gen. counsel, 1979-81, counsel, 1981-82, counsel, sec., 1982-88, sr. counsel, sec., 1988—. Office: May Dept Stores Co 611 Olive St Saint Louis MO 63101-1721

BRIDENBAUGH, PHILLIP OWEN, anesthesiologist, physician; b. Sioux City, Iowa, Dec. 17, 1932; s. Lloyd Donald and Harriet (Anderson) B.; m. Kathleen Conway, June 22, 1957 (div. Apr. 1980); children: Sue, Tom, Dan; m. Diann Hurd, Mar. 7, 1981; children: Rob, Jeff. BA, U. Nebr., 1954; MD, U. Nebr., Omaha, 1960. Diplomate Am. Bd. Anesthesiology. Staff anesthesiologist Mason Clinic, Seattle, 1965-70, dir. dept. anesthesia, 1970-77; prof., chmn. dept. anesthesiology U. Cin. Med. Ctr., 1977—. Pres. UAA, Inc., Cin., 1977—. Co-editor: Neural Blockade, 1980, 2d edit., 1988, 3d edit., 1997: sect. editor Anesthesia and Analgesia, 1989-95; sr. editor Regional Anesthesia, 1989-97. Trustee Wood Libr. Mus. Anesthesiology, 1992-94. 1st lt. U.S. Army, 1954-56. Mem. Assn. Univ. Anesthetists, Soc. Acad. Anesthesia Chmn. (pres. 1988-90), Am. Soc. Anesthesiology (bd. dirs., v.p. sci. affairs 1992-94, 1st v.p. 1994-95, pres. elect 1995-96, pres. 1996-97, immediate past pres. 1997-98), Am. Soc. Regional Anesthesia (pres. 1990-91), Ohio Soc. Anesthesiologists (pres. 1991-92). Office: U Cin Dept Anesthesia 231 Bethesda Ave Cincinnati OH 45267-0001 E-mail: bridenpo@uc.edu.

BRIDGELAND, JAMES RALPH, JR. lawyer; b. Cleve., Feb. 16, 1929; s. James Ralph and Alice Laura (Huth) B.; m. Margaret Louise Bates, March 24, 1950; children: Deborah, Cynthia, Rebekah, Alicia, John. BA magna cum laude, U. Akron, 1951; MA, Harvard U., 1955, JD, 1957. Bar: Ohio 1957. Mem. internat. staff Goodyear Tire & Rubber Co., Akron, Ohio, 1953-56; ptnr. Taft, Stettinius & Hollister, Cin., 1957—; dir., mem. exec. com. Firstar Corp. and Star Bank Cin.; dir. SHV N.Am., Inc., The David J. Joseph Co., Robert A. Cline Co., Art Stamping, Inc., Seinau-Fisher Studios, Inc.; instr., lectr. in lit. U. Cin.. Pres., trustee Cin. Symphony Orch.; sec., trustee Louise Taft Semple Found.; trustee Cin. Opera Co., Hillside Trust, Jobs for Cin. Grads., Cin. Inst. Fine Arts; past bd. dirs. Legal Aid Soc.; mayor, mem. coun. City of Indian Hill, Ohio, 1985-91; pres. Indian Hill Sch. Bd., 1971-77. 1st lt. USAF, 1951-53, Korea. Mem. ABA, Ohio Bar Assn., Cin. Bar Assn., Am. Arbitration Assn., Harvard Law Sch. Assn. (past pres. Cin. chpt.), Harvard Alumni Assn. (nat. v.p. 1978-85). Harvard Club (pres. 1983-84), Queen City Club, Commonwealth Club (treas. 1984-86), Queen City Optimist Club, Recess Club, Assn. Literary Scholars and Critics, Cin. Optimist Club, Cin. Literary Club. Republican. Episcopalian. Home: 8175 Brill Rd Cincinnati OH 45243-3937

BRIDGES, JACK EDGAR, electronics engineer; b. Denver, Jan. 6, 1925; s. Byron Edgar and Edith Katherine (Kimmel) B.; m. Martha Jane Ernest, Dec. 22, 1951; children: Victoria Ann, Amelia Joan, Cynthia Sue. BSEE, U. Colo., 1945, MSEE, 1947. Instr. elec. engr. Iowa State Coll., Ames, 1947-48; antenna engr. Andrew Corp., Chgo., 1948-49; rsch. engr. Zenith Radio Corp., 1949-55; head of color TV rsch. Magnavox, Ft. Wayne, Ind., 1955-56; chief electronics engr. Warwick Mfg., Niles, Ill., 1956-61; sr. sci. adv. IIT Rsch. Inst., Chgo., 1961-92; chmn. Interstitial, Park Ridge, Ill., 1993—. Patentee in field; contbr. articles to profl. jours. With USN, 1943-46. Recipient Browder J. Thompson prize Inst. Radio Engrs., 1956, Disting. Engring. Alumnus award U. Colo., 1983. Fellow IEEE (life, cert. of achievement Group on EMC, 1976, Prize Paper award Power Engring. Soc., 1980); mem. Eta Kappa Nu, Tau Beta Pi, Sigma Xi. Home and Office: 1937 Fenton Ln Park Ridge IL 60068-1503

BRIDGES, ROGER DEAN, historical agency administrator; b. Marshalltown, Iowa, Feb. 10, 1937; s. Floyd F. and Beatrice Andrea (Pipher) B.; m. Karen Maureen Buckley, June 4, 1960; children: Patrick Sean, Kristin Joy, Jennifer Lynn. BA, Iowa State Tchrs. Coll., 1959; MA, State Coll. of Iowa, 1962; PhD, U. Ill., 1970; LHD, Lincoln (Ill.) Coll., 1987, Tiffin U., 1994. Tchr., libr. Keokuk (Iowa) Pub. Schs., 1959-62; instr. in history Bradley U., Peoria, Ill., 1967; asst. prof. history U. S.D., Vermillion, 1968-69; asst. editor Papers of Ulysses Grant, Carbondale, Ill., 1969-70; dir. rsch. Ill. State Hist. Libr., Springfield, 1970-76, head libr., 1976-85; dir. Ill. State Hist. Libr./Ill. Hist. Preservation Agy., 1985-87; dir., editor Lincoln legal papers project, asst. historian Ill. Hist. Preservation Agy, 1987-88; exec. dir. Rutherford B. Hayes Presdl. Ctr., Fremont, Ohio, 1988—. Part-time instr. Ill. State U., Normal, Ill., 1974-84; prof. Sangamon State U., Springfield, 1985-88, Bowling Green (Ohio) State U., 1989—. Author, editor: Illinois: It's History and Legacy, 1984; asst. editor: Papers of Ulysses S. Grant, vol. 4, 1972. Bd. dirs. Springfield Urban League, 1976-82, Gt. Am. People Show, New Salem, Ill., 1978-85; bd. dirs., sec., v.p. Birchard Pub. Libr. Sandusky County, Fremont, 1988-96, pres., 1996-99; bd. dirs., pres. Conv. and Visitors Bur. Sandusky County, Fremont, 1988-93. Nat. Hist. Publs. Commn. fellow, 1969-70; recipient Disting. Svc. awrd Springfield Urban League, 1977. Mem. Am. Hist. Assn., So. Hist. Assn., Abraham Lincoln Assn. bd. dirs. 1985—), Orgn. Am. Historians, Soc. for Historians of Gilded Age and Progressive Era (sec., treas. 1989—), Ill. State Hist. Soc. (Disting. Svc. award 1988), Ohio Acad. History (exec. coun. 1996-98), bd. trustees Ohioana Library Assn., 1998—, C. of C. of Sandusky County (bd. dirs. 1999-2002), Rotary Internat. Democrat. Baptist. Home: 1500 Buckland Ave Fremont OH 43420-3205 Office: Rutherford B Hayes Presdl Ctr Libr Presdl Ctr Spiegel Grove Fremont OH 43420-2796 E-mail: rdbridges@nwonline.net., rbridges@rbhayes.org.

BRIDGEWATER, BERNARD ADOLPHUS, JR. retired footwear company executive, consultant; b. Tulsa, Mar. 13, 1934; s. Bernard Adolphus and Mary Alethea (Burton) B.; m. Barbara Paton, July 2, 1960; children: Barrie, Elizabeth, Bonnie. AB, Westminster Coll., Fulton, Mo., 1955; LLB, U. Okla., 1958; MBA, Harvard, 1964. Bar: Okla. 1958, U.S. Supreme Ct. 1958, U.S. Ct. of Claims 1958. Asst. county atty., Tulsa, 1962; assoc. McKinsey & Co., mgmt. cons., 1964-68, prin., 1968-72, dir., 1972-73, 75; assoc. dir. nat. security and internat. affairs Office Mgmt. and Budget, Exec. Office Pres., Washington, 1973-74; exec. v.p. Baxter Travenol Labs., Inc., Chgo. and Deerfield, Ill., 1975-79, dir., 1975-85; pres. Brown Group, Inc., Clayton, Mo., 1979-87, 90-99, CEO, 1982-99, chmn., 1985-99, also dir.; now ret.; cons. TIAA-CREF, N.Y.C. Bd. dirs. FMC Corp., Phila., FMC Techs., Inc., Chgo., Mitretek Sys., Inc., McLean, Va., EEX Corp., Houston, ThoughtWorks Inc., Chgo.; adv. dir. Schroder Venture Ptnrs. LLC, N.Y.C.; cons. Office Mgmt. and Budget, 1973, 75; pvt. cons. Author: (with others) Better Management of Business Giving, 1965. Trustee Rush-Presbyn. St. Luke's Med. Ctr., 1974-84, Washington U., St. Louis, 1983-94, 95—, Barnes Hosp., St. Louis, 1987-90; bd. visitors Harvard U. Bus. Sch., 1987-93. Served to lt. USNR, 1958-62. Recipient Rayonier Found. award Harvard U., 1963; George F. Baker scholar, 1964 Mem. Beta Theta Pi, Omicron Delta Kappa, Phi Alpha Delta. Clubs: River (N.Y.C.); St. Louis Country, Log Cabin (St. Louis); Indian Hill Country (Winnetka, Ill.). Office: 7701 Forsyth Blvd Ste 1000 Saint Louis MO 63105-1841

BRIDGMAN, G(EORGE) ROSS, lawyer; b. New Haven, Dec. 27, 1947; s. George Ross Bridgman and Betty Jean (Soderquist) Burrows; m. Patricia Hess; children: Taylor Wilson, Katharine June, Elizabeth Honey. BA cum laude, Yale U., 1970; JD, Northwestern U., 1973. Bar: Ohio 1973, U.S. Dist. Ct. (so. dist.) Ohio 1974, U.S. Dist. Ct. (no. dist.) Ohio 1976, U.S. Ct. Appeals (6th cir.) 1984, U.S. Supreme Ct. 1990. Assoc. Vorys, Sater, Seymour & Paese, Columbus, Ohio, 1973-80, ptnr., 1980—. Mem. editorial bd. Northwestern U. Law Rev., Chgo., 1972-73. Trustee Columbus Jr. Theatre of the Arts, 1976-80, pres., 1978-80; trustee, v.p. London (Ohio) Pub. Libr., 1979-84; bd. dirs. Ctrl. Ohio Regional Coun. on Alcoholism, Columbus, 1987-89; trustee Kidscope, Columbus, 1988-89, Recovery Alliance, Columbus, 1989-97, Ohio Parents for Drug-Free Youth, 1991-99; mem. exec. bd. Simon Kenton coun. Boy Scouts Am., 1996—; mem. Columbus Symphony Chorus, 1999—. Mem. ABA, Columbus Bar Assn., Ohio Bar Assn., Nat. Assn. Coll. and Univ. Attys., Capital Club, Columbus Country Club. Republican. Episcopalian. Office: Vorys Sater Seymour & Pease PO Box 1008 52 E Gay St Columbus OH 43215-3161 E-mail: grbridgman@vssp.com.

BRIDGMAN, THOMAS FRANCIS, lawyer; b. Chgo., Dec. 30, 1933; s. Thomas Joseph and Angeline (Gorman) B.; m. Patricia A. McCormick, May 16, 1959; children: Thomas, Kathleen Ann, Ann Marie, Jane T., Molly. B.S. cum laude, John Carroll U., 1955; J.D. cum laude, Loyola U., Chgo., 1958. Bar: Ill. 1958, U.S. Dist. Ct. 1959. Assoc. McCarthy & Levin, Chgo., 1958, Baker & McKenzie, Chgo., 1958-62, ptnr., 1962—. Trustee John Carroll U., 1982-88. Fellow Am. Coll. Trial Lawyers, Am. Bd. Trial Advs. (adv.), Internat. Acad. Trial Lawyers (past pres.), Union Club, Beverly Country Club (Chgo., pres. 1983). Democrat. Roman Catholic. Home: 9400 S Pleasant Ave Chicago IL 60620-5646 Office: Baker & McKenzie 1 Prudential Plaza 130 E Randolph St Ste 3700 Chicago IL 60601-6342

BRIERLEY, GERALD P. physiological chemistry educator; b. Ogallala, Nebr., Aug. 14, 1931; s. Phillip and Myrtle (Shireman) B.; m. Miriam Grove, Apr. 17, 1971; children: David, Steven, Glenn, Lynn. B.S., U. Med.-Coll. Park, 1953, Ph.D., 1961. Asst. prof. U. Wis., Madison, 1962-64; faculty mem. Ohio State U., Columbus, 1964—, prof. physiol. chemistry, 1969—, chmn. dept., 1981-95, prof. emeritus, chmn. emeritus of dept. med. biochemistry, 1996—. Capt. USAF, 1953-56. USPHS grantee to study ion transport by heart mitochondra, 1965— ; USPHS grantee to study pathology mitchondria in ischemia, 1977— Mem. Am. Soc. Biol. Chemistry, Biophys. Soc., Am. Heart Assn. Office: Dept of Medical Biochemistry 333 Hamilton Hall 1645 Neil Ave Columbus OH 43210-1218

BRIGGS, JOHN, grocery retail executive; Internal auditor Hy-Vee Inc, West Des Moines, 1982-84, staff acct., 1984-86, asst. treas., 1986-88, dir.

office adminstrn., 1988-92, sec., controller, asst. v.p., 1992-97, v.p., CFO, treas., 1997—. Office: Hy-Vee Inc 5820 Westown Pkwy West Des Moines IA 50266

BRIGHT, MYRON H. judge, educator; b. Eveleth, Minn., Mar. 5, 1919; s. Morris and Lena A. Bright; m. Frances Louise Reisler, Dec. 26, 1947; children: Dinah Ann, Joshua Robert. BSL, U. Minn., 1941, JD, 1947. Bar: N.D. 1947, Minn. 1947. Assoc. Wattam, Vogel, Vogel & Bright, Fargo, ND, 1947, ptnr., 1949—68; judge 8th U.S. Cir. Ct. Appeals, 1968—85, sr. judge, 1985—; disting. prof. law St. Louis U., 1985—88, emeritus prof. of law, 1989—95. Capt. U.S. Army, 1942—46. Recipient Francis Rawle award, ALI-ABA, 1996, Lifetime Achievement award, U. N.D. Law Sch., 0198, Herbert Harley award, AJS, 2000. Mem.: ABA, U.S. Jud. Conf. (com. on adminstrn. of probation sys. 1977—83, adv. com. on appellate rules 1987—90, com. on internat. jud. rels. 1996—), N.D. Bar Assn. Office: US Ct Appeals 8th Cir 655 1st Ave N Ste 340 Fargo ND 58102-4952 E-mail: myron-bright@ca8.uscourts.gov.

BRIGHTFELT, ROBERT, diagnostic company executive; BS with distinction, MS with distinction, U. Nebr.; MBA, U. Ga. Various positions in healthcare and diagnostics DuPont Diagnostics, Dade Behring, Deerfield, Ill., group pres. for Chemistry products divsn., pres. Global Products. E-mail: brightrw@dadebehring.com.

BRIGHTON, GERALD DAVID, accounting educator; b. Weldon, Ill., May 14, 1920; s. William Henry and Geneva (Ennis) B.; m. Lois Helen Robbins, June 7, 1949; children: Anne, William, Joan, John, Jeffrey. B.S., U. Ill., 1941, M.S., 1947, Ph.D., 1953. C.P.A., Ill. Instr. accountancy U. Ill., Urbana, 1947-53, prof., 1954-83, Ernst & Whinney Disting. prof., 1983-88, prof. emeritus, 1988—, dir. undergrad. acctg. program, 1978-86; staff acct. Touche, Niven, Bailey & Smart, Chgo., 1953-54. Cons. G.D. Brighton, C.P.A., Urbana, 1954— ; vis. prof. U. Tex.-Austin, 1973; program specialist Dept. HUD, Washington, 1979; vice chmn. U. Ill. Athletic Assn., Urbana, 1982-86 Contbr. articles to profl. jours. Alderman City of Urbana, 1967-69; officer, bd. dirs. U. Ill. YMCA, Champaign, 1959-81, 89-95, Wesley Found., U. Ill., 1986—; treas. John Gwinn for Congress, Urbana, 1982-83, Green Meadows coun. Girl Scouts U.S., 1981-83. Served to maj. U.S. Army, 1941-46. AACSB Faculty fellow, 1978-79; recipient Bronze Tablet for high honors U. Ill., 1941 Mem. AICPA (hon.), Ill. Soc. CPAs (disting.), Am. Acctg. Assn., Assn. Govt. Accts., Govtl. Fin. Officers Assn., Nat. Tax Assn., Tax Inst. Am. Democrat. Methodist. Home: 501 Evergreen Ct Urbana IL 61801-5928 Office: U Ill 1206 S 6th St Champaign IL 61820-6978

BRILL, ALAN RICHARD, entrepreneur; b. Evansville, Ind., July 5, 1942; s. Gregory and Bernice Lucille (Froman) B.; children: Jennifer Leigh, Katherine Anne, Alison Elizabeth. AB, DePauw U., 1964; MBA, Harvard U., 1968. Mgmt. cons. Peace Corps, Ecuador, 1964-66; sr. acct., cons. Arthur Young & Co., N.Y.C., 1968-71; v.p. ops. Charter Med. Mgmt. Co., Inc., 1972-73; v.p. controller Hosp. Investors, Atlanta, 1972-73; v.p., treas., dir. Worrell Newspapers, Inc., Worrell Broadcasting, Inc., Charlottesville, Va., 1973-79; pres. Brill Assocs., Evansville, Ind., 1979—, Brill Media Co., Inc., Evansville, 1980—. Bd. visitors U. So. Ind. Sch. Bus. Mem. AICPA, N.Y. State Soc. CPAs, Evansville C. of C. (bd. dirs.), Jobs for S.W. Ind. (bd. dirs.), Beacon Group, Farmington Country Club (Charlottesville), Safari Internat. Club. Republican. Methodist. Home: PO Box 3517 Evansville IN 47734-3517 Office: Brill Media Co Inc PO Box 3353 Evansville IN 47732-3353

BRILL, LESLEY, literature and film studies educator; b. Chgo., Sept. 3, 1943; s. Walter Henry and Fay (Trolander) B.; m. Megan Parry, Jan. 18, 1970; children: Benjamin, Calista. BA, U. Chgo., 1965; MA, SUNY, Binghamton, 1967; Ph.D., Rutgers U., 1971. Asst. prof. English U. Colo., Boulder, 1970-80, assoc. prof., 1981-89, chmn. dept. English, 1981-85, grad. dir., 1985-87; prof. and chmn. dept. English Wayne State U., Detroit, 1989-94. Vis. lectr. U. Kent, Canterbury, Eng., 1978-79; vis. prof. U. Paul Valery, Montpellier, France, 1984, U. de Nantes, France, 1995. Author: The Hitchcock Romance: Love and Irony in Hitchcock's Films, 1988, John Huston's Filmmaking, 1997; contbr. articles on lit. and film to profl. jours. Rockefeller Found. fellow, 1977-78. Mem. Soc. Cinema Studies. Office: Wayne State U Dept English Detroit MI 48202 E-mail: aa4525@wayne.edu.

BRILL, WINSTON JONAS, microbiologist, educator, research director, publisher and management consultant; b. London, June 16, 1939; came to U.S., 1949; s. Walter and Irmgard (Levy) B.; m. Nancy Carol Weisburd, June 11, 1964; 1 child, Eric David B.A., Rutgers U., 1961; Ph.D. in Microbiology, U. Ill., 1965. Postdoctoral fellow MIT, Cambridge, 1965-67; asst. prof. dept. bacteriology U. Wis., Madison, 1967-70, assoc. prof., 1970-74, prof., 1974-79, Vilas research prof., 1979-83, adj. prof., 1983—, v.p., dir. research Agracetus, 1981-89; pres. Winston J. Brill & Assocs., Madison, 1989—. Panel mem. NSF, USDA, Pontifical Acad. Scis.; mem. recombinant DNA adv. com. NIH, 1979-83; mem. policy adv. com. USDA, 1985— ; mem. genetic engring. adv. panel to U.S. sec. state, 1981; mem. exec. bd. Nat. Inst. Emerging Tech. Pub., editor: Innovative Leader, 1992—; mem. editl. bd. Jour. Biotech., Trends in Biotech., Critical Revs. in Biotech.; contbr. articles to profl. jours. Recipient Eli Lilly award in microbiology and immunology, 1979, Alexander von Humboldt Found. award, 1979, Award of Distinction U. Wis., 1990; Henry Rutgers fellow Rutgers U., 1961. Fellow AAAS, Am. Acad. Microbiology; mem. NAS, Am. Soc. Microbiology, Am. Soc. Plant Physiologists, Am. Soc. Biochemistry and Molecular Biology, Internat. Soc. Plant Molecular Biology. E-mail: wbrill@winstonbrill.com.

BRIMIJOIN, WILLIAM STEPHEN, pharmacology educator, neuroscience researcher; b. Passaic, N.J., July 1, 1942; s. William Owen and Georgiana (Macklin) B.; m. Margaret Murray Ross, June 22, 1964; children: Megan Rebekkah Brimijoin Vaules, William Owen, Alexander. AB in Psychology, Harvard Coll., 1964; PhD in Pharmacology, Harvard U., 1969. Asst. prof Mayo Med. Sch., Rochester, Minn., 1972-76, assoc. prof., 1976-80, prof. pharmacology, 1980—, Winston and Iris Clement prof., 1989—; chair dept. pharmacology Mayo Clinic, 1993—. Assoc. cons. Mayo Clinic Rochester Minn., 1971-72, cons. 1972—; vis. scientist Karolinska Inst. Stockholm, Sweden, 1978-79, U. Würzburg, Germany, 1987-88; assoc. dir. dean Mayo Grad. Sch., Rochester, 1983-87; mem. behavioral and neurosci. study sect. NIH, 1989-93, sci. adv. panel U.S. EPA, 1993—; mem. Gulf War Grants Rev. Bd. Dept. Def., 1997-99. Mem. editl. bd. Muscle and Nerve Jour., 1980-88, Diabetes Jour., 1985-93; contbr. to numerous profl. jours.; patentee in field. With USPHS, 1969-71. Recipient Career Devel. award NIH, 1975, Javits Neuroscience Investigator award NINDS, 1987, Sr. Disting. U.S. Scientist award Humboldt Found., 1987-88, Mayo Disting. Investigator award Mayo Clinic, 1993. Mem. Soc. Neuroscience (social issues com. 1987), Internat. Soc. Neurochemistry, Am. Soc. Neurochemistry (program com. 1993-94), Am. Soc. Pharmacology and Exptl. Therapeutics. Office: Mayo Clinic Dept of Pharmacology 200 1st St SW Dept Of Rochester MN 55905-0002

BRIN, DAVID, writer, astronomer; b. Glendale, Calif., Oct. 6, 1950; s. Herbert Henry and Selma (Stone) B. B.S. in Astronomy, Calif. Inst. Tech., 1973; M.S. in Elec. Engring., U. Calif.-San Diego, 1977, Ph.D. in Space Sci., 1981. Electronics engr. Hughes Aircraft Co., Carlsbad, Calif., 1973-77; profl. novelist Bantam Books, N.Y.C., 1980—; postdoctoral fellow Calif. State Inst., LaJolla, Calif., 1984—. Instr. physics, astronomy, writing San Diego State U., San Diego Community Colls., 1982— Author: (novels) Sundiver, 1980, Startide Rising (Nebula award 1983, Hugo award 1983, Locus award), 1983, The Practice Effect (Balrog award), 1984, (with Gregory Benford) Heart of the Comet, 1986, Earth, 1990; (novellas and novellettes) The Tides of Kithrup, 1981, The Loom of Thessaly, 1981, The Postman (runner-up Hugo award 1983), 1982, Cyclops (nominee Hugo award 1985), 1984, Glory Season, 1993, Brightness Reef, 1996, Infinity's Shore, 1996, The Transparent Society, 1998, (series) Startride Rising (Nebula award), 1983, Sundiver, 1985, The Uplift War, 1987, Heaven's Reach, 1998, Foundation's Triumph, 1999, (collections) The River of Time, 1986, Otherness, 1994, (stories for anthologies) War of the Worlds: Global Dispatches, 1996; contbr. short stories, sci. fact articles, and sci. papers to profl. publs. Nominated for John W. Campbell award for best new author of 1982 Mem. Am. Assn. Aeronautics and Astronautics, Sci. Fiction Writers Am. (sec. 1982-84) Avocations: backpacking; music, science, general eclecticism. Office: care Phantasia Press 5536 Crispin Way Rd West Bloomfield MI 48323-3405

BRINK, DAVID RYRIE, lawyer; b. Mpls., July 28, 1919; s. Raymond Woodard and Carol Sybil (Ryrie) B.; m. Irma Lorentz Brink; children: Anne Carol, Mary Claire, David Owen, Sarah Jane. BA with honors, U. Minn., 1940, BSL with honors, 1941, JD with honors, 1947; LLD, Capital U., 1981, Suffolk U., 1981, Mitchell Coll. Law, 1982. Bar: Minn. 1947, U.S. Dist. Ct. Minn. 1947, U.S. Tax Ct. 1967, U.S. Supreme Ct. 1980, U.S. Ct. Appeals (D.C. Cir.) 1982. Assoc. firm Dorsey & Whitney, Mpls., 1947-53, ptnr., 1953-89, head Washington office, 1982-84, ret. ptnr. Trustee Lawyers Com. Civil Rights Under Law, 1978—; bd. dirs. Nat. Legal Aid and Defender Assn., 1978-80; U.S. panelist for Dispute Resolution under Free Trade Agreement with Can.; bd. visitors U. Minn. Law Sch., 1978-81; chmn. trust and estates dept. Dorsey & Whitney, 1956-82; qualified neutral for mediation and arbitration Supreme Ct. of Minn., 1996—. Bd. editors: U. Minn. Law Rev, 1941-42; contbr. numerous articles to law jours. Bd. govs. Am. Coll. Trust and Estate Counsel Found., 1987-95. Served to lt. comdr. USNR, 1943-46. Recipient Outstanding Achievement award U. Minn., 1982 Fellow Coll. Law Practice Mgmt. (hon.), Am. Coll. Trust and Estate Counsel (regent, exec. com.); mem. ABA (gov. 1974-77, 80-83, pres. 1981-82), Ctrl. and Ea. European Legal Initiative, Com. on Law and Nat. Security, Fund for Pub. Edn. of ABA (pres. 1981-82), Am. Bar Found. (state chmn. 1977-80, gov. 1980-83), Am. Bar Retirement Assn. (pres. 1976-77), Am. Judicature Soc. (bd. dirs. 1988—), Nat. Conf. Bar Pres., Inst. Jud. Adminstrn., Am. Arbitration Assn. (trustee 1981—), Can.-U.S. Law Inst. (adv. bd. 1987—), Minn. Bar Assn. (pres. 1978-79), Internat. Mgmt. and Devel. Inst., Hennepin County Bar Assn. (pres. 1967-68), Nat. Inst. Citizen Edn. in Law (nat. adv. bd. 1982-85, chmn. 1983-84), N.W. Racquet Club, Sr. Tennis Players Club, Inc. Office: Dorsey & Whitney # 50 S 6th St Minneapolis MN 55402

BRINK, MARION FRANCIS, trade association administrator; b. Golden Eagle, Ill., Nov. 20, 1932; s. Anton Frank and Agnes Gertrude B. BS, U. Ill., 1955, MS, 1958; PhD, U. Mo., 1961. Rsch. biologist U.S. Naval Radiol. Def. Lab., San Francisco, 1961-62; assoc. dir. div. nutrition rsch. Nat. Dairy Council, Chgo., 1962-65, dir. div. nutrition rsch., 1965-70, pres. Rosemont, Ill., 1970-85; exec. v.p. ops. United Dairy Industry Assn., 1985-88, chief exec. officer, 1988-91. Vice chmn. human nutrition adv. com. USDA, 1980-81. Contbr. articles to prof. jours. Recipient citation of merit U. Mo. Alumni Assn. Mem. Am. Soc. for Nutritional Scis., Am. Soc. Clin. Nutrition, Am. Dietetic Assn., Dairy Shrine Club, Soc. for Nutrition Edn., Chgo. Nutrition Assn., Alpha Tau Alpha, Gamma Sigma Delta. Home: 444 Highcrest Dr Wilmette IL 60091-2358

BRINKMAN, DALE THOMAS, lawyer; b. Columbus, Ohio, Dec. 10, 1952; s. Harry H. and Jean May (Sandel) B.; m. Martha Louise Johnson, Aug. 3, 1974; children: Marin Veronica, Lauren Elizabeth, Kelsey Renee. BA, U. Notre Dame, 1974; JD, Ohio State U., 1977. Bar: Ohio 1977, U.S. Dist. Ct. (so. dist.) Ohio 1979. Assoc. Schwartz, Shapiro, Kelm & Warren, Columbus, 1977-82; asst. tax counsel Am. Elect. Power, 1982; gen. counsel Worthington Industries, Inc., 1982-99, v.p. adminstrn., gen. counsel, sec., 1999—. Author: Ohio State U. Law Jour.,1975-76, editor, 1976-77. Trustee, officer Friends of Dahlberg Ctr., Columbus, 1980-86; dir., officer Assn. for Developmentally Disabled, Columbus, 1986-94. Mem. ABA, Ohio Bar Assn., Columbus Bar Assn. Republican. Roman Catholic. Office: Worthington Industries Inc 1205 Dearborn Dr Columbus OH 43085-4769 E-mail: dtbrinkm@worthingtonindustries.com.

BRINKMAN, JOHN ANTHONY, historian, educator; b. Chgo., July 4, 1934; s. Adam John and Alice (Davies) B.; m. Monique E. Geschier, Mar. 24, 1970; 1 son, Charles E. A.B., Loyola U., Chgo., 1956, M.A., 1958; Ph.D., U. Chgo., 1962. Rsch. assoc. Oriental Inst., U. Chgo., 1963, dir. inst., 1972-81, asst. prof. Assyriology and ancient history, 1964-66, assoc. prof., 1966—70, prof., 1970—84, Charles H. Swift disting. svc. prof., 1984—2001, chmn. dept., 1969—72, Charles S. Swift disting. svc. prof. emeritus, 2001—. Ann. prof. Am. Schs. Oriental Rsch., Baghdad, 1968-69; chmn. Baghdad Schs. Com., 1970-85, chmn. exec. com., 1973-75, trustee, 1975-90; chmn. vis. com. dept. Near Ea. langs. and civilizations Harvard U., 1995-2001. Author: Political History of Post-Kassite Babylonia, 1968, Materials and Studies for Kassite History, Vol. I, 1976; Prelude to Empire, 1984; editorial bd. Chgo. Assyrian Dictionary, 1977—, State Archives Assyria, 1985—; editor in charge Babylonian sect. Royal Inscriptions of Mesopotamia, 1979-91; contbr. numerous articles to profl. jours. Fellow Am. Research Inst., in Turkey, 1971; sr. fellow Nat. Endowment Humanities, 1973-74; Guggenheim fellow, 1984-85 Fellow Am. Acad. Arts and Scis.; mem. Am. Oriental Soc. (pres. Middle West chpt. 1971-72), Am. Schs. of Oriental Rsch., Brit. Inst. Persian Studies, Brit. Sch. Archaeology in Iraq, Deutsche Orient Gesellschaft, Brit. Inst. Archaeology at Ankara, Am. Coun. Learned Socs. Roman Catholic. Home: 1321 E 56th St Apt 4 Chicago IL 60637-1762 Office: U Chgo 1155 E 58th St Chicago IL 60637-1540

BRINZO, JOHN S. business executive; b. 1942; married. BS, Kent State U., 1964; MBA, Case Western Res. U., 1968. Sr. v.p. Cleve.-Cliffs, Inc., Cleve., until 1989, exec. v.p., 1989—. Office: Cleve-Cliffs Inc 1100 Superior Ave Cleveland OH 44114-2589

BRISBANE, ARTHUR SEWARD, newspaper publisher; b. N.Y.C., Sept. 30, 1950; s. Seward Scatcherd and Doris Mae (Fauser) B.; m. Jo Ellen Hull, Oct. 16, 1982; children: Allison Faith, Madeline Mariah, Laura Calista. AB, Harvard Coll., 1973. Child care worker McLean Hosp., Belmont, Mass., 1973-74; freelance musician, 1974-76; reporter Glen Cove (N.Y.) Guardian, 1976-77, Kansas City (Mo.) Star & Times, 1977-79, columnist, 1979-84; reporter Washington Post, 1984-87, asst. city editor, 1987-89; columnist Kansas City Star, 1990-92, editor, v.p., 1992-97, pub., pres., 1997—. Author: Arthur Brisbane's Kansas City, 1982. Avocations: tennis, reading. Office: The Kansas City Star 1729 Grand Blvd Kansas City MO 64108-1458

BRISCOE, JOHN W. lawyer; BA, Westminster Coll., 1963; JD, U. Mo., 1966. Bar: Mo. Ptnr. Briscoe, Rodenbaugh & Brannon, Hannibal, Mo.; prosecuting atty. Ralls County. Pres. Mo. Bar, bd. govs., 1990—. Pres. bd. dirs. Barkley Cemetery Assn.; active Boy Scout Am. Troop 106 Com.; bd. dirs. Hannibal C. of C.; active Truman State U. Parents Coun., 1995—97; apptd. bd. govs. Truman State U., 1997—; active Trinity Episcopal Ch. Mem.: Hannibal Elks Club, New London Lions Club. Office: Briscoe Rodenbaugh & Brannon PO Box 446 423 S Main St New London MO 63459 Office Fax: 573-221-3456.*

BRISCOE, MARY BECK, federal judge; b. Council Grove, Kans., Apr. 4, 1947; m. Charles Arthur Briscoe. BA, U. Kans., 1969, JD, 1973; LLM, U. Va., 1990. Rsch. asst. Harold L. Haun, Esq., 1973; atty.-examiner fin. divsn. ICC, 1973—74; asst. U.S. atty. for Wichita and Topeka, Kans. Dept. Justice, 1974—84; judge Kans. Ct. Appeals, 1984—95, chief judge, 1990—95; judge U.S. Ct. Appeals (10th cir.), Topeka, 1995—. Fellow: Kans. Bar Found., Am. Bar Found.; mem.: ABA, Women Attys. Assn. Topeka, Kans. Bar Assn. (Outstanding Svc. award 1992), Topeka Bar Assn., Nat. Assn. Women Judges, Am. Judicature Soc., U. Kans. Law Soc., Kans. Hist. Soc., Washburn Law Sch. Assn. (hon.). Office: US Ct Appeals 10th Cir 645 Massachusetts Ste 400 Lawrence KS 66044-2235

BRISTOL, NORMAN, lawyer, arbitrator, former food company executive; b. Bronx, N.Y., June 14, 1924; s. Lawrence and Bell (Allchin) B.; m. Doreen Kingan, Mar. 28, 1952; children: Charles L., Norman, Alexander, Barnaby. Grad., Phillips Exeter Acad., 1939-41; A.B., Yale, 1944; LLB, Columbia Law Sch., 1947-49. Bar: N.Y. bar 1950, Mich. bar 1954. Atty. Root, Ballantine, Harlan, Bushby & Palmer, N.Y.C., 1949-53; with Kellogg Co., Battle Creek, Mich., 1954-78, asst. gen. counsel, 1958-64, sec., 1960-78, gen. counsel, 1964-78, sr. v.p., 1968-75, dir., 1972-78, exec. v.p., 1975-78; atty. Howard & Howard, Kalamazoo, 1979-93. Mem. Gull Lake Comty. Schs. Bd. Edn., 1963-70, pres., 1965-67; trustee Kalamazoo Symphony Soc., Inc., 1983-94, pres., 1990-91; bd. dirs. Southwest Mich. Land Conservancy, Inc., 1996-2001. Lt. (j.g.) USNR, 1943-46. Mem. State Bar Mich., Kalamazoo Bar Assn., Am. Soc. Corp. Secs., SCORE (counsellor). Home and Office: 2962 Sylvan Dr Hickory Corners MI 49060-9319

BRITT, KEVIN M. bishop; b. Nov. 19, 1944; Ordained priest Roman Cath. Ch., 1970. Consecrated aux. bishop Archdiocese of Detroit, 1993-94, consecrated bishop, 1994—. Office: St Aloysius Downtown 1234 Washington Blvd Detroit MI 48226-1808

BRITTON, CLAROLD LAWRENCE, lawyer, consultant; b. Soldier, Iowa, Nov. 1, 1932; s. Arnold Olaf and Florence Ruth (Gardner) B.; m. Joyce Helene Hamlett, Feb. 1, 1958; children: Laura, Eric, Val, Martha. BS in Engring., U. Mich., Ann Arbor, 1958, JD, 1961, postgrad. Bar: Ill. 1961, U.S. Dist. Ct. (no. dist.) Ill. 1962, U.S. Ct. Appeals (7th cir.) 1963, U.S. Supreme Ct. 1970, Mich. 1989. Assoc. Jenner & Block, Chgo., 1961-70, ptnr., 1970-88; pres. Britton Info. Systems, Inc., 1991—. Lectr. DePaul U., 1988. Author: Computerized Trial Ntoebook, 1991; asst. editor Mich. Law Rev., 1960. Comdr. USNR, 1952-57. Fellow Am. Coll. Trial Lawyers; mem. ABA (litigation sect., antitrust com., past regional chmn. discovery com. 1961), Ill. State Bar Assn. (chmn. Allerton House Conf. 1984, 86, 88, chmn. rule 23 com. 1985-87, chmn. civil practice and procedure coun. 1987-88, antitrust com.), Chgo. Bar Assn. (past chmn. fed. civil procedure com., mem. judiciary and computer law coms., civil practice com.), 7th Cir. Bar Assn., Def. Rsch. Inst. (com. on aerospace 1984), Mich. Bar Assn., Ill. Assn. Trial Lawyers, Order of Coif, Law Club (Chgo.), Racine Yacht Club (Wis.), Macatawa Yacht Club (Mich.), Masons, Alpha Phi Mu, Tau Beta Pi. Republican. Lutheran. Office: 411 E Washington St Ann Arbor MI 48104-2015 E-mail: britton@ic.net.

BRITTON, SAM, state legislator; m. to Kaye Britton; 1 child, Samuel. BS, U. Cin. Real estate agt. Britton and Assocs., Cin.; treas. Avondale Redevelop. Corp.; mem. Ohio Ho. of Reps., Columbus. Mem. adv. bd. Cin. Comty. Devel. Mem. NAACP (life), Madisonville Comty. Coun. (past pres.), Cin. Area Bd. Realtors, Ohio Assn. Realtors (trustee), Black Male Coaliton, Kappa Alpha Psi Office: Ohio Ho of Reps Ohio State Bldg Columbus OH 43215

BRIZZOLARA, CHARLES ANTHONY, lawyer, director; b. Chgo., Nov. 20, 1929; s. Ralph D. and Florence H. (Hurley) B.; m. Audree Doyle, Aug. 24, 1968. B.A., Lake Forest (Ill.) Coll., 1951; J.D., Ill. Inst. Tech., 1957. Bar: Ill. 1959. Practiced law, Chgo., 1959-67; with Walter E. Heller & Co., also Walter E. Heller Internat. Corp. (later Amerifin Corp.), 1967-85; v.p., sec., gen. counsel Walter E. Heller & Co., also Walter E. Heller Internat. Corp., 1974-85, sr. v.p., 1980-85; v.p. Chgo. Bears Football Club, Inc., 1975-88; mem. firm Chadwell & Kayser Ltd., 1985-90; ptnr. Michael Best & Friedrich, LLC, Chgo., 1990—. Bd. dirs. Abacus Real Estate Fin. Co., Walter E. Heller & Co. S.E., Heller Factoring (Hong Kong) Ltd., Factoring Serfin, S.A., Chandler Leasing Corp., 1975-80; lectr. seminars Am. Mgmt. Assn. Editor: Chgo.-Kent Law Rev, 1956. Bd. dirs. Cath. Charities Archdiocese of Chgo., 1978-99, sec., 1991-94; bd. dirs. Ill. Inst. Tech. Chgo. Kent Alumni Assn., 1980-89. Served with AUS, 1952-54. Mem. Internat. Bar Assn., ABA, Ill. Bar Assn. Roman Catholic. Home: Apt 20G 253 E Delaware Pl Chicago IL 60611-1758

BROADIE, THOMAS ALLEN, surgeon, educator; b. St. Paul, June 26, 1941; s. Thomas Edward and Laura Marjorie (Allen) B.; m. Victoria Taylor, July 20, 1968; children: Frances, Thomas. AB, Princeton U., 1963; MD, Northwestern U., 1967; PhD, U. Minn., 1977. Diplomate Am. Bd. Surgery. Intern, resident Johns Hopkins Hosp., 1967-69; resident U. Minn., 1969-75; from asst. prof. to prof. surgery Ind. U., Indpls., 1978-92, prof., 1992—. Mem. at large Com. on Trauma, Chgo., 1990-97; chmn. Ind. State Com. on Trauma, Indpls., 1991-97. Fellow ACS (pres. Ind. chpt. 1989-90, gov. at large 1992-97); mem. Soc. Univ. Surgeons, Midwest Surg. Assn. (pres. 1995-96), Ctrl. Surg. Assn., Am. Assn. Surgery Trauma, Western Surg. Assn., Am. Assn. Endocrine Surgeons, Am. Thyroid Assn. Office: Wishard Meml Hosp Dept Surgery 1001 W 10th St Indianapolis IN 46202-2859

BROCK, THOMAS DALE, microbiology educator; b. Cleve., Sept. 10, 1926; s. Thomas Carter and Helen Sophia (Ringwald) B.; m. Mary Louise Louden, Sept. 13, 1952 (div. Feb. 1971); m. Katherine Serat Middleton, Feb. 20, 1971; children: Emily Katherine, Brian Thomas. B.S., Ohio State U., 1949, M.S., 1950, Ph.D., 1952. Research microbiologist Upjohn Co., Kalamazoo, 1952-57; asst. prof. Western Res. U., Cleve., 1957-59, Ind. U., Bloomington, 1960-61, assoc. prof., 1962-64, prof., 1964-71; E.B. Fred prof. natural scis. U. Wis., Madison, 1971-90, prof. emeritus, 1990—, chmn. dept. bacteriology, 1979-82; pres. Sci. Tech. Pubs., 1990-94, Savanna Oak Found., 2000—. Found. for Microbiology lectr., 1971-72, 78-79 Author: Milestones in Microbiology, 1961, Principles of Microbial Ecology, 1966, Thermophilic Microorganisms, 1978, Biology of Microorganism, 7th edit., 1994, Basic Microbiology with Applications, 3d edit., 1986, A Eutrophic Lake, 1985, Thermophiles: General, Molecular and Applied Microbiology, 1986, Robert Koch: A Life in Medicine and Bacteriology, 1988, The Emergence of Bacterial Genetics, 1990, Shorewood Hills: An Illustrated History, 1999. Recipient Research Career Devel. NIH, 1962-68 Fellow AAAS; mem. Am. Soc. for Microbiology (hon. mem., chmn. gen. div. 1970-71, Fisher award 1984, Carski award 1988) Home and Office: 1227 Dartmouth Rd Madison WI 53705-2213

BROCK, WILLIAM ALLEN, III, economics educator, consultant; b. Phila., Oct. 23, 1941; s. William Allen and Margaret Elizabeth (Holcroft) B.; m. Joan Elaine Loutenshlager, Aug. 31, 1962; 1 child, Caroline Christine AB with honors in Math., U. Mo., 1965; PhD, U. Calif., Berkeley, 1969. Asst. prof. econs. U. Rochester, N.Y., 1969-71; assoc. prof. econs. U. Chgo., 1972-75; vis. assoc. prof. econs. U. Rochester, 1973; assoc., full prof. econs. Cornell U., 1974-77; prof. econs. U. Chgo., 1975-81; Romnes prof. econs. U. Wis., Madison, 1981—, F.P. Ramsey prof. econs., 1984—, W.F. Vilas rsch. prof., 1990—. Cons. U.S. Dept. Justice, SBA, EPA, FTC. Assoc. editor Jour. Econ. Theory, Internat. Econ. Rev., 1972-99; contbr. articles to profl. jours.; co-author: (with A. Malliaris) Differential Equations, Stability and Chaos in Dynamic Economics, 1989, (with D. Hsieh, B. LeBaron) Nonlinear Dynamics, Chaos and Instability: Statistical Theory and Economic Evidence, 1991. NSF grantee, 1970—, Sherman Fairchild disting. scholar Calif. Inst. Tech., 1978, Guggenheim fellow, 1987-88; recipient Roger F. Murray 3rd pl. prize Inst. Quantitative Rsch. in Fin., 1989. Fellow Econometric Soc.; mem. NAS, Am. Acad. Arts and Scis. Office: U Wis Dept Econs 1180 Observatory Dr Madison WI 53706-1320

BROCKA, BRUCE, editor, educator, software engineer; b. Davenport, Iowa, Nov. 1, 1959; s. Donald H. and Daisy Ann (Robertson) B.; m. M. Suzanne St. Ledger, Mar. 17, 1984; children: Melinda Athena, Bennett Paul. BS, St. Ambrose U., 1981; MS, U. Iowa, 1984. Instr. Army Mgmt. Engring. Coll., Rock Island, Ill., 1984-90; exec. editor, assoc. pub. Exec. Scis. Inst., Davenport, 1986—. Editor: Quality Control and Applied Statistics, 1987—, Operations Research/Management Science, 1987—, Automation in Quality Assurance, 1988, Biostatistica, 1990—, Quality Management, 1992; contbr. articles on sci. tech. to profl. jours. Ptnr. Summit Lane Properties. Republican. Avocation: hist. preservation. Home and Office: 1005 Mississippi Ave Davenport IA 52803-3938

BROCKMANN, WILLIAM FRANK, medical facility administrator; b. South Bend, Ind., Nov. 14, 1942; s. Ervin William and Elizabeth Marie (Kassidy) B.; m. Ellen Meier, June 10, 1967; children: William Edward, Rebecca Jayne. BS in Mgmt., Ind. U., 1966; MHA, St. Louis U., 1968. Administrv. asst. St. Anthony Hosp., Okla. City, 1968; asst. hosp. adminstr. Caylor-Nickel Med. Ctr., Bluffton, Ind., 1972-77, hosp. adminstr., 1977-86, pres., 1986-89, chief exec. officer, 1989—, also mem. exec. com., 1985—. Bd. dirs. Old First Nat. Bank. Gen. campaign mgr. Wells County United Way, 1973; past pres. Bluffton United Meth. Ch., Wells County Found.; pres., bd. dirs. Wells County Coun. on Aging; spkr. in field. Capt. M.S.C., U.S. Army, 1969-71. Fellow Am. Coll. Healthcare Execs. (Regents award, 2001); mem. Ind. Hosp. Assn. (chmn. bd. 1990-91, PRO negotiating team, Disting. Svc. award, 2001), Am. Hosp. Assn. (ho. dels. 1991-93). Republican. Methodist. Avocations: scuba diving, pool, reading, golf. Home: 1127 Ridgewood Ln Bluffton IN 46714-3827 Office: Bluffton Regional Med 303 S Main Bluffton IN 46714 E-mail: wbrockmann@bluffton-regional.com.

BROCKWAY, LEE J. architect; b. Mecosta, Mich., Aug. 13, 1932; s. Byron Maxwell and Mildred Loro (Wolfe) B.; m. Mary Haglind, Aug. 4, 1956; children: David, Michael, Anne McDonough, Bill. BArch, U. Notre Dame, 1955. Archtl. intern Haughey, Black and Williams, Architects, Battle Creek, Mich., 1959-61; chief architect Charles W. Cole & Son, Engrs. and Architects, South Bend, Ind., 1961-65; ptnr. The Shaver Partnership, Architects and Engrs., Michigan City, 1965-73; owner, architect Brockway Assocs., Architects, 1974-76; prin., corp. dir. Fanning/Howey Assoc., Inc., Ind., 1976-98, prin. emeritus, 1998—. Pres. Ind. Soc. Architects, 1990. Recipient Outstanding Svc. award Ind. soc. Architects, 1987, 89, Mich. City C. of C., 1978. Mem. AIA (corp. mem., mem. nat. com. on architecture for edn. 1978—, chmn. 1988), Coun. for Archtl. Rsch., Nat. Coalition Edn. Facilities (chmn. 1991-92), Coun. Edn. Facility Planners (bd. dirs. 1986-92, pres. 1990-91). Home: 2922 Belle Plaine Trl Michigan City IN 46360-1777 Office: Fanning Howey Assoc Inc PO Box 584 Michigan City IN 46361-0584

BROD, STANFORD, graphic designer, educator; b. Cin., Sept. 29, 1932; s. Morris and Rebecca (Mitman) B.; m. McCrystle Wood; children: Deborah, Daniel, Michael. BS in Design, U. Cin., 1955. Graphic designer Rhoades Studio, Cin., 1955-62; tchr. exptl. typography Art Acad. Cin., 1960-75; graphic designer Lipson, Alport & Glass Assocs., Inc. and predecessor firm Lipson Jacob, Assocs. Inc., Cin., 1962-94, Wood/Brod Design, Cin., 1994—; prof. graphic design U. Cin., 1962—. Tchr. illustration and packaging Art Acad. Cin., 1991-92, 94, 96—, tchr. corp. identity, 1992-97, 2002, tchr. illustration, packaging, 1997-98, 2001-02, tchr. adv. design, corp. design, 1994-97, tchr. visual comms., 1997-98, exhbn. design, 1999, 2001. Exhibited in group shows at Mus. Modern Art, N.Y.C., 1966, Urban Walls, Cin., 1972, City Banners, Sao Paulo, Brazil, 1975, ITC Ctr., N.Y.C., 1981, Tel Aviv Mus., 1982, Internat. Art Exhbn., Dusseldorf, Germany, 1982, Calligraphia U.S.A./USSR, 1990-96, UN, 1994; one-man shows include Skirball Mus. Hebrew Union Coll., Cin., 1989. Recipient Communications Arts awards, 1959, 64, 66, 70, 73, 76, Creativity on Paper awards, 1960-67, Internat. Typographic awards, 1965, 70, N.Y. Type Dirs. Club award, 1968, Typographic Composition Assn. awards, 1970-76. Office: 3662 Grandin Rd Cincinnati OH 45226-1117

BRODELL, ROBERT THOMAS, internal medicine educator; b. Rochester, N.Y., Nov. 24, 1953; s. Harold Louis and Alma Jean (Moreland) B.; m. Linda P. Brodell, July 2, 1977; children: Lindsey Ann, Julie Lynn, David William, Erin Elizabeth, Nathan Thomas. BA, Washington and Jefferson Coll., 1975; MD, U. Rochester, 1979. Bd. cert. in dermatology and dermatopathology. Asst. prof. dermatology Washington U., St. Louis, 1984-85; asst. prof. internal medicine Northeastern Ohio U. Coll. Medicine, Rootstown, Ohio, 1986-90, 1990-94, prof. internal medicine, 1994—, master tchr., 1997—. Asst. clin. prof. dermatology Case Western Res. U., Cleve., 1986-94, assoc. clin. prof., 1994—; chmn. Midwest Congress Derm. Socs., Dayton, Ohio, 1995—. Trustee Ohio divsn. Am. Cancer Soc., Columbus, 1992—; bd. dirs. Warren (Ohio) Sports Hall of Fame, 1996. Named Cleve. Cavaliers Prof. Basketball Team Fan of Year, 1997. Fellow Am. Acad. Dermatology, Am. Soc. Dermatopathology; mem. AMA, Ohio State Med. Assn., Wilderness Med. Assn., Ohio Dermatol. Assn. (trustee 1994—), Am. Cancer Soc. (v.p. Ohio divsn. 1999-2000, pres. Ohio divsn. 2000—), Masons (Master Old Erie # 3), Phi Beta Kappa, Alpha Omega Alpha. Home: 2660 E Market St Warren OH 44483-6204 Office: Northeastern Ohio Univ Coll Med PO Box 95 4209 State Route 44 Rootstown OH 44272-9698 E-mail: rtb@neoucom.edu.

BRODEN, JOHN E. state legislator; m. Josephine Broden; children: Ana Marie, John Francis. BA, U. Notre Dame; JD, Ind. U. Atty. Botkin & Leone Attys. at Law; city atty. South Bend; mem. Ind. State Senate, 2000—, mem. corrections, criminal and civil procedures com., mem. environ. affairs com., mem. govtl. and regulatory affairs local govt. subcom., mem. pub. policy, pub. affairs subcom. Councilman South Bend City County, 1995-98; active St. Joseph's H.S. Alumni Bd.; bd. dirs. South Bend Ctr. for the Homeless, CHIARA Home. Mem. Ind. State Bar Assn., South Bend Kiwanis Club. Roman Catholic. Avocations: running, golf, reading. Office: 200 W Washington St Indianapolis IN 46204-2785

BRODERICK, B. MICHAEL, JR. state legislator, banker; Banker, Canton, S.D.; mem. S.D. Ho. of Reps., Pierre. Mem. agr., nat. resources and transp. coms. S.D. Ho. of Reps.

BRODERICK, DENNIS JOHN, lawyer, retail company executive; BA, U. Notre Dame, 1970; JD, Georgetown U., 1976. Bar: Ohio 1976. Assoc. Hahn Loeser Freidheim Dean & Wellman, 1976-81; from staff atty. to asst. gen. counsel Firestone Tire & Rubber Co., 1982-87; counsel for regions, v.p. Federated Dept. Stores, Inc. (formerly Allied Stores Corp.), Cin., 1987-88, v.p., gen. counsel, 1988-90, sr. v.p., gen. counsel, sec., 1990—. Mem. Am. Corp. Counsel Assn. (dir. NE Ohio chpt. 1986). Office: Federated Dept Stores Inc 7 W 7th St Cincinnati OH 45202-2424

BRODEUR, ARMAND EDWARD, pediatric radiologist; b. Penacook, N.H., Jan. 8, 1922; s. Felix and Patronyne Antoinette (Lavoie) B.; m. Gloria Marie Thompson, June 4, 1947; children: Armand Paul, Garrett Michael, Mark Stephen, Mariette Therese, Michelle Bernadette, Paul Francis. AB, St. Anselm Coll., 1945; MD, St. Louis U., 1947, M.Rd., 1952; LLD (hon.), St Anselm Coll., 1974. Intern St. Louis U. Hosps., 1947-48, resident in pediat., 1948-49; resident in radiology St. Louis U. Hosps. and St. Louis U. Grad. Sch., 1949-52; instr. St. Louis U. Sch. Medicine, 1952-60, sr. instr., 1960-62, asst. prof., 1962-65, assoc. prof., 1965-70, prof. radiology, 1970—, chmn. dept. radiology, 1975-78, vice chmn. dept., 1978-88, prof. pediat., 1979—, prof. juvenile law, 1979—; pvt. practice specializing in pediat. radiology St. Louis, 1954-56; radiologist-in-chief Cardinal Glennon Meml. Hosp. for Children, 1956-88, Shriners Hosp. for Children, 1988—; assoc. v.p., bd. govs. Cardinal Glennon Children's Hosp., St. Louis. Lectr. and cons. in field; med. dir. radiography Sanford Brown Coll., 1996—. Radio show host Doctor to Doctor, Sta. KMOX-CBS, St. Louis; host daily To Your Health; health reporter Sta. KMOV-TV, also Sta. WFUN-FM, Sta. KSIV-AM; TV host Sta. WCVB Channel 5, Boston; author: Radiologic Diagnosis in Infants and Children, 1965, Radiology of the Pediatric Elbow, 1980, Radiologic Pathology for Allied Health Professions, 1980, Child Maltreatment, 1993, also monographs; contbr. articles to profl. jours., numerous tchg. tapes. Bd. dirs. ARC, TB Soc., March of Dimes, 15 others. With U.S. Army, 1942-46, with USPHS, 1952-54. Decorated Knight Equestrian Order Holy Sepulchre Jerusalem; recipient Mo. Health Care Communicator of Yr. award, 1991, Welby award Nat. Acad. Radio and TV Health Communicators, Healthcare Leadership award Met. Hosp. St. Louis, 1994, Lifetime Achievement award Nat. Assn. Physician Broadcasters, numerous civic awards; Armand Brodeur Day proclaimed by City of St. Louis; named St. Paul Man of Yr., 1991; ann. lecture named in his honor dept. radiology St. Louis U. Sch. Medicine, 1998. Fellow Am. Coll. Radiology, Am. Acad. Pediat.; mem. AMA (Bronze medal, Golden Apple), Soc. Pediat. Radiology, Radio. Soc. N.Am., Nat. Assn. Med. Communicators (charter, co-founder, pres. 1987-88), Sigma Xi, Alpha Omega Alpha, Alpha Sigma Nu, Rho Kappa Sigma. Roman Catholic. Home: 6 Huntleigh Trails Ln Saint Louis MO 63131-4801 Office: 2001 S Lindbergh Blvd Saint Louis MO 63131-3504

BRODHEAD, WILLIAM MCNULTY, lawyer, former congressman; b. Cleve., Sept. 12, 1941; s. William McNulty and Agnes Marie (Franz) B.; m. Kathleen Garlock, Jan. 16, 1965; children: Michael, Paul. A.B., Wayne State U., 1965; J.D., U. Mich., 1967. Bar: Mich. 1968, D.C. 1983. Tchr., Detroit, 1964-65; atty. City of Detroit, 1969-70; mem. Mich. Ho. Reps., 1971-74, 94th-97th Congresses from 17th Dist., mem. com. on ways and means, 1977-82, mem. budget com., 1979-80; chmn. Democratic Study Group, 1981-82; ptnr. firm Plunkett & Cooney P.C., Detroit, 1982—. Trustee The Skillman Found., Michigan's Children; chair Focus: Hope-Covenant House of Mich.; dir. Citizens Rsch. Coun. of Mich. Home: 5096 Mirror Lake Ct West Bloomfield MI 48323-1534 Office: Plunkett & Cooney 38505 Woodward Ave Ste 2000 Bloomfield Hills MI 48304 E-mail: wbrodhead@plunketcooney.com.

BRODKEY, ROBERT STANLEY, chemical engineering educator; b. L.A., Sept. 14, 1928; s. Harold R. and Clara (Goldman) B.; m. Martha Mahr, Dec. 22, 1958 (div. Nov. 1971); 1 son, Philip Arthur; m. Carolyn Patch, Dec. 6, 1975. A.A., San Francisco City Coll., 1948; B.Chemistry with highest honors, M.S. in Chem. Engring, U. Calif.-Berkeley, 1950; Ph.D. in Chem. Engring. (Gulf Oil fellow), U. Wis., 1952. Rsch. chem. engr. Esso Rsch. & Engring. Co., Linden, N.J., 1952-56, Esso Std. Oil Co., Bayway, 1956-57; asst. prof. chem. engring. Ohio State U., Columbus, 1957-60, assoc. prof., 1960-64, prof., 1964-92, prof. emeritus, 1992—. Cons. on turbulent motion, mixing kinetics, rheology, 2-phase flow, fluid dynamics, image processing and analysis; expository lectr. GAMM Conf., 1975; vis. prof. Japan Soc. Promotion Sci., 1978; Clyde chair engring. U. Utah, fall 1994. Author: Transport Phemomena, A Unified Approach, 1988, The Phenomena of Fluid Motions, 1967, reprint edit., 1995; editor: Turbulence in Mixing Operations, 1975; contbr. articles to profl. jours.; patentee in field. Recipient Outstanding Paper of Yr. award Can. Jour. Chem. Engring., 1970; NATO sr. fellow in sci. Max Planck Institut für Strömungsforschung, Göttingen, Fed. Republic Germany, 1972; Alexander Von Humboldt Found. sr. U.S. scientist award, 1975, 83; sr. rsch. award Coll. Engring. Ohio State U., 1983, 86; Disting. Sr. Rsch. award Am. Soc. Engring. Edn., 1985; Chem. Engr. lectureship award Am. Soc. Engring. Edn., 1986; North Am. Mixing Forum award, 1994. Fellow AAAS, AIChE, Am. Phys. Soc., Am. Inst. Chemists; mem. Am. Chem. Soc., Am. Acad. Mech., Soc. Engring. Sci., Soc. Rheology, Sigma Xi, Phi Lambda Upsilon, Alpha Gamma Sigma, Phi Beta Delta. Office: Ohio St Univ 140 W 19th Ave Columbus OH 43210-1110 E-mail: brodkey.1@osu.edu.

BRODL, RAYMOND FRANK, lawyer, former lumber company executive; b. Cicero, Ill., June 1, 1924; s. Edward C. and Lillian (Cerny) B.; m. Ethel Jean Johnson, Aug. 15, 1953; children: Mark Raymond, Pamela Jean, Susan Marie. Student, Norwich U., Northfield, Vt., 1943, Ill. Coll., 1946-48; J.D., Loyola U., Chgo., 1951. Bar: Ill. 1951. Atty. law office Joseph A. Ricker, Chgo., 1951-58, Brunswick Corp., Chgo., 1958-62; sec., gen. atty. Edward Hines Lumber Co., 1962-84, atty., cons., 1985—, sr. counselor, 2001. Democratic candidate for local jud. office, 1953, 57. Served with AUS, 1943-46. Mem. Ill. Bar Assn. Home and Office: 366 Lance Dr Des Plaines IL 60016-2628

BRODSKY, PHILIP HYMAN, chemical executive, researcher; b. Phila., July 7, 1942; s. Herbert and Gladys (Ettenger) B.; m. Rita Kissen, Sept. 13, 1964 (div. 1974); children: Michelle, Andrew; m. Sunny Jo Kurn, Feb. 18, 1977; 1 child: Noah. BChemE, Cornell U., 1965, PhD, 1969; postgrad., MIT, 1988. Sr. research engr. Monsanto Co., Springfield, Mass., 1968-1973, Research specialist, 1973-77, research group leader, 1977-80, mgr. results mgmt. St. Louis, 1980-82, mgr. Lustran New Products Springfield, dir. Plastics Tech., 1984-87, dir. ctrl. rsch. labs. St. Louis, 1987-90, dir. corp. rsch. and environ. tech., 1991-95, corp. v.p., corp. rsch. and environ. tech., 1996-2000; v.p. Office Sci. and Tech. Pharmacia Corp., 2000—02. Mem. bd. chem. scis. and tech. NRC, 1992-98, mem. critical techs. com., 1992; mem. remediation techs. devel. forum EPA, 1992—; mem. groundwater remediation tech. rsch. and analytical ctr. guide com., 1993-99; bd. dirs. Metaphore Pharms., 1998—; mem. Ind. Rsch. Inst., 1987—, chair fin. com., 1994, chair rsch. com. 1991, bd. dirs. 1992-95; mem. adv. bd. dept. chem. and environ. engring. U. Ariz., 1994—; mem. adv. bd. dept. chem. engring. Cornell U., 1995-2001, Washington U., 1999—; mem. bd. visitors Idaho Nat. Engring. and Environ. Lab., 1998—; mem. com. on chem. and pub. affairs Am. Chem. Soc., 1996—, chair, 1999—. Patentee in field; contbr. articles to profl. publs. including Environ Sci. and Tech., Rsch. Tech. Mgmt., Clean Products and Processes, Chem. Engring., SPE Jour., Am. Inst. Chem. Engring. Reprints, Chem. Health and Safety. Pres. Cmty. Day Alternative Sch., Springfield, 1974-77, St. Louis Rsch. Coun., 1987—; mem. St. Louis Regional Commerce and Growth Assn., 1987—; bd. dirs. Inroads Inc., St. Louis, 1988-99. Mem. MIT Soc. Sr. Execs. (bd. dirs. 1988-95), Sigma Xi. Avocations: skiing, backpacking, tennis, golf.

BRODSKY, WILLIAM J. options exchange executive; b. N.Y.C., 1944; Student, Syracuse U., 1965, JD, 1968. Bar: N.Y. 1969, Ill. 1985. Atty. Model, Roland & Co., 1968-74; with Am. Stock Exch., 1974-82, exec. v.p. ops., 1979-82; exec. v.p., COO Chgo. Merc. Exch., 1982-85, pres., CEO, 1985-97; chmn., CEO Chgo. Bd. Options Exch., 1997—. Adv. mem. internat. capital mktgs. adv. com. Fed. Res. Bank N.Y.; mem. adv. coun. J.L. Kellogg Grad. Sch. Mgmt.; bd. dirs. Peoples Energy Corp. Bd. dirs. Northwestern Meml. Corp.; trustee Syracuse U. Mem. N.Y. State Bar Assn., Ill. Bar Assn., Swiss Futures and Options Assn. (bd. dirs.), Futures Industry Assn. (bd. dirs.), Econ. Club Chgo., Comml. Club Chgo. Achievements include: selection for inclusion into Derivatives Hall of Fame, 2000, Jr. Achievement Chgo. Bus. Hall of Fame, 2001. Office: Chgo Bd Options Exch LaSalle at Van Buren Chicago IL 60605-7413

BRODY, LAWRENCE, lawyer, educator; b. St. Louis, Aug. 12, 1942; s. Max and Jeannette (Cohen) B.; m. Janice Dobinsky, Dec. 25, 1967; 1 child, Michael Allen. BS in Econs., U. Pa., 1964; JD, Washington U., St. Louis, 1967; LLM in Tax, NYU, 1968. Bar: Mo. Assoc. atty. Husch, Eppenberger, Donohue, Elson & Cornfeld, St. Louis, 1968-74, ptnr., 1974-86, Bryan Cave, LLP, St. Louis, 1986—. Adj. prof. Washington U. Sch. Law, 1968—. Author: Missouri Estate Planning, 1988; author, editor Life Insurance Counsellor Series, 1990, 91. Fellow Am. Coll. of Trust and Estate Counsel, Am. Coll. Tax Counsel; mem. Adv. Bd. of Tax Mgmt. Office: Bryan Cave LLP 211 N Broadway Ste 3600 Saint Louis MO 63102-2733

BRODY, THEODORE MEYER, pharmacologist, educator; b. Newark, May 10, 1920; s. Samuel and Lena (Hammer) B.; m. Ethel Vivian Drelich, Sept. 7, 1947; children— Steven Lewis, Debra Jane, Laura Kate, Elizabeth. B.S., Rutgers U., 1943; M.S., U. Ill., 1949, Ph.D., 1952. Mem. faculty U. Mich. Med. Sch., Ann Arbor, 1952-66; prof. pharmacology Coll. Medicine, Mich. State U., East Lansing, 1966-90, prof. emeritus, 1990—, chmn. dept., 1966-86. Cons. NIH, 1969-73, NIDA, 1975-79, Internat. Soc. Heart Rsch., 1973—2002; mem. sci. adv. com. Pharm. Mfrs. Assn. Found., 1973—2002; U.S. rep. Internat. Union Pharmacology, 1973-76; mem. bd. Fedn. Am. Socs. for Exptl. Biology, 1973-76; mem. Com. Sci. Soc. Presidents. Mem. editl. bd. Jour. Pharmacology and Exptl. Therapeutics, 1965-80, specific field editor, 1981-92; mem. editl. bd. Rsch. Comm. in Chem. Pathology and Pharmacology, Molecular Pharmacology, 1972-90; editor: Human Pharmacology Molecular to Clinical, 1991, 94, 97; cons. Random House Dictionary of English Lang., 1964—; contbr. 300 articles to profl. jours. Served with AUS, 1943-46. Scholar Disting. scholar, NSF-U. Hawaii, 1974. Mem. Am. Soc. Pharmacology and Exptl. Therapeutics (John Jacob Abel award 1955, mem. council 1969-72, sec.-treas. 1970, pres. elect 1973, pres. 1974, past pres. 1975, Torald Sollmann award in pharmacology 1995), Internat. Soc. Biochem. Pharmacology, Am. Coll. Clin. Pharmacology, Assn. Med. Sch. Pharmacologists (sec. 1984-86), Soc. Toxicology, Soc. Neurosci., Japanese Pharmacology Soc., AAUP, Sigma Xi, Rho Chi, Phi Kappa Phi. Home: 842 Longfellow Dr East Lansing MI 48823-2444 Office: Mich State U Dept Pharmacology East Lansing MI 48824 E-mail: brodyt@msu.edu.

BROECKER, SHERRY, state legislator; b. Feb. 14, 1951; m. Jerry Broecker; 3 children. Student, U. Minn. Self-employed custom picture framer; rep. Dist. 53B Minn. Ho. of Reps., 1994—.

BROEG, BOB (ROBERT WILLIAM BROEG), writer; b. St. Louis, Mar. 18, 1918; s. Robert Michael and Alice (Wiley) B.; m. Dorothy Carr, June 19, 1943 (dec.); m. Lynette A. Emmenegger, July 23, 1977. BJ, U. Mo., 1941. With A.P., Columbia, Mo., 1939-40, Jefferson City, 1941, Boston, 1941-42; reporter St. Louis Star-Times, 1942; staff sports dept. St. Louis Post-Dispatch, 1945-85, sports editor, 1958-85, asst. to pub., 1977-85. Author: Don't Bring That Up, 1946, Stan Musial: The Man's Own Story, 1964, Super Stars of Baseball, 1971, Ol' Missou, a Story of Missouri Football, 1974, We Saw Stars, 1976, The Man Stan...Musial, Now and Then, 1977, Football Greats, 1977, The Pilot Light and the Gas House Gang, 1980, Bob Broeg's Redbirds, 1981, My Baseball Scrapbook, 1983, Front Page, 1984, Baseball From a Different Angle, 1988, Baseball's Barnum, 1989, Ol' Mizzou, A Century of Tiger Football, 1990, Bob Broeg's Redbirds, A Century of Cardinals Baseball, 1992, Super Stars of Baseball No. 2, 1993, Autobiography, Bob Broeg, Memories of Hall of Fame Sportswriter, 1995; co-author: That's a Winner, Jack Buck Autobiography, 1997, St. Louis Cardinals' Encyclopedia, 1998, The 100 Greatest Moments in St. Louis Sports, 2000; contbr. articles to profl. publs. Bd. dirs. Vets. com. Baseball Hall of Fame, 1972-2000, bd. dirs. 1975-2000; bd. dirs. Honors Ct., Nat. Football Found., 1975. Served with USMCR, 1942-45. Recipient Nat. Sportscasters, Sportswriters awards Mo., 1962-65, 67; Journalism medal U. Mo., 1971; Faculty-Alumni award U. Mo., 1969, Hall of Fame Writing award, 1980; elected to Mo. Sports Hall of Fame, 1978, Nat. Sportscasters/Sportswriters Hall of Fame, 1997, Nat. Baseball Congress Hall of Fame, 1998, Mo. Sports Legend, 2000. Mem. Baseball Writers Assn. Am. (pres. 1958), Kappa Tau Alpha, Sigma Delta Chi, Sigma Phi Epsilon, Omicron Delta Kappa. Home: 60 Frontenac Estates Dr Saint Louis MO 63131-2602 Office: Pulitzer Pub Co 900 N Tucker Blvd Saint Louis MO 63101-1069

BROMBERG, ROBERT SHELDON, lawyer; b. Bklyn., May 3, 1935; s. Jack and Bertha (Toskey) B.; m. Barbara W. Schwartz, Apr. 1, 1978; children: Jason, David. AB, Columbia U., 1956, LLB, 1959; LLM in Taxation, NYU, 1966. Bar: N.Y. 1960, D.C. 1972, Ohio 1972, U.S. Ct. Claims 1976, U.S. Supreme Ct 1975. Practiced law, N.Y.C., 1960-66; atty. exempt orgns. br. IRS, Washington, 1966-70, Office Chief Counsel, 1970-72; partner firm Baker, Hostetler & Patterson, Cleve., 1972-79; prin. Robert S. Bromberg, L.P.A., 1979-81, Paxton & Seasongood, Cin., 1981-85; sole practice, 1985—. Lectr. tax and health law confs. Author: Tax Planning for Hospitals and Health Care Organizations, 2 vols., 1979; cons. editor: Prentice Hall Tax Exempt Organizations Service, 1973-84; nat. adv. bd. Integrated Healthcare Report; adv. bd. The Exempt Organization Tax Review; contbr. articles to profl. jours. Recipient award (5) Dept. Treasury, 1966-72, citation Am. Assn. Homes for Aged, 1973 Mem. Am. Health Lawyers Assn. (pres. 1986-87, program chmn. Am. Tax Inst. 1975-95). Home: 1144 E Rookwood Dr Cincinnati OH 45208-3334 Office: 36 E 4th St Ste 1119 Cincinnati OH 45202-3810

BROMM, CURT, state legislator; b. Oakland, Nebr., Mar. 19, 1945; m. Vicki Nodlinski, 1968; children: Jason, Jenefer, John, Jina, Jaron. Student, U. Nebr. Past county atty. Saunders County; mem. Nebr. Legislature from 23rd dist., Lincoln, 1992—; mem. bus. and labor com. Nebr. Legislature, mem. natural resources and urban affairs com., vice chmn. rules com., speaker of the legislature, 2002—. Chmn. bd. dirs. Saunders County Sch. Reorgn. Bd.; mem., pres. Wahoo Pub. Sch. Bd. Mem. Nebr. State Bar Assn. Home: 1448 N Pine St Wahoo NE 68066-1449 Office: Nebraska Unicameral Legislature State Capitol PO Box 94604 Lincoln NE 68509-4604

BRONSON, DAVID LEIGH, physician, educator; b. Bath, Maine, Mar. 24, 1947; s. Frank Edgar Bronson and Edna Louise (Sullivan) Belanger; m. Susan Kylei McEvoy, May 27, 1973 (div. Dec. 1988); children: Chad Devin, Carly Anne, Jaclyn Ruth, Jonathan David; m. Kathleen Susan Franco, Jan. 30, 1993; children: Roberto Anthony Franco, John Carlos Franco. BA, U. Maine, 1969; MD, U. Vt., 1973. Diplomate Am. Bd. Internal Medicine, Am. Bd. Geriatrics. Med. resident U. Wis., Madison, 1973-74, U. Vt., Burlington, 1974-76, asst. prof. medicine, 1977-83, assoc. prof. medicine, 1983-92, vice chmn. dept. medicine, 1990-92; chmn. dept. internal medicine Cleve. Clinic Found., 1992-96, chmn. regional med. practice, 1995—; assoc. prof. internal medicine Ohio State U., Columbus, 1992—; clin. prof. medicine Pa. State U., Hershey, 1995—. Pres. med. staff, trustee Med. Ctr. Hosp. Vt., Burlington, 1989-90; trustee Univ. Health Ctr., Burlington, 1987-92. Contbr. numerous articles to profl. jours. Fellow ACP; mem. Am. Coll. Physician Execs., Am. Mgmt. Assn., Med. Group Mgmt. Assn., Am. Fedn. for Clin. Rsch., Soc. Gen. Internal Medicine. Office: Cleve Clinic Found 9500 Euclid Ave # S13 Cleveland OH 44195-0001

BRONSTEIN, FRED, orchestra executive; b. Boston; MMus, Manhattan Sch. Music, N.Y.C.; DMus, SUNY, Stony Brook. Co-founder Aequalis, Boston, 1985-93; orch. mgmt. fellow Am. Symphony Orch. League, 1995-96; exec. dir. Civic Orch. Chgo., 1996-98; CEO, pres. Omaha Symphony Orch., 1998—. Office: Omaha Symphony Orch 1605 Howard St Omaha NE 68102-2797

BROOKE, JOHN L. history educator; b. Mass., May 19, 1953; m. Sara C. Balderston, July 31, 1979. BA in History and Anthropology, Cornell U., 1976; MA in History, U. Pa., 1977, PhD in History, 1982. Vis. asst. prof.

Amherst (Mass.) Coll., 1982-83; asst. prof. to prof. Tufts U., Medford, Mass., 1983-2001; dept. chair, 1996-97; prof. Ohio State U., Columbus, 2001—. Author: The Heart of the Commonwealth: Society and Political Culture in Worcester County, Massachusetts, 1713-1861, 1989, The Refiner's Fire: The Making of Mormon Cosmology, 1644-1844, 1994; contbr. articles to scholarly jours. Recipient award Nat. Soc. Daus. Colonial Wars, 1989, E. Harold Hugo Meml. Book prize Old Sturbridge Village Rsch. Libr. Soc., 1989, Merle Curti award for intellectual history, 1991, book prize for Am. history Nat. Hist. Soc., 1991, Bancroft prize Columbia U., 1995, ann. book prize Soc. for Historians of Early Am. Republic, 1995, ann. book award New Eng. Hist. Assn., 1995; S.F. Haven fellow Am. Antiquarian Soc., 1982, faculty rsch. fellow Tufts U., 1983, 88, Charles Warren fellow Harvard U., 1986-87, jr. fellow NEH, 1986-87, sr. fellow Commonwealth Ctr., 1990-91, fellow Am. Coun. Learned Socs., 1990-91, NEH fellow 1997-98, Guggenheim fellow, 1997-98. Mem. AAUP, Am. Antiq. Soc., Am. Hist. Assn., Orgn. Am. Historians, Mass. Hist. Soc. Democrat. Office: Ohio State U Dept History Dulles Hall Columbus OH 43210

BROOKER, THOMAS KIMBALL, oil company executive; b. L.A., Oct. 1, 1939; s.Robert Elton and Sally Burton Harrison (Smith) B.; m. Nancy Belle Neumann, 1966; children: Thomas Kimball Jr., Isobel, Vanessa. BA in French Lit., Yale U., 1961; MBA, Harvard U., 1968; MA in Art History, U. Chgo., 1989, PhD in Art History, 1996. Assoc. in corp. fin. Morgan Stanley & Co., Inc., N.Y.C., 1968-73, v.p., 1973-75, mng. dir., 1976-88, head Chgo. office, 1978-88; pres. Barbara Oil Co., Chgo., 1989—, also bd. dirs. Bd. dirs. Arthur J. Gallagher & Co., Miami Corp., Cutler Oil & Gas Corp.; bd. govs. Midwest Stock Exch., 1980-88, vice chmn., 1986-88. Contbr. articles to profl. jours. Chmn. vis. com. libr. U. Chgo., mem. vis. com. visual arts dept.; mem., chmn. com. on libr. Yale U. President's Coun., 1980-84; trustee Pierpont Morgan Libr., Newberry Libr., Gov. John Carter Brown Libr., Yale U. Libr. Assn.; bd. dirs. Lyric Opera Chgo.; v.p. Alliance Francaise Chgo. Recipient Sir Thomas More medal U. San Francisco, 1992; assoc. fellow Saybrook Coll., Yale U. Mem. Adminstrv. Coun. (v.p.), Assn. Internat. de Bibliophilie, Bibliotheca Wittockiana (mem. sci. com.), Bandar-Log, Caxton Club, Chgo. Club, Comml. Club, Econ. Club, River Club (N.Y.C.), Knickerbocker Club (N.Y.C.), Grolier Club (N.Y.C.), The Casino, Saddle and Cycle Club, Edgartown (Mass.) Yacht Club, The Reading Room (Edgartown), Quadrangle Club, Racquet Club, Rockaway Hunt Club, Wayfarers Club. Home: 1500 N Lake Shore Dr Chicago IL 60610-6657 Office: Barbara Oil Co 1 S First National Plz Ste 5030 Chicago IL 60603-2000

BROOKS, BENJAMIN RIX, neurologist, educator; b. Cambridge, Mass., Dec. 1, 1942; s. Frederic Manning and Miriam Adelaide (Rix) B.; m. Susan Jane Whitmore, May 31, 1970; children: Nathaniel Phillips, Alexander Whitmore, Joshua Cushing. AB cum laude, Harvard U., 1965, MD magna cum laude, 1970. Diplomate Am. Bd. Psychiatry and Neurology, Am. Bd. Internal Medicine. Intern, asst. resident Harvard Med. Svc., Boston City Hosp., 1970-72; resident in neurology Mass. Gen. Hosp., Boston, 1972-74; clin. assoc. med. neurology br. Nat. Inst. Neurolog. Diseases and Stroke, Bethesda, Md., 1974-76; rsch. fellow neurovirology div. Johns Hopkins Med. Sch., Balt., 1976-78, asst. prof. neurology dept., 1978-82; assoc. prof. neurology and med. microbiology U. Wis. Med. Sch., Madison, 1982-87, prof., 1987—; staff neurologist William S. Middleton Meml. VA Hosp., 1982-84, chief neurology svc., 1984—. Examiner Am. Bd. Psychiatry and Neurology, Evanston, Ill., 1980—; chmn. neuropharmacologic drugs adv. com. FDA, Rockville, Md., 1982-85; vis. prof. various schs., U.S., Eng., Fed. Republic Germany, Japan, Spain. Editor: Amyotrophic Lateral Sclerosis, 1987, Brain Rsch. Bull., 1980-90; contbr. papers, revs., abstracts to profl. publs., chpts. to books. Mem. ushers com. Grace Episcopal Ch., Madison, 1983—; mem. talented and gifted evaluation com. Madison Sch. Bd., 1986; mem. com. on VA manpower of the Inst. of Medicine of the Nat. Acad. Scis. Lt. comdr. USPHS, 1974-76. Recipient Nat. Rsch. award Nat. Inst. Neurolog. and Communicative Disorders and Stroke, 1976-78, Tchr.-Investigator Devel. award, 1978-82. Mem. Am. Acad. Neurology (chair govt. svcs. sect. 1995—, mem. animal rsch. com. 1990-95), Am. Neurolog. Assn., Wis. Neurolog. Soc. (sec.-treas. 1985-87, v.p. 1988, pres.-elect 1989, pres. 1990), Soc. for Neurosci., N.Am. ALS Care Registry (adv. com.), Soc. Exptl. Neuropathology, Am. Soc. Microbiology, Internat. Soc. Neuroimmunology, Assn. VA Neurologists (pres. 1994-96, councilor 1996—), Soc. In Vitro Biology, Tissue Culture Assn., World Fedn. Neurology Rsch. Group on Motor Neuron Diseases (steering com.). Republican. Avocations: running, sailing, swimming, bicycling, hiking. Office: Wm S Middleton Meml VA Hosp 2500 Overlook Ter Madison WI 53705-2254

BROOKS, KENNETH N. forestry educator; m. Pamela Naylor; children: Marianne, Robin, Cherie, Nicole. BS in Range Sci., Utah State U., 1966; MS in Watershed Mgmt., U. Ariz., 1969, PhD in Watershed Mgmt., 1970. Hydrologist North Pacific Divsn. Corps of Engrs., Portland, Oreg., 1971-73, Tng. and Methods br. Hydrologic Engrng. Ctr., Davis, Calif., 1973-75; asst. prof. dept. forest resources U. Minn., St. Paul, 1975-79, assoc. prof., 1979-85, prof., 1985—, dir. grad. studies in forestry Coll. Natural Resources, 1987—; fellow Environment and Policy Inst. East-West Ctr., Honolulu, 1983-84. Cons. nat. and internat. agencies and firms including Food and Agrl. Orgn. of UN, U.S. Agy. for Internat. Devel., World Bank; condr. workshops in field; Fulbright lectr., Taiwan, 1997-98. Co-author: Guidelines for Economic Appraisal of Watershed Management Projects, 1987, Watershed Management Project Planning, Monitoring and Evaluation: A Manual for the ASEAN Region, 1989, Hydrology and the Management of Watersheds, 1991, 2d edit. 1997, Challenges in Upland Conservation: Asia and the Pacific, 1993, Dryland Forestry, 1995; contbr. articles to profl. jours. Am. Inst. Hydrology (chmn. bd. registration 1995—, sec. 1992), Soc. Am. Foresters (chmn. water resources working group 1991-93), Am. Water Resources Assn. (dir. West North Ctrl. dist. 1987-90), Western Snow Conf., Internat. Soc. Tropical Foresters, Xi Sigma Pi, Sigma Xi, Phi Kappa Phi. E-mail: kbrooks@umn.edu.

BROOKS, MARION, newscaster; BA English, Spelman Coll. Weekend anchor Sta. WABG-TV, Greenville, Miss., anchor weekday 6 pm and 11 pm newscasts; gen. assignment reporter, morning anchor Sta. WJKS-TV, Jacksonville, Fla., 1991—93; gen. assignment reporter Sta. KTVI-TV, St. Louis, 1993—96, weekend anchor; anchor noon newscast, reporter 5 pm and 6 pm newscasts Sta. WSB-TV, Atlanta, 1996—98; co-anchor 5 pm and 10 pm weekend newscasts Sta. WMAQ-TV, Chgo., 1998—, co-anchor 4:30 pm and 5 pm weekday newscasts, healthwatch reporter. Mem.: Nat. Assn. Black Journalists. Office: NBC 454 N Columbus Dr Chicago IL 60611*

BROOKS, PETER, radio director; m. Lynette Brooks; children: Megan, Kirsten. Mgr. Family Life Radio stas., Albuquerque, Mason; with Family Life Comms. WUGN, Midland, Mich., 1977—, gen. mgr. Avocations: community theater, racquetball. Mailing: 510 E Isabella Rd Midland MI 48640

BROOKS, PHILLIP, advertising executive; b. 1955; With Affiliate of Excellence Co., Mpls., 1976—, now pres.; with Excellence Co., pres., CEO. Office: Excellence Co 2601 E Hennepin Ave Minneapolis MN 55413-2913

BROOKS, RANDY, research company executive; BS, U. Maryland, 1973; MBA, U. Cin., 1975. Pres., founder Directions Rsch., 1988—. Speaker at industry events, ARF, AMA, AMA Tutorial Conf., CASRO, MRA; bd. mem. U. Ga. MMR program; bd. mem. MRA-CBOK com. Office: Directions Rsch Inc 401 E Court St Ste 200 Cincinnati OH 45202-1379

BROOKS, RICHARD DICKINSON, lawyer; b. Daytona Beach, Fla., Sept. 17, 1944; s. Richard D. Brooks and Violet (Hamilton) Christenson; m. Betty Jane Huba, Aug. 28, 1971; children: Hillary Ann, Richard Jason. BA, Marietta (Ohio) Coll., 1967; JD, Case Western Res. U., 1972. Bar: Ohio 1972, U.S. Dist. Ct. (so. dist.) Ohio 1975, U.S. Ct. Appeals (6th cir.) 1993. Assoc., ptnr. Bridgewater Robe Brooks & Keifer, Athens, Ohio, 1972-87; of counsel Arter & Hadden, Columbus, 1987, ptnr., 1988—. Coach Upper Arlington Cub Scout Baseball, Columbus, 1989-90; pres. A.T.C.O. Inc. Sheltered Workshop, Athens, 1986; chmn. com. Athens Kiwanis, 1977-87; bd.d irs. Athens C. of C., 1984-87. Sgt. U.S. Army, 1968-70, Vietnam. Fellow Am. Bar Found., Ohio Bar Found. (pres. 1988); mem. ABA, Ohio Bar Assn. (exec. com. 1979-83), Columbus Bar Assn. (environ. law com.), Athens County Bar Assn. (pres. 1978-79), Ohio CLE Inst. (bd. dirs. 1989-90), Ohio State Legal Svcs. Assn. (bd. dirs. 1982—). Avocations: basketball, tennis, fishing, furniture restoration. Office: Arter & Hadden 10 W Broad St Ste 2100 Columbus OH 43215-3422

BROOKS, ROGER, state legislator; Rep. S.D. State Ho. Reps. Dist. 10, until 2000, mem. agr. and natural resources and edn. coms.; ret. Computer cons. Home: 1800 Sylvan Cir Brandon SD 57005-1518

BROOKS, ROGER KAY, insurance company executive; b. Clarion, Iowa, Apr. 30, 1937; s. Edgar Sherman and Hazel (Whipple) B.; m. Marcia Rae Ramsay, Nov. 19, 1955 (div. Sept. 1989); children: Michael, Jeffrey, David; m. Saulene Richer, Mar. 17, 1990. B.A. magna cum laude, U. Iowa, 1959. With AmerUs Grp., Des Moines, 1964—; asst. sec. Central Life Assurance Co., 1964-68, v.p., 1968-70, exec. v.p., 1970-72, pres., 1972-92, chmn., 1992—. Mem. Des Moines Devel. Com. Fellow Soc. Actuaries; mem. Greater Des Moines C. of C. (past chmn.), Actuaries Club of Des Moines (past pres.), Iowa Ins. Hall of Fame, Phi Beta Kappa. Presbyterian (elder). Club: Des Moines (past pres.). Home: 5205 Woodland Des Moines IA 50312 Office: AmerUs Group PO Box 1555 Des Moines IA 50306-1555 E-mail: roger.brooks@amerus.com.

BROOTEN, DOROTHY, dean, nursing educator; b. Hazleton, Pa. married; two children. BSN, U. Pa., 1966, MSN, 1970, PhD in Ednl. Adminstrn., 1980. Assoc. prof. nursing Thomas Jefferson U., 1972-77; from asst. to assoc. prof. nursing U. Pa., 1977-88, prof. nursing, chair Health Care of Women & Childbearing, 1980-93, dir. Ctr. for Low Birthweight, Sch. Nursing, 1990-96, Overseers prof. perinatal nursing, 1990-96; dean, prof. nursing Frances Payne Bolton Sch. Nursing Case Western Res. U., Cleve., 1998—. Cons. Sch. Medicine, U. Utrecht, The Netherlands, 1989, Ministry of Health, Malawi, Africa, 1991. Recipient Contbrn. to Nursing Sci. award ANA, 1988. Mem. Inst. Medicine-NAS, Am. Acad. Nursing (mem. gov. coun. 1988-91). Achievements include research on low birthweight prevention, postdischarge care of low birthweight infants, health care delivery. Office: Case Western Res Univ FP Bolton Sch Nursing 10900 Euclid Ave Cleveland OH 44106-4901

BROPHY, JERE EDWARD, education educator, researcher; b. Chgo., June 11, 1940; s. Joseph Thomas and Eileen Marie (Sullivan) B.; m. Arlene Marie Pintozzi, Sept. 21, 1963; children: Cheryl, Joseph. BS in Psychology, Loyola U., Chgo., 1962; MA in Human Devel., U. Chgo., 1965, PhD in Human Devel., 1967. Rsch. assoc., asst. prof. U. Chgo., 1967-68; from asst. to assoc. prof. U. Tex., Austin, 1968-76; staff devel. coord. S.W. Ednl. Devel. Lab., 1970-72; prof. Mich. State U., East Lansing, 1976-92, co-dir. Inst. for Rsch. on Tchg., 1981-93, univ. disting. prof., 1993—. Co-author: Teacher-Student Relationships: Causes and Consequences, 1974; editor (book series) Advances in Research on Teaching, 1989—. Fellow Ctr. for Advanced Study in the Behavioral Scis., 1994. Fellow: APA, Internat. Soc. Edn., Am. Psychol. Soc.; mem.: Nat. Soc. for the Study of Edn., Nat. Coun. for the Social Studies, Nat. Acad. Edn., Am. Ednl. Rsch. Assn. (Palmer O. Johnson award 1983, Presdl. citation 1995). Office: Mich State U 213B Erickson Hall East Lansing MI 48824-1034

BROPHY, JERE HALL, manufacturing company executive; b. Schenectady, Mar. 11, 1934; s. Gerald Robert and Helen Dorothy (Hall) B.; m. Joyce Elaine Wright, Aug. 18, 1956; children: Jennifer, Carolyn, Jere. B.S. in Chem. Engring, B.S. in Metall. Engring, U. Mich., 1956, M.S., 1957, Ph.D., 1958. Asst. prof. Mass. Inst. Tech., 1958-63; sect. supr. nickel alloys sect. Paul D. Merica Research Lab., Inco, Inc., Suffern, N.Y., 1963-67, research mgr. non-ferrous group, 1967-72, asst. mgr., 1972-73, mgr., 1973-77; dir. research and devel. and dir. Paul D. Merica Research Lab., Inco, Inc. (Inco Research and Devel. Center), 1978-80; dir. advanced tech. initiation INCO Ltd., N.Y.C., 1980-82; v.p., dir. Materials and Mfg. Tech. Ctr. TRW Inc., Cleve., 1982-86, v.p. mfg. and materials devel. automotive sect., 1986-88; v.p technology Brush Wellman Inc., 1988-96; cons., 1996—. Author: (with J. Wolff) Thermodynamics of Structure; Contbr. (with J. Wolff) tech. articles to profl. jours. Fellow Am. Soc. Metals, AAAS; mem. Am. Inst. Mining and Metall. Engrs. (dir. IMD div. 1973-76), Am. Mgmt. Assn. (research and devel. council 1975-87). Episcopalian. Club: Edgewater Yacht. Home and Office: 31905 Jackson Rd Chagrin Falls OH 44022-1707

BROSILOW, COLEMAN BERNARD, chemical engineering educator; b. Phila., Nov. 14, 1934; s. Samuel and Ethel (Stein) B.; m. Rosalie Ziegleman, Feb. 18, 1962; children— Rachelle, Benjamin. B.S., Drexel U., 1957; M.Ch.E., Poly. Inst. N.Y., 1959, Ph.D., 1962. Systems engr. Am. Cyanamid Co., Process Analysis Group, Wayne, N.J., 1962-63; asst. prof. chem. engring. Case Western Res. U., Cleve., 1963-67, assoc. prof., 1967-73, prof. chem. engring., 1973—2001, prof. emeritus, 2001—, chmn. dept. chem. engring., 1980-84. Chmn. bd. Control Soft Corp., 1985-2001, now bd. dirs.; vis. prof. chem. engring. The Technion, Haifa, Israel, 1971-72, Ben Gurion U., Israel, 2000; cons. in field. Contbr. articles to profl. jours.; editorial bd.: Am. Inst. Chem. Engrs. Jour, 1980-85; patentee in field. Founding mem. bd. trustees Solomon Schecter Day Sch. of Cleve., 1978— , pres., 1978-84. . Fellow AIChE (computing in chem. engring. award 1989); mem. Sigma Xi, Tau Beta Pi, Phi Lambda Upsilon. Jewish. Home: 25 Shoham St Rehovot 76227 Israel Office: Ben Gurion U of the Negev Dept Chem Engring PO Box 653 Beer-Sheva 84105 Israel E-mail: cbb@po.cwru.edu.

BROSNAHAN, ROGER PAUL, lawyer; b. Kansas City, Mo., Aug. 9, 1935; s. Earl and Helen (Mottin) B.; m. Jill Farley, Aug. 2, 1958; children: Paul, Connor, Helen, Farley, Tracy, Hugh, Lee. BS, St. Louis U., 1956; LLB, Mich. U., 1959. Bar: Mo. 1959, Minn. 1959, U.S. Ct. Appeals (6th cir.) 1984, U.S. Ct. Appeals (10th cir.) 1999, U.S. Ct. Appeals (8th cir.) 1975, U.S. Supreme Ct. 1971. Ptnr. Streater, Murphy, Brosnahan & Langford, Winona, Minn., 1959-78, Kutak, Rock & Huie, Mpls., 1979-82, Robins, Kaplan, Miller & Ciresi, Mpls., 1982-93, Brosnahan, Joseph & Suggs P.A., Mpls., 1993-99; prin. Law Offices of Roger P. Brosnahan, 1999—. Mem.: ATLA, ABA (state del. 1976—88), Nat. Conf. Bar Pres. (pres. 1980—81), Minn. Bar Assn. 1974—75, Minn. Trial Lawyers Assn., Am. Bd. Trial Advocates. Democrat. Roman Catholic. Office: Law Offices of Roger P Brosnahan 116 Center St Winona MN 55987 Fax: 507-457-3001. E-mail: rpbros@mwt.net.

BROSZ, DON, retired state legislator; b. Alpena, S.D., Sept. 17, 1931; Salesperson Procter & Gamble Dist. Co., 1962-82, sales and unit mgr., 1982-90; mem. S.D. Ho. of Reps., Pierre, 1995-97, S.D. Senate, Pierre, 1998—, mem. agr. and taxation coms., 1998—, mem. agr. com., chair edn. com. and taxation com. Mem. edn. and judiciary coms. S.D. Ho. of Reps. Bd. visitors S.D. U. Med. Sch.; mem. adv. bd. Sr. Companions for Eastern S.D.

BROTMAN, BARBARA LOUISE, columnist, writer; b. N.Y.C., Feb. 23, 1956; d. Oscar J. and Ruth (Branchor) Brotman; m. Chuck Berman, Aug. 28, 1983; children: Robin, Nina. BA, Queens Coll., 1978. Writer, columnist Chgo. Tribune, 1978—. Recipient Ill. Newspapers Column Writing award UPI, 1984, Peter Lisagor award Sigma Delta Chi, 1984. Avocation: broomball. Office: Chgo Tribune Co 435 N Michigan Ave Chicago IL 60611-4066

BROUDER, GERALD T. academic administrator; Interim chancellor, provost Columbia (Mo.) Coll., 1992-95, pres., 1995—. Office: Columbia Coll 1001 Rogers St Columbia MO 65216-0001

BROUS, THOMAS RICHARD, lawyer; b. Fulton, Mo., Jan. 7, 1943; s. Richard Pendleton and Augusta (Gilpin) B.; m. Patricia Catlin, Sept. 12, 1964; (dec. Sept. 1999); children: Anna Catlin Brous, Joel Pendleton Brous; m. Mary Lou McClelland Kroh, Sept. 8, 2001. BSBA, Northwestern U., 1965; JD cum laude, U. Mich., 1968. Bar: Mo. 1968, U.S. Dist. Ct. (we. dist.) Mo. 1968, U.S. Ct. Mil. Appeals 1968, U.S. Supreme Ct. 1971. Assoc. Watson & Marshall L.C., Kansas City, Mo., 1968-78, ptnr., 1978-96, mng. ptrn., 1992-94; shareholder Stinson, Mag & Fizzell, P.C., 1996—2002; ptnr. Stinson Morrison Hecker LLP, 2002—. Mem. steering com. U. Mo. Kansas City Law Sch. Employee Benefits Inst., 1990—2001, chmn. 1992-93; mid-states key dist. EP/EO coun. IRS, 1997—. Author: Chapter 26, III Missouri Business Organizations, 1998; asst. editor Mich. Law Rev., 1966-68. Mem. vestry St. Andrews Episcopal Ch., Kansas City, 1974-77, Grace & Holy Trinity Cathedral, 1994—, chancellor, 1998—; trustee Mo. Repertory Theatre, Inc., Kansas City, 1990—, pres., 1995-98; v.p., treas. Barstow Sch., Kansas City, 1982-86; dir. Met. Orgn. to Counter Sexual Abuse, Kansas City, 1992-95. Capt. U.S. Army, 1968-72. Mem. ABA, Univ. Club (pres. 1988-89), Greater Kansas City Soc. Hosp. Attys., Kansas City Met. Bar Assn., Heart of Am. Employee Benefit Conf., The Mo. Bar Assn. (vice-chair employee benefits com. 1997-2000), Mo. Soc. Hosp. Attys., Delta Upsilon, Beta Gamma Sigma. Episcopalian. Avocations: reading, hiking, gardening. Office: Morrison Hecker LLP 1204 Walnut Ste 2800 Kansas City MO 64106 E-mail: tbrous@stinsonmoheck.com.

BROWAR, LISA MURIEL, librarian; b. N.Y.C., Jan. 22, 1951; d. Elliott Andrew and Shirley (Kahn) B. B in English Lit., Ind. U., 1973, MLS, 1977; M in English Lit., U. Kans., 1976; postgrad., Ind. U./Purdue. U., Indpls., 2001. Cert. in fund raising mgmt., 2001. Asst. curator Beinecke Libr. Yale U., New Haven, 1979-81, archivist Sterling Meml. Libr., 1981-82; curator spl. collections Vassar Coll. Libr., Poughkeepsie, N.Y., 1982-87; asst. dir. rare books and manuscripts N.Y. Pub. Libr., N.Y.C., 1987-96; dir. The Lilly Libr., Ind. U., Bloomington, 1996-2001; libr. for English and Am. lit., philosophy and film studies Main Libr., Ind. U., 2001—. Editor RBM: A Jour. of Rare Books, Manuscripts, and Cultural Heritage, 1999—. Mem. ALA, Assn. Coll. and Rsch. Librs. (sec. rare books and manuscripts sect. 1987-89, chair, 1994-95, editor 1999—), Soc. Am. Archivists, Bibliog. Soc. Am., Grolier Club. Democrat. Avocations: opera, theatre, motion pictures, photography, singing. Office: E10 60 Main Libr Indiana Univ Bloomington IN 47405 E-mail: lbrowar@indiana.edu.

BROWDER, OLIN LORRAINE, legal educator; b. Urbana, Ill., Dec. 19, 1913; s. Olin Lorraine and Nellie (Taylor) B.; m. Edna Olive Forsythe, Sept. 9 1939 (dec. Nov. 1993); children: Ann Browder Sorensen, Catherine Browder Morris, John; m. Aleeta Swantner, May 17, 1997. A.B., U. Ill., 1935, LL.B., 1937; S.J.D., U. Mich., 1941. Bar: Ill. 1939. Practiced in Chgo., 1938-39; asst. prof. bus. law U. Ala., 1939-41; asst. prof. law U. Tenn., 1941-42; mem. legal dept. TVA, 1942-43; spl. agt. FBI, 1943-45; prof. law U. Okla., 1946-53, U. Mich., Ann Arbor, 1953-79, James V. Campbell prof. law, 1979-84, prof. emeritus, 1984—. Author: (with others) American Law of Property, 1953, (with L.W. Waggoner) Family Property Transactions, 1965, 3d edit., 1980, (with R. A. Cunningham, G.S. Nelson, W.B. Stoebuck, D.A. Whitman) Basic Property Law, 1966, 5th edit., 1989, (with L. W. Waggoner and R. V. Wellman) Palmer's Cases on Trusts and Succession, 4th edit., 1983. Mem. Order of Coif, Phi Beta Kappa, Beta Theta Phi, Phi Alpha Delta, Phi Kappa Phi. Home: 1520 Edinborough Rd Ann Arbor MI 48104-4128

BROWER, JAMES CALVIN, graphic artist, painter; b. Clarksburg, W.Va., Dec. 30, 1914; s. Leroy Cooper and Margaret Wood (Watkins) B.; m. Elsie Margaret Day, Sept. 19, 1936; children: James Lawrence, Sandra Joan, Margaret, Linda Ann, Beth. Grad. high sch., Charleston, W.Va., 1932. Pvt. practice, Huntington, W.Va., 1933-43, Toledo, 1952—; ptnr., art dir. Brower, Brownsberger and Burda, 1944-51; dir. art and design Meeks Heit Pub. Co., 1992-99. Illustrator: Education for Sexuality, 1970, Human Sexuality, 1982, Education for Sexuality and HIV/AIDS, 1993; paintings featured in The Creative Artist, 1990, The Best of Watercolor 2, 1997, The Best of Watercolor Composition, 1997. Recipient Pres. award Okla. Watercolor Soc., 1987, Past Pres. award San Diego Watercolor Soc. Internat. Exhbn., 1989. Mem. Ohio Watercolor Soc. (hon.; signature mem., bd. dirs. 1986-92, publicity chmn. 1986-92, Gold medal 1984, Charles Burchfield Meml. award 1991, Exhbn. award 1992, made hon. mem. 2001), Northwestern Ohio Watercolor Soc. (pres. 1983-84), Nat. Water Color Soc. (signature mem., Artist's Mag./Liquitex award 1990, Mem.'s Exhbn. awards 1996, 98), Ky. Watercolor Soc. (artist mem.), Ga. Watercolor Soc. (signature mem., Gold award Nat. Exhbn. 1990), Midwest Watercolor Soc. (signature mem.), Toledo Fedn. Art Soc. (pres. 1987-88), Tile Club Toledo, Toledo Artists Club (gold medal 1998). Republican. Presbyterian. Avocations: chess, bridge. Home and Office: 2222 Grecourt Dr Toledo OH 43615-2918

BROWMAN, DAVID L(UDVIG), archaeologist; b. Dec. 9, 1941; s. Ludvig G. and Audra (Arnold) B.; m. M. Jane Fox, Apr. 24, 1965; children: Lisa, Tina, Becky. BA, U. Mont., 1963; MA, U. Wash., 1966; PhD, Harvard U., 1970. Hwy. archeologist Wash. State Hwy. Dept., Olympia, 1964-66; field dir. Yale U., New Haven, 1968-69; tutor Harvard U., 1969-70; mem. faculty Washington U., St. Louis, 1970—, prof. archeology, 1984—, chmn., 1986—. Dir. Cons. Survey Archeology, St. Louis, 1976—, Inst. Study of Plants, Food and Man, Kirkwood, Mo. 1979-84: cons. St. Louis Dept. Parks and Recreation, 1978—. Editor/author: Advances in Andean Archaeology, 1978, editor/author: Economic Organization of Prehispanic Peru, 1984, editor/author: Risk Management and Arid Land Use Strategies in the Andes, 1986, editor/author: New Perspectives on Americanist Archaeology, 2002; editor: Cultural Continuity in Mesoamerica, 1979, Early Native Americans, 1980. Charter mem. Confluence St. Louis, 1983; mem. Gov.'s Adv. Coun. Hist. Preservation, 1982-89, sec. 1989-91. NSF fellow, 1967, grantee, 1974-75, 85—. Fellow AAAS; mem. Soc. Profl. Archeologists (sec.-treas. 1981-83, grievance coord. 1997-98), AAUP (chpt. pres. 1980-82), Registry Profl. Archaeologists (grievance coord. 1998-99), Mo. Assn. Profl. Archeologists (v.p. 1981-82), Mo. Archeology Soc. (trustee 1977—), Sigma Xi (chpt. pres. 1985-). Roman Catholic. Avocations: hiking, gardening. Office: Washington U PO Box 1114 Saint Louis MO 63188-1114

BROWN, A. DEMETRIUS, metal products executive; CEO FUCI Metals USA Inc., Northbrook, Ill., now pres. Office: FUCI Metals USA Inc 495 Central Ave Ste 200 Northfield IL 60093-3044

BROWN, ALAN CRAWFORD, lawyer; b. Rockford, Ill., May 12, 1956; s. Gerald Crawford and Jane Ella (Herzberger) B.; m. Dawn Lestrud, Apr. 16, 1998; children: Parker Crawford, Sydney Danielle, Sarah Kate, Drew Kristen, Connor Austin. BA magna cum laude, Miami U., Oxford, Ohio, 1978; JD with honors, U. Chgo., 1981. Bar: Ill. 1981, U.S. Dist. Ct. (no.

dist.) Ill. 1981, U.S. Tax Ct. 1986. Assoc. Kirkland & Ellis, Chgo., 1981-87; sr. assoc. Coffield Ungaretti Harris & Slavin, 1987-89; ptnr. McDermott, Will & Emery, 1989—2001, Neal, Gerber & Eisenberg, Chgo., 2001. Deacon Northminster Presbyn. Ch., Evanston, Ill., 1989-92; apiarist Chgo. Botanic Garden, Glencoe, Ill., 1988-97; active Kenilworth (Ill.) Union Ch. Mem. Order of Coif, Phi Beta Kappa. Office: Neal Gerber & Eisenberg Ste 2200 Two North LaSalle St Chicago IL 60602-3801 E-mail: acbrownesq@aol.com ., abrown@ngelaw.com.

BROWN, ARNOLD LANEHART, JR. pathologist, educator, university dean; b. Wooster, Ohio, Jan. 26, 1926; s. Arnold Lanehart and Wilda (Woods) B.; m. Betty Jane Simpson, Oct. 2, 1949; children— Arnold III, Anthony, Allen, Fletcher, Lisa. Student, U. Richmond, 1943-45; M.D., Med. Coll. Va., 1949. Diplomate: Am. Bd. Pathology. Intern Presbyn.-St. Luke's Hosp., Chgo., 1949-50, resident, 1950-51, 53-56, asst. attending pathologist, 1957-59; practice medicine specializing in pathology Rochester, Minn., 1959-78; cons. exptl. pathology, anatomy Mayo Clinic, 1959-78, also prof., chmn. dept., 1968-78; prof. pathology U. Wis., Madison, 1978—, dean Med. Sch., 1978-91. Mem. nat. cancer adv. council NIH, 1971-74, HEW, 1972-74; chmn. clearing house on environ. carcinogens Nat. Cancer Inst., 1976-80, chmn. com. to study carcinogenicity of cyclamate, 1975-76; mem. Nat. Com. on Heart Disease, Cancer and Stroke, 1975-79; mem. com. on safe drinking water NRC, 1976-77; mem. award assembly Gen. Motors Cancer Research Found., 1978-83, vice chmn., 1982-83; co-chmn. panel on geochemistry of fibrous materials related to health risks Nat. Acad. Scis.-NRC, 1978-80; chair working group Internat. Agy. for Research on Cancer, Lyon, France, 1979, 83, 87. Contbr. articles to profl. jours. Bd. sci. counselors Nat. Inst. Environ. Health Scis., NIH Nat. Toxicology Program, 1992—. With USNR, 1943-45, 51-53. Nat. Heart Inst. postdoctoral fellow, 1956-59 Mem. Am. Soc. Exptl. Pathology, Internat. Acad. Pathology, Assn. Am. Med. Colls. (chmn. council deans 1984-85). Home: 2822 Marshall Ct Madison WI 53705-2271 Office: 1300 University Ave Madison WI 53706-1510 E-mail: albrown1@facstaff.wisc.edu.

BROWN, ARNOLD M. state legislator; b. Sherman, S.D., Mar. 5, 1931; Mem. S.D. Ho. Reps. Dist. 7, Pierre, 1993-96; mem. health and human svc. and transp. coms. S.D. Ho. Reps.; mem. S.D. Senate from 7th dist., Pierre, 1997—. Home: 1718 Teton Pass Brookings SD 57006-3626

BROWN, BOB OLIVER, retired manufacturing company executive; b. Ft. Dodge, Iowa, June 5, 1929; s. Frank Arthur and Winona (Thietje) B.; m. JoAnn Louise Brown, Sept. 7, 1963 (div. Oct. 1989); children: Scott, Douglas. BSBA, U. Omaha, 1950; MS, U. Ill., 1951. CPA, Mo. Auditor Price Waterhouse, St. Louis, 1954-58, E A Rothaus, St. Louis, 1958-62; treas. Hazell Machine, 1962-64, Troug Nichols, Kansas City, Mo., 1964-66; v.p. Unitog Co., 1966-94; ret., 1994. Capt. USMC, 1951-54, Korea. Mem. AICPA, Mo. Soc. CPA, Tax Execs. Inst., Smithsonian Assocs., VFW, Am. Legion, Kansas City C. of C. Republican. Episcopalian. Home: 527 S 36th Ct Omaha NE 68105-1253

BROWN, CHARLES EARL, lawyer; b. Columbus, Ohio, June 6, 1919; s. Anderson and Ruth (Keeran) B.; m. Mary Elizabeth Hiett, May 23, 1959; children: Douglas Charles, Rebecca Ruth. AB, Ohio Wesleyan U., 1941; JD, U. Mich., 1949. Bar: Ohio 1949. Pvt. practice, Toledo; assoc. Zachman, Boxell, Bebout & Torbet, 1950-53; ptnr. Brown, Baker, Schlageter & Craig (and predecessors), 1953-90, of counsel, 1990-95, Shindler, Neff, Holmes & Schlageter, 1996—. Chmn. steering and exec. coms. Auto Trim Wholesalers div. Automotive Service Industry Assn., 1960-68 Lucas County Rep. Exec. Com., 1968-92; trustee, sec. Joseph J. and Marie P. Schedel Found., 1963-93, pres., 1993—. Capt. AUS, 1941-46; col. Res. ret. Decorated Bronze Star; recipient John J. Pershing award U.S. Army Command and Gen. Staff Coll., 1963 Fellow Am. Bar Found. (state chmn. 1978-84), Ohio State Bar Found. (trustee 1987-92), Am. Coll. Trust and Estate Counsel; mem. ABA, Ohio Bar Assn. (bd. govs. real property sect. 1953-76, coun. of dels. 1973-84, exec. com. 1984-87), Toledo Bar Assn. (past mem. exec. com.), Sixth Cir. Jud. Conf. (life), Toledo Area C. of C. (past trustee, com. chmn.), Res. Officers Assn., Assn. U.S. Army, Phi Beta Kappa. Congregationalist (past chmn. trustees). Lodge: Masons (32 deg.). Home: 3758 Brookside Rd Toledo OH 43606-2614 Office: 1200 Edison Plaza 300 Madison Ave Toledo OH 43604-1561

BROWN, CHARLES ERIC, health facility administrator, biochemist; b. Nov. 23, 1946; s. Charles E. and Dorothy R. (Riddle) B.; m. Kathy Louise Houck, July 24, 1971; 1 child, Eric Nathaniel. BA in Chemistry, SUNY, Buffalo, 1968; PhD in Biochemistry, Northwestern U., 1973. Instr., fellow depts. chemistry, biochemistry, molec. biol. Northwestern U., Evanston, Ill., 1973-75; rsch. fellow Roche Inst. Molecular Biology, Nutley, N.J., 1975-77; from asst. prof. biochemistry to assoc. prof. Med. Coll. Wis., Milw., 1977-88; analytical bus. devel. coord. BP Rsch., 1988-92; analytical rsch. mgr. BP Chems. Ltd., 1992-94; dir. Rsch. Resources Ctr. U. Ill., Chgo., 1994—, Adj. prof. chemistry U. Ill., Chgo., 1994—, adj. prof. mech. engring., 1998—; cons. Nicolet Instrument Corp., Metriflow, Inc., 1984-88. Contbr. articles in field to profl. jours., chpts. to books; developer biomedical and petrochemical equipment and techniques; patentee in field. Recipient Tech. Merit award Johnson Wax, 1987; NIH predoctoral fellow, 1968-72; Cottrell Rsch. grantee, 1979-82, Arthritis Found. grantee, 1984, Retirement Rsch. Found. grantee, 1987-88. Fellow Royal Soc. Chemistry; mem. AAAS, Internat. Soc. Magnetic Resonance, Soc. Neurosci., Am. Chem. Soc., Am. Soc. Pharmacology and Exptl. Therapeutics, Am. Soc. for Mass Spectrometry, Microscopy Soc. Am., Sigma Xi, Phi Lambda Upsilon. Office: Rsch Resources Ctr U Ill 901 S Wolcott Ave # E102 Msb Chicago IL 60612-7307 E-mail: charlieb@uic.edu.

BROWN, CHARLIE, state representative; b. Williston, S.C., Mar. 8, 1938; m. Angela Baker; 1 child, Charlisa. BS, Cheyney U.; MPA, Ind. U. Founder Mayor Hatcher's Youth Found., Gary, Ind.; CEO Gary (Ind.) Cmty. Mental Health Ctr.; risk mgr. City of Gary; state rep. dist. 3 Ind. House of Reps., 1982—, chmn. pub. health com., local govt. com., environ. affairs com., ins. and corp. com., family and children com., ranking minority mem. pub. health com. Bd. dirs. Lake County Hosp. Bldg. Authority; cons. mgmt. and health; mem. Med. Ctr. of Gary, Nat. Civil Rights Mus. and Hall Fame & Benson & Taylor Ensemble Co. Mayor Hatcher's Youth Found., Gary. Mem. Gary Frontiers Svc. Club, Black Minority Health Adv. Coun., Nat. Black Caucus State Legislators, Interagency Coun. on Black and Minority Health. Democrat. Home: 9439 Lake Shore Dr Gary IN 46403-1609

BROWN, COLLEEN, broadcast executice; Grad., U. Colo. Gen. mgr. Sta. KPNX-TV, Phoenix, till 1998; v.p. broadcast Lee Enterprises, 1998-99, pres., 1999. Mem. March of Dimes. Mem. Young Press Assn. Office: Lee Enterprises 215 N Main St Ste 400 Davenport IA 52801-1924

BROWN, CRAIG J. printing company executive; BA, MBA, Bowling Green State U. Various positions Std. Register Co., Dayton, Ohio, 1975-94, v.p. fin., treas., CFO, 1994-98, sr. v.p. adminstrn., treas., CFO, 1998—. Office: Std Register Co 600 Albany St Dayton OH 45408

BROWN, DALE, electronics executive; CEO Micro Electronics, Inc., Hilliard, Ohio. Office: Micro Electronics Inc 4119 Leap Rd Hilliard OH 43026-1117

BROWN, DAVID MITCHELL, physician, educator, dean; b. Chgo., Nov. 11, 1935; m. Sandra Miriam Brown B.S., U. Ill., Urban, 1956; M.D., U. Ill., Chgo., 1960. Intern U. Ill. Research-Edn. Hosp., Chgo., 1960-61; resident in pediatrics U. Minn., Mpls., 1961-63, fellow in endocrinology and metabolism, 1963-65; attending staff pediatric eoncrinology USAF Hosp., San Antonio, 1965-67; asst. prof. pediatrics, lab. medicine and pathology U. Minn., Mpls., 1967-70, assoc. prof., 1970-73, dir. clin. labs., 1970-84, prof. pediatrics, lab. medicine and pathology, 1974—, dean. Med. Sch., 1984-93, dir. Gen. clin. Rsch. Ctr., med. dir. clin. trials unit. Mem. adv. com. on rsch. on women's health NIH, 1995-99; co-chair orgainzing com. 7th Internat. Symposium on Basement Membranes, 1995; mem. planning com. NIH 3d Internat. Symposium on Kidney Disease of Diabetes Mellitus, 1991. With USAF, 1965-67. Recipient USPHS Research Career Devel. award, 1968-73 Mem. AAAS, Acad. Clin. Lab. Physicians and Scientists, Am. Diabetes Assn., Am. Pediatric Soc., Am. Physiol. Soc., Am. Soc. Clin. Pathology, Am. Soc. Nephrology, Am. Soc. Pediatric Nephrology, Central Soc. for Clin. Research, Endocrine Soc., Internat. Soc. Nephrology, Lawson Wilkins Soc. Pediatric Endocrinology, Mpls. Pediatris Soc., Orthopaedic Research Soc., Soc. Pediatric Nephrology, Soc. Pediatric Research, Am. Assn. Pathologists, Am. Soc. Bone and Mineral Research, Internat. Acad. Pathology, Assn. Am. Med. Colls. (chmn. council acad. Socs.), Am. Assn. Pathologists, Am. Soc. Cell Biology, Minn. Soc. Clin. Pathology, Alpha Omega Alpha. Home: 2571 Abbey Hill Dr Hopkins MN 55305-2332 Office: PO Box 404 516 Delaware St SE Minneapolis MN 55455-0356

BROWN, DONALD JAMES, JR. lawyer; b. Chgo., Apr. 21, 1948; s. Donald James Sr. and Marian Constance (Scimeca) B.; m. Donna Bowen, Jan. 15, 1972; children: Megan, Maura. AB, John Carroll U., 1970; JD, Loyola U., Chgo., 1973. Bar: Ill. 1973, U.S. Dist. Ct. (no. dist.) Ill. 1973, U.S. Tax Ct. 1982. Asst. to state's atty. Cook County, Ill., 1973-75; assoc. Baker & McKenzie, Chgo., 1975-82, ptnr., 1982-95, Donohue, Brown, Mathewson & Smyth, Chgo., 1995—. Office: Donohue Brown et al 140 S Dearborn St Chicago IL 60603-5202

BROWN, EDWIN WILSON, JR. physician, educator; b. Youngstown, Ohio, Mar. 6, 1926; s. Edwin Wilson and Doris (McClellan) B.; m. Patricia Ann Currier, Aug. 9, 1952; children: Edwin Wilson, John Currier, Wende Patricia. Student, Carnegie Inst. Tech., 1943, Houghton Coll., 1946-47, Amherst Coll., 1943-44; M.D., Harvard U., 1953, M.P.H. (Nat. Found. fellow), 1957. Research fellow U. Buffalo, 1953-54; intern E.J. Meyer Meml. Hosp., Buffalo, 1954-55; resident pub. health Va. Dept. Health, 1955-56; tchr. medicine specializing in preventive medicine Boston, 1958-61, Hyderabad, India, 1961-63; assoc. med. dir. People-to-People Health Found., Washington, 1965-66; assoc. prof. medicine Ind. U.-Purdue U., Indpls., 1966-85, dir. div. internat. affairs, 1966-74, assoc. dean student services, dir. internat. services, 1979-85; pres. Global Health Svcs., Inc., 1986—. Med. dir. Ind. Dept. Correction, 1974-76; sr. med. edn. advisor King Faisal U., Dammam, Saudi Arabia, 1977-78; field dir. Harvard Epidemiol. Project, Egedesminde, Greenland, 1956-57; asst. prof. preventive medicine Sch. Medicine Tufts U., 1958-61; dep. chief staff Boston Dispensary, 1961; vis. prof. preventive medicine Osmania Med. Coll., Hyderabad, India, 1961-63; asst. dir. div. internat. med. edn., dir. AAMC-AID project internat. med. edn. Assn. Am. Med. Colls., Evanston, 1963-65; exec. sec. Study Group on Childhood Accidents, Boston, 1959-61; research asso. Sch. Pub. Health, Harvard U., 1959-60; dir. Curtis Pub. Co., Inc.; cons. Boston City Health Dept., 1959-60, WHO, 1973-74; chmn. bd. dirs. Med. Assistance Programs, Inc. Contbr. articles to profl. jours. Bd. dirs. Paul Carlson Found., Campus Teams, Iran Found., CARE/MEDICO, Internat. Students Inc. Served with AUS, 1944-46, ETO. Recipient Pub. Svc. award Vets. Day Coun. Indpls., 1996, Patriarch of Antioch's award Knight Comdr. of Order of St. Mark, 1998. Fellow Am. Pub. Health Assn.; mem. Assn. Tchrs. Preventive Medicine, Indian Assn. Advancement Med. Edn., Mass. Med. Soc., Internat. Policy Forum (bd. govs.), Nat. Policy Coun., Rotary Internat., Sigma Xi. Home: 8153 Oakland Rd Indianapolis IN 46240-2747 Office: PO Box 40951 Indianapolis IN 46240-0951 E-mail: Ed@TheBrowns.com.

BROWN, ELI MATTHEW, anesthesiologist, department chairman; b. Balt., Apr. 24, 1923; s. Morris and Dora (Poliakoff) B.; m. Estelle Tamus Neidish, May 26, 1948; children: Otto, Morris, Jacqueline Brown Rosenblatt, Barbara Brown Smith. BS, U. Md., 1943; MD, U. Md., Balt., 1946. Diplomate Am. Bd. Anesthesiologists. Intern Jewish Hosp. Bklyn., 1946-47, resident, 1947-48, Valley Forge Gen. Hosp., Phoenixville, Pa., 1948-49; asst. prof. anesthesiology SUNY-Downstate, Bklyn., 1952-54; clin. asst. prof. Wayne State U., Detroit, 1957-61, clin. assoc. prof., 1961-73, prof., 1975-76, chmn., 1976-98, prof. emeritus, 1998—. Chmn. dept. anesthesia Sinai Hosp. Detroit, 1954-91. Contbr. articles to profl. jours. Maj. U.S. Army, 1948-51. Mem. AMA, Am. Soc. Anesthesiologists (pres. Ill. chpt. 1980-81), World Fedn. Soc. Anesthesiologists (del. 1978—), Am. Coll. Grad. Med. Edn., Assn. Univ. Anesthetists, Soc. Acad. Anesthesia Chmn. Avocations: golf, tennis. E-mail: ETMBrown@aol.com.

BROWN, ERIC A. food products executive; Group v.p. prepared foods Hormel Foods Corp., Austin, Minn., 1999—. Office: Hormel Foods Corp One Hormel Pl Austin MN 55912-3680

BROWN, FAITH A. communications executive; BA in English with distinction, U. Mich., 1969. Editl. asst., prodn. mgr. Music Educators Jour., Washington, 1970-74; prodn. editor Social Edn., 1974-75, Big Farmer, Frankfort, Ill., 1976; mng. editor Am. Printer, 1976-79; dir. pub. rels., pubs. mgr. Triton Coll., River Grove, Ill., 1979-84; employee comm. mgr. Chgo. Tribune Co., 1984-90, Tribune Co., 1990-92, corp. comm. mgr., 1992-98, corp. comm. dir., 1998-2000, ret., 2000. Office: Tribune Co 435 N Michigan Ave Chicago IL 60611-4066

BROWN, FREDERICK LEE, health care executive; b. Clarksburg, W.Va., Oct. 22, 1940; s. Claude Raymond and Anne Elizabeth (Kiddy) B.; m. Shirley Fiille Brown; children: Gregory Lee, Michael Owen-Price, Kyle Stephen, Kathryn Alexis. BA in Psychology, Northwestern U., 1962; MBA in Health Care Adminstrn., George Washington U., 1966; LHD (hon.) , U. Mo., 1995. Vocat. counselor Cook County Dept. Pub. Aid, Chgo., 1962-64; adminstrv. resident Meth. Hosp. Ind., Inc., Indpls., 1965-66, adminstrv. asst., 1966, asst. adminstr., 1966-71, assoc. adminstr., 1971-72, v.p. ops., 1972-74; exec. v.p., chief operating officer Meml. Hosp. DuPage County, Elmhurst, Ill., 1974-82, Meml. Health Svcs., Elmhurst, 1980-82; pres., CEO Christian Hosp. NW-NW, St. Louis, 1982-89, CH Health Techs., Inc., St. Louis, 1983-93; CEO Christain Health Svcs., 1986-93; pres., CEO CH Allied Svcs., Inc., 1988-93, BJC Health System, St. Louis, 1993—98, vice-chmn., 1999—2000. Adj. instr. Washington U. Sch. Medicine, St. Louis, 1982—2001; mem. chancellor's coun. U. Mo., 1990—94; mem. exec. com. HealthLink, Inc., 1986—92; pres., chief exec. officer Village North, Inc., 1986—93; chmn. shareholder comm. com. Am. Healthcare Systems, Inc., 1985—86, vice chmn., 1992; bd. dirs. Commerce Bank St. Louis, Am. Excess Inc. Ltd.; mem. corp. assembly Blue Cross Blue Shidle Mo., 1991—95; vis. scholar, exec. in residence The George Washington U., 2001—02. Contbr. articles to profl. jours. Co-chmn. hosp. divsn. United Way Greater St. Louis, 1983, chmn., 1984, chmn. health svcs. divsn., 1985—86, vice chmn. region, 1988, bd. dirs., 1986—2001, exec. com., 1991—, chmn. audit com., 1992—2001; active Kammergild Chamber ORch., 1984—88, v.p., 1985—88, bd. dirs., 1987—91; active Mo. Heart Inst., 1988—92, Alton Meml. Hosp., 1987—91, bd. dirs., 1987—91; mem. exec. bd. St. Louis Area coun. Boy Scouts Am., 1989—2000, activities coun. chmn., 1993—95; chmn. Friends of Scouting Campaign, 1991—92; mem. medicaid budget trak force Mo. Dept. Social Svcs., 1990; mem. emergency rm. svcs. task force St. Louis Regional Med. Ctr., 1985; mem. corp. assembly Blue Cross Blue Shield of Mo., 1991; bd. dirs. Sold on St. Louis, 1991—93, St. Louis Reg. Commerce & Growth Assn., 1993—98; bd. trustees Webster Hills Math. Ch., 1990—92, commuunion steward, 1987. Fellow Am. Coll. Healthcare Execs. (chmn. credentials com. 1978, task force governance and constituencies 1986-88; mem. Gold Medal award com. 1985, chmn. task force on governance and constituencies 1986-87, com. on ethics 1989-91, chmn. awards & testimonials com., 1992-93, bd. regents 1991-93); gov. dist V, 1993-98; mem. Am. Acad. Med. Adminstrs. (life, state dir. 1988—, Health Care Exec. of Yr. 1990, Statesman in Healthcare, 1992), Hosp. Pres.'s Assn., Advt. Club Greater St. Louis, Am. Hosp. Assn. (coun. on mgmt. 1987, alt. del. for healthcare systems 1988-90, del. to ho. of dels. for health care systems 1991, fin. com. chair 1995, chair-elect 1998, chmn. 1999-2000, immediate past chmn. 2000), Am. Pub. Health Assn., George Washington U. Alumni Assn. for Health Svcs. Adminstrn. (preceptor 1975-93, Alumnus of Yr. award 1981, Frederick Gibbs award, 1993), Hosp. Assn. Met. St. Louis (bd. dirs. 1984-94, chmn. bd. 1988-89, sec. 1985-86, treas. 1987, chmn. coun. on pub. affairs and communications 1985, vice chmn. 1987, various coms.), Greater St. Louis Health Care Alliance (co-chair 1992-96), Mo. Hosp. Assn. (mem. coun. on rsch. and policy devel. 1983-88, chmn. coun. on multi-instnl. hosps. 1986-88, mem. dist. coun. pres.'s 1986-89, bd. dirs. 1988-92, chmn. bd. trustees 1990), Cen. Ea. Profl. Rev. Orgn. (bd. dirs. 1982-85, various coms.), St. Louis Met. Med. Soc. (lay advisor 1990-92), Healthcare Execs. Study Soc., Internat. Health Policy and Mgmt. Inst. (bd. dirs. 1988—), Am. Protestant Health Assn. (bd. dirs. 1988-93, chmn. 1992-93), Pinnacle Pech Country Club, Algonquin Golf Club. Republican. Home and Office: 8409 E La Junta Scottsdale AZ 85255-2859 Fax: 480-513-4550. E-mail: FredLBrown@prodigy.net.

BROWN, GENE W. steel company executive; b. Warsaw, Feb. 16, 1936; s. Dean L. and Ilean (Clase) B.; m. Beverly A. Sink, Feb. 25, 1956; children: Lisa Jo, Scott Eugene. BSME, Purdue U., 1960; MBA, Northwestern U., 1967. Engr. Ill. Tool Works, Chgo., 1957-67; gen. mgr. Chgo. Gasket Co., 1967-69; ops. mgr. Maremont Corp., Harvey, Ill., 1969-74; gen. mgr. Marmon Group, Chgo., 1974-77; pres. Whittar Steel Strip, Detroit, 1977-88, Lisco Inc., Detroit, 1979—. Home: 6322 Palma Del Mar Blvd S # 9024 Saint Petersburg FL 33715-2700 also: 677 N 175 W Valparaiso IN 46385-8542 Office: Browneo Inc 277 Melton Rd Chesterton IN 46304-9746

BROWN, GLENN F. transportation executive, department chairman; Pres. Contract Freighters, Inc., Joplin, Mo., 1986—. Office: Contract Freighters, Inc 4701 E 32nd St Joplin MO 64804-3482 Fax: 417 782-3723.

BROWN, GRANT CLAUDE, retired state legislator; m. Linda Landes. Farmer, rancher, 1959—; state rep. dist. 36, 1991-98. Chmn. constrn. rev. com., 1993—; vice chmn. joint constrn. rev. com.; mem. fin. and taxation com. N.D. Ho. Reps. Sec. Ch. Trust Fund. Recipient Outstanding Young Men Am. award, 1970. Mem. County Farm Bur. (pres.), Stockmen's Legion, Masons (past master), Elks. Republican. Home: HC 1 Box 69 Dunn Center ND 58626-9782

BROWN, GREGORY K. lawyer; b. Warren, Ohio, Dec. 9, 1951; s. George K. and Dorothy H. (Gaynor) B.; m. Joy M. Feinberg, Apr. 10, 1976. BS in Bus. & Econs., U. Ky., 1973; JD, U. Ill., 1976. Bar: Ill. 1976. Assoc. atty. McDermott, Will & Emery, Chgo., 1976-80, Mayer, Brown & Platt, Chgo., 1980-84; ptnr. Keck, Mahin & Cate, 1984-93, Oppenheimer Wolff & Donnelly, Chgo., 1994-97, Seyfarth, Shaw, Fairweather & Geraldson, Chgo., 1997-2000, Gardner, Carton & Douglas, Chgo., 2000—. Contbg. author: The Handbook of Employee Ownership Plans, 1989, Employee Stock Ownership Plans, 1989 Active Chgo. Coun. Fgn. Rels. Named One of the Top Benefits Lawyers Nat. Law Jour., 1998. Mem. ABA (chair Employee Stock Ownership Plan com. real property, probate and trust law sect., Nat. Ctr. Employee Ownership, Employee Stock Ownership Plan Assn. (chair legis. and regulatory adv. com.), Chgo. Bar Assn. (chmn. employee benefits com. 1988-89). Avocations: basketball, bicycling, golf, opera, theatre. Office: Gardner Carton & Douglas 321 N Clark St Ste #3400 Chicago IL 60610-4795 E-mail: gkbrown@gcd.com.

BROWN, HERBERT CHARLES, chemistry educator; b. London, May 22, 1912; arrived in U.S., 1914; s. Charles and Pearl (Gorinstein) Brown; m. Sarah Baylen Brown, Feb. 6, 1937; 1 child Charles Allan. AS, Wright Jr. Coll., Chgo., 1935; BS, U. Chgo., 1936, PhD, 1938, DSc (hon.) , 1968; doctorate (hon.) , Wayne State U., 1980, Lebanon Valley Coll., 1980, L.I. U., 1980, Hebrew U. Jerusalem, 1980, Pontificia Universidad de Chile, 1980, Purdue U., 1980; doctorates (hon.) , U. Wales, 1981, U. Paris, 1982, Butler U., 1982, Ball State U., 1985. Asst. chemistry U. Chgo., 1936—38, Eli Lilly post-doctorate rsch. fellow, 1938—39, instr., 1939—43; asst. prof. chemistry Wayne U., 1943—46, assoc. prof., 1946—47; prof. inorganic chemistry Purdue U., 1947—59, Richard B. Wetherill prof. chemistry, 1959, Richard B. Wetherill rsch. prof., 1960—78, emeritus, 1978—. Vis. prof. UCLA, 1951, Ohio State U., 1952, U. Mex., 1954, U. Calif. at Berkeley, 1957, U. Colo., 1958, U. Heidelberg, 1963, SUNY, Stony Brook, 1966, U. Calif., Santa Barbara, 1967, Hebrew U., Jerusalem, 1969, U. Wales, Swansea, 1973, U. Cape Town, South Africa, 1974, U. Calif., San Diego, 1979; Harrison Howe lectr., 53; Friend E. Clark lectr., 53; Freud-McCormack lectr., 54; Centenary lectr., England, 55; Thomas W. Talley lectr., 56; Falk-Plaut lectr., 57; Julius Stieglitz lectr., 58; Max Tishler lectr., 58; Kekule-Couper Centenary lectr., 58; E.C. Franklin lectr., 60; Ira Remsen lectr., 61; Edgar Fahs Smith lectr., 62; Seydel-Wooley lectr., 66; Baker lectr., 69; Benjamin Rush lectr., 71; Chem. Soc. lectr., Australia, 72; Armes lectr., 73; Henry Gilman lectr., 75; others; hon. prof. Organomet Chem. Chinese Acad. Scis., 1994; chem. cons. to indsl. corps.; rschr. phys., organic and inorganic chemistry relating chem. behavior to molecular structure, selective reductions, hydroboration and chemistry of organoboranes. Author: Hydroboration, 1962, Boranes in Organic Chemistry, 1972, Organic Synthesis via Boranes, 1975, The Nonclassical Ion Problem, 1977; author: (with A.W. Pelter and K. Smith) Borane Reagents, 1988; contbr. articles to chem. jours. Bd. govs. Hebrew U., 1969—90; co-dir. war rsch. projects for U.S. Army, Nat. Def. Rsch. Com., Manhattan Project U. Chgo., 1940—43. Decorated Order of the Rising Sun, Gold and Silver Star Japan; named one of Top 75 Disting. Contbrs. to Chem. Enterprise, Chem. & Engring. News, 1998; recipient Purdue Sigma Xi rsch. award, 1951, Nichols medal, 1959, award, Am. Chem. Soc., 1960, S.O.C.M.A. medal, 1960, H.N. McCoy award, 1965, Linus Pauling medal, 1968, Nat. medal of Sci., 1969, Roger Adams medal, 1971, Charles Frederick Chandler medal, 1973, Chem. Pioneer award, 1975, CUNY medal for sci. achievement, 1976, Elliott Cresson medal, 1978, C.K. Ingold medal, 1978, Nobel prize in Chemistry, 1979, Priestley medal, 1981, Perkin medal, 1982, Gold medal award, Am. Inst. Chemists, 1981, G.M. Kosolapoff medal, 1987, NAS award in chem. scis., 1987, Oesper award, Cin. sect. Am. Chem. Soc., 1990, Herbert C. Brown medal and award for creative rsch. in synthetic methods, Am. Chem. Soc., 1998; fellow (hon.) U. Wales Swansea, 1994. Fellow: AAAS, Indian Nat. Sci. Acad. (fgn.), Royal Soc. Chemistry (hon.); mem.: NAS, Chinese Acad. Sci. (hon. prof. 1994), Indian Acad. Sci., Chem. Soc. Japan, Pharm. Soc. Japan (hon.), Am. Chem. Soc. (chmn. Purdue sect. 1955—56), Am. Acad. Arts and Sci., Sigma Xi, Phi Beta Kappa, Alpha Chi Sigma, Phi Lambda Upsilon (hon.). Office: Purdue U Dept Chemistry Lafayette IN 47907

BROWN, HERBERT RUSSELL, lawyer, writer; b. Columbus, Ohio, Sept. 27, 1931; s. Thomas Newton and Irene (Hankinson) B.; m. Beverly Ann Jenkins, Dec. 2, 1967; children: David Herbert, Andrew Jenkins. BA, Denison U., 1953; JD, U. Mich., 1956. Assoc. Vorys, Sater, Seymour and Pease, Columbus, Ohio, 1956, 60-64, ptnr., 1965-82; treas. Sunday Creek Coal Co., 1970-86; assoc. justice Ohio Supreme Ct., 1987-93. Examiner Ohio Bar, 1967-72, Multi-State Bar, 1971-76, Dist. Ct. Bar, 1968-71; commr. Fed. Lands, Columbus, 1967-68, Lake Lands, Columbus, 1981; bd. dirs. Thurber House, 1992-94, Sunday Creek Coal Co.; adj. prof. Ohio

State U. Coll. Law, 1997-2000; panelist Am. Arbitration Assn., 1993—. Author: (novels) Presumption of Guilt, 1991, Shadows of Doubt, 1994, (plays) You're My Boy, 1999, Peace with Honor, 2000, Mano A Mano, 2000, Power of God, 2002; mem. editl. bd. U. Mich. Law Rev., 1955-56. Trustee Columbus Bar Found., 1993—, pres., 2001—; candidate Ohio State Legis.; deacon, mem. governing bd. 1st Cmty. Ch., 1966—80; bd. dirs. Ctrl. Cmty. House Columbus, 1967—75. Capt. JAGC U.S. Army, 1956—57. Fellow Am. Coll. Trial Lawyers; mem. Ohio Bar Assn., Columbus Bar Assn. Democrat. Office: 145 N High St Columbus OH 43215-3006

BROWN, JACK WYMAN, architect; b. Detroit, Oct. 17, 1922; s. Ernest E. and Mary Morse (Jones) B.; m. Joan M. Graham, Oct. 4, 1971; 1 dau., Elizabeth. B.S., U. Mich., 1945. Designer Odell, Hewlett & Luckenbach, Inc., Birmingham, Mich., 1952-57; pres. Brown Assocs. Architects, Inc., Bloomfield Hills, 1957—; part-time instr. design Lawrence Inst. Tech., 1959. Mem. Mayor Detroit Task Force, 1969-70. Served with USNR, 1943-46. Co-recipient 1st prize nat. competition design Nat. Cowboy Hall Fame, 1967; recipient Institutions mag. award, 1980 Mem. AIA (chmn. working coms.), Am. Soc. Ch. Architecture (dir. 1960-64, 72—), Mich. Soc. Architects (design award St. Regis Ch. 1969, Fox Hills Elem. Sch. 1970, Andor Office Bldg. 1972, CAM Design award 1992). Home: 5980 Braemoor Rd Bloomfield Hills MI 48301-1419 Office: Brown Teefey Assocs Archs PC 4190 Telegraph Rd Bloomfield Hills MI 48302-2079 E-mail: jandjbrown@aol.com.

BROWN, JAMES WARD, mathematician, educator, author; b. Phila., Jan. 15, 1934; s. George Harold and Julia Elizabeth (Ward) B.; m. Jacqueline Read, Sept. 3, 1957; children: Scott Cameron, Gordon Elliot. AB, Harvard U., 1955; AM, U. Mich., 1958, PhD (Inst. Sci and Tech. predoctoral fellow), 1964. Asst. prof. math. U. Mich., Dearborn, 1964-66, assoc. prof., 1968-71, prof., 1971—, acting chmn. dept., 1974, 85. Asst. prof. Oberlin Coll., 1966-68; editorial cons. Math. Rev., 1970-85; dir. NSF Grant, 1969 Author: (with R.V. Churchill) Complex Variables and Applications, 6th edit., 1996, Internat. Student edit., 1996, Japanese edit., 1995, Spanish edit., 1978, Chinese edit., 1985, Korean edit., 1992, Greek edit., 1993, Fourier Series and Boundary Value Problems, 6th edit., 2001, internat. student edit., 1993, Japanese edit., 1980; contbr. articles to U.S. and fgn. sci. jours. Recipient Disting. Faculty award U. Mich.-Dearborn, 1976, Disting. Faculty award Mich. Assn. Governing Bds. Colls. and Univs., 1983 Mem. Am. Math. Soc., Research Club of U. Mich., Sigma Xi. Home: 1710 Morton Ave Ann Arbor MI 48104-4522 Office: 4901 Evergreen Rd Dearborn MI 48128-2406

BROWN, JARED, theater director, educator, writer; BFA, Ithaca Coll., 1960; MA Theatre, San Francisco State Coll., 1962; PhD Theatre, U. Minn., 1967. Instr. creative writing St. Paul Pub. Sch. System, 1962-63; teaching asst. U. Minn., 1963-64, instr. Communication Dept., 1964-65; from asst. prof. to prof. dept. theatre Western Ill. U., 1965-89, acad. dir. Semester in London, 1979-80; dir. Sch. Theatre Arts, Prof. Theatre Arts Ill. Wesleyan U., 1989—. Aided devel. (policies, curriculum), Theatre Dept. Western Ill. U., 1971; panel discussant Western Ill. U., 1973, 1974; chmn. panel Ill. Theatre Assn. Convention, 1976; panel discussant Assn. Theatre in Higher Edn. Convention, 1987; disting. faculty lectr. Western Ill. U., 1986, dir. grad. program dept. theatre, 1975-89, chmn. directing, theatre history and playwriting programs, dept. theatre, 1972-89; mem. panel judges to award NEH Summer Stipends, Ill., 1990; judge Am. Coll. Theatre Festival, 1973-74, 89-90; mem. various theatre coms. Ill. Wesleyan U.; mem. various coms. Univ., Coll. Fine Arts, Dept. Theatre Western Ill. U.; spkr., presenter in field. Author: The Fabulous Lunts, A Biography of Alfred Lunt and Lynn Fontanne, 1986, (Barnard Hewitt award 1987), Zero Mostel: A Biography, 1989, The Theatre in America During the Revolution, 1995; dir. plays including The Merchant of Venice, Hedda Gabler, Henry IV, La Ronde, Death of a Salesman, Cat on a Hot Tin Roof, A Streetcar Named Desire, Who's Afraid of Virginia Woolf, You Can't Take It With You, Brighton Beach Memoirs, Inherit the Wind, Peter Pan, Bye Bye Birdie, Guys and Dolls, Kiss Me Kate, 110 In The Shade, Annie, Funny Girl, Broadway Bound, Tartuffe, Antigone, She Loves Me, Noises Off, Sight Unseen, Bedroom Farce, Once in a Lifetime; appeared in My Fair Lady, Western Ill. U., 1978, On The Twentieth Century, 1986, various radio and TV programs; contbr. chpts. to texts, articles to profl. jours. Recipient stipend NEH, 1988, DuPont award for tchg. excellence, 1997; named Best Dir., The Pantagraph, 1991, 92, 94, 96; grantee Ill. Arts Coun., 1980, 81, 87, Western Ill. U., 1983-85, 86-87, 89, Cultural Arts Devel. Fund, 1980-89, Ill. Wesleyan U., 1990, Artistic/Scholarly Devel. grantee, 1999, 2002. Mem. Nat. Collegiate Players, Phi Kappa Phi, Theta Alpha Phi. Home: 18 Chatsford Ct Bloomington IL 61704-6220 Office: Sch Theatre Arts Ill Wesleyan U Bloomington IL 61702 E-mail: jbrown@titan.iwu.edu.

BROWN, JEANETTE GRASSELLI, retired university official; b. Cleve., Aug. 4, 1928; d. Nicholas W. and Veronica (Varga) Gecsy; m. Glenn R. Brown, Aug. 1, 1987. BS summa cum laude, Ohio U., 1950, DSc (hon.), 1978; MS, Western Res. U., 1958, DSc (hon.), 1995, Clarkson U., 1986; D Engring. (hon.), Mich. Tech. U., 1989; DSc (hon.), Wilson Coll., 1994, Notre Dame Coll., 1995, Kenyon Coll., 1995, Mt. Union Coll., 1996, Cleveland State U., 2000, Kent State U., 2000, Ursuline Coll., 2001. Project leader, assoc. Infrared Spectroscopist, Cleve., 1950-78; mgr. analytical sci. lab. Standard Oil (name changed to BP Am., Inc. 1985), 1978-83, dir. technol. support dept., 1983-85, dir. corp. rsch. and analytical scis., 1985-88; disting. vis. prof., dir. rsch. enhancement Ohio U., Athens, 1989-95; ret., 1995. Bd. dirs. AGA Gas, Inc., USX Corp., McDonald Investments, BDM Internat., BF Goodrich Co., Nicolet Instrument Corp.; mem. bd. on chem. sci. and tech. NRC, 1986-91; chmn. U.S. Nat. Com. to Internat. Union of Pure and Applied Chemistry, 1992-94; mem. joint high level adv. panel U.S.-Japan Sci. and Tech., 1994-2001, Ohio Bd. Regents, 1995—, chmn., 2000—; vis. com. Nat. Inst. Stds. and Tech., 1988-91. Author, editor 8 books; editor: Vibrational Spectroscopy; contbr. numerous articles on molecular spectroscopy to profl. jours.; patentee naphthalene extraction process. Bd. dirs. N.E. Ohio Sci. and Engring. Fair, Cleve., Martha Holden Jennings Found., Cleve. Clinic Found.; chair bd. dirs. Cleve. Scholarship Programs, Inc., 1994—; trustee Holden Arboretum, Cleve., 1988—, Edison Biotech Ctr., Cleve., 1988-95, Cleve. Playhouse, 1990-96, Garden Ctr. Greater Cleve., 1990-93, Mus. Arts Assn., 1991—, Gt. Lakes Sci. Ctr., 1991—, Rainbow Babies and Children's Hosp., 1992-95, Nat. Inventors' Hall of Fame, 1993—, Ohio U., 1985-94, chmn. 1991-92; chair Cleve. Scholarship Programs, 1995—; chair steering com. Mellen Ctr. Cleve. Clinic, 1996—. Recipient Disting. Svc. award Cleve. Tech. Soc. Coun., 1985; named Woman of Yr. YWCA, 1980; named to Ohio Women's Hall of Fame State of Ohio, 1989, Ohio Sci. & Tech. Hall of Fame, 1991. Mem. Am. Chem. Soc. (chair analytical divsn. 1990-91, Garvan medal 1986, Analytical Chem. award 1993, Encouraging Women into Careers in Sci. award 1999), Soc. for Applied Spectroscopy (pres. 1970, Disting. Svc. award 1983), Coblentz Soc. (bd. govs. 1968-71, William Wright award 1980), Royal Soc. Chemistry (Theophilus Redwood lectr. 1994), Phi Beta Kappa, Iota Sigma Pi (pres. fluorine chpt. 1957-60, nat. hon. mem. 1987). Republican. Roman Catholic. Avocations: swimming, dance, music. Home: 150 Greentree Rd Chagrin Falls OH 44022-2424

BROWN, JOBETH GOODE, food products executive, lawyer; b. Oakdale, La., Sept. 15, 1950; d. Samuel C. Goode and Elizabeth E. (Twiner) Baker; m. H. William Brown, Aug. 4, 1973; 1 child, Kevin William. BA, Newcomb Coll. Tulane U., 1972; JD, Wash. U., 1979. Assoc. Coburn, Croft & Putzell, St. Louis, 1979-80; staff atty. Anheuser-Busch Cos. Inc., 1980-81, exec. asst. to v.p. sec., 1982-83, asst. sec., 1983-89, sec., v.p., 1989—. Trustee Anheuser-Busch Found., St. Louis, 1989—, St. Louis Sci. Ctr., Girls, Inc. of St. Louis; bd. dirs. St. Louis Zoo Friends. Mem. ABA, Mo. Women's Forum, Mo. Bar Assn., Bar Assn. Met. St. Louis, Am. Soc. Corp. Secs. (pres. 1992), Met. Assn. Philanthropy, Algonquin Golf Club, Order of Coif. Republican. Presbyterian. Office: Anheuser-Busch Cos Inc 1 Busch Pl 202-6 Saint Louis MO 63118-1852

BROWN, JOHN WILFORD, surgical/medical company executive; b. Paris, Sept. 15, 1934; s. Albert T. and Treva (Moody) B.; m. Rosemary Kopel, June 7, 1957; children: Sarah Beth, Janine. BSChemE, Auburn U., 1957. Process engr. Ormet Corp., Hannibal, Ohio, 1958-62; sr. engr. Thiokol Chem. Corp., Marshall, Tex., 1962-65; with Squibb Corp., Princeton, n.J., 1965-72, asst. to pres., 1970-72; pres. Edward Weck & Co. divsn. Squibb Corp., N.Y.C., 1972-77; chmn. bd. dirs., pres., CEO Stryker Corp., Kalamazoo, 1979—. Mem. Am. Chem. Soc., Health Industries Mfg. Assn. (bd. dirs.). Democrat. Mem. Ch. of Christ. Office: Stryker Corp 2725 Fairfield Ave Kalamazoo MI 49048-2605

BROWN, KIRK, secretary of transportation; b. Harriburg, Ill., 1946; BCE, Vanderbilt U. Registered profl. engr., Ill. Deputy dir. planning, programming Ill. Dept. Transp., Springfield, dir. planning, programming, 1985-91, sec., 1991—. Mem. Nat. Soc. Profl. Engrs. (Ill. chpt.). Office: Illinois Dept Transportation Office of Public Affairs 2300 S Dirksen Pkwy Springfield IL 62764-0001

BROWN, LAURENCE DAVID, retired bishop; b. Fargo, N.D., Feb. 16, 1926; s. John Nicolai and Ada Amelia (Johnson) B.; m. Virginia Ann Allen, Sept. 6, 1950; children: Patricia Ann, Julia Louise, Claudia Ruth. BS, U. Minn., 1946; BA, Concordia Coll., 1948; M of Theology, Luther Theol. Sem., 1951. Ordained to ministry Evang. Luth. Ch., 1951. Pastor Our Savior's Luth. Ch., New Ulm, Minn., 1951-55; nat. assoc. youth dir. Evang. Luth. Ch., Mpls., 1955-60; nat. youth dir. Am. Luth. Ch., 1960-68; instn. dir. Tchr. Tng., U. Minn., 1968-69; exec. dir. Freedom from Hunger Found., Washington, 1969-73; sr. pastor St. Paul Luth. Ch., Waverly, Iowa, 1973-79; bishop Iowa Dist. Am. Luth. Ch., Des Moines, 1979-89, N.E. Iowa Synod, Evang. Luth. Ch. in Am., Waverly, 1989-92; prof. religion Wartburg Coll., Iowa, 1992-93; interim sr. pastor Ctrl. Luth. Ch., Mpls., 1994-95, Calvary Luth. Ch., Mpls., 1996-97; ret. Bd. regents Luther Coll., Decorah, Iowa, 1989-92, Wartburg Coll., 1988-92, Wartburg Theol. Sem., Dubuque, Iowa, 1988-91, Self-Help, Inc., 1989-94. Author: Take Care: A Guide for Responsible Living, 1983; contbr. articles to profl. jours. Lt. USN, 1943-46. Lutheran. Avocation: reading. Home: 7201 York Ave S Apt 514 Edina MN 55435-4444

BROWN, MARK E. manufacturing executive; b. Peosta, Iowa; BA, U. Iowa. Acct. Whirlpool, 1973; controller, v.p. procurement N. Am. Appliance Group/Whirlpool; gen. mgr. product mgmt. N. Am. Whirlpool, 1991; CFO Whirlpool Asia, Hong Kong; corp. controller Whirlpool, 1997, exec. v.p., CFO, 1999. Office: Whirlpool Corp 2000 M-63 Benton Harbor MI 49022

BROWN, MELVIN F. corporate executive; b. Carlinville, Ill., June 4, 1935; s. Ben and Selma (Frommel) B.; m. Jacqueline Sue Hirsch, Sept. 2, 1962 (dec.); children: Benjamin Andrew, Mark Steven; m. Pamela Turken, Sept. 12, 1992. AB, Washington U., 1957, JD, 1961. Bar: Mo. 1961. Pvt. practice, St. Louis, 1961-62; asst. to gen. counsel Union Elec. Co., 1962-65; sec., atty. ITT Aetna Corp., 1965-72, v.p., gen. counsel, 1972; also dir.; corp. sec., gen. counsel ITT Fin. Corp., 1974-77, exec. v.p., 1977-95; pres. ITT Comml. Fin. Corp., 1977-95, St. Louis, 1977-95; pres., CEO Deutsche Fin. Svcs., 1995-96, vice chmn., 1997-98. Bd. dirs. Falcon Products, Founders Bancshares. Mem. Mo. Commn. Dem. Party Constn. By-Laws and Party Structure, 1969-70, Mo. Dem. Platform Com., 1966, 68; mem. bd. adjustment City of Clayton, Mo., 1974—; chmn. St. Louis chpt. Am. Jewish Com., 1968—; mem. nat. coun. Washington U. Sch. Law; bd. trustees Mo. Hist. Soc.; trustee Whitaker Charitable Found.; trustee Maryville U., St. Louis Symphony Soc.; pres. Gateway chpt. Leukemia Soc.; mem. Rsch. Hon. col. Mo. Gov.'s Staff. Capt. AUS, 1957-64. Mem. Bar Assn. Met. St. Louis (pres. young lawyers sect. 1965-66), Mo. Bar Assn.. Office: Deutsche Fin Svcs 655 Maryville Centre Dr Saint Louis MO 63141-5815

BROWN, MICHAEL RICHARD, minister; b. Columbus, Ohio, Mar. 2, 1959; s. Cornelius Paul Brown and Pearl Elizabeth (Baker) Buck; m. Christine Elaine Stanley, Aug. 23, 1980; 1 child, Stephanie Nicole. BA in Bible and Religion, Huntington Coll., 1981, M in Ministry, 1983, postgrad., 1984. Ordained to ministry Ch. of United Brethren in Christ, 1983. Minister Monroe (Ind.) United Brethren Ch., 1982-89, Franklin United Brethern Ch., New Albany, Ohio, 1989—. Dir. Adams County Soccer Clinic, Decatur, Ind., 1984—85; chmn. Adams County Child Protection Team, 1985; mem. Hoosiers for Better Schs., A-Plus Program; soccer coach New Albany Mid. Sch., 1989—2001; chmn. bd. dirs. Ch. Planting Ctr.; bd. dirs. Camp COTUBIC, 1996—; v.p. Adams County Energy Assistance Inc., 1986. Named one of Outstanding Young Men of Am., 1985. Mem. New Albany Ministerial Assn. (v.p. 1994, pres. 1991, 94, conf. supt. Columbus dist. 1995-97). Republican. Avocations: soccer coach, running. Home: 6695 Albanyview Rd Westerville OH 43081-9236 Office: Franklin United Brethren Ch 7171 Central College Rd New Albany OH 43054-9303

BROWN, MIKE, professional sports team executive; Gen. mgr., v.p. Cin. Bengals, pres., CEO. Address: 1 Paul Brown Stadium Cincinnati OH 45202-3418

BROWN, MORTON B. biostatistics educator; b. Montreal, Que., Can., Dec. 15, 1941; s. Israel I. and Leah (Shaikovitch) B.; m. Raya Sobol, Oct. 16, 1969; children— Danit, Alon B.Sc., McGill U., 1962; M.A., Princeton U., 1964, Ph.D., 1965. Asst. research statistician UCLA, 1965-68, assoc. research statistician, 1975-77; vis. lectr. Tel Aviv U., 1968-69, sr. lectr., 1969-75, assoc. prof. stats., 1975-81; prof. biostatistics U. Mich., Ann Arbor, 1981—, chmn. dept., 1984-87; interim dir. biometrics core Ctr. for Clin. Investigation and Therapeutics, 1998—. Editor: BMDP Statistical Software, 1977 Fellow Royal Statis. Soc.; mem. Internat. Statis. Inst., Am. Statis. Assn., Biometric Soc., Inst. Math. Stats. Office: U Mich Dept Biostats Ann Arbor MI 48109-2029

BROWN, NANCY FIELD, editor; b. Troy, N.Y., Feb. 20, 1951; d. Robert Grant and Barbara Katherine (Field) B. BS in Journalism, Mich. State U., East Lansing, 1974. Asst. editor Mich. Am. Legion, Lansing, 1974-76, State Bar of Mich., Lansing, 1976-78, editor, 1976—, sr. dir. pubs., 1995-98, asst. exec. dir. publs., 1998—. Mem. Nat. Assn. Bar Execs. (cons. pubs. com. Chgo. chpt. 1989—), Mich. State U. Alumni Assn., Nat. Assn. Desktop Pubs., Am. Soc. Assn. Execs. Presbyterian. Avocations: reading, writing, photography, travel. Office: State Bar of Mich 306 Townsend St Lansing MI 48933-2012

BROWN, OLEN RAY, medical microbiology and toxicology research educator, consultant, writer; b. Hastings, Okla., Aug. 18, 1935; s. Willis Edward and Rosa Nell (Fulton) B.; m. Pollyana June King, Aug. 30, 1958; children: Barbara Kathryn, Diana Carol, David Gregory. BS in Lab. Tech., Okla. U., 1958, MS in Bacteriology, 1960, PhD in Microbiology, 1964. Diplomate Am. Bd. Toxicology. Instr. Sch. Medicine, U. Mo., Columbia, 1964-65, asst. prof., 1965-70, assoc. prof., 1970-77, prof. dept. molecular microbiology and immunology, 1981-96, rsch. prof., 1996—2001; joint appointments, prof. depts. microbiology and biomed. scis. Coll. Vet. Medicine, U. Mo., 1977-96, prof. biomed. scis., 1987-96. Guest lectr. Ross U., St. Kitts, W.I., 1984, 88; asst. dir. Dalton Rsch. Ctr., U. Mo., 1974-78, Dalton rsch. investigator grad. sch., 1968—; grant peer reviewer for program projects SCOR and Superfund grants NIH, 1979, Nat. Inst. Environ. Health Scis., Dept. Commerce, EPA, 1986, 90-99, Am. Inst. Biol. Scis. for Dept. Def., USAMRMC, Fund for Improvement of Secondary Edn., 2002; cons. drug abuse policy office White House, 1982, Immunol. Vaccines, Inc., Columbia, 1984—, Lab. Support, Inc., Chgo., 1988-89, Ea. Rsch. Group, Lexington, Mass., 1991—, Teltech, Mpls., 1992—, Scis. Internat., Inc., Alexandria, Va.; judge top 100 products for 1996, 99, Rsch. and Devel. Mag. Author: Laboratory Manual for Veterinary Microbiology, 1973, The Art and Science of Expert Witnessing, 2002; co-author: elem. and advanced lab. manuals for med. microbiology, 2 vols., 1978, 79; contbr. Progress in Clinical Research, Vol. 21, 1978, 79, Oxygen, 5th Internat. Hyperbaric Conf., Vols. I, II, 1974, 79, numerous articles to profl. jours.; book and film critic AAAS, Washington, 1986—; item preparer Am. Coll. Test, Med. Coll. Admissions Test, 1981—; mem. editorial staff Biomed. Letters, 1981—; responder Sci. and Math. Helpline for Mus. Sci. Discovery, Harrisburg, Pa., 1996—, reviewer profl. jours. Track and field ofcl. U. Mo. and Big Eight Conf., Columbia, 1979-86. Investigative rsch. grantee Office Naval Rsch., Dept. Def., 1968-81, NIH, 1976-88, NIEHS, 1981-94, 95—, USAID, 1983-86, Nat. Inst. Dental Health Scis., 1989-92. Fellow Am. Inst. Chemists (cert. chemistry and chem engring., profl. program bd. 1989-90, sd com. chemistry and environ. concerns); mem. Top One Percent Soc., Soc. Toxicology, Internat. Soc. Study Xenobiotics, Am. Chem. Soc., Am. Heart Assn., Internat. Soc. Exposure Analysts, Nat. Space Soc., Oxygen Soc., Columbia Track Club (sec.-treas. 1979-82). Avocations: long-distance running, oil painting. Office: U Mo Dalton Rsch Ctr Columbia MO 65211-0001

BROWN, PAM, state legislator; b. San Antonio, Sept. 12, 1952; m. F. Steve Brown; 1 child, Paul D. BA, U. Nebr., Lincoln. Mem. Nebr. Legislature from 6th dist., Lincoln, 1995—. Mem. Nebr. human genetics tech. commn. Bd. dirs. United Way of the Midlands, Westside Schs. Found. Office: State Capitol Rm 1012 Lincoln NE 68509

BROWN, PAUL, former publishing executive; MA, Cambridge U., 1976. With Butterworth Group Reed Elsevier, U.K., South Africa, N.Am., 1976-94; v.p., gen. mgr. legal info. svcs. Lexis-Nexis, Dayton, Ohio, 1994-96, COO legal info. svcs., 1996-99; pres., CEO Matthew Bender Pub., N.Y.C., 1999-00.

BROWN, PHILIP ALBERT, lawyer; b. Gettysburg, Pa., June 12, 1949; s. Clyde Raynor and Jean (McCullough) B.; m. Donna Leslie Lohr, May 25, 1985; 1 child, Andrew Raynor. BA in History, George Washington U., 1971; JD, U. Mich., 1974. Bar: Ohio 1974. Assoc. Vorys, Sater, Seymour & Pease, Columbus, Ohio, 1974-81, ptnr., 1981—. Arbitrator Nat. Assn. Security Dealers: mem. Ohio civil legal needs assessment implementation com. Ohio Supreme Ct., 1991-94. Trustee Legal Aid Soc. Columbus, 1985-91, pres. 1989-90; trustee Ohio State Legal Svcs. Assn., 1994—; mem. Nat. Coun. for Arts and Scis. of George Washington U. Fellow Columbus Bar Found.; mem. Phi Beta Kappa. Avocation: fishing. Office: Vorys Sater Seymour & Pease 52 E Gay St Columbus OH 43215-3161

BROWN, RICHARD ELLSWORTH, state legislator; Gen. agt. Luth. Brotherhood, Sioux Falls, S.D.; mem. S.D. Ho. of Reps., Pierre. Chmn. edn. com., S.D. Ho. of Reps., mem. state affairs com.

BROWN, RICHARD HOLBROOK, library administrator, historian; b. Boston, Sept. 25, 1927; s. Joseph Richard and Sylvia (Cook) B. B.A., Yale U., 1949, M.A., 1952, Ph.D., 1955. Instr. history U. Mass., Amherst, 1955-59, asst. prof., 1959-62; assoc. prof. history No. Ill. U., De Kalb, 1962-64; dir. The Amherst Project, Amherst and Chgo., 1964-72; dir. research and edn. Newberry Library, Chgo., 1972-83, acad. v.p., 1983-94; sr. rsch. fellow, 1994—. Mem. Ill. Humanities Council., 1980-86, chmn., 1982-83; cons. Nat. Endowment Humanities, 1977—; bd. dirs. Chgo. Metro History Fair, 1977—, pres., 1984-91; cons. Ctr. Study of So. Culture, U. Miss., 1979—; vis. prof. history and edn. Northwestern U., Evanston, Ill., 1971-84. Author: The Hero and the People, 1964, The Missouri Compromise: Political Statesmanship or Unwise Evasion?, 1964; gen. editor: Amherst Project Units in American History, 25 vols., 1964-75. Recipient George Washington Eggleston prize Yale U., 1955; Andrew Mellon post doctoral fellow, 1960-61 Mem. Am. Antiquarian Soc., Social Sci. Edn. Consortium (pres. 1975-77), Orgn. Am. Historians. Democrat. Roman Catholic. Office: The Newberry Libr 60 W Walton St Chicago IL 60610-3380 E-mail: brownr@newberry.org.

BROWN, ROBERT GROVER, engineering educator; b. Shenandoah, Iowa, Apr. 25, 1926; s. Grover Whitney and Irene (Frink) B. BS, Iowa State Coll., 1948, MS, 1951, PhD, 1956. Instr. Iowa State Coll., Ames, 1948-51, 53-55, asst. prof., 1955-56, assoc. prof., 1956-59, prof., 1959-76, Disting. prof., 1976-88, Disting. prof. emeritus, 1988—; research engr. N. Am. Aviation, Downey, Calif., 1951-53. Cons. various aerospace engring. firms., 1956— Author: (with R.A. Sharpe, W.L. Hughes) Lines, Waves and Antennas, 1961, (with J.W. Nilsson) Linear Systems Analysis, 1962, (with Patrick Y.C. Hwang) Introduction to Random Signals and Applied Kalman Filtering with MATLAB Exercises and Solutions, 3d edit., 1997. Fellow IEEE, Inst. Navigation (Burka award 1978, 84, Weems award 1994). Office: Iowa State U Dept Engring Ames IA 50011-0001

BROWN, ROGER WILLIAM, manufacturer's representative, real estate developer; b. Lansing, Mich., Feb. 25, 1940; s. Gustave Adolph and Beulah Alice (Bates) B.; m. Janet Rose Neiman, Apr. 16, 1977. BA, Denison U., 1961; commerce diploma, U. Birmingham, Eng., 1962; MBA, U. Chgo., 1966. Instr. Dept. Econs. Denison U., Granville, Ohio, 1966-67; lectr. Dept. Econs. Ohio State U., Columbus, 1966-67; cons. Boston Cons. Group, Boston and London, 1967-69; mgr. mktg. services Graflex div. Singer Co., Rochester, N.Y., 1969-70; v.p. Gustave Brown and Assoc., Inc., Oak Brook, Ill., 1970-87; pres. Roger Brown and Assoc., Inc., Elburn, 1987—. Author: Study to Learn, 1965; contbr. articles on USAF programmed instrn., econs, corp. strategy. Mem. land use com. Campton Twp., Kane County, Ill., 1978-81. Served to 1st lt. USAF, 1962-65. Mem. Omicron Delta Epsilon, Rho Beta Chi, Omicron Delta Kappa. Republican. Methodist. Clubs: Upton Country (Jamaica), Runaway Bay Country (Jamaica). Avocation: grain and cattle farmer. Home and Office: PO Box 428 Elburn IL 60119-0428 also: Tranquillity PO Box 224 Ocho Rios Jamaica E-mail: rwbrown@elnet.com.

BROWN, RONALD DELANO, endocrinologist; b. Grosse Pointe, Mich., Dec. 28, 1936; s. Carroll Bradley and Alice Ruth (Chapper) B.; m. Marylee Ethel Lucas, July 27, 1957; children: Linda Diane, Kent William, Mark Steven. BS with distinction, U. Mich., 1959, MD with distinction, 1963. Diplomate Am. Bd. Internal Medicine, subspecialty in endocrinology and metabolism; lic. physician Mich. Intern Detroit Gen. Hosp., 1963-64; asst. resident in medicine U. Calif. Med. Ctr., San Francisco, 1966-68; chief resident in medicine San Francisco Gen. Hosp., 1968-69; fellow in endocrinology Vanderbilt U., Nashville, 1969-71, instr. medicine, 1969-71, asst. prof. medicine, 1971-73; assoc. prof. medicine Baylor Coll. Medicine, Houston, 1973-74, Mayo Med. Sch., Rochester, Minn., 1975-80; prof. medicine Health Scis. Ctr., U. Okla., Oklahoma city, 1980-93; clin. staff St. Joseph's Mercy Hosp., Clintown Twp., Mich., 1993—. Dir. U. Okla. Hypertension Ctr., 1986-93; chief clin. hypertension Health Scis. Ctr., U. Okla., 1980-93; chief hypertension VA Hosp., Oklahoma City, 1980-86; dir. multidisciplinary hypertension rsch. tng. program (NIH), Mayo Clinic, Rochester, 1977-80; chief endocrinology Ben Taub Hosp., Houston, 1973-74, assoc. dir. clin. rsch. ctr., 1973-74; coord. Tenn. Mid-South Regional Hyper-Control Program, Vanderbilt U., 1971-73; lectr. in field.

Editl. bd. Jour. Clin. Endocrinology and Metabolism, 1987-91; reviewer for Life Scis., Annals of Internal Medicine, Jour. Lab. Clin. Medicine, Am. Jour. Medicine, Endocrinology, Mayo Clinic Proceedings, Steroids; contbr. 58 articles to profl. jours. Capt. USAF, 1964-66. Fellow ACP. Am. Coll. Endocrinologists; mem. Am. Soc. Hypertension, Am. Diabetes Assn., Am. Assn. Clin. Endocrinologists, Phi Kappa Phi, Phi Lambda Upsilon, Alpha Omega Alpha. Avocation: nursery. Office: 43171 Dalcoma Dr Ste 1 Clinton Township MI 48038-6307

BROWN, ROWLAND CHAUNCEY WIDRIG, information systems, strategic planning and ethics consultant; b. Detroit, Oct. 11, 1923; s. Rowland Chauncey and Rhea (Widrig) B.; m. Kathleen Heather Sayre, May 18, 1946; children: Stephanie Anne, Geoffrey Rowland Sayre (dec.), Kathleen Heather. BA cum laude, Harvard U., 1947, JD, 1950; sr. mgmt. Sloan Sch., MIT, 1969; D. Humane Letters (hon.), Ohio Dominican Coll., 1999. Bar: D.C. 1951. Counsel Econ. Sablzn. Agy., 1950-52; staff counsel SBA, 1954; counsel Machinery and Allied Products Inst., Washington, 1955-59; with Dorr Oliver, Stamford, Conn., 1959-70, pres., 1968-70; pres., chief exec. officer Buckeye Internat., Inc., Columbus, Ohio, 1970-80; chief exec. officer Online Computer Libr. Ctr., 1980-89; with R. Brown & Assocs. Adv. bd. tchg. and learning Ohio State U. Sr. internat. cons. Coun. for Ethics and Econs.; hon. trustee Columbus Cmty. Cable Access; bd. dirs., visitor's bd. Ohio Dominican Coll.; mem. race rels. vision coun. United Way; trustee Coun. for Pub. Deliberation, Civic Life Inst., Edn. Coun. Found. Decorated Air medal (3), Purple Heart, Korean Republic citation. Mem. ALA, Am. Soc. Info. Sci., Am. Assn. for Higher Edn., N.Y. Harvard Club, Columbus Club, Torch Club, Scioto Country Club, Rotary. Home and Office: R Brown & Assoc 2711 Edington Rd Columbus OH 43221-2502 E-mail: rcwbrow@columbus.rr.com.

BROWN, SANDRA LEE, art association administrator, watercolorist; b. Chgo., July 9, 1943; d. Arthur Willard and Erma Emily (Lange) Boettcher; m. Ronald Gregory Brown, June 21, 1983; 1 child, Jon Michael. BA in Art and Edn., N.E. Ill. U., 1966; postgrad., No. Ill. U. Cert. K-9 tchr., Ill. Travel agt. Weiss Travel Bur., Chgo., 1959-66; tchr. Chgo. Sch. Sys., 1966-68, Schaumburg (Ill.) Sch. Dist. 54, 1968-94, creator coord. peer mentoring program for 1st-yr. tchrs., 1992-96; cons. Yardstick Ednl. Svcs., Monroe, Wis., 1994—; exec. dir. Monroe Arts Ctr., 1996—2001, Monroe Area Coun. for the Arts , Madisonville, Tenn., 2002—. Mem. adv. bd. Peer Coaching and Mentoring Network, Chgo. suburban region, 1992-94; peer cons. Schaumburg Sch. Dist. 54, 1988-94. Exhibited in group shows Court House Gallery, Woodstock, Ill., Millburn (Ill.) Gallery, Gallerie Stefanie, Chgo., Monroe Arts Ctr., 1997. Campaign chmn. for mayoral candidate, Grayslake, Ill., 1989; campaign chmn. for trustee Citizens for Responsible Govt., Grayslake, 1991. Mem. Lakes Region Watercolor Guild, Delta Kappa Gamma (chmn. women in arts Gamma chpt. Ill. 1992-94, Alpha Mu chpt. 1995-97). Avocations: gardening, musician for barn dances, pre-war Appalachian, blues and Cajun music, research collecting 78 RPM records. Home and Office: Yardstick Ednl Svcs PO Box 1456 Athens TN 37371

BROWN, SEYMOUR R. lawyer, director; b. Cleve., Oct. 24, 1924; s. Leonard and Ella (Rubinstein) B.; m. Madeline Kusevich, July 8, 1956; children: Frederic M., Thomas R., Barbara L. N. Rybicki. B.A., Case-Western Res. U., 1948; J.D., Cleve. State U., 1953. Bar: Ohio 1953. Prin. Seymour R. Brown & Assocs., Cleve.; pres. Carnegie Fin. Corp., 1961—; ptnr. Brown-McCallister Real Estate, Residential & Comml. Constrn., Melbourne, Fla., 1973-81. Spl. counsel to atty. gen. State of Ohio, 1963-70. Editor, pub.: Gt. Lakes Architecture, 1955-59. Chmn. CSC, University Heights, Ohio, 1978-82, 84-86, mem., 1976—; mem. exec. com. Cuyahoga County Rep. Orgn., 1966—; pres. Nat. Permanent Endowment Fund, Inc., 1988-92. With AUS, 1943-45. Decorated Purple Heart, Bronze Star. Mem. ABA, Ohio Bar Assn., Cleve. Bar Assn., Am. Arbitration Assn. (comml. arbitration panel), Zeta Beta Tau (nat. dir., nat. pres. 1978-80), Masons. Home: 3718 Meadowbrook Blvd Cleveland OH 44118-4422

BROWN, SHERROD, congressman, former state official; b. Mansfield, Ohio, Nov. 9, 1952; s. Charles G. and Emily (Campbell) B.; children: Emily, Elizabeth. B.A., Yale U., 1974; M.A. in Edn., Ohio State U., 1979, M.A. in Pub. Adminstrn., 1981. Mem. Ohio Ho. of Reps., Mansfield, 1975-82; Sec. of State State of Ohio, Columbus, 1983-91; mem. U.S. Congress from 13th Ohio dist., Washington, 1993—; mem. energy and commerce com., internat. rels. com. Instr. Ohio State U., Mansfield, 1978-79 Author: Congress from the Inside, 1999. Active India Caucus. Recipient Eagle Scout Am. 1966, Friend of Edn. award, 1978 Mem. Nat. Assn. Secs. State Democrat. Lutheran. Office: US Ho of Reps 2438 Rayburn Ho Office Bldg Washington DC 20515-3513*

BROWN, THEODORE LAWRENCE, chemistry educator; b. Green Bay, Wis., Oct. 15, 1928; s. Lawrence A. and Martha E. (Kedinger) B.; m. Audrey Catherine Brockman, Jan. 6, 1951; children: Mary Margaret, Karen Anne, Jennifer Gerarda, Philip Matthew (dec.), Andrew Lawrence. BS in Chemistry, Ill. Inst. Tech., 1950; PhD, Mich. State U., 1956. Mem. faculty U. Ill., Urbana, 1956—, prof. chemistry, 1965-93, prof. chemistry emeritus, 1993—, vice chancellor for rsch., dean Grad. Coll., 1980-86, dir.Beckman Inst. for Advanced Sci. and Tech., 1987-93. Vis. scientist Internat. Meteorol. Inst., Stockholm, 1972; Boomer lectr. U. Alta., Edmonton, Can., 1975; Firth vis. prof. U. Sheffield, Eng., 1977; mem. bd. govs. Argonne Nat. Lab., 1982-88, Mercy Hosp., Urbana, 1985-89, Chem. Abstracts Svc., 1991-96, Arnold and Mabel Beckman Found., 1994—, Am. Chem. Soc. Pub., 1996-2001. Author: (with R.S. Drago) Experiments in General Chemistry, 3d edit., 1970, General Chemistry, 2d edit., 1968, Energy and the Environment, 1971, (with H.E. LeMay and B.E. Bursten) Chemistry: The Central Science, 1977, 8th edit., 2000; assoc. editor Inorganic Chemistry, 1969-78; contbr. articles to profl. publs. Mem. Govt.-Univ.-Industry Roundtable Coun., 1989-94; bd. dirs. Champaign County Opportunities Industrialization Ctr., 1970-79, chmn. bd. dirs., 1975-78. With USN, 1950-53. Sloan rsch. fellow, 1962-66, NSF sr. postdoctoral fellow, 1964-65, Guggenheim fellow, 1979. Fellow AAAS, Am. Acad. Arts and Scis.; mem. Am. Chem. Soc. (award in inorganic chemistry 1972, award for disting. svc. in advancement of inorganic chemistry 1993), Sigma Xi, Alpha Chi Sigma. Home: 10741 Crooked River Rd Unit 101 Bonita Springs FL 34135-1726

BROWN, THOMAS D. pharmaceutical executive; Divsnl. v.p. diagnostic comml. opers. Abbott Labs., Abbott Park, Ill., 1993, v.p. diagnostic comml. opers., 1993-98, sr. v.p. diagnostic opers., 1998—, corp. officer, 1993. Office: Abbott Labs 100 Abbott Park Rd Abbott Park IL 60064-3502

BROWN, TIMOTHY N. state legislator; BA, Ill. Wesleyan U.; MD, U. Ill. Physician Crawfordsville (Ind.) Family Care; rep. Dist. 41 Ind. Ho. of Reps., mem. fin. inst., ins., corp. and small bus. coms., pub. safety com., vice chmn. pub. health com. Asst. clin. prof. medicine Ind. U. Mem. Ind. State Med. Assn. Address: PO Box 861 Crawfordsville IN 47933-0861

BROWN, TREVOR, dean; Dean journalism Ind. U., Bloomington. Office: Ind U Sch Journalism Ernie Pyle Hall Rm 200 940 E 7th St Bloomington IN 47405-7108

BROWN, WENDY WEINSTOCK, nephrologist, educator; b. N.Y.C., Dec. 9, 1944; d. Irving and Pearl (Levack) Weinstock; m. Barry David Brown, May 2, 1971 (div. Sept. 1995); children: Jennifer Faye, Joshua Reuben, Julie Aviva, Rachel Ann. BA, U. Mass., 1966; MD, Med. Coll. of Pa., 1970; MPH, St. Louis U., 1999. Am. Bd. Internal Medicine, 1977. Intern U. Ill. Affiliated Hosps., Chgo., 1970-71; resident in internal medicine The Med. Coll. Wis. Affiliated Hosps., Milw., 1971-74; gen. practitioner Vogelweh (W. Germany) Health Clinics, 1975-76; fellow in nephrology Med. Coll. of Wis. Milw. County Med. Complex, Milw., 1976-78; staff physician St. Louis VA Med Ctr., 1978—, acting chief, hemodialysis sect., 1983-85, chief dialysis/renal sect., 1985-90; dir. clin. nephrology, 1990—; staff physician St. Louis U. Hosps., 1978—, St. Louis City Hosp., 1982-85, St Mary's Health Ctr., St. Louis, 1994—. Assoc. prof. internal medicine St. Louis U. Health Sci. Ctr., 1985-98, prof. internal medicine, 1998—. Reviewer Clin. Nephrology, Nephrology, Dialysis & Transplantation, Am. Jour. Nephrology, Am. Jour. Kidney Disease, Jour Am. Geriatric Soc., Jour. Renal Replacement Therapy, Jour. Am. Soc. Nephrology, Geriatric Nephrology and Urology; med. editor NKF Family Focus; mem. editl. bd. Clin. Nephrology, Geriatric Nephrology, Advances in Renal Replacement Therapy, Internat. Urology & Nephrology; contbr. articles to profl. jours. Mem. adv. coun. Mo. Kidney Program, 1985-91, chmn., 1988-89; numerous positions Nat. Kidney Found., 1984—, nat. chmn., 1995-97; bd. dirs. United Way, St. Louis, 1994—, Nat. Kidney Found. Ea. Mo. and Metro East, Inc., 1980-94; bd. dirs. Combined Health Appeal Greater St. Louis, Inc., 1988, pres., 1989-92; bd. dirs. Combined Health Appeal Am., 1991-98, sec., 1992-96, vice chmn., 1996-98. Named Casual Corner Career Woman of Yr., 1986, Combine Health Appeal of Am. Vol. of Yr., 1991, Olympic Torch Bearer, 1996, St. Louis Health Profl. of Yr., 1997; recipient Upjohn Achievement award, Med. Coll. Wis. Affiliated HOsps., 1972, Cert. of Leadership, St. Louis YWCA, 1989, Chmn.'s award, Nat. Kidney Found. of Ea. Mo. and Metro East, 1990, award of excellence, 2002, Chmn.'s award, Nat. Kidney Found., Washington, 1990, Martin Wagner award, Nat. Kidney Found., 1999, award of excellence, Nat. Kidney Found. Ea. Mo. and Metro East, 2002. Fellow ACP; mem. Am. Soc. Nephrology, Internat. Soc. Nephrology, Coun. on Kidney in Cardiovascular Disease, Am. Heart Assn., St. Louis Soc. Am. Med. Women's Assn., St. Louis Internists (v.p. 1983-84, pres. 1984-85), Women in Nephrology (pres.-elect 1999-00, pres. 2000—), Internat. Soc. for Peritoneal Dialysis, Am. Geriatrics Soc., Soc. for Exec. Leadership in Acad. Medicine (bd. dirs., program chair 1999—), Alpha Omega Alpha. Home: 100 Frontenac Frst Saint Louis MO 63131-3235 Office: Saint Louis VAMC 915 N Grand Blvd Saint Louis MO 63106-1621 E-mail: wendy.brown@med.va.gov.

BROWN, WESLEY ERNEST, federal judge; b. Hutchinson, Kans., June 22, 1907; s. Morrison H. H. and Julia (Wesley) B.; m. Mary A. Miller, Nov. 30, 1934 (dec.); children: Wesley Miller, Loy B. Wiley; m. Thadene N. Moore. Student, Kans. U., 1925-28; LLB, Kansas City Law Sch., 1933. Bar: Kans. 1933, Mo. 1933. Pvt. practice, Hutchinson, 1933-58; county atty. Reno County, Kans., 1935-39; referee in bankruptcy U.S. Dist. Ct. Kans., 1958-62, judge, 1962-79, sr. judge, 1979—. Apptd. Temporary Emergency Ct. of Appeals of U.S., 1980-93; dir. Nat. Assn. Referees in Bankruptcy, 1959-62; mem. bankruptcy divsn. Jud. Conf., 1963-70; mem. Jud. Conf., U.S., 1976-79. With USN, 1944-46. Mem. ABA, Kans. Bar Assn. (exec. council 1950-62, pres. 1964-65), Reno County Bar Assn. (pres. 1947), Wichita Bar Assn., S.W. Bar Kan., Delta Theta Phi. Office: US Dist Ct 414 US Courthouse 401 N Market St Wichita KS 67202-2089

BROWNBACK, SAM, senator; b. Parker, Kans. m. Mary; children: Abby, Andy, Liz. BS in Agrl. Econs. with honors, Kan. State U.; JD, U. Kans. Farm broadcaster KKSU; ptnr. law firm, N.Y.C.; instr. law Kans. State U.; city atty. Ogden and Leonardville, Kans.; sec. agr., Washington; mem. 104th Congress from 2nd Kans. dist., 1994-96; U.S. Senator from Kans., 1996—. Mem. com., sci.. and transp., fgn. rels., govtl. affairs, joint econ. coms.; fellow U.S. Trade Rep. Carla Hills, 1990-91, mem. intergovtl. adv. com.; spkr. on trade, agr., leadership, motivation, mem. com. health, edn., labor and pensions. Co-author: 2 books; contbr. numerous articles. Pres. Kans. Prayer Breakfast; developer Family Impact Statement; vice chmn. Riley County Rep. Com. Recipient Hon. Am. Farmer degree, FFA; named Outstanding Young Person, Osaka, Japan Jaycees, Kansan of Distinction, 1988. Office: US Senate 303 Hart Senate Office Bldg Washington DC 20510-0001*

BROWNE, DONALD ROGER, speech communication educator; b. Detroit, Mar. 13, 1934; s. A. and L. Browne; m. Mary Jo Rowell, Aug. 23, 1958; children: Mary Kathleen, Stuart Roger, Steven Rowell. BA, U. Mich., 1955, MA, 1958, PhD, 1961. Corr. Voice of Am., fgn. service officer U.S. Info. Agy., Tunis, Tunisia and Conakry, Guinea, 1960-63; asst. prof. broadcasting Boston U., 1963-65; asst. prof. speech Purdue U., West Lafayette, Ind., 1965-66; assoc. prof. U. Minn., Mpls., 1966-70, prof., 1970—, dept. chair, 1989-93, 96-99. Fulbright lectr., Beirut, 1973-74; vis. lectr. Lund U., Sweden, spring 1993. Author: International Radio Broadcasting, 1982, Comparing Broadcast Systems, 1989 (BEA/NAB Electronic Media Book of Yr. award 1989, Outstanding Acad. Book in Comm. Category, Choice, 1990), Television/Radio News & Minorities, 1994, Electronic Media and Indigenous Peoples, 1996, Electronic Media and Industrialized Nations, 1999. Mem.Civic Orch. Mpls., 1966—. Served with U.S. Army, 1955-57. NATO fellow, Brussels, 1980. Mem. Broadcast Edn. Assn., Assn. for Edn. in Journalism and Mass Comm., Civic Orch. Mpls. Episcopalian. Avocation: playing trombone. Office: Univ of Minn 224 Church St SE Ford Hall Minneapolis MN 55455

BROWNE, RAY BROADUS, popular culture educator; b. Millport, Ala., Jan. 15, 1922; s. Garfield and Annie Nola (Trull) B.; m. Olwyn Orde, Aug. 21, 1952 (dec.); children— Glenn, Kevin; m. Alice Pat Matthews, Aug. 25, 1965; 1 child, Alicia. A.B., U. Ala., 1943; A.M., Columbia U., 1947; Ph.D., UCLA, 1956. Instr. U. Nebr., Lincoln, 1947-50; instr. U. Md., College Park, 1956-60; asst. prof., assoc. prof. Purdue U., Lafayette, Ind., 1960-67; prof. popular culture Bowling Green (Ohio) State U., 1967—, Univ. disting. prof., 1975—. Author, editor over 50 books, including Melville's Drive to Humanism, 1971, Popular Culture and the Expanding Consciousness, 1973, The Constitution and Popular Culture, 1975, Dominant Symbols in Popular Culture, 1990, The Many Tongues of Literacy, 1992, Continuities in Popular Culture, 1993, The Cultures of Celebrations, 1994, Preview 2001: Popular Culture Studies in the Future, 1996, Lincoln-Lore: Lincoln in Contemporary Popular Culture, 1996, Pioneers in Popular Culture Studies, 1998, The Defining Guide to United States Popular Culture, 2000, The Detective as Historian, 2000, Mission Underway: The History of the Popular Culture Association/American Culture Association and Popular Culture Movement, 2002; creator, editor Jour. Popular Culture, 1967—, Jour. Am. Culture, 1977. Served with U.S. Army, 1942-46 Mem. Popular Culture Assn. (founder, sec., treas. 1970—), Am. Culture Assn. (sec.-treas. 1977—). Democrat. Avocation: scholarly research. Home: 210 N Grove St Bowling Green OH 43402-2335 Office: Bowling Green U Jour Popular Culture Bowling Green OH 43403-0001 E-mail: rbrowne@bgnet.bgsu.edu.

BROWNE, WILLIAM BITNER, lawyer; b. Springfield, Ohio, Nov. 23, 1914; s. John Franklin and Etta Blanche (Bitner) B.; m. Dorothy Ruth Gilbert, Aug. 31, 1939; children: Franklin G., Dale Ann Browne Compton. AB, Wittenberg U., 1935, LLD (hon.), 1970; postgrad., U. Bordeaux, 1935-36; JD cum laude, Harvard U., 1939. Bar: Ohio 1939, U.S. Dist. Ct. (so. dist.) Ohio 1941, U.S. Ct. Appeals (6th cir.) 1950, U.S. Supreme Ct. 1970. Assoc. Donovan, Leisure, Newton & Lumbard, N.Y.C., 1939-40; assoc. Corry, Durfey & Martin, Springfield, Ohio, 1940-48; ptnr. Corry, Durfey, Martin & Browne and successors, 1948-88; of counsel Martin, Browne, Hull & Harper, 1988-94. Contbr. (articles to legal jours.). Bd. dirs. Wittenberg U., 1955-89; pres. Greater Springfield & Clark County Assn., 1948-49; vice chmn. Clark County Republican Central and Exec. coms., 1948-52; mem. Springfield City Bd. Edn., 1950-53; mem. exec. com. United Appeals Clark County, 1956-62. Capt. OSS Signal Corps, U.S. Army, 1942-46. Decorated Bronze Star; decorated Croix de Guerre with palm, Medaille de Reconnaissance Francaise; laureate Springfield Area Bus. Hall of Fame, 1993. Fellow Am. Coll. Trial Lawyers (ret.), Am. Bar Found., Am. Coll. Trust and Estate Counsel (ret.), Ohio Bar Found. (pres. 1979, Fellows rsch. and svc. award 1976); mem. ABA (del. 1971-76), Ohio Bar Assn. (pres. 1969-70, medal of honor 1973), Springfield Bar Assn. (pres. 1967), Springfield C. of C. (pres. 1961-62), Zanesfield Rod and Gun Club, Springfield Country Club, Rotary, Masons. Episcopalian. Office: Martin Browne Hull & Harper 1 S Limestone St PO Box 1488 Springfield OH 45501-1488

BROWNELL, BLAINE ALLISON, university administrator, history educator; b. Birmingham, Ala., Nov. 12, 1942; s. Blaine Jr. and Annette (Holmes) B.; m. Mardi Ann Taylor, Aug. 21, 1964; children— Blaine, Allison BA, Washington and Lee U., 1965; MA, U. N.C., 1967, PhD, 1969. Asst. prof. Purdue U., West Lafayette, Ind., 1969-74; assoc. prof., chmn. dept. U. Ala., Birmingham, 1974-78, prof., 1980-90, dean grad. sch., 1978-84, dean social and behavioral scis., 1984-90; provost, v.p. for acad. affairs U. North Tex., Denton, 1990-98; exec. dir. Ctr. Internat. Programs and Svcs. U. Memphis, 1998-2000; pres. Ball State U., Muncie, Ind., 2000—. Sr. fellow Johns Hopkins U., Balt., 1971-72; Fulbright lectr. Hiroshima U., Japan, 1977-78; dir. U. Ala. Ctr. Internat. Programs, 1980-90. Author: The Urban Ethos...., 1975, City in Southern History, 1977, Urban America, 1979, 2d edit., 1990, The Urban Nation 1920-80, 1981; editor Jour. Urban History, 1976-90, assoc. editor, 1990-95. Mem. Birmingham City Planning Commn., 1975-77, Jefferson County Planning Commn., 1975-77, Dallas Com. Fgn. Rels., 1990-98; chmn. Birmingham Coun. on Fgn. Rels., 1988-90. Mem. Am. Hist. Assn., Orgn. Am. Historians, So. Hist. Assn., Philos. Soc. Tex. Presbyterian Office: Ball State U Office Of Pres Muncie IN 47306-0001

BROWNING, DON SPENCER, religious educator; b. Trenton, Mo., Jan. 13, 1934; s. Robert Watson and Nelle Juanita Browning; m. Carol LaVeta Browning, Sept. 28, 1958; children: Elizabeth Dell, Christopher Robert. AB, Ctrl. Meth. Coll., Fayette, Mo., 1956; DDiv, Ctr. Meth. Coll., Fayette, Mo., 1984; BD, U. Chgo., 1959, PhD, 1964; DDiv, Christian Theol. Sem., Indpls., 1990; DDiv (hon.), U. Glasgow, Scotland, 1998. Asst. prof. Phillips U., Enid, Okla., 1963-65; instr. Div. Sch., U. Chgo., 1965-66, asst. prof., 1966-69, assoc. prof., 1969-77, prof., 1977-79, Alexander Campbell prof. of ethics and social sci., 1979—. Author: Atonement and Psychotherapy, 1966, Generative Man: Society and Good Man in Philip Rieff, Norman Borwn, Erich Fromm and Erik Erikson, 1973, The Moral Context of Pastoral Care, 1976, Pluralism and Personality: William James and Some Contemporary Cultures of Psychology, 1980, Religious Ethics and Pastoral Care, 1983, Religious Thought and the Modern Psychologies, 1987, A Fundamental Practical Theology, 1991; co-author: From Culture Wars to Common Ground: Religion and the American Family Debate, 1997; co-author: Reweaving the Social Tapestry: Toward a Public Philosophy and Policy of Families, 2001; sr. advisor PBS documentary Marriage--Just a Piece of Paper?. Recipient Oskar Pfister Award Lecture, Am. Psychiat. Assn., 1999; Cadbury Lectr., U. Birmingham, Eng., 1998; Guggenheim fellow, 1975-76; Lilly Endowment grantee, 1991-97, 97, 99. Home: 5513 S Kenwood Ave Chicago IL 60637-1713 Office: Univ of Chicago Divinity Sch Chicago IL 60637

BROWNLEE, KARIN S. state legislator; m. Doug Brownlee; 4 children. BS in Microbiology, Kans. State U. Co-owner Patrons Mortgage Co.; mem. Kans. Senate, Topeka, 1996—, mem. commerce com., mem. fin. instns. and ins. com., 1996—, mem. utilities com., mem. claims against the state com., mem. arts and cultural resources com. Mem. steering com. Leadership Olathe, 1994—; mem. QPA issues com. Olathe Sch. Dist., 1993; mem. adv. com. Mahaffie Farmsted; women's ministry leader Olathe Bible Ch.; del. Rep. Nat. Conv., 1996; vice chair Johnston Rep. Party, 1994-96; chair Olathe Rep. Party, 1992-94. Mem. Olathe Area C. of C. Republican. Office: 300 SW 10th Ave Rm 143-n Topeka KS 66612-1504

BROWNLEE, ROBERT HAMMEL, lawyer; b. Chester, Ill., Dec. 15, 1951; s. Robert Mathis and Geneva (Hammel) B.; m. Sue F., June 17, 1978. BS, So. Ill. U., Carbondale, 1973; JD, Vanderbilt U., Nashville, 1976. Bar: Mo. 1976, Ill. 1977, U.S. Dist. Ct. (ea. and we. dists.) Mo. 1976, U.S. Dist. Ct. (so. and cen. dists.) Ill. 1977, U.S. Ct. Appeals (8th cir.) 1979, Ky. 1999, U.S. Supreme Ct. 1999. Assoc. Thompson & Mitchell, St. Louis, 1976-82; ptnr. Thompson Coburn, 1982—. Mng. editor Vanderbilt Law Review, Nashville, 1975-76; mem. Bar Assn. of Met. St. Louis, 1976—, Ill. State Bar Assn., Springfield, Ill., 1977—, Am. Bankruptcy Inst., 1988—, Ky. Bar, 1999—. Co-author: (books) Rights of Secured Creditors in Bankruptcy, 1987, Lender Liability in Missouri, 1988, Protection of Secured Interests in Bankruptcy, 1989, Litigation in Bankruptcy Proceedings, 1994, Interlocutory Appeal Issues Before the Bankruptcy Reform Commission, 1996, Bankruptcy Impact on Commercial Leases, Advanced Missouri Real Estate Law, 1997, updated, 1999, Impact of the Bankruptcy Review Commissions Report on Creditor Issues, 1997. Mem. Friends of the St. Louis Zoo., 1986—, St. Louis Bot. Garden Sponsors, 1987—; builder of the community United Way of Greater St. Louis, 1988—. Mem. ABA (litigation sec. 1976—, co-chair jury instrn. subcom. of bankruptcy and insolvency com. 1994-99, bus. sec. 1976—, vice-chair claims trading subcom. bus. bankruptcy com. 1998—), Mo. Athletic Club, Mo. Bankers Assn. (chmn. legal adv. bd. 1997-98). Avocations: fishing, american art pottery, antiques, gardening. Office: Thompson Coburn 1 Firstar Plz Ste 3500 Saint Louis MO 63101-1643 E-mail: rbrownlee@thompsoncoburn.com.

BROWNRIGG, JOHN CLINTON, lawyer; b. Detroit, Aug. 7, 1948; s. John Arthur and Sheila Pauline (Taffe) B.; children: Brian M., Jennifer A., Katharine T. BA, Rockhurst Coll., 1970; JD cum laude, Creighton U., 1974. Bar: Nebr. 1974, U.S. Dist. Ct. Nebr. 1974, U.S. Tax Ct. 1977, U.S. Ct. Appeals (8th cir.) 1990. Ptnr. Eisenstatt, Higgins, Kinnamon, Okun & Brownrigg, P.C., Omaha, 1974-80, Erickson & Sederstrom, P.C., Omaha, 1980—. Lectr. law trial practice Creighton U. Sch. Law, Omaha, 1978-83; dir. Legal Aid Soc., Inc., Omaha, 1982-88, pres., 1987-88, devel. coun., 1989—; dir. Nebr. Continuing Legal Edn., Inc., 1991-93. Chmn. law sect. Archbishop's Capital Campaign, Omaha, 1991. Sgt. USAR, 1970-76. Fellow Nebr. State Bar Found. (dir. 1991-93); mem. Nebr. State Bar Assn. (pres. 1992-93), Nebr. Assn. Trial Attys., Omaha Bar Assn. (pres. 1990-91). Avocations: golf, bicycling, hiking. Office: Erickson & Sederstrom PC Ste 100 10330 Regency Parkway Dr Omaha NE 68114-3761 E-mail: brownrigg@eslaw.com.

BROXMEYER, HAL EDWARD, medical educator; b. Bklyn., Nov. 27, 1944; s. David and Anna (Gurman) B.; m. C. Beth Biller, 1969; children: Eric Jay, Jeffrey Daniel. BS, Bklyn. Coll., 1966; MS, L.I. U., 1969; PhD, NYU, 1973. Postdoctoral student Queens U., Kingston, Ont., Can., 1973-75; assoc. researcher, rsch. assoc. Meml. Sloan Kettering Cancer Ctr., N.Y.C., 1975-78, assoc., 1978-83, assoc. mem., 1983; asst. prof. Cornell U. Grad. Sch., 1980-83; assoc. prof. Ind. U. Sch. Medicine, Indpls., 1983-86, prof. medicine, microbiology and immunology, 1986—; sci. dir. Walther Oncology Ctr., 1988—, chmn. microbiology and immunology, 1997—. Mem. hematology II study sect. NIH, Bethesda, Md., 1981-86, 95-2000, chair, 1997-2000; adv. com. NHLBI, NIH, Bethesda, 1991-94; chmn. bd. sci. counselors Nat. Space Biomed. Rsch. Inst., 1998—; mem. coun. Nat. Space Biomed. Rsch. Inst., 1999—; ; bd. sci. advisers Viacell Corp.; bd. dirs. Nat. Disease Rsch. Interchange. Assoc. editor Exptl. Hematology, 1981-90, Jour. Immunology, 1987-92, Stem Cells, 1996-97, Brit. Jour. Haematology, 1998—, Am. Soc. Hematology, 2001-; editor Jour. LeuKocyte Biology, 1995—; sr. editor Jour. Hematotherapy and Stem Cell Rsch., 2000—; mem. editl. bd. Blood, 1983-87, Biotech. Therapeutics, 1988-95, Internat. Jour. Hematology, 1991—, Jour. Lab. Clin. Medicine, 1992—, Jour. Exptl. Medicine, 1992—, Annals Hematology, 1993—, Cell Transplantation, 1994—, Critical Rev. Oncology/Hematology, 1995—, Stem Cells, 1998—, Jour. Blood and Marrow Transplantations, 1998—, Cytokines, Cellular and Molecular Therapy, 1998—I contbr. over 500 papers to profl. publs. Mem. ednl. com. Leukemia Soc. Am., Indpls., 1983—, nat. career devel. study sect., N.Y., 1991-95, 2000—. Recipient Merit award Nat. Cancer Inst., 1987-95, Spl. Fellow award, 1976-78, and Scholar award, 1978-83, Leukemia Soc. Am. Mem. AAAS, N.Y. Acad. Scis., Soc. for Leukocyte Biology, Am. Assn. Cancer Rsch., Am. Assn. Immunologists, Internat. Soc. Exptl. Hematology (pres. 1990-91), Am. Soc. Hematology, Am. Fedn. Clin. Rsch., Am. Soc. Blood and Marrow Transplantation. Avocations: competitive Olympic-style weightlifting (nat. master's champion 50-54 age group 76 kg. class, 1994, 97). Home: 1210 Chessington Rd Indianapolis IN 46260-1630 Office: Ind U Sch Medicine 1044 W Walnut St Rm 302 Indianapolis IN 46202-5254 Fax: 317-274-7592. E-mail: hbroxmey@iupui.edu.

BRUBAKER, ROBERT LORING, lawyer; b. Louisville, May 22, 1947; s. Robert Lee and Betty (Brock) B.; m Jeannette Marie Montgomery, Dec. 21, 1968; children: Benjamin Brock, Anne Montgomery. BA, Earlham Coll., 1969; JD, U. Chgo., 1972. Bar: Ohio 1972, U.S. Dist. Ct. (so. dist.) Ohio 1973, U.S. Ct. Appeals (6th cir.) 1975, U.S. Supreme Ct. 1978, U.S. Ct. Appeals (D.C. cir.) 1979, U.S. Ct. Appeals (3d, 4th and 7th cirs.) 1995. Asst. atty. gen. Atty. Gen.'s Office State of Ohio, Columbus, 1972-76; assoc. Porter Wright Morris & Arthur, 1976-78, ptnr., 1979—. Editor: Ohio Environmental Law Handbook, 1990, 2d edit., 1992, 3d edit., 1994, Deposition Strategy, Law and Forms: Environmental Law; mem. editl. bd. Ohio Environ. Law Letter, 1991. Mem. ABA (natural resources, energy and environ. law sect., pub. utility sect.), Ohio Bar Assn. (environ. law com.), Air and Waste Mgmt. Assn. (chmn. S.W. Ohio chpt. 1990-91, chmn. East Ctrl. sect. 1991-92), Columbus Bar Assn. (environ. law com.), Nat. Coal Coun. Home: 2661 Wexford Rd Columbus OH 43221-3217 Office: Porter Wright Morris & Arthur 41 S High St Ste 2800 Columbus OH 43215-6194 E-mail: rbrubaker@porterwright.com.

BRUCE, ISSAC ISIDORE, football player; b. Ft. Lauderdale, Florida, Nov. 10, 1972; Postgrad in phys. edn., Memphis State, 1992. Winner Super Bowl 35, 2000; wide receiver St. Louis Rams, 1995—, L.A. Rams, 1994—95. Bd. dirs. Childhaven; donator children orgn., homeless. Recipient Daniel F. Reeves Memorial award, 1996, Carroll Rosenbloom award, 1994. Achievements include first Rams receiver to earn consecutive Pro Bowl invitations;ranked fifth in NFL's all-time single season reception list;first player in history to record three consecutive games with at least 170 receiving yards. Office: 1 Rams Way St. Louis MO 63045*

BRUCE, JACKSON MARTIN, JR. lawyer; b. Milw., Apr. 10, 1931; s. Jackson Martin and Harriet (Edgell) B.; m. Lilias M. Morehouse, June 30, 1954; children: Lilias Stephanie, Andrew Edgell. AB magna cum laude, Harvard U., 1953, JD cum laude, 1957; MA with 1st class honors in Law, Cambridge U., 1955. Bar: Wis. 1957, Fla. 1973. Assoc. Quarles & Brady, Milw., 1957-64, ptnr., 1964-96; shareholder Dunwody, White & Landon, Naples, Fla., 1996—; counsel Michael Best & Friedrich, Milw., 1996—. Mem. joint editl. bd. Uniform Trusts and Estates Acts; contbr. articles to profl. jours. Bd. dirs. Living Ch. Found., Inc., 1965-98; trustee Univ. Sch. Milw., 1973-79. Fellow Am. Coll. Trust and Estate Counsel (bd. regents 1976-82, treas. 1990-91, sec. 1991-92, v.p. 1992-93, pres. 1994-95); mem. ABA (bd. govs. 1994-97, chmn. sect. real property, probate and trust law 1984-85, ho. dels., ethics com. 1998-2001), State Bar Wis. (chmn. bd. govs. 1979-80), Am. Bar Found., Am. Law Inst., Internat. Acad. Estate and Trust Law (mem. exec. coun. 1980-86), Nat. Conf. Bar Pres., Nat. Conf. Lawyers and Corp. Fiduciaries (chmn. 1984-90), Town Club, Milw. Club (bd. dirs. 1985-2001), The Club Pelican Bay. Home: 6101 Pelican Bay Blvd Apt 1201 Naples FL 34108-8183 also: 9008 N Bayside Dr Milwaukee WI 53217-1913 Office: Dunwody White & Landon 4001 Tamiami Trl N Ste 200 Naples FL 34103-3591 also: Michael Best & Friedrich 100 E Wisconsin Ave Ste 3300 Milwaukee WI 53202-4107 Business E-Mail: jbruce@dwl-law.com., jmbruce@mbf-law.com.

BRUCE, PETER WAYNE, lawyer, insurance company executive; b. Rome, July 12, 1945; s. G. Wayne and Helen A. (Hibling) B.; m. Joan M. McCabe, Sept. 20, 1969; children: Allison, Steven. B.A., U. Wis., 1967; J.D., U. Chgo., 1970; postgrad., Harvard Bus. Sch., 1986. Bar: Wis. 1970. Atty. Northwestern Mut. Life Ins. Co., Milw., 1970-74, asst. gen. counsel, 1974-80, gen. counsel, sec., 1980—, v.p., 1983-87, sr. v.p., gen. counsel, sec., 1987-90, sr. v.p. ins. ops., 1990-95, exec. v.p. ins. ops. & adminstrn., chief compliance officer, 1995-98, exec. v.p. accumulation products and long term care, 1998-2000, sr. exec. v.p. ins. ops. and long term care, 2000, sr. exec. v.p., 2000—. Bd. dirs. Northwestern Mut. Life Ins. Co., Milw., Alverno Coll. Badger Meter Found., Growth Design Corp. Former chmn. Alverno Coll., Curative Rehab. Ctr., former mem. Shorewood Civic Improvement Found.; chair Milw. Archdiocese Resource Devel. Coun.; bd. dirs., chair Curative Found.; mem. Milw. Archdiocese Cath. Cmty. Found.; mem. Village of Shorewood (Wis.); mem. Village Shorewood Cmty. Devel. Assn., Equal Justice Coalition, Jesuit Partnership Coun.; former mem. Planning and Devel. Commn. Mem. Wis. Bar Assn., Milw. Bar Assn., Am. Law Inst. Office: Northwestern Mut Life Ins Co 720 E Wisconsin Ave Milwaukee WI 53202-4703

BRUCKEN, ROBERT MATTHEW, lawyer; b. Akron, Ohio, Sept. 15, 1934; s. Harold M. and Eunice B. (Boesel) B.; m. Lois R. Gilbert, June 30, 1960; children: Nancy, Elizabeth, Rowland, Gilbert. AB, Marietta Coll., 1956; JD, U. Mich., 1959. Bar: Ohio 1960. Assoc. Baker & Hostetler, Cleve., 1960-69; ptnr., 1970—. Trustee Lakeside Assn., 1979-97, Marietta Coll., 1983—; sec., treas. Leader Shape, Inc., 1990—. Served with AUS, 1959-60. Mem. ABA, Ohio State Bar Assn. (chmn. probate and trust law sect. 1981-83), Cleve. Bar Assn. (chmn. probate ct. com. 1973-75), Am. Coll. Trust and Estate Counsel, Phi Beta Kappa. Congregationalist. Office: Baker & Hostetler 3200 Nat City Ctr 1900 E 9th St Ste 3200 Cleveland OH 44114-3475 E-mail: rbrucken@bakerlaw.com.

BRUENING, RICHARD P(ATRICK), lawyer; b. Kansas City, Mo., Mar. 17, 1939; s. Arthur Louis, Jr. and Lorraine Elizebeth (Gamble) B.; m. Jane Marie Egender, Aug. 25, 1962; children: Christiana G., Paul R., Erin E. AB, Rockhurst Coll., 1960; JD, U. Mo. at Kansas City, 1963. Bar: Mo. 1963. Since practiced in, Kansas City; law clk. U.S. Dist. Judge R.M., Duncan, 1963-65; assoc. firm Houts, James, McCanse & Larison, 1965-68; gen. atty. Kansas City So. Ry. Co., 1969; asst. gen. counsel Kansas City So. Industries, Inc., 1970-76, gen. counsel, 1976-82, v.p., gen. counsel, 1982—, sr. v.p., gen. counsel Transp. Group, 1992—. Bd. dirs. Kansas City So. Ry. Co.; mem. Mo. Press-Bar Commn., 1981-85, Mo. Rail Improvement Authority, 1984-86, chmn., 1984-85; mem. bd. commrs. Port Authority Kansas City, 1995-98; mem. Mo. Total Transp. Commn., 1997—. Bd. dirs. Friends of Zoo, Inc., 1987-98, Heart of Am. Shakespeare Festival, 1995—, Brain Injury Assn., 1999—; bd. dirs. Performing Arts Found./Folly Theatre, 1983-90, sec., 1984-90; mem. exec. com., trustee Conservatory Music, U. Mo., Kansas City. Mem. ABA, Mo. Bar Assn., Kansas City Bar Assn., Lawyers Assn. Kansas City, Nat. Assn. R.R. Trial Counsel (exec. com.), Practising Law Inst., Kansas City Country Club, Kansas City Club, River Club, Phi Delta Phi, Omicron Delta Kappa. Roman Catholic. Home: 606 W Meyer Blvd Kansas City MO 64113-1544 Office: Kans City So Industries Inc 114 W 11th St Kansas City MO 64105-1804

BRUESCHKE, ERICH EDWARD, physician, researcher, educator; b. nr. Eagle Butte, S.D., July 17, 1933; s. Erich Herman and Eva Johanna (Joens) B.; m. Frances Marie Bryan, Mar. 25, 1967; children: Erich Raymond, Jason Douglas, Tina Marie, Patricia Frances, Susan Eva. B.S. in Elec. Engring, S.D. Sch. Mines and Tech., 1956; postgrad., U. So. Calif., 1960-61; M.D., Temple U., 1965. Diplomate Am. Bd. Family Practice, also cert. in geriatrics. Intern Germantown Dispensary and Hosp., Phila., 1965-66; mem. tech. staff Hughes Research and Devel. Labs., Culver City, Calif., 1956-61; practiced gen. medicine Fullerton, 1968-69; dir. research Ill. Inst. Tech. Research Inst., Chgo., 1970-76; research asst. prof. Temple U. Sch. Medicine, 1965-69; mem. staff Mercy Hosp. and Med. Center, Chgo., 1970-76; vis. prof. Rush Med. Coll., 1974-76, prof., chmn. dept. family practice, 1976—, program dir. Rush. Christ family practice residency, 1978-93, vice dean, 1992—, acting dean, 1993-94, dean, 1994-2000, v.p. univ. affairs, 2000—; trustee Anchor HMO, 1976-81, v.p. med. and acad. affairs, 1981—; trustee Synergon Health Systems, 1993-98; vice chmn., bd. dirs. Rush Presbyn. St. Lukes Health Assocs. Sr. attending Presbyn.-St. Luke's Hosp., Chgo., 1976—; med. dir. Chgo. Bd. of Health West Side Hypertension Ctr., 1974—78; bd. dirs. Comprehensive Health Planning Met. Chgo., 1971—74, Fedn. of Ind. Ill. Colls. and Univs., West Suburban Higher Edn. Consortium; adv. com. Edn. to Careers, Health and Medicine/Chg. Bd. Edn. Editor-in-chief Disease-a-Month, 1998—; assoc. editor Primary Cardiology, 1979-85; cons. editor for family practice Hosp. Medicine, 1986—; med. editor World Book/Rush Presbyn. St. Lukes/Med. Ency., 1987—; contbr. articles to profl. jours. Served with USAF, 1966-68. Named Physician Tchr. of Yr. Ill. Acad. Family Physicians, 1988, alumni of yr. Temple U. Sch. Medicine, 1996. Fellow Am. Acad. Family Physicians, Inst. of Medicine of Chgo.; mem. IEEE (chmn. Chgo. sect. Engring. in Medicine and Biology group 1974-75), Internat. Soc. for Artificial Internal Organs, Am. Fertility Soc., Am. Occupational Med. Assn. (recipient Physician's recognition award 1969, 72, 75), Chgo. Med. Soc., Am. Heart Assn., Assn. for Advancement Med. Instrumentation, N.Y. Acad. Scis., Sigma Xi, Phi Rho Sigma, Eta Kappa Nu, Alpha Omega Alpha. Home: 319 N Lincoln St Hinsdale IL 60521-3442 Office: Rush Medical College of Rush Univ 600 S Paulina St Chicago IL 60612-3806

BRUMBACK, CHARLES TIEDTKE, retired newpaper executive; b. Toledo, Sept. 27, 1928; s. John Sanford and Frances Hannah (Tiedtke) B.; m. Mary Louise Howe, July 7, 1951; children: Charles Tiedtke Jr., Anne Meyer, Wesley W., Ellen Allen. BA in Econs., Princeton U., 1950; postgrad., U. Toledo, 1953-54. CPA, Ohio, Fla. With Arthur Young & Co., CPAs, 1950-57; bus. mgr., v.p., treas., pres., CEO Sentinel Star Co. subs. Tribune Co., Orlando, Fla., 1957-81; pres., CEO Chgo. Tribune subs. Tribune Co., 1981-88, pres., COO, 1988-90, CEO, 1990-95, chmn., 1993-95, bd. dirs., 1981-96. Bd. dirs. Avid Tech., Inc. Bd. dirs. Robert R. McCormick Tribune Found.; life trustee Northwestern U., Chgo. Hit. Soc.; trustee Culver Ednl. Found.; trustee Northwestern Meml. Hosp., chmn., 1987-90. 1st lt. U.S. Army, 1951-53. Decorated Bronze star. Mem. AICPA, Fla. Press Assn. (treas. 1969-76, pres. 1980, bd. dirs.), Am. Newspaper Pubs. Assn. (bd. dirs., treas. 1991-92), Newspaper Assn. Am. (bd. dirs., sec., 1992-93, vice chmn. 1993-94, chmn. 1994-95), Comml. Club Chgo., Chgo. Club, Tavern Club. Home: 1500 N Lake Shore Dr Chicago IL 60610-6657 Office: Tribune Co 435 N Michigan Ave Chicago IL 60611-4066 E-mail: cbrumback@tribune.com., charlie435@aol.com.

BRUMFIELD, JIM, news executive; Bur. chief Detroit Met. Network News, 1997—. Office: 5032 Rochester Rd Ste 200 Troy MI 48085-3454

BRUMMEL, MARK JOSEPH, magazine editor; b. Chgo., Oct. 28, 1933; s. Anthony William and Mary (Helmreich) B. BA, Cath. U. Am., 1956, STL, 1961, MSLS, 1964. Joined Order of Claretians, Roman Cath. Ch., 1952; ordained priest Order of Caretians, Roman Cath. Ch., 1960; librarian, tchr. St. Jude Sem., Momence, Ill., 1961-70; asso. editor U.S. Cath. mag., Chgo., 1971-72; editor U.S. Cath. Mag., 1970—; dir. St. Jude League, Chgo., 1970—. Treas. Eastern Province Claretians, 1998—, also bd. dirs.; bd. dirs. Chgo. Family Health Ctr. Editor Today mag., 1970-71; contbr. article to publ. Chmn. bd. Eighth Day Ctr. for Justice, Chgo., 1988-92; bd. dirs. Assn. of Chgo. Priests, 1994-96; mem. Ill. Cath. Conf., 1993-96. Mem. Cath. Press Assn. (St. Francis De Sales award 1996), Associated Ch. Press. (v.p. 1985-87). Avocation: photography. E-mail: mark. Home: 7760 S South Shore Dr Chicago IL 60649-4434 Office: US Cath 205 W Monroe St Fl 7 Chicago IL 60606-5033 E-mail: markbrummel@claret.org.

BRÜN, HERBERT J. composer, educator; b. Berlin, 1918; m. Marianne Kortner; children: Michael, Stefan. Student piano composition with, Stefan Wolpe, Eli Friedmann, Frank Pelleg, Tel-Aviv; student piano composition, Jerusalem Conservatory Music, Columbia U. Prof. composition, then prof. emeritus U. Ill. Sch. Music, Urbana, 1963—. Composer: Mobile for Orch., Sonoriferous Loops, Gestures for Eleven, Non-Sequitur VI, Gesto for Piccolo and Piano, Trio for Flute, Double Bass and Percussion, Trio for Trumpet, Trombone and Percussion, Futility 1964, Mutatis Mutandis: Computer Graphics for Interpreters, Infraudibles, Nonet, Piece of Prose, Three String Quartets, "at loose ends:, In and...and Out, Dust, More Dust, Dustiny, A Mere Ripple, U-Turn-To, I Told You So, Twice Upon Three Times, SNOW 1984, Six for Five by Two in Pieces; per contra: serenata: bassa; just seven for drum; The Laughing Third for Piano, 1993, Come, Scenario and Go for 13 Players, 1994, On Stilts Among Ducks for viola and tape, 1995, Floating Hierarchies for various small ensembles, 1995, for double-bass solo...yet with a heart of gold!, 1997; also scores for theatre; author: Über Musik und zum Computer, 1971, My Words and Where I Want Them, 1986, 2d edit., 1990, Drawing Distinctions Links Contradictions, 1997; contr. articles to profl. jours. Founder The Performers' Workshop, 1978, The Performers' Workshop Ensemble, 1980. Recipient Norbert Wiener medal Am. Soc. for Cybernetics, 1993. Achievements include research in computer composition, designer computer project SAWDUST.

BRUNER, PHILIP LANE, lawyer; b. Chgo., Sept. 26, 1939; s. Henry Pfeiffer and Mary Marjorie (Williamson) B.; m. Ellen Carole Germann, Mar. 21, 1964; children: Philip Richard, Stephen Reed, Carolyn Anne AB, Princeton U., 1961; JD, U. Mich., 1964; MBA, Syracuse U., 1967. Bar: Wis. 1964, Minn. 1968. Mem. Briggs and Morgan P.A., Mpls., St. Paul, 1967-83; founding shareholder Hart and Bruner P.A., Mpls., 1983-90; ptnr. Faegre & Benson, 1991—, head constrn. law group, 1991—2001. Adj. prof. William Mitchell Coll. Law, St. Paul, 1970-76; lectr. law seminars, univs., bar assns. and industry; chmn. Supreme Ct. Minn. Bd. Continuing Legal Edn., 1994-98. Co-author: Bruner and O'Conner on Construction Law, 7 vols., 2002; contbr. articles to profl. jours. Mem. Bd. Edn., Mahtomedi Ind. Sch. Dist. 832, 1978-86; bd. dirs. Mahtomedi Area Ednl. Found., 1988-94, pres., 1988-91; bd. dirs. Minn. Ch. Found., 1975—, pres., 1989-97; chmn. constrn. industry adv. bd. West Group, 1991—. Capt. USAF, 1964-67. Decorated Air Force Commendation Medal; recipient Disting. Service award St. Paul Jaycees, 1974; named One of Ten Outstanding Young Minnesotans, Minn. Jaycees, 1975. Fellow Am. Coll. Constrn. Lawyers (founding mem., bd. govs.), Nat. Contract Mgmt. Assn., Am. Bar Found.; mem. ABA (chmn. internat. constrn. divsn. forum com. on constrn. industry 1989-91, chmn. fidelity and surety law com. 1994-95, regional chmn. pub. contract law sect. 1990-96), Internat. Bar Assn., Inter-Pacific Bar Assn. (vice chmn. internat. constrn. com. 1995-97), Fed. Bar Assn., Minn. Bar Assn. (vice chmn. litigation sect. 1979-81), Wis. Bar Assn., Hennepin Bar Assn., Internat. Assn. Def. Counsel, Am. Arbitration Assn. (nat. panel arbitrators), Mpls. Club. Presbyterian. Home: 8432 80th St N Stillwater MN 55082-9331 Office: Faegre & Benson 2200 Wells Fargo Ctr 90 S 7th St Minneapolis MN 55402-3901 E-mail: pbruner@faegre.com., Philipbruner@hotmail.com.

BRUNER, STEPHEN C. lawyer; b. Chgo., Nov. 11, 1941; s. Henry Pfeiffer and Mary Marjorie (Williamson) B.; m. Elizabeth Erskine Osborn, Apr. 7, 1973; children: Elizabeth, David. B.A. summa cum laude, Yale U., 1963; J.D. cum laude, Harvard U., 1967. Bar: Ill. 1967, U.S. Dist. Ct. (no. dist.) Ill. 1971, U.S. Ct. Appeals (7th cir.) 1983, U.S. Supreme Ct. 1988. Assoc. Winston & Strawn, Chgo., 1971-76, ptnr., 1976-82, capital ptnr., 1982-01. Lectr. Northwestern U. Sch. of Law, 1983-84; cons. Commn. on Govt. Procurement, 1972; mem. Landmarks Commn., Oak Park, Ill., 1978-81; bd. govs. Oak Park-River Forest Community Chest, 1985-90; elected mem. Bd. Edn. Oak Park and River Forest High Sch., 1993-01. Served to lt. USN, 1968-71. Recipient Navy Achievement medal; Corning Found. travelling fellow, 1963-64. Mem. ABA (litigation and pub. contracts sects.), Chgo. Bar Assn., Am. Arbitration (panel of arbitrators), Chgo. Coun. on Fgn. Rels., Econ. Club, Univ. Club, Yale Club, Harvard Club (Chgo.). Office: Winston & Strawn 35 W Wacker Dr Chicago IL 60601-1695

BRUNETTI, WAYNE H. utility company executive; BSBA, U. Fla.; grad. degree, Harvard U. With treasury dept. Fla. Power & Light, from 1964; pres., CEO Mgmt. Sys. Internat. Inc., 1991-94; pres., COO Pub. Svc. Co. Colo., Denver, 1994-2000; pres., CEO Xcel Energy Inc, Mpls., 2000—. Bd. dirs. Sun Bank Miami. Bd. dirs. Fla. Power & Light, United Way, Assoc. Industries Fla., Fla. C. of C., South Miami Hosp., Dade Found.; pres. bd. dirs. Haven Ctr. for Mentally Retarded; mem. various coms. Elec. Power Rsch. Inst., Edison Elec. Inst. Office: Xcel Energy Inc 414 Nicollet Mall Minneapolis MN 55401

BRUNETTI, WAYNE HENRY, utilities executive; b. Cleve., Oct. 13, 1942; s. Henry Joseph and Lillian (Lupo) B.; m. Mary Kelly, Aug. 17, 1963; children: Kelly Christine, Andrew Wayne. BSBA in Acctg., U. Fla., 1964; program for mgmt. devel., Harvard U., 1974. Acct. Fla. Power and Light Co., Miami, Fla., 1964-68, systems analyst, 1968-69, project coordinator, 1969-72, mgr. property acctg., 1972-73, mgr. corp. acctg., asst. comptroller, 1973-77, asst. to v.p. pub. affairs, 1977-80, dir. energy mgmt., 1980, v.p. energy mgmt., 1980-83, v.p. divs., 1983-84, group v.p., 1984-87, exec. v.p., 1987-91; pres., CEO Mgmnt. Systems Internat., 1991-94; pres., COO Public Svc. Co. of Colo., 1994-96, pres., CEO, 1996—; chmn., pres., CEO New Century Energies, Inc., Denver, 2000—; pres., CEO Xcel Energy, 2001—. Bd. dirs. Sun Bank Miami, Fla. Power & Light Co. United Way of Dade County, Miami (bd. dirs. 1986—). Mem. Associated Industries Fla. (bd. dirs. 1986—), Dade Found. (bd. gov. 1988—), Fla. C. of C. (bd. dirs. 1989—), Edison Electric Inst. Democrat. Roman Catholic. Office: Xcel Energy 800 Nicollet Mall Minneapolis MN 55402

BRUNGARDT, PETE, state legislator; m. Rosie Brungardt. Mem. Kans. State Senate, 2001—, vice chair fed. and state affairs com., mem. commerce com., mem. corrections and juvenile justice oversight com., mem. fin. instns. and ins. com., mem. pub. health and welfare com. Home: 522 Fairdale Rd Salina KS 67401 Office: 436 S Ohio St Salina KS 67401 E-mail: peterose@midusa.net., brungardt@senate.state.ks.us.

BRUNING, JAMES LEON, university official, educator; b. Bruning, Nebr., Apr. 1, 1938; s. Leon G. and Delma Dorothy (Middendorf) B.; m. E. Marlene Schaff, Aug. 24, 1958; children: Michael, Stephen, Kathleen. B.A., Doane Coll., 1959; M.A., U. Iowa, 1961, Ph.D., 1962. Chmn. dept psychology Ohio U., Athens, 1972-76, acting dean arts and scis., 1976-77, assoc. dean, 1977-78, vice provost, 1978-81, provost, 1981-93, trustee prof., 1993—; provost Shawnee (Ohio) State U., 1996; v.p. regional higher edn. Ohio U., 1998-99. Planning cons. NCHEMS, Boulder, Colo., 1979-80 Author: Computational Handbook of Statistics, 1968, Research in Psychology, 1970; contbr. over 70 articles to profl. jours. Chair task force Ohio Bd. Regents, 1994-95. Grantee Esso, 1963-64, NIMH, 1963-66, EPDA, 1974-75, OBOR, 1989-91. Mem. AAAS, APA (vis. scientist), Midwestern Psychol. Assn., Sigma Xi. Democrat. Lutheran. Home: 6148 Melnor Dr Athens OH 45701-3577 Office: Ohio U Psychology Dept Athens OH 45701 E-mail: bruningj@ohio.edu.

BRUNING, JON CUMBERLAND, state legislator; b. Lincoln, Nebr., Apr. 30, 1969; s. Roger Howard and Mary Genevieve (Cumberland) B.; m. Deonne Leigh Niemack, July 8, 1995, two children, Lauren Caroline, Jon Cumberland Jr. BA with high distinction, U. Nebr., 1990, JD with distinction, 1994. Bar: Nebr. 1994, U.S. Dist. Ct. Nebr. 1994, U.S. Ct. Appeals (8th cir.) 1994. Pvt. practice, Papillion, Nebr., 1993-97; mem. Nebr. Legislature from 3rd dist., Lincoln, 1997—. Mem., Gretna United Methodist Church, Nebr. State Bar Assoc., Phi Beta Kappa. Republican. Methodist. Home: 17501 Riviera Dr Omaha NE 68136-1951 Office: Nebraska Unicameral Legislature Rm 2104 State Capitol Lincoln NE 68509

BRUNKHORST, ROBERT JOHN, computer programmer, analyst; b. Waverly, Iowa, Dec. 5, 1965; s. John Blaine and Edna C. (Atkins) B.; m. Kris Nielsen, Sept. 12, 1992; 1 child, Karalynn Kristine. BS in Computer Sci., Loras Coll., 1989. Computer programmer Century Cos. Am., Waverly, 1990—, computer analyst. Press intern Sen. Charles Grassley, Washington, fall 1986. State rep. State of Iowa, 1992—; organizer Solid Waste Adv. Com., Waverly, 1990—; active Boy Scouts Am., N.E. Iowa, 1982—. Mem. Jaycees, Farm Bur. Home: 419 3rd Ave SW Waverly IA 50677-3114

BRUNNER, GORDON F(RANCIS), household products company executive; b. Des Plaines, Ill., Nov. 6, 1938; s. Frank Anthony and Alfreida Elizabeth (Eslinger) B. ; m. Nadine Marie Slosar, Aug. 10, 1963; children: Christine Marie Conselyea, Pamela Ann, Meggan Therese. BChemE, U. Wis., 1961; MBA, Xavier U., Cin., 1965. With Procter & Gamble Co., 1961—, mgr. product coordination European Ops., Brussels, 1977-81, mgr. research and devel. European Ops., 1981-83, mgr. research and devel. U.S., 1983-85, v.p. R&D U.S., 1985-87, sr. v.p. R&D U.S., 1987—, also bd. dirs. Mem. exec. com. Campaign for Chemistry, Am. Chem. Soc., 1990. Patentee in field. Corp. chmn. United Way, 1990-91; mem. adv. coun. Citizens Against Substance Abuse, 1990; trustee The Christ Hosp., Cin. Mus. Natural History, Xavier U., Ohio U., com. econ. devel.; mem. Govt.-Univ.-Industry Rsch. Roundtable; nat. adv. com. Coll. Engring., U. Mich.; mem. Mgmt. Policy Coun., Conf. Bd. Internat. Coun. Mgmt. Innovation & Tech.; mem. tour equipment adv. com. PGA; chmn. Cin. Campaign for U. Wis.; mem. selection com. Evals Scholarship; sci. adv. bd. Bowling Green State U.; Cin. chmn. Habitat for Humanity; Cin. chmn. BIO/START; mem. Ohio Sci. and Tech. Coun.; mem. Evans Scholarship selection com. Western Golf Assn. Recipient Exec. Achievement award Xavier U., 1991, Disting. Svc. award U. Wis., 1992; Evans scholar Western Golf Assn., 1956. Mem. Am. Oil Chemists Soc., Engring. Soc. Cin., Cin. Coun. on World Affairs, Am. Chem. Soc., Mgmt. Policy Coun., Evans Scholar Alumni Assn., Comml. Club, Queen City Club, Hyde Park Country Club Cin., Crystal Downs Country Club (Frankfort, Mich.). Roman Catholic. Avocations: golf, tennis, woodworking, gardening. Home: 7300 Sanderson Pl Cincinnati OH 45243-4045 Office: Procter & Gamble Co 1 Procter And Gamble Plz Cincinnati OH 45202-3393

BRUNNER, KIM M. insurance company executive; Chief counsel Ill. Ins. Dept.; atty. Nationwide Ins. Co.; with State Farm Ins. Cos., Bloomington, Ill., 1987—, assoc. gen. counsel, 1991-93, v.p.-counsel, 1993-97, sr. v.p., gen. counsel, 1997—. Office: State Farm Ins Cos 1 State Farm Plz Bloomington IL 61710-0001

BRUNNER, VERNON ANTHONY, marketing executive; b. Chgo., Aug. 9, 1940; s. Frank Anthony and Alfrieda (Eslinger) B.; divorced; children: Jack Daniel, Amanda Josephine; m. Sharon Ann Walschon, July 1, 1972; 1 child, Suzanne Marie. BS in Pharmacy, U. Wis., 1963. Registered pharmacist. Mgr. store Walgreen Co., Chgo., 1963-71, dist. mgr. Deerfield, Ill., 1971-75, dir. merchandising, 1975-77, dir. mktg., 1977-78, v.p. mktg.,

1978-82, sr. v.p. mktg., 1982-90, exec. v.p. mktg., 1990—. Bd. dirs. Walgreen. Mem. Evans Scholar Alumni Assn. Roman Catholic. Office: Walgreen Co 200 Wilmot Rd Deerfield IL 60015-4616

BRUNNGRABER, ERIC HENRY, banker; b. Madison, Wis., Feb. 12, 1957; s. Eric G. and Lois M. (Ihde) B.; m. Ann M. Roberson, May 30, 1987. BSBA in Fin., U. Mo., 1979; MBA in Fin., St. Louis U., 1982; diploma, U. Del., 1991. Asst. to chmn. Cass Bank & Trust Co., St. Louis, 1979-82, mgr. spl. projects, 1982-84, asst. v.p. comml. lending, 1986-88, v.p., treas., 1989-92, exec. v.p., 1993—; mgmt. cons. Cass Bus. Cons., 1984-86; v.p., sec. & CFO Cass Comml. Corp., Bridgeton, Mo. Mem. Robert Morris Assocs. Office: Cass Comml Corp 13001 Hollenberg Dr Bridgeton MO 63044

BRUNO, GARY ROBERT, lawyer; b. Green Bay, Wis., Oct. 7, 1951; s. Robert John and Mary Lois (Epparviar) B.; m. Terry Lynn Ott, Oct. 22, 1977. BBA in Fin. and Regional Planning, U. Wis., Green Bay, 1973; JD, John Marshall Law Sch., 1977. Bar: Wis. 1977, U.S. Dist. Ct. Wis. 1978. Sole practice, Green Bay and Shawano, Wis., 1977-78; prosecutor Code of Fed. Regulation Ct., Keshena, 1978; asst. dist. atty. Menominee and Shawano Counties, Shawano, 1978-82, dist. atty., corp. counsel, adminstr. child support agy., 1982—. Mem. exec. com. Fed. Law Enforcement Coordinating Com. Ea. Dist. Wis., Milw., 1985—. V.p. Big Bros./Big Sisters, Shawano, 1981-83, bd. dirs. 1980—; bd. dirs. Alcohol and Drug Ctr. Shawano, 1979-82; mem. exec. bd. Reps., Shawano, 1985—. Mem. ABA, Wis. Bar Assn., Shawano County Bar Assn. (sec., treas. 1982, v.p. 1983, pres. 1984), Nat. Dist. Atty. Assn., Wis. Dist. Atty. Assn. Club: Shawano. Lodge: Optimists (2d v.p. Shawano 1985—, bd. dirs. 1979-85, optimist of yr. award 1984). Avocations: community service, scuba diving, hunting. Home: 1413 E Lieg St Shawano WI 54166-3613 Office: Dist Atty Office 311 N Main St Shawano WI 54166-2100

BRUNS, BILLY LEE, electrical engineer, consultant; b. St. Louis, Nov. 21, 1925; s. Henry Lee and Violet Jean (Williams) B.; m. Lillian Colleen Mobley, Sept. 6, 1947; children: Holly Rene, Kerry Alan, Barry Lee, Terrence William. BA, Washington U., St. Louis, 1949; postgrad., Sch. Engring., St. Louis, 1959-62; EE, ICS, Scranton, Pa., 1954. Registered profl. engr., Mo., Ill., Wash., Fla., La., Wis., Minn., N.Y., N.C., Iowa, Pa., Miss., Ind., Ala., Ga., Va., R.I., Wyo. Supt., engr., estimator Schneider Electric Co., St. Louis, 1950-54, Ledbetter Electric Co., St. Louis, 1954-57; tchr. indsl. electricity St. Louis Bd. Edn., 1957-71; pres. B.L. Bruns & assocs. Cons. Engrs. Inc., St. Louis, 1963-72; v.p., chief engr. Hosp. Bldg. & Equipment Co., 1972-76; pres., prin. B.L. Bruns & Assocs. Cons. Engrs., 1976—. Tchr. elec. engring. U. Mo. St. Louis extension, 1975-76. Tech. editor The National Electrical Code and Blueprint Reading, Am. Tech. Soc., 1959-65. Mem. Mo. Adv. Coun. on Vocat. Edn., 1969-76, chmn., 1975-76; leader Explorer post Boy Scouts Am., 1950-57. Served with AUS, 1944-46, PTO, Okinawa. Decorated Purple Heart. Mem. NSPE, Mo. Soc. Profl. Engrs., Profl. Engrs. in Pvt. Practice, Am. Soc. Heating, Refrigeration and Air Conditioning Engrs., Illuminating Engrs. Soc., Am. Mgmt. Assn., Nat. Fire Protection Assn. (health care divsn., archtl./engr. divsn.), Masons. Baptist. Home: 1243 Hobson Dr Ferguson MO 63135-1422

BRUNSVOLD, JOEL DEAN, state legislator, educator; b. Mason City, Iowa, Feb. 26, 1942; s. Burnell Raymond and Esther Agusta (Geilendeld) B.; m. Barbara Louise Bashaw, Feb. 22, 1964; children: Timothy, Theodore. BA, Augustana Coll., 1964; student, Black Hawk Coll./We. Ill. U., 1969-71. Tchr. Sherrard (Ill.) Cmty. Unit # 200, 1969-83; mem. Ho. of Reps., Rock Island, Ill., 1982—. Trustee, Milan, Ill., 1973-77, mayor, 1977-83. Mem. NEA, Ill. Edn. Assn., C. of C., Ducks Unlimited, Pheasants Forever, Phi Omega Phi. Democrat. Lutheran. Avocation: hunting. Home: 12810 25th Street Ct Milan IL 61264-4984

BRUSHABER, GEORGE KARL, college-theological seminary president, minister; b. Milw., Dec. 15, 1938; s. Ralph E. and Marie C. (Meister) B.; m. N. Darleen Dugar, Jan. 27, 1962; children: Deanna Lyn Dalberg, Donald Paul. BA, Wheaton Coll., 1959, MA, 1962; MDiv, Gordon-Conwell Theol. Sem., 1963; PhD, Boston U., 1967. Ordained to ministry Bapt. Gen. Conf., 1966. Prof. philosophy, chair dept. Gordon Coll., Wenham, Mass., 1963-72; dir. admissions and registration Gordon-Conwell Theol. Sem., 1970-72; v.p., acad. dean Westmont Coll., Santa Barbara, Calif., 1972-75; v.p., dean of coll. Bethel. Coll., St. Paul, 1975-82; pres. Bethel Coll. & Theol. Sem., St. Paul and San Diego, 1982—. Staley Found. lectr. Anderson U., Sioux Falls Coll.; sec. for higher edn. Bapt. Gen. Conf., Arlington Heights, Ill., 1982—; cons., evaluator Minn. Humanities Commn., St. Paul. Editor Gordon Rev., 1965-70; pub., founding editor Christian Scholar's Rev., 1970-79; exec. editor Christianity Today, 1985-90, chmn. sr. editors, 1990—; contbr. articles to religious jours. Bd. dirs. Youth Leadership, Mpls., 1982—, Fairview Elders' Enterprises Found., 1989—, Scripture Press Ministries Found., 1994—; adv. bd. Mpls./St. Paul Salvation Army, 1992--; chair bd. Scripture Press Ministries, 1994—; adv. coun. Evang. Environ. Network, 1994—; mem. Commn. on Minorities in Higher Edn. Am. Coun. Edn., 1995-99. Mem. Christian Environ. Assn., Christian Coll. Consortium (bd. dirs.), Nat. Assn. Evangs. (trustee 1982—), Minn. Pvt. Coll. Coun. (bd. dirs. 1982—), Minn. Consortium Theol. Sems. (bd. dirs. 1982—), Cook Comm. Internat. (bd. dirs. 1998--), Coun. Ind. Colls. (bd. dirs. 1984-89), Am. Philos. Assn., Evang. Theol. Soc., Am. Assn. Higher Edn., Swedish Coun. Am. (bd. dirs. 1992--), Soc. Christian Philosophers, Fellowship Evang. Sem. Pres., Minn. Club, North Oaks Country Club. Home and Office: Bethel Coll and Theol Sem 3900 Bethel Dr Saint Paul MN 55112-6902

BRUSTAD, ORIN DANIEL, lawyer; b. Chgo., Nov. 11, 1941; s. Marvin D. and Sylvia Evelyn (Peterson) B.; m. Ilona M. Fox, July 16, 1966; children: Caroline E., Katherine L., Mark D. BA in History, Yale U., 1963, MA, 1964; JD, Harvard U., 1968. Bar: Mich. 1968, U.S. Dist. Ct. (so. dist.) Mich. 1968. Assoc. Miller, Canfield, Paddock and Stone, Detroit, 1968-74, sr. ptnr., 1975—, chmn. employee benefits practice group, 1989-96, dep. chmn. tax dept., 1989-93. Bd. dirs. Electrocon Internat., Inc., Ann Arbor, Mich. Mem. editl. adv. bd. Benefits Law Jour.; contbr. articles to profl. jours. Fellow Am. Coun. Employee Benefits Counsel (charter); mem. ABA, Mich. Bar Assn., Detroit Bar Assn., Mich. Employee Benefits Conf. Avocations: sailing, skiing, reading, piano. Home: 1422 Macgregor Ln Ann Arbor MI 48105-2836 Office: Miller Canfield Paddock & Stone 150 W Jefferson Ave Fl 25th Detroit MI 48226-4432 E-mail: odbrusta@aol.com., brustad@millercanfield.com.

BRUVOLD, KATHLEEN PARKER, lawyer; BS in Math., U. Denver, 1965; MS in Math., Purdue U., 1967; JD, U. Cin., 1978. Bar: Ohio 1978, U.S. Dist. Ct. (so. dist.) Ohio 1978, U.S. Dist. Ct. (ea. dist.) Ky. 1979. Mathematician bur. rsch. and engring. U.S. Post Office, 1967; instr. math. Purdue U., West Lafayette, Ind., 1967-68, asst. to dir., tng. coord., programmer Administrv. Data Processing Ctr., 1968-71; instr. math. Ind. U., Kokomo, 1969-70; pvt. practice Cin., 1978-80; asst. dir. Legal Adv. Svcs. U. Cin., 1980-89, assoc. gen. counsel, 1989—; asst. atty. gen. State of Ohio, 1983—. Chair Ohio pub. records com. Inter-univ. Coun. Legal Advisors, 1980-84; presenter various confs. and symposiums. Active com. group svcs. allocation United Way and Community Chest; v.p. Clifton Recreation Ctr. Adv. Coun., 1983-84; vice chair Cin. Bilingual Acad. PTA, 1989-90. U. Denver scholar, Jewel Tea Co. scholar. Mem. ABA, Nat. Assn. Coll. and Univ. Attys. (bd. dirs., co-chair taxation sect., com. ann. meeting arrangements, program com., publs. com., bd. ops. com., JCUL editl. bd. nominations com., honors and award com., intellectual property sect., com. continuing legal edn. 1992—), Cin. Bar Assn. (com. taxation, program chmn. 1985-86, sec. 1986-87, com. computer law). Home: 536 Evanswood Pl Cincinnati OH 45220-1527 Office: U Cin Office of Gen Counsel 300-a Adminstrn Bldg Cincinnati OH 45221-0001

BRUYN, KIMBERLY ANN, public relations executive, consultant; b. Grand Rapids, Mich., Jan. 25, 1955; BA in English, Calvin Coll., Grand Rapids, 1977; MS in Journalism, U. Kans., 1979. Advt. copywriter, acct. exec. Mendenhall, Jones & Leistra Advt., Grand Rapids, 1979-81; advt. copywriter Johnson & Dean Advt., 1981-82; pub. rels. analyst Amway Corp., Ada, Mich., 1982-84, sr. pub. rels. analyst, 1984-85, sr. pub. rels. specialist, 1986-87, pub. rels. supr., 1987-88, pub. rels. mgr., chief corp. spokesperson, 1988-93, sr. mgr. pub. rels., chief corp. spokesperson, 1993-98; v.p. comms. The Windquest Group, Grand Rapids, 1998-2000; exec. dir. Straightline Pub. Rels., 2000—01; sr. cons. The Grey Stone Group, Grand Rapids, Mich., 2001—. Mem. pub. rels. and mktg. com. Grand Rapids Symphony Orch., 1992; mem. planning com. Spl. Olympics Festival of Trees, Grand Rapids, 1990-92, Gerald R. Ford Presdl. Mus. 10th Anniversary Celebration, Grand Rapids, 1992; bd. dirs. Celebration on the Grand, 1989-96, co-chair, 1993, 94; co-chair pub. rels. Heart Ball, Am. Heart Assn., 1996-2001; chair pub. rels. Van Andel Arena Grand Opening, 1996, Presdl. Tribute to Gerald R. Ford, 1997. Mem. PRSA (Spectrum award 1990-98), Direct Selling Assn. (chair comm. com. 1997-98). Office: Greystone Group Inc 678 Front NW Ste 159 Grand Rapids MI 49504 E-mail: kimb@greystonegp.com.

BRYAN, DAVID, radio personality; b. Brinnell, Iowa, Feb. 8, 1952; 2 children. Student, North West Mo. State U. Radio host WDAF, Westwood, Kans., 1981—. Avocation: exercise. Office: WDAF 4935 Belinder Rd Westwood KS 66205*

BRYAN, JOHN HENRY, food and consumer products company executive; b. West Point, Miss., 1936; BA in Econs. and Bus. Adminstrn, Rhodes Coll., Memphis, 1958. Joined Bryan Foods, 1960; with Sara Lee Corp. (formerly known as Consol. Food Corp.), Chgo., 1960—; from exec. v.p. to pres. Sara Lee Corp. (formerly known as Consol Food Corp.), 1974, CFO, 1975—, chmn. bd., 1976—, also bd. dirs. Bd. dirs. Gen. Motors Corp., BP Amoco Corp., Bank One. Chmn. bus. adv. coun. Chgo. Urban League; bd. govs. Nat. Women's Econ. Alliance, Chgo.; trustee, vice-chmn., exec. com. U. Chgo., Rush-Presbyn.-St. Luke's Med. Ctr.; trustee Com. Econ. Devel.; trustee, treas. Art Inst. Chgo.; chmn. Catalyst; bd. dirs. Bus. Com. for Arts; chmn. Chgo. com. Chgo. Coun. on Fgn. Rels.; mem. trustee's coun. Nat. Gallery Art, Washington; mem. pres.'s com. on the arts and humanities; dir. bus. com. for the arts. Decorated Legion of Honor (France), Order of Orange Nassau (The Netherlands), Order of Lincoln Medallion; recipient Nat. Humanitarian award NCCJ, William H. Albers award Food Mktg. Inst., Man of Yr. award Harvard Bus. Sch. Club Chgo.; named Exec. Yr. Crain's Chgo. Bus., 1992, Jr. Achievement Chgo. Bus. Hall of Fame, 1992, Miss. Hall of Fame, 1992. Mem. Grocery Mfrs. Assn. (sr., past. chmn. bd.), Bus. Coun., Bus. Roundtable. Office: Sara Lee Corp 3 1st Nat Plz 70 W Madison St Ste 4500 Chicago IL 60602-4260

BRYAN, LAWRENCE DOW, college president; b. Barberton, Ohio, Jan. 30, 1945; s. W. Richard and Celia A. (Evans) B.; m. Marjorie Napier, June 15, 1968; children: Mark Evans, Alexa Marie. BA, Muskingum Coll., 1967; MDiv., Garrett Theol. Sem., 1970; PhD, Northwestern U., 1973. Tchg. asst. Nat. Coll. Edn., Evanston, Ill., 1969-71; biog. rsch. fellow Garrett Theol. Sem., 1972-73; asst. prof. religious studies, chaplain McKendree Coll., Lebanon, Ill., 1973-77, asst. v.p. acad. affairs, 1977-78, dean, 1978-79, assoc. prof., 1978-79; prof. philosophy and religion, v.p., dean Franklin (Ind.) Coll., 1979-90; pres. Kalamazoo Coll., 1990-96, MacMurray Coll., Jacksonville, Ill., 1997—. Trustee Parkstone Group of Funds, 1994-98. Mem. Forum for Kalamazoo County, 1990-94, Kalamazoo Symphony Orch. Bd., 1990-96; pres. Heyl Found., Kalamazoo, 1990-96; bd. dirs. Bronson Hosp., 1991-96; trustee Interlochen Ctr. for Arts, 1994-97; pres. Jacksonville Main St. Bd. Dirs. Mem. Internat. Bonhoeffer Soc., Fed. Ind. Ill. Colls. and Univs., Rotary, Phi Sigma Tau, Delta Sigma Rho-Tau Kappa Alpha, Alpha Psi Omega, Theta Alpha Phi. Methodist.

BRYAN, NORMAN E. dentist; b. South Bend, Ind., Jan. 20, 1947; s. Norman E. and Frances (Kuhn) B.; m. Constance C. Cook, Feb. 23, 1974 (div. Apr. 1985); m. Linda Markley, Dec. 31, 1986; 1 child, Noelle. AB, Ind. U., 1969; DDS, Ind. U. Purdue U., Indpls., 1973. Sr. dentist Downtown Dental Svcs., Elkhart, Ind., 1973—. Specialist Temporomandibular Joint Disfunction. Author: Canine Endodontics, 1982. Mem. ADA, Ind. Dental Assn., Elkhart Dental Assn. (pres. 1976-77, 84-86), Am. Acad. Head, Neck and Facial Pain, Great Lakes Cruising Club (Chgo.), Elcona Country Club, Great Lakes Cruising Club (Chgo.). Republican. Avocations: sailor, photography, painter. Office: 505 Vistula St Elkhart IN 46516-2809

BRYAN, WAYNE, producer; Producing dir. Music Theatre of Wichita, Kans. Office: Music Theatre of Wichita 225 W Douglas Ave Ste 202 Wichita KS 67202-3100

BRYANT, BARBARA EVERITT, academic researcher, market research consultant, former federal agency administrator; b. Ann Arbor, Mich., Apr. 5, 1926; d. William Littell and Dorothy (Wallace) Everitt; m. John H. Bryant, Aug. 14, 1948; children: Linda Bryant Valentine, Randal F., Lois. AB, Cornell U., 1947; MA, Mich. State U., 1967, PhD, 1970; HonD, U. Ill., 1993. Editor art Chem. Engring. mag. McGraw-Hill Pub. Co., N.Y.C., 1947-48; editl. rsch. asst. U. Ill., Urbana, 1948-49, free-lance editor, writer, 1950-61; with continuing edn. adminstrn. dept. Oakland Univ., Rochester, Mich., 1961-66; grad. rsch. asst. Mich. State U., East Lansing, 1966-70; sr. analyst to v.p. Market Opinion Rsch., Detroit, 1970-77, sr. v.p., 1977-89; dir. Bur. of the Census, U.S. Dept. Commerce, 1989-93; rsch. scientist Sch. Bus. Adminstrn., U. Mich., 1993—. Author: High School Students Look at Their World, 1970, American Women Today & Tomorrow, 1977, Moving Power and Money: The Politics of Census Taking, 1995; contbr. articles to profl. jours. Mem. U.S. Census Adv. Com., Washington, 1980—86, Mich. Job Devel. Authority, Lansing, 1980—85; state editor LWV of Mich., 1959—61; bd. dirs. Roper Ctr. for Pub. Opinion Rsch., 1993—; mem. nat. adv. com. Inst. for Social Rsch., U. Mich., 1993—. Fellow: Am. Statis. Assn.; mem.: Am. Assn. Pub. Opinion Rsch., Am. Mktg. Assn. (pres. Detroit 1976—77, midwestern v.p. 1978—80, v.p. mktg. rsch. 1982—84, found. trustee 1993—2001), Cornell Club N.Y., Cosmos Club. Republican. Presbyterian. Avocation: swimming. Home: 1505 Sheridan Dr Ann Arbor MI 48104-4051 Office: U Mich Sch Bus Ann Arbor MI 48109-1234 E-mail: bryantb@umich.edu.

BRYANT, KEITH LYNN, JR. history educator; b. Oklahoma City, Nov. 6, 1937; s. Keith Lynn and Elsie L. (Furman) B.; m. Margaret A. Burum, Aug. 14, 1962; children: Jennifer Lynne, Craig Warne. BS, U. Okla., 1959, MEd, 1961; PhD, U. Mo., 1965. From asst. prof. to prof., assoc. dean U. Wis., Milw., 1965-76; prof. Coll. Liberal Arts Tex. A&M U., College Station, 1976-88, head dept. history Coll. Liberal Arts, 1976-80, dean, 1980-84; prof. history U. Akron, Ohio, 1988-2000, head dept., 1988-95, prof. emeritus, 2000—. Cons. So. Ry., NEH. Author: Alfalfa Bill Murray, 1968, Arthur E. Stilwell, Promoter with a Hunch, 1971, History of the Atchison, Topeka and Santa Fe Railway, 1974, William Merritt Chase: A Genteel Bohemian, 1991, Culture in the American Southwest, 2001; co-author: A History of American Business, 1983; bd. editors Western Hist. Quar., 1984-87, Southwestern Hist. Quar., 1980-87; editor Railroads in the Age of Regulation, 1900-1980, 1988. Various offices local Rep. Party, Okla., Tex.; chmn. Bush for Pres., Brazos County, 1979-80. Served to 1st lt. U.S. Army, 1959-60. Recipient William H. Kiekhofer award U. Wis., 1968, George W. and Constance M. Hilton book award Ry. and Locomotive Hist. Soc., 1990, David P. Morgan Article award Ry. and Locomotive Hist. Soc., 1998; grantee Am. Philos. Soc., 1968, NEH, 1984. Mem. So. Hist. Assn. (chmn. Frank Owsley book award com. 1988), Western History Assn., Tex. Hist. Assn., Lexington Group, S.W. Conf. Humanities Consortium (pres. 1982-83). Presbyterian. Home: PO Box 5366 Bryan TX 77805-5366

BRYCHTOVA, JAROSLAVA, sculptor; b. Semily, Czechoslovakia, 1924; m. S. Libensky. Student, Acad. Applied Arts, Prague, Czechoslovakia, 1945-51, Acad. Fine Arts, Prague, 1947-50. Designer Zeleznobrodské sklo, Zelezny Brod, Czechoslovakia, 1950-84. Guest lectr. Pilchuck Summer Sch., Stanwood, Wash., Ctr. Creative Studies, Detroit, others; presenter in field. Office: 7 N Saginaw St Pontiac MI 48342-2148 also: Heller Gallery 420 W 14th St New York NY 10014-1064

BRYFONSKI, DEDRIA ANNE, publishing company executive; b. Utica, N.Y., Aug. 21, 1947; d. Lewis Francis and Catherine Marie (Stevens) B.; m. Alexander Burgess Cruden, May 24, 1975 B.A., Nazareth Coll., Rochester, N.Y., 1969; M.A., Fordham U., 1970. Editorial asst. Dial Press, N.Y.C., 1970-71; editor Walker & Co., 1971-73, Gale Research Co., Detroit, 1974-79, sr. editor, 1979, v.p., assoc. editorial dir., 1979-84, sr. v.p., editorial dir., 1984-86, exec. v.p., pub., 1986-94, pres., CEO, 1995-98; pres. Gale Pub. The Gale Group, Farmington Hills, Mich., 1999—. Author: The New England Beach Book, 1974; editor: Contemporary Literary Criticism, Vols. 7-14, 1977-80, Twentieth Century Literary Criticism, vols. 1-2, 1977-78, Contemporary Issues Criticism, vol. 1, 1982, Contemporary Authors Autobiography Series, vol. 1, 1984 Bd. dirs. Friends of Detroit Pub. Libr., 1980-89, pres., 1984-86; bd. dirs. Friends of Librs. U.S.A., 1995—. Mem. ALA, Assn. Am. Pubs. (chmn. libraries com. 1983-85, exec. council gen. pub. div. 1985-87, co-chmn. joint com. resources and tech. services div. 1983-85). Home: 546 Lincoln Rd Grosse Pointe MI 48230-1218 Office: The Gale Group 27500 Drake Rd Farmington Hills MI 48331-3535

BRZEZINSKI, ROB, professional sports team executive; m. Leah Brzezinski. BS in Edn., Nova Southeastern U., 1992, JD, 1995. Bar: Fla. Staff counsel Miami Dolphins, 1993—98; dir. football adminstrn. Minn. Vikings, 1999—2000, v.p. football adminstrn. Office: Minn Vikings 9520 Vikings Dr Eden Prairie MN 55344

BUA, NICHOLAS JOHN, retired federal judge; b. Chgo., Feb. 9, 1925; s. Francesco and Lena (Marino) B.; m. Camille F. Scordato, Nov. 20, 1943; 1 dau., Lisa Annette. JD, DePaul U., 1953; LLD (hon.), Govs. State U., 1992. Bar: Ill. 1953. Trial atty., Chgo., 1953-63; judge Village Ct., Melrose Park, Ill., 1963-64; assoc. judge Cir. Ct. Cook County, Chgo., 1964-71, cir. judge, 1971-76; justice Appellate Ct. Ill., 1st Dist., 1976-77; judge U.S. Dist. Ct., Chgo., 1977-91; with Burke, Weaver & Prell, 1991—. Spl. counsel to U.S. atty. gen., 1991-93; mem. exec. com. Jud. Conf. Ill., also mem. supreme ct. rules com., 1970-77; lectr. DePaul U.; mem. faculty Def. Tactics Seminar, Ill. Def. Counsel Seminar, 1971; fellow Nat. Coll. State Trial Judges, U. Nev., 1966. Contbr. articles to legal publs. Bd. govs. Gottlieb Meml. Hosp., 1978-79; trustee Schwab Rehab. Hosp., 1977-78; chmn. Mayor of City of Chgo.'s Gaming Commn., 1992. With AUS, World War II. Named Man of Yr. Justinian Soc. Lawyers, 1977, Best Fed. Judge No. Dist. Ill. Chgo. Lawyer, 1989; recipient Alumni award DePaul U., 1977. Mem. Am. Justinian Soc. Jurists (pres. 1978) Clubs: Nat. Lawyers (Chgo.), Legal (Chgo.), Union League (Chgo.), Lex Legio DePaul U. (Chgo.). Office: Burke Weaver & Prell Xerox Centre 55 W Monroe St Chicago IL 60603-5001

BUBENZER, GARY DEAN, agricultural engineering educator, researcher; b. Bicknell, Ind., Aug. 21, 1940; s. Ernest and Nelda (Telligman) B.; m. Sandra Lee Capehart, June 10, 1962; children— Nathan Edward, Brian Peter A.S., Vincennes U., 1960; B.S., Purdue U., 1962, M.S., 1964; Ph.D., U. Ill., 1970. Registered profl. engr., Wis. Instr. agrl. engring. U. Ill., Urbana, 1964-69; asst. prof. U. Wis., Madison, 1969-74, assoc. prof., 1974-79, prof., 1979—, chmn. dept. agrl. engring., 1983-88; guest scholar Kyoto U., Japan, 1981. Contbr. articles to profl. jours. Named Outstanding Instr., Coll. Agr. and Life Sci., U. Wis., 1983; recipient faculty-alumni citation Vincennes U., 1984 Fellow Am. Soc. Agrl. Engrs. (chmn. soil and water div. 1983-84, engr. of the yr. Wis. sect. 1988, Hancor Honor award 1998). United Methodist. Home: 5105 Sherwood Rd Madison WI 53711-1019 E-mail: gdbubenz@facstaff.wisc.edu, bubenzer@chorus.net.

BUBRICK, MELVIN PHILLIP, surgeon; b. Chgo., June 2, 1944; m. Barbara Lynn Jacobs, Jan. 26, 1969; children: Jerome Bradley, Ellen Jeanne, Dena Beth. BA with honors, U. Ill., 1964, MD, 1968. Diplomate Am. Bd. Surgery, Am. Bd. Colon and Rectal Surgery; lic. Minn. Intern in surgery Univ. Hosps., Madison, Wis., 1968-69; resident in gen. surgery Hennepin County Gen. Hosp., Mpls., 1969-74; postdoctoral fellow colon and rectal surgery U. Minn. Health Scis. Ctr., 1974-75; clin. instr. div. colon and rectal surgery U. Minn., 1975-77, clin. asst. prof., 1977-78, clin. asst. prof. dept. surgery, 1978-80, asst. prof., 1980-87, assoc. prof., 1987—; chief surgery, program dir. surg. residency Hennepin County Med. Ctr., 1988-94; pres., CEO Hennepin Facility Assocs., 1995—. V.p. Mpls. Med. Rsch. Found., 1991-95; chmn. bd. dirs. Hennepin Faculty Assocs., 1991—, pres., CEO, 1995—. Author: (with others) Conn's Therapy, 1985, The Pancreas. Principles of Medical and Surgical Practice, 1985, Applied Therapeutics: The clinical use of drugs, 4th rev. edit., 1988; contbr. over 90 articles to Minn. Med. jour., Am. Surg. jour., Diseases of Colon and Rectum, Surgery, others. Bd. dirs. Mpls. Med. Rsch. Found., Inc., 1981-89. Mem. AMA, ACS, Am. Assn. Surgery of Trauma, Am. Soc. Colon and Rectal Surgeons (co-chair Self Assessment Exam. Com. 1984-85), Am. Soc. Microbiology, Assn. Program Dirs. of Surgery, Cen. Surg. Assn., Collegium Internat. Chirurgiae Digestivae, Soc. Surgery of Alimentary Tract, Minn. Assn. Pub. Teaching Hosps., Minn. Surg. Soc., Minn. Med. Assn., Mpls. Surg. Soc., Hennepin County Med. Soc. (mem. and chair various coms. 1975—, Hennepin faculty assoc. 1983—). Achievements include rsch. in assessment of bursting strength and healing of intestinal anastomoses, predictive value of surface oximetry in assessing healing in irradiated bowel, use of antibiotic microspheres for infected vascular grafts and peritonitis, clinical and anatomic assessment of first rib-clavicular decompression on subclavian catheters and pacemaker leads, influence of nutritional deficits in intestinal anastomotic strength, iron chelation with a Deferoxamine (DFO) conjugate in hemorrhagic shock.

BUBULA, JOHN, chef; Chef de cuisine Morton's of Chgo., Boston; chef Boston Harbor Hotel, Boston Four Seasons; owner, chef Thyme, Chgo. Office: Thyme 464 N Halsted Chicago IL 60622

BUCHELE, WESLEY FISHER, retired agricultural engineering educator; b. Cedar Vale, Kans., Mar. 18, 1920; s. Charles John and Bessie (Fisher) B.; m. Mary Jagger, June 12, 1945 (dec. 2000); children: Rod, Marybeth, Sheron, Steven. BS, Kans. State U., 1943; MS, U. Ark., 1951; PhD, Iowa State U., 1954. Registered profl. engr., Iowa, Calif. Jr. engr. John Deere Tractor Works, Waterloo, Iowa, 1946-48; asst. prof. U. Ark., Fayetteville, 1948-51; agrl. engr. USDA, Ames, Iowa, 1954-56; assoc. prof. Mich. State U., East Lansing, 1956-63; prof. Iowa State U., Ames, 1963-89, prof. emeritus, 1989—. Vis. prof. U. Ghana, Legon, 1968-69, Beijing Agrl. Engring. U., 1983-84; vis. scientist Commonwealth Sci. and Indsl. Rsch. Orgn., Australia, Internat. Inst., Tropical Agr., Ibadan, Nigeria, 1979-80, Internat. Rice Rsch. Inst., Manila, 1991-92; cons. engr. Detroit Arsenal, Ordnance Corps, Waterways Exptl. Sta., Corps of Engrs., U.S. Steel Corp., GM, Detroit, 1974-76; bd. dirs. Farm Safety 4 Just Kids,

Earlham, Iowa, Self-Help, Inc., Waverly, Iowa, JAC Tractor Co. Author 18 books; inventor 23 patents. Mem. Ames Energy Com., 1974-75; advisor Living History Farm, Urbandale, Iowa, 1965—, bd. govs., 1984—. Maj. U.S. Army, 1943-46, PTO; maj. Ordnance Corps, USAR, 1946-69, ret. Named Eminent Engineer Iowa Engring. Soc., 1989 Fellow Am. Soc. Agrl. Engrs. (bd. dirs. 1978-80, McCormick-Case award 1988), Nat. Inst. Agrl. Engrs.; mem. AAAS, Soc. Automotive Engrs., Am. Soc. Agronomy (mem. com. 1961-65), Steel Ring, Internat. Assn. Mechanization of Field Experiments (v.p. 1964-93), Internat. Platform Assn., Osborne Club, Toastmasters. Avocations: photography, travel, golf, inventing, writing. Home and Office: 239 Parkridge Cir Ames IA 50014-3645 E-mail: wbuchele@com.net.

BUCHENROTH, STEPHEN RICHARD, lawyer; b. Bellefontaine, Ohio, Feb. 8, 1948; s. Richard G. and Patricia (Muller) B.; m. Vicki Anderson, June 6, 1974; children: Matthew Brian, Sarah Elizabeth. BA, Wittenburg U., Springfield, Ohio, 1970; JD, U. Chgo., 1974. Bar: Ohio 1974, U.S. Dist. Ct. (so. and no. dists.) Ohio 1974, U.S. Ct. Appeals (6th cir.) 1974. Ptnr. Vorys, Sater, Seymour & Pease, Columbus, Ohio, 1974—. Author: Ohio Mortgage Foreclosures, 1986, Ohio Franchising Law, 1990, also chpts. in books. Trustee, v.p. Godman Guild Assn., Columbus, 1977-83; trustee, sec. Neighborhood Homes, Inc., Columbus, 1977-85; mem. bd. rev. Worthington Pers., 1981—; pres. Worthington Alliance for Quality Edn., 1989-91; chmn. bd. advisors paralegal program Capitol U. Law Sch., 1991; pres. bd. trustees Worthington Edn. Found., 1997-98; mem. Ohio Supreme Ct. Commn. on CLE, 1994-2000, chmn., 1999; bd. advisors C.H.A.D.D. of Ctrl. Ohio, 1993-97; bd. trustees Wittenberg U., 2000—. Recipient Cmty. Svc. award Legal Assts. Ctrl. Ohio, 1987. Mem.: ABA (forum com. franchising), Am. Coll. Real Estate Lawyers, Columbus Bar Assn. (bd. govs., pres. 1992—93, Bar Svc. medal 2000), Ohio State Bar Assn. (coun. dels., chmn. legal assts. com., bd.govs. real property sect.). Republican. Lutheran. Home: 2342 Collins Dr Columbus OH 43085-2810 Office: Vorys Sater Seymore & Pease 52 E Gay St PO Box 1008 Columbus OH 43215-3161 E-mail: SRBuchenroth@vssp.com.

BUCHKO, GARTH, broadcasting executive; b. Winnipeg, MB, Canada, 1958; m. Lesley; 1 child. From acct. exec. to retail and gen. sales mgr. CJOB AM, Winnipeg, 1982-95, pres., gen. mgr., 1995—. Bd. dirs. Children's Hosp. Rsch. Found., Manitoba Spl. Olympics, Big Brothers of Manitoba; chmn. fundraising com. 1997 Manitoba Spl. Olympics Summer Games. Avocations: football, travel, golf. Office: CJOB AM 930 Portage Ave Winnipeg MB Canada R3G 0P8

BUCHSIEB, WALTER CHARLES, orthodontist, director; b. Columbus, Ohio, Aug. 30, 1929; s. Walter William and Emma Marie (Held) b.; m. Betty Lou Risch, June 19, 1955; children: Walter Charles II, christine Ann. BA, Ohio State U., 1951, DDS, 1955, MS, 1960. Pvt. practice dentistry specializing in orthodontics, Dayton, Ohio, 1959-93. Cons. orthodontist Miami Valley Hosp., Children's Med. Ctr., Dayton; orthodontic cons. Columbus Children's Hosp.; assoc. prof. dept. orthodontics Ohio State U. Coll. Dentistry, 1984—, clinic dir., 1993—98, mem. dean's adv. com.; mem. fin. and program com. United Health Found., 1971—73. Bd. dirs. Hearing and Speech Ctr., 1968-82, 2d v.p., 1976-78, pres., 1978-79; orthodontic advisor State of Ohio Dept. Health, Bur. Crippled Children's Svcs., 1983-84; elder Luth. ch., 1965-68, v.p. 1974. Capt. AUS, 1955-58. Fellow Am. Coll. Dentists (pres. Ohio sect. 1988); mem. ADA (alt. del. 1968, del. 1991, coun. on ann. sessions and internat. rels. 1984-88), Am. Assn. Dental Schs., Am. Cleft Palate Assn., Am. Assn. Dental Schs., Internat. Assn. Dental Rsch., Ohio Dental Assn. (sec. coun. legis. 1969-78, v.p. 1978-79, pres.-elect 1979-80, pres. 1980-81, polit. action com. 1987-95, Coun. on constn. and By- Laws 1988-92, Achievement award 1989), Dayton Dental Soc. (pres. 1970-71), Am. Bd. Orthodontics, Gt. Lakes Soc. Orthodontists (sec.-treas. 1972-75, pres. 1977-78), Internat. Coll. Dentists,Am. Assn. Orthodontists (chmn. coun. legis. 1976, speaker of house 1982-85, ad hoc com. to revise by-laws, coun. on govtl. affairs 1988-96, recipient James E. Brophy Dist. Svc. award 1992, bd. mem. polit. action com.), Pierre Fauchard Acad., Coll. of Diplomats Am. Bd. Orthodontics (pres. 1990-91), Ohio State U. Alumni Assn. (advocates group), Delta Upsilon (pres. Ohio State U. alumni chpt. 1997-99, alumni advisor 2000—), Psi Omega, Masons, Rotary (pres. 1973-74, Paul Harris fellow). Republican. Lutheran. Home: 1212 Harrison Pond Dr New Albany OH 43054-9553 Office: Ohio State U Orthodontics Dept 305 W 12th Ave Columbus OH 43210-1267 E-mail: buchsieb.1@osu.edu.

BUCHWALD, HENRY, surgeon, educator, researcher; b. Vienna, Austria, June 21, 1932; came to U.S., 1939; naturalized; s. Andor and Renee (Franzos) B.; m. Emilie D. Bix, June 6, 1954; children: Jane Nicole, Amy Elizabeth, Claire Gretchen, Dana Alexandra. BA summa cum laude, Columbia U., 1954, MD, 1957; MS in Biochemistry, PhD in Surgery, U. Minn., 1967. Diplomate Am. Bd. Surgery. Intern Columbia/Presbyn. Med. Ctr., N.Y.C., 1957-58; resident fellow in surgery U. Minn., Mpls., 1960-67; asst. prof. surgery U. Minn. Med. Sch., 1967-70, assoc. prof., 1970-77, prof. surgery, prof. biomed. engring., 1977—, dir. grad. surg. tng., resident tng. program, in-tng. exam.; chmn. credentials com. Pres. Minn. Inventors Hall of Fame, 1989-92, chmn. bd. dirs. 1992-94; vis. prof., lectr. McLaren Gen. Hosp., Flint., Mich., 1979, Buffalo Surg. Soc., Mpls., 1980, G.P. Wratten Surg. Symposium, Washington, 1980, Frontiers of Medicine Series, Chgo., 1980, Minn. Endocrine Club, Mpls., 1980, Symposium on Surgery, Tokyo, 1980, Northwestern Med. Assn., Sun Valley, Idaho, 1981, Mayo Clinic, Rochester, Minn., 1981, BSG/Glaxo Internat. Teaching Day, Norwich, Eng., 1982, Mass. Gen. Hosp., Boston, 1983, SUNY Stony Brook, 1984, D.C. Gen. Hosp., Washington, 1984, L.A. Surg. Soc., 1987, Sch. Dentistry, Dept. Continuing Edn., U. Minn., 1988, others; Alfred Strauss vis. lectr., Chgo., 1989; spkr., cons. in field.; presenter numerous confs. and symposia. Author: (with others) Hepatic, Biliary and Pancreatic Surgery, 1980, Lipoproteins and Coronary Atherosclerosis, 1982, Atherosclerosis: Clinical Evaluation and Therapy, 1982, Nutrition and Heart Disease, 1982, Advances in Vascular Surgery, 1983, Advances in Surgery, 1984, others; contbr. Gibbon's Surgery of the Chest, 4th edit., 1983, Hardy's Textbook of Surgery, 1983, Implantable Pumps: ASAIO Primers in Artificial Organs, 1987; contbr. over 250 articles to profl. jours., trans.; mem. editorial bd. Chirurgia Generale, Jour. Clin. Surgery, Infu-Systems Internat., Diabetes, Nutrition and Metabolism, Obesity Surgery Jour. Am. Soc. Artificial Int. Orgn., Jour. Bacteriol. Surgery, Online Jour. Current Clin. Trials, also guest editor other jours. Capt. SAC, USAF, 1958-60. Recipient Inventor of Yr. award Minn. Inventors Hall of Fame, 1988, 90, Clin. Scholar award U.Minn., 1991; recipient numerous rsch. grants univs., Nat. Heart and Lung Inst., Nat. Cancer Inst., Nat. Inst. Arthritis, Metabolism and Digestive Diseases, NIH, med. founds., pharm. cos., corps., 1956—. Fellow ACS (Samuel D. Gross award 1969), Am. Surg. Assn., Soc. Univ. Surgeons, Cen. Surg. Assn. (program com. 1982-85, chmn. 1984-85, treas. 1992-94, pres. 1997-98), Assn. Acad. Surgery (Disting. Svc. award 1976), Epidemiology Coun. and Cardiovascular Coun. Am. Heart Assn. (established investigator), Am. Coll. Cardiology, Soc. Surgery Alimentary Tract, Soc. Clin. Trials (program com. 1984-85); mem. AAAS, Minn. Surg. Assn. (First Clin. Rsch. award 1965), Mpls. Surg. Assn., Minn. Heart Assn., Am. Assn. History Medicine, Am. Soc. Artificial Internal Organs (program com. 1984-87, sect. editor Trans.), Internat. Study Group Diabetes Treatment with Implantable Insulin Delivery Devices (sec.-gen. 1984-88, chmn. 1989-94), St. Paul Surg. Soc. (hon.), Am. Coll. Nutrition (mem. editorial bd.), Am. Soc. Bariatric Soc. (pres. 1998-99), Paleopathology Club, Alpha Omega Alpha. Avocations: running, riding, tennis, reading, chess. Home: 6808 Margarets Ln Minneapolis MN 55439-1019 Office: U Minn Dept Surgery PO Box 290 Minneapolis MN 55440-0290

BUCHY, JIM, state legislator, packing company executive; b. Greenville, Ohio, Sept. 24, 1940; s. George Jacob and Amba (Armbruster) B.; m. Sharon Lynn Steinvall, 1965; children: Kathryn, John. BS, Wittenberg U., 1962. Pres. Charles G. Buchy Packing Co., Greenville, 1977—; mem. Ohio Ho. of Reps., Columbus, 1983—. Mem. Greenville Bd. Edn., 1980-82; dist. del. Rep. Nat. Conf.; mem. Darke County (Ohio) Rep. Exec. Com.; chmn. Darke Econ. Found., 1977-82; bd. dirs. Greenville Indsl. Park; past pres. Darke County Rep. Men's Club. Mem. Darke County C. of C., Rotary, Phi Mu Delta. Home: North Broadway PO Box 899 Greenville OH 45331-0899

BUCK, EARL WAYNE, insurance investigator, motel owner; b. La Porte City, Iowa, Jan. 15, 1939; s. Edwin Earl and Uleta Pearl (Purdy) B.; m. Maxine E. Parker, Oct. 19, 1969; children: Brian, Douglas, Stuart, Teresa. LLB, La Salle U., 1969. Asst. mgr. Chgo. br. Atwell, Vogel & Sterling, Scarsdale, N.Y., 1965-70; pvt. detective, Sioux City, Iowa, 1968-74; mgr. Milw. br. Atwell, Vogel & Sterling, Scarsdale, N.Y., 1970; sr. auditor Comml. Union Ins. Co., Chgo., 1970-74; police chief McHenry Shores (Ill.) Police Dept., 1973-79; self-employed ins. investigator McHenry, Ill., 1980-88, Rapid City, S.D., 1988—; owner Corral Motel, 1988—. Liquor liability investigator for various ins. cos., 1980-88; farm owner, 1986-96; owner High Plaines Detective Agy., 1990—; ptnr. Juke Boxes, Western Fla. Chmn. McHenry Shores (Ill.) Zoning Commn., 1972, Police Support Subcom., C. of C. Pub. Safety Com.; key contact Help Abolish Legal Tyranny; active Rapid City Police Res., 1989-90, North Rapid Civic Assn., 1991—, pres., chmn. bd., 1993-94; active Pennington County Air Quality Bd., 1990-93, chmn., 1992-93. With U.S. Army, 1957-61. Recipient Police Meritorius Service award Vill. of McHenry Shores, 1979. Mem. Midwest Ins. Auditors Assn., McHenry County Police Chief's Assn., Rapid City Police Officers Assn., Rapid City Area Hospitality Assn. (bd. dirs.), Rapid City Area C. of C. (safety com. 1989-91), Black Hills Badlands & Lakes Assn., Fed. Weed and Seed Program Rapid City (steering com.), NRA, Moose. Republican. Lutheran. Avocations: flying, amateur archaeology, photography, fishing, hunting.

BUCK, JAMES RUSSELL, state legislator; m. Judith Ann Buck. BA, BS, MBA, Ind. Wesleyan Coll. Mem. Ind. State Ho. of Reps. Dist. 38, mem. commerce & econ. devel., ins., corp. & small bus. coms., mem. roads and transp. com., vice-chmn. labor and employment com. Mem. Nat. Assn. Realtors, Ind. Assn. Realtors, Kokomo Bd. Realtors. Home: 4407 Mckibben Dr Kokomo IN 46902-4719

BUCK, JOHN A. business executive; Chmn., CEO The John Buck Co., 1989—. Office: The John Buck Co 233 S Wacker Dr Ste 550 Chicago IL 60606-6417 Fax: 312-627-7570.

BUCKLER, ROBERT J. energy distribution company executive; Sr. v.p. energy mktg. & distbn. Detroit Edison, 1974-97; pres. energy distbn. DTE Energy Corp., Detroit, 1998—. Office: DTE Energy Co 2000 2d Ave Detroit MI 48226-1279

BUCKLEY, GEORGE W. sporting goods executive; PhD in Engring., U. Southhampton (Eng.). Various mgmt. positions Brit. Railways Bd., GEC Turbine Generators Ltd., Detroit Edison Co.; past pres. elec. motors divsn. Emerson Elec. Co.; pres. Mercury Marine unit Brunswick Corp., Fond du Lac, Wis., 1997-2000, chmn. & CEO Lake Forest, Ill., 2000—. Office: Brunswick Corp 1 N Field Ct Lake Forest IL 60045-4811

BUCKLEY, JOHN JOSEPH, JR. health care executive; b. Evanston, Ill., Oct. 5, 1944; s. John Joseph and Mary Ruth (Smith) B.; m. Sarah Amelia Puceloski, May 16, 1970; children— Ruth Mary, Patricia Kimberly, John Joseph III A.B., Kenyon Coll., 1966; M.B.A., George Washington U., 1969. Asst. adminstr. Maricopa County Gen. Hosp., Phoenix, 1969-71, St. Joseph's Hosp. and Med. Ctr., Phoenix, 1971-74, assoc. adminstr., 1974-76, v.p., 1976-79, pres., 1984-88, St. Anthony's Hosp., Amarillo, Tex., 1979-84, St. Anthony's Devel. Corp., Amarillo, 1982-84; chief operating officer Harrington Cancer Ctr., 1982-84; sr. v.p. Mercy Health System, Cin., 1988-91; pres. So. Ill. Healthcare Enterprises, Carbondale, Ill., 1992—2001, Jack Buckley & Assocs., Herrin, 2001—; interim pres., CEO St. Mary's Hosp. of East St. Louis, 2002—. Pres. So. Ill. Hosp. Svcs., Health Svcs. of So. Ill., Regional Health Plan, 1992-2001. Active Amarillo Alliance of Cmty. Svc. Execs., Amarillo Area Acad. Health Ctr. Corp., Amarillo Area Hosp. Home Care, Amarillo Found. Health and Sci., Panhandle chpt. Tex. Soc. to Prevent Blindness, Amarillo Jr. League, Children's Oncology Svcs. of Tex. Panhandle; Amarillo diocesan coord. health affairs; mem. adminstrv. com. Amarillo; pres. Mercy Svcs. Corp., 1984-88; bd. dirs. Greater Phoenix Affordable Health Care Found., 1984-88; trustee Kenyon Coll., Gambier, Ohio, 1991-95, mem. alumni coun., 1998—, pres., 2001—; mem. SI Edge, 1995—. Fellow: Am. Coll. Healthcare Execs. (regent Ariz. 1984—88, regent So. Ill. 1998—2002); mem.: Ariz. Hosp. Assn., Ariz. Kidney Found., Cath. Health Assn. U.S., Ill. Hosp. and Health Sys. Assn. (trustee 1995—2001, chmn. 2000), Tex. Hosp. Assn. (trustee 1983—84), Alumni Assn. of George Washington U. Health Svcs. Mgmt. and Policy (pres. 1995—97), Delta Phi (pres. alumni assn. 1988—2000). Republican. Roman Catholic. Office: Jack Buckley & Assocs 1907 S 27th St Herrin IL 62948 E-mail: jackbuckleyjr@earthlink.net.

BUCKLEY, JOSEPH PAUL, III, polygraph specialist; b. Chgo., July 6, 1949; s. Joseph Paul and Helen (Lavelle) B.; m. Patricia Nemeth, June 17, 1972; children: Megan, Michael, Patrick, Thomas. B.A., Loyola U., Chgo., 1971; M.S. in Detection of Deception, Reid Coll. Detection of Deception, Chgo., 1973. Lic., Ill. Detection of deception examiner John E. Reid & Assocs., Inc., Chgo., 1971—, chief polygraph examiner, 1978-80, dir. Chgo. office, 1980-82, pres. corp. Chgo., Milw., 1982—. Chmn. Ill. Detection of Deception Examiner Com., 1978-82; mem. adv. com. Office of Tech. Assessment, 1983 Co-author: Criminal Interrogation and Confessions, 1st edit., 1962, 4th edit., 2001, The Investigator Anthology, 1999; contbr. articles to profl. jours. Mem. Am. Polygraph Assn. (v.p. 1979-80, chmn. pub. rels. com. 1979-80, 84-95, awards), Ill. Polygraph Soc. (v.p. 1981, pres. 1982-83), Am. Acad. Forensic Scis., Am. Mgmt. Assn., Am. Soc. Indsl. Security (investigations com. 1983-89), Spl. Agts. Assn., Internat. Pers. Mgmt. Assn., Internat. Assn. Chiefs Policy, Chgo. Crime Commn. Office: 250 S Wacker Dr Ste 1200 Chicago IL 60606-5841 E-mail: jbuckley@reid.com.

BUCKLO, ELAINE EDWARDS, United States district court judge; b. Boston, Oct. 1, 1944; married. AB, St. Louis U., 1966; JD, Northwestern U., 1972. Bar: Calif. 1973, U.S. Dist. Ct. (no. dist.) Calif. 1973, Ill. 1974, U.S. Dist. ct. (no. dist.) Ill. 1974, U.S. Ct. Appeals (7th cir.) 1983. Law clk. U.S. Ct. Appeals (7th cir.), Chgo.; pvt. practice, 1973-85; U.S. magistrate judge U.S. Dist. Ct. (no. dist.) Ill., Chgo., 1985-94, judge, 1994—. Spkr. in field. Contbr. articles to profl. jours. Mem. jud. conf. com. on adminstrn. Magistrate Judge Sys., 1998—; mem. vis. com. No. Ill. U. Sch. Law, 1994—; mem. Northwestern U. Law Bd., 1996-99. Mem. ABA (standing com. law and literacy 1995-98), FBA (v.p. 1990-92, pres. Chgo. chpt. 1992-93), Women's Bar Assn. Ill. (bd. dirs. 1994-96), Chgo. Coun. Lawyers (pres. 1977-78). Office: US Dist Ct No Dist Everett McKinley Dirksen Bldg 219 S Dearborn St Ste 1988 Chicago IL 60604-1794

BUCKSBAUM, JOHN, real estate development company executive; BS in Econs., U. Denver. Pres. Gen. Growth Calif.; CEO Gen. Growth Properties, Inc., 1999—, also bd. dirs. Mem. exec. com. Wharton Sch. Adv. Bd., Urban Land Inst., bd. govs.; bd. dirs. World TEAM Sports, U.S. Ski Team Found. Mem. Internat. Coun. Shopping Ctr. (bd. dirs. Ednl. Found.), Nat. Assn. Real Estate Investment Trusts, Nat. Realty Coun. (exec. com.), U. Calif. Real Estate Ctr. Office: Gen Growth Properties inc 110 N Wacker Dr Chicago IL 60606-1511

BUCKSBAUM, MATTHEW, real estate investment trust company executive; b. Marshalltown, Iowa, Feb. 20, 1926; s. Louis and Ida (Gerwin) B.; m. Carolyn Swartz, Aug. 3, 1952; children: Ann B. Friedman, John. BA in econ., U. Iowa, 1949. Owner, operator Regional Supermarket Chain, Marshalltown, 1949-54; owner, developer Pvt. Real Estate, Iowa, 1954-64; chmn. Gen. Growth Properties, Des Moines, 1964—. Trustee, chmn. Aspen (Colo.) Music Festival & Sch.; Sgt. USAF, 1944-46, PTO. Mem. Internat. Coun. Shopping Ctrs. (past chmn.), Urban Land Inst., Nat. Assn. Real Estate Investment Trusts. Jewish. Office: General Growth Properties Inc 110 N Wacker Dr Chicago IL 60606-1511 Fax: (312) 960-5463.

BUCKWALTER, JOSEPH ADDISON, orthopedic surgeon, educator; b. Ottumwa, Iowa, June 21, 1947; s. Joseph Addison and Carole Ann (Kelly) B.; m. Kathleen Coen, May 31, 1975; children: Jody, Andrea, Abigail. BS with high distinction, U. Iowa, 1969, MS, 1972, MD, 1974. Diplomate Am. Bd. Orthopaedic Surgery (recert., oral examiner 1988—, dir. 1990—, mem. examinations com. 1992—, chmn. examinations com. 1992-93, chmn. cert. renewal com. 1992—); lic. surgeon Iowa. Intern in internal medicine U. Iowa, Iowa City, 1974-75, resident in orthopaedics, 1975-77, 78-79, Nat. Rsch. Svc. Award rsch. fellow, 1977-78, from asst. prof. to assoc. prof. orthopaedic surgery, 1979-85, prof. orthopaedic surgery, 1985—. Mem. R&D devel. com. VA Med. Ctr. Com., 1985-88; mem. orthopaedic tumor therapy group U. Iowa Cancer Ctr., 1981—, cancer edn. subcom., 1982-90; mem. grants and fellowships adv. com. Iowa City Vets. Med. Ctr., 1983-86, chief orthopaedic surgery, 1987-91; mem. Arthritis Found. Rsch. Com., 1985-86; mem. panel NIH Consensus Devel. Confs., Bethesda, Md., 1984, 88; mem. rheumatology rsch. adv. bd. Syntex Corp., 1987-94; mem. adv. bd. WHO Multinational Collaborative Study on Predictors of Osteoarthritis, 1992; mem. sci. adv. com. Specialised Ctr. Rsch. on Osteoarthritis Rush-Presbyn.-St. Luke's Med. Ctr., Chgo., 1993—; mem. Nat. Arthritis and Musculoskeletal and Skin Diseases Adv. Coun., NIH, 1993—; disting. lectr. Hosp. Spl. Surgery, N.Y.C., 1982, Coll. Physicians and Surgeons-N.Y. Orthopaedic Hosp., 1988, U. N.Mex., 1989; guest lectr. Wilford Hall Med. Ctr., San Antonio, 1983, vis. prof., 1984; vis. prof. U. Miami, Fla., 1986, Cath. Med. Colls., Seoul, Republic of Korea, 1989, U. Pitts., 1993, Ohio State U., Columbus, 1994; vis. orthopaedic prof. U. So. Calif., L.A., 1990; Am. Orthopaedic Assn. 1991 Internat. vis. prof. Nuffield Orthopaedic Ctr., Oxford (Eng.) U., 1991, vis. prof. orthopaedics, 1991; vis. prof. orthopaedics, U. N.C., 1991; OREF Hark lectr. and vis. prof. U. Wash., Seattle, 1992; Watson Jones lectr. Royal Coll. Surgeons (Gt. Britain), 1992; A.M. Rechtman lectr. Phila. Orthopaedic Soc., 1993; Predl. guest spkr. 1993 Japanese Orthopaedic Assn. Rsch. Meeting, Matsumoto, Japan, 1993; Kelly Rsch. Award vis. prof. Mayo Clinic, Rochester, Minn., 1993; participant numerous workshops and confs. Cons. reviewer: Jour. Bone and Joint Surgery, 1979—, cons. editor for rsch., 1989—; bd. assoc. editors: Jour. Orthopaedic Rsch., 1982-85, mem. editl. adv. bd., 1985-88, co-editor-in-chief, 1993—; mem. editl. adv. bd. Orthopaedics, 1986-90; reviewer: The Lancet, 1993—; contbr. articles to profl. jours. Student rsch. fellow U. Iowa Coll. Medicine, 1970. Fellow Am. Inst. Med. and Biol. Engring. (founding), Am. Acad. Orthopaedic Surgeons (mem. com. basic scis. 1983-85, chmn. com. evaulation 1985-90, mem. at large, bd. dirs. 1988-89, mem. steering com. for devel. Musculoskeletal Conditions in U.S. 1990-92, chmn. coun. for rsch. and sci. affairs 1990-93, 94—, sec. 1993-94); mem. AAAS, Internat. Soc. Limb Salvage, Brit. Orthopaedic Assn. (companion mem.), Orthopaedic Rsch. Soc. (sec.-treas. 1985-88, bd. dirs. 1985-91, pres. 1989-90), Am. Orthopaedic Assn. (exch. fellowship com. 1989-90, chmn. internat. vis. prof. com. 1993—), Am. Orthopaedic Soc. for Sports Medicine (chmn. rsch. awards com. 1988-90, rsch. com. 1989-91), Internat. Skeletal Soc., Iowa Orthopaedic Soc., Johnson County Med. Soc., Musculoskeletal Tumor Soc., 20th Century Orthopaedic Assn., Girdlestone Orthopaedic Soc., Phi Beta Kappa, Alpha Omega Alpha. Office: U Iowa Hosps Dept Orthopaedics 200 Hawkins Dr Iowa City IA 52242-1009

BUCKWALTER, KATHLEEN C. academic administrator, educator; Assoc. dir. Gerontological Nursing Interventions Rsch. Ctr., dir. Ctr. on Aging U. Iowa, Found. Disting. Prof. Elected to Inst. of Medicine Nat. Acad. of Sciences. Contbr. over 200 articles to profl. jours., 75 chpts. to books; editor: Nursing Diagnosis and Intervention for the Elderly (Maas, M., Buckwalter, K.C., Hardy, M.A.), 1991, Geriatric Mental Health: Current and Future Challenges, 1992, others. Office: U Iowa Coll Nusing 101 Nursing Bldg 234 CMAB Iowa City IA 52242

BUCZAK, DOUGLAS CHESTER, financial advisor, lawyer; b. Detroit, Feb. 6, 1949; s. Chester and Rose Marie (Czech) B. BA in English, U. Mich., 1971; JD, U. Detroit, 1975. Bar: Mich. 1975. Pvt. practice, Lansing, Mich., 1978-80; bus. cons. Dynamic Learning Systems, Farmington Hills, 1981-82; fin. planner Pacific Fin. Cos., 1982-86, Pacific Fin. Group, Birmingham, 1986—. Pres. Pacific Adv. Svcs., Inc., 1986—. Fin. columnist Detroit Legal News, 1992-94. Named one of Best 200 Fin. Advisors in Am., Worth Fin. Mag., 1996, 97, 98, 99. Mem. Mich. Bar Assn., Internat. Assn. Fin. Planning (bd. dirs. 1988-91, 96-99, v.p. 1990-91), Optimist Club Farmington Hills (pres. 1984-85), Sigma Phi Epsilon (pres. alumni bd. Ann Arbor, Mich. 1983-93). Home: 6426 Heritage West Bloomfield MI 48322-1336 Office: Pacific Fin Group Ste 126 380 N Old Woodward Birmingham MI 48009-5307

BUDAK, MARY KAY, state legislator; b. Phila. m. Michael S. Budak, 1953; children: Kathy Budak Norred, Michael S. III, Patricia A. Budak Jones. Student, Temple U., 1950-51, Purdue U., 1968, 80. Owner, mgr. Budak Memls. Inc., 1960-81; sec. to campaign coord. Michigan City Mayor Campaign, Ind., 1966-79; mem. Ind. Ho. of Reps., 1980—, mem. various coms., ranking majority mem. judiciary com., former ranking Rep. mem. family and children com., asst. Rep. whip. Pres. Miss Ind. Scholar Pageant, 1970-74, former mem. exec. bd.; mem. exec. bd. Michiana Sheltered Workshop, 1981-86, Parents & Friends of Handicapped; asst. Rep. WAIP; bd. dirs. Stepping Stone for Spousal Abuse. Named Outstanding Woman in Politics, 1982, Outstanding Legislator, Fraternal Order Police and State Employees, 1983. Mem. LWV, LaPorte County Grange, LaPorte GOP Women's Club (v.p. 1979-81), Bus. & Profl. Women's Club, LaPorte Rep. Women's Club, LaPorte Homemakers Ext. Club, VFW Aux., Rotary. Roman Catholic. Home: 5144 N Pawnee Trl La Porte IN 46350-7565 Office: State House State Capital Indianapolis IN 46204

BUECHE, WENDELL FRANCIS, agricultural products company executive; b. Flushing, Mich., Nov. 7, 1930; s. Paul D. and Catherine (McGraw) B.; m. Virginia M. Smith, June 14, 1952 (dec. May 12, 1992); children: Denise, Barbara, Daniel, Brian; m. Nancy Bird Jacobson, June 24, 1994; children: Meredith, Stuart, Julia. B.S.M.E., U. Notre Dame, 1952. With Allis-Chalmers Corp., 1952-88, dist. mgr., 1961-64, sales and mktg. mgr., 1964-69, group exec. v.p. West Allis, Wis., 1973-76, exec. v.p. elec. groups, 1976-77, exec. v.p., chief adminstrv. and fin. officer, 1977-80, exec. v.p., head solids process equipment sector and fluids processing group, chief fin. officer, 1980-81, pres., chief operating officer, dir., 1981-83, pres., CEO, dir., 1984-86, chmn., 1986-88, ret., 1988; CEO IMC Global, Northbrook, Ill., 1993-97, chmn. bd. dirs., 1994-98, bd. dirs. Bd. dirs. M&I Marshall Illsley Bank, M&I Corp., Integrated Solutions, Inc., Integra; advisor to Am. Indsl. Ptnrs., LPP, Windpoint Ptnrs. Fund III and IV, LP, K-B Ptnrs. I & II, L.P. Mem. council Med. Coll. Wis., 1983—, engring. adv. coun., past chmn., U. Notre Dame. Mem. Mid-Am. Com. for Internat. Bus. (chmn.

exec. com.), Nat. Assn. Mfgrs. (past dir.), TFI (past chmn.), Longboat Key Club, The Chgo. Racquet Club. Office: IMC Global 919 N Michigan Ave Ste 520 Chicago IL 60611-1602 E-mail: wfbueche@aol.com.

BUECHLER, BRADLEY BRUCE, plastic processing company executive, accountant; b. St. Louis, Dec. 5, 1948; s. Phillip Earl and Mildred M. (Braun) B.; m. Stephanie A. Walker, June 20, 1969; children: Sheila, Lisa, Brian. BSBA, U. Mo., St. Louis, 1971. CPA, Mo. Audit mgr. Arthur Andersen & Co., St. Louis, 1971-81; corp. controller Spartech Corp., 1981-83, exec. v.p., COO, 1984-87, pres., COO, 1987-91, pres., CEO, 1991—, chmn., 1999—. Bd. regents St. Louis U., 1994—; mem. corp. bd. St. Joseph Inst. for the Deaf, 1995—; bd. dirs. Boy Scouts Am., 1998. With Mo. Army N.G., 1969-75. Mem. AICPA, Soc. Plastics Industry (chmn. sheet prodrs. divsn., bd. dirs. 1993-95, mem. exec. com. color and additive compounders divsn.). Methodist. Avocations: golf, baseball. Office: Spartech Corp 120 S Central Ave Ste 1700 Clayton MO 63105-1735

BUEHRLE, MARK, baseball player; b. St. Charles, Mo., Mar. 23, 1979; Pitcher Chgo. White Sox, 2000—. Office: Chgo White Sox 333 W 35th St Chicago IL 60616*

BUETOW, DENNIS EDWARD, physiologist, educator; b. Chgo., June 20, 1932; s. Earl Frank and Helen Anna (Roeske) Buetow; m. Mary Kathleen Carney, Oct. 29, 1960; children: Katherine, Thomas(dec.) , Michael, Ellen. BA, UCLA, 1954, MS, 1957, PhD, 1959. Biologist NIH, Bethesda, Md., 1959-65; biochemist Balt. City Hosps., 1959-65; assoc. prof. physiology U. Ill., Urbana, 1965-70, prof., 1970—, head dept. physiology and biophysics, 1983-88. Cons. in field. Contbr. articles to profl. jours. Grantee, NIH, NSF, Life Ins. Med. Rsch. Fund, Am. Heart Assn., USDA. Fellow: AAAS, Gerontol. Soc.; mem.: Am. Soc. Plant Biology, Am. Fedn. Aging Rsch., Soc. Protozoologists, Am. Physiol. Soc., Am. Soc. Cell Biology. Home: 2 Eton Ct Champaign IL 61820-7602 Office: Univ Ill 524 Burrill Hall Urbana IL 61801 E-mail: d-buetow@uiuc.edu.

BUFE, NOEL CARL, program director; b. Wyandotte, Mich., Dec. 25, 1933; s. Carl Frederick and Alcha D. (Brumfield) B.; m. Nancy Carolyn Sinclair, Mar. 23, 1957; children: Kevin, Lynn, Bruce, Carol. BS, Mich. State U., 1956, MS in Criminal Justice, 1971, PhD, 1974. Exec. trainee and security investigation J.L. Hudson Co., Detroit, 1956-57, office mgr., 1960-62; rsch. investigator Wayne State U., 1962; admisntrv. asst. to sec. bd. police commrs. Met. Police Dept., St. Louis, 1964; mgmt. cons. hwy. safety divsn. Internat. Assn. Chiefs of Police, Washington, 1964-66; exec. sec. Mich. Law Enforcement Officers Tng. Coun., Lansing, 1966-67; exec. dir. office hwy. safety planning Mich. Govs.' Hwy. Safety Rep., 1967-74; dep. adminstr. Nat. Hwy. Traffic Safety Adminstrn., 1974-75; adminstr. office criminal justice programs Mich. Dept. Mgmt. and Budget, Lansing, 1975-78; dir. traffic inst. Northwestern U., Evanston, Ill., 1978-99; chmn. nat. safety Itasca, 1999—. Bd. mem. com. for strategic transp. rsch. study Nat. Rsch. Coun. Transp. Rsch. Bd., 1989-91; chairperson, vice chairperson injury rsch. grant rev. com. Ctr. for Disease Control, 1986-91; chairperson police equipment tech. adv. com. U.S. Dept. Justice, 1987; bd. dirs. Nat. Commn. Against Drunk Driving, 1986; presdl. appointee Nat. Hwy. Safety Adv. Com. U.S. Dept. Transp., 1986; mem. Pres.-elect Ronald Reagan's Task Force on Adminstrn. Justice, 1980; mem. traffic safety adv. coun. Ill. Sec. State. Contbr. articles to profl. jours. Chairperson bd. elders Community Christian Ch., Lincolnshire, Ill., 1983-85; pres. Okemos (Mich.) Sch. Bd., 1975-78; chairperson Okemos Community Recreation Program, 1971-74. Inducted into Football Hall of Fame Roosevelt High Sch., 1992, Disting. Grads. Hall of Fame, 1993, Wyandotte, Mich. Sports Hall of Fame, 1995. Mem. Nat. Safety Coun. (bd. dirs., v.p. for traffic safety, exec. com. 1987, 88, chairperson traffic divsn. 1984-87, chair fin. com., 1995-96, vice chmn. bd., 1996—), Mich. State U. Sch. Criminal Justice Alumni Assn. (pres. 1984-86), Il. Assn. Chiefs of Police, Univ. Club, Nat. Sheriffs Assn. (hwy. safety com.), Internat. Assn. Chiefs of Police (vice chairperson enforcement equipment adv. com. 1975-76, chairperson weapons subcom. 1977, chairperson phys. security 1979, hwy. safety com. 1974-78), Mich. State U. S. Club (life.). Avocations: golf, boating, cross country skiing, professional and college sports. Office: Northwestern U Traffic Inst 1121 Spring Lake Dr Itasca IL 60143-3200 Home: 4385 Turfway Trl Harbor Springs MI 49740-8853

BUFFETT, WARREN EDWARD, entrepreneur; b. Omaha, Aug. 30, 1930; s. Howard Homan and Leila (Stahl) B.; m. Susan Thompson, Apr. 19, 1952; children: Susan, Howard, Peter. Student, U. Pa., 1947-49; B.S., U. Nebr., 1950; M.S., Columbia, 1951. Investment salesman Buffett-Falk & Co., Omaha, 1951-54; security analyst Graham-Newman Corp., N.Y.C., 1954-56; gen. partner Buffett Partnership, Ltd., Omaha, 1956-69; now chmn. Berkshire Hathaway Inc., 1970—, also CEO. Chmn. bd. Berkshire Hathaway, Inc., Nat. Indemnity Co., Nat. Fire & Marine Ins. Co., See's Candy Shops, Inc., Columbia Ins. Co., Buffalo Evening News; bd. dirs. Capital Cities/ABC, Salomon, Inc., Coca-Cola Co., Gillette Co., Fechheimer Bros. Co., Associated Retail Stores, Scott and Fetzer Co., Home & Auto Ins. Co., Omaha World Herald, Precision Steel Warehouse, Inc. Life trustee Grinnell Coll., 1968—, Urban Inst. Office: Berkshire Hathaway Inc 1440 Kiewit Plz Omaha NE 68131

BUGGE, LAWRENCE JOHN, lawyer, educator; b. Milw., June 1, 1936; s. Lawrence Anthony and Anita (Westenberg) B.; m. Mary Daly, Nov. 28, 1959 (div.); m. Elaine Andersen, Jan. 29, 1977; children: Kristin, Laura, Jill, David, Carol. AB, Marquette U., 1958; JD, Harvard U., 1963. Bar: Wis. 1963. Assoc. Foley and Lardner, Milw., Madison, Wis., 1963-70, ptnr., 1970-96, of counsel, 1996—. Pres. Nat. Conf. Commrs. on Uniform State Laws, 1989-91; adj. prof. law U. Wis. Law Sch., Madison, 1997—. Mem. Wis. Bar Assn. (pres. 1980-81), Mil. Bar Assn. (pres. 1974-75), Milw. Young Lawyers Assn. (pres. 1969-70). Home: 313 Walnut Grove Dr Madison WI 53717-1228 Office: Foley & Lardner PO Box 1497 150 E Gilman St Madison WI 53701-1497 E-mail: ljbugge@itis.com.

BUGHER, ROBERT DEAN, professional society administrator; b. Lafayette, Ind., Oct. 17, 1925; s. Walter Earl and Lillie Victoria (Feldner) B.; m. Patricia Jean McConnell, Sept. 7, 1945; children: Vickie Leigh, Robert James. Student, Millsaps Coll., 1943, Miami U., Oxford, Ohio, 1944; BS in Civil Engring, Purdue U., 1948; MPA, U. Mich., 1951. Staff engr. Mich. Mcpl. League, 1948-53; mgr. Mcpl. Purchasing Svc., 1951-53; sec.-treas. Mich. Mcpl. Utilities Assn., 1951-53; asst. dir. Am. Pub. Works Assn., 1953-58, exec. dir., 1958-89, exec. dir. emeritus, 1990—. Lectr. Internat. Seminar on Ekistics, Athens, Greece, 1970; chmn. nat. adv. coun. Keep Am. Beautiful, Inc., 1974-75; chmn. Nat. Conf. on Solid Waste Disposal Sites, Washington, 1971; advisor pub. mgmt. program Northwestern U., 1977-82; bd. dirs. Pub. Adminstrn. Svc., Chgo., 1958-73; trustee Nat. Acad. Code Adminstrs.; chmn. Coun. Internat. Urban Liaison, 1982-84; trustee Nat. Tng. and Devel. Svc., Am. Consortium for Internat. Pub. Adminstrn.; adv. com. internat. divsn. GAO, 1979-80. Editor: pub. works sect. Municipal Yearbook Internat. City Mgmt. Assn., 1953-58, People Making Public Works History-A Century of Progress 1894-1994, 1998 ; cons. editor pub. works sect., Mcpl. Pub. Works Adminstrn., 1957; chmn. adv. bd. Internat. Ctr. Acad. State and Local Govts., 1985-87. Served to 1st lt. USMCR, 1943-45. Mem. ASCE (life), Am. Pub. Works Assn. (hon.), Internat. Pub. Works Fedn. (treas. 1985-89, sec.-gen. 1990), Am. Soc. Assn. Execs., Am. Soc. Pub. Adminstrn., Internat. Union Local Authorities (pres. U.S. sect. 1977-79, v.p. 1968-70, 75-77), Internat. Solid Wastes and Pub. Cleansing Assn. (v.p. 1968-70), Internat. Fedn. Mcpl. Engrs. (treas. 1976-79), Pub. Works Hist. Soc. (hon., treas. 1975-89), Sigma Alpha Epsilon. Baptist. Home: 8238 E Del Cadena Dr Scottsdale AZ 85258-2319 Office: 2345 Grand Blvd Ste 500 Kansas City MO 64108-2641 E-mail: rdpjbugher@msn.com.

BUGIELSKI, ROBERT JOSEPH, state legislator; b. Chgo., June 5, 1947; s. Edward Leon and Lottie Regina (Ptak) B.; m. Dona Rosalie Obrzut, Aug. 2, 1980. BS in Bus. Edn., Chgo. State U., 1971. Tchr. Weber High Sch., Chgo., 1971-83; asst. athletic dir., 1973-78; dir. devel. Weber High Sch., Chgo., 1974-83, adminstrv. bd. dirs., 1975-83; rep. Ill. Gen. Assembly, 1987—. Named Legislator of Yr. Am. Legis. Exch. Coun., 1991. Democrat. Roman Catholic. Office: 6839 W Belmont Ave Chicago IL 60634-4646

BUHR, FLORENCE D. county official; b. Strahan, Iowa, Apr. 7, 1933; d. Earnest G. and May (Brott) Wederquist; m. Glenn E. Buhr, 1955; children: Barbara, Lori Lynn, David. BA, U. No. Iowa, 1954. Precinct chair Polk County Dem. Ctrl. Com., Iowa, 1974-79; clerk, sec. Iowa Ho. Reps., 1974-79, 81-82; rep. dist. 85 State of Iowa, 1983-90, asst. majority leader Ho. Reps., 1985-90; state senator Iowa State Senate, 1991-95, asst. majority leader, 1992-95; Polk County supr. Des Moines, 1995—. Chairwoman Polk County Bd. Suprs., 1997. Democrat. Presbyterian. Home and Office: 4127 30th St Des Moines IA 50310-5946

BUHRMASTER, ROBERT C. company executive; b. 1947; B in Mech. Engring., Rensselaer Poly. Inst.; MBA, Dartmouth Coll. With Corning Inc., Corning, N.Y.; exec. v.p. Jostens, Inc., Mpls., 1992-93, pres., COO, 1993, CEO, 1994, chmn. bd. dirs., 1998—. Bd. dirs. Toro Corp., Nat. Alliance of Bus. Pres. Viking coun. Boy Scouts. Am.; past bd. dirs. Exec. Coun. Fgn. Diplomats, Marietta Corp. Mem. U.S. Advanced Ceramics Assn. (founding mem.). Office: 5501 Norman Center Dr Minneapolis MN 55437-1040 Office Fax: 952-897-4116.

BUHROW, WILLIAM CARL, religious organization administrator; b. Cleve., Jan. 18, 1934; s. Philip John and Edith Rose (Leutz) B.; m. Carole Corinne Craven, Feb. 14, 1959; children: William Carl Jr., David Paul, Peter John, Carole Lynn. Diploma, Phila. Coll. Bible, 1954; B.A., Wheaton (Ill.) Coll., 1956, M.A., 1959. Ordained to ministry Gen. Assn. Regular Bapt. Chs., 1958. Asst. pastor (Hydewood Park Bapt. Ch.), N. Plainfield, N.J., 1959-63; with Continental Fed. Savs. & Loan Assn., Cleve., 1963-81, sr. v.p., 1971-75, pres., chief exec. officer, dir., 1975-81; chmn. bd. Security Savs. Mortgage Corp., Citizens Service Corp., New Market Corp., CFS Service Corp., 1975-81; trustee Credit Bur. Cleve., 1975-81, Bldg. Expositions, Inc., 1974-84; registered rep. IDS/Am. Express, Cleve., 1982-83; gen. credit mgr. Forest City Enterprises, Inc., 1983-85; pres. Forest City Ins. Agy., Inc., 1983-85; asst. v.p. Mellon Fin. Services Corp., 1985-87; exec. adminstr. The Gospel Ho. Ch. and Evangelistic Ctr., Walton Hills, Ohio, 1988—. Trustee Bapt. Bible Coll. and Theol. Sem., Clarks Summit, Pa., 1977-90; vice chmn. bd. deacons Cedar Hill Bapt. Ch., Cleveland Heights, Ohio, 1981-87; trustee, sec. and treas. Gospel House Prison Ministry Found., 1992—. Mem. Christian Bus. Men's Com. Internat., Nat. Assn. Ch. Bus. Adminstrn. Home: 1044 Linden Ln Lyndhurst OH 44124-1051 Office: 14707 Alexander Rd Cleveland OH 44146-4924

BUJOLD, TYRONE PATRICK, lawyer; b. Duluth, Minn., Dec. 4, 1937; s. Dewey J. and Lucille C. (Donahue) B.; m. Delia H. Goulet, Sept. 17, 1960; children: Christopher Andrew, Anne Elizabeth, Lara Suzanne. BS, Marquette U., 1959; JD, U. Minn., 1962. Bar: Minn. 1962, U.S. Dist. Ct. Minn. 1963, U.S. Ct. Appeals (8th cir.) 1964, Wis. 1983, U.S. Dist. Ct. (we. dist.) Wis. 1985, N.D. 1987. Assoc. Furuseth & Bujold, International Falls, Minn., 1962-63, Sullivan, MacMillan, Hanft & Hastings, Duluth, 1963-68, ptnr., 1968-85, Robins, Kaplan, Miller & Ciresi, Mpls., 1985—. Mem. faculty CLE program, Minn., 1965—, Inst. CLE, Ann Arbor, Mich., 1975—, Nat. Inst. Trial Advocacy, 1983—. Mem. Commn. Fair Housing and Employment Practices, Duluth, 1970-78, City Charter Commn., Duluth, 1983-85, Plymouth, Minn., 1991—. Mem. Am. Coll. Trial Lawyers, Internat. Soc. Barristers, Am. Bd. Trial Advocates. Roman Catholic. Avocations: reading, theatre, guitar, swimming.

BUKATY, MICHAEL EDWARD, manufacturing company executive; b. Kansas City, Mo., Aug. 2, 1936; s. Nicholas Martin and Anna Marie (Walsh) B.; m. Dale Patricia, Aug. 13, 1960; children: Lynne, Jill, Brad. BS in Engring., U. Kans., 1961; MBA, U. Mo., 1965. Design engr. Vendo Co., Kansas City, 1961-65, sales mgmt., 1965-74, v.p. sales, 1975-78; v.p. mktg. Wescon Products Co., Wichita, Kans., 1978-82, pres., 1982—. Avocations: golf, tennis, reading. Home: 1202 N Shefford St Wichita KS 67212-5667 Office: Latshaw Enterprises Inc PO Box 7710 Wichita KS 67277-7710

BUKOVAC, MARTIN JOHN, horticulturist, educator; b. Johnston City, Ill., Nov. 12, 1929; s. John and Sadie (Fak) B.; m. Judith Ann Kelley, Sept. 5, 1956; 1 dau., Janice Louise. BS with honors, Mich. State U., 1951, MS, 1954, PhD, 1957; D honoris causa, U. Bonn, Germany, 1995. Asst. prof. horticulture Mich. State U., East Lansing, 1957-61, assoc. prof., 1961-63, prof., 1963; NSF sr. postdoctoral fellow Oxford U., U. Bristol, Eng., 1965-66; univ. disting. prof., 1992—. Vis. lectr. Japan Atomic Energy Rsch. Inst., 1958; adviser IAEA, Vienna, 1961; NAS exch. lectr. Coun. Acads., Yugoslavia, 1971; vis. scholar Va. Poly. Inst., Blacksburg, 1973; guest lectr. Polish Acad. Scis., 1974; disting. vis. prof. N.Mex. State U., 1976; vis. prof. Japan Soc. Promotion Sci., Osaka Prefecture U., 1977; guest lectr. Serbian Sci. Coun., Fruit Rsch. Inst., Cacak, Yugoslavia, 1979; John A. Hannah Disting. lectr. Mich. State Hort. Soc., 1980; vis. prof. U. Guelph, Ont., Can., 1982, Ohio State U., 1982, U. Zagreb, Yugoslavia, 1983, Ohio State U., 1990; collaborator Agrl. Rsch. Svc. USDA, 1982—; guest rschr. Hort. Rsch. Inst., Budapest, Hungary, 1983, Inst. Obstbau und Gemusebau U. Bonn, Fed. Republic Germany, 1986; Batjer Meml. lectr. Wash. State Hort. Soc., 1985; mem. agrl. rsch. adv. com. Eli Lilly Co., Indpls., 1971-88; cons. Dept. Agr.; disting. lectr. Dept. Sci. and Tech. Peoples Republic China, 1984; commencement spkr. Mich. State U., 1986; mem. internat. adv. bd. divsn. life scis. Ctr. for Nuclear Studies, Atomic Energy Commn., Grenoble, France, 1993-2000; Monselise Meml. lectr. Hebrew U., 1994; Agrl. Rsch. Svc. B.Y. Morrison Meml. lectr., 1994, Kermit Olson Meml. lectr. Univ. Minn., 1997; pres. Martin J. Bukovac Inc., 1996—; Donald L. Reichard Meml. lectr., Ohio State U., 1999; sci. exch. lectr. Nara (Japan) Inst. Sci. and Tech., 2000. Mem. exec. adv. bd. Ency. of Agrl. Scis., 1991-96; mem. editl. adv. bd. Ctr. for Agr. and Bioscis. Internat., 1989—; internat. editl. bd. Horticultural Sci., Budapest; mem. editl. bd. Ency. of Agrl. Sci., 1991-96. Pres. Okemos Music Patrons, Mich., 1973-74; bd. dirs. Mich. State U. Press, 1983-92. 1st lt. U.S. Army, 1951-53. Recipient citation meritorious rsch. Am. Hort. Soc., 1970, Disting. Faculty award Mich. State U., 1971, Disting. Svc. award Mich. Hort. Soc., 1974, Disting. Faculty award Mich. Assn. Governing Bds., 1986, Hatch Meml. Medallion award USDA, 1987, Industry Man of Yr. award Nat. Cherry Festival, 1987, Alexander von Humboldt Rsch. prize, 1995, Am. Soc. Agrl. Engring. Outstanding Paper award, 1995; Bukovac Disting. Lectr. established in his honor Mich. State Horticultural Soc., 1995. Fellow AAAS, Am. Soc. Hort. Sci. (hon. life, pres. 1974-75, Joseph Harvey Gourley award 1969, 76, Marion Meadows award 1975, citation of appreciation 1975, Carroll R. Miller award 1980, Outstanding Researcher award 1988, M.A. Blake award for disting. grad. teaching 1975, Hall of Fame inductee 2001); mem. NAS, Am. Chem. Soc., Am. Soc. Plant Physiologists (Dennis R. Hoagland award 1988), Bot. Soc. Am., Scandinavian Soc. Plant Physiologists, Japanese Soc. Plant Physiologists, Internat. Soc. Hort. Sci., Soc. Exptl. Biology, Sigma Xi (pres. 1978-79 research award Kedzie chpt.), Phi Kappa Phi, Gamma Sigma Delta. Club: Mich. State U. Faculty. Home: 4428 Seneca Dr Okemos MI 48864-2946 Office: Mich State U Dept Horticulture East Lansing MI 48824 E-mail: bukovacm@msu.edu.

BULGER, BRIAN WEGG, lawyer; b. Chgo., May 27, 1951; s. John Burton and Mary Jane (Wegg) B.; m. Laura Ellen McErlean, Sept. 12, 1981; children: Burton, Kevin. AB cum laude, Georgetown U., 1972, JD, 1977. Bar: Ill. 1977, U.S. Dist. Ct. (no. dist.) Ill. 1977, U.S. Ct. Appeals (4th, 7th and 8th cirs.) 1977, U.S. Supreme Ct. 1980. From assoc. to ptnr. Pope Ballard Shepard & Fowle, Chgo., 1977-87; ptnr., dept. head Katten Muchin & Zavis, 1987-94; founding ptnr. Meckler, Bulger & Tilson, 1994—. Adj. prof. U. Wis. Mgmt. Inst., Milw., 1980—. Contbr. articles to profl. jours. Bd. dirs. Anixter Ctr., Chgo., James Electronics, Chgo. Mem. ABA (chair pub. employer labor rels. com. sect. on urban state and govt. law), Ill. State Bar Assn., Georgetown Law Alumni (bd. dirs. 1984-93). Roman Catholic. Avocations: baseball, reading, boating, skeet shooting. Office: Meckler Bulger Tilson 8300 Sears Tower 233 S Wacker Dr Chicago IL 60606-6306

BULLARD, GEORGE, newspaper editor; b. Middlesboro, Ky., Feb. 8, 1945; s. George Kibert and Frances Rose (Costanzo) B.; m. Donna DeVoe, Nov. 29, 1980 (div. May 1989); m. Susan Burzynski, Mar. 21, 1992. BA in Journalism, Mich. State U., 1971. Editor-in-chief Mich. State News, East Lansing, 1970-71; reporter The Detroit News, 1971-86, dep. city editor, 1986-87, city editor, 1987-95, asst. mng. editor/religion writer, 1995-98. Contbr. articles to newspapers and mags., 1975-86. Mem. Leadership Detroit, 1988-89. Sgt. U.S. Army, 1963-66, Korea. Fellow Religious Pub. Rels. Coun. Avocations: flying private plane, ham radio, skiing. Office: Detroit News 615 W Lafayette Blvd Detroit MI 48226-3197

BULLARD, WILLIS CLARE, JR. state legislator; b. Detroit, July 12, 1943; s. Willis C. and Virginia Katherine (Gilmore) B.; children: Willis C. III, Melissa Ann, Kaila Michelle. AB, U. Mich., 1965; JD, Detroit Coll. Law, 1971. Bar: Mich. 1971. Practice of law, Detroit, 1971-77, Troy, 1977-80, Milford, 1983—; supr. Highland Twp., 1980-82; mem. Mich. Ho. of Reps., 1983-96, Mich. Senate from 15th dist., Lansing, 1996—2002. Asst. Rep. caucus chmn., 1983-84, asst. Rep. floor leader, 1985-88, chmn. House Rep. campaign, 1987-90; chmn. House taxation com., 1993-96; chmn. task force Midwe stern Legis. Conf. Coun. State Govts., 1985-86, Mich. Ho. of Reps., 1983-96, Mich. State Senate, 1996-2002; mediator cir. and dist. cts., 1988—. Bd. dirs. Dunham Lake Property Owners Assn., 1975-78, treas., 1975-76, pres., 1976-78; mem. Dunham Lake Civic Com., 1982-87; trustee Highland Twp., 1978-80, mem. zoning bd. appeals, 1979. Named Legislator of Yr. Mich. Twp. Assn., 1984, Nat. Rep. Legislator of Yr., 2000. Mem. Oakland County Bar Assn., State Bar Mich., Oakland County Assn. Twp. Suprs. (sec.-treas. 1981), Michigamua. Clubs: U. Mich. of Greater Detroit, Highland Republican, Highland Men's (sec. 1979, pres. 1980). Home: 1849 Lakeview Dr Highland MI 48357-4817 Office: State Capitol Lansing MI 48909

BULLOCK, JOSEPH DANIEL, pediatrician, educator; b. Cin., Jan. 23, 1942; s. Joseph Craven and Emilie (Woide) B.; m. Martha Foss, June 20, 1964; children: Jennifer Zane, Sarah Harrison. BA, Wittenberg U., 1963; MD, Ohio State U., 1967, degree in pediatrics, 1969; degree in immunology, allergy, U. Calif., San Francisco, 1971. Diplomate Am. Bd. Pediatrics, Am. Bd. Allergy and Immunology. Clin. prof. pediatrics Ohio State U., Columbus, 1971—; pres. Midwest Allergy Assocs., Inc., Worthington, Ohio, 1971—. Contbr. articles to profl. jours. Active fund raising Wittenberg U., Springfield, Ohio, 1980-83, Columbus Sch. for Girls, 1977-86. Served to capt. USAF, 1967-71. Recipient Mead Johnson award, 1965. Fellow Am. Acad. Pediatrics, Am. Acad. Allergy, Am. Coll. Allergists (Bd. Regents 1979-82, Clemens von Pirquet award 1968, 69, 70, 71), Am. Thoracic Soc., Interasma, Ohio Soc. Allergy and Immunology (pres. 1985-87). Republican. Lutheran. Clubs: Columbus Country; The Golf (New Albany, Ohio); Indian Creek Country (Miami Beach, Fla.), The Surf (Surfside, Fla.). Home: 189 N Parkview Ave Columbus OH 43209-1435 Office: Midwest Allergy Assocs Inc 85 E Wilson Bridge Rd Columbus OH 43085-2392

BULLOCK, STEVEN CARL, lawyer; b. Anderson, Ind., Jan. 19, 1949; s. Carl Pearson and Dorothy Mae (Colle) B.; m. Debra Bullock; children: Bradford, Christine, Justin, Evan. BA, Purdue U., 1971; JD, Detroit Coll., 1985. Bar: Mich. 1985, U.S. Dist. Ct. (ea. dist.) 1985, Ct. of Appeals (6th cir.) 1993, U.S. Supreme Ct. 1993. Pvt. pracitce, Inkster, Mich., 1985—. With USAF, 1971-75. Mem. Mich. Bar Assn. (criminal law sect.), Detroit Bar Assn., Detroit Funder's Soc., Recorder's Ct. Bar Assn., Suburban Bar Assn., Criminal Def. Lawyers of Mich. Avocations: golf, travel. Office: 2228 Inkster Rd Inkster MI 48141-1811 E-mail: lawone123@aol.com.

BULLOCK, WILLIAM HENRY, bishop; b. Maple Lake, Minn., Apr. 13, 1927; s. Loren W. and Anne C. (Raiche) B. B.A., Notre Dame U., 1948, M.A., 1962; Ed.S., St. Thomas Coll., St. Paul, 1969; HHD (hon.), St. Ambrose U., Davenport, Iowa, 1989. Ordained priest Roman Catholic Ch., 1952, ordained bishop Roman Catholic Ch., 1980. Assoc. pastor Ch. of St. Stephens, Mpls., 1952-55, Ch. of Our Lady of Grace, Edina, Minn., 1955-56, Ch. of Incarnation, Mpls., 1956-57; instr. St. Thomas Acad., Mendota Heights, Minn., 1957-61, headmaster, 1968-71; pastor Ch. of St. John the Baptist, Excelsior, 1971-80; former pastor Ch. of Our Lady of Perpetual Help, Mpls., from 1980; aux. bishop Archdiocese of St. Paul and Mpls., 1980-87; apptd. bishop Diocese of Des Moines, 1987, installed, 1987-93; apptd. bishop Madison, Wis., 1993—. V.p. Wis. Cath. Conf.; mem. Cath. Relief Svcs. Bd. Trustee St. Francis Sem. Mem. U.S. Bishops-Region II, Nat. Conf. Cath. Bishops (NCCB/USCC com. evangelization), KC (4th degree), Knights of Holy Sepulchre, Cath. Relief Svcs. (exec. com., Africa com., com. overseas programs and ops.) Lodges: KC; Knights of Holy Sepulchre. Office: Diocese of Madison Cath Pastoral Ctr PO Box 44983 Madison WI 53744-4983

BULLOFF, JACK JOHN, physical chemist, consultant; b. N.Y.C., Dec. 9, 1914; s. John Stevens and Selma (Lyadova) B.; m. Gertrude Scher, Nov. 11, 1942 (dec. Oct. 1951); 1 child, Eric Douglas (dec.); m. Florence Gutin, Oct. 4, 1952 (dec. May 1996); children: Dorie Lee, Aaron Harley, Steven Marc. BS in Chemistry, CUNY, 1939; PhD in Phys. Chemistry, Rensselaer Poly. Inst., 1953. Asst. prof. chemistry Associated Colls. Upper N.Y., Ovid/Plattsburgh, 1946-50; teaching fellow Rensselaer Poly. Inst., Troy, N.Y., 1950-52; project supr. Commonwealth Engring. Co., Dayton, Ohio, 1953-56; rsch. assoc. Battelle Meml. Inst., Columbus, 1956-68; prof., dir. sci. and tech. studies SUNY, Albany, 1968-76; author-revisor Fla. State U., Tallahassee, 1977-78; cons. safety and wastes J.T. Baker Chem. Co., Phillipsburg, N.J., 1978-84; chief cons. scientist N.Y. State Legis. Commn. on Sci. Tech., Albany, 1985-92; prin. J. Bulloff Chem. and Environ. Cons., Schenectady, N.Y., 1968—. Jr. scientist Los Alamos Nat. Lab., N.M., 1946; vis. lectr. NSF, 1960-66; Kimberley Clark ann. lectr., 1963; cons., expert witness, Schenectady, N.Y., 1968—. Co-author 18 books in field; co-editor: Semiconductor Abstracts, 1959-62, Foundations of Mathematics, 1969; contbr. over 100 articles to profl. jours. With U.S. Army chem. corps. 1942-44, med. corps. 1944-46, ETOUSA. Recipient Best Paper award Tech. Assn. Graphic Arts, 1961. Fellow AAAS (emeritus), Am. Inst. Chemists (emeritus, chair safety in the chemists' workplace com., 1993-94, co-chair coms. in chemistry and environ. concerns, govt. activities and safety in the chemists' workplace 1995-96, govt. activities com. 1995—), Am. Chem. Soc. (emeritus 1989—, various positions 1953-78); mem. N.Y. Acad. Scis. (emeritus 1993—), Ohio Acad. Sci. (v.p. 1966). Achievements include 29 patents for volatile compound metals deposition, air odor control, metallic soaps, and dextran chemistry, others; innovation in xerography and lithography, image-wise photopolymerization, technological forecasting and environmental impact and technology assessment. Home and Office: Ste 5220 8140 Township Line Rd Indianapolis IN 46260-5866 E-mail: bulloff@indy.net.

BULRISS, MARK, chemicals executive; BSCE, Clarkson U., 1973. Process engr. Procter & Gamble, 1973-77; gen. mgr. GE Plastics, 1977-93; pres. laminates divsn. AlliedSignal Inc., 1993-95, pres. electronics materials divsn., 1995-96, pres. polymers divsn., 1996-98; pres., CEO Great Lakes Chem., Indpls., 1998—, chmn. bd. dirs., 2000—. Office: Great Lakes Chem 500 E 96th St Indianapolis IN 46240

BUNCH, HOWARD MCRAVEN, ship production educator, consultant, researcher; b. Texarkana, Tex., Aug. 20, 1926; s. Howard Phillips and Truby Electra (Lowrance) B.; m. Frances Findlater, Dec. 19, 1953; children: James Allday, John Findlater, Howard Carscaden, Helen Clare. BA, U. Tex., 1949, MBA, 1958. Cert. mgmt. acct., mfg. engr., tech. observer. V.p. Bunch Riesen Co., San Angelo, Tex., 1949-56; sec.-treas. United Butone Co., 1956-57; sr. engr. S.W. Rsch. Inst., San Antonio, 1957-63, head indsl. econs. Houston, 1963-68; v.p. Olson Labs., Dearborn, Mich., 1968-73; cons. Ann Arbor, 1973-76; rsch. scientist U. Mich., 1976—, Navsea prof., 1981—. Hon. prof. (life) Zhenziang (China) Shipbuilding Inst., 1987, vis. prof., 1983; vis. lectr. MIT, 1984-86. Author: Ship Production, 1988; contbr. articles to profl. jours. Fellow Soc. Naval Archs. and Marine Engrs. (William H. Webb medal 1993). Office: U Michigan Dept Naval Arch 2600 Draper Dr Ann Arbor MI 48109-2145

BUNCHER, CHARLES RALPH, epidemiologist, educator; b. Dover, N.J., Jan. 18, 1938; BS, MIT, 1960; MS, Harvard U., 1964, ScD, 1967. Statistician Atomic Bomb Casualty Comsn., NAS, 1967-70; chief biostatistician Merrell-Nat. Labs., 1970-73, asst. prof. stats., 1970-73; prof. and dir. divsn. epidemiology and biostats. Med. Coll., U. Cin., 1973-96, prof. biostats. and epidemiology, 1973—, dir. grad. edn., 2001—. Fellow Am. Stats. Assn., Am. Coll. Epidemiology; mem. APHA, Biometrical Assn., Soc. Epidemiol. Rsch., Soc. Med. Decision Making, Soc. Clin. Trials, Tau Beta Pi. Achievements include research in cancer epidemiology; screening, diagnosis and treatment, as well as occupational and environmental epidemiology; risk analysis; statistical research; clinical trials; design of experiments; pharmaceutical research; biostatistical analysis, pharmaceutical statistics, ALS epidemiology. Office: U Cincinnati Div of Epidemiology & Biostatistics PO Box 670183 Cincinnati OH 45267-0183 E-mail: charles.buncher@uc.edu.

BUNDY, BILL, radio personality; b. Menomonie, Wis. Grad. broadcasting, Brown Inst., Mpls.; postgrad., U. Wis. With CNN, CBS; radio host, news anchor Sta. WCCO Radio, Mpls. Office: WCCO 625 2nd Ave S Minneapolis MN 55402*

BUNDY, DAVID DALE, librarian, educator; b. Longview, Wash., Sept. 27, 1948; s. Cedric Dale and Florence (Prichard) B.; m. Consuelo Ann Briones, Dec. 19, 1969 (div. 1982); children: Keith Dale, Cheryl Ann; m. Melody Lynn Garlock, June 14, 1986; children: Rachel Lynn, Lydia Marie, Joel David. BA, Seattle Pacific U., 1969; MDiv, ThM, Asbury Theol. Sem., Wilmore, Ky., 1973; Licentiate, Cath. U. Louvain, Louvain-la-Neuve, Belgium, 1978. Dean Inst. Univ. Ministry Louvain, 1977-81; rsch. asst. Cath. U. Louvain, 1978-85; assoc. prof. Christian Origins, collection devel. libr. Asbury Theol. Sem., Wilmore, 1985-91; libr., assoc. prof. ch. history Christian Theol. Sem., Indpls., 1991—. Dir. Wesleyan Holiness Studies Ctr., Wilmore, 1990-91. Author: Keswick, 1985; editor: Pietist and Wesleyan Studies; contbr. articles to profl. jours. Grantee Fondation Universitaire, Belgium, 1977-84, Pew Charitable Trusts, 1988, Wesleyan/Holiness Studies Ctr., 1992, NEH, 1989—. Mem. N.Am. Patristic Soc., Symposium Syriacum (internat. dir. 1988—), Am. Acad. Religion, Assn. Christian Arabic Studies (editor Mid. Ea. Christian Studies), Wesleyan Theol. Soc. Democrat. Mem. United Meth. Ch. Office: Christian Theol Sem 1000 W 42d St PO Box 88267 Indianapolis IN 46208-0267

BUNGE, CHARLES ALBERT, library science educator; b. Kimball, Nebr., Mar. 18, 1936; s. Louis Herman and Leona Hazel (Cromwell) B.; m. Joanne C. VonStoeser, Aug. 20, 1960; children: Lorraine A., Jeffrey C. Stephen L. AB, U. Mo., 1959; MSLS, U. Ill., 1960, PhD, 1967. Reference librarian Daniel Boone Regional Library, Columbia, Mo., 1960-62; Ball State Tchrs. Coll., Muncie, Ind., 1962-64; research assoc. Library Research Center, U. Ill., 1964-67; mem. faculty Sch. Library and Info. Studies U. Wis., Madison, 1967-98, prof. emeritus, 1998—. Author: Professional Education and Reference Efficiency, 1967; columnist: Wilson Library Bull, 1972-81. Mem. ALA (pres. ref. and adult svcs. divsn. 1987-88, chair com. on accreditation 1990-92, Mudge award 1983, mem. coun. 1993-96, Beta Phi Mu award 1997), Assn. Libr. and Info. Sci. Edn. (pres. 1980-81, Prof. Contribution award 1997), Wis. Libr. Assn. (pres. 1972-73, Libr. of Yr. 1983), Phi Beta Kappa, Beta Phi Mu. Home: 509 Orchard Dr Madison WI 53711-1316 Office: Univ Wis Sch Libr and Info Studies 600 N Park St Madison WI 53706-1403

BUNKOWSKE, EUGENE WALTER, religious studies educator; b. Wecota, S.D., July 3, 1935; s. Walter Adolph and Ottille Sophie (Richter) B.; m. Bernice Bock; children: Barbara, Nancy, Walter, Joel. AA, Concordia Acad. and Jr. Coll., St. Paul, 1955; BA, Concordia Seminary, 1958, BD, MDiv, 1960; MA in Linguistics, UCLA, 1964, C Phil in Linguistics, 1968, PhD in Linguistics, 1976; LittD, Concordia Coll., 1983; DD, Christ Coll., 1991; DLitt, Concordia U., St. Paul, 1997. Missionary Luth. Ch.-Mo. Synod, Africa, 1960-82, congl. pastor, pioneer ch. planter Africa, 1960-74, chmn. Nung Udoe dist. Africa, 1960-61, builder chs., schs., hosp. Africa, 1960-67, medical worker Ogoja Province Africa, 1961-66, justice of peace Ogoja Province Africa, 1962-74, chmn. Ogoja dist. Africa, 1964-69, chmn. Evang. Luth. Mission in Nigeria Africa, 1965-67, analyzer Yala lang., orthography devel. & Bible translator Africa, 1967-71, counselor to Yala Paramount Chief Africa, 1969-74, fourth v.p., 1989-92, 95-98, third v.p., 1992-95; dir. mission Concordia Theol. Seminary, Ft. Wayne, Ind., 1982-88, mission prof., 1982—, mission chair prof., 1986—, grad. prof. mission, 1990—, chmn. dept. pastoral ministries, 1985-88; chmn. mission dept., 1988-90; supr. D Missiology program, chmn. Mission and Comm. Congress Concordia Theol. Seminary, Ft. Wayne, Ind., 1984—. Ling. cons. and adminstr. Luth. Bible Translators, Liberia, Sierra Leone, 1970-74; dir. Vacation Inst. for Tng. in Applied Linguistics and Bible Translation, U. Liberia, Monrovia, 1971-74; cons. United Bible Soc., 1974-80, regional translations coord., 1980-82; cons. Near West Side Cleve. Cluster, St. Paul Internat. Mission Bd. Author: Orede, 1973, Woka yi Ijona, 1974, Topics in Yala Grammar, 1976, God's Mission in Action, 1986, The Body of Christ in Mission, 1987, God's Communicators in Mission, 1988, Receptor Oriented Gospel Communication, 1989, The State of Gospel Communication Today, 1990, Church Growth: A Biblical Perspective, 1991, The Role of the Laity in Gospel Communications, 1992, The Christian Family: Nurture and Outreach, 1993, Multicultural Outreach: Bridging Cultures - Theirs and Ours, 1995, Struggling with Change: Reaching the Lost in Changing Times, 1999, The Lutherans in Mission, 2000; translator Yala Bible, 1967-74; contbr. articles to religious and profl. publs., chpts. to books. Mem. God's Word to Nations Bible Soc. (bd. dirs., trans. and tech. cons.), World Mission Prayer League (bd. dirs.), All Nations Mission (bd. dirs., cons.), Luth. Soc. for Missiology (founding organizer). Republican. Avocations: travel, reading, hiking. Home: 5724 Lancashire Ct Fort Wayne IN 46825-5910 Office: Concordia Theol Seminary 6600 N Clinton St Fort Wayne IN 46825-4916

BUNN, RONALD FREEZE, political science educator, lawyer; b. Jonesboro, Ark., Aug. 1, 1929; s. S. Neal and Velma (Freeze) B.; m. Rita E. Hess, Mar. 29, 1955; children: Robin Gail, Katharine Sue, Lisabeth Joann. BA, Rhodes Coll., 1951; LLD, Southwestern at Memphis, 1973; MA, Duke U., 1953, PhD, 1956; postgrad., U. Cologne, Fed. Republic Germany, 1954-55; JD, U. Mo., 1989. Bar: Mo. 1990. Instr. U. Tex., Austin, 1956-59, asst. prof., 1960-64; asso. prof. La. State U., Baton Rouge, 1964-67, U Houston, 1967-69; prof., dean U Houston (Grad. Sch.), 1969-74, interim dean arts and scis., 1972-74, asso. dean faculties, 1974-75, acting v.p., dean faculties, 1975-76; v.p. acad. affairs State U. N.Y. at Buffalo, 1976-80; provost U. Mo., Columbia, 1980-86, prof. polit. sci., 1986—; ptnr. Shurtleff, Froeschner, Bunn and Aulgur, 1992—; adj. prof. law, 2001. Vis. lectr. Ind. U., 1962; cons. Coun. Grad. Schs. Author: Politics and Civil Liberties in Europe, 1967, German Politics and the Spiegel Affair: A Case Study of the Bonn System, 1968; Contbr. articles profl. jours. Bd. dirs. S.W. Center for Urban Research, Houston, chmn. bd., 1975-76. Fulbright predoctoral scholar, 1954-55, Fulbright rsch. scholar, 1963; NATO sr. fellow in sci., 1973. Mem. Mo. Bar Assn. (labor law com.), So. Polit. Sci. Assn. (past mem. exec. coun.), Southwestern Polit. Sci. Assn. (past v.p.), Am. Coun. on Germany, Phi Beta Kappa (pres. Mo. Alpha chpt. 1986-88), Omicron Delta Kappa. Office: U Mo Dept Polit Sci Columbia MO 65211-0001 also: 25 N 9th St Columbia MO 65201-4845

BUNN, WILLIAM BERNICE, III, physician, lawyer, epidemiologist; b. Raleigh, N.C., June 28, 1952; s. William Bernice Jr. and Clara Eva (Ray) B.; m. Shirley Welch, July 31, 1982; children: Ashley Howell, Elizabeth Jordan. AB, Duke U., 1974, MD, JD, 1979; MPH, U. N.C., 1983. Diplomate Am. Bd. Internal and Occupational Medicine. Intern, then resident in internal medicine Duke U. Med. Ctr., 1981-83, fellow in occupational medicine dept. community medicine, 1983; asst. prof. Sch. of Medicine Duke U., Durham, N.C., 1984-86, dir. rsch. in occupational medicine Sch. of Medicine, 1985-86; dir. occupational health and environmental affairs Bristol Myers Co., Wallingford, Conn., 1986-87, sr. dir. occupational health and environ. affairs, 1987-88; asst. clin. prof. Yale U., New Haven, 1986—; clin. asst. prof. U. Colo., Boulder, 1989; assoc. clin. prof. U. Cin., 1989—; corp. med. dir. Manville Sales Corp., Denver, 1988, v.p., corp. med. dir., 1988-89, sr. dir. for health safety and environ., v.p., 1989-92; dir. internat. med. affairs Mobil Corp., Princeton, N.J., 1992—; med. dir., dir. health, workers compensation, health benefits & safety Navistan Internat. Corp., Chgo., v.p. health safety and productivity, 1998—. Cons. author, co-editor Dellacorte Publs., N.Y.C., 1984-87; sci. adv. bd. U.S. EPA, Washington, 1991—; chmn. radiation epidemiology com. NAS, Washington, 1991-95; assoc. prof. clin. preventive medicine Northwestern Sch. Medicine; bd. sci. counselors Nat. Inst. Occupl. Safety and Health. Author: (with others) Effects of Exposure to Toxic Gases, 1986; author, editor: Poisoning, 1986, Occupational Problems in Clinical Practice; editor: Occupational and Environmental Medicine; editor, author: Issues in International Occupational and Environmental Medicine, 1997, International Occupational and Environmental Medicine, 1998. Bd. dirs. Colo. Safety Assn., Denver, 1988-90, Gaylord Hosp., Wallingford, 1987-88, Meriden-Wallingford Hosp., 1986-88, Chem. Industry Inst. Toxicology, 1989-91, Am. Coll. Occupational and Environ. Medicine, 1993—. NIOSH scholar, 1980; NIH fellow, 1982-83, Nat. Inst. Occupational Safety and Health fellow, 1983-84. Fellow Am. Occupl. Medicine Assn. (co-chmn. acad. affairs com. and publs. com. 1985-90, nat. affairs com. 1985-86, chmn. pubs. com. 1990, bd. dirs. 1993—, chair internat. coun. 1994, sec. 1995, mem. exec. com. 1995), Am. Coll. Occupl. and Environ. Medicine; mem. ACP, AMA, APHA, Occupl. Medicine Assn. Conn. (sec., pres.-elect 1986-88), Internat. Coll. Occupl. Health, Phi Beta Kappa, Phi Eta Sigma. Office: 455 N Cityfront Plaza Dr Chicago IL 60611-5503 also: Yale U Dept Epidemiology & Pub Health New Haven CT 06520 also: U Colo Sch Pharmacy Dept Toxicology Boulder CO 80309-0001 also: U Cin Dept Occupational Med Cincinnati OH 45267-0001

BUNTROCK, DEAN LEWIS, retired waste management company executive; b. Columbia, S.D., June 6, 1931; BA, St. Olaf Coll., Northfield, Minn., 1955. Founder Waste Mgmt. Inc., Oak Brook, Ill., 1968—; chmn. bd., dir. Waste Mgmt. Inc. (changed to WMX Technologies in 1993), 1968—; also chmn. bd., bd. dirs. WMI Internat., until 1997. Bd. dirs. Wheelabrator Techs., Inc., First Nat. Bank Chgo., Waste Mgmt. Internat., Plc. Trustee Chgo. Symphony Orch.; mem. adv. bd. J.L. Kellogg Grad. Sch. Nortwestern U., Evanston, Ill. Named Outstanding CEO, Fin. World Mag., Wall St. Transcript; appointed to Pres.'s Coun. on Environ. Quality. Mem. Am. Pub. Works Assn., Environ. Industries Assn. (co-founder, past pres., sec.-treas., dir.), Bus. Roundtable. Office: Oakbrook Terrace Tower One Tower Ln Ste 2242 Oakbrook Terrace IL 60181-4636

BUOEN, ROGER, newspaper editor; Nat. news editor Star Tribune. Office: Star Tribune 425 Portland Ave Minneapolis MN 55488-0002

BURACK, ELMER HOWARD, management educator; b. Chgo., Oct. 21, 1927; s. Charles and Rose (Taerbaum) B.; m. Ruth Goldsmith, Mar. 18, 1930; children— Charles Michael, Robert Jay, Alan Jeffrey BS, U. Ill., 1950; MS, Ill. Inst. Tech., 1956; PhD, Northwestern U., 1964. Prodn. supt. Richardson Co., Melrose Park, Ill., 1953-55; prodn. control mgr. Fed. Tool Corp., Lincolnwood, 1955-59; mgmt. cons. Booz, Allen & Hamilton, Chgo, 1959-60; mem. faculty Ill. Inst. Tech., 1960-78, prof. mgmt., 1978; prof. mgmt., chair U. Ill.-Chgo., 1978—, head dept., dir. doctoral studies CBA, 1990-96, prof. mgmt. emeritus, 1997. Pres. Ill. Mgmt. Tng. Inst., 1975-77; mem. Ill. Gov. Adv. Coun. Employment and Tng., 1976-83, vice chmn., 1980-83; mem. NSF mission to Russia, 1979. Author: Manpower Planning, 1972, Personnel Management, 1982, Growing-Careers for Women, 1980, Introduction to Management, 1983, Career planning and Management, 1983, Planning for Human Resources, 1983, Creative Human Resource Planning, 1988, Career Management, 1990, Corporate Resurgence and the New Employment Relationships, 1993, Human Resource Planning, 4th edit., 2001, Retiring Retirement, 2002; contbr. articles to profl. jours. With USAAF, 1945-47 Research grantee Dept. Labor, 1965-68; recipient Alumni award for disting. svc. Coll. Bus. U. Ill., Chgo., 1996. Mem. Nat. Acad. Mgmt. (chmn. pers./human resource divsn. 1974-75, health divsn. 1978-79), Human Resource Mgmt. Assn. Chgo. (pres. 1974-75), Soc. Human Resource Mgmt., Pers. Accreditation Inst. (bd. dirs. 1978-89), Midwest Human Resource Planners Group (founding mem., bd. dirs. 1984-95), B'nai B'rith. Office: U Ill MC243 601 S Morgan St Rm 718 Chicago IL 60607-7100

BURATTI, DENNIS P. lawyer; b. Madison, Wis., 1949; JD, U. Wis., 1973. Bar: Wis. 1973, Minn. 1973. Gen. counsel Ryan Cos., Mpls. Office: Ryan Companies Ste 300 50 S 10th St Minneapolis MN 55403

BURBANK, GARY, radio personality; b. July 29, 1941; Radio host 700 WLW, Cin. Office: 700 WLW 1111 St Gregory St Cincinnati OH 45202*

BURBANK, JANE RICHARDSON, Russian and European studies educator; b. Hartford, Conn., June 11, 1946; d. John and Helen Lee (West) B.; m. Frederick Cooper, Sept. 3, 1985. BA, Reed Coll., 1967; MLS, Simmons Coll., 1969; MA, Harvard U., 1971, PhD, 1981. Asst. prof. Harvard U., Cambridge, Mass., 1981-85, U. Calif., Santa Barbara, 1985-86, assoc. prof., 1986-87, U. Mich., Ann Arbor, 1987-95, prof., 1995—2002, NYU, 2002—. Reviewer Kritika, 1983, Russian Rev., 1984, 98, Am. Hist. Rev., 1988, 91, 96, Jour. Modern History, 1989, 92, 94, Slavic Rev., 1990, Harvard Ukrainian Studies, 1991; presenter in field; dir. ctr. Russian E. European studies U. Mich., 1992-95, 98. Author: Intelligentsia and Revolution: Russian Views of Bolshevism, 1917-1922, 1986; editor: Perestroika and Soviet Culture, 1989, Imperial Russia, New Histories for the Empire, 1998; editor Kritika, 1978-80; mem. editl. bd. Ind.-Mich. Series in Russian and East European Studies, Kritika, 1999—; contbr. articles to profl. jours. Fulbright-Hayes Rsch. award, 1991, Krupp Found. fellow, Ctr. for European Studies, Harvard U., 1977-78, Whiting fellow, 1980-81, Am. Coun. Learned Socs. fellow, 1983-84, Hoover Inst. Postdoctoral fellow, 1990-91; grantee NEH, 1984, 97, Harvard U., 1982-84, Internat. Rsch. and Exchs. Bd., Acad. Exch. with the USSR, 1987-88, 91, Fulbright-Hays, 1991, U. Mich., 1990, 91, 93, 94, 97. Mem. Am. Hist. Assn., Am. Assn. for the Advancement of Slavic Studies, Social Sci. Rsch. Coun. (joint com. on Soviet studies 1988-93), Nat. Coun. for Eurasia and East European Rsch., Phi Beta Kappa. Office: NYU 53 Washington Sq South New York NY 10012 E-mail: jburbank@umich.edu.

BURCH, AMY, communications media executive; Bur. chief Springfield Gannett News Svc., 1999—. Office: Gannett News Svc State Capital Bldg Press Rm-Mezzanine Springfield IL 62706

BURCH, STEPHEN KENNETH, financial services company executive, real estate investor; b. Fairmont, W.Va., Feb. 1, 1945; s. Kenneth Edward and Gloria Lorraine (Wilson) B.; m. Juliana Yuan Yuan, June 17, 1972 (div. Feb. 1985); children: Emily, Adrien. AB in Econs., Washington U., St. Louis, 1969. V.p. TSI Mgmt., Los Angeles, 1970-71; pres. Investors Choice Cattle Co., 1972-76; v.p. Clayton Brokerage Co., St. Louis, 1976-84; pres. Yuan Med. Lab., 1976-78; v.p. Restaurant Assocs., 1982-83, Am. Capital Equities, St. Louis, 1984-89; pres., owner Burch Properties, Inc., 1984—; owner Clayton-Hanley, Inc., 1987-88; pres., owner Clayton Securities Services, Inc., 1988—; CEO Huntleigh Securities Corp., 2000—, also bd. dirs. Mng. ptnr. 600 S. Ptnrs., St. Louis, 1976-87, Midvale Ptnrs., St. Louis, 1979—; mng. mem. Del Coronado Investment Co., LLC, 1997—. Bd. dirs. AMC Cancer Rsch. Ctr., 1989-91. Mem. Sigma Phi Epsilon (pres. alumni bd. 1981-87). Avocation: wine, movies. Office: Clayton Securities Svcs Inc 112 S Hanley Rd Ste 102 Saint Louis MO 63105-3418 E-mail: sburch@hntlgh.com.

BURCHAM, EVA HELEN (PAT BURCHAM), retired electronics technician; b. Bloomfield, Ind., Apr. 11, 1941; d. Paul Harold and Hazel Helen (Buzan) B. Grad., Blackstone Sch. of Law, 1988, Paralegal Inst., Phoenix, 1991; grad. paralegal, So. Career Inst., Boca Raton, Fla., 1991. With Naval Weapons Support Ctr./Crane Div. Naval Surface Warfare, Crane, Ind., 1967-76, 78-80; electronics technician Naval Weapons Support Ctr., 1980-97. With U.S. Army, 1976-77, with Res. 1977-81. Named to Am. Women's Hall of Fame. Mem. NAFE (exec. bd. chair), NOW, Am. Soc. Naval Engrs., Soc. Logistics Engrs., Am. Legion, Federally Employed Women, Fed. Women's Program, Profl. Women's Network (pres. 1993, bd. dirs.), Blacks in Govt., Nat. Paralegal Assn. (registered paralegal), Nat. Fedn. Paralegal Assn., Inc., Toastmasters (gov.). Roman Catholic. Home: 200 W Washington St Loogootee IN 47553-2324

BURDI, ALPHONSE ROCCO, anatomist; b. Chgo., Aug. 28, 1935; s. Alphonse Rocco and Anna (Basilo) B.; m. Sandra Shaw, Mar. 22, 1968; children— Elizabeth Anne, Sarah Lynne. B.S., No. Ill. U., DeKalb, 1957; M.S., U. Ill., 1959, U. Mich., 1961, Ph.D., 1963; Doctorate (hon.), U. Athens, Greece, 2000. Predoctoral fellow physiology U. Ill., 1957-59; NSF summer fellow U. Mich., 1960, NIH trainee, 1960-61, NIH predoctoral research fellow, 1962, mem. faculty, 1962—, prof. cell and devel. biology, 1974—; rsch. scientist Center for Human Growth and Devel. Dir. integrated pre-med.-med. program U. Mich. Mem. editorial bd.: Cleft Palate Jour. 1972-88 , Am. Jour. Phys. Anthropology, 1971-75, C.C. Thomas Am. Lectr. Series in Anatomy, 1971-88 , Jour. Dental Research, 1977-87 . Grantee NIH. Mem. Internat. Assn. Dental Research, Am. Assn. Dental Research, Am. Cleft Palate Assn., Teratology Soc., Am. Assn. Anatomists, Am. Assn. Phys. Anthropology, Sigma Xi. Home: 2600 Page Ct Ann Arbor MI 48104-6249 Office: U Mich Dept Cell & Devel Biology Med Sci Bldg 2 Ann Arbor MI 48109-0616

BURG, H. PETER, financial executive; b. Akron; BS, MBA, U. Akron; postgrad., Harvard U. Fin. analyst trainee Ohio Edison, assoc. fin. analyst, econ. analyst, dir. fin. studies, treas., 1974, v.p., 1985, sr. v.p., CFO, 1989, FirstEnergy Corp., pres., COO OH, 1998-99, pres. & CEO, 1999-00; chmn. & CEO FirstEnergy Corp, 2000—. Interim pres. Pa. Power, 1994-95; pres. Ohio Edison, The Illuminating Co., Toledo Edison Co.; mem. fin. com. Edison Elec. Inst.; bd. dirs. Energy Ins. Mutual, Key Bank. Bd. dirs. Summit County chpt. ARC; past pres. U. Akron Alumni Assn.; past bd. dirs. Akron Child Guidance Ctr.; active various coms. United Way. Office: FirstEnergy Corp 18th Fl 76 S Main St Fl 18 Akron OH 44308-1812

BURG, JAMES ALLEN, state agency administrator, farmer; b. Mitchell, S.D., Apr. 22, 1941; s. Albert Leo and Pearl Margaret (Linafelter) B.; m. Bernice Marie Kaiser, July 22, 1967; children: Jeff, Cory, Casey, Julie, Lisa. BS, S.D. State U., 1963. Fieldman Fed. Land Bank, Yankton, S.D., 1964-67; farmer Wessington Springs, 1967—; mem. S.D. Ho. Reps., Pierre, 1975-83, S.D. State Senate, Pierre, 1984-86; pub. utility commr. State of S.D., 1987—. Served to maj. USNG, 1963—. Mem. S.D. Retailers Assn. (bd. dirs. 1983—), Jaycees (pres. Wessington Springs chpt.), S.D. C. of C. (bd. dirs. 1983-84), Gamma Sigma Delta. Democrat. Roman Catholic. Lodge: KC. Home and Office: RR 1 Wessington Springs SD 57382-9801

BURG, RANDALL K. federal judge; b. Mpls., Apr. 11, 1951; BA, U. Minn., 1973, JD, 1976. Part-time magistrate judge U.S. Dist. Ct. Minn., Bemidji, 1990—. Office: US Courthouse 207 4th St NW Bemidji MN 56601-3114

BURGER, HENRY G. vocabulary scientist, anthropologist, publisher; b. N.Y.C., June 27, 1923; s. B. William and Terese R. (Felleman) B.; m. Barbara G. Smith, Nov. 29, 1991. BA with honors (Pulitzer scholar), Columbia Coll., 1947; MA, Columbia U., 1965, Ph.D. in Cultural Anthropology (State Doctoral fellow), 1967. Indsl. engr. various orgns., 1947-51; Midwest mfrs. rep., 1952-55; social sci. cons. Chgo. and N.Y.C., 1956-67; anthropologist Southwestern Coop. Ednl. Lab., Albuquerque, 1967-69; assoc. prof. anthropology and edn. U. Mo., Kansas City, 1969-73, prof., 1973-93, prof. emeritus, 1994—, founding mem. univ. wide doctoral faculty, 1974-93; founder, pub. The Wordtree, Overland Park, Kans., 1984—. Lectr. CUNY, 1957-65; adj. prof. ednl. anthropology U. N.Mex., 1969; anthrop. cons. U.S. VA Hosp., Kansas City, 1971-72; speaker in field. Author: Ethno-Pedagogy, 1968, 2d edit., 1968; editor, compiler: The Wordtree, a Branching Dictionary for Solving Physical and Social Problems, 1984; selected for exhibit at 3 insts.; selected as a topic in Cambridge Ency. of the English Lang., 1995—; 7-time citee in Oxford English Dictionary; mem. editl. bd. Coun. Anthropology and Edn., 1975-80; author linguistic periodical column New Times, New Verbs, 1988—; contbr. to anthologies; author articles. Capt. AUS, 1943-46. NSF Instl. grantee, 1970 Fellow World Acad. Art and Sci., Am. Anthrop. Assn. (life), Royal Anthrop. Inst. Gt. Britain (life); mem. European Assn. for Lexicography, Internat. Assn. Semiotic Studies, English-Speaking Union (v.p. Kansas City chpt. 1995-96), Dictionary Soc. N.Am. (life, terminology com.), Kans. Acad. Sci. (life), Assn. Internationale de Terminologie, Academie Europeenne des Scis., Arts et Lettres (corr.), Soc. Conceptual and Content Analysis by Computer, Columbia U. Club, Phi Beta Kappa. Achievements include discovery of the branchability of processes (corresponding, for materials, to the periodic table of elements); research on computerized causality and reasoning. Office: The Wordtree 10876 Bradshaw St Overland Park KS 66210-1148 E-mail: burger@cctr.umkc.edu.

BURGESS, JAMES EDWARD, newspaper publisher, executive; b. LaCrosse, Wis., Apr. 5, 1936; s. William Thomas and Margaret (Forseth) B.; m. Catherine Eleanor, Dec. 20, 1958; children: Karen E. Burgess Hardy, J. Peter, Sydney Ann, R. Curtis Student, Wayland Acad.; BS, U. Wis. Pub. Ind. Record, Helena, Mont., 1969-71, Tribune, LaCrosse, Wisc., 1971-74; v.p. newspapers Lee Enterprises, Davenport, Iowa, 1974-81, exec. v.p., 1981-84, dir., 1974-85, Madison (Wis.) Newspapers, Inc., 1975-93, pres., 1984-93; pub. Wis. State Jour., Madison, 1984-94. Chmn. Edgewood Coll., Madison, 1984—; founder Future Madison, Inc.; chmn. SAVE Commn.; bd. dirs. Madison Cmty. Found., U. Wis. Med. Found. Mem. Wis. Newspaper Assn. (past pres.), Inland Daily Press Assn. (pres., chmn. 1982-84), Wis. Assn. Lakes (bd. dirs., pres., chair). Home: 6102 S Highlands Ave Madison WI 53705-1113 Office: PO Box 55060 Madison WI 53705-8860

BURGESS, JAMES HARLAND, physics educator, researcher; b. Portland, Oreg., May 11, 1929; s. Harland F. B. and Marion U. (Burgess); m. Dorothy R. Crosby, June 10, 1951; children: Karen, Donald, Joanne. B.S., Wash. State U., 1949, M.S., 1951; Ph.D., Washington U., St. Louis, 1955. Sr. engr. Sylvania Electric Products, Mountain View, Calif., 1955-56; research assoc. Stanford U., Palo Al to, 1956-57, asst. prof. physics Palo Alto, 1958-62; assoc. prof. Washington U., St. Louis, 1962-73, prof., 1973-98, prof. emeritus, 1998—. Cons. in field, 1956-66. Mem. Am. Phys. Soc., Am. Assn. Physics Tchrs., Phi Beta Kappa, Sigma Xi Office: Washington U Physics Dept 1 Brookings Dr Saint Louis MO 63130-4899

BURGESS, RICHARD RAY, oncology educator, molecular biology researcher, biotechnology consultant; b. Mt. Vernon, Wash., Sept. 8, 1942; s. Robert Carl and Irene Marjorie (Wegner) B.; m. Ann Baker, June 17, 1967; children— Kristin, Andreas B.S. in Chemistry, Calif. Inst. Tech., 1964; Ph.D. in Biochemistry and Molecular Biology, Harvard U., 1969. Helen Hay Whitney fellow Inst. Molecular Biology, Geneva, Switzerland, 1969-71; asst. prof. oncology McArdle Lab. Cancer Research U. Wis., Madison, 1971-77, assoc. prof., 1977-82, prof., 1982—, dir. Biotech. Ctr., 1984-96, James D. Watson Prof. Oncology, 2001—. Cons. in field; mem. NSF study sect. in biochemistry, 1979-84; chmn. bd. Consortium for Plant Biotech. Rsch., Inc., 1992-96. Series editor U. Wis. Biotech. Ctr. Resource Manuals; editor-in chief Jour. Protein Expression and Purification, 1990—; contbr. articles to profl. jours. Bd. dirs. Coun. Biotech. Ctrs., 1991-93; mem. Gov.'s Coun. on Biotech. Grantee NSF, 1978-80, 85-90, NIH, 1980—, Nat. Cancer Inst., 1971—; Guggenheim fellow, 1983-84; recipient medal Waksman Inst., 1999. Mem. Am. Soc. Biochemistry and Molecular Biology, Am. Chem. Soc. (Pfizer award 1982), Am. Assn. Cancer Research, Am. Soc. Microbiology, Protein Soc. Home: 10 Knollwood Ct Madison WI 53713-3479 Office: U Wis McArdle Lab Cancer Rsch 1400 University Ave Madison WI 53706-1526

BURGHART, JAMES HENRY, electrical engineer, educator; b. Erie, Pa., July 18, 1938; s. Chester Albert and Mary Virginia (Burke) B.; m. Judith Ann Hoff, July 8, 1961; children— Jill Kathryn, Mark Alan. B.S. in Elec. Engring, Case Inst. Tech., 1960, M.S. (U.S. Steel Found. fellow 1961-63), 1962, Ph.D., 1965. Asst. prof., then assoc. prof. elec. engring. SUNY, Buffalo, 1969-75; prof. elec. engring. Cleve. State U., 1975—, chmn. dept., 1975-85, 89-97. Served as officer USAF, 1965-68. Mem. IEEE (chmn. Cleve. sect. 1980-81, sec. region 2 1989-96, profl. activities coord. region 2 1997-2000, Ohio area chair region 2 2001—), Am. Soc. Engring. Edn., Sigma Xi, Eta Kappa Nu. Home: 5501 Strathaven Dr Cleveland OH 44143-1970 Office: 1983 E 24th St Cleveland OH 44115-2403 E-mail: j.burghart@ieee.org.

BURHOE, BRIAN WALTER, automotive service executive; b. Worcester, Mass., Apr. 9, 1941; s. Walter De Forest and Dorothy Merrium (Gould) B.; m. Lynda Clayton, May 28, 1960 (div. May 1972); children: Mark S., Ty C., Scott M.; m. Joan Elaine Bredenberg, Oct. 21, 1989. Arts Baccalaureate, Clark U., Worcester, 1963, MA in History, Internat. Relations, 1971; cert. advanced mgmt. program, Northwestern U., 1985. Tchr. Orleans (Mass.) Sch. System, 1965-67; mgr. labor rels. Ill. Central R.R., Chgo., 1967-74, exec. asst., 1974-77; dir. human resources Midas Internat. Corp., 1977-79, v.p. human resources, 1979-89, sr. v.p. human resources, 1989-98; pres. The Old Bookseller, Inc., 1998—. Mem. Ill. Safety Coun. (chmn. 1992-94). Avocation: collecting out of print books. Home: 325 Nebraska St Frankfort IL 60423 Office: The Old Bookseller Inc 11 S White St Frankfort IL 60423

BURICK, LAWRENCE T. lawyer; b. Dayton, Ohio, May 15, 1943; s. Lee and Doris (Brenner) B.; m. Cynthia Joy Rosen, Aug. 31, 1969; children: Carrie R., Samuel J. BA, Miami U., 1965; JD, Northwestern U., 1968. Bar: Ohio 1968. Assoc. Smith & Schnacke, Dayton, 1969-78, ptnr., 1978-89, Thompson Hine LLP, Dayton, 1989—. Chmn. Dayton Jewish Ctr., Ohio, 1982—83, Jewish Cmty. Rels. Coun., 1980—81; pres. Jewish Fedn. Greater Dayton, Ohio, 1989—93, bd. dir., 1977—; chmn. United Jewish Campaign, 1997—99, Nat. Conf. Cmty. and Justice, 2002—; bd. dir. Jewish Edn. in Svc. to N.Am., 1994—99, v.p., 1997—99; bd. dir.. Nat. Conf. of Cmty. & Justice, 1997—, treas., 1998—, v.p., 1999—; bd. dir. Beth Abraham Synagogue, 1997—. Recipient Wasserman Leadership award, Jewish Fedn. Greater Dayton, 1978. Mem. Ohio State Bar Assn., Dayton Bar Assn., Am. Bankruptcy Law Forum, Am. Bankruptcy Inst. Office: Thompson Hine LLP PO Box 8801 2000 Courthouse Plz NE Dayton OH 45401-8801 E-mail: larry.burick@thompsonhine.com.

BURK, ROBERT S. lawyer; b. Mpls., Jan. 13, 1937; s. Harvey and Mayme (Cottle) B.; m. Eunice L. Silverman, Mar. 22, 1959; children: Bryan, Pam, Matt. BBA in Indsl. Rels., U. Minn., 1959; LLB, William Mitchell Coll. Law, 1965. Bar: Minn. 1966; qualified neutral under Rule 114 of the Minn. Gen. Rules of Practice, 1995—. Labor rels. cons. St. Paul Employers Assn., 1959-66; labor rels. mgr. Koch Refining Co., St. Paul, 1966-72, mgr. indsl. rels., 1972-75, mgr. indsl. rels., environ. affairs, 1975-77; sr. atty. Popham, Haik, Schnobrich & Kaufman, Ltd., Mpls., 1977-95, pres., CEO, 1986-90; ptnr. Burk & Seaton, P.A., Edina, Minn., 1995-2001, Burk & Landrum, P.A., Edina, 2001—. Chair bd. trustees William Mitchell Coll. Law, St. Paul, 1994-96, sec. 1991. Recipient Hon. Ronald E. Hachey Outstanding Alumnus award William Mitchell Coll. Law Alumni Assn., 1993. Mem. ABA (labor sect.), Minn. Bar Assn. (labor sect.). Office: Burk & Landrum PA 7400 Metro Blvd Ste 100 Edina MN 55439 Office Fax: 952-835-1867. E-mail: rburk@burklandrum.com.

BURKE, BRIAN B. state legislator, lawyer; b. Milw., Apr. 19, 1958; s. Thomas Joseph and Mary White (Higgins) B.; m. Patricia J. Coorough, Aug. 7, 1982; children: Colleen Marie, Kathleen Clare, Erin Elizabeth. BA magna cum laude, Marquette U., 1978; JD, Georgetown U., 1981; grad., FBI Citizen's Acad., Milw., 1999. Bar: Wis. 1981, U.S. Dist. Ct. (ea. and we. dists.) Wis. 1981, U.S. Ct. Appeals (7th cir.) 1983, U.S. Supreme Ct. 1984. Asst. dist. atty. Milwaukee County, Milw., 1981-84; alderman Milw. Common Coun., 1984-88; mem. Wis. Senate, Madison, 1988—. Mem. editl. bd. Georgetown Internat Law Jour.; contbr. articles to profl. jours. Trustee Milw. Pub. Libr., 1984-88, Pabst Theatre Bd., Milw., 1984-88, Milw. County Federated Libr. Sys., 1997—; commr. Milw. Met. Sewerage Dist., 1990—, Milw. Redevel. Authority, 1985-88, Wis. Ctr. Dist. Bd., 1996—, Hist. Preservation Commn., Milw., 1987-88; exec. bd. Wis. Pub. Utility Inst., 1993—; mem. State Capitol and Exec. Residence Bd., 1996—, Wis. Trust for Hist. Preservation, 1992—; mem. Dem. Leadership Coun., Nat. Conf. State Legis. Environ. Com.; mem. Wis. Environ. Edn. Bd., 1995—; mem. U. Wis. Hosps. and Clinics Authority, 1996—. Named Legislator of Yr. Wis. Urban Transit Assn., 1997, Vietnam Vets. Am., 1997-2000, Wis.'s Environ. Decade Clean 16 award, 1989-00, Bridge Builder's award Nature Conservancy, 1994, Profl. Firefighters Wis., 2001; recipient Cesar Chavez Humanitarian award Hispanic Leadership Coun., 1994, Friend of Wis. Jewish Cmty. award Wis. Jewish Conf., 1994, Friend of Hispanic Cmty. award United Cmty. Ctr., 1994, Hon. Riverkeeper award Friends of the Menomonee River, 1996, Disting. Svc. award Wis. Alliance of Cities, 1992-98, Atty. Gen.'s award for outstanding leadership on law enforcement issues, 1999, Clean Energy Leadership award, 1999, Voices of Courage in Public Policy award Wisc. Coalition Against Sexual Assault, 2000, Comdr.'s award for pub. svc Dept. of Army, 1999, Ptnrs. for Survival award Equal Justice Coalition of State Bar of Wis., 2000, Gaylord Nelson award 1000 Friends of Wis., 2000, Promise to the Earth Award, Greening Milw., 2001, Svc. to Marquette award Marquette Alumni, 2001, Lifetime Achievement award Wis. Environ. Decade, 2002; named to Washington H.S. Hall of Fame, 2001. Mem. Washington Heights Neighborhood Assn., State Hist. Soc., Hispanic C. of C., Greater Mitchell Street Assn., Shamrock Club of Wis., Phi Beta Kappa. Democrat. Roman Catholic. Avocation: tennis. Office: Wis Senate PO Box 7882 Madison WI 53707-7882 E-mail: sen.burke@legis.state.wis.us.

BURKE, DANIEL J. state legislator; b. Chgo., Dec. 17, 1951; Student, Loyola U., Berlitz Sch. Lang., DePaul U. Dep. city clk., Chgo, 1979—; Ill. state rep. Dist. 23, 1991—. Mem Edn. Appropriations, Election Law, Elem. & Secondary Edn., Labor and Commerce, Transp. & Vehicles Coms., Ill. Ho. of Reps. Mem. Internat. Mcpl. Clks. Assn. (legis. co-chmn.), Gov. Fin. Officers Assn. Address: 2650 W 51st St Chicago IL 60632-1560

BURKE, DERMOT, artistic director; m. Karen Russo; children: Daniel, Kevin, Margaret Kathleen. Ballet master, resident choreographer, artistic dir. Am. Repertory Ballet Co., 1979-92; exec. dir. Dayton (Ohio) Ballet, 1992—. Choreographer Pacific Northwest Ballet, Am. Repertory Ballet, Dayton Ballet. Office: Dayton Ballet 140 N Main St Dayton OH 45402-1750

BURKE, EDWARD MICHAEL, alderman; b. Chgo., Dec. 29, 1943; s. Joseph and Ann (Dolan) B.; m. Anne Marie McGlone, 1968; children: Jennifer, Edward, Emmett, Sarah. BA, DePaul U., 1965, JD, 1968. Atty. Klafter & Burke; underwriter Lloyd's of London, 1980—; alderman Chgo. City Coun., 1969—. Mem. com. on budget and govt. ops., vice chair rules and ethics com., mem. energy, environ. protection and pub. utilities com., police and fire com., zoning com.; former chmn. Dem. com. and alderman 14th ward, Chgo. Mem. Chgo. and Cook County Criminal Justice Commn., 1975; counsel Ill. Mcpl. Problems Commn., 1975; mem. Econ. Devel. Commn.; mem. Chgo. Plan Commn.; bd. dirs. Navy Pier Devel. Authority, USO; mem. Ill. Com. for Employer Support of the Guard and Res., One Hundred Club of Cook County, Military Order of World Wars, Southwest Realty Bd., Back of the Yards Businessman's Assn., SW Parish Neighborhood Fedn., Chgo. Lawn C. of C.; chmn. Police and Firemen's Death Benefit Fund; hon. mem. Chgo. Conv. and Tourism Bd. 1st lt. U.S. Army Res. Recipient Order of the Holy Family Evangelical Catholic Diocese of the Northwest, 1999, Public Svc. awrd Mex. Am. C. of C., 1999, Leadership award Kelly H.S. Cmty. Coun., 1999, Brighton Park Neighborhood Coun. Svc. award, 1999, Support for Bosnian Peace Keepers Appreciation award NATO, 1999, Catholic Lawyer of Yr. award Catholic Lawyers Guild of Chgo., 1998, Achievement in Gov. award Aspira, 1998, Rerum Novarum award St. Joseph Seminary Archdiocese of Chgo., 1998, Man of Yr. award Ill.-Ireland C. of C., 1995, Advocate of Yr. award AHA, Father Terme award for Outstanding Civic Leadership Cenacle Retreat House, 1992, Loyalty Day award VFWUS, 1992, Legislative Svc. award, Chgo. Lung Assn, 1991, Statesman of Yr. award Internat. Union of Operating Engrs. Local 150, 1991, Recognition award Soc. Human Resource Professionals, 1991, Pax et Bonum award, St. Peter's Catholic Ch., 1991, Brotherhood award for Outstanding Civic Svc. Nat. Conf. of Christians and Jews, 1991, Appreciation award Am. Cancer Soc., 1991, Disting. Citizen award Mt. Carmel H.S., 1991, Chgo. Father of Yr. award Chgo. Father's Day Com., 1990, Irishman of Yr. award, Chgo. Limerick Assn., 1990, Gratitude award Chgo. Firefighters Union Local No. 2, 1989, Ill. Enterprise Zone award Ill. Dept. of Commerce and Cmty. Affairs, 1989, Man of Yr. award Men of Tolentine, 1985, Ill. Assn. of Retarded Citizens award, 1981, Man of Yr. award Chgo. Police Capts. Assn., 1975. Mem. ABA, Ill. Bar Assn., Chgo. Bar Assn., Moose, K of C (4th degree, Leo XIII coun.), Celtic Lawyers' Assn. Am., Order of Holy Sepulchre, Irish Fellowship Club (chmn. bd. dirs.), Am. Legion (Frank Leahy Post 1974), Sovereign Military Order of Malta, Ill. Com. for Employer Support of the Guard and Reserve. Roman Catholic. Office: 2650 W 51st St Chicago IL 60632-1560

BURKE, JAMES DONALD, museum administrator; b. Salem, Oreg., Feb. 22, 1939; s. Donald J. and Ellin (Adams) B.; m. Diane E. Davies, May 17, 1980 B.A., Brown U., 1961; M.A., U. Pa., 1966; Ph.D., Harvard U., 1972. Curator Yale U. Art Gallery, New Haven, 1972-78; asst. dir. St. Louis Art Mus., 1978-80, dir., chief exec. officer, 1980-99, dir. emeritus, 1999—. Cons., panel mem. IRS, Washington, 1980—; scholar-in-residence Washington U., St. Louis, 1999—, Mercantile Libr., U. Mo., St. Louis, 1999—. Author: Jan Both, 1974, Charles Meyron, 1974; contbr. articles to profl. jours.; organizer in field. Pres. St. Louis Art Mus. Found., 1985—99, Gateway Found., 1986—. Fulbright fellow, 1968-69 Mem. Coll. Art Assn., Print Council Am., Am. Assn. Mus., Assn. Art Mus. Dirs. Office: Saint Louis Art Mus One Fine Arts Dr Forest Park Saint Louis MO 63110

BURKE, KATHLEEN B. lawyer; b. Bklyn., Sept. 2, 1948; BA, St. John's U., 1969, JD, 1973. Bar: Ohio 1973. Ptnr. Jones, Day, Reavis & Pogue, Cleve. Vice chair Notre Dame Coll. of Ohio, 2000—. Pres. Cleve. Skating Club, 2000—; vice chmn. Notre Dame Coll. Ohio, 2000—. Fellow Ohio State Bar Found. (pres. 2000); mem. Ohio State Bar Assn. (pres. 1993-94). Office: Jones Day Reavis & Pogue North Point 901 Lakeside Ave E Cleveland OH 44114-1190

BURKE, KENNETH ANDREW, advertising executive; b. Sept. 9, 1941; s. Frank Flory and Margret Anne (Tomè) B.; m. Karen Lee Burley, July 1, 1968; children: Allison Leigh, Aric Jason. BSBA in Mktg., Bowling Green (Ohio) State U., 1965. Mem. Green Bay Packers Nat. Football League, Sask. Roughriders, Can. Football League; acct. exec. lang, Fisher, Stashower, Cleve., 1967-69; v.p., acct. supr. Tracy-Locke, Dallas, 1969-72; v.p. Grey Advt., N.Y.C., 1972-76, Griswold Eshleman, Cleve., 1976-79; sr. v.p., gen. mgr. Simpson Mktg., Columbus, Ohio, 1979-81; pres., CEO, chmn. Martcom Inc., 1981-91; chmn. ret. Ad Factory, Inc., Advt. and Mktg., Ad Factory Outlets, 1991-98; exec. v.p. Berkshire Product Inc., Tampa, Fla., 1983-89. Author: Bordini and the Black Knight, 1975. Mem. adv. bd. columbus chpt. Am. Cancer Soc., 1980-88. Recipient USN Achievement award, 1975. Mem. Am. Mktg. Assn., Columbus Advt. Fedn., NFL Alumni Assn., Cleve. Advt. Club (Merit award 1968), Columbus C. of C., Upper Arlington C. of C., Theta chi. Republican. Roman Catholic. Home: 1753 Bedford Rd Columbus OH 43212-2004 Office: Ad Factory Corp Offices 22 Gay Street Columbus OH 43215 E-mail: kenburke@adfactoryinc.com.

BURKE, PAUL BRADFORD, lawyer, manufacturing executive; b. Detroit, Mar. 3, 1956; s. Donald Joseph and Janet Cottrell (Davis) B.; m. Shannon Louise Egan, Aug. 12, 1978; children: Kelly Marie, Clayton Davis. BA, Yale U., 1978; JD, U. Mich., 1981. Bar: Minn. 1981. Assoc. Oppenheimer Wolff et al, Mpls., 1981-83, Delaney & Solum, Mpls., 1983; assoc. gen. counsel BMC Industries, Inc., St. Paul, 1983-85, v.p., sec., gen. counsel, 1985-87, pres., CEO Mpls., 1991—, now also chmn.; v.p. Ft. Lauderdale (Fla.) ops. Vision-Ease Lens div. BMC Industries, Inc., 1987-89, pres., 1989-91. Lectr. Minn. Inst. Legal Edn., Mpls., 1986, Advanced Legal Edn., St. Paul, 1983. Mem. ABA (fed. regulation of securities com. 1983—), Minn. Bar Assn., Hennepin County Bar Assn., Am. Soc. Corp. Secs., Midwest Corp. Counsel Ctr. Methodist. Clubs: Mpls. Golf; St. Paul Athletic. Office: BMC Industries Inc 1 Meridian Xing Ste 850 Richfield MN 55423-3938

BURKE, PAUL E., JR. governmental relations consultant; b. Kansas City, Mo., Jan. 4, 1934; s. Paul E. and Virgnia (Moling) B.; m. Debbie Weihe; children: Anne Elizabeth, Kelly Patricia, A. Catherine, Jennifer Marie. BSBA, U. Kans., 1956. Mem. Kans. Ho. of Reps., 1972-74, Kans. Senate, 1975-97, majority leader, 1985-89; pres. Issues Mgmt. Group, Inc., Lawrence, Kans., 1996—. Chmn. Legis. Coordinating Coun., 1995; pres.-elect Nat. Conf. State Legislatures, 1990-91, pres., 1992; pres. Nat. Conf. State Legislatures Found., 1994; mem. Fed. Adv. Commn. Intergovtl. Rels., 1993-96. Councilman City of Prairie Village, Kans., 1959-63; mem. Kans. Turnpike Authority, 1965-69, chmn., 1969; mem. adv. bd. Sect. Corrections, 1973-78; mem. Gov.'s Mil. Adv. Coordinating Coun., 2002--. Capt. USAF, 1956-59; capt. USNR, 1963-88. Mem. Kans. Assn. Commerce and Industry, Masons, Shriners, Rotary. Republican. Episcopalian. Address: 2009 Camelback Dr Lawrence KS 66047

BURKE, RAYMOND L. bishop; ordained June 29, 1975. Bishop Diocese of La Crosse, 1994—. Office: PO Box 4004 La Crosse WI 54602-4004

BURKE, ROBERT HARRY, surgeon, educator; b. Cambridge, Mass., Dec. 22, 1945; s. Harry Clearfield and Joan Rosalyn (Spire) B.; m. Margaret Cauldwell Fisher, May 4, 1968; children: Christopher David, Catherine Cauldwell. Student, U. Mich. Coll. Pharmacy, 1964-67; DDS, U. Mich., 1971, MS, 1976; MD, Mich. State U., 1980. Diplomate Am. Bd. Oral and Maxillofacial Surgery, Am. Bd. Cosmetic Surgery. Pvt. practice cosmetic and reconstructive surgery, Ann Arbor, Mich. House officer oral and maxillofacial surgery U. Mich. Sch. Dentistry, U. Mich. Hosp., Ann Arbor, 1973-76; clin. asst. prof. dept. oral surgery U. Detroit Sch. Dentistry, 1976-77; adj. asst. rsch. scientist Ctr. Human Growth and Devel. U. Mich., 1976-77, adj. rsch. investigator, 1982-85; clin. asst. prof. Mich. State U., East Lansing, 1978-80, 1987—; house officer surg. emphasis St. Joseph Mercy Hosp., Ann Arbor, 1980-81; adj. rsch. investigator dept. anatomy U. Mich. Med. Sch., 1982-85; clin. asst. prof. oral and maxillofacial surgery U. Mich., 1984-86; lectr. U. Detroit Sch. Dentistry, 1986, assoc. clin. prof. oral and maxillofacial surgery, 1987-90; cons., lectr. dept. occlusion U. Mich. Sch. Dentistry, 1986; head sect. dentistry and oral surgery dept. gen. surgery St. Joseph Mercy Hosp., 1982-87, mem. exec. com. dept. gen. surgery, 1984-87; chmn. com. emergency care rev. Beyer Meml. Hosp., Ypsilanti, Mich., 1986, also active, 1987, 1990-2000; active staff St. Joseph Meml. Hosp.; courtesy staff Saline (Mich.) Cmty. Hosp., 1978-88; Chelsea (Mich.) Med. Ctr., 1978-88, 90-92, McPherson Cmty. Hosp., Howell, Mich., 1984-87, Herrick Meml. Hosp., 1998—, Bixby Hosp., 1998—, Annapolis Hosp., 2000—, Oakwood Hosp., 2000—; dir. Mich. Ctr. Cosmetic Surgery. Mem. editl. bd. Topics in Pain Mgmt., 1985—; contbg. editor Am. Jours. Cosmetic surgery, 1990-91; sect. editor Internat. Jour. Aesthetic and Restorative Surgery, 1992-95, 96-2000, Internat. Jour. Cosmetic Surgery and Aesthetic Dermatology, 2000—. Campaign chmn. med. and dental sects. United Way Washtenaw County, Ann Arbor, 1982, dental sect. 1983; profl. adv. com. March of Dimes Genesee County Valley Chpt., Flint, 1979; pres. Huron Pkwy. Pla. Condominium, 1984—. Fellow: Am. Acad. Aesthetic and Restorative Surgery, Am. Coll. Oral and Maxillofacial Surgeons, ACS, Internat. Coll. Surgeons; mem.: Inst. Study Profl. Risk, Washtenaw County Med. Soc., European Assn. for Cranio-Maxillofacial Surgery, Chalmers Lyons Acad. oral Surgery, European Soc. Aesthetic Surgery and Liposuction, Brit. Soc. for Oral and Maxillofacial Surgeons, Internat. Soc. Cosmetic Laser Surgeons, Am. Assn. Craniomaxillofacial Surgeons, Am. Assn. Cosmetic Maxillofacial Surgeons, AMA, Pres.'s Club, Victor's Club, Omicron Kappa Upsilon. Congregationalist. Avocations: triathlon, chang moo kwan, tae kwon do. Home: 5207 Red Fox Run Ann Arbor MI 48105-9364 Office: 2260 S Huron Pky Ann Arbor MI 48104-5151 E-mail: info@robertburke.com.

BURKE, STEVEN FRANCIS, organization executive; b. St. Paul, May 23, 1952; s. Paul Stanley and Irene Marie (Wagner) B.; m. Kathleen Mary Frost, Mar. 24, 1974; children: Susan, Kathleen, Elizabeth, Michael, Thomas. BS, U. Minn., 1974; owner pres. mgmt. program, Harvard U., 1991. V.p. N.Am. Outdoor Group Inc., Minnetonka, Minn., 1978-84, exec. v.p., 1984-88, pres., 1988-90, pres. and chief exec. officer, 1990—, also bd. dirs., 1978—; pres. N.Am. World Travel Inc., 1989-91, also bd. dirs., 1989-91. Bd. dirs. Larson and Burke Inc., Hopkins, Minn., Comml. Banl Chaska, Minn. Mem. pastoral coun. St. Hubert Cath. Ch., Chanhassen, Minn., 1984-85; pres. Wildlife Forever Inc., Hopkins, 1987—. Capt. USMC, 1974-78. Mem. NRA, N. Am. Hunting Club (pres. 1978—), N. Am. Fishing Club (pres. 1988—). Avocations: hunting, fishing, golfing, racquetball. Office: Comml Bank Chaska 507 N Walnut St Chaska MN 55318-2075

BURKE, THOMAS JOSEPH, JR. lawyer; b. Oct. 23, 1941; s. Thomas Joseph and Violet (Green) B.; m. Sharon Lynne Forke, Aug. 29, 1964; children: Lisa Lynne, Heather Ann. BA, Elmhurst Coll., 1963; JD, Chgo.-Kent Coll. Law, 1966. Bar: Ill. 1966, U.S. Dist. Ct. (no. dist.) Ill. 1967, U.S. Ct. Appeals (7th cir.) 1972, U.S. Supreme Ct. 1972, U.S. Ct. Appeals (11th cir.) 1994, U.S. Ct. Appeals (6th cir.) 1995. Assoc. Lord, Bissell & Brook, Chgo., 1966-74, ptnr., 1974—. Fellow: Am. Coll. Trial Lawyers; mem.: Assn. Advancement Automotive Medicine, Soc. Automotive Engrs., Product Liability Adv. Coun., Ill. Assn. Def. Trial Counsel, Def. Rsch. Inst., Trial Lawyers Club Chgo., Soc. Trial Lawyers, Chgo. Bar Assn., Mid-Day Club, Phi Delta Phi, Pi Kappa Delta. Republican. Roman Catholic. Office: Lord Bissell & Brook 115 S La Salle St Ste 3300 Chicago IL 60603-3801 E-mail: tburke@lordbissell.com.

BURKE, THOMAS RICHARD, community college administrator; b. St. Louis, Oct. 2, 1944; s. Lloyd Richard and Frances Elizabeth (Yelton) B.; m. Sara Lou Janes, July 3, 1969; 1 child, Kimberly Ayre. BA, U. Miss., 1970, MA, 1972, PhD, 1981. Instr. Mountain Empire C.C., Big Stone Gap, Va., 1972-74, asst. prof., 1974-77, assoc. prof. history, 1977-80, acting pres., 1977, dean instrn., 1976-80; v.p. Three Rivers C.C., Poplar Bluff, Mo., 1980-86; pres. Independence C.C., 1986—, Kansas City (Kans.) C.C. Chmn. City of Poplar Bluff Hist. Commn. Served with USAF, 1965-69. Edn. Professions Devel. Act fellow, 1970-72. Mem. Am. Assn. Cmty. and Jr. Colls. (chmn. 1984-85), Kans. Assn. C.C. (chmn.), S.E. Kans. Consortium Colls. and Univs., Mo. Hist. Assn., Phi Delta Kappa, Masons, Shriners. Methodist. Office: Kansas City CC Office of Pres 7250 State Ave Kansas City KS 66112-3003

BURKEMPER, SARAH B. state agency administrator; m. Ben Burkemper; 2 children. B Econs. and Bus. Adminstrn. Fin. cum laude, Truman State U., 1992, M Acctg., 1992, Washington U., St. Louis, 1997. CPA Mo. Pub. adminstr. Lincoln County, Mo., 1996—, also registered guardian. Active Trinity Luth. Ch.; bd. govs. Truman State U., 2001—. Office: 201 Main St Troy MO 63379

BURKEN, RUTH MARIE, utility company executive; b. Kenosha, Wis., Sept. 25, 1956; d. Richard Stanley and Anne Theresa (Steplyk) Wojtak; m. James H. Burken, Oct. 15, 1988. AAS, Gateway Tech. Inst., 1976; BA, U. Wis., Parkside, 1980; AAS, Coll. of DuPage, 1995. Transp. aide Kenosha Achievement Ctr., 1977; libr. clk. U. Wis.-Parkside, Kenosha, 1978-80, lifeguard, 1980; asst. mgr. K Mart Corp., Troy, Mich., 1980-88, regional office supr., 1988, internal auditor, 1989-92, sr. field auditor, 1992-98; gen. auditor Nicor Gas, Naperville, Ill., 1998-2000, billing splst., 2000—.

Mem. VFW, NAFE, Distributive Edn. Clubs Am. (parliamentarian 1976), U. Wis.-Parkside Alumni Assn., Am. Gas Assn. Roman Catholic. Office: Nicor Gas 1844 W Ferry Rd Naperville IL 60563-9600 E-mail: rburken@nicor.com.

BURKETT, RANDY JAMES, lighting designer; b. DuBois, Pa., Nov. 12, 1955; s. Lloyd John and Helen Louise (North) B.; m. Carol Jeanne Collins, Aug. 22, 1981; 1 child, Meredith. B in Archtl. Engring., Pa. State U., 1978. Application engr. Johns-Manville, Denver, 1978-80; lighting designer HOK, St. Louis, 1980-82, assoc., 1982-85, v.p., 1986-88; pres. Randy Burkett Lighting Design, Inc., 1988—. Contbr. articles to profl. jours. Recipient Internat. Illumination Design Award of Excellence, 1987, 89, 93, 96, Edison award, 1993. Mem. Illuminating Engring. Soc., Internat. Assn. Lighting Designers (pres. 1996--97). Home: 5334 Chapelford Ln Saint Louis MO 63119-5017 Office: Randy Burkett Lighting Design Inc 127 Kenrick Plz Ste 207 Saint Louis MO 63119-4416

BURKEY, LEE MELVILLE, lawyer; b. Beach, N.D., Mar. 21, 1914; s. Levi Melville and Mina Lou (Horner) B.; m. Lorraine Lillian Burghardt, June 11, 1938; 1 child, Lee Melville, III B.A., U. Ill., 1936, M.A., 1938; J.D. with honor, John Marshall Law Sch., 1943. Bar: Ill., 1944, U.S. Dist. Ct., 1947, U.S. Ct. Appeals, 1954, U.S. Supreme Ct.; 1983; cert. secondary tchr., Ill. Tchr. Princeton Twp. High Sch., Princeton, Ill., 1937-38, Thornton Twp. High Sch., Harvey, 1938-43; atty. Office of Solicitor, U.S. Dept. Labor, Chgo., 1944-51; ptnr. Asher, Gubbins & Segall and successor firms, 1951-94; of counsel, 1995—. Lectr. bus. law Roosevelt Coll., 1949-52; bd. dirs., pres. West Suburban Fin. Corp., 1975-94. Contbr. numerous articles on lie detector evidence. Trustee, Village of La Grange, Ill., 1962-68, mayor, 1968-73, village atty., 1973-87; commr., pres. Northeastern Ill. Planning Commn., Chgo., 1969-73; mem. bd. dirs. United Ch. Christ, Bd. of Homeland Ministries, 1981-87; mem. exec. com. Cook County Coun. Govts., 1968-70; life mem. La Grange Area Hist. Soc.; bd. dirs. Better Bus. Bur. Met. Chgo., Inc., 1975-82, Plymouth Place, Inc., 1973-82; mem. exec. bd., v.p. S.W. Suburban Ctr. on Aging, 1993—. Brevet 2nd Lt. Ill. Nat. Guard, 1932. Recipient Disting. Alumnus award John Marshall Law Sch., 1973, Good Citizenship medal S.A.R., 1973, Patriot medal S.A.R., 1977, Meritorious Svc. award Am. Legion Post 1941, 1974, Honor award LaGrange Area Hist. Soc., 1987, Cmty. Svc. award S.W. Suburban Ctr. on Aging, 2000; named to Order of Ky. Cols. Fellow Coll. Labor and Employment Lawyers (charter); mem. ABA (coun., sect. labor and employment law 1982-86, governance officer 1986-96), Ill. Bar Assn., Chgo. Bar Assn., SAR (state pres. 1977), S.R., La Grange Country Club, Masons, Order of John Marshall, Theta Delta Chi. Mem. United Ch. of Christ. Office: 125 S Wacker Dr Chicago IL 60606-4402

BURKHARDT, EDWARD ARNOLD, railway executive; b. N.Y.C., July 23, 1938; s. Edward Arnold Burkhardt Sr. and Kathryn C. (Pfister) Dow; m. Sandra Kay Schwaegel, June 9, 1967; 1 child, Cynthia Kay. BS Indsl. Adminstrn., Yale U., 1960. Various operating positions Wabash R.R., St. Louis, 1960-64, Norfolk and Western Rlwy., St. Louis, 1964-67; asst. to gen. mgr. Chgo. Northwestern Transp. Co., 1967-68, gen. supt. transp., 1968-70, asst. v.p. transp., 1970-76, v.p. mktg., 1976-79, v.p. transp., 1979-87; bd. dirs., pres., CEO Wis. Ctrl. Transp. Corp., Chgo., 1987-99; chmn. Tranz Rail Ltd., 1993-99; bd. dirs., pres. Algoma Ctrl. Rlwy. Inc., 1995-99; bd. dirs., chmn., CEO English, Welsh and Scottish Ry. Ltd., 1995-99; bd. dirs., chmn. Australian Transport Network, 1997-99; pres./CEO Rail World, Inc., 1999—; pres. RailPolska, 1999—. Pres. CargoCentral Europe, 2000—; chmn. Baltic Rail Svc., 2000—. Trustee Village of Kenilworth, Ill., 1984-93; bd. dirs. Wheeling & Lake Erie Rlwy. Co., Nat. Railway Mus., York, England, Lake Superior Mus. Transp., Duluth, Minn., John W. Barringer R.R. Libr., St. Louis, Nat. Railroad Mus., Green Bay, Wis. Hon. consul New Zealand, Chgo. Mem. Am. Assn. R.R. Supts. (bd. dirs.), Western Ry. Club , Kenilworth Club, Union League Club. Republican. Episcopalian. Office: Rail World Inc Ste 500N 8600 W Bryn Mawr Ave Chicago IL 60631-3579 E-mail: eaburkhardt@railworld-inc.com.

BURKHOLDER, DONALD LYMAN, mathematician, educator; b. Octavia, Nebr., Jan. 19, 1927; s. Elmer and Susie (Rothrock) B.; m. Jean Annette Fox, June 17, 1950; children: Kathleen, Peter, William. BA, Earlham Coll., 1950; MS, U. Wis., 1953; PhD, U. N.C., 1955. Asst. prof. math. U. Ill., Urbana, 1955-60, assoc. prof., 1960-64, prof., 1964-98, prof. Ctr. for Advanced Study, 1978-98, prof. emeritus, 1998—. Sabbatical leaves U. Calif., Berkeley, 1961-62, Westfield Coll., U. London, 1969-70; vis. prof. Rutgers U., 1972-73; researcher Stanford U., 1961, Hebrew U., 1969, Mittag-Leffler Inst., Sweden, 1971, 82, U. Paris, 1975, Institut des Hautes Études Scientifiques, 1986, U. Edinburgh, 1986, Tel Aviv U., 1989, U. New South Wales, 1991; Mordell lectr. Cambridge U., 1986; Zygmund lectr. U. Chgo., 1988; trustee Math. Scis. Rsch. Inst., 1981-84; bd. govs. Inst. Math. and Its Applications, 1983-85, chmn., 1985. Editor: Annals Math. Statistics, 1964-67. Fellow Inst. Math. Statistics (Wald lectr. 1971, pres. 1975-76); mem. NAS, Am. Math. Soc. (mem. editorial bd. Trans. 1983-85), London Math. Soc., Am. Acad. Arts and Scis. Achievements include research in probability theory and its applications to other branches of analysis. Home: 506 W Oregon St Urbana IL 61801-4044

BURKHOLDER, WENDELL EUGENE, retired entomology educator, researcher; b. Octavia, Nebr., June 24, 1928; s. Elmer and Susie (Rothrock) B.; m. Leona Rose Flory, Aug. 18, 1951; children: Paul Charles, Anne Carolyn, Joseph Kern, Stephen James. A.B., McPherson Coll., 1950; M.Sc., U. Nebr., 1956; Ph.D., U. Wis., 1967. Rsch. entomologist U.S. Dept. Agr., 1956-96, Madison, Wis., 1965-96; asst. prof. U. Wis.-Madison, 1967-70, asso. prof., 1970-75, prof. entomology, 1975-96; prof. emeritus, 1996—. Lectr. in field. Mem. editorial bd.: Jour. Chem. Ecology, 1980-96, Jour. Stored Products Rsch., 1992-98; contbr. chpts. to books and articles to profl. jours. Served with U.S. Army, 1951-53. NSF grantee, 1972-75, 79; Rockefeller Found. grantee, 1974-77; Nat. Inst. Occupational Safety and Health grantee, 1977-79 Mem. AAAS, Entomol. Soc. Am., Wis. Entomol. Soc., Wis. Acad. Sci. Arts, and Letters, Internat. Soc. Chem. Ecology, Sigma Xi. Achievements include patents in field. Home: 1726 Chadbourne Ave Madison WI 53705-4108 Office: U Wis Entomology Dept 545 Russell Lab Madison WI 53706-1598 E-mail: Burkhold@entomology.wisc.edu.

BURKS, KEITH W. pharmaceutical executive; Exec. v.p. Bindley Western Industries, Inc., Indpls., 1993-2001; pres. Bindley Western a Cardinal Health Co., 2001—. Office: Bindley Western Industries a Cardinal Health Co 8909 Purdue Rd Indianapolis IN 46268-3146

BURLEIGH, WILLIAM ROBERT, newspaper executive; b. Evansville, Ind., Sept. 6, 1935; s. Joseph Charles and Emma Bertha (Wittgen) B.; m. Catherine Anne Husted, Nov. 28, 1964; children: David William, Catherine Anne, Margaret Walden. BS, Marquette U., Milw., 1957; LLD (hon.), U. So. Ind., 1979. From reporter to editor, pres. Evansville Press, 1951-77; editor Cin. Post, 1977-83; v.p., gen. editl. mgr. Scripps-Howard Newspapers, Cin., 1984-86, sr. v.p. newspapers and publs., 1986-90, exec. v.p., 1990-94, pres., COO, 1994-96, pres., CEO, 1996-99; chmn., CEO E.W. Scripps Co., 1999-2000, chmn., 2000—. With AUS, 1957-58. Mem. Queen City Club, Cin. Lit. Club, Cin. Country Club, Cin. Comml. Club, Alpha Sigma Nu. Roman Catholic. Office: E W Scripps 312 Walnut St Cincinnati OH 45202-4024

BURMASTER, ELIZABETH, school system administrator; B Music Edn., M Ednl. Adminstrn., U. Wis. Music and drama tchr.; state supt. pub. instrn. State of Wis., Madison, 2001—; prin. Madison West H.S., 1999—2001. Mem. bd. regents U. Wis., Wis.; mem. Edn. Commn. U.S., Wis. Tech. Coll. Sys. Bd., Ednl. Comms. Bd., Very Spl. Arts Wis., Gov.'s Work-Based Learning Bd., Wis. Tobacco Control Bd.; bd. dirs. TEACH Wis. Mem.: Coun. of Chief State Sch. Officers, SAI-Music Assn., Tempo Internat., Assn. Wis. Sch. Adminstrs., Tempo. Mailing: PO Box 7841 Madison WI 53707-7841

BURNER, DAVID L. aerospace services company executive; b. Lodi, Ohio; m. Rosemary Burner; 3 children. BS in Commerce, Ohio U., 1962. Various postions aerospace industry; with B.F. Goodrich Co., Richfield, Ohio, 1983—, pres. aerospace divsn., 1987, pres., 1995—, CEO, chmn. and pres., 1996—. Bd. dirs. B.F. Goodrich Co., bd. govs. Aerospace Inst. Am., Washington. Bd. dirs. The Greater Cleve. Growth Assn.; active Cleve. Scholarship Programs Inc., Summit Edn. Initiative, Salvation Army Greater Cleve., Ohio U. Found., Cleve. Orch. Office: The BF Goodrich Co Four Coliseum Ctr 2730 W Tyvola Rd Ste 600 Charlotte NC 28217-4578

BURNETT, JEAN BULLARD (MRS. JAMES R. BURNETT), biochemist; b. Flint, Mich., Feb. 19, 1924; d. Chester M. and Katheryn (Krasser) Bullard; B.S., Mich. State U., 1944, M.S., 1945, Ph.D. (Council fellow), 1952; m. James R. Burnett, June 8, 1947. Research assoc. dept. zoology Mich. State U., East Lansing, 1954-59, dept. biochemistry, 1959-61, acting dir. research biochem. genetics, dept. biochemistry, 1961-62, assoc. prof., asst. chmn. dept. biomechanics, 1973-82, prof. dept. anatomy, 1982-84, prof. dept. zoology, Coll. Natural Sci. and Coll. Osteo. Medicine, 1984— ; assoc. biochemist Mass. Gen. Hosp., Boston, 1964-73; prin. research assoc. dermatology Harvard, 1962-73, faculty medicine, 1964-73, also spl. lectr., cons., tutor Med. Sch.; vis. prof. dept. biology U. Ariz., 1979-80. USPHS, NIH grantee, 1965-68; Gen. Research Support grantee Mass. Gen. Hosp., 1968-72; Ford Found. travel grantee, 1973; Am. Cancer Soc. grantee, 1971-73; Internat. Pigment Cell Conf. travel grantee, 1980; recipient Med. Found. award, 1970. Mem. AAAS, Am. Chem. Soc., Am. Inst. Biol. Sci., Genetics Soc. Am., Soc. Investigative Dermatology, N.Y. Acad. Scis., Sigma Xi (Research award 1971), Pi Kappa Delta, Kappa Delta Pi, Pi Mu Epsilon, Sigma Delta Epsilon. Home: PO Box 805 Okemos MI 48805-0805 Office: Mich State Univ Dept Zoology Natural Sci Bldg East Lansing MI 48824

BURNETT, ROBERT A. retired publisher; b. Joplin, Mo., June 4, 1927; s. Lee Worth and Gladys (Plummer) B.; m. Gloria M. Cowden, Dec. 25, 1948; children: Robert A., Stephen, Gregory, Douglas, David, Penelope. AB, U. Mo., 1948. Salesman Cowden Motor Co., Guthrie Center, Iowa; then Equitable Life Assurance Soc., Joplin, Mo.; retired chmn., CEO Meredith Corp.; ret., 1991. Bd. dirs. Hartford Fin. Svcs., ITT Industries. Served with AUS, 1945-46. Congregationalist. Home: 2942 Sioux Ct Des Moines IA 50321-1446 Office: Regency West 6 4600 Westown Pkwy Ste 115 West Des Moines IA 50266-1000

BURNHAM, JOHN CHYNOWETH, historian, educator; b. Boulder, Colo., July 14, 1929; s. William Allds and Florence (Hasbrouck) B.; m. Marjorie Ann Spencer, Aug. 31, 1957; children: Leonard, Abigail, Peter, Melissa. BA, Stanford U., 1951, PhD, 1958; MA, U. Wis., 1952. Lectr. Claremont Men's Coll., Calif., 1956-57; mem. faculty Stanford U., 1956, 57-58; postdoctoral fellow Founds. Fund for Research in Psychiatry, New Haven, 1958-61; asst. prof. San Francisco State Coll., 1961-63; from mem. faculty to rsch. prof. history Ohio State U., Columbus, Ohio, 1963—2002, rsch. prof. history, 2002—. Sr. Fulbright lectr. U. Melbourne, Australia, 1967, U. Tasmania, Australia, 1973, U. New Eng., Australia, 1973; Tallman vis. prof. history and psychology Bowdoin Coll., Brunswick, Maine, 1982; cons. panelist NEH, 1974—, dir. nat. seminar for professions, 1975, 76, 79; assoc. area adv. Coun. on Internat. Exch. of Scholars, 1975-78; mem. spl. study sect. NIH, 1978-79, 84-85, 92. Author: Psychoanalysis and American Medicine 1894-1918, 1967, Jelliffe: American Physician and Psychoanalyst, 1983, How Superstition Won and Science Lost: Popularizing Science in the United States, 1987, Paths into American Culture: Psychology, Medicine, and Morals, 1988, Bad Habits: Drinking, Smoking, Taking Drugs, Gambling, Sexual Misbehavior, and Swearing in American History, 1993, How the Idea of Profession Changed the Writing of Medical History, 1998; (with Buenker and Crunden) Progressivism, 1977; editor: Science in America-Historical Selections, 1971; editor Jour. of History of Behavioral Scis., 1997—2000. Recipient Publ. award Ohio Acad. History, 1993. Fellow AAAS, APA; mem. Am. Assn. for History of Medicine (v.p. 1988-90, pres. 1990-92), Orgn. Am. Historians, Am. Hist. Assn., History of Sci. Soc., Midwest History of Sci. Junto (pres. 1982-83), Cheiron Internat. Soc. for History of Behavioral and Social Scis. (presiding officer 1977-78) Home: 4158 Kendale Rd Columbus OH 43220-4136 Office: Ohio State U Dept History 230 W 17th Ave Columbus OH 43210-1367

BURNITZ, JEROMY, professional baseball player; b. Westminster, Calif., Apr. 15, 1969; Baseball player N.Y. Mets, 1993-94, Cleve. Indians, 1995-96, Milw. Brewers, 1996—. Office: Milw Brewers County Stadium PO Box 3099 Milwaukee WI 53201-3099*

BURNS, C(HARLES) PATRICK, hematologist-oncologist; b. Kansas City, Mo., Oct. 8, 1937; s. Charles Edgar and Ruth (Eastham) B.; m. Janet Sue Walsh, June 15, 1968; children— Charles Geoffrey, Scott Patrick. BA, U. Kans., 1959, MD, 1963. Diplomate Am. Bd. Internal Medicine, subsplty. bds. hematology, med. oncology. Intern Cleve. Met. Gen. Hosp., 1963-64; asst. resident in internal medicine Univ. Hosps., Cleve., 1966-68, sr. resident in hematology, 1968-69; instr. medicine Case Western Res. U., 1970-71; asst. chief hematology Cleve. VA Hosp., 1970-71; asst. prof. medicine U. Iowa Hosps., Iowa City, 1971-75, assoc. prof. medicine, 1975-80, prof., 1980—, dir. sect. med. oncology, co-dir. divsn. hematatol./oncology, 1980-85, dir. div. hematology, oncology, blood marrow transplantation, 1985-99. Vis. scientist Imperial Cancer Rsch. Fund Labs., London, 1982-83; cons. U.S. VA Hosp.; mem. study sect. on exptl. therapeutics NIH, Cancer Ctr. Support Rev. Commn. Nat. Cancer Inst., NIH, NIH Cancer Clin. Investigation Rev. Com., Com. H Nat. Cancer Inst., VA Med. Rsch. Svc. Career Devel. Com.; mem. external adv. com. U. Oreg. Cancer Ctr., 1994—. Mem. bd. assoc. editors Cancer Rsch., 1988—; rsch. and publs. on hematologic malignancies, tumor lipid biochemistry, leukemia and oncology, role of oxidation in cancer treatment. Served to capt. M.C., AUS, 1964-66. Am. Cancer Soc. fellow in hematology-oncology, 1968-69, USPHS fellow in medicine, 1969-70; USPHS career awardee, 1978 Fellow ACP; mem. AAAS, Am. Bd. Internal Medicine (Subsplty. bd. hematology 1992-98), Am. Soc. Hematology, Am. Assn. Cancer Rsch., Internat. Soc. Hematology, Ctrl. Soc. Clin. Rsch., Am. Soc. Clin. Oncology, Soc. Exptl. Biology and Medicine, Oxygen Soc., Royal Soc. Medicine, Am. Fedn. Clin. Rsch., Internat. Soc. for the Study of Fatty Acids and Lipids, Phi Beta Pi, Lambda Chi Alpha, Alpha Omega Alpha. Home: 2046 Rochester Ct Iowa City IA 52245-3246 Office: U Iowa Univ Hosps Dept Medicine Iowa City IA 52242 E-mail: c-burns@viowa.edu.

BURNS, DANIEL T. corporate lawyer; BA, Brown U., 1973; JD, Vanderbilt U., 1976. Bar: Ill. 1976, Fla. 1977. Gen. atty. Roper Corp., 1976-80; atty. Cotter & Co., Chgo., 1980-88, gen. counsel, 1988-90, v.p., 1990—. Address: Cotter & Co 8600 W Bryn Mawr Ave Chicago IL 60631-3579

BURNS, SISTER ELIZABETH MARY, hospital administrator; b. Estherville, Iowa, Mar. 3, 1927; d. Bernard Aloysius and Viola Caroline (Brennan) B. Diploma in Nursing, St. Joseph Mercy Sch. Nursing, Sioux City, Iowa, 1952; B.S. in Nursing Edn, Mercy Coll., Detroit, 1957; M.Sc. in Nursing, Wayne State U., 1958; Ed.D., Columbia U., 1969. Joined Sisters of Mercy, Roman Cath. Ch., 1946; nursing supr. Mercy Med. Center, Dubuque, Iowa, 1952-55; supr. orthopedics and urology St. Joseph Mercy Hosp., Sioux City, 1955-56; dir. Sch. Nursing, 1958-63; chmn. dept. nursing Mercy Coll. of Detroit, 1963-73; dir. health services Sisters of Mercy, Province of Detroit, 1973-77; pres., chief exec. officer Marian Health Center, Sioux City, 1977-87; sabbatical leave, 1988. Coord. life planning Sisters of Mercy, 1989-90, mem. province adminstrv. team, 1990-98; cons. Trinity Health, 2001—. Bd. dirs. Mercy Sch. Nursing of Detroit, 1968-77; mem. exec. com. Greater Detroit Area Hosp. Council, 1973-77; trustee St. Mary Coll., Omaha, 1981-82, Briar Cliff Coll., Sioux City, 1981-87; chmn. Mercy Health Adv. Council, 1978-80. Mem. Western Iowa League for Nursing (pres. 1960-62), Nat. League for Nursing, Sisters of Mercy Shared Svcs. Coordinating Com., Cath. Hosp. Assn. (trustee 1977-80), Sisters of Mercy Health Corp. (trustee 1988-90, governance coord. 1998-2001), Mercy Health Svcs. (chair bd. 1990-95, membership bd. 1995-98, historian 1998-2001). Office: 27870 Cabot Dr Novi MI 48377-2920 E-mail: eburns@mercydetroit.org., burnse@trinity-health.org.

BURNS, ELIZABETH MURPHY, media executive; b. Superior, Wis., Dec. 4, 1945; d. Morgan and Elizabeth (Beck) Murphy; m. Richard Ramsey Burns, June 24, 1984. Student, U. Ariz., 1963-67. Promotion and programming sec. Sta. KGUN-TV, Tucson, 1967-68; programming and traffic sec. Sta. KFMB-TV, San Diego, 1968-69; owner, operator Sta. KKAR, Pomona, 1970-73; co-owner, pres. Evening Telegram Co. (parent co. Murphy Stas.); pres. Morgan Murphy Stas., Madison, Wis., 1976—. Bd. dirs. Nat. Guardian Life Ins. Co., Republic Bank, various media stas. and corps. Mem. Nat. Assn. Broadcasters, Wis. Broadcasters Assn., Madison Club, Nakoma Country Club, Northland Country Club (Duluth), Boulders Country Club (Carefree, Ariz.). Roman Catholic. Avocations: golf, travel. Home: 180 Paine Farm Rd Duluth MN 55804-2609 Office: Sta WISC-TV 7025 Raymond Rd Madison WI 53719-5053

BURNS, JAMES B. prosecutor; b. Quincy, Ill., Sept. 21, 1945; married; 3 children. BA in History, Northwestern U., 1967, JD, 1971. Former profl. basketball player Chgo. Bulls, Dallas Chaparrals; asst. U.S. atty., then dep. chief and chief criminal litigation divsn. U.S. Dept. Justice, Chgo., 1971-78; assoc. Isham, Lincoln & Beale, 1978-80, ptnr., 1980-88, Keck, Mahin & Cate, Chgo., 1988-93; U.S. atty. for no. dist. Ill. U.S. Dept. Justice, 1993-97; pvt. practice Sibley & Austin, 1997-00; Inspector General State of Illinois, Springfield, 2000—. Bd. trustees Northwestern U., Evanston, Ill., 1981-83; Dem. candidate for lt. gov. State of Ill., 1990. Office: Office of the Sec of State 213 State Capitol Springfield IL 62706-0001

BURNS, LARRY WAYNE, marshall; b. May 5, 1949; m. Donna Swords, Aug. 20, 1975; 2 children. AA, Okaloosa Walton C.C., Valparaiso, Fla., 1972; BS in Criminology, Fla. State U., 1974. With Scranton Office, Mid. Dist. Pa., 1975-77; with hdqrs. office Columbia, 1977-78; dep. marshal in charge U.S. Marshal Svc., Florence, S.C., 1978-82, supr. no. dist. Ga. Atlanta, 1982-85; chief dep. U.S. marshal Office of U.S. Marshal for No. Dist. Ind., South Bend, 1985—. Mem. Masons, Phi Theta Kappa.

BURNS, PETER C. science educator, engineering educator; came to U.S., 1995; BSc with honors, U. New Brunswick, Can., 1988; MSc in Geology, U. Western Ont., Can., 1990; PhD in Geology, U. Man., Can., 1994. Rsch. fellow Univ. Cambridge, Cambridge, England, 1994-95; post doctoral fellow Univ. N.Mex., 1995-96; vis. ass. prof. Univ. Ill., Urbana-Champaign, 1996-97; from asst. prof. to assoc. prof., dir. graduate studies Univ. Notre Dame, 1997-99, assoc. prof., 1999—. Contbr. articles to profl. jours. Recipient Donath medal Geol. Soc. Am., 1999. Achievements include research in mineralogy and crystallography, mineralogy of nuclear waste disposal, environmental mineralogy, mineral crystal structures and crystal chemistry, mineral structure energetics, mineral paragenesis. Office: U Notre Dame 160 Fitzpatrick Engring Notre Dame IN 46556 Fax: 219-631-9236. E-mail: pburns@nd.edu.

BURNS, RICHARD RAMSEY, lawyer; b. Duluth, Minn., May 3, 1946; s. Herbert Morgan and Janet (Strobel) B.; Jennifer, Brian; m. Elizabeth Murphy, June 15, 1984. BA with distinction, U. Mich., 1968, JD magna cum laude, 1971. Bar: Calif. 1972, U.S. Dist. Ct. (no. dist.) Calif. 1972, U.S. Ct. Appeals (9th cir.) 1972, Minn. 1976, U.S. Dist. Ct. Minn. 1976, Wis. 1983, U.S. Tax. Ct. 1983. Assoc. Orrick, Herrington, Rowley & Sutcliffe, San Francisco, 1971-76; ptnr. Hanft, Fride, P.A., Duluth, 1976—. Gen. counsel Murphy, McGinnis Media, Duluth, Minn.,1982—, Murphy TV Stas., Madison, Wis., 1982—. Chmn. Duluth-Superior Area Comty. Found., 1988-90; chair United Way of Greater Duluth, Inc., 1998-99; bd. dirs. Miller Dwan Found., Northland Coll., Ashland, Wis. Fellow Am. Coll. Trust and Estate Counsel; mem. Calif. Bar Assn., Wis. Bar Assn., Minn. Bar Assn. (exec. com. bd. govs., past chmn. probate and trust coun.), 11th Dist. Bar Assn. (past pres., past chmn. ethics com.), Arrowhead Estate Planning Coun. (pres. 1980), Northland Country Club (pres. 1982), Boulders Club, Kitchi Gammi Club (bd. dirs.). Republican. Avocations: travel, golf, tennis, fishing. Home: 180 Paine Farm Rd Duluth MN 55804-2609 Office: Hanft Fride PA 1000 First Bank Pl 130 W Superior St Ste 1000 Duluth MN 55802-2056 E-mail: rrb@hanftlaw.com.

BURNS, ROBERT ARTHUR, lawyer; b. Independence, Iowa, 1944; BS, Iowa State U., 1966; JD, U. Iowa, 1972. Bar: Minn. 1972, Iowa 1972. Ptnr. Dorsey & Whitney L.L.P., Mpls., 1978—. Office: Dorsey & Whitney LLP Ste 1500 50 S Sixth St Minneapolis MN 55402-1498 E-mail: burns.bob@dorseylaw.com.

BURNS, TERRENCE MICHAEL, lawyer; b. Evergreen Park, Ill., Mar. 2, 1954; s. Jerome Joseph Burns and Eileen Beatrice (Collins) Neary; m. Therese Porucznik, Mar. 24, 1979; children: David, Steven, Theresa, Daniel. BA, Loyola U., Chgo., 1975; JD, DePaul U., 1978. Bar: Ill. 1978, U.S. Dist. Ct. (no. dist.) Ill. 1978, U.S. Ct. Appeals (7th cir.) 1979, U.S. Supreme Ct. 1985, U.S. Dist. Ct. (no. dist.) Ind. 1989. Asst. state's atty. Cook County, Chgo., 1979-85; ptnr. Rooks, Pitts & Poust, 1985—. Mem. inquiry bd. Ill. Supreme Ct. Atty. Registration and Disciplinary Commn., Chgo., 1986-90, chair hearing bd., 1990—. Mem. ABA (ann. meeting adv. com.), Chgo. Bar Assn. (treas. 1997-99, 2d v.p. 1999-2000, 1st v.p. 2000-01, pres. 2001—, bd. mgrs. 1995-97, chair fin. com. 1997-99, criminal law com. 1979-83, jud. candidate evaluation com. 1981-86, 87-95, chmn. investigation divsn. evaluation com. 1991-92, chmn. hearing divsn. evaluation com. 1992-93, gen. chmn. 1993-95, ct. liaison com. 1993-95, tort reform subcom. 1997), Chgo. Bar Found. (bd. dirs. 1999-2000). Roman Catholic. Office: Rooks Pitts & Poust 10 S Wacker Dr Ste 2300 Chicago IL 60606-7407

BURNS, THAGRUS ASHER, manufacturing company executive, former life insurance company executive; b. Columbia City, Ind., Feb. 19, 1917; s. Harlow A. and Hazlette (Wise) B.; m. Dorothy Kimble, May 1, 1942; children: Steven L., Gerald A. A.B., Wabash Coll., 1939. With Lincoln Nat. Life Ins. Co., Ft. Wayne, Ind., 1939-80, treas., 1967-80, Lincoln Nat. Life Co., 1967-80, Lincoln Nat. Corp., 1968-80; pres. Burns Mfg. Inc., Ft. Wayne, 1980—. Treas., dir. Lincoln Nat. Life Found. Served to lt. USNR, 1942- 45. Mem. Financial Execs. Inst., Phi Beta Kappa. Achievements include inventor automatic feeder for typewriter, inserting machine and clipping catcher for hedge trimmer. Home and Office: 2118 Heritage Park Dr Fort Wayne IN 46805-5802

BURR, BROOKS MILO, zoology educator; b. Toledo, Aug. 15, 1949; s. Lawrence E. and Beverly Joy (Herald) B.; m. Patti Ann Grubb, Mar. 5, 1977 (div. July 1987); 1 child, Jordan Brooks. BA, Greenville Coll., 1971; MS, U. Ill., 1974, PhD, 1977. Cert. scuba diver, Nat. Assn. Underwater Instrs. Lab. instr. dept. biology Greenville (Ill.) Coll., 1971-72; rsch. asst.

Ill. Natural History Survey, Champaign, 1972-77, affiliate scientist Ctr. for Biodiversity Urbana, 1989—; from asst. prof. to prof. dept. zoology So. Ill. U., Carbondale, 1977—. Mem. adv. panel U.S. Fish and Wildlife Svc., 1990—; adj. prof. dept. biology U. N.Mex., Albuquerque, 1991—; adj. prof. dept. ecology, ethology and evolution U. Ill., 1993—. Co-author: A Distributional Atlas of Kentucky Fishes, 1986, A Field Guide to Fishes, North America North of Mexico, 1991 (selected as one of Outstanding Acad. Books of 1992 by Choice Mag.); contbr. more than 120 articles to profl. jours. Recipient Paper of Yr. award Ohio Jour. Sci., 1986, Coll. Sci. Rsch. award, So. Ill. Univ., 2001. Mem. AAAS, Am. Soc. Ichthyologists and Herpetologists (sec., mem. exec. com. 1990-94, pres.-elect 2000—), Soc. Systematic Zoology, Biol. Soc. Washington, Assn. Systematic Collections, Sigma Xi (Leo M. Kaplan award 1990). Achievements include the discovery and description of 9 species of fish new to science from North American fresh waters. Home: 203 S Wedgewood Ln Carbondale IL 62901-2147 Office: So Ill Univ Dept Zoology Carbondale IL 62901-6501 E-mail: burr@zoology.siu.edu.

BURR, DAVID BENTLEY, anatomy educator; b. Findlay, Ohio, June 28, 1951; s. Willard Bentley and Dorothy Eleanor (Beiler) B.; m. Lisa Marie Pedigo; children: Kathryn Lise, Michael David, Erik Johan. BA, Beloit Coll., 1973; MA, U. Colo., 1974, PhD, 1977. Instr. anatomy U. Kans. Med. Ctr., Kansas City, 1977-78, asst. prof. anatomy, 1978-80; asst. prof. anatomy and orthop. surgery W.Va. U., Morgantown, 1980-83, assoc. prof., 1983-86, prof., 1986-90; chmn. dept. anatomy and cell biology, prof. anatomy and orthopedic surgery Ind. U., Indpls., 1990—, chmn. dept. cell biology. Mem. adv. bd. dirs. Primate Found. Am., Tempe, Ariz., 1978—; cons. County Med. Examiner, Morgantown, 1983-89; mem. Adv. Group for the Treatment Human Remains, USDA, Monongahela Nat. Forest Svc., 1989; cons. NASA, 1990-91, Am. Inst. Biol. Sci., NAS, 1990—, U.S. Congress Office Tech. Assessment, 1990; mem. biochemistry study sect. Arthritis found., 1992-95; spl. grants rev. com. NIH, 1996-2000. Author: Structure, Function & Adaptation of Compact Bone, 1989, Skeletal Tissue Mechanics, 1998, Musculoskeletal Fatigue and Stress Fracture, 2001; mem. editl. bd. Bone, 1993—, Jour. Bone and Mineral Metabolism, 1994—, Jour. Biomech., 1999—, Calcif. Tiss. Int., 2000—; contbr. articles to profl. jours. Pres. First Ward Sch. PTA, Morgantown, 1987—88; sec. Cub Scout Pack Com., 1989; chmn. troop com. Boy Scouts Am., 1993—95; linesman Morgantown Soccer League, 1988; sec. Classic Ragtime Soc., 1997—98; clk. witness and svc. First Friends Meeting, 1999—2001; mem. adminstrv. bd. Epworth United Meth. Ch., Indpls., 1992—93. Rsch. grantee NIH, 1988—, Orthopedic Rsch. and Edn. Found., 1985-86. Mem.: Assn. Anatomy, Cell Biology and Neurobiology Chairpersons (pres. 2001—02), Am. Anatomy Assn. (exec. com. 1998—2001), Orthop. Rsch. Assn., Internat. Soc. Bone Mineral Rsch., Am. Soc. Bone Mineral Rsch. Avocations: piano, softball, racquetball, stamps, reading. Office: Ind U Sch Medicine Dept Anat & Cell Biology 635 Barnhill Dr Indianapolis IN 46202-5126 E-mail: dburr@iupui.edu.

BURRELL, THOMAS J. marketing communication executive; m. Joli Burrell. Founder, chmn. Burrell Comms. Group, Chgo., 1971—. Office: Burrell Comm Group Inc 20 N Michigan Ave Chicago IL 60602-4811

BURRIS, JOHN EDWARD, biologist, educator, academic administrator; b. Feb. 1, 1949; s. Robert Harza and Katherine (Brusse) Burris; m. Sally Ann Sandermann, Dec. 21, 1974; children: Jennifer, Margaret, Mary. AB, Harvard U., 1971; postgrad., U. Wis., 1971—72; PhD, U. Calif., San Diego, 1976. Asst. prof. biology Pa. State U., University Park, 1976—83, assoc. prof. biology, 1983—85, adj. assoc. prof., 1985—89, adj. prof., 1989—2001; pres. Beloit College, Beloit, Wis., 2000—. Dir. bd. biology NRC, Washington, 1984—89; exec. dir. Commn. Life Scis., 1988—92, mem., 1993—97; dir., CEO Marine Biol. Lab., Woods Hole, Mass., 1992—2000; pres.-elect Am. Inst. Biol. Scis., 1995, pres., 96; chmn. adv. com. student sci. enrichment program Burroughs Wellcome Fund, 1995—; life and microgravity scis. and applications adv. com. NASA , 1997—2001; trustee Krasnow Inst., Moscow, 1999—2002; bd. dirs. Radiation Effects Rsch. Found. Bd. trustees Grass Found., 2001—. Mem.: AAAS (bd. dirs. 2002—), Naples Stazione Zoologica, Consiglio Sci., Phi Beta Kappa. Home: 709 College St Beloit WI 53511-5571 Office: 700 College St Beloit WI 53511 E-mail: burrisj@beloit.edu.

BURRIS, JOSEPH STEPHEN, agronomy educator; b. Cleve., Apr. 18, 1942; s. Charles Richard and Catherine T. (Pravica) B.; m. Joan Peterson; children: Jeffery S., John C., Jennifer K., Jason R. B.S., Iowa State U., 1964; M.S., Va. Poly. Inst., 1965, Ph.D., 1967. Research asst., Nat. Def. fellow Va. Poly. Inst., Blacksburg, 1964-67, dir. tobacco analysis lab., 1967; asst. prof. Iowa State U., Ames, 1968-72, assoc. prof., 1972-76, prof. agronomy and seed sci., 1976-99, prof. emeritus, 1999—; pres. Burris Cons., 1999—. Internat. cons. on seed prodn. FAO/UN Devel. Program, World Bank. Contbr. articles to profl. publs. Pres. PTA, Ames, 1980-81. Mem. Am. Soc. Agronomy, Crop Sci. Soc. Am. (Seed Sci. award 1998), Assn. Ofcl. Seed Analysts Presbyterian. Office: Burris Cons 1707 Burnett Ave Ames IA 50010-5338

BURROUGHS, CHARLES EDWARD, lawyer; b. Milw., June 9, 1939; s. Edward Albert and Ann Monica (Bussman) B.; m. Kathleen Walton, Jan. 30, 1965; children— James, Michael, Lauri, Stephanie. B.S., U. Wis.-Madison, 1962, LL.B., 1965; LL.M., George Washington U., 1968. Bar: Wis. 1965, U.S. Dist. Ct. (ea. and we. dists.) Wis. 1965, U.S. Ct. Clms. 1967, U.S. Ct. Mil. Apls. 1967, U.S. Ct. Apls. (7th cir.) 1969, U.S. Supreme Ct. 1968. Assoc., Porter & Porter, Milw., 1969-71, Purtell, Purcell, Wilmot & Burroughs, 1971-86; ptnr. VonBriesen & Purtell, 1986-91, Hinshaw & Culbertson, Milw. Served to capt. U.S. Army, 1965-69. Mem. ABA, AHLA, HFMA, State Bar Wis. (pres. health law sect.). Roman Catholic. Club: Milw. Athletic. Home: 10937 N Hedgewood Ln Mequon WI 53092-4907

BURROWS, BRIAN WILLIAM, research and development manufacturing executive; b. Burnie, Tasmania, Australia, Nov. 15, 1939; came to U.S., 1966; s. William Henry and Jean Elizabeth (Ling) B.; 1 child, Karin; m. Penny Nathan Kahan, 1998. BSc, U. Tasmania, 1960, BSc with honors, 1962; PhD, Southampton U., 1966. Staff scientist Tyco Labs., Inc., Waltham, Mass., 1966-68; lectr. Macquarie U., Sydney, Australia, 1969-71; chef de sect. Battelle-Geneva, Switzerland, 1971-75; group leader Inco, Ltd., Mississauga, Ont., Can., 1976-77; program mgr., lab. dir. Gould, Inc., Rolling Meadows, Ill., 1977-86; v.p. rsch. and tech. USG Corp., Chgo., 1986—. Co. rep., Indsl. Rsch. Inst., Washington. Contbr. articles to tech. jours.; patentee in field. Fellow AAAS; mem. IEEE, Am. Chem. Soc., Materials Rsch. Soc., Union League Club. Home: 927 Longmeadow Ct Barrington IL 60010-9391 Office: USG Rsch Ctr 700 N Us Highway 45 Libertyville IL 60048-1268

BURROWS, PAUL A. consumer products executive; Various sr. mgmt. positions Broadway Stores, chief info. officer, 1993-96, Coldwell Banker Corp., L.A.; sr. v.p., chief info. officer ShopKo Stores, Inc., Green Bay, Wis., 1997—. Office: ShopKo Stores Inc 700 Pilgrim Way Green Bay WI 54304-5276

BURSTEIN, RICHARD JOEL, lawyer; b. Detroit, Feb. 9, 1945; s. Harry Seymour and Florence (Rosen) B.; m. Gayle Lee Handmaker, Dec. 21, 1969; children: Stephanie Faith, Melissa Amy. Grad., U. Mich., 1966; JD, Wayne State U., 1969. Bar: Mich. 1969, U.S. Ct. Appeals (ea. dist.) Mich. 1969. Ptnr. Smith Miro Hirsch & Brody, Detroit, 1969-81, Honigman Miller Schwartz & Cohn, Detroit, 1981-96. Bd. dirs. Sandy Corp., Troy, Mich.; bd. dirs. Met. Affairs Corp., Detroit; co-chmn. Artrain. Mem. Am. Coll. Real Estate Lawyers. Office: Honigman Miller Schwartz & Cohn 32270 Telegraph RdSuite 225 Bingham Farms MI 48025

BURT, ROBERT NORCROSS, retired diversified manufacturing company executive; b. Lakewood, Ohio, May 24, 1937; s. Vernon Robert and Mary (Norcross) B.; m. Lynn Chilton, Apr. 19, 1969; children: Tracy, Randy, Charlie. BSChemE, Princeton U., 1959; MBA, Harvard U., 1964. With Mobil Oil Corp., N.Y.C. and Tokyo, 1964—68; dir. corp. planning and acquisitions Chemetron Corp., Chgo., 1968—70, mgr. internat. div., 1970—73; dir. corp. planning FMC Corp., 1973—76, v.p. agrl. chems. group Phila., 1976—83, v.p. def. group San Jose, Calif., 1983—88, exec. v.p. Chgo., 1988—90, pres., 1990—91, chmn., CEO, 1991—2001. Bd. dirs. Phelps Dodge, Pfizer. Bd. dirs. Rehab. Inst. Chgo., 1991—; trustee Orchestral Assn. of Chgo. Symphony Orch., 1992—, vice chmn., 1995-99. Lt. USMC, 1959-62. Mem. Bus. Roundtable (policy com., chmn. environ. task force 1993-99, chmn. 1999-2001), Ill. Bus. Roundtable (vice chmn. 1999-2001). Avocations: reading, golfing, spectator sports. Home: 5 Kent Rd Winnetka IL 60093-1815

BURTON, CHARLES VICTOR, physician, surgeon, inventor; b. N.Y.C., Jan. 2, 1935; s. Norman Howard and Ruth Esther (Putziger) B.; m. Joy Burton; children— Matthew, Timothy, Andrew, Dawn, Stacy, Chad. Student, Johns Hopkins U., Balt., 1952-56; MD, N.Y. Med. Coll., 1960. Diplomate Am. Bd. Neurol. Surgery, Nat. Bd. Med. Examiners, Am. Bd. Forensic Medicine, Am Bd. Spinal Surgery. Intern surgery Yale U. Med. Ctr., 1961-62; asst. resident neurol. surgery Johns Hopkins Hosp., Balt., 1962-66, chief resident, 1966-67; assoc. chief surgery, chief neurosurgery USPHS Hosp., Seattle, 1967-69; vis. research affiliate Primate Ctr., U. Wash., 1967-69; asst. prof. neurosurgery Temple U. Health Scis. Ctr., Phila., 1970-73, assoc. prof., 1973-74, neurol. research coordinator, 1970-74; dir. dept. neuroaugmentive surgery Sister Kenny Inst., Mpls., 1974-81, med. dir. Low Back Clinic, 1978-81; med. dir. Inst. for Low Back Care, 1981-96; sr. med. dir. Inst. Low Back and Neck Care, 1996—. Biomed. Instrumentations Internat., Ltd., 1988-92; co-chmn. Joint Neurosurg. Com. on Devices and Drugs, 1973-77; chmn. adv. panel on neurologic devices FDA, 1974-77, Internat. Standards Orgn., 1974-76; mem. U.S. Biomed. Instrumentation Del. to Soviet Union, 1974. Editor Neuroorthopedics jour., 1987—. Patentee surgical devices, operating room fiberophic headlights, clin. therapy systems and techniques. Research fellow Nat. Polio Found., 1956, HEW, 1958; neurosurg. fellow Johns Hopkins Hosp., 1960-61, 62-67, 69-70 Fellow ACS (exec. com. Minn. chpt. 1989-92); mem. Congress Neurol. Surgeons (chmn. com. materials and devices 1972-79), Am. Assn. Neurol. Surgeons, Minn. Neurosurg. Soc., AAAS, ASTM (chmn. com. materials 1973-78), Internat. Soc. Study of Lumbar Spine (exec. com. 1986-89), N.Am. Spine Soc. (exec. com. 1987-91, chmn. com. on profl. conduct 1991-92, dir. coun. mem. affairs 1992-94, bd. dirs. 1990-94), Am. Nat. Standards Inst. (med. device tech. adv. bd. 1973-78), Am. Bd. Spine Surgery (bd. dirs. 1997—, chair ethics com. 1998—), Philadelphia County Med. Soc. (med.-legal com. 1970-74), Minn. Med. Assn. (Gold medal award for best sci. presentation at 1975 meeting, subcom. on med. testimony 1978—), Hennepin County Med. Soc. (med.-legal com. 1975—), Mpls. Acad. Medicine, Cor et Manus Soc., Profl. Assn. Diving Instrs. (underwater photography splty. diver), Am. Back Soc., Twin Cities Spine Soc. (pres. 1994-95), Back Pain Assn. Am. (hon. chmn. 1995—), bd. dirs. Am. Bd. Sinal Surgery, 1997, Chmn. Com. on Ethics, Am. Bd. of Spinal Surgery, 1998, Johns Hopkins U. Alumni Assn. (pres. Minn. chpt. 1988-92), Yale Surg. Soc., Alpha Epsilon Delta. Home: 148 W Lake St Excelsior MN 55331-1744 Office: Inst Low Back and Neck Care 2800 Chicago Ave Minneapolis MN 55407-1318

BURTON, DAN L. congressman; b. Indpls., June 21, 1938; m. Barbara Jean Logan, 1959; children: Kelly, Danielle Lee, Danny Lee II. Mem. Ind. Ho. Reps., Indpls., 1967-68, 77-80, Ind. State Senate, 1969-70, 81-82; owner ins. and real estate firm, 1968—; mem. U.S. Congress from 6th Ind. dist., 1983—. Mem. internat. rels. com.; chmn. govt. reform and oversight com. Pres. Vols. of Am.; pres. Ind. Christian Benevolent Assn., Com. for Constl. Govt., Family Support Ctr. Served with U.S. Army, 1957-58. Republican. Office: US Ho of Reps 2185 Rayburn Ofc Bldg Washington DC 20515-0001*

BURTON, DONALD JOSEPH, chemistry educator; b. Balt., July 16, 1934; s. Lawrence Andrew and Dorothy Wilhelmina (Koehler) B.; m. Margaret Anna Billing, June 21, 1958; children— Andrew, Jennifer, David, Julie, Elizabeth. B.S., Loyola Coll., Balt., 1956; Ph.D., Cornell U., 1961; postgrad., Purdue U., 1961-62. Asst. prof. chemistry dept. U. Iowa, Iowa City, 1962-67, assoc. prof., 1967-70, prof., 1970—, Roy Carver/Ralph Shriner prof. chemistry, 1989—. Recipient Gov.'s Sci. Medal for Sci. Achievement, 1988; Japanese Soc. for Promotion Sci. fellow, 1979 Mem. Am. Chem. Soc. (chmn. fluorine div. 1978, award for creative work in fluorine chemistry 1984, Midwest Chemistry award 1990), Chem. Soc. London, Sigma Xi, Alpha Chi Sigma. Home: 4304 Oakridge Trl NE Iowa City IA 52240-7735 Office: U Iowa Dept Chemistry Iowa City IA 52242 E-mail: donald-burton@uiowa.edu.

BURTON, GARY L. state legislator; b. Knoxville, Iowa, Aug. 26, 1945; m. Jennifer Grant; children: Dianne, Todd, Lance, Melinda, Tye, Nathan. BS, Ea. N.Mex. U., 1968. Former mem. Joplin (Mo.) City Coun.; Mo. State rep. Dist. 128, 1988—; ins. agt. Mem. energy and environ. com., budget com., appropriations/edn. and transp. coms., ins. com., mines and mining com., state parks com., recreation and natural resources com. Mo. Ho. Reps.; former mem. Joplin Exec. Call Program, econ. devel. market, area solid waste, chamber govt. affairs and Joplin mote tax coms. Mem. Elks, Joplin C. of C., Mo. Life Underwriters, Mo. Spl. Olympics (state treas.). Home: 1101 S Willard Ave Apt D Joplin MO 64801-3780

BURTON, RAYMOND CHARLES, JR. retired transportation company executive; b. Phila., Aug. 29, 1938; s. Raymond Charles and Phyllis (Clifford) B.; m. Madeline Ann Starmann, Feb. 13, 1999; children: Carolyn Starmann, Raymond Starmann. BA, Cornell U., 1960; MBA, U. Pa., 1963. Various operating positions Santa Fe Ry. Co., 1963-68, asst. controller, 1968-69; asst. treas. Santa Fe Industries, Chgo., 1969-74; asst. v.p. planning, treas. Burlington No., Inc., 1974-79, v.p. and treas., 1979-82; v.p. planning Internat. Harvester Co., Chgo., 1982; chmn., pres., CEO, TTX Co., 1982-2000; pres., CEO, Railbox Co., Railgon Co., Chgo., 1982-2000; ret., 2000. 1st lt. U.S. Army, 1960-61. Mem.: Met. Club. Republican. Presbyterian.

BURTON, WOODY, state legislator; b. Indpls., June 11, 1945; m. Volly Burton; children: Woody Lee, Jeff, April Stirling. Student, Ind. U. Real estate broker, mgr., carpenter Better Homes & Gardens; mem. Ind. State Ho. of Reps. Dist. 58, 1988—, mem. elections and apportionment com., mem. ins., corp. and small bus., roads and transp. coms., mem. ways and means com., chmn. fin. com. Mem. Johnson County Coun., 1980-84, County Planning Commn., 1983, County Coun. on Aging, 1983-85. Mem. Nat. Assn. Realtors, Ind. Assn. Realtors, Met. Indpls. Bd. Realtors, Ind. Auctioneers Assn., Greenwood Masonic Lodge, Scottish Rite, Murat Shrine.

BURWELL, ROBERT LEMMON, JR. chemist, educator; b. Balt., May 6, 1912; s. Robert Lemmon and Anne Hume (Lewis) B.; m. Elise Frank, Dec. 23, 1939 (dec. Nov. 2001); children: Mary Elise, Augusta Somervell. A.B., St. John's Coll., Annapolis, Md., 1932; Ph.D. (Procter fellow), Princeton U., 1936. Instr. chemistry Trinity Coll., 1936-39; instr. Northwestern U., 1939-45, asst. prof., 1946, asso. prof., 1946-52, prof., 1952—, Ipatieff prof. chemistry, 1970-80, Ipatieff prof. emeritus, 1980—, chmn. dept. chemistry, 1952-57; Humboldt sr. scientist Tech. U. Munich, 1981; vis. prof. U. Pierre et Marie Curie, Paris, 1982. Dir. Internat. Congress Catalysis, 1956-65; chmn. Gordon Research Conf. Catalysis, 1957; sec. Council Internat. Congress Catalysis, 1968-72, v.p., 1972-76, pres., 1980-84; cons. Amoco Corp., 1949-92. Served as lt. USNR, 1942-45. Mem. Am. Chem. Soc. (chmn. div. phys. chemistry 1958-59, mem. council policy com. 1969-72, Kendall award in colloid and surface chemistry 1973, Lubrizol award in petroleum chemistry 1983, Langmuir award 1985), Catalysis Soc. (dir. 1977-81, pres. 1973-77, First Burwell lectr. 1983), Internat. Union Pure and Applied Chemistry (titular mem. colloid and surface chemistry commn. 1969-77). Achievements include research in heterogeneous catalysis and surface chemistry. Avocations: history, art. Home: #302 5700 Williamsburg Ldg Dr Williamsburg VA 23185-3775 Office: Dept of Chemistry Northwestern Univ Evanston IL 60208-0001 E-mail: rburl@widomaker.com.

BURZYNSKI, JAMES BRADLEY, state legislator; b. Christopher, Ill., July 13, 1955; m. Judy Burzynski; 2 children. BA, Ill. Wesleyan Coll. Ill. state sen. Dist. 35, 1990. Chair licenced activities com.; mem. state govt.ops. com., exec. appts. com. Address: 505 Dekalb Ave Sycamore IL 60178-1719

BURZYNSKI, SUSAN MARIE, newspaper editor; b. Jackson, Mich., Jan. 1, 1953; d. Leon Walter and Claudia (Kulpinski) B.; m. James W. Bush, May 22, 1976 (div. 1989); children: Lisa M., Kevin J.; m. George K. Bullard, Jr., Mar. 21, 1992. AA, Jackson C.C., 1972; BA, Mich. State, 1974. Reporter Saratogian, Saratoga Springs, N.Y., 1974, Gongwer News Svc., Lansing, Mich., 1975, The State Jour., Lansing, 1975-79; Metro editor Port Huron (Mich.) Times Herald, 1979-82, mng. editor, 1982-86; asst. city editor Detroit News, 1986-87, Sunday news editor, 1987, news editor, 1988-91, asst. mng. editor/news, 1991-96, asst. mng. editor, recruiting and tng., 1996-98, asst. mng. editor, adminstr., 1998-2000, assoc. editor, 2000—. Roman Catholic. Avocations: swimming, skiing, tennis, biking. Office: Detroit News 615 W Lafayette Blvd Detroit MI 48226-3197

BUS, JAMES STANLEY, toxicologist; b. Kalamazoo, June 27, 1949; s. Charles J. and Sena (Wolthuis) B.; m. Gerda W. Hekman, Apr. 20, 1974; children: Sara E., Timothy J., Brian M. BS in Medicinal Chemistry, U. Mich., 1971; PhD in Pharmacology, Mich. State U., 1975. Diplomate Am. Bd. Toxicology (v.p., pres. 1985-87). NIH predoctoral trainee Dept. Pharmacology, Mich. State U., East Lansing, 1971-75; asst. prof. environ. health U. Cin., 1975-76; scientist I (biochem. toxicologist) Chem. Industry Inst. Toxicology, Research Triangle Park, N.C., 1977-84, scientist II (biochem. toxicologist), 1984-86; assoc. dir. pathology/toxicology, dir. drug metabolism rsch. The Upjohn Co., Kalamazoo, 1986-89; toxicology rsch. lab. Dow Chem. Co., Midland, 1989-91, project mgr., 1992-93, rsch. mgr., tech. dir., 1994—2001, dir. external tech., 2001—. Adj. assoc. prof. curriculum in toxicology U. N.C., Chapel Hill, 1984-88; adj. prof. pharmacology/toxicology Mich. State U. East Lansing, 1987—; toxicology expert Am. Conf. for Govtl. Indsl. Hygienists, Cin., 1993—; mem. safety assessment bd. advisors Merck, Sharp & Dohme Lab., West Point, Pa., 1985-86; mem. bd. sci. counselors EPA, 1996—; mem. bd. sci. counselors NTP, 1997-2001; bd. dirs. CIIT, 1997—. Co-editor: Patty's Industrial Hygiene and Toxicology, Vol. 3B, 1995; assoc. editor Toxicology and Applied Pharmacology, 1989-92; editl. bd. Reproductive Toxicology, 1986-96; contbr. articles to profl. jours. Bd. trustees Covenant Coll., Lookout Mountain,. Ga., 1984-87. Recipient Robert A. Scala award, Environ. Occupl. Health Sci. Inst., Rutgers U., 1999, Disting. Alumni award, Mich. State U. Dept. Pharmacol. Toxicology, 2001. Mem. Soc. Toxicology (pres. 1996-97, Achievement award 1987), Am. Soc. for Pharmacology and Exptl. Therapeutics, Teratology Soc., Am. Conf. Govt. Indsl. Hygiene (mem. chem. substances threshold limit value com.). Republican. Achievements include research dealing with mechanisms of chemical toxicity, including oxidant and glutathione mediated toxicities. Office: Dow Chemical Co Toxicology Rsch Lab 1803 Bldg Midland MI 48674-0001 E-mail: jbus@dow.com.

BUSCH, ANNIE, library director; b. Joplin, Mo., Jan. 6, 1947; d. George Lee and Margaret Eleanor (Williams) Chancellor; 1 child, William Andrew Keller. BA, Mo. U., 1969, MA, 1976. Br. mgr. St. Charles (Mo.) City Coun. Libr., 1977-84, Springfield/Greene County (Mo.) Libr., 1985-89, exec. dir., 1989—. Exec. bd. Mo. Libr. Network Corp., St. Louis, 1991-96. Mem. adv. bd. Springfield Pub. Sch. Found., 1992-94; pres. Ozarks Regional Info. On-Line Network, Springfield, 1993—; mem. Gov.'s Commn. on Informational Tech.; exec. bd. Mo. Rsch. and Edn. Network, pres., 1996-97; bd. dirs. Ozarks Pub. TV, 1994-2000; mem. task force Mo. Goals 2000, 1995, Mo. Census 2000 Complete Count commn., 1999-00; coord. com. Springfield Vision 20/20; mem. Cmty. Task Force, Springfield, 1993-98, Cmty. Partnership of the Ozarks, 1998; adv. bd. St. John's Health Sys., Boys and Girls Town, Good Cmty. Task Force, 1999-2000; chair Sec. of State Adv. Coun., 2001—. Mem.: ALA, Springfield Rotary (pres. 1998—99), Springfield Area C. of C. (bd. dirs.), Pub. Libr. Assn., Mo. Libr. Assn. (pres. 1993—94, exec. bd. 1990—94). Office: Springfield-Greene Cty Libr PO Box 760 Springfield MO 65801-0760 E-mail: annie@orion.org.

BUSCH, ARTHUR ALLEN, lawyer, educator; b. Flint, Mich., July 25, 1954; s. William Allen and Anna Elizabeth (York) B.; m. Bernadette Marie-Therese Regnier, Aug. 28, 1982. BA, Mich. State U., 1976, MLIR, 1977; JD, T.M. Cooley Law Sch., 1982. Bar: Mich. 1982, U.S. Dist. Ct. (ea. dist.) Mich. 1984. Supr. pers. Nat. Gypsum Co., Gibsonburg, Ohio, 1977-78; instr. Mich. State U., East Lansing, 1980-82; pvt. practice Flint, 1982-92; instr. C.S. Mott C.C., 1978—. Counsel Flint City Coun., 1982-84; cons. labor atty. City of Flint, 1984; prosecutor Genesee County, 1993—. Commr. Genesee County, 1986-92, mem. planning com., pks. and recreation; active Valley Area Agy. on Aging. Mem. Mich. Bar Assn., Genesee County Bar Assn. Democrat. Baptist. Office: 200 Courthouse Flint MI 48502

BUSCH, AUGUST ADOLPHUS, III, brewery executive; b. St. Louis, June 16, 1937; s. August Anheuser and Elizabeth (Overton) B.; m. Susan Marie Hornibrook, Aug. 17, 1963 (div. 1969); children: August Adolphus IV, Susan Marie II; m. Virginia L. Wiley, Dec. 28, 1974; children: Steven August, Virginia Marie. Student, U. Ariz., 1957-58, Siebel Inst. Tech., 1960-61. With Anheuser-Busch, Inc., St. Louis, 1957—, pres., 1974-75; chmn. bd., pres., CEO Anheuser Busch Cos., Inc. Bd. dirs. SBC Comms., Emerson Electric Co. Exec. bd. St. Louis Boy Scouts Am.; bd. dirs. United Way Greater St. Louis. Mem. St. Louis Country Club, Log Cabin Club. Office: Anheuser-Busch Cos Inc 1 Busch Pl Saint Louis MO 63118-1852

BUSCH, JOHN ARTHUR, lawyer; b. Indpls., Mar. 23, 1951; s. John L. and Betty (Thomas) B.; m. Barbara Ann Holt, June 23, 1973; children: Abigail, Elizabeth, Amanda, Rachel. BA, Wabash Coll., 1973; JD, Duke U., 1976. Bar: Wis. 1976, U.S. Dist. Ct. (ea. we. dists.) Wis., U.S. Ct. Appeals (5th and 7th cirs.) 1976. Assoc. Michael, Best & Friedrich, Milw., 1976-83, ptnr., 1983—; chmn. litigation dept. Michael Best & Friedrich, 1990-95, mgmt. com., 1995-2001. Mem. ad hoc com. on alternative dispute resolution Milw. Cir. Ct., ad hoc com. on multidisciplinary practices State Bar, gov. bd. govs., 2001—. Treas. North Shore Rep. Club, Milw., 1984-85, vice chmn., 1985-86, chmn., 1987-89; del. Rep. State Conv., Milw., 1986; mem. local rules adv. com. Ea. dist., Wis.; mem. com. Fed. Bench Bar. Master Am. Inns of Ct.; mem. ABA, Wis. Bar Assn., Milw. Bar Assn. Home: 1660 N Prospect Ave #2507 Milwaukee WI 53202 Office: Michael Best & Friedrich 100 E Wisconsin Ave Ste 3300 Milwaukee WI 53202-4108

BUSCH, ROBERT HENRY, geneticist, researcher; b. Jefferson, Iowa, Oct. 22, 1937; s. Henry and Lena Margaret (Osterman) B.; m. Mavis Ann Bushman, Nov. 23, 1958; children: Shari Lynne, Todd William. BSc, Iowa State U., 1959, MSc, 1963; PhD, Purdue U., 1967. Asst. prof. N.D. State U., Fargo, 1967-72, assoc. prof., 1973-77, prof., 1977-78; rsch. geneticist USDA-ARS/U. Minn., St. Paul, 1978—. Cons. Nat. Hail Ins. Coun., Ill. and Colo., 1969-75, Internat. Atomic Energy Agy., UN. Developer 9 wheat varieties; contbr. chpts. to books, articles to profl. jours. Recipient Dedicated Svc. award Polk County Crop Improvement Assn., East Grand Forks, Minn., 1984; named Premier Seedsman Minn. Crop Improvement Assn., St. Paul, 1985. Fellow Crop Sci. Soc. Am. (editor 1976-78, com. chair 1988-90, bd. dirs. 1989-90), Am. Soc. Agronomy (Achievement award, Midwest Sr. Sci. 1998). Methodist. Avocations: sailing, fishing. Home: 2485 Galtier Cir Saint Paul MN 55113-3609 Office: U Minn Dept Agronomy Saint Paul MN 55108

BUSCHBACH, THOMAS CHARLES, geologist, consultant; b. Cicero, Ill., May 12, 1923; s. Thomas Dominick and Vivian (Smiley) B.; m. Mildred Merle Fletcher, Nov. 26, 1947; children— Thomas Richard, Susan Kay, Deborah Lynn B.S., U. Ill., 1950, M.S., 1951, Ph.D., 1959. Geologist, structural geology, stratigraphy, underground storage of natural gas Ill. Geol. Survey, 1951-78; coordinator New Madrid Seismotectonic Study, U.S. Nuclear Regulatory Commn., 1976-85; research prof. geology St. Louis U., 1978-85; geologic cons. Champaign, Ill., 1985—. Served to lt. comdr. USNR, 1942-47 Fellow Geol. Soc. Am. Home: 604 Park Lane Dr Champaign IL 61820-7631 Office: PO Box 1608 Champaign IL 61824-1608 E-mail: tcbusch@aol.com.

BUSCHMANN, SIEGFRIED, manufacturing executive; b. Essen, Germany, July 12, 1937; s. Walter and Frieda Maria (von. Stamm) B.; m. Rita Renate Moch, May 7, 1965; children: Verena, Mark. Diploma, Wilhelms U. Various exec. positions Thyssen AG, Duesseldorf, Germany, 1964-82; pres. Thyssen Holding Corp., Troy, Mich., 1982-99; chmn., pres. ThyssenKrupp USA, Inc., 1999—; sr. v.p. The Budd Co., Troy, 1982-83, sr. v.p., CFO, 1983-86, vice chmn., CFO, 1986-89, chmn., CEO, 1989—2001, chmn. bd., 2001—. Chmn. exec. bd. Thyssen Budd Automotive GmbH, Essen, Germany, 1997—99; v.chmn., exec. bd. Thyssen Krupp Automotive AG, Bochum, Germany, 1999—2001, mem. supervisory bd., 2001—. Avocation: golf. Office: The Budd Co PO Box 2601 3155 W Big Beaver Rd Troy MI 48007-2601

BUSDICKER, GORDON G. lawyer, retired; b. Winona, Minn., Oct. 12, 1933; s. Harry John and Edna Mae (Rogers) B.; m. Noreen Decker; children— Karla E., Pamela J., Alison G., Neal A. B.A., Hamline U., St. Paul, 1955; J.D., Harvard U., 1958. Bar: Minn. Atty. Aluminum Co. of Am., Pitts., 1958-61; assoc. Faegre & Benson, Mpls., 1961-67, ptnr., 1967-99, ret., 1999. Trustee Hamline U., St. Paul, 1973— Mem. Minn. Bar Assn., ABA Republican. Congregationalist. Club: Minneapolis Avocations: boating, geanealogy; Clubs: Mpsl. Club, Interlachen Golf Club. Home: 3833 Abbott Ave S Minneapolis MN 55410-1036 E-mail: busdicki@mn.rr.com.

BUSELMEIER, BERNARD JOSEPH, insurance company executive; b. Detroit, Feb. 10, 1956; s. Bernard August and Rita Mathilda (Cook) B.; m. Sharon Lynette Hoffman, Nov. 28, 1975; 1 child, Andrew Joseph. BBA in Acctg., U. Detroit, 1980, MBA, 1990. Various fin. positions ins. group Auto Club Mich., Dearborn, Mich., 1974-81; various fin. positions Motors Ins. Corp., Detroit, 1981-89, treas., 1989-98, v.p., treas., 1993-98; exec. v.p., CFO, Integon Corp., Winston-Salem, N.C., 1998-99; CFO GMAC Ins. Personal Lines, St. Louis, 1999—. Office: GMAC Ins Personal Lines One GMAC Insurance Plaza Earth City MO 63045

BUSEY, ROXANE C. lawyer; b. Chgo., June 15, 1949; BA cum laude, Miami U., 1970; MAT, Northwestern U., 1971, JD, 1975. Bar: Ill. 1975. Ptnr. Gardner, Carton & Douglas, Chgo. Mem. ABA (chair health com., antitrust sect. 1989-92, antitrust sect. coun. 1992-95, antitrust sect. vice-chair 1995-96, 98-99, fin. office 1996-98, vice chair 1999-2000, chair-elect 2000-2001, chair 2001-2002), Ill. State Bar Assn. (chair antitrust coun. 1984-85), Chgo. Bar Assn. (chair antitrust sect. 1990-91). Office: Gardner Carton & Douglas 321 N Clark St Ste 3000 Chicago IL 60610-4718 E-mail: rbusey@gcd.com.

BUSHEE, WARD, newspaper editor; b. Redding, Calif., 1949; m. Claudia Bushee; children: Ward Gardiner, Mary Standish. BS in History, San Diego State U., 1971. Sports editor Gilroy (Calif.) Dispatch, 1972-75; asst. city editor/sports editor/reporter/copy editor Salinas (Calif.) Californian, 1975-80; sports editor Marin County (Calif.) Ind. Jour., 1980-82; startup staff, including asst. sports editor profl. sports USA Today, Arlington, Va., 1982-85; asst. mng. editor Westchester (N.Y.) Suburban Newspapers, 1985-86; exec. editor Sioux Falls (S.D.) Argus Leader, 1986-90; editor Reno (Nev.) Gazette-Jour., 1990-99, Cinncinnati Enquirer, OH. Named Editor of Yr., 1992, 97, Gannett Co., Inc., Pres.'s Ring winner 1992-97, 99-2001. Mem. Nev. Press Assn. (pres. 1993, 94, API discussion leader 1996). Office: Cinncinnati Enquirer 312 Elm St Fl 18 Cincinnati OH 45202-2724 E-mail: wbushee@cincinna.gannett.com.

BUSHMAN, MARY LAURA JONES, developer, fundraiser; b. Mpls., 1946; d. William Ray and Emily Mary H. Jones; m. Donald Otto Bushman, Dec. 5, 1971; children: Donald Aaron, Justin David, Mark Joseph. BA in English, U. S.C., 1968. Assoc. dir. Funding & Devel., Chgo., 1971-75, The Inst. of Cultural Affairs, Chgo.; dir. Cleve. Region, 1975-79, Pacific, Oceania Region, Apia, Western Samoa, 1979-83. Co-creator Human Devel. Tng. Curriculum, 1984-85. Dir. pilot project for Uptown Community Resource Ctr. Inst. of Cult. Affairs, Chgo., 1986-2001. Mem. Uptown C. of C. (pres.), Internat. Women Entrepreneurs. Lutheran. Home and Office: Inst Cultural Affairs 4750 N Sheridan Rd Chicago IL 60640-5042

BUSHNELL, GEORGE EDWARD, JR. lawyer; b. Detroit, Nov. 15, 1924; s. George E. and Ida Mary (Bland) B.; children: George Edward III, Christopher Gilbert Whelden, Robina McLeod Bushnell Hogan. Mil. student, U. Kans., 1943; BA, Amherst Coll., 1948; LLB, U. Mich., 1951; LLD, Detroit Coll. Law, 1995. Bar: Mich. 1951, D.C. 1980, U.S. Dist. Ct. (ea. dist.) Mich. 1951, U.S. Dist. Ct. (we. dist.) Mich. 1971, U.S. Ct. Appeals (6th cir.) 1955, U.S. Ct. Appeals (fed. cir.) 1995, U.S. Ct. Appeals for the Armed Forces 1995, U.S. Supreme Ct. 1971, U.S. Ct. Internat. Trade 1995. From assoc. to sr. ptnr. Miller, Canfield, Paddock and Stone, Detroit, 1953-77, of counsel, 1989-2001; sr. ptnr. Bushnell, Gage, Doctoroff & Reizen, Southfield, Mich., 1977-89. Commr. Mich. Jud. Tenure Commn., 1969-83, chmn., 1978-80; pres. State Bar Mich., 1975-76; bd. dirs. Nat. Jud. Coll., 1985-89; mem. Mich. Atty. Discipline Bd., 1990-96; lectr. in field. Elder Grosse Pointe Meml. Ch.; moderator Detroit Presbytery, United Presbyn. Ch. U.S.A., 1972, pres. program agy. bd., 1972-76; bd. dirs. Econ. Devel. Corp. of Detroit, 1976—, Econ. Growth Corp. of Detroit, 1978-96, Tax Increment Fin. Authority, Detroit, 1984—, Econ. Devel. Authority, Detroit, 1988-98, Mich. Partnership to Prevent Gun Violence, 1995—, pres.-elect, 1999-2000; bd. trustees New Detroit, Inc., 1972—, chmn., 1974-75. Served with USAR, 1942-56. Decorated Bronze Star, Army Commendation medal. Mem. NAACP (life, co-chmn. fight for freedom fund dinner 1968), ABA (ho. of dels. 1976—, chmn. ho. of dels. 1988-90, pres.-elect 1993-94, pres. 1994-95, past pres. 1995-96, others, Trial Attys. of Am. (pres. 1971-89), State Bar Mich. . bd. of bar commrs. 1970-76, pres. 1975-76, John Hensel award for svcs. to the arts 1990, Roberts P. Hudson award for spl. svcs. to the bar and the people of Mich., 1979, 85, Cooley Law Sch. Louis A. Smith (disting. jurist award 1995), Detroit Bar Assn. (bd. dirs. 1958-65, pres. 1964-65, past pres. com. 1980—, bench & bar award for svc. to the judicial sys., the legal profession and the cmty. 1989), Nat. Conf. of Bar Pres. (pres. 1984-85), 6th Jud. Cir. Conf. (life), Am. Law Inst., Am. Arbitration Assn. (bd. dirs. 1970-82), Am. Coll. Trial Lawyers, Am. Bar Found. (life), Am. Judicature Soc. (bd. dirs. 1977-82), Can. Bar Assn. (hon.), Internat. Soc. Barristers, Fed. Bar Assn., Masons (33 deg.), Met. Club (N.Y.C.) Phi Delta Phi, Psi Upsilon. Democrat. Office: Miller Canfield Paddock & Stone 150 W Jefferson Ave Ste 2500 Detroit MI 48226-4416 E-mail: bushness@millermanfield.com.

BUSHNELL, WILLIAM RODGERS, agricultural research scientist; b. Wooster, Ohio, Aug. 19, 1931; s. John and Dyllone (Hempstead) B.; m. Ann Holcomb, Sep. 20, 1952; children: Thomas H., John A., Mary D. AB, U. Chgo., 1951; BS, Ohio State U., 1953, MS, 1955; PhD, U. Wis., 1960. Plant physiologist agrl. rsch. svc. U.S. Dept. Agr., St. Paul, 1960—. Adj. prof. U. Minn., St. Paul, 1973—. Contbr. numerous rsch. articles in plant sci. jours.; editor books in field. Named U.S. Sr. Scientist Alexander Von Humboldt Found., Germany, 1984. Fellow Am. Phytopathological Soc. Avocations: vineyard, folk music. Office: USDA Cereal Disease Lab 1551 Lindig St Saint Paul MN 55108-1050

BUSKIRK, PHYLLIS RICHARDSON, retired economist; b. Queens, N.Y., July 19, 1930; d. William Edward and Amy A. Richardson; m. Allen V. Buskirk, Sept. 13, 1950; children: Leslie, William, Carol, Janet. AB cum laude, William Smith Coll., 1951. Rsch. asst. W.E. Upjohn Insst. for Employment Rsch., Kalamazoo, 1970-75, rsch. assoc., 1976-83, sr. staff economist, 1983-87; co-editor Bus. Conditions in the Kalamazoo Area, Quar. Rev., 1979-84; asst. editor Bus. Outlook for West Mich., 1984-87; mem. civil svc. bd. City of Kalamazoo, 1977-91, chmn., 1981-91; trustee First Presbyn. Ch., Kalamazoo, 1984-87, chmn., 1985, 86, mgr. adminstrn. and fin., 1987-92, co-chair 150th ann., 1997-98, chair 150th ann., 1999-2000. Trustee Sr. Citizens Fund, Kalamazoo, 1984-88, exec. bd. 1986-88; bd. dirs. Heritage Cmty. Kalamazoo, 1988—, chair 1995-96, exec. com., 1997; Kalamazoo County Futures Coms., 1985-86, bd. dirs., 1987-89. Fellow Presbyn. Ch. Bus. Adminstrn. Assn.; mem. Nat. Assn. Ch. Bus. Adminstrn., P.E.O., Kalamazoo Network, YWCA; bd. dirs. Friends of Univ. Librs. Western Mich. U., 2000—. Mem. Phi Beta Kappa. Home: 3324 Saint Antoine Ave Kalamazoo MI 49006-5522

BUSS, DANIEL FRANK, environmental scientist; b. Milw., Jan. 13, 1943; s. Lynn Charles and Pearl Elizabeth (Ward) B.; m. Ann Makal, Jan. 22, 1977. B.S., Carroll Coll., 1965; M.S. in Biology, U. Wis., 1972, M.S. in Environ. Engring., 1977, P.D.D. in Environ. Engring., 1985. Registered profl. engr., Wis. Dir. limnological studies Aqua-Tech, Inc., Waukesha, Wis., 1969-72; project mgr. environ. studies Point Beach Nuclear Plant, Two Creeks, 1972-76; assoc., dir. aquatic studies environ. sci. div. Camp Dresser & McKee, Inc., Milw., 1977—, dir. indsl. service, 1978-90, office mgr., coord. for environ. assesments, 1990—. Lectr. on nuclear power and environ., environ. auditing; mgr. hazardous waste superfund projects, dredge disposal planning projects; asbestos insp., mgmt. planner EPA, 1988, also nat. accounts mgr. for performance of environ. site assessments for property trans. Author: An Environmental Study of the Ecological Effects on Lake Michigan of the Thermal Discharge from the Point Beach Nuclear Plant, 1976, Environmental Auditing-- A Systematic Approach, 1984; contbr. articles to profl. jours, chpts. to books and environmental site investigation protocols for ASTM, ASCE and other soc. guidance documents. Mem. ASCE (chmn. site constrn. and remediation implementation manual task com.),Am. Nuclear Soc. (sec.-treas. Wis. sect., program mgr. waste disposal studies, program mgr. for remedial programs involving jet fuel and deicer contamination at Gen. Mitchell Internat. Airport), Midwest Soc. Electron Microscopists, Internat. Soc. Theoretical and Applied Limnology and Oceanography, Internat. Assn. Gt. Lakes Rsch., Am. Indsl. Hygiene Soc., Nat. Assn. Environ. Profls., Fed. Water Pollution Control Adminstrn., Cons. Engrs. Coun. (chmn. liaison com. Ill. and Chgo. Bar Assn., mem. com. for devel. site investigation manual ASCE, sec. ASCE com. to develop remedial design, feasibility study manual), Am. Assn. Environ. Engrs. (diplomate 1990, cert. hazardous materials mgr. 1988, hazard control mgr. 1988), Program mgr. design, construction mgmt., oper. UV/Oxidation system (used for treating herbicide contaminated ground water in Wisconsin), Am. Acad. Environ. Engrs. (Wis. state rep.), Glendale Wis. Econ. Devel. Com. and Bus. Coun., Sigma Xi. Home: 5543 N Shasta Dr Milwaukee WI 53209-4924 also: 312 E Wisconsin Ave Ste 500 Milwaukee WI 53202-4305

BUSSMAN, DONALD HERBERT, lawyer; b. Lakewood, Ohio, July 15, 1925; s. Herbert L. and Hilda L. (Henrichs) B. PhB, U. of Chgo., 1947, JD, 1951. Bar: Ill. 1951. Atty. Swift & Co., Chgo., 1950-84; pvt. practice, 1985—. With U.S. Army, 1944-46. Mem. ABA, Chgo. Bar Assn., Am. Assn. of Individual Investors, Club Internat. (Chgo.). Office: Ste 2102 860 N Dewitt Pl Chicago IL 60611-5780

BUTCHVAROV, PANAYOT KRUSTEV, philosophy educator; b. Sofia, Bulgaria, Apr. 2, 1933; s. Krustyu Panayotov and Vanya (Tsaneva) B.; m. Sue Graham, Sept. 28, 1954; children: Vanya, Christopher. BA, Robert Coll., Istanbul, 1952; MA, U. Va., 1954, PhD, 1955. Instr. philosophy U. Balt., 1955-56; asst. prof. U. S.C., 1956-59; asso. prof. Syracuse U., 1959-66, prof., 1966-68; vis. prof. U. Iowa, 1967-68, prof., 1968—, chmn. dept. philosophy, 1970-77; univ. found. disting. prof., 1995—. Vis. prof. U. Miami, Coral Gables, Fla., 1979-80; Simon lectr. U. Toronto, 1984; guest prof. Akad. für Philosophie, Liechtenstein, 1997. Author: Resemblance and Identity, 1966, The Concept of Knowledge, 1970, Being Qua Being, 1979, Skepticism in Ethics, 1989, Skepticism About the External World, 1998; editor: Jour. Philosophical Rsch., 1993—; mem. editl. bd.: Midwest Studies in Philosophy, Philos. Monographs; contbr. numerous articles and revs. to profl. jours. Mem. Am. Philos. Assn. (program com. 1971, chmn. 1975, nominating com. 1978, chmn. 1993-94, pres. ctrl. div. 1992-93), Ctrl. States Philos. Assn. (v.p. 1987-88, pres. 1988-89), Phi Beta Kappa. Home: 2507 Princeton Rd Iowa City IA 52245-3721 E-mail: panayot-butchvarov@uiowa.edu.

BUTLER, JAMES E. automotive executive; CFO Venture Ind., Fraser, Mich. Office: Venture Industries 33662 James J Pampo Dr Fraser MI 48026 Office Fax: (810) 296-8863.

BUTLER, JOHN MUSGRAVE, financial consultant, consultant; b. Bklyn., Dec. 6, 1928; s. John Joseph and Sabina Catherine (Musgrave) Butler; m. Ann Elizabeth Kelly, July 9, 1955; children: Maureen, John, Ellen, Suzanne. BA cum laude, St. John's U., 1950; MBA, NYU, 1951. CPA N.Y., Ill. Sr. acct. Lybrand, Ross Bros. & Montgomery (CPAs), N.Y.C., 1953-59; sr. auditor ITT Corp., 1959-62; asst. to contr. Dictaphone Corp., Bridgeport, Conn., 1962-63, contr. Bridgeport, Rye, NY, 1964-68; v.p. acctg. Chgo. & North Western Ry. Co., 1968-69, v.p. fin. and acctg., 1969-72, Chgo. and North Western Transp. Co., 1972-79, sr. v.p. fin. and acctg., 1979-89, dir., 1976-89, trustee, 1978-82, acting sr. v.p. fin. and acctg., 1994; sr. v.p. fin. and acctg., dir. CNW Corp., 1985-89; cons. in fin. and acctg. for bus., 1989—; instr. fin. DePaul U., Chgo., 1989—2001. Dir. Cath. Med. Mission Bd., N.Y.C., 1998—2000. Mem.: Fin. Execs. Inst. Roman Catholic. Office: 119 E Palatine Rd Ste 206 Palatine IL 60067-5132

BUTLER, MARGARET KAMPSCHAEFER, retired computer scientist; b. Evansville, Ind., Mar. 7, 1924; d. Otto Louis and Lou Etta (Rehsteiner) Kampschaefer; m. James W. Butler, Sept. 30, 1951; 1 child, Jay. AB, Ind. U., 1944; postgrad., U.S. Dept. Agr. Grad. Sch., 1945, U. Chgo., 1949, U. Minn., 1950. Statistician U.S. Bur. Labor Statistics, Washington, 1945-46, U.S. Air Forces in Europe, Erlangen and Wiesbaden, Germany, 1946-48, U.S. Bur. Labor Statistics, St. Paul, 1949-51; mathematician Argonne (Ill.) Nat. Lab., 1948-49, 51-80, sr. computer scientist, 1980-92; dir. Argonne Code Ctr. and Nat. Energy Software Ctr. Dept. Energy Computer Program Exch., 1960-91; spl. term appointee Argonne Nat. Lab., 1993—. Cons. AMF Corp., 1956-57, OECD, 1964, Poole Bros., 1967. Author: Careers for Women in Nuclear Science and Technology, 1992; editor Computer Physics Communications, 1969-80; contbr. (chpt.) The Application of Digital Computers to Problems in Reactor Physics, 1968, Advances in Nuclear Sci. and Technology, 1976; contbr. articles to profl. publs. Treas. Timberlake Civic Assn., 1958; rep. mem. nomination com. Hinsdale (Ill.) Caucus, 1961-62; coord. 6th dist. ERA, 1973-80; del. Rep. Nat. Conv., 1980; bd. mgr. DuPage dist. YWCA Met. Chgo., 1987-90; mem. computer and info. sys. adv. bd. Coll. DuPage, 1987-95; mem. industry adv. bd. computer sci. dept. Bradley U., 1988-91; vice chair Ill. Women's Polit. Caucus, 1987-90; chair voter's svc. LWV, Burr-Ridge-Willowbrook, 1991-93; vol. Morton Arboretum, 1997—, Friends of Indian Prairie Pub. Libr., 2000—. Recipient cert. of leadership Met. YWCA, Chgo., 1985, Merit award Chgo. Assn. Technol. Socs., 1988; named to Fed. 100, 1991; named Outstanding Woman Leader of DuPage County Sci., Tech. and Health Care, 1992. Fellow Am. Nuclear Soc. (mem. publs. com. 1965-71, bd. dirs. 1976-79, exec. com. 1977-78, chmn. bylaws and rules com., 1979-82, profl. women in ANS com. 1991-93, reviewer for publs., spl. award math. and computer divsn. 1992); mem. Assn. Computing Machinery (exec. com., sec. Chgo. chpt. 1963-65, publs. chmn. nat. conf. 1968, reviewer for publs.), Assn. Women in Sci. (pres. Chgo. area chpt. 1982, nat. exec. bd. 1985-87), Nat. Computer Conf. (chmn. Pioneer Day com. 1985, tech. program chmn. 1987). Independent. Home: 107 Brewster Lane La Grange Park IL 60526 E-mail: MargaretKButler@cs.com.

BUTLER, MERLIN GENE, physician, medical geneticist, educator; b. Atkinson, Nebr., Aug. 2, 1952; s. Garold Melvin and Berdena June (Sandall) B.; m. Ranae Ilene Kisker, Oct. 2, 1976; children: Michelle Ranae, Brian Gene. BA with very high distinction, Chadron State Coll., 1974, BS with very high distinction, 1975; MD, U. Nebr., Omaha, 1978; MS, U. Nebr., Lincoln, 1980; PhD, Ind. U., Indpls., 1984. Supervising physician Med. Info. Svcs., Omaha, 1978-80; rsch. assoc. dept. biology U. Notre Dame, South Bend, Ind., 1983-84; med. dir. North Ctrl. Ind. Regional Genetics Ctr., 1983-84; dir. cytogenetics Meml. Hosp., 1983-84; NIH postdoctoral fellow dept. med. genetics Sch. Medicine Ind. U., Indpls., 1980-83, adj. asst. prof. dept. med. genetics Sch. Medicine, 1984; asst. prof. dept. pediatrics Sch. Medicine Vanderbilt U., Nashville, 1984-90, dir. regional genetics program Sch. Medicine, 1984-98, dir. Cytogenetics Lab. dept. pediatrics Sch. Medicine, 1989-98, assoc. prof. dept. pediatrics, 1990-98, assoc. prof. dept. pathology, 1991-98, investigator John F. Kennedy Ctr. Rsch. on Edn. and Human Devel., Peabody Coll., 1987-98; assoc. dir. Inst. Behavior and Genetics; assoc. prof. dept. orthopedics Vanderbilt U., 1994-98. Adj. assoc. prof. dept. pediatrics Meharry Med. Coll., Nashville, 1988-98; genetics cons. Baptist Hosp., Nashville, 1985-98, Westside Hosp., Nashville, 1985-98, Nashville Gen. Hosp., 1985-98, chief, section of Med. Genetics and Molecular Medicine, Children's Mercy Hosp., Kansas City, Mo., 1998—, William R. Brown prof., chmn., 1998—, prof. dept. pediats., U. Mo.-Kansas City Sch. Medicine; mem. epidemiology genetic diseases subcom. Ind. State Bd. Health, 1983-84; faculty interviewer Vanderbilt U., 1987; peer reviewer Am. Jour. Human Genetics, Am. Jour. Med. Genetics, Clin. Genetics, Am. Jour. Diseases of Children, Dysmorphology and Clin. Genetics, Am. Jour. Mental Retardation, Jour. Pediatrics, So. Med. Jour., Human Mutations, Cancer Genetics and Cytogenetics, Pediatrics, Genomics, Prader-Willi Perspectives; mem. ad-hoc grant review com. NIH, 1990—, craniofacial assessment team Vanderbilt U., 1992-98; lectr., presenter in field. Author: Fragile X Syndrome: A Major Cause of X-Linked Mental Retardation, 1988, 1989; author: (with others) Genetics for the Medically Oriented, 1983, Novak's Textbook of Gynecology, 11th edit., 1988, Birth Defects Encyclopedia, 1990, Prader-Willi Syndrome and Other Chromosome 15q Deletion Disorders, 1992, Human Genetics: New Perspectives, 1994, 1992 International Fragile X Conference Proceedings, 1992, Prader-Willi and Angelman Syndromes Examples of Genetic Imprinting in Man, 1994, Prader-Willi Syndrome: A Guide for PArents and Physicians, 1995, Prader-Willi Syndrome: Clinical and Genetic Findings, 2000; mem. editorial bd. Prader-Willi Perspectives, 1992—; contbr. numerous articles to profl. jours. including Nature and New England Jour. Medicine. Grant reviewer March of Dimes Birth Defects Found., 1985—. Recipient Disting. Svc. award Chadron State Coll., 1986, Teaching award Osler Inst., 1989; grantee Univ. Rsch. Coun., 1985, 92-93, Tenn. Dept. Mental Health and Mental Retardation, 1986-91, Clin. Nutrition Rsch. Unit, 1986-88, Joseph P. Kennedy, Jr. Found., 1988, Clin. Rsch. Ctr. Meharry Med. Coll., 1989-98, Dept. Pathology, 1992-93, Orthopedic Rsch. Edn. Found., 1993-95, NIH, 1995—; Cancer Rsch. grantee Ind. U. Med. Ctr., 1980, Biomed. Rsch. Support grantee, 1985, 88, 89—, Clin. Rsch. grantee March of Dimes Birth Defects Found., 1987, 88, 90-92, Lyle V. Andrews Meml. scholar, 1974. Fellow Am. Coll. Med. Genetics (founder, diplomate, lab. practice subcom. 1993); mem. AMA (Physician Recognition award 1984, 87), AAAS, Am. Bd. Med. Genetics (cert. clin. genetics and clin. cytogenetics), Am. Genetics Assn., Am. Soc. Human Genetics (cytogenetics resource com. 1992-97), Am. Fedn. Clin. Rsch., Coll. Am. Pathologists (cytogenetics resource com. 1992-97, molecular pathology resource com. 1993-97), So. Med. Assn., Davidson County Pediatric Soc., Metro. Med. Soc., Prader-Willi Syndrome Assn. (med. rsch. task force 1985—, diagnostic task force 1991—, sci. adv. bd. 1991—, chair 2000—), N.Y. Acad. Scis., Sigma Xi, Phi Chi. Avocations: gardening, camping, fishing, collecting sports memorabilia. Home: 6410 Hillside St Shawnee KS 66218-9070 Office: Children's Mercy Hosp 2401 Gillham Rd Kansas City MO 64108-4698 E-mail: mgbutler@cmh.edu.

BUTLER, RICHARD D. state treasurer; b. Rapid City, S.D., Mar. 2, 1946; m. Karen Henry, Nov. 29, 1968; children: Adrian, Paul, Adriana, Cornelia. BA, U. S.D. Owner comml. ins. agy.; flour miller; treas. State of S.D., 1995—. Mem. State Bd. Fin., S.D. Pub. Deposit Protection Commn.; ex-officio mem. S.D. Investment Coun. Mem. Assn. Operative Millers. Anglican Catholic. Democrat. Office: Office of State Treas 500 E Capitol Ave Ste 212 Pierre SD 57501-5070 Fax: 605-773-3115. E-mail: dickb@st-treas.state.sd.us.

BUTLER, WILLIAM E. retired manufacturing company executive; b. 1931; With Eaton Corp., Cleve., 1957-95, pres. and chief ops. officer, 1989-91, CEO, 1991, chmn., CEO, 1992-95. Office: Eaton Corp 1111 Superior Ave E Cleveland OH 44114-2507

BUTT, EDWARD THOMAS, JR. lawyer; b. Chgo., Oct. 27, 1947; s. Edward T. and Helen Kathryn (Guy) B.; m. Leslie Laidlaw Hilton, Oct. 20, 1972; children: Julie Guy, Andrew McNaughton. BA, Lawrence U., 1968; JD, U. Mich., 1971. Bar: Ill. 1971, U.S. Dist. Ct. (no. dist.) Ill. 1971, Wis. 1975, U.S. Dist. Ct. (ea. dist.) Wis. 1978, U.S. Ct. Appeals (7th cir.) 1978, U.S. Ct. Claims 1982, U.S. Ct. Appeals (6th cir.) 1986, U.S. Ct. Appeals (6th cir.) 1987, Mich. 1997. Assoc. Wildman, Harrold, Allen & Dixon, Chgo., 1971-75, 76-78, ptnr., 1979-94, Lund & Butt, S.C., Minocqua, Wis., 1975-76; of counsel Swanson, Martin & Bell, Chgo. and Wheaton, Ill., 1994—. Bd. dirs. Constl. Rights Found., Chgo. Mem. ABA, State Bar Wis., State Bar Mich., 7th Cir. Bar Assn., Def. Rsch. Inst., Crystal Lake Yacht Club, Crystal Downs Country Club. Avocations: distance running, sailing, golf. Home: Michabou Shores 1006 Tiba Rd Frankfort MI 49635-9216 also: 3903 Forest Ave Western Springs IL 60558-1049 Office: Swanson Martin & Bell 2100 Manchester Rd Ste 1420 Wheaton IL 60187-4534

BUTTERBRODT, JOHN ERVIN, real estate executive; b. Beaver Dam, Wis., Feb. 14, 1929; s. Ervin E. and Josephine M. (O'Mare) B.; m. June Rose Bohalter, Sept. 27, 1952; children— Claire, Daniel, Larry. U.

Agriculture short course, 1946-47. Cert. tchr. real estate, rental weatherization inspector, real estate appraiser, sr. profl. appraiser; internat. cert. farm appraiser; cert. gen., lic. appraiser, Wis. Vice-pres. Pure Milk Assn., 1967-69; pres. Asso. Milk Producers, Inc. Chgo., 1969-75, State Brand Creameries, Madison, Wis., 1970—, Wis. Real Estate Co., Wis. Real Estate of Burnett Inc., 1978—, Sunset Hills Golf & Supper Club Inc., 1979—; chmn. bd. Realty World-Wis. Real Estate, Inc., 1985—; treas. Real Estate Cons., 1983—. Dir. Town Mut. Ins. Co., Central Milk Sales, Central Milk Producers Coop. Pres. Sch. Bd., 1968; Bd. dirs. Nat. Milk Producers Fedn., Central Am. Coop. Fedn., World Dairy Expo. Recipient Am. Farmer degree Future Farmers of Am., 1949, hon. degree, 1973; Outstanding Wis. Farmer award, 1965; Outstanding Wis. 4-H Alumni award, 1973; named Realtor of Yr., 1979 Mem. United Dairy Industry Assn. Republican. Office: 1708 N Spring St Beaver Dam WI 53916-1106

BUTTERFIELD, JAMES T. small business owner; b. Galion, Ohio, July 9, 1951; s. Carlos and Ethel Louise (Miller) B.; m. Mary Anne Shaffo, May 17, 1986; children: Jacob Alan, Emily Lauren. Cert. plumbing insp., backflow insp., cert. pipe welder, EPA cert. refrigerant handling technician, lic. low pressure steam operator, cert. automatic sprinkler installer, lic. plumbing contractor, Ohio; lic. hydronics contractor, Ohio, N.C., elec. contractor, Ohio. Apprentice Don Barnett Plumbing, Galion, Ohio, 1968-69, Rinehart Plumbing and Heating, Galion, 1969-71; owner Butterfield Plumbing and Heating, 1972—, Galion Sheet Metal, 1982—. Mem. Am. Soc. Sanitary Engrs., Ohio Assn. Plumbing Insps. Home: 375 W Atwood St Galion OH 44833-2553 Office: Butterfield Plumbing and Heating PO Box 33 Galion OH 44833-0033 E-mail: bfield@richnet.net., Mengdu@netscape.net.

BUTTIGIEG, JOSEPH J. banking executive; BBA, U. Notre Dame; JD, Detroit Coll. Various to sr. v.p. Manufacturer's Bank, Detroit, 1972-89, exec. v.p., 1989-91; exec. v.p. global corp. banking Comerica, Inc., 1995-99, vice-chmn. bus. bank, 1999—. Office: Comerica Inc Comerica Twr/500 Woodward A Detroit MI 48226

BUTTREY, DONALD WAYNE, lawyer; b. Terre Haute, Ind., Feb. 6, 1935; s. William Edgar and Nellie (Vaughn) B.; children: Greg, Alan, Jason; m. Karen Lake, Mar. 23, 1985. BS, Ind. State U., 1956; JD, Ind. U., 1961. Bar: Ind. 1961, U.S. Dist. Ct. 1961, U.S. Ct. Appeals (7th cir.) 1972, U.S. Tax Ct. 1972, U.S. Supreme Ct. 1972. Law clk. to chief judge Steckler, U.S. Dist. Ct. So. Dist. Ind., 1961-63; mem. McHale, Cook & Welch, P.C., Indpls., 1963—2001, pres., 1986-93, chmn., 1993—2001. Chmn. Ctrl. Region IRS-Bar Liaison Com., 1984; mem. jud. nominating com. Marion County Mcpl. Ct., 1993-96; mem. Estate Planning Coun. Indpls., 1990—. Note editor Ind. Law Jour., 1960-61. Trustee Ind. State U., 1992-2000, v.p. bd., 1997-2000; bd. dirs. Ind. State U. Found., 1991—. With AUS, 1956-58, Korea. Fellow Am. Coll. Tax Counsel, Am. Bar Found., Ind. State Bar Found., Indpls. Bar Found. (pres. 1993-96, Buchanan award 1999); mem. ABA (taxation, real property, probate and trust sect., liaison IRS-Bar Liaison com., taxation sect. 1995-96), Ind. State Bar Assn. (bd. govs. 1994-96, taxation, real property, probate and trust sect., chmn. taxation sect. 1982-83), Indpls. Bar Assn. (pres. 1990, mem. probate, taxation sects.), Highland Golf and Country Club, Indpls. Athletic Club (bd. dirs. 1982-88), Skyline Club, Univ. Club (bd. dirs. 1997-2000). Presbyterian. E-mail: dbuttrey@woodmaclaw.com.

BUTTS, VIRGINIA, corporate public relations executive; b. Chgo. BA, U. Chgo. Writer Dave Garroway radio show NBC, N.Y.C., 1953; writer, producer, talent Sta. WBBM-TV, Chgo.; midwest dir. pub. relations for mags. Time, Fortune, Life and Sports Illustrated, Time Inc., 1956-63; dir. pub. relations Chgo. Sun-Times and Chgo. Daily News, 1963-74; v.p. pub. relations Field Enterprises Inc., Chgo., 1974-84; v.p. pub. rels. The Field Corp., 1984-90; pub. rels. counsel Marshall Field V, Chgo., 1991—. Pub. affairs com. Art Inst. Chgo., exec. prodn. assoc., 1985; instr. TV Columbia Coll. Contbr. Lesly's Public Relations Handbook, 1978, 83, World Book Ency. Recipient Clarion award Women in Communications, Inc., 1975-76, Businesswoman of the Yr. award Lewis U., 1976. Mem. Pub. Rels. Soc. Am. (nat. bd. ethics 1987-93), Publicity Club Chgo. (Golden Trumpet award 1968-69, 75-76, 80), Nat. Acad. TV Arts and Scis., The Chgo. Network. Achievements include the Lion at Lincoln Park Zoo named for her public relations work; late Milton Caniff's character in Steve Canyon Comic Strip named for her; for work in the film Continental Divide "the producer wishes to thank Virginia Butts and the editors and staff of the Chicago Sun-Times for their generous cooperation and assistance in the filming of this motion picture".

BUTZBAUGH, ALFRED M. lawyer; b. Benton Harbor, Mich., July 25, 1940; AB, U. Mich., 1963, JD, 1966; MBA, U. Chgo., 1983. Bar: Mich. 1967, Tex. 1991. Ptnr. Butzbaugh & Dewane, St. Jospeh, Mich. Mem. ABA, State Bar Mich. (rep. assembly 1973-79, commr. 1992—, treas. 1996-97), State Bar Tex., Berrien County Bar Assn. (pres. 1982-83). Office: Butzbaugh & Dewane PLC Law and Title Bldg 811 Ship St Saint Joseph MI 49085-1171 E-mail: Al.bdlaw@parrett.net.

BUXTON, WINSLOW HURLBERT, paper company executive; Degree in Chem. Engring., U. Washington, 1961. Pres. Niagara of Wis. Paper Corp., 1986-89; with Pentair Inc., St. Paul, 1986—, v.p. paper group, 1989-90, pres., COO, dir., 1990-92, chmn., pres., 1993-99, chmn., CEO, 1999-2000, chmn., 2000—.

BUYER, STEVE EARLE, congressman, lawyer; b. 1958; m. Joni Buyer; children: Colleen, Ryan. BS in Bus. Adminstrn., The Citadel, 1980; JD, Valparaiso U., 1984. Officer Med. Svc. Corps U.S. Army, 1980, spl. att to U.S. Atty. Va., 1984-87; atty., 1988—; dep. atty. gen. Ind., 1987-88; legal counsel 22nd Theater Army, Saudi Arabia, 1990-91; legal advisor U.S Armed Forces/Western Enemy Prisoner of War Camps/War Crimes Interrogations, Saudi Arabia, 1991; mem. 103d Congress from 5th Ind. Dist., 1993—. Mem. com. on energy & commerce, U.S. Ho. of Reps.; mem. health, commerce, trade and consumer protection, environment & hazardous materials subcoms.; mem. com. on vet.'s affairs, chmn. subcom. oversights & investigations. Decorated Bronze Star. Republican. Office: US Ho Reps 2443 Rayburn HOB Washington DC 20515-0001*

BUZARD, JAMES ALBERT, healthcare management consultant; b. Warren, Ohio, Nov. 2, 1927; s. Milton Vogan and Mary Cora (Matthews) B.; m. Caroline L. Jansen, July 28, 1951; children: Catherine A. Sazdanoff, James M. BS, Kent (Ohio) State U., 1949; MA, U. Buffalo, 1951, PhD, 1954. Rsch. biochemist, then dir. R & D Norwich (N.Y.) Pharmacal Co., 1954-68; dir. devel., then exec. v.p. G.D. Searle & Co., Skokie, Ill., 1968-79, also bd. dirs.; exec. v.p. Merrell Internat./Richardson Merrell Inc., Wilton, Conn., 1979-81, Merrell Dow Pharm., Inc., Cin., 1981-89; v.p. corp. affairs, mergers & acquisitions Marion Merrell Dow Inc., 1989-90; ret., 1990; mgmt.-health care cons., 1990—. Bd. dirs. Meridian Diagnostics Inc., Cin.; bd. trustees Biostart, Cin.; bd. dirs. Stolle Milk Biologics Internat., Cin. Contbr. 40 articles to profl. jours. With USNR, 1945-46, 51-55. Republican. Roman Catholic. Avocations: woodworking, golf, gardening, painting.

BYAL, NANCY LOUISE, food editor; b. Plainfield, N.J., Mar. 12, 1944; d. Albert William and Anna Marie (Goering) Zeiner; m. Wayne Ole Byal, May 2, 1967; 1 child, Jason David. BS, Iowa State U., 1965. Cert. home economist; cert. culinary prof. Product counselor Gen. Mills, Inc., Mpls., 1965-67; assoc. food editor Better Homes & Gardens Books Meredith Corp., Des Moines, 1968-72, assoc. food editor Better Homes & Gardens, 1972-74, sr. food editor, 1974-83, sr. dept. head Food and Nutrition, 1983-86, exec. food editor Better Homes and Gardens, 1986—. Chair, com. mem. Iowa State U. Coll. Family and Consumer Scis. Adv. Com., Ames; chmn., exec. mem. Julia Child Cookbook Awards Com. Editor, author: Better Home and Gardens Fondue Cook Book, 1970, Better Home and Gardens Salad Book, 1969. Named Home Economist in Bus. of Yr., Iowa Home Economists in Bus., 1992. Mem. Internat. Assn. Culinary Profls., Am. Inst. Food and Wine (mem. tast and health com.), Am. Assn. Family and Consumer Scis., Luth. Women's Missionary League. Avocations: gardening, crafting, reading. Office: Meredith Corp 1716 Locust St Des Moines IA 50309-3023

BYARS, DENNIS M. state legislator; b. Beatrice, Nebr., Aug. 23, 1940; m. Janet A. Busboom, Apr. 10, 1981; children: Mark, Jonathan. Student, U. Nebr., Doane Coll. Former small bus. owner; mem. Nebr. Legislature from 30th dist., Lincoln, 1988-94, 98—. Dir. cmty. support, govt. rels. Martin Luther Home Found.; mem. Beatrice Sch. Bd., 1970-72; chmn. Gage County Bd. Suprs., 1976-83; former chmn. Nat. Conf. State Legislatures Task Force on Devel. Disabilities; mem. Gov.'s Planning Coun. on Devel. Disabilities; faculty mem. pres. com. Mental Retardation Nat. Collaborative Acad.; pres. Beatrice Retail Coun.; chmn. Gage County Indsl. Devel. Bd.; bd. dirs. Gage County United Way, Gage County Red Cross; mem. capital campaign adv. com. YMCA Found.; mem. adv. bd. Nebr. Dept. Social Svcs.; bd. trustees Pershing Coll. With Nebr. Army NG. Recipient Pub. Svc. award City of Beatrice, Meritorious Svc. Recognition, Gage County, Outstanding Leadership award Nat. Conf. State Legislatures; named Legislator of Yr., Nebr. Hosp. Assn., Nebr. County Ofcl. of Yr., Pub. Ofcl. of Yr., Assn. Retarded Citizens. Mem. U. Nebr.--Lincoln Alumni Assn. (life mem.), Beatrice C. of C. (Good Neighbor award), Beatrice Sertoma Club, Beatrice Cmty. Hosp. Centurian Club, Rotary (hon. mem.) Home: 823 N 8th St Beatrice NE 68310-2344 Office: State Capitol Dist 30 PO Box 94604 Rm 1208 Lincoln NE 68509

BYE, KERMIT EDWARD, federal judge, lawyer; b. Hatton, N.D., Jan. 13, 1937; s. Kermit Berthrand and Margaret B. (Brekke) Bye; m. Carol Beth Soliah, Aug. 23, 1958; children: Laura Lee, William Edward, Bethany Ann. BS, U. N.D., 1959, JD, 1962. Bar: N.D. 1962, U.S. Dist. Ct. N.D. 1962, U.S. Ct. Appeals (8th cir.) 1969, U.S. Supreme Ct. 1974, Minn. 1981. Dep. securities commr. State of N.D., 1962—66, spl. asst. atty. gen., 1962—66; asst. U.S. atty. U.S. Atty.'s Office, Dist. N.D., 1966—68; ptnr. Vogel Brantner Kelly Knutson Weir & Bye, Fargo, ND, 1968—2000; judge U.S. Ct. Appeals (8th cir.), 2000—. Contbr. articles. Chmn. Red River Human Svcs. Found., 1980—83; S.E. Mental Health and Retardation Ctr., Inc. Mem.: ABA, Cass County Bar Assn., State Bar Assn. N.C. (pres. 1983—84). Democrat. Lutheran. Office: Quentin Burdick US Courthouse 655 1st Ave N Rm 300 Fargo ND 58102

BYERLY, REX R. state legislator; m. Linda Byerly; 1 child. BS, Nat. Coll., Rapid City, Mich. Computer cons.; state rep. dist. 1, 1991—. Mem. appropriations com.; chmn. human resources com. N.D. Ho. Reps. Mem. CAP. Mem. Exptl. Aviation Assn., Williston Basin Racing Assn., Moose. Republican. Home: PO Box 968 Williston ND 58802-0968

BYERS, GEORGE WILLIAM, retired entomology educator; b. Washington, May 16, 1923; s. George and Helen (Kessler) B.; m. Martha Esther Sparks, Feb. 25, 1945 (div. 1953); children: George William, Carolyn Sylvia; m. Gloria B. Wong, Dec. 16, 1955; children: Bruce Alan, Brian William, Douglas Eric BS, Purdue U., 1947; MS, U. Mich., 1948, PhD, 1952. Asst. prof. dept. entomology U. Kans., Lawrence, 1956-60, curator Snow Entomol. Mus., 1956-83, dir., sr. curator, 1983-88, assoc. prof., 1960-65, prof. entomology, 1965-88, prof. dept. systematics and ecology, 1969-88, chmn. dept. entomology, 1969-72, 84-87, ret., 1988. Vis. prof. Mountain Lake Biol. Sta. U. Va., alt. summers, 1961-92, U. Minn., 1970. Author: several book chpts.; contbr. articles to profl. jours. With U.S. Army, 1942-46, 53-56, WWII and Korea; lt. col. M.S.C., USAR, ret. Rackham fellow U. Mich., 1952-53; NSF grantee, 1958-87, 97-99. Mem. Entomol. Soc. Am. (editl. bd. Annals 1967-72, chmn. 1971-72), Entomol. Soc. Can., Ctrl. States Entomol. Soc. (pres. 1958-59), Entomol. Soc. Washington, Soc. Systematic Biology (editor Syst. Zool. jour. 1963-66), Phi Beta Kappa, Phi Kappa Phi, Sigma Xi. Avocations: invertebrate paleontology; photography; ornithology. Home: 909 Holiday Dr Lawrence KS 66049-3006 Office: U Kans Entomology Divsn Natural History Mus Lawrence KS 66045-7523 E-mail: ksem@ku.edu.

BYL, WILLIAM, state legislator; b. May 11, 1946; BS, Calvin Coll. County commr., Kent, Mich.; rep. Mich. State Dist. 75, 1995—. Transp. com. Mich. Ho. Reps., conservation com., environ. & Great Lakes com., vice chmn. urban policy com. Address: 619 Old Plaza Bldg Lansing MI 48909

BYRD, JAMES EVERETT, lawyer; b. Cin., Aug. 1, 1958; BS, U. Dayton, Ohio, 1980, JD cum laude, 1984. Law clk. U.S. Dist Ct. (so. dist.), Ohio, 1983; assoc. Smith & Schnacke, Dayton, 1984-89; v.p., gen. counsel Internat. Cargo Svcs., Virginia Beach, Va., 1989-91; assoc. Beale, Balfour et al., Richmond, 1991-92; corp. counsel Huffy Corp., Dayton, 1992-94; ind. corp. legal cons., 1994-95; assoc. gen. counsel Lexis-Nexis divsn. Reed Elsevier, Inc., Dayton, 1995—. Pres. Condominium Owners Assn., Dayton, 1995-99. Mem. ABA, Ohio Bar Assn., Va. Bar Assn. Office: Lexis-Nexis 9443 Springboro Pike Miamisburg OH 45342-4425 E-mail: james.e.byrd@lexis-nexis.com.

BYRD, VINCENT C. food products company executive; With J. M. Smucker Co., Orrville, Ohio, 1977—, treas., v.p. procurement and tech. svcs., 1988-95, v.p., gen. mgr. consumer market, 1995—. Office: J M Smucker Co 1 Strawberry Ln Orrville OH 44667-1241

BYRNE, C. WILLIAM, JR. athletics program director; b. Boston; m. Marilyn Kent; children: Bill, Greg. BBA, Idaho State U, 1967, MBA, 1971. Dir. alumni rels. Idaho State, 1971—76; exec. dir. Lobo Club, U. N.Mex., Albuquerque, 1976-79; asst. athletic dir. San Diego State U., 1980-82; assoc. dir., adminstr. Duck Athletic Fund, U. Oreg., Eugene, 1983-84, dir. athletic dept., 1984-92; dir. athletics U. Nebr., Lincoln, 1992—. Named Ctrl. Region NACDA/Continental Athletic Dir. Yr., Hall of Champions dedicated in his honor, Autzen Stadium, 1993, Nat. Fundraiser Yr., Nat. Athletic Fundraisers Assn. Mem. Nat. Assn. Collegiate Dirs. of Athletics (exec. com., pres.), U.S. Collegiate Sports Coun. (v.p., bd. dirs.), All-Am. Football Found. (v.p.), Football Assn. (bd. dirs.), NCAA (spl. events com., mktg. com., cert. com.). Office: U Nebr Athletics Dept 103 South Stadium PO Box 880120 Lincoln NE 68588-0120

BYRNE, MICHAEL JOSEPH, business executive; b. Chgo., Apr. 3, 1928; s. Michael Joseph and Edith (Lueken) B.; B.Sc. in Mktg., Loyola U., Chgo., 1952; m. Eileen Kelly, June 27, 1953; children— Michael Joseph, Nancy, James, Thomas, Patrick, Terrence. Sales engr. Emery Industries, Inc., Cin., 1952-59; with Pennsalt Chem. Corp., Phila., 1959-60; with Oakton Cleaners, Inc., Skokie, Ill., 1960-70, pres., 1960-70; pres. Datatax Inc., Skokie, 1970-74, Midwest Synthetic Lubrication Products, 1978—, Pure Water Systems, 1984—, Superior Tax Service, 1984—. Served with ordnance U.S. Army, 1946-48. Mem. A.I.M., VFW, Alpha Kappa Psi. Club: Toastmasters Internat. Home: PO Box 916 Prospect Heights IL 60070-0916

BYRNES, CHRISTOPHER IAN, academic dean, researcher; b. N.Y.C., June 28, 1949; s. Richard Francis and Jeanne (Orchard) B.; m. Catherine Morris, June 24, 1984; children: Kathleen, Alison, Christopher. BS, Manhattan Coll., 1971; MS, U. Mass., 1973, PhD, 1975; D (hon.) of Tech., Royal Inst. Tech., Stockholm, 1998. Instr. U. Utah, Salt Lake City, 1975-78; asst. prof. Harvard U., Cambridge, Mass., 1978-81, assoc. prof., 1981-85; rsch. prof. Ariz. State U., Tempe, 1985-89; prof., chmn. dept. systems sci. and math. Washington U., St. Louis, 1989-91, dean engring. and applied sci., 1991—. Adj. prof. Royal Inst. Tech., Stockholm, 1985-90; cons. Sci. Sys., Inc., Cambridge, 1980-84, Sys. Engring., Inc., Greenbelt, Md., 1986; sci. advisor Sherwood Davis & Geck, 1996-98, Aucsyn Venture Capital Cernium Inc., 2002-; mem. NRC; bd. dirs., chmn. compensation com. Belden Inc.; chmn. bd. dirs. Ctr. for Emerging Techs.; pres., bd. dirs. WUTA, Inc. Editor: (book series) Progress in Systems Control, 1988—01, Foundations of Systems and Control, 1998—2001; Nonlinear Synthesis, 1991, 13 other books; contbr. numerous articles to profl. jours., book revs. Recipient Best Paper award, IFAC, 1993. Fellow: IEEE (Geroge Axelby award 1991), Acad. Sci. St. Louis, Japan Soc. for Promotion Sci.; mem.: AAAS, Regional Chamber for Growth Assn. (vice chmn. tech., chmn Tech. Gateway Alliance), Royal Swedish Acad. Engring. Sci. (fgn.), Am. Math. Soc., Soc. Indsl. Applied Math. (program com. 1986—89), Tau Beta Pi, Sigma Xi. Avocations: cooking, fishing, travel. Office: Washington U Sch Engring and Applied Sci 1 Brookings Dr Saint Louis MO 63130-4899 E-mail: Chrisbyrnes@seas.wustl.edu.

BYRON, RITA ELLEN COONEY, travel executive, publisher, real estate agent, photojournalist, writer; b. Cleve.; d. Harry James and Marie (Hakey) Cooney; m. Carl James Byron Jr., Nov. 27, 1954 (dec.); children: Carey Lewis, Carl James, Bradford William. Student Cleve. Coll., 1954, Western Res. U., 1955, John Carroll U., 1956; PhD (hon.), Colo. State Christian Coll., 1972. Mgr. European Immigration dept. U.S. Steamship Lines, Cleve., 1956; real estate agt. W.I. White Realtor Inc., Shaker Heights, Ohio, 1965-67, J.P. Malone Realtors Inc., Shaker Heights, 1967-70, Thomas Murray & Assocs., 1971-76, Mary Anderson Realty, Shaker Heights, 1978-79, Barth Brad & Andrews Realtors Inc., Shaker Heights, 1979—, Heights Realty, 1986—; v.p., co-owner Your Connection To Travel, Kent, Ohio, 1980—; v.p., gen. mgr. World Class Travel Agy., 1985—; dir. Travel One div. Quaker Sq., Akron, Travel Trends for Singles, 1985, Playhouse Sq. Travel, 1986, World Class Internat., 1986. Mem. U.S. Figure Skating Assn., 1960—, Wightman Cup Women's Com., 1965—; mem. women's com. Cleve. Mus. of Art, 1969—, Friendship Force Ohio, 1986 ; co-chmn. Cleve. Invitational Figure Skating Competition, 1972—; chmn. Gold Rush Rush, U.S. Ski Team, 1982, Cleve. benefit U.S. Olympic Teams, Midas Touch, 1983, Gran Apres-Ski Prix, 1981, blue ribbon ball Hunt Club for Handicapped; patron Cleve. 500, 1983; originator Benefits Unltd., Exceptional Single Person's, Connections Unltd., 1983; founder, coordinator Singled Out Club, 1983; co-ptnr., adv. bd. The Service Service, 1984; benefit chmn., patroness various balls and fund-raising events; vol. Foster Parents Inc., 1983; vol. Council on World Affairs, 1983, Bellefaire Home for Spl. Children, 1983, Big Sisters Greater Cleve., 1983, Camp Cheerful, 1983, Chisholm Ctr., 1983, Children's Diabetic Camp Ho Mita Koda, 1984, Young Audiences, 1985; adv. trustee Friends of Fairmount Theatre of the Deaf, 1983; mem. Greater Cleve. Growth Assn., 1983. Mem. Western Res. Hist. Soc., Garden Ctr. Greater Cleve., Friends Cleve. Pub. Library, UN Assn. of U.S., Cleve. Council World Affairs, U.S. Ski Ednl. Fund (chmn. benefits), English Speaking Union (jr. bd.), Travel Age Exchange, Globetrotters Internat. Fedn. Women's Travel Orgns., North Coast Exec. Women's Network, Growth Assn., Council on Small Enterprises. Cleve. Real Estate Bd., Cleve. Photographic Soc. (bd. dirs. 1989—), Camera Guild (exec. bd. trustees 1989), Associated Photographers, Photographic Soc. Am. Clubs: Cleve. Skating, Broadmoor World Arena Figure Skating, Colony Beach and Racquet, Suburban Ski, Cleve. Advertising, Communicator's, Towne Hall, Women's City, Gilmour Acad. Women's, Mid-Day, Cleve. Wellesley, Arctic Circle, Intrepid Traveler, Tibet, Mongolia and China Explorers', Himalaya Yeti (1987 Nepal Expdn.), Internat. Chagrin Valley Camera, Nat. Hist. Mus. Photo Soc., Kodochrome Adventure Soc., Nature Artists Soc., Cleve. Astronomical Soc., Archeol. Soc., Holden Aborteum Soc., East Berlin Photo Club, Chagrin Valley Photo Club, Shaker Lakes Nature Club, Met. Parks, Photography Club, Photocrafters, Sanctuary Marsh Photo, Cuyahoga Valley Nat. Pk. Photo Club (assoc. photographer, various photography awards). Co-pub., exec. editor The Single Register (pub. documentary book The Fall of the Wall 1989), other publs.; featured in numerous publs. Home: 18126 Lomond Blvd Cleveland OH 44122-5012 Office: World Class Travel 3520 Ingleside Rd Cleveland OH 44122-5002 also: Es Turo Edificio Kontiki Majorica Balearic Islands Spain

BYRUM, DIANNE, state legislator, small business owner; b. Mar. 18, 1954; d. Cecil Dershem and Mary D.; m. James E. Byrum; children: Barbara Anne, James Richard. AA, Lansing Cmty. Coll.; BS cum laude, Mich. State U. Rep. dist. 68 Mich. Ho. of Reps. from 68th dist., Lansing, 1991-94; mem. Mich. Senate from 25th dist., 1995—; owner Blackhawk Hardware, Leslie, Mich., 1983—, Panther Hardware, Stockbridge, 1991—. Minority vice chair agr. and forestry, health policy and sr. citizens; mem. tech. and energy com., capitol com.; chair dem. caucus. Recipient Disting. Citizen award Ingham County Soil Conservation Dist., 1991, Disting. Alumnus award Lansing Cmty. Coll., 1993. Mem. Mich. Retail Hardware Assn., Lansing Regional C. of C., South Lansing Bus. Assn., South Lansing-Everett Kiwanis. Democrat. Office: Mich State Senate 125 W Allegan PO Box 30036 Lansing MI 48909-7536 E-mail: sendbyrum@senate.state.mi.us.

BYRUM-SUTTON, JUDITH MIRIAM, accountant; b. Bismarck, N.D., Sept. 24, 1943; d. Adolph Mathew and Gertrude Cecelia (Lechner) H.; m. Richard W. Byrum, July 30, 1965 (div. Oct. 1984); children: Thomasin Jane, Toby Oliver; m. Danny D. Jansen, Oct. 21, 1989 (dec. Nov. 1989); m. Jack N. Sutton, June 26, 1993. BS in Acctg., Ariz. State U., 1967. CPA, Ariz., Kans. Underwriter Gt. SW Fire Ins. Co., Mesa, Ariz., 1963-65; staff auditor Touche Ross & Co., London, 1967-69, Arthur Andersen & Co., Kansas City, Mo., 1970-71; treas. John J. Peterson Real Estate, Overland Park, Kans., 1971-75; internal auditor Bus. Men's Assurance Co., Kansas City, 1975-78; owner Judith H. Byrum, CPA, Chartered, 1978—; ptnr. G.R. Starbuck & Co. P.A., Leawood, Kans., 1996—. Contbr. articles to newsletter. Mem. adv. bd. Rockhurst Coll. Women's Ctr., Kansas City, 1977; mem. Congressman Larry Winn II Small Bus. Com., Washington, 1977-80; treas. Trinity Luth. Ch., Mission, Kans., 1990-94. Mem. AICPA (legis. liaison), Am. Woman's Soc. CPAs (treas., v.p. Chgo. 1977-83), Am. Soc. Women Accts. (pres. Kansas City 1980-81), Kans. Soc. CPAs (com. mem. 1977—, pres., v.p., treas. Metro chpt. 1989—, bd. dirs. 1994-97), Kansas City Women's C. of C. (v.p. 1980), Beta Alpha Psi. Avocations: skiing, golf, reading, gardening, hunting. Office: 4601 College Blvd Ste 160 Leawood KS 66211-1678

CACCHIONE, PATRICK JOSEPH, health association executive; b. Syracuse, N.Y., Mar. 19, 1959; s. Nicholas Phillip and Ruth Helen (Liadka) C.; m. Pamela Carol Zurkowski, Oct. 8, 1988. BA, Hobart Coll., 1981; MPA, Am. U., 1983. Rsch. asst. Brookings Instn., Washington, 1982-83; field organizer Mondale for Pres. Campaign, 1983-84; legis. asst. Office of Congressman Tom Luken, 1985-86; cons. Am. Express Co., 1986, Francis, McGinnis and Rees Assocs., Washington, 1986; legis. asst. Law Office of Raymond D. Cotton, 1987-88; dir. legis. affairs Nat. Assn. Med. Equipment Suppliers, Alexandria, Va., 1988-90; v.p. govt. affairs Daus. of Charity Nat. Health System, St. Louis, 1991-98; v.p. advocacy/comm. Carondelet Health System, 1998—. Cons. Cardondelet Health System, St. Louis, 1992—; candidate U.S. House Rep., First Dist. Mo., 1993—. Contbr. articles to profl. publs. Vol. Harriet Woods for Senate, St. Louis, 1986, Guardian Angels Settlement, St. Louis, 1991-92, Jack Garvey for Cir. Atty., St. Louis, 1992; campaign mgr. Dianne Smith for County Coun., Silver Spring, Md., 1990; bd. dirs. Compton Heights Civic Assn., St. Louis, 1992. Mem. St. Louis Ambassadors, Women in Govt. Rels., Democratic Club, Healthcare Fin. Mgrs. Assn., Network. Democrat. Roman Catholic. Avocations: golf, reading, movies, antiques, travel. Office: Cardondelet Health System 13801 Riverport Dr Maryland Heights MO 63043-4828 Home: 3419 Hawthorne Blvd Saint Louis MO 63104-1622

CACIOPPO, JOHN TERRANCE, psychology educator, researcher; b. Marshall, Tex., June 12, 1951; s. Cyrus Joseph and Mary Katherine (Kazimour) Cacioppo; m. Barbara Lee Andersen, May 17, 1981 (div. 1998); children: Christina Elizabeth, Anthony Cyrus; m. Wendi L. Gardner, Sept. 8, 2001. BS in Econs., U. Mo., Columbia, 1973; MA in Psychology, Ohio State U., 1975, PhD in Psychology, 1977. Asst. prof. psychology U. Notre Dame, Ind., 1977-79, U. Iowa, Iowa City, 1979-81, assoc. prof., 1981-85, prof. psychology, 1985-89, Ohio State U., 1989-98, Univ. chaired prof. psychology, 1998-99; Tiffany-Margaret Blake disting. svc. prof. U. Chgo., 1999—. Vis. faculty Yale U., 1986, U. Hawaii, 1990, U. Chgo., 1998—99; tng. grant dir. NIMH Social Psychology, 1993—98; co-dir. Inst. for Mind and Biology, 1999—; dir. Social Psychology Program, 1999—. Author (& editor): 6 books; editor: Psychophysiology, 1994—97; mem. editl. bd.: various prof. jours.; contbr. articles over 270 to profl. jours. Active John D. and Catherine T. MacArthur Found. Network on Mid-Body Integrations, 1995-98; bd. dirs. Ohio State U. Rsch. Found., 1993-98 Recipient Early Career Contbn. award Psychophysiology, 1981, Troland Rsch. award NAS, 1989, Disting. Sci. Contbr. Psychophysiol., Soc. Psychophysiol. Rsch., 2000; NSF grantee, 1979—, Campbell award Soc. Personality and Social Psychology, 2000. Fellow: APA (past pres. 2 divsns., Disting. Sci. Contbn. award 2002), Acad. Behavioral Medicine; mem.: AMA, Soc. Exptl. Social Psychology, Soc. Personality and Social Psychology (pres. 1995), Soc. Psychophysiol. Rsch. (bd. dirs. 1985—88, 1998—, officer 1991—94, pres. 1992—93), Acad. Behavioral Medicine Rsch., AM. Psychol. Soc. (keynote spkr. ann. meeting 2002), Sigma Xi (nat. lectr. 1996—98). Office: U Chgo Dept Psychology Chicago IL 60637

CADOGAN, WILLIAM J. telecommunications company executive; b. 1948; With AT&T, 1971-86, Intelsat, 1986-87, ADC Telecomm. Inc., Mpls., 1987—, pres., COO, 1990—, CEO, 1991—, chmn., 1994—. Office: ADC Telecomm Inc PO Box 1101 Minneapolis MN 55440

CADY, MARK S. state supreme court justice; b. Rapid City, S.D. married; 2 children. Undergrad. degree, Drake U., JD, 1978. Law clk. 2d Jud. Dist. Ct., 1978-79; asst. Webster County atty.; with law firm Ft. Dodge; dist. assoc. judge, 1983; dist. ct. judge, 1986; judge Iowa Ct. Appeals, 1994, chief judge, 1994; justice Iowa Supreme Ct., 1998—. Chmn. Supreme Ct. Task Force on Ct.'s and Cmty.'s Response to Domestic Abuse. Mem.: Webster County Bar Assn., Iowa State Bar Assn. Office: Iowa Supreme Ct State House Des Moines IA 50319-0001 E-mail: MarkS.Cady@jb.state.ia.us.

CAFARO, ANTHONY M. corporate executive; Prin., owner The Cafaro Co., Youngstown, Ohio, 1995—. Office: The Cafaro Co PO Box 2186 2445 Belmont Ave Youngstown OH 44504-0186 Fax: 330-743-2902.

CAHILL, DAVID G. materials science educator, engineering educator; b. Feb. 15, 1962; BS in Engring. Physics, Ohio State U., 1984; PhD in Exptl. Condensed Matter Physics, Cornell U., 1989. Grad. rsch. asst. Cornell U., Ithaca, N.Y., 1984-89; postdoct. rsch. assoc. IBM Watson Rsch. Ctr., 1984-89; asst. prof. dept. materials sci. and engring. U. Ill., Urbana-Champaign, 1989-91, assoc. prof. dept. materials sci. and engring., 1997—. Coord. materials sci. and engring. component Jr. Engr. Technical Soc., minority intro. to engring. program, 1992-95; workshop co-chair heat trasport in amorphous solids 7th Internat. Conf. Phonon Scattering in Condensed Matter, Ithaca, N.Y., 1992; mem. pre-proposal rev. panel Optical Sci. Engring. Initiative NSF, 1996, Career award rev. panel DMR Electronic Materials, 1997, nanotechnology proposal review panel, 1998; mem. scientific adv. com. Dynamic Crystal Surfaces and Interfaces, 1996; co-organizer March meeting nanometer-scale morphology of surfaces and interfaces divsn. of material physics Am. Phys. Soc., Kansas City, 1997, sessions on thermo-phys. properties of thin films 13th Symposium on Thermophys. Properties, 1997; lead organizer Evolution of Surface and Thin Film Microstructure Mateials Rsch. Soc., Boston, 1997; cons. INRAD, Northvale, N.J., 1991, Hoechst Celanese, Summit, N.J., 1993, United Technologies, East Hartford, Conn., 1993-96, Pratt & Whitney, West Palm Beach, Fla., 1994-96, HiPatent, Chgo., 1996-98, Read-Rite, Fremont, Calif., 1998, Sumitomo Metal Industries, Kyoto, Japan, 1998; presenter in field. Contbr. numerous articles to profl. jours., chpts. to books. Advisor electronic materials group materials tech. workshop for high sch. tchrs. NSF, 1995. Grad. fellow NSF, 1984-87; recipient Charles Luck award Internat. Thermal Conductivity Conf., 1989. Fellow Am. Vacuum Soc. (Peter Mark meml. award 1998, mem. exec. bd. nanometer-scale sci. and tech. divsn. 1995-97). Office: U Il Dept Material Sci & Engring 1101 W Springfield Ave Urbana IL 61801-3005 Fax: 217-244-1631. E-mail: d-cahill@vive.edu.

CAHILL, PATRICIA DEAL, radio station executive; b. St. Louis, Oct. 9, 1947; d. Richard Joseph and Dorothy (Deal) C.; m. children: Lindsay Cahill, Jessica Cahill Crump. BA, U. Kans., 1969, MA, 1971. Continuity dir. Sta. KANU-FM, Lawrence, Kans., 1970, audio reader dir., 1970-73; reporter Sta. KCUR-FM, Kansas City, Mo., 1973-75; news dir. Sta. KMUW-FM, Wichita, Kans., 1975, gen. mgr., 1976-87, Sta. KCUR-FM, Kansas City, 1987—. Asst. prof. communications studies U. Mo. Kansas City, 1987—; dir. Nat. Pub. Radio, 1982-88, exec. com., 1983-88, chair tech. and distbn., 1985-88. Chmn. Wichita Free U., 1979-81; v.p. Planned Parenthood Kans., 1986-87; bd. dirs. Kansas City Cultural Alliance. Recipient Matrix award Wichita chpt. Women in Commn., 1986, Alumni Honor citation U. Kans., 1993. Mem. Pub. Radio Mid. Am. (pres. 1979-80, 89-93), Radio Rsch. Consortium (bd. dirs. 1981—), Kans. Pub. Radio Assn. (bd. dirs. 1980-87). Office: Sta KCUR 4825 Troost Ave Ste 202 Kansas City MO 64110-2030

CAIN, J. MATTHEW, prosecutor; b. Cleve., Oct. 3, 1943; m. Karen, 1965 J. Telliard; 4 children. BSBA, Ohio State U., 1966; postgrad., Golden Gate Coll., 1968-70; JD cum laude, Ohio State U., 1966. Bar: Ohio 1972, U.S. Supreme Ct. 1979, U.S. Dist. Ct. (no. dist.) Ohio 1981, U.S. Ct. Appeals (6th cir.) 1983. Employee rels. & ins. Diamond Shamrock Corp., 1966-73; asst. county prosecutor Cuyahoga County, Ohio, 1973-80; asst. U.S. atty. Cleve., 1980—; chief criminal divsn. Office of U.S. Atty. (no. dist.) Ohio, 1987—. With USN, 1960-63. Avocation family. Office: US Atty Rm 1800 Bank One Ctr 600 Superior Ave E Ste 1800 Cleveland OH 44114-2600

CAIN, MADELINE ANN, mayor; b. Cleve., Nov. 21, 1949; d. Edward Vincent and Mary Rita (Quinn) C. BA, Ursuline Coll., 1973; MPA, Cleve. State U., 1985. Tchr. St. Augustine Acad., Lakewood, Ohio, 1973-75; clk. coun. legis. aide Lakewood City Coun., 1981-85; legis. liaison Cuyahoga County Bd. Commrs., Cleve., 1985-88; mem. Ohio Ho. of Reps., Columbus, 1989-95; mayor City of Lakewood, Lakewood, Ohio, 1995—. Mem. Cudell Neighborhood Improvement Corp., West Blvd. Neighborhood Assn.; trustee Malachi House. Mem. Lakewood Bus. and Profl. Women, Lakewood C. of C., City Club. Democrat. Roman Catholic. Office: Lakewood City Hall 12650 Detroit Ave Lakewood OH 44107-2891

CAIN, R. WAYNE, sales, finance and leasing company executive; b. 1937; BA, Wayne State U., 1959; LLB, N.Y.U., 1962. Lawyer Cleary, Gottlieb, Steen & Hamilton, 1962-63; with Chrysler Corp., Chrysler Fin. Corp., 1965-81; asst. treas. Navistar Internat. Corp., 1981-85; v.p., treas. Navistar Fin. Corp., 1985—, Harco Leasing Co., Inc. Del.; treas. Harco Nat. Ins. Co. With USAF, 1963-65. Office: Navistar Fin Corp 2850 W Golf Rd Rolling Meadows IL 60008-4050

CAIN, TIM J. lawyer; b. Angola, Ind., July 12, 1958; s. Nancy J. (Nichols) C.; m. Debra J. VanWagner, Feb. 28, 1976; children: Christine M., Stephanie L., Katherine S., Jennifer A. BA in Polit. Sci. with honors, Ind. U., 1980; JD, Valparaiso U., 1984; MBA, Ind. Wesleyan U., 1991; LLM in Internat. Bus. and Trade, John Marshall Law Sch., 2001. Bar: Ind. 1984, U.S. Dist. Ct. (no. and so. dists.) Ind. 1984. Assoc. Hartz & Eberhard, LaGrange, Ind., 1984-85; pub. defender LaGrange Cir. Ct., 1985-86; sr. assoc. Eberhard & Assocs., LaGrange, 1985-86; chief dep. to Pros. Atty.'s Office, 1986-87; ptnr. Eberhard & Cain, 1986-89; pvt. practice, 1989-95. Asst. atty. La Grange County, La Grange, 1984-89, prosecuting atty., 1991—; atty. Town of Shipshewana, Ind., 1984-93. Coach Orland (Ind.) Little League, 1977-79, Prairie Hts. Baseball, LaGrange, 1986-90; pres. Prairie Hts. H.S. Dollars for Scholars, LaGrange, 1989; active LaGrange County Coun. on Aging, 1989-91, Prairie Hts. At-Risk Students Com., 1989—, LaGrange County 4-H Fair Assn., 1993-97. Mem. ATLA, Ind. Bar Assn., LaGrange County Bar Assn. (sec.-treas. 1986-87, v.p. 1987-89, pres. 1990-93). Republican. Club: Exchange (pres. 1988-89). Home: 360 S 900 E Lagrange IN 46761-9529 Office: 114 W Michigan St Lagrange IN 46761-1853

CAINE, STANLEY PAUL, college administrator; b. Huron, S.D., Feb. 11, 1940; s. Louis Vernon and Elizabeth (Holland) C.; m. Karen Anne Mickelson, July 11, 1964; children: Rebecca, Kathryn, David. BA, Macalester Coll., 1962; MS, U. Wis., 1964, PhD, 1967; LLD, Hanover Coll., 2000. Asst. prof. history Lindenwood Coll., St. Charles, Mo., 1967-71; from asst. to assoc. prof. history DePauw U., Greencastle, Ind., 1971-77; prof. history, v.p. for acad. affairs Hanover (Ind.) Coll., 1977-89; pres. Adrian (Mich.) Coll., 1989—. Bd. dirs. NCAA Coun., 1995-96, vice chair mgmt. coun. divsn. III, 1997-99, pres.'s coun., 1999-2002; cons., evaluator North Ctrl. Assn., 1984—. Author: The Myth of a Political Reform, 1970; contbr. to book The Progressive Era, 1974; co-editor: Political Reform in Wisconsin, 1973. Bd. dirs. Nat. Assn. Schs., Colls. and Univs. of United Meth. Ch., 1994-97, 2000—; mem. Lenawee Tomorrow, Adrian, 1989—. Recipient D.C. Everest prize Wis. State Hist. Soc., 1968; Woodrow Wilson fellow, 1962-63, Nat. Presbyn. fellow Presbyn. Ch. U.S., 1963-65 Mem. Orgn. Am. Historians, Nat. Assn. Ind. Colls. Univs. (bd. dirs. 1997-2000), Rotary. Methodist. Avocations: sports, reading. Office: Adrian Coll Office of Pres 110 S Madison St Adrian MI 49221-2518

CAIRNS, JAMES DONALD, lawyer; b. Chelsea, Mass., Aug. 7, 1931; s. Stewart Scott and Kathleen (Hand) C.; m. Alice Crout Cairns, June 18, 1988; children from previous marriage: Douglas S., Timothy H., Pamela S., Heather M. AB, Harvard U., 1952; JD, Ohio State U., 1958. Bar: Fla. 1974, Ohio 1958, U.S. Dist. Ct. (no. dist.) Ohio 1975, U.S. Tax Ct. 1963. Ptnr. Squire, Sanders & Dempsey, Cleve., 1958-95, Spieth, Bell, McCurdy & Newell, Cleve., 1995—. Served to lt. (j.g.) USNR, 1952-55. Mem. ABA, Am. Coll. Trust and Estate Counsel, Fla. Bar Assn., Ohio State Bar Assn., Bar Assn. Greater Cleve., Union Club, Edgewater Yacht Club, Shoreby Club. Democrat. Episcopalian. Office: Spieth Bell McCurdy Newell 2000 Huntington Bldg 925 Euclid Ave Cleveland OH 44115-1408 E-mail: dcairns@spiethbell.com.

CAIRNS, JAMES ROBERT, mechanical engineering educator; b. Indpls., Feb. 4, 1930; s. John Joseph and Agatha Bertha (Krebs) C.; m. Catherine I. DiCicco, Feb. 6, 1954; children: James Robert, Steven J., Michael P., Daniel F., Timothy E., Robert B. B.S. in Mech. Engring, U. Detroit, 1954; M.S. in Engring, U. Mich., 1959, Ph.D., 1963. Registered profl. engr., Mich. cert. energy mgr. Instr. U. Detroit, 1954-57, U. Mich., Ann Arbor, 1957-63, asst. prof. Dearborn, 1963-65, asso. prof., 1965-68, prof. mech. engring., 1968—, chmn. engring. div., 1964-73, acting dean, 1973-75, dean, 1975-81. Cons. and expert witness in product liability litigation. Contbr. articles to profl. jours. Ford Faculty fellow, 1960-63 Mem. ASME, ASHRAE, Assn. Energy Engrs., Am. Soc. Engring. Edn., Common Cause, Tau Beta Pi, Pi Tau Sigma. Roman Catholic. Home: 836 Dover Dr Dearborn Heights MI 48127-4144 Office: 4901 Evergreen Rd Dearborn MI 48128-2406 E-mail: bcairns@dhol.org.

CALAHAN, DONALD ALBERT, electrical engineering educator; b. Cin., Feb. 23, 1935; s. Joseph Dexter and Loretta Margaret (Reichling) C.; m. Martha Meyer, Aug. 22, 1959; children: Donald Theodore, Patricia Susan, Mary Susan, Judith Lynn. B.S., U. Notre Dame, 1957; M.S., U. Ill., 1958, Ph.D., 1960. Asst. prof. elec. engring. U. Ill., 1961-65; prof. elec. engring. U. Ky., 1965-66; prof. computer engring. U. Mich., Ann Arbor, 1966—. Indsl. cons. in high speed computation, 1976— Author: Modern Network Synthesis, 1964, Computer-Aided Network Design, 1967, rev. edit., 1972, Introduction to Modern Circuit Analysis, 1974. Served to 1st lt. U.S. Army, 1961-62. Fellow IEEE. Roman Catholic. Home: 3139 Lexington Dr Ann Arbor MI 48105-1461 Office: U Mich Dept Elec Engring & Computer Sci Ann Arbor MI 48109

CALCATERRA, EDWARD LEE, construction company executive; b. St. Louis, Mar. 26, 1930; s. Frank John and Rose Theresa (Ruggeri) C.; m. Patricia Jean Marlow, July 4, 1953; children— Christine, Curtis, David, Richard, Tracy B.S.C.E., U. Mo., Rollo, 1952. Registered profl. engr., Mo. Estimator J.S. Alberici Constrn. Co., St. Louis, 1955-57, mgr. project, 1957-63, v.p. ops., 1963-71, sr. v.p., 1971-76, exec. v.p., 1976-91, pres., 1991-96; exec. dir. J.S. Albenci Constrn. Co., 1996—. Bd. dirs. Cardinal Ritter Inst., St. Louis, 1980-83; bd. regents Rockhurst Coll., Kansas City, Mo., 1983— . Served with U.S. Army, 1953-55 Mem. Assoc. Gen. Contractors St. Louis (pres. 1980) Roman Catholic

CALDWELL, CHARLES M. federal judge; b. 1954; BS, Evansville U., 1976; JD, Northwestern U., 1979. Asst. U.S. trustee U.S. Dist. Ct. (so. dist.) Ohio, 1988-93; staff atty. bankruptcy divsn. Adminstrv. Office U.S. Cts., Washington, 1986-88; bankruptcy judge U.S. Bankruptcy Ct., Columbus, 1993—. Office: US Bankruptcy Ct 170 N High St Columbus OH 43215-2403 Fax: (614) 469-2478.

CALDWELL, WILEY NORTH, retired distribution company executive; b. L.A., Apr. 24, 1927; s. Wiley North and Jean (Clarke) C.; m. Joanne Humphrey, Mar. 25, 1950; children: David, Wendy, Charles, Thomas. BSME, Stanford U., 1950; MBA, Harvard U., 1952. Mgr. prodn. control Waste King Corp., L.A., 1952-54; v.p., co-founder Poroloy Equipment, Inc., Van Nuys, Calif., 1954-58, dir. sales and mktg. Bendix Filter div., 1958-60; v.p. Jamieson Labs., Inc., 1960-61; v.p. mktg., exec. v.p. McGaw Labs., Am. Hosp. Supply Corp., L.A., Chgo., 1961-69; v.p. internat. Am. Hosp. Supply Corp., Chgo., 1969-72, pres. Midwest Dental div., 1972-77; v.p. ops. distbn. group W.W. Grainger, Inc., Skokie, Ill., 1977-78, pres. distbn. group, 1978-81, exec. v.p., 1981-84, pres., 1984-92; ret., 1992; also bd. dirs. W.W. Grainger, Inc., Skokie, Ill., 1979-93; ret., 1993. Bd. dirs. Kewaunee Sci. Corp., Statesville, N.C., Alliant Exch. Inc., Deerfield, Ill., Evanston Northwestern Healthcare, Inc., Ill.; chmn. bd. dirs. Presbyn. Homes, Evanston, Chgo. Found. for Edn. Mem. adv. bd. J.L. Kellogg Grad. Sch., Northwestern U., mem. Northwestern U. Assocs. With USN, 1945-46. Mem. Indian Hill Club, Chgo. Club, Old Elm Club, The Econ. Club Chgo., The Chgo. Com. Home: 125 Woodstock Ave Kenilworth IL 60043-1231 Office: 5215 Old Orchard Rd Ste 440 Skokie IL 60077-1047

CALENOFF, LEONID, radiologist; b. Vienna, Austria, Aug. 24, 1923; arrived in U.S., 1957, naturalized, 1962; s. Albert and Anna (Prover) C.; m. Miriam Arnon, Oct. 30, 1955; children— Jean Zucker, Deborah Lipoff. M.D., U. Paris, 1955. Diplomate Am. Bd. Radiology. Intern Jewish Hosp., Cin., 1958; resident in radiology U. Ill. Med. Center, Chgo., 1959-61; asst. radiologist Ill. Research and Ednl. Hosp., 1961-64; chief radiology Chgo. State Hosp., 1963-68; dir. radiology Sheridan Gen. Hosp., Chgo., 1964-68; attending radiologist West Side VA Hosp., 1963-68, Rehab. Inst. Chgo., 1974-89, chief diagnostic radiology, 1974-86; attending radiologist Northwestern Meml. Hosp., Chgo., 1968—, chief outpatient diagnostic radiology, 1979—, vice chmn. dept. radiology, 1991-96; chief diagnostic radiology Passavant Pavillion of Northwestern Meml. Hosp., 1972-79; asst. prof. radiology Northwestern U. Med. Sch., 1970-73, asso. prof., 1973-78, prof., 1978—. Author articles in field, chpts. in books.; Editor: Radiology of Spinal Cord Injury, 1981. Fellow Am. Coll. Radiology; mem. Radiol. Soc. N.Am., Am. Roentgen Ray Soc. Home: 1515 N Astor St #18A Chicago IL 60610-1627 Office: Galter 4-321 675 N Saint Clair St Chicago IL 60611-5975 E-mail: l-calenoff@northwestern.edu.

CALFEE, JOHN BEVERLY, retired lawyer; b. Cleve., May 2, 1913; s. Robert M. and Alwine (Haas) C.; m. Nancy Leighton, Feb. 8, 1944; children: John Beverly Jr., David L., Peter H., Mark E. Grad., Hotchkiss Sch., 1931; BA, Yale U., 1935; LLB, Western Res. U., 1938. Bar: Ohio 1939. Sr. ptnr. Calfee, Halter & Griswold, Cleve., 1939-86, ret., 1987. Dir. civil def., Cleveland Heights, 1951; active Cuyohoga County Rep. Fin. Com., 1978—81; mem. Ohio N.W. Ordinance Bicentennial Commn., 1986. Mem. ABA, Ohio Bar Assn., Cleve. Bar Assn., Ohio Hist. Soc. (trustee 1988-97 Presbyterian. Home: 4892 Clubside Rd Cleveland OH 44124-2539

CALFEE, WILLIAM LEWIS, lawyer; b. Cleveland Heights, Ohio, July 12, 1917; s. Robert Martin and Alwine (Haas) C.; m. Eleanor Elizabeth Bliss, Dec. 6, 1941; children: William R., Bruce K., Cynthia B. B.A., Harvard Coll., 1939; LL.D., Yale U., 1946. Bar: Ohio 1946. Assoc. Baker & Hostetler, Cleve., 1946-56, ptnr., 1957-90, of counsel, 1990-92. Bd. dirs. Growth Assn. Greater Cleve., 1979-92; trustee Greater Cleve. United Appeal; pres. Health Fund Greater Cleve. Served to lt. col. M.I., U.S. Army, 1941-45. Decorated Legion of Merit; decorated Order of Brit. Empire Mem. ABA (ho. of dels. 1980-93), Ohio Bar Assn., Bar Assn. Greater Cleve. (trustee 1980-93, pres. 1979-80), Nat. Conf. Bar Pres. (exec. coun. 1982-85), Ohio C. of C. (bd. dirs. 1993), Mayfield Country Club (pres.), Union Club, Pepper Pike Club. Republican. Episcopalian. Home: 2845 SOM Center Rd Chagrin Falls OH 44022-6653

CALHOUN, DONALD EUGENE, JR. federal judge; b. Columbus, Ohio, May 15, 1926; s. Donald Eugene and Esther C.; m. Shirley Claggett, Aug. 28, 1948; children: Catherine C., Donald Eugene III, Elizabeth C. BA in Polit. Sci., Ohio State U., 1949, JD, 1951. Bar: Ohio 1951. Pvt. practice, 1951-68; ptnr. Folkerth, Calhoun, Webster, Maurer & O'Brien, 1968-82, Guren, Merritt, Feibel, Sogg & Cohen, 1982-84; of counsel Lane, Alton, Horst, 1984-85; judge U. S. Bankruptcy Ct., Columbus, 1985-99, ret., 1999, recalled, 2000—. Gen. counsel Ohio Conf. United Ch. of Christ, 1964-85 Chmn. City-wide Citizens Com. for Neighborhood Seminars on Sch. Program and Fin., 1963; mem. Columbus Bd. Edn., 1963-71, pres., 1966, 70. With USNR, 1944-46. Mem. Columbus Bar Assn. (pres. 1967-68, Community Svc. award 1972), Nat. Conf. Bar Pres., Am. Arbitration Assn., Columbus Jaycees (life), Athletic Club, Masons. Congregationalist. Office: US Bankruptcy Ct 170 N High St Columbus OH 43215-2403

CALINESCU, ADRIANA GABRIELA, museum curator, art historian; b. Bucharest, Romania, Dec. 30, 1941; came to U.S., 1973; d. Nicolae and Tamara Gane; m. Matei Alexe Calinescu, Apr. 29, 1963; children: Irena, Matthew. BA, Cen. Lycée, Bucharest, 1959; MA in English, U. Bucharest, 1964; MLS, Ind. U., 1976, MA in Art History, 1983. Asst. prof. Inst. Theater and Cinema, Bucharest, 1967-73; rsch. assoc. Ind. U. Art Mus., Bloomington, 1979-83, Thomas T. Solley curator ancient art, assoc. scholar, 1992—. Vis. assoc. mem. Am. Sch. Classical Studies, Athens, Greece, 1984. Author: The Art of Ancient Jewelry, 1994; author, co-editor: Ancient Art from the V. G. Simkhovitch Collection, 1988; editor: Ancient Jewelry and Archaeology, 1996. NEA fellow, 1984; grantee Salzburg Seminar, 1970, NEA, 1987, 93, Kress Found., 1991, Internat. Rsch. and Exchanges Bd., 1991. Mem. Am. Inst. Archaeology, Classical Art Soc., Beta Phi Mu. Office: Ind U Art Mus E 7th St Bloomington IN 47405

CALISE, WILLIAM JOSEPH, JR. lawyer; b. N.Y.C., May 22, 1938; s. William Joseph and Adeline (Rota) C.; m. Elizabeth Mae Gagne, Apr. 16, 1966; children: Kimberly Elizabeth, Andrea Elizabeth. BA, Bucknell U., 1960; MBA, JD, Columbia U., 1963. Bar: N.Y. 1963, D.C. 1981. Assoc., then ptnr. Chadbourne & Parke, NYC, 1967—94; sr. v.p., gen. counsel, sec. Rockwell Automation, Inc., Milw., 1994—. Dir. Henry St. Settlement, N.Y.C., 1977-94; mem. Allendale (N.J.) Sch. Bd., 1977-80. Capt. U.S. Army, 1964-66. Mem. Assn. Bar N.Y.C., Milw. Club. Roman Catholic. Office: Rockwell Automation Inc 777 E Wisconsin Ave Milwaukee WI 53202-5300 E-mail: wjcalise@corp.rockwell.com.

CALKINS, HUGH, foundation executive; b. Newton, Mass., Feb. 20, 1924; s. Grosvenor and Patty (Phillips) C.; m. Ann Clark, June 14, 1955; children: Peter, Andrew, Margaret, Elizabeth. AB, LLB, Harvard U., 1949, D in Law (hon.), 1985. Bar: Ohio 1950. Law clk. to presiding judge U.S. Ct. Appeals (2d cir.), N.Y.C., 1949-50; law clk. to justice Felix Frankfurter U.S. Supreme Ct., Washington, 1950-51; from assoc. to ptnr. Jones, Day, Reavis & Pogue, Cleve., 1951-90; tchr. elem. schs. Cleve. City Sch. Dist., 1991-94. Contbr. articles on fed. income tax to profl. jours. Mem. Cleve. Bd. Edn., 1965-69; assoc. dir. Pres.'s Commn. on Nat. Goals, Washington, 1960; mem., pres., fellow Harvard U., 1968-85; mem. task forces Cleve. Summit on Edn., 1990-94; pres., trustee Initiatives in Urban Edn., 1991—. Capt. USAF, 1943-46. Mem. ABA (chmn. tax sect. 1985-86), Am. Law Inst. (coun.), City Club, Cleve. Skating Club, Phi Beta Kappa. Democrat. Unitarian. Home and Office: 3345 N Park Blvd Cleveland OH 44118-4258

CALKINS, RICHARD W. former college president; b. June 3, 1939; BA in Music, Albion Coll., 1960; MA in Edn., Mich. State U., 1966, MA, 1971, postgrad., 1972—; Doctorate (hon.), Ferris State U., 1992. Vocal music tchr. Ridgeview Jr. High Sch., 1961-64, Creston High Sch., 1964-68, asst. dir. pers., 1968-71, gen. assoc. supt., 1971-74, asst. supt. pers. and community svcs., 1974-75; pres. Grand Rapids (Mich.) C.C., 1975-98; ret., 1998. Cons. in field. Bd. dirs. religious activities Epworth Assembly, Ludington, Mich., 1960-82; mins. music Eastminster Presbyn. ch., Grand Rapids, 1964-93; v.p. planning, mem. exec. com. Downtown Mgmt. Bd., 1985-91; pres. Grand Rapids C.C. Found., 1978—; bd. dirs. Mich. Info. Tech. Network, 1988—; mem. Mid Am. Training Group, 1989—, Downtown Planning Com., 1991, Nat. Modernization Forum, 1990-91, Nat. Coalition Advance Tech. Ctrs., 1990—, Alliance for Mfg. Productivity, 1990—, IBM CIM Higher Edn., 1990—; bd. dirs., mem. pub. policy and pers. coms. YMCA, 1989-92; chair edn. div. United Way Kent County, chair major accounts, 1992; founding bd. dirs. Noorthoek Acad., 1989—; bd. dirs. edn. and summer facility coms. Grand Rapids Symphony, 1989— Mem. Indsl. Tech. Inst., Am. Assn. Community and Colls., Assn. C.C. Trustees, Assn. Tchr. Educators, Mich. Assn. Sch. Adminstrs., Mich. Assn. Pub. Adult Continuing Educators, Mich. Assn. Tchr. Educators, Mich. C.C. Assn. (chair polit. action com. 1983—, exec. com. 1987-90, v.p. 1987-88, past pres. 1989-90, treas. 1990-91), C.C. Assn. for Tech. Transfer, Grand

Rapids Dunkers Club, Peninsular Club Grand Rapids, Phi Delta Kappa. Home: 2519 Riveredge Dr SE Grand Rapids MI 49546-7450 Office: Grand Rapids Community Coll 143 Bostwick Ave NE Grand Rapids MI 49503-3201

CALKINS, STEPHEN, law educator, lawyer; b. Balt., Mar. 20, 1950; s. Evan and Virginia (Brady) C.; m. Joan Wadsworth, Oct. 18, 1981; children: Timothy, Geoffrey, Virginia. BA, Yale U., 1972; JD, Harvard U., 1975. Bar: N.Y. 1976, D.C. 1977, U.S. Dist. Ct. D.C. 1979. Law clk. to FTC commr. S. Nye, Washington, 1975-76; assoc. Covington & Burling, 1976-83; assoc. law prof. Wayne State U., Detroit, 1983-88, prof., 1988—; gen. counsel FTC, Washington, 1995-97; of counsel Covington & Burling, 1997—, program dir. conf. and annual antitrust conf., 2001—. Vis. assoc. prof. law U. Mich., Ann Arbor, 1985, U. Pa., Phila., 1987; vis. prof. law U. Utrecht, Netherlands, 1989; chair career devel. Wayne State U., 1990-91. Editor: Antitrust Law Developments, 1984, 86, 88, (legal book revs.) The Antitrust Bulletin, 1986—, (articles) Antitrust, 1991-95. Counsel Ind. Commn. on Admissions Practices in Cranbrook Sch., Detroit, 1984-85; mem. Northville Zoning Bd. Appeals, 1987-95; rep.-at-large Assn. Yale Alumni Assembly, 1989-92; elder First Presbyn. Ch. of Northville, 1989-92. Research fellow Wayne State U., 1984; USAID grantee, 1999-2000. Mem. ABA (coun. antitrust sect. 1988-91, 97-2000, counsel to com. on FTC 1988-89, co-chair 50th Anniversary com., adminstrv. law sect. 1997-2000, council 1999—, antitrust section 50th anniversary pub. award 2002, FTC award for disting. svc. 1997), Am. Law Inst., Am. Assn. Law Schs. (sec. antitrust sect. 1987-91, chair-elect, 1991-93, chair, 1993-95), Harvard Club, Yale Club (Detroit), Northville Swim Club. Avocations: reading, skiing. Home: 317 W Dunlap St Northville MI 48167-1404 Office: Wayne State U Law Sch 471 W Palmer Detroit MI 48202 E-mail: calkins@wayne.edu.

CALL, LAWRENCE MICHAEL, consumer products company executive; b. Little Rock, Mar. 27, 1942; s. Cornelius Kelton and Emma F. (Kling) C.; m. Patricia Elizabeth Popp, Nov. 25, 1961; children: Lawrence Jr., Terrence D., Elizabeth A., Alexander D. BBA, Loyola U., 1964. CPA, N.Y., Pa. Various Deloitte, Haskins & Sells, N.Y.C., 1964-70, mgr., 1970-71, Madrid, Spain, 1971-75, N.Y.C., 1975-77, Pitts., 1977-79; mgr., fin. policy PPG Industries, Inc., 1979-81, dir. risk mgmt., 1981-83, asst. treas., 1983-84, treas., 1984-91; chief fin. officer Amway Corp., Ada, Mich., 1991—2000. Bd. dirs. Davenport Coll. Found. Mem. AICPA, Mich. Inst. CPAs. Roman Catholic. Avocations: golf, fishing. Home: 2216 Rolling Dove Rd Seabrook Island SC 29455-6601

CALLAHAN, FRANCIS JOSEPH, manufacturing company executive; b. Lima, Ohio, July 8, 1923; s. Francis J. and Bertha E. (Falk) C.; m. Mary Elizabeth Krouse, June 30, 1945; children: Francis Joseph III, Cornelia S. Callahan Richards, Timothy J. Student, U. Dayton, 1941; BS, U.S. Naval Acad., 1945; B.S.E.E., MIT, 1948; MS in Nuclear Engring., 1953. Commd. ensign USN, 1945; project officer USS Nautilus, USS Sea Wolf, 1954-58; pres. Nupro Co., Willoughby, Ohio, 1958-99; v.p. Crawford Fitting Co., Solon, 1959-81; pres. Swagelok Co. (formerly Crawford Fitting), 1981-99, Whitey Co., Cleveland Heights, Ohio, 1960-99; chmn. Swagelok Co., until 1999; ret. Dir. Midwest Bank & Trust Co., 1969—, Midwestern Nat. Life Ins. Co., 1970—, Tappan Co., 1977-80, Invacare Co., 1980—, Environ. Growth Control Co., 1970—, Royal Appliance Co., 1984—, Applied Concrete Tech., 1984—. Patentee for valves, fittings. Chmn. bd. trustees Gilmoor Acad., 1973-79; chmn. bd. dirs. Marymoutn Hosp., 1983; trustee cleve. Boys Clubs, 1970—; bd. dirs. Jr. Achievement, 1963—. Capt. USNR, 1976. Recipient Man of Yr. award Gilmoor Acad., 1973. Mem. NAM, ASME, Atomic Indsl. Forum, Kirtland Country, Pepper Pike, Union, Hillbrook (Cleve.), Quail Creek Country (Naples, Fla.). Roman Catholic. Home: 3195 Roundwood Rd Chagrin Falls OH 44022-6635

CALLAHAN, J(OHN) WILLIAM (BILL CALLAHAN), judge; b. Rockville Centre, N.Y., Feb. 8, 1947; s. Peter Felix and Catherine Lucille (Walbroehl) C. BA, Mich. State U., 1971, JD cum laude, 1974. Atty. Bank of Commonwealth, Detroit, 1974-76; assoc. Hoops & Hudson, P.C., 1976-79, Tyler & Canham, P.C., Detroit, 1979-80, Stark & Reagan, P.C., Troy, Mich., 1980-81; pvt. practice Farmington Hills, 1981-86; mem. Plunkett & Cooney, P.C., Detroit, 1986-96; judge Wayne County Cir. Ct., 1996—. Bd. dirs. Vietnam Vets. Am. Chpt. 9, Detroit, 1981-85. With USMC, 1967-69, Vietnam. Mem. ABA, Detroit Bar Assn. Office: 1813 City-County Bldg Detroit MI 48226

CALLAHAN, PATRICK, communication media executive; Bur. chief Pierre UP Internat., Pierre, S.D., 1999—; state bur. chief Dakota News Network. Office: UP Internat 214 W Pleasant Dr Pierre SD 57501-2472

CALLAHAN, RICHARD G. prosecutor; b. St. Louis, Apr. 22, 1947; s. George G. and Doris M. (Ohmer) C.; children: Maureen, Jerry, Mary Kay, Tim, Mike. AB, Georgetown U., Washington, 1968, JD, 1972. Asst. prosecutor St. Louis Cir. Attys. Office, 1972-78, Cole County, Jefferson City, Mo., 1979-86, pros. atty., 1987—. Office: 311 E High St # 3 Jefferson City MO 65101-3250

CALLAHAN, WILLIAM E., JR. federal judge; b. Evanston, Ill., Sept. 15, 1948; BA, Marquette U., 1970, JD, 1973. Atty. Goldberg, Previant and Uelman, 1973-75; asst. U.S. atty. Eastern Dist. Wis., 1975-82, 1st asst. U.S. atty., 1982-84; atty. Davis & Kuelthau, S.C., 1984-95; magistrate judge U.S. Dist. Ct. (ea. dist.) Wis., Milw., 1995—. Office: 247 US Courthouse 517 E Wisconsin Ave Milwaukee WI 53202-4500

CALLANDER, KAY EILEEN PAISLEY, business owner, retired education educator, writer; b. Coshocton, Ohio, Oct. 15, 1938; d. Dalton Olas and Dorothy Pauline (Davis) Paisley; m. Don Larry Callander, Nov. 18, 1977. BSE, Muskingum Coll., 1960; MA in Speech Edn., Ohio State U., 1964, postgrad., 1964-84. Cert. elem., gifted, drama, theater tchr., Ohio. Tchr. Columbus (Ohio) Pub. Schs., 1960-70, 80-88, drama specialist, 1970-80, classroom, gifted/talented tchr., 1986-90, ret., 1990; sole prop. The Ali Group, Kay Kards, 1992—. Coord. Artists-in-the Schs., 1977-88; cons., presenter numerous ednl. confs. and sems., 1971—; mem., ednl. cons. Innovation Alliance Youth Adv. Coun., 1992—. Producer-dir., Shady Lane Music Festival, 1980-88; dir. tchr. (nat. distbr. video) The Trial of Gold E. Locks, 1983-84; rep., media pub. relations liason Sch. News., 1983-88; author, creator Trivia Game About Black Americans (TGABA), exhibitor of TGABA game at L.A. County Office Edn. Conf., 1990; presenter for workshop by Human Svc. Group and Creative Edn. Coop., Columbus, Ohio, 1989. Benefactor, Columbus Jazz Arts Group; v.p., bd. dirs. Neoteric Dance and Theater Co., Columbus, 1985-87; tchr., participant Future Stars sculpture exhibit, Ft. Hayes Ctr., Columbus Pub. Schs., 1988; tchr. advisor Columbus Coun. PTAs, 1983-86, co-chmn. reflections com., 1984-87; mem. Columbus Mus. Art, Citizens for Humane Action, Inc.; mem. supt.'s adv. coun. Columbus Pub. Schs., 1967-68; presenter Young Author Seminar, Ohio Dept. Edn., 1988, Illustrating Methods for Young Authors' Books, 1986-87; cons. and workshop leader seminar/workshop Tchg. About the Constitution in Elem. Schs., Franklin County Ednl. Coun., 1988; sponsor Minority Youth Recognition Awards, 1994. Named Educator of Yr., Shady Lane PTA, 1982, Columbus Coun. PTAs, 1989, winner Colour Columbus Landscape Design Competition, 1990; Sch. Excellence grantee Columbus Pub. Schs.; Commendation Columbus Bd. Edn. and Ohio Ho. of Reps. for Child Assault Prevention project, 1986-87; first place winner statewide photo contest Ohio Vet. Assn., 1991; recipient Muskingum Coll. Alumni Disting. Svc. award, 1995. Mem. ASCD, AAUW, Assn. for Childhood Edn. Internat., Ohio Coun. for Social Studies, Franklin County Ret. Tchrs. Assn., Nat. Mus. Women in the Arts, Ohio State U. Alumni Assn., U.S. Army Officers Club, Navy League, Liturgical Art Guild Ohio, Columbus Jazz Arts Group, Columbus Mus. Art, Nat. Coun. for Social Studies, Columbus Art League, Columbus Maennerchor (Damen sect.). Republican. Avocations: painting, photography, swimming, golfing, playing piano and organ. Home: 2323 Colts Neck Rd Blacklick OH 43004-9003 Office: The Ali Group Kay Kards PO Box 13093 Columbus OH 43213-0093 E-mail: pais1609@aol.com.

CALLAWAY, KAREN A(LICE), journalist; b. Daytona Beach, Fla., Sept. 5, 1946; d. Robert Clayton III and Alice Johnston (Webb) C. (deceased). BS in Journalism, Northwestern U., 1968. Copy editor Detroit Free Press, 1968-69; asst. woman's editor, features copy editor, news copy editor, asst. makeup editor Chgo. Am. and Chgo. Today, 1969-74; asst. makeup editor Chgo. Tribune, 1974-76, asst. news editor, 1976-81, assoc. news editor spl. sect., 1981-2000, assoc. news editor vertical publs., 1993-2000, asst. news editor spl. sect., 2000—. Adviser Jr. Achievement Tribune sponsored co., Chgo., 1976-77; editor Infant Mortality sect., 1989; vis. prof. student chpt. Soc. Profl. Journalists, Northwestern U., 1989. Chmn. class of 1968 20th reunion Northwestern U., 1989, mem. seminar day com., 1989-90, chmn., 1991, mem. alumni bd. dirs. Medill Sch. Journalism, Northwestern U., Evanston, Ill., 1991-99; vol. Northwestern U. Settlement House. Mem. Soc. of Profl. Journalists, Sigma Delta Chi, Kappa Delta. Methodist. Avocations: scuba diving; swimming; cooking; traveling. Office: Chicago Tribune 435 N Michigan Ave Ste 500 Chicago IL 60611-4041 Business E-Mail: kcallaway@tribune.com.

CALLEN, JAMES DONALD, nuclear engineer, plasma physicist, educator; b. Wichita, Kans., Jan. 31, 1941; s. Donald Dewitt and Bonnie Jean (Walton) C.; m. Judith Carolyn Chinn, Aug. 26, 1961; children: Jeffrey Scott, Sandra Jean. BS in Nuclear Engring., Kans. State U., 1962, MS in Nuclear Engring., 1964; PhD in Nuclear Engring., MIT, 1968. Postdoctoral fellow Inst. for Advanced Study, Princeton, N.J., 1968-69; asst. prof. aeros. and astronautics MIT, Cambridge, 1969-72; mem. rsch. staff fusion energy div. Oak Ridge (Tenn.) Nat. Lab., 1972-74, group leader, 1974-75, head plasma theory sect., 1975-79; prof. nuclear engring. and physics U. Wis., Madison, 1979-86, D.W. Kerst prof. engring. physics, and physics, 1986—. Mem. editor. bd. Nuclear Fusion Jour., 1978-97; assoc. editor divsn. plasma physics Phys. Rev. Letters Jour., 1980-85; contbr. over 150 articles to profl. jours. Fulbright fellow Tech. Hogesch. to Eindhoven, Netherlands, 1962-63; recipient Dept. of Energy Disting. Assoc. award, 1988; named to Coll. Engring. Hall of Fame, Kans. State U., 1991; Guggenheim fellow, 1986. Fellow Am. Phys. Soc. (chmn. div. plasma physics 1986), Am. Nuclear Soc.; mem. NAE, AAAS. Office: Univ. of Wisconsin 1500 Engr. Dr. 521 ERB Madison WI 53706-1687

CALLOW, WILLIAM GRANT, retired state supreme court justice; b. Waukesha, Wis., Apr. 9, 1921; s. Curtis Grant and Mildred G. C.; m. Jean A. Zilavy, Apr. 15, 1950; children: William G., Christine S., Katherine H. PhB in Econs, U. Wis., 1943, JD, 1948. Bar: Wis.; cert. for Fla. mediation. Asst. city atty., Waukesha, 1948-52; city atty., 1952-60; county judge Waukesha, 1961-77; justice Supreme Ct. Wis., Madison, 1978-92. Asst. prof. U. Minn., 1951-52; mem. faculty Wis. Jud. Coll., 1968-75; Wis. commr. Nat. Conf. Commrs. on Uniform State Laws, 1967—; arbitrator Wis. Employment Rel. Commn.; arbitrator-mediator bus. disputes; arbitration and mediation nat. and internat. res. judge, 1992—. With USMC, 1943-45; with USAF, 1951-52, Korea. Recipient Outstanding Alumnus award U. Wis., 1973 Fellow Am. Bar Found.; mem. ABA, Dane County Bar Assn., Waukesha County Bar Assn. Episcopalian. Fax: 608-241-9923, 715-588-3452, 941-642-8889. E-mail: wgc@mymailstation.com., justice4@newnorth.net.

CALLSEN, CHRISTIAN EDWARD, medical device company executive; b. 1938; married. AB, Miami U., 1959; MBA, Harvard U., 1966. With Cole Nat. Corp., Cleve., 1966-87, various mgmt. and v.p. positions, 1966-87, exec. v.p., 1983-87; pres. Hyatt Legal Svcs., 1987-90, Profl. Vet. Hosps., Detroit, 1991, Profl. Med. Mgmt., Cleve., 1992—, Applied Med. Tech., Cleve., 1993-96; chmn., CEO Allen Med. Sys., 1995-99; pres. Polymer Concepts, Inc., 1999; dir. Sight Resources Corp. Lt. USN, 1959-64. Home: 235 College St Hudson OH 44236-2908 Office: 7561 Tyler Blvd Ste 8 Mentor OH 44060-4867 E-mail: cec235@aol.com.

CAMACCI, MICHAEL A. commercial real estate broker, development consultant; b. Youngstown, Ohio, Feb. 6, 1951; s. Martin B. and Viola F. (Conti) C.; m. Susan Hawkins, Oct. 18, 1985; 1 child, Michael Philip. BBA, Youngstown Coll., 1974. Cert. bus. analyst. Acct. U.S. Steel Corp., Youngstown, 1969-80; mgr. sales Soc. Realty, Boardman, Ohio, 1980-81; dir. sales Pop-ins Maid Services, Columbiana, 1981-82; bus. broker Eranco Assocs., Girard, 1982-86; pres. JMC Realty, Inc., Youngstown, 1986-99; pres., broker Camacci Real Estate, 1986—; pres. Hillview Nursing Home, 1988-99, Valley View Nursing Home, 1990-99, Pyramid Printing, Inc., 1991-99; dir. Crestview Nursing & Rehab. Facility, 1999—; CEO Van Fossan & Assoc., 2000—. Pres. Wedgewood Property Mgmt., Inc., 4682 North, LLC, 55 West, LLC, 1997—, 19th Hole Investments, 1997—; pres. CRE Holding Corp., 1996; pres. 20 West, LLC, 1998—, pres. Goldco Internat., 1997—, Downtown Partners, Landmark Real Estate Svcs, Inc., 1998—. Mem. Youngstown-Warren Regional Growth Alliance; v.p. Austintown Growth Found., 1994-96. Served with U.S. Army, 1971-77. Mem. Am. Health Care Assn., Ohio Health Care Assn., Nat. Assn. Printers and Lithographers, Internat. Coun. Shopping Ctrs., Youngstown-Warren Area C. of C., Columbiana Area C. of C., Mahoning County Home Builders Assn., Downtown Ptnrs. Democrat. Roman Catholic. Office: Camacci Real Estate Inc 5533 Mahoning Ave Youngstown OH 44515-2316

CAMBRIDGE, WILLIAM G. federal judge; b. Atlantic, Iowa, Dec. 13, 1931; m. Jean C. Burford; two children. BS, U. Nebr., 1953, JD, 1955. With Madgett, Hunter and Cambridge, 1957-63; pvt. practice law Hastings, Nebr., 1964-81; judge 10th Jud. Dist. Nebr., 1981-88, U.S. Dist. Ct. Nebr., Omaha, 1988—. Hon. trustee Hastings (Nebr.) Coll. 1st lt. U.S. Army, 1955-57, USAR, 1957-65. Mem. ABA, Nebr. Bar Assn., Omaha Bar Assn., 10th Jud. Dist. Bar Assn., Adams County Bar Assn. Office: US Dist Ct PO Box 1076-dts Omaha NE 68101-1076

CAMDEN, CARL T. human resources company executive; BA in Psychology/Speech, Southwest Baptist Coll., 1975; MA in Clin. Psychology/Speech Comm., Central Mo. State U., 1977; DCom., Ohio State U., 1980. Assoc. prof. comms. Cleve. State U.; co-founder, co-owner North Coast Behavioral Rsch. Group; co-pres. Wyse Advt.; sr. v.p., dir. corp. mktg. KeyCorp.; exec. v.p., field ops. sales & mktg. Kelly Svcs., Inc., Troy, Mich. Office: Kelly Svcs Inc 999 W Big Beaver Rd Troy MI 48084-4716

CAMERIUS, JAMES WALTER, marketing educator, corporate researcher; b. Chgo., June 14, 1939; s. Wilbert Albert and Violet Elna (Johnson) C. BS, No. Mich. U., 1961; MS, U. N.D., 1963; postgrad., U. Okla., 1974-77. From instr. to assoc. prof. No. Mich. U., Marquette, 1963-90, prof. mktg., 1990—. Lectr. in field; mem. adv. bd. S.E. Advanced Tech. Edn. Consortium. Newsletter editor N.Am. Case Rsch. Assn.; bd. rev., editl. rev. bd. Bus. Case Jour.; mem. internat. editl. adv. bd. Jour. SMET Edn. Cir. lay rep. Luth. Ch.-Mo. Synod, 1987-89; pres. Redeemer Luth. Ch., Marquette, 1989-90, sec. to ch. coun., 1990-92, bd. elders, 1993-98, v.p., 2000-2001, pres. 2001-02; mktg. track chair N.Am. Case Rsch. & Mktg. Assn., 1997-2001. Recipient MAGB Disting. Prof. award, 1995; Rsch. grantee Direct Selling Edn. Found., 1987—, Walker L. Cisler Sch. No. Mich. U., 1990, Filene Rsch. Inst., 1994; named Outstanding Case Reviewer, Case Rsch. Jour., 1998. Fellow Acad. Mktg. Sci.; mem. Am. Mktg. Assn., Soc. Case Rsch. (v.p. 1990-91, case workshop dir. 1999, pres.-elect 2000, pres. 2001—), N.Am. Case Rsch. Assn. (midwest rep.), World Assn. for Case Method Rsch. and Application (case colloquium dir. 1997-2000), Econ. Club, Alpha Kappa Psi (Alumni award). Democrat. Home: 171 Lakewood Ln Marquette MI 49855-9543 Office: No Mich U Mktg Dept Marquette MI 49855

CAMERON, JOHN M. nuclear scientist, educator, science administrator; b. Aug. 9, 1940; BSc, Queens U., Ireland, 1962; MSc, UCLA, 1965, PhD, 1967. Tech. asst. U.K. Atomic Energy Authority, Eng., 1962-63; asst. prof. UCLA, 1967-68; rsch. assoc. U. Wash., Seattle, 1968-70; asst. prof. to prof. U. Alta., 1970-87; dir. Cyclotron Facility, prof. dept. physics Ind. U., Bloomington, 1987—. Asst. dir. initial ops. TRIUMF, Vancouver, 1973-74; vis scientist U. Paris, SIN Switzerland, 1977-78; staff scientist Nat. Saturne Lab., France, 1981-82; dir. Nuclear Rsch. Ctr., U. Alta., 1985-87. Fellow Am. Phys. Soc. Office: IN Univ Bloomington Cyclotron Facility 2401 Milo Sampson Ln Bloomington IN 47408-1368

CAMERON, OLIVER GENE, psychiatrist, educator, psychobiology researcher; b. Evanston, Ill., Aug. 28, 1946; s. Gene Oliver and Elizabeth Marie (Burns) C.; m. Susan Linda Friedman, June 22, 1972; children—Leah Victoria, Peter Sean. B.A., U. Notre Dame, 1968; Ph.D., U. Chgo., 1972, M.D., 1974. Diplomate Am. Bd. psychiatry and Neurology. Med. intern U. Mich., Ann Arbor, 1974-75, psychiatry resident, 1975-78, psychiatry fellow, 1978-79, asst. prof. psychiatry, 1979-86, assoc. prof., 1986-92, prof., 1992—; dir. anxiety disorders program, dept. psychiatry, 1984-85, dir. adult psychiatry outpatient program, dept. psychiatry, 1985-90, Combined Mood & Anxiety Program, 1994—. Contbr. articles to profl. jours. Mem. Am. Psychiatric Assn., Am. Psychosomatic Soc., AAAS, Sigma Xi. Avocations: photography; travel; golf. Home: 1215 Southwood Ct Ann Arbor MI 48103-9735 Office: U Mich 1500 E Medical Center Dr Ann Arbor MI 48109-0005

CAMERON, PATRICIA, advertising executive; Exec. v.p. Campbell Mithun Esty, Mpls. Office: Campbell Mithun Esty 222 S 9th St Minneapolis MN 55402-3803

CAMP, DAVE, congressman; b. Midland, Mich., July 9, 1953; m. Nancy Keil, Sept. 10, 1994; children: Andrew David, Lauren. BA, Albion (Mich.) Coll., 1975; JD, U. San Diego, 1978. Bar: Mich., Calif., D.C., U.S. Supreme Ct., U.S. Dist. Ct. (ea. dist.) Mich., U.S. Dist. Ct. (so. dist.) Calif. With Riecker, Van Dam, Looby & Barker, 1978-90; spl. asst. atty. gen., 1980-84; adminstrv. asst. to Congressman Bill Schuette, 1985-87; state rep. 102nd Dist. Mich., 1989-91; mem. U.S. Congress from 10th (now 4th) Mich. dist., 1991—; mem. ways and means com., asst. minority whip. Chmn. Spkrs. Correction Day Com. Mem. ABA, Midland County Bar Assn. Republican. Office: US Ho of Reps 137 Cannon Bldg Washington DC 20515-2204*

CAMPBELL, BRUCE CRICHTON, hospital administrator; b. Balt., July 21, 1947; s. James Allen and Elda Shaffer (Crichton) C.; m. Linda Page Cottrell, June 28, 1969; children: Molly Shaffer, Andrew Crichton. B.A., Lake Forest Coll., 1969; M.H.A., Washington U., St. Louis, 1973; D.P.H., U. Ill., 1979. Adminstrv. asst. Passavant Meml. Hosp., Chgo., 1970-71; adminstrv. resident Albany (N.Y.) Med. Center Hosp., 1972-73; adminstrv. asst. Rush-Presbyn.-St. Luke's Med. Center, Chgo., 1973-75, asst. adminstr., 1975-77, asst. v.p., 1977-79, v.p. adminstrv. affairs, 1979-83; chmn. dept. health systems mgmt. Rush U., Chgo., 1977-81, dean Coll. Health Scis., 1981-83; exec. dir. U. Chgo. Hosps. and Clinics, 1983-85; lectr. Grad. Sch. Bus., U. Chgo., 1983-85; pres. Campbell Assocs., Chgo., 1985-92; exec. v.p. Ill. Masonic Med. Ctr., 1993, pres., 1993-2000; chief exec. Advocate Luth. Gen. Hosp., Park Ridge, Ill., 2000—. W.K. Kellogg Found. fellow, 1977; Leadership Greater Chgo. fellow, 1984-85 Fellow Am. Coll. Healthcare Execs.; mem. Young Adminstrs. Chgo. (pres. 1977), Assn. Univ. Programs in Health Adminstrn., Am. Hosp. Assn., Ill. Hosp. Assn., Chgo. Hosp. Council. Office: Advocate Luth Gen Hosp 1775 Dempster St Park Ridge IL 60668

CAMPBELL, BRUCE IRVING, lawyer; b. Mason City, Iowa, July 7, 1947; s. E. Riley Jr. and Donna May (Andresen) C.; children: Anne, John; m. Beverly J. Evans. BA, Upper Iowa U., 1969; JD, Harvard U., 1973. Bar: Iowa 1973, U.S. Dist. Ct. (so. dist.) Iowa 1973, U.S. Dist. Ct. (no. dist.) Iowa 1974, U.S. Tax Ct. 1976, U.S. Ct. Appeals (8th cir.) 1977, U.S. Ct. Claims 1982. Shareholder Davis, Brown, Koehn, Shors & Roberts, P.C., Des Moines, 1973—. Adj. prof. law Drake U., Des Moines, 1974-90. Trustee Upper Iowa U., Fayette, 1978—, chair bd. trustees, 1992—; sec., dir Iowa Natural Heritage Found., 2001—. Mem. ABA, Iowa State Bar Assn., Polk County Bar Assn. Republican. Home: 62 Meadowbrook Cir Cumming IA 50061-1014 Office: Davis Brown Koehn Shors & Roberts PC 666 Walnut St Ste 2500 Des Moines IA 50309-3904 E-mail: bruce.campbell@lawiowa.com.

CAMPBELL, COLE C. journalist, educator; b. Roanoke, Va. BA in English, U. N.C.; postgrad., Poynter Inst. Media Studies. Obituary writer The News and Observer, Raleigh, reporter city hall news; reporter Chapel Hill News; editor The Tar Heel mag., Norfolk, Va.; reporter city hall news Greensboro (N.C.) News & Record, asst. city editor, metro editor, asst. mng. editor, Va. Pilot and the Ledger-Star, Norfolk, 1990-91, mng. editor, 1991-93, editor, 1993-97, St. Louis Post Dispatch. Instr. journalism Guilford Coll., U. N.C., Greensboro; journalism adv. bd. Norfolk State U. Bd. dirs. Goodwill Industries South Hampton Roads, United Way; alumni Leadership Hampton Roads. John S. Knight Journalism fellow, 1989-90. Office: St Louis Post Dispatch 900 N Tucker Blvd Saint Louis MO 63101-1099

CAMPBELL, COLIN, obstetrician, gynecologist, school dean; b. Washington, June 24, 1927; s. Colin and Margaret (Kingsland) Masters C.; m. Catherine Marian Hayden, Aug. 20, 1952; children: Catherine, Janet, Philip. AB, Stanford U., 1949; MD, CM, McGill U., 1953; EdM, Temple U., 1967; DHL, U. Akron, 1991. Diplomate Am. Bd. Ob-Gyn. Intern George Washington Hosp., Washington, 1953-54; asst. resident in pathology U.S. VA Hosp., Coral Gables, Fla., 1954; gen. practice resident Dade County Hosp., Kendall, 1955; gen. practice medicine Perrine, 1955-57; asst. resident, resident in ob-gyn. Hosp. for the Women of Md., Balt., 1957-60; practice medicine specializing in ob-gyn., 1960-61; instr. ob-gyn. Temple U., Phila., 1961-64; asst. prof. ob-gyn. U. Mich., Ann Arbor, 1964-67, assoc. prof., 1967-71, prof., 1971-78, asst. dean Med. Sch., 1972-76, assoc. dean, 1976-78; prof. ob-gyn., dean U. Ala. Sch. Primary Med. Care, Huntsville, 1978-83; prof. ob-gyn., pres., dean Northeastern Ohio Univs. Coll. Medicine, Rootstown, 1983-92, pres., dean emeritus, 1992—. Contbr. numerous articles to profl. jours. Fellow ACOG. Home: 4741 Mint Dr Memphis TN 38117-4010 Office: Northeastern Ohio Us Coll Medicine 4209 State Route 44 Rootstown OH 44272-9698

CAMPBELL, DOROTHY MAY, management consultant; d. George S. May. V.p. George S. May Intl Co Del, Park Ridge, Ill., 1962—; also bd. dirs. Office: George S May Intl Co Del 303 S Northwest Hwy Park Ridge IL 60068-4232

CAMPBELL, DUGALD K. automotive company executive; b. St. Thomas, Ont., Can., 1946; BA, U. West Ont., 1970. Pres., CEO Tower Automotive, Inc., Mpls. Office: Tower Automotive 4508 IDS Ctr Minneapolis MN 55402

CAMPBELL, EDWARD JOSEPH, retired machinery company executive; b. Boston, Feb. 21, 1928; s. Edward and Mary (Doherty) C.; divorced; children: Gary, Kevin, Diane. BSME, Northwestern U., 1952, MBA, 1959. With Am. Brakeshoe Co., 1952-58, Whirlpool Corp., 1958-65; gen. mgr. Joy Mfg. Co., 1965-67; exec. v.p. J.I. Case Co. subs. Tenneco, Inc., 1968-78; pres., chief exec. officer Newport News Shipbuilding & Dry Dock Co. subs. Tenneco, Inc., Va., 1979-91; pres. J.I. Case Co. subs. Tenneco Inc., Racine, Wis., 1992-94. Bd. dirs. Global Marine, Zurn Industries, Titan Internat., ABS Group; chmn. Campbell Enterprises. Mem. bds. and adv. coun. Webb Inst., Northwestern U., William & Mary Coll., U. Wis. Vet. Medicine Sch., Hampden & Sydney Coll.; chmn. Navy League U.S. Found. With USNR, 1945-48. Home: 1 Deepwood Dr Unit A1 Racine WI 53402-2868 Office: PO Box 8 Racine WI 53401-0008

CAMPBELL, F(ENTON) GREGORY, college administrator, historian; b. Columbia, Tenn., Dec. 16, 1939; s. Fenton G. and Ruth (Hayes) C.; m. Barbara D. Kuhn, Aug. 29, 1970; children: Fenton H., Matthew W., Charles H. AB, Baylor U., 1960; postgrad., Philipps U., Marburg/Lahn, Germany, 1960-61; MA, Emory U., 1962; postgrad., Charles U., Prague, Czechoslovakia, 1965-66; PhD, Yale U., 1967; postgrad., Harvard U., 1981. Rsch. staff historian Yale U., New Haven, 1966-68, spl. asst. to acting pres., 1977-78; asst. prof. history U. Wis., Milw., 1968-69; asst. prof. European history U. Chgo., 1969-76, spl. asst. to pres., 1978-87, sec. bd. trustees, 1979-87, sr. lectr., 1985-87; pres., prof. history Carthage Coll., Kenosha, Wis., 1987—. Fellow Woodrow Wilson Internat. Ctr. for Scholars, Smithsonian Instn., Washington, 1976-77; participant Japan Study Program for Internat. Execs., 1987; bd. dirs. AAL Mut. Funds, Johnson Family Mut. Funds., Prairie Sch., United Health Systems, Wis. Author: Confrontation in Central Europe, 1975; joint editor Akten zur deutschen auswartigen Politik, 1918-1945, 1966-96; contbr. articles and revs. to profl. jours. Fulbright grantee, 1960-61, 73-74; Woodrow Wilson fellow, 1961-62; U.S.A.-Czechoslovakia Exch. fellow, 1965-66, 73-74, 85. Mem. Mid-Day Club (Chgo.), Coun. on Fgn. Rels. (NYC), Phi Beta Kappa, Omicron Delta Kappa. Home: 623 17th Pl Kenosha WI 53140-1360 Office: Carthage Coll Kenosha WI 53140-1360 E-mail: poc@carthage.edu.

CAMPBELL, JOHN CREIGHTON, political science educator; b. N.Y.C., June 12, 1941; s. Charles Edward and Ruth (Creighton) C.; m. Ruth Zimring, Sept. 21, 1962; children: David Riggs, Robert Charles, Judy Fredericka. BA, Columbia Coll., 1965; Cert. East Asian Inst., PhD in Polit. Sci., Columbia U., 1973; postgrad., Interuniv. Ctr. Japanese Lang., Tokyo, 1965-66. Staff assoc. Social Sci. Rsch. Coun., N.Y.C., 1970-73; asst. prof. polit. sci. U. Mich., Ann Arbor, 1973-80, assoc. prof., 1980-91, prof., 1991—, dir. Ctr. Japanese Studies and East Asia Nat. Resource Ctr., 1982-87, dir. East Asia Bus. Program, 1984-88, 90—, dir. Japan Tech. Mgmt. Program, 1991-93, co-dir., 1993—. Fellow Woodrow Wilson Internat. Ctr. for Scholars, Washington, 1980-81; vis. prof. law Keio U., Tokyo, 1989-90, vis. prof. medicine, 1997-99; sec., treas. Assn. for Asian Studies, 1994-2000; vis. prof., acting dir. Kyoto Ctr. Japanese Studies; vis. prof. Doshisha U., Kyowo, 2001; chmn. governing bd. Kyoto Ctr. for Japanese Studies, 2001—. Author: Contemporary Japanese Budget Politics, 1977, How Policies Change: The Japanese Government and the Aging Society, 1992; (with Naoki Ikegami) The Art of Balance in Health Policy, 1997; editor: (with Naoki Ikegami) Containing Health Care Costs in Japan, 1996, Long-Term Care for Frail Older People: Reaching for the Ideal System, 1999; contbr. articles to profl. jours., chpts. to books. With U.S. Army, 1959-62, Japan. Ford Found. travel and study fellow, 1972, Fulbright-Hayes fellow U.S. Dept. State, Japan, 1976-77, 89-90, Japan Found. fellow, 1980, Abe fellow, 1997-98; recipient Masayoshi Ohira Meml. prize, 1993. Mem. Assn. Asian Studies (bd. dirs. 1994-2000, chair Bibliography of Asian Studies adv. com. 2000-01, Disting. Lectr. 1994), Am. Polit. Sci. Assn., Internat. House of Japan. Democrat. Avocations: reading novels, listening to music. Office: Univ Mich Dept Polit Sci Corner House 202 S Thayer St Ann Arbor MI 48104-1608 Home: # 1212 800 Victors Way Ann Arbor MI 48108-1767 E-mail: jccamp@umich.edu.

CAMPBELL, JOSEPH LEONARD, trade association executive; b. Independence, Mo., 1938; BS in Acctg., U. Kans., 1960, MS in Acctg., 1963. CPA, Mo. Audit mgr. Arthur Young & Co., Kansas City, Mo., 1962-75; v.p., sec., treas. Assoc. Wholesale Grocers, Kans., 1975—. Active Boy Scouts Am., Overland Park, Kans., 1983-93. Mem. AICPA. Office: Associated Wholesale Grocers Inc PO Box 2932 Kansas City KS 66110-2932

CAMPBELL, KARLYN KOHRS, speech and communication educator; b. Blomkest, Minn., Apr. 16, 1937; d. Meinhard and Dorothy (Siegers) Kohrs; m. Paul Newell Campbell, Sept. 16, 1967 (dec. Mar. 1999). BA, Macalester Coll., 1958; MA, U. Minn., 1959, PhD, 1968. Asst. prof. SUNY, Brockport, 1959-63; with The Brit. Coll., Palermo, Italy, 1964; asst. prof. Calif. State U., L.A., 1966-71; assoc. prof. SUNY, Binghamton, 1971-72, CUNY, 1973-74; prof. comms. studies U. Kans., Lawrence, 1974-86, dir. women's studies, 1983-86; prof. comms. studies U. Minn., Mpls., 1986—, dept. chair, 1993-96, 99—. Inaugural Gladys Borchers lectr. U. Wis., Madison, 1974. Author: Critiques of Contemporary Rhetoric, 1972, rev. edit., 1997, Form and Genre, 1978, The Rhetorical Act, 1982, rev. edit. 1996, The Interplay of Influence, 1983, rev. edits., 1987, 92, 96, 2000, Man Cannot Speak for Her, 2 Vols., 1989, Deeds Done in Words, 1990, Women Public Speakers in the United States, 1800-1925: A Bio-Critical Sourcebook, 1993, Women Public Speakers in the United States, 1925—: A Bio-Critical Sourcebook, 1994; editor Quar. Jour. Speech, 2001--; co-editor: Guilford Revisioning Rhetoric series, 1995—; mem. editl. bd. Communication Monographs, 1977-80, Quar. Jour. Speech, 1981-86, 92-94, editor, 2001—, Critical Studies in Mass Commn., 1993-99, Rhetoric and Pub. Affairs, 1997-2000, Philosophy and Rhetoric, 1988-93; contbr. articles to profl. jours. Recipient Woolbert Rsch. award, 1987, Winans-Wichelns book award, 1990, Ehninger Rsch. award, 1991; Tozer scholar Macalester Coll., 1958, Tozer fellow, 1959; Fellow Shorenstein Barone Ctr., JFK Sch. of Govt., Harvard, 1992. Mem. Nat. Comm. Assn. (disting. scholar award 1992, Francine Merritt award for significant contbns. to the lives of women in comm. 1996 Women's Caucus), Ctrl. States Speech Comm. Assn., Rhetoric Soc. Am., Phi Beta Kappa, Pi Phi Epsilon. Office: U Minn Dept Comm Studies 225 Ford Hall 224 Church SE Minneapolis MN 55455 E-mail: campb003@umn.edu.

CAMPBELL, KEVIN PETER, physiology and biophysics educator, researcher; b. Bklyn., Jan. 19, 1952; s. Miller Jerome and Anna L. (Telesco) C.; m. Anna A. Derragon, Jan. 5, 1974; children: Colleen, Kerry, David. BS in Physics, Manhattan Coll., 1973; MS, U. Rochester, 1976, PhD, 1979. Grad. fellow U. Rochester (N.Y.), 1973-77, teaching asst., 1976-78; Elon Huntington Hooker fellow dept. radiation biology and biophysics, U. Rochester (N.Y.), 1977-78; Med. Rsch. Coun. postdoctoral fellow U. Toronto, Ont., Can., 1978-81; asst. prof. dept. physiology and biophysics U. Iowa, Iowa City, 1981-85, assoc. prof., 1985-88, prof., 1988—, Found. Disting. prof., 1989—, Howard Hughes Med. Inst. investigator, 1989—. Mem. editorial bd. Jour. Biol. Chemistry, Circulation Rsch., Cell Calcium; reviewer for Nature, Jour. Clin. Investigation, Jour. Cell Biology, Proc. NAS, Archives Biochem. and Biophysics, Molecular Pharmacology, Biophys. Jour.; contbr. numerous articles and abstracts to profl. jours. Patentee immunogen conjugates and use; co-patentee in field. Grantee NIH, NSF, NATO, Muscular Dystrophy Assn., 1981—; recipient Amgen award Am. Society of Biochemistry and Molecular Biology, 1994 Mem. AAAS, Biophys. Soc. (officer 1988—), N.Y. Acad. Scis., Soc. Gen. Physiologists, Am. Physiology Soc., Am. Soc. Cell Biology, Am. Soc. Biochem. Chemists, Am. Heart Assn. (established investigator, coun. high blood pressure rsch., cell transport and metabolism rsch. study com. 1989—), Sigma Xi (Bendix award), Phi Beta Kappa. Roman Catholic. Office: U Iowa HHMI 400 Eckstein Med Rsch Ctr Iowa City IA 52242

CAMPBELL, TERRY M. food products executive; BSc in Finance, St. Joseph's Coll. Asst. treas. Burger King Corp.; v.p., asst. treas. Harcourt, Brace, Jovanovich; pres. Pheonix Resources, Inc.; exec. v.p., CFO Farmland Industries, Inc., Kansas City, Mo., until 2000. Mem. Nat. Assn. Corp. Treas., Coop. Finance Assn. (bd. dirs.), Heartland Wheat Growers Inc. (bd. dirs.). Office: Farmland Industries Inc 3315 N Oak Traffic Way Kansas City MO 64116

CAMPBELL, WILLIAM EDWARD, mental hospital administrator; b. Kansas City, Kans., June 30, 1927; s. William Warren and Mary (Bickerman) C.; m. Joan Josselyn Larimer, July 26, 1952; children: William Gregory, Stephen James, Douglas Edward. Student, U. Nebr., 1944-45, M.S., 1975; student, U. Mich., 1945, Drake U., 1948; B.A., U. Iowa, 1949, M.A., 1950; Ph.D. in Psychology, U. Nebr., Lincoln, 1980. Psychologist Dept. Pub. Instrn., State of Iowa, 1951-52; hosp. adminstr. Mental Health Inst., Cherokee, Iowa, 1952-68; dir. planning and rsch. Dept. Social Svcs., State of Iowa, 1968-69; supt. Glenwood Rescource Ctr. (formerly Glenwood State Hosp. Sch.), Iowa, 1969—, Clarinda Mental Health Inst., 1979—; assoc. prof. mental health adminstrn. Northwestern U., Chgo., 1982—; pres., bd. dirs. River Bluffs Cmty. Mental Health Ctr. Dir. Shared Mental Health Svcs., Clarinda/Glenwood; founder, chmn. Regional Drug Abuse Adv. Coun.; adj. prof. Sch. Pub. Health U. Minn., also preceptor grad. students in mental health adminstrn.; vis. faculty Avepane U., Caracas, Venezuela; adj. prof. Coll. Medicine and Health Adminstrn. Tulane U.; mem. vis. staff dept. psychiatry U. Nebr. Med. Ctr.-Creighton U. St. Joseph Med. Ctr. Author works in field. UN spl. cons. to Venzuela for UNESCO; bd. dirs. Polk County Mental Health; v.p., bd. dirs. Mercy Hosp., Coun. Bluffs, Iowa; state pres. United Cerebral Palsy; charter mem., bd. dirs. Pub. Broadcasting Sta. KIWR, Council Bluffs, Iowa, Glenwood-Mills County Econ. Devel. Found., Inc., 1985—; chartered mem., bd. dirs. Mills County Econ. Devel., 1987, Glenwood Resource Ctr., 1993—; apptd. State of Iowa Dept. Human Svcs. Exec. Mgmt. Team, 1997; charter mem., organizer Loess Hills Alliance, 1998—, mem. land protection, econ. devel. and long range planning coms., 1999—. Served with AUS, 1944-46; col. Res. Decorated Army Commendation medal; recipient Meritorious Service medal U.S. Army, 1982. Fellow Assn. Mental Health Adminstrs. (nat. com. chmn. 1970); mem. Assn. Med. Adminstrs., Am. Hosp. Assn. (nat. governing bd. psychiat. services sect., charter panelist nat. adv. panel on mental health services, mem. governing body psychiat. services sect.), Iowa Hosp. Assn., Health Planning Council of Midlands, Assn. Univ. Programs in Health Adminstrn. (mem. nat. task force on edn. of mental health adminstrs.), Am. Assn. on Mental Deficiency (chmn. adminstrn. sect. Region 8), Nat. Rehab. Assn., Assn. for Retarded Children, Mental Health Assn., Phi Beta Kappa. Office: Office of Supt Glenwood Resource Ctr Glenwood IA 51534

CAMPER, JOHN JACOB, speech writer; b. Toledo, Sept. 8, 1943; m. Cleraine Uguccioni, Mar. 27, 1971 (div. May 1981); 1 child, Sarah; m. Mary C. Galligan, Jan. 9, 1988; 1 child, Joseph. BA, Kenyon Coll., 1964. Reporter Detroit News, 1965-68; reporter, critic Chgo. Daily News, 1968-78; editorial writer Chgo. Sun-Times, 1979-84; dept. head external relations Regional Transp. Authority, Chgo., 1984-85; media coord. Chgo. World's Fair Authority, 1985; reporter Chgo. Tribune, 1985-90; assoc. chancellor for pub. affairs U. Ill., Chgo., 1990-97; dep. press sec., speech writer Mayor of Chgo., 1997—; v.p. Chgo. Pub. Rels. Forum, 1995-97, pres., 1997-98. Bd. dirs. Family Svc. Mental Health Ctr. of Oak Park and River Forest, 1990-97. Recipient Peter Lisagor award Chgo. Headline Club, 1983, UPI award, Chgo., 1983, Stick-O-Type, Chgo. Newspaper Guild, 1983, Nat. Assn. Black Journalists award, 1987. Home: 1846 W Newport Ave Chicago IL 60657-1024 Office: 502 City Hall 121 N Lasalle St Chicago IL 60602-1202 E-mail: jcamper@cityofchicago.org.

CAMSTER, BARON OF **See WIEMANN, MARION RUSSELL JR.**

CANADY, ALEXA IRENE, pediatric neurosurgeon; b. Lansing, Mich., Nov. 7, 1950; d. Clinton Jr. and Hortense (Golden) C.; m. George Davis, June 18, 1988. BS, U. Mich., 1971, MD cum laude, 1975; DHL (hon.), Marygrove Coll., 1994, U. Detroit, 1997; DSc (hon.), Ctrl. Mich. U., 1999, U. So. Conn., 1999. Diplomate Am. Bd. Neurol. Surgery. Intern in surgery Yale U., New Haven, 1975-76; resident in neurosurgery U. Minn., Mpls., 1976-81; fellow in pediatric neurosurgery Children's Hosp. Pa., Phila., 1981-82; instr. neurosurgery U. Pa., 1981-82; staff neurosurgeon, instr. neurosurgery Henry Ford Hosp., Detroit, 1982-83; asst. dir. neurosurgery Children's Hosp. Mich., 1986-87, chief of neurosurgery, 1987-97; assoc. prof. neurosurgery Wayne State U., Detroit, 1988-91, vice chmn. neurosurgery, 1991—2001; prof. neurosurgery, 1997—2001. Clin. instr. neurosurgery Wayne State U. Sch. Medicine, 1985, mem. internal rev. com. dept. anatomy, 1988, chmn. search com. dept. neurosurgery, 1989, internal rev. com. dept. neurology, 1991-92, 125th anniversary celebration com., 1992, internal rev. com. dept. pediat., 1993, chmn. search com. dept. ophthalmology, 1992-93, internal rev. com. dept. neurosurgery, 1994; chmn. neurobil. devices panel, FDA; vis. prof. Med. Coll. S.C., 1990; cons. neurol. devices panel Med. Devices Adv. Com., FDA, 1994; mem. surg. com. Children's Hosp. Mich., chmn. operating room subcom. surg. com., intensive care unit com., med. record com., med. exec. com.; mem. med. staff Children's Hosp. Mich., William Beaumont Hosp, Royal Oak and Troy, Mich., Harper-Grace Hosps., Detroit, Hutzel Hosp., Detroit, Sinai Hosp., Detroit, Huron Valley Hosp., Milford, Mich., Crittenton Hosp., Rochester Hills, Mich., St. John Hosp. and Med. Ctr., Detroit; presenter various profl confs. in U.S. and internat. Contbr. chpts. to books. Mem. Mich. Head Injury Alliance, Mich. Myelodysplasia Assn.; bd. dirs. Inst. Am. Bus., 1986-88. Recipient Citation Women's Med. Assn., 1975, Candace award Nat. Coalition 100 Black Women, N.Y., 1986, Golden Heritage award, 1989, Leonard F. Sain Esteemed Alumni award U. Mich., 1990, Disting. Alumni award Everett H.S., Pres.'s award Am. Med. Women's Assn., 1993, Variety Heart award for Med., Sci. and Tech. Variety Club, 1994, Shining Star award Colgate-Palmolive Co./Starlight Found., 1994, Golden Apple award Roeper Sch., 1995, Athena award Alumni Assn. U. Mich., 1995; named Outstanding Young Woman in Am., 1977, Top 100 Bus. & Profl. Women of Am., 1985, Woman of Yr. Detroit Club Nat. Assn. Negro Bus. & Profl. Women's Club, Inc., 1986; named to Mich. Woman's Hall of Fame, 1989; grantee Am. Cancer Soc., 1979, Minn. Med. Found., 1979, Am. Cancer Soc., 1981-82, Widman Found. Early Intervention Treatment and Follow-Up of Infants with Post-hemorrhagic Hydrocephalus, 1984-85, Neuropsychol. Recovery and Family Adaptation to CHI Children's Hosp. Mich., 1987-88, Hydrocephalus Induced Endocrinopathies: Morphologic Correlates Children's Hosp. Mich., 1989, 91. Mem. AMA, ACS, Am. Assn. Neurol. Surgeons, Congress Neurol. Surgeons, Am. Soc. Pediatric Neurosurgery, Nat. Med. Assn. Detroit Med. Soc., Mich. Assn. Neurol. Surgeons (sec. 1992-93, v.p. 1994-95, pres. 1995-96), Transplantation Soc. Mich. (adv. bd. 1993-94), Mich. State Med. Soc. (child abuse and neglect divsn. 1986), Southeastern Mich. Surg. Soc. (sec. 1986-87), Soc. Crit. Care Medicine, Wayne County Med. Soc. (ethics com., pub. affairs com., law com.), U. Mich. Med. Ctr. Alumni Soc., Delta Sigma Theta. Office: 6064 Forest Green Rd Pensacola FL 32505

CANARY, NANCY HALLIDAY, lawyer; b. Cleve., Apr. 21, 1941; d. Robert Fraser and Nanna (Hall) Halliday; m. Sumner Canary, Dec. 1975 (dec. Jan. 1979). BA, Case Western Res. U., 1963; JD, Cleve. State U., 1968. Bar: Ohio 1968, Fla. 1972, U.S. Dist. Ct. (no. dist.) Ohio 1975, U.S. Supreme Ct. 1974, U.S. Dist. Ct. (so. dist.) Fla. 1994. Law clk. to presiding judge Ohio Ct. Appeals, Cleve., 1968-69; ptnr. McDonald, Hopkins & Hardy, 1969-83, Thompson, Hine, LLP, Cleve., 1984—2002. Trustee Beck Ctr. for Cultural Arts, Lakewood, Ohio, 1980—90, Ohio Motorists Assn., 1989—95, Ohio Chamber Orch.; trustee, mem. devel. adv. com. Fairview Gen. Hosp., Cleve., 1980—96; chairperson Sumner Canary Lectureship com. Case Western Res. U. Law Sch.; sec. bd. govs. Churchill Ctr., Washington, 2000—; bd. dirs. Comerica Bank & Trust Co., F.S.B., 1993—2000. Mem. Ohio State Bar Assn., Cleve. Bar Assn., Palm Beach County Bar Assn., Estate Planning Coun. Cleve., Estate Planning Coun. Palm Beach County, Gulf Stream (Fla.) Golf Club, Westwood Country Club (Cleve.). Republican. Avocations: music, horseback riding, collecting Churchill books. Home: Unit 1806 12500 Edgewater Dr Cleveland OH 44107-1677 also: 200 N Ocean Blvd Delray Beach FL 33483-7126

CANDLER, JAMES NALL, JR. lawyer; b. Detroit, Jan. 25, 1943; s. James Nall and Lorna Augusta (Blood) C.; m. Jean Ward McKinnon, Mar. 8, 1974; children: Christine, Elizabeth, Anne. AB, Princeton U., 1965; JD, U. Mich., 1970. Bar: Mich. 1970. Assoc. Dickinson Wright PLLC, Detroit, 1970-77, ptnr., 1977—. Adj. prof. real estate planning U. Detroit Sch. of Law, 1975-80. Bd. dirs. Detroit Inst. Ophthalmology Grosse Pointe Park, Mich., 1983—, chmn., 1994—. Lt. USNR, 1965-67. Mem. Internat. Assn. Attys. and Execs. in Corp. Real Estate, State Bar Mich. (chmn. real property law sect. 1998-99), Am. Coll. of Real Estate Lawyers, Grosse Pointe Club (chmn. 1987-89), Country Club of Detroit. Republican. Avocations: sailing, golf, platform tennis. Home: 211 Country Club Dr Grosse Pointe Farms MI 48236-2901 Office: 500 Woodward Ave Ste 4000 Detroit MI 48226-3416 E-mail: jcandler@dickinson-wright.com.

CANEPA, JOHN CHARLES, banking consultant; b. Newburyport, Mass., Aug. 26, 1930; s. John Jere and Agnes R. (Barbour) C.; m. Marie Olney, Sept. 13, 1953; children: Claudia, John J., Peter C., Milissa L. A.B., Harvard U., 1953; M.B.A., NYU, 1960. With Chase Manhattan Bank, N.Y.C., 1957-63; sr. v.p. Provident Bank, Cin., 1963-70; past pres., chmn. bd., CEO Old Kent Fin. Corp., Grand Rapids, Mich., 1970-95; past pres., past chief exec. officer Old Kent Bank & Trust Co., 1970-95; consulting prin. Crowe Chizek, Mich., 1995—. Served with USN, 1953-57. Office: Crowe Chizek 400 Riverfront Plaza Grand Rapids MI 49503 E-mail: jcanepa@crowechizek.com.

CANFIELD, ROBERT CLEO, lawyer; b. St. Joseph, Mo., Sept. 10, 1938; s. Robert Charles Canfield and Nadine (Ressler) Thomas; m. Patricia Joan Harms, June 8, 1958; children: Tamara, Robert, Michael. AB, DePauw U., 1960; LLB, U. Mich., 1963. Bar: Mo. 1963, U.S. Dist. Ct. (we. dist.) Mo. 1964. Assoc. Watson, Ess, Marshall & Enggas, Kansas City, Mo., 1963-72, ptnr., 1972-92; sr. v.p., gen. counsel, sec. DST Sys., inc., 1992—. Am. exec. bd. Boy Scouts Am., Kansas City, 1982—. Mem. ABA, Mo. Bar Assn., Kansas City Club. Republican. Methodist. Home: 9722 Sagamore Rd Shawnee Mission KS 66206-2314 Office: DST Systems Inc 333 W 11th St Kansas City MO 64105-1634

CANNING, JOHN RAFTON, urologist; b. Evanston, Ill., Dec. 5, 1927; s. Claude E. and Martha C. Canning; m. Elizabeth Learned, Sept. 11, 1948; 1 dau., Sarah Blee; m. Jacqueline Maartense, Apr. 3, 1970; children— John R., Richard, Roberta. B.A., Lake Forest (Ill.) Coll., 1951; M.D., Northwestern U., 1955, M.S., 1956. Diplomate: Am. Bd. Surgery, Am. Bd. Urology. Intern St. Luke's Hosp., Chgo., 1955; resident in gen. surgery VA Hosp., Hines, 1956-60, resident in urology, 1966-68; chest fellow Presbyn.-St. Luke's Hosp., Chgo., 1963; asst. chief vascular surg. sect. VA Hosp., Hines, 1960-66, asst. chief urology surg. sect., 1968, chief urology, 1969—86; asst. prof. urology Loyola U. Stritch Sch. Medicine, Maywood, Ill., 1969-82, prof. urology, 1982—, chmn. dept., 1979-86; attending urologist Cook County Bur. Health, 1995—. Fellow A.C.S.; mem. AMA, Ill. Urol. Soc. (exec. com.), Chgo. Urol. Soc. (pres. exec. com.), Chgo. Med. Soc., Soc. Univ. Urologists. Club: Chgo. Yacht. Office: Loyola U Stritch Sch Medicine Dept Urology Maywood IL 60153

CANNON, DAVID JOSEPH, lawyer; b. Milw., Aug. 6, 1933; s. George W. and Florence (Dean) c.; m. Carol Nevins, Mar. 10, 1962; children: Charles, Courtney. BS, Marquette U., 1955, JD, 1960. Bar; Wis. 1960, U.S. Dist. Ct. (ea. dist.) Wis. 1960, U.S. Ct. Appeals (7th cir.) 1969, U.S. Ct. Appeals (8th cir.) 1976, U.S. Dist. Ct. (we. dist.) Wis. 1976, U.S. Ct. Appeals (5th cir.) 1978, U.S. Ct. Appeals (4th cir.) 1997. Atty. Cannon & Cannon, Milw., 1960-66; asst. dist. atty. Milw. County Dist. Atty., 1966-68, dist. atty., 1968; U.S. atty. Dept. Justice Ea. Dist. Wis., Milw., 1969-73; ptnr. Michael, Best & Friedrich, 1973—. Home: 1520 Sunset Dr Elm Grove WI 53122-1629 Office: Michael Best & Friedrich 100 E Wisconsin Ave Ste 3300 Milwaukee WI 53202-4108

CANNON, PATRICK D. federal offical, broadcaster; married; five children. Comm. specialist Mich. Dept. Labor, Bur. Workers' Disability; staff rsch. specialist; dir. Senate Ctrl. Office, Audio Comm. Divsn.; exec. dir. Mich. Commn. Disability Concern, Lansing, 1988-97, Mich. Commn. Blind, Lansing, 1997—. Bd. dirs. Capital Area Transp. Authority; mem. Pres.'s Com. Employment People with Disabilites; apptd. U.S. access Bd., 1995; presentor in field. Mem. Pres.'s com. Employment of People with Disabilities, Gov.'s com. People with Disabilities, Access Bd., 1995—, Advanced Am. with Disabilities Act Tng. Network, Capital Area Ctr. Indep. Living, All Peoples' Theater, Riverwalk Theater; bd. trustees BoarsHead Theater, Capitol Area Transp. Authority; co-chair Gov.'s State Am. with Disabilites Act Implementation Task Force; chair Mich. Am. with Disabilities Act Steering Com.; trainer Windmills; active People's Theatre, Easter Seal Soc., St. Vincent Home. Mem. Nat. Rehab. Assn.. Avocations: baseball, movies, theater, hotdogs, sunshine. Office: Mich Commn Blind PO Box 30652 Lansing MI 48909-8152

CANNON, PATRICK FRANCIS, public relations executive; b. Braddock, Pa., Mar. 2, 1938; s. Peter J. and Kathleen (Donnelly) C.; children by previous marriage: Patrick F. Jr., Elizabeth Kathleen; m. Jeanette Krema, Nov. 22, 1986. BA, Northwestern U., 1969. Ops. mgr. Compact Industries, Albert Lea, Minn., 1968-72; pub. info. dir. Dept. Pub. Works, Chgo., 1970-72; acct. exec. Humes & Assocs., 1972-77; freelance journalist, cons. Oak Park, Ill., 1977-79; mgr. pub. rels. and prodn. Lions Clubs Internat., Oak Brook, 1979-2001; pvt. comms. cons., writer, 2001—. Editor: Water in Rural America, 1973, Wastewater in Rural America, 1974, We Serve: A History of the Lions Clubs, 1991; contbr. articles to profl. jours. and mags.; exec. producer, writer (pub. TV documentaries) With Very Little...Blindness Prevention in Developing Countries, 1991, The Search for Light, 1993, A Dangerous Time for Kids, 1997. Exec. dir. Civic Arts Coun. Oak Park, 1977-79; bd. dirs. interpreter coun. Oak Park Tour Ctr., 1978-82, mem. vol. svc. com. Frank Lloyd Wright Home and Studio Found., 1988-94, mem. pub. programs com., 1995-96, chmn. Wright Plus Housewalk, 1996; mem. bd. advisors U.S. Internat. Film and Video Festival; mem. internat. bd. advisors World Media Festival. Named PR All Star 1996, Inside PR Mag. Mem. Lions (pres. 1983-84). Roman Catholic. Avocations: history, horse racing. Home and Office: 243 Iowa St Oak Park IL 60302-2347 E-mail: patnette@aol.com.

CANO, JUVENTINO, manufacturing company executive; b. Estapillo, Mex., 1956; cam to U.s., 1974; m. Hermila Cano; 3 children. Grad., Benito Juarez H.S., Tecoman, Mex. Pres., CEO Cano Container Corp., Aurora, Ill., 1986—. Mem. adv. bd. Merchants Bank, Aurora, Joseph Corp., Aurora. Mem. Aurora Sch. Bus. Partnership; bd. dirs. Aurora Econ. Devel. Commn., Mercy Svc. Found., Waubonsee C.C. Found.; mem. exec. bd. Aurora Cmty. Mobilization Adv. Bd. Recipient Mfg. Firm of Yr. award, 1993, Hispanic 500 award Hispanic bus. Mag., 1994. Mem. USHCC (bd. dirs. Region IV 1997, Region IV Hispanic Businessman of Yr. 1995),

Aurora Hispanic C. of C. (pres. bd. dirs.), Greater Aurora C. of C. (bd. dirs.), Urban League (bd. dirs.). Office: Cano Container Corp 2300 Raddant Rd Ste A Aurora IL 60504-9101 Fax: 630-585-7501.

CANTALUPO, JAMES RICHARD, restaurant company executive; b. Oak Park, Ill., Nov. 14, 1943; s. James Francis and Eileen Patricia (Goggin) C.; m. Jo Ann Lucero, June 16, 1973; children: Christine, Jeffrey. B.S. in Acctg., U. Ill.-Champaign, 1966. C.P.A., Ill. Staff acct. Arthur Young & Co., Chgo., 1966-71, mgr., 1971-74; controller McDonald's Corp., Oak Brook, Ill., 1974-75, sr. v.p., controller, 1981-85, sr. v.p., zone mgr., 1985-87, pres. McDonald's Internat., 1987—; dir. No. Trust Bank-Oak Brook, 1983—. Treas. McDonald Polit.. Action Com., Oak Brook, 1979-85; chmn., dir. Nat. Multiple Sclerosis Soc., Chgo.-No. Ill. chpt., 1981— . Mem. Am. Inst. C.P.A.'s, Ill. Soc. C.P.A.'s, Inst. Corp. Controllers Roman Catholic. Office: McDonald's Corp 1 Kroc Dr Oak Brook IL 60523-2275 also: McDonald's Corp 1 McDonald's Plaza Oak Brook IL 60523

CANTOR, BERNARD JACK, patent lawyer; b. N.Y.C., Aug. 18, 1927; s. Alexander J. and Tillie (Henzeloff) C.; m. Judith L. Levin, Mar. 25, 1951; children— Glenn H., Cliff A., James E., Ellen B., Mark E. B. Mech. Engring., Cornell, 1949; J.D., George Washington U., Washington, 1952. Bar: D.C. 1952, U.S. Patent Office 1952, Mich. 1953; registered patent atty. U.S., Can. Examiner U.S. Patent Office, Washington, 1949-52; pvt. practice Detroit, 1952-88; ptnr. firm Harness, Dickey & Pierce, Troy, Mich., 1988—. Lectr. in field. Contbr. articles on patent law to profl. jours. Mem. exec. coun. Detroit Area Boy Scouts Am., 1972—. Served with U.S. Army, 1944-46. Recipient Ellsworth award patent law George Washington U., 1952, Shofar award Boy Scouts Am., 1975, Silver Beaver award, 1975, Disting. Eagle award, 1985. Fellow Mich. State Bar Found.; mem. ABA, Mich. Bar Assn. (dir. econs. sect., arbitrator State of Mich. grievance com.), Detroit Bar Assn., Oakland Bar Assn., Mich. Patent Law Assn., Am. Intellectual Property Law Assn., Am. Arbitration Assn. (arbitrator), Cornell Engring. Soc., Am. Technion Soc. (bd. dirs. Detroit 1970—), Pi Tau Sigma, Phi Delta Phi, Beta Sigma Rho. Home: 5685 Forman Dr Bloomfield Hills MI 48301-1154 Office: Harness Dickey & Pierce 5445 Corporate Dr Troy MI 48098-2683

CANTOR, GEORGE NATHAN, journalist; b. Detroit, June 14, 1941; s. Harold and Evelyn (Grossman) C.; m. Sheryl Joyce Bershad, Dec. 7, 1975; children: Jaime, Courtney. B.A., Wayne State U., 1962. Reporter, editor Detroit Free Press, 1963-77; columnist Detroit News, 1977—; commentator WWJ-Radio, Detroit, 1981-90, WXYZ-TV, Detroit, 1982-90; editl. page writer Detroit News. Author: The Great Lakes Guidebook, 3 vols., 1978-80. Bd. dirs. Greater Detroit Area Hosp. Council, 1983. Recipient Malcolm Bingay Wayne State U., 1962; recipient Paul Tobenaw Meml. Columbia U., 1980, Disting. Achievement UPI, 1982 Mem. Phi Beta Kappa Jewish. Office: Detroit News 615 W Lafayette Blvd Detroit MI 48226-3197

CAPALDO, GUY, obstetrician, gynecologist; b. Bisaccia, Italy, Jan. 1, 1950; came to U.S., 1958; s. Arturo Nunziante and Maria Carmela (Ciani) C.; m. Kathy Nicita, Apr. 20, 1985. BSEE magna cum laude, U. Dayton, 1972; MS, Ohio State U., Columbus, 1973; MD, Med. Coll. Ohio, 1978. Diplomate Am. Bd. Ob-Gyn; cert. clin. densitometrist Internat. Soc. Clin. Densitometry. Research asst. Ohio State U., 1973-75; resident in ob-gyn Med. Coll. Ohio, Toledo, 1978-82; practice medicine specializing in ob-gyn Mansfield, Ohio, 1982—. Chief ob-gyn. dept. Mansfield Gen. Hosp., 1985—; lab. dir. Mansfield (Ohio) Ob-Gyn Assocs. Contbr. articles to profl. jours. Clinic physician Plan Parenthood, Mansfield, 1982—. Pres. scholar U. Dayton, 1968-72, Univ. fellow Ohio State U., 1972-75. Fellow Am. Coll. Ob-Gyn; mem. AMA, Ohio State Med. Assn., Richland County Med. Soc. Avocations: reading, fishing, traveling, golfing. Office: Mansfield Ob-Gyn Assocs 500 S Trimble Rd Mansfield OH 44906-3483

CAPE, JAMES ODIES E. fashion designer; b. Detroit, Nov. 18, 1947; s. Odies E. and Juanita K. (Brandon) C. Student, Henry Ford C.C., 1973-75, Am. Acad. Dramatic Arts, N.Y.C., 1975-76, Pace U., 1977-78. Trapeze artist Mills Bros. Circus, 1962; skater Ice Capades, 1971-72; creator, dir., instr. skating program City of Southfield, Mich., 1972, 73; haute couture designer James E. Cape & Assocs., Dearborn, 1986—. Mem. Marji Kunz scholarship award com. Wayne State U., Detroit. Film reviewer Times-Herald Newspapers, 1989-90; clothing designs pub. in various mags. and newspapers; creations for TV and stage including the Emmys, The Am. Music Awards, Dick Clark-ABC Prodns., Showtime Spl. "Aretha", Trump Castle, Atlantic City, The Chgo. Theater, Kennedy Ctr., Washington, Radio City Music Hall; co-prodr. Eartha Kitt, A Night in Paris; spl. commd. designs various celebrities; spl. publicity creations for Detroit Inst. Arts, Am. Lung Assn.; producer, host TV show "Town Talk." Recipient Pre-silver, bronze medals U.S. Figure Skating Assn., 1969, Citation award City of Dearborn, 1994, Wayne County (Mich.) Resolution award, 1993, Spl. Tribute award State of Mich. Ho. of Reps., 1994, Page award Herald Newspapers, 1999-2000. Mem. AFTRA, Actors Equity, Soc. for Cinephiles. Home: James E. Cape and Associates 500 N Rosevere Dearborn MI 48128 E-mail: JamesECape@aol.com.

CAPEN, CHARLES CHABERT, veterinary pathology educator; b. Tacoma, Sept. 3, 1936; s. Charles (Kenneth) and Ruth (Chabert) C.; m. Sharron Lee Martin, June 27, 1968. DVM, Wash. State U., 1960; MS, Ohio State U., 1961, PhD, 1965. Instr. dept. vet. pathology Ohio State U., Columbus, 1962—65, asst. prof. dept. vet. pathology 1965—67, assoc. prof., 1967—70, prof., 1970—, prof. endocrinology Coll. Medicine, 1972—, chmn. dept. vet. pathobiology, 1981—94, chmn., 1982—94, interim chmn. dept. bioscis., 1994—97; chmn., 1997—2002. Israel Doniach Meml. lectr. Brit. Endocrine Soc. meeting, Manchester, 1989; plenary lectr. Italian Soc. Endocrinology Congress, Pisa, 1995. Editor: (series) Animal Models of Human Disease, 1979—96; (mem. editl. bd.): Lab. Investigation, 1988—; Vet. Pathology, 1986—87; Am. Jour. Pathology, 1984—88; Exptl. and Toxicologic Pathology, 1990—; Food and Chem. Toxicology, 1993—; Drug and Chem. Toxicology, 1994—; Toxicology and Ecotoxicology News, 1993—; Handbook on Rat Tumor Pathology WHO/IARC, 1991—96. Mem. Opera Columbus, 1982—, Columbus Symphony Assn., 1972—. Named Disting. U. prof., Ohio State U., 2001; recipient Disting. scholar award, 1993, Dean's Tchg. Excellence award for grad. edn., Coll. Vet. Medicine, 1993, Disting. Vet. Alumnus award, Wash. State U., 1997, Career Achievement award in canine rsch., Am. Vet. Med. Found., 1997. Mem.: AVMA (Nat. Borden rsch. award 1975, small animal rsch. award 1984, Gaines rsch. award 1987, excellence in canine rsch. award 1995, George Scott Meml. award of Toxicology Forum 1997), Soc. Toxicol. Pathologists (pres. 1997—98), U.S. Can. Acad. Pathology (coun. 1989—92), Inst. Medicine/NAS, Am. Coll. Vet. Pathologists (disting. mem., diplomate) 1975—81, (pres. 1978—79). Avocations: traveling, wildlife and nature photography. Office: The Ohio State U Dept Vet Biosci 1925 Coffey Rd Columbus OH 43210-1005

CAPERS, CYNTHIA FLYNN, dean, nursing educator; Diploma, Freedman's Hosp., Washington, 1965; BSN, U. Md., 1968; MSN, U. Pa., 1981, PhD in Culture and Nursing, 1986. Assoc. prof., course coord. Thomas Jefferson U., Phila., 1989-93; dir. undergrad. programs, assoc. prof. LaSalle U. Sch. Nursing, 1993-96, interim dean, assoc. prof., 1996-97; dean, prof. U. Akron Coll. of Nursing, 1997—. M. Elizabeth Carnegie vis. prof. in nursing rsch. Howard U., 1998; recipient Outstanding Achievement, Leadership and Svc. Med. Soc. of Ea. Pa., 1997, Disting. Nurse award Pa. Nurses Assn., 1995, Nurse Excellence award Pa. Nurses Assn., 1991; named Woman of Yr. YWCA of Germantown, 1992. Contbr. articles to profl. jours. Bd. trustees Am. Heart Assn., 1998-2000, Coming Together Project, Akron, 1998—, The Akron Cmty. Found., 1999—, Summa Health Sys. Hosp. Bd., 2000—; adv. bd. LaSalle U. Neighborhood Nursing Ctr., 1997-98, Coll. of Health, Edn., and Human Resources U. Scranton, 1992-96, Govs. Sch. of Health Care Professions in Pa., 1990-97; vice chmn. Pa. State Bd. of Nursing, 1991, chmn., 1992, 93; bd. mgrs. The Phila. Found., 1993-97. Office: U Akron Coll Nursing Mary E Gladwin Hl Akron OH 44325-0001 Fax: 330-972-5737.

CAPERTON, ALBERT FRANKLIN, retired newspaper editor; b. Hemphill, W.Va., Dec. 31, 1936; s. Albert Harrison and Viola (Hicks) C.; m. Elizabeth Moreland, Jan. 29, 1960; children— Catherine Elizabeth, Robert Harrell B., Northwestern State U., 1962; M.Jour., Columbia U., 1965; cert. Advanced Mgmt. Program, Harvard U., 1982. Reporter Richmond News Leader, Va., 1962-64; reporter St Petersburg Times, Fla., 1965-67, Tampa Tribune, 1967-69; asst. city editor Miami Herald, 1969-72, Broward County editor, 1972-75; exec. editor Macon Telegraph & News, Ga., 1975-78, Virginian-Pilot & Ledger Star, Norfolk, 1978-84; mng. editor Indpls. News, 1984-90, Indpls. Star, 1990-95; exec. editor Indpls. Star and News, 1995-99, Indpls. Star, 1999-2000. Pres. Crossroads of Am. Coun. Boy Scouts of Am., Indpls., 1991-92; chmn., bd. trustees Christian Theol. Sem. With USAF, 1954-57. Mem. Rotary, Indpls. Athletic Club (pres. 1999—). Mem. Diciples of Christ. Avocations: reading, tennis. Home: 6432 Landborough North Dr Indianapolis IN 46220-4351 E-mail: acape1066@aol.com.

CAPLAN, ARNOLD I. biology educator; b. Chgo., Jan. 5, 1942; s. David and Lillian (Diskin) C.; m. Bonita Wright, July 4, 1965; children: Aaron M., Rachel L. BS, Ill. Inst. Tech., 1963; PhD, Johns Hopkins U., 1966. Asst. prof. Case Western Res. U., Cleve., 1969-75, assoc. prof., 1975-81, prof. devel. genetics, anatomy, 1981-88, dir. cell molecule basis aging tng. program, 1981—, dir. skeletal rsch. ctr., 1986—, prof. biophysics, physiology, 1989—. Vis. prof. U. Calif., San Francisco, 1973, Inst. de Chimie Biologique, Strasbourg, France, 1976-77; Erna and Jakob Michael vis. prof. Weizmann Inst. Sci., Rehovot, Israel, 1984-85. Contbr. articles to profl. jours. Recipient Career Devel. award NIH, 1971-76; Am. Cancer Soc. fellow, 1967-69; Josiah Macy Faculty scholar Case Western Res. U., 1976-77. Mem. Am. Assn. Orthopaedics Surgery (Elizabeth Winston Lanier Kappa Delta award 1990), Orthopaedics Rsch. Soc., Soc. Devel. Biology, AAAS, Am. Soc. Cell Biology. Office: Case Western Res U Dept Biology 2080 Adelbert Rd Cleveland OH 44106-2623

CAPONIGRO, JEFFREY RALPH, public relations counselor; b. Kankakee, Ill., Aug. 13, 1957; s. Ralph A. and Barbara Jean (Paul) C.; m. Ellen Colleen Kennedy, Oct. 15, 1982; children: Nicholas J., Michael J. BA, Ctrl. Mich. U., 1979. Sports reporter Observer and Eccentric newspaper, Rochester, Mich., 1974-75, Mt. Pleasant (Mich.) Times, 1975-77, Midland (Mich.) Daily News, 1977-79; acct. exec. Desmond & Assocs., Oak Park, Mich., 1979-80; v.p. Anthony M. Franco, Inc., Detroit, 1980-84; chmn., pres., CEO Shandwick USA (formerly Casey Comm. Mgmt., Inc.), Southfield, 1984—. Founder & CEO, Caponigro Public Relations Inc., Detroit. Contbr. author: Best Sports Stories, 1978. Mem. Pub. Rels. Soc. Am. (accredited, Detroit chpt., nat. accrediation bd.). Home: 5790 Springbrook Dr Troy MI 48098-5352 Office: Caponigro Public Relations 4000 Town Ctr Southfield MI 48075-1410

CAPORALE, D. NICK, lawyer; b. Omaha, Sept. 13, 1928; s. Michele and Lucia Caporale; m. Margaret Nilson, Aug. 5, 1950; children: Laura Diane Stevenson, Leland Alan. B.A., U. Nebr.-Omaha, 1949, M.Sc., 1954; J.D. with distinction, U. Nebr.-Lincoln, 1957. Bar: Nebr. 1957, U.S. Dist. Ct. Nebr. 1957, U.S. Ct. Appeals 8th cir. 1958, U.S. Supreme Ct. 1970. Judge Nebr. Dist. Ct., Omaha, 1979-81, Nebr. Supreme Ct., Lincoln, 1982-98; of counsel Baird Holm Law Firm, 1998—. Lectr. U. Nebr., Lincoln, 1982-84, 2000—. Pres. Omaha Community Playhouse, 1976. Served to 1st lt. U.S. Army, 1952-54, Korea. Decorated Bronze Star; recipient Alumni Achievement U. Nebr.-Omaha, 1972 Fellow Am. Coll. Trial Lawyers, Internat. Soc. Barristers; mem. Order of Coif. Office: Baird Holm Law Firm 1500 Woodmen Tower Omaha NE 68102 E-mail: ncaporale@bairdholm.com.

CAPP, DAVID A. former prosecutor; Criminal divsn. chief U.S. Atty.'s Office, Dyer, 1988-91, 1st asst. atty., U.S. Atty, no. dist Ind, 1999—2001.

CAPPARELLI, RALPH C. state legislator; b. Chgo., Apr. 12, 1924; s. Ralph and Mary (Drammis) C.; m. Cordelia Capparelli; children: Ralph, Valerie. BS, No. Ill. U. 1st v.p. 41st Ward Dem. Orgn., Chgo., 1965—; Ill. state rep. Dist. 13, 1971—. Asst. majority whip, ex officio mem. Com. Intergovt. Coop. Com., exec. mem. Fin. Inst. Com. and Transp. and Motor Vehicles Com., Ill. Ho. of Reps.; supr. recreation Chgo. Pk. Dist., 1953-67; advisor Columbia Bank, Chgo., 1967—; sec.-treas. Jefferson Travel, 1968—; former tchr. Decorated Battle Star. Mem. Nat. Recreation Soc., Ill. Recreation Soc., Lions, K.C. (4th degree), Eagles, Am. Legion, Sigma Nu. Office: 7452 N Harlem Ave Chicago IL 60631-4404

CAPPO, JOSEPH C. publisher; b. Chgo., Feb. 24, 1936; s. Joseph V. and Frances (Maggio) Cacioppo; m. Mary Anne Cappo, May 7, 1967; children: Elizabeth, John. BA, DePaul U., 1957. Reporter Hollister Publs., Wilmette, Ill., 1961-62, Chgo. Daily News, 1962-68, bus. columnist, 1968-78; columnist Crain's Chgo. Bus., 1978—, pub., 1979-89; v.p. Crain Comm., Inc., 1981-89, sr. v.p. group pub., 1989-95, sr. v.p. internat., 1996—; pres. Crain Comms. of Mex., 2001—. Pub. Advt. Age, 1989—92, publishing dir., 1992—99; dir. Assn. Area Bus. Publs., 1982—88, pres., 1985—86. Author: Future Scope: Success Strategies for the 1990's and Beyond, 1990. Bd. dirs. Off the Street Club, Chgo., 1981—, Chgo. Advt. Fedn., 1987-93, Mus. Broadcast Comm., 1984-90, Ill. Coun. on Econ. Edn., 1990-95. With U.S. Army, 1959-61. Recipient award Ill. Press Assn., 1962, (with other Daily News staffers) Nat. Headliner award, 1966, Disting. Alumni award DePaul U., 1975, Page One award Chgo. Newspaper Guild, 1978, Peter Lisagor award Sigma Delta Chi, 1978, Outstanding Achievement award in comm., Justinian Soc. Lawyers, 1979, Champion award YWCA of Met. Chgo., 1984, Media Svc. award Chgo. Lung Assn., 1990. Mem.: Bus. and Econ. Writers (bd. govs. 1984—89), Econ. Club (Chgo.), Internat. Advt. Assn. (world bd. 1994—, sr. v.p. 1996—98, world pres. 1998—2000), Delta Mu Delta (hon.). Roman Catholic. Office: Crain Communications Inc 360 N Michigan Ave Chicago IL 60601-3806

CAPSHAW, TOMMIE DEAN, judge; b. Oklahoma City, Sept. 20, 1936; m. Dian Shipp; 1 child, Charles W. BS in Bus., Oklahoma City U., 1958; postrad., U. Ark., 1958-59; JD, U. Okla., 1961. Bar: Okla. 1961, Wyo. 1971, Ind. 1975. Assoc. Looney, Watts, Looney, Nichols and Johnson, Oklahoma City, 1961-63, Pierce, Duncan, Couch and Hendrickson, Oklahoma City, 1963-70; trial atty., v.p. Capshaw Well Service Co., Liberty Pipe and Supply Co., Casper, Wyo.; adminstrv. law judge Evansville, Ind., 1973-75, 96-99; hearing office chief adminstrv. law judge Chgo., 1975-96; acting regional chief adminstrv. law judge, 1977-78; sr. adminstrv. law judge, 1999—. Acting appeals coun. mem., Arlington, Va., 1980, acting chief adminstrv. law judge, 1984; mem. faculty U. Evansville, 1977, Sch. Law Ill. U., 1988—, So. Ind. U., 1990; lectr. in field. Author: A Manual for Continuing Judicial Education, 1981, Practical Aspects of Handling Social Security Disability Claims, 1982, Judicial Practice Handbook, 1990, A Quest for Quality, Speedy Justice, 1991; contbr. numerous articles to profl. jours., chpt. to textbook. Mem. adv. coun. Boy Scouts Am., scoutmaster, den leader, 1969—, Nat. Jud. Coll. U. Nev.; bd. dirs. Casper Symphony, 1972-73, Casper United Fund, 1972-73, Midget Football Assn., Casper, 1972-73, German Twp. Water Dist., 1984-85; pres. Evansville Unitarian Universalist Ch., 1984-86; performer Evansville Philharmonic Orch., 1986-98; bd. dirs. German Twp. Vol. Fire Dept., 1998—. Recipient Kappa Alpha Order Ct. of Honor award, 1962, Silver Beaver award Boy Scouts Am., 1980, presentation for vol. svc. contbg. betterment of cmty. Office Hearings and Appeals, 1992, presentation outstanding jud. mentor tng. Supreme Ct. Iowa, 1992, presentation dising. mentor tng. Fla. Jud. Coll., 1992. Mem. Okla. Bar Assn., Okla. County Bar Assn. (v.p. 1967), Wyo. Bar Assn., Evansville Bar Assn. (jud. rep. 1986-87, James Bethel Gresham Freedom award 1988), Young Lawyers Assn., Assn. Adminstrv. Law Judges HHS (bd. dirs. 1979-82, Tic Vickery award 1998), Oklahoma City U. Alumni Assn. (bd. dirs. 1965). Home: 6105 School Rd # 6 Evansville IN 47720

CARBON, MAX WILLIAM, nuclear engineering educator; b. Monon, Ind., Jan. 19, 1922; s. Joseph William and Mary Olive (Goble) C.; m. Phyllis Camille Myers, Apr. 13, 1944; children: Ronald Allen, Jean Ann, Susan Jane, David William, Janet Elaine. BSME, Purdue U., 1943, MS, 1947, PhD, 1949. With Hanford Works divsn. GE, 1949-55, head heat transfer unit, 1951-55; with rsch. and advanced devel. divsn. Avco Mfg. Corp., 1955-58, chief thermodynamics sect., 1956-58; prof., chmn. nuclear engring. and engring. physics dept. U. Wis. Coll. Engring., Madison, 1958-92, emeritus prof., collateral faculty, 1992—, acting assoc. dean for rsch., 1995-96. Group leader Ford Found. program Singapore, 1967-68; mem. adv. com. on reactor safeguards, 1975-87; chmn. spl. com. for integral fast reactor U. Chgo., 1984-94, chmn. spl. adv. com. for nuclear tech. program Argonne (Ill.) Nat. Lab., 1995—; mem. INPO Nat. Nuclear Accrediting Bd., 1990-94; mem. nuclear safety rev. and audit com. Kewaunee Nuclear Power Plant, 1993-96. Author: Nuclear Power: Villain or Victim, 1997. Capt. ordnance dept. AUS, 1943-46. Named Disting. Engring. Alumnus, Purdue U. Fellow Am. Nuclear Soc.; mem. AAAS, Sigma Xi, Tau Beta Pi. Office: U Wis Engring Rsch Bldg Madison WI 53706 E-mail: carbon@engr.wisc.edu.

CARBONE, ANTHONY J. chemicals executive; m. Patricia; children: Christopher, Carolyn. BS in Mech. Engring., Yale U.; MBA, Ctrl. Mich. U. Various tech. svc. and devel. positions Dow Chem. Co., Midland, Mich., 1962-67, sect. head, 1967-69, group mgr. TS&D, 1969-70, product sales mgr. laminated and coated products, 1970-72, mktg. mgr. laminated and coated products, 1972-74, group v.p. Dow Plastics, Chems., Plastic bus. group, 1993-95, exec. v.p., 1996—; also bd. dirs., mem. exec. com.; mktg. dir. Dow Lat. Am., Coral Gables, Fla., 1974-76; bus. mgr. STYROFOAM brand functional products adn sys. dept. Dow U.S.A., Midland, 1976-80, dir. mktg. functional products and sys., 1980-83, gen. mgr. coatings and resins dept., 1983-87, gen. mgr. separation sys. dept., 1983-86, v.p. Dow Plastics, 1987-91; group v.p. Dow Plastics Dow N.Am., 1991-93. Mem. adv. coun. Heritage Found. Mem. Am. Plastics Coun.(mem. bd., exec. com.), Am. Chem. Soc., Soc. Plastic Industries. Office: The Dow Chem Co 2030 Dow Ctr Midland MI 48674

CARBONE, PAUL PETER, oncologist, educator, administrator; b. White Plains, N.Y., May 2, 1931; s. Antonio and Grace (Cappelieri) C.; m. Mary Iamurri, Aug. 20, 1954; children: David, Kathryn, Karen, Kim, Paul J., Mary Beth, Matthew. Student, Union Coll., Schenectady, 1949-52; M.D., Albany (N.Y.). Med. Coll., 1956. Diplomate: Am. Bd. Internal Medicine; cert. medical oncology. Joined USPHS Hosp., 1956, intern, 1956-57, resident in internal medicine San Francisco, 1958-60; resident NIH, Bethesda, Md., 1961-63; mem. staff Nat. Cancer Inst., NIH, 1960-76, chief medicine br., 1968-72, asso. dir. for med. oncology, div. cancer treatment, 1972-76, dep. clin. dir., 1972-76; clin. prof. Georgetown U. Med. Sch., 1971-76; lectr. hematology Walter Reed Army Inst. Research, 1962-76; prof. medicine and human oncology U. Wis., Madison, 1976—, dir. div. clin. oncology, 1976-80, chmn. dept. human oncology, 1977-87; dir. Wis. Comprehensive Cancer Ctr., 1978-97; assoc. dean for program devel. U. Wis. Med. Sch., from 1992. Assoc. dean program devel. U. Wis. Med. Sch.; vis. prof. Nat. U. Singapore. Contbr. profl. jours. Decorated USPHS Commendation medal; recipient Trimble Lecture award Md. Chirurgical Faculty, 1968; Lasker award clin. cancer chemotherapy, 1972; Rosenthal award for improvement in clin. cancer care, 1977, Medal of Honor Am. Cancer Soc., 1987, Jeffrey A. Gottlieb Meml. award M.D. Anderson Cancer Ctr., U. Tex., 1990, Folkert O. Belzer Lifetime Achievement medal U. Wis. Med. Sch., 2000; NIMMO vis. prof. Royal Adelaide Hosp., Adelaide, Australia, 1989. Master ACP (bd. govs. Wis. chpt. 1986-90); mem. AMA, Am. Soc. Clin. Oncology (pres. 1972-73, Outstanding Achievement award 1995), Am. Soc. Clin. Investigation, Assn. Am. Physicians, Am. Assn. Cancer Rsch. (pres. 1978-79), Am. Fedn. Clin. Rsch., Alpha Omega Alpha. Home: Middleton, Wis. Died Feb. 22, 2002.

CARDELLA, TOM, sales executive; Founder, pres. Access Direct Telemktg. Svcs. Inc., Cedar Rapids, Iowa, 1995—. Office: Access Direct Ste B 4515 20th Ave SW Cedar Rapids IA 52404-1290

CARDOZO, RICHARD NUNEZ, marketing, entrepreneurship and business educator; b. Mpls., Feb. 13, 1936; s. William Nunez and Miriam (Honig) C.; m. Arlene Rossen, June 29, 1959; children: Miriam, Rachel (dec.), Rebecca. AB, Carleton Coll., 1956; MBA, Harvard U., 1959; PhD (Ford Found. fellow, Kaiser fellow), U. Minn., 1964. Asst. prof. bus. adminstrn. Harvard U., 1964-67; assoc. prof. mktg. U. Minn., 1967-71, prof., 1971—, Curtis L. Carlson chair in entrepreneurial studies, 1987-2000, prof. entrepreneurial studies, strategic mgmt., 2000—02; dir. Center for Exptl. Studies in Bus., 1969-73, chmn. dept. mktg., 1975-78; dir. Case Devel. Ctr., 1980-2000, Entrepreneurial Studies Ctr., 1987-2000. Dir. Nat. Presto Industries, Brownstone Distbg.; Fulbright lectr. Hebrew U., Jerusalem, 1980; vis. prof. bus. adminstrn. Harvard U., Grad. Sch. Bus., 1982-83; cons. in field. Author: (with others) Problems in Marketing, 4th edit, 1968; Product Policy: Cases and Concepts, 1979; contbr. articles to profl. jours. Served with USAR, 1961. Fulbright fellow London Sch. Econ., 1956-57 Mem. Am. Mktg. Assn., AAAS, Product Devel. and Mgmt. Assn., Acad. Mgmt. Home: 1007 Pine Tree Trail Stillwater MN 55082-5918 Office: U Minn 3-306 Carlson Sch Mgmt Minneapolis MN 55455 E-mail: rcardozo@csom.umn.edu.

CAREY, CHRISTOPHER L. financial company executive; Sr. v.p., contr. holding co., CFO Corestates Bank; CFO Provident Fin. Group Inc., Cin., 1999—. Office: Provident Fin Group Inc 1 E 4th St Cincinnati OH 45202-3717

CAREY, JOHN LEO, lawyer; b. Morris, Ill., Oct. 1, 1920; s. John Leo and Loretta (Conley) C.; m. Rhea M. White, July 15, 1950; children: John Leo III, Daniel Hobart, Deborah M. BS, St. Ambrose Coll., Davenport, Ia., 1941; JD, Georgetown U., 1947, LLM, 1949. Bar: Ind. 1954, DC 1947, Ill. 1947. Legislative asst. Sen. Scott W. Lucas, 1945-47; spl. atty. IRS, Washington, 1947-54; since practiced in South Bend; ptnr. Barnes & Thornburg, 1954—, now of counsel; law prof. taxation Notre Dame Law Sch., 1968-90. Trustee LaLumire Prep. Sch., Laporte, Ind. Served with USAAF, World War II; to lt. col. USAF, Korean War. Decorated D.F.C., Air medal. Mem. ABA (bd. govs. 1986-89, treas. 1990-93), Ind. Bar Assn. (pres. 1976-77), St. Joseph County Bar Assn., Signal Point Country Club. Home: # 114 1250 W Southwinds Blvd Vero Beach FL 32963 Office: 600 1st Source Bank Ctr 100 N Michigan St South Bend IN 46601-1630

CAREY, PAUL RICHARD, biophysicist; b. Dartford, Kent, Eng., June 17, 1945; arrived in Can., 1969; s. Charles Richard and Winifred Margaret (Knight) C.; m. Julia Smith, Sept. 4, 1966 (div. May 1991); children: Emma, Sarah, Matthew; m. Marianne Pusztai, Mar. 7, 1992. BS in Chemistry with honors, U. Sussex, Eng., 1966, PhD, 1969. Postdoctoral fellow Nat. Rsch. Coun., Ottawa, Ont., Can., 1969-71, rsch. officer Can., 1971-94; mgr. Ctr. for Protein Structure Design, head protein lab. Inst. for Bio. Scis., Can., 1987-93; prof. dept. biochemistry Case Western Res. U.,

1995—, dir. Cleve. Ctr. Structural Biology, 2000—. Mem. internat. adminstrv. com. Internat. Conf. on Lasers and Biol. Molecules, 1987—, adj. prof. Dept. Biochemistry, U. Ottawa, 1987-94, prof., 1994; prof. dept. biochemistry Case Western Reserve U. Author: Biochemical Applications of Raman and Resonance Raman Spectroscopies, 1982; contbr. over 180 articles to profl. jours.; patentee in field. Mem., past pres. Ottawa br. Amnesty Internat., 1980—. Fellow Chem. Inst. Can.; mem. Am. Chem. Soc., Can. Protein Engring. Network (Adminstrv. body 1990-93), Internat. Network Protein Engring. Ctrs. Achievements include first demonstration of resonance Raman spectroscopy providing vibrational spectrum of a substrate or drug in active site of an enzyme; generation of first quantitative relationship between active site bond lengths and reactivity by combining resonance Raman spectroscopy, enzyme kinetics and x-ray crystallography; elucidation of mechanism of sunlight degradation of biological insecticide from B. thuringiensis; research on use of lasers in fingerprint detection. Avocations: literature, music, birding. Office: Case Western Res U Dept Biochemistry Cleveland OH 44106-4935 E-mail: carey@biochemistry.cwru.edu.

CARL, JOHN L. insurance company executive; b. Huntington, Ind., Feb. 22, 1948; m. Brook Swanson, Aug. 30, 1969; children: Brian, Erin. BS, Purdue U., 1970; MBA, Ind. U., 1972. Fin. analyst Am. Hosp. Supply Corp., Glendale, Calif., 1972-73, plant contr., 1973-74, Milledgeville, Ga., 1974-75, dir. fin. planning Irvine, Calif., 1975-76; v.p., contr. McGraw Labs divsn., 1976-81, Hosp. Sector divsn., Evanston, Ill., 1981-86; v.p., corp. contr. Kraft Foods Inc., Glenview, 1986-89; v.p., CFO Nat. Computer Sys., Mpls., 1989-90; v.p., corp. contr. Amoco Corp., Chgo., 1991-94, exec. v.p., CFO, 1994-99; sr. v.p., CFO Allstate Corp., Northbrook, 1999-. Active Dean's Adv. Coun., Sch. Bus., Ind. U.; bd. dirs. Evanston (Ill.) Hosp., United Way of Chicago Coun. Mem. Fin. Execs. Inst., Am. Petroleum Inst. Home: 377 E Woodland Rd Lake Forest IL 60045-1313 Office: Allstate 2775 Sanders Rd Northbrook IL 60062

CARLEN, SISTER CLAUDIA, librarian, consultant; b. Detroit, July 24, 1906; d. Albert B. and Theresa Mary (Ternes) C. AB in Library Sci., U. Mich., 1928, MA in Library Sci., 1938; LHD (hon.), Marygrove Coll., 1981, Loyola U., Chgo., 1983, Sacred Heart Major Sem., 1989; LittD (hon.), Cath. U. of Am., 1983. Asst. librarian St. Mary Acad., Monroe, Mich., 1928-29, Marygrove Coll., Detroit, 1929-44, librarian, 1944-69, library cons., 1970-71; on leave as index editor New Cath. Ency., 1963-67, Cath. Theol. Ency., 1968-70; library cons. grad. div. Casa Santa Maria, N.Am. Coll., Rome, 1971-72; libr. St. John's Provincial Sem., Plymouth, Mich., 1972-80, libr. emeritus, 1980-82, scholar-in-residence, 1982-85, archivist, 1985-88; rschr. Bentley Hist. Libr., U. Mich., Ann Arbor, 1989-97. Supr. orgn. and servicing Community Ctr. Libraries staffed by vols.; bd. dirs. Corpus Instrumentorum, Inc., v.p., 1969-70; mem. instructional materials com. Mich. Curriculum Study; cons. McGraw Hill Ency. World Biography, 1968-72, World Book Ency., 1969-70; mem. working group on uniform headings for liturgical works Internat. Fedn. of Libr. Assns., 1972-75. Author: Guide to Encyclicals of the Roman Pontiffs, 1939, Guide to the Documents of Pius XII, 1951, Dictionary of Papal Pronouncements, 1958; editor: Papal Encyclicals, 1740-1981, 1981, Papal Pronouncements, 1991; editor: column At Your Service, Cath. Library World, 1950-52; Reference Book Rev. Sect., 1952-64, 66-72; Books for the Home column; monthly news release, Nat. Cath. Rural Life Conf., 1952-61; mem. adv. bd.: The Pope Speaks (quarterly periodical), 1953-88; contbr.: Catholic Bookman's Guide, 1961, Dictionary Western Chs, 1969, Ency. Dictionary of Religion, 1979, Translatio Studii, 1973, Intellectual Life on the Michigan Frontier, 1985; contbr.: Vatican Archives: An Inventory and Guide, 1997, Transtalio Studio Festichrift. Trustee Marygrove Coll., Detroit, 1976-79, vice chmn. bd., 1977-79. Recipient Disting. Alumna award U. Mich. Sch. Libr. Sci., 1974, Domitilla award Marygrove Coll., 1991, Gabriel Richard award Mich. Cath. Libr. Assn., 1998. Mem. ALA (coun. 1958-61, 68-71), Cath. Libr. Assn. (chmn. com. membership 1946-49, chmn. Mich. unit 1952-54, chmn. coll. and univ. sect. 1954-56, chmn. publs. com. 1961-62, pres. 1965-67, Jerome award 1993), Mich. Libr. Assn. (chmn. coll. sect. 1956-57, chmn. recruiting com. 1959-60), Accademia Olubrense (Pietrabissara, Italy, charter), Am. Friends of Vatican Libr. (co-founder, v.p.), Phi Beta Kappa, Phi Kappa Phi, Beta Phi Mu. Home: 610 W Elm Ave # A107 Monroe MI 48162

CARLIN, CLAIR MYRON, lawyer; b. Sharon, Pa., Apr. 20, 1947; s. Charles William and Carolyn L. (Vukasich) C.; children: Eric Richard, Elizabeth Marie, Alexander Myron. BS in Econs., Ohio State U., 1969, JD, 1972. Bar: Ohio 1973, Pa. 1973, U.S. Dist. Ct. (so. dist.) Ohio 1973, U.S. Dist. Ct. (no. dist.) Ohio 1975, U.S. Supreme Ct. 1976, U.S. Ct. Claims, 1983, U.S. Tax Ct. 1985. Staff atty. Ohio Dept. Taxation, Columbus, 1972-73; asst. atty. City of Warren, Ohio, 1973-75; assoc. McLaughlin, DiBlasio & Harshman, Youngstown, 1975-80; ptnr. McLaughlin, McNally & Carlin, 1980-98, Carlin & Vasvari, LLC, Poland, Ohio, 1998-2000, Clair M. Carlin, LLC, 2000—. Mem. editl. bd. Ohio Trial mag. Mem. Trumbull County Bicentennial Commn., Ohio, 1976; v.p. Svcs. for the Aging, Trumbull County, 1976-77; mem. Pres.' Club Ohio State U. Maj. Ohio NG, 1972-82. Fellow Ohio State Bar Found.; mem. ATLA (bd. govs. 1996—, trustee PAC 1996-98), ABA, Ohio State Bar Assn. (negligence law com. 1991—), Ohio State Bar Coll., Mahoning County Bar Assn. (chmn. legal edn. com. 1985-86, counsel 1986-87), Ohio Acad. Trial Lawyers (trustee 1988-92, polit. action com. chmn. 1991, exec. com. 1991-97, treas. 1992-93, sec. 1993-94, pres.-elect 1994-95, pres. 1995-96), Mahoning-Trumbull Acad. Trial Lawyers (pres. 1991), Ohio State U. Alumni Assn. (pres. Trumbull County chpt. 1985—), Cath. War Vets. (Ohio state commdr., Vet. of Yr. 1988), Rotary. Democrat. Roman Catholic. Home: 3524 Hunters Hl Poland OH 44514-2034 Office: Clair M Carlin LLC PO Box 5369 Youngstown OH 44514-0369 E-mail: info@carlin-law.com.

CARLIN, DENNIS J. lawyer; b. Chgo., Aug. 23, 1941; s. Herbert E. and Lillian (Schnelder) C.; m. Fern Carlin, Nov. 25, 1964; children: Gregory A., H. David, Stuart B. BBA, U. Wis., 1963; JD, DePaul U., 1967; LLM in Taxation, Georgetown U., 1971. Bar: Ill. 1967; CPA. Auditor Checkers, Simon & Rosner, Chgo., 1963-67; assoc. tax ct. litigation divsn. IRS, Washington, 1967-71; ptnr. Frankel, McKay, Orlikoff, Denten & Kostner, Chgo., 1971-77, Horwood & Carlin, Chgo., 1977-82, Gardner, Carton & Douglas, Chgo., 1982—, vice-chmn., 1998—. Contbr. articles to profl. jours. Mem. atty. div. Jewish United Fund; bd. dirs. Coun. for Jewish Elderly. Mem. ABA, Am. Coll. Tax Counsel, Chgo. Bar Assn. (former chmn. fed. tax com.), Nat. Strategy Forum, NYU Inst. Fed. Taxation, DePaul U. Alumni Coun., Am. Israeli C. of C., Twin Orchard Country Club. Avocations: golf, skiing, reading, music, theatre. Office: Gardner Carton & Douglas Quaker Tower Suite 3400 321 N Clark St Ste 3000 Chicago IL 60610-4718

CARLIN, DONALD WALTER, retired food products executive, consultant; b. Gary, Ind., Aug. 27, 1934; s. Walter Joseph and Mabel (Ebert) C.; m. Kathleen Susan McCone, Jan. 21, 1961; children: Michael Scott, Karen Mary, Mark Steven. BS in Engring, U. Notre Dame, 1956; LLB, U. Mich., 1959; grad., Advanced Mgmt. Program, Harvard U., 1978. Bar: Ind. 1959, Ill. 1960. Assoc. to ptnr. Soans, Anderson Luedeka & Fitch, Chgo., 1960-72; sr. atty. Kraft Inc., Glenview, Ill., 1972-73, v.p., asst. gen. counsel, 1974-79, sr. v.p., gen. counsel, 1979-81, sr. v.p., gen. counsel, sec., 1981-86, v.p., assoc. gen. counsel, 1986-89; v.p., dep. gen. counsel Kraft Gen. Foods, Northfield, 1989-92. Mem. bd. visitors Sch. Medicine, U. Calif.-Davis, 1990—. Mem. ABA (hon.) (com. corp. law depts. sect. bus. law), Assn. Gen. Counsel (emeritus), Westmoreland Country Club (bd. dirs. 1989-94, pres. 1993-94), Notre Dame Club (Chgo.), Ironwood Country Club (pres. 2000-, bd. dirs. 2000—). Home and Office: 333 Regentwood Rd Northfield IL 60093-2762 also: 73-106 Galleria Ct Palm Desert CA 92260

CARLISLE, RICK, professional basketball coach; m. Donna Carlisle. Attended, U. Maine; BA in Psychology, U. Va., 1984. Role-player Celtics, 1984—87; NBA player, asst. coach Detroit Pistons, head coach, 2001—. Named winner NBA Championship, 1985—86. Achievements include teams that have ranked no lower than 16th in the league in scoring and have ranked in the top-10 during four of those seasons. Office: Detroit Pistons Palace Auburn Hills 3777 Lapeer Rd Auburn Hills MI 48326*

CARLISLE, RONALD DWIGHT, nursery owner; b. Bismarck, N.D., Oct. 28, 1940; m. Neva Carlisle, May 18, 1968. BS, Black Hills State Coll., 1966. Policy issue mgr. Provident Life Ins. Co., Bismarck, N.D., 1966-83; workers compensation commr., 1983-85; delivery driver Premium Beverage, 1985-86; owner trees N M Ore, 1986—; mem. N.D. Legislature. Chair Dist. 52-Dist. 30, Bismarck; del. Rep. State Conv., 1976, 78, 80, 82, 84, 86, 88, 90, 92, 94, 96, 98, 2000, 2002. With USN, 1958-62. Recipient Guardian of Small Bus. award NFIB, 1991. Mem. Am. Vets. (life), N.D. Nursery Assn., Elks, NRA. Address: PO Box 222 Bismarck ND 58502-0222

CARLOCK, MAHLON WALDO, financial consultant, former high school administrator; b. Plymouth, Ind., Sept. 17, 1926; s. Thorstine Clifford and Katheryn G. (Gephart) C.; m. Betty L. Dobbs, Aug. 27, 1954; children: Mahlon W. II, Rhena M., Shawn R. BS, Ind. U., 1951, MS, 1956. Tchr. jr. high Martinsville Schs. Corp., Brooklyn, Ind., 1952-53; tchr. high sch. Indpls. Pub. Schs., 1953-63, asst. to dean of boys, 1963-73, asst. dean of boys, 1973-75, bus. mgr., 1976-87; fin. cons. Indpls., 1987-93; property builder, owner Ind. Lectr. on fin. and real estate; condr. seminars on estate planning and trust; income tax preparer. Sgt. U.S. Army, 1945-47. Mem. NEA (life), Indpls. Adminstrs., Ind. Bus. Edn. Assn., Indpls. Edn. Assn. (rep. 1958-63). Republican. Baptist. Lodge: Masons. Avocation: investing in real estate. Home and Office: 9705 E Michigan St Indianapolis IN 46229-2564

CARLOTTI, RONALD JOHN, food scientist; b. Martins Ferry, Ohio, Sept. 20, 1942; s. John Peter and Mary Rose (Pilla) C.; m. Eileen Theresa Dorsey, May 17, 1969; children: Lori Ann, Christina Maria, Jennifer Ann, Theresa Maria. Student, Wheeling (W.Va.) Jesuit Coll., 1960-63; BS, Ohio State U., 1964; MS, W.Va. U., 1966, PhD, 1970; MM, Aquinas Coll., 1996. Postdoctoral fellow Dept. Biochemistry, U. Iowa, Iowa City, 1971-72; asst. rsch. scientist Pediatrics Dept., U. Iowa, 1973-74; corp. nutritionist Kellogg Co., Battle Creek, Mich., 1974-77; mgr. nutrition/basic rsch. Frito Lay div. Pepsico, Dallas, 1977-82, prin. scientist new products, 1982-85; sr. rsch. scientist Amway Corp., Ada, Mich., 1985-89; dir. food sci. and tech. Country Home Bakers, Grand Rapids, 1990-93; pres. Carlotti and Assocs., 1994; pres., CEO Natura Inc., Lansing, Mich., 1995—2001, corp. sec., 2002—, bd. dirs., 2002—. Tech. rep. Snack Food Assn., Crystal City, Va., 1978-82, Grocery Mfrs. of Am., Washington, 1975-77; nutritionist Am. Frozen Food Assn., Washington, 1990-93; bis. asst. prof. chemistry Grand Valley State U., Allendale, Mich., 2002-; v.p. Global Bus. Develop., Aviral Pharmachem, Grand Rapids, Mich., 2001-. Contbr. articles to profl. jours. Pres. Mary Immaculate Sch. Bd., Dallas, 1981-83. Recipient Lovable Spud award, Nat. Potato Promotion Bd., Denver, 1981. Mem. Am. Chem. Soc., Am. Assn. Cereal Chemists, Inst. Food Tech. Roman Catholic. Achievements include start-up of new biotechnology-based food and chemical ingredients company, development of patented taste-appealing shelf-stable blend of fruit juice and milk, development of first nutritionally improved (low fat/low calorie) prototype of Tostitos Baked tortilla chips, of new high potency dry dog food for Amway Corp., of a series of nutritionally improved fruit pies for diabetics, of a specially formulated pumpkin pie which will not allow for the growth of pathogenic bacteria innoculated after baking in testing required to verify that the product can be stored at ambient temperature for up to five days; initiation of tech. and regulatory functions for corporate products. Home: 6921 Maplecrest Dr SE Grand Rapids MI 49546-9208

CARLSON, ARNE HELGE, former governor; b. N.Y.C., Sept. 24, 1934; s. Helge William and Kerstin (Magnusson) C.; children by previous marriage: Arne H. Jr., Anne Davis; m. Susan Shepard, July 12, 1985; 1 child, Jessica Shepard. BA, Williams Coll., 1957; postgrad., U. Minn., 1957-58. Mem. advt. staff Control Data, Bloomington, Minn., 1962-64; councilman Mpls. City Council, 1965-67; ind. businessman Mpls., 1968-69; legislator Minn. Ho. Reps., St. Paul, 1970-78; state auditor State of Minn., 1979-90, gov., 1991-99; chmn. bd. Am. Express Funds, Mpls., 1999—. Bd. dirs. Minn. Land Exch. Bd., St. Paul; trustee Minn. State Bd. Investment, St. Paul, 1979-99. Bd. dirs. Exec. Coun., St. Paul; sec. Minn. Housing Fin. Agy., St. Paul, 1979-91; past pres. Pub. Employees Retirement Assn., St. Paul, 1985-88; mem. Nat. Gov.'s Assn., Midwest Gov.'s Assn., Great Lakes Govs.; mem. Nat. Ednl. Goals Panel of Nat. Gov.'s Assn. Bush Found. Leadership fellow, 1971; recipient Children's Champion award Minn. Children's Def. Fund, Nat. Audubon Soc. award, Small Bus. Guardian award Nat. Fedn. Ind. Businesses, 1994, Great Blue Heron award N.Am. Waterfront Mgmt. Plan/U.S. Fish & Wildlife Svc., 1995; named Rep. of Yr. Nat. Ripon Soc., 1993. Bd. dirs. Exec. Coun. St. Paul, sec. Minn. Housing Fin. Agy., St. Paul, 1979-91; past pres. Pub. Employees Retirement Assn., St. Paul, 1985-88; mem. Nat. Gov.'s Assn. (chmn. com. on human resources, mem. Nat. Ednl. Goals Panel), Rep. Gov.'s Assn., Midwest Gov.'s Assn., Great Lakes Govs. Republican. Avocations: reading, squash, University of Minnesota basketball and football games. Home: 22005 Iden Ave N Forest Lake MN 55025-9329 Office: Am Express Funds 901 Marquette Ave Ste 2810 Minneapolis MN 55402-3268

CARLSON, ARTHUR EUGENE, accounting educator; b. Whitewater, Wis., May 10, 1923; s. Paul Adolph and Dorothy Adeline (Cooper) C.; m. Lorraine June Bronson, Aug. 19, 1944; 1 child, George Arthur. EdB, U. Wis., Whitewater, 1943; MBA, Harvard U., 1947; PhD, Northwestern U., 1954. Instr. Ohio U., 1947-50; lectr. Northwestern U., 1950-52; from asst. prof. to prof. acctg. Washington U., St. Louis, 1952-88, prof. emeritus, 1988—. Vis. prof. U. Hawaii, 1963-64. Author: College Accounting, 1967, 7th edit., 1993, Accounting Essentials, 1973, 5th edit., 1991. Chmn. Robert Meml. Endowment Fund, University City, Mo., 1972-98, trustee Police and Fire Pension Bd., 1979-88. Mem. Inst. Mgmt. Accts. (past pres.), Assn. Sys. Mgmt. (past pres., Disting. Svc. award 1973), Soc. Profs. Emeriti Washington U. (pres. 1995, disting. bus. alumni awards com. 1998—), Kiwanis (pres. 1969). Republican. Episcopalian. Avocations: bowling, gardening. Home: 801 S Skinker Blvd # 9A Saint Louis MO 63105-3228 E-mail: carlson@olin.wustl.edu.

CARLSON, BRUCE MARTIN, anatomist; b. Gary, Ind., July 11, 1938; s. Martin E. and Esther (Granquist) C.; m. Jean Ann Hyslop, Aug. 18, 1968; children: Martin, James. BA, Gustavus Adolphus Coll., 1959; MS, Cornell U., 1961; MD, PhD, U. Minn., 1986. Exchange scientist Inst. of Devel. Biology, Moscow, 1965-66; Fulbright fellow Hubrecht (Netherlands) Inst., 1973-74; Joshiah Macy scholar U. Helsinki, Finland, 1981-82; exchange scientist Inst. of Physiology, Prague, Czechoslovakia, 1971; asst. prof. of anatomy to prof. U. Mich., Ann Arbor, 1966—, prof. biology, 1979—, chmn. dept. anatomy and cell biology, 1988-2000, rsch. scientist Inst. Gerontology, 1989—, dir. Inst. Gerontology, 2000—. Fellow Fetzer Inst., Kalamazoo, Mich., 1990-96, trustee, 1998—; mem. study sects. NIH, 1986-90, Nat. Bd. Med. Examiners, 1994-96; NIH Fogerty fellow, U. Otago, Dunedin, New Zealand, 1999-00. Author: The Regeneration of Minced Muscles, 1972, Patten's Foundations of Embryology, 1974, 4th edit. 1981, 5th edit. 1988, 6th edit. 1996, Regeneration (in Russian), 1986, Human Embryology and Developmental Biology, 1994, 99; editor: From Message to Mind, 1988, Regeneration and Transplantation, 1990, numerous others. Recipient Disting. Alumni award Gustavus Adolphus Coll., 1979, Newcomb-Cleveland prize AAAS, 1972, 650th Anniversary medal, Charles U., Prague. Fellow: AAAS, Russian Acad. Natural Scis.; mem.: Gerontol. Soc. Am., Internat. Soc. Devel. Biology, Soc. Devel. Biologists, Assn. of Anatomy, Cell Biology and Neurobiology Chairpersons (pres. 1995), Am. Soc. Ichthyologists and Herpetologists, Am. Soc. Zoologists (divsn. chmn. 1987—89), Am. Assn. Clin. Anatomists, Am. Assn. Anatomists (nominating com. 1991, exec. com. 1994, pres. 1997—99). Lutheran. Achievements include invention of techniques of free muscle transplantation. Home: 3838 Curlew Ln Ann Arbor MI 48103-9404 Office: U Mich Inst of Gerontology Ann Arbor MI 48109

CARLSON, CHRIS, company executive; Pres. The Carlson Co., Madison, Wis., 1994—. Office: The Carlson Co 2305 Daniels St Madison WI 53718-6705 Fax: 608-222-9087.

CARLSON, E. DEAN, state official; Sec. Dept. Transp., Topeka. Office: Transp Dept Docking State Office Bldg Fl 7 Topeka KS 66612-1568

CARLSON, EDWARD C. anatomy educator; b. Iron Mountain, Mich., Feb. 22, 1942; s. Clarence H. and Rachel O. (Olsen) C.; m. Pam R. Carlson, 1995; children: Scott Edward, Susan Rebecca. BA, Bethel Coll., 1964; PhD, U. N.D., 1970. Spl. instr. dept. biology Bethel Coll., St. Paul, 1964-66; instr. anatomy U. Ariz., Tucson, 1970-72, asst. prof., 1972-77; assoc. prof. human anatomy U. Calif., Davis, 1977-81, prof., 1981—; chmn. dept. anatomy and cell biology U. N.D., Grand Forks, 1981—, acting chmn. dept. pharmacology, physiology and therapeutics, 2001—. Rsch. anatomist Calif. Primate Rsch. Ctr., Davis, 1982-85, rsch. affiliate, 1985—; co-dir. N.D. Diabetes Ocular Rsch. Ctr., Grand Forks, 1988—. Contbr. articles to profl. jours. Rsch. grantee Juvenile Diabetes Found., Am. Heart Assn., NIH, EPSCOR, NSF. Mem. Am. Assn. Anatomists, Am. Soc. for Investigative Pathology, Am. Soc. Cell Biology, Microcirculatory Soc. Avocations: running, fishing, skiing. Office: U ND Dept Anatomy & Cell Biol Grand Forks ND 58202

CARLSON, JAMES R. food products executive; Asst. counsel Sara Lee Corp., 1973; sr. v.p., CFO Sara Lee Bakery; exec. v.p., COO PYA/Monarch, 1991-93; pres. PYA/Monarch, 1993; v.p. Sara Lee Corp., 1993-97, sr. v.p. corp. strategy, 1997—. Office: Sara Lee Corp Three 1st National Plz Chicago IL 60602-2600

CARLSON, JEFFREY, lawyer; b. Valley City, N.D., Sept. 24, 1954; BA magna cum laude, Concordia Coll., 1976; JD cum laude, U. Minn., 1979. Bar: Minn. 1979, U.S. Dist. Ct. Minn. Regional counsel Supervalu, Inc., Eden Prairie, Minn. Mem. Hennepin County Bar Assn., Minn. State Bar Assn. Office: Supervalu Inc 11840 Valley View Rd Eden Prairie MN 55344-3643

CARLSON, JENNIE PEASLACK, lawyer; b. Ft. Thomas, Ky., June 11, 1960; d. Roland A. and Shirley (Willen) Peaslack; m. Charles I. Michaels, Aug. 13, 1983 (div. May 1989); m. Richard A. Carlson, May 2, 1992. BA in English, Centre Coll., 1982; JD, Vanderbilt U., 1985. Bar: Ohio 1985. Atty. Taft, Stettinius & Hollister, Cin., 1985-91; sr. v.p., dep. gen. counsel Star Banc Corp., 1991—. Office: Firstar Corp 425 Walnut St Ste 9 Cincinnati OH 45202-3923 Home: 6425 Indian Hills Rd Minneapolis MN 55439-1160

CARLSON, LEROY THEODORE, JR. telecommunications industry executive; b. 1946; AB, Harvard U., 1968, MBA, 1971. Fin. analyst, mgr. fin. analysis and planning, mgr. acctg. Singer Corp., 1971-74; v.p. Telephone and Data Systems, Inc., 1974-78, exec. v.p., 1978-81, pres., 1981-86, pres., CEO, 1981—; chmn. bd. Am. Paging Sys., Inc., 1998. Chmn. bd. Am. Paging, Inc., TDS Telecomm., U.S. Cellular Corp., Am. Portable Telecom. Mem. U.S. Telephone Assn. (bd. dirs.), Nat. Rural Telecom. Assn. (bd. dirs.). Office: Telephone & Data Sys Inc 30 N La Salle St Ste 4000 Chicago IL 60602-2587

CARLSON, LOREN MERLE, political science educator; b. Mitchell, S.D., Nov. 2, 1923; s. Clarence A. and Edna M. (Rosenquist) C.; m. Verona Gladys Hole, Dec. 21, 1950; children: Catherine Ann, Bradley Reed, Nancy Jewel. BA, Yankton Coll., 1948; MA, U. Wis., 1952; JD, George Washington U., 1961. Bar: S.D. 1961, U.S. Supreme Ct. 1976. Asst. dir. Govt. Rsch. Bur., U. S.D., 1949-51; orgn. and methods examiner Dept. State, Washington, 1951-52; asst. dir. legis. rsch. State of S.D., 1953-55, dir., 1955-59, budget officer, 1963-68; rsch. asst. to U.S. Senator from S.D., 1959-60, adminstrv. asst., 1960-63; dir. statewide ednl. svcs. U. S.D., Vermillion, 1968-74, dean continuing edn., 1974-87, assoc. prof. polit. sci., 1968-79, prof., 1979-89, emeritus prof. polit. sci., 1989—; hwy. laws study dir. U. S.D. Law Sch., 1963; mng. editor U. S.D. Press, 1985-89, sr. editor, 1989-93. Chmn. Model Rural Devel. Commn., Dist. II, State of S.D., 1972-74; chmn. Region VII Planning Commn. on Criminal Justice, S.D., 1969-74; vice-chmn. South East Coun. of Govts., 1989-90, chmn., 1993-97. Author: (with W.O. Farber and T.C. Geary) Government of South Dakota, 1979; contbr. articles profl. publs. Mem. Vermillion City Coun., 1980-90, 91-92, pres. 1982-90; mem. S.D. Humanities Found., 1989-97; bd. dirs. Vermillion Devel. Co., pres., 1987; mem. Vermillion Golf Course/Rsch. Market Analysis Study Rev. Com., 1993-94; mem. Vermillion Facilities Task Force, 1996-97; Rep. candidate State Ho. of Reps., 1986; hon. life trustee U. S.D. Found., 1998. Named Outstanding Young Man Pierre Jaycees, 1959 Fellow: Nat. Univ. Continuing Edn. Assn.; mem.: Farber Found. (exec. bd. dirs. 1993-2001), Nat. Meml. Mt. Rushmore Soc., Spirit Mound Trust (v.p. 1984-2002), S.D. City Mgrs. Assn. (hon.), S.D. City Mgr. Assn. (hon.), Karl Mundt Found., S.D. Adult Edn. Assn. (chmn. 1973-74), ASPA, Pi Kappa Delta, Pi Sigma Alpha. Republican. Lutheran. Home: 229 Catalina Ave Vermillion SD 57069-3319 Office: U SD Dept Polit Sci Dept Polit Sci Vermillion SD 57069 E-mail: lmcarlso@usd.edu.

CARLSON, LYNDON RICHARD SELVIG, state legislator, educator; b. Mpls., Apr. 18, 1940; s. Lyndon C. and Shirley (Gittens) C.; m. Carole Moss, Dec. 7, 1968; children: Tonya, Lyndon Jr., Philip. BS, Minn. State U., Mankato, 1964. Mem. Minn. Ho. of Reps., St. Paul, 1972—. Recipient Pub. Svc. award Met. State U., 1983, Carroll award Minn. Vocat. Assn., 1990, Disting. Svc. award U. Minn. Extension Svc., 1990. Mem. Minn. Fedn. Tchrs. Office: Minn Ho of Reps 283 State Office Bldg Saint Paul MN 55155-0001

CARLSON, MARY ISABEL (MARIBEL CARLSON), county treasurer; b. Kinsley, Kans., July 26, 1931; d. Paul Doak and Minnie (Huser) Owen; m. Merle Dean Carlson, Aug. 16, 1952 (dec. 1984); children: James Dean, Gary Lee, Tommy Owen. Grad., Am. Bus. Coll., 1950; postgrad., Hays State U., 1992. Pvt. sec. Equitable of Iowa, Wichita, Kans., 1950-51; exec. sec. Wichita Jr. C. of C., 1951-52; sec. Etling & Beezley, Attys. at Law, Kinsley, 1952-55; dep. Edwards County Register of Deeds, 1967; ins. clk. Taylor & Sons, Ins., 1969-84; treas. County of Edwards, 1984—. Clk. election bd. Logan Twp., Edwards County, 1960-70, judge, 1960-70. Mem. Kans. County Treas. Assn., South Cen. Dist. Kans. County Treas. Assn. (pres. 1990-91, v.p. 1989-90, sec.-treas. 1988-89, hostess spring mtg. 1990, 99). Republican. Methodist. Avocations: reading newspapers, watching TV. Office: Edwards County Treas PO Box 246 Kinsley KS 67547-0246

CARLSON, RANDY EUGENE, insurance executive; b. Central City, Nebr., Jan. 5, 1948; s. Ned Conrad and Bonnie Lee (Norgard) C.; m. Lorraine Marie Cordsen, Sept. 16, 1967; children: Lance, Brent. BA in Edn., Wayne State Coll., 1970. Tchr., coach Elgin (Nebr.) Pub. Schs., 1970-72, Lewiston (Nebr.) Consol. Schs., 1972-74, North Platte (Nebr.) Pub. Schs., 1974-78; sales assoc. Franklin Life Ins. Co., North Platte, 1977-79; mng. gen. agt. Life Investors Ins. Co., 1979—. Trustee Fortunaires Found., Davenport, Iowa, 1980—; bd. dirs. Life Investors Ownership Trust, Cedar Rapids, Iowa, Life Investors Gen. Agt. Coun., 1993—; mem. Communicating for Agr. Scholarship and Edn. Found., 1985—. Contbr. articles to profl. jours. Mem. North Platte Booster Club, 1983—; designed plan for Nebr. High Sch. Football Playoff Sys., 1973; bd. dirs. Gt. Plains Regional Med. Ctr., 1997—, Physician-Hosp. Orgn., 1998—, Gt. Plains Regional Med. Ctr. Found. Mem. Nat. Assn. Life Underwriters (local pres. 1985-86, state membership chmn. 1986-87, local chmn. life underwriter polit. action com. 1993-95, mem. state lupac bd. 1997—), Nebr. State Life Underwriters Assn. (regional v.p. 1988-89), Gen. Agts. and Mgrs. Assn., North Platte C. of C. (bd. dirs. 1986-91, vice chmn. 1988-89, chmn. 1989-90, chamber amb. 1989—, chmn. bus. and edn. com. 1991-96), North Platte Am. Legion, North Platte Country Club. Republican. Lutheran. Avocations: golf, fishing, spectator sports. Home: 3301 W F St North Platte NE 69101-5866 Office: Carlson and Assocs Inc 717 S Willow St PO Box 969 North Platte NE 69103-0969

CARLSON, ROBERT JAMES, bishop; b. Mpls., June 30, 1944; s. Robert James and Jeanne Catherine (Dorgan) C. B.A., St. Paul Sem., 1964, M.Div., 1976; J.C.L., Catholic U. Am., 1979. Ordained priest Roman Catholic Ch. 1970. Asst. St. Raphael Ch., Crystal, 1970-72; assoc. St. Margaret Mary Ch., Golden Valley, 1972-73, adminstr., 1973-76; vice chancellor, dir. Vocation Office, 1976-79, dir., 1977; pastor St. Leonard of Port Maurice, Mpls., 1982-84; aux. bishop St. Paul and Mpls., 1983-94; vicar Eastern Vicariate Archdiocese of St. Paul and Mpls., 1984-94; apptd. coadjutor Bishop of Sioux Falls, S.D., 1994-95; apptd. bishop Sioux Falls, 1995—. Author: Going All Out: An Invitation to Belong, 1985 Pres. Nat. Found. Cath. Youth Ministry, Washington, 1989-97; bd. dirs. St. Paul Sem., 1993-2000; Episcopal moderator Nat. Cath. Com. on Scouting, 1993-97, USA/Can. coun. Serra Internat., 1996-2001; bd. dirs. Mt. Angel Sem., Portland, Oreg., 1995-2001; bd. dirs. St. John V. Coll. Sem., U. St. Thomas, St. Paul, 1997-; bd. govs. N.Am. Coll. Rome, 1997-; bd. dirs. Hennich-Glennon Sem., St. Louis, 1998-2001. Recipient Friendship award, Knights and Ladies of St. Peter Claver, 1990, St. De LaSalle Meml. awrd, Cretin H.S. Alumni Assn., 1990, Humanitarian of Yr. award, S.D. Right to Life, 1998. Mem. Canon Law Soc. Am. Avocation: hunting. Office: The Chancery 523 N Duluth Ave Sioux Falls SD 57104-2714 E-mail: rcarlson@sfcatholic.org.

CARLSON, STEPHEN CURTIS, lawyer; b. Mpls., Mar. 22, 1951; s. Curtis Harvey and Edna Mae (Pfunder) C.; m. Patricia Jane Brown, Aug. 21, 1976; children: Elizabeth Buckley, Susan Pfunder, Julie Desloge. AB magna cum laude, Princeton U., 1973; JD, Yale U., 1976. Bar: Minn. 1977, Ill. 1977, U.S. Dist. Ct. Minn. 1977, U.S. Dist. Ct. (no. dist.) Ill. 1977, U.S. Ct. Appeals (7th and 8th cirs.) 1977, U.S. Ct. Appeals (6th cir.) 1987, U.S. Ct. Appeals (9th cir.) 1989, U.S. Dist. Ct. (cen. dist.) Ill. 1991. Law clk. to presiding justice Minn. Supreme Ct., St. Paul, 1976-77; assoc. Sidley & Austin, Chgo., 1977-83, ptnr., 1983—. Rep. precinct capt. 1st Ward 11th Precinct, Chgo., 1985-91; pres. Dearborn Park Unit One Townhomes Condominium Assn., 1987-88; sec. Dearborn Park Prairie Single Family Homes Assn., 1997—. Mem. ABA, Ill. Bar Assn., Chgo. Bar Assn., Am. Inns of Ct., Legal Club (sec.-treas. 1997-99, v.p. 1999), Nordic Law Club (v.p. 1987-90, pres. 1990-91), Def. Rsch. Inst., Princeton Club, Lawyers Club Chgo. (v.p. 2000—), Yale Club, Mid-Day Club, Civil War Roundtable, Phi Beta Kappa. Presbyterian. Avocations: theater, opera, symphony. Home: 1323 S Federal St Chicago IL 60605-2716 Office: Sidley & Austin Bank One Plz 425 W Surf St Apt 605 Chicago IL 60657-6139 E-mail: scarlson@sidley.com.

CARLSON, THOMAS DAVID, lawyer; b. Mpls., Aug. 17, 1944; s. David W. and Grace M. (Laser) C.; m. Jane A. Gleeson; children: Amy A., Ryan T., Madeline Jane. BA, Colgate U., 1966; JD cum laude, U. Minn., 1969. Bar: Minn. 1969, U.S. Dist. Ct. Minn. 1969, U.S. Supreme Ct. 1973. Law clk. to Hon. Earl R. Larson U.S. Dist. Ct. (fed. dist.) Minn., Mpls., 1969-70; assoc. Best & Flanagan, 1970-74, ptnr., 1974-91, Lindquist & Vennum, Mpls., 1991—. Bd. trustees Groves Acad.; asst. varsity hockey coach Edina H.S. Fellow Am. Coll. Trust & Estate Counsel; mem. ABA, Minn. State Bar Assn., Hennepin County Bar Assn., Mpls. Club, Minikahda Club, Colgate Silver Puck Club (bd. trustees), Spring Hill Golf Club, Colgate U. Alumni (bd. trustees). Office: Lindquist & Vennum 4200 IDS Ctr Minneapolis MN 55402

CARLSON, THOMAS JOSEPH, real estate developer, lawyer, mayor; b. St. Paul, Jan. 12, 1953; s. Delbert George and Shirley Lorraine (Willardson) C.; m. Chandler Elizabeth Campbell, July 15, 1973; 1 child, Thomas Chandler. BA, George Washington U., 1975; JD, U. Mo., Kansas City, 1979. Reporter Springfield (Mo.) News-Leader, 1975-76; editor Buffalo (Mo.) Reflex, 1976-77; assoc. Woolsey Fisher, Springfield, 1980-83; pvt. practice law, 1983-86; ptnr. Carlson & Clark, 1986-93, Carmichael, Carlson, Gardner & Clark, Springfield, 1993-94; mayor City of Springfield, 1987-93, 2001—; U.S. Bankruptcy trustee Springfield, 1982-98; pvt. practice, 1994-98. CEO, Resorts Mgmt., Inc., 1995—; bd. dirs. ITEC Attractions, Inc., Greater So. Bank; lectr. in field. Contbr. articles to profl. jours. Mem. Springfield City Coun., 1983-87, 97—, Airport Bd. Springfield, 1994-97; chmn. Springfield-Branson Leadership Com., 1993—. Mem. Mo. Bar Assn. (Disting. Young Lawyer award 1989). Presbyterian. Office: 205 W Walnut Ste 200 Springfield MO 65806-2115

CARLSON, WALTER CARL, lawyer; b. Chgo., Sept. 14, 1953; s. LeRoy T. and Margaret (Deffenbaugh) C.; m. Debora M. DeHoyos, June 20, 1981; children: Amanda, Greta, Linnea. BA, Yale U., 1975; JD, Harvard U., 1978. Bar: Ill. 1978, U.S. Dist. Ct. (no. dist.) Ill. 1978, U.S. Supreme Ct. 1991. Law clk. to presiding justice U.S. Dist. Ct. No. Dist., Chgo., 1978-80; ptnr. Sidley, Austin, Brown & Wood, 1980—, mem. exec. com., 2002—. Bd. dirs. Telephone and Data Sys., Inc., Chgo., mem. audit com. 1989-2001, chmn., 2002-; bd. dirs. U.S. Cellular Corp., 1989—, chmn. audit com. 1989-2001; bd. dirs. Aerial Comm., Inc., 1996-2000. Mem. Dist. 65 Sch. Bd., Evanston, Ill., 1993-2001, pres., 1997-2001. Mem. ABA, U.S. Supreme Ct. Hist. Soc., Am. Judicature Soc., Chgo. United. Office: Sidley Austin Brown & Wood Apt 605 425 W Surf St Chicago IL 60657-6139

CARLSON ARONSON, MARILYN A. English language and education educator; b. Gothenburg, Nebr., July 24, 1938; d. Harold N. and Verma Elnora (Granlund) C.; m. Paul E. Carlson, July 31, 1959 (dec. Sept. 1988); 1 child, Andrea Joy; m. David L. Aronson, July 8, 1995. BS in Edn., English and Psychology, Sioux Falls Coll., 1960; MA in History, U. S.D., 1973, MA in English, 1992, EdD in Ednl. Adminstrn., 1997. Tchr. English and social scis. curriculum coord. Beresford (S.D.) Pub. Sch., 1960-78; tchr. English and social scis. Sioux Empire Coll., Hawarden, Iowa, 1979-85; instr. English and ESL, Midwest Inst. for Internat. Studies, Sioux Falls, S.D., 1985-89; asst. prof. English Augustana Coll., 1989-97, asst. prof. English and edn., 1997-2000; acad. affairs coord. acad. evaluation U. S.D., Vermillion, 2000—02; assoc. acad. dean Nat. Am. U., Sioux Falls, 2002—. Part time instr. psychology Northwestern Coll., 1985; part time instr. English and lit. Nat. Coll., 1985-88; part time instr. English and history Augustana Coll., 1986-89; presenter in field. Author: Visions of Light: Flannery O'Connor's Themes and Narrative Method, 1992, A Higher Education Perspective: Themes and Narrative Methods of Flannery O'Connor and Eudora Welty, 1997; Plains Goddesses: Heroines in Willa Cather's Prairie Novels, 1995; contbr. articles and revs. to profl. publs. including The Social Sci. Jour., others. Humanities Scholar evaluator Rainbow Project and Increasing Cultural Understanding Seminar, 2000; evaluator Profl. Devel. Conf. Native Am. Curriculum, Rapid City, S.Dak., 2001. Recipient Internat. Prof.'s Exch. award Sor Trondelag Coll., Trondheim, Norway, Jan. 1999; named Tchr. of Yr. Beresford (S.D.) Pub. Schs., 1976; S.D. Humanities scholar, 1993—; Bush mini-grantee, 1993, Internat. Studies grantee, 1994, 98, 99, S.D. Humanities Spkr.'s Bur. grantee, 1996—. Mem. Home: 29615 469th Ave Beresford SD 57004-6457 Office: Nat Am U 2801 S Kiwanis Ave Sioux Falls SD 57105 E-mail: mcarlson@national.edu.

CARLSSON, BO AXEL VILHELM, economics educator; b. Ulricehamn, Sweden, July 22, 1942; s. Carl Axel Valentin and Dagmar Elisabet (Karlsson) C.; m. Glenda Joyce Bishop, Dec. 28, 1965; children: Eric, Mark, Amy. BA, Harvard U., 1968; MA, Stanford U., 1970, PhD, 1972; Docent, Uppsala U., Sweden, 1980. Sr. rsch. assoc. Indsl. Inst. Econ. and Social Rsch., Stockholm, 1972-84, dep. dir., 1977-81; Umstattd prof. indsl. econs. Case Western Res. U., Cleve., 1984-2000, de Windt prof. indsl. econs., 2000—, chmn. dept. econs., 1984-87, assoc. dean rsch. and grad. programs Weatherhead Sch. Mgmt., 1996—, dir. PhD programs and rsch., 2001—. Vis. scholar MIT, 1982; cons. World Bank, Washington, 1983-87, Swedish Fedn. Industries, Stockholm, 1984-89; min. of fin. Stockholm, 1993-94, Econ. Commn. for L.Am., 1996; project dir. Sweden's Tech. Sys., Stockholm, 1987—; mem. Indsl. and Sci. Coun., Nat. Bd. Tech. Devel., 1987-98; chair sci. adv. bd. Danish Rsch. Unit for Indsl. Dynamics, 1996—. Author: Technology and Industrial Structure, 1979, Industrial Subsidies, 1980, Swedish Industry Facing the 80s, 1981; editor: Industrial Dynamics, 1989, Technological Systems and Economic Performance, 1995, Technological Systems and Industrial Dynamics, 1997, Technological Systems in the Bio Industries: An International Study, 2002. Mem. Swedish cultural orgns. Mem. Europe Assn. Rsch. Indsl. Econs. (pres. 1983-85, exec. com.), Am. Econ. Assn., Ea. Econ. Assn. (bd. dirs. 1989-92), Internat. J.A. Schumpeter Soc. (prize selection com. 1988-90, 94-96), Assn. Christian Economists. Methodist. Home: 2708 Rochester Rd Cleveland OH 44122-2167 Office: Case Western Res Univ Weatherhead Sch Mgmt Dept Econs Cleveland OH 44106-7206 E-mail: Bo.Carlsson@weatherhead.cwru.edu.

CARLSTROM, JOHN E. astronomy educator; b. Hyde Park, N.Y., Feb. 24, 1957; AB in Physics, Vassar Coll., 1981; PhD in Physics, U. Calif., Berkeley, 1981. Prof. dept. Astronomy and Astrophysics U. Chgo. Recipient Packard Found. fellow, 1994, MacArthur Found. fellow, 1998, James S. McDonnell Centennial fellow, 1999. Office: U Chgo Dept Astronomy and Astrophys 5640 S Ellis Ave Chicago IL 60637-1433

CARLTON, DENNIS WILLIAM, economics educator; b. Boston, Feb. 15, 1951; s. Jay and Mildred C.; m. Jane R. Berkowitz, 1971; children: Deborah, Rebecca, Daniel. BA summa cum laude, Harvard U., 1972; MS in Ops. Research, MIT, 1974, PhD in Econs., 1975. Instr. econs. MIT, Cambridge, Mass., 1975-76; asst. prof. econs. U. Chgo., 1976-79, assoc. prof., 1979-80; prof. U. Chgo. Law Sch., 1980-84, U. Chgo. Grad. Sch. Bus., 1984—; with Lexecon, Chgo., 1977—. Author: Market Behavior Under Uncertainty, 1984 (Outstanding Dissertation award 1984), (with J. Perloff) Modern Industrial Organization, 1999; co-editor Jour. Law and Econs., 1980—. Recipient P.W.S. Andrews prize Jour. Indsl. Econs., 1979. Mem. Am. Econ. Assn., Econometric Soc., Phi Beta Kappa. Jewish. Office: Univ Chgo Grad Sch Business 1101 E 58th St Chicago IL 60637-1511

CARLTON, TERRY SCOTT, chemist, educator; b. Peoria, Ill., Jan. 29, 1939; s. Daniel Cushman and Mabel (Smith) C.; m. Claudine Fields, 1960; children: Brian, David. B.S., Duke U., 1960; Ph.D. (NSF grad. fellow 1960-63), U. Calif., Berkeley, 1963. Mem. faculty Oberlin (Ohio) Coll., 1963—, prof. chemistry, 1976-2001, chmn. dept., 1980-83, prof. emeritus, 2001—. Vis. prof. chemistry U. N.C., Chapel Hill, 1976 Co-author: Composition, Reaction and Equilibrium, 1970. Mem. Am. Chem. Soc. Home: 143 Kendal Dr Oberlin OH 44074-1906 Office: Oberlin Coll Dept Chemistry Oberlin OH 44074-1085 E-mail: terry.carlton@oberlin.edu.

CARMEN, IRA HARRIS, political scientist, educator; b. Boston, Dec. 3, 1934; s. Jacob and Lida (Rosenman) C.; m. Sandra Vineberg, Sept. 6, 1958 (div. June 1999); children: Gail Deborah, Amy Rebecca. BA, U. N.H., 1957; MA, U. Mich., 1959, PhD, 1964. Asst. prof. Ball State U., 1963-66; assoc. prof. Coe Coll., 1966-68; prof. polit. sci. U. Ill., 1968—. Recombinant DNA adv. com. NIH, 1990-94; participant meetings on China-U.S. genetic engring. rsch. and policy rels., Beijing, 1991, European-U.S. human genetic experimentation and policy rels., London, Paris, Rome, 1995; program organizer Human Genome Orgn. internat. meeting, Heidelberg, 1996; vis. scholar Yale Law Sch., 1981; vis. lectr. Tamkang U., Taiwan, 1991. Author: Movies, Censorship, and the Law, 1966, Power and Balance, 1978, Cloning and the Constitution, 1985; co-prin. investigator Sociogenomics in Advanced Species, Consilience in Theory and Practice; contbr. articles to profl. jours. Sr. advisor Bush-Quayle Nat. Jewish Campaign Com., 1988; mem. Pres. George Bush's Inaugural Educators Adv. Com., 1989; guest del. Rep. Nat. Conv., 1992; active Rep. Nat. Com., Rep. Jewish Coalition, Empower Am. Recipient Clarence Berdahl award U. Ill., 1980, 87, 90, All-Campus award for excellence in undergrad. teaching, 1980, William F. Prokasy award, 1995, Harriet and Charles Luckman award, 1995; grantee U. Ill. Mem. AAAS, Am. Polit. Sci. Assn., Human Genome Orgn., Am. Soc. Gene Therapy, Assn. for Politics and Life Scis. (chmn. coun. 2000—), Phi Beta Kappa. Office: U Ill Dept Polit Sci Urbana IL 61801

CARMICHAEL, LLOYD JOSEPH, lawyer; BA, S.W. Mo. State U., 1969; JD, U. Ark., 1974. Atty. Carmichael, Gardner and Clark, Springfield, Mo., 1992. Chmn. Mo. State Dem. Party, 1994—. Office: Carmichael Gardner and Clark 901 Saint Louis St Ste 800 Springfield MO 65806-2560

CARNAHAN, BRICE, chemical engineer, educator; b. New Philadelphia, Ohio, Oct. 13, 1933; s. Paul Tracy and Amelia Christina (Gray) C. BS, Case Western Res. U., 1955, MS, 1957; PhD, U. Mich., 1965. Lectr. in engring. biostats. U. Mich., Ann Arbor, 1959-64, asst. prof. chem. engring. and biostatics, 1965-68, assoc. prof., 1968-70, prof. chem. engring., 1970—. Vis. lect. Imperial Coll., London, England, 1971-72; vis. prof. U. Pa., 1970, U. Calif.-San Diego, 1986-87; mem., chmn. Curriculum Aids for Chem. Engring. Edn. com. Nat. Acad. Engring., 1974-75 Author: (with H.A. Luther and J.O. Wilkes) Applied Numerical Methods, 1969, (with J.O. Wilkes) Digital Computing and Numerical Methods, 1973; Editorial bd.: Jour. Computers and Fluids, 1971—, Computers and Chemical Engineering, 1974—. Mem. communications com. Mich. Council for Arts, 1977—. Recipient Chem. Engr. of Yr. award Detroit Engring. Soc., 1987, 3M award Am. Soc. for Engring. Edn., 1990. Fellow AIChE (Computers in Chem. Engring. award 1980, chmn. CAST div. 1981); mem. AAAS, Assn. for Computing Machinery, Soc. for Computer Simulation, Sigma Xi, Sigma Nu. Home: 1605 Kearney Rd Ann Arbor MI 48104-4065

CARNAHAN, JEAN, senator; m. Mel Carnahan (dec. Oct. 16, 2000); children: Randy (dec.), Russ, Robin, Tom. BA in Bus. and Pub. Admin., George Washington U. Senator State of Mo., 2001—. Mem. armed svcs. com, small bus. and entrepreneurship com., gov. affairs com., commerce, sci. and transportation com., special com. aging, State of Mo.; co-founder Children in the Workplace; spkr. for domestic violence, cancer, osteoporosis, mental health, drug problems. Author: If Walls Could Talk, 1998, Christmas at the Mansion: Its Memories and Menus, 1999; contbr.: Vital Speeches of the Day, 1999, Will You Say a Few Words, 2000. Recipient Robert C. Goshorn award for pub. svc., State of Mo. Martin Luther King, Jr. Special Acheivement award, Child Adv. of Yr. award, Boys' and Girls' Town Mo., 1995, Citizen of Yr., March of Dimes, 1997, Woman of Yr., St. Louis Zonta Clubs Internat., 1999. Bd. mem. William Woods U. Office: 517 Hart Senate Office bldg Washington DC 20510

CARNAHAN, JOHN ANDERSON, lawyer; b. Cleve., May 8, 1930; s. Samuel Edwin and Penelope (Moulton) C.; m. Katherine A. Halter, June 14, 1958; children: Peter M., Allison E., Kristin A. BA, Duke U., 1953, JD, 1955. Bar: Ohio 1955. Pvt. practice, Columbus, Ohio, 1955-78; ptnr. Arter & Hadden, 1978-99; in-house counsel The Excello Splty. Co., Cleve., 2000—. Lectr. Ohio Legal Ctr. Inst., 1969, 73-74. Editor Duke Law Jour., 1954-55; chmn. bd. editors Ohio Lawyer, 1986-91; contbr. articles to profl. jours. Chmn. UN Day, Columbus, 1960; pres. Capital City Young Republican Club, 1960; bd. dirs. Columbus Cancer Clinic, pres., 1978-81; bd. dirs. Columbus chpt. ARC, 1979-87; mem. governing bd. Hannah Neil Mission, Inc., 1974-78; chmn. Duke Alumni Admissions Adv. Com., 1965-79. Named one of Outstanding Young Men of Columbus, 1965. Fellow Am. Bar Found. (life, chmn. Ohio fellows 1988-95), Columbus Bar Found. (life); mem ABA (ho. of dels. 1984-95), Ohio State Bar Found. (trustee 1986-90), Nat. Conf. Bar Pres., Ohio State Bar Assn. (coun. of dels. 1965-67, exec. com. 1977-81, 82-85, pres.-elect 1982-83, pres. 1983-84, Ritter award for outstanding contbns. adminstrn. justice 1987), Columbus Bar Assn. (bd. govs. 1970-72, sec.-treas. 1974-75, pres. 1976-77, Professionalism award 1996), Kit Kat Club (past pres.). Presbyterian. Home and Office: 767 S 5th St Columbus OH 43206-2145 E-mail: jac5830@aol.com.

CARNES, JAMES EDWARD, state legislator; b. Wheeling, W.Va., Feb. 19, 1942; s. Edward A. and Avis E. (Hoop) C.; m. Nancy Ann Taylor, 1962; children: Jeffrey, Karen. Student, Bethany Coll., Coll. of Commerce, Wheeling, W. Va. Book keeper C. V. & W. Coal Co., 1962-69; office mgr. Cravat Coal Co., Holloway, Ohio, 1969—; owner, mgr. Carnes Mobile Home and Appliances, Barnesville; sec.-treas. McCants Ins. Agy., Newcomerstown; mem. Ohio Senate from 20th dist., Columbus, 1994—. Former chmn. legis. com. Ohio State Senate, Columbus; mem. Bd. Electors, State of Ohio, 1970-82, Ohio Commn. on Aging; regional chmn. Ohio State Manpower Coun. Pres. Rep. Club, 1970; mem., chmn. Belmont County Ctrl. and Exec. Coms., 1970-82. Finalist in 1959, 60, Prince of Peace Contests, Ohio; named hon. Lt. Gov. State of Ohio. Mem. Belmont County Hist. Soc., Flushing (Ohio) Rotary Club. Office: 47403 Puskarich Rd Saint Clairsville OH 43950-9458

CARNEY, BRIAN P. retail executive; V.p., contr. Revco D.S., Inc. (acquired by CVS Corp.), 1992-96, sr. v.p. fin., 1996-97; exec. v.p., CFO Jo-Ann Stores, Inc., Hudson, Ohio, 1997—. Office: Jo-Ann Stores Inc 5555 Darrow Rd Hudson OH 44236

CARNEY, JEAN KATHRYN, psychologist; b. Ft. Dodge, Iowa, Nov. 10, 1948; d. Eugene James and Lucy (Devlin) C.; m. Mark Krupnick, Jan. 1, 1977; 1 child, Joseph Carney Krupnick. BA, Marquette U., Milw., 1970; MA, U. Chgo., Chgo., 1984; PhD, U. Chgo., 1986. Registered Clin. Psychologist, Ill. Reporter Milw. Jour., 1971-76, editorial writer, 1976-79; asst. prof. psychology St. Xavier Coll., Chgo., 1985-86; dir. Lincoln Park Clinic, 1986-87; pvt. practice psychotherapist, 1987—. Sci. staff Michael Reese Hosp. Med. Ctr., Chgo., 1987—; instr. Northwestern U. Med. Sch., 1991-95; clin. asst. prof. U. Ill. Coll. Medicine, 1993—. Recipient Best Series Articles, 1975, Best Editorial, 1978, Milw. Press Club, William Allen White Nat. Award for Editorial Writing, 1978, Robert Kahn Meml. Award for Research on Aging, Univ. Chgo., 1985. Mem. APA, Ill. Psychol. Assn., Chgo. Assn. Psychoanalytic Psychology. Office: Ste 1219 55 E Washington St Ste 1219 Chicago IL 60602-2115 E-mail: jkcarney@usa.net.

CARNEY, JOSEPH BUCKINGHAM, lawyer; b. Greensburg, Ind., July 8, 1928; s. Edward O. and Grace Rebecca (Buckingham) C.; m. Constance J. Caylor, July 8, 1950; children: Elizabeth, Joseph Buckingham Jr., Julia, Sarah. AB, DePauw U., 1950; LLB, Harvard U., 1953. Bar: D.C. 1953, Ind. 1953, U.S. Dist. Ct. (so. dist.) Ind. 1953, U.S. Supreme Ct. 1957, U.S. Ct. Appeals (7th cir.) 1961; ind. cert. mediator. Assoc. Hogg, Peters & Leonard, Ft. Wayne, Ind., 1953-54, Baker & Daniels, Indpls., 1957-62, ptnr., 1962-95, mem. mgmt. com., 1993-94, sec., 1994, of counsel, 1996—. Mem. lawyers com. Nat. Ctr. State Cts., Williamsburg, Va., 1985—; assoc. Environ. Law Inst., Washington. Chmn. bd. dirs. Parkinson Awareness Assn. Ctrl. Ind., Inc.; past pres. Interfaith Homes, Inc., Indpls.; past chmn., elder Northwood Christian Ch., Indpls. 1st lt. U.S. Army, 1954-57. Recipient Disting. Alumni award DePauw U., 1984. Mem. ABA, Ind. Bar Assn., Indpls. Bar Assn., Am. Judicature Soc., 7th Cir. Bar Assn. (pres. 1983-84), Univ. Club, Indpls. Athletic Club, Columbia Club, Contemporary, Lawyers Club Indpls. (past pres.), Phi Eta Sigma, Phi Gamma Delta (bd. dirs. 1974-78, sec. 1976-78, pres. 1980-82), Phi Gamma Delta Ednl. Found. (bd. dirs., pres. 1996-98). Avocations: scuba diving, travel, photography. Office: Baker & Daniels 300 N Meridian St Ste 2700 Indianapolis IN 46204-1782

CARNEY, ROBERT ALFRED, retired health care administrator; b. Winnipeg, Man., Can., Feb. 24, 1916; s. Thomas Alfred and Opal Edna (Fogle) C. (parents Am. citizens); m. Jacqueline Briscoe, May 15, 1943; children: Thomas A., Roberta L., Richard D. BA, Denison U., 1938. Lic. hosp. and nursing home adminstr. Accountant Nat. Cash Register Co., 1938-41; accountant, auditor, controller Miami Valley Hosp., Dayton, O., 1941-47; asst. dir. Ochsner Found. Hosp., New Orleans, 1947-48; adminstrv. dir. Jewish Hosp., Cin., 1948-61, assoc. exec. dir., 1961-68, exec. dir., 1968-78; cons. mgmt. and employee relations Children's Hosp. Med. Center, Cin., 1979; adminstr. Marjorie P. Lee Home for Aged, 1980-89; dir. spl. projects Twin Towers Retirement Community, 1989-92; interim adminstr. Auglaize Acres County Nursing Home, Wapakoneta, Ohio, 1990-91; adminstr. Lincoln Ave. and Crawford's Home for the Aged, 1993-96; cons. Drake Ctr., 1996-97; ret., 1998. Adj. assoc. prof. hosp. adminstrn. Coll. Pharmacy U. Cin., 1969-78; adj. faculty mem., grad. program hosp. adminstrn. Xavier U., Cin., 1970-78; trustee Health Careers Greater Cin., 1956-85, 1st v.p., 1970-85; mem. exec. com., trustee Health Careers of Ohio, 1973-81, treas., 1976-79; trustee Am. Nurses Assn. Nat. Retirement Plan, 1973-75; pres. Withrow H.S. PTA, 1969-71; mem. bd., pres. Bapt. Home Benevolent Soc., 1974-88; mem. bd. Jewish Fedn. Cin., 1969-70, 72-73; mem. racial isolation task force Cin. Pub. Schs., 1972-73, mem. adv. com. for sch. lic. practical nursing, 1973; mem. home health svcs. adv. com. Cin. Dept. Health, 1972—, chmn., 1974-76, 96-99; mem. adv. com. Lic. Practical Nurse Assn. Ohio, 1979-85; mem. Ohio Commn. Nursing, 1973-75, Am. Bd. Med. Specialists, 1977-80; sec. Ohio Coun. on Nursing Needs and Resources, 1978-81; bd. dirs., sec., treas. Fedn. for accessible Nursing Edn. and Licensure, 1984-98; chmn. Greater Cin. Nursing Home assn., 1985-98. Trustee emeritus Assn. Ohio Philanthropic Homes, 1993. Recipient Outstanding Preceptor award Xavier U., 1974 Mem. Am. Coll. Hosp. Adminstrs. (life), Am. Hosp. Assn. (life), Ohio Hosp. Assn. (life), Nat. League for Nursing (dir. 1977-81), Ohio League for Nursing (dir. 1968-76, v.p. 1973-76), Greater Cin. Hosp. Council, Am. Pub. Health Assn., Assembly of Hosp. Schs. Nursing (chmn. bd. 1977-78), Eagle Scout Assn. (life), Sigma Chi, Phi Mu Alpha. Baptist. Lodge: Masons. Home and Office: 2721 Grandin Rd Cincinnati OH 45208-3414

CARO, WILLIAM ALLAN, physician; b. Chgo., Aug. 16, 1934; s. Marcus Rayner and Adeline Beatrice (Cohen) C.; m. Ruth Fruchtlander, June 15, 1959 (dec.); children: Mark Stephen, David Edward; m. Joan Peters, Oct. 18, 1997. Student, U. Mich., 1952-55; BS in Medicine, U. Ill.,

1957, MD, 1959. Diplomate Am. Bd. Dermatology (bd. dirs. 1981-91, v.p. 1989-90, pres. 1990-91). Intern Cook County Hosp., Chgo., 1959-60; resident in internal medicine U. Ill. Research and Ednl. Hosps., 1960-61; resident in dermatology Hosp. of U. Pa., 1961-62, 64-66; Earl D. Osborne fellow dermal pathology Armed Forces Inst. Pathology, Washington, 1966-67; asst. in medicine U. Ill. Coll. Medicine, 1960-61; asst. instr. U. Pa. Med. Sch., 1961-62, 64-66; asst. prof. dermatology Northwestern U. Med. Sch., 1967-73, assoc. prof. clin. dermatology, 1973-81; practice medicine specializing in dermatology Chgo., 1967—. Chief dermatology sect. MacDonald Army Hosp., Fort Eustis, Va., 1962-64; attending physician Chgo. Wesley Meml. Hosp., 1969-72, Northwestern Meml. Hosp., 1972—, mem. med. exec. com., 1977-79; attending pathologist, cons. dermatologist VA Lakeside Hosp., Chgo.; cons. Children's Meml. Hosp., Rehab. Inst. Chgo.; Mcpl. Tb Sanitarium of Chgo., 1968-74; affiliate pathologist Evanston (Ill.) Hosp.; prof. clin. dermatology Northwestern U. Med. Sch., 1981—. Editor trans.: Chgo. Dermatol. Soc, 1971-73; editorial bd., Cutis, 1975— ; asso. editor Year Book Pathology and Clin. Pathology, 1977-80. Mem. medicine adv. bd. U. Ill. Coll. Medicine, 1988—; trustee Northwestern Meml. Hosp., Chgo., 1986-87, bd. dirs., 1988-91; bd. dirs. Northwestern Meml. Corp., 1987-2000, exec. com., 1988-91. Served as capt. M.C. USAR, 1962-64. Mem.: AMA, Dermatology Found., Pacific Dermatol. Assn., Internat. Soc. Dermatology, Am. Soc. Dermatopathology (bd. dirs. 1995—2000, pres.-elect 1995—96, pres. 1996—97), Am. Dermatol. Assn. (bd. dirs. 1993—98), Chgo. Dermatol. Soc. (pres. 1983—84), Am. Acad. Dermatology (Gold award sci. exhibit 1970), U. Ill. Med. Alumni Assn. (exec. bd. 1977—80), Phi Kappa Phi, Alpha Omega Alpha. Office: 676 N Saint Clair St Ste 1840 Chicago IL 60611-2927 E-mail: w-caro@northwestern.edu.

CAROLAN, DOUGLAS, wholesale company executive; BS, Western Mich. U., 1964. Store mgr. to dir. mktg. div. Nat. Tea Co., 1962-83; sr. v.p. Associated Wholesale Grocers, Inc., Kansas City, Kans., 1983-86, chief ops. officer, exec. v.p., sec., 1986—, CEO, pres., 1998—. Bd. dirs. UMB Bank, Food Mktg. Inst. Bd. dirs. Kans. City area food bank Harvesters. Office: Assoc Wholesale Grocers Inc PO Box 2932 Kansas City KS 66110-2932

CAROLLO, RUSSELL, journalist; b. New Orleans; B in History, Southeastern La. U., 1980; B in Journalism, La. State U., 1982; Journalism fellow, U. Mich., 1989-90. General assignment reporter The Spokesman-Rev., Spokane, Wash., 1986-90; spl. projects and computer assisted reporter Dayton (Ohio) Daily News, 1990-93; mil. and projects reporter The News Tribune, Tacoma, 1993-94; spl. projects reporter Dayton Daily News, 1994—. Reported refugee crisis in Goma, Zaire, 1994; reported Am. troop deployment in Bosnia, 1995-96; journalism fellowship to report in Japan, 1997. Reporter: (series) Flawed and Sometimes Deadly, 1997, Military Secrets, 1995, Prisoners on Payroll, 1994, Lives on the Line, 1992, A Trust Betrayed, 1988, Cashdance, 1984. Winner 1998 Pulitzer prize for nat. reporting; Pulitzer prize finalist, 1996, 92; U. Mich. Journalism fellow, 1989-90, Internat. Ctr. for Journalists fellow, Japan, 1997; recipient Investigative Reporters and Editors awards, 1992, 95, 96 (Gold medal), Harvard U. Goldsmith award, 1996, White House Corr. Assn. Edgar A. Poe award, 1995, Soc. Profl. Journalists Nat. Award for Investigative Reporting, 1995, John Hancock award, 1992, Polk award, 1998, Nat. Headliner Best of Show award, 1998. Office: Dayton Daily News Cox Newspapers Inc 45 S Ludlow St Dayton OH 45402-1858

CARP, LARRY (LARRY CARP), lawyer; b. St. Louis, Jan. 26, 1926; s. Avery and Ruth C. Student, U. Mo., Columbia, 1944; cert., Sorbonne U., Paris, 1946; BA, Washington U., St. Louis, 1947; postgrad., Grad. Inst. Internat. Studies, Geneva, 1949; JD, Washington U., St. Louis, 1951. Bar: Mo. 1951, U.S. Dist. Ct. (ea. dist.) Mo. 1951. Mem. U.S. Dept. of State, Washington, 1951-53; mem. staff Senator Paul H. Douglas (Dem. Ill.), 1953-54; assoc. Fordyce, Mayne, Hartman, Renard, and Stribling, St. Louis, 1954-63; sole practice, 1963-68; ptnr. Carp & Morris, 1968-90, Carp, Sexauer and Carr, St. Louis, 1990-94, Carp and Sexauer, St. Louis, 1994—. Assoc. counsel, acting chief counsel U.S. Senate Subcom. on Constitutional Rights, Washington, 1956; mem. St. Louis Regional U.S. Export Expansion Coun., 1964-74; mem. Mo. Commn. on Human Rights, 1966-78, vice chmn., 1977-78; vice chmn., bd. dirs. Pastoral Counselling Inst. for Greater St. Louis, 1964-91; mem. bd. trustees The Acad. Sci., St. Louis, 1984—, asst. treas., 1992—; mem. adv. bd. George Engelmann Math. and Science Inst., 1992-96; bd. dirs. St. Louis Ctr. for Internat. Rels.; advisor on immigration law matters Ethiopian Cmty. Assn. St. Louis, 1995—; legal advisor Image, Inc., St. Louis, 1998—; mem. cmty. adv. panel Double Helix (TV and Radio) Corp., 1999—. Co-author: (musicals) Pocahontas, The Pied Piper, Androcles; author: (musicals) For the Love of Adam, The Red Ribbon, Famous Last Words, God Knows!; contbr. articles to newspapers and mags. on subjects relating to immigration and nationality law. Mem. Common Cause, 1966-78, chmn. Mo. chpt., 1973-75; bd. dirs. Internat. Inst. of Metro St. Louis, 1980-86, English Speaking Union, St. Louis, 1985—, Mo. Prison Arts Program, 1999—; trustee St. Louis Ctr. for Internat. Rels., 1998—; U.S. presdl. appointee as sr. adviser and U.S. pub. del. to UN 55th Gen. Assembly, 2000-2001. With U.S. Army, 1944-46, ETO. Decorated (2) Battle Stars; Rotary Internat. fellow Grad. Inst. Internat. Studies, Geneva, 1948-49; award for Outstanding Service in Recognition of Spl. Needs of Hispanic Community IMAGE, St. Louis, 1984; selected in immigration and naturalization law by his peers as one in Best Lawyers in Am. Fellow Am. Acad. Matrimonial Lawyers (cert.); mem. ABA (immigration law coord. com., chmn. immigration law com. gen. practice sect. 1981-86), Mo. Bar Assn., Bar Assn. Met. St. Louis (chmn. internat. law and trade com. 1973-79, chmn. immigration law com. 1989-92), Am. Immigration Lawyers Assn., St. Louis Ctr. for Internat. Rels. (bd. dirs. 1998—), UNA-USA Assn. (bd. dirs. St. Louis chpt. 1999—), Phi Delta Phi. Office: Carp and Sexauer Ste 325 225 S Meramec Ave Saint Louis MO 63105-3511 Fax: 314-727-0308. E-mail: cands@i1.net.

CARPENTER, ALLAN, writer, editor, publisher; b. Waterloo, Iowa, May 11, 1917; s. John Alex and Theodosia (Smith) C. BA, U. No. Iowa, 1938. Founder, editor, publisher Tchrs. Digest mag., 1940-48; dir. pub. relations Popular Mechanics mag., 1943-62; founder, 1962, since pres. Carpenter Pub. House, Inc., Chgo.; founder Infordata Internat. Inc., 1970-89, chmn. bd., dir., 1970-89; partner, editor Index to U.S. Govt. Periodicals, 1972-90; ret. Historian of Cook County, 1999. Author over 231 nonfiction books including Between Two Rivers, Iowa Year By Year, 1940, 3d edit., 1997, 52 vol. Enchantment of America state series, 52 vol. New Enchantment of America, Enchantment of Africa, 38 vol. Enchantment of Latin America, 20 vol. Illinois, Land of Lincoln, 1968, All About the U.S.A., 1986, 7 vol. The Mighty Warriors, 1987, 4 vol. Encyclopedia of the Midwest, 1988, Encyclopedia of the Central West, 1990, Encyclopedia of the Far West, 1990, Facts About the Cities, 1992, 2d rev. edit., 1996, World Almanac of the U.S.A., 1993, 3rd rev. edit., 1999, Between Two Rivers Iowa Year By Year, 3rd rev. edit., 1999; creator, editor 16 vol. Popular Mechanics Home Handyman Ency., 1962; founder, pub. Index to Readers Digest, 1980-90, Index to Alternative Health Periodicals, 1998—. Pres., chmn. Chgo. Businessmen's Symphony Orch., 1942-65, prin. string bass sect.; founder, 1954; since pres. Music Council Met. Chgo.; prin. bass violist non-profl. symphony orchs., 1935—. Mem. Soc. Wilson Descendants, Inc. (pres. 1955-93, chmn. 1994, founder James "Tama Jim" Wilson award), Arts Club Chgo. Home and Office: 4919 N Glenwood Ave Chicago IL 60640-3554

CARPENTER, DAVID WILLIAM, lawyer; b. Chgo., Aug. 26, 1950; s. William Warren and Dorothy Susan (Jacobs) C.; m. Jane Ellen French, Aug. 18, 1973; children: Johanna Lindsay, Julie Rachel. BA, Yale U., 1972; JD, Boston U., 1975. Bar: Mass. 1975, U.S. Ct. Appeals (1st cir.) 1977, D.C., Ill., U.S. Dist. Ct. (no. dist.) Ill. 1979, U.S. Ct. Appeals (D.C. cir.) 1980, U.S. Ct. Appeals (3d and 7th cirs.), U.S. Supreme Ct. 1981, U.S. Ct. Appeals (10th cir.) 1985, (8th cir.) 1986, (9th and 11th cirs.) 1987, (2d and 5th cirs.) 1990. Law clk. to presiding justice U.S. Ct. Appeals (1st cir.), Portland, Maine, 1975-77, U.S. Supreme Ct., Washington, 1977-78; assoc. Sidley & Austin, Chgo., 1978-82, ptnr., 1982—. Lectr. Ill. Inst. Tech., Chgo., 1980-82. Bd. dirs., sec. Chgo. Coun. for Young Profls., 1985-90; bd. dirs., exec. com. Brennan Ctr. for Justice, N.Y.C., 1995—; bd. dirs. Lyric Opera Chgo., 1999—. Democrat. Mem. United Ch. Christ. Home: 1948 N Maud Ave Chicago IL 60614-4908 Office: Sidley & Austin Bank One Plz 425 W Surf St Apt 605 Chicago IL 60657-6139

CARPENTER, DOROTHY FULTON, retired state legislator; b. Ismay, Mont., Mar. 13, 1933; d. Daniel A. and Mary Ann (George) Fulton; m. Thomas W. Carpenter, June 12, 1955; children: Mary Ione, James Thomas. BA, Grinnell Coll., 1955. Elem. tchr., Houston and Iowa City, 1955-58; mem. Iowa Ho. of Reps., 1980-94, asst. minority fl. leader, 1982-88, chair ethics and state govt. coms., 1992-94; ret., 1994. Bd. dirs. Planned Parenthood Fedn. of Am., 1977—80; pres. Planned Parenthood of Iowa, 1970; active West Des Moines Human Rights Commn., 1999—; fin. chair Episcopal Diocese, Iowa, 1979—80. Recipient Grinnell Coll. Alumni award, 1980; named Citizen of Yr., West Des Moines C. of C., 1999.

CARPENTER, J. SCOTT, vocational educator; Supr. Penta County Career Ctr., Perrysburg, Ohio, supr. student svcs. & admissions. Named Nat. Vocat. Tchr. of Yr., 1993, Nat. Bus. Tchr. of Yr. Office: Penta County Career Ctr 30095 Oregon Rd Perrysburg OH 43551-4533 E-mail: scarpenter@pentanet.k12.oh.us.

CARPENTER, JOHN MARLAND, engineer, physicist; b. Williamsport, Pa., June 20, 1935; s. John Hiram and Ruth Edith (Johnson) Carpenter; m. Rhonda DeCardy, 1991; children: John Marland Jr., Kathryn Ann, Susan Marie, Janet Elaine. BS in Engring. Sci, Pa. State U., 1957; MS in Nuclear Engring, U. Mich., 1958, PhD, 1963. Fellow Oak Ridge Inst. Nuclear Studies, 1957-60; postdoctoral fellow Inst. Sci. and Tech., U. Mich., 1963-64, mem. faculty univ., 1964-75, prof. nuclear engring., 1973-75; vis. scientist nuclear tech. br. Phillips Petroleum Co., 1965; solid state sci. div. Argonne (Ill.) Nat. Lab., 1971-72, 73; physics div. Los Alamos Sci. Lab., 1973; sr. physicist solid state sci. div., mgr. intense pulsed neutron source project Argonne Nat. Lab., 1975-77, program dir., 1977-78, tech. dir., 1978—. Mem. U.S. del. to USSR on fundamental properties of matter, 1977; co-founder Internat. Collaboration on Advanced Neurton Sources, 1977; vis. scientist Japanese Lab. for High Energy Physics, 1982, 93; mem. indsl. and profl. adv. coun. Coll. Engring., Pa. State U., 1984—87; mem. nat. steering com. Advanced Neutron Source, 1986—95, mem. exec. com.; mem. grad. faculty Iowa State U., 1988—93; mem. internat. sci. coun. AUSTRON, Austria, 1993—; mem. external rev. com. Accelerator Prodn. Tritium Project Los Alamos Nat. Lab., N.Mex., 1995—98; mem. internat. adv. com.Scientific Coun. on Condensed Matter Investigations with Neutrons Russian Ministry of Sci. and Tech., 1996—; sr. tech. advisor exptl. facilities divsn. SNS Oak Ridge Nat. Lab., 1999—; vis. scientist Rutherford Appleton Lab., 1997—; mem. steering com. spallation neutron source Oak Ridge Nat. Lab., 1996—98, sci. adv. com. for spallation neutron source, 1996—2001. Author: (with Motoharu Kimura) Living with Nuclei, 1993, editor; patentee nuclear instrumentation, neutron scattering, time dependent neutron thermalization, pulsed spallation neutron sources, neutron scattering instrumentation, structure and dynamcs of amorphous solids. Presdl. appointee vis. com. dept. nuclear engring. MIT, 1989-95. Recipient Disting. Svc. award, U. Mich. Dept. Nuc. Engring., 1967, L.J. Hamilton Disting. Alumnus award, 1977, Disting. Performance award for work at Argonne Nat. Lab., U. Chgo., 1982, Ilja M. Frank prize, Joint Inst. Nuc. Rsch., 1998, merit award, Dept. Nuc. Engring. and Radiol. Scis., U. Mich. Alumni Soc., 2001. Fellow Condensed Matter Physics Divsn, Am. Phys. Soc.; mem. Am. Nuclear Soc. (sect. chmn. 1974-75), Neutron Scattering Soc. Am. (mem. subcom. on pulsed spallation sources 1993—, mem. pulsed source steering com.). Office: Argonne Nat Lab Intense Pulsed Neutron Source Argonne IL 60439 E-mail: jmcarpenter@anl.gov.

CARPENTER, JOT DAVID, landscape architect, educator; b. San Francisco, Mar. 19, 1938; s. Jot Thomas and Gretchen Marie (Johnston) C.; m. Claire Marie Dunn, Aug. 8, 1962; children: Jot David, Sean Michael, Kevin Patrick. B.L.A., U. Ga., 1960; M.L.A., Harvard U., 1962. Registered landscape architect, N.Y., Ohio. Landscape architect T.J. Wirth Assocs., Billings, Mont., 1965-68; asst. prof. dept. hort. Cornell U., Ithaca, N.Y., 1968-72; assoc. prof., chmn. dept. landscape architecture Ohio State U., Columbus, 1972-76, chmn. dept. landscape architecture, 1976-87, prof., 1987—. Vis. scholar Kyoto U., Japan, 1985, Chongqing Inst. Architecture and Engring., People's Republic of China, 1984, 87; dir. Landscape Arch. Found., Washington, 1977-87, v.p., 1981, sec., 1982-83; mem. Ohio Bd. Landscape Arch. Examiners, 1973-76, CLARB Uniform Nat. Examination Com., Syracuse, N.Y., 1975-77. Author: Landscape Construction Workbook, 1975; editor: Handbook of Landscape Architectural Construction, 1976; editl. adv. bd. Landscape Planning, 1978-85; chmn. editl. adv. com. Landscape Architecture Mag., 1984-87, 93-96. Bd. dirs. Columbus Conv. & Visitors Bur., 1977-92; mem. Planning Commn., Upper Arlington, Ohio, 1978-82, Ohio Land Use Planning Task Force, 1974, Ohio Motorists Svcs. Signing Adv. Bd., 1989-93. 1st lt. USAF, 1962-65. Fellow Am. Soc. Landscape Architects (treas. 1973-74, v.p. 1976-78, pres. 1978-79, Pres.'s medal 1982, Ohio chpt. medal 1982); mem. Coun. of Educators in Landscape Architecture, Internat. Fedn. Landscape Architects, Phi Kappa Phi, Sigma Lambda Alpha. Roman Catholic. Home: 1801 Elmwood Ave Columbus OH 43212-1111 Office: Ohio State-Knowlton Sch. Architecture Dept Landscape Architecture 190 W 17th Ave Columbus OH 43210-1320

CARPENTER, KENNETH RUSSELL, international trading executive; b. Chgo., May 22, 1955; s. Kenneth and Margaret (Lucas) C.; 1 child, Matthew. AS in Aviation, Prairie State Coll., Chicago Heights, Ill., 1979. Respiratory therapist, Harvey, Ill., 1980-83; dir., owner, ptnr. Pulmonary Therapy Inc., 1983-91; v.p. Home Air Joliet Ltd., 1984—; dir., owner Air Systems Internat. Export/Import Med. Equipment, Chicago Heights, 1981—, Air Systems, Ft. Lauderdale, 1991—, Home Ortho Ltd., Harvey, 1985—; pres., CEO Profl. Yacht Svcs., Inc., Chicago Heights, 1987-94; owner CLZ Exporting Inc., 1993-95; owner, CEO, Profl. Yacht Svcs., 1997—, Info. Plus Inc., Chicago Heights, 1997—. Acquisition and mgmt. of investment real estate KRLC, 1991—; dir. pub. rels. Lansing (Ill.) Med. Group, 1990; dir. pulmonary rehab. Cardio-Pulmonary Assocs., Munster, Ind., 1990—, CLZ Exporting, 1992—; maj. importer/exporter of durable med. oxygen equipment worldwide, KRLC Mktg., 1996—. Pilot CAP, 1979-86. With USN, 1973-77. Mem. Am. Assn. Respiratory Therapy (cert.), Nat. Assn. Med. Equipment Suppliers, Ill. Assn. of Med. Equipment Suppliers, Am. Biog. Inst., Steger C. of C., Ill. C. of C. Avocations: flying, boating, computer programming. Home and Office: 23030 Miller Rd Steger IL 60475-5932

CARPENTER, MICHAEL H. lawyer; b. Huntington, W.Va., Mar. 3, 1953; BA, Ohio State U., 1974, JD, 1977. Bar: Ohio 1977. Former ptnr. Jones, Day, Reavis & Pogue, Columbus, Ohio; ptnr. Zeiger & Carpenter, 1994—. Mem. Phi Beta Kappa, Order of Coif. Office: Zeiger & Carpenter 1600 Huntington Ctr 41 S High St Columbus OH 43215-6101

CARPENTER, NOBLE OLDS, retired bank executive; b. Cleve., May 8, 1929; s. John W. and Maribel (Olds) C.; m. Ann Lindemann, Oct. 13, 1956 (dec. Aug. 1987); children: John L., Noble Olds, Robert W.; m. Sharon D. D'Atri, Aug. 11, 1990. A.B. cum laude, Princeton, 1951. Cert. comml. lender. Comml. Lending div. Am. Bankers Assn. Vice pres. Central Nat. Bank, Cleve., 1951-65; chmn., pres., chief exec. officer, dir. Central Trust Co. of Northeastern Ohio, N.A., Canton, 1965-91; dir. Bank One, Akron, Ohio, 1991-97. Mem. Internat. Exec. Svc. Corps.; dir. Mountain Lake Tree & Land Co., Ltd. Dep. sheriff Stark County; bd. dirs. Aultman Hosp. Devel. Found., Blue Coats, Inc., Greater Canton Partnership; trustee State Troopers of Ohio. Named outstanding Young Man of Year Jr. C. of C., 1965 Mem. Cleve. Pres. Orgn., Brookside Country Club. Home: 3423 Croydon Dr NW Canton OH 44718-3221 E-mail: NC29@aol.com.

CARPENTER, SHARON QUIGLEY, municipal official; Tchr. history St. Louis Pub Schs.; elected recorder of deeds City of St. Louis, 1980—. Mem. Mo. Reapportionment Commn. Dem. Committeewoman 23rd ward St. Louis, 1964—; chair Dem. Ctrl. Com. St. Louis; founding mem, 1st chair, bd. dirs. Maria Droste Residence, St. Louis; mem. Mo. Commn. on Intergovernmental Rels, 1996—, adv. bd. Cath. Youth Coun., St. Louis., 1997—. Mem. Recorders' Assn. Mo. (past pres.). Office: City of St Louis Office Recorder of Deeds Market & Tucker Aves Rm 126 Saint Louis MO 63103

CARPENTER, SUSAN KAREN, public defender; b. New Orleans, May 6, 1951; d. Donald Jack and Elise Ann (Diehl) C. BA magna cum laude with honors in English, Smith Coll., 1973; JD, Ind. U., 1976. Bar: Ind. 1976. Dep. pub. defender of Ind. State of Ind., Indpls., 1976-81, pub. defender of Ind., 1981—; chief pub. defender Wayne County, Richmond, Ind., 1981. Bd. dirs. Ind. Pub. Defender Coun., Indpls., 1981—; Ind. Lawyers Comm., Indpls., 1984-89; trustee Ind. Criminal Justice Inst., INdpls., 1983—. Mem. Criminal Code Study Commn., Indpls., 1981—, Supreme Ct. Records Mgmt. Com., Indpls., 1983—, Ind. Pub. Defender Commn., 1989—, Ind. Supreme Ct. Commn. on Race and Gender Fairness, 2000—. Mem. Ind. State Bar Assn. (criminal justice sect.), Nat. Legal Aid and Defender Assn., Nat. Assn. Defense Lawyers, Phi Beta Kappa. E-mail: scarpenter@iquest.net.

CARPENTER, TIMOTHY W. state legislator; b. Milw., Feb. 24, 1960; BA, U. Wis., Milw., 1982. Former delivery svc. courier; rep. for dist. 20 Wis. Ho. of Reps., 1984-92, rep. for dist. 9, 1992—; chmn. health com. Wis. State Assembly. Mem. 4th Congl. Dist. Dem. Com., former chmn. Mem. Wilson Park Advancement Assn. Democrat. Home: 2957 S 38th St Milwaukee WI 53215-3519

CARPENTER, WILL DOCKERY, chemical company executive; b. Moorhead, Miss., July 13, 1930; s. Horace Aubrey and Celeste (Brian) C.; m. Hellen E. Dodd, Mar. 26, 1960; children: Celeste, Bill. BS in Agronomy, Miss. State U., 1952; MS in Plant Physiology, Purdue U., 1956, PhD in Plant Physiology, 1958, DSc (hon.), 1999; grad. exec. program in bus. adminstrn., Columbia U., 1980. Research biochemist Monsanto Co., St. Louis, 1958-60, agrl. research chemist, 1960-61, staff agrl. devel., 1961-65; mgr. market devel. Monsanto Agrl. Div., 1965-71; dir. product devel. Monsanto Agrl. Products Co., 1971-77, dir. environ. ops., 1977-80, dir. environ. mgmt./environ. policy staff, 1980-84, gen. mgr. tech., 1984-86; v.p. technology Monsanto Agrl. Co., 1986-90, v.p., gen. mgr. new products, 1990-92; chmn., bd. dirs. Agridyne Techs. Inc. Served to capt. U.S. Army, 1952-54, Korea. Fellow Weed Sci. Soc. Am. (treas. 1975, pres. 1980); mem. Indsl. Biotech. Assn. (bd. dirs. 1986—), Chem. Mfrs. Assn. (chmn. environ. mgmt. com. 1982-84, chmn. chem. warfare disarmament com. Washington 1985—), North Cen. Weed Control Conf. (pres. 1977, hon. mem. 1982). Office: 456 Conway Meadows Dr Chesterfield MO 63017-9625 E-mail: wdchdc@aol.com.

CARR, ANNE ELIZABETH, theology educator; b. Chgo., Nov. 11, 1934; d. Frank James and Dorothy Margaret (Graber) C. AB, Mundelein Coll., 1956; AM, Marquette U., 1963, U. Chgo., 1968, PhD, 1971. Instr. Mundelein Coll., Chgo., 1963-66, asst. prof., 1966-71, Ind. U., Bloomington, 1972-74; asst. prof., asst. dean U. Chgo. Divinity Sch., 1975-78, assoc. prof., assoc. dean, 1978-88, prof., 1988—. Donnelan vis. prof. Trinity Coll., Dublin, Ireland, 1983. Author: Theological Method of K. Rahner, 1977, Transforming Grace, 1988, Search for Wisdom and Spirit, 1988; editor: (with E.S. Florenza) Women, Work and Poverty, 1987, Motherhood: Experience, Institution, Theologu, 1989, Women's Special Nature?, 1991; bd. cons. Jour. of Religion, 1975-86, co-editor, 1987-94; assoc. editor Horizons, 1974—; editorial bd. Concilium, 1985-91. Trustee Mundelein Coll., Chgo., 1977-91. Postdoctoral fellow Harvard Divinity Sch., 1983-84. Mem. Am. Acad. Religion (program com. 1978-80), Cath. Theol. Soc. Am., Coll. Theology Soc. Roman Catholic. Office: U Chgo Divinity Sch 1025 E 58th St Chicago IL 60637-1509

CARR, BONNIE JEAN, professional ice skater; b. Chgo., Sept. 29, 1947; d. Nicholas and Agnes Marie (Moran) Musashe; m. James Bradley Carr, Dec. 8, 1984; children: Brittany Jean, James Bradley II, Brooke Anderson. BS, Northwestern U., 1969; JD (hon.), Loyola U., Chgo., 1978. Skater Adventures on Ice, Mpls., 1961; prin. skater Jamboree on Ice, Chgo., 1961-68; society editor The Free Press, Colorado Springs, Colo., 1969; prin. skater, publicist on tour, asst. lighting dir., tour ednl. tutor Holiday on Ice Internat., 1970-74; skating dir. William McFetridge Sports Ctr., Chgo., 1975-86; choreographer, prin. skater Ice Time, USA, Mundelein, Ill., 1975—. Skating coach St. Bronislava Athletic Club, Chgo., 1967-69; publicity dir. Amateur Skating Assn. Ill., Chgo., 1968; founder, dir. skating programs for blind, hearing impaired and mentally handicapped, Chgo., 1975-85; physical fitness advisor Exec. Health Seminars, Chgo., 1979; founder, dir. skating programs Fred Hutchinson Cancer Rsch. Ctr., Seattle, 1985-86; guest speaker Am. Cancer Soc., Columbia, S.C., 1973; conditioning coach Riverside Wellness and Fitness Ctr., Richmond, Va., 1989-91, Southampton Rec. Assn., Richmond, 1991-94; figure & speed skating coach Va. Spl. Olympics, 1991—. Recipient Key to City, Mobile, Ala., 1973, Service Recognition award Special Olympics, Chgo., 1984. Mem. Am. Guild Variety Artists, Am. Coun. on Exercise (cert. 1990-96). Roman Catholic. Avocation: writing, public speaking, choreography. Office: Ice Time USA 28800 N Gilmer Rd Mundelein IL 60060-9538 Home: 8 Fishing Point Elgin SC 29045-8636

CARR, GARY THOMAS, lawyer; b. El Reno, Okla., July 25, 1946; s. Thomas Clay and Bobbye Jean (Page) C.; m. Ann Elizabeth Smith, Jan. 5, 1985. AB, Washington U., St. Louis, 1968, BSCE, 1972, JD, 1975. Bar: Mo. 1975, U.S. Dist. Ct. (ea. and we. dists.) Mo. 1975, U.S. Ct. Appeals (8th cir.) 1977, U.S. Ct. Appeals (fed. cir.) 1980, U.S. Ct. Appeals (5th cir.) 1991. Jr. ptnr. Bryan, Cave, McPheeters & McRoberts, St. Louis, 1975-83, ptnr., 1984-99. Lectr. law Washington U., 1978-82, adj. prof., 1982-85; sec., dir. Bruton-Stroube Studios, Inc., 1978—, bd. dirs. Trustee Parkview Subdiv. Assn., St. Louis, 1982-90. 1st lt. U.S. Army, 1968-71, Vietnam. Mem. ABA, Mo. Bar Assn., St. Louis Bar Assn., Order of Coif. Avocations: woodworking, hunting, fishing, automobiles. Office: PO Box 3030 Saint Louis MO 63130-0430 E-mail: gtc10485@aol.com.

CARR, GEORGE FRANCIS FRANCIS, JR. lawyer; b. Bklyn., Feb. 11, 1939; s. George Francis and Edith Frances (Schaible) C.; m. Patricia Louise Shiels, Jan. 30, 1965; children: Frances Virginia, Anne McKenzie, Margaret Edith. BA, Georgetown U., 1961; LLB, Harvard U., 1964. Bar: Ohio 1964, U.S. Dist. Ct. Ohio 1964. Assoc. Kyte, Conlan, Wulsin & Vogeler, Cin., 1964-70, ptnr., 1970-78, Frost & Jacobs, Cin., 1978-82; sec., counsel Baldwin-United Corp., 1982-84, v.p., spl. counsel, 1984-85; sole practice, 1985-86; ptnr. Douglas, Carr and Pettit, Milford, 1987-88; staff v.p., assoc. gen. counsel Penn Cen. Corp., Cin., 1988-92, Gen. Cable Corp., Highland Heights, Ky., 1992-95, ret., 1995. Bd. dirs. Ctr. for Comprehensive Alcoholism Treatment, Cin., 1975-87, pres., 1980-83; bd. dirs. NCCJ, Cin., 1975-82. U.S. Army, 1965—67. Avocations: farming, geology, hiking, physical fitness. Home: 7150 Ragland Rd # 4 Cincinnati OH 45244-3148

CARR, JAMES GRAY, judge; b. Boston, Nov. 14, 1940; s. Edmund Albert and Anna Frances C.; m. Eileen Margaret Glynn, Dec. 17, 1966; children: Maureen M., Megan A., Darrah E., Caitlin E. AB, Kenyon Coll., 1962; LLB, Harvard U., 1966. Bar: Ill. 1966, Ohio 1972, U.S. Dist. Ct. (no. dist.) Ill. 1966, U.S. Dist. Ct. (no. dist.) Ohio 1970, U.S. Supreme Ct. 1980. Assoc. Gardner & Carton, et al., Chgo., 1966-68; staff atty. Cook County Legal Asst. Found., Evanston, Ill., 1968-70; prof. U. Toledo Law Sch., 1970-79; U.S. magistrate judge U.S. Dist. Ct., Toledo, 1979-94, U.S. dist. judge, 1994—. Adj. prof. law Chgo. Kent Law Sch., 1969, Loyola U., Chgo., 1970; reporter, juvenile rules com. Ohio Supreme Ct., Columbus, 1971-72; reporter, mem. nat. wiretap com. U.S. Congress, Washington, 1976-77. Contbr. articles to profl. law jours. Founder, bd. dirs. Child Abuse Ctr., Toledo, 1970-84; active Lucas County Mental Health Bd., Toledo, 1984-89, Lucas County Children Svcs. Bd., Toledo, 1989-94. Fulbright fellow, 1977-78. Mem. ABA (reporter, elec. survey stds. 1979-80, mem. task force on tech. and law enforcement 1995-99, mem. task force on jury initiatives 1995-98), Toledo Bar Assn. (bd. dirs.), Phi Beta Kappa. Roman Catholic. Office: US Dist Ct 203 US Courthouse 1716 Spielbusch Ave Toledo OH 43624-1363 E-mail: jcarr@ohnd.uscourts.gov.

CARR, PETER WILLIAM, chemistry educator; b. Bklyn., Aug. 16, 1944; s. Peter V. and Kathleen T. Carr; m. Leah Phillips, 1966; children: Sean, Erin, Kelly. BS in Chemistry, Polytech Inst. Bklyn., 1965; PhD in Analytical Chemistry, Pa. State U., 1969. Rsch. asst., assoc. Brookhaven Nat. Lab., 1965, 66; postdoctoral assoc. Stanford U. Med. Sch., 1968; faculty mem. U. Ga., 1969-77; prof. chemistry U. Minn., 1977—. Cons. Leeds and Northrup, Hewlett Packard, 3M Co., Cabot Inc.; pres. ZirChrom Separations, Inc.; pres. Symposium Analytical Chemistry in Environment, 1976. Mem. editl. adv. bd. Analytical Chemistry, Talanta, Jour. Chromatography, LC/GC, Chromatographia, Separation Sci. and Tech.; contbr. over 290 articles to profl. jours. Recipient L.S. Palmer award Minn. Chromatography Forum, 1984, Benedetti-Pichler award Am. Microchem. Soc., 1990, award in Fields Analytical Chemistry Ea. Analytical Symposium, 1993, S. Nogare award Del. Valley Chromatography Forum, 1996, award in chromatography ISCO, 1997, award in separation sci. Ea. Analytical Symposium, 2000. Mem. Am. Chem. Soc. (chmn. subdivsn. chromatography and separation sci. of Analytical Chemistry divsn. 1988-89, Chromatography award 1997), Minn. Chromatography Forum. Office: U Minn Dept Chemistry 207 Pleasant St SE Minneapolis MN 55455-0431 E-mail: carr@chem.umn.edu., carr@zirchrom.com.

CARR, ROBERT WILSON, JR. chemistry educator; b. Montpelier, Vt., Sept. 7, 1934; s. Robert Wilson and Marie (Soucy) C.; m. Betty Lee Elmer, June 21, 1958; children: Kevin, Terrell, Kathryn. B.S., Norwich U., 1956; M.S., U. Vt., 1958; Ph.D., U. Rochester, 1962. NIH fellow Harvard U., 1963-65; asst. prof. U. Minn., 1965-69, asso. prof., 1969-75, prof. dept. chem. engring. and materials sci., 1975—. Vis. prof. U. Cambridge, 1971-72, MIT, 1995; guest prof. U. Göttingen, Fed. Republic Germany, 1982. Asst. editor: Jour. Phys. Chemistry, 1970-80. Served to 1st lt. U.S. Army, 1963. NSF fellow, 1971-72; Fulbright fellow, 1982 Mem. Am. Chem. Soc., Am. Aviation Hist. Soc., Interam. Photochem. Soc., Am. Inst. Chem. Engrs., Sigma Xi. Mem. Congregational Ch. Home: 5722 Harriet Ave Minneapolis MN 55419-1807 Office: U Minn Dept Chem Engring & Material Scis Minneapolis MN 55455

CARR, STEPHEN HOWARD, materials engineer, educator; b. Dayton, Ohio, Sept. 29, 1942; s. William Howard and Mary Elizabeth (Clement) C.; m. Virginia W. McMillan, June 24, 1967; children: Rosamond Elizabeth, Louisa Ruth. BS, U. Cin., 1965; MS, Case Western Res. U., 1967, PhD, 1970. Coop. engr. Inland divsn. GM, Dayton, 1960-65; asst. prof. materials sci. and engring. and chem. engring. Northwestern U., Evanston, Ill., 1970-73, assoc. prof., 1973-78, prof., 1978—, dir. Materials Rsch. Ctr., 1984-90, asst. dean engring., 1991-93, assoc. dean engring., 1993—. Cons. in field. Contbr. articles to profl. jours. Recipient Outstanding Alumni Achievement award U. Cin. Coll. Engring., 1993. Fellow Am. Soc. for Metals Internat., Am. Phys. Soc.; mem. AIChE, Soc. Automotive Engrs. (Ralph R. Teetor award 1980), Plastics Inst. Am. (Ednl. Svc. award 1975), Am. Chem. Soc., Soc. Plastics Engrs., Materials Rsch. Soc. Achievements include patents in plastics and textiles fields. Home: 2704 Harrison St Evanston IL 60201-1216 Office: Northwestern U 2145 Sheridan Rd Evanston IL 60208-0834

CARR, STEVE, public relations executive; V.p. pub. rels. Cramer-Krasselt, Chgo., 1995-96, sr. v.p. pub. rels., 1996—. Office: Cramer-Krasselt 225 N Michigan Ave Chicago IL 60601-7601 Fax: 312-938-3157.

CARR, WILEY NELSON, hospital administrator; b. Dayton, Ohio, Dec. 29, 1940; s. Russell Earl and Anna Lee (Stroud) C.; m. Grace Elizabeth Brown, June 4, 1960 (div.); children: Wiley Nelson, Alison Mary Ann, G. Elizabeth, Joshua William, Joy Kathleen; m. Sharon L. Kersey, Aug. 22, 1997. Student, Miami U., Oxford, Ohio, l959-62; BSJ, Ohio U., l963, MS, l964; MBA, Xavier U., Cin., 1974. Lic. nursing home adminstr., Ky. Dir. pub. rels. Western Coll. for Women, Oxford, l964-67, dir. devel., 1967-70; dir. devel. and community rels. St. Elizabeth Med. Ctr., Covington, Ky., l970-74, asst. adminstr., 1974-83, v.p., chief operating officer Edgewood, 1983-90; pres., CEO, Porter Meml. Hosp., Valparaiso, Ind., 1990—. Bd. dirs. BetterCare, Inc., Cin.; sec. Tri-State Healthcare Laundry, Edgewood, l989-90. Pres. Tri-State Community Cancer Orgn., Cin., 1988—; bd. dirs. United Way Porter County, Community Devel. Corp., Valparaiso, N.W. Ind. Forum, YMCA Valparaiso. Fellow Am. Coll. Healthcare Execs.; mem. Ind. Hosp. Assn. Republican. Methodist. Avocations: golf, hiking, swimming. Home: 1716 Beachview Ct Crown Point IN 46307-9315 Office: Porter Memorial Hospital 814 Laporte Ave Valparaiso IN 46383-5898

CARRAHER, CHARLES JACOB, JR. professional speaker; b. Sept. 22, 1922; s. Charles Jacob and Marcella Marie (Hager) C.; m. Joyce Ann Root, June 13, 1947; children: Cynthia A., Craig J. Grad. pub. schs., Norwood, Ohio. With Cin. Enquirer, 1937-72, office mgr., circulation mgr., admin. asst. to exec. v.p., 1947-66, dir. employee cmty. rels., 1966-72, corp. sec., 1969-72; exec. v.p., ptnr. Cin. Suburban Newspapers Inc., 1973-77; asst. dir. devel. Sta. WCET-TV, 1977-79; v.p. Garrett Computer Inc., 1979-81. Participant numerous symposia. Mem. bd., v.p. Cin. Conv. and Visitors Bur., 1966-72; mem. Cin. Manpower Planning Coun., 1972; bd. dirs. Cen. Psychiat. Clinic, 1970-80, Mental Health Assn., 1970-72, Great Rivers coun. Girl Scouts U.S.A., 1969-74; v.p. bd. dirs. Neediest Kids of All, 1969-72; bd. dirs. Greater Cin. Urban League, 1971-74, 75-78. Lt. USAF, WWII, ETO. Decorated Air medal with cluster. Mem. Greater Cin. C. of C. (chmn. human resources devel. com. 1972), Beta Gamma Sigma. Republican Home and Office: 10848 Lake Thames Dr Cincinnati OH 45242-3105

CARRAWAY, MELVIN J. protective services official; m. Karen Carraway; children: Rachel, Maya. BMus, Heidelberg Coll., 1975; grad., FBI Nat. Acad., 1984. Comdr. enforcement divsn. Ind. State Police, supt., 1997—. Exec. dir. Ind. State Emergency Mgmt. Agy./Dept. of Fire and Bldg. Svcs. With U.S. Army. Office: Ind State Police 100 N Senate Ave Indianapolis IN 46204-2273

CARREN, JEFFREY P. lawyer; b. Chgo., Oct. 8, 1946; AB with high honors, U. Ill., 1968; JD, Northwestern U., 1972. Bar: Ill. 1973, U.S. Dist. Ct. (no. dist.) Ill. 1973, U.S. Ct. Appeals (7th cir.) 1976, U.S. Supreme Ct. 1980. Formerly ptnr. Winston & Strawn, Chgo.; ptnr. Laner, Muchin, Dombrow, Becker, Levin & Tominberg Ltd., 1994—. Editor notes and comments Northwestern U. Law Rev., 1971-72/ Edmund James scholar. Mem. ABA (tax and bus. sects.), Ill. State Bar Assn. (employee benefits sect.), Chgo. Bar Assn. (employee benefits com), Am. Arbitration Assn. (panel arbitrators), Phi Eta Sigma. Office: Laner Muchin et al 515 N State St Chicago IL 60610-4325 E-mail: jcarren@lmdblt.com.

CARRICK, KATHLEEN MICHELE, law librarian; b. Cleve., June 11, 1950; d. Michael James and Genevieve (Wenger) C. BA, Duquesne U., Pitts., 1972; MLS, U. Pitts., 1973; JD, Cleve.-Marshall U., 1977. Bar: Ohio 1977, U.S. Ct. Internat. Trade 1983. Rsch. asst. The Plain Dealer, Cleve., 1973-75; head reference SUNY, Buffalo, 1977-78, assoc. dir., 1978-80, dir., asst. prof., 1980-83; dir., assoc. prof. law Case Western Res. U., Cleve., 1983—. Cons. Mead Data Central, Dayton, Ohio, 1987-91. Author: Lexis: A Research Manual, 1989; contbr. articles to profl. jours. Fellow Am. Bar Found.; mem. ABA, Am. Law Inst., Am. Assn. Law Librs., Assn. Am. Law Schs., Scribes. Home: 1317 Burlington Rd Cleveland OH 44118-1212 Office: Case Western Res U 11075 East Blvd Cleveland OH 44106-5409

CARRICO, VIRGIL NORMAN, physician; b. Cumberland, Md., Aug. 28, 1940; s. Virgil Norman and Lucille E. (Gnagy) C.; m. Nina Lois Lemper, Aug. 17, 1963; children: Pamela Beth Carrico-Miller, Sandra Kelly (dec.). BA, Wabash Coll., 1962; MD, Ind. U., 1966. Diplomate Am. Bd. Family Practice. Intern Marion County Gen. Hosp., Indpls., 1966-67; resident in family practice Akron (Ohio) City Hosp., 1970-72, chief resident in family practice, 1972, assoc. dir. family practice residency, 1972; chief family practice Bryan Cmty. Hosp., past chmn. bd. dirs. home health care; past mem. undergrad. med. edn. subcom. Med. Coll. Ohio, Toledo, past preceptor cmty. medicine, clin. asst. prof. family medicine, clin. prof. family medicine; past preceptor preventive medicine and family practice Ohio State U.; chief of staff Bryan Cmty. Hosp., 1977-78, preceptor Bryan Area Health Edn. Ctr., chmn. continuing med. edn. com.; med. dir. Bryan Area Health Edn. Ctr. Past pres., bd. dirs. Bryan Med. Group, Inc. Contbr. articles to profl. jours. Trustee YWCA, Bryan, Ohio, v.p., 1990-92; bd. dirs. United Fund, pres., 1990-92; bd. dirs. Jr. Achievement, 1981-83, Bryan Area Found. Capt. USAF, 1967-70. Fellow Am. Acad. Family Physicians (bylaw coms. 1989, 90, 91, 92, nat. chmn. 1993, chmn. patient care svcs. commn. 1988-89, chmn. mem. svcs. commn. 1989-90); mem. Soc. Tchrs. Family Medicine, Ohio Acad. Family Medicine, Am. Acad. Family Medicine, Williams County Med. Soc. (rpes. 1976-79, sec.-treas., v.p. 1980-83), Ohio Acad. Family Physicians (del. to ho. of dels. 1972-85; pres. Fulton County chpt. 1973-85, chmn. resident affairs subcom., nominating com., student awards, fin. com., ref. com. of the ho. of dels.; treas. 1985-87, v.p. 1987-89, bd. dirs. 1983-92, pres.-elect 1990-91), Rotary Internat. Avocations: golf, traveling, reading. Office: Bryan Med Group 442 W High St Bryan OH 43506-1681

CARRINGTON, MICHAEL DAVIS, criminal justice administrator, educator, consultant; b. South Bend, Ind., Mar. 9, 1938; s. Herman Lakin and Margaret (Davis) C.; m. Lynn Ogden, Feb. 8, 1958; children: Michael O. (dec.), Jill A., Elizabeth A., Gretchen L. BA, Ind. U., 1970; MALS, Valparaiso U., 1971. Parole officer State of Ind., South Bend, 1970-71; chief probation officer St. Joseph County, 1971-74; dir. pub. safety City of South Bend, 1974-76, mayor's asst., 1976-80; adj. assoc. prof., dir. safety, security, police Ind. U., South Bend, 1979-94; presdl. appointment as U.S. Marshal Northern Dist. of Ind., Ind., 1994—2002; security dir. St. Mary's Coll., Notre Dame, 2002—. Cons. in pvt. security Pan Am. Games, Indpls., 1987; security advance agt. Olympic Torch Relay, Ind., 1984, Hands Across Am., Ind., 1986. Recipient Sagamore of Wabash award, 1984, 2002; named Ky. Col., 1984, Hon. Big. Brother of Yr., 1974, Outstanding Residential Faculty Mem. awrd Ind. U. South Bend Sch. Pub. and Environ. Affairs, 1992. Mem. Am. Soc. Indsl. Security, Assn. of Threat Assessment Profls. Presbyterian. Avocation: travel, reading, walking, working. Office: Security Dir St Marys Coll Notre Dame IN 46556 E-mail: mikecmarshal@netscape.net.

CARROLL, BARRY JOSEPH, manufacturing and real estate executive; b. Highland Park, Ill., Jan. 22, 1944; s. Wallace Edward and Lelia (Holden) C.; m. Barbara Ann Pehrson, July 16, 1965; children: Megan, Sean, Deirdre, Colleen, Oona. Student, Boston Coll., 1961-63; AB, Shimer Coll., 1966; MBA, Harvard U., 1969. Lic. real estate broker, Ill. Account rep. Amerad Advt. Service, Chgo., summers 1966, 67; staff analyst Jamesbury Valve Co., Worcester, Mass., 1968; asst. to pres. Am. Gage & Machine Co., Elgin, Ill., 1969; pres. J.C. Deagan Co., Chgo., 1969-77; v.p. Internat. Metals & Machines, Des Plaines, 1977-92, also bd. dirs.; v.p. Katy Industries, Elgin, 1984-94, also bd. dirs.; pres. Katy Comm., Inc. (WIVS-AM, WXRD-FM, WAIT AM/FM), 1986-92, Sta. W45AJ-TV, Rockford, Ill., 1989-92. V.p., bd. dirs. Pehrson-Long Assocs., Real Estate Mgmt., Am. Machine & Sci. Inc., CRL Inc., Carroll Internat. Corp. (chmn. 1992), GFS Holdings Co. Author: (monograph) Talking with Business, 1986; author of appendix/editor: What I Do Best: The Biography of Wallace Edward Carroll, 1992; editor/author: Private Means/Public Ends, 1987; author: Lake Forest, A Very Special Place, 1996; producer, dir. indsl. films, including In There Punching, 1965, Digging Lake County, 1999; dir./host (cable TV series) Area Arts, 2000—. Spl. asst. U.S. Sec. Edn., Washington, 1983-84; Presdl. Exch. exec., Washington, 1983-84; bd. govs. United Rep. Fund, Chgo., 1986-92; mem. Nat. Inst. Edn. Commn. Edn. and Tech., U.S. Dept. Edn., 1984-85; trustee Shimer Coll., 1970—, chmn. bd. trustees, 1975-78; trustee Barat Coll., Lake Forest, 1983—, life trustee, 1999—; trustee St. Xavier U., Chgo., 1988-94, Lake County Regional Sch. Bd., 1993—; bd. trustees Am. Ireland Fund, 1982-2001, sec., 1991—; bd. dirs. Lake Forest Symphony, 1970—, Pageant of Peace/Nat. Christmas Tree, 1987-2000, Lake Forest Music Inst., 1991—, Roosevelt U., Chgo., 1996—, U. Ill. Eye Rsch. Inst., 1996—; bd. dirs. Chgo. Crime Commn., 1993—, treas., 1994-98; mem., chmn. Lake Forest Cultural Arts Commn., 1997—; chair adv. bd. Inst. Metro. Affairs Roosevelt U., 1998—. Shimer fellow Shimer Coll., Mt. Carroll, Ill., 1972, Shimer Hero award Shimer Coll., Waukegan, Ill., 1980, Dr. Letters, 1995. Mem. Woods Hole Oceanographic Inst. Assn., Ill. Mfrs. Assn. (bd. dirs. 1989—), Assn. for Mfg. Tech. (bd. dirs. chmn. pub. affairs com. 1988-93), Onwentsia Club (Lake Forest), Chgo. Club, Met. Club (Washington), East Chop Beach Tennis and Yacht Clubs (Martha's Vineyard Island), Edgartown Yacht Club, Bath and Tennis Club (Palm Beach, Fla.), Soc. Colonial Wars in the State of Ill. (treas. 1988-94, gov. 1998-2000). Avocations: flying, sailing, skiing, scuba diving, photography. Office: Carroll Internat Corp 2340 Des Plaines Ave Des Plaines IL 60018-3212

CARROLL, CHARLES A. manufacturing executive; Sales rep. Rubbermaid, 1971, pres., gen. mgr. housewares product divsn., 1990, pres., COO, 1993-99; pres., CEO Amana Appliances, 2000—. Office: Amana Appliances 2800 220th Trail Amana IA 52204

CARROLL, FRANK JAMES, lawyer, educator; b. Albuquerque, Feb. 10, 1947; s. Francis J. and Dorothy (Bloom) C.; m. Marilyn Blume, Aug. 9, 1969; children: Christine, Kathleen, Emily. BS in Acctg., St. Louis U., 1969; JD, U. Ill., 1973. Bar: Iowa 1973, U.S. Dist. Ct. Iowa, U.S. Tax Ct., U.S. Ct. Appeals (8th cir.); CPA, Mo., Iowa. Acct. Arthur Young & Co., St. Louis, 1969-70; shareholder Davis, Brown, Koehn, Shors & Roberts, P.C., Des Moines, 1973—. Lectr. law Drake U. Law Sch., Des Moines, 1976-86, lectr. Sch. of Bus., 1988-92; bd. dirs. Newton Mfg. Co., Pella Plastics, Inc., Iowa Agr. Devel. Authority. Mem. commr.'s adv. group IRS, Washington, 1989; mem. grad. tax adv. bd. U. Mo. Kansas City Sch. Law, 1995. Mem. ABA, Iowa Bar Assn. (chair bus. law sect. 1995-98, chair corp. counsel sect. 2001—), Polk County Bar Assn., Des Moines C. of C., Wakonda Club, Des Moines Variety Club (bd. dirs. 1998), Beta Gamma Sigma. Home: 5725 Harwood Dr Des Moines IA 50312-1203 Office: Davis Brown Koehn Shors Roberts PC 666 Walnut St Ste 2500 Des Moines IA 50309-3904

CARROLL, HOWARD WILLIAM, state senator, lawyer; b. July 28, 1942; s. Barney M. and Lyla (Price) C.; m. Eda Stagman, Dec. 1, 1973; children: Jacqueline, Barbara. BBA, Roosevelt U., 1964; postgrad., Loyola U., 1964-65; JD, DePaul U., 1967. Bar: Ill. 1967. Staff atty. Chgo. Transit Authority, 1967-71; pvt. practice, 1971-74; ptnr. Carroll & Sain, Chgo., 1974—; mem. Ill. Senate, Springfield, 1973-99, asst. minority leader, 1993-99, chmn. appropriations com., 1977-93. Mem. Legis. Info. System Commn., Ill. Comprehensive Health Ins. Bd.; vice chmn. State Employees Suggestion Award Bd.; mem. fed. budget and taxation com. State-Fed. Assembly; mem. Assembly Com. on State's Legis. Fiscal Affairs and Oversight; prof. complemental faculty Rush U. Coll. Health Scis., Chgo.; lectr. in field. Mem. Ill. Ho. of Reps., 1971-72; chmn. fin. com. Chgo. and Cook County Dem. Crtl. Com., 1982-84, treas., 1984-2000; committeeman 50th Ward Dem. Orgn., 1980-2000; mem. platform com. Ill. Dem. Com., 1974—; former mem. youth adv. bd. Dem. Nat. Com.; del. nat. and Ill. Dem. convs.; v.p. Young Dem. Clubs Am., 1971-73, also former gen. counsel; mem. exec. bd. Atlantic Alliance Young Polit. Leaders, 1970-73; active numerous civic orgns.; mem. exec. com. Jewish Nat. Fund, 1977—; chair govt. affairs Jewish Fedn. Met. Chgo.; founder Howard W. Carroll Found. Recipient numerous awards, 1971, including cert. of appreciation Decalogue Soc. Lawyers, 1972, Hemophilia Found. Ill., 1988, City Colls. Chgo., 1992, Disting. Svc. award State of Israel Bonds, 1974, Self-Help Assn., 1986, citation for meritorious svc. DAV, 1986, Legislator of Yr. award Child Care Assn. Ill., 1988, Ill. Coun. on Long Term Care, 1988, Outstanding Legislator award Am. Acad. Ophthalmology, 1989, Legis. Advocacy award Ill. Coun. for Gifted, 1991, Founders medal Montay Coll., 1992; named Ill. Health Care Outstanding Legislator of Yr., 1995. Mem. Chgo. Bar Assn. (Disting. Lawyer and Legislator award 1974), Zionist Orgn. Chgo., Masons (32d degree), B'nai B'rith (bd. dirs. West Rogers Park, chmn. Anti-Defamation League 1978-80, mem. exec. com. and chmn. spl. events Greater Chgo. coun., bd. dirs. Budlong Woods chpt.) Home: 2929 W Albion Ave Chicago IL 60645-4203 Office: 7250 N Cicero Ave Lincolnwood IL 60712

CARROLL, JAMES J. lawyer; b. Chgo., Jan. 10, 1948; BS magna cum laude, DePaul U., 1969, JD summa cum laude, 1972. Bar: Ill. 1972, U.S. Tax Ct. 1980, U.S. Supreme Ct. 1981. Of counsel Sidley & Austin, Chgo., 1995-99, ptnr., 1978-95; dir., pres. Wrigley Mgmt. Inc., 1995-99; trust counsel Northern Trust Co., 1999—. Lectr. Ill. Inst. for Continuing Legal Edn. Editor-in-chief DePaul Law Rev., 1971-72. Sec. Lakewood Estates Homeowners Assn.; bd. dirs. David and Ruth Barnow Found., 1979, Wrigley Family Found., 1993-99; active Ill. Atty. Gen.'s Charitable Adv. Coun. With USAR, 1970-76. Mem. Ill. State Bar Assn. (chmn. children's rights subcom. 1972-73), Chgo. Bar Assn. (probate practice com. 1977-88, lectr.), Law Club Chgo., Legal Club Chgo., Phi Eta Sigma, Beta Alpha Psi. Office: Northern Trust Co 181 W Madison St M 9 Chicago IL 60675-0001 E-mail: jjc@notes.ntrs.com.

CARROLL, ROBERT WAYNE, mathematics educator; b. Chgo., May 10, 1930; s. Walter Scott and Dorothy (Le Monnier) C.; m. Berenice Jacobs, Sept. 7, 1957 (div. June 1974); children: David Leon, Malcolm Scott; m. Alice von Neumann, Sept. 1974 (div. Mar. 1977); m. Joan Miller, Jan. 1979. B.S., U. Wis., 1952; Ph.D., U. Md., 1959. Aero. research scientist NASA, Cleve., 1952-54; NSF postdoctoral fellow, 1959-60; asst. prof. Rutgers U., 1960-63, assoc. prof., 1963-64; assoc. prof. math. U. Ill., Urbana, 1964-67, prof., 1967-97, prof. emeritus, 1997—. Author: Abstract Methods in Partial Differential Equations, 1969, Transmutation and Operator Differential Equations, 1979, Transmutation, Scattering Theory and Special Functions, 1982, Transmutation Theory and Applications, 1985, Mathematical Physics, 1988, Topics in Soliton Theory, 1991, Quantum Theory, Deformation and Integrability, 2000; co-author: Singular and Degenerate Cachy Problems, 1976; assoc. editor Jour. Applicable Analysis, 1970—; contbr. over 170 articles to math. and physics jours. Served with U.S. Army, 1954-57. Mem. Am. Math. Soc., Am. Phys. Soc. Avocations: foreign languages, cello. Home: 1314 Brighton Dr Urbana IL 61801-6417 Office: Univ Ill Math Dept Urbana IL 61801

CARROLL, THOMAS JOHN, retired advertising executive; b. St. Paul, Aug. 15, 1929; s. William H. and Neva (Saller) C.; m. Eleanor Rose Schmid, Aug. 27, 1955; children: David G., Thomas John, Ann Catherine, Robert G., Paul William. BA, St. Mary's Coll., Winona, Minn., 1952; cert., Grad. Sch. Mgmt., UCLA, 1977. Pharm. salesman A.H. Robins, Davenport, Iowa, 1955-70; advt. salesman Modern Medicine mag., Chgo., 1970-72; advt. exec. D'Arcy, McManus & Massius, St. Paul, 1972-73; dir. mktg. communications AMA, Chgo., 1973-92; cons. Carroll Media Svcs., LaGrange Park, Ill., 1992—. Editor Synergy mag., 1975-92, The Voice Quar., 1996—. Dir. pub. rels. St. Francis Xavier Sch. Bd., La Grange, Ill., 1977-79, Organist St. Francis Xavier Ch., La Grange, 1964-91; bd. trustee La Grange Park Libr. Dist., 1994—, v.p.; adminstrv. assoc. St. Francis Xavier Ch., La Grange, 1996—. Mem. Phar. Advt. Coun., Midwest Healthcare Mktg. Assn. (bd. dirs.), Med. Mktg. Assn., Am. Guild Organists, Chgo. Area Theatre Orgn. Enthusiasts, La Grange Field Club, La Grange Tennis Assn. (past pres.), St. Francis Xavier Men's Club. Republican. Roman Catholic. Home and Office: 333 N Edgewood Ave La Grange Park IL 60526-5505

CARROLL, WILLIAM J. automotive executive; Pres. automotive systems group Dana Corp., Toledo. Office: Dana Corp 4500 Doxx St PO Box 1000 Toledo OH 43697-1000

CARROLL, WILLIAM KENNETH, law educator, psychologist, theologian; b. Oak Park, Ill., May 8, 1927; s. Ralph Thomas and Edith (Fay) C.; m. Frances Louise Forgue; children: Michele, Brian. BS in Edn., BA in Philosophy, Quincy Coll., 1950; MA, Duquesne U., 1964; STL, Catholic U., 1965; PhD, U. Strasbourg, France, 1968; JD, Northwestern U., 1972. Bar: Ill. 1972, U.S. Dist. Ct. (no. dist.) Ill 1972, U.S. Ct. Appeals (7th cir.) 1973; lic. clin. psychologist, Ill. Asst. editor Franciscan Press, Chgo., 1955-60; asst. prof. psychology and religion Carlow Coll., Pitts., 1962-65, Loyola U., Chgo., 1968-70; staff atty. Fed. Defender Program, 1972-75; prof. law John Marshall Law Sch., 1975—. Bd. dirs. Am. Inst. Adlerian Studies, 1982—; law reporter ABA Criminal Justice Mental Health Standards Project, 1981-83; cons. legal issues, Am. Psych. Assn.; standing com. on mental health law, Illinois. Author: (with Kosnik et al.) Human Sexuality, 1977; Eyewitness Testimony, Strategies and Tactics, 1984; contbg. author: By Reason of Insanity, 1983, Law for Illinois Psychologists, 1985. Bd. dirs. Chgo. Sch. Profl. Psychology, 1978-82; mem. bd. advisors Ill. Sch. Profl. Psychology, 1985. Recipient Am. Juris award, 1970; U. Chgo. scholar, 1968-69. Fellow Inst. Social and Behavioral Pathology (chmn. 1987—); mem. ABA, AAUP, APA (Outstanding Contbn. to Psychology award 1998, com. on legal issues 1995—), Ill. Psychol. Assn., Cath. Theol. Soc. Am. Avocation: pvt. pilot. Office: John Marshall Law Sch 315 S Plymouth Ct Chicago IL 60604-3968 E-mail: 7carroll@jmls.edu.

CARRUTHERS, PHILIP CHARLES, lawyer, public official; b. London, Dec. 8, 1953; s. J. Alex and Marie Carruthers. BA, U. Minn., 1975, JD, 1979. Bar: Minn. 1979, U.S. Dist. Ct. Minn. 1979, U.S. Ct. Appeals (8th cir.) 1979. Assoc. Nichols & Kruger, and predecessor firm, 1979-81; ptnr. Nichols, Kruger, Starks and Carruthers, Mpls., 1982-84, Luther, Ballenthin & Carruthers, Mpls., 1985-93; pvt. practice, 1994-2000; pros. atty. City of Deephaven, Minn., 1979-2000, City of Woodland, 1980-2000; mem. Minn.

Ho. of Reps., St. Paul, 1987-2000, majority leader, 1993-96, spkr. of house, 1997-98; dir. prosecution divsn. Ramsey County Attys. Office, 2000—. Co-author: The Drinking Driver in Minnesota: Criminal and Civil Issues, 1982; note and comment editor Minn. Law Rev., 1978-79. Mem. Met. Coun. of Twin Cities Area, St. Paul, 1983-87. Mem. Minn. Trial Lawyers Assn. (bd. govs. 1982-86), Minn. State Bar Assn., Ramsey County Bar Assn. Democratic Farmer-Labor Party. Roman Catholic. Home: 6018 Halifax Pl Brooklyn Center MN 55429-2440 Office: 315 Government Ctr W 50 W Kellogg Blvd Saint Paul MN 55102-1657 E-mail: Phil.Carruthers@Co.Ramsey.mn.us.

CARSON, GORDON BLOOM, retired engineering executive; b. High Bridge, N.J., Aug. 1, 1911; s. Whitfield R. and Emily (Bloom) C.; m. Beth Lacy, June 19, 1937 (dec. Mar. 1998); children: Richard Whitfield, Emily Elizabeth (Mrs. Lee A. Duffus), Alice Lacy (Mrs. William P. Allman), Jeanne Helen (Mrs. Michael J. Gable). BSMechE, Case Inst. Tech., 1931, D Engring., 1957; MS, Yale U., 1932, ME, 1938; LLD, Rio Grande Coll., 1973. With Western Electric Co., 1930; instr. mech. engring. Case Inst. Tech., 1932-37, asst. prof., 1937-40, asso. prof. indsl. engring. charge indsl. div., 1940-44; with Am. Shipbldg. Co., 1936; patent litigation, 1937; research engr., dir. research Cleve. Automatic Machine Co., 1939-44; asst. to gen. mgr. Selby Shoe Co., 1944, mgr. engring., 1945-49, sec. of corp., 1949-53; sec., dir. Pyrrole Products Co., 1948-53; dean engring. Ohio State U., Columbus, 1953-58, v.p. bus. and finance, treas., 1958-71; dir. Engring. Exptl. Sta., 1953-58, Accuray Corp., 1960-82, Cardinal Funds, Inc., 1962-98; exec. v.p. Albion (Mich.) Coll., 1971-76, exec. cons., 1976-77; asst. to chancellor, dir. fin. Northwood Inst., 1977-82; v.p. Mich. Molecular Inst., 1982-88; prin. Whitfield Robert Assocs., 1988—. Editor: The Production Handbook, 1958; cons. editor, 1972—; Author of tech. papers engring. subjects. Trustee White Cross Hosp. Assn., 1960-71; bd. dirs. Cardinal Funds, 1966-98; bd. d irs. Goodwill Industries, 1959-67, 1st v.p., 1963-64; bd. dirs. Orton Found., 1953-58; v.p. Ohio State U. Rsch. Found., 1958-71; v.p., chmn. adv. coun. Ctr. for Automation and Soc., U. Ga., 1969-71; Chmn. tool and die com. 5th Regional War Labor Bd., 1943-45; chmn. Ohio State adv. com. for sci., tech. and specialized personnel SSS, 1965-70; pres. Larkin Parking Condo Assn., Inc., 1992—. Fellow ASME, AAAS, Inst. Indsl. Engrs. (pres. 1957-58); mem. Columbus Soc. Fin. Analysts (pres. 1974-75), Fin. Analysts Fedn. (bd. dirs. 1964-65), C. of C. (bd. dirs., treas. 1952-53), Am. Soc. Engring. Edn., Assn. Univs. for Rsch. in Astronomy (bd. dirs. 1958-71), Midwestern Univs. Rsch. Assn. (bd. dirs. 1958-71), U.S. Naval Inst., Nat. Soc. Profl. Engrs. (life), Romophos, Sphinx, Rotary (Paul Harris fellow), Sigma Xi (fin. com. 1975-89, nat. treas. 1979-89), Masons (32 deg.), Tau Beta Pi, Zeta Psi, Phi Eta Sigma, Alpha Pi Mu, Omicron Delta Epsilon. Office: Whitfield Robert Assocs 5413 Gardenbrook Dr Midland MI 48642-3402 Fax: 989-631-0925.

CARSON, JULIA M. congresswoman; b. Louisville, July 8, 1938; 2 children. Ed., Ind. U., 1960-62, St. Mary of the Woods, 1976-78. Mem. Ind. Ho. of Reps., Indpls., 1972-76, Ind. Senate, 1976-90, U.S. Congress from 10th Ind. dist., 1997—. Mem. fin. svcs. com., 1997—, Vets. Affairs com., 1997—. V.p. Greater Indpls. Prog. Com.; nat. Dem. committeewoman; trustee YMCA; bd. didrs. Pub. Svc. Acad. Recipient Woman of Yr. Ind. award, 1974, Outstanding Leadership award AKA, Humanitarian award Christian Theol. Sem. Mem. NAACP, Urban League, Nat. Coun. Negro Women. Baptist. Office: 1339 Longworth HOB Washington DC 20515-0001*

CARSON, RICHARD MCKEE, chemical engineer; b. Dayton, Ohio, June 6, 1912; s. George E. and Gertrude (Barthelemy) C.; children: Joan Roderer, Linda McCartan. BS in Chem. Engring., U. Dayton (Ohio), 1934. Registered profl. engr., Ohio. Rsch. chemist Dayton Mall Iron Co., 1934-45; pres. Carson-Saeks, Inc., Dayton, 1945-80, Carson & Saeks Cons. Assocs. Inc., Dayton, 1980—; sec.-treas. Cecile Baird, Inc., Hillsboro, Ohio. Mem. AAAS, Am. Chem. Soc. Achievements include 6 patents for clinical test procedures, reagents, and closet accessories. Home: 2310 Kershner Rd Dayton OH 45414-1214

CARSON, ROGER, radio personality; 1 child Katie. Radio host Lake 93, The Lakd of The Ozarks, 1979—81, KMOX, St. Louis, 1981—82, WHB, Kansas City, 1982—89, local sta., 1989—93, KUDL, Westwood, Kans. Office: KUDL 4935 Belinder Westwood KS 66205

CARSON, SAMUEL GOODMAN, retired banker, company director; b. Glens Falls, N.Y., Oct. 6, 1913; s. Russell M.L. and Mary (Goodman) C.; m. Alice Williams, Oct. 14, 1939; children: Russell L., Frances Elizabeth (Mrs. Thomas E. Brady Jr.), Mary Goodman (Mrs. John A. Fedderke), Kathryn Williams (Mrs. Robert Richards), Samuel Goodman. B.A. magna cum laude, Dartmouth Coll., 1934. With Aetna Life Ins. Co., 1934-68; with Toledo Trust Co., 1967-84, exec. v.p., 1968, pres., 1969-84, chief exec. officer, 1970-84, chmn., 1976-84; chmn., dir. Toledo Trustcorp, Inc., 1976-84. Dir. Kiemle-Hankins Co., Plastic Technologies, Inc., Carson Assocs., Inc. Mem. Ottawa Hills Bd. Edn., 1954-64; pres. United Appeal Greater Toledo Area, 1969, campaign chmn., 1964; Bd. dirs., trustee Toledo chpt. ARC, 1950— , chmn., 1959-61; trustee Toledo Hosp., 1960— , v.p., 1963-65, pres., 1966-69; bd. dirs. Community Chest Greater Toledo, 1962-65, pres., 1965; pres. Boys' Club Toledo, 1961-64, trustee, 1957— ; trustee Toledo Mus. Art, 1967— , sec.-treas., 1969, v.p., 1973-78, pres., 1978-80. Recipient Service to Mankind award Sertoma Club Toledo, 1965, Man and Boy award Boys' Clubs Am., 1966, Pacemaker of Yr. award U. Toledo Coll. Bus. Adminstrn. Alumni Assn., 1969 Mem. Toledo Area C. of C. (trustee 1961-62, 73-76, pres. 1974-75), Phi Beta Kappa, Phi Gamma Delta. Republican. Conglist. Clubs: Rotarian, Toledo Country, Toledo. Lodge: Rotary. Office: 425 Madison Ave Toledo OH 43604-1229

CARTER, ADAM, radio personality; b. South St. Paul, Minn. BA Comms., St. Peter and Bustavus Adolphus Coll., 1998. News dir., morning show host Sta. KZAT-FM, Tama and Toledo, Ohio; morning anchor Stas. WAXX-FM and WAYY-AM, Eau Claire, Wis., 1999—2001; news anchor Sta. WCCO Radio, Mpls., 2001—. Recipient award, AP, Wis. Broadcasters Assn. Office: WCCO 625 2nd Ave S Minneapolis MN 55402*

CARTER, CRIS, professional football player; b. Middletown, Ohio, Nov. 25, 1965; Student, Ohio State U. With Phila. Eagles, 1987-89; wide received Minn. Vikings, 1990—. Selected to Pro Bowl, 1993, 95; named to The Sporting News NFL All-Pro team, 1994. Achievements include holding NFL single-season record for most pass receptions, 122, 1994. Office: Minn Vikings 9520 Viking Dr Eden Prairie MN 55344-3898

CARTER, JAMES H. state supreme court justice; b. Waverly, Iowa, Jan. 18, 1935; s. Harvey J. and Althea (Dominick) C.; m. Jeanne E. Carter, Aug. 1965; children: Carol, James. B.A., U. Iowa, 1956, J.D., 1960. Law clk. to judge U.S. Dist. Ct, 1960-62; assoc. Shuttleworth & Ingersoll, Cedar Rapids, Iowa, 1962-73; judge 6th Jud. Dist., 1973-76, Iowa Ct. Appeals, 1976-82; justice Iowa Supreme Ct., Des Moines, 1982—. Office: Iowa Supreme Ct State House Des Moines IA 50319-0001 E-mail: James.carter@jb.state.us.*

CARTER, MELINDA, municipal official; b. Springfield, Ohio; BA in English lit., Ohio U.; JD, Capital U. Assoc. Beatty and Roseboro, Columbus, Ohio; spl. counsel to Ohio Atty. Gen.; exec. dir. New Salem Cmty. Reinvestment Corp.; exec. asst. to the dir. Equal Bus. Opportunity Commn., City of Columbus, exec. dir., 1996—. Mem. New Salem Missionary Bapt. Ch. Mem. Ohio U. Alumni Assn., Nat. Coalition of 100 Black Women, Network of Black Women for Justice, Alpha Kappa Alpha. Office: Equal Bus Opportunity Commn City of Columbus 109 N Front St Fl 4 Columbus OH 43215-2806

CARTER, PAMELA LYNN, former state attorney general; b. South Haven, Mich., Aug. 20, 1949; d. Roscoe Hollis and Dorothy Elizabeth (Hadley) Fanning; m. Michael Anthony Carter, Aug. 26, 1971; children: Michael Anthony Jr., Marcya Alicia. BA cum laude, U. Detroit, 1971; MSW, U. Mich., 1973; JD, Ind. U., 1984. Bar: Ind. 1984, U.S. Dist. Ct. (no. dist.) Ind. 1984, U.S. Dist. Ct. (so. dist.) Ind. 1984. Rsch. analyst, treatment dir. U. Mich. Sch. Pub. Health and UAW, Detroit, 1973—75; exec. dir. Mental Health Ctr. for Women and Children, 1975—77; consumer litigation atty. UAW-Gen. Motors Legal Svcs., Indpls., 1983—87; securities atty. Sec. of State, 1987—89; Gov.'s exec. asst. for health and human svcs. Gov.'s Office, 1989—91, dep. chief of staff to Gov., 1991—92; with Baker & Daniels, 1992—93; atty. gen. State of Ind., Indpls., 1993—96; ptnr. Johnson & Smith, 1996—97; v.p., gen. counsel and sec. Cummins Engine Co., Inc., Columbus, Ind., 1998—. Author (numerous poems). Active Jr. League, Indpls., Dem. Precinct, Indpls., Cath. Social Svcs., Indpls. Named Breakthrough Woman of the Year, 1989; named one of Outstanding Young Woman of America, 1977; recipient Outstanding Svc. award, Ind. Perinatal Assn., 1991, Cmty. Svc. Coun. Ctrl. Ind., 1991, Non-profl. Healthcare award, Family Health Conf. Bd. Dirs., 1991, award for excellence, Women of the Rainbow, 1991. Mem.: Ind. Bar Assn., Nat. Bar Assn., Coalition of 100 Black Women. Avocations: gardening, hiking, travel, reading. Office: Cummins Engine Co Inc MC 60903 500 Jackson St Columbus IN 47201-6258

CARTER, PAULA J. state legislator; LLD, Lincoln U., 1999. Mem. Mo. Ho. of Reps from 61st dist., Jefferson City, 1986-2000, Mo. Senate from 5th dist., Jefferson City, 2000—. Vice chmn. Mo. State Dem. Party; pres. Mo. Legis. Blafk Caucus Found. Home: 5936 Summit Pl Saint Louis MO 63147-1119 Office: Mo Ho of Reps State Capitol Building Jefferson City MO 65101-1556

CARTER, ROY ERNEST, JR. journalist, educator; b. Ulysses, Kans., Apr. 7, 1922; s. Roy Ernest and Inez (Anderson) C.; m. Ruby Maxine Rice, Mar. 28, 1948; children: Phyllis Diane, Patricia Inez, Susan Dolores. BA, Ft. Hays State U., 1948; MA, U. Minn., 1951; PhD, Stanford U., 1954; Prof. h.c., U. Chile, 1982. Reporter, editor, editorial writer various newspapers, 1942-48, 51; high sch. tchr. Hutchinson, Kans., 1948-50; assoc. prof., chmn. dept. journalism Ohio Wesleyan U., 1951-52; acting assoc. prof. journalism Stanford U., 1952-54; research prof. journalism, mem. Inst. Research in Social Sci. of U. N.C., 1954-58; prof. journalism, sociology and internat. relations U. Minn., 1958-90, prof. emeritus, 1990—, prof. ind. and distance learning. Lectr., Quito, Ecuador, 1961, Chile, Argentina, Uruguay, 1991; vis. prof. U. Chile, 1962-63, 82, U. Concepción, Chile, 1964, 66-68, 91, U. Costa Rica, 1971, 84, U. Pernambuco, Brazil, 1972, U. P.R., 1978-79, 86, Cath. U. Uruguay, 1987, U. del Salvador, Buenos Aires, 1989, Fla. Internat. U., 1992-96, U. Md., 1996-98; cons. to mktg., pub. opinion rsch. firms, internat. orgns. Author: North Carolina Press-Medical Study, 1957, (with R.O. Nafziger, D.M. White et al.) Introduction to Mass Communication Research, 1963; Assoc. editor of: Journalism, Quarterly, 1958-63; Contbr. articles to sci. jours. Recipient Kellogg Found. grant Stanford, 1952-53, sr. Fulbright-Hays award Chile, 1962-63, sr. Fulbright-Hays award Costa Rica, 1971, sr. Fulbright award Argentina, 1989, Social Sci. Research Council grants, 1962, 68; Rotary fellow, Uruguay, 1987 Fellow Am. Sociol. Assn.; mem. Assn. Edn. Journalism, World Assn. Pub. Opinion Research, Sigma Delta Chi, Phi Kappa Phi. Episcopalian. Achievements include research in Costa Rica, 1975, 91, El Salvador and Chile, 1976, P.R., 1979, Uruguay, 1982-89, 93—, Colombia, 1993, Peru, 1994. Office: U of Minn Journalism Sch 206 Church St SE Minneapolis MN 55455-0488

CARTER, STEVE, state attorney general; b. Lafayette, Ind. BA in Econs., Harvard U., 1976; JD, MBA, Ind. U. Chief city-county atty. Indpls.-Marion County; atty. gen. State of Ind., 2001—. Office: Ind Govt Ctr S 5th Fl 402 W Washington St Indianapolis IN 46204*

CARTER, VALERIE, food products executive; d. John and Katherine Daniels. BA in Bus. Adminstrn., Lincoln U., 1978; Masters Degree, Cardinal Stritch Coll., 1982. Mgmt. trainee Firstar Bank (formerly First Wis. Nat. Bank), 1978; auditor MGIC Investment Corp., 1981; co-founder V&J Foods, 1984, CEO. Recipient Sacajawea award for creativity, 1997; named Entrepreneur of Yr., Ernst & Young and Merrill Lynch, 1994. Mem. Milw. World Festival Inc. (pres. bd.). Office: 6933 W Brown Deer Rd Milwaukee WI 53223-2103

CARTER, WILLIAM H. company executive; CFO Borden Inc., Columbus, Ohio. Office: Borden Inc 180 E Broad StFl 30 Columbus OH 43215

CARTIER, BRIAN EVANS, association executive; b. Providence, Apr. 12, 1950; s. Clarence Joseph and Mary Anna (Evans) C. BA, R.I. Coll., 1972; MEd, Springfield (Mass.) Coll., 1973. Exec. dir. Arthritis Found. Conn., Hartford, 1976-78, dep. exec. dir. N.Y. chpt. N.Y.C., 1979; exec. dir. Found. for Chiropractic Edn. and Rsch., Arlington, Va., 1979-90, Nat. Ct. Reporters Assn., 1990-98; CEO Nat. Assn. Coll. Stores, Oberlin, Ohio, 1998—. Mem. Am. Mgmt. Assn. (cert. assn. exec.), Am. Soc. Assn. Execs., Greater Washington Soc. Assn. Execs., U.S. C. of C. Republican. Roman Catholic. Office: NACS 500 E Lorain St Oberlin OH 44074-1238

CARTWRIGHT, BILL, professional basketball coach; b. Lodi, Calif. , July 30, 1957; m. Sheri Cartwright; children: Justin, Jason, James, Kristin. Student, U. San Francisco, MA in Orgnl. Devel. and Human Resources. Basketball player Chgo. Bulls, NBA World Championships; asst. coach Chgo. Bulls, 1996, head coach, 2001—. Named One time NBA All-Star, 1980, 3 time All Am. Player of Yr., WCC's 50 Greatest Student-Athletes of All-Time; named to NBA Ea. Conf. All-Star Team, 1980; recipient NBA All-Rookie Team honors, 3 time West Coast Conf. Player of Yr. . Achievements include Dons all-time leading scorer;helped the Bulls win 55 victories in each of his final five seasons in Chicago including the first back-to-back 60+ win seasons in Bulls history, 1990-92. Office: United Ctr 1901 W Madison St Chicago IL 60612*

CARTWRIGHT, CAROL ANN, university president; b. Sioux City, Iowa, June 19, 1941; d. Carl Anton and Kathryn Marie (Weishapple) Becker; m. G. Phillip Cartwright, June 11, 1966; children: Catherine E., Stephen R., Susan D. BS in Early Childhood Edn., U. Wis., Whitewater, 1962; MEd in Spl. Edn., U. Pitts., 1965, PhD in Spl. Edn., Ednl. Rsch., 1968. From instr. to assoc. prof. Coll. Edn. Pa. State U., University Park, 1968-72, from assoc. prof. to prof., 1972-79, dean acad. affairs, 1981-84, dean undergrad. program, vice provost, 1984-88; vice chancellor acad. affairs U. Calif., Davis, 1988-91, prof. human devel., 1988-91; pres. Kent (Ohio) State U., 1991—. Trustee Akron Reg. Devel. Bd., 1991—, Akron Gen. Med. Ctr., 1991—; bd. dirs. First Energy Corp. (formerly Ohio Edison), Akron, 1992—, Republic Engineered Steels, Inc., Massillon, Ohio, 1992—. Editorial bd. Topics in Early Childhood Special Education, 1982-88, Exceptional Education Quarterly, 1982-88. Pres., bd. dirs. Child Devel. Coun. of Center County, Title XX Day Care Contractor, 1977-80; bd. dirs. Center County United Way, State College, Pa., 1984-88, Urban League of Greater Cleve., 1997—; bd. mem. Davis (Calif.) Art Ctr., 1988-91, Davis Sci. Ctr., 1989-91; bd. dirs. Ohio divsn. Am. Cancer Soc., 1993-2000, nat. bd. dirs., 1993—. Mem. AAUW, Am. Coun. Edn., Am. Ednl. Rsch. Assn., Am. Assn. for Higher Edn., Nat. Assn. State Univs. and Land-Grant Colls., Coun. for Exceptional Children. Roman Catholic. Avocations: walking, reading, traveling. Home: 1703 Woodway Rd Kent OH 44240-5917 Office: Kent State U Office of the President PO Box 5190 Kent OH 44242-0001 E-mail: carol.cartwright@kent.edu.

CARUS, ANDRE WOLFGANG, educational publishing firm executive; b. LaSalle, Ill., June 24, 1953; s. Milton Blouke and Marianne (Sondermann) C. MA, U. St. Andrews (Scotland), 1977; PhD, U. Cambridge (Eng.), 1981; MBA, U. Chgo., 1990. Editor Ernst Klett Verlag, Stuttgart, Fed. Republic Germany, 1979-81; instr., asst. to dir. curriculum lab. sch. U. Bielefeld (Fed. Republic Germany), 1981-82; project dir. reading Open Ct. Pub. Co., Peru, Ill., 1983-85, dir. reading, 1985-86, v.p., gen. mgr., 1986-88, pres., 1988-90; pres., chief operating officer Carus Pub. Co., Chgo., 1990—, bd. dirs., chmn. Mem. Am. Ednl. Rsch. Assn., Nat. Coun. for the Social Studies, Nat. Coun. Tchrs. of Math., Assn. for Supervision and Curriculum Devel., Am. Econ. Assn., Univ. Club Chgo., Union League Club Chgo. Office: Open Court Pub Co 315 5th St Peru IL 61354-2859

CARUS, MILTON BLOUKE, publisher children's periodicals; b. Chgo., June 15, 1927; s. Edward H. and Dorothy (Blouke) C.; m. Marianne Sondermann, Mar. 3, 1951; children: Andre, Christine, Inga. BS in Elec. Engring, Calif. Inst. Tech., 1949; postgrad., Mexico City Coll., summer 1949, U. Freiburg, Germany, 1949-51, Sorbonne U., Paris, 1951. Devel. engr. Carus Chem. Co., Inc., LaSalle, Ill., 1951-55, asst. gen. mgr., 1955-61, exec. v.p., 1961-64, chmn., CEO, 1964—, Carus Corp., Peru, 1967—; editor Open Ct. Pub. Co., 1962-67, pub., pres., 1967-88, pub., 1988-89, sr. cons., 1989—; pub. Cricket mag., 1973-89; sr. cons. Cricket mag. group, 1990—. Treas. Bookbird Internat. Bd. Books Young People, 1994—. Chmn. Ill. Valley Cmty. Coll. Com., 1965-67; pres. Internat. Baccalaureat N.Am. Inc., 1977, chmn., 1980-89; mem. IBO Coun., Geneva, 1977-94; co-trustee Hegeler Inst., 1968-89; mem. employment and tng. com. U.S. Chamber, 1981-85; mem. Nat. Coun. on Ednl. Rsch. Nat. Inst. Edn., Dept. Edn., 1982-85, vice chmn., 1983-85; trustee Parliament of World's Religious, 1988—; mem. Ill. Gov.'s Task Force on Sch.-to-Work, 1994—. Mem. Ill. Valley Indsl. Assn. (pres. 1970—), Chem. Mfrs. Assn. (dir. 1977-80), Ill. Mfrs. Assn. (dir. 1972-77, 1988—, chmn. edn. com. 1988—), LaSalle County Hist. Soc. (dir. 1979-85), Phila Soc., Ill. State C. of C. (edn. com. 1973—). Office: Carus Corp Hdqrs 315 5th St Peru IL 61354-2859

CARUSO, FRED, plastics manufacturing company executive; Formerly CEO, pres. Comml. Fin. Svcs., Inc., Tulsa, Okla.; treas. Transilwrap Co., Inc., Franklin Park, Ill. Office: Transilwrap Co Inc 9201 Belmont Ave Franklin Park IL 60131

CARVER, MARTIN GREGORY, tire manufacturing company executive; b. Davenport, Iowa, May 10, 1948; s. Roy James and Lucille Avis (Young) C. B.A. in Math, U. Iowa, 1970; M.B.A., U. Ind., 1972. Asst. treas. Consol. Foods Corp. now Sara Lee, 1975-79; regional v.p. heavy duty parts, then vice chmn. Bandag, Inc., Muscatine, 1979-81; chief exec. officer Bandag, Inc. (retreaded tires mfrs.), 1982—, chmn. bd., 1981. Bd. dirs. Augustana Coll., 1986—; bd. visitors U. Iowa Sch. Bus. Named Chief Exec. Officer of Yr., rubber and plastics industry, Fin. World, 1986, Chief Exec. Officer of Decade, 1989. Mem. Nat. Assn. Mfrs. Office: Bandag Inc Bandag Ctr 2905 N Highway 61 Muscatine IA 52761-5886

CASAD, ROBERT CLAIR, legal educator; b. Council Grove, Kans., Dec. 8, 1929; s. Clair L. and Eula Imogene (Compton) C.; m. Sally Ann McKeighan, Aug. 20, 1955; children: Benjamin Nathan, Joseph Story, Robert Clair, Madeleine, Imogene. A.B., U. Kans., 1950, M.A., 1952; J.D. with honors, U. Mich., 1957; S.J.D., Harvard U., 1979. Bar: Kans. 1957, Minn. 1958, U.S. Dist. Ct. Kans. 1957; U.S. Ct. Appeals (10th cir.) 1985. Instr. law U. Mich., Ann Arbor, 1957-58; assoc. firm Streater & Murphy, Winona, Minn., 1958-59; asst. prof. law U. Kans., Lawrence, 1959-62, assoc. prof., 1962-64, prof., 1964-81, John H. and John M. Kane prof. law, 1981-97; John H. and John M. Kane prof. law emeritus, 1997. Vis. prof. UCLA, 1969—70, U. Ill., 1973—74, U. Calif., 1979—80, U. Colo., 1982, U. Vienna, 1986, U. Mich., 1986, U. Valladolid, 1988, Chuo U., 1992, U. Salamanca, 1995, Emory U., 2001—02. Author: Jurisdiction and Forum Selection, 1988, 2nd edit., 1999, Jurisdiction in Civil Actions, 1983, 2d edit., 1991, (with Richman) 3d edit., 1998, Expropriation Procedures in Central America and Panama, 1975, (with others) Kansas Appellate Practice, 1978, Civil Judgment Recognition and the Integration of Multiple State Associations, 1982, Res Judicata in a Nutshell, 1976; (with Fink and Simon) Civil Procedure: Cases and Materials, 2d edit., 1989, (with Gard) Kansas Code of Civil Procedure Annotated, 3rd edit., 1997, (with Clermont) Res Judicata: A Handbook on its Theory, Doctrine and Practice, 2001; contbr. numerous articles to legal jours. Mem. civil code adv. com. Kans. Jud. Coun. 1st lt. USAF, 1952-53. Recipient Coblentz prize Sch. Law, U. Mich., 1957, Rice prize U. Kans. Law Sch., 1976, 83, 84, 88, 89, medal Dana Fund for Internat. and Comparative Legal Studies, 1981, Balfour Jeffrey Rsch. prize U. Kans., 1984; Ford fellow, 1965-66, fellow in law Harvard U., 1965-66, OAS fellow, 1976, NEH fellow, summer 1978; grantee Dana Fund for Internat. and Comparative Legal Studies. Mem. Am. Law Inst., ABA, Kans. Bar Assn., Order of Coif. Democrat. Home: 1130 Emery Rd Lawrence KS 66044-2515 E-mail: casad@ku.edu., crobkan@cs.com.

CASALE, THOMAS BRUCE, medical educator; b. Chgo., Apr. 21, 1951; m. Jean M. Casale; 1 son, Jeffrey G. BS cum laude, U. Ill., 1973; MD, Chgo. Med. Sch., 1977. Diplomate Am. Bd. Internal Medicine, Am. Bd. Allergy and Immunology. Resident in internal medicine Baylor Coll. Medicine, Houston, 1977-80; med. staff fellow lab. clin. investigation NIAID, NIH, Bethesda, Md., 1980-84; from asst. prof. to prof. internal medicine U. Iowa, Iowa City, 1984-94, prof. internal medicine, 1994-96; dir. Nebr. Med. Rsch. Inst., 1996-99; adj. prof. pediatrics Coll. Medicine U. Nebr., 1996—; clin. prof. medicine Creighton U., Omaha, 1997-99, prof., asst. chair dept. medicine, dir. clin. rsch., 1999—, chief allergy/immunology, 2001—. Chief med. staff fellow lab. clin. investigation, NIAID, NIH, Bethesda, 1982-83; attending physician VA Med. Ctr., Iowa City, 1984-96, staff physician, 1986-96, clin. investigator, 1991-96; asst. dir. tchg. allergy/immunology divsn. dept. internal medicine U. Iowa, Iowa City, 1989-92, acting dir., 1992, dir., 1993-96, faculty inerdisciplinary immunology grad. degree program U. Iowa, 1993-96; bd. dirs. Am. Bd. Allergy and Immunology, Am. Acad. Allergy, Asthma and Immunology; reviewer over 15 profl. and sci. jours. Contbr. over 200 articles to profl. publs.; mem. editl. bd. Jour. Allergy Clin. Immunology, 1988-93, clin. asthma revs., 1996-99, Allergy & Clinical Immunology Internat., 1997—; editor Respiratory Digest, 1999—, Ann. Allergy, Asthma & Immunology, 1999—. Mem. asthma technical adv. group Am. Lung Assn., 1989-96. Lt. commdr. USPHS, 1980-83, USPHS Res., 1983—. Recipient Dr. John J. Sheinin Rsch. award Chgo. Med. Sch., 1977, Clin. Investigator VA, 1991-96, Am. Soc. Clin. Investigation, 1992; grantee Am. Acad. Allergy Immunology, 1981, Am. Coll. Allergy, 1984, Internat. Congress Allergology Clin. Immunology, 1985, 88, NIH, 1986-91, 87-90, 92-93, 93-94, VA Merit Rev., 1986-89, 89-92, 92-96, Environ. Health Sci. Core Ctr., 1990-96, Novartis Pharms., 1997—, Sepracor, Inc., 1997, others. Fellow ACP, Am. Acad. Allergy Immunology (cutaneous allergy com. 1985-90, postgrad. edn. com. 1988-91, chmn. 1989-90, program com. dermatologic diseases sect. 1988-93, sec. 1989-90, vice chmn. 1990-91, chmn. 1991-92, prof. edn. coun. 1998—, chair 1998—, sec. 1993-95, vice chair 1995—, chmn. bronchoalveolar lavage com. 1991-95, 98—, others), Am. Coll. Allergy Immunology (profl. allergy/immunology edn. com. 1989-94); mem. Am. Acad. Allergy Asthma Immunology (bd. dirs. 2001—), Am. Fedn. Clin. Rsch., Am. Thoracic Soc. (sec. allergy immunology and inflammation scientific assembly 1990-91, chair-elect 1991-93, chair program com. 1992-93, chair 1993-95, long-range planning and policy com. sci. assembly on allergy immunology and inflammation 1991-96, sci. conf. com. 1991-93, bd. dirs. 1993-95, chair asthma adv. com. 1995-99), Iowa Soc. Allergy Immunology (pres. 1987-89), Am. Assn. Immunologists, Midwest Sect. Am. Fedn. Clin. Rsch., Ctrl. Soc. Clin. Rsch., Am. Soc. Clin. Invest., Am. Lung Assn. (mem. rsch. coordinating com. 1996-99), European Respiratory Soc. Office: Creighton U Dept Medicine 601 N 30th St Ste 5850 Omaha NE 68131-2137 Fax: 402-280-4115. E-mail: tbcasale@creighton.edu.

CASCORBI, HELMUT FREIMUND, anesthesiologist, educator; b. Berlin, Germany, July 13, 1933; came to U.S., 1958; s. Gisbert and Isa (Ruckert) C.; m. Ann M. Morgan, Aug. 7, 1965; children: Alicia Maria, Kathryn Ann. M.D., U. Munich, W. Ger., 1957; Ph.D., U. Md., 1962. Prof., chmn. dept. anesthesiology Case Western Res. U., Cleve., 1980-2000. Mem. Am. Soc. Anesthesiologists, AMA, Assn. Univ. Anesthetists, Am. Soc. Pharmacology and Exptl. Therapeutics Home: 2844 Fairmount Blvd Cleveland OH 44118-4059 Office: Univ Hosps of Cleve 11100 Euclid Ave Cleveland OH 44106-1736 E-mail: helmut.cascorbi@uhms.com.

CASE, DONNI MARIE, investment company executive; b. Chgo., Feb. 20, 1948; d. Donald Milton and Felecia Virginia (Krantz) Schuette; m. Lawrence Lee Hewitt, Apr. 20, 1996. BA in Econs., U. Ill., 1970. Vice chmn., nat. dir. mktg. intelligence Fin. Rels. Bd., Inc., Chgo., 1972—. Bd. dirs. Inst. Bus. and Profl. Ethics Depaul U. Mem. Civil War Round Table Chgo. (trustee 1996—). Home: 2417 N Geneva Ter Chicago IL 60614-5914 Office: Fin Rels Bd Inc John Hancock Ctr 875 N Michigan Ave Chicago IL 60611-1803

CASE, ELDON DARREL, materials science educator; b. Logan, Kans., Aug. 23, 1949; s. Eldon George and Ila Marie (Lewis) C.; m. Linda Lee Lubken, Aug. 29, 1975 (div. Mar. 1993); 1 child, Carl Allen; m. Rebecca J. Ervin, 1996. BA in Physics and Math., U. Colo., 1971; PhD in Materials Sci., Iowa State U., 1980. Rsch. asst. dept. materials sci. Iowa State U., Ames, 1976-80; NRC postdoctoral assoc. Nat. Bur. Standards, Gaithersburg, Md., 1980-82; rsch. engr. in materials sci. and mining engring. U. Calif., Berkeley, 1982-85; asst. prof. metallurgy, mechanics and materials sci. Mich. State U., East Lansing, 1985-88, assoc. prof., 1988-99, prof., 1999—. Cons. Indsl. Tech. Inst., Ann Arbor, Mich., 1990, Westinghouse, West Mifflin, Pa., 1991-92; judge Nat. Am. Indian Sci. and Engring. Fair, 1993-2001; grand awards judge Internat. Sci. and Engring. Fair, 2000; mem. internat. sci. com. ACUN-3 Advanced Composites, Sydney, Australia, 2000-01. Contbr. more than 100 tech. articles to profl. jours. and conf. procs. including Jour. Materials Sci., Materials Sci. Engring., Applied Physics Letters. Speaker to sch. groups Okemos (Mich.) Pub. Schs., 1986-90; asst. with middle-sch. activities Episcopal Ch., East Lansing, 1988-92; judge Nat. Am. Indian Sci. and Engring. Fair, 1993-2001. Recipient Tchr.-Scholar award Mich. State U., 1989, Withrow Excellence in Tchg. award Engring. Coll. Mich. State U., 1993, 95, 98; Regents scholar U. Colo., 1967-71; NRC postdoctoral assoc., 1980-82; grantee NASA, 1987, NSF, 1987-90, Mich. State U., 1989. Mem. AAUP, ASM (chair advanced joining tech. com. 1999—, tech. programming bd. for joining critical tech. sector 1999—), Nat. Inst. Ceramic Engrs., The Metall. Soc. (sec. structural materials div. 1988-91, chair non-metall. com. 1988-91), Am. Ceramic Soc. (pres. Mich. sect. 1998—, officer nominating com. engring. ceramics divsn., internat. sci. adv. com. for ACMN-3 advanced composites symposium Sydney, Australia, 2000-01), Sigma Xi. Democrat. Achievements include first neutron scattering study from microcracks in a polycrystalline ceramic; statistical analysis of water drop impact damage cracks in infrared windows; microwave sintering and joining of ceramics and ceramic composites; adhesion studies of diamond thin-films on brittle substrates; thermal-shock and thermal fatigue studies on ceramics and ceramic composites, microwave sintering and joining of ceramics. Home: 4469 Fairlane Dr Okemos MI 48864-2407 Office: Materials Sci and Mechanics Sci Dept East Lansing MI 48824 E-mail: casee@egr.msu.edu.

CASE, KAREN ANN, lawyer; b. Milw., Apr. 7, 1944; d. Alfred F. and Hilda M. (Tomich) Case. BS, Marquette U., 1963, JD, 1966; LLM, NYU, 1973. Bar: Wis. 1966, U.S. Ct. Claims 1973, U.S. Tax Ct. 1973. Ptnr. Meldman, Case & Weine, Milw., 1973-85, Meldman, Case & Weine divsn. Mulcahy & Wherry, S.C., 1985-87; Sec. of Revenue State of Wis., 1987-88; ptnr. Case & Drinka, S.C., Milw., 1989-91, Case, Drinka & Diel, S.C., Milw., 1991-97, CoVac, 1997—. Lectr. U. Wis., Milw., 1974-78; guest lectr. Marquette U. Law Sch., 1975-78; dir. WBBC, 1998—. Contbr. articles to legal jours. Mem. gov.'s Commn. on Taliesin, 1988, gov.'s Econ. Adv. Commn., 1989-91, pres.'s coun. Alverno Coll., 1988-94, nat. coun., 1998-2000; bd. dirs. WBCC, 1998—. Fellow Wis. Bar Found. (dir. 1977-90, treas. 1980-90); mem. ABA, Milw. Assn. Women Lawyers (founding mem., bd. dirs. 1975-78, 81-82), Milw. Bar Assn. (bd. dirs. 1985-87, law office mgmt. chair 1992-93), State Bar Wis. (bd. govs. 1981-85, 87-90, dir. taxation sect. 1981-87, vice chmn. 1986-87, 90-91, chmn. 1991-92), Am. Acad. Matrimonial Lawyers (bd. dirs. 1988-90), Nat. Assn. Women Lawyers (Wis. del. 1982-83), Milw. Rose Soc. (pres. 1981, dir. 1981-83), Friends of Boerner Bot. Gardens (founding mem., pres. 1984-90), Profl. Dimensions Club (dir. 1985-87), Tempo Club (sec. 1984-85). Home: 2212 Harbour Ct Longboat Key FL 34228-4174 Office: 2212 Harbour Court Dr Longboat Key FL 34228-4174

CASEY, DONALD M. air transportation executive; Sr. v.p. mktg. TWA, exec. v.p. mktg., 1997—; prin. Deskey Luxon Carra. Office: TWA 1 City Ctr 515 N 6th St Saint Louis MO 63101-1842

CASEY, JOHN ALEXANDER, lawyer; b. Wisconsin Rapids, Wis., Apr. 7, 1945; s. Samuel Alexander and Ardean A. AB, Stanford U., 1967; JD, U. Mich., 1970. Ptnr. Quarles & Brady, Milw., 1970—. Office: Quarles & Brady 411 E Wisconsin Ave Ste 2550 Milwaukee WI 53202-4497 E-mail: jac@quarles.com.

CASEY, KENNETH LYMAN, neurologist; b. Ogden, Utah, Apr. 16, 1935; s. Kenneth Lafayette and Lyzena (Payne) C.; m. Jean Louise Madsen, June 21, 1958; children— Tena Jeanette, Kenneth Lyman, Teresa Louise. B.A., Whitman Coll., Walla Walla, Wash., 1957; M.D. with honors, U. Wash., Seattle, 1961. Diplomate: Am. Bd. Neurology and Psychiatry. Intern in medicine Cornell U. Med. Center-N.Y. Hosp., 1961-62; USPHS officer lab. neurophysiology NIMH, 1962-64; fellow in psychology McGill U., Montreal, Que., Can., 1964-66; mem. faculty U. Mich. Med. Sch., Ann Arbor, 1966—, prof. neurology and physiology, 1978—; resident in neurology U. Mich Hosp., 1971-74; chief neurology svc. VA Med. Center, Ann Arbor, 1979—. Sci. bd. dirs. Nat. Inst. Dental Rsch., 1984-88; sci. adv. com. Santa Fe Neurol. Inst., 1984—. Assoc. editor Clin. Jour. Pain, 1984—, Pain, 1991—; editor-in-chief Am. Pain Soc. Jour. Pain Forum, 1991-99; contbr. articles to profl. jours., chpts. to books. NIH Spl. fellow, 1964-66, grantee, 1966—; Bristol-Myers rsch. grantee, 1988-93. Fellow Am. Acad. Neurology; mem. Am. Physiol. Soc., Am. Acad. Neurology, Am. Neurol. Assn., Soc. Neurosci., Am. Pain Soc. (pres. 1984-85, F.W.L. Kerr Basic Sci. Rsch. award and lecture 1998), Wayne County Med. Soc. (Rhoades lectr. and medalist 2002), Internat. Assn. Study Pain, Phi Beta Kappa, Sigma Xi, Alpha Omega Alpha (J.J. Bonica disting. lectr. and awardee 1991). Unitarian. Home: 2775 Heatherway St Ann Arbor MI 48104-2852 Office: VA Med Ctr Neurology Svc 2215 Fuller Rd Ann Arbor MI 48105-2300 E-mail: kencasey@umich.edu.

CASEY, LYNN M. public relations executive; b. Bismark, N.D., June 18, 1955; BA, U. N.C., 1976; MA, U. Minn., 1979; MBA, Coll. St. Thomas. Comms. specialist Burlington Northern, 1979-80, asst. editor employee comms., 1980-81, asst. mgr. mktg. comms., 1981-82, mgr. mktg./comms., 1982-83; with Brum & Anderson, 1983-87; v.p. Padilla Speer, 1987-91; COO Padilla Speer Beardsley, 1991—. Mem. Pub. Rels. Soc. Am., Phi Beta Kappa. Office: Padilla Speer Beardsley 224 W Franklin Ave Minneapolis MN 55404-2394

CASILLAS, FRANK C. former state agency administrator; Assst. U.S. sec. labor Ronald Reagan, Washington; dir. financial institional dept. Financial Institutions Dept., Chgo., 1994—. Office: Financial Institutions Dept 100 W Randolph St Ste 15-700 Chicago IL 60601-3234

CASKEY, HAROLD LEROY, state legislator; b. Hume, Mo., Jan. 3, 1938; s. James Alfred and Edith Irnen (Anderson) C.; m. Kay Head, 1974; 1 child, Kyle James. AB, Ctrl. Mo. State U., 1960; JD, U. Mo., Columbia, 1963. Pros. atty. Bates County, 1967-72; city atty. Butler, Mo., 1973-76; pvt. practice; mem. from dist. 31 Mo. Senate, 1977—, chmn. ethics com., civil and criminal jurisprudence com., vice chmn. judiciary com. Asst. prof. NE Mo. State U., 1975-76. Mem. Mo. Bar Assn., Am. Judicature Soc., Fellowship Christian Politicians, Am. Criminal Justice Educators, Order Coif, Acacia, Phi Alpha Delta, Kappa Mu Epsilon, Alpha Phi Sigma. Democrat. Baptist. Office: Rm 320 State Capitol Building Jefferson City MO 65101-1556 also: PO Box 45 Butler MO 64730-0045

CASON, MARILYNN JEAN, technological institute official, lawyer; b. Denver, May 18, 1943; d. Eugene Martin and Evelyn Lucille (Clark) C.; married. BA in Polit. Sci., Stanford U., 1965; JD, U. Mich., 1969; MBA, Roosevelt U., 1977. Bar: Colo. 1969, Ill. 1973. Assoc. Dawson, Nagel, Sherman & Howard, Denver, 1969-73; atty. Kraft, Inc., Glenview, Ill., 1973-75; corp. counsel Johnson Products Co., Inc., Chgo., 1975-86, v.p., 1977-86, mng. dir. Lagos, Nigeria, 1980-83, v.p. internat. Chgo., 1986-88; v.p., gen. counsel DeVry, Inc., 1989-96; sr. v.p. adminstrn. gen. counsel, 1996—. Trustee Arthritis Found., Atlanta, 1993—96, Chgo. Symphony Orch., 1997—; bd. dirs. Ill. chpt. Arthritis Found., Chgo., 1979—, chmn., 1991—93; bd. dirs. Internat. House, 1986—92, Interfaith House, Chgo., 1996—, Ill. Humanities Coun., Chgo., 1987—96, chmn., 1993—96. Mem. ABA, Nat. Bar Assn., Cook County Bar Assn. (pres. community law project 1986-88). Club: Stanford (Chgo.) (pres. 1985-87). Home: 3108 Colfax St Evanston IL 60201-1842 Office: DeVry Inc 1 Tower Ln Ste 1000 Oakbrook Terrace IL 60181-4663 E-mail: mcason@devry.com.

CASPAR, JOHN M. manufacturing executive; BS, Drexel Inst. of Tech.; MBA, Okla. State U. Exec. v.p. internat., CFO Mitek, Inc., St. Louis, 1987-94; v.p., CFO Petrolite Corp.; fin. cons.; sr. v.p. fin., CFO DT Industries, Inc., Springfield, Mo., 2001—. Office: DT Industries Inc 907 W 5th St Dayton OH 45407-3306

CASPER, BARRY MICHAEL, physics educator; b. Knoxville, Tenn., Jan. 21, 1939; s. Barry and Florence (Becker) C.; m. Nancy Carolyn Peterson, Aug. 25, 1979; children: Daniel Casper, Benjamin Casper, Michael Casper, Aaron Syverson, Jay Syverson, Kaarin Madigan. B.A., Swarthmore Coll., 1960; Ph.D. in Physics, Cornell U., 1966. From asst. prof. to prof. physics Carleton Coll., Northfield, Minn., 1966—; rsch. fellow Stanford U., Calif., 1973-74, Harvard U., Cambridge, Mass., 1975-76, U. Minn., Mpls., 1976-77, MIT, Cambridge, Mass., 1980-81, U. Calif., San Diego, 1992-93. Policy advisor to U.S. Sen. Paul Wellstone, 1991. Co-author: Revolutions in Physics, 1972, Powerline: First Battle of America's Energy War, 1981; author: Lost in Washington: Finding the Way Back to Democracy in America, 2000. Dir. Nuclear War Graphics Project, Northfield, 1981-89, Minn. Nuclear Weapons Freeze Campaign, 1983-84 Recipient Pub. Citizen award Minn. Pub. Interest Research Group, 1984 Mem. Am. Phys. Soc. (nat. council 1980-83; Forum on Physics and Soc. prize 1984), Fedn. Am. Scientists (nat. council 1970-74, 80-84, 91-95). Home: 100 Nevada St Northfield MN 55057-2341 Office: Carleton College Dept Physics Northfield MN 55057 E-mail: mcasper@carleton.edu.

CASPER, JOHN M. financial executive; Exec. v.p. internat., CFO Mitek, Inc., St. Louis, 1987-94; v.p., CFO Petrolite Corp., 1994-97; ind. fin. cons., 1997-2001; sr. v.p. fin., CFO DT Industries, Springfield, Mo., 2001—. Office: DT Industries 1949 E Sunshine Ste Z-300 Springfield MO 65804

CASPER, RICHARD HENRY, lawyer; b. Chgo., Nov. 4, 1950; s. Edson Lee and Dorothy Ellen (Klemp) C.; m. Betty Gene Ward, Aug. 26, 1972; children: Terrance, Laura, Russell, Jeremy. AB, Bowdoin Coll., 1972; JD, Northwestern U., 1975. Bar: Wis. 1975, U.S. Dist. Ct. (ea. dist.) Wis. 1975. Assoc. Foley & Lardner, Milw., 1975-82, ptnr., 1982—. James Bowdoin scholar Bowdoin Coll, 1972. Mem. Wis. Bar Assn., Milw. Bar Assn., Order of the Coif. Office: Foley & Lardner Firstar 777 E Wisconsin Ave Milwaukee WI 53202-5367 E-mail: rcasper@foleylaw.com.

CASS, EDWARD ROBERTS (PETER CASS), hotel and travel marketing professional; b. La Porte, Ind., Nov. 21, 1941; s. Edward Smith and Shirley (Mazur) C.; m. Marilyn Brooks, Apr. 1, 1967; children: Edward Brooks Cass, Alexander Brooks Cass. AB in History, Hamilton Coll., 1964; MBA in Mktg./Fin., Syracuse U., 1970. Dir. mktg., gen. sales mgr. Mohawk Airlines Inc., N.Y.C., 1964-72; sr. v.p., gen. mgr. The Travel Industry Assn. Am., Washington, 1972-78; gen. mgr., COO Tri-Met, Oreg. and Wash., 1978-81; v.p. unregulated activities Pacific Telecom, subsidiary of Pacificorp, Vancouver, Wash., 1982-83; pres., founder Transax Data Corp., Falls Church, Va., 1983-85; pres., CEO Transax Data divsn. of Jour. of Commerce Knight-Ridder Inc., Bridgewater, N.J., 1985-94, Preferred Hotels & Resorts Worldwide, Chgo., 1994—. Home: 101 Woodland Dr Oak Brook IL 60523-1416 Office: IndeCorp Corp 311 S Wacker Dr Ste 1900 Chicago IL 60606-6676

CASSELL, SAMUEL JAMES, basketball player; b. Balt., Nov. 18, 1969; Grad., Dunbar H.S., Balt., San Jacinto Coll., 1993. Basketball player Houston Rockets, 1994-96, Pheonix Suns, 1996, Dallas Mavericks, 1996-97, N.J. Nets, East Rutherford, 1997-99, Milw. Bucks, Houston; co-owner shoe store. Mem. NBA championship team, 1994,95; won Fleer Shoot-Around during the 1996 All-Star Weekend, San Antonio, Tex; named NBA Player of Week from Apr. 6-12, 1998. Office: Milw Bucks 1001 N 4th St Milwaukee WI 53203-1314*

CASSIDY, EUGENE PATRICK, pathologist; b. N.Y.C., July 21, 1940; s. Eugene Zachary and Anita Hilda (Corsi) C.; m. Hollis Elizabeth Ward, Sept. 25, 1965; 1 child, Meredith. BA, Williams Coll., 1962; MD, Yale U., 1966. Diplomate Am. Bd. Pathology. Intern Yale-New Haven Hosp., Conn., 1966-67; resident then fellow in pathology and lab. medicine Yale U. Med. Ctr., 1967-70; dir. pathology Appalachian Lab. for Occupational Respitory Disease, Morgantown, Wis., 1970-72; pathologist Clarkson Hosp., Omaha, 1972-78, Scripps Hosp., Encinitas, Calif., 1978-84; dir. pathology Marshalltown (Iowa) Med. and Surgical Ctr., 1984—. Asst. prof. W.Va. U. Sch. Medicine, Morgantown, 1970-72, U. Nebr. Sch. Medicine, Omaha, 1974-78. Contbr. articles to profl. jours. Served with USPHS, 1970-72. Fellow Internat. Acad. Pathology, Coll. Am. Pathologists, Am. Soc. Clin. Pathologists; mem. AMA, Am. Assn. Blood Banks. Republican. Avocations: music, architecture. Home: Woodfield Rd Marshalltown IA 50158-3851 Office: Marshalltown Med & Surg Ctr 3 S Fouth Ave Marshalltown IA 50158-2924

CASSIDY, JAMES MARK, construction company executive; b. Evanston, Ill., June 22, 1942; s. James Michael and Mary Ellen (Munroe) C.; m. Bonnie Marie Bercker, Aug. 1, 1964 (dec. Dec. 1981); children: Micaela Marie, Elizabeth Ann, Daniel James; m. Patricia Margaret Mary Murphy, Sept. 15, 1984. BA, St. Mary's Coll., 1963. Estimator Cassidy Bros., Inc., Rosemont, Ill., 1963-65, project mgr., 1965-67, v.p., 1967-71, exec. v.p., 1971-77, pres., 1978—. Trustee Plasterer's Health & Welfare Trust, 1971-92; chmn. labor liaison com. Laborers Internat. Union N.Am. and Assn. Wall and Ceiling Industries, 1982-85, chmn. labor-mgmt. group, 1985-88; chmn. Chicagoland Assn. Wall and Ceiling Contractors' Carpenters Union Negotiating Team, 1983—; trustee, vice chmn. laborers dist. coun. Chgo. and Vicinity Laborers-Employers Cooperation and Edn. Trust Fund, 1999—. Area fund leader Constrn. Industry Salute to Boy Scouts Am., 1975; mem. president's coun. St. Mary's Coll. With U.S. Army, 1963-64, N.G., 1964-69. Mem. Chgo. Plastering Inst., Builder Uppers Club (pres. 1973-74), Chicagoland Assn. Wall and Ceiling Contractors (pres. 1976-79), Great Lakes Coun., Internat. Assn. Wall and Ceiling Contractors (chmn. 1977), Constrn. Employers Assn. Chgo. (bd. dirs. 1976—, pres.-elect 1989-90, pres. 1991-93, chmn. com. labor-mgmt. rels. 1983-93), Chicagoland Safety Coun. (bd. dirs. 1988-92), Joint Conf. Bd. Cook County (chmn. 1996-97, 98-99), Assn. Wall and Ceiling Industries Internat. (bd. dirs. 1978-81, 88-89, fin. v.p. 1990, 2d v.p. 1991, pres.-elect 1992, pres. 1993), Park Ridge County Club (Ill.) (bd. dirs. 1994-97), Eagle Creek Country Club (Naples, Fla.).

CASSIDY, JOHN HAROLD, lawyer; b. St. Louis, June 18, 1925; s. John Harold and Jennie (Phillips) C.; m. Marjorie Blair, Nov. 26, 1947; children: Patricia, John, Brian. AB, Washington U., 1949, JD, 1951. Bar: Mo. 1951, U.S. Dist. Ct. (ea. dist.) Mo. 1951, U.S. Ct. Appeals (8th crct.) 1951, U.S. Supreme Ct. 1955. Atty. U.S. Govt., St. Louis, 1951-56; pvt. practice, 1956-59; atty. Crown Zellerbach Corp., San Francisco, 1959-61, Ralston Purina Co., St. Louis, 1961-89, v.p., 1975-85, v.p., sec., sr. counsel, 1985-89. Served with U.S. Mcht. Marine, 1943-45. Mem. ABA, Mo. Bar Assn., St. Louis Bar Assn., Am. Soc. Corp. Secs. Republican.

CASSILL, HERBERT CARROLL, artist; b. Percival, Iowa, Dec. 24, 1928; s. Howard Earl and Mary Elizabeth (Glosser) C.; m. Jean Kuniko Kubota, Aug. 23, 1951; children: Sarah Eden, J. Aaron. Student, Purdue U., 1944-45; B.F.A., State U. Iowa, 1948, M.F.A., 1950. Instr. printmaking State U. Iowa, Iowa City, 1953-57; prof., head dept. printmaking Cleve. Inst. Art, 1957-91, prof. emeritus, 1991—. One man shows include Oakland (Calif.) Art Mus., Ohio State U., Columbus, Cleve. Inst. Art, U. Wis., William Busta Gallery, 1990, 93, 96, 2001; group shows include Library of Congress, Washington, Bklyn. Art Mus., Bradford Internat. Invitational, 1984; represented in permanent collections, Mus. Modern Art, N.Y.C., Cleve. Mus. Art, Oakland Art Mus., San Francisco Art Mus., and others. Tiffany fellow printmaking, 1953 Mem. Coll. Art Assn. Home: 3084 Coleridge Rd Cleveland OH 44118-3556 Office: 11141 East Blvd Cleveland OH 44106-1710

CASSINELLI, JOSEPH PATRICK, astronomy educator; b. Cin., Aug. 23, 1940; s. Herbert John and Louise (Schlottman) C.; m. Mary LeFever; children: Joseph Michael, Carolyn Marie, Mary Kathleen. BS in Physics, Xavier U., 1962; MS in Physics, U. Ariz., 1965; PhD in Astronomy, U. Wash., 1970. Research asst. Kitt Peak Nat. Obs., Tucson, 1963-65; research engr. Boeing Co., Seattle, 1965-66; postdoctoral research assoc. Joint Inst. for Lab. Astrophysics, Boulder, Colo., 1970-72; postdoctoral fellow U. Wis., Madison, 1972-73, asst. prof., 1973-77, assoc. prof., 1977-81, prof., 1981—, chmn. astronomy dept., 1986-89. Vis. scientist Space Astronomy Lab., Utrecht, the Netherlands, 1975-76, Space Telescope Sci. Inst., 1991, High Altitude Obs., 1998; Donders chair U. Utrecht, 1985; sr. vis. fellow dept. physics and astronomy U. Glasgow, Scotland, 1998. Co-author: Introduction to Stellar Winds, 1999. Langley Abbot research fellow Harvard Smithsonian Ctr. for Astrophysics, 1981; Fulbright research fellow Sonnenborgh Obs., 1986. Mem. Am. Astron. Soc., Internat. Astron. Union. Roman Catholic. Home: 1520 Chandler St Madison WI 53711-2210 Office: U Wis Astronomy Dept 475 N Charter St Madison WI 53706-1582 E-mail: cassinelli@astro.wisc.edu.

CASTELE, THEODORE JOHN, radiologist; b. New Castle, Pa., Feb. 1, 1928; s. Theodore Robert and Anne Mercedes (McNavish) C.; m. Jean Marie Willse, Oct. 20, 1951; children: Robert, Ann Marie, Richard, Mary Kathryn, Thomas, Daniel, John. BS, Case Western Res. U., 1951, MD, 1957. Diplomate Am. Bd. Radiology, 1962. Intern then resident U. Hosps. Cleve., 1957-61, fellow, 1961-62; dir. of radiology Luth. Med. Ctr., Cleve., 1968-75, 77-89, chief of staff, 1975-81; pres. Med. Ctr. Radiologists, Inc., Cleve., 1978-95; v.p. med. and copr. devel. Health Cleve. Inc., 1989-91; chmn. Lakeshore Radiology Inc., Cleve., 1991-96, emeritus chmn., 1996—. Med. editor sta. WEWS-TV-ABC, Cleve., 1975-99; chmn. bd. Med. Cons. Imaging Co., Cleve., 1981-97; asst. clin. prof. radiology Case Western Res. U., chmn. dean's tech. coun. Sch. Medicine, 1996—, chmn. vis. com. Cleve. Health Scis. Libr., chmn. campaign for future of acad. medicine, 1998—. Exec. editor Prime mag., 2000—. Chmn. Southwestern dist. Greater Cleve. coun. Boy Scouts Am., 1969, 73; mem. bd. med. cons. Cleve. Police Dept., pres., 1988-90; trustee Comty. Dialysis Ctr., chmn. 1997-99, chmn. emeritus, 2000—; active Luth. Med. Ctr. Found., chmn. bd. trustees, 1969-75, pres., 1988-90; trustee Case Western Res. U., Blue Cross/Blue Shield Ohio, Greater Cleve. Hosp. Assn., Fairview Health, Luth. Med. Ctr., 1975-80, Fairview Hosp. Found.; bd. trustees Fairview Luth. Hosp. Found., 1999—, No. Ohio Lung Assn.; chmn. Health Mus. Cleve., 1996—, Humility of Mary Healthcare Sys., 1995-98; dir. Coun. Pub. Reps. for NIH, 1999-2001. With USN, 1946-47. Recipient Order of Merit award Boy Scouts Am., 1971, Silver Beaver award, 1972, Nat. Disting. Eagle Scout award, 1984, Frances Payne Bolton Sch. of Nursing Disting. Svc. award, 1990, Outstanding Philanthropist award Nat. Soc. of Fundraising Execs., 1991, Alumnus of the Yr. award Dept. Radiology of Case Western Res. U., 1996, LMC Found. Women's Bd. award, 1996, Luth. Hosp. award Fairview Health Sys. Bd., 1996, Midwest Nursing Rsch. Soc. Media award, 1998, Lamplighter Humanitarian award 2001; named Knight of the Equestrian, Order of the Holy Sepulchre of Jerusalem, 1993—; recipient Magis award St. Ignatius H.S.; named to Med. Hall of Fame, Case Western Res. U., Cleve. Mag., 1999, No. Ohio Italian-Am. Found., 1999. Fellow Am. Coll. Radiology; mem. AMA (Physician Spkr. Gold award 1978, 80, Silver 1979, Bronze 1978, Benjamin Rush award 1989, Golden Achievement award Golden Age Ctrs., 1996, chmn. Ohio del. 1987-96), Ohio State Med. Assn. (5th dist. councilor 1977-79, Spl. award 1979, Disting. Svc. award 1997), Cleve. Radiol. Soc. (pres. 1969-70), Cleve. Med. Libr. Assn. (pres. 1996, 97-98), Case Western Res. U. Med. Alumni Assn. (pres. 1971-72, 91-92, Disting. Svc. award 1987, Spl. Trustees award 1997, Univ. medal 1998), Cleve. Acad. Medicine (pres. 1974-75, Disting. Mem. award 1990, Disting. Svc. award 1984, Spl. Honor award and portrait 1998), Ohio State Radiol. Soc. (Silver award 1990). Home: 18869 Canyon Rd Cleveland OH 44126-1703 Office: Case Western Reserve University School of Medicine Cleveland OH 44106

CASTELLINA, DANIEL J. financial executive; Degree in acctg., U. Notre Dame; MBA, Xavier U. CPA, Ohio. With Deloitte & Touche; asst. treas. E.W. Scripps Co., Cin., 1971-75, treas.-sec., 1975-79, v.p., contr., 1979-85, sr. v.p. fin. and adminstrn., 1986—. Trustee Greater Cin. for Econ. Edn., Gradison Growth Trust. Officer U.S. Army, 1962-64. Mem. AICPA, Fin. Execs. Inst., Internat. Newspaper Fin. Execs., Ohio Soc. CPAs. Office: 312 Walnut St Cincinnati OH 48202

CASTELLINO, FRANCIS JOSEPH, university dean; b. Pittston, Pa., Mar. 7, 1943; s. Joseph Samuel and Evelyn Bonita C.; m. Mary Margaret Fabiny, June 5, 1965; children— Kimberly Ann, Michael Joseph, Anthony Francis. BS, U. Scranton, 1964; MS, U. Iowa, 1966, PhD in Biochemistry, 1968; LLD, U. Scranton, 1983; DSc (hon.), U. Waterloo, Ont., Can., 1994. Postdoctoral fellow Duke U., Durham, N.C., 1968-70; mem. faculty dept. chemistry & biochemistry U. Notre Dame, Ind., 1970—, prof., 1977—; dean U. Notre Dame (Coll. Sci.), 1979—2002. Contbr. articles to profl.

jours. NIH fellow, 395201968-70 Fellow N.Y. Acad. Scis., AAAS; mem. Am. Heart Assn., Am. Chem. Soc., Am. Soc. Biol. Chemistry. Roman Catholic. Office: Univ Notre Damei Dept Chemistry & Biochemistry 256 Nieuwland Sci Hall Notre Dame IN 46556-5670

CASTILLO, RUBEN, judge; b. 1954; BA, Loyola U., 1976; JD, Northwestern U., 1979. Pvt. practice, Chgo., 1979-84, Kirkland & Ellis, 1991-93; dist. judge U.S. Dist. Ct. (no. dist.) Ill., 1994—. Adj. prof. Northwestern U., 1988—. Mem. ABA, Latin Am. Bar Assn., Chgo. Bar Found., Chgo. Coun. of Lawyers (v.p. 1991-93). Office: U S Courthouse 2378 Dirksen Bldg 219 S Dearborn St Chicago IL 60604-1702

CASTLE, HOWARD BLAINE, retired religious organization administrator; b. Toledo, July 15, 1935; s. Russell Wesley and Letha Belle (Hobbs) C.; m. Patricia Ann Haverty, Aug. 12, 1957; 1 child Kevin Blaine. AB, Marion Coll., 1958; postgrad., Valparaiso U., 1960. Pastor The Wesleyan Ch., Valparaiso, Ind., 1958-60, Toronto, Ohio, 1963-69; assoc. pastor Northridge Wesleyan Ch., Dayton, 1960-63; exec. dir. gen. dept. youth Wesleyan Ch. Hdqrs., Marion, Ind., 1968-72, dir. field ministries gen. dept. Sunday schs., 1972-74, exec. dir. curriculum, 1980-81; mng. editor WIN Mag., 1969-72; asst. gen. sec. Gen. Dept. of Local Ch. Edn., 1974-80; gen. dir. estate planning Wesleyan Ch. Internat Ctr., Indpls., 1982—2002, ret., 2002. Editor Ohio dist. The Wesleyan Ch., Columbus, 1961-69; gen. conf. del. The Wesleyan Ch., Anderson, Ind., 1968, Greensboro, N.C., 2000. Writer: Curriculum-Religious Adult Student/Teacher, 1982—, Light from the Word, 1982—. Mem. Christian Holiness Partnership, Christian Stewardship Assn., Christian Mgmt. Assn. Avocations: music, reading. E-mail: castleh@wesleyan.org.

CASTON, J(ESSE) DOUGLAS, medical educator; b. Ellenboro, N.C., June 16, 1932; s. Lemuel Joseph and Myrtice Elizabeth (Vassey) C.; m. Marry Ann Keeter, June 1, 1958; children: John Andrew, Elizabeth Anne, Mary Susan. A.B., Lenoir Rhyne Coll., 1954; M.A., U. N.C., 1958; Ph.D., Brown U., 1961. Fellow Carnegie Instn., Washington, Balt., 1961-62; asst. prof. anatomy Case Western Res. U., Cleve., 1962-71, assoc. prof., 1971-76, prof., 1976-98, co-dir. Devel. Biology Ctr., 1971-77, prof. emeritus, 1999—. Cons. Diamond Shamrock Corp., Cleve., 1975-77; coordinator Core Acad. Program, Sch. Medicine, 1985-94. Patentee folate assay, methotrexate assay; contbr. numerous articles to sci. jours., 1962—. Served with AUS, 1954-56. Fellow H.W. Wilson, 1956; grantee USPHS, 1963— , Cancer Soc., 1963— Mem. Am. Chem. Soc., AAAS, Am. Soc. Zoologists and Developmental Biologists, Biophys. Soc., Soc. Cell Biology, Am. Assn. Anatomists Episcopalian.

CASTORINO, SUE, communications executive; b. Columbus, Ohio, May 5, 1953; m. Randy Minkoff, Oct. 23, 1983. BS in Speech, Northwestern U., Evanston, Ill., 1975. Grad. fellow Ohio Gov.'s Sch., Columbus, 1975; producer, community affairs Sta. WBBM-TV, Chgo., 1975; news anchor, reporter Sta. WBBM, 1981-86; news reporter Sta. WHTH-AM/FM, Newark, 1975; news anchor, reporter Sta. WERE, Cleve., 1975-78, Sta. WWWE, Cleve., 1978-81; founder, pres. Sue Castorino: The Speaking Specialists, Chgo., 1986—. Leader media and presentation skills seminars; pvt. voice coach; active internat. exec. comm. tng. in media, crisis and issue mgmt.; lectr. in field. Author: North Shore Mag., 1987—92. Recipient Golden Gavel award, Chgo. Soc. Assn. Execs., 1991, various news reporting awards, AP. UPI, Chgo., 1981—86. Mem.: Sigma Delta Chi. Avocation: Avocations: sports, film, accomplished pianist. Office: The Speaking Specialists Ste 2602 435 N Michigan Ave Fl 2602 Chicago IL 60611-4001

CASTRO, JAN GARDEN, writer, arts consultant, educator; b. St. Louis, June 8, 1945; d. Harold and Estelle (Fischer) Garden; 1 child, Jomo Jemal. Student, Cornell U., 1963-65; BA, U. Wis., 1967; pub. cert., Radcliffe Coll., 1967; MA in Tchg., Washington U., St. Louis, 1974, MA, 1994. Life cert. tchr. secondary English, speech, drama and social studies, Mo. Tchr., writer, St. Louis, 1970—; dir. Big River Assn., 1975-85; adj. prof. humanities Lindenwood Coll., 1980—. Co-founder, dir. Duff's Poetry Series, St. Louis, 1975-81; founder, dir. River Styx P.M. Series, St. Louis, 1981-83; arts cons. Harris-Stowe State Coll., 1986-87; vis. scholar Am. Acad. in Rome, summer 2000. Contbg. author: rev. books San Francisco Rev. Books, 1982—85, Contbg. author: rev. books Am. Book Rev., 1990—93, Contbg. author: rev. books Mo. Rev., 1991, Contbg. author: rev. books New Letters, 1993, Contbg. author: rev. books, 1996, Contbg. author: rev. books Tampa Rev., 1994—2000, Contbg. author: rev. books The Nation, Am. Poetry Rev., Sculpture Mag., 1997—; author: (novels) Mandala of the Five Senses, 1975, The Art and Live of Georgia O'Keeffe, 1985, 1995, Memories and Memoirs...Contemporary Missouri Authors, 2000, (poetry) The Last Frontier, 2001—, Sonia DeLaunay: la moderne, 2002—; editor: (jours.) River Styx mag., 1975—86; co-editor: (novels) Margaret Atwood: Vision and Forms, 1988; co-prodr.(TV host, co-prodr.): (shows) The Writers Cir., Double Helix, 1987—89; contbg. editor: (jours.) Sculpture Mag. Seeking St. Louis, Voices from a River City, 1670—2000. Mem. University City Arts and Letters Commn., Mo., 1983-84. NEH fellow UCLA, 1988, Johns Hopkins U., 1990, Camargo Found. fellow (Cassis, France), 1996; recipient Arts and Letters award St. Louis Mag., 1985, Editor's award and editor during G.E. Younger Writers award to River Styx Mag., Coord. Coun. for Lit. Mags., 1986, Arts award Mandrake Soc. Charity Ball, 1988, Leadership award YWCA St. Louis, 1988. Mem. MLA, CAA, PEN Am. Ctr., Nat. Coalition Ind. Scholars, Margaret Atwood Soc. (founder). Home: 7420 Cornell Ave Saint Louis MO 63130-2914 Office: LCIE Coll Lindenwood U Saint Charles MO 63301 E-mail: jan_g_castro@mail.com.

CATALANO, GERALD, accountant; b. Chgo., Jan. 17, 1949; s. Frank and Virginia (Kreiman) C.; m. Mary L. Billings, July 4, 1970; children: James, Maria, Gina. BSBA, Roosevelt U., 1971. CPA, Ill. Jr. acct. Drebin, Lindquist and Gervasio, Chgo., 1971, Leaf, Dahl and Co., Ltd., Chgo., 1971-77, prin., 1978-80, ptnr., 1980-82; prin. Gerald Catalano, CPA, 1982-83; ptnr. Barbakoff, Catalano & Assocs., 1983-87; pres. Barbakoff, Catalano & Caboor Ltd., 1993—. V.p. Tri-City Oil, Inc., Addison, Ill., 1983-93; treas. Uncle Andy's, Inc., 1991-94; corp. officer Bionic Auto Parts, Inc.; bd. dirs. EDT, Inc., treas., 1993—; ptnr. PetCatMusic Publ., 1996—; owner IEP Record Group, 1996—, dir. United Community Lisle, IL, 2001-. Pres. Young Dems., Roosevelt U., 1967-71; trustee U. Ill. Russo Scholarship Fund, 1989—; dir. Elmhurst Jaycees, 1976. Mem. AICPA, ASCAP (assoc.), NARAS (assoc.), Ill. CPA Soc., Theosophical Soc. Roman Catholic. Office: 1 S 376 Summit Ave Oakbrook Terrace IL 60181 E-mail: jerryc@catboor.com.

CATALDO, C. A. hotel executive; b. Chgo., Oct. 23, 1933; Student, Loyola U.; grad. bus. mgmt. program, Harvard U., 1973. Founder Hostmark Hospitality Group, 1974—, chmn., CEO, 1994—. Past chmn., bd. dirs. Chgo. Convention and Tourism Bur. Active City of Hope Med. Ctr., Maryville Acad., Boy Scouts Am. Recipient Awards Nat. Restuarant Assn., award Holiday Inn's Top 10 Restaurant Mgrs., 1968, Innkeeper of Yr. award Holiday Inn, Spirit of Life award, Lifetime Achievement award Roosevelt U. Manfred Seinfeld Sch. in Hospitality Mgmt., 1998; med. rsch. fellowship established in his name City of Hope, 1982. Mem. Greater Chgo. Hotel/Motel Assn., Am. Hotel/Motel Assn. (bd. dirs.), Ill. Hotel and Motel Assn. (bd. dirs.). Office: Hostmark Hospitality Group 11 Plaza Dr Schaumburg IL 60173

CATALDO, ROBERT J. hotel executive; b. Chgo., Sept. 1, 1941; Pres., COO Hostmark Hospitality Group, 1996—. Office: Hostmark Hospitality Group 11 Plaza Dr Schaumburg IL 60173

CATHCART, RICHARD J. technology company executive; BA in Engring. Scis., U.S. Air Force Acad. V.p., gne. mgr. worldwide bldg. control divsn. Honeywell, v.p. bus. devel.; exec. v.p. corp. devel. Pentair Inc., St. Paul, exec. v.p., pres. water and fluid techs. group. Office: Pentair Inc 1500 County Road B2 W Ste 400 Saint Paul MN 55113-3105

CATIZONE, CARMEN A. health science association administrator, secretary; Grad., U. Ill., 1983. Exec. dir., sec. Nat. Assn. of Bds. of Pharmacy, Park Ridge. Office: Nat Assn of Bds of Pharmacy 700 Busse Hwy Park Ridge IL 60068-2402 Fax: 847-698-0124. E-mail: ceo@nabp.net.

CATTANEO, MICHAEL S. heating and cooling company executive; b. Detroit, May 30, 1948; s. Alex and Bernadine (Krause) C.; m. Nancy Lucille Horsch, Sept. 6, 1969; children: Michael Alex, Jason Ryan. Cert., Lawrence Inst. Tech., 1970, Macomb Coll., 1977. Service tech. Reliable Heating and Cooling, Detroit, 1965-69; service supr. Artic Air Inc., 1969-77; supt. Kropf Service Inc., 1977-78; owner Greater Detroit Heating and Cooling, Inc., 1978—, J.B. Air Conditioning Inc., 1978—. Mech., tech. educator, Career Prep. Ctr., Warren, Mich., 1982-83; tech advisor Macomb Prosecutor's Office div. consumer fraud, Mt. Clemens, Mich., 1985—; pres. Catt Enterprises Real Estate and Investments; ptnr. B.F.P.T. Investments LLC Named Republican of Yr., Mich., 2000, Republican Businessman of Yr., 2002. Mem. Italian Cultural Ctr. (Warren), Ams. Italian Origin, Mich. Italian C. of C. Republican. Roman Catholic. Avocations: fishing, hunting, competitive shooting and boating, bicycling, tennis, golf. Office: Greater Detroit Heating and Cooling Inc 31485 Groesbeck Fraser MI 48021-1961 E-mail: catt8484@aol.com.

CAUDILL, TOM HOLDEN, governmental policy and analysis executive; b. St. Augustine, Fla., June 21, 1945; s. Julian Terrill and Alta Jane (Holden) C.; m. Virginia Mary Kauss, June 26, 1971; 1 child, Mara Julia. BA in History, East Tenn. State U., 1967, MA in Internat. Rels., 1977; MA in Mgmt. Sci., Webster U., 1980. Instr. English as second lang., polit. sci., mgmt. sci. U.S. Peace Corps, Loei, Thailand, 1970-73; instr. English as second lang., polit. sci., mgmt. sci. Steed Coll., Johnson City, Tenn., 1973-76; instr. Internat. Ctr. U. Tex., Austin, 1976-77; tng. specialist Air Tng. Command USAF, Lackland AFB, Tex., 1977-80, tng. specialist Logistics Command Wright-Patterson AFB, Ohio, 1980-81, logistics mgmt. specialist, 1981-85, chief, policy and procedures Internat. Logistics Ctr., 1985-88, chief policy and analysis, 1986—, chief plans and devel., 1988; dir. Arabian programs Internat. Logistics Ctr., 1991-95; exec. fellow Woodrow Wilson Sch. Govt. Princeton U., 1995-96; dep. dir. internat. programs Air Force Security Assistance Ctr., 1996; chief prodn. policy Hdqtrs. Air Force Material Command, Wright Patterson AFB, Ohio, 1997-99; dir. ops. mgmt. Air Force Security Assistance Ctr., 1999-2000, dir. case mgmt., 2000—. Vis. instr. English as a second lang., polit. sci., mgmt. sci. Antioch Coll., Yellow Springs, Ohio, 1986—; asst. dep. plans policy mgmt. systems, 1988, dir. plans and policy, 1988, tech. lead integrated logistics support, acquisition logistics div., 1988—, instr. mgmt. sci. Author: Textbook in Logistics 1988, Policy Regulations/Procedural Instructions 1986—; contbr. articles to profl. jours., 1987—. Adminstr. Refugee Assistance Program, Greene County, Ohio, 1981-84, AFS chpt. v.p.; Scoutmaster Buckeye Trails coun. Girl Scout U.S., Yellow Springs, 1982-86; active Dayton (Ohio) Coun. on World Affairs, 1984—; pres. local chpt. Am. Field Svc., Greene County, 1988—. Mem LWV (fin. chm. Greene county chpt. 1987—). Democratic. Methodist. Avocations: traveling, scouting, reading, profl. rsch. writing. Home: 2381 Bluewing Dr Dayton OH 45431 Office: Hdqs Air Force Material Cmd Air Force Security Asst Ctr AFSAC/CO Wright Patterson AFB OH 45433 E-mail: tom.caudill@wpafb.af.mil.

CAVANAGH, MICHAEL FRANCIS, state supreme court justice; b. Detroit, Oct. 21, 1940; s. Sylvester J. and Mary Irene (Timmins) C.; m. Patricia E. Ferriss, Apr. 30, 1966; children: Jane Elizabeth, Michael F., Megan Kathleen BA, U. Detroit, 1962, JD, 1966. Bar: Mich. 1966. Law clk. to judge Ct. Appeals, Detroit, 1966-67; atty. City of Lansing, Mich., 1967-69; ptnr. Farhat, Story, et al., Lansing, 1969-73; judge 54-A Dist. Ct., 1973-75, Mich. Ct. Appeals, Lansing, 1975-82; justice Supreme Ct., 1983—, chief justice, 1991-94; Supreme Ct. liaison Mich. Indian Tribal Cts./Mich. State Cts. Supervising justice Sentencing Guidelines Com., Lansing, 1983-94, Mich. Jud. Inst., Lansing, 1986-94, 2001-02; bd. dirs. Thomas M. Cooley Law Sch., 1979-88; chair Mich. Justice Project, 1994-95, Nat. Interbranch Conf., Mpls., 1994-95. Bd. dirs. Am. Heart Assn. Mich., 1982—, chmn. bd. Am. Heart Assn. Mich., Lathrup Village, 1984-85; bd. dirs. YMCA, Lansing, 1978. Mem. ABA, Fed. Bar Assn., Ingham County Bar Assn., Inst. Jud. Adminstrn. (hon.), Inc. Soc. of Irish/Am. Lawyers (pres. 1987-88). Democrat. Roman Catholic Avocations: jogging, racquetball, fishing. Office: Mich Supreme Ct PO Box 30052 525 W Ottawa St Lansing MI 48933-1067

CECERE, ANDREW, bank executive; Sr. v.p. mgmt. acctg. U.S. Bancorp, Mpls., sr. v.p. acquisition integration and process mgmt., 1996-99, sr. v.p. ops. and adminstrn. wholesale banking, 1999, vice chmn. comml. svcs., 1999—. Office: US Bancorp 601 2d Ave S Minneapolis MN 55402-4302

CECERE, DOMINICO, company executive; b. June 10, 1949; BA in Fin. and Acctg., U. Okla. V.p. fin. indsl. controls Honeywell, Inc., v.p. fin. home and bldg. controlling bus., v.p. fin. European bus.; v.p., contr. Owens Corning, Toledo, 1993-95, pres. roofing sys. bus., 1995-98, sr. v.p., CFO, 1998-2000, exec. v.p., COO, 2000-01. Office: Owens Corning 1 Owens Corning Pkwy Toledo OH 43659-0001

CECI, LOUIS J. former state supreme court justice; b. N.Y.C., Sept. 10, 1927; s. Louis and Filomena C.; m. Shirley; children— Joseph, Geraldine, David; children by previous marriage: Kristin, Remy, Louis Ph.B., Marquette U., 1951, J.D., 1954. Bar: Wis. 1954, U.S. Dist. Ct. (ea. dist.) Wis. 1954, U.S. Dist. Ct. (we. dist.) Wis. 1987; cert. mediator-arbitrator. Sole practice, Milw., 1954-58, 63-68; asst. city atty. City of Milw., 1958-63; mem. Wis. Assembly, Madison, 1965-66; judge Milw. County Ct., 1968-73, Milw. Circuit Ct., 1973-82; justice Wis. Supreme Ct., Madison, 1982-93, retired, 1993; res. judge State of Wis., 1993—. Lectr. Wis. Jud. Confs., 1970-79 Lectr. Badger Boys State, Ripon, Wis., 1961, 1982-84; asst. dist. commr. Boy Scouts Am., 1962. Recipient Wis. Civic Recognition PLAV, Milw., 1970; recipient Community Improvement Pompeii Men's Club, Milw., 1971, Good Govt. Milw Jaycees, 1973, Community-Judiciary Pompeii Men's Club, 1982 Mem. ABA, Wis. Bar Assn., Dane County Bar Assn., Milw. County Bar Assn., Waukesha County Bar Assn., Am. Legion (comdr. 1962-63). E-mail: appeal301@aol.com.

CEDAR, PAUL ARNOLD, church executive, minister; b. Mpls., Nov. 4, 1938; s. Carl Benjamin and Bernice M. (Peterson) C.; m. Jean Helen Lier, Aug. 25, 1959; children: Daniel Paul, Mark John, Deborah Jean. BS, No. State Coll., Aberdeen, S.D., 1960; MDiv, No. Bap. Theol. Sem., 1968, Calif. State U., Fullerton, 1971; DMin, Am. Baptist Sem. of the West, 1973. Ordained to ministry Evang. Free Ch. of Am., 1966. Youth for Christ, crusade dir. Billy Graham Evang. Assn., Leighton Ford Team, 1960-65; pastor Evang. Free Ch., Naperville, Ill., 1965-67, Yorba Linda, Calif., 1969-73; exec. pastor 1st Presbyn. Ch. Hollywood, 1975-81; sr. pastor Lake Ave. Congl. Ch., Pasadena, 1981-90; pres. Evang. Free Ch. Am., Mpls., 1990-96; chmn., CEO Mission Am., 1995—. Guest dean Billy Graham Sch. Evangelism, Mpls., 1983—; vis. prof. Fuller Theol. Sem., Pasadena, Talbot Theol. Sem., La Habra, Calif., Trinity Div. Sch., Deerfield, Ill. Author: How to Make Love Your Motive, 1977, Becoming a Lover, 1978, Seven Keys to Maximum Communication, 1980, Sharing the Good Life, 1980, Communicators Commentary, 1983, Strength in Servant Leadership, 1987, Mastering the Pastoral Role, 1991, Where Is Hope?, 1992, A Life of Prayer, 1998. Mem. exec. com. Nat. Prayer Com. Mem. Christian TV and Film Commn., Internat. Students, Worldwide Leadership Coun., Caleb Ministries, Leadership Renewal Ctr., John M. Perkins Found., Revival Prayer Fellowship, Barnabas Internat., Pioneer Clubs. Avocations: athletics, music, writing, carpentry. Office: 77564 Country Club Dr # A Palm Desert CA 92211-0484 E-mail: PaulC@missionamerica.org.

CEDERBERG, JAMES, physics educator; b. Oberlin, Kans., Mar. 16, 1939; s. J. Walter and Edith E. (Glad) C.; m. Judith Ness, June 10, 1967; children: Anna Sook, Rachel Eun. BA, U. Kans., 1959; MA, Harvard U., 1960, PhD, 1963. Lectr., rsch. assoc. Harvard U., Cambridge, Mass., 1963-64; asst. prof. St. Olaf Coll., Northfield, Minn., 1964-68, assoc. prof., 1968-80, prof., 1980—, Grace A. Whittier prof. sci., 1992—. Councilor Coun. on Undergrad. Rsch., 1985-91, 92-95, pres. physics coun., 1985-88. Recipient Distinguished Service Citation awd., Am. Assn. of Physics Teachers, 1993. Fellow: Am. Phys. Soc.; mem.: Am. Assn. Physics Tchrs. (mem. coun. on undergraduate rsch.). Lutheran. Office: St Olaf Coll 1520 Saint Olaf Ave Northfield MN 55057-1098 Fax: 507-646-3968. E-mail: ceder@stolaf.edu.

CEDERBURG, BARBARA M. printing company executive; b. St. Paul, Sept. 22, 1953; BA in Chemistry and Biology, Macalester Coll.; MS in Chemistry, U. Minn. Wilver Halide Emulsion trainee Minn. 3M Rsch. Ltd., Harlow, Eng., 1979; tech. mgr. Color Proofing Lab., 1986; mgr. graphic rsch. lab. 3M, St. Paul, 1986-90, lab. mgr., tech. dir. Dry Imaging Tech. Ctr., 1991-93, tech. dir. printing and pub. sys. divsn., 1994; bus. dir. printing and pub. sys. Imation/3M, 1994-97; gen. mgr. printing and proofing bus. Imation Enterprises, 1997-98; pres. product techs., v.p. Imation Corp., 1998—. Active St. Paul Civic Symphony. Mem. Am. Chem. Soc., Graphic Arts Tech. Found., Soc. Imaging Sci. and Tech. Achievements include co-inventor of Matchprint II Negative. Office: Imation Corp Jason Thunstrom Pub Rels 1 Imation Pl Oakdale MN 55128-3414

CELESIA, GASTONE GUGLIELMO, neurologist, neurophysiologist, researcher; b. Genoa, Italy, Nov. 22, 1933; came to U.S., 1959, naturalized, 1970; s. Raffaele Amadeo and Ottavia (Tortrino) C.; m. Linda Irene Pike, Aug. 1, 1964; children— Gloria, Laura M.D., U. Genoa, 1959; M.S., McGill U., Montreal, 1965. Diplomate Am. Bd. Psychiatry and Neurology in Neurology, Am. Bd. Psychiatry and Neurology in Clin. Neurophysiology. Intern Madison Gen. Hosp., Wis., 1960; fellow neurophysiology U. Wis., Madison, 1960-62, asst. prof. neurology, 1966-69, assoc. prof., 1970-73, prof., 1974-79, 1979-83; resident in neurology Montreal Neurol. Inst./McGill U., Montreal, Que., Can., 1962-66; chief neurology service VA Hosp., Madison, 1979-83; chmn. dept. neurology Loyola U., Chgo., 1983-99. Editor in chief: Electroenceph. Clin. Neurophysiol., 1988-99; contbr. articles to profl. jours. Fellow Am. Acad. Neurology; mem. AMA, Am. EEG Soc., Am. Acad. Clin. Neurophysiology (pres. 1993-95), Am. Neurol. Assn., Ctrl. Assn. EEG, Wis. Neurol. Soc. Wis. Med. Alumni Assn., Wis. Neurol. Soc. (pres. 1975-76), Soc. Neurosci., Am. Epilepsy Soc., N.Y. Acad. Scis. AAAS, Royal Soc. Medicine, Am. Soc. Exptl. Med. Therapeutics. Office: Loyola Univ-Chgo Dept Neurology 2160 S 1st Ave Maywood IL 60153-3304 E-mail: gcelesi@lumc.edu.

CELLINI, WILLIAM F. hotel executive; b. Springfield, Ill., Nov. 5, 1934; married. Student, U. Ill., 1952—55, postgrad., 6061; BS in Physics, Ill. Coll., 1958. With Ill. Dept. Pub. Works, 1968—70; sec. transp. State of Ill., 1970—72; exec. v.p. Ill. Asphalt Paving Assn., Springfield, 1973—; pres., CEO New Frontier Mgmt. Corp., Springfield and Chgo., 1977—; chmn. bd. dirs., mem. nominating com. Argosy Gaming Co., 1993—. Office: Argosy Gaming Co 219 Piasa St Alton IL 62002-6232

CENTANNI, ROSS J. compressed air products manufacturing executive; b. 1946; With B.F. Goodrich Co., Hooker Chem. divsn. Occidental Petroleum; mgr. corp. planning Cooper Industries, Quincy, Ill., 1981, dir. mktg. Gardner-Denver Indsl. Machinery divsn., 1985-90, v.p., gen. mgr. Gardner-Denver Indsl. Machinery divsn., 1990-93; pres., CEO Gardner Denver, Inc., 1993—, chmn. bd., 1998—. Office: 1800 Gardner Expy Quincy IL 62305-9364 Office Fax: 217-228-8247.

CENTNER, CHARLES WILLIAM, lawyer, educator; b. Battle Creek, Mich., July 4, 1915; s. Charles William and Lucy Irene (Patterson) C.; m. Evi Rohr, Dec. 22, 1956; children: Charles Patterson, David William, Geoffrey Christopher. AB, U. Chgo., 1936, AM, 1938, 39, PhD, 1941; JD, Detroit Coll. Law, 1970; LLB, LaSalle Extension U., 1965. Bar: Mich. 1970. Asst. prof. U. N.D., 1940-41, Tulane U., New Orleans, 1941-42; liaison officer for Latin Am., Dept. State at Lend-Lease Adminstrn., 1942; assoc. dir. Western Hemisphere divsn. Nat. Fgn. Trade Coun., N.Y., 1946-52; exec. Ford Motor Co., Detroit, 1952-57, Chrysler Corp. and Chrysler Internat. S.A., Detroit and Geneva, Switzerland, 1957-70. Adj. prof. Pace U., N.Y.C., 1950-52, Wayne State U., Detroit, 1971-78, U. Detroit, 1970-72, Wayne County C.C., 1970-2001. Author: Great Britian and Chile, 1810-1914, 1941. Lt. comdr. USNR, 1942-45, Res., 1945-75. Mem. ABA, State Bar Mich., Oakland County Bar Assn., Masons. Republican. Episcopalian. Home: 936 Harcourt Rd Grosse Pointe Park MI 48230-1874

CENTO, WILLIAM FRANCIS, retired newspaper editor; b. St. Louis, Mar. 20, 1932; s. Frank and Augusta (Albietz) C.; m. Vera Ann Shaide, May 16, 1964. BS, St. Louis U., 1954. Gen. assignment reporter East St. Louis (Ill.) Jour., 1954-56; suburban editor Globe-Democrat, St. Louis, 1956-61; copyeditor Post-Dispatch, 1961-62; make-up editor Pioneer Press, St. Paul, 1962-65, wire editor, 1965-67, Sunday editor, 1967-73; graphics editor Pioneer Press & Dispatch, 1974-77; mng. editor St. Paul Dispatch, 1977-84; assoc. editor Pioneer Press, St. Paul, 1984-90. Owner Give Me Rewrite, West St. Paul, 1990—; editor, pub. Letter from Minn., West St. Paul, 1995—. Editor: Fifty and Feisty APME: 1933 to 1983, 1983. Recipient numerous awards including Twin Cities Newspaper Guild Page 1 award Makeup 1st pl. award, 1969, 71, 74, 2d pl., 1971, 72, Award of Appreciation, AP Mng. Editors Assn., 1983. Mem. Soc. Profl. Journalists, AP Mng. Editors Assn. (bd. dirs. 1982-88). Roman Catholic. Avocations: painting, graphic design. Home and Office: 111 Imperial Dr W Apt 103 West Saint Paul MN 55118-2249 E-mail: mnletter@aol.com.

CEPERLEY, DAVID MATTHEW, physics educator; BS in Physics and Maths., U. Mich., 1971; PhD in Physics, Cornell U., 1976. Postdoct. fellow Lab. Physique Theorique, Orsay, France, 1976-77, Rutgers U., N.J., 1977-78; staff scientist Nat Resource for Computation in Chemistry Lawrence Berkeley Lab., 1978-81; staff scientist Lawrence Livermore Nat. Lab., 1981-87; assoc. prof. physics U. Ill., 1987-91, prof. physics, 1991—. Rsch. scientist Nat. Ctr. for Supercomputing Applications, 1987—, assoc. dir. applications, 1997-98; on sabbatical U. Trento, Italy, 1985-86 IRRMA Ecole Poly. Lausanne, Switzerland, 1993; coord. workshop Inst. Theoretical Physics U. Calif., Santa Barbara, 1994; co-organizer numerous workshops. Contbr. numerous articles to profl. jours. Grad. fellow NSF, 1971-74, Joliot-Curie fellow, 1976-77; recipient Feenberg award for contributions to many-body physics, 1994. Fellow Am. Phys. Soc. (Aneesur Rahman prize for computational physics 1998); mem. AAAS, Am. Acad. Arts & Scis. Achievements include development and contributions to of fermion quantum Monte Carlo methods, contributions to understanding of physical or formal understanding of quantum many-body systems, mainly his calculation of the energy of electron gas; pioneer in the development and application of Path Integral Monte Carlo methods for quantum systems at finite temperatures. Office: U Ill Dept Physics 1110 W Green St Urbana IL 61801-9013 Fax: (217) 244-2909. E-mail: ceperley@uiuc.edu.

CERNUGEL, WILLIAM JOHN, consumer products and special retail executive; b. Joliet, Ill., Nov. 19, 1942; m. Laurie M. Kusnik, Apr. 22, 1967; children: Debra, James, David. BS, No. Ill. U., 1964. CPA, Ill. Sr. supr. KPMG LLP, Chgo., 1964-70; asst. corp. contr. Alberto-Culver Co., Melrose Park, Ill., 1970-71, corp. contr., 1972—, v.p., 1974-82, v.p. fin., 1982-93, sr. v.p. fin., 1993-2000, sr. v.p., CFO, 2000—. Mem. bd. govs., treas. Gottlieb Meml. Hosp., Melrose Park; assoc. mem. bd. advisors Coll. Bus., No. Ill. U. Mem. AICPA, Am. Mgmt. Assn. (fin. coun.), Inst. Mgmt. Accts., Ill. Soc. CPAs, Fin. Exec. Inst., Lions. Home: 8111 Lake Ridge Dr Burr Ridge IL 60527-5977 Office: Alberto-Culver Co 2525 Armitage Ave Melrose Park IL 60160-1163

CERNY, JOSEPH CHARLES, urologist, educator; b. Apr. 20, 1930; s. Joseph James and Mary (Turek) C.; m. Patti Bobette Pickens, Nov. 10, 1962; children: Joseph Charles, Rebecca Anne. BA, Knox Coll., 1952; MD, Yale U., 1956. Diplomate Am. Bd. Urology. Intern U. Mich. Hosp., Ann Arbor, 1956-57, resident, 1957-62; practice medicine specializing in urology Ann Arbor and Detroit, 1962—. Instr. surgery (urology) U. Mich., Ann Arbor, 1962-64, asst. prof., 1964-66, assoc. prof., 1961-77, clin. prof., 1971—; chmn. dept. urology Henry Ford Hosp., Detroit, 1971—, chmn. emeritus urology Henry Ford Hosp., 1998; pres. Resistors, Inc., Chgo., 1960—; cons. St. Joseph Hosp., Ann Arbor, 1973—; chief urology sect., dept. surgery Ann Arbor VA Hosp., 1999—. Mem. editl. bd. Am. Jour. Kidney Diseases, 1988—; contbr. articles to profl. jours., chpts. to books. Bd. dirs., trustee Nat. Kidney Found. Mich., Ann Arbor, 1988—, chmn. urology coun., 1987—, exec. com., 1987—, pres., 1988—, emeritus trustee, 1997; bd. dirs. Ann Arbor Amateur Hockey Assn., 1980-83; pres. PTO, Ann Arbor Pub. Schs., 1980. Lt. USNR, 1956-76. Recipient Disting. Svc. award Transplantation Soc. Mich., 1982, Disting. Svc. award Nat. Kidney Found. Mich., 1993, Champion of Hope award Nat. Kidney Found., 1997, Disting. Career award Henry Ford Hosp. Alumni, 2000. Fellow ACS (pres.-elect Mich. br. 1984-85, pres. 1985—); mem. Am. Acad. Med. Dirs., Am. Coll. Physician Execs., Internat. Soc. Urology, Am. Urol. Assn. (pres. Mich. br. 1980-81, pres. North Cen. sect. 1985-86, manpower com. 1987-88, 90-92, jud. rev. com. 1987-91, tech. exhibits 1987-88, fiscal affairs rev. commn. 1985-89, audit commn. 1992-96, chmn. 1995, exec. commn. 1993—, bd. dirs. 1994—, work force com., publs. com. 1995—, chmn. publs. com. 1999, Best Sci. Exhibit award 1978, Best Sci. Films award 1980, 82, audio-visual com. 1994—, program rev. com. 1994—, urology work force com. 1995—, jud. and ethics com. 1997—), Transplantation Soc. Mich. (pres. Mich. 1983-85), Am. Assn. Transplant Surgeons, Endocrine Surgeons, Soc. Univ. Urologists, Am. Assn. Urologic Oncology, Am. Fertilitiy Soc., Am. Coll. Physician Execs., Am. Acad. Med. Dirs., S.W. Oncology Group, Barton Hills Country Club, Ann Arbor Racquet Club. Avocations: tennis, fishing, Civil War. Home: 2800 Fairlane St Ann Arbor MI 48104-4110 Office: U Mich Health Sys Sect Urology Dept Surgery 1500 E Medical Center Dr Ann Arbor MI 48109-0005 E-mail: jocerny@umich.edu.

CERNY, WILLIAM F. state legislator; m. Patricia Cerny. Rep. S.D. State Ho. of Reps. Dist. 29, S.D. State Ho. of Reps. Dist. 25, 1993—, minority whip, mem. appropriations com. Farmer. Home: RR 1 Box 2 Burke SD 57523-9501

CEROKE, CLARENCE JOHN, engineer, consultant; b. Chgo., Dec. 1, 1921; s. Paul Anthony and Anne (Krieger) C.; m. Violet Marie Lobonc, Sept. 21, 1947; children: Paul, Donald, Robert, Marie, Louise, Karen. BS in mech. Engring., Ill. Inst. Tech., 1943. Reg. profl. engr., Ill. Supr. product devel. U.S.I. Clearing, Chgo., 1969-74; engr. Panduit Corp., Tinley Park, Ill., 1974-75; design engr. Interlake Steel, Chgo., 1975-76; mgr. engring. AFL Industries, West Chicago, 1976-77; design engr. Castle Engring., Chgo., 1977-80; supr. Dreis and Krump, 1980-81; project engr. Epstein Process Engring., 1981-83; cons. engr. Beacon Engring., Homewood, Ill., 1983-84; engr. Espo Engring., Canton, Ohio, 1984—. Owner Beacon Engring., Homewood, 1978—. Patentee in field; author books. Pres. St. Kilians Holy Name Soc., Chgo., 1960; coach Little League Baseball, Chgo., 1959. With USN, 1943-44. Mem. Mt. Carmel Alumni Assn., Pi Tau Sigma, Hall-Fame Racquet Club. Roman Catholic. Avocations: tennis, contract bridge, in plant safety and environmental research. Home: 755 Wood St Crown Point IN 46307-4910 Office: Beacon 755 Wood St Crown Point IN 46307-4910

CERONE, DAVID, academic administrator; Pres. Cleve. Inst. Music, 1985—. Office: Cleve Inst Music 11021 East Blvd Cleveland OH 44106-1705

CERRA, FRANK BERNARD, dean; b. Oneonta, N.Y., Feb. 13, 1943; m. Kathie Krieger; children: Josh, Christa, Nicole. BA in Biology, SUNY, Binghamton, 1965; MD, Northwestern U., 1969. Diplomate Nat. Bd. Med. Examiners, Am. Bd. Surgery. Intern, resident in surgery Buffalo Gen. Hosp., 1969-74; staff surgeon U. Minn. Hosp. Clinic, Mpls.; prof. U. Minn. Med. Sch., 1981—, dean, prof. surgery, 1995-96, sr. v.p. health scis., 1996—. Clin. asst. instr. surgery SUNY, Buffalo, 1969-75, asst. prof. 1975-80, assoc. prof. surgery and biophysics, 1980; interim head surgery U. Minn., 1994-95, dean med. sch., 1995-96, provost acad. health ctr., 1996—; rsch. asst. pharmacology Upstate Med. Ctr., 1963-64; rsch. asst. transplantation Northwestern U., 1967-69; rsch. assoc. immunology and cardiovascular rsch. labs. Buffalo Gen. Hosp., 1972-73, SUNY, Buffalo, 1974-75; dir. surg. critical care, dir. nutrition support svcs. U. Minn. Hosp. and Clinic; vis. lectr. in exptl. surgery Harvard U., 1991; vis. prof. Rush Presbyn.-St. Lukes Med. Ctr., 1991. Editor Perspective in Critical Care, 1988-91, Critical Care Outlook, 1988-90, Critical Care Medicine, 1990—; mem. editl. bd. Drug Intelligence & Clin. Pharmacy Panel onCritical Care, 1982-87, Nutrition, 1982—, Critical Care Medicine, 1983—, Circulatory Shock, 1987-93, Shock, 1993—, Jour. Parenteral and Enternal Nutrition, 1987-93, Am. Jour. Surgery, 1987—, Current Opinion in Gen. Surgery, 1992—, Jour. Critical Care Nutrition; contbr. articles to profl. jours.; patentee preparation for the prevention of catabolism, preparation for nutirtion support of immune function. Acute care com. Found. for Health Care Evaluation, 1983-86; adv. group Minn. Emerging Infections Program, 1995—. Clark Found. fellow, 1965-69, Kellogg Nutrition fellow, 1987-89, Surgical Infection Soc. Rsch. fellow, 1988-90, Soc. Critical Care Medicine Lilly Rsch. fellow, 1990-93, Svc. award fellow NIH, 1994-96; United Health Found. Rsch. Tng. grantee, 1972-73; recipient Owen Wangensteen award, 1987, Therapeutic Frontiers Rsch. award Am. Coll. Clin. Pharmacy, 1990, Disting. Investigator award Am. Coll. Critical Care Medicine, 1993. Fellow ACS (chmn. pre-postoperative care com. 1985-87), Am. Coll. Nutrition, Coll. Critical Care Medicine; mem. AMA, AAAS, Soc. Parenteral Alimentation, Soc. for Surgery the Alimentary Tract, Am. Soc. Parenteral and Enteral Nutrition (bd. dirs. 1987-88), Soc. Critical Care Medicine (treas. 1990, pres. 1991-92), Assn. for Acad. Surgery, Assn. Internat. Anesthesistes-Reanimateurs D'Expression, Soc. Univ. Surgeons (exec. coun. 1984-85), Ctrl. Surg. Assn., Am. Assn. for the Surgery Trauma, Assn. for Surg. Edn., St. Paul Surg. Soc., Surg. Biology Club, Shock Soc., Soc. Internat. Surgery, Internat. Assn. for the Surgery Trauma and Surg. Intensive Care, Am. Soc. for Artificial Internal Organs (membership com. 1994-95), Am. Soc. Home Care Physician, Hennepin County Med. Soc. Office: 420 Delaware St SE # 501 Minneapolis MN 55455-0374 also: U Minn Health & Scis Ctr PO Box 501 420 Delaware St SE Minneapolis MN 55455-0374 Fax: 612-625-5000.

CESARIO, ROBERT CHARLES, franchise executive, consultant; b. Chgo., Apr. 6, 1941; s. Valentino A. and Mary Ethel (Kenny) C.; m. Susan Kay DePouee; children: Jeffrey, Bradley. BS in Gen. Edn., Northwestern U., 1975; postgrad. in bus. adminstrn., DePaul U., 1975. Mgr. fin. ops. Midas Internat. Corp., Chgo., 1968-73; dir. staff ops. Am. Hosp. Supply Corp., McGaw Park, Ill., 1973-76; v.p. Car X Svc. Sys. Inc., Chgo., 1976-78, v.p. oil svcs., 1983-84; v.p. Chicken Unltd. Enterprises Inc., 1978-83; pres. Growth Strategies, Inc., 1984-87; pres., CEO Lube Pro's Internat., Inc., 1987—. With USMC, 1960-62. Office: Lube Pros Internat Inc 1630 W Colonial Pkwy Palatine IL 60067-1209

CHABOT, STEVEN J. congressman; b. Cin., Jan. 22, 1953; s. Gerard Joseph and Doris Leona (Tilly) C.; m. Donna Daly, June 22; children: Erica, Randy. BA, Coll. William & Mary, 1975; JD, Salmon P. Chase Coll. of Law, 1978. Bar: Ohio; cert. tchr., Ohio. Tchr. St. Joseph Sch., Cin., 1975-76; atty., 1978-95; mem. city coun. City of Cin., 1985-90; commr. Hamilton County, Ohio, 1990-94; mem. U.S. Congress from 1st Ohio Dist., Washington, 1995—; internat. rels., judiciary, sm. bus. coms. Mem. internat. rels. with Africa, internat. econ. policy & trade, comml. & adminstrv. law, crime, procurement, exports & bus. opportunities coms. Republican. Roman Catholic. Avocations: reading, spending time with family. Office: US House Reps 129 Cannon Bldg Washington DC 20515-3501*

CHADWICK, JOHN EDWIN, financial counselor; b. Mpls., Feb. 6, 1957; s. Edwin Bazley and Roberta Mae (Brown) Chadwick; m. Patti E. Anderson, June 20, 1997; 2 children. BA, Gustavus Adolphus Coll., St. Peter, Minn., 1979; cert., Am. Coll., Bryn Mawr, Pa., 1989. CFP. Feed ingredient merchandiser Pillsbury Co., Mpls., 1979-81; pres. Chadwick Co., Bloomington, Minn., 1982-84; v.p. sales Red Wing (Minn.) Bus. Systems, 1984-85; fin. counselor CIGNA, Mpls., 1985-88; prin. The Chadwick Group, Inc., Bloomington, Minn., 1989—. Bd. trustees Gustavus Adolphus Coll., 2000. Lutheran. Avocations: hunting, waterskiing. Office: The Chadwick Group Inc 9905 N 45th Ave N Plymouth MN 55442

CHAFFEE, PAUL CHARLES, newspaper editor; b. Racine, Wis., Aug. 10, 1947; s. Raymond Russell and Ellen Mary (Tiles) C.; m. Bonnie Louise Burmeister, Aug. 9, 1969. BA in Journalism, U. Minn., 1969. Reporter Grand Rapids (Mich.) Press, 1969-79, asst. met. editor, 1979-81; met. editor Saginaw (Mich.) News, 1981-88, editor, 1988—. Founding mem. adv. bd. dept. journalism Ctrl. Mich. U., Mt. Pleasant, 1987—; mem. Hispanic adv. bd. dept. journalism Mich. State U.; past pres. bd. dirs. Mich. Assoc. Press Editl. Assn.; bd. dirs. Mid Am. Press Inst. Bd. dirs. Salvation Army, Saginaw, 1986—, St. Charles (Mich.) Cmty. Schs. Found., 1994—, Westlund Child Guidance Clinic, 1995-99, Saginaw Bay Symphony, 1996—; mem. Leadership Saginaw Steering Bd.; mem. steering com. Bridge Ctr. Racial Harmony. Mem.: Nat. Assn. Hispanic Journalists, Soc. Profl. Journalists, Am. Soc. Newspaper Editors, Saginaw Country Club. Avocations: gardening, horses. Office: Saginaw News 203 S Washington Ave Saginaw MI 48607-1283

CHAFFIN, DON BRIAN, industrial engineering educator, research director; b. Sandusky, Ohio, Apr. 17, 1939; m. 1966; 3 children. B of Indsl. Engring., Gen. Motors Inst., 1962; MS in Indsl. Engring., U. Toledo, 1964; PhD in Engring., U. Mich., 1967. Registered profl. engr., Ohio; cert. prof. ergonomist. Quality ctrl. engr. New Departure Divsn. GM Corp., Ohio, 1960-62, inspection foreman, 1962-63; project engr. Micrometrical Divsn. Bendix Corp., Mich., 1963-64; asst. prof. phys. medicine U. Kans., 1967-68, asst. prof. indsl. engring., 1968-70, assoc. prof. indsl. engring., 1970-77; prof. indsl. and ops. engring. U. Mich., Ann Arbor, 1977-93, dir. Ctr. for Ergonomics, 1980-97, Johnson prof. indsl. engring. and biomedical engring., 1993—. Fellow Human Factors Soc. (Paul Fitts award 1992), Am. Indsl. Hygiene Assn. (Edward Baier award 1994), Ergonomics Soc., Am. Inst. Med. and Biol. Engring.; mem. NSPE, NAE, Am. Inst. Indsl. Engrs. (Baker Disting. Rschr. award 1991), Am. Soc. Biomechanics, Sigma Xi (Borrelli award). Achievements include research on effects and applications of electromyography for measuring human performance, concepts of biomechanics for injury prevention in skeletal-muscle system; expanding the teaching of physiological, neurological and anatomical concepts related to the simulation of human motions and exertions in the design of operated systems in manufacturing and service organizations, and in vehicle operation and maintenance. Office: U Mich Ctr Ergonomics 1656 IOE Bldg Ann Arbor MI 48109-2117

CHAFFIN, GARY ROGER, business executive; b. Satanta, Kans., June 6, 1937; s. Owen Charles and Leona Irene (Dale) C.; m. Charlotte Daisy Hawley, Aug. 17, 1958; children: Darcy Lea, Charla Cai, Darren Roger, Charles Dale. BA, U. Kans., 1960. Loan officer Limerick Fin., Lawrence, Kans., 1959-60; asst. mgr. Chaffin Grocery, Moscow, 1960-62; store mgr. Chaffin Inc. Gibson Discount Ctrs., 1962-68; gen. mgr. Chaffin Inc., Dodge City, Kans., 1968-85; pres. Chaffin, Inc., 1985—, Great S.W. BanCorp, 1978-97, Chaffin Acquisition Co., Inc., 1999—. Bd. dirs., sec. Dodge City C.C. Found., 1996-98; bd. dirs., v.p. Dodge City Area Cmty. Found. Republican. Methodist. Avocations: golf, travel. Home: 510 Clover St Dodge City KS 67801-2816 Office: Chaffin Inc 100 Chaffin Ind Park Dodge City KS 67801

CHAIT, JON FREDERICK, corporate executive, lawyer; b. Bakersfield, Calif., Aug. 9, 1950; s. Michael and Irene (Goddard) C.; m. Mary Lardner, Feb. 13, 1988; children: Jamie E., Meredith L. BA magna cum laude, UCLA, 1972, JD, 1975. Bar: Wis. 1975. Assoc. Foley & Lardner, Milw., 1975-79, Godfrey & Kahn, S.C., Milw., 1979-82, ptnr., 1982-89; exec. v.p., CFO, bd. dirs. Manpower Inc., 1989-98, mng. dir. internat. ops., 1995-98; chmn., CEO Magenta.com, 1998-2000, Spring Group PLC, London, 2000—. Bd. dirs. Marshall & Ilsley Corp., Milw., M&I Data Svcs., Milw., Krueger Internat., Inc., Green Bay, Wis. Mem. ABA, Am. Soc. Corp. Secs., Univ. Club, Milw. Country Club, Milw. Club, Phi Beta Kappa. Office: 388 Oxford St London England

CHAIT, WILLIAM, librarian, consultant; b. N.Y.C., Dec. 5, 1915; s. Max and Mollie (Miller) C.; m. Beatrice L. Faigelman, June 13, 1937; 1 son, Edward Martin. B.A., Bklyn. Coll., 1934; B.L.S., Pratt Inst., 1935; M.S. in L.S, Columbia U., 1938. Library asst., br. librarian Bklyn. Pub. Library, 1935-45; service command librarian 2d Service Command AUS, 1945-46; chief in- service tng., personnel control Milw. Pub. Library, 1946-48; dir. Kalamazoo Pub. Library, 1948-56, Dayton and Montgomery County Pub. Library, 1956-78, dir. emeritus, 1979—. Mem. Library Cons., Inc. Pres. Kalamazoo Council Social Agys., 1954-55, Dayton City Beautiful Com., 1968-69; treas. Montgomery County Hist. Soc., 1968-69; trustee On-Line Computer Library Center, 1974-85, treas., 1976-79. Fulbright lectr. library sci. U. Tehran, 1969-70 Mem. Pub. Library Assn. (pres. 1964-65), ALA (treas. 1976-80, council 1981-85, chmn. personnel adminstrn. sect. 1958-60), Mich. Library Assn. (pres. 1955-56), Ohio Library Assn. (pres. 1964-65), S.C. Library Assn. Home: 99 Birdsong Way D404 Hilton Head Island SC 29926-1387 Office: 215 E 3rd St Dayton OH 45402-2103

CHAKRABARTI, SUBRATA KUMAR, marine research engineer; b. Calcutta, India, Feb. 3, 1941; came to U.S., 1964, naturalized, 1981; s. Asutosh and Shefali C.; m. Prakriti Bhaduri, July 23, 1967; children: Sumita, Prabal. BSME, Jadavpur U., Calcutta, India, 1963; MSME, U. Colo., 1965, PhD, 1968. Registered profl. engr., Ill. Asst. engr. Kuljian Corp., Calcutta, 1963-64, Simon Carves Ltd., Calcutta, 1964; instr. engring. U. Colo., Boulder, 1965-66; hydrodynamicist CB&I Tech. Svcs. Co. (formerly Chgo. Bridge and Iron Co.), Plainfield, Ill., 1968-70, head analytical group, 1970-79, dir. marine rsch., 1979-95, dir. structural devel., 1995-96; pres. Offshore Structure Analysis, Inc., 1996—. Vis. prof. U.S. Naval Acad., Annapolis, Md., 1986, 88, Indian Inst. Tech., Madras, 1996; presenter in field. Author: Hydrodynamics of Offshore Structures, 1987, Nonlinear Methods in Offshore Engineering, 1990, Offshore Structure Modeling, 1994; editor: Fluid Structure Interaction in Offshore Engineering, 1994, Fluid Structure Interaction, 2001; tech. editor Applied Ocean Rsch., 1998, mem. editl. bd., Marine Structures, Topics in Engring., Advances in Fluid Mechanics series, assoc. editor Energy Resources Tech., 1983—86; contbr. articles, chapters to books. Recipient Jadavpur U. Gold medal, 1963; U. Colo. fellow, 1968; named Outstanding New Citizen, 1981-82. Fellow AAAS, ASCE (publ. com. waterway divsn., James R. Cross Gold medal 1974, Freeman scholar 1979), ASME (exec. com., editor jour. offshore mechanics and arctic engring. divsn. 1986-96, chmn. divsn., 1987-88, awards com. 1983-96, tech. session devloper, chmn. 1983—, chmn. tech. program com. 1988-89, Ralph James award 1984, co-editor proc. internat. symposium, Offshore Mechanics and Arctic Engring. achievement award 1990, Ten Paper award 1991, Disting. Svcs. award 1998); mem. NAS (design group, marine structures group 1989-91, chmn. 1992-95), Nat. Acad. Engring., Nat. Acad. Engring., Sigma Xi. Achievements include patents in field. Office: Offshore Structure Analysis Inc 13613 Capista Dr Plainfield IL 60544-7966 E-mail: chakrab@aol.com.

CHAKRABARTY, ANANDA MOHAN, microbiologist; b. Sainthia, India, Apr. 4, 1938; s. Satya Dos and Sasthi Bala (Mukherjee) C.; m. Krishna Chakraverty, May 26, 1965; children: Kaberi, Asit. BSc, St. Xavier's Coll., 1958; MSc, U. Calcutta, 1960, PhD, 1965. Sr. research officer U. Calcutta, 1964-65; research asso. in biochemistry U. Ill., Urbana, 1965-71; mem. staff Gen. Electric Research and Devel. Center, Schenectady, 1971-79; prof. dept. microbiology U. Ill. Med. Center, 1979-89; disting. prof., 1989—. Editor: Genetic Engineering, 1977, Biodegradation and Detoxification of Environmental Pollutants, 1982. Named Scientist of Yr. Indsl. Rsch. Mag., 1975, Univ. scholar U. Ill., 1989; recipient Inventor of Yr. award Patent Lawyers' Assn., 1982, Pub. Affairs award Am. Chem. Soc., 1984, Disting. Scientist award EPA, 1985, Merit award NIH, 1986, Pasteur award, 1991, Disting. Svc. award U.S. Army, 1993, Proctor & Gamble award, 1995. Mem. Am. Soc. Microbiology, Am. Soc. Biol. Chemists. Home: 206 E Julia Dr Villa Park IL 60181-3340 Office: U Ill Med Ctr Dept Microbiology M/C 790 835 S Wolcott Ave Chicago IL 60612-7340

CHALEFF, CARL THOMAS, brokerage house executive; b. Inpls., Nov. 21, 1945; s. Boris Carl and Betty J. (Miller) C.; m. Carolyn F. Heath, Apr. 26, 1970 (div. Apr. 1985); children: Fritz. Eric; m. Darlene Finkel, Dec. 13, 1987. BS in Econs., Purdue U., 1969; MBA in Fin., Xavier U., 1976. Asst. v.p. Am. Can Corp., N.Y.C., 1969-70, sales mgr. Cin., 1970-73; account exec. Merrill Lynch, 1973-76; v.p. Oppenheimer, Chgo., 1976-81; assoc. dir. Bear Stearns & Co., 1981-88; ptnr., mng. dir. CIBC Oppenheimer, 1988—. Pres. bd. dirs. Nat. Kidney Found. of Ill.; exec. coun. U. Chgo. Childrens Hosp., Boy Scouts Am., 1992-94; former bd. dirs. AIDS Care, bd. dir. Adler Planetarium & Mus., Chgo., bd. dir., Jobs for Youth. Mem. Chgo. Bond Club, Am. Arbitration Assn., Nat. Bd. Arbitrators, East Bank Club, Rainbows (bd. dirs. 1984-96), Met. Club, Chgo. Mercantile Exch. Club, Chgo. Yacht Club, Ctr. for Excellence in Edn. (bd. dirs. 1990-92), Chgo. Filmmakers (bd. dirs. 1986-98). Avocations: sailing, skiing, tennis. Home: 55 W Goethe St Chicago IL 60610-7406 Personal E-mail: chaleff@21stcentury.net. Business E-Mail: carl.chaleff@us.cibc.com.

CHALMERS, JANE, broadcast executive; News reporter, documentary prodr. ITV, Edmonton, Alta., Can., 1981; co-host current affairs program CBC, Calgary, sr. prodr. 24 Hours Manitoba, exec., area prodr. 24 Hours News and Current Affairs, 1989-93, dir. radio, 1994-96; dir. radio/regional dir. Man. CBC/SRC, Winnipeg, 1996-99, regional dir. Manitoba, 1999—. Recipient Gold medals Internat. Film and TV Festivals of N.Y. and Columbus, Ohio, Human Right awards B'nai B'rith, Prix Anik, Michener award for journalism. Office: CBC-SRC 541 Portage Ave Winnipeg MB Canada R3B 2G1

CHAMBERS, CHARLES MACKAY, university president; b. Hampton, Va., June 22, 1941; s. Charles McKay and Ruth Ellanora (Wallach) C.; m. Barbara Mae Fromm, June 9, 1962; children: Charles M., Catherine M., Christina M., Carleton M. BS, U. Ala., 1962, MS, 1963, PhD, 1964; JD, George Washington U., 1976. Bar: Va. 1977, D.C. 1978, U.S. Patent and Trademark Office, 1978, U.S. Supreme Ct. 1980, U.S. Dist. Ct. D.C. 1985, U.S. Ct. Appeals (D.C. cir.) 1987, U.S. Dist. Ct. (ea. dist.) Va. 1988, U.S. Ct. Appeals D.C., 1987, U.S. Ct. Appeals (4th cir.) 1990, Mich. 1994; cert. comml. pilot, multiengine, land and instrument. Aerospace engr. NASA, Huntsville, Ala., 1962-63; rsch., teaching asst. U. Ala. Rsch. Inst., 1963-64; research fellow NASA, Cambridge, Mass., 1964-65; assoc. prof. U. Ala., Tuscaloosa, 1965-69; mng. dir. Univ. Assocs., Washington, 1969-72; prof., assoc. dean George Washington U., 1972-77; v.p., gen. counsel Council on Postsecondary Accreditation, 1977-83; exec. dir. Am. Inst. Biol. Sci., 1983-87; pres. Am. Found. Biol. Scis., 1987-93, Lawrence Tech. U., Southfield, Mich., 1993—. Cons., evaluator, accreditation rev. coun. commn. on instns. of higher edn. Noth Ctrl. Assn. Colls. and Schs., Chgo.; bd. dirs. Automation Alley, Mich., Internat. Sci. and Engring. Fair 2000, Mich. Sci. and Math. Alliance, 2000—. Author: (with others) Understanding Accreditation, 1983; pub. BioScience; contbr. chpts. to books. Mem. Diocesan Adv. Coun., Arlington, Va., 1978-84, Fairfax County (Va.) Dem. Com., 1979-95; judge No. Va. Sci. Fair, 1976—; trustee, sec. Southeastern U., Washington, 1983-87; trustee BIOSIS, Inc., Phila. and London, 1991-93; mem. Oakland County (Mich.) Workforce Devel. Bd., 1996—; bd. dirs. Automation Alley, 1999—. Recipient Olive Branch award Editors and Writers Com., N.Y.C., 1986, Citizenship award Am. Legion, 1959; postdoctoral fellow Nat. Sci. Found., 1964. Fellow AAAS; mem. ABA, AAUP, Am. Assn. Univ. Adminstrs. (pres. 1984-85), Engring. and Sci. Devel. Found. (bd. dirs., pres. 1996-2000, fellow Engring. Soc. 1997), Am. Coun. Edn. (bus. and higher edn. forum), Soc. Automotive Engrs., Nat. Soc. Black Engrs. (hon.), ESD-The Engring. Soc. (bd. dirs. 1999—), Circumnavigators Club, Econ. Club of Detroit (bd. dirs.), Detroit Athletic Club, Cosmos Club, Phi Beta Kappa, Sigma Xi, Tau Beta Pi. Roman Catholic. Avocation: flying. Office: Lawrence Tech U 21000 W 10 Mile Rd Ste M351 Southfield MI 48075-1058 E-mail: mail@charleschambers.com.

CHAMBERS, DONALD ARTHUR, biochemistry and molecular medicine educator; b. N.Y.C., Sept. 24, 1936; AB, Columbia U., 1959, PhD, 1972. Rsch. biochemist dept. surgery Harvard Med. Sch./Mass. Gen. Hosp., Boston, 1961-66; rsch. fellow in hematology dept. surgery Harvard Med. Sch./Beth Israel Hosp., 1967-68; faculty fellow in chem. biology Columbia U., N.Y.C., 1969-71; asst. rsch. biochemist Ctr. for Med. Genetics dept. medicine U. Calif. Med. Ctr., San Francisco, 1972-74, lectr. in biochemistry and biophysics, 1972-74, asst. prof. molecular biology and biochemistry, 1974-75; asst. prof. biol. chemistry and dermatology U. Mich., Ann Arbor, 1975-79, assoc. prof. biol. chemistry, 1979; prof. molecular biology U. Ill., Chgo., 1979—, prof. biol. chemistry, 1980—, rsch. prof. dermatology, 1981—, prof. biol. psychiatry, 1996. Assoc. mem. Dental Rsch. Inst. U. Mich., 1978-79, adj. rsch. investigator Dept. Biol. Chemistry, 1979—; dir. Ctr. for Molecular Biology of Oral Disease, U. Ill., Chgo., 1979—, interim head dept. biochemistry, 1985, head dept. biochemistry, 1986—; vis. scholar Green Coll., Oxford U., 1989-93, hon. vis. fellow, 1993—; sr. rsch. assoc. Wellcome Unit History of Medicine, Oxford. 2000--; fellow Honors Coll., 1985—, Phi Kappa Phi lectr., 1991, Sigma Xi lectr., 2001; nat. action com. Am. Assn. Dental Rsch., 1981—; study sect. rev. NIH, 1983-86, 92, 98—. Mem. editl. bd. Perspectives in Biology and Medicine. Recipient James Howard McGregor prize Columbia U., 1971; named Inventor of Yr., U. Ill., 1990; fellow in hematology NIH, 1967-68, fellow in chem. biology, 1969-71; Rsch. grantee NIH, Am.

Cancer Soc., Office of Naval Rsch.,1986—, Helene Curtis, Inc., 1988—, Tng. grantee NIH-NIGMS, 1975-79, NIH-NIAMDD, 1976-79, 77-80, NIH-NIDR-NIAMDD, 1980—, NIH-NCI, 1982-88. Mem. AAAS, Am. Assn. Med. Colls., Am. Assn. Immunology, Am. Chem. Soc., Am. Fedn. Clin. Rsch., Am. Soc. Biol. Chemistry, Am. Soc. Cell Biology, Am. Soc. Microbiology, Internat. Assn. Dental Rsch. (com. on rsch. progress 1982-85, chmn. 1984-85, chmn. grad. tng. forum com. exptl. pathology sect. 1983), Assn. Dept. Chmn. Biol. Chemistry, Chgo. Assn. Immunologists, N.Y. Acad. Scis. (organizer meeting The Double Helix, 40 Yrs. 1993), Royal Soc. Medicine, Soc. Investigative Dermatology, Oxford Med. Alumni Assn. (N.Am. rep. 2000—), Green Coll. Oxford Soc. (N.Am. rep. 2000—), Athenaeum Club London, Phi Kappa Phi, Sigma Xi (NIDCR 1998, spl. emphisii panel), Sigma Xi (pres.-elect 2000, pres. 2001). Achievements include patents (U.S., Can.) for method of determining periodontal disease, (with other) method of quantifying aspartate amino transferase in periodontal disease; research in role of cyclic nucleotides, prostaglandins, hormones and other regulatory factors in the regulation of cell function, proliferation and differentiation, in molecular medicine in neural-immune interactions, the regulatory mechanisms of host-microbial interactions, in the history and devel. of concepts in the bio-med. scis. Office: U Ill Coll Med Dept Biochemistry 1819 W Polk St # C 536 Chicago IL 60612-7331 also: Ctr Molecular Biol Oral Diseases 801 S Paulina St # C 860 Chicago IL 60612-7210 E-mail: donc@uic.edu.

CHAMBERS, ERNEST, state legislator; b. July 10, 1937; Mem. Nebr. Legislature from 11th dist., Lincoln, 1970—; mem. agr., bus. and labor coms. Nebr. Legislature, vice chmn. judiciary com., exec. bd. Address: Nebr Legislature Rm 1107 PO Box 94604 Lincoln NE 68509-4604

CHAMPAGNE, RONALD OSCAR, academic administrator, mathematics educator; b. Woonsocket, R.I., Jan. 2, 1942; s. George Albert and Simone (Brodeur) C.; m. Ruth Inez DesRuisseux, Nov. 25, 1970 BA, Duquesne U., 1964; MA, Cath. U. Am., 1966, Fordham U., 1970, PhD, 1973. Instr. math. Sacred Heart U., Bridgeport, Conn., 1966-69; asst. prof. math. Manhattanville Coll., Purchase, N.Y., 1969-75, dir. advanced studies program, 1973-75; prof. math., v.p., dean of faculty Salem Coll., W.Va., 1975-82; prof. math., pres., trustee St. Xavier U., Chgo., 1982-94, pres. emeritus, 1994—; prof. philosophy, v.p. for devel. Roosevelt U., 1996—. Bd. dirs. Chgo., Tchrs. Acad. for Math. and Sci. Author: LP Spaces of Complex Valued Functions, 1966; A Formalization of the Dialectical Development of Intelligence, 1974 Mem. Mat. Assn. Am., Philosophy of Sci. Assn., Carlton Club, Econs. Club Chgo., Exec. Club Chgo. Roman Catholic. Office: Roosevelt Univ 430 S Michigan Ave Chicago IL 60605-1394

CHAMPION, NORMA JEAN, communications educator, state legislator; b. Oklahoma City, Jan. 21, 1933; d. Aubra Dell (dec.) and Beuleah Beatrice (Flanagan) Black; m. Richard Gordon Champion, Oct. 3, 1953 (dec.); children: Jeffrey Bruce, Ashley Brooke. BA in Religious Edn., Cen. Bible Coll., Springfield, Mo., 1971; MA in Comm., S.W. Mo. State U., 1978; PhD in Tech., U. Okla., 1986. Producer, hostess The Children's Hour, Sta. KYTV-TV, NBC, Springfield, 1957-86; asst. prof. Cen. Bible Coll., 1968-84; prof. broadcasting Evangel U., Springfield, 1978—; mem. Springfield City Coun., 1987-92, Mo. Ho. of Reps., Jefferson City, 1993—. Adj. faculty Assemblies of God Theol. Sem., Springfield, 1987—, pres. coun.; bd. dirs. Global U.; mem. Commn. on Higher Edn., Assemblies of God, 1998—; frequent lectr. to svc. clubs, ednl. seminars; seminar spkr. Internat. Pentecostal Press Assn. World Conf., Singapore, 1989; announcer various TV commls. Contbr. numerous articles to religious publs. Mem. bd Mo. Access to Higher Edn. Trust, 1990—, Boys & Girls Town of Mo.; regional rep. Muscular Dystrophy Assn.; mem. adv. bd. Chameleon Puppet Theater, 1987; mem. exec. bd. Univ. Child Care Ctr., 1987; hon. chmn. fund raising Salvation Army, 1986; also numerous other bds., hon. chairmanships.; judge Springfield City Schs. Recipient commendation resolution Mo. Ho. of Reps., 1988; numerous award for The Children's Hour; Aunt Norma Day named in her honor City of Springfield, 1976. Mem. Nat. Broadcast Edn. Assn., Mo. Broadcast Edn. Assn., Nat. League Cities, Mo. Mcpl. League (human resource com. 1989, intergovtl. rels. com. 1990), Nat. Assn. Telecom. Officers and Advisors, PTA (life). Republican. Mem. Assemblies of God Ch. Avocations: gardening, reading, interior decoration. Home: 3609 S Broadway Ave Springfield MO 65807-4505 Office: Evangel Univ 1111 N Glenstone Ave Springfield MO 65802-2125 E-mail: mchampio@servics.state.mo.us.

CHAMPLEY, MICHAEL E. electric power industry executive; b. 1949; With Detroit Edison, 1977-92; v.p. mktg. and sales DTE Energy Co., Detroit, 1992-97, sr. v.p., 1997—. Office: DTE Energy Co 2000 2nd Ave Detroit MI 48226-1203

CHAMPLIN, STEVEN KIRK, lawyer; b. Omaha, July 6, 1944; m. Marjorie Eckenberg, Mar. 15, 1969; children: Anne, Paul, Jane. BA, Vanderbilt U., 1966; JD, U. Minn., 1969. Bar: Minn. 1969, U.S. Dist. Ct. Minn., U.S. Ct. Appeals (8th cir.). Assoc. Dorsey & Whitney, Mpls., 1969-70, 71-72, 73-75, ptnr., 1976—; pub. defender Hennepin County, 1972-73. Capt. U.S. Army, 1970-71. Mem. USTA. Home: 50 Myrtlewood Rd Wayzata MN 55391-9679 Office: Dorsey & Whitney LLP 220 S 6th St Ste 2200 Minneapolis MN 55402-1498

CHAN, SHIH HUNG, mechanical engineering educator, consultant; b. Chang Hwa, Taiwan, Nov. 8, 1943; came to U.S., 1964; s. Ping and Fu Zon (Liao) C.; m. Shirley Shih-Lin Wang, June 14, 1969; children: Bryan, Erick. Diploma Taipei Inst. Tech., Taiwan, 1963; MS, U. N.H., 1966; PhD, U. Calif.-Berkeley, 1969. Registered profl. engr., Wis. Asst. to assoc. prof. NYU, N.Y.C., 1969-73; assoc. prof. Poly. Inst. N.Y., N.Y.C., 1973-74; research staff mem. Argonne Nat. Lab., Ill., 1974-75; assoc. prof. U. Wis., Milw., 1975-78, prof. mech. engring., 1978-88, chmn. dept., 1979-89, Wis. Disting. prof. mech. engring., 1989—, dir. thermal engring. rsch. lab., 1997—, dean Coll. Engring. & Applied Sci., 1991—, honor chair prof. Yuan-Tze Inst. Tech., 1993—; cons. Argonne Nat. Lab., Ill., 1975—, Allen-Bradley Co., Milw., 1984, Gen. Electric Co., Schenectady, 1980, Teltech Resource Network, 1986—, Eclipse, Inc., 1988. Contbr. articles to profl. jours. Bd. dirs. Orgn. Chinese Americans, State of Wis., 1983—; v.p. Civic Club, Milw., 1984—, pres., 1985—. Served to 2d lt. Taiwan M.C., 1963-64. Recipient Outstanding Research award U. Wis.-Milw. Research Found., 1983, Research citation Assembly State of Wis., Madison, 1984, 1st Coll. Research award, 1987, Coll. Outstanding Rsch. award, 1987, Disting. Alumni award, 1991 ; grantee NSF, Dept. Energy, Argonne Nat. Lab., Office of Naval Research NASA Gas Rsch. Inst., 1969—. Fellow ASME; mem. Am. Nuclear Soc. (pres. Wis. 1982-83), Profl. Ergrs. State of Wis. Avocations: fishing, Tae-Kwon-do. Home: 3416 W Meadowview Ct Thiensville WI 53092-5110 Office: U Wis-Milw Dept of Mech Engring PO Box 784 Milwaukee WI 53201-0784

CHANDLER, KENT, JR. lawyer; b. Chgo., Jan. 10, 1920; s. Kent and Grace Emeret (Tuttle) C.; m. Frances Robertson, June 19, 1948; children: Gail, Robertson Kent. BA, Yale U., 1942; JD, U. Mich., 1949. Bar: Ill. 1949, U.S. Dist. Ct. (no. dist.) Ill. 1949, U.S. Ct. Appeals (7th cir.) 1955, U.S. Ct. Claims 1958. Assoc. Wilson & McIlvaine, Chgo., 1949-56, ptnr., 1957-94, spl. counsel to firm, 1994-98; of counsel Bell Jones & Quinlisk, 1998—. Bd. dirs. No. Trust Bank, Lake Forest, Ill., 1969-90, A.B. Dick Co., 1971-79, Internat. Crane Found., 1988—. Mem. zoning bd. appeals City of Lake Forest, Ill., 1953-63, chmn., 1963-67, mem. plan commn., 1955-69, chmn., 1969-70, pres. bd. local improvements, 1970-73, mayor, 1970-73, mem. bd. fire and police commn., 1975-82, chmn., 1982-84. Served to maj. USMCR, 1941-46. Mem. ABA, Ill. State Bar Assn., Chgo. Bar Assn., Lake County Bar Assn., Legal Club Chgo., Law Club (pres. 1985-86), Univ. Club, Onwentsia Club (Lake Forest), Old Elm Club (Highland Park, Ill.). Republican. Presbyterian. Office: 200 W Adams St Ste 2600 Chicago IL 60606-5233

CHANDLER, KEVIN, former state legislator; b. Mar. 31, 1960; m. Kathleen Chandler; 1 child. BA, U. Minn.; JD, Cath. U. Am. State senator Dist. 55 Minn. State Senate, 1993-97; atty., 1996—. Home: 5339 W Bald Eagle Blvd White Bear Lake MN 55110-6410

CHANDLER, RICHARD GATES, lawyer; b. Stockton, Calif., July 6, 1952; s. Kensal Roberts and Barbara (Gates) C; m. Heidi Pankoke, Oct. 22, 1994. BA, Lawrence U., 1974; JD, U. Chgo., 1977. Bar: Wis. 1977. Assoc. Minahan & Peterson S.C., Milw., 1979-84; legis. counsel to State Rep. Tommy G. Thompson, Rep. leader, Wis. Assembly, Madison, 1985-86; legis. asst. Congressman Robert W. Kasten, Jr., Washington, 1977-78; budget dir. State of Wis., 1987-2001; sec. Dept. Revenue, Madison, 2001-. Mem. Phi Beta Kappa. Republican. Methodist. Home: 810 Ottawa Trail Madison WI 53711-2941 Office: Dept Revenue PO Box 8933 Madison WI 53708-8933 E-mail: richards.chandler@dor.state.wi.us.

CHANDRASEKARAN, BALAKRISHNAN, computer and information science educator; b. Lalgudi, Tamil Nadu, India, June 20, 1942; came to U.S., 1963; s. Srinivasan and Nagamani Balakrishnan; m. Sandra Mamrak, Oct. 21, 1978; 1 child, Mallika. B in Engring., Madras U., Karaikudi, India, 1963; PhD, U. Pa., 1967. Devel. engr. Smith Kline Instruments, Phila., 1964-65; rsch. specialist Philco-Ford Corp., Blue Bell, Pa., 1967-69; asst. prof. computer and info. sci. Ohio State U., Columbus, 1969-71, assoc. prof., 1971-77, prof., 1977-95; sr. rsch. scientist, 1995—; dir. Lab. for Artificial Intelligence Rsch., Columbus, 1983—. Co-chmn. Symposium on Potentials and Limitations of Mech. Intelligence, Anaheim, Calif., 1971; chmn. Norbert Wiener Symposium, Boston, 1974; sci. dir. Summer Sch. on Computer Program Testing, SOGESTA, Urbino, Italy, 1981; vis. scientist Lawrence Livermore Nat. Lab., Livermore, Calif., summer 1981, cons. fall 1981; vis. scientist MIT Computer Sci. Lab., 1983; dir. NIH Artificial Intelligence in Medicine Workshop, 1984; organizer panel discussion on artificial intelligence and engring. ASME, 1985; vis. scholar Stanford U., 1990-91; keynote spkr. World Congress on Expert Sys., Mexico City, 1998. Editor: Diagrammatic Reasoning, 1995; co-editor Computer Program Testing, 1981; editor ACM Sigart Spl. Issue on Structure, Function, and Behavior, 1985; assoc. editor Artificial Intelligence in Engring., 1986—; mem. bd. editors Internat. Jour. Pattern Recognition & Artificial Intelligence, Med. Expert Systems, Artificial Intelligence in Engring.; assoc. editor Internat. Jour. Human-Computer Interactions, 1996—. Recipient Outstanding Paper award Pattern Recognition Soc., 1976; Moore fellow U. Pa., 1964-67. Fellow IEEE (editor-in-chief Expert Jour. 1990-94), Am. Assn. for Artificial Intelligence (chmn. workshops on diagrammatic reasoning 1992), Assn. for Computing Machinery; mem. Sys. Man and Cybernetics Soc. IEEE (v.p. 1974-75, pattern recognition com. 1969-72, assoc. editor Trans. 1973—, guest editor spl. issue on distributed program solving 1981). Democrat. Avocation: travel. Home: 2053 Iuka Ave Columbus OH 43201-1415 Office: Ohio State U Dept Computer and Info Sci 2015 Neil Ave Columbus OH 43210-1210 E-mail: chandra@cis.ohio-state.edu.

CHANEY, WILLIAM ALBERT, historian, educator; b. Arcadia, Calif., Dec. 23, 1922; s. Horace Pierce and Esther (Bowen) C. AB, U. Calif., Berkeley, 1943, PhD, 1961. Mem. faculty Lawrence U., Appleton, Wis., 1952-99, George McKendree Steele prof. Western culture, 1966-99, Steele prof. emeritus, 1999—, chmn. dept. history, 1968-71, 95-96. Vis. prof. Mich. State U., summer 1958. Author: The Cult of Kingship in Anglo-Saxon England: The Transition from Paganism to Christianity, 1970, reprinted 1999; contbr. articles to profl. jours. and encys. Jr. fellow Harvard Soc. Fellows, 1949-52; grantee Am. Council Learned Socs., 1966-67 Fellow Royal Soc. Arts; mem. MLA, AAUP, Am. Hist. Assn., Mediaeval Acad. Am., Am. Soc. Ch. History, Conf. Brit. Studies, Archeol. Inst. Am. Episcopalian. Home: 215 E Kimball St Appleton WI 54911-5720

CHANG, R. P. H. materials science educator; b. Chung King, Peoples Republic China, Dec. 22, 1941; s. Joseph K. Cho; m. Bennie Chang; children: Vivian, Samuel. BS in Physics, MIT, 1965; PhD in Plasma Physics, Princeton U., 1970. Postdoctoral fellowship Princeton Plasma Physics Lab., 1970-71; mem. tech. staff AT&T Bell Labs., Murray Hill, N.J., 1971-86; prof. Material Sci. & Engring. Northwestern U., 1986—. Dir. Materials Rsch. Ctr., 1989—. 7 original inventions 1977—; author over 170 sci. publs.; co-author chpts. in Plasma Diagnostics and Material Sci. & Engring.; co-editor: Plasma Synthesis & Etching of Electronic Materials, 1985. Fellow Am. Vacuum Soc.; mem. Am. Physics Soc., Materials Rsch. Soc. (pres. 1989), Internat. Union of Materials Rsch. Socs. (pres. 1991-92). Office: Northwestern U Dept Materials Sci Engring 2225 N Campus Dr Evanston IL 60208-0876

CHANG, Y. AUSTIN, materials engineer, educator; m. P. Jean Ho, Sept. 15, 1956; children: Vincent D., Lawrence D., Theodore D. B.S. in Chem. Engring, U. Calif., Berkeley, 1954; Ph.D. in Metallurgy, U. Calif., 1963; M.S. in Chem. Engring, U. Wash., 1955. Chem. engr. Stauffer Chem. Co., Richmond, Calif., 1956-59; postdoctoral fellow U. Calif.-Berkeley, 1963; metall. engr. Aerojet-Gen. Corp., Sacramento, 1963-67; assoc. prof. U. Wis.-Milw., 1967-70, prof., 1970-80, chmn. materials dept., 1971-78, assoc. dean research Grad. Sch., 1978-80; prof. dept. materials sci. and engring. U. Wis., Madison, 1980—, chmn. dept., 1982-91, Wis. Disting. prof., 1988—. Mem. summer faculty Sandia Labs., Livermore, Calif., 1971; vis. prof. Tohuku U., Sendai, Japan, fall 1987, MIT, Cambridge, fall 1991; NRC Disting. lectr. in material sci. Nat. Cheng Kung U., Tainan, Taiwan, 1987-88; adj. prof. U. Sci. Tech., Beijing, 1987—, hon. prof., 1995-96, adv. bd., 1996—; hon. prof. Ctrl. South U. Technology, Changsha, Hunan, 1996—, S.E. U., Nanjing, 1997, N.E. U., Shenyang, 1998; Winchell Lectr., Purdue U., 1999; summer faculty Quantum Structure Resh. Initiative, Hewlett-Packard Laboratories, Palo Alto, 1999; Belton Lectr. CSIRO, Clayton, Victoria, Australia, 2000. Co-author four books on phase equilibria and thermodynamic properties; co-editor four books; contbr. 300 scholarly articles in metall. and materials field to profl. jours. Mem. bd. Goodwill Residential Cmty., Inc., Milw., 1978-80; mem. Wis. Gov.'s Asian Am. Adv. Coun., 1980-82, Nat. Acad. Engring., 1996. Recipient Outstanding Instr. award U. Wis., Milw., 1972, Byron Bird award U. Wis., Madison, 1984, Alloy Phase Diagram Internat. Comm. Best Paper award, 1999, John Bardeen award TMS, 2000; named hon. prof. Southeast U. Nanjing, 1997, Northeast U., Shenyang, 1998. Fellow Am. Soc. Metals Internat. (Fellow award 1978, trustee 1981-84, Hall of Fame award Milw. chpt. 1986, Albert Easton White Disting. Tchr. award 1994, Albert Sauveun Achievement award 1996), Minerals, Metals and Materials Soc. (William Hume-Rothery award 1989, Educator award 1990, Fellow award 1991, Extraction and Processing lectr. award 1993, Mathewson award 1996); mem. NSPE, NAE, Orgn. Chinese Ams. (chpt. pres. 1979-81), Nat. Assn. Corrosion Engrs., Electrochem. Soc., Materials Rsch. Soc., Am. Phys. Soc., Sigma Xi, Tau Beta Pi, Phi Tau Phi, Alpha Sigma Mu (pres. 1984-85, hon. life), Chinese Acad. of Sci. (fgn. mem.). Office: U Wis 1509 University Ave Madison WI 53706-1538

CHANG, YOON IL, nuclear engineer; b. Seoul, Korea, Apr. 12, 1942; came to U.S., 1965; s. Paul Kun and In Sil (Hahn) C.; m. Ok Ja Kim, Dec. 19, 1966; children: Alice, Dennis, Eugene. BS in Nuclear Engring., Seoul Nat. U., 1964; ME, Tex. A & M U., 1967; PhD, U. Mich., 1971; MBA, U. Chgo., 1983. Mgr. spl. projects Nuclear Assurance Corp., Atlanta, 1971-74; asst. nuclear engr. Argonne (Ill.) Nat. Lab., 1974-76, group leader, 1976-77, sect. head, 1977-78, assoc. div. dir., 1978-84, gen. mgr. IFR program, 1984-94, dep. assoc. lab. dir. for engring. rsch., 1994-96, assoc. lab. dir. for engring. rsch., 1997—. Recipient E. O. Lawrence award U.S. Dept. Energy, 1994. Fellow Am. Nuclear Soc. (Walker Cisler award 1997—). Home: 2020 Palmer Dr Naperville IL 60564-5664 Office: Argonne Nat Lab 9700 Cass Ave Argonne IL 60439-4803

CHAO, BEI TSE, mechanical engineering educator; b. Soochow, China, Dec. 18, 1918; came to U.S., 1948, naturalized, 1962; s. Tse Yu and Yin T. (Yao) C.; m. May Kiang, Feb. 7, 1948; children: Clara, Fred Roberto. B.S. in Elec. Engring. with highest honor, Nat. Chiao-Tung U., China, 1939; Ph.D. (Boxer Indemnity scholar), Victoria U., Manchester, Eng., 1947. Asst. engr. tool and gage div. Central Machine Works, Kunming, China, 1939-41, asso. engr., 1941-43, mgr. tool and gage div., 1943-45; research asst. U. Ill., Urbana, 1948-50, asst. prof. dept. mech. engring., 1951-53, assoc. prof., 1953-55, prof., 1955-87, prof. emeritus, 1987—, head thermal sci. div., 1971-75, head dept. mech. and indsl. engring., 1975-87; assoc. mem. U. Ill. (Center for Advanced Study), 1963-64. Cons. to industry and govtl. agys., 1950-94; vis. Russell S. Springer prof. mech. engring. U. Calif., Berkeley, 1973; mem. reviewing staff Zentralblatt für Mathematik, Berlin, 1970-82; mem. U.S. Engring. Edn. Del. to Visit People's Republic of China, 1978; mem. adv. screening com. in engring. Fulbright-Hays Awards Program, 1979-81, chmn., 1980, 81; mem. com. U.S. Army basic sci. rsch. NRC, 1980-83; Prince disting. lectr. Ariz. State U., 1984; bd. dirs. Aircraft Gear Corp., 1989-94. Author: Advanced Heat Transfer, 1969; tech. editor Jour. Heat Transfer, 1975-81; mem. adv. editl. bd. Numerical Heat Transfer, 1977-95; mem. hon. edit. bd. Internat. Jour. Heat and Mass Transfer, 1987-97, Internat. Comm. in Heat and Mass Transfer, 1987-97; contbr. numerous articles on mech. engring. to profl. jours. Recipient Outstanding Tchr. award Ill. Mech. Engring. Alumni, 1978, Max Jakob Meml. award ASME/Am. Inst. Chem. Engring., 1983; Tau Beta Pi Daniel C. Drucker eminent faculty award, 1985; Univ. scholar, 1985 Fellow AAAS, ASME (Blackall award 1957, Heat Transfer award 1971, William T. Ennor Mfg. Tech. award 1992), Am. Soc. Engring. Edn. (Outstanding Tchr. award 1975, Western Electric Fund award 1973, Ralph Coats Roe award 1975, Benjamin Garver Lamme award 1984, Centennial Medallion 1993); mem. Nat. Acad. Engring., Academia Sinica, Chiao-Tung U. Alumni Assn. (pres. Midwest sect. 1975-76), Tau Beta Pi, Pi Tau Sigma (hon.). Home: 101 W Windsor Rd Apt 6103 Urbana IL 61802-6663 Office: Univ Ill 264 Mech Engring Bldg 1206 W Green St Urbana IL 61801-2906 E-mail: beitsechao@hotmail.com.

CHAO, MARSHALL, chemist; b. Changsha, Hunan, China, Nov. 20, 1924; came to U.S., 1955; s. Heng-ti and Hwei-yng C.; m. Patricia Hu, July 20, 1968; 1 dau., Anita A. B.S., Nat. Central U., Nanking, China, 1947; M.S., U. Ill., 1958, Ph.D., 1961. Tech. asst. Taiwan Fertilizer Co., Taipei, 1949-55; research chemist Dow Chem. Co., Midland, Mich., 1960-72, research specialist, 1973-80; research leader Dow chem. Co., 1980-86; sr. assoc. Omni Tech Internat., Ltd., 1986—. Author: Taiwan Fertilizers, 1951; editor newsletter Midland Chinese Christian Fellowship, 1987-94; contbr. articles to profl. jours.; patentee in field. Mem. Ch. Council Grace Bapt. Ch., Taipei, 1951-55; deacon 1st Baptist Ch., Midland, 1974-76. Univ. fellow U. Ill., 1957-60 Fellow Am. Inst. Chemists; mem. Am. Chem. Soc., Electrochem. Soc. (sect. chmn. 1973-74, 83-84, councilor 1974-76, 85—, vice chmn. 1964-65), Soc. Electroanalytical chemistry (charter), N.Y. Acad. Scis., Mensa, Sigma Xi, Phi Lambda Upsilon Clubs: Midland Chinese (chmn. 1975-76), Tittabawassee Toastmasters (sec.-treas. 1976-77). Home: 1206 Evamar Dr Midland MI 48640-7213 Office: Omni Tech Internat Ltd 2715 Ashman St Midland MI 48640-4449

CHAPDELAINE, ROLAND JOSEPH, academic administrator; b. Springfield, Mass., Aug. 23, 1946; s. Roland George and Therese Rose (LaRose) C.; m. Pamela Jeanne Mearns, Aug. 24, 1968; children: Eric Roland, Denise Elizabeth. BA, Providence Coll., 1968; MS, Ball State U., 1969, EdD, 1976. Instr. biology Ball State U., Muncie, Ind., 1969-72; assoc. prof. Howard Community Coll., Columbia, Md., 1972-78, div. chmn., 1975-80, coordinator faculty devel., 1978-80, acting dean students, 1982-83, dean instrn., 1980-86; v.p. acad. affairs Mohave Community Coll., Kingman, Ariz., 1986—. Co-chmn. adv. com. Columbia Assn. Urban Lake Water Quality Project, 1976-86; advisor Solar Energy Ednl. Project State of Md., 1977; cons. various community colls., Md., Pa., N.J., 1974—; lectr. Md. Acad. Scis., Balt., 1976-80; mem. Project Cooperation Task Force on Value added Instrn., 1988—. Contbr. articles to profl. jours. Vice-chmn. AYRA Youth Baseball, Howard County, Md., 1982; bd. dirs. St. John's Parish, Howard County, 1980-84; co-chmn. Citizens Adv. Com. Critical Areas Planning, Howard County, 1976-77; edn. coordinator Middle Patuxent Environ. Assn., Howard County, 1974-78; appointed State Commn. for Study of Future of Md. Community Coll., 1985-86; bd. dirs. Industry Edn. Alliance Council, Howard County, 1984-86, Hist. Savage Mill Mus., 1985-86; mem. Cholesterol Edn. Task Force, 1988—; selected participant Rising Star League for Innovation Leadership Inst., 1988; mem. Ariz. Task Force on Awarding Credit, 1988-89. Recipient Cert. Appreciation, Md. Dept. Vocat. Edn., 1982, Spl. Achievement award Howard Community Coll., 1986; grantee NSF, 1981, FIPSE, 1984, 85. Mem. Ariz. Acad. Adminstrs. (exec. com. 1988-89), Nat. Council Staff Program and Orgnl. Devel. (regional dir. 1984-85, Cert. Appreciation 1985), Nat. Council Instructional Adminstrs. (regional dir. 1980-85, dir. nat. issues 1985-86, sec. 1986, v.p., pres. elect 1987-88, pres. 1988—, co-chair Project Cooperation, 1988-89), Council Md. Deans (pres. 1983-84), Nat. Council for Staff, Program and Orgnl. Devel. (regional dir.), Md. Consortium of Biol. Scientists (steering com. 1973-80), Howard County C. of C. (leadership tng. program 1986); Ariz. Media Assn. (adminstr. of Yr. 1987). Democrat. Roman Catholic. Lodges: Rotary (sec. Kingman Rt.66, 1988—, program chair 1987-88, mem. exec. leadership inst. 1988—), Elks (Kingman Lodge 468, chaplain 1988-89). Home: 3705 Martingale Dr Kingman AZ 86401-2926 Office: Rock Valley College 3301 N Mulford Rd Rockford IL 61114-5699

CHAPLIN, DAVID DUNBAR, medical research specialist, medical educator; b. London, Aug. 28, 1952; came to U.S., 1952; s. Hugh Jr. and Alice Elizabeth (Dougherty) C.; m. Jane Ellen Bryant; children: Vernon H., Rosalind K., Daniel B. AB, Harvard U., 1973; MD, PhD, Washington U., St. Louis, 1980. Intern, then resident Parkland Meml. Hosp., Dallas, 1980-82; post-doctoral fellow dept. genetics Harvard U. Med. Sch., Boston, 1982-84; asst. prof. medicine Washington U. Sch. Medicine, St. Louis, 1984-91, prof. medicine, 1995—; assoc. investigator Howard Hughes Med. Inst., 1984—. Assoc. editor: The New Biologist, 1990-92, Diabetes, 1992-96; contbr. articles to profl. jours. Mem. grants com. Arthritis Found., Atlanta, 1989-92, NIAID AITR, 1998—. Scholar Harvard U., 1972, 73; Jane Coffin Childs Fund for Med. Rsch. fellow, 1982-84. Mem. Am. Soc. Clin. Investigation, Am. Fedn. Clin. Rsch., Am. Assn. Immunologists, Am. Soc. Human Genetics, Assn., Assn. Am. Physicians, Alpha Omega Alpha. Democrat. Roman Catholic. Office: Howard Hughes Med Inst 10050 Clin Scis Res Bldg 660 S Euclid Ave # 8022 Saint Louis MO 63110-1010 E-mail: cahplin@im.wustl.edu.

CHAPLIN, HUGH, JR. physician, educator; b. N.Y.C., Feb. 4, 1923; m. Alice Dougherty, June 16, 1945; 4 children; m. Lee Nelken Robins, Aug. 5, 1998. A.B., Princeton U., 1943; M.D., Columbia U., 1947. Diplomate Am. Bd. Internal Medicine, Nat. Bd. Med. Examiners. Intern Mass. Gen. Hosp., Boston, 1947-48, resident, 1948-50; fellow in hematology Brit. Postgrad. Med. Sch., London, 1951-53; physician in charge Clin. Center Blood Bank, NIH, Bethesda, Md., 1953-55; Commonwealth Fund fellow Wright Fleming Inst. Microbiology, London, 1962-63, Josiah Macy Faculty scholar, 1975-76. Instr. in medicine Washington U. Sch. Medicine, St. Louis, 1955-56, asst. prof. medicine and preventive medicine, 1956-62, asso. dean, chmn. admissions com., 1957-62, asso. prof., 1963-65, prof., 1965, William B. Kountz prof. preventive medicine, 1965-83; dir. IWJ Inst.

of Rehab., St. Louis, 1964-72; prof. pathology, dir. Barnes Hosp. Blood Bank, St. Louis, 1983-91; emeritus prof. pathology and medicine, 1991—; mem. Am. Standards Com. for Blood Transfusion Equipment; mem. subcom. on transfusion problems NRC, 1959-62, mem. com. on blood and transfusion problems, 1963-67; chmn. ad hoc blood program research com. ARC, 1967-73, bd. govs., 1978-84 Assoc. editor Transfusion, 1960-98; contbg. editor Vox Sanguinis, 1960-79. Served with USNR, 1942-45. Mem. Am. Fedn. Clin. Research, Central Soc. Clin. Research, Am. Soc. Clin. Investigation, Assn. Am. Physicians, Am., Internat. socs. hematology, Brit. Med. Research Soc., Brit. Royal Soc. Medicine, Am. Assn. Blood Banks (sci. program com. 1959-60, Emily Cooley award 1968, Morton Grove-Rasmussen award 1985), Phi Beta Kappa, Alpha Omega Alpha, Sigma Xi. Office: Washington U Sch Medicine Box 8118 4949 Barnes Hospital Plz Saint Louis MO 63110-1003

CHAPMAN, ALGER BALDWIN, finance executive, lawyer; b. Portland, Maine, Sept. 28, 1931; s. Alger Baldwin Sr. and Elizabeth (Ives) C.; m. Beatrice Bishop, Oct. 30, 1983; children: Alger III, Samuel P., Andrew I., Henry H. BA, Williams Coll., 1953; JD, Columbia U., 1956. Bar: N.Y. 1957. Pres. Shearson, Hammill & Co., 1970-74; co-chmn. Shearson & Co., 1974-81; vice chmn. Am. Express Bank, 1982-85; chmn., chief exec. officer Chgo. Bd. Options Exchange, 1986-97; vice chmn. ABN Amro, Inc., 1996-2001; chmn., CEO ABN Amro Fin. Svcs, 2001—. Vice chmn. ABN AMRO Inc., 1997—; bd. dirs. ISO New Eng., HDO, Current Assets LLC. Clubs: Chgo., Racquet Club Chgo.; Metropolitan (N.Y.C.), Chgo. Club. Avocations: golf, skiing, reading. Home: 1500 N Lake Shore Dr Chicago IL 60610-6657 Office: ABN AMRO Fin Svcs 208 S Lasalle St 2d Fl Chicago IL 60604-1065

CHAPMAN, DARRIAN, sportscaster; children from previous marriage: Marrisa, Jordan. Student, U. Mass. Sports dir. Sta. WGR Newsradio 55, Buffalo; broadcast analyst Buffalo Bisons Baseball Club; with NBC4, Washington, 1995—, sports segment prodr., weekend morning sports anchor, sports reporter, subs. host for The George Michael Sports Machine; weekend sports anchor, sports reporter NBC 5, Chgo., 2000, lead sports anchor for evening and nightly news broadcasts; host NBC5's Sports Sunday at 10:30 pm. Avocations: baseball, classical music, biking, cooking. Office: NBC 454 N Columbus Dr Chicago IL 60611*

CHAPMAN, KATHLEEN HALLORAN, state legislator, lawyer; b. Estherville, Iowa, Jan. 19, 1937; d. Edward E. and Meryl (McConoughey) Halloran; m. Allen Ray Chapman, Apr. 29, 1961 (div. May 1999); children: Christopher, Stuart. BA, U. Iowa, 1959, JD, 1974. Bar: Iowa 1974, U.S. Ct. Appeals (8th cir.) 1974. Prin. Booth & Chapman, Cedar Rapids, Iowa, 1974-99; mem. Iowa Ho. of Reps., Des Moines, 1983-92, 97-99, vice chmn. judiciary com., 1983-86, vice chmn. ethics com., 1985-88, vice chmn. ways and means com., 1987-88, chmn. rules and adminstrn. com., 1987-88, asst. majority leader, 1989-90, chmn. edn. appropriations, 1991-92; adminstr. profl. licensing divsn. Dept. Commerce, State of Iowa, 1999—. Legis. Coun. Iowa Gen. Assembly, 1987-92, 97-99; participant Atlantic Exch., 1989. Trustee East Cen. Regional Libr., Cedar Rapids, 1974-80, Tanager Place, Cedar Rapids, 1978-99. Toll fellow Coun. State Govts., 1988; named Woman of Yr. Linn County, 1995. Mem. Iowa Bar Assn. (chair adminstrv. law sect. 1995-96). Democrat. Roman Catholic. Office: 1918 SE Hulsizer Rd Ankeny IA 50021-3941

CHAPMAN, LOREN J. psychology educator; b. Muncie, Ind., Jan. 5, 1927; s. Herbert L. and Lurana Gertrude (Treff) C.; m. Jean Marilyn Paulsen, June 6, 1953; children: Nancy, Laurence. AB cum laude, Harvard U., 1948; MS, Northwestern U., 1952, PhD, 1954. USPHS postdoctorate research fellow U. Chgo., 1954-56, instr., asst. prof., 1956-59; assoc. prof. U. Ky., Lexington, 1959-62; from assoc. prof. to prof. Southern Ill. U., Carbondale, 1962-67; prof. U. Wis., Madison, 1966-93, NIMH rsch. scientist, 1988-93; prof. emeritus, 1994—. Author: Disordered Thought in Schizophrenia, 1973; contbr. over 100 articles to profl. jours. Recipient Disting. Scientist award Soc. for Sci. Clin. Psychology, 1992; NIMH research grantee, 1952-97. Fellow AAAS, APA (Disting. Sci. award for application of psychology 1999); mem. Am. Psychopathol. Assn., Soc. Rsch. Psychopathology (pres. 1989, Joseph Zubin award 1992), Am. Psychol. Soc. (William James fellow 1995). Home: 129 Richland Ln Madison WI 53705-4834 Office: Univ Wis Dept Psychology 1202 W Johnson St Madison WI 53706-1611 E-mail: ljchapm1@facstaff.wisc.edu.

CHAPPEL, DONALD R. waste management executive; Grad., U. Ill. CPA, Ill. With Arthur Andersen & Co., Chgo.; dir. bus. devel. Beatrice Cos., Inc./Esmark, Inc., dir. N.Am. ops. analysis, dir. fin./ops. analysis and audit; v.p., contr. chem. waste mgmt. divsn. Waste Mgmt., Inc., v.p., contr. West and Mountain groups, v.p., contr. N.Am. solid waste ops., 1995-97, v.p., acting CFO, 1997-2000. Office: Waste Mgmt Inc 720 E Butterfield Rd Oak Brook IL 60148

CHAREWICZ, DAVID MICHAEL, photographer; b. Chgo., Feb. 17, 1932; s. Michael and Stella (Pietrzak) C.; student DePaul U., 1957, Northwestern U., 1952; MA in Photography, Profl. Photographers Am. Inc., 1986; m. Catherine Uccello, Nov. 8, 1952; children: Michael, Karen, Daniel. Trainee, Merill Chase, Chgo., 1950-51; dark room technician Maurice Seymour, Chgo., 1951-52; photographer Oscar & Assos., Chgo., 1955-63; owner Dave Chare Photography, Park Ridge, Ill., 1963—; pres., owner C&C Duplicating, Inc., 1978-93. Pres. Oakton Parent Tchr. Club, 1968-69, del. dist. 64 caucus, 1970, 73; mem. centennial photo com., Park Ridge, Ill., 1973; mem. sponsoring com. Park Ridge Men's Prayer Breakfast 1982—. Served with AUS, 1952-54. Mem. Am. Soc. Photographers, Profl. Photographers Assn., Midstate Indsl. Photographers Assn. (treas. 1981, pres. 1984-85). Home: 739 N Northwest Hwy Park Ridge IL 60068-2541 Office: 739 N Northwest Hwy Park Ridge IL 60068-2541

CHARFOOS, LAWRENCE SELIG, lawyer; b. Detroit, Dec. 7, 1935; s. Samuel and Charlotte (Salkin) C.; m. Jane Emerson. Student, U. Mich., 1953-56; LLB, Wayne State U., 1959. Bar: Mich. 1959, Ill. 1965. Pvt. practice, Detroit, 1960-63; pres., partner Charfoos & Christensen, (P.C.), 1967—; theatrical producer, legitimate theater mgr. Chgo., 1963-67. Cons. med.-legal problems Mich. Med. Soc., Mich. Hosp. Coun., State Bar Mich., ATLA; mem. Com. U.S. Cts., 1995; lead counsel N.W./Detroit Met. Airport. Author: The Medical Malpractice Case: A Complete Handbook, 1974, Daughters at Risk, 1981, Personal Injury Practice, Technique and Technology, 1986; contbr. articles to profl. jours. Trustee Lawrence S. Charfoos Found. Elected to Inner Circle of Advocates, 1973 Mem. ABA, Mich. Bar Assn., Detroit Bar Assn. (past dir.), Am. Bd. Profl. Liability Attys. (founder, past pres.), Internat. Acad. Trial Lawyers, Plaintiff's Steering Com./Breast Implant Cases, Com. on U.S. Cts., State Bar Mich., 1995—. Office: 5510 Woodward Ave Detroit MI 48202-3804

CHARLA, LEONARD FRANCIS, lawyer; b. New Rochelle, N.Y., May 4, 1940; s. Leonard A. and Mary L. Charla; m. Kathleen Gerace, Feb. 3, 1968 (div. Dec. 1988); children: Larisa, Christopher; m. Elizabeth A. Du Mouchelle, Aug. 27, 1993. BA, Iona Coll., 1962; JD, Cath. U., 1965; LLM, George Washington U., 1971. Bar: D.C. 1967, N.J. 1970, Mich. 1971. Tech. writer IRS, Washington, 1966-67; atty. adv. ICC, 1967, atty., 1968-69; mgmt. intern HEW, 1967-68; atty. Bowes & Millner, Transp. Cons., Newark, 1969-71; atty. legal staff GM, Detroit, 1971-85, sr. counsel, 1985-87, asst. gen. counsel, 1987-89; sr. v.p. Clean Sites Inc., Alexandria, Va., 1989-90; shareholder Butzel Long, Detroit, Bloomfield Hills, Ann Arbor, and Lansing, Mich., 1990—. Mem. faculty Ctr. for Creative Studies, Coll. Art and Design, Detroit, 1978-89, adj. asst. prof., 1982-89; faculty art U. Mich., 1980, 84-89, adj. asst. prof. 1988-89. Author: Never Cooked Before/Gotta Cook Now!, 1999. Bd. dirs. Gt. Lakes Performing Artists Assocs., 1983-85; bd. dirs. Mich. Assn. Cmty. Arts Agys., 1983-89, 92-93, vice-chair, 1986-88, chair, 1988-89; bd. govs. Cath. U. Am. Alumni, 1982, v.p., 1993-99; active Info. Network Superfund Settlements, 1988—; bd. regents Cath. U. Am., 1992—, Birmingham Bloomfield Art Assn., 1987-88, 94-95; bd. dirs. Friends of Modern Art, Detroit Inst. Arts, 1996—, v.p., 1998—; bd. Art Ctr. Mt. Clemens, Mich., 1997-99, 99—, chair bldg. com., 2001—. Fellow N.Y. State Regents, 1962; scholar Cath. U. Law Sch., 1962-65. Mem. ABA, Mich. State Bar Assn. (chmn. arts sect. 1980-81, chair arts comm. entertainment and sports sect. 1980-81, arts comm. entertainment and sports sect. coun. 1979-88, 92—). Office: Butzel Long 150 W Jefferson Ave Ste 900 Detroit MI 48226 E-mail: charla@butzel.com.

CHARLES, ALLAN G. physician, educator; b. N.Y.C., Nov. 15, 1928; s. Harry G. and Alice (Grotzky) C.; m. Phyllis V. J. Vail, June 28, 1957; children: Della Marie, Aaron Joseph, David Jonathan. AB cum laude, NYU, 1948, MD, 1952. Diplomate: Am. Bd. Obstetrics and Gynecology. Intern Phila. Gen. Hosp., 1952-53; resident in obstetrics and gynecology Mt. Sinai Hosp., N.Y.C., 1955-57, Michael Reese Hosp., Chgo., 1957-60, clin. asst., 1960-61, assoc. attending physician, 1961-69, attending physician, 1969—; co-dir. Michael Reese Hosp. (Rh-Investigative Clinic), 1963—, vice-chmn. dept. obstetrics and gynecology, 1971, pres. staff, 1978, bd. dirs., 1981-84; chief obstetrics and gynecology Michael Reese Hosp., 1990-99; chmn. rsch. and edn. found. Michael Reese Hosp. Med. Staff, 1996-2000; pvt. practice specializing in office gynecology Chgo., 1960—. Courtesy staff Chgo. Lying-In-Hosp.; clin. asst. prof. ob-gyn. U. Ill. Coll. Medicine, Chgo., 1960-64, Chgo. Med. Sch., 1964-72; clin. prof. Pritzker Sch. Medicine, U. Chgo., 1972-84; attending physician Northwestern Meml. Hosp., 1984-90; prof. clin. ob-gyn. Northwestern U., 1983; clin. prof. ob-gyn. U. Ill. Coll. Medicine, 1991. Author: Rh Iso Immunization and Erythroblastosis Fetalis, 1969; Contbr. articles to profl. jours. Fellow Am. Coll. Obstetricians and Gynecologists, Internat. Coll. Surgeons (chmn. Am. sect. obs. and gynec. 1979-83, sec., asst. treas. Am. sect.), Central Assn. Obstetricians and Gynecologists; mem. AMA, Ill., Chgo. med. socs., Chgo. Gynecol. Soc. (v.p. 1980—, sec. 1988-90, pres.-elect, 1992, pres. 1993-94). Achievements include developing substitute for uterine tube, Rh-sensitization. Home: 1150 N Lake Shore Dr Apt 22GH Chicago IL 60611 Office: 55 E Washington St Fl 37 Chicago IL 60602-2103 E-mail: agcobg@aol.com.

CHARLES, GERARD, performing company executive, choreographer; b. Folkstone, Eng. m. Catherine Yoshimura; 1 child Max. Student, Royal Ballet Sch. Master ballet BalletMet, Les Grands Ballets Canadiens; profl. dancer Milw. Ballet, Ballet Internat. , London; assoc. artistic dir. BalletMet Columbus, artistic dir., 2001—. Choreographer, tchr., rearranger works internationally in field. Artistic dir. The Sleeping Beauty, Coppelia. Fellow choreography, Nat. Endowment for Arts. Office: BalletMet Columbus 322 Mount Vernon Ave Columbus OH 43215 Office Fax: 614-229-4858.*

CHARLSON, ALAN EDWARD, corporate lawyer, retail company executive; b. 1948; BS, U. Mich.; JD, U. Pitts. Bar: Pa. 1973. Exec. v.p., gen. counsel May Department Stores Co., St. Louis. Mem. ABA. Office: May Dept Stores Co 611 Olive St Ste 1750 Saint Louis MO 63101-1721

CHARLTON, BETTY JO, retired state legislator; b. Reno County, Kans., June 15, 1923; d. Joseph and Elma (Johnson) Canning; BA, U. Kans., 1970, MA, 1976; m. Robert Sansom Charlton, Feb. 24, 1946 (dec. 1984); children: John Robert, Richard Bruce. Asst. instr. polit. sci. and western civilization U. Kans., Lawrence, 1970-73; legis. adminstrv. svcs. employee State of Kans., Topeka, 1977-78, legis. aide gov's. office, 1979; mem. Kans. Ho. of Reps., 1980-95, ret., 1995.

CHARNAS, LAWRENCE, neurologist; MD, U. Pa. Diplomate Am. Bd. Med. Genetics, Am. Bd. Neurology. With Harvey Inst. for Human Genetics, Balt. Office: Divsn Ped Neurology Box 486 Mayo 420 Delaware St SE Minneapolis MN 55455-0374 Fax: 410-828-2919. E-mail: charnas@gbmc.org.

CHARNAS, MICHAEL (MANNIE CHARNAS), investment company executive; b. Cleve., Sept. 24, 1947; s. Max and Eleanor (Gross) C.; m. Mimi F. Stein, June 10, 1990; 1 child from previous marriage, Matthew; 1 child, Max. BBA, Ohio State U., 1969, MBA, 1971. Page Ohio Ho. of Reps., 1969; mem. Ohio Staters, Inc., 1969; fin. analyst Addressograph-Multigraph, Inc., Cleve., 1971-73; asst. to pres., dir. planning and budget 1st Nat. Supermarkets, Inc. (Pick-N-Pay), 1975-78, asst. to pres., v.p. planning and budgets, 1978-79, sr. v.p. fin., adminstr., 1979-81, sr. v.p., CFO, adminstrv. officer Hartford, Conn., 1981-86; founder Charnas Mktg. and Investment Co., 1986—; pres., owner Indsl. Pallet and Packaging Co., Beachwood, Ohio, 1986-94; regional v.p. Pallet Pallet, Inc. (formerly Indsl. Pallet and Packaging Co.), Toronto, 1995-97; co-owner Samm Properties and Samm Mgmt. Svcs., Ltd., 1998—. Bd. dirs. Gorman-Lavelle Corp.; owner/CEO Pallet Distbrs., Inc., 1999-2001; fin. adv. bd. Gooey Industries, 2000. Jewish. Avocations: tennis, reading, collecting modern classic cars. Office: Ste 217 3659 Green Rd Cleveland OH 44122-5715 E-mail: bizwiz924@cs.com.

CHARO, ROBIN ALTA, law educator; b. Bklyn., June 6, 1958; d. Jon and Ethel (Munach) C. BA, Harvard U., 1979; JD, Columbia U., 1982. Bar: N.Y. 1983. Assoc. dir. Legis. Drafting Rsch. Fund, N.Y.C., 1982-85; lectr. Columbia Law Sch., 1983-85, U. Paris, Paris, 1985-86; legal analyst Congl. Office of Tech. Assessment, Washington, 1986-88; fellow U.S. Agy. for Internat. Devel., 1988-89; assoc. prof. law U. Wis., Madison, 1989-98, prof. law, 1998—. Cons. Congl. Office of Tech. Assessment, 1988-92, U.S. AID, 1989-91, Can. Law Reform Commn., Ottawa, Can., 1989-90, NAS, 1989—. Contbr. articles to profl. jours. Active U. Wis. Human Subjects Com., Madison, U. Wis. Hosp. Ethics Com., Madison, Abortion Strategy Group, Madison; cons. Rural South Cen. Wis. Perinatal Substance Abuse Project, 1989—. Fulbright grantee, 1985-86. Fellow AAAS; mem. Internat. Bioethics Assn., Am. Soc. Law and Medicine. Democrat. Jewish. Avocations: travel, folk music, foreign languages. Office: U Wis Law Sch 975 Bascom Mall Madison WI 53706-1399

CHARPENTIER, MARTI RAY, accountant, financial executive; b. Oakes, N.D., Feb. 28, 1955; s. Donald Alexander and Marcia Deloris (Remillard) C. BBA cum laude, U. N.D., 1977. CPA, Minn., N.D. Staff acct. Touche Ross & Co., Mpls., 1978-82, supr., 1982-83; mgr. fin. systems Dyco Petroleum Corp., 1983-85; asst. controller Best Products Co., Inc., 1985-87; contr. The King Cos. Inc., St. Paul, 1987-89; contr., asst. treas. Analysts Internat. Corp., Mpls., 1989—99, v.p. fin., treas., 1999—. Mem. Am. Inst. CPA's, N.D. Soc. CPA's, Minn. Soc. CPA's. Roman Catholic. Avocations: sports, fishing, hunting, camping. Home: 18934 Radford St Minnetonka MN 55345-6036 Office: Analysts Internat Corp 3601 W 76th St Minneapolis MN 55435

CHASE, ALYSSA ANN, editor; b. New Orleans, Dec. 23, 1965; d. John Churchill and Alexandra Andra (de Monsabert) C.; m. Robert Brian Rebein, July 1, 1995; 1 child, Alexandra Maria Rebein. BA in Lit. in English, U. Kans., 1988; BA in Studio Art magna cum laude, SUNY, Buffalo, 1994. Asst. editor Dial Books for Young Readers, N.Y.C., 1989-90; assoc. editor Holiday House, Inc., 1990-92, Buffalo (N.Y.) Spree Mag., Buffalo, 1992-95; copy editor, writer The Riverfront Times and St. Louis Mag., St. Louis, 1995-97; mng. editor St. Louis Mag., 1997-98; editor RCI Premier Mag., Indpls., 1998—. Freelance copy writer, proofreader, copy editor and/or rschr. Harper Collins Children's Books, N.Y.C., 1990-92, Morrow Jr. Books, N.Y.C., 1990-92, Tambourine Books, N.Y.C., 1990-92, Lothrop, Lee & Shepherd Books, N.Y.C., 1990-92, Dorling Kindersley, Inc., N.Y.C., 1990-92, The Humanist: Prometheus Books, 1993, Printing Prep, Buffalo, 1994, Georgette Hasiotis, Buffalo, 1994, August Tavern Creek Developers, St. Louis, 1996; tchg. artist, docent coord., tour guide The Arts in Edn. Inst. of Western N.Y., Cheektowaga, N.Y., 1995. Mem. Phi Beta Kappa. Avocations: painting, writing childrens books, travel, gardening, running. Home: 306 N Ridgeview Dr Indianapolis IN 46219-6127

CHASE, CLINTON IRVIN, psychologist, educator, business executive; b. Aug. 14, 1927; m. Patricia Cronenberger; 1 child. B.S. in Psychology with honors, U. Idaho, 1950, M.S. in Adminstrn., 1951; Ph.D. in Ednl. Psychology, U. Calif.-Berkeley, 1958. Asst. to dean students Wash. State U., 1951-52; sch. psychologist Piedmont Pub. Schs., Calif., 1957-58; asst. prof. ednl. psychology Idaho State U., 1958-61, Miami U., Oxford, 1961-62, Ind. U., Bloomington, 1962-64, assoc. prof., 1964-68, prof., 1968-95; prof. emeritus Indiana U., 1995—; assoc. dir. Bur. Evaluative Studies and Testing Ind. U., 1962-70, dir., 1970-89, chmn. dept. ednl. psychology, 1970-74; dir. Ind. Testing and Evaluation Svc., 1976-87, Ind. Ctr. for Evaluation, 1988-94; owner, mgr. Ind. Testing and Evaluation Svc., 1990—. Author: (with H. Glenn Ludlow) Readings in Educational and Psychological Measurement, 1966, Elementary Statistical Procedures, 1967, 3d edit., 1984, Measurement for Educational Evaluation, 1974, 2d edit., 1978, (with L.C. Jacobs) Developing and Using Tests Effectively, 1992, Contemporary Assessment for Educators, 1999. Served with USN, 1945-46; to capt. USAF, 1952-55. Named Ky. Col., 1998. Fellow Am. Psychol. Assn., Am. Ednl. Research Assn., Nat. Council on Measurement in Edn., Phi Beta Kappa, Kappa Delta Pi E-mail: chase@indiana.edu.

CHATO, JOHN CLARK, mechanical and bioengineering educator; b. Budapest, Hungary, Dec. 28, 1929; s. Joseph Alexander and Elsie (Wasserman) C.; m. Elizabeth Janet Owens, Aug. 1954; children: Christine B., David J., Susan E. ME, U. Cin., 1954; MS, U. Ill., 1955; PhD, MIT, 1960. Co-op student, trainee Frigidaire div. GMC, Dayton, Ohio, 1950-54; grad. fellow U. Ill., Urbana, 1954-55; grad. fellow, inst. MIT, Cambridge, 1955-58, asst. prof., 1958-64; assoc. prof. U. Ill., Urbana, 1964-69, prof., 1969-96, prof. emeritus, 1996—, chmn. exec. com. bioengring. faculty, 1972-78, 82-83, 84-85, asst. dean of engring., 1997-98. Cons. Industry and Govt., 1958—; dir., founder Biomed. Engring. Systems Team, Urbana, Ill, 1974-78; assoc. editor Jour. Biomech. Engring., 1976-82. Patentee in field; contbr. articles to profl. jours., chpts. to books on heat transfer, bio-heat transfer, refrigeration, air conditioning, cryogenics, and thermal systems. Trustee 1st Presbyn. Ch., Urbana, 1976-78, 99-2001, edler, 1982-85; bd. dirs. Univ. YMCA, Champaign, Ill., 1976-78, 87-90; com. mem. troop 6 Boy Scouts Am., Urbana, 1984-86, Urbana Planning Commn., 1973-78; mem. adv. com. Urbana Park Dist., 1981-84, 2d v.p. Champaign County Izaak Walton League, 1986, 1st v.p., 1987, pres., 1988-92, bd. dirs., state dir., 1992—. Recipient Tobin award Champaign County Izaak Walton League, 1992, Cmty. Svc. award Urbana Park Dist., 1996; named Disting. Engring. Alumnus, U. Cin., 1972, NSF fellow 1961, Fogarty Sr. Internat. fellow 1978-79; Japan Soc. Promotioin of Sci. fellow, 1997. Fellow ASME (exec. com. bioengring. divsn. 1992-96, sec. 1993-94, chmn. 1994-95, Charles Russ Richards Meml. award 1978, N.R. Lissner award 1992, Dedicated Svc. award 2000), Am. Inst. Med. and Biol. Engrs.; mem. ASHRAE (treas. East Ctrl. Ill. chpt. 1984, sec. 1985, 87, 1st v.p. 1988, pres. 1989), IEEE (sr.), Am. Soc. for Engring. Edn., Internat. Inst. Refrigeration (assoc.), Audubon Soc. (bd. dirs. 1988-89, 2000--, v.p. 1990, 95-96, treas. 1991-93, 98-99, pres. 2000-01, 02-), Exch. Club (bd. dirs. 1989-91, 95-96, pres.-elect 1996-97, pres. 1997-98, dist. dir. 2001—). Achievements include research in fields of heat transfer, bio-heat transfer, refrigeration, air conditioning, cryogenics, and thermal systems. Avocations: tennis, photography, bird watching, hiking, kayaking. Office: U Ill Dept Mech Indsl Engring 1206 W Green St Urbana IL 61801-2906 E-mail: j-chato@uiuc.edu.

CHATTERJEE, JAYANTA, academic administrator; b. Calcutta, India, Mar. 19, 1936; came to U.S., 1959; s. Hari Charan and Asha (Mukherjee) C.; m. Janet Ley Smith, Aug. 31, 1968; children: Eric, Brinda. BArch, Indian Inst. Tech., 1958; M in Regional Planning, U. N.C., 1962; MArch in Urban Design, Harvard U., 1965. Asst. prof. U. of Cin., 1967-72, assoc. prof., 1972-77, assoc. dean, 1975-77, prof., 1977—, dir. sch. planning, 1977-82, acting dean, 1982-83, dean, 1982-2001. Regional designer Met. Area Planning Commn., Boston, 1965-67; urban scholar Cities Recovery Program, Cleve., 1981-82. Co-author: The Partnership Planning, 1982, Rebuilding American Cities, 1983, Breaking the Boundaries, 1989; co-editor/founder: Jour. Planning, Education and Research, 1981-84. Mem. Ohio Eminent Scholar Rev. Panel, 1985, Urban Design Rev. Bd., Cin., 1988—; bd. dirs. Arts Consortium, 1983—87, Contemporary Arts Ctr., Cin., 1983—, Hillside Trust, Cin., 1983—84, Bethesda Hosp., Inc., Cin., 1982—95, Total Living Concept, Inc., Cin., 1976—88, Ctr. Mediation of Disputes, Cin., 1989—92, The Emery Ctr., Cin., 1988—90, Better Housing League, Cin., 1989—92, Archtl. Found., Cin., 1990—. Recipient Apple award Archtl. Fedn. Cin., 1996, Disting. Alumnus award U. N.C., 1996, Disting. Svc. award Assn. Coll. Schs. of Planning, 1991. Fellow Am. Inst. Cert. Planners (editl. bd. AICP Casebook 1991-93, tech. adv. bd. 1993-96); mem. AIA (assoc.; Thomas Jefferson award pub. arch. 2000), Am. Planning Assn. (pres. Ohio chpt. 1970-72, editorial adv. bd. Jour. APA), Ptnrs. of Ams. (Ohio-Parana), Assn. Collegiate Schs. of Planning (pres. 1983-85, Jay Chatterjee Svc. award 1998--), Internat. Coun. Fine Arts Deans, Cin. Post/Corbett Found. (Lifetime achievement award in Arts 1999). Office: U Cin Coll of Design Architecture Art and Planning PO Box 210016 Cincinnati OH 45221-0016 Fax: 513.556.3288. E-mail: Jay.Chatterjee@uc.edu.

CHATTERTON, ROBERT TREAT, JR. reproductive endocrinology educator; b. Catskill, N.Y., Aug. 9, 1935; s. Robert Treat and Irene (Spoor) Chatterton; m. Patricia A. Holland, June 24, 1956 (div. 1965); children: Ruth Ellen, William Matthew, James Daniel; m. Astrida J. Vanags, June 4, 1966 (div. 1977); 1 child Derek Scott ; m. Carol J. Lewis, May 24, 1985. BS, Cornell U., 1958, PhD, 1963; MS, U. Conn., 1959. Postdoctoral fellow Med. Sch. Harvard U., 1963-65; rsch. assoc. div. oncology Inst. Steroid Rsch. Montefiore Hosp. and Med. Ctr., N.Y.C., 1965-70; asst. prof. Coll. Medicine U. Ill., 1970-72, assoc. prof. Coll. Medicine, 1972-79; prof. Med. Sch. Northwestern U., Chgo., 1979—. Mem. sci. adv. com. AID, chairperson Instnl. Rev. Bd. Northwestern U., 1982—83, mem. intellectual properties com., 1987—95, chairperson radiation safety com., 2000—; dir. Immunoassay Facility, R. H. Lurie Cancer Ctr. Northwestern U. Med. Sch., 1997—; dir. clin. labs., dept. ob-gyn. Northwestern Med. Facutly Found., 1996—99, dir. shared clin. labs., 1999—. Contbr. articles to profl. jours. Grantee, NIH, 1972—90, 1995—, NSF, 1975, 1995—98, AID, 1971—86, Army Office Rsch., 1987—94. Mem.: AAAS, Chgo. Assn. Reproductive Endocrinologists (pres. 1987—88), Soc. Study Reproduction, Soc. Gynecologic Investigation, Endocrine Soc., Am. Chem. Soc., N.Y. Acad. Scis., Phi Kappa Phi, Sigma Xi. Presbyterian. Achievements include patents for method of totally suppressing ovarian follicular devel. and method of ovulation detection. Home: 6001 N Knox Ave Chicago IL 60646-5821 Office: Northwestern U Prentice 1516 333 E Superior St Chicago IL 60611-3015 E-mail: chat@northwestern.edu.

CHAUDHARY, SATVEER, state senator; b. June 12, 1969; BA, St. Olaf Coll., 1991; JD, U. Minn., 1995. Mem. Minn. Ho. Reps., 1996-2000, Minn. State Senate, 2000—, vice chair transp. com., mem. crime prevention com., edn. com., E-12 edn. budget divsn. com., fin. com., transp. and pub. safety budget divsn. com.; owner Chaudhary Cons. Law clk., intern Hennepin County Atty.'s Office, Minn.; aide Minn. Atty. Gen. Hubert H. Humphrey

Ill. Co-chair Anoka County Legis. Delegation; hon. adv. coun. Asian-Pacific Endowment for Cmty. Devel.; mem. Coalition of Labor Union Women, Minn. Outdoor Heritage Alliance; hon. chair Minn. Cricket Assn.; mem. Minn. Welcome Com. for The Dalai Lama, U. Minn. Indsl. Rels. Adv. Coun., Twin Cities Internat. Citizen Award Com.; Fridley Human Resources Commn.; vol. Mounds View Festival in the Park; mem. New Brighton Hist. Soc., New Brighton Sportsmen's Club, Minn. Pheasants Forever Soc.; state affirmative action officer Minn. DFL Party; co-founder, chair Minn. Asian-Indian Dem. Assn.; bd. dirs. World Trade Ctr., St. Paul, A Blanket of Hope. Named Legislator of the Yr., Coll. Dems. of Minn., 1999; recipient Cert. of Commendation, Legal Aid Soc. of Minn., Cert. of Appreciation, DFL Party, 1995, Achievement award, Indian Assn. Minn. Mem.: New Brighton Eagles, Bass Anglers Soc. Am., Columbia Hts. Lions. Home: 1601 N Innsbruck Dr Fridley MN 55432 Office: 325 Capitol 75 Constitution Ave Saint Paul MN 55155-1206 E-mail: sen.satveer.chaudhary@senate.leg.state.mn.us.

CHAVERS, BLANCHE MARIE, pediatrician, educator, researcher; b. Clarksdale, Miss., Aug. 2, 1949; d. Andrew and Mildred Louise C.; m. Gubare Mpambara, May 21, 1982; 1 child, Kaita. BS in Zoology, U. Wash., 1971, MD, 1975. Diplomate Am. Bd. Pediatrics. Intern U. Wash., Seattle, 1975-76, resident in pediatrics, 1976-78; instr. U. Minn., Mpls., 1982, asst. prof. pediatrics, 1983-90, assoc. prof. pediatrics, 1990-99, prof. pediatrics, 1999—. Attending physician dept. pediatrics, U. Minn. Sch. Medicine, Mpls., 1982. Contbr. articles to profl. jours. Recipient Clin. Investigator award NIH, 1982; Pediatric Nephrology fellow U. Minn., 1978-81. Mem. Am. Soc. Nephrology, Am. Soc. Pediatric Nephrology, Internat. Soc. Nephrology, Internat. Soc. Pediatric Nephrology, Am. Soc. Transplantation. Democrat. Methodist. Avocations: tennis, reading, collecting African artifacts, art. Office: Univ Minn MMC 491 420 Delaware St SE Minneapolis MN 55455-0348

CHECCHI, ALFRED A. airline company executive; b. 1948; m. BA, Amherst Coll., 1970; MBA, Harvard Univ., 1974. V.p. Marriott Corp., 1975-82; with Bass Bros., 1982-86; pres. Alfred Checchi Assocs., Inc., 1986—; co-chmn., bd. dirs. NWA Inc., 1997—, Northwest Airlines Inc., 1997—, Wings Holdings Inc., 1997—; bd. dirs. Northwest Airlines, Inc., St. Paul, 1997—. Office: NW Airlines Inc 5101 Northwest Dr Saint Paul MN 55111-3034

CHEE, CHENG-KHEE, artist, educator; b. Xienyou, Fujian, China, Jan. 14, 1934; came to the U.S., 1962, naturalized, 1980; s. Ya-Jie and Xien-chun (Zheng) C.; m. Sing-Bee Ong, Aug. 28, 1965; children: Yi-Hung, Yi-Min, Wan-Ying, Yen-Ying. BA, Nanyang U., Singapore, 1960; MA, U. Minn., 1964. Asst. libr. Nanyang U., 1961-62; tchg. asst. U. Minn., Mpls., 1963-64, libr. Duluth, 1965-68, instr., 1968-80, asst. prof., 1981-88, assoc. prof., 1988—. One-man shows include Zhejiang Acad. Fine Arts, 1984, 87, Tweed Mus. Art, U. Minn., 1982-83, 91-92, Shanghai U. Acad. Fine Arts, China, 1987, Tianjin Acad. Fine Arts, China, 1988, Phipps Ctr. for Arts, Wis., 1991, Cannon Rotunda U.S. Ho. Office Bldg., Washington, 1993, Singapore Nat. Art Mus., 1997, Minn. Mus. Am. Art, 1997; exhibited in group shows Am. Watercolor Soc. Ann., Nat. Acad. and Salmagundi Club, N.Y.C., 1975, 78, 79, 81, 91, 94, 95, 98, 2001, Rocky Mountain Nat. Watermedia Exhbn., Foothills Art Ctr., Golden, Colo., 1976, 78, 80, 84, 90, 92, 93, Allied Artists Am. Ann. Exhbn., Nat. Arts Club, N.Y.C., 1980, 82, 91, 92, 93, 94, 95, 96, 97, 99, 2000, Adirondacks Nat. Exhbn. Am. Watercolors, Cmty. Arts Ctr., Old Forge, N.Y., 1982, 83, 86, 89, 91, 92, 95, 96, 97, 98, 2000, Nat. Watercolor Soc. Ann. Exhbn., 1983, 84, 85, 92, 96, Knickerbocker Artists USA Ann. Exhbn., 1980-81, 89-93, Sumi-e Soc. Am. Ann. Exhbn., 1979-84, 86, Mitchell Mus., Ill., 1983, Mpls. Inst. Arts, 1978, Nat. Taiwan Art Edn. Inst. Watercolor Exhbn. Artist of Taiwan, U.S. and Australia, 1994; author portfolio Cheng-Khee Chee Watercolors, 1984, 87, 91, 94, 96, (book) The Watercolor World of Cheng-Khee Chee, 1997; author exhbn. catalog, 1973-82, Retrospective Exhbn., 1982, China Exhbn. Tour, 1987, Singapore Nat. Art Mus. Exhbn., 1997; contbr. to books: Watercolor Energies, 1983, Learn Watercolor, The Edgar Whitney Way, 1994, Splash 3: Ideas and Inspirations, 1994, The Best of Watercolor, 1995, Splash 4: The Splendor of Light, 1996; illustrator: (children's books) Old Turtle, 1992 (AABBY award, Internat.Reading Assn. award 1993), Splash 5: The Glory of Color, 1998, The Best of Watercolor, Vol. 3, 1999. Recipient Gold medal of honor Allied Artists of Am. exhibit, 1980, Knickerbocker Artists Exhbn., 1989, Silver medal of honor Am. Watercolor Soc. Exhbn., 1991, High Winds medal Am. Watercolor Soc. Exhbn., 1994, Grand award Akron Soc. Artists Grant Nat. Exhbn., 1994, Colo. Centennial award Rocky Mountain Nat. Watermedia Exhbn., 1976, Grumbacher Gold medal Midwest Watercolor Soc. Exhbn., 1984, 85, 98, Gold award Ga. Watercolor Soc. Exhbn., 1985, 98, Gold medal and Purchase prize Knickerbocker Artists 43rd Ann. Grand Nat. Open Juried Exhbn., 1993, Chancellor's Disting. Svc. award U. Minn., 1994, Silver award Calif. Watercolor Assn., 1998; named Best in Show Sumi-e Soc. Am., 1984, 86, New Orleans Art Assn. 11th Nat. Art Exhbn., 1986, Western Colo. Watercolor Soc. Ann. Nat. Exhbn., 1993, Red River Watercolor Soc. 1st Nat. Art Exhbn., 1994, La. Watercolor Soc. 26th Ann. Internat. Exhbn., 1996, Duluth's Cultural Amb. to the World, Mayor Doty, 1994. Mem. Am. Watercolor Soc. (Dolphin fellow), Nat. Watercolor Soc., Rocky Mountain Nat. Watermedia Soc., Allied Artists Am., Knickerbocker Artists USA, Midwest Watercolor Soc. (Master Watercolorist), Watercolor USA Honor Soc., Sumi-e Soc. Am., others. Home: 1508 Vermilion Rd Duluth MN 55812-1526 Fax: 218-724-6153.

CHEELY, DANIEL JOSEPH, lawyer; b. Melrose Park, Ill., Oct. 24, 1949; s. Walter Hubbard and Edith Arlene (Orlandino) C.; m. Patricia Elizabeth Dorsey, May 14, 1977; children: Mary Elizabeth, Daniel, Katherine, Laura, Anne-Marie, Thomas, Susan, Michael, William. AB, Princeton U., 1971; JD, Harvard U., 1974. Bar: Ill. 1974, U.S. Dist. Ct (no. dist.) Ill. 1975, U.S. Ct. Appeals (7th cir.) 1975. Ptnr. Baker & McKenzie, Chgo., 1974-81, ptnr. litigation, 1981-85, capital ptnr. litigation, 1985-94; ptnr. Mauck, Bellande & Cheely, 1994-2000; ptnr. Bellande, Cheely & O'Flaherty, 2000—. Liaison counsel Asbestos Claims Facility, Chgo., 1985-88, bus. devel. com., 1987-90, Chgo. assoc. train com., 1988-91, chmn. Chgo. assoc. evaluation; liaison coun. Com. for Claims Resolution, 1988-89. Advisor Midtown Sports and Cultural Ctr., Chgo., 1974—; mem. River Forest Regular Reps., Ill., 1980-88, Ill. Rep. Assembly, Chgo., 1984—; pres. Cath. Evidence Forum, 1984—; pres. Ch. History Forum, 1994—; dir. Cath. Citizens of Ill., 1997—; bd. dirs. Cath. Lawyers Guild, 2000—. Mem. ABA (vice chmn. environ. law sect. 1989-97), Ill. Bar Assn., Appellate Lawyers Soc. Ill., Chgo. Bar Assn., Trial Lawyers Club. Chgo., Serra Club (v.p. Chgo. chpt. 1988-89, 92-94, 96—, treas. 1989-92), United Rep. Fund, Phi Beta Kappa. Roman Catholic. Avocations: history, parent effectiveness training, education, Christian apologetics, travel consulting. Office: Bellande Cheely & O'Flaherty 19 S La Salle St Ste 1203 Chicago IL 60603-1406

CHEFITZ, JOEL GERALD, lawyer; b. Boston, Aug. 27, 1951; s. Melvin L and Bernice L (Kahn) Chefitz; m. Sharon P Garfinkel, June 18, 1972; children: Sandra Beth, Meira Sarah, Michael Hanan. AB cum laude, Boston U., 1972, JD magna cum laude, 1976. Bar: Ill 1976, US Dist Ct (no Dist) Ill 1977, US Ct Appeals (3d cir) 1981, US Supreme Ct 1983, US Ct Appeals (7th cir) 1984, US Ct Appeals (9th cir) 1993, US Ct Appeals (2d cir) 1994, US Ct Appeals (5th cir) 1996, US Ct Appeals (4th cir) 1998, US Ct Appeals (fed cir) 2000, US Ct Appeals (DC cir) 2001. Law clk. to presiding justice U.S. Dist. Ct. Mass., Boston, 1976-77; assoc. Kirkland & Ellis, Chgo., 1977-82, ptnr., 1982-86, Katten Muchin & Zavis, Chgo., 1986—. Editor: (jour) Boston Univ Law Rev, 1975—76; contbr. articles to profl jours. Bd dirs Legal Assistance Found Met Chicago. Scholar Am Jurisprudence, Boston Univ, 1973—76, CJS, 1975, Bigelow, 1976. Mem.: ABA, 7th Cir Asn, Chicago Bar Asn, East Bank Club. Office: Howrey Simon Arnold & White LLP 321 North Clark Street Ste 800 Chicago IL 60610 E-mail: chefitzj@howrey.com.

CHELBERG, BRUCE STANLEY, holding company executive; b. Chgo., Aug. 14, 1934; s. Stanlye Andrew and Josephine Marie (Mohn) C.; children: Stephen E., david M., Kimberly Anne. BS in Commerce, U. Ill., 1956; LL.B., 1958. Bar: Ill. 1958. Atty. Trans Union Corp., Chgo., 1958-64; asst. gen. counsel, 1964-68; pres. Getz Corp., San Francisco, 1968-71; v.p. Trans Union Corp., Chgo., 1971-78; pres., COO, 1978-81; sr. v.p. Whitman Corp. (formerly IC Industries, Inc.), Chgo., 1982-85; exec. v.p., 1985-92; chmn., CEO, 1992—; also bd. dirs. Bd. dirs. First Midwest Bank corp., Northfield Labs, Snap-On-Tools, Inc. Bd. dirs. Arlington Heights Pub. Sch. Dist. 25, Ill., 1974-83, higher edn. State Ill., 1988—. Mem. Ill. State Bar Assn., Chgo., Met. (Chgo.), World Trade (San Francisco).

CHELETTE, TAMARA LYNNE, biomedical engineer; b. Morgantown, W.Va., July 11, 1962; d. Charles Caruthers and Nancy Ruth (Williams) Cook; m. Murry René Chelette, June 1, 1985; children: Murry René Jr., Andrew John. BS in Engring., Boston U., 1984; PhD of Biomed. Scis., Wright State U., 1994. Registered profl. engr., Ohio. Intern clin. engring. Mass. Eye and Ear Infirmary, Boston, 1983-84; biomed. engr. VA, Little Rock, 1984-86, Dayton, Ohio, 1986-87; biomed. sys. engr. Krug Internat., 1987-89; biomed. engr. human effectiveness directorate Air Force Rsch. Lab., Wright-Patterson AFB, Ohio, 1989—. Adj. prof. Wright State U., Dayton, 1994—. Patentee in field; contbr. articles to profl. jours. Treas. Wright-Patt Young Heroes Assn., Dayton, 1992—. Recipient Outstanding Achievement award Soc. Women Engrs., 1982, Arthur Flemming award, Washington JayCees, 1995, Dayton English and Sci. Found. outstanding engr. of Miami Valley award, 2000. Fellow Aerospace Human Factors Assn.; mem. IEEE (Fritz Russ award in biomedical engring. 2000) Aerospace Med. Assn. (assoc. fellow, Innovative Rsch. award 1994, pres. life scis. br. 1996, Eric Liljencrantz award 1997, Paul Bert award 1998), Engring. in Medicine and Biology Soc., SAFE Assn. (v.p. Wright Bros. chpt. 1994-95, pres. 1998-99). Avocation: gardening. Office: Air Force Rsch Lab Bldg 824 Rm 206 2800 Q St Wright Patterson AFB OH 45433-7008

CHELIOS, CHRISTOS K, professional hockey player; b. Chgo., Jan. 25, 1962; Student, U. Wis. With Montreal Canadiens, 1981-90; defenseman Chgo. Blackhawks, 1990-99, Detroit Red Wings, 1999—. Mem. NHL All-Rookie team, 1984-85, NHL All-Star 1st team, 1988-89, 92-93, NHL All-Star 2nd team, 1990-91, WCHA All-Star 2nd team, 1982-83. Recipient James Norris Meml. trophy, 1988-89, 92-93; named to NCAA All-Tournament Team, 1982-83, Sporting News All-Star first team, 1988-89, Sporting New All-Star second team, 1990-91, 91-92. Office: Detroit Red Wings 600 Civic Center Dr Detroit MI 48226-4419

CHELLE, ROBERT FREDERICK, entrepreneurial leadership educator; b. New Brunswick, N.J., July 18, 1948; s. Robert and Frances (Brown) C.; m. Karen Ann Cederburg, Aug. 7, 1971; children: Robert, Pamela. BA, Bethany Coll., 1970; MBA, U. Dayton, 1972. Asst. contr. Tait Mfg. Co., Dayton, Ohio, 1972-73; pres. High Voltage Maintenance Corp., 1973-99; dir. Crotty Ctr. for Entrepreneurial Leadership, U. Dayton, 1999—. Bd. dirs. The Siebenthaler Co., Dayton; adv. bd. U. Dayton Sch. Bus., 1994—. Contbr. articles to profl. jours. Chmn. Dayton C. of C., 1993, County Corp., Dayton, 1995. Recipient Cert. Appreciation Montgomery County Commn., Dayton, 1984-85, Up and Comer award for engring. City of Dayton, 1988. Mem. Nat. Elect. Testing Assn., Ohio Bar Assn. (mem. profl. ethics com. 2001—), Rotary (pres. 1984-85). Presbyterian. Avocations: yachting, fishing.

CHELLINE, WARREN HERMAN, English educator, clergy member; b. Jonesport, Maine, Sept. 26, 1923; s. Herman Albert and Olive Viola (Yarwood) C.; m. Bonnibelle Nelson, Jan. 1, 1950 (dec. June 1991); 1 child, Eric Warren; m. Frances Nadine Woodside, Aug. 7, 1993. Student, Brown U., 1941-43; DD, Am. Div. Sch., 1956; BA, MA, U. Mo., 1969, 70; MPhil, PhD, U. Kans., 1979, 82. Cert. secondary education tchr., Mo., Kans. Clergy member Remnant LDS Ch., Independence, Mo., 1942—; prof. English lang. and lit. Mo. We. State U., St. Joseph, 1971-97, prof. emeritus English lang. and lit., 1997—. Insp. U.S. Lighthouse Soc., 1997—. Author: John Milton and Roger Williams, 1982; contbg. editor Herald House Pubs., 1940-69; contbr. articles to profl. jours. Chmn. adv. bd. The Salvation Army, 1989—; bd. dirs. Boy Scouts Am., Can. and U.S.A., 1946— (Wood Badge award 1956, Silver Beaver award 1990), St. Joseph Pub. Libr., 1975—, St. Joseph Symphony, 1994—, Allied Arts Coun., 1995—. Chaplain USN, 1941-43. James E. West fellow, 1998. Mem. Am. Legion, Moila Shrine, Soc. Profl. Journalists, Milton Soc. Internat., Kiwanis Internat. (disting. lt. gov. 1982—), Am. Mason (32nd degree, chaplain 1988—). Avocations: clowning, lighthouses, circus lore, Scottish bagpipe band. Home: Apt 1 421 N 25th St Saint Joseph MO 64501-2653 Office: 620 Francis St Saint Joseph MO 64501-2653 E-mail: chelline@magiccablepc.com.

CHEMA, THOMAS V. government official, lawyer; b. East Liverpool, Ohio, Oct. 31, 1946; s. Stephen T. and Dorothy Grace (McCormack) C.; m. Barbara Burke Orr, Aug. 15, 1970; children: Christine, Stephen. A.B., U. Notre Dame, 1968; J.D., Harvard U., 1971. Bar: Ohio 1971, U.S. Supreme Ct. 1977. Assoc. Arter and Hadden, Cleve., 1971-79, ptnr. 1979-85, 1989—; pres. Gateway Cons. Group, Inc., 1995--; exec. dir. Ohio Lottery Commn., Cleve., 1983-85, Gateway Econ. Devel. Corp. Greater Cleveland, 1990-95; chmn. Pub. Utilities Commn. Ohio, Columbus, 1985-89; chmn. Ohio Bldg. Authority, 1990-96. Candidate for Ohio Senate, 1980; campaign mgr., Senator Howard M. Metzenbaum, 1976; co-chmn. task force on violent crime, Cleve., 1981-83; trustee Hiram Coll., 1994—, Cleve. Works, Inc., 1995-98, Cleve. City Club, 1993-96, Sisters of Charity of St. Augustine Health Sys., 1994—, Historic Gateway Neighborhood, Inc., 1995—; dir. Transtechnology, Inc., Fairport Funds. Mem. ABA (adv. council), Nat. Assn. Regulatory Utility Commrs., Nat. Assn. State Lotteries (bd. dirs.), Greater Cleve. Bar Assn., Ohio State Bar Assn., Cleve. Legal Aid Soc., Ohio Legal Assistance Found. (chmn. 1996-99), Electric Power Research Inst., Sr. Citizens Resources Inc. (trustee), Hospice Council No. Ohio (sec., trustee, legal counsel), Citizens League, NAACP, League Women Voters, Am. Soc. Pub. Adminstrs. Trustee, St. Ignatius High Sch., Prospect Vision, Inc., Downtown Devel. Coordinators Cleve. Found. Arch.. Democrat. Roman Catholic. Club: City (Cleve., trustee 1993—). Avocation: skiing. Home: 18580 Parkland Dr Cleveland OH 44122-3469 Office: Arter & Hadden 925 Euclid Ave 1100 Huntington Bldg Cleveland OH 44115-1475

CHEMBERLIN, PEG, clergy, religious organization administrator; Ordained deacon Moravian Ch. of Am., 1982, consecrated presbyter, 1986. BA cum laude, U. Wis., Parkside; grad., United Theol. Sem. Twin Cities, 1982. Formerly dir. campus ministries, tchr., youth min.; also outreach min., parish intern pastor; exec. dir. Minn. Coun. Chs., 1995—. Former pres., former program chaqir Nat. Assn. Ecumenical and Interfaith Staff, 1992, 97. Recipient Women of Excellence award Minn. Gov., 1994, NOVA Peace and Justice award, 1985. Office: Minn Coun Chs 122 W Franklin Ave Minneapolis MN 55404-2447

CHEMERS, ROBERT MARC, lawyer; b. Chgo., July 24, 1951; s. Donald and Florence (Weinberg) C.; m. Lenore Ziemann, Aug. 16, 1975; children: Brandon J., Derek M. BA, U. So. Calif., 1973; JD, Ind. U.-Indpls., 1976. Bar: Ind. 1976, Ill. 1976, U.S. Dist. Ct. (so. dist.) Ind. 1976, U.S. Dist. Ct. (no. and so. dists.) Ill. 1977, U.S. Ct. Appeals 7th cir.) 1977, U.S. Ct. Appeals (5th cir.) 1985. Assoc. Pretzel & Stouffer, Chgo., 1976-79, officer, 1979-81, dir., 1981—. Author: IICLE - Civil Practice, 1978, rev. edit. 1982, 87; IICLE Settlements, 1984. Mem. ABA, Ill. State Bar Assn., Chgo. Bar Assn., Def. Rsch. Inst., Ill. Def. Counsel, Appellate Lawyers Assn. Office: Pretzel & Stouffer One S Wacker Dr Chicago IL 60606

CHEN, DI, electro-optic company executive, consultant; b. Chekiang, China, Mar. 15, 1929; came to U.S., 1954, naturalized, 1972; s. Hsun Yu and chien (Wang) C.; m. Lynn C. Wang, June 14, 1958; children: Andrew A.J., Daniel T.Y. BS, Nat. Taiwan U., 1953; MS, U. Minn., 1956; PhD, Stanford U., 1959. Asst. prof. U. Minn., Mpls., 1959-62; rsch. fellow Honeywell Co., Bloomington, Minn., 1962-80; tech. dir. Optical Peripherals Lab., Colorado Springs, Colo., 1980-84; co-founder, exec. v.p. tech. Optotech, Inc., 1984-89; pres. Chen and Assocs. Cons., 1989—. V.p. tech. and engring. Literal Corp., Colorado Springs, 1990-91; chmn., then co-chmn., advisor, sr. advisor Optical Data Storage, 1983-98. Topical editor Applied Optics Jour., 1991-97; contbr. articles to profl. jours.; patentee in field. Recipient Honeywell Sweatt Scientists and Engrs. award, 1972. Fellow IEEE (chmn. IEEE-MAG Twin Cities chpt. 1974); mem. SPIE, Optical Soc. Am., Sigma Xi, Eta Kappa Nu. E-mail: dichen2127@cs.com.

CHEN, KUN-MU, electrical engineering educator; b. Taiwan, China, Feb. 3, 1933; came to U.S., 1957, naturalized, 1969; s. Tsa-Mao and Che (Wu) C.; m. Shun-Shun Chen, Feb. 22, 1962; children: Margaret, Katherine, Kenneth, George. B.S., Nat. Taiwan U., 1955; M.S., Harvard, 1958, Ph.D., 1960. Research asso. U. Mich., 1960-64; vis. prof. Chao-Tung U., Taiwan, 1962; asso. prof. elec. engring. Mich. State U., 1964-67, prof., 1967-95, Richard M. Hong Endowed prof. elec. engring., 1995—, dir. elec. engring. grad. program, 1967-70. Vis. prof. Tohoku U., Japan, 1989, Nat. Taiwan U., 1989. Author articles on electromagnetic radiation, plasma physics, electromagnetic bioeffects. Recipient Disting. Faculty award Mich. State U., 1976, Outstanding Achievement award in sci. and engring. Taiwanese Am. Found., 1984; Withrow Disting. scholar Coll. Engring., Mich. State U., 1993; C.T. Loo fellow, 1957; Gordon McKay fellow, 1958-60. Fellow IEEE, AAAS; mem. Internat. Union Radio Sci. (commn. A, B and C), AAUP, Sigma Xi, Phi Kappa Phi, Tau Beta Pi. Home: 4433 Comanche Dr Okemos MI 48864-2071 Office: Mich State U Dept Elec Engring East Lansing MI 48824 E-mail: chen@msu.edu.

CHEN, MICHAEL MING, mechanical engineering educator; b. Hankow, China, Mar. 10, 1933; came to U.S., 1953, naturalized, 1965; s. Kwang Tzu and Hwei Chuing (Deng) C.; m. Ruth Hsu, Oct. 15, 1961; children: Brigitte (dec.), Derek, Melinda. BS, U. Ill., 1955; SM, MIT, 1957, PhD, 1961. Sr. staff scientist research and devel. Avco Corp., Wilmington, Mass., 1960-63; asst. prof. engring. and applied sci. Yale U., 1963-69; asso. prof. mech. engring. N.Y. U., 1969-73; prof. mech. engring. and bioengring., dept. mech. and indsl. engring. U. Ill., Urbana-Champaign, 1973-91; prof. mech. engring. and applied mechanics U. Mich., Ann Arbor, 1991—. Dir. thermal systems program NSF, 1991-93; cons. A.D. Little Co., NIH, Argonne Nat. Lab., Bell Labs. Asso. editor: Applied Mechanics Rev.; contbr. to profl. publs. Fellow ASME (Heat Transfer Meml. award 1990); mem. AIChE, Minerals, Metals and Materials Soc., Am. Phys. Soc., Sigma Xi, Phi Kappa Phi, Tau Beta Pi, Pi Tau Sigma. Office: U Mich Dept Mech Engring 2350 Hayward St Ann Arbor MI 48109-2125

CHEN, SHOEI-SHENG, mechanical engineer; b. Taiwan, Jan. 26, 1940; s. Yung-cheng and A-shu (Fang) C.; m. Ruth C. Lee, June 28, 1969; children: Lyrice, Lisa, Steve. B.S., Nat. Taiwan U., 1963; M.S., Princeton U., 1966, M.A., 1967, Ph.D., 1968. Research asst. Princeton U., 1965-68; asst. mech. engr. Argonne (Ill.) Nat. Lab., 1968-71, mech. engr., 1971-80, sr. mech. engr., 1980—2001. Cons. to Internat. Atomic Energy Agy. to assist developing countries in R & D of nuclear reator systems components, 1977, 79, 80, 94; cons. NASA, NRC, Rockwell Internat., others. Author: Flow-Induced Vibration of Circular Cylinderical Structures, 1987; mem. internat. adv. editorial bd. Acta Mechanica Solida; adv. bd. JSME Internat. Jour.; assoc. editor Applied Mechs. Rev., Jour. of Pressure Vessels Tech.; contbr. articles to profl. jours. Recipient Disting. Performance award U. Chgo., 1986, ASME pressure vessel and piping medal, 2001. Fellow ASME (chmn. tech. subcom. on fluid and structure interactions pressure vessels and piping divsn. 1987-90, honors chmn. 1990-94, mem. exec. com. 1990-96, organizer symposia, tech. program chmn. 1994, conf. chair ASME/JSME pressure vessels and piping conf. 1995, pressure vessels and piping divsn., chmn. 1995-96, senate pres. 1997-98, honors and awards chair of materials and structures tech. group 1996-99), Instn. Diagnostic Engrs.; mem. Am. Acad. Mechanics, Acoustical Soc. Am., Sigma Xi. Home: 27721 Manor Hill Rd Laguna Niguel CA 92677 Office: 9700 Cass Ave Lemont IL 60439-4803 E-mail: sschen88@aol.com.

CHENEVICH, WILLIAM L. bank executive; Grad., City Coll. N.Y.; master's, CUNY. Chief indsl. engr. space programs Grumman Aerospace; with Carte Blanche Corp. Citicorp, L.A.; pres., COO Security Pacific Automation Co., Inc.; exec. v.p., dir. info. svcs. Home Savings of Am.; group exec. v.p., head sys. group and software devel. Visa Internat., San Francisco; vice chmn., dir. info. svcs. and ops. Firstar Corp., Milw., 1999—. Office: Firstar Corp 777 E Wisconsin Ave Milwaukee WI 53202-5300

CHENEY, JEFFREY PAUL, manufacturing executive; b. Laona, Wis., Feb. 28, 1956; s. Joseph C. and Gordie Lee (Bodoh) C.; m. Rhoda L. Mueller, Feb. 14, 1981; children: Lisa Marie, Mathew Steven. BS in Bus., U. Wis., Green Bay, 1979; MBA, Marquette U., 1986. CPA. Fin. analyst Kohler (Wis.) Co., 1979-81, sr. planning analyst, 1981-82, mgr., planning, 1982-83, mgr., corp. planning, 1984-86, controller, 1986-90, treas., 1990—; sr. v.p. fin. Kohler, 1999—. Treas., Kohler Found. Trust, 1990, Kohler Preservation Trust, 1991. Republican. Office: Kohler Co 444 Highland Dr Kohler WI 53044

CHENEY, PAUL D. physiologist , educator; b. Jamestown, N.Y., Oct. 10, 1947; married; 2 children. BS, SUNY, Fredonia, 1969; PhD, SUNY, Syracuse, 1975. Fellow in physiology U. Wash. Sch. Medicine, Seattle, 1974-77; rsch. asst. prof. dept. physiology and biophysics U. Wash., 1977-78; asst. prof. physiology U. Kans. Med. Ctr., Kansas City, 1978-88, prof. physiology, 1988—. Mem. Soc. Neurosci, Sigma Xi. Office: U Kansas Med Ctr R L Smith Rsch Ctr 3901 Rainbow Blvd Kansas City KS 66160-0004

CHENG, HERBERT SU-YUEN, mechanical engineering educator; b. Shanghai, China, Jan. 15, 1929; came to U.S., 1949; s. Chung-Mei and Jing-Ming (Xu) C.; m. Lily D. Hsiung, Apr. 11, 1953; children: Elaine, Elise, Edward, Earl. BSME, U. Mich., 1962; MSME, Ill. Inst. Tech., 1956; PhD, U. Pa., 1961. Jr. mech. engr. Internat. Harvester Co., Chgo., 1952-53; project engr. Machine Engring. co., 1953-56; instr. Ill. Inst. Tech., 1956-57, U. Pa., Phila., 1957-61; asst. prof. Syracuse (N.Y.) U., 1961-62; rsch. engr. Mech. Tech. Inc., Latham, N.Y., 1962-68; assoc. prof. Northwestern U., Evanston, Ill., 1968-74, prof., 1974—, Walter P. Murphy prof., 1987—, dir. Ctr. for Engring. Tribology, 1984-88, 92—. V.p. Gear Rsch. Inst., Naperville, Ill., 1985-90; cons. GM, Chrysler Corp., Deere Co., Nissan, E.T.C., 1970—. Contbr. articles to profl. jours. Deacon South Presbyn. Ch., Syracuse, 1961-62, 1st Presbyn. Ch. Schenectady, N.Y., 1962-68. Named a hon. prof. Nat. Zhejiang (People's Republic of China) U., 1985. Fellow ASME (hon., Mayo D. Hersey award 1990, D.F. Wilcock award 1999), Soc. Tribologists & Lubrication Engrs. (hon., Nat. award 1987, CAP Alfred

Hunt award 1997); mem. NAE, Inst. Mech. Engrs. (U.K., Tribology gold medal 1992), Am. Gear Mfrs. Assn. (acad. mem.). Avocations: Peking opera, tennis. Office: Northwestern U 219 Catalysis Bldg 2145 Sheridan Rd Evanston IL 60208-0834

CHENG, H(WEI) H(SIEN), soil scientist, agronomic and environmental science educator; b. Shanghai, China, Aug. 13, 1932; came to U.S., 1951, naturalized, 1961; s. Chi-Pao and Anna (Lan) C.; m. Jo Yuan, Dec. 15, 1962; children: Edwin, Antony. BA, Berea Coll., 1956; MS, U. Ill., 1958, PhD, 1961. Rsch. assoc. Iowa State U., Ames, 1962-64, asst. prof. agronomy, 1964-65; asst. prof. dept. agronomy and soils Wash. State U., Pullman, 1965-71, assoc. prof., 1971-77, prof., 1977-89, interim chmn., 1986-87, chmn. program environ. sci. and regional planning, 1977-79, 88-89, assoc. dean Grad. Sch., 1982-86; prof., head dept. soil, water, and climate U. Minn., St. Paul, 1989—. Vis. scientist Juelich Nuclear Rsch. Ctr., Fed. Republic Germany, 1971-73, 79-80, Academia Sinica, Taipei, Republic of China, 1978, Fed. Agrl. Rsch. Ctr., Braunschweig, Fed. Republic Germany, 1980; mem. acad. adv. coun. Inst. Soil Sci., Academia Sinica, Nanjing, People's Republic China, 1987—; mem. adv. bd. Inst. Botany, Academia Sinica, Taipei, 1991—; mem. first sci. adv. bd. Dept. Ecology State of Wash., 1988-89; chioef tech. advisor project on water-saving agr. for N.W. China, UNDP, 2001--. Editor: Pesticides in the Soil Environment: Processes, Impacts, and Modeling, 1990; assoc. editor Jour. Environ. Quality, 1983-89; mem. editorial bd. Bot. bull. Academia Sinica, 1988—, Jour. Environ. Sci. and Health, Part B-Pesticides, Food Contaminants, and Agrl. Wastes, 2000—; cons. editor: Pedosphere, 1991—; contbr. articles to profl. jours. Fulbright rsch. scholar State Agrl. U., Ghent, Belgium, 1963-64. Fellow AAAS, Am. Soc. Agronomy (bd. dirs. 1990-2000, exec. com. 1994-2000, pres. 1998-99), Soil Sci. Soc. Am. (divsn. chair 1985-86, bd. dirs. 1990-93, exec. com. 1994-97, pres. 1995-96); mem. Am. Chem. Soc., Soc. Environ. Toxicology and Chemistry, Internat. Soc. Chem. Ecology, Internat. Humic Substances Soc., Internat. Soc. Soil Sci., Coun. for Agrl. Sci. and Tech., Soil and Water Conservation Soc., Inst. Internat. Devel. in Edn. and Agrl. and Life Scis. (chair bd. dirs. 2000—), Sigma Xi (pres. U. Minn. chpt. 1995-96), Phi Kappa Phi, Gamma Sigma Delta (pres. Wash. State chpt. 1988-89, Award of Merit U. Minn. chpt. 2000). Methodist. Office: U Minn Dept Soil Water and Climate 1991 Upper Buford Cir Saint Paul MN 55108-0010 E-mail: hcheng@soils.umn.edu.

CHENG, STEPHEN ZHENG DI, chemistry educator, polymeric material researcher; b. Shanghai, Aug. 3, 1949; came to U.S., 1981, naturalization, 1992; s. Luzhong and Jingzhi (Zhang) C.; m. Susan Lian Zhi Xue, June 28, 1978; 1 child, Wendy D.W. BS in Math., East China Normal U., 1977; MS in Polymer Engring., China Textile U., 1981; PhD in Polymer Chemistry, Rensselaer Poly. Inst., 1985. Postdoctoral and rsch. assoc. Rensselaer Poly. Inst., Troy, N.Y., 1985-87; asst. prof. polymer sci. U. Akron, Ohio, 1987-91, assoc. prof. polymer sci., 1991-95, prof. polymer sci., trustee, 1995—. Faculty rsch. assoc. Maurice Morton Inst. of Polymer Sci., U. Akron, 1987—, faculty rsch. assoc. Inst. Polymer Engring., 1988—; vis. prof. sci, U. of Tokyo, 1994; vis. prof. polymer sci. and engring. Sichun Union U., China, 1994—; fgn. mem. acad. steering com. Nat. Polymer Physics Open Lab., Chinese Acad. Sci., 1994—, guest prof. polymer sci. Guangzhou Inst. Chemistry, 1994—, guest prof. polymer sci. Changchun Inst. Applied Chemistry, 1995—; guest prof. polymer materials and engring. Zhengzhou U., China, 1994—; guest prof. polymer sci. and engring. Peking U., 1996—, Zhejiang U., 1996—; guest prof. U. Sci. and Tech. of China, 1996—; mem. orgn. com. The First Conf. Worldwide Young Chinese Chemists, Beijing, 1995; adv. prof. polymer sci. Chinese Textile U., 1995—, Fudan U., 1996—, Hebei U. of Tech., 1996—; cons., spkr. in field; project dir. thin film optics Sci. and Tech. Ctr. for Advanced Liquid Crystalline Optical Materials, NSF, 1994—, assoc. dir. Ctr. for Molecular and Microstructure of Composites, 1996—; hon. mem. acad. steering com. Nat. Key Lab. of Chem. Fiber Structure Modification, China Textile U., 1995—; internat. lectr. in field. Editor: Jour. Macromolecular Sci. Part B, Physics, 1995—; adv. bd. Polymer Internat. Jour., 1990—, Marcromolecules, 1996—, Trends in Polymer Sci., 1992—; editl. bd. Jour. Macromolecular Sci., Rev. of Macromolecular Chemistry and Physics, 1992—, Thermochemica Acta,, 1992—, Macromolecular Chemistry and Physics, 1994—, Macromolecular Rapid Communications, 1994—, Jour. Polymer Rsch., 1995—, Internat. Jour. Analysis and Characterization, 1995—; vol. editor: Liquid-Crystalline Polymer Systems: Technological Advances, 1996, Handbook of Thermal Analysis and Calorimetry, Vol. 3, 1997; contbr. chpts. to books and more than 180 articles to profl. jours.; patentee in field. Bd. trustees Akron Internat. Inst., 1995—. Grantee in field; recipient Presdl. Young Investigator award NSF and White House, 1991, Appreciation cert. U. Akron Bd. Trustees, 1992, 94, John H. Dillon Medal, Am. Phys. Soc., 1995, Outstanding Rschr. award U. Akron, 1997; named Disting. corp. Inventor, Am. Soc. Patent Holders, Inventure Place and Home of the Nat. Inventors Hall of Fame, 1995. Fellow Am. Phys. Soc., N.Am. Thermal Analysis Soc. (exec. coun. 1991-93, 94-96, awards vice chmn. 1991-92, awards chmn. 1992-93, meeting vice chmn. 1994, meeting chmn. 1995, others); mem. Am. Chem. Soc. (Akron Sect. award 1994), Soc. Plastics Engrs. (awards com. 1991-94), Materials Rsch. Soc., Soc. Advancement Material and Process Engring., Internat. Confedn. for Thermal Analysis (edn. com. 1996—), Material Rsch. Soc., Internat. Liquid Crystal Soc. Achievements include research on solid state of polymeric materials including phase transition thermodynamics, kinetics, molecular motion, crystal structure and morphology, liquid crystal polymers, surface and interface structures, high-performance polymer fibers, films for microelectronic and optical applications, high temperature composites, computer simulation of molecular dynamics and modeling. Office: U Akron Morton Inst Polymer Sci Akron OH 44325-0001

CHERNEY, JAMES ALAN, lawyer; b. Boston, Mar. 19, 1948; s. Alvin George and Janice (Elaine) Cherney; m. Linda Bienenfeld. BA, Tufts U., 1969; JD, Columbia U., 1973. Bar: Ill. 1973, U.S. Supreme Ct. 1977, U.S. Ct. Appeals (7th cir.) 1979, U.S. Ct. Appeals (3d cir.) 1982, U.S. Ct. Appeals (10th cir.) 1984, U.S. Ct. Appeals (8th and 9th cirs.) 1987. Assoc. Kirkland & Ellis, Chgo., 1973-76, Hedlund, Hunter & Lynch, Chgo., 1976-79, ptnr., 1979-82, Latham & Watkins, Chgo., 1982—. Mem. ABA, Chgo. Bar Assn. Office: Latham & Watkins Sears Tower Ste 5800 Chicago IL 60606-6306

CHERRY, DANIEL RONALD, lawyer; b. Mpls., Dec. 31, 1948; s. Clifford D. and Ruby E. (Norman) C.; m. Dianne Brown, Jan. 24, 1971 (dec.); children: Matthew A., Kathryn E.; m. Q. Rhea Walker, Oct. 25, 1998. SB, MIT, 1970; JD cum laude, Harvard U., 1976. Bar: Ohio 1976, U.S. Dist. Ct. (no. dist.) Ohio 1976, U.S. Patent and Trademark Office 1978, U.S. Ct. Appeals (6th and Fed. cirs.) 1982, Ill. 1987, U.S. Dist. Ct. (no. dist.) Ill. 1987. Assoc. Squire, Sanders & Dempsey, Cleve., 1976-85, ptnr., 1985-87, Welsh & Katz, Ltd., Chgo., 1987—. Co-author: Patent Practice, 1997. With USCG, 1970-73. Mem. ABA, Ohio State Bar Assn., Ill. State Bar Assn., Chgo. Bar Assn., Am. Intellectual Property Law Assn., Intellectual Property Law Assn. Chgo., Licensing Execs. Soc. Home: 1046 Vine St Winnetka IL 60093-1834 Office: Welsh & Katz Ltd 120 S Riverside Plz # 22 Chicago IL 60606-3913

CHERRY, JOHN D., JR. state legislator; b. Sulphur Springs, Tex., May 5, 1951; s. John D. Sr. and Margaret L. (Roark) C.; m. Pamela M. Faris, 1979; children: Meghan M., John D. BA, U. Mich., 1973, MA, 1984. Chmn. 7th Cong. Dist. Dem. Com., Mich., 1973-75; adminstrv. asst. Mich. State Sen. Gary Corbin, 1975-81; Mich. polit. dir. Am. Fedn. State, County & Munic Employees AFL-CIO, 1981-82; mem. Mich. Ho. Reps. from 79th dist., Lansing, 1983-86, Mich. Senate from 29th dist., 1987-95, Mich. Senate from 28th dist., lansing, 1995—; senate minority leader, mem. legis. coun. Mem. Oakland county Dem. Exec. Bd., 1995—; mem. Mich. Jobs Commn. Bd., 1996—; del. Dem. Nat. Conv., 1996. Address: 4116 Orme Cir Clio MI 48420-8527 also: State Senate PO Box 30036 Lansing MI 48909-7536

CHERRY, PETER BALLARD, electrical products corporation executive; b. Evanston, Ill., May 25, 1947; s. Walter Lorain and Virginia Ames (Ballard) C.; m. Crissy Hazard, Sept. 6, 1969; children: Serena Ames, Spencer Ballard. B.A., Yale U., 1969; M.B.A., Stanford U., 1972. Analyst Cherry Elec. Products Corp., Waukegan, Ill., 1972-74, data processing and systems mgr., 1974, treas., 1974-77; v.p. fin. and bus. devel. Cherry Elec. Products Corps., 1977-80; exec. v.p. Cherry Elec. Products Corp., 1980-82, pres., chief oper. officer, 1982-86; pres., chief exec. officer Cherry Corp., 1986-92, chmn., pres., 1992—. Trustee Lake Forest Coll., Ill., 1982-90; trustee Lake Forest Hosp., 1982—, chmn., 1989-92. Mem. Chgo. Coun. Fgn. Rels., Econ. Club, Comml. Club, Chgo. Club, Commonwealth Club, Onwentsia Club. Office: Cherry Corp 3600 Sunset Ave Waukegan IL 60087-3214

CHESLEY, STANLEY MORRIS, lawyer; b. Cin., Mar. 26, 1936; s. Frankl and Rachel (Kinsburg) C.; children: Richard A., Lauren B. BA, U. Cin., 1958, LLB, 1960. Bar: Ohio 1960, Ky. 1978, W.Va. 1981, Tex. 1981, Nev. 1981. Ptnr. Waite, Schneider, Bayless & Chesley Co., Cin., 1960—. Contbr. articles to profl. jours. Past chmn. bd. commrs. on grievances and discipline Supreme Ct. Ohio; past pres. Jewish Fedn. Cin.; nat. vice chair, bd. govs., trustee, joint distbn. com. United Jewish Coms.; exec. bd., nat. bd. govs. Am. Jewish Com.; nat. bd. govs. Hebrew Uninon Coll.; exec. com. U.S. Holocaust Meml. Mus. Mem. ABA, ATLA, FBA, Am. Judicature Soc., Melvin M. Belli Soc., Ohio Bar Assn., Ky. Bar Assn., W.Va. Bar Assn., Tex. Bar Assn., Nev. Bar Assn., Cin. Bar Assn. Office: Waite Schneider Bayless & Chesley 1513 Central Trust Towers Cincinnati OH 45202 E-mail: wsbclaw@aol.com.

CHESTER, JOHN JONAS, lawyer, educator; b. Columbus, Ohio, July 13, 1920; s. John J. and Harriet Bonnadine (Rice) C.; m. Cynthia Johnson, Apr. 18, 1959; children: John, James, Joel, Cecily. AB cum laude, Amherst Coll., 1942; JD, Yale U., 1948. Bar: Ohio 1948. Ptnr. Chester & Chester, Columbus, 1948-57, Chester & Rose, Columbus, 1958-70, Chester Willcox and Saxbe and predecessor firm, Columbus, 1971—. Spl. counsel Pres. of U.S., 1974. adj. prof. Ohio State U. Coll. Law. Emeritus bd. dirs. Grand Riverside Meth. Hosps.; former chmn. Doctor's Hosp.; chmn. bd. dirs. Ohio Health, 2001—; former trustee Doctor's Hosp., Columbus Sch. for Girls, Columbus Acad., Shepherd Hill Hosp., Ohio Hist. Found.; trustee emeritus Ohio Hist. Soc.; mem. Ohio Gen. Assembly, 1953-58. Lt. USNR, 1942-46. Mem. ABA, Ohio State Bar Assn., Columbus Bar Assn., Am. Coll. Trial Lawyers, Columbus Club (bd. dirs.),Columbus Athletic Club, Rocky Fork Hunt and Country Cub, Masons. Republican. Episcopalian. Home: 4906 Riverside Dr Columbus OH 43220-2876 Office: Chester Willcox & Saxbe 17 S High St Ste 900 Columbus OH 43215-3442

CHIANG, HUAI CHANG, entomologist, educator; b. Sunkiang, China, Feb. 15, 1915; came to U.S., 1945, naturalized, 1953; s. Wentse Chiang and Hsiu Hsiu C.; m. Zoh Ing Shen, Sept. 8, 1946; children: Jeanne, Katherine, Robert. B.S., Tsing Hua U., Peking, China, 1938; M.S., U. Minn., 1946, Ph.D., 1948; D.Sc. (hon.), Bowling Green State U., 1979. Asst. instr. entomology Tsing Hua U., Peking, 1938-40, instr., 1940-44; asst. prof. U. Minn., St. Paul and Duluth, 1954-57, assoc. prof. St. Paul, 1957-60, prof., 1960-83, prof. emeritus, 1984—. Cons. UNDP FAO, 1970, 72, 75, 76, 80, 82, 85-88, USDA, 1975-83; mem. sci. del. Am. Entomol. Soc., 1974, NAS, 1975, USDA/EPA, 1978, 81, USDA, 1979, 81, FAO, 1980, 82; sci. panel Coun. Environ. Quality, 1977, U.S. Internat. Comm. Agy., 1979, Internat. Centre Insect Physiology and Ecology, Nairobi, Kenya, 1980, Taiwan Coun. Agr., 1979, 84, Chinese Ministry Agr., 1982. Editor 3 publs.; contbr. over 230 rsch. papers to profl. jours. Recipient Cert. Appreciation USDA, 1975, Disting. Svc. award Am. Inst. Biol. Scis., 1979, Regents Cert. Merit U. Minn., 1984, Disting. Svc. award Ministry Agr. and Coops., Thailand, 1988; named Tchr. of yr. Student Assn., U. Minn-Duluth Campus, 1961; Guggenheim fellow, 1955; Phi Kappa Phi nat. scholar, 1983. Mem. Can. Royal London Entomol. Socs., Am. Entomol. Soc. (hon. mem., sect. chmn., chpt. pres., C.V. Riley award, Master Entomologist award), Hungarian Entomol. Soc. (hon. mem.), Japanese Soc. Population Rsch., Internat. Assn. Ecologists, Internat. Orgn. Biol. Control (pres. Western hemisphere, pres., hon. pres. working group), AAAS, Minn. Acad. Scis., Sigma Xi, Gamma Sigma Delta (Merit award 1983), Phi Kappa Phi (scholar of Yr. award 1982, Minn. chpt.). Home: 139 Westview Ln Ithaca NY 19850-6262

CHIAPPETTA, ROBERT A. manufacturing executive; BS in Acctg., No. Ill. U.; MBA, Loyola U. CPA, Ill. Internal auditor Amsted Industries Inc., Chgo., 1973-75; staff asst., supr. treasury & taxes Griffin Wheel (divsn. of Amsted Industries Inc.), 1975-76, mgr. info. sys., 1976-77; sr. acct. Amsted Industries Inc., 1977-78, asst. mgr. gen. acctg., 1978-80, mgr. gen. acctg., 1980-82, dir. gen. acctg., 1982-84, asst. controller, 1984-90; controller Griffin Pipe (divsn. of Amsted Industries Inc.), 1990-98; treas. Amsted Industries Inc., 1998-99, v.p., CFO, 1999—. Office: Amsted Industries Inc 205 N Michigan Ave Chicago IL 60601

CHICOINE, ROLAND ALVIN, farmer, former state legislator; b. Rural Elk Point, S.D., Dec. 10, 1922; s. Elmire Joseph and Louise Marie (Ryan) C.; m. Evelyn Marie Lyle, June 18, 1945; children: Jeffrey R., David L., Marcia M. Quinn, Daniel B., Timothy K., Brian Elmire, Ellen Little, Nicole Louise Klein. Owner, farmer, Elk Point, 1942-90; state rep. S.D. State Legislature, 1980—86, 1993—2000, state senator, 1987—92. Mem. Elk Point Local Dist. Sch. Bd., 1971-80; bd. dirs. Union County Farmers Home Adminstrn.; 4-H leader (40 yrs.) Sioux Livestock 4-H Club, state past pres. Named Family of Yr., S.D. State U., 1989, Eminent Farmer of Yr., S.D. State U., 1998. Mem. County Crop Improvement Assn. (past chmn. bd. dirs.), County Livestock Improvement Assn. (past chmn. bd. dirs.), S.D. State Irrigators Assn. (past state chmn. and organizer), S.D. Water Congress (past bd. dirs.), Union County Livestock Assn. (resolutions com. 1980—), Fed. Land Bank Assn. (Sioux Falls area chmn., bd. dirs. 1970-84, Omaha 4 state adv. bd. 1976-80), S.C. State 4-H Leaders Assn. (state chmn.), Eminent Farmers Assn. (pres. 2001-02) Lions(pres. Elk Point chpt. 2002). Democrat. Roman Catholic. Avocation: golf. Address: 32648 480th Ave Elk Point SD 57025-6833

CHIEGER, KATHRYN JEAN, recreation company executive; b. Detroit, July 13, 1948; d. George and Goldie Caroline (Payor) C. BA, Purdue U., 1970; MA, U. Mich., 1974; MBA, U. Denver, 1983. Libr. U. Mich., Ann Arbor, 1970-74; staff aide U.S. Sen. Gary Hart, Denver, 1974-79; dir. fin. rels. Petro-Lewis Corp., 1979-86; dir. investor rels. Kraft Inc., Glenview, Ill., 1987-89; v.p. corp. affairs Gaylor Container Corp., Deerfield, 1989-96; v.p. corp. and investor rels. Brunswick Corp., Lake Forest, 1996—. Mem. Nat. Investor Rels. Inst. (chpt. bd. dirs. 1979-84, v.p. mem. 1982-83, pres. 1983-84, nat. bd. dirs. 1984-88), Chgo. Execs. Club, Investor Rels. Assn., Sr. Investor Rels. Roundtable. Office: Brunswick Corp 1 N Field Ct Lake Forest IL 60045-4811 E-mail: kchieger@brunswick.com.

CHILCOTE, GARY M. museum director, reporter; b. St. Joseph, Mo., Nov. 2, 1934; s. Merrill and Mary Thelma C.; m. Mary Carolyn Abmeyer, April 2, 1958; children: Douglas A., Carolyn D. BA, Northwest Mo. State U., 1956. News-press spl. corr. St. Joseph News-Press/Gazette, 1954—; mus. dir. Patee House Mus. and Jesse James Home Mus., St. Joseph, 1963—. Vocat. tchr. Hillyard Tech. Sch., St. Joseph, 1964-91. Author, editor Pony Express Mail, 1972—. Staff sgt. Mo. Air Guard, 1957-63. Mem. Nat. Pony Express Assn. (nat. dir., nat. v.p. 1990—), Pony Express Hist. Assn. (bd. dirs., co-founder 1963), James-Younger Gang (nat. pres. 1997—, 98-99). Republican. Home: 1910 N 32nd St Saint Joseph MO 64506-2313 Office: Patee Ho Mus/Jesse James Ho Mus 1202 Penn St Saint Joseph MO 64503-2560

CHILDERS, L. DOYLE, state legislator; b. Ironton, Mo., Nov. 25, 1944; s. Lawrence Arlin and Jewel Nicks C. AS, Sch. Ozarks, 1964, BS, 1972; postgrad., Southwestern Mo. State U. Active U.S. Peace Corps., Cen. Am., 1965-69; sci. chmn. Reeds Spring RIV Sch. System, 1972-82; Mo. State rep. Dist. 29, 1983-96, Mo. state sen., 1996—. Active Reeds Spring Comm. Betterment Assn. Mem. Lions, Delta Kappa Phi. Home: PO Box 127 Reeds Spring MO 65737-0127

CHILES, STEPHEN MICHAEL, lawyer; b. July 15, 1942; s. Daniel Duncan and Helen Virginia (Hayes) C.; m. Deborah E. Nash, June 13, 1964; children: Stephen, Abigail. BA, Davidson Coll., 1964; JD, Duke U., 1967. Bar: N.Y. 1970, Pa. 1978, Wis. 1981, Ill. 1986, U.S. Dist. Ct. (ea. dist.) Pa. 1978, U.S. Tax Ct. 1978, U.S. Supreme Ct. 1978. Officer trust dept. Irving Trust Co., N.Y.C., 1970-75, v.p., 1975-77; assoc. atty. Stassen Kostos & Mason, Phila., 1978-79, mem., shareholder, 1979-85; ptnr. McDermott, Will & Emery, Chgo., 1986—. Contbr. articles to profl. jours. Served to capt. U.S. Army, 1967-69. Decorated Bronze Star, Army Commendation medal. Mem. ABA, State Bar Wis., Exmoor Country Club (Highland Park, Ill.). Republican. Episcopalian. Office: McDermott Will & Emery 227 W Monroe St Ste 3100 Chicago IL 60606-5096

CHIN, NEE OO WONG, reproductive endocrinologist; b. Hong Kong, Nov. 27, 1955; came to U.S., 1958; s. Bing Leong and Din Sui (Gee) C.; m. Shelly Loraine Crumrine, June 25, 1977; children: Jason Lei, Taryn Mae. BA, U. Cin., 1977; MD, Ohio State U., 1981. Diplomate Am. Bd. Ob-Gyn. Resident Duke U. Med. Ctr., Durham, N.C., 1981-84, chief resident, 1984-85; fellow Ohio State U. Coll. Medicine, Columbus, Ohio, 1985-87; teaching staff Good Samaritan Hosp., Cin., 1987—; clin. asst. prof. U. Cin. Med. Ctr., 1987—; dir. assisted reproductive techs. The Christ Hosp., Cin., 1992—. Mem. High Sch. for the Health Profl. subcom., Cin., 1989—. Author: (with others) Current Therapy in Obstetrics, 1988; contbr. articles to profl. jours. Named to Honorable Order of Ky. Cols., Gov. Martha Collins of Ky., 1987. Fellow Am. Coll. Ob-Gyn.; mem. AAAS, Am. Fertility Soc., Soc. Assisted Reproductive Tech., Soc. for Immunology Repro., Cin. Ob-Gyn. Soc. (med. malpractice com. 1989—), Acad. Medicine Cin. Avocations: tennis, karate. Office: Ste 220 11503 Spring Field Pike Cincinnati OH 45246-3550

CHING, WAI YIM, physics educator, researcher; b. Shaoshing, China, Oct. 18, 1945; came to U.S., 1969; s. Di-Son and Hung-Wong (Sung) C.; m. Mon Yin Lung, Dec. 27, 1975; children: Tianyu, Kunyu. BSc, U. Hong Kong, 1969; MS, La. State U., 1971, PhD, 1974. Rsch. assoc., lectr. U. Wis., Madison, 1974-78; asst. prof. U. Mo., Kansas City, 1978-81, assoc. prof., 1981-84, prof. physics, 1984-88, curators' prof., 1988—, chmn. physics dept., 1990-98. Cons. Argonne (Ill.) Nat. Lab., 1978-82, vis. scientist, 1985-86; vis. prof. U. Sci. and Tech., Hefei, China, 1983; guest scientist Max-Planck Inst. für Metallforschung, Stuttgart, Germany, 1997. Contbr. articles to profl. jours. Recipient N.T. Veatch award for disting. rsch., 1985; Trustee fellow U. Mo., 1984, 90. Fellow: Am. Ceramic Soc.; mem.: AAAS, Materials Rsch. Soc., Am. Vacuum Soc., Am. Phys. Soc., Sigma Xi. Achievements include the study of theoretical dondensed matter physics and materials sciences; electronic, magnetic, optical, dynamical structural and superconducting properties of ordered and disordered solids. Home: 2809 W 119th St Leawood KS 66209-1104 Office: U Mo Dept Physics Robert H Flarsheim Hall 5100 Rockhill Rd Kansas City MO 64110-2481 E-mail: chingw@umkc.edu.

CHINN, REX ARLYN, chemist; b. Bosworth, Mo., Apr. 5, 1935; s. Loren Herbert and Lima (Stanton) C.; m. Wanda June Williams, May 31, 1959 (dec.); children: Timothy Michael, Sharon Rose Chinn-Heritch, Jonathan Daniel; m. Victoria Loraine Hunter. BS in Chemistry, S.W. Mo. State Coll., 1961; grad., Cleve. Inst. Electronics. Lic. Bapt. minister. Rsch. asst. U. Mo. Med. Ctr., Columbia, 1961-65, William S. Merrell Co., Cin., 1965-67; lab. supr. U.S. Indsl. Chem. Co., Rsch. div., 1967-72; mgr. quality assurance Cloudsley Co., 1972-74; dir. tech. affairs Woodson Tenent Labs., Memphis, 1974-77; quality engr. Nat. Ind. for the Blind, Earth City, Mo., 1977-96; owner/mgr. The Master's Image, Maryland Hts., 1987—. Freelance field prodns. KNLC, Channel 24, St. Louis, 1987—; freelance audo rec. for ACTS Inc., 1996-2000; dir. video ops. Mission Gate Prison Ministry, 2000-2001; video cons.; environ. control sys. cons. Contbr. articles to profl. jours; producer/dir.: More Than a Fighting Chance, 1989. With U.S. Army, 1954-56. Mem. Media Comms. Assn. Republican. Avocations: art, photography, electronics, motorcycling, guitar. Home and Office: The Masters Image 12079 Ameling Rd Maryland Heights MO 63043-4148

CHIPMAN, JOHN SOMERSET, economist, educator; b. Montreal, Que., Can., June 28, 1926; s. Warwick Fielding and Mary Somerset (Aikins) C.; m. Margaret Ann Ellefson, June 24, 1960; children: Thomas Noel, Timothy Warwick. Student, Universidad de Chile, Santiago, 1943-44; BA, McGill U., Montreal, 1947, MA, 1948; PhD, Johns Hopkins U., 1951; postdoctoral, U. Chgo., 1950-51; Doctor rerum politicarum honoris causa, U. Konstanz, Germany, 1991, U. Würzburg, 1998; Doctor social and econ. scis., U. Graz, Austria, 2001. Asst. prof. econs. Harvard U., Cambridge, Mass., 1951-55; assoc. prof. econs. U. Minn., Mpls., 1955-60, prof., 1961-81, Regents' prof., 1981—. Fellow Ctr. for Advanced Study in Behavioral Scis., Stanford, Calif., 1972-73; Guggenheim fellow, 1980-81; vis. prof. econs. various univs.; permanent guest prof. U. Konstanz, 1985-91; bd. dirs. Leuthold Funds, Inc., 1995—. Author: The Theory of Intersectoral Money Flows and Income Formation, 1951; editor: (with others) Preferences, Utility, and Demand, 1971, Preferences, Uncertainty and Optimality, 1990, (with C.P. Kindleberger) Flexible Exchange Rates and the Balance of Payments, 1980; co-editor Jour. Internat. Econs., 1971-76, editor, 1977-87; assoc. editor Econometrica, 1956-60, Can. Jour. Stats., 1980-82; mem. adv. bd. Jour. Multivariate Analysis, 1988-92. Recipient James Murray Luck award Nat. Acad. Scis., 1981, Humboldt Rsch. award for Sr. U.S. Scientists, 1992. Fellow AAAS, Econometric Soc. (coun. 1971-76, 81-83), Am. Statis. Assn., Am. Acad. Arts and Scis., Am. Econ. Assn. (disting.); mem. NAS (chair sect. econ. scis. 1997-2000), Internat. Statis. Inst., Am. Philosophical Soc., Inst. Math. Stats., Can Econ. Assn., Royal Econ. Soc., History of Econs. Soc. Home: 2121 W 49th St Minneapolis MN 55409-2229 Office: U Minn Dept Econs 1035 Heller Hall 217 19th Ave S Minneapolis MN 55455-0400 E-mail: jchipman@econ.umn.edu.

CHIPPARONI, GUY, communications company executive; married; two children. BS in Journalism, Ill. State U., 1981. Sr. mng. dir. of pub. affairs Hill & Knowlton, Chgo., 1992-97; pres., pub. affairs KemperLesnik Comms., 1997—. Apptd. to bd. Met. Pier and Exposition Authority to oversee Navy Pier and McCormick Place, Chgo., 1998. Office: Kemper-Lesnik Comms Ste 1500 455 N Cityfront Plaza Dr Chicago IL 60611-5313 Fax: 312-755-0274.

CHISHOLM, MALCOLM HAROLD, chemistry educator; b. Bombay, India, Oct. 15, 1945; came to U.S., 1972; s. Angus MacPhail and Gweneth (Robey) C.; m. Cynthia Ann Truax, May 1, 1982; children: Calum R.I., Selby Scott, Derek Adrian. BS in Chemistry, Queen Mary Coll., London, 1966, PhD in Chemistry, 1969; DSc (hon.), London U., 1981. Postdoctoral fellow U. Western Ont., London, 1969-72; asst. prof. Princeton (N.J.) U., 1972-78; assoc. prof. chemistry Ind. U., Bloomington, 1978-80, prof.,

1980-85, Disting. prof. chemistry, 1985-99; disting. prof. math., phys. scis. Ohio State U., 2000—. Cons. in field. Editor: Polyhedron, Chem. Comm., Dalton Transactions; mem. editl. bd. Inorganic Chemistry, Organometallics, Inorganic Chimica Acta, Inorganic Syn. Inc., Jour. Cluster Sci., Chem. European Jour., Can. Jour. Chemistry, Chem. Record; contbr. over 500 rsch. articles to profl. jours. Fellow AAAS, Ind. Acad. Scis., Royal Soc. (London, Davy medal), Royal Soc. for Chemistry (Corday Morgan medal 1981, award for Transition Metal Chemistry, Centenary Lectr. and medal, Mond Lectr. and medal), Am. Chem. Soc. (Akron sect. award 1982, Buck Whitney award 1987, Inorganic Chemistry award, Disting. Svc. award). Home: 100 Kenyon Brook Dr Worthington OH 43085-3629 also: 38 Norwich St Cambridge CB2 1NE England Office: Ohio State U Dept Chemistry 100 W 18th Ave Columbus OH 43210-1185 E-mail: chisholm@chemistry.ohio-state.edu.

CHITWOOD, JULIUS RICHARD, librarian; b. Magazine, Ark., June 1, 1921; s. Hoyt Mozart and Florence (Umfrid) C.; m. Aileen Newsom, Aug. 6, 1944. A.B. cum laude, Ouachita Bapt. Coll., Ark., 1942; M.Mus., Ind. U., 1948; M.A., U. Chgo., 1954. Music supr. Edinburgh (Ind.) Pub. Schs., 1946-47; music and audiovisual librarian Roosevelt Coll., Chgo., 1948-51; humanities librarian Drake U., 1951-53; spl. cataloger Chgo. Tchrs. Coll., 1953; asst. circulation librarian Indpls. Pub. Library, 1954-57, coordinator adult services, 1957-61; dir. Rockford (Ill.) Pub. Library, 1961-79, No. Ill. Library System, Rockford, 1966-76. Chmn. subcom. library system devel. Ill. Library Adv. Com., 1965— ; adv. com. U. Ill. Grad. Sch. Library Sci., 1964-68; cons. in field, participant workshops Pres. Rockford Regional Academic Center, 1974-76; Mem. history com. Ill. Sesquicentennial Commn.; mem. Mayor Rockford Com. for UN, 1962-70; sect. chmn. Rockford United Fund, 1966-70; exec. Rockford Civic Orch. Assn., 1962-70. Served to maj., inf. AUS, 1942-45, ETO. Recipient Ill. Librarian of Year award, 1974 Mem. ALA (chmn. subcom. revision standards of materials, pub. library div. 1965-66, pres. bldg. and equipment sect. library adminstrn. div. 1967-68, chmn. staff devel. com. personnel adminstrn. sect., library adminstrv. div. 1964-68, pres. library adminstrn. div. 1969-70), Ill. Library Assn. (v.p. 1964-65, pres. 1965-66). Unitarian. Home: 3662 E Covenanter Dr Bloomington IN 47401-4681

CHIVETTA, ANTHONY JOSEPH, architect; b. St. Louis, Dec. 7, 1932; s. Anthony Joseph and Antoinette (Piazza) C.; m. Dolores Krekeler; children: Anthony Joseph III, Victoria, Christopher. BArch, Washington U., St. Louis, 1955. V.p. Hastings & Chivetta Architects, Inc., St. Louis, 1961-95, chmn., 1995—. Mem. alumni bd. Washington U. Sch. Architecture, St. Louis, 1987-88. Bd. dirs. Chaminade Coll. Prep., St. Louis, 1975-78, St. Joseph's Inst. for the Deaf, St. Louis, 1993—. Mem. AIA. Club: St. Louis. Office: Hastings & Chivetta Architects Inc 700 Corporate Park Dr Ste 400 Saint Louis MO 63105-4209

CHLEBOWSKI, JOHN FRANCIS, JR. business executive; b. Wilmington, Del., Aug. 19, 1945; s. John Francis and Helen Ann (Cholewa) C.; m. Mary L. Ahern, Sept., 1997; children: J. Christopher, Lauren R. B.S., U. Del., Newark, 1967; M.B.A., Pa. State U., State College, 1971. Fin. analyst Jones & Laughlin Steel, Pitts., 1971-74; mgr. fin. analysis W.R. Grace & Co., N.Y.C., 1974-75, mgr. fin. planning Dallas, 1975-77; v.p. planning Polumbus Co., Denver, 1977-78; asst. treas. W.R. Grace & Co., N.Y.C., 1978-83; v.p. fin. planning GATX Corp., Chgo., 1983-84, v.p. fin., 1984-86, v.p. fin., chief fin. officer, 1986-94; pres. GATX Terminals Corp., 1994—97, pres., CEO, 1995-97, Lakeshore Operating Ptnrs. LLC, Chgo., 1998—. Bd. dirs. Heartland Alliance, pres. bd. dirs., 1992-93. Leadership Greater Chgo. fellow, 1984-85 Mem.: The Racquet Club, Anglers Club, Beta Gamma Sigma. Roman Catholic.

CHO, WONHWA, biomedical researcher; b. Seoul, Korea, Apr. 27, 1958; BS in Chemistry, Seoul Nat. U., 1980, MS in Chemistry, 1982; PhD in Chemistry, U. Chgo., 1988. Postdoctoral fellow Calif. Inst. Tech., Pasadena, 1988-90; assoc. prof. chemistry U. Ill., Chgo., 1990-96, assoc. prof., 1996—; arthritis investigator, 1992-95; investigator Am. Heart Assn., 1999—. Mem. Am. Soc. Biochemistry & Molecular Biology, Am. Chem. Soc. Office: U Ill Chgo Dept Chemistry 845 W Taylor St Chicago IL 60607-7056

CHODOS, DALE DAVID JEROME, physician, consumer advocate; b. Mpls., June 5, 1928; s. John H. and Elvira Isabella (Lundberg) C.; m. Joyce Annette Smith, Sept. 9, 1951; children: John, Julie, David, Jennifer. A.B., Carroll Coll., Helena, Mont., 1950; M.D., St. Louis U., 1954. Diplomate Am. Bd. Pediatrics. Intern U. Utah, Salt Lake City, 1954-55, resident in pediatrics, 1955-57, chief resident in pediatrics, 1957, NIH fellow in endocrinology and metabolism, 1957-58; practice medicine specializing in pediatrics Idaho Falls, Idaho, 1958-62; staff physician Upjohn Co., Kalamazoo, 1962-64, head clin. pharmacology, 1964-65, research mgr. clin. pharmacology, 1965-68, research mgr. clin. services, 1968-73, group research mgr. med. therapeutics, 1973-81, med. dir. domestic med. affairs, 1981-85, exec. dir. domestic med. affairs, 1985-87; chief pediatrics Latter-day Saints Hosp., Sacred Heart Hosp., Idaho Falls, 1962; cons. to pharm. industry, 1988-91. Pres. Am. Health Advocacy, 1991—; chmn. med. rels. oper. com. Nat. Pharm. Coun., 1977-80; mem. med. sect. steering com. Pharm. Mfrs. Assn., 1977-87, chmn., 1984-86; sci. advisor Am. Coun. on Sci. and Health, 1991—. Contbr. articles to med. and pharm. jours. Bd. dirs. Family Service Ctr., Kalamazoo, 1965-71. Served with AUS, 1945-46. Recipient W.E. Upjohn award for excellence, 1969, Physician's Recognition award AMA, 1969, 73, 76, 79, 82, 85, 88. Fellow: Am. Acad. Pediat.; mem.: Advancement of Sound Sci. Coalition (mem. scientist). Republican. Home: 619 Aquaview Dr Kalamazoo MI 49009-9652 E-mail: dalekazoo@aol.com.

CHOKEL, CHARLES B. insurance company executive; Formerly CFO Progressive Corp., Cleve.; CFO Conseco, Inc., Carmel, Ind., 2001—. Office: Conseco Inc 11825 N Pennsylvania St Carmel IN 46032

CHOKEY, JAMES A. lawyer; b. Pitts., Sept. 2, 1943; AB, U. Pitts., 1965; JD, Duquesne U., 1969. Bar: Pa. 1969, U.S. Dist. Ct. (we. dist.) Pa., Wis. 1973. Atty. Westinghouse Electric Corp., 1972-73; v.p., gen. counsel, sec. Joy Mfg., 1973-87, RTE Corp., 1987-88, A.O. Smith Corp., 1989-91; v.p., gen. counsel Cooper Industries Inc., Houston, 1991—; v.p. corp. affairs, gen. counsel Beloit (Wis.) Corp.; exec. v.p., sec. and gen. counsel Harnischfeger Industries Inc., Milw. and St. Francis, Wis., 1997—. Mem. ABA, Am. Corp. Counsel Assn. (pres. we. Pa. chpt. 1985-86). Office: Harnischfeger Industries Inc PO Box 554 Milwaukee WI 53201-0554 E-mail: jchokey@HII.com.

CHOLDIN, MARIANNA TAX, librarian, educator; b. Chgo., Feb. 26, 1942; d. Sol and Gertrude (Katz) Tax; m. Harvey Myron Choldin, Aug. 28, 1962; children: Kate and Mary (twins). BA, U. Chgo., 1962, MA, 1967, PhD, 1979. Slavic bibliographer Mich. State U., East Lansing, 1967-69; Slavic bibliographer, instr. U. Ill., Urbana, 1969-73, Slavic bibliographer, asst. prof., 1973-76, Slavic bibliographer, assoc. prof., 1976-84, head Slavic and East European Libr., 1982-89, head, prof., 1984—, dir. Russian and East European Ctr., 1987-89, C. Walter and Gerda B. Mortenson Disting. prof., 1989—, dir. Mortenson Ctr. for Internat. Libr. Programs, 1991—. Author: Fence Around the Empire: Russian Censorship, 1985; editor: Red Pencil: Artists, Scholars and Censors in the USSR, 1989, Books, Libraries and Information in Slavic and East European Studies, 1986. Chair Soros Found. Network Libr. Program Bd., 1997—2000. Recipient Pushkin gold medal for contbns. to culture, Russian Presdl. Coun. on Culture, 2000. Mem. ALA, Am. Assn. for Advancement of Slavic Studies (pres. 1995), Internat. Fedn. Libr. Assns. and Instns., Phi Beta Kappa. Jewish. Home: 1111 S Pine St Champaign IL 61820-6334 Office: U Ill Libr 1402 W Gregory Dr Urbana IL 61801-3607

CHOLE, RICHARD ARTHUR, otolaryngologist, educator; b. Madison, Wis., Oct. 12, 1944; s. Arthur Steven and Wendy Elveyn (Danielczyk) C.; m. Cynthia Beiseker, Dec. 27, 1969; children: Joseph Michael, Timothy Thomas, Katharine, Melinda. Student, U. Calif., Berkeley, 1962-65; MD, U. So. Calif., 1969; PhD in Otolaryngology, U. Minn., 1977. Diplomate Am. Bd. Otolaryngology (sr. bd. examiner). Rotating intern U. So. Calif. Med. Ctr., 1969-70; med. fellow dept. surgery Sch. Medicine U. Minn., 1972-73, med. fellow dept. otolaryngology Sch. Medicine, 1973-77; asst. prof. dept. otolaryngology-head and neck surgery Sch. Medicine U. Calif., Davis, 1977-81, assoc. prof., 1981-84, prof., 1984-98, acting chmn. dept., 1985, chmn., 1985-88; chmn. dept. otolaryngology Washington U., St. Louis, 1998—. Mem. sci. rev. com. Deafness Rsch. Found., 1986—; mem. communicative disorders rev. com. Nat. Inst. Deafness and Communication Disorders, 1989—94; staff cons. Dept. Air Force, David Grant USAF Med. Ctr., Travis AFB, Calif., 1981—98; keynote spkr. 92d Japan Oto-Rhino-Laryngol. Soc. Meeting, Fukuoka City, Japan, 1990—; faculty mem. 4th Internat. Cholesteatoma Conf., Niigata City, Japan, 1992; bd. dirs. Am. Bd. Otolaryngology, 2000—; adv. coun. Nat. Deafness and Other Communication Disorders, 2001—; lectr. in field. Mem. editorial bd. Laryngoscope, 1985-87; mem. exec. editorial bd. Otolaryngology-Head and Neck Surgery, 1990—; contbr. numerous articles to profl. jours., book chpts., revs.; patentee in field. Mem. profl. edn. com. Am. Cancer Soc., 1977-78, Sacramento Noise Control Hearing Bd., 1977—, Greater Sacramento Profl. Standards Rev. Orgn., 1978-79; deacon 1st Bapt. Ch., Davis, 1979-82, elder, 1983-88. Recipient 1st pl. award Am. Acad. Ophthalmology and Otolaryngology, 1977, care recognition awards U. Calif., Davis, 1988-91; rsch. grantee NIH, Nat. Inst. Aging, Nat. Inst. Neurol. and Communicative Disorders and Stroke, Nat. Inst. on Deafness and Other Communication Disorders, Deafness Rsch. Found., Am. Otol. Soc., U. Calif., 1978-91. Mem. Collegeum Otorhinolaryngologicum Amicitiae Sacrum (U.S. group), Am. Acad. Otolaryngology-Head and Neck Surgery (Honors award 1984, com. on rsch. 1987—, rsch. coordinating coun. 1987—, continuing edn. com. 1991—), Am. Otol. Soc. (trustee rsch. fund 1986—, sec.-treas. 1989—, pres. 2001—), Assn. for Rsch. in Otolaryngology (pres. 1999-2000, award of merit com. 1988—), Am. Laryngol., Rhinol. and Otol. Soc., Am. Soc. for Bone and Mineral Rsch., Assn. Acad. Depts. Otolaryngology-Head and Neck Surgery (coun. 1986—), Calif. Med. Assn. (sci. adv. panel, sect. on otolaryngology-head and neck surgery 1986-98), Sacramento Soc. Otolaryngology and Maxillofacial Surgery, Soc. Univ. Otolaryngologists-Head and Neck Surgeons. Achievements include research in experimental cholesteatoma, experimental otosclerosis, the aging auditory system, osteoclast cell biology. E-mial. Office: Washington U Sch Med CB8115 660 S Euclid Ave # 8115 Saint Louis MO 63110-1010 E-mail: choler@msnotes.wustl.edu.

CHOOKASZIAN, DENNIS HAIG, retired financial executive; b. Chgo., Sept. 19, 1943; s. Haig Harold and Annabelle (Kalkanian) C.; m. Karen Margaret Genteman, Mar. 18, 1967; children: Jeffrey, Michael, Kerry. BS in Chem. Engring., Northwestern U., 1965; MBA in Fin., U. Chgo., 1967; MS in Econs., London Sch. of Econs., 1968. CPA, Ill.; cert. mgmt. cons. Mgmt. cons. Touche Ross & Co., Chgo., 1968-75; CFO, CNA Fin. Corp., 1975-90; pres., COO CNA, 1990-92; chmn., CEO, CNA Ins., from 1992, now bd. dirs. Bd. dirs. Loews Corp., Mercury Fin. Pres. Found. for Health Enhancement; bd. dirs. Nat. Boy Scouts Am., Northwestern Meml. Hosp., Nat. Merit Scholarship Corp.; mem. adv. coun. U. Chgo. Grad. Sch. of Bus.; mem. adv. bd. Northwestern U. Kellogg Grad. Sch. of Bus., Inroads; trustee Northwestern U., 1996—. Mem. AICPAs, Ill. Soc. CPAs, Westmoreland Country Club (Wilmette), East Bank Club (Chgo.), The Econ. Club of Chgo., The Execs. Club of Chgo. (dirs.' table), Am. Inst. Assn., Am. Coun. of Life Ins., Ins. Svcs. Office, Beta Gamma Sigma. Republican. Avocations: skiing, tennis, triathlons, golf. Home: 1100 Michigan Ave Wilmette IL 60091-1976 Office: CNA Cna Plz Chicago IL 60685-0001

CHOPLIN, JOHN M., II, lawyer; b. Cedar Rapids, Iowa, Nov. 10, 1945; s. John M. and Joyce G. (Mickelson) C.; m. Linda H. Kutchen, Feb. 14, 1969; children: Julie, John, James. BA, Drake U., 1967; JD, U. Mich., 1974. Bar: Ind. 1974, U.S. Dist. Ct. (so. dist.) Ind. 1974, U.S. Ct. Appeals (7th cir.) 1976, U.S. Supreme Ct. 1977, U.S. Ct. Appeals (6th cir.) 1983, U.S. Dist. Ct. (no. dist.) Ind. 1991. Assoc. Wilson, Tabor & Holland, Indpls., 1974-80; ptnr. Norris, Choplin & Schroeder, 1980—. Committeeman precinct Carmel Reps., Ind., 1982-84. Served to capt. USAF, 1969-73. Mem. ABA, Ind. Bar Assn., Indpls. Bar Assn., 7th Fed. Cir. Bar Assn., Lawyers-Pilots Bar Assn., Ind. Trial Lawyers Assn., Assn. Trial Lawyers Am., Christian Legal Soc., Phi Beta Kappa, Omicron Delta Kappa. Baptist. Avocations: water sports, tennis, flying. Home: 8553 Twin Pointe Cir Indianapolis IN 46236-8903 Office: Norris Choplin & Schroeder 101 W Ohio St Ste 900 Indianapolis IN 46204-4213

CHORENGEL, BERND, international hotel corporation executive; Pres. Hyatt Internat. Corp., Chgo. Office: Hyatt Internat Hotels Corp Madison Plz 200 W Madison St Chicago IL 60606-3414

CHOU, CLIFFORD CHI FONG, research engineering executive; b. Taipei, Taiwan, Dec. 19, 1940; came to U.S., 1966, naturalized, 1978; s. Ching piao and Yueh li (Huang) C.; m. Chu hwei Lee, Mar. 23, 1968; children: Kelvin Lin yu, Renee Lincy. Ph.D., Mich. State U., 1972. Research asst. Mich. State U., East Lansing, 1967-70, Wayne State U., Detroit, 1970-72, research assoc., 1972-76; research engr. Ford Motor Co., Dearborn, 1976-81, sr. research engr., 1981-82, prin. research engr. assoc., 1982-89, prin. staff engr., 1989-93; sr. engring. specialist, 1993-95; staff tech. specialist, 1995—. Adj. prof. Mich. Technol. U., 1997—; lectr. to China under UN Devel. Program, 1987, 93, 95, lectr. to Taiwan under Automotive Rsch. and Test Ctr., 1991, 97, 98; organizer Safety Test Methodology, SAE session chair, 1997, 98, 99, 00, 01, 02, IBEC session chair 1999, 2000; coord. Detroit Automobile Tech. Conf., 1993, session chair, 1997; mem. safety and environ. systems planning com. IBEC '98, 1997-2000, 01-02; indsl. acad. adv. to PhD Coms., U. Mich., 1995-98, U. Va., 1997—, Mich. Tchrs. U., 1997-2000, Wayne State U., 1999—; tchr. in field; co-organizer 6th U.S. Nat. Conf. on Computational Mechs., crashworthiness session, Dearborn, 2001. Five patents in field; contbr. chpts. to books, articles to profl. jours. Recipient Safety Engring. Excellence award Nat. Hwy. Traffic Safety Adminstrn., 1980, Innovation award Engring. and Mfg. Staff Ford Motor Co., 1986, 95, 96, 97, 98, Tech. Accomplishment awards, 1989, 91, 92, 93, 94, Henry Ford Tech. award, 1995, 2000, Customer Quality Driven award, 1995, 96, 2000, Product and Analysis Verification Tech. award, 2000; grantee Soc. Automotive Engrs. Fellow: Soc. Automotive Engrs. (Forest R. McFarland award 2000); mem.: AIAA, ASME, Detroit Chinese Am. Assn., Mich. Chinese Acad. Profl. Assn. (bd. dirs. 1992—93, pres. 1993—94, advisor 1994—, seminar spkr. 2000), Ford Chinese Club (pres. 1991—92), Sigma Xi. Achievements include patents. Home: 28970 Forest Hill Dr Farmington MI 48331-2439 E-mail: cchou@ford.com.

CHOU, KUO-CHEN, biophysical chemist; b. Guangdong, China, Aug. 14, 1938; came to U.S., 1980; s. Hsiu-Chi Chou and Bi-Kun Luo; m. Wei-Zhu Zhong, Apr. 12, 1968; 1 child, James Jeiwen Chou. BS, Nanking (Peoples Republic China) U., 1960, MS, 1962; PhD, Shanghai (Peoples Republic China) Inst. Biochemistry, 1976; DSc, Kyoto (Japan) U., 1983. Jr. scientist Shanghai Inst. Biochemistry, Chinese Acad. Sci., 1976-78, assoc. prof., 1978-79; vis. assoc., prof. Chem. Ctr. Lund (Sweden) U., 1979-80; vis. assoc. prof. Max-Planck Inst. Biophys. Chemistry, Göttingen, Fed. Republic Germany, 1979-80; vis. assoc. prof. chemistry Cornell U., Ithaca, N.Y., 1980-83, sr. scientist Baker Lab., 1984-85; prof. biophysics U. Rochester, 1985-86; sr. scientist Eastman Kodak Co., Rochester, 1986-87, Upjohn Labs., Kalamazoo, 1987—92, sr. prin. scientist, 1993—99, rsch. advisor, 1993—99, sr. rsch. advisor, 1999—; sr. scientist Pharmacia & Upjohn, 1995—. Editor Jour. Molecular Sci., 1983-86, Progress in Physics, 1981-85; mem. editl. bd. Current Peptide and Protein Sci., 2000—; contbr. more than 200 rsch. articles and rev. papers to profl. jours. Recipient Sci. and Tech. award Shanghai Com. of Sci. and Tech., 1977, Nat. medal of Sci., Nat. Acad. of Sci., China, 1978, Disting. Leadership award Am. Biog. Inst., N.C., 1989, Commemorative medal of Honor, Am. Biog. Inst., 1991; named for Leadership and Achievement, Internat. Biog. Ctr., Cambridge, U.K., 1990. Fellow Am. Inst. Chemistry; mem. AAAS, N.Y. Acad. Scis., Biophysical Soc., Am. Chem. Soc., Sigma Xi. Achievements include rsch. in protein conformation and folding; graph theory in chem. reaction systems; enzyme kinetics; DNA codon usage analysis; prediction of protein cellular location and structural class; structure and function of antifreeze protein; prediction of HIV protease cleavege site; low-frequency collective motions of biomacromolecules and their biol. functions; structures of growth hormone and membrane proteins, proton-pumping mechanism of membrane proteins, inhibition kinetics of HIV reverse transcriptase, structure and binding site of adhesion proteins, apoptosis, g-protein couple receptors; GABA receptors, cyclin-dependent kinases, molecular mechanism of Alzheimer's Disease, prediction signal peptides and their cleavage sites. Home: 7088 Arbor Valley Ave Kalamazoo MI 49009-8540 Office: Pharmacia & Upjohn Labs Computer-Aided Drug Discov 301 Henrietta St Kalamazoo MI 49007-4940 E-mail: kuo-chen.chou@am.pru.com.

CHOW, CHI-MING, retired mathematics educator; b. Tai-Yuan, Shansi, Republic of China, Nov. 15, 1931; came to U.S., 1959; s. Wei-Han Chow and Lu-Tsen Hsu. Cert. tech. officer, Chinese Air Force Tech. Inst., Republic of China, 1954; BS in Math., Ch. Coll. Hawaii, 1962; MS in Math., Oreg. State U., 1965. Tech. officer Chinese Air Force, Republic of China, 1954-59; prof. math. Oakland C.C., Mich., 1965-92, ret., 1992. Author (first author of the proof of the theorem): The sight area A of a moving body is inversely proportional to the square of the distance D between the body and observing point, i.e. A=C/(DxD), where C is a constant; contbr. articles to profl. jours. including The Math. Tchr. 1st Lt. Air Force of Republic of China, 1954-59. Mem. Pi Mu Epsilon. Avocation: piloting aircraft. Home: PO Box 903 Novi MI 48376-0903

CHOW, POO, wood technologist, scientist; b. Shanghai, China, Apr. 27, 1934; arrived in U.S., 1960, naturalized, 1971; s. Kai and Yung-Kwan (Hsieh) C.; m. Ai-Yu Kuo, July 17, 1965; children— Eugenia, Andrew E. M.S. in Forest Products, La. State U., 1961; Ph.D. in Wood Sci. and Tech., Forestry, Mich. State U., 1969. Lab. dir. Pope and Talbot, Inc., Oakridge, Oreg., 1962-67; asst. prof. wood sci. U. Ill., Urbana, 1969-74, assoc. prof., 1974-80, prof., 1980—. Sr. Fulbright scholar, Fed. Republic Germany; cons. to industry; external examiner U. Ibadan, Nigeria; expert witness. Contbr. numerous articles to profl. jours.; patentee in field. Mem. ASTM, Forest Products Soc., Am. Chem. Soc., Soc. Wood Sci. and Tech., Am. Railway Engrs. and Maintenance-of-Way Assn., Internat. Rsch. on Wood Preservation Group, German Wood Technology Soc., RR Tie Assn., TAPPI, Am. Wood Preservatives Assn., Nat. Forensic Ctr., Sigma Xi, Gamma Sigma Delta, Xi Sigma Pi. Office: Univ Ill 1102 S Goodwin Ave Urbana IL 61801-4730 E-mail: P-Chow2@uiuc.edu.

CHOY, PATRICK C. biochemistry educator; b. China, June 16, 1944; 1 child. BSc, McGill U., 1969; MSc, U. N.D., 1972, PhD, 1975, MD (hon.) , 1999. Teaching fellow biochemistry U. B.C., Canada, 1975-79; from asst. prof. to assoc. prof. U. Man., Canada, 1979-86, prof. biochemistry Canada, 1986—, head dept. Canada, 1992—, assoc. dean facilty of medicine Canada; scientist Med. Rsch. Coun. Can., 1984—. Mem. Am. Soc. Biol. Chemists, Can. Biochem. Soc., Can. Cardiovascular Soc. Achievements include rsch. in lipid metabolism in mammalian hearts; pathogenesis of heart failure. Office: U Man Dept Biochem Fac Med Winnipeg MB Canada R3E 0W3

CHRISMAN, BRUCE LOWELL, physicist, administrator; b. Stillwater, Okla., Mar. 16, 1943; s. Everett Lowell and Lavinia Evelyn (Roether) C.; m. Barbara JoAnn Karnuth, May 17, 1975; children: Brenden Lowell, Brady Kenneth. SB, MIT, 1964; MS, U. Ill., 1965, PhD, 1971; MBA, U. Chgo., 1975; MA (hon.), Yale U., 1983. With Fermi Nat. Accelerator Lab., Batavia, Ill., 1970-88, physicist, 1970-75, exec. asst., 1975-79, bus. mgr., 1979-83, assoc. dir. adminstrn., 1984-88, 91—; v.p. adminstrn. Yale U., New Haven, 1983-84; assoc. dir. adminstrn. Superconducting Super Collider, Dallas, 1988-89; dir. adminstrn. Wildman, Harrold, Allan & Dixon, Chgo., 1989-91. Bd. dirs. Sch. Dist. 41, Glen Ellyn, Ill., 1986-95; bd. overseers Ill. Inst. Tech. Rice Campus, 1997—. Mem. Sigma Xi (pres. 1981-83). Home: 701 Forest Ave Glen Ellyn IL 60137-3905 Office: Fermi Nat Accelerator Lab PO Box 500 Batavia IL 60510-0500 E-mail: chrisman@fnal.gov.

CHRISMER, RICH, state legislator; b. Apr. 9, 1946; m. Mary Margaret Parson, 1972; children: Richard, Anna, Laura, Mark. AA, St. Louis C.C., Florissant Valley. Mo. State rep. Dist. 16; svc. technician. Bd. dirs. Pro-Life Citizen Mo. Mem. K.C. (4th degree). Home: Apt 605 275 Union Blvd Saint Louis MO 63108-1234

CHRISTENSEN, A(LBERT) KENT, anatomy educator; b. Washington, Dec. 3, 1927; s. Albert Sherman and Lois (Bowen) C.; m. Elizabeth Anne Reynolds Sears, Aug. 26, 1952; children: Anne, Kathleen Martha, Albert David, Jennifer, John Sears. AB, Brigham Young U., 1953; PhD, Harvard U., 1958. Postdoctoral fellow Cornell Med. Coll., 1958-59, Harvard Med. Sch., Boston, 1959-60, instr. dept. anatomy, 1960-61; asst. prof. dept. anatomy Stanford Sch. Medicine, Palo Alto, Calif., 1961-68, assoc. prof., 1968-71; prof., chmn. dept. anatomy Temple U. Sch. Medicine, Phila., 1971-78; prof. anatomy and cell biology U. Mich. Med. Sch., Ann Arbor, 1978-99, chmn. dept. anatomy and cell biology, 1978-82, prof. emeritus, 1999—. Contbr. articles to profl. jours. With USMC, 1946-47. Mem. AAAS, Am. Soc. Cell Biology, Am. Assn. Anatomists (pres. 1984-85), Microscopy Soc. Am. Office: U Mich Med Sch Dept Cell & Devel Biology Med Sci II Bldg Ann Arbor MI 48109-0616 E-mail: akc@mich.edu.

CHRISTENSEN, DAVID ALLEN, manufacturing company executive; b. 1935; BS, S.D. State U., 1957. With John Morrell & Co., 1960-62, Raven Industries Inc., Sioux Falls, S.D., 1962—, product mgr., 1964-71, pres., chief exec. officer, 1971-2000; ret., 2000. Served with AUS, 1957-60. Office: Raven Industries Inc PO Box 5107 Sioux Falls SD 57117-5107

CHRISTENSEN, DOUGLAS, state education commissioner; BA, Midland Luth. Coll., 1965; MA, U. Nebr., 1970, PhD, 1978. Tchr. Holdrege (Nebr.) Sr. H.S., 1965-70; h.s. prin. Bloomfield (Nebr.) Cmty. Schs., 1970-74, supt. of schs., 1974-76; county supt. of schs. Knox County Ctr., Nebr., 1975-76; supt. of schs. Colby Pub. Schs. Unified Sch. Dist. #315, 1978-85, North Platte (Nebr.) Pub. Schs., 1985-90; assoc. commr. of edn. Nebr. Dept. of Edn., Lincoln, 1990-92, dep. commr. of edn., 1992-94, commr. edn., 1994—. Presenter, cons. in field. Contbr. articles to profl. jours. Chair North Platte Area Econ. Devel. Task Force, 1986-90, Coun. for Inter-Agy. Cooperation, 1986-90; liturgist First Luth. Ch., 1986-90, chair fin. com., 1988-90; bd. dirs. Mid-Nebr. Cmty. Found., 1989-90; bd. dirs. Mari Sandoz Soc., 1990—; mem. Nebr. Commn. for the Protection of Children, 1994—; advanced planning com. Southwood Luth. Ch., 1994—. Recipient Spirit of PTA award Nebr. PTA, 1997, 98, Cornerstone award Future Farmers Am., 1998, Walter Turner award Am. Assn. Ednl. Svc. Agys., 1998, David Hutchinson award U. Nebr., 1998, Burnham Yates award Nebr. Coun. Econ. Edn., 1999. Mem. ASCD (pres. Kans. affiliate 1984-85), Am. Assn. of Sch. Adminstrs. (Nebr. Supt. of Yr. 1990), Coun. Chief State Sch. Officers (bd. dirs. 1997—), Nebr. Coun. of Sch. Adminstrs., Rotary Internat. (pres. 1981-82), Nebr. Ctr. for Ednl. Excellence (chair 1985-90, bd. dirs. 1989-90), Midland Luth. Coll. Alumni Assn. (pres. 1992-93). Office: Commrs Office Dept of Edn PO Box 94987 Lincoln NE 68509-4987

CHRISTENSEN, GARY M. building materials company executive; Various sr. mgmt. positions GE, Trane Corp.; joined Pella Corp., Iowa, 1990, now pres., CEO, also bd. dirs.

CHRISTENSEN, JOHN WILLIAM, lawyer; b. Roselawn, Ind., Mar. 14, 1914; s. Henry Julius and Caroline Belle (Conrad) C.; m. Eleanor Schwerak, Sept. 2, 1939; children: William J., Amy Christensen Fox, Martha Christensen Rand, Nancy Christensen Couyoumjian; m. Beth Pinkley, Nov. 9, 1996. AB, DePauw U., 1935; JD, U. Ind., 1939. Bar: Ind. 1939, U.S. Supreme Ct., 1945, Ohio 1947. Acct. GE Co., Schnectady, N.Y., 1935-36; atty. SEC, Washington, 1939-44, spl. counsel utilities divsn., 1944-46; assoc., then ptnr. Dargusch, Caren, Greek & King, Columbus, Ohio, 1946-53; ptnr. Gingher & Christensen, 1953-86; of counsel Baker & Hostetler, 1986—; gen. counsel Brodhead-Garrett Co., Cleve., 1955-86, also bd. dirs.; v.p., gen. counsel Columbus Mut. Life Ins. Co., 1962-84. V.p., gen. counsel, sec., bd. dirs. O.M. Scott & Sons Co., Marysville, Ohio, 1951-84; chmn., pres., CEO Nat. Extrusion and Mfg., Bellefontaine, Ohio, 1978-87; bd. dirs. State Automobile Mut. Ins. Co., United McGill Corp., Taylor Woodcraft Inc.; adj. prof. law Ohio State U., 1964-72. Trustee DePauw U., Greencastle, Ind., 1962—. With USCGR, 1943-45. Mem. ABA, Ohio Bar Assn., Columbus Bar Assn., Ind. U. Law Acad. of Fellows, Order of Coif, Phi Beta Kappa, Phi Delta Phi. Presbyterian. Home: 8240 Round Hills Cir Las Vegas NV 89113-1230 Office: 65 E State St Columbus OH 43215-4213 E-mail: torch44@lvcm.com.

CHRISTENSEN, JON, finance company executive, former congressman; b. St. Paul, Feb. 20, 1963; s. Harlan and Audrey C.; m. Meredith Stewart Maxfield, 1987. Degrees in biology & bus., Midland Lutheran Coll., 1985; JD, South Tex. Coll. of Law, 1989. V.p. corp. divsn. COMReP, Inc., 1989-91; mktg. dir. Conn. Mutual Ins. Co., 1991; founder The Aquila Group, Inc. (holding co. for Old McDonald's); mem. U.S. Ho. of Reps., Washington, 1994-98, mem. ways & means com., subcoms. health and social security; sr. v.p. Wuantim Alliance, Omaha, 1999—. Mem. Am. Diabetes Assn.'s Celebrity Breakfast. Mem. Nebr. Farm Bureau, Nebr. Cattlemen's Assn. Nat. Fedn. Ind. Bus., Nat. Assn. of Life Underwriters, Omaha Assn. Life Underwriters, ABA (mem real estate, probate & trust divsn.), Nebr. Bar Assn., Omaha Bar Assn., Northwest Rotary Club. Republican. Office: Quantum Applaice 1 Valmont Plz Fl 4 Omaha NE 68154-5214

CHRISTENSEN, MARVIN NELSON, venture capitalist; b. W. Branch, Iowa, July 15, 1927; s. Peter Ancher and Martha Henrietta (Neilsen) C.; m. Mary Lou Miller, Dec. 17, 1949 (dec. June 1999); children: Stephen R., Barbara. BS, U. Iowa, 1950. Pvt. practice ins. and real estate, Iowa City, 1955-69; asst. to pres. Gen. Growth Cos., Des Moines, 1970-72; acquisitions dir. Life Investors of Iowa, Cedar Rapids, 1972-80; chmn. and chief exec. officer Bus. Comml. Realty, Denver, 1980—; chmn., CEO Colo. Internat. Devel., Colorado Springs, 1984—; chmn. Byers (Colo.) State Bank, 1987-89, Farmer's State Bank, Waubun, Minn., 1988-96. Founder, adminstr. Waubun Area Devel. Enterprises, 1988—. Columnist: View from My Window (monthly newspaper); contbr. many articles to nat. pubs. Lt. (j.g.) USNR, 1944-46. Mem. Am. Bankers Assn., Minn. Bankers Assn., Masons, Elks, Eagles, VFW. Avocations: writing, cabinet making, fishing. Home: RR 2 Waubun MN 56589-9802

CHRISTENSEN, NIKOLAS IVAN, geophysicist, educator; b. Madison, Wis., Apr. 11, 1937; s. Ivan Rudolph and Alice Evelyn (Ethen) C.; m. Karen Mary Luberg, June 18, 1960; children— Kirk Nathan, Signe Kay. BS, U. Wis., 1959, MS, 1961, PhD, 1963. Rsch. fellow in geophysics Harvard U., Cambridge, Mass., 1963-64; asst. prof. geol. scis. U. So. Calif., 1964-66; prof. U. Wash., Seattle, 1966-83, Purdue U., Lafayette, Ind., 1983-97; Weeks disting. prof. U. Wis., Madison, 1997—. Mem. Pacific adv. panel Joint Oceanographic Instns. for Deep Earth Sampling, Seattle, 1973-75, mem. igneous and metamorphic petrology panel, 1973-75, mem. ocean crust panel, 1974-77; mem. adv. panel on oceanography NSF, 1976-78, mem. adv. panel on earth scis. 1994-97; mem. adv. panel on continental lithosphere NRC, 1979-83; mem. adv. panel Internat. Assn. Geodesy, 1980-88. Contbg. author: Geodynamics of Iceland and the North Atlantic Area, 1974; Contbr. numerous articles to profl. jours. NSF grantee, 1968-98. Fellow Geol. Soc. Am. (chmn. geophysics divsn. 1984-86, assoc. editor Geology 1985-89, George P. Woollard award 1996), Am. Geophys. Union (assoc. editor Jour. Geophys. Rsch. 1998—). Achievements include research on nature of Earth's interior. Home: 2390 Highway AB Mc Farland WI 53558 Office: U Wisc Dept Geology and Geophys U Wisc Madison WI 53706

CHRISTENSON, GORDON A. law educator; b. Salt Lake City, June 22, 1932; s. Gordon B. and Ruth Arzella (Anderson) C.; m. Katherine Joy deMik, Nov. 2, 1951 (div. 1977); children: Gordon Scott, Marjorie Lynne, Ruth Ann, Nanette; m. Fabienne Fadeley, Sept. 16, 1979. BS in Law, U. Utah, 1955, JD, 1956; SJD, George Washington U., 1961. Bar: Utah 1956, U.S. Supreme Ct. 1971, D.C. 1978. Law clk. to chief justice Utah Supreme Ct., 1956-57; assoc. firm Christenson & Callister, Salt Lake City, 1956-58; atty. Dept. of Army, Nat. Guard Bur., Washington, 1957-58; atty., acting asst. legal adviser Office of Legal Adviser, U.S. Dept. State, 1958-62; asst. gen. counsel for sci. and tech. U.S. Dept. Commerce, 1962-67, spl. asst. to undersec. of commerce, 1967, counsel to commerce tech. adv. bd., 1962-67, chmn. task force on telecommunications missions and orgn., 1967, counsel to panel on engring. and commodity standards, tech. adv. bd., 1963-65; assoc. prof. law U. Okla., Norman, 1967-70, exec. asst. to pres., 1967-70; univ. dean for ednl. devel., central adminstrn. State U. N.Y., Albany, 1970-71; prof. law Am. U. Law Sch., Washington, 1971-79, dean, 1971-77; on leave, 1977-79; Charles H. Stockton prof. internat. law U.S. Naval War Coll., Newport, R.I., 1977-79; dean, Nippert prof. law U. Cin. Coll. Law, 1979-85, univ. prof. law, 1985-99, prof. emeritus, dean emeritus, 1999—. Assoc. professorial lectr. in internat. affairs George Washington U., 1961-67; vis. scholar Harvard U. Law Sch., 1977-78, Yale Law Sch., 1985-86, Law Sch. U. Maine, Portland, 1997; Wallace S. Fujiyama vis. disting. prof. law Univ. Hawaii Law Sch., 1997; participant summer confs. on internat. law Cornell Law Sch., Ithaca, N.Y., 1962, 64; cons. in internat. law U.S. Naval War Coll., Newport, R.I., 1969; faculty mem., reporter seminars for experienced fed. dist. judges Fed. Jud. Center, Washington, 1972-77. Author: (with Richard B. Lillich) International Claims: Their Preparation and Presentation, 1962, The Future of the University, 1969; Contbr. articles to legal jours. Cons. to Center for Policy Alternatives Mass. Inst. Tech., Cambridge, 1970-81; mem. intergovtl. com. on Internat. Policy on Weather Modification, 1967; Vice pres. Procedural Aspects of Internat. Law Inst., N.Y.C., 1962-2001, trustee, 1962—. Served with intelligence sect. USAF, 1951-52, Japan. Recipient Silver Medal award Dept. Commerce, 1967; fellow Grad. Sch. U. Cin. Mem. Am. Soc. Internat. Law (mem. panel on state responsibility), Utah Bar Assn., Cin. Bar Assn., Order of Coif, Phi Delta Phi, Kappa Sigma. Clubs: Literary (Cin.); Cosmos (Washington). Home and Office: 3465 Principio Ave Cincinnati OH 45208-4242 E-mail: christga@msn.com.

CHRISTENSON, GREGG ANDREW, bank executive; b. Kalamazoo, June 11, 1958; s. Elmer J. and Marie E. (Durrstein) C.; m. Karen Peterson. BA, Mich. State U., 1980. CPA. Auditor Price Waterhouse, N.Y.C., 1980-82; with Bankers Trust Co., 1982-92, v.p., 1987-92; sr. v.p. Huntington Nat. Bank, Columbus, Ohio, 1992-2000, sr. v.p. retail market Troy, Mich., 2000—. Bd. trustees, v.p. Worthington Pub. Libr.; treas. Far North Columbus Communities Coalition. Mem. Jr. Achievement Alumni Assn. (charter), Mich. State Alumni Assn., Phi Kappa Phi, Beta Gamma Sigma. Republican. Roman Catholic. E-mail: gregg.christenson@huntington.com.

CHRISTENSON, LE ROY HOWARD, insurance consultant; b. Rochester, N.Y., Oct. 28, 1948; s. Howard Le Roy and Sigrid (Anderson) Christenson; m. Pamala Jean Mattson, Jan. 26, 1974; children: Nathan Lee, David Wayne. BS, Valparaiso U., 1970; MS, Purdue U., 1972. CLU. Corp. actuary Western Life Ins. Co., St. Paul, 1972-84; v.p., reins. actuary Am. United Life Ins. Co., Indpls., 1984—99, exec. v.p., 1999—2000; pvt. practice cons. Fishers, 2001—. Fin. cons. Mgmt. Assistance Program, Mpls., 1982. Mission conf. chmn. Faith Missionary Ch., Indpls., 1987—89, elder, 1991—93, 1999—, elder chmn., 1993, 2000—02, mission com. chmn., 1995—2000; bd. dirs. Lake Wapogasset Bible Camp, Mpls., 1982—83, Christian Businessman's Com., Indpls., 1985—88, Interserve, chmn. nominating com., 1999—, mem. exec. com., 1999—2001; age group leader Pioneer Club, Indpls., 1983, 1987. Fellow: Soc. Actuaries (chmn. audit working group reins. sect. 1985—88, vice chmn. reins. sect. 1988—89, 1995—96, chmn. 1989—90, 1996—97, sec.-treas. reins. sect. 1994—95); mem.: Indpls. Actuarial Club (pres. 1987—88), Tri-State Actuarial Club (Indpls. rep. 1984—90, chmn. 1989—90), Am. Acad. Actuaries. Avocation: Avocations: tennis, bible study, biking, motorcycling. Home and Office: 10955 Knightsbridge Lane Fishers IN 46038 E-mail: lhchristenson@iquest.net.

CHRISTENSON, LINDA, state legislator; m. Duane Christenson; 4 children. BA, MS, Minot State U. English tchr.; mem. N.D. Ho. of Reps. from 18th dist., Bismarck, 1994-98; mem. judicary, govt. and vet. affairs coms. N.D. Ho. of Reps.; mem. N.D. Senate from 18th dist., 2000—. Bd. dirs. Firehall Cmty. Theater, United Health Svc. Named Martin Luther King Educator of Yr., N.D., 1991. Mem. Grand Forks Edn. Assn. Address: 812 Belmont Rd Grand Forks ND 58201-4930

CHRISTIAN, EDWARD KIEREN, broadcasting station executive; b. Detroit, June 26, 1944; s. William Edward and Dorothy Miriam (Kieren) C.; m. Judith Dallaire, Nov. 25, 1966; children: Eric, Dana. BA, Wayne State U., 1966, postgrad.; MA, Cen. Mich. U., 1980. Mgr. John C. Butler Co., Detroit, 1968-69; nat. sales mgr. WCAR Radio, WSUN Radio, St. Petersburg, Fla., 1969-70; v.p., gen. mgr., ptnr. WCER Radio, Charlotte, Mich., 1970-74; pres. Josephson Internat. Broadcast, 1975-86; pres., CEO Saga Comm., Inc., Detroit, 1986—. Pres., CEO, bd. dirs. Stas. WSNY-FM, WVKO-FM, Columbus, Ohio, Sta. WNOR-FM, Norfolk, Va., Sta. WAFX, Norfolk, WJOI AM Norfolk, Stas. WKLH-FM, WLZR-FM, WJYI-AM, WFMR-FM, WJMR-FM Milw., Stas. KRNT, KSTZ-FM, KIOA-AM/FM, KAZR FM, KLTI FM, Des Moines, Stas. WLRW-FM and WIXY-FM, WKIO-FM, Champaign, Ill., Stas. WYMG-FM, WQQL-FM, WDBR-FM, WMXH-FM, WTAX-AM, WLLM-Am, Springfield, Ill., Stas. WGAN-AM/WMGX, WZAN-AM/WYNZ-FM, WPOR/FM, WBAE-AM Portland, Maine, Sta. WFEA-AM/WZID-FM, WQLL-FM, Manchester, N.H., Sta. WAQY-FM, WHNP-AM, Springfield, Mass., WHMP-AM, WLZX-FM, Northampton, Mass., WHMQ-AM, WHAI-AM, Greenfield, Mass., KOAM TV, Joplin, Mo., WNAX-AM/FM, Yankton, S.D., KGMI, KISM-FM, Bellingham, Wash., KBAI-AM, KAFE FM, Bellingham, Wash., Victoria Tex., KUNU TV, KXTS TV, KAVU TV, KVCT TV, Victoria, WXVT TV, Greenville, Miss., KICD AM-FM, Spencer, Iowa, KLLT, Spencer, WXDN, WJMR-AM, WZZP-FM, WCVQ-FM, WVVR-FM, Clarkesville, Tenn., Mich. Radio Network, Ill. Radio Network, others; Mich. Farm Radio Network; vice-chmn. Mut. Broadcasting Affiliates Coun., 1977-79; chmn. Arbitron Radio Adv. Coun., 1978-79; bd. dirs. All Industry Music Licensing Com. Pres. United Way, Charlotte, 1973-74; del. Rep. State Conv., 1974; bd. dirs. Am. Auto Immune Related Disease Found., 1995—; consul Republic of Iceland for Mich., Ohio and Ind., 1996—. Mem. Alpha Epsilon Rho (nat. adv. coun. 1980—). Home: 21 Newberry Pl Grosse Pointe Farms MI 48236-3749 also: 3310 Sabal Cove Dr Longboat Key FL 34228-4154 Office: Saga Communications Inc 73 Kercheval Ave Grosse Pointe Farms MI 48236-3603 E-mail: echristian@sagacommunications.com.

CHRISTIAN, JOE CLARK, medical genetics researcher, educator; b. Marshall, Okla., Sept. 12, 1934; s. Roy John and Katherine Elizabeth (Beeby) C.; m. Shirley Ann Yancey, June 5, 1960; children: Roy Clark, Charles David. BS, Okla. State U., 1956; MS, U. Ky., 1959, PhD, 1960, MD, 1964. Cert. clin. geneticist, Am. Bd. Med. Genetics. Resident internal medicine Vanderbilt U., Nashville, 1964-66; asst. prof. med. genetics Ind. U., Indpls., 1966-69, assoc. prof., 1969-74, prof., 1974-99, assoc. dean basic scis. and regional ctrs., 1996-98, prof. emeritus, assoc. dean emeritus, 1999—. Served with USAR, 1953-60. Mem. AMA, Am. Soc. Human Genetics. Democrat. Methodist. Avocations: bicycling, farming. Office: Ind U Dept Med/Molecular Genetics 975 W Walnut St Dept Med Indianapolis IN 46202-5181 E-mail: jcristi@iupui.edu.

CHRISTIAN, JOHN EDWARD, health science educator; b. Indpls., July 12, 1917; s. George Edward and Okel Kandus (Waltz) C.; m. Catherine Ellen Spooner, July 23, 1948; 1 dau., Linda Kay. BS, Purdue U., 1939, PhD, 1944. Control chemist Upjohn Co., 1939-40; faculty Purdue U., Lafayette, Ind., 1940—, prof. pharm. chemistry, 1950-59, head dept. radiol. control, 1956-59, prof. bionucleonics, head dept., 1959-82; chmn. adminstrv. com. Trace Level Research Inst., 1960-88; dir. Inst. for Environmental Health, 1965-88; head Sch. Health Scis., 1979-82, Hovde Disting. prof., 1979-88, Hovde Disting. prof. bionucleonics and health scis. emeritus, 1988—. Vis. prof. radiation therapy Ind. U. Sch. Medicine, 1970-88; Harvey Washington Meml. lectr. Purdue U., 1955; Edward-Kremers Meml. lectr. U. Wis., 1956; vis. lectr. U. Tex., 1959, Taylor U. Ann. Sci. Lecture Series, Upton, Ind., 1960; Julius A. Koch Meml. lectr. U. Pitts., 1961 Assoc. editor Radiochem. Letters. Mem. revision com. U.S. Pharmacopeia, 1950-60, mem. adv. panel on radioactive drugs, 1960-70; adv. com. isotope distbn. AEC, 1952-58, mem. med. adv. com., 1967-75; mem. radiation and chem. def. sect. Ind. Dept. Civil Def., 1954— ; vice chmn. Radiation Control Adv. Commn., Ind., 1958— ; mem. exec. com. Ind. Comprehensive Health Planning Council, 1972-76; mem. adv. com. radiopharms. FDA, 1970-75; mem. Ind. Gov.'s Pesticide Council, 1970-73; Alumni research councilor Purdue Research Found., 1964-88; mem. Ind. Environmental Mgmt. Bd., 1972-87, Nat. Energy Policy Task Force, Dept. Energy, 1981-83; mem. Bd. Grants Am. Found. for Pharm. Edn., 1989—. Recipient award Chilean Iodine Ednl. Bur., 1956, Julius Sturmer award Phila. Coll. Pharmacy and Sci., 1958, Leather medal Purdue U., 1971, Hovde Faculty Purdue U. fellow, 1988. Fellow AAAS (past sec. and chmn. pharm. sci. sect., mem. council), Ind. Acad. Sci.; mem. AMA (spl. affiliate), AAUP, Am. Inst. Architecture (bd. dirs. 1998—, Gibson award 1999), Am. Assn. Colls. Pharmacy (past mem. exec. com., chmn. conf. tchrs., chmn. conf. grad. study and grad. tchrs., chmn. com. study grad. edn. in pharmacy), Am. Chem. Soc. (past chmn. Purdue sect.), Am. Pharm. Assn. (Ebert medal 1957, Justin L. Powers Research Achievement award 1963, past chmn. sci. sect.), Acad. Pharm. Sci. (past v.p.), Ind. Pharm. Assn., Am. Pub. Health Assn., Am. Nuclear Soc., Am. Soc. Bacteriology, Health Phys. Soc., Historic Landmarks Found. of Ind. (bd. dirs., exec. com. 1997—), Frank Lloyd Wright Bldg. Conservancy (Wright Spirit award 1997), Sigma Xi (past pres. Purdue chpt., research award Purdue chpt. 1950), Rho Chi, Phi Lambda Upsilon, Sigma Pi Sigma., Eta Sigma Gamma, Gamma Sigma Delta. Home: 1301 Woodland Ave West Lafayette IN 47906-2371 Office: Purdue U Sch Health Scis Civil Engring Bldg West Lafayette IN 47907

CHRISTIAN, JOHN M. lawyer; b. Wichita, Kans., Sept. 15, 1948; AB with honors, Princeton U., 1970; JD with honors, U. Mich., 1973. Bar: Ill. 1974. Mem. Cahill, Christian & Kunkle, Ltd., Chgo. Adj. prof. law IIT/Chgo.-Kent Coll. Law. Mem. ABA, Chgo. Bar Assn. (mem. spl. task force ins. 1985-86, spl. com. lawyers profl. liability ins. 1987-88, chmn. tort litigation com. 1986-87). Office: Cahill Christian & Kunkle Ltd Santa Fe Bldg 224 S Michigan Ave Ste 1300 Chicago IL 60604-2583

CHRISTIAN, RICHARD CARLTON, university dean, former advertising agency executive; b. Dayton, Ohio, Nov. 29, 1924; s. Raymond A. and Louise (Gamber) C.; m. Audrey Bongartz, Sept. 10, 1949; children: Ann Christian Carra, Richard Carlton Jr. B.S. in Bus. Adminstrn, Miami U., Oxford, Ohio, 1948; MBA, Northwestern U., 1949; LLD (hon.), Nat.-Louis U., 1986; postgrad., Denison U., The Citadel, Biarritz Am. U. Mktg. analyst Rockwell Mfg. Co., Pitts., 1949-50; exec. v.p. Marsteller Inc., Chgo., 1951-60, pres., 1960-75; bd. dirs., exec. com. Young and Rubicam, Inc., 1979-84; chmn. bd. Marsteller Inc., 1975-84, chmn. emeritus, 1984—; assoc. dean Kellogg Grad. Sch. Mgmt. Northwestern U., 1984-91, assoc. dean Medill Sch. Journalism, 1991-99. Dir., chmn. Bus. Publs. Audit Circulation, Inc., 1969-75; Speaker, author marketing, sales mgmt., marketing research and advt. Trustee Northwestern U., 1970-74, Nat.-Louis U., Evanston, Ill., 1970-92, James Webb Young Fund for Edn., U. Ill., 1962-95; pres. Nat. Advt. Rev. Coun., 1976-77; bd. adv. coun. mem. Miami U.; mem. adv. coun. J.L. Kellogg Grad. Sch. Mgmt., Northwestern U.; v.p., dir. Mus. Broadcast Comm.; dir. Can. U.S. Ednl. Exch. (Fulbright Found.), 1988-92. With inf. AUS, 1942-46, ETO. Recipient Ohio Gov.'s award 1977, Alumni medal, Alumni, Merit and Svc. awards Northwestern U.; named to the Advt. Hall of Fame, 1991. Mem. Am. Mktg. assn., Indsl. Mktg. Assn. (founder, chmn. 1951), Bus. Profl. Advt. Assn. (life mem. Chgo., pres. Chgo. 1954-55, nat. v.p. 1955-58, G. D. Crain award 1977), U. Ill. Found., Northwestern U. Bus. Sch. Alumni Assn. (founder, pres.), Am. Assn. Advt. Agys. (dir., chmn. 1976-77), Am. Acad. Advt. (1st disting. svc. award 1978), Northwestern U. Alumni Assn. (nat. pres. 1968-70), Mid-Am. Club, Comml. Club, Econ. Club Chgo., Kenilworth Club, Westmoreland Country Club, Alpha Delta Sigma, Beta Gamma Sigma, Delta Sigma Pi, Phi Gamma Delta. Baptist.

CHRISTIANS, CLIFFORD GLENN, communications educator; b. Hull, Iowa, Dec. 22, 1939; s. Arnold and Verbena Janette (Geerdes) C.; m. Priscilla Jean Kreun, June 13, 1961; children: Glenn Clifford, Ted Arnold, Paul Raymond. AB, Calvin Coll., 1961; ThM, Fuller Theol. Sem., 1965; MA, U. So. Calif., 1966; PhD, U. Ill., 1974. Dir. comms. Christian Ref. Home Ministries, Grand Rapids, Mich., 1966-70; rsch. asst. prof. comms. U. Ill., Urbana, 1974-80, rsch. assoc. prof. comms., 1980-87, rsch. prof. comms., 1987—. Rsch. fellow Calvin Ctr. for Christian Scholarship, Grand Rapids, 1983-84; vis. scholar in ethics Princeton (N.J.) U., spring, 1979; inst. fellow U. Chgo., 1986-87; Pew Evangel. scholar in ethics Oxford U., spring, 1995; dir. Inst. Rsch. Comms., Urbana, 1987—. Co-author: Jacques Ellul: Interpretive Essays, 1981, Good News: Social Ethics and The Press, 1993, Media Ethics: Cases and Moral Reasoning, 1998, Communication Ethics and Universal Values, 1997; editor: Critical Studies in Mass Communication, 1992-95. Bd. dirs. Empty Tomb, Inc., Champaign, Ill., 1986—; elder Christian Ref. Ch., Champaign, 1974-82; bd. dirs. Univ. YMCA, Champaign, 1974-77, Judah Christian Sch., Champaign, 1984-90. Rsch. fellow Program for Cultural Values and Ethics, 1990. Mem. Soc. for Philosophy and Tech., Assn. for Edn. in Journalism and Mass Comm. (chair qualitative studies divsn. 1980-81), Internat. Assn. Mass Comm. Rsch. (program co-chair 1991-94), Ellul Studies Forum, Nat. Comm. Assn. Democrat. Avocations: fishing, travel, reading. Home: U Ill Inst Comm Rsch 1002 W William St Champaign IL 61821 Office: U Ill Comm Dept 810 S Wright St Urbana IL 61801

CHRISTIANSEN, JAY DAVID, lawyer; b. Slayton, Minn., Mar. 22, 1952; s. Holger K. and Dagny (Fjelstad) C.; children: Tyler, Carrie, Jayne. BA, Luther Coll., 1974; JD, Vanderbilt U., 1977. Ptnr. Faegre & Benson, Mpls., 1977—. Mem. ABA (chair 1997-99, health law sect., mem. ho. dels. 1999—), Nat. Health Lawyers Assn., Am. Acad. Hosp. Attys., Order of the Coif. Avocations: golf, canoeing. Office: Faegre & Benson 90 S 7th St Ste 2200 Minneapolis MN 55402-3901 E-mail: jchristi@faegre.com.

CHRISTIANSEN, KEITH ALLAN, lawyer; b. Madison, Wis., Dec. 14, 1943; s. Herman Louis and Faith Louise (Haase) C.; m. Sheila Irene Stangel, Apr. 11, 1966; children: Douglas, Jeffrey. BS, U. Wis., 1965, JD, 1968. Bar: Wis. 1968, Fla. 1973, U.S. Dist. Ct. (ea. dist.) Wis. 1968. Assoc. Foley & Lardner, Milw., 1968-74, ptnr., 1975—. Co-author: Marital Property Law in Wisconsin, 1984, supplements. Active Potawatomi Coun. Boy Scouts Am. (past pres.), 1975—; v.p. Ctrl. Region Boy Scouts. Am., 1992—. Fellow Am. Coll. Trust & Estate Counselors; mem. Mid-winter Estate Planning Clinic, Estate Counselors Forum. Republican. Office: Foley & Lardner 777 E Wisconsin Ave Ste 3800 Milwaukee WI 53202-5367 E-mail: kchristiansen@foleylaw.com.

CHRISTIANSEN, RAYMOND STEPHAN, librarian, educator; b. Oak Park, Ill., Feb. 15, 1950; s. Raymond Julius and Anne Mary (Fusek) C.; m. Phyllis Anne Dombkowski, Nov. 25, 1972; 1 child, Mark David. BA, Elmhurst Coll., 1971; MEd, No. Ill. U., 1974. Dept. dir. Elmhurst Coll., Ill., 1971-73; asst. law librarian media services Lewis U., Glen Ellyn, Ill., 1974-77; asst. prof. edn. Aurora U., Ill., 1977-90, assoc. prof., 1990—, media librarian, 1977-82, instructional developer, 1982-89, dir. univ. media svcs., 1985—; media cons., 1977—. Author video series: Rothblatt on Criminal Advocacy, 1975; book: Index to SCOPE the UN Magazine, 1977. Lic. lay min. Episcopal Ch., 1990—. Mem. Assn. Ednl. Communications and Tech., Assn. Tchr. Educators, Assn. Supervision and Curriculum Devel. Home: 424 S Gladstone Ave Aurora IL 60506-5370 Office: Aurora U Libr 347 S Gladstone Ave Aurora IL 60506-4877

CHRISTIANSEN, RICHARD DEAN, retired newspaper editor; b. Berwyn, Ill., Aug. 1, 1931; s. William Edward and Louise Christine (Dethlefs) C. BA, Carleton Coll., Northfield, Minn., 1953; postgrad., Harvard U., 1954; LHD (hon.), DePaul U., 1988. Reporter, critic, editor Chgo. Daily News, 1957-73, 74-78; editor Chicagoan mag., 1973-74; critic-at-large Chgo. Tribune, 1978-83, entertainment editor, 1983-91, chief critic, sr. writer, 1991—2002; ret., 2002. Served to cpl. U.S. Army, 1954-56. Recipient award Chgo. Newspaper Guild, 1969, 74, Joseph Jefferson award, 1996, Excellence in the Arts award DePaul U., 1998; named to Chgo. Journalism Hall of Fame, 1998. Mem. Am. Theatre Critics Assn., Chgo. Acad. TV Arts and Scis., Soc. Midland Authors, Headline Club Chgo. (Peter Lisayor award for exemplary journalism 2002), Arts Club Chgo. (dir.), Phi Beta Kappa, Sigma Delta Chi. Republican. Lutheran.

CHRISTIANSEN, RICHARD LOUIS, orthodontics educator, research director, former dean; b. Denison, Iowa, Apr. 1, 1935; s. John Cornelius and Rosa Katherine C.; m. Nancy Marie Norman, June 24, 1956; children— Mark Richard, David Norman, Laura Marie DDS, U. Iowa, 1959; MSD, Ind. U., Indpls., 1964; PhD, U. Minn., 1970; hon. doctorate, Nippon Dental U., Tokyo, 2000. Prin. investigator Nat. Inst. Dental Research NIH, Bethesda, Md., 1970-73, chief craniofacial anomalies program br., 1973-81, dir. extramural Nat. Inst. Dental Research, 1981-82; prof. dept. orthodontics U. Mich., Ann Arbor, 1982—, dean, Sch. Dentistry and dir. W.K. Kellogg Found. Inst., 1982—2001, prof., dean emeritus, 2001—. Organizer state-of-the -art workshops in field of craniofacial anomalies and other aspects of oral health; founder Internat. Union Schs. Oral Health, 1985; organizer oral health conf. in Poland, 1989, Jordan, 1995. Contbr. chpts. to books and articles to profl. jours. Chmn. Region III United Way, U. Mich., Ann Arbor, 1984; chmn., v.p. Trinity Luth. Ch., Rockville, Md., 1975; v.p. and chmn. planning task force Trinity Luth. Ch., Ann Arbor, chmn. bd. Sequois Sr. Housing; bd. dirs. Luth. Soc. Svcs. Mich., 1997—. With USPHS, 1959-82. Recipient Commendation medal USPHS, 1980; Cert. of Recognition NIH, 1982, numerous internat. awards. Fellow Internat. Coll. Dentists, Am. Coll. Dentists, Pierre Fauchard Acad.; mem. Am. Assn. Orthodontists, Am. Assn. Dental Sch., ADA (rsch. coun.), Mich. Dental Assn., Am. Assn. Dental Research (dir. craniofacial biology group 1975-79, v.p. 1979-80, pres. 1981-82), Omicron Kappa Upsilon (mem. numerous nat. and internat. coms. and bds.). Avocations: reading, jogging, tennis, sailing, econs. Home: 5612 N Dixboro Rd Ann Arbor MI 48105-9415 E-mail: vista@umich.edu.

CHRISTIANSON, DARCEY K. broadcast engineer; b. Albert Lea, Minn., Sept. 13, 1958; s. Darrell D. and Darla L. (Jensen) C.; m. Renae A. Rue. Student, Austin (Minn.) Vocat. Tech., 1979. Asst. chief engr. Sta. KWOA-AM-FM, Worthington, Minn., 1979-80; chief engr. Stas. KATE/KCPI-FM, Albert Lea, 1980—. Contract engr. Sta. KJLY-FM, Blue Earth, Minn., 1986-88. Mem. Nat. Assn. Radio and Telecommunications Engrs. Republican. Avocations: softball, fishing. Office: Stas KATE/KCPI-FM 305 S 1st Ave Albert Lea MN 56007-1777

CHRISTIANSON, JAMES D. real estate developer; b. Bismarck, N.D., Aug. 18, 1952; s. Adolph M. and Elizabeth M. (Barnes) C.; m. Deborah Jaeger, Oct. 10, 1987. Student, Bismarck Jr. Coll., 1970, 1971-72, U. N.D., 1971. Lic. pvt. pilot; lic. realtor. Gen. mgr. and supr. Nutrition Search, Bismarck, 1974-76; gen. mgr. Home Still, Inc., 1976-78; v.p. Good Heart Assocs., 1978-82; pres. N. W. Devel. Group, 1982—, First Realty Bismark Inc., 1990-93, N.W. Realty Group, Bismarck, 1994—. Chmn. bd. Basin State Bank, Stanford, Mont., 1986-94; mem., vice chair Ctr. City Partnership, 1994—; mng. prin. N.W. Lodging Group, LLC. Supr. editor: Nutrition Almanac, 1975. Mem. Bismarck Centennial Com., 1986-89, Bismarck Parking Authority, 1996—; bd. trustees Bismarck State Coll., 1999—. Recipient Outstanding Citizen award Mayor and City Commn., Bismarck, 1982. Mem. Downtown Bus. and Profl. Assn. (bd. dirs. 1989—, pres. 1991). Avocations: traveling, reading, computers, golf. Office: N W Devel Group Inc PO Box 1097 Bismarck ND 58502-1097

CHRISTIANSON, STANLEY DAVID, corporate executive; b. Chgo., Dec. 8, 1931; s. Stanley Olai and Emma Josephine (Johnson) D.; m. Elin J. Ballantyne, July 25, 1959; children: Erica Joanna, David Ballantyne. BS, U. Ill., 1954; MBA, U. Chgo., 1960. Auditor Price Waterhouse & Co., Chgo., 1956-58; asst. to controller Miehle-Goss-Dexter, Inc., 1960-67, v.p. adminstrn. Goss Div., 1967-69; dir. mgmt. systems MGD Graphics Systems-N.Am. Rockwell (formerly Miehle-Goss-Dexter), 1969-70; v.p. fin. Duchossois/Thrall Group (formerly Thrall Car Mfg. Co.), Chicago Heights, Elmhurst, Ill., 1970-83; vice chmn., bd. dirs. Thrall Enterprises, Inc., Chgo., 1983—. Bd. dirs. Midwestern Univ., chmn., 1997-98, mem., 1992—. Bd. govs. Internat. House, U. Chgo., 1988-2000, chmn. 1997-2000; bd. trustees Cmty. Theatre Guild, Nalparaiso, Ind., 2001-; mem. Hobart (Ind.) Plan Commn., 1986-92, pres., 1988-92. Capt. U.S. Army, 1954-56. Home: 141 Beverly Blvd Hobart IN 46342-4346 Office: Thrall Enterprises Inc 180 N Stetson Ste 3020 Chicago IL 60601-6223

CHRISTIE, JAMES R. technology company executive; BS in Applied Chemistry, Heriot-Watt U., Edinburgh, Scotland; diploma in bus. adminstrn., PhD in Chem. Engring., U. Edinburgh. With Atlantic Richfield Co., Occidental Petroleum Corp.; chmn., CEO applied chems. divsn. Hickson Internat., 1987-93; pres. Valenite Milacron Inc., Cin., 1993-97, corp. officer, v.p. Valenite and Widia, 1997-2000, group v.p. metalworking techs., 2000—. Office: Milacron Inc 2090 Florence Ave PO Box 63716 Cincinnati OH 45206-3716

CHRISTMAN, RICHARD M. manufacturing executive; BS in Mech. Engring., Rose Hulman Inst. Tech.; MBA in Mktg. and Fin., U. Mich. Various sales and mktg. positions Case Corp., Racine, Wis., 1975, sr. v.p. European sales and mktg., sr. v.p. N.Am. sales and mktg., v.p. product mgmt., strategic planning, 1995—. Office: Case Corp 700 State St Racine WI 53404-3392

CHRISTMANN, RANDEL DARVIN, state legislator; b. Hazen, N.D., June 16, 1960; B in Bus. Adminstrn., N.D. State U., 1982. Truck driver, rancher, Hazen, N.D.; mem. N.D. Senate from 33rd dist., Bismark, 2000—. Mem. fin. and taxation com. N.D. State Senate, vice-chmn. natural resources com., vice chmn. interim N.D./S.D. Commn. Mem. NRA, Farm Bur. N.D., Stockmen's Assn. Office: Rte 1 Box 120A Hazen ND 58545-9726

CHRISTNER, THEODORE CARROLL, architect; b. Quincy, Ill., Oct. 3, 1932; s. Thornton Carroll and Mable Irene (Trogdon) C.; m. Jo Hartmann, 1957 (div. 1980); children: Eric, Kitsy, Caellen, Erin; m. Claudia Trautman, Oct. 4, 1986; 1 child: Adrienne. BArch, Culver-Stockton Coll., 1952, Washington U., St. Louis, 1957. Registered architect, Mo. Staff architect Fischer, Frichtel Design and Constrn., St. Louis, 1961-62; assoc. Gale and Cannon, 1962-63; pres. The Christner Partnership, Inc., 1963-95; chmn. bd. dirs. Christner, Inc., 1995—. Bd. dirs. Ecumencial Housing Prodn. Corp., mem exec. com. Bd. dirs., v.p. Ecumenical Housing Corp., St. Louis, 1988—; bd. dirs. Mt. St. Rose Hosp., 1967-75; chmn. bd. St. Joseph's Hosp. Hospice, 1988—; mem. Commn. for Future Washington U., 1988; mem. nat. coun. Wash. U. Sch. Architecture, 1988—. Mem. AIA (dir. 1986), Am. Arbitration Assn. Avocations: golf, tennis, skiing, flying. Home: 6319 San Bonita Ave Saint Louis MO 63105-3115 Office: Christner Inc 7711 Bonhomme Ave Clayton MO 63105-1908

CHRISTOFFEL, KATHERINE KAUFER, pediatrician, epidemiologist, educator; b. N.Y.C., June 28, 1948; d. George and Sonya (Firstenberg) Kaufer; m. Tom Christoffel, 1970 (div. 1992); children: Kevin, Kimberly. BA, Radcliffe Coll., 1969; MD, Tufts U., 1973; MPH, Northwestern U., 1981. Diplomate Am. Bd. Pediat., Nat. Bd. Med. Examiners. Intern Columbus (Ohio) Children' Hosp., 1972-73; resident then fellow Children's Meml. Hosp., Chgo., 1973-76; asst. prof. Sch. Medicine U. Chgo., 1976-79; asst. prof., then assoc. prof. Northwestern U. Med. Sch., Chgo., 1979-91, prof., 1991—; dir. Nutrition Evaluation Clinic Children's Meml. Hosp., 1982-2000; med. dir. violent injury prevention ctr. Children's Meml. Med. Ctr., 1993—. Chmn. steering com. Handgun Epidemic Lowering Plan, Chgo., 1993—; dir. then assoc. dir. Pediatric Practice Rsch. Group, Chgo., 1984-97; dir. statis. scis. and epidemiology program Children's Meml. Inst. for Edn. and Rsch., 1994—. Contbr. numerous articles to med. jours. Recipient M. Fay Spencer Disting. Woman Physician Scientist award Nat. Bd. Hahnemann Med. Sch., 1997. Fellow Am. Acad. Pediatrics (spokesperson on firearms 1985—, injury com. 1985-93, coun. on pediatric rsch. 1996-2000, chair adolescent violence task force 1994, 1st Injury Control award 1992); mem. APHA (Disting. Career award 1991), Am. Coll. Epidemiology, Soc. for Pediatric Rsch., Ambulatory Pediatric Assn. (bd. mem. 2000—, Rsch. award 2000). Avocations: hiking, creative writing, photography. Office: Childrens Meml Hosp 2300 N Childrens Plz # 208 Chicago IL 60614-3394

CHRISTOFORIDIS, A. JOHN, radiologist, educator; b. Greece, Dec. 24, 1924; s. John P. and Ada A. C.; m. Ann Dimitriadis, Nov. 11, 1961; children: John, Gregory, Alex, Jimmy. M.D. summa cum laude, Nat. U. Athens, Greece, 1949; M.M.Sc., Ohio State U., 1957; Ph.D., Aristotelian U., Greece, 1969. Instr. to prof. Ohio State U., Columbus, 1956-74, clin. prof., 1974—; chmn. dept. radiology Aristotelian U., Salonika, Greece, 1971; prof., chmn. dept. radiology Med. Coll. Ohio, Toledo, until 1982; prof., chmn. dept. Ohio State U., Columbus, 1982—. Researcher in chest and gastrointestinal radiology; cons. Greek Ministry Health, Batelle Meml. Inst., Columbus. Contbr. to textbook Atlas of Axial Sagittal and Coronal Anatomy with Computed Tomography and Magnetic Resonance; author: Radiology for Medical Students, 4th edit., 1988, Diagnostic Radiology-Thorax, 1989; contbr. several chpts. to books, over 100 articles to med. jours. Served to lt. M.C. Greek Army, 1950-52. Recipient Silver award Ohio Med. Assn., 1969, awards Heart Assn., 1960, awards Batelle Meml. Inst., 1965, awards Astra Co., 1967, awards Lung Assn., 1970-71; named Hon. Citizen City of Thessalonike, 1973; Ohio Geriatrics Med. grantee, 1980; NSF grantee, 1980 Fellow Am. Coll. Chest Physicians, Am. Coll. Radiology; mem. AAA, AMA, AAUP, Ohio Radiol. Soc., Assn. Univ. Radiologists, Radiol. Soc. N. Am., Soc. Chmn. Acad. Radiology Depts., Fleishner Soc. (charter), Am. Hellenic Ednl. Progressive Assn., Greek-Am. Progressive Assn., Acad. of Athens (corr. mem.). Greek Orthodox. Office: Ohio State U 410 W 10th Ave Columbus OH 43210-1240

CHRISTOPHER, DAVID L. bank executive; Chmn., CEO Wayne Bancorp, Inc., 1989—. Office: 112 W Liberty St Wooster OH 44691-4802

CHRISTOPHER, DORIS, kitchen tools sales and demonstration company executive; m. Jay Christopher, 1967; children: Julie, Kelley. BS in Home Econs., U. Ill., 1967. Cert. in family and consumer svcs. H.S. home econs. tchr.; with U. Ill. Coop. Extension Svc.; founder, chmn. The Pampered Chef Ltd., Addison, Ill., 1980—. Appeared on various TV programs, including Oprah Winfrey Show, NBC Weekend Today. Author: Come to the Table: A Celebration of Family Life, 1999. Company named one of country's Top Women-Owned Businesses, Working Woman. Mem. Am. Assn. Family and Consumer Scis., Com. of 200. Office: The Pampered Chef 350 S Rohlwing Rd Addison IL 60101-3079

CHRISTOPHER, SHARON A. BROWN, bishop; b. Corpus Christi, Tex., July 24, 1944; d. Fred L. and Mavis Lorraine (Krueger) Brown; m. Charles Edmond Logsdon Christopher, June 17, 1973. BA, Southwestern U., Georgetown, Tex., 1966; MDiv, Perkins Sch. Theology, 1969; DD, Southwestern U., 1990; DST, McMurray Coll., 1996. Ordained to ministry United Meth. Ch., 1970; elected bishop 1988. Dir. Christian Edn. First United Meth. Ch., Appleton, Wis., 1969-70, assoc. pastor, 1970-72; pastor Butler United Meth. Ch., Butler, 1972-76, Calvary United Meth. Ch., Germantown, 1972-76, Aldersgate United Meth. Ch., Milw., 1976-80; dist. supt. Ea. Dist. Wis. Conf. United Meth. Ch., 1980-85; asst. to bishop Wis. Conf. Wis. Conf. United Meth. Ch., Sun Prairie, Wis., 1986-88; bishop North Cen. jurisdiction United Meth. Ch., Minn., 1988-96, bishop Ill. area, 1996—, resident bishop Ill. area Springfield, 1996—. Contbr. articles and papers to religious publs. Bd. dirs. Nat. Coun. Chs. of Christ, 1988—, United Meth. Ch. Bd. of Ch. & Soc., 1988-92, bd. discipleship, 1992—; trustee Hamline U., St. Paul, 1988-96; gen. and jurisdictional conf. del., 1976, 80, 84, 88; mem. N. Cen. Jurisdiction Com. on Episcopacy, 1984-88, Com. on Investigation, 1980-88, Gen. Bd. Global Ministries, 1980-88, chmn. Mission Pers. Resources Program Dept., 1984-88. Named one of Eighty for the Eighties, Milw. Jour., 1980.

CHRISTOPHERSON, AL, farm association executive; m. Diane Christopherson; children: Todd, Scott. BS in Agrl. Econs., U. Minn. Owner, operator diversidifed crop and livestock farm, Pennock, Minn.; v.p. Minn. Farm Bur. Fedn., 1978—88, pres., 1988—. Bd. dirs. Midwestern Farm Bur. Mem. agrl. bd. Agrl. Utilization and Rsch. INst.; chmn. River Resource Alliance; bd. advisors and govs. Ctr. for Internat. Food and Agrl. Policy, U. Minn., Minn. Office: PO Box 64370 Saint Paul MN 55164

CHROMIZKY, WILLIAM RUDOLPH, accountant; b. Chgo., Jan. 21, 1955; s. Rudolph Joseph and Helen M. (Gniewek) C.; m. Laura Lee Lamoureux, Oct. 24, 1992. BS, No. Ill. U., 1977; M of Mgmt., Northwestern U., 1987. CPA, Ill. Sr. auditor Arthur Andersen & Co., Chgo., 1977-83; supr. internal audit AM Internat., 1983-84, mgr. fin. reporting, 1984-85, dir. acctg., 1985; mgr. bus. analysis Premark Internat., Inc., Deerfield, Ill., 1985-87, dir. fin. reporting, 1987-2000; v.p., sec. and external reporting Aon Corp., Chgo., 2001—. Vol. CPAs for the Pub Interest, Chgo., 1990-92; mem. fin. com. Brother Rice H.S., 1995—, bd. dirs., 1999—. Mem. AICPA, Fin. Execs. Inst., Ill. CPA Soc. Avocations: skiing, tennis, bowling, competitive running. Office: Aon Corp 200 E Randolph St Chicago IL 60601 E-mail: william_chromizky@asc.aon.com.

CHRONISTER, ROCHELLE BEACH, former state legislator; b. Neodesha, Kans., Aug. 27, 1939; m. Bert Chronister, 1961; children: Pam, Phillip. AB, U. Kans. State rep. dist. 13 Kans. Ho. of Reps., until 1999; former asst. majority leader; sec. for social and rehab. svcs. Kans. Cabinet, 1995-99. Chmn. Kans. Rep. Party, 1989—. Named Woman of Yr., Neodesha C. of C. Mem. AMA (aux.), Bus. and Profl. Women. Methodist. Home: RR 2 Box 321 A Neodesha KS 66757-9562

CHRYSLER, RICHARD R. former congressman; b. St. Paul, Apr. 29, 1942; m. Katie; children: Richard R., Phil, Christie Ann. With Chevrolet divsn. Gen. Motors Corp., 1960-64, Hurst Performance, Inc., Brighton, Mich., 1966-76; founder, chmn. Cars & Concepts, Inc., 1976-86, RCI; U.S. congressman Mich. 8th Dist., 1995-96; pres. JPE, Inc., 1998-99; vice chmn. ASCET, Inc., 1999; pres. Ideal Steel, Hamburg, Mich., 1999—. Bd. dirs. Mich. Nat. Bank. Patentee skylite T-roof.

CHU, JOHNSON CHIN SHENG, retired physician; b. Peiping, China, Sept. 25, 1918; came to U.S., 1948, naturalized, 1957; s. Harry S.P. and Florence (Young) C.; m. Sylvia Cheng, June 11, 1949; children: Stephen, Timothy M.D., St. John's U., 1945. Intern Univ. Hosp., Shanghai, 1944-45; resident, research fellow NYU Hosp., 1948-50; resident physician in charge State Hosp. and Med. Ctr., Weston, W.Va., 1951-56; chief services, clin. dir. State Hosp., Logansport, Ind., 1957-84, ret., 1998. Active mem. Meml. Hosp., Logansport, Ind., 1968—. Research in cardiology and pharmacology; contbr. articles to profl. jours. Fellow Am. Psychiat. Assn., Am. Coll. Chest Physicians; mem. AMA, Ind. Med. Assn., Cass County Med. Soc., AAAS Home: 36 E Lake Shafer Monticello IN 47960 Office: Southeastern Med Ctr Walton IN 46994

CHUGH, YOGINDER PAUL, mining engineering educator; came to U.S., 1965, naturalized, 1975; s. Atma Ram and Dharam (Devi) C.; m. Evangeline Negron, July 18, 1970; children: Anjeli K., Shirmilee M., Pauline E. BS, Banaras Hindu U., 1961; MS, Pa. State U., 1968, PhD, 1970. Cert. 1st class mine mgr., India. Instr. Banaras Hindu U., India, 1961-64; asst. mgr. Andrew Yule Coal Co., India, 1961-64; research asst. Pa. State U., University Park, 1965-70; rsch. assoc. Henry Krumb Sch. Mines Columbia U., N.Y.C., 1971, research assoc., 1971; research engr. Ill. Inst. Tech. Research Inst., Chgo., 1971-74; planning engr. Amax Coal Co., Indpsl., 1974-76; assoc. prof. Dept. Mining Engrng. So. Ill. U., Carbondale, 1977-81, prof. Dept. Mining Engring., 1981—. Acting chmn., Dept. Mining Engring., So. Ill. U., 1981-82, chmn., 1984—; dir. Coal Combustion Residues Mgmt. Program; chmn. PhD. com., 1983-86, active numerous other univ. coms; cons. to nat. and internat. coal cos., state and fed. mining and mineral agys.; dir. Coal Combustion Residues Mgmt. Program, 1990—; bd. dirs. Accreditation Bd. for Engring. and Tech., 1989-92. Author: (with K.V.K. Prasad) Workshop on Design of Coal Pillars in Room-and-Pillar Mining, Workshop on Design of Mine Openings in Room-and-Pillar Mining, 1984; editor (with others) Proceedings of the First Conference on Ground Control Problems in the Illinois Coal Basin, 1980, Proceedings First International Conference on Ground Control in Longwall Mining and Mining Subsidence, 1982, Proceedings of the Polish-American Conference on Ground Control in Room-and-Pillar Mining, 1983; editor Ground Control Room and Pillar Mining, 1983 (Soc. Mining Engrs. award 1983), Longwall Mining Subsidence, 1983 (Soc. Mining Engrs. award 1984), Proceedings of the Second Conference on Ground Control Problems in the Illinois Coal Basin, 1985, Proceedings of the Third and Fourth Conference on Ground Control Problems in the Midwestern U.S., 1990, 92; contbr. over 50 articles to profl. jours., also many research reports; inventor roof truss, 1990. V.p. India Assn., Indpls., 1975. Recipient numerous research grants state and fed. agys., pvt. coal cos.; named Disting. Alumnus Banaras Hindu U., 1985, Outstanding Alumnus Achievement award Pa. State U., 1996. Mem. AIME (active rock mechanics unit com. 1978-82, various pubs. coms.1979-85, geomechanics com. 1984-85), ASTM, ASCE, Internat. Soc. Rock Mechanics (coordinator 1986—), Internat. Bur. Strata Mechanics, Ill. Mining Inst. (bd. dirs.), Ind. Mining Inst., Soc. Geologists and Mining Engrs. (faculty advisor 1977-78, 80-84), Soc. Exptl. Stress Analysis, Am. Soc. Higher Edn., Sigma Xi. Lodge: Rotary. Avocations: tennis, boating, badminton, computers. Office: So Ill U-Carbondale Mining & Mineral Resources Rsch Inst Coal Extraction Rsch Ctr Carbondale IL 62901

CHUNG, DO SUP, agricultural engineering educator; b. Inchon, Korea, Mar. 20, 1935; married, 1961; 2 children. BS, Purdue U., 1958; MS, Kans. State U., 1960, PhD in Chem. Engring., Food Sci., 1966. From instr. to assoc. prof. agrl. engring. Kans. State U., Manhattan, 1965-80, prof. agrl. engring., 1980—. Mem. agrl. rsch. svc. divsn. USDA, 1967-70. Fellow Am. Soc. Agrl. Engrs.; mem. AICE, Am. Assn. Cereal Chemists, Inst. Food Tech. Achievements include research in adsorption, desorption and absorption of water by cereal products, heat transfer in grain investigations, physical properties of grains and handling of grain for minimizing damage investigations. Office: Kansas State Univ Agricultural Engineering Dept Seaton Hall Rm 148 Manhattan KS 66506

CHUNG, PAUL MYUNGHA, mechanical engineer, educator; b. Seoul, Dec. 1, 1929; came to U.S., 1947, naturalized, 1956; s. Robert N. and Kyungsook (Kim) C.; m. E. Jean Judy, Mar. 8, 1952; children: Maurice W., Tamara P. BSME, U. Ky., 1952, MS, 1954; Ph.D., U. Minn., 1957. Asst. prof. mech. engring. U. Minn., 1957-58; aero. research scientist Ames Research Center, NASA, Calif., 1958-61; head fluid physics dept. Aerospace Corp., San Bernardino, 1961-66; prof. mech. engring. U. Ill., Chgo., 1966-95, head dept. energy engring., 1974-79, dean engring., 1979-94, prof., dean emeritus, 1995—. Mem. tech. adv. com. Ill. Inst. Environ. Quality, 1975-77; corp. mem. Underwriters Lab., 1983-95; cons. to industry, 1966—. Author numerous papers in field; author: Electric Probes in Stationary and Flowing Plasmas, 1975, Russian edit., 1978; contbr. chpt. to Advances in Heat Transfer, 1965, to Dynamics of Ionized Gases, 1973. Bd. govs. Redlands (Calif.) YMCA, 1965-67. Fellow AIAA (nat. tech. com. on plasmadynamics 1972-74, com. on propellants and combustion 1976-80); mem. AIChE (nat. com. on internat. activities 1992-94), Am. Soc. Engring. Edn. (exec. bd. engring. dean's coun. 1983-84), Sigma Xi, Tau Beta Pi, Pi Tau Sigma, Phi Kappa Phi. Home: 2003 E Lillian Ln Arlington Heights IL 60004-4215 Office: Univ Ill Off of Dean Chicago IL 60680

CHUPP, TIMOTHY EDWARD, physicist, educator, academic administrator; b. Berkeley, Calif., Nov. 30, 1954; AB, Princeton U., 1977; PhD in Physics, U. Wash., 1983. Instr., asst. prof. physics Princeton U., 1983-85; from asst. prof. to assoc. prof. physics Harvard U., 1985-91; assoc. prof U. Mich., Ann Arbor, 1991-94, prof. physics, 1994—. Fellow Alfred P. Sloan Found., 1987. Recipient Presdl. Young Investor award NSF, 1987. Fellow Am. Phys. Soc. (I.I. Rabi prize 1993). Achievements include research in low energy particle physics particularly by study of symmetries accessible with polarization; weak interactions: CP violation and time reversal violation; fundamentals of quantum mechanics; structure of nucleons; biomedical and technological applications of lasers and optical pumping. Office: U Mich Dept Physics Ann Arbor MI 48109

CHURCHILL, JAMES PAUL, federal judge; b. Imlay City, Mich., Apr. 10, 1924; s. Howard and Faye (Shurte) C.; m. Ann Muir, Aug. 30, 1950; children: Nancy Ann Churchill Nyquist, David James, Sally Jo. BA, U. Mich., 1947, JD, 1950. Bar: Mich. Pvt. practice law, Vassar, Mich., 1950-65; judge 40th Jud. Cir. Mich., 1965-74, U.S. Dist. Ct. (ea. dist.) Mich., Detroit, 1974—; now sr. judge. Ct. commr. Tuscola County Cir., 1963-65; adj. prof. Detroit Coll. Law, 1980-81. Served with U.S. Army, 1943-46. Mem. Fed. Judges Assn., Fed. Bar Assn., 40th Jud. Cir. Bar Assn. Office: PO Box 913 Bay City MI 48707-0913

CHURCHILL, ROBERT WILSON, state legislator, lawyer; b. Waukegan, Ill., Apr. 10, 1947; s. George Oliver and Helga C. (Carlson) Churchill; children: Abigail Lee, Lulia Aubrey, Christine Lizbeth. BA, Northwestern U., Evanston, Ill., 1969; JD, U. Iowa, 1972. Elected del. Rep. Nat. Conv., 1980, 92, 96, alt. del., 1984; trustee Lake Villa (Ill.) Township, 1981-83; rep. Ill. Ho. Reps., 1983-99; minority whip Ill. Gen. Assembly, 1987-89, asst. minority leader, 1989-91, dep. minority leader, 1991-94, 97-99; majority leader, 1995-97; chmn. Rep. Ctrl. Com. for Lake County, Ill., 1990-94. Co-chmn. Ill. Econ. and Fiscal Commn., Springfield, 1991-95, Space Needs Commn., 1997-99; mem. Ill. Prisoner Review Bd., 1999-2001; chief counsel, dir. legis. Ill. Ho. Reps., 2001-02. Mem. ABA, Lake County, Ill. Bar Assn., Ducks Unlimited, Lake Villa Lions, Exchange Club, Moose. Republican.

CHURCHILL, STEVEN WAYNE, former state legislator, marketing professional; b. Akron, Ohio, May 8, 1963; s. Wayne Stevenson and Carol Sue (Gurney) C. BA, Iowa State U., 1985. Fin. asst. The Governor Branstad Com., Des Moines, 1986, fin. dir., 1988-90; mktg. mgr. Iowa Dept. Econ. Devel., 1987; devel. officer Simpson Coll., Indianola, Iowa, 1990-93; fundraising cons. The Churchill Group, Johnston, 1993-97; v.p. mktg. Mid-Am. Group, West Des Moines, 1997—. State Rep., Johnston, Iowa, 1993-99; commr. Iowa Civil Rights Commn., Des Moines, 1991-92; deacon Plymouth Congl. Ch., 1988-91, 96-99; admissions amb. Iowa State U., 1990-92; mem. Greater Des Moines Leadership Inst., 1998-99; chmn. Chef's Auction Dinner, March of Dimes, 1999. Recipient Comdr.'s Award for Pub. Svc., Dept. of the Army, 1991; named one of 10 Outstanding Young Iowans, Iowa Jaycees, 1995, one of Forty under 40 Ctrl. Iowans for Profl. Accomplishments and Cmty. Involvement Des Moines Bus. Record, 2000. Mem. Bull Moose Club (pres. 1990-91), Rotary of Des Moines (pres. 1991-92, team leader group study exch. to The Netherlands 2000), Sigma Alpha Epsilon (pres. 1989-90, Order of the Lion 1990, 96, 99, Merit Key award 2000, chmn. Robert D. Ray scholarship golf benefit 2002). Avocations: history, travel, stand-up comedy. Home: 6140 Nottingham Johnston IA 50131-8713 Office: Mid-Am Group 4700 Westown Pkwy Ste 303 West Des Moines IA 50266-6718 E-mail: swc@midamericagroup.com.

CHURCHWELL, EDWARD BRUCE, astronomer, educator; b. Sylva, N.C., July 9, 1940; s. Doris L. Churchwell; m. Dorothy S. Churchwell, June 24, 1964; children: Steven T., Beth M. BS, Earlham Coll., 1963; PhD, Ind. U., 1970. NASA fellow Ind. U., Bloomington, 1963; postdoctoral fellow Nat. Radio Astronomy Obs., Charlottesville, Va., 1970; Heinrich Hertz postdoctoral fellow Max Planck Inst. Radioastronomie, Bonn, Germany, 1970-72, staff scientist Germany, 1972-77; asst. prof. U. Wis., Madison, 1977-79, assoc. prof., 1979-83, prof., 1983—. Fellow NASA, 1985, Fulbright Rsch., 1988—89. Mem.: Union Concerned Scientists, Internat. Astron. Union, Am. Astron. Soc. Office: U Wis Washburn Observatory 475 N Charter St Madison WI 53706-1507

CHVALA, CHARLES JOSEPH, state legislator; b. Merrill, Wis., Dec. 5, 1954; s. John Patrick and Mary Ann (Severt) C.; children: Ted, Jessica. BA, JD, U. Wis., 1978. Bar: Wis. Atty. DeWitt, Sundby, Huggett & Schumacher, 1979-81, Smith, Chvala & Merg, 1981-83, Boushea, Newton & Seagall, 1983-92; lobbyist Citizen's Utility Bd., 1981-82; mem. Wis. State Assembly, 1983-85, Wis. Senate from 16th dist., Madison, 1985—; majority leader Wis. Senate, 1995—; pvt. practice Madison, Wis., 1996—. Mem. Citizens Utility Bd., Wis. Environ. Decade, Wis. Farmers Union; bd. dirs. World Dairy Ctr. Authority Nat. Merit scholar. Mem. State Bar Wis., Dane County Bar Assn. Democrat. Office: State Senate State Capitol Rm 211 S PO Box 7882 Madison WI 53707-7882

CIANI, ALFRED JOSEPH, language professional, associate dean; b. N.Y.C., June 29, 1946; s. Joseph Alfred and Aurora Smiles (VanOver) C.; m. Sharon Skolkey, Aug. 16, 1968 (div. 1979); children: Mieke Jo, Gabriel Wolf; m. Lesley Lockwood, Aug. 9, 1980; children: Joseph Alfred, Clinton Lockwood. BA, U. Albany, 1969; MA, Coll. of St. Rose, 1972; EdD, Ind. U., 1974. Tchr. Greater Amsterdam (N.Y.) Schs., 1969-72; rsch. asst. Ind. U., Bloomington, 1972-73, assoc. instr., 1973-74; asst. prof. U. Cin., 1974-79, assoc. prof., 1979—; vis. prof. U. Wis., Milw., 1980; assoc. dean, info. officer U. Cin., 1988-92. Pres. Ohio Internat. Reading Assn., Columbus, 1981-82; outside cons. State of Miss., Jackson, 1982-84, State of Ky., 1996-99, State of W.Va., 1972-74, 97-98, City of N.Y. Pub. Schs.; cons., U. Oreg. Profl. Devel., Eugene, 1979-80, Nashville Schs., 1982-83, State of W.Va., N.Y.C. Pub. Schs.; mem. Dean's Cabinet; mem. Urban Schs. Task Force. Author: Motivating Reluctant Readers, 1981; editor: (book series) Reading in Content Areas, 1979-81; rev. editor: Rsch. in Mid. Level Edn., 1995—. Grantee Ford Found., 1990, IBM, 1990. Mem. AAUP, Internat. Reading Assn., Am. Ednl. Rsch. Assn. (nat. coms.), Assn. Tchr. Educators (nat. coms.), Nat. Coun. Tchrs. English (nat. coms.), , Nat. Mid. Sch. Assn. (nat. coms.), Nat. Reading Coun., Phi Delta Kappa, Kappa Delta Pi (counselor). Democrat. Roman Catholic. Avocations: reading, walking, family oriented activities. Office: U Cin Mail Location 02 Cincinnati OH 45221-0001 E-mail: alfred.ciani@uc.edu.

CIARAMITARO, NICK, prosecutor; b. Detroit, Dec. 17, 1951; s. Sam and Catherine (Sorentino) C.; m. Peggy Houlihan. BA cum laude, U. Detroit, 1974; JD, Wayne State U., 1979. City clk. City of Roseville (Mich.), 1977-78; law clk. Mich. Atty. Gen. Frank Kelley & Atty. Michael P. Long, 1977; state rep. Mich. Ho. Reps., Dist. 27, 1979-98; asst. prosecutor Macomb County, Mt. Clemens, Mich., 1991—. Mem. appropriations com., Mich. Ho. Reps., 1991-98. Chmn. Macomb County Young Dem., Mich., 1972, vice chmn., 1972-73, officer-at-large, 1972-74; dir. registration Macomb Voters Registrar Com., 1972; alt. del. Dem. State Ctrl. Com., 1971-72; vice chmn. Mich. Young Dem., 1973-75; exec. bd. 12th Congl. Dist. Dem. Com., 1972; assoc. field staff reporter Mich. State Dem. Party, 1973-76; staff mem. U.S. Rep. James O'Hara, 1973-77; del. Dem. Nat. Mid-Term Conf., 1974; mem. exec. bd. Macomb County Dem. Conm., 1974—; mem. Friends Roseville Libr., Roseville Bicentennial Com., treas., 1976—; officer-at-large Mich. Dem. Party, 1997—. Mem. Lions, Jaycees, Alpha Sigma Nu. Office: Prosecutors Office Macomb County Bt Bldg 40 N Main St Fl 6 Mount Clemens MI 48043-5658

CICCARELLI, JOHN A. manufacturing executive; b. Boston, 1939; Grad., Northeastern U., 1963. Pres., CEO, bd. dirs. Dayton (Ohio) Superior Corp. Office: Dayton Superior Corp Ste 130 7777 Washington Village Dr Dayton OH 45459

CICCHINO, SAMUEL, deputy marshal; b. Newark, June 15, 1944; m. Zabel Kazanjian, Sept. 6, 1965; 3 children. AS in Police Sci., Brookdale C.C., Lynchcross, N.J., 1981. Enlisted USMC, 1961, advanced through ranks to sgt., 1971; dep. U.S. Marshal, Trenton, N.J., 1971-81, supervisory dept. Cin., 1981-83, Miami, Fla., 1983-84, chief dep. L.A., 1984-88, marshal Cen. Dist. Calif., 1988-90, chief dep., 1990-92, chief dep. So. Dist. Ohio Columbus, 1992—, acting marshal Western Dist. Louisville, 1997-98. Master sgt. USMCR, 1971—. Decorated Purple Heart, Vietnamese Cross of Gallantry; recipient Disting. Svc. Plaque, Nat. Mgmt. Negotiating Team, 1985, Letter of Appreciation, Pres. Ronald Reagan, 1990, award Atty. Gen.'s Commn. on Pornography, 1986, Calif. Atty. Gen. Van De Camp, 1990, Gov. Dukmajian of Calif., 1990, Disting. Achievement award Fed. Bar Assn., 1992. Mem. NRA, Fraternal Order Police. Mil. Order Purple Heart, Spl. Agts. Assn., Rep. Presdl. Trust. Baptist. Avocations: collecting coins, pistol and rifle shooting, archery. Office: Office of US Marshal So Dist Ohio 85 Marconi Blvd Rm 460 Columbus OH 43215-2835

CICCONE, F. RICHARD, retired newspaper editor; b. Sewickley, Pa., Feb. 23, 1940; s. Samuel C. and Mary (Thomas) C.; m. Joan M. Garrity, Nov. 18, 1967; children: Cristin, Richard. Reporter Chgo. Bur. AP, 1962-63, 66-74, news editor, 1974-76; reporter Chgo. Tribune, 1976-77, polit. editor, from 1976, mng. editor, assoc. editor, 1995-98; ret., 1998. Co-author: Who's Running Chicago, 1979. With USMC, 1963-66, Vietnam. Decorated Bronze star.

CICERO, FRANK, JR. lawyer; b. Nov. 30, 1935; s. Frnk and Mary (Balma) Cicero; m. Janice Pickett, July 11, 1959; children: Erica, Caroline. AB with hons., Wheaton Coll., 1957; M in Pub. Affairs, Woodrow Wilson Sch. of Pub. & Internat. Affairs, 1962; JD, U. Chgo., 1965. Bar: Ill., U.S. Supreme Ct. 1965, various U.S. Ct. of Appeals and Dist. Cts. Polit. sci. instr. Wheaton Coll., Ill., 1957—58; spl. asst. Gov. Richard J. Hughes , NJ, 1962; assoc. Kirkland & Ellis, Chgo., 1965—70, ptnr., 1970—. Mem. vis. com. U. Chgo. Law Sch., 1971—74, 1996—99, lectr., 1989—90, 1991—92; del. 6th Ill. Constl. Conv., 1969—70. Bd. editors: law rev. U. Chgo. Law Rev.; contbr. articles to profl. jours. Recipient Joseph Henry Beale prize, U. Chgo., 1963, Outstanding Young Man award, Evanston Jaycees, 1970. Fellow: Internat. Acad. Trial Lawyers, Am. Coll. Trial Lawyers; mem.: ABA, Am. Acad. Polit. and Social Sci., Am. Polit. Sci. Assn., Bar Assn. 7th Fed. Cir., Ill. State Bar Assn., Internat. Bar Assn., Saddle and Cycle Club (gov. 1984), Mid-Am. Club 1981—84, Ventana Canyon Golf Club, Cherry Hill Country Club, Glen View Club, Chgo. Club. Office: Kirkland & Ellis 200 E Randolph Dr Ste 6000 Chicago IL 60601-6636

CICIRELLI, VICTOR GEORGE, psychologist; b. Miami, Fla., Oct. 1, 1926; s. Felix and Rene (DeMaria) C.; m. Jean Alice Solveson, Aug. 9, 1953; children: Ann Victoria, Michael Felix, Gregory Sheldon. B.S., Notre Dame U., 1947; M.A., U. Ill., Urbana, 1950; M.Ed., U. Miami, 1956; Ph.D. (Univ. fellow), U. Mich., 1964; Ph.D., Mich. State U., 1971. Asst. prof. ednl. psychology U. Mich., 1963-65; dir. student teaching for elem., secondary and M.A.T. programs U. Pa., 1965-67; assoc. prof. early childhood edn. Ohio U., 1967-68; dir. research Nat. Evaluation of Head Start Westinghouse Learning Corp. at Ohio U., 1968-69; Office Edn. postdoctoral fellow U. Wis. Inst. Cognitive Learning, 1969-70; prof. human devel. Purdue U., 1970-73, prof. devel./aging psychology, 1974—, dir. devel. psychology program, 1977-78, 80-81, 82-83, 92-93, 96, 99-2001. Vis. sci. fellow Max Planck Inst. for Human Devel. and Edn., Berlin, 1991; fellow Ctr. for Health Policy Rsch., J. Hillis Miller Health Sci. Ctr., Sch. Medicine, U. Fla., Gainesville, summer 1991; cons. in field; mem. research adv. bd. Calif. Commn. for Tchr. Preparation and Licensing, 1973-78; scholar NSF Inst., Ohio U., 1956, Am. U., 1958, U. Fla., 1960. Author: Helping Elderly Parents: Role of Adult Children, 1981, Family Caregiving: Autonomous and Paternalistic Decision Making, 1992, Sibling Relationships Across the Life Span, 1995, Older Adults' Views on Death, 2002; mem. editl. bd.: Jour. Marriage and the Family, 1990—; contbr. articles to profl. publs. Bd. dirs. Nat. Com. on Prevention of Elder Abuse, 1988-91; mem. adv. com. Ind. Geriatric Edn. Ctr., U. Ind., 1991. Grantee OEO, 1968-69, 71-73, U.S. Office Edn., 1971-73; Nat. Inst. Edn., 1973-74, NIH, 1973-74, Office Child Devel., 1973-74, Nat. Ret. Tchrs. Assn./Am. Assn. Ret. Persons Andrus Found., 1978-82, 90-91, 92, 95, Retirement Rsch. Found., 1984-85, 87-89; fellow Andrew Norman Inst. Advanced Study, Andrus Gerontology Ctr., U. So. Calif., 1984, Gerontology Soc., 1983, 84. Fellow APA, Gerontol. Soc.; mem. Internat. Soc. Study Behavioral Deve., Am. Psychol. Soc., Am. Assn. Aging, Nat. Coun. on Family Rels. Soc. for Chaos Theory, Phi Kappa Phi. Roman Catholic. Home: 1221 N Salisbury St West Lafayette IN 47906-2415 Office: Purdue U Dept Psychol Sci West Lafayette IN 47907 E-mail: victor@psych.purdue.edu.

CIERPIOT, CONNIE, state legislator; Mem. from dist. 52 Mo. Ho. of Reps., Jefferson City. Republican.

CIFELLI, JOHN LOUIS, lawyer; b. Chicago Heights, Ill., Aug. 19, 1923; s. Antonio and Domenica (Liberatore) C.; m. Irene Romandine, Jan. 4, 1948; children— Carla, David, John L., Bruce, Thomas, Carol. Student, Bowdoin Coll., 1943, Norwick Mil. Acad., 1943, Mt. Piliar Acad., 1943, U. Ill. Extension Ctr., 1946-47; LLB, DePaul U., 1950, JD (hon.), 1975. Bar: Ill. 1950, U.S. Supreme Ct. 1960. Ptnr. Piacenti, Cifelli & Sims, Chicago Heights, 1950-78; pres. John L. Cifelli & Assocs., 1978-85; sr. ptnr. Cifelli Baczynski & Scrementi Ltd. (now Cifelli & Scrementi), 1985—; spl. counsel City of Chicago Heights, 1961-72; village atty. Village of Richton Park, Ill., 1962-77, Village of Ford Heights, 1984-89. Counsel Maj. League Umpires Assn., 1973-78, Ill. High Sch. Baseball Coaches Assn., 1975-89. Sec. Bd. Fire and Police, Chicago Heights, 1959-65; co-founder Small Fry Internat. Basketball, 1969, pres., 1969— ; coach, baseball coordinator Chicago Heights Park Dist., 1970-75; coach Babe Ruth League Baseball, 1972, 74, 75, asst. Ill. dir., 1973; dir. Ill. tournament, 1973. Served to 2d lt. USAAF, 1942-45, ETO. Mem. ABA, Ill. Bar Assn., Ill. Trial Lawyers Assn., Asns. Trial Lawyers Am., Justinian Soc. Lawyers, Isaac Walton League, Italo Am. Vets. Group, VFW (judge adv. 1951-72), Cath. War Vets. (judge adv. 1951-70), Am. Legion. Republican. Clubs: Chicago Heights Country (bd. dirs. 1972-76), Mt. Carmel; Pike Lake Fishing (Wis.). Lodges: Moose, Amaseno. Avocations: hunting, fishing, golf. Home: 879 Amico Dr Chicago Heights IL 60411 Office: Cifelli & Scrementi 100 1st National Plz Chicago Heights IL 60411-3555 E-mail: cifellilawfirm@msn.com.

CILELLA, SALVATORE GEORGE, JR. museum director; b. Chgo., Oct. 19, 1941; s. Salvatore G. and Mary Genevieve (LaRocque) C.; m. Mary Winifred Broucek, Aug. 29, 1970; children: Salvatore G. III, Peter Dominic. BA, U. Notre Dame, 1963, MA in Am. History, 1966; MA in museum adminstrn., Univ. N.Y., Oneonta, 1971. Community amb. Experiment in Internat. Living, Iran, 1965; exec. dir. No. Ind. Hist. Soc., South Bend, 1970-72; registrar, asst. dir. N.Y. State Hist. Assn., Cooperstown, 1973-76; exec. dir. Historic Bethlehem (Pa.) Inc., 1976-79; dir. devel. and membership Old Sturbridge (Mass.) Village, 1979-81; devel. officer Smithsonian Instn., Washington, 1981-87; exec. dir. Columbia (S.C.) Mus. Art, 1987-2001; pres., CEO Ind. Hist. Soc., Indpls., 2001—. Cons. various mus., 1979—; overseer Old Sturbridge Village, 1982-89; lectr. Seminar for Hist. Adminstrn., Williamsburg, Va., 1983—, Mus. Mgmt. Program, Boulder, Colo., 1993. Contbr. articles to profl. jours. Co-chmn. United Black Fund, 1999; chmn. search com. Hist. Columbia; vice chair Gov.'s Commn. on Heritage; bd. dirs. Indpls. Conv. and Visitors Assn. Decorated Army commendation medal, 1969. Mem.: Am. Assn. for State and Local History, Am. Hist. Print Collections Assn., Am. Assn. Mus. (chmn. devel. and membership com. 1984—89, bd. dirs. 1989—92), Rotary. Roman Catholic. Avocations: collecting 18th and 19th century American prints and maps, antiques, Civil War artifacts and rugs. Office: Ind Hist Soc 450 W Ohio St Indianapolis IN 46202-3269

CIOFFI, MICHAEL LAWRENCE, lawyer; b. Cin., Feb. 2, 1953; s. Patrick Anthony and Patricia (Schroeder) C.; children: Michael A., David P., Gina M. BA magna cum laude, U. Notre Dame, 1975; JD, U. Cin., 1979. Bar: Ohio 1979, U.S. Dist. Ct. (so. dist.) Ohio 1980, U.S. Dist. Ct. (no. dist.) Ohio 1983, U.S. Ct. Appeals (6th cir.) 1985. Asst. atty. gen. Ohio Atty. Gen., Columbus, 1979-81; from assoc. to ptnr. Frost & Jacobs, Cin., 1981-87; staff v.p., asst. gen. counsel Penn Cen. Corp., 1988-93; v.p., asst. gen. counsel Am. Fin. Group, 1993-2000; ptnr. Blank Rome Comisky & McCauley, 2001—. Adj. prof. law U. Cin. Coll. Law, 1983—. Author: Ohio Pretrial Litigation, 1991; co-author: Sixth Circuit Federal Practice Manual, 1993. Bd. dirs. Charter Com. of Greater Cin., 1985—88. Recipient Goldman Prize for Tchg. Excellence U. Cin. Coll. Law, 1995, Nicholas Longworth Disting. Alumni award, 1996. Mem. ABA, Fed. Bar Assn. (mem. exec. com., pres.1994), Ohio Bar Assn., Cin. Bar Assn. Avocations: tennis, travel. Office: Blank Rome Comisky & McCauley LLP 201 E 5th St Cincinnati OH 45202

CIPLIJAUSKAITE, BIRUTE, humanities educator; b. Kaunas, Lithuania, Apr. 11, 1929; came to U.S., 1957; d. Juozas and Elena (Stelmokaite) C. B.A., Lycee Lithuanien Tubingen, 1947; M.A., U. Montreal, 1956; Ph.D., Bryn Mawr Coll., 1960. Permanent mem. Inst. Rsch. in Humanities U. Wis., Madison, 1974, asst. prof., 1961-65, assoc. prof., 1965-68, prof., 1968-73, John Bascom prof., 1973—. Author: La Soledad y la poesia española contemporánea, 1962, El poeta y la poesia, 1966, Baroja, un estilo, 1972, Deber de plenitud: La poesia de Jorge Guillén, 1973, Los noventayochistas y la historia, 1981, La mujer insatisfecha, 1984, La novela femenina contemporánea (1970-85), 1988, Literaturos eskizai, 1992, De signos y significaciones. I: Juegos con a vanguardia, 1999, Carmen Martin Gaite, 2000, Guilleniana, 2002; editor: Luis de Gongora, Sonetos completos, 1969, critical edit., 1981, Jorge Guillén, 1975, (with C. Maurer) La voluntad de humanismo: Homenaje a Juan Marichal, 1990, Novisimos, postnovisimos, clásicos: la poesia de los 80 en España, 1991; translator: Juan Ramón Jiménez, Sidabrinukas ir as, 1982, María Victoria Atencia, Svenciausios Karalienes Ekstazes, 1989, Voces en el silencio: Poesia lituana contemporánea, 1991, Birute Pukeleviciute, Planto, 1994, (with Nicole Laurent-Catrice) Vingt poètes lituaniens d'aujourd'hui, 1997. Guggenheim fellow, 1968 Mem. Assn. For Advancement Baltic Studies (v.p. 1981), Asociación Internacional de Hispanistas. Office: U Wis Inst Rsch in Humanities 1401 Observatory Dr Madison WI 53706-1209

CIRESI, MICHAEL VINCENT, lawyer; b. St. Paul, Apr. 18, 1946; s. Samuel Vincent and Selena Marie (Bloom) Ciresi; m. Ann Ciresi; children: Dominic, Adam. BBA, U. St. Thomas; JD, U. Minn.; LLD, Southwestern U., 2001. Bar: Minn. 1971, U.S. Dist. Ct. Minn. 1974, U.S. Ct. Appeals (8th cir.) 1971, U.S. Supreme Ct. 1981, U.S. Ct. Appeals (2d cir.) 1986, U.S. Ct. Appeals (9th cir.) 1987, U.S. Ct. Appeals (10th cir.) 1990, NY 1995, Fed. Cir. 1998, U.S. Ct. Appeals (5th cir.) 1999. Assoc. Robins, Kaplan, Miller & Ciresi, Mpls., 1971—78, ptnr., 1978—, exec. bd., 1983—, chmn. exec. bd., 1995—. Adv. bd. Ctr. Advanced Litig. Nottingham (Eng.) Law Sch. Trustee U. St. Thomas. Named Product Liability Lawyer of Yr., Australian Nat. Consumer Law Assn., 1989, Trial Lawyer of Yr., Trial Lawyers for Pub. Justice Found., 1998. Mem.: ABA, Trial Lawyers for Pub. Justice (bd. dirs.), Inner Cir. of Advocates, Internat. Bar Assn., Am. Bd. Trial Advocates, Assn. Trial Lawyers Am., Ramsey County Bar Assn., Hennepin County Bar Assn., Minn. State Bar Assn. Roman Catholic. Avocations: sports, U.S. history. Home: 1247 Culligan Ln Saint Paul MN 55118-4151 Office: Robins Kaplan Miller & Ciresi 2800 Lasalle Plz Minneapolis MN 55402

CISSELL, JAMES CHARLES, lawyer; b. Cleve., May 29, 1940; s. Robert Francis and Helen Cecelia (Freeman) C; children: Denise, Helene-Marie, Suzanne, James. Student, Sophia U., Tokyo, 1961; AB, Xavier U., 1962; JD, U. Cin., 1966; postgrad., Ohio State U., 1973-74; D. Tech. Letters, Cin. Tech. Coll., 1979. Bar: Ohio 1966, U.S. Dist. Ct. (so. dist.) Ohio 1967, U.S. Ct. Appeals (6th cir.) 1978, U.S. Supreme Ct. 1980, U.S. Dist. Ct. (ea. dist.) Ky. 1981. Pvt. practice law, 1966-78, 82—; asst. atty. gen. State of Ohio, 1971-74; first v.p. Cin. Bd. Park Commrs., 1973-74; vice mayor City of Cin., 1976-77; U.S. atty. So. Dist. Ohio, Cin., 1978-82. Adj. instr. law No. Ky. U., 1982-86; pres. Nat. Assn. Former U.S. attys., 2001—. Author: Oil and Gas Law in Ohio, 1964, Federal Criminal Trials, 5th edit., 1999; editor; Proving Federal Crimes. Gen. chmn. amateur pub. links championship U.S. Golf Assn., 1987; mem. coun. City of Cin., 1974-78, 85-87, 89-92; clk of cts., Hamilton County, 1992—, commr. Recreation Bd. Cin., 1974, Planning Bd. Cin., 1977; pres. Ohio Clk. of Cts. Assn., 1998; mem. Ohio Bicentennial Commn., 1998—; mem. Ohio Cts. Futures Commn., 1998-2000; mem. Ohio Supreme Ct. Adv. Com. on Tech. and the Cts., 2000—. Recipient Econ. Opportunity award, Dr. Martin Luther King Jr. Holiday Commn., 2002; fellow, Ford Found., 1973—74. Mem. Ohio Bar Assn., Cin. Bar Assn., Fed. Bar Assn., Former U.S. Attys. Assn. Avocations: golf, jogging. Home: 201B Belvedere 3900 Rose Hl Cincinnati OH 45229 Office: 602 Main St Ste 320 Cincinnati OH 45202-2521 E-mail: jcissell@cms.hamilton-co.org.

CIZEK, DAVID JOHN, sales engineer, small business owner; b. Chgo., Sept. 29, 1959; s. John Jacob and Cecelia Ursula (Shway) C.; m. Kimberly Ann Kral, May 12, 1984. BSEE, U. Ill., 1981. Asst. sales engr. control divsn. Westinghouse Electric Co., Chgo., 1981-83, product line engr. control divsn. Fayetteville, N.C., 1983-85, sales engr. field sales divsn. Chgo., 1985-86, aerospace and def. automation specialist, 1987-88, engr. distbn. support sales, 1988-94; field sales divsn. sales engr. Cutler-Hammer, 1994-95; pres., owner Lakeridge Electric Supply Co., Inc., Romeoville, Ill., 1995—. Mem. U. Ill. Alumni Assn., Girl Scouts of Am., Kappa Sigma Alumni Assn. Republican. Presbyterian. Avocations: real estate investing, fishing, hunting, tennis. Home: 8409 Willow West Dr Willow Springs IL 60480-1139 Office: Lakeridge Electric Supply 734 Oakridge Dr Romeoville IL 60446-1395

CLACK, FLOYD, former state legislator; b. Houston, Dec. 21, 1940; m. Brenda J. Jones; children: Michael, Mia. BS, Tex. So. U., 1965; MA, Ea. Mich. U., 1972. State rep. Mich. Ho. Reps., Dist. 80, 1983-94, Mich. Ho. Reps., Dist. 48, 1995-97. Vice chmn. Dem. black caucus, majority whip, mem. standing com. labor, standing con. coll. & univs., standing com. constrn. rev. & women's rights, chmn. standing com. corrections, ad hoc spl. com. alternatives fo rhigh risk students, 2d vice chmn. majority caucus, mahority vice chmn., standing com. civic rights, mem. standing com. mental health, standing com. corp. & fin., standing com. ins., criminal justice com., ad hoc spl. com. studying Mich. fin. inst., Mich. Ho. Reps. Mem. exec. bd. Genesee County Dem. Com., Mich.; co-chmn. Mayor's Hail Task Force; del. Dem. Nat. Conv.; chmn. Genesee County Jackson for Pres. Caucus, Jesse Jackson for Pres. com., Flint, 1988; founder Floyd Clack Cmty Project; chmn. Mott Found. Tribute Com. & Floyd J. McCree Tribute Com.; mem. New Paths, Inc. Adv. Coun.; bd. dirs. Eastside Teen Ctr.; bd. trustees Don Haley Scholar; founder, bd. dirs. Youth Leadership Ins., Flint. Recipient Svc. award Concerned Pastors Assn., 1982, Greater Flint Afro-Am. Hall of Fame, Toll Fel., 1987, David McMahon award Mech. Edn. Assn., 150% Achiever Lansing Stae Jour. Mem. NEA, Am. Corrections Assn., Mich. Corrections Assn., United Tchrs. Flint (chmn. human rels. com.), John W. Stevenson Lodge No. 56, Lions (charter, past v.p., Man of Yr. 1982), Met. C. of C., Urban League, Kappa Alpha Psi. Home: 3120 Helber St Flint MI 48504-2921

CLAPPER, LYLE NIELSEN, magazine publisher; b. Evanston, Ill., Apr. 24, 1941; s. John Marion and Edna (Nielsen) C.; m. Lynn Dewey, Sept. 1, 1962 (div. June 1978); children: John Scott, Susan Louise; m. Marie Petersen, Jan. 1, 1980; children: Jeffrey Leland, Anne Reinke. Student, Cornell U., 1959-60; BS in Quantative Econs., U. Ill., 1964. Chief exec. officer Clapper Communications (pubs. Crafts 'N Things mag., Pack-O-Fun mag., Decorative Arts Painting mag., Cross Stitcher Mag., Bridal Crafts mag.), Des Plaines, Ill., 1960—. Dir. AirLifeLine Midwest, 1995-2000. Avocations: teaching flying, photography, computer programming.

CLAPPER, MARIE ANNE, magazine publisher; b. Chgo., Nov. 21, 1942; d. Chester William and Hazel Alice (Gilso) Reinke; m. William Neil Petersen, Aug. 17, 1963 (div. 1975); children: Elaine Myrtice, Edward William; m. Lyle N. Clapper, Jan. 1, 1980; children: Jeffrey Leland, Anne Reinke; stepchildren: John Scott, Susan Louise Student, Augustana Coll., Rock Island, Ill., 1960-63; EdB, Northeastern U., 1964. Writer Pack-o-Fun mag., Park Ridge, Ill., 1976-77, editor Des Plaines, 1977-78, pub., 1990—; asst. to pub., circulation dir. Crafts 'n Things mag., 1978-82, pub., 1982—, Decorative Arts Painting mag., Des Plaines, 1990—, The Cross Stitcher mag., Des Plaines, 1991—, 101 Bridal Ideas mag., Des Plaines, 1991—; pub., pres. Clapper pub. Host TV show The Crafts 'n Things Show, 1984-86, Crafting for the 90s, 1990-94; author: EveryDay Matters, 1996. Mem. TEC, Mag. Pubs. Am. (bd. dirs.), Hobby Industry Am. (bd. dirs., treas. 1998-99), Soc. Craft Designers. Office: Crafts 'n Things 2400 E Devon Ave Ste 375 Des Plaines IL 60018-4618

CLAREY, JOHN ROBERT, executive search consultant; b. Waterloo, Iowa, June 5, 1942; s. Robert J. and Norma (Knox) C.; m. Kathleen Ann Kingsley, June 5, 1965; children: Sharon Diane, Suzanne Marie. BSBA, Iowa Sate U., 1965; MBA, U. Pa., 1972. Fin. analyst Ford Motor Co., Dearborn, Mich., 1972-74; cons. Price Waterhouse, Chgo., 1974-75, mgr., 1975-76; assoc. Heidrick & Struggles, 1976-81, v.p., ptnr., 1981-82; pres. Clarey & Andrews Inc., Northbrook, Ill. Served to lt. USN, 1965-70, Vietnam. Mem. Stick and Rudder, Assn. Exec. Search Cons., Lifeline Pilots, Mid-Am. Club (Chgo.), Sunset Ridge Country Club (Northbrook). Republican. Roman Catholic. Avocations: flying, microcomputers, tennis. Home: 1347 Hillside Rd Northbrook IL 60062-4612 Office: Clarey & Andrews Inc 1200 Shermer Rd Ste 108 Northbrook IL 60062-4563 E-mail: jackc@clarey-andrews.com.

CLARK, BEVERLY ANN, lawyer; b. Davenport, Iowa, Dec. 9, 1944; d. F. Henry and Arlene F. (Meyer) C.; m. Richard Floss; children: Amy and Barry (twins); stepchildren: Heather, Gretchan. Student, Mich. State U., 1963-65; BA, Calif. State U., Fullerton, 1967; MSW, U. Iowa, 1975, JD, 1980; grad., Iowa Massage Inst., 1999. Bar: Iowa 1980; lic. social worker, Iowa; nat. cert. lic. massage therapist. Probation officer County of San Bernardino, San Bernardino, Calif., 1968, County of Riverside, Riverside, 1968-69; social worker Skiff Hosp., Newton, Iowa, 1971-73, State of Iowa, Mitchellville, 1973-74, planner Des Moines, 1976-77, law clk., 1980-81; corp. counsel Pioneer Hi-Bred Internat., Inc., 1981-2000; pvt. practice, 2000—. Instr. Des Moines Area C.C., Ankeny, Iowa, 1974—75, Ankeny, 2001—; adj. prof. Drake Law Sch., 1993—96; pub. Sweet Annie Press; owner Annie's Place, The B&B Connection Gift Catalog. Editor: Proceedings: Bicentennial Symposium on New Directions in Juvenile Justice, 1975; contbr. articles to prof. jours. Founder Mother of Twins Club, Newton, 1971; co-chmn. Juvenile Justice Symposium, Des Moines, 1974-75; mem. Juvenile Justice Com., Des Moines, 1974-75; mem. Nat. Offender Based State Corrections Info. System. Com., Iowa rep., 1976-78; incorporator, dir. Iowa Dance Theatre, Des Moines, 1981; mem. Pesticide User's Adv. Com., Fort Collins, Colo., 1981-88; co-developer Iowa Migrant Ombudsmen Project, Pioneer, Inc. and Proteus, Inc. Recipient Disting. Alumni award U. Iowa, 1990, Nat. award Ctr. for Pub. Resources. Mem.: ABA (subcom. on devel. individual rights in work place, termination-at-will subcom. 1982—), Polk County Women Attys., Am. Assn. Agrl. Lawyers, Jasper County Bar Assn., Polk County Bar Assn., Iowa Bar Assn., Iowa Orgn. Women Attys. (bd. dirs., sec. 2001).

CLARK, CHARLES M., JR. research institution administrator; b. Greensburg, Ind., Mar. 12, 1938; s. Charles Malcolm and Mary Louise (Christian) C.; m. Julia Berg Freeman, Jan 27, 1963 (div. 1982); children: Margaret Louise, Brian Alexander; m. Eleanor DeArman Kinney, June 25, 1983; 1 child, Janet Marie Clark. BA, Ind. U., 1960, MD, 1963. From asst.

prof. to prof. medicine Ind. U., Indpls., 1969—, from asst. prof. to prof. pharmacology, 1970—; assoc. chief staff rsch. and devel. VA Hosp., 1988—; dir. Diabetes Rsch. and Tng. Ctr., 1977—; co-dir. Regenstrief Inst., 1993-97. Chmn. Safety and Quality com. DCCT, 1982-93, Nat. Diabetes adv. bd., 1987-88; chair Nat. Diabetes Edn. Program, 1995—; vis. prof. Facultad de Ciencias Medicas, U. Nacional de la Plata, Argentina, 1999-2000. Editor Diabetes Care, 1996-2001; contbr. numerous articles to profl. jours. Lt comdr. USPHS, 1967-69. Mem. ACP, Am. Soc. Clin. Investigation, Internat. Diabetes Fedn., Am. Diabetes Assn. (Banting award 1989). Office: VA Med Ctr (151) 1481 W 10th St Indianapolis IN 46202 E-mail: chclark@iupui.edu.

CLARK, CLIFFORD EDWARD, JR. history educator; b. BayShore, N.Y., July 13, 1941; s. Clifford Edward and Helen C.; m. Grace Williams, Aug. 20, 1966; children: Cynthia Williams, Christopher Allen, Susan McGrath. BA, Yale U., 1963; MA, Harvard U., 1964, PhD in Am. Civilization, 1968. History tutor Harvard U., Cambridge, Mass., 1966-67; instr. Amherst (Mass.) Coll., 1968-69, asst. prof., 1969-70; from asst. to assoc. prof. Carleton Coll., Northfield, Minn., 1970-80, prof. history, 1980—, M.A. & A.D. Hulings Prof. of Am. Studies, 1982—, dir. summer acad. programs, 1984—, chmn. history dept., 1986-89. Cons. Minn. Humanities Commn., Mpls., 1976—, Minn. Hist. Soc., Mpls., 1982—; Northfield Sch. Bd., 1978-87; editl. cons. Winterthur Portfolio, Del., 1983-92. Author: Henry Ward Beecher, Spokesman for a Middle-Class America, 1978, The American Family Home, 1800-1960, 1986, (with others) The Enduring Tradition, 4th edit. 1999; editor: Minnesota in a Century of Change: The State and Its People Since 1900, 1989. Mem. Northfield Heritage Preservation Commn., 1986—. Fellow Woodrow Wilson Found., 1964, 67; Demonstration grantee NEH, 1978, sr. fellow NEH, 1980; recipient Younger Humanist Summer Stipend, NEH, 1973. Mem. Am. Studies Assn., Am. Hist. Assn., Orgn. Am. Historians, Northfield Hist. Soc. Episcopalian. Avocations: tennis, squash. Home: 718 4th St E Northfield MN 55057-2316 Office: Carleton Coll Dept History One N College St Northfield MN 55057 E-mail: cclark@cameton.edu.

CLARK, DAVID LEIGH, marine geologist, educator; b. Albuquerque, June 15, 1931; s. Leigh William and Sadie (Ollerton) C.; m. Louise Boley, Aug. 31, 1951; children: Steven, Douglas, Julee, Linda. BS, Brigham Young U., 1953, MS, 1954; PhD in Geology, U. Iowa, 1957. Geologist Standard Oil Calif., Albuquerque, 1954; asst. geologist Columbia U., 1954-55; asst. U. Iowa, 1955-57; asst. prof. So. Meth. U., Dallas, 1957-59; asst. to assoc. prof. Brigham Young U., Provo, Utah, 1959-63; assoc. prof. U. Wis., Madison, 1963-68; prof. geology and geophysics U. Wis.-Madison, 1968—, chmn. dept. geology and geophysics, 1971-74, assoc. dean natural scis., 1986-91. Chmn. polar rsch. bd. NAS, 1995—. Author Fossils, Paleontology, Evolution, 1968,72; author and coordinator: Treatise on Invertebrate Paleontology-Conodonts, 1981. Recipient Fulbright award Bonn, W.Ger., 1965-66; Disting. Professorship U. Wis., 1974 Fellow Geol. Soc. Am.; mem. Paleontol. Soc., Am. Assn. Petroleum Geologists, Soc. Econ. Paleontologists and Mineralogists, Am. Geophys. Union, Pander Soc., Paleontol. Assn., N.Am. Micropaleontology Soc., AAAS Mem. LDS Ch. Home: 612 Canyon Oak Ct Santa Rosa CA 95409-5915 Office: U Wis Dept Geology and Geophysics Weeks Hall 1215 W Dayton St Madison WI 53706

CLARK, DWIGHT EDWARD, sports team executive, former professional football player; b. Kinston, N.C., Jan. 8, 1957; B.A., Clemson U., 1979. Wide receiver San Francisco 49ers, NFL, 1979-87, exec. v.p., dir. football ops., 1995-98, played in Super Bowl, 1981, 84; v.p., dir of football ops. Cleveland Browns, 1998—. Mem. NFL All-Star Team, 1981, 82 Office: c/o Cleveland Browns 76 Lou Groza Blvd Berea OH 44017-1238

CLARK, ELOISE ELIZABETH, biologist, educator; b. Grundy, Va., Jan. 20, 1931; d. J. Francis Emmett and Ava Clayton (Harris) C. BA, Mary Washington Coll., 1951; PhD in Zoology, U. N.C., 1958; DSc, King Coll., 1976; postdoctoral rsch., Washington U., St. Louis, 1957-58, U. Calif. at Berkeley, 1958-59. Rsch. asst., then instr. U. N.C., 1952-55; instr. physiology Marine Biol. Lab., Woods Hole, Mass., 1958-62; asst. prof. Columbia U., 1960-65, assoc. prof. biol. sci., 1966-69; with NSF, Washington, 1969-83, head molecular biology, 1971-73, div. dir. biol. and med. scis., 1973-75, dep. asst. dir. biol., behavioral and social scis., 1975-76, asst. dir. biol., behavioral and social scis., 1976-83; v.p. acad. affairs, prof. biol. sci. Bowling Green (Ohio) State U., 1983-96, acting pres., 1992, interim chair, 2000-01; trustee prof. Biol. Sci., 1996—. Contbr. articles to profl. jours. and congl. hearings. Mem. alumnae bd. Mary Washington Coll., U. Va., 1967—70; bd. regents Nat. Libr. of Medicine, 1973—83; mem. policy group competitive grants program U.S. Dept. Agr.; mem. White House Interdepartmental Task Force on Women, 1978—80, Task Force for Com. on Families, 1980, Com. on Health and Medicine, 1976—80; vice chmn. Com. on Food and Renewable Resources, 1977—80; mem. selective excellence task force Ohio Bd. Regents, 1984—85; mem. Ohio Adv. Coun., Coll. Prep. Edn., 1983—84, Ohio Inter-Univ. Coun. for Provosts, 1983—96, chmn., 1984—85, 1995—96; nat. adv. rsch. resources coun. NIH, 1987—89; mem. informal sci. edn. panel NSF, 1986—88, adv. com., social, behavioral and econ. scis., 1997—2000; program adv. coun. sci., tech. and pub. policy Harvard U., 1988—90, mem. editl. bd. Forum, 1997—2001; mem. governing bd. OhioLink, 1990—96, vice chair, 1992, chair, 1993—94. Named Disting. Alumnus Mary Washington Coll., 1975; Wilson scholar, 1956; E.C. Drew scholar, 1956; USPHS postdoctoral fellow, 1957-59; recipient Disting. Service award NSF, 1978 Mem. AAAS (coun. 1969-71, bd. dirs. 1978-82, pres.-elect, 1992, pres., 1993, chmn. bd. 1994), Soc. Gen. Physiology (sec. 1965-67, coun. 1969-71), Biophys. Soc. (coun. 1975-76), Am. Soc. Cell Biology (coun. 1972-75), Am. Inst. Biol. Scientists, Marine biol. Lab. (trustee 1993), NASULGC (higher edn. and tech. com. 1988-93, com. on info. tech. 1994-96), Consortium of Social Sci. Assn. (bd. dirs. 1993-96), Ohio Coun. rsch. and Econ. Devel., Assn. Women in Sci. (bd. dirs. 1998-2001), Phi Beta Kappa (com. on qualifications 1995—, chair 1998—, senate 1996—, exec. com. 1997--), Sigma Xi, Omicron Delta Kappa. Home: 1222 Brownwood Dr Bowling Green OH 43402-3503 Office: Bowling Green State U Dept Biol Scis Bowling Green OH 43403-0001

CLARK, GARY R. newspaper editor; b. Cleve., June 27, 1946; s. Dale Francis and Mary Louise (Rozeski) C.; m. Caryn Elaine Helm, Dec. 18, 1976; children: Jessica Lynn, Brian Michael. BA, Ohio State U., 1973, MA, 1978. Reporter Chronicle-Telegram, Elyria, Ohio, 1973-77, The Plain Dealer, Cleve., 1978-88, state editor, 1988-89, nat. editor, 1989, city editor, 1989-90, mng. editor, 1990—. Tchg. assoc. Ohio State U., Columbus, 1977-78. Sgt. USMC, 1966-69, Vietnam. Mem. AP Mng. Editors, Am. Soc. Newspaper Editors, Investigative Reporters and Editors, Cleve. City Club. Office: The Plain Dealer 1801 Superior Ave E Cleveland OH 44114-2198

CLARK, JAMES MURRAY, state legislator; b. Indpls., Nov. 3, 1957; m. Janet Campbell. BA, Kenyon Coll., 1979; JD, Ind. U., 1982. Mem. Clark, Quinn, Moses & Clark, Attys. at Law, 1982; mem. from dist. 29 Ind. Senate, Indpls., 1994—, mem. govt. and regulatory affairs, mem. health and environ. affairs com., mem. fin. inst. com., judiciary coms. Address: 1 Indiana Sq Ste 2200 Indianapolis IN 46204-2011

CLARK, JAMES NORMAN, insurance executive; b. Decatur, Ill., Jan. 30, 1932; s. John W. and Pearl (Allen) C.; m. Marlene F. Geason, Oct. 10, 1953; children— Paul R., Donald A., Robert S., Christine A. Tax and acctg. mgr. Caterpillar Tractor Co., 1957-66; mgr. tax dept. Towmotor Corp., 1966-68; with Western & So. Life Ins. Co., Cin., 1968—, exec. v.p., 1980—, also bd. dirs. Dir. Columbus (Ohio) Life Ins. Co. Former trustee Good Samaritan Hosp. Found. Capt. USAF, 1954-57. Mem. Life Office Mgmt. Assn. (prin. rep.), Fin. Exec. Inst. (former nat. chmn.), Tax Execs. Inst. Office: Western & So Life Ins Co 400 Broadway St Cincinnati OH 45202-3312

CLARK, JAMES RICHARD, lawyer; b. Madison, Wis., Mar. 30, 1946; s. James F. and Gloria J. Clark; m. Martha C. Conrad, Mar. 18, 1950; children: Lindsey Kelley, Chad. BA, Ripon Coll., 1968; JD, U. Wis., 1971. Bar: Wis. 1971, U.S. Dist. Ct. (we. and ea. dists.) Wis. 1972, U.S. Ct. Appeals (7th cir.) 1973, U.S. Dist. Ct. (no. dist.) Ill. 1974, U.S. Supreme Ct. 1976. Assoc. Foley & Lardner, Milw., 1971-78, ptnr., 1978—. Editor-in-chief Wis. Law Rev., 1971. Trustee Ripon Coll., 1985—. 1st lt. U.S. Army, 1971. Mem. ABA, Am. Coll. Trial Lawyers, Am. Bd. Trial Advs., 7th Cir. Bar Assn., Wis. Bar Assn., Ripon Coll. Alumni Assn. (past pres.), Milw. Athletic Club, Tripoli Country Club, Order of Coif, Phi Beta Kappa. Home: 9719 N Dalewood Ln Mequon WI 53092-6210 Office: Foley & Lardner Firstar Ctr 777 E Wisc Ave Milwaukee WI 53202

CLARK, JUDY, newscaster; m. Tom Clark; 2 children. Grad., U. Wis., Eau Claire. Reporter, anchor WAXX-WAYY; noon anchor NewsCenter 13 WEAU-TV, Eau Claire, Wis., 1992—98, anchor at five and ten, 1998—. Avocations: reading, fishing, gardening. Office: WEAU-TV PO Box 47 Eau Claire WI 54702

CLARK, KAREN, state legislator; BS, Coll. St. Teresa, Winona, Minn.; MPA, Harvard U. Mem. Minn. Ho. of Reps., 1981—, mem. jobs and econ. devel. com., commerce com. Recipient Martin Luther King, Jr. award, 1987, Minn. Alliance Progressive Leadership award, 1991, Leadership award Nat. Gay & Lesbian Task Force. Office: Minn State House Office Bldg 100 Constitution Ave Saint Paul MN 55155-1232

CLARK, LELAND CHARLES, JR. biochemist, medical products executive; b. Rochester, N.Y., Dec. 4, 1918; married, 1939; 4 children. BS, Antioch Coll., 1941; PhD in Biochemistry, U. Rochester, 1944. Chmn. biochem. dept. Fels Rsch. Inst., 1944-58; asst. prof. biochem. Antioch coll., 1944-56, prof., 1956-58; from assoc. prof. to prof. surg. Med. Ctr. Univ. Ala., 1958-68; prof. rsch. pediat. Children's Hosp. Rsch. Found. Med. Coll., U. Cin., 1968—; cons. Synthetic Blood Internat. Inc., Kettering, Ohio. Sr. rsch. assoc. surg. and pediats. U. Cin., 1955-58; cons. Wright-Patterson AFB, 1956-58, NIH, 1961—; vis. prof. Cardiovasc. Rsch. Inst., San Francisco, 1967. Editor: Symp. Oxygen Transport. Recipient Disting. Lectr. award Am. Coll. chest Physicians, 1975, Rsch. Career award NIH, 1962-68. Mem. NAE, AAAS, Am. Heart Assn. (fellow coun. cerebrovasc. disease 1967—), Artificial Organs Soc., N.Y. Acad. Sci., Sigma Xi. Achievements include research in vitamin, steroid and oxygen metabolism; polarography; cardiovascular disease; hydrogen and oxygen electrodes in diagnosis; ion exchange resins in biology; glucose electrodes. Office: Synthetic Blood Internat Inc 2685 Culver Ave Kettering OH 45429-3721

CLARK, MAURA J. oil, gas industry executive; CFO Clark Refining & Mktg. Inc.(now Premcor), Glen Ellyn, Ill. Office: Premcor 8182 Maryland Avenue Saint Louis MO 63105

CLARK, NOREEN MORRISON, behavioral science educator, researcher; b. Glasgow, Scotland, Jan. 12, 1943; came to U.S., 1948; d. Angus Watt and Anne (Murphy) Morrison; m. George Robert Pitt, Dec. 3, 1982; 1 child, Alexander Robert. BS, U. Utah, 1965; MA, Columbia U., 1972, MPhil, 1975, PhD, 1976. Rsch. coord. World Edn. Inc., N.Y.C., 1972-73; asst. prof. Sch. Pub. Health Columbia U., 1973-80, assoc. prof., 1980-81, Sch. Pub. Health U. Mich., Ann Arbor, 1981-85, prof., chmn. dept. health behavior and health edn., 1985-95, Marshall H. Becker prof. of pub. health, 1995—, dean, 1995—. Adj. prof. health adminstrn. Sch. Pub. Health Columbia U., 1988—; prin. investigator NIH, 1977—; mem. adv. com. pulmonary diseases Nat. Heart, Lung & Blood Inst., Rockville, Md., 1983-87, mem. adv. com. for prevention, edn. and control, 1987-91, coordinating com. Nat. Asthma Edn. Program, 1991—; assoc. Synergos Inst., N.Y.C., 1987-99; nat. adv. environ. health scis. coun. NIH, 1999—. Co-author: Evaluation of Health Promotion, 1984; editor Health Edn. and Behavior, 1985-97; mem. editorial bd. Women in Health, Advances in Health Edn. and Promotion, Home Health Care Services Quarterly; contbr. articles to profl. jours. Hon. dir. Freedom from Hunger Found., Davis, Calif., 1980-94; bd. dirs. Aaron Diamond Found., 1990-97, Family Care Internat., N.Y.C., 1987—, Internat. Asthma Coun., Am. Lung Assn., N.Y.C., 1988—, World Edn., Inc., The Healthtrak Found. Prize. Fellow Soc. Pub. Health Edn. (pres. 1985-86, Disting. Fellow award 1987); mem. APHA (chair health edn. sect. 1982-83, Derryberry award in behavioral sci. 1985, Disting. Career award 1994), Am. Thoracic Soc. (Health Edn. Rsch. award Nat. Asthma Edn. Program 1992, Healthtrak Edn. prize 1997), Internat. Union Health Edn., Soc. Behavioral Medicine, Coun. Fgn. Rels., Overseas Devel. Coun., Nat. Acad. Sci. Inst. Medicine, Pi Sigma Alpha. Office: U Mich Sch Pub Health 109 Observatory St Ann Arbor MI 48109-2029

CLARK, ROBERT ARTHUR, mathematician, educator; b. Melrose, Mass., May 3, 1923; s. Arthur Henry and Persis (Kidder) C.; m. Jane Burr Croftut Kinder, June 25, 1966. Student, Colo. Coll., 1940-42; BA, Duke, 1944; MA, MIT, 1946, Ph.D., 1949. Instr., research asso. MIT, 1946-50, vis. asst. prof., 1956-57; faculty Case Inst. Tech. (now Case Western Res. U.), Cleve., 1950—, prof. math., 1964-85, prof. emeritus, 1985—, acting head dept. math., 1960-61, assoc. chmn. dept. math., 1974-79, 82-84, exec. officer, 1981-82. Vis. mem. U.S. Army Math. Research Center, Madison, Wis., 1961-62 Mem. AAAS, Am. Math. Soc., Math. Assn. Am., Soc. Indsl. and Applied Math., Phi Beta Kappa, Sigma Xi. Achievements include spl. research asymptotic integration theory of differential equations and theory thin elastic shells. Home: 7469 Sherman Rd Gates Mills OH 44040-9769 Office: Case Western Res Univ Dept Math Cleveland OH 44106

CLARK, ROBERT KING, communications educator emeritus, lecturer, consultant, actor, model; b. Springfield, Mass., Apr. 12, 1934; s. Harry Robert and Alice (McClure) C.; m. Suzanne Chapin, Apr. 9, 1966; children— Jennifer, Jeffrey, Anne Elizabeth B.A., U. Wyo., 1956; M.A., U. Tenn., 1960; Ph.D., Ohio State U., 1971. Instr. journalism U. Tenn., Knoxville, 1958; instr. speech Westminster Coll., New Wilmington, Pa., 1959-61; faculty Bowling Green State U., Ohio, 1963—, prof. radio-TV film, 1980-84, prof. emeritus, 1985—; gen. mgr. Sta. WBGU-FM, 1976-85. Cons. in field; lectr. in field; seminar leader in field; yoga instr./therapist. Contbr. articles to profl. jours. Mem. Broadcast Edn. Assn., Ohio Assn. Broadcasters. Presbyterian. Office: 1064 Village Dr Bowling Green OH 43402-1231

CLARK, RONALD DEAN, newspaper editor; b. Millersburg, Ohio, Aug. 29, 1943; s. Dean Eli and Lavaun Lurline (Glasgo) C.; m. Carole Ann Smith, Oct. 15, 1983; children from previous marriage— Kelly Jay, Carrie Anne, Courtney Erin B.A., Kent State U., 1965; M.S. in Journalism, Northwestern U.-Evanston, Ill., 1966; MPA, Humphrey Inst. of Pub. Affairs, U. Minn., 1999. Reporter Akron Beacon Jour., Ohio, 1966-67, asst. city editor, 1967-68, city editor, 1968-70, met. editor, 1970-71, statehouse bur. chief, 1971-76, chief editorial writer, 1976-81; editorial page editor St. Paul Pioneer Press, 1981—. Past pres. Minn. Newspaper Found. Recipient Pulitzer Prize (shared) Columbia U., 1971. Mem. Soc. Profl. Journalists, Nat. Conf. Editorial Writers, World Press Inst. (bd. dirs.), Informal Club (St. Paul). Luth. Avocations: cycling, music. Home: 13823 Tomahawk Dr S Afton MN 55001-9706 Office: Saint Paul Pioneer Press 345 Cedar St Saint Paul MN 55101-1004 E-mail: rclark@pioneerpress.com.

CLARK, RUSSELL GENTRY, retired federal judge; b. Myrtle, Mo., July 27, 1925; s. William B. and Grace Frances (Jenkins) C.; m. Jerry Elaine Burrows, Apr. 30, 1959; children: Vincent A., Viki F. LLB, U. Mo., 1952. Bar: Mo. 1952. Mem. firm Woolsey, Fisher, Clark, Whiteaker & Stenger, Springfield, Mo., 1952-77; judge U.S. Dist. Ct. (we. dist.) Mo., Kansas City, 1977-91, sr. judge, 1991-2000; ret., 2000. 2d lt. U.S. Army, 1944-46. Fellow Am. Bar Found.; mem. ABA, Internat. Platform Soc., Mo. Bar Assn. (continuing legal edn. com. 1969), Greene County Bar Assn. (dir. 1968-71), Kiwanis (past pres. Springfield chpt.). Democrat. Methodist. Club: Kiwanis (past pres. Springfield chpt.).

CLARK, STAN W. state legislator; b. Oakley, Kans., Dec. 9, 1954; married; 1 child. Student, Colby C.C. Photographer; mem. Kans. Senate from 40th dist., Topeka, 1994—; chmn. arts and cultural resources com. Kans. Senate, chair joint computer com., vice chmn. utilities com., mem. agr. com., mem. rules and regulations com., mem. fin. instns. com. Past pres. Oakley Industries, Inc.; pres. Oakley Planning Commn.; past vice chair Oakley Bd. Zoning Appeals; past vice chair Kans. Agrl. Value-Added Ctr.'s Leadership Coun. Mem. Nat. Fedn. Ind. Bus., Oakley C. of C. (past pres.). Republican. Office: 300 SW 10th Ave Rm 128-s Topeka KS 66612-1504

CLARK, TONY, state commissioner; Student, Mich. State U., 1990-91; BS in Polit. Sci., N.D. State U., 1994, BS in History Edn., 1996. Mem. Dist. 44 N.D. Ho. of Reps., 1994-97; adminstrv. officer N.D. Tax Dept., 1997-99; commr. N.D. Dept. Labor, 1999-2000, N.D. Pub. Svc., 2001—, 2001—. Adult leader Boy Scouts Am. Named Eagle Scout Boy Scouts Am. Mem. Elks, Phi Kappa Phi. Office: 600 E Boulevard Ave Bismarck ND 58505-0480

CLARK, TRUDY H. career officer; BA sociology, U. MD, 1972; MS guidance and counseling, Troy State U., Montgomery, Al, 1987; Distinguished graduate, Squadron Officer Sch., Maxwell AFB, Al, 1980, Air Command and Staff Coll., Maxwell AFB, 1987, Armed Forces Staff Coll., Norfolk, Va, 1992, Air War Coll., Maxwell AFB, 1993. Second lt. USAF, 1973, first lt., 1975, cptn., 1977, major, 1985, lt. col., 1989, col., 1994, brigadier general, 1999; dir., command, control, communications and computer systems US Strategic Command, Offutt AFB, Nebr., 1999—. Office: Dir C4 Sys J-6 USSTRATCOM Offutt A F B NE 68113

CLARK, WILL (WILLIAM NUSCHLER CLARK JR.), professional baseball player; b. New Orleans, Mar. 13, 1964; Student, Miss. State U. Baseball player San Francisco Giants, 1986-93, Texas Rangers, 1994-99; infielder Balt. Orioles, 1999, St. Louis Cardinals, 2000—. Mem. U.S. Olympic baseball team, 1984. Recipient Golden Spikes award USA Baseball, 1985, Gold Glove award Nat. League, 1991, Silver Slugger, 1989, 91; named to Sporting News Nat. League All-Star team, 1988-89, 91, Coll. All-Am. Team Sporting News, 1984-85, Nat. League All-Star team, 1988-92, Am. League All-Star team, 1994; Nat. RBI leader, 1988. Achievements include playing in World Series, 1989. Office: St Louis Cardinals 250 Stadium Plz Saint Louis MO 63102-1722*

CLARK, WILLIAM ALFRED, federal judge; b. Dayton, Ohio, Aug. 27, 1928; s. Webb Rufus and Dora Lee (Weddle) C.; m. Catherine C. Clark, Apr. 5, 1952; children: Mary Clark Youra, Jennifer Clark Kinder, Cynthia S., Andrea G. AB, U. Mich., 1950, JD, 1952. Bar: Ohio 1952, Mich. 1953. Pvt. practice, Dayton, 1954-57; assoc. Frank J. Svoboda, 1957-73; ptnr. Legler, Lang & Kuhns, 1973-82, Pickrel, Schaeffer & Ebeling, Dayton, 1982-85; judge so. dist. Ohio U.S. Bankruptcy Ct., 1985-99, chief judge, 1993-99; apptd. recalled bankruptcy judge, 1999—. Judge Montgomery County Ct., Dayton, 1958-63; trial counsel in eminent domain Asst. Atty. Gen. Ohio, Dayton, 1963-70; tchr. bus. law Dayton chpt. Cert. Property and Casualty Underwriters, 1963-83; arbitrator Montgomery County Common Pleas Ct., Am. Arbitration Assn., Better Bus. Bur. Contbr. to Ohio Practice and Procedure Handbook, 1962. Lt. USAF, 1952-54. Named Alumnus of Yr., U. Mich. Club, Dayton, 1965. Mem. ABA, Ohio State Bar Assn. (chmn. eminent domain 1979-82), Dayton Bar Assn. (treas. 1964-65), Nat. Conf. Bankruptcy Judges, Lawyers Club. Republican. Avocations: tennis, other sports, reading, travel. Office: US Bankruptcy Ct Federal Bldg 120 W 3rd St Dayton OH 45402-1872

CLARKE, CHARLES FENTON, lawyer; b. Hillsboro, Ohio, July 25, 1916; s. Charles F. and Margaret (Patton) C.; m. Virginia Schoppenhorst, Apr. 3, 1945 (dec. July 1989); children: Elizabeth, Margaret, Jane, Charles Fenton, IV; m. Lesley Wells, Nov. 13, 1998. AB summa cum laude, Washington and Lee U., Lexington, Va., 1938; LLB, U. Mich., 1940; LLD (hon.), Cleve. State U., 1971. Bar: Mich. 1940, Ohio 1946. Pvt. practice, Detroit, 1942, Cleve., 1946—; ptnr. firm Squire, Sanders & Dempsey, 1957—, adminstr. litigation dept., 1979-85. Trustee Cleve. Legal Aid Soc., 1959-67; pres. Nat. Assn. R.R. Trial Counsel, 1966-68; life mem. 6th Circuit Jud. Conf.; chmn. legis. com. Cleve. Welfare Fedn., 1961-68; master bencher Celebrezze Inn of Ct., 1991—; bd. dirs. Wheeling and Lake Erie R.R. Co. Pres. alumni bd. dirs. Washington and Lee U., 1970-72; pres. bd. dirs. Free Med. Clinic Greater Cleve., 1970-86; trustee Cleve. Citizens League, 1956-62, Cleve. chpt. ACLU, 1986-93, Cleve. Works Inc., 1995—; bd. dirs. citizens adv. bd. Cuyahoga County (Ohio) Juvenile Ct., 1970-73; bd. dirs. George Jr. Republic, Greenville, Pa., 1970-73, Bowman Tech. Sch., Cleve., 1970-91; vice chmn. Cleve. Crime Commn., 1973-75; exec. com. Cuyahoga County Rep. Orgn., 1950—; councilman Bay Village, Ohio, 1948-53; pres., trustee Cleve. Hearing and Speech Ctr., 1957-62, Laurel Sch., 1962-72, Fedn. Cmty. Progress, 1984-90; mem. planning commn. Cleveland Heights, 1994—. Fellow Am. Coll. Trial Lawyers; mem. Greater Cleve. Bar Assn. (trustee 1983-86), Cleve. Civil War Round Table (pres. 1968), Cleve. Zool. Soc. (dir. 1970), Phi Beta Kappa. Presbyterian. Clubs: Skating, Union (Cleve.); Tavern, Rowfant. Home: 2262 Tudor Dr Cleveland Heights OH 44106-3210 Office: Squire Sanders & Dempsey 4900 Key Tower 127 Public Sq Cleveland OH 44114-1304 E-mail: cclarke@ssd.com.

CLARKE, CORNELIUS WILDER, religious organization administrator, minister; b. White Plains, N.Y., May 11, 1935; s. Cornelius Wilder and Margaret (Sutherland) C. BS, Nyack Coll., 1957; B D Div., Gordon Divinity Sch., 1960; MDiv, Gordon Conwell Theol. Sem., 1978. Ordained minister 1964. Pastor Missionary Alliance Ch., Bennington, Vt., 1960-65, Rock Hill Alliance Ch., Boston, 1965-73; sr. pastor Cranford (N.J.) Alliance Ch., 1973-76; dir. personnel Christian & Missionary Alliance, Nyack, N.Y., 1976-78; sr. pastor Simpson Meml. Ch., 1978-89; dist. supt. New Eng. Dist. of Christian & Missionary Alliance, South Easton, Mass., 1989-97; pastor Hillside Chapel, Beaver Creek, Ohio, 1998—. Trustee Nyack Coll., 1989-95. Avocations: golf, sailing, backpacking, fishing, travel. Office: Hillside Chapel 3515 Shakertown Rd Beavercreek OH 45430-1423 E-mail: nclarke@hillsidecma.org.

CLARKE, JAMES T. financial company excutive; b. Mich. BA, Coll. Wooster; MBA, U. Mich. CPA. With Coopers & Lybrand L.L.P., McLeans, Va., 1961, deputy chmn.; ptnr. Price Waterhouse Coopers, Detroit, 2000—. Trustee Coll. Wooster, Ohio. Pres. San Francisco C. of C.; chmn. San Francisco Econ. Devel. Corp.; mem. exec. com. San Francisco Bay Area Coun.; chmn. San Francisco Summer Jobs Program; bd. dirs. San Francisco Bay Area Pvt. Industry Coun.; mem. bd. regents Santa Clara (Calif.) U.; chmn. profl. accounting adv. com. U. Calif., Berkeley; asst. sec. mgmt. U.S. Dept. Interior, 1973-76. Office: Pricewaterhouse Coopers 400 Renaissance Ctr Detroit MI 48243

CLARKE, KENNETH STEVENS, insurance company executive; b. South Bend, Ind., Aug. 18, 1931; s. Walter Robert and Mattie Marie (Boley) C.; m. Vivian Elizabeth Long, July 5, 1958; children— Patrick Stevens, Mary Elizabeth, Margaret Christine, Daniel Whitman. M.S., U. Ill., 1957, Ph.D., 1963. Program cons. Chgo. Heart Assn., 1957-59; supr. recreation and athletics U. Ill. div. rehab.-edn., 1959-63; cons. health and fitness AMA, Chgo., 1963-68; coordinator continuing edn. Am. Acad. Orthopedic Surgeons, 1968-70; prof. health scis. Mankato (Minn.) State U., 1970-73; prof., chmn. health edn. Pa. State U., 1973-77; dean Coll. Applied Life Studies U. Ill., Urbana, 1977-81; asst. sec. gen. U.S. Olympic Com., Colorado Springs, Colo., 1981-89; sr. v.p. risk analysis SLE Worldwide, Inc., Ft. Wayne, Ind., 1989—. Cons. athletic injury prevention; founder Nat. Athletic Injury/Illness Reporting System; active Pa. Emergency Med. Svcs. Coun., 1974-77; chmn. NCAA Med. Aspects of Sports, 1974-79; v.p. Nat. Safety Coun., 1987-89. Editor: Standard Nomenclature of Athletic Injuries, 1966, (with J.C. Hughston) Bibliography of Sports Medicine, 1970, Fundamentals of Athletic Training, 1971, Drugs and the Coach, 1972, 2d edit., 1976; contbr. profl. articles to ednl. and med. jours. Served with CIC U.S. Army, 1953-55. Recipient Spl. citation Nat. Fedn. State High Sch. Assns., Achievement award U.S. Baseball Fedn., Disting. Service to Safety award Nat. Safety Council; named to Nat. Wheelchair Athletic Assn. Hall of Fame; named Safefy Profl. of Yr., Hoosier Safety Coun.. Fellow Am. Coll. Sports Medicine (past chair ethics com.); mem. AAHPER, Am. Acad. Phys. Edn., Assn. for Advancement Health Edn., Am. Orthopedic Soc. for Sports Medicine (hon.), U. Ill. Alumni Assn. (Merit award), Rotary Internat. Roman Catholic. Home: 27751 Calle Rabano Sun City CA 92585-3949 Office: 1712 Magnavox Way Fort Wayne IN 46804-1538 E-mail: Kenneth_clarke@asg.aon.com.

CLARKE, MILTON CHARLES, lawyer; b. Chgo., Jan. 31, 1929; s. Gordon Robert and Senoria Josephine (Carlisa) C.; m. Dorothy Jane Brodie, Feb. 19, 1955; children: Laura, Virginia, Senoria K. BS, Northwestern U., 1950, JD, 1953. Bar: Ill. 1953, Mo. 1956, U.S. Dist. Ct. (we. dist.) Mo. 1961, U.S. Ct. Appeals (8th cir.) 1961. Assoc. Swanson, Midgley, Gangwere, Clarke & Kitchin, Kansas City, Mo., 1955-61, ptnr., 1961-91; of counsel Olsen & Talpers, P.C., 1994—. Served with U.S. Army, 1953-55. Mem. Rotary. Office: Olsen and Talpers PC 2100 City Center Square 1100 Main St Kansas City MO 64105-2125 E-mail: miltonclarke@hotmail.com.

CLARKE, PHILIP REAM, JR. retired investment banker; b. Chgo., Feb. 10, 1914; s. Philip Ream and Louise (Hildebr) C.; m. Valerie Mead, Oct. 20, 1939 (dec. Sept. 1965); children: Barbara Foster, Philip Ream III; m. Jan Finan, Dec. 2, 1967; m. Barbara Schroeder, Apr. 15, 1977. AB, U. Chgo., 1937. With Glore, Forgan & Co., Chgo., 1937-42, City Nat. Bank & Trust Co., Chgo., 1946-57, asst. v.p., 1947-51, v.p., 1951-57; with Lehman Bros., Chgo., 1957-65, mgr. indsl. dept., 1957-62, dir. new bus., 1962-65; v.p., treas., dir. Hinsdale Cemetery Co., 1946-66; from sr. v.p. to vice-chmn Chgo. Corp., 1965-86, vice-chmn. emeritus, 1986-96, vice chmn. emeritus, 1997-98, dir., 1965-86; pres., CEO Hollymatic Corp., 1978-79, chmn., CEO, 1979-81, dir., 1969-81. Mem. Midwest Stock Exchange, 1954-56; pres., treas., dir. Bronswood Cemetery, Inc., 1966-89, chmn., 1990—; vice-chmn. emeritus ABN Amro Inc., 1998-2001. Bd. dirs., exec. com. Cook County Sch. of Nursing, 1958-68, v.p., 1965-68; treas., dir. Chgo. Com. on Alcoholism, 1952-56, v.p., 1957, exec. v.p., 1958, pres., 1959, chmn., 1960-61; charter mem. bd. assocs., Chgo. Theol. Sem., 1980-84; vice chmn. Chgo. Non Partisan Com. to Bring Rep. Nat. Conv. to Chgo.; Mem. Rep. Nat. Conv., 1959-60; treas. Citizens Com. to Bring Rep. and Dem. convs. to Chgo., 1952, 56; bd. govs. Hinsdale Community House, 1968-70, vice chmn., 1969, chmn., 1970, life trustee 1993—; trustee, chmn. fin. com., 1951-55, Village of Clarendon Hills, Ill., 1956-60, pres., 1961-65; bd. govs. United Rep. Fund of Ill., 1948-74, treas., 1948-62, v.p., exec. com., 1955-69; bd. dirs. Ill. council Trout Unltd., 1972-75; trustee U. Chgo. Alumni Found., 1958-61, citizens bd., 1955-80; mem. exec. com. Citizens of Greater Chgo., 1960-61. Lt. comdr. USNR, 1942-46. Mem. Chgo. Assn. Commerce and Industry (dir., treas. 1952-53), Chgo. Zool. Soc. (governing mem. 1956-69, 79—), Nat. Council on Alcoholism (v.p. 1959-62), Alpha Delta Phi. Republican. Episcopalian. Clubs: Chicago (Chgo.), Bond (Chgo.); Hinsdale Golf; Coleman Lake (dir. 1972-84, v.p. 1982) (Wis.); Plaza (Chgo.). Home: 404 Burr Ridge Clb Burr Ridge IL 60527-5207

CLARKE, RICHARD LEWIS, health science association administrator; b. Indpls., Sept. 9, 1948; s. John Richard and Opal (Emmons) C.; m. Linda DeMattia, Aug. 12, 1972; children: John, Laura, R. Bradley. BS, Bradley U., 1971; MBA, U. Miami, 1972. Bus. mgr. Jackson Meml. Hosp., Miami, 1973-76; controller Palmetto Gen. Hosp., Hialeah, Fla., 1976-80; sr. v.p. fin. Swedish Med. Ctr., Englewood, Colo., 1980-86; pres. Healthcare Fin. Mgmt. Assn., Westchester, Ill., 1986—. Bd. dirs., treas. Colo. Hosp. Assn. Trust, Denver. Fellow Healthcare Fin. Mgmt. Assn.; mem. Am. Soc. Assn. Execs., Econ. Club of Chgo. Avocations: sailboat racing, skiing. Office: Healthcare Fin Mgmt Assn 2 Westbrook Corp Ctr Ste 700 Westchester IL 60154

CLARKE, ROY, physicist, educator; b. Bury, Lancashire, England, May 9, 1947; BSc in Physics, U. London, PhD, 1973. Rsch. assoc. Cavendish Lab., Cambridge, U.K., 1973-78; James Franck fellow U. Chgo., 1978-79; prof. U. Mich., Ann Arbor, 1979-86; dir. applied physics program, 1986—. Co-founder k-Space Assocs. Inc. Editor: Synchrotron Radiation in Materials Research, 1989. Fellow Am. Phys. Soc. Achievements include development of novel methods for real-time x-ray and electron diffraction studies; patent for quasiperiodic optical coatings. Office: U Mich Randall Lab Ann Arbor MI 48109

CLARKSON, WILLIAM MORRIS, children's pastor; b. Newport, R.I., Feb. 23, 1954; s. George and Lois Ruth (Terwilligar) C.; m. Janice Aiko Enoki, June 16, 1978; children: Kyle Hideo, Keith Hiroshi. BA, Muhlenberg Coll., Allentown, Pa., 1976; MPA, Ball State U., Muncie, Ind., 1977. Advanced cert. in Employee Relations Law, Mich., Ind.; cert. Rev., Assemblies of God, Springfield, Mo., 1997. Research asst. Ball State U. Bur. Govtl. Research, Muncie, Ind., 1977; field staff cons. Ind. U., Div. Pub. Service, Indpls., 1977-78; adminstrv. asst. City of Midland, Mich., 1978-81, pers. dir., 1981-91; asst. city mgr. for pers. and risk mgmt., 1991-96; children's pastor Christian Celebration Ctr., Midland, 1996—. Adj. instr. pub. adminstrn. Ctrl. Mich. U., Mt. Pleasant, 1982-91, mem. MPA program adv. bd., 1988-91; mem. planning and evaluation com. Mich. Inst. for Pub. Adminstrn., 1989-91; dir. apptd. com. on act 312/PERA Det., Mich. Employment Rels. Commn., 1987-91; chmn. edn. and tng. com. Mich. Mcpl. League, 1991-95; mem., govtl. sector chmn. Midland Area Chamber Quality Coun., 1992-96; mem. Dow Chem. Cmty. Adv. Panel, 1994-98; exec. dir. Mid-Mich. Royal Family Kids Camp, 1996—. Co-author: Manual Indiana Counties Model Personnel Policies, 1978. Bd. dirs. Salvation Army Adv. Bd., Midland Mich., 1978-81, trustee Meml. Presbyn. Ch., Midland Mich., 1984-87, Loaned Exec. United Way Midland Mich., 1985; vice-chair Midland County Drug Abuse Resistance Edn. Project, 1989-95; bd. dirs. Midland County Camping Coun., 1999—. Recipient Mcpl. Achievement award Mich. Mcpl. League 1984; named one of Outstanding Young Men of Am., 1981. Mem. Assembly of God. Avocations: guitar, soccer, Bible study, religious retreat leadership, directing children's church camp. Home: 3806 Westbrier Ter Midland MI 48642-6656 Office: Christian Celebration Ctr 6100 Swede Ave Midland MI 48642-3199 E-mail: pastorbil@aol.com.

CLARY, BRADLEY G. lawyer, educator; b. Richmond, Va., Sept. 7, 1950; s. Sidney G. and Jean B. Clary; m. Mary-Louise Hunt, July 31, 1982; children: Benjamin, Samuel. BA magna cum laude, Carleton Coll., 1972; JD cum laude, U. Minn., 1975. Bar: Minn. 1975, U.S. Dist. Ct. Minn. 1975, U.S. Ct. Appeals (10th cir.) 1977, U.S. Ct. Appeals (8th cir.) 1979, U.S. Ct. Appeals (6th cir.) 1980, U.S. Ct. Appeals (7th cir.) 1981, U.S. Supreme Ct. 1986, U.S. Ct. Appeals (4th cir.) 1989, U.S. Ct. Appeals (9th cir.) 1991. Assoc. Oppenheimer Wolff & Donnelly, St. Paul, 1975-81, ptnr., 1982-2000; legal writing dir. Law Sch. U. Minn., 1999—, clin. prof. Law Sch., 2000—. Adj. prof. Law Sch. U. Minn., Mpls., 1985-99; adj. instr. William Mitchell Coll. Law, St. Paul, 1995-96, 98, adj. prof., 1997, 99. Author: Primer on the Analysis and Presentation of Legal Argument, 1992; co-author: Advocacy on Appeal, 2001, Successful First Depositions, 2001. Vestryman St. John Evangelist Ch., St. Paul, 1978-81, 98-00, pledge drive co-chmn., 1989-90, sr. warden, 2000-2002; mem. alumni bd. Breck Sch., Mpls., 1981-85, 89-96, exec. com., 1991-96, dir. emeritus, 1996—; mem. adv. bd. Glass Theatre Co., West St. Paul, Minn., 1982-87; mem. antitrust adv. panel dept. health State of Minn., 1992-93. Mem. ABA (adv. group antitrust sect. 1987-89, corp. counseling com.), Minn. Bar Assn. (program chmn. antitrust sect. 1986-87, treas. 1987-88, vice-chmn. 1989-90, co-chmn. 1990-92, governing coun. appellate practice sect. 2001--), Phi Beta Kappa. Avocations: tennis, sailing. Office: U Minn Law Sch 229 19th Ave S Rm 444 Minneapolis MN 55455-0400

CLARY, ROSALIE BRANDON STANTON, timber farm executive, civic worker; b. Evanston, Ill., Aug. 3, 1928; d. Frederick Charles Hite-Smith and Rose Cecile (Liebich) Stanton; m. Virgil Vincent Clary, Oct. 17, 1959; children: Rosalie Marian Hawley, Frederick Stanton, Virgil Vincent, Katheleen Elizabeth. BS, Northwestern U., 1950, MA, 1954. Tchr. Chgo. Pub. Schs., 1951-61; faculty Loyola U., Chgo., 1963; v.p. Stanton Enterprises, Inc., Adams County, Miss., 1971-89; timber farmer, trustee, 1975—. Author Family History Record, geneaology record book, Kenilworth, Ill., 1977—. Lectr. Girl Scouts U.S., Winnetka, Ill., 1969-71, 78-86, Cub Scouts, 1972-77; badge counselor Boy Scouts Am., 1978-87; election judge Rep. Com., 1977—; vol. Winnetka Libr. Geneaology Projects Com., 1995—. Mem. Nat. Soc. DAR (Ill. rec. sec. 1979-81, nat. vice chmn. program com. 1980-83, state vice regent 1986-88, state regent 1989-91, rec. sec. gen. 1992-95, state parliamentarian 1999—), Am. Forestry Assn., Forest Farmers Assn., North Suburban Geneal. Soc. (governing bd. 1979-86, 99—, pres. 1997-99), WInnetka Hist. Soc. (governing bd. 1978-90, 95—), Internat. Platform Assn., Delta Gamma (mem. nat. cabinet 1985-89). Roman Catholic. Home: 509 Elder Ln Winnetka IL 60093-4122 Office: PO Box 401 Kenilworth IL 60043-0401

CLASPILL, JAMES LOUIS, finance company executive; b. St. Louis, Dec. 31, 1946; s. Rufus Ira and Alma Elizabeth (Holzum) C.; m. Bonnie Lee Roth, Feb. 13, 1971; 1 child, Jennifer Yvonne. BA in Polit. Sci., S.W. Mo. State U., Springfield, 1968; MBA in Fin., St. Louis U., 1974. Dept. mgr. Venture Stores, St. Louis, 1970-74, J.C. Penny Co., St. Louis, 1974-77; ins. broker, agy. mgr. Aetna Life and Casualty, 1977-82; pres., CEO Claspill Fin. Group, St. Charles, Mo., 1982—; CEO Winterhawk Corp., Channel Islands, 1990—; exec. v.p. Bi-Golden Mfg. Co., 1991—. Cons. Bank of Eng., London, 1986—, Garwick Mortgage Bankers, Sydney, Australia, 1986—, Internat. C. of C., 1986-88; advisor, bus. mgr. United Health Care Workers Greater St. Louis, 1996. Candidate Mo., State Senate, 1978, Dem. candidate 2d dist. Mo. U.S. House of Reps., 1996; campaign organizer Litton for U.S. Senator, 1974; troop leader Boy Scouts Am.; bd. dirs. Am. Diabetes Assn. Sgt. U.S. Army, 1968-70, Vietnam. Recipient Million Dollar Round Table award Nat. Assn. of Life Underwriters, 1979, 80, 81. Mem. VFW, Regional Commerce Growth Assn., Better Bus. Bur., St. Charles C. of C., Nat. Hist. Soc., Internat. Assn. Financiers (v.p. 1985-86), Am. Legion, Lions Club. Roman Catholic. Avocations: fishing, baseball, football, swimming, reading.

CLAUSING, ALICE, state legislator; b. June 7, 1944; BA, U. Wis., Oshkosh. Property mgr.; mem. from dist. 10 Wis. State Senate, Madison, 1992—, mem. child abuse and neglect prevention bd., mem. Minn.-Wis. boundary area com., mem. Miss. River Pkwy. com. Mem. Wis. Assn. of Lakes, John Muir Sierra Club. Office: 1314 Wilson Ave Menomonie WI 54751-2927

CLAUSING, ARTHUR MARVIN, mechanical engineering educator; b. Palatine, Ill., Aug. 17, 1936; s. Arthur Fred and Emma Marie (Opfer) C.; m. Willa Louise Spence, Dec. 19, 1964; children— Erin, Kimberly B.S. in Mech. Engring., Valparaiso U., 1958; M.S. in Mech. Engring., U. Ill., 1960, Ph.D. in Mech. Engring., 1963. Research asst. U. Ill., Urbana, 1962-63, asst. prof., 1963-68, assoc. prof., 1968-84, asst. dean coll. engring., 1982-83, 98—, prof. mech. engring., 1984-98, assoc. head. dept. mech. and indsl. engring., 1987-98, prof. emeritus mech. and indsl. engring., 1998—; cons. Solar Energy Research Inst., 1984-86, M.A.N. Neve Technologie, Munich, Fed. Republic Germany, 1980-87, Ill. Power Co., 1979-81. Author: Numerical Methods in Heat Transfer, 1969; editor Am. Soc. Mech. Engrs. Jour. of Solar Energy Engring., 1984-88; contbr. articles to profl. jours. Recipient Instructional award U. Ill., 1967; Standard Oil award for devel. of heat transfer lab., 1968; Fulbright scholar, 1983; Valparaiso U. Disting. Alumnus award, 1985; ASME fellow, 1997. Mem. ASME, ASHRAE, Am. Soc. Engring. Edn., Internat. Solar Energy Soc. Lutheran. Avocations: running; bicycling; photography; music. Home: 613 Hessel Blvd Champaign IL 61820-6328 Office: Univ Ill Dept Mech Engring Room 152 1206 W Green St Urbana IL 61801-2906

CLAVER, ROBERT EARL, television director, producer; b. Chgo., May 22, 1928; s. Louis E. and Sara M. (Sosna) C.; 1 child, Nancy Beth. BS in Journalism, U. Ill., 1950. Prodr.-writer: first 1000 Captain Kangaroo shows (Sylvania award, Peabody award); prodr., dir.: (TV shows) Here Comes the Brides, 1968-70, The Interns, 1970-71, Partridge Family, 1970-74, Gloria, CBS-TV, 1982-83, Small Wonder, 1985, New Love American Style, 1985, New Leave It to Beaver, 1986-87, Charles in Charge, 1987, Out of This World, 1987-91, numerous other series; dir.: (TV shows) Welcome Back Kotter, ABC-TV, 1977-78, All's Fair, CBS-TV, Housecalls, CBS-TV, 1979-80, Mork and Mindy, ABC-TV, 1981-82. With U.S. Army, 1951-53. Mem. Dirs. Guild Am.

CLAY, CLARENCE SAMUEL, acoustical oceanographer; b. Kansas City, Mo., Nov. 2, 1923; s. Clarence Samuel and Mary Else (Hall) C.; m. Andre Jane Edwards, Mar. 27, 1945; children: Arnold, Jo, David, Michael. BS, Kans. State U., 1947, MS, 1948; PhD in Physics, U. Wis., 1951. Asst. prof. U. Wyo., Laramie, 1950-51; physicist Carter Oil Co., Tulsa, 1951-55; rsch. scientist Columbia U., Dobbs Ferry, N.Y., 1955-67; prof. dept. geol. geophysics U. Wis., Madison, 1967-89, emeritus prof., 1989—. Author: Elementary Exploration Seismology, 1990, (with I. Tolstoy) Ocean Acoustics, 1966, (with H. Medwin) Acoustical Oceanography, 1977, Fundamentals of Acoustical Oceanography, 1997; (with I. Tolstoy) Ocean Acoustics, 1987. Fellow Acoustical Soc. Am. (Silver medal in Acoustical Oceanography, 1993); mem. Sigma Xi. Home: 5033 Saint Cyr Rd Middleton WI 53562-2424 Office: U Wis Weeks Hall 1215 W Dayton St Madison WI 53706-1600

CLAY, ERIC L. judge; b. Durham, N.C., Jan. 18, 1948; BA, U. N.C., 1969; JD, Yale U., 1972. Bar: Mich. 1972, U.S. Dist. Ct. (ea. dist.) Mich. 1972, U.S. Supreme Ct. 1977, U.S. Ct. Appeals (6th cir.) 1978, U.S. Dist. Ct. (we. dist.) Mich. 1987, U.S. Ct. Appeals (DC cir.) 1994. Law clk. to Judge Damon J. Keith U.S. Dist. Ct. (ea. dist.) Mich., 1973—97; shareholder, dir. Lewis, White & Clay, P.C., Detroit, 1997; now judge U.S. Ct. Appeals (6th cir.), 1997—. Fellow John Hay Whitney, Yale U. Mem.: ABA, Wolverine Bar Assn., Detroit Bar Assn., Nat. Assn. Railroad Trial Counsel, Nat. Bar Assn., U.S. Sixth Jud. Conf. (life), Phi Beta Kappa. Office: US Courthouse 231 W LafayetteRm 619 Detroit MI 48226-2700

CLAY, WILLIAM LACY, JR. congressman; b. St. Louis, July 27, 1956; s. William L. and Carol Ann (Johnson) C.; m. Ivie Lewellen, Jan. 24, 1992. BS in Polit. Sci., U. Md., Coll. Park, 1983. Cert. paralegal; lic. real estate salesman, Mo. State senator Mo. Gen. Assembly, Jefferson City, 1983-2000; mem. U.S. Ho. of Reps., 2001—, U.S. Congress from 1st Mo. dist., 2001—; mem. fins svcs. com. and govt. reform com. Chmn. Mo. Jesse Jackson 1988 Presdl. Campaign; Jackson del. to 1988 Dem. Nat. Conv.; committeeman to Dem. Nat. Com.; bd. dirs. William L. Clay Scholarship and Rsch. Fund. Mem. Ams. Dem. Action (Outstanding Legis. Mo. chpt. 1985, 86). Roman Catholic. Office: US Ho of Reps 415 Cannon HOB Washington DC 20515

CLAY, WILLIAM LACY, former congressman; b. St. Louis, Apr. 30, 1931; s. Irving C. and Luella (Hyatt) C.; m. Carol A. Johnson, Oct. 10, 1953; children: Vicki, Lacy, Michelle. B.S. in Polit. Sci, St. Louis U., 1953. Real estate broker, from 1964; mgr. life ins. co., 1959-61; alderman 26th Ward, St. Louis, 1959-64; bus. rep. state, county and municipal employees union, 1961-64; edn. coord. Steamfitters local 562, 1966-67; mem. U.S. Congress from 1st. Mo. dist., Washington, 1969-2001; former ranking minority mem. edn. and the workforce. Served with AUS, 1953-55. Mem. NAACP (past exec. bd. mem. St. Louis), CORE, St. Louis Jr. C. of C. Democrat.*

CLAYBORNE, JAMES F., JR. state legislator; b. St. Louis, Dec. 29, 1963; Sen. from dist. 37 Ill. State Senate, 1995—. Office: First Ill Bank Bldg 327 Missouri Ave # 422 East Saint Louis IL 62201-3088

CLAYBURGH, RICHARD SCOTT, state tax commissioner; m. Jane Clayburgh; 2 children. BA, Concordia Coll., Moorhead, Minn., 1982; MBA, U. N.D., 1990, JD, 1994. Bar: N.D. 1994, Minn. 1994. Atty.; state rep. dist. 17, 1989-96; atty. Warcup & Clayburgh, Grand Forks, 1994-96; state tax commr. State of N.D., Bismarck, 1997—. Sec. N.D. State Bd. Equalization; pub. mem. Nat. Bd. for Cert. of Orthopaedic Technologists. Past bd. dirs. Spl. Olympics, past chmn. State Summer Games. Mem. Fedn. Tax Adminstrs. (trustee), Minn. Bar Assn., N.D. Bar Assn. (info. and svc. com.), Nat. Fedn. Ind. Bus., N.D. Industrial Devel. Assn., Sons of Norway, Bismarck-Mandan C. of C., Rotary, Elks. Republican. Home: 601 Augsburg Ave Bismarck ND 58504-7008 Office: State Capitol 600 E Boulevard Ave Bismarck ND 58505-0599

CLAYPOOL, DAVID L. lawyer; b. Springfield, Ill., 1946; BA in History, Ill. Coll., 1968; JD with high distinction, U. Iowa, 1975. Bar: Iowa 1975. Ptnr. Dorsey & Whitney, LLP, Des Moines. Editor notes and comments Iowa Law Review, 1974-75. Capt. U.S. Army, 1968-72 Mem. Iowa State Bar Assn., Pol County Bar Assn., Nat. Assn. Bond Lawyers, Iowa Mcpl. Attys. Assn., Order of Coif. Office: Dorsey & Whitney LLP 801 Grand Ave Ste 3900 Des Moines IA 50309-2790 E-mail: claypool.david@dorseylaw.com.

CLAYTON, JOHN ANTHONY, radio broadcast executive; b. St. Louis, Dec. 3, 1958; s. James Dale and Sharon Lee (Sack) C.; m. Lynn Marie Staley, Oct. 24, 1992. BA in Bus. Adminstrn., BA in German and Radio TV, Film, U. Mo., 1981. Radio announcer KHMO, Hannibal, MO, 1981-82; prodn. dir. KSIV, St. Louis, 1982-83; news dir. KPCQ-FM, Powell/Cody, Wyo., 1983-84; ops. mgr./interim gen. mgr. KVOK-KJJZ-FM, Kodiak, Alaska, 1984-85; asst. program dir. KFUO-FM Classic 99, St. Louis, 1985—. Author critical rev. St. Louis Guitar Soc. Newsletter, 1990—. Bd. mem. Alaska Visitors Assn., Kodiak br., 1984-85; bd. mem. Guitar Found. Am., St. Louis Consortium, 1996. Avocations: guitar study, golf, fishing, woodworking, wine. Office: Classic 99 KFUO-FM 85 Founders Ln Saint Louis MO 63105-3059

CLAYTON, ROBERT MORRISON, III, state legislator; b. Hannibal, Mo., Aug. 20, 1969; s. Robert M. II and Frances (Price) C. BA, So. Meth. U., 1991; JD, U. Mo., Kansas City, 1994. Ptnr. Clayton & Curl LLC, Hannibal, 1994—; mem. Mo. Ho. of Reps. from 10th dist., 1995—; mem. exec. com. So. Legisl. Conf. and Coun. State Govts. Sr. articles editor: The Urban Lawyer, 1993. Mem. Historic Bethel German Colony, Hannibal Arts Coun. Recipient Pres.'s award Kansas City Met. Bar Assn, 1994. Mem. Mo. Bar Assn., Hannibal C. of C., Jaycees, Delta Theta Phi. Democrat. Office: Robert M Clayton III PO Box 1032 Hannibal MO 63401-1032

CLAYTON, VERNA LEWIS, retired state legislator; b. Hamden, Ohio, Feb. 28, 1937; d. Matthews L. and Yail (Miller) Lewis; m. Frank R. Clayton, Feb. 4, 1956; children: children: Valerie S., Barry L. Office mgr. Village of Buffalo Grove, Ill., 1972-78, village clk., 1971-79, village pres., 1979-91; mem. Ill. Ho. of Reps., Springfield, 1993-99. Bd. dirs. Savannah Lakes Property Owners Assn., 2000. Mem. Lake County Solid Waste Planning Agy., chmn. tech. com., chmn. agy., Nat. League of Cities, chmn. transp. and comms. steering com. Recipient Disting. Svc. award Amvets, 1981; named Libr. Legislator of the Yr. 1997. Mem. N.W. Mcpl. Conf. (pres. 1983-84), Chgo. Area Transp. Study Coun. Mayors (vice chmn. 1981-83, chmn. 1985-91), Mcpl. Clks. Ill. (treas. 1978-79), Mcpl. Clks. Lake County (pres. 1977-78), Ill. Mcpl. League (bd. dirs., v.p. 1985-90, pres. 1989-90), Buffalo Grove Rotary Club (hon. mem.), Buffalo Grove C. of C. (bd. dirs.). Republican. Methodist. Home: 11 Overlook Dr Mc Cormick SC 29835-2850 E-mail: frclayton9@wctel.net.

CLEAR, JOHN MICHAEL, lawyer; b. St. Louis, Dec. 16, 1948; s. Raymond H. and Marian (Clark) Clear; m. Isabel Marie Bone, May 10, 1980; 1 child Thomas Henry. BA summa cum laude, Washington U., St. Louis, 1971; JD with honors, U. Chgo., 1974. Bar: Mo. 1974, D.C. 1975, U.S. Ct. Appeals (5th and D.C. cirs.) 1975, U.S. Supreme Ct. 1977, U.S. Ct. Appeals (3d cir.) 1978, U.S. Ct. Appeals (8th cir.) 1980, U.S. Ct. Appeals (9th cir.) 1990, U.S. Dist. Ct. (so. dist.) Ill. 1995, U.S. Ct. Appeals (7th cir.) 1997. Law clk. to judge U.S. Ct. Appeals (5th cir.), Atlanta, 1974-75; assoc. Covington & Burling, Washington, 1975-80; jr. ptnr. Bryan, Cave, McPheeters & McRoberts, St. Louis, 1980-81, ptnr., 1982—. Mem. ABA, Mo. Bar Assn., D.C. Bar Assn., St. Louis Met. Bar Assn., Am. Law Inst., Order of Coif., Racquet Club, Noonday Club, Fox Run Golf Club, Phi Beta Kappa. Office: Bryan Cave LLP One Metropolitan Sq Saint Louis MO 63102-2750 E-mail: jmclear@bryancave.com.

CLEARY, JOHN WASHINGTON, lawyer; b. Milw., Feb. 22, 1911; s. Peter A. and Mathilda A. (Borning) C.; m. Alice M. Shinners, Jan. 15, 1938; children: Terrence P., Mary E., Peter J., Margaret A., John T., Catherine A. J.D., Marquette U., 1933. Bar: Wis. 1933. Since practiced in Milw.; partner Erbstoeszer, Cleary & Misey, 1936-82, Fiorenza & Hayes, 1982—. Sec. Hopkins Savs. & Loan Assn., Milw., 1936-65, pres., 1965—; faculty Savs. and Loan Inst., Milw., 1961-63 Vice chmn. Milw. Commn. Community Relations, 1959-63; savs. and loan commr., Wis., 1963-65; mem. pres.'s senate Marquette U., 1977— ; bd. dirs. Greater Milw. chpt. ARC, pres., 1961-63; trustee Marquette U. High Sch.; gov. nat. ARC. Mem. Wis. Legis. Council, Milw. Savs. and Loan Council (pres. 1948-50), Wis. Savs. and Loan League (pres. 1954-55), U.S. Savs. and Loan League (dir. 1962-63) Home: 2728 N 98th St Milwaukee WI 53222-4513 Office: 7901 W Burleigh St Milwaukee WI 53222-4916

CLEARY, MARTIN JOSEPH, real estate company executive; b. N.Y.C., July 27, 1935; s. Patrick Joseph and Kathleen Theresa (Costello) C.; m. Peggy Elizabeth McIntyre, June 22, 1957; children: Patrick Francis, Eileen Ann, Michael Thomas, Kathleen Marie, Maureen Elizabeth. B.S., Fordham U., 1960; M.B.A., N.Y. U., 1963. With Tchrs. Ins. and Annuity Assn. and Coll. Retirement Equities Fund, N.Y.C., 1953-81; pres. Richard E. Jacobs

Group, Westlake, Ohio, 1981—2001, ret., 2001. Bd. dirs. Guardian Life Ins. Co., Lamson & Sessions, CBL & Assocs. Mem. Internat. Coun. Shopping Ctrs. (trustee 1980—, pres. 1983-84). Office: 619 Ocean Ave Sea Girt NJ 08750

CLEARY, MICHAEL J. educational administrator; Exec. dir. Nat. Assn. Collegiate Dirs. Athletics. Office: NACDA PO Box 16428 Cleveland OH 44116-0428

CLEASBY, JOHN LEROY, civil engineer, educator; b. Madison, Wis., Mar. 1, 1928; s. Clarence Allen and Othelia Amanda (Swanson) C.; m. Donna Jean Haugh, Sept. 2, 1950; children: Teresa, Richard, Lynne. B.S., U. Wis., 1950, M.S., 1951; Ph.D., Iowa State U., 1960. Diplomate: Am. Acad. Environ. Engrs.; registered profl. engr., Iowa. Inspection engr. Standard Oil Co. Ind., Whiting, 1951—52; project engr. Consoer Townsend & Assocs., Chgo., 1952—54; instr. Iowa State U., Ames, 1954—56, asst. prof., 1956—61, assoc. prof., 1961—83, prof., 1983—93, disting. prof. emeritus, 1994—. Vis. prof. Univ. Coll. London, 1975-76; cons. World Bank, Washington, Pan Am. Health Orgn., WHO, U. Sao Paulo Co-author: Water Supply Engineering, 1962; contbr. articles to profl. jours. Served with USN, 1945-46. Recipient Outstanding Tchr. award, Iowa State U., 1977, David R. Boylan Eminent Faculty award for rsch., 1989. Mem. ASCE (sec. Environ. Engring. divsn. 1969-73, pres. Iowa sect. 1966, Hering medal 1968, 70, 83, Norman medal 1980), NAE (life.), Am. Water Works Assn. (trustee Water Quality divsn. 1981-87, chmn. 1985, chmn. Iowa sect. 1982, hon., Publs. awards 1962, 80, Divsn. Best Paper awards 1970, 92, 95, Rsch. award 1982, Abel Wolman award 1997), Kiwanis. Am. Baptist. Home: 4805 Dover Dr Ames IA 50014-4586 Office: Iowa State U 487 Town Engring Ames IA 50011-0001

CLEAVER, EMANUEL, II, former mayor, minister; b. Waxahachie, Tex., Oct. 26, 1944; s. Lucky and Marie (McKnight) Cl; m. Dianne Donaldson, June 1970; children: Evan Donaldson, Emanuel III and Emiel Davenport (twins), Marissa Dianne. BA, Prairie View (Tex.) A&M Coll.; ThM, St. Paul Sch. Theology, Kansas City, Mo.; DD (hon.), Baker U., 1988. Ordained to ministry United Meth. Ch. Pastor St. James-Paseo United Meth. Ch.; mayor pro-tem City of Kansas City, 1987-91, mayor, 1991-98. Lectr. to chs., schs., civic and social orgns. nationwide. Councilman Fifth Dist. City, 1979-91; chmn. City Coun. Plans and Zoning Com., 1984-87, Policy and Rules Com., 1987-91; mid-cen. regional v.p. So. Christian Leadership Conf., Drum Major for Justice award, 1991; founder, co-chair Kansas City Harmony In A World of Difference. Recipient Centurions Leadership award Greater Kansas City C. of C., 1987, William Yates Disting. Svc. Medallion William Jewel Coll., 1987, Pub. Svc. award Am.-Jewish Com., 1991, Junteenth Man of Yr. award Black Archives of Mid-Am. Inc., 1991, Disting. Citizen award Greater Kansas City Urban Affairs Coun., 1991, Community Svc./Leadership award Webster U., 1991, Disting. Svc. award Park Coll., 1991, Drum Major of Justice award Nat. SCLC, 1991, Friend of Youth award Boys & Girls Clubs, 1991, Outstanding Contbns. to Black Cmty. award Concerned Citizens Black Clergy of Atlanta, 1991, Rainbow award, 1992, 100 Most Influential Kansas Citians award Kansas City Globe, 1991, 92, 93, Bridge Builders award Kansas City Globem 1992, Harold L. Holiday Sr. Civil Rights award NAACP, 1992, Disting. Grad. award St. Paul Sch. Theology, 1993, Kansas City Anti-Apartheid award, 1993, James C. Kirkpatrick Excellence for Govt. award, 1993, Disting. Citizen of Midwest award NCCJ, 1993, Gov. award for local elected ofcl. of yr. State of Mo., 1994. Mem. NAACP, Greater Kansas City C. of C. (Centurions Leadership award 1987), Alpha Phi Alpha. Founder and co-chmn., Harmony In A World of Difference program.

CLEGG, KAREN KOHLER, lawyer; b. Junction City, Kans., Jan. 7, 1949; d. John Emil and Delores Maxine (Letkeman) Kohler; m. Stephen J. Clegg Jr., Mar. 28, 1970. BS, Emporia State U., 1970; JD, U. Kans., 1975; MBA, Rockhurst Coll., 1989. Bar: Kans. 1975, U.S. Dist. Ct. Kans. 1975, Mo. 1977, U.S. Dist. Ct. (we. dist.) Mo. 1977. Asst. atty. gen. State of Kans., Topeka, 1975-77; atty. The Bendix Corp., Kansas City, Mo., 1977-81, sr. atty., 1981-84; counsel Allied Corp. (now Allied Signal, Inc.), 1984-90, v.p. adminstrn., 1990—; pres. Honeywell Fed. Mfg. and Technologies Honeywell Internat., 1999—. Mem. council human resources mgmt. adv. bd. Commerce Clearing House, Chgo., 1985-88. Sec. Assn. Greater Devel. Coll. Blvd., Shawnee Mission, Kans., 1986-87; bd. dirs. adv. council Avila Coll. Bus., Kansas City, 1984—, Dimension's Unltd., Kansas City, 1985-86. Mem. ABA, Mo. Bar Assn., Am. Soc. Personnel Adminstrn. (v.p., bd. dirs. EEO 1985, profl. services 1986-87), Greater Kansas City C. of C. (centurian leadership program). Avocations: music, theatre, art, reading, travel. Office: Honeywell 2000 E 95th St Kansas City MO 64131-3030 Home: 6909 Burnt Sienna Cir Naples FL 34109-7828

CLELAND, ROBERT HARDY, federal judge; b. 1947; BA, Mich. State U., 1969; JD, U. N.C., 1972. Pvt. practice, Port Huron, Mich., 1972-75; chief trial atty. County Prosecuting Atty.'s. Office, 1975-80; prosecuting atty. St. Clair County, 1981-90; judge U.S. Dist. Ct. (ea. dist.) Mich., Detroit, 1990—. Positions with Port Huron Hosp., 1989-91, United Way of St. Clair County, 1988-90, Civic Theater of Port Huron, Blue Water YMCA, First Congl. Ch. of Port Huron, MADD, St. Clair Rep. Party. Mem. ABA, Mich. Bar Assn., St. Clair County Bar Assn., Prosecuting Atty's. Assn. Mich. (pres. 1988-89). Office: US Dist Ct Theodore Levin US Courthous 231 W Lafayette Blvd Rm 707 Detroit MI 48226-2775

CLELAND, W(ILLIAM) WALLACE, biochemistry educator; b. Balt., Jan. 6, 1930; s. Ralph E. and Elizabeth P. (Shoyer) C.; m. Joan K. Hookanson, June 18, 1967 (div. Mar. 1999); children: Elsa Eleanor, Erica Elizabeth. A.B. summa cum laude, Oberlin Coll., 1950; M.S., U. Wis., 1953, Ph.D., 1955. Postdoctoral fellow U. Chgo., 1957-59; asst. prof. U. Wis., Madison, 1959-62, assoc. prof., 1962-66, prof., 1966—, M.J. Johnson prof. biochemistry, 1978—, Steenbock prof. chem. sci., 1982—2002. Contbr. articles to profl. biochem. and chem. jours. Served with U.S. Army, 1957-59. Grantee NIH, 1960—, NSF, 1960-94; recipient Stein and Moore award Protein Soc., 1999. Mem. NAS, Am. Acad. Arts and Scis., Am. Soc. Biochemistry and Molecular Biology (Merck award 1990), Am. Chem. Soc. (Alfred R. Bader Bioinorganic or Bioorganic Chem. award 1993, Repligen award 1995). Achievements include development of dithiothreitol (Cleland's Reagent) as reducing agent for thiol groups; development of application of kinetic methods for determining enzyme mechanism. Office: Enzyme Inst 1710 University Ave Madison WI 53726-4087 E-mail: cleland@biochem.wisc.edu.

CLEM, ALAN LELAND, political scientist, educator; b. Lincoln, Nebr., Mar. 4, 1929; s. Remey Leland and Bernice (Thompson) C.; m. Mary Louise Burke, Oct. 24, 1953; children: Andrew, Christopher, Constance, John, Daniel. BA, U. Nebr., 1950; MA, Am. U., 1957, PhD, 1960. Copywriter, research dir. Ayres Advt. Agy., Lincoln, 1950-52; press sec. to Congressman Carl Curtis of Nebr., 1953-54, Congressman R. D. Harrison of Nebr., 1955-58; info. specialist Fgn. Agrl. Service, Dept. Agr., 1959-60; asst. prof. polit. sci. U. S.D., Vermillion, 1960-62, assoc. prof., 1962-64, prof., 1965—; assoc. dir. Govtl. Research Bur., 1962-76, chmn. dept. polit. sci., 1976-78; ptnr. Opinion Survey Assocs., 1964-88. State analyst Comparative State Elections Project, U. N.C., 1968-73; dir. Mt. Rushmore Presdl. Inst., 1970-71; mem. U.S. Census Bur. Adv. Com. on State and Local Govt. Stats., 1970-74 Author: several books, including Prairie State Politics: Popular Democracy in South Dakota, 1967, The Making of Congressmen: Seven Campaigns of 1974, 1976, American Electoral Politics: Strategies for Renewal, 1981, Law Enforcement: The South Dakota Experience, 1982, The Government We Deserve, 1985, 5th edit., 1995, Congress: Powers, Processes and Politics, 1989, Government by the People? South Dakota Politics in the Last Third of the 20th Century, 2001; contbr. articles to profl. jours.; editor: Contemporary Approaches to State Constitutional Revision, 1969. Mem. Vermillion City Coun., 1965-69; sr. warden St. Paul's Episcopal Ch., Vermillion, 1971-73, treas., 1996—. Named Outstanding Alumnus, U. Nebr. Coll. Arts and Scis., 1998; Nat. Conv. faculty fellow, 1964 Mem. Mensa, Midwest Polit. Sci. Assn. (exec. council 1970-72, editorial bd. Am. Jour. Polit. Sci. 1971-72), Am. Polit. Sci. Assn., Phi Beta Kappa, Phi Alpha Theta, Pi Sigma Alpha (nat. coun. 1986-89), Sigma Delta Chi. Republican. Club: Vermillion Golf Assn. (pres. 1986-87). Home: 608 Colonial Ct Vermillion SD 57069-3424 Office: U SD Dept Polit Sci Vermillion SD 57069

CLEM, JOHN RICHARD, physicist, educator; b. Waukegan, Ill., Apr. 24, 1938; s. Gilbert D. and Bernelda May (Moyer) C.; m. Judith Ann Paulsen, Aug. 27, 1960; children: Paul Gilbert, Jean Ann BS, . Ill., 1960; MS, U. Ill., 1962, PhD, 1965. Rsch. assoc. U. Md., College Park, 1965-66; vis. rsch. fellow Tech. U., Munich, Ger., 1966-67; asst. prof. physics Iowa State U., Ames, 1967-70, assoc. prof., 1970-75, prof. physics, 1975—, chmn. dept. physics, 1982-85, disting. prof. in liberal arts and scis., 1989—. Vis. staff mem. Los Alamos Nat. Lab., 1971-83; cons. Argonne Nat. Lab., Ill., 1971-76, Oak Ridge (Tenn.) Nat. Lab., 1981, Brookhaven Nat. Lab., Upton, N.Y., 1980-81, Allied-Signal, Torrance, Calif., 1990-92, Am. Superconductor Corp., Westborough, Mass., 1996-97,, Pirelli Cable Corp., Lexington, S.C., 1996-97, Los Alamos Nat. Lab., 1997-2001; guest prof. U. Tuebingen, Fed. Republic Germany, 1978; cons. IBM Watson Rsch. Ctr., Yorktown Hts., N.Y., 1982-85, vis. scientist, 1985-86; vis. scientist Electric Power Rsch. Inst., Palo Alto, Calif., 1992-93; vis. prof. applied physics Stanford U., 1992-93. Sci. editor newsletter High-Tc Update; contbr. articles to profl. jours.; patentee in field Recipient award for sustained outstanding rsch. in solid state physics, U.S. Dept. Energy; Fulbright sr. rsch. fellow, 1974-75; NATO grantee, 1979-82 Fellow Am. Phys. Soc. (chair divsn. condensed matter physics 1994-95); mem. AAUP, Iowa Acad. Sci., Sigma Xi, Tau Beta Pi, Phi Kappa Phi. Democrat. Presbyterian Avocation: singing. Home: 2307 Timberland Rd Ames IA 50014-8251 Office: Iowa State Univ A517 Physics Ames IA 50011-3160 E-mail: clem@ameslab.gov.

CLEMENCE, ROGER DAVIDSON, landscape architect, educator; b. Worcester, Mass., Jan. 20, 1936; s. Luther Davidson and Dorothy (Kay) C.; m. Margaret Ann Weinandy, Aug. 19, 1961; children: Peter, Benjamin, Ellsabeth. AB, Amherst Coll., 1957, MArch, U. Pa., 1960, M in Landscape Architecture, 1962. Registered landscape architect, Minn. Instr., asst. prof. Coll. Architecture and Design U. Mich., Ann Arbor, 1962-66; assoc. prof. Sch. Architecture and Landscape Architecture U. Minn., Mpls., 1966-73, dir. Urban Edn. Ctr., Sch. Architecture and Landscape Architecture, 1970-77, interim head Sch. Architecture and Landscape Architecture, 1984, mem. urban studies faculty Coll. Liberal Arts, 1973—, mem. Am. studies faculty Coll. Liberal Arts, 1986—, dir. grad. studies in architecture Sch. Architecture and Landscape Architecture, 1978-85, prof. dept. architecture, 1973, assoc. dean Coll. of Architecture and Landscape Architecture, 1989-95, acting dean, spring 1993, interim dean, 1995-96. Landscape arch., planner, Mpls., 1963; collegiate program leader Minn. Ext. Svc., 1993-97, prof. emeritus, summer 1997. Co-creator 10-part TV series The Meanings of Place, 1986. Mem. Minn. Com. on Urban Environment, 1979-88, Designer Selection Bd., 1980-85, chmn., 1983-84; mem. Mpls. Fed. Cts. Master Plan Com., 1991-92. Recipient Morse-Alumni Disting. Tchg. award, 1974, Pub. Svc. award Minn. Soc. Landscape Architects, 1982, Lob Pine award, 1996, CALA Disting. Svc. award, 1995; T.P. Chandler fellow U. Pa. Grad. Sch. Fine Arts, 1960-62; HWS Cleveland Vis. scholar U. Minn., 2000-01. Fellow Am. Soc. Landscape Architects; mem. AIA (prof. affiliate Minn. chapt. 1979), MASLA, Tau Sigma Delta. Democrat. Mem. Unitarian Universalist Assn. Avocations: photography, writing, golf, reading, gardening. Office: U Minn CALA 89 Church St SE Minneapolis MN 55455-0109

CLEMENS, DEB FISCHER, state legislator, nursing administrator; DON; mem. S.D. Ho. of Reps., Pierre, 1995—, mem. health and human svcs., local govt. coms., 1995—. Democrat. Office: Queen of Peace Hosp 525 N Foster St Mitchell SD 57301-2999

CLEMENS, RICHARD GLENN, lawyer; b. Chgo., Oct. 8, 1940; s. James Ralston and Jeanette Louise (Moellering) C.; m. Judith B. Clemens, Aug. 19, 1967; 1 child, Kathleen. BA, U. Va., 1962, JD, 1965. Bar: Ill. 1965. Assoc. Sidley Austin Brown & Wood, Chgo., 1965—66, Washington, 1968—71, Brussels, 1972—73, ptnr. Chgo., 1973—. Served to capt. U.S. Army, 1966-68. Mem. ABA, Chgo. Bar Assn., Lawyers Club, Mid-Day Club. Office: Sidley Austin Brown & Wood Apt 605 425 W Surf St Chicago IL 60657-6139 E-mail: rclemens@sidley.com.

CLEMENS, T. PAT, manufacturing company executive; b. Hibbing, Minn., July 26, 1944; s. Jack LeRoy and Mildred (Coss) C.; m. 1966 (div. 1992); children: Patrick Michael, Heather Kristen. BS in Econs. and Mgmt., St. Cloud State U., 1968; student of theology, Coll. St. Thomas, 1985-87. Sales adminstr. Transistor Electronics Co., Eden Prarie, Minn., 1969; head instnl. sales Chiquita Brands, Edina, 1970; dist. sales mgr. Menley & James Labs., Phila., 1971-75; owner, pres. T.P. Clemens Labs., Eagan, Minn., 1975—. Instr community edn. Rosemount, Minn., 1977-78; bd. dirs. Rosemount Hockey, 1977-78, Relocation Assistance Assn. Am., 1984-85; v.p. Sch. Dist. #196 Booster Club, 1984-85; lectr. econs. to corps., high schs. and colls. in U.S., Scotland, Ireland, and Jamaica, 1979—. Author, editor: How Prejudice and Narcissism Control Economics of the United States and the World, 1979. Mem. Rosemont Cmty. Edn. Bd., 1985, chmn., 1986-87; chmn. speakers bur. Citizens Steering Com., 1984-85; coach Little League, 1970-82, 88-91; coach high sch. weight lifting team, 1975-95; vol. worker with comatose children, 1975-96, 97—. Recipient letter of recognition for stopping armed robbery Dakota County Atty.'s Dept., 1979, 93. Mem. Internat. Platform Assn., Kids-N-Kinship Program 1988-92. Home and Office: 1276 Vildmark Dr Eagan MN 55123-2801

CLEMENT, DANIEL ROY, IV, accountant, assistant nurse, small business owner; b. Kirtland, Ohio, Apr. 2, 1943; s. Roy A. Jr. and Evelyn Violet (Hale Chase) C.; m. Jennifer Ilean Handley, July 10, 1965 (div. 1975); children: Elizabeth Ann Clement Baitt, Catherine Lynn Clement Holder; m. Barbara Jane Griffiths, Dec. 10, 1985. Student, Fenn Coll., 1961-63, Alexander Hamilton Inst., 1963-67, Am. Inst. of Banking, 1963-65, Lakeland Coll., 1965-70, Case Western Res. U., 1970-73, Lake Erie Coll., 1973-85; PhD, Case Western Res. U., 1999. Shipping and cost acctg. Mentor (Ohio) Products, 1961; acctg. asst. N.Y. Cen. Transport, Cleve., 1963-65; acct. mgr. Am. Soc. of Metals, Novelty, Ohio, 1965-67; corp. fleet mgr. Addressograph Multigraph, Euclid, 1967-72; treas. Debevec Salo & Assocs., Painesville, 1972-74; with sales Pontiac Cadillac-Record Shack, Mentor, 1974-78; shipping coord. Ajax Mfg., Euclid, 1978-82. Notary pub. Active Jr. C. of C., Mentor, Willoughby, Brunswick, Novelty, Lake County, 1962-78; mem. Congl. Task Force Pres. Bush, 1981-94. Republican. Methodist. Avocations: gardening, dogs, cats, tropical fish. Office: 344 N Saint Clair St Painesville OH 44077-4039 Home: 258 North St Chagrin Falls OH 44022

CLEMENT, HENRY JOSEPH, JR. diversified building products executive; b. New Orleans, May 14, 1942; s. Henry Joseph Sr. and Margaret (Dowd) C.; m. Kathleen Erin Shean; children: Colleen and Collette (twins). BS, Loyola U., 1973. Sales rep. GE, New Orleans, 1972-77, mgr. product planning Louisville, 1977-79, mgr. internat. market Tyler, Tex., 1979-83; v.p. internat. sales Phillips Industries, Inc., Dayton, Ohio, 1983-84, pres. internat. div., 1984-88; pres. internat. group Tomkins Industries, 1988-94; pres. Crescent Group, Inc., Dublin, 1994—. Vice chmn., bd. dirs. Shaanxi-Hytec, Ltd., Xian, Chila, 1988-89. Loan exec. United Way, New Orleans, 1974, Tyler, 1979. Mem. Miami Valley (Ohio) Internat. Trade Assn. (trustee), Blue Key (Cross Key Svc. award 1973). Republican. Roman Catholic. Home: 4666 Chatham Ct Dublin OH 43017-8607

CLEMENTS, DONALD M. utilities executive; With Am. Electric Power Co. Inc., Columbus, Ohio, 1994-98, pres. comms., resources, 1998—. Pres. Am. Electric Power Resourced Svc. Co., 1998—. Office: Am Electric Power Co Inc 1 Riverside Plz Columbus OH 43215-2355

CLEMONS, JOHN ROBERT, lawyer; b. Oak Park, Ill., June 9, 1948; BA, U. Iowa, 1970; JD, DePaul U., 1975. Asst. village mgr. Village of Riverside, Ill., 1970-72; co-dir. dist. 208 Youth Ctr., Riverside, 1970-73; area dir. S.W. area Cook County OEO, 1972-73; clk., legal researcher Klein, Thorpe & Jenkins, attys., Chgo., 1974-75; asst. state atty.'s Jackson County, Murphysboro, 1975-80, state's atty., 1980-88; asst. prof. So. Ill. U., Carbondale, 1977-79, lectr., 1987—; ptnr. Clemens & Hood, 1991—. Home: 375 Mount Joy Rd Murphysboro IL 62966-4464 Office: 813 W Main St Carbondale IL 62901-2537

CLEVELAND, CLYDE, city official; b. Detroit, May 22, 1935; m. Mary; 1 child. Student, Wayne State U. Pub. aid worker City of Detroit, 1958, 60-64; supervisor cmty. svc. Mayor's Com. Human Resources Devel., Detroit, 1965-68; cmty. planner Inner City Bus. Improvement Forum, 1968-71; city councilman City of Detroit, 1974—. Del. Dem. Nat. Conv., 1980; former vice chair Mich. State Dem. Party; co-campaign mgr. Jesse Jackson Victory in Mich., 1988; vice chair Southeastern Mich. Coun. Govts.; cmty. orgn. specialist New Detroit, Inc., 1971-73. Served in U.S. Army, Korea. Mem. NAACP, Elks, People's Cmty. & Civic League, Assn. Study Negro Life & History, Booker T. Washington Bus. Assn., Shriners, Masons. Baptist. Office: Coleman A Young Mcpl Ctr 2 Woodward Ave Detroit MI 48226-3437

CLEVERT, CHARLES NELSON, JR. federal judge; b. Richmond, Va., Oct. 11, 1947; s. Charles Nelson and Ruby Clevert. BA, Davis and Elkins Coll., 1969; JD, Georgetown U., 1972. Bar: Wis. 1972, U.S. Dist. Ct. (ea. dist.) Wis. 1974, U.S. Ct. Appeals (7th cir.) 1975. Adminstrv. aide D.C. Dept. Corrections, 1970-71; law clk. Law Enforcement Assistance Adminstrn., Washington, 1972; asst. dist. atty. for Milw. County (Wis.), Milw., 1972-75; asst. U.S. atty. Eastern Dist. Wis., Dept. Justice, Milw., 1975-77; spl. asst. U.S. atty. No. Dist. Ill., Chgo., 1977; chief judge U.S. Bankruptcy Ct. Eastern Dist. Wis., Milw., 1977—; lectr. law sch. U. Wis., 1987-89; judge Nat. Moot Ct. Competition; judge trial practice Marquette U. Bd. dirs. Milw. Council on Alcoholism and Drug Dependence, 1982-94, Local Edn. Agy., Inc., Milw., 1975, Milw. Forum, 1981-83; v.p. Milw. Club Frontiers Internat., 1981; mem. budget com. of the Jud. Conf. of the U.S. and Bankruptcy; mem. judges adv. com. Adminstrv. Office U.S. Cts. Fellow Am. Coll. Bankruptcy; mem. ABA (mem. exec. bd. nat. conf. fed. trial judges), Am. Judicature Soc. (bd. dirs.), Am. Bankruptcy Inst. (bd. dirs.), Nat. Conf. Bankruptcy Judges (pres. 1989-90, chair endowment edn.), Nat. Bar Assn. (jud. council), Milw. Bar Assn., Wis. Assn. of Minority Attys., 7th Cir. Bar Assn., Thomas E. Fairchild Am. Inn Ct. (pres.), Alpha Phi Alpha, Alpha Sigma Phi. Mem. African Methodist Episcopal Ch. Office: Rm 208 US Courthouse 517 E Wisconsin Ave Milwaukee WI 53202-4500

CLIFF, JOHNNIE MARIE, mathematics and chemistry educator; b. Lamkin, Miss., May 10, 1935; d. John and Modest Alma (Lewis) Walton; m. William Henry Cliff, Apr. 1, 1961 (dec. 1983); 1 child, Karen Marie. BA in Chemistry, Math., U. Indpls., 1956; postgrad., NSF Inst., Butler U., 1960; MA in Chemistry, Ind. U., 1964; MS in Math., U. Notre Dame, 1980; postgrad., Martin U., 2000. Cert. tchr., Ind. Rsch. chemist Ind. U. Med. Ctr., Indpls., 1956-59; tchr. sci. and math. Indpls. Pub. Schs., 1960-88; tchr. chemistry, math. Martin U., Indpls., 1989—, chmn. math. dept., 1990—, divsn. chmn. depts. sci. and math., 1993—. Adj. instr. math. U. Indpls., 1991. Contbr. rsch. papers to sci. jours. Grantee NSF, 1961-64, 73-76, 78-79, Woodrow Wilson Found., 1987-88; scholarship U. Indpls., 1952-56, NSF Inst. Reed Coll., 1961, C. of C., 1963. Mem. AAUW, NAACP, NEA, Assn. Women in Sci., Urban League, N.Y. Acad. Scis., Am. Chem. Soc., Nat. Coun. Math. Tchrs., Am. Assn. Physics Tchrs., Nat. Sci. Tchrs. Assn., Am. Statis. Assn., Am. Assn. Ret. Persons, Neal-Marshall-Ind. U. Alumni Assn., U. Indpls. Alumni Assn., U. Notre Dame Alumni Assn., Ind. U. Chemist Assn., Notre Dame Club Indpls., Kappa Delta Pi, Delta Sigma Theta. Democrat. Baptist. Avocations: gardening, sewing. Home: 405 Golf Ln Indianapolis IN 46260-4108 Office: Martin U 2171 Avondale Pl Indianapolis IN 46218-3878

CLIFTON, DOUGLAS C. newspaper editor; b. Bklyn., July 14, 1943; s. Norman Stanton and Anne Frances (Montesano) C.; m. Margaret E. Clifton, Dec. 18, 1965; children: Amy Elizabeth Clifton Gallup, Clay Norman. BA Polit. Sci., Dowling Coll., 1965. Reporter, editor Miami Herald, 1970-87; news editor Knight Ridder, Washington, 1987-89; mng. editor Charlotte (N.C.) Observer, 1989-91; sr. v.p., exec. editor Miami Herald, 1991-99; exec. editor Plain Dealer, Cleve., 1999—. Lt. U.S. Army, 1966-69, Vietnam. Home: 19 Shoreby Dr Bratenahl OH 44108-1161 Office: Plain Dealer 1801 Superior Ave E Cleveland OH 44114-2198

CLIFTON, JAMES ALBERT, physician, educator; b. Fayetteville, N.C., Sept. 18, 1923; s. James Albert Jr. and Flora M. (McNair) Clifton; m. Katherine Rathe, June 25, 1949; children: Susan M.(dec.) , Katherine Y., Caroline M. BA, Vanderbilt U., 1944, MD, 1947. Diplomate Am. Bd. Internal Medicine (mem. 1972-81, mem. subsplty. bd. gastroenterology 1968-75, chmn. 1972-75, mem. exec. com. 1978-81, chmn. 1980-81). Intern U. Hosps., Iowa City, 1947—48, resident dept. medicine, 1948—51; staff dept. medicine Thayer VA Hosp., Nashville, 1952—53; asst. clin. medicine Vanderbilt Hosp., 1952—53; cons. physician VA Hosp., Iowa City, 1965—93; assoc. medicine dept. internal medicine Coll. Medicine, U. Iowa, 1953—54, chief divsn. gastroenterology, 1953—71, asst. prof. medicine, 1954-58, assoc. prof., 1958—63, prof., 1963—91, prof. emeritus, 1991—, traveling fellow, 1964, vis. prof. dept. physiology, 1964, vice chmn. dept. medicine, 1967—70, chmn. dept. medicine Coll. Medicine, 1970—76, Roy J. Carver prof. medicine, 1974—91, Roy J. Carver prof. emeritus, 1991—, dir. James A. Clifton Ctr. Digestive Diseases, 1985—90, interim dean, 1991—93. Investigator Mt. Desert Isle Biol. Lab., Salisbury Cove, Maine, 1964; vis. faculty mem. Mayo Found. and Mayo Clinic, 1966; vis. prof. dept. medicine U. N.C. Chapel Hill, 1970; cons. gastroenterology and nutrition tng. grants com. Nat. Inst. Arthritis and Metabolic Diseases, NIH, 1964—68, chmn., 1965—68; mem. Nat. Adv. Arthritis and Metabolic Diseases Coun., 1970—73; mem. gastroenterology tng. com. VA, Washington, 1967—71, chmn. tng. grants com., 1971—73; mem. med. adv. bd. Digestive Disease Found., 1969—73; vis. prof. gastroenterology U. London (St. Marks Hosp.), 1984—85; mem. sci. adv. com. Ludwig Inst. Cancer Rsch., Zurich, 1984—95. Internat. editl. bd. Italian Jour. Gastroenterology, 1970—90, Gastroenterology, 1964—68. Recipient Disting. Alumnus of Yr. award, Vanderbilt U. Sch. Medicine, 1984, Disting. Alumnus of Yr. Achievement award, U. Iowa Coll. Medicine, 2000; fellow spl. rsch., NIH, USPHS, 1955—56, in medicine, Evans Meml. Hosp., Mass. Meml. Hosps., also Boston U. Sch. Medicine, 1955—56; scholar Phi Connell, Vanderbilt U., 1943—44. Fellow: ACP (bd. regents 1972—79, pres. 1977—78, Alfred Stengel award 1984, Laureate award 1989); mem.: AAUP, AAAS, AMA (liaison com. grad. med. edn. 1976—77), Internat. Soc. Internal Medicine (exec. com. 1978—80), Assn. Profs. Medicine (councillor 1972—73, sec.-treas. 1973—75), Assn. Am. Med. Colls., Am. Physiol. Soc., Soc. Exptl. Biology and Medicine, Assn. Am. Physicians, Am. Clin. and Climatol. Assn. (v.p. 1984), Am. Fedn. Clin. Rsch., Am. Soc. Internal Medicine (Internist of Yr. award Iowa chpt. 1986), Am. Assn.

Study Liver Disease, Am. Heart Assn., Am. Gastroent. Assn. (pres. 1970—71), Inst. Medicine NAS, U. Iowa Assn. Emeritus Faculty 1999—2000, U. Iowa Retirees Assn. 1999—2000. Home: 39 Audubon Pl Iowa City IA 52245-3437 Office: U Iowa Hosp and Clinics 4 JCP Hawkins Dr Iowa City IA 52242 E-mail: jclifton@uiowa.edu., zylumjim@home.com.

CLIFTON, JAMES K. market research company executive; CEO mktg. Gallup, Inc., Lincoln, Nebr., chmn., CEO, 2000—. Office: Gallup Inc 300 S 68th Street Pl Lincoln NE 68510-2449

CLIFTON, THOMAS E. seminary president, minister; m. Audrey Vought; children: Sandra, Jill Clifton Mallard. Student, Duke Divinity Sch.; M in Divinity, Crozer Theol. Sem., Rochester, N.Y.; MS in Personnel Counseling, Wright State U., Dayton; D in Ministry, Princeton Theol. Sem. Pastor First Bapt. Ch., Perry, Ohio, 1967-70, Sidney, 1970-73; assoc. pastor Binkley Bapt. Ch., Chapel Hill, N.C., 1973-77; pastor First Bapt. Ch., Lafayette, Ind., 1977-85, Penifield, N.Y., 1985-93; pres. Ctrl. Bapt. Theol. Sch., Kansas City, Kans., 1993—. Writer: Bapt. Leader, Capitol Report; (curriculum) Judson Press. Office: Ctrl Bapt Theol Sem 741 N 31st St Kansas City KS 66102-3964

CLIFTON-SMITH, RHONDA DARLEEN, art center director; b. Dyersburg, Tenn., Mar. 19, 1954; d. Charles Burton Clifton and Mary Opal (Carter) Harris; m. Michael Frederick Smith, Feb. 14, 1980 (dec. Sept. 1981). BS in Art Edn., Columbus Coll., 1977; MA in Hist. Administrn., Eastern Ill. U., 1986. Asst. cataloging libr. Lawton (Okla.) Pub. Libr., 1978-79; registrar Mus. of the Great Plains, Lawton, 1979-82; curator Boot Hill Mus., Dodge City, Kans., 1982-94; exec. dir. Carnegie Ctr. for Arts, 1994—. Author: (booklet) Dodge City: The Early Years, 1985; co-author: (booklet) Cattle and Wheat: Agricultural Growth in 19th Century Dodge City, 1985. Mem. Am. Assn. Mus., Am. Assn. State & Local History (c-chair mem. com. 1990-92), Kan. Mus. Assn. (treas. 1989—, area rep. 1982-85), Mt. Plains Mus. Assn., Soroptimists Internat. Avocations: painting and drawing, theater. Office: Carnegie Ctr for Arts 701 2d Ave Dodge City KS 67801 E-mail: carnegie@dodgecity.net.

CLINE, THOMAS WILLIAM, real estate leasing company executive, management consultant; b. Flint, Mich., Oct. 17, 1932; s. Leo D. and Helen (Wolohan) C.; m. Joanne Greiner, July 18, 1959; children: Robert Arthur, Thomas John, Mary Elizabeth. BS, U. Detroit, 1954, JD, 1956. Bar: Mich. 1957. Gen. atty. Wickes Corp., Saginaw, Mich., 1958-61, sec., gen. counsel, 1961-69, sr. v.p., gen. counsel, 1969-71, sr. v.p., sec., 1971-80, dir., 1964-70, 74-80; sr. v.p., group officer, dir. Wickes Cos. Inc., 1980-83; pres. Cline Mgmt. Co., 1983—; pres., chief oper. officer Signature Corp., Chgo., 1984-85; exec. v.p., chief oper. officer Seitner Bros. Inc., Saginaw, 1986—. Bd. dirs. Mid-Am. Life Assurance Co., Mich. Nat. Bank, Saginaw, Can. West Fin. Svcs.(U.S.) Inc., Aristar Inc. Chmn. fin. com. Diocese of Saginaw, 1970-72; chmn. Saginaw Cath. Schs. Study Com., 1969, Nat. assn. Boys Clubs Am.; bd. dirs. San Diego Symphony Assn., 1975-78, Econ. devel. Corp. San Deigo County, 1975-78, Saginaw Japanese Cultural Ctr. and Tea House; vice chmn. Boys Clubs San Diego, 1975-77; trustee Saginaw Gen. Hosp. Assn., 1971-72, 73-75; trustee, fin. chmn. Saginaw Coop. Hosp. Inc., 1972; trustee, v.p. United Way of Saginaw County; bd. fellows Saginaw Valley Coll., 1973-75, chmn. bus. fund dr., 1978; mem. adv. bd. Delta Coll., U. San Diego, 1975-78, San Diego State U. Bus. Sch., 1975-78, Saginaw Art Mus., 1986-94; mem. fin. com. Diocese San Diego, 1975-78; bd. dirs. Mich. State C. of C., 1973-75; chmn. Saginaw Met. Area Nat. Alliance of Bus., 1979-80; bd. dirs. San Diego C. of C., 1976-77; ann. programs fund stategic advisor Rotary Found., 2001; pres. Big Creek Fishing Lodge, 2000—. With U.S. Army, 1956-58. Mem. Mich. Bar Assn., Mich. Mfrs. Assn. (bd. dirs. 1980-88), U.S. C. of C. (adv. com.), Saginaw Club (bd. dirs., v.p. 1991), Serra Club Saginaw County (pres., bd. dirs.), Rotary (pres. Saginaw 1990-91, dist. gov. 1994-95, chair dist. found.1996-2000, del. coun. on legis. 1998), Blue Key Soc., Delta Sigma Pi, Beta Alpha Psi, Delta Theta Pi. Home and Office: 4640 Ashland Dr Saginaw MI 48603-4605

CLIPPERT, CHARLES FREDERICK, lawyer; b. Detroit, May 21, 1931; s. Harrison Frank and Ethelyn (Reuss) C.; m. Lynne Davison, June 6, 1959; children: Martha G. Shannon, Charles Frederick III, Thomas Harrison. BA, U. Mich., 1953, LLB, 1959. Bar: Mich. 1959. Assoc. Dickinson, Wright, Moon, Van Dusen & Freeman, Bloomfield Hills, Mich., 1959-67, ptnr., 1967-97, mem. exec. com., 1986-89; mem. Dickinson Wright PLLC, 1998-2000, cons. mem., 2001—. Commr. City of Birmingham, Mich., 1964-70, mayor, 1969-70; gov. Cranbrook Schs., Bloomfield Hills, 1978-99; trustee Cranbrook Ednl. Community, Bloomfield Hills, 1980-98, sec., 1989-93. Lt. (j.g.) USNR, 1953-56; mem. endowment com. The Consortium of Endowed Episcopal Parishes, 1998—. Fellow Am. Bar Found., Mich. Bar Found.; mem. ABA, State Bar Mich. (real property law coun. 1980-85, mem. select com. on professionalism 1992-99, mem. Alternate dispute resolution com. 1999—), Oakland County Bar Assn. (bd. dirs. 1985-91, pres. 1990-91), Orchard Lake Country Club (gov. 1986-92, pres. 1991-92), Am. Arbitration Assn. (panel of neutral arbitrators 1997—), Pi Sigma Alpha. Office: Dickinson Wright PLLC Ste 2000 525 N Woodward Ave Bloomfield Hills MI 48304-2971 E-mail: cclippert@dickinson-wright.com.

CLONINGER, CLAUDE ROBERT, psychiatric researcher, educator, genetic epidemiologist; b. Beaumont, Tex., Apr. 4, 1944; s. Morris Sheppard and Marie Concetta (Mazzagatti) C.; m. Sharon Lee Rogan, July 11, 1969; children: Bryan Joseph, Kevin Michael. BA U. Tex., 1966; MD, Washington U., St. Louis, 1970, (hon.) U. Umea, Sweden, 1983. Diplomate Am. Bd. Psychiatry and Neurology. Instr. psychiatry Washington U., St. Louis, 1973-74, asst. prof. 1974-78, assoc. prof., 1978-81, prof., 1981—, prof. genetics, 1978—, prof. psychology, 1989—, Wallace Renard prof. psychiatry, 1991—, head dept. psychiatry, 1989-94, dir. ctr. psychobiology personality, 1994—; psychiatrist-in-chief Barnes and Renard Hosps., St. Louis, 1989-94; vis. prof. U. Hawaii, Honolulu, 1978-79, U. Umea, Sweden, 1980; chmn. NIMH psychopathology Review Com., Washington, 1980-84; cons. WHO, Geneva, 1981—, Am. Psychiatric Assn., Washington, 1978—, Nat. Inst. on Alcohol Abuse and Alcoholism, 1984-99, Inst. Medicine, 1986; chmn. genetics initiative schizophrenia NIMH, 1989-97; mental health commr. State of Mo., 1990-95. Author 6 books; editor: Jour. Behavior Genetics, 1980-86, Am. Jour. Human Genetics, 1980-83; assoc. editor Genetic Epidemiology, 1983-92, Human Heredity, 1989—; mem. editl. bd. Arch. Gen. Psychiatry, Comprehensive Psychiatry, Neuropsychopharmacology, Jour. Comprehensive Psychiatry, Jour. Psychiat. Rsch., Jour. Med. Genetics; contbr. articles to profl. jours. Recipient Rsch. Scientist award NIMH, 1975, 80, 85, Strecker award Inst. Pa. Hosp., 1988, James B. Isaacson award, ISBRA, 1992, Lifetime Achievement award Am. Soc. of Addiction Medicine, 2000, Finnish Psychiatry Assn. Annual Medal. Fellow AAAS, Am. Psychiat. Assn. (Adolph Meyer award, 1993), Am. Psychopathol. Assn. (treas. 1984-89, v.p. 1990, pres. 1991-93, sec. 1994-96, Samuel Hamilton award 1993); mem. Am. Soc. Human Genetics (editl. bd. 1980-83), Behavior Genetics Assn. (editl. bd. 1980—), Inst. Medicine of NAS, Rsch. Soc. Alcoholism (bd. dirs. 1987-90). Avocations: gardening, reading, travel. Home: 7100 Delmar Blvd Saint Louis MO 63130-4303 Office: Washington U Dept of Psychiatry 4940 Childrens Pl Saint Louis MO 63110-1002

CLOONAN, JAMES BRIAN, investment executive; b. Chgo., Jan. 28, 1931; s. Bernard V. and Lauretta D. (Maloney) C.; m. Edythe Adrianne Ratner, Mar. 26, 1970; children: Michele, Christine, Mia; stepchildren: Carrie Madorin, Harry Madorin. Prof. Sch. Bus. Loyola U., Chgo., 1966-71; pres. Quantitative Decision Sys., Inc., 1972-73; chmn. bd. Heinold Securities, Inc., 1974-77; prof. grad. sch. bus. DePaul U., 1978-82; chmn. Investment Info. Svcs., 1981-86; pres. Mktg. Sys. Internat. Inc., 1985-87, Analytics Sys. Inc., 1987—. Bd. dirs., chmn. Mktg. Svcs. Internat., Inc., Wizeup.com, Inc. Author: Estimates of the Impact of Sign and Billboard Removal Under the Highway Beautification Act of 1965, 1966, Stock Options-The Application of Decision Theory to Basic and Advanced Strategies, 1973, An Introduction to Decision Making for the Individual Investor, 1980, Expanding Your Investment Horizons, 1983, A Lifetime Strategy for Investing in Common Stocks, 1988. Mem. Am. Fin. Assn., Am. Mktg. Assn., Am. Assn. Individual Investors (pres. 1979-92, chmn. 1992—). Home: 1242 N Lake Shore Dr Chicago IL 60610-2361 Office: Am Assn Individual Investors 625 N Michigan Ave Chicago IL 60611-3110 E-mail: jbcaaii@aol.com.

CLOSEN, MICHAEL LEE, law educator; b. Peoria, Ill., Jan. 25, 1949; s. Stanley Paul and Dorothy Mae (Kendall) C. BS, MA, Bradley U., 1971; JD, U. Ill., 1974. Bar: Ill. 1974; notary pub., Ill. Instr. U. Ill., Champaign, 1974; jud. clk. Ill. Appellate Ct., Springfield, 1974-76, 77-78; asst. states atty. Cook County, Chgo., 1978; prof. law John Marshall Law Sch., 1976—. Vis. prof. No. Ill. U., 1985—86, adj. prof., 1990, St. Thomas U., 1991; vis. prof. U. Ark., 1993, 96; reporter Ill. Jud. Conf., Chgo., 1981—; arbitrator Am. Arbitration Assn., Chgo., 1981—, Cook County Cir. Ct. Mandatory Arbitration Program, 1990—, Will County Cir. Ct. Mandatory Arbitration Program, 1996—; lectr. Ill. Inst. Continuing Legal Edn., Chgo., 1981—; dir. Ctr. for Legal Edn., Ltd., 1995—96; adj. prof. Loyola U., Chgo., 1999—. Author: (casebooks) Agency and Partnership Law, 1984, 3d edit., 2000, (with others) Contracts, 1984, 3d edit., 1992, AIDS Cases and Materials, 1989, 3d edit., 2002, Notary Law and Practice, 1997, Contract Law and Practice, 1998; co-author: The Shopping Bag: Portable Art, 1986, AIDS Law in a Nutshell, 1991, 2d edit., 1996, Legal Aspects of AIDS, 1991; contbr. articles to profl. jours. Recipient Svc. award Am. Arbitration Assn., 1984, 5-Yr. Comty. Achievement award Ill. Politics Mag., 1998; named one of Outstanding Young Men in Am., 1981. Mem. ABA, Ill. Bar Assn., Appellate Lawyers Assn., Chgo. Coun. Lawyers, Nat. Notary Assn. (Achievement award 1998), Am. Soc. Notaries, Notary Law Inst. Home: 17640 S Mccarron Rd Lockport IL 60441-9774 Office: John Marshall Law Sch 315 S Plymouth Ct Chicago IL 60604-3968

CLOUGH, BARRY, marketing executive; b. June 19, 1941; married; 3 children. BS in Bus. Adminstrn., BS in Applied Math. Engring., U. Colo., 1964; M in Computer Sci., Bradley U., 1970. Mgr. sales, customer svc. engine divsn. Caterpillar, Inc., Peoria, Ill. Chmn. bd. WTVP-Channel 47, Peoria; bd. trustees Mt. Hawley C.C.; bd. trustees., chmn. bd. Advanced Filter Sys. Inc. Mem. parents bd. Internat. Sch. Brussels.

CLOUSE, JOHN DANIEL, lawyer; b. Evansville, Ind., Sept. 4, 1925; s. Frank Paul and Anna Lucille (Frank) C.; m. Georgia L. Ross, Dec. 7, 1978; 1 child, George Chauncey. AB, U. Evansville, 1950; JD, Ind. U., 1952. Bar: Ind. 1952, U.S. Supreme Ct. 1962, U.S. Ct. Appeals (7th cir.) 1965. Assoc. Firm of James D. Lopp, Evansville, 1952-56; pvt. practice law James D. Lopp, 1956—. Guest editorialist Viewpoint, Evansville Courier, 1978—86, Evansville Press, 1986—98, Focus, Radio Sta. WGBF, 1978—84; 2d asst. city atty. Evansville, 1954—55; mem. Com. for Implementation of Criminal Justice Act of 1964, 1965; mem. appellate rules sub-com. Ind. Supreme Ct. Com. on Rules of Practice and Procedure, 1980. Pres. Civil Svc. Commn. Evansville Police Dept., 1961-62, v.p., 1988; pres. Ind. War Memls. Com., 1963-69; mem. jud. nominating com. Vanderburgh County, Ind., 1976-80; dir. Ind. Fed. Cmty. Defender Project, Inc., 1993-98. With inf. U.S. Army, 1943-46. Decorated Bronze Star; named one of World's Most travelled Man Guinness Book of Records, 1993, Most Travelled Man, 1995-2001. Fellow Ind. Bar Found.; mem. Evansville Bar Assn. (v.p. 1972, James Bethel Gresham Freedom award 1997), Ind. Bar Assn. (chmn. com. on civil rights 1991-92), Travelers Century Club (L.A.), Pi Gamma Mu. Republican. Methodist. Office: 123 NW 4th St Ste 317 Evansville IN 47708-1712 E-mail: JDCMJS@aol.com.

COAR, DAVID H. federal judge; b. Birmingham, Ala., Aug. 11, 1943; s. Robert and Lorayne C.; children: Chinyelu, Kamau, Jamila. BA, Syracuse U., 1964; JD, Loyola U., 1969; LLM, Harvard U., 1970. Bar: Ill. 1969, Ala. 1971. Atty.-extern NAACP Legal Def. and Edn. Fund, Inc., N.Y.C., 1970-71, Crawford & Cooper, Mobile, Ala., 1971-72, Adams, Baker & Clemon, Birmingham, 1972-74; prof. DePaul U. Law Sch., Chgo., 1974-79, 82-86; U.S. trustee U.S. Justice Dept., 1979-82; bankruptcy judge U.S. Bankruptcy Ct., 1986-94; dist. ct. judge U.S. Dist. Ct., 1994—. Bd. dirs. Boys and Girls Club, Chgo. Mem. ABA, Am. Coll. Bankruptcy, Law Club, Legal Club Chgo., Chgo. Inns of Ct. Office: US Dist Ct 219 S Dearborn St Ste 1478 Chicago IL 60604-1705

COASE, RONALD HARRY, economist, educator; b. Willesden, Eng., Dec. 29, 1910; arrived in U.S., 1951; s. Henry Joseph and Rosalie (Giles) Coase; m. Marian Ruth Hartung, Aug. 7, 1937. B of Commerce, London Sch. Econs., 1932, DSc, 1951; Dr. Rer. Pol. honoris causa, Cologne U., Fed. Republic Germany, 1988; D of Social Sci. (hon.) , Yale U., 1989; LLD (hon.) , Washington U., St. Louis, 1991; LLD (hon.) , U. Dundee, Scotland, 1992; DSc (hon.) , U. Buckingham, Eng., 1995; DHL (hon.) , Beloit Coll., 1996; docteur honoris causa, U. Paris, 1996. Sir Ernest Cassel Travelling scholar, 1931—32; asst. lectr. Dundee Sch. Econs., 1932—34, U. Liverpool, England, 1934—35; from asst. lectr. to lectr. to reader London Sch. Econs., 1935—51; prof. U. Buffalo, 1951—58, U. Va., Charlottesville, 1958—64, U. Chgo., 1964—, now Clifton R. Musser prof. emeritus, sr. fellow in law and econs. Law Sch. Sr. fellow in law and econs. Law Sch. Statistician, then chief statistician Ctrl. Statis. Office, Offices War Cabinet, England, 1941—46. Author: British Broadcasting, A Study in Monopoly, 1950, The Firm, the Market and the Law, 1988, Essays on Economics and Economists, 1994; editor: Jour. Law and Econs., 1964—82. Mem. hon. com. Eurosci.; chmn. adv. bd. Contracting and Orgns. Rsch. Facilities U. Mo., Columbua. Recipient Nobel prize in Econs., 1991; fellow Rockefeller fellow, 1948, Ctr. for Advanced Study Behavioral Scis., 1958—59, sr. rsch. fellow, Hoover Instn., Stanford U., 1977, hon. fellow, London Sch. Econs. Fellow: European Acad., Am. Econ. Assn. (disting.), Brit. Acad. (corr.), Am. Acad. Arts and Scis.; mem.: Contracting and Orgns. Rsch. Inst. (chmn. adv. bd.), Internat. Soc. for New Instnl. Econs. (founding pres. 1997), Mont Pelerin Soc., Royal Econ. Soc. Office: U Chgo Laird Bell Law Quadrangle 1111 E 60th St Chicago IL 60637-2776 Home: Apt 1100 2960 N Lake Shore Dr Chicago IL 60657-5647

COATS, JAMES O. state legislator; m. Alice Coats. BS, N.D. State U. Tchr.; ret.; state rep. dist. 34, 1991-99; ret. Mem. industry, bus. and labor, polit. subdvsns. coms. N.D. Ho. Reps. Recipient Golden Rule award, 1991. Mem. VFW, Am. Legion (dept. comdr.), Mandan Golden Age Club (pres.), Elks, Eagles, Amvets. Democrat. Home: 1704 Sunset Dr Mandan ND 58554-1628

COBEY, RALPH, industrialist; b. Sycamore, Ohio, Aug. 15, 1909; m. Hortense Kohn, Feb. 28, 1944; children: Minnie, Susanne. ME, Carnegie Inst. Tech., 1932; D.Sc. (hon.), Findlay Coll., 1958. Pres. Perfection Steel Body Co., Galion, Ohio, 1945-70, Perfection-Cobey, Co., Galion, 1949-70, Eagle Crusher Co., 1954-90, chmn. bd., 1990—; pres. Philips-Davies Co., 1965-70, Cobey Co., 1946-70, Diamond Iron Works, 1972-90, Austin-Western Crusher Co., 1974-90, Scoopmobile Co., 1978-90, Madsen Co., 1979-90, World Wide Investment Co., 1950—. Aide in preparation of prodn. and design of Army tanks OPM, 1939-42. Mem. contbg. com. NCCJ, 1951-55, now area chmn. spl. gifts com.; founder, pres. Harry Cobey Found.; area chmn. U.S. Savs. Bonds; mem. pres.'s adv. coun. for devel. Ashland Coll., Ohio, mem. Ohio Gov.'s Citizens' Task Force on Environ. Protection, 1971-72, Pres.'s Tax Com., 1962-66; pioneer chaplain svcs. in indsl. plants; mem. Ohio Expns. Commn., 1964, Radio Free Europe Com.; chmn. Cmty. Heart Fund Campaign, 1971-72; pres., spl. gifts chmn. Crawford County Heart Fund, 1972-78; mem. Ohio fin. bd. Heart Fund, 1973—; mem. Ohio Rep. Fin. Com.; mounted dep. sheriff, Morrow County (Ohio), 1974-84; bd. dirs., chmn. long range planning com. Johnny Appleseed Area coun. Boy Scouts of Am.; hon. life mem. Galion Cmty. Ctr.; trustee Galion City Hosp. Found. Bd.; mem. pres.'s coun. Ohio State U.; chmn., founder Minnie Cobey Meml. Libr.; founder, chmn. bd. trustees Louis Bromfield Malabar Farm Found.; bd. dirs. Morrow County United Appeals; State of Ohio amb. of natural resources; numerous other civic activities. Capt. USAAF, 1942-46, 51, Korea. Baden-Powel World fellow King Carl Gustaf of Sweden, 1992; recipient Disting. Citizen of Yr. award Heart of Ohio Coun., Boy Scouts Am., 1995, Lifetime Commitment to Humanitarianism award from Rep. Joan Lawrence, Ohio Ho. Reps., 1996, award Louis Bromfield Soc., 2001; named to Ohio Agrl. Hall of Fame, 1999, Ohio Nat. Resources Hall of Fame, 2001; Ralph Cobey Day in City of Galion, 1995, City of Bucyrus, 1999. Mem. NAM, Nat. Assn. 4-H Clubs, Future Farmers Am., U.S. C. of C. (mem. taxation, fgn. affairs, labor rels. coms.), Masons (32 degree), Shriners (sec.-treas.). Home: 4270 State Route 309 Galion OH 44833-9618 Office: Eagle Crusher Co Inc PO Box 537 Galion OH 44833-0537

COBLE, YANK DAVID, JR. internist, endocrinologist; b. Burlington, N.C., 1937; m. Shereth Landrum; 2 children. MD, Duke U., 1962; degree in clin. medicine of the tropics, London Sch. Hygiene/Trop Med. Diplomate Am. Bd. Internal Medicine, Am. Bd. Endocrinology. Intern N.Y. Hosp.-Cornell Med. Ctr., N.Y.C., 1962-63, resident, 1963-64; resident in internal medicine London Sch. Trop Medicine Hygiene, 1966-67; resident in endocrinology NIH, Bethesda, Md., 1967-68; fellow in endocrinology Vanderbilt Med. Sch., Nashville, 1968-69; pvt. practice; clin. prof. medicine U. Fla., Jacksonville, chair dept. cmty. health and family medicine, prof. medicine and family medicine. Hosp. staff Univ. Hosp., 1970—, St. Luke's Hosp., 1970—, Bapt. Med. Ctr., 1970—, St. Vincents Med. Ctr., Jacksonville, Fla., 1970—; bd. dirs. Blue Cross/Blue Shield of Fla., Inc.; chmn. FLAMEDCO, Inc., Fla. Med. Ins. Trust; bd. dirs., exec. com. Fla. Physicians Ins. Co., Koger Equity Co.; mem. dirs. adv. com. NIH; mem. nat. guidelines clearing house policy bd. AHRQ. Pres. Jacksonville Cmty. Coun.; bd. dirs. Leadership Jacksonville, Big Bros., Arts Assembly, Jacksonville Enterprise Ctr. for Health Care Tech., Wesley Manor Retirement Village; bd. dirs. Rsch.! Am., 2001—, Nat. Osteoporosis Found., 2001—, Hospice NEF, 2001—. Master ACP, Am. Coll. Endocrinology (pres.); mem. AMA (trustee 1994—, commr. joint commn. on accreditation of healthcare orgns., chair practice parameters partnership, clin. quality improvement forum governing bd., sec.-treas. bd. trustees, pres. edn. and rsch. found. exec. com. 1995-97, chair audit com., fin. com., EVP search, town and gown com., continuing med. edn. adv. com. 1986-88, coun. sci. affairs 1988-94, vice chair, chair, pres. elect 2001—), Am. Soc. Internal Medicine (past pres.), Fla. Med. Assn. (past pres.), Am. Assn. Clin. Endorcrinologists (1st pres.), Fla. Med. Assn. (Cert. of Merit), Jacksonville C. of C. Office: AMA 515 N State St Chicago IL 60610-4325

COCHRAN, DALE M. state agency administrator; b. Ft. Dodge, Iowa, Nov. 20, 1928; s. Melvin and Gladys C.; m. Jeannene Hirsch, 1952; children: Deborah, Cynthia, Tamara. BS, Iowa State U., 1950. Rep. Iowa State Rep. Dist. 14, 1965-86; spkr. of house Iowa Ho. of Reps., 1975-78, exec. com. mem. nat. conf. state legis. and coun. state govt.; sec. agrl. Iowa, 1987—; owner of farm. Pres. Midwestern Assn. State Depts. Agrl. and Mid-Am. Int. Agrl. Trade Coun. Farm editor: Ft. Dodge Messenger. Recipient Altig award Nat. Fedn. Blind, Sweepstakes award Friends of Agrl. Mem. Iowa Assn. Soil (hon. life), Iowa Soybean Assn. (bd. dirs. 1969-75), Lions, Pi Kappa Phi, Gamma Sigma Delta. Office: Agr & Land Stewardship Dept 9th And Grand Des Moines IA 50319-0001

COCHRAN, JOHN R. bank executive; b. Council Bluffs, IA, 1943; m. Bette Chochran; 3 children. B.A. econ. and fin., U. Iowa; Stonier Grad. Sch. of Banking, Rutgers U., NJ. Teller Hawkeye State Bank, Iowa City, 1966-67; with Norwest Bancorporation, Minneapolis, MN, 1967-95; pres. and CEO 5th Norwestern Bank, 1976-79, various Norwest Banks, 1979-84; regional pres. Norwest Corp., NE, 1984-86; pres. and CEO Norwest Bank, Omaha, 1986-95, FirstMerit Corp., Akron, OH, 1996—, now chmn. CEO. Office: FirstMerit Corp 7th Fl 3 Cascade Plz Ste 7 Akron OH 44308-1124

COCHRAN, LESLIE HERSCHEL, university administrator; b. Valparaiso, Ind., Apr. 24, 1939; s. Robert H. and Dellcena (Marquart) C.; m. Linda Stockman, May 20, 1978; children: Troy, Kirt, Leslee. B.S., Western Mich. U., 1961, M.A., 1962; Ed.D., Wayne State U., 1968. Mem. faculty Central Mich. U., Mt. Pleasant, 1968-80, assoc. dean, 1970-75, dean fine and applied arts, 1975-76, vice provost, 1976-80; provost S.E. Mo. State U., Cape Girardeau, 1980-92; pres. Youngstown (Ohio) State U., 1992—. Mem. accreditation team North Ctrl. Assn., Chgo., 1982—. Author: Advisory Committee in Action, 1980, Innovative Program in Industrial Education, 1970, Administrative Commitment to Teaching, 1989, Publish or Perish: The Wrong Issue, 1992. Trustee Butler Inst. Am. Art, Western Res. Health Care System, N.E. Ohio Med. Coll. Japan Soc. Promotion of Sci. fellow Tokyo, 1976. Mem. Nat. Assn. Indsl. and Tech. Tchr. Edn. (pres. 1976), Rotary. Office: Youngstown State U Todd Hall Office Of Pres Youngstown OH 44555-0001

COCHRAN, WILLIAM C. state legislator; b. New Albany, Ind., Aug. 25, 1934; m. Judith Ann Bocard; children: Sherry Lee, Rex Charles, Richard Paul. Student, Ind. U. Realtor Brooks Realtors; rep. Dist. 72 Ind. Ho. of Reps., 1974—, vice chmn. interstate coop. com., mem. from dist. 72, mem. judiciary com., ways and means com. Clk. Cir. Ct., Floyd County, 1967-74; vol. March of Dimes. Recipient Outstanding Cmty. Svc. award, 1970. Mem. VFW, FOB, Manzanita Tribe Redmen, Elks, Masons. Home: 4330 Green Valley Rd New Albany IN 47150-4258

COCKBURN, EVE GILLIAN, newsletter editor; b. Astley, Eng., Mar. 3, 1924; came to U.S., 1948; d. Thomas and Alice (Speakman) Fairhurst; m. Aidan Cockburn, June 26, 1945 (dec. 1981); children: Gillian Margaret, Erika June, Vivien Jo, Alistair Aidan, Alison Francesca. BA with honours, Oxford U., 1945, MA, 1958. Sci. and health columnist Berkshire Evening Eagle, 1954-55; syndicated sci. and health columnist Pakistani newspapers, including Civil and Mil. Gazette, 1958-60; founder, editor Dance Newsletter, Detroit, 1969-74; co-founder, editor newsletter Paleopathology Assn., 1973-99, dir., 1981-99, immediate past pres., 2000-01, pres. emerita, 2001—. Vice chmn. antiquaries bd., Detroit Inst. of Arts, 1997—. Editor Woman and Health, 1959-60, Mummies, Disease, and Ancient Cultures, 1980 (Med. Writers Am. award 1981); mem. editl. bd. Jour. Paleopathology, 1988—, contbg. editor, 1991; mem. sci. com. Cronos, 1990-92. Mem. World Coun. on Mummy Studies, 1992—, hon. com. The Origin of Syphilis in Europe, Toulon, France, 1993; mem. sci. com. The Evolution and Paleoepidemiology of Tb, Szeged, Hungary, 1996—. Fellow Zool. Soc. London; mem. Am. Assn. Phys. Anthropologists. Avocations: walking, birdwatching, travel.

CODY, THOMAS GERALD, lawyer; b. N.Y.C., Nov. 4, 1941; s. Thomas J. Cody and Esther Mary Courtney; m. Mary Ellen Palmer, Nov. 26, 1966; children: Thomas Jr., Mark, Amy, Anne. BA in Philosophy, Maryknoll Coll., 1963; JD, St. John's U., 1967; LLD (hon.), Cen. State U., Wilberforce, Ohio, 1985. Bar: N.Y. 1967. Assoc. Simpson Thacher & Bartlett, N.Y., 1967-72; asst. prof. law sch. St. John's U., 1972-76; sr. v.p., gen. counsel, sec. Pan Am. Airways, 1976-82; sr. v.p. law and pub. affairs Federated Dept. Stores, Cin., 1982-88, exec. v.p. legal & human resources, 1989—. Trustee Xavier U., Cin., Children's Hosp. Med. Ctr., Cin. Mem. ABA, Bankers Club, Queen City Club, Hyde Park Country Club, Commonwealth Club of Cin. Roman Catholic. Office: Federated Dept Stores Inc 7 W 7th St Cincinnati OH 45202-2424

COE, FREDRIC L. physician, educator, researcher; b. Chgo., Dec. 25, 1936; s. Lester J. and Lillian (Chaitlen) C.; m. Eleanor Joyce Brodny, May 5, 1965; children: Brian, Laura. A.B., U. Chgo., 1955; M.S., U. Chgo., 1957; M.D., U. Chgo., 1961. Diplomate Am. Bd. Internal Medicine. Intern Michael Reese Hosp., Chgo., 1961-62, resident, 1962-65, U. Tex. S.W. Med. Sch., 1967-69; chmn. nephrology Michael Reese Hosp., 1972-82; prof. medicine U. Chgo., 1977—, prof. physiology, 1979—; chmn. nephrology A.M. Billings Hosp., Chgo., 1982—; founder, pres. Litholink Corp., 1995—. Author: Nephrolithiasis, 1978, 2d edit. (with J. Parks), 1987, (with B. Brenner and F.C. Rector) Renal Physiology, 1986, Clinical Nephrology; editor: Renal Therapeutics, 1978, Nephrolithiasis, 1980, Hypercalciuric States, 1983, (with M. Favus) Disorders of Bone and Mineral Metabolism, 1993, 2d edit., 2001; editor-in-chief Yearbook of Nephrology, 1991-96; editor: (with others) Kidney Stones: Medical and Surgical Management, 1996. Served to capt. USAF, 1961-67. Recipient Belding Scribner medal for lifetime achievement in clin. rsch. Am. Soc. Nephrology, 2000; grantee NIH, 1977— . Fellow ACP; mem. Am. Soc. Clin. Investigation, Am. Physiol. Soc., Assn. Am. Physicians Jewish. Achievements include first evidence for hyperuricosuria as cause of calcium renal stones; discovery of nephro calcin a protien inhibitor of crystal growth; first demonstration that human idiopathic hypercalciuris is hereditary. Home: 5490 S South Shore Dr Chicago IL 60615-5984 Office: U Chgo Med Ctr 5841 S Maryland Ave Chicago IL 60637-1463

COFFEY, CHARLES MOORE, communication research professional, writer; b. Chgo., July 8, 1941; s. Charles Adams and Helen Marie (Moore) C. BA in Econs., Beloit Coll., 1963; postgrad., Purdue U., 1980. WDBJ radio and TV reporter Times-World Corp., Roanoke, Va., 1964-65; reporter, anchor, prodr. WHAS AM FM TV, Louisville, 1967-72; asst. to chancellor Ind. U. S.E., New Albany, 1972-77; dir. spl. events Ind. U., Bloomington, 1977-82; dir. alumni affairs Ind. U.-Purdue U., Inpdls., 1982-88; comm. advisor Bayh-O'Bannon Campaign, 1988; comm. asst. Lt. Gov. of Ind., 1989-97; dir. comm. rsch. Ind. Dept. Adminstrn., 1997—. Lt. gov.'s rep. INTELENET Commn., Indpls., 1990-97, gov.'s rep., 1997—; gov.'s rep. Enhanced Data Access Rev. Com., Indpls., 1997—. Contbr. articles to profl. jours. Pres. Coun. for Retarded Children, Clark County, Ind., 1975-76, Bloomington Restorations, 1982; founding chmn. Clark-Floyd Conv. Bur., Jeffersonville, Ind., 1977; bd. dirs. YMCA Greater Indpls., 1989-95, 97-98, 2000—, sec. bd. 1998-2000, trustee 1999—. With USAF, 1963. Recipient AP award for comprehensive reporting Va. AP Broadcasters, 1964-65. Mem. Rotary Club Indpls. Democrat. Home: 3922 Alsace Pl Indianapolis IN 46226-5413 Office: Ind Dept Adminstrn 402 W Washington St Indianapolis IN 46204-2739 E-mail: ccoffey@idoa.state.in.us., coffeyc@iquest.net.

COFFEY, FRANK W. food products executive; MBA in Fin. Mgmt. CPA, Kans. With My Bread Baking Co., New Bedford, Mass.; v.p. corp. devel. Interstate Bakeries Corp., Kansas City, Mo., sr. v.p., CFO. Office: Interstate Bakeries Corp 12 E ARmour Blvd Kansas City MO 64111

COFFEY, JOHN LOUIS, judge; b. Milw., Apr. 15, 1922; s. William Leo and Elizabeth Ann (Walsh) Coffey; m. Marion Kunzelmann, Feb. 3, 1951; children: Peter, Elizabeth Mary Coffey Robbins. BA, Marquette U., 1943, JD, 1948; MBA (hon.) , Spencerian Coll., 1964. Bar: Wis. 1948, U.S. Dist. Ct. 1948, U.S. Supreme Ct. 1980. Asst. city atty. City of Milw., 1949—54; judge Civil Ct., Milw. County, 1954—60, Milw. County Mcpl. Ct., 1960—62; judge criminal divsn. Cir. Ct., Milw. County, 1962—72, sr. judge criminal divsn., 1972—75, chief presiding judge criminal divsn., 1976, judge civil divsn., 1976—78; justice Wis. Supreme Ct., Madison, 1978—82; cir. judge U.S. Ct. Appeals (7th cir.), Chgo., 1982—; mem. Wis. Bd. Criminal Ct. Judges, 1960—78, Wis. Bd. Circuit Ct. Judges, 1962—78. Mem. adv. bd. St. Mary's Hosp., 1964—70; bd. dirs., mem. exec. bd. Milw.-Waukesha chpt. ARC; mem. Milw. County coun. Boy Scouts Am.; mem. vol. svc. adv. com. Milw. County Dept. Pub. Welfare; chmn. St. Eugene's Sch. Bd., 1967—70; pres. St. Eugene's Ch. Coun., 1974. With USNR, 1943—46. Named Outstanding Man of Yr., Milw. Jr. C. of C., 1951, One of 5 Outstanding Men in the the State, 1957, Outstanding Law Alumnus of Yr., Marquette U., 1980, Outstanding Man of Yr., Milw. Jr. C. of C., 1951, Outstanding Law Alumnus of Yr., Marquette U., 1980; named one of 5 Outstanding Men in State of Wis., 1957; recipient Marquette Univ. H.S. Alumni Merit award, 2001. Fellow: Am. Bar Found.; mem.: Marquette U. Law Alumni Assn. (Disting. Profl. Achievement Merit award 1985), Ill. State Bar Assn., 7th Cir.Bar Assn., Wis. Bar Assn., Marquette U. M Club (former dir.), Nat. Lawyers Club, Am. Legion (Disting. Svc. award 1973), Alpha Sigma Nu, Phi Alpha Delta (hon.). Roman Catholic.

COFFMAN, JAMES RICHARD, academic administrator, veterinarian; b. Lyndon, Kans., July 19, 1938; s. Harry Thomas and Eleanor Louise (Lowe) C.; m. Sharon Sue Neill, June 10, 1960; children: David Neill, Michael James, Scott Thomas. BS, Kans. State U., 1960, DVM, 1962, MS, 1969. Pvt. practice equine vet., Wichita, Kans., 1962-65, Oklahoma City, 1969-71; inst. vet. medicine Kans. State U., Manhattan, 1965-69, prof., head dept. surgery and medicine, vet. medicine, 1981-84, prof. vet. medicine, dean, 1984-87, provost, 1987—; assoc. prof. vet. medicine and surgery U. Mo., Columbia, 1971-75, prof., 1975-81, dir. Equine Ctr., 1973-78; prof., head dept. surgery and medicine Sch. Vet. Medicine Kans. State U., Manhattan, 1981-84, prof., dean, 1984-87, provost, 1987—. Chair Nat. rsch. Coun., Bd. on Agr. subcom., 1999. Author: Equine Chemistry and Pathophysiology, 1991; equine editor Compendium on Continuing Edn. 1980-83, mem. editorial bd., 1980-85; editor in chief Equine Sportsmedicine, 1981-85; mem. editorial bd. Jour. Equine Medicine and Surgery, 1979-80; adv. bd. Equine Vet. Jour., 1980—; contbr. numerous articles to profl. jours. Bd. dirs. St. Mary Hosp., Manhattan, 1989—. Recipient Disting. Tchr. award Norden Labs., 1969. Mem. Am. Coll. Vet. Internal Medicine (diplomate, pres. 1978-79, chmn. bd. regents 1979-80), Am. Assn. Equine Practitioners (dir. at large 1982-83, v.p. 1984, pres. 1986-87), Am. Vet. Med. Assn. (trustee profl. liability ins. trust 1978-85, chmn. 1980-82), Nat. Acads. Practice Vet. Medicine (exec. bd. 1985-87, founding com. mem. 1985—), Kans. Vet. Med. Assn., Nat. Assn. State Univs. and Land Grant Colls. (coun. chief acad. officers 1987—, exec. coun. on acad. affairs), Rotary (bd. dirs. 1989-90), Phi Kappa Phi, Gamma Sigma Delta, Phi Zeta. Avocation: oil painting. Home: 3727 Anderson Ave Manhattan KS 66503-2512

COFFMAN, TERRENCE J. academic administrator; Pres. Milw. Inst. Art & Design. Office: Milw Inst Art & Design 273 E Erie St Milwaukee WI 53202-6003

COFIELD, ROBERT HAHN, orthopedic surgeon, educator; b. Cin., Oct. 24, 1943; s. Robert Hedrick and Virginia (Hahn) C.; m. Pamela Joyce Haarbauer, Aug. 12, 1967; children: Robert, Stacey, Virginia. BA, Washington and Lee U., 1965; MD, U. Ky., 1969; MS, Mayo Grad. Sch. Medicine, 1976. Diplomate Am. Bd. Orthopedic Surgery. Intern Charity Hosp./Tulane U., New Orleans, 1970; cons. Mayo Clinic, Rochester, Minn., 1975—; from instr. to assoc. prof. Mayo Med. Sch., 1975-88, prof., 1988—; vice chmn. dept. orthopedics Mayo Clinic, 1992-97, Frank R. and Shari Caywood prof. orthopedic surgery, 1993; assoc. dean Mayo Grad. Sch., 1992-94, dean, 1994-98; chmn. dept. orthopedics Mayo Clinic, 1997—; pres. Am. Bd. Orthopaedic Surgery, Chapel Hill, 1999-2000. Editor-in-chief Jour. Shoulder and Elbow Surgery, 1990-96; contbr. chpts. to books, more than 150 articles to profl. jours.; co-inventor humeral resect. guide; co-designer Cofield total shoulder sys. Lt. comdr. USNR. Mem. ACS, AMA, Am. Acad. Orthopedic Surgery, Am. Bd. Orthopedic Surgery (dir. 114—), Am. Orthopedic Assn., Am. Shoulder and Elbow Surgeons (founding sec.-treas. 1982-87, pres. 1988-89). Republican. Presbyterian. Office: Mayo Clinic 200 1st Ave NW Rochester MN 55901-3004

COGGS, G. SPENCER, state legislator; b. Milw., Aug. 6, 1949; s. Calvin Jr. and Erma (Bryant) C.; m. Gershia Christina Brown, 1971; children: Mariama, Kijana. AA, Milw. Area Tech. Coll., 1975; BS, U. Wis., Milw., 1976. Former health officer, postal worker, printer City of Milw.; mem. from dist. 16 Wis. State Assembly, Madison, 1982-92, 93—, chmn. spkr.'s task force on gang violence, mem. com. on urban and local affairs, com. on rules, mem. com. on children and human svcs., com. on colls./univs., mem. coms. on employment and tng.; mem. com. on criminal justice and pub. safety; vice chmn. majority caucus, 1985, 87, 89. Mem. Wis. State Job Tng. Coord. Coun., Job Tng. Partnership Act, 1983—. Mem. Milw. Truancy Com.; mem. N.W. Corridor Rapid Transit Adv. Com., Sherman Park Rapid Transit Adv. Com.; bd. dirs. Isaac Coggs Cmty. Health Ctr. Mem. NAAPC, Urban League (bd. dirs., health and social svc. com.), Wis. Pub. Health Assn., Nat. Conf. State Legislators (mem. transp. and comms. com.). Home: 3732 N 40th St Milwaukee WI 53216-3027 Office: State Capitol Rm 214 N PO Box 8952 Madison WI 53708

COHAN, LEON SUMNER, lawyer, retired electric company executive; b. Detroit, June 24, 1929; s. Maurice and Lillian (Rosenfeld) C.; m. Heidi Ruth Seelmann, Jan. 22, 1956; children: Nicole, Timothy David, Jonathan Daniel. B.A., Wayne State U., 1949, J.D., 1952. Bar: Mich. 1953. Pvt. practice, Detroit, 1954-58; asst. atty. gen. State of Mich., Lansing, 1958-61, dep. atty. gen., 1961-72; v.p. legal affairs Detroit Edison Co., 1973-75, v.p., 1975-79, sr. v.p., gen. counsel, 1979-93; counsel Barris, Sott, Denn & Driker, Detroit, 1993—. Bd. dirs. Oakland Commerce Bank. Trustee Mich. Cancer Found.; bd. dirs. Concerned Citizens for Arts in Mich., U. Mich. Musical Soc.; mem. arts commn. Detroit Inst. Arts; mem. Race Rels. Coun. Met. Detroit. With U.S. Army, 1952-54. Recipient Disting. Alumni award Wayne State U. Law Sch., 1972, Disting. Svc. award Bd. Govs., Wayne State U., 1973, Judge Ira W. Jayne award NAACP, 1987, Israel Histadrut Menorah award, 1987, Knights of Charity award Pontifical Inst. for Fgn. Missions, 1989, Fellowship award Am. Arabic and Jewish Friends of Met. Detroit, Judge Learned Hand Human Rels. award, 1991, Gov.'s Arts award for Civic Leadership in the Arts, Michiganian of Yr. award Detroit News, 1993. Mem. ABA, Detroit Bar Assn., State Bar Mich. (Champion of Justice award 1993), Mich. Gen. Counsel Assn., Detroit Club. Democrat. Jewish. Home: 17 Eastbury Ct Ann Arbor MI 48105-1402 Office: Barris Sott Denn & Driker 15th Fl 211 W Fort St Lbby 15 Detroit MI 48226-3244 E-mail: icohan@aol.com.

COHEN, ALBERT DIAMOND, retail executive; b. Winnipeg, Man., Can., Jan. 20, 1914; s. Alexander and Rose (Diamond) C.; m. Irena Kankova, Nov. 6, 1953; children: Anthony Jan, James Eduard, Anna-Lisa. LLD (hon.), U. Man., 1987. Pres. Gendis Inc., Winnipeg, 1953-87; chmn., chief exec. officer, 1987-99; chmn., 1999—. Chmn. exec. com. Gendis Realty Inc., Winnipeg, 1961-88, also bd. dirs.; bd. dirs. SAAN Stores Ltd., Gendis Realty Inc. Author: The Entrepreneurs (Cert. of Merit Nat. Bus. Book award 1986). Past pres. Winnipeg Clin. Rsch. Inst., 1975-80, Paul H.T. Thorlakson Rsch. Found., 1978-80, Man. Theatre Ctr., 1968-71, 76-81; past hon. chmn. St. John's Ravenscourt Sch., 1984-94; commr. Metric Bd. Ottawa, 1978. Named mem. Order of Can., 1983, promoted to officer, 1995; recipient Internat. Disting. Entrepreneur award U. Man., 1983, Man. of Yr. award Sales and Advt. Club, Winnipeg, 1974, Commemorative medal 125th Ann. Can. Fedn., 1992, Sony Lifetime Achievement award, 2000; inducted into Can. Bus. Hall of Fame, 1994. Office: Gendis Inc 1370 Sony Pl Winnipeg MB Canada R3T 1N5 E-mail: finance@gendis.ca.

COHEN, ALLAN RICHARD, broadcasting executive; b. Bklyn., Dec. 27, 1947; s. Ike and Fae C.; m. Roberta Segal, July 12, 1970; children: Evan, Stacie. BS, Hofstra U., 1970; MM, Poly. Inst. Bklyn., 1976. Electronics engr. Sperry Systems Mgmt. Div., Great Neck, N.Y., 1970-74; with CBS/Viacom, 1974—; dir. planning and adminstrn. WCBS-TV, 1977-79; v.p. personnel CBS Broadcast Group, 1979-80; v.p., gen. mgr. Sta. KMOX-TV, St. Louis, 1980-86, Sta. KMOV-TV, St. Louis, 1986—. Lectr. in comm. and journalism Washington U., St. Louis; mem. affiliates adv. bd. CBS. Restaurant critic, travel editor St. Louis Bus. Jour. Vice chmn. bd. dirs. St. Louis Symphony; bd. dirs. Paraquad, Jewish Hosp., United Way, Variety Club; mem. adv. bd. Nat. Coun. Jewish Women, St. Louis. Recipient Flair awards, Emmy awards. Mem. NATAS (v.p. St. Louis chpt. 1987-88, pres. 1989-91), Mo. Broadcasters Assn. (bd. dirs.), Ill. Broadcasters Assn., Nat. Assn. Broadcasters, St. Louis Jr. League (adv. bd.), Westwood Club, St. Louis Variety Club (bd. dirs.).

COHEN, BURTON DAVID, franchising executive, lawyer; b. Chgo., Feb. 12, 1940; s. Allan and Gussy (Katz) C.; m. LInda Rochelle Kaine, Jan. 19, 1969; children: David, Jordana. BS in Bus. and Econs., Ill. Inst. Tech., 1960; JD, Northwestern U., 1963. Staff atty. McDonald's Corp., Oak Brook, Ill., 1964-69, asst. sec., 1969-70, asst. gen. counsel, 1970-76, asst. v.p., 1976-78, dep. dir. legal dept., 1978-80, v.p. franchising, asst. gen. counsel, asst. sec., 1980-89, sr. v.p., chief franchising officer, 1989-98. Adv. dir., 1992-93, McDonald's Corp., 1992—; lectr. Practising Law Inst.; guest lectr. grad. sch. of bus. U. Chgo.; adv. bd. La. State U. Franchise U.; dir. Goodwill Enterprises Devel. Corp.; franchise mediator CPR Inst. for Dispute Resolution; cons. Exec. Svc. Corps Chgo.; adj. prof. Kellogg Grad Sch. of Mgmt., Northwestern U.; dir. The Owyer Group. Author: Franchising: Second Generation Problems, 1969. With AUS, 1963-64. Mem. ABA, Ill. Bar Assn., Chgo. Bar Assn., Internat. Franchise Assn. (lectr.), Assn. Nat. Advertisers, Chgo. Coun. Fgn. Rels., Execs. Club (Chgo.), Tau Epsilon Phi, Phi Delta Phi. Office: 300 Cedar Ave Highland Park IL 60035

COHEN, CHRISTOPHER B. lawyer; b. Washington, July 10, 1942; m. Judith Calder; 2 children. BA, U. Mich., 1964, JD, 1967. Bar: Ill. 1968, Wis. 1986, D.C. 1972, U.S. Dist. Ct. D.C. 1969, U.S. Dist Ct. (no. dist.) Ill. 1968, U.S. Ct. Mil. Appeals 1977, U.S. Supreme Ct. 1974; lic. real estate broker, cert. real estate continuing edn. instr., Ill. Clerk, lawyer Legal Aid Bur.-United Charities of Chgo., 1967-68; adminstrv. asst. to pres. Cook County Bd. Commrs., 1969-71; hearing officer Liquor Commn. Cook County, Chgo., 1970-71; alderman 46th ward Chgo. City Coun., 1971-77; atty. Schwartzberg, Barnett & Cohen, Chgo., 1973-77; midwest regional dir. U.S. Dept. HHS, 1977-81; atty. Hinshaw, Culbertson, Moelmann, Hoban & Fuller, 1981-82, Cassiday, Shade & Gloor, Chgo., 1982-85; ptnr. Holleb & Coff, 1985-98; of counsel Buyer & Rubin, 1998—; prin. Cohen Law Firm, 1998—. Lectr. Northwestern U., 1973, DePaul U., Chgo., 1981, U. Ill., Chgo., 1981, 82; adult edn. tchr. Francis Parker Sch., Chgo., 1979, 80, 81; bd. dirs. State of Ill. Hosp. Licensing Bd., 1987-97; bd. dirs. State of Ill. Med. Ctr. Commn., 1985-90; mem. fed. regional coun. 1977-81; nursing home adv. coun. Office of Ill. Atty. Gen., 1988-94; Dem. candidate U.S. Ho. Reps., 10th Congressional Dist. Ill., 1999. Contbr. articles to profl. jours. and nat. newspapers. Field organizer Humphrey for Pres., Chgo., 1968; asst. to Ill. field dir. Jimmy Carter for Pres., Chgo., 1976; active spl. projects, polit. unit Clinton/Gore Campaign, Little Rock, 1992; mem. govt. affairs com. Jewish Fedn. Met. Chgo., 1988—; mem. U. Mich. Law Sch. Alumni Fund, Glenview Concert Band; fin. exec. bd. New Trier Township Dem. Orgn., 1993-98; bd. dirs. UNICEF Chgo., 1996-97. Mem. ABA (adminstrv. law and regulatory practice sect. 1990-95), Ill. State Bar Assn. (founding mem., chair health care sect. coun. 1986-87, mem. legis. com. 1988-90, assembly 1991-97, local govt. sect.), Chgo. Bar Assn. (vice chair urban affairs com. 1991, chair health law com. 1983, mem. real estate tax com.), D.C. Bar Assn., State Bar Wis. Office: Cohen Law Firm 185 Franklin Glencoe IL 60022-1259

COHEN, EDWARD, state official; Commr. Dept. Correction, Indpls. Office: IGCS Rm E334 302 W Washington St Indianapolis IN 46204-4701

COHEN, EDWARD PHILIP, microbiology and immunology educator, physician; b. Glen Ridge, N.J., Sept. 28, 1932; s. Harry and Rae (Berke) C.; m. Toba Joy Gold, Mar. 24, 1963; children— Mark L., Lauren L., Jennifer L., Jonathan M. Tuition scholarship student, U., Miami (Fla.), 1950-53; M.D., Washington U., St. Louis, 1957. Diplomate: Am. Bd. Allergy and Immunology, Nat. Bd. Med. Examiners. Intern. U. Chgo. Hosps., 1957-58; research asso. Nat. Inst. Allergy and Infectious Diseases, NIH, 1958-60; resident in medicine U. Colo. Med. Center, 1960-61, instr. dept. medicine, 1962-74; instr., then asst. prof. microbiology U. Colo., 1963-65; asso. prof. Inst. Microbiology, Rutgers U., 1965-67; asso. prof. microbiology and medicine Rutgers Med. Sch., 1967-68; asso. prof. La Rabida-U. Chgo. Inst. and dept. medicine U. Chgo. Sch. Medicine, 1968-69, asso. prof. depts. medicine and microbiology, 1969-77, prof. microbiology, 1977-79, asst. dean, 1971-73; prof. microbiology and immunology, dean Sch. Basic Med. Scis., Coll. Medicine U. Ill., 1979-82, also prof. Ctr. Edn. and Research in Genetics, 1979-82, dir. Office of Research and Devel., 1982-84, prof. dept. microbiology and immunology, 1985—, research prof. dept. medicine, 1986—; dir. MD/PhD program U. Ill. Coll. Medicine, 1993—. Editor: Immune RNA, 1976, Medicine in Transition: The Centennial of the University of Illinois College of Medicine, 1981; co-editor: Membranes, Receptors and the Immune Response, 1980; contbr. over 200 articles and revs. to profl. jours. Sci. adv. bd. Leukemia Research Found., 1978-83 ; chmn. Biotech. Contact Group City of Chgo., 1982-83 . Served with USPHS, 1958-60. Spl. postdoctoral fellow USPHS, 1961-63; Research Career Devel. grantee, 1963-65 Mem. Am. Assn. Immunologists, Am. Soc. Cell Biology, Am. Acad. Allergy, Acad. Medicine N.J., Am. Soc. Microbiology, Central Soc. Clin. Research, Chgo. Assn. Immunologists (pres. 1974-75), Chgo. Soc. Allergy, Inst. Medicine Chgo., Reticuloendothelial Soc. Home: 4737 S Kimbark Ave Chicago IL 60615-1901 Office: 835 S Wolcott Ave Chicago IL 60612-7340

COHEN, GABRIEL MURREL, editor, publisher; b. Louisville, Aug. 31, 1908; s. Isaac and Jenny (Rosenbaum) C.; m. Helen Aronovitz, Sept. 22, 1938; children: Lawrence, Theodore, Miriam, Debbie, Ben-Zion, Jennie, Hermine, Rena. A.B., U. N.C., 1930. Reporter Louisville Herald-Post, 1927-28, 30-31; founder, editor, pub. Ky. Jewish Chronicle (now Ky. Jewish Post and Opinion), Louisville, 1931—, Ind. Jewish Post, Indpls., 1935—, Mo. Jewish Post and Opinion, St. Louis, 1948-92, Nat. Jewish Post (now Nat. Jewish Post and Opinion), Indpls., 1948—. Founding chmn. Am. Jewish Press Assn., 1944—. Home: 7984 Lieber Rd Indianapolis IN 46260-2835 Office: Nat Jewish Post & Opinion 238 S Meridian St Indianapolis IN 46225-1024

COHEN, HARLEY, civil engineer, science educator; b. Winnipeg, Man., Can., May 12, 1933; s. Joseph and Ettie (Gilman) C.; m. Estelle Brodsky, Dec. 25, 1956; children: Brent, Murray, Carla. B.Sc. hons., U. Man., 1956; Sc.M., Brown U., 1958; Ph.D., U. Minn., 1964. Registered profl. engr., Man. Research engr. Boeing Co., Seattle, 1958-60; sr. research scientist Honeywell, Inc., Mpls., 1960-64; asst. prof. aero. and engring. mechanics U. Minn., 1965-66; assoc. prof. civil engring. U. Man., Winnipeg, 1966—, prof., 1968-89, disting. prof., 1983—, head dept., 1984-89, prof. applied math., 1989-94, dean faculty of sci., 1989-94, prof. applied math. and civil engring., 1994-98, disting. prof. math. emeritus, 1998—. J.L. Record prof. U. Minn.; invited vis. prof. U. Pisa, Italian Rsch. Coun., 1987; bd. dirs. Man. Rsch. Coun., 1989-94, Tri-Univ.-Meson Facility, U. B.C., 1989-94, Premier's Econ. Innovation and Tech. Coun., 1989-94. Co-author: Theory of Psuedo-Rigid Bodies, 1988; contbr. over 100 articles to profl. jours. Killam scholar, 1982; Brit. sci. fellow, 1985 Fellow Am. Acad. Mechanics (bd. dirs. 1988-91); mem. Soc. Natural Philosophy, Soc. Engring. Sci. Home: 55 Tanoak Park Dr Winnipeg MB Canada R2V 2W6 Office: U Man Dept Applied Math Faculty of Sci Winnipeg MB R3T 2N2 Canada R3T 2N2 E-mail: hcohen@cc.umanitoba.ca.

COHEN, IRA, legislative staff member; b. Chgo., Sept. 6, 1947; With Rep. Danny K. Davis, Washington, 1979—, issues and comm. dir., 1996—. Office: Office of Rep Danny K Davis 3333 W Arthington St Ste 130 Chicago IL 60624-4102

COHEN, JEROME, psychology educator, electrophysiologist; b. Pitts., May 27, 1925; s. Abraham Wolfe and Dorothy (Middleman) C.; m. Florence A. Chanock, Oct. 28, 1945; children— Marcus, Mara, Aaron. AA, Princeton U., 1943; BA, U. Pitts., 1947; MA, Cornell U., 1949; PhD, U. Pitts., 1951. Instr. U. Pitts., 1950-51; asst. prof., assoc. prof. Antioch Coll., Yellow Springs, Ohio, 1951-57; prof. psychiatry and behavioral sci. and neurology Northwestern U. Med. Sch., Chgo., 1957-93, prof. emeritus, 1993—. Dir. Electroencephalography Lab. Presbyn.-St. Lukes Hosp., Chgo., 1967-72, Cook County Hosp., Chgo., 1973-99; vis. scientist Neurol. Inst., U. London, 1963-64; vis. prof. Hebrew U., 1972-73, Stanford U., winter 1984. Lt. (j.g.) USNR, 1943-46. Commonwealth Fund fellow, 1963-64 Mem. Am. EEG Soc., Am. Psychol. Assn., Psychophysiol. Research Soc., Internat. Brain Research Soc., AAUP, AAAS, Am. Soc. for Applied Psychophysiology and Biofeedback, Sigma Xi.

COHEN, MALCOLM STUART, economist, research institute director; b. Mpls., Jan. 17, 1942; s. Jack Alvin and Lorraine Ethel (Hill) C.; m. Judith Ann Arenson, Sept. 25, 1965; children: Laura, Randall, Ilona. BA in Econs. summa cum laude, U. Minn., 1963; PhD in Econs., MIT, 1967. Labor economist U.S. Bur. Labor Stats., Washington, 1967-68; lectr. U. Md., College Park, 1968; asst. to v.p. state rels. and planning U. Mich., Ann Arbor, 1968-70, various tchr. positions, 1968-85; co-rsch. dir. U. Mich. Inst. of Labor and Indsl. Rels., 1973-80, dir., 1980-93; cons. Corp. Pub. Broadcasting, 1994-97; vis. prof. indsl. rels. ctr. U. Minn., 1994-96; pres. Employment Rsch. Corp., Ann Arbor, 1997—. Cons. U.S. Dept. Labor, 1995—, EEOC, 1996—, Money Mag., 1995—, Mich. Senate Fiscal Agy., Lansing, 1988; project dir. various projects Washington, 1968-92; expert witness discrimination and econs. various clients, 1982—. Author: Labor Shortages: As America Approaches the 21st Century, 1995, Global Skill Shortages, 2002; co-author: A Micro Model of Labor Supply, 1970; contbr. articles to profl. jours. Pres. Jewish Community Ctr., Ann Arbor, 1991-93. Mem. Nat. Assn. Forensic Economists, Indsl. Rels. Rsch. Assn., Internat. Indsl. Rels. Assn., N.Am. Econs. and Fin. Assn. Avocations: jogging, geneology. Office: Employment Rsch Corp Ste 250 3820 Packard Rd Ann Arbor MI 48108-3348 also: U Mich Inst Labor and Indsl Rels Ann Arbor MI 48109-2054 E-mail: malco@umich.edu.

COHEN, MARK A. retail executive; Chmn., pres.,ceo Lazarus Divsn., Cin. Office: Lazarus Div 690 Race St Cincinnati OH 45202-2323

COHEN, MARYJO R. manufacturing executive; BS in Bus. Adminstrn., U. Mich., 1973, JD, 1976. Bar: Mich. 1976. Assoc. resident counsel Nat. Presto Industries, 1976-82, asst. to treas., 1982-83, treas., 1983-86, v.p., 1986-89, pres., 1989—, CEO, 1995—, COO, CFO. V.p. subsidiaries and divsns. Canton Sales & Storage Co., Century Leasing & Liquidating, Inc., Jackson Sales and Storage Co., Nat. Def. Corp., Nat. Holding Investment Co., Presto Export Ltd., Presto Mfg. Co., Presto Products Mfg. Co. Office: Nat Presto Industries 3925 N Hastings Way Eau Claire WI 54703

COHEN, MELANIE ROVNER, lawyer; b. Chgo., Aug. 9, 1944; d. Millard Jack and Sheila (Fox) Rovner; m. Arthur Wieber Cohen, Feb. 17, 1968; children: Mitchell Jay, Jennifer Sue. AB, Brandeis U., 1965; JD, DePaul U., 1977. Bar: Ill. 1977, U.S. Dist. Ct. (no. dist.) Ill., U.S. Ct. Appeals (7th cir.). Law clk. to Justice F.J. Hertz U.S. Bankruptcy Ct.,

1976-77; ptnr. Altheimer & Gray, Chgo., 1977-89, 89—, Antonow & Fink, Chgo., 1977-89. Mem. Supreme Ct. of Ill. Atty. Registration and Disciplinary Commn. Inquiry Bd., 1982-86, hearing bd., 1986-94; instr. secured and consumer transactions creditor-debtor law DePaul U., Chgo., 1980-90; bd. dirs. Bankruptcy Arbitration and Mediation Svcs., 1994-96; instr. real estate and bankruptcy law John Marshall Law Sch., Chgo., 1996-98. Contbr. articles to profl. jours. Panelist, spkr., bd. dirs., v.p., fellow Brandeis U. Nat. Alumni Assn., 1981—; life mem. Nat. Women's Com., 1975—, pres. Chgo. chpt., 1975-82; mem. Glencoe (Ill.) Caucus, 1977-80; chair lawyers com. Ravinia Festival, 1990-91, chmn. sustaining com., 1991, mem. annual fund, 1991—. Fellow: ABA (co-chair com. on enforcement of creditors' rights and bankruptcy), Am. Coll. Bankruptcy; mem.: Internat. Insolvency Inst., Turnaround Mgmt. Assn. (pres. Chgo./midwest chpt. 1990—92, internat. bd. dirs. 1990—, mem. mgmt. com. 1995—, pres. internat. bd. dirs. 1999—2000, chmn. internat. bd. dirs. 2000—01), Comml. Fin. Assn. Edn. Found. (bd. govs.), Ill. Trial Lawyers Assn., Comml. Law League, Chgo. Bar Assn. (chmn. bankruptcy reorgn. com. 1983—85), Ill. State Bar Assn. Home: 167 Park Ave Glencoe IL 60022-1351 Office: Altheimer & Gray 10 S Wacker Dr Ste 4000 Chicago IL 60606-7407 E-mail: cohenm@altheimer.com.

COHEN, MELVIN SAMUEL, manufacturing company executive; b. Mpls., Jan. 16, 1918; s. Henry and Mary (Witebsky); m. Eileen Phillips; children: Amy, Maryjo. BS, U. Minn., 1939, JD, 1941. Bar: Minn. 1941, U.S. Supreme Ct. 1944. Pvt. practice, Mpls., until 1942; with legal div., rationing sect. Office Price Adminstrn., Washington, 1942-43; pub. counsel Civil Aero. Bd., 1943-44; with Nat. Presto Industries, Inc., Eau Claire, Wis., 1944—, treas., 1950-51, v.p. adminstrn., treas., 1951-54, exec. v.p., 1954-60, pres., 1960-75, chmn. bd., 1975—. Chmn. bd. dirs., pres., dir. Nat. Holding Investment Co., Jackson (Miss.) Sales & Storage Co., Presto Mfg. Co., chmn. bd., pres., dir., Nat. Presto Industries Export Corp., Eau Claire, Presto Internat. Ltd., Hong Kong; pres., dir. Presto Products Mfg. Co., Canton Sales and Storage Co.; v.p., dir. Nat. Pipeline Co., Cleve. Nat. Automatic Pipeline Ops., Inc., Escanaba, Mich.; bd. dirs. 1st Nat. Bank, Eau Claire; mem. industry adv. com. for aluminum industry and internat. combustion engine industry during Korean War for Nat. Prodn. Authority. Editor Minn. Law Rev., 1939-41. Office: Nat Presto Industries Inc 3925 N Hastings Way Eau Claire WI 54703-0485

COHEN, MORTON A. venture capitalist; b. Montreal, Can., Apr. 13, 1935; s. Lillian (Bloom) C.; m. Rosalie Cohen, June 5, 1960; children: Carl, Joanne, Margaret. AB, Concordia U., Montreal, 1957; MBA, U. Pa., 1959. Salesman, analyst Merrill Lynch, Montreal, 1960-65, Baker Weeks, Montreal, 1965-70, Kippen & Co., Montreal, 1970-72; pres. Yorkton Securities, 1972-77, MAC Mgmt. Assocs., Montreal, 1977-80, Bel-Fran Investments, Toronto, Ont., Can., 1980-82; chmn., chief exec. officer Clarion Capital Corp., Cleve., 1982—, First City Technology Ventures, Cleve., 1982—. Bd. dirs. Monitek, Hayward, Calif., Environ. Protection Sys., Inc., Atlanta, Abaxis, Inc., Sunnyvale, Calif., Small's Oilfield Svcs. Corp., Big Springs, Tex., Zemex Corp. Mem. Fin. Analysts Soc. Avocations: tennis, golf. Office: Cohesant Technologies Inc 5845 W 82nd St Ste 102 Indianapolis IN 46278

COHEN, NEAL, airline executive; Various positions in internat. fin., banking, planning GM, N.Y.C., 1984-91; dir. corp. planning Northwest Airlines Corp., St. Paul, 1991, from dir. mkt. planning to v.p. fin. and contr., 1992-99, sr. v.p., treas., 1999—. Office: Northwest Airlines Corp 5101 Northwest Dr Saint Paul MN 55111-3027

COHEN, RAYMOND, mechanical engineer, educator; b. St. Louis, Nov. 30, 1923; s. Benjamin and Leah (Lewis) C.; m. Katherine Elise Silverman, Feb. 1, 1948 (dec. May 1985); children— Richard Samuel, Deborah, Barbara Beth; m. Lila Lakin Cagen, Nov. 30, 1986. B.S., Purdue U., 1947, M.S., 1950, Ph.D., 1955. Instr. mech. engring. Purdue U., 1948-55, asst. prof., 1955-58, assoc. prof., 1958-60, prof., 1960-98, asst. dir. Ray W. Herrick Labs., 1970-71, dir., 1971-93, acting head Sch. Mech. Engring., 1988-89, Herrick prof. engring., 1994-99, Herrick prof. emeritus engring., 1999—. Cons. to industry. Departmental editor: Ency. Brit., 1957-62; editorial bd. Jour. Sound and Vibration, 1971-87; editor Internat. Jour. of Heating, Ventilating, Air Conditioning and Refrigerating Rsch., 1994-98. Served as sgt. inf. AUS, 1943-46. Recipient Kamerlingh Onnes gold medal, 1995; NATO sr. fellow in sci., 1971 Fellow ASME, ASHRAE; mem. NSPE, Am. Soc. Engring. Edn., Soc. Exptl. Mechanics, Internat. Inst. Refrigeration (chmn. U.S. nat. com. 1992-95, U.S. del. 1992-99), Acoustical Soc. Am., Inst. Noise Control Engring. (pres. 1990), Sigma Xi, Pi Tau Sigma, Tau Beta Pi. Home: 2501 Spyglass Dr Valparaiso IN 46383 Office: Purdue U Ray W Herrick Labs Sch Mechanical Engring West Lafayette IN 47907-1077

COHEN, RICHARD J. state legislator; b. Oct. 5, 1949; BA, Northwestern U.; JD, William Mitchell Coll. Law. Mem. Minn. Ho. of Reps., St. Paul, 1977-78, 1983-86, Minn. Senate from 64th dist., St. Paul, 1986—; atty., 1996—. Chmn. State Govt. Divsn. Fin. Com.; mem. Crime Prevention com., Ethics & Campaign Reform & Judiciary coms. Office: 517 Capitol Bldg 75 Constitution Ave Saint Paul MN 55155-1601 also: State Senate State Capital Building Saint Paul MN 55155-0001

COHEN, RONALD S. accountant; b. Lafayette, Ind., July 13, 1937; s. William and Stella (Fleischman) C.; m. Nancy Ann Plotkin, May 29, 1960; children: Philip, Douglas. BS in Acctg., Ind. U., 1958. CPA, Ind. Staff acct. Crowe, Chizek & Co., South Bend, Ind., 1958-65, ptnr., 1965-82, mng. ptnr., 1982-94, chmn. bd. dirs., 1994-2000. Mem. dean's adv. coun. Ind. U. Sch. Bus., 1996—. Commr. Housing Authority of South Bend, 1976-85, also vice-chmn.; pres. Jewish Fedn., 1979-82; bd. dirs. United Way of South Bend, 1987-90. Served to lt. USAR, 1958-66. Mem. AICPA (bd. dirs. 1990-97, vice-chmn. 1994, chmn. 1995), Ind. Soc. CPAs, Ind. U. Sch. Bus. Alumni Assn. (bd. dirs. 1992-95). Democrat. Jewish. Office: Crowe Chizek & Co PO Box 7 330 E Jefferson Blvd South Bend IN 46601-2366 E-mail: rcohen@crowechizek.com.

COHEN, SANFORD NED, pediatrics educator, academic administrator; b. N.Y.C., June 12, 1935; s. George M. and Fannie Leah (Epstein) C.; m. Judith Luskind, June 22, 1958 (div. 1984); 1 child, Andrew B.; m. Elizabeth Prevot(div. 1991); m. Sandra Hoffmann, June 13, 1992. AB, The Johns Hopkins U., 1956, MD, 1960. Diplomate Am. Bd. Pediat. Intern in pediat. Johns Hopkins Hosp., 1960-61, resident, 1961-63; instr. to assoc. prof. NYU Sch. Medicine, N.Y.C., 1965-74; chmn., prof. pediat. Wayne State U. Sch. Medicine, Detroit, 1974-81, assoc. dean, 1981-86, sr. v.p. for acad. affairs, provost, 1986-91, prof. pediat., 1991-98, prof. emeritus, 1998—. Dir. Wayne State U. Devel. Disability Inst., 1983-86, Child Rsch. Ctr., Detroit, 1975-81; pediatrician-in-chief Children's Hosp. Mich., Detroit, 1974-81; adj. faculty U. Mich. Sch. Pub. Health, Ann Arbor, 1980-90; chair steering com. NIH Network of Pediat. Pharmacology Rsch. Units, 1994-98, mem. adv. com., 1999—; reviewer Inst. of Medicine Nat. Acad. Sci.; mem. profl. adv. coun. Children's Med. Rsch. Inst., Oklahoma City, 1999—; vol. cons. Lee Meml. Health Sys., Ft. Myers, Fla., 2000—. Editor: Progress in Drug Therapy in Children, 1981; contbr. articles to profl. jours. Mem. bd. health, Leonia, N.J., 1972-74; mem. Bd. Police Commrs., Detroit, 1995-99, chmn., 1997-98. John and Mary R. Markle scholar acad. medicine, 1968-74. Mem.: Soc. Pediat. Rsch. (v.p. 1980—81), Sr. & Ret. Physicians Assn. (pres. 2001—), Midwest Soc. Pediat. Rsch. 1979—80, Am. Pediat. Soc. Avocations: reading, golf. Office: Children's Hosp Mich 3901 Beaubien St Detroit MI 48201-2119 E-mail: scohen@med.wayne.edu.

COHEN, TED, philosophy educator; b. Danville, Ill., Dec. 13, 1939; s. Sam and Shirley E. (Nimz) C.; m. Julie Simon, Apr. 18, 1940 (div. 1992); children: Shoshannah, Amos; m. Ann Rutherfurd Collier Austin, 1994. AB, U. Chgo., 1962; MA, Harvard U., 1965, PhD, 1972. Prof. philosophy U. Chgo., 1967—, chmn. dept. philosophy, 1974-79. Author: Jokes, 1999; editor: Essays in Kant's Aesthetics, 1982, Pursuits of Reason, 1993; contbr. articles to profl. jours. in German, Polish, Italian, French, Norwegian, Spanish, Finnish, Russian, and Dutch, 1972—. Bd. dirs. Ctr. for Rehab. and Tng. of Disabled, B'nai Brith Hillel Found. of U. Chgo., KAM Isaiah Israel Congregation, Chgo., 1980—, mem. faculty religious sch.; chmn. com. on gen. studies in humanities U. Chgo., 1991—. Named William R. Kenan Jr. Disting. Prof. Humanities Coll. of William and Mary, 1986-87; grantee Am. Council Learned Socs., 1980, 85. Mem. Am. Soc. Aesthetics (v.p., pres.-elect, pres. 1997—), Phi Beta Kappa (vis. scholar 2000-2001). Avocation: baseball theory and practice. Office: U Chgo Dept Philosophy 1050 E 59th St Chicago IL 60637-1559 Home: # 2 5816 S Blackstone Ave Chicago IL 60637-1839 E-mail: tedcohen@midway.vebicago.edu.

COHEN, WILLIAM BENJAMIN, historian, educator; b. Jakobstad, Finland, May 2, 1941; came to U.S., 1957; s. Walter Israel and Rosi (Hirschberg) C.; m. Christine Matheu; children: Natalie, Leslie, Laurel. B.A., Pomona Coll., 1962; M.A., Stanford U., 1963, Ph.D., 1968. Vis. lectr. Northwestern U., Evanston, Ill., 1966-67; instr. history Ind. U., Bloomington, 1966-68, asst. prof., 1968-71, assoc. prof., 1971-80, prof., 1980—, chmn. West European studies, 1978-80, chmn. dept. history, 1980-87, acting chmn. dept. history, 2001—02. Author: Rulers of Empire, 1971, Robert Delavignette, 1977, French Encounter, 1980, European Empire Building, 1980, (with Thomas F. Noble et al) Western Civilization: The Continuing Experiment, 1994, 2d edit., 1998, Urban Government and the Rise of the French City, 1998, The Transformation of Modern France, 1997. NEH fellow, 1972, Fulbright fellow, 1983-84. Mem. Am. Hist. Assn. (mem. nominating com. 1987-90, George Louis prize com. 1997-00), Coun. for European Studies, Soc. French Hist. Studies (pres. 1980-81, exec. com. 1980-83) Democrat. Home: 1016 S Highland Ave Bloomington IN 47401-6016 Office: Ind Univ History Dept Ballantine Hall Bloomington IN 47405 E-mail: cohenw@indiana.edu.

COHLER, BERTRAM JOSEPH, social sciences educator, clinical psychologist; b. Chgo., Dec. 3, 1938; s. Jonas Robert and Betty (Cahn) C.; m. Anne Meyers, June 11, 1962 (dec. Dec. 1989); children: Jonathan Richard, James Joseph. BA, U. Chgo., 1961; PhD, Harvard U., 1967; cert. in adult analysis, Inst. Psychoanalysis, 1989. Diplomate Am. Bd. Psychoanalysis, Am. Bd. Examiners in Profl. Psychology. Lectr. social relations Harvard U., Cambridge, Mass., 1967-69; assoc. dir. Sonia Shankman Orthogenic Sch., 1969-72, 94-96; dir. Orthogenic Sch. U. Chgo., 1969-72, 94—; asst. prof. U. Chgo., 1969-75, assoc. prof., 1975-81, prof. depts. psychology, edn. and psychiatry, 1981—. Co-dir. Univ. Ctr. Health and Aging Soc., 1987—; sci. and profl. staff dept. psychiatry Michael Reese Hosp., Chgo., 1980-90; cons. The Tresholds, Chgo., 1972-81, Inst. Psychoanalysis, Chgo., 1972—, Ill. State Psychiat. Inst., Chgo., 1977-82; pres. bd. Ctr. Religion and Psychotherapy, Chgo. Author: (with H. Grunebaum et al) Mentally Ill Mothers and Their Children, 1975, 82, Mothers, Grandmothers, and Daughters, 1981, (with others) Parenthood as an Adult Experience, 1983, The Invulnerable Child, 1987, Handbook of Clinical Research on Adolescence, 1993, (with R. Galatzer-Levy) The Essential Other, 1993, The Course of Gay and Lesbian Lives, 2000, (with R. Galatzer Levy) The Psychoanalytic Study of Lives Over Time, 1999. Mem. initial rev. group in aging NIMH, Washington, 1982-86, Mental Health Spl. Projects, 1988-96; bd. dirs. Horizons Cmty. Svcs., Chgo. Recipient Quantrell prize U. Chgo., 1975, Lily Gondor award Postgrad. Ctr. for Mental Health, 2000; fellow Inst. Medicine, 1975; named William Rainey Harper chair U. Chgo., 1978. Fellow Gerontol. Soc., Soc. Projective Techniques Am. Orthopsychiat. Assn. (bd. dirs. 1981-84, pres. elect 1991, pres. 1992), Am. Psychol. Assn. (chmn. profl. affairs com. divsn. 39 1981-83, editor Psychoanalytic Psychology 1987-97, pres. sect. II 1992); mem. Am. Sociol. Assn., Am. Anthrop. Assn., Am. Assn. Psychiat. Svcs. to Children (Alexander Gralnick award), Soc. Rsch. in Child Devel., Chgo. Assn. Psychoanalytic Psychology (pres. 1983-84), Am. Psychoanalytic Assn. Home: 5408 S Blackstone Ave Chicago IL 60615-5407 Office: U Chgo 5730 S Woodlawn Ave Chicago IL 60637-1603

COHN, AVERN LEVIN, district judge; b. Detroit, July 23, 1924; s. Irwin I. and Sadie (Levin) C.; m. Joyce Hochman, Dec. 30, 1954 (dec. Dec. 1989); m. Lois Pincus Cohn, June 1992; children: Sheldon, Leslie Cohn Magy, Thomas. Student, John Tarleton Agrl. Coll., 1943, Stanford U., 1944; J.D., U. Mich., 1949. Bar: Mich. 1949. Practiced in, Detroit, 1949-79; mem. firm Honigman Miller Schwartz & Cohn, 1961-79; sr. judge U.S. Dist. Ct., 1979—. Mem. Mich. Civil Rights Commn., 1972-75, chmn., 1974-75; Mem. Detroit Bd. Police Commrs., 1975-79, chmn., 1979; bd. govs. Jewish Welfare Fedn., Detroit, 1972—. Served with AUS, 1943-46. Mem. ABA, Mich. Bar Assn., Am. Law Inst. E-mail: avern_cohn@mied.uscourts.gov.

COHN, EDWARD L. commissioner corrections department; BA in History, Polit. Sci., Culver-Stockton Coll., 1961; MA in Forensic Studies, Ind. U., 1977. From parole agent to commr. Gary (Ind.) Dept. Correction, 1965-1996; commr. Ind. Dept. Correction, Indpls., 1996—. Active Special Olympics Ind., Law Enforcement Torch Run, Optimist Club Plainfield (past pres.), Lake County Assn. Crime, Delinquency (past pres.), Govs. Council Impaired, Dangerous Driving, Advisory Resource Council Culver-Stockton Coll. Mem. A.S.C.A. (juvenile issues com., technol. com.), Nat. Inst. Justice Am. Correctional Assn. (Ind. chpt., past pres.), Criminal Justice Inst. (bd. trustees), Assn. State Correctional Adminstrs., Correctional Accreditation Mgrs. Assn., Law Enforcement Tech. Advisory Council, Fraternal Order Police. Office: Indiana Dept of Correction E334 Ind Govt Ctr South 302 W Washington St Indianapolis IN 46204-4701

COHN, GERALD B. federal judge; b. 1939; BA, Ill. Coll., 1961; JD, U. Chgo., 1964. Magistrate judge Ill. So. Dist., East St. Louis, 1981—. Served with U.S. Army, 1965-67, Res., 1967-71. Office: US Courthouse 750 Missouri Ave East Saint Louis IL 62201-2954 E-mail: gcohn@aol.com.

COHODES, ELI AARON, publisher; b. Iron Mountain, Mich., Sept. 12, 1927; s. Joseph Harry and Esther Ida (Albert) C.; m. Phyllis Hersh, Jan. 4, 1953; children: Stephen Eliot, David Bruce, Mitchell Joseph, Paul Andrew (dec.) BA, Harvard U., 1950. Assoc. editor Hosp. Mgmt. mag., 1953-54; mng. editor Trustee mag., 1957-59, Modern Hosp. mag., 1959-63; editor Nation's Schs. mag., Chgo., 1963-68, chmn. editorial adv. bd., columnist, 1968-75; v.p. Instructional Dynamics, Inc., Chgo., 1968-70; chmn. Teach'em, Chgo, 1970—; pres. Bonus Books, Inc., Chgo., 1985—2002. Lectr. profl. writing U. Chgo., 1959-63 Co-author: Planning Flexible Learning Places, 1977; mem. editorial bd. Coll. and Univ. Bus. mag, 1973-75. With AUS, 1945-46. Home: 37 Turnbull Woods Ct Highland Park IL 60035-5135

COLANDER, PATRICIA MARIE, newspaper editor; b. Chgo., Oct. 25, 1952; d. Charles L. Colander and Mary Elizabeth Connors; m. Paul Michael Ansell, Aug. 18, 1980 (div. Jan. 1993); children: Charles Thomas, Ida Kay Ansell; m. Jeffery A. Kumorek, Dec. 12, 1997. BJ, U. Ill., 1973. Staff writer Chgo. Tribune, 1973-77, Chgo. Reader, 1977-81; adj. prof. Medill Sch. Journalism Northwestern U., 1982-87; editor Copley Newspapers, Chgo. suburbs, No. Ill., 1987-92; asst. mng. editor The Times, 1992-93, pub. Ill. edits., 1993-96, mng. editor Ind., 1996—. Exec. devel. program Am. Press Inst., Reston, Va., 1994. Author: Thin Air: The Life and Mysterious Disappearance of Helen Brach, 1982, Hugh Hefner's First Funeral and Other True Tales of Love and Death in Chicago, 1985. Recipient awards AP, 1987, 88, 89, Suburban Newspapers Am., 1988. Mem. Inland Press Assn. (award 1991), Hoosier State Press, Tavern Club Chgo. Office: The Times 601 45th Ave Munster IN 46321-2819

COLBERT, VIRGIS WILLIAM, brewery company executive; b. Jackson, Miss., Oct. 13, 1939; s. Quillie and Eddi C.; grad. Exec. Inst., Earlham Coll.; BS, Ctrl. Mich. U. With Toledo Machining Plant, Chrysler Corp., 1966-79, foreman, 1968-70, gen. foreman, 1970-73, mfg. supt., 1973-77, gen. mfg. supt., 1977-79; asst. to plant mgr. Miller Brewing Co., Reidsville, N.C., 1979-80, prodn. mgr., Ft. Worth, Tex., 1980-81, plant mgr. Milw. Container Plant, 1981-87, asst. dir. can mfg., 1987-88, dir. container and support mfg., 1988-90, v.p. materials mfg. and plant ops., 1990-91, v.p. plant ops., 1991-93, sr. v.p. ops., 1993-95, sr. v.p. worldwide ops., 1995-97, exec. v.p., 1997—; bd. dirs. Delphi Automotive Sys., Inc., Weyco Group, Inc., The Manitowoc Co., Inc., Bradley Ctr., Sports and Entertainment Corp., Miller Brewing Co., Milw., Fisk Univ., Greater Milw. Open, Thurgood Marshall Scholarship Fund. Mem. NAACP, Nat. Urban League's Black Exec. Exchange Program. Mem. Frontiers Internat. Club, Masons, Shriners, Omega Psi Phi, Sigma Pi Phi. Office: Miller Brewing Co 3939 W Highland Blvd Milwaukee WI 53208-2866

COLBY, JOY HAKANSON, critic; b. Detroit; d. Alva Hilliard and Eleanor (Radtke) Hakanson; m. Raymond L. Colby, Apr. 11, 1953; children: Sarah, Katherine, Lisa. Student, Detroit Soc. Arts and Crafts, 1945; BFA, Wayne State U., 1946; DFA (hon.) , Coll. Art & Design, 1998, Ctr. for Creative Studies, 1998. Art critic Detroit News, 1947—; originator exhibit Arts and Crafts in Detroit, 1906-1976; with Detroit Inst. Arts, 1976. Author: (book) Art and A City, 1956; contbr. articles to art periodicals. Mem. visual arts adv. panel Mich. Coun. Arts, 1974—79; mayor's appointment Detroit Inst. Arts, 1974; mem. Bloomfield Hills Arts Coun., 1974. Recipient Alumni award, Wayne State U., 1967, Art Achievement award, 1983, Headliner award, 1984, award arts reporting, Detroit Press Club, 1984, Art Leadership award, Ctr. Creative Studies, 1989. Office: 615 W Lafayette Blvd Detroit MI 48226-3124

COLE, BRUCE MILAN, Federal Agency Administrator, Art Historian; b. Cleve., Aug. 2, 1938; s. Jerome I. and Selma (Kaufman) C.; m. Doreen Luff, July 15, 1962; children: Stephaine Wren, Ryan Lawrence. BA, Western Res. U., 1962; MA, Oberlin Coll., 1964; PhD, Bryn Mawr Coll., 1969. Asst. prof. U. Rochester, 1969-73; assoc. prof. Ind. U., Bloomington, 1973-77, prof., 1973-88, disting. prof. fine arts, 1988—; mem. Nat. Found. on the Arts and the Humanities, Washington, 2001—. Author: Giott and Florentine Painting 1280-1575, 1976, paperback edit., 1977, Agnolo Gaddi, 1977, Italian Majolica from Midwestern Collections, 1977, Masaccio and the Art of Early Renaissance Florence, 1980, Sienese Painting from Its Origins to the Fifteenth Century, 1969, The Renaissance Artist at Work, 1983, London, John Murray, 1983, Sienese Painting in the Age of Renaissance, 1985, Italian Art 1250-1550: The Relation of Renaissance Art to Life and Soc., 1987, Art of the Western World, Piero della Francesca, 1991, Giotto: The Scrovegni Chapel, Padua, 1993, Studies in Italian Art 1250-1550, 1996, Titian and Venetian Painting, 1450-1590, 1998, The Informed Eye, 1999. Recipient Pres.' award Am. Assn. Italian Studies, 1987; NEH fellow, 1972, Guggenheim Found. fellow, 1975, Am. Coun. Learned Socs. fellow, 1981. Fellow Accademia Senese degli Intronati; mem. Nat. Coun. on the Humanities. Avocation: walking. Office: Nat Found on the Arts and Humanities NEH 1100 Pennsylvania Ave NW Washington DC 20506 Office Fax: 202-682-5603.

COLE, DAVID EDWARD, university administrator; b. Detroit, July 20, 1937; s. Edward Nicholas and Esther Helen (Engman) C.; m. Carol Hutchins, July 9, 1965; children: Scott David, Christopher Carl. BS in Mech. Engring. and Math., U. Mich., 1960, MS in Mech. Engring., 1961, PhD, 1966. Engr. GM, Detroit, 1960-65; prof. U. Mich., Ann Arbor, 1967—, dir. Office for Study of Automotive Transp., 1978-2000; entrepreneur 6 cos., 1975-95; dir. Ctr. Auto Rsch. and Mgmt., ptnr. Environment Inst. Mich, 2000—. Bd. dirs. MSX Internat., Detroit, Mech. Dynamics, A Arbor, Thyssen U.S., Detroit, Saturn Electronics, Detroit, Plastech, Detroit, R.L. Polk, Southfield, Mich.; energy engring. bd. NRC, 1989-94; select panel U.S.-Can. Free trade Pact, 1988-91. Author: Elementary Vehicle Dynamics, 1972; contbr. articles to profl. jours. Bd. trustees Hope Coll., 1994-98. Fellow Soc. Automotive Engrs. (dir. 1980-83, 85-88, Teetor award 1969), Engring. Soc. Detroit (Horace H. Rackham medal 2000); mem. Chevalier of the Nat. Order of Merit from France, 1999, Soc. Mktg. Execs. (Mktg. Educator of Yr. 1998, Rene Dubos Environ. award 1998), Nat. Auto Dealers Assn. Found. (Freedom of Mobility award 1993), Swedens Royal Order of the Polar Star. Republican. Presbyterian. Avocations: hunting, fishing, boating, running, tennis. Office: Ctr Auto Rsch PO Box 134004 Ann Arbor MI 48113-4004 E-mail: dcole@erim.org.

COLE, DOUGLAS, retired English literature educator; b. N.Y.C., July 25, 1934; s. Ronald and Helen Elizabeth (Bladykas) C.; m. Virginia Ann Ford, Nov. 28, 1957; children: David, Stephen, Karen, Kristin. BA, U. Notre Dame, Ind., 1957; MA, U. Chgo., 1957; PhD, Princeton U., 1961. Instr. English, Yale U., New Haven, 1960-64, asst. prof., 1964-67, assoc. prof., 1967-69; prof. Northwestern U., Evanston, Ill., 1969-98, prof. emeritus, 1998—, chmn. dept. English, 1974-77, acting chmn., 1993, master Humanities Residential Coll., 1981-84, dir. major program in drama, 1980-93, 95-97. Author: Suffering and Evil in the Plays of Christopher Marlowe, 1962, Christopher Marlowe and the Renaissance of Tragedy, 1995; editor: 20th Century Views of Romeo and Juliet, 1970, Renaissance Drama XI: Tragedy, 1980; contbr. numerous articles to profl. jours. Morse fellow, 1966-67; Woodrow Wilson fellow, Danforth fellow Princeton U., 1957-61. Office: Northwestern U English Dept Evanston IL 60208-0001 E-mail: d-cole@northwestern.edu.

COLE, ELSA KIRCHER, lawyer; b. Dec. 5, 1949; d. Paul and Hester Marie (Pellegrom) Kircher; m. Roland J. Cole, Aug. 16, 1975; children: Isabel Ashley, Madeline Aldis. AB in History with distinction, Stanford U., 1971; JD, Boston U., 1974. Bar: Wash. 1974, Mich. 1989, Kans. 1997, Ind. 1999, U.S. Supreme Ct. 1980. Asst. atty gen., rep. dept. motor vehicles State of Wash., Seattle, 1974-75, asst. atty. gen., rep. dept. social and health svcs., 1975-76, asst. atty. gen., rep. U. Wash., 1976-89; gen. counsel U. Mich., Ann Arbor, 1989-97, NCAA, Indpls., 1997—. Presenter ednl. issues various confs. and workshops. Contbr. articles to profl. jours. Mem. Nat. Assn. Coll. and Univ. Attys. (chair profl. devel. com. 1990-91, mem. nominations and site selection coms. 1987-88, 95-96, program 1988-89, 89-90, 91-92, 92-93, 95-96, board ops. 92-93, fin., articles and by-laws coms. 1988-89, CLE com. 1995-96, 96-97, 2000-01, co-chair student affairs sect. 1987-88, 88-89, honors and awards ethics com. 1991-92, continuing legal edn. com. 1995-97, pub. com. 1996-97, bd. dirs. 1988-91), Wash. State Bar Assn. (chair law sch. liaison com. 1988-89), Wash. Women Lawyers (pres. Seattle-King County chpt. 1986, v.p. membership, state bd. 1987, 88, state chair candidate endorsement com. 1987, 88), Seattle-King County Bar Assn. Office: NCAA PO 6222 Indianapolis IN 46206-6222 E-mail: ecole@ncaa.org.

COLE, KENNETH DUANE, architect; b. Ft. Wayne, Ind., Jan. 23, 1932; s. Wolford J. and Helen Francis (McDowell) C.; m. Carolyn Lou Meyer, Apr. 25, 1953; children: David Brent, Denelle Hope, Diana Faith, Dawn Love. Student, Ft. Wayne Art Inst., 1950-51; BS in Architecture, U. Cin., 1957. Draftsman/intern Humbrecht Assocs., Ft. Wayne, 1957-58; ptnr./arch. Cole-Matott, Archs./Planners, 1959-94, Cole & Cole Archs., 1995—. Mem. adv. bd. Gen. Services Adminstrn., Region 5, 1976, 78. Archtl. works include: Weisser Pk. Jr. H.S., 1963, Brandt Hall, 1965, Bonsib Bldg., 1967, Lindley Elem. Sch., 1969, Young Elem. Sch., 1972, Study Elem. Sch., 1975, Old City Hall Renovation, 1978, Peoples Trust

Bank Adminstrv. Svcs. Ctr., 1979, Cole Residence (Design award 1988), Ossian Office Old 1st Nat. Bank, 1988, Perimeter Security Wall, Ind. State Prison. Bd. dirs. Ft. Wayne Art Inst., 1969-74, Arch, Inc., Ft. Wayne, 1975-77, Downtown Ft. Wayne Assn., 1977-82, Hist. Soc. Ft. Wayne and Allen County, 1982-88, Izaak Walton League Am., Ft. Wayne, 1970-76. Recipient citation Ind. Soc. Archs. for remodeling of Bonsib Bldg., 1978. Mem. Ft. Wayne C. of C., AIA (bd. dirs. No. Ind. 1971-74, pres. 1974), Ind. Soc. Archs. (bd. dirs. 1973-76, sec. 1976), Ft. Wayne Soc. Archs. (pres. 1970-71), Am. Arbitration Assn. (panel of arbitrators 1980-96). Lutheran. Home: 11602 Stellhorn Rd New Haven IN 46774-9775 Office: Cole & Cole Architects 927 S Harrison St Fort Wayne IN 46802-3672 E-mail: Arch2Cole@aol.com.

COLE, MONROE, neurologist, educator; b. N.Y.C., Mar. 21, 1933; s. Harry and Sylvia (Firman) C.; m. Merritt Ellen Frindel, June 15, 1958; children: Elizabeth Anne, Victoria, Scott Frindel, Pamela Catherine. A.B. cum laude, Amherst Coll., 1953; M.D. magna cum laude, Georgetown U., 1957. Diplomate Am. Bd. Psychiatry and Neurology. Intern in medicine Seton Hall Coll. Medicine, Jersey City, 1957-58, asst. resident in medicine, 1958-59; asst. resident in neurology Mass. Gen. Hosp., Boston, 1959-60, rsch. fellow in neuropathology, 1960-61, rsch. fellow in neurology, 1961-62; teaching fellow in neurology Harvard U., Cambridge, 1959-60, 61-62, teaching fellow in neuropathology, 1960-61; clin. instr. in neurology Georgetown U., Washington, 1962-65; asst. prof. neurology, assoc. in anatomy Bowman Gray Sch. Medicine, Wake Forest U., Winston-Salem, N.C., 1965-69, assoc. prof., assoc. in anatomy, 1969-70; assoc. prof. neurology Case Western Res. U., Cleve., 1970, clin. assoc. prof., 1972—, assoc. prof., 1989-93, prof., 1993—2000; chief neurology Highland View Hosp., 1970-72; neurologist U. Hosps. Cleve.; prof. emeritus Case Western Res. U., Cleve., 2000—. Contbr. chpts. and articles to med. publs. Served to capt. U.S. Army, 1962-65 Fellow ACP, Am. Acad. Neurology, AHA Stroke Coun.; mem. N.Y. Acad. Scis., Acad. of Aphasia, Assn. for Rsch. in Nervous and Mental Disease, Am. Assn. Neuropathologists (assoc.), Am. Neurol. Assn., Alpha Omega Alpha Office: Univ Hosps Cleve Dept Neurology 11100 Euclid Ave Cleveland OH 44106-1736 E-mail: mcole@nacs.net.

COLE, RANSEY GUY, JR. judge; b. Birmingham, Ala., May 23, 1951; s. Ransey Guy and Sarah Nell (Coker) Cole; m. Kathleine Kelley, Nov. 26, 1983; children: Justin Robert Jefferson, Jordan Paul, Alexandra Sarah. BA, Tufts U., 1972; JD, Yale U., 1975. Bar: Ohio 1975, D.C. 1982. Assoc. Vorys, Sater, Seymour and Pease, Columbus, Ohio, 1975—78, ptnr., 1980—87, 1993—; trial atty. U.S. Dept. Justice, Washington, 1978—80; judge U.S. Bankruptcy Ct., Columbus, 1987—93; circuit judge U.S. Ct. Appeals (6th cir.) Ohio, Cinn., 1996—. Mem.: ABA, Columbus Bar Assn., Nat. Bar Assn. Office: US Courthouse 85 Marconi Blvd Rm 127 Columbus OH 43215-2823

COLE, THEODORE JOHN, osteopathic and naturopathic physician; b. Covington, Ky., May 30, 1953; s. John N. and Florence R. (Bruener) C.; m. Ellen Cole; children: Joren, Emily, Kevin, Aidan, Ronan. BA, Centre Coll., Danville, Ky., 1975; MA, Western Ky. U., 1978; DO, Ohio U., 1986. Diplomate Am. Osteo. Bd. Gen. Practice, Nat. Bd. Osteo. Examiners, Am. Naturopathic Med. Assn. Psychologist Comprehensive Mental Health Svcs., St. Petersburg, Fla., 1978-82; intern Detroit Osteo. Hosp., 1986-87; resident Doctors Hosp., Columbus, Ohio, 1987-88; pvt. practice, West Chester, 1989—. Preceptor Ohio U. Coll. Osteo. Medicine, Athens, 1990—, U. Cin. Med. Sch., 1990-99; dir. So. Ohio Coll. Nursing. Coach, Soccer Assn. for Youth, West Chester, 1989, 90, Liberty Sports Orgn., West Chester, 1990. Mem. Am. Osteo. Assn., Am. Assn. Osteopathy, Am. Coll. Gen. Practitioners, Am. Acad. Environ. Medicine, Am. Acad. Advancement of Medicine, Occidental Inst. Rsch. Found. Avocations: collecting art, hunting, camping, farming, Tai Chi. Office: West Chester Family Practice Ste 228 11974 Lebanon Rd Cincinnati OH 45241-1700

COLEMAN, JOHN JOSEPH, III, surgery educator; b. Boston, Nov. 15, 1947; MD, Harvard U., 1973. Intern Emory U. Affiliated Hosp., Atlanta, 1973-74, resident in gen. surgery, 1974-78, residentin plastic surgery, 1978-80; fellow in surg. oncology U. Md., Balt., 1980; prof. surgery Ind. U., Indpls., 1980—; chief plastic surgery Ind. U. Med. Ctr., 1980—. Office: U Plastic Surg Assocs 235 Emerson Hall 565 Barnhill Dr Indianapolis IN 46202-5112

COLEMAN, MARY SUE, academic administrator; b. Richmond, Ky, Oct. 2, 1943; BA, Grinnell Coll., 1965; PhD, U. N.C., 1969. NIH postdoctoral fellow U. N.C., Chapel Hill, 1969-70, U. Ky., 1971-72, instr., rsch. assoc. depts. biochemistry and medicine, 1972-75, asst. prof. dept. biochemistry, 1975-80, assoc. prof. dept. biochemistry, 1980-85, prof. dept. biochemistry, 1985-90; prof. dept. biochemistry and biophysics U. N.C., Chapel Hill, 1990-93; provost, v.p. for academic affairs, prof. biochemistry U. N.Mex., 1993-95; pres., prof. biochemistry, prof. biol. scis. U. Iowa, Iowa City, 1995—. Pres. Iowa Health Sys., 1995—; vice chancellor for grad. studies and rsch. U. N.C., 1992-93; assoc. provost, dean rsch. U. N.C., 1990-92; trustee U. Ky. (elected by faculty), 1987-90; assoc. dir. rsch. L.P. Markey Cancer Ctr., U. Ky., 1983-90; dir. grad. studies in biochemistry U. Ky., 1984-87; acting dir. basic rsch. U. Ky. Cancer Ctr., 1980-83; NSF summer trainee Grinnell Coll., 1962; scientific cons. Abbott Labs., 1981-85, Collaborative Rsch., 1983-88, Life Techs., Inc., 1992; mem. gov.'s ACCESS Edn. Commn. State of Iowa, 1997; bd. trustees Univs. Rsch. Assn., 1998—; mem. Gov.'s Strategic Planning Coun., 1998-2000, Imagining Am. Pres.'s Coun., 1999—, Bus.-Higher Edn. Forum, 1999—, Knight Commn., 2000-01; mem. rsch. accountability task force Am. Assn. Univs., 2000—, chair undergrad. edn. com., 1997—; mem. task force on tchr. edn. Am. Coun. Edn., 1998—; editl. bd. Jour. Biol. Chemistry, 1989-93; bd. dirs. Norwest Bank Iowa N.A., 1996-99, Gaylord Container Corp., 1996—, Meredith Corp., 1997—; mem. Big Ten Coun. Pres.'s, 1995—; mem. stds. for success adv. bd. Am. Assn. Univs. and the Pew Charitable Trusts, 2000—; co-chair Inst. Medicine Com. on the Consequences of Uninsurance, 2000—. Contbr. numerous articles to profl. jours.; presenter in field. Trustee Grinnell Coll., 1996—; mem. bd. govs. Warren G. Magnuson Clin. Ctr., NIH, 1996-2000, State of Iowa Gov.'s ACCESS Edn. Commn., 1997, Inst. Medicine, 1997; bd. dirs. Albuquerque United Way, 1995. Recipient Clayton Found. Biochem. Inst. postdoctoral fellowship U. Tex., 1970-71. Fellow AAAS, Am. Acad. Arts and Scis.; mem. Am. Assn. for Cancer Rsch., Am. Soc. Biochemistry and Molecular Biology, Nat. Assn. State Univs. and Land Grant Colls. Coun. Chief Acad. Officers (exec. com. 1993-95). Office: Office of the President 101 Jessup Hall U Iowa Iowa City IA 52242-1316

COLEMAN, MICHAEL B. mayor; s. John and Joan Coleman. Student, U. Cin.; JD, U. Dayton, 1980. Pvt. practice; mem. City Coun. Columbus, Ohio; mayor Columbus, 1999—. Office: Mayors Office 90 W Broad St Rm 247 Columbus OH 43215-9014*

COLEMAN, NORM, mayor; BA, Hofstra U.; JD, U. Iowa. Bar: Minn. Asst. atty. gen., solicitor gen., dir. crim. justice policy Minn. Atty. Gen.'s Office, 17 yrs.; mayor City of St. Paul, 1994—. Active in creation of Minn. Drug Abuse Resistance Edn. program, also The Partnership for a Drug Free Minn. Humphrey fellow U. Minn. Office: Office of the Mayor 15 W Kellogg Blvd 390 City Hall Saint Paul MN 55102

COLEMAN, PAUL DARE, electrical engineering educator; b. Stoystown, Pa., June 4, 1918; s. Clyde R. and Catharine (Livengood) C.; m. Betty L. Carter, June 20, 1942; children— Susan Dare, Peter Carter. A.B., Susquehanna U., 1940; M.S., Pa. State U., 1942; Ph.D., Mass. Inst. Tech., 1951, D.Sc. (hon.), 1978. Asst. physics Susquehanna U., 1938-40, Pa. State U., 1940-42; physicist USAF-WADC, Wright Field, Ohio, 1942-46, Cambridge Air Research Center, also; grad. research assoc. Mass. Inst. Tech., 1946-51; prof. elec. engring., dir. electro-physics lab. U. Ill. at Urbana, 1951—. Recipient meritorious civilian award USAAF, 1946 Fellow IEEE-MTT (Disting. Educator award 1994, Centennial medal 1984), Optical Soc. Am., Am. Phys. Soc.; mem. Sigma Xi, Pi Mu Delta, Pi Mu Epsilon, Eta Kappa Nu. Achievements include research on millimeter waves, submillimeter waves, relativistic electronics, far infrared molecular lasers, beam wave guides and detectors, chem. lasers, nonlinear optics, solid state electronics. Home: 710 Park Lane Dr Champaign IL 61820-7633 Office: Univ Ill 133 Everitt Lab 1406 W Green St Urbana IL 61801-2918

COLEMAN, ROBERT LEE, retired lawyer; b. Kansas City, June 14, 1929; s. William Houston and Edna Fay (Smith) C. BMus in Edn., Drake U., 1951; LLB, U. Mo., 1959. Bar: Mo. 1959, Fla. 1973. Law clk. to judge U.S. Dist. Ct. (we. dist.) Mo., Kansas City, 1959-60; assoc. Watson, Ess, Marshall & Engas, 1960-66; asst. gen. counsel Gas Svc. Co., 1966-74; v.p., corp. counsel H & R Block, Inc., 1974-94; retired, 1994. With U.S. Army, 1955-57. Mem. ABA.

COLES, GRAHAM, conductor, composer; b. London, May 7, 1948; arrived in Canada, 1951; s. Walter Harold and Phyllis Irene Gwendoline (Conn) C. MusB, U. Toronto, 1972, MusM, 1974, EdB, 1991. Music dir. Kitchener-Waterloo (Ont.) Chamber Orch., 1985—. Mem. coll. of examiners Royal Conservatory of Music, Toronto. Composer numerous instrumental and vocal compositions. Mem. Can. League Composers, Can. Music Ctr. (assoc. composer), Assn. Can. Orchs. Home: 1803 - 81 Church St Kitchener ON N2G 4M1 Canada N2G 4M1 Office: Kitchener Waterloo Chamber Orch PO Box 34015 Kitchener ON Canada N2N 3G2 E-mail: kwchamberorchest@aol.com.

COLESCOTT, WARRINGTON WICKHAM, artist, printmaker, educator; b. Oakland, Calif., Mar. 7, 1921; s. Warrington W. and Lydia (Hutton) C.; m. Frances Myers, Mar. 15, 1971; children by previous marriage: Louis Moore, Julian Hutton, Lydia Alice. A.B., U. Calif. at Berkeley, 1942, M.A., 1947; postgrad., Acad. de la Grand Chaumiere, Paris, France, 1950, 53, Slade Sch. Art, U. London (Eng.), 1957. Mem. faculty U. Wis., Madison, 1949-86, prof. art, 1957-86, Leo Steppat chair, prof., 1979-85, emeritus prof., 1986—. Printmaker emeritus So. Graphics Coun., 1991; academician Nat. Acad. Design. One-man shows include Perimeter Gallery, Chgo., 1985, 87, 88, 91, 93, 95, 99, 2002, Milw. Mus. Art, 1996, Rockford (Ill.) Art Mus., Bradley U., Peoria, Ill.; print retrospective Elvehjem Mus., Madison, Wis., 1989, Nelson-Atkins Mus., Kansas City, 1990, U. Oreg. Art Mus., Eugene, 1992, SUNY, Albany, N.Y., 1995; represented in permanent collections Mus. Modern Art, Victoria and Albert Mus., London, Bibliotechque Nat., Paris, Met. Mus., Chgo. Art Inst., Bklyn. Mus., Phila. Mus. Art, Milw. ARt Mus., Elvehjem Art Mus.; co-author (with Arthur Hove) Progressive Printmakers, 1999. Recipient Print award NAD, 1991, 92, 95, 97, NSAL Award of Excellence, 1993, 99; named Koopman disting. chair in visual arts Hartford Sch. Art, 1995, award Internat. Triennial of Print, Cracow, Poland, 1997; Fulbright fellow, 1957, Guggenheim fellow, 1965, Nat. Endowment Arts Printmaking fellow, 1975, Artist fellow, 1979, 83-84, 93-94. Fellow Wis. Acad. Sci. Arts and Letters. Office: 8788 County Hwy A Hollandale WI 53544-9801

COLETTA, JOHN, chef; Chef Four Seasons, N.Y.C., Waldorf-Astoria, N.Y.C., Atlanta Hilton Hotel; exec. chef Fairmont Hotel, Chgo.; chef Entre Nous, Primavera; exec. chef Sheraton Chgo. Hotel, 1991, Caesar's Palace, Las Vegas, Nev., Caliterra, Chgo.; regional exec. chef Whydham Hotels & Resorts, Itasca. Mem. Visiting Masters from the World of Food Program Epcot Internat. Food and Wine Festival, 1997. Named one of 15 America's Rising Star Chefs; recipient gold megal, Culinary Olympics, 1984. Office: Caliterra 633 N Saint Clair St Chicago IL 60611

COLGATE, S. EDWARD, mechanical engineering educator; Prof. dept. mech. engring. Northwestern U., Evanston, Ill. Recipient Henry Hess award ASME, 1995. Office: Northwestern U Dept Mech Engring 2145 Sheridan Rd Dept Mech Evanston IL 60208-0834

COLLADAY, ROBERT S. trust company executive, consultant; b. Flint, Mich., Sept. 24, 1940; s. Robert Harold and Mary Elizabeth (Strong) C.; m. Joan M. Hartsock; children: David, Jill, James, Christopher. B.A., Alma Coll., 1962; postgrad., Nat. Trust Sch., Northwestern U., 1967. Asst. trust officer Comerica Bank-Detroit, 1968-71, trust officer, 1971-74, v.p., 1974-80, 1st v.p., 1980-83, sr. v.p., 1983-91, Comerica Inc., 1984-91; pres., prin. cons. Trust Consulting Svcs., Inc., Bloomfield Hills, Mich., 1991—. Cons. to bd. dirs. Found. Southeast Mich. Trustee, chmn. investment com. Alma Coll., Mich. Republican. Presbyterian. Avocations: photography; fishing. Home: 22241 Village Pines Dr Franklin MI 48025-3568 Office: Trust Consulting Svcs Inc PO Box 1131 Bloomfield Hills MI 48303-1131

COLLEN, JOHN, lawyer; b. Chgo., Dec. 26, 1954; s. Sheldon and Ann Collen; m. Lauren Kay Smulyan, Sept. 20, 1986; children: Joshua, Benjamin, Sarah, Joel. AB summa cum laude, Dartmouth Coll., 1977; JD, Georgetown U., 1980. Bar: Ill. 1980, U.S. Dist. Ct. (no. dist.) Ill. 1980, Trial 1982, U.S. Ct. Appeals (7th cir.) 1984, U.S. Supreme Ct. 1990. Ptnr. Duane & Morris LLP, Chgo. Mem. editl. adv. bd. Journal of Bankruptcy Law & Practice. Author: Buying and Selling Real Estate in Bankruptcy, 1997; contbr. articles to profl. jours.; lectr. in field. Mem. ABA, Chgo. Bar Assn., Am. Bankruptcy Inst. (chmn. com. real estate bankruptcy), Phi Beta Kappa. Avocations: water sports, magic, biographies. Office: Duane & Morris LLP 227 W Monroe St Chicago IL 60606-5016 Fax: 312-499-6701. E-mail: jcollen@duanemorris.com.

COLLENS, LEWIS MORTON, university president, legal educator; b. Chgo., Feb. 10, 1938; BS, U. Ill., Urbana, 1960, MA, 1963; JD, U. Chgo., 1966. Bar: Ill. 1966. Assoc. Ross, Hardies, Chgo., 1966-67; spl. asst. to gen. counsel EEOC, Washington, 1967-68; asst. prof. Ill. Inst. Tech., Chgo. Kent Coll. Law, 1970-72, assoc. prof., 1972-74, prof., 1975—90; dean Coll. Law, Ill. Inst. Tech., 1974-90, pres., 1990—. Bd. dirs. Amsted Industries, Inc., Dean Foods Co., Inc. Chmn. Ill. Gov.'s Commn. on Y2K; mem. Chgo. Mayor's Coun. Tech. Advisors; bd. dirs. Latin Sch., Chgo.; dir. Ill. Coalition. Mem. ABA, Ill. Bar Assn., Chgo. Bar Assn., Am. Law Inst., Econ. Club of Chgo. (dir.), Order of Coif. Office: Ill Inst Tech 10 W 33rd St Rm 223 Chicago IL 60616-3730

COLLETT, LAWRENCE, diversified financial service company executive; b. 1943; With Cass Bank & Trust Co., 1963-83; chmn., pres., CEO Cass Comml. Corp., St. Louis, 1983—. Office: Cass Comml Corp 13001 Hollenberg Dr Bridgeton MO 63044

COLLEY, KAREN J. medical educator, medical researcher; b. Nov. 3, 1958; BS in Chemistry, Duke U., 1981; PhD in Molecular Biology, Washington U., St. Louis, 1987. Postdoctoral fellow dept. biol. chemistry UCLA, 1987—91; postdoctoral fellow NIH, 1990; asst. prof. dept. biochemistry U. Ill., Chgo., 1991—97, assoc. prof., 1997—. Mem. med. adv. bd. Leukemia Rsch. Found., 1994—, reviewer study sect., 1994—; outside reviewer NSF Grants, 1995—, VA Rsch. Grants, 1995—; mem. pathiobiochemistry study sect. NIH, 1998—. Reviewer: Jour. Biol. Chemistry, reviewer: Jour. Cell Biology, reviewer: Molecular and Chem. Neuropathology, reviewer: Jour. Cell Sci., reviewer: Devel. Biology; contbr. articles to profl. jours.; patentee in field. Recipient Established Investigator award, Am. Heart Assn., 1996; fellow (Sr.), Am. Cancer Soc., 1991; grantee, 1992, U. Ill., 1992, 1996, Leukemia Rsch. Found., Inc., 1993. Mem.: AAAS, Soc. Glycobiology, Am. Soc. Biochemistry and Molecular Biology, Am. Soc. Cell Biology, Sigma Xi. Office: U Ill Dept Biochemistry and Molecular Biology 1819 W Polk St Chicago IL 60612-7331

COLLIE, JOHN, JR. insurance agent; b. Gary, Ind., Apr. 23, 1934; s. John and Christina Dempster (Wardrop) C.; m. Jessie Fearn Shaw, Aug. 1, 1964; children: Cynthia Elizabeth Lunsford, Douglas A.H., Jennifer F. Student, Purdue U., 1953; AB in Econs., U. Ind., 1957; assoc. risk mgmt. (A.R.M.). Operator Collie Optical Lab., Gary, 1957-62; owner, operator Collie Ins. Agy., 1962—. Pres. Collie Realty and Investment, Ins. and Fin. Advisory, Lake Mich. Global Industries; lectr. High Frontier; dist. chmn. 1st dist. Ind. for com. to secure High Frontier; mem. employer support Guard & Res., Dept. Def.; affiliated broker Pickart Ins. Agy. Inc., Merrillville. Lt. col. U.S. Army Res., 1957-86; instr. Command and Gen. Staff Coll., 1973-77. Mem. Ind. Ins. Agts. Assn., Mil. Order World Wars, Res. Officers Assn. (sec., pres. N.W. Ind. chpt., v.p. Ind. chpt.), Ret. Officers Assn., Leadership Coun. Am., Nat. Fedn. Ind. Bus. (guardian, state adv. bd., NW-IN adv. bd.), Masons (32 degree), Shriners, Phi Kappa Psi. Republican. Methodist. Home: 871 Camelot Mnr Portage IN 46368-6632 Office: 500 W Lincoln Hwy Ste #C PO Box 10148 Merrillville IN 46411-0148

COLLIER, BARRY S. coach; m. Annette Collier, 1975; children: Casey, Brady, Clay. BS, Butler, 1973; MS, Ind. State U., 1977. Asst. coach Rose Hulman Inst., Seattle Ctrl. C.C., U. Idaho, U. Oreg., Stanford U.; head coach men's basketball Butler U., U. Nebr., Lincoln. Office: U Nebr 106 Devaney Sports Ctr Lincoln NE 68588*

COLLIER, JAMES WARREN, lawyer; b. Dallas, July 31, 1940; s. J.W. and Mary Gertrude (Roberts) C.; m. Judith Lane, Dec. 27, 1964; children: Anne Elizabeth, Jennifer Susan. BA, U. Mich., 1962, JD, 1965. Bar: N.Y. 1966, Mich. 1968. Assoc. Simpson Thacher & Bartlett, N.Y.C., 1965-66; tax atty. office gen. counsel Ford Motor Co., 1966-67; assoc. Dykema Gossett, Detroit, 1967-73, ptnr., 1973—. Mem. Dykema Gossett. Contbr. articles to profl. jours. Mem. ABA, Mich. Bar Assn., Econ. Club Detroit, Lochmoor Club. Office: Dykema Gossett 400 Renaissance Ctr # 3500 Detroit MI 48243-1603 E-mail: jcollier@dykema.com.

COLLIER, KEN O. editor; b. Mpls., Oct. 7, 1952; BA, Carleton Coll., 1976; MSc, UCLA, Santa Barbara, 1978. Instr. geology Carleton Coll., Northfield, Minn., 1980; owner Custom Furniture, Mpls., 1980-87; assoc. editor The Family Handyman Mag., 1987-91; exec. editor Custom Furniture, 1995—; sr. editor New Bus. Devel., 1991-95; chief editor Am. Woodworker Mag./Home Svc. Publ., Eagan, Minn., 1998—. Office: Home Svcs Publ 2915 Commers Dr Ste 700 Eagan MN 55121-2398

COLLIN, THOMAS JAMES, lawyer; b. Windom, Minn., Jan. 6, 1949; s. Everett Earl and Genevieve May (Wilson) C.; m. Victoria Gatov, Oct. 11, 1985; children: Arielle, Elise, Sarah. BA, U. Minn., 1970; AM, Harvard U., 1972; JD, Georgetown U., 1974. Bar: Ohio 1975, U.S. Dist. Ct. (no. dist.) Ohio 1975, U.S. Ct. Appeals (10th cir.) 1977, U.S. Supreme Ct. 1980, U.S. Ct. Appeals (6th cir.) 1981, U.S. Ct. Appeals (8th cir.) 1982, U.S. Ct. Appeals (7th cir.) 1997, U.S. Ct. Appeals (11th cir.) 1999. Law clk. to Judge Myron Bright U.S. Ct. Appeals, 8th Cir., St. Louis, 1974-75; assoc. Thompson, Hine & Flory, LLP, Cleve., 1975-82, ptnr., 1982--. Author: Ohio Business Competition Law, 1994, (with others) Criminal Antitrust Litigation Manual, 1983; editor: Punitive Damages and Business Torts: A Practitioner's Handbook, 1998; contbr. articles to profl. jours. Active Citizens League, Cleve., bd. trustees, 1994-99, v.p., 1995-97, pres. 1997-99; bd. trustees Citizens League Rsch. Inst., Cleve., 1999—. Mem. ABA (chair bus. torts and unfair competition com., antitrust sect. 1995-98, chair annual mtg. com. antitrust sect., 2001-), Ohio State Bar Assn. (bd. govs. antitrust sect. 1988-98). Republican. Avocations: book collecting, music. Home: 7879 Oakhurst Dr Cleveland OH 44141-1123 Office: Thompson Hine LLP 127 Public Sq Cleveland OH 44114-1216

COLLINS, ARTHUR D., JR. medical products executive; Pres. Medtronics Internat., 1992; exec. v.p. Medtronics Inc., Mpls., 1992, COO, pres., COO, 1994—. Office: Medtronics 7000 Central Ave NE Minneapolis MN 55432-3576

COLLINS, CARDISS, former congresswoman; b. St. Louis, Sept. 24, 1931; m. George W. Collins (dec.); 1 child, Kevin. Ed., Northwestern U.; hon. degree, Winston-Salem State U., Spelman Coll., John Marshall Law Sch., Rosary Coll., Forest Inst. Profl. Psychology. Barber Scotia Coll.; mem. 93d-104th Congresses from 7th Ill. Dist., 1973-97; ret., 1997. Ranking minority mem. govt. reform & oversight com.; former chair. govt. activity and transp. subcom.; former chair commerce, consumer protection and competition subcom.; former majority whip-at-large; former asst. regional whip; former chair Congl. Black Caucus, sec.; former chair Congl. Black Caucus Found.; former chair Mems. Congress for Peace through Law. Recipient award Roosevelt U., Loyola U. Mem. NAACP, Nat. Coun. Negro Women (v.p.), Chgo. Urban League, Black Women's Agenda, The Chgo. Network, The Links, Dem. Nat. Com., Alpha Kappa Alpha. Democrat. Baptist. Home: 1110 Roundhouse Ln Alexandria VA 22314-5934

COLLINS, DANA JON, financial executive; b. Grand Rapids, Mich., July 15, 1956; s. Daniel Hiltz and JoAnne M. (Smee) C. BBA with honors, U. Mich., 1978. CPA, Mich. Staff acct. Ernst & Whinney, Jackson, Mich., 1978-82, mgr., 1982-86; CFO, treas. Fetzer Broadcasting Svc., Inc., Kalamazoo, 1986—, also bd. dirs.; asst. sec., asst. treas. Jacobson Stores Inc., Jackson, Mich., 1997—. Exec. v.p., treas., bd. dirs. W.C.A. Holdings, Inc. Mem. AICPA, Mich. Assn. CPAs, Inst. Mgmt. Accts. (treas. 1984-86, exec. v.p. 1989, pres. 1990-91, 2000—, bd. dirs. local chpt. 1984-92, nat. bd. dirs. 1992—). Republican. Avocations: golf, tennis, sports, square dancing. Home: 7094 Jamaica Ln Portage MI 49002-9400 Office: Jacobson Stores Inc 3333 Sargent Rd Jackson MI 49201-8800

COLLINS, DANIEL W. accountant, educator; b. Marshalltown, Iowa, Sept. 1, 1946; s. Donald E. and Lorine R. (Metge) C.; m. Mary L. Packer, June 27, 1970; children— Melissa, Theresa BBA with honors, U. Iowa, 1968, PhD, 1973. Asst. prof. acctg. Mich. State U., East Lansing, 1973-76, assoc. prof., 1976-77; vis. assoc. prof. U. Iowa, Iowa City, 1977-78, assoc. prof., 1978-81, prof., 1981-83, Murray chaired prof. acctg., 1983-88, Henry B. Tippie prof. of acctg., 1989—; vis. IBM prof. bus. Fuqua Sch. Bus., Duke U., 1988-89, chmn. dept. acctg., 1995—. Mem. Fin. Acctg. Stds. Adv. Coun., acad. adv. bd. Deloitte & Touche; mem. Arthur Andersen doctoral dissertation awards com., 1996—; bd. dirs. Ira B. McGladrey Inst., U.S. Bank, Iowa City, Christian Ret. Svcs., Iowa City. Assoc. editor Acctg. Rev., 1980-86; mem. editl. bd. Jour. Acctg. and Econs., 1978—, Jour. Acctg., Auditing and Fin., 1986—; contbr. articles to profl. jours. 2d lt. U.S. Army, 1972 Recipient All Univ. Tchr. scholar award Mich. State U., 1976, Gilbert Maynard Excellence in Tchg. award U. Iowa, 1985, Collegiate Tchg. award, 1998; Univ. Faculty scholar U. Iowa, 1980-82, Faculty Excellence award Iowa Bd. Regents, 2000. Mem. Am. Acctg. Assn. (disting. vis. faculty mem. Doctoral Consortium 1980, 89, dir. Doctoral Consortium 1987, program dir. ann. conv. 1988, dir. publs. 1989-91, exec. com. 1989-91, Outstanding Acctg. Educator award 2001), Acctg. Rschrs. Internat. Avocations: jogging, gardening. Home: 11 Wildberry Ct NE Iowa City IA 52240-9173 Office: U Iowa Coll Bus W252 PBAB Iowa City IA 52242-1000

COLLINS, DUANE E. manufacturing executive; BSME, U. Wis.; post-grad., Harvard U. Sales engr. Parker Hannifin Corp., Cleve., 1961, gen. sales mgr., ops. mgr. hose products divsn., gen. mgr., 1973-76, v.p. ops. fluid connectors group, 1976-80, pres. fluid connectors group, 1980-83, corp. v.p., 1983-87, pres. internat., 1987-88, corp. exec. v.p., pres. internat., 1988-92, vice chmn., 1992-93, CEO, 1993-2000, 2000—01, chmn., 2001; ret., 2001. Bd. dis. Nat. City Bank, Sherwin-Williams Co. Bd. dirs. Greater Cleve. Growth Assn.; bd. trustees Cleve. YMCA. Office: Parker Hannifin Corp 6035 Parkland Blvd Cleveland OH 44124-4141

COLLINS, GARY L. human resources professional, automotive executive; Sr. v.p. human resources Meritor Automotive, Inc., Troy, Mich., 1997—. Office: Meritor Automotive Inc 2135 W Maple Rd Troy MI 48084-7121

COLLINS, LARRY WAYNE, small business owner, information systems specialist; b. Plainville, Ind., Mar. 23, 1941; s. Virgil Raymond and Eva Pauline (Hedden) C.; m. Donna Kay Miller, July 25, 1961 (div. Apr. 1983); children: Rex Aaron, Jill Renee; m. Mary Ellen McConn, Dec. 15, 1983; 1 child, Ann Marie. AS, Vincennes U., 1961; BS, U. Indpls., 1968, MBA, 1981. Computer programmer State of Ind., Indpls., 1963-64, systems analyst, 1964-65, asst. ops. mgr., 1965-66; mgr. systems and programming Community Hosp. of Indpls., 1966-67, dir. data processing, 1967-77, v.p. hosp. systems, 1977-84; v.p., mgr. Bethesda N. Hosp., Cin., 1984-85, group v.p., 1985-86; sr. v.p. Bethesda Oak Hosp., 1986-91; sr. v.p., chief info. officer Bethesda Hosp., Inc., 1991-95; ptnr. RHI, Inc., Maineville, Ohio, 1995-98; prin. Collins Cons., 1998—. Bd. dirs. Tri-State Community Cancer Orgn., 1986-92, chmn., 1989-92; chmn. bd. dirs. Hospice of Cin., Inc., 1987-91; bd. dirs. Interfaith Hospitality Network Warren County, 2000—. Mem. Ind. Cen. U. Alumni Assn. (bd. dirs. 1984-88), Am. Coll. Healthcare Execs., Tri-State Health Adminstrs. Forum, Am. Mgmt. Assn., Am. Acad. Med. Adminstrs. (bd. dirs. 1993-98, chmn. elect 1996, chmn. 1997), Kiwanis (bd. dirs. Montgomery chpt. 1984-87). Methodist. Avocations: golf, photography. Home and Office: 7667 Hopkins Rd Ste 101 Maineville OH 45039-8682 E-mail: lwc7667@aol.com.

COLLINS, MARTHA, English language educator, writer; b. Omaha, Nov. 25, 1940; d. William E. and Katheryn (Essick) C.; m. Theodore M. Space, Apr. 1991. AB, Stanford U., 1962; MA, U. Iowa, 1965, PhD, 1971. Asst. prof. N.E. Mo. U., Kirksville, Kirksville, 1965-66; instr. U. Mass., Boston, 1966-71, asst. prof. English, 1971-75, assoc. prof., 1975-85, prof. English, 1985—, co-dir. creative writing, 1979—, chair dept. English, 1994-96; Pauline Delaney prof., co-dir. creative writing Oberlin (Ohio) Coll., 1997—. Author (poetry): The Catastrophe of Rainbows, 1985, The Arrangement of Space, 1991, A History of Small Life on a Windy Planet, 1993, Some Things Words Can Do, 1998. Fellow Bunting Inst., 1982-83, Ingram Merrill Found., 1988, NEA, 1990; recipient Pushcart prize, 1985, 96, 98, Di Castagnola award, 1990. Mem. Poetry Soc. Am., Assoc. Writing Programs. Democrat. Office: Oberlin Coll Rice Hall Oberlin OH 44074

COLLINS, MARY ELLEN, retired human resources executive; b. Indpls., Jan. 24, 1949; d. Carl William and Hester (Dawson) McConn; m. Thomas N. Wininger, June 19, 1971 (div. 1981); m. Larry Wayne Collins, Dec. 15, 1983; 1 child, Ann Marie. Diploma in nursing, Holy Cross Coll., 1969; BS, Coll. of St. Francis, 1981; MS, Ind. U., 1984; PhD in Orgnl. Behavior, Union Inst., Cin., 1993. Edn. coord. Cmty. Hosp., Indpls., 1969-84; dir. tng. Middletown (Ohio) Regional Hosp., 1984-87; pres. People Power Cons. Svc., Cin., 1987—. Adj. prof. Coll. Mt. St. Joseph, Ohio, 1988-93; faculty MBA program Xavier U., Cin., 1996—. Editl. bd. Strategic Governance for Non Profit Orgns., (newsletters) Teamwork, Quality One. Adminstrv. chair Deerfield Ch., Maineville, 1987-89. Mem. ASTD (bd. dirs. Cin. chpt. 1988-89), Assn. for Psychol. Type (pres., founder Greater Cin. chpt. 1992—, bd. dirs. Gt. Lakes region, Internat. New Leader award 1993, internat. conf. chair 1997, dir. membership com. 1997—), Assn. Quality Participation (healthcare adv. bd., Disting. Faculty mem.), Internat. Visitors Ctr., Women Entrepreneurs, Inc. Methodist. Avocation: gourmet cooking.

COLLINS, MICHAEL J. medical company executive; BS in Econs., Northwestern U., 1974, MS in Adminstrn., 1976. Various bus. mgmt. positions drug and cosmetic chems. divsn. Mallinckrodt, 1976-81, bus. dir. drug and cosmetic chems. divsn., 1981-84, asst. gen. mgr. drug and cosmetic chems. divsn., 1985-86, gen. mgr., 1986-88, v.p., gen. mgr., 1988-89, sr. v.p., gen. mgr., 1990-91, group v.p. analgesics and pharm. specialties group, 1992, group v.p. pharm. specialties, 1992-95, pres. pharm. specialties divsn., 1995-98, pres. pharms. group, 1998—. Home: PO Box 5840 Saint Louis MO 63134-0840

COLLINS, THOMAS WILLIAM, caterer, consultant; b. Lewiston, Idaho, Nov. 4, 1926; s. William James and Mary (Egan) C.; m. Mary Charlene Tracy, Aug. 1, 1947 (dec. Apr. 1984); children: Kathleen, William, Charles. Grad. high sch., Staples, Minn., 1944. Owner Collins Cafe, Park Rapids, Minn., 1947-63, Tom Collins Restaurant, Walker, 1963-83, Tom Collins Catering, Walker, 1983—. Author: Collins Cooking Secrets, 1981. Fundraiser DFL, 1976-83; adv. bd. Lake Country Food Bank, Mpls., 1981-86. Served with USN, 1945-46, 51-52. Recipient Recognition award Mont. Gov., 1978, cert. of Spl. Congl. Recognition, 1995; Tom Collins Day proclaimed by Minn. Gov., 1977. Mem. Assn. Great Lakes Outdoor Writers, Am. Legion. Lodge: Masons (sr. warden 1958), Shriners. Avocations: hunting, fishing, photography. Home and Office: PO Box 33 Walker MN 56484-0033

COLLISON, JIM, business executive; b. Blue Earth, Minn., May 24, 1933; s. Elliott Eugene and Rosa Theresa (Whitcomb) C.; m. Valerie Ann Thul, Oct. 28, 1954; children: Judith, Michelle, Daniel, Michael, Rebecca, David. BA, St. John's Univ., 1955. Sports editor Blue Earth Post and Faribault County Register, 1953; staff writer St. Cloud (Minn.) Daily Times, 1953-55, Waterloo (Iowa) Courier, 1955-57, Mason City (Iowa) Globe Gazette, 1958-63; bus. and edn. cons. Jim Collison Assocs., Mason City, 1963-77; exec. dir. Employers of Am., 1978-81, pres., 1981—; pres., pub. Sunburst Publ., 1990—. Co-founder Employers of Am., 1978; chmn. bd. ISBE Ins. Alliance, Mason City, 1986—, Select Advantage, Inc., ISBE Bus. Ins. Assn., ISBE Employer Benefits Assn.; pres. Am. Corp. Advisors, Inc.; workshop presenter. Author: Skill Building in Advanced Raeding, 1968, Mental Power in Reading, 1970, Complete Employee Handbook Made Easy, 1994, 97, 2001, The Employer Protection Workshop, 1996, No-How Coaching, 2001, Complete Suggestion Program Make Easy, 2001; pub., sr. editor (newsletter) Smart Workplace Practices. Asst. min. Orchard (Iowa) Congreg. Ch., 1985—; designer Adult Literacy and Employment Reading Training Program. Democrat. Avocations: flower gardening, hiking. Home: 310 Meadow Ln Mason City IA 50401-1717 Office: Employers of Am 520 S Pierce Ave Ste 224 Mason City IA 50401-2751

COLLOTON, JOHN WILLIAM, university health care executive; b. Mason City, Iowa, Feb. 20, 1931; s. Harold and Miriam (Kelly) Colloton; m. Mary Ann Hagglund, Oct. 8, 1960; children: Steven, Laura, Ann. B.A. with high honors, Loras Coll., 1953; M.A., U. Iowa, 1957. Hosp. relations rep. Hosp. Service Inc. of Iowa, Des Moines, 1957—58; with U. Iowa, Iowa City, 1958—; assoc. dir. U. Iowa Hosps. and Clinics, 1969—71, dir., asst. to univ. pres. for statewide health svcs., 1971—93; v.p. statewide health svcs. U. Iowa, 1993—. Bd. dirs. Baxter Internat., Inc., Nat. Med. Waste Inc., Iowa State Bank & Trust Co., MidAm. Energy Co., Premier Anesthesia, Atlanta, Assn. Health Svcs. Rsch.; cons. HIH; pres. adminstrv. bd. Assn. Am. Med. Colls. Coun. of Tchg. Hosps., 1979—80; mem. presdl. search com. Assn. Am. Med. Colls., 1984; mem. adv. bd. Duke U. Hosp., 1985; mem. task force on acad. health ctrs. Commonwealth Fund, chmn. selection com. exec. nurse leadership program, 1983; mem. prospective payment commn. Congl. Office Tech. Assessment, 1983; chmn. bd. dirs. Iowa-S.D. Health Svcs. Corp. (now Blue Cross/Blue Shield Iowa, Blue Cross S.D.), 1993—. Contbr. articles. Served with Fin. Corps U.S. Army, 1953—55. Fellow: Am. Coll. Hosp. Adminstrs.; mem.: U. Iowa Alumni Assn., Johnson County Med. Soc., Assn. Am. Med. Colls. (chmn. 1987—88, disting. svc. mem.), Am. Assn. Hosp. Planning, Iowa Hosp. Assn. (chmn. bd. trustees 1977—78, trustee 1978—), Am. Hosp. Assn. (coun. on financing 1977, med. edn. com. 1984—87), Inst. Medicine of NAS, Rotary. Roman Catholic. Office: U Iowa Hosps & Clinics 200 Hawkins Dr Ste 8820 Iowa City IA 52242-1009

COLOM, VILMA, alderman; b. San Juan, P.R., June 7, 1954; d. Andres and Niza (Miranda) C.; divorced; 1 child, Omar Otero. BA, Northeastern U., 1978; MA, U. Ill., 1980. Mem. U.S. Sen. Task Force, Washington, 1983-90; chmn. Nat. Puerto Rican Forum, N.Y.C., 1986-89; pres. Colom Internat. & Assocs., 1986-88; bilingual educator Richard Yate Pub. Sch., 1993-95; alderman, committeeman 35th ward City of Chgo., 1995—. With nat. Hispanic affairs Allstate Ins., 1983-90. Asst. dir. U. Ill., Chgo., 1990-93; mem. adv. bd. LeadershipAm., 1994—; bd. dirs. Nat. Network Latino Women, 1995—; chmn. Chgo. office Nat. Puerto Rican Forum, N.Y.C., 1986-89, mem. adv. bd. nat. hqrs.; mem. aux. bd. Golden Apple Found., fundraising chmn., 1995—; mem. corp. nat. bd. Nat. Svc. Jobs for Progress. Recipient Signature award Leadership Am., 1994, Hispanic State Law Enforcement award, 1996, Law Enforcement award Hispanic Inst., 1996, Internat. award Logan Sq. Lions Club, 1996; named Hispanic of Yr., 1996. Mem. Nat. Women's C. of C., Omega Sigma Alpha. Democrat. Office: 2535 N Kedzie Blvd Chicago IL 60647-2655

COLONNA, ROCCO J. state legislator; m. Shirley J. Colonna; children: Tina Marie Colonna Rini, Lavaine Anne Colonna Cates, Danny V.M. BA, U.S. Armed Forces Inst.; postgrad., Internat. Data Processing Inst., Cuyahoga C.C., Baldwin Wallace Coll. Mem. Ohio Ho. of Reps., Columbus, 1975-98. Chmn. econ. devel. and small bus. com., labor-mgmt. com., mem. rules com., ways and means com., devel. financing adv. bd., select com. for tech., linked deposit adv. com., rep. to speaker on econ. devel. policy bd., mem. turnpike oversight com., motor vehicle inspection and maintenance program and policy planning com. Former mem. Brook Park (Ohio) Planning Commn., Brook Park Zoning and Bldg. Bd. Appeals; mem. Brook Park City Coun., 1970-74; mem. Ohio Gov.'s Tripartite Labor and Mgmt. Adv. Commn. Recipient Outstanding Leadership award Ohio C. of C., 1986, Legislator of Yr. award food industry com. Ohio Coun. Retail Mchts., 1980, AMVETS, 1990. Mem. Ohio Aerospace Inst., Am. Legion, Holy Name Soc., Eagles. Democrat. Home: 6477 Wolf Rd Brookpark OH 44142-3873

COLTON, VICTOR ROBERT, real estate developer, investor; b. Detroit, Apr. 30, 1930; s. McArthur Colton, Lottie S. Colton. BA, Wayne State U., 1952; DDS, U. Detroit, 1956. Owner V. Robert Colton, DDS Dental Clinic, Detroit, 1956-84; owner, dir. Lakewood Devel. Co., Inc., Southfield, 1974-81, Monetary Investment Group Inc., Southfield, 1975-90, Clean Rooms Internat., Grand Rapids, Mich., 1984-90, Macomb Biotech., Inc., Romeo, 1984-90, Polymeric Processes Inc., Tecumseh, 1984-97, Toth Aluminium Corp., Vacherie, La., 1986—, Strong Point, Inc., Detroit, 1986—, IMPCO Technologies, Inc., Seattle and Cerritos, Calif., 1988-2000, Accor Tech., Inc., Bellevue, Wash., 1988—, Clifton Engrig. Co., Inc., Three Rivers, Mich., 1989-91, Movie Am. Corp., Atlanta, 1989-91, RCM Internat., Inc., Sylvan Lake, Mich., 1991-96, Am. Artists Film Corp., Atlanta, 1991-97, RCH Investments, Inc., Wellington, Fla., 1994—, Marco Aquisitions Inc., Wellington, 1998—, Marco Aquisitions Ltd., LP., Wellington, 1998—, Key West (Fla.) Aquisitions, LLC, 1998—. Owner, dir. Marco Acquisitions, Inc., Wellington, 1998, Marco Acquisitions, Ltd., L.P., Wellington, Key West Acquisitions, LLC, 1998, Sea Horse Adventures, Ltd., Key West, 1999—, Tartar Acquisitions, Ltd., Wellington, 1999—, Montego's Inc., Wellington, 1999—, Key West Acquisitions Inc., 1999—, Key West Oceanfront, LP, 1999—; trustee Monetary Realty Trust, Southfield, 1978—82; owner, dir. Primus Fin. Svcs., Inc., Grand Rapids, 1983—88; owner cons. Cartrex Corp., Grand Rapids, 1984—88, PDVR, LLC, Wellington, 2000—, TARTAR, LP, Wellington, 2000—.

COLVIN, THOMAS STUART, agricultural engineer, farmer; b. Columbia, Mo., July 17, 1947; s. Charles Darwin and Miriam Elizabeth (Kimball) C.; m. Sonya Marie Peterson, Sept. 11, 1982; children: Christopher, Kristel. BS, Iowa State U., 1970, MS, 1974, PhD, 1977. Registered profl. engr., Iowa. Farmer, Hawkeye and Cambridge, Iowa, 1970—; rsch. assoc. Iowa State U., Ames, 1972-77; agrl. engr. USDA/Agrl. Rsch. Svc., 1977—. Cons. WillowCreek Cons., Manning, Iowa, 1978-85. Sgt. USAF, 1970-72, Vietnam. Recipient Air Force Commendation medal USAF, 1971. Mem. Am. Soc. Agrl. Engrs. (power machinery stds. com. St. Joseph, Mich. 1989—, Iowa sec., Young Engr. of Yr. 1986), Soil and Water Conservation Soc., Iowa Acad. Sci. (chair agrl. scis. sect. 1991-92), Sigma Xi, Alpha Epsilon (pres. 1978), Gamma Sigma Delta, Phi Mu Alpha. Achievements include design and development of first computer program to help farmers manage tillage and residue cover for erosion control. Office: Nat Soil Tilth Lab USDA ARS 2150 Pammel Dr Ames IA 50011-3120

COLWILL, JACK MARSHALL, physician, educator, dean; b. Cleve., June 15, 1932; s. Clifford V. and Olive A. (Marshall) Colwill; m. Winifred Stedman, 1954; children: James F., Elizabeth Ann, Carolyn. BA, Oberlin Coll., 1953; MD (George Whipple scholar), U. Rochester, 1957. Diplomate AM. Bd. Med. Examiners, Am. Bd. Internal Medicine, Am. Bd. Family Practice. Intern Barnes Hosp., Washington U. Sch. Medicine, St. Louis, 1957—58; resident in medicine U. Washington Affiliated Hosps., Seattle, 1958—60; chief resident U. Hosp., 1960—61; instr. medicine, dir. med. outpatient dept. U. Rochester (N.Y.) Sch. Medicine and Dentistry, 1961—62, sr. instr. medicine, dir. med. outpatient dept., 1962—64; asst. dean, asst. prof. medicine, asst. prof. community health and med. practice U. Mo. Sch. Medicine, Columbia, 1964—67, assoc. dean, asst. prof., 1967—69, assoc. dean for acad. affairs, asst. prof., 1969—70, assoc. dean, assoc. prof., 1970—76, interim chmn. dept. family and community medicine, 1976—77, prof., 1976—97, prof. emeritus, 1999—, chmn. dept., 1977—97, interim dean, 2000. Cons. Bur. Health Manpower, NIH, 1969—75, Office Divsn. Dir. USPHS, 1977—; mem. Coun. on Grad. Med. Edn. Health Resources and Svcs. Adminstrn., 1990—96; bd. dirs. Am. Bd. Family Practice, 1998—. Contbr. articles to profl. jours. Chair commn. on Gulf War and Health Inst. of med., Nat. Acad. Scis., 1999—2001; dir. Robert Wood Johnson Found. Generalist Physician Initiative, 1991—2000. Mem.: AMA, Inst. Medicine NAS, Am. Acad. Family Physicians (commn. on govtl. legis. affairs 1984—87), Soc. Tchrs. Family Medicine (bd. dirs. 1978—82, 1983—87, pres.-elect 1987—88, pres. 1988—89), Assn. Med. Am. Colls. (chmn. Midwest-Gt. Plains Group on Student Affairs 1971—73, nat. vice chmn. group 1973—74, chmn. working group on non-cognitive assessment 1974—77, adv. to com. on admissions assessment 1974—77), Alpha Omega Alpha. Office: U Mo-Columbia Sch Medicine Dept Family And Medicine Columbia MO 65212-0001

COMBS, ROBERT KIMBAL, museum director; b. Oklahoma City, Mar. 5, 1955; s. Harold Lee and Joanna Jane (Barton) Combs; m. Lynn Marie Robison, June 9, 1979 (div. 1984); 1 child, Caitlyn. BA in History, San Francisco State U., 1978; cert. in museology, U. Calif., Berkeley, 1979; MA in Museology, John F. Kennedy U., 1980. Curator San Mateo (Calif.) County Mus., 1978-79; intern Smithsonian Instn., Washington, 1979; San Francisco Fine Arts Mus., 1979-81; curator Presidio Army Mus., San Francisco, 1981-83; dir. U.S. Army Engr. Mus., Ft. Leonard Wood, Mo., 1983—2001; prof. history Columbia Coll., 1984—2001; dir. 2d Inf. Div. Mus., Republic of Korea, 2001—. Cons. Nat. Park Svc., San Francisco, 1978; dir. mus. educators forum, 1983-85; historian 2d Inf. Divsn., 1994-96; guest lectr. Kookmin U., Seoul, 1995. Editor: Fort Leonard Wood, 1941, 1991; contbr. articles and monographs to mags. and newspapers; appeared in numerous TV documentaries and programs. Bd. dirs. South Ctrl. Mo. Arts Coun., Rolla, 1991. Mem. Am. Assn. Mus., Am. Assn. State and Local History, Internat. Commn. on Mus., Commn. on Mil. Mus. in Am., Rolls Royce Owners Club. Avocations: travel, archaeology, theatre. E-mail: combsk@usfk.korea.army.mil.

COMISAR, MICHAEL E. restaurant manager; Mng. ptnr. Maisonette Restaurant, Cin. Office: Maisonette 114 E 6th St Cincinnati OH 45202-3202*

COMISAR, NAT, restaurant manager; Mng. ptnr. Maisonette Restaurant, Cin. Office: Maisonette 114 E 6th St Cincinnati OH 45202-3202*

COMISKEY, MICHAEL PETER, lawyer; b. Oak Park, Ill., Oct. 13, 1948; s. John B. and Jeanne M. (Platt) C.; m. Barbara A. Twardowski, Apr. 24, 1981; children: Julianne, Bridget, Eleanor, Michael Patrick. BA, U. Notre Dame, 1970; JD, Harvard U., 1975. Bar: Ill. 1975, U.S. Dist. Ct. (no. dist.) Ill. 1975. Ptnr. Lord, Bissell & Brook, Chgo., 1983—. Office: Lord Bissell & Brook 115 S La Salle St Ste 3200 Chicago IL 60603-3902

COMISKEY, NANCY, newspaper editor; Mng. editor features The Indpls. News; dep. mng. editor features and readership The Star & The News, Indpls., 1998—. Office: The Indpls News PO Box 145 Indianapolis IN 46206-0145

COMPTON, RALPH THEODORE, JR. electrical engineering educator; b. St. Louis, July 26, 1935; s. Ralph Theodore and Ethel (Evans) C.; m. Lorraine Fielding, Nov. 9, 1957; children: Diane Marie, Ralph Theodore III, Richard Thomas. S.B., MIT, 1958; M.Sc., Ohio State U., 1961, Ph.D., 1964. Jr. engr. DECO Electronics, Leesburg, Va., 1958-59; sr. engr. Battelle Meml. Inst., Columbus, Ohio, 1959-62; asst. supr. Antenna Lab., 1962-65; asst. prof. Case Inst. Tech., Cleve., 1965-67; fellow, guest prof. Tech. Hochschule, Munich, W. Ger., 1967-68; assoc. prof. Ohio State U., Columbus, 1968-78, prof. elec. engring., 1978-91; pres. Compton Rsch., Inc., 1992—. Cons. to various orgns., U.S., Europe, Israel, 1969—. Author: Adaptive Antennas-Concepts and Performance, 1988; contbr. chpts. to books, articles to profl. jours. Fellow Battelle Meml. Inst., 1961; NSF fellow, 1967; recipient Outstanding Paper awards Ohio State Electro-Sci. Lab., 1978, 80, 82, M. Barry Carlton award IEEE Aerospace and Electric Systems Soc., 1983, Sr. Research award Ohio State U. Engring. Coll., 1983 Fellow IEEE (assoc. editor Jour. Trans. on Antennas Propagation 1970); mem. Antenna and Propagation Soc. (chmn. Columbus chpt. 1971-72), Sigma Xi (sec.-treas. Case Inst. Tech. chpt. 1965-67), Pi Mu Epsilon Home and Office: 477 Poe Ave Worthington OH 43085-3036 E-mail: compton@ieee.org.

COMPTON, WILLIAM F. air transportation executive; m. Dreana Compton. Flight instr., 1966; pilot TWA, 1968; exec. v.p. ops. Trans World Airlines, Inc., St. Louis, 1996—, pres., COO, 1997—, now pres., CEO. Chmn. Air Lines Pilots Assn. TWA Master Exec. Coun., 1991-95, mem. exec. bd.; guest lectr. Stanford U. Grad. Sch. Bus./Law Sch., Midwest Acad. Mgmt. Office: Transworld Airlines Inc One City Ctr 515 N 6th St Saint Louis MO 63101-1842

COMSTOCK, REBECCA ANN, lawyer; b. Mpls., Mar. 13, 1950; d. Clark Franklin and Ruth Carolyn (Sundt) C. Student, Conn. Coll., 1968-70; BA summa cum laude, U. Minn., 1973; JD Order of St. Ives, U. Denver, 1977. Bar: Minn. 1978, U.S. Dist. Ct. Minn., U.S. Ct. Appeals (8th cir.). Ptnr. Dorsey & Whitney, Mpls., 1982—. Bd. dirs. St. Paul Chamber Orch., 1996-2001. Mem. ABA, Internat. Bar Assn., Minn. Bar Assn. (chmn. adminstrv. law sect. 1989-90, exec. coun. environ. and natural resources law sect. 1992-94, coun. computer law sect. 2001—), Hennepin County Bar Assn. (co-chmn. environ. law com. 1998-2000), Legal Aid Soc. of Mpls. (bd. dirs. 1988-93), Minn. Women Lawyers (bd. dirs. 1979-81), Nat. Assn. of Women Bus. Owners, Licensing Exec. Soc. (USA and Can.), Minn. Women's Econ. Roundtable. Avocations: skiing, sailing, golf, music, theatre. Office: Dorsey & Whitney LLP 50 S 6th St Minneapolis MN 55402-1498

CONANT, HOWARD ROSSET, steel company executive; b. Chgo., Sept. 30, 1924; s. Louis J. and Fredericka (Rosset) Cohn; m. Doris S. Kaplan, Dec. 14, 1947; children: Alison Sue, Howard R., Meredith Ann. B.S., U. Pa., 1947. Pres., dir. Interstate Steel Co., Des Plaines, Ill., 1947-71, chmn. bd., 1971-90; pres., dir. Elliott Paint & Varnish Co., Chgo., 1961-76. Dir. The Valspar Corp., 1977-91; chmn. bd. dirs. White Products Corp., 1965-67. Discussion leader Center Study of Continuing Edn., 1955-62; dir. Com. for Sane Nuclear Policy, 1964-69; mem. Bus. Execs. Move for Vietnam Peace, 1965-73. Served with AUS, 1943-46, PTO. Mem. World Pres.' Orgn., Ridge and Valley Tennis Club, Carlton Club, East Bank Club, North Shore Racquet Club. Home: 736 Greenacres Ln Glenview IL 60025-3204 Office: 445 N Wells St Ste 403 Chicago IL 60610-4534

CONARD, NORMAN DALE, secondary education educator; Tchr. social studies Uniontown (Kans.) High Sch., 1987—. Recipient State Tchr. of Yr. Social Studies award, Kans., 1992. Office: Uniontown High Sch 601 E 5th St Uniontown KS 66779-0070

CONATON, MICHAEL JOSEPH, financial service executive; b. Detroit, Aug. 3, 1933; s. John Martin and Margaret Alice (Cleary) C.; m. Nancy D. Kelley, June 13; children: Catherine, Macaira (dec.), Michael, Margaret, Elizabeth. B.S., Xavier U., 1955. Public accountant Stanley A. Hitter, C.P.A., Cin., 1956-58; controller The Moloney Co., Albia, Iowa, 1958-61; v.p. fin. The Midland Co., Cin., 1961-80, sr. v.p., chief fin. officer, 1980-83, exec. v.p., chief fin. officer, 1983-88, pres., chief operating officer, 1988—, also dir., vice-chmn., 1998—. Interim pres. Xavier U., 1990-91. City councilman, Albia, 1959-61; trustee, chmn. bd. Xavier U., 1983—. Served to lt. USMC, 1955-56. Mem. Fin. Execs. Inst., New Ohio Inst. (chmn.), Cin. Soc. Fin. Analysts, Athenaeum of Ohio (trustee), Met. Club (chmn. bd.). Home: 736 Elsinboro Dr Cincinnati OH 45226-1706 Office: The Midland Company PO Box 1256 Cincinnati OH 45201-1256

CONAWAY, CHARLES C. retail company executive; Exec. v.p., chief operating officer Reliable Drug Stores, Inc., 1989-92; sr. v.p. pharmacy CVS Corp., Woonsocket, RI, 1992-95, exec. v.p., CFO, 1995-99, pres., chief operating officer, 1999-2000; chmn., CEO Kmart Corp., Troy, Mich. Bd. dirs. Linens 'n Things. Office: KMart Corp CVS Corp 3100 W Big Beaver Rd Troy MI 48084

CONCANNON, JAMES M. law educator, university dean; b. Columbus, Ga., Oct. 2, 1947; s. James M. Jr. and Mary Jane (Crow) C.; m. Melissa P. Masoner, June 9, 1988. BS, U. Kans., 1968, JD, 1971. Law clk. Kans. Ins. Commn., Topeka, 1971; rsch. atty. Kans. Supreme Ct., 1971-73; asst. prof. law Washburn U., 1973-75, assoc. prof. law, 1976-81, prof., 1981—, dean, 1988-2001. Vis. prof. law Washington U., St. Louis, 1979; active Kans. Commn. on Pub. Understanding of Law, 1983-89, Task Force on Law Enforcement Consolidation, Topeka, 1991-92; mem. Nat. Conf. Commrs. on Uniform State Laws, 1998—; mem. Pattern Instrns. for Kans.-Civil Com., Kans. Jud. Coun., 2001—. Co-author: Kans. Appellate Practice Manual, 1978, Kansas Statutes of Limitations, 1988; sr. contbn. editor: Evidence in America-Federal Rules in the States, 1987. Coord. Citizens to

Keep Politics Out of Our Courts, Topeka, 1984; co-reporter Citizens Justice Initiative, 1997-99; chmn. legal com. Concerned Citizens Topeka, 1995-99; bd. dirs. Mut. Funds Waddell and Reed, Inc., 1997—. Master: Topeka Am. Inn. of Ct.; fellow: Kans. Bar Found., Am. Bar Found.; mem.: Assn. Am. Law Schs. (com. on bar admission, lawyer performance 1994—97), Kans. Bar Assn. (CLE com. 1976—2001, Outstanding Svc. award 1982), Washburn Law Sch. Alumni Assn. (life), Order of Coif. Office: Washburn U Law Sch 1700 SW College Ave Topeka KS 66621-0001

CONDRON, BARBARA O'GUINN, metaphysics educator, school administrator, publisher; b. New Orleans, May 1, 1953; d. Bill Gene O'Guinn and Marie Gladys (Newbill) Jackson; m. Daniel Ralph Condron, Feb. 29, 1992; 1 child, Hezekiah Daniel. BJ, U. Mo., 1973; MA, Coll. Metaphysics, Springfield, Mo., 1977, DD, D in Metaphysics, 1979. Cert. counselor; ordained min. Interfaith Ch. Metaphysics. Field rep. Sch. Metaphysics, New Orleans, 1978-80; dir. Interfaith Ch. Metaphysics, 1884-89; pres. Nat. Hdqs., Sch. Metaphysics, Windyville, Mo., 1980-84, prof., 1989—, chmn. bd. dirs., 1991-98, mem. coun. elders, bd. govs. internat. edn., 1998—; CEO SOM Pub., 1989-98. Guest lectr., instr. Wichita State U., 1977, U. New Orleans, 1979, La. State U., 1981, Am. Bus. Womens Assn., 1982, U. Mo., Kansas City, 1984, Unity Village, 1985, Kans. Dept. Social Svcs. Conf., Topeka, 1986, U. Mo., Columbia and St. Louis, 1986, Mo. Tchrs. Conf., St. Louis, 1991, U. Okla., Norman, 1988-89, Parliament of World's Religions, Chgo., 1993, many others; creator Sch. Metaphysics Assocs., 1992; initiator Universal Hour Peace, 1995; initiator, internat. coord. Nat. Dream Hotline, 1988—; radio and TV guest, 1977—; creator Maker's Dozen-Visionary Schs. Recognition, 1999. Author: What will I do Tomorrow?, Probing Depression, 1977, Search for a Satisfying Relationship, 1980, Strangers in My Dreams, 1987, Total Recall: An Introduction to Past Life & Health Readings, 1991, Kundalini Rising, 1992, Dreamers Dictionary, 1994, The Work of the Soul: Past Life Recall & Spiritual Enlightenment, 1996, Uncommon Knowledge, 1996, First Opinion: 21st Century Wholistic Health Care, 1997, Spiritual Renaissance Elevating Your Conciousness for the Common Good, 1999, The Bible Interpreted in Dream Symbols, 2000, Every Dream is About the Dreamer, 2001, Remembering Atlantis: The History of the World Vol. 1, 2001; author series When All Else Fails; editor-in-chief Thresholds Jour., 1990—; editor Wholistic Health and Healing Guide, 1992-2000; also numerous poems. Mem. Internat. Platform Assn., Am. Bus. Women's Assn., Interfaith Ministries, Kundalini Rsch. Network, Planetary Soc., Heritage Found., Mo. Writers Guild, Sigma Delta Chi. Office: Sch Metaphysics World Hdqs Windyville MO 65783

CONDRON, DANIEL RALPH, academic administrator, metaphysics educator; b. Chillicothe, Mo., Jan. 30, 1953; s. Ralph Wesley and Rosa Irene (Garber) C.; m. Barbara Gail O'Guinn, Feb. 29, 1992; 1 child, Hezekiah Daniel. BS, U. Mo., 1975, MS, 1978; DDiv, Coll. Metaphysics, Springfield, Mo., 1982, D in Metaphysics, 1985. Cert. counselor; ordained to ministry Interfaith Ch. of Metaphysics. Dir. Sch. Metaphysics, Des Moines, 1980, Kansas City, Mo., 1981, regional dir. Colo., 1982-85, Chgo. and Detroit, 1985-90, pres. bd. nat. hdqs. Windyville, Mo., 1988—; chancellor, prof. Coll. Metaphysics, 1990—. Tchg. asst. U. Mo., Columbia, 1977; sales and mgmt. cons. Am. Media, Des Moines, 1980-83; speaker in field including Parliament of the World's Religions, Chgo., 1993. Author: Dreams of the Soul, 1991, Permanent Healing, 1992, Universal Language of Mind, 1994, Understanding Your Dreams, 1994, Uncommon Knowledge, Seven Secret Keys to Prosperity and Abundance, 1996, Superconscious Meditation, 1997; pub. jour. Thresholds Quar., 1988—; internat. radio and TV guest including BBC, Radio Hong Kong, Voice of Am., 1979—. Mem. Sch. Metaphysics Assocs. (pres.), Nat. Space Soc., Planetary Soc., Alpha Gamma Rho, Alpha Zeta. Republican. Achievements include implementer and designer of organic and bio-dynamic farming and agriculture at the 1500 acre College of Metaphysics campus, landscape designer and artist for 1500 acre college of metaphysics campus, discoverer and developer of the Universal language of mind as it applies to dreams, to the Bible and other holy works; discoverer of specific attitudes that cause specific disease and disorders in the body. Avocations: photography, horticulture, landscaping, designing and inventing, space research. Home: Box 15 Windyville MO 65783-9703 Office: Sch Metaphysics Nat Headquarters Windyville MO 65783

CONGALTON, SUSAN TICHENOR, lawyer; b. Mt. Vernon, N.Y., July 12, 1946; d. Arthur George and M. Marjorie (McDermott) Tichenor; m. Christopher William Congalton, May 29, 1971. BA summa cum laude, Loretto Heights Coll., 1968; JD, Georgetown U., 1971. Bar: N.Y. 1972, Ill. 1986, Colo. 1990. Assoc. Reavis & McGrath (now Fulbright & Jaworski), N.Y.C., 1971-78, ptnr., 1978-85; v.p., gen. counsel, sec. Carson Pirie Scott & Co., Chgo., 1985-87, sr. v.p. fin. and law, 1987-89; mng. dir. Lupine LLC (formerly known as Lupine Ptnrs.), 1989—. Bd. dirs. Harris Trust & Savs. Bank, Harris Bankcorp, Inc., Bankmont Fin. Corp.; chmn. Community Reinvestment Act Com., 1990-97, chmn. audit com., 1997—; bd. dirs. Pulitzer Inc., St. Louis. Mem. editorial staff Georgetown U. Law Jour., 1969-70, editor, 1970-71. Mem. bd. overseers Ill. Inst. Tech., Chgo., Chgo. Kent Coll. Law, 1985-89; mem. bus. adv. coun. Bus. Sch., U. Ill., Chgo., 1987-90; mem. planning com. Ann. Corp. Counsel Inst., 1986-89; bd. dirs. Ill. Inst. Continuing Legal Edn., 1992-95; mem. Chgo. Workforce Bd., 1995-98; chmn. Strategic Planning Task force, 1995-96, chmn. Performance Rev. Com., 1996-98. Mem. ABA, Econ. Club Chgo., Chgo. Club (bd. dirs. 1996—, treas. 1999-). Office: Lupine LLC 1520 Kensington Rd Ste 112 Oak Brook IL 60523-2140 E-mail: lupineLLC@aol.com.

CONGER, WILLIAM FRAME, artist, educator; b. Dixon, Ill., May 29, 1937; s. Robert Allen and Catherine Florence (Kelly) C.; m. Kathleen Marie Onderak, May 23, 1964; children: Sarah Elizabeth, Clarisa Lynn. Student, Art Inst. Chgo., 1954, 56-57, 60, 62; BFA, U. N.Mex., 1960; MFA, U. Chgo., 1966. Asst. prof. Rock Valley Coll., Rockford, 1966-71; vis. lectr. Beloit Coll., 1969; prof., chmn. dept. art DePaul U., Chgo., 1971-85; vis. artist U. Chgo., 1976, 83, Cornell U., 1980; Sch. Art Inst. Chgo., 1985, Univ. Iowa; adj. prof. So. Ill. U., 1984; chmn. dept. art theory and practice Northwestern U., Evanston, Ill., 1985-99, prof., 1985— ; numerous lectures; cons. Puresol. One man shows Burpee Mus., Rockford, Ill., 1971, Douglas Kenyon Gallery, Chgo., 1974, 75, Krannert Ctr. for Arts, Urbana, Ill., 1976, Zaks Gallery, Chgo., 1978, 80, 83, Roy Boyd Gallery, Chgo., 1985, 87, 90, 92, 94, 96, 97, 98, 99 Janus Gallery, Santa Fe, 1992, Tarbel Mus., Ill., 1993, Univ. Club Chgo., 1998, Jonson Mus., Albuquerque, 1998, Walters Art Ctr., Tulsa, 2000, 2001; group shows include Art Inst. Chgo., 1963, 71, 73, 78, 80, 84-85, Mus. Contemporary Art, Chgo., 1976, 96-97, Krannert Mus., Urbana, 1976, Ill. State Mus., 1978, 88-89, E.B. Crocker Gallery, Sacramento, 1977, Phoenix Mus., 1977, Mitchell Mus., 1980, Notre Dame U., 1981, Sonoma State U., 1983, Cowles Mus., 1983, Arts Club Chgo., 1983-97, Sheldon Meml. Gallery, U. Nebr., 1984, Anchorage Fine Arts Mus., 1985, Ark Art Ctr., 1985, Block Gallery, Northwestern U., 1986, 90, 96-97, Smart Mus., 1996; represented in permanent collections Art Inst. Chgo., Mus. Contemporary Art, Chgo., Smart Mus., U. Chgo., Ill. State Mus., Chgo., No. Ill. U., DePaul U., Jonson Mus., U. N.Mex., Block Gallery, others; also pvt. collections U.S. and worldwide; numerous catalogs, revs. and commentary in Arts mag., Art Forum, Art in Am., Ciamese, Art News, Art Criticism, Art & Antiques; others; author essays in Whitewalls, Chicago/Art/Write, Psychoanalytic Perspectives on Art, Psychoanalytic Studies of Biography, Critical Inquiry, other jours. Bd. dirs. Ox Bow Art Sch., 1982-86; adv. bd. Renaissance Soc., 1988—; bd. trustees St. Benedict H.S., Chgo., 1994—; referee NEH, 1989; interviewee TV and radio programs including Am. Art Forum. Recipient Bartels award Art Inst. Chgo., 1971; Clusmann award, 1973; Friedman awards U. Chgo., 1965, 66. Mem. Coll. Art Assn. Am., Phi Sigma Tau. Office: Northwestern U Dept Art Theory & Practice Rm 244 Kresge Hall Evanston IL 60201 Home: 3500 N Lake Shore Dr Chicago IL 60657-1815 Studio: 3711 N Ravenswood Chicago IL 60613 E-mail: w-conger@nwu.edu.

CONIDI, DANIEL JOSEPH, private investigation agency executive; b. Chgo., Mar. 11, 1957; s. Joseph Frank and Gloria (Zimmerman) C. BS, SUNY, Albany, 1983; MA, Chgo. State U., 1987. Lic. pvt. detective, Ill. Owner, mgr. Conidi Enterprises, Chgo., 1979-81; pres. Daniel J. Conidi-Assocs., 1981—; cons. Office Cook County Sheriff, 1983-90. Freelance lectr., 1983—. Author: Professional Investigative Methods, 1984, Private Investigators Training Manual, 1986. Del. Cook County Rep. Conv., 1987. Recipient cert. of appreciation Boys Town, 1982; named Ky. col. State of Ky., 1987. Mem. World Assn. Detectives, Internat. Police Congress, Coun. Internat. Investigators, Nat. Assn. Investigations and Security, Fraternal Order Police, NRA (life), Navy League (life), Univ. Club, Masons, Shriners. Presbyterian. Avocations: flying, writing. Home: 500 Ashland Ave River Forest IL 60305-1825 Office: 734 N La Salle Dr Ste 1082 Chicago IL 60610-3530

CONKLIN, MARA LORAINE, public relations executive; b. Vallejo, Calif., July 28, 1962; d. Kenneth J. and Laura T. (Siegrist) Cichosz; m. Rex D. Conklin, Sept. 6, 1986; children: Elisabeth, Emily, Margaret. BA, Marquette U., 1984. Nat. news editl. staff Nat. Safety Coun., Chgo., 1984-85; corp. comm. specialist Household Internat., Prospect Hgts., Ill., 1985-86; acct. supr. Posner McGrath Ltd., Lincolnshire, 1986-90, v.p., 1990-92, sr. v.p., 1992-94, exec. v.p., 1994-97, pres., 1997-98, Clarus Comms. Ltd., Libertyville, 1998—. Recipient Spectra award Internat. Assn. Bus. Communicators, 1992, 94, Silver Trumpet award Publicity Club Chgo., 1993. Mem. Marquette Club Chgo. (chair alumni com. 1986-94, pres. 1994-96). Office: Clarus Comms Ltd 620 Mullady Pkwy Libertyville IL 60048-3729

CONKLIN, THOMAS WILLIAM, lawyer; b. Chgo., Mar. 1, 1938; s. Clarence Robert and Ellen Pauline (Gleason) C.; children: Thomas William, Sarah Adrienne. BA, Yale U., 1960; JD, U. Chgo., 1963. Bar: Ill. 1964, Mich. 1997. Ptnr. Upton, Conklin & Leahy, Chgo., 1969-72, Conklin, Leahy & Eisenberg, Chgo., 1972-79, Conklin & Adler, Ltd., Chgo., 1979-87, Conklin & Roadhouse, Chgo., 1988-95; Rivkin, Radler & Kremer, 1995-97; ptnr. Conklin Murphy & Conklin, 1997—. Contbr. numerous articles to legal jours. With USAF, 1963-64. Mem. ABA, Fed. Bar Assn., Am. Arbitration Assn., Internat. Assn. Ins. Counsel, Chgo. Bar Assn., Maritime Law Assn., Mich. Bar Assn., Ill. State Bar Assn., Chgo. Bar Assn., Union League Club Chgo. Home: PO Box 189 Bangor MI 49013-0189 Office: Conklin Murphy Conklin & Snyder 53 W Jackson Blvd Ste 1150 Chicago IL 60604-3790 E-mail: tconk@msn.com.

CONLEY, EUGENE ALLEN, retired insurance company executive; b. Nebraska City, Nebr., Oct. 3, 1925; s. Melville Evans and Margaret (Allen) C.; m. Erma Grace Fuller, June 27, 1948; children: Tom, Roger, John, Carol Sue. B.S., U. Nebr., 1949; D.Sc. (hon.), U. Nebr. Med. Ctr.; LL.D. (hon.), Nebr. Wesleyan U. C.L.U. Agt. Am. Mut. Life Ins. Co., Omaha, 1948-54, supr., supt. agts., v.p., dir. agts., dir. Des Moines, 1954-72; exec. v.p., dir. Guarantee Mut. Life Co., Omaha, 1972-76, pres., 1976-89, chmn. bd., 1989-90; retired, 1990. Bd. dirs. Omaha Zool. Soc.; trustee, past chmn. Nebr. Ind. Coll. Found.; bd. trustees U. Nebr. Found., Lincoln; civilian aide to sec. Army; mem. pres.'s adv. coun. Creighton U.; past chmn. bd. govs. Nebr. Wesleyan U.; co-chmn. fund drive United Way Midlands, 1976-77, pres., 1979-80; past crusade chmn. Am. Cancer Soc.; co-chmn. NCCJ; chmn. bd. Bishop Clarkson Coll., 1990; chmn. Omaha Community Found., 1991.. Served with USNR, 1943-46. Recipient Americanism citation B'Nai B'rith, 1982, Builder award U. Nebr.; named Citizen of Yr. United Way, 1983 Mem. Nat. Assn. Life Underwriters, Coll. Life Underwriters, Omaha C. of C. (chmn. dir.), Phi Kappa Psi. Clubs: Omaha, Omaha Country, Plaza, Masons, Shriners. Office: Guarantee Centre 8801 Indian Hills Dr Omaha NE 68114-4059 Home: Apt 1Q 17120 Cedar Plz Omaha NE 68130-2376

CONLEY, MICHAEL L. food products executive; CFO McDonald's Corp., Oak Brook, Ill., 60523. Office: McDonalds Corp One Kroc Dr Oak Brook IL 60523

CONLEY, SARAH ANN, health facility administrator; b. Richmond, Ind., Sept. 14, 1942; d. Harry Herbert and Mary Janet Kercheval; m. Philip Howard Conley, Apr. 5, 1963 (dec.); children: Christine L., Philip Douglas. BS, Purdue U., 1964; postgrad., U. Cin., 1965. Elem. tchr. Southwest Local Schs., Harrison, Ohio, 1964-66; svc. office mgr. Renault of Dayton (Ohio), 1970-73; mgr. Office of Charlotte Ames, Xenia, Ohio, 1974-77; bus. mgr. Radiol. Physicians, Inc., Dayton, 1977-79, Nat. Tractor Pullers Assn., Columbus, Ohio, 1979-85; HMO adminstr. Cen. Benefits Mutual Ins. Co., 1985-90; adminstr. Orthopedic and Neurol. Cons., 1990-97, Peripheral Vascular Surgery, Columbus, 1997-99; owner Conley Mgmt. Svc., Westerville, Ohio. Mem. Am. Coll. Med. Practice Execs. (cert.), Ohio Med. Group Mgmt. Assn. (pres. 1993-94), MidOhio Med. Mgmt. Assn., Med. Group Mgmt. Assn., Licking County Bus. and Profl. Women (pres. 1989-91). Democrat. Methodist. Avocations: piano, organ, church choir, teaching sunday school. E-mail: conleyserv.@cs.com.

CONLIN, ROXANNE BARTON, lawyer; b. Huron, S.D., June 30, 1944; d. Marion William and Alyce Muraine (Madden) Barton; m. James Clyde Conlin, Mar. 21, 1964; children: Jacalyn Rae, James Barton, Deborah Ann, Douglas Benton BA, Drake U., 1964, JD, 1966, MPA, 1979; LLD (hon.), U. Dubuque, 1975. Bar: Iowa 1966. Assoc. Davis, Huebner, Johnson & Burt, Des Moines, 1966-67; dep. indsl. commr. State of Iowa, 1967-68, asst. atty. gen., 1969-76; U.S. atty. So. Dist. Iowa, 1977-81; ptnr. Conlin, P.C., Des Moines, 1983—. Adj. prof. law U. Iowa, 1977-79; chmn. Iowa Women's Polit. Caucus, 1973-75, del. nat. steering com., 1973-77; cons. U.S. Commn. on Internat. Women's Year, 1976-77; gen. counsel NOW Legal Def. and Edn. Fund, 1985-88, pres., 1986-88; lectr. in field. Contbr. articles to profl. jours. Nat. committeewoman Iowa Young Dems.; pres. Polk County Young Dems., 1965-66; del. Iowa Presdl. Conv., 1972; Dem. candidate for gov. of Iowa, 1982; bd. dirs. Riverhills Day Care Ctr., YWCA; chmn. Drake U. Law Sch. Endowment Trust, 1985-86; bd. counselors Drake U., 1982-86; pres. Civil Justice Found., 1986-88, Roscoe Pound Found., 1994-97; chair Iowa Dem. Party, 1998-99. Named one of Top Ten Litigators, Nat. Law Jour, 1989, 100 Most Influential Attys., 1991, 50 Most Powerful Women Attys., Nat. Law Jour., 1998, 10 Most Influential Women, Nat. Law Jour., 2002; recipient award, Iowa ACLU, 1974, Alumnus of Yr. award, Drake U. Law Sch., 1989, ann. award, Young Women's Resource Ctr., 1989, Verne Lawyer award as Outstanding Mem., Iowa Trial Lawyers Assn., 1994, Rosalie Wahl award, Minn. Women Lawyers, 1998, Marie Lambert award, 2000, Mary Louise Smith award, YWCA, 2001; grantee scholarship established in her homor Kansas City Women Lawyers; scholar Reader's Digest scholar, 1963—64, scholar, Fishcher Found, 1965—66. Mem.: ATLA (chmn. consumer and victims coalition com. 1985—87, chmn. edn. dept 1987—88, parliamentarian 1988—89, sec. 1989—90, v.p. 1990—91, pres.-elect 1991—92, pres. 1992—93), ABA, NOW, Trial Lawyers Care (bd. dirs.), Inner Circle of Advocates, Higher Edn. Commn. Iowa (co-chmn. 1988—90), Iowa Acad. Trial Lawyers, Internat. Acad. Trial Lawyers, Assn. Trial Lawyers Iowa (bd. dirs.), Iowa Bar Assn., Chi Omega, Alpha Lambda Delta, Phi Beta Kappa. Office: Griffin Bldg 319 7th St Ste 600 Des Moines IA 50309-3826

CONLIN, THOMAS (BYRD), conductor; b. Arlington, Va., Jan. 29, 1944; BMus, Peabody Conservatory Music, 1966, MMus, 1967; studied with Leonard Bernstein, Erich Leinsdorf, Sir Adrian Boult. Artistic dir. Chamber Opera Soc., Balt., 1966-72; assoc. condr. N.C. Symphony Orch., 1972-74; music dir. Queens (N.Y.) Orchestral Soc., 1974-76; condr. Amarillo (Tex.) Symphony Orch., 1976-84, W.Va. Symphony Orch., 1983-2001, condr. laureate, 2001—; prin. condr. Toledo Opera, 2002—. Asst. prof. mus. CUNY, 1974-76. Condr. recs. of contemporary orchestral music Bridge Records, 1999—, Grammy award 2001, Indie nomination, 2001. Mem. Am. Symphony Orch. League, Nat. Opera Assn., Condrs. Guild, Opera America. Office: 8440 Augusta Ln Holland OH 43528 E-mail: thconmusic@aol.com.

CONLON, HARRY B., JR. banking company executive; b. Green Bay, Wis., May 15, 1935; s. Harry B. and Alice (O'Neil) C.; m. Margaret Sullivan. BS in Bus., U. Notre Dame, 1957; JD, U. Wis., 1963. With Continental Ill. Nat. Bank, Chgo., 1963-65; v.p. Kellogg-Citizens Nat. Bank, Green Bay, 1965-75, also bd. dirs.; chmn., chief exec. officer Associated Banc-Corp., 1975—. Served to lt. USNR, 1957-63. Mem. Wis. Bankers Assn. (bd. dirs. exec. counsel 1984-87), Bankers Round Table, Am. Bankers Coun.

CONLON, JAMES CHARLES, former state legislator; m. Janice D. Winters; 7 children. BS, U. Notre Dame; MEd, Pa. State U. Tchr.; rep. Dist. 19 Ind. Ho. of Reps., 1990-97, mem. cities and towns, edn. coms., mem. local govt. and natural resources coms., mem. urban affairs com., dep. spkr. pro tem. Mem. Crown Point (Ind.) City Coun., 1980-90; bd. mem. works and Pub. Safety, Crown Point, 1985-90, mem. planning com., 1987-90. Home: 341 Maple Ln Crown Point IN 46307-4544

CONLON, SUZANNE B. federal judge; b. 1939; AB, Mundelein Coll., 1963; JD, Loyola U., Chgo., 1968; postgrad., U. London, 1971. Law clk. to judge U.S. Dist. Ct. (no. dist.) Ill., 1968-71; assoc. Pattishall, McAuliffe & Hostetter, 1972-73, Schiff Hardin & Waite, 1973-75; asst. U.S. atty. U.S. Dist. Ct. (no. dist.) Ill., 1976-77, 82-86, U.S. Dist. Ct. (cen. dist.) Calif., 1978-82; exec. dir. U.S. Sentencing Commn., 1986-88; spl. counsel to assoc. atty. gen., 1988; judge U.S. Dist. Ct. (no. dist.) Ill., 1988—. Asst. prof. law De Paul U., Chgo., 1972-73, lectr., 1973-75; adj. prof. Northwestern U. Sch. Law, 1991-95; vice chmn. Chgo. Bar Assn. Internat. Inst., 1993—; vis. com. U. Chgo. Harris Grad. Sch. Pub. Policy, 1997—. Mem. ABA, FBA, Am. Judicature Soc., Internat. Bar Assn. Judges Forum, Lawyers Club Chgo. (pres. 1996-97). Office: US Dist Ct No Dist Everett McKinley Dirksen Bldg 219 S Dearborn St Ste 2356 Chicago IL 60604-1878

CONMY, PATRICK A. federal judge; b. 1934; BA, Harvard U., 1955; JD, Georgetown U., 1959. Bar: Va. 1959, N.D. 1959. Ptnr. Lundberg, Conmy et al, Bismarck, N.D., 1959-85; mem. Bismarck City Commn., 1968-76; state rep. N.D. House Reps., Bismarck, 1976-85; judge U.S. Dist. Ct. N.D., 1985—. Office: US Dist Ct Fed Bldg 220 E Rosser Ave Rm 411 PO Box 1578 Bismarck ND 58502-1578

CONN, GORDON BRAINARD, JR. lawyer; b. St. Louis, Dec. 20, 1944; BA, Macalester Coll., 1967; JD, U. Mich., 1970. Bar: Minn. 1970, U.S. Supreme Ct. 1986; cert. in bus. bankruptcy law Am. Bd. Certficiation. Law clk. to Chief Justice Minn. Supreme Ct., St. Paul, 1970-71; ptnr. Faegre & Benson, Mpls., 1971-99, Kalina, Wills, Gisvold & Clark, P.L.L.P., Mpls., 1999—. Mem. ABA, Am. Bankruptcy Inst., Minn. State Bar Assn., Comml. Law League Am., Nat. Assn. Bankruptcy Trustees. Office: # 560 6160 Summit Dr N Minneapolis MN 55430-2100

CONNEALY, MATT J. state legislator; b. Oakland, Nebr., Dec. 11, 1951; m. Judith Scherer Connealy, May 25, 1974; children: Maggie, Mick. Student, Coll. St. Thomas, St. Paul, U. Nebr., 1970-73. Farmer; mem. Nebr. Legislature from 16th dist., Lincoln, 1998—. Former mem. Lyons-Decatur N.E. Sch. Bd., Gov.'s Agr. Adv. Com., Nebr. Ethanol Authority and Devel. Bd., Archdiocesan Pastoral Coun., Archdiocese Omaha, Biomass to Energy Adv. Group, U.S. Dept. Energy, We. Area Power Adminstrn., Am. Corn Growers Bd., Elm Creek Task Force, Burt County Farm Crisis Com.; mem. coun. exec. com. and market devel. com. U.S. Feed Grains Coun.; mem. ctrl. com. and exec. com. agr. rep. Nebr. Dem. Party; mem. utilization and mktg. bd. Nebr. Corn Devel.; bd. dirs. Burt County Pub. Power; treas. Nebr. Farmers Union; mem. parish coun., instr. youth edn. Holy Family Cath. Ch. Home: 2999 Old Highway 118 Decatur NE 68020-2046 Office: State Capitol Dist 16 PO Box 94604 Rm 1101 Lincoln NE 68509

CONNELLY, JOHN JAMES, retired oil company technical specialist; b. Lima, Ohio, Aug. 14, 1935; s. Robert Vincent and Helen Josephine (Hay) C.; m. Aug. 22, 1959 (dec. Aug. 1991); children: Thomas, Kathleen, Joseph, Patrick; m. Virginia Connelly, July, 1993. BSChemE, Ohio State U., 1958; MBA with honors, Baldwin Wallace U., 1975. Registered profl. engr., Ohio. Engr. Std. Oil of Ohio, Lima, 1958-63; rsch. assoc. Battelle Meml. Inst., Columbus, Ohio, 1963-65; tech. specialist Owens Corning Fiberglas, Granville, 1965-67; sr. engr. Std. Oil of Ohio, Lima, 1967-71, tech. program analyst Cleve., 1971-74, linear program specialist, 1974-78, fed. affairs analyst, 1978-81; project leader Std. of Ohio/Brit. Petroleum Am., 1981-92; tech. specialist BP Am., 1992-95; retired, 1995; part time technical specialist Paramount Tech. Svcs., 1995—. Instr. Ohio State U., Lima, 1961-63. Advisor Jr. Achievement, Lima, 1960-62; treas. Harding Middle Sch. PTA, Lakewood, Ohio, 1975-77, Music Parents Assn., Lakewood, 1978-80, Sch. Bd. Candidate Treas., Lakewood, 1981; mem. Vols. for Internat. Tech. Assistance, 1988—. Mem. Soc. of Friends. Avocations: reading, biking, needlework. Home: 23749 Wonneta Pkwy Westlake OH 44145-2733 E-mail: johnjconnelly@stratos.net.

CONNELLY, MARK, writer, educator; b. Phila., July 8, 1951; s. Edward James and Hilda Virginia (Pfleger) C. BA in English and History, Carroll Coll., 1973; MA in Creative Writing, U. Wis., Milw., 1974, PhD in English, 1984. Instr. English Milw. Area Tech. Coll., 1986—. Cons. Great Lakes Precision Products. Author: The Diminished Self: Orwell and the Loss of Freedom, 1987, The Sundance Reader, 1997, Orwell and Gissing, 1997, The Sundance Writer, 1999, Deadly Closets, 2000. V.p. Irish Cultural and Heritage Ctr. of Wis., 2000—. Recipient Ann. Fiction award Milw. Mag., 1982, 1st Place Fiction award Ind. Mag., 1982. Presbyterian. Avocations: reading, travel, Irish studies. Office: Milw Area Tech Coll 700 W State St Milwaukee WI 53233-1419 E-mail: markconn@earthlink.net.

CONNETT, JIM, radio director; b. Effingham, Ill. BA in Comms., So. Ill. U., Edwardsville. Program dir. Classic 99, St. Louis. Office: Classic 99 85 Founders Ln Saint Louis MO 63105

CONNOLLY, GERALD EDWARD, lawyer; b. Boston, Oct. 13, 1943; s. Thomas E. and Grace J. (Fitzgerald) C.; m. Elizabeth Heidi Eckert, Jan. 6, 1968; children: Matthew F., Dennis F., David D., Edward F. BS, Coll. of Holy Cross, 1965; JD, U. Va., 1972. Bar: Wis. 1972, U.S. Tax Ct. 1973. From assoc. to ptnr. Whyte & Hirschboeck S.C., Milw., 1972-78; ptnr. Minahan & Peterson S.C., 1978-91, Quarles & Brady, 1991—. V.p., bd. dirs., sec. Reinhart FoodService, Inc.; bd. dirs., sec. Reinhart Real Estate Group, Inc., Reinhart Retail Group; v.p., sec., bd. dirs. Bernstein Comm., Inc.; sec. Hometown Inc.; bd. dirs. Viterbo U., LaCrosse, Wis., Hatco Corp., Milw., Adaptive Engring. Lab., Inc., Diversatek, Inc., Medovations, Sunlite Plastics, Inc., Milw.; sec. The Medalcraft Mint, Inc., Radisson LaCrosse Hotel, Water Blasting. Trustee Emory T. Clark Family Charitable Found., D.B. Reinhart Family Found.; chmn. Circle of Care Children's Hosp. Wis.; bd. dirs. Children's Hosp. Wis. Found. Lt. USN, 1966-69. Mem. ABA, Milw. Club, Milw. Athletic Club, North Shore Country Club,

Order of Coif. Home: 10134 N Range Line Rd # 27W Mequon WI 53092-5435 Office: Quarles & Brady 411 E Wisconsin Ave Ste 2550 Milwaukee WI 53202-4497 E-mail: gec@quarles.com.

CONNOLLY, MIKE W. state legislator; b. Dubuque, Iowa, Oct. 31, 1945; m. Martha Fessler. BA, Loras Coll., 1967, MA, 1976. Tchr. Dubuque Sr. H.S., sch. adminstr.; mem. Iowa Ho. of Reps., Iowa Senate from 18th dist., 1988—. Mem. Greater Dubuque Devel. Corp. Mem. St. Joseph's Ch., Duuque County Dem. Party, Regional Coord. Coun. With U.S. Army Res. Mem. Dubuque Edn. Assn., Four Mounds Assn., Loras Club. Home: 3458 Daniels St Dubuque IA 52002-5121 Office: State Capitol Dist 18 3 9th And Grand Des Moines IA 50319-0001 E-mail: mike_connolly@legis.state.ia.us.

CONNOLLY, WILLIAM M. state supreme court justice; Undergrad., Creighton U. , 1956—59; JD, Creighton U., 1963. Dep. atty. Adams County, 1964—66, atty., 1967—72; pvt. law practice Hastings, 1972—91; former judge Nebr. Ct. of Appeals, Lincoln, 1992—94; assoc. justice Nebr. Supreme Ct., justice, 1994—. Office: Nebr Supreme Ct PO Box 98910 2413 State Capitol Bldg Lincoln NE 68509 Office Fax: 402-471-3480.*

CONNOR, CAROL J. library director; BA in History, Molloy Coll., 1964; MA in History, Georgetown U., 1970; MS in Libr. Sci., Drexel U., 1972. Various adminstrv. positions in ednl. fields, various U.S. Cities, 1964-72; spl. asst. tech. processes divsn. Lincoln (Nebr.) City Librs., 1972-73, coord. tech. processes divsn., 1973-76, asst. dir., 1976-78, dir., 1978—. Mem. Mayor's Com. for Internat. Friendship, Lincoln, 1973—; adv. com. U. Nebr., search for dean of librs., 1984-85; del. to cmty. retreat, Star Venture, 1986, edn. task force, 1987-88, vocat. edn. task force, 1988-89, downtown child care task force, 1988-89; mem. cmty. adv. com. Lincoln Pub. Schs. Search for English Cons., 1991, Search for Media Dir., 1992; mem. Nebr. Ctr. for Book Bd., 1990-95, Nebr. Libr. Commn. state adv. coun. 1985-86, Nebr. Lit. Festival Com., 1990-92; bd. dirs. Postsecondary Ednl. Librs. and Resource Ctrs. of Nebr. 1981-84, chair 1982; mem. edn. com. Am. Cancer Soc., Lancaster County, Nebr., 1989-91, Family Svcs. Bd., 1991—, vice chair chair elect 1992, chair, 1994; leadership Lincoln VI 1990-91; mem. Lincoln Cancer Ctr. adv. bd., 1988-94, vice chair 1991-94. Mem. ALA, (bylaws com., membership com., LITA/LAMA conf. com. 1996-97), Mountain Plains Libr. Assn. (chair continuing edn. com. 1984-85; membership devel. com. 1986-87, vice chair and chair of pub. libr. sect. 1975-77, v.p./ pres. elect 1996-97, pres. 1997-98), Nebr. Libr. Assn. (chair intellectual freedom com. 1975-76, state rep. to Mountain Plains Libr. Assn., 1984-86, vice chair and chair of pub. libr. sect. 1987-89), Urban Librs. Coun. (leadership programs 1994-95), Capitol Bus. and Profl. Women (v.p. 1983), Downtown Lincoln Assn. (mktg. com. 1988-89). Office: Lincoln City Librs 136 S 14th St Lincoln NE 68508-1899

CONNOR, CHRISTOPHER M. textiles executive; Grad., Ohio State U. Dir. advt. Sherwin-Williams' Paint Stores Group, 1983, pres., gen. mgr. western divsn., sr. v.p. mktg. group, pres., gen. mgr. diversified brands divsn., pres., 1997, vice chmn., CEO, 1999, also bd. dirs. Office: Sherwin-Williams Co 101 Prospect Ave NW Cleveland OH 44115-1075

CONNOR, LAURENCE DAVIS, lawyer, director; b. Columbus, Ohio, May 14, 1938; s. Laurence R. and Gladys C. (Davis) C.; m. Clare Elizabeth Hartwick, Aug. 8, 1964; children: Jeffrey H., Lynne D. Scoville. BA, Miami U., Oxford, Ohio, 1960; JD, U. Mich., 1965. Bar: Mich. 1966, U.S. Dist. Ct. (ea. dist.) Mich. 1966, U.S. Ct. Appeals (6th cir.) 1973, U.S. Supreme Ct. 1979. Assoc. Dykema Gossett, Detroit, 1965-73, ptnr., 1973—2002, mem. exec. com., 1984-90, dir. litigation sect., 1987-91. Mem. coun. sect. on alternative dispute resolution State Bar of Mich., 1992—, chairperson, 1996-97; pres. Vis. Nurse Assn. Met. Detroit, 1980-81, Vist. Nurse Corp., Detroit, 1986-88; asst. clin. prof. law U. Mich., 2002-. Mem. ABA, Am. Judicature Soc., Country Club Detroit, Detroit Athletic Club, Yondotega Club. Office: Dykema Gossett 400 Renaissance Ctr Ste 3500 Detroit MI 48243-1602 E-mail: lconnor@dykema.com.

CONNORS, DORSEY, television and radio commentator, newspaper columnist; b. Chgo. d. William J. and Sarah (MacLain) C.; m. John E. Forbes; 1 dau., Stephanie. BA cum laude, U. Ill. Fl. reporter WGN-TV Rep. Nat. Conv., Chgo., Dem. Nat. Conv., L.A., 1960. Conducted: Personality Profiles, WGN-TV, Chgo., 1948-49, Dorsey Connors Show, WMAQ-TV, Chgo., 1949-58, 61-63, Armchair Travels, WMAQ-TV, 1952-55, Homeshow, NBC,1954-57, NBC Today Show, Dorsey Connors program, WGN, 1958-61, Tempo Nine, WGN-TV, 1961, Society in Chgo, WMAQ-TV, 1964; writer: column Hi! I'm Dorsey Connors, Chgo. Sun Times, 1965—; Author: Gadgets Galore, 1953, Save Time, Save Money, Save Yourself, 1972, Helpful Hints for Hurried Homemakers, 1988. Founder Ill. Epilepsy League; mem. woman's bd. Children's Home and Aid Soc., mem. women's bd. USO. Named one of Am.'s Outstanding Irish Am. Women, World of Hibernia mag., 1995. Mem. AFTRA, NATAS (Silver Cir. award 1995), SAG, Mus. Broadcast Comm. (founding mem.), Soc. Midland Authors, Chgo. Hist. Soc. (guild com., costume com.), Chi Omega. Roman Catholic. Office: Chgo Sun Times 401 N Wabash Ave Chicago IL 60611-5642

CONNORS, KENNETH ANTONIO, retired chemistry educator; b. Torrington, Conn., Feb. 19, 1932; s. Peter Francis and Adeline (Gioia) C.; m. Patricia R. Smart, Dec. 30, 1972. B.S., U. Conn., 1954; M.S., U. Wis., 1957, Ph.D., 1959. Rsch. assoc. dept. chemistry Ill. Inst. Tech., Chgo., 1959-60, Northwestern U., Evanston, Ill., 1960-61; asst. prof. U. Wis. Sch. Pharmacy, Madison, 1962-65, assoc. prof., 1965-72, prof., 1972-97, prof. emeritus, 1997—, acting dean, 1991-93. Author: A Textbook of Pharmaceutical Analysis, 3d edit., 1982, Reaction Mechanisms in Organic Analytical Chemistry, 1973, Chemical Stability of Pharmaceuticals, 2d edit., 1986, Binding Constants, 1987, Chemical Kinetics, 1990. Served with U.S. Army, 1961. Fellow AAAS, Acad. Pharm. Scis., Am. Assn. Pharm. Scis.; mem. Am. Chem. Soc., N.Y. Acad. Scis. Office: U Wis Sch Pharmacy 777 Highland Ave Madison WI 53705-2222

CONRAD, GEOFFREY WENTWORTH, archaeologist, educator; b. Boston, Dec. 24, 1947; s. Albert Austin and Ruth Wentworth (Cadieux) C.; m. Karen Ann Hildebrant, June 12, 1971; children: Matthew, Peter, Marc. AB, Harvard U., 1969, PhD, 1974. Curatorial asst. Smithsonian Inst., Washington, 1974-75; asst. prof. and asst. curator Harvard U., Cambridge, Mass., 1976-81, assoc. prof. and assoc. curator, 1981-83; dir. William Hammond Mathers Mus. Ind. U., Bloomington, 1983—, assoc. prof. anthropology, 1983-91, prof., 1991—, chair, 1991-95. Cons. Nat. Geog. Soc., Washington, 1982-83. Co-author (books): Religion and Empire, 1984, The Andean Heritage, 1982; co-editor (book) Ideology and Precolumbian Civilizations, 1992; contbr. articles to profl. jours.; mem. editl. bd. Jour. of Field Archaeology, 1986-96. Bd. dirs. Monroe County Hist. Soc., Bloomington, 1989-92. Grantee NSF, 1978, 85, Ind. Humanities Coun., 1983, 86, 88, 95, Wenner-Gren Found., 1987, Inst. Mus. and Libr. Svcs., 2000. Fellow AAAS; mem. Archaeol. Inst. Am. (pres. Cen. Ind. chpt. 1989-91, acad. trustee 1994-97), Soc. Am. Archaeology, Assn. for Field Archaeology, Am. Assn. Mus., Midwest Mus. Conf., Assn. Coll. and Univ. Mus. and Galleries (Midwest rep. 1990-91). Home: 3130 Saint James Ct Bloomington IN 47401-7105 Office: Mathers Mus Ind U 601 E 8th St Bloomington IN 47408-3812 also: Ind U Dept Anthropology Student Bldg Bloomington IN 47405 E-mail: conrad@indiana.edu.

CONRAD, JOHN R. corporate executive; b. Chgo., Dec. 3, 1915; s. Nicholas John and Irene Edna (Billups) C.; m. Ruth Osborne Good, June 14, 1940 (div. 1957); children: Lynn, Joanne, Catherine; m. Arlys Mafra Streitmatter, Apr. 11, 1958. Student, Yale U., 1934-36; BS in Econs., U. Chgo., 1937; postgrad., Boeing Sch. Aeros., 1938; LHD (hon.), Ill. Inst. Tech., 1991. Mem. staff engring. and mfg. Douglas Aircraft, Santa Monica, Calif., 1938-44, mgr. properties Long Beach, 1944-45; v.p. S&C Electric Co., Chgo., 1945-52, pres., 1952-88, CEO, chmn. bd. dirs., 1988-97, chmn. bd. dirs., 1997—. Bd. dirs. S&C Electric Can. Ltd., Toronto, Ont. Patentee terminal constrn. 1957. Mem. Mid-Am. Com., Chgo., 1983—, Chgo. Com. Chgo. Coun. on Fgn. Rels., 1980—; life mem. Ill. Coalition; mem. Northwestern U. J.L. Kellogg Grad. Sch. Mgmt. Adv. Bd.; mem. Pres. Coun. U. Ill.; mem. adv. bd. Exec. Club Chgo.; gov. mem. John G. Shedd Aquarium Soc.; mem. St. Francis Hosp. of Evanston Founders Soc. (Founders' Day award 1983). Recipient Progress award Soc. Mfg. Engrs., 1972, Bus. in the Arts award Esquire/Bus. Com. for Arts, 1975, Spl. award for support and contbns. to switchgear industry IEEE Power Engring. Soc. Switchgear Com., 1990, Citizen's Coun. Cmty. Svc. award Gateway Found., 1991, 25th Anniversary Cmty. Svc. award Gateway Found., 1992, Civic award Loyola U., 1993, award for excellence in power distbn. engring. IEEE, Inc. Power Engring. Soc., 1994. Mem. IEEE (life), Conf. Internat. Grandes Reseaux Electriques (U.S. nat. com., U.S. v.p. 1971-72), Ill. Bus. Roundtable, Mid-Am. Club. Avocations: charitable and civic activities. Office: S&C Electric Co 6601 N Ridge Blvd Chicago IL 60626-3925

CONRAD, KENT, senator; b. Bismarck, N.D., Mar. 12, 1948; m. Lucy Calautti, Feb. 1987; 1 child, Jessamyn Abigail. Student, U. Mo., 1967; BA, Stanford U., 1972; MBA, George Washington U., 1975. Asst. to tax commr. State of N.D. Tax Dept., Bismarck, 1974-80, tax commr., 1981-87; U.S. senator from N.D. Washington, 1987—. Mem. agr. nutrition and forestry com., mem. budget com. and fin. coms., ethics com., Indian affairs com., senate Dem. steering and coord. com., forestry com. Democrat Office: US Senate 530 Hart Senate Office Bldg Washington DC 20510-0001*

CONRAD, WILLIAM MERRILL, architect; b. Sapulpa, Okla., Sept. 5, 1926; s. William Samuel and Lillian Lorraine (Strain) C.; m. Esther Marian Lenz, Nov. 8, 1952. BS in Architecture, U. Kans., 1950, BSBA, 1951. Lic. architect. Prin., architect William M. Conrad, F.A.I.A., Kansas City, Mo., 1956—; asst. prof., Sch. of Architecture and Urban Design U. Kans., Lawrence, 1956-59. Mem. adv. com. U. Kans. Sch. of Architecture and Urban Design, 1974-86; vis. Fulbright prof., U. Helsinki, 1958-59. Mem. Kans. City-St. Joseph Bldg. Commn., 1970-82; leader People to People Internat. Peace Mission Overseas Tours, 1994-2002. Recipient Patriotic Svc. award Dept. Army, 1974, 84, Nat. Friend of Park and Recreation award Nat. Assn. Park and Recreation Ofcls., 1982, Urban Design award Mcpl. Art Com., Kansas City, 1976, Disting. Alumnus award U. Kans. Sch. Arch. and Urban Design, 1993, Achievement award PTP Philippines, 1999, PTP Taiwan, 1999. Fellow AIA (treas. nat. conv. 1979, Kansas City chpt. pres. 1968, past sec., other offices, mem. numerous coms., Cmty. Svc. award 1990, numerous other awards); mem. SAR (Good Citizenship award 1997), Mo. Coun. Architects (past dir. and treas.), People to People Internat. (pres. Greater Kansas City chpt. 1972-74, chmn. Gt. Plains regional coun. 1974-77, chmn. bd. dirs., trustee 1985-89, internat. pres. 1988-91, Disting. Mem. award 1986, Eisenhower Lifetime Achievement award 1996), Optimists (past pres. Honor Club), Masons, Shriners (pres. 1990), Sertoma Kans. dist. gov. 1984-86, pres. Honor Club 1982-84, Sertoman of Yr. 1987, Outstanding Regional Sec. award 1995), Christian the Fourth Guild (hon.), Tau Beta Pi (life), Tau Sigma Delta. Methodist. Home: 6120 W 69th St Overland Park KS 66204-1411

CONRAN, JOSEPH PALMER, lawyer; b. St. Louis, Oct. 4, 1945; s. Palmer and Theresa (Bussmann) C.; m. Daria D. Conran, June 8, 1968; children: Andrew, Lisabeth, Theresa. BA, St. Louis U., 1967, JD with honors, 1970. Bar: Mo. 1970, U.S. Ct. Mil. Appeals 1971, U.S. Ct. Appeals (8th cir.) 1974. Assoc. Husch and Eppenberger, St. Louis, 1974-78, ptnr., 1978—, chmn. litigation dept., 1980-95, chmn. mgmt. com., 1995—. Mem. faculty Trial Practice Inst. Capt., JAGC, USAF, 1970-74. Mem. Bar Assn. Met. St. Louis (Merit award 1976, 77), Mo. Bar Assn. (bd. govs. 1987-92), Mo. Athletic Club (pres. 1986-87), Norwood Hills Country Club, St. Louis Club. Roman Catholic. Home: 53 Hawthorne Est Saint Louis MO 63131-3035 Office: Husch & Eppenberger 100 N Broadway Ste 1300 Saint Louis MO 63102-2789 E-mail: joe.conran@husch.com.

CONROY, JOE, former state legislator; m. Mary Ann Macksood; children: Kevin, Kelly, Tim, Christine, Colleen. State senator Mich. State Senate, Dist. 25, 1985-94, Mich. State Senate, Dist. 29, 1995-98. Mem. appropriations com., higher edn. & tech. com., Mich. State Senate; mem. human svc. com. & health com. Nat. Conf. State Legis. Office: 6095 Mapleridge Dr Flint MI 48532-2119

CONRY, THOMAS FRANCIS, mechanical engineering educator, consultant; b. West Hempstead, N.Y., Mar. 7, 1942; s. Thomas and Bridget Anne (Walsh) C.; m. Sharon Ann Silverwood, June 10, 1967; children: Christine Elizabeth, Carolyn Danielle, Anne Marie. BS, Pa. State U., 1963; MS, U. Wis.-Madison, 1967, PhD, 1970. Registered profl. engr., Wis., Ill. Engr. Gen. Motors Corp., Milw., 1963-66, sr. research engr. Indpls., 1969-71; asst. prof. gen. engring. U. Ill., Urbana, 1971-75, assoc. prof. gen. and mech. engring., 1975-81, prof. gen. and mech. engring., 1981—; co-dir. mng. engring. program Coll. Engring., 1986-89, head dept. gen. engring., 1987-98, coord. program in tech. and bus., 1995-98. Sr. visitor U. Cambridge (Eng.), 1978; cons. Zurn Industries, 1974-83; staff cons. Sargent & Lundy, Engrs., 1977, 79; cons.-evaluator commn. on instns. of higher edn. North Ctl. Assn., 1983—; cons. indsl. firm on machine dynamics, optimization and tribology. NSF trainee, 1968-69; NASA/ASEE summer faculty fellow, 1974-75. Contbr. articles to profl. jours. Mem. Bd. Edn. St. Matthews Parish Roman Catholic Ch., Champaign, 1981-84. Fellow ASME (chmn. design engring. divsn. 1979-80, tech. editor Jour. Vibration, Acoustics, Stress and Reliability in Design, 1984-89, mem. bd. on comm. 1989-93, 96-2000, mem. com. on fin. and investment 1999—); mem. Am. Soc. Engring. Edn., Rotary, Sigma Xi, Lambda Chi Alpha, Phi Kappa Phi. Home: 3301 Lakeshore Dr Champaign IL 61822-5205 Office: 104 S Mathews Ave Urbana IL 61801-2925

CONSIDINE, JOHN JOSEPH, advertising executive; b. Jersey City, Sept. 6, 1941; s. Joseph Patrick and Helen (Hrezak) C.; m. Catherine Christine Noone, Nov. 26, 1966; children: Elizabeth, Laura, Adam, Kate. BA, St. Peter's Coll., Jersey City, 1963. Rsch. analyst Prudential Ins. Co., Newark, 1964-66; asst. rsch. mgr. The Mennen Co., Morristown, N.J., 1966-68; rsch. mgr. The Gillette Co., Boston, 1968-69; rsch. dir. W. B. Doner & Co., Detroit, 1969-74, sr. v.p., corp. rsch. dir., 1974-82, exec. v.p., corp. dir. strategic planning, 1982-94, vice chmn., 1994—. Mem. Pine Lake Country Club (West Bloomfield, Mich.). Home: 3652 Erie Dr West Bloomfield MI 48324-1524 Office: W B Doner & Co 25900 Northwestern Hwy West Bloomfield MI 48075-1067

CONSTABLE, JOHN, advertising executive; b. 1943; Pvt. practice, London, 1964-76; with Cramer Krasselt Co., Milw., 1976-78; ptnr. Laughlin/Constable Inc., 1978—, now v.p., sec., ptnr., creative dir., art dir., 1978—. Office: Laughlin/Constable Inc 207 E Michigan St Stop 1 Milwaukee WI 53202-4996

CONSTANT, ANITA AURELIA, publisher; b. Youngstown, Ohio, Jan. 5, 1945; d. Sandu Nicholas and Erie Marie (Tecau) C. BA, Ind. U., 1967; postgrad., Northwestern U., Evanston, Ill., 1991. Sales rep. Economy Fin. Inc., St. Louis, 1967-69; recruiter Case Western U. Hosp., Cleve., 1969-70; sales rep. Internat. Playtex Inc., Chgo., 1970-71, John Wiley & Sons, Inc., Chgo., 1971-77; sr. product mgr. CBS Pub. Inc., The Dryden Press, Chog., 1977-80; exec. editor Dearborn Fin. Pub., Inc., Chgo., 1980-81, v.p., 1981-89, sr. v.p., prin., 1989-97; cons. to pub. industry, 1997-98; prin. Ea. European investment venture EUROTEC, 1997-99; sr. v.p., editor-in-chief Southwestern Coll. Pub. divsn. ITP Inc., 1998-94; sr. v.p. new bus. devel. South-Western/Thomson Learning, 2000—. Bd. dirs. Romanian Heritage Ctr., Detroit, 1988—, Orthodox Brotherhood of Am., Detroit, 1985—. Mem. Chgo. Women in Pub. (keynote speaker 1988), Real Estate Educators Assn. (conv. coord. 1989), Internat. Assn. of Fin. Planners, Chgo. Book Clinic (bd. dirs. 1987-88, v.p. 1988-90), pres. 1990-91, past pres. 1991-92, Mary Alexander award 1995), Nat. Assn. Women Bus. Owners. Eastern Orthodox. Avocations: property development and renovation, hiking, bicycling. Office: 1047 W Wolfram Chicago IL 60657 E-mail: aaconst@interaccess.com.

CONTE, LOU, artistic director, choreographer; b. DuQuoin, Ill., Apr. 17, 1942; s. John and Floy Mae (Saunders) C. Student, Ellis DuBoulay Sch. Ballet, Chgo., 1961-68, So. Ill. U., 1960-62, Am. Ballet Theatre Sch., N.Y.C., 1964-66. Choreographer musicals Mame, 1972, Boss, 1973; choreographer Milw. Melody Top, 1966; dir. Lou Conte Dance Studio, Chgo., 1974—; artistic dir. Hubbard St. Dance Co., Chgo., 1977—; lectr. Mem. Actors Equity Assn., AFTRA. Office: Hubbard St Dance Co 1147 W Jackson Blvd Chicago IL 60607-2905

CONTI, LEE ANN, lawyer; b. Astoria, Oreg. BA with honors, So. Ill. U., 1970; JD summa cum laude, De Paul U., 1976. Bar: Ill. 1976, U.S. Dist. Ct. (no. dist.) Ill. 1976. Ptnr. Mayer, Brown & Platt, Chgo., 1983-94; assoc. gen. counsel Citizens Comm. Co., Stamford, 1994—. Contbr. articles to profl. jours. Mem. Bd. Edn. Cmty. Consol. Sch. Dist. 89, Du Page County, 1987-93. Recipient Am. Jurisprudence awards in Torts, Remedies. Mem. ABA, Am. Corp. Counsel Assn., Ill. State Bar Assn., Du Page County Bar Assn., Chgo. Bar Assn., Phi Kappa Phi, Pi Sigma Alpha, Phi Lambda Pi. Office: Citizens Comm Co 1000 Internationale Pkwy Woodridge IL 60517-4924

CONTI, PAUL LOUIS, management consulting company executive; b. Utica, N.Y., Sept. 3, 1945; s. Louis Joseph and Dorothy Mae (Kellogg) C.; m. Lee Ann Scheuerman, Apr. 18, 1970; children: Meghan Elizabeth, Dawn Michelle. BA, So. Ill. U., 1972, MBA, 1974. Sr. cons. Lester B. Knight & Assocs., Chgo., 1974-76; dir. pers. Applied Info. Devel., Oak Brook, Ill., 1976-80; v.p. Comsi, Inc., 1980-82; CEO Prestige Mgmt. Sys., Inc., Glen Ellyn, Ill., 1982-86; v.p. human resources Rand McNally & Co., Skokie, 1986-87; assoc. dir. Ernst & Young (formerly Ernst & Whinney), Chgo., 1987-93; regional v.p. Alexandria Alexander, Inc., 1993-97; COO, sr. v.p. AON Corp., 1997-99; sr. v.p. Apropos Tech., Inc., Oak Brook, Ill., 1999—. Bd. dirs. So. Ill. U. Coll. Bus. Adminstrn. Lobbyist Invest in the Future, Invest in Edn., State of Ill., 1988; bd. dirs., exec. com. So. Ill. U.-Carbondale Found., 1991—, pres., 1994-97. Named to So. Ill. U. COBA Hall of Fame, 1988; named Cmty. Ambassador So. Ill. U., 1980. Mem. Soc. Human Resource Profls., Soc. Human Resources Mgmt., Human Resources Mgmt. Assn. of Chgo., Employment Mgmt. Assn., Pontikes Ctr. for Mgmt. Info. (bd. dirs. 1989—), So. Ill. U. Alumni Assn. (pres. 1986-88, bd. dirs. 1986—, exec. com. 1991—), Ideal Club (pres. 1986-88), McCullom Lake Club. Republican. Roman Catholic. Avocations: hunting waterfowl and upland game, golf, various participative sports, coaching women's fast pitch softball. Home: 635 S Park Blvd Glen Ellyn IL 60137-6977 E-mail: paul.conti@apropos.com.

CONTRENI, JOHN JOSEPH, JR. humanities educator, educator; b. Savannah, Ga., Aug. 31, 1944; s. John Joseph Sr. and Elfriede Johanna (Hille) C.; m. Margarita Lee Partridge, July 3, 1986; children: Judith, Rachel, Daniel, Maureen, Jennifer Rogers, Paul Rogers. BA, St. Vincent Coll., 1966, HHD (hon.), 1996; PhD, Mich. State U., 1971. From asst. prof. to prof. history Purdue U., West Lafayette, Ind., 1971—, head dept. history, 1985-97, asst. dean Sch. Humanities, Social Sci. and Edn., 1981-85, interim head dept. fgn. langs. and lits., 1983-85. Pres. Midwest Medieval Conf., 1980-81. Author: The Cathedral School of Laon from 850 to 930: Its Manuscripts and Masters, 1978, (John Nicholas Brown prize 1982), Codex Laudunensis 468: A Ninth-Century Guide to Virgil, Sedulius, and the Liberal Arts, 1984; co-author: Glossae Divinae Historiae: The Biblical Glosses of John Scottus Eriugena, 1997: translator: Education and Culture in the Barbarian West, Sixth Through Eighth Centuries (Pierre Riché), 1976, Carolingian Learning, Masters, and Manuscripts, 1992; co-editor: Religion, Culture, and Society in the Early Middle Ages: Studies in Honor of Richard E. Sullivan, 1987, French Historical Studies, 1991-2000; mem. editl. bd. Internat. History Rev., 2001—; contbr. articles to profl. jours. and chpts. to books. Pres., bd. trustees Brookston-Prairie Twp. Pub. Libr., 1995-01. Grantee Am. Philos. Soc., 1973, 76, 82, 86, NEH, 1973, 86, Am. Coun. Learned Socs., 1975, 77-79, 83, 89, Purdue U., 1973, 75-76, 81, 83, 89. Mem. Soc. for Promotion Eriugenian Studies, Medieval Acad. Am. (councillor 1987-90, grantee 1973), Phi Beta Kappa. Home: 504 W 5th St Brookston IN 47923-8100 Office: Purdue Univ Dept of History Univ Hall West Lafayette IN 47907-1358 E-mail: contreni@purdue.edu.

CONVERSE, JAMES CLARENCE, agricultural engineering educator; b. Brainerd, Minn., Apr. 2, 1942; s. James L. and Doris E. (Beck) C.; m. Marjorie A. Swanson, Aug. 6, 1965; children— James, Julie, Mark, Katherine AA, Brainerd Jr. Coll, 1962; BS in Agrl. Engring., N.D. State U., 1964, MS in Agrl. Engring., 1966; PhD in Agrl. Engring., U. Ill., 1970. Asst. prof. agrl. engring. U. Wis., Madison, 1970-75, assoc. prof., 1975-80, prof., 1980—, chmn. dept., 1988-96. Fellow Am. Soc. Agrl. Engring. (Gunlogson countryside engring. award 1984). Roman Catholic Avocations: scouts, soccer. Office: U Wis Dept Agrl Engring 460 Henry Mall Madison WI 53706-1533

CONVISER, RICHARD JAMES, law educator, lawyer, publications company executive; b. Chgo., Apr. 4, 1938; s. Jack and Florence Conviser; 1 child, Ryan Elizabeth BA, U. Calif.-Berkeley, 1959, JD, 1962; Dr. Jur, U. Cologne, Fed. Republic Germany, 1964. Bar: Calif. 1962, Ill. 1965. Assoc. Baker & McKenzie, Chgo., 1965-67; dep. European dir. European Office of Ill., Brussels, Belgium, 1968-69; prof. law DePaul U., Chgo., 1969-73, Chgo.-Kent Coll. Law, Ill. Inst. Tech., 1973—; sr. v.p. Harcourt Brace Pubs., N.Y.C., from 1980; chmn., chief exec. officer Harcourt Profl. Edn. Group, Chgo., 1967—. Founder, dir. BAR/BRI Bar Rev., Chgo.; founder, dir. Conviser & Duffy CPA Rev., Chgo.; bd. dirs. Harcourt Profl. Edn., Exchange Nat. Bank, Chgo., Conviser-Duffy CPA Rev. Author: The Modern Philanthrophic Foundation: A Comparative Legal Analysis, 1965, The Law of Agency and Partnership, 1993; mng. editl. dir. Gilbert Law Summaries, L.A., 1978—. Mem. North Dearborn Pk. Assn.; trustee Emory U. Sch. Law, Atlanta, Libr. Internat. Rels., Inst. Internat. Edn. Fellow Col. W. Dinkelspiel Found., 1960-62, Newhouse Found., 1960-62; Ford Found. internat. law fellow, 1962-64 Mem. ABA, Calif. Bar Assn., Ill. Bar Assn., Chgo. Bar Assn. Clubs: Racquet of Chgo., Saddle and Cycle (Chgo.) Office: Harcourt Profl Edn Group 111 W Jackson Blvd Fl 7 Chicago IL 60604-3502

CONWAY, EDWIN MICHAEL, priest, church administrator; b. Chgo., Mar. 6, 1934; s. Edwin Michael and Nellie Veronica (Rooney) C. ThM, St. Mary of the Lake Sem., Mundelein, Ill., 1960; MSW, Loyola U., Chgo., 1970. Ordained priest Roman Cath. Ch.; lic. social worker, Ill. Assoc. pastor St. Bonaventure Parish, Chgo., 1960-65, St. Mary of the Lake Parish, Chgo., 1965-67, priest-in-residence, 1967—; dir. dept. human svcs. Archdiocese of Chgo., 1991—. Assoc. adminstr. Cath. Charities, Archdiocese of Chgo., 1967-83, dept. dir., 1970-78, divsn. mgr., 1978-83, adminstr., 1983—, nat. treas., 1985-91. Editor manuals. Bd. dirs. citizens com. Juvenile Ct., Chgo., 1985-90; bd. dirs. planning com. United Way Chgo.,

1985-88; mem. planning com. Crusade of Mercy, met. Chgo., 1988—; mem. Mayor's Com. for a Clean Chgo., 1990. Decorated knight comdr. Order of Holy Sepulcher (Italy); award South Chgo. Legal Clinic, 1988, Outstanding Svc. award United Way Chgo., 1988, Alumni Citation award Loyola U. Alumni Assn., 1989. Mem. Cath. Conf. Ill. (social svc. com. 1971—), Coun. Cmty. Svcs. (adv. vol. com. 1971-75), Nat. Conf. Cath. Charities (bd. dirs. 1973-78). Office: Cath Charities 1651 W Diversey Pkwy Chicago IL 60614-1027

CONWAY, JAMES JOSEPH, physician; b. Chgo., July 1, 1933; s. Frank and Mary (Tuohy) Conway; m. Dolores Mazer, June 30, 1956; children: Laurie, John, Cheryl. BS, DePaul U., 1959; MD, Northwestern U., 1963. Asst. instr. U. Pa., 1964—68; assoc. in radiology McGaw Med. Ctr. Northwestern U., Chgo., 1968—71, asst. prof. to assoc. prof. radiology, 1974—80; attendant radiology Children's Meml. Hosp., 1968—98, prof. radiology, 1980—. Contbr. articles over 110 to profl. jours. With U.S. Army, 1953—55. Recipient Gold medal, Chgo. Radiol. Soc., 1993. Fellow: Soc. Nuclear Medicine (pres. 1994—95), Radiol. Soc. N.Am. (Scroll of Appreciation award 1983), Am. Coll. Radiology, Am. Coll. Nuclear Physicians, P.R. Soc. Nuclear Medicine (hon.). Avocation: collector of Chicago memorabilia. Office: Children's Meml Hosp 2300 N Childrens Plz Chicago IL 60614-3394 E-mail: nukedr@hotmail.com.

CONWAY, JOHN K. lawyer; Gen. counsel Kemper Ins. Co., Long Grove, Ill. Office: Lumbermens Mutual Casualty Co 1 Kemper Dr Long Grove IL 60049-0001

CONWAY, LYNN, computer scientist, electrical engineer, educator; b. Mt. Vernon, N.Y., Jan. 2, 1938; BS, Columbia U., 1962, MSEE, 1963; D (hon.), Trinity Coll., 1997. Rsch. staff IBM Corp., Yorktown Heights, N.Y., 1964-68; sr. staff engr. Memorex Corp., Santa Clara, Calif., 1969-73; rsch. staff Xerox Corp., Palo Alto, 1973-78, rsch. fellow, mgr. VLSI systems area, 1978-82, rsch. fellow, mgr. knowledge systems area, 1982-83; asst. dir. for strategic computing Def. Advanced Research Projects Agy., Arlington, Va., 1983-85; prof. elec. engring. and computer sci., assoc. dean U. Mich. Coll. Engring., Ann Arbor, Mich., 1985—. Vis. assoc. prof. elec. engring. and computer sci. MIT, Cambridge, Mass., 1978-79; sci. adv. bd. USAF, 1987-90. Co-author: textbook Introduction to VLSI Systems, 1980; contbr. articles to profl. jours.; patentee in field. Mem. coun. Govt.-Univ.-Industry Rsch. Roundtable, 1993-98; mem. corp. Charles Stark Draper Lab., 1993—; mem. bd. visitors USAF Acad., 1996-2000, presdl. appt.; mem. Air Force Sci. and Tech. Bd., Nat. Acads., 2000—. Recipient Ann. Achievement award Electronics mag., 1981, Harold Pender award U. Pa., 1984, Wetherill Medal Franklin Inst., 1985, Sec. of Def. Meritorious Civilian Svc. award, 1985. Fellow IEEE; mem. NAE, AAAS, Soc. Women Engrs. (Ann. Achievement award 1990), Assn. Computing Machinery. Avocations: motocross racing, whitewater canoeing, natural landscaping. Office: U Mich 146 ATL Bldg Ann Arbor MI 48109-2110 E-mail: conway@engin.umich.edu.

CONWAY, MICHAEL MAURICE, lawyer; b. St. Joseph, Mo., Mar. 11, 1946; s. Michael Maurice and Genevieve (Hepburn) C.; m. Kathleen Stevens; children: Michael, Cara, Mary. BS in Journalism, Northwestern U., 1968; JD, Yale U., 1973. Bar: Ill. 1973, U.S. Dist. Ct. (no. dist.) Ill. 1973, U.S. Tax Ct. 1975, U.S. Ct. Claims 1976, U.S. Ct. Appeals (7th cir.) 1976, U.S. Ct. Appeals (1st cir.) 1979, U.S. Supreme Ct. 1980, U.S. Ct. Appeals (5th and 11th cirs.) 1981, U.S. Ct. Appeals (fed. cir. 1982). Ptnr. Hopkins & Sutter now Foley & Lardner, Chgo., 1979—. Counsel U.S. Ho. Reps. com. on judiciary impeachement inquiry Richard M. Nixon, 1974. Chmn. Ill. Lawyers Com. Clinton/Gore, Chgo., 1992; alt. del. Dem. Nat. Conv., 1992, del., 1996. Mem. Am. Coll. Trial Lawyers, Union League Club. Roman Catholic. Avocation: baseball coaching. Office: Foley & Larndner 3 1st Nat Plz Chicago IL 60602 E-mail: mconway@foleylaw.com.

CONYERS, JOHN, JR. congressman; b. Detroit, May 16, 1929; s. John and Lucille (Simpson) C.; m. Monia Estes; children: John Jr., Carl Edward. B.A., Wayne State U., 1957, J.D., 1958; LL.D., Wilberforce U., 1969. Bar: Mich. 1959. Legis. asst. to Congressman John Dingell, 1959-61; sr. ptnr. firm Conyers, Bell & Townsend, 1959-61; referee Mich. Workmen's Compensation Dept., 1961-64; mem. U.S. Congress from 14th Mich. dist., 1964—; former chmn. Govt. Ops. Com., former chmn. subcom. on legis. and nat. security; ranking mem. Judiciary Com. Past dir. edn. Local 900, United Auto Workers; mem. adv. council Mich. Liberties Union; gen. counsel Detroit Trade Union Leadership Council; vice chmn. nat. bd. Ams. for Democratic Action; vice chmn. adv. council ACLU; an organizer Mems. Congress for Peace through Law; bd. dirs. numerous other orgns. including African-Am. Inst., Commn. Racial Justice, Detroit Inst. Arts, Nat. Alliance Against Racist and Polit. Repression, Nat. League Cities. Sponsor, contbg. author: Am. Militarism, 1970, War Crimes and the American Conscience, 1970, Anatomy of an Undeclared War, 1972; contbr. articles to profl. jours. Trustee Martin Luther King Jr. Ctr. for Non-Violent Social Change. Served to 2d lt. U.S. Army, 1950-54, Korea. Recipient Rosa Parks award SCLC. Mem. NAACP (exec. bd. Detroit), Kappa Alpha Psi. Democrat. Baptist. Office: 2426 Rayburn Bldg Washington DC 20515-2214 also: District Office 669 Federal Building, 231 W. Lafayette Detroit MI 48226*

COOK, DEBORAH L. state supreme court justice; BA in English, U. Akron, 1974, JD, 1978, LLD (hon.), 1996. Ptnr. Roderick & Linton, Akron, 1976-91; judge 9th dist. Ohio Ct. Appeals, 1991-94; justice Ohio Supreme Ct., 1995—. Bd. trustees Summit County United Way, Vol. Ctr., Stan Hywet Hall and Gardens, Akron Sch. Law, Coll. Scholars, Inc.; bd. dirs. Women's Network; vol. Mobile Meals, Safe Landing Shelter. Named Woman of Yr., Women's Network, 1991. Fellow Am. Bar Found.; mem. Omicron Delta Kappa, Delta Gamma (pres., Nat. Shield award). Office: Ohio Supreme Ct 30 E Broad St Fl 3 Columbus OH 43215-0001*

COOK, DWIGHT C. state legislator; b. Moorhead, Minn., Dec. 14, 1951; m. Shirley; 3 children. , N. D. State U. Owner Cook Indsl. Sales; mem. N. D. Senate from 34th dist., Bismark, 1997—. Chmn. Morton County Housing Authority; mem. Kiwanis, Am. Legion. Republican. Lutheran. Office: Dist 34 1408 17th St SE Mandan ND 58554-4895 E-mail: dcook@state.nd.us.

COOK, GARY L. state legislator; m. Cheryl Cook. Grad., Ind. Law Enforcement Acad. Police officer/patrolman Plymouth (Ind.) Police Dept.; rep. Dist. 17 Ind. Ho. of Reps., 1990—, mem. county and twp. govt. affairs, environ. affairs com., mem. pub. safety, rds. and transp. coms., chmn. internstate coop. com., rds. transp. com., ranking minority mem. Mem. Marshall County Right to Life, Plymouth Arts Commn. Mem. FOB, Lions. Home: 11385 9th Rd Plymouth IN 46563-8324

COOK, HARRY EDGAR, engineering educator; b. Americus, Ga., Feb. 14, 1939; m. 1961; 2 children. BS, Case Inst. Tech., 1960; MS, Northwestern U., 1962, PhD in Materials Sci., 1966. Sr. rsch. scientist Ford Motor Co., Detroit, 1967-69, sr. engr., 1969-70, prin. engr. chassis, engine, 1970-71, supr., 1971-72, sr. rsch. scientist metallurgy, 1977-78, mgr. materials engring., 1978-79, body component engr., 1979-81, mgr. body component engring. and metallurgy dept., 1981-85; from assoc. prof. to prof. metallurgy and mech. engring. U. Ill., Champaign-Urbana, 1972-77; dir. auto rsch. Chrysler Motors, Detroit, 1985-90; J. Gauthier prof. dept. mech. and indsl. engring. U. Ill., Champaign-Urbana, 1990-98, head dept. gen. engring., 1998—. Recipient Robert Lansing Hardy medal Am. Inst. Mining and Metall. Engrs. Fellow Am. Soc. Metals, Am. Soc. Automitive Engrs. (Teetor award 1977); mem. Nat. Acad. Engring. Achievements include research contributing to knowledge of phase transformation and friction materials; studies in competitiveness and leadtime. Home: 4004 Pinecrest Dr Champaign IL 61822-9216 Office: U Ill Dept Gen Engring Transp Bldg 104 S Mathews Ave Rm 117 Urbana IL 61801-2925

COOK, JACK MCPHERSON, hospital administrator; b. Liberty, N.C., Jan. 7, 1945; married BA, U. N.C., 1967; M Health Adminstrn., Duke U., 1969. Adminstrv. res. Durham (N.C.) County Gen. Hosp., 1968, Duke U. Med. Ctr., Durham, 1968-69; asst. adminstr. Cabarrus Meml. Hosp., Concord, N.H., 1969-74; v.p. profl. svcs. Meml. Med. Ctr., Springfield, Ill., 1974-76, pres., 1976-83, Christ Hosp., Cincinnati, Ohio, 1984-95; pres., ceo Health Alliance of Greater Cincinnati, 1995-. Contbr. articles to profl. jours. Fellow, Amer. Coll. of Healthcare Execs., 1981, recertified, 1992; Healthcare Execs. Study Soc., 1989-; pres., 1997; chair. Ohio Hosp. Assoc., 1997; Strategic Planning Com., Greater Cincinnati Hosp. Council Trustee, 1983-; chair., 1987; Trustee, Work & Rehab. Ctrs of Greater Cincinnati, 1993-95; Board of Advisors, Univ. of Cinn. Coll. of Bus. Admin., 1988-; Board of Dirs., Provident Ban Corp., 1992-; mem. Metro. Hosp. Governing Council of Amer. Hosp. Assoc., 1992-95; House of Delegates and Regional Policy Board, 1997; Board of dirs., Voluntary Hosp. of Amer., 1988-92; Physician Advisory Comm., 1988-89; chair., Shareholder Evaluation Comm., 1989-92; VHA Central Exec. Comm., 1986-92; Founder and first pres., Healthspan, 1991-1993. Home: 650 Reisling Knls Cincinnati OH 45226-1735

COOK, JAMES IVAN, clergyman, religion educator; b. Grand Rapids, Mich., Mar. 8, 1925; s. Cornelius Peter and Cornelia (Dornbos) C.; m. Jean Rivenburgh, July 8, 1950; children: Mark James, Carol Jean, Timothy Scott, Paul Brian (dec.). BA, Hope Coll., 1948; MA, Mich. State U., 1949; BD, Western Theol. Sem., 1952; ThD, Princeton Theol. Sem., 1964. Ordained to ministry Reformed Ch. America, 1953. Pastor Blawenburg Reformed Ch., N.J., 1953-63; from instr. to asst. prof. bibl. langs. Western Theol. Sem., Holland, Mich., 1963-67, prof. bibl. langs. and lit., 1967-77, Anton Biemont prof. New Testament, 1977-95, prof. emeritus, 1995—; chmn. Theol. Commn., Reformed Ch. Am. N.Y.C., 1980-85; pres. Gen. Synod-Reformed Ch. Am., N.Y.C., 1982-83. Author: Edgar Johnson Goodspeed, 1981, Shared Pain and Sorrow: Reflections of a Secondary Sufferer, 1991, One Lord/One Body, 1991; editor Reformed Rev., 1987-2002; contbg. editor: Grace Upon Grace, 1975, Saved by Hope, 1978, The Church Speaks, 1985; contbg. editor Perspectives: A Jour. of Reformed Thought, 1986-90. Served with U.S. Army, 1943-45, ETO. Home: 1004 S Shore Dr Holland MI 49423-4539 Office: Western Theol Sem 101 E 13th St Holland MI 49423-3622

COOK, JULIAN ABELE, JR. federal judge; b. Washington, June 22, 1930; s. Julian Abele and Ruth Elizabeth (McNeill) C.; m. Carol Annette Dibble, Dec. 22, 1957; children: Julian Abele III, Peter Dibble, Susan Annette. BA, Pa. State U., 1952; JD, Georgetown U., 1957, LLD (hon.), 1992; LLM, U. Va., 1988; LLD (hon.), U. Detroit, 1996, Wayne State U., 1997. Bar: Mich. 1957. Law clk. to judge, Pontiac, Mich., 1957-58; pvt. practice Detroit, 1958-78; judge U.S. Dist. Ct. (ea. dist.) Mich., 1978, chief judge, 1989-96, sr. judge, 1996—. Spl. asst. atty. gen. State of Mich., 1968-78; adj. prof. U. Detroit Sch. Law, 1971-74; gen. counsel pub. TV Sta. WTVS, 1973-78; labor arbitrator Am. Arbitration Assn. and Mich. Employment Rels. Commn., 1975-78; mem. Mich. State Bd. Ethics, 1977-78; instr. trial advocacy workshop Harvard U., 1988—, trial advocacy program U.S. Dept. Justice, 1989-90; com. on fin. disclosure Jud. Conf. U.S., 1988-93, chmn., 1990-93; screening panel NYU Root-Tilden-Snow Scholarship Program, 1991, 96—; mem. U.S. Sentencing Commn. Judicial Adv. Group, 1996-98; mem. nat. bd. trustees Am. Inn Ct., 1996—; mem. adv. com. Nat. Publs., 1994-96, chmn. nat. nominations and election com., 1994-95; pres. chpt. XI, Master of Bench, 1984-95. Contbr. articles to profl. jours. Exec. bd. dirs. Child and Family Svcs. Mich., 1968-89, past pres., 1975-76; bd. dirs. Am. Heart Assn. Mich., 1968-89, Hutzel Hosp., 1984-95; chmn. Mich. Civil Rights Commn., 1968-71; co-chair exec. com. Walter P. Reuther Libr. Labor and Urban Affairs, Wayne State U.; mem. bd. visitors Georgetown U. Law Ctr., 1992—. With Signal Corps, U.S. Army, 1952-54. Recipient Merit citation Pontiac Area Urban League, 1971, Pathfinders award Oakland U., 1977, Svc. award Todd-Phillips Home, Inc., 1978, Disting. Alumnus award Pa. State U., 1987, Georgetown U., 1989, Focus and Impact award Oakland U., 1985; resolution Mich. Ho. of Reps., 1971, Outstanding Community Svc. award Va. Park Community Investment Assocs., 1992, 1st Ann. Trailblazers award D. Augustus Straker Bar Assn., 1993, Renowned Jurist award Friends of African Art, 1993, Brotherhood award Jewish War Vets. U.S., 1994, Paul R. Dean award Georgetown U. Law Sch., 1997; named Boss of Yr., Oakland County Legal Secs. Assn., 1974, one of Mich. Most Respected Judges, Mich. Law Weekly, 1990-91; named one of the Best Judges, Detroit Monthly, 1991; named Disting. Citizen of Yr., NAACP Oakland County, Mich., 1970. Fellow Am. Bar Found., Mich. Bar Found. (vice-chmn. 1992-93, chmn. 1993—); mem. NAACP (mem. state constl. revision and legal redress com. 1963, Disting. Citizen of Yr. 1970, Presdl. award North Oakland County, Mich. chpt. 1987), ABA, Fed. Bar Assn. (fed.-state ct. seminar lectr. Detroit chpt. 1981—), Mich. Bar Assn. (chmn. constl. law com. 1969, vice-chmn. civil liberties com. 1970, co-chmn. profl. devel. task force 1984-87, U.S. cts. com. 1988-95, com. on professionalism 1991—, Champion of Justice 1994), Mich. Tribunal Assn. (bd. dirs. 3rd cir. 1992-98), Detroit Bar Assn. (Bench-Bar award 1987), Oakland County Bar Assn. (chmn. continuing legal edn. com. 1968-69, jud. liaison Dist. Ct. com. 1977, unauthorized practice law com. 1977), Wolverine Bar Assn. (Bench-Bar award 1987, D. Augustus Straker award 1988), Mich. Assn. Black Judges, Am. Inn of Ct. (founder Met. Detroit chpt., pres., master of bench, chmn. 6th cir. com. on standard jury instructions 1986—), Am. Law Inst., Union Black Episcopalians (Detroit chpt., Absalom Jones award 1988), Justice Frank Murphy Honor Soc.

COOK, RICHARD BORRESON, architect; b. Harvard, Ill., May 23, 1937; s. Ernest Keller and Clara Matilda (Borreson) C.; m. Shirley Jean Antrup,; children: Alan Blair, Elizabeth Ann, Rebecca Alica. BArch, U. Ill., 1962. Registered architect, Calif., Fla., Ill., Ind., Mich., Mo., N.D., N.Y., Ohio, Wis. Intern architect Skidmore, Owings & Merrill, Chgo., 1962-64, Ulrich Franzen & Assocs., N.Y.C., 1964-65; assoc. I.W. Colburn & Assocs., Chgo., 1965-70, Metz, Train, Olson & Youngren, Chgo., 1970-78; pres. Orput Assocs., Wilmette, Ill., 1978-81, Stowell Cook Frolichstein, Chgo., 1981—, Green Cook Ltd., Chgo., 1981. Bd. dirs., pres. Chgo. Archtl. Assistance Ctr., 1983; chmn. handicapped subcom. Mayor's Commn. Bldg. Code Amendments, Chgo., chmn. constrn. industry affairs com.; speaker, presenter papers in field. Prin. projects with Stowell Cook Frolichstein and Cook, Hiltscher Assoc. include Countryside Mall, Fla., Orange Park Mall, Fla., Trinity Evangel. Div. Sch., Rolfing Libr. addition and renovation, Deerfield, Ill, renovation main br. U.S. Postal Svc., Chgo., City Colls. of Chgo., Main St. Sq. Shopping Ctr., Downers Grove, Ill., Chgo. Bd. Edn.; with Orput Assocs. Kenosha (Wis.) County Pub. Safety Bldg., Burnham Terr. Apts. for Elderly, Rockford, Ill., addition and renovation Garrett-Evangel. Sem. Libr., addition Elmhurst (Ill.) Pub. Libr., addition Lake Forest (Ill.) Sch. Mgmt., apt. bldg. renovation Gt. Lakes (Ill.) Naval Sta., Hickory Hills (Ill.) Mcpl. Bldg.; with Metz Train, Olson & Youngren, Inc. office and computer ctr. Lumbermen's Mut. Casualty Co., Long Grove, Ill., Safeguards Analytical Lab. Bldg. Argonne (Ill.) Nat. Lab., Cancer Virus Rsch. Lab. U. Chgo., pub. bldg. commn. John Hope Middle Sch., Chgo.; with I.W. Colburn & Assocs. Geophys. Sci. Bldg. U. Chgo, Cathedral Christ the King, Kalamazoo, dormitory complex and dining facilities Bryn Mawr Coll, Pa., lab. and office bldg. Standard "T" Chem. Co., Lisle, Ill., Temple Jeremiah, Northbrook, Ill. Mem. plann commn. Evanston, 1997. Fellow AIA (dir. Ill. region 1988-89, chmn. T6B documents com., chmn. 1987 nat. conv., chmn. membership svcs. task force, mem. goals and grassroots '82 com.); mem. Ill. Council AIA (bd. dirs., pres., co-chmn. Midwest Regional Conf., mem. fin. and nominating coms.), Chgo. chpt. AIA (sec., v.p., 1st v.p., pres., mem. 1992 World's Fair Rev. Com., chmn. nominating com., mem. Logan Sq. Design Ctr.), Am. Arbitration Assn., Chgo. chpt. AIA Found. (pres.). Democrat. Congregationalist. Avocations: sculpture, photography. Home: 1330 Wesley Ave Evanston IL 60201-4141 Office: Stowell Cook & Frolichstein 33 W Grand Ave Chicago IL 60610-4306

COOK, STANTON R. media company executive; b. Chgo., July 3, 1925; s. Rufus Merrill and Thelma Marie (Borgerson) C.; m. Barbara Wilson, Sept. 23, 1950 (dec. Nov. 1994). BS in Mech. Engring., Northwestern U., 1949. With Shell Oil Co., 1949-51, Chgo. Tribune Co., 1951-81, v.p., 1967-70, exec. v.p. and gen. mgr., 1970-72, pres., 1972-74, pub., 1973-90, CEO, 1974-76, chmn., 1974-81; dir. Tribune Co., 1972-96, v.p., 1972-74, pres., 1974-88, chmn., 1989-92, CEO, 1974-90; chmn. Chgo. Nat. League Ball Club, Inc., 1990-94. Bd. dirs. AP, 1975-84, 2d vice chmn., 1979-84; bd. dirs. Newspaper Adv. Bur., 1973-92, Am. Newspaper Pubs. Assn., 1974-82; dep. chmn., bd. dirs. Fed. Res. Bank Chgo., 1980-83, chmn., 1984-85; bd. dirs. Robert R. McCormick Tribune Found., 1990-2001. Trustee Robert R. McCormick Trust, 1972-90, Savs. and Profit Sharing Fund of Sears Employees, 1991-94, U. Chgo., 1973-87, Mus. Sci. and Industry, Chgo., 1973—, Field Mus. Natural History, Chgo., 1973—, Gen. Douglas MacArthur Found., 1979—, Northwestern U., 1987—, Shedd Aquarium Soc., 1987—, Am. Newspaper Pubs. Assn. Found., 1973-82. Mem. Newspaper Assn. Am. (bd. govs. 1992), Chgo. Coun. Fgn. Rels. (bd. dirs. 1973-93), Comml. Club (past pres.), Econ. Club (past pres., life mem.), Glen Lake Assn. (pres. 2001-). Home: 224 Raleigh Rd Kenilworth IL 60043-1209

COOKE, MICHAEL, editor-in-chief; Former editor-in-chief The Vancouver Province , 2000; editor-in-chief Chgo. Sun Times, 2000—. Office: Chgo Sun Times 401 N Wabash Ave Chicago IL 60611 Office Fax: 312-321-3084.*

COOKS, R(OBERT) GRAHAM, chemist, educator; b. Benoni, South Africa, July 2, 1941; came to U.S., 1968; s. Audrey Owen Eva Mitchie; m. Maria-Luisa Raduan Ripoll, Aug. 19, 1967; children: Owen, Barry, Jude. BSc, U. Natal, 1961, PhD, 1965, Cambridge U., 1967. Asst. prof. Kansas State U., Manhattan, 1968-71; from assoc. dir. to disting. prof. Purdue U., Lafayette, Ind., 1971—. Author: Metastable Ions, 1973; contbr. articles to profl. jours.; patentee in field. Recipient ACS award in analytical chemistry Am. Chem. Soc., 1997. Mem. Am. Soc. Mass Spectrometry (pres. 1984-86), Internat. Mass Spectrometry Soc. (pres. 1997-2000). Home: 177 Prophet Dr West Lafayette IN 47906-1235 Office: Purdue U Dept Chemistry West Lafayette IN 47907 E-mail: cooks@purdue.edu.

COOLEY, CHARLES P. chemicals executive; married; 3 children. BA in Philosophy, Yale Coll.; MBA, Dartmouth Coll. With nat. banking div. Mfrs. Hanover Trust Co., N.Y.C.; various positions Atlantic Richfield; controller and v.p. fin. and adminstrn. ARCO Products Co.; asst. treas. corp. fin. Atlantic Richfield Co., L.A.; v.p., treas., CFO The Lubrizol Corp., Wickliffe, Ohio, 1998—. Office: The Lubrizol Corp 29400 Lakeland Blvd Wickliffe OH 44092

COOLEY, WILLIAM EDWARD, regulatory affairs manager; b. St. Louis, Mar. 7, 1930; s. Charles Frederic and Lillian Marie (Williams) C.; m. Marion Grace Sherman, June 5, 1952; children: Charles, Marilyn, Harold, Noele. AB, Cen. Coll., 1951; PhD, U. Ill., 1954. Rsch. chemist Procter & Gamble Co., Cin., 1954-61, product devel. chemist, 1961-65, product devel. group leader, 1965-75, product devel. regulatory sect. mgr., 1975-90, regulatory affairs sect. mgr., 1990-91; worldwide regulatory coordination sect. mgr., 1991-94; pres. Cooley Cons., Inc., 1994—. Contbr. articles to profl. jours.; inventor, patentee in field. Mem. Am. Assn. Dental Rsch., Internat. Assn. Dental Rsch., Drug Info. Assn., Assn. Food Drug Ofcls., Regulatory Affairs Profl. Soc. (bd. editors 1990), Consumer Healthcare Products Assn. (bd. dirs. 1987-91), Food and Drug Law Inst. Republican. Avocations: music, motorcycling, railroading, flying, astronomy. Home and Office: Cooley Cons Inc 531 Chisholm Trail Wyoming OH 45215-2517

COOLIDGE, CHARLES H., JR. career officer; BS in Basic Sci., USAF Acad., 1968; student undergrad. pilot tng., Moody AFB, Ga., 1968-69; M in Physics, Air Force Inst. Tech., 1974; student, Air Command and Staff Coll., 1979, Nat. War Coll., 1988. Commd. 2d lt. USAF, 1968, advanced through grades to maj. gen., 1996, various pilot/instr. pilot assignments, 1969-72; instr. and assoc. prof. dept. physics USAF Acad., Colorado Springs, Colo., 1974-77, br. chief cadet parachute program airmanship div., 1977-78; KC-135 pilot 4017th Combat Crew Tng. Squadron, Castle AFB, Calif., 1979; stationed at 911th Air Refueling Squadron, Seymour Johnson AFB, N.C., 1979-83; various assignments USAF, 1983-87; vice comdr. then comdr. 301st Air Refueling Wing, Malmstrom AFB, Mont., 1988-91; asst. dep. chief staff requirements and test Hdqs. Strategic Air Command, Offutt AFB, Nebr., 1991-92; vice comdr. Tanker Airlift Control Ctr. Hdqs. Air Mobility Command, Scott AFB, Ill., 1992-93; various comdr. positions USAF, 1993-96; dir. plans and ops. then dir. ops. Hdqs. Air Edn. and Tng. Command, Randolph AFB, Tex., 1996-97; dir. ops. and logistics U.S. Transp. Command, Scott AFB, 1997—; vice comdr. HQ Air Force Material Commd., Wright-Patterson AFB, OH, 2000—. Decorated Legion of Merit with oak leaf cluster, D.F.C., Air medal with four oak leaf clusters, Rep. Vietnam Gallantry Cross with Palm.

COOLLEY, RONALD B. lawyer; b. Manchester, N.H., Feb. 15, 1946; s. Mace A. and Ruth A. C. BS, Iowa State U., 1969; MBA, JD, U. Iowa, 1972. Bar: Ill. 1974, Tex. 1987. Assoc. Mason, Kolehmainen, Chgo., 1973-87, Arnold, White & Durkee, Chgo., 1987—. Contbr. articles to profl. jours. Recipient Gerald Rose award John Marshall Law Sch., 1985, Rossman award, Patent and Trademark Office Soc., 1985. Mem. ABA (bd. dirs. 1988-90), Patent Law Assn. Chgo. (pres.1988-89). Office: Arnold White & Durkee 321 N Clark St Chicago IL 60610-4714

COOMBE, V. ANDERSON, retired valve manufacturing company executive; b. Cin., Mar. 5, 1926; s. Harry Elijah and Mary (Anderson) C.; m. Eva Jane Romaine, Sept. 26, 1957; children— James, Michael, Peter. B.E., Yale, 1948. Asst. to pres. Wm. Powell Co., Cin., 1953-57, v.p., 1957-63, exec. v.p., 1963-69, pres., treas., 1969-91, chmn. bd., 1991—. Mem.: Cin. Country Club, Queen City Club (Cin.), Camargo Club (Cin.). Home: 6 Corbin Dr Cincinnati OH 45208-3302 Office: 2503 Spring Grove Ave Cincinnati OH 45214-1729

COONEY, PATRICK RONALD, bishop; b. Detroit, Mar. 10, 1934; s. Michael and Elizabeth (Dowdall) C. B.A., Sacred Heart Sem., 1956; S.T.B., Gregorian U., Rome, 1958, S.T.L., 1960; M.A., Notre Dame U., 1973. Ordained priest Roman Cath. Ch., 1959 ordained bishop, 1983. Assoc. pastor St. Catherine Ch., Detroit, 1960-62; asst. chancellor Archdiocese of Detroit, 1962-69, dir. dept. worship, 1969-83; rector Blessed Sacrament Cathedral, 1977-83; regional bishop Roman Cath. Ch., Detroit, 1983-89; apptd. bishop Diocese of Gaylord, Mich., 1989—. Office: Diocese of Gaylord Pastoral Ctr 611 W North St Gaylord MI 49735-8349

COONS, JAMES WILLIAM, economist; b. Glen Ellyn, Ill., Oct. 8, 1957; s. Richard and Barbara (Hirt) C.; m. Margaret Ellen Sims, May 21, 1983; children: Sarah Ann, Katherine Elizabeth, Charles William. BA in Econs. and Math., DePauw U., 1979; MA in Econs., Ohio U., 1980. Staff economist Am. Electric Power, Columbus, Ohio, 1980-84; sr. economist Borden, Inc., 1984-85; chief economist Huntington Nat. Bank, 1985—. Mem. Fed. Res. Bank of Cleve. Econ. Roundtable, 1987—; dir. Cen. Ohio Coun. Econ. Edn., 1990—. Mem. Ohio Gov.'s Econ. Adv. Coun., Columbus, 1986—. Recipient grad. assistantship Ohio U., 1979-80. Mem. Nat. Assn. Bus. Economists, Am. Economy Assn., Capital Club, Beta Theta Pi. Avocations: golf, running, reading. Office: Huntington Ctr Huntington Ctr Columbus OH 43287-0001

COOPER, ARNOLD COOK, management educator, researcher; b. Chgo., Mar. 9, 1933; s. Millard and Sarah Ellen C.; m. Jean Phillips Lord, Sept. 12, 1959; children: Katherine Lord, David Andrew. BS in Chem. Engring., Purdue U., 1955, MS in Mgmt., 1957; D in Bus. Adminstrn., Harvard U., 1962. Engr. Proctor & Gamble, Cin., 1957-58; asst. prof. Harvard U., Cambridge, Mass., 1961-63; assoc. prof. Purdue U., West Lafayette, Ind., 1963-70, prof., 1970-84, Weil prof. mgmt., 1984—. Vis. assoc. prof. Stanford Univ., Palo Alto, Calif., 1967-68; vis. prof. Manchester (Eng.) Bus. Sch., 1972, IMEDE Mgmt. Devel. Inst., Lausanne, Switzerland, 1977-78; past dir. Grad. Profl. Programs, chmn. Mgmt. Policy Com., Purdue U., West Lafayette; mem. Ind. Employment Devel. Commn., 1982-89, Fed. Adv. Com. on Indsl. Innovation, 1978-79. Author: The Founding of Technologically Based Firms, 1971; co-author: Small Business Management, 1966, Technical Entrepreneurship: A Symposium, 1972, The Entrepreneurial Function, 1977, New Business in America, 1990; contbr. numerous articles to profl. jours. and bus. publs.; mem. editorial bd. Stategic Mgmt. Jour., 1979—, Jour. of Bus. Venturing, 1985—, Acad. of Mgmt. Jour., 1978-84, Jour. High Tech. Mktg., 1986-87. 2nd lt. U.S. Army, 1956. Recipient Honeywell Master Tchr. award, 1990, Disting. Scholar award, Intenat. Coun. on Small Bus., 1987, Ten Year Author award, Babson Entrepreneurship Conf., 1990, John S. Day Disting. Alumni Acad. Svc. award, 2001. Mem. Acad. Mgmt. (chmn. bus. policy and strategy divsn. 1978-79, Outstanding Paper award Entrepreneurship Divsn. 1991, 92, Coleman Entrepreneurship Mentor award, 1993), Soc. Fellows (Richard D. Irwin outstanding educator award, 1999, Internat. award for entrepreneurship and small bus. rsch. 1997), Internat. Coun. Small Bus., Strategic Mgmt. Soc. (bd. govs. 1984-86). Home: 616 Ridgewood Dr West Lafayette IN 47906-2367 Office: Purdue Univ Krannert Sch of Mgmt 1310 Krannert West Lafayette IN 47907-1310 E-mail: coopera@mgmt.purdue.edu.

COOPER, CHARLES GILBERT, toiletries and cosmetics company executive; b. Chgo., Apr. 4, 1928; s. Benjamin and Gertrude Cooper; m. Miriam Meyer, Feb. 11, 1951 (dec. Oct. 17, 1984); children: Debra, Ruth, Janet, Benjamin; m. Nancy Cooper BS in Journalism, U. Ill., 1949. With sales promotion dept. Maidenform Co., N.Y.C., 1949-51; with circulation promotion dept. Esquire mag., Chgo., 1951-52; with Helene Curtis Industries Inc., 1953-96, pres. salon div., 1971-75, pres. consumer products div., 1975-82, corp. exec. v.p., 1982-85, exec. v.p., COO, 1985-93, sr. v.p., 1993-96; sr. ptnr. GCG Ptnrs. Bd. dirs. Devon Bank. Bd. dirs. Coun. for Jewish Elderly. With AUS, 1952-53. Office: 225 W Wacker Dr Ste 1800 Chicago IL 60606-1274

COOPER, CHARLES GORDON, insurance consultant, former executive; b. Providence, May 31, 1927; s. Irving and Helen Christina (Skog) C.; m. Barbara Caroline Termohlen, June 17, 1950; 1 dau., Marie Suzanne. B.A., Ohio Wesleyan U., 1949. C.L.U. Group rep. Washington Nat. Ins. Co., 1949-53, asst. mgr., 1953-58, mgr., 1958-63, dir. assn. field services, 1963-65, asst. sec., 1965-67, 3d v.p., 1967-72, 2d v.p., 1972-77, v.p., 1977-79, sr. v.p., 1979-83, exec. v.p. Ill., 1983-85, dir., mem. exec. com., 1979-85; sr. v.p.-mktg. Washington Nat. Corp., parent co. Washington Nat. Ins. Co., Evanston, 1983-85, cons., 1985—. Dir. Washington Nat. Trust Co., 1974-85, chmn. exec. com., 1979-85; chmn., dir. Washington Nat. Fin. Services, Inc., 1979-85; pres., dir. Washington Nat. Equity Co., 1973-85, chmn. bd., 1983-85 Bd. dirs. North Shore Assn. for Retarded, Evanston, 1983— . Served with USNR, 1945-46, PTO. Mem. Am. Coll. Life Underwriters, Chartered Life Underwriters, Nat. Assn. Life Underwriters, Chgo. Life Underwriters Assn., Nat. Assn. Health Underwriters, Chgo. Health Underwriters Republican. Club: Ivanhoe (Ill.). Lodges: Masons, Shriners.

COOPER, CORINNE, communications consultant, lawyer; b. Albuquerque, July 12, 1952; d. David D. and Martha Lucille (Rosenblum) C. BA magna cum laude, U. Ariz., 1975, JD summa cum laude, 1978. Bar: Ariz. 1978, U.S. Dist. Ct. Ariz. 1978, Mo. 1985. Assoc. Streich, Lang, Weeks & Cardon, Phoenix, 1978-82; asst. prof. U. Mo., Kansas City, 1982-86, assoc. prof., 1986-94, prof., 1994-2000, prof. emerita, 2000—; pres. Profl. Presence, Comm. Cons., Mo., 2001—. Vis. prof. U. Wis., Madison, 1985, 91, U. Pa., Phila., 1988, U. Ariz., 1993, U. Colo., 1994. Author: (with Bruce Meyerson) A Drafter's Guide to Alternative Dispute Resolution, 1991; editor: The Portable UCC, 1993, 3d edit., 2001, Getting Graphic I and II, 1993, 94, The New Article 9, 1999, 2d edit., 2000; editor in chief Bus. Law Today, 1995-97; mem. editl. bd. ABA Jour., 1999—; contbr. articles to profl. jours., chpts. to books. Legal counsel Mo. for Hart campaign, 1984; dir. issues Goddard for Gov. campaign, 1990; bd. dirs. Com. for County Progress, Kansas City, 1985—. Mem. ABA (mem. coun. bus. sect. 1992-96, uniform comml. code com., chmn. membership com. 1992-94, editl. bd. Bus. Law Today, 1991-97, sect. of bus. law pubs. 1998-2002, ABA jour. editorial bd. 1999—), Am. Law Inst., Am. Assn. Law Schs. (comml. law 1982-2000, chair 1992-93, alternative dispute resolution com.), Ariz. Bar Assn., Mo. Bar Assn. (comml. law com.), Order of Coif, Phi Beta Kappa, Phi Kappa Phi. Democrat. Jewish. Office: Profl Presence 6412 Morningside Dr Kansas City MO 64113 also: 1323 E Renfrew Pl Tucson AZ 85719

COOPER, EDWARD HAYES, lawyer, educator; b. Highland Park, Mich., Oct. 13, 1941; s. Frank Edward and Margaret Ellen (Hayes) C.; m. Nancy Carol Wybo, June 29, 1963; children: Lisa, Chandra. A.B., Dartmouth Coll., 1961; LL.B., Harvard U., 1964. Bar: Mich. 1965. Law clk. Hon. Clifford O'Sullivan, U.S. Ct. of Appeals, 1964-65; practice law, Detroit, 1965-67; adj. prof. Wayne State U. Law Sch., 1965-67; assoc. prof. U. Minn. Law Sch., 1967-72; prof. law U. Mich. Law Sch., Ann Arbor, 1972-88, assoc. dean for acad. affairs, 1981-94; Thomas M. Cooley prof. of law, 1988—. Advisor Restatement of the Law, 2d Judgments, 1976-80, Complex Litigation Project, Restatement of the Law, 3d Torts-Apportionment, Fed. Jud. Code Project, Transnational Procedure Project, Internat. Jurisdiction Judgment; reporter fed. state jurisdiction com. Jud. Conf. U.S., 1985-91; mem. civil rules adv. com., 1991-92, reporter, 1992—; reporter Uniform Transfer of Litigation Act, 1989-91. Author: (with C.A. Wright and A.R. Miller) Federal Practice and Procedure: Jurisdiction, Vols. 13-19, 1975-81, 3d edit., 1999—; contbr. articles to law revs. Mem. ABA, Mich. Bar Assn., Am. Law Inst. (council). Office: U Mich 330 Hutchins Law Sch Ann Arbor MI 48109-1215 E-mail: coopere@umich.edu.

COOPER, HAL DEAN, lawyer; b. Marshall County, Iowa, Dec. 8, 1934; s. Truman Braton and Golda Frances (Chadwick) C.; m. Constance Bellinger Simms, Dec. 31, 1960; children: Shannon, Charles, Ellen. Student, Neb. U., 1952-54; BS in Mech. Engring., Iowa State U., 1957; JD with honors, George Washington U., 1963. Bar: Iowa 1963, Ohio 1963, U.S. Supreme Ct. 1971. Assoc., ptnr. Fay & Fay, Cleve., 1962-67; ptnr. Meyer, Tilberry & Body, 1967-69, Yount, Tarolli, Weinshenker & Cooper, Cleve, 1969-72; trial judge U.S. Ct. Claims, Washington, 1972-75; ptnr. Jones, Day, Reavis & Pogue, Cleve., 1975-95; owner Halco Enterprises, Ltd., Austinburg, Ohio, 1995—; pvt. arbitrator, mediator, 1996—. Served with AUS, 1957-59. Mem. Cleve. Intellectual Property Law Assn., Rowfant Club, Clifton Club, Rotary. Episcopalian. E-mail: halco@apk.net.

COOPER, ILENE LINDA, magazine editor, author; b. Chgo., Mar. 10, 1948; d. Morris and Lillian (Friedman) C.; m. Robert Seid, May 28, 1972 (div. 1995). BJ, U. Mo., 1969; MLS, Rosary Coll., 1973. Head of children's svcs. Winnetka (Ill.) Libr. Dist., 1974-80; editor children's books Booklist Mag., ALA, Chgo., 1981—. Author: Susan B. Anthony, 1983, Choosing Sides, 1990 (Internat. Reading Assn.-Children's Book Coun. choice 1990), Mean Streak, 1991, (series) Frances in the Fourth Grade, 1991, The Dead Sea Scrolls, 1997, numerous others. Mem. Soc. Midland Authors, Soc. Children's Book Writers, Children's Reading Roundtable. Jewish. Office: Booklist Mag 50 E Huron St Chicago IL 60611-5295

COOPER, JAMES ALBERT, JR. electrical engineering educator; b. Columbus, Miss., Feb. 5, 1946; s. James Albert and Juanita (Perkins) C.; m. Barbara Crowder, Aug. 3, 1968; children: David Alan, Katherine Liann. BSEE, Miss. State U., 1968; MSEE, Stanford U., 1969; PhD, Purdue U., 1973. Mem. tech. staff Sandia Labs., Albuquerque, 1968-69; grad. rsch. asst. Sch. Elec. Engring. Purdue U., West Lafayette, Ind., 1970-72, prof., 1983—, dir. Purdue Optoelectronics Rsch. Ctr., 1986-89; mem. tech. staff Bell Labs., Murray Hill, N.J., 1973-83. Contbr. numerous articles to jours., chpts. to books; patentee in field. Fellow IEEE (assoc. editor Trans. on Electron Devices 1983-86). Republican. Mem. United Methodist Ch. Achievements include 10 patents in field; co-origination of the Time-of-Flight measurement technique for the study of high-field transport of electrons along semiconductor/insulator interfaces; design of Bell System's first microprocessor chip; co-development of first silicon carbide nonvolatile memory chips, first silicon carbide monolithic integrated circuits and first SiC DMOS power transistors. Office: Purdue U Sch Elec & Computer Engring 1285 EE Bldg West Lafayette IN 47907-1285

COOPER, JANIS CAMPBELL, public relations executive; b. Laurel, Miss., July 26, 1947; d. Clifton B. and Hilna Mae (Welch) Campbell; m. William R. Cooper, Sept. 18, 1971; 1 child, Emily Susanne. BS, U. So. Miss., 1969. Certified home economist. Staff home economist Maytag Co., Newton, Iowa, 1969-73, supr. home econs., 1973-81, mgr. consumer edn., 1981-86; mgr. corp. pub. affairs Maytag Corp., 1986-87, asst. dir. corp. pub. affairs, 1987-88, corp. dir. pub. affairs, 1988-89, corp. v.p. pub. affairs, 1989-96, dir. found. programs, 1996—. Chmn. bd. trustees Newton Cmty. Edn. Found., 1992-95; campaign vice chmn. United Way, Newton, 1996, campaign chmn., 1997, bd. dirs., 1998—, pres., 1998, mem. exec. com., 1998-99; bd. dirs. YMCA, 1997-2000; mem. Newton Chamber Edn. Com. 1999—, chair 2000; edn. com. Newton Chamber Alliance, 1999—, chmn. 2000—. Mem. Assn. Family and Consumer Scis., Pub. Rels. Soc. Am., Home Economists in Bus. (nat. chmn. 1981-82, Disting. Svc. award 1986, Nat. Bus. Home Economist of Yr. 1991), Iowa Assn. Bus. and Industry (bd. dirs., mem. exec. com. 1990-96), Assn. Home Appliance Mfrs. (treas. 1988-89, 1st vice chmn. 1989-90, chmn. 1990-92, chmn. Major Appliance Divsn. Bd. 1993-95), Consumer Sci. Bus. Profls., Maytag Mgmt. Club (Cmty. Svc. award 1997), Kiwanis Internat. Avocations: golfing, reading, travel. Office: Maytag Corp PO Box 39 403 W 4th St N Newton IA 50208-0039

COOPER, JOHN MILTON, JR. history educator, author; b. Washington, Mar. 16, 1940; s. John Milton and Mary Louise (Porter) C.; m. Judith Karin Widerkrantz, June 9, 1962; children: John Milton III, Elizabeth Karin Doyle. AB summa cum laude, Princeton U., 1961; MA, Columbia U., 1962, PhD, 1968. Instr. history Wellesley (Mass.) Coll., 1965-67, asst. prof., 1967-70; asst. prof. history U. Wis., Madison, 1970-71, assoc. prof., 1971-76, prof., 1976-87, William Francis Allen prof. history, 1987-99, E. Gofdon Fox prof. Am. instns., 1999—, chmn. dept., 1988-91. Fulbright prof. Coun. Internat. Exch. Scholars, Moscow, 1987. Author: Vanity of Power, 1969, Walter Hines Page, 1977, Warrior and Priest, 1983, Pivotal Decades, 1990, Breaking the Heart of the World: Woodrow Wilson and the Fight for the League of Nations, 2001; editor: Causes and Consequences of World War I, 1971, The Wilson Era, 1991. Woodrow Wilson Found. fellow, 1961, NEH fellow, 1969, 91, Guggenheim Found. fellow, 1979. Mem.: Ctr. for Nat. Policy, State Hist. Soc. Wis. (bd. curators), Woodrow Wilson Birthplace Found. (hon. pres.), Coun. Fgn. Rels., So. Hist. Assn., Orgn. Am. Historians, Am. Hist. Assn., Rotary, Phi Beta Kappa. Democrat. Congregationalist. E-mail: jmcooper@facstaff.wisc.edu.

COOPER, KEN ERROL, retired management educator; b. Bryan, Ohio, Mar. 10, 1939; s. George Wayne and Agnes Anibel (Fisher) C.; m. Karen Cremean, June 17, 1961; children: Kristin, Andrew. BS, Bowling Green State U., 1961; MBA, Miami U., Oxford, Ohio, 1962; PhD, U. Minn., 1984. Instr. Miami U., 1962-63; lectr. U. Minn., 1965-67, 84-86; group v.p. Land O'Lakes, Inc., Mpls., 1967-82; v.p. fin. and adminstrn. Hamline U., 1982-84; dean Coll. Bus., Ohio No. U., Ada, 1986-90, prof., 1990-2000; prof., post chair for ethics and professions Am. Coll., Bryn Mawr, Pa., 1994-95, retired, 1995. Vis. prof. (on leave) Coll. of St. Thomas, St. Paul, 1981-82. Trustee Westmar Coll., 1980-86; bd. dirs., sec.-treas. Acad. Mgmt., 1989-95; mem. Iowa Supreme Ct. Adv. Coun., 1972-75, North Ctrl. Devel. Found. Republican. Methodist. Office: Ohio No U Coll Bus Adminstrn Ada OH 45810

COOPER, REGINALD RUDYARD, orthopedic surgeon, educator; b. Elkins, W.Va., Jan. 6, 1932; s. Eston H. and Kathryn (Wyatt) C.; m. Jacqueline Smith, Aug. 22, 1954; children: Pamela Ann, Douglas Mark, Christopher Scott, Jeffrey Michael. BA with honors, W.Va. U., 1952, BS, 1953; MD, Med. Coll. Va., 1955; MS, U. Iowa, 1960. Diplomate Am. Bd. Orthopedic Surgeons (examiner 1968-70). Orthopedic surgeon U.S. Naval Hosp., Pensacola, Fla., 1960-62; assoc. in orthopedics U. Iowa Coll. Medicine, Iowa City, 1962-65, asst. prof. orthopedics, 1965-68, assoc. prof. orthopedics, 1968-71, prof. orthopedics, 1971-99, chmn. orthopedics, 1973-99. Rsch. fellow orthopedic surgery Johns Hopkins Hosp., Balt., 1964-65; exch. fellow to Britain for Am. Orthopedic Assn., 1969. Trustee Jour. Bone and Joint Surgeons, 1989-94, chmn. 1993-94. Trustee Nat. Easter Seals Rsch. Found., 1977-81, chmn., 1979-81. Served to lt. comdr. USNR, 1960-62. Mem. Iowa, Johnson County Med. Socs., Orthopedic Rsch. Soc. (sec.-treas. 1970-73, pres. 1974-75), Am. Acad. Orthopedic Surgeons (Kappa Delta award for outstanding rsch. in orthopedics 1971), Can. Orthopedic Assn., Am. Orthopedic Assn., N.Y. Acad. Sci., Assn. Bone and Joint Surgeons, AMA, Am. Rheumatism Assn., Am. Acad. Cerebral Palsy, Am. Acad. Orthopedic Surgeons (chmn. exams. com. 1978-82, sec. 1982, 2d v.p. 1985-86, 1st v.p. 1986-87, pres. 1987-88, ortho residency rev. com. 1989-95, chmn. 1993-95). Home: 201 Ridgeview Ave Iowa City IA 52246-1625 Office: U Iowa Hosps & Clinics 450 Newton Rd Iowa City IA 52242

COOPER, RICHARD ALAN, hematologist, college dean, health policy analyst; b. Milw., Sept. 23, 1936; s. Peter and Annabelle (Schlomovitz) C.; m. Jaclyn Koppel, June 22, 1958 (dec.); children: Stephanie, Jonathan; m. Andrea Pastor, Aug. 20, 1988. BS, U. Wis., 1958; MD, Washington U., St. Louis, 1961. Intern Harvard U. med. svcs. Boston City Hosp., 1961-63, resident in medicine, 1965-66, fellow in hematology Thorndike Meml. Lab., 1966-69; asst. prof. medicine Harvard U. Med. Sch., 1969-71; chief hematology divsn. Thorndike Meml. Lab. and Harvard Med. Svcs., Boston City Hosp., 1969-71; prof. medicine, dir. Cancer Ctr., chief hematology-oncology sect. U. Pa., Phila., 1971-85; prof. medicine, exec. v.p., dean Med. Coll. Wis., Milw., 1985-94, dir. health policy inst., 1992—. Mem. editl. bd. Blood, 1979-84, Lipid Research, 1983-84. Served with USPHS, 1963-65. NIH grantee. Mem. Am. Soc. Hematology, Am. Fedn. Clin. Rsch., Am. Soc. Clin. Investigation, Assn. Am. Physicians, Am. Clin. Climatol. Assn., Phi Beta Kappa., Alpha Omega Alpha. Office: 8701 W Watertown Plank Rd Milwaukee WI 53226-3548

COOPER, RICHARD LEE, agronomist, educator; b. Rensselaer, Ind., Feb. 28, 1932; married, 1952; 4 children. BS, Purdue U., 1957; MS, Mich. State U., 1958, PhD in Plant Breeding and Genetics, 1962. Rsch. assoc. soybean breeding and genetics dept. agronomy and plant genetics U. Minn., 1961-67; from assoc. prof. to prof. agronomy U. Ill., Urbana-Champaign, 1969-77, rsch. leader USDA-ARS Regional Soybean Lab., 1967-76; USDA-ARS rsch. agronomist, prof. plant breeding Ohio Agrl. R & D Ctr. Ohio State U., Wooster, 1977—. Mem. adv. coun. Potash & Phosphate Inst., 1981-83; ARS fellow Agrl. Rsch. Assignment, Brisbane, Australia, 1990-91. Sr. Fulbright scholar, Australia, 1990-91; recipient Agronomic Rsch. award Am. Soc. Agronomy, 1997. Fellow Am. Soc. Agronomy (Agronomy Achievement award 1993, Agronomic Rsch. award 1997), Crop Science Soc. Am.; mem. Am. Soybean Assn. (Soybean Rsch. recognition award 1981, Meritorious Svc. award 1987). Achievements include research in solid seeding of soybeans with increases of 10-30% in yield; development of semidwarf soybean cultivars; maximum yield research in soybeans; breeding methodology (early generation testing); development of abiotic stress tolerant cultivars; subirrigation/drainage research. Office: Ohio Agrl R & D Ctr Dept Horticulture and Crop Science Wooster OH 44691

COOPER, ROBERT JAMES, purchasing consultant; b. St. Louis, Dec. 27, 1929; s. William McKinley and Lucille Evelyn (Floyd) C.; m. Joan Kathleen Gray, Nov. 20, 1932; children: Bruce John, Anne Muriel. Student, Ruskin Coll., Oxford, Eng., 1954-55. Asst. purchasing agt. Absorbant Cotton Co., St. Louis, 1960-65; purchasing agt. Christian Hosp., 1965-67; dir. purchasing St. John's Mercy Med. Ctr., 1967-86; purchasing cons., 1986—. Lectr. in field; condr. seminars/workshops in field. Contbr. articles to profl. jours. With USAF, 1950-54. Mem. Nat. Assn. Purchasing Mgmt., Nat. Assn. Hosp. Purchasing Mgmt. (pres. 1974-76, fellow), Assn. Hosp. Purchasing Agts. of Greater St. Louis (pres. 1968). Democrat. Episcopalian. Avocations: oil painting, stained glass, sculpture. Home: 9118 Clydesdale Dr Saint Louis MO 63126-2536

COOPER, ROGER, educator former state legislator; b. Nov. 8, 1944; m. Margie. BA, Rockford Coll.; postgrad., Mankato State U. State rep. Minn. Ho. Reps., Dist. 15B, 1986-97; tchr. Bold High Sch., Olivia, Minn. Vice chmn. econ. devel. com., mem. govt. oper. com., vice chmn. health & human svc. com., mem. gen. legis., bet affairs & elec. agrl., hyman svcs. fin. divsn. & local govt. & met. affairs com., Minn. Ho. Reps. Home: 55345 County Road 38 Buffalo Lake MN 55314-2072

COOPER, STUART LEONARD, chemical engineering educator, researcher, consultant; b. N.Y.C., Aug. 28, 1941; s. Jacob and Anne (Bloom) C.; m. Marilyn Portnoy, Aug. 29, 1965; children: Gary, Stacey. B.S., MIT, 1963; Ph.D., Princeton U., 1967. Asst. prof. chem. engring. U. Wis., Madison, 1967-71, assoc. prof., 1971-74, prof., 1974, chmn. dept., 1983-89, 92, Paul A. Elfers prof., 1989-93; dean, H. Rodney Sharp prof. Coll of Engring. U. Del., Newark, 1993-98; v.p., chief acad. officer, P. Danforth prof. engring. Ill. Inst. Tech., 1998-2001; provost, vice chancellor for acad. affairs N.C. State U., 2001—. Vis. assoc. prof. U. Calif.-Berkeley, 1974; vis. prof. Technion, Haifa, Israel, 1977; cons. in field; trustee Argonne Univs. Assn., Argonne Nat. Lab., 1975-81 Editor: Multiphase Polymers, 1979, Biomaterials: Interfacial Phenomena and Applications, 1982, The Vroman Effect, 1992, Polymer Biomaterials: In Solution as Interfaces and as Solids, 1995; author: Polyurethanes in Medicine, 1986, Polyurethanes in Biomedical Applications, 1998; contbr. numerous articles in field to profl. jours. Lady Davis fellow, 1977 Fellow AIChE (Charles M.A. Stine award 1987), AAAS, Am. Phys. Soc., Am. Inst. Med. and Biol. Engrs. (founding), Soc. for Biomaterials (pres. 1996-97, Clemson award for basic rsch. 1987); mem. Am. Chem. Soc. (best paper award 1976), Am. Soc. Artificial Internal Organs, Soc. Rheology, Soc. Plastics Engrs. Office: Provost Office NC State Univ 109 Holladay Hall Box 7101 Raleigh NC 27695 E-mail: stuart_cooper@ncsu.edu.

COOPER, THOM R. transportation executive; Chmn. Jack Cooper Transport Co., Inc., Kansas City, 1938—. Office: Jack Cooper Transport Co Inc 2345 Grand Blvd Ste 400 Kansas City MO 64108-2625

COOPER, WILLIAM ALLEN, banking executive; b. Detroit, July 3, 1943; BS in Acctg., Wayne State U., 1967. CPA, Mich. With Touche, Ross & Co., Detroit, 1967-71; chm. Minn. Rep Party. Sr. v.p. Mich. Nat. Bank of Detroit, 1971-72; sr. v.p. Mich. Nat. Corp., 1971-78; exec. v.p. Huntington Nat. Bank, Columbus, Ohio, 1978-83, pres., 1983-84; pres., Am. Savs. & Loan Assn. of Fla., Miami, 1984-85 , also dir.; chmn. bd., chief exec. officer TCF Bank, FSB, Mpls., 1985—; chmn., TCF Fin. Corp., Mpls., from 1987, now chmn. bd., past chief exec. officer, bd. dirs. Mem. AICPA. Office: TCF Bank Office of Chmn Bd 801 Marquette Ave Minneapolis MN 55402-3475 also: Minn Rep Party 480 Ceder Street Ste 560 Castle Rock MN 55010

COORDSEN, GEORGE, state legislator; b. Fairburg, Nebr., Aug. 13, 1935; m. Janice Fegter, 1956; children: Debra (Mrs. David Fangmeier), Kevin, Valerie (Mrs. Brice). Farmer, Nebr.; mem. Nebr. Legislature from 32nd dist., Lincoln, 1987—; mem. banking, comml. and com. com. Nebr. Legislature, vice chmn. revenue and bldg. maintenance com., chmn. exec. bd. Chmn. Nebr. Grail & Sorghum Bd., 1981-86; dir. U.S. Feed Grains Coun., 1981-86. Named to Hall of Fame, Nebr. Agr., 1989. Address: RR 1 Box 122 Hebron NE 68370-9780 also: State Legislature State Capitol Lincoln NE 68509

COPELAND, EDWARD JEROME, lawyer; b. Chgo., Oct. 29, 1933; s. Harvey and Lilyan (Rubin) C.; m. Ruth Caminer, Sept. 2, 1962; children: Ellyn, Bradley. BA, Carleton Coll., 1955; JD, Northwestern U., 1958. Bar: Ill. 1959, N.Y. 1981. Mem. Ill. Ho. of Reps., Springfield, 1967-71; ptnr. Foss, Schuman, Drake & Barnard, Chgo., 1971-86, Wood, Lucksinger & Epstein, Chgo., 1986-88, Shefsky & Froelich, Ltd., Chgo., 1988-89, Schuyler, Roche & Zwirner, Chgo., 1989—. Chmn. Bank of North Shore, Northbrook, Ill., 1976-81. Mem. Ill. Bd. Edn., 1975-83, chmn., 1981-83. Mem. ABA, Ill. Bar Assn., Chgo. Bar Assn. Republican. Office: One Prudential Plaza Ste 3800 Schuyler Roche & Zwirner 130 E Randolph St Chicago IL 60601-6312 E-mail: ecopeland@srzlaw.com.

COPELAND, FRED E. state legislator; b. Cooter, Mo., June 12, 1932; m. Patricia Ann Weber, 1952 (div.); m. Ginna Lee Hequembourg, 1980; children: Fred, Lisa Ann, Leslie Ann. Student, Ark. State Coll. State rep. dist. 161 Mo. Ho. of Reps., 1960-98, chmn. maj. caucus, 1985-96, mem. deferred compensation commn., fed. funds and block grant oversight com., tourism commn., alt. mem. coun. state govts.-so. legis. conf. exec. com. Real estate exec. and farmer. With USN, 1952-56. Baptist. Home: 4306 Kendallwood Ct Jefferson City MO 65109-7119

COPELAND, HENRY JEFFERSON, JR. former college president; b. Griffin, Ga., June 13, 1936; s. Henry Jefferson and Emory (Drake) C.; m. Laura Harper, Dec. 21, 1958; children: Henry Drake, Eleanor Harper. BA, Baylor U., 1958; PhD, Cornell U., 1966. Instr. Cornell U., Ithaca, N.Y., 1965-66; asst. prof. history Coll. Wooster, Ohio, 1966-69, assoc. dean, 1969-74, dean, 1974-77, pres., 1977-95, prof. history, 1995-98. Woodrow Wilson fellow, 1960 Presbyterian

COPPER, JAMES ROBERT, manufacturing company executive; b. St. Louis, Aug. 19, 1939; s. Charles Alva and Cora Imogene (Shifley) Copper; m. Patricia Leeper, Aug. 12, 1961; children: Susan, Robin, Julie. A.B., Culver-Stockton Coll., 1961; M.S., U. Tenn.-Knoxville, 1969. Tchr. Mo. Mil. Acad., Mexico, 1961-63; mgr. applications analysis Nuclear div.

Union Carbide, Oak Ridge, Tenn., 1963-69; mgr. corp. mgmt. scis. Coca-Cola Co., Atlanta, 1969-76; v.p. strategic planning and analysis Pillsbury Co., Mpls., 1976-80; v.p. strategic planning IC Industries, Inc., Chgo., 1980-86, sr. v.p. corp. planning and devel., 1986-88; pres., COO Pet, Inc., St. Louis, 1988, pres., CEO, 1989—. Mem. Civic Progress; bd. dirs. YMCA Greater St. Louis, St. Louis area counc. Boy Scouts Am., United Way St. Louis, Boatmen's Nat. Bank of St. Louis, Christmas in St. Louis, St. Louis Variety Club, Culver-Stockton Coll. Mem. Mo. Athletic Club, St. Louis Club, Old Warson Country Club. Home: 5777 Gene Sarazen Dr Braselton GA 30517-4057

COPPERSMITH, SUSAN NAN, physicist; b. Johnstown, Pa., Mar. 18, 1957; d. Wallace Louis and Bernice Barbara (Evans) C.; m. Robert Daniel Blank, Dec. 20, 1981. BS in Physics, MIT, 1978; postgrad., Cambridge U., 1979; MS in Physics, Cornell U., 1981, PhD in Physics, 1983. Rsch. assoc. Brookhaven Nat. Labs., 1983-85; postdoctoral mem. tech. staff AT&T Bell Labs., Murray Hill, N.J., 1985-86, mem. tech. staff, 1987-90, disting. mem. tech. staff, 1990-95; prof. physics U. Chgo., 1995—. Vis. lectr. Princeton U., 1986-87; vis. professorship for women NSF, 1986-87; gen. mem. Aspen Ctr. for Physics, 1991—; chancellor's disting. lectr. U. Calif., Irvine, 1991. Trustee Aspen Ctr. for Physics, 1993-96. Winston Churchill scholar, 1978-79, Bell Labs. GRPW fellow, 1979-83. Fellow Am. Phys. Soc. Home: 1826 Camelot Dr Madison WI 53705-1008

COPPOCK, BRUCE, orchestra executive; m. Linda Marder. Cellist Boston Symphony Orch.; ops. & orch. mgr. St. Louis Symphony Orch., exec. dir., 1992-97; dep. dir. Carnegie Hall, N.Y.C., 1997-98; v.p. Am. Symphony Orch. League, Washington, 1998-99; dir. Orch. Leadership Acad., 1998-99; pres., mng. dir. St. Paul Chamber Orch., 1999—. Mem. Boston Chamber Music Soc. (founder). Office: St Paul Chamber Orch 408 Saint Peter St Saint Paul MN 55102-1130

COPPS, MICHAEL WILLIAM, retail and wholesale company executive; b. Stevens Point, Wis., Aug. 29, 1939; s. Donald William and Mary Jane (Krembs) C.; B.S., U. Wis., 1963, LL.B., 1967; m. Priscilla Lynn Reichardt, July 10, 1971; children— Clinton, Carolyn. Legis. analyst Wis. Taypayers Alliance, Madison, 1967-68; intern Supermarket Inst., Chgo., 1968-70; with Copps Corp., Stevens Point, Wis., 1970— , successively warehouse supt., exec. v.p., vice chmn. bd., now chmn. bd. Bd. dirs. YMCA, Stevens Point, 1978—. Republican. Lutheran. Office: Copps Corp 2828 Wayne St Stevens Point WI 54481-4100

COQUILLETTE, WILLIAM HOLLIS, lawyer; b. Boston, Oct. 7, 1949; s. Robert McTavish and Dagmar (Bistrup) C.; m. Mary Katherine Templeton, June 19, 1971 (div. Oct. 1984); 1 child, Carolyn Patricia; m. Janet Marie Weiland, Dec. 8, 1984; children: Benjamin, Weiland, Madeline Marie, Elizabeth Charlotte. BA, Yale U., 1971, Oxford U., 1973; JD, Harvard U., 1975. Bar: Ohio 1976, Mass. 1976. Law clk. to presiding justice Mass. Supreme Ct., Boston, 1975-76; assoc. Jones, Day, Reavis & Pogue, Cleve., 1976-83, ptnr., 1984—. Trustee Cleve. Foodbank, Playhouse Sq. Found., Greater Cleve. Com. on Hunger. Mem. Kirtland Club, Yale Club (N.Y.C.), Union Club (Cleve.), Cleve. Skating Club, Rowfant Club, N.Y. Yacht Club. Office: Jones Day Reavis & Pogue 901 Lakeside Ave E Cleveland OH 44114-1190

CORAN, ARNOLD GERALD, pediatric surgeon; b. Boston, Apr. 16, 1938; s. Charles and Ann (Cohen) C.; m. Susan Myra Williams, Nov. 17, 1960; children: Michael, David, Randi Beth. AB, Harvard U., 1959, MD, 1963. Diplomate Am. Bd. Surgery, Am. Bd. Thoracic Surgery, Am. Bd. Pediat. Surgery. Intern in surgery Peter Bent Brigham Hosp., Boston, 1963-64, resident in general and thoracic surgery, 1964-69; resident in pediatric surgery Children's Hosp., 1966-68; chief pediat. surgery, assoc. prof. surgery U. South Calif. Med. Sch., L.A., 1972-74; chief pediat. surgery, prof. surgery U. Mich., Ann Arbor, 1974—; surgeon in chief C.S. Mott Childrens Hosp., 1981—. Contbr. articles to profl. jours. Lt. comdr. USN, 1970-72. Mem.: Am. Pediat. Surg. Assn. (pres. 2001—02). Avocations: skiing, golf, running. Home: 505 E Huron St Apt 802 Ann Arbor MI 48104-1553 Office: CS Mott Childrens Hosp Rm F3970 Ann Arbor MI 48109-0245

CORBALLY, JOHN EDWARD, foundation director; b. South Bend, Wash., Oct. 14, 1924; s. John Edward and Grace (Williams) C.; m. Marguerite B. Walker, Mar. 12, 1946; children: Jan Elizabeth, David William. BS, U. Wash., 1947, MA, 1950; PhD, U. Calif., Berkeley, 1955; LLD, U. Md., 1971; LL.D., Blackburn Coll., 1972, Ill. State U., 1977, Ohio State U., 1980; Litt.D., U. Akron, 1979. Tchr. Clover Park High Sch., Tacoma, 1947-50; prin. Twin City High Sch., Stanwood, 1950-53; asst. prof., then assoc. prof. edn. Ohio State U., Columbus, 1955-60, prof., 1960-69, dir. pers. budget, exec. asst. to pres., 1960-64, v.p. adminstrn., 1964-66, provost, v.p. acad. affairs, 1966-69; chancellor, pres. Syracuse (N.Y.) U., 1969-71; pres. U. Ill., Chgo. and Urbana-Champaign, 1971-79, pres. emeritus, 1979—, disting. prof. higher edn., 1979-82, disting. prof. emeritus, 1982—; pres. John D. and Catherine T. MacArthur Found., 1979-89, dir., 1979—2002, chmn., 1995—2002; cons. Heidrick & Struggles, 1989-90. Chmn. Nat. Coun. Ednl. Rsch., Nat. Inst. Edn., 1973-79; trustee Mus. Sci. and Industry, Chgo., 1971-79; chmn. Commn. Curricular Outcome, Ill. Bd. Edn., 1985-88; chmn. Chgo. Sch. Reform Authority, 1988-89. Author: Introduction to Educational Adminstration, 6th edit, 1983, Educational Administration: The Secondary School, 2d edit, 1965, School Finance, 1962. Bd. dirs. U. Wash. Found., 1989-93, Ill. Ednl. Consortium, 1973-79, Zion Prep. Acad. (Seattle), Snohomish County Comty. Found., Rural Devel. Inst., Seattle, Philanthropy NW, Exec, Svc. Corps of Wash., 1990-96, 98-2000, Snonet, Everett, Wash., 1994-2002. Lt. (j.g.) USNR, 1943-46. Recipient Centennial medal U. Calif. Alumni Assn. and Sch. Edn. Alumni Soc., 1976, Disting. Eagle award Boy Scouts Am., 1978, Van Miller award Ill. Assn. Sch. Adminstrs. and Ednl. Adminstrn. Alumni Assn. U. Ill., 1986, Humanitarian award No. Ill. U., 1986, Disting. Alumnus award U. Wash. Coll. Edn., 1987, Disting. Achievement award U. Wash. Coll. Arts and Sci., 1995; named Alumnus Summa Laude Dignatus, U. Wash., 1988, Laureate, Lincoln Acad. Ill., 1989. Mem. U. Ill. Alumni Assn. (life, Disting. Svc. award 1986), U. Wash. Alumni Assn. (life), Tavern Club, Wayfarers Club, Phi Beta Kappa. Home: 1507 151st Pl SE Mill Creek WA 98012-1591

CORBATO, CHARLES EDWARD, geology educator; b. Los Angeles, July 12, 1932; s. Hermenegildo and Charlotte Carella (Jensen) C.; m. Patricia Jeanne Ferg, May 18, 1957; children: Steven, Barbara, Susan. BA, UCLA, 1954, PhD, 1960. Instr. geology U. Calif., Riverside, 1959, Los Angeles, 1959-60, asst. prof., 1960-66; assoc. prof. Ohio State U., Columbus, 1966-69, prof., 1969-92, chmn. dept. geology and mineralogy, 1972-80, assoc. provost office of acad. affairs, 1987-92, prof., assoc. provost emeritus, 1992—. Geophysicist U.S. Geol. Survey, 1966-74; dir. State Postsecondary Rev. Entity, Ohio Bd. Regents, 1994-95, dir. info. svcs., 1995-99. Fellow: Geol. Soc. Am.; mem.: Inst. Profl. Geologists, Am. Geophys. Union, Delta Tau Delta. Home: 2400 Buckley Rd Columbus OH 43220-4616 Office: Ohio State U 125 S Oval Mall Columbus OH 43210-1308 E-mail: corbato.1@osu.edu., ccorbato@columbus.rr.com.

CORBETT, FRANK JOSEPH, advertising executive; b. N.Y.C., July 5, 1917; s. Daniel and Frances (Manson) C.; m. Dolores Pierce, May 23, 1959; children: Kenneth, Beverly. PhD, Columbia U., 1938; postgrad., U. So. Calif., 1947, UCLA, 1947, NYU, 1945-46. Pharmacy mgr., N.Y.C., 1938-41; sales rep. Upjohn, Inc., 1941-43; dist. sales mgr., mgr. market research dept. William R. Warner Co., 1944-46; dir. product devel. and market research, advt. mgr., also asst. to dir. sales Harrower Lab., Inc., Glendale, Calif., 1946-51, Jersey City, 1946-51; account exec. Jordan-Sieber Advt. Agy., Chgo., 1951-55; ptnr., v.p. Jordan, Sieber & Corbett (advt.), 1955-60; cons. pharm. field, 1960-61; founder, pres. Frank J. Corbett, Inc. (advt.), 1961-78, chmn. bd., 1978-93, vice chmn., 1993—. Inductee Med. Advt. Hall of Fame, 1998. Mem. Nat. Wholesalers Drug Assn., Midwest Pharm. Advt. Club, Pharm. Mfrs. Assn. Home: 1320 N State Pky Chicago IL 60610-2118 Office: Frank J Corbett Inc 211 E Chicago Ave Ste 1600 Chicago IL 60611-2660

CORBIN, DAVID R. state legislator; b. July 20, 1944; m. Betty Corbin. Mem. Kans. Ho. of Reps., Topeka, 1990-92; mem. from dist. 16 Kans. Senate, 1993—. Chmn. energy and natural resources com., agrl. com.; mem. assessment and taxation coms.; farmer and commodity broker; market analyst Kans. Agrl. Network, 1983—. Mem. Farm Bur., Livestock Assn., Nat. Assn. Farmbroadcasters, El Dorado and Augusta C. of C., Lions, Kiwanis. Republican. Home: 5079 SW Fulton Rd Towanda KS 67144-9097

CORBIN, ROBERT L. state legislator; b. Appleton, Wis., Dec. 8, 1922; s. Lyle Dalton and Minnie (Yokers) C.; m. Edith Peters, 1948; children: Carol, Lynn Corbin. BA, Otterbein Coll. Buyer Rike Kumler, 1940-53; exec. pres. Foodcraft Mgmt. Corp., 1953-64, pres., 1964-79; mem. Oho Ho. of Reps. Columbus, 1977-2000, asst. majority floor leader, 1996. Named Restaurateur of Yr., Miami Valley Restaurant Assn., 1963. Mem. Ohio Restaurant Assn. (past pres.), Walnut Grove C. of C., Otterbein Coll. Alumni Assn. (past pres.), Dayton Agonis Club (past pres.), Pi Kappa Phi. Methodist. Home: 135 Shadybrook Dr Dayton OH 45459-1930

CORBY, FRANCIS MICHAEL, JR. financial executive; b. Chgo., Feb. 2, 1944; s. Francis M. and Jean (Wolf) C.; m. Diane S. Orselli, Aug. 5, 1972; children: Francis Michael III, Brian A., Christopher S. BA, St. Mary of the Lake, 1966; MBA, Columbia U., 1969. With Chrysler Corp., 1969-80; treasury mgr. Chrysler Peru S.A., Lima, 1973-74; fin. dir. Chrysler Wholesale Ltd., London, 1974-76; mng. dir. Chrysler Comml. S.A. de C.V., Mexico City, 1976-77; v.p., treas. Chrysler Fin. Corp., Troy, Mich., 1977-80; treas. Joy Mfg. Co., Pitts., 1980-83, contr., 1983-86, v.p., 1984-86; sr. v.p. fin., CFO Harnischfeger Industries, Inc., Milw., 1986-94, exec. v.p. fin. and adminstrn., 1994-99; exec. v.p. Frederick & Co., 2000-2001; exec. v.p., CFO Guide Corp., Pendleton, Ind., 2001—. Bd. dirs. Ultra Visual Med. Sys., Inc., Magnasphere Corp. Mem.: Westmoor Country Club. Office: Guide Corp Tech Customer Ctr 600 Corp Dr TC26 Pendleton IN 46064

CORCORAN, PHILIP E. wholesale distribution executive; CEO, co-founder, chmn. Comark, Inc., Bloomingdale, Ill.

CORDES, EUGENE HAROLD, pharmacy and chemistry educator; b. York, Nebr., Apr. 7, 1936; s. Elmer Henry and Ruby Mae (Hofeldt) C.; m. Shirley Ann Morton, Nov. 9, 1957; children: Jennifer Eve, Matthew Henry James. BS, Calif. Inst. Tech., 1958; PhD, Brandeis U., 1962. Instr. chemistry Ind. U., Bloomington, 1962-64, asst. prof., 1964-66, assoc. prof., 1966-68, prof., 1968-79, chmn., 1972-78; exec. dir. biochemistry Merck, Sharp and Dohme Research Labs., Rahway, N.J., 1979-84, v.p. biochemistry, 1984-87; v.p R & D Eastman Pharms., Malvern, Pa., 1987-88; pres. Sterling Winthrop Pharms. Rsch. divsn. Sterling Winthrop Inc., Collegeville, 1988-94; prof. U. Mich., Ann Arbor, 1995—. Author: (with Henry Mahler) Biological Chemistry, 1966, 2d. edit., 1971, Basic Biological Chemistry, 1969, (with Riley Schaeffer) Chemistry, 1973; also articles. NIH Career Devel. award, 1966; Alfred P. Sloan Found. fellow, 1968 Mem. AAAS, Am. Soc. Biol. Chemists. Home: 220 Barton North Dr Ann Arbor MI 48105-1016

COREY, JUDITH ANN, retired educator; b. Peoria, Ill., Dec. 1, 1937; d. Lyle William and Eileen A. (Zigrang) Springston; m. Thomas W. Corey, Aug. 12, 1961; children: John William, Jeffrey Michael, Gregory Lyle, Mark Andrew. BA in Bus., English, Marycrest Coll., 1960; MA in Counseling, Bradley U., 1972. Lic. tchr. K-12, Ill.; lic. clin. profl. counselor. Tchr. Riverview Sch., Spring Bay, Ill., 1960-61, Lincoln Sch., East Peoria, 1963-64; counselor Bradley U., Peoria, 1972-73; clin. psychologist intern Zeller Zone Ctr., 1973; dean students Morton (Ill.) High Sch., 1974-85; tchr. Jefferson Sch., Morton, 1985—2002. Contbr. poem to Worlds Greatest Contemporary Poems, 1981 (Hon. Mention). Campaign work Grace Bunn Lievens Ill. Rep., 89th Dist. Ill., Morton, 1994; mem. exec. bd. Ill. State Deans' Assn., 1980-84, historian, 1980-82, membership com., 1982-84. Named to Outstanding Young Women in Am., 1973. Mem. NEA, Ill. Edn. Assn., Morton Edn. Assn. (newsletter editor 1987-90, mem. exec. com. and maj. negotiator, 1987-2000, v.p. 1993-95), Assn. Play Therapy, Phi Kappa Phi (life), Kappa Gamma Pi, Pi Lambda Theta. Roman Catholic. Avocations: reading, writing, photography, music, nature. Home: 20432 Tennessee Ave Morton IL 61550-9777

COREY, KENNETH EDWARD, urban planning and geography educator, researcher; b. Cin., Nov. 11, 1938; s. Kenneth and Helen Ann (Beckman) C.; m. Marie Joann Fye, Aug. 26, 1961; children: Jeffrey Allen, Jennifer Marie. BA with honors, U. Cin., 1961, MA, 1962, M of Cmty. Planning, 1964, PhD, 1969. Instr. U. Cin., 1962-65, asst. prof. cmty. planning, 1965-69, assoc. prof., 1969-74, prof., 1974-79, head grad. comty. planning and geography, 1969-78; assoc. prof. cmty. planning and geography U. R.I., 1966-67; prof. geography, planning, chmn. dept. geography, dir. urban studies U. Md., 1979-89; prof. geography and urban and regional planning, dean Coll. Social Sci. Mich. State U., East Lansing, 1989-99, sr. rsch. advisor to v.p. for rsch. and grad. studies, 1999—. Vis. prof. geography Univ. Wales, Aberystyth, 1974-75, Peking U., 1986; chmn. Cin. Model Cities Bd., 1974; Fulbright rsch. scholar Inst. S.E. Asian Studies, Singapore, 1986, Fulbright group study abroad, Sri Lanka, 1983; trustee Met. Washington Housing Planning Assn., 1980-82. Author: The Local Community, 1968, Community Internships for Undergraduate Geography Students, 1973, The Planning of Change, 3d edit., 1976, Information Tectonics, 2000. Bd. dirs. Potomac River Basin Consortium, Washington, 1982-85. Recipient Svc. award Cmty. Chest and Coun. Cin., 1979; recipient Svc. award Planning Divsn., 1979, Svc. award Coalition of Neighborhoods, Cin., 1979, 83, medal of city Mayor of Seoul, South Korea, 1980. Fellow Royal Geog. Soc.; mem. Am. Inst. Cert. Planners, Am. Planning Assn., Assn. Am. Geographers (award spl. group on planning and regional devel. 1985), Assn. Asian Studies, Asia Soc., Pacific Rim Coun. on Urban Devel., World Future Soc. Democrat.

CORK, DONALD BURL, electrical engineer; b. Terre Haute, Ind., Aug. 10, 1949; s. Clay Jr. and Margaret M. (Ellis) C.; m. Carolyn R. Lewis, Nov. 18, 1978. BSEE, U. Evansville, Ind., 1971. Owner Ellcor Electric, West Union, Ill., 1971-73; test engr. Zenith Radio, Paris, 1973-78, mfg. engr., 1978-81; design engr. TRW Electronics, Marshall, 1981-84, electrical engr. coord., 1984-88, program mgr., 1988—. Mem. West Union (Ill.) Fire Dept., 1969—, trustee, 1995—; elder West Union Christian Ch. Mem. Eta Kappa Nu, Ea. Ill. Hamateurs (pres. 1971-73), West Union Firemans Assn. (v.p. 1977-78, treas. 1989), Old Nat. Trail Firefighters'. Republican. Avocation: amateur radio. Home: 321 S Walnut St West Union IL 62477-1045 Office: TRW TED PO Box 279 Marshall IL 62441-0279

CORLETT, ED, automotive executive; CFO Meridian Automotive Sys., Dearborn, Mich. Office: Meridian Automotive Systems 550 Town Center Dr Dearborn MI 48126 Office Fax: (313) 356-4184.

CORLEY, WILLIAM EDWARD, hospital administrator; b. Pittsburgh, Sept. 2, 1942; s. Robert Ray and Helen (Wise) C.; m. Angela Irvine Blose, Mar. 22, 1969; children: Laura, Matt BA in Bus. and Econs., Coll. of William and Mary, 1964; MHA in Hosp. Adminstrn., Duke U., Durham, 1966. Adminstrv. asst. Duke U., Durham, N.C., 1965-66; mgmt. cons. Booz, Allen & Hamilton, Chicago, 1968-71; assoc. hosp. dir. U. Ky., Lexington, 1971-75; hosp. dir. Milton S. Hersey Med. Ctr. of Pa. State U., Hershey, 1975-78; pres. Akron Gen. Med. Ctr., Ohio, 1978-84; pres., CEO Community Hosps. of Ind., Inc., 1984—. Bd. dirs. Vol. Hosps. Am. Tri-State, Indpls., Indpls. C. of C., Nat. City Bank, Indpls., Ind. Pro Health; tri-state chmn.; chmn. United Hosp. Svcs., Indpls., 1986-88; lectr. Ind. U.-Purdue U. at Indpls., 1984-98; high sch. basketball referee. Co-author: Ray E. Brown-A Manager's Manager: Lectures, Messages, Memoirs, 1990; contbr. articles to profl. jours. Chmn. United Hosp. Svc., 1986-88, Vol. Hosp. Am. Tri-State, 1989-91; vice chmn. Indpls. Children's Mus. Bd.; active United Way Bd.; pres. 400 and 500 Festival Bd. Named Sagamore of the Wabash, Gov. of Ind. Presbyterian. Avocations: photography, basketball, coaching, running. Home: 13570 N Gray Rd Carmel IN 46033-9708 Office: Community Hosps 1500 N Ritter Ave Indianapolis IN 46219-3095

CORLEY, WILLIAM GENE, engineering research executive; b. Shelbyville, Ill., Dec. 19, 1935; s. Clarence William and Mary Winifred (Douthit) C.; m. Jenny Lynd Wertheim, Aug. 9, 1959; children: Anne Lynd, Robert William, Scott Elson. BS, U. Ill., 1958, MS, 1960, PhD, 1961. Lic. profl. engr., Ill., Va., Wash., Calif., Miss., Fla., La., Pa., Ala., Hawaii, Tenn., Tex., Utah, Mich., Mo., S.D., S.C., Tenn., Kans., Ohio; lic. structural engr., Ill.; chartered structural engr., U.K. Devel. engr. Portland Cement Assn., Skokie, Ill., 1964-66, mgr. structural devel. sect., 1966-74, dir. engring. devel. divsn., 1974-86; sr. v.p. Constrn. Tech. Labs., Inc. (formerly Portland Cement Assn.), 1986—. Adv. panels NSF. Contbr. articles to profl. jours. Pres. caucus Glenview (Ill.) Sch. Bd., 1971-72; elder United Presbyn. Ch., 1975-79; sec. bd. dirs. Assn. Ho., Glenview, Ill., 1976, treas., 1977, pres., 1978-79; chmn. bd. dirs. North Cook dist. ARC, bd. dirs. Mid-Am. chpt., chmn. North Region Coun., 1988-92; mem. Gov.'s (Ill.) Earthquake Preparedness Task Force. Recipient Wason medal for rsch., 1970, Nat. Acad. Engring., 2000; Martin Korn award Prestressed Concrete Inst., 1978, Authur J. Boase award Reinforced Concrete Rsch. Coun., 1986. Fellow Inst. Structural Engrs., Am. Concrete Inst. (Bloem award 1978, Reese Structural Rsch. award 1986, Henry C. Turner award 1988, Lindau award, 1999, Ferguson lectr. 1991, bd. dirs. 1994-97, Henry Crown award 1997, Alfred E. Lindau award 2000); mem. NSPE, Reunion Internat. des Laboratoires d'Essais et Rsch. sur Materiaux Constrn., Nat. Acad. Engring., Earthquake Engring. Rsch. Inst. (chpt. sec., treas. 1980-82, chmn. 1984-86), Internat. Assn. Bridge and Structural Engring., Structural Engrs. Assn. Ill. (pres. 1986-87, meritorious publ. award 1993, 97, John Parmer award 1997), Nat. Coun. Structural Engrs. Assns. (pres. 1996-97, Best Paper award 1999, Disting. Svc. award 1999), Nat. Coun. Examiners Engring. and Surveying (Disting. Svc. award 2000), Post-Tensioning Inst., Chgo. Com. High-Rise Bldgs. (vice-chmn. 1978-82, chmn. 1982-84), Bldg. Seismic Safety Coun. (vice-chmn. 1983-85, sec. 1985-87), ASCE (hon.; T.Y. Lin award 1979, lifetime achievement award 1994), Presbyterian. Home: 744 Glenayre Dr Glenview IL 60025-4411 Office: Construction Tech Labs Inc 5420 Old Orchard Rd Skokie IL 60077-1053

CORLIN, RICHARD F. gastroenterologist; b. Newark; m. Catherine Corlin. Grad., Rutgers U.; MD, Hahnemann Med. Coll. Pvt. practice, Santa Monic, Calif. Mem. adv. com. Dir. of the NIH; asst. clin. prof. UCLA Sch. of Medicine. Lt. comdr. USPHS, 1968-70. Fellow ACP; mem. AMA (spkr. ho. of dels. 1997, mem., then chair coun. on long range planning and devel., chair commn. on svcs. to young physicians, chair study com. on hosp. med. staff, mem., chair reference coms., ad hoc com. on physician manpower 1987-88, spokesperson, Spkrs. Bur. award 1980, 81), Am. Gastroenterology Assn., Am. Soc. of Internal Medicine, So. Calif. Soc. of Gastrointestinal Endoscopy (past pres.), Calif. Med. Assn. (pres. 1992-93, vice spkr. and spkr. ho. of dels., bd. trustees), L.A. County Med. Assn. (pres. 1978-79). Office: AMA 515 N State St Chicago IL 60610-4325

CORNE, TODD, lawyer; b. Evansville, Ind., Aug. 5, 1966; s. George Butch and Patricia Sue Corne; m. Michelle Holweger. BS in Polit. Sci., U. Evansville, 1988; JD, Ind. U., 1991. Prosecutor Warrick County, Ind., 1995—. Mem. Ind. Prosecuting Atty. Death Penalty Com., Warrick County Bar Assn., Warrick County Domestic Violence Task Force. Republican. Avocations: hiking, reading. Office: Warrick County Prosecutor 1 County Sq Ste 180 Boonville IN 47601-1817 E-mail: wcpo@evansville.net.

CORNELIUS, KENNETH CREMER, JR. finance executive; b. Plainwell, Mich., Sept. 7, 1944; s. Kenneth Cremer and Hollie Jane (Tupper) C.; m. Mary Patricia Hagen, Aug. 19, 1967; children: Kari, Jay, Lee Ann. BA, Carleton Coll., 1966; MBA, U. Mich., 1967. Mgr. acctg. divsn. Maremont Corp., Nashville, 1972-74, mgr. regional acctg. divsn., 1974-75, divsn. contr., 1975-79, corp. contr., 1979-89, v.p., CFO Chgo., 1980-89, M-C Industries, Ann Arbor, Mich., 1989-92, Prestolite Electric Inc., Ann Arbor, 1992—. Capt. USAF, 1968-72. Mem. Phi Beta Kappa. Home: 4281 Pine Ridge Ct Ann Arbor MI 48105-2784 Office: Prestolite 2311 Green Rd Ann Arbor MI 48105-1593

CORNELL, EDWARD L. consumer products company executive; Exec. v.p. non-retail stores and internat. devel. Office Max, Inc., Shaker Heights, Ohio, 1997—. Office: Office Max Inc 3605 Warrensville Center Rd Shaker Heights OH 44122-5248

CORNELL, HARRY M., JR. furnishings company executive; b. 1928; married Grad., U. Mo., 1950. With Leggett & Platt, Inc., 1950—, salesman, 1950-53, gen. mgr., 1953-55, v.p., 1955-60, pres., chief exec. officer, from 1960, now chmn., chief exec. officer Mo. Office: Leggett & Platt Inc PO Box 757 1 Leggett Rd Carthage MO 64836-9649

CORNELL, HELEN W. manufacturing company executive; b. 1959; V.p. compressor ops., sec. Gardner Denver, Inc., Quincy, Ill. Office: 1800 Gardner Expy Quincy IL 62305-9364 Fax: 217-228-8247.

CORNELL, ROB, hotel executive; Sr. v.p. Preferred Hotels and Resorts Worldwide, Chgo., 1994—. Office: Preferred Hotels & Resorts Worldwide 311 S Wacker Dr Ste 1900 Chicago IL 60606-6676

CORNELL, WILLIAM DANIEL, mechanical engineer; b. Valley Falls, Kans., Apr. 17, 1919; s. Noah P. and Mabel (Hennessy) C.; m. Barbara L. Ferguson, Aug. 30, 1942; children: Alice Margaret, Randolph William. BS in Mech. Engring., U. Ill., 1942. Registered profl. engr., N.Y. Rsch. engr. Linde Air Products Co., Buffalo, 1942-48, cons. to Manhattan Dist. project, 1944-46; project engr. devel. of automatic bowling machine Am. Machine and Foundry, 1948-55; cons. Gen. Electric Co., Hanford, Wash., 1949-50; project engr. devel. of automatic bowling machine Brunswick Corp., Muskegon, Mich., 1955-59, mgr. advanced engring., 1959-72; mgr. advanced concepts and tech. Sherwood Med. Industries divsn. Am. Home Products Corp., St. Louis, 1972-85; mem. faculty Coll. Engring., U. Buffalo, 1946-47; cons. Cornell Engring., St. Louis, 1985—; mem. faculty Coll. Engring. Washington U., 1993-94. Patentee numerous inventions, including automatic golf and bowling game apparatus, med. instruments; developer new method of measuring hemoglobin and new method of counting platelets in whole blood. Recipient Navy E award, 1945, Manhattan Project Recognition award, 1945, Merit award Maritime Commn., 1945. Republican. Presbyterian Home and Office: 907 Camargo Dr Ballwin MO 63011-1506 E-mail: bbcornell@msn.com.

CORNELL, WILLIAM HARVEY, clergyman; b. Pitts., May 27, 1934; s. Floyd Anderson and Audrey Fern (Wasson) C.; m. Betty Jean Yates, July 24, 1954; children: Deborah Jean, William Mark, Darla Ruth. AA, Central (S.C.) Wesleyan Coll., 1953; AB in Religion, Ind. Wesleyan U., 1956. Ordained to ministry Wesleyan Meth. Ch., 1958. Clergyman Wilgus Wesleyan Meth. Ch., Gypsy, Pa., 1956-59, Wolf Summit (W.Va.) Wesleyan Meth. Ch., 1959-63, Canal Wesleyan Meth. Ch., Utica, Pa., 1968-73, Greenville (Pa.) Wesleyan Meth. Ch., 1973-76, Salem (Ohio) Wesleyan Meth. Ch., 1976-78, Sagamore (Pa.) Wesleyan Meth. Ch., 1963-68, 78-95, Niles (Ohio) Wesleyan Meth. Ch., 1995-2000, ret., 2000—. Mem. mission bd. Allegheny Wesleyan Meth. Connection, 1965—, sec., 1973-98, editor ann. jour., 1973-98, mem. adv. bd., 1978-98; sec. N.W. Indian Bible Sch., Alberton, Mont., 1969—. Republican. Avocations: hunting, travel. Home and Office: PO Box 115 7695 Rte 85 Beyer PA 16211

CORNELSEN, PAUL FREDERICK, manufacturing and engineering company executive; b. Wellington, Kans., Dec. 23, 1923; s. John S. and Theresa Albertine (von Klatt) C.; m. Floy Lila Brown, Dec. 11, 1943; 1 son, John Floyd. Student, U. Wichita, 1939-41, 45-46; BS in Mech. Engring., U. Denver, 1949. With Boeing Airplane Co., 1940-41, Ralston Purina Co., St. Louis, 1946—, v.p. internat. divsn., 1961-63, adminstrv. v.p., gen. mgr. internat. divsn., 1963-64, v.p., 1964-68, dir., 1966—, exec. v.p., 1968-78, vice-chmn. bd., COO, 1978-81, pres. internat. group, 1964-77; pres., CEO Moehlenpah Industries Inc., St. Louis, 1981-82; chmn., CEO Mitek Inc. (formerly Moehlenpah), 1982-93; cons. Cornelsen Assocs., 1993—. Founding mem. L.Am. Agribus. Investment Corp., 1970—; founding mem. industry coop. program UN Agys., Rome; chmn. Point Of Purchase Corp., St. Louis. 1st lt. AUS, World War II, AUS, Korea. Decorated Silver Star. Home: 506 Fox Ridge Rd Saint Louis MO 63131-3402 Office: 1001 Craig Rd Ste 260 Saint Louis MO 63146-6212 E-mail: plcornelsen@earthlink.net.

CORNFELD, DAVE LOUIS, lawyer; b. St. Louis, Dec. 24, 1921; s. Abraham and Rebecca (David) C.; m. Martha Herrmann, May 30, 1943; children: Richard Steven, James Allen, Lawrence Joseph. AB, Washington U., St. Louis, 1942, LLB, 1943. Bar: Mo. 1943. Practice law, St. Louis; ptnr. Husch & Eppenberger, 1954—2001, of counsel, 2001—. Adj. prof. Washington U., 1966-87. Co-author: Missouri Estate Planning, Will Drafting and Estate Administration, 2 vol., 1988, supplement, 2001; editor Law Quar. 1943. Bd. dirs. Jewish Fedn., St. Louis, 1977-80, 83-88, Jewish Ctr. for Aged, 1981-88; mem. adv. com. U. Miami Inst. Estate Planning, 1979—. Served with AUS, 1945-46. Mem. ABA (past chmn. com. taxation income estates and trusts, vice chmn. sect. taxation 1977-80, editor-in-chief Tax Lawyer 1977-80, sr. assoc. editor Probate and Property), St. Louis Bar Assn. (past chmn. taxation com), Am. Law Inst., Am. Coll. Trust and Estate Counsel (regent 1984-90), Am. Coll. Tax Counsel (regent 1980-88), Internat. Acad. Estate and Trust Law, Order of Coif. Jewish (trustee temple 1967-91). Club: Masons. Home: 834 Oakbrook Ln Saint Louis MO 63132-4812 Office: Husch & Eppenberger LLC 190 Carondelet Plz Ste 600 Saint Louis MO 63105-3441 E-mail: doornfel@mvp.net, dave.cornfeld@husch.com.

CORNING, JOY COLE, former state official; b. Bridgewater, Iowa, Sept. 7, 1932; d. Perry Aaron and Ethel Marie (Sullivan) Cole; m. Burton Eugene Corning, June 19, 1955; children: Carol, Claudia, Ann. BA, U. No. Iowa, 1954; hon. degree, Allen Coll. Nursing. Cert. elem. tchr., Iowa. Tchr. elem. sch. Greenfield (Iowa) Sch. Dist., 1951-53, Waterloo (Iowa) Cmty. Sch. Dist., 1954-55; mem. Iowa Senate, Des Moines, 1984-90, asst. Rep. leader, 1989-90; lt. gov. State of Iowa, 1991-99. Past chmn. Nat. Conf. Lt. Govs. Bd. dirs. Inst. for Character Devel.; mem. policy bd. Performing Arts Ctr., U. No. Iowa, also trustee UNI Found.; bd. dirs. Nat. Conf. Cmty. and Justice, Des Moines Symphony, Planned Parenthood of Greater Iowa. Named Citizen of Yr., Cedar Falls C. of C., 1984; recipient ITAG Disting. Svc. to Iowa's Gifted and Talented Students award, 1991, Pub. Svc. award Iowa Home Econs. Assn., 1994, Friend of Math. award Iowa Coun. Tchrs. of Math., 1995, Iowa State Edn. Assn. Human Rights award, 1996, Govs. Affirmative Action award, Spl. Recognition award Nat. Foster Parent Assoc., Des Moines Human Rights Commn. award, Pub. Svc. award Coalition for Family and Children's Svcs in Iowa, Friends of Iowa Civil Rights, Inc. award, Martin Luther King Jr. Lifetime Svc. award, 1999, Svc. award Des Moines Area Religious Coun., 2002; recognized for Extraordinary Advocacy for Children of Iowa chpt. Nat. Com. for Child Abuse, award for leadership Early Care and Edn. Congress, Alumni Achievement award U. No. Iowa; named among YWCA Women of Achievement, 2000. Mem. AAUW, LWV, PEO, Nat. Assn. for Gifted Children (mem. adv. bd. 1991-99), Delta Kappa Gamma, Alpha Delta Kappa. Republican. Mem. United Ch. of Christ. Home: 4323 Grand Ave No 324 Des Moines IA 50312-2443 E-mail: corningj@aol.com.

CORNISH, KENT M. television executive; b. Topeka, Nov. 29, 1954; BS in Journalism, U. Kans., 1976. V.p., gen. mgr. KTKA TV, Topeka, 1991—. Address: KTKA TV PO Box 4949 Topeka KS 66604-0949

CORNWELL, PAUL M., JR. architect; b. Wheeling, W.Va., Jan. 28, 1966; s. Paul M. Sr. and Penny S. (Kain) C. BS, Kent State U., 1988, BArch, 1989. Registered architect, Ohio. Estimator/field rep. Evick Cons., Inc., St. Clairsville, Ohio, summer 1987, summer 1988; intern architect Brubaker/Brandt, Inc., Columbus, 1989-92, Maddox-NBD/Brubaker-Brandt, Inc., Dublin, 1992-93, NBBJ, Columbus, 1993-95, Fanning/Howey Assocs., Dublin, 1995—; ind. contractor Amway Corp., Ada, Mich., 1991—. Architect/engr. C.H.K. Degvel., Belmont, Ohio. Scolar Ruritan Internat., Am. Inst. Architects, Honors Coll. Kent State U. Republican. Lutheran. Avocations: 20th century U.S. history, transportation history, aviation/space flight, model railroading. Home: 2624 Deming Ave Columbus OH 43202 Office: Fanning/Howey Assocs Inc 4930 Bradenton Ave Dublin OH 43017-7599 E-mail: pvcornell@yahoo.com.

CORRADINI, MICHAEL L. engineering educator; BSME, Marquette U., 1975; MS, MIT, 1976, PhD, 1978. With tech. staff Sandia Nat. Labs.; with faculty U. Wis., Madison, 1981—, Wis. disting. prof., assoc. dean for acad. affairs. Cons. adv. com. on reactor safeguards NRC. Named Presdl. Young Investigator in Reactor Safety, 1984. Fellow Am. Nuclear Soc.; mem. NAE. Office: U Wis 2630 Engineering Hall 1415 Engineering Dr Madison WI 53706 E-mail: corradini@engr.wisc.edu.

CORRIGAN, MAURA DENISE, judge; b. Cleve., June 14, 1948; d. Peter James and Mae Ardell (McCrone) Corrigan; m. Joseph Dante Grano, July 11, 1976 (dec.). BA with honors, Marygrove Coll., 1969; JD with honors, U. Detroit, 1973; LLD (hon.) , No. Mich. U., 1999; JD (hon.) , Mercy Law Sch., 2002. Bar: Mich. 1974. Jud. clk. Mich. Ct. Appeals, Detroit, 1973-74; asst. prosecutor Wayne County, 1974-79, asst. U.S. atty., 1979-89, chief appellate divsn., 1979-86, chief asst. U.S. Atty., 1986-89; ptnr. Plunkett & Cooney PC, Detroit, 1989-92; judge Mich. Ct. Appeals, 1992-98, chief judge, 1997-98; justice Mich. Supreme Ct., Detroit, 1999-2001, chief justice, 2001—. Vice chmn. Mich. Com. to formulate Rules of Criminal Procedure, Mich. Supreme Ct., 1982-89; mem. Mich. Law Revision Commn., 1991-98; mem. com. on standard jury instrns., State Bar Mich., 1978-82; lectr. Mich. Jud. Inst., Sixth cir. Jud. Workshop, Inst. CLE, ABA-Cin. Bar Litigation Sects., Dept. Justice Advocacy Inst. Contbr. chpt. to book, articles to legal revs. Vice chmn. Project Transition, Detroit, 1976-92; mem. citizens Adv. Coun. Lafayette Clinic, Detroit, 1979-87; bd. dirs. Detroit Wayne County Criminal Advocacy Program, 1983-86; pres., bd. dirs. Rep. Women's Bus. and Profl. Forum, 1991. Recipient award of merit Detroit Commn. on Human Rels., 1974, Dir.'s award Dept. Justice, 1985, Outstanding Practitioner of Criminal Law award Fed. Bar Assn., 1989, award Mich. Women's Commn., 1998, Grano award, 2001. Mem. Mich. Bar Assn., Detroit Bar Assn., Fed. Bar Assn. (pres. Detroit chpt. 1990-91), Inc. Soc. Irish Am. Lawyers (pres. 1991-92, Achievment award 2001), Federalist Soc. (Mich. chpt.). Office: Mich Supreme Ct 500 Woodward Ave Fl 20 Detroit MI 48226-5498

CORSIGLIA, ROBERT JOSEPH, electrical construction company executive; b. Chgo., Jan. 22, 1935; s. John Robert and Marie Virgina Corsiglia; m. Patricia Ann Ryan, Jan. 26, 1960 (div. Jan. 1984); children: Nancee, Thomas, Karen; m. Emilie Joe Clementz, Sept. 10, 1989. BSEE, Ill. Inst. Tech., Chgo., 1963. Registered profl. engr., Ill., Ind., Calif., Tex., Fla. CEO, pres. Hyre Electric Co. Ind., Highland, 1970-90, JWP/Hyre Electric Co. Ind., Highland, 1990—; CEO Midwestern region JWP Mech./Elec. Svcs. Inc., Oak Brook, Ill., 1991-93; chmn. C & H Engring. Co., Inc., Highland, 1984-90; sec.-treas. Adventures in Travel, 1984-95. Bd. dirs. Bank One, Highland. Bd. dirs. No. Ind. Arts Assn., Munster, 1989-93, v.p. devel., 1990; bd. dirs. N.W. Ind. United Way, Highland, 1985, Chgo. Engring. Found., 1991-97; bd. dirs. IIT Alumni Bd., Chgo., 1985, v.p. adminstrn., 1986; mem. IIT Pres.' Coun., 1985—; mem. Legacy Found. Inc. Lake County, Griffith, Ind., 1993—; mem. exec. bd. Boy Scouts of Am. Calumet Coun., 1993—; pres. Nat. Elec. Contractors Assn., 1975, 76, 77. Served with U.S. Army, 1964-70. Mem. Internat. Brotherhood of Elec. Workers (hon.), Chgo. Pres. Orgn., Young Pres. Orgn., World Pres. Orgn., Union League Club. Republican. Roman Catholic. Avocations: collecting, golf. Home: 8701 Northcote Ave Munster IN 46321-2726

CORSON, KEITH DANIEL, business executive; b. South Bend, Ind., Oct. 27, 1935; Student, Wichita State U., 1958-59. Mgmt. trainee Sears Roebuck & Co., Wichita, Kans., 1959-60; product mgr. Taylor Products div. Tecumseh Products, Inc., Elkhart, Ind., 1960-64; pres., chief ops. officer, coachmen Coachmen Industries, Middlebury, 1964-82; chief exec. officer Robertson's Dept. Stores, South Bend, 1982-83; pres., chief exec. officer Koszegi Products, Inc., 1983-90; pres., chief oper. officer Coachman Industries, Elkhart, Ind., 1990—. Office: Coachman Industries Inc PO Box 3300 Elkhart IN 46515-3300

CORSON, THOMAS HAROLD, manufacturing company executive; b. Elkhart, Ind., Oct. 15, 1927; s. Carl W. and Charlotte (Keyser) C.; m. Dorthy Claire Scheide, July 11, 1948; children: Benjamin Thomas, Claire Elaine. Student, Purdue U., 1945-46, Rennsselaer Poly. Inst., 1946-47, So. Meth. U., 1948-49. Chmn. bd. dirs. Coachmen Industries, Inc., Elkhart, 1965-97, chmn. emeritus, dir., 1997—. Bd. dirs. 1st State Bank, Middlebury, R.C.R. Sci. Inc., Goshen, Ind., Micrology Labs., Inc., Goshen, Great Lakes Capital, L.L.C., Morristown, N.J., Elkhart County Econ. Devel. Corp., Elkhart, Ind.; chmn., sec. Greenfield Corp., Middlebury. Adv. coun. U. Notre Dame; past trustee Ball State U.; dir., past trustee, past vice chmn. Interlochen (Mich.) Arts Acad. and Nat. Music Camp. With U.S. Naval Air Force, 1945-47. Mem. Ind. Mfrs. Assn. (past dir.), Elkhart C. of C. (past bd. dirs.), Ind. C. of C. (past bd. dirs.), Ind. Hist. Soc. (past dir.), Royal Poinciana Golf Club, Elcona Club (past bd. dirs.), 33 Degrees, Mason, Shriners. Methodist. Home: PO Box 340 Middlebury IN 46540-0340 Office: Coachmen Industries Inc PO Box 3300 Elkhart IN 46515-3300 E-mail: tcorson@coachmen.com.

CORTS, JOHN RONALD, minister, religious organization executive; b. Hammond, Ind., Jan. 26, 1936; s. Charles Harold and Hazel (Vernon) Corts; m. Jo-Ann Ketchum, 1956; 1 child, Alicia Beth. BA, Trinity Coll., Clearwater, Fla., 1956. Ordained to ministry Gospel Tabernacle Ch., 1957. Pastor Christian Fellowship Ch., Tampa, Fla., 1957-58; registrar Trinity Coll., Clearwater, 1957; pastor First Evang. Bapt. Ch., St. Petersburg, Fla., 1958-62; exec. dir. Youth for Christ, Tampa, 1962-64; crusade assoc. Billy graham Assn., 1964-80; pastor Idlewild Bapt. Ch., Tampa, 1980-83; pres., COO Billy Graham Evangelistic Assn., Mpls., 1983—. Avocations: sports, drama, journalism. Office: Billy Graham Evangelistic Assn 1300 Harmon Pl Minneapolis MN 55403-1925

CORWELL, ANN ELIZABETH, public relations executive; b. Battle Creek, Mich. d. James Albert Corwell and Marion Elizabeth (Petersen) Shertzer. BA, Mich. State U., 1971, MBA, 1981; cert. fin., Wharton Sch., 1986. Sr. publicist City of Dearborn, Mich., 1972-76; sr. assoc. GM, Detroit, 1976-77, media coord. N.Y.C., 1977, mgr. cmty. rels. Pontiac, Mich., 1977-81, mgr. internal comm., 1981-82; dir. pub. rels. Pillsbury Co., Mpls., 1982-85, Avon Products Inc., N.Y.C., 1985-87; exec. v.p. MECA Internat., Flat Rock, Mich., 1987-95; v.p. coll. rels. William Tyndale Coll., Farmington Hills, 1995—. Dir. Mich. State U. Nat. Alumni Bd. Mem. Pub. Rels. Soc. Am., Women In Comm., Oakland County C. of C. (dir. 1988-91), Dearborn C. of C. (dir. 1989-91). E-mail: acorwell@williamtyndale.edu.

CORWIN, BERT CLARK, optometrist; b. Rapid City, S.D., Oct. 4, 1930; s. Meade and Adeline (Clark) C.; m. Lydia M. Forehand; children: B. Clark II, Kelley Linette Fromm. AS, S.D. State U., 1952; BS, Ill. Coll. Optometry, Chgo., 1956, OD, 1957. Pvt. practice, Rapid City, 1957—. Projects chmn. S.D. Lions Sight and Svc. Found., 1964; chmn. med. adv. com. to S.D. Dept. Pub. Welfare, 1968-76; mem. S.D. Adv. Coun. for Regional Med. and Health Planning, 1971; cons. S.D. Dept. Human Svcs., 1989—; adv. bd. S.D. Dept. of Svc. to Visual Impaired; bd. dirs. Super 8 Motel Developers, Rapid City Regional Airport, v.p., 1999-2000, pres., 2000—; chmn. bd. dirs. Transaction Network, Inc., 1997—; mng. ptnr. Right Line Lake, 1999—. Contbr. articles to profl. jours. Pres. Cleghorn PTA, Rapid City, 1968-70; bd. dirs. Am. Optometric Found., 1989-90, v.p., 1990-94, pres., 1994-96. Recipient Presdl. medal of honor Pres. of Ill. Coll. of Optometry, 1999, Spl. honor Am. Optometric Found. Fellow Am. Acad. Optometry (diplomate contact lens sect., sec.-treas. 1985-86, pres.-elect 1987-88, pres. 1988-90, chmn. 1st internat. meeting 1992, nom. com. 2000-01); mem. Am. Optometric Assn. (exec. com. 1974-76, Am. Optometrist of the Yr. 1993), S.D. Optometric Soc. (pres. 1970-71), North Ctrl. State Optometric Conf. (bd. dirs. 1970-71), Black Hills Optometric Soc. (sec.-treas. 1958-69), S.D. State Bd. Examiners (pres. 1982-85), Nat. Acad. Practice Optometry (sec.-treas. 1990-94, Disting. Practitioners award, co-chmn. 1994-96). Republican. Methodist. Club: Black Hills Water Ski (pres. 1963). Lodges: Masons, Elks, Lions (pres. Rushmore chpt. 1961-62, Robert Tyler award 1998). Avocations: skiing, water skiing, hunting, piloting, public speaking. Home: 5436 Timberline Trl Rapid City SD 57702-1806 Office: 810 Mountain View Rd Rapid City SD 57702-2520

CORWIN, SHERMAN PHILLIP, lawyer; b. Chgo., June 29, 1917; s. Louis C. and Becky (Goodman) Cohen; m. Betty C. Corwin (dec. Jan. 1998); children: Susan M. Rothberg, Laurie L. Grad. valedictorian, Wilson Jr. Coll., 1937; B.A., U. Chgo., 1939, J.D. cum laude, 1941. Bar: Ill. 1941, Mich. 1946, Colo. 1946. Assoc. Lederer, Livingston Kahn & Adsit, Chgo., 1941-43; assoc. Sonnenschein Nath & Rosenthal, 1946-60, ptnr., 1960—, head estate planning and probate group, 1970-88. Editor: Estate Planning Handbook for Lawyers, 6th edit., 1976, 7th edit., 1980 Bd. dirs., officer North Suburban Synagogue Beth El, Highland Park, Ill., 1959-80; bd. dirs. Congregation Moriah, Deerfield, Ill., 1980-84; chmn. profl. adv. com. (estate planning) Jewish Fedn. Met. Chgo., 1985-87. Served to 1st lt. U.S. Army, 1944-46 Fellow Am. Coll. Trust and Estate Counsel; mem. Chgo. Bar Assn. (chmn. trust law com. 1970, chmn. Am. citizenship com. 1955), Chgo. Estate Planning Coun. (pres. 1983), Nu Sigma Kappa (past pres. local chpt.), Nu Beta Epsilon (past pres. local chpt.). Home: 400 E Ohio St Apt 2104 Chicago IL 60611-4615 Office: Sonnenschein Nath Et Al 8000 Sears Tower 233 S Wacker Dr Ste 8000 Chicago IL 60606-6491

COSBEY, ROGER B. federal magistrate judge; b. 1950; BA, Western Mich. U., 1972; JD, U. Toledo, 1975. Bar: Ind. 1975. With Heckner & Assocs., Ligonier, Ind., 1975-81; judge Superior Ct., Noble County, 1982-90; magistrate judge U.S. Dist. Ct. (no. dist.) Ind., Ft. Wayne, 1990—. Presenter in field. Contbr. articles to profl. jours. Maj. JAGC, USAR, 1972-92. Fellow Allen County Bar Assn.; mem. Ind. State Bar Assn., Allen County Bar Assn., Fed. Magistrate Judges Assn., Am. Judicature Soc., Benjamin Harrison Am. Inns of Ct. (pres. Fort Wayne Ind. chpt. 1995-96), Supreme Ct. Historical Soc. E-mail: roger_cosbey.innd.uscourts.gov. Office: 1130 Adair Federal Bldg 1300 S Harrison St Fort Wayne IN 46802-3495

COSCO, JOHN ANTHONY, health care executive, educator, consultant; b. Cin., July 13, 1947; s. Adolph John and Pasqualina Marie (Saluppo) C.; m. Anne Patricia Ward, Aug. 5, 1978; children: Stephen Ward, Justin Thomas. BS, Xavier U., Cin., 1969, MEd, 1972, MBA, 1975; postgrad., U. Cin., 1972; PhD in Health Svcs. and Mgmt., Columbia-Pacific U., 1986. Asst. dir. edn. and staff devel. Jewish Hosp., Cin., 1972-77; exec. dir. Region IX Peer Rev. Systems, Inc., Portsmouth, Ohio, 1977-78, Region II Med. Rev. Corp., Dayton, 1978-81; asst. adminstr., sr. v.p. Mercy Hosp., Tiffin, 1981-87; adminstr. Grafton (W.Va.) City Hosp., 1987-89; sr. v.p., COO The St. Francis Acad., Inc., Salina, Kans., 1989—. Bd. dirs. Sunflower Network, Inc., Salina, Kans., WSFA, Phila.; ptnr. Hos-Con & Assocs., 1974-79; pres. & CEO hale foster & stunning, 1993—; adj. assoc. prof. bus. and health svcs. adminstrn. Kans. Wesleyan U., 1997—. Lt. AUS, 1969-71. Fellow Am. Coll. Health Care Execs. Roman Catholic. Office: St Francis Academy Inc 509 E Elm St Salina KS 67401-2348

COSGRIFF, JAMES ARTHUR, physician; b. Lamberton, Minn., Mar. 18, 1924; s. James Arthur and Elsie Ann (Forster) C. BS summa cum laude, Coll. St. Thomas, 1944; MD, U. Minn., 1946. Diplomate Am. Bd. Family Practice. Intern St. Mary's Hosp., Duluth, Minn.; pvt. practice Olivia, 1949—. With USN, 1947-49. Fellow Am. Acad. Family Physicians; mem. Minn. Acad. Family Physicians (pres. 1963, Merit award 1964), Alpha Omega Alpha. Roman Catholic. Avocations: travel, photography, reading, music. Home: 802 E Park Ave Olivia MN 56277-1361 Office: Olivia Clinic 619 E Lincoln Ave Olivia MN 56277-1349

COSIER, RICHARD A. dean, business educator, consultant; b. Jackson, Mich., May 18, 1947; s. Roy A. and Wilma M. (Braund) C.; m. Rae L. Pettelle, June 14, 1969 (div. Feb. 1985); children: Jeffrey R., Nathan R.; m. Lynn M. Hays, Aug. 30, 1986; children: Courtney M., Kelsey L. BS, Mich. State U., 1969; MBA, Loyola U., 1972; PhD, U. Iowa, 1976. From asst. to assoc. prof. mgmt. Ind. U., Bloomington, 1976-86, prof. mgmt., 1986-92, chairperson, prof. mgmt., 1983-90, assoc. dean for acads., prof. mgmt., 1990-92; dean, Fred E. Brown chair U. Okla., Norman, 1993-99; dean and Leeds prof. mgmt. Purdue U., 1999—. Cons. in field. Contbr. over 75 articles and book chpts. to profl. jours.; inventor patented packaging technique. Mem. Acad. Mgmt., Decision Scis. Inst. Republican. Office: Krannert Sch Mgmt Purdue U West Lafayette IN 47907-1310 Home: 3523 Chancellor Way West Lafayette IN 47906-8808 E-mail: rcosier@mgmt.purdue.edu.

COSLET, BRUCE N. professional football coach; b. Oakdale, Calif., Aug. 5, 1946; s. James A. and Mae C. (Coon) C.; m. Kathleen Joseph; children: Jonathan James, Amy Kathleen. BA, U. of Pacific, 1968. Player Edmonton (Alta., Can.) Eskimos, CFL, 1968; player, capt. Cinn. Bengals, NFL, 1969-76, coach spl. teams, 1981-83, coach wide receivers, 1984-85, coach, offense coord., 1986-89, 95-96; coach spl. teams San Francisco 49ers, 1980; head coach N.Y. Jets, 1990-93, Cincinnati Bengals, 1996—. Owner Coslet Devel., Stockton, Calif., 1977-80. Author: Youth Passing and Receiving, 1989 Named to Pacific Sports Hall of Fame U. Pacific, 1984, Oakdale (Calif.) Sports Hall of Fame, (charter) 1987. Mem. LDS Ch. Avocations: golf, fishing, reading, music. Office: Cincinnati Bengals 1 Paul Brown Stadium Cincinnati OH 45202-3418

COSS, JOHN EDWARD, archivist; b. Spring Valley, Ill., Apr. 2, 1947; s. Edward Francis and Doris (Leonard) C.; m. Sherry Lee Ushman, June 4, 1973 (div. May 1979); 1 child, Stephen John; m. Brenda Lynn Gibson, May 30, 1981; 1 stepchild, Anthony Robert. AA, Ill. Valley C.C., 1967; BA, Northwest Mo. State U., 1970. Sr. archivist Ill. State Archives, Springfield, 1971—2002; ret., 2002. Mem. Ill. Fedn. Archivists, Archival Technicians & Photographers, Springfield Trades & Labor Coun. (del.). Methodist. Avocations: music, reading, golf. Home: 10470 E State Route 54 Buffalo IL 62515-7148 E-mail: jcoss@springnet1.com.

COSS, ROCKY ALAN, lawyer; b. Dayton, Ohio, Apr. 6, 1951; s. Vernon F. and Necia Lea (Shaw) C.; m. Cheryl Sue Kelch, Sept. 9, 1972; children— : Tracey, Derek. B.A., Ohio State, 1973, J.D., 1976. Bar: Ohio, 1976, U.S. Supreme Ct., 1979, U.S. Dist. Ct. (so. dist.) Ohio 1982, U.S. Ct. Appeals (6th cir.) 1983. Sole practice, Hillsboro, Ohio, 1976-81; ptnr. Coss & Greer, Hillsboro, 1982— ; pros. atty. Highland County, Ohio, 1977— . Mem. Steering com. City of Hillsboro, 1980-85; county chmn. Highland County Fund Drive; pres. Highland County Soc. Crippled Children and Adults, 1985-86; mem. enrollment com. Highland County Boy Scouts Am., 1977-78. Fellow Ohio State Bar Found.; mem. Ohio State Bar Assn., Highland County Bar Assn. (pres. 1982), Ohio Pros. Atty's. Assn. (v.p.), Nat. Dist. Atty's. Assn., ABA, Ohio Council Sch. Bd. Attys., Nat. Council Sch. Bd. Attys., Hillsboro Jaycees (v.p. 1978-83). Democrat. Methodist. Lodges: Rotary (pres. 1983-84), Masons, Elks. Home: PO Box 258 Hillsboro OH 45133-0258 Office: 14612 E Main St Hillsboro OH 45133

COSTA, ERMINIO, pharmacologist, cell biology educator; b. Cagliari, Italy, Mar. 9, 1924; s. Oreste and Gigina (Murgia) Costa; divorced; children: Max, Robert Henry, Michael John; m. Ingeborg Hanbauer, July 13, 1973. MD, U. Cagliari, 1947, PhD in Pharmacology, 1953; PhD in Biol. Sci. (hon.) , U. Cagliari, Italy, 1986; DSc (hon.) , Georgetown U., 1992; MD (hon.) , U. Tampere, Finland, 1992. Asst. prof., assoc. prof. U. Cagliari, 1948—54, prof. pharmacology, 1954—56; physician II, med. rsch. assn. Thudichum Psychology Rsch., Galesburg, Ill., 1956—60; vis. scientist NIH, Bethesda, Md., 1960—61; dep. chief lab. chem. pharmacology Nat. Heart Inst., 1961—63, head sect. clin. pharmacology, 1963—65; assoc. prof. pharmacology Columbia U., N.Y.C., 1965—68; chief lab. preclin. pharmacology St. Elizabeth's Hosp., Washington, 1968—85; dir. Fidia-Georgetown Inst. for the Neuroscis. Georgetown U., 1985—94, 1996—; McDonnel vis. prof. neurology Washington U. Sch. Medicine, St. Louis, 1994—; sci. dir., prof. biochemistry in psychiatry U. Ill. at Chgo. Psychiat. Inst., 1996—. Editor Neuropharmacology, 1967, Advanced Biochem. Psychopharmacology, 1968, contbr. 915 articles to profl. jours. Recipient Bennet award and Gold medal, Soc. Biol. Psychiatry, 1990, Gold medal Fed. II Univ., Naples, 1990, Premio Fiuggi award, Fiuggi Rsch. Found., 1988. Mem.: NAS, Am. Soc. Biol. Chemistry and Molecular Biology, Am. Soc. Physiology, Am. Soc. Pharmacology and Exptl. Therapeutics, Academia Nazionale Lincei, Peripatetic Club, Cosmos Club. Office: Psychiatric Ins Univ of Illinois at Chicago 1601 W Taylor St Chicago IL 60612-4310

COSTAS, BOB (ROBERT QUINLAN COSTAS), sportscaster; b. N.Y.C., Mar. 22, 1952; s. John George and Jayne (Quinlan) C.; m. Carole Randall Krummenacher, June 24, 1983; children: Keith Michael, Taylor. Student, Syracuse U., 1970-74. Sportscaster Sta. KMOX-AM, St. Louis, 1974-81; sportscaster, host sports programs NBC Sports, N.Y.C., 1980—. Former host Later with Bob Costas. Recipient 12 Emmy awards, 8 for outstanding sports broadcaster, 2 Emmy awards for writing, 1 Emmy award for interview show, 1996, one for play-by-play broadcast of 1997 World Series; named Nat. Sportscaster of Yr., Nat. Sportscasters and Sportwriters Assn., 1985, 87, 88, 91, 92, 95, 97.

COSTELLO, JERRY F., JR. congressman, former county official; b. Sept. 25, 1949; County bd. chmn. St. Clair County, Ill.; dir. ct. svcs. and probation 20th Jud. Cir. Campaign; chmn. Heart Assn., Belleville, Ill., 1983; vice chmn. Ill. div. United Way, 1984, chmn., 1985; mem. U.S. Congress from 21st (now 12th) Ill. Dist., 1988—; mem. budget com.; mem. transp., infrastructure and sci. coms. Bd. dirs. Ill. Ctr. for Autism; active St. Clair County Big Bros./Big Sisters, Belleville Women's Crisis Ctr., Children's Ctr. for Behavioral Devel.; helped establish St. Clair County chpt. Vets. Outreach Info. Ctr.; mem. East St. Louis Econ. Opportunity Commn., Ill.; vice chmn. Southwestern Ill. Bus. Devel. Fin. Corp., 1985—; bd. dirs. So. Ill. Leadershp Council; pres. Urban Counties Council of Ill. Recipient cert. of Appreciation, Bus. and Profl. Women's Assn., 1985; honored Citizens League for Adequate Social Services; 1985 AAHMES Court #84, Daus. ISIS Ann. Humanitarian award, Gene Hughes award Ill. Ct. Services and Probation Assn. Office: US Ho of Reps 2454 Rayburn House Off Bldg Washington DC 20515-0001*

COSTELLO, JOHN WILLIAM, lawyer; b. Chgo., Apr. 16, 1947; s. William John and June Ester (O'Neill) C.; m. Maureen Grace Matthews, June 13, 1970; children— Colleen, William, Erin, Owen. BA, John Carroll U., 1969; JD, DePaul U., 1972. Bar: U.S. Dist. Ct. (no. dist.) Ill. 1982. Assoc. Arvey, Hodes, Costello & Burman, Chgo., 1972-76; ptnr., 1976-90, ptnr. Wildman, Harrold Allen & Dixon, 1990—. Co-author: (manual) The Bankrupcy Reform Act of 1978, 1981. Served to capt. U.S. Army, 1972-73. Mem. ABA (bus. bankruptcy com., jurisdiction and venue and secured creditors subcoms.), Ill. State Bar Assn. (former vice chmn., chmn. comml. banking and bankrupcy law sect. 1979-81), Am. Bankruptcy Inst., Turnaround Mgmt. Assn. (former bd. dirs. Midwest sect.). Democrat. Roman Catholic. Office: Wildman Harrold Aller & Dixon 225 W Wacker Dr Chicago IL 60606-1224

COSTIGAN, EDWARD JOHN, investment banker; b. St. Louis, Oct. 31, 1914; s. Edward J. and Elizabeth Keane; m. Sara Louise Guth, Mar. 30, 1940 (dec. Nov. 1988); children: Sally, Edward John, James (dec.), Betsy, Robert, David, Louise; m. Mildred F. Fabick, Dec. 27, 1995. AB, St. Louis U., 1935; MBA, Stanford U., 1937. Analyst, v.p. Whitaker & Co., St. Louis, 1937-43; ptnr. Edward D. Jones & Co., 1943-72; sr. v.p. Stifel Nicolaus & Co. Inc., St. Louis, 1972-74, pres., 1974-79, vice chmn., 1979-83, emeritus, 1983, ret., 2001. Gov. Nat. Assn. Securities Dealers, 1967-70, Investment Bankers Assn., 1968-69, Midwest Stock Exch., Chgo., 1962-64; bd. dirs. 12 cos. Trustee Calvary Cemetery Assn., St. Louis, 1956— Mem. St. Louis Soc. Fin. Analysts (pres. 1956), Harvard Club St. Louis (pres. 1955), Bellerive Country Club, Mo. Athletic Club, Old Warson Country Club, Noonday Club, University Club. Republican. Roman Catholic. Office: 501 N Broadway Fl 8 Saint Louis MO 63102-2102

COSTIN, JAMES D. performing arts company executive; BA in Theater, U. Calif., L.A., 1959; MA in Theater, U. Mo., Kansas City, 1966. Cert. German linguist, 1956. Mgr. Fox West Coast Theatres, L.A., Calif., 1954-56; German linguist Army Security Agency, U.S. Army, 1956-59; editor Great Lakes News, 1960-61; asst. stage mgr to stage mgr. Am. Ballet Theatre, 1961-62, co. mgr., 1962-63; asst. gen. mgr. Washington D.C. Ballet Guild/Am. Ballet Theatre, 1963-64; co-founder, adminstrv. dir. Mo. Repertory Theatre, U. Mo., Kansas City, 1964-67; playwright in residence U. Mo., 1966-67, adminstrv. dir. of theatre, 1968-72, asst. to the provost, dir. office of cultural events, 1972-76, asst provost for performing arts mgmt., 1976-79, vice provost, chief academic fiscal officer, 1979—; exec. dir./playwright in residence Mo. Repertory Theatre, Inc., 1979—. Cons. Internat. Theatre Inst., Great Lakes Shakespeare Festival, Kansas City Ballet. Author: (play) Laity, 1964, Lee, 1966, Ageina, 1969, The Curious Adventures of Alice, 1988, Jekyll, 1989; (stage productions) Ageina, The Curious Adventures of Alice, Jekyll; (co-author play with James Lee) The Holy Terror, 1967. Com. mem. Mayor's Com. Save The Starlight Theater, Save the Phiharmonic Orchestra; bd. dirs. State Ballet Mo., Kans. City Arts Coun. Lt. USNR 1968-71. Recipient Best Playwright award UCLA, 1959, Pirouette award, 1987, Mo. Arts award, 2000. Office: Mo Repertory Theatre 4949 Cherry St Ste 307 Kansas City MO 64110-2269

COTHORN, JOHN ARTHUR, lawyer; b. Des Moines, Dec. 12, 1939; s. John L. and Marguerite (Esters) C.; m. Connie Cason, Aug. 6, 1996; children: Jeffrey, Judith. BS in Math., BS in Aero. Engring., U. Mich., 1961, JD, 1980. Bar: Mich. 1981, U.S. Dist. Ct. (ea. dist.) Mich. 1981, U.S. Ct. Appeals (6th cir.) 1981, U.S. Dist. Ct. (we. dist.) Mich. 1986, U.S. Supreme Ct. Exec. U.S Govt., 1965-78; asst. prosecutor Washtenaw County, Ann Arbor, Mich., 1981-82; ptnr. Kitch, Saurbier, Drutchas, Wagner & Kenney P.C., Detroit, 1982-94, Meganck & Cothorn P.C., Detroit, 1994-97, Meganck, Cothorn & Stanczyk P.C., Detroit, 1997-98, Cothorn & Stanczyk, P.C., Detroit, 1998-2000, Cothorn & Braceful, Detroit, 2000—02, Cothorn & Assocs., P.C., Detroit, 2002—. Served to capt. U.S. Army, 1961-65. Mem. ABA, Nat. Bar Assn. (numerous fed. and state coms.), Soc. Automotive Engrs., Assn. Def. Trial Counsel, Phi Alpha Delta. Republican. Avocations: bridge, golf. Office: 535 Griswold St Ste 1525 Detroit MI 48226-3696

COTSONAS, NICHOLAS JOHN, JR. physician, medical educator; b. Boston, Jan. 28, 1919; s. Nicholas John and Louise Catherine (Lapham) C.; m. Betty Borge, Nov. 21, 1970; children by previous marriage: Nicholas III, Bruce, Elena. AB, Harvard, 1940; MD cum laude, Georgetown U., 1943. Intern D.C. Gen. Hosp., Washington, 1944, resident in chest diseases, 1946-47, asst. med. resident, 1947-48, chief med. resident, 1948-49; asst. prof. medicine Georgetown U. Sch. Medicine, 1949-53; chief med. officer, med. divsn. D.C. Gen. Hosp., 1951-53; asst. prof. medicine U. Ill. Coll. Medicine, Chgo., 1953-57, assoc. prof., 1957-62, prof., 1962-70; dean, prof. medicine Peoria Sch. Medicine, U. Ill., 1970-79; prof. medicine U. Ill., Chgo., 1979-90, prof. emeritus, 1989—, assoc. vice chancellor for acad. affairs, 1979-82. Mem. Bradley Assocs., 1972-79; bd. dirs. Ill. Heart Assn., 1972-79, pres., 1976-77; bd. dirs. Ill. Ctrl. Health Sys. Agy., 1976-79, Planned Parenthood Assn. Greater Peoria Area, 1971-79; mem. Statewide Health Coordinating Council, 1978-79; bd. dirs. Chgo. Heart Assn., 1980-82, Inst. Religion and Medicine, 1980; mem. task force on older women Ill. Council on Aging, 1985-86; chmn. Commn. on Health Resources Allocation, Peoria, Ill., 1985-87. Asst. editor: Disease-A-Month, 1960-77; asso. editor, 1977-80, editor, 1980-86, emeritus, 1987. Served to capt. AUS, 1944-46. Recipient Raymond Allen award U. Ill. Coll. Medicine, 1955, Faculty of Yr. award, 1978 Fellow ACP, Am. Heart Assn. (coun. clin. cardiology 1963), Am. Coll. Cardiology, Inst. Medicine Chgo., Am. Geriatrics Soc.; mem. Am. Fedn. Clin. Rsch., Chgo. Soc. Internal Medicine, Harvard Soc. Chemists, Sigma Xi, Alpha Omega Alpha.

COTTER, DANIEL A. diversified company executive; b. Duluth, Minn., Dec. 26, 1934; B.A., Marquette U., 1957; M.B.A., Northwestern U., 1960. With Truserv Corp., Chgo., 1959-99, chmn., CEO; retired, 1999. Office: Truserv Corp 8600 W Bryn Mawr Ave Chicago IL 60631-3579

COTTON, LARRY, ranching executive; Pres. Cotton & Assocs., Howell, Mich. Office: Cotton and Assocs 131 Robin Ct Howell MI 48843-8776

COTTON, W(ILLIAM) PHILIP, JR. architect; b. Columbia, Mo., July 11, 1932; s. William Philip and Frances Barbara (Harrington) C. AB, Princeton U., 1954; MArch, Harvard U., 1960. Registered architect, Mo., Ill. Pvt. practice architecture, St. Louis, 1964—. Author (book) 100 Historic Buildings in St. Louis County, 1970. Treas. New Music Circle, St. Louis, 1968-96, Pub. Revenue Edn. Coun., St. Louis, 1977—; v.p. Music Diversions Soc., St. Louis, 1993—; pres. Collegium Vocale, 1999—. Mem. AIA (Ctrl. States Spl. Honor award 1981, Rozier award for Hist. Preservation 1991), Valley Sailing Club (commodore 1985). Roman Catholic. Home: 5145 Lindell Blvd Saint Louis MO 63108-1221 Office: W Philip Cotton Jr Arch ste 1410 1221 Locust St Saint Louis MO 63103-2364

COTTRELL, DAVID ALTON, school system administrator; b. Lima, Ohio, Sept. 8, 1941; s. Hiram David and Clara Marie (Williams) C.; m. Barbara Jean Campbell, Dec. 28, 1963; children: Richard, Deanna, Lynda. AA, Graceland Coll., 1961; BS in Edn., Bowling Green State U., 1964; MA, Kent State U., 1967; EdD, U. Akron, 1970. Cert. supt., Ohio. Social studies tchr. Fairview High Sch., Fairview Park, Ohio, 1964-68; curriculum rsch. specialist Geauga County Schs., Chardon, 1968-70; asst. supt. Girard (Ohio) City Schs., 1970-75; supt. Northwood (Ohio) Local Schs., 1975-82, Franklin County Ednl. Svc. Ctr., 1982-87, 1987—. Mem. Berea Cable TV Commn., 1987—; chair suburban schs. Greater Cleve. United Way, 1989. Mem. Am. Assn. Sch. Adminstrn., Buckeye Assn. Sch. Adminstrs. (chair profl. rights and responsibility com.), Mid-Am. Assn. Sch. Adminstrs. Avocations: sailing, jogging, golf, tennis. Office: Franklin County Ednl Svc Ctr Edn Dept 1717 Alum Creek Dr Columbus OH 43207-1708

COTTRELL, FRANK STEWART, former lawyer, manufacturing executive; b. Boulder, Colo., July 11, 1942; s. Frank Stewart Sr. and Dorris Mary (Payne) C.; m. Janet Anne Goode, Jan. 8, 1966; children: Kristin, Jeffrey, Steven. AB, Knox Coll., 1964; JD, U. Chgo., 1967. Bar: Ill. 1967. Atty. Deere & Co., Moline, Ill., 1967-77, internat. atty., 1977-80, sr. atty., 1980-82, asst. gen. counsel, 1982-87, assoc. gen. counsel, corp. sec., 1987-91, gen. counsel, sec., 1991-93, v.p., gen. counsel, sec., 1993-98, sr. v.p., gen. counsel, sec., 1998—99. Mem. adv. bd. Butterworth Trust; trustee Knox Coll. Mem. ABA, Ill. Bar Assn., Assn. Gen. Counsel. Office: Deere & Co One John Deere Pl Moline IL 61265-8098

COUCH, DANIEL MICHAEL, healthcare executive; b. Chgo., July 1, 1937; s. Arthur Daniel and Helen Margret (Kreamer) C.; m. Marilee Hermon, Sept. 12, 1958; children: Laura Ann, Mark Allen, Kristina Lynn, Michelle Louise, Daniel Michael Jr. BS in Bus., Ind. U., 1958; MBA, Butler U., 1977. Field examiner Ind. State Bd. Accounts, Indpls., 1959-61; controller Community Hosp., Anderson, Ind., 1961-67; field rep. Am. Hosp. Assn., Chgo., 1967-68; treas./controller Health & Hosp. Corp. of Marion County, Indpls., 1968-71; assoc. adminstr. Winona Meml. Hosp., 1971-78; pres. Huntington (Ind.) Meml. Hosp., 1978-80; dep. exec. dir. Truman Med. Ctr., Kansas City, Mo., 1980-99. Bd. dirs. Nat. Pub. Health and Hosp. Inst., Washington, 1987-90, chmn., 1989. Bd. dirs, mem. exec. com. Labor-Mgmt. Coun., Kansas City, Mo., 1982—, co-chmn, 1991—97; bd. dirs. Greater Kans.City Mental Health Found., 1984—93, pres., 1992—93; bd. dirs. Kans. City Care Ctr., 1990—, treas., 1999—; bd. dirs. Resource Devel. Inst., Kans. City, 1998—; pres., 2002—; bd. dirs. Vis. Nurse Home Care Svcs, Kans. City, 1991—98; chmn., 1993—98. 1st lt. USAR, 1958—67. Fellow Am. Coll. Healthcare Execs. (life fellow, nominating com. 1995-99); mem. Am. Hosp. Assn. (ho. of dels. and Regional Policy Bd. 7 1989-92, governing coun. sect. met. hosps. 1990-93, chmn. 1993), Nat. Assn. Pub. Hosps. (bd. dirs. 1981-99, chmn. 1989), Kansas City Area Hosp. Assn. (bd. dirs. 1990-96), Greater Kansas City C. of C. (various coms. 1985-99), Healthcare Fin. Mgmt. Assn. (advanced), Kansas City Care Network (bd. dirs. 1995-99, pres. 1995-99), Family Health Ptnrs. (bd. dirs. 1995-99), Masons, Rotary. Episcopalian. Avocations: golf, bowling, reading.

COUCH, TIM, professional football player; b. July 31, 1977; s. Elbert and Janice. Football player Cleve. Browns, 1999—. Participant DARA prog., Leslie County; guest spkr. two youth football leagues, 1996-97; guest Chldn's Miracle Network t.v. show. Mailing: Cleveland Browns 76 Lou Groza Blvd. Berea OH 44017

COUGHLAN, GARY PATRICK, pharmaceutical company executive; b. Fresno, Calif., Feb. 14, 1944; s. Edward Patrick and Elizabeth Claire (Ryan) C.; m. Mary Cary Kelley, Dec. 21, 1967; children: Christopher, Sarah, Laura, Claire, Moira. BA, St. Mary's Coll., 1966; MA in Econs., UCLA, 1967; MBA, Wayne State U., 1971. Sr. fin. analyst Burroughs Corp., Detroit, 1969-72; with Dart Industries, L.A., 1972-81, group v.p. field services, 1978-81, v.p. ops. services, 1981, Dart & Kraft Inc., Northbrook, Ill., 1981-82, v.p. fin., contr., 1984-85, sr. v.p. fin. affairs, 1985-86, sr. v.p., CFO, 1986; v.p. fin. retail food group Kraft Inc., Glenview, 1982-84, sr. v.p., CFO, 1986-88; sr. v.p. fin. Kraft Gen. Foods, 1989-90; sr. v.p. fin., CFO Abbott Labs., Abbott Park, Ill., 1990-2001, ret., 2001. Instr. prof. fin. ext. program UCLA, 1974—80; bd. dirs. Arthur J. Gallagher, Itasca, Ill., Gen. Binding Corp., Northbrook, Ill., Hershey (Pa.) Corp., Chgo. Hort. Soc., Glencoe, Ill.; mem. chancellor's adv. bd. U. Ill., Chgo.; mem. adv. coun. Coun. Fgn. Rels., Chgo. Com.; bd. dirs. Hershey Foods, Hershey, Pa. Mem. Fin. Execs. Inst., Econ. Club Chgo. Republican. Roman Catholic. Home: 1135 Central Rd Glenview IL 60025-4432 Office: Abbott Labs 1200 Central Ave Ste 306 Wilmette IL 60091 E-mail: gcoughlan@earthlink.com.

COUGHLAN, KENNETH L. lawyer; b. Chgo., July 8, 1940; s. Edward James and Mary Virginia (Lewis) C.; m. Therese Koziol, Oct. 11, 1981; 1 child, Kevin Edward. BA, U. Notre Dame, 1962; JD, Northwestern U., Chgo., 1966. Bar: Ill. 1967. Trust officer Am. Nat. Bank & Trust Co., Chgo., 1969-72; sec. bd., sr. v.p., gen. counsel, cashier Ctrl. Nat. Bank., 1972-82; sec., gen. counsel Ctrl. Nat. Chgo. Corp., 1976-82; sr. v.p., gen. counsel Exch. Nat. Bank, Chgo., 1982-83; gen. counsel Exch. Internat. Corp., 1982-83; chmn. bd., pres. Union Realty Mortgage Co., Inc., 1981-83; shareholder DeHaan & Richter P.C., 1983-2000; mem. Kelly, Olson, Michod, DeHaan & Richter, L.L.C. Capt. U.S. Army, 1966-68. Fellow Ill. Bar Found.; mem. ABA, Ill. State Bar Assn. (chmn. sect. on comml., banking and bankruptcy law 1981-82), Chgo. Bar Assn. (chmn. fin. instns. com. 1980-81, chmn. comml. fin. com. 1979-80), Lawyers Club (Chgo.). E-mail: kcoughlan@komdr.com.

COULMAN, GEORGE ALBERT, chemical engineer, educator; b. Detroit, June 29, 1930; s. William John Thompson and Mary (Dega) C.; m. Annette Marie Felder, Sept. 1, 1956; children: Karl, Paula. B.S., Case Inst. Tech., 1952, Ph.D. (Ford Found. fellow), 1962; M.S., U. Mich., 1958. Process devel. engr. Dow Corning Corp., Midland, Mich., 1954-57; mgr. devel. Am. Metal Products Co., Ann Arbor, 1958-60; asst. prof. chem. engring. U. Waterloo (Ont., Can.), 1961-64; mem. faculty Mich. State U., East Lansing, 1964-76, prof. chem. engring., 1974-76, Cleve. State U., 1976—, chmn. dept., 1976-85, interim dean engring., 1988-89, dean Coll. of Engring., 1989-96, prof. emeritus, 1996—. Cons. in field. Author numerous papers in field. Served with AUS, 1952-54. Named Engr. of Yr., Nat. Engrs. Week Com., 1995. Mem. AICE, Am. Soc. Engring. Edn., Cleve. Engring. Soc. (bd. govs., 1st v.p.), Ohio Soc. Profl. Engrs. (outstanding engring. educator 1992), Cleve. Tech. Soc. Coun. (Disting. Svc. award 1992). Office: 1963 E 24th St Cleveland OH 44115-2403

COULSON, CHARLES ERNEST, lawyer; b. Belleville, Ill., Oct. 29, 1944; s. Charles Henry and Genevieve (Bell) C.; B.A., Kent State U., 1970; J.D. U. Akron, 1974. Bar: Ohio 1974, U.S. Dist. Ct. (no. dist.) Ohio 1976. Asst. prosecutor Lake County Prosecutor's Office, Painesville, Ohio, 1975-77, chief asst. prosecutor, 1977-79; ptnr. Coulson and Perez, Mentor, Ohio, 1979-82, Davies, Rosplock, Coulson, Perez, Deeb, and Harrell, Willoughby, Ohio, 1982— ; law dir. City of Kirtland, Ohio, 1980— ; parttime instr. bus. and real estate law Lakeland Community Coll., Mentor, 1979— . Served to 1st lt. U.S. Army, 1968-70, Vietnam. Mem. Assn. Trial Lawyers Am., Ohio Acad. Trial Lawyers, Ohio State Bar Assn., Lake County Bar Assn. Office: Davies Rosplock Coulson Perez Deeb and Harrell 4230 State Route 306 Willoughby OH 44094-9274

COULTER, CHARLES ROY, lawyer; b. Webster City, Iowa, June 10, 1940; s. Harold L. Coulter and Eloise (Wheeler) Harrison; m. Elizabeth Bean, Dec. 16, 1961; 1 child, Anne Elizabeth. BA in Journalism, U. Iowa, 1962, JD, 1965. Bar: Iowa 1965. Assoc. Stanley, Bloom, Mealy & Lande, Muscatine, Iowa, 1965-68; v.p. Stanley, Lande & Hunter, 1969—, also bd. dirs. County fin. chmn. Leach for Congress, 1980-96; county coord. George Bush for Pres. , 1980, 88, Reagan-Bush Campaign, 1984. Fellow Coll. of Law Practice Mgmt., Am. Bar Found., Iowa State Bar Found., Am. Coll. Trust and Estate Counsel; mem. ABA (mem. coun. law practice mgmt. sect. 1984-88, sec. 1988-89, vice chair 1989-90, chair 1991-92, chair coord. commn. legal tech. 1994-97, mem. standing com. on tech. and info. sys. 1997-98), Iowa Bar Assn., Muscatine County Bar Assn., Thirty-Three Club (pres. 1981), Rotary, Order of Coif. Episcopalian. Avocation: tennis. Office: Stanley Lande & Hunter 301 Iowa Ave Ste 400 Muscatine IA 52761-3881 E-mail: chuckcoulter@slhlaw.com.

COUNSELL, PAUL S. former advertising executive, counselor; Former CEO, Cramer-Krasselt Co., Milw.; now semi-ret., also counselor. Office: Cramer-Krasselt Co 733 N Van Buren St 4th Fl Milwaukee WI 53202-4799

COUNTRYMAN, DAYTON WENDELL, lawyer; b. Sioux City, Iowa, Mar. 31, 1918; s. Cleve and Susie (Schaeffer) Countryman; m. Ruth Hazen, Feb. 2, 1941 (dec.); children: Karen, Joan, James, Kay. BS, Iowa State Coll., 1940; LLB, State U. Iowa, 1948, JD, 1969. Bar: Iowa 1948. Practiced in, Nevada; ptnr. Hadley & Countryman, Iowa, 1949-64; mem. Countryman & Zaffarano P.C., 1984-87, Dayton Countryman Law Offices, P.C., 1987—; county atty. Story County, Iowa, 1950-54; atty. gen. State of Iowa, 1954-56. Candidate for U.S. Senate, 1956, 1960, 68. Air Force Res. pilot USAAF, 1941-46. Mem. ABA, Iowa Bar Assn., Story County Bar Assn., VFW, Am. Legion, Iowa State U. Alumni Assn. (pres. 1970-71), Iowa 2B Jud. Dist. Assn., Masons, Lions (pres. 1975-76). Methodist. Office: PO Box 28 Nevada IA 50201-0028 E-mail: dcountryman@midiowa.net.

COUNTS, DONALD R. furniture maker; b. St. Louis, May 26, 1961; m. Elizabeth Ann Counts; 5 children. H.S., Salem H.S., 1979. Rep. nom. for U.S. House of Reps., 1994; Rep. candidate 1st dist. Mo. U.S. House Reps., 1996. Apostolic Pentacostal.

COURANT, PAUL NOAH, economist, educator, academic administrator; b. Ithaca, N.Y., Jan. 5, 1948; s. Ernest David and Sara (Paul) Courant; m. Katherine Olive Johnson, Sept. 21, 1969 (dissolved 1984); children: Ernest Mendel, Noah Albert; m. Marta Ann Manildi, Jan. 30, 1988; 1 stepchild Samuel Robinson Manildi. BA, Swarthmore Coll., 1968; MA, Princeton U., 1972, PhD, 1973. Jr. economist Coun. Econ. Advisers, Washington, 1969—70, sr. economist, 1979—80; asst. prof. econs., pub. policy U. Mich., Ann Arbor, 1973—78, assoc. prof., 1978—84, prof. econs. and pub. policy, 1984—, dir. Inst. Pub. Policy Studies, 1983—87, 1989—90, chmn. econs. dept., 1995—97, assoc. provost, 1997—2001, interim provost, exec. v.p. acad. affairs, 2002—. Mem. task force long-term econ. growth State of Mich., 1983—84; cons. Mich. Dept. Commerce, Lansing, 1984—85, Congl. Budget Office, Washington, 1988—89; bd. dirs. Mich. Future. Author: (book) America's Great Consumption Binge, 1986; co-author: Economics, 1973, Economics, 11th edit., 1996; contbr. articles to profl. jours. Bd. dirs. Ctr. Watershed and Cmty. Health, Eugene, Oreg., 1997—. Grantee, NSF, 1976—77, 1979—81, 1994—97, Rockefeller Found., 1985—87, Nat. Cancer Inst., 1992—95. Mem.: Nat. Tax Assn., Assn. Pub. Policy Analysis and Mgmt. (mem. policy coun. 1994—98), Am. Econ. Assn. Avocations: sailing, skiing, tennis, hiking, clarinet. Office: Univ Mich 3060 Fleming Bldg Ann Arbor MI 48109-1340 E-mail: pncourant@netscape.net.

COURTICE, THOMAS BARR, academic administrator; b. Dayton, Ohio, Oct. 31, 1943; s. Allyn J. and Mary Louise (Barr) C.; children: Heather, Ryan, Lindsey; m. Lisa Schweitzer. BS, U. Pitts, 1965; MBA, Ind. U., 1967; PhD, U. Minn., 1974; cert. Inst. Edn. Mgmt., Harvard U., 1977. Dir. placement, instr. Econs. Hamline U., St. Paul, 1967-69, asst. to pres., 1969-75, v.p. for univ. affairs, 1975-77; pres. Westbrook Coll., Portland, Maine, 1977-86, W.Va. Wesleyan Coll., Buckhannon, 1986-94, Ohio Wesleyan U., Delaware, 1994—. Accreditation evaluator North Ctrl. and New Eng. Assn. Schs. and colls., 1980—; mem. exec. com. Found. for Ind. Higher Edn., 1994—, NCAA Pres. Commn. Divsn. III, 1998-2002; bd. dirs. Ednl. and Instnl. Ins. Adminstrs., Inc. Trustee Waynflete Sch., Portland, 1980-86, Portland Symphony Orch, 1982-86, Delaware Cmty. Found., 1996— Bush Found. summer fellow, St. Paul, 1977. Mem. Nat. Assn. Ind. Colls. and Univs. (bd. dirs. and exec. com. 1993), Nat. Assn. Schs. and Colls. of the United Meth. Ch. (bd. dirs., pres. 1996-97), Appalachian Coll. Assn. (pres. 1992-94). Home: 135 Oak Hill Ave Delaware OH 43015-2519 Office: Office of Pres Ohio Wesleyan Univ Delaware OH 43015 E-mail: tbcourti@cc.owu.edu.

COURTNEY, DAVID W. chemical company executive; Exec. v.p., dir. mktg. Chemcentral, Bedford Park, Ill., exec. v.p., COO, 1997-98, CEO, 1998—. Office: Chemcentral 7050 W 71st St Bedford Park IL 60638-5902

COURTNEY, EUGENE WHITMAL, computer company executive; b. East St. Louis, Ill., Jan. 3, 1936; s. Eugene and Goldie Genell (Mitchell) C.; m. Barbara Ann Beckwith, Aug. 1, 1959; children: Kevin Eugene, Kyle Patrick. BSEE, Princeton U. with honors, 1957. Exec. v.p., gen. mgr., dir. Digital Sci. Corp., San Diego, 1970-75, pres., CEO, 1975-79; dir. Digital Sci./Europe, 1975-79; v.p. corp. devel. Topaz, Inc., San Diego, 1979, Nat. Computer Sys., Mpls., 1980-81, v.p., gen. mgr. scanning divsn., 1981-83, group v.p., 1983-88; exec. v.p., COO, dir. HEI Inc., Victoria, 1988-90, pres., CEO, 1990-99; dir., 1989-2000; prin. and dir. Triangle Industries, Inc., 1988—; pres., CEO RSI Sys., Edina, Minn., 1999-2001; prin. E.W. Courtney & Assocs., 2001—. Bd. dirs. DRS Data and Rsch. Svcs. plc, Milton Keynes, Eng., SFT Solutions From Tech., Mpls., Datakey, Inc., Mpls.; mem. Minn. Software Tech. Com., 1985-86. Contbr. articles to profl. jours. Trustee, v.p. engring. San Diego Hall of Sci., 1974-79; mem. State of Calif. gov.'s task force on edn. and industry, 1977-78; mem. Rancho Santa Fe (Calif.) Park and Recreation Bd., 1978; mem. tech. adv. bd. Minn. Dept. Corrections, Shakopee, 1985-86. Am. Electronics Assn. (nat. bd. dirs., chmn. San Diego coun. 1976-79, chmn. Minn. coun. 1993-96), Princeton Club (N.Y.C.). Republican. Avocation: print collecting. Home and Office: 7312 Claredon Dr Minneapolis MN 55439-1722

COUSINS, WILLIAM, JR. judge; b. Swiftown, Miss., Oct. 6, 1927; s. William and Drusilla (Harris) C.; m. Hiroko Ogawa, May 12, 1953; children: Cheryl Akiko, Noel William, Yul Vincent, Gail Yoshiko. BA, U. Ill., 1948; LLB, Harvard U., 1951. Bar: Ill. 1953, U.S. Dist. Ct. (no. dist.) Ill. 1961, U.S. Supreme Ct. 1975. Title examiner Chgo. Title & Trust Co., 1953-57; asst. state's atty. Cook County, Ill., 1957-61; sole practice Chgo., 1961-67; judge Circuit Ct. Cook County, 1976-92; justice Ill. Appeallate Ct., 1992—. Chair exec. com. 1st Dist. Appellate Ct., 1997—; lectr. DePaul Law Sch., Chgo.; bd. dirs. Nat. Ctr. State Cts., 1996—; faculty advisor Nat. Jud. Coll., 1987; mem. exec. com. Ill. Jud. Conf., 1983, former chmn. exec.

com.; liaison assoc. judge coordinating com.; former chmn. Ill. Jud. Coun. Bd. dirs. Ind. Voters Ill., 1964-67, Ams. for Dem. Action, 1968, Operation PUSH, 1971-76, Nat. Ctr. for State Cts.; mem. Chgo. City Coun., 1967-76; del. Dem. Nat. Conv., 1972; asst. moderator United Ch. of Christ, N.Y.C., 1981. Served with U.S. Army, 1951-53. Decorated Army Commendation medal; named Judge of Yr., John Marshall Law Sch., Chgo., 1980; recipient Thurgood Marshall award Ill. Jud. Coun., 1992, Earl Burris Dickerson award Chgo. Bar Assn., 1998, C. Francis Stradford award, 2001. Mem. ABA, Nat. Bar Assn. (jud. coun., Raymond Pace Alexander award 1999, Hall of Fame 1994), Ill. Bar Assn., Cook County Bar Assn. (former bd. dirs., Edward N. Wright award 1968, William R. Ming award 1974, Hall of Fame 1997), Alpha Kappa Alpha (Monarch award for Statesmanship 1995), Kappa Alpha Psi, Sigma Pi Phi, Delta Sigma Rho. Home: 1745 E 83rd Pl Chicago IL 60617-1714 Office: Ill Appellate Ct 160 N La Salle St Rm 1905 Chicago IL 60601-3103

COVALT, ROBERT BYRON, chemicals executive; b. Chgo., Nov. 8, 1931; s. Byron L. and Thelma A. (Adams) C.; m. Virginia, Aug. 17, 1952; children: Karen Elizabeth Ryberg, David Byron. BSChemE, Purdue U., 1953, DEng (hon.), 1992; MBA, U. Chgo., 1967. Devel. engr. B.F. Goodrich Chem. Co., Avon Lake, Ohio, 1953-54; with Morton Chem. div. Morton Thiokol, Inc., 1956—, v.p. engring. and mfg., 1973-78, group v.p., 1978-79, pres., 1979-87; pres. specialty chems. group, group v.p. Morton Thiokol, Inc., 1987-89; pres. splty. chems. group, group v.p. Morton Internat. Inc., 1989-90, exec. v.p., 1990-94; pres., CEO, chmn. Sovereign Specialty Chems., Inc., 1994—. Bd. dirs. CFC Internat. Trustee N. Cen. Coll., Naperville, Ill. Served as 1st lt. USAF, 1954-56. Recipient Disting. Engring. Alumnus award Purdue U. Mem. AIChE, Am. Chem. Soc. Home: 7517 Bull Valley Rd Mchenry IL 60050-7493 Office: Sovereign Splty Chems Inc 225 W Washington St Ste 2200 Chicago IL 60606-3408

COVAULT, LLOYD R., JR. retired hospital administrator, psychiatrist; b. Troy, Ohio, Feb. 3, 1928; s. Lloyd R. and Anne Marie (Grisez) C.; m. Janet Eileen Davidson, June 12, 1951; children: Sheryl Ann, Jane Helen, Michael Lee, Roger Ken. BA, Miami U., Oxford, Ohio, 1950; MD, Ohio State U., 1954. From extern to asst. supt. Orient (Ohio) State Inst., 1953-70; pvt. practice, Columbus, 1968-75; psychiat. trainee Ctrl. Ohio Psychiat. Hosp., 1966-68, psychiatrist, 1982-85; supt. Columbus State Inst., 1970-74; med. dir. North Ctrl. Cmty. Mental Health Ctr., Columbus, 1974-79, cons. psychiatry, 1985-90; assoc. prof. psychiatry Ohio State U. Med. Sch., 1975-76; cons. psychiatry North Ctrl. Cmty. Mental Health Ctr., Columbus, 1985-90; from dir. to cons. psychiatrist S.E. Mental Health Ctr., 1979-97, cons. psychiatrist, 1986-97; med. dir. Charles B. Milles Mental Health Ctr., Marysville, Ohio, 1989-95; psychiat. cons. Union Manor Nursing Home, 1996-98; ret., 1999. Mem. Franklin County Mental Health and Retardation Bd., 1970-74, Ohio Dept. Mental Health, ret. 1984; cons. psychiatrist Madison County Mental Health Ctr., London, 1984-85, Chillecothe VA Hosp., 1995-99; staff psychiatrist Ohio Correction Complex, Orient, 1988-89; 1st med. coord. Netcare Admission Unit Ctrl. Ohio Psychiat. Hosp., 1985-87; founding father Physicians Assn. Ohio Dept. Mental Health, 1956-68, pres. 1957; psychiatrist, cons. Buckeye Ranch for Children and Adolescents, Grove City, Ohio, 1998-99. Recipient Union County Pillar award, 1991; named Ohio's Disting. Rural Practitioner, Ohio State Dept. Health, 1993. Fellow Am. Assn. Mental Retardation (life, chmn. adminstrn. state chpt. 1974-75), Am. Psychiat. Assn. (life); mem. Ohio Psychiat. Assn., Neuropsychiat. Soc. Ctrl. Ohio (pres. 1973-74), Mental Health Supts. Assn. (pres. Ohio chpt. 1973-74). Home: 11092 Darby Creek Rd Orient OH 43146-9797

COVINGTON, ANN K. former state supreme court justice; b. Fairmont, W.Va., Mar. 5, 1942; d. James R. and Elizabeth Ann (Hornor) Kettering; m. James E. Waddell, Aug. 17, 1963 (div. Aug. 1976); children: Mary Elizabeth Waddell, Paul Kettering Waddell; m. Joe E. Covington, May 14, 1977. BA, Duke U., 1963; JD, U. Mo., 1977. Bar: Mo. 1977, U.S. Dist. Ct. (we. dist.) Mo. 1977. Asst. atty. gen. State of Mo., Jefferson City, 1977-79; ptnr. Covington & Maier, Columbia, Mo., 1979-81, Butcher, Cline, Mallory & Covington, Columbia, 1981-87; justice Mo. Ct. Appeals (we. dist.), Kansas City, 1987-89, Mo. Supreme Ct., 1989—2001, chief justice, 1993-95. Bd. dirs. Mid Mo. Legal Services Corp., Columbia, 1983-87; chmn. Juvenile Justice Adv. Bd., Columbia, 1984-87. Bd. dirs. Ellis Fischel State Cancer Hosp., Columbia, 1982-83, Nat. Ctr. for State Cts., 1998—; chmn. Columbia Indsl. Revenue Bond Authority, 1984-87; trustee United Meth. Ch., Columbia, 1983-86, Am. Law Inst., 1998—. Recipient Citation of Merit, U. Mo. Law Sch., 1993, Faculty-Alumni award U. Mo., 1993; Coun. of State Govt. Toll fellow, 1988. Fellow Am. Bar Found.; mem. ABA (jud. adminstrv. divsn., mem. adv. com. on Evidence Rules, U.S. Cts.), Mo. Bar Assn., Boone County Bar Assn. (sec. 1981-82), Am. Law Inst., Acad. Mo. Squires, Order of Coif (hon.), Mortar Bd. (hon.), Phi Alpha Delta, Kappa Kappa Gamma. Home: 1201 Torrey Pines Dr Columbia MO 65203-4825 Office: 101 High St Jefferson City MO 65101*

COVINGTON, GEORGE MORSE, lawyer; b. Lake Forest, Ill., Oct. 4, 1942; s. William Slaughter and Elizabeth (Morse) C.; m. Shelagh Tait Hickey, Dec.28, 1966 (div. May 1995); children: Karen Morse, Jean Tait, Sarah Ingersoll Covington; m. Barbara Schilling Trentham, Dec. 19, 1998. AB, Yale U., 1964; JD, U. Chgo., 1967. Assoc. Gardner, Carton & Douglas, Chgo., 1970-75, ptnr., 1976-95; atty. pvt. practice, Lake Forest, Ill., 1995—. Lectr. in field. Contbr. articles to profl. jours. Active Grant Hosp. of Chgo., 1974-95, chmn. of bd. 1990-95; bd. dirs. Grant Healthcare Found., 1995—, chmn. 1999—; trustee Chgo. Acad. Sci., 1974-85, pres., 1980-82; trustee, chmn. Ill. chpt. Nature Conservancy, Chgo., 1974-88; bd. dirs. Latin Sch Chgo., 1979-80, Open Lands Project, Chgo., 1972-86, Chgo. Farmers, 1994-96; bd. dirs., sec. Lake Forest Open Lands Assn., 1984—; bd. dirs., sec., treas. Les Cheneaux Found., 1978—; bd. dirs. Student Conservation Assn., 1996—, Little Traverse Conservancy, 1998—, vice chmn., 1999—; mem. Bd. Fire and Police Commrs., Village of Lake Bluff, Ill., 1991—. With U.S. Army, 1967-69. Mem. ABA, Ill. Bar Assn., Lake County Bar Assn., Chgo. Bar Assn., Univ. Club (bd. dirs. 1985-88), Commonwealth Club, Legal Club, Shoreacres (Lake Bluff, Ill.), Les Cheneaux Club (Cedarville, Mich.), Lambda Alpha. Office: 500 N Western Ave Ste 204 Lake Forest IL 60045-1955

COWEN, ROY CHADWELL, JR. language educator, educator; b. Kansas City, Mo., Aug. 2, 1930; s. Roy Chadwell and Mildred Frances (Schuetz) Cowen; m. Hildegard Bredemeier, Oct. 6, 1956 (dec.); 1 child Ernst Werner (dec.). BA, Yale U., 1952; PhD, U. Gottingen, Federal Republic of Germany, 1960. Instr. U. Mich., Ann Arbor, 1960-64, asst. prof., 1964-67, assoc. prof., 1967-71, prof., 1971—, chmn. dept. Germanic langs., 1979-85. Author: (book) Christian Dietrich Grabbe, 1972, Naturalismus Kommentar zu einer Epoche, 1973, Hauptmann Kommentar zum dramatischen Werk, 1981, Poetischer Realismus: Kommentar zu einer Epoche, 1985, Das deutsche Drama im 19. Jahrhundert, 1988, Christian Dietrich Grabbe-Dramatiker ungeloster Widersprueche, 1998. With USN, 1952—56. Decorated Sr. Officer's Cross Federal Republic of Germany; recipient Williams Tchg. award, U. Mich., 1967; fellow Sr., NEH, 1972—73. Mem.: MLA, Internationale Vereinigung fur Germanistik. Democrat. Methodist. Home: 2874 Baylis Dr Ann Arbor MI 48108-1764 Office: U Mich Dept Germanic Langs/Lits Ann Arbor MI 48109 E-mail: rcowen@umich.edu.

COWLES, JOHN, JR. publisher, women's sports promoter; b. Des Moines, May 27, 1929; s. John and Elizabeth (Bates) C.; m. Jane Sage Fuller, Aug. 23, 1952; children: Tessa Sage Flores, John, Jane Sage, Charles Fuller. Grad., Phillips Exeter Acad., 1947; AB, Harvard U., 1951; LittD (hon.), Simpson Coll., 1965. With Cowles Media Co. (formerly Mpls. Star and Tribune Co.), 1953-83, v.p., 1957-68, editor, 1961-69, pres., 1968-73, 79-83, editorial chmn., 1969-73, chmn., 1973-79, dir., 1956-84; pres. Harper's Mag., Inc., 1965-68, chmn. bd., 1968-72; dir. Harper & Row, Pubs., Inc., N.Y.C., 1965-81, chmn., 1968-79. Dir. Des Moines Register & Tribune Co., 1960-84, Farmers & Mechanics Savs. Bank, Mpls., 1960-65, Cowles Comms., Inc., N.Y.C., 1960-65, Equitable Life Ins. Co. Iowa, Des Moines, 1964-66, 1st Bank Systems, Inc., Mpls., 1964-68, A.P., N.Y.C., 1966-75, Midwest Radio-TV, Inc., Mpls., 1967-76; fitness instr. Sweatshop Fitness Ctr., St. Paul, 1989-93; guest artist Bill T. Jones/Arnie Zane & Co., 1990-92; vice chmn. Women's Pro. Softball League, Denver, 1994—. Mem. adv. bd. on Pulitzer Prizes, Columbia U., 1970-83; campaign chmn. Mpls. United Fund, 1967; bd. dirs. Guthrie Theatre Found., 1960-71, pres., 1960-63, chmn., 1964-65; trustee Phillips Exeter Acad., 1960-65; bd. dirs. Walker Art Ctr., 1960-69, 87-92, Minn. Civil Liberties Union, 1956-61, Urban Coalition Mpls., 1968-70, Mpls. Found., 1970-75, German Marshall Fund U.S., 1975-78; bd. dirs. Am. Newspaper Pubs. Assn., 1975-77, mem. govt. affairs com., 1976-79. Served to 2d lt. AUS, 1951-53. Named one of Ten Outstanding Men of Yr. U.S. Jr. C. of C., 1964. Mem. Greater Mpls. C. of C. (dir. 1978-81, chmn. stadium site task force 1977-82). Clubs: Minneapolis (Mpls.). Office: 123 N 3rd St Ste 804 Minneapolis MN 55401-1668

COWLES, JOHN, III, management consultant, investor; b. Mpls., Nov. 1, 1953; s. John Jr. and Jane Sage (Fuller) C.; m. Elizabeth Page Knudsen, Sept. 8, 1984; children: Lucia, Colin, Maxwell. BA in Govt. cum laude, Harvard U., 1981, MBA, 1983. Pres., CEO Classic Printers, Prescott, Ariz., 1975-79, chmn., 1979-96; cons. Office Cable Comm. Boston City Hall, 1980-81; dir. planning Cowles Media Co., Mpls., 1985-88, vice chmn. bd. dirs., 1991-93, chmn. bd. dirs., 1993-98; dir. fin. analysis United Satellite Comm., Inc., N.Y.C., 1983-85; v.p. Sentinel Pub. (divsn. Cowles Media Co.), Denver, 1988-91, Book Ventures, Inc., Mpls., 1992-93; pres., CEO Women's Pro Softball, 1993-95, chmn. bd., 1993—. Bd. dirs. St. Paul Riverfront Corp., chmn., 1998—; bd. dirs. Capital City Partnership. Bd. dirs. Minn. Ctr. Book Arts, Mpls., 1991-98, chmn. bd. dirs., 1995-98, acting exec. dir., 1995-97; bd. dirs. Prescott Coll., 1976-82, Mpls. Found., 1987-88, Guthrie Theater, Mpls., 1993-98. Mem. Harvard Bus. Sch. Club. Minn., Mpls. Club, Minn. Club. Office: Unity Ave Assoc Ste 804 123 N 3d St Minneapolis MN 55401

COWLES, ROBERT L. state legislator; b. July 31, 1950; BS, U. Wis., Green Bay, 1975. Mem. from dist. 75 Wis. State Assembly, Madison, 1983-87; mem. from dist. 2 Wis. Senate, 1987—. Mem. Gov.'s Coun. on Recycling and Environ. Edn. Bd.; mem. joint com. on fin. Wis. House Reps. Office: 300 W Saint Joseph St Green Bay WI 54301-2328

COWLES, RONALD EUGENE, church administrator; b. Ottumwa, Iowa, Jan. 30, 1941; s. Fred Howard and Bertha Ilela (Sammons) C.; m. Rowena Rae Miller, Apr. 30, 1959; children: Richard Eric, David Allen, Rebecca Ruth. BA, Ottawa (Kans.) U., 1963; BD, MDiv, Ctrl. Bapt. Theol. Sem., Kansas City, Kans., 1966; D of Ministry, U. Bibl. Studies, 1991. Pastor Dry Ridge Bapt. Ch., Uniontown, Kans., 1961-63, First Bapt. Ch., Easton, 1963-66, Renwick (Iowa)-Corwith Parish, 1966-72, First Bapt. Ch., Pella, Iowa, 1972-86; assoc. exec. min. S.D. Bapt. Conv., Sioux Falls, 1986-91; exec. min. Am. Bapt. Chs. Dakotas, 1991—. Bd. trustees Sioux Falls Coll., Ctrl. Bapt. Theol. Sem., Kansas City. Mem. Lions (pres. 1971), Rotary (bd. dirs. 1980-82). Avocations: fishing, hunting, photography, canoe camping. Office: Am Bapt Chs 1524 S Summit Ave Sioux Falls SD 57105-1632

COWLEY, ALLEN WILSON, JR. physiologist, educator; b. Harrisburg, Pa., Jan. 21, 1940; m. Theresa Ann Malinoski BA, Trinity Coll., Hartford, Conn., 1961; MS, Hahnemann Med. Coll., Phila., 1965, PhD, 1968. Instr. physiology and biophysics U. Miss. Med. Ctr., Jackson, 1968-69, asst. prof. physiology and biophysics, 1969-72, assoc. prof. physiology and biophysics, 1973-75, prof. physiology and biophysics, 1975-80; prof. physiology, chmn. physiology dept. Med. Coll. Wis., Milw., 1980—; chmn. dept. physiology Marquette U., 1990—. Lectr. and invited spkr. in field; organizer various confs. Mem. editl. bd. Clin. and Exptl. Hypertension, 1977—, Am. Jour. Physiology: Circulation Sect., 1979-83, Hypertension, 1980-91, 93—, Am. Jour. Physiology: Regulatory, Integrative and Comparative Physiology, 1984-88, Internat. Jour. Cardiology, 1985—, Am. Jour. Physiology: Heart and Circulatory Physiology, 1987-89, Clin. Exptl. Pharmacology Physiology, 1993-96, Jour. Hypertension, 1993-96, Physiol. Revs., 1997—, News in Physiol. Scis., 1997—, assoc. editor 1988-91; guest editor Hypertension, Ann. Supplement Procs. Coun. for High Blood Pressure Rsch., 1981-84; contbr. 30 chpts. to books and symposia, over 180 articles to profl. jours. and conf. procs. Recipient numerous NIH rsch. grants, 1971—; recipient Established Investigatorship award Am. Heart Asnsn., 1973-78, Alumnus of Yr. award Hahnemann Med. Coll., 1975, MERIT award NIH, 1996. Fellow Am. Heart Assn. Coun. High Blood Pressure Rsch. (chmn. publs. com. 1982-84, mem. various coms., Disting. Achievement award 1996, Novartis award 1997), Am. Heart Assn. Coun. on Circulation (various coms.), Am. Physiol. Soc. Cardiovasc. Sect.; mem. Am. Physiol. Soc. (various coms., pres.-elect 1996-97, pres. 1997—, Ernest H. Starling Disting. lectureship 1996, Wiggers award 1997), Internat. Soc. Hypertension, Am. Soc. Nephrology, Microcirculation Soc., Assn. Chairmen Depts. Physiology (various offices and coms., pres. 1990), Hungarian Physiol. Soc. (hon.), Brazilian Acad. Sci. (hon.), Sigma Xi. Office: Med Coll Wisconsin Dept Physiology 8701 W Watertown Plank Rd Milwaukee WI 53226-3548

COWLISHAW, MARY LOU, state legislator; b. Rockford, Ill., Feb. 20, 1932; d. Donald George and Mildred Corinne (Hayes) Miller; m. Wayne Arnold Cowlishaw, July 24, 1954; children: Beth Cowlishaw McDaniel, John, Paula Cowlishaw Rader. BS in Journalism, U. Ill., 1954; DHL, North Ctrl. Coll., 1999; DHL (hon.), Benedictine U., 2000. Mem. editorial staff Naperville (Ill.) Sun newspaper, 1977-83; mem. Ill. Ho. of Reps., Springfield, 1983—, chmn. elem. and secondary edn. com., 1995—, vice-chmn. pub. utilities com., 1995—, mem. joint Ho.-Senate edn. reform oversight com., 1985—. Mem. Ill. Task Force on Sch. Fin., 1990—; vice chmn. Ho. Rep. Campaign Com., 1990—; co-chair Ho. Rep. Policy Com., 1991—; chmn. edn. com. Nat. Conf. State Legislatures, 1993—; mem. Joint Com. Adminstrv. Rules, 1992—; commr. Edn. Commn. of the States, 1995—; chair, Ill. Women's Agenda Task Force, 1994—; mem. Nat. Edn. Goals Panel, 1996—, bd. govs. Lincoln Series for Excellence in Pub. Svc., 1996—. Author: This Band's Been Here Quite a Spell, 1983. Mem. Naperville Dist. 203 Bd. Edn., 1972-83; co-chmn. Ill. Citizens Coun. on Sch. Problems, Springfield, 1985—. Recipient 1st pl. award Ill. Press Assn., 1981, commendation Naperville Jaycees, 1986, Golden Apple award Ill. Assn. Sch. Bds., 1988, 90, 92, 94, Outstanding Women Leaders of DuPage County award West Suburban YWCA, 1990, Activator award Ill. Farm Bur., 1996, 1998, Bd. of Dirs. award Little Friends, Inc., 1998; named Best Legislator, Ill. Citizens for Better Care, 1985, Woman of Yr., Naperville AAUW, 1987, Best Legislator, Ill. Assn. Fire Chiefs, 1994, Outstanding Edn. Adv. Indian Prairie Sch. Dist. 204, 1994, Legislator of Yr., Ill. Assn. Pk. Dists., 1995; commr. Edn. Commn. of the States, 1994—; Mary Lou Cowlishaw Elem. Sch. named in her honor, 1997, Legislator of Yr., Ill. Assn. Mus., 1998. Mem. Am. Legis. Exch. Coun., Conf. Women Legislators, Nat. Fedn. Rep. Women, DAR, Naperville Rep. Women's Club (pres. 1994—), Jr. League of Greater DuKane (cmty. adv. bd. 1997—). Methodist. Avocation: the violin. Home: 924 Merrimac Cir Naperville IL 60540-7107 Office: 552 S Washington St Ste 119 Naperville IL 60540-6669

COX, ALLAN JAMES, management consultant; b. Berwyn, Ill., June 13, 1937; s. Brack C. and Ruby D. C.; m. Jeanne Begalke, 1961 (div. 1966); 1 child, Heather; m. Bonnie Lynne Welden, 1966 (div. 1990); 1 child, Laura; m. Cheryl Patric, 1991. B.A., No. Ill. U., 1961, M.A., 1962; postgrad., McCormick Theol. Sem., Chgo., 1962-63, Alfred Adler Inst. of Chgo., 1965-67, Gestalt Inst. of Chgo., 1994-96. Instr. Wheaton (Ill.) Coll., 1963-65; assoc. Case and Co., Inc., Chgo., 1965-66, Spencer Stuart & Assos., Inc., Chgo., 1966-68; v.p. Westcott Assos., Inc., 1968-69; founder, pres. Allan Cox & Assocs., Inc., 1969—; chmn. Berryman Comm. Co., Chgo., 1994-98; chmn. of the bd. Amateur Baseball, Inc., 1992-96, CEO, 1996-98; chmn., CEO Assn. for Internat. Youth Sports, Inc., 1998-99. Adj. staff Ctr. for Creative Leadership, Greensboro, N.C., 1985-90; mem. vis. com. U. Chgo. Div. Sch.; chancellor's associate Univ. Calif., San Diego. Author: Confessions of a Corporate Headhunter, 1973, Work, Love and Friendship, 1974, The Cox Report on the American Corporation, 1982, The Making of the Achiever, 1985, The Achiever's Profile, 1988, Straight Talk for Monday Morning, 1990, Redefining Corporate Soul: Linking Purpose and People, 1996; columnist L.A. Times Syndicate, 1986-90; contbr. articles to profl. jours. Chmn. bd. Ctr. for Ethics and Corp. Policy, 1987-92; Elder Fourth Presbyn. Ch. of Chgo. Mem. Am. Sociol. Assn., N.Am. Soc. Adlerian Psychology, Midwest Human Resources Planners Group, Human Resources Planning Soc., Chgo. Club, San Diego Press Club, Alpha Kappa Delta. Presbyterian. Office: 45 East Bellevue Pl Chicago IL 60611-1133 E-mail: allan@allancox.com.

COX, CHARLES C. economist; b. Missoula, Mont., May 8, 1945; m. Monica Lewis, 1984. BA magna cum laude, U. Wash., 1967; AM, U. Chgo., 1970, PhD, 1975. Asst. prof. econs. Ohio State U., Columbus, 1972-80; nat. fellow Hoover Instn., 1977-78; asst. prof. mgmt. Tex. A&M U., College Station, 1980-82; chief economist SEC, Washington, 1982-83, commr., 1983-89, acting chmn., 1987; prin., sr. v.p. Lexecon, Inc., Chgo., 1989—. Nat. fellow Hoover Institution, 1977-78. Mem. Am. Econ. Assn., United Shareholders Assn. (chmn. 1990-93), Mt. Pelerin Soc., Phi Beta Kappa. Office: Lexecon Inc 332 S Michigan Ave Ste 1300 Chicago IL 60604-4397

COX, DAVID JACKSON, biochemistry educator; b. N.Y.C., Dec. 22, 1934; s. Reavis and Rachel (Dunaway) C.; m. Joan M. Narbeth, Sept. 6, 1958 (dec. Oct. 8, 1982); children: Andrew Reavis, Matthew Bruce, Thomas Jackson; m. Tamara L. Compton, Nov. 26, 1983. B.A., Wesleyan U., 1956; Ph.D., U. Pa., 1960. Instr. biochemistry U. Wash., 1960-63; asst. prof. chemistry U. Tex., 1963-67, assoc. prof., 1967-73; prof., head dept. biochemistry Kans. State U., 1973-89; prof. chemistry Ind. U./Purdue U., Ft. Wayne, 1989-2000, prof. emeritus, 2000—. Vis. prof. U. Va., 1970-71; dean arts scis. Ind. U./Purdue U., Ft. Wayne, 1989-96. NSF predoctoral fellow, 1956-59; NSF sr. postdoctoral fellow, 1970-71 Mem. AAAS, Am. Soc. Biol. Chemists, Am. Chem. Soc., Phi Beta Kappa, Sigma Xi. Democrat. Presbyterian. Home: 309 Crown Ln Bellingham WA 98226-5929 E-mail: moody@gte.net.

COX, JAMES ALLAN, chemistry educator; b. Chisholm, Minn., Sept. 19, 1941; s. Robert Earl and Mary Jean (Berdey) C.; m. Kersti Suik, Aug. 21, 1965; children: Kaila Ann, Alison Jean. AA, Hibbing State Coll., 1961; BChem, U. Minn., 1963; PhD, U. Ill., 1967. Lectr., rsch. assoc. U. Wis., Madison, 1967-69; faculty, prof. chemistry So. Ill. U., Carbondale, 1969-86; prof., chair chemistry Miami U., Oxford, Ohio, 1987-94, prof. chemistry, 1994—. Cons. NIH, Washington, 1988—; environ. chem. cons. various industries, 1980—. Author book chpts. on coal chemistry; contbr. more than 150 articles to environ., chem., and electrochemistry jours. Named Cin. Chemist of Yr., 2002. Mem. Internat. Soc. Electrochemistry, Am. Chem. Soc., Electrochemistry Soc., Soc. Electroanalytical Chemists. Achievements include discovery of catalysts for oxidation of environmental pollutants and various biological compounds including insulin and various amino acids. Office: Miami U Chemistry-Hughes Hall Oxford OH 45056

COX, JEROME ROCKHOLD, JR. electrical engineer; b. Washington, May 24, 1925; s. Jerome R. and Jane (Mills) Cox; m. Barbara Jane Lueders, Sept. 2, 1951; children: Nancy Jane Cox Battersby, Jerome Mills, Randall Allen. SB, MIT, 1947, SM, 1949, ScD, 1954. Faculty Washington U., St. Louis, 1955—61, prof. elec. engring., 1961—2000, dir. Biomed. Computer Lab., 1964—75, prof. biomed. engring. in physiology and biophysics, Sch. Medicine, 1965—2000, chmn. computer labs., 1967—83, program dir. tng. program tech. in health care, 1970—78, chmn. dept. computer sci., 1975—91, prof. biomedicine, Inst. for Biomed. Computing, 1983—2000, Harold and Adelaide Welge prof. computer sci., 1989—98, dir. Applied Rsch. Lab., 1991—95, sr. prof., 1999—; v.p. Growth Networks, 1999—2000. Co-chmn. computers in cardiology conf., , 1974—78; cardiology adv. com. Nat. Heart and Lung Inst., 1975—78; epidemiology biostatistics and bioengring. cluster Pres.'s Biomed. Rsch. Panel, 1975—76; chmn. divsn. computer rsch. and tech. rev. com. NIH, 1983—96, PROPHET adv. com. , 1983—88; adv. com. Harvard-MIT Health Scis. and Tech., Boston, 1988—92; nat. neural circuitry database com. Inst. of Medicine, NAS, 1989—91; mem. Nat. Adv. Coun. Human Genome Rsch., 1990—95. Mem. editl. bd.: Computers and Biomed. Rsch., 1967—2000, mem. editl. bd.: Applied Mathematics Letters, 1987—96. Bd. dirs. Ctrl. Inst. Deaf, 1993—. With U.S. Army, 1943—44. Fellow: IEEE (mem. editl. bd. Trans. Biomed. Enring. 1969—71), St. Louis Acad. Sci. (bd. dirs. 1997—99), Am. Coll. Med. Informatics, Acoustical Soc. Am.; mem.: Inst. Medicine, Tau Beta Pi, Eta Kappa Nu, Sigma Xi. Achievements include patents for air traffic control;patents for computerized tomography;patents for medical display technology. Office: Washington U Dept Computer Sci Campus Box 1045 One Brookings Dr Saint Louis MO 63130-4899 E-mail: jrc@cs.wustl.edu.

COX, MITCHEL NEAL, editor; b. Portsmouth, Ohio, Sept. 8, 1956; s. Walter Eugene and Mary Agnes (Orlett) Cox; m. Lisa Renee LaLonde, Sept. 8, 1979 (dec. May 2001); children: Harmony, Leigh Ann, Katie. BS in Journalism, Ohio State U., 1985. Mng. editor The Puller, Columbus, Ohio, 1984-87; editor Bicycles Today, 1985-87, Fur-Fish-Game, Columbus, 1987—. Mem. Outdoor Writers Assn. Am. Office: Fur-Fish-Game 2878 E Main St Columbus OH 43209-2698 E-mail: ffgcox@netwalk.com.

COY, PATRICIA ANN, special education director, consultant; b. Beardstown, Ill., Apr. 2, 1952; d. Ben L. and Dorothy Lee (Hubbell) C. BS in Elem. and Spl. Edn., No. Ill. U., 1974; MS in Spl. Edn., Northeastern Ill. U., 1976, MA in Spl. Edn., 1978; MEd in Spl. Edn., Northeastern U., 1984; postgrad., No. Ill. U., 1988—. Cert. elem. and spl. edn. tchr.; cert. counselor. Mental health supr. Waukegan (Ill.) Devel. Ctr., 1974-77; ednl. therapist Grove Sch. and Residential Program, Lake Forest, Ill., 1977-78; dir. residential svcs. N.W. Suburban Aid for the Retarded, Park Ridge, 1978-83; exec. dir. The Learning Tree, Des Plaines, 1983—; dir. residential svcs. Augustanan Ctr. Luth. Social Svcs. of Ill., Chgo., 1984-86, dir. planning and evaluation, 1986-93, dir. cmty. svc., 1993-95; CEO Visions Network (formerly Blare House Inc.), Des Plaines, Ill., 1995—. Behavior advisor Habilitative Systems, Inc., Chgo., 1985-88; program coord. Human Resource Devel. Inst., Chgo., 1986-89; project dir. Support Svcs. Ill., Inc., Chgo., 1987-91; dir. TranSteps Inc. Steps for Success for Adults with Learning Differences, 1991—. Contbr. articles to profl. jours. Mem. Coun. for Exceptional Children, Am. Assn. Mental Deficiency, Chgo. Assn. Behavioral Analysis, Behavior Analysis Soc. Ill., Assn. for Supervision and Curriculum Devel., Nat. Rehab. Assn., Coun. for Disability Rights, Assn. for Learning Disability, Profls. in Learning Disabilities, Cwens, Echoes, Mortar Bd., Kappa Delta Pi. Democrat. Mem. United Ch. of Christ. Home: 8936 N Parkside Ave Apt 118 Des Plaines IL 60016-5517 Office: 7144 N Harlem Ave Ste 344 Chicago IL 60631-1005 also: Blare Inc 960 Rand Rd Ste 216 Des Plaines IL 60016-2355 E-mail: coycondo@aol.com.

COYLE, MICHAEL J. medical administrator; Pres. Daig divsn. St. Jude Med. Inc. Office: 14901 Deveau Pl Minnetonka MN 55345-2126

COYNE, PATRICK IVAN, physiological ecologist; b. Wichita, Kans., Feb. 26, 1944; s. Ivan Lefranz and Ellen Lucille (Brown) C.; m. Mary Ann White, Aug. 22, 1964; children: Shane Barrett, Shannon Renee. BS, Kans. State U., 1966; PhD, Utah State U., 1970. R & D coord. U.S. Army Cold Regions Rsch. and Engring. Lab., Hanover, N.H., 1970-72; asst. prof. forestry U. Alaska, Fairbanks, 1973-74; plant physiologist, environ. scientist Lawrence Livermore (Calif.) Nat. Lab., 1975-79, cons., 1980—; rsch. plant physiologist USDA/ Agrl. Rsch. Svc., Woodward, Okla., 1979-85; prof., head Agrl. Rsch. Ctr. Kansas State U., Hays, 1985-94, prof., head Western Kans. Agrl. Rsch. Ctrs., 1994—. Mem. adv. coun. Kans. Geol. Survey, Lawrence, 1986-91. Contbr. 33 articles to profl. jours. Capt., U.S. Army, 1970-72. Mem. AAAS, Am. Soc. Agronomy, Soil Sci. Soc. Am., Crop Sci. Soc. Am., Soc. Range Mgmt., Coun. Agriculture Sci. and Tech., Hays Area C. of C. (bd. dirs. 1988-90), Rotary, Phi Kappa Phi, Gamma Sigma Delta, Sigma Xi. Republican. Mennonite Brethren Ch. Office: Kans State U Agrl Rsch Ctr 1232 240th Ave Hays KS 67601-9228

COZAD, JOHN CONDON, lawyer; b. Portland, Maine, Dec. 18, 1944; s. Francis E. and Arlyn Odell (Condon) C.; m. Linda Hickerson, Feb. 18, 1978. B.A. in Polit. Sci., Westminster Coll., Fulton, Mo., 1966; J.D., U. Mo.-Columbia, 1972. Bar: Mo. 1972. Assoc. & ptnr. Field, Gentry, Benjamin, & Robertson, Kansas City, Mo., 1972-83; ptnr. Morrison & Hecker, 1983—; chmn. Mo. Rep State Party, 1995-99. Chmn. Mo. Hwy. and Transp. Commn., 1985-91; mem. desegregation monitoring com. U.S. Dist. Ct. (we. dist.) Mo., 1989-91; bd. curators U. Mo. Sys., 1991-96; bd. trustees U. Kansas City, 1991—; mem. Rep. Nat. Com., 1995-99. Lt. USNR, 1967-69, Vietnam. Decorated Bronze Star. Navy Commendation medals, Presdl. Unit Citation. Mem. Mo. Bar Assn., Kansas City Bar Assn., Carriage Club. Republican. Mem. Disciples of Christ Ch. Avocations: politics, pheasant hunting, reading. Home: RR 2 Box 140 Platte City MO 64079-9805 Office: Morrison & Hecker 2600 Grand Blvd Ste 1200 Kansas City MO 64108-4606

CRABB, BARBARA BRANDRIFF, federal judge; b. Green Bay, Wis., Mar. 17, 1939; d. Charles Edward and Mary (Forrest) Brandriff; m. Theodore E. Crabb, Jr., Aug. 29, 1959; children: Julia Forrest, Philip Elliott. A.B., U. Wis., 1960, J.D., 1962. Bar: Wis. 1963. Assoc. Roberts, Boardman, Suhr and Curry, Madison, Wis., 1962-64; legal rschr. Sch. Law, U. Wis., 1968-70, Am. Bar Assn., Madison, 1970-71; U.S. magistrate, 1971-79; judge U.S. Dist. Ct. (we. dist.) Wis., 1979—, chief judge, 1980-96, dist. judge, 1996—. Mem. Gov. Wis. Task Force Prison Reform, 1971-73 Membership chmn., v.p. Milw. LWV, 1966-68; mem. Milw. Jr. League, 1967-68. Mem. ABA, Nat. Assn. Women Judges, State Bar Wis., Dane County Bar Assn., U. Wis. Law Alumni Assn. Office: US Dist Ct PO Box 591 120 N Henry St Madison WI 53701-0591

CRADDOCK, CAMPBELL (JOHN CAMPBELL CRADDOCK), geologist, educator; b. Chgo., Apr. 3, 1930; s. Alice Phillips; adopted by John and Bernice (Campbell) C.; m. Dorothy Dunkelberg, June 13, 1953; children: Susan, John, Carol. BA, DePauw U., 1951; MA, Columbia U., 1953, PhD, 1954. Geologist Shell Oil Co., N.Mex., Tex., Colo., Wyo., 1954-56; asst. prof. U. Minn., Mpls., 1956-60, assoc. prof., 1960-67; prof. geology U. Wis., Madison, 1967-96; prof. emeritus, 1996—; chmn. dept. U. Wis., 1977-80; leader Antarctic geologic field rsch. programs, 1959-69, geologist, 1980; leader Alaskan Range field rsch. programs, 1968-81; leader Svalbard field rsch. programs, 1977-86. Cons. C.E. AUS, 1957—58, N. Star Rsch. Inst., 1965—68, Dept. State, 1976, Phillips Petroleum Co., 1980, Texaco, 1985; vis. scientist N.Z. Geol. Survey, 1962—63; lectr. Nanjing (China) U., 1981, Beijing U., 1981; chmn. panel polar geology and geophysics NRC, 1967—71, com. on polar rsch., 1967—71, mem. polar rsch. bd., 1978—82; U.S. mem. working group on geology Sci. Com. on Antarctic Rsch., 1967—81, chmn. group, 1973—80; co-chief scientist Leg 35 Deep Sea Drilling Project, 1974; chmn. Antarctic panel Circum-Pacific Map Project, 1979—90; leader Antarctic geologic field rsch. programs, 1959—69, geologist, 1980; leader Alaskan Range field rsch. programs, 1968—81, Svalbard field rsch. programs, 1977—86. Editor: Antarctic Geoscience, 1982; co-editor: Geologic Maps of Antarctica, Folio 12, Antarctic Map Folio Series, 1970, Initial Reports of the Deep Sea Drilling Project, Vol. 35, 1976, Geology and Paleontology of the Ellsworth Mountains, Antarctica, Geol. Soc. of Am. Memoir 170, 1992; contbr. articles to profl. jours. Higgins fellow, 1951-52, NSF fellow, 1952-53; Rsch. grantee, 1957-95; recipient U.S. Antarctic Service medal, 1968, Bellingshausen-Lazarev medal Soviet Acad. Scis., 1970, Alumni citation DePauw U., 1976 Fellow AAAS (steering com. geology and geography sect. 1996-98), Geol. Soc. Am. (chmn. North Ctrl. sect. 1982-83, chmn. structural geology and tectonics divsn. 1983-84, books editor 1982-88, Disting. Svc. award 1988); mem. Internat. Union Geol. Scis. (commn. on structural geology 1968-76, mem. commn. on tectonics 1976-85, del. Sci. Com. on Antarctic Rsch. 1974-87, mem. commn. on geologic map of world 1974-91, commn. v.p. for Antarctica 1979-91), Am. Geophys. Union, Am. Assn. Petroleum Geologists, Groupe Francais d'Etude de Gondwana (hon.), Phi Beta Kappa, Sigma Xi. Office: U Wis Dept Geology and Geophysics 1215 W Dayton St Madison WI 53706-1600

CRAFT, EDMUND COLEMAN, automotive parts manufacturing company executive; b. Plainfield, N.J., Dec. 23, 1939; s. Edmund Coleman and Ruth Irene (Morrell) C.; m. Gail Christensen; children: Edmund Coleman III, Elisabeth Gordon, William Todd. BS, Lycoming Coll., 1963; postgrad., Syracuse U., 1963-64; grad. exec. program, U. Minn., 1984. With Borg-Warner Corp., Detroit, adminstrv. asst. to chmn. Chgo., 1969-70; with Borg-Warner Ltd., Letchworth, Hertfordshire, Eng., 1970-75; v.p. hydraulics div. Borg-Warner, Wooster, Ohio, 1975-79; dir. hydraulics div. Donaldson Co. Inc., Mpls., 1979-83, v.p., 1983-2000; sr. advisor Global Aftermarket, 2000-2001; ret., 2001. Bd. dirs. Jr. Achievement of Upper Midwest Inc., 1993-2000, mem. exec. com., 1994-2000; divsn. chmn. United Way, Wooster, 1974. Mem. Automotive Filter Mfrs. Coun. (vice chmn. 1985-89, chmn. 1989-91, bd. dirs. 1991-2000), Dataw Island Club. Republican. Presbyterian. Avocations: golf, power boating.

CRAHAN, JACK BERTSCH, retired manufacturing company executive; b. Peoria, Ill., Aug. 24, 1923; s. John F. and Ann B. (Bertsch) C.; m. Peggy Furey, Sept. 9, 1944; children: Patrick Michael, Colleen Mary, Kevin Furey. BS, U. Minn., 1948. With Flexsteel Industries, Inc., Dubuque, Iowa, 1948—50, plant mgr., 1950-54, gen. mgr., v.p., 1955-70, exec. v.p., 1970-84, pres., 1985-89, vice-chmn., COO, 1989-90, chmn., CEO, 1990-99; ret., 1999. Bd. dirs. Dubuque Racing Assn.; trustee United Steel Workers Am. Pension Fund, 1960-99. Bd. regents Loras Coll., 1967-80, 81— ; bd. dirs. Xavier Hosp., 1969-78, Boys Club Am., 1981-99 . Served with USNR, 1942-43; with USMC, 1943-46, 51-52. Decorated D.F.C. (1), Air medal (4). Mem. Am. Furniture Assn. (bd. dirs. 1967-74). Republican. Roman Catholic. Home: 1195 Arrowhead Dr Dubuque IA 52003-8594 Office: Flexsteel Industries Inc Brunswick Indsl Block PO Box 847 Dubuque IA 52004-0847

CRAIG, CLIFFORD LINDLEY, orthopaedic pediatric surgery educator; b. Detroit, Mar. 25, 1944; s. Paul Forrest and Dorothy Madeline (Denhart) C.; m. Laura Ann Hackley, June 20, 1976; children: Paul Edward, Julia Marie. BS, Tufts U., 1965; MD, U. Mich., 1969. Diplomat Am. Bd. Orthopaedic Surgery. Asst. prof. orthopaedic surgery Tufts U. Sch. Medicine, Boston, 1979-94, assoc. prof. orthopaedic surgery, 1994-99; clin. assoc. prof. orthopedic surgery U. Mich. Med. Sch., Ann Arbor, 1999—. Fellow Am. Coll. Surgery; mem. AMA, Am. Acad. Orthopaedic Surgery, Am. Acad. Pediatrics, Am. Acad. Cerebral Palsy, Am. Assn. Clin. Anatomy, Pediatric Orthopaedic Soc. of N.Am. Office: Univ Mich Med Ctr Taubman Center 2912 PO Box 328 Ann Arbor MI 48106-0328 E-mail: clcraig@umich.edu.

CRAIG, JAMES LYNN, physician, consumer products company executive; b. Columbia, Tenn., Aug. 7, 1933; s. Clifford Paul and Maple (Harris) C.; m. Suzanne Anderson, July 20, 1957; children: James Lynn, Margaret; m. Roberta Anne, May 17, 1980. Ed., Mid. Tenn. State U., 1953; MD, U. Tenn., 1956; MPH, U. Pitts., 1963. Diplomate Am. Bd. Preventive Medicine, Am. Bd. Family Practice. Intern U. Tenn. Meml. Hosp., Knoxville, 1957; resident in occupl. medicine U. Pitts., 1962-64, TVA, Chattanooga, 1964-65, physician, 1966-69, chief med. officer, 1969-74; corp. med. dir. Gen. Mills Corp., Mpls., 1974-76, v.p. corp. med. dir., 1976-80, v.p., dir. health and human svcs., 1980-98; adj. clin. prof. U. Minn., 1979—, chmn. cmty. adv. com. Ctr. for Environ. and Health Policy, 1994-97, mem. adv. coun. health in scis., 1992-95, chmn. adv. bd. Ctr. for Environ. and Health Policy, 1994-97; pres. Family and Preventive Health Svcs., Inc., 1998—. Clin. instr. U. Tenn., Memphis, 1970-74, Meharry Med. Sch., Nashville, 1972-74; bd. dirs. Inst. Rsch. and Edn. Health Sys. Minn.; mem. adv. bd. to dir. Ctr. Disease Control and Prevention; nat. adv. bd. Internat. Health and Media Awards, 1996—. Contbr. articles to profl. jours. Bd. dirs. Mpls. Blood Bank, 1976-88, Minn. Bible Coll., Rochester, 1978-83, Minn. Safety Coun., 1981-90, Minn. Heart Assn., Mpls., 1976-87, Children's Heart Fund, 1976-88, Meth. Hosp. Found., 1979-87, Park Nicolett Med. Found., 1987-93, Altcare, 1983-95, Meth. Hosp. Health Assn., 1987-93, Minn. Wellness Coun., 1986-91, Health Sys. Minn. Assocs., 1993-94; bd. dirs. Health Systems Minn. Inst. for Rsch. and Edn., 1996-2000, chmn., 1997-2000, chmn. Park Nicollet Inst., 2000-01; trustee Minn. Med. Found., 2001--. Recipient Physician Recognition award AMA, 1975, 78,81, 85, 89, 93, 96, 99, Cmty. Svc. award Park Nicollet Med. Ctr., 1995, Knudsen award in Occupl. Medicine, Am. Coll. Occupl. and Environ. Medicine, 2000, Legacy Laureate U. Pitts., 2000. Fellow Am. Occupl. Medicine Assn. (bd. dirs. 1974-78), Am. Acad. Occupl. Medicine (treas. 1982-83, sec. 1983-84, v.p. 1984-85, prs. 1986-87), Am. Acad. Family Practice; mem. AMA (alt. del. Ho. Dels. 1990-92, del. 1992-96), Occupl. Health Inst. (chmn. 1983-84), North Ctrl. Occupl. Medicine Assn. (pres. 1977), Minn. Acad. Medicine, Mpls. Acad. Medicine (sec. 1983-85, pres. 1985-86), Emergency Physicians Assn. (bd. dirs. 1984-92). Home: 10008 S Shore Dr Minneapolis MN 55441-5011 Office: PO Box 270330 Minneapolis MN 55427-6330 E-mail: jimlcraig@aol.com.

CRAIG, JUDITH, bishop; b. Lexington, Mo., June 5, 1937; d. Raymond Luther and Edna Amelia (Forsha) C. BA, William Jewell Coll., 1959; MA in Christian Edn., Eden Theol. Sem., 1961; MDiv, Union Theol. Sem., 1968; DD, Baldwin Wallace Coll., 1981; DHL, Adrian Coll., 1985, Otterbein Coll., 1993, Lebanon Valley Coll., Baldwin Wallace Coll. Youth dir. Bellefontaine United Meth. Ch., St. Louis, 1959-61; intern children's work Nat. Coun. of Chs. of Christ, N.Y.C., 1961-62; dir. Christian edn. 1st United Meth. Ch., Stamford, Ct., 1962-66; inst. adult basic edn. N.Y.C. Schs., 1967; dir. Christian edn. Epworth Euclid United Meth. Ch., Cleve., 1969-72, assoc. pastor, 1972-76; pastor Pleasant Hills United Meth. Ch., Middleburg Heights, Ohio, 1976-80; conf. council dir. East Ohio Conf. United Meth. Ch., Canton, 1980-84; bishop United Meth. Ch., Mich. area, 1984-92, West Ohio area, 1992-2000; ret. Mem. United Meth. Gen. Coun. Mins., 1976-80, 88-92, United Meth. Commn. Status Role Women, 1984-88; gen. conf. del., 1980, 84; mem. United Meth. Publ. House Bd., 1992—; bd. dirs. U.S. Health Corp.; frequent lectr. and preacher; bd. trustees 27 institutions in West Ohio. Contbr. articles to ministry mags. Bd. dirs. YWCA, Middleburg Heights, 1976-80. Recipient Citation of Achievement William Jewell Coll., 1985, Woman of Achievement award YWCA, 1995.

CRAIG, L. CLIFFORD, lawyer; b. Ohio, Aug. 29, 1938; Student, Stanford U., 1957-59; BA, Duke U., 1961, LLB, 1964. Bar: Ohio. Ptnr. Taft, Stettinius & Hollister, Cin., 1971—. Fellow Am. Coll. Trial Lawyers; mem. ABA, Ohio Bar Assn., Cin. Bar Assn. Office: 1800 Firstar Tower 425 Walnut St Cincinnati OH 45202-3957

CRAIG, ROBERT GEORGE, dental science educator; b. Charlevoix, Mich., Sept. 8, 1923; s. Harry Allen and Marion Ione (Swinton) C.; m. Luella Georgine Dean, Sept. 29, 1945; children: Susan Georgine, Barbara Dean, Katherine Ann. BS, U. Mich., 1944, MS, 1951, PhD in Phys. Chemistry, 1955; MD (hon.), U. Geneva, Switzerland, 1989. Rsch. chemist Linde Air Products Co., Tonawanda, N.Y., 1944-50, Texaco, Inc., Beacon, 1954-55; rsch. assoc. U. Mich. Engring. Rsch. Inst., 1955-57; faculty dept. dental materials Sch. Dentistry, U. Mich., Ann Arbor, 1957-87, asst. prof., 1957-60, assoc. prof., 1960-64, prof., 1964-87, chmn. dept., 1969-87, prof. biologic and material sci., 1987-93, Marcus Ward prof. dentistry, 1990-93, prof. emeritus, 1993—; dir. Specialized Materials Sci. Ctr. Nat. Inst. Dental Rsch., 1989-93; exec. com. Sch. Dentistry, U. Mich., 1972-75; budget priorities com. U. Mich., 1978-81, chmn. budget priorities com., 1979-81. Sci. adv. com. Dental Rsch. Inst., U. Mich., Ann Arbor, 1980-89, chmn., 1984-89; cons. Walter Reed Army Hosp., 1969-75; assessor for Nat. Health and Med. Rsch. Coun., Commonwealth Australia. Co-author (with K.A. Easlick, S.I. Seger and A.L. Russell): Communicating in Dentistry, 1973; co-author: (with W.J. O'Brien, J.M. Powers) Dental Materials-Properties and Manipulation, 6th edit., 1966; co-author: (with J.M. Powers) Workbook for Dental Materials, 1979; co-author: (with J.M. Powers, J.C. Wataha) Dental Materials-Properties and Manipulation, 7th edit. , 2000; contbr. ; editor (with J.M. Powers): Restorative Dental Materials, 11th edit., 2002; editor: Mich. State Dental Jour., 1973—77, Oral Implantology Jour., 1988—. Prin. investigator specialized material Scis. Rsch. Ctr. (funded by Nat. Inst. Dental Rsch. 1989-94). Rsch. grantee Nat. Inst. Dental Rsch., 1965-76, 84-94, Nat. Scis. Res. Svc. Tng., 1976-93; Rsch. fellow E.I. du Pont, 1952-53. Mem. ADA (cons. coun. on dental materials and devices 1983-95), Am. Nat. Stds. Inst. (chmn. spl. com. 1968-77, subcom. with ADA on mouth protectors and materials 1996—), Internat. Assn. Dental Rsch. (pres.-elect dental materials group 1972-73, pres. 1973-74, Wilmer Souder award 1975), Am. Assn. Dental Schs. (chmn. biomaterials sect. 1977-79), Am. Chem. Soc., Soc. Biomaterials (Clemson award for basic rsch. in biomaterials 1978, program chmn. 1983, fellow 1994), Acad. Operative Dentistry (George Hollenbach Meml. prize 1991), Sigma Xi (sec. U. Mich chpt. 1978-81), Phi Kappa Phi, Phi Lambda Upsilon, Omicron Kappa Upsilon. Home: 1503 Wells St Ann Arbor MI 48104-3914 Office: U Mich Sch Dentistry 1011 N University Ave Ann Arbor MI 48109-1078

CRAMBLETT, HENRY GAYLORD, pediatrician, virologist, educator; b. Scio, Ohio, Feb. 8, 1929; s. Carl Smith and Olive (Fulton) C.; m. Donna Jean Reese, June 16, 1960; children: Deborah Kaye, Betsy Diane. BS, Mt. Union Coll., 1950; MD, U. Cin., 1953. Diplomate Am. Bd. Pediatrics, Am. Bd. Microbiology, Am. Bd. Med. Specialists. Intern in medicine Boston City Hosp., Harvard Med. Svc., 1953-54; resident in pediatrics Children's Hosp., Cin., 1954-55; clin. rsch. assoc. Nat. Inst. Allergy and Infectious Diseases, Clin. Ctr., Bethesda, Md., 1955-57; chief resident, instr. dept. pediat. State U. Iowa, Iowa City, 1957-58, faculty, 1957-60, asst. prof., 1958-60; faculty Bowman Gray Sch. Medicine, 1960-64, prof. pediat., 1963-64, dir. virology lab., 1960-64; prof. pediat. Ohio State U., Columbus, 1964-95, prof. med. microbiology, 1966-95, exec. dir. Children's Hosp. Rsch. Found., 1964-73, chmn. dept. med. microbiology, 1966-73, dean Coll. Medicine, 1973-80, acting v.p. for med. affairs, 1974-80, v.p. health scis., 1980-83, Warner M. and Lora Kays Pomerene chair in medicine, 1982-95, assoc. to v.p. health svcs., to dean and prof. emeritus, 1984-95. Mem. Ohio State U. bd. trustees Cancer Hosp. Oversight Com., 1991-96, mem. Ohio Med. Bd., sec. 1984-92, past pres.; hosp. surveyor Joint Com. on Accreditation of Health Care Orgns., 1985-95; chmn. com. on cert., subcert. and recert. Am. Bd. Med. Specialists; mem. coms. on written exam., comprehensive qualifying evaluation program Nat. Bd. Med. Examiners; mem. Accreditation Coun. Continuing Med. Edn., chmn., 1980-83, 93-94, also mem. fin. com., 1993—, mem. strategic plan implementation com., 1993—, mem. external monitoring com., 1993—; mem. adv. com. on undergrad. med. evaluation; mem. Fedn. State Med. Bds., pres., 1976-82 (mem. Flex bd. 1983-91, chmn. 1985-91), mem. fin. audit com., 1991; chmn. Fed. Exam. Bd., 1991-92, cons., 1992—; mem. composite com. Fedn. of State Med. Bds. and Nat. Bd. of Med. Examiners, U.S. Med. Licensing Exam., 1990-96; Fedn. of State Med. Bds. observer Clin. Skills Assessment Alliance, 1990-95; bd. dirs. Ohio State U. Hosp., 1979-80; dir. med. and postgrad. med. edn. King Faisal Specialist Hosp., Riyadh, Saudi Arabia, 1983-84; mem. strategic planning task force CSAA, 1992-94; med. dir. Columbus Health Plan, 1995—. Trustee Children's Hosp. Rsch. Found., 1973-84, Children's Hosp., 1973-84, Children's Hosp., Inc., 1982-84. Recipient Hoffheimer prize U. Cin., 1953, Eben J. Carey award in anatomy, 1950, Rsch. Career Devel. award NIH, 1961-63; Henry G. Cramblett chair in medicine established at Ohio State U., 1988; Henry G. Cramblett Hall dedicated at Ohio State U., 1999. Fellow Am. Acad. Microbiology, AAAS; mem. So. Soc. Pediatric Rsch. (past pres.), Soc. Pediatric Rsch., Am. Pediatric Soc., Am. Acad. Pediat., Midwest Soc. Pediatric Rsch., Soc. Exptl. Biology and Medicine, Am. Soc. Microbiology, Alpha Omega Alpha. Achievements include research, publs. on medical licensure, medical staff hospital standards, etiologic assn. virus infections in illnesses of infants and children, estimation of importance of various viruses in morbidity and mortality in pediatric age group. Home: 2480 Sheringham Rd Columbus OH 43220-4274 Office: Ohio State U 1024 Cramblett Hall 456 W 10th Ave Columbus OH 43210-1240

CRAMER, KEVIN, foundation administrator; b. Rolla, N.D. m. Kris Cramer; children: Ian, Isaac, Rachel, Annie. BA in Social Work, Concordia Coll. Dir. tourism; dir. N.D. Dept. Econ. Devel. and Fin., 1997-2001; found. dir. U. Mary, Bismarck, N.D., 2001—. Supporter, mem. Growing N.D. Programs; com. mem. Growing N.D. III, 1994. Chmn., exec. dir. N.D. Rep. Party; active Rep. Nat. Com.; Rep. nominee U.S. Ho. of Reps. Office: U Mary 7500 University Dr Bismarck ND 58504

CRAMER, ROBERT, retail executive; CEO, pres. FareWay Stores, Inc., Boone, Iowa. Office: FareWay Stores Inc PO Box 70 Boone IA 50036-0070

CRAMER, TED, radio personality; b. Kansas City, Sept. 22; m. Linda Cramer. Radio host WDAF, Westwood, Kans., 1977—80, 1992—. Office: WDAF 4935 Belinder Westwood KS 66205*

CRAMER, WILLIAM ANTHONY, biochemistry and biophysics researcher, educator; b. N.Y.C., June 11, 1938; s. Robert and Sylvia (Blumstein) C.; m. Hanni Aebersold, Sept. 11, 1964; children: Rebecca, Jean-Marc, Gabrielle, Nicholas. BS, MIT, 1959; MS, U. Chgo., 1960, PhD, 1965. NSF post doctoral fellow U. Calif., San Diego, 1965-67, rsch. assoc., 1967-68; asst. prof. dept. biol. scis. Purdue U., West Lafayette, Ind., 1968-73, assoc. prof., 1973-78, prof., 1978—, assoc. head dept., 1984-86, Henry Koffler prof. biol. scis. Ind., 1995-2001, Henry Koffler Disting. prof. biol. scis., 2001—. Head panel predoctoral fellowships in biophysics and biochemistry NSF, 1979, mem. molecular biology panel, 1980-82, mem. cellular biochemistry panel, 1989-91; mem. panel competitive grants USDA, 1983-84; chmn. Gordon Confs. on Photosynthesis, 1990, Bioenergetics, 2001; mem. phys. biochemistry study sect. NIH, 1991-95. Author textbook on bioenergetics; editor: Archives Biochemistry and Biophysics, 1979—91, Biochim. Biophys. Acta, 1983—, Photosynthesis Rsch., 1989—98, Jour. Bioenergetics Biomembranes, 1991—, Biophys. Jour., 1999—, Biochem. Jour., 2001—, Jour. Biol. Chemistry, 2002—; contbr. articles to profl. jours. Finalist EMBO fellow, U. Amsterdam, 1974—75; recipient Rsch. Career Devel. award, NIH, 1970—75, H.N. McCoy award for sci. achievement, Purdue U., 1988, Charles F. Kettering award, Am. Soc. Plant Physiologists, 1996; fellow Alexander von Humboldt fellow, Max-Planck Inst., Frankfurt, 1992, John Simon Guggenheim fellow, 1992—93. Mem.: Biophys. Soc. (chmn. bioenergetics subgroup 1989—92, organizing com. "Biophys. Discussions" 1992, program chair 40th ann. meeting 1996, coun. 1997—2001, exec. coun. 1999—2001, rep. Fedn. Am. Socs. Exptl. Biology com. ethical issues genetic rsch. 1998, pub. policy com. 1999—), Protein Soc., Am. Soc. Biol. Chemists. Office: Purdue U Dept Biol Sci Lilly Hall of Life Sciences West Lafayette IN 47907

CRAMES, PAUL F. writer, lawyer; b. Miami, Fla., Dec. 4, 1945; s. Albert A. and Marguerite R. Crames; m. Betty Bloomer, July 17, 1970; children: Todd, Michelle, Katie. BS, U. Fla., 1967; JD, U. Miami, 1972. Bar: Fla., U.S. Dist. Cts. (so. and mid. dist.) Fla., U.S. Ct. Appeals (5th cir.). Pvt. practice, 1972-86; city atty. City of St. Petersburg, Fla., 1973-74. Mem. ABA, ATLA.

CRANDELL, DWIGHT SAMUEL, retired museum executive; b. Parke County, Ind., Nov. 30, 1943; s. Terence Wesley and Alice Ruth (Cox) C.; m. Rachel Louise Wentworth, June 14, 1965; children: Jeremy, Abigail, Joanna, Joshua. BA, Principia Coll., 1965; MA, SUNY-Oneonta, 1974. Asst. in rsch. and adminstrn. Mt. Vernon (Va.) Ladies Assn. of the Union, 1965-66; exhibits coord., ednl. docent Children's Mus., Indpls., 1972-73, curator exhibits rsch. and planning, 1973-77, collections dir., 1977-81; dir. devel., asst. dir. St. Louis Sci. Ctr., 1981-82, exec. dir., 1982-94, v.p. programs and ops., 1992-95, v.p. ops., 1996-2001; ret., 2001. Bd. dirs. Wild Canid Rsch. and Survival Ctr., 1983-88, 91-95. Served to capt. USAF, 1966-71. Nat. Mus. Act travel grantee, 1973 Mem. Am. Assn. Museums, Midwest Museums Conf., Mo. Museums Assocs. (v.p. 1983-85, pres. 1986-87, 94-95), Assn. Sci-Tech. Ctrs. (bd. dirs. 1983-85), St. Louis Area Mus. Collaborative, Rotary. Christian Scientist. Office: Saint Louis Sci Ctr 5050 Oakland Ave Saint Louis MO 63110-1460 E-mail: dcrandel@slsc.org.

CRANE, GARY E. financial executive; BBA, U. Mich. CPA, Ohio, Fla. With Camco Fin. Corp., Cambridge, Ohio, 1996—, now CFO, treas. Office: Camco Fin Corp 6901 Glenn Hwy Cambridge OH 43725-8685

CRANE, MARK, lawyer; b. Chgo., Aug. 27, 1930; s. Martin and Ruth (Bangs) C.; m. Constance Bird Wilson, Aug. 18, 1956; children: Christopher, Katherine, Stephanie. AB, Princeton U., 1952; LLB, Harvard U., 1957. Bar: U.S. Dist. Ct. (no. dist.) Ill. 1957, U.S. Ct. Appeals (7th cir.) 1968, U.S. Ct. Appeals (9th cir.) 1972, U.S. Supreme Ct. 1978, U.S. Ct. Appeals (10th cir.) 1982, U.S. Ct. Appeals (fed. cir.) 1983, U.S. Ct. Appeals (6th cir.) 1995, U.S. Ct. Appeals (8th cir.) 1998. Assoc. Hopkins & Sutter, Chgo., 1957-63, ptnr., 1963-2001; of counsel Foley & Lardner, 2001—. Adj. prof. Loyola U. Law Sch., 2000—; comml. arbitrator, mediator complex case panel Am. Arbitration Assn., Chgo., 1997—. Served to lt. (j.g.) USNR, 1952-54. Fellow Am. Bar Found., Am. Coll. Trial Lawyers (chmn. upstate Ill. com. 1997-99); mem. ABA (chmn. antitrust sect. 1986-87), Ill. Bar Assn. (chmn. fed. jud. appointments com. 1978-79, chmn. antitrust sect. 1970), Chgo. Bar Assn., 7th Cir. Bar Assn. (pres. 1984-85). Republican. Episcopalian. Home: 520 Hoyt Ln Winnetka IL 60093-2623 Office: Foley & Lardner 3 1st National Plz Chicago IL 60602

CRANE, PHILIP MILLER, congressman; b. Chgo., Nov. 3, 1930; s. George Washington III and Cora (Miller) C.; m. Arlene Catherine Johnson, Feb. 14, 1959; children: Catherine Anne, Susanna Marie, Jennifer Elizabeth, Rebekah Caroline, George Washington V, Rachel Ellen, Sarah Emma, Carrie Esther. Student, DePauw U., 1948-50; BA, Hillsdale Coll., 1952; postgrad., U. Mich., 1952-54, U. Vienna, Austria, 1953, 56; MA, Ind. U., 1961; PhD, 1963; LLD, Grove City Coll., 1973, Nat. Coll. Edn., 1987;

Doctor en Ciencias Politicas, Francisco Marroquin U., 1979. Advt. mgr. Hopkins Syndicate, Inc., Chgo., 1956-58; tchg. asst. Ind. U., Bloomington, 1959-62; asst. prof. history Bradley U., Peoria, Ill., 1963-67; dir. schs. Westminster Acad., Northbrook, 1967-68; mem. 91st-106th Congresses from 13th, 12th (now 8th) Ill. Dist., Washington, 1969—, vice chmn. ways and means com. Author: Democrat's Dilemma, 1964, The Sum of Good Government, 1976, Surrender In Panama: The Case Against the Treaty, 1978; contbr.: Continuity in Crisis, 1974, Crisis in Confidence, 1974, Case Against the Reckless Congress, 1976, Can You Afford This House?, 1978, View from the Capitol Dome (Looking Right), 1980, Liberal Cliches and Conservative Solutions, 1984. Dir. rsch. Ill. Goldwater Orgn., 1964; mem. nat. adv. bd. Young Ams. for Freedom, 1965—; bd. dirs. Am. Conservative Union, 1965-82, chmn., 1976; bd. dirs., chmn. Intercollegiate Studies Inst.; bd. advisors Ashbrook Ctr., Ashland U., 1983—, univ. trustee, 1988-93; founder Rep. Study Com., 1972—, chmn., 1984; commr. Commn. on Bicentennial U.S. Constn., 1986-91; trustee Hillsdale Coll. Recipient Distinguished Alumnus award Hillsdale Coll., 1968, Independence award, 1974, William McGovern award Chgo. Soc., 1969, Freedoms Found. award, 1973; named Ill. Statesman's Father Yr., 1979. Mem. ASCAP, VFW (award 1978), Am. Hist. Assn., Orgn. Am. Historians, Acad. Polit. Sci., Am. Acad. Polit. and Social Scis., Am. Legion, Phila. Soc., B'nai B'rith (award 1978), Phi Alpha Theta, Pi Gamma Mu. Office: US Ho of Reps 233 Cannon House Bldg Washington DC 20515-0001*

CRANG, RICHARD FRANCIS EARL, plant and cell biologist, research center administrator; b. Clinton, Ill., Dec. 2, 1936; s. Richard Francis and Clara Esther (Cummins) Crang; m. Linda L. Crang, Aug. 10, 1958 (div.). B.S., Eastern Ill. U., 1958; M.S., U. S.D., 1962; Ph.D., U. Iowa, 1965. Asst. prof. biology Wittenberg U., 1965-69; assoc. prof. biol. sci. Bowling Green State U., 1969-74, prof., 1974-80; prof. plant biology U. Ill., Urbana-Champaign, 1980—, assoc. head dept. plant biology, 1995-97, faculty fellow in acad. adminstrn., 1997-99, dir. Ctr. Elec. Microsci., 1980-92. Adj. prof. anatomy Med. Coll. Ohio, 1974—80; summer rsch. prof. Lehman Coll., CUNY, Bronx, vis. prof. biol. sci., 1999—2001; vis. scientist in botany Cambridge U., England, 1978—79; vis. scientist in botany Komarov Bot. Inst., Warsaw U., Poland, 1993; rschr., collaborator in fungal adhesion Kaohsiung Med. Coll., Taiwan, China, 1988—90; lectr., China, 1990. Author: (with A. Vassilyev) CD-ROM Text on Plant Anatomy, 2002; rschr., contbr. numerous publs. in field of air pollution effects on plant, fungal, and lichen ultrastructure, 1967—; early developer asynchronous learning techs. by means of networked computers on World-Wide Web, 1995—. Mem. Statewide Democratic Support Group, Ill. Recipient Outstanding Faculty Rsch. Recognition awards Bowling Green State U., 1973, 75; grantee Paint Rsch. Inst., 1976-83, NSF, 1981-83, EPA, 1984-86, USDA, 1986-89, Internat. Plant and Pollution Lab., 1993-98; lifetime assoc. fellow Clare Hall, Cambridge, Eng. Mem. AAAS, Bot. Soc. Am., Internat. Soc. Environ. Botanists (advisor, life mem., inaugurated 1st internat. meeting, Lucknow, India, 1996), Microscopy Soc. Am. (nat. chmn. cert. bd. 1982-89, dir. USA local affiliates 1990-93, Disting. Svc. award 1994, Cecil Hall award for outstanding rsch. in biology with analytical microscopy 1994), Sigma Xi. Mem. Christian Ch. (Disciples of Christ) Home: 3901 Farhills Dr Champaign IL 61822-9305 Office: U Ill Plant Biology 505 S Goodwin Ave 155 Morrill Hall Urbana IL 61801-3707 E-mail: r-crang@life.uiuc.edu.

CRANGLE, ROBERT D. lawyer, management consultant, entrepreneur, manufacturing executive; b. Putnam, Conn., May 5, 1943; s. Dale E. and Libbie S. (Krepela) C.; m. S. Jeanne Rose, June 6, 1968; children: Rob, Scott, Elenor, Bill, Kimball, Susan, Sara, Paul, Hally. BS in Nuclear Engring., Kans. State U., 1966; JD, Harvard U., 1969. Bar: Mass. 1969, Ill. 1974, Kans. 1987, U.S. Dist. Ct. Kans. 1987. Sr. v.p. Harbridge House, Inc., Boston, 1969-84; pres., dir. Rose & Crangle, Ltd., Lincoln, 1984—; dir. Helisys Inc., L.A., 1985-99; ptnr. Metz and Crangle, Chartered, Lincoln, Kans., 1987—; elected atty. Lincoln County, 1997—2001. Mem. faculty Bus. Sch., Ill. Inst. Tech., Chgo., 1984-87, dir. Ctr. Rsch. on Indsl. Strategy and Policy, Chgo., 1984-87. Bd. dirs. Lake Bluff (Ill.) Sch. Bd., 1982-87, Farmers Nat. Bank, 1992—; mem. Kans. Sci. and Tech. Coun., 1992-96; mem. Natural History Mus. Bd., 1995-98, Kans. Geol. Survey Adv. Com., 1995—. Recipient Meritorious Pub. Service award NSF, 1985. Fellow AAAS; mem. ABA, Kans. Bar Assn. (officer bus. law sect. 1993-97), N.W. Kans. Bar Assn., Kans. Math and Sci. Edn. Coalition (bd. dirs.), Inst. Mgmt. Cons. (cert. 1980). Republican. Mem. Soc. of Friends. Avocations: science policy, entrepreneurship. Office: Metz and Crangle Chartered PO Box 36 116 S 4th St Lincoln KS 67455-0036 also: Rose & Crangle Ltd PO Box 285 102 E Lincoln Av Lincoln KS 67455-0285 E-mail: rcltd@nckcn.com., mcc@nckcn.com.

CRANSTON, STEWART E. career officer; BA in Math., U. So. Calif., 1966; MBA, Auburn U., 1979; Grad., Air Command and Staff Coll., 1979; Diploma, Indsl. Coll. of Armed Forces, 1986; postgrad., Carnegie-Mellon U., 1989. Commd. 2d lt. USAF, 1966, advanced through ranks to lt. gen., 1997; various assignments to dep. chief of staff, test and opers. Hdqtrs. Air Force Material Command, Wright-Patterson AFB, Ohio, 1992-93; comdr. Air Force Devel. Test Ctr./Air Force Material Command, Eglin AFB, Fla., 1993-97; vice-comdr. Hdqtrs. Air Force Material Comman, Wright-Patterson AFB, Ohio, 1997—. Decorated Disting. Svc. medal, Legion of Merit, Disting. Flying Cross, Meritorious Svc. medal with four oak leaf clusters, Air medal with 15 oak leaf clusters, Air Force Commendation medal with oak leaf cluster, Republic of Vietnam Gallantry Cross with Palm, Vietnam Svc. medal with four svc. stars, others. Office: AFMC/CV 4375 Chidlaw Rd Ste 1 Wright Pat OH 45433-5066

CRAVEN, GEORGE W. lawyer; b. Louisville, Mar. 11, 1951; s. Mark Patrick and Doris Ann Craven; m. Jane A. Gallery, Aug. 16, 1980; children: Charles, Francis. Student, Sophia U., Tokyo, Japan, 1970-71; BA, U. Notre Dame, 1973; JD, Harvard U., 1976. Bar: Ill. 1976, U.S. Dist. Ct. (no. dist.) Ill. 1976, U.S. Tax Ct. 1977. Assoc. Sidley & Austin, Chgo., 1976—80; ptnr. Ogden & Robertson, Louisville, 1980—81; assoc. Mayer, Brown, Rowe & Maw, Chgo., 1981—82, ptnr., 1983—. Sec., United Way/Crusade of Mercy, Inc., 1997—, bd. dirs., 2001-. Mem. ABA (sect. taxation), Coun. on Fgn. Rels. (Chgo. com. 1996—). Roman Catholic. Office: Mayer Brown Rowe & Maw 190 S La Salle St Ste 3100 Chicago IL 60603-3441 E-mail: gcraven@mayerbrown.com.

CRAWFORD, BRYCE LOW, JR. retired chemist, educator; b. New Orleans, Nov. 27, 1914; s. Bryce Low and Clara Hall (Crawford) C.; m. Ruth Raney, Dec. 21, 1940; children: Bryce, Craig, Sherry Ann. A.B., Stanford U., 1934, M.A., 1935, Ph.D., 1937; Nat. Research fellow, Harvard U., 1937-39. Instr. chemistry Yale U., 1939-40; asst. prof. U. Minn., Mpls., 1940-43, assoc. prof., 1943-46, prof. phys. chemistry, 1946-82, Regents' prof. chemistry, 1982-85, emeritus, 1985—, chmn. dept., 1955-60, dean grad. sch., 1960-72. Mem. Grad. Record Exam. Bd., 1968-72; chmn. Council Grad Schs. in U.S., 1962-63; pres. Assn. Grad. Schs., 1970; dir. research on rocket propellants under Div. 3 Nat. Def. Research Com., 1942-45 Editor: Jour. Phys. Chemistry, 1970-80. Trustee Midwest Research Inst., 1963-92. Guggenheim fellow, 1950-51, 72-73; Fulbright grantee Oxford, 1951; Fulbright grantee, Tokyo, 1966; recipient Presdl. Cert. of Merit. Fellow Optical Soc. Am. (Pitts. Spectroscopy award, Ellis Lippincott award), Am. Phys. Soc.; mem. Am. Chem. Soc. (bd. dirs. 1969-77, Priestley medal 1982), AAAS, AAUP, Nat. Acad. Scis. (council 1975-78, home. sec. 1979-87), Coblentz Soc., Am. Philos. Soc., Soc. for Applied Spectrosopy, Am. Acad. Arts and Scis., Phi Beta Kappa, Sigma Xi, Phi Lambda Upsilon, Alpha Chi Sigma. Episcopalian. Clubs: Campus, Cosmos. Achievements include specializing in molecular structure and molecular spectra. Home: 1666 Coffman St Apt 114 Saint Paul MN 55108-1326 Office: U Minn Dept Chemistry 207 Pleasant St SE Minneapolis MN 55455-0431 E-mail: crawford@chemsun.chem.umm.edu.

CRAWFORD, DANIEL J. biologist, educator; PhD, U. Iowa. Prof. evolution, ecology and orgnl. biology Ohio State U., Columbus. Recipient Asa Gray award Am. Soc. Plant Taxonomists, 1997. Office: Ohio State U 386 B&Z Bldg 1735 Neil Ave Columbus OH 43210

CRAWFORD, DEWEY BYERS, lawyer; b. Saginaw, Mich., Dec. 22, 1941; s. Edward Owen and Ruth (Wentworth) C.; m. Nancy Elizabeth Eck, Mar. 24, 1974. AB in Econs., Dartmouth Coll., 1963; JD with distinction, U. Mich., 1966. Bar: Ill. 1967, U.S. Dist. Ct. (no. dist.) Ill. 1969. Assoc. Gardner, Carton & Douglas, Chgo., 1969-74, ptnr., 1975—. Adj. prof. law, ITT, Kent Sch. Law, 1992—. Contbr. articles to profl. jours. Chmn. Winnetka (Ill.) Caucus Coun., 1988-89. With U.S. Army, 1966-68, Vietnam. Mem. ABA, Chgo. Bar Assn., Am. Coll. Investment Counsel, Law Club Chgo., Legal Club Chgo. Republican. Congregationalist. Avocations: running, reading, music. Office: Gardner Carton & Douglas 321 N Clark St Ste 3000 Chicago IL 60610-4718 E-mail: dcrawford@ged.com.

CRAWFORD, EDWARD E. consumer products company executive; Owner Cleve. Steel Container, 1963; pres., CEO Pk.-Ohio Industries Inc., Cleve., 1992—, also chmn. bd. dirs. Office: Pk Ohio Holdings 23000 Euclid Ave Cleveland OH 44117-1729

CRAWFORD, HOWARD ALLEN, lawyer; b. Stafford, Kans., Aug. 4, 1917; s. Perry V. and Kate (Allen) C.; m. Millie Houseworth, Oct. 9, 1948; children: Catherine, Edward BS, Kans. State U., 1939; JD, U. Mich., 1942. Bar: Kans. 1942, Mo. 1943, U.S. Ct. Appeals (8th, 10th and D.C. cirs.), U.S. Supreme Ct. Mem. firm Lathrop and Gage, Kansas City, Mo., 1950-91; mng. ptnr. Lathrop and Norquist, 1970-85, ret., 1991. Dir. various cos. Mem. coun. City of Mission Hills, Kans., 1965-70 Mem. Lawyers Assn. Kansas City, Kansas City Club, Mission Hills Country Club. Home: 3103 W 67th Ter Shawnee Mission KS 66208-1857 Office: Lathrop and Gage 25th Fl 2345 Grand Blvd Fl 25 Kansas City MO 64108-2603

CRAWFORD, JAMES WELDON, psychiatrist, educator, administrator; b. Napoleon, Ohio, Oct. 27, 1927; s. Homer and Olga (Aderman) C.; m. Susan Young, July 5, 1955; 1 child, Robert James A.B., Oberlin Coll., 1950; M.D., U. Chgo., 1954, Ph.D., 1961. Intern Wayne County Hosp. and Infirmary, Eloise, Mich., 1954-55; resident Northwestern U., Chgo., 1958-59, Mt. Sinai Hosp./Chgo. Med. Sch., 1959-60; practice medicine specializing in occupational, individual and family psychiatry Chgo., 1961—. Mem. staff Mt. Sinai Hosp., Chgo, Ravenswood Hosp. Med. Ctr., Chgo., St. Lukes-Presbyn. Med. Ctr.; clin. assoc. prof. dept. psychiatry Sch. of Medicine, U. Ill. at Chgo., 1970—; chair and assoc. prof. dept. psychiatry Ravenswood Hosp. Med. Ctr., 1973-79; chmn. J.W. Crawford Assocs., Inc., 1979-82; assoc. prof. depts. psychology and psychiatry Rush Med. Co.. Contbr. articles to profl. jours. Bd. dirs. Pegasus Player, Chgo., 1978—, chmn. bd. dirs., 1979-84; bd. dirs. Bach Soc., 1985-98; del. to Russia and the Ukraine with People-to-People Internat., 1993, del. to Kenya, Africa, 1995, del. to China, 1998. NIH Inst. Neurol. Diseases postdoctoral fellow, 1955-59 Fellow Am. Psychiat. Assn. (life), Am. Orthopsychiat. Assn.; mem. AAAS, AAUP, Assn. Am. Med. Colls., Nat. Coalition Mental Health Profls. and Consumers, Ill. Coalition Mental Health Profls. and Consumers (steering com.), Inc. Psychiat. Soc., Chgo. Assn. for Psychoanalytic Psychology, Nat. Coun. on Family Rels., Sigma Xi. Lodge: Rotary (various coms. profl. rep.). Home and Office: 2418 Lincoln St Evanston IL 60201-2151 E-mail: sjcrawf@aol.com.

CRAWFORD, LEWIS CLEAVER, engineering executive, researcher; b. Salina, Kans., Dec. 7, 1925; s. Percival Wallace and Viva Estelle (Beichle) C.; m. Helen Alleyne Henry, May 28, 1950; children: Dorothy Caroline, Lewis Henry. B in Engring., Yale U., 1946. Registered profl. engr., Kans. Engr. Cemenstone Corp., Pitts., 1946-47; engr., then assoc. Wilson & Co. (engrs. and architects), Salina, 1947-67, ptnr., 1967-87, Western Properties and Cenwest Partnerships, 1992—. Served with USNR, 1943-46. Fellow ASCE; mem. NSPE, SAR, Flagon and Trencher, Kans. Cons. Engrs. (past chmn.), Kans. Engring. Soc. (past. dir.), Salina Country Club. Republican. Methodist. Office: Board of Trade Bldg 1700 E Iron Salina KS 67401-5101

CRAWFORD, RICHARD DWIGHT, biology educator, wildlife biology researcher; b. Kirksville, Mo., Nov. 16, 1947; s. John Barton and Ethel May (Kirkpatrick) C.; m. Glinda Carol Bloskovich, Dec. 30, 1966; 1 child, Melanie Contessa. BS in Edn., N.E. Mo. State U., 1968, MS, 1969; PhD, Iowa State U., 1975. Instr. Iowa State U., Ames, 1973-75; asst. prof. U. N.D., Grand Forks, 1975-80, assoc. prof., 1980-81, assoc. prof., biology chmn., 1981-82, assoc. prof., 1982-88, prof. and chair, 1988-91, prof., 1991—. Cons. U.S. Fish and Wildlife Svc., Jamestown, N.D., 1977, Three Tribes Indian Reservation, New Town, N.D., 1982. Author: (with others) Wildlife in Southwest North Dakota, 1978; editor: Wildlife Values of Sand and Gravel Pits, 1982; contbr. articles to profl. jours. Served with U.S. Amry, 1969-71. Recipient B.C. Gamble award U. N.D. Alumni Found., 1983. Mem. Wildlife Soc. (assoc. editor 1981-83, pres. N.D. chpt. 1981-82, nat. com. wetland mitigation and categorization 1993, N.D. Profl. award 1992), Am. Ornithologists Union (life), Wilson Ornithol. Soc. (life). Avocations: wood carving, gardening, fishing. Office: U ND Dept Biology Grand Forks ND 58202-9019 E-mail: richard_crawford@und.nodak.edu.

CRAWFORD, ROBERT W., JR. furniture rental company executive; b. Yonkers, N.Y., Oct. 19, 1938; BS, Dickinson Coll., 1960; MBA, U. Pa., 1963. Chmn., CEO Brook Furniture Rental, Inc., Lake Forest, Ill. Mem. adv. coun. on agr. and bus. Fed. Res. Bank of Chgo. Active Chgo. Coun. Fgn. Rels., Art Inst. Chgo., Lyric Opera Chgo.; mem. adv. bd. Lake Forest Symphony; bd. dirs. Greater Chgo. Home Bldrs. Assn.; governing mem. John G. Shedd Aquarium; trustee Field Mus.; divsn. chair United Way; co-founder Lincolnshire troop Boy Scouts Am. Inductee Chicagoland Entrepreneurial Hall of Fame, 1998. Mem. Nat. Recreation Found. (pres., trustee), Internat. Furniture Rental Assn. (chmn., pres., bd. dirs., com. chmn.), Chicagoland C. of C. (bd. dirs.), The Chgo. Club, Union League Club, Exmoor Country Club, The CEO Club, Execs. Club Chgo., Comml. Club Chgo., Econ. Club Chgo. (chmn.), Phi Kappa Sigma (Alumnus of Yr. award). Avocations: travel, athletics, reading, music, art. Office: Brook Furniture Rental Inc 100 Field Dr Ste 220 Lake Forest IL 60045 E-mail: rwc@bfn.com.

CRAWLEY, VERNON OBADIAH, academic adminstrator; b. Oct. 22, 1936; s. Joseph and Ruth (Adkins) C.; m. Betty W. Wood, July 9, 1966; children: V. Alan, Vonda, Keith. BS in Chemistry, Va. State U., 1958; postgrad., Coll. William and Mary, 1962, Am. U., 1964; MEd, U. Va., 1965; EdD, Pa. State U., 1971. Chemist Stuart Products Co., Richmond, Va., 1958-61; tchr. sci. and math. Ruthville (Va.) High Sch., 1961-64; asst. prof. sci. dept. Morgan State U., Balt., 1965-69; instr. phys. sci. Towson State Coll., 1969; assoc. prof. chemistry, chmn. sci., math. and technologies Dundalk C.C., 1971-74; assoc. dean acad. affairs Mercer County C.C., Trenton, N.J., 1974-78; pres. St. Louis C.C. at Forest Park, 1978-91, Moraine Valley C.C., Palos Hills, Ill., 1991—. Acting dean James Kerney campus Mercer County C.C., Trenton, 1976-77; adminstrv. specialist in sci. NASA, Washington, summer 1966, 67, 68; cons. N. Cen. Assn., Coro Found. Adv. bd. mem. St. Francis Hosp., Blue Island, Ill.; fin. adv. com. mem. Ill. C.C. Bd.; chmn. Ill. Coun. C.C. Pres.; bd. dirs. Southwest YMCA, Alsip, Ill. Recipient Outstanding Svc. to Williams Cmty. Sch. award 8th Dist. Police Cmty.Youth Network Com., 1990, Assistance with Minority Tchr. Recruitment Program award St. Louis Area Pers. and Place Adminstrs., 1989, Outstanding Leadership award Nat. Coun. Black Am. Affairs, 1987, Citizenship award Wellston Sch. Dist., 1983, NSF Acad. Yr. award, 1964-65, Southern fellowship, 1965. Mem. League for Innovation in C.C. (bd. dirs.), Expanding Leadership Opportunities for Minorities in C.C. (nat. adv. group), Am. Assn. C.C. (bd. dirs., exec. bd.), Nat. Coun. on Black Am. Affairs (bd. dirs.), Econ. Devel. Corp. for Southwest Suburbs (bd. dirs.), Rotary Club Oak Lawn, Moraine Valley C.C. Found. (bd. dirs.), Mo. Assn. Community and Jr. Colls. (bd. dirs.), Mo. Coun. C.C. Pres./Chancellors (chmn. 1986-87, v.p. 1985-86, sec. treas. 1984-85), Sigma Xi, Phi Theta Kappa. Avocations: travel, reading, gardening. Home: 7841 Sioux Rd Orland Park IL 60462-1894 Office: Moraine Valley CC 10900 S 88th Ave Palos Hills IL 60465-2175

CRAYCRAFT, ALLIE V., JR. state legislator; b. Mt. Sterling, Ky., May 30, 1932; m. Juanita Craycraft. Material mgr. Detroit Diesel Allison; with Hydra-Matic, Muncie, Ind.; mem. Ind. Senate from 26th dist., 1979—; ranking minority mem., ethics com.; mem. govt. and regulatory affairs com. Ind. State Senate, mem. transp. and interstate coop. com., mem. legis. appointment and elec. com., ranking minority mem. pensions/labor com., pub. policy com. Precinct committeeman, 1968—; trustee Liberty Twp., 1970-74; mem. Delaware County Welfare Bd., 1970-78; chmn. Delaware County chpt. Am. Heart Assn.; mem. Liberty-Perry Athletic Booster Club. Mem. Amvets (chmn. Delaware County chpt.), Muncie Lions. Office: 9501 E Jackson St Selma IN 47383-9599 also: State Senate State Capitol Indianapolis IN 46204

CRAYPO, CHARLES, labor economics educator; b. Jackson, Mich., Jan. 3, 1936; s. Norman Laverne and Ann Marie (Bogdan) C.; m. Mary Louise Vaclavik, Sept. 6, 1958; children: Jack, Carrie, Susan. BA in Econs., Mich. State U., 1959, MA in Econs., 1961, PhD in Econs., 1966. Asst. prof. econs. U. Maine, Orono, 1966-67; assoc. prof. Mich. State U., East Lansing, 1967-72, Pa. State U., University Park, 1972-78, U. Notre Dame, Ind., 1978-82, prof., 1984-2000, prof., chmn. dept. econs., 1984-93; prof. Cornell U., Ithaca, N.Y., 1982-84. Bd. dirs. Bus. Devel. Com., South Bend, Ind.; dir. Bur. Workers Edn., U. Maine, Orono, 1966-67, Higgins Labor Rsch. Ctr., U. Notre Dame, 1993; mem. acad. evaluating com. Labor Studies Ctr., Empire State Coll., SUNY, 1980; mem. labor studies dept. Ramapo Coll., 1981; mem. indsl. rels. dept. LeMoyne Coll., Syracuse, N.Y., 1983, Bur. of Labor Edn., U. Maine, Orono; external rev. mem. Divsn. Labor Studies Ind. U., 1998-99; mem. Labor Rsch. Adv. Coun., Bureau Labor Statistics, U.S. Dept. Labor, 2000; lectr. in field; expert witness. Author: Economics of Collective Bargaining, 1986, Grand Designs, 1993; mem. editl. bd., bus. mgr. Labor Studies Jour., 1976-80, chmn. editl. bd., 1980-85; mem. editl. bd. Contbns. to Labor Studies, 1989—; internat. mem. editl. bd. Indsl. Rels. Jour., 1989—; contbr. articles to profl. jours. Mem. acad. adv. com. Divsn. Labor Studies Ind. U., 1978-82, 84-92, 95-96. Served with USMC, 1953-55. Grantee NEH, 1981; rsch. grantee Dept. Commerce, 1984, Lilly Endowment, 1992-93, D. Dority Labor Rsch. Fund. Mem. Indsl. Rels. Rsch. Assn. Home: 50600 Sorrel Dr Granger IN 46530-8506

CREEK, PHILLIP G. real estate development executive; Sr. v.p., treas. M/I Schottenstein Homes, Columbus, Ohio, 1995—. Office: M/I Schottenstein Homes 3 East St Ste 500 Columbus OH 43228-1107

CREGG, ROGER A. construction executive; BS in Acctg., Northeastern U.; M in Mgmt., Northwestern U. CFO Sweetheart Cup Co.; Exec. v.p., CFO Zenith Electronics Corp.; sr. v.p., CFO Pulte Homes Corp., 1998—. Office: Pulte Homes Corp 33 Bloomfield Hills Pkwy Bloomfield Hills MI 48304-2944

CREIGH, THOMAS, JR. utility executive; b. Evanston, Ill., Jan. 3, 1912; s. Thomas and Frances (Connor) C.; m. Dorothy Claire Weyer, July 17, 1948; children: Mary Elizabeth, Thomas III, John, James. Grad., Mercersburg (Pa.) Acad., 1929; A.B., Wabash Coll., 1933. With No. Natural Gas Co., 1933-36; with KN Energy, Inc. (formerly Kans.-Nebr. Natural Gas Co., Inc.), 1936-86; v.p. KN Energy, Inc., 1951-61, pres., 1961-78, chmn. bd., 1978-85, chmn. emeritus, 1985-93, also dir.; v.p., dir. Excelsior Oil Corp., 1955-68, pres., 1968-84; pres., dir. Western Gas Corp., 1967-84. V.p., dir. Helium, Inc., 1960-85; sec., dir. Western Plastics Corp., 1953-69; dir. Dunne Gardner Drilling Co., City Nat. Bank, Hastings, Western Alfalfa Corp., Cap-Con Internat Inc., Cape Constrn. Co., Energy Transmission System, Inc., Advanced Fuel Systems, Inc., Slurry Transport Assos., Mem. Nebr. Gov.'s Task Force for Govt. Improvemenet, 1980-82, Nebr. Bd. Ednl. Lands and Funds, 1987-91; trustee Hastings Coll., Inst. Gas Tech., U. Nebr. Found., Nebr. State Hist. Found.; bd. dirs. Nebr. Art Collection, Nebr. chpt. Nature Conservancy, Nebraskans for Pub. TV, 1994—; mem. Nebr. Hist. Preservation Bd., 1991—, Adams County Hist. Soc., Nebr. Ind. Coll. Found., Crane Meadows Nature Ctr. Mem. Am. Gas Assn. (dir. 1969-73), Midwest Gas Assn. (dir. 1965-68), Interstate Natural Gas Assn. (dir. 1967-71, 74-82), Nebr. Assn. Commerce and Industry (past pres.), Nebr. Coun. Econ. Edn. (chmn. 1967-70), Nebr. State Hist. Soc. (exec. bd. 1990-91). Presbyterian (trustee). Office: Ste 204 Burlington Ctr 747 N Burlington Ave Hastings NE 68901

CREIGHTON, NEAL, retired army officer; b. Ft. Sill, Okla., July 11, 1930; s. Neal and Charlotte (Gilliam) C.; m. Joan Hicks, Aug. 1, 1958; children: Linda, Lisa, Neal. B.S., U.S. Mil. Acad., 1953; student, U. Madrid, 1959-60; M.A., Middlebury Coll., 1961; grad., U.S. Army Command and Staff Coll., 1967, U.S. Army War Coll., 1970. Commd. 2d lt. U.S. Army, 1953, advanced through grades to maj. gen.; troop assignments U.S., Germany, 1953-59; from instr. to asst. prof. fgn. lang. U.S. Mil. Acad., 1960-63; staff officer So. Command Panama, 1964-66; squadron comdr. Vietnam, 1967-68; mil. asst. Office of Sec. Army Washington, 1970-72; comdr. Combined Arms Tng. Center Germany, 1973-74; brigade comdr. Germany, 1974-76; dep. dir. Ops. and Readiness Directorate, Dept. Army, 1977-78; comdr. 1st Inf. Divsn. Germany, 1978-80; dep. chief of staff Allied Forces Central Europe, Brunssum, Netherlands, 1980; comdg. gen. 1st Inf. Divsn. Ft. Riley, Kans., 1982-84; ret. U.S. Army, 1984; administrator Robert R. McCormick Trust Founds., Chgo., 1985; pres., CEO R.R. McCormick Tribune Found., 1986-99; pres. Westminster Coll., Fulton, MO, 1999-2000; exec. dir. Liberty Meml., Kansas City, Mo., 2001—02. Decorated Disting. Service Medal, Silver Star medal, Bronze Star medal, Air medal. Mem. Chgo. Coun. on Fgn. Rels., Nat. Strategy Forum. Episcopalian. Office: 4600 E 63rd Trfy Kansas City MO 64130-4629 E-mail: nealc@crosslink.net.

CREMIN, SUSAN ELIZABETH, lawyer; b. Chgo., July 2, 1947; d. William Amberg and Rosemary (Brennan) C. AB cum laude, Vassar Coll., 1969; JD, Northwestern U., Chgo., 1976. Bar: Ill. 1977. Assoc. Winston & Strawn, Chgo., 1976-83, ptnr., 1983-93, capital ptnr., 1993—. Co-author: Registration and Reporting Under the Exchange Act, 1995, 2nd edit., 1996. Trustee The Shedd Aquarium, Chgo., The Masters Sch., Dobbs Ferry, N.Y. Office: Winston & Strawn 35 W Wacker Dr Ste 4200 Chicago IL 60601-1695

CRENSHAW, CAROL, charitable organization administrator; b. Chgo., July 3, 1956; BS in Acctg., Fin., No. Ill. U., 1978. CPA, Ill. Auditor CPMG Peat Marwick, Chgo., 1978-83, asst. contr., 1983, contr., 1983-94; CFO The Chgo. Cmty. Trust, 1994—. Mem. fin. acting practice com. Com. for the Found. Sector, 1997—. Office: The Chicago Community Trust 222 N Lasalle St Ste 1400 Chicago IL 60601-1088

CREWS, TERRELL, agricultural products executive; BS in Acctg., Freed Hardeman U.; M in Mgmt., Kelloggs Exec. M Program. Cost analyst acctg., bus. analysis lead Latin Am. Monsanto, controller Latin Am., fin. lead Asia Pacific; gen. auditor, global fin. lead Monsanto Global Seed Ops.; CFO Monsanto. Bd. trustees Freed Hardeman U.; bd. dirs. Jr. Achievement of Miss. Valley, Inc.; nat. council John M. Olin Sch. Bus., Washington U. Office: Monsanto 800 N Lindbergh Blvd Saint Louis MO 68167

CRIANCAMILLI, ANDREW A. retail executive; Pres., COO Perry Drug Stores; with U.S. Kmart, Troy, Mich., 1995—, pres., gen. merchandise mgr., 1997—. Office: Kmart Corp 3100 W Big Beaver Rd Fl 4 Troy MI 48084

CRIBBET, JOHN EDWARD, law educator, former university chancellor; b. Findlay, Ill., Feb. 21, 1918; s. Howard H. and Ruth (Wright) C.; m. Betty Jane Smith, Dec. 24, 1941; children: Carol Ann, Pamela Lee. BA, Ill. Wesleyan U., 1940, LLD, 1971; JD, U. Ill., 1947. Bar: Ill. 1947. Pvt. practice in law, Bloomington, Ill., 1947—; prof. law U. Ill., Urbana, 1947-67, dean. Coll. Law, 1967-79; chancellor Urbana-Champaign Campus, U. Ill., 1979-84, Corman prof. law, 1984-88, prof. emeritus, 1988—. Author: Cases and Materials on Judicial Remedies, 1954, Cases on Property, 7th edit., 1996, (with others) Principles of the Law of Property, 1975, (with Prof. Corwin Johnson), 3d edit., 1989; editor: U. Ill. Law Forum, 1947-55; contbr. articles to profl. jours. Chmn. com. on jud. ethics Il. Supreme Ct.; pres. United Fund Champaign County, (Ill.), 1962-63; trustee Ill. Wesleyan U.; mem. exec. com. Assn. Am. Law Schs., 1973-75, pres., 1979. Served to maj. AUS, 1941-45. Decorated Bronze Star; decorated Croix de Guerre Mem. ABA, Ill. State Bar Assn., Champaign County Bar Assn., Order of Coif Lodge: Rotary. Office: U Ill Coll of Law 504 E Pennsylvania Ave Champaign IL 61820-6909

CRIDER, ROBERT AGUSTINE, international financier, law enforcement official; b. Washington, Jan. 3, 1935; s. Rana Albert and Terasa Helen (Dampf) C.; m. Debbie Ann Lee, Feb. 1960. Student, U. Md., 1959-63. Police officer Met. Police Dept., Washington, 1957-67; substitute tchr., bldg. trades instr. Maries R-1 Sch., Vienna, 1968-70; vets. constrn. tng. officer VA Dept. Edn., 1968-70; constrn. mgr. Tectonnics Ltd., Vienna, 1970-79; owner, dir. R-A Crider & Assocs., St. Louis, 1979—. Bd. dirs. TI-CO Investment Corp., Langcaster Corp. With USAF, 1952-56. Mem. Assn. Ret. Policemen, Internat. Conf. Police, Internat. Assn. Chiefs of Police, Nat. Police Assn., World Future Soc., Internat. Platform Assn., Mo. Police Chiefs Asn., Mo. Sheriff's Assn., Am. Correctional Assn., Law Enforcement Intelligence Assn., Internat. Drug Enforcement Assn., Nat. Assn. Fin. Cons., Internat. Soc. Financiers, Am. Legion, St. Louis Honor Guard, Lions, K.C. (4th degree). Roman Catholic. Home: PO Box 109 Vienna MO 65582-0109 Office: R-A Crider & Assocs 2644 Roseland Ter Saint Louis MO 63143-2304 E-mail: p9468w@aol.com.

CRIHFIELD, PHILIP J. lawyer; b. Chgo., Oct. 3, 1945; BS with highest distinction, Purdue U., 1967; JD with honors, John Marshall Law Sch., 1971. Bar: Ill. 1971, U.S. Patents and Trademark Office 1972. Ptnr. Sidley & Austin, Chgo. Adj. prof. mktg. and pub. policy Northwestern U., 1986—. Mem. Chgo. Bar Assn. (chmn. law, sci., tech. com. 1975). Office: Sidley & Austin 1 S First National Plz Chicago IL 60603-2000

CRIM, FORREST FLEMING, JR. chemist, educator; b. Waco, Tex., May 30, 1947; s. Forrest Fleming Sr. and Almanor Adair (Chapman) C.; m. Joyce Ann Wileman, June 21, 1969; 1 child, Tracy F. BS, Southwestern U., 1969; PhD, Cornell U., 1974. Staff mem. Engrng. Rsch. Ctr. Western Electric Co., Princeton, N.J., 1974-76; postdoctoral staff mem. Los Alamos (N.Mex.) Sci. Lab., 1976-77; from asst. prof. to assoc. prof. Dept. Chemistry U. Wis., Madison, 1977-84, prof. Dept. Chemistry, 1984—. Mem. rev. panel, Dept. of Energy Combustion Rsch. Facility, 1983-85, chmn., 1985, review com., Chemistry Dept., Brookhaven Nat. Lab., 1989; mem. Nat. Rsch. Coun. Workshop on the Chemistry Dept. of the Future, 1987; chmn. Gordon Rsch Conf. on Atomic and Molecular Interactions, 1988; external adv. com. of the Chemical and Laser Scis. Divsn., Los Alamos Nat. Lab., 1990—; rev. com. Associated Univs. Chemistry Dept., Brookhaven Nat. Lab., 1990—; mem. Nat. Rsch. Coun. Panel on Future Opportunities in Atomic, Molecular, and Optical Sci., 1991—. Editorial bd. internat. revs. Phys. Chemistry, 1990—, editorial adv. bd. Ency. of Applied Physics, 1989—, Jour. Phys. Chemistry, 1987-93; contbr. articles to profl. jours. Fellow Alfred P. Sloan Rsch., 1981-83, fellow AAAS, 1995, fellow Am. Acad. Arts and Scis., 1998; named Camille and Henry Dreyfus Tchr.-Scholar, 1982, Helfaer Prof. Chemistry, 1985-91, Robert A. Welch Foun. lectr., 1989, Bayer-Mobay lectr., U. N.H., 1991, Malcolm Dole Disting. lectr., Northwestern U., 2000; recipient Alexander von Humnboldt Sr. U.S. Scientist award, 1986, Southwestern Univ. Alumni Assn. Citation of Merit, 1987, Max Planck award Alexander von Humboldt Soc., 1993. Fellow Am. Phys. Soc. (Earl K. Plyler Prize Selection Com. 1992—, Earle K. Plyler Molecular Physics prize 1998); mem. AAAS, NAS, Am. Chem. Soc. (chmn. Symposium on State-to-State Chemistry 1986, vice-chmn. Phys. Chemistry Div. 1986-87, chmn.-elect 1987-88, chmn. 1988-89, chmn. Task Force to Monitor Jour. of Physical Chemistry 1990-91), Optical Soc. of Am. (Quantum Electronics and Laser Scis. com. 1990-91). Office: Univ Wis Dept Chemistry 1101 University Ave Madison WI 53706-1322

CRISHAM, THOMAS MICHAEL, lawyer; b. Chgo., June 7, 1939; s. John and Ellen (Moore) C.; m. Catherine Marie Schaab, Oct. 2, 1965; children: Catherine Marie, Megan, Maura. BBA, Loyola U., 1962, JD cum laude, 1965. Bar: Ill. 1965, U.S. Dist. Ct. (no. dist.) Ill. 1965, U.S. Supreme Ct. 1971, U.S. Ct. Appeals (7th crct.) 1978. Ptnr. Hinshaw & Culbertson, Chgo., 1965-95; sr. ptnr. Quinlan & Crisham, Ltd., 1996—2001, Crisham & Kubes, Ltd., Chgo., 2001—. Mem. editl. bd. Ins. Outlook, Colorado Springs, Colo., 1990; pres. Def. Rsch. and Trial Lawyers Inst., Chgo., 1989, chmn. bd., 1990; mem. advisors Expert Evidence Reporter, Colorado Springs, 1990. Contbg. author: Abortion and Social Justice, 1973, Human Life: Our Legacy and Our Challenge, 1975, Architect and Engineer Liability: Claims Against Design Professional, 1987, Prosecuting and Defending Insurance Claims, 1989. Bd. dirs. Wendy Will Case Cancer Rsch. Found., Boys' Hope Scholars. With USMCR, 1959-60. Fellow Am. Coll. Trial Lawyers, Internat. Soc. Barristers; mem. ABA, Am. Bd. Trial Advs. (diplomate), Def. Rsch. Inst. (pres. 1989-90, chair 1990-91), Internat. Assn. Def. Counsel, Ill. Bar Assn., Trial Lawyers Club Chgo. (pres. 1975-76), Soc. Trial Lawyers Ill., Appellate Lawyers Assn., Assn. Def. Trial Lawyers, Am. Inns of Ct., Chgo. Bar Assn. Roman Catholic. Office: Crisham & Kubes Ltd 30 N Lasalle St Ste 2800 Chicago IL 60602-2511 E-mail: tcrisham@crishamlaw.com.

CRISSMAN, PENNY M. state legislator; b. Nov. 20, 1943; m. Charles; children: Mitzi, Mark. Student, Ea. Mich. U., Oakland U. Mayor, Rochester, Mich., 1989-92; rep. Mich. Dist. 45, 1993-98; mem. Rochester City Coun., 1999—. Mem. Rochester City Coun., 1985-92; asst. Rep. whip Mich. Ho. Reps., 1993—, co-chair com. on civil rights & women's issues, edn. com., higher edn. com., local govt. coms., pub. health coms. Recipient disting. citizenship award Rochester Elks, 1992. Mem. Rochester C. of C., Optimists, Oakland U. Press Club. Office: 400 6th St Rochester MI 48307-1400

CRIST, PAUL GRANT, lawyer; b. Denver, Sept. 9, 1949; s. Max Warren and Marjorie Raymond (Catland) C.; m. Christine Faye Clements, June 4, 1972; children: Susan Christine, Benjamin Warren, John Willis. BA, U. Nebr., 1971; JD cum laude, NYU, 1974. Bar: Ohio 1974, U.S. Ct. Mil. Appeals 1975, Calif. 1976, U.S. Dist. Ct. (no. dist.) Ohio 1979, U.S. Ct. Appeals (6th cir.) 1982. Assoc. Jones, Day, Reavis & Pogue, Cleve., 1974, 78-83, ptnr., 1984—. Rsch. editor NYU Law Rev., 1972-74. Capt. JAGC, USAF, 1974-78. Decorated Meritorious Svc. medal. Fellow Am. Coll. Trial Lawyers; mem. Ohio State Bar Assn., Cleve. Bar Assn., State Bar Calif., Order of Coif, Am. Inns of Ct. Democrat. Presbyterian. Home: 6565 Canterbury Dr Hudson OH 44236-3484 Office: Jones Day Reavis & Pogue N Point 901 Lakeside Ave E Cleveland OH 44114-1190

CRITTENDEN, BRUCE A. finance company executive; Exec. v.p. Green Tree Fin. Group, St. Paul, pres., 1998—. Office: Green Tree Fin Corp 1100 Landmark Towers 345 Saint Peter St 11th Fl Saint Paul MN 55102

CRITZER, SUSAN L. health products company executive; BSME, Gen. Motors Inst.; MBA, U. Mich. Mgmt., info. sys., quality assurance and engrng. positions GM, until 1986; various mgr. engrng. and quality assurance positions Becton-Dickinson Corp., 1986-89; various mgmt. positions Davis and Geck divsn. Am. Cyanamid Corp., 1989-95, dir. engrng. endosurgery divsn., until 1995; v.p. ops. Integ Inc., St. Paul, 1995-99, pres., CEO, 1999—. Office: Ingeg Inc 2800 Patton Rd Saint Paul MN 55113-1100 Fax: 651-639-9042.

CROCKER, DOUGLAS, II, real estate executive; Pres., CEO Equity Residential Properties Trust, Chgo. Mem. Urban Land Inst., Nat. Multi-Housing Coun., Nat. Multifamily Inst., Nat. Real Estate Com. Mem. Nat. Assn. Real Estate Investment Trusts. Office: Equity Residential Properties Trust 2 N Riverside Plz Ste 450 Chicago IL 60606-2600

CROCKER, STEPHEN L. federal magistrate judge; BA, Wesleyan U., 1980; JD, Northwestern U., 1983. Law clk. to Hon. Barbara Crabb U.S. Dist. Ct. (we. dist.) Wis., Madison, 1983-84; trial atty. D.O.J., 1984-86; asst. U.S. atty. No. Dist. Ill., 1986-90; assoc. Michael, Best & Friedrich, 1990-92; magistrate judge U.S. Dist. Ct. (we. dist.) Wis., Madison, 1992—. Office: US Courthouse 120 N Henry St Madison WI 53703-2559

CROCKETT, JOAN M. human resources executive; , John Carroll Univ., 1972. Sr. v.p. human resources Allstate Ins. Co. Bd. dirs. INROADS; adv. bd. Univ. Ill. Chgo. Internat. Student Exchange Program; ptnr., bd. dirs. Ctr. for Human Resource Mgmt. Univ. Ill., gov. coun. Good Shepherd Hosp., Barrington, Ill. Named Human Resource Exec. of Yr., Human Resource Exec. mag., 1997. Office: Allstate 2775 Sanders Rd Northbrook IL 60062-6127

CROFTS, ANTONY RICHARD, biochemistry and biophysics educator; b. Harrow, Eng., Jan. 26, 1940; came to U.S., 1978; s. Richard Basil Iliffe and Vera Rosetta (Bland) C.; m. Paula Anne Hinds-Johnson, June 7, 1969 (div. 1981); 1 child, Charlotte Victoria Patricia; 1 adopted child, Rupert Charles; m. Christine Thompson Yerkes, Dec. 23, 1982; children: Stephanie Boynton, Terence Spencer. BA, U. Cambridge, Eng., 1961, PhD, 1965. Asst. lectr. dept. biochemistry U. Bristol, Eng., 1964-65, lectr. Eng., 1966-72, reader Eng., 1972-78; prof. biophysics U. Ill., Urbana-Champaign, 1978—, prof. microbiology, 1992-99, chmn. biophysics divsn., 1978-91, assoc. dean Coll. Liberal Arts & Scis., 1996-98, prof. biochemistry, 1998—. Mem. organizing com. 4th Internat. Congress Photosynthesis, Reading, Eng., 1977, 7th Internat. Congress Photosynthesis, Providence, 1986, Table Ronde, Rousel-UCLA Forum, Paris, 1985; vis. prof. Coll. de France, 1983; Melandri lectr. European BioEnergetics Conf., Lyon, France, 1982. Contbr. numerous articles, revs., etc., in area of biophysics, photosynthesis and bioenergetics; mem. editl. bd. Biochem. Jour., U.K., 1971-72, Biochimica Biophysica Acta, Holland, 1972-77, jour. Bacteriology, 1979-83, Archives Biochemistry and Biophysics, 1980-85. Major scholar nat. sci. U. Cambridge, 1958-61, U. Ill. scholar, 1989-92; grantee U.S. Dept. Energy, 1982-96, Guggenheim Found., 1985, NSF, NIH, U.S. Dept. Agr., 1979-2001. Fellow AAAS; mem. Biophys. Soc., Am. Soc. Biochemistry and Molecular Biology, Am. Soc. Plant Physiologists (Charles F. Kettering award 1992). Avocations: windsurfing, skiing, fishing, sailing. Office: U Ill Dept Biochemistry 419 Roger Adams Lab Box B4 600 S Mathews Ave Urbana IL 61801-3602 E-mail: a-crofts@life.uiuc.edu.

CROIS, JOHN HENRY, local government official; b. Chgo., Jan. 13, 1946; s. Henry F. and Dorothy M. (Priebe) C. BA, Elmhurst Coll., 1969; MA, U. Notre Dame, 1972. Asst. village mgr. Village of Oak Lawn, Ill., 1975-85; village mgr. Village of Westchester, 1985; dir. West Cook County Solid Waste Agy., 1990—. Coord. Oak Lawn Swine Flu Immunization Program, 1976; bd. dirs. Ill. Met. Investment Fund. Mem. ASPA, West Ctrl. Mcpl. Conf. (chmn. intergovtl. com. 1991, exec. bd. 1991—), Ill. Met. Investment Fund (dir. 1996—), Chgo. Area Transp. Study Coun. Mayors (North Ctrl. region), Internat. City Mgmt. Assn., Ill. City Mgmt. Assn., Metro-Mgrs. Assn., St. Germaine's Men's Club. Home: 10233 Karlov Ave Oak Lawn IL 60453-4235 Office: 10300 W Roosevelt Rd Westchester IL 60154-2568

CROMLEY, JON LOWELL, lawyer; b. Riverton, Ill., May 23, 1934; s. John Donald and Naomi M. (Mathews) C. JD, John Marshall Law Sch., 1966. Bar: Ill. 1966. Real estate title examiner Chgo. Title & Trust Co., 1966-70; pvt. practice Genoa, Ill., 1970—; mem. firm O'Grady & Cromley, 1970-96. Bd. dirs. Citizen's First Nat. Bank, 1984-92, Kingston Mut. Ins. Co., Genoa Main St., Inc. Mem.: ABA, Am. Judicature Soc., DeKalb County Bar Assn., Chgo. Bar Assn., Ill. State Bar Assn. Home: 130 Homewood Dr Genoa IL 60135-1260 E-mail: jcromley@msn.com.

CROMWELL, AMANDA CARYL, former soccer player, coach; b. Washington, June 15, 1970; BS in Biology, U. Va., 1992. Head women's soccer coach U. Md.; head coach U. Central Fla. Mem. U.S. Women's Nat. Soccer Team, 1991—; mem. U.S. Team CONCACAF Qualifying Tournament, Haiti, 1991, Montreal, Can., 1994; mem. silver medal U.S. Team, 1993 World Univ. Games, Buffalo, N.Y.; alternate gold medal U.S. Olympic Team, 1996; mem. 3d place U.S. Team, 1995 FIFA Women's World Cup, Sweden; mem. Hammarby Soccer Club, Stockholm, 1994; mem. SA United Soccer Club of Fairfax (Va.), 1997. Named NSCAA All-Am. (twice); named Soccer Am. Freshman of Yr., h.s. Rookie of Yr., 1990. Office: US Soccer Fedn 1801-1811 S Prairie Ave Chicago IL 60616

CRONIN, DAN, state legislator; b. Elmhurst, Ill., Nov. 7, 1959; BA, Northwestern U., 1981; JD, Loyola U., 1985. Campaign coord. Congressman John E. Porter, 1981; law clk. spl. prosecution divsn. Ill. Atty. Gen. Office, 1983; minority leader Ill. Ho. of Reps., 1985-87; with DuPage County State's Atty.'s Office, 1987-89; Ill. State sen. Dist. 39, 1993—. Mem. Elem. and Secondary Edn., Gen. Svcs. Appropriations and Health Care Coms.; atty. Kemp & Capanna, Ltd., Oak Brook, Ill. Mem. YMCA. Mem. ABA, ATLA,Ill. Bar Assn., DuPage County Bar Assn., Am. Cancer Soc., Lions, KC. Address: 105 E 1st St Elmhurst IL 60126-2801

CRONIN, JAMES WATSON, physicist, educator; b. Chicago, Ill., Sept. 29, 1931; s. James Farley and Dorothy (Watson) Cronin; m. Annette Martin, Sept. 11, 1954; children: Catheryn, Emily, Daniel Watson. A.B., So. Methodist U. (1951); Ph.D., U. Chgo.; D (hon.) , U. Paris, 1995, U. Leeds, 1996, Univ. Pierre & Marie Curie, 1994; DSc (hon.) , U. Leeds, 1996. Asst. physicist Brookhaven Nat. Lab., 1955—58; asst. prof. Princeton, 1958—65, prof. physics, 1965—71; prof. physics and astronomy U. Chgo., 1971—, prof. emeritus physics and astronomy. Loeb lectr. physics Harvard U., 1967; participant early devel. spark chambers; co-discoverer CP-violation, 64; lectr. Nashima Found., 1993. Recipient Rsch. Corp. Am. award, 1967, John Price Wetherill medal, Franklin Inst., 1976, E.O. Lawrence award, ERDA, 1977, Nobel prize for Physics, 1980, Nat. medal of Sci., 1999; fellow Sloan, 1964—66, Guggenheim, 1970—71, 1982—83. Mem.: NAS (coun. mem.), Am. Phys. Soc., Am. Acad. Arts and Scis., Am. Philos. Soc. Office: U Chgo Enrico Fermi Inst 5630 S Ellis Ave Chicago IL 60637-1433

CRONIN, PATRICK G. financial executive; BS in Math. and Computer Scis., Moravian Coll., 1982. Ea. region dist. mgr. AT&T CS; v.p. worldwide profl. svcs. NCR Corp., Dayton, Ohio, 1991—, now sr. v.p. fin. solutions group. Office: NCR Corp 1700 S Patterson Blvd Dayton OH 45479-0002

CRONIN, PATTI ADRIENNE WRIGHT, state agency administrator; b. Chgo., May 25, 1943; d. Rodney Adrian and Dorothy Louise (Thiele) Wright; m. Kevin Brian Cronin, May 1, 1971; 1 child, Kevin. BA, Beloit (Wis.) Coll., 1965; JD with honors, U. Wis., 1983. Vol. Peace Corps, Turkey, 1965-67, recruiter, 1967-68; tchr. English Kamehameha III Sch., Lahaina, Hawaii, 1968-70, Evansville (Wis.) High Sch., 1972-77; tchr. math. and history Killian Sch., Hartford, Wis., 1977-78; tchr. English Kaiser High Sch., Honolulu, 1979-80; intern Wis. Ct. Appeals, Madison, 1983; exec. dir. Wis. Waste Facility Siting Bd., 1983—. Founder, v.p., bd. dirs. Justice Ctr. Honolulu, 1979-82; sec., treas. Cronin Constrn. Co., Inc., Madison, 1986—. Editor: Internat. Law Jour., 1982. Bd. dirs. Neighborhood Bd., Honolulu, 1979-82; chmn. United Way, 1989—; active Parent Citizens Adv. Coun. Recipient Mayor's award of outstanding achievement, City of Honolulu, 1980. Mem. Soc. Profls. in Dispute Resolution, ABA, State Bar Wis. Avocations: family, real estate, travel. Office: Waste Facility Siting Bd 201 W Washington Ave Madison WI 53703-2760 E-mail: patti.cronin@wfs.state.wi.us.

CRONON, WILLIAM, history educator; b. New Haven, Sept. 11, 1954; m. Nancy Elizabeth Fey. BA in History, English with honors, U. Wis., 1976; MA in Am. History, Yale U., 1979, M of Philosophy in Am. History, 1981, PhD in Am. History, 1990; DPhil in Brit. History, Oxford U., 1981. Asst. prof. history Yale U., New Haven, 1981-86, assoc. prof., 1986-91, prof., 1991-92, mem. studies in environment program creation com., 1983-84, co-chair studies environment program, 1989-92, dir. grad. studies, history dept., 1990-92; Frederick Jackson Turner chair of history, geography, and environ. studies U. Wis., Madison, 1992—, dir. honors program Coll. Letters and Sci., 1996-98; found. fac. dir. Chadbourne Residential Coll., 1997-2000. Asst. Am. sec. Rhodes Scholarship Trust, 1978-80, Wis. state sec., 1993-98; cons. in field; mem. adv. bd. The History Tchr., 1986-2000. Author: Changes in the Land: Indians, Colonists and the Ecology of New England, 1983 (Valley Forge honor cert. 1984, Soc. Colonial award citation of honor 1984, Francis Parkman prize 1984), Nature's Metropolis: Chicago and the Great West, 1991 (Chgo. Tribune Heartlaand prize 1991, Bancroft prize 1992, George Perkins Marsh prize 1993); editor: (with Miles and Gitlin) Under an Open Sky: Rethinking America's Western Past, 1992, Uncommon Ground: Rethinking the Human Place in Nature, 1995; mem. bd. editors Forest and Conservation History, 1986-91; also articles; gen. editor Weyerhaeuser Environ. Books, U. Wash. Press, 1993—. Bd. dirs. Conn. Fund for Environ., 1986-91, v.p., 1987-89; mem. adv. bd. TV series Am. Experience Sta. WGBH-TV; trustee Conn. Nature Conservancy, 1989-91; bd. dirs., mem. com. on problems and policy Social Sci. Rsch. Coun., 1991-96, chairperson com. on problems and policy, 1994-96. Rhodes scholar Oxford U., 1976-78; fellow Danforth Found., 1976-82, Newberry Libr., 1980, Mellon Found., 1982-83, Morse fellow Yale U., 1985-86, MacArthur Found., 1985-90, Whitney Humanities Ctr., 1987-89, fellow U. Calif. Humanities Rsch. Inst., 1994, Guggenheim fellow, 1995. Mem. AAAS, Am. Hist. Assn. (Robinson prize com. 1990), Am. Philos. Soc., Orgn. Am. Historians (chmn. Curti prize com. 1987-88), Forest History Soc. (bd. dirs.), Econ. History Assn., Agrl. History Soc., Ecol. Soc. Am., Western Hist. Assn. (conv. program com. 1987, chmn. 1991-92), Assn. Am. Geographers, Am. Studies Assn., Am. Anthrop. Assn., Wilderness Soc. (gov. coun. 1995—), Am. Soc. for Ethnohistory, Chgo. Hist. Soc., Am. Antiquarian Soc., Soc. Am. Historians, Phi Beta Kappa (William C. DeVane award Yale chpt. 1988), Phi Kappa Phi, Phi Eta Sigma. Office: U Wis Dept History 3211 Humanities 455 N Park St Madison WI 53706-1405 Home: 2027 Chadbourne Ave Madison WI 53726

CROOKS, N(EIL) PATRICK, state supreme court justice; b. Green Bay, Wis., May 16, 1938; s. George Merrill and Aurelia Ellen (O'Neill) C.; m. Kristin Marie Madson, Feb. 15, 1964; children: Michael, Molly, Kevin, Kathleen, Peggy, Eileen. BA magna cum laude, St. Norbert Coll., 1960; JD, U. Notre Dame, 1963. Bar: Wis. 1963, U.S. Supreme Ct. 1969. Assoc. Cohen and Parins, Green Bay, 1963; ptnr. Cohen, Grant, Crooks and Parins, 1966-70; sr. ptnr. Crooks, Jerry, Norman and Dilweg, 1970-77; judge Brown County (Wis.) Ct., 1977-78, Brown County (Wis.) Cir. Ct., 1978-96; justice Wis. Supreme Ct., Madison, 1996—. Instr. bus. law U. Wis., Green Bay, 1970-72; mem. faculty Wis. Jud. Coll., 1982. Editor Law Rev. Notre Dame, 1962-63. Pres. Brown County United Way, 1976-78; chmn. Brown County Legal Aid, 1971-73; mem. Northeast Criminal Justice Coord. Coun., 1973-85; pres. St. Joseph Acad. Sch. Bd., 1987-89. Capt. U.S. Army, 1963-66. Recipient Human Rights award Baha'i Community of Green Bay, 1971, Disting. Achievement award in Social Sci. St. Norbert Coll., 1977 award of Yr. U. Notre Dame, 1978, Brown County Vandalism Prevention Assn. award, 1982, W. Heraly MacDonald award Brown County United Way, 1983, Community Svc. award St. Joseph Acad., 1989, Alma Mater award St. Norbert Coll., 1992, Disting. Alumnus of Yr. award notre Dame Acad., 2002; named Wis. Trial Judge of the Year Wis. Chpt. Am. Bd. of Trial Advocates, 1994. Mem. ABA, FBA, State Bar Wis., Brown County Bar Assn. (pres. 1977), Wis. Acad. Trial Lawyers, Wis. Law Found. (bd. dirs., mem. exec. com.), Nat. Conf. of Appellate Ct. Judges, Assn. of Women Lawyers for Brown County, Dane County Bar Assn., James E. Doyle Am. Inn of Ct., Wis. Jud. Coun. Roman Catholic. Home: 5329 Lighthouse Bay Dr Madison WI 53704-1113 Office: PO Box 1688 State Capitol 16 E Madison WI 53701

CROPSEY, ALAN LEE, state legislator, lawyer; b. Paw Paw, Mich., June 13, 1952; s. Harmon George and Ruth Marian (Lindsay) C.; m. Erika Lynn Rumminger, Nov. 24, 1979; children: Joel Daniel, Gabriel Michael, Nathaniel Samuel, Evamarie Barbara. B of Math. Edn., Bob Jones U., 1975; JD, Cooley Law Sch., 1978. Bar: Mich., 1978. State senator 30th dist. Mich. Senate, 1983-86; state rep. 88th dist. Mich. Ho. of Reps., 1981-82, state rep. 86th dist., 1993-98; internet svc. provider, polit. cons. Freedom ISP, Lansing, Mich., 1999—. Home: 7730 Loomis Rd Dewitt MI 48820-8482 Office: Freedom ISP 205 W Saginaw St Lansing MI 48933-1216

CROPSEY, JOSEPH, political science educator; b. N.Y.C., Aug. 27, 1919; s. Gustave and Margaret (Dirnfeld) C.; m. Lilian Crystal Levy, Nov. 4, 1945; children— Seth, Rachel Cropsey Simons A.B., Columbia U., 1939, A.M., 1940, Ph.D., 1952; DHL (hon.), Colo. Coll., 1989. Tutor, asst. prof. CCNY, 1946-57; instr. polit. sci. New Sch. Social Rsch., N.Y.C., 1949-54; asst. prof. U. Chgo., 1958-64, assoc. prof., 1964-70, prof., 1970-85, Disting. Svc. prof., 1985-89, prof. emeritus, 1989—. Author: Polity and Economy, 1957, Political Philosophy and the Issues of Politics, 1977, Plato's World, 1995; editor: Ancients and Moderns, 1964; co-editor, co-author: History of Political Philosophy, 1963. Served to 1st. lt. U.S. Army, 1941-46, PTO, ETO Office: U Chgo 5828 S University Ave Chicago IL 60637-1515

CROSBIE, ALFRED LINDEN, mechanical engineering educator; b. Muskogee, Okla., Aug. 1, 1942; s. Alfred Henry and Jacquetta Hope (Stoneburner) C.; m. Ann Frances Cirou, July 18, 1963; children: Mark, Jacqueline. BSME, U. Okla., d1964; MSME, Purdue U., 1966, PhD, 1969. Asst. prof. U. Mo., Rolla, 1968-72, assoc. prof., 1972-75, prof., 1975-91, curators' prof., 1991—. Editor: Aerothermodynamics and Planetary Entry, 1981, Heat Transfer and Thermal Control, 1981; editor-in-chief Jour. Thermophysics and Heat Transfer, 1986—; assoc. editor Jour. Quantitative Spectroscopy and Radiative Transfer, 1979—; mem. editl. bd. Heat Transfer-Recent Contents, 1996-2000; mem. adv. bd. Internat. Jour. Thermal Scis., 2000—; contbr. over 80 articles on radiative heat transfer to profl. jours. Fellow AIAA (chmn. thermophysics com. 1984-86, tech. program chmn. 15th Thermophysics Conf. 1980, assoc. editor AIAA Jour. 1981-83, Thermophysics award 1987, Tech. Contbn. award, 1988), ASME (heat transfer com. on theory and fundamentals 1983—, heat transfer com. on numerical heat transfer 1993—, Heat Transfer Meml. award 1990), AAAS; mem. Optical Soc. Am., Phi Eta Sigma, Sigma Pi Sigma, Tau Beta Pi, Pi Tau Sigma, Sigma Tau, Pi Mu Epsilon, Sigma Xi. Lutheran. Avocation: fishing. Home: 8 Mcfarland Dr Rolla MO 65401-3805 Office: U Mo 233 Mech Engring Rolla MO 65401 E-mail: crosbie@umr.edu.

CROSBY, FRED MCCLELLAN, retail home and office furnishings executive; b. Cleve., May 17, 1928; s. Fred Douglas and Marion Grace (Naylor) C.; m. Phendalyné D. Tazewell, Dec. 23, 1958; children: Fred, James, Llionicia. Grad. H.S. V.p. Seaway Flooring & Paving Co., Cleve., 1959-63; chmn., CEO Crosby Furniture Co., Inc., 1963—. Vice chmn. bd. First Bank Nat.; bd. dirs. Budget Rent-A-Car Systems, Greater Cleve. Growth Assn.; dir., chmn. First Intercity Banc Corp.; trustee Better Bus. Bur. Bd. dirs. Forest City Hosp. Found., Cleve. State U. Found., Greater Cleve. Growth Assn., 1971-90, 93—, Coun. Smaller Enterprise, 1973-80, Goodwill Industries, 1973-80, 97—, Woodruff Hosp., 1975-82, Cleve. Devel. Found., Pub. TV, Surveyors Telecom., Inc., Sta. WVIZ-TV, Cleve.-Cuyahoga Port Authority, 1986-90; dir. adv. coun. Ohio Bd. Workmen's Compensation, 1974-82; chmn. Minority Econ. Devel. Corp., 1972-83; chmn. bd. dirs. Glenville YMCA, 1973-76; trustee BBB, 1995—, Cleve. Play House, 1979-87, Eliza Bryant Health Care Ctr., 1984-86, Cleve. Small Bus. Incubator, 1986-90; bd. dirs., treas. Urban League Cleve., 1971-78; mem. adv. coun. Small Bus. Assn.; mem. adv. bd. Salvation Army, 1980; commr. Ohio State Boxing Commn., 1984-94, Pvt. Industry Coun., 1985, Nat. Small Bus. Adv. Coun., 1980; bd. advs. Antioch Coll.; county commrs. appointee to Cmty. Adv. Bd., 1987—; mem. Cleve. Opera Coun., 1987-89, Forest City Hosp. Found., 1985—; trustee Ohio Motorist, 1993—, Murtis H. Taylor Mental Health; Gov. Voinovich appointee to minority devel. fin. adv. bd., 1996—; bd. trustee Metro Hosp. Systems Found. With AUS, 1950-52. Recipient award bus. excellence Dept. Commerce, 1972; Presdl. award YMCA, 1974; Gov. Ohio award community action, 1973; First Class Leadership Cleve., 1977. named Family of Yr. Cleve. Urban League, 1971 Mem. Cleve. C. of C., NAACP (v.p. Cleve. 1969-78, exec. dir.), Ohio Coun. Retail Mchts. (chmn. 1991-93), Ohio Home Furnishings and Appliance Assn. (pres. 1981-87), Exec. Order Ohio Commodore, Am. Auto Assn. (corp. mem.), Mid-Day Club, Cleve. Play House, Harvard Bus. Sch. Club, Clevelander, Bratenahl Club, Univ. Club (Cleve.), Rotary. Clubs: Mid-Day, Cleve. Play House, Harvard Bus. Sch., Clevelander, Bratenahl, Univ. (Cleve.). Lodge: Rotary. Office: 12435 Saint Clair Ave Cleveland OH 44108-2013 E-mail: crosbyfurniture@msn.com.

CROSBY, JACQUELINE GARTON, newspaper editor, journalist; b. Jacksonville, Fla., May 13, 1961; d. James Ellis and Marianne (Garton) Crosby. ABJ, U. Ga., 1983; MBA, U. Cen. Fla., 1987. Staff writer Macon Telegraph & News, Ga., 1983-84; copy editor Orlando Sentinel, Fla., 1984-85; dir. spl. projects Ivanhoe Communications, Inc., Orlando, 1987-89; producer spl. projects Sta. KSTP-TV, Mpls., 1989-94; asst. news editor Star Tribune Online, 1994—. Recipient award for best sports story Ga. Press Assn., 1982; award for best series of yr. AP, 1985, Pulitzer prize, 1985 Mem. Quill Avocations: competing in triathlons, playing electric bass, tutoring, reading. Home: 5348 Drew Ave S Minneapolis MN 55410-2006 Office: Star Tribune Online 425 Portland Ave Minneapolis MN 55488-0001

CROSBY, LAVON KEHOE STUART, state legislator, civic leader; b. Hastings, Nebr., Apr. 25, 1924; d. Charles William and Kathryn Marie (Farrell) Kehoe; m. Lester Stuart, Oct. 9, 1948 (dec. 1970); children: Mary Stuart Bolin, Michael, Timothy, Frederick Stuart; m. Robert B. Crosby, May 22, 1971. BA, U. Nebr., 1987. Asst. to pres. Hastings Tribune Corp., Nebr., 1941-68; mem. staff U.S. Senator Roman Hruska, Washington, 1968-71; mem. Nebr. State Legislature, 1988—, Appropriations Com., 1988—, Nebr. Retirement Systems com., 1992—, chmn. com. on coms., 1994—. Civic leader; b. Hastings, Nebr., Apr. 25, 1924; d. Charles William and Kathryn Marie (Farrell) Kehoe; m. Lester Stuart, Oct. 9, 1948 (dec. 1970); children— Mary Stuart Bolin, Michael, Timothy, Frederick Stuart; m. Robert B. Crosby, May 22, 1971. BA, U. Nebr., 1987. Asst. to pres. Hastings Tribune Corp., Nebr., 1941-68; mem. staff U.S. Senator Roman Hruska, Washington, 1968-71; mem. Nebr. State Legislature, 1988—; mem. Appropriations Com., 1988—, mem. Nebr. Retirement Systems com., 1992—, chmn. com. on coms., 1994—. Chmn. music com. Cathedral of Risen Christ Choir, Lincoln, Nebr.; pres. Lincoln Community Playhouse Guild; bd. dirs., chmn. membership com. Lincoln Community Playhouse; v.p., bd. dirs. Lincoln Symphony Guild; bd. dirs. Lincoln Symphony Orch. Assn., 1972-82; founder Nebr. Found. for Humanities; mem. Lincoln Symphony Found. Bd., 1984—; bd. dirs. Friends of Ctr. for Great Plains Studies, 1984—; vice chmn. Nebr. Arts Council, 1981-82, chmn., 1982-85; past mem. and sec. Pershing Auditorium Bd.; pres. Nebr. Legis. Ladies League, 1977-78; adv. bd. Cath. social services Bur.; budget chmn. Nebr. Mother's Assn.; chmn. legis. affairs Diocesan Council Cath. Women; v.p. Heritage League, Lincoln, 1985—; pres. Cornhusker Republican Women, 1974-75. Recipient Mayor's Arts award, Lincoln, 1985, Gov.'s Arts award, Nebr., 1986, YWCA Tribute to Women award, 1993. Mem. Nebr. Club (Lincoln). Chmn. music com. Cathedral of Risen Christ Choir, Lincoln, Nebr.; pres. Lincoln Community Playhouse Guild; bd. dirs., chmn. membership com. Lincoln Community Playhouse; v.p., bd. dirs. Lincoln Symphony Guild; bd. dirs. Lincoln Symphony Orch. Assn., 1972-82; founder Nebr. Found. for Humanities; mem. Lincoln Symphony Found. Bd., 1984—; bd. dirs. Friends of Ctr. for Great Plains Studies, 1984—; vice chmn. Nebr. Arts Council, 1981-82, chmn., 1982-85; past mem. and sec. Pershing Auditorium Bd.; pres. Nebr. Legis. Ladies League, 1977-78; adv. bd. Cath. social Services Bur.; budget chmn. Nebr. Mother's Assn.; chmn. legis. affairs Diocesan Council Cath. Women; v.p. Heritage League, Lincoln, 1985—; pres. Cornhusker Republican Women, 1974-75. Recipient Mayor's Arts award, Lincoln, 1985, Gov.'s Arts award, Nebr., 1986, YWCA Tribute to Women award, 1993. Mem. Nebr. Club (Lincoln). Office: State Legislature Rm 1010 State Capitol Lincoln NE 68509

CROSBY, THOMAS MANVILLE, JR. lawyer; b. Mpls., Oct. 9, 1938; s. Thomas M. and Ella (Pillsbury) C.; m. Eleanor Rauch, June 12, 1965; children: Stewart, Brewster, Grant, Brooke. BA, Yale U., 1960, LLB, 1965. Bar: Minn. 1965. Assoc. Faegre & Benson, Mpls., 1965-72, ptnr., 1965—. Served to lt. USNR, 1960-62. Office: Faegre & Benson 2200 Norwest Ctr 90 S 7th St Ste 2200 Minneapolis MN 55402-3901

CROSS, AUREAL THEOPHILUS, geology and botany educator; b. Findlay, Ohio, June 4, 1916; s. Raymond Willard and Myra Jane (Coon) C.; m. Christina Aleen Teyssier, Mar. 11, 1945; children: Timothy Aureal, Christina Avonne Cross Collier, Jonathan Ariel, Cheryl Aleen (Mrs. Richard M. Bowman), Christopher Charles. BA, Coe Coll., 1939; MS in Botany, U. Cin., 1941, PhD in Botany and Paleontology, 1943. Instr. to asst. prof. U. Notre Dame, 1943-46; NRC fellow in geology, 1943-44; paleobotanist; Ctrl. Expt. Sta., U.S. Bur. Mines, Pitts., 1945; asst. prof. dept. geology U. Cin., 1946-49, asst. prof. dept. botany, 1948-49; part-time geologist Geol. Survey Ohio, 1946-51; coal geologist and paleobotanist W.Va. Geol. and Econ. Survey, 1949-57; assoc. prof. to prof. dept. geology U. W.Va., 1949-57; sr. rsch. engr. Pan Am. Petroleum Corp. Rsch. Center, Tulsa, 1957-61, supr. tech. group and rsch. group, 1959-61; prof. dept. geology Mich. State U., East Lansing, 1961-86, prof. dept. botany and plant pathology, 1961-86, prof. emeritus, 1987—. Prof. ecology U. Alaska, 1971; research palynologist U. So. Calif., 1972; Morton vis. prof. Ohio U., Athens Ohio, 1981; Nathaniel S. Shaler Disting. lectr. U. Ky., 1991; UNESCO adviser U. grants commn. India Coal Programs, 1983; Calcutta adviser geology dept. Jadavpur U., India, 1983. Editor: Palynology in Oil Exploration, 1964, Compte Rendu 9th Internat. Congress Carboniferous Stratigraphy and Geology, vol. 4, Econ. Geology: Coal, Oil and Gas, 1985; co-editor: Coal Resources and Research in Latin America, 1978, World Class Coal Deposits, Internat. Jour. Coal Geology, 1993; assoc. editor: Fossil Spores and Pollen, 41 vols, 1956-87; contbr. numerous articles, abstracts and revs. to profl. jours. Chmn. citywide rally Fellowship Christian Athletes, Tulsa, 1960; mem. nat. council U.P. Men, 1966-68, 74-84 ; active Boy Scouts Am., YMCA, others. Named Seward Meml. lectr. Sahni Inst. Palaeobotany, 1985, J. Sen Meml. lectr., 1985; named Disting. lectr. Am. Assn. Petroleum Geologists, 1964, Outstanding Educator Am. Assn. Petroleum Geologists Ea. Sect., 1987; recipient Gordon H. Wood Jr. Meml. award, 1993, John T. Galey medal, 1995. Mem. Am. Assn. Stratigraphic Palynologists (hon.; medal of Excellence in Edn. 1999), Bot. Soc. Am. (chmn. paleobotany sect. 1953, 77, grantee 1954, Disting. Svc. Paleobotany award 1985), Geol. Soc. Am. (Gilbert H. Cady Coal Geology award 1987, chmn. coal geology divsn. 1966, chmn. North Ctrl. sect. 1969-70, exec. sec. sect. 1971-80, grantee 1951), Soc. Econ. Paleontologists and Mineralogists (chmn. rsch. com. 1961-62, councillor in paleontology 1971-73, numerous other internat., nat. and regional profl. assns. Presbyterian. Home: 529 N Harrison Rd East Lansing MI 48823-3015 Office: Mich State Univ Dept Geol Scis East Lansing MI 48824 Fax: 517-353-8787. E-mail: cross1@msu.edu.

CROSS, BRUCE A. food service company executive; Grad., Calif. State U., Sacramento. Technology dir. Safeway; mgr. large info. technology outsourcing contracts IBM Global Svcs.; sr. v.p., pres., chief info. officer Nash Finch Co., Mpls., 1999—. Office: Nash Finch Co 7600 France Ave S Minneapolis MN 55435-5924

CROSS, ROBERT CLARK, journalist; b. Cheboygan, Mich., May 12, 1939; s. Warren Clark and Maryle M. (Allaire) Cross; m. Juju Lien; children: Gabriel Francis, Amy Lien. B.A. in Journalism, Wayne State U., 1962. Writer, researcher Newsweek mag., 1962; reporter, editor Chgo. Tribune, 1962-66, 67-82, assoc. editor mag., 1973-82, writer, 1982—; reporter Newsday, 1966-67; travel writer, 1992—. Recipient Gold and Silver Lowell Thomas awards Soc. of Am. Travel Writers, 1995, 2000. Office: 435 N Michigan Ave Chicago IL 60611-4066 E-mail: bcross@tribune.com.

CROSS, W. THOMAS, investment company executive; b. Knoxville, Tenn., Sept. 1, 1949; s. Joseph Eugene and Wanda (Price) C.; children: Joseph, Victoria. BS, U. Tenn., 1971; CLU, Am. Coll., Bryn Mawr, Pa., 1983, ChFC, 1987. Sales rep. John Hancock Fin. Svcs., Knoxville, 1971-72, sales mgr., 1972-78, regional supr. Washington, 1978-79, agy. mgr. Appleton, Wis., 1979-84, Memphis, 1984-95; sr. v.p. product distbn. Securities Am., Inc., Omaha, 1995—; pres. Fin. Dynamics Am., Inc., 1997—. Chair troop com., scoutmaster Boy Scouts Am., Germantown, Tenn., 1991-95. Mem. Am. Soc. CLU and ChFC (bd. dirs. 1992-95), Am. Health Ins. Assn., Gen. Agts. and Mgrs. Assn. (pres. Appleton chpt. 1977-78, pres. Memphis chpt. 1988-89, pres. 1993-94), Memphis Life Underwriters (bd. dirs. 1985-88). Avocations: golf, scouting. Office: Securities Am Inc 7100 W Center Rd Ste 500 Omaha NE 68106-2798 E-mail: tcross@§aionline.com.

CROSS, WILLIAM DENNIS, lawyer; b. Tulsa, Nov. 7, 1940; s. John Howell and Virginia Grace (Ferrell) C.; m. Peggy Ruth Plapp, Jan. 30, 1982; children: William Dennis Jr., John Frederick. BS, U.S. Naval Acad., 1962; JD, NYU, 1969. Bar: N.Y. 1970, U.S. Dist. Ct. (so. and ea. dists.) N.Y. 1970, U.S. Ct. Appeals (2d cir.) 1970, U.S. Supreme Ct. 1974, Calif. 1977, U.S. Dist. Ct. (ctrl. dist.) Calif. 1977, U.S. Ct. Appeals (9th cir.) 1977, U.S. Ct. Appeals (5th, 10th and 11th cirs.) 1981, Mo. 1982, U.S. Dist. Ct. (we. dist.) Mo. 1982, U.S. Ct. Appeals (8th cir.) 1989, U.S. Ct. Appeals (fed. cir.) 1992, U.S. Dist. Ct. Ariz. 1997, U.S. Dist. Ct. Colo. 1997, U.S. Dist. Ct. Kans. 1998. Commd. ensign USN, 1962, advanced through ranks to lt., 1965, resigned, 1966; assoc. Cravath, Swaine & Moore, N.Y.C., 1969-76, Lillick, McHose & Charles, L.A., 1976-77; asst. gen. counsel FTC, Washington, 1977-82; of counsel Morrison & Hecker, Kansas City, Mo., 1982-83, ptnr., 1983—2002, Stimson Morrison Hecker, 2002—. Staff mem. NYU Law Rev., 1967-69, editor, 1968-69; assoc. editor Antitrust Mag. Mem. ABA, Calif. Bar Assn., Mo. Bar Assn., Assn. Bar City N.Y., Kansas City Bar Assn., Lawyers Assn. Kansas City. Home: 1223 Huntington Rd Kansas City MO 64113-1347 Office: Stinson Morrison Hecker 2600 Grand Blvd Kansas City MO 64108-4606 E-mail: wdcross@moheck.com.

CROSSAN, JOHN ROBERT, lawyer; b. Buckhannon, W.Va., May 31, 1947; s. Thomas Benjamin Jr. and Margaret Windsor (Hicks) C.; m. Monique Margaretha Scheen, Dec. 22, 1973; children: Ashley Margaret, Aubry Kelly. BS with honors, U. Va., 1969; JD, U. Chgo., 1974. Bar: Ill. 1974, U.S. Dist. Ct. (no. dist.) Ill. 1974, (ctrl. dist.) Ill. 1998, U.S. Ct. Appeals (4th and 10th cirs.) 1978, U.S. Ct. Appeals (7th cir.) 1979, U.S. Ct. Appeals (fed. cir.) 1983, U.S. Supreme Ct. 1985, U.S. Ct. Appeals (6th cir.) 1989. Staff atty. Ill. Task Force N.E. Ill. Pub. Transp., Chgo., 1972-73; assoc. Hill, Van Santen, Steadman, Chiara, 1973-77; assoc., then ptnr. Cook, Wetzel and Egan, Ltd., 1978-88; counsel Willian, Brinks, Hofer, Gilson and Lione, 1989-90; ptnr. Brinks, Hofer, Gilson & Lione, 1991-97, Chapman and Cutler, Chgo., 1998—. Bd. dirs. Va. Engring. Found., 1996—, v.p., 1998—2000, pres., 2000—02. Author: Quick Guide to the Patent Law, 1994; contbr. articles to profl publs. Pres. aux. bd. Chgo. Architecture Found., 1983-85. Mem. ABA, Am. Intellectual Property Lawyers Assn., Chgo. Yacht Club. Home: 2825 N Cambridge Ave Chicago IL 60657-6018 Office: Chapman and Cutler 111 W Monroe St Ste 1700 Chicago IL 60603-4006 E-mail: crossan@chapman.com., jrcrossan@hotmail.com.

CROSSER, RICHARD H. real estate company executive; Pres., CEO Crossman Cmtys., Indpls., 1973—. Office: Crossman Communities Inc 9202 N Meridian St Ste 300 Indianapolis IN 46260-1833

CROSSON, FREDERICK JAMES, former university dean, humanities educator; b. Belmar, N.J., Apr. 27, 1926; s. George Leon and Emily (Bennett) C.; m. Mary Patricia Burns, Sept. 5, 1953; children: Jessica, Christopher, Veronica, Benedict, Jennifer. BA, Cath. U. Am., 1949, MA, 1950; postgrad., U. Paris, 1951-52; PhD, U. Notre Dame, 1956. Instr. U. Notre Dame, 1953-56, asst. prof., 1956-62, assoc. prof., 1962-66, prof., 1966—; dean Coll. Arts and Letters, 1968-76, O'Hara Disting. prof. philosophy, 1976-84, Cavanaugh Disting. prof. humanities, 1984—98. Author: The Modeling of Mind, 1963, Philosophy and Cybernetics, 1967, Science and Contemporary Society, 1967; Editor: Review of Politics, 1976-83. With USN, 1943-46. Mem.: North Ctrl. Assn. (exec. commr. 1984—89), Am. Cath. Philos. Assn. (pres. 1990—91), Am. Philos. Assn., Phi Beta Kappa (senator 1982—2000, v.p. 1994—97, pres. 1997—2000). Home: 51997 Heather Cv South Bend IN 46635-1074 Office: Coll Arts and Letters U of Notre Dame Notre Dame IN 46556

CROUCH, STEVEN L. mining engineer; b. L.A., Apr. 25, 1943; BS, U. Minn., 1966, MS in Mineral Engring., 1967, PhD in Mineral Engring., 1970. Rsch. officer Mining Rsch. Lab. Chamber of Mines of South Africa, Johannesburg, 1968-70; from asst. to assoc. prof. civil and mineral engring. U. Minn., Mpls., 1970-81, prof., 1981—, acting head dept., 1987-88, head, 1988—. Vis. lectr. dept. applied math. U. Witwatersrand, Johannesburg, South Africa, 1976-77, People's Republic of China, 1983; mem. U.S. NAS Com. on Feasibility of Returning Coal Mine Waste Underground, 1973; mem. NAS Task Force on Underground Engring. at Basalt Waste Isolation Project, 1987; active Sandia Nat. Labs. Yucca Mtn. Site Characterization Project Rock Mechanics Rev. Panel, 1989—; cons. in field. Author: (with A.M. Starfield) Boundary Element Methods in Solid Mechanics, 1983; contbr. articles to profl. jours. Recipient U.S. Nat. Com. for Rock Mechanics Applied Rsch. award, 1992. Mem. AIME (Rock Mechanics award 1991), ASCE, Internat. Soc. Roch Mechanics, Minn. Soc. Surveyors and Engrs., Engrs. Club Mpls. Office: U Minn 105 Walter Libr 117 Pleasant St SE Minneapolis MN 55455-0291

CROUTER, RICHARD EARL, religion educator; b. Washington, Nov. 2, 1937; s. Earl Clinton and Neva J. (Crain) C.; m. Barbara Jean Williams, Jan. 30, 1960; children— Edward, Frances A.B., Occidental Coll., 1960; B.D., Union Theol. U., N.Y.C., 1963, Th.D., 1968. Asst. prof. religion Carleton Coll., Northfield, Minn., 1967-73, assoc. prof., 1973-79, prof., 1979-92, Bryn-Jones disting. tchg. prof. humanities, 1993-96, Musser prof. religious studies, 1997—. Translator, editor: On Religion (F. Schleiermacher), 1988, 96; co-editor Jour. for the History of Modern Theology, 1993—. Chmn. parents adv. coun. Greenvale Sch. Northfield, 1977-78; resident dir. A Better Chance Program, Northfield, 1968-70. Fulbright scholar, 1976-77, 87, 91-92; Am. Council Learned Socs. fellow, 1976-77, Wallin fellow, 2001, DAAD fellow, 2001. Mem. Am. Acad. Religion (steering com. 19th century theol. group 1982-92, chmn. 1987-92), Hegel Soc. Am., Troeltsch Soc., German Studies Assn., Kierkegaard Soc., Schleiermacher Gesellschaft. Democrat. Avocations: hiking, travel, biking, piano. Home: 808 2d St E Northfield MN 55057-2307 Office: Carleton Coll Dept Religious Studies Northfield MN 55057 E-mail: rcrouter@carleton.edu., rcrouter@charter.net.

CROW, SAM ALFRED, judge; b. Topeka, May 5, 1926; s. Samuel Wheadon and Phyllis K. (Brown) Crow; m. Ruth M. Rush, Jan. 30, 1948; children: Sam A., Dan W. BA, U. Kans., 1949; JD, Washburn U., 1952. Ptnr. Rooney, Dickinson, Prager & Crow, Topeka, 1953—63, Dickinson, Crow, Skoog & Honeyman, Topeka, 1963—70; sr. ptnr. Crow & Skoog, 1971—75; part-time U.S. magistrate, 1973—75; U.S. magistrate, 1975—81; judge U.S. Dist. Ct. Kans., Wichita, 1981—92, sr. judge Topeka, 1992—. Bd. rev. Boy Scouts Am., 1960—70, cubmaster, 1957—60; chmn. Kans. March of Dimes, 1959, bd. dirs., 1960—65, Topeka Coun. Chs., 1960—70; mem. Kans. Hist. Soc., 1960—; pres., v.p. PTA; bd. govs. Washburn Law Sch. Alumni Assn., 1993—99; mem. vestry Grace Episcopal Ch., Topeka, 1960—65. Col. JAGC USAR, ret. Named to, Topeka H.S. Hall of Fame, 2000; recipient Washburn U. Sch. Law Disting. Svc. award, 2000. Fellow: Kans. Bar Found.; mem.: ABA (del. Nat. Conf. Spl. Ct. Judges 1978), Topeka Lawyers Club (sec. 1964—65, pres. 1965—66), Wichita Bar Assn., Topeka Bar Assn. (chmn. jud. reform com., chmn. bench and bar com., chmn. criminal law com., Disting. Svc. award 2000), Nat. Assn. U.S. Magistrates (com. discovery abuse), Kans. Trial Lawyers Assn. (sec. 1959—60, pres. 1960—61), Kans. Bar Assn. (chmn. mil. law sect. 1965, 1967, 1970, trustee 1970—76, chmn. mil. law sect. 1972, 1974, 1975), Shawnee Country Club, Shriners, Am. Legion, Sigma Alpha Epsilon, Delta Theta Phi. Office: US Dist Ct 444 SE Quincy St Topeka KS 66683

CROWDER, MARJORIE BRIGGS, lawyer; b. Shreveport, La., Mar. 26, 1946; d. Rowland Edmund and Marjorie Ernestine (Biles) Crowder; m. Ronald J. Briggs, July 11, 1970 (div. Nov. 2000); children: Sarah, Andrew. BA, Carson-Newman Coll., 1968; MA, Ohio State U., 1969, JD, 1975. Bar: Ohio 1975, U.S. Ct. Appeals (6th cir.) 1983, U.S. Ct. Claims 1992, U.S. Supreme Ct. 2001. Asst. dean of women Albion Coll., Mich., 1969-70; dir. residence hall Ohio State U., Columbus, 1970-71, acad. counselor, 1971-72; assoc. Porter, Wright, Morris, Arthur, 1975—83, ptnr., 1983-2000; AmeriCorps atty. Southeastern Ohio Legal Svs., Portsmouth, 2000—. Legal aide Community Law Office, Columbus, 1973-74. Contbg. author: Going to Trial, A Step-By-Step Guide to Trial Practice and Procedure, 1989. Trustee, pres. Epilepsy Assn. Central Ohio, Columbus, 1977-84; bd. dirs. Columbus Speech & Hearing, 1977-82, Scioto County Domestic Violence Task Force, v.p. 2001-; mem. allocation com. United Way Franklin County, 1984-88. Fellow Columbus Bar Found. (trustee 1993-95); mem. ABA (mem. gavel awards com. 1989-96, gen. practice sect. 1983—, chair litigation com. 1987-89, exec. coun. 1989-93, dir. bus. com. group 1990-91, chair program com. 1991-93, torts and ins. practice sect. 1993—, vice chair health ins. law com. 1993-96), Ohio Bar Assn. (Joint Task Force on Gender Fairness 1991-93), Columbus Bar Assn. (com. chmn. 1979-83, docket control task force 1989-91, editor 1981-83), Scioto County Bar Assn.; Women Lawyers Franklin County. Home: 2106 Summit St Portsmouth OH 45662 Office: Southeastern Ohio Legal Svcs 800 Gallia St Ste 700 Portsmouth OH 45662-4035 E-mail: mcrowder@oslsa.org.

CROWE, JAMES QUELL, communications company executive; b. Camp Pendleton, Calif., July 2, 1949; s. Henry Pierson and Mona (Quell) C.; m. Pamela L. Powell, June 20, 1986; children: Sterling, Angela, James Michael. BS in Mech. Engring., Rensselaer Poly. Inst., 1972; MBA, Pepperdine U., 1982. Project engr. Cozzolino Constrn. Co., Port of Albany, N.Y., 1971-73; ind., cons. engr. Albany, 1973-74; engr. Morrison-Knudsen, Saratoga, N.Y., 1974-75, project engr. Washington, 1975-76, project mgr. various cities, 1976-80, v.p. ops. Boise, 1980-83, group v.p. power, 1983-86; pres. Kiewit Indsl. Co., Omaha, 1986—. Chmn., CEO MFS Comms. Co., Inc., Omaha, 1988-97; chmn. WorldCom, Inc., 1997; CEO, dir. Level 3 Comms., Inc., 1997—. Mem. Am. Nuclear Soc.

CROWE, JAMES WILSON, university administrator, educator; b. Churubusco, Ind., June 27, 1934; s. James A. and Ruth Crowe; m. Barbara Jones; children: Michael James, Monica Sue Crowe Black. BS, Purdue U., 1959; MS, U. Fla., 1960; Dir. Degree, Ind. U., 1970, EdD, 1979. Grad. asst. in health and safety edn. U. Fla., Gainesville, 1959-60; health edn. tchr., coach, dir. driver edn. program Edinburg (Ind.) Cmty. H.S., 1960-65; dir. health and safety edn. Atterbury Job Corps Ctr., Columbus, Ind., 1965-66; asst. prof. applied health sci. Ind. U., Bloomington, 1966-80, assoc. prof. applied health sci., 1980-96; prof., 1996—; dir. Ctr. for Health and Safety Studies Ind. U., Bloomington, 1992—, co-dir. Inst. for Drug Abuse Prevention, 1992—, acting chair dept. applied health sci., 1992-93, chair dept. applied health sci., 1993—. Bd. dirs. Monroe County chpt. ARC, 1991-94. Recipient Svc. award ARC, 1986, 87, 88, 89, Instr. of Yr. award ARC, 1985, 87, 88, Outstanding Tchg. award Amoco, 1977. Mem. AAHPERD (v.p. cmty./safety divsn. Midwest dist. 1989-90), Am. Assn. Active Lifestyles and Fitness (bd. dirs. 1994—), Am. Driver and Traffic Edn. Assn. (Visions of Tomorrow award 1992), Am. Sch. Health Assn., Nat. Safety Coun. (mem.-at-large ednl. rsch. sect. 1993, cert. in recognition of outstanding contbn. 1994), Sch. and Cmty. Safety Soc. Am. (bd. dirs. 1991—, pres.-elect 1992-94, pres. 1994-96, past pres. 1996-98, scholar award 1996, C.P. Yost Disting. Svc. award 1998).

CROWE, ROBERT WILLIAM, lawyer, mediator; b. Chgo., Aug. 20, 1924; s. Harry James and Miriam (McCune) C.; m. Virginia C. Kelley, Mar. 25, 1955 (dec. Feb. 1976); children— Robert Kelley, William Park; m. Elizabeth F. Roenisch, Oct. 22, 1977. A.B., U. Chgo., 1948, J.D., 1949. Bar: Ill. 1949. Practice in, Chgo., 1949-57; with R.R. Donnelley & Sons Co., 1957-83, sec., 1965-83, v.p., 1970-83; chmn. Resolve Dispute Mgmt. Inc., Chgo., 1983-92; pres. Dearborn Inst. for Conflict Resolution, 1992-94. Dir. Peoria Jour. Star, Inc., 1972-95. Bd. dirs. Chgo. Child Care Soc., 1963—; trustee Christian Century Found., 1966— ; vis. com. U. Chgo. Divinity Sch. Served to 1st lt. USAAF, 1943-45. Decorated Air medal with

5 oak leaf clusters. Mem. ABA, Chgo. Bar Assn., Lawyers Club Chgo., Econ. Club (Chgo.), Univ. Club (Chgo.). Presbyterian. Home and Office: 1228 Westmoor Rd Winnetka IL 60093-1845 E-mail: RWCROWE@aol.com.

CROWE, WILLIAM JOSEPH, librarian; b. Boston, Feb. 27, 1947; s. William J. and Mary (Dawley) C.; m. Nancy P. Sanders, June 10, 1978; children: Katherine. BA in European history with highest honors, Boston State Coll., 1968; MLS, Rutgers U., 1969; PhD in Adminstrn. Acad. Librs., Ind. U., 1986. Cataloger Boston Pub. Libr., 1969-70, asst. to acquisitions libr., 1970-71; coord. processing Ind. U. Librs., Bloomington, 1971-76, asst. to dean univ. librs., 1977-79; mgmt. intern U. Mich. Libr., Ann Arbor, 1976-77; asst. to dir. librs. Ohio State U., Columbus, 1979-83, asst. dir. librs. adminstrn. and tech. svcs., 1983-90; dean librs. U. Kans., Lawrence, 1990-96, vice chancellor, dean, 1996-99, libr. Spencer Rsch. Libr., 1999—. Cons. Newberry Libr., Chgo., 1989; alternate del. Ind. Gov.'s Conf. Librs. and Info. Svcs., 1978; co-prin. investigator Am. fiction 1901-25 Dept. Edn., 1983-85; tech. mgr. project Am. fiction 1901-25 NEH, 1988-90; trustee Online Computer Lit. Ctr., 1996—. Contbr. articles to profl. jours. Sr. fellow UCLA, 1991. Mem. ALA, Kans. Libr. Assn., Beta Phi Mu, Phi Alpha Theta. Home: 910 E 850th Rd Lawrence KS 66047-9578 Office: U Kans Spencer Rsch Libr Lawrence KS 66045-7616

CROWL, SAMUEL RENNINGER, former university dean, English language educator, author; b. Toledo, Oct. 9, 1940; s. Lester Samuel and Margaret Elizabeth (Renninger) C.; m. Susan Richardson, Dec. 29, 1963; children: Miranda Paine, Samuel Emerson. AB, Hamilton Coll., 1962; MA, Ind. U., 1969, PhD, 1970. Resident lectr. Ind. U., Indpls., 1967-69; asst. prof. English, Ohio U., Athens, 1970-75, assoc. prof., 1975-80, prof., 1980—, dean Univ. Coll., 1981-92, trustee prof. Eng., 1992—; cons. NEH, Washington, 1980—; observer Royal Shakespeare Co. Mem. Ohio Humanities Coun., 1985-91, Ohio Student Loan Commn., 1985-88. Author: Shakespeare Observed: Studies in Performance on Stage and Screen, 1992; co-author: Ohio University's Educational Plan, 1977-78; contbr. articles to profl. and Shakespearian jours. Recipient O'Bleness award for pub. broadcasting Ctr. Telecommunications, Ohio U., 1976, several awards disting. teaching. Fellow Royal Soc. Arts (London); mem. Nat. Assn. Univ. and Gen. Coll. Deans (pres. 1991—), Nat. Humanities Faculty, Ohio Shakespeare Assn. (founding mem.), Ohio U. Alumni Assn. (hon.), Univ. Club (Chgo.), Phi Kappa Phi. Avocations: Royal Shakespeare Co., Detroit Tigers. Office: Ohio U Eng Dept Ellis Hall Athens OH 45701

CROWLEY, DALE ALAN, prosecutor; b. Saginaw, Mich., May 29, 1951; s. Lester Robert and Esther Irene C.; m. Deanne Kay Westendorp, Dec. 30, 1983; children: Jessica Erin, Leslie Ann, Kelsey Jo. BA in Econs. with honors, Mich. State U., 1973; JD, Wayne State U., 1976. Bar: Mich. 1976, U.S. Dist. Ct. (we. dist.) Mich. 1981. Counsel trust dept. Security Nat. Bank, Battle Creek, Mich., 1976-78; counsel claims dept. Transamerica Ins. Group, 1978-80; asst. pros. atty Barry County, Mich., 1980, chief asst. pros. atty., 1980-88, pros. atty., 1989—. Vice chmn. Barry County Cmty. Corrections Bd.; legal advisor Barry County E-911 Central Dispatch Bd.; served as spl. pros. atty. in Allegan, Kalamazoo and Eaton Counties. Recipient Profl. Excellence citation Mich. State Police, 1989, 92. Mem. Nat. Dist. Attys. Assn., Pros. Attys. Assn. Mich., Barry County Bar Assn. (past pres., vice pres., treas., sect.), Kiwanis Club, Exchange Club (treas.) Republican. Lutheran. Avocations: sports, reading, computers, bicycling. Office: Barry County Pros Atty 220 W Court St Ste 201 Hastings MI 49058-1857

CROWLEY, GEOFFREY THOMAS, airline executive; b. St. Catherines, Ont., Can., Oct. 8, 1952; arrived in U.S., 1959; s. Douglas Geoffrey and Joan Margaret (Ratley) C.; m. Linda Anne Buckelew, Jan. 30, 1986; 4 children. BS in Engring., Purdue U., 1974; MBA, Xavier U., 1977. Sr. cons. Booz, Allen & Hamilton TCD, Cin., 1974-77; dir. customer svc. quality assurance Tex. Internat. Airlines, Houston, 1977-80; gen. mgr. People Express Airlines, Newark, 1980-85; sr. v.p. mktg. and planning Presdl. Airways, Washington, 1985-89; v.p. sales and svc. Trump Shuttle, Inc., N.Y.C., 1989-91; v.p. mktg. alliances Northwest Airlines, Inc., St. Paul, 1991-93; chmn., pres., CEO Air Wisconsin Airlines Corp., Appleton, 1993—. Apptd. by Pres. Clinton to FAA Mgmt. Adv. Coun., 2000—. Mem. Regional Airline Assn. (chmn. 1995-96, dir. 1994-97), Wings Club (gov. 1995-98). Office: Air Wisconsin Airlines Corp W6390 Challenger Dr Ste 203 Appleton WI 54914-9120

CROWN, JAMES SCHINE, investment executive; b. Chgo., June 25, 1953; s. Lester and Renée (Schine) Crown; m. Paula Ann Hannaway, June 27, 1985; children: Victoria, Hayley, Andrew, Summer Olivia. BA, Hampshire Coll., 1976; JD, Stanford U., 1980. Bar: Ill. 1980. V.p. Salomon Bros. Inc., N.Y.C., 1980-85; gen. ptnr. Henry Crown and Co., Chgo., 1985—. Bd, durs, Gen. Dynamics Corp., Falls Church, Va., Bank One Corp., Sara Lee Corp. Trustee U. Chgo., Mus. Sci. and Industry, Chgo., Orchestral Assn., Chgo. Mem.: Ill. State Bar Assn. Office: Henry Crown and Co 222 N La Salle St Chicago IL 60601-1003

CROWN, LESTER, manufacturing company executive; b. Chgo., June 7, 1925; s. Henry and Rebecca (Kranz) C.; m. Renee Schine, Dec. 28, 1950; children: Steven, James, Patricia, Daniel, Susan, Sara, Janet. BS in Chem. Engring., Northwestern U., 1946; MBA, Harvard U., 1949. Instr. math. Northwestern U., 1946-47; v.p., chem. engr. Marblehead Lime Co., 1950-56, pres., 1956-66, also bd. dirs.; v.p. Material Svc. Corp. subs. Gen. Dynamics Corp., Chgo., 1953-66, pres., 1970-83, chmn., 1983—, also bd. dirs.; chmn. exec. com. Gen. Dynamics Corp., 1982—2001, also bd. dirs.; pres. Henry Crown & Co., Chgo., 1969—2002, chmn., 2002—, also bd. dirs. Bd. dirs. Maytag Corp.; ptnr. N.Y. Yankees Partnership, from 1973. Trustee Aspen Inst. Humanistic Studies, Northwestern U., Michael Reese Found.; bd. dirs. Lyric Opera Corp., Children's Meml. Med. Ctr., Jewish Theol. Sem., Jerusalem Found.; mem. bd. govs. Weizmann Inst. of Sci./Tel Aviv U. Mem. Am. Acad. Arts & Scis., Lake Shore Country Club, Northmoor Country Club, Standard Club, Econ. Club (dir. 1972), Chgo. Club, Comml. Club, Mid-Am. Club (Chgo.), John Evans Club of Northwestern U., Tau Beta Pi, Pi My Epsilon, Phi Eta Sigma. Office: Material Svc Corp 222 N La Salle St Ste 1200 Chicago IL 60601-1087 also: Gen Dynamics Corp 3190 Fairview Park Dr Fl 1 Falls Church VA 22042-4510

CROWN, WILLIAM H. manufacturing executive; Pres., CEO CC Industries. Office: CC Industries 222 N LaSalle St Chicago IL 60601

CRUDEN, ROBERT WILLIAM, botany educator; b. Cleve., Mar. 18, 1936; m. Diana Benedict Loeb, Dec. 21, 1967; children: Nathalie Rebecca, Lyda Marie; m. Diana Ruth Gannett, July 1996. AB, Hiram (Ohio) Coll., 1958; MS, Ohio State U., Columbus, 1960; PhD, U. Calif., Berkeley, 1967. Asst. prof. U. Iowa, Iowa City, 1967-71, assoc. prof., 1971-78, prof., 1978-99, prof. emeritus, 1999—. Acting dir. Iowa Lakeside Lab., Wahepton, 1989-94, past asst. dir.; adj. prof. U. Mich, Ann Arbor, 2001- Editor Ecol. Soc. Am., 1983-86; editl. bd. Madrono; contbr. numerous articles to profl. jours. Mem. pres.'s coun. on sci. initiatives Hiram Coll., 1994—. Recipient J.J. Turner award Hiram Coll., 2001. Fellow Iowa Acad. Sci.; mem. AAAS, Am. Soc. Plant Taxonomists, Bot. Soc. Am., Ecol. Soc. Am., Iowa Acad. Sci., Soc. for the Study of Evolution, Assn. for Tropical Biology, New Eng. Bot. Soc. Office: U Iowa Dept Biol Scis Iowa City IA 52242 Home: 4194 Thorn Oaks Dr Ann Arbor MI 48104-4256 E-mail: robert-cruden@uiowa.edu.

CRUIKSHANK, JOHN W., III, life insurance underwriter; b. Sharon, Pa., Aug. 22, 1933; s. John W. and Jeannette Sprague (Lane) C.; m. Myrna Jean Wright, Nov. 25, 1960; children— Nancy Lynn, David Wright BA, Princeton U., 1955. CLU. Group ins. sales rep. Conn. Gen. Life Ins. Co., Hartford, also Chgo., 1955-56; spl. agt. Northwestern Mut. Life Ins. Co., Chgo., 1959—, pres. Spl. Agts., Inc., 1983-84, faculty advanced planning sch. Northbrook, Ill., 1978-97; pres. Assn. of Agts. Northwestern Mut. Life, 1994-95. Pres. Million Dollar Round Table Found., 1988-89; divisional v.p. Million Dollar Round Table, 1976-77, 86-87, 92-93, exec. com., 1994-98, pres., 1996-97; trustee Life Underwriter Tng. Coun., 1997-2001, Am. Coll., 2001-02. Elder United Presbyn. Ch. in U.S.A., 1975—, mem. gen. assembly mission coun., 1972-78; pres. Nat. Coun. United Presbyn. Men, 1971-72; chmn. mission divsn. Presbytery of Chgo., gen. coun., 1966-67, 80-84; bd. dirs. Vocation Agy., Presbyn. Ch. in U.S.A., 1982-87, Life and Health Ins. Found. for Edn., chair-elect, 2000, chmn., 2002, North Shore Sr. Ctr.; bd. dirs. Life and Health Ins. Found. for Edn., chair, 2002; trustee Pikeville (Ky.) Coll., 1969-75, The Am. Coll., 2001-02. Recipient Circle of Life award Million Dollar Round Table Found., 1998, Huebner Scholar award Am. Soc. CLU and ChFC, Chgo., 1995, Distinguished Citizen award Ill. St. Andrew Soc., 1998, Grauer Disting. Svc. award Chgo. Chpt. Fin. Svc. Profls., 2000; named one of Most Outstanding Life Underwriters in the U.S. for decade of 1990s, Leaders Mag., 1999. Home: 1412 Ridge Rd Northbrook IL 60062-4628

CRUM, JAMES FRANCIS, waste recycling company executive; b. Pitts., July 23, 1934; s. Frank J. and Martha (Huffman) C.; m. Madeleine Jones, July 3, 1957 (dec. Feb. 2001); children: Cynthia Anne, James Joseph. BMechE, U. Rochester, 1956. Trainee to supt. transp. U.S. Steel Corp., Braddock, Pa., 1959-74, supt. transp. South Chgo., Ill., 1974-75, supt. operating maintenance, 1975-76, asst. divsn. supt. iron Gary, Ind., 1976-83; divsn. mgr. iron. U.S. Steel div. USX, 1983-88; exec. v.p., COO McGraw Construction Co., Middletown, Ohio, 1988-92; from dir. bus. devel. to v.p. ops. Nat. Recovery Systems, East Chicago, Ind., 1992-99, pvt. practice Flossmoor, Ill., 1999—. Adv. coun. South Suburban Hosp., 1993—; cons. in field. Vol. U. Rochester Admissions Network, N.Y., 1987—; cons. Clean City Coalition, Gary, 1988-90; bd. dirs. South Suburban Hosp. Found. Mem. AIME, Eastern States Blast Furnace Assn., Western States Blast Furnace Assn. (bd. dirs. 1985-88), Assn. Iron & Steel Engrs. Republican. Roman Catholic. Avocations: golf, photography, foreign travel, stained glass. Home: 736 Central Park Ave Flossmoor IL 60422-2220 E-mail: jfcrum@aol.com.

CRUMP, WAYNE F. state legislator; b. Belleville, Ill., June 26, 1950; m. Nancy C. Allen, 1974. Student, Belleville Area Coll. Former dep. sheriff Washington County, Mo., 1975-82; state rep. dist. 152 Mo. Ho. of Reps., 1983—. Mem. rules com., joint rules com., bills perfected and printed com. (chmn.); cattle farmer. Named Outstanding Legislator Coalition for Alternatives to Imprisonment, 1986, Oustanding Performer Meramec Regional Planning Commn., 1986, Outstanding Legislator, Mo. Assn. of Counties, 1990, 91, 95, State Rep. of Yr. Mo. Deputy Sheriffs' Assn., 1995, Statesman of Month Jefferson City News Tribune, 1995, 98. Democrat. Home: 606 Pine St Potosi MO 63664-1644

CRUTCHER, RICHARD METCALF, astronomer, educator; b. Lexington, Ky., Apr. 18, 1945; BS, U. Ky., 1967; MA, UCLA, 1969, PhD in Astronomy, 1972. Rsch. fellow Calif. Inst. Tech., 1972-74; prof., chmn. dept. astronomy U. Ill., Urbana. Mem. Am. Astron. Soc., Internat. Astron. Union, Union Radio Sci. Internat. Achievements include research on physics and chemistry of the interstellar medium, star formation, advanced scientific computing. Office: U Ill Dept Astronomy 1002 W Green St Urbana IL 61801

CRUZ, DEIVI, professional baseball player; b. Nizao de Bani, Dominican Republic, Nov. 6, 1975; Baseball player Detroit Tigers, 1997—. Office: Detroit Tigers 2100 Woodward Detroit MI 48201*

CRUZ, JOSE BEJAR, JR. engineering educator, educator; b. Bacolod City, The Philippines, Sept. 17, 1932; came to U.S., 1954, naturalized, 1969; s. Jose P. and Felicidad (Bejar) C.; m. Stella E. Rubia; children by previous marriage: Fe E. Cruz Langdon, Ricardo A., Rene L., Sylvia C. Cruz Loebach, Loretta C. Cruz Spray. BSEE summa cum laude, U. Philippines, 1953; MS, MIT, 1956; PhD, U. Ill., 1959. Lic. profl. engr., Ill., Ohio. Instr. elec. engring. U. Philippines, Quezon City, 1953-54; rsch. asst. MIT, Cambridge, 1954-56, vis. prof., 1973; from instr. to assoc. prof. U. Ill., Urbana-Champaign, 1956-65, prof. elec. engring., 1965-86, assoc. mem. Ctr. Advanced Study, 1967-68; rsch. prof. Coordinated Sci. Lab., 1965-86; prof. dept. elec. and computer engring. U. Calif., Irvine, 1986-92, chmn. dept., 1986-90; prof. elec. engring. Ohio State U., Columbus, 1992—, dean Coll. Engring., 1992-97, Howard D. Winbigler chair in engring., 1997—. Vis. assoc. prof. U. Calif., Berkeley, 1964-65; vis. prof. Harvard U., 1973; pres. Dynamic Sys.; mem. theory com. Am. Automatic Control Coun., 1967; gen. chmn. Conf. on Decision and Control, 1975; mem. profl. engring. exam. com. State of Ill., 1984-86; mem. Nat. Coun. Engring. Examiners, 1985-86; mem. project adv. group on engring. and sci. edn. project Dept. Sci. and Tech., Republic of The Philippines, 1993-98. Author: (with M.E. Van Valkenburg) Introductory Signals and Circuits, 1967, (with W.R. Perkins) Engineering of Dynamic Systems, 1969, Feedback Systems, 1972, translated into Chinese, 1976, Polish, 1977, System Sensitivity Analysis, 1973, (with M.E. Van Valkenburg) Signals in Linear Circuits, 1974, translated into Spanish, 1978; Assoc. editor: Jour. Franklin Inst, 1976-82, Jour. Optimization Theory and Applications, 1980—; series editor Advances in Large Scale Systems Theory and Applications; contbr. articles on network theory, automatic control systems, system theory, sensitivity theory of dynamical systems, large scale systems, dynamic games and dynamic scheduling in mfg. systems to sci., tech. jours. Recipient Purple Tower award Beta Epsilon U., Philippines, 1969, Diamond award, 1999, Curtis W. McGraw Rsch. award Am. Soc. for Engring. Edn., 1972, Halliburton Engring. Edn. Leadership award, 1981, Most Outstanding Alumnus award U. of the Philippines Alumni Assn. Am., 1989, Most Outstanding Overseas Alumnus Coll. Engring., U. of the Philippines Alumni Assn., 1990, Richard E. Bellman Control Heritage award Am. Automatic Control Coun., 1994. Fellow AAAS (sect. com. for sect. on engring. 1991-94, sec. 1998—), IEEE (chmn. linear sys. com., group on automatic control 1966-68, assoc. editor Trans. on Circuit Theory 1962-64); mem. Control Sys. Soc. (adminstrv. com. 1966-75, 78-80, v.p. fin. and adminstrv. activities 1976-77, pres. 1979, chmn. awards com. 1973-75, ednl. activities bd. 1973-75, editor Trans. on Automatic Control 1971-73, mem. tech. activities bd. 1979-83, chmn. 1982-83, v.p. tech. activities 1982-83, edn. med. com. 1977-79, dir. 1980-85, vice-chmn. publs. bd. 1981, chmn. 1984-85, chmn. panel of tech. editors 1981, chmn. TAB periodicals com. 1981, chmn. PUB. Soc. publs. com. 1981, v.p. publ. activities 1984-85, exec. com. 1982-85, Richard M. Emberson award 1989), Philippine Engrs. and Scientists Orgn., Am. Soc. Engring Edn. (awards policy com.), U.S. Nat. Acad. Engring. (mem. peer com. for electronics engring. 1982, 2000—, com. on nat. agenda for career-long edn. for engrs. 1986-88, membership com. 1987-90, acad. adv. bd. 1994-97, com. on diversity in engring. workforce 1999-2001), Philippine-Am. Acad. Sci. and Engring. (founding mem. 1980, pres. 1982, chmn. bd. dirs. 1998-00), Internat. Fedn. Automatic Control (chmn. theory com. 1981-84, vice-chmn. tech. bd. 1984-87, policy com. 1987-93, vice-chmn. 1993, 99, chmn. 1996, congress internat. program com.), Philippine Engrs. and Scientists Orgn., Sigma Xi, Phi Kappa Phi, Eta Kappa Nu. Achievements include introduction of concept of comparison sensitivity in dynamical feedback systems, of leader-follower strategies in hierarchical engineering systems; development of synthesis methods for time-varying systems. Office: Ohio State U Dept Elec Engring Columbus OH 43210-1272 E-mail: jbcruz@attglobal.net.

CRYER, PHILIP EUGENE, medical educator, scientist, endocrinologist; b. El Paso, Ill., Jan. 5, 1940; s. Clifford Eugene and Carol Ruth (Cherry) C.; m. Susan Odette Shipman, Dec. 23, 1963 (div. May 1990); children: Philip Clifford, Justine Laurel; m. Carolyn Elizabeth Havlin, Sept. 16, 1994. BA, Northwestern U., 1962, MD, 1965; MD (hon.), U. Copenhagen, 2000. Diplomate Am. Bd. Internal Medicine, diplomate Am. Bd. Endocrinology and Metabolism. Intern Barnes Hosp., St. Louis, 1965-67; fellow in endocrinology Barnes Hosp./Washington U., 1967-68, resident in medicine, 1968-69, 71-72; investigator Naval Med. Rsch. Inst., Bethesda, Md., 1969-71; from instr. to assoc. prof. Washington U. Sch. Medicine, St. Louis, 1971-80, prof., 1981—, Irene E. and Michael M. Karl prof. endocrinology/metabolism, 1995—, dir. gen. clin. rsch. ctr., 1978—, dir. div. endocrinology, diabetes and metabolism, 1985—. Connaught-Novo lectr. Can. Diabetes Assn., 1987; Pimstone lectr. Soc. Endocrinology, Metabolism and Diabetes, South Africa, 1989; Kellion lectr. Australian Diabetes Soc., 1992; Plenary lectr. Japan Diabetes Soc., 1994, plenary lectr. Argentine Diabetes Assn., 1998, plenary lectr. Asean Fed. Endocrine Socs., 1999. Author: Diagnostic Endocrinology, 1976, Diagnostic Endocrinology, 2d edit., 1979, Hypoglycemia, 1997, also 74 book chpts.; editor: Diabetes; mem. editl. bd.: Clin. Investigation, mem. editl. bd.: Am. Jour. Physiology, mem. editl. bd.: Jour. Clin. Endocrinology and Metabolism; contbr. over 300 articles to profl. jours. Recipient Rorer Clin. Investigator award Endocrine Soc., 1988, Rumbough Sci. award Juvenile Diabetes Found., 1989, Banting medal Am. Diabetes Assn., 1994, Excellence in Clin. Rsch. award NIH, 1994, Claude Bernard medal European Assn. Study Diabetes, 2001; Am. Diabetes Clin. Rsch. grantee, 1996, NIH Rsch. grantee, 1980—. Fellow ACP; mem. Am. Fedn. Clin. Rsch. (councilor 1979-80), Am. Soc. Clin. Investigation (v.p. 1985-86), Assn. Am. Physicians, Am. Diabetes Assn. (pres. 1996-97), Phi Beta Kappa, Alpha Omega Alpha. Office: Washington U Sch Medicine 660 South Euclid Ave PO Box 8127 Saint Louis MO 63156-8127 E-mail: pcryer@im.wustl.edu.

CSAR, MICHAEL F. lawyer; b. Chgo., May 26, 1950; s. Frank J. and Rosaria (Motto) C.; children: Cordelia, Christian. BA, Yale U., 1972, Kings Coll., Cambridge, 1974; JD, Yale U., 1977. Bar: Ill. 1977, U.S. Dist. Ct. (no. dist.) Ill. 1977. Assoc. Wilson & McIlvaine, Chgo., 1977-83; ptnr. Quarles & Brady (formerly Wilson & McIlvaine), 1983-98, Gardner, Carton & Douglas, Chgo., 1998—. Office: Gardner, Carton & Douglas 321 N Clark St Ste 3400 Chicago IL 60610-4795

CSERE, CSABA, magazine editor; b. Cleve., June 16, 1951; s. Zoltan and Theresa (Balazs) C.; m. Mary Patricia O'Brien, July 6, 1975; 1 child, Madeline Christine. SB, MIT, 1975. Design engr. Data Gen. Corp., Southboro, Mass., 1975-77, Ford Motor Co., 1978-80; tech. editor Car and Driver mag., 1980-87, tech. dir., 1987-93, editor-in-chief, 1993—. Mem. Soc. Automotive Engrs., Am. Soc. Mag. Editors. Office: Car and Driver Hachette Filipacchi Mags Inc 2002 Hogback Rd Ste 1 Ann Arbor MI 48105-9795

CUCCO, ULISSE P. obstetrician, gynecologist; b. Bklyn., Aug. 19, 1929; s. Charles and Elvira (Garafalo) C.; m. Antoinette DeMarco, Aug. 31, 1952; children— Carl, Richard, Antoinette Marie, Michael, Frank, James B.S. cum laude, L.I. U., 1950; M.D., Loyola U., Chgo., 1954. Diplomate Am. Bd. Ob-Gyn. Intern Nassau County Hosp., Hempstead, N.Y., 1954-55; resident in ob-gyn Lewis Meml. Mercy Hosp., Chgo., 1955-58; practice medicine specializing in ob-gyn Des Plaines, Ill., 1960—. Past pres. med. staff, chmn. dept. ob-gyn. Holy Family Hosp., Des Plaines, Ill.; clin. asst. prof. Stritch Sch. Medicine, Loyola U. Contbr. articles to med. jours. Mem. ACS, Am. Fertility Soc., Ctrl. Assn. Ob-Gyn., Ill. Med. Soc., Chgo. Med. Soc., Chgo. Gynecol. Soc. (past pres.), Chgo. Inst. Medicine, Sunset Ridge Country Club. Roman Catholic. Home: 665 Midfield Ln Northbrook IL 60062-5507

CUCUZ, RANKO (RON CUCUZ), manufacturing executive; BSME, MBA, Purdue U. Formerly with LaSalle Steel Co., Hammond, Ind., U.S. Steel Corp., Gary; plant mgr. Am. Chain & Cable Co.'s Cable Control Worldwide, Fairfield, Conn., 1976-87, pres., CEO, 1987-91; group pres. Kelsey Hayes Wheels Unit Hayes Wheels Internat. (subs. Hayes Lammerz), Romulus, Mich., 1991-92, pres., CEO, 1992-99; CEO Hayes Lemmerz, 1999—. Bd. dirs. Nat.-Standard Co. Office: 15300 Centennial Dr Northville MI 48167

CUDABACK, JIM D. state legislator; b. Riverdale, Nebr., Apr. 12, 1938; Student, Kearney State Coll., Lincoln Sch. Commerce, USAF Schs. Rental property mgr., Nebr.; mem. Nebr. Legislature from 36th dist., Lincoln, 1990—; vice chair exec. bd., vice chair reference com. Nebr. Legislature, vice chair gen. affairs, mem. govt., mil. and vets. affairs com., mem. bldg. maintenance com., mem. com. on coms. Former mem. Buffalo County Bd. Commrs., Riverdale Village Bd., Ctrl. C.C. Adv. Bd.; pres. Buffalo County Hist. Soc. Adv. Bd., Cmty. Concert Assn.; active Gibbon Good Samaritan Village, Buffalo County Econ. Devel. Visitors Promotion Com., Kearney Vol. Fire Dept. Mem. Rotary, IOOF Lodge, Elks. Office: Nebr State Senate State Capitol Rm 1124 Lincoln NE 68509

CUDAHY, RICHARD D. judge; b. Milwaukee, Wisc., Feb. 2, 1926; s. Michael F. and Alice (Dickson) Cudahy; m. Ann Featherston, July 14, 1956 (dec. 1974); m. Janet Stuart, July 17, 1976; children: Richard D., Norma K., Theresa E., Daniel M., Michaela A., Marguerite L., Patrick G. BS, U.S. Mil. Acad., 1948; JD, Yale U., 1955; LLD, Ripon Coll., 1981, DePaul U., 1995, Wabash Coll., 1996, Stetson U., 1998. Bar: Conn. 1955, D.C. 1957, Ill. 1957, Wis. 1961. Commd. 2d. lt. U.S. Army, 1948, advanced through grades to 1st lt., 1950; law clk. to presiding judge U.S. Ct. Appeals (2d cir.), 1955—56; asst. to legal adv. Dept. State, 1956—57; assoc. Isham, Lincoln & Beale, Chgo., 1957—60; pres. Patrick Cudahy, Inc., Wis., 1961—71, Patrick Cudahy Family Co., 1968—75; ptnr. firm Godfrey & Kahn, Milw., 1972; commr., chmn. Wis. Pub. Svc. Commn., 1972—75; ptnr. Isham, Lincoln & Beale, Chgo. and Washington, 1976—79; judge U.S. Ct Appeals (7th cir.), Chgo., 1979—94, sr. judge, 1994—. Lectr. law Marquette U. Law Sch., 1962; vis. prof. law U. Wis., 1966—67; prof. lectr. law George Washington U., Washington, 1978—79; adj. prof. DePaul U. Coll. Law, 1995—. Commr. Milw. Harbor, 1964—66; pres. Milw. Urban League, 1965—66; trustee Environ. Def. Fund, 1976—79; chmn. DePaul Human Rights Law Inst., 1990—98; mem. adv. com. Ctr. for Internat. Human Rights, Northwestern U., 2000—; chmn. Wis. Dem. Party, 1967—68; Dem. candidate for Wis. atty. gen., 1968. Mem.: ABA (spl. com. on Energy Law 1978—84, 1990—96, pub. utility/sect. coun. group), Am. Inst. for Pub. Svc. (bd. selectors), Fed. Judges' Assn. (bd. dirs.), Chgo. Bar Assn., Milw. Bar Assn., Wis. Bar Assn., Am. Law Inst., Cath. Theol. Union (trustee), Lawyers Club Chgo. (pres. 1992—93, spl. divsn. D.C. cir. for appt. ind. counsel 1998—). Office: US Ct Appeals 219 S Dearborn St Ste 2648 Chicago IL 60604-1874

CUDAK, GAIL LINDA, lawyer; b. Bellville, Ill., July 13, 1952; d. Robert Joseph and Margaret Lucille C.; m. Thomas Edward Young, Sept. 15, 1979. BA, Kenyon Coll., 1974; JD, Case Western Res. U., 1977, MBA, 1991. Bar: Ohio 1977, U.S. Dist. Ct. (no. dist.) Ohio 1977, U.S. Ct. Appeals (6th cir.) 1977, U.S. Ct. Appeals (fed. cir.) 1989. Assoc. Fuerst, Leidner, Dougherty & Kasdan, Cleve., 1977-79; staff atty. The B.F. Goodrich Co., Akron, Ohio, 1979-84, sr. corp. counsel Independence, 1985-89, divsn. counsel Brecksville, 1990-98, group counsel, 1998-99; sr. attorney Eaton

Corp., Cleve., 1999—. Trustee Great Lakes Theater Festival, 1996—, mem. exec. com.; fundraiser Ohio Found. Ind. Colls., 1993—. Mem.: ABA, Cleve. Internat. Lawyers Group, Cleve. Bar Assn. (chair corp. sect.), Ohio State Bar Assn. Home: 12520 Edgewater Dr Apt 1405 Lakewood OH 44107-1639 Office: Eaton Corp 1111 Superior Ave E Cleveland OH 44114-2507

CULL, ROBERT ROBINETTE, electric products manufacturing company executive; b. Cleve., Sept. 24, 1912; s. Louis David and Wilma Penn (Robinette) C.; m. Gay Cornwell, Oct. 4, 1986. B.S. in Physics, M.I.T., 1934. Supr. Eastman Kodak Co., Rochester, N.Y., 1934-39; asst. to gen. mgr. Cleve. Chain & Mfg. Co., 1940-45; partner Tenna Mfg. Co., Cleve., 1945-56; pres. Tenatronics Ltd., Newmarket, Ont., Can., 1956—, Sterling Mfg. Co., Cleve., 1960—. Trustee Garden Center Greater Cleve., 1975-80, pres., 1979-80; trustee Musical Arts Assn. of Cleve. Orch., 1976— . Mem. IEEE, Cleve. Engring. Soc., Sigma Psi. Clubs: Hermit, Union.

CULLEN, CHARLES THOMAS, historian, librarian; b. Gainesville, Fla., Oct. 11, 1940; s. Spencer L. and Blanche J. Cullen; m. Shirley Harrington, June 13, 1964; children: Leslie Lanier, Charles Spencer Harrington. BA, U. of South, 1962; MA, Fla. State U., 1963; PhD, U. Va., 1971; HHD (hon.), Lewis U., 1987; DLitt (hon.), U. South, 1994; LLD (hon.), John Marshall Law Sch., 1995; DHist (hon.), Lincoln Coll., 2000. Asst. prof. history Averett Coll., 1963-66; assoc. editor Papers of John Marshall Inst. Early Am. History and Culture, Williamsburg, Va., 1971-74, co-editor, 1974-77, editor, 1977-79; lectr. history Coll. William and Mary, 1971-79; sr. research historian, editor Papers of Thomas Jefferson Princeton (N.J.) U., 1979-86; pres., librarian Newberry Library, Chgo., 1986—. Mem. N.J. Hist. Commn., 1985-86, Nat. Hist. Publs. and Records Com., 1990—. Nat. Hist. Publs. and Records Commn. fellow, 1970-71. Mem. Assn. Documentary Editing (pres. 1982-83), Orgn. Am. Historians, Am. Hist. Assn., Am. Antiquarian Soc., Heartland Lit. Soc. (pres. 1994—), Modern Poetry Assn. (trustee 1987—, v.p. 1998—), Ind. Rsch. Librs. Assn. (pres. 2000—), Caxton Club, Grolier Club. Office: Newberry Libr 60 W Walton St Chicago IL 60610-3380

CULLEN, DAVID A. state legislator; b. Milw., Feb. 1, 1960; married; 1 child. BA, U. Wis., 1981; JD, Marquette U., 1984. Mem. from dist. 13 Wis. State Assembly, Madison, 1990—. Mem. Milw. Sch. Bd., 1983-90, pres., 1987-90; bd. dirs. Friends of Sch. Edn., U. wis.; mem. Statewide Presch.-Grade 5 Adv. Coun. Mem. Wis. Bar Assn. Home: 2845 N 68th St Milwaukee WI 53210-1206 Office: State Capitol PO Box 8952 Madison WI 53708-8952

CULLERTON, JOHN JAMES, state senator, lawyer; b. Chgo., Oct. 28, 1948; s. John James and Mary Patricia (Tyrrell) C.; m. Pamela J. Wilson, Sept. 8, 1979; children: Maggie, John, Garritt, Kyle, Josephine. BS, Loyola U., 1970, JD, 1974. Bar: Ill. 1974. Asst. pub. defender Cook County, Chgo., 1974-79; state rep. State of Ill., Springfield, 1979-91, state senator, 1991—; from assoc. to ptnr. Fagel & Haber, Chgo., 1987—. With U.S. Nat. Guard, 1970-76. Democrat. Roman Catholic. Office: Fagel & Haber 140 S Dearborn St Ste 1400 Chicago IL 60603-5293

CULLIS, CHRISTOPHER ASHLEY, dean, biology educator; b. Harrow, Eng., Nov. 20, 1945; s. Jack Douglas Bungard and Isette Sarah (Cullis) Giles; m. Margaret Angela Webb, Sept. 4, 1971; children: Benjamin, Oliver, Thomas, Bethia, Tristan, Camilla. BS, London U., 1966; MS in Biophysics, U. East Anglia, Norwich, Eng., 1968, PhD, 1971. Higher sci. officer John Innes Inst., Norwich, 1971-73, sr. sci. officer, 1973-81, prin. sci. officer, 1981-85; prof. biology Case Western Res. U., Cleve., 1986—, dean, math. and natural scis., 1989-93; Francis Hobart Herrick prof. biology U. Cleve., 1994—. Vis. prof. Case Western Res. U., 1985-86, Stanford U., Palo Alto, Calif., 1982-83; adj. prof. plant biotech. ctr. Bond U., Queensland, Australia, 1990-93; founder, gen. ptnr. Novomark Technols. LLC.; mem. rsch. com. Holden Arboretum, 1992—. Editor: The Nucleolus, 1981, John Innes Symposium, 1983; author chpts. in books. Cubmaster Boy Scouts Am., Winding River, 1988, 89, com. chair, 1990-94. Nuffield and Leverhulme fellow Civil Svc. Commn., 1982-83; Assn. Commonwealth Univs. scholar, 1967-70. Mem. AAAS, Genetical Soc. Am., Bot. Soc. Am., Soc. for Plant Molecular Biology, Soc. for Exptl. Biology (coun. 1979-81, chair com. for cell biology 1980-81). Avocations: sports, reading. Office: Case Western Res U 2040 Adelbert Rd Cleveland OH 44106-2623

CULP, KRISTINE ANN, dean, theology educator; B in Gen. Studies with distinction, U. Iowa, 1978; MDiv, Princeton Theol. Sem., 1982; PhD in Religion, U. Chgo., 1989. Vis. instr. theology St. Paul Sch. Theology, Kansas City, Mo., 1985-86, instr. theology, 1986-89, asst. prof. theology, 1990-91; dean Disciples Div. House U. Chgo., 1991—, sr. lectr. theology Div. Sch., 1991—. Contbr. articles to profl. jours. Office: U Chgo Disciples Divinity House 1156 E 57th St Chicago IL 60637-1536 also: The Divinity Sch-U Chgo Swift Hall S-406 1025 E 58th St Chicago IL 60637-1509

CULP, MILDRED LOUISE, corporate executive; b. Ft. Monroe, Va., Jan. 13, 1949; d. William W. and Winifred (Stilwell) C. BA in English, Knox Coll., 1971; AM in Religion and Literature, U. Chgo., 1974, PhD The Com. on History of Culture, 1976. Faculty, adminstr. Coll., 1976-81; dir. Exec. Résumés, Seattle, 1981—; pres. Exec. Directions Internat., Inc., 1985—. MBA mgmt. skills adv. com. U. Wash. Sch. Bus. Adminstrn., 1993; spkr. in field; contract rschr. U.S. Army Recruiting Command, 1997. Author: Be WorkWise: Retooling Your Work for the 21st Century, 1994; columnist Seattle Daily Jour. Commerce, 1982-88; writer Singer Media Corp., 1991-98, Worldwide Media, 1999—, WorkWise syndicated column, 1994—, Universal Press Syndicate, 1997-2001, syndicated in U.S., in print and online svcs., WorkWise Registered, 1992 (radio), 96 (print), 2000 (Internet audio); WorkWise syndicated Internet audio program, 2000—; featured on TV and radio; contbr. articles and book revs. to profl. jours.; presenter WorkWise Report, Sta. KIRO, 1991-96. Admissions counselor U. Chgo., 1981—; mem. Nat. Alliance Mentally Ill, 1984—, mem. adv. bd., 1988; mem. A.M.I. Hamilton County, 1984—; founding mem. People Against Telephone Terrorism and Harassment, 1990; co-sponsor WorkWise award, 1999-2000. Recipient Alumni Achievement award Knox Coll., 1990, 8 other awards; named Hon. Army Recruiter. Mem. Knox Coll. Alumni Network, U. Chgo. Puget Sound Alumni Club (bd. dirs. 1982-86).

CULPEPPER, DAUNTE, football player; b. Jan. 28, 1977; Football player Minn. Vikings, 1999—. Office: Minn Vikings 9520 Viking Dr Eden Prairie MN 55344

CULVER, CHESTER J. state official, educator; m. Mari Thinnes Culver. BA in Polit. Sci., Va. Polytechnic Inst. and State U., 1988; MA in Tchg., Drake U., 1994. Tchr. HS govt., history, coach Hoover HS, Des Moines; investigator Atty. Gen.'s Office; Sec. of State State of Iowa, 1999—. Established Iowa Student Polit. Awareness Club; elder mem. Ctrl. Presbyn. Ch. Mem.: Iowa State Edn. Assn. (Fulbright Meml. Fund Tchrs. scholarship 1997), Coun. State Govts., Elections Task Force, New Millenium Youth Initiative, Presdl. Caucuses and Primaries Com., Elections and Voter Participation Com., Nat. Assn. Secs. State, State Records Mgmt. Com., State Voter Registration Commn. (chmn.), Exec. Coun. Office: Office of Secretary of State State House Des Moines IA 50319-0001 Business E-Mail: sos@sos.state.ia.us.*

CULVERWELL, ROSEMARY JEAN, principal, elementary education educator; b. Chgo., Jan. 15, 1934; d. August John and Marie Josephine (Westermeyer) Flashing; m. Paul Jerome Culverwell, Apr. 26, 1958; children: Joanne, Mary Frances, Janet, Nancy, Amy. BEd, Chgo. State U., 1955, MEd in Libr. Sci., 1958; postgrad., DePaul U., 1973. Cert. supr., tchr. Tchr. Otis Sch., Chgo., 1955-59; tchr., libr. Yates Sch., 1960-61, Nash Sch., Chgo., 1962-63, Boys Chgo. Parental, 1969-72, Edgebrook and Reilly Schs., Chgo., 1965-67; counselor, libr. Reilly Sch., 1968, tchr., libr., asst. prin., 1973, prin., 1974—. Reviewer Ill. State Bd. Edn. Quality Review Team. Pres. Infant Jesus Guild, Park Ridge, Ill., 1969-70; troop leader Girl Scouts U.S., Park Ridge, 1967-69; sec. Home Sch. Assn., Park Ridge, 1969, v.p. spl. projects, 1970; mem. Ill. Svc. Ctr. Six Governing Bd., 1994; vol. Ctr. of Concern, Park Ridge, Ill., 1997; quality reviewer Ill. State Bd. Edn., 1998; mem. Ill. Quality Edn. Rev. Team, 1998; v.p. Renaissance Art Club, 1999—. Recipient Outstanding Prin. award Citizens Schs. Com., Chgo., 1987, For Character award, 1984-85, Whitman award for Excellence in Edn. Mgmt., 1990, Local Sch. Coun. award Ill. Bell Ameritech, 1991, Ill. Disting. Educator award Milken Family Found. Nat. Educators, 1991, Ill. Edn./Bus. Partnership award, 1994, 96. Mem. AAUW, LWV (chmn. speakers bur. 1969), Delta Kappa Gamma, Phi Delta Kappa. Avocations: acrylic painting, reading, swimming, making doll houses and furniture. Home: 1929 S Ashland Ave Park Ridge IL 60068-5460 Office: FW Reilly Sch 3650 W School St Chicago IL 60618-5358 E-mail: rosemary.culverwell@mciworldcom.net.

CUMMINGS, JOAN E. health facility administrator, educator; BA, Trinity Coll., 1964; MD, Loyola U., 1968. Diplomate Am. Bd. Internal Medicine, Geriatric Medicine. Med. internship St. Vincent Hosp., Worcester, Mass., 1968-69; med. residency Hines VA Hosp., Hines, Ill., 1969-71, sr. residency Nephrology, 1971-72, ambulatory care svc. chief gen. med. section, 1971-84, med. dir., hosp. based home care, 1972-87, chief, intermediate care svc., 1984-87, assoc. chief of staff, extended care and geriatrics, 1987-90, med. dir., extended care center, 1987-90, dir., 1990—; asst. prof. Clinical Medicine U. Ill., 1976-82, Loyola U., 1983-91, assoc. prof. Clinical Medicine, 1991—; network dir. Dept. Vet. Affairs, Hines, Ill. Mem. ad hoc com. on primary care U. Ill., 1980-82, coll. edn. policy com. U. Ill., 1980-82, State Ill. Emergency Med. Svc. Coun., 1981-83, Comprehensive Health Ins. Plan Bd. State Ill., 1990—, Med. Licensing Bd. State Ill., 1992—, exec. com. Chgo. Fed. Exec. Bd. State Ill., 1992—; program dir. Loyola/Hines Geriatric Fellowship Program, 1987-90. Contbr. to profl. mags. and jour. Recipient Disting. Svc. award Abraham Lincoln Sch. Med. Univ. Ill., 1979, 81, Leadership award VA, 1980, Certificate of Appreciation award VA, 1980, Laureate award Am. Coll. Physicians, 1990. Fellow Am. Coll. Physicians; mem. AMA (Ill. delegation 1985—, vice speaker ho. delegates 1987-89), Chgo. Med. Soc. (pres. Hines-Loyola Branch 1982-83), Ill. State Med. Soc. (trustee 1984—, chmn. com. on Ill. med., 1988—, speaker ho delegates 1989-91, exec. com., 1989-91, policy com., 1989—), Am. Coll. Physicians (councilor Ill. chpt. 1984—), Chgo. Geriatric Soc., Am. Geriatric Soc. Office: Bldg 18 PO Box 5000 5th Ave & Roosevelt Rd Hines IL 60141-5000 E-mail: joan.cummings@med.va.gov.

CUNEO, NGAIRE E. corporate development executive; b. Oct. 24, 1950; BA in Econs., Coll. New Rochelle, N.Y.; MBA, Iona Coll. Deputy dir. Metropolitan Transit Authority, N.Y.C., 1972-75; mem. staff Gen. Acctg. Office, 1975-86; sr. v.p. Gen. Electric Capital Corp., 1986-92; executive v.p. Conseco Inc., Carmel, Ind., 1992—. Bd. dirs. Bankers Life Holding Corp., Am. Life Holdings, Inc., Am. Life Holding Co., Duke Realty Investments, Inc., NAL Financial Group Inc. Office: Conseco Inc 11825 N Pennsylvania St Carmel IN 46032-4604

CUNNINGHAM, BILL, radio personality; b. Covington; Radio host 700 WLW, Cin. Recipient Marconi award for large market personality of yr., 2001. Avocation: golf. Office: 700 WLW 111 St Gregory St Cincinnati OH 45202

CUNNINGHAM, CHARLES BAKER, III, manufacturing company executive; b. St. Louis, Oct. 1, 1941; s. Charles Baker C. and Mary Blythe (Cunningham); m. Georganne Rose, Sept. 17, 1966; children: Margaret B., Charles B. IV. B.S., Washington U., St. Louis, 1964; M.S., Ga. Inst. Tech., 1966; M.B.A., Harvard U., 1970. Dir. fin. The Cooper Group, Raleigh, N.C., 1972-75, v.p. adminstrn., 1975-77; v.p. devel. Cooper Industries Inc., Houston, 1977-79, v.p. ops., 1980-82, exec. v.p., 1982-93, pres. Indsl. Equipment Group, 1979-80; chmn., pres., CEO Belden Inc., 1993—. Served to 1st lt. U.S. Army, 1966-68, Iran. Decorated Army Commendation medal Office: Belden Inc 7701 Forsyth Blvd Ste 800 Saint Louis MO 63105-1861 E-mail: baker.cunningham@belden.com.

CUNNINGHAM, DOUGLAS D. state legislator; b. Osmond, Nebr., Oct. 13, 1954; m. Deb Cunningham; 1 child, John. Owner, operator D&D Foodliner, Wausa, Nebr.; mem. Nebr. Legislature from 18th dist., 2001—. Bd. dirs. Osmond Gen. Hosp. Found., Knox County Block Grant; mem. com. Wausa Appreciation Day; mem. strategic planning com. Wausa Pub. Schs.; coun. treas., Sunday sch. prin. Thabor Luth. Ch.; mem. Vol. Fire Dept.; del. Rep. State Conv.; co-chairperson Knox County Hagel for Senate campaign; vice chmn. Knox County Reps., 1996. Mem. Nat. Grocers Assn. (mem. govt. rels. coun., mem. polit. edn. com., Spirit of Am. award 2000), Nat. Grocery Industry (bd. dirs.), Knox County Pork Prodrs. (assoc.), Knox County Cattle Feeders (assoc.), Wausa Cmty. Club. Home: Box 160 Wausa NE 68786 Office: Rm 1010 State Capitol Lincoln NE 68509

CUNNINGHAM, GUNTHER, professional football coach; m. Rene Cunningham; children: Natalie, Adam. Grad., U. Oreg. Football coach U. Oreg., 1969-71, U. Kar., 1972, Stanford (Calif.) U., 1973-76, U. Calif., 1977-80; coach defensive line, linebackers CFL's Hamilton Tiger Cats, 1981; defensive line coach Balt. Colts, 1982-84; mentor defensive line San Diego Charters, 1985-90; coach linebackers Oakland Raiders, 1991, defensive coord., 1992-93, tutor defensive line, 1994; defensive coord. Kansas City Chief, 1995-98, coach, 1999—. Office: c/o Kansas City Chiefs One Arrowhead Dr Kansas City MO 64129

CUNNINGHAM, MILAMARI ANTOINELLA, anesthesiologist; b. Cody, Wyo., Oct. 4, 1949; d. Milo Leo and Mary Madeline (Haley) Olds; m. Michael Otis Webb, June 4, 1970 (div. Feb. 1971); m. James Kenneth Cunningham, June 14, 1975. BA with honors, U. Mo., 1971, MD, 1975. Diplomate Am. Bd. Anesthesiologists. Intern and resident U. Mo., Columbia, 1975-78; jr. ptnr. Anesthesiologist, Inc., 1979-82, ptnr., 1982-86; owner Cunningham Anesthesia, 1986—; dir. anesthesia dept. Ellis Fischel Cancer Ctr., 1991-92; acting chief anesthesia Harry S. Truman Meml. Vets. Hosp., 1994-95. Mem. med. staff Columbia Regional Hosp., U. Mo. Hosp. and Clinics, Columbia; mem. rev. com. Mo. Health Facilities, 2001—. Mem. editl. bd.: Mo. Medicine Jour., 2001. Active Mo. Med. Polit. Action Com., 1991-2000, Friends of Music, Friends of Libr., Boone County Fair, 1978-94, with ham breakfast divsn., 1978-85, with draft horse and mule show, 1986-88; bd. dirs. A Call to Serve Mo., 1996. Fellowship Am. Coll. Anesthesiologists, 1977. Mem.: AMA (Physicians Recognition award 1978, 1985, 1987, 1991, 1995), Vis. Nurses Assn. (bd. dirs. 1982—89, chair 1984—86, adv. bd. 1989—93), Mo. State Med. Assn. (commn. econs. third party payors 1986—89, chair 1989, Mo. health facilities rev. com. 2001—), Boone County Med. Soc. (membership chair 1982—84, alt. del. 1986, del. 1987—89, pres. 1988—98, sec.-treas. 1996, bd. dirs. 1996—99, del. 1997), Mo. Soc. Anesthesiologists (v.p. 1986—87, pres. elect 1987—88, pres. 1988—89, Am. Soc. Anesthesiologists del. 1989—98, 2000), Am. Med. Women's Assn., Phi Beta Kappa. Home: 8202 S Bennett Dr Columbia MO 65201-9178 Office: PO Box 1301 Columbia MO 65205-1301 E-mail: mila@tranquility.net.

CUNNINGHAM, PAUL GEORGE, minister; b. Chgo., Aug. 27, 1937; s. Paul George Sr. and Naomi Pearl (Anderson) C.; m. Constance Ruth Seaman, May 27, 1960; children: Lori, Paul, Connie Jo. BA, Olivet Nazarene U., 1960; BDiv., Nazarene Theol. Sem., 1964; DD, Mid Am. Nazarene Coll., 1975. Sr. pastor Coll. Ch. of the Nazarene, Olathe, Kans., 1964-93; gen. supt. Internat. Ch. of the Nazarene, 1993—. Adv. bd. Kansas City Dist. Ch. of the Nazarene, Overland Park, Kans., 1971-93; trustee Mid Am. Nazarene Coll., Olathe, 1971—; chmn. book com. Nazarene Pub. House, Kansas City, Mo., 1974-90; pres. gen. bd. Internat. Ch. of the Nazarene, Kansas City, 1985-93. Police chaplain Olathe (Kans.) Police Dept., 1975-93; adv. bd. Good Samaritan Ctr., Olathe, 1990—. Recipient Disting. Svc. award Jaycees, Olathe, 1967, Paul Harris fellow Rotary Internat., Olathe, 1989. Mem. Nat. Assn. Evangs., Rotary. Home: 12543 S Hagan Ln Olathe KS 66062-6075 Office: Ch of the Nazarene 6401 Paseo Blvd Kansas City MO 64131-1213

CUNNINGHAM, RAYMOND LEO, retired research chemist; b. Easton, Ill., Jan. 5, 1934; s. Raymond J. and Minnie G. (Vaughn) C. BA, St. Ambrose U., Davenport, Iowa, 1955. Phys. sci. aid in chemistry Nat. Ctr. Agrl. Utilization Rsch USDA Agrl. Rsch. Svc., Peoria, Ill., 1957-61, chemist Nat. Ctr. Agrl. Utilization Rsch., 1961-78, rsch. chemist Nat. Ctr. Agrl. Utilization Rsch., 1978-97; ret., 1997. Contbr. articles to profl. jours. With U.S. Army, 1958. Co-recipient R&D 100 award R&D mag., 1988. Fellow Am. Inst. Chemists; mem. AAAS, Am. Chem. Soc., Ill. State Acad. Sci. Home: 1108 W MacQueen Ave Peoria IL 61604-3310 E-mail: raymond.cunningham@att.net.

CUNNINGHAM, ROBERT JAMES, lawyer; b. Kearney, Nebr., June 27, 1942; m. Sara Jean Dickson, July 22, 1967. BA, U. Nebr., 1964; JD, NYU, 1967, LLM in Taxation, 1969. Bar: N.Y. 1967, Ill. 1969, U.S. Dist. Ct. (no. dist.) Ill. 1969, U.S. Ct. Claims 1970, U.S. Tax Ct. 1970, U.S. Ct. Appeals (D.C. cir.) 1972, U.S. Ct. Appeals (9th cir.) 1975, U.S. Ct. Appeals (7th cir.) 1979, U.S. Ct. Appeals (fed. cir.) 1982. Instr. law NYU, N.Y.C., 1967-69; assoc. Baker & McKenzie, Chgo., 1969-74, ptnr., 1974—. Spkr. in field. Contbr. articles to profl. jours. Mem. ABA, Ill. Bar Assn., Chgo. Bar Assn. Office: Baker & McKenzie One Prudential Plz 130 E Randolph Dr Ste 3700 Chicago IL 60601-6342 E-mail: robert.j.cunningham@bakernet.com.

CUNNINGHAM, THOMAS B. aerospace engineer; b. Washington, May 8, 1946; BS, U. Nebr., 1969; MS, Purdue U., 1972, PhD in Engring., 1973. Dir. rsch. engring. automatic control Honeywell, Inc., 1973—. Adj. prof. U. Minn., 1978—. Mem. IEEE, Am. Inst. Aeronaut. & Astronaut., Sigma Xi. Achievements include applications of modern control and estimation theory to aerospace and industrial problems. Office: Honeywell Tech Ctr 3660 Technology Dr Minneapolis MN 55418-1096

CUNNINGHAM, WES, radio personality; b. Harrisonville, Mo., Aug. 16; m. Lois Cunningham; 1 child Ryan 4 stepchildren. Student, Mich. State U. Radio host WDAF, Westwood, Kans., 1993—. Avocations: music, golf, bowling, singing. Office: WDAF 4935 Belinder Rd Westwood KS 66205*

CUPICH, BLASE, bishop; b. Mar. 19, 1949; Bishop of Rapid City Roman Cath. Ch., S.D., 1998—. Office: Rapid City Diocese 606 Cathedral Dr Rapid City SD 57701-5407

CUPP, DAVID FOSTER, photographer, journalist; b. Derry Twp., Pa., Feb. 4, 1938; s. Foster Wilson and Elizabeth (Erhard) C.; m. Catherine Lucille Lum, Nov. 20, 1965; children: Mary Catherine, David Patterson, John. B.A. in Journalism, U. Miami (Fla.), 1960. Staff photographer Miami News, 1960-63, Charlotte (N.C.) Observer, 1963-66; photographer, writer Internat. Harvesters, Chgo., 1966-67; picture editor Nat. Geog. Mag., Washington, 1967, photographer, 1967-69; picture editor Detroit Free Press, 1969; writer, photographer Denver Post, 1969-77; freelance writer, photographer, 1977-88; dir. photography Press-Enterprise, Riverside, Calif., 1988-90; instr. photojournalism, dept. journalism U. Mo., Columbia, 1990; instr. Sch. Vis. Communication Ohio U., Athens, 1991-92; working book author Cupp Design, Inc., Atlanta, 1993; graphics editor Ft. Lauderdale (Fla.) Sun-Sentinel, 1993-94; freelance writer & photographer Hilliard, Ohio, 1994—; pres., creative dir. Photos Online, Inc., OH, 1995—. Tchr. jr. and sr. h.s.-adult classes, including Journalist-in-the-schs., pilot program, Aurora, Colo., 1974-76, Nat. Endowment Arts poet-in-residence 5 Colo. schs.; photography aboard Voyager Spacecraft Co-author Search and Rescue Dogs, 1988; contbg. author: Nat. Geog. books; co-author: Cindy, a Hearing Ear Dog, The Animal Shelter, All Wild Creatures Welcome; contbr. article, photographs to popular mags. Bd. dirs. Friends of Children of Vietnam, adoption agy., 1973. Mem. Nat. Press Photographers Assn. (recipient numerous awards, citations, including, named Nat. runner-up Photographer of Year 1965, 72, named Regional Photographer of Year 1974, recipient 2nd Place News Picture Story award 1974, 3rd Place Sports Picture Story award 1974, McWilliams award for picture story 1974, McWilliams award for single picture 1974, 75, 2d Home, Family Picture Story award 1972, co-chmn. nat. conv.), Colo. Press Photographers Assn. (v.p.), Am. Soc. Mag. Photographers. Home: 4508 Swenson St Hilliard OH 43026-3811

CUPP, ROBERT RICHARD, state senator, attorney; b. Bluffton, Ohio, Nov. 9, 1950; s. William Henry and Pearl Margaret (Keifer) C.; m. Lisbeth Ann Cochran, July 29, 1978; children: Matthew R., Ryan W. BA, Ohio Northern U., 1973, JD, 1976. Bar: Ohio. Prosecutor, asst. city law dir. City of Lima, Ohio, 1976-80; county commr. Allen County, Lima, 1981-84; ptnr. Cupp and Smith, Attys., 1983-86; mem. Ohio Senate, 1985-2000; ptnr. Cupp and Jenson, Attys., Lima, 1986-93; commnr. Allen County, Ohio, 2001—. Pres. Bd. County Commrs., Allen County, Ohio, 1981, 82, 84; chmn. Gilmor Commn. Sch. Funding, 1987-88; commerce and labor com. chmn. Ohio Senate 1989-94; com. chmn. Fin. Instns. Ins. and Commerce, 1995-96; majority whip Ohio Senate, 1995-96, pres. pro tem, 1997-2000; vis. prof. applied politics Ohio Northern U., 2001—. Co-author: Ethics and Discipline in Ohio, 1977 Co-chmn. Midwest Fedn. Coll. Reps., 1974; pres. exec. bd. Black Swamp coun. Boy Scouts Am.; chmn. League of Coll. Republican Clubs, 1972-73. Mem. Allen County and Ohio State Bar Assn. Methodist. Office: 2021 Allentown Rd Ste 3 Lima OH 45805-1897

CURFMAN, FLOYD EDWIN, engineering educator, retired; b. Gorin, Mo., Nov. 16, 1929; s. Charles Robert and Cleo Lucille (Sweeney) C.; m. Eleanor Elaine Fehl, Aug. 5, 1950; children: Gary Floyd, Karen Elaine. BSCE, U. Mo., 1958; BA in Math. Edn., Mt. Mary Coll., 1988. Registered profl. engr., Wis., Mo.; cert. tchr., Wis. Forest engr. U.S. Forest Svc., Rolla and Harrisburg, Mo., Ill., 1958-70, engring. dir. Milw., 1970-84, chief tech. engr. Washington, 1984-86; tchr. Wauwatosa (Wis.) High Sch., 1987-89, Our Lady of Rosary, Milw., 1989-96; retired, 1996. Author: (booklet) Forest Roads-R-9, 1973; co-author: (tng. manual) Transportation Roads, 1966. Co-leader Boy Scouts Am., Harrisburg, 1958-62; activities coord. Cmty. Action Com., Brookfield, 1970-76; bike and hiking trails com. City of Brookfield (Wis.), 1982-83; program chair Math Counts, 1982. With U.S. Army, 1952-54. Mem. ASCE (program chair, Letter Nat. award 1970), NSPE (coms. 1970-86), Nat. Coun. Tchrs. Math., Wis. Soc. Profl. Engrs. (pres. Milw. chpt. 1982-83, State Recognition award 1983). Avocations: travel, auto trips, reading. Home: 1755 N 166th St Brookfield WI 53005-5114

CURIEL, CAROLYN, ambassador; b. Hammond, Ind. BA in Radio-TV-Film, Purdue U., 1976. Chief Caribbean Divsn. UPI; editor Late Editions Fgn. Desk N.Y. Times, N.Y.C., Washington Post; writer, prodr. ABC News Nightline, 1992; spl. asst. to pres., sr. presdl. speechwriter White House, Washington; apptd. U.S. amb. to Belize Dept. State, 1997—. Office: 6710 Ohio Ave Hammond IN 46323-1914

CURLER, JEFFREY H. packaging manufacturing executive; Various positions Bemis Co., Inc., Mpls., 1973—, pres., 1995—, COO, 1998-2000, CEO, 2000—. Office: Bemis Co Inc 222 S 9th St Ste 2300 Minneapolis MN 55402-4099

CURLEY, EDWIN MUNSON, philosophy educator; b. Albany, N.Y., May 1, 1937; s. Julius Edwin and Gertrude E.; m. Ruth Helen Snyder, Dec. 12, 1959; children: Julia Anne, Richard Edwin. BA, Lafayette Coll., 1959; PhD, Duke U., 1963. Asst. prof. philosophy San Jose State Coll., 1963-66; research fellow Australian Nat. U., Canberra, 1966-68, fellow, 1968-72, sr. fellow, 1972-77; prof. philosophy Northwestern U., 1977-83, U. Ill.-Chgo., 1983-93, U. Mich., 1993—. Author: Hellenistic Philosophy, 1965, Spinoza's Metaphysics, 1969, Descartes Against the Skeptics, 1978, The Collected Works of Spinoza, vol. 1, 1985, Behind the Geometrical Method, 1988, A Spinoza Reader, 1994, Hobbes' Leviathan, 1994; Am. co-editor Archiv für Geschichte der Philosophie, 1979-95; contbr. articles to profl. jours. Fellow AAAS; mem. Am. Philos. Assn. (v.p. ctr. divsn., 1989-90, pres. 1990-91). Home: 2645 Pin Oak Dr Ann Arbor MI 48103-2370 Office: U Mich Dept Philosophy 2215 Angell Hall Ann Arbor MI 48109

CURRAN, BARBARA ADELL, retired law foundation administrator, lawyer, writer; b. Washington, Oct. 21, 1928; d. John R. and Beda Curran. BA, U. Mass., 1950; LLB, U. Conn., 1953; LLM, Yale U., 1961. Bar: Conn. 1953. Atty. Conn. Gen. Life Ins. Co., 1953-61; mem. rsch. staff Am. Bar Found., Chgo., 1961-93, assoc. exec. dir., 1976-86, rsch. atty., 1986-93, rsch. fellow emeritus, 1993—. Vis. prof. U. Ill. Law Sch., 1965, Sch. Social Svc., U. Chgo., 1966-68, Ariz. State U., 1980; cons. in field. Author of eight books in field; contbr. articles to profl. jours. Mem. Ill. Gov.'s Consumer Credit Adv. Com., 1962-63; consumer credit adv. com. Nat. Conf. Commns. on Uniform State Laws, 1964-70; credit legis. subcom. Mayor Daley's Com. on New Residents, 1966-69; cons. Pres.'s Commn. on Consumer Interests, 1966-70, Ill. Commn. on Gender Bias in the Cts., 1987-92. Mem. ABA, Pi Beta Phi. Office: Am Bar Found 750 N Lake Shore Dr Chicago IL 60611-4403

CURRAN, ED, meteorologist, reporter; Cert. broadcast meterorology, Miss. State U.; grad., Columbia Coll. Weathercaster Sta. WIND, Sta. WGCI-FM; with Sta. WGN Radio, Chgo., 1986—94, Sta. WGN-TV, Chgo., 1996, weathercaster, 1997; weather anchor, reporter NBC 5 Weather Team, 2000—. Office: NBC 454 N Columbus Dr Chicago IL 60611*

CURRAN, JOHN MARK, military career officer; b. West Palm Beach, Fla., Jan. 27, 1952; m. Cindy Templon; children: Jennifer, Jessica, Julia. Grad., Fla. So. Coll.; M in Mil. Arts and Scis.; grad., Command & Gen. Staff Coll., Nat. War Coll. Commd. officer U.S. Army, advanced through grades to brig. gen., 1998, evaluation officer 1st ROTC region, armored cavalry platoon leader, trans sect. leader, officer Ft. Bliss, Tex., hdqrs. co. exec. officer, aeroscout platoon leader, bn. S1 Germany, flight comdr., ops. officer, br. comdr., dept. flight tng., tng. devel. officer dept. combined arms tactics, co. comdr. Ala., G3 air, attack bn. exec. officer Aviation Brigade S3 Ft. Campbell, Ky., dep. aviation brigade comdr. 101st Airborne Divsn.; dept. of the Army programs, priorities & requirements divsn. Office Dep. Chief Staff for Ops. and Plans, Force Devel.; comdr. aviation brigade 2nd Inf. Divsn. U.S. Army, Republic of Korea, dep. chief staff ops. USAREUR Forward, Germany, asst. divsn. comdr. for support 1st Inf. Divsn., asst. dep. chief of staff for tng. west Kans., 1998—. Decorated Bronze Star, Legion of Merit with oak leaf cluster, Meritorious Svc. medal with three oak leaf clusters, Army Commendation medal, two Air medals, Army Achievement medal, Nat. Def. Svc. medal, NATO medal, Kuwait Liberation medal Govts. of Saudi Arabia and Kuwait.

CURRAN, MICHAEL WALTER, research scientist, director; b. St. Louis, Dec. 6, 1935; s. Clarence Maurice and Helen Gertrude (Parsons) Curran; m. Jeanette Lucille Rawizza, Sept. 24, 1955 (div. 1977); children: Kevin Michael, Karen Ann, Kathleen Marie(dec.) , Kimberly Elizabeth; m. Mary Jane Lemanek, Aug. 18, 0981. BS, Washington U., St. Louis, 1964. With Monsanto Co., St. Louis, 1953-65, supervisory positions dept. adminstrv. services, 1956-64, rsch. technician inorganic chems. divsn., 1964-65; sr. ops. rsch. analyst Pet Inc., 1965-68; pres. Decision Scis. Corp., 1968—, dir. Former mem. adv. bd. Entrepreneurial Bus. Ctr., U. Mo., St. Louis; judge Tech. Awards, St. Louis, 2002. Co-author: (book) Handbook of Budgeting, 1981, Handbook of Budgeting, 4th edit., 1999, Effective Project Management Through Applied Cost and Schedule Control, 1996; editor: Professional Practice Guide to Risk, Vols. 1-3, 1998; contbr. articles to profl. jours.; developer theories of bracket budgeting and range estimating. Adviser Jr. Achievement, St. Louis, 1958—59; active United Way, 1958—62. Mem.: Soc. Cost Estimating and Analysis, Project Mgmt. Inst., Assn. Advancement Cost Engring. (chmn. risk mgmt. com. 1991—, mem. editl. adv. com. 1997—, Tech. Excellence award 2000), Ops. Rsch. Soc. Am., Inst. Mgmt. Scis. (chmn. St. Louis chpt. 1971—72), Intertel, Mensa, Alpha Sigma Lambda, Sigma Xi. Office: Decision Scis Corp PO Box 28848 Saint Louis MO 63123-0048

CURRAN, RAYMOND M. paper-based packaging company executive; b. 1948; CEO Smurfit Paribas Bank, until 1991; with Jefferson Smurfit Group plc, from 1981, CFO, 1991-98; with Data Exch. Corp., sr. v.p. ops., until 1996, pres., gen. mgr. U.S. ops. N.Am. divsn., 1996; exec. v.p., dep. chief exec. Smurfit-Stone Container Corp., Chgo., 1998-99, pres., CEO, 1999—. Office: Smurfit-Stone Container Corp 150 N Michigan Ave Chicago IL 60601-7553

CURRAN, THOMAS J. federal judge; b. 1924; B of Naval Scis., Marquette U., 1945, LLB, 1948. Ptnr. Curran, Curran and Hollenback, Mauston, Wis., 1948-83; judge U.S. Dist. Ct. (ea. dist.) Wis., Milw., 1983—, now sr. judge. Mem. Gov's Commn. on Crime and Law Enforcement, State of Wis. With USN, 1943-46. Mem. ABA, Am. Coll. Trial Lawyers. Office: US Dist Ct 250 US Courthouse 517 E Wisconsin Ave Milwaukee WI 53202-4500

CURRIE, BARBARA FLYNN, state legislator; b. LaCrosse, Wis., May 3, 1940; d. Frank T. And Elsie R. (Gobel) Flynn; m. David P. Currie, Dec. 29, 1959; children: Stephen Francis, Margaret Rose. AB cum laude, U. Chgo., 1968, AM, 1973. Asst. study dir. Nat. Opinion Rsch. Ctr., Chgo., 1973-77; part time instr. polit. sci. DePaul U., 1973-74; mem. Ill. Ho. of Reps., 1979—, chmn. House Dem. Study Group, 1980-83, asst. majority leader, 1993, asst. minority leader, 1995, majority leader, 1997. Contbr. article to publ. Mem. adv. bd. Harriet Harris YWCA; v.p. Chgo. LWV, 1965-69; mem. Hyde Park-Kenwood Cmty. Conf., Ind. Voters of Ill. Ind. Precinct Orgn., Hyde Park Coop. Soc., Ams. for Dem. Action. Named Best Legislator Ind. Voters of Ill., 1980, 82, 84, 86, 88, 90, 92, 94, 96, 98, Best Legislator Ill. Credit Union League, Outstanding Legislator Ill. Hosp. Assn., 1987; Legislator of Yr. Ill. Nurses Assn., 1984, Nat. Assn. Social Workers, 1984, Ill. Women's Substance Abuse Coalition, 1984; recipient Leon Despres award, 1991, Ill. Environ. Coun. award, Ill. Women's Polit. Caucus Lottie Holman O'Neill award, Susan B. Anthony award, honor award Nat. Trust Historic Preservation; awards Welfare Rights Coalition of Orgns., Ill. Pub. Action Coun., Chgo. Heart Assn., BEST BETS award Nat. Ctr. Policy Alternatives, 1988, Svc. award Nat. Ctr. for Freedom of Info. Studies, 1989, Beautiful Person award Chgo. Urban League, 1989, Friend of Labor award Ill. AFL-CIO, 1990, Ill. Maternal and Child Health Coalition award, 1990, Ill. Hunger Coalition award, 1991, Cert. of Appreciation SEIU Local 880, 1989, March of Dimes, 1988, Chgo. Tchrs. Union, Ill. Hosp. Assn., Ptnr. Vision award Families' and Children's AIDS Network, Woman of Vision award Womens' Bar Assn. Ill., 1997, Nat. Elected Pub. Offcl. award Nat. Assn. Social Workers, 1997, Outstanding Working Woman of Ill. award Ill. Fedn. Bus. and Profl. Women, Dist. Pub. Health Legislator award Am. Pub. Health Assn., 1999. Mem. ACLU (bd. dirs. Ill.), Ill. Conf. Women Legislators, Nat. Order Women Legislators. Office: Ill Gen Assembly 300 State House Springfield IL 62706-0001

CURRIE, DAVID PARK, lawyer, educator; b. Macon, Ga., May 29, 1936; s. Gillette Brainerd and Elmyr (Park) C.; m. Barbara Suzanne Flynn, Dec. 29, 1959; children: Stephen Francis, Margaret Rose. BA, U. Chgo., 1957; LLB, Harvard U., 1960. Bar: Ill. 1963. Law clk. to Hon. Henry J. Friendly U.S. Ct. Appeals (2d cir.), N.Y.C., 1960-61; to Hon. Felix Frankfurter U.S. Supreme Ct., Washington, 1961-62; asst. prof. law U. Chgo., 1962-65, assoc. prof., 1965-68, prof., 1968—, now Edward H. Levi Disting. Svc. prof., 1991—. Vis. prof. Stanford (Calif.) U. Law Sch., 1965, U. Mich. Law Sch., Ann Arbor, 1964, 68, U. Hanover, Germany, 1981, U. Frankfurt, Germany, 1986, U. Heidelberg, Germany, 1989, U. Tubingen, Germany, 1996, U. Aix-Marseille, France, 1998; coord. environ. quality State of Ill., Chgo., 1970; chmn. Ill. Pollution Control Bd., Chgo., 1970-72. Author: Cases and Materials on Federal Courts, 1968, 4th edit., 1990, On Pollution, 1975, On Conflict of Laws, 1968, 6th edit., 2001, Federa Jurisdiction in a Nutshell, 1976, 81, 90, 99, Air Pollution: Federal Law and Analysis, 1981, Constitution in the Supreme Court, (2 vols.), 1985, 1990, Constitution of the Federal Republic of Germany, 1994, Constitution in Congress, 2 vols., 1997, 2001. Mem. Am. Acad. Arts and Scis. E-mail: david. Office: U Chgo Law Sch 1111 E 60th St Chicago IL 60637-2776 E-mail: currie@law.uchicago.edu.

CURRIE, EARL JAMES, transportation company executive; b. Fergus Falls, Minn., May 14, 1939; s. Victor James and Calma (Hammer) C.; m. Kathleen P. Phalen, June 3, 1972; children: Jane, Joseph. BA, St. Olaf Coll., 1961; cert. in transp., Yale U., 1963; P.M.D., Harvard U., 1974. With Burlington No. Inc., 1964-85; asst. v.p. St. Paul, 1977-78, Chgo., 1978-80; v.p., gen. mgr. Seattle, 1980-83; sr. v.p. Overland Park, Kans., 1983-85; pres. Camas Prairie R.R., Lewiston, Idaho, 1982-83, Longview Switching Co., Wash., 1982-83, Western Fruit Express Co., 1984-85; exec. v.p. ops. Soo Line R.R. Co. & Rail Units, 1986-89; v.p. engring. CSX Transp. Co., Jacksonville, Fla., 1989-92, v.p., chief transp. officer, 1992-95; v.p. planning, chief safety officer Wis. Ctrl. Ltd., 1996-99; sr. v.p. ops. Rail World, Inc., 1999—2001; mng. dir. Estonian Rlwy. Sys., Tallinn, Estonia, 2001—. Bd. dirs. Belt Ry. Co. Chgo., Terminal R.R. Assn. St. Louis, Norfolk and Portsmouth Ry. Co. Bd. dirs. United Way, King County, Wash., 1980-83, Corp. Council for Arts, Seattle, 1980-83, Jr. Achievement, 1980-82, Lake Superior Mus. Transp., 1986-89, 1999—, pres., 2001-, North Shore Scenic Railroad, 1999—, James J. Hill Reference Libr.; trustee St. Martins Coll., Lacey, Wash., 1982-83; mem. Mpls. Neighborhood Employment Network. Mem. Am. Rlwy. Engring. Assn. (bd. dirs. 1989-92), Am. Rlwy. Engring. and Maintenance Assn., Am. Assn. R.R. Supts. (bd. dirs. 1979-80), Seattle C. of C. (bd. dirs. 1980-83), St. Olaf Coll. Alumni Assn. (bd. dirs. 1993-97), Internat. Assn. of Railroad Operating Officers, Roadmasters Assn. Home: PO Box 2827 Warba MN 55793-2827 Office: Estonian Rlwy Sys 36 Pikk St Tallinn 60631Estonia

CURRIE, WILLIAM G. forest products executive; b. Youngsville, N.Y., 1947; Degree, Hope Coll., 1969. Vice chmn., CEO Universal Forest Products Inc., Grand Rapids, Mich. Office: Universal Forest Products Inc 2801 E Beltline NE Grand Rapids MI 49525

CURRIVAN, JOHN DANIEL, lawyer; b. Paris; s. Gene and Rachel Currivan; m. Patrice Salley; children: Christopher, Melissa. BS with distinction, Cornell U.; MS , U Calif.-Berkeley; MS, U. West Fla.; JD summa cum laude, Cornell Law Sch., 1978. Bar: Ohio 1978. Mng. ptnr. S.W. Devel. Co., Kingsville, Tex., 1971-76; note editor Cornell Law Rev., Ithaca, N.Y., 1977-78; prosecutor Naval Legal Office, Norfolk, Va., 1978-79, chief prosecutor, 1979-81; sr. atty. USS Nimitz, 1981-83; trial judge Naval Base, Norfolk, 1983-84; tax atty. Jones, Day, Reavis & Pogue, Cleve., 1984-88, ptnr., 1989—. Adj. prof. law Case Western Res. U. Sch. Law, 1997—. Author: (with Rickert) Ohio Limited Liability Companies, 1999. Comdr. USN, 1969-84. Recipient Younger Fed. Lawyer award FBA, 1981. Mem. ABA, Nat. Assn. Bond Lawyers, Order of Coif, Tau Beta Pi, Eta Kappa Nu, Phi Kappa Phi. Home: 12700 Lake Ave Ste 2105 Lakewood OH 44107-1506 Office: Jones Day Reavis & Pogue 901 Lakeside Ave E Cleveland OH 44114-1190

CURRY, JULIE A. state legislator; Ill. state rep. Dist. 101, 1995—. Office: 101-A Ashland Ave Mount Zion IL 62549-1272

CURTIN, MICHAEL FRANCIS, printing company executive, publisher; b. Columbus, Ohio, Oct. 23, 1951; s. Robert Edward and Marie (Cummins) C.; m. Sharon Rhodes, May 26, 1976; children: Matthew, Christy. BA in Journalism, Ohio State U., 1973. Reporter The Columbus (Ohio) Dispatch, 1973-85, pub. affairs editor, 1985-94, exec. mng. editor, 1994-95, editor, 1995-99, assoc. pub., 1998—; pres. The Dispatch Printing Co., 1999—. Bd. dirs. The Columbus Dispatch, Ohio Mag. Author: (book) The Ohio Politics Almanac, 1996. Bd. dirs. YMCA, Columbus, 1996-97, Prevent Blindness/Ohio, Columbus, 1997. Mem. Soc. Profl. Journalists, Athletic Club. Roman Catholic. Office: The Columbus Dispatch 34 S 3rd St Columbus OH 43215-4241

CURTIN, TIMOTHY JOHN, lawyer; b. Detroit, Sept. 21, 1942; s. James J. and Irma Alice (Sirotti) C.; m. B. Colleen Lindsey, July 11, 1964; children: Kathleen, Mary. BA, U. Mich., 1964, JD, 1967. Bar: Ohio 1968, Mich. 1970, U.S. Dist. Ct. (no. dist.) Ohio 1968, U.S. Dist. Ct. (we. dist.) Mich. 1970, U.S. Dist. Ct. (ea. dist.) Mich. 1980, U.S. Dist. Ct. Del. 1996, U.S. Dist. Ct. (no. dist.) Ill. 1999, U.S. Ct. Appeals (6th cir.) 1968. Assoc. Taft, Stettinius & Hollister, Cin., 1967-70, McCobb, Heaney & Van't Hof, Grand Rapids, Mich., 1970-72; ptnr. Schmidt, Howlett, Van't Hof, Snell & Vana, 1972-83, Varnum, Riddering, Schmidt & Howlett, Grand Rapids, 1983—. Contbr. articles to legal publs. Treas. Kent County Dem. Com., 1976-78, chmn. 3rd Dist. Dem. Com., 1993—. Mem. ABA, Mich. Bar Assn., Grand Rapids Bar Assn., Fed.. Bar Assn., Am. Bankruptcy Inst., Egypt Valley C.C. Roman Catholic. Avocations: travel, fishing. Office: Varnum Riddering Schmidt & Howlett 333 Bridge St SW Grand Rapids MI 49501-0352 E-mail: tjcurtin@varnumlaw.com.

CURTIS, CANDACE A. former state legislator; m. Michael Curtis; 1 child, Jameson. BA, Mich. State U., 1982. Environ. health Genesee County Health Dept. Mich.; dep. ct. clk. 67th Dist. Ct., Mich.; chair Genesee County Commrs.; rep. Mich. Dist. 51, 1993-98. Mem. Genesee County Dem. Com. Mem. Farm Bur., South End Dem. Club.

CURTIS, CHARLES EDWARD, Canadian government official; b. Winnipeg, Man., Can., July 28, 1931; s. Samuel and May (Goodison) C.; m. Hilda Marion Simpson, Oct. 30, 1954; 1 dau., Nancy Maude. C.A., U. Manitoba, 1955. Chartered acct. Dunwoody & Co., Winnipeg, 1949-54; chief assessor nat. revenue, income tax bd. Province of N.B., Can., 1954-67; asst. dep. min. budget fin. and adminstrn. Province of Man., Winnipeg, 1967-75, dep. min., 1976-96. Past CEO Man. Energy Authority; acting CEO MTX subs. Man. Telephone Sys.; mem. Man. Hydro-Electric Bd.; bd.mem. Man. Commodity Exch.; mem. investment coms. Superannuation Bd., WPG Found., Manitoba Mus. Man & Nature, Law Soc. Manitoba; fin. advisor Min. of Fin.; exec.-in-residence faculty of mgmt. U. Man.; dir. Indsl. Bank of Japan (Can.); bd. dirs. WPG Commodity Exch. Fellow Can. Inst. Chartered Accts. (past chmn. pub. sector acctg. and audit standards com.); mem. Man. Inst. Chartered Accts. (pres. 1975-76), Law Soc. of Man. (lay bencher), Rotary (hon. treas. 1974-2000), Man. Club. Home: 596 South Dr Winnipeg MB Canada R3T 0B1 Office: Provincial Govt Province MN 109-450 Broadway Ave Winnipeg MB Canada R3C 0V8

CURTIS, DOUGLAS HOMER, small business owner; b. Jackson, Mich., July 19, 1934; s. Homer K. and Luella D. (Hall) C.; m. Jean A. Breaux; children: Rebecca, Linda, Colleen, Robert. BA, Park Coll., Parkville, Mo., 1956. With Gen. Electric Co., 1958-69, mgr. Boston region Gen. Electric Supply Co. div., 1967-69; v.p. fin. and adminstrn. internat. Data Corp., Boston, 1969; v.p. fin. Franklin Electric Co. Inc., Bluffton, Ind., 1969-80; pres. Curtis Assocs., Inc., 1980-82; pres., COO Satelco, Inc., San Antonio, 1983-84; v.p. adminstrn. Lyall Electric Co., Kendallville, Ind., 1984-86; pres., owner Flexible Personnel Group of Cos., Inc., Ft. Wayne, 1987-97, Nat. On-Site Pers., 1991-2001, HR America, 1992—, On-Site Med. Staffing, 2000—. Bd. dirs. Wabash Valley Mfg., Inc., Silver Lake, Ind.; pres. Wells County (Ind.) Hosp. Authority, 1974-75 Served to capt. USMCR, 1956-58. Mem. Nat. Assn. Securities Dealers (vicechmn. fin. 1980, chmn. fin. com. 1980), Fin. Execs. Inst. (chpt. dir. 1975) Home: 3206 Covington Lake Dr Fort Wayne IN 46804-2516 Office: 1833 Magnavox Way Fort Wayne IN 46804-1539

CURTISS, ROY, III, biology educator; b. May 27, 1934; m. Josephine Clark, Dec. 28, 1976; children: Brian, Wayne, Roy IV, Lynn, Gregory Clark, Eric Garth, Megan Kimberly. B.S. in Agr., Cornell U., 1956; Ph.D. in Microbiology, U. Chgo., 1962. Instr., research asst. Cornell U., 1955-56; jr. tech. specialist Brookhaven Nat. Lab., 1956-58; fellow microbiology U. Chgo., 1958-60, USPHS fellow, 1960-62; biologist Oak Ridge Nat. Lab., 1963-72; lectr. microbiology U. Tenn., 1965-72, lectr. Grad. Sch. Biomed. Scis., 1967-69; prof. U. Tenn. (Grad. Sch. Biomed. Scis.), 1969-72, assoc. dir., 1970-71, interim dir., 1971-72; Charles H. McCauley prof. microbiology U. Ala., Birmingham, 1972-83; sr. scientist Inst. Dental Rsch., 1972-83, Comprehensive Cancer Ctr., 1972-83; dir. molecular cell biology grad. program, 1973-82; dir., sr. scientist Cystic Fibrosis Rsch. Ctr., 1981-83; prof. cellular and molecular biology Sch. Dental Medicine Washington U., St. Louis, 1983-91; George William and Irene Koechig Freiberg prof. biology Wash. U., 1984—, chmn. dept. biology, 1983-93, dir. Ctr. Plant Sci. and Biotech., 1991-94. Mem. Ctr. for Infectious Disease, Wash. U., St. Louis; vis. prof. Instituto Venezolana de Investigaciones Cientificas, 1969, U. P.R., 1972, U. Católica de Chile, 1973, U. Okla., 1982; Mem. NIH Recombinant DNA Molecule Program Adv. Com., 1974-77, NSF Genetic Biology Com., 1975-78; mem. NIH Genetic Basis of Disease Rev. Com., 1979-83, chmn., 1981-83. Editor: Jour. Bacteriology, 1970-76, Infection and Immunity, 1985-92, Escherichia coli and Salmonella: Cellular and Molecular Biology, 1993-96, exec. editor, 2000—. Mem. Oak Ridge City Coun., 1969-72, Cystic Fibrosis Found. (rsch. devel. program rev. com. 1984-89), Conf. Rsch. Workers on Animal Diseases, Heiser Found. Scientific Adv. Bd., 1996—; bd. dirs. Am. Type Culture Collection, 1989-99, Whitfield Sch., 1997—; founder, dir. and sci. adv. MEGAN Health, Inc., 1992-2000, v.p. rsch., 1998-99; mem. Mo. Seed Capital Investment Bd., 2000—. Named Mo. Inventor of Yr., 1997. Fellow: AAAS, Acad. Sci. St. Louis, Am. Acad. Microbiology; mem.: NAS, Internat. Soc. Vaccines, World Health Orgn. (steering com. immunology of TB 1982—85), Coun. Advancement Sci. Writing (dir. 1976—82, v.p. 1978—82), N.Y. Acad. Scis., Am. Soc. Microbiology (parliamentarian 1970—75, dir. 1977—80, 1989—94, 1999—, editl. bd. ASM News 1987—99), Soc. Gen. Microbiology, Internat. Soc. Mucosal Immunology, Am. Assn. Avian Pathologists, Genetics Soc. Am. (chmn. genetics stock ctrs. com. 1987—89), Gateway Strikers Soccer Club (founder, pres. 1995—2001), Sigma Xi. Home: 6065 Lindell Blvd Saint Louis MO 63112-1009 Office: Washington U Dept Biology Saint Louis MO 63130

CURTRIGHT, ROBERT EUGENE, newspaper critic and columnist; b. Kansas City, Mo., Aug. 27, 1944; s. Leslie Odean and Wilma Jean (Kraus) C. BA in Journalism, U. Kans., 1966, MA in Journalism, 1968. Reporter Coffeyville (Kans.) Jour., 1969-74, Wichita (Kans.) Eagle-Beacon (name changed to The Wichita Eagle 1990), 1974-76, spl. bicentennial editor, 1976, movie critic, 1976—, TV columnist, 1981—. Mem. TV Critics Assn. (sec. 1993-95, newsletter editor 1993-2000, v.p. 1995-97, pres. 1997-99, pres.'s coun. 1999—). Office: Wichita Eagle 825 E Douglas Ave Wichita KS 67202-3594

CURWEN, RANDALL WILLIAM, journalist, editor; b. Hazel Green, Wis., Apr. 18, 1946; s. Charles William and Theda (Hillary) C. BS, U. Wis., 1968. Reporter Rockford (Ill.) Morning Star, 1968-69, copy editor/asst. city editor, 1969-72; copy editor Chgo. Today, 1972-74; copy editor/asst. sect. editor Chgo. Tribune, 1974-80, assoc. features editor, 1980-91, co-editor evening edit., 1992, travel editor, 1992—. Recipient 1st place headline writing award Ill. UPI, 1977, Johnrae Earl award Chgo. Tribune, 1979, 96, Soc. Am. Travel Writers Ctrl. States award for best travel sect., 1994, 99, 2000, Lowell Thomas award for best travel sect., 1995, 97. Mem. Soc. Am. Travel Writers, Nat. Lesbian and Gay Journalists Assn. Avocations: travel, baseball, video. Home: 930 W Roscoe Rear Coachhouse Chicago IL 60657 Office: Chgo Tribune Co 435 N Michigan Ave PO Box 25340 Chicago IL 60625-0340

CUSACK, JOHN THOMAS, lawyer; b. Oak Park, Ill., June 22, 1935; s. Thomas Jr. and Clare (Hock) C.; m. Mary Louise Coughlin, Nov. 1, 1969; children: John, James, Mary Helen, Cathleen. AB cum laude, U. Notre Dame, 1957; JD, U. Mich., 1960; postgrad., Harvard U., 1961-62. Bar: Ill. 1960, U.S. Dist. Ct. (no. dist.) Ill. 1961, U.S. Dist. Ct. (no. dist.) Ind. 1983, U.S. Tax Ct. 1984, U.S. Ct. Appeals (7th cir.) 1973, U.S. Ct. Appeals (5th and 9th cirs.) 1975, U.S. Ct. Appeals (3d cir.) 1986, U.S. Ct. Appeals (10th cir.) 1987, U.S. Ct. Appeals (11th cir.) 1988, U.S. Supreme Ct. 1966. Trial atty. antitrust div. U.S. Dept. Justice, 1962-70; assoc. Gardner, Carton & Douglas, Chgo., 1970-74, ptnr., 1974—, chmn. litigation dept., 1978-86, chmn. antitrust practice group, 1986—. Contbr. articles to legal jours. Trustee Fenwick H.S. 1st lt. JAGC, USAR, 1963-67. Mem. ABA (antitrust and litigation sect., health law com. 1960—), Chgo. Bar Assn., Law Club City Chgo. Roman Catholic. Home: 1030 Franklin Ave River Forest IL 60305-1340 Office: Gardner Carton & Douglas 321 N Clark St Ste 3400 Chicago IL 60610-4795 E-mail: jcusack@gcd.com.

CUSANO, CRISTINO, mechanical engineer, educator; b. Sepino, Italy, Mar. 22, 1941; s. Crescenzo and Carmela (D'Anello) C.; m. Isabella Pera, Aug. 7, 1974 B.S., Rochester Inst. Tech., 1965; M.S., Cornell U., 1967, Ph.D., 1970. Asst. prof. mech. engring. U. Ill., Urbana, Ill., 1970—74, assoc. prof., 1974—83, prof., 1983—99, prof. emeritus, 1999—. Cons. Carrier Corp., Copeland Corp., Whirlpool Corp. Contbr. articles to profl. jours. NSF fellow, 1965-69, ASME fellow; recipient Capt. Alfred E. Hunt award, Al Sonntag award, Xerox award Mem. Soc. Tribologists and Lubrication Engrs., Am. Soc. Engring. Edn., Sigma Xi, Phi Kappa Phi, Pi Tau Sigma. Roman Catholic Home: 110 E Stoughton St Champaign IL 61820-4103 Office: Univ Ill Dept Mech Engring 1206 W Green St Urbana IL 61801-2906

CUSMANO, J. JOYCE, public relations executive; b. Mich. BA, Eastern Mich. U.; MA, U. Md., 1972. Asst. dir. Detroit Youtheatre Detroit Inst. Arts; spl. events dir. Detroit Renaissance; v.p. Franco Pub. Rels. Group, Detroit, 1985-90, sr. v.p., 1991—, dir., consumer group. Mem. Women's Econ. Club. Office: Franco Pub Rels Group 400 Renaissance Ctr Ste 1050 Detroit MI 48243-1605

CUSTER, CHARLES FRANCIS, lawyer; b. Hays, Kans., Aug. 19, 1928; s. Raymond Earl and Eva Marie (Walker) C.; m. Irene Louise Macarow, Jan. 2, 1950; children: Shannon Elaine, Charles Francis, Murray Maxwell, Kelly Sue. AB, U. Chgo., 1948, JD, 1958. Bar: Ill. 1958, U.S. Dist. Ct. (no dist.) Ill. 1971, U.S. Supreme Ct. 1991. Assoc. Meyers & Matthias, Chgo., 1958-72; pvt. practice, 1972-78; ptnr. Vedder, Price, Kaufman & Kammholz, 1978-98, of counsel, 1998—. Arbitrator, mediator. Bd. dirs. Family Care Svcs., Chgo., 1959-81 Mem. ABA (mem. fed. regulation of securities and devels. in investment svcs. coms., dispute resolution sect.), Chgo. Bar Assn. (mem. securities law com., mem. investment cos. subcom., alternative dispute resolution com.), Cliff Dwellers (past officer and dir.). Avocations: music, theater . Home: 5210 S Kenwood Ave Chicago IL 60615-4006 Office: Vedder Price Kaufman & Kammholz 222 N La Salle St Ste 2600 Chicago IL 60601-1100

CUTCHINS, CLIFFORD ARMSTRONG, IV, lawyer; b. Norfolk, Va., May 13, 1948; s. Clifford Armstrong III and Ann (Woods) C.; m. Jane McKenzie, Aug. 14, 1971; children: Sarah Helen, Ann Woods. BA, Princeton U., 1971; JD, MBA, U. Va., 1975. Bar: Va. 1975, U.S. Dist. Ct. (ea. dist.) Va. 1975, U.S. Ct. Appeals (4th cir.) 1975. Ptnr. McGuire, Woods, Battle & Boothe, Richmond, Va., 1975-90; sr. v.p., gen. counsel, sec. James River Corp. Va., 1990-97, Ft. James Corp., Deerfield, Ill., 1997-2000; ptnr. McGuireWoods LLP, Richmond, 2001—. Bd. dirs. Arts Coun. Richmond, 1980-86, Richmond Heart Assn., 1980-83, St. Catherine's Sch., Richmond, 1983-86, Richmond Ballet, 1986-88, Richmond Children's Mus., 1986-94, Richmond on the James, 1986-88, Henrico Drs. Hosp., 1986—, Hist. Richmond Found., 1990-94, Richmond Met. Blood Svc., 1995-97, Kohl Children's Mus., Wilmette, Ill., 1998-2000; chmn. Fort James Found., 1997-2000, Richmond First Tee, 2001-, Nature Conservancy of Va., 2002-. Mem. ABA, Va. Bar Assn., Country Club Va. (bd. dirs. 1990-93), Commonwealth Club (bd. dirs. 1983-86, 96-97), Kinloch Golf Clubs. Republican. Baptist. Avocations: golf, travel, photography. Home: 118 Tempsford Ln Richmond VA 23226-2319 Office: McGuireWoods LLP 901 E Cary St Richmond VA 23219 E-mail: ccutchins@mcguirewoods.com.

CUTLER, ALEXANDER MACDONALD, manufacturing company executive; b. Milw., May 28, 1951; s. Richard Woolsey and Elizabeth (Fitzgerald) C.; m. Sarah Lynn Stark, Oct. 11, 1980; children: David Alexander, William MacDonald. BA, Yale U., 1973; MBA, Dartmouth Coll., 1975. Fin. analyst Cutler-Hammer, Milw., 1975-77, bus. group contr., 1977-79; contr. custom distbn. and control divsn. Eaton Corp., Atlanta, 1979-80, plant mgr. custom distbn. and control divsn., 1981-82, mgr. custom distbn. and control divsn., 1982-83, mgr. power distbn. divsn. Milw., 1984-85, gen. mgr. indsl. control and power distbn., 1985-86, pres. controls group Cleve., 1986-91, exec. v.p. ops., 1992-93, exec. v.p., COO controls, 1993-95, pres., COO, 1995-2000, chmn., CEO, 2000—, also bd. dirs. Bd. dirs. Axcelis Techs. Bd. dirs. United Way Svcs. Cleve., N.E. Ohio Coun. on Higher Edn., 1993-97, Mus. Arts Assn., 2000—; class agt. alumni fund Loomis Chaffee Sch., Windsor, Conn., 1969—; bd. dirs. alumni fund Yale U., New Haven, 1974-89; trustee The Cleve. Play House, 1987-94, 95—, Gt. Lakes Mus., Inc., 1988-91, Mus. Natural History, Cleve., 1989-97; mem. bd. overseers Amos Tuck Sch. Bus. Dartmouth Coll., 1996—; mem. Keycorp., 2000—. Mem. Nat. Elec. Mfrs. Assn. (bd. govs. 1987-99, indsl. automation divsn. 1986-90, treas. 1993-95, bd. govs. 1996-99), Elec. Mfrs. Club (bd. dirs.), Yale U. Alumni Assn. (pres. Cleve. chpt. 1991-93, exec. com. of vis. com. Weatherhood Sch. Mgmt. 1993—, Yale devel. bd. 1998—), Chagrin Valley Hunt Club. Avocation: tennis. Office: Eaton Corp 1111 Superior Ave Eaton Ctr Cleveland OH 44114-2584

CUTLER, RICHARD WOOLSEY, lawyer; b. New Rochelle, N.Y., Mar. 9, 1917; s. Charles Evelyn and Amelia (MacDonald) C.; m. Elizabeth Fitzgerald, Oct. 18, 1947; children: Marguerite Blackburn, Alexander MacDonald, Judith Elizabeth. BA, Yale U., 1938, LLB, 1941. Bar: Conn. 1941, N.Y. 1942, Wis. 1950, D.C. 1975, U.S. Supreme Ct. 1980. Practiced in, NYC, 1941—49, Milw., 1949—87; assoc. Donovan, Leisure, Newton & Lumbard, 1941—42; atty. Legal Aid Soc., 1946—47, RCA Comm., Inc., 1947—49; ptnr. Quarles & Brady, and predecessors, 1954—87; gen. ptnr. Sunset Investment Co., Milw. Author: Zoning Law and Practice in Wisconsin, 1967, Greater Milwaukee's Growing Pains, 1950-2000: An Insider's View, 2001. Chmn. Milw. br. Fgn. Policy Assn., 1951-53; pres. Childrens Service Soc. Wis., 1961-63, Neighborhood House, 1971-74; sec. Southeastern Wis. Regional Planning Commn., 1960-84, Yale Devel. Bd., 1973-79; bd. dirs. Wis. Dept. Resource Devel., 1967-68; Met. Milw. Study Commn., 1957-61; bd. dirs. Milw. Innovation Ctr., 1985-89, pres., 1984-85, exec. v.p., 1985-89; bd. dirs. Greater Milw. Com., 1982-89. Capt. USAAF, 1943-46 and OSS, 1944-46. Recipient Disting. Leadership award Am. Planning Assn., 1992. Mem. ABA, Wis. Bar Assn., Milw. Club, Milw. Country Club, Town Club, Phi Beta Kappa. Republican. Presbyterian. Home: 938 W Shaker Cir Mequon WI 53092-6032 Office: 411 E Wisconsin Ave Milwaukee WI 53202-4461 E-mail: rwc@quarles.com.

CUTLER, STEVE KEITH, state legislator; b. Britton, S.D., June 2, 1948; s. Keith and Kathryn (Olson) C.; m. Penny Louise Jones, 1969; children: Jennifer, Shanda. BS, S.D. State U., 1970, MS, 1971. Asst. material engr. S.D. Dept. Transp., 1971-74; rep. S.D. State Ho. of Reps. Dist. 2, 1984—, vice chmn. Taxation Com., mem. legis. procedure, state affairs and taxation coms. Named Outstanding Freshman Civil Engr., ASCE, 1967, Outstanding Sr. Civil Engr., ASCE, 1972. Mem. Am. Legion (legis. officer 1985), Claremont Cmty. Club, Claremont Sportsman Club, Sigma Tau, Chi Epsilon. Office: 12057 411th Ave Claremont SD 57432-7302

CUTSHALL-HAYES, DIANE MARION, elementary education educator; b. Pitts., Jan. 15, 1954; d. William Edward and Irma Delores (Marion) Snowden; m. John Steven Baran, Jan. 11, 1975 (div. 1982); 1 child, Allison Rae; m. Dean F. Cutshall, Dec. 17, 1989. BA, Eureka Coll., 1975; BS, Ind. U., Ft. Wayne, 1986. First grade tchr. Hoover Elem. Sch., Schaumburg, Ill., 1976-79, Indian Meadows Elem. Sch., Ft. Wayne, Ind., 1979-80, 82-86, Perry Hill Elem. Sch., Ft. Wayne, 1981-82; second grade tchr. Indian Meadows Elem. Sch., 1986—. Tchr. rep. State Ill. Rsch. Adv. Coun., 1991; active ISTEP Blue Ribbon Commn., Ill., 1989, State Ill. Lang. Arts Adv. Commn., 1988, Project REAP Adv. Bd., 1988. Spl. events chair Greater Ft. Wayne (Ind.) Crime Stoppers, 1992-95; active YMCA Camp Potawotami, Ft. Wayne, 1993—, Eureka Coll. Alumni Assn., 1992—, pres., 1995—. Christa McAuliffe fellow State of Ind., 1987; recipient Excellence in Edn. award Inst. Copy Corp., 1988, Outstanding Young Alumna award Eureka Coll., 1990, Armstrong Tchr. Educator award, 1998; named Ind. State Elem. Tchr. of Yr., 1993. Mem. Nat. Coun. Tchrs. Math., Internat. Reading Assn., Tchrs. Applying Whole Langs. Lutheran. Avocations: inline skating, racquetball, reading, walking. Home: 5809 Eagle Creek Dr Fort Wayne IN 46814-3207 Office: Indian Meadows Elem Sch 4810 Homestead Rd Fort Wayne IN 46814-5461

CUTTS, CHARLES EUGENE, civil engineering educator; b. Sioux Falls, S.D., May 15, 1914; s. Charles Clifford and Ethel May (Gardner) C.; m. Jane Bebensee, Mar. 16, 1946; children: George Gardner, Elizabeth Anne. B.C.E., U. Minn., 1936, M.S. in Civil Engring, 1939, Ph.D., 1949. Registered profl. engr., Minn., Fla., Mich. Instrumentman Milw. R.R., 1936- 38; teaching asst. dept. civil engring. U. Minn., 1938-39, instr., asst. prof., 1946-50; engr. C.F. Haglin & Sons, summer 1939; asst. prof. dept. civil engring. Robert Coll., Istanbul, Turkey, 1939-42; engr. Braithwaite Co., Ltd., Iskenderun, Turkey, summer 1942, 43; assoc. prof., assoc. rsch. engr. U. Fla., 1950-53; engr. Engring. Scis. Program NSF, Washington, 1953-56; profl. lectr. civil engring. George Washington U., 1955-56; prof., chmn. dept. civil engring. Mich. State U., 1956-69, prof., 1969-84, prof. emeritus, 1984—. Cons. U. Minn. Morocco Project, 1986. Author: Structural Design in Reinforced Concrete, 1954, other tech. publs. Served to maj. C.E. AUS, 1943-46; lt. col. Res. ret. Mem. Nat. Acad. Scis. (fellowship com. 1961-63), ASCE (chmn. com. on mech. properties of materials 1965, pres. Mich. sect. 1967, chmn. com. on engring. edn. 1969-70), Am. Concrete Inst., Am. Soc. Engring. Edn. (chmn. civil engr. div. 1965-66, v.p. 1970—, chmn. constn. and bylaws com. 1981-83), Engrs. Coun. Profl. Devel. (chmn. region 5 1972-73), Nat. Soc. Profl. Engrs., Column Rsch. Coun., Tau Beta Pi, Chi Epsilon. Home: 4599 Ottawa Dr Okemos MI 48864-2028 Office: Civil Engring Mich State Univ East Lansing MI 48824

CVETANOVICH, DANNY L. lawyer; b. Wheeling, W.Va., Oct. 2, 1952; s. Louis J. and Nila J. (Hall) C.; m. Sharon M. Smith, Sept. 8, 1979; children; Gregory L., Steven W. BA, West Liberty State Coll., 1974; JD, Harvard U., 1977. Bar: Ohio 1977, U.S. Dist. Ct. (so. dist.) Ohio 1978, U.S. Ct. Appeals (6th cir.) 1980, U.S. Dist. Ct. (no. dist.) Ohio 1984, W.Va. 1985, U.S. Dist. Ct. (so. dist.) W.Va. 1985, U.S. Ct. Appeals (4th cir.) 1986, U.S. Dist. Ct. (we. dist.) Tex. 1998, U.S. Dist. Ct. (no. dist.) W.Va. 2001. Assoc. Bricker & Eckler, Columbus, Ohio, 1977-82, ptnr., 1983-87, Arter & Hadden LLP, Columbus, 1987—. Mem.: ABA, Columbus Bar Assn., W.Va. State Bar, Ohio State Bar Assn. Republican. Avocations: hunting, fishing, golf. Office: Arter & Hadden LLP One Columbus 10 W Broad St Columbus OH 43215-3422

CYGAN, THOMAS S. metal products executive; Sales trainee Joseph T. Ryerson & Son subs. Inland Steel Industries Inc., inside sales mgr., 1976-81, gen. mgr. Kansas City, 1981-95; pres., COO Ryerson W. subs. Inland Steel Industries Inc., 1995—. Office: Ryerson Tull Inc 2621 W 15th Pl Chicago IL 60608-1752

CYR, ARTHUR I. political science educator, economics educator; b. L.A., Mar. 1, 1945; s. Irving Arthur and Frances Mary Cyr; m. Betty Totten (div.); children: David Arthur, Thomas Harold, James Price. BA, UCLA, 1966, MA, 1967; AM, Harvard U., 1969, PhD, 1971. Teaching fellow Harvard U., 1970-71; program officer internat. and edn.-rsch. divs. Ford Found., 1971-74; asst. prof. polit. sci., adminstr. UCLA, 1974-76; program dir. Chgo. Coun. Fgn. Rels., 1976-81, v.p., 1981-96; pres., CEO, World Trade Ctr. Assn., Chgo., 1996-98; Clausen disting. prof. polit. econ. and world bus. Carthage Coll., Kenosha, Wis., 1998—; dir. Clausen Ctr. World Bus., 2000—. Author: Liberal Politics in Britain, 1977, rev. edit., 1988, British Foreign Policy and the Atlantic Area, 1979, U.S. Foreign Policy and European Security, 1987, After the Cold War—American Foreign Policy, Europe and Asia, 1997, rev. edit., 2000; contbr. articles to profl. jours. Capt. USAR, 1966—73. Mem. Internat. Inst. Strategic Studies, Royal Inst. Internat. Affairs, Am. Econ. Assn., Am. Polit. Sci. Assn., Coun. Fgn. Rels., Century, Econ. Club Chgo., Nat. Liberal Club (London), Cosmos Club (Washington), Phi Beta Kappa. Office: Carthage Coll Chair Polit Econ World Bus Kenosha WI 53140-1994 E-mail: a-cyr@carthage.edu.

CYRUS, MICHAEL J. electric power industry executive; m. Mariet Cyrus; children: Maura, Audrey, Marshall. BA, MBA, U. Ark.; grad., Mahler Sch. Advanced Mgmt. Skills Program. With Conoco, Inc., 1982-88, Kottke Assocs., Chgo., 1988-93; joined Natural Gas Clearinghouse NGC Corp., 1993; pres. NGC Canada; exec. v.p. Novagas Clearinghouse Ltd.; sr. v.p. trading and ops. Electric Clearinghouse, 1997; exec. v.p. Cinergy Capital and Trade, Inc., 1998; pres. Energy Commodities Bus. Unit Cinergy Corp. Bd. mem. PanAlberta Gas Ltd., Novagas Clearinghouse Ltd.; del. advisor NYMEX, Canadian Gas Assn. Office: 139 E 4th St Cincinnati OH 45202-4003

CZARNECKI, WALTER P. truck rental company executive; Exec. v.p. Penske Corp., Detroit, 1978—. Office: Penske Corp 13400 W Outer Dr Detroit MI 48239-1309

DABERKO, DAVID A. banker; b. Hudson, Ohio, 1945; BA, Denison U., 1967; MBA, Case Western Res. U., 1970. Mgmt. trainee Nat. City Bank, Cleve., 1968-72, asst. v.p., 1972-73, v.p. bank investment divsn., dept. head met. lending divsn., 1973-80, sr. v.p. corp. banking, 1980-82, pres., 1987-93; exec. v.p. corp. banking Nat. City Corp., Nat. City Bank, 1982-85; pres., bd. dirs. Nat. City Bank (formerly BancOhio Nat. Bank), Columbus, 1985-87; dep. chmn. Nat. City Corp., Cleve., 1987-93, pres., CEO, 1993-95, chmn., CEO, 1995—. Dir. Fed. Res. Bank, Cleve. Trustee Cleve. Tomorrow, Greater Cleve. Growth Assn., Case Western Res. U., Hawken Sch., Neighborhood Progress, Univ. Cir. Inc., Univ. Hosp. Health Sys.; co-chair Harvest for Hunger Campaign, 1992, 93. Mem. Bankers Roundtable. Office: Nat City Corp National City Center 1900 E 9th St Cleveland OH 44114-3401

DABERKOW, DAVE, historic site director; b. Windom, Minn., Nov. 16, 1945; BS, S.D. State U., 1968. Park mgr. Richmond & Mina Recreation Area, Aberdeen, S.D., 1971-86; dist. park mgr. Ft. Sisseton State Park, Lake City, 1986—. Office: Fort Sisseton State Hist Park 11545 Northside Dr Lake City SD 57247-6142

DAEHN, GLENN STEVEN, materials scientist; b. Chgo., July 4, 1961; s. Ralph Charles and Beverly S. (Shanske) D.; m. Margaret A. Burkhart, Oct. 25, 1987; children: Andrew Joseph, Katrin Ellen, Matthew Charles. BS, Northwestern U., 1983; MS, Stanford U., 1985, PhD, 1988. Rsch. asst. Stanford U., Palo Alto, Calif., 1983-87; asst. prof. dept. materials sci. and engring. Ohio State U., Columbus, 1987-92, assoc. prof. dept. materials sci. and engring., 1992-96, Fontana prof. dept. materials sci. and engring., 1996—. V.p. BFD, Inc., 1992—. Co-editor: Modeling the Deformation of Crystalline Solids, 1991. Named Nat. Young Investigator, NSF, 1992; recipient Young Investigator award Army Rsch. Office, 1992, R.L. Hardy Gold medal TMS, 1992, Marcus Grossman award ASM Internat., 1990. Mem. ASM Internat., Am. Ceramic Soc., Materials Rsch. Soc., Minerals, Metals and Materials Soc. Achievements include description and practical applications of how temperature changes accelerate the deformation of composite materials; co-development of new class of ceramic-metal composites; development of hyperplasticity --practical application of extended metal ductility observed at high velocity. Home: 2076 Fairfax Rd Upper Arlington OH 43221-4319 Office: Ohio State U Materials Sci Dept 2041 N College Rd Columbus OH 43210-1124 E-mail: Daehn.1@osu.edu.

DAGES, PETER F. manufacturing executive; BA, U. Ill.; MBA, U. Chgo. Supt., Chgo. plant Stone Container Corp., 1980, gen. mgr. Ill., 1985-91, dir. mfg., corrugated container divsn., 1991-96, divsn. v.p., regional mgr., 1996-99, v.p., gen. mgr., corrugated container divsn., 1999—. Office: Smurfit-Stone Container Corp 150 N Michigan Ave Chicago IL 60601-7553

DAGGETT, ROXANN, state legislator; b. Mar. 10, 1947; m. Dave Daggett, Aug. 20, 1967; 2 children. Student, Concordia Coll., 1965-67; BS, U. N.D., 1968. Motivational spkr.; rep. Dist. 11A Minn. Ho. of Reps., 1994—.

DAHL, GERALD LUVERN, psychotherapist, educator, psychotherapist, consultant, psychotherapist, writer; b. Nov. 10, 1938; s. Lloyd F. and Leola J. (Painter) Dahl; m. Judith Lee Brown, June 24, 1960; children: Peter, Stephen, Leah. BA, Wheaton Coll., 1960; MSW, U. Nebr., 1962; PhD in Psychotherapy (hon.) , Internat. U. Found., 1987. Cert. diplomate Am. Psychotherapy Assn., 1998. Juvenile probation officer Hennepin County Ct. Svcs., 1962—65; cons. Citizens Coun. on Delinquency and Crime, Mpls., 1965—67; dir. patient svcs. Mt. Sinai Hosp., 1967—69; clin. social worker Mpls. Clinic of Psychiatry, 1969—82, G.L. Dahl & Assocs., Inc., Mpls., 1983—. Assoc. prof. social work Bethel Coll., St. Paul, 1964—83; spl. instr. sociology Golden Valley Luth. Coll., 1974—83; pres. Strategic Team-Makers, Inc., 1985—; adj. prof. U. Wis., River Falls, 1988—90. Author: Why Christian Marriages Are Breaking Up, 1979, Everybody Needs Somebody Sometime, 1980, How Can We Keep Christian Marriages from Falling Apart, 1988, The Sandwich Generation, 1995; contbr. articles to profl. jours. Founder Family Counseling Svc., Minn. Bapt. Conf., bd. stewards, 1994—; bd. dirs. Edgewater Bapt. Ch., 1972—75, chmn., 1974—75; vice chmn. bd. stewards Minnetonka Bapt. Ch., 1995. Mem.: AAUP, Am. Assn. Behavioral Therapists, Pi Gamma Mu. Office: 4825 Highway 55 Ste 140 Minneapolis MN 55422-5155 E-mail: jerryd@strategicteammakers.com., stmi@strategicteammakers.com.

DAHL, LAWRENCE FREDERICK, chemistry educator; b. Evanston, Ill., June 2, 1929; s. Lawrence Gustave and Anne (Stuessy) D.; m. June Lomnes, Sept. 1, 1956; children: Larry, Eric, Christopher (dec.). BS in Chemistry, U. Louisville, 1951; PhD, Iowa State U., 1956; DSc (hon.), U. Louisville, 1991. Postdoctoral fellow Ames (Iowa State U.) Lab. AEC, 1957; from instr. to assoc. prof. chemistry U. Wis., Madison, 1957-64, prof., 1964—, R. E. Rundlechair, 1978—, Hilldale chair and prof., 1991—. Brotherton rsch. prof. U. Leeds, 1983 Recipient Inorganic Chemistry award Am. Chem. Soc., 1974, Disting. Alumnus award U. Louisville Coll. Letters and Sci., 1990, Sr. U.S. Scientist Humboldt award Alexander von Humboldt Stiftung, 1985, R.S. Nyholm medal Royal Soc. Chemistry, 1985, P. Chini medal Italian Soc. Chemistry, 1989, J.C. Bailar Jr. medal U. Ill., 1990, F. Basolo medal Northwestern U., 1995, Hilldale award in phys. scis. U. Wis., 1994, Willard Gibbs medal, Chgo. sect. Am. Chem. Soc., 1999, Pioneer award, Am. Inst. Chemists, 2000; named to Hon. Order Ky. Cols., 1982; Alfred P. Sloan fellow, 1963-65, U. Louisvlle Coll. Letters and Sci. fellow, 1990. Fellow AAAS, N.Y. Acad. Sci., Am. Acad. Arts and Scis.; mem. NAS. Home: 4817 Woodburn Dr Madison WI 53711-1345 Office: Univ of Wis Madison Dept of Chemistry 1101 University Ave Madison WI 53706-1322 Fax: 608-262-6143. E-mail: dahl@chem.wisc.edu.

DAHL, REYNOLD PAUL, applied economics educator; b. Willmar, Minn., Feb. 19, 1924; s. Paul Efrain and Margaret Elizabeth (Peterson) D.; m. Alyce Rosalind Druskis, Sept. 11, 1948; children— John, Ann Student, North Park Coll., Chgo., 1942-43; B.S., U. Minn., 1949, M.S., 1950, Ph.D., 1954. Instr. agrl. econs. U. Minn., St. Paul, 1950-54, asst. prof., 1954-58, assoc. prof., 1958-63, prof., 1963-94, prof. emeritus Tunisia, 1994—, chief of party, economist Tunis, Tunisia, 1967-70. Agrl. economist Soybean Coun. of Am., Brussels, 1962-63; dir. Mpls. Grain Exchange, 1972-80; agrl. economist U.S. AID, Port-au-Prince, Haiti, 1972, 74 Contbr. articles to profl. jours., chpts. to books. Served with USAAF, 1943-46; PTO Mem. Am. Agrl. Econs. Assn., Am. Inst. Coop. (trustee 1981-84), Xi Sigma Pi, Alpha Zeta Roman Catholic Avocations: gardening; fishing; outdoor activities. Home: 1666 Coffman St Apt 326 Saint Paul MN 55108-1344 Office: U Minn Dept Applied Econs 1994 Buford Ave Saint Paul MN 55108-6038 E-mail: dahlx008@maroon.tc.umn.edu.

DAHLBERG, BURTON FRANCIS, real estate corporation executive; b. Ashland, Wis., Dec. 14, 1932; s. Oscar A. and Estelle (Bratton) D.; m. Gloria Dahlberg, Aug. 23, 1957 (div. Nov. 1982); children: Michael, Andrea, David; m. Sandy Sieverson, Jan. 22, 1985 BA, U. Minn., 1960. Cert. property mgr. Property mgr., leasing Oneida Realty, Duluth, Minn.; real estate analyst Control Data Corp., Bloomington, 1965-68; v.p., real estate mgr. Kraus-Anderson Realty Co., 1968-84, pres., 1984—. Bd. dirs. Am. State Bank, Bloomington, 1985-94. Bd. dirs. Minn. Taxpayers Assn., 1984—. Mem. Minn. C. of C. (bd. dirs. 1994—), Blomington C. of C. (bd. dirs. 1983-80), Nat. Assn. Office and Indsl. Parks (bd. dirs.), Mpls. Bldg. Onwers and Mgrs. Assn. (past pres.), Internat. Council Shopping Ctrs. (bd. dirs.), Inst. Real Estate Mgmt. Club: Decathlon Athletic (Bloomington, bd. dirs. 1983-86). Avocations: racquetball, hunting, cooking, race horses. Office: Kraus-Anderson Inc 523 S 8th St Minneapolis MN 55404-1030

DAHLIN, DONALD C(LIFFORD), academic administrator; b. Ironwood, Mich., June 18, 1941; married; 2 children. BA magna cum laude in history, Carroll Coll., 1963; PhD in Govt. (Univ. Departmental fellow), Claremont Grad. Sch., 1969; fellow in ct. mgmt., Inst. Ct. Mgmt., 1980. Asst. prof. govt. U. S.D., Vermillion, 1966-70, assoc. prof., 1970-75, prof., 1975—, dir. criminal justice studies program, 1972-75, 78-89, chmn. dept. polit. sci., 1978-89, 95-98, fellow Pres.'s office, 1984-85, interim v.p. acad. affairs, 1988-90, acting dean continuing edn., 1995, v.p. acad. affairs, 1997—, acting pres., 2002—. Mgmt. analyst Law Enforcement Assistance Adminstrn., Dept. Justice, Washington, 1970-71; sec. S.D. Dept. Public Safety, Pierre, 1975-78; lectr., cons. in field; mem. S.D. Human Resource Cabinet Sub-Group, 1975-78, chmn., 1977-78; mem. S.D. Planning Commn., 1975-78; adv. bd. Criminal Justice Statis. Analysis Center, 1975-78; chmn. S.D. Criminal Justice Commn., 1976-78; mem. U. So. Calif. Criminal Justice Tng. Center Planning Com., 1977-79, U. S.D. Research Inst. Adv. Panel, 1978-80, Gov.'s Corrections Task Force, 1987; mem. acad. resource council S.D. Planning Agy., 1978-79; chmn. S.D. County Commr.'s Juvenile Justice Com., 1986-89; chmn. S.D. Youth Advocacy Project; mem. Commn. on Advancement of Fed. Law Enforcement, 1997-99. Author: Models of Court Management, 1986; contbr. articles to profl. publs. Recipient Sustained High Performance award Law Enforcement Assistance Adminstrn., 1971, Disting. Safety Svcs. award S.D. Auto Club, 1978, Disting. Faculty award U. S.D., 1980, Friend of Law Enforcement award S.D. Peace Officers, 1983; Haynes Found. rsch. fellow, 1965-66; ASPA fellow, 1970-71; Bush Leadership fellow, summer 1975; Law Enforcement Edn. Program grantee, 1972-75; S.D. Criminal Justice Commn. grantee, 1972-74, 72-75; Criminal Justice Standards and Goals for S.D. grantee, 1974-75; Criminal Justice Data Collection grantee, 1974-75. Mem. ASPA (pres. Siouxland chpt. 1980-81, exec. bd. dirs. and sec./treas. criminal justice adminstrn. sect.), Am. Polit. Sci. Assn., Am. Judicature Soc. Home: 608 Poplar St Vermillion SD 57069-3529 Office: U SD Acad Affairs Vermillion SD 57069 E-mail: ddahlin@usd.edu.

DAILEY, DONALD HARRY, adult education educator, volunteer; b. Sommerville, Mass., Mar. 26, 1949; s. Walter Merle Dailey and Shirley Esma (Clarke) Davidson; m. Janet Lynn Johnson, May 25, 1974; children: Catherine Shirley, Amanda Margaret. AS in Behavioral Scis., SUNY, Albany, 1978, BS in Liberal Arts, 1987; MPA, Ball State U., 1991, M in Adult Edn., 1995. Substitute Tchrs.' Cert., Ind. Career non-commissioned U.S. Army, 1968-88; field enumerator U.S. CENSUS Dept., Indpls., 1990, 2000; course developer Veteran's Upward Bound, 1994. Demographic cons. DataSource, Indpls., 1985—; com. mem. at large INCONJUCTION; spokesman Parents Adv. Coun. Author, critical reviews: Sherlock Holmes Review, 1990—; author, editor: Media Newsletter INTERCOM: 1705, 1983-88 (Best in Orgn. 1983-85). Polit. cons. Ind. State Senate, Indpls., 1994-95; mem. sci.-fiction rsch. group First Fandom. With U.S. Army, 1968-88. Recipient Appreciation Plaque INCONJUNCTION, Indpls., 1991, 94, Cert. of Appreciation Salvation Army, Indpls., 1990-94. Mem. VFW, Mensa, Mutual Unidentified Flying Object Network, First Fandom. Republican. Lutheran. Avocations: newsletter editing/publishing, media fan organizations, literary history. Home: 8003 Maple Grove Dr Georgetown IN 47122-9047 E-mail: fadmdon@otherside.com.

DAILEY, FRED L. state agency administrator; m. Rita Dailey; children: Dawn, Shawn, Calley. BA in Polit. Sci. and History, Anderson U., Ind.; MPA, Ball State U. Formerly rodeo cowboy and amateur mountaineer; with Ind. Dept. Corrections; later with U.S. Treasury; dir. Ind. Divsn. Agr., 1975-82; exec. v.p. Ohio Beef Coun., 1982-91; exec. sec. Ohio Cattlemen's Assn., 1982-91; dir. Ohio Dept. Agr., 1991—. Served with U.S. Army, Vietnam. Recipient numerous awards include Agri-Marketer of Yr., Industry svc. awards, Golden Boot award, Nat. Outstanding State Agrl. Exec. award, 1998; named Man of Yr. Progressive Farmer mag. Mem. Nat. Assn. State Depts. Agr. (pres. 1999—2001), Midwest Assn. State Depts. Agr. (past pres.), Mid-Am. Internat. Agri-Trade Coun. Office: Ohio Dept Agr Divsn Adminstrn 8995 E Main St Reynoldsburg OH 43068-3399 E-mail: agri@odant.agri.state.oh.us.

DAILY, FRANK J(EROME), lawyer; b. Chgo., Mar. 22, 1942; s. Francis Jerome and Eileen Veronica (O'Toole) D.; m. Julianna Ebert, June 23, 1996; children: Catherine, Eileen, Frank, William, Michael. BA in Journalism, Marquette U., 1964, JD, 1968. Bar: Wis. 1968, U.S. Dist. Ct. (ea. dist.) Wis. 1968, U.S. Dist. Ct. (we. dist.) Wis. 1971, U.S. Dist. Ct. (ctrl. dist.) Ill. 1990, U.S. Dist. Ct. (ea. dist.) Mich. 1994, U.S. Ct. Appeals (7th cir.) 1977, U.S. Ct. Appeals (3d and 5th cirs.) 1985, U.S. Ct. Appeals (4th, 6th, 8th, 9th, 10th, 11th cirs.) 1990, U.S. Supreme Ct. 1998, U.S. Dist. Ct. (no. dist.) Ill. 1999. Assoc. Quarles & Brady, Milw., 1968-75, ptnr., 1975—. Lectr. in product liability law and trial techniques Marquette U. Law Sch., U. Wis., Harvard U.; lectr. seminars sponsored by ABA, State Bar Wis., State Bar S.D., State Bar S.C., Product Liability Adv. Coun., Chem. Mfrs. Assn., Wis. Acad. Trial Lawyers, Trial Attys. Am., Marquette U., Southeastern Corp. Law Inst., Risk Ins. Mgmt. Soc., Inc.; life mem. pres.'s coun. Wake Forest U., Dayton Coll., Boston Coll. Author: Your Product's Life Is in the Balance: Litigation Survival-Increasing the Odds for Success, 1986, Product Liability Litigation in the 80s: A Trial Lawyer's View from the Trenches, 1986, Discovery Available to the Litigator and Its Effective Use, 1986, The Future of Tort Litigation: The Continuing Validity of Jury Trials, 1991, How to Make an Impact in Opening Statements for the Defense in Automobile Product Liability Cases, 1992, How Much Reform Does Civil Jury System Need, 1992, Do Protective Orders Compromise Public's Right to Know, 1993, Developments in Chemical Exposure Cases: Challenging Expert Testimony, 1993, The Spoliation Doctrine: The Sword, The Shield and The Shadow, 1997, Trial Tested Techniques for Winning Opening Statements, 1997, Litigation in the Next Millennium -- A Trial Lawyer's Crystal Ball Report, 1998, What's Hot and What's Not in Non-Daubert Products Liability In the Seventh Circuit, 1998. Ct. commr. Milwaukee County, Wis., 2001; bd. visitors Wake Forest U. Law Sch. Named Marquette U. Law Alumnus of Yr., 2000. Fellow Internat. Acad. Trial Lawyers; mem. ABA (past co-chair discovery com. litigation sect., vice chmn. products, gen. liability and consumer law com. of sect. tort and ins. practice, litigation sect. and mfrs. liability subcom.), ATLA, AAAS, Trial Atty. of Am., Wis. Bar Assn., Chgo. Bar Assn., Milw. Bar Assn., 7th Cir. Bar Assn., Am. Judicature Soc., Def. Rsch. Inst., Supreme Ct. Hist. Soc., Indsl. Truck Assn. (lawyers com.), Am. Law Inst., Product Liability Adv. Coun., Am. Agrl. Law Assn., Wis. Acad. Trial Lawyers, Assn. for Advancement of Automotive Medicine (life), Nat. I-Club U. Iowa, U. Ala. Nat. Alumni Assn., Circle of Champions. Roman Catholic. Office: Quarles & Brady 411 E Wisconsin Ave Ste 2550 Milwaukee WI 53202-4497 E-mail: fjd@quarles.com.

DALEY, CLAYTON CARL, JR. cosmetics company executive; b. Canton, Ohio, Nov. 6, 1951; s. Clayton and Jane Daley; m. Meredythe Lee Gray, Mar. 10, 1979; children: Clayton III, Graeme. AB in Econs., Davidson Coll., 1973; MBA, Ohio State U., 1974. Mgr. cost dept. Procter & Gamble Co., Green Bay, Wis., 1974-76, acctg. and office mgr. Cape Girardeau, 1976-78, forecaster paper divsn., 1978-79, fin. analysis supr. tissue brands, 1979-80, mgr. fin. analysis dept. paper divsn., 1980-82, mgr. soap cost acctg. dept. PS&D divsn., 1982-84, dir. fin. info. systems project, comptr.'s divsn., 1984-86, dir. corp. planning, 1986-88, divsn. comptr. PS&D divsn., 1988-89, divsn. comptr. PS&D divsn., BS&HCP divsn., 1989-90, comptr. soap products, 1990-91; comptr. U.S. ops. Procter & Gamble USA, 1991-92; v.p., comptr. Procter & Gamble Internat., 1992-93, team leader, v.p., compt., 1993-94; v.p., treas. Procter & Gamble Co., 1994-98, CFO, 1998—. Trustee Fin. Execs. Inst., 1994, Fin. Execs. Rsch. Found., 1994. Bd. dirs. Boy Scouts Am., Dan Beard Coun., 1997, Am. Cancer Soc., Hamilton County Unit, Cancer Family Care, Inc. Mem. Cin. Rotary. Office: Procter & Gamble Co 1 Procter And Gamble Plz Cincinnati OH 45202-3393

DALEY, RICHARD MICHAEL, mayor; b. Chgo., Apr. 24, 1942; s. Richard J. and Eleanor (Guilfoyle) D.; m. Margaret Corbett, Mar. 25, 1972; children: Nora, Patrick, Elizabeth. B.A., DePaul U., Chgo., 1964, J.D., 1968. Bar: Ill. 1969. Ptnr. Simon and Daley, Chgo., 1970-72, Daley, Riley & Daley, Chgo., 1972-80; mem. Ill. State Senate, 1973-80, chmn. Judiciary I Com., 1975, 77; state's atty. Cook County, Ill., 1980-89; mayor Chgo., 1989—; pres. U.S. Conf. Mayors , 1996. Bd. dirs. Little City Home; mem. Citizens Bd. U. Chgo.; mem. adv. bd. Mercy Hosp., Chgo.; bd. mgrs. Valentine Boys Club; active Nativity of Our Lord Parish, Chgo. Recipient Golden Rule plaque Chgo. Boys Club Am.; named Outstanding Legislator of Yr., Lt. Gov's. Sr. Legis. Forum, 1979, Outstanding Leader in Revision of Ill. Mental Health Code, Ill. Assn. Retarded Citizens, 1979, Outstanding Leader, Ill. Assn. Social workers, 1978. Mem. Chgo. Bar Assn., Ill. State Bar Assn., ABA, Cath. Lawyers Guild. Democrat. Roman Catholic Office: Office of the Mayor City Hall Rm 507 121 N La Salle St Chicago IL 60602-1202*

DALEY, ROBERT EMMETT, retired foundation executive; b. Cleve., Mar. 13, 1933; s. Emmett Wilfred and Anne Gertrude (O'Donnell) D.; m. Mary Berneta Fredericks, June 7, 1958; children: Marianne Fredericks, John Gerard. BA in English, U. Dayton, 1955; MA in Polit. Sci., Ohio State U., 1968, MA in Pub. Adminstrn., 1976. Local govt. reporter, Washington corr., fin. editor Jour. Herald, Dayton, Ohio, 1957-65, pub. affairs reporter, 1967; staff writer Congressional Quar., Inc., Washington, 1966; pub. affairs reporter Dayton Daily News, Dayton, 1969; dir. pub. affairs & comm. Charles F. Kettering Found., 1977-94, ret., now assoc., 1994—. Part-time copy boy, sports reporter Jour. Herald, Dayton, 1953-55. Past pres., bd. trustees St. Joseph Home for Children; former mem. adv. bd. Ctr. for Religious Telecomms., U. Dayton; traveling press sec. sen. candidate John J. Gilligan, 1968, for gubernatorial candidate, 1970-71, asst. to Gov. Gilligan, 1971-75; media rels. dir. Nat. League of Cities, Washington, 1976-77; mem. Montgomery County Hist. Soc.; past mem. Ind. Sector Pub. Info. & Edn. Com. With U.S. Army, 1955-57. Mem. Pub. Rels. Soc. Am., Soc. Profl. Journalists, Nat. Press Club, KC, Ancient Order Hibernians. Roman Catholic. Home: 888 Cranbrook Ct Dayton OH 45459-1525 Office: Charles F Kettering Found 200 Commons Rd Dayton OH 45459-2788 E-mail: daley@kettering.org.

DALEY, SUSAN JEAN, lawyer; b. New Britain, Conn., May 27, 1959; d. George Joseph and Norma (Woods) D. BA, U. Conn., 1978; JD, Harvard U., 1981. Bar: Ill. 1981. Assoc. Altheimer & Gray, Chgo., 1981-86, ptnr., 1986—. Mem. ABA (real property, probate and trust law sect. 1983—, chmn. welfare plans com. real property, probate and trust law sect. 1989-95, employee benefits com. taxation sect. 1984—, chmn. EEOC issues subcom. employee benefits com. taxation sect. 1990—, chmn. fed. securities law subcom. employee benefits com. taxation sect. 2001--), Nat. Assn. Stock Plan Profls. (pres. Chgo. chpt. 1995—), Ill. Bar Assn. (chmn. employee benefits divsn. fed. taxation sect. 1984-86, chmn. employee benefits sect., 1995-96, mem. employee benefits sect. 1990-97), Chgo. Bar Assn. (chmn. employee benefits divsn. fed. taxation com. 1985-86, chmn. employee benefits com. 1990-91, chmn. fed. taxation com. 1992-93), Chgo. Coun. on Fgn. Rels. Avocation: marathons. Home: 1636 N Wells St Apt 415 Chicago IL 60614-6009 Office: Altheimer & Gray 10 S Wacker Dr Ste 4000 Chicago IL 60606-7407 E-mail: daleys@altheimer.com.

DALLAS, DANIEL GEORGE, social worker; b. Chgo., June 8, 1932; s. George C. and Azimena P. (Marines) D.; B.A., Anderson (Ind.) Coll., 1955; B.D., No. Bapt. Theol. Sem., 1958; M.S.W., Mich. State U., 1963; M.Div., No. Bapt. Theol. Sem., 1972, D.Min., 1981; m. G. Aleta Leppien, May 26, 1956; children— Paul, Rhonda. Mem. faculty Mich. Dept. Corrections, Mich. State U., 1963-66; med. social adminstr. Med. Svcs. divsn. Mich. Dept. Social Svcs., 1966-68; cons. Outreach Ctr. of DuPage County, 1976— , also dir. social service Meml. Hosp. of DuPage County, Elmhurst, Ill., 1968— ; therapist, lectr. Traffic Sch., Elmhurst Coll.; pvt. practice; indsl. cons. Mem. Elmhurst Sr. Citizen Commn., 1976— . Recipient Outstanding Service award Mental Health Assn. Ill., 1978. Mem. Nat. Assn. Social Workers, Soc. Hosp. Social Work Dirs., Am. Hosp. Assn., Nat. Registry of Health Care Providers, Mental Health Assn. Chgo. Club: Rotary. Contbr. articles to profl. jours. Office: 242 N York St Ste 203 Elmhurst IL 60126-2747

DALLA-VICENZA, MARIO JOSEPH, steel company executive; b. Sudbury, Ont., Can., Oct. 30, 1938; s. Mario Valentino and Cecilia (Bonaldo) D.-V.; m. Deanna Karen Leblanc, July 15, 1961; children: Janice, Peter, Mark. Grad. in acctg., Queens U., Kingston, Can., 1962, McMaster U., Can., 1969; MBA, Lake Superior State U., 1983. Chartered acct., Can.; cert. mgmt. acct., Can. Acct. Tessier, Massicotte & Co., Sault Ste Marie, Ont., 1957-63; with Algoma Steel Corp., 1963-83, gen. mgr. corp. acctg. svcs., 1981-83; treas. IPSCO Inc., Regina, Sask., Can., 1983-87, v.p., CFO Can., 1987-88, sr. v.p., CFO Can., 1988-96, sr. v.p. corp. affairs Can., 1996-97; pres. Demar Enterprises, Sault Ste Marie, Ont., Can., 1998—. Pres., bd. dirs. Sault Ste Marie C. of C., 1974-79; chmn. econ. devel. coun. City of Sault Ste Marie, 1981-83. Fellow Inst. Chartered Accts. (nat. coun., nat. exec. com. 1994-95, provincial coun. 1990-96, pres. 1996); mem. Soc. Mgmt. Accts. (pres., provincial coun. 1984-88, fellow 1993, nat. bd. 1989-90), Fin. Execs. Inst. (bd. dirs. Regina chpt. 1985-90, chpt. pres. 1989-90), Ranch Ehrlo Soc. (bd. dirs. 1992-99, chmn. 1997-99). Office: Algoma Steel PO Box 1400 Sault Sainte Marie ON Canada P6A 5P2

DALLEPEZZE, JOHN RAYMOND, lighting company executive; b. Princeton, N.J., May 27, 1943; s. Angelo Peter and Yolanda Irene (Micai) D.; m. Joanne Rita McGuinn, June 19, 1965; children: Christina Maria, John Raymond Jr., Peter Angelo. BS in Engring., Princeton U., 1965; SM, MIT, 1967. Scheduling supr. Corning Glass Works, Danville, Va., 1967, plant controller, 1967-69, plant mfg. engr., 1969-71, market specialist, tech. products Corning, N.Y., 1971-73, sales mgr., indsl. products, 1973-77, div. controller, tech. products, 1977-80, gen. mgr., lighting products, 1980-83; pres. N.L. McCullough, Houston, 1983-89; pres., chief exec. officer Holophane Co., Inc., Newark, 1989—. Mem. Petroleum Equipment Suppliers Assn., Soc. Profl. Well Log Analysts, Soc. Petroleum Engrs. Republican. Club: Raveneaux Country (Houston). Address: 214 Oakwood Ave Newark OH 43055-6716 Home: 4308 Harlem Rd Galena OH 43021-9347 Office: Holophane Co Inc 214 Oakwood Ave Newark OH 43055-6700

DALLMAN, ROBERT EDWARD, lawyer; b. Shawano, Wis., Apr. 16, 1947; BA, Valparaiso U., 1970; JD, U. Kans., 1973; LLM, Georgetown U., 1977. Bar: Kans. 1973, U.S. Tax Ct. 1973, U.S. Supreme Ct. 1978, Wis. 1980. Chief counsel IRS, Washington, 1973-77, Milw., 1977-80; shareholder Reinhart, Boerner, Van Deuren, Norris & Rieselbach S.C. Instr. corp. tax. planning and advanced real estate tax planning U. Wis., Milw., 1981—; cons. to chief counsel IRS, Washington, 1980. Co-author: Tax Planning for Real Estate Transactions, 1983; contbr. articles to profl. jours. Mem. ABA, State Bar Wis., Milw. Bar Assn. Office: Reinhart Boerner Van Deuren PO Box 92900 1000 N Water St Ste 2100 Milwaukee WI 53202-3197 E-mail: rdallman@reinhartlaw.com.

DALLOS, PETER JOHN, neurobiologist, educator; b. Budapest, Hungary, Nov. 26, 1934; came to U.S., 1956, naturalized, 1962; s. Ernest and Maria Dallos; m. Joan Usis, Aug. 18, 1977; 1 child by previous marriage, Christopher. Student, Tech. U. Budapest, 1953-56; BS, Ill. Inst. Tech., 1958; MS, Northwestern U., 1959, PhD, 1962. Rsch. engr. Am. Machine and Foundry Co., 1959; cons. engr., 1959-60; mem. faculty Northwestern U., 1962—, prof. audiology and elec. engring., 1969—, prof. neurobiology and physiology, 1981—, chmn., 1981-84, 86-87, assoc. dean Coll. Arts and Scis., 1984-85, John Evans prof. neurosci., 1986—, Hugh Knowles prof. audiology, 1994—. Vis. scientist Karolinska Inst., Stockholm, 1977-78; chmn. behavioral and neurosci. rev. panel No. 5 Nat. Inst. Neurol., Communicative Disorders and Stroke, NIH, 1982-85, mem. nat. adv. council, 1984-87 Author: The Auditory Periphery: Biophysics and Physiology, 1973; editor: The Cochlea, 1996; contbr. articles to profl. jours. Recipient 12th ann. award Beltone Inst. Hearing Rsch., 1977, Internat. prize Amplifon Rsch. and Study Ctr., 1984, Senator Jacob Javits Neurosci. Investigator award, 1984, Honors of Assn. award Am. Speech-Lang.-Hearing Assn., 1994, Bekesy medal of Acoustical Soc. Am., 1995, Sigma Xi Disting. Nat. lectr., 1997-98, Acta Otolaryngologica Internat. prize, 1997, Kresge-Mirmelstein prize La. State U., 2000; Guggenheim fellow, 1977-78; McKnight sr. fellow, 1997-2000. Fellow IEEE (life), AAAS, Acoustical Soc. Am., Am. Acad. Arts and Scis.; mem. Soc. for Neurosci., Assn. for Rsch. in Otolaryngology (pres. 1992-93, award of merit 1994), Collegium Otolaryngologium Amicitae Sacrum, Sigma Xi, Tau Beta Pi, Eta Kappa Nu. Office: Northwestern U 2299 N Campus Dr Evanston IL 60208-0837 E-mail: p-dallos@northwestern.edu.

DALRYMPLE, JACK, lieutenant governor; m. Betsy Dalrymple; 4 children. BA, Yale U., 1970. Farmer, 1970—; state rep. dist. 22, 1985—2001; lt. gov. State of N.D., 2001—. Chmn. appropriations com. N.D. Ho. Reps.; bd. dirs. Prairie Pub. TV, N.D. State u. Devel. Found., Golden Growers Coop.; mem. Edn. Broadcasting Coun.; co-founder Share House Inc. Recipient Outstanding Young Farmer award, 1983. Mem. Cass County Rural Water Users Assn. (past bd. dirs.), Casselton Econ. Devel. Found., Univ. Pres. Agr. Club (pres.), Durum Growers Assn. (bd. dirs.), Jaycees. Republican. Address: PO Box 220 Casselton ND 58012-0220*

DALTON, DAN R. college dean; PhD, U. Calif. Mem. staff Gen. Telephone & Electronics; dean Kelley Sch. Ind. U., Bloomington, Ind., 1997—. Contbr. over 160 articles to profl. jours.; cons. editor Jour. Applied Psychology; editor Jour. Mgmt. Recipient of 25 awards and citations for excellence in tchg.; nat. recognized by Bus. Week for excellence in tchg. Office: Indiana Univ Kelley School Business 1309 E 10th St Bloomington IN 47405-1701 Fax: 812-855-8983. E-mail: dalton@indiana.edu.

DALY, SIMEON PHILIP JOHN, retired librarian; b. Detroit, May 9, 1922; s. Philip T. and Marguerite I. (Ginzel) D. BA, St. Meinrad Coll., 1945; Licentiate in Sacred Theol., Cath. U., 1949, MLS, 1951; MDiv, St. Meinrad Sch. Theol., 1985. Joined Benedictines, 1943, ordained priest Roman Cath. Ch., 1948. Libr. dir. St. Meinrad (Ind.) Coll. and St. Meinrad Sch. Theol., 1951-2000; pres. Four Rivers Area Libr. Svcs. Authority, Ind., 1974-75, Am. Theol. Libr. Assn., St. Meinrad, 1979-81, exec. sec., 1985-90. Mem. ALA, Ind. Libr. Assn., Am. Theol. Libr. Assn. (bd. dirs., pres., exec. sec.), Am. Benedictine Acad. Home: St Meinrad Archabbey 100 Hill Dr Saint Meinrad IN 47577

DALY, WALTER JOSEPH, physician, educator; b. Michigan City, Ind., Jan. 12, 1930; s. Walter Hayes and Nellie Martha (Stipp) D.; m. Joan Brown, June 12, 1953; children: Lois Kay, Alice Louise. AB, Ind. U., 1951, MD, 1955, ScD, 1998. Diplomate Am. Bd. Internal Medicine. Intern Ind. U., 1955-56, resident, 1956-57, 59-62, instr. medicine, 1962-63, asst. prof., 1963-65, assoc. prof., 1965-68, prof., 1968-77, John B. Hickam prof., 1977-80, J.O. Ritchey prof., 1980-95, J.O. Ritchey prof. emeritus, 1995—; chmn. dept. medicine, 1970-83; dean Sch. Medicine, 1983-95; dean emeritus Ind. U., 1995—. Dir. Regenstrief Inst. Health Rsch., 1976-83. Capt. M.C., U.S. Army, 1957-59. Master ACP (gov. 1980-84), Am. Physiol. Soc., Ctr. Soc. Clin. Rsch. (pres. 1980-81), Am. Soc. Clin. Investigation, Am. Clin. and Climatol. Assn., Assn. Am. Physicians. Home: 1120 South Dr Indianapolis IN 46202-5135 Office: Ind U Sch Medicine 1120 South Dr Indianapolis IN 46202-5135

DAM, KENNETH W. lawyer, law educator, federal agency administrator; b. Marysville, Kans., Aug. 10, 1932; s. Oliver W. and Ida L. (Hueppelsheuser) D.; m. Marcia Wachs, June 9, 1962; children: Eliot, Charlotte. BS, U. Kans., 1954; JD, U. Chgo., 1957; LLD (hon.), New Sch. Social Rsch., 1983. Bar: N.Y. State 1959. Law clk. to justice U.S. Supreme Ct., 1957-58; assoc. Cravath, Swaine & Moore, N.Y.C., 1958-60; faculty U. Chgo. Law Sch., 1960-82, prof., 1964-71, 74-82, Harold J. and Marion F. Green prof., 1976-82, provost, 1980-82; dep. sec. of state Dept. State, 1982-85; v.p. law and external rels. IBM Corp., 1985-92; pres., CEO United Way Am., 1992; Max Pam prof. of Am. and fgn. law U. Chgo. Law Sch., 1992—2001; dep. sec. Dept. Treasury, Washington, 2001—. Asst. dir. nat. security and internat. affairs Office Mgmt. and Budget, 1971-73; exec. dir. Coun. Econ. Policy, 1973; vis. prof. U. Freiburg, Germany, 1964; adv. bd. BMW of N.Am., 1990-95. Author: The GATT: Law and International Economic Organization, 1970, Oil Resources: Who Gets What How?, 1976, The Rules of the Game: Reform and Evolution in the International Monetary System, 1982, The Rules of the Global Game: A New Look at U.S. International Economic Policymaking, 2001; co-author: Federal Tax Treatment of Foreign Income, 1964, Economic Policy Beyond the Headlines, 1977, 2d edit., 1998; co-editor: Crytography's Role in Securing the Information Society, 1996; chair bd. advisors Fgn. Affairs jour., 1997-2001. Bd. dirs. Am. Coun. on Germany, 1986-95, Am.-China Soc., 1989-99, Coun. on Fgn. Rels., 1992-2001, Chgo. Coun. on Fgn. Rels., 1992-2001; trustee Brookings Inst., 1989-2001; co-chmn. Aspen Strategy Group, 1991-2001. Mem. Am. Acad. Arts and Scis., Am. Acad. Diplomacy, Am. Law Inst., Met. Club (Washington), Quadrangle Club. Office: Dept Treasury Office of the Secy 1500 Pennsylvania Ave NW Washington DC 20220

DAMASIO, ANTONIO R. physician, neurologist; b. Lisbon, Portugal, Feb. 25, 1944; came to U.S., 1975; m. Hanna Damasio. MD, U. Lisbon, 1969, DMS, 1974. Intern U. Hosp., Lisbon, 1969-72; prof. auxiliar in neurology Med. Sch., U. Lisbon, 1971; assoc. prof. dept. neurology U. Iowa, Iowa City, 1976-80, prof. neurology, 1980-86, prof. neurology, head dept., 1986—, M.W. Van Allen Disting. prof., 1989—, chief divsn. behavioral neurology and cognitive neurosci., 1977—. Adj. prof. Salk Inst., San Diego, 1989—; mem. planning subcom. Nat. Adv. Neurol. Disorders Stroke Coun. Author: Lesion Analysis in Neuropsychgology, 1989 (award Assn. Am. Pubs. 1990); mem. editorial bd. Trends in Neuroscis., 1986-91, Behavioral Brain Rsch., 1988—, Cerebral Cortex, 1990—, Jour. Neurosci., 1990, Cognitive Brain Rsch., Learning and Memory, spl. brain issue Sci. Am, 1992, Descartes' Error: Emotion, Reason, and the Human Brain, 1994, The Feeling of What Happens: Body and Emotion in the Making of Consciousness, 1999. Recipient Disting. prof. award U. So. Calif., Prix Plasticite' Neuronale, Ispen Found., 1997, Golden Brain award, 1995, The Reenpää prize, Finland, 2000, Dr. William Beaumont award AMA, 1990, Pessoa prize Portuguese govt., 1992. Fellow Am. Acad. Neurology, Am. Neurol. Asns.; mem. NAS Inst. Medicine, Soc. for Neurosci., Acad. Aphasia (pres. 1983), Behavioral Neurology Soc., (pres. 1985), Royal Soc. Medicine Belgium (elected), European Acad. Arts and Scis. (elected), Am. Acad. Arts and Scis. Office: U Iowa Hosp & Clinic Dept Neurology 200 Hawkins Dr Iowa City IA 52242-1009

DAMICO, JOSEPH F. medical company executive; BS, MS in Mgmt. and Mktg., James Madison U. Sales rep. to various mgmt. positions Am. Hosp. Supply Corp. (now merged with Baxter), 1979-87; former group v.p. to pres. divsns. Baxter Internat., Inc., 1987-93; former pres., CEO Allegiance Corp.; group pres. Cardinal Health, Dublin, 1996—. Bd. dirs. Xillix Technologies Corp., Richmond, B.C., Lake Forest Hosp., Ill., Health Industry Mfrs. Assn., Washington, The Baxter Allegiance Found., Deerfield, Ill., Coll. of Lake County, Grayslake, Ill. Office: Cardinal Health 5555 Glendon Ct Dublin OH 43016-3249 also: Cardinal Health Co Allegiance Healthcare Corp 1430 Waukegan Rd Mc Gaw Park IL 60085-6726

DAMJANOV, IVAN, pathologist, educator; b. Subotica, Yugoslavia, Mar. 31, 1941; came to U.S., 1967; s. Milenko and Ana (Pavkovic) D.; m. Andrea Zivanovic, Jan. 18, 1964; children: Nevena, Ivana, Milena. MD, U. Zagreb (Croatia), 1964, PhD, 1971. Lic. physician, Croatia; diplomate Am. Bd. Pathology. Intern Gen. Hosp., Zagreb, 1964-65; resident in pathology U. Zagreb, 1966-67; intern in pathology Cleve. Met. Gen. Hosp., 1967-68; resident in pathology Mt. Sinai Hosp., N.Y.C., 1968-69; asst. in pathology U. Zagreb, 1969-71; postdoctoral fellow Fels Rsch. Inst., Temple U., Phila., 1971-72; asst. prof. pathology U. Zagreb, 1972-73; from asst. prof. to assoc. prof. U. Conn., Farmington, 1973-77; from assoc. prof. to prof. Hahnemann Med. Coll. and Hosp., Phila., 1977-86; prof. pathology Jefferson Med. Coll. of Thomas Jefferson U., 1986-94; prof. pathology, chmn. U. Kans. Sch. Med., Kansas City, 1994-98, prof. pathology, 1998—. Cons. pathologist VA Hosp., Newington, Conn., 1975-77, Cancer Info. Dissemination and Analysis Ctr. for Virology, Immunology and Cancer-Related Biology, Franklin Inst., Phila., 1977-82, VAMC, Kansas City, Mo., 1995--; mem. group for rsch. in pathology edn. U. Iowa, 1977-82; ad hoc reviewer, mem. site vis. teams and study sects. NIH, Bethesda, Md., 1978—; mem. basic sci. merit award bd. VA, 1989-92; mem. Croatian Acad. Arts and Scis., 1992; mem. coun. U.S.-Can. Acad. Pathology, 1996-99. Mem. editl. bd. Ultrastructural Pathology, 1985-96, Virchows Archiv, 1986—, In Vivo, 1988—, Modern Pathology, 1989—, Hosp. Physician, 1990-96, Human Pathology, 1991—, Lab. Investigation, 1994—, Jour. Urologic Pathology, 1991-2000, editor-in-chief, 2000-2002; assoc. editor Lab. Investigation, 1982-94; regional editor N.Am. Differentiation, 1985-96, Pathology Rsch. Practice, 1998-2002; co-editor Anderson's Pathology, 10th edit., 1996; mem. editl. rev. group chairperson for pathology/surg. pathology Doody's Health Sciences Book Rev. Jour., 1998—. Recipient Christian R. and Mary F. Lindback award for disting. teaching Jefferson Med. Coll., Phila., 1988. Mem. Am. Soc. Investigative Pathology, Internat. Acad. Pathology, European Soc. Pathology, Am. Soc. Clin. Pathologists. Office: U Kansas Sch of Med Dept Pathol & Lab Med 3901 Rainbow Blvd Kansas City KS 66160-0001 E-mail: idamjano@kumc.edu., idamjanov@kc.rr.com.

DAMMEYER, RODNEY FOSTER, distribution company executive; b. Cleve., Nov. 5, 1940; s. Frederick and Marion (Foster) D.; m. Diane Newins, Feb. 8, 1975; children: Paul, Scott, Tom, Kimberley, Alice. BS in Acctg., Kent State U., 1962. With Arthur Andersen & Co., Ohio, 1952-70, ptnr. audit practice, 1970-74, mng. ptnr. N.C., 1974-75, with Cleve., 1975-79; ptnr. audit practice Arthur Anderson & Co., 1970-74, mng. dir. Greensboro, N.C., 1974-, mng. ptnr. Seattle, 1975—; exec. v.p. fin. Northwest Industries, Inc., Chgo., 1979-83; sr. v.p., chief fin. officer Household Internat., Prospect Heights, Ill., 1983-85; pres., CEO Anixter Internat. Corp., Chgo., 1985—, also bd. dirs.; vice chmn. Anixter Corp. Pres., CEO, dir. Great Am. Mgmt. Investments, Inc.; bd. dirs. Antec,

Capsure Holdings, Falcon Bldg. Products, Inc., Jacor Comm., Inc., Lukens, Inc., Revco D.S., Inc., Sealy Inc., IMC Global, Inc., various Van Kampen Merritt Trusts; mem. nat. adv. bd. Chase Bank; mem. nat. and econ. policy couns. UN Assn. of U.S. Bd. dirs. Kent State U. Found., Inc. Presbyterian. Club: Econs. Chgo. Office: Ste 2800 676 N Michigan Ave Chicago IL 60611-2861

DAMON, JOHNNY, professional baseball player; b. Ft. Riley, Kans., Nov. 5, 1973; Baseball player Kansas City (Mo.) Royals, 1995—. Office: Kansas City Royals PO Box 419969 Kansas City MO 64141-6969*

DAMSCHRODER, REX, state legislator; m. Rhonda Damschroder; children: Alex, Anthony. BA, Bowling Green State U., 1974; MBA, Tiffin U., 1994. Mem. Ho. of Reps. State of Ohio, Columbus, 1994—. Mem. Sandusky County Rep. Ctrl. Com.; mem. bd. Terra C.C. Mem. Farm Bur., Twp. Trustees Assn., Fremont (Ohio) C. of C., Kiwanis. Republican.

DANCEWICZ, JOHN EDWARD, investment banker; b. Boston, Feb. 12, 1949; s. John Felix and Teresa Sophia (Lewandowski) D.; m. Barbaragail Jarrett, Jan. 23, 1971; children: John Lawrence, Jill Elizabeth, Jenna Gail. BA in Econs., Yale U., 1971; MBA, Harvard U., 1973. Project adminstr., cons. Nat. Shawmut Bank Boston, 1972-73; v.p., mgr. U.S. investment banking Continental Ill. Nat. Bank Chgo., 1973-82; sr. mng. dir., mgr. corp. fin. Bear Stearns & Co. Inc., Chgo., 1982-96; founder, mng. ptnr. DN Ptnrs. LP, 1996—. Chmn. bd. dirs. Aztec Outdoor Advt. Co. Contbr. articles to profl. jours. Active Yale U. Schs. Com., Spl. Gifts Com. (chmn. 25th Reunion Fundraising, sec. Yale class 1971); sec. Harvard Bus. Sch. sect.; mem. spl. gifts com. Harvard Bus. Sch. Fund. Mem. Scholarship and Guidance Assn. (bd. dirs., v.p. 1982—), Lake Forest H.S. Hockey Assn. (pres.), Harvard Bus. Sch. Club Chgo., Econ. Club, Univ. Club, East Bank Club, Mid-Am. Club. Home: 969 Spring Ln Lake Forest IL 60045-2302 Office: 77 W Wacker Dr Ste 4550 Chicago IL 60601 Business E-Mail: info@dupartners.com.

DANCO, LÉON ANTOINE, management consultant, educator; b. N.Y.C., May 30, 1923; s. Leon A. and Alvira T. (Gomez) D.; m. Katharine Elizabeth Leck, Aug. 25, 1951; children: Suzanne, Walter Ten Eyck. AB, Harvard, 1943, MBA, 1947; PhD, Case Western Res. U., 1963. Asst. to divsn. pres. Interchem. Corp., N.Y.C., 1947-50; sales promotion mgr. Risdon Mfg. Co., Waterbury, Conn., 1950-55; mgmt. cons. Cheshire, 1955-57; prof., assoc. dir. mgmt. program Case Inst. Tech., Cleve., 1957-58, lectr., 1959—; mgmt. cons. L.A. Danco & Co., 1957—; lectr. John Carroll U., Cleve., 1959-66, prof., dir. mgmt. confs., 1966—. Vis. prof. econs. Cleve. Inst. Art, 1966-69, Kent State U., 1966-67; exec. dir. Univ. Svcs. Inst., Cleve., 1967-69, pres., 1969—, chmn., 1989—; pub. The Family in Business (newsletter), 1978—; pres. Center for Family Bus., 1978—, chmn. Ctr.for Family Bus., 1991. Author: Beyond Survival-A Business Owners Guide for Success, 1975, Inside the Successful Family Business, 1979, Outside Directors in the Family Owned Business, 1981, Someday It'll All Be...Whose?, 1990; (in French) L'Entreprise Familiale, 1998; (in Spanish) La Empresa Familiare, 1998; syndicated columnist: It's Your Business, 1973—. Lt. (j.g.) USCG, 1942-46, PTO. Mem. Am. Econ. Assn. Home: 28230 Cedar Rd Pepper Pike Cleveland OH 44124 Office: Ctr for Family Bus PO Box 24219 Cleveland OH 44124-0219 E-mail: grummi@aol.com.

DANFORTH, JOHN CLAGGETT, former senator, lawyer, clergyman; b. St. Louis, Sept. 5, 1936; s. Donald and Dorothy (Claggett) D.; m. Sally B. Dobson, Sept. 7, 1957; children: Eleanor, Mary, Dorothy, Johanna, Thomas. BA with honors, Princeton U., 1958; BD, LLB, Yale U., 1963, MA (hon.); LHD (hon.), Lindenwood Coll., 1970, Ind. Central U.; LLD (hon.), Drury Coll., 1970, Maryville Coll., Rockhurst Coll., Westminster Coll., Culver-Stockton Coll., St. Louis U.; DD (hon.), Lewis and Clark Coll.; HHD (hon.), William Jewell Coll.; STD (hon.), Southwest Bapt. Coll.; hon. deg., Va. Theol. Sem., 1990, Holy Cross Coll., 1992, Harris Stowe Coll., 1992, Wash. U., 1995, U. Mo., 1995. Bar: N.Y. 1964, Mo. 1966, D.C. 1994. With firm Davis Polk Wardwell Sunderland & Kiendl, N.Y.C., 1964-66; ptnr. Bryan, Cave, McPheeters and McRoberts (now Bryan Cave LLP), St. Louis, 1966-68, 95—; atty. gen. State of Mo., 1969-76; U.S. senator from Mo., 1976-94; ordained deacon Episc. Ch., 1963, priest, 1964; asst. rector N.Y.C., 1963-66; assoc. rector Clayton, Mo., 1966-68, Grace Ch., Jefferson City, 1969; hon. assoc. St. Alban's Ch., Washington, 1977-94. Chmn. Mo. Law Enforcement Assistance Council, 1973-74; asst. chaplain Meml. Sloan-Kettering Cancer Ctr. of N.Y.C.; asst. rector Ch. of Epiphany in N.Y.C., Ch. of St. Michael and St. George, Clayton, Mo.; hon. canon Christ Ch. Cathedral, St. Louis. Republican nominee U.S. Senate, 1970; assoc. rector Ch. of the Holy Communion, Univ. City, Mo., 1995—. Recipient Disting. Svc. award St. Louis Jr. C. of C., 1969, Disting. Missourian and Brotherhood awards NCCJ, Presdl. World Without Hunger award, 1985, Disting. Lectr. award Avila Coll., Chancellors medal UMKC, 1995; named Outstanding Young Man Mo. Jr. C. of C., 1968, St. Louis Man of Yr., 1994; Alumni fellow Yale U., 1973-79 Mem. Mo. Acad. Squires, Alpha Sigma Nu (hon.) Republican.

DANFORTH, WILLIAM HENRY, retired academic administrator, physician; b. St. Louis, Apr. 10, 1926; s. Donald and Dorothy (Claggett) D.; m. Elizabeth Anne Gray, Sept. 1, 1950; children: Cynthia Danforth Prather, David Gray, Maebelle Danforth Reed, Elizabeth D. Sankey. A.B., Princeton U., 1947; M.D., Harvard U., 1951. Intern Barnes Hosp., St. Louis, 1951—52, resident, 1954—57; now mem. staff; asst. prof. medicine Washington U., St. Louis, 1960—65, assoc. prof., 1965—67, prof., 1967—, vice chancellor for med. affairs, 1965—71, chancellor, 1971—95, chmn., bd. trustees, 1995—99, vice-chmn. bd. trustees, chancellor emeritus, 1999—. Pres. Washington U. Med. Sch. and Assoc. Hosps., 1965-71; program coord. Bi-State Regional Med. Program, 1967-68; dir. Energizing Holdings; chmn. bd. dirs. Donald Danforth Plant Sci. Ctr. Trustee Danforth Found.; trustee Am. Youth Found., 1963—, Princeton U., 1970-74; pres. St. Louis Christmas Carols Assn., 1958-74, chmn., 1975—; co-chair Barnes/Jewish Hosp., 1996-2002; bd. dirs. BJC Health Systems, 1996-2002. Named Man of Yr., St. Louis Gloe-Democrat, 1978, St. Louis Globe-Democrat, 1978. Fellow: AAAS, Am. Acad. Arts and Scis.; mem.: Inst. Medicine. Home: 10 Glenview Rd Saint Louis MO 63124-1308 Office: Washington U West Campus Campus Box 1044 7425 Forsyth Blvd Ste 262 Saint Louis MO 63105-2161

DANIEL, DAVID EDWIN, civil engineer, educator; b. Newport News, Va., Dec. 20, 1949; s. David Edwin and Betty Ruth (Aschenback) D.; m. Frances Louise Locker, June 12, 1971 (div.); children: Katherine Ruth, William Monroe; m. Susan Nielsen Brady, May 12, 1989; 1 child, Alexander David. BS, U. Tex., 1972, MS, 1974, PhD, 1980. Staff engr. Woodward-Clyde, San Francisco, 1974-77; asst. prof. U. Tex., Austin, 1981-85, assoc. prof., 1985-91, prof., 1991-96; prof., head dept. civil engring. U. Ill., Urbana, 1996-2001, dean, engring., 2001—. Recipient Richard R. Torrens award Am. Soc. of Civil Engineers, 1995 Mem. ASCE (Norman medal 1975, Cross medal 1984, 2000, Middlebrooks award 1995), NAE. Office: U Ill Dept Civil Engring Urbana IL 61801

DANIEL, MICHAEL EDWIN, insurance agency executive; b. Indpls., Sept. 8, 1948; s. Richard E. and Margret A. (Phillips) D.; m. Jeanne L. Nobbe, Sept. 29, 1979; children: Whitney Marie, Lindsay Michelle, Tyler Edwin. BA, Principia Coll., Elsah, Ill., 1970; German lang. degree, Dept. Def., Monterey, Calif., 1971. Sales mgr. Mr. Ins. of Ind., Indpls., 1973-77; pres. Ind. Ins. Svcs., Inc., Greenwood, 1977—, Ins. Svc., Inc., 5, 1990—. V.p. Brown County Water Utility, Helmsburg, Ind., 1982-85. Leader Johnson County 4-H, 1993-97, cub scout pack 218 Boy Scouts Am., 1999—. With U.S. Army, 1970-73. Mem. Ind. Ins. Agts. Assn., Profl. Ins. Agt. Assn. (treas. Indpls. region 1990), Ind. Trail Riders Assn., BMW Motorcycle Owners Am. Christian Scientist. Avocations: Appaloosa and quarter horses, camping. Office: Ind Ins Svcs 3115 Meridian Parke Dr Ste P Greenwood IN 46142-9414 E-mail: mdaniel@principia.edu., insure@indymall.com.

DANIEL, T. mime performer, theater director, choreographer; b. Chgo., Aug. 23, 1945; s. Theodore Charles and Thelma L. (Soderlind) Heagstedt; m. Laurie Willets, July 14, 1976. BS, Ill. State U., 1967, postgrad., 1969. Cert. Ecole Internat. de Mime. Performer, creator, artistic dir. T. Daniel Productions (Movement & Movement Theatre), Winnetka, Ill., 1971—. Choreographer (film) Poltergeist III, 1988; choreographer, performer (video) Sweets for the Sweet, 1984; performer, creator (plays) Fantasmia, 1984, Merlin & The Color of Magic, 1986, Structures on Silence, 1988, The Magic of Mime, 1973, A World of Mime, 1971, ImVentionS, musical mims quartet, 2000 Home and Office: 6619 N Campbell Chicago IL 60645

DANIELS, DAVID WILDER, conductor, music educator; b. Penn Yan, N.Y., Dec. 20, 1933; s. Carroll Cronk and Ursula (Wilder) D.; m. Jimmie Sue Evans, Aug. 11, 1956; children: Michael, Abigail, Andrew. AB, Oberlin Coll., 1955; MA, Boston U., 1956; MFA, PhD, U. Iowa, 1963. Instr. music Culver-Stockton Coll., Canton, Mo., 1956-58; music libr. Berkshire Athenaeum, Pittsfield, Mass., 1958-61; asst. prof. U. Redlands, Calif., 1963-64, Knox Coll., Galesburg, Ill., 1964-69, Oakland U., Rochester, Mich., 1969-71, assoc. prof., 1971-85, prof., 1985-97, chmn. dept., 1982-88, prof. emeritus, 1997—. Music dir. Warren Symphony, Mich., 1974—, Pontiac-Oakland Symphony, Pontiac, Mich., 1977-97; prin. condr. Detroit Symphony Civic Orch., 1997-98. Author: Orchestral Music, 1972, 3rd edit., 1996; editor Avanti newsletter, 1982-86. Mem. Am. Symphony Orch. League, Condrs. Guild (bd. dirs. 1986-94, sec. 1989-91, v.p. 1991-94), Mich. Orch. Assn. (pres. 1981-83). Home: 1215 Gettysburg Ct Rochester Hills MI 48306-3819

DANIELS, LEE ALBERT, state legislator; b. Lansing, Mich., Apr. 15, 1942; s. Albert Lee and Evelyn (Bousfield) D.; m. Pamela Mesha; children: Laurie Lynn, Rachael Lee, Julie, Thomas, Christina. BA, U. Iowa, 1965; JD, John Marshall Law Sch., 1967. Rep. precinct committeeman, 1965-74; mem. bd. auditors York Twp., Ill., 1966-73; vice chmn. York Twp. Rep. Comty. Orgn., 1973-74; former minority spokesman judiciary com. Ill. Ho. of Reps.; spl. asst. atty. gen., 1973-75; Ill. state rep. 46th Dist., 1975—, majority whip, 1981-82, minority leader, 1983-94; speaker of the House, 1995—. Full ptnr. Katten, Muchin & Zavis, 1984-91; ptnr. Bell, Boyd & Lloyd, Chgo., 1992— Trustee Elmhurst Hosp. Recipient Everett McKinley Dirksen award, 1995; named one of Outstanding Legislators in Country, Nat. Rep. Legis. Assn., 1991, Legislator of Yr., Ill. Hosp. Assn., 1986, DuPage Mayors and Mgrs. Conf., 1995. Mem. ABA, Ill. Bar Assn., DuPage County Bar Assn., Shriners, Masons, Moose. Home: 611 N York Rd Elmhurst IL 60126-1903 Office: 316 State House Springfield IL 62706-0001*

DANIELS, PRESTON A. mayor; b. Des Moines; B in Psychology, MS in Health Sci. and Counseling, Drake U. Probation officer 5th jud. dist. Dept. Corrections, tech. assistance to cmty.-based programs; dir. ct. and cmty. rels. Employee and Family Resources Iowa Managed Substance Abuse Care Plan; city councilman at large Des Moines; mayor. Chmn. Des Moines Police Subcom. Mem. U. Iowa Adv. Bd. for Addiction Tech. Transfer Ctr.; mem. Tng. Adv. Bd. for Substance Abuse, State of Iowa; pres. Drake Neighborhood Assn.; active numerous neighborhood activities; mem. Nat. Conf. Black Mayors, Nat. Conf. Mayors. Sgt. U.S. Army. Named Hon. Lt. Col. Ala. State Guard. Office: 400 E 1st St Des Moines IA 50309-1809 E-mail: padaniels@ci.des-moines.ia.us.

DANIELS-CARTER, VALERIE, food franchise executive; d. John and Katherine Daniels. Degree, Lincoln U., 1978; MS, Cardinal Stritch Coll., 1982. With Firstar Bank, 1978-81; auditor MGIC Investment Corp., 1981-84; co-founder V & J Foods, Milw., 1984—. Owner 37 Burger King restaurants, 61 Pizza Hut restaurants. Pres. bd. dirs. Milw. World Festival Inc. Named Entrepreneur of Yr., Ernst & Young and Merrill Lynch, 1994; recipient award Black Women's Network of Milw., 1997, Sacajawea award for creativity Midwest Express Airlines, 1997. Office: V & J Holding Cos 6933 W Brown Deer Rd Milwaukee WI 53223-2103

DANNEMILLER, JOHN C. transportation company executive; b. Cleve., May 17, 1938; s. John Charles and Jean I. (Bage) D.; m. Jean Marie Sheridan, Sept. 22, 1962; children— David, Peter B.S., Case Western Res. U., 1960, M.B.A., 1964; postgrad., Stanford U., 1975, Columbia U., 1974, Tuck Exec. program Dartmouth Coll., 1976. Vice pres. foods div. Diamond Shamrock, 1978-81, dir. planning, 1981-83; v.p. SDS Biotech Corp., Cleve., 1984-85; group v.p. leasing group Leaseway Transp., 1984-85, pres., chief operating officer, 1985-88, exec. v.p., chief oper. officer, 1988—; exec. v.p. Bearings Inc., 1988—, now chmn., ceo, b d. dirs. Bd. dirs. Lamson & Sessions, Cleve., Star Bank, Cleve. Bd. dirs., advisor Jr. Achievement, Cleve., 1962-64; bd. dirs. Luth. Med. Found.; fund raiser United Way, Cleve. and St. Louis Mem. Bearing Speciality Assn., Cleve. Athletic Club, Lakewood Country Club, Union Club, Univ. Club, Beta Gamma Sigma. Republican. Presbyterian. Avocations: tennis; water skiing; boating; snow skiing; golf. Office: Bearings Inc PO Box 6925 3600 Euclid Ave Cleveland OH 44115-2515

DANNER, DEAN WILSON, electrical engineer, manufacturing executive; b. Milw., June 9, 1950; s. George Wilson and Hazel B. (Damisch) D.; m. Bonita Mae Albert, June 19, 1971; children: Elizabeth, Matthew, Jonathan. BSEE, Marquette U., 1976; MBA, U. Wis., Whitewater, 1990. Registered profl. engr., Wis. Field engr. GTE Automatic Electric, Waukesha, Wis., 1972-74, purchasing agt. and tech. liason, 1974-76, mgr. product shop, 1976-78, mgr. engring., 1978-80; v.p. and dir. engring. Electronic Tele-Communications, Inc., 1980-86, exec. v.p., 1986-89, pres., 1989—, also bd. dirs. Patentee in field. Bd. dirs. Waukesha United Way, 1986—. Mem. IEEE, Nat. Soc. Profl. Engrs., Wis. Soc. Profl. Engrs., Independent Telephone Pioneer Assn., Roadrunners Internat. Republican. Roman Catholic. Lodge: Rotary (pres. 1983-84). Office: Electronic Tele-Communications Inc. 1915 Macarthur Rd Waukesha WI 53188-5702

DANNER, GEORGE WILSON, telecommunications executive; b. Chgo., Aug. 13, 1919; s. George L. and Lucille (Knott) D.; m. HAzel B. Damisch, Aug. 25, 1934; children: George M., Cynthia K., David L., Dean W., Lynne F. BS, Purdue U., 1965. Registered engr. Wis., 1970. Engr. Milw. Gas. & Light, 1941-47; ptnr. Wis. Instrument & Control, Milw., 1947-49; pres. Elec. Sec. Inds., Waukesha, Wis., 1949-59; v.p. Automatic Electric, 1959-80; chief exec. officer Electronic Tlee-Communications, 1980-93, chmn., 1980—. Bd. dirs. Barre-Ruth, Orlando, Fla., Electronic Tele-Communications. Bd. dirs. Waukesha C. of C., mem. fire & policy commn.; bldg. chmn. St. Mary Ch., Waukesha; bd. dirs. Merrill Country Club, Waukesha. Republican. Roman Catholic. Avocations: golf, bowling. Office: Electronic Telecom 1915 Mac Arthur Rd Waukesha WI 53188-5702

DANNER, KATHLEEN FRANCES STEELE, federal official; b. Kansas City, Mo., Oct. 28, 1960; m. Steve Danner, Jan. 18, 1996. Admissions counselor N.E. Mo. State U., Kirksville, 1980-83, assoc. dir. admissions, 1983-86, programming coord. dept. pub. svcs., 1986-87; Iowa, N.H. dir. Gephardt for Pres., St. Louis, 1987-88; mem. Mo. Ho. of Reps., Jefferson City, 1988-94; state dir. Clinton for Pres., 1991-92; regional dir. U.S. Dept. HHS, Kansas City, Mo., 1994—, acting dir. intergovtl. affairs Washington, 1998—. Pres. Greater Kansas City Fed. Exec. Bd. Pres. Greater Mo. Found.; exec. com. Heart of Am. United Way; mem. White House Outreach Task Force on CHIP. Recipient Hammer award V.P. Gore, 1999, award for disting. svc. Sec. Shalala, 1998. Mem. Ctrl. Exch., Nat. Women's Polit. Caucus. Roman Catholic. Avocations: sports enthusiast, dancing, reading, politics. Home: 6 Nantucket Ct Smithville MO 64089-9605 Office: US Dept Health and Human Svcs 601 E 12th St Ste 210 Kansas City MO 64106-2826

DANNER, PATSY ANN (MRS. C. M. MEYER), former congresswoman; b. Louisville, Jan. 13, 1934; d. Henry J. and Catherine M. (Shaheen) Berrer; children: Stephen, Stephanie, Shane, Shavonne.; m. C.M. Meyer, Dec. 30, 1982. Student, Hannibal-LaGrange Coll., 1952; B.A. in Polit. Sci. cum laude, N.E. Mo. State U., 1972. Dist. asst. to Congressman Jerry Litton, Kansas City, Mo., 1973-76; fed. co-chmn. Ozarks Regional Commn., Washington, 1977-81; mem. Mo. State Senate, 1983-1992, 103rd-106th Congress from 6th Mo. dist., 1993-2001. Mem. internat. rels. com., transp. and infrastructure com. Roman Catholic.*

D'ARCY, JOHN MICHAEL, bishop; b. Brighton, Mass., Aug. 18, 1932; Student, St. John's Sem., Brighton, 1949-57; ThD, Angelicum U., Rome, 1968. Ordained priest Roman Cath. Ch., 1957. Spiritual dir., prof. theology St. John's Sem., 1968-85; ordained titular bishop of Mediana and aux. bishop of Boston Archdiocese of Boston, 1975-85; bishop Diocese of Ft. Wayne-South Bend Ind., 1985—. Office: Diocese of Ft Wayne-South Bend PO Box 390 1103 S Calhoun St Fort Wayne IN 46801

DARKE, RICHARD FRANCIS, lawyer; b. Detroit, June 17, 1943; s. Francis Joseph and Irene Anne (Potts) D.; m. Alice Mary Renger, Feb. 14, 1968; children: Kimberly, Richard, Kelly, Sean, Colin. BBA, U. Notre Dame, 1965; JD, Detroit Coll. Law, 1969. Bar: Mich. 1969. Atty. AAA, Detroit, 1969-72; assoc. Oster & Mollett P.C., Mt. Clemens, Mich., 1972-73; ptnr. Small, Darke, Oakes P.C., Southfield, 1973-77; v.p., gen. counsel, sec. Fruehauf Corp., Detroit, 1977-92; ptnr. Darke & Wilson, Grosse Pointe Woods, Mich., 1993—. Mem. ABA, Mich. Bar Assn., Detroit Bar Assn., Machinery and Allied Products Inst. (counsel), Mich. Gen. Counsel Group, Essex Country Club, Lockmoor Club. Roman Catholic. Avocation: golfing. Home: 5700 N Pinnacle West Bloomfield MI 48322-1353

DARLING, ALBERTA STATKUS, state legislator, marketing executive, former art museum executive; b. Hammond, Ind., Apr. 28, 1944; d. Albert William and Helen Anne (Vaicunas) Statkus; m. William Anthony Darling, Aug. 12, 1967; children— Elizabeth Suzanne, William Anthony. BS, U. Wis., 1967. English tchr. Nathan Hale High Sch., West Allis, Wis., 1967-69, Castle Rock High Sch., Castke Rock, Colo., 1969-71, community vol. worker West Allis, Milw., 1971—; mem. Wis. State Assembly, 1990-92, Wis. Senate from 8th dist., Madison, 1992—. Cons. orgn. devel., Milw., 1982— ; dir. mktg. and communications Milw. Art Mus., 1981-88; exec. dir. mktg. architectural firm, 1988-90; State Rep. Wis., 1990—, mem. urban edn. com., children and human svcs. com., tourism com., homelessness com., teeenage pregnancy com., vice chmn. gov.'s housing policy commn., assembly coms. Pres. Community Action Seminar for Women, 1979-80; a founder Goals for Greater Milw. 2000, 1980-84; co-chair Action 2000, 1984-86; co-chmn. Icebreaker Am. Winterfestival; chmn. Community Action Seminar for Women, 1988; bd. dirs., exec. com. United Way, Milw., 1982-1992, chair project 1985, 1984-85, chmn. policy com. 1988; founder Today's Girls/Tomorrow's Women, Milw., pres. Jr. League Milw., 1980-82, Planned Parenthood Milw., 1982-84, Future Milw., 1983-85; vice chmn. State of Wis. Strategic Planning Council, 1988—, chmn. small bus./entrpreneur com.; mem. Greater Milw. Com.'s Mktg. Task Force, 1987-88; chmn. United Way Policy Com., 1987-88; participant Bus. Ptnrs. White House Conf., 1987; mem. summerfest adv. com. on Winter Festivals, 1989; founder Women's Fund of Milw. Found; actuve Juvenile Justice Leadership Com. Recipient Vol. Action award Milw. Civic Alliance, 1984, Community Service award United Way, 1984, Leader of Future award Milw. Mag., 1988, Nat. Assn. Community Leadership Orgn. award, 1986, Today's Girls/Tomorrow's Women Leadership award, 1987, Future Milw. Community Leadership award, 1988, Friend of Edn. Leadership award Head Start, 1994, William Steiger Humanitarian award, 1994. Mem. Greater Milw. Com., TEMPO Profl. Women, Am. Mktg. Assn. (Marketer of Yr. 1984), Pub. Relations Soc. Am., Ctr. for Pub. Representation (state bd. 1988), ARC (bd. dirs., exec. fin. coms. 1987—), Women's Fund (steering com. 1988), Internat. Assn. Bus. Communicators, Greater Milw. Com. Republican. Avocations: travel, art history, contemporary American literature, golf, tennis. Home: 1325 W Dean Rd Milwaukee WI 53217-2537 Office: State Capitol PO Box 7882 Madison WI 53707-7882

DARLING, JOHN ROTHBURN, JR. business educator; b. Holton, Kans., Mar. 30, 1937; s. John Rothburn and Beatrice Noel (Deaver) D.; m. Melva Jean Fears, Aug. 20, 1958; children: Stephen, Cynthia, Gregory. BS, U. Ala., 1959, M.S., 1960; Ph.D., U. Ill., 1967; Ph.D. (hon.), Chung Yuan Christian U., Taiwan, 1998. Divisional mgr. J.C. Penney Co., 1960-63; grad. teaching asst. U. Ill., Urbana, 1965-66; asst. prof. mktg. U. Ala., Tuscaloosa, 1966-68; assoc. prof. mktg. U. Mo., Columbia, 1968-71; prof. adminstrn., coord. mktg. Wichita State U., 1971-76; dean, prof. mktg. Coll. Bus. Adminstrn. So. Ill. U., Carbondale, 1976-81; v.p. acad. affairs and rsch., prof. internat. bus. Tex. Tech U., Lubbock, 1981-86; provost, v.p. acad. affairs, prof. mktg. and internat. bus. Miss. State U., Mississippi State, 1986-90; chancellor, disting. prof. internat. bus. La. State U., Shreveport, 1990-95; pres. Pittsburg (Kans.) State U., 1995-99, prof. mktg. and internat. bus., 1995-2000; vis. disting. prof. mktg. Rockhurst U., 2000—. Mktg. rsch. cons. Southwestern Bell, 1970; sr. v.p. Boothe Advt. Wichita, 1972; pres. Bus. Rsch. Assocs., 1972-76; cons. Bus. Rsch. Assocs., 1976-82; spl. cons. FTC, Washington, 1972-75, U.S. Dept. Justice, 1973-74, Atty. Gen., State of Kans., 1972-76, Dist. Atty. 18th Jud. Dist., Wichita, 1972-76, Maya Internat. Inc., Houston, 1995—, Morrison and Assocs., Inc., Shreveport, 1995-97; vis. disting. prof. internat. mktg. Helsinki Sch. Econs. and Bus. Adminstrn., 1993—. Author: (with Harry A. Lipson) Marketing Fundamentals, Text and Cases, 1980, (with Raimo Nurmi) International Management Leadership: The Primary Competitive Advantage, 1997; mem. bd. cons. editors Jour. Advt., 1984—; mem. editl. rev. bd. Jour. Internat. Bus. Studies, 1991—, Jour. Entrepreneurship, 1997—; contbr. articles to profl. jours. Bd. dirs. Outreach Found., 1973-79, v.p., 1975-77; trustee Graceland Coll., Lamoni, Iowa, 1976-82; mem. mgmt. com. Park Coll., Kansas City, 1976-79. Dist. Eagle Scout Awd., Boy Scouts Amer., 1998. Mem. Internat. Coun. Small Bus., Am. Mktg. Assn., Am. Mgmt. Assn., Acad. Internat. Bus., Am. Econs. Assn., Am. Arbitration Assn., (mem. nat. panel arbitrators and mediators 1993—), Nat. Assn. Intercollegiate Athletics (mem. governing bd. 1994-95), So. Bus. Adminstrn. Assn., So. Mktg. Assn., So. Econs. Assn., So. Assn. Colls. and Schs. (chair reaccreditation com. 1982-95, chair faculty qualifications criteria com. 1989-90, com. to rev. criteria for accreditation 1990-92, commr. 1992-95, Nat. Assn. State Univs. and Land-Grant Colls. (chair regional accreditation rev. com. 1989-90), Sales and Mktg. Execs. Internat., Beta Gamma Sigma, Phi Kappa Phi, Omicorn Delta Kappa, Phi Delta Kappa, Kappa Delta Phi, Mu Kappa Tau, Pi Sigma Epsilon, Alpha Kappa Psi, Chi Alpha Phi, Alpha Phi Omega, Phi Eta Sigma, Delta Mu Delta, Alpha Mu Gamma. Home: 12705 E 37th Terr Ct Independence MO 64055-3179 Office: Office of the President Pittsburg State Univ 1701 S Broadway St Pittsburg KS 66762-5856

DARLOW, JULIA DONOVAN, lawyer; b. Detroit, Sept. 18, 1941; d. Frank William Donovan and Helen Adele Turner; m. George Anthony Gratton Darlow (div.); 1 child, Gillian; m. John Corbett O'Meara. AB, Vassar Coll., 1963; postgrad., Columbia U. Law Sch., 1964-65; J.D. cum laude, Wayne State U., 1971. Bar: Mich. 1971, U.S. Dist. Ct. (ea. dist.)

Mich. 1971. Assoc. Dickinson, Wright, McKean, Cudlip & Moon, Detroit, 1971-78; ptnr. Dickinson, Wright, Moon, Van Dusen & Freeman and predecessor, 1978—2001; sr. v.p. Detroit Med. Ctr., 2001—01; cons. Dickinson, Wright, Moon, Van Dusen & Freeman and predecessor, Detroit, 2002—. Adj. prof. Wayne State U. Law Sch., 1974-75, 96; commr. State Bar Mich., 1977-87, mem. exec. com., 1979-83, 84-87, sec. 1980-81, v.p., 1984-85, pres.-elect 1985-86, pres. 1986-87, coun. corp. fin. and bus. law sect. 1980-86, coun. computer law sect. 1985-88; mem. State Officers Compensation Commn., 1994-96; chair Mich. Supreme Ct. Task Force on Gender Issues in the Cts., 1987-89. Reporter: Mich. Nonprofit Corp. Act, 1977-82. Bd. dirs. Hutzel Hosp., 1984—, chair, 2002-; bd. dirs. Mich. Opera Theater, 1985—, Mich. Women's Found., 1986-91, Detroit Med. Ctr., 1990—, Marygrove Coll., 1996—; trustee Internat. Inst. Met. Detroit, 1986-92, Mich. Met. coun. Girl Scouts U.S., 1988-91, Detroit coun. Boy Scouts Am., 1988—; mem. exec. com. Mich. Coun. for Humanities 1988-92; mem. Blue Cross-Blue Shield Prospective Reimbursement Com., Detroit, 1979-81; v.p., mem. exec. com. United Found., 1988-95; mem. Mich. Gov.'s Bilateral Trade Team for Germany, 1992-98. Fellow Am. Bar Found. (Mich. State chairperson 1990-96; mem. state officers compensation commn., 1994-96); mem. Detroit Bar Assn. Found. (treas. 1984-85, trustee 1982-85), Mich. Bar Found. (trustee 1987-94), Am. Judicature Soc. (bd. dirs. 1985-88), Internat. Women's Forum (global affairs com. 1994—), Women Lawyers Assn. (pres. 1977-78), Mich. Women's Campaign Fund (charter), Detroit Athletic Club. Democrat. Office: Dickinson Wright PLLC 500 Woodward Ave Ste 4000 Detroit MI 48226-3416

DAROFF, ROBERT BARRY, neurologist, educator; b. N.Y.C., Aug. 3, 1936; s. Charles and May (Wolin) D.; m. Jane L. Abrahams, Dec. 4, 1959; children: Charles II, Robert Barry, Jr., William Clayton BA, U. Pa., 1957, MD, 1961. Intern Phila. Gen. Hosp., 1961-62; resident in neurology Yale-New Haven Med. Center, 1962-65; fellow in neuro-ophthalmology U. Calif. Med. Center, San Francisco, 1967-68; prof. neurology, assoc. prof. ophthalmology U. Miami (Fla.) Med. Sch.; also dir. ocular motor neurophysiology lab. Miami VA Med. Center, 1968-80; Gilbert W. Humphrey prof., chmn. dept. neurology Case Western Res. U. Med. Sch.; also dir. dept. neurology Univ. Hosps., Cleve., 1980-93; prof. neurology, assoc. dean Case Western U., 1994—; staff neurologist Cleve. VA Med. Ctr., 1980-93; chief of staff, sr. v.p. acad. affairs U. Hosp., Cleve., 1994-2001. Med. sci. adv. bd., chmn. sci. program com. Myasthenia Gravis Found., 1984-87, exec. com., 1992—, sec., 1995-96, vice chair, 1997-99, chair, 1999-2001; med. adv. bd. Nat. Multiple Sclerosis Found., 1988-90, Soc. for Progressive Supranuclear Palsy, 1991-94; mem. nat. adv. eye coun. sensory and motor disorders vision panel NIH, 1980-83; mem. steering com. neurological disorders in comml. drivers U.S. Dept. Transp., chmn. task force, 1987; lectr. T.S. Srinivasan Endowment, Madras, India, 1994; Cumings lectr. Migraine Trust, London, 1994; lectr. Am. Coun. for Headache Edn., San Diego, 1996, vice chair, 2000—; hon. prof. Astana-State Med. Acad., Kazakhstan, 1999; mem. bd. advisors Capnia, Inc., 2000--. Book rev. editor: Neuro-ophthalmology, 1981-86, mem. editl. bd., 1987—; assoc. editor Jour. Biomed. Systems, 1970-72; editor Neurol. Progress, Anns. of Neurology, 1981-84; editor-in-chief Neurology, 1987-96; co-editor World Neurology, 1991-98, editl. adv. bd. 1998—; mem. editl. bd. Annals of Neurology, 1977-86, Archives of Neurology, 1976, Neurology and Neurosurgery Update Series, 1978-93, Headache, 1980-86; mem. editl. coun. Neurologia Croatica, 1991—; mem. editl. bd. Contemporary Neurology Series, 1989-93; contbr. numerous articles to profl. jours. Chmn. Young Tae Kwon Do Acad., North Miami, 1977-80; bd. dirs. Benign Essential Blepharospasm Rsch. Found., 1983—; trustee Fairhill Ctr. for Aging, 1988—, The Learning Corp., 1992-2000, Edison Bio Tech. Ctr., 1994-2001, Great Lakes Sci. Ctr., 1994—, Myasthenia Gravis Found. Am., 1999-2001; mem. tech. adv. coun. BIOMEC, Inc., 1999—; bd. trustees Greater Cleve. chpt. ARC, 1999--, mem. exec. com., 2000. Served with M.C. USAR, 1965-67. Recipient Ernst Jung-Medaille Für Medizin in Gold, 1993; Silver Jubilee Oration award Med. Coll. Trivandrum, India, 1994. Mem. AMA, Am. Neurol. Assn. (program adv. com. 1977-78, chmn. 1978, membership adv. com. 1980-83, chmn. 1981-83, nominating com. 1984, chmn. Annals of Neurology oversight com. 1984-86, councillor 1980-82, sec. 1985-89, pres.-elect 1989-90, pres. 1990-91, past pres. 1991-92, chair hon. membership com. 1994, hon. mem.), Am. Acad. Neurology (chmn. sci. program com. 1973-75, exec. bd. 1987-96, pub. com. 1993—, Netter lectr. 1989, hon. mem.), Rocky Mountain Neuro-ophthalmology Soc. (bd. dirs. 1980-86), N.Am. Neuro-ophthalmology Soc. (bd. dirs. 1986-94, chair cert. and accreditation com. 1997-98, publs. com. 1999—, Disting. Svc. award 1999), Internat. Neuro-Ophthalmology Soc. (mem. organizing com. 1986), Barany Soc., Am. Headache Soc. (bd. dirs., sec., chmn. membership com. 1998-2000, pres. 2002—), Internat. Headache Soc., Clin. Eye Movement Soc. (founder), World Fedn. Neurology (fin. com. 1985—, chmn. 1990-2001, chmn. pubs. com. 1987-2001, exec. com. Rsch. Group on Neuro-Ophthalmology 1987-95), Coun. Sci. Editors, Alliance for Brain Initiatives (founding mem.), Vietnam Vets. Inst. (bd. scholars 1998—), Assn. Columbiana de Neurologia (hon.), Acad. Med. Scis. Kazakhstan, Neuromuscular Disease Assn. Romania (internat. sci. com. 1991-93), Alpha Omega Alpha. Office: U Hosps Cleve 11100 Euclid Ave Cleveland OH 44106-1736 E-mail: rbd2@po.cwru.edu.

DARR, ALAN PHIPPS, curator, historian; b. Kankakee, Ill., Sept. 30, 1948; s. Milton Freeman, Jr. and Margaret (Phipps) D.; m. Mollie Hayden Fletcher, June 28, 1980; children: Owen, Alexander. BA, Northwestern U., 1970; MA, Inst. Fine Arts, NYU, 1975, PhD in Art History, 1980; Cert., Mus. Tng., Met. Mus. Art, 1976, Mus. Mgmt. Inst., U. Calif. Berkeley, 1980. Grad. intern Met. Mus. Art, N.Y.C., 1976; instr. NYU, 1976; asst. curator Detroit Inst. Arts, 1978-80, assoc. curator, 1980-81, curator in charge European sculpture and decorative arts, 1981—, Walter B. Ford II Family curator European sculpture and decorative arts, 1997—; postdoctoral fellow Harvard U. Ctr. for Italian Renaissance Studies at Villa I Tatti, Florence, 1988-89; adj. prof. Wayne State U., Detroit, 1982—; Paul Mellon vis. sr. scholar Ctr. Advanced Study in Visual Arts, Nat. Gallery, Washington, 1994. Co-editor/co-author: Italian Renaissance Sculpture in the Time of Donatello, 1985-86, Donatello Studien, 1989, Verrocchio and Late Quattrocentro Italian Sculpture, 1992, The Dodge Collection of Eighteenth Century French and English Art in the Detroit Institute of Arts, 1996, Woven Splendor: Five Centuries of European Tapestry in the Detroit Institute of Arts, 1996, Catalogue of the Italian Scuplture Collectionin the Detriot Inst. of Art, 2002, The Medici Michelangelo and the Art of Late Renaissance Florence, 2002, others; contbr. articles to profl. jours. Nat. Endowment Arts Mus. Profls. Fellow, 1983; John J. McCloy fellow, 1980-81, Ford Found. fellow, 1975-78, Met. Mus. Art fellow, 1975. Office: Detroit Inst Arts 5200 Woodward Ave Detroit MI 48202-4094

DARR, MILTON FREEMAN, JR. banker; b. Oak Park, Ill., Oct. 30, 1921; s. Milton Freeman and Frances Anna (Kaiser) D.; m. Margaret Claire Phipps, Jan. 27, 1945; children: Alan Phipps, Bruce Milton. B.S., U. Ill., 1942. With LaSalle Nat. Bank, Chgo., 1946-80, asst. cashier, 1950-53, asst. v.p., 1953, v.p., 1954-62, exec. v.p., dir., 1962-64, pres., 1964-68, chmn. bd., chief exec. officer, 1968-73, pres., 1974-77, vice chmn. bd., 1977-80. Organizer, founding dir. Buffalo Grove (Ill.) Nat. Bank, 1975; pres. Park Shore Tower Assn., Naples, Fla. Mem. Bd. Edn. Dist. 88 Community High Sch., 1963-68, Nat. Bd. YMCA's, 1973-77; past chmn., mem. Ill. Gov.'s Adv. Bd. on Cancer Control; chmn. commerce and industry com., treas. Chgo. Com. for Project Hope; state crusade chmn. Ill. div. Am. Cancer Soc., 1967, 68, chmn. bd., 1973-75, nat. bd. dirs., 1975-78; chmn. bd. mgrs., v.p. bd. trustees YMCA Met. Chgo., 1970-72; chmn. bd. trustees Elmhurst Coll., 1982-87, hon. life trustee, 1998—; chmn. YMCA Retirement Fund, 1986-92, trustee emeritus, 1994; trustee Ill. Cancer Council, Better Govt. Assn.; life trustee Union League Boys and Girls Clubs; chmn. Armed Forces Week, 1987; bd. dirs. Chgo. Crime Commn., United Charities of Chgo., Mid-Am. chpt. ARC; pres. Park Shore Tower Assn., Naples, Fla., 2001. Served to maj. USAAF, 1942-46. Recipient Distinguished Service award Am. Cancer Soc., 1976, Founders medal Elmhurst Coll., 1987; Citizen fellow Inst. Medicine of Chgo. Mem. Am. Inst. Banking (pres. Chgo. chpt. 1955-56, mem. exec. council 1956-59, nat. v.p. 1959-60, nat. pres. 1960-61), Am. Bankers Assn. (mem. adminstrv. com., exec. council 1960-61), Assn. Res. City Bankers (treas. 1969-72), Robert Morris Assos. (pres. Chgo. chpt. 1965-66), Chgo. Clearing House Assn. (past chmn.), Theta Chi. Presbyterian. Clubs: Rotarian (pres. 1973-74, Paul Harris fellow, Ches Perry fellow), Chicago, Bankers (pres. 1973), Economic, Executives, Union League (pres. 1968-69), Commerical (life, treas.) (Chgo.); Glen Oak Country; Moorings Country Club of Naples, Fla. Home: Residence N206 5 Oakbrook Club Dr Oak Brook IL 60523-6860 Office: 135 S La Salle St Chicago IL 60603-4159

DARROW, RUSSE M. corporate executive; CEO Russ Darrow Group, West Bend, Ind. Office: Russ Darrow Group PO Box 515 West Bend WI 53095-0515

DART, KENNETH, food container manufacturing executive; Pres., CEO Dart Container Corp., Mason, Mich. Office: Dart Container Corp 500 Hogsback Rd Mason MI 48854-9547

DART, THOMAS J. state legislator; b. May 22, 1962; BA, Providence Coll., 1984; JD, Loyola U., 1987. Former asst. state atty., Ill.; Ill. state rep. Dist. 28; fl. leader, minority spokesman Rev. Com. Mem. Judiciary I Com. and Legis. Com. on Juvenile Justice; lectr. St. Xavier Coll. Recipient Disting. Svc. award Com. for Honest Govts., Disting. Lectr. award DeBoer Com. for Children's Rights, Exceptional Legis. award Office of Pub. Guardians. Address: 10231 S Western Ave Chicago IL 60643-1917

DARWIN, DAVID, civil engineering educator, researcher, consultant; b. N.Y.C., Apr. 17, 1946; s. Samuel David and Earle (Rives) D.; m. Diane Marie Mayer, June 29, 1968; children: Samuel David, Lorraine Marie. BS, Cornell U., 1967, MS, 1968; PhD, U. Ill., 1974. Registered profl. engr., Kans. Asst. prof. civil engring. U. Kans., Lawrence, 1974-77, assoc. prof., 1977-82, prof., 1982—, Deane E. Ackers disting. prof. civil engring., 1990—, dir. Structural Engring. and Materials Lab., 1982—; dir. Infrastructure Rsch. Inst., 1998-2001. Cons. David Darwin, Lawrence, 1976—. Author: Steel and Composite Beams with Web Openings, 1990; also numerous articles. Mem. Uniform Bldg. Code Bd. Appeals, Lawrence, 1978-84. Capt. U.S. Army, 1967-72, Vietnam. Grantee NSF, 1976—, Kans. Dept. Transp., 1980-82, 90—, Air Force Office Sci. Rsch., 1985-92, Civil Engring. Rsch. Found., 1991-95, Fed. Hwy. Adminstrn., 1994-98, S.D. Dept. Transp., 2001—, Nat. Cooperative Hwy. Rsch. Program, 1994-95; recipient Miller award U. Kans., 1986, Irvin Youngberg Rsch. Achievement award, 1992; Bellows scholar, 2001—02. Fellow ASCE (editor Jour. Structural Engring. 1994-2000, bd. govs. Structural Engring. Inst. 2000—, Kans. sect. v.p./pres.-elect 2001—, Huber rsch. prize 1985, Moisseiff award 1991, state-of-the-art of civil engring. award 1996, 2000, Richard R. Torrens award 1997), Am. Concrete Inst. (pres. Kans. chpt. 1975, bd. dirs. 1988-91, Bloem Disting. Svc. award 1986, Arthur R. Anderson award for disting. rsch. 1992, Structural Rsch. award 1996); mem. AAAS, Am. Soc. Engring. Edn., ASTM, Am. Inst. Steel Constrn. (profl.), Prestressed Concrete Inst. (profl.), Post-Tensioning Inst. (profl.), Concrete Rsch. Coun. (chmn. 1990-96), Structural Engring. Inst. (bd. govs. 2000—), Phi Kappa Phi (pres. U. Kans. chpt. 1976-78). Democrat. Unitarian. Avocations: swimming, walking. Office: U Kans Civil Environ and Archtl Engring Dept 2006 Learned Hall 1530 W 15th St Lawrence KS 66045-7609 E-mail: daved@ku.edu.

DASBURG, JOHN HAROLD, quick service restaurant executive; b. N.Y.C., Jan. 7, 1943; s. Jean Henry and Alice Etta Dasburg; m. Mary Lois Diaz, July 6, 1968; children: John Peter, Kathryn. AA, U. Miami, 1963; BS in Indsl. Engring., U. Fla., 1966, MBA, 1971, JD, 1973. Bar: Fla. 1974; CPA, Fla., Md. Staff Peat Marwick Mitchell & Co., Jacksonville, Fla., 1973-78, tax ptnr. in charge, 1978-80; v.p. tax Marriott Corp., Washington, 1980-82, v.p. fin., 1982-84, sr. v.p., 1984-85, exec. v.p., CFO, chief real estate officer, 1985-88, pres. lodging group, 1988-89; pres., CEO Northwest Airlines, 1990-2001; chmn., CEO, pres. Burger King Corp., Miami, Fla., 2001—. Bd. dirs. St. Paul Cos., Genuity. Contbr. articles to profl. jours. Lt. (j.g.) USN, 1966-69, Vietnam. Republican. Roman Catholic.

DASCHLE, THOMAS ANDREW, senator; b. Aberdeen, S.D., Dec. 9, 1947; m. Linda Hall Daschle; children: Kelly, Nathan, Lindsay. B.A., S.D. State U., 1969. Fin. investment rep.; chief legis. aide, field coordinator Sen. James Abourzek, 1973-77; mem. 96th-97th Congresses from 1st S.D. Dist., U.S. Ho. of Reps., 1978—86, 98th-99th Congresses at large, 1983-87; U.S. senator from S.D., 1986—; senate minority leader 104th, 105th, 106th, 107th Congress, 1996—2001; majority leader, 2001. Mem. agrl. nutrition and forestry com., mem. fin. com., rules com., co-chmn. Sen. Dem. steering and coord. com., co-chair Sen. Dem. tech. and comm. com., chmn. Sen. Dem. conf. com., co-chmn. Sen. Dem. policy com.; leader bipartisan effort ; author, enforcer Agent Orange Act, 1991; authored, reformulated gasoline provisions of Clean Air Act Amendment 1990. Founder Am. Grown Found., 1987. Served to 1st lt. USAF, 1969-72. Recipient Nat. Commdr.'s award Disabled Am. Vets., 1980, Disting. Alumni award S.D. State U., 1997, VFW Congl. award VFW, 1997, Legislator of Yr. award Vietnam Vets. Am., 1997, Cert. Appreciation, Nat. Assn. Federally Impacted Sch., 1997, Congl. Leadership award Cmty. Anti-Drug Coalitions Am., 1997, Golden Triangle award Nat. Farmer's Union, 1997-98, Outstanding Vets. Adv. of Yr. award Disabled Am. Vets. Dept. S.D., 1998, Pres. Recognition award Nat. Indian Impacted Schs. Assn., 1998, Cert. Appreciation, Nat. Assn. Alcoholism and Drug Abuse Counselors, 1998, Diplomat award Rapid City C. of C., 1998, Disting. Svc. award Nat. Rural Electric Coop. Assn., 2000; named Outstanding Young Man of Yr., U.S. Jaycees, 1981, Friend of Edn., S.D. Edn. Assn., 1997, Person of the Yr., Nat. Assn. Concerned Vets., 1997, Legislator of Yr., Renewable Fuels Assn., 1998, Maj. Gen. Williamson's S.D. Nat. Guard Militia Man of 1998, S.D. Nat. Guard. Democrat. Roman Catholic. Office: US Senate 509 Hart Senate Bldg Washington DC 20510-0001

DASH, LEON DECOSTA, JR. journalist; b. New Bedford, Mass., Mar. 16, 1944; s. Leon DeCosta and Ruth Elizabeth (Kydd) D. BA, Howard U., 1968; DHD, Lincoln U., 1996. Reporter Washington Post, 1966-68, 71-79, African bur. chief, 1979-83, with investigations desk, 1984-98; prof. journalism & afro-Am. studies U. Ill., Champaign, 1998-99, Swanlund chair prof. journalism and Afro-Am. studies, 2000—01, Swanlund prof. journalism, 2001—. Vis. prof. U. Calif.-San Diego, 1978 Author: (with Ben H. Bagdikian) The Shame of the Prisons, 1972, When Children Want Children: The Urban Crisis of Teenage Childbearing, 1989, Rosa Lee: A Mother and Her Family in Urban America, 1996 (Polit. Book award Washington Monthly Mag. 1997, 1st prize Harry Chapin Best Book award World Hunger Year Orgn. 1997). Peace Corps vol., Kenya, 1969-70. Recipient George Polk Meml. award Overseas Press Club, 1974, award for internat. news reporting Washington-Balt. Newspaper Guild, 1974, hon. mention Washington-Balt. Newspaper Guild, 1975, Internat. Reporting awards Africare, 1984, Capitol Press Club, 1984, 1st Place Journalism award Gen. News, Nat. Assn. Black Journalists, 1986, Investigative Reporters and Editors award, 1987, Editl. award for news series Chesapeake Associated Press (co-winner), 1987, 1st Prize award Washington-Balt. Newspaper Guild, 1987, Pres.'s award Washington Ind. Writers Assn., 1989, Editl. award Chesapeake Associated Press (co-winner), 1989, Martha Albrand Spl. Citation for Nonfiction PEN, 1990, Pulitzer Prize for explanatory journalism, 1995, 1st prize Robert F. Kennedy award for print journalism, 1995, Emmy award for pub. affairs NATAS, 1996, Polit. Book award The Washington Monthly Mag., 1997, Prevention for a Safer Soc. award Nat. Coun. on Crime and Delinquency for Rosa Lee book, 1997; fellow Henry J. Kaiser Family Found., 1995-96; Washington Post 8-part series Rosa Lee's Story selected one of Best 100 Works iin 20th Century Am. Journalism, 1999. Office: U Ill Dept Journalism 119 Gregory Hall 810 S Wright St Urbana IL 61801-3644 E-mail: leondash@uiuc.edu.

DASKIN, MARK STEPHEN, civil engineering educator; b. Balt., Dec. 3, 1952; s. Walter and Betty Jane (Fax) D.; m. Babette Reva Levy, July 2, 1978; children: Tamar, Keren. BSCE, MIT, 1974; postgrad. study in Engring., Cambridge, England, 1975; PhD in Civil Engring., MIT, 1978. Tchg. asst. trans. sys. divsn. civil engring. MIT, Cambridge, 1976-77; asst. prof. civil engring. Univ. Tex., Austin, 1978-79, Northwestern U., Evanston, Ill., 1980-83, assoc. prof. civil engring., 1983-89, prof., 1989—, chair dept. indsl. engring. and mgmt. scis., 1995—2001. Author: Network and Discrete Location: Models, Algorithms and Applications, 1995; editor-in-chief Transp. Sci., 1991-94; assoc. editor Location Sci., 1991-2000; contbr. articles to profl. jours. Bd. dirs. North Suburban Synagogue Beth El, Highland Park, Ill., 1991-94. Univ. Tex. Bur. Engring. Rsch. grant, 1978-79, Northwestern Univ. Transp. Ctr. grant, 1980, 81, NSF grant, 1980-82, 84-90, 93-97, 96-99, Urban Mass Transp. Adminstr. grant, 1982-84, 84-85, United Parcel Svc. grant, 1983-86, 91-92, Thermo-King Corp. grant, 1990-91, 92-94, Heartland Blood Ctr. grant, 1992, 96; recipient Fulbright Rsch. award, 1989-90, Burlington Northern Found. Faculty Achievement award, 1985, NSF Presdl. Young Investigator award, 1984, Scott Paper Leadership award, 1973-75, IIE Tech. Innovation award in indusl. engring. Mem. ASCE, Inst. Indsl. Engrs. (editor-in-chief IEE Transactions 2001—), INFORMS (v.p. publs. 1996-99), Ops. Rsch. Soc. Am. (jour. editor 1991-94), Inst. Mgmt. Sci., Sigma Xi, Tau Beta Pi, Chi Epsilon. Avocations: swimming, photography. Office: Northwestern U Dept Indsl Engring Mgmt Sci Evanston IL 60208-0001 E-mail: daskin@iems.nwu.edu.

DATTILO, THOMAS A. diversified corporation executive; B.A., OH State U.; LLB, U. Toledo. Mem., corporate legal staff Dana Corp., 1977-82, with ins. operations dvsn., 1982-85, v.p. then gen. mgr., Precision Control Divsn. NC, 1985—; pres. and CEO Hayes-Dana Inc., St. Cahtarines, Ont., Can.; pres. Victor Reinz Products, N. Am., Lisle, IL, 1997-; pres., sealing products group Dana Corp., Toledo, 1997-98; pres. and COO Cooper Tire and Rubber Co., Findlay, 1999—. Mem. Young President's Orgn., Automotive Parts Manufacturer's Assoc. Office: Cooper Tire & Rubber Co. 701 Lima Ave Findlay OH 45840-2388

DAUB, PEGGY ELLEN, library administrator; b. Bluffton, Ohio, Oct. 15, 1949; d. Perry J. and Olive L. (Hoover) D.; m. Jeffrey H. Cooper, Dec. 13, 1975; 1 child, William P. Cooper-Daub. MusB summa cum laude, Miami U., 1972; MA, Cornell U., 1975; MSLS, U. Ill., 1980; PhD, Cornell U., 1985. Acting asst. music libr. Yale U., 1980-81, head of music tech. svcs., rare books libr. Music Libr., 1981-82; head Music Libr. U. Mich., Ann Arbor, 1982-89, head Spl. Collections & Arts Librs., 1989-99, head Spl. Collections Libr., 2000—. Presenter Rare Books and Manuscript Sect. Pre-Conf., New Orleans, 1993, Bloomington, 1995 and others. Contbr. articles to profl. jours. Co-clk. Ann Arbor Friends Meeting, 1997-2001. Travel grantee Ctr. for Internat. Studies, Cornell U., 1977. Mem. ALA (Assn. Coll. and Rsch. Librs. rare books and manuscripts sect., mem. task force on interlibr. loan 1991-93, mem. preconf. program planning com. 1992-94), Music Libr. Assn. (bd. dirs. 1985-87, mem. resource sharing and collection devel. com. 1982-91), Rsch. Librs. Group (chairperson music program com. 1985-87, mem. steering com. 1982-87), Am. Musicol. Soc. (mem. coun. 1988-91, mem. coun. com. on minorities/diversity 1988-91), Phi Beta Kappa. Mem. Soc. of Friends. Office: U of Mich Spl Collections Libr 711 Graduate Libr Ann Arbor MI 48109-1205 E-mail: pdaub@umich.edu.

DAUCH, RICHARD E. automobile manufacturing company executive; b. 1942; BS, Purdue U., 1964. With Gen. Motors Corp., 1964-75; group v.p. mfg. Volkswagen of Am., 1976-80; v.p. Chrysler Corp., 1980, exec. v.p. diversified ops., 1980-81, exec. v.p. stamping assembly diversified ops., 1981-84, exec. v.p. mfg., 1984-1994; pres., CEO Am. Axle & Mfg., 1994-97, chmn., CEO, pres., 1997—. Recipient Eli Whitney Meml. award Soc. Mfg. Engrs., 1987, Ellis Island medal of honor, 1997; named industry leader of yr. Automotive Hall of Fame, 1997, mfr. of yr. Mich. Mfg. Assn., 1997, newsmaker of yr. Crain's Detroit Bus., 1998, world trader of yr. Detroit Regional Chamber, 2002. Office: American Axle & Mfg 1840 Holbrook St Detroit MI 48212-3442

DAUGAARD, DENNIS M. state legislator, professional society administrator; b. Garretson, S.D., June 11, 1953; m. Linda Kay Schmidt; 3 children. BS, U. S.D., 1975; JD, Northwestern U., 1978. Bar: S.D. Atty. Supena & Nyman, 1978-79, Shand Morahan & Co., 1979-81; bank trust offier 1st Bank S.d., 1981-90; devel. dir. Children's Home Soc., 1990—; mem. S.D. Senate from 9th dist., Pierre, 1996—. Mem. Nat. Soc. Fund Raising Execs., S.D. Bar Assn., S.D. Planned Giving Coun., Siox Falls (S.D.) Estate Planning Coun., Rotary. Republican. Lutheran. Office: State Capitol Bldg 500 E Capitol Ave Pierre SD 57501-5070

DAUNER, MARVIN K. former state legislator; b. Dec. 4, 1927; m. Shirley Ann; 5 children. County commr., 1974-86; state rep. Minn. Ho. Reps., Dist. 9B, 1986-97. Vice chmn. health & human svc., mem. agrl. housing, taxes & transp. & transit coms., Minn. Ho. Reps. Named Outstanding Young Farmer, 1960. Mem. Farm Bur. Fedn. Home: RR 2 Box 21 Hawley MN 56549-9506

DAUPHINAIS, GEORGE ARTHUR, import company executive; b. Waterbury, Conn., Apr. 11, 1918; s. Arthur J. and Nell (Phillips) D.; m. Sarah McConnell, Dec. 27, 1942; children: Carol Joe, George William, Sarah Marie. B.S. in Mech. Engring., La. State U., 1942. Advanced engrng. program Gen. Electric Co., Schenectady, 1942, engr., 1942-47; with H.K. Porter Co., Inc., Phila., 1947-59, successively plant engr., works mgr., 1947-52, v.p., gen. mgr., 1952-59; v.p. Electric Autolite Co., Toledo, 1960—; pres. Prestolite Internat. Co. div. Eltra Corp., 1964—; group v.p. Sangamo Electric Co., Springfield, 1965-76; pres. Dauphin Company. Mem. ASME, Tau Beta Pi, Sigma Alpha Epsilon. Home and Office: 933 111th Ave NE Bellevue WA 98004-4486 E-mail: geodau4@aol.com.

D'AURORA, JAMES JOSEPH, psychologist, consultant; b. Canton, Ohio, Feb. 10, 1949; s. James Joseph Sr. and Arsilia (Lombardi) D'A.; m. Denise Marie Linkenhoker, Dec. 28, 1974; children: Andrew David, Elizabeth Clare. BA, U. Notre Dame, 1971; MEd, Kent State U., 1974; PhD, U. Minn., 1984. Lic. psychologist, Minn.; cert. Nat. Register Health Svc. Providers in Psychology. Pre-major adv. Coll. of Liberal Arts U. Minn., Mpls., 1974-75; intern Bach Inst., 1975-77, staff psychologist, 1977-79; psychologist Loring Family Clinic, 1979-81; pvt. practice, 1981-86; cons. psychologist Solstice: A Ctr. for Psychotherapy and Learning, St. Paul, 1986-89; pvt. practice, 1989—. Cons. in field, 1975—; researcher Family Renewal Ctr., Mpls., 1982-85, Golden Valley Health Ctr. Psychology Subsect., 1988-92. Lectr., lay homilist, choir Christ the King Ch., mem. parish pastoral coun., 1991—96; interim sch. bd. Christ the King-St. Thomas the Apostle Sch., 1992; bd. dirs., 1992—96; mem. governance com., 1992. Mem.: APA, Minn. Psychol. Assn. (chmn. ins. com. 1988—94), Minn. Soc. Clin. Hypnosis, Nat. Register Health Svcs. Providers in Psychology, N.W. Athletic Club (adv. bd. club run 1997—2000, chair 1999—2000, bd. dirs. Twin Cities Marathon 2001, sec. 2001—02), Notre Dame Club Minn. (bd. dirs. 1986—91, sec. 1987—88, v.p. 1988—89, pres. 1989—90). Mem. Democratic Farm Labor Party.

Roman Catholic. Achievements include being qualifier, finisher 100th Boston marathon, 1996;104th Boston marathon, 2000. Home: 5536 Merritt Cir Edina MN 55436-2026 Office: 91 Snelling Ave N Ste 200 Saint Paul MN 55104-6753

DAVENPORT, PAUL, university president, economics educator; BA in Econs. with gt. distinction/honors, Stanford U., 1969; MA, U. Toronto, 1970, PhD, 1976, LLD (hon.), 2000, U. Alta., 1994. Prof. econs. McGill U., Montreal, Que., Can., 1972-89, assoc. dean grad. studies Can., 1982-86, vice prin. planning and computer svcs. Can., 1986-89; pres., vice chancellor U. Alta., Edmonton, Alta., Can., 1989-94, U. Western Ont., London, Can., 1994—. Chair Assn. Univs. and Colls. Can., 1997-99, Coun. Ont. Univs., 1999-2001. Editor: (with Richard H. Leach) Reshaping Confederation: The 1982 Reform of the Canadian Constitution, 1984. Mem. policy program adv. com. on econ. growth Can. Inst. for Advanced Rsch.; mem. bd. govs. London Health Scis. Ctr., Loncon Econ. Devel. Corp.; bd. dirs. Nat. Ballet Sch. Decorated chevalier Legion of Honor (France). Mem. Can. Assn. Economists, Am. Econ. Assn., Phi Beta Kappa. Office: U Western Ont-Off of President Stevenson-Lawson Bldg London ON Canada N6A 5B8 E-mail: pdavenpo@uwo.ca.

DAVIDO, SCOTT, retail executive; b. 1961; BS in Acctg. and Econs., JD, Case Western Reserve U. Ptnr. Jones, Ray, Reavis & Pogue, Pittsburgh; sr. v.p., gen. counsel/sec. Elder-Beerman, Dayton, Ohio, 1997-99, exec. v.p., CFO, treas., 1999—. Contbr. articles to profl. jours. Office: Elder-Beerman Stores Corp PO Box 1448 Dayton OH 45401-1448

DAVIDS, GREGORY M. state legislator; b. Aug. 28, 1958; m. Bonnie; 3 children. BS, Winona State U., 1979; postgrad., Mankato State U. Mayor City of Preston (Minn.), 1987-91; state rep. Minn. Ho. Reps., Dist. 31B, 1991—. Mem. fin. instr. & ins., health & human svc., human svc. fin. divsn. & housing coms., Minn. Ho. Reps. Mem. Lions. Home: PO Box 32 Preston MN 55965-0032

DAVIDSON, ERNEST ROY, chemist, educator; b. Terre Haute, Ind., Oct. 12, 1936; s. Roy Emmette and Opal Ruth (Hugunin) D.; m. Reba Faye Minnich, Jan. 27, 1956; children: Michael Collins, John Philip, Mark Ernest, Martha Ruth. BSc, Rose-Hulman Inst. Tech., 1958, DEng (hon.), 1998; PhD, Ind. U., 1961; PhD (hon.), Uppsala U., 2000. NSF Postdoctoral fellow U. Wis.-Madison, 1961-62; asst. prof. chemistry U. Wash., 1962-65, assoc. prof., 1965-68, prof., 1968-84, Ind. U., Bloomington, 1984-86, disting. prof., 1986—2002, chmn. chem. dept., 1999—. Disting. vis. prof. Ohio State U., 1974-75; vis. prof. IMS, Japan, 1984, Technion, Israel, 1985; Boys-Rahman lectr. Royal Soc. Chemistry, 2002. Editor: Jour. Computational Physics, 1975-98, Internat. Jour. Quantum Chemistry, 1975—, Jour. Chem. Physics, 1976-78, 98—, Chem. Physics Letters, 1977-84, Jour. Am. Chem. Soc., 1978-83, Jour. Phys. Chemistry, 1982-90, Accounts of Chem. Rsch., 1984-92, Theoretica Chimica Acta, 1985-98, Chem. Revs., 1986—; contbr. numerous articles on density matrices and quantum theory of molecular structure to profl. jours. Union Carbide fellow Rose-Hulman Inst. Tech., 1958; NSF fellow Ind. U., 1961; recipient Hirschfelder prize in theoretical chemistry, 1997-98, Schrodinger medal, 2001, Nat. medal of sci., 2002; Sloan fellow, 1967-68; Guggenheim fellow, 1974-75; laureate l'Academie Internationale des Sciences Moleculaires Quantiques, 1971. Fellow Am. Phys. Soc., Sigma Xi; mem. NAS, Am. Chem. Soc. (Computers in Chemistry award 1992, Theoretical Chemistry award 2000), Am. Acad. Arts and Scis., Ind. Acad. Sci. (Chemist of Yr. award 1999), Phi Lambda Upsilon, Tau Beta Pi. Home: 1013 Woodbine Ct Bloomington IN 47401-5445 Office: Ind U Chemistry Dept 800 E Kirkwood Ave Bloomington IN 47405-7102

DAVIDSON, JO ANN, state legislator; children: Julie, Jenifer. Mem. Ohio Ho. of Reps., Columbus, 1981—, minority whip, speaker. Mem. fin., ethics and stds. and rules coms., house speaker, minority leader, mem. joint com. on mental retardation and devel. disabilities. Mem. Reynoldsburg (Ohio) City Coun., 1968-77; former vice chmn. Ohio Turnpike Commn.; trustee Franklin U., U. Findlay, Ohio; mem. Columbus Area Women's Polit. Caucus. Named Legislator of Yr., Nat. Rep. Legislators Assn., 1991; named to Ohio Women's Hall of Fame, 1991. Mem. Oho C. of C. (v.p. spl. programs), Rotary. Home: 6639 Forrester Way Reynoldsburg OH 43068-4315 Office: Ohio Ho of Reps State House 77 S High St Fl 14 Columbus OH 43266-0001

DAVIDSON, RICHARD K. railroad company executive; b. Allen, Kans., Jan. 9, 1942; s. Richard B. and Thelma (Rees) D.; m. Lynne P. Durham, July 11, 1998; children: Richard Byron, Elizabeth Ann. BA in History, Washburn U., 1965, D of Commerce (hon.), 1984. Brakeman, conductor Mo. Pacific R.R., St. Louis, 1960-66, transp. tng. program, 1966, asst. trainmaster, trainmaster, 1966-75, asst. supt. to asst. v.p. ops., 1975-76; v.p. ops. Mo. Pacific Railroad, 1976-85, Union Pacific R.R., Omaha, 1985-89, exec. v.p. ops., 1989-91, chmn., CEO, 1991—; pres. Union Pacific Corp., 1994—, COO, 1995-97, chmn., pres., COO, 1997—. Mem. Happy Hollow Club. Office: Union Pacific RR 1416 Dodge St Omaha NE 68179-0002

DAVIDSON, RICHARD LAURENCE, geneticist, educator; b. Cleve., Feb. 22, 1941; B.A., Case Western Res. U., 1963, Ph.D., 1967. Asst. prof. Harvard Med. Sch., Boston, 1970-73, assoc. prof. microbiology and molecular genetics, 1973-81; research assoc. human genetics Children's Hosp. Med. Ctr., 1970-81; head dept. molecular genetics U. Ill. Med. Ctr., Chgo., 1981—, Benjamin Goldberg prof. genetics, 1981—. Co-dir. Cell Cult Ctr., MIT, Boston, 1975-81; mem. mammalian genetics study sect. NIH, 1975-81; mem. human cell biology adv. panel NSF, 1973-75. Editor-in-chief: Somatic Cell Genetics. U.S. Air Force Office Research-NRC fellow, 1967-68, Ctr. Molecular Genetics, Paris, 1967-70. Mem. AAAS, Tissue Culture Assn., Cell Biology Assn. Office: U Ill at Chicago Head Dept Mol Gen (M/7 669) 900 S Ashland Ave Ste 669 Chicago IL 60607-4046

DAVIDSON, STANLEY J. lawyer; b. Chgo., Oct. 22, 1946; BA with honors, U. Ill., 1968; JD, Loyola U., 1971. Bar: Ill. 1971, U.S. Dist. Ct. (no. dist.) Ill. 1973, U.S. Ct. Appeals (7th cir.) 1982, U.S. Supreme Ct. 1982. Law clk. to Hon. Thomas J. Moran Ill. Appellate Ct. (2nd dist.), 1971-73; ptnr. Hinshaw & Culbertson, Chgo. Mem. ABA, Am. Soc. Hosp. Attys., Ill. State Bar Assn., Chgo. Bar Assn., Appellate Lawyers Assn. (bd. dirs. 1978-80, treas. 1982-83, sec. 1983-84, v.p. 1984-85, pres. 1985-86), Soc. Trial Lawyers, Am. Bd. Trial Advocates, Def. Rsch. Inst., Decalogue Soc. Lawyers. Office: Hinshaw & Culbertson 222 N La Salle St Ste 300 Chicago IL 60601-1081

DAVIDSON, WILLIAM M. diversified company executive, professional basketball executive; b. 1921; divorced. LL.B., Wayne State U.; B.B.A., U. Mich.; JD, Wayne State U. Pres. CEO Guardian Glass Co., Northville, Mich., 1957-68; pres., CEO, dir. Guardian Industries Corp., 1968—; majority owner Detroit Pistons, NBA, 1974—, mng. ptnr. Served with USN. Office: Guardian Industries Corp 2300 Harmon Rd Auburn Hills MI 48326 also: care Detroit Pistons 2 Championship Dr Auburn Hills MI 48326-1753

DAVIS, BARBARA SNELL, college educator; b. Painesville, Ohio, Feb. 21, 1929; d. Roy Addison and Mabelle Irene (Denning) Snell; children: Beth Ann Davis Schnorf, James L., Polly Denning Davis Spaeth. BS, Kent State U., 1951; MA, Lake Erie Coll., 1981; postgrad., Cleve. State U., 1982-83. Cert. reading specialist, elem. prin., Ohio. Dir. publicity Lake Erie Coll., Painesville, 1954-59; tchr. Mentor (Ohio) Exempted Village Sch. Dist., 1972-86, prin., 1986-97; mem. faculty Lake Erie Coll., 1997—. Contbr. articles to profl. jours. Former trustee Mentor United Meth. Ch. Mem. Delta Kappa Gamma (pres. 1982-84), Phi Delta Kappa (pres. 1992-93), Theta Sigma Phi (charter). Home: 7293 Beechwood Dr Mentor OH 44060-6305 Office: 326 College Hall Lake Erie Coll Painesville OH 44077 E-mail: beachbumbarb@aol.com.

DAVIS, BUTCH, professional football coach; Former asst. coach Dallas Cowboys; head coach U. Miami Hurricaines, 1995—. Office: Cleveland Browns 76 Lou Groza Blvd. Berea OH 44017

DAVIS, COLE, recreational vehicle manufacturing executive; CEO, pres. Keystone RV, Goshen, Ind. Office: Keystone RV 3819 Augusta Ln Elkhart IN 46517

DAVIS, DANNY K. congressman; b. Parkdale, Ark., Sept. 6, 1941; m. Vera Davis; children: Jonathon, Stacey BA, Ark. A. M. & N. Coll., 1961; MA, Chgo. State U., 1968; PhD, Union Inst., 1977. Mem. U.S. Congress from 7th Ill. dist., 1997—; mem. com. on govt. reform and oversight, com. on small bus.; mem. subcom. of census. Chgo. alderman, 1979-90; commr. Cook. County, 1990-96; candidate Chgo. mayor, 1991; founder, pres. Westside Assn. for Community Action; pres. Nat. Assn. Community Health Ctrs.; co-chmn. Clinton/Gore/Moseley-Braun Ill. campaigns, 1992; bd. dirs. Nat. Housing Partnership. Office: 3333 W Arthington St Ste 130 Chicago IL 60624-4102 also: 1222 Longworth Bldg Washington DC 20515-1307*

DAVIS, DAVID, newscaster; Degree, U. Tenn., Knoxville, 1977. Broadcast reporter KREX-TV, Grand Junction, Colo.; anchor KLAS-TV, Las Vegas, Nev., KATV-TV, Little Rock; morning anchor, reporter WISN 12, Milw., 1988—. Telethon vol. Children's Miracle Network; co-emcee telethon Briggs and Stratton Run/Walk for Children's Hosp. Wis., Cerebral Palsy. Recipient award for best newscast and spot news coverage, AP, Emmy award. Office: WISN PO Box 402 Milwaukee WI 53201-4020

DAVIS, DAVID AARON, journalist; b. San Diego, Feb. 8, 1959; m. M. Caroline Berry, Sept. 5, 1987; children: Anne Elizabeth, Caroline Camille, Aaron Edward. BA, Colo. Coll., 1983; MSJ, Columbia U., 1985. Reporter The Gazette, Charleston, W.Va., 1986, The Dayton (Ohio) Daily News, 1987-90, The Plain Dealer, Cleve., 1990—. Paul Miller Journalism lectr. Okla. State U., 1996. Recipient Best Consumer Journalism award Nat. Press Club, Washington, 1987, Sigma Delta Chi award for investigative reporting Soc. Profl. Journalists, Greencastle, Ind., 1993, Freedom of Info. award AP Mng. Editors Assn., 1993, Max Karant award excellence in aviation reporting Aircraft Owners & Pilots Assn., 1993, 94, George Polk award L.I. U., 1995, Heywood Broun award Comms. Workers of Am., 1998. Mem. Investigative Reporters & Editors Inc. (IRE medal 1993), Soc. Environ. Journalists. Office: The Cleveland Plain Dealer 1801 Superior Ave E Cleveland OH 44114-2198

DAVIS, DEFOREST P. architectural engineer; From staff cons. to chmn., CEO Lester B. Knight & Assocs., Inc., Chgo., 1966-91, pres., CEO, 1987-91, chmn., CEO, 1991—. Trustee Knight Charitable Trust, Chgo., 1989—, Lake Forest (Ill.) Coll., 1992—, St. George's Sch., Newport, R.I., 1988-97, Grant Hosp. and Healthcare Ctr. Found., Chgo., 1992—; mem. adv. bd. dirs. Code, Hennessy & Simons, Chgo., Fiduciary Mgmt. Assocs., Chgo., Constrn. Bus. Rev., McLean, Va.; bd. dirs. Surgipath Med. Industries, Inc., Richmond, Ill. Mem. Chgo. Club (pres.), Econ. Club Chgo. (membership com.), Exec.'s Club Chgo. Office: Lester B Knight & Assocs 549 W Randolph St Ste 701 Chicago IL 60661-2208

DAVIS, DON H., JR. multi-industry high-technology company executive; Engring. sales trainee Allen-Bradley (aquired by Rockwell 1985), 1963-66, dist. mgr. Ala., 1966-79, gen. mgr. programmable contr. divsn., 1979-80, v.p. programmable contr. divsn., 1980-82, v.p., gen. mgr. indsl. control divsn., 1982-85, sr. v.p., 1985-86, head indsl. control group, 1986-87, sr. v.p., gen. mgr. indsl. computer and comm. group, 1987-89, pres., 1989-93, corp. sr. v.p., pres. automation, 1993-95, pres., COO, 1995-97, pres., CEO, 1997-98; chmn., CEO Rockwell Internat. Corp., 1998—. Bd. dirs. Sybron Internat., Ingram Micro, Inc. Nat. trustee Boys and Girls Clubs Am.; chmn. bd. L.A. Mfg. Learning Ctr.; regent Milw. Sch. Engring. Mem. Internat. Soc. for Measurement and Control (hon. chmn.), Nat. Elec. Mfrs. Assn. (past chmn. bd. govs.), Bus. Roundtable, The Conf. Bd. (sr.). Office: Rockwell Internat Corp 777 E Wisconsin Ave Ste 1400 Milwaukee WI 53202-5302

DAVIS, DORATHEA, state legislator; State rep. dist. 63 Mo. Ho. of Reps. Democrat. Office: 2017 Menard St Saint Louis MO 63104-3929

DAVIS, EDGAR GLENN, science and health policy executive; b. Indpls., May 12, 1931; s. Thomas Carroll and Florence Isabelle (Watson) Davis; m. Margaret Louise Alandt, June 20, 1953; children: Anne-Elizabeth Davis Polestra, Amy Alandt, Edgar Glenn Davis Jr. AB, Kenyon Coll., 1953; MBA, Harvard U., 1955. With Eli Lilly & Co., Indpls., 1958—63, mgr. budgeting and profit planning, 1963—66, mgr. econ. studies, 1966—67, mgr. Atlanta sales dist., 1967—68, dir. market rsch. and sales manpower planning, 1968—69, dir. mktg. plans, 1969—74, exec. dir. pharm. mktg. planning, 1974—75, exec. dir. corp. affairs, 1975—76, v.p. corp. affairs, 1976—90, v.p. health care policy, 1990; pres., chmn. bd. dirs. Centre for Health Sci. Info., Boston, 1990—; fellow Ctr. for Bus. and Govt. Kennedy Sch. of Govt. Harvard U., 1991—; adj. prof. Butler U., Indpls. Exec. in residence Butler U. Coll. Bus.; mem. Inst. Ednl. Mgmt., Harvard U. Grad. Sch. Edn., 1987; chmn. staff Bus. Roundtable Task Force on Health, 1981—85; U.S. rep. UN Indsl. Devel. Orgn. Conf., Lisbon, 1980, Casablanca, 81, Budapest, 83, Madrid, 87; participant meeting of experts on pharms UNIDO , 1981; rep. to UN Commn. on Narcotic Drugs, Vienna, 1981, UN Econ. and Social Coun., N.Y.C., 1981, UN Indsl. Devel. Orgn. Conf. ; Ctr. for Bus. and Govt. fellow Kennedy Sch. Govt., Harvard U.; co-chmn. Harvard Conf. on Govt. Role in Civilian Tech., 1992, Harvard Conf. Pharmaceutical Rsch., Innovation and Pub. Policy, 1993, Harvard Biotech. Roundtable, 1991—; vis. scholar, advisor Health and Welfare Unit, Inst. for Econ. Affairs, London; vis. scholar Green Coll. Oxford (Eng.) U., 1994—; chmn. Nat. Fund for Med. Edn., 1994—; dir. English Speaking Union, Indpls.; gov. Soc. Indiana Pioneers; lectr. in field. Contbr. articles to profl. jours. Pres. Eli Lilly and Co. Found., 1976—88; pres., chmn. bd. Indpls. Health Inst., 1988—91; trustee Kenyon Coll., Gambier, Ohio, Ind. Hist. Soc.; pres. bd. trustees Boston Biomed. Rsch. Inst.; chmn. Nat. Fund for Med. Edn., 1996—; bd. dirs. Carnegie Coun. on Ethics and Internat. Affairs, 1985—92; accredited nongovtl. observer rep. to UN Goodwill Found. Ind. Inc., 1987—95; bd. dirs. Sta. WFYI Pub. TV, Indpls., 1983—91, Indpls. Mus. Art, Am. Symphony Orch. League, 1987—92, Nat. Health Coun., 1984—91, Pub. Affairs Coun., Washington, Nat. Fund for Med. Edn.; bd. advisors Christian Theol. Sem., N.C. Schl Arts, Bishops Sch., LaJolla, Calif.; chmn. bd. dirs. Ind. Repertory Theatre, 1979—85; vice chmn., exec. com., bd. dirs. Indpls. Symphony Orch. and Ind. State Symphony Soc., 1977—91; chmn. task force on fine arts Commn. for Future of Butler U.; chmn. exec. com. Pan Am. Econ. Leadership Conf. 10th Pan Am. Games, Indpls.; mem. Chgo. Coun. on Fgn. Rels.; bd. govs. Soc. Ind. Pioneers; trustee Boston Biomed. Rsch. Inst., 1991—. Fellow: The Hudson Inst. (sr. adj. Indpls.); mem.: Inst. Medicine NAS, Ind. Soc. Pioneers (bd. govs.), NAM (vice-chmn. health policy com. 1987—91, bd. dirs.), Literary Club Indpls., Reform Club London, Traders Point Hunt Club, N.Y. Yacht Club, Edgartown Golf Club, Chappaquiddick Beach Club, Crooked Stick Golf Club, Lambs Club, Contemporary Club, Woodstock Club, Yacht Club, Edgartown Yacht Club , Naples (Fla.), Met. Club (Washington). Office: Butler U Coll Bus Adminstrn 4600 Sunset Ave Indianapolis IN 46208-3487 Fax: 317-940-9455.

DAVIS, ERIC KEITH, professional baseball player; b. L.A., May 29, 1962; m. Erica D. Baseball player Cin. Reds, 1980-91, 96, L.A. Dodgers, 1991-93, Detroit Tigers, 1993-94, Balt. Orioles, 1997-98, St Louis Cardinals, 1998—. Mem. Nat. League All-Star Team, 1987, 89, Nat. League Silver Slugger team, 1987,89, NL Gold Glove 1987-89; named to Sporting News Nat. League. All-Star team, 1987, 89; named Nat. League Comeback Player of Yr., 1996. Achievements include playing in World Series, 1990. Office: St Louis Cardinals 250 Stadium Plz Saint Louis MO 63102-1722*

DAVIS, ERROLL BROWN, JR. utility executive; b. Pitts., Aug. 5, 1944; s. Erroll Brown and Eleanor Margaret (Boykin) D.; m. Elaine E. Casey, July 13, 1968; children: Christopher, Whitney Diploma in elec. engring., Carnegie-Mellon U., 1965; MBA in Fin., U. Chgo., 1967. Corp. fin. staff Ford Motor Co., Detroit, 1969-73, Xerox Corp., Rochester, N.Y., 1973-78; v.p. fin. Wis. Power and Light Co., Madison, 1978-82, v.p. fin and pub. affairs, 1982-84, exec. v.p., 1984-87, pres., 1987, pres., CEO, 1988-98; pres. WPH Holdings, 1990—98; pres., CEO Alliant Energy, Madison, 1998—, chmn., 2000—. Bd. dirs. BP plc, PPG Industries. Active Selective Svc. Bd., Madison, 1982-2001; mem. bd. regents U. Wis., 1987-94; bd. dirs. United Way Dane County, 1984-89, chmn. bd. dirs., 1987; life trustee Carnegie Mellon U., chmn. bd. trustees, 2000—; bd. dirs. Competitive Wis., 1989—, Ednl. Comm. Bd., 1992-94; chmn. Start Smart of Dane County. Mem. Am. Soc. Corp. Execs., Wis. Mfg. and Commerce (bd. dirs. 1986—, chmn. 1994-95), Am. Gas Assn. (bd. dirs. 1990-95), Electric Power Rsch. Inst. (bd. dirs. 1990—), Assn. Edison Illuminating Cos. (bd. dirs. 1993—), Edison Electric Inst. (bd. dirs. 1995—, chmn. 2002--, DOE electricity adv. bd.). Avocations: tennis, golf. Office: Alliant Energy 4902 N Biltmore Ln Madison WI 53718

DAVIS, EVELYN MARGUERITE BAILEY, artist, organist, pianist; d. Philip Edward and Della Jane (Morris) Bailey; m. James Harvey Davis, Sept. 22, 1946. Student pub. schs., Springfield; student art, Drury Coll.; piano, organ student of Charles Cordeal. Sec. Shea and Morris Monument Co., before 1946; past mem. sextet, soloist Sta. KGBX. Tchr. Bible, organist, pianist, vocal soloist, dir. youth choir Bible Bapt. Ch., Maplewood, Mo., 1956-69; pvt. instr. piano and organ, voice Croma Harp, Affton, Mo., 1960-71, St. Charles, Mo., 1971-83; Bible instr. 3d Bapt. Ch., St. Louis, 1948-54; pianist, soloist, tchr. Bible Temple Bapt. Ch., Kirkwood, Mo., 1969-71; asst. organist-pianist, vocal soloist, tchr. Bible, Bible Ch., Arnold, Mo., 1969; faculty St. Charles Bible Bapt. Christian Sch., 1976-77; organist for Dr. Jack Van Impe Crusades and Dr. Oliver B. Green Crusades; organist, pianist, soloist, Bible tchr., dir. youth orch., music arranger, floral arranger Bible Bapt. Ch., St. Charles, 1971-78; organist, vocal soloist, floral arranger, Bible tchr. Faith Missionary Bapt. Ch., St. Charles, 1978-82; organist, floral arranger, vocal soloist Belleview Bapt. Ch., Springfield, Mo., 1984-90; tchr. piano, organ, voice, organist, Springfield, 1983—; pianist Golden Agers Pk. Crest Bapt. Ch., Springfield, 1991; interior decorator, floral arranger, organist, vocal soloist for weddings and funerals. Composer: I Will Sing Hallelujah, (cantata) I Am Alpha and Omega, Prelude to Prayer, My Shepherd, O Sing unto the Lord a New Song, O Come Let Us Sing unto the Lord, The King of Glory, The Lord Is My Light and My Salvation, O Worship the Lord in the Beauty of Holiness, The Greatest of These Is Love, Prayer to the Lord Our God, We Will Sing Praises, His Name Is Jesus, From Bethlehem's Manger to the Cross, The King of Kings Is Coming! Alleluia! To the Throne You Go, The Eyes of God, also numerous hymn arrangements for organ and piano. Past pianist, Sunday sch. tchr., mem. choir East Ave. Bapt. Ch. Fellow Internat. Biog. Assn. (life), Am. Biog. Inst. Rsch. Assn. (life); mem. Nat. Guild Organists, Nat. Guild Piano Tchr. Auditions, Internat. Platform Assn. Home: 5135 E Farm Road 174 Rogersville MO 65742-8220

DAVIS, F(RANCIS) KEITH, civil engineer; b. Bloomington, Wis., Oct. 23, 1928; s. Martin Morris and Anna (Weber) D.; m. Roberta Dean Anderson, May 25, 1957; 1 child, Mark Francis. BSCE, S.D. State U., 1950. Registered profl. engr., Mo., Ind., Nebr., Mich., Colo., Ariz., Oreg. With firm Howard, Needles, Tammen & Bergendoff, Kansas City, Mo., 1950—, asst. chief structural designer, 1960-65, project mgr., sect. chief, 1965-76, dep. chief structural engr., 1976-79, chief engr., 1979—. Mem. bd. advisers N.W. Kans. Area Vocat. Tech. Sch., 1977-80, chmn., 1979-80. With U.S. Army, 1951-53. Fellow ASCE; mem. NSPE, Mo. Soc. Profl. Engrs., Am. Ry. Engring. Assn. (tech. com. 1981—), Homestead Country Club. Home: 5024 Howe Dr Shawnee Mission KS 66205-1465 Office: PO Box 419299 1201 Walnut St Kansas City MO 64106-2117 E-mail: kdavis@hntb.com.

DAVIS, GEORGE CULLOM, historian; b. Aurora, Ill., May 2, 1935; s. George Cullom and Mary Elizabeth (Scripps) D.; m. Marilyn Louise Whittaker, June 22, 1957 (div. Mar. 1974); children: Catherine, Lesa, Charles; m. Ann Elizabeth Chapman, May 27, 1976. AB, Princeton U., 1957; MA, U. Ill., Urbana, 1961, PhD, 1968; Dr of History (hon.) , Lincoln Coll., 1999; Diploma of Honor, Lincoln Meml. U., 1995; DHL (hon.) , Knox Coll., 2000. Instr. Punahou Sch., Honolulu, 1957-59, U. Ill., Urbana, 1962-64; asst. prof. Ind. U., Bloomington, 1964-70, assoc. dean, 1967-70; assoc. prof. Sangamon State U., Springfield, Ill., 1970-74, prof., 1974-95; prof. emeritus, 1995—; prof. history U. Ill.-Springfield, 1974—; dir., sr. editor Lincoln Legal Papers Documentary Edit., 1988—. Bd. dirs. Bank One, Springfield; cons. John Nuveen & Co., Chgo., 1989—, Meml. Med. Ctr., Springfield, 1991—. Author: History With a Tape Recorder: An Oral History Handbook, 1972, 4th edit., 1985; co-author: Oral History: From Tape to Tape, 1977, Bench and Bar on the Illinoir Frontier, 1979, The Prairie Bondman, 1996, Memorial Days, 1997; editor: Bicentennial Studies in Sangamon History, 1973-78; co-editor: The Public and the Private Lincoln: Contemporary Perspectives, 1979, Abraham Lincoln Association Papers, 1981-86, The Law Practice of Abraham Lincoln: Complete Documentary Edit. (DVD-ROM), 2000; contbr. numerous articles to profl. jours.; editl. advisor Scholar Book Revs. on CD-ROM, 1991-93. Del. Dem. Nat. Conv., 1972; pres. Springfield Pub. Schs. Found., 1987-88. Recipient Pelzer award Orgn. Am. Historians, 1962, award of Merit Ill. State Hist. Soc., 1975, Writer of Yr. award Friends of Lincoln Libr., 1989; Fulbright Rsch. scholar, 1987-88; fellow Newberry Libr., 1977, NEH/Woodrow Wilson Found. Inst., 1980, NEH Summer Inst. on Pub. History, 1984; grantee Ill. Bicentennial Commn., 1974-75, Ill. State Libr., 1975, 79-81, Ill. Legis. Coun., 1979-87, Ill. Humanities Coun., 1980-82, NEH, 1990-92, 94—, Nat. Hist. Publs. and Records Commn., 1990—, Ill. Bar Found., 1990-91, Ency. Britannica, 1991, Shelby C. Davis Found., 1991—, William Nelson Cromwell Found., 1992—. Mem. Manuscript Soc., Assn. for Documentary Editing (chmn. constitution com. 1990-94, pres. 1997-98), Ill. Coalition of Libr. Advocates (bd. dirs. 1982-84), Ill. Humanities Coun. (bd. dirs. 1983-89, vice chair 1985-87, chair 1987-89), Ill. State Hist. Soc. (v.p. 1974-75, 82-83, bd. dirs. 1979-82, exec. com. 1979-82, adv. bd. 1994—), Sangamon County Hist. Soc. (bd. dirs. 1971-74, 79-82, v.p. 1981-82, 90-91, pres. 1991-92), Orgn. Am. Historians (treas. 1984-93), Oral History Assn. (nominating com. 1978-79, 85-87, colloquium program com. 1978, chmn. nat. workshop 1979, nat. coun. 1980-85, v.p. 1982-83, pres. 1983-84), Abraham Lincoln Assn. (bd. dirs. 1977—, chmn. publs. com. 1981-87, v.p. 1984-86, pres. 1995-96). Democrat. Home: 2624 E Lake Shore Dr Springfield IL 62707-5533 Office: Lincoln Legal Papers Old State Capitol Springfield IL 62701

DAVIS, GLENN CRAIG, psychiatrist; b. Columbia, Mo., Apr. 26, 1946; s. Morris S. and Dorothy (Hall) D.; children: Jason Michael, Galen Brent. BA, Reed Coll., 1968; MD, Duke U., 1972. Diplomate Am. Bd. Psychiatry and Neurology. Intern, then resident Duke U. Med. Ctr., Durham, N.C., 1972-75; clin. assoc. NIMH, Bethesda, Md., 1975-77, chief of drug abuse unit, biological psychiatry br., 1977-79; assoc. prof. U. Tenn. Ctr. Health Scis., Memphis, 1979-81; assoc. prof. then prof. Sch. of Medicine Case Western Reserve U., Cleve., 1981-87; dir. psychiat. rsch. to chief of staff Cleve. VA Med. Ctr., 1981-87; chair psychiatry Henry Ford Med. Ctr., Detroit, 1987-92; v.p. behavioral svcs. Henry Ford Health System, 1991-94, v.p. acad. affairs, 1992—2001, chief med. officer suburban regions, 1996-98, assoc. dean Case Western Reserve U., 1993—2001; prof. psychiatry Case Western Reserve U., Cleve., 1994—2001; pres. Am. Bd. Psychiatry & Neurology, Deerfield, IL; dean coll. of human medicine Mich. State U., East Lansing, Mich., 2001—. Clin. prof. U. Mich. Sch. Medicine, Ann Arbor, Mich., 1988—. Author numerous scientific rsch. papers and book chpts.; contbr. articles to profl. jours. Lt. comdr. USPHS U.S. Army, 1975—79. Fellow Am. Psychiat. Assn., Am. Psychopathological Assn.; mem. AAAS, AMA, Biol. Psychiatry, Am. Bd. Psychiatry and Neurology (dir. 1996—, pres. 2000), Am. Bd. Med. Specialties, Sigma Xi, Alpha Omega Alpha. Office: Mich State U A-110 East Fee Hall East Lansing MI 48824 E-mail: gdavis@msu.edu.

DAVIS, GREGORY THOMAS, marine surveyor; b. Evergreen Park, Ill., Jan. 19, 1952; s. Bernard Thomas and Helen Therese (Keehan) D.; m. Christine Ellen Luka, Aug. 25, 1975; children: Brian Thomas, Bonnie Jean. BA, Coll. of Santa Fe, 1973. Cert. marine surveyor, fire and explosion investigator, bd. cert. forensic examiner. Adjuster Gen. Adjustment Bur., Chgo., 1973-74; marine surveyor Graham Miller Ltd., London, 1974-76; marine surveyor, pres. Davis and Co. Ltd., Lisle, Ill., 1977—. Guest lect. Tec Core, Wheeling, Ill., 1990—; mem. ad hoc com. on marine fuel U.L. Marine, Northbrook, Ill., 1986—; mem. Am. Bd. Forensic Examiners. Contbr. articles to profl. jours. Parents adv. bd. U. San Diego, 2000-2001. Mem. Nat. Assn. Marine Surveyors (chmn. ins. com. 1982-95, chair yachts and small crafts tech. com. 2000—), Am. Boat and Yacht Coun. (bd. dirs. 1999—), Nat. Fire Protection Assn. (permanent mem. 303 com. 1997—), Am. Soc. for Non-destructive Testing, Nat. Assn. Fire Investigators, Internat. Assn. Arson Investigators, Internat. Assn. Marine Investigators, Soc. of Naval Architects and Marine Engrs. (mem. 0-45 panel 1997—), Nat. Marine Mfrs. Assn. (mem. boating industry risk mgmt. com., edn. com.). Avocations: computer, boats, fishing, golf. Office: Davis and Co Ltd 1989 University Ln Ste I Lisle IL 60532-4132 E-mail: gdavis@daviscoltd.com.

DAVIS, HARRY REX, political science educator; b. Ozona, Tex., Nov. 9, 1921; s. Rex Otis and Mima (Gowin) D.; m. Ruth Elizabeth Greenlee, Sept. 6, 1947; children: Peter Gowin, Scott Andrew, Martha Greenlee. BA summa cum laude, Tex. Christian U., 1942; AM, U. Chgo., 1949, PhD, 1951; postdoctorate, Union Theol. Sem., 1952-53. Teaching fellow Tex. Christian U., 1945-46; mem. faculty dept. govt. Beloit (Wis.) Coll., 1948-90, assoc. prof., 1956-59, prof., 1959-90, chmn. dept., 1959-84, prof. emeritus, 1990—. Cons. ch. and soc. dept. World Council Chs., 1969 Author: (with others) Small City Government, 1962, Colleges and Commitments, 1971; Editor: (with others) Reinhold Niebuhr on Politics, 1960. Mem. Beloit City Coun., 1959-60; chmn. Beloit Dem. Com., 1956, 61-63; local mgr. campaigns congl. candidates; mem. Beloit Bd. Ethics, 1975-81, Wis. Gov.'s Coun. on Jud. Selection, 1983-86; mem. Beloit Bd. Health, 1996—, chmn., 1996-98. With USAAF, 1942-45. Ford faculty fellow, 1952-53; Social Sci. Research Council grantee; Rockefeller Found. grantee. Mem. Midwest Polit. Sci. Assn. (sec.-treas. 1959-65, mem. exec. coun. 1966-68), Am. Polit. Sci. Assn. (chmn. Burdette award com. 1979), Am. Soc. Polit. and Legal Philosophy, Soc. Christian Ethics. Democrat. Presbyterian (elder, coun. on ch. and society 1965-72, Gen. Assembly commr. 1991). Home: 735 Harrison Ave Beloit WI 53511-5529 Office: Beloit Coll Dept Government Beloit WI 53511

DAVIS, HENRY BARNARD, JR. lawyer; b. East Grand Rapids, Mich., June 3, 1923; s. Henry Barnard and Ethel Margaret (Turnbull) D.; m. Margaret Lees Wilson, Aug. 27, 1946; children: Caroline Dellenbusch, Laura Davis, George B. BA, Yale U., 1945; JD, U. Mich., 1950; LLD, Olivet Coll., 1983. Bar: MIch. 1951, U.S. Dist. Ct. (we. dist.) Mich. 1956, U.S. Ct. Appeals (6th cir.) 1971, U.S. Supreme Ct. 1978. Assoc. Allaben, Wiarda, Hayes & Hewitt, 1951-52; ptnr. Hayes, Davis & Dellenbusch PLC, Grand Rapids, Mich., 1952—. Mem. Kent County Bd. Commrs., 1968-72; mem. Cmty. Mental Health Bd., 1970-94, past chmn.; trustee, sec. bd. Olivet Coll., 1965-91, trustee emeritus, 1991—; bd. dirs. Jr. Achievement Grand Rapids, 1960-65; chair Grand Rapids Historic Preservation Com., 1977-79; trustee East Congregational Ch., 1979-81. Served with USAAF, 1943-46, Philippines. Mem. ABA, Mich. Bar Assn., Grand Rapids Round Table (pres. 1969), Masons. Republican. Home: 30 Mayfair Dr NE Grand Rapids MI 49503-3831 Office: 535 Fountain St NE Grand Rapids MI 49503-3421 E-mail: DavisHBdr@aol.com.

DAVIS, HOWARD TED, engineering educator; b. Hendersonville, N.C., Aug. 2, 1937; s. William Howard and Gladys Isabel (Rhodes) D.; m. Eugenia Asimakopoulos, Sept. 15, 1960 (dec. July 1996); children: William Howard II, Maria Katherine. BS in Chemistry, Furman U., 1959; PhD in Chem. Physics, U. Chgo., 1962. Postdoctoral fellow Free U. of Brussels, 1962-63; asst. prof. U. Minn., Mpls., 1963-66, assoc. prof., 1966-69, prof., 1969-80, prof., head chem. engring. and materials sci., 1980-95, dean Inst. Tech., 1995—, Regent's prof., 1997—. Editor: Springs of Creativity, 1981; author: Statistical Mechanics of Phases, Interfaces and Thin Films, 1995, (with K. Thomson) Linear Algebra and Linear Operators in Engineering, 2000; contbr. over 500 articles to sci. and engring. jours. Fellow Sloan Found., 1967-69, Guggenheim Found., 1969-70. Mem. AAAS, AIChE (Walker award for excellence in publs. 1990), NAE, Am. Chem. Soc., Soc. Petroleum Engrs., Minn. Fedn. Engring. Socs. (Disting. Engr. 1998). Democrat. Methodist. Avocations: tennis, golf, reading, movies. Home: 1822 Mount Curve Ave Minneapolis MN 55403-1018 Office: U Minn 421 Washington Ave SE Minneapolis MN 55455-0373 E-mail: davis@itdean.umn.edu.

DAVIS, H(UMPHREY) DENNY, publisher; b. Fayette, Mo., May 8, 1927; s. Lionel Winchester and Sarah Elizabeth (Denny) D.; m. Barbara Ellen Hartsgrove, June 6, 1954; 1 child, Thomas Shackelford. Student, Central Meth. Coll., Fayette, 1944-45, 46-47; BJ, U. Mo., 1949. Reporter, wire editor S.E. Missourian, Cape Girardeau, 1949-54; corr. UPI, Oklahoma City, Tulsa, Denver, 1954-55, exec. Albuquerque, 1955-56, bur. mgr. Lima, Peru, 1955-58, mgr. for Brazil Rio de Janeiro, 1958-68; mgr. no. div. Latin Am. Mexico City, 1968-75; regional exec. Charlotte, N.C., 1975-78; founder, owner pub. Wood Creek Corp., Fayette, 1978—; editor Fayette Advertiser and Democrat-Leader, 1984—2001. Author profl. manual; contbr. articles to mags. and newspapers. Chmn. Fayette Planning and Zoning Commn., 1980-87; chmn. Howard County Rep. Cen. Com., Fayette, 1982-98; pres. Franklin or Bust, Inc., Fayette, 1988-2000; mem. Santa Fe Trail Nat. Hist. Trail Nat. Adv. Coun., 1991-97. With USN, 1945-46, 50-51. Mem. NRA, Santa Fe Trail Assn., Fayette Round Table Club (pres. 1989-90), Fayette Area Heritage Assn. (v.p. 1989-91), Am. Legion. Republican. Episcopalian. Avocation: local history. Home: 400 N Church St Fayette MO 65248-1125 Office: Wood Creek Corp PO Box 132 Fayette MO 65248-0132 E-mail: hddavis@mcmsys.com.

DAVIS, IRVIN, advertising, public relations, broadcast executive; b. St. Louis, Dec. 18, 1926; s. Julius and Anna (Rosen) D.; m. Adrienne Bronstein, Apr. 25, 1968; 1 child, Jennifer Alison. BSBA, Washington U., 1950; postgrad., St. Louis U., 1952; D Humanities (hon.), Nat. Coll., 1981. Pres. Clayton-Davis & Assoc., Inc., St. Louis, 1953—, Admiral Broadcasting Corp., St. Louis, 1983—. C.p., bd. dirs. Nat. Acad. TV Arts and Scis., 1982—; bd. dirs. Truman Bank; pres. Galtex Broadcasting; pres. Celebrities Prodns. Author: (books) Room for Three, Comprehensive Tng. in Advt. and Pub. Relations; producer (film) Family Album, 1974, Use It in Good Health, Charlie, 1975. Pres. Child Assistance Program, 1986—92; v.p. Boys and Girls Town Mo., St. James, 1976—99, Make Today Count, 1985—86; bd. dirs. Jackie Joyner Kersee Found., 1997—2001, Crusade Against Crime, St. Louis, 1984—; v.p. St. Louis Artists Guild, 2002—. Sgt. USAF, 1945—47, PTO. Recipient Freedom Found. award, 1975, Internat. Film and TV Festival award, 1973-75, Internat. Broadcasting award Hollywood Advt. Club, 1965, 77, 82, 83, Cinegolden Eagle award Coun. on Internat. Non-Theatrical Events, 1975, Nat. Emmy award, 1991. Mem.: Am. Fedn. TV and Radio Arts, Am. Med. Writers Assn., Pub. Rels. Soc. Am. (accredited), St. Louis Club, Press Club, Advt. Club. Office: Clayton-Davis & Assoc Inc 8229 Maryland Ave Saint Louis MO 63105-3697

DAVIS, JACK WAYNE, JR. b. Toledo, May 21, 1947; s. Jack Wayne and Virginia (Moore) D.; m. Amélie Claiborne Matthews, June 24, 1977; 1 child, Claiborne Levering. Grad., Harvard Coll., 1969. Mng. editor Figaro, New Orleans, 1972-73; reporter, columnist, asst. city editor, city editor Item, 1973-80; metro editor The Times - Picayune, 1980-83; assoc. metro editor, night metro editor, metro editor The Chgo. Tribune, 1983-87; editor, v.p. Daily Press, Newport News, Va., 1987-94, pres., pub., CEO, 1994-98; pres. Tribune Interactive Inc., 1998-00, pub.,v.p. planning, 2000—. Frank Knox fellow U. Rajasthan, India, 1971, Profl. Journalism fellow Stanford U., 1977-78. Mem. Am. Soc. Newspaper Editors. Avocations: sculling, reading. Office: Hartford Courant 285 Broad Street Hartford CT 06115-2510

DAVIS, JAMES FREDERICK, chemical engineer, researcher, educator, consultant; b. Urbana, Ill., Aug. 8, 1952; BSCE, U. Ill., 1974; MSCE, Northwestern U., Evanston, Ill., 1978, PhD in Chem. Engring., 1981. Rsch. engr. Amoco Chems., Naperville, Ill., 1974-76; postdoctoral rsch. assoc. Northwestern U., Evanston, 1981-82; lectr. U. Wis., Madison, 1982-83; asst. prof. Ohio U., Columbus, 1983-89, assoc. prof., 1989-94, prof., 1994—, assoc. dir. rsch. computing, 1992-95, dir. univ. tech. svcs., 1995—. Cons. numerous chem. and refining cos., 1983—; bd. trustees Computer Aids in Chem. Engring. Corp., Austin, Tes., 1987—. Author: (chpt.) Neural Networks in Process Operation, 1994; contbr. over 90 articles to profl. jours. Mem. IEEE, AIChE (dir. computer and system tech. 1991-94). Achievements include patent in portable infusate heating device; development of intelligent systems technology area in chemical and process engineering. Office: Ohio State Univ Univ Tech Svcs 320 Baker Systems Bldg 1971 Neil Ave Columbus OH 43210-1210

DAVIS, JAMES ROBERT, cartoonist; b. Marion, Ind., July 28, 1945; s. James William and Anna Catherine (Carter) D.; m. Jill Carol Davis; 1 son, James Alexander. B.S., Ball State U., Muncie, Ind., 1967. Artist, Groves & Assocs., advt., Muncie, 1968-69; asst. to cartoonist: Tumbleweeds comic strip, 1969-78; cartoonist: Garfield comic strip, 1978— ; TV script Here Comes Garfield, 1982, Garfield on the Town, 1983 (Emmy award 1984), Garfield in the Rough, 1984 (Emmy award 1985), Garfield's Halloween Adventure, 1985 (Emmy award 1986), Garfield in Paradise, 1986, Garfield Goes Hollywood, 1987, The Garfield Christmas Special, 1987; author: Garfield at Large, 1980, Garfield Gains Weight, 1981, Garfield Bigger Than Life, 1981, Garfield Weighs In, 1982, Garfield Takes the Cake, 1982, Garfield Treasury, 1982, Here Comes Garfield, 1982, Garfield Sits Around the House, 1983, Garfield Second Treasury, 1983, Garfield Eats His Heart Out, 1983, Garfield Tips the Scale, 1984, Garfield Loses his Feet, 1984, Garfield: His Nine Lives, 1984, Garfield Makes It Big, 1985, Garfield Rolls On, 1985, Third Garfield Treasury, 1985, Garfield Out to Lunch, 1986, The Unabridged, Uncensored, Unbelieveable Garfield Book, 1986, Garfield Food for Thought, 1987, The 4th Garfield Treasury, 1987, The Garfield Cat Naming Book, 1988, Garfield Chews the Fat, 1989, The 5th Garfield Treasury, 1989, Happy Birthday, Garfield, 1989, Garfield, Tiens Bon La Rampe, 1989, Garfield's Longest Catnap, 1989, Garfield The Big Star, 1989, Garfield in the Park, 1989, Garfield and the Tiger, 1989, Mini-Mysteries featuring Garfield, 1990, Garfield: The Me Book: A Guide to Superiority, How to Get It, Use It, and Keep It, 1990, Garfield's Judgement Day, 1990, Garfield's Feline Fantasies, 1990, Garfield Stories, 1990, Garfield on the Farm, 1990, Garfield Hangs Out, 1990, Garfield Goes to Waist, 1990, The Sixth Garfield Trasury, 1991, Garfield: The Truth About Cats, 1991, Garfield: Seasons Greetings, 1991, Garfield Thanksgiving Special, 1991, Garfield Takes Up Space, 1991, Garfield Says a Mouthful, 1991, Garfield Gets a Life, 1991, Garfield's Ghost Stories, 1992, Garfield Vacation Greetings, 1992, Garfield Learns About Thoughtfulness: Don't Be Late!, 1992, Garfield Learns About Planning: Surprize Party, 1992, Garfield Learns About Money: Money Madness!, 1992, Garfield Learns About Fire Safety: Where's the Fire?, 1992, Garfield Learns About Cooking: Any Cat Can Cook, 1992, Garfield Learns about Conservation: Endangered Odie?, 1992, Garfield Keeps His Chin Up, 1992, Garfield By the Pound, 1992, Garfield Birthday Greetings, 1992, The Seventh Garfield Treasury, 1993, Garfield's Big Fat Hairy Joke Book, 1993, Garfield Takes His Licks, 1993, Garfield Hits the Big Time: His 25th Book, 1993, Garfield's Tales of Mystery, 1994, Garfield's Night Before Christmas, 1994, Garfield's Insults, 1994, Garfield's Haunted House: And Other Spooky Tales, 1994, Garfield's Furry Tales, 1994, Garfield's Big Fat Scary Joke Book, 1994, Garfield's Big Fat Holiday Joke Book, 1994, Garfield Insults, Put-Downs, 1994, Garfield Fat Cat, 1994, Garfield Discovers America, 1994, Garfield's Son of Big, Fat Hairy Jokes, 1994, Big Hairy Garfield, 1994, Garfield, The Easter Bunny?, 1995, Garfield's Stupid Cupid: And Other Silly Stories, 1995, Garfield Fat Cat 3 Pack, 1995, Garfield Dishes It Out, 1995, Mr. Potato Head, 2001. Mktg. Hall of Fame award Am. Mktg. Assn., 1982; recipient Disting. Alumnus award Am. Assn. State Colls. Univs. Mem. Nat. Cartoonists Soc. (Best Humor Strip of 1981, 86, Segar award 1985, Cartoonist of Yr. 1990), Newspaper Comics Council. Protestant. Republican. Office: Universal Press Syndicate 4520 Main St Ste 700 Kansas City MO 64111-7701

DAVIS, JOHN CHARLES, lawyer; b. Kansas City, Mo., Mar. 4, 1943; s. Ralph B. Jr. and Helen M. (Schneider) D.; m. C. Jane Reusser, June 18, 1966; children: Tracy A., Matthew S. BA, U. Kans., 1965; JD, U. Mich., 1968. Bar: Mo. 1968, Kans. 1983. Stockholder Stinson, Mag & Fizzell, P.C., Kansas City, 1968—. Chmn. Fed. Estate Tax Symposium, 1986-87. Chmn. Bacchus Found., Kansas City, 1974; bd. dirs. Crittenten, Kansas City, 1988-94, vice chmn., 1990-92; trustee Schutte Found., Kansas City, 1986—, U. Kansas City, 1989—, treas., 1994-96, counsel, 1996—; trustee Village Presbyn. Ch. Found., chmn., 1991-93; elder Village Presbyn. Ch., 1994-97; bd. dirs. Gamma O Edn. Found., 1991—, Heart of Am. Counsel, Boy Scouts Am., 1995—, exec. com., 1996—; dir. John Cty. C.C. Found., 2000—. Fellow Am. Coll. Trust and Estate Counsel (by-laws com. 1987-96, chmn. 1996-99, 2002-, program com. 1993-96); mem. ABA, Mo. Bar Assn., Kans. Bar Assn., Estate Planning Soc. Kansas City (pres. 1990-91), Nelson-Atkins Mus. Soc. Fellows, Kansas City Club (v.p. 1989-90), Indian Hills Country Club (Mission Hills, Kans.), Rotary, Gamma Omicron (pres., bd. dirs. 1979-85). Presbyterian. Avocations: squash, Hopi art, Marklin trains, travel, photography. Home: 6421 High Dr Shawnee Mission KS 66208-1935 Office: Stinson Morrison Hecker LLP 1201 Walnut St PO Box 419251 Kansas City MO 64141-6251

DAVIS, JOHN JAMES, religion educator; b. Phila., Oct. 13, 1936; s. John James and Cathryn Ann (Nichols) D.; m. Carolyn Ann. BA, Trinity Coll., Dunedin, Fla., 1959, DD (hon.), 1968; MDiv, Grace Coll. & Grace Theol. Sem., Winona Lake, Ind., 1962, ThM, 1964, ThD, 1967. Instr. Grace Coll. & Grace Theol. Sem., 1963-65, prof. of Old Testament, 1965—, exec. v.p., 1976-82, pres., 1986-93; exec. dean Near East Sch. Archaeology, Jerusalem, 1970-71. Area supr. Tekoa Archeol. Expdn., Jordan, 1968, 70, Raddana Expdn., Jordan, 1974, Heshbon Expdn., Jordan, 1976, Abila Archeol. Expdn., Jordan, 1982, 84, Khirbet el-Maqatir Expdn., Israel, 2000. Author: Paradise to Prison, 1975 (Book of Yr.), The Perfect Shepherd, 1979 (Book of Yr.), 16 other books. Chmn., bd. dirs. Kosciusko Comty. Hosp., 1994-2000. Recipient Gold award United Way, 1980, Conservation award Barbee Property Owners Assn., 1983; named Outdoor Writer of Yr., Ind. Dept. Natural Resources, 1986, to the Koscivsko County Rep. Hall of Fame, 1992. Mem. Am. Schs. of Oriental Research, Near East Archeol. Soc., Outdoor Writers Assn., Hoosier Outdoor Writers Assn. (pres. 1984-86). Avocations: fishing, hunting, photography. Home: PO Box 557 Winona Lake IN 46590-0557 Office: Grace Theol Sem 200 Seminary Dr Winona Lake IN 46590-1224

DAVIS, KATHERINE LYON, state official; b. Boston, June 24, 1956; d. Richard Harold and Joy (Hallum) Winer; m. John Marshall Davis, Feb. 22, 1992; 1 child, Madeline Felton. BS, MIT, 1978; MBA, Harvard U., 1982. Engr. Cambridge (Mass.) Collaborative, 1978-80; mfg. mgr. Cummins Engine Co., Columbus, Ind., 1982-87, bus. dir., 1987-89; dep. commr. Ind. Dept. Transp., Indpls., 1989-95; budget dir. State of Ind., 1995-97; exec. sec. Ind. Family and Social Svcs. Commn., 1997-99; city contr. City of Indpls., 1999—. Mem. Transp. Rsch. Bd., 1990-93. Recipient commendation Dept. Transp., Fed. Hwy. Adminstrn., 1991. Democrat. Avocations: running, swimming, bicycling, hiking, photography. Home: 621 E 9th St Indianapolis IN 46202-3408 Office: 200 E Washington St Ste 2222 Indianapolis IN 46204

DAVIS, KAY, state legislator; Mem. S.D. Ho. of Reps., Pierre; mem. edn. and retirement laws coms. Democrat.

DAVIS, KENNETH WAYNE, English language educator, business communication consultant; b. Chariton, Iowa, June 22, 1945; s. Wayne Pitman and Jeanne Frances (West) D.; m. Bette Hargrove, Nov. 28, 1970; Cassandra Alice, Evan Thomas. BA, Drake U., 1967; MA, Columbia U., 1968; PhD, U. Mich., 1975. From asst. prof. English to assoc. prof. U. Ky., Lexington, 1975-88; assoc. prof. to prof. Ind. U.-Purdue U., Indpls., 1988—, dept. chair, 1998-2001; edn. dir. Am. Cabaret Theatre, 2001—. Bus. cons., Lexington, 1977-88; pres. Komei, Inc., 1994—. Author: Better Business Writing, 1983, (with others) Business Communication for the Information Age, 1988, Rehearsing the Audience, 1988, (with others) Writing: Process, Product, and Power, 1993; prodr.: 2001: Lessons in Leadership videoconf., 1991; numerous other books and articles. Bd. dirs. Shepherd's House, Inc., Lexington, 1986-88, Waycross Camp and Conf. Ctr., 1995-2000, World Trade Club Ind., 1998-2001. Sgt. U.S. Army, 1968-71. Woodrow Wilson fellow, 1967; recipient Faculty Service award Nat. Univ. Continuing Edn. Assn., 1987. Mem. ASTD, Nat. Coun. Tchrs. English, Assn. Bus. Comm., Assn. Profl. Comm. Cons., Amnesty Internat. Episcopalian. Avocations: theater, travel. Office: Ind U-Purdue U Dept English 425 University Blvd Indianapolis IN 46202-5148

DAVIS, KENNETH BOONE, JR. dean, law educator; b. Louisville, Sept. 1, 1947; s. Kenneth Boone and Doris Edna (Gordon) D. m. Arrietta Evoline Hastings, June 2, 1984; children: Peter Hastings, Mary Elizabeth, Kenneth Boone III. AB, U. Mich., 1969; JD, Case Western Res. U., 1974. Bar: D.C. 1975, Ohio 1974. Law clk. to chief judge U.S. Ct. Appeals (9th cir.), San Francisco, 1974-75; assoc. Covington & Burling, Washington, 1975-78; prof. law U. Wis., Madison, 1978—, dean Law Sch., 1997—. Contbr. numerous articles on corp. and securities law to profl jours. Mem. ABA, Am. Fin. Assn., Am. Law Inst., Wis. Bar Assn. (reporter, corp. and bus. law com.). Office: U Wis Law Sch 975 Bascom Mall Madison WI 53706-1399

DAVIS, LAWRENCE EDWARD, church official; b. Louisville, Aug. 14, 1939; s. George Edward and Isabel (Gerow) D.; m. Joan Cynthia Rhodes, June 20, 1959 (dec. Mar. 1984); children: Terri L., Todd E., Cynthia Davis Kennedy, Wendy J.; m. Barbara Irene Oldford, Mar., 1985. BS, Nyack Coll., 1961; MDiv, New Brunswick Theol. Sem., 1968; DDiv (hon.), King Coll., 1991. Pastor Christian Missionary Alliance, Detroit; exec. pastor World Presbyn., Livonia, Mich., 1974-82; stated clk. Evang. Presbyn. Ch., 1981—. Adj. prof. Reformed Theol. Sem., Jackson, Miss., 1988—. Mem. Nat. Assn. Evangelicals (bd. adminstrn. 1983—). Home: 38646 Silken Glen Dr Northville MI 48167-8960 Office: Ward Presbyn Ch 4000 Sixth Mile Rd Northville MI 48167

DAVIS, LAWRENCE O. federal magistrate judge; LLB, JD, U. Mo., 1958. Atty. Jenny, Cole & Davis, Union, Mo., 1963-71; pros. atty., 1967-70; magistrate judge Franklin County, 1971-74; jduge Mo. Cir. Ct., 20th Jud. Cir. Mo., 1975-92; magistrate judge U.S. Dist. Ct. (ea. dist.) Mo., St. Louis, 1993—. Served to capt. USAF, 1959-62, USAFR, 1962-65. Office: 111 S 10th St Rm 9144 Saint Louis MO 63102-1125

DAVIS, LYNN J. telecommunications executive; MSEE, Iowa State U.; MBA, U. Minn. With prodn. engring. and ops. dept. Honeywell, Mpls.; joined ADC Telecom., Inc., 1973—, dir. internat. ops., dir. domestic sales, gen. mgr. telecom. and electronic divsn., v.p. mfg., sr. v.p., gen. mgr. broadband connectivity divsn., pres. broadband connectivity divsn., sr. v.p. Bd. dirs. Lion Precision. Mem. Internat. Engring. Consortium. Office: ADC Telecom Inc 12501 Whitewater Dr Minnetonka MN 55343-9498

DAVIS, MARGARET BRYAN, paleoecology researcher, educator; b. Boston, Oct. 23, 1931; d. Melvin Arthur and Betty Lou (Wenholz) Timm; m. David Joseph Murphy, July 28, 1984; 2 children. AB, Radcliffe Coll., 1953; PhD in Biology, Harvard U., 1957. NSF fellow dept. biology Harvard U., Cambridge, Mass., 1957-58; dept. geosci. Calif. Inst. Tech., Pasadena, 1959-60; rsch. fellow dept. zoology Yale U., New HAven, 1960-61, prof. biology, 1973-76; rsch. asoc. dept. botany U. Mich., Ann Arbor, 1961-64, assoc. rsch. biologist Gt. Lakes Rsch. divsn., 1964-70, rsch. biologist, assoc. prof. dept. zoology, 1966-70, rsch. biologist, prof. zoology, 1970-73; head dept. ecology and behavioral biology U. Minn., Mpls., 1976-81, prof. dept. ecology, evolution and behavior, 1976-82, Regents prof. ecology, 1982-2000. Vis. prof. Quaternary Rsch. Ctr., U. Wash., 1973; vis. investigator environ. studies program U. Calif., Santa Barbara, 1981-82; adv. panel ecology NSF, 1976-79; sci. adv. com. biology, behavior and social scis., 1989-91; adv. panel geol. record of global change, NRC, 1991-92, planetary biology com., 1981-82, global change com; 1987-90, mem. screening com. in plant scis., internat. exch. of persons com., 1972-75, sci. and tech. edn. com., 1984-86, vis. rsch. scientist scholarly exch. com. NAS/NRC, People's Republic China, mem. grand challenges in environ. sci. com., 1999-2000; U.S. nat. com. internat. Union Quaternary Rsch., 1966-74; bd. trustees IES, 2000—. Mem. editl. bd. Quaternary Rsch., 1969-82, Trends in Ecology and Evolution, 1986-92, Ecosystems, 2000—. Recipient Sci. Achievement award Sci. Mus. Minn., 1988, alumnae Recognition award Radcliffe Coll., Merit award Botanical Soc. Am., 1998, award for Contbn. Grad. Edn., U. Minn., 1999. Fellow: AAAS, Geol. Soc. Am., Am. Acad Arts and Scis.; mem.: NAS, Brit. Ecol. Soc., Am. Soc. Naturalists (hon.), Am. Quaternary Assn. (councillor 1969—70, 1972—76, pres. 1978—80, Dist. Career award 2001), Ecol. Soc. Am. 1987—88, (Eminent Ecologist award 1993), Nature Conservancy (bd. dirs. Minn. chpt. 1979—85), Internat. Assn. Gt. Lakes Rsch. (bd. dirs. 1970—73), Sigma Xi, Phi Beta Kappa. Office: U Minn Dept Ecology 100 Ecology Bldg 1987 Upper Buford Cir Saint Paul MN 55108-1051 E-mail: mbdavis@ecology.umn.edu.

DAVIS, MICHAEL J. judge; b. 1947; BA, Macalester Coll., 1969; JD, U. Minn., 1972; LLD (hon.) , Macalester Coll., 2001. Law clk. Legal Rights Ctr., 1971-73; with Office Gen. Counsel Dept. Health, Edn. and Welfare, Social Security Adminstrn., Balt., 1973; criminal def. atty. Neighborhood Justice Ctr., 1974, Legal Rights Ctr., 1975—78; pub. defender Hennepin

County, 1978-83; judge Hennepin County Mcpl. Ct., 1983-84, Hennepin County Dist. Ct. (4th jud. dist.), 1984-94; atty., commr. Mpls. Civil Rights Commn., 1977-82; judge U.S. Dist. Ct. Minn., St. Paul, 1994—. Constnl. law instr. Antioch Mpls. C.C., 1974; criminal def. trial practice instr. Nat. Lawyer's Guild, 1977; trial practice instr. William Mitchell Coll. Law, 1977-81, Bemidji Trial Advocacy Course, 1992, 93; adj. prof. U. Minn. Law Sch., 1982—, Hubert H. Humphrey Sch. Pub. Affairs, 1990; instr. Minn. Inst. Legal Edn., Civil Trial Practice Inst., 1991-92; lectr. FBI Acad., 1991, 92. Mem. Minn. Superior Ct. Racial Bias Task Force, 1990—93, U.S. Dist. Ct.; chmn. Pretrial Release & Bail Evaluation Com., 1997—. Recipient Outstanding Alumni award Macalester Coll., 1989, Good Neighbor award WCCO Radio, 1989, Disting Svc. award William Mitchell Coll. of Law, 2000. Mem. ABA, Nat. Bar Assn., Minn. Minority Lawyers Assn., Am. Inns. of Ct., Fed. Bar Assn., Fed. Judges Assn., Hennepin County Bar Assn., Minn. State Bar Assn., Minn. Lawyers Internat. Human Rights Com. (past mem. bd. dirs.), Internat. Acad. Trial Judges, Nat. Assn. for Pub. Interest Law (bd. dirs.), 8th Cir. Jury Instruction Com., U.S. Assn. Constitutional Law. Office: US Dist Ct Minn 300 S 4th St Ste 14E Minneapolis MN 55415-2251 E-mail: mjdavis@mnd.uscourts.gov.

DAVIS, MICHAEL W. lawyer; b. N.Y.C., Nov. 12, 1950; BA magna cum laude, SUNY, Binghamton, 1972; JD cum laude, Northwestern U., 1975. Bar: Ill. 1975, U.S. Supreme Ct. 1981. Ptnr. Sidley & Austin, Chgo., sec. exec. com. Prof. products liability law Chgo. Kent Coll. Law, 1984-88. Mem. drug and med. device steering com. Def. Rsch. Inst. Mem. Internat. Assn. Defense Coun., Legal Club Chgo. Office: Sidley & Austin Bank One Plz 10 S Dearborn Chicago IL 60603

DAVIS, MONIQUE D. (DEON DAVIS), state legislator; b. Chgo., Aug. 19, 1936; d. James and Constance (Dutton) McKay; divorced; children: Robert Jr., Monique C. Conway. BS in Edn., Chgo. State U., 1967, MS in Guidance and Counseling, 1976. Tchr. Chgo. Bd. Edn., 1967-86, coordinator, 1986—; mem. Ill. Ho. of Reps. from 27th dist., 1987—, vice chmn. elem. and secondary edn. com. Mem. legis. com. Chgo. Area Alliance Black Sch. Edn., 1982-84, Independent Voters of Ill.-Independent Precinct Orgns., Chgo., 1982-83; coordinator 21st ward, Citizens for Mayor Washington, 1985, 87. Recipient GRIT award Roseland Womens Orgn., 1987; named a Tchr. Who Makes a Difference PTA, 1978, 85, 2002 March Monique Davis Named best Legislature of the year by Chicago Area Proseet Mem. Chgo. Area Tchrs. Alliance (chmn.), Christian Bd. Edn. (bd. dirs. 1978-82), Phi Delta Kappa. Mem. United Ch. of Christ. Office: Ill Ho of Reps 2040-j Stratton Bldg Springfield IL 62706-0001

DAVIS, MULLER, lawyer; b. Chgo., Apr. 23, 1935; s. Benjamin B. and Janice (Muller) D.; m. Jane Lynn Strauss, Dec. 28, 1963 (div. July 1998); children: Melissa Davis Muller, Muller Jr., Joseph Jeffrey; m. Lynn Straus, Jan. 23, 1999. Grad. with honors, Phillips Exeter (N.H.) Acad., 1953; BA magna cum laude, Yale U., 1957; JD, Harvard U., 1960. Bar: Ill. 1960, U.S. Dist. Ct. (no. dist.) Ill. 1961. Practice law, Chgo., 1960—; assoc. Jenner & Block, 1960-67; ptnr. Davis, Friedman, Zavett, Kane, MacRae, Marcus & Rubens, 1967—. Lectr. continuing legal edn., matrimonial law and litigation; legal adviser Michael Reese Med. Research Inst. Council, 1967-82. Author: (with Sherman C. Feinstein) The Parental Couple in a Successful Divorce, Illinois Practice of Family Law, 1995, 97, 98-99, (with Jody Meyer Yazici) 4th edit., 2000-01; contbg. author Marriage, Health and the Professions; mem. editl. bd. Equitable Distbn. Jour., 1984—; contbr. articles to law jours. Bd. dirs. Infant Welfare Soc., 1975-96, hon. bd. dirs., 1996—, pres., 1978-82; co-chmn. gen. gifts 40th and 45th reunions Phillips Exeter Acad., chair class capital giving, 1994-98. Capt. U.S. Army, Ill. N.G., 1960-67. Fellow Am. Acad. Matrimonial Lawyers (bd. mgrs. Ill. chpt. 1996-99), Am. Bar Found.; mem. ABA, FBA, Ill. Bar Assn., Chgo. Bar Assn. (matrimonial com. 1968-83, sec. civil practice com. 1979-80, vice chmn. 1980-81, chmn. 1981-82), Am. Soc. Writers on Legal Subjects, Chgo. Estate Planning Coun., Legal Aid Soc. (vice chmn. matrimonial bar 1991-95, vice chmn. 1995-97, chmn. 1997-99), Lawyers Club Chgo., Tavern Club, Lake Shore Country Club, Chgo. Club. Republican. Jewish. Home: 161 E Chicago Ave Apt 34 E Chicago IL 60611-2601 Office: Davis Friedman Zavett Kane MacRae Marcus & Rubens 140 S Dearborn St Ste 1600 Chicago IL 60603-5288 E-mail: mdavis@davisfriedman.com.

DAVIS, PAMELA BOWES, pediatric pulmonologist; b. Jamaica, N.Y., July 20, 1949; d. Elmer George and Florence (Welsch) Bowes; m. Glenn C. Davis, June 28, 1970 (div. Mar. 1987); children: Jason, Galen. AB, Smith Coll., 1968; PhD, Duke U., 1973, MD, 1974. Internal medicine intern Duke Hosp., 1973-74, resident in internal medicine, 1974-75; sr. investigator NIAMD/NIH, Bethesda, Md., 1977-79; asst. prof. U. Tenn. Coll. Medicine, Memphis, 1979-81, Case Western Res. U. Sch. Medicine, Cleve., 1981-85, assoc. prof., 1985-89, prof., 1989—, chief pediatric pulmonary divsn., 1985—, vice chmn. rsch. dept., 1994-96. Pres. Am. Fedn. for Clin. Rsch., Thorofare, NJ, 1989—90; trustee Rsch. Am, Arlington, Va., 1989—90; mem. adv. coun. Nat. Inst. Diabetes, Digestive and Kidney Diseases, 1992—96; mem. bd. sci. counselors NHLBI, 2001—. Contbr. articles to profl. jours. Chmn., med. adv. coun. Cystic Fibrosis Found., Bethesda, 1988-90. Named to, Clevel. Med. Hall of Fame, 2001; recipient Samuel Rosenthal award in acad. pediat., 1996, Maurice Saltzman award, Mt. Sinai Health Care Found., 1998, Smith Coll. medal, 2001. Fellow ACP; mem. Am. Pediatric Soc., Am. Acad. Pediatrics, Am. Physiol. Soc., Am. Thoracic Soc., Am. Soc. Gene Therapy, Biophys. Soc., Soc. for Pediatric Rsch., Phi Beta Kappa, Sigma Xi, Alpha Omega Alpha. Office: Rainbow Babies/Child Hosp 2101 Adelbert Rd Cleveland OH 44106-2624 E-mail: pbd@po.cwru.edu.

DAVIS, RICHARD CARLTON, rehabilitation services administrator; b. Salem, Mass., June 10, 1948; s. William Montgomery and Ruth Wiley (Durkee) D.; m. Patricia Lynn Paquette, Apr. 6, 1974; children: Susannah, Amanda, Adam. BA, Concord Coll., 1969; postgrad., U. Iowa. Orientation tchr. Iowa Dept. for the Blind, Des Moines, 1971-73, rehab. tchr., 1973-77, rehab. counselor, 1977-80, sr. svc. specialist, 1980-86; so. area supr. N.Mex. Commn. for the Blind, Alamogordo, 1987-91, orientation ctr. adminstr., 1987-92; asst. commr. State Svcs. for the Blind, Minn. Dept. of Econ. Security, St. Paul, 1992-2000; cons. on blindness and rehab. Circle Pines, Minn., 2000—; asst. dir. BLIND, Inc., Mpls., 2000—. Cons. Nebr. Svcs. for the Visually Impaired, Lincoln, 1980, Am. Printing House for the Blind, Louisville, 1992. Coord./vol. field svc. rep. Job Opportunities for the Blind, Balt., 1979-86; chair, vice chair Mayor's com. for the Handicapped, Alamogordo, 1990-92; bd. dirs. White Sands Press Club, Alamogordo, 1988-92. Recipient Silver award United Way, 1991, over 100% Goal award, 1990, Founders award N.Mex. Commn. for the Blind, 1992, Wayne E. Bonnell award Nat. Fedn. of the Blind, 1982, Gov.'s commendations, 1998, 2000, Cert. of Appreciation, Red Lake Nation's divsn. Rehab. Svcs. Mem. Nat. Coun. of State Agencies for the Blind (bd. dirs. 1994-98, treas. 1999-2000), Coun. of State Adminstrs. of Vocat. Rehab., Nat. Fedn. of the Blind (Des Moines Chpt. award 1983), Alamogordo Rotary Club. Avocations: camping, canoeing, snowshoeing, woodworking. Home: 136 Canterbury Rd Circle Pines MN 55014-1777

DAVIS, RICHARD FRANCIS, city government official; b. Providence, Aug. 18, 1936; s. Walter Francis and Mary Elizabeth (Gearin) D.; m. Virginia Catherine Oates, Aug. 27, 1960; children: Walter Douglas, John Richard, Theresa Catherine. BS, U. Ark., Little Rock, 1964; student city and regional planning, MIT, summer, 1964; postgrad., Carnegie Mellon U., 1973. Planner Met. Area Planning Commn., Little Rock, 1964-66; mem. Met. Planning Commn. Kansas City, Mo., 1966-67, dir. econs., 1967-69, dir. ops., 1969-71; exec. dir. Mid-Am. Regional Council, Kansas City, 1972-77; gen. mgr. Kansas City Area Transp. Authority, 1977-2000; instr. city planning U. Mo., Kansas City, 1973-74; Planning commr. City of Gladstone, Mo., 1967-69, 81-90, city councilman, 1969-71, mayor, 1971-72, chmn. park bd., 1972-76, mem. bd. zoning adjustment, 1993—; gen. mgr. bus. devel. Olsson Assocs., 2002—. Mem. Clay County (Mo.) Indsl. Devel. Commn., 1972-77, Council on Edn., Kansas City, 1974-82, treas., chmn. interdist. rels. com.; bd. dirs. Mo. Pub. Transit Assn., 1979-2000, pres., 1987-89, 1999-2000; bd. dirs. Kans. Pub. Transit Assn., 1979-2000; trustee Black Econ. Union, 1984-88; bd. dirs., treas. Heart of Am. United Way Vol. Ctr., 1985-87. Mem. coun. advisers, Major League Baseball Players Trust for Children, 2000—; v.p. Brooktree Homeowners Assn., 1979-80; mem. Total Transp. adv. com., MidAmerica Regional Coun., 1977-2000, chmn. transit adv. com., 1997-2000; mem. Northland Regional C. of C., 2000-. Served with USAF, 1955-59. Recipient Transp. Svc. award Kansas City chpt. Conf. of Minority Transit Officials, 1987. Mem. Am. Soc. Pub. Adminstrn. (pres. Kansas City chpt. 1980, Pub. Adminstr. of Yr. award 1973, L.P. Cookingham award 1991), Am. Planning Assn., Am. Pub. Transit Assn. (bd. dirs. 1980-93, 94—, mem. govtl. affairs and legis. steering com., v.p. mgmt. and fin. com. 1984-86, v.p. govt. affairs com. 1991-93, Outstanding Pub. Transp. Mgr. award 2000), Kansas City Royal Lancers (v.p. 2001-2002. pres. 2002-). Home: 3612 NE Brooktree Cir Kansas City MO 64119-2229 Office: 1200 E 18th St Kansas City MO 64108-1606

DAVIS, ROBERT A. data storing company executive; Sr. v.p., chief quality officer Ideon Group, Inc.; with NCR, Inc., Dayton, Ohio, 1995-99, 1999—. Office: NCR Corp 1700 S Patterson Blvd Dayton OH 45479-0002

DAVIS, ROBERT EDWARD, state supreme court justice; b. Topeka, Aug. 28, 1939; s. Thomas Homer and Emma Claire (Hund) D.; m. Jana Jones; children: Edward, Rachel, Patrick, Carolyn, Brian. BA in Polit. Sci., Creighton U., 1961; JD, Georgetown U., 1964. Bar: Kans. 1964, U.S. Dist. Ct. Kans. 1964, U.S. Tax Ct. 1974, U.S. Ct. Mil. Appeals 1965, U.S. Ct. Mil. Review, 1970, U.S. Ct. Appeals (10th cir.) 1974, U.S. Supreme Ct. 1982. Pvt. practice, Leavenworth, Kans., 1967-84; magistrate judge Leavenworth County, 1969-76, county atty., 1980-84, judge dist. ct., 1984-86; judge Kans. Ct. Appeals Jud. Br. Govt., Topeka, 1986-93; justice Kans. Supreme Ct., 1993—. Lectr. U. Kans. Law Sch., Lawrence, 1986-95. Capt. JAGC, U.S. Army, 1964-67, Korea. Mem. Am. Judges Assn., Kans. Bar Assn., Leavenworth County Bar Assn. (pres. 1977), Judge Hugh Means Am. Inn of Ct. Charter Orgn. Lawrence. Roman Catholic. Office: 301 W 10th Ave Topeka KS 66612

DAVIS, SAMUEL BERNHARD, manufacturing executive; b. Dayton, Ohio, Feb. 9, 1942; s. Samuel Spencer and Jeanette Louise (Albiez) D.; children: Samuel N., Krista A. BA, Ohio State U., Columbus, 1970. Chmn., chief exec. officer Liqui-Box Corp., Worthington, 1977—. Bd. dir. Liqui-Box Corp., Worthington, 1976, Central Benefits Mutual Ins., Columbus, 1987, Wendy's Internat., Dublin, 1988. Bd. dirs. Greater Columbus Arts Coun., I Know I Can, Columbus, JASAM Found., Worthington. Mem. Pres's. Club Ohio State Univ. (exec. com.), Rio Grande Coll., World Pres. Orgn. (mgr.), Soc. of Plastics Engrs., Scioto Country Club, Ocean Reef Club, Muirfield Country Club. Avocations: photography, jogging, travel. Home: PO Box 494 Columbus OH 43085-0494 Office: Liqui-Box Corp 6950 Worthington-Galena Rd Worthington OH 43085-2360

DAVIS, SCOTT JONATHAN, lawyer; b. Chgo., Jan. 8, 1952; s. Oscar and Doris (Koller) D.; m. Anne Megan, Jan. 4, 1981; children: William, James, Peter. BA, Yale U., 1972; JD, Harvard U., 1976. Bar: Ill. 1976, U.S. Dist. Ct. (no. dist.) Ill. 1976, U.S. Ct. Appeals (7th cir.) 1977, U.S. Ct. Appeals (8th cir.) 1986. Law clk. to judge U.S. Ct. Appeals (7th cir.), Chgo., 1976—77; assoc. Mayer, Brown, Rowe & Maw, 1977—82, ptnr., 1983—. Bd. editors Harvard Law Rev., 1974-76; contbr. articles to profl. jours. V.p. Chgo. Police Bd. Home: 838 W Belden Ave Chicago IL 60614-3236 Office: Mayer Brown Rowe & Maw 190 S La Salle St Ste 3100 Chicago IL 60603-3441

DAVIS, STEPHEN HOWARD, applied mathematics educator; b. N.Y.C., Sept. 7, 1939; s. Harry Carl and Eva Leah (Axelrod) D.; m. Suellen Lewis, Jan. 15, 1966. BEE, Rensselaer Poly. Inst., 1960, MS in Math, 1962, PhD in Math., 1964; BSc honoris causa, U. Western Ont., 2001. Research mathematician Rand Corp., Santa Monica, Calif., 1964-66; lectr. in math. Imperial Coll., London U., 1966-68; asst. prof. mechanics and materials sci. Johns Hopkins U., 1968-70, assoc. prof., 1970-75, prof., 1975-78; prof. engring. sci. and applied math. Northwestern U., 1979—, Walter P. Murphy prof., 1987—, McCormick Sch. prof., 2000—. Dir. Ctr. for Multiphase Fluid Flow and Transport, 1986-88; cons. in field; vis. prof. math. Monash U., Australia, 1973; vis. prof. chem. engring. U. Ariz., 1977; vis. prof. aerospace and mech. engring., 1981; vis. scientist Institut für Aerodynamik-ETH, Zurich, Switzerland, 1971; vis. scientist Dept. Math. Ecole Polytechnique Federale, Lausanne, Switzerland, 1984, 85, vis. prof. 1987, 88, 91; mem. U.S. Nat. Com. for Theoretical and Applied Mechanics, 1978-87. Asst. editor Jour. Fluid Mechanics, 1969-75, assoc. editor, 1975-89, editor-in-chief, 2000—; contbr. articles to profl. jours. Recipient Alexander von Humboldt award, 1994, Fluid Dynamics prize Am. Phys. Soc., 1994, G.I. Taylor medal Soc. for Engring. Sci., 2001. Fellow Am. Phys. Soc. (chmn. divsn. fluid dynamics 1978-79, 87-88, councillor divsn. fluid dynamics 1980-82); mem. NAE, Am. Acad. Arts and Scis., Soc. Indsl. and Applied Math. (coun. 1983-87), Sigma Xi, Pi Mu Epsilon. Home: 1199 Edgewood Rd Lake Forest IL 60045-1308 Office: Northwestern U McCormick Sch Engring/Applied Scis Sheridan Rd Evanston IL 60208-0001

DAVIS, STEVE, state legislator; b. Sept. 22, 1949; m. Carol Keck; children: Shane, Shelly. Student, Lewis and Clark C.C., So. Ill. U. Hwy. commr. Wood River Twp., Ill., 1981-94; former mem., treas. Madison County Dem. Cen. Com.; Ill. state rep. Dist. 111, 1995—. Mem. Aging, Appropriations-Edn., Environ. and Energy and Transp. Coms., 1995—, Ill. Ho. of Reps.; draftsman R. W. Booker and Assocs., 1970; sr. civil engr. Sterling Engring. Co., 1970-73, Volz Engring. and Survey, 1973-75, PHO Inc., 1975-78; operator Amoco Oil Co., 1978-80; pres. Steve Davis and Assocs., 1980-82. Bd. dirs. Family Svc. and Vis. Nurse Assn. Mem. Moose, Am. Legion (post 214), Ill. Legis. Sportsmans Caucus. Office: 2 Terminal Dr Ste 18B East Alton IL 62024-2289

DAVIS, SUSAN F. human resources specialist; BS, MS, Beloit Coll.; MBA, U. Mich. From strategic planner to corp. mgr. tng. and devel. Hoover Universal Corp., 1983-85; various positions Johnson Controls, Inc., Milw., 1985-94, corp. officer, v.p. human resources, 1994—. Bd. dirs. Quanex Corp. Office: Johnson Controls Inc 5757 N Green Bay Ave Milwaukee WI 53209-4408

DAVIS, THOMAS WILLIAM, computer company executive; b. Belvidere, Ill., Mar. 14, 1946; s. Thomas William and Charlotte Ann (Schildgen) D.; m. Lyndel Etta Schuettpelz, Apr. 3, 1971; 1 child, Bryan William. BSEE, Milw. Sch. Engring., 1968; MSEE, U. Wis., Milw., 1971. Registered profl. engr., Wis. From asst. prof. to assoc. prof. elec. engring. Milw. Sch. Engring., 1971-75, head computer engring. tech., 1975-77, prof. 1976-94, chmn. dept. elec. engring., 1977-84, dean rsch., 1981-84, dean acads. and rsch., 1984-87, v.p. academics, dean faculty, 1987-89, sr. v.p. 1989-94; exec. v.p. Super Steel Products Corp., Milw., 1994-96, sr. v.p., 1996-98; pres. Milw. Rehab. Ctr., 1997—; pres. Prophet Tech. LLC, 1998—; lectr. U. Wis., Milw., 1973-76. Author: Problems in Measurements, 1968, (textbooks) Computer Aided Analysis, 1973, Introduction to Interactive Programs, 1978, Experimentation with Microprocessor Applications, 1981; patentee in field. Warning and communications officer Ozaukee County Emergency Govt., Wis., 1981-82; sgt. reserves Grafton Police Dept., Wis., 1976—; corp. mem. svcs. Curative Rehab. Ctr, Gov.'s Quality Improvement Task Force, Gov.'s Sci. and Tech. Coun.; bd. dirs. Jordan Controls, Inc., Jagemann Stamping, Mechanical Industries Inc., Amalga Composites Co, Curative Rehab. Svcs., Inc., Resolute Sys., Inc.; past pres. Milw. Coun. Engring. and Sci. Socs., MSOE Alumni Assn., Inc. Mem. IEEE (sr., student activity dir. 1972-73), Engrs. and Scis. Milw. (past pres.), Robotics Internat., Soc. Mfg. Engrs. (sr.), Am. Soc. Engring. Edn. (membership policies com.), Milw. Sch. Engring. Alumni Assn. (achievement award 1968, 25th ann. Outstanding Alumnus award 1993, pres. 1997-98), UWM Alumni Assn. (outstanding alumnus award 1995), Wis. Soc. Profl. Engrs. (past pres. Milw. chpt.), Phi Kappa Phi, Tau Alpha Pi, Eta Kappa Nu. Avocation: flying, amateur radio. Home: 5590 Gray Log Ct Grafton WI 53024-9622 Office: Prophet Technologies 1550 N Prospect Ave Milwaukee WI 53202-6501

DAVIS, THOMAS WILLIAM, insurance company executive; b. Hinsdale, Ill., May 28, 1943; s. Charles K. and Ann (Bovy) D.; m. Loretta Marie Resutko, Dec. 28, 1969; children: Todd Arthur, Lauren Elizabeth. BA, Lewis U., Lockport, Ill., 1967. Tchr. St. Francis High Sch., Wheaton, Ill., 1964-66, Providence High Sch., New Lenox, 1966-68, Highland (Ind.) Pub. High Sch., 1968-70; mktg. rep. Employers Ins. Warsaw, River Forest, Ill., Boockford and Co., Oakbrook, 1973-76; pres., owner Davis-Am., Ltd., 1976--, Corp. Assurance Services, Cary, 1983--. Bd. mem. Utica Natl. Ins. Co.,Columbus, Ohio, 1988--; bd. mem. Uniigard Ins. Co., Seattle, Wash., 1987. Contbr. articles to Big Savings Corp. Ins., 1983. Named Guest Lecturer, Columbia U. Sch. Journalism, N.Y., 1969; guest lecturer, Valporaise U.-Journalism Dept. Ind., 1970. Mem. Ill. Ins. Agents Inc. Republican. Roman Catholic. Avocations: painting, golf, writing. Office: Davis-American Ltd 1010 Jorie Blvd Ste 112 Oak Brook IL 60523-4446

DAVIS, W. JEREMY, dean, law educator, lawyer; b. Pitts., Apr. 13, 1942; s. Winthrop Neuffer and Eleanor (Power) D.; m. Jacqueline Dvoracek, June 11, 1966; children: Jeremy Michael, Sarah Elizabeth. BSBA, U. Denver, 1964, JD, 1970; LLM, Yale U., 1980. Bar: Colo. 1970, N.D. 1973. Pvt. practice law, Denver, 1970-71; asst. prof. U. N.D., Grand Forks, 1971-74, assoc. prof., 1975-82, dean, prof. law, 1983—, gen. counsel, 1993-2000, dir. legal affairs, 2000—. With U.S. Army, 1965-68. Fellow Bush Found., 1979-80. Mem. State Bar Assn. N.D. (bd. govs. 1982—), N.D. Trial Lawyers Assn. (bd. govs. 1986—). Home: 131 Conklin Ave Grand Forks ND 58203-1622 Office: U ND Sch Law PO Box 9003 Grand Forks ND 58202-9003 E-mail: wjd@law.und.edu.

DAVIS, WAYNE KAY, medical educator; b. Findlay, Ohio, Mar. 23, 1946; s. Albert Wayne and Freida Evelyn (Winkle) D.; m. Patricia Ann Krimmer, May 26, 1967; 1 child, J Brandon. B.A., Central Bible Coll., 1967; M.A., U. Mich., 1969, Ph.D., 1971. Research scientist Ctr. Research Learning and Teaching, Ann Arbor, Mich., 1971-73; asst. prof. U. Mich. Med. Sch., 1973-77, assoc. dir. edn. resources and research, 1976-78, assoc. prof., 1977-82, dir. edn. resources and rsch., 1978-98, prof., 1982—, asst. dean, 1982-86, assoc. dean, 1991-98. Adv. mem. ad hoc study sect. Nat. Heart, Lung and Blood Inst., NIH, Bethesda, Md., mem. site visit team Nat. Inst. Arthritis, Metabolic and Digestive Diseases, NIH, Bethesda, 1978-91; cons. Multipurpose Arthritis Ctr., NIH, Bethesda, 1981-83; vis. scholar U. Calif. Med. Sch., San Diego, 1984-85. Author: A Guide to MTS and Remote Terminal Operation, 1972, Moving Medical Education from the Hospital to the Community, 1997; mem. edit. bd. Diabetes Care, 1983-86; assoc. editor Acad. Medicine, 1988-89; contbr. chpts. and articles to med. jours. Bd. dirs. Washtenaw County unit Mich. Hearth Assn., 1977-79. Recipient Best Article award Assn. Diabetes Educators, 1982; Med. Informatics fellow Nat. Libr. Medicine, 2000. Mem. Am. Ednl. Research Assn. (program chmn. div. I, v.p. 1985-87), Assn. Am. Med. Colls. (nat. chair group on ednl. affairs 1994-95), Am. Diabetes Assn., Soc. Dirs. Rsch. in med. Edn. (pres. 1990-91, 93-94), Phi Delta kappa, Gt.Lakes Cruising Club, Seven Seas Cruising Assn. Office: U Mich Dept Med Edn G1215 Towsley Centre 1515 Hospital Dr Ann Arbor MI 48109-0201 E-mail: wkdavis@umich.edu.

DAVIS, WILLIAM ALBERT, theme park director; b. New Haven, Sept. 10, 1946; s. Arthur Wilson Davis and Dorothy May (Hellyer) Jordan; m. Rebecca Marsden Haile, Apr. 8, 1965; children: William Albert Jr., Anna Catherine. BA in Profl. Arts, Brooks Inst. Photography, 1971; BSBA, San Diego State U., 1980. Photographer, owner Davis-Hixon Photography, Santa Ana, Calif., 1971-73; photographer Sea World, Inc., San Diego, 1973, sales rep., 1974-76, sales mgr., 1976-78, mktg. mgr. fast food subs., 1978-80, corp. planning assoc., 1980-81; dir. mktg. Sea World Ohio, Aurora, 1981-85, v.p. mktg., 1985-86, pres., 1986-88, Sea World Fla., Orlando, 1988-97; exec. v.p., gen. mgr. Sea World of Calif., 1997-2001; corp. v.p. guest svcs. Busch Entertainment Corp., St. Louis, 2001—. Bd. dirs. Hubbs-Sea World Rsch. Inst., San Diego, Marine Rsch. Ctr., Sea World, Orlando, Calif. Travel and Tourism Commn. Bd. dirs., exec. com. Conv. and Visitors Bur. Orange County, Orlando, 1988-97, pres.-elect, 1990, pres., 1991, chmn., 1992-93; mem. bd. Efficient Transp. for Community Orlando, 1988-97; mem. adv. coun. Dick Pope Sr. Inst. Tourism Studies, Orlando, 1989-97; commr. Fla. Tourism Commn., 1991—; trustee United Arts of Ctrl. Fla., 1992—; mem. U. Ctrl. Fla. Found., 1994-97; mem. White House Com. on Tourism, 1995, mem. exec. com. San Diego Conv. and Visitors Bur., 1997—, Super Bowl XXXII Host com. Staff sgt. USAF, 1965-69, Vietnam. Fellow Am. Assn. Zool. Parks and Aquariums; mem. San Diego C. of C. Roundtable, Brooks Inst. Alumni Assn., Kiwanis (bd. dirs. Aurora club 1985-87, 1st v.p. 1987—) Avocations: golf, photography, family. Office: Busch Entertainment Corp Ste 600 231 S Benniston Clayton MO 63105

DAVIS, WILLIAM L. publishing company executive; BA in Polit. Sci., Princeton U., 1965. With Sears, Roebuck and Co.; pres. Appleton Electric; group v.p. Emerson, 1983-85, pres. skills divsn., 1985-88, exec. v.p., 1988-93, sr. exec. v.p., 1993-95, head process control group, 1995, CEO, chmn., 1997—. Office: RR Donnelley & Sons Co 77 W Wacker Dr Fl 19 Chicago IL 60601-1604

DAVISON, RICHARD, physician, educator; b. Buenos Aires, Nov. 7, 1937; came to U.S., 1966; s. Charles Edward and Matilde (Muller) D.; m. Lisette Glusberg, July 1, 1965; 1 child, Sebastian. MD, U. Buenos Aires, 1963. Diplomate Am. Bd. Internal Medicine, Am. Bd. Cardiovascular Diseases, Am. Bd. Critical Care Medicine. Intern Inst. Med. Rsch., Buenos Aires, 1964; resident Passavant Meml. Hosp., Chgo., 1966-68, chief resident, 1968-69; cardiology fellowship VA Hosp., 1969-71; asst. prof. Northwestern U. Sch. Medicine, 1973-81, assoc. prof., 1981—, chief sect. critical care medicine, 1982—, chief sect. cardiology, 1988-92; dir. med. intensive care area Northwestern Meml. Hosp., 1973—. Contbr. articles to profl. jours. Recipient Thrombolysis in Myocardial Infarction award NIH. Fellow Am. Coll. Cardiology, Am. Coll. Physicians, Council of Clin. Cardiology (Am. Heart. Assn.), Soc. Critical Care Medicine; mem. Am. Heart Assn., Alpha Omega Alpha. Office: Northwestern Meml Hosp Divsn Critical Care 201 E Huron St Galter 10-240 Chicago IL 60611-2908

DAWES, ALAN S. automotive company executive; B in Applied Math., Harvard U., 1977, MBA, 1981. Asst. treas. Chase Manhattan Bank, 1977-80; fin. analyst GM, N.Y.C., 1981-83, mgr. overseas borrowings, 1984, dir. overseas fin. analysis, 1985, dir. financing, investments and fin. planning, 1986, gen. dir. Treasurer's Office, 1987, asst. treas., 1988-91, asst. comptr. Detroit, 1991; fin. dir. Automotive Components Group, 1992; GM v.p., gen. mgr. Delphi Chassis Systems (formerly Delco Chassis Systems); CFO Delphi Chassis Systems, 1998; CFO, exec. v.p. Delphi

Automotive Systems Corp., Troy, Mich., 1998—. Named Fin. Exec. of Yr. Automotive News Industry All Stars, 1999. Mem. Harvard Bus. Club. Office: Delphi Automotive Systems Corp 5725 Delphi Dr Troy MI 48098-2815

DAWKINS, RUSTY, meteorologist; Student, Chadron State Coll.; BS in Meteorlolgy and Climatology, U. Nebr. With KLKN, Lincoln, Nebr.; mem. weather WEAU-TV Channel 13, Eau Claire, Wis. Office: WEAN-TV PO Box 47 Eau Claire WI 54702

DAWN, CLARENCE ERNEST, history educator; b. Chattanooga, Dec. 6, 1918; s. Fred Hartman and Hettie Lou (Gibson) D.; m. Pansie Mozelle Dooley, July 8, 1944; children: Julia Anne, Carolyn Louise. B.A., U. Chattanooga, 1941; M.A., Princeton U., 1947, Ph.D., 1948. Instr. history U. Ill., Urbana, 1949-52, asst. prof., 1952-55, assoc. prof., 1955-60, prof., 1960—, prof. emeritus, 1989—; dir. U. Ill. Tehran Rsch. Unit, Iran, 1972-74. Fellow Inst. Advanced Studies, Hebrew U., Jerusalem, 1981-82 Author: From Ottomanism to Arabism, 1973; contbr. articles to profl. jours. Served with AUS, 1942-46, with U.S. Army, 1951-52. Social Sci. Rsch. Coun. World Area fellow, 1948-49; fellow joint com. on Near and Mid. East Social Sci. Rsch. Coun. and Am. Coun. Learned Socs., 1966-67; Fulbright-Hays fellow, 1966-67. Mem. Mid. East Studies Assn., Mid. East Inst. Home: 1628 72d•Ave SE Mercer Island WA 98040

DAWSON, DENNIS RAY, lawyer, manufacturing company executive; b. Alma, Mich., June 19, 1948; s. Maurice L. and Virginia (Baker) D.; m. Marilynn S. Gordon, Nov. 26, 1971; children: Emily Lynn, Brett Thomas. AA, Gulf Coast Coll., 1968; AB, Duke U., 1970; JD, Wayne State U., 1973. Bar: Mich. 1973, U.S. Dist. Ct. (ea. dist.) Mich. 1973, U.S. Dist. Ct. (we. dist.) Mich. 1975. Assoc. Watson, Wunsch & Keidan, Detroit, 1973-75; mem. Coupe, Ophoff & Dawson, Holland, Mich., 1975-77; staff atty. Amway Corp., Ada, 1977-79; corp. counsel Meijer, Inc., Grand Rapids, 1979-82; sec., corp. counsel Tecumseh Products Co., 1982-92; corp. counsel, asst. sec. Holnam Inc., Dundee, Mich., 1992-93; v.p., gen. counsel, sec. Denso Internat. Am. Inc., Southfield, 1993-2000, sr. v.p., gen. counsel, sec., 2000—. Exec. com. Bank of Lenawee, Adrian, Mich., 1984-93, also bd. dirs.; adj. prof. Aquinas Coll., Grand Rapids, 1978-82; govt. regulation and litigation com. Outdoor Power Equipment Inst. Inc., Washington, 1982-92. Trustee Herrick Meml. Hosp., 1988-91, Tecumseh Civic Auditorium, 1986-89; mem. adv. coun. Montessori Children's House and Acad., Adrian, 1987-93. Mem. ABA, Mich. State Bar Assn., Am. Soc. Corp. Secs., Am. Corp. Counsel Assn., Mich. Mfrs. Assn. (lawyers com. 1987-92), Lenawee C. of C. (bd. dirs. 1988-92). Office: Denso Internat America Inc PO Box 5133 24777 Denso Dr Southfield MI 48034-5244

DAWSON, KIM, reporter; Degree, Howard U. Reporter WISN, Milw., 2001—. Recipient Michele Clark fellowship, Radio and TV News Dirs. Assn. Office: WISN PO Box 402 Milwaukee WI 53201-0402

DAWSON, STEPHEN EVERETTE, lawyer; b. Detroit, May 14, 1946; s. Everette Ivan and Irene (Dresser) D.; m. Consiglia J. Bellisario, Sept. 20, 1974; children: Stephen Everette Jr., Gina C., Joseph J. BA, Mich. State U., 1968; MA, U. Mich., 1969, JD, 1972. Bar: Mich. 1972, U.S. Dist. Ct. (ea. dist.) Mich. 1972, U.S. Supreme Ct. 1978, U.S. Ct. Appeals (6th cir.) 1980. Assoc. Dickinson, Wright, Moon, Van Dusen & Freeman, Detroit, 1972-79; ptnr. Dickinson, Wright, PLLC, Bloomfield Hills, Mich., 1979—. Adj. prof. law U. Detroit, 1986-88. Mem. ABA, Am. Coll. Real Estate Lawyers, Mich. State Bar Assn. (mem. coun. real property law sect. 1986-93, chair 1992-93, land title stds. com. 1999—), Mich. State Bar Found., Phi Beta Kappa. Republican. Avocations: jogging, reading. Office: Dickinson Wright PLLC 38525 Woodward Ave Ste 2000 Bloomfield Hills MI 48304-5092 E-mail: sdawson@dickinson-wright.com.

DAWSON, SUZANNE STOCKUS, lawyer; b. Chgo., Dec. 29, 1941; d. John Charles and Josephine (Zolpe) Stockus; m. Daniel P. Dawson Sr., Sept. 1, 1962; children: Daniel P. Jr., John Charles, Michael Sean. BA, Marquette U., 1963; JD cum laude, Loyola U., Chgo., 1965. Bar: Ill. 1965, U.S. dist. Ct. (no. dist.) Ill. 1965. Assoc. Kirkland & Ellis, Chgo., 1965-71, ptnr., 1971-82, Arnstein & Lehr, Chgo., 1982-89, Foley & Lardner, Chgo., 1989-94; spl. counsel publicly held corps. Glenview, Ill., 1995-97; corp. counsel Baxter Healthcare Corp., Deerfield, 1997-98, sr. counsel, 1998—. Mem. various coms. United Way Chgo.; corp. adv. bd. Sec. State of Ill., 1973; past mem. bd. advisors Loyola of Chgo. Law Sch.; trustee Lawrence Hall Youth Svcs., Chgo., 1983-98, pres., 1991-93, chair 1993-96; mem. adv. bd. Cath. Charities Chgo., 1985—; mem. exec. com., bd. governance Notre Dame High Sch., Niles, Ill., 1990-97. Recipient Founder's Day award Loyola U., 1980, St. Thomas More award Loyola of Chgo. Law Sch., 1983. Mem. ABA, Am. Arbitration Assn. (appointed mem. nat. panel of comml. arbitrators 1996—), Ill. Bar Assn. Roman Catholic. Avocations: piano, choir singing, gardening, skiing, gourmet cooking. Home: 2113 Valley Lo Ln Glenview IL 60025-1724 Office: Baxter Healthcare Corp One Baxter Pkwy Deerfield IL 60015-4633 E-mail: suzanne_dawson@baxter.com.

DAWSON, VIRGINIA SUE, retired newspaper editor; b. Concordia, Kans., June 6, 1940; d. John Edward and Wilma Aileen (Thompson) Morgan; m. Neil S. Dawson, Nov. 28, 1964; children: Shelley Diane Dawson Sedwick, Lori Ann Dawson Hughes, Christy Lynn. BS in Home Econs. and Journalism, Kans. State U., 1962. Asst. publs. editor Ohio State U. Coop. Extension Svc., Columbus, 1962-64; home editor Ohio Farmer mag., 1964-78; food editor Columbus Dispatch, 1978-2000; ret. Recipient Commn. award Ohio Poultry Assn., 1980. Mem. Assn. Food Journalists, Ohio Newspaper Women's Assn. (several writing and newspaper design awards 1985-94). Avocations: biking, running, reading, cooking.

DAWSON, WILLIAM RYAN, zoology educator; b. Los Angeles, Aug. 24, 1927; s. William Eldon and Mary (Ryan) D.; m. Virginia Louise Berwick, Sept. 9, 1950; children: Deborah, Denise, William. Student, Stanford, 1945-46; BA, UCLA, 1949, MA, 1950, PhD, 1953; DSc, U. Western Australia, 1971. Faculty zoology U. Mich., Ann Arbor, 1953-94, prof., 1962-94, D.E.S. Brown prof. biol. scis., 1981-94, chmn. div. biol. scis., 1974-82, dir. Mus. Zoology, 1982-93, D.E.S. Brown prof. emeritus, 1994—. Lectr. Summer Inst. Desert Biology, Ariz. State U., 1960-71, Maytag prof., 1982; rschr. Australian-Am. Edn. Found., U. Western Australia, 1969-70; Carpenter lectr. San Diego State U., 1996; mem. Speakers Bur., Am. Inst. Biol. Sci., 1960-62; mem. adv. panel NSF environ. biology program, 1967-69; mem. adv. com. for rsch. NSF, 1973-77; adv. panel NSF regulatory biology program, 1979-82; mem. R/V Alpha Helix New Guinea Expdn., 1969; chief scientist R/V Dolphin Gulf of Calif. Expdn., 1976; mem. R/V Alpha Helix Galapagos Expdn., 1978. Editorial bd.: Condor, 1960-63, Auk, 1964-68, Ecology, 1968-70, Ann. Rev. Physiology, 1973-79, Physiol. Zoology, 1976-86; co-editor: Springer-Verlag Zoophysiology and Ecology series, 1968-72; assoc. editor: Biology of the Reptilia, 1972, Birds of N.Am., 1997—. Served with USNR, 1945-46. USPHS Postdoctoral Research fellow, 1953; Guggenheim fellow, 1962-63; Recipient Russell award U. Mich., 1959, Distinguished Faculty Achievement award, 1976; Wheeler Lectr. U. N.D., 1986. Fellow AAAS (council del. 1984-86), Am. Ornithol. Union (Brewster medal 1979); mem. Soc. Integrative Comparative Biology, Am. Physiol. Soc., Ecol. Soc. Am., Cooper Ornithol. Soc. (hon., Painton award 1963, Miller Rsch. award 1996), Phi Beta Kappa, Sigma Xi, Kappa Sigma. Home: 1376 Bird Rd Ann Arbor MI 48103-2351 E-mail: wrdawson@umich.edu.

DAY, BOBBY, radio personality; Radio host KUDL-AM, Kansas City, 1970, WHB-AM, KBEQ-FM, Oldies 95, Mission, Kans., 1991—. Avocations: hockey, soccer. Office: Oldies 95 5800 Foxridge Dr 6th Fl Mission KS 66202

DAY, COLIN LESLIE, publisher; b. St. Albans, Eng., July 19, 1944; came to U.S., 1978; s. Archibald William Dagless and José (Greenfield) D.; m. Jennifer Ann Jones, July 30, 1966; children: Matthew, Gudrun. B.A., Oxford U., 1966, M.A., 1968; Ph.D., U. Stirling, 1973. Research officer N.I.E.S.R., London, 1966-68; research fellow Stirling U., Scotland, 1968-71, lectr. in econs. Scotland, 1971-75; sr. econs. editor Cambridge Univ. Press, U.K., N.Y.C., 1976-81, editor-in-chief, 1981-82, editorial dir., 1982-87; dir. U. Mich. Press, 1988—. Bd. dirs. Assn. Am. Univ. Presses, 1986-89, 92-95, pres., 1993-94. Co-author: Company Financing in United Kingdom, 1974; contbr. articles to prof. jours. Justice of peace County of Perthshire, Scotland, 1970-75; chmn. West Perthshire Labour Party, 1972-75. Home: 276 Sumac Ln Ann Arbor MI 48105-3013 Office: U Mich Press PO Box 1104 839 Greene St Ann Arbor MI 48104-3209

DAY, DELBERT EDWIN, ceramic engineering educator; b. Avon, Ill., Aug. 16, 1936; s. Edwin Raymond and Doris Jennings (Main) D.; m. Shirley Ann Foraker, June 2, 1956; children: Lynne Denise, Thomas Edwin. BS in Ceramic Engring., Mo. Sch. Mines and Metallurgy, 1958; MS in Ceramic Tech., Pa. State U., 1960, PhD in Ceramic Tech., 1961. Registered profl. engr., Mo. With U. Mo., Rolla, 1961—, dir. Indsl. Rsch. Ctr., 1965-72, dir. Grad. Ctr. Materials Rsch., 1983-92, Curators' prof. ceramic engring., 1981—; founder, chmn., CEO Mo-Sci Corp., Mo., 1985—; dir. State of Mo. Tech. Corp., 1999—. Vis. prof. chemistry Miss. Coll., 1963, Eindhoven Tech. U., The Netherlands, 1971; mem. tech. staff Sandia Nat. Labs., Albuquerque, 1981, 91; sr. vis. faculty scientist Battelle Pacific N.W. Labs., Richland, Wash., 1990; asst. dean grad. studies Mo. Sch. Mines and Metallurgy, 1979-81; chmn. acad. coun. U. Mo., Rolla, 1978-79, active numerous other coms.; cons. Los Alamos Nat. Labs., 1983-95, NASA, 1974-88, numerous other glass and refractories cos., 1958—; vice-chmn. Gordon Rsch. Conf. on Glass, 1990-92, chmn., 1992-94; tech. program dir. confs. on glass including Baden-Baden, Germany, 1973, Rolla, 1975, XII Internat. Glass Congress, Albuquerque, 1980, Internat. and 7th U. Conf. Glass Sci., Clausthal-Zellerfeld, Germany, 1983; founder, CEO MO-Sci. Corp., Rolla. Contbr. over 275 articles to profl. jours. Bd. chmn. Wesley Found.; chmn. United Ministries Higher Edn. Bd. Dirs., 1969; adv. Explorer Scout Post 82, 1964-69; bd. dirs. Rolla Community United Fund, 1975-81, Mo. Incutech Found., 1984-87; mem. bd. adjustment City of Rolla, 1973-79; fin. chmn. United Meth. Ch., 1978-80; pres., bd. dirs. Rolla Community Devel. Corp., 1967-61, 82-90. 1st lt. CE US Army, 1958-64. Recipient Outstanding Young Man award Clinton (Miss.) Jaycees, 1963, Rolla (Mo.) Jaycees, 1968, Cmty. Builder award Fraternal Order of Eagles, 1971, Pres.'s award for rsch. and creativity U. Mo., 1996. Fellow Am. Ceramic Soc. (Outstanding Educator award edni. coun. 1991, v.p. rsch. 1990-91, trustee 1986-98, trustee glass divsn. 1986-89, chmn. glass divsn. 1982-83, fellows com. 1987-92, publs. com. 1980-82, 90-95, v.p. Publs. 1992-93, treas. 1993-94, pres.-elect 1994-95, pres. 1995-96, others); mem. ASTM, Am. Soc. Engring. Edn. (chmn. mineral engring. div. 1968-69, program chmn. mineral engring. div. 1967-68), Nat. Inst. Ceramic Engrs. (Profl. Achievement in Ceramic Engring. award 1971), Brit. Soc. Glass Tech., Materials Rsch. Soc., Mo. Acad. Sci. (corp. mem. com. 1989-90), Keramos, Blue Key, Tau Beta Pi, Phi Kappa Phi, Sigma Gamma Epsilon, Sigma Xi (treas. U. Mo.-Rolla chpt. 1966-67, sec. 1967-68, v.p. 1968-69, pres. 1969-70). Achievements include first to include 41 U.S. and foreign patents (with others) for Alumina Zircon Bond for Refractory Grains, Chemically Durable Nitrogen Containing Phosphate Glasses USeful for Sealing to Metals;first to include Radioactive Biologically Compatible Glass Microspheres, Radioactive Glass Microspheres, iron phosphate glasses for vitrifying hazardous materials, others;invention of TheraSphere used for treatment of liver cancer. Home: PO Box 357 Rolla MO 65402-0357 Office: U Mo-Rolla Grad Ctr Material Rsch 109 Straumanis Hl Rolla MO 65409-1170 E-mail: day@umr.edu.

DAY, JULIAN C. retail executive; BA, MA, Oxford U.; MBA, London Bus. Sch. Sr. engagement mgr. McKinsey & Co., 1980-85; v.p., European devel. mgr. Chase Manhattan Bank, 1985-87; exec. mgmt. cons. Kohlberg, Kravis, and Roberts, 1987-93; exec. v.p., CFO Safeway, Inc., 1993-98, Sears, Roebuck and Co., Hoffman Estate, Ill., 1999—. Office: Sears Roebuck and Co 333 Beverly Rd Hoffman Estates IL 60179-0001

DAY, RICHARD H. state legislator; b. Owatonna, Minn., Mar. 9, 1937; m. Janet; 4 children. BA, Winona State U., 1968. Mem. Minn. Senate from 28th dist., St. Paul, 1991—. Mem. agrl. & rural com., con. com. & health & human svc. com., Minn. State Senate. Mem. Eagles, Elks, KC. Office: Minn Senate 117 State Ofc Bldg 100 Constitution Ave Saint Paul MN 55155-1232 Address: 277 Cedar Cove Ln Owatonna MN 55060-4224

DAYS, RITA DENISE, state legislator; b. Minden, La., Oct. 16, 1950; d. Marion and Juliette (Mitchell) Heard; m. Frank S. Days, June 17, 1972; children: Elliott Charles, Natalie Rechelle, Evelyn Jeanine. BMus, Lincoln U., 1972. Tchr. Webster Parish Sch. Bd., Minden, La., 1972; clk. typist Urban League of St. Louis, 1973-74, asst. dir. pub. info., 1974, placement interviewer, 1974-76; office supr. Burroughs Corp., St. Louis, 1976-80; sec., admissions counselor Jewish Coll. of Nursing, 1989-93; mem. Mo. Ho. of Reps., 1993—. Chair elections com. Mo. Ho. of Reps., St. Louis, treas. Mo. Legis. Black Caucus, mem. Supreme Ct. Task Force on Children and Families; mem. Interagy. Coordinating Coun. part H. Active Ptnrs. for Kids, 1993—, New Sunny Mount Bapt. Ch.; sec. Women Legislators Mo.; bd. mem. Project Respond.; past bd. dirs. Normandy Sch. Dist. Mem. Alpha Kappa Alpha. Democrat. Office: Mo Ho of Reps State Capitol Building Jefferson City MO 65101-1556

DAYTON, MARK, senator; b. Mpls., Jan. 26, 1947; 2 children: Eric, Andrew. Grad. cum laude, Yale U., 1969. Tchr. gen. sci. N.Y.C. Pub. Sch., 1969-71; counselor, adminstr. Social Svc. agency, Boston, 1972-76; legis. asst. to Minn. Senator Walter Mondale; staff mem. for Govr. Rudy Perpich, Minn., 1977; commr. econ. devel. State of Minn., 1978, commr. energy and econ. devel., 1983, state auditor, 1990, U.S. senator, 2001—. Mem. Senator Paul Wellstone's re-election campaign, 1995-96; agr., armed svcs., rules, gov. affairs com., state of Minn. Office: SR-346 Russell Senate Office bldg Washington DC 20510*

DAZE, ERIC, professional hockey player; b. Montreal, Can., July 2, 1975; Selected 4th found NHL entry draft Chgo. Blackhawks, 1993; left wing Beauport QMJ Hockey League, 1992-95; right wing Chgo. Blackhawks, 1995—. Named to QMJ Hockey League All-Star first team, 1993-94, 94-95. Recipient Can. Hockey League Most Sportsmanlike Player of Yr. award, 1994-95, Frank J. Selke Trophy, 1994-95; named Sporting News Rookie of Yr., 1996. Office: c/o Chicago Blackhawks 1901 W Madison St Chicago IL 60612-2459*

D'AZZO, JOHN JOACHIM, electrical engineer, educator; b. N.Y.C., Nov. 30, 1919; s. Domenick and Jacqueline (Cappello) D'A.; m. Betty G. McBride, June 13, 1953; 1 child, Dennis. BEE, CCNY, 1941; MSEE, Ohio State U., 1950; PhD, Salford U., Eng., 1978. Registered profl. engr., Ohio. Quality control engr. Western Electric Co., Kearney, N.J., 1941-42; devel. engr. Air Materiel Command, Wright Patterson AFB, Ohio, 1942-46; prof. elec. engring. Air Force Inst. Tech., 1947-98, prof. emeritus, 1998—. Head dept. elec. and computer engring. Air Force Inst. Tech., Wright Patterson AFB, 1984-95. Co-author: Feedback Control System Analysis and Synthesis, 1960, 2d edit., 1966, Linear Control System Analysis and Design, 1975, 4th edit., 1995. Served to 2d lt. U.S. Army, 1945-46. Named Outstanding Engr. Affiliate Socs. Ohio, 1962, 86. Fellow IEEE, AIAA (assoc.); mem. Am. Soc. for Engring. Edn., Sigma Xi, Tau Beta Pi, Eta Kappa Nu. Roman Catholic. Home: 3923 Winthrop Dr Beavercreek OH 45431-3148 Office: Air Force Inst Tech 2950 P St Wright Patterson AFB OH 45433-7765 E-mail: john.dazzo@afit.edu.

DE ACOSTA, ALEJANDRO DANIEL, mathematician, educator; b. Buenos Aires, Feb. 1, 1941; came to U.S., 1981; s. Wladimiro and Telma (Reca) de A.; m. Martha Callejo, Aug. 19, 1966; children: Alejandro Elias, Diego Andrés. Lic. in math. scis., U. Buenos Aires, 1965; PhD, U. Calif., Berkeley, 1969. Instr. math. MIT, Cambridge, 1970-71; asst. prof. U. La Plata, Argentina, 1972-75; assoc. prof. U. Buenos Aires, 1975; rschr. Venezuelan Inst. Sci. Investigation, Caracas, 1976-82; vis. prof. U. Wis., Madison, 1981-82; vis. prof. dept. math. and stats. Case Western Res. U., Cleve., 1983, prof., 1984—. Assoc. editor Annals Probability, 1985-90; mem. editl. bd. Jour. Theoretical Probability, 1987—; contbr. articles to math. jours. Recipient prize in math. Nat. Rsch. Coun. Venezuela, 1978. Fellow Inst. Math. Stats.; mem. Am. Math. Soc. Office: Case Western Res U Dept Maths Cleveland OH 44106

DEACY, THOMAS EDWARD, JR. lawyer; b. Kansas City, Mo., Oct. 14, 1918; s. Thomas Edward and Grace (Scales) D.; m. Jean Freeman, July 10, 1943 (div. 1988); children: Bennette Kay Deacy Kramer, Carolyn G., Margaret Deacy Vickrey, Thomas, Ann Deacy Krause; m. Jean Holmes McDonald, 1988. J.D., U. Mo., 1940; M.B.A., U. Chgo., 1949. Bar: Mo. 1940, Ill. 1946. Practice law, Kansas City, 1940-42; ptnr. Taylor, Miller, Busch & Magner, Chgo., 1946-55, Deacy & Deacy, Kansas City, 1955—. Lectr. Northwestern U., 1949-55, U. Chgo., 1950-55; dir., mem. exec. com. St. L.-S.F. Ry., 1962-80; dir. Burlington No. Inc., 1980-86; mem. U.S. team Anglo-Am. Legal Exchange, 1973, 77. Mem. Juv. Protective Assn. Chgo., 1947-55, pres., bd. dirs., 1950-53; mem. exec. bd. Chgo. coun. Boy Scouts Am., 1952-55; pres. Kansas City Philharmonic Orch., 1961-63, chmn. bd. trustees, 1963-65; trustee Sunset Hill Sch., 1963-73; trustee, mem. exec. com. u. Kansas City, 1963—; trustee Mo. Law Sch. Found., pres., 1973-77, Kans. chpt. The Nature Conservancy, 1994-99. Capt. AUS, 1942-45. Fellow Am. Coll. Trial Lawyers (regent 1968— , treas. 1973-74, pres. 1975-76), Am. Bar Found; mem. Am. Law Inst., Jud. Conf. U.S. (implementation com. on admission of attys. to fed. practice 1979-86), ABA (commn. standards jud. adminstrn. 1972-74, standing com. fed. judiciary 1974-80), Ill. Bar Assn., Chgo. Bar Assn., Mo. Bar, Kansas City Bar Assn., Lawyers Assn. Kansas City, Chgo. Club, La Jolla (Calif.) Country Club, La Jolla Beach and Tennis Club, Kansas City Club, Kansas City Country Club, River Club, Q.E.B.H. Sr. Hon. Soc. of Mo. Univ., Beta Gamma Sigma, Sigma Chi. Home: 2724 Verona Cir Mission Hills KS 66208-1265 Office: 920 Main St Ste 1900 Kansas City MO 64105-2010 E-mail: ted@deacylaw.com.

DEAL, WILLIAM THOMAS, school psychologist; b. Dec. 18, 1949; s. Richard Lee and Rheta Lucille (Gerber) D.; m. Paula Nespeca, AUg. 5, 1972. BS, Bowling Green State U., 1972; MA, John Carroll U., 1977; postgrad., Kent State U., 1979—. Sci. tchr. Westlake Schs., 1972-76; intern sch. psychologist Garfield Heights Schs., 1976-77; sch. psychologist, 1977—; pvt. practice psychology Parma Heights, Ohio, 1982-84. Alternate mem. adv. council Cuyahoga COunty Spl. Edn. Svc. Ctr., 1977—. Recipient Cert. of Recognition, Garfield Heights Bd. Edn., 1980; Outstanding Achievement award Cleve. Assn. for Children with Learning Disabilities, Inc., 1980; named Psychologist of Yr., Cleveland Sch., 1990. Mem. Nat. Assn. Sch. Psychologists, United Teaching Profession, Ohio Sch. Psychology Assn., Cleve. Assn. Sch. Psychologists, Phi Delta Kappa. Republican. Methodist. Home: 5290 Kings Hwy Cleveland OH 44126-3059 Office: 5275 Turney Rd Cleveland OH 44125-2501

DEAN, GEORGE R. state legislator; b. Kansas City, Kans., Sept. 12, 1933; m. Ethel J. Haley, 1957. BSEE, U. Kans., 1959; MSEE, Wichita State U., 1969. Aerospace engr. Missile System divsn. Beech Aircraft, until 1992; mem. Kans. Ho. of Reps. Topeka, 1978-2000. Bd. dirs. Kans. Tech. Enterprise Corp. Bd. dirs. Spl. Olumpics, 1986-87, Very Spl. Arts Kans.; adv. bd. University Kans. EECS. Mem. Inst. Elec. and Electronic Engrs. (dir. 1997-99, Region 5 Profl. award 1983, Centenial award 1984, Profl. Acheivement award 1988), Am. Legion, Aircraft Owners and Pilots Assn. Democrat. Home: 2646 Exchange St Wichita KS 67217-2928

DEAN, HOWARD M., JR. food company executive; b. 1937; married. BBA, So. Meth. U., 1960; MBA, Northwestern U., 1961. With Dean Foods Co., Inc., Franklin Park, Ill., 1955—, internal auditor, 1965-68, asst. to v.p. fin., 1968-70, pres., 1970-89, CEO, 1987—, chmn., 1989—. Served to lt. (j.g.) USN, 1962-65. Office: Dean Foods Co 3600 River Rd Franklin Park IL 60131-2185

DEAN, WARREN MICHAEL, design and construction company executive; b. Great Falls, Mont., Apr. 27, 1944; s. Warren Earl and Mary Amelia (Sankovich) D.; m. Pamela Carol House, June 18, 1977; children: Marc, Drew, Molly, Anna. BArch, Mont. State U., 1969; MArch in Urban Design, U. Colo., Denver, 1973; MBA, U. Denver, 1982. Registered architect, Colo. Architect Davis Partnership, Denver, 1973-74; project mgr. CRS Constructors/Mgrs., 1974-78, v.p., 1978-82, group v.p., 1982-83; pres. CRSS Constructors Inc., 1983-88; exec. v.p. CRSS Commercial Group, Inc., 1988-90; v.p. CRSS, Inc., Greenville, S.C., 1990-92; chmn., CEO CRSS Constructors, Inc. (subs. Jacobs Engring. Group), Houston, 1993—; group v.p., corp. officer Jacobs Engring. Group, Inc., Houston and St. Louis, 1997—; chmn. Jacobs Facilities Inc., 1999—. Contbr. articles to profl. jours.; speaker in field. Mem. Denver Concert Chorale, 1974-77; bd. dirs. Jr. Achievement Metro Denver, 1985-88, chmn., 1987-88; bd. dirs. Jr. Achievement Southeast Tex., Inc., 1998-99, Jr. Achievement Mississippi Valley, Inc., 2000—; bd. dirs. Denver Opera Co., 1976-77. Served to lt. USNR, 1969-72. Advanced Acad. scholar Mont. St. U., 1967-69. Mem. AIA (com. architecture for edn. 1982—), Soc. Am. Milit. Engrs., Constrn. Industry Inst., Planning Execs. Inst., Denver C. of C. (chmn. com. econ. devel.), Colo. Soc. Architects, Rotary. Roman Catholic. Office: Jacobs Engring Group Inc 501 N Broadway Saint Louis MO 63102-1815

DEARDEN, DICK L. state legislator; b. Des Moines, June 3, 1938; m. Sharon Dearden; 3 children. With Polk County Ctrl. Com., 1972—; chmn. Polk County Dems., 1980-82; job developer fifth jud. dist., 1986—; supr. AMF Lawn and Garden; bus. rep. Almalgated Meat Cutters; mem. Iowa Senate from 35th dist., 1994—. Del. Dem. Nat. Convention, 1996. With Iowa NG, 1956-62. Mem. AFSCME (local 3289), AMVETS, Nat. Wild Turkey Fedn., Pheasants Forever, Ducks Unltd., Izaak Walton League. Democrat. Lutheran. Home: 3113 Kinsey Ave Des Moines IA 50317-6603 Office: State Capitol Dist 35 3 9th And Grand Des Moines IA 50319-0001 E-mail: dick_dearden@legis.state.ia.us.

DE ARMAS, FREDERICK ALFRED, foreign language educator; b. Havana, Cuba, Feb. 9, 1945; came to U.S., 1959, naturalized, 1968; s. Alfredo and Ana Maria (Galdos) De A. B.A. magna cum laude, Stetson U., DeLand, Fla., 1965; Ph.D. (Carnegie fellow 1965-68), U. N.C., 1968. Mem. faculty La. State U., Baton Rouge, 1968-88, prof. Spanish, 1978-88, acting chmn. dept., 1979-80, dir. grad. studies, 1980-85; prof. Spanish and comparative lit. Pa. State U., 1988-91, Disting. prof. Spanish and comparative lit., 1991-98, Edwin Erle Sparks prof. Spanish and Comparative Lit., 1998-2000, fellow Inst. for Arts and Humanities, 1989-2000; prof. Spanish U. Chgo., 2000-01, Andrew W. Mellon prof. of humanities, 2001—. Vis. assoc. prof. U. Mo., Columbia, summer 1977, vis. prof., fall

1986; vis. prof. Duke U., spring 1994. Author: The Four Interpolated Stories in the Roman Comique, 1971, Paul Scarron, 1972, The Invisible Mistress, 1976, The Return of Astraea, 1986, The Prince in the Tower, 1993, Heavenly Bodies, 1996, A Star-Crossed Golden Age, 1998, Cervantes, Raphael and the Classics, 1998, also articles; editor: Pa. State U. Studies in Romance Literatures, 1991-2001; mem. editorial adv. bd. Bull. Comediantes, 1981—, Hispanófila, 1981-88, 2001—, PMLA, 1985-89, Hispania, 1993-95, Jour. Interdisciplinary Lit. Studies, 1993—; assoc. editor South Central Rev., 1987-89, Comparative Literature Studies, 1989-2001. NEH grantee, summer 1979; NEH fellow, 1985, 95, summer inst., 1989, dir. summer isnt., 1994. Mem. MLA, Comparative Lit. Assn., Renaissance Soc. Am., Am. Assn. Tchrs. Spanish and Portuguese, Assn. Internat, Hispanistas, Hispanic Soc. Am. (Corr.) Office: U Chgo Dept Romance Lang 1050 E 59th St Chicago IL 60637 E-mail: fdearmas@uchicago.edu.

DEASON, HEROLD MCCLURE, lawyer; b. Alton, Ill., July 24, 1942; s. Ernest Wilburn and Mildred Mary (McClure) D.; m. Wilma Lee Kaemmerle, June 18, 1966; children: Sean, Ian, Whitney. BA, Albion Coll., 1964; JD, Northwestern U., 1967. Bar: Mich. 1968. Assoc. Bodman, Longley & Dahling, LLP, Detroit, 1967-74, ptnr., 1975—. City atty. Grosse Pointe Pk., Mich., 1978—. Vice chmn. Detroit, Windsor Freedom Festival, 1978-92; bd. dirs. Spirit of Detroit Assn., 1980—. Recipient Spirit of Detroit award, Detroit City Coun., 1986. Mem. ABA, Mich. Assn. Mcpl. Attys. (pres. 1995-97), Detroit Bar Assn., Can.-U.S. Bus. Assn. (v.p. 1997—), Grosse Pointe Yacht Club (commodore 1992-93), Detroit Racquet Club, Windsor Club, Clinton River Boat Club. Home: 1044 Kensington Ave Grosse Pointe Park MI 48230-1437 Office: Bodman Longley & Dahling 100 Renaissance Ctr 34th Fl Detroit MI 48243-1001 E-mail: hdeason@bodmanlongley.com.

DEBARTOLO, EDWARD JOHN, JR. professional football team owner, real estate developer; b. Youngstown, Ohio, Nov. 6, 1946; s. Edward J. and Marie Patricia (Montani) DeB.; m. Cynthia Ruth Papalia, Nov. 27, 1968; children: Lisa Marie, Tiffanie Lynne, Nicole Anne. Student, U. Notre Dame, 1964-68. With Edward J. DeBartolo Corp., Youngstown, Ohio, 1960—, v.p., 1971-76, exec. v.p., 1976-79, chief adminstrv. officer, 1979-94; pres., CEO, 1995—; owner San Francisco 49ers, 1977-97; chmn. bd. DeBartolo Realty Corp., 1994—; chmn., CEO DeBartolo Entertainment, Inc. Trustee Youngstown State U., 1974-77; nat. adv. coun. St. Jude Children's Rsch. Hosp., 1978—, local chmn., 1979-80; chmn. local fund drive Am. Cancer Soc., 1975—; mem. Nat. Cambodia Crisis Com., 1980—; chmn. 19th Ann. Victor Warner award, 1985, City of Hope's Spirit of Life Banquet, 1986; apptd. adv. coun. Coll. Bus. Adminstrn. U. Notre Dame, 1988; adv. coun. Nat. Assn. People with AIDS, 1992; bd. dirs. Cleve. Clinic Found., 1991; lifetime mem. Italian Scholarship League. With U.S. Army, 1969. Recipient Man of Yr. award St. Jude Children's Hosp., 1979, Boy's Town of Italy in San Francisco, 1985, Sportsman of Yr. award Nat. Italian Am. Sports Hall of Fame, 1991, Cert. of Merit, Salvation Army, 1982, Warner award, 1986, Silver Cable Car award San Francisco Conv. and Visitors Bur., 1988, Nat. Football League Man of Yr. award Football News, 1989, Svc. to Youth award Cath. Youth Orgn., 1990, Hall of Fame award Cardinal Mooney High Sch., 1993. Mem. Internat. Coun. Shopping Ctrs., Italian Scholarship League (life), Tippecanoe Country Club, Fonderlac Country Club, Dapper Dan Club (dir. 1980—). Office: Edward J DeBartolo Corp PO Box 9128 Youngstown OH 44513-0128

DEBAT, DONALD JOSEPH, media consultant, columnist; b. Chgo., Sept. 29, 1944; s. Chester Louis and Marie Dorothy (Mehok) DeB.; m. Heidi Loretta Meinhardt, Sept. 3, 1966 (div. Aug. 1984); children: Aimee Lisa, Erik Andreas; m. Sara Elizabeth Benson, Aug. 20, 1994 (div. Oct. 2001); children: Donald Edward, Herbert Lankford. AA, Wright Jr. Coll., 1963; BJ, U. Mo., 1966, MA, 1968. Editl. asst. Ency. Brit., Chgo., summer 1965; reporter, Sunday editor Columbia Missourian, 1966-67; fin. reporter Chgo. Daily News, 1968-73, sports copy editor, 1974-75, real estate editor, 1976-78, Chgo. Sun-Times, 1978-88, asst. mng. editor, real estate, 1988-94; real estate columnist Crain News Svc., Chgo., 1995—; pres. Donald J. DeBat & Assocs., Inc., 1995—2001; CEO DeBat Media, Inc., 2001—. Author: The Mortgage Manual, 1986, 2d edit., 1989, Home Refinancing, 1986; author, editor: Living in Greater Chicago, 1988-94. Recipient numerous awards for articles in real estate field; inductee Chgo. Sixteen-inch Softball Hall of Fame, 1999. Mem. Nat. Assn. Real Estate Editors (bd. dirs., editor of best real estate sect. award 1978, 83, 84, 92), Nat. Trust for Hist. Preservation. Avocations: softball, handball, real estate investing and renovation, travel, skiing. Office: Crane Comm Inc 360 N Michigan Ave Chicago IL 60601-3806 Fax: (312) 944-8877. E-mail: debatnet@aol.com.

DEBAUGE, JANICE B. musician; MusB magna cum laude, Southern Mo. U. Classical musician, soprano. Bd. regents Washburn U., 2001—. Home: 1966 Morningside Dr Emporia KS 66801

DEBEAR, RICHARD STEPHEN, library planning consultant; b. N.Y.C., Jan. 18, 1933; s. Arthur A. and Sarah (Morrison) deB.; m. Estelle Carmel Grandon, Apr. 27, 1951; children: Richard, Jr., Diana deBear Fortson, Patricia deBear Talkington, Robert, Christopher, Nancy deBear Naski. BS, Queens Coll., CUNY, 1953. Sales rep. Sperry Rand Corp., Blue Bell, Pa., 1954-76; pres. Libr. Design Assocs., Plymouth, Mich., 1976-97, Am. Libr. Ctr., Plymouth, 1981—. Bldg. cons. to numerous librs., 1965—; mem. interior design program profl. adv. com. Wayne State U. Mem. ALA, Mich. Libr. Assn. (oversight com. Leadership Acad. 1990—). Office: Am Libr Ctr Inc 1149 S Main St Plymouth MI 48170-2213 E-mail: ddebear@americanlibrary.com.

DEBEAUSSAERT, KENNETH JOSEPH, state legislator; b. Mt. Clemens, Mich., Apr. 10, 1954; Aide U.S. Rep. David Bonior; mem. Mich. Ho. of Reps from 75th dist., Lansing, Mich. Senate from 11th dist., Lansing, 1995—. Chmn. consumers com. Mich. Ho. Reps., agriculture, conservation, recreation & environ. com., liquor control com., transp. com. Mem. New Baltimore Hist. Soc., Macomb County Farm Bur., Oakland U. Alumni Assn., Friends of Catholic Social Svc. Address: 310 Farnum Bldg PO Box 30036 Lansing MI 48909-7536

DEBICKI, ANDREW PETER, foreign language educator; b. Warsaw, Poland, June 28, 1934; came to U.S., 1948, naturalized, 1955; s. Roman and Jadwiga (Dunin) D.; m. Mary Jo Tidmarsh, Dec. 29, 1959 (dec. 1975); children: Mary Beth, Margaret; m. Mary Elizabeth Gwin, May 16, 1987. BA, Yale U., 1955, PhD, 1960. Instr. Trinity Coll., Hartford, Conn., 1957-60; asst. prof. Grinnell (Iowa) Coll., 1960-62, assoc. prof., 1962-66, prof., 1966-68; prof. Spanish U. Kans., Lawrence, 1968-76; Univ. Disting. prof. Univ. Kans., 1976—. Dir. Hall Ctr., 1989-93; dean Grad. Sch. and Internat. Programs, 1993-2000. Author: La poesia de Jose Gorostiza, 1962, Estudios sobre poesia espanola contemporanea, 1968, 81, Damaso Alonso, 1970, 74, La poesia de Jorge Guillen, 1973, Poetas hispanoamericanos contemporaneos: Punto de vista, perspectiva, experiencia, 1976, Poetry of Discovery, 1982, 87, Angel Gonzalez, 1989, Spanish Poetry of the Twentieth Century, 1994, 97; contbr. articles to various publs. Guggenheim fellow, 1970-71, 80, Nat. Humanities Ctr. fellow, 1980, 92-93, Am. Coun. Learned Socs. fellow, 1966-67, NEH sr. rsch. fellow, 1992-93; ADFL Career award 1999. Mem. MLA (exec. coun. 1989-93), Am. Assn. Tchrs. Spanish and Portuguese. Home: 1445 Applegate Ct Lawrence KS 66049-2937 Office: U Kans Dept of Spanish/Portuguese Lawrence KS 66045-0001 E-mail: adebicki@ukans.edu.

DE BLASIS, JAMES MICHAEL, artistic director, producer, stage director; b. N.Y.C., Apr. 12, 1931; s. James and Sarah (de Felice) de B.; m. Ruth Hofreuter, Aug. 25, 1957; 1 child, Blythe. BFA, Carnegie Mellon U., 1959, MFA, 1960. Mem. drama faculty Carnegie Mellon U., 1960-62; head drama dept. Onondaga C.C., Syracuse, N.Y., 1963-72; head Opera Workshop, 1969-70; adv. of opera Corbett Found., Cin., 1971-76; gen. dir. Cin. Opera Assn., 1973-87, artistic dir., 1988-96. Internat. ind. stage dir. of opera, 1962—; pvt. coach, Dramatic Interpretation of Operatic Roles, 1995—. Artistic advisor, Pitts. Opera, Inc., 1979-83. With U.S. Army, 1951-53. Recipient award Omicron Delta Kappa, 1959, Alumni award Bellaire High Sch., 1974, award in arts adminstrn. Gov. Ohio, 1989, Post/Corbett award for performing artist Corbett Found./Cin. Post, 1989. Mem. Actors Equity, Am. Guild Mus. Artists, Drama Alumni Carnegie Mellon U., Beta Theta Pi, Omicron Delta Kappa. Republican. Episcopalian.

DE BOOR, CARL, mathematician; b. Stolp, Germany, Dec. 3, 1937; m. Matilda C. Friedrich, Feb. 6, 1960 (div. Sept. 12, 1984); children: C. Thomas, Elisabeth, Peter, Adam; m. Helen L. Bee, Jan. 2, 1991. Student, Universitaet Hamburg, 1956-59, Harvard U., 1959-60; Ph.D., U. Mich., 1966. Rsch. mathematician Gen. Motors Research Labs., 1960-64; asst. prof. math., computer sci. Purdue U., 1966-68, assoc. prof., 1968-72; prof. math., computer sci. U. Wis.-Madison, 1972—. Vis. staff mem. Los Alamos Sci. Labs., 1970— Author: (with S. Conte) Elementary Numerical Analysis, 1972, 1980, A Practical Guide to Splines, 1978, (with J.B. Rosser) Pocket Calculator Supplement for Calculus, 1979, (with K. Höllig and S. Riemenschneider) Box Splines, 1993. Named John Von Neumann lectr. Soc. Indsl. and Applied Math., 1996. Fellow Am. Acad. Arts and Scis.; mem. Nat. Acad. Engring., NAS, Soc. Indsl. and Applied Math., Polish Acad. Sci., Leopoldina, Phi Beta Kappa. Office: U Wis Depts Computer Scis Math Madison WI 53706 E-mail: carl@deBoor.de.

DE BRANGES DE BOURCIA, LOUIS, mathematics educator; b. Paris, Aug. 21, 1932; s. Louis and Diane (McDonald) deB.; m. Tatiana Jakimow, Dec. 17, 1980; 1 child, Konstantin. BS, MIT, 1953; PhD, Cornell U., 1957. Prof. Purdue U., Lafayette, Ind., 1962-88, disting. prof. of math., 1989—. Fellow Sloan Found., 1963-66, Guggenheim Found., 1967-68; recipient Humboldt prize Alexander Humboldt Found., 1986-88, Ostrowski prize Alexander Ostrowski Found., 1989. Home: Hameau de l'Yvette Batiment D Chemin des Graviers F-91190 Gif Sur Yvette France Office: Purdue U Dept Math Lafayette IN 47907-1395 E-mail: branges@math.purdue.edu.

DEBRUCE, PAUL, agricultural food products company executive; Founder DeBruce Grain Inc., Kansas City, Mo., 1978, now CEO; also DeBruce Grain de Mex., Queretaro.

DEBUS, ALLEN GEORGE, history educator; b. Chgo., Aug. 16, 1926; s. George Walter William and Edna Pauline (Schwenneke) D.; m. Brunilda Lopez-Rodriguez, Aug. 25, 1951; children: Allen Anthony George, Richard William, Karl Edward. B.S., Northwestern U., 1947; A.M., Ind. U., 1949; Ph.D., Harvard U., 1961; postgrad., U. Coll. London, 1959-60; D.Sc. h.c., Cath. U. Louvain, 1985. Research chemist Abbott Labs., North Chicago, Ill., 1951-56; asst. prof. U. Chgo., 1961-65, assoc. prof. history, 1965-68, prof., 1968-78, Morris Fishbein prof. history sci. and medicine, 1978-96, Morris Fishbein prof. emeritus, 1996—; dir. Morris Fishbein Ctr. for Study History Sci. and Medicine, 1971-77. Disting. vis. prof. Ariz. ctr. for medieval and renaissance studies Ariz. State U., 1984; vis. prof. Inst. Chemistry, U. São Paulo, Brazil, 1990; mem. internat. adv. com. Tel-Aviv U. The Cohn Inst. History and Philosophy of Sci. and Ideas, Ctr. for History and Philosophy of Sci. of Hebrew U. of Jerusalem; mem. internat. adv. bd. Annali dell'Istituto e Museo di Storia della Scienza di Firenze; cons. lit. and sci. curriculum Ga. Inst. Tech. Author: The English Paracelsians, 1965, 66, (with Robert P. Multhauf) Alchemy and Chemistry in the 17th Century, 1966, The Chemical Dream of the Renaissance, 1968, 2d edit., 1972, Science and Education in the 17th Century, 1970, (with Brian Rust) The Complete Entertainment Discography, 1973, 2d rev. edit., 1989, The Chemical Philosophy, 2 vols., 1977, 2d edit., 2002, Japanese transl., 1999, Man and Nature in the Renaissance, 1978, 15th rev. edit., 1995, Italian transl., 1982, Spanish transl., 1985, 86, 2d edit., 1995, Japanese transl., 1986, Chinese transl., 1988, 2000, Greek transl., 1997, Robert Fludd and His Philosophical Key, 1979; Science and History: A Chemist's Appraisal, 1984, Chinese transl., 1999, Chemistry, Alchemy and the New Philosophy, 1550-1700, 1987, The French Paracelsians: The Chemical Challenge to Medical and Scientific Tradition in Early Modern France, 1991, Paracelso e la Tradizione Paracelsiana, 1996, Chemistry and Medical Debate: Van Helmont to Boerhaave, 2001; editor: World Who's Who in Science from Antiquity to the Present, 1968, Science, Medicine and Society in the Renaissance, 2 vols, 1972, Medicine in Seventeenth-Century England, 1974; editor reprint: Theatrum Chemicum Britannicum (1652), 1967, John Dee's Mathematicall Praeface (1570), 1975; editor: (with Ingrid Merkel) Hermeticism and the Renaissance: Intellectual History and the Occult in Early Modern Europe, 1988, (with Michael T. Walton) Reading the Book of Nature: The Other Side of the Scientific Revolution, 1998; essayist: Festschrift: Experiencing Nature: Essays for Allen G. Debus (edited by Paul Theerman and Karen Parshall, 1997); mem. bd. adv. editors Physis Rivista internazionale de storia della scienza, Nuncius, The 16th Century Jour.; adv. editor: History of Science; hon. bd. editors Incognita; programmed 3 records released by Smithsonian Instn. Music of Victor Herbert, 1979; contbr. articles to profl. jours.; patentee in field. Social Sci. Rsch. Coun. fellow, 1959-60; Fulbright fellow, 1959-60; Fels Found. fellow, 1960-61; Guggenheim fellow, 1966-67; overseas fellow Churchill Coll. Cambridge (Eng.) U., 1966-67, 69; mem. Inst. Advanced Study Princeton, N.J., 1972-73; NEH fellow Newberry Libr., Chgo., 1975-76; fellow Inst. for Rsch. in Humanities U. Wis., Madison, 1981-82, NEH, 1987, Folger Shakespeare Libr., Washington; rsch. grantee Am. Philos. Soc., 1961-62, Wellcome Trust, 1962, NIH, 1962-70, 74-75, 77-78, 92-97, NSF, 1961-63, 71-74, 80-83, Am. Coun. Learned Socs., 1966, 70, 71. Fellow AAAS (mem. electorate nominating com., sect. L 1974-77, chmn. com. 1974); mem. History of Sci. Soc. (council 1962-65, 87-90, program chmn. 1972, Pfizer award 1978, Sarton medal 1994, Disting. lectr. 1996), Soc. Study Alchemy and Early Chemistry (mem. council 1967—), Am. Assn. for History Medicine (program com. 1975), Brit. Soc. for History Sci., Internationale Paracelsus Gesellschaft, Am. Chem. Soc. (asso. mem. history of chemistry div., exec. com. 1969-72, Dexter award 1987), Soc. Med. History of Chgo. (sec.-treas. 1971-72, v.p. 1972-74, pres. 1974-76, mem. council), Académie Internat. d'Histoire de la Medecine, Société Internationale d'Histoire de la Medecine, Academie Internat. d'Histoire des Scis. (corr. 1971, membre effectif 1991), Am. Inst. History of Pharmacy (Edward Kremers award 1978, adv. panel hist. activity 1979-81, awards com. 1981—), Am. Soc. Reformation Research, Assn. Recorded Sound Collections., Midwest Junto for History of Sci. (pres. 1983-84), Academia das Ciencias de Lisboa. Office: U Chgo Dept History Chicago IL 60637 E-mail: adebus@midway.uchicago.edu.

DECAIRE, JOHN, electronics executive, aerospace engineer; BS in Appied Physics, Mich. Tech. U., 1962; MS in Engring. Space Physics, PhD in Aerospace Engring., Air Force Inst. Tech.; grad. mgt. devel. program, Harvard U. Bus. Sch. Commd. 2d. lt. USAF, 1962, resigned, 1975; mgr. electronic mfg. Wright-Patterson AFB, Dayton, Ohio, 1975-78; program mgr. Bedford engring. labs. Raytheon Co., 1979-80; founder, mgr. Westinghouse Mfg. Systems and Tech. Ctr., Balt., 1980-84; gen. mgr. design and producibility engring. divsn. Westinghouse Electonics Systems Group, 1985-88, exec. dir. systems and tech., 1989-91; prin. John Decaire and Assocs., Cons., 1991-93; pres. Nat. Ctr. for Mfg. Scis., Ann Arbor, Mich., 1993—. Bd. dirs. NACFAM and CIMS. Mem. adv. bd. Mich. Tech. U. Coll. Engring., U. Md. MIPS, U. Mich. Tauber Mfg. Inst. Office: Nat Ctr for Mfg Sciences 3025 Boardwalk St Ann Arbor MI 48108-3230

DECANNIERE, DAN, human resources executive; CFO Hewitt Assocs., Lincolnshire, Ill. Office: Hewitt Assocs 100 Half Day Rd Lincolnshire IL 60069 Fax: ((847) 883-9019.

DECARLO, WILLIAM S. lawyer; b. Bayonne, N.J., Apr. 11, 1950; BS, U. Pa., 1971, MA, 1976; JD, Georgetown U., 1976. Bar: N.J. 1977, N.Y. 1977, Ill. 1986. Ptnr. Sidley & Austin, Chgo. Office: Sidley & Austin Bank One Plaza 425 W Surf St Apt 605 Chicago IL 60657-6139

DECASTRO, FERNANDO JOSE, pediatrics educator; b. Havana, Cuba, Nov. 11, 1937; s. Fernando R. and Maria A. (Freyre) deC.; m. Catalina, June 9, 1962; children: Maria, Ana, Fernando, Ramon, Teresa, Pablo, Jose Manuel. MD, Tulane U., 1962; MPH, U. Mich., 1966. Intern, resident, fellow U. Mich., 1962-66; clin. prof. pediatrics St. Louis U., 1976—; dir. toxicology Arcadia Valley Hosp., Pilot Kove, Mo., 1992—. Contbr. articles to profl. jours. Fellow APHA, Am. Acad. Pediatrics, Am. Coll. Emergency Physicians, Am. Coll. Med. Toxicology, Am. Acad. Clin. Toxicology, Am. Fedn. Clin. Rsch. Office: Arcadia Valley Hosp Hwy 21 Pilot Knob MO 63663

DECAVEL, JEAN-ROBERT, chef; b. France; Recipient award, James Beard Found., 2001. Office: Jean-Robert at Pigall's 127 W 4th St Cincinnati OH 43202

DECIO, ARTHUR JULIUS, manufacturing company executive; b. Elkhart, Ind., Oct. 19, 1930; s. Julius A. and Lena (Alesia) D.; m. Patricia George, Jan. 6, 1951; children: Terrence, Jamee, Linda, Jay, Leigh Allison. Student, DePaul U., 1949-50; DBA (hon.), Salem Coll., W.Va., 1973; LLD, U. Notre Dame, 1975, Ind. State U., Terre Haute, 1978; LLD (hon.), Saint Mary's Coll., Notre Dame, Ind., 1996; D. Bus. (hon.), Vincennes U., 1991; D Humanitarian Svc. (hon.), Hillsdale Coll., 1993; DHL (hon.), Purdue U., 1999. Pres. Skyline Corp., Elkhart, 1956-72, chmn. bd., chief exec. officer, 1959-98, chmn. bd., 1998—. Bd. dirs. Schwarz, Morton Grove, Ill., NiSource (formerly NIPSCO Industries, Inc.), Merrillville, Ind.; past dir. adv. council Coll. Commerce DePaul U.; past mem. adv. coun. Coll. Engring., U. Notre Dame, also Coll. Bus. Adminstrn.; past bd. govs. NFL Alumni; founding dir. Elkhart (Ind.) Community Found.; dir. Ara Parseghian Med. Rsch. Found.; past dir. Quality Dining, Mishawaka, Ind. Past dir. Spl. Olympics Internat., Washington; fellow, trustee U. Notre Dame; trustee emeritus, past chmn. Holy Cross Coll., Notre Dame, Ind., trustee Hillsdale Coll., Mich.; past mem. adv. bd. Goshen (Ind.) Coll., Ind. U., South Bend; past mem. coun. advisors Ctr. for the Homeless, South Bend; past mem., pres. coun. Ind. U.; past mem. Logan Cmty. Adv. Coun., South Bend; past chmn. Elkhart Urban League Membership Drive, Elkhart Gen. Hosp. Major Capital Campaign, Bicentennial Commn. Elkhart County, Salvation Army New Hdqrs. Bldg. Drive, 1975; hon. chmn. Salvation Army Christmas Fund Drive, 1972-2000; past mem. Commn. on Presdl. Scholars, Presdl. appointment, 1978; pres. Elkhart Gen. Hosp. Found.; past dir. Nat. Italian-Am. Found., Washington; past chmn. adv. coun. United Way, Elkhart, past dir., campaign chmn., 1966; past dir. Cath. Diocese of Ft. Wayne-South Bend, bd. dirs. diocesan fin. coun.; past dir. Banc One Ind. Corp., Indpls., Bank One., Indpls., Midwest Commerce Banking Co., Elkhart, Ind., Fed. Reserve Bank Chgo., dir. emeritus, St. Joseph Capital Corp. (Bank), South Bend, Ind.; founding mem., trustee Aux Chandelles Trust for Mentally Retarded, Elkhart; life mem., past chmn., past chmn. exec. com. nat. adv. bd. Salvation Army, Washington; chmn. planning com., Salvation Army Adv. Orgns. Conf., London, 1989; life mem. NAACP, exec. bd. Elkhart County chpt., 1980-82; chmn. for special gifts/bldg. campaign St. Thomas the Apostle Ch., Elkhart, Ind., 1963; co-chmn. capital campaign Elkhart Conf. Superblock, 1976, Goshen Coll. Uncommon Cause Campaign, 1983, hon. co-chmn. capital campaign Marmion Acad., Aurora, Ill., 1998-99; chmn. Salvation Army capital campaign, 1990; co-chmn. capital campaign Sta. WNIT-TV Pub. TV, 1991; chmn. Living Faith Campaign, Congregation Holy Cross, Ind. Province; chmn. Sign of Hope campaign Congregation Holy Cross, Ind. Province; life trustee. Marmion Acad., Aurora, Ill.; past mem., bd. advisors Mundelein (Ill.) Sem. of U. St. Mary of the Lake; past dir. Elkhart Urban League, Elkhart Gen. Hosp., No. Ctrl. Ind. Med. Edn. Found., South Bend, Nat. Jr. Achievement, Greencroft Found., Elkhart; past dir. Jr. Achievement Elkhart, pres. 1965-66; past trustee Stanley Clark Sch., South Bend, LaLumiere Sch., Laporte, Ind.; mem. Coun. on Devel. Choices for the 80's, Urban Land Inst.; Presdl. appointment Low Income Housing task force, 1970; past Presdl. appointee as commr. Christopher Columbus Quincentenary Jubilee Commn., Washington; mem. Internat. Summer Spl. Olympics Com., Inc., 1987; co-chmn. capital campaign Assn. for Disabled of Elkhart County, 1985; hon. chmn. capital campaign for Elkhart Cmty. Day Care Ctr., 1987; bd. govs. Ind. Colls. of Ind.; 1st chmn. annual bishop's appeal fund drive Diocese of Ft. Wayne-South Bend, 1987; bd. dirs., past chmn. Regional Approach for Progress, South Bend; past pres. Elkhart Park Found., Elkhart; founding dir., charter bd. dirs. Michiana Pub. Broadcasting Corp., Elkhart. Recipient U. Portland (Oreg.) medal, 1972, Golden Plate award Acad. Achievement Dallas, 1967, Others award Salvation Army, 1972, William Booth award Salvation Army, 1987, Alexis de Tocqueville Soc. award United Way Am., 1987, Sagamore of the Wabash award State of Ind., 1977, 85, Community Service award Elkhart County br. NAACP, 1980, Marmion Centurion award Marmion Mil. Acad., 1979, Achievement award Jr. Achievement, 1974, Humanitarian award Elkhart Urban League, 1981, Community Service award Elkhart Urban League, 1977 Disting. Am. award Moose Krause chpt. NFL Found. and Hall of Fame, 1984, Book of Golden Deeds award Elkhart Noon Exchange Club, 1984, E. M. Morris award Div. Bus. and Econs., Ind. U.-South Bend, 1985, Alumni Leadership award Marmion Mil. Acad., 1964, Wall of Fame award Assn. for the Disabled, 1985; Salvation Army Hon. Adv. Bd. Mem. award, 1971, Columbus Day award for outstanding Italian-Am., 1973, Elkhart Bar Assn. Liberty Bell award, 1976, Aux Chandelles Village Found. OK award, 1976, Life Hon. Membership award Elkhart Urban League, 1980, Outstanding Contbn. award Elkhart Urban League, 1982, Nat. Italian-Am. Found. Career Achievement award, Washington, 1984, Disting. Citizen of Yr. award No. Ind. council Boy Scouts Am., 1988, Ind. Individual Philanthropist of Yr. award, 1984, Mobile Home Hall of Fame, 1975, Industry Man of Yr. award Iowa Manufactured Housing Assn., 1976, Calif. Manufactured Housing Assn., 1977, N.J. Manufactured Housing Assn., 1977. Arthur J. Decio Vol. of Yr. award established by Elkhart United Way, 1984, Journi Industrialist of Yr. award The Exec. Jour. Bd. Dirs., 1989, Howard J. Kenna, C.S.C. award Congregation of Holy Cross, Ind. Province U. Notre Dame, 1989, John J. Cavanaugh award U. Notre Dame Alumni Assn., 1989, Business Hall of Fame Awd., Jr. Achievement of Elkhart County, Inc., 1989, James R. Price/Automated Builder Achievement in Housing award Automated Builder mag., 1990, Man of Yr. award Notre Dame Club of St. Joseph Valley, 1990, Ind. Spl. Cause award Ind. Assn. Rehab. Facilities, 1991, Helping Hands award Hospice St. Joseph County, Inc., 1991, Labor Humanitarian award United Labor Agy., Elkhart, Ind., 1991, Alumni of Yr. award St. Vincent's Sch., Elkhart, 1993, John W. Meaney Founders award Michiana Pub. Broadcasting Corp., 1993, Disting. Aux. Svc. Cross Salvation Army Internat. Hdqrs., London, 1995, Cross of Hope award Bros. of Holy Cross and Holy Cross Coll., Notre Dame, 1996, outstanding kindness award ADEC, 1997, special internat. olympics award, 1997, Citizen of the Yr. award, The Elkhart Lions Club 75th Anniversary, 1999, Lifetime Achievement award, WNIT-TV, Ind., 1999, 2000 Disting. Am. award Nat. Football Found. and Coll. Hall of Fame, Morristown, N.J., 2000, The Herman B. Wells Visionary award Ind. U. Found., Bloomington, Ind., 2000. Past mem. and past chmn. Manufactured Housing Inst.

Washington, Ind. Acad. (apptd. 1978), Chgo. Pres. Assn., Chief Execs. Orgn., World Bus. Coun., Marmion Benedictine Abbey (life affiliate, Aurora, Ill.), Knights of Malta; hon. mem. Elkhart Rotary Club. Roman Catholic. Home: 3215 Greenleaf Blvd Elkhart IN 46514-4357 Office: Skyline Corp 2520 Bypass Rd Elkhart IN 46514-1584

DECKER, RAYMOND FRANK, technology transfer executive, metal products executive, scientist; b. Afton, N.Y., July 20, 1930; s. Bernett Hurd and Mildred (Bisbee) Decker; life ptnr. Mary Birdsall, Dec. 27, 1951; children: Susan, Elizabeth, Catherine, Laura. BS, U. Mich., 1952, MS, 1955, PhD, 1958. With Inco Ltd., 1958-82, v.p. corp. tech. and diversification ventures, 1978-82; v.p. rsch. and corp. rels. Mich. Technol. U., Houghton, 1982-86; pres., CEO Univ. Sci. Ptnrs., Inc., 1986-98; pres. ASM Internat., 1986-87; founding chmn. Thixomat, Inc., 1988—, also bd. dirs.; founding chmn. Wavemat, Inc., 1987-88. Bd. dirs. Spl. Metals Corp.; adj. prof. Poly. Inst. Bklyn., 1962—66, NYU, 1968, U. Mich., 1997—; cons. KMS Fusion, Inc., Howmet turbine Components, Alcoa, GE, GM, 1985—; Van Horn Disting. lectr. Case-Western Res. U., 1975; mem. materials adv. bd. NASA, 1969, Nat. Bur. Stds., 1973, NSF, 1985—86; mem. Nat. Materials Adv. Bd., 1982—88; mem. exec. com. Strategic Hwy. Rsch. Program, 1986—93; long-range planning com. Metall. Soc., 1985—87, State Rsch. Fund Panel Mich., 1983—86; chmn. rsch. & tech. coordinating com. Fed. Hwy. Adminstrn., 1995—98; trustee Foundry Ednl. Found., 1975—77, Welding Rsch. Coun., 1975—80; chmn. bd. trustees Mich. Energy and Resource Rsch. Assn., 1985—86; keynote spkr. on superalloys Seven Springs Conf., 1980, NAE, 1980—. Author: (book) Strengthening Mechanisms in Nickel-Base Superalloys; editor: Maraging Steels. Chmn. alumni com. dept. material sci. and engring. U. Mich., Ann Arbor. Recipient IR-100 award, 1964, Sesquicentennial award, U. Mich., 1967, Disting. Grad. award, 1994, Innovation award, Mobile Computing, 1999, Inc 500 award, 1999. Fellow: Am. Soc. Metals Internat. (chmn. materials sys. and design divsn. 1971—73, trustee 1976—79, chmn. organizing com. World Materials Congress 1988, Campbell Meml. lectr. 1985, chmn. diamond decade com. 1980—81, hon. mem. 1991, Alpha Simga Mu lectr. 2001, Gold medal 1981); mem.: NAE, AAAS, AIME (lectr. Inst. Metals divsn. 1973, R. F. Mehl medal 1973). Congregationalist. Achievements include co-inventing maraging steels, Thixomolding machine. Home: 3065 Provincial Dr Ann Arbor MI 48104-4117 E-mail: rdecker@thixomat.com.

DECKER, RICHARD KNORE, lawyer; b. Lincoln, Nebr., Sept. 15, 1913; s. Fred William and Georgia (Kilmer) D.; m. Fern Iona Steinbaugh, June 12, 1938. AB, U. Nebr., 1935, JD, 1938. Bar: Nebr. 1938, U.S. Supreme Ct. 1941, D.C. 1948, Ill. 1952. Trial atty. antitrust div. Dept. Justice, 1938-52; ptnr. Lord, Bissell & Brook, Chgo., 1953-84, of counsel, 1984—. Trustee Village of Clarendon Hills (Ill.), 1960-64; chmn. bd. elders Community Presbyn. Ch., Clarendon Hills, 1963-66; mem. Union Ch. of Hinsdale; chmn. bd. Community House, Hinsdale, Ill., 1976, Robert Crown Center Health Edn., Hinsdale, Ill., 1981-83, also bd. dirs, 1976—. With USNR, 1942-45, lt. comdr. ret. Mem. ABA (chmn. antitrust sect. 1971-72), Ill. Bar Assn. (gov. 1969-73, chmn. antitrust sect. 1964-66), Chgo. Bar Assn. (chmn. antitrust law com. 1956-59), Law Club Chgo., Met. Club, Hinsdale Golf Club (pres. 1968), Five Seasons Country Club. Republican. Home: 196 Pheasant Hollow Dr Burr Ridge IL 60527 Office: 115 S La Salle St Ste 2900 Chicago IL 60603-3801

DECKER, RUSSELL S. state legislator; b. May 25, 1953; married; 2 children. Grad., No. Ctrl. Tech. Coll., 1980. Mem. from dist. 29 Wis. Senate, Madison, 1990—. Mem. rural econ. devel. bd. Active Habitat for Humanity; mem. apprentice com. United Way; rep. for bricklayers union. Mem. Bricklayers Intl. Union. Democrat. Home: 6803 Lora Lee Ln Schofield WI 54476-4369

DECKER, WALTER JOHNS, toxicologist; b. Tannersville, N.Y., June 13, 1933; s. H. Russell and Leola May (Coons) D.; m. Barbara Allen Hart, Aug. 19, 1961; children: Karl Hart, Reid Johns, Sam Travis. BA, SUNY, Albany, 1954, MA, 1955; PhD, George Washington U., 1966. Commd. 2d lt. U.S. Army, 1955, advanced through grades to lt. col., 1970, ret., 1975; assoc. prof. U. Tex. Med. Br., Galveston, 1976-83; pres. Toxicology Cons. Svcs., El Paso, Tex., 1984-97. Adj. clin. prof. Tex. Tech. U., El Paso, 1991—. Contbr. articles to jours. Clin. Toxicology, Vet. and Human Toxicology, Toxicology and Applied Pharmacology, others. Mem. sci. rev. panel Nat. Libr. Medicine's Hazardous Substance Data Bank, Bethesda, Md., 1985-2000; chair steering com. West Tex. Poison Ctr., El Paso, 1994-96. Recipient Aesculapius award, Tex. Med. Assn., 1977, Career Achievement award, Am. Acad. Clin. Toxicology, 2001. Fellow: Am. Acad. Clin. Toxicology (Career Achievement award 2001); mem.: Soc. Toxicology. Episcopalian. Achievements include research in toxicology. E-mail: barbwaltlax@msn.com.

DECKER, WAYNE LEROY, meteorologist, educator; b. Patterson, Iowa, Jan. 24, 1922; s. Albert Henry and Effie (Holmes) D.; m. Martha Jane Livingston, Dec. 29, 1943; 1 dau., Susan Jane. B.S., Central Coll., Pella, Iowa, 1943; postgrad., UCLA, 1943-44; M.S., Iowa State U., 1947, Ph.D., 1955. Meteorologist U.S. Weather Bur., Washington and Des Moines, 1947-49; mem. faculty U. Mo. at Columbia, 1949—, prof. atmospheric sci., 1958-67, prof., chmn. dept. atmospheric sci., 1967-91; prof. emeritus U. Mo., Columbia, 1992—; dir. coop. inst. applied meteorology U. Mo. at Columbia, 1985-92; cons. climatologist, 1992—. Chmn. com. climatic fluctuations and agrl. prodn. NRC, 1975-76; bd. dirs. Council for Agrl. Sci. and Tech., 1978-85, mem. exec. com., 1981-85; chair organizing com. 16th Internat. Congress Biometeonology. Fellow Am. Meteorol. Soc.; mem. Internat. Soc. Biometeorology (treas. 1990-99), Am. Geophys. Union, Am. Agronomy Soc., Sigma Xi, Gamma Sigma Delta. Home: 1007 Hulen Dr Columbia MO 65203-1414 Office: U Mo 116 Gentry Hall Columbia MO 65211-7040 E-mail: deckerw@missouri.edu.

DECKROSH, HAZEN DOUGLAS, retired state agency educator and administrator; b. Defiance, Ohio, Apr. 13, 1936; s. Lawrence L. and Martha L. Deckrosh; m. Carol Ann Everett, Nov. 25, 1970; children: Stephanie, Todd, Douglas, Nadia Nicole. BS, Ohio No. U., 1959; MEd, U. Toledo, 1980. Cert. tchr., Ohio. Phys. edn. and history tchr., coach Waynesfield (Ohio)-Goshen Jr. High Sch., 1959-61; coach, history, phys. edn. tchr. Coshocton (Ohio) Sacred Heart High Sch., 1961-63; health-phys. edn. tchr., coach West Holmes Jr. High Sch., Millersburg, Ohio, 1965-70; tchr. history and govt., coach Elida High Sch., 1970-73; occupational work experience tchr.-coord., coach Spencerville (Ohio) High Sch., 1973-77; occupational work edn. tchr., coord. Four County Vocat. Sch., Archbold, Ohio, 1977-82, 99—; vocat. supr. Jefferson County Vocat. Sch., Steubenville, 1986-87; occupational work experience tchr., coord. Ohio Dept. of Youth Svcs., Columbus, 1987-94; ret., 1994. Pres. DYS Coordinators, Columbus, 1990-94; ski instr. Swiss Valley, Mich., 1995—; GED instr. Correction Ctr. Northwest Ohio. Editor: Threaded Fasteners, 1987; contbr. articles to profl. publs. Mem. Am. Youth Hostels, Lima, 1972—. Mem. NEA, Ohio Edn. Assn., Am. Vocat. Assn., Ohio Vocat. Assn., Occupl. Work Experience Coords. Assn. (state adv. coun., Lima rep. 1977-80, Columbus rep. 1991-94), Full Gospel Bus. Men's Fellowship Internat., Gideons Internat. (treas., then sec.), 5th Dist. Ofcls. Assn. (v.p., rules interpreter), Capitol West Umpires Assn. (rules interpreter 1991-93), Lima Umpires Assn. (sec.-treas. 1973-77), Ret. Tchrs. Assn. (pres.), Alpha Sigma Phi. Republican. Avocations: sports officiating, high school and college sports, teaching skiing. Home: 12265 County Road 150 Montpelier OH 43543-9613

DE COURTEN-MYERS, GABRIELLE MARGUERITE, neuropathologist; b. Fribourg, Switzerland, Aug. 8, 1947; came to U.S., 1979; d. Maurice Edmond and Margrit (Wettstein) De Courten; m. Ronald Elwood Myers, Apr. 18, 1981; 1 child, Maximilian. BSBA, Akademikergemeinschaft, Zurich, Switzerland, 1967; MD, U. Zurich, 1974. Resident in psychiatry Hopital Psycho-Geriatrique, Gimel, Switzerland, 1974-75; resident in pediatrics U. Hosp. Zurich, 1977; resident in neuropathology U. Hosp. of Lausanne, Switzerland, 1976-78; rsch. assoc. NIH, Bethesda, Md., 1979-80; fellow in neuropathology Coll. of Medicine U. Cin., 1980-83, asst. prof. neuropathology Coll. of Medicine, 1983-88, assoc. prof. neuropathology Coll. of Medicine, 1988-89, tenured assoc. prof. Coll. of Medicine, 1989—. Cons. Vets. Affairs Med. Ctr., Cin., 1983—, Children's Hosp. Med. Ctr., Cin., 1984—, Good Samaritan Hosp., Cin., 1990—. Grantee VA, 1985—, NIH, 1986-90, 93—, Am. Heart Assn., 1991-94, Am. Diabetes Assn., 1995. Mem. AAAS, Am. Assn. Neuropathologists, Am. Acad. Neurology, AAUP, Soc. Acad. Emergency Medicine, Soc. Exptl. Neuropathology. Office: U Cin Coll of Medicine Dept Pathology PO Box 670529 231 Bethesda Ave Cincinnati OH 45267-0529

DEDERICK, ROBERT GOGAN, economist; b. Keene, N.H., Nov. 18, 1929; s. Frederic Van Dyck and Margaret (Gogan) D.; m. Margarida N. Magalhaes, Aug. 24, 1957; children: Frederic, Laura, Peter. AB, Harvard U., 1951, AM, 1953, PhD, 1958; postgrad., Cornell U., 1953-54. Econ. research mgr. New Eng. Mut. Life Ins. Co., Boston, 1957-64; assoc. economist No. Trust Co., Chgo., 1964, v.p., assoc. economist, 1965-69, v.p., economist, 1969-70, sr. v.p., chief economist, 1970-81, exec. v.p., chief economist, 1983-94, econ. cons., 1994—; mem. panel of econ. advisers Congl. Budget Office; mem. econ. adv. bd. U.S. Commerce Dept., 1968-70, 75-76, 83-85, asst. sec. commerce for econ. affairs, 1981-82, under sec. commerce for econ. affairs, 1982-83; prin. RGD Econs., Hinsdale, 1994—. Fellow: Nat. Assn. Bus. Economists (pres. 1973—74, governing coun. 1969—75); mem.: Internat. Conf. Comml. Bank Economists, Am. Bankers Assn. (alumni coun.), Harvard Discussion Group Indsl. Economists, Conf. Bus. Economists (chmn. 1984—85), Tech. Cons. Bus. Coun., Capital Hill Club (Washington), Hinsdale Golf Club, Harvard Club (Chgo., Boston, Cape Cod), Econ. Club (Chgo.). Home: 113 S County Line Rd Hinsdale IL 60521-4722 Office: RGD Economics 113 S County Line Rd Hinsdale IL 60521-4722 also: Northern Trust Company 50 S Lasalle St Chicago IL 60675-0001 E-mail: dederick_robert@ntrs.com.

DEDONATO, DONALD MICHAEL, obstetrician/gynecologist; b. Bridgeport, Conn., Apr. 25, 1952; s. Michael Anthony and Mary Jane (Zawacki) DeDonato; m. Susan Mary Naulty, June 15, 1974; children: Mark Dominic, David Nicholas. BA in Chemistry cum laude, Coll. Holy Cross, 1974; MD, Loyola U., Maywood, Ill., 1977. Intern Loyola Foster McGaw Hosp., Maywood, Ill., 1977-78; resident Ohio State U. Hosp., Columbus, Ohio, 1978-81; ob-gyn. Ob-Gyn. Assocs., Arlington Heights, Ill., 1981-87, DeDonato, Goodnough and Geittmann, Ob-Gyn., Arlington Heights, 1987-92; pres., CEO N.W. Women's Cons., 1993—. Clin. instr. Northwestern U. Med. Ctr., Chgo., 1981—; chmn. dept. ob-gyn. N.W. Cmty. Healthcare, 1998—2000. Mem. alumni bd. Loyola Stritch Sch. of Medicine, Maywood, Ill. Recipient CIBA award. Mem. AMA, Am. Assn. Med. Colls. (Loyola rep.), Chgo. Med. Soc., Ill. State Med. Soc., Am. Bd. Ob-Gyn., Am. Assn. Gyn. Laparoscopists, Garden Camera (pres. 1985-86, 92-93), Phi Beta Kappa, Alpha Sigma Nu. Avocation: photography. Office: NW Womens Cons 1630 W Central Rd Arlington Heights IL 60005-2407

DEE, IVAN RICHARD, book publisher; b. Chgo., Mar. 11, 1935; s. Jack Arthur and Jeanette Rose (Melcher) D.; m. Sandra Cohen, June 21, 1959 (div. 1973); m. Phyllis Kirz, Aug. 3, 1977 (div. 1981); m. Barbara Burgess, Apr. 15, 1989; children: Alexander, Sara, Jacob, Gabriel. BJ, U. Mo., 1956, MA, 1957. Pres. Ardivan Press, Macon, Ga., 1960-61; v.p., editor-in-chief Quadrangle Books, Chgo., 1961-72; assoc. editor Chgo. Tribune Book World, 1972-73; exec. editor Pubs.-Hall Syndicate, 1973-74; editor-in-chief Chicagoan Mag., 1974-75; dir. pub. affairs Michael Reese Hosp. and Med. Ctr., 1975-89; pres. Ivan R. Dee, Inc., 1989—. V.p. South Side Planning Bd., Chgo., 1975-89; commr. Chgo. Baseball League, 1978-00. Lt. (j.g.) USN, 1957-60. Office: Ivan R Dee Inc 1332 N Halsted St Chicago IL 60622-2624

DEEMS, NYAL DAVID, lawyer, mayor; b. Cleve., Jan. 24, 1948; s. Nyal Wilbert and Octavia C. (Roush) D.; m. Jody Deems; children: Brooke Elizabeth, Nyal Christopher, Holly Jean, Eric Wellington, Georgia Octavia, Susannah Irma Genevieve. BA in Internat. Studies, Miami U., 1969; JD, U. Ga., 1976. Bar: Ga. 1976, Mich. 1976, U.S. Dist. Ct. (we. dist.) Mich., U.S. Dist. Ct. (no. dist.) Ga. Assoc. then ptnr. Varnum, Riddering, Wierengo & Christenson now Varnum, Riddering, Schmidt & Howlett, Grand Rapids, Mich., 1976—. Co-author: Michigan Real Estate Sales Transactions, 1983, Real Estate Development, 4 vols., 1988, A Practical Guide to Winning Land Use Approvals and Permits, 1989, Michigan Real Estate Practice and Forms, 1989, Michigan Business Formbook, 1989, Michigan Basic Practice Handbook, 1989. Commr. City of East Grand Rapids, Mich., 1982-85, mayor, 1985-95; chmn. Grand Rapids Met. Coun., 1990-95. Lt. USN, 1969-73. Mem. ABA, Ga. Bar Assn., Mich. Bar Assn. (chmn. water law com. 1984-86, real property coun. 1984—, chairperson 1989), Grand Rapids Bar Assn., Am. Coll. Real Estate Lawyers, Am. Coll. Mortgage Attys. Home: 431 Cambridge Blvd SE Grand Rapids MI 49506-2806 Office: Varnum Riddering Schmidt Howlett 333 Bridge St NW Ste 1700 Grand Rapids MI 49504-5356

DEER, RICHARD ELLIOTT, lawyer; b. Indpls., Sept. 8, 1932; s. Leon Leslie and Mary Jane (Ostheimer) D.; m. Lee Todd, Feb. 22, 1958; children: William K., Laura A., Susannah T., Thomas E. A.B., DePauw U., 1954; LL.B. magna cum laude, Harvard U., 1957. Bar: Ind. 1957, U.S. Dist. Ct. (no. and so. dists.) Ind. 1957, U.S. Ct. Appeals (7th cir.) 1957, U.S. Ct. Appeals (9th cir.) 1990, U.S. Supreme Ct. 1962. Assoc. firm Barnes & Thornburg and predecessor firm, Indpls., 1957-65, ptnr., 1965—, chmn. mgmt. com., 1990-93; dir. Flagship Capital Corp., Indpls. Author: Indiana Corporation Law and Practice, 1990, Supplement, 1994; co-author: Indiana Limited Liability Company Forms and Practice Manual, 1996, Supplement, 1997; bd. editors Harvard Law Rev., 1956-57; contbr. articles to legal jours.; chief reporter: The Lawyer's Basic Corporate Practice Manual, 3d edit., 1984. Mem. Indpls. Coun. Fgn. Relations, Ind. Corps. Survey Commn., 1983—. Fellow Am. Bar Found., Ind. Bar Found.; mem. Indpls. Bar Assn., Ind. State Bar Assn. (past chmn. corp., banking and bus. law sect.), ABA (drafting com., exec. planning group of legal opinion project sect. bus. law, 3d party legal opinion report 1991), Am. Law Inst. Clubs: Hillcrest Country, Players, Columbia. Office: Barnes & Thornburg 11 S Meridian St Ste 1313 Indianapolis IN 46204-3535

DEES, STEPHEN PHILLIP, agricultural finance executive, lawyer; b. Tulsa, Feb. 21, 1943; s. Jesse Raymond and Mary Adelia (Ledbetter) D.; m. Mary Louise Porter, June 26, 1966 (div. Oct. 1986); children: Emily Ann, Daniel Ledbetter, Matthew Louis; m. Kristine Ann Odenwald, Oct. 10, 1987 (div. Apr. 1992); 1 child, Charles Jesse; m. Linda Petsch, Sept. 3, 1995. BA, Washington U., 1965, JD, 1967. Bar: Mo. 1967. Assoc. Stinson, Mag, Thomson, McEvers & Fizzell, Kansas City, Mo., 1967-71; ptnr. Stinson, Mag & Fizzell, 1971-84; v.p., gen. counsel Farmland Industries Inc., 1984-87, sec., 1986-91, v.p. law and adminstrn., 1987-93, now exec. v.p. bus. development & internat. mktg., dir. gen., 1993-98; dir. gen. Farmland Industries, S.A. de C.V. of Mex., 1993-95; ptnr. Rochdale Prins., 1998—; of counsel Shook, Hardy & Bacon, Kansas City, Mo., 2000—. Officer, bd. dirs. Gt. Am. Basketball League, Shawnee Mission, Kans., 1979-86, commr., 1983-86; mem. Sister Cities Commn., Kansas City, 1982-90; mem. leadership com. Legal Aid Western Mo. Served with USAF, 1967, then with Res. Mem. ABA, Mo. Bar (vice chmn. labor law com. 1977-80, chmn. 1980-81), Lawyers Assn. Kansas City (bd. dirs. 1983-86, treas. 1989-91), Kansas City Met. Bar Assn., Order of Coif. Republican. Jewish. Avocations: stamp collecting, racquetball, travel. Home: 4511 N Mulberry Dr Kansas City MO 64116-4652 Office: Shook Hardy & Bacon PO Box 15607 1010 Grand Blvd Fl 5 Kansas City MO 64106-2220

DE FRANCESCO, JOHN BLAZE, JR. public relations company executive; b. Stamford, Conn., May 22, 1936; s. John Blaze and Mae (Matyscyk) DeF.; m. Louise C. Terlizzo, Nov. 1, 1958 (div. 1983); children: Daryl, Jay, Dana, Dorian; m. Diana Picchietti, Oct. 20, 1990. B.S., U. Conn., 1958. Sr. v.p. Daniel J. Edelman, Inc., Chgo., 1967-77; exec. v.p. Ruder Finn & Rotman, Inc., 1977-85; prin., CEO DeFrancesco/Goodfriend Pub. Relations, 1985-2001; exec. v.p. L.C. Williams & Assoc., Chgo., 2001—. Bd. dirs. Ill. Divsn. Vocat. Rehab., 1976-78; mem. pub. rels. adv. bd. Gov.'s State U., 1994-98. Comdr. USN, 1958-67; comdr. USNR; ret. 1979. Recipient 3 Silver Anvil awards Pub. Rels. Soc. Am., 6 Golden Trumpet awards Publicity Club, Chgo. Mem. Pub. Rels. Soc. Am., Navy League U.S., Naval Res. Assn. Mil. Assn. of World Wars. Roman Catholic. Home: 18785 Saint Andrews Dr Monument CO 80132-8824 Office: LC Williams & Assoc 150 N Michigan Ave Chicago IL 60601-3903

DEGENHARDT, ROBERT ALLAN, architectural and engineering firm executive; b. Kearney, Nebr., May 29, 1943; s. Robert Franklin and Florence Elizabeth (Spohnheimer) D.; m. Elizabeth Scholl; children: Barry, Christopher, Kathleen. BSME, U. Nebr., 1965, MSME, 1968. Registered profl. engr., D.C. and all states except Alaska and Hawaii. Project engr. Davis & Wilson Architects and Engrs., Lincoln, Nebr., 1964-68, White Sands (N.Mex.) Missile Range, 1968-70, Sundstrand Aviation, Rockford, Ill., 1970-74; dir. engring. Davis, Fenton, Stange, Darling, Architects and Engrs., Lincoln, 1974-77; v.p. mech. engring. Durrant Engrs. Inc., Madison, Wis., 1977-1980; dir. mech. engring . Ellerbe Assocs. Inc., Mpls., 1980-82, dir. archtl./engring. svcs., 1982-83, v.p., dir. ops., 1983-85; sr. v.p., dir. Ellerbe Becket Inc., Washington, 1985-89; exec. v.p., COO Ellerbe Becket Co., Mpls., 1989-93, pres., COO, 1993-94, pres., CEO, 1994-98, CEO, 1998-2001, pres., 2001—. Mem. Ctr. for Ethical Bus. Cultures, 1993—. 1st lt. U.S. Army, 1968-70. Mem. Constrn. Industry Roundtable, U.S. C. of C. (internat. polic com.), Sigma Xi, Pi Tau Sigma. Republican. Lutheran. Avocations: backpacking, fly-fishing.

DEGROOT, LESLIE JACOB, medical educator; b. Ft. Edward, N.Y., Sept. 20, 1928; B.S., Union Coll., 1948; M.D., Columbia U., 1952. Intern, asst. resident in medicine Presbyn. Hosp., N.Y.C., 1952-54; health physician Nat. Cancer Inst., 1954-55; physician U.S. Mission, Afghanistan, 1955-56; clin. and research fellow medicine Mass. Gen. Hosp., Boston, 1956, 58-60, resident, 1957-58, asst., 1960-64, asst. physician, 1964-66; assoc. prof. exptl. medicine MIT, 1966-68, assoc. dir. dept. nutrition and food sci. Clin. Research Ctr., 1966-68; prof. endocrinology Pritzker Sch. Medicine, U. Chgo., 1968—, chief thyroid study unit, 1968—, chief endocrinology sect., 1980-87. Nat. Cancer Inst. clin. fellow, 1954-55 Mem. Assn. Am. Physicians, Am. Thyroid Assn., Endocrine Soc., Am. Soc. Clin. Investigation, Am. Fedn. Clin. Research Office: Univ Chgo Med Ctr MC3090 5841 S Maryland Ave Chicago IL 60637-1463 E-mail: ldegroot@medicine.bsd.uchicago.edu.

DEGROOTE, MICHAEL G. management consulting company executive; Pres., CEO Laidlaw Inc., 1959-90, Republic Industries Inc., 1991-96, also chmn. bd. dirs.; pres. Century Bus. Svcs. Inc., Cleve., 1997-99, CEO, 1999—, also chmn. bd. dirs. Office: Century Bus Svcs Inc Ste 330 6480 Rockside Woods Blvd S Cleveland OH 44131-2222

DEGROW, DAN L. state legislator; b. Ann Arbor, Mich., Jan. 28, 1953; m. Cheryl L. Simpson, 1981; children: Allison, Kelsie Sue, Stephen. Grad., Mich. State U., 1975; JD, Wayne State U., 1978. Mem. Mich. Ho. of Reps., Lansing, 1980-82, Mich. Senate from dist. 28, Lansing, 1982-94, Mich. Senate from 27th dist., Lansing, 1995—; sen. majority leader, 1999—. Vice chair appropriations com. Mich. State Senate, chmn. K-12 & edn. subcom., cmty. coll. com., capital outlay, budget and oversight com., jud. com., legis coun; ptnr. Nicholson, Fletcher, West & DeGrow, 1979—. Active St. Clair County Rep. Com. Mem. NAACP, Assn. Retarded Citizens, Mich. Bar Assn., St. Clair County Bar Assn., Phi Beta Kappa. Office: State Senate Office State Capitol Lansing MI 48909-7536

DEGUILIO, JON E. lawyer; b. Hammond, Ind., June 15, 1955; s. Ernest Michael and Jeanne (Hochis) D.; m. Barbara Jo Wieser, Oct. 3, 1981; 1 child, Suzanne Jeanne. BA, U. Notre Dame, 1977; JD, Valparaiso U., 1981. Bar: Ind. 1981, U.S. Dist. Ct. (so. dist.) Ind. 1981, U.S. Dist. Ct. (no. dist.) Ind. 1981. Pub. defender Lake County Ct., Crown Point, Ind., 1984-87; dep. prosecutor Lake County Prosecutor's Office, 1981-84; 87-94; assoc. James Wieser Law Offices, Highland, Ind., 1981-93; U.S. atty. no. dist. Ind. Dept. Justice, Dyer, 1993-99. Atty. Highland Police Commn., Highland, Ind., 1987— and Highland Water Bd., 1987—; legal advisor, Lake County Sheriff, Crown Point, Ind., 1986-87; atty. Hammond and East Chgo. Fedn. of Tchrs., 1986—. Councilman Hammond City Council, 1984-87; mem. Lake County Med. Ctr. Devel. Agy., 1988—, Greater Hammond Community Services, 1987—; treas. Little Calumet River Basin Com., 1986. Mem. Lake County Bar Assn. (bd. dirs. 1988-90), Justinian Soc. Democrat. Avocations: basketball, bolf, reading. Home: 8944 Liable Rd Hammond IN 46322-2248 Office: 1001 Main St Ste A Dyer IN 46311-1234

DEHART, EILEEN, state legislator; b. Sept. 15, 1948; Grad., Mich. State U. Staff Rep. Justine Barns; rep. Mich. State Dist. 18, 1995—. Conservation, environ. and Great Lakes com. Mich. Ho. Reps., sr. citizens com., vet. affairs com. Address: Mich Ho of Reps PO Box 30014 Lansing MI 48909-7514

DEHAYES, DANIEL WESLEY, management executive, educator; b. Columbus, Ohio, Sept. 23, 1941; s. Daniel Wesley and June Rosiland (Page) DeH.; married Lisa A. Gregoline; children: Sarah Baxter, Benjamin Wesley. BA in Math. and Computer Sci., Ohio State U., 1963, MBA, 1964, PhD in Bus. Adminstrn., 1968. Asst. prof. systems analysis Naval Postgrad. Sch., Monterey, Calif., 1967-69; asst. prof. sch. bus. Ind. U., Bloomington, Ind., 1969-72, assoc. prof.sch. bus., 1972-79, prof. sch. bus., 1979—, dean of acad. computing, 1981-86, asst. v.p. info. tech., 1987-88; dir. Ctr. For Entrepreneurship and Innovation, Ind. U., 1989-98. Exec. dir. Inst. Rsch. on the MIS, 1989-92, chmn. exec. edn., 1992-93; cons. in field. Textbook author; contbr. articles to profl. jours. Served to capt. U.S. Army, 1967-69 Recipient fellowships and grants Mem. Decision Scis. Inst., Acad. Mgmt. Republican. Methodist Office: Indiana University Kelley School of Business Bloomington IN 47405

DEHLER, STEVE, state legislator; b. 1950; m. Jean; 2 children. Student, St. John's U. State rep. Minn. Ho. Reps., Dist. 14A, 1993—. Home: PO Box 337 Saint Joseph MN 56374-0337

DEHNER, JOSEPH JULNES, lawyer; b. Cin., Nov. 28, 1948; s. Walter Joseph and Bess (Humphries) D.; m. Noel Julnes, Nov. 19, 1983; children: Holly Julnes, Sara Julnes. AB, Princeton U., 1970; JD, Harvard Law Sch., Cambridge, Mass., 1973. Bar: Ohio 1973, U.S. Dist. Ct. (no. and so. dists.) Ohio 1975, Fla. 1986, U.S. Dist. Ct. (ea. dist.) Ky. 1988, U.S. Ct. Internat. Trade 1992. Law clk. to judge U.S. Court Appeals, Cleve., 1973-75; assoc. Kyte, Conlan, Wulsin & Vogeler, Cin., 1975-78, Frost Brown Todd LLC, Cin., 1978—; chmn. Universal Transactions Inc., 1991-95. Co-mgr. Ukraine Investments Ltd., 1995-99. Author: Structured Settlements and Periodic Payment Judgments, 1986, A Guide to Soviet Businesspeople on American Business Law, 1991, Doing Business in Russia, 1992, Dispute Resolution and China, 1994, A Foreign Investors Guide to Ukraine, 1995;

contbr. articles to profl. publs. Sec., v.p. Cin. Preservation Assn., 1978-86; mem. Cin. Planning Commn., 1984-85; pres. Charter Com. Greater Cin., 1982-86; chmn. Cin.-Kharkiv Sister City Project, 1988-91; trustee Princeton U., 1970-74, Ohio Hist. Soc., 1974-78; chancellor Episcopal Diocese of So. Ohio, 1997—. Mem. ABA, Internat. Bar Assn., Pub. Investors Arbitration Bar Assn., Ohio State Bar Assn. (chmn. internat. law com. 1989-91), Cin. Bar Assn., Sixth Cir. Jud. Conf. Episcopal. Avocations: tennis, family, reading. Home: 822 Yale Ave Terrace Park OH 45174-1258 Office: Frost Brown Todd LLC 2500 PNC Ctr 201 E 5th St Ste 2500 Cincinnati OH 45202-4182

DE HOYOS, DEBORA M. lawyer; b. Monticello, N.Y., Aug. 10, 1953; d. Luis and Marion (Kinney) de Hoyos; m. Walter C. Carlson, June 20, 1981; children: Amanda, Greta, Linnea. BA, Wellesley Coll., 1975; JD, Harvard U., 1978. Bar: Ill. 1978, U.S. Dist. Ct. (no. dist.) Ill. 1980. Assoc. Mayer, Brown & Platt, Chgo., 1978—84, ptnr., 1985—, mng. ptnr., 1991—. Bd. dirs. Evanston Northwestern Healthcare; bd. trustees Providence St. Mel. Sch. Contbr. chpt. to Securitization of Financial Assets. Trustee Chgo. Symphony Orch. Office: Mayer Brown & Platt 190 S La Salle St Ste 3100 Chicago IL 60603-3441

DEININGER, DAVID GEORGE, judge; b. Monroe, Wis., July 9, 1947; s. Wilbur Emerson and Anna Emilie (Karlen) D.; m. Mary Carol Nussbaum, June 4, 1969; children: Jonathan David, Christopher Jacob, Emilie Joanne. BS, U.S. Naval Acad., 1969; JD, U. Wis., 1978. Bar: Wis. 1978, Ill. 1978, U.S. Dist. Ct. (we. dist.) Wis. 1978. Ptnr. Benkert, Spielman, Asmus & Deininger, Monroe, 1978-87; legislator Wis. State Assembly, Madison, 1987-94; of counsel Brennan, Steil, Basting & MacDougall, S.C., Monroe, 1988-94; cir. ct. judge Green County, 1994-96. Active Monroe Sch. Bd., 1986-89, Monroe Theatre Guild, 1980—; chmn. Green County Rep. Cen. Com., Monroe, 1982-84. Lt. USN, 1969-75. Mem. Green County Bar Assn. (pres. 1982-83), Wis. State Bar Assn., Am. Legion, VFW, Optimists (pres. Monroe chpt. 1984-85). Avocations: bridge, cross country skiing, boating. Home: 814 19th Ave Monroe WI 53566-1661 Office: Ct Appeals Dist IV Madison WI 53703-3330

DEISSLER, ROBERT GEORGE, fluid dynamicist, researcher; b. Greenville, Pa., Aug. 1, 1921; s. Victor Girard and Helen Stella (Fisher) D.; m. June Marie Gallagher, Oct. 7, 1950; children— Robert Joseph, Mary Beth, Ellen Ann, Anne Marie BS, Carnegie Inst. Tech., 1943; MS, Case Inst. Tech., 1948; PHD, Case Western Res. U., 1989. Researcher Goodyear Aircraft Corp., Akron, OH, 1943-44; aero. rsch. scientist NASA Lewis Rsch. Ctr., Cleve., 1947-52, chief fundamental heat transfer br., 1952-70, staff scientist, sci. cons. fluid physics, 1970-94, disting. rsch. assoc., 1994—. Fellow Lewis Rsch. Acad., 1983—; staff scientist sr. level emeritus, 1994. Author: Turbulent Fluid Motion, Taylor and Francis, 1998; contbr. articles to profl. jours.; areas of rsch. fluid turbulence, turbulent heat transfer, turbulent solutions of equations of fluid motion, nonlinear dynamics and chaos, meteorol. and astrophysical flows, radiative heat transfer in gases, heat transfer in powders. Served as lt. (j.g.) USNR, 1944-46 Recipient NACA/NASA Exceptional Svc. award, 1957, Outstanding Publ. award, 1978, Wisdom Soc. award of honor, 2000; Lewis Rsch. Acad. fellow, 1983—. Fellow AIAA (Best Paper award 1975, Tech. Achievement award 1981), ASME (Heat Transfer Meml. award 1964, Max Jacob Meml. award 1975, Wisdom Hall of Fame 2000); mem. Am. Phys. Soc., Sigma Xi. Roman Catholic Avocations: violin, reading, walking, natural theology. Home: 4540 W 213th St Fairview Park OH 44126-2106 Office: NASA Glenn Rsch Ctr 21000 Brookpark Rd Cleveland OH 44135-3191

DEITCH, LAURENCE B. lawyer; AB, U. Mich., 1969, JD, 1972. Ptnr. Bodman, Longley & Dahling LLP, Detroit. Vice chmn. Mich. Civil Svc. Commn.; bd. regents U. Mich., Ann Arbor, 1992—; treas. Mich. Dem. Party; pres. Temple Beth El, Bloomfield Hills. Office: Bodman Langley & Dahling LLP 100 Renaissance Ctr 34th Fl Detroit MI 48243

DEITRICK, WILLIAM EDGAR, lawyer; b. N.Y.C., July 30, 1944; s. John English and Dorothy Alice (Geib) D.; m. Emily Jane Posey, June 22, 1968; children: William Jr., Elizabeth, Peter. BA, Johns Hopkins U., 1967; JD, Cornell U., 1971. Bar: Ill. 1972, U.S. Dist. Ct. (no. dist.) Ill. 1972, U.S. Ct. Appeals (7th cir.) 1976, D.C. 1981. Ptnr. Gardner, Carton and Douglas, Chgo., 1972—85; sr. v.p., dep. gen. counsel, mgr. litigation divsn. Continental Bank N.A., 1985—91; ptnr. Mayer, Brown, Rowe & Maw, Chgo., 1991—. Contbr. articles to profl. jours. Trustee North Shore Country Day Sch., 1992-97; gov. mem. Shedd Aquarium; With U.S. Army, 1968-70. Mem. ABA, Ill. Bar Assn., Chgo. Bar Assn., Johns Hopkins U. Alumni Assn. (class agt. 1967-95), Cornell Law Sch. Chgo. Alumni Assn. (chmn. 1985-87). Clubs: Legal, Univ. (Chgo.); Indian Hill (Winnetka, Ill.). Home: 365 Greenwood Ave Glencoe IL 60022-2045 Office: Mayer Brown Rowe & Maw 190 S La Salle St Ste 3100 Chicago IL 60603-3441

DEKKER, EUGENE EARL, biochemistry educator; b. Highland, Ind., July 23, 1927; s. Peter and Anne (Hendrikse) D.; m. Harriet Ella Holwerda, July 5, 1958; children: Gwen E., Paul D., Tom R. A.B., Calvin Coll., 1949; M.S., U. Ill., 1951, Ph.D., 1954. Instr. U. Louisville Med. Sch., 1954-56; instr. biol. chemistry U. Mich. Med. Sch., Ann Arbor, 1956-58, asst. prof., 1958-65, assoc. prof., 1965-70, prof., 1970-94, assoc. chmn. dept., 1975-88, emeritus prof., 1994—. Served with USN, 1945-46 Mem. AAAS, Am. Chem. Soc., Am. Soc. Biol. Chemists, Am. Soc. Plant Physiologists, Oxygen Soc., Protein Soc., Sigma Xi, Phi Lambda Upsilon. Mem. Christian Reformed Ch. Home: 2612 Manchester Rd Ann Arbor MI 48104-6500 Office: U Mich Med Sch Dept Biol Chemistry Ann Arbor MI 48109-0606

DEKOOL, L.M. (THEO), food products executive; With CPC Benelux, B.V., Buhrmann Tetterode; v.p. fin. Household and Pers. Care divsn. Sara Lee/DE, Netherlands, 1990—93, CFO Netherlands, 1995—96, Blokker retail chain; v.p. Sara Lee Corp., Chgo., 1996—2001, sr. v.p., 2001, exec. v.p., 2002—. Office: 3 First Nat Plz Chicago IL 60602-4260

DEKREY, DUANE LEE, farmer, rancher; b. Jamestown, N.D., June 20, 1956; s. John Edward and Alpha Ann (Whitman) DeK.; m. Jan M. DeKrey, June 18, 1983; children: Tyler John, Peder Robert, RoxAnne Marie. BS in Agr., N.D. State U., 1978. Tchr. agrl. edn. Devils Lake (N.D.) Sch., 1979; farmer, rancher JD Acres, Tappen, N.D., 1979—; mem. N.D. Senate, Bismarck, 1990-92, N.D. House, Bismarck, 1994—; vice chair jud. com. N.D. Senate, 1997—. Mem. judiciary com. (chmn.), natural resources com. 2d lt. USAR, 1978—, maj. N.D. Nat. Guard, 1993. Mem. N.D. Stockmen Assn., Farm Bur. (past pres.), Res. Officers Assn., LAND (state dir., sec.), Farmers Union, Nat. Guard Assn. Republican. Congregationalist. Home: RR 1 Box 94 Tappen ND 58487-9514 Office: 4323 27th St SE Pettibone ND 58475-9357

DE LA CHAPELLE, ALBERT, education educator; Prof., chair dept. of med. genetics U. Helsinki; dir. Human Cancer Genetics Program Comp Cancer Ctr. Arthur G James Cancer Hosp. and Rsch. Inst., Ohio State U., Columbus, 1998—; prof., chair divsn. human cancer genetics d dept. molecular biology, virology, immunology, med. genetics Ohio State U., 1998—. Office: Ohio State Univ Human Cancer Genetics Rm 646 Med Rsch Facility 420 W 12th Ave Columbus OH 43210-1214

DE LA IGLESIA, FELIX ALBERTO, pathologist, toxicologist; b. Cordoba, Argentina, Nov. 27, 1939; s. Andres Avelino and Rosalia (Figueroa) De La Iglesia; m. Graciela Moreno, May 19, 1964; children: Felix Andres, Jose Vicente, Alberto Victor, Michele, Stephanie. MD, U. Cordoba, 1964. Dir. Warner-Lambert Rsch. Inst., Toronto, Ont., 1972-79; dir. toxicology Warner-Lambert/Parke-Davis, Ann Arbor, Mich., 1979-83, v.p. pathology and exptl. toxicology Parke-Davis Pharm. Rsch., 1983-2000; prof. pathology U. Toronto Sch. Medicine, 1981—. Adj. prof. toxicology, prof. pathology U. Mich. Med. Sch. Pub. Health, 1982—; cons. pharm. rsch. and devel., 2000—; founder, prin. FIP-Cons., Mich., 2001—; founder, sr. cons. Cambridge (Eng.) Biotech. Ltd., 2001—; mem. sci. adv. bd. Cellonics, Pitts., WaraFah Pharma, Boston. Author: Molecular Biochemistry of Human Disease, 1985, Drug Toxicokinetics, 1993, Drug-Induced Hepatotoxicity, 1996. Served to 1st lt. Argentine Army Inf., 1954-56. Fellow Acad. Toxicological Scis. Avocations: collecting antique microscopes, vintage sports cars, commercial real estate development. Home and Office: 2307 Hill St Ann Arbor MI 48104-2651

DELANEY, CORNELIUS FRANCIS, philosophy educator; b. Waterbury, Conn., June 30, 1938; s. Patrick Francis and Margaret (Gavigan) D.; 1 child, Cornelius Francis Jr. MA, Boston Coll., 1961; PhD, St. Louis U., 1967. Prof. philosophy U. Notre Dame, Notre Dame, Ind., 1967—, chmn. philosophy dept., 1972-82, dir. honors program, 1989—. Author: Mind and Nature, 1969m The Synoptic Vision, 1977, Science, Knowledge and Mind, 1993, The Liberalism-Communitarianism Debate, 1994, New Essays on the Philosophy of C.S. Pierce, 2000. Recipient Madden award U. Notre Dame, 1974, Bicentennial award Boston Coll., 1976, Pres.'s award U. Notre Dame, 1984, Sheedy award U. Notre Dame,1987. Mem. Am. Cath. Philos. Assn. (pres. 1985), C.S. Peirce Soc. (pres. 1986), Am. Philos. Assn. (exec. com. 1983-85). Office: U Notre Dame Dept Philosophy 336 O'Shaughnessy Hall Notre Dame IN 46556-5639

DELANEY, JAMES M. business executive; V.p. specialty metals group Ryerson Tull Inc., Chgo., 1999—, pres. Ryerson Ctrl., 1999—. Office: Ryerson Tull Inc 2621 W 15th Pl Chicago IL 60608-1752 Fax: 773-762-0437.

DELANEY, ROBERT VERNON, logistics and transportation executive; b. Passaic, N.J., Mar. 16, 1936; s. Edward Aloysius and Helen Margaret (Gauthier) D.; m. Elissa Ornato, June 15, 1963; children: Edward, James. BBA, NYU, 1963, MBA, 1966; postgrad., St. Louis U., 1967-69, Am. U., 1971-72. Registered practitioner Surface Transp. Bd. formerly ICC. Transp. mgr. Nabisco, N.Y.C., 1958-62; distbn. mgr. Monsanto Co., St. Louis, 1963-70; dir. phys. distbn. Md. Cup Corp., Owings Mills, 1970-74; mgr. internal cons. Pet Inc., St. Louis, 1974-78; mgr. distbn. planning Internat. Paper Co., N.Y.C., 1978-83; sr. v.p. Leaseway Transp. Co., Cleve., 1983-87; practice leader for transp. Arthur D. Little, Inc., Cambridge, Mass., 1988-89; exec. v.p. Cass Info. Sys., St. Louis, 1990—. Founder Warehousing Edn. and Rsch. Coun., Oak Brook, Ill., 1977; bd. dirs. Pvt. Carrier Conf., Inc.; faculty Acad. Advanced Traffic, 1966; guest lectr., frequent spkr. ednl. and profl. orgns. Co-author Transportation Strategies for the Eighties, 1982, The Distribution Handbook, 1984; mem. editl. rev. bd. Transportation Quar., Internat. Jour. Phys. Distbn. and Materials Mgmt.; contbr. articles to newpapers and bus. pubs. Mem. transp. com. The New England Coun., Boston, 1978-82. St. Louis Regional Commerce & Growth Assn., 1975-78; bus. advisor Norman Thomas H.S., N.Y.C., 1979-82. Staff sgt. U.S. Army, 1953-56. Recipient Salzberg Medallion award for transp., Syracuse U., 1988. Mem. Am. Soc. Transp. and Logistics (cert., Joseph Scheleen award for excellence 1992), Coun. Logistics Mgmt. (exec. com. 1976-84, sec. 1983-84, Disting. Svc. award 1981), Nat. Coun. Phys. Distbn. Mgmt. (John Drury Sheahan Disting. Svc. award 1981), Nat. Press Club (Washington, author ann. State of Logistics report). Republican. Avocation: education. Office: Cass Info Systems 13001 Hollenberg Dr Bridgeton MO 63044-2410 Business E-Mail: bdelaney@cassinfo.com.

DELANGE, WALTER J. former state legislator; b. Grand Rapids, Mich., Nov. 9, 1931; s. Walter and Harriet DeL.; m. Lois A. Lindhout, 1951; three children. Mem. Kentwood City (Mich.) Bd. Rev., 1981; commr. Kent County, Mich., 1982; rep. Mich. Dist. 72, 1983-96. Majority caucus chmn. Mich. Ho. Reps., chmn. Rep. policy com., chmn. human resources & labor com., transp. com., regulatory com. Dir. Grand Rapids Home Builders Assn.; v.p. Mich. Assn. Home Builders, 1979-82, bd. dirs.; bd. dirs. Millbrook Christian Sch.; Sunday sch. tchr. Millbrook Christian Reformed Ch., former deacon, elder, tchr. catechism, clk. Home: 5815 Lindenwood Ct SE Kentwood MI 49512-9668

DE LA RIVA, JUAN L. automotive company executive; BA, N.Y.U.; MBA, U. Detroit. Mng. dir., Light Vehicles Systems Wheels Meritor, Limeira, Brazil, v.p., bus. devel. comm., sr. v.p., bus. devel. comm., 1999—. Office: Meritor Auto Inc 2135 W Maple Rd Troy MI 48084-7121

DE LASA, JOSÉ M. lawyer; b. Havana, Cuba, Nov. 28, 1941; came to U.S., 1961; s. Miguel and Conchita de Lasa; m. Maria Teresa Figueroa, Nov. 23, 1963; children: Maria Teresa, José, Andrés, Carlos. BA, Yale U., 1968, JD, 1971. Bar: N.Y. 1973. Assoc. Cleary, Gottlieb, Steen & Hamilton, N.Y.C., 1971-76; legal dept. Bristol-Myers Squibb Co., 1976-94; sr. v.p., sec. and gen. counsel Abbott Labs., 1994—. Lectr. internat. law, various locations. Bd. dirs. Am. Arbitration Assn., Chgo. Children's Mus., The Resource Found., Chgo. Coun. Fgn. Rels., The Stovir Found. Mem. ABA, Assn. of Bar of City of N.Y., Assn. Gen. Counsel, North Shore Gen. Counsel Assn., Ill. State Bar Assn. Roman Catholic. Office: Abbott Laboratories D-364 AP6D-2 100 Abbott Park Rd North Chicago IL 60064-3500

DE LAWDER, C. DANIEL, company executive; BA, Ohio U., 1971. With Park Nat. Corp., Newark, 1971-98, CEO, 1998—. Office: 50 N 3d St Newark OH 43055

DE LERNO, MANUEL JOSEPH, electrical engineer; b. Jan. 8, 1922; s. Joseph Salvador and Elizabeth Mabry (Jordan) De L.; m. Margery Ellen Eaton, Nov. 30, 1946 (div. Oct. 1978); children: Diane, Douglas. BEE, Tulane U., 1941; MEE, Rensselaer Poly. Inst., 1943. Registered profl. engr., Ill., Mass. Devel. engr. indsl. control dept. Gen. Electric Co., Schenectady, N.Y., 1941-44; design engr. Lexington Electric Products Co., Newark, 1946-47; asst. prof. elec. engring. Newark Coll. Engring., 1948-49; test engr. Maschinenfabrik Oerlikon, Zurich, Switzerland, 1947-48; application engr. Henry J. Kaufman Co., Chgo., 1949-55; pres. Del Equipment Co., 1955-60; v.p. Del-Ray Co., 1960-67; pres. S-P-D Svcs. Inc., Forest Park, 1967-81, S-P-D Industries, Inc., Berwyn, 1981—2001, S-P-D Inc., Schaumburg, 2001—. Mem. standards making coms. Nat. Fire Protection Assn. Internat. Lt. (j.g.) USNR, 1944-45. Fellow Soc. Fire Protection Engrs.; mem. IEEE (sr. life), Ill. Soc. Profl. Engrs., Am. Water Works Assn. Home: 36w760 Stonebridge Ln Saint Charles IL 60175-4931 Office: 1161 Tower Rd Schaumburg IL 60173 E-mail: manny@spdinc.com.

DELFS, ANDREAS, conductor, musical director; b. Flensburg, Germany; Grad., Hamburg Conservatory, 1981; MA, Juilliard Sch., 1984. Staff conductor Lüneburg Stadttheater; music dir. Hamburg U. Orch.; musical asst. Hamburg State Opera; guest conductor Bremen State Theater, 1981; dir. Pitts. Youth Symphony; resident conductor Pitts. Symphony, 1986-90; music dir. Orch. Suisse Jeunes, 1984-95, Bern Opera, 1991-94; conductor N.Y. City Opera, 1995-96; music dir. Milw. Symphony Orch., 1997—; gen. music dir. Hannover State Opera and Orch. Guest conductor Phila. Orchestra at Carnegie Hall, 1998, London Philharmonic, 1997, Dallas Symphony Orch., 1997, Houston Symphony, 1996-98., Junge Deutsche Philharmoni, Germany, 1995-98, others; guest conductor Bern Symphony Orch., Minn. Orch., Detroit Symphony, Rochester Philharmonic, others. Bruno Walter scholar Juilliard Sch.; Steinburg fellow Pitts. Symphony. Office: Milw Symph Orch 330 E Kilbourn Ave Ste 900 Milwaukee WI 53202-3141

DELLACORTE, CHRISTOPHER, engineer, tribologist; b. Port Jefferson, N.Y., Dec. 10, 1963; s. Franklin Alfred and Suzanne DellaCorte; m. Patricia DellaCorte. BS, Case Western Res. U., 1986, MS, PhD, Case Western Res. U., 1987. Rsch. engr. Case Western Res. U., Cleve., 1986-87, NASA, Cleve., 1987—. Contbr. over 50 articles to profl. jours. Bd. dirs. Medina (Ohio) County Bd. Mental Retardation and Devel. Disabilities, 1992-96. Mem. ASME (Burt L. Newkirk award 1996, conf. planning com. 1995—), Soc. Tribologists and Lubrication (assoc. editor, solid lubricants com. chair 1989-92). Avocations: mechanical devices, technical history, natural history. Office: NASA Glenn Rsch Ctr MS 23-2 21000 Brookpark Rd Cleveland OH 44135-3191

DELLEUR, JACQUES WILLIAM, civil engineering educator; b. Paris, Dec. 30, 1924; came to U.S., 1952, naturalized, 1957; s. Georges Leon and Simone (Rossum) D.; m. DeLores Ann Horne, June 18, 1957; children: James Robert, Ann Marie. Civil and Mining Engr., Nat. U. Colombia, 1949; M.S. in Civil Engring., Rensselaer Poly. Inst., 1950; D.Engring. Sci., Columbia U., 1955. Civil engr. R.J. Tipton and Assocs., 1950-52; from research asst. to instr. civil engring. and engring. mechanics Columbia U., 1952-55; mem. faculty Purdue U., 1955-95, prof. hydraulic engring. and hydrology, 1963-95, prof. emeritus hydraulic engring., 1995—, head hydromechanics and water resources area, 1965-76, head hydraulic and systems engring. area, 1981-90, 91-92; assoc. dir. Purdue U. Water Resources Rsch. Ctr., 1971-89, acting dir., 1983. Researcher fluid mechanics U. Grenoble, Fance, 1961-62, hydrology and environ. fluid mechanics French Nat. Hydraulics Lab., Chatou, France, 1968-69, 76-77, statis. hydrology U. Brussels, Belgium, 1991; NSF sr. exch. scientist U. Grenoble, France, 1983-84; vis. prof. U. Quebec, Canada, 1996—, Vrije U., Brussels, 1995—; scientific coun. Revue des Sciences de L'eau Water Scis. Scientific Interest Group/Nat. Inst. Scientific Rsch., Quebec, 1988—; vis. lectr. Ecole Polytechnique Federale de Lausanne, Switzerland, 1991, 93, 95, 97; coord. Consortium of U.S. and European Cmty. Univs. for Scholar and Multimedia Exchs. in Environ. and Water Resources Engring. and Scis., 1998—. Author and co-author 2 books on statis. hydrology; co-author book on urban hydorlogy; editor: Handbook of Groundwater Engineering, 1999; assoc. editor: Handbook of Civil Engineering, 1995, 2d edit., 2002; also articles, reports in field. Fellow Ind. Acad. Sci.; mem. ASCE (Freeman fellow 1961-62, chmn. fluid dynamics com. 1964-66, task com. mechanics of turbulence 1964-69, task com. hydraulics of bridges 1963-68, task com. on rehab. urban drainage infrastructure 1988-90, co-chmn. task com. on urban drainage rehab. & techniques 1990-94, chmn. com. urban water resources 1994-95, chmn. com. sediment movement in urban drainage sys. 1998—, internat. bd. advisors Jour. Hydrologic Engring. 1996—, Svc. to the Profession award 2000, Ven Te Chow Hydrology award 2002), Am. Geophys. Union (chmn. urban hydrology com. 1978-83), Am. Water Resources Assn., Am. Soc. Engring. Edn., Internat. Assn. Hydraulic Rsch. (U.S. del. joint com. on urban storm drainage with Internat. Assn. Water Quality 1987-93), Internat. Assn. Sci. Hydrology, Ind. Water Resources Assn. (Charles Harold Bechert award 1992). Home: 124 Mohican Pl West Lafayette IN 47906-2159 Office: Purdue U Sch Civil Engring West Lafayette IN 47907-1284

DELL'OSSO, LOUIS FRANK, neuroscience educator; b. Bklyn., Mar. 16, 1941; s. Frank and Rose (Perrone) Dell'O.; m. Aquilina Marie Ferlo, May 22, 1965 (div. 1976); single ptnr. Charlene Hale Morse, Sept. 30, 1977. BEE, Bklyn. Poly. Inst., 1961, postgrad., 1961-63; PhD, U. Wyo., 1968. Co-dir. Ocular Motor Neurophysiology Lab. VA. Med. Ctr., Miami, Fla., 1972-80; asst. prof. biomed. engring. and surgery U. Miami, 1970-72, asst. prof. neurology, 1972-75, assoc. prof. neurology, 1975-79, prof. neurology, 1979-80; dir. Ocular Motor Neurophysiology Lab. VA Med. Ctr., Cleve., 1980—; prof. neurology and biomed. engring. Case Western Res. U., 1980—. Cons. Westinghouse Research Lab, Pitts, 1966-67, 70-71, Mt. Sinai Hosp., Miami, Fla., 1972-75. Bd. dirs. Vineland Galloway Civic Assn., Miami, 1973-76. Grantee NIH, 1971-77, VA Med. Ctr., 1972—, NSF, 1970. Fellow N.Am. NeuroOphthalmology Soc.; mem. IEEE, Engring. in Medicine and Biology Soc. (sr., chpt. chmn. 1977-78), Assn. Rsch. in Vision and Ophthalmology, Soc. Neurosci., NY Acad. Scis., Train Collectors Assn., CCCC Rod & Gun Club. Democrat. Home: 2356 Tudor Dr Cleveland OH 44106-3212 E-mail: lfd@po.cwru.edu.

DELMORE, LOIS M. state legislator; m. Michael Delmore; 2 child. Student, U. N.D. Tchr. English Red River H.S.; mem. Dist. 43 N.D. Ho. of Reps.; mem. judiciary and polit subdivsn. coms. N.D. State Senate. Mem. N.D. State Tchrs. Assn. Home: 714 S 22nd St Grand Forks ND 58201-4138

DELONG, DEBORAH, lawyer; b. Louisville, Sept. 5, 1950; d. Henry F. and Lois Jean (Stepp) D.; children: Amelie DeLong, Samuel Prentice. BA, Vanderbilt U., 1972; JD, U. Cin., 1975. Bar: Ohio 1975, Ky. 1999, U.S. Dist. Ct. (so. dist.) Ohio 1975, U.S. Ct. Appeals (Fed. cir.) 1990, (11th cir.), 1995, U.S. Ct. Appeals (6th cir.) 1991, U.S. Supreme Ct. 1982. Assoc. Paxton & Seasongood, Cin., 1975-82, ptnr., 1982-88, Thompson, Hine & Flory, 1989—. Contbr. articles to profl. jours. Bd. dirs. Cin. Opera, People Working Cooperatively, Inc. Mem. ABA, Ohio State Bar Assn., Cin. Bar Assn., Arbitration Tribunal U.S. Dist. Ct., Ohio, 1984. Republican. Episcopalian. Office: Thompson Hine & Flory 312 Walnut St Ste 1400 Cincinnati OH 45202-4089

DELONG, RAY, editor; Copy editor Dayton (Ohio) Jour. Herald, 1972-73; editor, reporter Chgo. Daily News, 1973-78; city editor Columbia Missourian, summer 1980; freelance writer, 1978—; with ABA, 1986—, now editor Bus. Law Today, Litigation Docket. Asst. prof. journalism U. Ill., 1978-84; asst. prof. Medill Sch. Journalism, Northwestern U., 1984-86; lectr. Univ. Coll., Northwestern U., 1985—. Office: ABA Publishing 750 N Lake Shore Dr Chicago IL 60611-4403

DELOREY, JOHN ALFRED, printing company executive; b. Malden, Mass., July 13, 1924; s. John Alfred and Alice Gertrude (Collins) D.; m. Ann M. Abbott, Dec. 27, 1952; children— Debra Ann, Michael John, David Abbott BS in Econs., Boston Coll., 1950; MBA, Harvard U., 1953. Plant mgr. Container Corp. Am., Renton, Wash., 1965-69, mgf. mgr. Carol Stream, Ill., 1969-73, gen. mgr. St. Louis, 1973-77, Carol Stream, 1977-81, v.p., divsn. gen. mgr. St. Louis, 1981-82; exec. v.p. W.F. Hall Printing Co., Chgo., 1982-87; v.p. Container Corp. Am., 1987-93; pres. DeLorey & Assocs., Oak Brook, Ill., 1993—. Dir. Container Corp. Am. Polit. Action Com., Chgo., 1981-86. Author: (with others) Consumer Packaging, 1953 Served to maj. USAF, 1942-53, ETO. Decorated DFC, Air medal with 3 oak leaf clusters, European Theater medal with 3 battle stars. Mem.: Paperboard Packaging Assn. (dir. midwest region 1977—81), Boston Coll. Club (Naples, Fla.), Kensington Country Club, Harvard Bus. Club, Butterfield Country Club. Avocations: golf; swimming; skiing; bridge; reading. Home and Office: DeLorey & Assocs 194 Briarwood Loop Oak Brook IL 60523-8714

DELP, WILBUR CHARLES, JR. lawyer; b. Cedar Rapids, Iowa, Oct. 26, 1934; s. Wilbur Charles and Irene Frances (Flynn) D.; m. Patricia Lynn Vesely, June 22, 1963; children: Marci Lynn, Melissa Kathryn, Derek Charles. B.A., Coe Coll., 1956; LL.B., NYU, 1959. Bar: Ill. 1960, U.S. Supreme Ct. 1962. Assoc. Sidley Austin Brown & Wood, Chgo., 1959—68, ptnr., 1968—. Lectr. securities law seminars With USAF, 1959-65. Mem. ABA (securities com.), Chgo. Bar Assn., Law Club

(Chgo.), Legal Club (Chgo.), Mid-Day Club (Chgo.), Phi Beta Kappa, Phi Kappa Phi. Home: PO Box 97 Wayne IL 60184-0097 Office: Sidley Austin Brown & Wood Bank One Plz Chicago IL 60603-0001 E-mail: wdelp@sidley.com.

DELPH, DONNA JEAN (MAROC), education educator, consultant, university administrator; b. Hammond, Ind., Mar. 7, 1931; d. Edward Joseph and Beatrice Catherine (Ethier) Maroc; m. Billy Keith Delph, May 30, 1953 (div. 1967); 1 child, James Eric. BS, Ball State U., 1953, MA, 1963, EdD, 1970. Cert. in ednl. adminstrn./supervision, reading specialist, Ind.; cert. elem. sch. tchr., Ind., Calif. Elem. tchr. Long Beach (Calif.) Community Schs., 1953-54; elem. tchr., reading specialist, asst. dir. elem. edn. Hammond Pub. Schs., 1954-70; prof. edn. Purdue U. Calumet, Hammond, 1970-84, 88-90, prof. emeritus, 1990—, head dept. edn., dir. tchr. edn., 1984-88. Cons. pub. schs., Highland, Ind., 1970-88, Gary, Ind., 1983-88, East Chicago, Ind., 1987-88, Hammond, 1970-88; speaker/workshop presenter numerous profl. orgns., Hammond, 1964—; mem. exec. coun. Nat. Coun. Accreditation Tchr. Edn., 1991-97. Author: (with others) Individualized Reading, 1967; contbr. articles, monographs to profl. jours. Bd. dirs. Bethany Child Care and Devel. Ctr., Hammond, 1972-77. Recipient Outstanding Teaching award Purdue U. Calumet, 1981. Mem. Assn. Tchr. Educators, Assn. for Supervision and Curriculum Devel. (rev. coun. 1987-91, bd. dirs. 1974-85), Internat. Reading Assn., Ind. Reading Profs. (pres. 1985-86), Pi Lambda Theta. Office: Purdue Univ Calumet Dept Education Hammond IN 46323 E-mail: delnjohn@otherside.com.

DE LUCIA, FRANK CHARLES, physicist, educator; b. St. Paul, June 21, 1943; s. Frank Charles and Muriel Ruth (Rinehart) D.; m. Shirley Ann Wood, June 25, 1966; children: Frank Charles, Elizabeth Ann. BS, Iowa Wesleyan Coll., 1964; PhD, Duke U., 1969. Instr, research assoc. Duke U., Durham, N.C., asst. prof., assoc. prof.; program mgr. Army Research Office, Research Triangle Park; prof. Duke U., Durham, chmn. physics dept.; prof., chmn. dept. physics Ohio State U., Columbus, 1990-98, prof., 1998—. Recipient Max Planck Rsch. prize, 1992, William F. Meggers award, 2001; named Disting. rsch. scholar, 1999, Disting. Univ. prof., 2000. Mem. Am. Phys. Soc., IEEE, Optical Soc. Am., Phi Beta Kappa. Office: Ohio State U Dept Of Physics Columbus OH 43210

DELUHERY, PATRICK JOHN, state legislator; b. Birmingham, Ala., Jan. 31, 1942; s. Frank B. and Lucille (Donovan) D.; m. Margaret Morris, 1973; children: Allison, Norah, Rose. BA with honors, U. Notre Dame, 1964; BSc in Econs. with honors, London Sch. Econs., 1967. Legis. asst. U.S. Senator Harold Hughes, Washington, 1969-74, U.S. Senator John Culver, Washington, 1975; asst. prof. econs. and bus. adminstrn. St. Ambrose U., Davenport, Iowa, 1975—. Mem. Iowa State Senate, 1979—; ins. agt., 1989—. Democrat. Roman Catholic. patrick. Home: 11839 100th Ave Davenport IA 52804-9110 Office: Iowa Senate Statehouse Des Moines IA 50319-0001 E-mail: pdeluhery@saunix.sau.edu., patrick_deluhery@legis.state.ia.us.

DEL VALLE, MIGUEL, state legislator; b. P.R., July 24, 1951; m. Lupe; 4 children. BA, MA, Northeastern Ill. U. Mem. dist. 2 Ill. State Senate, 1987—; chmn. consumer affairs, vice chmn. com. and econ. devel., mem. appropriations II, higher edn., revenue and elections and reapportionment coms. also: Ill State Senate Capitol Bldg Springfield IL 62706-0001

DELZER, JEFF W. state legislator; Student, Dawson C.C. Farmer/rancher; rep. Dist. 8 N.D. Ho. of Reps., 1991-92, 95—, mem. indsl., bus. and labor and transp. coms., mem. appropriations com., 1997, 99, chmn. interim budget com. on human svcs., 1999. Home: 2919 5th St NW Underwood ND 58576-9603 Office: ND Ho of Reps State Capitol 600 E Boulevard Ave Bismarck ND 58505-0660

DE MAIN, JOHN, artistic director of opera company; b. Youngstown, Ohio, Jan. 11, 1944; BMus, Juilliard Sch. Music, 1966, MusM, 1968; studies in conducting with, Leonard Bernstein, Peter Adler. Assoc. condr. St. Paul Chamber Orch., 1972-74; music dir. Tex. Opera Theater, 1974-76; former music dir. Houston Grand Opera, Opera Omaha; artistic dir. Madison Symphony Orch. & Opera, WI. Prin. guest condr. Chautauqua Opera Inst., 1985. Rec. performances; Piano Concerto (Frances Thorne), CRI, 1975, Porgy and Bess, RCA, 1976, Nocturnes (Miriam Gideon), CRI, 1978. Recipient Julius Rudel award, 1971, Grammy award, 1977, Grand Prix, 1977; Juilliard Sch. Music scholar 1964-68. Office: Madison Symphony Orch 211 N Carroll St Madison WI 53703-2211 Home: 52 White Oaks Ln Madison WI 53711-6216

DE MARCO, THOMAS JOSEPH, periodontist, educator; b. Farmingdale, N.Y., Feb. 12, 1942; s. Joseph Louis and Mildred Nora (Cifarelli) De M.; children: Todd Gordon, Kristin Alice, Lisa Anne. B.S., U. Pitts., 1962; D.D.S., 1965; Ph.D., certificate in Periodontology, Boston U., 1968; cert. in fin. planning, Coll. Fin. Planning, Denver, 1976. Certificate in clin. hypnosis. Practice dentistry specializing in periodontics and implants, Cleve., 1968—; mem. staff Met. Gen. Hosp., Univ. Hosp., Cleve., VA Hosp., Cleve.; asst. prof. periodontics and pharmacology Case-Western Res. U., 1968-70, assoc. prof., 1970-73, prof., 1973-84; asso. dean Case-Western Res. U. (Sch. Dentistry), 1972-76, dean, 1976-84; pvt. practice periodontia, 1984—. Author review books in dentistry, book on fin. planning, also articles on periodontology, pharmacology, fin. planning. Grantee Air Force Office Sci. Research, 1969; grantee Upjohn Co., 1970; grantee Columbus Dental Mfg. Co., 1971. Mem. Am. Acad. Periodontology, Internat. Assn. Dental Research, Am. Soc. for Preventive Dentistry (past pres. Ohio chpt.) Home: 12370 Rockhaven Rd Chesterland OH 44026-2744 Office: 29001 Cedar Rd Cleveland OH 44124

DE MARIA, PAOLO, state governor policy advisor; Grad. in econ. and polit. sci., Furman U.; M in Pub. Adminstrn., Ohio State U., 1996. Sr. fiscal analyst fin. com. Ohio Senate, Columbus; mem. gubernatorial transition team Gov. George V. Voinovich; asst. dir. Office Budget and Mgmt., dir., 1998-2000; chief polity adv. Gov. Ohio Office, 2000—. Office: 77 S High Sch 30th Fl Columbus OH 43215-6117

DEMBER, WILLIAM NORTON, retired psychologist, educator; b. Waterbury, Conn., Aug. 8, 1928; s. David and Henrietta Dember; m. Cynthia Fox, Dec. 21, 1958; children: Joanna, Laura, Gregory. AB, Yale U., 1950; MA, U. Mich., 1951, PhD, 1955. Instr. dept. psychology U. Mich., 1954-56; asst. prof. Yale U., 1956-59; faculty U. Cin., 1959-98, prof. psychology, 1965-98, asst. dean, grad. sch., 1965-67, head dept. psychology, 1968-76, 79-81, dean Coll. Arts and Scis., 1981-86, disting. rsch. prof., 1989, prof., dean emeritus, 1998; ret. Author: Psychology of Perception, 1960, 2d edit., 1979, Visual Perception, 1964, General Psychology, 1970, 2d edit., 1984, Exploring Behavior and Experience, 1971, Spontaneous Alternation Behavior, 1989; contbr. articles to profl. jours. Fellow APA, Am. Psychol. Soc.; mem. Midwest Psychol. Assn. (pres. 1976). Achievements include developing and testing theory of motivation applying to behavior of human beings and animals; rsch. in visual metacontrast, optimism/pessimism, and sustained attention. Home: 920 Oregon Trl Cincinnati OH 45215-2536 E-mail: Drsdember@aol.com.

DEMBO, LAWRENCE SANFORD, English educator; b. Troy, N.Y., Dec. 3, 1929; s. Irving and Mildred (Spiwak) D.; m. Royce Benderson, Mar. 15, 1953. B.A., Syracuse U., 1951; M.A., Columbia, 1952; Ph.D., Cornell U., 1955. Instr. English Cornell U., 1959-60; asst. prof. UCLA, 1960-65; Fulbright lectr. Montpellier, France, 1963-64; prof. English U. Wis., Madison, 1965-90, prof. emeritus, 1990—. Author: Hart Crane's Sanskrit Charge, A Study of the Bridge, 1960, The Confucian Odes of Ezra Pound, A Critical Appraisal, 1963, Conceptions of Reality in Modern American Poetry, 1966, The Monological Jew, A Literary Study, 1988, Detotalized Totalities: Synthesis and Disintegration in Naturalist, Existential, and Socialist Fiction, 1989; editor: Nabokov, The Man and His Work, 1967, Criticism, Speculative and Analytical Essays, 1968; co-editor: The Contemporary Writer: Interviews with Sixteen Novelists and Poets, 1972, Doris Lessing, Critical Studies, 1974, Directions for Criticism, 1977, Interviews with Contemporary Writers, Second Series, 1972-82, 83; editor in chief: Contemporary Literature, 1966-90; mem. editorial bd. Am. Lit., 1973-76; author poetry/contbr. regional jours. Served to lt. USNR, 1955-65. Guggenheim fellow, 1968-69; Am. Council Learned Socs. fellow, 1977-78 Home: 3434 Valley Creek Cir Middleton WI 53562-1990 Office: U Wis Madison 7164 Helen White Hall Madison WI 53706-1416

DEMBOWSKI, PETER FLORIAN, foreign language educator; b. Warsaw, Poland, Dec. 23, 1925; came to U.S., 1966, naturalized, 1974; s. Wlodzimierz and Henryka (Sokolowski) D.; m. Yolande Jessop, June 29, 1954; children: Anne, Eve, Paul. B.A. with honors, U. B.C., 1952; Doctorat d'Universite, U. Paris, France, 1954; Ph.D., U. Calif. at Berkeley, 1960. Instr. French U. B.C., 1954-56; asst. prof. French U. Toronto, 1960-63, assoc. prof., 1963-66; mem. faculty U. Chgo., 1966-95, prof. French, 1970-95, Disting. Svc. prof., 1989-95, prof. emeritus, 1995—, dean students div. humanities, 1968-70, chmn. dept. Romance langs. and lits., 1976-83, resident master Snell-Hitchcock halls, 1973-79; vis. mem. Sch. Hist. Studies, Inst. Advanced Study, Princeton, N.J., 1979-80. Author: La Chronique de Robert de Clari, 1963, Jourdain de Blaye, 1969, Ami et Amile, 1969, La Vie de sainte Marie l'Egyptienne, 1977, Jean Froissart and his Meliador, 1983, Jean Froissart, Le Paradis d'Amour et l'Orloge Amoureus, 1986, Erec et Enide, 1994, L'Estrif de Fortune et Vertu, 1999. Served with Polish Army, 1944-46. Decorated Cross of Valor, Cross of Service with swords (Poland), Chevalier des Palmes Academiques (France); Guggenheim fellow, 1970-71; Danforth Found. assoc., 1976-84 Fellow Am. Acad. Arts and Scis.; mem. Sociètè de Linguistique Romane (councillor 1995—), Medieval Acad. Am. (councillor 1980-82). Office: U Chgo Dept Romance Langs and Lit 1050 E 59th St Rm 205B Chicago IL 60637-1559

DEMBSKI, STEPHEN MICHAEL, composer, university music composition professor; b. Boston, Dec. 13, 1949; s. Theodore Arthur and Minna Morris (Baldauf) D.; m. Sonja Sullivan, July 9, 1988; children: Melissa Leonora, Rachel Michalena. BA, Antioch Coll., 1973; MA, SUNY, Stony Brook, 1975; MFA, Princeton U., 1977, PhD, 1980. Dir. advanced composition program U. Wis., Madison, 1982—; prof., 1982—. Bd. dirs. Composers' Recordings, Inc., N.Y.C., Internat. Soc. Contemporary Music, N.Y.C., N.Y. New Music Ensemble, Phantom Arts, Boston; vis. asst. prof. Dartmouth Coll., Hanover, N.H., 1978-81, Bates Coll., Lewiston, Maine, 1982; mem. editl. bd. Spectrum. Composer musical scores including Pterodactyl, 1974, Of Mere Being, 1975, 82, Tender Buttons, 1977, Trio, 1977, Hard Times, 1978, Singles, 1980, Caritas, 1980, Alba, 1980, Alta, 1981, String Quartet, 1984, At Baia, 1984, Spectra, 1985, The Show, 1986, Sonata for Violin and Piano, 1987-88, Digit, 1978, Stacked Deck, 1979, Altamira, 1983, On Ondine, 1991-2000, Two Scenes from Elsaveta, 1992, So Fine, 1993, For Five, 1994, Hornbill, 1994, Memory's Minefield, 1994, Needles & Pins, 1994, Out of My System, 1995, Sonotropism, 1996, Brass Attacks, 1998, Le Monde Merengue, 1999, Contemplations, 2000, Tu m'hai si piena, 2000; composer recordings including CRI, 1988, 90, Vienna Modern Masters, 1990, Music and Arts, 1997; condr. recordings include Scott Fields' 48 Motives, Cadence, 1996, (books) Internat. Music Lexicon, 1979, 84; editor: (with others) Milton Babbitt-Words About Music, 1987. Fellow Howard Found., Providence, 1986-87, Nat. Endowment for the Arts, Washington, 1979, 81, 86; recipient Goddard Lieberson award Am. Acad. and Inst. of Arts and Letters, 1982, Segnalazione: Premio Musicale award Citta di Trieste, 1990. Mem. ASCAP, Soc. for Music Theory, Am. Music Ctr. Home: 96 Perry St Apt B22 New York NY 10014-5506 Office: U Wis Sch of Music 455 N Park St Madison WI 53706-1405 E-mail: sdembski@facstaff.wisc.edu.

DEMERDASH, NABEEL ALY OMAR, electrical engineer; b. Cairo, Apr. 26, 1943; came to U.S., 1966; s. Aly Omar and Aziza D.; m. Esther Adel Feher, Feb. 22, 1969; children: Yvonne, Omar, Nancy. BScEE with 1st class honors, Cairo U., 1964; MSEE, U. Pitts., 1967, PhD, 1971. Tchg. asst. in elec. engring. Cairo U., 1964-66, U. Pitts., 1966-68; engr. Westinghouse Electric Corp., Pitts., 1968-72; asst. prof. elec. engring. Va. Poly. Tech. Inst. and State U., Blacksburg, 1972-77, assoc. prof. elec. engring., 1977-81, prof., 1981-83; prof. dept. elec. and computer engring. Clarkson U., Potsdam, N.Y., 1983-94; prof., chmn. dept. elec. and computer engring. Marquette U., Milw., 1994-97, prof. dept. elec. and computer engring., 1994—. Cons. Sundstrand Corp., Rockford, Ill., 1985-98. Contbr. articles to profl. jours. Recipient cert. recognition NASA, 1979, cert. of teaching excellence Va. Poly. Inst. and State U., 1980. Fellow IEEE (subcom. chmn. 1988-92, 94-97, Nikola Tesla award 1999); mem. IEEE Power Engring. Soc. (disting. lectr. 1987—, Elec. Machinery Com. prize paper award 1993, working group award 1994, PES prize paper award 1993, working group award 1994), Indsl. Electronics Soc. (Disting. Spkr. program 1990—), Electromagnetics Acad. Achievements include development of three dimensional finite element vector potential and coupled 3D vector potential-scalar potential methods of solution of electromagnetic fields in electric devices; time-stepping coupled finite element-state space computer simulation models and design of electronically operated/controlled AC and DC motor drives. Office: Marquette Univ Elec Computer Engring Dept PO Box 1881 Milwaukee WI 53201-1881 E-mail: nabeel.demerdash@marquette.edu.

DEMERITT, STEPHEN R. food products executive; Various consumer food mktg. positions General Mills Inc., 1969—, pres. Internat. Foods, 1991-93, CEO Cereal Ptnrs. Worldwide, vice chmn., 1999—. Office: General Mills Inc PO Box 1113 One General Mills Blvd Minneapolis MN 55440-1113

DEMERS, JUDY LEE, former state legislator, university dean; b. Grand Forks, N.D., June 27, 1944; d. Robert L. and V. Margaret (Harming) Prosser; m. Donald E. DeMers, Oct. 3, 1964 (div. Oct. 1971); 1 child, Robert M.; m. Joseph M. Murphy, Mar. 5, 1977 (div. Oct. 1983). BS in Nursing, U. N.D., 1966; MEd, U. Wash., 1973; postgrad., 1973-76. Pub. health nurse Govt. D.C., 1966-68; Combined Nursing Svc., Mpls., 1968-69; instr. pub. health nursing U. N.D., Grand Forks, 1969-71; assoc. dir. Medex program, 1970-72; dir. family nurse practitioner program, 1977-82; assoc. dir. rural health, 1982-85; dir. undergrad. med. edn., 1982-83; assoc. dean, 1983—; rsch. assoc. U. Wash., Seattle, 1973-76; mem. N.D. Ho. of Reps., 1982-92, N.D. Senate, 1992-2000. Cons. Health Manpower Devel. Staff, Honolulu, 1975-81, Assn. Physician Asst. Programs, Washington, 1979-82; site visitor cons. AMA Com. Allied Health Edn. Accreditation, Chgo.,1979-81. Author: Educating New Health Practitioners, 1976; mem. editl. bd.: P.A. Jour., 1976-78; contbr. articles to profl. jours. Sec., bd. dirs. Valley Family Health, Grand Forks, N.D., 1982—; mem. exec. com., bd. dirs. Agassiz Health Systems Agy., Grand Forks, 1982-86; mem. N.D. State Daycare Adv. Com., 1983-93, Mayor's Adv. com. on Police Policy, Grand Forks, 1983-85, N.D. State Foster Care Adv. Com., 1985-87, N.D. State Hypertension Adv. Com., 1983-85, Gov.'s Com. on DUI and Traffic Safety, 1985-91, Statewide Adv. Com. on AIDS, 1985-90; bd. dirs. Casey Found., Families First Initiative, 1988-97, Comprehensive Health Assn. N.D., 1993-95, United Health Found., 1990-97, Northern Valley Mental Health Assn., 1994—, Grand Forks Girl's and Women's Hockey Assn., 1999-2002; bd. dirs., exec. com., program com. Devel. Homes, 1999--; mem. adv. bd. Mountainbrooke (formerly Friendship Place), 1992-96; mem. adv. com. Ruth Meiers Adolescent Ctr., Grand Forks, 1988—, Altru Health Sys. Corp. Bd., 1997—; mem. Commn. on Future Structure of VA Health Care, 1990-91; bd. dirs. Red River Valley Cmty. action Program, 1991—; mem. Resource and Referral Bd. Dirs., 1990—; mem. caring coun. N.D. Blue Cross and Blue Shield Caring Program for Children, 1995-99; coun. mem. N.D. Health Task Force, 1992-94; mem. healthcare subcom. Northern Gt. Plains Econ. Devel. Commn., 1995-96; mem. adv. com. on telecomms. and healthcare FCC, 1996; mem. Grand Forks City-County Bd. Health, 2000—. Recipient Pub. citizen of Yr. award N.D. chpt. Nat. Assn. Social Workers, 1986, Golden Grain award N.D. Dietetic Assn., 1988, Person of Yr. award U. N.D. Law Women Caucus, 1990, Legislator of Yr. award No. Valley Labor Coun., 1990, N.D. Martin Luther King Jr. award, 1990, Legislator of Yr. award Mental Health Assn., N.D., 1993, Libr. Assn., 1999, Friend of Medicine award N.D. Med. Assn., 1999, Legislator of Year award N.D. Pub. Employees Assn., 1999, Friend of Counseling award N.D. State Counseling Assn., 2000, Legislative Svc. award ARC of N.D. Mem. N.D. Nurses Assn. (nurse of yr. 1983), Alpha Lambda Delta. Home: Unit 92N 2200 S 29th St Apt 92N Grand Forks ND 58201-5869 Office: U ND Sch Medicine PO Box 9037 501 N Columbia Rd Grand Forks ND 58202-9037

DEMETS, DAVID L. medical educator, biomedical researcher; b. Austin, Minn., Nov. 27, 1944; married; 2 children. BA in Math., Gustavus Adolphus Coll., St. Peter, Minn., 1966; MS in Biostats., U. Minn., 1968, PhD in Biostats., 1970. Statistician, divsn. computer rsch. and tech. NIH, Bethesda, Md., 1970-72, math. statistician, Nat. Heart, Lung and Blood Inst., 1973-79, chief, mathematical and applied statistics br., 1979-82; dir. biostats. Ctr., prof. stats. and biostats. U. Wis., Madison, 1982-91, assoc. dir. Clin. Cancer Ctr., 1982-91, chair dept. biostats., prof. stats. and biostats., 1991—, assoc. dir. Comprehensive Cancer Ctr., 1991—. Lectr., cons. in field; bd. scientific counselors Nat. Cancer Inst., 1993-96. Co-author: Fundamentals of Clinical Trials, 1981, 2d edit. 1985, 3d edit. 1995; contbr. numerous articles to profl. jours., chpts. to books; presenter in field; mem. adv. bd. jour. Controlled Clin. Trials, 1993—, editl. bd. 1994—; assoc. editor Jour. Clin. Rsch. and Drug Devel., 1987-90. Recipient Disting. Alumni award Gustavus Adolphus Coll., 1990, Gaylord Anderson Leadership award U. Minn. Sch. Pub. Health Alumni Soc., 1993. Fellow Am. Statis. Assn. (bd. dirs. 1987-89), Internat. Statis. Inst.; mem. Biometrics Soc. (regional adv. bd. 1975-77, 80-82, exec. com. Ea. N.Am. region 1992-94, pres. 1993), Soc. for Controlled Clin. Trials (bd. dirs. 1983-87, program com. 1984, 85, program chmn. 1988, v.p. 1988-89, pres. 1989-90, joint program com. with Internat. Soc. Clin. Biostats., Brussels, 1991, policy com. 1993—), Internat. Soc. Clin. Biostats. Office: U Wis Clin Science Ctr Dept Biostatistics & Med In 600 Highland Ave K61446 Madison WI 53792-0001

DEMING, DAVID LAWSON, art educator, educator; b. Cleve., May 26, 1943; s. Lawson Joseph and Mary Rita (Basile) D.; m. Ann Elizabeth Haldeman, Sept. 4, 1965; children: Matthew Lawson, Lisa Ann, Michael David. BFA, Cleve. Inst. Art, 1967; MFA, Cranbrook Acad. Art, Bloomfield Hills, Mich., 1970. Instr. Boston U., 1967-68, U. Tex., El Paso, 1970-72, asst. prof., assoc. prof. art Austin, 1972, prof., 1985, chmn. art dept., Marguerite Fairchild prof. art, 1991-96; interim dean Coll. of Fine Arts U. Tex., 1996-97, dean, 1997-98; pres. Cleve. Inst. Art, 1998—. Sculptures represented in permanent collection Columbus (Ohio) Mus. Art, Ark. Art Ctr., Little Rock, U. Tex. Southwestern Regional Med. Ctr. Dallas; included in White House Garden Exhbn. of Am. Sculptors, 1995. Recipient award of honor Austin chpt. AIA, 1983. Mem. Internat. Sculpture Assn. Roman Catholic. Office: Cleveland Inst of Art 11141 East Blvd Cleveland OH 44106-1700 E-mail: ddeming@gate.cia.edu.

DEMITRA, PAVOL, professional hockey player; b. Dubnica, Slovakia, Nov. 29, 1974; Drafted left wing/ctr. Ottawa (Can.), 1993-96; traded left wing/ctr. St. Louis Blues, 1996—. Represented Slovia in 1998 Winter Olympics, Nagano, Japan. Office: c/o St Louis Blues 1401 Clark Ave Saint Louis MO 63103-2700

DEMLOW, DANIEL J. lawyer; b. Ludington, Mich., Oct. 16, 1944; s. Richard M. and Nan (Jager) D.; m. Catherine M. Jerzak, Aug. 7, 1982; children: Sara Beth, Michelle Catherine. BA, Mich. State U., 1966; JD, U. Mich., 1969. Atty. Fraser Trebilock Davis & Foster, Lansing, Mich., 1969-70, Securities Bur., Lansing, State of Mich., 1970-71; dep. dir. Mich. Dept. Commerce, 1971-73; commr. ins. Ins. Bur., 1973-75; chmn. Mich. Pub. Svc. Commn., 1975-81; assoc. Honigman Miller Schwartz & Cohn, 1985—. Fellow Mich. State Bar Found. Republican. Presbyterian. Avocations: tennis, boating, grouse hunting. Home: 3773 Yosemite Dr Okemos MI 48864-3838 Office: Honigman Miller Schwartz & Cohn 222 N Washington Sq Ste 400 Lansing MI 48933-1800

DEMOREST, ALLAN FREDERICK, retired psychologist; b. Omaha, Dec. 20, 1931; s. Byron Peter and Minerva Gladys (Heine) D.; 1 child, Steven M. BA, U. Omaha, 1957; MA, U. Mich., 1959, postgrad., 1960. Lic. psychologist, Iowa, Nat. Register Health Svc. Providers. Counselor Mayor's Com. on Skid Row Problems, Detroit, 1959-61; psychologist Macomb County Schs., Mt. Clemens, Mich., 1961-64; chief psychologist Jasper County Mental Health Ctr., Newton, Iowa, 1964-68; exec. dir. North Cen. Iowa Mental Health Ctr., Ft. Dodge, 1968-75; pvt. practice, 1968-85; psychologist Iowa Luth. Hosp., Des Moines, 1985-87; clin. dir. United Behavioral Systems, 1987-94, sr. psychologist, 1994-96; cons. pvt. practice, 1996—. Adj. prof. psychology Buena Vista U., Ft. Dodge, 1974—. Contbr. articles on rational therapy to profl. jours. Founding bd. dirs. Rape and Sexual Assault Victim Program, Ft. Dodge, 1976-85, Family Violence Ctr., Ft. Dodge, 1976-85, Youth Shelter Svcs., Ft. Dodge, 1979. With U.S. Army, 1952-54, Korea. Recipient appreciation award Community Mental Health Ctrs. Assn., 1968, community svc. award Iowa Dept. Human Svcs., 1985. Fellow Albert Elias Inst.; mem. APA., Iowa Psychol. Assn., Adminstrv. Mgmt. Soc. (pres. Ft. Dodge 1979-80, 84-85), Iowa Assn. for Advancement Psychology (pres. 1984, appreciation award 1988), Elks (exalted ruler 1979, trustee 2002). Home and Office: 4225 Hickman Rd Des Moines IA 50310-3334 E-mail: ademorest@aol.com.

DEMOS, DAVE, marketing executive; V.p. sales, mktg. Am. Axle & Mfg., Detroit, v.p. sales and bus. devel., 1997-99, v.p. strategic planning, 1999—. Office: Am Axle & Mfg 1840 Holbrook Ave Detroit MI 48212-3442

DEMOSS, JON W. insurance company executive, lawyer; b. Kewanee, Ill., Aug. 9, 1947; s. Wendell and Virginia Beth DeMoss; m. Eleanor T. Thornley, Aug. 9, 1969; 1 child, Marc Alain. BS, U. Ill., 1969, JD, 1972. Bar: Ill. 1972, U.S. Dist. Ct. (cen. dist.) Ill. 1977, U.S. Supreme Ct. 1978, U.S. dist. Ct. (no. dist., trial bar) Ill. 1983. In house counsel Assn. Ill. Electric Coop., Springfield, 1972-74; registered lobbyist Ill. Gen. Assembly, 1972-74; asst. dir. Ill. Inst. for CLE, 1974-85; exec. dir. Ill. State Bar Assn., 1986-94; pres., CEO ISBA Mut. Ins. Co., Chgo., 1994—. Bd. dirs. Bar Plan Surety & Fidelity Co., St. Louis, 1999-. Bd. dirs. Springfield Symphony Orch., 1982-87, Ill. Inst. for CLE, 1986-89, Nat. Assn. of Bar Related Ins. Cos., 1989, pres., elect., 1998-99, pres. 1999—; bd. dirs. Lawyers Reins. Co., 1997—; bd. visitors John Marshall Law Sch., 1990—. Capt. U.S. Army, 1972. Fellow Am. Bar Found. (life, co-chmn. projects to prepare Appellate Handbook 1978, 90), Ill. Bar Found. (life, bd. dirs. 1983-85); mem. ABA (ho. of dels. 1979-85, 89, 91, 93-94), Nat. Conf. Bar Pres., Am. Judicature Soc. (bd. dirs. Ill. state chpt.), Ill. State Bar Assn. (pres. 1984-85, bd. govs. 1975-85, chmn. com. on scope and correlation of work 1982-83, chmn. budget com. 1983-85, chmn. legis. com. 1983-84, 85, chmn. com. on merit selection of judges 1977, del. long-range planning conf. 1972, 78, liaison to numerous coms. and sects.), Chgo. Bar Assn., Lake County Bar Assn., U. Ill. Coll. Dean's Club, La Chaine des Rotisseurs (Chgo.), Ordre Mondial des Gourmet Degustateurs (Chgo.), Les Gourmets

(Chgo.). Home: 180 Norwich Ct Lake Bluff IL 60044-1914 Office: ISBA Mutual Ins Co 223 W Ohio St Chicago IL 60610-4101

DEMPSEY, CEDRIC W. sports association administrator; b. Apr. 14, 1932; m. June Dempsey, Aug. 22, 1953; children: Linda, David, Marcia. BA in Phys. Edn. and History, MA in Edn., Albion Coll.; PhD in Phys. Edn., U. Ill.; LLD (hon.), Albion Coll. Grad. asst., asst. football and basketball coach, head tennis coach Albion (Mich.) Coll., 1954-56, head basketball & cross country coach, phys. edn. instr., 1959-62, dean of men, 1962-63; grad. asst., counselor profl. students, dir. placement svc. U. Ill., Urbana, 1956-59; asst. basketball coach, supr. undergrad. health, phys. edn. & recreation, asst. prof. U. Ariz., Tucson, 1963-65, asst. dir. health, phys. edn., recreation & athletics, assoc. prof., 1965-67, dir. athletics, 1982-93; dir. athletics, chair phys. edn. & recreation U. of the Pacific, Stockton, Calif., 1967-79; dir. athletics San Diego State U., 1979, U. Houston, 1979-82; pres. NCAA, Overland Park, Kans., 1993—. Sec.- treas. exec. com. NCAA, adminstrn. com., coun. and joint policy bd., chair budget subcom., mem. numerous other coms. Recipient Kathy Miller Courage award Phoenix Press Box Assn., 1988, Disting. Alumni award Albion Coll., 1993; named to Albion Coll. Inaugural Hall of Fame, 1989, U. Pacific Sports Hall of Fame, 1991. Address: NCAA PO Box 6222 Indianapolis IN 46206-6222

DEMPSEY, JERRY, state legislator; m. Joanne; 4 children. BA, U. St. Thomas; MA, U. Wis., River Falls. State rep. Minn. Ho. Reps., Dist. 29A, 1993—. Mem. capital investment, econ. devel., infrastructure & regulation fin. govt. ops., gaming, regulated indsl. & energy coms., Minn. Ho. Reps., 1993—. Address: 2025 Creekview Ct Red Wing MN 55066-4215

DEMPSEY, MARY A. library commissioner, lawyer; m. Philip Corboy, Sept. 4, 1992. BA with honors, St. Mary's Coll., Winona, Minn., 1975; MLS, U. Ill., 1976; JD, DePaul U., 1982. Bar: Ill. 1982. Libr. Hillside (Ill.) Pub. Libr., 1976-78; assoc. Reuben & Proctor, Chgo., 1982-85; assoc. gen. counsel Michael Reese Hosp. and Med. Ctr., 1985-86; pvt. practice, 1987-89; counsel Sidley & Austin, 1990-93; commr. Chgo. Pub. Libr., 1994—. Adj. prof. law DePaul U. Coll. Law and Health Inst., Chgo., 1986-90; spl. counsel Chgo. Bd. Edn., 1987-89; mem. adv. bd. Dominican U. Grad. Sch. Libr. and Info. Sci., River Forest, Ill. Mem. State Street Commn., Chgo.; bd. dirs. Big Shoulders Fund (for inner city Cath. schs.); bd. govs. Cath. Extension Soc.; trustee DePaul U., Chgo.; mem. Ill State Libr. Adv. Coun. Libr. scholar State of Ill. Mem. ALA, Pub. Libr. Assn., Ill. Libr. Assn., Chgo. Bar Assn. (bd. mgrs.), Chgo. Network (bd. dirs.). Office: Chgo Pub Libr 400 S State St Chicago IL 60605-1203

DEMUZIO, VINCE THOMAS, state legislator; b. Gillespie, Ill., May 7, 1941; s. Vince and Catherine McKnight (Murphy) D.; m. Deanna Joan Clemonds, June 23, 1962; children: Bradley, Stephanie. Student, Sangamon State U.; JD (hon.), Lewis & Clark C.C.; BA, Sangamon State U.; MA, U. Ill., Springfield, 1996. Investigator Office of Sec. of State, Springfield, Ill.; exec. dir. Ill. Valley Econ. Devel. Corp., Carlinville; state senator Springfield, 1974—; asst. majority leader, 1983-92; asst. minority leader, 1992—. State ctrl. committeeman 20th Congl. Dist., Springfield, 1982—; state chmn. Ill. Dem. Ctrl. Com., 1986-90; precinct committeeman Macoupin County Dem. Ctrl. Com., Carlinville, 1992—, chmn., 1992—. Named Friend of Agriculture Ill. Extension Adviser's Assn., 1993, Legislator of Yr. Ill. Edn. Assn., 1976; recipient Ill. Agriculture award Ill. Assn. Vocat. Agriculture Tchrs., 1993. Mem. K. of C., Elks. Roman Catholic. Avocations: historical, biographical and political reading. Office: 309-d Capitol Bldg Springfield IL 62706-0001

DENBO, JERRY L. state legislator; b. Bradford, Ind., Apr. 24, 1950; m. Donna Denbo; children: Robbie, Marey. BS, Ind. U., 1972, MS, 1975. Owner Denbo & Assocs.; rep. Dist. 62 Ind. Ho. of Reps., 1990—, mem. aging com., mem. environ. affairs, edn., ins. coms., corps. and small bus., rds. and transp. com. Mem. bd. Spring's Valley Sch.; active Dist. Club Scout Coun. Mem. NRA, Sons of Am. Legion, Ind. U. Alumni Assn., Masons, Gideons. Home: RR 1 Box 329 French Lick IN 47432-9801

DENEVAN, WILLIAM MAXFIELD, geographer, ecologist; b. San Diego, Oct. 16, 1931; s. Lester W. and Wilda M. D.; m. Patricia Sue French, June 21, 1958; children: Curtis, Victoria. PhD, U. Calif., Berkeley, 1963. Faculty dept. geography U. Wis., Madison, 1963-94, prof., 1972-94, chmn. dept., 1980-83, dir. L.Am. Ctr., 1975-77, prof. emeritus, 1994—. Author/co-author: The Upland Pine Forests of Nicaragua, 1961, The Aboriginal Cultural Geography of the Llanos de Mojos of Bolivia, 1966, The Biogeography of a Savanna Landscape, 1970, Adaptive Strategies in Karinya Subsistance, Venezuelan Llanos, 1978, Campos Elevados en los Llanos Occidentales de Venezuela, 1979, Cultivated Landscapes of Native Amazonia and the Andes, 2001; editor: The Native Population of the Americas in 1492, 1976, Pre-Hispanic Agricultural Fields in the Andean Region, 1987, Swidden-Fallow Agroforestry in the Peruvian Amazon, 1988, Hispanic Lands and Peoples, 1989, Las Chacras de Coporaque, 1994; contbr. articles to profl. jours. With USN, 1953-55. Grantee Fulbright, 1957, NRC, 1961-62, Ford Found., 1965-66, NSF, 1972-73, 84-86, Nat. Geog. Soc., 1985-86, NEH, 1989-90; Guggenheim fellow, 1977-78. Mem. Assn. Am. Geographers (Honors award 1987), Am. Geog. Soc., Am. Anthrop. Assn., Soc. for Am. Archaeology, Am. Acad. Arts and Scis. E-mail: sbden@saber.net.

DENGLER, ROBERT ANTHONY, professional association executive; b. Upper Darby, Pa., Aug. 23, 1947; s. Anthony William and Harriet Josephine (Schneider) D.; m. Renee Faith Aird, Oct. 26, 1985. BS, Drexel U., 1970, MBA, 1972; MS in MIS, Benedictine U., 2000, postgrad., 2000—. Cert. assn. exec., mtg. profl. Cons. Orgn. Devel., Phila., 1972-73; dir. tng. & edn. Parkview Meml. Hosp., Ft. Wayne, Ind., 1973-76; dir. human resource mgmt. Americana Healthcare Corp., Chgo., 1976-82; corp. mgr. Human Resource Tng. and Devel. Means Svc. Inc., 1982-83; dir. physician services West Suburban Hosp. Med. Ctr., Oak Park, 1983-85; assoc. dir. Assoc. Equipment Distributors, Oak Brook, 1985-88; exec. v.p. Internat. Reprographic Assn., 1988-92; exec. dir. Data Processing Mgmt. Assn., Park Ridge, Ill., 1993-94; pres. R.A. Dengler & Assocs., 1994—; exec. dir. Nat. Assn. Med. Staff Svcs., Lombard, Ill., 1996-98; engring. leadership devel. adminstr. Commonwealth Edison/Exelon Corp., 2001—. Capt. USAR, 1972-80. Mem. Inst. Mgmt. Cons., Project Mgmt. Inst., Am. Soc. Assn. Execs., Acad. of Mgmt., Midwest Acad. Mgmt., Orgn. Devel. Network, Orgn. Devel. Inst., Mensa. Home and Office: 294 Lionel Rd Riverside IL 60546-2204

DENLOW, MORTON, federal magistrate judge; b. 1947; BA, Washington U., 1969; JD, Northwestern U., 1972. Pvt. practice, Chgo., 1972-96; sr. lectr. Loyola U. Sch. Law, 1983-95; adj. prof. trial advocacy Northwestern U. Sch. Law, 1990-91; magistrate judge U.S. Dist. Ct. (no. dist.) Ill., 1996—. With USAR, 1970-76. Office: US Dist Ct 219 S Dearborn St Ste 1356 Chicago IL 60604-1802 Fax: 312-554-8547.

DENNEEN, JOHN PAUL, lawyer; b. N.Y.C., Aug. 18, 1940; s. John Thomas Denneen and Pauline Jane Ludlow; m. Mary Veronica Murphy, July 3, 1965 (dec. Dec. 2000); children: John Edward, Thomas Michael, James Patrick, Robert Andrew, Daniel Joseph, Mary Elizabeth. BS, Fordham U., 1963; JD, Columbia U., 1966. Bar: N.Y. 1966, U.S. Ct. Appeals (2d cir.) 1974, U.S. Dist. Ct. (so. and ea. dists.) N.Y. 1975, Mo. 1987. Assoc. Seward & Kissel, N.Y.C., 1966-75; sr. v.p., gen counsel, sec. GK Techs., Inc., Greenwich, Conn., 1975-83; exec. v.p., gen. counsel, sec. Chromalloy Am. Corp., St. Louis, 1983-87; ptnr. Bryan Cave LLP, 1987-99; exec. v.p. corp. devel. and legal affairs, sec. NuVox, Inc., 1999—. Mem. ABA, Internat. Bar Assn., N.Y. State Bar Assn., N.Y.C. Bar Assn., Bar Assn. Met. St. Louis. Office: NuVox Inc Ste 500 16090 Swingley Ridge Rd Chesterfield MO 63017-6029

DENNER, MELVIN WALTER, retired life sciences educator; b. North Washington, Iowa, Aug. 27, 1933; s. Norbert William and Petronella Nettie (Eischeid) D.; m. N. Anne Greer, June 19, 1965; children: Mark Andrew, Michael Alan (twins). BS, Upper Iowa U., 1961; MS (NSF fellow), U. Ky., 1963; PhD, Iowa State U., 1968. Asst. prof. life scis. U. So. Ind., Evansville, 1968-71, assoc. prof., 1971-76, prof., 1976-95, Disting. prof., 1989-90, pre-med. advisor, chmn. dept., 1969-95, assoc. chmn. div. scis. and math., 1975-77, acting chmn. div. scis. and math., 1976-77, chmn., 1979-87; dean Sch. of Sci. and Engring. Tech., 1994; coord. univ. self-study U. So. Ind., Evansville, 1976, 86, 96; ret., 1996. Eucharistic minister Corpus Christi Ch., 1981—; panelist Ind. Com. Higher Edn., 1993. Contbr. articles to profl. jours.; editor USI Ret newsletter. Vice chmn. Iowa Young Dems., 1958-60; bd. dirs. Deaconess Hosp. Allied Health Programs, chmn. radiation tech. adv. com., 1987-95; bd. dirs. Evansville Mus. Arts and Scis.; mem. alumni adv. bd. U. So. Ind., 1982—; spl. minister Corpus Christi Ch., 1981—; mem. facilcom. Ludington (Mich.) H.S., 2000—. With USN, 1953-57. Named Ind. Prof. of Yr., 1989, Sagamore of the Wabash, 1989; NSF fellow 1962, 64, NIH fellow, 1966-67, Alumni Achievement fellow, 1967-68. Fellow AAAS (film critic); mem. Internat. Soc. Invertebrate Pathology (founding), Am. Soc. Parasitologists, Am. Micros. Soc. (nat. treas.), North Ctrl. Assn. Colls. and Secondary Schs. (visitation team 1976-94), Am. Inst. Biol. Scis., Sigma Xi (pres. So. Ind. chpt.), Sigma Zeta. Home: 215 S Lakeshore Dr Apt 20 Ludington MI 49431-2076

DENNERT, H. PAUL, state legislator; b. June 25, 1937; Mem. S.D. Ho. of Reps. Dist. 2, Pierre, 1993-96; mem. Transp., Agr. and Natural Resources Com., Appropriations Com. S.D. of Reps.; mem. S.D. Senate from 2nd dist., 1997—. Farmer, cattleman. Democrat. Home: 11853 391st Ave Columbia SD 57433-7002 Office: 109 River Pl Pierre SD 57501

DENNIS, FRANK GEORGE, JR. retired horticulture educator; b. Lyons, N.Y., Apr. 12, 1932; s. Frank George and Corinne Isabel (Smith) D.; m. Katharine Ann Merrell, June 5, 1954. BS in Agriculture, Cornell U., 1955, PhD in Pomology, 1961. Postdoctoral fellow NSF, Gif-sur-Yvette, France, 1961-62; asst. prof. Cornell U., Geneva, 1962-68, assoc. prof., 1968—, Mich. State U., East Lansing, 1968-72, prof., 1972-96. Contbr. articles to profl. jours. Fulbright fellow, Morocco, 1990. Fellow Am. Soc. for Hort. Sci. (v.p. 1985-86, Gourley award 1985, sci. editor HortScience 1997-2000); mem. Internat. Soc. Hort. Sci. (chmn. working group 1984-90), Sigma Xi. Office: Mich State U Dept Horticulture East Lansing MI 48824-1325 E-mail: fgdennis@msu.edu.

DENT, THOMAS G. lawyer; b. Chgo., May 2, 1942; Student, U. Ill., De Paul U., LLB, 1970. Bar: Ill. 1970. Ptnr. Seyfarth, Shaw, Fairweather & Geraldson, Chgo. Office: Seyfarth Shaw Fairweather & Geraldson Mid Continental Plz 55 E Monroe St Ste 4200 Chicago IL 60603-5863

DENTON, D. KEITH, management educator; b. Paducah, Ky., June 28, 1948; s. Derward and Bonnie Denton; children: Shane, Taylor. BS, Murray State U., 1971; M in Pub. Adminstrn., Memphis State U., 1974; PhD, So. Ill. U., 1981. Supr. Shelby Pre-Casting, Memphis, 1971-72; safety engr. Md. Casualty Corp., 1972-76; instr. Draughn's Bus. Coll., Paducah, 1977; safety trainer Union Carbide Corp., 1977-78; prof. So. Ill. U., Carbondale, 1978-83, S.W. Mo. State U., Springfield, 1983—. Cons. Small Bus. Research Ctr., Springfield, 1985—, Springfield Remfg. Corp., 1986. Author: Safety Management, 1982; (with others) Safety Performance, 1985, Quality Service in America, 1989, The Production Game, 1990, Handling Employee Complaints, 1990, Horizontal Management, 1991, The Service Trainer, 1992, Recruitment Retention and Employee Relations, 1992, Did You Know?, Fascinating Facts and Fallacies, 1994, Enviro-Management: How Companies Turn Pollution Cost into Profits, 1994, The Toolbox for the Mind, 1999; contbr. over 120 articles to profl. jours. Mem. Acad. Mgmt., Nat. Assn. Purchasing, Am. Soc. Prodn. and Inventory Control, Inst. Indsl. Engrs. Office: SW Mo State U 901 S National Ave Springfield MO 65804-0088

DENTON, FRANK M. newspaper editor; b. Tulsa, Mar. 30, 1945; s. Frank McCray and Eydith (Langley) D.; m. April Murphy, June 18, 1983 (div. 2000); children: Langley Sara, Allegra Murphy. BA, U. Tex., 1968; MS, Columbia U., 1970; MBA, U. Wis., 1994, PhD, 1996. Sportswriter Austin Am. Statesman, 1964-66; reporter Stuart Long News Svc., Austin, Tex., 1966-69, Anniston (Ala.) Star, 1970-72, Cin. Enquirer, 1972-75; asst. lifestyle editor Detroit Free Press, 1976-78, lifestyle editor, 1978-81, asst. mng. editor, 1981-86; editor Wis. State Journal, Madison, 1986—. Bd. dirs. Mid-Am. Press Inst. Mem. Am. Soc. Newspaper Editors (bd. dirs.), Phi Kappa Phi. Home: 3046 Irvington Way Madison WI 53713-3414 Office: Wis State Journal 1901 Fish Hatchery Rd Madison WI 53713-1297 E-mail: fdenton@madison.com.

DEPASCO, RONNIE NICK, state legislator; b. Kansas City, Mo., Mar. 19, 1943; s. Nick and Mildred Anderson DePasco; m. Martha McAdam; children: Carrie E., Kelly L., Kacie A. Grad., Maple Wood Jr. Coll., 1966. Mem. Mo. Ho. of Reps. from 37th dist., Jefferson City, 1976-80, 82-92, Mo. Senate from 11th dist., Jefferson City, 1993—. Chmn. accounts com., budget and local govt. com. Mo. Ho. of Reps., co-chmn. redistricting and appropriations coms.; vice chmn. consumer protection and environ. com. Mo. State Senate, mem. fin. and govt. inst., ins. and housing, labor and indsl. rels., transp. and tourism coms. Recipient Appreciation award Mo. C. of C., 1984, Fraternal Order of Police, 1985, Sch. Dist. Greater Kansas City, 1986, Recognition award Mo. U., 1987. Mem. KC, Mo. Liquor Assn., Entrepreneur and Small Bus. Com., Nat. Com. State Legislators, Moose, Allied Dem. Assn. (chmn.). Home: 2917 Grand Ave Kansas City MO 64108-3221

DEPOY, PHIL E. special studies think-tank executive; Pres. Nat. Opinion Rsch. Ctr., Chgo. Office: National Opinion Research Ctr 1155 E 60th St Chicago IL 60637-2799

DERLACKI, EUGENE L(UBIN), otolaryngologist, physician; b. Chgo., Mar. 16, 1913; s. Walter and Jadwiga (Pamulowna) D. BS, Northwestern U., 1936, MD, 1939; postgrad. otolaryngology, Rush Med. Coll., 1940, U. Ill., 1941-42. Diplomate: Am. Bd. Otolaryngology. Intern Cook County Hosp., Chgo., 1939-40, jr. resident, 1941, sr. resident, 1942-43; sr. attending staff Northwestern Meml. Hosp., 1946—; prof. otolaryngology Northwestern U. Med. Sch., from 1957, now prof. emeritus. Contbr. articles to profl. jours. Pres. Am. Hearing Research Found. Served with M.C. AUS, 1943-46. Mem. AMA, Am. Acad. Otolaryngology (past pres.), Coll. Allergists, Am. Otol. Soc. (past pres.), Am. Laryngol., Rhinol. and Otol. Soc. Home: 700 W Fabyan Pkwy Apt 22A Batavia IL 60510-1479 Office: Northwestern Med Faculty Found 675 N Saint Clair St Chicago IL 60611-5975

DEROMEDI, HERB WILLIAM, athletic director; b. May 26, 1939; m. Marilyn Long, Aug. 19, 1961; children: David, Tom, Lori. BS, U. Mich., 1960, MS, 1961. Asst. football coach Ctrl. Mich. U., Mt. Pleasant, 1967-78, head coach, 1978-94, athletic dir., 1994—. Office: Ctrl Mich U Rose Ctr 100A Mount Pleasant MI 48859-0001

DEROUSIE, CHARLES STUART, lawyer; b. Adrian, Mich., May 24, 1947; s. Stuart J. and Helia I. (Juntunen) DeR.; m. Patricia Jean Fetzer, May 31, 1969; children: Jennifer, Jason. BA magna cum laude, Oakland U., 1969; JD magna cum laude, U. Mich., 1973. Bar: Ohio, 1973, U.S. Dist. Ct. (so. dist.) Ohio 1974. Ptnr. Vorys, Sater, Seymour and Pease, LLP, Columbus, Ohio, 1973—. Trustee Ballet Met., Inc., Columbus, 1978-90, pres., 1986-88; trustee Gladden Community House, Columbus, 1975-81, pres., 1979-81; mem. Children's Hosp. Devel. Bd., Columbus, 1987—, pres. 1995-96; trustee Elder Choices of Ctrl. Ohio, Columbus, 1989-95, Heritage Day Health Ctrs., Columbus, 1992-98. Fellow Columbus Bar Found.; mem. ABA, Am. Health Lawyers Assn., Columbus Bar Assn., Ohio Bar Assn., Order of Coif. Office: Vorys Sater Seymour and Pease LLP PO Box 1008 52 E Gay St Columbus OH 43215-3161

DERRICK, MALCOLM, physicist; b. Hull, Eng., Feb. 15, 1933; came to U.S., 1963, naturalized, 1976; s. Arthur Henry and Gladys (Hopkinson) D.; m. Kathleen Allen, 1957; 1 child, Matthew; m. Christa Zars Baumgardner; 1966; m. Eva Krebbers, 1995. B.Sc. with 1st class honours, U. Birmingham, 1954, Ph.D., 1959; M.A., Oxford U., 1961. Instr. Carnegie Inst. Tech., 1957-60; asst. prof. Oxford U., 1960-63; asst. physicist Argonne (Ill.) Nat. Lab., 1963-67, sr. physicist, 1967—, dir. high energy physics div., 1974-81. Vis. prof. U. Minn., 1969-70, Univ. Coll., London, 1972-73; adv. com. Stanford U. Accelerator Center, Fermi Nat. Accelerator Lab.; mem. high energy physics adv. panel Dept. Energy. Author numerous research papers on high energy physics. Fellow Am. Phys. Soc. Home: 20 Equestrian Way Lemont IL 60439-9785 Office: Argonne Nat Lab Bldg 362 Argonne IL 60439 E-mail: mxd@hep.anl.gov.

DERSTADT, RONALD THEODORE, health care administrator; b. Detroit, June 9, 1950; s. Theodore Edward and Dorothy J. (Semko) D.; m. J. Gail Adamson, June 9, 1990. BA, U. Detroit, 1971; M of Hosp. Healthcare Adminstn., Xavier U., 1975. Mgr. shared svcs. Bethesda Hosp. North, Cin., 1975-76; asst. adminstr. McCullough-Hyde Meml. Hosp., Oxford, Ohio, 1977-79; pres. Hospice of Cin., Inc., 1979-82; dir. strategic planning St. Francis-St. George Hosp., Cin., 1982-84; v.p. Mgmt. Dynamics, Inc., 1984-85; sr. v.p. St. Francis-St. George Mgmt. Co., 1986-88; v.p. Franciscan Health System of Cin., 1988-91; dir. hosp. affairs ChoiceCare, Cin., 1991-95; CEO Medquest, Owensboro, Ky., 1995-98; COO Ctr. for Chem. Addictions Treatment, Cin., 1998—. Vice-chmn., bd. dirs. Franciscan Health Network, Cin., Franciscan Health Ventures, Cin. Treas., bd. dirs. Ohio Easter Seals Soc., Columbus, 1987-93; bd. dirs. S.W. Ohio Easter Seal Soc., Cin., 1986-92; adv. bd. Dater Jr. H.S., Cin., 1984-88. Fellow Am. Coll. Healthcare Execs.; mem. Healthcare Fin. Mgmt. Assn., Am. Hosp. Assn., Ohio Hosp. Assn. Avocations: boating, golf, radio control model building. Home: 7363 Dogtrot Rd Cincinnati OH 45248 Office: 830 Ezzard Charles Dr Cincinnati OH 45214-2525

DERTIEN, JAMES LEROY, librarian; b. Kearney, Nebr., Dec. 14, 1942; s. John Ludwig and Muriel May (Cooley) D.; m. Elaine Paulette Mohror, Dec. 26, 1966; children— David Dalton, Channing Lee AB, U. S.D., 1965; MLS, U. Pitts., 1966; MPA, U. S.D., 1995. Head librarian Mitchell Pub. Library, S.D., 1966-67; head librarian Sioux Falls Coll., 1967-69; acting dir. libraries U. S.D., Vermillion, 1969-70; head librarian Vets. Meml. Pub. Library, Bismarck, N.D., 1970-75, Bellevue Pub. Library, Nebr., 1975-81; libr. dir. Siouxland Librs., S.D., 1981—. Pres., bd. dirs. Vol. and Info. Ctr., Sioux Falls, 1991-93. Mem. ALA, Mountain Plains Library Assn. (pres. 1978-79, editor newsletter 1982—), S.D. Library Assn. (pres. 1986-87). Unitarian. Lodge: Rotary Avocations: backpacking, reading, fishing. Home: 2501 S Kiwanis Ave Apt 303 Sioux Falls SD 57105-0161 Office: Siouxland Librs 201 N Main Ave Sioux Falls SD 57104-6002 E-mail: jimd@siouxland.lib.sd.us.

DERUSHA, JASON, reporter; m. Alyssa DeRusha. Degree in polit. sci. and broadcast/electronic comms., Marquette U. Intern ABC World News Tonight, Prime Time Live; anchor, reporter KWQC-TV, Davenport, Ind.; assoc. prodr. WISN, Milw., 1995—96, news reporter, 2000—. Recipient First Place award for best continuing series, Ill. AP, 1998, award for gen. reporting, Iowa AP, 1999, 2d place for news reporting, 2000, Gold medal media award, Ill. Pub. Health Assn., 1999. Office: WISN Po Box 402 Milwaukee WI 53201-0402

DERVIN, BRENDA LOUISE, communications educator; b. Beverly, Mass., Nov. 20, 1938; d. Ermina Diluiso; adopted d. John Jordan and Marjorie (Sullivan) D. BS, Cornell U., 1960; MA, Mich. State U., 1968, PhD, 1972; PhD (hon.), U. Helsinki, 2000. Pub. info. asst. Am. Home Econ. Assn., Washington, 1960-62; pub. info. specialist Ctr. Consumer Affairs, U. Wis., Milw., 1962-65; instr., rsch. and teaching asst. dept. communications Mich. State U., E. Lansing, 1965-70; asst. prof., Sch. Info. Transfer Syracuse (N.Y.) U., 1970-72; asst. to assoc. prof. U. Wash., Seattle, 1972-85; prof. comm. Ohio State U., Columbus, 1985—. Co-author: The Mass Media Behavior of the Urban Poor, 1980; editor: Rethinking Communication, 1989; editor jour. Progress in Communication Sci., 1981-92; contbr. numerous articles to profl. publs. Grantee U.S. Office Edn., 1974-76, Calif. State Libr., 1974-84, Nat. Cancer Inst., 1984, Ameritech, 1992. Fellow Internat. Communication Assn. (pres. 1986-87); mem. Internat. Assn. Mass Communications Rsch. (governing coun. 1988-97). Home: 4269 Kenridge Dr Columbus OH 43220-4157 Office: Ohio State U 3016 Derby 154 N Oval Mall Columbus OH 43210-1330 E-mail: dervin.1@osu.edu.

DERZON, GORDON M. hospital administrator; b. Milw., Dec. 28, 1934; married. BA, Dartmouth Coll., 1957; MHA, U. Mich., 1961. Adminstrv. resident Bklyn. Hosp., 1960-61, adminstrv. asst., 1961-63, asst. exec. dir., 1963-65, exec. dir., 1966-67, State U. Hosp., Bklyn., 1967-68, Kings County Hosp. Center, Bklyn., 1968-74; CEO U. Wis. Hosps. and Clinics, Madison, 1974-2000; assoc. prof. SUNY, 1967-74; clin. prof. U. Wis. Bd. dir. U. Hosp. Consortium, Indep. Living, Hospice Care, MATC Found., Madison Cmty. Health Ctr. Hospice, Combat Blindness Found., Perinatal Found., Ctr. Health Emotions. Contbr. articles to profl. jours. Mem. Am. Hosp. Assn. (past chmn. pub. gen. hosp. sect.). Home: 3440 Topping Rd Madison WI 53705-1439 Office: U Wis Hosp & Clinics 600 Highland Ave Madison WI 53792-0001 E-mail: gm.derzon@hosp.wisc.edu.

DESIMONE, ALFRED S. insurance agent; BA, U. Wis.; MA, Northwestern U.; postgrad., U. Wis., Milw. Life ins. agt. Equitable, Kenosha, Wis.; classroom tchr. Port Washington (Wis.) schs.; prin. Waukegan (Ill.) schs.; supt. Mattoon (Wis.) Sch. Dist. Mem. bd. regents U. Wis., 1995—; charter pres. U. Wis.-Parkside Found.; bd. dirs. U. Wis. Found., Wis. Mem.: U. Wis. Alumni Assn. (past pres.). Office: Equitable 7514 30th Ave Kenosha WI 53142

DESIMONE, LIVIO DIEGO, retired diversified manufacturing company executive; b. Montreal, Que., Can., July 16, 1936; s. Joseph D. and Maria E. (Bergamin) De S.; m. Lise Marguerite Wong, 1957, children: Daniel J., Livia D., Mark A., Cynthia A. B.Chem. Engring., McGill U., Montreal, 957. Process engr. 3M Can., 1957-61; With 3M Co., St. Paul, 1961—; exec. v.p. life scis. sector 3M Can., 1981, exec. v.p. indsl. and consumer sector, 1984-86, exec. v.p. indsl. and consumer sector and pvt. svcs., 1986-89, exec. v.p. indsl. and electronic sector and corp. svcs., 1989-91, exec. v.p. info., imaging and electronic sector & pvt. svcs., 1991, exec. v.p., 1991; chmn. bd., CEO 3M Co., 1991-2000. Bd. dirs. Cray Rsch. Inc., Dayton Hudson Corp., Gen. Mills Inc., Vulcan Materials Co. Bd. dirs. Jr. Achievement Inc. (nat.), Minn. Bus. Partnership, 3M Found.; trustee U. Minn. Found. Mem. Bus. Roundtable. Office: Minn Mining & Mfg Co 3 M Ctr Bldg 22014w05 Saint Paul MN 55144-0001

DESJARDINS, CLAUDE, physiologist, dean; b. Fall River, Mass., June 13, 1938; s. Armand Louis and Marguerite Jean (Mercier) D.; m. Jane Elizabeth Campbell, June 30, 1962; children: Douglas, Mark, Anne. BS, U. R.I., 1960; MS, Mich. State U., 1964, PhD, 1967. Asst. prof. dept. physiology Okla. State U., Stillwater, 1968-69, assoc. prof., 1969-72; assoc. prof. physiology U. Tex., Austin, 1970-75; prof. physiology Inst. Reproductive Biology, Patterson Labs., 1975-86, U. Va. Med. Sch., Charlottesville, 1987-96, dir. Ctr. Rsch. Reprodn., 1990-96; prof. physiology & biophysics, sr. assoc. dean med. coll. U. Ill., Chgo., 1996—. Mem. Ctr. for Advanced Studies, 1986; cons. NIH, ASA, VA, FDA. Author: Cell and Molecular Biology of the Testis, 1993, Molecular Physiology of Testicular Cells, 1996; editor-in-chief Am. Jour. physiology: Endocrinology and Metabolism, 1991-95; editor-in-chief Jour. Andrology, 1989-91, Ency. of Reprodn., 1997-98; mem. editl. bd. Biology Reprodn., Endocrinology; contbr. articles to profl. jours.; patentee techs. for male contraception, mechanisms of peptide hormone transport in the microcirculation and ligand-dependent and ligand ind. action of steroid hormones in peripheral vasculature. Fellow The Jackson Lab., Bar Harbor, Maine, 1967, NIH Sr. fellow U. Va. Med. Sch., 1983-84, Danforth Found. fellow, 1960; C.F. Wilcox Found. scholar, 1958. Mem. Am. Physiol. Soc., Soc. Neurosci., Soc. study Reprodn. (pres. 1982-83), Endocrine Soc., Am. Soc. Cell Biology, The Microcirculatory Soc. Office: U Ill at Chgo Office of Dean M/C 784 1853 W Polk St Chicago IL 60612-4316 E-mail: clauded@uic.edu.

DESMARAIS, CHARLES JOSEPH, museum director, writer, editor; b. N.Y.C., Apr. 21, 1949; s. Charles Emil and Helen Barbara (Young) D.; m. Sharon McLeod, May 1, 1970; m. Patricia Jon Carroll, June 15, 1979; m. Katherine Ann Morgan, Dec. 31, 1985 Student, Western Conn. State Coll., Danbury, 1967-71; B.S., SUNY-Rochester, 1975; M.F.A., SUNY-Buffalo, 1977. Curator Friends of Photography, Carmel, Calif., 1973-74; asst. editor Afterimage, Rochester, 1975-77; editor Exposure, Chgo., 1977-81; dir. Art Gallery, Columbia Coll., 1977-79, Calif. Mus. Photography, U. Calif.-Riverside, 1981-88, Laguna Art Mus., Laguna Beach, Calif., 1988-94; Contemporary Arts Ctr., Cin., 1995—. Guest curator Mus. Contemporary Art, Chgo., 1980, L.A. Ctr. Photog. Studies, 1981; arts adv. com. Riverside County Bd. Suprs., 1981-86; chair Orange County Arts Coun., 1989-91; bd. mem. Regional Cultural Alliance, 2000—. Author, editor: Roger Mertin: Records 1976-1978, 1978, Michael Bishop, 1979, The Portrait Extended, 1980, Why I Got Into TV and Other Stories: The Art of Ilene Segalove, 1990, Proof: Los Angeles Art and the Photograph, 1960-1980, 1992, Humongolous: Sculpture and Other Works by Tim Hawkinson, 1996, Jim Dine Photographs, 1999, Stephan Balkenhol, 2000; arts columnist Riverside Press Enterprise, 1987-88. Art Critic's fellow Nat. Endowment Arts, 1979 Mem. Assn. Art Mus. Dirs., Soc. Photog. Edn. (dir. 1979-83), Am. Assn. Museums, Coll. Art Assn. Office: Contemporary Arts Ctr 115 E 5th St Cincinnati OH 45202-3998 E-mail: director@spiral.org.

DESOMBRE, NANCY COX, academic administrator, consultant; b. Lake City, Minn., Sept. 7, 1939; d. Ray Ronald and Marjorie Mae (Lipa) C.; m. Eugene DeSombre, Sept. 10, 1960; children: Elizabeth DeSombre, Michael DeSombre. BA, U. Chgo., 1961, MA, 1962. Prof. English dept. Wilbur Wright Coll., Chgo., 1962—, chair English dept., 1976—, dean vocat. program, 1981-82, dean of instrn., 1982-86, v.p. faculty, instr., 1987-94; pres. Harold Washington Coll., 1994—. Cons. evaluator North Cen. Assn. of Coll./Schs., Chgo., 1987—; dir. LaSalle Bank, N.A., Chgo., 1994—; mem. bd. dirs. Greater State St. Coun., Chgo., 1995—, State Univ. Retirement System, Champaign, Ill., 1995—. Mem. bd. dirs. Frank Lloyd Wright Found., Oak Park, 1987—. Recipient Inst. Ednl. Mgmt. award Harvard U., 1990, Project Enhance award Wright Coll., 1991, Woman of the Yr. award Exec. Leadership Inst.-League for Innovation, 1993, 94. Avocation: gardening. Office: Harold Washington Coll 30 E Lake St Chicago IL 60601-2403

D'ESPOSITO, JULIAN C., JR. lawyer; b. N.Y.C., Aug. 6, 1944; BS, Loyola U., 1966; JD cum laude, Northwestern U., 1969. Bar: Ill. 1969, U.S. Dist. Ct. (no. dist.) 1969. Counsel to Gov. Ill., 1977-81; ptnr. Mayer, Brown, Rowe & Maw, Chgo. Chmn. Winnetka Plan Commn., 1985-89; mem. Ill. Med. Ctr. Commn., 1987-94; dir. Taxpayers Fedn. Ill.; dir. Ill. Capital Devel. Bd., 1994-95; chmn. Ill. State Toll Hwy. Authority, 1995-99. Co-editor-in-chief Jour. Criminal Law, Criminology & Police Sci., Northwestern U., 1968-69. Mem. Gov. George Ryan Transition Team. Mem. ABA. Office: Mayer Brown Rowe & Maw 190 S La Salle St Ste 3100 Chicago IL 60603-3441

DESPRES, LEO ARTHUR, sociology and anthropology educator, academic administrator; b. Lebanon, N.H., Mar. 29, 1932; s. Leo Arthur and Madeline (Bedford) D.; m. Loretta A. LaBarre, Aug. 22, 1953; children—Christine, Michelle, Denise, Mary Louise, Renee. B.A., U. Notre Dame, 1954, M.A., 1956; Ph.D., Ohio State U., 1960. Research assoc. Columbia Psychiat. Inst. and Hosp., 1957-60; postdoctoral fellow Social Sci. Research Council, Guyana, 1960-61; asst. prof. Ohio Wesleyan U., 1961-63; faculty Case Western Res. U., Cleve., 1963-74, prof. anthropology, 1967-74, chmn. dept., 1968-74; prof. sociology, anthropology U. Notre Dame, Ind., 1974-97, chmn. dept., 1974-80, fellow Kellogg Inst. Internat. Studies, 1982—, prof. emeritus, 1997—. Cons. in field. Author: Cultural Pluralism and Nationalist Politics in British Guyana, 1968; editor: Ethnicity and Resource Competition in Plural Societies, 1975, Manaus: Social Life and Work in Brazil's Free Trade Zone, 1991. Fulbright scholar U. Guyana, 1970-71, Brazil, 1986; research grantee NSF, 1984. Mem. Am. Anthrop. Assn., Am. Ethnol. Soc., Latin Am. Studies Assn., Cen. States Anthrop. Soc. (pres. 1976-77), AAUP. Office: U Notre Dame Dept Anthropology Notre Dame IN 46556 Home: PO Box 6752 South Bend IN 46660-6752 E-mail: hdespres@nd.edu.

DESPRES, LEON MATHIS, lawyer, former city official; b. Chgo., Feb. 2, 1908; s. Samuel and Henrietta (Rubovits) D.; m. Marian Alschuler, Sept. 10, 1931; children— Linda Baskin, Robert Leon. PhB, U. Chgo., 1927, JD, 1929; DLitt, Columbia Coll., 1990, U. Ill., 2000. Bar: Ill. 1929. Ptnr. Despres, Schwartz and Geoghegan, Chgo.; trial examiner NLRB, 1935-37; instr. U. Chgo., 1936, U. Wis., summers 1946-49; alderman 5th Ward Chgo. City Council, 1955-75, parliamentarian, 1979-87. Mem. Chgo. Plan Commn., 1979-89. Mem. Am., Ill., Chgo. bar. assns., Chgo. Council Lawyers, Order of Coif, Phi Beta Kappa. Home: 5830 S Stony Island Ave Apt 10A Chicago IL 60637-2024 Office: 77 W Washington St Chicago IL 60602-2801 E-mail: DSG777@aol.com.

DESROSIERS, ANNE BOOKE, performing arts administrator, consultant; b. Bradford, Pa., Sept. 30, 1938; d. Benjamin and Twila Mae (Schwab) Booke; m. Roger Isadore DesRosiers, Dec. 27, 1960 (div. 1994); children Marc (dec.), Diana, Berinthia. BA in English, U. Fla., 1960. Tchr. Rantoul (Ill.) Elem. Sch., 1961-63, Oogontz Jr. H.S., Phila., 1969-73; dir. adult edn. Guadaloupe Ctr., Salt Lake City, 1974-77; dir. devel. Repertory Theater of St. Louis, 1977-85, St. Louis Zoo, 1985-88; pres. DesRosiers & Assocs., Cleve., 1988—; mng. dir. Great Lakes Theater Festival, 1993-98; acting exec. dir. Cleve. Cultural Coalition, 1999-2000. Mem. Nat. Soc. Fund Raising Execs. (cert., Exec. Leadership Inst. 1990, Outstanding Fund Raising St. Louis chpt. 1988), Cleve. Cultural Coalition (vice chair 1995-98). Republican. Jewish. Avocations: golf, travel, sailing. Home and Office: 1 Bratenahl Pl Apt 1102 Bratenahl OH 44108-1155 Fax: 216-541-0344. E-mail: abdesr@megsinet.net.

DETHOMASIS, BROTHER LOUIS, college president; b. Bklyn., Oct. 6, 1940; s. Costantino and Anna (Maggio) DeT. B.S. in Fgn. Service, Georgetown U., 1963; Ph.D., Union Grad. Sch., 1982. Tchr. LaSalle Acad., Providence, 1969-71; assoc. headmaster LaSalle Mil. Acad., Oakdale, N.Y., 1971-73, pres., 1976-84; v.p. for fin. The Christian Brothers, Narragansett, R.I., 1973-76; pres. St. Mary's U., Winona, Minn., 1984—. Author: The Finance of Education, 1978; Investing With Options, 1981; Social Justice, 1982; My Father's Business, 1984 Recipient Pres.'s medal for Christian edn., St. John's Coll. High Sch., 1985, Christian Edn. award Franz W. Sichel Found., 1974 Roman Catholic Home and Office: St Marys U 700 Terrace Hts Box 30 Winona MN 55987-1321

DETTMER, HELENA R. classics educator; d. Terry Stone; children: Dan, Heather, Mike, Anne, Alex. BA in Classics, Ind. U., 1972; MA/PhD, U. Mich., 1976. Asst. prof. U. Iowa, Iowa City, 1976-83, assoc. prof., 1983-97, chair, 1993—, prof., 1997—, dir. interdisciplinary program, 2001—; co-editor Syllecta Classica, 1989—98. Author: Horace: A Study in Structure, 1983, Love By the Numbers: Form and Meaning in the Poetry of Catullus, 1997; contbr. articles to profl. jours. Mellon fellowship Duke U., 1977-78; faculty scholarship, 1986-89. Mem. Classical Assn. of Middle West and South (pres.-elect 1995-96, pres. 1996-97). Am. Philolog. Assn. Office: Univ Iowa 212 Schaeffer Hall Iowa City IA 52242-1409

DETTMER, MICHAEL HAYES, former prosecutor; b. Detroit, June 6, 1946; s. Frank Arthur and Mary Frances (Conway) D.; m. Teckla Ann Getts, Aug. 15, 1969; children: Bryn Patrick, Janna Hayes. BS, Mich. State U., 1968; JD, Wayne State U., 1971. Bar: Mich. 1971, U.S. Dist. Ct. (we. dist.) Mich. 1992. Atty. Dettmer Thompon Parsons, Traverse City, Mich., 1972-90; pres., CEO Mich. Lawyer Mutual Ins. Co., Southfield, Grand Rapids, 1990-93; U.S. atty. we. dist. Mich. U.S. Dept. Justice, Grand Rapids, 1994—2001. Lectr. in field. Contbr. articles to profl. jours. Pres. Traverse City Montessori Ctr., 1978-83; commr. Traverse City Human Rights Commn.; chmn. Grand Traverse County Dem. Party, 1986. Fellow Am. Bar Found., Mich. State Bar Found.; mem. ABA, State Bar of Mich. (pres. 1993-94, commr. No. Mich. and Upper Peninsula 1986-94, exec. com. bd. commrs. 1988-94, com. on legislation 1990-91, task force on professionalism 1988-90, co-chair standing com. on professionalism 1992—, chair Upper Mich. lawyers com. 1986-94, rep. assembly 1977-80, 88-94, atty. discipline bd. hearing panelist 1980-88), Am. Bd. Trial Advocates, Nat. Bd. Trial Advocacy (cert. 1981—). Democrat. Presbyterian.

DEUCHLER, SUZANNE LOUISE, former state legislator; b. Chgo., July 21, 1929; m. Walter E. Deuchler Jr.; children: Mark, Maryll. BA, U. Ill. Mem. Ill. Ho. of Reps., Springfield, 1980—. Mem. Aurora reg. adv. com., Ill. Dept. Children and Family Svcs., 1976, citizens adv. bd., Aurora U., 1981; bd. dirs. Copley Meml. Hosp., 1982. Mem. AAUW, Altrusa, Bus. and Profl. Women. Republican. Avocations: painting, travelling, reading.

DEUTSCH, JAMES BERNARD, lawyer; b. St. Louis, Aug. 24, 1948; s. William Joseph and Margaret (Klevorn) D.; m. Deborah Marie Hallenberg, June 26, 1976; children: Michael, Gabriel. BA, Southeast Mo. State U., 1974; JD, U. Mo., 1978. Bar: Mo. 1978, U.S. Dist. Ct. (we. dist.) Mo. 1978, U.S. Ct. Appeals (8th cir.), 1989, U.S. Supreme Ct., 1990. Assoc. Gt. Plains Legal Found., Kansas City, Mo., 1978-79; pvt. practice, 1979-81; gen. counsel Mo. Dept. Revenue, Jefferson City, Mo., 1981-83; commr. Mo. Adminstrv. Hearing Commn., 1983-89; dep. atty.-gen State of Mo., 1989-93; ptnr. Riezman & Blitz, P.C., Mo., 1993-99; Ptnr. Blitz Bardgett & Deutsch LC, 2000—. Served to lance cpl. USMC, 1968-70, Vietnam. Named one of Men of Yr. in Constrn. Industry, Engring. News, McGraw-Hill Pub., N.Y.C., 1985. Mem. ABA (jud. adminstrn. com.), ASCE (hon. fellow), Mo. Bar Assn. (council mem. taxation com. 1985—, adminstrn. law and jud. adminstrn. coms.), Mo. Inst. for Justice (bd. dirs. 1977—), VFW, Marine Corps League. Office: Blitz Bardgett & Deutsch LC 308 E High St Jefferson City MO 65101-3237 E-mail: jdeutsch@blitzbardgett.com.

DEUTSCH, THOMAS ALAN, ophthalmologist, educator; b. Nagoya, Japan, Aug. 11, 1954; (parents U.S. citizens); William E. and Natasha S. (Sobotka) D.; m. Judith Silverman, Dec. 6, 1986. AB, Washington U., 1975; MD, Rush Med. Coll., Chgo., 1979. Diplomate Am. Bd. Ophthalmology. Intern Presbyn.-St. Luke's Hosp., Chgo., 1979-80; resident U. Ill. Eye and Ear Infirmary, 1980-83; asst. prof. ophthalmology U. Ill., 1983-84, Rush Med. Coll., Chgo., 1984-87, assoc. prof., 1987-94, prof., 1994—, chmn. ophthalmology, 1996—, assoc. dean grad. med. edn., 2000—02, acting dean, 2002—. Lectr., U. Ill., Chgo., 1984-96; adj. asst. prof. biomed. engri., Northwestern U. Evanston, Ill., 1986-87, adj. assoc. prof., 1987-94, adj. prof., 1994-97. Assoc. editor Key Ophthalmology, 1986-88, Year Book Ophthalmology, 1986-88; author 6 books; contbr. articles to profl. jours. Recipient Chancellor's award Washington U., 1975, Henry Lyman award Rush Med. Coll, 1978, Mark Lepper tchg. award, 1994, Disting. Alumnus award Rush Med. Coll., 1998. Fellow: ACS, Am. Acad. Ophthalmology (sec. for instrn. 2001—02, sec. for new ophthalmic info. 2002—, Honor award 1990); mem.: Rush Alumni Assn. (pres. 1990—93, James A. Campbell award 1990), Chgo. Ophthalmol. Soc. (chmn. clin. conf. 1986, councillor 1988—89, sec.-treas. 1989—91, pres. 1994—95), Assn. Rsch. Vision Ophthalmology. Office: Rush Presbyn St Luke's Med Ctr 1725 W Harrison St Ste 918 Chicago IL 60612-3835

DEVANEY, DENNIS MARTIN, lawyer, educator; b. Cheverly, Md., Feb. 25, 1946; s. Peter Paul and Alice Dorothy (Duffy) D.; children: Jeanne Marie, Susan Theresa. BA in History, U. Md., 1968, MA in Govt. Politics, 1970; JD, Georgetown U., 1975. Bar: Md. 1976, D.C. 1976, Fla. 1977, Mich. 1999, U.S. Supreme Ct. 1980. Instr. European div. U. Md., Bremerhaven, Fed. Republic Germany, 1971-72; legis. asst. Md. Senate Jud. Commn., Annapolis, 1973-74; asst. gen. counsel U.S. Brewers Assn., Washington, 1975-77; counsel Food Mktg. Inst., 1977-79; ptnr. Randall, Bangert & Thelen, 1979-81; assoc. Tighe, Curhan & Piliero, 1981-82; mem. U.S. Merit System Protection Bd., 1982-88; gen. counsel Fed. Labor Relations Auth., 1988; mem. NLRB, 1988-94; commr. US Internat. Trade Commn., 2001; of counsel Winston & Strawn, 1995-97, Butzel Long, 1997—2001; ptnr. Williams, Mullen Clark and Dobbins, 2002—. Adj. prof. George Washington U., Washington, 1982—90, Boston U., 1992—94, 2002, Cornell U., 1995, Tulane U., 1995; assoc. prof. Wayne State U., 1995—2001. Served with USN, 1970-72, ETO. Mem. ABA, Md. Bar Assn., D.C. Bar Assn., Fla. Bar Assn., Mich. State Bar, Fed. Bar Assn., Phi Alpha Theta, Pi Sigma Alpha, Delta Theta Phi, Omicron Delta Kappa. Roman Catholic. Office: Williams Mullen 535 Griswold Fl 11 Buhl Bldg Detroit MI 48226 Home: 2661 Hidden Woods Dr Canton MI 48188-2477

DEVANNY, E.H. (TRACE) III, healthcare informatics executive; Grad., U. of the South. With IBM, 1977-94; corp. v.p. Cerner Corp., Kansas City, Mo., 1994-97, pres., 1999—; pres. health care info. sys. divsn. ADAC Labs., Houston, 1997-99. Office: Cerner Corp 2800 Rockcreek Pkwy Kansas City MO 64117-2521

DEVANTIER, PAUL W. communications executive, broadcaster; b. Wausau, Wis., Mar. 25, 1946; w. Walter Herman and Ella Marie (Mundt) D.; m. Ellen Stapel, Aug. 2, 1970; children: Richard, John, Andrew, Katie, Susan. BA, Concordia Coll., 1968; M in Divinity, Concordia Seminary, 1972; M in Mass Comm., So. Ill. U., Edwardsville, 1993; LLD, Concordia U., 1998. Radio announcer Sta. WXCO, Wausau, 1965-68, Sta. KRCH, St. Louis, 1968-72; dir. devel. Sta. KFUO-AM-FM, 1972-74, gen. mgr., 1974-82; exec. dir. comms. Luth. Ch.-Mo. Synod, 1982-2000; chief comm. officer Bethesda Luth. Homes and Svcs., Watertown, Wis., 2000—02; nat. dir. Infant Adoption Awareness Tng. Program, Washington, 2002—. Speaker By the Way (internat. syndicated radio program) 1974—. Author: By the Way, 1993, By the Way, Encore, 1999; exec. prodr.: (religious documentary film) Hymn A Celebration of Change, 1984 (Angel award), (TV spl.) Easter Alive 'Round the World, 1993 (Emmy award nomination), (TV spl.) Not Without Hope, 1994 (Angel award), Martin Luther Promo, 1998 (Telley award), Message of Hope, 1998 (Angel award DeRose Hinkhouse award), Just in Time For Christmas, 1999 (Angel award De Rose Hinkhouse award), Message of Love, 2000 (Angel award); (radio) Lutheran School Spots, 1999 (Angel award), Classical Radio Station of the Year in America, 1999 (Marconi award), (video) Free to Voice the Gospel, 2000 (Angel award), By The Way, 2001 (Angel award), So Much Like Us, 2002 (Angel award); exec. dir. Lutheran Witness mag., 1999 (Associated Ch. Press Best of Class award). Trustee, pres. Luth. Film Assocs., N.Y.C., 1982-2000; bd. dirs. Excellence in Media, Hollywood, 2001—. Mem. Religious Comm. Coun., World Assn. Christian Communicators, Nat. Religious Broadcasters, Phi Kappa Phi. Office: Nat Coun for Adoption 225 N Washington St Alexandria VA 22314-2520 E-mail: pdevantier@infantadopt.org.

DEVELLANO, JAMES CHARLES, professional hockey manager, baseball executive; b. Toronto, Ont., Can., Jan. 18, 1943; came to U.S., 1979; s. James Joseph and Jean (Piter) D. Ont. scout St. Louis Blues NHL, Toronto, 1967-72; eastern Can. scout N.Y. Islanders, 1972-74, dir. scouting, 1974-82; asst. gen. mgr. Islanders, L.I., N.Y., 1981-82; gen. mgr. Detroit Red Wings, 1982-90, sr. v.p., 1990—; v.p., gen. mgr. Indpls. Checkers, 1979-81; sr. v.p. Detroit Tigers, 2001—. Alternate gov. for Detroit Red Wings. Winner Stanley Cup with N.Y. Islanders, 1979-80, 80-81, 81-82, with Detroit Red Wings, 1996-97, 97-98, Pres.'s Trophy with Detroit Red Wings, 1994-95, 95-96. Mem. Nat. Hockey League (bd. govs.). Office: Detroit Red Wings Hockey Club Joe Louis Arena 600 Civic Center Dr Detroit MI 48226-4419

DEVER, DICK, state legislator; m. Pam Dever; 3 children. B, U. N.D. Owner DEVCO; mem. N.D. Senate from 32d dist., Bismark, 2001—. Elder Boy Scouts Am. With U.S. Army. Mem. VFW. Republican. Lutheran. Office: State Capitol 600 East Blvd Bismarck ND 58505 E-mail: ddever@state.nd.us.

DEVEREUX, TIMOTHY EDWARD, advertising executive; b. Chgo., Jan. 13, 1932; s. James Matthew and Nellie (Fitzmaurice) D.; m. Ann Sullivan, Apr. 2, 1956; children: Timothy Jr., Colette Marie, Jennifer Ann, Peter Gerard, Nora Marie, Matthew. BA in Communication Arts, U. Notre Dame, 1955. Copywriter Montgomery Ward & Co., Chgo., 1957-58; pub. relations dir. Victor Comptometer Corp., 1958-60; sales promotion mgr. Bankers Life & Casualty Co., 1960-61; dir. advt. and pub. relations Mid-America Foods, Inc., River Forest, 1961-62; mdse. mgr. Marshall John & Assos., Chgo. also Northbrook, 1962-65; acct. supr. Marshall John/Action Advt., Northbrook, 1965-70, exec. v.p., chief exec. officer, 1970-77, also dir.; pres. Devereux Direct, Ltd., 1977-79; v.p. direct response group Frankel & Co., Chgo., 1979-85; pres. Timothy E. Devereux & Assocs., Oak Park, 1985—. Served to 1st lt. USMCR, 1955-57. Roman Catholic. Roman Catholic. Home and Office: 1185 S Oak Park Ave Oak Park IL 60304-2048

DEVINATZ, ALLEN, mathematician, mathematics educator; b. Chgo., July 22, 1922; s. Victor and Kate (Bass) D.; m. Pearl Moskowitz, Sep. 16, 1956; children: Victor Gary, Ethan Sander. B.S., Ill. Inst. Tech., 1944; A.M., Harvard U., 1947, Ph.D., 1950. Instr. Ill. Inst. Tech., 1950-52; NSF Postdoctoral fellow, 1952-53; fellow Inst. Advanced Study, Princeton, 1953-54; asst. prof. U. Conn., 1954-55; mem. faculty Washington U., St. Louis, 1955-67, prof. math., 1961-67, acting chmn. dept., 1963-64; prof. math. Northwestern U., Evanston, Ill., 1967-92, prof. emeritus, 1992—, asst. chmn. dept., 1968-70, acting chmn. dept., 1991. Vis. mem. Weizmann Inst., Israel, 1980, Inst. Hautes Etudes Sci., Paris, 1982, Inst. for Applications of Calculus-Mauro Picone, Rome, 1988; vis. scholar U. Calif., Berkeley, 1985; Disting. lectr. Hebrew U., Jerusalem, 1993. Contbr. articles profl. jours. Sr. NSF Postdoctoral fellow, 1960-61 Mem. Am. Math. Soc. (translation com. for Russian 1985-88), Sigma Xi, Tau Beta Pi. Office: Northwestern U Dept Math Lunt Bldg Evanston IL 60208-0001

DEVINE, DICK, lawyer; b. Chgo., July 5, 1943; m. Charlene DeVine; children: Matt, Karen, Tim, Pete. BA cum laude, Loyola U., 1966; JD cum laude, Northwestern U., 1968. Bar: Ohio 1968, Ill. 1969, U.S. Dist. Ct. (no. dist.) Ill. 1973, U.S. Ct. Appeals (7th cir.) 1983, U.S. Supreme Ct. 1983. Assoc. Squire, Sanders & Dempsey, Cleve., 1968-69; adminstrv. asst. to mayor of Chgo., 1969-72; assoc. Pope, Ballard, Shepard & Fowle, 1972-74; assoc., ptnr. Foran, Wiss & Schultz, 1974-80, ptnr., 1983-85; 1st asst. state's atty. Cook County State's Atty.'s Office, 1980-83; ptnr. Phelan, Pope, Cahill, DeVine & Ouinlan, Ltd., 1985-95, Shefsky Froelich & DeVine Ltd., 1995-96; state's atty. Cook County, 1996—. Lectr. continuing legal edn. IIT Kent Coll. Law, John Marshall U.; co-chair courses on damages in bus. litigation Law Jour. Seminar; judge moot ct. programs Northwestern Law Sch., John Marshall Law Sch.; appointed mem. State Commn. on Accreditation of Criminal Justice; appointed mem. Spl. Commn. on Adminstrn. of Justice in Cook County, chmn. task force on misdemeanor and preliminary hearing cts., chmn. task force on jud. adminstrn.; appointed mem. profl. adv. com. Office of State's Atty. of Cook County, 1984-89; bd. dirs. Cook County Criminal Justice Project; mem. Chgo.-Cook County Criminal Justice Commn., 1971-78; hearing officer Chgo. Bd. Election Commrs., 1984. Mem. editl. bd. Northwestern U. Law Rev., 1966-68, mng. editor, 1967-68; contbr. to law jours. Bd. commrs. Chgo. Park Dist., 1989-93, pres. bd., 1990-93; bd. trustees Loyola Acad., 1982-88, St. Scholastica H.S., 1992—; bd. dirs. Chgo. Hist. Soc., 1990-93, Adler Planetarium. Russell Sage fellow in law and social scis. Mem. ABA, Am. Coll. Trial Lawyers (elected), Ill. State Bar Assn., Chgo. Bar Assn. (com. jud. evaluation 1983-88, chmn. legis. assistance and evaluation com., young lawyers sect. 1973-74, vice-chmn. 1974-76, chmn. 1976-77, urban affairs com., mem. local govt. com. 1974-76, faculty young lawyers sect. trial advocacy program, lectr. on continuing legal edn.), Northwestern Law Sch. Alumni Assn. (bd. dirs. 1993—). Office: 50 W Washington St Rm 500 Chicago IL 60602-1356

DEVINE, EDMOND FRANCIS, lawyer; b. Ann Arbor, Mich., Aug. 9, 1916; s. Frank B. and Elizabeth Catherine (Doherty) DeV.; m. Elizabeth Palmer Ward, Sept. 17, 1955; children: Elizabeth Palmer, Stephen Ward, Michael Edmond, Suzanne Lee. AB, U. Mich., 1937, JD, 1940; LLM, Cath. U. Am., 1941. Bar: Mich. 1940, U.S. Dist. Ct. (ea. dist.) Mich. 1940, U.S. Ct. Appeals (6th cir) 1974, U.S. Supreme Ct. 1975. Spl. agt. FBI, 1941-43; chief asst. prosecutor Washtenaw County (Mich.), Ann Arbor, 1947-53, prosecuting atty., 1953-58; ptnr. DeVine & DeVine, 1958-74, DeVine, DeVine, Kantor & Serr, Ann Arbor, 1974-84; sr. ptnr. Miller, Canfield, Paddock & Stone, 1984-92, of counsel, 1992—. Asst. prof., adj. prof. U. Mich. Law Sch., 1949-79. Co-author: Criminal Procedure, 1960. Lt. USNR, 1943—46, PTO. Decorated Bronze Star with combat v. Fellow Am. Bar Found. Am. Coll. Trial Lawyers, Mich. Bar Found.; mem. ABA, State Bar Mich. (bd. commrs., chmn. judiciary com. 1976-85, mem. rep. assembly, chmn. rules and calendar com.1971-76, co-chair U.S. Cts. com. 1986-87), Internat. Assn. Def. Counsel, U.S. Supreme Ct. Hist. Soc., Ann Arbor C. of C. (chmn. bd. 1971), Detroit Athletic Club, Barton Hills Country Club, Pres.'s Club. U. Mich., Varsity M Club, Order of Coif, Barristers, Phi Delta Phi, Phi Kappa Psi. Republican. Roman Catholic. Avocations: golf, running, reading. Home: 101 Underdown Rd Ann Arbor MI 48105-1078 Office: Miller Canfield Paddock & Stone 101 N Main St Fl 7 Ann Arbor MI 48104-5507

DEVINE, JOHN MARTIN, automotive company executive; b. Pitts., May 13, 1944; s. John Patrick and Camilla (Durkin) D.; m. Patricia McGee Devine; children: Sean, Bridget. BS in Econs., Duquesne U., 1967; MBA, U. Mich., 1972. Various fin. positions Ford Motor Co., 1968-80, contr.

product devel. Europe Europe, 1981-83; staff dir. fin. Asia, Asia, 1983-85; v.p. no. Pacific ops. Ford Motor Co., Asia, 1985-86, exec. dir. no. Pacific bus. devel. Asia, 1986-87; contr. truck ops. U.S., U.S., 1988; CFO Ford Motor Co., U.S., 1994—; pres. First Nationwide Bank, 1988-91; contr. Ford Motor Co., 1994, chief fin. officer, 1994-99; CFO Gen.Motors Corp., Detroit, 2000—. Office: Gen Motors Corp 300 Renaissance Ctr Detroit MI 48265

DEVINE, TERRY MICHAEL, newspaper editor; b. Watertown, S.D., Dec. 13, 1945; s. Russell LeRoy and Margaret Evelyn (Adams) DevV.; m. Patricia Rae Engler, July 25, 1969; children: Taylor Alan, Nathan Lee, Erin Renae. BS, S.D. State U., 1972. Reporter Watertown Pub. Opinion, 1963-65, Sioux Falls (S.D.) Argus Leader, 1969-70; newsman AP, Sioux Falls, 1970-72, Pierre, S.D., 1972-73, newsman-supr. Mpls., 1973-74, corr. Sioux Falls, 1974-75, broadcast exec. Mpls., 1975-78, news editor, 1978-81, Forum Fargo (N.D.)-Moorhead, 1981-85; mng. editor Forum Fargo (N.D.)-Moorehead, 1985-98; reporter Forum Fargo (N.D.) - Moorehead. Sgt. USMC, 1965-69, Vietnam. Mem. AP Mng. Editors Assn. (nat. edn. com. 1986--), Am. Legion (post baseball com. 1986--), Shanley Quarterback Club (pres. 1987--). Republican. Roman Catholic. Avocations: reading, fishing, writing, military history, golf. Home: 2807 32d St SW Fargo ND 58103-7875 Office: Forum Pub Co 101 N 5th St PO Box 2020 Fargo ND 58107-2020

DEVLIN, BARBARA JO, school district administrator; b. Milw., Oct. 6, 1947; d. Raymond Peter Seeley and Lois Elsa Young; m. John Edward Devlin, June 23, 1973; children: Christine Elizabeth, Kathleen Megan. BA, Gustavus Adolphus Coll., 1969; MA, U. Mass., 1971; PhD, U. Minn., 1978. Cert. tchr., sch. prin., supt., Minn.; cert. supt., Ill., Minn. Tchr. Worthington (Minn.) High Sch., 1971-75; rsch. assoc. Ednl. R & D, Mpls.-St. Paul, 1975-76, 76-77; coord. edn. svcs. Ednl. Coop. Svc., 1977-79; dir. personnel Minnetonka Pub. Schs., Excelsior, Minn., 1979-85, asst. supt., 1985-87; supt. Sch. Dist. 45, Villa Park, Ill., 1987-95, Ind. Sch. Dist. 280, Richfield, Minn., 1995—. Editor working papers Gov.'s Coun. on Fluctuating Enrollments, St. Paul, 1976. Contbr. articles to ednl. jours. Bd. dirs. Richfield Found., 1995—. Ednl. Policy fellow George Washington U., 1977-78; mem. fellow program Bush Found. Pub. Schs., 1984-85; named Ill. Supt. of the Yr., 1994; recipient Disting. Alumni award Gustavus Adolphus Coll., 1994. Mem. Richfield C. of C. (bd. dirs. 1996-99), Rotary Internat. (membership chair Villa Park unit 1989-91, vocat. dir. 1991-92, sec. 1992-93, pres. 1994-95), Optimists Internat. (pres. elect Richfield unit 1998-99, pres. 1999-2000). Methodist. Office: Richfield Pub Schs 7001 Harriet Ave Richfield MN 55423-3061 E-mail: Barbara.Devlin@richfiedl.k12.mn.us.

DEVLIN, JAMES RICHARD, lawyer; b. Camden, N.J., July 7, 1950; s. Gerald William and Mary (Hand) D.; children: Grace, Jennifer, Kristen. BS in Indsl. Enginrg., N.J. Inst. Tech., 1972; JD, Fordham U., 1976. Bar: N.J. 1976, N.Y. 1977, U.S. Ct. Appeals (D.C. cir.) 1982. Various mgmt. positions in Long Lines Sect. AT&T, N.Y.C., 1972-76, counsel Long Lines Sect. Bedminster, N.J., 1976-82, counsel N.Y.C., 1982-83, gen. atty. comm. sect. Basking Ridge, N.J., 1983-86; v.p., gen. counsel telephone United Telecomm., Inc., Westwood, Kans., 1987-88; exec. v.p. gen. counsel and external affairs Sprint Corp., 1989—. Past pres., bd. dirs. Ctr. for Mgmt. Assistance, Kansas City, Mo., 1993-96; Mem. ABA (past chmn. comm. com. pub. utility law sect.), Am. Arbitration Assn., Fed. Comm. Bar Assn. Home: 12300 Catalina Leawood KS 66209-2220 Office: Sprint Corp Eisenhower A 6200 Sprint Pkwy Shawnee Mission KS 66251-2090

DEVOE, ROBERT DONALD, visual physiologist; b. White Plains, N.Y., Oct. 7, 1934; s. Frank Kenneth and Martha (Josselyn) DeV.; m. Joanne Mattson, July 9, 1960 (div. 1986); children: Catherine Ellen, Edward Edgar; m. Gwendolyn Latta Berghorn, May 20, 1989 (div. 1992); m. Elizabeth Strong Gitlitz, Aug. 9, 1997. AB, Oberlin Coll., 1956; PhD, The Rockefeller U. From asst. to assoc. prof. Med. Sch. Johns Hopkins U., Balt., 1961-83; prof. Sch. of Optometry Ind. U., Bloomington, 1983-99, emeritus prof., 1999—. Grantee referee NIH, Washington, 1968—, NSF, Med. Rsch. Coun., Eng., 1973—, B.C. Health Rsch. Found., 1993—, Australian Rsch. Coun., 1993—; manuscript referee to numerous jours., 1960—; rsch. sabbatical Max-Planck Inst. für Biol. Kybernetic, Tübingen, Germany, 1973-74, Sch. Optometry, U. New South Wales, Australia, 1993. Mem. adv. bd. Jour. Comparative Physiology, Berlin, 1983-86; contbr. articles to profl. jours. Recipient Sr. Sci. award Alexander von Humboldt Found., Bonn, Germany, 1973-74; grantee NIH, 1962-91. Mem. AAAS, Assn. for Rsch. in Vision and Ophthalmology, Soc. for Neurosci., Serious Macintosh User's Group (treas.), Alpine Ski Club, Sigma Xi, Phi Beta Kappa. Democrat. Avocations: gardening, camping, skiing, hiking, music. Office: Ind U Sch Optometry 800 E Atwater Ave Bloomington IN 47405-3635

DEVORE, C(ARL) BRENT, college president, educator; b. Zanesville, Ohio, Sept. 3, 1940; s. Carl Emerson and Helen Elizabeth (Van Atta) DeV.; m. Linda Mospens, July 2, 1966; children— Krista, Matthew B.S.J., Ohio U., 1962; M.A., Kent State U., 1971, Ph.D., 1978. Dir. devel. Am. Heart Assn., Cleve., 1965-68; exec. dir. Kent State U. Found., Ohio, 1968-72; v.p. Hiram Coll., 1972-82; pres. Davis and Elkins Coll., Elkins, W.Va., 1982-84, Otterbein Coll., Westerville, Ohio, 1984—. Pres. Higher Edn. Coun., Columbus, 1985; trustee Nationwide Investing Found., 1990. Producer and moderator film series on liberal arts edn. Pres. Hiram (Ohio) Village Council, 1981; chmn. E. Cen. Colls., 1990; pres. Nat. Assn. Schs. and Colls., United Meth. Ch., 1991. Mem. Am. Assn. Advancement of Humanities, AAUP, Ohio Council of Fund Raising Execs. (pres. 1976), Ohio Coll. Assn. (pres. 1987), W.Va. Assn. Coll. and Univ. Pres. (pres. 1984), Westerville C. of C. (pres.). Clubs: University (Columbus, Ohio); University (N.Y.C.). Lodge: Rotary Office: Otterbein Coll Pres Office 27 S Grove St Westerville OH 43081-2004

DEVOS, ELISABETH, political association executive; b. Holland, Mich., Jan. 8, 1958; d. Edgar Dale and Elsa D. (Zwiep) Prince; m. Richard M. DeVos Jr., 1979; four children. BS, Calvin Coll., 1979. Co-chmn. Kent County (Mich.) Rep. Finance Com., 1983-84, chmn., 1985-88, 96—; Rep. Nat. Committeewoman State of Mich., 1992-97; chmn. Mich. State Rep. Party, 1996—; mem. Nat. Rep. Com., 1996—. Market rsch. analyst Amway Corp., 1979-81; pres. Windquest Group. Bd. dirs. Blodgett Meml. Med. Ctr., 1986—, Ada (Mich.) Christian Sch., 1992—; mem. Rep. Congl. Leadership Coun. Mem. Econ. Club of Grand Rapids.

DEVOS, RICHARD MARVIN, SR. former network marketing company executive; b. Grand Rapids, Mich., Mar. 4, 1926; s. Simon C. and Ethel R. (Dekker) DeV.; m. Helen J. Van Wesep, Feb. 7, 1953. Student, Calvin Coll., 1946; LL.D. (hon.), Oral Roberts U., 1976, Grove City (Pa.) Coll., Northwood Inst., Midland, Mich., 1977, Dickinson Sch. Law, Carlisle, Pa., 1980, Pepperdine U., 1980, Lubbock Christian Coll., 1981; D.Litt. (hon.), Hope Coll., 1982; LHD (hon.), Grand Valley State U., 1992; LLD (hon.), Regent U., 1992; D business (hon.) , Northern Mich. U., 1998. Ptnr. Wolverine Air Service, 1945-48; co-founder, pres. Ja-Ri Corp., 1949, Amway Corp., 1959-92. Author: Believe!, Compassionate Capitalism, Hope From My Heart: Ten Lessons For Life. Chmn. Gospel Films, Muskegon, Mich.; owner, chmn. Orlando Magic NBA Basketball Team; co-founder, pres. Amway Environ. Found.; bd. dirs., chmn. Midwest region BIPAC, Nat. Orgn. Disability; past co-chair Salvation Army Campaign, Grand Rapids, Mich., 1993; dir. Grand Rapids Econ. Club; past pres. Grand Rapids Jr. Achievement, 1966-67; past mem. bd. control Grand Valley State Coll.; past bd. dirs. United Way Kent County; past bd. dirs. Nat. Legal Ctr. for Pub. Interest; chmn., bd. dirs. Butterworth Health Corp., Grand Rapids, Nat. Adv. Bd. Coral Ridge Ministries, Fla. Bd. Govs. Northwood U.; trustee Gerald R. Ford Found.; past chmn. New Grand Rapids Com.; spl. advisor Pres. Coun. on Phys. Fitness and Sports; mem. Close-Up Found. Hon. State Bd. Adv.; mem. coun. trustees Freedoms Found.; past chmn. Nat. Adv. Bd. Nat. Rep. Com.; past fin. chmn. Rep. Nat. Com.; past mem. Presdl. Commn. AIDS; past pres. Coun. Nat. Policy; fellow World Fellowship for Duke of Edinburgh's Award; named to Jr. Achievement Nat. Bus. Hall of Fame, 1998. With USAAF, 1944-46. Recipient Alexander Hamilton award Econ. Edn. from Freedoms Found.; Disting. Salesman of Year award Grand Rapids Sales and Mktg. Assn., Bus. Leader of Yr. award Religious Heritage Am., Industry Week Excellence in Mgmt. award, Thomas Jefferson Freedom of Speech award Kiwanis Internat., Mich. Week Vol. Leadership award, Am. Spirit Award, Repub. House and Senate, 1998, House of Hope Humanitarian Award, 1999, Excellence in Business Award, Davenport U., 2000, Mktg. Man of Yr. award West Mich. chpt. Am. Mktg. Assn., Edison Achievement award, 1994, Horatio Alger award, 1996, Am. Enterprise Exec. award Nat. Mgmt. Assn., Golden Plate award Acad. of Achievement, George Washington Honor Medal award Freedoms Found., Free Enterprise award Americanism Ednl. League, Patron award Mich. Found. for the Arts, 1982, Am. Entrepreneur Yr. award U. Mo., 1988, Disting. Alumni award Calvin Coll., 1982, Exec. Yr. award U. Ariz., 1991, Napoleon Hill Gold medal, 1989, Outstanding Bus. Leader award Northwood U., 1983, Outstanding Am. award Nat. Future Farmers Am., 1990, Environ. Programme Achievement award UN, 1989, William Booth award Salvation Army, 1990, Adam Smith Free Enterprise award Am. Legis. Exch. Coun., 1993, Donald J. Porter Humanitarian award YMCA Heritage Club, 1993; named Greater Grand Rapids Hall of Fame, 1989, Sales & Mktg. Execs. Internat. Acad. Achievement, 1990, Socially Responsible Entrepreneur of Yr. Mem. NAM (past dir.), Direct Selling Assn. (past chmn., dir., Champion of Free Enterprise and Knights of Royal Way awards, Hall of Fame award, Circle of Honor award), Direct Selling Edu. Found., Newcomen Soc., Grand Rapids Econ. Club (dir.), Round Table Internat. (hon. knight for life 1992) , Omicron Delta Kappa (hon.). Mem. Christian Reformed Ch. (former elder, chmn. fin. com.; past pres. missionary soc.). Clubs: Economic (Grand Rapids) (dir.), Rotary (Disting. Service award) (Grand Rapids); Pillars bd. dirs. Office: Alticor 7575 Fulton St E Ada MI 49355-0001

DEVOS, RICHARD MARVIN, JR. (DICK DEVOS), direct sales company executive, sports team executive; b. Grand Rapids, Mich., Oct. 21, 1955; s. Richard Marvin and Helen June (Van Wesep) DeV.; m. Elisabeth Dee Prince, Feb. 24, 1979. BBA, Northwood U., 1981. Coordinator sales Amway Corp., Ada, Mich., 1973-75, coordinator meetings, 1975-77, mgmt. trainee, 1977-82, dir. spl. events, 1982-84, v.p. internat., 1984-89; bd. dirs. The Windquest Group, Inc., Grand Rapids, 1989—; pres.,CEO Amway Corp., Ada, 1993-00; pres., bd. dirs. Alticor, Inc., 2000—. Bd. dirs. USA DSA, 1993-98, vice chmn. 1995-97, chmn. 1997, Old Kent Fin. Corp., 1994-01; bd. dirs. Fifth Third Bank W. Mich., 2001—, pres., CEO Orlando Magic NBA, 1991-93; chmn. Amway Japan Ltd., 1995—. Chmn. Kent Ottawa Muskegon Fgn. Trade Zone Bd., 1989-96, chmn. Coalition for Better Schs., 1993-94; bd. dirs. Mackinac Ctr., 1990-95 (hon. chair bd. adv. 1995—), Kent Hosp. Fin. Authority, 1980-93, West Mich. Boy Scouts Am., 1985-93, chmn. Blodgett Health Care, Butterworth Found., 1994—; co-chmn. Grand Rapids Area Negro Coll. Fund, 1989-92; mem. by appointment of Pres. Bush Commn. on Presdl. Scholars, 1991-93; elected mem. Mich. State Bd. Edn., 1991-93; bd. trustees Davenport Coll. Bus., 1991—, apptd. mem. bd. of control Grand Valley State U., 1995—; bd. dirs., exec. com. Project Rehab, 1978-84; mem. bd. dirs. Bus. Industry Political Action Com., 1995—, co-chmn. Grand Action Com., 1992—, bd. dirs., Right Place Prog., 1994—, chmn. Edn. Freedom Fund, 1994—, bd. dirs. Willow Creek Assoc., 1997—, chmn. Restoring the Am. Dream, 1998—. Recipient Grand Rapids Jaycees Disting. Svc. award 1985, Disting. Svc. Citation Northwood U., 1991, Assn. Ind. Colls. and Univs. Mich. Disting. Svc. award, 1992. Mem. Nat. Assn. of Mfgs. (bd. dirs. 1994—), Federalist Soc. (trustee), 1990-93, me Lodge: Rotary. Avocations: sailing, skiing. Office: Alticor Inc 7575 Fulton St E Ada MI 49355-0001

DEVRIES, ROBERT ALLEN, foundation administrator; b. Chgo., May 12, 1936; s. Robert and Mildred (Burgess) DeV.; m. Eleanor Rose Siems, Aug. 16, 1958; children: Susan E., Robert S., Laura H., Steven P. BS in Physiology, U. Chgo., 1958, MBA in Hosp. Adminstrn., 1961. Adminstrv. resident, asst. Miami Valley Hosp., Dayton, Ohio, 1959-61, asst. dir., 1961-67; adminstr. McPherson Community Health Ctr., Howell, Mich., 1967-71; program dir. W.K. Kellogg Found., Battle Creek, 1971-88, program dir., dir. Kellogg Internat. Fellowship Programs, 1988-90, program dir., dir. Internat. Study Grants and Exchanges, 1990-97, mem. adminstrv. coun., 1995-97, program dir., mem. fellowship com., 1997-99; ret., 1999. Cons. on domestic and internat. programs W.K. Kellogg Found., 1999—; mem. com. vis. Sch. Nursing, U. Mich., 2000—; chmn. quality com. bd. trustees Battle Creek Health Sys., 2001—; bd. dirs. Lifecare Ambulance, Mich. Health Coun., Leila Auboretum Soc.; lectr. nursing orgn., adminstrn. Sch. Nursing Miami Valley Hosp., 1961-67, Grad. Sch. Pub. Health U. Mich., 1967—; adj. prof. Coll. Health and Human Svcs., Western Mich. U., 1986—; advisor Sch. Pub. Health Beijing Med. U., 1986—, Med. Coll. Health Staff, Shanghai, 1986—, 1st People's Hosp., Shanghai, 1986—; mem. nat. adv. com. on rural health U.S Dept. Health and Human Svcs., Washington, 1988-92; mem. adv. panel acad. health scis. ctr. U.N.C., Chapel Hill, 1992-94; mem. policy coun. Nat. Inst. Rural Health Policy, 1987-90; mem. health planning and cert. of need workgroup Mich. Dept. Mgmt. & Budget, Mich. Dept. Pub. Health, 1986-87; vice chmn. adv. coun. Hosp. Rsch. & Ednl. Trust, Chgo., 1974-85; treas. coun. practice Am. Assn. Nurse Anesthetists, 1978-84; mem. Southwest Mich. Health Sys. Agy. Bd., 1980-83; guest lectr. King's Fund Coll., London, U. Leeds, Eng., French Nat. Sch. Pub. Health, Rennes, U. Toronto, Pan Am. Health Orgn., Washington and Brasilia, Brazil, Katholieke Universiteit Leuven, Belgium, Internat. Hosp. Fedn., London, Elton Mayo Sch. Mgmt., Adelaide, Australia, Ministry Pub. Health, Beijing, Indian Hosp. Assn., New Delhi. Editorial bds. Inquiry, Hosp. & Health Svcs.; contbr. articles to profl. jours., also book chpts. Counselor Baxter Am. Found. Prize in Health Svcs. Rsch., 1986—; assoc. trustee Florence Nightingale Mus. Trust, London; chair quality com. bd. trustees Battle Creek Health Sys., 2001—. Recipient Disting. Svc. award Am. Soc. Allied Health Professions, 1989, Med. Group Mgmt. Assn., Denver, 1990, Ohio State U. Alumni Assn., 1998; Monsignor Griffin award for disting. writing Ohio Hosp. Assn., 1965, Civic Achievement award Jr. C. of C., Chgo., 1955, recognition award for contbns. to svcs. to handicapped Commn. on Accreditation of Rehab. Facilities, 1976, Cmty. Health Leadership award Hosp. Rsch. and Ednl. Trust, 1994, Spl. Recognition award Mich. Health and Hosp. Assn., 1999; named Outstanding Young Men in Am. Howell, Mich. Area C. of C. and Jaycees, 1970; Nat. Health Svcs. rsch. fellow U. Mich., 1970-71. Fellow Am. Coll. Healthcare Execs.(life), U.S. China Ednl. Inst., Can. Sch. Mgmt. (hon.); mem. APHA, Am. Hosp. Assn. (hon. life, vice chair R&D coun. 1974-85, adv. panel multi-hosp. systems 1977-85, Living the Vision award 1999), Internat. Hosp. Fedn., Nat. Rural Health Assn., Mich. Hosp. Assn. (assn. governance and strategic planning com. 1986-89, pub. policy and govt. com. 1981-83), U. Chgo. Hosp. Adminstrn. Alumni Assn. (pres. 1982-83), Leila Arboretum Soc. (bd. dirs.). Lutheran. Avocations: music, writing, travel, gardening.

DE VRIES, ROBERT JOHN, investment banker; b. Pella, Iowa, Aug. 18, 1932; s. John G. and Anna (Kool) m. Patricia Lynn Jackson, Dec. 22, 1962 (dec.); children: Robert John Jr., Garrett Andrew. BBA, U. Tex., Austin, 1958; MBA, Harvard Grad. Sch. of Bus., Boston, 1960. Registered principal. Security analyst Cyrus J. Lawrence & Sons, N.Y.C., 1960-64, Jas. H. Oliphant and Co., N.Y.C., 1964-66; investment banker William D. Witter Inc., N.Y., 1966-68; v.p. Mgmt. Planning Inc., Princeton, N.J., 1968-73; pres. Cryomed Devices, Inc., 1973-80; v.p. Smith Barney, Harris Upham, 1981-84; pres., dir., founder Robert J. De Vries and Co., Inc., Kansas City, 1984—. Served with USAF, 1952-56. Inst. of Chartered Fin. Analyst, Harvard Club of N.Y., Beta Gamma Sigma. Republican. Presbyterian. Avocations: photography, marathon running. Home: 24805 W 190th St Gardner KS 66030 Office: De Vries and Co 800 W 47th St Ste 319 Kansas City MO 64112-3022

DEVRIES, ROBERT K. religious book publisher; b. Sully, Iowa, July 6, 1932; s. Fred G. and Selena Irene (Willetts) DeV.; m. Carolyn Jo Schroeder, June 2, 1962 (div. 1978); children: Stephen Robert, Suzanne Mishael Dahill; m. Carolyn Gail Bergmans, May 26, 1979; children: Staci Ann McKellar, Keri Gail Bailey. AB, Wheaton Coll., 1954; ThM, Dallas Theol. Sem., 1958, ThD, 1969. Asst. registrar Dallas Theol. Sem., 1959-63; editor-in-chief Moody Press, Chgo., 1963-68; dir., v.p. pubs. Zondervan Pub. House, Grand Rapids, Mich., 1968-76, exec. v.p. book div., 1976-85; exec. v.p., publisher Zondervan Book Group, Zondervan Corp., 1985-86; pub., bd. dirs. Discovery House Pubs., 1987-2000, sr. publisher, bd. dirs., 2000—; cons., bd. dirs. Serendipity House, Littleton, Colo., 1990-99; bd. dirs. Serendipity House Found., 1999—. Bd. dirs. Oswald Chambers Pub. Assn. Ltd., Eng. Bd. dirs. Ligonier Valley Study Ctr., Stahlstown, Pa., 1979-83, Bd. Publ., Evang. Covenant Ch. Am., Chgo., 1989-94, chmn., 1992-94; advisor Internat. Coun. Bibl. Inerrancy, Walnut Creek, Calif., 1978-87. Recipient Outstanding Young Man in Am. award Jaycees, 1965 Mem. Evang. Christian Pubs. Assn. Republican. Mem. Evangelical Covenant Ch. Avocation: model railroading. Home: 7554 Lime Hollow Dr SE Grand Rapids MI 49546-7439 Office: 3000 Kraft Ave SE Grand Rapids MI 49512-2024 E-mail: rdevries@rbc.org.

DEWALD, PAUL ADOLPH, psychiatrist, educator; b. N.Y.C., Mar. 12, 1920; s. Jacob Frederick and Elsie (Wurzburger) D.; m. Eleanor Whitman, Sept. 1, 1961; children: Jonathan S., Ellen F. B.A., Swarthmore Coll., 1942; M.D., U. Rochester, 1945; cert. psychoanalysis, SUNY, 1960. Intern, Strong Meml. Hosp., Rochester, N.Y., 1945-46, resident, 1948-52; instr. U. Rochester, 1952-57, asst. prof. psychiatry, 1957-61; pvt. practice psychoanalysis St. Louis, 1961-99; asst. clin. prof. psychiatry Washington U., 1961-65, 96—; asso. clin. prof. St. Louis U., 1965-69, clin. prof. psychiatry, 1969—. Dir. treatment svc. Psychoanalytic Found. St. Louis, 1961-72, med. dir., 1972-83 St. Louis Psychoanalytic Inst., 1973-83, supervising and tng. analyst, 1973—; mem. faculty Chgo. Inst. Psychoanlysis, 1961-75, supervising and tng. analyst, 1965-73; vis. prof. U. Cin., 1968-80; mem. Mo. State Mental Health Commn., 1978-83, chmn., 1981-83; asst. prof. clin. psychiatry Washington U., 1995—. Author: Psychotherapy: A Dynamic Approach, 1964, 2d edit., 1969, The Psychoanalytic Process, 1972, Learning Process in Psycho-analytic Supervision, 1987; co-editor: Ethics Case Book of the American Psychoanalytic Assn., 2001; contbr. articles to profl. jours. Served to capt. M.C., AUS, 1946-48. Fellow Am. Psychiat. Assn. (life); mem. Mo. Psychiat. Assn. (pres. 1970-71), Eastern Mo. Psychiat. Assn. (pres. 1969-70), Am. Psychoanalytic Assn. (life), St. Louis Psychoanalytic Soc. (pres. 1970-71, 86-88) Home: 60 Conway Ln Saint Louis MO 63124-1203 Office: 8820 Ladue Rd Saint Louis MO 63124 E-mail: padewald@mindspring.com.

DEWERD, LARRY ALBERT, medical physicist, educator; b. Milw., July 18, 1941; s. Anthony Lawrence and Dorothy M. (Heling) DeW.; m. Vada Mary Anderson, Sept. 14, 1963; children: Scott, Mark, Eric. BS, U. Wis., Milw., 1963; MS, U. Wis., 1965, PhD, 1970. Rsch. assoc. U. Wash., Seattle, 1970-72, rsch. asst. prof., 1973-75; vis. asst. prof. U. Wis., Madison, 1975-76, clin. asst. prof., 1976-79, clin. assoc. prof., 1979-86, prof., 1990—. Mgr. product devel. Radiation Measurements, Middleton, Wis., 1986-90; dir. Radiation Calibration Lab., Madison, 1983-86, 90—; cons. Instrumentarium, Milw., 1990; v.p. Standard Imaging, Madison, 1990—; presenter in field to sci. confs., seminars and workshops; cons. various projects IAEA. Contbg. author: Brachytherapy, Ionization Chambers and Dosimetry, Thermoluminescence and Mammography; also numerous articles. Science chmn. Am. Cancer Soc. State of Wis., 1986-90. Grantee Nat. Cancer Inst., 1979-86, 94-98. Fellow Am. Assn. Physicists in Medicine (pres. 1990-92), Health Physics Soc., Am. Phys. Soc., Coun. Ionizing Radiation Measurements and Standards (pres. 1995-98), Sigma Xi (bd. dirs. 1984-86). Avocations: golf, fishing, backpacking, hunting. Home: 13 Pilgrim Cir Madison WI 53711-4033 Office: U Wis 1530 Med Sci Ctr 1300 University Ave Madison WI 53706-1510 E-mail: ladewerd@facstaff.wisc.edu.

DEWHURST, CHARLES KURT, museum director, curator, folklorist, English language educator; b. Passaic, N.J., Dec. 21, 1948; s. Charles Allaire and Minn Jule (Hanzl) D.:; m. Marsha MacDowell, Dec. 15, 1972; 1 dau., Marit Charlene. B.A., Mich. State U., 1970, M.A., 1973, Ph.D., 1983. Editorial asst. Carlton Press, N.Y.C., 1967; computer operator IBM, 1968; project dir. Mich. State U. Mus., 1975, curator, 1976-83, dir., 1982—. Guest curator Mus. Am. Folk Art, N.Y.C., 1978—83, Artrain, Detroit, 1980—83; dir. Festival of Mich. Folklife, 1987—95, Ctr. for Great Lakes Culture, 2000—. Author: Reflections of Faith, 1983, Artists in Aprons, 1979, Rainbows in the Sky, 1978, Michigan Folk Art, 1976 (Am. Assn. State and Local History award 1977), Art at Work: Folk Pottery of Grand Ledge, Michigan, 1986, Michigan Quilts, 1987, Michigan Folklife Reader, 1988, To Honor and Comfort: Native Quilting Traditions, 1998. Coord. South African-U.S. Partnership Project, 1967—; mem. adv. com. Smithsonian Ctr. for Folklife and Cultural Heritage; vice chair Mich. Humanities Coun., 1995—; mem. Mich. Coun. for Arts and Cultural Affairs; v.p. bd. dirs. Fund for Folk Culture. Recipient Disting. Svc. and Humanities award, 1994. Mem. Am. Folkore Soc., Mich. Folklore Soc., Midwest Soc. Lit., Popular Culture Assn., Mich. Hist. Soc., Mich. Mus. Assn., Am. Assn. Mus., Internat. Coun. Mus. Home: 1804 Cricket Ln East Lansing MI 48823-1225 Office: Mich State U Mus W Circle Dr East Lansing MI 48824

DEWINE, R. MICHAEL, senator, lawyer; b. Springfield, Ohio, Jan. 5, 1947; s. Richard and Jean DeWine; m. Frances Struewing, June 3, 1967; children: Patrick, Jill, Rebecca, John, Brian, Alice, Mark, Anna. BS in Edn., Miami U., Oxford, Ohio, 1969; JD, Ohio No. U., 1972. Bar: Ohio 1972, U.S. Supreme Ct. 1977. Asst. pros. atty. Greene County, Xenia, Ohio, 1973-75, pros. atty., 1977-81; mem. Ohio Senate, 1981-82, 98th, 99th, 100th, 101st Congress from 7th Ohio dist., Washington, 1983-90; lt. gov. State of Ohio, Columbus, Ohio, 1991-94; U.S. senator from Ohio, 1995—. Mem. judiciary com., labor and human resources com., intelligence com., Health Edn. Com., Labor and Pensions Com. Republican. Roman Catholic Home: 2587 Conley Rd Cedarville OH 45314-9525 Office: US Senate 140 Russell Senate Bldg Washington DC 20510-0001*

DEWITT, DAVID J. computer scientist; PhD, U. Mich., 1976. Prof., Romnes fellow computer scis. U. Wis., Madison. Mem. NAE. Office: U Wis Dept Computer Sci 1210 W Dayton St Madison WI 53706-1685 E-mail: dewitt@cs.wisc.edu.

DEWITT, THOMAS, pediatrician, educator; MD, U. Rochester, 1976. Diplomate Am. Bd. Pediatrics. Resident in pediatrics Yale-New Haven (Conn.) Hosp.; fellowship gen. acad. pediatrics Robert Wood Johnson Found., Yale U. Sch. Medicine; with Cin. Children's Hosp. Med. Ctr. Office: Cin Childrens Hosp Med Ctr 3333 Burnet Ave Cincinnati OH 45229-3026

DEWITT, WILLIAM O., JR. professional sports team executive; b. St. Louis, Aug. 31, 1941; s. William O. and Margaret H. DeW.; m. Katharine Cramer; children: Katie, Bill, Andrew, Margot. BA in Econs., Yale U., 1963; MBA, Harvard U., 1965. Pres. Reynolds, DeWitt & Co.; owner St.

Louis Cardinals, 1996—; chmn. bd. dirs., CEO Gateway Group Inc., 1996—. Co-chmn. Restaurant Mgmt. Inc.; bd. dirs. Sena Weller Rohe, Williams Inc., U.S. Playing Card Co. Pres. Fund for Ind. Schs. Cin., William O. and Margaret H. DeWitt Found.; pres. Rep. fin. com. Hamilton County; bd. dirs. Semple Found., Cin. Art Mus., Taft Mus., Salvation Army; mem. devel. bd. Yale U.; regional chmn. Yale Campaign; cabinet mem. Cin. Fine Arts Fund, United Way Cin., Multiple Sclerosis Soc. Office: St Louis Cardinals 250 Stadium Plz Saint Louis MO 63102-1722

DEWITZ, LOREN, former state legislator; m. Judith DeWitz; 2 children. BS, N.D. State U. Farmer; state rep. dist. 14, 1991-97. Mem. appropriations, human resources divsn. coms. N.D. Ho. Reps.; bd. dirs. Kidder Co. Water Resource. Recipient Great Am. Family award, 1980. Mem. VFW, 4-H (leader), Farm Bur., Am. Legion. Republican.

DEWOLFE, JOHN CHAUNCEY, JR. lawyer; b. Chgo., June 9, 1913; s. John Chauncey and Mabel (Spafford) DeW.; m. Dorothy Fulton, May 9, 1942; children: John Chauncey, III, George F. B.S., U. Ill.; J.D., U. Wis., 1939. Bar: Wis. 1939, Ill. 1940. Ptnr. firm DeWolfe, Poynton & Stevens and predecessor firms, 1946—. Contbr. articles to profl. jours. Trustee Village of Riverside, Ill., 1963-70; Chmn. West Suburban Mass Transit Dist., 1974-76. Served from lt. to maj. AUS, 1942-45, 51-52; lt. col. USAR ret. Mem. Am., Ill., Wis. bar assns., Chgo. Bar Assn. (chmn. corp. law com. 1973-74), Bar Assn. 7th Fed. Circuit, Assn. Trial Lawyers Am., Sigma Phi Epsilon. Republican. Episcopalian. Club: University (Chgo.). Home: 1448 N Lake Shore Dr Chicago IL 60610-6655 Office: 135 S La Salle St Chicago IL 60603-4159

DEWULF NICKELL, KAROL, editor; m. Don Nickell; 2 children. Editor-in-chief Traditional Home mag., Better Homes and Gardens mag., 2001—. Office: 1716 Locust St Des Moines IA 50309-3023*

DIAMOND, EUGENE CHRISTOPHER, lawyer, hospital administrator; b. Oceanside, Calif., Oct. 19, 1952; s. Eugene Francis and Rosemary (Wright) D.; m. Mary Theresa O'Donnell, Jan. 20, 1984; children: Eugene John, Kevin Seamus, Hannah Rosemary, Seamus Michael, Maeve Therese. BA, U. Notre Dame, 1974; MHA, St. Louis U., 1978, JD, 1979. Bar: Ill. 1979. Staff atty. AUL Legal Def. Fund, Chgo., 1979-80; adminstrv. asst. Holy Cross Hosp., 1980-81, asst. adminstr., 1981-82, v.p., 1982-83, counsel to adminstr., 1980—, exec. v.p., 1983-91; exec. v.p., COO, St. Margaret Mercy Healthcare Ctrs., Hammond, Ind., 1991-93, pres., CEO, 1993—, regional COO, 2001—. Cons. Birthright of Chgo., 1979—, mem. benefit com., 1981—; bd. dirs. Hammond C. of C., 1993, North West Ind. Forum. Mem. Ill. State Bar Assn., Chgo. Bar Assn. Roman Catholic. Office: St Margaret Mercy Healthcare Ctrs 5454 Hohman Ave Hammond IN 46320-1999

DIAMOND, SEYMOUR, physician; b. Chgo., Apr. 15, 1925; s. Nathan Avruum and Rose (Roth) D.; m. Elaine June Flamm, June 20, 1948; children: Judi, Merle, Amy. Student, Loyola U., 1943-45; MB, Chgo. Med. Sch., 1948, MD, 1949. Intern White Cross Hosp., Columbus, Ohio, 1949-50; gen. practice medicine Chgo., 1950—; dir. Diamond Headache Clinic, Ltd., 1970—; dir. inpatient headache unit St. Joseph Hosp.; prof. neurology Finch U. Health Scis. Finch U. Health Scis., Chgo. Med. Sch., 1970-82, 85—, adj. prof. cellular and molecular pharmacology, 1985—, clin. professor family medicine, 1999—; clin. prof. dept. family medicine U. Medicine and Dentistry N.J. Sch. Osteo. Medicine, Stratford, N.J., 1994-98; cons. mem. FDA Orphan Products Devel. Initial Rev. Group. Lectr. dept. cmty. and family medicine Loyola U. Stritch Sch. Medicine, 1972-78; lectr. Falconbridge lecture series Laurentian U., Sudbury, Ont., Can., 1987; disting. lectr. neurology U. Tenn., 1992; AMA cons. on drug evaluation, 1993; mem. sci. com. neurology Internat. Jour. Pain Therapy, 1993. Author: A Pain Specialist's Approach to the Headache Patient, 1994; (with Bill and Cynthia Still) The Hormone Headache, 1995, Diagnosing and Managing Headaches, 1994, 3d edit., 2001; (with Donald J. Dalessio) The Practicing Physician's Approach to Headache, 5th edit., 1992, More Than Two Aspirin: Help for Your Headache Problem, 1976, Advice from the Diamond Headache Clinic, 1982; (with Judi Diamond-Falk) Coping with Your Headaches, 1982, 2d edit.; (with Mary Franklin Epstein), 1987; (with Arnold P. Friedman MD) Headache in Contemporary Patient Management series, 1983; (with Amy Diamond Vye) Headache and Diet, 1990; (with Michael Maliszewski) Sexual Aspects of Headaches, 1992; (with Mary A. Franklin) Conquering Your Migraine, 2001; (with Amy Diamond) Headache and Your Child, 2001; (with Merle L. Diamond) Contemporary Diagnosis and Management of Headache and Migraine, 2d edit., 2000; contbg. author: Wolff's Headache and Other Head Pain, 6th edit., 1993, Handbook of Pain Management, 2d edit., 1994, Nonsteroidal Anti-Inflammatory Drugs, 2d edit., 1994, Current Review of Pain, 1994, New Advances in Headache Research, 1994, Conn's Current Therapy, 1998, Advanced Therapy of Headache, 1999, Diamond and Dalessio's Practicing Physician's Approach to Headache, 6th edit., 1994; editor: Migraine Headache Prevention and Management; editor-in-chief Headache Quar., 1990—; editl. cons. BIOSIS, 1986-90; contbr. numerous articles on headache and related fields to profl. jours. Bd. govs. Finch U. of Health/Chgo. Med. Sch. Recipient Disting. Alumni award Chgo. Med. Sch., 1977; Nat. Migraine Found. lectureship award, 1982, award Headache Consortium of New Eng., 1997, Cert. Appreciation, Chgo. Med. Soc., 1998; 1st recipient Migraine Trust lectureship, 1988; Brit. Migraine Trust 7th Internat. Migraine Symposium, London; Nat. Headache Found. Seymour Diamond fellow, 1993; Disting. lectr. in neurology U. Tenn., 1992. Fellow Royal Soc. Medicine; mem. AMA (Physicians Recognition awards 1970-73, 74, 77, 79, 82, 87, del. sect. clin. pharmacology and therapeutics 1987-89, mem. health policy agenda for Am. People, mem. Cost Effectiveness Conf., del. reference com. "C" on edn., reference com. C, 1988), mem. Bd. of Scientific and Policy Advs. for The Am. Council on Sci. and Health, So. Med. Assn., Am. Assn. Study of Headache (exec. dir. 1971-85, pres. 1972-74, #1 regent mem. 1984, svc. award 1971-85, Lifetime Achievement award 1999), Nat. Headache Found. (pres. 1971-77, exec. dir. 1977-95, exec. chmn. 1995—, 1st recipient cert. of added qualification in headache mgmt. Nat. Bd. Cert. in Headache Mgmt. 2001), World Fedn. Neurology (exec. officer 1980-95, research group on migraine and headache), Ill. Acad. Gen. Practice (chmn. mental health com. 1966-70), Ill. Med. Soc., Chgo. Med. Soc., Biofeedback Soc. Am., Internat. Assn. Study of Pain, Am. Soc. Clin. Pharmacology and Therapeutics (chmn. headache sect. 1982-89, mem. com. coordination sci. sects. 1983-89), Postgrad. Med. Assn. (pres. 1981). Office: 467 W Deming Pl Ste 500 Chicago IL 60614-1726

DIAMOND, SHARI SEIDMAN, law and psychology educator, law researcher; b. Chgo., Mar. 17, 1947; d. Leon Harry and Rita (Wolff) S.; m. Stewart Howard Diamond, Nov. 1, 1970; 1 child, Nicole. BA in Psychology, Sociology, U. Mich., 1968; MA in Psychology, Northwestern U., 1970, PhD in Social Psychology, 1972; JD with honors, U. Chgo., 1985. Bar: Ill. 1985. Rsch. assoc. Sch. Law U. Chgo., 1972-73; asst. prof. psychology and criminal justice U. Ill., Chgo., 1973-79, assoc. prof., 1979-90, prof., 1990-2000; assoc. Sidley & Austin, 1985-87; sr. rsch. fellow ABF, 1987—; lectr. U. Chgo. Law Sch., 1994-96; prof. law and psychology Northwestern U., 1999—, Stanton Clinton sr. rsch. prof., 2000-01. Cons. govtl. and pub. interests groups including Rsch. Adv. Panel for U.S. Sentencing Commn., 1987-91; acad. visitor dept. law London Sch. Econs., 1981; hon. fellow Ctr. for Urban Affairs Northwestern U., Evanston, Ill., 1973-73; hon. rsch. assoc. U. London, 1970; speaker, lectr. in field; mem. NAS panel on sentencing rsch., 1981-83, panel on forensic DNA evidence, 1994-96. Editor Law and Soc. Rev., 1988-91; past mem. editorial bd. Law and Soc. Rev., 1983-88, Law and Human Behavior, Crime and Justice Annual, Evaluation Rev.; reviewer NSF; contbr. articles to profl. jours. Chair Coll. Edn. Policy Com., 1979-80; dir. tng. grant NIMH Crime and Delinquency, 1979-80. Fellow Northwestern U., 1968-69, NIMH, 1969-71; grantee Spencer Found., 1972-74, disting. scholar, grantee, U. Ill., 1995-98, Law Enforcement Assistance Adminstrn., 1974-76, Ctr. for Crime and Delinquency NIMH, 1976-81, NSF, 1980-83, 90-92, 99—; B. Kenneth West U. scholar, 1995-98. Fellow APA (Award for Disting. Contbns. to Rsch. in Pub. Policy 1991), Am. Psychol. Soc.; mem. ABA, Am. Psychology-Law Soc. (pres. 1987-88), Law and Soc. Assn. (trustee 1979-82). Office: Northwestern U Law Sch 357 E Chicago Ave Chicago IL 60611

DIAMOND, SIDNEY, chemist, educator; b. N.Y.C., Nov. 10, 1929; s. Julius and Ethel D.; m. Harriet Urish, May 2, 1953; children: Florence, Julia. B.S., Syracuse U., 1950; M.F., Duke U., 1951; Ph.D., Purdue U., 1963. Research engr. U.S. Bur. Public Rds. (now Fed. Hwy. Adminstrn.), Washington, 1953-61, research chemist, 1961-65; assoc. prof. engring. materials Purdue U., 1965-69, prof., 1969—; pres. Sidney Diamond and Assocs., Inc., engring. materials cons. Mem. Nat. Materials Adv. Bd. Com. on Status of Research in U.S. Cement and Concrete Industries; chmn. Internat. Symposium on Durability of Glass Fiber Reinforced Concrete, Chgo., 1985; mem. adv. com. NSF Ctr. for Advanced Cement-Based Materials, 1989—. Contbr. numerous articles on cement and concrete to profl. jours.; editor: Cement and Concrete Research. Served with U.S. Army, 1951-53. Fellow Am. Ceramic Soc. (past trustee, Copeland award), Am. Concrete Inst., Am. Concrete Inst. (anderson award 1993); mem. ASTM, Internat. Congress on Chemistry of Cement (pres. sect. 6 of 8th congress), Materials Rsch. Soc. Home: 819 Essex St West Lafayette IN 47906-1534 Office: Purdue U Sch Civil Engring West Lafayette IN 47907

DIAMOND, SUSAN ZEE, management consultant; b. Okla., Aug. 20, 1949; d. Louis Edward Diamond, Henrietta (Wood) Diamond; m. Allan T. Devitt, July 27, 1974. AB, U. Chgo., 1970; MBA, DePaul U., 1979. Dir. study guide prodn. Am. Sch. Co., Chgo., 1972—75; supr. publs. Allied Van Lines, Broadview, 1975—78, sr. account svcs. rep., 1978—79; pres. Diamond Assocs. Ltd., Bensenville, Ill., 1978—. Author: Records Management:A Practical Guide, 3d edit., 1995; editor: The Serpentine Muse, 1996—. Mem.: Assn. Record Mgrs. and Adminstrs., Inst. Mgmt. Accts., Baker St. Irregulars, Adventuresses of Sherlock Holmes.

DI CHIERA, DAVID, general director of opera company; b. McKeesport, Pa., Apr. 8, 1935; s. Cosimo and Maria (Pezzaniti) DiC.; m. Karen VanderKloot, July 20, 1965 (div. 1992); children: Lisa Maria, Cristina Maria. BA in Music summa cum laude, UCLA, 1956, MA in Composition (scholar), 1958, PhD in Musicology, 1962; certificate in composition and piano (Fulbright Research grantee), Naples Conservatory of Music, 1959; D (hon.), U. Mich., 1998. Instr. music U. Calif., Los Angeles, 1960-61; asst. prof. music, asst. dean Oakland U., Rochester, Mich., 1962-65, chmn. music dept., 1966-73; founding gen. dir. Mich. Opera Theatre, Detroit, 1971—; founding dir. Music Hall Center for the Performing Arts, 1973—. Artistic dir. Dayton Opera Assn., 1981-92; founding gen. dir. Opera Pacific, Costa Mesa, Calif., 1985-97; trustee Nat. Opera Inst.; adj. prof. Oakland U., Wayne State U. Producer, dir.: Overture to Opera series for, Detroit Grand Opera series, 1963-71; Composer various works for piano, violin, orch., voice; author articles on Italian opera for various encyclopedias; contbr. revs. and articles to music jours. Mem. Arts Com. New Detroit, Inc.; trustee, mem. exec. com. Music Center for Performing Arts; mem. Arts Task Force City of Detroit. Recipient Atwater Kent award U. Calif., Los Angeles, 1961; Certificate of Appreciation City of Detroit, 1970; citation Mich. Legislature, 1976; Michaelangelo award Boys' Town of Italy, 1980; award Arts Found. of Mich., 1981; President's Cabinet award U. Detroit, 1982; George Gershwin fellow, 1958; named A Michiganian of Yr., 1980; cavaliere della Repubblica Italiana. Mem. Am. Arts Alliance (exec. com.), Nat. Opera Assn., Internat. Assn. Lyric Theatre (v.p.), Am. Symphony League, Am. Musicol. Soc., OPERA Am. (pres. 1979-83), AAUP, Phi Beta Kappa, Phi Mu Alpha Sinfonia. Club: Detroit Athletic. Office: Mich Opera Theatre 1526 Broadway St Detroit MI 48226-2115

DICK, HAROLD LATHAM, manufacturing executive; b. Wichita, Kans., Oct. 24, 1943; s. Harold G. and Evelyn (Spines) D.; m. Jeanne Marie Luczai, Aug. 25, 1973; children: Harold Campbell, Edward Latham. BA, Washburn U., 1966; MBA, Harvard U., 1968. Exec. asst. to treas. Skelly Oil Co., Tulsa, 1968-70; mgmt. cons. McKinsey & Co. Inc., Chgo., Dallas, Houston, 1970-77; dir. planning Frito-Lay Inc., Dallas, 1977-80; v.p. Norton Simon Inc., N.Y.C., 1980-83; founder Summit Ptnrs., Wichita, Kans., 1983-85; pres., chief exec. officer Doskocil Cos. Inc., Hutchinson, 1985-88; founder, pres. The Summit Group, 1988—. Adv. bd. dirs. Garvey Industries, Wichita, 1987-94, Petroleum Inc., Wichita, 1993—. Trustee Kanza coun. Boy Scouts Am., 1989-97, exec. bd., 1995-97, v.p. 1997—, exec. bd. dirs. Quivira coun., 1997—, v.p., 1997-98, coun. commr., 1998-2002, coun. pres., 2002-; Stephen minister, 1987-94; mem. bd. regents Washburn U., 1995—, chmn. bd. regents, 2001—, chmn. fin. com., 1998-2001; trustee Washburn Endowment Assn., 1990-; mem. presdl. search com. Washburn U., 1987-88. Mem. Washburn Alumni Assn. (bd. dirs. 1986-89). Republican. Episcopalian. Office: The Summit Group 405 First Nat Ctr Hutchinson KS 67501

DICK, ROLLIN MERLE, insurance company executive; b. Sanborn, Iowa, Aug. 9, 1931; s. Laurence I. and Lillian M. (Reisser) D.; m. Helen E. Dodds, May 20, 1951; children: Jeri L., Lawrence E., Tami S. CPA, Ind. Ptnr. Coopers & Lybrand, Indpls., 1965-86; exec. v.p., chief fin. officer Conseco Inc., Carmel, Ind., 1986—, vice chmn., cfo, until 2000. Office: Conseco Inc PO Box 1911 Carmel IN 46082-1911

DICKE, JAMES FREDERICK, II, manufacturing company executive; b. San Angelo, Tex., Nov. 9, 1945; s. James Frederick and Eilleen (Webster) D.; m. Janet St. Clair, July 6, 1968; children: James F. III, Jennifer S. BS, Trinity U., 1968. Intern U.S. Ho. of Reps., Washington, 1966; sales coord. Crown Controls Corp., New Bremen, Ohio, 1968-69, v.p. internat., 1970-78; exec. v.p. Crown Equipment Corp., 1979-80, pres., CEO, 1980—. Chmn. Crown Australia Pty. Ltd., Sydney, 1980—, Crown Ltd., Galway, Ireland, 1980—; bd. dirs. Dayton (Ohio) Power and Light Co. Chmn. bd. trustees Trinity U., San Antonio, 1980—, Dayton (Ohio) Art Inst., 1998—; trustee, sec. Culver (Ind.) Ednl. Found., 1981—; Midwest dir. Boys and Girls Clubs Am., Chgo., 1987—; co-chmn. Ohio Rep. Fin. Com., 1995—. Recipient Disting. Svc. award Culver Acads., 1989, Disting. Alumnus award Trinity U., 1991; honoree Nat. Acad. Design, 1999. Mem. Young Pres.' Orgn. (bd. dirs. 1985-94, internat. pres. 1992-93), Cum Laude Soc. Culver Acads., Key Largo Anglers CLub (chmn. bd. dirs. 1999—). Mem. United Ch. of Christ. Office: Crown Equipment Corp PO Box 97 New Bremen OH 45869-0097

DICKENSON-HAZARD, NANCY ANN, pediatric nurse practitioner, consultant; b. Ashland, Ky., Sept. 25, 1946; m. John H. Hazard Jr., May 28, 1977; 2 children. BSN, U. Ky., 1968; cert., U. Mo., 1971, U. Va., 1976, MSN, 1977. RN, Md.; PNP. Asst. program dir., instr. nursing Ea. Ky. U., Richmond, Va., 1973-75; PNP Cen. Va. Community Health Plan, New Canton, 1976-77; PNP nurse coord. Georgetown U. Health Plan, Kensington, Md., 1977-79; PNP Kaiser Health Plan, 1979-81; exec. dir. Nat. Cert. Bd. PNP/Nurses, Rockville, 1981—. Ind. nurse cons. Continuing Edn. and Quality Assurance, Rockville, 1978-81; cons. to Student Nurse Assn., Ea. Ky. U., Richmond, 1974-75; speaker numerous convs. and confs. Contbg. author: Fundamentals of Nursing, 1989, Basic Nursing: Theory and Practice, 1987, Community Health Nursing, 1991; mem. editorial bd. Ped. Nursing Jour., 1986—, Jour. Pediatric Health Care, 1987; chmn. humanitarian award com. Pediatric Nursing Jour.; contbr. articles to profl. jours. Pres., Home and Sch. Assn., Rockville, 1990; mem. com. St. Elizabeth Parish and Sch., Rockville, 1984-92. Fellow Nat. Assn. Pediatric Nurse Assocs. and Practitioners (Henry K. Silver award for nat. excellence 1983), Am. Acad. Nursing; mem. ANA, Leadership Roundtable for Advanced Nursing Practice, Sigma Theta Tau. Roman Catholic. Avocations: crafts, sewing, reading, gardening. Office: Sigma Theta Tau Intl 550 W North St Indianapolis IN 46202-3191

DICKERSON, BRIAN, columnist; b. Rochester, N.Y., Dec. 25, 1956; s. Donald Thomas and Shirley Wright D.; 1 child, Zachary. BA History, Princeton U., 1979. Editor, reporter Miami (Fla.) Herald, 1979-88; editor mag. Detroit Free Press, 1988-97, columnist, 1997—. Pres. Sunday Magazine Editors Assn., Phila., 1991-92. Office: Detroit Free Press 600 W Fort St Detroit MI 48226-2706 E-mail: dicker@freepress.com.

DICKESON, ROBERT CELMER, retired university president, foundation executive, political science educator; b. Independence, Mo., June 28, 1940; s. James Houston and Sophie Stephanie (Celmer) D.; m. Ludmila Ann Weir, June 22, 1963; children: Elizabeth Ann, Cynthia Marie. AB, U. Mo., 1962, MA, 1963, PhD, 1968; postgrad., U. No. Colo., 1971, 72; postgrad. inst. ednl. mgmt., Harvard U., 1973. Adminstrv. asst. U. Mo., Columbia, 1962-64, dir. student activities, 1964-68, asst. dean students, 1968-69; dean student affairs No. Ariz. U., Flagstaff, 1969-70, assoc. prof. polit. sci., 1970-76, prof., 1976-81, on leave, 1979-81, v.p. student affairs, 1970-79, v.p., univ. relations, 1973-79; dir. Ariz. Dept. Adminstrn., Phoenix, 1979-81; pres. U. No. Colo., Greeley, 1981-91, prof. polit. sci., 1981-87, 88-91; chief of staff to gov., exec. dir. Office of State Planning and Budgeting State of Colo., 1987; pres. Noel/Levitz Ctrs. Inc., Iowa City, 1991-97; divsn. pres. Lumina Found. for Edn., Indpls., 1995-97. Sr. v.p. Lumina Found. for Edn., 1997—; adj. prof. U. Colo., Denver, 1987, Ariz. State U., Tempe, 1979-81; nat. vice-chmn. Cert. Public Mgr. Policy Bd., 1980-81; planning and mgmt. cons.; mem. univ. adv. council Am. Council on Life Ins.; dir. United Bank of Greeley; mem. Pres.' Commn. NCAA, 1989-91; mem. Nat. Commn. on Minorities in Higher Edn., 1989-91; nat. cons. Office of Women in Higher Edn., Am. Coun. on Edn., 1989-97. Author: Prioritizing Academic Programs and Services, 1999; contbr. articles to profl. jours. Active Boy Scouts Am., v.p. Grand Canyon council, Flagstaff, 1974-76, pres., 1976-79, mem. nat. council, 1976-81, T. Roosevelt council, 1979-81, v.p. Long's Peak Council, 1981-87; mem. state com. Ariz. Democratic Com., 1970-72; chmn. Gov.'s Commn. on Merit System Reform, 1979-80, Gov.'s Regulatory Rev. Council, 1980-81, Gov.'s Commn. Higher Edn., 1983-86; mem. Gov.'s Commn. Excellence in Edn., 1983-86, Gov.'s Coun. on Creative Schs., 1989-91; commr. from Colo. to Edn. Commn. of the States, 1987-91; internat. trustee Sigma Alpha Epsilon Found., 1993-97. Recipient Dist. award of Merit., 1973, Silver Beaver award, 1975, Disting. Service award Sigma Alpha Epsilon, 1969, Merit Key award 1997, Disting. Alumnus award U. Mo.-Columbia, 1988, Outstanding Pres. award Am. Assn. Colls. of Tchrs. Edn, 1991, Bus. Excellence award U. No. Colo., 1996, Faculty-Alumni U. Mo. award, 1999, Disting. Svc. award Am. Coun. Edn., 2000; named to N. Crtrl. Athletic Conf. Hall of Fame, 1991. Mem. Am. Polit. Sci. Assn., Am. Soc. Public Adminstrn. (Ariz. exec. bd., Superior Svc. award 1981), Am. Acad. Polit. and Social Sci., Coll. Student Pers. Inst. (acad. coun. 1969-73), Assn. Pub. Coll. and Univ. Pres. (pres. 1985-87), Assn. Pub. Coll. and Univ. Pres. (pres. 1985-87), Nat. Assn. Student Pers. Adminstrs. (regional coun. 1974-79), Am. Assn. State Colls. and Univs. (chmn. coun. on doctoral granting instns., Meritorious Svc. award 1991), Columbia Club (Indpls.), Newcomen Soc., Phi Kappa Phi. United Methodist (pres. bd. trustees 1974). Lodges: Kiwanis (pres. 1975-76); Rotary. E-mail: rdickeso@luminafoundation.org.

DICKEY, L. ROBERT, state senator; b. Ponca, Nebr., Sept. 5, 1939; m. Mary Sellwock, Aug. 6, 1965; children: Julie, Jim, June. Cert. in gen. agr., U. Nebr., 1960. Farmer; state senator Nebr. Legislature, Lincoln, 1999—. Mem. Gov. Mike Johanns' Adv. Cabinet on Agr., U.S. Rep. Doug Bereuter's Agrl. Adv. Com., Nebr. Farm Bur., Nebr. Pork Prodrs., Ag Builders Nebr., Ag Coun. Am.; past chmn. congregation Evang. Free Ch.; former mem. utilization and mktg. bd. Nebr. Corn Devel.; former mem. Nebr. Arbor Day Found.; mem. Laurel-Concord Sch. Bd., 1988-93; dir., chmn. Farm Credit Bank Bd., Omaha, 1983; leader 4-H, 1984-94. With U.S. Army, 1961-62. Mem. Am. Legion. Home: 87081 Hwy 20 Laurel NE 68745-1965 Office: State Capitol Dist 18 PO Box 94604 Rm 1115 Lincoln NE 68509

DICKINSON, MAE, state legislator; b. Feb. 8, 1933; Student, Ind. U., Martin Coll., Ivy Tech. Coll. Retired quality inspector GM; rep. Dist. 95 Ind. Ho. of Reps., 1992—, mem. elections and apportionment, cities and towns com., mem. families, children and human affairs, pub. safety coms., vice chmn. labor and employment com. Precinct committeewoman; del. Dem. Nat. Conv.; ward chmn. Named Breakthrough woman in Area of Polit. Coalition of 100 Black Women. Mem. NAACP, Urban League, United Auto Workers, A. Philip Randolph Inst. (Pres.'s award 1990), Flamingo Social and Charity Club, Coalition of Black Trade Unionists. Home: 5455 N Arlington Ave Indianapolis IN 46226-1607 Office: Ind Ho of Reps State Capitol Indianapolis IN 46204

DICKINSON, WILLIAM BOYD, JR. editorial consultant; b. Kansas City, Mo., Feb. 21, 1931; s. William Boyd and Aileen (Robinson) D.; m. Betty Ann Landree, Feb. 1, 1953; children: William Boyd IV, David Alan. A.B., U. Kans., 1953; student, George Washington U. Law Sch., 1957-58. With U.P.I., 1955-59, mem. staff overnight desk, 1957-59; staff writer Editorial Research Reports, 1959-66, editor, 1966-73; editor, v.p. Congl. Quar., Inc., 1972-73; gen. mgr., editorial dir. Washington Post Writers Group, 1973-91; cons., 1991-96, Biocentric Inst., 1991—. Resident profl. Journalism Sch. U. Kans., 1993-99; manship chair Journalism Sch. La. State U., 1999—; Winston Churchill Traveling fellow, summer 1968. Supervisory editor: Congl. Quar.'s Complete Guide to Congress. Served with AUS, 1953-55. Press fellowship Knight Internat., 1998. Mem. William Allen White Found. (trustee), Alpha Tau Omega, Omicron Delta Kappa. (Washington). Home and Office: 1617 Alvamar Dr Lawrence KS 66047-1715 also: LSU 221B Journalism Bldg Baton Rouge LA 70803-0001 E-mail: wdicki2@lsu.edu.

DICKOW, JAMES FRED, management consultant; b. Chgo., Mar. 27, 1943; s. Fred H. and Margaret I. (Arnold) D.; m. Yvonne A. Zabilka, Aug. 20, 1966; children: Michael J., Christine Y. BSME, Purdue U., 1965, MSME, 1967. Cert. mgmt. cons. Mech. engr. CPC Internat., Argo, Ill., 1965-66; engr. dynamics McDonnell-Douglas Corp., St. Louis, 1967-70; cons. Drake Sheahan/Steward Dougal, Chgo., 1970-71; dir. distbn. planning Will Ross Div. G.D. Searle, Milw., 1971-80; dir. distbn. Gentec Healthcare, 1980-82, R&J Med. Supply, Milw., 1982-83; exec. v.p., ptnr. Kowaski-Dickow Assoc. Inc., Mequon, Wis., 1983—. Mem. Coun. Logistics Mgmt. (pres. Milw. roundtable 1978-79), Phi Kappa Theta (bd. dirs., nat. pres., pres. Ind. alumni 1980—). Home: 10011 N Miller Ct Thiensville WI 53092-6180

DICKSON, BRENT E(LLIS), state supreme court justice; b. July 18, 1941; m. Jan Aikman, June 8, 1963; children: Andrew, Kyle, Reed. BA, Purdue U., 1964; JD, Ind. U., Indpls., 1968; LittD, Purdue U., 1996. Bar: Ind. 1968, U.S. Ct. Appeals (7th cir.) 1972, U.S. Supreme Ct. 1975; cert. civil trial adv., NBTA. Pvt. practice, Lafayette, Ind., 1968-85; sr. ptnr. Dickson, Reiling, Teder & Withered, 1977-85; assoc. justice Ind. Supreme Ct., Indpls., 1986—. Adj. prof. Sch. of Law Ind. U., 1992-98. Past pres. Tippecanoe County Hist. Assn.; mem. dean's adv. coun. Sch. Liberal Arts Purdue U., 1990-94; mem. adv. bd. Heartland Film Festival, 1995—. Mem. Am. Inns Ct. (founding pres. Sagamore chpt.), Am. Law Inst. Office: Ind Supreme Ct 306 Statehouse Indianapolis IN 46204-2213*

DICKSON, EDGAR ROLLAND, gastroenterologist; b. Hackensack, N.J., June 10, 1933; MD, Ohio State U., 1959. Diplomate Am. Bd. Internal Medicine, Am. Bd. Gastroenterology. Intern Ohio State U. Hosp., Columbus, 1959-60; resident in internal medicine Mayo Clinic, Rochester, N.Y., 1960-63; asst. prof. medicine Mayo Med. Sch., 1973-77, assoc. prof., 1977-80, prof., 1980—, Mary Lowell Leary prof. medicine, 1992—; dir. devel. Mayo Found. Edn. and Rsch., 1994—. Mem. staff St. Mary's Hosp., Meth. Hosp.; mem. digestive disease adv. bd. NIH. Chair bd. dirs. Am. Liver Found., 1988-90. Fellow ACP; mem. Am. Gastroenterol. Assn., Am. Assn. Study of Liver Diseases (mem. fiscal audit com. 1991-94, ad hoc clinic com. 1992-96, chair fiscal com. 1994-97, mem. subcom. health care policy 1996—, abstract selection com.), Am. Fedn. Clin. Rsch., Internat. Assn. Study of the Liver, Sigma Xi. Office: Mayo Clinic 200 1st St SW Rochester MN 55905-0002

DICKSTEIN, BETH J. lawyer, accountant; BS with highest honors, U. Ill., 1985; JD cum laude, U. Pa., 1988. Bar: Ill. 1988; CPA, Ill. Ptnr. Sidley & Austin, Chgo. Office: Sidley & Austin 1 S First National Plz Chicago IL 60603-2000 Fax: 312-853-7036.

DI COSIMO, JOANNE VIOLET, museum director; b. Winnipegosis, Man., Can., Feb. 2, 1953; d. Bui Oscar and Lois Dawn (Tomes) Fredrickson. BA (Hons.), U. Winnipeg, 1974; MPA, Harvard U., 1995. Program coord. Can. studies Dept. Edn., Man., 1974-78; sch. program officer Man. Mus. of Man and Nature, Winnipeg, 1978-81, head edn., 1981-84, chief pub. programs, 1984-86, dir. programs, planning and evaluation, 1986-88, exec. dir., 1988—. Contbr. articles to profl. jours. Bd. pres. West End Cultural Ctr., Winnipeg, 1987-90; bd. dirs. Can. Learning Materials Ctr., Halifax, N.S., 1986-92. Mem. Can. Mus.'s Assn. (councillor/sec.-treas. 1988-90), Internat. Coun. Mus.'s, Assn. Man. Mus.'s. Avocations: reading, music. Office: Manitoba Mus of Man & Nature 190 Rupert Ave Winnipeg MB Canada R3B 0N2

DICUS, JOHN CARMACK, savings bank executive; b. Hutchinson, Kans., May 16, 1933; s. George Byron and Desda (Carmack) D.; m. Barbara Elizabeth Bubb, Feb. 4, 1956; children: Debra Elizabeth Kennedy, John Bubb. BS, U. Kans., 1955; HDL (hon.), Washburn U., 2000. With Capitol Fed. Savs. Bank, Topeka, 1959—, exec. v.p., 1963-69, pres., 1969—, chmn., 1989—. Bd. dirs. Columbian Nat. Title Co., Topeka, Security Benefit Life Ins. Co., Topeka, Western Resources Inc., Topeka; treas. Scottish Rite Bodies Valley of Topeka; mem. Fed. Savs. and Loan Adv. Coun., 1973; mem. Fed. Res. Bd. Thrift Instns. Adv. Coun., 1986-87. Chmn. Shawnee County chpt. ARC, 1965; treas. Jayhawk area coun. Boy Scouts Am., 1967-68; pres. Topeka United Way, 1972-73; trustee Stormont-Vail Healthcare Inc., chmn. 1991-92; chmn. Menninger Fund; trustee Menninger Found.; vice chmn. Kans. U. Endowment Assn.; past pres. Native Sons of Kans. Lt. (j.g.) USN, 1956-59. Recipient Fred Ellsworth medallion U. Kans., 1990, Disting. Alumnus award U. Kans. Bus. Sch., 1998; Paul Harris fellow, 1992. Mem. Am.'s Comty. Bankers (past exec. com., past dir.), Heartland Comty. Bankers Assn. (pres. 1974-75), Topeka C. of C. (dir. 1962, v.p. 1965-66, 71, pres. 1978, pres. Indsl. Devel. Corp.), U. Kans. Alumni Assn. (nat. pres. 1987-88), Masons (33 degree), Kans. C. of C. and Industry (past dir.), Shriners (potentate Arab Temple 1975), Jesters, Rotary (past dir.), Topeka Country Club (dir., pres. 1972). Episcopalian (sr. warden, vestryman). Office: Capitol Fed Savings Bank 700 S Kansas Ave Topeka KS 66603-3894

DIDONATO, GREGORY L. state legislator; b. Dennison, Ohio, May 22, 1961; Student, Kent State U. Mayor City of Dennison, 1984-90; mem. Ohio Ho. Reps., 1991-94, Ohio Senate from 30th dist., Columbus, 1997—. Mem. Tuscarawas County C. of C., Twin City C. of C., Rotary. Democrat. Office: Senate Bldg Rm 48, Ground Fl Columbus OH 43215

DIEBOLT, JUDITH, newspaper editor; b. Atchison, Kans., Oct. 6, 1948; d. George Edward and Mary Lou (Hill) D.; m. John C. Aldrich, Oct. 25, 1985. BSJ, U. Kans., 1970. Reporter Detroit Free Press, 1970-80, columnist, 1980-82, asst. city editor, 1982-85; reporter Detroit News, 1986-88, asst city editor, 1988-89, suburban editor, 1989-91; mng. editor Burlington (Vt.) Free Press, 1991-94; city editor Detroit News, 1994-98. Recipient Pub. Svc. award AP, 1978. Mem. AP Mng. Editors, Detroit Press Club (bd. govs., 1990-91), Univ. Club Detroit. Roman Catholic. Office: The Detroit News 615 W Lafayette Blvd Detroit MI 48226-3197

DIEDERICHS, JANET WOOD, public relations executive; b. Libertyville, Ill. d. J. Howard and Ruth (Hendrickson) Wood; m. John Kuensting Diedrichs, 1953. BA, Wellesley Coll, 1950. Sales agt. Pan Am. Airways, Chgo., 1951-52; regional mgr. pub. relations Braniff Internat., 1953-69; pres. Janet Diederichs & Assocs., Inc.; pub. rels. cons. Chgo., 1970—. Lectr. Harvard U.; mem. exec. com. World Trade Conf., 1983, 84. Com. mem. Nat. Trust for Historic Preservation, 1975-79, Marshall Scholars (Brit. Govt.), 1975-79; trustee Sherwood Conservatory Music, 2000—, Northwestern Meml. Hosp., 1985—, mem. exec. com., 1995-2000; trustee Fourth Presbyn. Ch., mem. bd. dirs. 1990-93; bd. dirs., mem. exec. com. Chgo. Conv. and Visitors Bur. 1978-87; bd. dirs. Internat. House, U. Chgo., 1978-84; bd. dirs., founder Com. of 200, 1982—; bd. dirs. Latino Inst., 1986-89, Chgo. Network, Albert Pick Jr. Found.; founders coun. Field Mus., 1999—; com. mem. Art Inst. Chgo., 1980-83; mem. exec. com. Vatican Art Coun. Chgo., 1981-83; pres. Jr. League Chgo., 1968-69. Mem. Chgo. Assn. Commerce and Industry (bd. dirs. 1982-89, exec. com. 1985-88), Internat. Women's Forum, Pub. Rels. Soc. Am., Pub. Rels. Exch. Internat. (founder), Publicity Club Chgo., Chgo. Network, Econ. Club, Woman's Athletic Club of Chgo., Comml. Club of Chgo., The Casino Club (Chgo.), The River Club (N.Y.), The Exec. Svc. Corps. (mem. adv. com. 1993-97), Chgo. Club. Office: Diederichs & Assocs 333 N Michigan Ave Ste 1205 Chicago IL 60601-4002

DIEDTRICH, ELMER, state legislator; b. Glenross, S.D., Mar. 31, 1927; m. Deloris Diedtrich; children: Dehain, Melanie. BS, No. State U., 1956. Territory sales Std. Oil Co. Ind., 1952-54; pres., owner ins. co./ins. brokerage, 1956-2000; mem. S.D. Ho. Reps., Pierre, 1989-2000, S.D. Senate from 3d dist., Pierre, 2001—. Petty officer USN, 1945-47. Mem. Eagles, Elks, Moose, Shriners. Republican. Lutheran. Office: 819 E Broadway Apt B2 Pierre SD 57501 E-mail: eandd@nvc.net.

DIEFENBACH, VIRON LEROY, dental, public health educator, university dean; b. Balt., Feb. 9, 1922; s. William Louis and Ardie Gertrude (Von Wachter) D.; m. Virginia Kent, Dec, 3, 1944 (div. Jan. 1956); children: Kathryn Louise, Arthur Karl; mem. Adele Larson Henderson, Apr. 18, 1956; children: William Henderson, Sue Henderson. Student, Western Md. Coll., 1940-42, Pratt Inst. Engring., 1943, Harvard U., 1944; DDS, U. Md., 1949; MPH, U. Pitts., 1954. Diplomate Am. Bd. Dental Pub. Health. Dental intern USPHS Hosp., Norfolk, Va., 1949-50, various clin. assignments, 1950-52, dental pub. health field tng., 1954-55; asst. regional dental cons. USPHS, Chgo., Office Personnel, Office Surgeon Gen., USPHS, Washington, 1955-56; information dir. USPHS Dental Public Health, 1957-59; regional dental cons. USPHS, Denver, 1959-61; dep. chief div. USPHS (Dental Health), Bethesda, Md., 1962-65, acting chief and dir., 1966; asst. surgeon gen. USPHS, 1966-70; asst. exec. dir. Am. Dental Assn., 1970-72; prof. health resources mgmt. Grad. Sch. Public Health, U. Ill., 1973-88, prof. emeritus, 1988—, assoc. dean, 1977, dean, 1978-83. With AUS, 1942-44; USPHS, 1949-70. Recipient Scholarship Gold medal U. Md., 1949, Meritorious Service medal USPHS, 1966; Disting. Dental Alumnus award Balt. Coll. Dental Surgery, U. Md., 1999. Fellow APHA (past sect. chmn., sec., John W. Knutson award 1999), AAAS, Am. Coll. Dentists; mem. Commd. Officers Assn. USPHS (mem. exec. bd., past chmn. bd.), ADA, Am. Assn. Pub. Health Dentists, Fedn. Dentaire Internationale. Achievements include early scientific studies on use of fluorides in preventive dentistry, innovations in dental education and feasibility of dental care insurance. Office: U Ill at Chgo Grad Sch Pub Health Chicago IL 60612 Home: 3122 Gracefield Rd Apt 311 Silver Spring MD 20904-5804

DIEHL, ANN, radio personality; m. Bob Diehl; 2 children. Adminstrv. asst. Family Life Radio WUGN, Midland, Mich., 1990—96, sports reader, 1996—2001, radio personality, 1997—, cohost Morning Show, 2001—. Office: WUGN 510 E Isabella Rd Midland MI 48640

DIEHL, JAMES HARVEY, church administrator; m. Dorothy Diehl; 4 children. BA, Olivet Nazarene U., 1959; DD, N.W. Nazarene U., 1990. Adminstr. MidAm. Nazarene U., 1973-76; dist. supt. Ch. of Nazarene, Nebr. and Colo., 1979-89; pastor Atlanta First Ch., 1976-79, Nazarene chs. in Iowa, Denver First Ch. of Nazarene, 1989-93; gen. supt. Ch. of the Nazarene, Kansas City, Mo., 1993—. Contbr. articles to Herald of Holiness, Preacher's Mag., Bread, World Mission, others; condr. daily radio program, weekly TV broadcast. Bd. trustees MidAm. Nazarene U., Nazarene Theol. Sem., Nazarene Bible Coll., N.W. Nazarene U.; chmn. bd. N.W. Nazarene U. Office: Ch of the Nazarene 6401 Paseo Blvd Kansas City MO 64131-1213

DIEKEMA, ANTHONY J. college president emeritus, educational consultant; b. Borculo, Mich., Dec. 3, 1933; m. Jeane Waanders, Dec. 20, 1957; children: Douglas, David, Daniel, Paul, Mark, Maria, Tanya. BA, Calvin Coll., Grand Rapids, Mich., 1956; MA in Sociology and Anthropology, Mich. State U., 1958, PhD in Sociology, 1965. Field interviewer Bur. Bus. Research Mich. State U., East Lansing, 1955-56, asst. dir. housing, 1957-59, instr., lectr. sociology and anthropology, 1959-64, admissions counselor, 1959-61, asst. dir. admissions and scholarships, 1961-62, asst. registrar, 1962-64; asst. dean admissions and records, research assoc. in med. edn. and asst. prof. sociology U. Ill. Med. Center, Chgo., 1964-66, dir. admissions and records, asst. prof. sociology and edn., 1966-70, asso. chancellor, asso. prof. med. edn., 1970-76; pres. Calvin Coll., 1976-96, pres. emeritus. Mem. adv. bd. NBD Grand Rapids, 1983-95 Trustee Blodgett Meml. Med. Center, Grand Rapids, 1979-91; bd. dirs. Met. YMCA, 1979-93, Project Rehab, 1978-84; treas. Back-to-God Hour Radio Com., 1970-76; chmn. Synodical Com. on Race Relations, 1973-75; pres. Strategic Christian Ministry Found., 1969-73; mem. bd. curators Trinity Christian Coll., 1969-73, chmn., 1972-73, mem. presdl. search com., 1972-73, NCAA coun. 1983-87, Pres'. commn. 1987-91. Mem. Am. Assn. Pres.'s Ind. Coll. and Univs. (bd. dirs. 1978-84, 88-91), Nat. Assn. Ind. Colls. and Univs. (bd. dirs. 1991-94), Assn. Ind. Colls. and Univs. Mich. (exec. com. 1979-84), Am. Assn. Higher Edn., Am. Sociol. Assn., Soc. Health and Human Values, Soc. Values in Higher Edn., Nat. League Nursing (accreditation com. 1974-79), Alpha Kappa Delta, Rotary. Office: Calvin Coll Grand Rapids MI 49546 E-mail: ajdiek@aol.com.

DIERBERG, JAMES F. bank executive; BS, BA, Univ. Mo.; JD, Univ. Wash. Chmn., CEO First Bank, Inc., Clayton, Mo., 1995—. Office: 135 N Meramec Ave Clayton MO 63105-3751

DIERCKS, EILEEN KAY, educational media coordinator, elementary school educator; b. Lima, Ohio, Oct. 31, 1944; d. Robert Wehner and Florence (Huckemeyer) McCarty; m. Dwight Richard Diercks, Dec. 27, 1969; children: Roger, David, Laura. BS in Edn., Bluffton Coll., 1966; MS, U. Ill., 1968. Tchr. elem. grades Kettering City Schs., Ohio, 1966-67; children's libr. St. Charles County, Mo., 1968-69; libr. Rantoul (Ill.) H.S., 1970-71; elem. tchr. Elmhurst (Ill.) Sch. Dist., 1971-72; media coord. Plainfield (Ill.) Sch. Dist., 1980—2001. Evaluator Rebecca Caudill Young Readers' Book Award, 1990-97. Founder, treas. FISH orgn., Plainfield, 1975-78; pres. Ch. Women United, 1974; sec. Plainfield Cmty. TV Access League, 1987-89; treas. Plainfield Congl. Ch., 1983-88; bd. dirs. Cub Scouts, 1983-86; leader, mem. Girl Scouts USA, Plainfield, 1985—; mem. Bolingbrook (Ill.) Cmty. Chorus, 1986-90, Plainfield Area Cmty. Chorus, 1999—. Mo. State Libr. scholar, 1967, Naperville chpt. Valparaiso U. Guild, treas., 1993-95. Mem.: ALA, Am. Assn. Sch. Librs., Ill. Sch. Libr. Media Assn. (membership chmn. 1992—93, mem. awards com. 1994—96, disaster relief chmn. 1996—97, treas. 2001—), Plainfield Assn. Tchrs., Plainfield Athletic Club, Rotary (treas. 1994—95, bd. dirs. 1994—, v.p. 1995—96, pres.-elect 1996—97, pres. 1997—98, Plainfield chpt.), Beta Phi Mu, Pi Delta, Delta Kappa Gamma (Beta Rho) (treas. 1993—97). Home: 13440 S Rivercrest Dr Plainfield IL 60544-8979 Office: Plainfield Sch Dist # 202 611 Fort Beggs Dr Plainfield IL 60544-1877

DIERKS, MERTON L. state legislator; b. July 2, 1942; m. Gloria L. Zoeller, Dec. 27, 1959; children: john Martin, Thomas Lyle, Christopher Joseph, Mary Sephanie. , U. Nebr., 1954; DVM, Kansas State U., 1961. Veterinarian; rancher; mem. Nebr. Legislature from 40th dist., Lincoln, 1986—. Mem. Nebraska Vet. Medical Assn. (pres.). Mem. Am. Legion, Knights Columbus, Weing Pub. Sch. Bd. Edn. Roman Catholic. Office: State Capitol (Dist 40) Room 1019 PO Box 96404 Lincoln NE 68509-4604

DIERKS, MERTON LYLE, veterinarian; b. Ewing, Nebr., July 2, 1932; s. Lyle P. and Alys G. (Sanders) D.; m. Gloria Lee Zoeller, Dec. 27, 1958; children: Jon Martin, Thomas Lyle, Christopher Joseph, M. Stephanie. BS in Agriculture, U. Nebr., 1954; DVM, Kans. State U., 1961. Pvt. practice, Ewing, 1961-73; ptnr. practice O'Neill, Nebr., 1973-92; mem. 40th dist. Nebr. Legislature, Lincoln, 1986—; chmn. com. on agr. Nebr. Legislature, 1993—. Bd. dirs. St. Anthony's Hosp. Pres. Bd. Edn., Ewing, 1970-84. Lt. USAF, 1954-56. Recipient Outstanding Grassland Conservation award Nebr. Assn. Resource Dists., 1987, 96. Mem. Nebr. Vet. Med. Assn. (Nebr. Veterinarian of Yr 1986, pres. 1983), AVMA, U.S. Animal Health Assn., Comml. Club (pres. 1962-63). Democrat. Roman Catholic. Avocations: flying. Home: RR ! Box 131 Ewing NE 68735-0038 Office: State Legislature State Capital Lincoln NE 68516

DIESCH, STANLEY LA VERNE, veterinarian, educator; b. Blooming Prairie, Minn., May 16, 1925; s. John Herman and Emma Lillian (Erickson) D.; m. Darlene Ardis Witty; July 22, 1956; children: Lauren, Stephanie. BS, U. Minn., 1951, DVM, 1956, MPH, 1963. Diplomate Am. Coll. Vet. Preventive Medicine and Epidemiology. Asst. prof. Coll. Vet. Med., U. Iowa, Iowa City, 1963-66; asst. prof. U. Minn. Coll. Vet. Medicine, St. Paul, 1966-69, assoc. prof., 1969-73, prof., 1973-95, prof. emeritus, 1995—, dir. internat. programs, 1985-98; prof. Sch. Pub. Health, U. Minn., Mpls., 1973-95. Advisor Pan Am. Health Orgn., Washington, 1971— Contbr. more than 100 articles to profl. jours., 4 chapters to books. Mem. East Buchanan County Sch. Bd., Winthrop, Iowa, 1960; Rep. del., Minn., 1970-85; co-chair nat. Outdoor Speedskating, St. Paul, 1973; dir. CENSHARE, Mpls., 1981-82; chmn. Veterinarians for Re-election of Durenberger, Minn., 1982, 88; bd. dirs. Minn.-Uruguay Ptnrs. Ams., 1981—, pres., 1990-94, chmn. bd., 1995-99; hon. consul of Uruguay in Minn., 1991-96. Recipient Am. Express award Nat. Assn. Ptnrs. Ams., 1984, Internat. Castricone U. Linkage award Nat. Assn. Ptnrs. Ams., 1998; WHO travel fellow, 1974; grantee EPA, 1968-71, USDA, 1978. Mem. AVMA (Pub. Svc. award 1987, Internat. Vet. Congress award 1998), APHA (coun. 1971-84), U.S. Animal Health Assn. (com. chair, Appreciation award 1986), Internat. Soc. Animal Hygiene (exec. bd. 1988-2000, pres. 1991-94, Internat. soc. for Animal Hygiene Hon. award 2000), Minn. Vet. Medicine Assn. (com. chair 1970-75, Disting. Svc. award 1996). Lutheran. Avocations: fishing, hunting, boating. Home and Office: 743 Heinel Dr Saint Paul MN 55113-2152 E-mail: diesc001@tc.umn.edu.

DIETCH, HENRY XERXES, judge; b. Bklyn., Nov. 13, 1913; s. Isadore J. and Mary (Krieg) D.; m. Shirley Friedman, Jan. 11, 1941; children: William A., Nancie I., James T. AA, Crane Coll., 1933; JD, John Marshall Law Sch., 1937; grad., Nat. Jud. Coll. Bar: Ill. 1937. Ptnr. Davis, Dietch & Ryan, Chgo., 1954-77; assoc. judge Circuit Ct. Cook County, 1977-84; ret., 1984. Hearing officer Dept. of Labor, Chgo., 1937-46; v.p., dir. Unity Savs. of Park Forest, Ill., to 1977, arbitrator, mediator, 1987—. Columnist: Judiciously Speaking, 1979—; Contbr. articles to profl. jours. Mayor City of Park Forest, 1949-55, corp. counsel, 1958-77, vice chmn. Chgo. adv. bd., Salvation Army, 1969-89, hon. bd. dirs. 1989—. Lt. USAAC, 1942-45, ETO. Recipient Citation of Merit John Marshall Law Sch., 1972. Mem. ABA, Ill. Bar Assn., Chgo. Bar Assn., Am. Judicature Soc., Nat. Inst. Mcpl. Law Officers, Rotary, B'nai B'rith. Clubs: Rotary, B'nai B'rith. Office: 18161 Morris Ave Homewood IL 60430-2108 Fax: 708-799-8805.

DIETER, RAYMOND ANDREW, JR. physician, surgeon; b. Chebanse, Ill., June 19, 1934; s. Raymond Augustus Sr. and Emma Rose Mayme (Witt) D.; m. Bette René Myers, Sept. 29, 1961; children: Raymond III, David, Lisa, Lynn, Deanna, Robert. Student, U. Ill., 1952-56, Olivet Nazarene Coll., 1954; MA in Physiology, U. Ill., 1966, BS in Chemistry, 1994; MD, Loyola U., 1960. Diplomate Am. Bd. Thoracic Surgery, Am. Bd. Surgery. Intern Cook County Hosp., Chgo., 1960-61; resident in gen. surgery VA Hosp., Hines, Ill., 1963-67, sr. resident in cardiopulmonary surgery, 1967-69; practice specializing in thoracic, cardiovascular surg. Glen Ellyn (Ill.) Clinic, 1969—, pres., 1982-85, also bd. dirs.; mem. staff Hines (Ill.) VA Hosp., 1963-74, Cen. DuPage Hosp., Winfield, Ill., 1969—, pres. staff, 1987-89; mem. staff Loyola U. Med. Ctr., Maywood, 1969-80, Meml. Hosp. DuPage County, Elmhurst, 1969—, Delnor Hosp., St. Charles, 1970-79, Community Hosp., Geneva, 1970—, Alexian Bros. Med. Ctr., Elk Grove Village, 1975-79, 93—, Good Samaritan Hosp., Downers Grove, 1976—, pres. staff, 1979; mem. staff Glendale Heights (Ill.) and Glen Oaks Cmty. Hosp., 1980—, St. Mary's Hosp., Streator, Ill., 1997—. Clin. instr. Stritch Sch. Medicine Loyola U., 1966-71, clin. asst. prof., 1971-80; trustee Ctr. Bank, Glen Ellyn, 1978-90, Lake Shore Bank, Glen Ellyn Found.; internat. lectr. on med. topics; chmn. Glen Ellyn Clinic Facilities, 1987-98, Physicians Benefit trust, 1988-92; pres., chmn. bd. No. Ill. Surg. Ctr., 1989—; pres. DuPage Doctors, Inc., Ctr. for Surgery; bd. dirs., co-founder Cmty. Bank of Wheaton, Glen Ellyn, 1993—, Cmty. Bank Wheaton-Glen Ellyn, 1998; co-founder, pres. Northeast DuPage Surgicenter, 1997—; chmn. bd. dirs., CEO Masterile, Inc., 1997-99; mem., chmn. negotiating com. Glen Ellyn Clinic, 1999. Author: (with B.R. Dieter and A.C. Mickelson) Mickelson and Peterson Family Sketch, 1970, (with M.C. Sorensen and E.R. Dieter) A Sorensen and Jensen Family Tree, 1975, (with B.R. Dieter, C. Myers, U. Myers, and D. Dieter) A Myers and Remley Family Tree, 1978, (with others) A Witt and (von) Ruehle Family Sketch, 1976, A Hofeling, Janssen, Lehnert, and Meier Family Sketch, 1979, A Dieter Family Tree: Sketches of German Families, 1981, Thoracoscopy for Surgeons, 1994; editor: Thoracoscopy for Surgeons-Diagnostic and Therapeutic, 1995; contbr. numerous articles to profl. jours. and chpts. in med. book. Mgr. Glen Ellyn baseball team, 1970, 71, 78-82; asst. leader 4-H Club, 1975-83; mem. Glenbard South High Sch. Boosters, World Fedn. Drs. Who Respect Human Life, 1980—; pres., bd. dirs. DuPage Med. Found. Served with USPHS, 1961-63, with R es. 1982—. Fellow ACS, Internat. Coll. Angiology (editl. bd. 1995—), Internat. Coll. Surgeons (exec. com. 1991—, treas. 1993-94, pres. elect 1995-96, pres. 1997-98, U.S. sect., corp. sec. 1997-2000, pres.-elect 2001-02, World body); mem. AMA (Physician's Recognition awards, mem. ho. dels.), Internat. Mus. Surg. Sci. (chmn. bd. dirs. 1991—), Internat. Soc. Circumpolar Health, Internat. Soc. Outdoor Health, Am. Coll. Angiology, Am. Coll. Chest Physicians, Assn. Acad. Surgeons, Am. Soc. Circumpolar Health (charter), Assn. Mil. Surgeons, Assn. Res. Officers, Am. Heart Assn. (coun. 1974—), Nat. Assn. Interns and Residents, Soc. Med. Hist. Chgo., Soc. Critical Care Medicine, Soc. Thoracic Surgeons (membership com.), Ill. State Med. Soc. (trustee 1983-92, chmn. Ill. hosp. med. staff sect. 1985-87, pres., med. adminstrs. ctr. for surgery 1994—), Ill. Thoracic Surg. Soc. (sec. 1981-83, pres. 1984-85), DuPage County Med. Soc. (pres. 1977, mem. numerous coms.), Chgo. Med. Soc., Charles B. Puestow Surg. Soc. (sec., treas. 1966-67, v.p. 1968), Good Samaritan Soc., Ala. Geographic Soc., Kankakee Valley Geneal. Soc., Ill. Geneal. Soc., U. Ill. Alumni Assn., Am. Rabbit Breeders Assn., Silver Marten Club. Republican. Roman Catholic. Club: Century (Elmhurst). Lodge: Lions (charter). Avocations: Alaska, large game animals, outdoor health, farming, fishing. Home: 22w240 Stanton Rd Glen Ellyn IL 60137-7111 Office: Glen Ellyn Clinic 454 Pennsylvania Ave Glen Ellyn IL 60137-4496 Fax: (630) 858-4575. E-mail: brdrad@aol.com.

DIETMEYER, DONALD LEO, retired electrical engineer, educator; b. Wausau, Wis., Nov. 20, 1932; s. Henry Joseph and Erna M. (Zastrow) D.; m. Carol White, Jan. 26, 1957; children: Karl Peter, Elizabeth Mary, Anne Katherine, Diana Lee. BSEE, U. Wis., Madison, 1954, MS, 1955, PhD, 1959. Mem. faculty U. Wis., Madison, 1958-63, 64-98, prof. elec. and computer engring., 1967-98, prof. emeritus, 1998—, assoc. dean Coll. Engring., 1983-95. Sr. engr. IBM Corp., Poughkeepsie, N.Y., 1964 Author: Logic Design of Digital Systems, 1978, 3rd rev. edit., 1988, Conlan Report, 1983. With AUS, 1957. Recipient Western Electric Fund award, 1972 Fellow IEEE; mem. Computer Soc., Assn. Computing Machinery, Sigma Xi. Home: 2211 Waunona Way Madison WI 53713-1619 Office: 1415 Engineering Dr Madison WI 53706-1607 E-mail: dld@engr.wisc.edu.

DIETRICH, JOSEPH JACOB, retired chemist, research executive; b. Bismark, N.D., Oct. 31, 1932; s. Jacob Peter and Elizabeth (Janzer) D.; m. Florence Kolodziejczak, June 27, 1959; children: Ann Marie, Michael, John, James. BA in Chemistry, St. John's U., Collegeville, Minn., 1953; PhD in Organic Chemistry, Iowa State U., 1957. Rsch. chemist PPG, Inc., Barberton, Ohio, 1957-59, Spencer Chem. Co., Kansas City, Kans., 1960-64; with Diamond-Shamrock Corp., Cleve., 1964-82, dir. rsch., 1973-78, dir. tech. devel., 1978-82; dir. tech. Eltech Systems Corp., Painesville, Ohio, 1982-85, dir. tech. and comml. devel./ Europe, Chardon, Ohio, 1986-90; pres. Eltech Internat. Corp., 1990-94, Elgard Corp., 1994; ret., 1994. Contbr. articles to profl. jours; patentee in field. Mem. Am. Chem. Soc., Soc. Plastic Engrs., Serra Club. Republican. Roman Catholic. Home: 6958 Pennywhistle Cir Painesville OH 44077-2141

DIETRICH, RICHARD VINCENT, geologist, educator; b. LaFargeville, N.Y., Feb. 7, 1924; s. Roy Eugene and Mida Amy (Vincent) D.; m. Frances Elizabeth Smith, Dec. 28, 1946; children: Richard Smith, Kurt Robert, Krista Gayle Brown. AB, Colgate U., 1947; MS, Yale U., 1950, PhD, 1951. Geologist Iowa Geol. Survey, 1947, N.Y. State Sci. Service, summers 1949-50; asst. prof. geology Va. Poly. Inst., Blacksburg, 1951, assoc. prof., 1952-56, prof., 1956-69, mineral technologist Va. Engring. Exp. Sta., 1951-58; fulbright rsch. prof. Oslo U., Norway, 1959-60; asso. dean arts and scis. Va. Poly. Inst., 1966-69, dean, 1969; prof. geology Central Mich. U., Mt. Pleasant, 1969-86, prof. emeritus, 1986—, dean arts and scis., 1969-75. Dir. Econ. Geol. Pub. Co., 1966-72 Author or co-author over 20 sci. books and textbooks in field (transl. into German, Malaysian, Russian, and Japanese); also poems, haiku, essays, cartoons; editor Mineral Industries Jour., 1953-61; mng. editor Bull. Econ. Geology, 1966-73; exec. editor Rocks and Minerals, 1980-88, petrology adv. editor, 1988—; mem. editl. bd. Mineral Record, 1969-74; contbr. over 300 articles to profl. jours.; composer, performer music. Organizer N. Am. for Mineral. Abstracts, 1976-80. Served with U.S. Air Corps, 1943-46. Recipient Acad. Citation Mich. Acad. Sci., Arts and Letters, 1978, Children's Sci. Book award N.Y. Acad. Scis., 1981; Fulbright rsch. prof. U. Oslo, 1958-59; Pres.'s scholar, 1941-42, Austin Colgate scholar Colgate U., 1943, Newton Lloyd Andrews scholar, 1943, Colgate U. scholar, 1946; Edward S. Binney fellow, 1948-49, James Dwight Dana fellow Yale U., 1950-51. Fellow Am. Mineral. Soc. (assoc. life), Soc. Econ. Geol. (sr.); mem. Norsk Geologisk

Forening (life), Geol. Soc. Finland (life), Am. Geol. Inst. (gov. 1972-74), Assn. Earth Sci. Editors (pres. 1972-73), Phi Beta Kappa, Sigma Xi, Phi Kappa Phi, Sigma Gamma Epsilon. Presbyterian. Home: 1323 Center Dr Mount Pleasant MI 48858-4103 E-mail: dietr1rv@cmich.edu., r.v.dietrich@cmich.edu.

DIETRICH, SUZANNE CLAIRE, instructional designer, communications consultant; b. Granite City, Ill. d. Charles Daniel and Evelyn Blanche (Waters) D. BS in Speech, Northwestern U.; MS in Pub. Comm., Boston U., 1967; postgrad., So. Ill. U., 1973-83. Intern prodn. staff Sta. WGBH-TV, Boston, 1958-59; asst. dir., 1962-64; asst. dir. program invitation to art, 1958; cons. producer dir. dept. instructional tv radio Ill. Office Supt. Pub. Instrn., Springfield, 1969-70; dir. program prodn. and distbn., 1970-72; instr. faculty call staff, speech dept. Sch. Fine Arts So. Ill. U., Edwardsville, 1972-73; grad. asst. for doctoral program office of dean Sch. Edn., 1975-78; rsch. asst. Ill. pub. telecomms. study for Ill. Pub. Broadcasting Coun., 1979-80; cons., rsch. in comm., 1980—. Pub. advisor Bradly Pub., Inc., 1996. Exec. prodr., dir. tv programs Con-Con Countdown, 1970, The Flag Speaks, 1971. Mem. sch. bd. St. Mary's Cath. Sch., Edwardsville, 1991-92; cable tv adv. com. City of Edwardsville, 1994—, co-chair, 1996-98; bd. dirs. Goshen Preservation Alliance, Edwardsville, 1992-94, pres., 1995-97; dir. Madison County Hist. Mus. and Archival Libr., 1999—. Mem. Mdison County Hist. Soc. (bd. dirs. 1997-99). Roman Catholic. Home: 1011 Minnesota St Edwardsville IL 62025-1424 Office: 715 N Main St Edwardsville IL 62025-1111

DIETRICH, THOMAS W. corporate lawyer, insurance company executive; b. 1948; BA, Adrian Coll.; JD, Capital U. Bar: 1976. V.p., assoc. gen. counsel Nationwide Ins. Enterprise, Columbus, Ohio. Office: Nationwide Ins Enterprise 1 Nationwide Plz Columbus OH 43215-2239

DIETRICH, WILLIAM GALE, lawyer, real estate developer, consultant; b. Kansas City, Mo., Mar. 6, 1925; s. Roy Kaiser and Gale (Gossett) D.; m. Marjorie Nell Reich, July 14, 1945; children: Meredith G. Dietrich Steinhaus, Ann. E. Dietrich Cooling, Walter R. AB with high honors, Yale U., 1948, LLB, 1951. Bar: Mo. 1951. Ptnr. Dietrich, Davis, Dicus, Rowlands, Schmitt & Gorman (and predecessors), 1953-73; project dir., gen. counsel Blue Ridge Shopping Ctr., Inc., Kansas City, 1955-73, pres., gen. mgr., 1964-73, Blue Ridge Tower, Inc., Kansas City, 1967-73; sec.-treas. A. Reich & Sons, Inc., 1973-88, chmn., 1988—; pvt. practice law, 1973—; sec., treas. A. Reich & Sons Gardens, Inc., 1973-89; pres. J&D Devel., Inc., 1987—; gen. ptnr. J & D Enterprises, 1986—; gen. mgr. The Farm Shopping and Office Ctr., 1994-98; pres. BBJ Treats, L.L.C., 1994-98; mem. WGD Properties, LLC, 1999—. Sec., bd. dirs. Rsch. Med. Ctr., Kansas City, 1977, vice-chmn., 1980-83, chmn., 1983-87; bd. dirs. The Rsch. Found., 1980-91, vice-chmn., 1989-91; bd. dirs. Rsch. Health Svcs., 1980-81, vice chmn., 1983-87, chmn. 1987-89; bd. dirs. Mahana Condominium Assn., Maui, Hawaii, 1977-96, Blue Ridge Bank and Trust Co., Kansas City, 1982-94; vestry mem. Grace & Holy Trinity Cathedral, Kansas City, 1972-95, former treas. 1st lt. AUS, 1943-46, PTO. Mem. ABA, Mo. Bar Assn., Kansas City Bar Assn., Blue Ridge Mall Mchts. Assn. (dir. 1958-73), Internat. Coun. Shopping Ctrs. (past dir. for Mo., Kans, Iowa, cert. shopping ctr. mgr.), Lawyers Assn. Kansas City, Mission Hills Country Club, Yale Club, Kansas City (Mo.) Club, Rotary (bd. dirs., sec. found. Kansas City 1978—), Phi Beta Kappa (pres. Kansas City chpt. 1989-91), Phi Delta Phi. E-mail: Bus. Pers. Home: 1000 Huntington Rd Kansas City MO 64113-1346 Office: 6155 Oak St Profl Bldg Ste A Kansas City MO 64113-2266 E-mail: wgdlo@aol.com., wgdlooo@aol.com.

DIETZ, WILLIAM RONALD, management company executive; b. Seattle, Nov. 25, 1942; s. William Phillip and Helen Mae (Wilson) D.; m. Elizabeth R. Daoust; 1 child, David Phillip. BA, U. Wash., 1964; MBA, Stanford U., 1968. Fin. cons. 1st Nat. City Bank, N.Y.C., 1968-70; v.p., mgr. Citicorp Subs. Mgmt. Office, Citicorp, 1971-74; chmn. Citicorp Factors, Inc., 1974-75; v.p., mgr. N.Y., N.J. and Conn. comml. banking Citibank N.A., 1976-78, sr. v.p., gen. mgr. Eastern region corp. banking, 1978-81, sr. v.p., head Caribbean Basin div., 1982-84; pres. Charter Assocs. Ltd., 1985-89; chmn. and chief exec. officer CorEast Savs. Bank, Richmond, Va., 1989-91; pres., CEO Am. Savs. Bank, White Plains, N.Y., 1991-92, Mo. Bridge Bank, Kansas City, 1992-93, Anthem Fin., Inc., Indpls., 1993-96; ptnr. Concord Ptnrs., 1997—; mng. ptnr. Customer Contact solutions, LLC, 1999—; pres. W.M. Putnam Co., 2001—. Bd. dirs. Capital One Fin. Corp., Stratis Corp., Baker Hill; mem. policy com. Bank Mgmt. Inst., SUNY-Buffalo. Contbg. author: Customer-Focused Marketing of Financial Services. Trustee Children's Mus. of Indpls.; bd. advisors Ind. U./Purdue U., Indpls.; bd. trustees Indpls.-Marion County Pub. Libr. Found. Lt. USNR, 1964-66. Mem. Univ. Club (N.Y.C.), Woodstock Country Club, Delta Tau Delta. Home: 7925 Ridge Rd Indianapolis IN 46240-2539 Office: Customer Contact Solutions 135 N Pennsylvania St Ste 1400 Indianapolis IN 46204-2489 E-mail: contactsolutions@earthlink.net.

DIFEO, SAMUEL X. automotive executive; Exec. v.p. DiFeo Group United Auto Group, Inc., Detroit, 1992-98, pres., COO DiFeo Group, 1998—. Office: United Auto Group Inc Ste 36B 1340 Outer Dr West Detroit MI 48239-4001

DIFONZO, KENNETH W. financial officer; BS in Acct., U. Ill. CPA. Various fin. positions H.J. Heinz Co., 1981-91; v.p. fin. and controller internat. divsn. ConAgra, Inc., Omaha, 1991-94, v.p., corp. controller to sr. v.p. profit improvement, 1994-2000, sr. fin. officer, 2000—. Office: ConAgra Inc One ConAgra Dr Omaha NE 68102-5001

DIGANGI, AL, marketing executive; V.p. mktg. Montgomery Ward & Co., Chgo., exec. v.p. Elec. Ave. and Auto Express, 1997—. Office: Montgomery Ward & Co Montgomery Ward Plz 535 W Chicago Ave Chicago IL 60610-2430

DIGANGI, FRANK EDWARD, academic administrator; b. West Rutland, Vt., Sept. 29, 1917; s. Leonard and Mary Grace (Zafonti) DiG.; m. Genevieve Frances Colignon, June 27, 1946; children— Ellen (Mrs. Philo David Hall), Janet (Mrs. W. Dale Greenwood). B.S. in Pharmacy, Rutgers U., 1940; M.S., Western Res. U., 1942; Ph.D., U. Minn., 1948. Asst. prof. U. Minn. Coll. Pharmacy, 1948-52, asso. prof., 1952-57, prof. medicinal chemistry, 1957—, also asso. dean adminstrv. affairs. Author: Quantitative Pharmaceutical Analysis, 7th edit, 1977; Contbr. articles to pharm. jours. Served with USNR, 1943-46, PTO. Recipient Alumni Assn. Disting. Pharmacist award, 1977, Faculty Recognition award Coll. of Pharmacy Alumni Soc., 1981, Lawrence and Delores M. Weaver medal, 1997. Mem. Am. Pharm. Assn., Minn. Pharm. Assn. (pres. 1971, chmn. bd. 1972-73, Pharmacist of Yr. award 1972, Harold R. Popp Meml. award 1979, hon. mem. 1994), Mpls. Soc. Profl. Pharmacists (hon.), AAUP, Am. Chem. Soc., Am. Assn. Colls. Pharmacy, Sigma Xi, Phi Beta Phi, Phi Lambda Upsilon Rho Chi. Clubs: University Campus (Mpls.), University Faculty Golf (Mpls.), Gown-in-Town (Mpls.). Home: 1666 Coffman St Apt 234 Saint Paul MN 55108-1343 Office: Univ Minn Coll of Pharmacy Minneapolis MN 55455

DIGESO, AMY, mail order company executive; BS in Behavioral Sci., Pa. State U., 1974; MBA in Internat. Mgmt., Fordham U., 1982. Former mgmt. positions Am. Express, Estee Lauder, Banker's Trust; various positions including CEO Mary Kay, 1991-98; pres. Popular Club Plan Fingerhut Cos. Inc., Minnetonka, Minn., 1999—. Office: Fingerhut Cos Inc 4400 Baker Rd Minnetonka MN 55343-8684

DIGGS, MATTHEW O'BRIEN, JR. air conditioning and refrigeration manufacturing executive; b. Louisville, Jan. 11, 1933; s. Matthew O'Brien and Dorothy (Leary) D.; m. Nancy Carolyn Brown, Nov. 5, 1955; children: Elizabeth, Joan, Judith, Matthew III. Student, Hanover Coll., 1950-52; BSME, Purdue U., 1955; MBA, Harvard U., 1961. With Lincoln Electric, Cleve., 1957-59, Toledo Scale Corp., 1961-63; cons., assoc., v.p., then v.p. and mng. officer East Cen. Region Booz, Allen & Hamilton, Inc., Cleve., 1963-72; v.p. mktg. Copeland Corp., Sidney, Ohio, 1972-74, exec. v.p., 1974, pres., chief exec. officer, 1975-87, vice chmn., 1987-90; CEO The Diggs Group McClintock Ind., Dayton, 1990—. Bd. dirs. Helix Tech. Corp., Dayton Superior Corp., Ripplewood Holdings L.L.C. Cmty. bd. trustees Wright State U., 1995—; chmn. adv. bd. Herrick Labs. Perdue U., 1980—; former sr. warden St. Paul's Episcopal Ch. 1st lt. U.S. Army, 1955-57. Home: 1160 Lytle Ln Dayton OH 45409-2112 Office: 1630 Kettering Tower Dayton OH 45423-1005

DIGIROLAMO, VINCENT A. retired banking services executive; Vice-chmn. Nat. City Corp., Cleve., 1995-2001; ret. Office: 1900 E 9th St Cleveland OH 44114-3401

DILIDDO, RONALD C. automotive executive; BS in Ceramic Engring., MS in Ceramic Sci., Alfred U. Various mfg. positions GM and Delphi; pres., CEO Hansford Mfg.; v.p. ops. automotive elec. sys. group ITT; gen. mgr. N.Am. wiper sys. and elec. motor group Valeo S.A.; pres. Amcast Automotive, N.Am. Amcast Indsl. Corp. Office: PO Box 98 7887 Washington Village Dr Dayton OH 45401-0098

DILL, CHARLES ANTHONY, manufacturing and computer company executive; b. Cleve., Nov. 29, 1939; s. Melville Reese and Gladys (Frode) D.; m. Louise T. Hall, Aug. 24, 1963 (dec. Sept. 28, 1983); children: Charles Anthony, Dudley Barnes; m. Mary M. Howell, Jan. 17, 1987. BSME, Yale U., 1961; MBA, Harvard U., 1963. With Emerson Electric Co., 1963-88, corp. v.p. internat., 1973-77; pres. A.B. Chance Co. subs. Emerson Electric Co., 1977-80; corp. group v.p. Emerson Electric Co., St. Louis, 1980-82, sr. v.p. office of chief exec., adv. dir., 1982-88; pres., COO, bd. dirs. AVX Corp., N.Y.C., 1988-90; pres., CEO, bd. dirs. Bridge Info. Systems, Inc., St. Louis, 1990-95; gen. ptnr. Gateway Equity Ptnrs. IV, 1995—. Bd. dirs. Maryville Technologies Inc., Neovision Hypersystems, V-Brick Inc., Digital Concepts of Mo., Zoltec Inc., Stifel Nicholaus Inc., Transact Techs., DT Industries, Potter Elec. Mem. St. Louis Country Club, Log Cabin Club. Republican. Home: 807 S Warson Rd Saint Louis MO 63124-1258 Office: Gateway Equity Partners 8000 Maryland Ave Ste 1190 Saint Louis MO 63105-3910 E-mail: cdill@gatewayventures.com.

DILL, SHERI, publishing executive; With Wichita (Kans.) Eagle, v.p. mktg. Office: The Wichita Eagle PO Box 820 Wichita KS 67201-0820

DILLARD, KIRK WHITFIELD, state legislator, lawyer; b. Chgo., June 1, 1955; s. Edward Floyd and Martina Raye (Whitfield) D.; m. Carol E. Crumbaugh, Mar. 16, 1985. BA, Western Ill. U., 1977; JD, DePaul U., 1982. Bar: Ill. 1983, U.S. Dist Ct. (no. dist.) Ill. 1983, U.S. Dist Ct. (cen. dist.) Ill. 1984, U.S. Dist. Ct. (ea. dist.) Mich. 1988. Staff cons. Ill. State Senate, Springfield, 1977-81; atty., dir. legis. affairs Ill. Office Gov., civingfield, 1982-87, chief of staff Springfield, 1991-93; judge State of Ill. Ct. of Claims, 1987-90; ptnr. Lord, Bissell & Brook, Chgo., 1987—; mem. Ill. Senate, 1993—. Legal writing and moot ct. tutor DePaul U. Coll. Laws, 1981-82; guest lectr. Loyola and DePaul U. Coll. Law, Chgo. Rep. precinct committeeman DuPage County, Wheaton, Ill., 1988; mem. Union League Chgo., Bi-State 3rd Airport for Chgo. Study Commn., Ill. Coalition. Named Legislator of the Yr. for Civil Justice, Am. Legis. Exch. Coun., 1995. Mem. ABA (Best performance in land use and local govt. law courses award Urban, State and Local Govt. sect. 1982), Ill. Assn. Def. Trial Counsel, Ill. State Bar Assn., Western Ill. U. Alumni Coun. (pres. 1989-92), Blue Key, Phi Alpha Delta. Methodist. Avocations: golf, tennis, travel, politics. Home: 120 Rosalie Ct Hinsdale IL 60521-3165 Office: Lord Bissell & Brook 115 S La Salle St Ste 3200 Chicago IL 60603-3902

DILLE, ROLAND PAUL, college president; b. Dassel, Minn., Sept. 16, 1924; s. Oliver Valentine and Eleanor (Johnson) D.; m. Beth Hopeman, Sept. 4, 1948; children— Deborah, Martha, Sarah, Benjamin. B.A. summa cum laude, U. Minn., 1949, Ph.D., 1962, LHD (hon.), 1995. Instr. English U. Minn., 1953-56; asst. prof. St. Olaf Coll., Northfield, Minn., 1956-61; asst. prof. English Calif. Lutheran Coll., Thousand Oaks, Calif., 1961-63; mem. faculty Moorhead (Minn.) State U., 1964-94, pres., 1968-94; ret., 1994. Chmn. Commn. on Instns. Higher Edn. of N. Cen. Assn. of Colls. and Schs., 1991. Author: Four Romantic Poets, 1969; contbr. numerous articles and revs. to profl. jours. Treas. Am. Assn. State Colls. and Univs., 1977-78, bd. dirs., 1978-80, chmn., 1980-81; mem. Nat. Coun. for Humanities, 1980-86; vice-chair Commn. on Higher Edn., North Cen. Assn., 1989-91, chair, 1991-93. With inf. AUS, 1944-46. Disting. Svc. to Humanities award given by Minn. Humanities Commn. named in his honor; named one of 100 most effective Am. coll. pres., 1987. Mem. Phi Beta Kappa. Home: 516 9th St S Moorhead MN 56560-3519 Office: Moorhead State U 11th St S Moorhead MN 56560-9980

DILLE, STEPHEN EVERETT, state legislator, farmer, veterinarian; b. Mpls., Mar. 16, 1945; s. Donald Everett and Bonnie Marie (Anderson) D.; m. Pamela Jane Johnson, July 5, 1975; children: Nicholas, Kaisa, Spencer, Mitchell. BS, U. Minn., 1967, DVM, 1969. Vet. advisor USAID, South Vietnam, 1969-72; mem. faculty Coll. Vet. Medicine U. Minn., St. Paul, 1973-75; pvt. vet. practice Litchfield, Minn., 1975—; crop livestock farmer Dassel, 1975—; twp. supr., 1977-84; county commr. Meeker County, 1985-86; mem. Minn. Ho. of Reps. from dist. 21A, St. Paul, 1987-92, Minn. Senate from 20th dist., St. Paul, 1993—. Republican. Home: 69800 305th St Dassel MN 55325-2912 Office: Minn State Senate 103 SOB Saint Paul MN 55155-0001

DILLER, EDWARD DIETRICH, lawyer; b. Pandora, Ohio, Aug. 7, 1947; s. Hiram D. and Selma G. (Warkentin) D.; m. Karen Esmonde, June 1, 1968; children: Jason, Anna. BA, Bluffton Coll., 1969; postgrad., U. Oreg., 1969-70; JD cum laude, Harvard U., 1976. Assoc. Taft, Stettinius & Hollister, Cin., 1976-84, ptnr., 1984—, chmn. dept. bus. & fin., 1998—. Chmn. Gen. Conf. Coun. on Higher Edn., 1990-93, 96—, vice chmn., 1993-94; lectr. numerous seminars; mem. women's initiative adv. bd. Deloitte & Touche, Cin., 2000—. Tchr. Mennonite Ctrl. Com., Frankfield, Jamaica, 1970-73; chmn. edn. integration com. Mennonite Ch. USA, 1997—; trustee Mental Health Svcs. East, 1977-85, Bluffton Coll., 1979—, mem. exec. com., 1987—, chmn. bd., 1991—; mem. Family Svc. of Greater Cin. Area, 1989-96, chmn., 1992-95; trustee Habitat for Humanity (Southwestern Ohio and No. Ky. affiliate), 1995-2000; trustee Working in Neighborhoods, 1991-94, Dan Beard Coun. Boy Scouts of Am., 1996—, Leadership Cin. Alumni Assn., 2001—; mem. Leadership Cin. Class XVI; trustee Found. Family Svc., 1997—. Mem. Ohio State Bar Assn., Cin. Bar Assn., Ohio Harvard Law Sch. Assn. Office: 1800 Firstar Tower 425 Walnut St Cincinnati OH 45202-3923 E-mail: diller@taftlaw.com.

DILLIN, S. HUGH, federal judge; b. Petersburg, Ind., June 9, 1914; s. Samuel E. and Maude (Harrell) D.; m. Mary Eloise Humphreys, Nov. 24, 1940; 1 child, Patricia Wright. A.B. in Govt, Ind. U., 1936, LLB, 1938, LLD, 1992; D of Civil Law (hon.), Ind. State U., 1990. Bar: Ind. 1938. Ptnr. Dillin & Dillin, Petersburg, 1938-61; U.S. dist. judge So. Dist. Ind., 1961—, chief judge, 1982-84. Mem. Jud. Conf. U.S., 1979-82, mem. exec. com., 1980-82, mem. Jud. Conf. Com. on Ct. Adminstrn., 1983-89, chmn. subcom. on fed.-state rels., 1983-89; mem. Jud. Panel on Multidist. Litigation, 1983-92; sec. Pub. Svc. Commn. Ind., 1942; mem. Interstate Oil Compact Commn., 1949-52, 61. Mem. Ind. Ho. of Reps. from Pike and Knox Counties, 1937, 39, 41, 51, floor leader, 1951; mem. Ind. Senate from Pike and Gibson Counties, 1959-61, pres. pro tem, 1961. Capt. AUS, 1943-46. Recipient Disting. Alumnus award Ind. U. Coll. Arts and Scis., 1985, Ind. U. Sch. Law, 1987, 2001 Am. Inns of Ct. Professionalism award in the 7th Cir. Mem. Am. Bar Assn., Ind. State Bar Assn., Fed. Bar Assn., 7th Cir. Judges Assn. (pres. 1977-79), Am. Judicature Soc., Delta Tau Delta, Phi Delta Phi. Democrat. Presbyn. Club: Indianapolis Athletic. Office: US Dist Ct 255 US Courthouse 46 E Ohio St Indianapolis IN 46204-1903

DILLINGHAM, JOHN ALLEN, marketing professional; b. Kansas City, Mo., Jan. 9, 1939; s. Jay B. and Frances (Thompson) D.; m. Nancy Jane Abbott, Sept. 4, 1965; children: Allen Edwards, William Kemp. AS, Wentworth Mil. Acad., 1958; AB in Polit. Sci., U. Mo., 1961, MS in Pub. Adminstrn., 1962. Br. mgr. Rudy-Patrick divsn. W.R. Grace Co., Mt. Vernon, Ill., 1964-68; pres. Sho-Hawk Industries, Kansas City, Mo., 1968-72; v.p. comml. loans Traders Nat. Bank, 1972-79; sr. v.p. sales and mktg. Garney Constrn. Co., 1979-95; pres., bd. dirs. Jo Dill, Inc., 1985—, Dillingham Enterprises, 1997—. Bd. dirs. United Funds, Inc., Kansas City; chmn. Clay County Indsl. Devel. Authority, 1980—, Clay County EDC, 1972-74; mem. pres. adv. bd. for extension U. Mo., 1972-80; cons. CMSU Grad. Sch., Warrensberg, Mo., 1996-97; dir., cons. McDougal Constrn., Kansas City, 1996-97; adv. dir. Northland Bd. United Mo. Bank, 1998—, Synergy Svcs. Trustee Wentworth Mil. Acad., Lexington, 1978-80, 93—; state chmn. Mo. 4H Found., Columbia, 1985-90; mem. ctrl. governing bd. Children's Mercy Hosp., Kansas City, 1987-92; bd. dirs. Kansas City Conv. and Vis. Bur., 1976-80, Northland Cmty. Fund, Kansas City, 1988-97, Kansas City Sports Commn., 1990-93; treas. Harry S. Truman Scholarship Nat. Alumni Assn., 1979-90; mem., v.p. Kansas City Bd. Police Commrs., 1990-95; chmn. Kansas City Mcpl. Asst. Corp., 1984—, Alex Doniphan Meml. Hwy. Naming, 1998; hon. co-chair St. Plus X H.S. Capital campaign, 1997-98; coordinating bd. task force on affordability of higher edn. State of Mo., 1999; mem. Nat. 4H Resource Devel. Com., 1990-92, Kansas City Mayor's Fast Forward Commn., 1996—; mem. exec. com. Metro C. C. Found., Kansas City, 1996—; exec. bd. Heart of Am. coun. Boy Scouts Am., 1993—; 1st bd. dirs. alumni assn. U.S. Command and Gen. Staff Coll., Ft. Leavenworth, Kans., 1993—; dir. DARE of Greater Kansas City, 1995-98, CMSU Found. Warrensburg, 1995-97, Am. Royal, Kansas City, Mo., 1997—; co-chmn. K.C. Storm runoff campaign, 1998. With U.S. Army, 1964. Recipient Faculty Alumni award U. Mo., Columbia, 1981, Silver Beaver award Boy Scouts Am. Heart Am. coun., 1992, Harry S. Truman Scholarship Appreciation plaque, 1993, Cmty. Svc. award Park Coll., 1993, Pub. Svc. award Ctrl. Mo. State Univ., 1994; named one of 100 Most Influential Kans. Citizens, Ingrams Mag., 1993, Spirit award Kansas City, 1999. Mem. SAR, VFW, Am. Legion, Sons of the Confederate Officers, Decendents of Magna Charta, Plantenegent Soc., Northland C. of C. (Quality of Life award 1990), KC Kings, Gold Coaters (pres. 1979-89), Mt. Vernon Ill. C. of C. (pres. 1968), Native Sons Kansas City (bd. dirs. 1991-92, 98—), Sigma Alpha Epsilon (KC Alumni Assn. pres. 1976, Honor Man 1988, trustee Nat. Found. 1987-93, Nat. Disting. Svc. award 1993). Democrat. Mem. Disciples of Christ Ch. Avocations: fishing, landscaping, family geneaology. Home: 4040 NW Claymont Dr Kansas City MO 64116-1751 Office: 924 Livestock Exch Bldg Kansas City MO 64102 Fax: 816-842-6803.

DILLON, COREY, professional football player; b. Oct. 24, 1975; Student, U. Wash. Football player Cin. Bengals, 1997—. Office: Cin Bengals 1 Paul Brown Stadium Cincinnati OH 45202-3492

DILLON, DAVID BRIAN, retail grocery executive; b. Hutchinson, Kans., Mar. 30, 1951; s. Paul Wilson and Ruth (Muirhead) D.; m. Dee A. Ehling, July 29, 1973; children: Jefferson, Heather, Kathryn. BS, U. Kans., 1973; JD, So. Meth. U., 1976. V.p. Fry's Food Stores of Ariz. Inc. div. Dillon Cos. Inc., Phoenix, 1978-79, exec. v.p., 1979-83; v.p. Dillon Cos. Inc. (subs. of Kroger Co.), Hutchinson, 1983-86, pres., 1986-95; exec. v.p. Kroger Co., Cin., 1990-95; chmn. bd. Dillon Cos., Inc. (subs. Kroger Co.), 1993—; pres., COO The Kroger Co., 1995—; also bd. dirs., 1995—. Bd. dirs. Convergys. Chmn. Leadership Hutchinson, 1986-87, Leadership Kans., 1988; bd. dirs. Bethesda Hosp., Cin., 1996—; bd. trustees U. Kans. Endowment Assn., 1993—, U. Cin. Found., 1997—, Den Beard Coun. of Boy Scouts Am., 1996—; bd. advisors U. Kans. Bus. Sch., 1990—. Recipient Brotherhood-Sisterhood award Kans. region NCCJ, 1992. Mem. U. Kans. Alumni Assn., Urban League of Greater Cin. (trustee 1998—), Order of Coif, Sigma Chi (Balfour award 1973). Republican. Presbyterian. Office: The Kroger Co 1014 Vine St Cincinnati OH 45202-1100

DILLON, HOWARD BURTON, civil engineer; b. Hardyville, Ky., Aug. 12, 1935; s. Charlie Edison and Mary Opal (Bell) D.; m. Bonny Jean Garard, May 19, 1962; 1 child, Robert Edward. BCE, U. Louisville, 1958, MCE, 1960; postgrad., Okla. State U., 1962, Mich. State U., 1962-65. Registered profl. engr., Ind. Instr. U. Louisville, Ky., 1958-60; from assoc. prof. to prof. Ind. Inst. Tech., Ft. Wayne, 1960-62; NSF fellow Okla. State U., Stillwater, 1962; NSF grantee, instr. Mich. State U., East Lansing, 1962-67; head civil engring. dept. MW Inc. Cons. Engrs., Indpls., 1967-83; project mgr. civil divsn. SEG Engrs. & Cons., 1983-91; pvt. practice Howard B. Dillon, Cons. Engr., 1991—. Asst. dir. to local pub. road needs study for Ind., 1970; mem. design com. for dams in Ind., 1974—; spl. cons. to Ind. Dept. Nat. Resources on dams, 1980—; mem. infrastructure com. for State of Ind., 1984—. Contbr. articles to profl. jours. Committeeman Wayne 52 precinct, Indpls., 1972-86; vice-ward chmn. Wayne South Twp., Indpls., 1986-87. Hazelett and Erdal scholar, 1957-58, W.B. Wendt scholar U. Louisville; recipient Order of Engr. award Purdue U., 1993. Mem. ASCE (life), NSPE (life), Am. Soc. Engring. Edn. (life), ASTM, Internat. Soc. Found. Engrs., Mil. Engrs., Internat. Acad. Sci. Ind. Water Resources Assn., Am. Water Works Assn., Nat. Audubon Soc., Optimists (pres. Suburban West chpt. 1972-74, bd. dirs. 1974-78, sec. 1992-94, lt. gov. ind. dist. 1972-74, Optimist of Yr., 1995); Chi Epsilon. Democrat. Baptist. Avocations: fishing, travel, photography, lecturing, coin collecting. Home and Office: 6548 Westdrum Rd Indianapolis IN 46241-1843 Fax: (317 244-1428.

DILLON, MERTON LYNN, historian, educator; b. nr. Addison, Mich., Apr. 4, 1924; s. Henry J. and Cecil Edith (Sanford) D. B.A., Mich. State Normal Coll., 1945; M.A., U. Mich., 1948, Ph.D., 1951. Asst. prof. history N.Mex. Mil. Inst., Roswell, 1951-56; asst. prof. Tex. Tech. Coll., Lubbock, 1956-59, asso. prof., 1959-63, prof., 1963-65; asso. prof. Northern Ill. U., DeKalb, 1965-67; prof. Ohio State U., Columbus, 1967-91, prof. emeritus, 1991—. Author: Elijah P. Lovejoy, Abolitionist Editor, 1961, Benjamin Lundy and the Struggle for Negro Freedom, 1966, The Abolitionists, the Growth of a Dissenting Minority, 1974; Ulrich Bonnell Phillips, Historian of the Old South, 1985, Slavery Attacked: Southern Slaves and Their Allies, 1619-1865, 1990; contbr. articles to profl. jours. NEH fellow, 1973-74 Mem.Orgn. Am. Historians, So. Hist. Assn. (bd. editors 1959-63). Home: 10460 Addison Rd Jerome MI 49249-9723 Office: Ohio State U Dept History Columbus OH 43210

DI LORENZO, JOHN FLORIO , JR. retired lawyer (corporate); b. Paterson, N.J., May 18, 1940; s. John F. and Ida (Cona) Di L.; m. Ernestine R. De Rose, Nov. 15, 1969; children: Christina P., Roberta J. BA, Seton Hall U., 1962; LLB, MBA, Columbia U., 1966. Bar: N.J. 1967, N.Y. 1968, Ohio 1981. Assoc. Stryker, Tams & Dill, Esqs., Newark, 1966-68; atty. Am. Electric Power Svc. Corp., N.Y.C., 1968-79, asst. gen. counsel, asst. v.p., exec. asst. to pres., 1979-81, assoc. gen. counsel, v.p., sec. Columbus, Ohio, 1981-2001; ret., 2001. Sec. various Am. Electric Power Sys. cos., 1987-2001, asst. sec. 1979. Trustee Ballet Met. Columbus, 1981-87. Mem.

ABA (chmn. subcom. on pub. utility holding co. act of fed. regulation of securities com. 1985-94), Scioto Country Club. Roman Catholic. Avocations: skiing, travel. Home: 2756 Elginfield Rd Columbus OH 43220-4248

DIMON, JAMES, bank executive; b. N.Y.C., Mar. 13, 1956; s. Theodore and Themis Dimon; m. Judith Kent, May 21, 1983; children: Julia, Laura, Kara. BA, Tufts U., 1978; MBA, Harvard U., 1982. V.p., asst. to pres. Am. Express Co., N.Y.C., 1982-85; pvt. practice investor, 1985-86; sr. v.p., CFO Comml. Credit Co., Balt., 1986-88; exec. v.p., CFO Primerica Corp., N.Y.C., 1991-93, pres., 1993—; pres., COO Travelers Inc.; pres., COO, CFO The Travelers Inc, 1993—; pres. Citigroup Inc; chmn. & CEO Bank One Corp., Chicago, 2000—.

DIMOND, EDMUNDS GREY, medical educator; b. St. Louis, Dec. 8, 1918; s. Edmunds Grey and Gertrude Ruth (Schmidt) D.; m. Mary Dwight Clark, Nov. 28, 1968 (dec. June 1983); children: Sherri Grey Byrer, Lea Grey, Lark Grey Dimond-Cates. Student, Purdue U., 1938-39; BS, Ind. U., 1942, MD, 1944. Mem. faculty Med. Ctr., U. Kans., Kansas City, 1950-60, prof., chmn. dept. medicine, 1953-60, dir. cardiovascular lab., 1950-60; mem., dir. Inst. for Cardiopulmonary Diseases, Scripps Clinic and Rsch. Found., 1960-67; rsch. assoc. physiology Scripps Inst. Oceanography, La Jolla, Calif., 1960-68; prof. in residence Sch. Medicine, U. Calif., San Diego, 1967-68; scholar in residence Nat. Libr. Medicine, 1967; spl. asst. to asst. sec. HEW, Washington, 1968; Disting. univ. prof. medicine U. Mo., Kansas City, 1968-98, provost for health scis., 1968-79. Fulbright prof., The Netherlands, 1956; vis. prof., Israel, 1978; scholar in residence Rockefeller Found. Study Ctr., Bellagio, Italy, 1978; chmn. overseas edn. team Dept. State, 1962, 64-66, 73; guest lectr. Chinese Med. Assn., 1971-73, 76-80, 82-92; pres. Edgar Snow Fund, Inc., Diastole-Hospital Hill, Inc. Author: Electrocardiography, 1952, rev. edits., 1955, 60, 64, Digitalis, 1957, Exercise Electrocardiograms, 1961, More Than Herbs and Acupuncture, 1975, Inside China Today, 1981, Take Wing, 1991, Dr. Horse of China, 1992, Reverend Whitehead, Missionary Pioneer, 1987, Letters from Forest Place, 1993, Essays By An Unfinished Physician, 1995, Milestone Eighty, 2000; editor: Diastole on Hospital Hill Audiotape, 1980-86; editor-in-chief Accel, 1968-77; contbr. articles to profl. jours. Bd. dirs. Truman Med. Ctr., Kansas City, Mo., Eye Found., Kansas City, Sci. Edn. Partnership, Kansas City. With M.C., AUS, 1945-47. Paul Dudley White Traveling scholar, 1956-57. Master Am. Coll. Cardiology (pres. 1962, Disting. Svc. award 1969). Home and Office: 2501 Holmes St Kansas City MO 64108-2742 E-mail: gdimond@planetkc.com.

DIMOND, ROBERT EDWARD, publisher; b. Washington, Dec. 12, 1936; s. James Robert and Helen Marie (Murphy) D.; m. Patricia Berger (div.); children: Mark Edward, Michele Lynn Keating, Melinda Ann. B.A. in Journalism, George Washington U., 1961. Mng. editor Nat. Automobile Dealers Assn. Mag., Washington, 1955-63; editor, pub. Bus. Products Mag., 1963-69; v.p. Hitchcock Pub. Co.; pub. Infosystems Mag., Office Products Mag., Wheaton, Ill., 1969-81; pres. R.E. Dimond & Assocs., Hinsdale, 1981-83; pub. Networking Mgmt. Mag., Westford, Mass., 1983-89, Home Improvement Ctr. Mag., Lincolnshire, Ill., 1989-90; v.p., pub. dir. mining and constrn. group Intertec; pub. Coal, Rock Products, Internat. Construction, Concrete Products, Engring. and Mining Jour., C&D Materials Recycling and Keystone Directory, 1990-96; group v.p. Intertec Pub. Co., 1996-99; pres. R.E. Dimond & Assocs., 1999—. Keynote spkr. COMDEX, 1979. Served with USAF, 1961-62. Democrat. Roman Catholic. Home and Office: 400 Bentley Pl Buffalo Grove IL 60089-2500 E-mail: dimondre@attbi.com.

DINARDO, DANIEL N. bishop; b. Steubenville, Ohio, May 23, 1949; BA, Master's degree, Cath. U. Am.; BST, Gregorian U., Rome, 1975. Ordained priest Roman Cath. Ch., 1977. Asst. pastor St. Pius X Ch., Brookline, Pa., 1977-80; asst. chancellor Diocese of Pitts., 1980-83; mem. staff Congregation of Bishops, Rome, 1983-89; asst. sec. edn. Diocese of Pitts., 1991; pastor Sts. John and Paul Parish; consecrated bishop, 1997; co-adjutor bishop Diocese of Sioux City, Iowa, 1997-98, bishop, 1998—. Office: PO Box 3379 1821 Jackson St Sioux City IA 51102-3379

DINGELL, CHRISTOPHER DENNIS, state legislator; b. Washington, Feb. 23, 1957; s. John David and Helen (Henebry) D.; 1 child, Gabrielle. BSc, U. Mich., 1978; JD, Detroit Coll. Law., 1986. Engr. Ford Motor Co., Detroit, 1979-80, Rouge Steel Co., 1980-86; mem. Mich. Senate from 7th dist., Lansing, 1987—. Appropriations com. Mich. State Senate, career devel. com., strategic fund com., judiciary com., state policy and mil. affairs com., retirement com.; atty. Sommers, Schwartz, Silver & Schwartz, 1989—. Vol. Dem. Nat. Conv. Mem. Engring. Soc. Detroit, Econ. Club Detroit, Mich. Jaycees, Polish Roman Catholic Union, Mich. United Conservation Club, K. of C. Office: 910 Farnum Bldg PO Box 30036 Lansing MI 48909-7536 Fax: 517 373 9310. E-mail: sencdingell@senate.state.mi.us.

DINGELL, JOHN DAVID, congressman; b. Colorado Springs, Colo., July 8, 1926; s. John D. and Grace (Bigler) D. BS in Chemistry, Georgetown U., 1949, JD, 1952. Bar: D.C. 1952, Mich. 1953. Pk. ranger U.S. Dept. Interior, 1948-52; asst. pros. atty. Wayne County, Mich., 1953-55; mem. U.S. Congress from 15th Mich. dist., 1955-65, U.S. Congress from 16th Mich. dist., 1965—. Mem. migratory bird conservation commn.; ranking mem. energy and commerce com. 2nd lt. inf. AUS, 1945-46. Office: US Ho of Reps 2328 Rayburn Bldg Washington DC 20515-2216*

DINOS, NICHOLAS, engineering educator, administrator; b. Tamaqua, Pa., Jan. 15, 1934; s. Christophoros and Calliope (Haralambos) D.; m. Lillian Gravell, June 18, 1955; children: Gwen Elizabeth, Christopher Nicholas, Janet Kay. BS, Pa. State U., 1955; MS, Lehigh U., 1966, PhD., 1967. Engr. E.I. duPont Co., Terre Haute, Ind., 1955-57, rsch. engr. Augusta, Ga., 1957-64; assoc. prof. Ohio U., Athens, 1967-72, prof., 1972—, chmn., 1976-89. Vis. prof. Chubu U., Nagoya, Japan, 1976. Contbr. articles to profl. jours. Elder Presbyn. Ch., Athens, 1967—; Danforth Found. assoc., Ohio U., 1978—. NASA fellow Lehigh U., Stanford U., 1966, 72, 74, U.S. Steel fellow Lehigh U., 1965. Mem. AAUP, AAAS, AIChE, Am. Chem. Soc., Am. Soc. Engring. Edn., Sigma Xi, Phi Kappa Phi, Tau Beta Pi. Democrat. Avocations: reading, music, outdoors, travel. Home: 29 Briarwood Dr Athens OH 45701-1302 Office: Ohio U Dept Chem Engring Athens OH 45701 E-mail: dinos@ohio.edu.

DINSMOOR, JAMES ARTHUR, psychology educator; b. Woburn, Mass., Oct. 4, 1921; s. Daniel Stark and Jean Erskine (Masson) D.; m. Anne Darrow Berninger, July 17, 1943 (div. Mar. 1953); 1 son, Daniel Stark; m. Marise Kay Sawyer, Jan. 1, 1956; children: Mara Jean, Robert Scott. B.A., Dartmouth Coll., 1943; M.A., Columbia U., 1945, Ph.D., 1949. Instr. Newark Colls., Rutgers U., 1945-46; lectr. Columbia U., N.Y.C., 1946-51; asst. prof. Ind. U., Bloomington, 1951-58, assoc. prof., 1958-63, prof. psychology, 1963-86, prof. emeritus psychology, 1987—. Author: Operant Conditioning: An Experimental Analysis of Behavior, 1970. Mem. nat. bd. Nat. Com. for a Sane Nuclear Policy, Washington, 1966-68. Fellow APA (divsn. v.p. 1977-80, divsn. pres. 1992-93); mem. Soc. Exptl. Analysis of Behavior (pres. 1979-81), Midwestern Psychol. Assn. (coun. 1973-82, pres. 1980-81), Assn. for Behavior Analysis (orgnl. com. 1974-76). Home: 1511 E Maxwell Ln Bloomington IN 47401-5144 Office: Ind U Dept Psychology 1101 E 10th St Bloomington IN 47405-7007 E-mail: dinsmoor@indiana.edu.

DIONISOPOULOS, GEORGE ALLAN, lawyer; b. Santa Monica, Calif., July 31, 1954; s. P. Allan and Christine (Nassios) D.; m. Sandra Doreen Jordan, June 11, 1977; children: Sarah, Elaina. BA summa cum laude, U. Ill., 1976; JD cum laude, Harvard U., 1980. Bar: Wis. 1980, U.S. Dist. Ct. (ea. and we. dists.) Wis. 1980. Ptnr. Foley & Lardner, Milw., 1980—. Mem. ABA (real property and probate sect., taxation sect.), Wis. Bar Assn. (speaker 1984—), Milw. Young Lawyers Assn., Phi Beta Kappa. Greek Orthodox. Home: W304n2978 Hawksnest Ct Pewaukee WI 53072-4279 Office: Foley & Lardner 777 E Wisconsin Ave Ste 3800 Milwaukee WI 53202-5367 E-mail: gdionisopoulos@foleylaw.com.

DIONNE, NEAL, radio personality; Radio host Neal Dionne Show, Wood 1300, Grand Rapids, Mich. Office: Newsradio Wood 1300 77 Monroe Ctr Ste 1000 Grand Rapids MI 49503

DIPERSIO, JOHN F. oncologist; b. Boston; BA magna cum laude, Williams Coll.; MD, PhD, U. Rochester, 1980. Resident Parkland Meml. Hosp., chief resident; fellow hematology-oncology UCLA; chief divsn. bone marrow transplantation & stem cell biology Barnes-Jewish Hosp., Lewis T. and Rosalind B. Apple chair oncology; full prof. depts. medicine, pathology, pediat. Sch. Medicine; acting chief divn. med. oncology Med. Sch.; asst. prof. medicine U. Rochester, N.Y.; dir. bone marrow transplantation program Strong Meml. Hosp. Contbr. articles to profl. jours. Mem. Internat. Soc. for Exptl. Hematology (councilor, chair nomating com.), Alpha Omega Alpha.

DIPKO, THOMAS EARL, retired minister, national church executive; b. St. Michael, Pa., June 26, 1936; s. John and Sarah Jane (Gittins) D.; m. Sandra Jane Faust, Nov. 19, 1960; children: Lisa Renee, Sarah Marie. BA, Otterbein Coll., 1958; MDiv, United Theol. Sem., 1961; PhD in Ecumenical Theology, Boston U., 1969; LLD (hon.), Heidelberg Coll., 1987; DD (hon.), United Theol. Sem. of the Twin Cities, 1992; LHD (hon.), The Defiance Coll., 1992; DD (hon.), Elmhurst Coll., 1993, Ursinus Coll., 1994. ordained min. Youth min. First United Methodist Ch., Dayton, Ohio, 1958-61; ecumenical intern social action office Ch. Rhineland-Westphalia, Germany, 1962; asst. pastor First Ch. Congregational, Swampscott, Mass., 1963-64; pastor First United Methodist Ch., East Conemaugh, Pa., 1964-66; asst. pastor South Ch. Congregational, Andover, Mass., 1966-68; sr. pastor Christ Ch. United in Lowell, Mass., 1969-77, Grace Congregational Ch., Framingham, Mass., 1977-84; conf. min. and exec. Ohio conf. United Ch. of Christ, Columbus, 1984-92; exec. v.p. United Ch. Bd. for Homeland Ministries, Cleve., 1992-2000. Mem. bd. trustees The Defiance Coll., 1985—; mem. exec. com. Consultation on Church Union, 1989—2002; del. Seventh Assembly World Coun. Churches, Canberra, Australia, 1991; mem. bd. dirs. Ryder Meml. Hosp., Humacao, Puerto Rico, 1993-96. Author: (first draft, book) United Church of Christ Book of Worship, 1986; contbr. chpts. to books, articles to profl. jours. Chmn. Lowell Drug Action Com., 1971-74; mem. bd. dirs. Internat. Inst., 1971-77. Samaritans (suicide intervention), 1983-84; del. gen. coun. World Alliance Reformed Chs., Debrecen, Hungary, 1997; bd. trustees LeMoyne-Owen Coll. Fellow Coll. Preachers, 1983. Mem. N.Am. Acad. Ecumenists (mem. exec. com. 1981-83), Christians Associated for Rels. in Eastern Europe, Consultation on Common Texts. Avocations: swimming, perennial gardening, canoeing.

DIRECTOR, STEPHEN WILLIAM, electrical and computer engineering educator, academic administrator; b. Bklyn., June 28, 1943; s. Murray and Lillian (Brody) D.; m. Lorraine Schwartz, June 20, 1965; children: Joshua, Kimberly, Cynthia, Deborah. BS, SUNY, Stony Brook, 1965; MS, U. Calif., Berkeley, 1967, PhD, 1968. Prof. elec. engring. U. Fla., Gainesville, 1968-77; vis. scientist IBM Rsch. Labs., Yorktown Heights, N.Y., 1974-75; prof. elec. and computer engring. Carnegie-Mellon U., Pitts., 1977-96, U.A. and Helen Whitaker Univ. prof. electrical and computer engring., 1980-96, prof. computer sci., 1981-96, head dept. elec. and computer engring., 1982-91; univ. prof., 1992-93; dean Carnegie Inst. Tech. Carnegie-Mellon U., Pitts., 1991-96; Robert J. Vlasic Dean of Engring. U. Mich., Ann Arbor, 1996—, prof. elec. engring. and computer science, 1996—. Cons. Intel. Corp., Santa Clara, Calif., 1977—84, Digital Equipment Corp., Hudson, Mass., 1982—88, Calma Corp., 1985—86, Mentor Graphics Corp., 1988—91, Lutron Electronics Co., Inc., 1999—; advisor info. and comm. tech. Techno Venture Mgmt., 1999—; mem. tech. adv. bd. Nextwave, Inc., 1990—95, Job Gravity; sr. rsch. fellow IC2 Inst., 1996—; sr. cons. editor McGraw-Hill Book Co., N.Y.C., 1976—; dir. Rsch. Ctr. Computer-Aided Design, Pitts., 1982—89. Author: Introduction to System Theory, 1972, Circuit Theory, 1975, VLSI Design for Manufacturing: Yield Enhancement, 1989, Principles of VLSI System Planning: A Framework for Conceptual Design, 1991; editor: Computer-Aided Design, 1974; co-editor: Advances in Computer-Aided Design for VLSI: vol. 8, Statistical Approach to VLSI, 1994. Chair bd. dirs. Am. Soc. Engring. Edn., Engring. Deans Coun., 1999-2001. Recipient Frederick Emmons Terman award Am. Soc. Engring. Edn., 1976; named Distinguished Alumnus, SUNY, Stony Brook, 1984; Aristotle Award Semiconductor Rsch. Corp., 1996, Outstanding Alumnus award in Elec. Engring. U. Calif., Berkeley, 1996, Berkeley Disting. Engring. Alumnus award, U. Calif., 1999, IEEE Circuits and Sys. Soc. Golden Jubilee award, 1999. Fellow IEEE (W.R.G. Baker prize 1979, Centennial medal 1984, Edn. Soc. Outstanding Achievement award 1995, Edn. medal 1998, Millennium medal 2000); mem. NAE (chair com. on engring. edn.), IEEE Cirs. and Sys. Soc. (pres. 1981, assoc. editor jour. 1973-75, best paper award 1970, 85, 89, 92, soc. award 1992, Golden Jubilee medal 1999). Office: Univ Michigan Coll Engring Robert H Lurie Engring Ctr Ann Arbor MI 48109 E-mail: director@umich.edu.

DISHMAN, CRIS EDWARD, professional football player; b. Louisville, Aug. 13, 1965; Student, Purdue U. Cornerback Houston Oilers, 1988-96, Washington Redskins, 1997-98, Kansas City Chiefs, 1998—. Achievements include playing in Pro Bowl, 1991. Office: c/o Kansas City Chiefs One Arrowhead Dr Kansas City MO 64129

DI SIMONE, ROBERT NICHOLAS, radiologist, educator; b. Canton, Ohio, Nov. 15, 1937; s. Nicholas Joseph and Margaret Elizabeth (Karas) DiS.; m. Patricia Anne Zwigard, June 22, 1963; children: Christopher, Angela, Elizabeth. BSc summa cum laude, Ohio State U., 1959, MSc, MD cum laude, Ohio State U., 1963. Diplomate Am. Bd. Radiology, Am. Bd. Nuclear Medicine. Intern, fellow Johns Hopkins U. Hosp., Balt., 1963-64, asst. resident, fellow in internal medicine, 1964-65, asst. resident, fellow in radiology, 1967-70, instr., radiologist, 1970-71; dir. nuclear medicine Aultman Hosp., Canton, 1971-95, pres., med. staff, 1986-87, vice-chmn. dept. radiology, 1988-96, sec.-treas. med. staff, 1977-79; chmn. nuclear medicine sect. Northeastern Ohio Univs. Coll. Medicine, Rootstown, 1979-97; chmn. dept. radiology Northeastern Ohio Univs. Coll. of Medicine (NEOUCOM), 1992-93; diagnostic radiologist Aultman Health Found., Canton, Ohio, 1971-2000; radiology cons. North Canton, 2000—. Author: Imaging of the Endocrine System in Organ System Radiology, 1984; contbr. articles to profl. jours. Fellow Am. Coll. Radiology; mem. AMA, Soc. Nuclear Medicine, Ohio State Med. Soc. (del. 1983-95), Radiol. Soc. N.Am., Stark County Med. Soc. (trustee 1979-95, chmn. bd. censors 1980-82, pres. 1993), Unique Club Stark County, Phi Beta Kappa, Sigma Xi, Alpha Omega Alpha, Phi Lambda Upsilon. Avocations: playing bluegrass guitar music, collecting antique old trains, traveling, hiking. Home and Office: 2465 Oakway St N North Canton OH 44720-5886 E-mail: rnd@neoucom.edu.

DISINGER, JOHN FRANKLIN, natural resources educator; b. Lockport, N.Y., July 7, 1930; s. Allan Eugene and Grace (Meeks) D.; m. Norma Jean Vescovi, June 25, 1960; children: David C., Douglas A. BS, SUNY, Brockport, 1952; MEd, U. Rochester, 1960; PhD, Ohio State U., 1971. Lic. sci. tchr., N.Y. Tchr., chmn. mid. sch. sci. dept. West Irondequoit Cen. Sch. Dist., Rochester, N.Y., 1955-70; prof. Sch. Natural Resources Ohio State U., Columbus, 1971-95, prof. emeritus, 1995—, acting dir., 1988-89; faculty Ohio State U. Coll. Edn., 1971-95. Assoc. dir. Ednl. Resources Info. Ctr. Clearinghouse for Sci., Math, Environ. Edn., Columbus, 1971-91; cons. TVA, Knoxville, 1985-88, N. Am. Assn. Environ. Edn., 1993. Mem. editl. bd. The Environmentalist, 1984—; book rev. editor Jour. Environ. Edn., 1999—; contbr. articles to profl. jours. Mem. Environ. Lit. Coun., 1996—. Recipient Pres.' award Ohio Alliance for Environ., 1984, Alumni award for disting tchg. Ohio State U., 1995. Fellow Ohio Acad. Sci.; mem. N.Am. Assn. Environ. Edn. (pres. 1985-86, Walter Jeske award 1984, Pres. award, 1991). Presbyterian. Office: Ohio State Univ Sch Natural Resources 2021 Coffey Rd Columbus OH 43210-1044 E-mail: disinger.1@osu.edu.

DISTELHORST, GARIS FRED, trade association executive; b. Columbus, Ohio, Jan. 21, 1942; s. Harold Theodore and Ruth (Haywood) D.; m. Helen Cecilla Gillen, Oct. 28, 1972; children: Garen, Kristen, Alison. BSc, Ohio State U., 1965. V.p. Smith, Bucklin & Assocs., Washington, 1969-80; chief staff exec., CEO, pres. Nat. Assn. Coll. Stores, Oberlin, Ohio, 1980-98; pres. Assn. Initiatives, Inc., Westlake, 1998—2001; pres., CEO Conv. Industry Coun., 1999-2000; pres., COO RecTech Assn. Directories, 2000—02; pres., CEO Marble Inst. Am., 2002—. Mem. book and libr. adv. com. USIA, 1990-93; bd. dirs. First Merit Corp., Holcombs, Inc. Pres. Oberlin Cmty. Improvement Corp., 1985-88; bd. dirs. Leadership Lorain County, 1988-89, Access Program, 1994-97, Conv. and Visitors Bur. Greater Cleve., Lorain County C.C. Found., Lorain County United Way, 1991-97, v.p., 1993-94, pres., 1994-96, campaign chmn., 1993. Decorated USN Achievement medal, 1969 Mem. Inst. Assn. Mgmt. Soc. (treas. 1979-80, award of merit), Am. Soc. Assn. Execs. (bd. dirs. 1981-84, vice chmn. 1985, chmn.-elect 1994, chmn. 1995-96, bd. dirs. found. 1990-94, vice chmn. found. 1991-92, chmn. found. 1992-93, Key award 1984, chmn. Assn. Advance Am. 1993-94), Oberlin Area C. of C. (pres. 1987-90, bd. dirs. 1987-90), Greater Cleve. Soc. Assn. Execs. Republican. Roman Catholic. Office: Marble Inst Am 28901 Clemens Rd Ste 100 Cleveland OH 44145 E-mail: gdistelhorst@attbi.com.

D'ITRI, FRANK MICHAEL, environmental research chemist; b. Flint, Mich., Apr. 25, 1933; s. Dominic and Angelina (Costanza) D'I.; m. Patricia Ann Ward, Sept. 10, 1955; children: Michael Payne, Angela Kathryn, Patricia Ann, Julie Lynn. BS in Zoology, Mich. State U., 1955, MS in Analytical Chemistry, 1966, PhD, 1968. Lab. technician Dow Industry Service Labs., Midland, Mich., 1960-62; research asst. dept. chemistry Mich. State U., East Lansing, 1963-68, asst. prof. dept. fisheries and wildlife, 1968-72, assoc. prof. dept. fisheries and wildlife, 1973-76, prof. dept. fisheries and wildlife, 1977—; assoc. dir. Inst. Water Rsch., 1987—; asst. dir. Mich. Agrl. Exptl. Sta., 1996—. Cons. U.S. Dept. Energy, Washington, 1983-85, EEC, UN, Geneva, 1982—; vis. prof. U. Bahia, Brazil, 1978, Tokyo U. Agr., 1980, 84-85, 87, 94, 2000, 01; mem. adv. bd. Lewis Pubs., Inc., Springer-Verlag. Author: The Environmental Mercury Problem, 1972, (with P.A. D'Itri) Mercury Contamination: A Human Tragedy, 1977, (with A.W. Andren, R.A. Doherty, J.M. Wood), Assessment of Mercury in the Environment, 1978, Acid Precipitation, 1982, Artificial Reefs, 1985; editor (with J. Aguirre M., M. Athie L.), Municipal Wastewater in Agriculture, 1981, Land Treatment of Municipal Wastewater: Vegetation Selection and Management, 1982, Acid Precipitation: Effects on Ecological Systems, 1982, (with M.A. Kamrin) PCBs: Human and Environmental Hazards, 1983, Artificial Reefs: Marine and Freshwater Applications, 1985, A System Approach to Conservation Tillage, 1985, (with H.H. Prince) Coastal Wetlands, 1985; (with L.G. Wolfson) Rural Groundwater Contamination, 1987, Chemical Deicers And The Environment, 1992, (with H.W. Belcher) Subirrigation and Controlled Drainage, 1995, Zebra Mussels and Aquatic Nuisance Species, 1997, (with Y. Itakura) Integrated Environmental Management, 1999; contbr. numerous articles to profl. jours. Mem. critical materials adv. subcom. Mich. Water Resources Commns. Mich. Dept. Natural Resources, 1971-79, mem. solid waste com., 1971-79; mem. subcom. Mich. State U. Waste Control Authority Chem. Waste, 1971—; mem. tech. adv. com. Great Lakes Protection fund tech. adv. com., 1990-93; mem. Great Lakes Commn., 1992—; mem. subirrigation steering com. Mich. Soil Conservation Svc., 1986—; mem. fluctuating lake levels com. Internat. Joint Commn., 1992-93; mem. internat. rsch. group mercury pollution in Amazon, Brazil, 1992—. NIH summer fellow, 1964-67, Socony-Mobil fellow Mich. State U., 1967-68, Japan Soc. Promotion Sci. fellow, 1980; Rockefeller Found. Bellagio Resident scholar, 1972, 75. Mem. Am. Chem. Soc., Am. Soc. Limnology and Oceanography, Assn. Analytical Chemists, Water Pollution Research Soc., Midwest Univs. Analytical Chemists Conf., Mich. Acad. Sci., Arts and Letters, Sigma Xi, Setac. Home: 4395 Elmwood Dr Okemos MI 48864-3034 Office: Mich State U 115 Manly Miles 1405 S Harrison Rd East Lansing MI 48823-5289 E-mail: ditri@msu.edu.

DITTMAN, WILLIAM A. company executive; BS, Miami U., Oxford, Ohio. V.p. sales and mktg. A.H. Hoffman; with Miracle-Gro, 1992; key mgr. Consumer Gardens Group The Scotts Co., sr. v.p. growing media bus. group, 1998—. Office: 41 S High St Ste 3500 Columbus OH 43215-6110

DITTMER, JOHN AVERY, history educator; b. Seymour, Ind., Oct. 30, 1939; s. J. Avery and Melba Roberta (Ahlbrand) D.; m. Ellen Ann Tobey, June 3, 1961; children: Julia Susan, John David. BS in Edn., Ind. U., 1961, MA in History, 1964, PhD in History, 1971. Asst. prof. Tougaloo (Miss.) Coll., 1967-68, acad. dean, 1968-70, assoc. prof., 1971-79; assoc. prof. history DePauw U., Greencastle, Ind., 1985-92, prof., 1993—. Vis. assoc. prof. Brown U., Providence, R.I., 1979-80, 81-82, 83-84, MIT, Cambridge, 1982-84; cons. NEH, Washington, 1980-83, PBS Series, Eyes on the Prize, Boston, 1986. Author: Black Georgia in the Progressive Era, 1900-1920, 1977, Local People: The Struggle for Civil Rights in Mississippi, 1994 (Lillian Smith book award, 1994, Bancroft prize Columbia Univ. 1995); contbr. articles to profl. jours. Younger Humanist fellow NEH, 1973-74, fellowship-in-residence NEH, Vanderbilt U., 1976-77, Rockefeller Found., 1980-81, Am. Coun. Learned Socs., 1983-84, Ctr. for Study of Civil Rights, U. Va., 1988-89, NEH, 2000-01, Nat. Humanities Ctr., 2001—. Mem. Orgn. of Am. Historians (Frederick Jackson Turner award finalist 1972), So. Hist. Assn., Am. Hist. Assn. Avocations: tennis, golf, jazz music. Home: 230 Westwood Rd Fillmore IN 46128-9621 Office: DePauw U Dept History Greencastle IN 46135 E-mail: rip@depauw.edu.

DIX, ROLLIN C(UMMING), mechanical engineering educator, consultant; b. N.Y.C., N.Y., Feb. 8, 1936; s. Omer Houston and Ona Mae (Cumming) D.; m. Elaine B. VanNest, June 18, 1960; children: Gregory, Elisabeth, Karen. BSME, Purdue U., 1957, MSME, 1958, PhD, 1963. Registered profl. engr., Ill. Asst. prof. mech. engring. Ill. Inst. Tech., Chgo., 1964-69, assoc. prof., 1969-80, prof., 1980—, assoc. dean for computing, 1980-96; pres. Patpending Mktg., Inc., 1996—. Bd. dirs. USI Capital Corp., Reformteh, Inc., Romania. Patentee road repair vehicle, method for vestibular test. Chmn. bd. dirs. Pilsen affiliate Habitat for Humanity, Chgo. 1st lt. U.S. Army, 1960—61. Fellow: ASME. Home: 10154 S Seeley Ave Chicago IL 60643-2037 Office: Ill Inst Tech 10 W 32d St Chicago IL 60616-3729 E-mail: patpending@aol.com.

DIXON, BILLY GENE, academic administrator, educator; b. Benton, Ill., Oct. 25, 1935; s. John and Stella (Prowell) D.; m. Judith R. McCommons, June 7, 1957; children: Valerie J., Clark A. BS, So. Ill. U., 1957, PhD, 1967; MS, Ill. Wesleyan U., 1961. Tchr. math., chmn. dept. Cahokia (Ill.) High Sch., 1960-61; tchr. Univ. Sch., So. Ill. U., Carbondale, 1961-67, chmn. dept. math., 1963-67; dir. rsch. and evaluation ESEA Title II Project Uplift, Mt. Vernon, Ill., 1967-69; coordinator profl. edn. experiences Coll. Edn. So. Ill. U., Carbondale, 1968-75, mem. faculty, coord. grad. program in secondary edn., 1975-78, departmental exec. officer curriculum and instrn., 1978—2001, asst. to dept. exec. officer for spl. projects, 2001—. Pres. Benton Cmty. Pk. Dist., 1974—95; bd. dirs. The Holmes Partnership, 2000—. Named Citizen of Yr., Benton C. of C., 1982; recipient Liberty Bell award, 1995. Mem. Ill. Assn. Tchr. Educators (pres. 1973, exec. coun. 1976-79, Disting. mem. 1984), Assn. Tchr. Educators (chmn. nat. rev. panel Disting. Program in Tchr. Edn. 1976-86, exec. bd. 1983-86, pres. 1988-89, Pres.'s award 1983, 84, 95, 99, Disting. mem. 1992), Pi Mu Epsilon, Phi Kappa Phi, Phi Delta Kappa, Kappa Delta Pi. Democrat. Methodist. Home: 9793 Stuyvesant St Benton IL 62812-5916 Office: So Ill U Dept Curriculum Instrn Carbondale IL 62901-4610

DIXON, GERALD AUTHUR, aerospace manufacturing company executive; b. Lowell, Mass., Mar. 4, 1946; s. Lester French and Frances (Whitely) D.; m. Roberta Packard, Aug. 1, 1968 (div. May 26, 1980; children: Christy Lynn, Kelly; m. Blanche Sue, May 28, 1980; children: Joshua Stark, Jason Whitely (dec.); m. Rhonda Kim, Dec. 30, 1998. BS, Lowell (Mass.) Tech. Inst., 1970. Prodn. mgr. Fiber Materials Inc., Lowell, 1972-75; sales engr. TEK Specialties, Inc., Winchester, Mass., 1975-80; mktg. mgr. Exxon Enterprises, Green, S.C., 1980-82; bus. mgr. Airco Carbon, St. Mary's, Pa., 1982-87; program mgr. BF Goodrich, Cedar Knolls, N.J., 1987-98; sales and mktg. mgr. TRW Aeronautical Sys. Group (formerly Lucas Aerospace), Aurora, Ohio, 1998-2001, Goodrich Corp., Vergennes, Vt., 2001—. Commanding officer USNR Navsen 1006, Washington, 1993-96. Coach Little League, Brandville, N.Y., 1995. Home: 114 Wildflower Ln Waterbury Center VT 05677 Office: Goodrich Corp 100 Panton Rd Vergennes VT 05491-8026 E-mail: Gerry.Dixon@Goodrich.com.

DIXON, JACK EDWARD, biological chemistry educator, consultant; b. June 16, 1943; BA, UCLA, 1966; PhD, U. Calif., Santa Barbara, 1971. NSF Found. postdoctoral rsch. fellow U. Calif., San Diego, 1971—73; from asst. prof. to assoc. prof. biochemistry Purdue U., West Lafayette, Ind., 1973—82, prof. biochemistry, 1982—86, Harvey W. Wiley disting. prof. biochemistry, 1986—91; Minor J. Coon prof. biol. chemistry, chmn. dept. U. Mich., Ann Arbor, 1991—. Adj. asst. prof. biochemistry Ind. U. Sch. Medicine, 1976—78, assoc. prof. biochemistry, 1978—91, adj. prof. biochemistry, 1983—91, part-time prof. medicine, 1985—91; vis. lectr. Wash. State U., 1985; cons. Wyeth-Ayurst Co., Phila., 1985—, Monsanto Chem. Co., St. Louis, 1985—, Mitotix Inc., Cambridge, Mass., 1993—98, Ceptyr, 1997—; P.T. Varandani Meml. lectr. Wright State U., Dayton, Ohio, 1987; chmn. rsch. rev. com. Ind. affiliate Am. Heart Assn., 1983; spl. reviewer alcohol study NIH, 1983, 84, endocrine study sect., 1985—90; Nathan O. Kaplan lectr. U. Calif., San Diego, 1991; Vestling lectr. U. Iowa, 1991; Edmund Fischer lectr. U. Wash., Seattle, 1993; Årets Novo Nordisk lectr. U. Copenhagen, 1994; presenter in field. Recipient Rsch. award, Ind. affiliate Am. Diabetes Assn., 1985—86, Merit award, NIH, 1987, 1996, Lions award for cancer rsch., 1990. Fellow: Am. Acad. Arts and Sci., Mich. Soc. Fellows U. Mich. (sr.); mem.: Am. Soc. Neurosci., Am. Soc. Cell Biology, Am. Soc. Biochemistry and Molecular Biology (program chmn. 1994—, pres. 1996—97), Am. Physiol. Soc., Am. Chem. Soc., NAS (elected mem. Inst. Medicine 1993), AAAS, Phi Kappa Phi, Sigma Xi. Office: U Mich Biochem Dept M5416 Med Sci 1 0606 Ann Arbor MI 48109-0606

DIXON, JOHN FULTON, village manager; b. Bellingham, Wash., Dec. 17, 1946; s. Fulton Albert and Patricia (Broderick) D.; m. Karen Elizabeth Creagh, May 19, 1973; children: Neil, Craig. BS, Bradley U., 1971; M in Mgmt., Vanderbilt U., 1973. Asst. village mgr. Village of Hoffman Estates, Ill., 1974-76, village mgr., 1980-86; dir. village svcs. Village of Roselle, 1976-79; asst. village mgr. Village of Schaumburg, 1979-80; village adminstr. Village of Lake Zurich, 1986-87; village mgr. Village of Mt. Prospect, 1987-92; village adminstr. Village of Lake Zurich, 1992—. Mem. exec. bd. dirs. N.W. Suburban Mcpl. Joint Action Water Agy., Hoffman Estates, 1980-92; mem. exec. bd. dirs. N.W. Cen. Dispatch, Arlington Heights, Ill., 1987-92. Troop com. chmn. Boy Scouts Am., 1989-93; bd. dirs. Marklund Chilren's Home, 1999—. Recipient Chief Scout's award Gov. Gen. of Jamaica, Kingston, 1970; Adminstrv. fellow Woodrow Wilson Found., 1973-74, Houston fellow Vanderbilt U., 1972-73; Baker scholar Vanderbilt U., 1971-73. Mem. Met. Chgo. City Mgrs. Assn. (bd. dirs., pres. 1986-87), Ill. City Mgmt. Assn. (bd. dirs., pres. 1990-91), Rotary (bd. dirs. 1989—, pres. Lake Zurich chpt. 1997-98). Roman Catholic. Avocations: golf, travel. Home: 248 Sebby Ln Lake Zurich IL 60047-1358 Office: Village of Lake Zurich 70 E Main St Lake Zurich IL 60047-2416

DIXON, LORRAINE, city official; b. Chgo., June 18, 1950; BS in Secondary Edn., Chgo. State U., 1972. Alderman, ward 8, Chgo., 1991—. Chmn. Com. on Budget and Govt. Ops., 1994—; pres. pro-tempore Chgo. City Coun.; bd. dirs. Open Hands Chgo. and Jackson Park Hosp. Mem. United Negro Coll. Fund, Cook County Dem. Women, Ill. Majority Women's Caucus, Operation PUSH, 87th St. C. of C. (bd. dirs.). Office: 8539 S Cottage Grove Ave Chicago IL 60619-6115

DIXON, STEWART STRAWN, lawyer, consultant; b. Chgo., Nov. 5, 1930; s. Wesley M. and Katherine (Strawn) D.; m. Romayne Wilson, June 24, 1961 (dec. July 1993); children: Stewart S. Jr., John W., Romayne W. Thompson; m. Ann Wilson Grozier, Sept. 15, 1997. BA, Yale U., 1952; JD, U. Mich., 1955. Bar: Ill. 1957, U.S. Dist. Ct. 1957, U.S. Ct. Appeals 1974, U.S. Supreme Ct. 1974. Ptnr. Kirkland & Ellis, Chgo., 1957-67, Wildman, Harrold, Allen & Dixon, Chgo., 1967—. Dir. Lord, Abbett & Co. Managed Mut. Funds, N.Y.C., 1976—; dir. Otho Sprague Inst., Chgo. Trustee, past chmn. Chgo. Hist. Soc., 1982-87. 1st lt. U.S. Army, 1955-60. Mem. Am. Bar Assn., Am. Law Inst., Ill. Bar Assn., Chgo. Bar Assn. Republican. Episcopalian. Clubs: Chgo., Commonwealth, Commercial, Met., Univ., Old Elm, Onwentsia, Rolling Rock. Office: Wildman Harrold Allen & Dixon 225 W Wacker Dr Chicago IL 60606-1224

DIXON, WHEELER WINSTON, film and video studies educator, writer; b. New Brunswick, N.J., Mar. 12, 1950; s. Percival Vincent and Hilda-Barr (Wheeler) D.; m. Gwendolyn Audrey Foster, Dec. 23, 1985. AB, Livingston Coll., 1972; MA, MPhil, Rutgers U., 1980, PhD, 1982. Instr. English Rutgers U., New Brunswick, 1974-84; lectr. film studies The New Sch. for Social Rsch., 1983, 97, 98; asst. prof. English and art U. Nebr., Lincoln, 1984-88, chmn. film studies program, assoc. prof. English, 1988-92, chmn. film studies program, prof. English, 1992—; series editor Cultural Studies in Cinema Video Series SUNY Press, 1995—, endowed chair, Ryan prof. of film studies, 2000—. Guest programmer, lectr. Nat. Film Theatre of Brit. Film Inst. and Mus. of Moving Image, London, 1991; guest programmer Nat. Film Theatre of Brit. Film Inst., London, 1992; mem. ad hoc curriculum rev. com. dept. English, U. Nebr., Lincoln, 1992, mem. faculty devel. fellowship com., 1992-95, chmn. Robinson Prize com., spring 1994, chmn. faculty devel. fellowship com., 1994, mem. various MA thesis and PhD coms.; panelist NEH, 1993—; presenter papers in field; lectr. Lincoln Ctr., Mus. Modern Art, N.Y.C., New Sch. Univ., N.Y.C., 1997; guest lectr. on digital prodn., U. Amsterdam, 1999. Author: The "B" Directors: A Bibliographical Directory, 1985, The Cinematic Vision of F. Scott Fitzgerald, 1986, The Films of Freddie Francis, 1991, The Charm of Evil: The Films of Terence Fisher, 1991, The Films of Reginald Le Borg: Interviews, Essays and Filmography, 1992, The Early Film Criticism of François Truffaut, 1993, Re-Viewing British Cinema 1900-1992: Essays and Interviews, 1994, It Looks at You: The Returned Gaze of Cinema, 1995, The Films of Jean-Luc Godard, 1997, The Exploding Eye: A Re-visionary History of 1960s Experimental Cinema, 1997, The Transparency of Spectacle, 1998, Disaster and Memory, 1999, The Second Century of Cinema, 2000, Film Genre 2000, 2000, Collected Interviews: Voices from 20th Century Cinema, 2001; editor-in-chief Quarterly Review of Film and Video, 1999—; guest editor Film Criticism, Fall-Winter 1991-92, mem. editl. bd., 1991—, article reviewer, 1991—; article reviewer Jour. of History of Sexuality, 1991-93, Cinema Jour., 1993—; mem. adv. bd. Jour. Popular Brit. Cinema; manuscript reviewer SUNY Press, 1993—; contbr. articles and revs. to profl. jours. and essays to various publs., including Film Criticism, Films in Rev., Cineaste, Interview, others; writer, dir., prodr. Coming Attractions: A History of the Motion Picture Trailer, 1986-88, (feature film) What Can I Do?, 1993 (Layman Fund award 1993-94); co-prodr., co-dir., co-writer: Women Who Made The Movies, 1988-90; dir./prodr.: (feature film) Squatters, 1994; exhibited in group shows at U. Nebr.-Lincoln, 1985-86, 87-88, 89-90, Syracuse U., 1986, W.Va. U., 1986, Lincolnshire Coll. Art, Lincoln, Eng., 1988-89; performances include That's Different: Tales of Nebraska, 1987; exhibitions of films include Whitney Mus. Am. Art, 1972, Mus. Modern Art, 1994, Mus. Moving Image, London, 1994, Millennium Film Workshop, 1997, and others. Grantee Royal Film Archive of Belgium, 1974, N.J. State Arts Coun., 1972, Rsch. Coun., U. Nebr., 1984-85, Ind. Filmmaker, S.W. Alt. Media Project, 1985, Interdisciplinary Arts Fellowship Program, Rockefeller Found. and NEA, 1987, Rsch. Coun., 1987, 89, S.W. Alt. Media Project Ind. Prodn. Fund, 1993; George Holmes Faculty fellow, 1989. Office: U Nebraska Dept English 202 Andrews Hall Lincoln NE 68588-0333 E-mail: wdixon@unlserve.unl.edu.

DIXSON, J. B. communications executive; b. Norwich, N.Y., Oct. 19, 1941; d. William Joseph and Ann Wanda (Teale) Barrett. BS, Syracuse U., 1963; postgrad. in bus. adminstrn., Wayne State U., 1979-81; MBA, Ctrl. Mich. U., 1984. Pub. rels. editl. asst. Am. Mus. Natural History, N.Y.C., 1963-64; writer, prodr. Norman, Navan, Moore & Baird Advt., Grand Rapids, Mich., 1964-67; prin. J.B. Dixson Comm. Cons., Detroit, 1967-74; dir. Pub. Info. Svcs. divsn. Mich. Employment Security Commn., 1974-82; news rels. mgr. Burroughs Corp., 1982-83, dir. creative svcs., 1983-85, dir. pub. rels., 1985-86; prin. Dixson Comm., Detroit, 1986-93, Durocher Dixson Werba, LLC, Detroit, 1994—. Lectr., spkr. in field at colls, univs., cmty. orgns. Author: Guidelines for Non-Sexist Verbal and Written Communication, 1976, Sexual Harassment on The Job, 1979, The TV Interview: Good News or Bad?, 1981; contbg. columnist Detroit News, 1995-99. Mem. Detroit Mayor's Transition Com. of 100, 1972; mem. bd. mgmt. Detroit YWCA, 1974; chmn. Detroit Women's Equality Day Com., 1975; bd. dirs., founding mem. Feminist Fed. Credit Union, Detroit, 1976; centennial chair Indian Village Assn., 1993-95; founding mem. Mich. Women's Campaign Fund, 1980; active Mich. Task Force on Sexual Harassment in Workplace, Mich. Women's Com. of 100, Mich. Women's Polit. Caucus, Mich. Women's Found. Named Outstanding Sr. Woman in Radio and TV, Syracuse U., 1963; recipient Five Watch award Am. Women in Radio and TV, Mich., 1969, 75, Outstanding Women in Comm. Women's Advt. Club, 1998, cert. of recognition Detroit City Coun., 1976, Feminist of Yr. award NOW, 1977, City of Detroit Human Rights Commn., 1988, Design in Mich. award Mich. Coun. of Arts/Gov. William G. Milliken, 1977, Achievement award U.S. Dept. Labor, 1979, Spirit of Detroit award Detroit City Coun., 1980, PR Casebook, 1983, PR News Case Study, 1986, Pinnacle award Mich. Hosp. Pub. Rels. Assn., 1987, award Nat. Sch. Pub. Rels. Assn., 1992, 21st Century award Corp. Detroit Mag., 1995, Creativity in Advt. award Detroit Newspapers Assn., 2000; subject of Mich. Senate Resolution 412, 1979. Fellow Pub. Rels. Soc. Am. (accredited, pres. chpt. 1983-84, Dist. award and citation 1984, 86, 87, 93, exec. com. corp. sect. 1996-2001, Disting. Svc. award 1999), Internat. Assn. Bus. Communicators (Silver Quill award chpt. 1987, 88, 91, 93, dist. 1987, Renaissance award 1988, 91, Mercury award 1987), Nat. Assn. Govt. Communicators (Blue Pencil award 1977, Gold Screen award 1980), Automotive Press Assn., Women's Advt. Club (Top 75 Women in Comm. 1999), Econ. Club Detroit, Maple Grove Gun Club, Detroit Athletic Club. Office: Durocher Dixson Werba LLC 16th Fl Buhl Bldg 535 Griswold St Detroit MI 48226-3604 E-mail: dixson@ddwpr.com.

DLOTT, SUSAN JUDY, judge, lawyer; b. Dayton, Oh., Sept. 11, 1949; d. Herman and Mildred (Zemboch) D.; m. Austin E. Knowlton, July 11, 1986 (div. 1988); m. Stanley M. Chesley, Dec. 7, 1991. BA, U. Pa., 1971; JD, Boston U., 1973. Bar: Oh. 1973, U.S. Dist. Ct. (so. dist.) Oh. 1975, U.S. Ct. Appeals (6th cir.) 1976, U.S. Supreme Ct. 1980, U.S. Dist. Ct. (ea. dist.) Ky. 1984, U.S. dist. Ct. (no. dist.) Oh. 1989, Ky. 1990. Law clk. Oh. Ct. of Appeals, Cleveland, 1973-74; asst. U.S. atty. U.S. Dist. Ct. (so. dist.) Ohio, Dayton, 1975-79; ptnr. Graydon, Head & Ritchey, Cincinnati, Oh., 1979-95; dist. judge U.S. Dist. Ct. for So. Dist. Ohio, Cin., 1995—. Master of the bench Potter Stewart Am. Inn of Ct., 1984-98; legal reporter Multimedia Program Prodn., Inc., 1982-84. Mem. Ohio Bldg. Authority, 1988-93, vice chmn., 1990-93, Jewish Fedn. Cin., trustee and mem. com. 1979-93, Jewish Cmty. Rels. Coun. Cin., 1980-90, Hamilton County Park Dist. Vol. in Parks, 1985-86. Recipient U.S. Postal Serv. Commendation, 1977, Service award, Dayton Bar Assoc., Oh., 1975-76. Mem. ABA, FBA (asst. treas. 1981-82, treas. 1982-83, sec. 1983-84, v.p. 1984-86), Ohio Bar Assn., Ky. Bar Assn., Dayton Bar Assn., Dayton Women's Bar Assn., Cin. Bar Assn., Leadership Cin. Alumni Assn., Queen City Dog Tng. Club, 6th Cir. Jud. Conf. (life), NAACP (life), Hadassah (life). Jewish. Office: 100 E 5th St Cincinnati OH 45202-3927

DOAN, HERBERT DOW, technical business consultant; b. Midland, Mich., Sept. 5, 1922; s. Leland Ira and Ruth Alden (Dow) D.; m. Donalda Lockwood, 1946 (div.); children: Jeffrey W., Christine Mary, Ruth Alden, Michael Alden; m. Anna Junia Cassell, July 16, 1979; 1 child, Alexandra Anne Alden. B Chem. Engring., Cornell U., 1949. Founder, owner Doan Assocs., Midland, 1971-85; chmn., dir. Neogen Corp., Lansing, Mich., 1983-99; pres. Mich. High Tech. Task Force, 1981-90; nat. adv. com. dept. engring. U. Mich., Ann Arbor, 1984-95; chmn. Midland Molecular Inst., 1971—; dir. Mich. Materials and Processing Inst., Ann Arbor, 1984-92; trustee, sec. Herbert H. and Grace A. Dow Found., Midland, 1951—; researcher Dow Chem. Co., 1949-60, exec. v.p., 1960-62, pres., 1962-71, The Herbert H. and Grace A Dow Found., Midland, 1996—, chmn., 2000—. Dir. Applied Intelligent Systems, Inc., Ann Arbor, Chem. Bank and Trust Co., Arch Devel. Corp., Chgo.; mem. engring. coun. Cornell U., Ithaca, N.Y., 1964-85, emeritus, 1985—; mem. Nat. Sci. Bd., Washington, 1976-82, vice chmn., 1981-82; mem. Commn. on Phys. Scis., Math. and Applications, NRC of NAS, Washington, 1987-91; bd. govs. Argonne Nat. Lab., U. Chgo., 1984-90; tech. assessment adv. coun. Office Tech. Assessment, Washington, 1992-95. Staff sgt. USAF, 1942-45; PTO. Mem. Am. Inst. Chem. Engrs., Am. Chem. Soc., Sigma Xi. Home: 3801 Valley Dr Midland MI 48640-6601 Office: Neogen Corporation 620 Lesher Pl Lansing MI 48912

DOANE, J. WILLIAM, physics educator and researcher, science administrator; b. Bayard, Nebr., Apr. 26, 1935; married, 1958; 2 children. BS, U. Mo., 1956, MS, 1962, PhD in Physics, 1965. From asst. to assoc. prof. Kent State U., 1965-74, prof. physics, 1974-96, prof. emeritus, 1996—, assoc. dir. Liquid Crystal Inst., 1979-83, dir. Liquid Crystal Inst., 1983-96, dir. emeritus, 1996—; v.p. R&D, chief sci. officer Kent Displays, Inc., Ohio, 1996-99. Prin. investigator def. agy. and industry grants NSF. Contbr. over 200 articles to profl. jours.; holder of 10 patents. Fellow Am. Phys. Soc.; mem. Am. Assn. Physics Tchrs., Sigma Xi. Achievements includes research on liquid crystal display and nuclear magnetic resonance in liquid crystals. Office: Kent State U Liquid Crystal Inst Kent OH 44242-0001

DOBIS, CHESTER F. state legislator; b. Gary, Ind., Aug. 15, 1942; s. Jack F. and Veronica (Kordys) D.; m. Darlene Zimmerman, 1971. Student, Ind. U. N.W., 1961. Sales rep. Standard Liquors; v.p. govt. svc. Gainer Bank, 1972—; banker, v.p. govt. svc. NBD Bank; rep. Dist. 13 Ind. Ho. of Reps., 1970—, vice chmn. fin. inst., mem. house adminstrn. com., mem. pub. policy, vet. affairs, ethics com., mem. interstate coop. com., rules and legis. procedure com., spkr. pro tem, asst. minority floor leader. Mem. exec. bd. N.w. Ind. Regional Planning Commn.; vice pres. Ross Twp. Dem. Club, Merrillville, Ind., 1968—; bd. dirs. Lake County Young Dems., 1969-70; pres. Ross Twp. Young Dems., 1970—; vol. Lake Area United Way, Lake County Assn. Retarded, Polish Am. Dem. Club. With Ind. N.G. Named One of Top Freshman Legislators, Ind. Gen. Assembly, 1971. Mem. Nat. Coun. State Legislators, Gary Sportsmen Club, PNA Silver Bell. Home: 6565 Marshall Ct Merrillville IN 46410-2859

DOCKHORN, ROBERT JOHN, physician, educator; b. Goodland, Kans., Oct. 9, 1934; s. Charles George and Dorotha Mae (Horton) D.; m. Beverly Ann Wilke, June 15, 1957; children: David, Douglas, Deborah. AB, U. Kans., 1956, MD, 1960. Diplomate Am. Bd. Pediat. Intern Naval Hosp., San Diego, 1960-61, resident in pediat. Oakland, Calif., 1963-65; resident in pediat. allergy and immunology U. Kans. Med. Ctr., 1967-69, adj. asst. prof. pediat., 1969—; resident in pediat. allergy and immunology Children's Mercy Hosp., Kansas City, Mo., 1967-69, chief divsn., 1969-83, practice medicine specializing in allergy and immunology Prairie Village, Kans., 1969-94, U. Mo. Med. Sch., Prairie Village, 1969-94; pres. Internat. Med. Tech. Cons., Inc., Kansas City, 1979—; with D&B Med. Consulting, LLC, Overland Park, Kans., 1999—. Pres. I.M.T.C.I. (Internat. Med. Tech. Cons., Inc.), Kansas City, 1979-99; founder, CEO Internat. Med. Tech. Cons., Inc., Lenexa, Kans., subs. Immuno-Allergy Tech. Cons., Inc., Clin. Rsch. Cons., Inc. Contbr. articles to med. jours.; co-editor: Allergy and Immunology in Children, 1973. Fellow Am. Acad. Pediatrics, Am. Coll. Allergists (bd. regents 1976—, v.p. 1978-79, pres. 1981-82), Am. Assn. Cert. Allegists (pres. 1991—), Am. Acad. Allergy; mem. AMA, Kans. Med. Soc., Johnson County Med. Soc., Kans. Allergy Soc. (pres. 1976-77), Mo. Allergy Soc. (sec. 1975-76), Joint Coun. Socio-Econs. of Allergy (bd. dirs. 1976—, pres. 1978-79). Home: 8510 Delmar Ln Shawnee Mission KS 66207-1926 Office: D&B Med Consulting LLC 8220 Travis St Ste 117 Overland Park KS 66204-3963 Fax: 913-649-0464.

DOCKING, THOMAS ROBERT, lawyer, former state lieutenant governor; b. Lawrence, Kans., Aug. 10, 1954; s. Robert Blackwell and Meredith (Gear) D.; m. Jill Sadowsky, June 18, 1977; children: Brian Thomas, Margery Meredith BS, U. Kans., 1976, MBA, JD, 1980. Bar: Kans. 1980. Assoc. Regan & McGannon, Wichita, Kans., 1980-82, ptnr., 1983-90, Ayesh, Docking, Herd & Theis, Wichita, 1990, Morris, Laing, Evans, Brock & Kennedy, Wichita, 1990—; lt. gov. State of Kans., Topeka, 1983-87. Dem. nominee for Gov. of Kans., 1986; chmn. adv. bd. Docking Inst. Pub. Affairs, Ft. Hays State U. Mem. steering com. Campaign Kans.; chmn. campaign com. Coll. Liberal Arts and Sci., 1988-91; bd. dirs. Kans. Easter Seals-Goodwill Industries, 1987-93, chmn. 1989 Telethon, vice-chair, 1991-93; bd. dirs. Wichita Conv. and Visitors Bur., chmn.; bd. dirs. St. Francis Found., 1988-94; trustee Emporia State U. Sch. Bus.; chmn. Wichita Water Conservation Task Force, 1991—; mem. Wichita/Brookes Water Task Force, 1997; vice chmn. allocation com. United Way of the Plains, 1997—, vice chair, 2002--; mem. bd. govs. U. Kans. Sch. Law, 1998—2000; bd. dirs. Wichita Downtown Devel. Corp., 2001—, Fin. Fitness Found., 1999—. Mem. ABA, Kans. Bar Assn., Pi Sigma Alpha, Beta Gamma Sigma, Beta Theta Pi. Presbyterian. Home: 125 S Crestway St Wichita KS 67218-1309 Office: Morris Laing Evans Brock & Kennedy 200 W Douglas Ave Fl 4 Wichita KS 67202-3013

DOCKTERMAN, MICHAEL, lawyer; b. Davenport, Iowa, Dec. 14, 1954; s. Jerome and Elaine (Epstein) D.; m. Laura Di Giantonio, Sept. 25, 1983; 1 child, Eliana. BA, Yale U., 1975; JD, Duke U., 1978. Bar: Ill. 1978, U.S. Dist. Ct. (no. dist.) Ill. 1978, U.S. Dist. Ct. (ea. dist.) Mich. 1986, U.S. Dist. Ct. (ctrl. dist.) Ill. 1988, U.S. Dist. Ct. (so. dist.) Ill. 1991, U.S. Dist Ct. (we. dist.) Mich. 1995, U.S. Dist. Ct. (ea. dist.) Mo. 1996, U.S. Ct. Appeals (7th cir.) 1978, U.S. Ct. Appeals (4th, 6th and fed. cirs.) 1990, U.S. Ct. Appeals (2d cir.) 1993, U.S. Supreme Ct. 1992. Ptnr. Wildman, Harrold, Allen and Dixon, Chgo., 1978—. Co-author: IICLE Class Actions, 1986, 92, 2000; contbg. author: ABA Criminal Antitrust Litigation Manual; contbr. articles on corp. governance and compliance to profl. jours. Active Chgo. Vol. Legal Svcs., 1983—; adult bd. dirs. Greater Midwest region B'nai B'rith Youth Orgn., 1985—; bd. dirs. KAM Isaiah Israel Congregation, 1993-96, 2002--, Duke Law Alumni Assn., pres., 2000—; trustee Max and Gretel Janowski Fund, Chgo., 1992-99; active The Chgo. Com., Chgo. Coun. on Fgn. Rels., Am. Refugee Com. Recipient Award for Advocacy Internat. Acad. Trial Lawyers, Leadership Devel. award B'nai B'rith Youth Orgn. Fellow Pvt. Adjudication Found.; mem. ABA (chair corp. governance subcom. Corp. Counsel com. Bus. Law Sect.), Chgo. Bar Assn., Lawyers Club Chgo., B'nai B'rith Justice Lodge. Office: Wildman Harrold Allen Dixon 225 W Wacker Dr Chicago IL 60606-1229 E-mail: dockterm@wildmanharrold.com.

DODD, GERALDA, metal products executive; children: T. Edward Sellers III, Madison Dodd Sellers. , U. Toledo, Ohio. Receptionist Heidtman Steel, Toledo, 1978-79, various positions, 1979-88, dir. purchasing, 1988; vp HS Processing (subs. Heidtmann Steel), Balt., 1988-90; pres., CEO Thomas Madison Inc., Detroit. Bd. dirs. Detroit Regiional Chamber, Detroit Econ. Growth Corp., Workforce Devel. Music Hall, Nataki Talibath Sch., United Way Cmty. Svcs., Nat. Kidney Found. of Mich. and New Detroit, Inc. Mem. Womens Econ. Club, Nat. Assn. Women Bus. Owners, Nat. Assn. Black Automotive Suppliers, Assn. Women in Metals Industry, Greater Wayne County chpt. of The Links, Inc. Office: Thomas Madison Inc PO Box 20318 Ferndale MI 48220-0318 Fax: 313-273-8052.

DODERER, MINNETTE FRERICHS, retired state legislator; b. Holland, Iowa, May 16, 1923; d. John A. and Sophie S. Frerichs; m. Fred H. Doderer, Aug. 5, 1944 (dec. 1991); children: Dennis, Kay Lynn. BA, U. Iowa, 1948. Chair standing com. public health Iowa Ho. of Reps., 1965-66, mem., 1964-69, 81-01, minority whip, 1967-68, chairperson ways and means com., 1983-88, chair small bus. and commerce com., 1989-90, chair small bus., econ. devel. and trade com., 1991-92; mem. Iowa Senate, 1968-78, pres. pro tem, 1975-76; ret., 2001. Vis. prof. Stephens Coll., Iowa State Univ. (both 1979); vice-chairwoman Iowa Interstate Cooperation Commn., 1965-66; vice-chairwoman Democratic Party Johnson County, 1957-60; vice chairperson com. on budget and taxation Nat. Conf. State Legislatures, 1989-90; mem. Dem. Nat. Com., 1968-70, Dem. Nat. Policy Council Elected Ofcls., 1973-76; chairwoman Iowa del. Internat. Women's Yr. Del. Bd. fellows Iowa Sch. Religion; Senate activities: chair subcom. Election Law Revision, 1975-76, Legislative Census Liaison Commn., Legislative Interim Study of Juvenile Justice, Senate State Govt. Standing com., 1977-78; vice chair Legislative Coun.; mem. Departmental Rules Review com., 1975-76, Interim Study com. on Prison Reform, Child Abuse Coun. Recipient Disting. Legis. Svc. award Iowa State Edn. Assn., 1969, Iowa Fedn. Bus. & Profl. Women's Clubs recognition, 1972, Iowa Civil Liberties award, 1978, Special award Midwest Race and Sex Desegregation Fed. Assistance Ctrs., 1979, Good Citizenship medal Sons of Am. Revolution, Friend of Edn. award Iowa City, 1986, Christine Wilson award for Equality and Justice Commn. on Status of Women, 1989, Gold Seal award Iowa Coalition Against Domestic Violence, 1995, Friend of Nursing award, 1996, citation Am. Acad. Pediat., 1996, Feminist of Yr. award, 1996, Friend of Nursing award, 1996, Woman of Achievement award Bus. and Profl. Women, 1997, Reproductive Rights Advocate award, 1998, medal of honor Vet. Feminists Am., 1999; named to Iowa Women's Hall of Fame, 1978, Woman of Yr. Iowa City Sr. Ctr., 1995. Mem. LWV, Pioneer Lawnmakers (pres. 1993-95), Delta Kappa Gamma (hon.). Democrat. Methodist.

DODGE, EDWARD JOHN, retired insurance executive; b. Malone, N.Y., Mar. 28, 1935; s. Harry Gilman and Marjorie Dietz (Wright) D.; m. Ann Louise Cupps, Aug. 21, 1932. Grad., Phoenix Union H.S., 1953. Map clk. N.Y. Underwriters, San Francisco, 1956-57; underwriter Reliance Ins.,

1957-58; agt. Am. Hardware Mut., 1958; investigator Retail Credit Co., 1963-68; claims adjuster Allstate Ins., Arlington Heights, Ill., 1968-70, Epiic Ins., Phoenix, 1974; claims examiner GEICO, Chgo., 1970-73; multi-line adjuster Ariz. Adjustment, Phoenix, 1973-74; investigator Equifax, Chgo., 1974-78; sales br. mgr. Hooper Holmes, Chgo. and Springfield, Ill., 1978-80; multi-line agt. Met. Ins., Springfield, 1980-81; subrogation examiner Horace Mann Ins., 1982-97; ret., 1997. Author: Relief is Greatly Wanted, The Battle of Fort William Henry, 1998; contbr. articles to hist. publs. Commr. Boy Scouts Am., Arlington Heights, Ill., 1971-78, Springfield, 1981-92, Phoenix, 1983-84, vice chmn. scouting, Arlinton Heights, 1977-79, vice chmn. exploring, 1988-90. Sgt. USMC, 1952-56, USAF, 1958-62. Recipient Dist. Commrs. award Boy Scouts Am., 1978, Bronze Big Horn award Boy Scouts Am., 1989, Scouter of Month award Boy Scouts Am., 1978. Mem. Masons, The Queen's Regimental Assn. (hon. life mem.), The Princess of Wale's Royal Regimental Assn. (hon. life mem.). Republican. Methodist. Avocations: historical research, historical writing. Home: 1223 N Rutledge St Springfield IL 62702-2524

DODGE, PAUL CECIL, academic administrator; b. Granville, N.Y., Mar. 25, 1943; s. Cecil John Paul and Elsie Elizabeth Dodge Rogers; m. Margaret Mary Kostyun, June 6, 1964 (div. Sept. 1985); 1 child, Cynthia Ruth; m. Cynthia Dee Bennett, Apr. 26, 1986; children: Michelle Lynn, Jason Paul, Benjamin Charles. BA in Math., U. Vt., 1967. Mgr. data processing Thermal Wire & Electronics, South Hero, Vt., 1967-70, DDSV divsn. Vt. Cos., Burlington, 1970-73, Revere Copper & Brass, Clinton, Ill., 1973-78, Angelica Corp., St. Louis, 1978-81; pres. chief ops. officer Dodge Mgmt., 1981-82; mgr. systems and programming Terra Internat., 1982-87; pres. chief ops. officer Mo. Tech. Sch., 1987—. Mem. Mo. Assn. Pvt. Career Schs. (pres. 1993-94), Nat. Rehab. Assn., Mo. Rehab. Assn. Republican. Presbyterian. Avocations: amatuer radio, chess. Office: Mo Tech Sch 1167 Corporate Lake Dr Saint Louis MO 63132-1716

DODGE, PHILIP ROGERS, physician, educator; b. Beverly, Mass., Mar. 16, 1923; s. Israel R. and Anna (McCarthy) D.; children: Susan, Judith. Student, U. N.H., 1941-43, Yale, 1943; M.D., U. Rochester, 1948. Diplomate: Am. Bd. Psychiatry and Neurology. Intern Strong Meml. Hosp., 1948-49; asst. resident neurology Boston City Hosp., 1949-50, resident, 1950, sr. resident, 1951-52; practice medicine, specializing in child neurology Boston, 1956-67, St. Louis, 1967—; teaching fellow neurology Harvard Med. Sch., 1950, 51-53, instr. neurology, 1956-58, assoc. in neurology, 1958-61, asst. prof., 1962-67; asst. neurologist Mass. Gen. Hosp., 1956-59, dir. pediatric neurology program, 1958-67, assoc. neurologist, 1959-63, neurologist, 1963-67, assoc. pediatrician, 1961-62, pediatrician, 1962-67; investigator Joseph P. Kennedy, Jr. Meml. Labs. for Study Mental Retardation, 1962-67; pediatric neurologist Boston Lying-In Hosp., 1961-67; cons. in neurology Walter E. Fernald State Sch. for Retarded Children, 1963-67; med. dir. St. Louis Children's Hosp., 1967-84, pediatrician-in-chief, 1967-86; assoc. neurologist Barnes Hosp., 1967—; chmn. Mallinckrodt Dept. Pediatrics, Washington U. Sch. Medicine, 1967-86, prof. pediatrics and neurology, 1967-93; prof. emeritus pediatrics and neurology Washington U. Sch. Medicine, 1993—; lectr. in pediatrics, 1993-99. Vis. scientist Clin. Research Center, U. P.R., 1965-66, hon. vis. prof. physiology, 1967; cons. collaborative project on cerebral palsy Nat. Inst. Neurol. Diseases and Blindness, 1958; bd. dirs., chmn. research adv. com. Mass. Soc. for Prevention Cruelty to Children, 1961-67; mem. sci. research adv. bd. Nat. Assn. for Retarded Children, 1963-67; bd. dirs. Central Midwestern Regional Lab., Inc., 1968-70; mem. gen. clin. research centers adv. com. USPHS, 1971-74; mem. Mo. Gov.'s Council on Developmental Disabilities, 1971-74; chmn. Mo. Mental Health Commn., 1974-78; mem. nat. adv. child health and human devel. council NIH, 1974-77; chmn. panel on neurol. disorders, developmental, long-range program strategies NINCDS, 1977-79; panel chmn., consensus devel. conf. on diagnosis and treatment of Reye's Syndrome, 1981; vis. prof. pediatrics and adolescent medicine, Royal Postgrad. Med. Sch., U. London, 1986—; hon. vis. fellow dept. pathology U. Western Australia, Nedlands, Australia, 1986-87; vis. prof. neurology Columbia U. Coll. Physicians and Surgeons, N.Y.C., 1987-88; spl. asst. to dir. for mental retardation Nat. Inst. Child Health and Human Devel., NIH, Washington, 1987-88. Author: (with others) Nutrition and the Developing Nervous System, 1975; Editorial bd.: (with others) Jour. Developmental Medicine and Child Neurology, 1965—, Jour. Pediatrics, 1970-80, Pediatric Research, 1970-78, Current Problems in Pediatrics, 1969-84, Neurology, 1973-76; Contbr. (with others) articles to profl. jours. Served from 1st lt. to maj. M.C. U.S. Army, 1950-56. Mem. Am. Pediatric Soc. (coun. 1972-78, chmn. coun. 1978-79), Am. Acad. Neurology (past com. chmn.), Am. Neurol. Assn., Child Neurology Soc., Assn. for Rsch. in Nervous and Mental Disease, Soc. Pediatric Rsch., Soc. Biol. Psychiatry, St. Louis Soc. Neurol. Scis., Assn. Med. Sch. Pediatric Dept. Chmn. (pres. 1975-77), Alpha Omega Alpha. Home: 410 N Newstead Ave Saint Louis MO 63108-2654 Office: 1 Childrens Pl Saint Louis MO 63110-1002

DODSON, VERNON NATHAN, physician, educator; b. Benton Harbor, Mich., Feb. 19, 1923; m. Shirley Jane Wheelihan: children: Martha Ione, Kathryn Anne, Christine Louise, John Nathan, Elizabeth Marie. Student, Mich. State Coll., 1941-43, 46, Northwestern U., summer 1942, Compton (Calif.) Coll., 1943, U. Oreg., 1943-44, Corpus Christi Coll., U. Oxford, Eng., 1945, U. Mich., 1946-47, 48, 51-52, BS, 1952; MD, Marquette U., 1951. Intern in surgery Henry Ford Hosp., Detroit, 1952-53; asst. in pathology Johns Hopkins U. Hosp., Balt., 1953-54, asst. pathologist, 1953-54; resident in internal medicine Univ. Hosp., Ann Arbor, Mich., 1954-57; rsch. assoc. U. Mich. Med. Sch., 1957-60, 60-71, lectr., 1959, from jr. clin. instr. to assoc. prof., 1956-64, assoc. prof. Dept. Indsl. Health, Sch. Pub. Health, 1965-71; attending physician U.S. VA Hosp., 1961-70; mem. med. staff Milw. County Gen. Hosp., 1971-72; rsch. assoc. U.S. VA Ctr., Wood, Wis., 1971-72; prof. medicine and environ. medicine Med. Coll. Wis., Milw., 1971-72; vis. prof. dept. preventive medicine U. Wis. Med. Sch., Madison, 1973-74, prof. medicine, sect. internal medicine, and preventive medicine, 1977-94, prof. emeritus medicine and preventive medicine, 1994—. Lectr. Sch. Dentistry, U. Mich., Ann Arbor, 1957-58, Sch. Nursing, U. Mich., 1958-60, Coll. Lit., Sci. and Arts, Inst. Social Work, U. Mich., 1957-58; cons. staff physician Rochester, Minn. Meth. Hosp., 1974-77; dir. Univ. Employee Health Svc., U. Wis., Madison, 1977-80, mem. staff Ctr. Health Sci., 1978-95, hon. staff, 1995—; physician cons. VA Hosp., Madison, 1978-95; mem. interdepartmental program in toxicology, U. Mich., 1965-71, vice chair, 1969-71; mem. Environ. Toxicology Ctr., Divsn. Health Scis., U. Wis., Madison, 1972-74, 77-94, acting dir., 1974-76, 78-79, assoc. dir. Sch. Biotron., 1979-84; vis. prof. U. Tex. Health Sci. Ctr., Sch. Pub. Health, Houston, 1986, So. Occupational Health Ctr., U. Calif., Irvine, 1986; mem. com. on edn. and libr., Trinity Meml. Hosp., Cudahy, Wis., 1971-71, assoc. med. staff, 1972-73; mem. assoc. med. staff St. Lukes Hosp., Milw., 1972-73; cons. Joint Commn. on Hosp. Accreditation, Chgo., 1974-76; cons. in preventive medicine and internal medicine, Mayo Clinic, Mayo Found., Rochester, 1974-77; cons. GM, Warren, Mich., 1963-65, 72-84, med. dir. GM, Oak Creek, Wis., 1971-72; cons. Oscar Mayer Co., 1973-74; cons. plant physician, IBM, Rochester, 1976-77; cons. med. dir. George A. Hormel co., Austin, Minn., 1977; mem. occupational health adv. bd. GM, UAW, 1982-85; cons. Owens-Corning Fiberglas, Toledo, 1968—, Gen. Mills, Mpls., 1980—; bd. dirs. Nat. Biogerontology Inst., 1984—; cons. USPHS, Dept. Natural Resources, Wis., Dept. Health and Social Svcs., Wis., U.S. Dept. Agr., OSHA, Wis., Nat. Inst. Occupational Safety and Health, Ctr. for Disease Control, Dept. Industry, Labor and Human Rels., Wis.; mem. Gov.'s Task Force on Occupational Health and Safety, State of Wis., Extramural Ctr. Adv. Rev. Panel, Nat. Inst. for Occupational Health and Safety, Sentinel Event Notification System for Occupational Risks, Divsn. Health, State Dept. Health and Social Svc., Madison, Wis.; vice chair Residency Rev. Com. for Preventive Medicine, Coun. Health & The Pub., Accreditation Coun. for Gen. Med. Edn., State of Wis. Occupl. Disease and Illness Ctr. Edn. cons. editor Am. Jour. Occupational Medicine, 1979-89; assoc. editor Am. Jour. Indsl. Medicine, 1986-80; author 5 books, 17 book chpts., 44 sci. rsch. papers, 119 abstracts and presentations, 4 TV programs; co-editor 1 book. Mem. spl. citizen's adv. com. on safety Ann Arbor Bd. Edn., 1969, gov.'s com. on crime detection and law enforcement, ad hoc com. on lab. svcs., State of Mich., 1969; chmn., mem. com. on sch. safety, King Sch., Ann Arbor, 1969-70; mem. Kettle Moraine High Sch. Band Parents, Wales, Wis., 1972-74, v.p., 1973-74, citizen's com. on drug abuse, Waukesha County, Wis., 1973-74. With U.S. Army, 1942-45, ETO. Recipient Disting. Svc. award, Occupational Health award UAW, GM, 1988. Fellow ACP, Am. Coll. Occupl. Medicine (bd. dirs. 1987—, award 1988), Am. Coll. Medicine, Am. Occupl. Medicine Assn. (bd. govs. 1985, award 1988), Am. Coll. Occupl. and Environ. Medicine, Am. Coll. Preventive Medicine, Soc. Occupl. and Environ. Health; mem. AAAS, AMA (rep. residency rev. com., vice chair accreditation coun. for gen. med. edn., Physician's Recognition award 1981-2002), Am. Fedn. for Clin. Rsch., The Biochem. Soc. (London), Wis. State Med. Soc. (environ./occupl. health commn., legis. affairs commn., continuing med. edn. commn. coun. on health of the pub., coun. on med. edn., coun. on the health and the pub., 1999—, Meritorious Svc. award 1991, 96), Ctrl. States Occupl. Medicine Assn. (bd. govs.), Dane County Med. Soc., Am. Pub. Health Assn., Wis. Pub. Health Assn., Am. Cancer Soc. (award 1987), Internat. Commn. for Occupl. Health (Geneva), alumnae orgns. Mich. State U., U. Mich., Marquette U., Johns Hopkins U., Mayo Clinic, Med. Coll. Wis., U. Wis., Henry Ford Hosp., VFW, 11th Armored Divsn. Assn., Friends of WHA-TV, Smithsonian Instn., Nat. Geog. Soc., World Wildlife Fund, Sierra Club, Natural Resource Def. Coun., Sigma Xi. Office: U Wis Dept Medicine 504 Walnut St Madison WI 53705-2335

DOERMANN, HUMPHREY, economics educator; b. Toledo, Nov. 13, 1930; s. Henry John and Alice (Robbins Humphrey) D.; m. Elisabeth Adams Wakefield, Jan. 7, 1956; children: Elisabeth M., Eleanor H., Julia L. AB, Harvard U., 1952, MBA, 1958, PhD, 1967; LLD (hon.), Xavier U., La., 1990, U. Minn., 1997; LHD (hon.), Coll. St. Scholastica, 1993, U. St. Thomas, 1996, Ctrl. Coll., 1998. Asst. to com. on admissions and scholarships Harvard, 1955-56; reporter Mpls. Star, 1958-60; asst. to bus. mgr. Mpls. Star & Tribune Co., 1960-61; dir. admissions Harvard, 1961-66; asst. to dean Harvard (Faculty of Arts and Scis.), 1966-69, asst. dean for financial affairs, 1970-71; lectr. on edn. Harvard (Grad. Sch. Edn.), 1967-71; exec. dir. Bush Found., St. Paul, 1971-78, pres., 1978-97; vis. prof. Macalester Coll., 1997-2000, rsch. assoc., asst. to pres., 2000—. Cons. Coun. Higher Edn. Va., 1969, W. Va. Bd. Regents, 1970; bd. overseers Harvard Coll., Harvard U., 1973-79; trustee St. Paul Acad. and Summit Sch., 1997—; bd. dirs. Coun. on Founds., Washington, 1985-92, chmn. bd. 1990-92; trustee Found. Ctr., N.Y.C., 1975-83, chmn. bd. 1982-83; chmn. Minn. Coun. on Founds., 1981-85, Coll. Bd., N.Y.C., 1994-99; chmn. Minn. Legis. Task Force on Student Aid, 1993; chair regents candidate adv. coun. U. Minn., 1997-99; trustee Minn. Humanities Commn., 2000—. Author: Crosscurrents in College Admissions, rev. edit, 1970, Toward Equal Access, 1978; co-author (with Henry N. Drewry) Stand and Prosper, 2001; cons. editor Change mag., 1991—; contbr. articles to profl. jours. Mem. Belmont (Mass.) Town Meeting, 1969-70; dist. chmn. Rhodes Scholarship Selection Com., 1995. Served to lt. (j.g.) USN, 1952-55. Home: 736 Goodrich Ave Saint Paul MN 55105-3524 Office: Macalester Coll 1600 Grand Ave Saint Paul MN 55105-1801 E-mail: doermann@macalester.edu.

DOERSHUK, CARL FREDERICK, physician, pediatrics educator; b. Warren, Ohio, Dec. 24, 1930; s. Carl Frederick and Eula Blanche (Mahan) D.; m. Emma Lou Plummer, Aug. 21, 1954; children: Rebecca Lee, John Frederick, David Plummer. BA, Oberlin Coll., 1952; MD, Case Western Res. U., 1956. Intern U.S. Naval Hosp., Camp Pendleton, Ohio, 1956-57; resident in pediat. Cleve. Met. Gen. Hosp. and Babies and Children's Hosp., Cleve., 1959-61; postdoctoral pulmonary fellow Babies and Children's Hosp. USPHS, 1961-63; sr. instr. to prof. pediatrics specializing in academic pediatric pulmonary medicine Case Western Res. U., 1963-98, emeritus prof., 1998—. Co-editor Pediatric Respiratory Therapy, 1974, 3d edit., 1986; contbr. articles to profl. jours. Chmn. med. adv. coun. Cystic Fibrosis Found., Washington, 1966-72, bd. trustees, 1969-81, exec. com., 1969-74, v.p. med. affairs Cleve. chpt., 1965-90. Lt. M.C., USN, 1957-59. Named Young Man Yr. Cystic Fibrosis Found., 1970; recipient Richard C. Talamo Clinician Scientist award Cystic Fibrosis Found., 1997. Mem. Am. Pediatric Soc., Soc. Pediatric Research, Am. Acad. Pediatrics (exec. com. chest sect.), Am. Thoracic Soc. (chmn. pediatric pulmonary sect. 1971), No. Ohio Pediatric Soc., Acad. Medicine. Avocations: sailing, raising dahlias. Office: Rainbow Babies and Childrens Hosp 11100 Euclid Ave Cleveland OH 44106

DOHERTY, SISTER BARBARA, religious institution administrator; b. Chgo., Dec. 2, 1931; d. Martin James and Margaret Eleanor (Noe) D. Student, Rosary Coll., 1949-51; BA in Latin, English and History, St. Mary-of-the-Woods Coll., 1953; MA in Theology, St. Mary's Coll., 1963; PhD in Theology, Fordham U., 1979; LittD (hon.), Ind. State U., 1990, Dominican U., Ill., 2002. Enter order of the Sisters of Providence. Tchr. Jr. and Sr. High Schs., Ind. and Ill., 1953-63; asst. prof. religion St. Mary-of-the-Woods Coll., Ind., 1963-67, 71-75, pres., 1984-98; provincial supr. Chgo. Province of Sisters of Providence, 1975-83; dir. Inst. of Religious Formation at Cath. Theol. Union, Chgo., 1998—. Summer faculty NCAIS-KCRCHE, Delhi, India, 1970. Author: I Am What I Do: Contemplation and Human Experience, 1981, Make Yourself an Ark: Beyond the Memorized Responses of Our Corporate Adolescence, 1984; editor: Providence: God's Face Towards the World, 1984; contbr. articles to New Cath. Ency. Vol. XVII, 1982, Dictionary of Catholic Spirituality, 1993. Pres. Leadership Terre Haute, Ind., 1985-86; bd. regents Ind. Acad., 1987-98; bd. dirs. 8th Day Cen. for Justice, Chgo., 1978-83, Family Svcs., Swope Art Mus., Terre Haute, Ind., 1988-98. Arthur J. Schmidt Found. grantee, 1967-71. Mem. Women's Coll. Coalition (nat. bd. dirs. 1984-90), Ind. Colls. Ind., Ind. Colls. Found. (exec. bd.), Ind. Conf. Higher Edn. (chair), Leadership Conf. Women Religious of USA (program chairperson nat. assembly 1982-83, chair Neylan commn. 1993-97). Democrat. Roman Catholic. Avocation: walking, reading, traveling. Office: Cath Theol Union 5401 S Cornell Ave Chicago IL 60615-5664 E-mail: bdoherty@ctu.edu.

DOHERTY, BRIAN GERARD, alderman; b. Chgo., Oct. 25, 1957; s. Daniel Joseph and Kathleen (McDonagh) D.; m. Rose Mary Gillespie, 1986; children: Kathleen Marie, Kevin Michael. BA, U. N.E. Ill., 1984. Alderman 41st Ward, Chgo., 1991—. Boxing champ Chgo. Pk. Dist., 1972, 73, Chgo. Golden Gloves champion Tribune Charities, 1973. Mem. Alpha Chi Honor Soc. Roman Catholic. Home: 7805 W Catalpa Ave Chicago IL 60656-1640 Office: 6650 N Northwest Hwy Chicago IL 60631-1307

DOHERTY, CHARLES VINCENT, investment counsel executive; b. Pitts., Dec. 17, 1933; s. Charles V. and Emma (Lager) D.; m. Marilyn Bongiorno, Oct. 17, 1964; children: Charles, Michelle, Kristen. BS, U. Notre Dame, 1955; MBA, U. Chgo., 1967. CPA, Ill. Tax specialist Haskins & Sells, CPA, Chgo., 1960-67; ptnr. Lamson Bros. & Co., 1968-73; pres. Doherty Zable & Co., 1974-85, Chgo. Stock Exch., Inc., 1986-92; mng. dir. Madison Adv. Group, Chgo., 1993—. Bd. dirs. Lakeside Bank, Howe Barnes Securities, Inc., Banc of Am. Fin. Products, Brauvin Capital Corp., Knight Trading Group, Inc; trustee Wayne Hummer Investment Trust, CCM Advisors Funds. Mem. chancellor's adv. coun. U. Ill., Chgo., 1991—. E-mail: cdoherty@ameritech.net.

DOHERTY, VALERIE, employment services professional, lawyer; Chief ops. officer, gen. counsel Doherty Employment Group, Edina, Minn. Office: Doherty Employment Group 7625 Parklawn Ave Minneapolis MN 55435-5123 Fax: 612-832-8355.

DOHMEN, FREDERICK HOEGER, retired wholesale drug company executive; b. Milw., May 12, 1917; s. Fred William and Viola (Gutsch) D.; m. Gladys Elizabeth Dite, Dec. 23, 1939 (dec. 1963); children: William Francis, Robert Charles; m. Mary Alexander Holgate, June 27, 1964. BA in Commerce, U. Wis., 1939. With F. Dohmen Co., Milw., 1939-82, successively warehouse employee, sec., v.p., 1944-52, pres., 1952-82, dir., 1947—, chmn. bd., 1952-82. Travel lectr. various orgns., 1980—. Bd. dirs. St. Luke's Hosp. Ednl. Found., Milw., 1965-83, pres., 1969-72, chmn. bd., 1972-73; bd. dirs. U. Wis. Milw. Found., 1976-79, bd. visitors, 1978-88, emeritus mem., 1988—; assoc. chmn. Nat. Bible Week, Laymen's Nat. Bible Com., N.Y.C;., 1968-82, mem. coun. of advisors, 1983—; elder Presbyn. Ch.; bd. dirs. Riveredge Nature Ctr., Newburg, Wis., 1993-94. Mem. Nat. Wholesale Druggists Assn. (chmn. mfr. rels. com. 1962, resolutions com. 1963, bd. control 1963-66), Nat. Assn. Wholesalers (trustee 1966-75), Druggists Svc. Coun. (dir. 1967-71), Wis. Pharm. Assn., Miss. Valley Drug Club, Univ. Club Town Club (Milw.), Beta Gamma Sigma, Phi Eta Sigma, Delta Kappa Epsilon. Home: 3903 W Mequon Rd Mequon WI 53092-2727

DOHMEN, MARY HOLGATE, retired primary school educator; b. Gary, Ind., July 28, 1918; d. Clarence Gibson and Margaret Alexander (Kinnear) Holgate; m. Frederick Hoeger Dohmen, June 27, 1964; children: William Francis, Robert Charles. BS, Milw. State Tchrs. Coll., 1940; M of Philosophy, U. Wis., 1945. Cert. tchr., Wis. Tchr. primary grades Baraboo (Wis.) Pub. Schs., 1940-43, Whitefish Bay (Wis.) Pub. Schs., 1943-64. Contbr. articles, story, poems to various pubs. Bd. dirs. Homestead H.S. chpt. Am. Field Svc., Mequon, Wis., 1970-80; mem. Milw. Aux. VNA, 1975—, 2d v.p., 1983-85, Milw. Pub. Mus. Enrichment Club, 1975—, Boys and Girls Club of Greater Milw., 1986—; vol. Reading is Fun program, 1987—, Milw. Symphony Orch. League, 1960—, Ptnrs. in Conservation, World Wildlife Fund, Washington, 1991—, Milw. Art Mus. Garden Club, 1979—, com. chmn., 1981-86; mem. Chancellor's Soc. U. Wis.-Milw., 1991—; travel lectr. various orgns., 1980—. Mem. AAUW, Milw. Coll. Endowment Assn. (v.p. 1987-90, pres. 1991-93), Bascom Hill Soc. (U. Wis.), Woman's Club Wis., Alpha Phi (pres. Milw. alumnae 1962-64), Pi Lambda Theta (pres. Milw. alumnae 1962-64), Delta Kappa Gamma. Republican. Presbyterian. Avocations: writing, travel, nature. Home: 3903 W Mequon Rd Mequon WI 53092-2727

DOHNÁNYI, CHRISTOPH VON, musician, conductor; b. Berlin, Sept. 8, 1929; s. Hans and Christine (Bonhoeffer) von D. Student, U. Munich, Hochschule fuer Musik, Munich, Fla. State U., Berkshire Music Ctr.; doctorate (hon.), Oberlin Coll., Cleve. Inst. Music, Kent State U., Case Western Res. U., Eastman Sch. Music, 1998. Coach, condr., asst. to Sir George Solti Frankfurt (Germany) Opera, 1952-57, gen. music dir., artistic dir., 1968-77; gen. music dir. Lubeck, Germany, 1957-63, Kassel, Germany, 1963-66; chief conductor West German Radio Symphony Orch., Cologne, 1964-70; artistic dir., chief condr., intendant Hamburg (Germany) State Opera, 1977-84; music dir. designate Cleve. Orch., 1982-84, music dir., 1984—2002; prin . guest conductor Philharmonia Orch., London, 1995—97, prin. condr., 1997—. Guest conductor Salzburg Festival, Chatelet Paris, Zurich Opera House, Israel Philharm., Orchestre de Paris, Vienna Philharm., Berlin Philharm. Recordings with Vienna Philharmonia include opera: Wozzeck, Lulu, Fidelio, Flying Dutchman, Salome, 5 Mendelssohn symphonies, works by Stravinsky, Tschaikovsky, Glass, Schnittke; recordings with Cleve. orch. include symphonies of Beethoven, Brahms, Schumann, Bruckner, Dvorak, Mahler, Mozart, Schubert; orchestral works by Bartok, Lutoslawski, R. Strauss, Webern, Ives, Ruggles, Birtwistle; opera Rheingold, Walkure. Recipient Scopus award Am. Friends of Hebrew U. in Jerusalem, 1996, Scroll of Remembrance for Von Dohnányi and Bonhoeffer Families in German resistance U.S. Holocaust Mus., Washington, 1995, Condr. of Yr. award Musical Am., 1992, Comdr.'s Cross Republic of Austria, 1992, Comdr. de L'Ordre des Arts et des Lettres, France, Cross Order of Merit, Germany, Bartok prize, Hungary, 1982, Goethe medal City of Frankfurt, 1979, Richard Straus prize Munich, 1951, Torch of Liberty award Anti Defamation League, 2001. Address: Colbert Artists Mgmt 111 W 57th St Ste 1416 New York NY 10019-2211

DOHRMANN, RUSSELL WILLIAM, manufacturing company executive; b. Clinton, Iowa, June 29, 1942; s. Russell Wilbert and Anita Doris (Miller) D.; m. Rita Marie Meade, Dec. 26, 1964 (dec. Feb. 1978); m. M. Jean Stapleton, Aug. 18, 1979. BS, Upper Iowa U., 1965; MBA, Drake U., 1971. Acct. Chamberlain Mfg. Corp., Clinton, 1965-66, plant controller Derry, Pa., 1967-68; fin. analyst Frye Copysystems Inc., Des Moines, 1968-71, v.p., controller, 1971-77, pres., 1980-97, also bd. dirs.; internat. controller Wheelabrator-Frye, N.Y.C., 1977-78; pres. FryeTech, Inc., Des Moines, 1997-98; group controller Wheelabrator-Frye, 1978-80; cons., 1998—. Mem. Nat. Assn. Accts., Des. Moines C. of C. Republican. Methodist. E-mail: dohrmann@mchsi.com.

DOLAN, BOB, radio personality; married; 2 children. Mng. editor weekly newspaper, Mo.; radio host 1130 WISN, Greenfield, Wis. Avocations: golf, racquetball, travel, horse racing, writing, reading. Office: WISN Radio 12100 W Howard Ave Greenfield WI 53228*

DOLAN, JAMES VINCENT, lawyer; b. Washington, Nov. 11, 1938; s. John Vincent and Philomena Theresa (Vance) D.; m. Anne McSherry Reilly, June 18, 1960; children: Caroline McSherry, James Reilly. AB, Georgetown U., 1960, LLB, 1963. Bar: U.S. Dist. Ct. 1963, U.S. Ct. Appeals (D.C.) cir. 1964, U.S. Ct. Appeals (4th cir.) 1976. Law clk. U.S. Ct. Appeals D.C., 1963-64; assoc. Steptoe & Johnson, Washington, 1964-71, ptnr., 1971-82; mem. Steptoe & Johnson Chartered, 1982-83; v.p. law Union Pacific R.R., Omaha, 1983—. Co-author: Construction Contract Law, 1981; contbr. articles to legal jours.; editor-in-chief: Georgetown Law Jour., 1962-63. Mem. ABA, Nebr. Bar Assn., D.C. Bar Assn., Barristers, Congl. Country Club (v.p. 1982, pres. 1983), Omaha Country Club. Republican. Roman Catholic. Home: 1909 County Road 8 Yutan NE 68073-5013 Office: Union Pacific RR 1416 Dodge St Omaha NE 68179-0002

DOLAN, JAN CLARK, former state legislator; b. Akron, Ohio, Jan. 15, 1927; d. Herbert Spencer and Jean Risk Clark; m. Walter John Dolan, Apr. 22, 1950 (dec. July 1986); children: Mark Raymond, Scott Spencer, Gary Clark, Todd Alvin. BA, U. Akron, 1949. Home svc. rep. East Ohio Gas Co., Akron, 1949-50; dietitian Akron City Hosp., 1950-51; tchr. Brecksville (Ohio) Sch. Dist., 1962-66; adminstr. Orchard Hills Adult Day Ctr., West Bloomfield, Mich., 1978-83; mem. Farmington Hills (Mich.) City Coun., 1975-88, Mich. Ho. of Reps., Lansing, 1989-96. Mayor City of Farmington Hills, 1978, 85; elder Presbyn. Ch. Republican. Home: 22587 Gill Rd Farmington Hills MI 48335-4037

DOLAN, TERRENCE RAYMOND, neurophysiology educator; b. Huron, S.D., May 24, 1940; s. Buell Ellery and Mary Lucille (Engler) D.; m. Mary Ann Mechtenberg, Apr. 23, 1962; children: Katherin, Patrick, Elizabeth, Meaghan. BA, Dakota Wesleyan U., Mitchell, S.D., 1962; MS, Trinity U., San Antonio, 1963; PhD in Psychology and Physiology, U. Tex., Austin, 1966; postdoctoral study, Ctr. Neuroscis., Ind. U., Bloomington, 1966-68. Rsch. assoc. Ctr. Neuroscis., Ind. U., Bloomington, 1968-70; assoc. prof. psychology Loyola U., Chgo., 1970-74, prof. dept. psychology, 1974-76, asst. dean Grad. Sch., 1974-76, dir. Parmly Rsch. Inst., 1970-76;

program dir. NSF Neuroscis. Sect., 1976-82; prof. dept. neurophysiology U. Wis., Madison, 1982—, dir. Waisman Ctr. Mental Retardation and Human Devel., prof. dept. neurology, 1997—, prof. dept. psychology, 1997—. NSF rep. to Nat. Inst. Neurol. and Communicative Disease, NIH, 1976-77, liaison rep. to Nat. Eye Coun., NIH, 1976-82; mem. exec. coun. com. on vision NAS-NRC, 1977-82, mem. exec. coun. com. on hearing, acoustics and biomechanics, 1977-84; chmn. NSF task force on Support of Young Investigators-Young Scientists, 1979-80; mem. Fed. Noise Effects Steering Com. EPA, 1977-80; chmn. Assn. Mental Retardation Rsch. Ctr. Dirs., 1984-88; mem. nat. adv. coun. Air Force Office Sci. Rsch., 1984—; pres. Am. Assn. U. Affiliated Programs, 1984-88; pres.-elect Internat. Assn. Sci. Study Mental Deficiency, 1988-92, pres., 1992—; exec. dir. Prince Salman Ctr. for Disability Rsch., Riyadh, Saudi Arabia, 2001—. Contbr. numerous articles to profl. publs. Von Humboldt fellow, Fed. Republic Germany; grantee Nat. Inst. Child Health and Human Devel., 1982-93, Wis., 1984-85, wis. Devel. Disability Coun., 1985-93, others. Mem. Assn. Rsch. in Otolaryngology, Acoustical Soc. Am., Am. Assn. Univ. Affiliated Progs. (pres. 1988-89, Internat. Assn. Sci. Study Mental Deficiency (pres. 1992-96). Office: U Wis-Madison Waisman Ctr Mental Retardation & Human Devel 1500 Highland Ave Madison WI 53705-2274

DOLAN, THOMAS CHRISTOPHER, professional society administrator; b. Chgo., Dec. 31, 1947; s. Thomas Christopher and Bernice Mary (Doyle) D.; m. Georgia Ann Siebke, Feb. 14, 1983; children: William, Barbara, Lauren. BBA, Loyola U., Chgo., 1969; PhD, U. Iowa, 1977. Instr. U. Iowa, Iowa City, 1971-72; vis. fellow U. Wash., Seattle, 1973-74; asst. prof. U. Mo., Columbia, 1974-79; assoc. prof., dir. St. Louis U., 1979-86; v.p. Am. Coll. Healthcare Execs., Chgo., 1986-87, exec. v.p., 1987-91, pres., 1991—. Mem. Accrediting Commn. on Edn. for Health Svcs. Adminstrn., Washington, 1985-86; chmn. Assn. Univ. Programs in Health Adminstrn., Washington, 1983-84; cons. HEW, Kansas City, Mo., 1974-79, State of Mo., Jefferson City, 1974-79. Author: Systems for Health Care Administration: A Model for the Education of Health Manpower, 1975; contbr. articles to profl. jours. Pres. Mental Health Assn. Boone County, Columbia, Mo., 1977-78, Mental Health Assn. Mo., Jefferson City, 1980-82; bd. dirs. Nat. Mental Health Assn., Washington, 1982-83, Alexian Bros. Hosp., St. Louis, 1980-86, Inst. for Diversity in Health Mgmt., 1994—; chair Assn. Forum, 1999-2000; chair Am. Soc. Assn. Execs. Found., Washington, 1999-2000. Fellow Am. Coll. Healthcare Execs., Am. Soc. Assn. Execs. (cert. assn. exec.); mem. APHA. Roman Catholic. Avocations: golf, motorcycling, reading. Office: Am Coll Healthcare Execs 1 N Franklin St Ste 1700 Chicago IL 60606-3421

DOLD, ROBERT BRUCE, journalist; b. Newark, Mar. 9, 1955; s. Robert Bruce and Margaret (Noll) D.; m. Eileen Claire Norris, July 10, 1982; children: Megan, Kristen. BS in Journalism, Northwestern U., 1977, MS in Journalism, 1978. Reporter Suburban Trib, Hinsdale, Ill., 1978-83, Chgo. Tribune, 1983-90, mem. editl. bd., 1990-95, dep. editl. page editor, columnist, 1995-2000, editl. page editor, 2000—. Pulitzer prize juror, 1997-98. Columnist Chgo. Enterprise, 1991-95; critic: Downbeat Mag., 1980-84; commentator: Chgo. Week in Rev., 1987—. Bd. dirs. Jazz Inst. Chgo., 1980-83. Recipient Peter Lisagor award Sigma Delta Chi, 1988, Pulitzer prize for editorial writing, 1994, Scripps Howard Found. Nat. award Commentary, 1999. Mem. Am. Soc. Newspaper Editors. Roman Catholic. Avocations: golf, basketball, jazz music. Home: 501 N Park Rd La Grange Park IL 60526-5516 Office: Chgo Tribune 435 N Michigan Ave Chicago IL 60611-4066 E-mail: bdold@tribune.com.

DOLLENS, RONALD W. pharmaceuticals company executive; b. Ind., Dec. 17, 1946; s. William Franklin and Louise Anna (Davis) D.; m. Susan Stanley, Aug. 30, 1969; children: Stephanie, Grant. BS, Purdue U., 1970; MBA, Ind. U., 1972. From sales rep. to dir. bus. devel. Eli Lilly & Co., Indpls., 1972-85; from sr. v.p. to ceo Advanced Cardiovasc. Sys., Santa Clara, 1985-91; pres. med. devices divsn. Eli Lilly & Co., 1991-94; pres., ceo Guidant Corp., Indpls., 1994—. Office: Guidant Corp PO Box 44906 Indianapolis IN 46244-0906

DOLLIVER, ROBERT HENRY, psychology educator; b. Fort Dodge, Iowa, Oct. 15, 1934; B.A., Cornell Coll., 1958; M.A., Ohio State U., 1963, Ph.D., 1966. Social worker Bd. Child Welfare, Elyria, Ohio, 1958-59; social worker Cleve. Boys Sch., 1959-61; asst., then assoc. prof. psychology U. Mo., Columbia, 1966-77, prof., 1977-99, prof. emeritus, 1999—. Office: U Mo Dept Psychology Columbia MO 65211-0001

DOMINGUEZ, KATHRYN MARY, educator; b. Santa Monica, Calif., Nov. 26, 1960; d. Frederick A. and Margaret M. (McGauren) D. AB, Vassar Coll., 1982; MA, Yale U., 1984, M in Philosophy, 1985, PhD, 1987. Researcher Congl. Budget Office, Washington, summer 1984; rsch. scholar bd. of govs. FRS, 1985-86; asst. prof. pub. policy Kennedy Sch. Govt. Harvard U., Cambridge, Mass., 1987-91, assoc. prof. pub. policy, 1991-97; assoc. prof. pub. policy and econs. U. Mich., Ann Arbor, 1997—. Rsch. cons IMF, Washington, 1989; vis. asst. prof., asst. dir. internat. fin. sect. dept. econs. Princeton U., 1990-91; Nat. Bur. Econs. Rsch. Olin fellow, 1991-92. Author: (monograph) Oil and Money, 1989; Exchange Rate Efficiency and the Behavior of International Asset Markets, 1992; (with Jeff Frankel) Does Foreign Exchange Intervention Work?, 1993. Mem. Nat. Bur. Econ. Rsch. (rsch. assoc. 2000—), Am. Econ. Assn., Am. Fin. Assn., Phi Beta Kappa. Democrat. Office: U Mich Sch Pub Policy Lorch Hall 611 Tappan Ave Ann Arbor MI 48109-1220

DOMINSKI, MATTHEW S. property manager; Pres., CEO Urban Retail Properties Co., Chgo., 1990—. Office: Urban Retail Properties Co 900 N Michigan Ave Chicago IL 60611-1542

DOMJAN, LASZLO KAROLY, newspaper editor; b. Kormend, Hungary, Apr. 19, 1947; came to U.S., 1956; s. Frank and Violet Domjan; m. Louise Replogle, June 6, 1969; children: Andrew P., Eric S. BJ, U. Mo., 1969. Copy editor St. Louis Globe-Democrat, 1969; reporter, bureau chief UPI, St. Louis, 1969-81; reporter, night city editor St. Louis Post-Dispatch, 1981-87, exec. city editor, 1987-96, projects editor, 1996-97, asst. mng. editor, 1997-99, sr. editor, 1999—. Author, editor: Dioxin: Quandary for the 80s, 1983 (numerous awards); author: (reporter series) Hungary: Thirty Years After, 1986; editor: (series) Prosecutorial Corruption (1993 Pulitzer prize finalist). Active Leadership St. Louis. Recipient Herb Trask award Sigma Delta Chi, St. Louis, 1968. Mem. Press Club of Met. St. Louis, Investigative Reporters and Editors. Roman Catholic. Avocations: reading, freelance writing, music. Office: St Louis Post-Dispatch 900 N Tucker Blvd Saint Louis MO 63101-1099 E-mail: ldomjan@post-dispatch.com.

DOMMERMUTH, WILLIAM PETER, marketing consultant, educator; b. Chgo. s. Peter R. and Gertrude Dommermuth; m. H. Joan Hasty, June 6, 1959; children: Karin, Margaret, Jean. BA, U. Iowa; PhD, Northwestern U., 1964. Advt. copywriter Sears, Roebuck & Co., Chgo., sales promotion mgr.; asst., then asso. prof. mktg. U. Tex., Austin, 1961-67; asso. prof. U. Iowa, Iowa City, 1967-68; prof. So. Ill. U., Carbondale, 1968-86, U. Mo., St. Louis, 1986—; CEO Optiphonics, Inc. Cons. in field. Author (with Kernan and Sommers): Promotion: An Introductory Analysis, 1970, (with Andersen) Distribution Systems, 1972, (with Marcus and others) Modern Marketing, 1975, Modern Marketing Management, 1980, Promotion: Analysis, Creativity and Strategy, 1984, 2d edit., 1989; contbr. articles to profl. jours. Mem. Am. Mktg. Assn., Am. Psychol. Assn., So. Mktg. Assn., Midwest Mktg. Assn., Phi Beta Kappa, Beta Gamma Sigma, Theta Xi, Delta Sigma Pi. Home: 11 Paris Ct Lake Saint Louis MO 63367-1506 E-mail: optomizer@consultant.com.

DOMPKE, NORBERT FRANK, retired photography studio executive; b. Chgo., Oct. 16, 1920; s. Frank and Mary (Manley) D.; m. Marjorie Gies, Dec. 12, 1964; children: Scott, Pamela. Grad., Wright Jr. Coll., 1939-40; student, Northwestern U., 1946-49. CPA, Ill. Cost comptr., budget dir. Scott Radio Corp., 1947; pres. TV Forecast, Inc., 1948-52; editor Chgo. edit. TV Guide, 1953, mgr. Wis. edit., 1954; pres. Root Photographers, Inc., Chgo., 1955-91; also chmn. bd. dirs.; bd. dirs. Root Studio, Inc., 1991-96, ret., 1996. Adv. com. photography & audiovisual tech., So. Ill. U., 1980-81; adv. bd. Gordon Tech. High Sch., 1979-86; co-founder TV Guide, 1947. With USAAC, 1943-47. Mem. NEA, Nat. Sch. Press Assn., Nat. Collegiate Sch. Press Assn., United Photographers Orgn. (pres. 1970-71), Profl. Photographers Am., Profl. Sch. Photographers Am. (v.p. 1966-67, 87-88, sec.-treas. 1967-69, pres. 1969-70, dir. 1971-78, treas. 1985-86, sec. 1986-87, pres. 1988-89), Photo Mktg. Assn. (Disting. Svc. award 1992), Photographic Art and Sci. Found. (Hall of Fame elector 1969-96), Ill. Small Bus. Men's Assn. (dir. 1970-73), Chgo. Assn. Commerce and Industry (edn. com. 1966-94), Ill. H.S. Press Assn., North Cen. Assn. (visitation com. 1986), Chgo. Bible Soc. (bd. advisors), Ill. C. of C., Internat. Club, Briar Ridge Country Club. Home: 918 Cornwallis Ln Munster IN 46321-2877

DONABEDIAN, AVEDIS, physician, educator; b. Beirut, Lebanon, Jan. 7, 1919; arrived in U.S., 1955, naturalized, 1960; s. Samuel and Maritza (Der Hagopian) Donabedian; m. Dorothy Salibian, Sept. 15, 1945; children: Haig, Bairj, Armen. BA, Am. U., Beirut, 1940, MD, 1944; MPH, Harvard U., 1955. Physician, acting supt. English Mission Hosp., Jerusalem, 1945—47; instr. physiology, clin. asst. dermatology and venereology Am. U. Med. Sch., 1948—51, univ. physician, dir. univ. health service, 1949—54; med. assoc. United Community Services Met. Boston, 1955—57; asst. prof., then assoc. prof. preventive medicine N.Y. Med. Coll., 1957—61; mem. faculty U. Mich. Sch. Pub. Health, Ann Arbor, 1961—, prof. med. care orgn., 1964—79, Nathan Sinai disting. prof. public health, 1979—89, emeritus. Author: A Guide to Medical Care Administration: Medical Care Appraisal--Quality and Utilization, 1969, Aspects of Medical Care Administration, 1973, Benefits in Medical Care Programs, 1976, The Definition of Quality and Approaches to Its Assessment, 1980, Medical Care Chartbook, 1986, The Criteria and Standards of Quality, 1982, Methods and Findings of Quality Assessment and Monitoring, 1985; co-author: Striving for Quality in Health Care: An Inquiry into Policy and Practice, 1991. Recipient Dean Conley award, Am. Coll. Hosp. Adminstrs., 1969, Norman A. Welch award, Nat. Assn. Blue Shield Plans, 1976, Elizur Wright award, Am. Risk and Ins. Assn., 1978, Nat. Merit award, Delta Omega, 1978, Richard B. Tobias award, Am. Coll. Utilization Rev. Physicians, 1984, Outstanding Contbns. in Health Svcs. Rsch. award, Assn. Health Svcs. Rsch., 1985, Baxter Am. Found. Health Svcs. Rsch. prize, 1986, Gold medal award, Med. Alumni Assn., Am. U. Beirut, 1986, The Ernest A. Codman award, Joint Commn. on Accreditation of Healthcare Orgns., 1997. Fellow: APHA (Sedgewick Meml. medal 1999), Am. Coll. Med. Quality, Am. Coll. Healthcare Execs. (hon.), Am. Coll. Utilization Rev. Physicians (hon.), Royal Coll. Gen. Practitioners (hon.); mem.: Inst. Medicine NAS, Internat. Soc. Quality Assurance in Health Care (hon.), Nat. Acad. Medicine of Mex. (hon.), Avedis Donabedian Found. (Barcelona, hon. pres. 1990—, Buenos Aires, hon. pres. 1994—). Home: 1739 Ivywood Dr Ann Arbor MI 48103-4523 Office: HMP-SPH II 109 Observatory St Ann Arbor MI 48109-2029

DONAHUE, LAURA KENT, state legislator; b. Quincy, Ill., Apr. 22, 1949; d. Laurence S. and Mary Lou Kent; m. Michael A. Donahue, July 16, 1983. BS, Stephens Coll., 1971. Mem. Ill. State Senate, Quincy, 1981—. State senator; b. Quincy, Ill., Apr. 22, 1949; d. Laurence S. and Mary Lou (McFarland) Kent; m. Michael A. Donahue, July 16, 1983. B.S., Stephens Coll., 1971. Mem. Ill. State Senate, Quincy, 1981—. Mem. Lincoln Club of Adams County, Ill. Fedn. Republican Women. Mem. P.E.O. Lodge: Altrusa. Mem. Lincoln Club of Adams County, Ill. Fedn. Rep. Women. Mem. PEO, Altrusa Lodge. Office: 640 Maine St Quincy IL 62301-3908

DONALD, ARNOLD W. company executive; m. Hazel Donald; children: Radiah, Alicia, Zachary. BA, Carleton Coll.; BSME, Washington U., St. Louis. Sr. v.p. Monsanto Co., St. Louis, 1998-99; chmn., CEO Merisant Co., 2000—. Home: 1 N Brentwood Saint Louis MO 63105

DONCHIN, EMANUEL, psychologist, educator; b. Tel Aviv, Apr. 3, 1935; came to U.S., 1961; s. Michael and Guta D.; m. Rina Greenfarb, June 3, 1955; children: Gill, Opher, Ayala. BA, Hebrew U., 1961, MA, 1963; PhD, UCLA, 1965. Tchg. and rsch. asst. dept. psychology Hebrew U., 1958-61; rsch. asst. dept. psychology UCLA, 1961-63, rsch. psychologist, 1964-65; rsch. assoc. div. neurology Stanford U. Med. Sch., 1965-66, asst. prof. in residence, 1966-68; rsch. assoc. neurobiology br. NASA, Ames Rsch. Ctr., Moffett Field, Calif., 1966-68; assoc. prof. dept. psychology U. Ill., Urbana-Champaign, 1968-72, prof. psychology, mem. Beckman Inst., 1972—2001, head dept. psychology, 1980-94, prof. emeritus, 2001—; prof., chair dept. psychology U. South Fla., Tampa, 2001—. Author: (with Donald B. Lindsley) Averaged Evoked Potentials, 1969; editor: Cognitive Psychophysiology, 1984, (with M.G.H. Coles and S.W. Porges) Handbook of Psychophysiology, 1986; contbr. articles to profl. jours. Served with Israeli Army, 1952-55. Fellow AAAS, APA; mem. Soc. Psychophysiol. Research (pres. 1980, Disting. Sci.Cont. award), Fedn. Behavioral, Cognitive and Psychol. Socs. (v.p. 1981-85), Psychonomic Soc., Am. Psychol. Soc. (W. James fellow), Soc. Exptl. Psychology. Office: U So Fla Dept Psychology 4202 E Fowler Ave PCD4118 Tampa FL 33620

DONELSON, JOHN EVERETT, biochemistry educator, molecular biologist; b. Ogden, Iowa, May 23, 1943; s. Mervin E. and Christine (James) D.; m. Linda Meyers, Sept. 16, 1966; children: Christina, Loren, Lyn, Emory. BS, Iowa State U., 1965; PhD, Cornell U., 1971. Postdoctoral fellow MRC Lab. Molecular biology, Cambridge, Eng., 1971-74, Stanford (Calif.) U., 1974; from asst. prof., assoc. prof. to prof. biochemistry U. Iowa, Iowa City, 1975-89, Disting. prof. biochemistry, 1989—, chmn. dept. biochemistry, 1998—; investigator Howard Hughes Med. Ctr. Howard Hughes Med. Inst., Iowa City, 1989-97. Contbr. numerous articles to profl. jours., sci. mags. Vol. Am. Peace Corps, Dormaa, Ghana, 1965-67. Recipient Molecular Parasitology award Burroughs-Wellcome Found., N.C., 1983, Medal of Sci. Achievement award Iowa Gov., 1990. Office: U Iowa Dept Biochemistry Iowa City IA 52242

DONEY, BART J. manufacturing executive; BS in Indsl. Engring., U. Ill., 1973. Various Temple-Inland Inc., Indpls., 1986-00, group v.p. packaging, 2000—; exec. v.p. Inland Paperboard & Packaging, Inc. subs. Temple-Inland Inc. Office: Temple Inland Inc 4030 Vincennes Rd Indianapolis IN 46268-3007

DONIGER, WENDY, history of religions educator; b. N.Y.C., Nov. 20, 1940; d. Lester L. and Rita (Roth) Doniger; m. Dennis M. O'Flaherty, Mar. 31, 1964; 1 child, Michael Lester O'Flaherty. BA summa cum laude, Radcliffe Coll., 1962; PhD, Harvard U., 1968. Lectr. U. London Sch. Oriental and African Studies, 1968-75; vis. lectr. U. Calif., Berkeley, 1975-77; prof. history of religions Div. Sch., dept. South Asian langs., com. on social thought U. Chgo., 1978-85, Mircea Eliade prof., 1986—. Author: (under name of Wendy Doniger O'Flaherty) Asceticism and Eroticism in the Mythology of Siva, 1973, Hindu Myths, 1975, The Origins of Evil in Hindu Mythology, 1976, Women, Androgynes and Other Mythical Beasts, 1980, The Rig Veda: An Anthology, 1981, Karma and Rebirth in Classical Indian Traditions, 1980, Dreams, Illusion and Other Realities, 1984, Other Peoples' Myths, 1988, (under name of Wendy Doniger), The Laws of Manu, 1991, Mythologies, 1991, Purana Perennis, 1993, The Implied Spider, 1998, Splitting the Difference, 1999, The Bedtrick, 2000, The Kamasutra, 2002; editor Jour. Am. Acad. Religion, 1977-80, History of Religions, 1979—; mem. editl. bd. Ency. Britannica, 1987-98, Daedalus, 1990--. Recipient Lucy Allen Paton prize, 1961, Phi Beta Kappa prize, 1962; Jonathan Fay Fund scholar, 1962, Am. Inst. Indian Studies fellow, 1963-64, NEH summer stipend, 1980, Guggenheim fellow, 1980-81. Fellow: Am. Acad. Arts and Scis., Am. Philos. Soc.; mem.: Assn. Asian Studies (pres. 1998), Am. Acad. Religion 1984, Phi Beta Kappa. Home: 1319 E 55th St Chicago IL 60615-5301 Office: U Chgo Div Sch 1025 E 58th St Chicago IL 60637-1509

DONKER, NORMAN WAYNE, prosecutor; b. Shelby, Mich., Apr. 16, 1955; s. Marvin C. and N. Lorrene (Miller) D.; m. H. Maureen, July 10, 1987; children: Erin Elizabeth, Jonathan Russell. BS in Polit. Sci., magna cum laude, BS in History, magna cum laude, Grand Valley State, 1977; JD cum laude, Wayne State U., 1980. Bar: Mich.; U.S. Dist. Ct. (ea. dist.) Mich.; U.S. Ct. Appeals (6th cir.); U.S. Supreme Ct. Asst. prosecuting atty. Clare County, Harrison, Mich., 1980, Midland (Mich.) County, 1981, sr. asst. prosecuting atty., 1981-85, chief asst. prosecuting atty., 1985-88, prosecuting atty., 1989—. Bd. dirs. Voluntary Action Ctr., Midland, 1985-91, Ernie Wallace Meml. Blood Bank, 1994—, ARC, Midland, 1995—; mem. Mich. Cmty. Corrections Bd. Mem. Pros. Atty. Assn. Mich. (pres. 1997, bd. dirs. 1990—). Office: Midland Co Prosecutor Offc 301 W Main St Midland MI 48640-5162

DONLEVY, JOHN DEARDEN, lawyer; b. Chgo., May 29, 1933; s. Frank and Alice Genevieve (O'Connor) D.; m. Kristin Bach Minnick, Apr. 20, 1963 (div. Sept. 1985); 1 son, John Dearden. Student, Stanford U., 1950-52; BS, Northwestern U., 1954; JD, U. Chgo., 1957; postgrad., Northwestern U., 1958. Bar: Ill. 1957, U.S. Dist. Ct. (no. dist.) 1957, U.S. Ct. Appeals (7th cir.) 1969, U.S. Supreme Ct. 1972. Asst. state's atty. Cook County Criminal Divsn., Chgo., 1958-61; city prosecutor City of Evanston, Ill., 1961; assoc. Mayer, Brown & Platt, Chgo., 1962-73, ptnr., 1973-90; pvt. practice law, 1990—. Participant Hinton Moot Ct. Competition U. Chgo., 1955-56, judge, 1972 Bd. dirs. English-Speaking Union, Chgo., 1964-65; active Rep. Orgn., 1958-60. Recipient Disting. Legal award Am. Legion, Chgo., 1960; named spl. prosecutor-labor racketeering Cook County State's Atty., Chgo., 1959-61; profiled in Lindberg "Summerdale--35 Year Anniversary", 1995. Mem. ABA, Ill. Bar Assn., Chgo. Bar Assn. (criminal law com., chair def. of prisoners com.), Chgo. Athletic Assn. Office: 30 N La Salle St Ste 2140 Chicago IL 60602-2504

DONNELL, HAROLD EUGENE, JR. professional society administrator; b. Balt., Mar. 12, 1935; s. Harold Eugene and Ruth Elizabeth (Meeth) D.; m. Rosemary Gatch, Apr. 25, 1959; children— David Crawford, Laurette Butler. BA, Amherst Coll., 1957. Field asst., agt. Equitable Life Assurance Soc., Balt., 1958-61; salesman Eastern Products Corp., 1961-64, asst. nat. sales mgr., 1964-66; exec. dir. Md. State Dental Assn., Towson, 1966-74, Acad. Gen. Dentistry, Chgo., 1974—. Trustee Am. Fund for Dental Health, 1976-84 . Served with U.S. Army, 1957-58. Recipient Disting. Service award N.C. Acad. Gen. Dentistry, 1980; ann. Walter E. Levine Meritorious Service award Alpha Omega, 1970 Fellow Acad. Gen. Denistry (hon.); mem. ADA, Am. Soc. Assn. Execs. (cert. assn. exec.), Assn. Forum, Acad. Gen. Dentistry. Republican. Lutheran. Office: Academy of General Dentistry 211 E Chicago Ave Chicago IL 60611-2637 E-mail: haroldd@agd.org.

DONNELL, JON M. real estate executive; BS Acctg., U. Ariz. CPA, Ohio. V.p., assoc. gen. mgr. Del Webb Corp.; treas., CFO, Dominion Homes, Dublin, 1995-96, exec. v.p., COO, 1996-99, pres., COO, 1999—, also bd. dirs. Mem. AICPAs, Ohio Soc. CPAs. Office: Dominion Homes Inc 5501 Frantz Rd Dublin OH 43017-7502

DONNELLEY, JAMES RUSSELL, printing company executive; b. Chgo., June 18, 1935; s. Elliott and Ann (Steinwedell) D.; m. Nina Louis Herrmann, Apr. 11, 1980; children: Niel J., Nicole C. BA, Dartmouth Coll., 1957; MBA, U. Chgo., 1962. With R.R. Donnelley & Sons Co., Chgo., 1962-2000, v.p., 1974-75, group pres. fin. svcs. group, 1985-87, group pres. corp. devel., 1987-90, vice chmn. bd., 1990-2000, also bd. dirs. Bd. dirs. Sierra Pacific Resources, PMP Inc., Melbourne, Australia. Office: Stet & Query LTD Partnership Ste 1009 360 N Michigan Ave Chicago IL 60601-3803

DONNELLY, GERARD THOMAS, arboretum director; b. Detroit, Nov. 2, 1954; s. Merlin Joseph and Ruth Helen (Scherrer) D.; m. Pamela Lewis, June 16, 1990; children: Jason, Whitney, Parker. BA, Oakland U., 1976; PhD, Mich. State U., 1985. Instr. Mich. State U., East Lansing, 1981-84; asst. prof. Coe Coll., Cedar Rapids, Iowa, 1985-86; curator, asst. prof. Beal Bot. Garden Mich. State U., East Lansing, 1986-90; dir. The Morton Arboretum, Lisle, Ill., 1990—. Vice chmn. Mich. Natural Areas Coun., 1988-89; mem. woody plant crop adv. com. USDA, 1989-92. Mem. AAAS, Am. Assn. Bot. Gardens and Arboreta (chmn. plant collections com. 1989-92, N.Am. plant collections consortium 1989—, editorial adv. com. 1989—), Ecol. Soc. Am., Am. Inst. Biol. Scis., Internat. Soc. Arboriculture, Am. Soc. for Hort. Sci. Office: Morton Arboretum Rte 53 Lisle IL 60532

DONNELLY, JOHN F. automotive part company executive; m. Barbara Donnelly; children: JOhn, Aisling, Saraid. BA, U. Mich.; M Sci. Mgmt., MIT. With Donnelly Corp., Holland, Mich., 1967—, mfg. mgr., current bus. group mgr. automotive vision sys., bus. group mgr. modular windows, v.p. modular window sys., sr. v.p. modular window sys. group, 1992—. Bd. dirs. Lakeshore Boys and Girls Club, Holland Hist. Trust. Office: Donnelly Corp 49 W 3d St Holland MI 49423

DONNELLY, PAUL E. lawyer; b. Kansas City, Mo., Jan. 12, 1948; AB, St. Louis U., 1970, JD, 1973. Bar: Mo. 1973. Law clerk to Hon. William H. Becker U.S. Dist. Ct. (we. dist.) Mo., 1973-75; counsel U.S. Senator Stuart Symington, 1975-77; mem. Stinson, Mag & Fizzell, Kansas City, Mo. Editorial bd. St. Louis U. Law Jour., 1972-73. Mem. ABA, Mo. Bar, Kansas City Met. Bar Assn. Office: Stinson Mag & Fizzell PO Box 419251 Kansas City MO 64141-6251

DONNELLY, ROBERT, bishop; b. Mar. 22, 1931; Ordained priest Roman Cath. Ch., 1957. Consecrated bishop, 1984; bishop Archdiocese of Toledo, 1984—. Office: PO Box 985 Toledo OH 43697-0985

DONNELLY, ROBERT WILLIAM, bishop; Attended, St. Meinard (Ind.) Sem. Coll., Mt. St. Mary's West Sem., Norwood, Ohio. Ordained priest Roman Cath. Ch., 1957; ordained titular bishop Gasba, aux. bishop, Toledo, 1984. Home: 2544 Parkwood Ave Toledo OH 43610-1317 Office: PO Box 985 Toledo OH 43697-0985 also: 1933 Spielbusch Ave Toledo OH 43624-1360

DONNEM, ROLAND WILLIAM, retired lawyer, real estate owner, developer; b. Seattle, Nov. 8, 1929; s. William Roland and Mary Louise (Hughes) D.; m. Sarah Brandon Lund, Feb. 18, 1961; children: Elizabeth Donnem Sigety, Sarah Madison. BA, Yale U., 1952; JD magna cum laude, Harvard U., 1957. Bar: N.Y. 1958, U.S. Dist. Ct. (ea. and so. dists.) N.Y. 1959, U.S. Ct. Appeals (2d cir.) 1959, U.S. Ct. Claims 1960, U.S. Tax Ct. 1960, U.S. Supreme Ct. 1963, U.S. Ct. Appeals (3d cir.) 1969, D.C. 1970, U.S. Ct. Appeals (D.C. cir.) 1970, Ohio 1976, U.S. Dist. Ct. (no. dist.) Ohio 1980, U.S. Ct. Appeals (7th cir.) 1980, U.S. Ct. Appeals (6th cir.) 1984. With Davis Polk & Wardwell, N.Y.C., 1957-63, 64-69; law sec. appellate divsn. N.Y. Supreme Ct., 1963-64; dir. policy planning antitrust divsn. Justice Dept., Washington, 1969-71; v.p., sec., gen. counsel Standard Brands Inc., N.Y.C., 1971-76; from v.p. law to sr. v.p. law and casualty prevention Chessie System, Cleve., 1976-86; ptnr. Meta Ptnrs., real estate devel., 1984—2002, mng. ptnr., 1989—2002, registered security rep., 1985-90; bd. dirs., gen. counsel Acorn Properties, Inc., Cleve., 1985—2002, pres., 1989—2002; bd. dirs., gen. counsel Meta Devel. Corp., 1985—2002, pres., 1989—2002; bd. dirs., gen. counsel Meta Properties, Inc., 1988—2002, pres., 1989—2002. Founding mem., bd. dirs. Assn. Sheraton Franchisees N.Am., 1997—2002. Mem. editl. bd. Harvard Law Rev., 1955-57. Bd. dirs., fin. v.p. Presbyn. Home for Aged Women, N.Y.C., 1972-76; bd. dirs., treas. James Lenox Ho., Inc., 1972-76; trustee Food and Drug Law Inst., 1974-76; trustee, sec. Brick Presbyn. Ch., N.Y.C., 1974-76; sec. class of 1952, Yale U., 1992-97; bd. dirs. Yale Alumni Fund, 1990-95; chmn. Cleve. Area Yale Campaign, 1991-97. Lt. (j.g.) USNR, 1952-54. Fellow Timothy Dwight Coll., Yale U., 1987—. Mem. D.C. Bar Assn., Greater Cleve. Bar Assn., Am. Law Inst. (life), Am. Arbitration Assn. (nat. panel arbitrators), Def. Orientation Conf. Assn. (bd. dirs. 1996-99), Yale U. Alumni Assn. Cleve. (treas. 1982-84, del. 1984-87, trustee 1984-93, adv. coun. 1993—), Yale U. Alumni Assn. (bd. govs. 1987-90), Union Club (N.Y.C. and Cleve.), Capitol Hill Club (Washington), Washington Chevy Chase Club, Cleve. Racquet Club, Kirtland Club (Cleve.), Met. Club (Washington), Phi Beta Kappa. Republican. Presbyterian. Home: 2945 Fontenay Rd Shaker Heights OH 44120-1726

DONNER, THOMAS BENJAMIN, lawyer; b. Yankton, S.D., Mar. 8, 1957; BA, U. Nebr., 1979, JD, 1982. Bar: Nebr. Assoc. Samison & McNalley, Franklin, Nebr., 1982-83; atty. County Atty.'s Office, West Point, 1986—; pvt. practice Wisner and West Point. Mem. C. of C., Lions. Avocations: hunting, fishing, outdoors. Office: 137 S Main St # 2 West Point NE 68788-1832

DONOHOE, JEROME FRANCIS, lawyer; b. Yankton, S.D., Mar. 17, 1939; s. Francis A. and Ruth D.; m. Elaine Bush, Jan. 27, 1968; 1 child, Nicole Elaine. BA, St. John's U., 1961; JD cum laude, U. Minn., 1964. Bar: Ill. 1964, S.D. 1964. Atty. Atchison, Topeka & Santa Fe Ry. Co., Chgo., 1967-73, gen. atty., 1973-78; gen. counsel corp. affairs Santa Fe Industries Inc., 1978-84; v.p. law Santa Fe Industries, Inc., 1984-90, Santa Fe Pacific Corp., Chgo., 1984-94; ptnr. Mayer, Brown, Rowe & Maw, 1990-99, sr. counsel, 1999—. Bd. dirs. Better Govt. Assn., 1989—, Evanston Cmty. Found., 2000—; Capt. JAGC. U.S. Army, 1964-67. Fellow: Ill. Bar Found.; mem.: ABA (sect. chair, pub. utility, comm. and transp. law sect.), Northwestern U. Assocs., Mich. Shores Club (Wilmette, Ill.), Chgo. Athletic Assn., Chgo. Club. Office: Mayer Brown Rowe & Maw 190 S La Salle St Ste 3100 Chicago IL 60603-3441 E-mail: jdonohoe@mayerbrown.com.

DONOHUE, CARROLL JOHN, lawyer; b. St. Louis, June 24, 1917; s. Thomas M. and Florence (Klefisch) D.; m. Juanita Maire, Jan. 4, 1943 (div. July 1973); children: Patricia Carol, Christine Ann Donohue Smith, Deborah Lee Donohue Wilucki; m. Barbara Lounsbury, Dec., 1978. AB, LLB/JD magna cum laude, Washington U., 1939. Bar: Mo. 1939. Ptnr. Husch, Eppenberger, Donohue, Cornfeld & Jenkins, St. Louis, 1949—. Contbr. articles to profl. jours. Campaign chmn. ARC, St. Louis County, 1950; mem. ad. com. Child Welfare, St. Louis, 1952-55; mem. exec. com. Slum Clearance, 1949, bond issues coms., 1995; mem. bond issue com. St. Louis County Bond Issue, screening and supervisory coms., 1955-61, county citizen's com. for better law enforcement, 1953-56, chmn. com. on immigration policy, 1954-56; mayor City of Olivette, Mo., 1953-56; chmn. St. Louis County Bd. Election Commrs., 1960-65; chmn. com. Non-Partisan Ct. Plan; vice chmn. bd. Regional Commerce and Growth Assn. (lifetime recognition award 1996); pres. St. Louis C.C. Found.; bd. dirs. Downtown St. Louis, Inc. (leadership award 1996), Civil Entrepreneurs Orgn., Caring Found., Gateway Mayors Emeritus Inc., Anti-Drug Abuse Edn. Fund, P.T. Boat. Comdr. USN, WWII. Decorated Bronze Star medal, Navy and Marine Corps medal; recipient Disting. Alumni award Washington U., 1991, Good Guys award NOW, 1995. Mem. ABA, Mo. Bar Assn. (past bd. govs., chmn. ann. meeting, editor jour. 1940-41), St. Louis Bar Assn. (past pres., v.p., treas., Disting. Lawyer award 1992), Order of Coif, Mo. Athletic Club, Univ. Club, Omicron Delta Kappa, Sigma Phi Epsilon, Delta Theta Phi. Office: Husch & Eppenberger LLC 100 N Broadway Ste 1300 Saint Louis MO 63102-2706

DONOVAN, DIANNE FRANCYS, journalist; b. Houston, Sept. 30, 1948; d. James Henry and Doris Elaine (Simerly) D.; m. Anthony Charles Burba; children: Donovan Anthony, James Donovan. Student, Trinity Coll., Dublin, Ireland, 1969; BA, Spring Hill Coll., 1970; MA, U. Mo., 1975, U. Chgo., 1982. Copy editor Chgo. Sun-Times, 1977-79; fgn./nat. copy desk supr. Chgo. Tribune, 1979-80, asst. editor for news/features, 1980-83, lit. editor, 1985-93, mem. editorial bd., 1993-99, sr. editor for recruitment, 2000—. Vis. prof. U. Oreg. Sch. Journalism, Eugene, 1983-85; adj. faculty Northwestern U. Sch. Journalism, 1980-81, 89-90; bd. dirs. Chgo. Tribune Found. Bd. dirs. Nelson Algren/Heartland lit. awards, Chgo., 1986-93; judge Nat. Headliners' Club Awards, Atlantic City, N.J., 1983. Recipient award for editl. writing Am. Soc. Newspaper Editors, 1999, Media award Chgo. Bar Assn., 1999. Episcopalian. Office: Chgo Tribune Co 435 N Michigan Ave Chicago IL 60611-4066

DONOVAN, JOHN VINCENT, consulting company executive; b. Chgo., May 13, 1924; s. Timothy Vincent and Mabel (Hederman) D.; m. Patricia Hasselhorn, Dec. 29, 1950; children: James, Timothy, Walter. AB, DePauw U., 1947, postgrad. in law, 1947-48; postgrad. in bus., Northwestern U., 1949-54. Mem. adminstrv. staff Swift-Brazil, 1947-50; asst. treas. Mid State Corp. Mobil Homes, Union City, Mich., 1951-55; gen. mgr. Bailey Corp., cosmetics, Chgo., 1955-58; sales mgr. Dole Corp., Honolulu, 1961-63; chmn. Intercon Rsch. Assocs. Ltd., Lincolnwood, 1963—. Past bd. dirs. Ind. Voters Ill., Chgo. Lt. (j.g.) USNR, 1942-45. PTO. Mem. AAAS, Licensing Execs. Soc., Assn. Corp. Growth, World Future Soc., Chgo. Athletic Assn., Mich. Shores Club. Home: 431 Laurel Ave Wilmette IL 60091-2809 Office: Intercon Rsch Assocs Ltd 6865 N Lincoln Ave Lincolnwood IL 60712-4612

DONOVAN, LAURIE B. former state legislator; b. Little Falls, N.Y., Dec. 14, 1932; m. William Donovan, 1958; four children. BA, Pratt Inst.; MA, Syracuse U. State rep. dist. 74 Mo. Ho. of Reps., 1983-99. Active Coun. Mental Retardation. Home: 7 Ipswich Ct Florissant MO 63033-4816

DONOVAN, LESLIE D., SR. state legislator; m. Mary (Sissy) Donovan. Kans. state rep. Dist. 94, 1993—; auto dealer, investor. Home: 314 N Rainbow Lake Rd Wichita KS 67235-8533

DONOVAN, PAUL V. former bishop; b. Bernard, Iowa, Sept. 1, 1924; s. John J. and Loretta (Carew) D. Student, St. Joseph Sem., Grand Rapids, Mich.; BA, St. Gregory Sem., Cin., 1946; postgrad., Mt. St. Mary Sem. of West, Cin.; JCL, Pontifical Lateran U., Rome, 1957. Ordained priest Roman Catholic Ch., 1950; asst. pastor St. Mary Ch., Jackson, Mich., 1950-51; sec. to bishop of Lansing; adminstr. St. Peter Ch., Eaton Rapids, 1951-55; sec. to bishop, 1957-59; pastor Our Lady of Fatima Ch., Michigan Center, Mich.; and St. Rita Mission, Clark Lake, 1959-68; pastor St. Agnes Ch., Flint, 1968-71; bishop of Kalamazoo, 1971-94. Mem. liturgical commn. Diocese of Lansing, chmn., 1963; mem. Cath. Bd. Edn., Jackson and Hillsdale counties; mem. bishop's personnel com., priests' senate. Bd. dirs. Family Services and, Mich. Children's Aid. Office: 2131 Aberdeen Dr Kalamazoo MI 49008-1759 Address: 238 Falkirk Ct Kalamazoo MI 49006-4355

DOODY, MARGARET ANNE, English language educator; b. St. John, N.B., Can., Sept. 21, 1939; came to U.S., 1976; d. Hubert and Anne Ruth (Cornwall) D. B.A., Dalhousie U., Can., 1960; B.A. with 1st class hons., Lady Margaret Hall-Oxford U., Eng., 1962, M.A., 1965, D.Phil., 1968; LLD (hon.), Dalhousie U., 1985. Instr. English U. Victoria (B.C., Can.), 1962-64, asst. prof. English, 1968-69; lectr. Univ. Coll. Swansea, Wales, 1969-76; assoc. prof. English U. Calif.-Berkeley, 1976-80; prof. English dept. Princeton U., N.J., 1980-89; Andrew W. Mellon prof. humanities, prof. English Vanderbilt U., Nashville, 1989-99, dir. comparative lit. program, 1992-99; John and Barbara Glyn Family prof. lit. U. Notre Dame, 2000—. Author: A Natural Passion: A Study of the Novels of Samuel Richardson, 1974; (novels) Aristotle Detective, 1978, The Alchemists, 1980, Aristotle e la giustizia poetica, 2000; (play) (with F. Stuber) Clarissa, 1984; The Daring Muse: Augustan Poetry Reconsidered, 1985; Frances Burney: The Life in the Works, 1988, The True Story of the Novel, 1996; editor: (with Peter Sabor) Samuel Richardson Tercentenary Essays, 1989; co-editor: (with Douglas Murray) Catharine and Other Writings by Jane Austen, 1993, (with Wendy Barry and Mary Doody Jones) Anne of Green Gables, 1997. Guggenheim postdoctoral fellow, 1979; recipient Rose Mary Crawshay award Brit. Acad., 1986. Episcopalian. Office: U Notre Dame Dept English Notre Dame IN 46556 E-mail: Doody.y@md.edu.

DOOLEY, DAVID J. elementary school principal; Prin. Aquila Primary Ctr., St. Louis Park, Minn., 1984-99, Field's Sch., Mpls., 1999—. Recipient Elem. Sch. Recognition award U.S. Dept. Edn., 1989-90. Office: Field's Sch 4645 4th Ave S Minneapolis MN 55409-2699

DOOLEY, DONALD JOHN, retired publishing executive; b. Des Moines, Aug. 16, 1921; s. Martin and Anne Marguerite (Barger) D.; m. Beverly Frederick, Dec. 21, 1955 (div. 1977); children: Nancy Elizabeth, Katherine Anne(dec.) , Mary Bridget, Robert Frederick; m. Patricia Connell, Dec. 28, 1996. B.A., U. Iowa, 1947; postgrad., Drake U., 1949-50. Gen. Promotion and pub. relations mgr. Meredith Corp., Des Moines, 1953-59, dir. pub. relations, 1960-65; art and editorial dir. Better Homes & Gardens Books & Spl. Interest Publs., 1965-77; dir. editorial planning and devel. Better Homes and Gardens Books (Meredith Corp.), 1977-84; cons., 1985. Chmn. bd. adv. com. Sch. Vol. Program, Des Moines; steering com. Intercultural Affairs program to Desegregate Dist. Schs., 1975-77; treas. Iowa U. Parents Assn., 1977-79; bd. dirs. Iowa Cystic Fibrosis Found., 1979-87, v.p., 1981-85; trustee Citizens Scholarship Found. Am., 1976-85, Iowa Freedom of Info. Council, 1977-87; adv. bd. Adult and Community Edn., Des Moines Pub. Sch., 1982— ; cons. White House Conf. on Families, 1981. Served as officer USAAF, 1942-46. Decorated 2 battle stars; recipient Dorothy Dawe award Home Furnishings Industry, 1973. Mem. Pub. Rels. Soc. Am. (accredited, pres. chpt. 1969, dir. chpt. 1965-76), ACLU, Beyond War (co-dir. Iowa office 1987-88), Friendship Force, Ams. for Dem. Action, Sigma Nu (comdr. chpt. 1946-47), Found. for Global Community, 1991—. Democrat. Club: Echo Valley Country Home and Office: 3711 Oak Creek Pl West Des Moines IA 50265-7968

DOOLEY, PATRICK JOHN, graphic designer, design educator; b. Cleve., May 29, 1950; s. John William and Edna Ann (Mellick) D.; m. Mary Leah Spicer, Apr. 3, 1982; children: Claire Adele, Grace Ellen, James Joseph. BFA, U. Iowa, 1975, MA, 1977, MFA, 1978. Designer J. Paul Getty Mus., L.A., 1980-89; design mgr. J. Paul Getty Mus., J. Paul Getty Trust, 1987-89; designer, owner Patrick Dooley Design, Santa Monica, Calif., 1989-93, Lawrence, Kans., 1993—; mem. faculty Otis Parsons Sch. Art and Design, L.A., 1988-93; assoc. prof. dept. design Sch. Fine Art U. Kans., Lawrence, 1993—, Gretchen Van Bloom Budig tchg. prof., 1997. Freelance graphic designer, L.A., 1978-80, designer, cons. Walt Disney Co., Burbank, Calif., 1989-93, Lannan Lit. Found., L.A., 1991—, The Lapis Press, Venice, Calif., 1989-93, Nelson-Atkins Mus., Kansas City, Mo., 1995-96; spkr. Assn. Am. U. Presses ann. conf., 1994, Art Dirs. Club Tulsa, 1996; judge 42nd Art Dirs. Club L.A. Show, 1988 Designer: (poster) Illuminated Manuscripts, 1984 (N.Y. Type Dirs. Club award of excellence 1985), (books) Whisper of the Muse, 1986 (N.Y. Art Dirs. Club award of merit 1987), Pierre Dubreuil, 1988 (Am. Inst. Graphic Arts Book Show cert. of excellence 1989), The Surrealists Look at Art, 1990 (N.Y. Art Dirs. Club award of merit 1991), Explorations, 1992 (Am. Inst. Graphic Arts 50 Books of 1992), Pacific Wall, 1992 (Am. Inst. Graphic Arts Cover Show 1994), Walter Evans: The Getty Museum Collection, 1996 (Assn. Am. Univ. Presses cert. of excellence 1996). Recipient over 60 awards from Comm. Arts Mag., Print Mag., Am. Assn. Museums, Art Mus. Assn. Am., Am. Fedn. Arts, Univ. and Coll. Designer's Assn., others. Mem. Am. Inst. Graphic Arts, Univ. and Coll. Designers Assn. Avocation: gardening. Office: U Kans Dept Design 300 Art And Design Bldg Lawrence KS 66045-0001

DOOLITTLE, SIDNEY NEWING, retail executive; b. Binghamton, N.Y., Sept. 7, 1934; s. Raymond Luvurn and Helen Esther (Newing) D.; m. Barbara Mae Colsten, Sept. 12, 1954; children: Scott Sidney, Craig Francis, Sally Anne. Student, Rensselaer Poly. Inst., 1954-56; A.A. in Advanced Mgmt, Harvard U., 1977. With Montgomery Ward & Co., 1955-83, dir. internat. ops., 1970-73; v.p., dir. Montgomery Ward & Co. (Montgomery Ward Internat. Inc.), 1972; corp. v.p., div. mgr. catalog mdse. Montgomery Ward & Co., Chgo., 1978-83; exec. v.p., mdse. mgr., dir. Warehouse Club, Inc., 1983-84; pres. SND Enterprises, 1984-85; founding ptnr. McMillan/Doolittle, 1986—. Bd. dirs., chmn. compensation and audit com. Otasco Inc., 1986-88; bd. dirs. High Performance Appliances, 1992-96. Vice chmn. bd. dirs. Henrotin Hosp., Chgo., 1980-97; vice-chmn. Mid-Am. chpt. Red Cross., chmn. bd. Greater Chgo. chpt., 1999—. Mem. Mail Order Assn. Am. (chmn. bd. 1981-83), Chgo. Fgn. Relations Council. Presbyterian. Office: McMillan Doolittle 350 W Hubbard St Chicago IL 60610-4098

DORAN, THOMAS GEORGE, bishop; b. Rockford, IL, Feb. 20, 1936; Licentiate in Sacred Theology, Pontifical Gregorian U., Rome, 1962, Ph.D. in Canon Law, 1975-78. Ordained priest, 1961, ordained bishop, 1994. Asst. pastor St. Joseph Parish, Elgin, IL, St. Peter Parish, South Beloit; various admin. duties Diocese of Rockford, rector diocesan cathedral; prelate auditor Roman Rota, 1986-1994; bishop Rockford, Ill., 1994—. Mem. Supreme Tribunal of the Apostolic Signatura, 2000. Mem. Congregation for the Clergy. Office: Diocese of Rockford PO Box 7044 Rockford IL 61125-7044

DORGAN, BYRON LESLIE, senator; b. Dickinson, N.D., May 14, 1942; s. Emmett P. and Dorothy (Bach) D.; m. Kimberly Olson Dorgan; children: Scott, Shelly (dec.), Brendon, Haley. BBA, U. N.D., 1965; MBA, U. Denver, 1966. Exec. devel. trainee Martin Marietta Corp., Denver, 1966-67; dep. tax commr., then tax commnr. State of N.D., 1967-80; mem. 97th-102nd congresses from N.D., Washington, 1981-92, U.S. Senate from N.D., Washington, 1992—; asst. Dem. floor leader U.S. Senate, 1996—. Mem. commerce, sci. and transp. com., select com. on Indian affairs, Dem. policy com., 1992—, appropriations com., energy and natural resource com.; instr. econs. Bismarck (N.D.) Jr. Coll., 1969-71. Contbr. articles to profl. jours. Recipient Nat. Leadership award Office Gov. N.D., 1972 Mem. Nat. Assn. Tax Adminstrs. (exec. com. 1972-75) Office: US Senate 713 Hart Senate Off Bldg Washington DC 20510-0001*

DORIS, ALAN S(ANFORD), lawyer; b. Cleve., June 18, 1947; s. Sam E. and Rebecca (Sunshine) D.; m. Nancy Rose Spitzer, Jan. 10, 1976; children: Matthew, Lisa. AB and BS in Bus. cum laude, Miami U., Oxford U., 1969; JD cum laude, Harvard U., 1972. Bar: Ohio 1972, U.S. Dist. Ct. (no. dist.) Ohio 1972, U.S. Tax Ct. 1972, U.S. Ct. Appeals (6th cir.) 1972. Assoc. Stotter, Familo, Cavitch, Elden & Durkin, Cleve., 1972-77; ptnr. Elden & Ford, 1978-79, Benesch, Friedlander, Coplan & Aronoff, Cleve., 1980-2000, Squire, Sanders & Dempsey, 2000—. Editor: Ohio Transaction Guide. Treas. Hawthorne Valley Country Club, Cleve., 1984-85; chmn. Cleve. Tax Inst., 1994. Mem. ABA (chmn. capital recovery com. taxation sect. 1994-96). Avocation: golf. Office: Squire Sanders & Dempsey LLP 4900 Key Tower Cleveland OH 44114

DORMAN, JEFFREY LAWRENCE, lawyer; b. Akron, Ohio, Feb. 6, 1949; s. Milton and Belle (Handler) D.; m. Bernadette Marie Pawlik, Sept. 2, 1988. BA, U. Mich., 1971; JD, Case Western Res. U., Cleve., 1974; MS, U. Wis., 1976. Bar: Ohio 1975, Ill. 1979, U.S. Dist. Ct. (no. dist.) Ill. 1980. Staff atty. U.S. Dept. Justice, Washington, 1976-79; assoc. Sonnenschein Nath & Rosenthal, Chgo., 1979-82, ptnr., 1982-2000, Freeborn & Peters, 2000—. Mem. ABA, Ohio Bar Assn., Chgo. Bar Assn. Avocation: mountain climbing. Home: 2639 N Southport Ave Chicago IL 60614-1227 Office: Freeborn & Peters 8000 Sears Tower 311 S Wacker Dr Ste 3000 Chicago IL 60606-6677

DORN, JOHN, state legislator; b. Dec. 28, 1943; m. Kathleen; 3 children. BA, John's U.; MA, U. Wis. State rep. Minn. Ho. Reps., Dist., 24A, 1986—. Vice chmn. appropriations com., mem. edn.-higher edn. fin. divsn., environ. & natural resources & local govt. & met. affairs coms., Minn. Ho. Reps. Home: 1021 Orchard Rd Mankato MN 56001-4522

DORNETTE, W(ILLIAM) STUART, lawyer, educator; b. Washington, Mar. 2, 1951; s. William Henry Lueders and Frances Roberta (Hester) D.; m. Martha Louise Mehl, Nov. 19, 1983; children: Marjorie Frances, Anna Christine, David Paul. AB, Williams Coll., 1972; JD, U. Va., 1975. Bar: Va. 1975, Ohio 1975, U.S. Dist. Ct. (so. dist.) Ohio 1975, D.C. 1976, U.S. Ct. Appeals (6th cir.) 1977, U.S. Supreme Ct. 1980. Assoc. Taft, Stettinius & Hollister, Cin., 1975-83, ptnr., 1983—. Instr. law U. Cin., 1980-87, adj. prof., 1988-91. Co-author: Federal Judiciary Almanac, 1984-87. Mem. Ohio Bd. Bar Examiners, 1991-93, Hamilton County Rep. Exec. Com., 1982—; bd. dirs. Zool. Soc. Cin., 1983-94, Cin. Parks Found., 1995—. Mem. FBA, Ohio State Bar Assn., Cin. Bar Assn., Am. Phys. Soc. Methodist. Home: 329 Bishopsbridge Dr Cincinnati OH 45255-3948 Office: 1800 Firstar Tower 425 Walnut St Cincinnati OH 45202-3923 E-mail: dornette@taftlaw.com.

DORSMAN, PETER A. printing company executive; Various positions Nat. Cash Register Corp., 1978-96; sr. v.p., gen. mgr. Std. Register Co., Dayton, Ohio, 1996-99, COO, exec. v.p., 1999—. Office: Std Register Co 600 Albany St Dayton OH 45408

DORSO, JOHN, state legislator; b. Mpls., June 12, 1943; s. Carmen T. and Jean D. Dorso; m. Susan James, 1987; children: Victor, Louis, Carmen, Danielle, Amy, Todd. BA, Coll. St. Thomas, 1967. V.p. Dorso Trailer Sales, Fargo, pres. semi trailer sales and leasing; mem. N.D. Ho. of Reps. Dist. 46, 1984—; majority leader N.D. Ho. of Reps. Mem. sts. and hwys. com., transp. com.; chmn. industry, bus. and labor com., majority leader N.D. Ho. Reps.; bd. dirs. Behavioral Health Care, Inc.; pres. N.D. Drivers. Chmn. dist. 46 N.D. Rep. Com., 1981-83, United Rep. Com., Fargo, 1983-84. Recipient Legislative Vision award, 1991, 93, Lignite Pub. Svc. award, 1993. Mem. N.D. State U. Teammakers (pres. 1982-83), N.D. Motor Carriers Assn., Fargo C. of C. Home: 1121 26th Ave S Fargo ND 58103-5728

DORWART, DONALD BRUCE, lawyer; b. Zanesville, Ohio, Dec. 12, 1949; s. Walter G. and Katherine (Kachmar) D.; children: Claire Lauren, Hillary Beth. BA, Vanderbilt U., 1971; JD, Washington U., St. Louis, 1974. Bar: Mo. 1974, U.S. Dist. Ct. (ea. dist.) Mo. 1974. Assoc. Thompson Coburn LLP, St. Louis, 1974-79, ptnr., 1980—; dir. New Energy Corp. Ind., 1992-95. Contbr. articles to profl. jours. Mem.: ABA, Focus St. Louis (mem. selection com. 1990—91, mem. fin. com. 1990—, chmn. 2001—, mem. cmty. police com. 2000—, bd. dirs. 2000—, treas. 2001—), Bar Assn. Met. St. Louis (chair securities regulation com. 1979), Maritime Law Assn. U.S. (proctor, mem. maritime fin. com. 1980—), Noonday Club. Office: Thompson Coburn LLP One US Bank Plz Ste 3300 Saint Louis MO 63101-1643 E-mail: ddorwart@thompsoncoburn.com.

DOTSON, JOHN LOUIS, JR. newspaper publisher; b. Paterson, N.J., Feb. 5, 1937; s. John Louis and Evelyn Elizabeth (Nelson) D.; m. Peggy Elaine Burnett, Apr. 4, 1959; children: John, Damon, Christopher, Brandon, Leslie. B.S., Temple U., 1958, Doctor of Journalism (hon.), 1981. Reporter Newark News, 1959-64; gen. assignment reporter Detroit Free Press, 1965; with Newsweek Mag., 1965-83; corr. Detroit, 1965-69, L.A., 1969-70; bur. chief, 1970-75; news editor N.Y.C., 1976-77; sr. editor, 1977-83; asst. to exec. editor Phila. Inquirer, 1983-84; exec. asst. to pres. Phila. Newspapers, Inc., 1984-85, dir. night ops., 1986-87; pres., pub. Daily Camera, Boulder, Colo., 1987-92; pub. Akron Beacon Journal, Akron, OH. Bd. dirs. Robert C. Maynard Inst. Journalism Edn., 1974—, treas., 1974-78, chmn., 1980-84, 93-99; mem. Pulitzer Prize Bd., 1991-2000; mem. nat. adv. bd. Poynter Inst. for Media Studies, 1994-2000; bd. dirs. Nat. Conf. for Cmty. Justice, Mus. Arts Assn. Mem. bd. visitors John S. Knight Fellowships, Stanford U., 1983—, Sch. Journalism, U. N.C., Chapel Hill, 1987—; mem. adv. bd. Sch. Journalism and Mass Comms., U. Colo., Boulder, 1988—; trustee Akron Cmty. Found., 1993—, chmn., 1995-96; mem. exec. com. Akron Regional Devel. Bd.; mem. governing bd. Summit Edn. Initiative. Office: Akron Beacon Jour 44 E Exchange Place PO Box 640 Akron OH 44309-0640

DOTT, ROBERT HENRY, JR. geologist, educator; b. Tulsa, June 2, 1929; s. Robert Henry and Esther Edgerton (Reed) Dott; m. Nancy Maud Robertson, Feb. 1, 1951; children: James, Karen, Eric, Cynthia, Brian. Student, U. Okla., 1946-48; BS, U. Mich., 1950, MS, 1951; PhD, Columbia U., 1956. Exploration geologist Humble Oil & Refining Co., Ariz., Oreg., Wash., 1954-56, So. Calif., 1958; mem. faculty U. Wis.-Madison, 1958-94, prof. geology, 1966-84, Stanley A. Tyler Disting. prof., 1984—, chmn. dept. geology and geophysics, 1974-77, emeritus prof., 1994—. Vis. prof. U. Calif., Berkeley, 1969; Cabot disting. vis. prof. U. Houston, 1986—87; NSF sci. faculty fellow Stamford U. and U.S. Geol. Survey, 1978, U. Colo., 1979; acad. visitor Imperial Coll., Oxford U., London, 1985—86, Adelaide U., Australia, 1992; cons. Roan Selection Trust, Ltd., Zambia, 1967, Atlantic-Richfield Co., 1983—85, Hubbard Map Co., 1984—86; lectr. Bur. Petroleum and Marine Geology, China, 1986; Erskine fellow, vis. prof. Canterbury U., New Zealand, 1987; Woodford-Ellis lectr. Pomona Coll., 1994. Co-author: Evolution of the Earth, 6th edit., 2001; contbr. 1st lt. USAF, 1956—57. Recipient Outstanding Tchr. award, Wis. Student Assn., 1969, Ben. H. Parker award, Am. Inst. Profl. Geologists, 1992; fellow AEC, Columbia U., 1956. Fellow: Edinburgh Geol. Soc. (hon. corr. 1997), Geol. Soc. Am. (chmn. history of geology divsn. 1990, councilor 1992—94, History of Geology award 1995, L.L. Sloss award 2001); mem.: AAAS, History of Earth Sci. Soc. (pres. 1990), Internat. Assn. Sedimentologists, Soc. Econ. Paleontologists and Mineralogists (sec.-treas. 1968—70, v.p. 1972—73, pres. 1981—82, hon., William H. Twenhofel medal 1993), Am. Assn. Petroleum Geologists (Pres.'s award 1956, Disting. Svc. award 1984, Disting. lectr. 1985), Sigma Xi (Disting. lectr. 1988—89). Unitarian. Office: U Wis Dept Geology and Geophysics 1215 W Dayton St Madison WI 53706-1600 E-mail: rdott@geology.wise.edu.

DOTY, DAVID SINGLETON, federal judge; b. Anoka, Minn., June 30, 1929; BA, JD, U. Minn., 1961; LLD (hon.) , William Mitchell Coll. Law. Bar: Minn. 1961, U.S. Ct. Appeals (8th and 9th cirs.) 1976, U.S. Supreme Ct. 1982. V.p., dir. Popham, Haik, Schnobrich, Kaufman & Doty, Mpls., 1962-87, pres., 1977-79; instr. William Mitchell Coll. Law, 1963-64; judge

U.S. Dist. Ct. for Minn., 1987—. Mem. Adv. Com. on Civil Rules, 1992-98, Adv. Com. on Evidence Rules, 1994-98; trustee Mpls. Libr. Bd., 1969-79, Mpls. Found., 1976-83. Fellow ABA Found.; mem. ABA, Minn. Bar Assn. (gov. 1976-87, sec. 1980-83, pres. 1984-85), Hennepin County Bar Assn. (pres. 1975-76), Am. Judicature Soc., Am. Law Inst. Home: 23 Greenway Gables Minneapolis MN 55403-2145 Office: US Dist Ct 14 W US Courthouse 300 S 4th St Minneapolis MN 55415-1320 E-mail: dsdoty@mnd.uscourts.gov.

DOTY, KAREN M. county official; b. N.Y.C., Oct. 16, 1948; d. Printon A. and Mary A. Doty. BS, Old Dominion U., Norfolk, Va., 1973; MA in Urban Studies, U. Akron, Ohio, 1977; JD, U. Akron, 1981. Atty., ptnr. Buckingham, Doolittle & Burroughs LLP, Akron, 1981-99; state rep. State of Ohio, 1993-96; chief staff Summit County, Akron, 1999—2000, dir. dept. law, 2001—. Mem. Leadership Akron, 1985; trustee Ardmore, Inc., 1980—85, pres., 1983—85; trustee Leadership Akron Alumni Assn., 1985—87, chmn. tng. com., 1988—90; mem. Akron Health Commn., 1984—89, pres., 1986—89; chair City of Akron 1990 Charter Rev. Commn.; mem. Children Svcs. Bd., 1990—92; Mayor's Task Force on Juvenile Violence, 1994—95; trustee Akron Law Libr. Assn., 1997—98; chair by-laws com. Women's Network, 1998—; chair grants adv. com. Women's Endowment Fund, 1998—2001, trustee, 1998—, Cuyahoga Valley Scenic R.R., 1997—; trustee, vice chair Scenic Ohio, 1997—; trustee Akron Gen. Med. Ctr., 1997—99. Named Woman of Yr., Akron Bus. and Profl. Women, 1994. Mem.: NASW (Ascending Achiever award 1994), Akron Bar Assn. Home: 1345 Jefferson Ave Akron OH 44313-7621 Office: Summit County 175 S Main St Rm 206 Akron OH 44308-1354 E-mail: kdoty@exec.summitoh.net.

DOUGHERTY, CHARLES HAMILTON, pediatrician; b. St. Louis, June 1, 1947; s. Charles Joseph and Suzanne Louise (Hamilton) D.; m. Mary Laverty Peckham, July 7, 1972; children: Bridget, Matthew, Erin, Kelly. BA in Biology, Coll. of the Holy Cross, 1969; MD, U. Rochester Sch. of Medicine, N.Y., 1973. Pediatric resident St. Louis Children's Hosp., 1973-76; pvt. practice pediatrics Primary Pediatric Care Group, St. Louis, 1976-86, Esse Health, St. Louis, 1986—. Fellow Am. Acad. Pediatrics. Roman Catholic. Avocations: marathon running, adventure vacations, computers, water sports, powered parachute pilot. Office: Esse Health 13303 Tesson Ferry Rd Saint Louis MO 63128-4062 E-mail: cdougher@essehealth.com., cdoughe103@aol.com.

DOUGHERTY, CHARLES JOHN, university administrator, philosophy and medical ethics educator; b. N.Y.C., June 28, 1949; s. Charles Aloysius and Mary Elizabeth (Quinn) D.; m. Sandra Lee Drabik; children: Constance Marie, Justin Charles. BA, St. Bonaventure U., 1971; MA, U. Notre Dame, 1973, PhD in Philosophy, 1975. Prof. philosophy Creighton U., Omaha, 1975-88, dir., Ctr. for Health Policy and Ethics, 1988-95, v.p. acad. affairs, 1995-2001; pres. Duquesne U., Pitts., 2001—. Author: Ideal, Fact, and Medicine, 1985, (with R.P. Heaney) Research for Health Professionals, 1988, American Health Care: Realities, Rights and Reforms, 1988, (with Jerry Cederblom) Ethics at Work, 1990, (with A. Haddad and B. Edwards) Ethical Dilemmas in Perioperative Nursing, 1990, Back to Reform, 1996; contbr. articles to profl. jours.; mem. bd. editors Health Progress, 1989—. Chmn. Nebr. Com. for the Humanities, Lincoln, 1987-88; bd. dirs. Fedn. of State Humanities Couns., 1986-89; mem. disciplinary rev. bd. Nebr. Supreme Ct., 1988—, Nebr. Accountability and Disclosure Commn., 1991—; bd. dirs. Sisters of Charity Health Sys. of Cin., 1994-96; bd. trustees Cath. Health Assn., 1995—. Mem. Am. Philos. Assn., Am. Catholic Philos. Assn. (exec. council mem. 1987-90), Alpha Sigma Nu. Democrat. Roman Catholic. Office: Duquesne Univ 600 Forbes Ave Pittsburgh PA 15282

DOUGHERTY, J. PATRICK, state legislator; b. Decatur, Ill., June 30, 1948; s. James Francis and Bernadine Brennan Dougherty; m. Beverly Anne Martin, 1973; children: Erica Maureen, Bridget Colleen, Elizabeth Kathleen. BA, Quincy Coll., 1970; postgrad., Kenrick Theol. Sem., 1970-72. State rep. dist. 98 Mo. Ho. of Reps., 1979-82, dist. 67, 1983—; caseworker divsn. family svc. St. Louis County, Mo., 1974-78; devel. dir. Marianist Apostolic Ctr.; mem. adv. bd. Fanning Cmty. Sch.; mem. adv. com. Crippled Children; mem. legis. com. United Way Greater St. Louis. Named Outstanding Freshman Legislator Mo. Assn. Pub. Employees, 1979—; recipient Citizen Labor Energy award, 1984, Rutherford T. Phillips award Humane Assn., 1984, Svc. award Mo. Humane Soc., 1984. Home: 4031 Parker Ave Saint Louis MO 63116-3719

DOUGHERTY, RICHARD MARTIN, library and information science educator; b. East Chicago, Ind., Jan. 17, 1935; s. Floyd C. and Harriet E. (Martin) D.; m. Ann Prescott, Mar. 24, 1974; children— Kathryn E., Emily E.; children by previous marriage— Jill Ann, Jacquelyn A., Douglas M. B.S., Purdue U., 1959, LHD honoris causa, 1991; M.L.S., Rutgers U., 1961, Ph.D., 1963; LHD honoris causa, U. Stellenbosch, South Africa, 1995. Head acquisitions dept. Univ. Library, U. N.C., Chapel Hill, 1963-66; assoc. dir. libraries U. Colo., Boulder, 1966-70; prof. library sci. Syracuse U., N.Y., 1970-72; univ. librarian U. Calif-Berkeley, 1972-78; dir. univ. library U. Mich., Ann Arbor, 1978-88, acting dean. Sch. Library Sci., 1984-85, prof. sch. info., 1978-98, prof. emeritus, 1999—; pres. Dougherty & Assocs., 1994—. Cons., change mgmt. librs.; founder, pres. Mountainside Pub. Corp., 1974—. Author: Scientific Management of Library Organizations, 2d edit., 1982; co-author: Preferred Futures for Libraries II, 1993; editor Coll. and Research Libraries jour., 1969-74, Jour. Acad. Librarianship, 1975-94, Library Issues, 1981—. Trustee Ann Arbor Dist. Libr., 1995—2002, pres. bd. trustees, 1998—2000. Recipient Esther Piercy award, 1968, Disting. Alumnus award Rutgers U., 1980, Acad. Librarian Yr., Assn. Coll. and Research Libraries, 1983, ALA Hugh C. Atkinson Meml. award, 1988, Blackwell Scholarship award, 1992, Joseph Lippincott medal, 1997; fellow Council on Library Resources. Mem. ALA (coun. 1969-76, 89-92, exec. bd. 1972-76, 89-92, endowment trustee 1986-89, pres. 1990-91), Assn. Rsch. Librs. (bd. dirs. 1977-80), Rsch. Librs. Group, Inc. (exec. com. 1984-88, chmn. bd. govs. 1986-87), Soc. Scholarly Pub. (bd. dirs. 1990-92, exec. com. 1991-92), Internat. Fedn. Libr. Assns. (round table of editors of library jours. 1985-87, standing com. univ. libr. sect. 1981-87). Home: 6 Northwick Ct Ann Arbor MI 48105-1408 Office: Dougherty & Assoc PO Box 8330 Ann Arbor MI 48107-8330 E-mail: rmdoughe@umich.edu.

DOUGHERTY, ROBERT ANTHONY, retired manufacturing company executive; b. St. Louis, May 3, 1928; s. Joseph A. and Venita E. (Gretline) D.; m. Rosemary Schmertmann, Jan. 29, 1955; children: Kevin, Patrick, Michael, Mary Ann, Timothy. B.S. in Mech. Engring, U. Notre Dame, 1952. Registered profl. engr., Calif. cert. mfg. engr. Sales engr. Robert R. Stephens Machinery Co., St. Louis, 1952-60, dist. mgr., 1961-72; pres. Dougherty & Assos., Prairie Village, Kans., 1972-99, ret., chmn. bd. dirs. Bd. dirs. Tech-Industry Cons., Lenexa, Kans.; exec. com. Kans. Industry/Univ./Govt. Engring. Edn. Consortium. Mem. adv. com. Pittsburg, Kans. Sch. Sci. and Tech., 1987—; coord. cons. Kans. U. Ctrs. Excellence for Kans. Tech. Enterprise Corp., 1991—. Served with U.S. Army, 1946-48. Recipient Productivity award Coll. and Univ. Mfg. Edn. Council, 1979, Soc. Mfg. Engrs. Joseph A. Siegel Meml. honor award, 1992; Outstanding Engring. Achievements award San Fernando Valley Engrs. Council, 1980. Fellow Instn. Prodn. Engrs. Gt. Britain (life); mem. ASME (state legis. fellow), Am. Soc. for Metals, Soc. Mfg. Engrs. (pres. 1980-81, dir. 1971-82, Region 5 award of merit 1969), Serra Club of Kansas City Kans. (pres.-elect 2002--). Roman Catholic. Clubs: Round Hill Bath and Tennis (pres. 1971), Hillcrest Country (v.p. 1982, pres. 1983—).

DOUGLAS, ANDREW, state supreme court justice; b. Toledo, July 5, 1932; 4 children J.D., U. Toledo, 1959. Bar: Ohio 1960, U.S. Dist. Ct. (no. dist.) Ohio 1960. Former ptnr. Winchester & Douglas; judge Ohio 6th Dist. Ct. Appeals, 1981-84; justice Ohio Supreme Ct., 1985—. Mem. nat. adv. bd. Ctr. for Informatics Law John Marshall Law Sch., Chgo.; former spl. counsel Atty. Gen. of Ohio; former instr. law Ohio Dominican Coll. Served with U.S. Army, 1952-54 Recipient award Maumee Valley council Girl Scouts U.S., 1976, Outstanding Service award Toledo Police Command Officers Assn., 1980, Toledo Soc. for Autistic Children and Adults, 1983, Extra-Spl. Person award Central Catholic High Sch., 1981, Disting. Service award Toledo Police Patrolman's Assn., 1982, award Ohio Hispanic Inst. Opportunity, 1985, Disting. Merit award Alpha Sigma Phi, 1988, Gold "T" award U. Toledo, First Amendment award Cen. Ohio Chpt. Soc. Profl. Journalists Sigma Delta Chi, 1989; named to Woodward High Sch. Hall of Fame. Mem. Toledo Bar Assn., Lucas County Bar Assn., Ohio Bar Assn., Toledo U. Alumni Assn., U. Toledo Coll. Law Alumni Assn. (Disting. Alumnus award 1991), Internat. Inst., North Toledo Old Timers Assn., Old Newsboys Goodfellow Assn., Pi Sigma Alpha, Delta Theta Phi. Office: Ohio Supreme Ct 30 E Broad St Fl 3 Columbus OH 43215*

DOUGLAS, CHARLES W. lawyer; b. Chgo., Apr. 1, 1948; BA, Northwestern U., 1970; JD, Harvard U., 1974. Bar: Ill. 1974, U.S. Dist. Ct. (no. dist.) Ill. 1974, U.S. Ct. Appeals (6th cir.) 1978, U.S. Ct. Appeals (9th cir.) 1981, U.S. Ct. Appeals (2nd cir.) 1983, U.S. Ct. Appeals (7th cir.) 1984. Ptnr. Sidley & Austin, Chgo. Office: Sidley & Austin Bank 1 Plz 425 W Surf St Apt 605 Chicago IL 60657-6139

DOUGLAS, GEORGE HALSEY, writer, educator; b. East Orange, N.J., Jan. 9, 1934; s. Halsey M. and Harriet Elizabeth (Goldbach) D.; m. Rosalind Braun, June 19, 1961; 1 son, Philip. AB with honors in Philosophy, Lafayette Coll., 1956; MA, Columbia U., 1966; PhD, U. Ill., 1968. Tech. editor Bell Tel. Labs., Whippany, N.J., 1958-59; editor Agrl. Expt. Sta., U. Ill., Urbana, 1961-66, instr. dept. English, 1966-68, asst. prof. English, 1968-77, assoc. prof. English, 1977-88, prof. English, 1988—. Author: H.L. Mencken Critic of American Life, 1978, The Teaching of Business Communication, 1978, Rail City: Chicago and Its Railroads, 1981, Edmund Wilson's America, 1983, Women of the Twenties, 1986, The Early Days of Radio Broadcasting, 1987, The Smart Magazines, 1991, All Aboard: The Railroad in American Life, 1992, Education Without Impact: How Our Universities Fail the Young, 1992, Skyscraper: A Social History of the Tall Building in America, 1996, Postwar America, 1998, The Golden Age of the Newspaper, 1999; editor numerous books; contbr. articles to profl. jours., reference books, television documentaries. Mem. MLA, Am. Studies Assn., Am. Bus. Comm. Assn. (editor jour. bus. comm. 1968-80). Home: 809 Mendota Dr Champaign IL 61820-7566

DOUGLAS, JANICE GREEN, physician, educator; b. Nashville, July 11, 1943; d. Louis D. and Electa Green. BA magna cum laude, Fish U., 1964; MD, Meharry Med. Coll., 1968. Intern Meharry Med. Coll., 1968-71; NIH tng. fellow in endocrinology, instr. internal medicine Vanderbilt U., Nashville, 1971-73; sr. staff fellow sect. on hormonal regulation NIH, 1973-76; asst. prof. medicine Case Western Res. U. Sch. Medicine, Cleve., 1976-81, assoc. prof. medicine, 1981-84, prof. medicine, 1984—; dir. hypertension renal ambulatory care svc. Univ. Hosps. Cleve., 1976-80; dir. divsn. endocrinology and hypertension dept. medicine Univ. Hosps. Cleve. and Case Western Res. U., 1988-93, vice chair acad. affairs dept. medicine, 1991-99, dir. divsn. hypertension dept. medicine, 1993—. Mem. numerous grant rev. coms.; lectr., presenter in field; atteding physician in medicine and endicrinology U. Hosps., 1987; vis. prof. SUNY, Kings County Hosp. and Health Sci. Ctr., Bklyn., 1987, Med. U. S.C., 1989, Harlem Hosp., N.Y.C., 1993, N.Y. Med. Coll., Valhalla, 1994. Mem. editl. rev. bd. Jour. Clin. Investigation, 1990—, Am. Jour. Physiology, Renal Fluid and Electrolytes, 1989-91; editl. bd. Hypertension, 1994—, Am. Soc. Clin. Investigation, 1990—, Ethnicity and Disease, 1990—, Circulation, 1993—; guest editor Jour. Clin. Investigation, U. Calif., San Diego, 1992—; assoc. editor Jour. Lab. and Clin. Medicine, 1986-90; reviewer numerous manuscripts and abstracts.; contbr. numerous articles, abstracts to profl. publs., chpts. to books. Fellow High Blood Pressure Coun., Am. Heart Assn., 1993—. Mem. Assn. Am. Physicians, Cleve. Med. Assn., Am. Soc. Hypertension, Kidney Found. Ohio, Women in Endocrinology, Inter-Am. Soc. Hypertension, Women in Nephrology, Assn. for Acad. Minority Physicians, Am. Physiology Soc., Endocrine Soc., Ctrl. Soc. for Clin. Rsch., Internat. Soc. Hypertension in Blacks, Inst. Medicine of NAS, Internat. Soc. Nephrology, Am. Soc. Nephrology, Am. Soc. Clin. Investigation, Am. Fedn. Clin. Rsch., Am. Heart Assn., Phi Beta Kappa, Alpha Omega Alpha (pres. Meharry chpt. 1968), Beta Kappa Chi. Office: Case Western U Sch Medicine 10900 Euclid Ave # 165 Cleveland OH 44106-1712

DOUGLAS, KENNETH JAY, food products executive; b. Harbor Beach, Mich., Sept. 4, 1922; s. Harry Douglas and Xenia (Williamson) D.; m. Elizabeth Ann Schweizer, Aug. 17, 1946; children: Connie Ann, Andrew Jay. Student, U. Ill., 1940-41, 46-47; J.D., Chgo. Kent Coll. Law, 1950; grad., Advanced Mgmt. Program, Harvard, 1962. Bar: Ill. 1950, Ind. 1952. Spl. agt. FBI, 1950-54; dir. indsl. relations Dean Foods Co., Franklin Park, Ill., 1954-64, v.p. fin. and adminstrn., 1964-70, chmn. bd., chief exec. officer, 1970-87, chmn. bd., 1987-89, vice-chmn., 1989-92. Bd. dirs. Andrew Corp. Mem. Chgo. Com. With USNR, 1944-46. Mem. Chgo. Club, Econ. Club, Execs. Club, Comml. Club (Chgo.), Oak Park Country Club, River Forest Tennis Club, Old Baldy Country Club (Wyo.). Republican. Office: 1440 W North Ave Ste 207 Melrose Park IL 60160-1425 E-mail: kenmilk@aol.com.

DOUGLAS, WILLIAM, dental educator, biomedical research administrator; b. Belfast, No. Ireland, Aug. 18, 1938; Am. citizen; married; 2 children. BS, Queen's U., Belfast, 1960, MS, 1961, PhD in Chemistry and Biomaterials, 1965; BDS, Guy's Hosp., London, 1970. Asst. lectr. in chemistry Queen's U., 1961-65; tchr. clin. dentistry Sch. Dentistry, Cardiff, Wales, 1965-67, lectr. dental materials Wales, 1971-78; assoc. prof. U. Minn., Mpls., 1978-85, dir. dental materials Sch. Dentistry, 1978—, H.L. Anderson endowed prof., 1985—. Cons. in field. Recipient IR-100 award Jour. Rsch. and Devel., 1983; NIH grantee, 1984—. Fellow Acad. Dental Materials; mem. Internat. Assn. Dental Rsch. Office: U Minn Dental Rsch Ctr Biomaterials and Biomechanics 16-212 Moos Tower Minneapolis MN 55455

DOUGLASS, BRUCE E. physician; b. Berwyn, Ill., Sept. 26, 1917; s. Frank Lionel and Helen Mary (Eccles) D.; m. Charlotte Maurer Natwick, Oct. 14, 1942; children: Jean N., Bruce G., John F. B.A., U. Wis., 1938, M.D., 1942; M.S. in Medicine, U. Minn., 1949. Intern Med. Coll. of Va., Richmond, 1942-43; resident in internal medicine Mayo Clinic, Rochester, Minn, 1947-50, mem. staff, 1949—, chmn. div. preventive medicine, 1962—; dir. Mayo Clinic (Mayo sect. of Patient and Health Edn.), 1976—. Dir. Occupational Health Inst., Chgo., 1968— Author: Anatomy of the Portal Vein and Its Tributaries, 1949, The Problem of Benign Bronchial Obstruction, 1954, Predicting Disease: Is It Possible? 1971, Health Problems of Hospital Employees, 1971, Examining Healthy Persons: How and How Often? 1980. Chmn. Rochester Music Bd., 1960-70; v.p. Minn. Zool. Soc., 1974-77. Served to capt. M.C. AUS, 1944-47. Fellow Am. Acad. Occupational Medicine (Keogh award 1981), Am. Occupational Med. Assn. (pres. 1977-78, Meritorious Service award 1979); mem. AMA (Physician's Recognition award 1974-77, chmn. sect. council on preventive medicine 1978-80, del. for occupational med. to ho. of dels. 1978-85), Minn. Med. Assn. (chmn. com. on public health edn. 1979), Ramazzini Soc., Assn. Tchrs. Preventive Medicine, Am. Coll. Preventive Medicine, Minn. Zool. Soc., Sigma Xi, Phi Kappa Phi, Sigma Phi, Nu Sigma Nu. Office: Mayo Clinic Rochester MN 55905-0001 Home: Charter House 211 2d St NW Rochester MN 55901

DOULL, JOHN, toxicologist, pharmacologist; b. Baker, Mont., Sept. 13, 1922; s. John G. and Vivian (Kelling) D.; m. Vera Orsborn, Mar. 1, 1958; children: Ellen, John, James. BS, Mont. State U., 1944; MD, PhD, U. Chgo., 1953. From asst. to assoc. prof. U. Chgo., 1946-67, asst. dir. Toxicity Lab.; prof. Med. Sch. U. Kans., Kansas City, 1967—, dir. Ctr. for Environ. Health, 1985-89, now prof. emeritus. Chair com. on toxicology NRC/Nat. Acad. Sci., Washington, 1985-93; mem. sci. adv. panel EPA, Washington, 1980-89. Editor: Textbook of Toxicology, 1975, 2d edit., 1980, 3d edit., 1986, 4th edit., 1991. With USN, 1944-46, PTO. Recipient Disting. Med. Alumni award U. Chgo., 1991, Founder's award Chem. Inst. of Toxicology, 1996. Mem. Am. Bd. Toxicology (pres. 1982-83), Soc. of Toxicology (pres. 1986-87). Office: U Kans Med Ctr Dept Pharmacology Rainbow At 39th Kansas City KS 66160-0001 E-mail: jdoull@kume.edu.

DOW, SIMON, artistic director; b. Australia; Diploma, Australian Ballet Sch. Joined Australian Ballet, Stuttgart (Germany) Ballet; joined, prin. dancer Wash. Ballet, 1979; prin. dancer Australan Ballet, 1982-85, San Francisco Ballet, 1985-88, Boston Ballet, 1988-90; freelance guest artist and master tchr., 1990; assoc. artistic dir. Wash. Ballet, 1992-93, 96-97; art dir. Milw. Ballet Co., 1999—. Master tchr. Australian Ballet, Australian Ballet Sch., Sydney Dance Co., NSW Coll. Dance, Am. Ballet Theatre, Boston Ballet, Met. Opera Ballet, Feld Ballet, Milw. Ballet, Internat. Tanz Wochen, Vienna, Austria, Frankfurt (Germany) Ballet, Les Grands Ballet Cans.; tchr. Wash. Sch. Ballet, David Howard Sch. Dance, N.Y. Guest appearances include Mann Performing Arts Ctr., Phila., Spoleto Festival, Wolf Trap Farm park, Jacob's Pillow Dance Festival, Pendleton Music Festival, Detroit Symphony; choreographed ballets Wash. Ballet, N.Y. Festival Ballet, Boston Ballet, Theater Artaud, San Francisco, Cin. Dance Pl. Recipient Cecchetti Jr. medal. Office: Milw Ballet 504 W National Ave Milwaukee WI 53204-1746

DOWD, DAVID D., JR. federal judge; b. Cleve., Jan. 31, 1929; m. Joyce; children— Cindy, David, Doug, Mark B.A., Coll. Wooster, 1951; J.D., U. Mich., 1954. Ptnr. Dowd & Dowd, Massillon, Ohio, 1954-55, ptnr., 1957-75; asst. pros. atty. Stark County, 1961-67, pros. atty., 1967-75; judge Ohio 5th Dist. Ct. Appeals, 1975-80, Ohio Supreme Ct., 1980-81; ptnr. Black, McCuskey, Souers & Arbaugh, Canton, Ohio, 1981-82; judge U.S. Dist. Ct. (no. dist.) Ohio, 1982—, now sr. judge, 1996—. Office: US Dist Ct 2 S Main St Akron OH 44308-1813

DOWD, EDWARD L., JR. lawyer, former prosecutor; s. Edward L. Dowd; m. Jill Goessling; 3 children. JD with distinction, St. Mary's Univ. With Dowd, Dowd & Dowd; from asst. U.S. atty. to chief narcotics sect., regional dir. south cen. region Pres.'s Organized Crime Drug Enforcement Task Force U.S. Atty.'s Office, 1979-84; pvt. practice, 1984-93; U.S. atty. ea. dist. of Mo. U.S. Dept. Justice, St. Louis, 1993-99; dep. spl. counsel to John C. Danforth Spl. Counsel Waco Investigation, 1999; ptnr. Bryan Cave, LLP, St. Louis, 1999—. Office: Bryan Cave LLP One Metropolitan Square 211 N Broadway Ste 3600 Saint Louis MO 63102-2733 Office Fax: 314-259-2020. E-mail: eldowd@bryancave.com.

DOWD, THOMAS F. lawyer; b. Boston, 1943; AB, Harvard U., 1965; JD, Case Western Reserve U., 1974. Bar: Ohio 1974, D.C. 1989. Ptnr. Bryan Cave, Washington. Editor articles Case Western Reserve Law Review, 1973-74. Mem. Order of Coif. Office: Bryan Cave 700 13th St NW Fl 7 Washington DC 20005-5921

DOWDLE, JAMES C. cable television executive; b. Oklahoma City, Oct. 21, 1963; s. James Charles and Sally Dowdle; m. Mary Joan Dowdle, Sept. 22, 1990; children: Erin, Charlie, Colin. BA, John Carroll U., Cleve., 1986. Account exec. WSBK TV, Boston, 1986-89, Turner Broadcasting, Chgo., 1989-94; sales mgr. TV Food Network, 1994—, v.p., midwest sales mgr., 1994—. Pres. RoDan Fest, Inc., Chgo., 1996—; bd. dirs. Chgo. Youth Ctrs., 1990—. Office: TV Food Network 333 N Michigan Ave Chicago IL 60601-3901

DOWELL, MICHAEL BRENDAN, chemist; b. N.Y.C., Nov. 18, 1942; s. William Henry and Anne Susan (Cannon) D.; m. Gail Elizabeth Renton, Mar. 16, 1968; children: Rebecca, Margaret. BS, Fordham U., 1963; PhD, Pa. State U., 1967. Physicist U.S. Army Frankford Arsenal, Phila., 1967-69; rsch. scientist Parma (Ohio) Tech. Ctr., Union Carbide Corp., 1969-74, devel. mgr. carbon fiber applications, 1974-76, group leader metals and ceramics rsch., 1976-80, sr. group leader process rsch., 1980-82, mgr. market devel., 1982-92, Praxair Advanced Ceramics Inc. (formerly Union Carbide Corp), Ohio, 1992-93, Advanced Ceramics Corp., Cleve., 1993—, v.p. tech., 1999—. Mem. materials tech. adv. com. U.S. Dept. Commerce, 1994—2001; lectr. ops. mgmt. Case Western Res. U. Contbr. articles to profl. jours. Chmn. 14th Congressional Dist. steering com. Common Cause, 1974-76; officer, trustee Hudson Montessori Assn., 1974-79. Served to capt. ordnance AUS, 1967-69. Mem. Am. Chem. Soc., Am. Phys. Soc., U.S. Advanced Ceramics An. (bd. dirs. 1988-96), Am. Soc. Metals Internat. (govt. and pub. affairs com. 1989—), Soc. Prof. Fellows Case Western Res. U., Phi Lambda Upsilon. Roman Catholic. Home: 368 N Main St Hudson OH 44236-2246 Office: Advanced Ceramics Corp PO Box 94924 Cleveland OH 44101-4924

DOWLING, THOMAS ALLAN, mathematics educator; b. Little Rock, Feb. 19, 1941; s. Charles and Esther (Jensen) D.; m. Nancy Lenthe D.; children: Debra Lynn, David Thomas. B.S., Creighton U., 1962; Ph.D., U. N.C., 1967. Research assoc. U. N.C.-Chapel Hill, 1967-69, asst. prof., 1969-72; assoc. prof. math. Ohio State U., Columbus, 1972-82, prof., 1982—. Ops. researcher U.S. Govt., Patrick AFB, Fla., 1963-64; faculty fellow NASA at UCLA, Pasadena, summer, 1968; conf. organizer U. N.C., 1967, 70, Ohio State U., 1978, 82, 88, 92, 94, 98, 00. Editor: Combinatorial Mathematics and its Applications, 1967, 70; contbr. article to profl. jours.; discoverer Dowling lattices. NSF grantee, 1972-79 Mem. AAUP, Am. Math. Soc., Math. Assn. Am., Inst. Combinatorics and Applications. Democrat. E-mail: tdowling@math.ohio_state.edu; tdowling@columbus.rr.com. Home: 2565 Sandover Rd Columbus OH 43220-2848 Office: Ohio State U Dept Math 231 W 18th Ave Columbus OH 43210-1101

DOWNEY, CHRISTINE, state legislator; b. Abilene, Kans., Mar. 26, 1949; children: Amy, Matthew, Erin. Elem. and mid. sch. tchr., 1975-93; mem. Kans. Senate from 31st. dist., Topeka, 1996—. Adj. prof. Bethel Coll., 1990-93; mem. edn. com. Kans. Senate, agriculture com., chldn's issues com., legis. ednl. planning com., ways and means com. Pres., bd. dirs. Newton Cmty. Children's Choir, 1991-92. Mem. Kans. Nat. Edn. Assn. (pres. 1990), Newton Nat. Edn. Assn. (pres. 1989). Home: 10320 N Wheat State Rd Inman KS 67546-8109

DOWNEY, DEBORAH ANN, systems specialist; b. Xenia, Ohio, July 22, 1958; d. Nathan Vernon and Patricia Jaunita (Ward) D. Assoc. in Applied Sci., Sinclair C.C., 1981, student, 1986-91; BA, Capital U., 1994. Jr. programmer, project mgr. Cole-Layer-Trumble Co., Dayton, Ohio, 1981-82; sr. programmer, analyst, project leader Systems Architects Inc., 1982-84, Systems and Applied Sci. Corp. (now Computer Sci. Corp.), Dayton, 1984; analyst Unisys, 1984-87; systems programmer Computer Sci. Corp., Fairborn, Ohio, 1987—. Cons. computer software M&S Garage/Body Shop, Beavercreek, Ohio, 1986-87. Mem. NAFE, Am.

Motorcyclist Assn., Sinclair C. C. Alumni Assn., Cherokee Nation Okla., Cherokee Nat. Hist. Soc. Democrat. Mem. United Ch. of Christ. Avocations: motorcycles, miniatures, sports, needlework.

DOWNEY, JAMES ERWIN, retired government official; b. Melita, Man., Can., Aug. 10, 1942; s. Wallace Archibald and Mabel Elizabeth (Bambridge) D.; m. Linda Rowene Johnson, July 27, 1968; 1 child, Ryan James. Agr. Diploma, U. Man., 1964; Auctioneer, Western Coll. Auctioneering, Billings, Mont., 1972. Minister agr. Govt. of Man., Winnipeg, 1977-81, mem. govt. opposition, 1982-88, minister no. affairs, 1988-93, dep. premier, 1989-99, minister energy and mines and rural devel., 1989-93, minister industry, trade and tourism, 1993-99. Recipient Pres.'s medal U. Man., 1964, Silver Eagle award Indigenous Women's Collective, Golden Dragon award Chinese Cultural. Home: PO Box 636 Melita MB Canada R0M 1LO Office: James E Downey Internat Ltd Box 636 Melita MB Canada R0M 1LO E-mail: jimdowney@jediltd.com.

DOWNEY, JOHN WILHAM, composer, pianist, conductor, educator; b. Chgo., Oct. 5, 1927; s. James Bernard and Augustina (Haas) D.; m. Irusha Czuszakivna; children: Lida, Marc. MusB, DePaul U., 1945; MusM, Chgo. Mus. Coll., 1951; Docteur es Lettres (PhD), U. Paris-Sorbonne, 1957; Prix de Composition (scholar), Paris Conservatory, 1956. Assoc. prof. Chgo. City Coll., 1958-64; prof. music U. Wis., Milw., 1964-86, disting. prof., 1986-98, prof. emeritus, 1999—, 1998—. Lectr. music theory De Paul U., Chgo., 1960-64, Roosevelt U., Chgo., 1961. Author: La Musique Populaire dans l'Oeuvre de Bela Bartok, 1966; composer Eastlake Terrace (piano solo), 1959 (recorded by Master Musician's Collectif, 1998), Chant to Michelangelo, 1959, Edges (piano solo, 1960), Pyramids (piano solo, 1961), Portrait No. 1 (piano solo, 1980), Gasparo Records, Jingalodeon for Orchestra, 1968, recorded with Cala Records, 1991, Harp Concerto, 1968 (recorded by Musician's Collectif 1998, Gasparo Records), Cello Sonata, CRI label, 1968, Symphonic Modules, 1972, Agort, woodwind quintet, recorded with Gasparo label, 1973, Gasparo Records, 1989, Adagio Lyrico: 2 pianos, 1953, What If? (composition for mixed choir, solo timpany and brass octet), 1973, Octet for Winds, 1954, A Dolphin, voice and chamber ensemble, 1974, recorded with Orion Label, 1974, Gasparo Records, 1989, Lydian Suite, 1975, Gasparo Records, Cala Records, 1998, String Quartet II, 1975, Gasparo Records, 1976, Crescendo (for large percussion ensemble), 1977, High Clouds and Soft Rain (for mixed flute choir), 1977, The Edge of Space (Fantasy for Bassoon and Orch.), 1977, CD recorded with Chandos Records, 1989, Silhouette (solo Doublebass), 1980, Qu'en Avez-vous Fait? (for voice and piano), 1984, CD recording for Gasparo Records, 1995, Prayer for string trio, 1984, Piano Trio, 1984, Declamations for Large Orch., 1985, recorded with Cala Records, 1991, Discourse for Oboe with String Orch. and Harpsichord, 1986, recorded with Cala Records, 1991, Recombinance for Doublebass and Piano, 1987, Concerto for Doublebass and Orch., 1987, recorded with Cala Records, 1991, Suite of Psalms for a cappella mixed choir, 1988, Fanfare For Freedom for symphonic winds, 1990, Call for Freedom for symphonic winds, 1991, Yad Vashem-An Impression (piano solo), 1991, Memories (piano solo) 1991, Ode to Freedom, for symphony orchestra, 1992, Symphony No. 1, 1993, Rough Road (guitar and flute), 1994, Angel Talk (for eight cellos), 1995, Rememberance-The Swing Set, Reminder-Hungry Squirrel, Reaffirmation-Red Rose, 1995, Song Suite (high voice and piano), 1995, CD recorded by VAI Recordings, 1997, Ghosts (for 12 violins), 1995, Soliloquy (for solo English Horn, recorded for Cala Records) 1997, For Those Who Suffered (for chamber orch.), 1996, recorded on CD by Master Musicians Collective, 1998, Irish Sonata (for violin and piano) 1998, Mountains and Valleys (solo piano), 2000, incidental music for The Winter's Tale, Bassoon Quintet for bassoon and string quartet, 2001, also electronic and computer music; resident artist, MacDowell Colony, summers 1971, 75-77, 82-83, 92, 94, falls 1978, 85, Millay Colony, summer 1991; rec. artist (album) John Downey Plays John Downey, 1987; 5 orchestral works recorded by the London Symphony Orch.: Jingalodeon, Declamations, Concerto for Double Bass and Orch., Discourse for Oboe, Harpsichord and String Orch., The Edge of Space. Decorated Chevalier de l'Ordre des Arts et des Lettres, France, 1980; scholar Fulbright France, 1952-54, winter, 1979, 80, Fulbright Australia, summer, 1987, French Govt., 1954-55; teaching fellow, 1955-56; German Govt. teaching fellow, 1956-57; Copley Found. grantee, 1956-57, 57-58; recipient awards U. Wis., 1971, 73, 75, 77, 79, 83, 87, 93, 95, Ford Found., 1976, Ctr. for L.Am. Studies of the U. Wis.-Milw. award, 1988, NEA, 1977, 83, 94, Moebius award, 1985, New Music for Young Ensembles award, 1986, Walter Heinrichsen award Am. Acad. and Inst. Arts and Letters, 1990, Meet the Composer awards, 1988, 90, 92, 93; named Music Citizen of Yr. Civic Music Assn. of Milw., 1980, Musician of the Yr. Milw Sentinel, 1993; Wis. Arts Bd. Composition fellow, 1991. Mem. Am. Soc. Univ. Composers, Am. Music Ctr., ASCAP (awards 1974—), Am. Fedn. Musicians, Wis. Contemporary Music Forum (founder, chmn. 1970—), Soc. of Composers, Ctr. 20th Century Studies, De Paul U. Alumni Assn. (Disting. Alumni award 1969), Phi Kappa Phi, Delta Omicron (nat. patron), Mu Phi Alpha (Disting. Musician award 1987, other awards 1974-86), Sigma Alpha Iota (Extraordinary Mus. Achievement award Milw. Alumnae chpt. 1986). Avocations: jogging, bicycling. Office: U Wis Sch Fine Arts Music PO Box 413 Milwaukee WI 53201-0413 E-mail: jwdowney@uwm.edu.

DOWNING, JOAN FORMAN, editor, writer; b. Mpls., Nov. 16, 1934; d. W. Chandler and Marie A. (Forster) Forman; children: Timothy Alan, Julie Marie Downing Giesen, Christopher Alan. BA, U. Wis., 1956. Editl. asst. Sci. Research Assocs., Chgo., 1960-61, asst. editor, 1961-63, Childrens Press, Chgo., 1963-66, assoc. editor, 1966-68, mng. editor, 1968-78, editor-in-chief, 1978-81, sr. editor, 1981-95; propr. Downing Pub. Svcs., Evanston, Ill., 1995—. Dir. Chgo. Book Clinic, 1973-75, publicity chmn., 1973-74 Author: (with Eugene Baker) Workers Long Ago, 1968, Baseball Is Our Game, 1982, Junior CB Picture Dictionary, 1978; project editor: 15 vol. Young People's Story of Our Heritage, 1966 (Graphic Arts Council of Chgo. award), 20 vol. People of Destiny (Chgo. Book Clinic award 1967-68), 20 vol. Enchantment of South and Central America, 1968-70, 36 vol. Open Door Books, 1968, 42 vol. Enchantment of Africa, 1972-78, Hobbies for Everyone: Collecting Toy Trains, 1979 (Graphic Arts award Printing Industries Am.), (multi-vol.) World at War, 1980-87, (52 vol.) America the Beautiful, 1987-91, (52 vol.) From Sea to Shining Sea, 1991-95, (multi-vol.) Rookie Read-About Science, 1994-97, (multi-vol.) Cities of the World, 1995-2001, (multi-vol.) Encyclopedia of First Ladies, 1997-2000. Election judge, Cook County (Ill.), 1974— . Mem. Authors Guild, Authors League Am., Alpha Phi. Democrat. Home and Office: 2414 Brown Ave Evanston IL 60201-2526 E-mail: jd2414@aol.com.

DOWNING, ROBERT ALLAN, lawyer; b. Kenosha, Wis., Jan. 6, 1929; s. Leo Vertin and Mayme C. (Kennedy) D.; m. JoAnn C. Cramton, Apr. 14, 1951 (div. Sept. 1977); children: Robert A., Kevin C., Tracey Downing Clark, Gregory E.; m. Joan Govan, Oct. 29, 1977; 1 child, Charles E. Reiter III. B.S., U. Wis., 1950, J.D., 1956. Bar: Wis. 1956, Ill. 1956, U.S. Supreme Ct. 1965. Assoc. Sidley & Austin, Chgo., 1956-64, ptnr., 1964-94, counsel, 1994-97, Ruff, Weidenaar & Reidy, Ltd., Chgo., 1997—. Trustee (life), former pres. Episcopal Charities and Cmty. Svcs., Chgo. Diocese. Served to lt. USN, 1950-53, Korea. Fellow Am. Coll. Trial Lawyers; mem. ABA, Soc. Trial Lawyers, Ill. Bar Assn., Chgo. Bar Assn., Wis. Bar Assn., 7th Cir. Bar Assn., Union League Club, Law Club, Legal Club, MidDay Club, Westmoreland Country Club. Republican. Episcopalian. Office: Ruff Weidenaar & Reidy Ltd 222 N Lasalle St Ste 1525 Chicago IL 60601-1003

DOWNS, THOMAS K. lawyer; b. New Albany, Ind., Jan. 10, 1949; BA, Ind. U., 1977, JD magna cum laude, 1980. Bar: Ind. 1980. Ptnr., mcpl. fin. chmn. Ice Miller, Indpls. Ethics update editor Mcpl. Fin. Jour., 1999—; editor Fundamentals of Mcpl. Bond Law: General Law and Professional Responsibility sects., 1994—; exec. editor Ind. Law Jour., 1979-80; contbr. articles to profl. jours. Pres. Ind. Assn. Cities and Towns Found., 1994—; mem. Lt. Gov.'s Jobs Coun. Fellow Am. Coll. Bond Counsel (founding mem., govt. rels. com., co-chmn. bond buyer midwest pub. fin. conf. 1998); mem. Nat. Assn. Bond Lawyers (steering com. 1985-86, 90, 92, chmn. bond banks workshop 1985-86, tax increment workshop 1989, panelist various workshops, faculty fundamentals mcpl. bond law, opinions and profl. responsibility 1989-90, chair Ann. Washington Conf. 1996, chmn. prof. responsibitly com.), Ind. Continuing Legal Edn. Forum (chmn. mcpl. law seminars 1984-92, practical impact tax reform act of 1986, panelist mcpl. utility fin. 1988, pub. law 10 1991), Ind. Mcpl. Lawyers Assn., Inc. (bd. dirs. 1983—), Order of Coif, Assn. Ind. Counties (adv. com.), Ind. Comn. for the Purchase of Products and Svcs. of Persons with Disabilities (bd. dirs.). Office: Ice Miller Box 82001 1 American Sq Indianapolis IN 46282-0020 E-mail: downs@icemiller.com.

DOWTY, ALAN KENT, political scientist, educator; b. Greenville, Ohio, Jan. 15, 1940; s. Paul Willard and Ethel Lovella (Harbaugh) D.; m. Nancy Ellen Gordon, Sept. 8, 1961 (div. 1972); children: Merav Aurli, Tamar Eliea, Gidon Yair; m. Gail Gaynell Schupack, Jan. 1, 1973; children: Rachel Miriam, Rafael Jonathan; 1 stepchild, David Freeman. BA, Shimer Coll., 1959; MA, U. Chgo., 1960, PhD, 1963. Lectr. Hebrew U., Jerusalem, 1965-72, sr. lectr., 1972-75; assoc. prof. U. Notre Dame, Ind., 1975-78, prof. polit. sci., 1978—. Exec. dir. Leonard Davis Inst., Jerusalem, 1972-74; editl. bd. Middle East Rev., N.Y.C., 1977-90; project dir. Twentieth Century Fund, N.Y.C., 1983-85; reporter experts meeting Internat. Inst. Human Rights, Strasbourg, France, 1989. Author: The Limits of American Isolation, 1971, Middle East Crisis, 1984 (Quincy Wright award 1985), The Arab-Israel Conflict (with others), 1984, Closed Borders, 1987, The Jewish State, 1998; book reviewer Jerusalem Post, 1964-75; contbr. numerous articles to topical publs. Exec. com. Am. Profs. for Peace in Mid. East, 1976-90; witness U.S. Senate Fgn. Rels. Com., Washington, 1976; nat. adv. com. Union of Couns. for Soviet Jews, Washington, 1980-91. Woodrow Wilson fellow, 1959-60; Rothschild fellow Hebrew U., 1963-64; resident fellow Adlai Stevenson Inst., Chgo., 1971-72; Skirball fellow Oxford Ctr. for Hebrew and Jewish Studies, 2000; recipient Charles W. Ramsdell award So. Hist. Assn., 1966; grantee Twentieth Century Fund, N.Y.C., 1983. Mem. Am. Polit. Sci. Assn., Internat. Polit. Sci. Assn., Internat. Studies Assn. (exec. com. 1977-79, Quincy Wright award 1985), Assn. Israel Studies. Jewish. Avocations: travel, Jewish studies. Office: U Notre Dame 313 Hesburgh Ctr Notre Dame IN 46556-5677 E-mail: dowty.1@nd.edu.

DOYLE, JAMES E(DWARD), state attorney general; b. Washington, Nov. 23, 1945; s. James E. and Ruth (Bachhuber) Doyle; m. Jessica Laird, Dec. 21, 1966; children: Augustus, Gabriel. Student, Stanford U., 1963—66; AB in History, U. Wis., 1967; JD cum laude, Harvard U., 1972. Bar: Ariz. 1973, Wis. 1975, U.S. Dist. Ct. N.Mex. 1973, U.S. Dist. Ct. Ariz. 1973, U.S. Dist. Ct. Utah 1973, U.S. Dist. Ct. (we. dist.) Wis. 1975, U.S. Dist. Ct. (ea. dist.) Wis. 1976, U.S. Ct. Appeals (10th cir.) 1974, U.S. Ct. Appeals (7th cir.) 1985, U.S. Supreme Ct. 1989. Vol. Peace Corps, Tunisia, 1967—69; atty. DNA Legal Svcs., Chinle, Ariz., 1972—75; ptnr. Jacobs & Doyle, Madison, Wis., 1975—77; dist. atty. Dane County, 1977—83; ptnr. Doyle & Ritz, 1983—90; of counsel Lawton & Cates, 1990—91; atty. gen. State of Wis., 1991—. Mem.: ABA, 7th Cir. Bar Assn. (chmn. criminal law sect. 1988—89), Wis. Bar Assn. (bd. dirs. criminal law sect. 1988). Democrat. Roman Catholic. Office: Office Atty Gen Dept Justice PO Box 7857 Madison WI 53707-7857*

DOYLE, JILL J. elementary school principal; Prin. George P Way Elem. Sch., Bloomfield Hills, Mich., 1987—. Recipient Elem. Sch. Recognition award U.S. Dept. Edn., 1989-90. Office: George P Way Elem Sch 765 W Long Lake Rd Bloomfield Hills MI 48302-1552

DOYLE, JOHN ROBERT, lawyer; b. Chgo., May 12, 1950; s. Frank Edward and Dorothy (Bolton) D.; m. Kathleen Julius, June 14, 1974; children: Melissa, Maureen. BA magna cum laude, St. Louis U., 1971; JD summa cum laude, DePaul U., 1976. Bar: Ill. 1976, U.S. Dist. Ct. 1976, U.S. Dist. Ct. (no. dist.) Ill. 1982, Ill. Trial Bar 1982, U.S. Ct. Appeals (7th cir.) 1982. Ptnr. McDermott, Will & Emery, Chgo., 1976—. Mem. ABA, Chgo. Bar Assn. (jud. investigative hearing panel 1986-88), Phi Beta Kappa. Office: McDermott Will & Emery 227 W Monroe St Ste 3100 Chicago IL 60606-5096

DOYLE, REBECCA CARLISLE, state agency administrator; m. Ken Doyle; children: Eric, Ben. BS, U. Ill., 1975, MS, 1977. Pvt. practice, Ill.; dir. Ill. Agriculture Dept., Springfield, 1991—. Mem. Internat. Agriculture Mgmt. Assn., Nat. Assn. State Depts. Agriculture (officer), Mid-Am. Internat. Agri-Trade Council (officer), Women Execs. State Govt. Office: Illinois Dept Agriculture State Fairgrounds PO Box 19281 Springfield IL 62794-9281

DRACH, JOHN CHARLES, scientist, educator; b. Cin., Sept. 25, 1939; s. Charles Louis and Edrie B. Drach; m. Elda Jean Flamm, June 20, 1964; children: Laura J., Diane E. BS in Pharmacy, U. Cin., 1961, MS in Pharm. Chemistry, 1963, PhD in Biochemistry, 1966. From assoc. rsch. scientist to rsch. scientist Parke, Davis and Co., Ann Arbor, Mich., 1966-70; asst. prof. U. Mich. Dental Sch., 1970-74; assoc. prof. U. Mich., 1974-80; assoc. prof. medicinal chemistry U. Mich. Coll. Pharmacy, 1978-80; prof. U. Mich., 1980—; chmn. dept. oral biology U. Mich. Dental Sch., 1985-87, chmn. dept. biologic and materials scis., 1987-95; vis. prof. divsn. virology Burroughs Wellcome Co., Research Triangle Park, N.C., 1994. Cons. Adria Labs., Am. Inst. Chem., Am. Pharm. Assn., AMA, Chartwell, Kimberly-Clark, 1976-83. Author: Clinical Pharmacology, 1986; contbr. numerous articles and revs. to profl. jours.; mem. editorial bd. Elsevier Sci. Pubs., 1984—, Antiviral Chemistry & Chemotherapy, 1996—; patentee antiviral drugs. NSF summer fellow, 1963; NIH grad. fellow, 1964-66; NIH grantee, 1970—. Fellow: AAAS; mem.: Internat. Soc. Antiviral Rsch. (archivist 1992—, chair awards com. 1998—2002, pres. elect 2000—02, pres. 2002—), Am. Soc. Microbiology (mem. editl. bd. 1982—91), Am. Chem. Soc., Am. Assn. Oral Biology, Dental Edn. Assn. (pres. oral biology sect. 1990—91), Am. Assn. Dental Rsch., Sigma Xi, Omicron Kappa Upsilon, Rho Chi. Avocations: jogging, skiing, sailing. Home: 1372 Barrister Rd Ann Arbor MI 48105-2875 Office: U Mich 1011 N University Ave Ann Arbor MI 48109-1078 E-mail: jdrach@umich.edu.

DRAFT, HOWARD CRAIG, advertising executive; m. Elvy L. Leake; children: Andrew, Anna, Margaret. BA in Philosophy and Art History, Ripon Coll., 1974. With Draft Worldwide, Chgo., 1978—, gen. mgr. N.Y., 1982-86, pres., 1986-88, chmn., CEO, 1988—. Mem. adv. coun. Response TV; bd. mem. Direct Mktg. Assn. Ednl. Found.; spkr. in field. Active Pedia. AIDS Chgo., Herbert G. Birch Svcs.; bd. mem. Chgo. Old Town Sch. Folk Music; trustee Ripon Coll. Named one of 100 Best and Brightest, Advt. Age, one of The Best, The Brightest, The Most Powerful, Target Mktg., Direct Marketer of the Yr., Chgo. Assn. Direct Mktg., 1999. Office: Draft Worldwide 633 N Saint Clair St Chicago IL 60611-3234

DRAHMANN, BROTHER THEODORE ROBERT, education educator; b. Perham, Minn., June 7, 1926; s. Vincent Henry Drahmann and Louise Cecile Speiser. BS in History, St. Mary's Coll., Winona, Wis., 1949, DEd (hon.), 1981; M in Social and Indsl. Relations, Loyola U., Chgo., 1956; degree in edn. adminstrn., Coll. St. Thomas, St. Paul, 1974. Joined Cath. order Bros. of the Christian Schs. Tchr. De La Salle High Sch., Chgo., 1949-56, prin., 1956-62; counselor St. Mary's Coll., 1963-66; prin. Cretin High Sch., St. Paul, 1966-70; supr. schs. Christian Bros., 1970-72; supt. schs. Archdiocese of St. Paul/Mpls., 1972-78; dir. grad. studies Coll. St. Thomas, 1978-80; pres. Christian Bros. U., Memphis, 1980-93; dir. edn. Christian Bros. Conf., Landover, Md., 1993-98; prof. edn. St. Mary's U. of Minn., Mpls., 1998—. Mem. U.S. Cath. Conf. Com. on Edn., Washington, 1993-99; mem. adv. com. Coun. Am. Pvt. Edn., Washington, 1993-98; mem. Chief Adminstrs. Cath. Edn., 1993—; exec. dir. Lasallian Assn. Univs. and Colls., 1993-98. Author: (manual) Catholic School Principal-Outline for Action, 1980, rev. 1989, (brochure) Governance & Administration in Catholic Schools, 1985. Trustee St. Mary's Coll., 1972-81, Lewis U., Romeoville, Ill., 1982-93, Coll. Santa Fe, 1995-2002, De La Salle Inst., 1995-2002; charter mem. Hall of Fame, Sch. Edn., U. St. Thomas, 2001—. Named Disting. Grad. Coll. St. Thomas, 1984, Oustanding Tennessean Gov. of Tenn., Nashville, 1988, Most Influential Cath. Educator for Past 25 Yrs., Today's Cath. Tchr. jour., 1997. Mem. Nat. Cath. Ednl. Assn. (Outstanding Educator of Yr. award 1985, bd. dirs. 1986-94), Assn. Cath. Colls. and Univs. (bd. dirs. 1985-94), NCCJ (chmn. bd. Memphis chpt. 1980-93, Humanitarian award 1990), Econ. Club of Memphis (bd. dirs. 1988-93), Rotary (bd. dirs. Memphis club 1984-89, pres. 1987-88), KC, Mil. and Hospitaller Order St. Lazarus Jerusalem (knight comdr. 1991—, Martyrs of Memphis award 1994), Pi Gamma Mu, Alpha Kappa Delta, Delta Epsilon Sigma. Avocations: reading, swimming. Office: St Marys Univ Minn 2500 Park Ave Minneapolis MN 55404-4403 E-mail: brted3456@aol.com.

DRAKE, GEORGE ALBERT, college president, historian; b. Springfield, Mo., Feb. 25, 1934; s. George Bryant and Alberta (Stimson) D.; m. Susan Martha Ratcliff, June 25, 1960; children: Christopher George, Cynthia May, Melanie Susan. AB, Grinnell Coll., 1956; Fulbright scholar, U. Paris, 1956-57; AB (Rhodes scholar), Oxford U., 1959, MA, 1963; BD, U. Chgo., 1962, MA, 1963, PhD (Rockefeller fellow), 1965; LLD (hon.), Colo. Coll., 1980, Ripon Coll., 1982; LHD (hon.), Ill. Coll., 1985, Ursinus Coll., 1988, Doane Coll., 1995, Morningside Coll., 1998. Instr. history Grinnell Coll., Iowa, 1960-61, pres., 1979-91, prof., 1979—, trustee, prof., 1991—. Asst. prof., assoc. prof., prof. history Colo. Coll., Colorado Springs, 1964-79, acting dean of Coll., 1967-68, dean, 1969-73 Trustee Grinnell Coll., 1970-79, Penrose Hosp., 1976-79, 80-84, Grinnell Gen. Hosp., 1980-86; mem. Doane Coll. Bd. Trustees, 1995—, Iowa Peace Inst. Bd., 1994—, chair, 1996-99, vol. U.S. Peace Corps, Lesotho, 1991-93; commr. North Ctrl. Assn. Colls. and Schs., 1998-2001; mem. FINE Found. bd., 1998—. NEH fellow, 1974. Mem. Am. Hist. Assn., Am. Ch. History Soc., Nat. Coll. Athletic Assn. (pres. commn. 1984-89), Nat. Merit Scholarship Corp. E-mail: Drake@Grinnell.edu.

DRAKE, GRACE L. retired state senator, cultural organization administrator; b. New London, Conn., May 25, 1926; d. Daniel Harvey and Marion Gertrude (Wiech) Driscoll; m. William Lee Drake, June 9, 1946 (dec.); 1 child Sandra DeNobile. With Am. Photographic Corp., N.Y.C., 1944-72; senator State of Ohio, Columbus, 1984—2001; dir. Ohio Ctr. Advancement Women in Pub. Svc., 2001—. Mem. Carmelite Guild Cleve., 1973—, Tech. Leadership Coun., Leadership Cleve., Cleve. Music Sch. Settlement. Named Legislator of the Yr., Rep. Legis.'s Assn., 1988, Pub. Ofcl. of the Yr., Ohio chpt. NASW, 1989, Outstanding Legislator of the Yr., Ohio Speech and Hearing Assn., 1989; named to, Ohio Women's Hall of Fame, 1995; recipient Outstanding Woman award, Nat. Fedn. Rep. Women, 1984, Pub. Affairs award, March of Dimes, 2001. Roman Catholic. Avocations: bridge, golf. Home: 5954 Briardale Ln Solon OH 44139-2302 Office: Ohio Senate 2nd Fl Senate Bldg Rm 220 Columbus OH 43215-4276

DRAKE, JOHN WARREN, aviation consultant; b. Chgo., July 5, 1930; s. Robert Warren and Winifred Elizabeth (Bramhall) D.; m. Miriam Anna Engleman, Dec. 19, 1960 (div. Dec. 1985); 1 child, Robert Warren; m. Mary Pat O'Kelly, Sept. 24, 2000. B.S., Rensselaer Poly. Inst., 1952; M.B.A., Harvard U., 1954, D.B.A., 1972. Research asso. Aero. Research Found., Cambridge, Mass., 1956-57; prin. United Research, Inc., 1957-61; v.p. Systems Analysis and Research Corp., 1961-69; prof. emeritus, air transp. area Sch. Aeros. and Astronautics, Sch. Engring., Purdue U., 1972-92, mem. president's council. Cons. in field; mem. Transp. Research Bd. NRC. Author: The Administration of Transportation Modeling Projects, 1973. Served with U.S. Army, 1954-56. Mem. Air Transp. Rsch. Internat. Forum (coun.), AIAA, Soc. Automotive Engrs. Club: University (Washington). Home and Office: 341 Riverview Dr Ann Arbor MI 48104-1847

DRAKE, RICHARD FRANCIS, state legislator; b. Muscatine, Iowa, Sept. 28, 1927; s. Frank and Gladys (Young) R.; m. Shirley Jean Henke; children: Cheryll Dee, Ricky Lee. Student, Iowa State U.; BS, U.S. Naval Acad., 1950. Enlisted man USN, WWII, commd. ensign, 1950; advanced through grades to lt. comdr., 1954; comdg. officer minesweeper USS Crow, 1953—54; ret., 1954; farmer, mgr. Muscatine, 1954—; mem. Iowa Senate from 24th dist., Des Moines, 1968—. Chmn. Young Rep. Orgn. Iowa, 1954-56; adminstrv. asst. Muscatine County Rep. Com., 1956-57, chmn., 1958-66; chmn. 1st Dist. Rep. Com., 1966-72, Nat. Task Force on Rail Line Abandonment and Curtailment; chmn. states and rai problems Midwestern Coun. State Govts., 1978-79. Named One of 10 Outstanding Legislators of Yr., Nat. Rep. Legislators Assn. Mem. VFW, Am. Legion, Farm Bur., Masons, Elks, Order Ea. Star. Lutheran. Office: State Senate State Capitol Des Moines IA 50319-0001

DRAKE, ROBERT ALAN, state legislator, animal nutritionist, mayor; b. Canton, S.D., July 6, 1957; s. Theodore Francis and LaRayne Margaret (Hoffman) D.; m. Pamela Sue Wiechmann, 1977; children: R. Ryan, Kimberly Margaret, Kendra Kay. BS, S.D. State U., 1979, MS, 1981. Animal nutritionist McFleeg Feeds, Bowdle, S.D., 1981—; mayor City of Bowdle, 1988-96; mem. S.D. Ho. of Reps., Pierre, 1995-96, S.D. Senate, 1997—. Supr. Edmunds County Conservation Dist., 1984-96; chmn. N.E. Coun. Govts., Aberdeen, S.D., 1992-93; pres. Bowdle Cmty. Club, 1985-86, Bowdle Devel. Corp., 1985-89. Republican.

DRAPER, E(RNEST) LINN, JR. electric utility executive; b. Houston, Feb. 6, 1942; s. Ernest Linn and Marcia L. (Saylor) D.; m. Mary Deborah Doyle, June 9, 1962; children: Susan Elizabeth, Robert Linn, Barbara Ann, David Doyle. Student, Williams Coll., 1960-62; BAChemE, Rice U., 1964, BSChemE, 1965; PhD in Nuclear Engring., Cornell U., 1970. Asst. prof. nuclear engring. U. Tex., Austin, 1969-72, assoc. prof., 1972-79; tech. asst. to CEO Gulf States Utilities Co., Beaumont, Tex., 1979, v.p. nuclear tech., 1980-81, sr. v.p. engring. tech. services, 1981-82, sr. v.p. external affairs, 1982-84, sr. v.p. external affairs and prodn., 1984-85, exec. v.p. external affairs and prodn., 1985-86, vice chmn., 1985-87, COO, 1986, pres., CEO, 1986-92, chmn. bd. dirs., 1987-92; pres. AEPCo., Inc.; pres., COO Am. Electric Power Svc. Corp., Columbus, Ohio, 1992-93; chmn., pres., CEO Am. Electric Power Co. and Svc. Corp., 1993—. Bd. dirs. Borden Chems. and Plastics. Fellow NSF, 1965-66, AEC, 1967-68. Mem. NAE, Am. Nuclear Soc. (pres. 1984-85), Nuclear Energy Inst. (chmn. 1993-95), Edison Electric Inst. (chmn. 1996-97). Office: Am Electric Power Inc 1 Riverside Plz Columbus OH 43215-2355

DRAPER, GERALD LINDEN, lawyer; b. Oberlin, Ohio, July 14, 1941; s. Earl Linden and Mary Antoinette (Colloto) Draper; m. Barbara Jean Winter, Aug. 26, 1960; children: Melissa Leigh Price, Stephen Edward. BA, Muskingum Coll., 1963; JD, Northwestern U., 1966. Bar: Ohio 1966, US Dist Ct (so dist) Ohio 1966, US Ct Appeals (6th cir) 1975, US Supreme Ct 1980, US Dist Ct (no dist) Ohio 2000. Ptnr. Bricker & Eckler, Columbus, Ohio, 1966-88, Thompson, Hine & Flory, Columbus, 1989-95, Draper, Hollenbaugh, Briscoe, Yashko & Carmany, Columbus, 1996-99, Roetzel & Andress, Columbus, 1999—. Trustee, pres Wesley Glen Retirement Ctr, Columbus, Ohio, 1979—95; trustee Meth Elder Care Servs, Inc,

1995—, Muskingum Coll., New Concord, Ohio, 1988—92, 1993—, vice chair, 1994—; trustee, pres Wesley Ridge Retirement Ctr, 1995—2000, treas, 2001—. Fellow: Am Bd Trial Advs (trustee Ohio chpt. 2001), Am Col Trial Lawyers; mem.: ABA (House Dels 1991—97, 1999—2001), Def Research Inst, Ohio Asn Hosp Attys, Ohio Continuing Legal Educ Inst (trustee 1992—98, chair 1997—98), Nat Conf Bar Found (trustee 1987—90, 1991—94), Columbus Bar Found (pres 1984—86), Columbus Bar Asn 1982—83, (Bar Serv Medal 1998), Ohio State Bar Found (trustee 1992—97), Ohio State Bar Asn (pres 1990—91). Avocations: travel, golf, photography. Office: Roetzel & Andress 155 E Broad St Columbus OH 43215-3609 E-mail: gdraper@ralaw.com.

DRAPER, JAMES WILSON, lawyer; b. Detroit, Dec. 26, 1926; s. Kenneth Draper and Dorothy (Wilson) Barker; m. Alice Patricia Sullivan, May 16, 1953; children: Catherine Draper Clain, Julie Draper Fazekas, James P., Martha Draper Grossman. BA, U. Mich., 1949, JD, 1951. Bar: Mich. 1951, U.S. Dist. Ct. (so. dist.) Mich. 1951, U.S. Ct. Appeals (6th cir.) 1951. Assoc. Dykema, Jones & Wheat and successor firms, Detroit, 1951-61; ptnr. Dykema Gossett, and predecessor firms, 1961—. Past chmn. real property law sect. council State Bar Mich. Served with USN, 1944-46 Fellow Am. Coll. Real Estate Lawyers; mem. Mich. State Bar (past chmn. real property law sect., land title stds. com.), Detroit Club, Country Club Detroit (Grosse Point Farms, Mich.). Republican. Presbyterian. Home: 113 Merriweather Rd Grosse Pointe Farms MI 48236-3622 Office: Dykema Gossett 400 Renaissance Ctr Detroit MI 48243-1603

DRAPER, NORMAN RICHARD, statistician, educator; b. Eng., Mar. 20, 1931; came to U.S., 1955; s. Norris and Helen (Draper). BA, Cambridge (Eng.) U., 1954, MA, 1958; PhD, U. N.C., 1958. Tech. officer, statistician plastics div. Imperial Chem. Industries, 1958-60; mem. Math. Research Center, U. Wis.-Madison, 1960-61, mem. faculty, 1961—, prof. statistics, 1966-99, prof. emeritus, 1999—, chmn., 1967-73, 94-97. Vis. prof. Imperial Coll., London, fall 1967, 68 Author: (with H. Smith) Applied Regression Analysis, 1966, 3d edit., 1998, (with G.E.P. Box) Evolutionary Operation, 1969, (with W. E. Lawrence) Probability: An Introductory Course, 1970, (with G.E.P. Box) Empirical Model Building and Response Surfaces, 1987. Recipient Max-Planck-Forschungs-Preis, Alexander von Humboldt-Stiftung, 1994. Fellow Royal Statis. Soc., Am. Statis. Assn., Inst. Math. Statistics, Am. Soc. Quality Control (lectr. 1963—); mem. Internat. Statis. Inst. Address: Univ of Wisconsin 1210 W Dayton St Madison WI 53706-1685

DRAUT, ERIC J. insurance company executive; Degree, U. Ill., 1979, Northwestern U., 1989. Sr. v.p., CFO, treas. Unitrin Inc., Chgo. Office: 1 E Wacker Dr Chicago IL 60601-1802

DREBUS, RICHARD WILLIAM, pharmaceutical company executive; b. Oshkosh, Wis., Mar. 30, 1924; s. William and Frieda (Schmidt) D.; m. Hazel Redford, June 7, 1947; children: William R., John R., Kathryn L. Belin. BS, U. Wis., 1947, MS, 1949, PhD, 1952. Tcr. Madison East H.S., 1947-48; Bus. trainee Marathon Paper Corp., Menasha, Wis., 1951-52; tng. mgr. Ansul Corp., Marinette, 1952-55, asst. to v.p., 1955-58, marketing mgr., 1958-60; dir. personnel devel. Mead Johnson & Co., Evansville, Ind., 1960-65, v.p. corporate planning, 1965-66, internat. pres., 1966-68; v.p. internat. div. Bristol-Myers Co. (merger Mead Johnson & Co. with Bristol-Myers Co.), N.Y.C., 1968-77, sr. v.p., 1977-78, v.p. parent co., 1978-85, sr. v.p. pharm. research and devel. div., 1985-89, ret., 1989. Past bd. dirs. Jr. Achievement S.E. Conn., Meriden Silver Mus.; past bd. dirs. Meriden-Wallngford United Way, chmn. fund raising drive, 1988-89; trustee emeritus Quinnipiac Coll. Served with AUS, 1943-45. Decorated Combat Inf. Badge, Purple Heart, Bronze Star. Mem. APA, N.Y. Acad. Scis., U. Wis. Bascom Hill Soc., Oshkosh Country Club, North Shore Country Club, Phi Delta Kappa. Home: 3720 Pau Ko Tuk Ln Oshkosh WI 54902-7332 E-mail: rwdrebus@aol.com.

DREHER, DARRELL L. lawyer; b. Coshocton, Ohio, Dec. 16, 1944; BA, Ohio State U., 1966; JD, George Washington U., 1973. Bar: Ohio 1974. Ptnr. Dreher Langer & Tomkies L.L.P., Columbus, Ohio. Founding mem., bd. regents Am. Coll. Consumer Fin. Svcs. Lawyers; sec., v.p. governing com. of Conf. on Consumer Fin. Law. Mem. Order of Coif. Office: Dreher Langer & Tomkies LLP 2250 Huntington Ctr Columbus OH 43215

DREHER, MELANIE CREAGAN, dean, nursing educator; BSN magna cum laude, L.I. U.; D in Anthropology, Columbia U. Mem. faculty Columbia U., N.Y.C.; dean Sch. Nursing, William Ryan disting. prof. U. Miami; dean Sch. Nursing, prof. U. Mass.; dean Coll. Nursing, prof. U. Iowa. Mem. editl. bds. various profl. jours. Recipient May A. Brunson award, CASE award. Mem. Sigma Theta Tau (pres. Beta Zeta chpt. 1995). Office: U Iowa Office Dean 101F NB Iowa City IA 52242

DRENGLER, WILLIAM ALLAN JOHN, lawyer; b. Shawano, Wis., Nov. 18, 1949; s. William J. and Vera J. (Simmonds) D.; m. Kathleen A. Hintz, June 18, 1983; children: Ryan, Jeffrey, Brittany. BA, Am. U., 1972; JD, Marquette U., 1976. Bar: Wis. 1976, U.S. Dist. Ct. (ea. and we. dists.) Wis. 1976. Assoc. Herrling, Swain & Drengler, Appleton, Wis., 1976-78; dist. atty. Outagamie County, 1979-81; corp. counsel Marathon County, Wausau, Wis., 1981-96, Drengler Law Firm, Wausau, 1997—. Vice chmn. Wis. Equal Rights Coun., 1978-83, Wis. Coun. on Criminal Justice, Madison, 1983-87. Nat. pres. Future Bus. Leaders Am., 1967-68; mem. nat. Dem. delegation, 1974-76; mem. adminstrv. com. Wis. Dems., Madison, 1977-81, 86-88; chmn. local Selective Svc. Bd., Wausau, 1982-89; mem. adv. bd. Wausau Salvation Army, 1986—; judge adv. officer Wis. Army N.G., 1989-96; bd. dirs. Wausau Youth/Little League Baseball, 1988—, team mgr., 1994—. Mem. ABA (chair com. on govt. lawyers, sect. state and local govt. 1991-93, bylaws com. govt. and pub. sect. lawyers divsn. 1993-98), KC, Nat. Assn. County Civil Attys. (dir. 1986-88, v.p. 1988-91, pres. 1991-92), Nat. Assn. Counties (bd. dirs. 1991-92, taxation and fin. steering com. 1991-93, deferred compensation adv. com. 1993-95, justice and pub. safety steering com. 1993-94), State Bar Wis. (govt. lawyers divsn., bd. dirs. 1982-86, sec. 1986-87, pres. 1989-91, professionalism com. 1987-91, 92-2000, solo and small firm practice com. 2001--), Kiwanis (lt. gov. 1985-86, club pres. 1989-90, chair past lt. govs. coun. 1990-91), Wausau Elks (parliamentarian 2000—), Kiwanis Internat. Found. (Hixon Fellowship Award 2001). Roman Catholic. Avocations: baseball, camping, fishing, gardening, tennis. Office: PO Box 5152 609 Scott St Wausau WI 54402-5152

DRESCHHOFF, GISELA AUGUSTE MARIE, physicist, educator; b. Moenchengladbach, Germany, Sept. 13, 1938; came to U.S., 1967, naturalized, 1976; d. Gustav Julius and Hildegard Friederike (Krug) D. Ph.D., Tech. U. Braunschweig (Ger.), 1972. Staff scientist Fed. Inst. Physics and Tech. Ger., 1965-67; research assoc. Kans. Geol. Survey, Lawrence, 1971-72; vis. asst. prof. physics U. Kans., 1972-74; dep. dir. radiation physics lab. Space Tech. Ctr., 1972-78, assoc. dir., 1979-84, co-dir., 1984-86, dir., 1996—; sr. sci. geology U. Kans., 1991, adj. assoc. prof. physics and astronomy, 1992. Assoc. program mgr. NSF, Washington, 1978-79. Patentee identification markings for gemstones and method of making selective conductive regions in diamond layers. Named to Women's Hall of Fame, U. Kans., 1978; recipient Antarctic Service medal U.S.A., 1979; recipient NASA Group Achievement award, 1983. Fellow Explorers Club; mem. AAAS, Am. Phys. Soc., Am. Geophys. Union, Am. Polar Soc. (pres.), Antarctican Soc., Sigma Xi. Home: 2908 W 19th St Lawrence KS 66047-2301 Office: U Kans Dept Physics & Astronomy Lawrence KS 66045-7541 E-mail: giselad@ku.edu.

DREW, RICHARD ALLEN, retired electrical and instrument engineer; b. Milw., Jan. 10, 1941; s. Frank Emmons and Irene Louise Drew. BSEE, Milw. Sch. Engring., 1970. Registered profl. engr., Wis. Instrument engr. Nekoosa Papers Inc., Port Edwards, Wis., 1970-74, sr. instrument engr., 1974-85, Specialty Systems Inc., Mosinee, Wis., 1985-87; chief elec. and instrument engr. Zimpro Environ. Inc., Rothschild, 1988-96, ret., 1997. With USAF, 1963-67. Recipient Outstanding Svc. award Pulp and Paper Industry Div., Instrument Soc. Am., 1983, Outstanding Alumnus award Milw. Sch. of Engring., 1985. Mem. Instrument Soc. Am. (sr. mem. chpt. pres. 1974-75), Am. Radio Relay League (life mem.), Milw. Sch. of Engring. Alumni Orgn. (chpt. pres. 1991-95). Achievements include research in pulp and paper indsl. control systems and waste treatment control systems. Home: 2610 5th St S Wisconsin Rapids WI 54494-6263

DREWS, ROBERT CARREL, retired physician; b. St. Louis, Sept. 9, 1930; s. Leslie C. and Sarah (Carrel) D.; m. Lorene Ruth Lowenguth, June 2, 1951; children: Pamela, Belinda, Carl, Jeanmarie. AB, Washington U., 1952, MD, 1955. Diplomate Am. Bd. Ophthalmology. Intern St. Luke's Hosp., St. Louis, 1955-56; resident Washington U., 1956-58, chief resident, 1958-59; practice medicine specializing in ophthalmology, 1961-97; lectr. ophthalmology Washington U., 1956-66, asst. clin. prof. ophthalmology, 1966-74, asst. prof. clin. ophthalmology, 1966-74, assoc. prof., 1974-79, prof., 1979-98, prof. emeritus, 1998; asst. ophthalmologist to med. staff Barnes Hosp. Group, 1961—. Mem. attending staff Bethesda Gen. Hosp., St. Louis, 1958—; mem. staff St. Luke's Hosp., St. Louis, 1971-97, mem. emeritus, 1997—; mem. courtesy staff St. Mary's Hosp., St. Louis, 1961-97, mem. emeritus, 1997—; cons. Faith Hosp., St. Louis, 1961-91, Frisco Employees Hosp., St. Louis, 1961-68; attending ophthalmologist St. Louis Childrens Hosp., 1961-80; attending staff ophthalmology St. Louis County Hosp., 1972-85; supervising ophthalmologist divsn. welfare State Mo., 1963-81; bd. dirs. St. Louis Soc. Blind, sec., 1966-67, v.p., 1967-68, pres., 1968-70, 84-85; cons. Spl. Sch. Dist. St. Louis County, Mo., 1967-80, Nat. Eye Inst. Program Staff, ataract Panel, The Nat. Plan Vision Rsch., 1983; mem. Am. Bd. Ophthalmology, 1985-93; pres. Highlights Ophthalmology, Inc., 1990—. Mem. editl. bds. Ophthalmology, 1984-98, Pakistan Jour. Ophthalmology, 1984-98. Trustee Washington U., 1984-92. Fellow Royal Coll. Ophthalmologists; mem. AMA, Am. Ophthalmol. Soc., So. Med. Assn., Mo. State Med. Assn., Mo. Ophthalmol. Soc., St. Louis Soc. Blind, St. Louis Med. Soc., St. Louis Ophthalmol. Soc., Contact Lens Assn. Ophthalmologists, Pan-Am. Assn. Ophthalmology, Am. intra-Ocular Implant Soc., Internat. Intraocular Implant Club, Internat. Ophthalmic Microsurgery Study Group, Washington U. Faculty Club, others. Republican. Lutheran. Avocations: photography.

DREXLER, MARY SANFORD, financial executive; b. Pontiac, Mich., Apr. 19, 1954; d. Arthur H. and Kathryn S. (Sherda) Sanford; m. Brian Day, 1975 (div. 1978); m. York Drexler, 1980. BS, Ea. Mich. U., Ypsilanti, 1976, MA, 1979; postgrad., Walsh Coll., Troy, Mich., 1983. CPA, Mich. Spl. edn. tchr. Oakland Schs., Pontiac, Mich., 1976-83; staff auditor Coopers & Lybrand, Detroit, 1983—84, sr. auditor, 1984—86; asst. contr. Webasto Sunroofs Inc., Rochester Hills, 1986-88; contr. Inalfa Roof Systems, U.S.A., Farmington Hills, Mich., 1988-92; v.p. fin., controller Inalfa Roof Sys., 1992-96, CFO, exec. v.p., 1997—. Bd. dirs. Inalfa Roof Systems, Inc., Inalfa Holding Inc. Bd. dirs. Neighborhood Civic Assn., Troy, 1986—, Coun. for Exceptional Children, Oakland County, 1976-83. Mem. Inst. Mgmt. Accts., Oakland County, Mich. Assn. CPA Mich., Forest Lake Country Club. Avocations: photography, painting, golf, swimming. Office: Inalfa Roof Systems USA 1370 Pacific Dr Auburn Hills MI 48326-1569

DREXLER, RICHARD ALLAN, manufacturing company executive; b. Chgo., May 14, 1947; s. Lloyd A. and Evelyn Violet (Kovaloff) D.; m. Clare F. Stunkel, Aug. 24, 1990; children by previous marriage: Dan Lloyd, Jason Ian. BS, Northwestern U., 1968, MBA, 1969. Staff v.p. Allied Products Corp., Chgo., 1971-75, sr. v.p. adminstrn., 1975-79, exec. v.p., COO, CFO, 1979-82, pres., COO, 1982-86, pres., CEO, 1986-93, chmn., pres., CEO, 1993—. Office: Allied Products Corp 10 Riverside Plaza Chicago IL 60606

DREXLER, RUDY MATTHEW, JR. professional law enforcement dog trainer; b. Elkhart, Ind., Jan. 16, 1941; s. Rudy Matthew Sr. and Elaine Irene (Hardman) D.; m. Patricia Ann Overmyer, Apr. 4, 1981; children: Scott M., Tina S. Thode. Student, Purdue U., 1960-63. V.p. Custom Booth Mfg. Corp., Elkhart, Ind., 1962-80; pres. Orchard Kennels, 1964-79; pres., treas. Rudy Drexler's Sch. for Dogs, Inc., 1980—. Lectr. civic orgns.; instr. U. Del. Continuing Edn., Wilmington, 1978. Named to Honorable Order of Ky. Colonels, 1989; named hon. dep. Middlesex County Sheriff's Dept., New Brunswick, N.J., 1984, Daviess County Sheriff's Dept., Owensboro, Ky., 1988, Fairfield County Sheriff's Dept., Lancaster, Ohio, 1982. Mem. Midwest Police K-9 Assn. (founder 1984, tng. dir. 1984-87), Am. Soc. Law Enforcement Trainers (charter mem.), Internat. Narcotics Enforcement Officers Assn. (assoc. mem.), Can. Police K-9 Assn. (assoc. mem.), Nat. Police Res. Officers Assn. (hon. mem.), Moose. Office: Rudy Drexler's Sch for Dogs 50947 County Road 7 Elkhart IN 46514-8853

DRIGGS, CHARLES MULFORD, lawyer; b. East Cleveland, Ohio, Jan. 26, 1924; s. Karl Holcomb and Lila Vandeveer (Wilson) D.; children: Ruth, Rachel, Carrie, Karl H., Charles M.; m. Ann Eileen Zargari, Oct. 25, 1991. BS, Yale U., 1947, JD, 1950. Bar: Ohio 1951. Assoc. Squire, Sanders & Dempsey, Cleve., 1950-64, ptnr., 1964-88, of counsel, 1988-91; pvt. practice civil law, 1991-95; ptnr. Driggs, Lucas, Brubaker & Hogg Co., LPA, Mentor, Ohio, 1995—. Pres. Bratenahl (Ohio) Sch. Bd., 1958-62; mem. adv. coun. Cleve. Ctr. for Theol. Edn., 1978—. Mem. ABA, Ohio Bar Assn., Lake County Bar Assn., Cleve. Bar Assn., Greater Cleve. Growth Assn., Cleve. Law Libr. Assn. (trustee 1977-91), Ct. Nisi Prius (judge 2000), Citizens League Greater Cleve., Geauga County Bar Assn., Phi Delta Phi, Tau Beta Pi, Phi Gamma Delta. Home: 9181 Hidden Glen Dr Mentor OH 44060-7359 Office: 8522 East Ave Mentor OH 44060

DRINFELD, VLADIMIR GERSHONOVICH, mathematician, educator; b. Kharkov, Ukraine, 1954; Grad., Moscow U., 1974, PhD, 1978. With B. Verkin Inst. Low Temperature Physics, Acad. Scis. Ukraine, 1981-98; sr. prof. dept math. U. Chgo., 1998—. Recipient Fields medal Internat. Congress Mathematicians, Kyoto, Japan, 1990. Mem. Acad. Scis. Ukraine. Achievements include research on quantum groups and number theory; proff. of the langlands conjecture for GL (2) over a functional field. Office: U Chgo Dept Math 5734 S University Ave Chicago IL 60637-1514

DRINKO, JOHN DEAVER, lawyer; b. St. Marys, W.Va., June 17, 1921; s. Emery J. and Hazel (White) D.; m. Elizabeth Gibson, May 14, 1946; children: Elizabeth Lee Sullivan, Diana Lynn Martin, John Randall, Jay Deaver. AB, Marshall U., 1942; JD, Ohio State U., 1944; postgrad., U. Tex. Sch. Law, 1944; LLD (hon.), Marshall U., 1980, Ohio State U., 1986, John Carroll U., 1987, Capital U., 1988, Cleve. State U., 1990; DHL (hon.), David N. Myers Coll., 1990, U. N.H., 1992, Baldwin-Wallace Coll., 1993, Ursuline Coll., 1994, Notre Dame Coll., 1997, U. Rio Grande, 1999, Marietta Coll., 2001. Bar: Ohio 1945, D.C 1946, U.S. Dist. Ct. (no. dist.) Ohio 1958. Assoc. Baker & Hostetler, Cleve., 1945-55, ptnr., 1955-69, mng. ptnr., from 1969, sr. adviser to mng. com. Chmn. bd. Cleve. Inst. Electronics Inc., Double D Ranch Inc., Ohio; bd. dirs. Cloyes Gear and Products Inc., McGean-Rohco Worldwide Inc., Orvis Co. Inc., Preformed Line Products Inc. Trustee Elizabeth G. and John D. Drinko Charitable Found., Orvis-Perkins Found., Thomas F. Peterson Found., Mellen Found., The Cloyes-Myers Found., Marshall U. Found.; founder Consortium of Multiple Sclerosis Ctrs., Mellen Conf. on Acute and Critical Care Nursing, Case Western Res. U. Disting. fellow Cleve. Clinc Found., 1991; Ohio State Law Sch. Bldg. named in his honor, 1995, libr. at Marshall U. named in his honor, 1997; inducted into Bus. Hall of Fame, Marshall Univ., 1996. Mem. ABA, Am. Jud. Assn., Bar Assn. Greater Cleve., Greater Cleve. Growth Assn., Ohio State Bar Assn., Jud. Conf. 8th Jud. Dist. (life), Soc. Benchers, Case Western Res. U. Law Sch. Assn., Cleve. Play House, Cleve. Civil War Round-table, Mayfield Country Club, Union Club, The Club at Soc. Ctr., O'Donnell Golf Club, Order of Coif, 33o Scottish Rite Mason, Knight Templar, York Rite, Euclid Blue Lodge No. 599 (Jesters, Shrine, Grotto). Republican. Presbyterian. Home: 4891 Middledale Rd Cleveland OH 44124-2522 also: 1245 Otono Dr Palm Springs CA 92264-8445 Office: Baker & Hostetler LLP 1900 E 9th St Ste 3200 Cleveland OH 44114-3475

DRISCOLL, CHARLES FRANCIS, financial services company executive, investment adviser; b. Dubuque, Iowa, July 8, 1943; s. Francis Clarence and Grace Ellen (Shanahan) D.; m. Marie Kathleen McGowan, Aug. 19, 1967; children: Sean, Erin. BA in Econs., Loras Coll., 1968. CLU; registered investment advisor; accredited estate planner. Sr. account mgr. NCR Corp., Davenport, Iowa, 1968-74, St. Louis, 1974-76; fin. planner Mass. Mut. Life Ins. Co., 1976—; pres. Driscoll and Assocs., 1989—. Equity sales coord. MML Investor Svcs., Inc., St. Louis, 1983-88. Chmn. Edgewood Program Alumni Recovery Fund, St. John's Mercy Hosp., St. Louis, 1988-90. Mem. Nat. Assn. Life Underwriters, Soc. Fin. Svc. Profls., Estate Planning Coun. St. Lo. Republican. Roman Catholic. Avocations: golf, fishing, nature photography, reading, travel. Home: 2324 Manor Lake Ct Chesterfield MO 63017-7817 Office: 16690 Swingley Ridge Rd Ste 150 Chesterfield MO 63017-0758 E-mail: cdriscoll@finsvcs.com., cdriscoll@mindspring.com.

DRNEVICH, VINCENT PAUL, civil engineering educator; b. Wilkinsburg, Pa., Aug. 6, 1940; s. Louis B. and Mary (Kutcel) D.; m. Roxanne M. Hosier, Aug. 20, 1966; children: Paul, Julie, Jenny, Marisa. BSCE, U. Notre Dame, 1962, MSCE, 1964; PhD, U. Mich., 1967. Registered profl. engr., Ky., Ind. Asst. prof. civil engring. U. Ky., Lexington, 1967-73, assoc. prof., 1973-78, prof., 1978-91; chmn. civil engring., 1980-84; acting dean engring. U. Ky., Lexington, 1989-90; prof., head Sch. Civil Engring. Purdue U., West Lafayette, Ind., 1991-2000. Dir. joint hwy. rsch. project Purdue U., 1991-95; pres. Soil Dynamics, Instruments, Inc., West Lafayette, 1974—. Inventor in field. Fellow ASCE (chmn. dept. heads coun. exec. com. 1996-2000, vice chmn. com. on edn.-practitioner interface, 1994-98, Norman medal 1973, Huber Rsch. prize 1980), ASTM (exec. com., tech. editor Geotech. Testing Jour. 1985-89, C.A. Hogentogler award 1979, Merit award 1993, Woodland Shockley award 1996); mem. NSPE, Am. Soc. Engring. Edn. (sec./treas. civil engring. divsn. 1995-98, dir. 1999—), Transp. Rsch. Bd., Earthquake Engring. Rsch. Inst., Ind. Soc. Profl. Engrs. (pres. A.A. Potter chpt.), Chi Epsilon (Harold T. Larson award 1985, James M. Robbins award 1989). Roman Catholic. Avocations: golf, fishing. Office: Purdue U 1284 Civil Engineering West Lafayette IN 47907-1284

DROHAN, DAVID F. medical products company executive; BS in Indsl. Rels., Manhattan Coll., N.Y. With Baxter Healthcare Corp., 1965—, territory mgr. N.Y., various positions, v.p. sales parenteral divsn., 1983-87, pres. pharmacy divsn., 1987-96, pres. intravenous systems, corp. v.p., 1996—. Bd. trustees St. Louis Coll. of Pharmacy. Chmn. Wake County Econ. Devel. Bd., dir. Riverside Found, dir. Baxter Credit Union. Office: Baxter Healthcare One Baxter Pkwy Deerfield IL 60015-4633

DROVDAL, DAVID (SKIP DROVDAL), state legislator; m. Kathy Wright; 4 children. Student, Minot Col. Bus., 1967; diploma, Western Coll. Auctioneering, 1992. Owner, mgr. Drovdal's Hardware, Watford, N.D., 1972—; mem. N.D. Ho. of Reps., 1993—. Mem. edn. and natural resources com., intreim edn. fin. com., vice chmn. edn. com., 1997. Bd. dirs. Good Shepherd Home; coun. pres. Zoar Ch., 1982-84. Named Watford City Fireman of Yr., 1991. Mem. Watford City C. of C. (past pres.), Sons of Norway (past pres. Watford), Lions (Lion of Yr. award 1993). Republican. Home: HC 1 Box 22 Arnegard ND 58835-9726

DRUMMOND, ROBERT KENDIG, lawyer; b. Phila., Feb. 9, 1939; s. Winslow Shaw and Dorothy (Moore) D.; m. Carol Young, Sept. 3, 1960; children: Anne Elizabeth, Robert Young D. BA, Coll. Wooster, 1961; JD, Duke U., 1964. Bar: Wis. 1964. Assoc. Foley & Lardner, Milw., 1964-71, ptnr., 1971—. Bd. dirs. Bandag Inc., Muscatine, Iowa, Custom Heat Treat Inc., Iron Mountain, Mich. Presbyterian. Office: Foley & Lardner Firstar Ctr 777 E Wisconsin Ave Ste 3800 Milwaukee WI 53202-5367

DRURY, CHARLES LOUIS, JR. hotel executive; b. Cape Girardeau, Mo., Nov. 4, 1955; s. Charles Louis Sr. and Shirley Jean (Luebbers) D.; m. Michelle Marguerite Swenson, Apr. 28, 1979; children: Charles L. III, Thomas Michael. BSBA, St. John's U., Collegeville, Minn., 1978. Gen. mgr. Drury Inns, Inc., St. Louis, 1978-79, regional mgr., 1979-81, v.p. ops., 1981-85, pres., 1985—, chief exec. officer, 1988—, also bd. dirs. Bd. dirs. Drury Industries, Inc., Cape Girardeau, Drury Displays, Inc., St. Louis, Druco, Inc., St. Louis; mem. exec. bd. Enterprise Bank, St. Louis, 1989— Bd. dirs. Dismas House of St. Louis, 1987—, Cardinal Glennon Children's Hosp. Devel. Bd. Mem. Pres. Assn., Am. Mgmt. Assn. Roman Catholic. Office: Drury Inns Inc 10801 Pear Tree Ln Saint Ann MO 63074-1450

DRURY, DAVID J. insurance company executive; Chmn. The Prin. Fin. Group, Des Moines. Office: The Principal Financial Grp 711 High St Des Moines IA 50392-0002

DRUSHAL, MARY ELLEN, educator, former university provost; b. Peru, Ind., Oct. 24, 1945; d. Herrell Lee and Opal Marie (Boone) Waters; m. J. Michael Drushal, June 12, 1966; children: Lori, Jeff. B of Music Edn., Ashland Coll., 1969; MS, Peabody Coll., 1981; PhD, Vanderbilt U., 1986. Dir. music and spl. edn. projects Smithville (Ohio) Brethren Ch., 1969-74; tchr. music Orrville (Ohio) Pub. Schs., 1969-74; seminar leader Internat. Ctr. for Learning, Glendale, Calif., 1974-76; dir. Christian edn. First and then Christ Presbyn. Ch., Nashville, 1976-84; asst. prof., then assoc. prof. Ashland (Ohio) Theol. Sem., 1984-91, acad. dean, 1991-95; provost Ashland U., 1995—2001; dir. instnl. effectiveness, prof. edn., 2001—. Cons. in strategic planning for not-for-profit orgns. Author: On Tablets of Human Hearts: Christian Education with Children, 1991; co-author: Spiritual Formation: A Personal Walk Toward Emmaus, 1990; contbr. articles to profl. jours. Trustee Brethren Care Found., Ashland, 1989-99, Ashland Symphony Orch., 1986-87; pres., fundraiser Habitat for Humanity, Ashland, 1990-94; bd. dirs. JOY Day Care Ctr., 1988-90. Grantee Lilly Endowment Inc., 1991, 93, Brethren Ch. Found., 1989, 90. Mem. Assn. Theol. Schs. (com. under-represented constituencies 1994-96), Am. Assn. for Higher Edn., Nat. Assn. Ch. Bus. Adminstrs., N.Am. Assn. Profs. of Christian Edn., Assn. Profs. and Rschrs. in Religious Edn., Nat. Assn. Evangelicals, Nat. Assn. Black Evangelical Assns., Epiphany Assn. (bd. dirs. 1994-98). Republican. Episcopalian. Avocations: stained glass, sailing, skiing. Office: Ashland U 401 College Ave Ashland OH 44805-3799 E-mail: medrusha@ashland.edu.

DRUTEN, ROBERT S. greeting card company executive; CFO Hallmark Cards Inc., Kansas City, Mo. Office: 2501 Mcgee St Kansas City MO 64108-2615

DRVOTA, MOJMIR, cinema educator, author; b. Prague, Czechoslovakia, Jan. 13, 1923; came to U.S., 1958, naturalized, 1963; s. Jan and Zdenka (Krejcikova) D.; m. Jana Kratochvilova, May 18, 1957; 1 child, Monica. Student, Charles U., 1945-48; PhD, Palacky U., 1953; MS, Columbia U., 1961. Stage dir. state theaters, Czechoslovakia, 1952-56; libr. Bklyn. Pub. Libr., 1958-62; asst. prof. dramatic arts Columbia U., N.Y.C., 1962-69;

assoc. prof. cinema NYU, 1969-72; prof. cinema Ohio State U., Columbus, 1972-92, prof. emeritus, 1992—. Script writer Czechoslovak State Film, Prague, 1948-52; author: Short Stories, 1946, Boarding House for Artists, 1947, Solitaire, 1974, Triptych, 1980, Solitaire, Triptych in Czech, 1993; The Constituents of Film Theory, 1973, in Czech, 1994, How Many ANgels Can Dance on the Tip of a Needle?, in Czech, 2002. Mem. Univ. Film Assn., AAUP, Phi Kappa Phi. Home: 3541 Prestwick Ct Columbus OH 43220-5097

DRYMALSKI, RAYMOND HIBNER, lawyer, banker; b. Chgo., June 1, 1936; s. Raymond P. and Alice H. (Hibner) D.; m. Sarah Fickes, Apr. 1, 1967; children: Robert, Paige. BA, Georgetown U., 1958; JD, U. Mich., 1961. Bar: Ill. 1962. Lawyer Chgo. Title & Trust Co., 1963-65; asst. sec., atty. No. Trust Co., Chgo., 1965-68; ptnr. Boodell, Sears, Giambalvo & Crowley, 1968-87; mem. Bell Boyd & Lloyd LLC, 1987—. Contbr. articles to profl. jours. Bd. dirs. Northwestern Meml. Hosp., Chgo., 1978—, Northwestern Meml. Healthcare, 1987—, vice chmn., sec., 1998—99, chmn., 2000—; bd. dirs. McGaw Med. Ctr. of Northwestern U., 2000—, Lincoln Park Zool. Soc., 1972—, pres., 1980—84; bd. dirs., officer Offield Family Found., 1990—; mem. coun. govs. Northwestern Healthcare Network, 1990—, bd. dirs., 1999. Mem. ABA, Econ. Club Chgo. Roman Catholic. Home: 443 W Eugenie St Chicago IL 60614-5674 Office: Bell Boyd & Lloyd LLC 70 W Madison St Ste 3300 Chicago IL 60602-4244 E-mail: rdrymalski@bellboyd.com.

DRZEWIECKI, GARY FRANCIS, state legislator; b. Pulaski, Wis., Oct. 29, 1954; s. Wallace and Marcella Drzewiecki; m. Julie Pakanich, 1982; children: Eric, Matthew, Michelle, Tiffany. Student, U. Wis., Stout, 1972-73. Owner, perator Pulaski Fin. Ctr.; pres. Pulaski Econ. Devel. Corp.; mem. from dist. 30 Wis. State Senate, Madison; chair state govt. ops. and corrections coms. Bd. dirs. Tri County Res. Squad, 1989—; past pres. Village of Pulaski; Bd. dirs. Brown County Planning Commn. Mem. Optimists, Lions. Home: 419 Washington St Pulaski WI 54162-0313

DUARTE, GLORIA, chef; Student, Dumas Pere Culinary Sch., Glenview, Ill. Chef Ritz-Carlton Hotel, Chgo., The Drake hotel, Chgo.; wner, chef Las Bellas Artes, Elmhurst, 1987—. Host Mexico's Day of the Dead celebration James Beard Found.; guest chef Jalisco Culinary Arts resort, Mexico. Named one of Top Ten Restaurants, Chgo. Sun Times. Office: Las Bellas Artes 112 W Park Ave Elmhurst IL 60126

DUBACK, STEVEN RAHR, lawyer; b. Washington, Sept. 4, 1944; s. Paul Hewitt and Natalie (Rahr) D.; children: David, Peter, Andrew. BA, Princeton U., 1966; JD, U. Mich., 1969. Bar: Wis. 1969, U.S. Dist. Ct. (ea. dist.) Wis. 1969, U.S. Ct. Claims 1969, U.S. Tax Ct. 1969. Ptnr. Quarles & Brady LLP, Milw., 1969—. Bd. dirs. Oshkosh (Wis.) B'Gosh, Inc., Commerce Indsl. Chems., Inc., Brady Fin. Co., L.M. Becker & Co., Inc. Dir. Ctr. for the Deaf and Hard of Hearing, Milw. Estate Planning Coun. Mem. Estate Counselors Forum, Town Club, Milw. Athletic Club, Wis. State and Local Tax Club, Am. Soc. Corp. Secs., Order of Coif, Phi Beta Kappa. Avocations: golf, tennis. Office: Quarles & Brady LLP 411 E Wisconsin Ave Ste 2550 Milwaukee WI 53202-4497 E-mail: srd@quarles.com.

DUBES, MICHAEL JOHN, insurance company executive; b. Dubuque, Iowa, Oct. 19, 1942; s. Wilmar C. and Cleo (Lenz) D.; m. Glenda Ra. Ackerlund, July 31, 1965; children: Scot (dec.), Heather. BS, Iowa State U., 1966; MS, Am. Coll., Bryn Mawr, Pa., 1981; postgrad., Harvard U., 1987, 90, LIMRA Strategies Inst., 1990. CLU, LLIF; cert. fin. planner; chartered fin. cons. Agt. Northwestern Nat. Life Ins. Co., Des Moines, 1967-68, staff asst., Mpls., 1968-70, tng. mgr., St. Paul, 1970-72, supt. agys., Mpls., 1972-73, asst. mgr., Des Moines, 1973-78, br. mgr., 1978-83, regional mgr., 1983-84, 2d v.p. individual ins. sales, Mpls., 1984-85, v.p. indiv. ins. sales, 1985-87, sr. v.p. individual ins., 1987—; exec. v.p. Northwestern Nat. Life Ins. Sales Co., Mpls., 1984-85, pres., 1985-87; vice chmn., CEO Washington Square Securities, Inc., 1984-87; chmn. Washington Sq. Securities, 1987—. Bd. dirs. Mpls., NWNL Found., Washington Sq. Securities Inc., Relia Star Lite, Corp. Coun. of the Arts; mem. NWNL cos. Enterprise Coun., mgmt. com.; bd. dirs. No. Life Ins. Co. (a Relia Star co.), Seattle. Amb. Iowa State U.; bd. dirs. Seattle C. of C., 1995—, Seattle Corp. Coun. of the Arts, 1995, Ind. Colls. of Wash., 1995; bd. govs. Iowa State U. With USAR, 1967. Recipient Gene Helton award Des Moines Life Underwriters, 1982. Mem. Nat. Assn. Life Underwriters (bd. dirs. 1983-84), Am. Soc. CLUs, Life Ins. Mktg. and Rsch. Assn. (exec. devel. com. 1985-91, ops. com. 1989—, bd. dirs. 1991-93, chmn. membership com.), Agy. Officer Round Table (meeting chmn. 1994), Gen. Agts. and Mgrs. Assn. (pres. 1983-84), Cert. Fin. Planners, MBA Ins. Mgmt. Adv., U. St. Thomas, Ind. Colls. Wash. (bd. dirs.), Met. Breakfast Club (bd. dirs. 1988-94), Interlachen Country Club (bd. govs.), Desert Mountain Country Club, Rainier Club, Amb. Club (Iowa State U.), Variety Club of Iowa (bd. dirs. 1983-84), Sahalee Country Club, Harvard Bus. Sch. Club Minn., Mpls. Club, Boys and Girls Club Mpls. (bd. dirs., exec. com., devel. com.), Rotary (Paul Harris fellow 1988, bd. dirs.), Seattle C. of C. (bd. dirs.). Home: 5816 Vernon Ln Edina MN 55436-2250 Office: ING/ReliaStar Lite 20 Washington Ave Minneapolis MN 55401-2900 E-mail: dubesg@aol.com.

DUBIN, HOWARD VICTOR, dermatologist; b. N.Y.C., Mar. 28, 1938; s. Meyer and Blanche D.; m. Patricia Sue Tucker, June 10, 1962; children—Douglas Scott, Kathryn Sue, David Andrew, Michael Stonier. A.B., Columbia U., 1958, M.D., 1962. Diplomate: Am. Bd. Dermatology, Am. Bd. Internal Medicine. Intern U. Mich., 1962-63, resident in internal medicine, 1963-64, resident in dermatology, 1968-70, asst. prof., 1970-72, asso. prof., 1972-75, clin. asso. prof., 1975-77, clin. prof., 1977—. Resident in internal medicine Columbia-Presbyn. Med. Center, N.Y.C., 1966-68; practice medicine specializing in dermatology, Ann Arbor, Mich., 1970— Contbr. articles to profl. jours. Trustee Greenhills Sch., Ann Arbor, 1979-87, pres. bd. trustees, 1981-84. Served with U.S. Army, 1964-66. Fellow ACP; mem. Am. Acad. Dermatology, Am. Dermatol. Assn., Soc. Investigative Dermatology, Dermatology Found. (mem. exec. com. 1987-2001, sec.-treas. 1988-91, pres. 1991-98), Mich. Dermatol. Soc. (pres. 1985-87), AMA, Mich. Med. Soc., Washtenaw County Med. Soc., Rotary, Sigma Xi. Office: 3250 Plymouth Rd Ann Arbor MI 48105-2592

DUCAR, TRACY, former soccer player; b. Lawrence, Mass., June 18, 1973; m. Chris Ducar, 1997. BS in Biology, U. N.C., 1995. Mem. U.S. Nat. Women's Soccer Team, 1996—, including Nike Victory Tour, 1997, U.S. Women's Cup, 1997. Named Team Most Valuable Player, U. N.C., 1995. Mem. Phi Beta Kappa. Office: US Soccer Fedn 1801-1811 S Prairie Ave Chicago IL 60616

DUCHOSSOIS, CRAIG, manufacturing executive, heavy; BBA, MBA, So. Meth. U. CEO, pres. Duchossois Industries, Elmhurst, Ill. Office: Duchossois Industries 845 N Larch Ave Elmhurst IL 60126

DUCHOSSOIS, RICHARD LOUIS, manufacturing executive, racetrack executive; b. Chgo., Oct. 7, 1921; s. Alphonse Christopher and Erna (Hessler) D.; children: Craig J., Dayle, R. Bruce, Kimberly. Student, Washington and Lee U. Chmn. bd. dirs. Duchossois Industries, Inc., Elmhurst, Ill., chmn.; chmn., dir. Chamberlain Tech. Cos.; chmn. Arlington Park Racecourse, Ltd., Arlington Heights, Ill. Bd. dirs. Chamberlain Consumer Products, Hill 'n Dale Farm. Served with U.S. Army, 1942-46, ETO. Decorated Purple Heart, Bronze Star. Mem. Chief Execs. Orgn., Economic Club, Execs. Club (bd. dirs.), Jockey Club N.Y.C. Republican. Methodist. Office: Duchossois Industries Inc 845 N Larch Ave Elmhurst IL 60126-1196 E-mail: duchossois@arlingtonpark.com.

DUCK, STEVE WEATHERILL, communications educator; b. Keynsham, Somerset, Engl., Jan. 4, 1946; s. Kenneth W. and Joan (Stickler) D.; m. Sandra Mariela Allen (div. 1987); children: Christina Louise, James Edward; m. Joanna Margaret Lawson, Dec. 30, 1987; children: Benjamin Lawson-Duck, Gabriel Lawson-Duck. PhD, Sheffield U., Eng., 1971; MA, Oxford U., Eng., 1972. Lectr. Glasgow (Scotland) U., 1970-73, Lancaster U., Eng., 1973-78, sr. lectr. Eng., 1978-85; prof. U. Iowa, Iowa City, 1986—; chair dept. comm. studies, 1994-98. Founder Internat. Confs. on Personal Relationships, Internat. Network Personal Relationships. Author: Relating to Others, 1999, Understanding Relationships, 1991, Human Relationships, 3rd edit., 1992; editor: Handbook of Personal Relationships, 1988, 2d edit., 1997, Meaningful Relationships, 1994; co-editor: Studying Interpersonal Interaction, 1991; editor Jour. Social and Personal Relationships, 1984-98. Fellow APA, Am. Psychol. Soc., Interpersonal Comm. Assn. Office: U Iowa Dept Comm Studies 105B CSB Iowa City IA 52242

DUDERSTADT, JAMES JOHNSON, academic administrator, engineering educator; b. Ft. Madison, Iowa, Dec. 5, 1942; s. Mack Henry and Katharine Sydney (Johnson) D.; m. Anne Marie, June 24, 1964; children: Susan Kay, Katharine Anne. B in Engring. with highest honors, Yale U., 1964; MS in Engring. Sci, Calif. Inst. Tech., 1965, PhD in Engring. Sci. and Physics, 1967. Asst. prof. nuclear engring. U. Mich., 1969—72, assoc. prof., 1972—76, prof., 1976—81; dean U. Mich. (Coll. Engring.), 1981—86; provost, v.p. acad. affairs U. Mich., 1986—88, pres. univ., 1988—96, pres. emeritus, prof. sci. engring., 1996—. Dir. Millennium Project, 1996—. AEC fellow, 1964-68; recipient E. O. Lawrence award U.S. Dept. Energy, 1986, Nat. medal of Tech., 1991; named Nat. Engr. of Yr., NSPE, 1991. Fellow Am. Nuclear Soc. (Mark Mills award 1968, Arthur Holly Compton award 1985); mem. NAE (coun.), Am. Phys. Soc., Nat. Sci. Bd. (chair 1991-94), Am. Acad. Arts & Scis., Sigma Xi, Tau Beta Pi, Phi Beta Kappa. Office: Millennium Project 2001 Media Union Ann Arbor MI 48109

DUDLEY, DURAND STOWELL, librarian; b. Cleve., Feb. 28, 1926; s. George Stowell and Corinne Elizabeth (Durand) D.; m. Dorothy Woolworth, July 3, 1954; children: Jane Elizabeth, Deborah Anne. BA, Oberlin Coll., 1948; MLS, Case Western Res. U., 1950. Librarian, Marietta (O.) Coll. Library, 1953-55, Akron (O.) Pub. Library, 1955-60; librarian Marathon Oil Co., Findlay, O., 1960-74, sr. law librarian, 1974-86; supr. tech. services dept. Findlay-Hancock County Pub. Library, Findlay, 1986-88. Mem. Spl. Libraries Assn. Presbyterian (deacon). Home: 807 Red Maple Ct Bluffton OH 45817-8551

DUDLEY, JOHN HENRY, JR. lawyer; b. Lansing, Mich., June 22, 1941; s. John Henry and Elizabeth (Dean) D.; m. Elizabeth Merrill Casgrain, Dec. 27, 1975; 1 child, John. BA, Denison U., 1963; LLB, Stanford U., 1966; MA, U. Mich., 1968. Bar: Mich. 1968, U.S. Ct. Appeals (6th cir.) 1972, U.S. Ct. Appeals (2d cir.) 1987. Assoc. Devine & Devine, Ann Arbor, Mich., 1968-69; ptnr. Butzel Long, Detroit, 1969—. Adj. prof. law sch. U. Detroit, 1991. Chair, bd. dirs. Ann Arbor YMCA, 1997-99. Named Master of Bench U. Detroit-Mercy. Fellow Mich. State Bar Found.; mem. ABA (litig. sect.), Mich. State Bar Assn. (rep. assembly 1974-77), Detroit Bar Assn. (vol. lawyers com. 1989—), Washtenaw County Bar Assn., Am. Inn of Ct. Office: Butzel Long 150 W Jefferson Ave Fl 9th Detroit MI 48226-4430

DUDLEY, KENNETH EUGENE, manufacturing company executive; b. Bellville, Ohio, Nov. 26, 1937; s. Kenneth Olin and Ethel Elizabeth (Poorman) D.; m. Judith Ann Brown, Apr. 15, 1972; children: Camaron J. McCluggage, Kenneth Alan. Inventory control mgr. Gorman-Rupp Industries, Bellville, 1958-67, prodn. mgr., 1967-69, mgr. data processing, 1969-74, cost mgr., 1974-78, contr., 1978-82; treas., chief fin. officer Gorman-Rupp Co., Mansfield, Ohio, 1982—. With USAF, 1962-63. Republican. Lutheran. Office: Gorman-Rupp Co PO Box 1217 Mansfield OH 44901-1217 Home: 1855 Chapelwood Blvd Mansfield OH 44907-2205

DUDLEY, PAUL V. retired bishop; b. Northfield, Minn., Nov. 27, 1926; s. Edward Austin and Margaret Ann (Nolan) D. Student, Nazareth Coll., St. Paul Sem. Ordained priest Roman Cath. Ch., 1951. Titular bishop of Ursona, aux. bishop of St. Paul-Mpls, 1977-78; bishop of Sioux Falls S.D., 1978-95; pastor Northfield (Minn.) St. Dominic, 1995-97; ret., 1997. Office: 2500 320th St W Northfield MN 55057-4564

DUDUKOVIC, MILORAD P. chemical engineering educator, consultant; b. Beograd, Yugoslavia, Mar. 25, 1944; arrived in U.S., 1968; s. Predrag R. and Melita Maria Dudukovic; m. Judith Ann Reiff, Dec. 27, 1969; children: Aleksandra Anne, Nicole Maria. BS in Engring., U. Beograd, 1967; M.S., Ill. Inst. Tech., 1970, PhD, 1972. Rsch. engr. Process Design Inst., Beograd, 1967-68; instr. Ill. Inst. Tech., Chgo., 1970-72; asst. prof. Ohio U., Athens, 1972-74; assoc. prof. Washington U., St. Louis, 1974-80, prof., dir., 1980—, Laura and William Jens prof. environ. engring., 1993—, chmn. dept. chem. engring., 1998—. Cons. in field. Assoc. editor: Indsl. and Engineering Chemistry Research, 1991—; contbr. articles to profl. jours. Recipient Burlington No. Found. Tchg. award, 1986, Nat. Catalyst award Chem. Mfrs. Assn., 1988, St. Louis award ACS, 1995, Malcolm E. Pruitt award Coun. Chem. Rsch., 1999; 2 NASA certs. of recognition and citations; Fulbright scholar Inst. for Higher Edn., 1968. Fellow AIChE (R.H. Wilhelm award 1994), St. Louis Acad. Scis.; mem. AAAS, Am. Chem. Soc., Am. Assn. Engring. Edn., Yugoslav Acad. Engring. (fgn. mem.), Sigma Xi, Century Club (St. Louis). Achievements include pioneering work on trickle bed reactors, bubble columns; research in Czochralski crystal growth, novel experimental techniques for multiphase reactors; environmentally benign processing. Office: Washington U Dept Chem Engring Campus Box 1198 One Brookings Dr Saint Louis MO 63130-4899 E-mail: dudu@poly1.che.wustl.edu.

DUDYCZ, WALTER W. state legislator; b. Chgo., Mar. 11, 1950; m. Oksana; 2 children. Grad., Chgo. Citywide Coll., Chgo. Police Acad. Police detective City of Chgo., 1971-84; mem. dist. 7 Ill. State Senate, 1985—; mem. appropriations I com., exec. appointment com., vet affairs and admin. com., minority spokesman, elec and reapportionment com.; legis. rsch. unit com., Alzheimers task force com., mem. state gov. orgn. ad admin., transp. com., asst. rep. leader. Office: 6143 N Northwest Hwy Chicago IL 60631-2127 also: Office of Senate Members State Capitol Springfield IL 62706-0001

DUE, JEAN MARGARET, agricultural economist, educator; b. Peterborough, Ont., Can., Sept. 19, 1921; d. Allan B. and Katherine Jean (Calder) Mann; m. John F. Due, Aug. 18, 1950; children— Allan Malcolm, Kevin John Burritt. B.Com., U. Toronto, 1946; M.S., U. Ill., 1950, Ph.D., 1953. Economist Dept. Agr., Ottawa, Ont., 1946-49; research asso. in home econs. U. Ill., 1959-61, vis. prof., 1965-70, prof. dept. agr. econs., 1970-90. Contbr. articles to profl. jours. Mem. African Studies Assn., Am. Econ. Assn., Am. Agrl. Econs. Assn., Internat. Assn. Agrl. Econs., Assn. Women Internat. Devel. Home: 1208 Clark Lindsey Village 101 W Windsor Rd Urbana IL 61802-6663 Office: Univ Illinois 305MH 1301 W Gregory Dr # 305mh Urbana IL 61801-9015 E-mail: jdue@uiuc.edu.

DUE, JOHN FITZGERALD, economist, educator emeritus; b. Hayward, Cal., July 11, 1915; s. Jackson Angelo and Emmarene (Hurd) D.; m. Margaret Jean Mann, Aug. 18, 1950; children: Nancy, Allan, Kevin. A.B., U. Calif.-Berkeley, 1935, Ph.D., 1939; A.M., George Washington U., 1936. Instr. U. Utah, 1939-42, asst. prof., 1945-48; economist Treasury Dept., 1942; faculty U. Ill., 1948-86, prof. econs., 1951-86, prof. emeritus, 1986—, chmn. dept. econs., 1963-67, 71-72; acting dean Coll. Commerce U. Ill., 1976, 85-86. Author: Taxation and Economic Development in Tropical Africa, 1963, Indirect Taxation in Developing Economies, 2d edit., 1988; co-author: Sales Taxation: State and Local Structure and Operation, 1983, rev., 1994, The Electric Interurban Railway in America, 1960, Rails to The Ochoco Country-The City of Prineville Railway, 1968, Government Finance, 7th edit, 1981, Rails to the Mid Columbia Wheatlands, 1979, Roads and Rails South from the Columbia, 1991. Served with USMCR, 1942-45. Mem. Am. Econ. Assn., Nat. Tax Assn., Phi Beta Kappa. Home: 101 W Windsor Rd Apt 1208 Urbana IL 61802-6663 Office: Univ Ill Wohlers Hall 1206 S 6th St Champaign IL 61820-6978 E-mail: jdue@uiuc.edu.

DUECKER, ROBERT SHELDON, retired bishop; b. Medina County, Ohio, Sept. 4, 1926; s. Howard LaVerne and Sarah Faye (Simpson) D.; m. Marjorie Louise Clouse, June 13, 1948; children: Philip Lee, Christine Cay Duecker Isle. B in Religion, AB, Indiana Wesleyan U., 1948; BD, MS, Christian Theol. Sem., Indpls., 1952, DD (hon.), 1969; D in Pub. Svc. (hon.), Kendall Coll., 1996. Ordained to ministry United Meth. Ch., 1952. Pastor Dyer (Ind.) United Meth. Ch., 1952-54; sr. pastor Gethsemane United Meth. Ch., Muncie, Ind., 1954-62, Grace United Meth. Ch., Hartford City, 1962-65, 1st United Meth. Ch., Warsaw, 1965-70, Simpson United Meth. Ch., Ft. Wayne, 1970-72; dir. No. Ind. Conf. Coun. Ministries United Meth. Ch., Marion, 1973-77, dist. supt. No. Ind. Conf. Ft. Wayne, 1977-82; sr. pastor High St. United Meth. Ch., Muncie, 1982-88; bishop Chgo. area United Meth. Ch., 1988-96; ret., 1996; instr. Christian Theol. Sem., Indpls., 1998. Trustee United Theol. Sem., Dayton, Ohio, 1985-88, Kendall Coll., Evanston, Ill., 1988-96, North Ctrl. Coll., Naperville, Ill., 1988-96, Garrett Theol. Sem., Evanston, 1988-96; mem. gen. bd. publ. United Meth. Ch., 1988-92, gen. bd. higher edn. and ministry, 1992-96, univ. senate, 1992-96, mem. adv. coun. Ams. United for Separation of Ch. and State; instr. Christian Theol. Sem., Indpls., 1998. Author: Tensions in the Connection, 1982; also monographs. Mem. Kosciusko County Health Planning Coun., Warsaw, 1968—70; former pres. Delaware County Mental Health Assn., Muncie; bd. dirs. Goodwill Industries, Ft. Wayne, Ind., 1977—88, Parkview Hosp. Found., 1997—. Named Sagamore of the Wabash Gov. of Ind., 1988. Mem. Coun. of Religious Leaders of Met. Chgo. (pres. 1996—), Coun. Bishops United Meth. Ch., North Ctrl. Jurisdiction Coll. Bishops, Kiwanis, Rotary, Theta Phi. Avocations: stamp collecting, golf. E-mail: rsduecker@aol.com.

DUEHOLM, ROBERT M. state legislator; b. June 7, 1945; BA, U. Wis. Assemblyman Wis. State Dist. 28. Bd. dirs. Inter-County Leaders; acct. mgr. Honeywell Corp.; adv. bd. Indianhead Tech. Coll. Democrat. Address: 904 State Road 48 PO Box 260 Luck WI 54853-5104

DUERINCK, LOUIS T. retired railroad executive, attorney; b. Chgo., Aug. 1, 1929; s. Aloys L. and Thais E. (De Backer) D.; m. Patricia A. Bird, June 27, 1953; children: Louis M., Kathleen M. Lutgen, Kevin F., Mark V., Lynn P. Dressel, Brian T., Paul S. Student, U. Notre Dame, 1947-48; JD, DePaul U., Chgo., 1952. Bar: Ill. 1952. Commerce atty. N.Y. Cen. R.R., Chgo., 1955-65; gen. atty. Nat. Ry. Labor Conf., 1967-68; with C&NW Ry. Co., 1965-67, 68-89; sr. v.p. law and real estate C&NW Transp. Co., 1979-83, sr. v.p. traffic, 1983-88, sr. v.p., 1988-89, also bd. dirs. Served with AUS, 1952-55. Mem. ABA, Assn. Transportation Law, Logistics and Policy, Ill. Bar Assn., Glen Oak Country Club, Wyndemere Country Club (Naples). Roman Catholic. Home and Office: 718 Midwest Club Pky Oak Brook IL 60523-2531

DUERKSEN, GEORGE LOUIS, music educator, music therapist; b. St. Joseph, Mo., Oct. 29, 1934; s. George Herbert and Louise May (Dalke) D.; m. Patricia Gay Beers, June 3, 1961; children— Mark Jeffrey, Joseph Scott, Cynthia Elizabeth Student, Tabor Coll, 1951-52; BMusEdn, U. Kans., 1955, MMusEdn, 1956, PhD, 1967. Cert. music edn., Kans., Mo.; bd. cert. music therapist, Nat. Certification Bd. for Music Therapy (CBMT). Tchr. music Tonganoxie High Sch., Kans., 1955-56, Stafford Jr. and Sr. High Sch., 1959-60, Labette County High Sch., Altamont, 1960-62, Shawnee Mission (Kans.) North High Sch., 1962-63; asst. prof., dir. psychology of music lab. Mich. State U., East Lansing, 1965-69; prof., chmn. dept. art and music edn. and music therapy U. Kans., Lawrence, 1969-93, dir. Singing Jayhawks, 1979-83, prof., dir. music edn. and music therapy divsn., 1993—, prof., interim chair dept. music and dance, 2000-01, dir. Ctr. for Rsch. on Music Behavior, 2001—; assoc. dir. Kans. North Ctrl. Assn. Colls. and Schs., 1992-2000. Cons., vis. prof. U. Hawaii, Honolulu, summer 1978; cons., vis. prof. U. Melbourne, Australia, summer 1981; cons., lectr. N.Z. Soc. for Music Therapy, Wellington, 1983, Ctr. for Contemporary Music Rsch., Athens, 1991, U. Thessaloniki, Greece, 1993, Korean Assn. for Music Therapy, 1994, 97, Sook Myung U., Seoul, 1997; cons. functional music applications, 1967—, Deakin U., Geelong, Victoria, Australia, 1990. Author: (monograph) Teaching Instrumental Music, 1973; Music for Exceptional Children, 1981; contbr. articles to profl. jours. Fulbright scholar Inst. for Internat. Edn., Australia, 1956-57; U.Kans. fellow, Lawrence, 1963-64; U.S. Office Edn. grantee, 1966-67, 73-75, 78-81 Mem. AAAS, Music Educators Nat. Conf., Am. Music Therapy Assn., Music Edn. Rsch. Coun. (chmn. 1980-82), Brit. Soc. for Music Therapy, Coun. for Rsch. in Music Edn., Pi Kappa Lambda, Phi Mu Alpha, Phi Delta Kappa. Avocations: photography, boating, travel. Office: U Kans Music Edn and Music Therapy Div 448 Murphy Hall 1530 Naismith Dr Lawrence KS 66045-3102 E-mail: gduerksen@ku.edu.

DUESENBERG, RICHARD WILLIAM, lawyer; b. St. Louis, Dec. 10, 1930; s. (John August) Hugo and Edna Marie (Warmann) D.; m. Phyllis Evelyn Buehner, Aug. 7, 1955; children: Karen, Daryl, Mark, David. BA, Valparaiso U., 1951, JD, 1953, LLD, 2001; LLM, Yale U., 1956. Bar: Mo. 1953. Prof. law NYU, N.Y.C., 1956-62, dir. law ctr. publs., 1960-62; sr. atty. Monsanto Co., St. Louis, 1963-70, asst. gen. counsel, asst. sec., 1975-77, sr. v.p., sec., gen. counsel, 1977-96. Dir. law Monsanto Textiles Co., St. Louis, 1971-75; corp. sec. Fisher Controls Co., Marshalltown, Iowa, 1969-71, Olympia Industries, Spartanburg, S.C., 1974-75; vis. prof. law U. Mo., 1970-71; faculty Banking Sch. South, La. State U., 1967-83; vis. scholar Cambridge U., England, 1996; vis. prof. law St. Louis U., 1997-98. Author: (with Lawrence P. King) Sales and Bulk Transfers Under the Uniform Commercial Code, 2 vols, 1966, rev., 1984, New York Law of Contracts, 3 vols, 1964, Missouri Forms and Practice Under the Uniform Commercial Code, 2 vols, 1966; editor: Ann. Survey of Am. Law, NYU, 1961-62; mem. bd. contbg. editors and advisors: Corp. Law Rev, 1977-86; contbr. articles to law revs., jours. Mem. lawyers adv. coun. NAM, Washington, 1980, Adminstrv. Conf. U.S., 1980-86, legal adv. com. N.Y. Stock Exch., 1983-87, corp. law dept. adv. coun. Practising Law Inst., 1982; bd. dirs. Bach Soc., St. Louis, 1985-86, pres., 1973-77; bd. dirs. Valparaiso U., 1977—, chmn. bd. visitors law sch., 1966—, Luth. Charities Assn., 1984-87, vice chmn., 1986-87; bd. dirs. Luth. Med. Ctr., St. Louis, 1973-82, vice chmn., 1975-80; bd. dirs. Nat. Jud. Coll., 1984-90, St. Louis Symphony, 1988-2002, Opera Theatre St. Louis, 1988—, Luth. Brotherhood, Mpls., 1992-2000, Liberty Fund, Inc., Indpls., 1997—. Served with U.S. Army, 1953-55. Decorated officer's cross Order of Merit (Germany); named Disting. Alumnus, Valparaiso U., 1976. Fellow Am. Bar Found.; mem. ABA (chmn. com. uniform comml. code 1976-79, coun. sect. corp., banking and bus. law 1979-83, sec. 1983-84, chmn. 1986-87), Mo. Bar Assn., Am. Law Inst., Mont Pelerin Soc., Nat. Jud. Coll. (bd. dirs.

1984-90), Order of Coif, Bach Soc., Am. Soc. Corp. Sec. (bd. chmn. 1987-88), Assn. Gen. Coun., Am. Arbitration Assn., St. Louis Club. Home: 1 Indian Creek Ln Saint Louis MO 63131-3333 E-mail: rwduesenberg@worldnet.att.net.

DUFF, BRIAN BARNETT, federal judge; b. Dallas, Sept. 15, 1930; s. Paul Harrington and Frances Ellen (FitzGerald) D.; m. Florence Ann Buckley, Nov. 27, 1953; children: F. Ellen, Brian Barnett Jr., Roderick FitzGerald, Kevin Buckley, Daniel Harrington. AB in English, U. Notre Dame, 1953, postgrad., 1997—; JD, DePaul U., Chgo., 1962. Bar: Ill. 1962, Mass. 1962, U.S. Dist. Ct. (no. dist.) Ill. 1962, U.S. Supreme Ct. 1968. Mgmt. trainee, multiple line underwriter Continental Casualty Co., Chgo., 1956-60; mgmt. cons. Booz, Allen and Hamilton, 1960-62; asst. to chief exec. officer Bankers Life and Casualty Co., 1962-67; atty. Sloan & Bragiel, 1965-68; exec. v.p., gen. counsel R.H. Gore Co., 1968-69; atty. Brian B. Duff & Assocs., 1969-76; judge Cir. Ct. Cook County Ill., 1976-85, U.S. Dist. Ct. (no. dist.) Ill., Chgo., 1985—, now sr. judge. Rep. Ill. Gen. Assembly, Springfield, 1971-76; chmn. House Judiciary Com., 1973-74, minority whip, 1975-76; vis. com. Coll. Law U Chgo., 1977-79; lectr. Law Sch. Loyola U., 1978-79; adj. prof. John Marshall Law Sch., 1985-90, DePaul U. Sch. Law, 1990. Served to lt (j.g.) USN, 1953-56. Mem. ABA, Chgo. Bar Assn., Fed. Judges Assn., Am. Judicature Soc., Nat. Lawyers Club, Inc., (hon.)., Legal Club Chgo. (hon.), Law Club, Ill. State Bar Assn. Roman Catholic. Avocations: fishing, reading, travel, writing. Office: US Dist Ct 219 S Dearborn St Ste 2050 Chicago IL 60604-1800

DUFF, CRAIG, agricultural products executive; Pres. Beef Belt Feeders, Inc., Scott City, Kansas, mgr. Office: Beef Belt Feeders Inc PO Box 528 Scott City KS 67871-0528

DUFF, JOHN BERNARD, college president, former city official; b. Orange, N.J., July 1, 1931; s. John Bernard and Mary Evelyn (Cunningham) D.; m. Helen Mezzanotti, Oct. 8, 1955 (div.); children: Michael, Maureen, Patricia, John, Robert, Emily Anne; m. Estelle M. Shanley, July, 1991. BS, Fordham U., 1953; MA, Seton Hall U., 1958; PhD, Columbia U., 1964; DHL (hon.), Seton Hall U., 1976, Northeastern U., 1982, Emerson Coll., 1983, Lincoln Coll., 1993. Sales rep. Remington-Rand Corp., 1955-57, dist. mgr., 1957-60; mem. faculty Seton Hall U., 1960-70, prof. history, 1968-70, acad. v.p., 1970-71, exec. v.p., acad. v.p., 1971-72, provost, acad. v.p., 1972-76; pres. U. Lowell, Mass., 1976-81; chancellor of higher edn. State of Mass., 1981-86; commr. Chgo. Pub. Libr. System, 1986-92; pres. Columbia Coll., Chgo., 1992-2000, ret., 2000—. Mem. Gov.'s Commn. to Study Capital Punishment, 1972-73; chmn. bd. dirs. Mass. Corp. Ednl. Telecommunications, 1983— ; dir. Mass. Tech. Park Corp. Author: The Irish in the United States, 1971, also articles.; Editor: (with others) The Structure of American History, 1970, (with P.M. Mitchell) The Nat Turner Rebellion: The Historical Event and the Modern Controversy, 1971, (with L. Greene) Slavery: Its Origin and Legacy, 1975. Dem. candidate to U.S. Congress, 1968; mem. State Bd. Edn., 1981-86; chmn. Livingston Town Dem. Com., 1972-76; bd. dirs. Merrimack Regional Theatre, 1981-84, Mass. Higher Edn. Assistance Corp., 1981-86, Chgo. Metro History Fair ; trustee Essex County Coll., 1966-70, Mass. Community Coll. System., St. John's Prep. Sch., Danvers, Mass.; chmn. Lowell Hist. Preservation Commn., 1979-86; mem. adv. bd. Wang Inst., 1979-81; mem. bd. visitors Emerson Coll., 1986-90; pres. Nat. Coun. of Heads of Public Higher Edn. Systems; mem. nat. adv. com. on accreditation and indsl. eligibility U.S. Dept. Edn., 1981-82; mem. Ill. Lit. Coun., 1986-92, adv. com. Ill. State Libr., 1986-92; chmn. Fedn. Ind. Ill. Colls. and Univs., 1996-98. With U.S. Army, 1953-55. Mem. Univ. Club, Tavern Club.

DUFF, MARC CHARLES, state legislator; b. Port Washington, Wis., July 4, 1961; s. James Wayne and Marlyn (Hoffman) D. BS, U. Wis., Whitewater, 1983; MA, U. Wis., Madison, 1985. Legis. asst. Wis. State Rep. Tom Ourada, Madison, 1985-87; sr. analyst rep. caucus staff Wis. State Assembly, 1987-88, mem. from dist. 98, 1988-92, 93—, mem. joint com. fin. Chmn. New Berlin (Wis.) Roadway Beautification Com., 1987—; supr. Dist. 31, Waukesha County, 1988-89. Mem. Rotary Club. Home: 1811 S Elm Grove Rd New Berlin WI 53151-2605 Germany Office: PO Box 8952 Madison WI 53708-8952

DUFFIE, JOHN ATWATER, chemical engineer, educator; b. White Plains, N.Y., Mar. 31, 1925; s. Archibald Duncan and Lulie Adele (Atwater) Duffie; m. Patricia Ellerton, Nov. 22, 1947; children: Neil A., Judith A. Duffie Schwarzmeier, Susan L. Duffie Buse. B.Ch.E., Rensselaer Poly. Inst., 1945, M.Ch.E., 1948; Ph.D., U. Wis., 1951. Registered profl. engr., Wis. Instr. chem. engring. Rensselaer Poly. Inst., 1946-49; research asst. U. Wis., 1949-51; research engr. DuPont Co., 1951; sci. liaison officer Office Naval Research, 1952-53; mem. faculty dept. chem. engring. U. Wis.-Madison, 1954—, prof., 1957-88, prof. emeritus, 1988—, dir. solar energy lab., 1956-88. Author (with W. A. Beckman, S. A. Klein): (book) Solar Heating Design, 1977. With USN, 1943—46, with USN, 1952—53. Fellow Hon. Sr. Research, U. Birmingham, 1984; scholar Fulbright, U. Queensland, Australia, 1964, Sr. Fulbright-Hays, Commonwealth Sci. and Indsl. Research Orgn., Australia, 1977. Fellow: Am. Inst. Chem. Engrs.; mem.: Internat. Solar Energy Soc. (past pres., editor Solar Energy Jour. 1985—93, Charles G. Abbott award Am. sect. 1976, Farrington Daniels award 1987). Office: Univ Wis 1500 Engineering Dr Madison WI 53706-1609

DUFFIELD, MICHAEL O. data processing executive; Various positions including plant mgr., mgr. mfg. bus. forms divsn., v.p. distbn. Wallace Computer Svcs., Inc., Lisle, Ill., v.p. ops., 1990-92, sr. v.p., 1992-98, pres., COO, 1998—, interim CEO, 2000—. Office: Wallace Computer Svcs 2275 Cabot Dr Lisle IL 60532

DUGGAN, PATRICK JAMES, federal judge; b. 1933; BS in Econs., Xavier U., 1955; LLB, U. Detroit, 1958. Pvt. practice Brashear, Duggan & Tangora, 1959-76; judge Wayne County Cir. Ct., 1977-86, U.S. Dist. Ct. (ea. dist.) Mich., Detroit, 1987—. Adj. prof. Madonna U., Livonia, Mich., 1975-93. Chmn. Livonia Family YMCA, 1970-71; bd. trustees Madonna U., 1970-79; pres. Livonia Bar Assn., 1975-76, Am. Inn of Ct. U. Detroit Law Sch. Mem. Mich. Jaycees (pres. 1967-68). Office: US Dist Ct 867 Theodore Levin Cthouse 231 W Lafayette Blvd Detroit MI 48226-2700

DUHL, MICHAEL FOSTER, lawyer; b. Chgo., July 12, 1944; s. Samuel Harold and Gertrude (Crodgen) D.; m. Judith Ann Currie, Jan. 30, 1970; children: Emilie Ann, Benjamin Currie. BBA, U. Mich., 1966; JD magna cum laude, Harvard U., 1969. Bar: Ill. 1969; CPA, Ill. Law clk. to presiding justice Ill. Supreme Ct., Chgo., 1969-70; assoc. Hopkins & Sutter, 1971-75, ptnr., 1976-96; prin. Deloitte & Touche, L.L.P., 1997—. Bd. editors Harvard Law Rev., 1967-69. Treas. Winnetka (Ill.) Pub. Libr. Dist. Bd., 1980-85; bd. dirs. Winnetka Hist. Soc., 1990-94, Winnetka Landmark Preservation Commn., 1992-96; bd. trustees Village of Winnetka, 1996-2000, pres., 2001—. Mem. ABA, Univ. Club Chgo. Jewish. Office: Deloitte & Touche LLP 2 Prudential Plz 180 N Stetson Ave Fl 19 Chicago IL 60601-6779

DUIM, GARY T. retired bank executive; Head corp. banking group U.S. Bancorp, Mpls., 1993-96, exec. v.p. retail banking group, 1996-97, vice-chmn. comml. and bus. banking and pvt. fin. svcs., 1997-2000, ret., 2000. Office: US Bancorp US Bank Pl 601 2nd Ave S Minneapolis MN 55402-4303

DUL, JOHN A. lawyer; b. 1961; BBA, U. Miami; JD, Northwestern U. Bar: Ill., 1986. Gen. counsel and sec. Anixter Internat., Skokie, Ill. Office: Anixter Internat 4711 Golf Rd Skokie IL 60076-1224

DULANY, ELIZABETH GJELSNESS, university press administrator; b. Charleston, S.C., Mar. 11, 1931; d. Rudolph Hjalmar and Ruth Elizabeth (Weaver) Gjelsness; m. Donelson Edwin Dulany, Mar. 19, 1955; 1 son, Christopher Daniel. BA, Bryn Mawr Coll., 1952. Editor, R.R. Bowker Co., 1948-52; med. editor U. Mich. Hosp., Ann Arbor, 1953-54; editorial asst. E.P. Dutton & Co., N.Y.C., 1954-55, U. Ill. Press, Champaign, 1956-59, asst. editor, 1959-67, assoc. editor, 1967-72, mng. editor, 1972-90, asst. dir., 1983-90, assoc. dir., 1990—. Democrat. Episcopalian. Home: 73 Greencroft Dr Champaign IL 61821-5112 Office: U Ill Press 1325 S Oak St Champaign IL 61820-6903 E-mail: e-dulany@uillinois.edu.

DULL, WILLIAM MARTIN, retired engineering executive; b. Buchanan, Mich., June 24, 1924; s. Curtis Frank and Daisy Julia (Sharp) D.; m. Margaret Ann McMillan, Apr. 10, 1976; children: Richard William, Beverly Ann, William McMillan. BSME, U. Mich., 1945. Registered profl. engr., Mich. Dir. tech. staff Detroit Edison, 1951-66, asst. gen. supt. cen. plants, 1966-70, gen. supt. underground lines, 1970-71, mgr. employee relations, 1971-74, mgr. orgn. planning and devel., 1974-89; pres. Charleston Engring. Cons., 1990-92; ret., 1992. Chmn. Charleston Engrs. Joint Coun., 1991—, chmn. 1993-94. Bd. dirs. World Med. Relief, Detroit, 1971-90, chmn., 1988-90; bd. dirs. Jr. Achivement, Southeastern Mich., 1971-90; trustee Detroit Sci. Ctr., Inc., 1979-85. Served to lt. (s.g.) USN, 1942-51, PTO. Recipient Gold Leadership award Jr. Achievement, 1985. Fellow Engring. Soc. Detroit (pres. 1970-71, Disting. Svc. 1980, life); mem. ASHRAE (pres. 1964-65, Outstanding Engr. award 1965, life), ASME (life), IEEE (chmn. nat. conf. 1971), NSPE (life), Architects, Engrs., Surveyors Registration Coun. (chmn. 1968-69), Mich. Soc. Profl. Engrs. (bd. dirs. 1973-75, Disting. Engr. 1980), S.C. Soc. Profl. Engrs. (bd. dirs. 1994-95), Charleston Engrs. Joint Coun. (chmn. 1993-94), U. Mich. Alumni Assn. (v.p., bd. dirs. 1964-71, Disting. Svc. award 1970), Charleston Navy League (v.p., bd. dirs. 1993—), Detroit Yacht Club. Republican. Methodist. E-mail: mwmdull@aol.com.

DUMARS, JOE, III, retired professional basketball player; b. Shreveport, La., May 24, 1963; m. Debbie Nelson, 1989; 1 child, Jordan. Grad. in bus. mgmt., McNeese State U., 1985. With Detroit Pistons, 1985-99. Mem. NBA Championship team, 1989, 90, Dream Team II, 1994. Named Most Valuable Player NBA finals, 1989; Mem. NBA All-Star team, 1990-93; mem. NBA All-Defensive first team, 1989-90, 92, 93, second team, 1991, 93; mem. NBA All-Rookie team, 1986; mem. All-NBA third team, 1990, 91; mem. Sporting News NCAA All-America second team, 1985; named to Dream Team II, 1994; recipient Citizenship award, 1994. Office: Detroit Pistons 2 Championship Dr Auburn Hills MI 48326-1753

DUMAS, RHETAUGH ETHELDRA GRAVES, university official; b. Natchez, Miss., Nov. 26, 1928; d. Rhetaugh Graves and Josephine (Clemmons) Graves Bell; m. A.W. Dumas, Jr., Dec. 25, 1950; 1 child, Adrienne. BS in Nursing, Dillard U., 1951; MS in Psychiat. Nursing, Yale U., 1961; PhD in Social Psychology, Union Grad. Sch., Union for Experimenting Colls. and Univs., Cinn., 1975; also various other courses; D Pub. Svc. (hon.), Simmons Coll., 1976, U. Cin., 1981; LHD (hon.), Yale U., 1989; LLD (hon.), Dillard U., 1990; LHD (hon.), U. San Diego, 1993, Georgetown U., 1996; DPub. Svc., Fla. Internat. U., Miami, 1996; DSc (hon.), Ind. U., Gary, 1996; JD (hon.), Bethune-Cookman Coll., 1997; LHD (hon.), U. Mass, 1997. Instr. Dillard U., 1957-59, 61; research asst., instr. Sch. Nursing Yale U., 1962-65, from asst. prof. nursing to assoc. prof., 1965-72, chmn. dept. psychiat. nursing, 1972; dir. nursing Conn. Mental Health Ctr., Yale-New Haven Med. Ctr., 1966-72; chief psychiat. nursing edn. br. Div. Manpower and Tng. Programs, NIMH, Rockville, Md., 1972-76; dep. dir. Div. Manpower and Tng. Programs NIMH, 1976-79, dep. dir. alcohol, drug abuse and mental health adminstrn., 1979-81; dean, prof. U. Mich. Sch. Nursing, 1981-94; vice provost health affairs U. Mich., 1994-97, Lucille Cole prof. sch. nursing, 1994—, vice provost emerita, 1997—, dean emerita, 1997—. Dir. Group Rels. Confs. in Tavistock Model; cons., speaker, panelist in field; fellow Helen Hadley Hall, Yale U., 1972, Branford Coll., 1972; dir. Community Health Care Ctr. Plan, New Haven, 1969-72; mem. U.S. Assessment Team, cons. to Fed. Ministry Health, Nigeria, 1982; mem. adv. com. Health Policy Agenda for the Am. People, AMA, 1983-86; cons. NIH Task Force on Nursing Rsch., 1984; mem. Nat. Commn. on Unemployment and Mental Health, Nat. Mental Health Assn., 1984-85; mem. com. to plan maj. study of nat. long-term care policy Inst. Medicine, 1985; mem. adv. com. to dir. NIH, 1986-87; mem. Sec.'s Nat. Commn. on Future Structure of VA Health Care System, 1990-91; mem. coun. on grad. med. edn. Nat. Adv. Coun. on Nurse Edn. and Practice Workgroup on Primary Care Workforce Projection, Divsn. Nursing, 1994; mem. com. to rev. breast cancer rsch. program U.S. Army Med. Rsch. and Material Command, Inst. of Medicine, 1996-97; mem. Pres.'s Nat. Bioethics Adv. Commn., 1996—. Author profl. monographs; contbr. over 40 articles to profl. pubs.; mem. editorial bd. Community Mental Health Rev., 1977-79, Jour. Personality and Social Systems, 1978-81, Advances in Psychiat. Mental Health Nursing, 1981. Bd. dirs. Afro Am. Ctr., Yale U., 1968-72; mem. New Haven Bd. Edn., 1968-71, New Haven City Demonstrations Agy., 1968-70, Human Rels. Coun. New Haven, 1961-63, Nat. Neural Circuitry Database Com., Inst. Medicine, Nat. Acad. Scis., mem. bd. scientific advisors, 1985—; mem. commn. on future structure of vets. health care U.S. Dept. Vets. Affairs, 1990; mem. Pres. Clinton's Nat. Bioethics Adv. Commn., 1996-01. Named Disting. Alumna, Dillard U., 1966; recipient various awards, including cert. Honor NAACP, 1970, Disting. Alumnae award Yale U. Sch. Nursing, 1976, award for outstanding achievement and service in field mental health D.C. chpt. Assn. Black Psychologists, 1980, Pres. 21st Century award The Nat. Women's Hall of Fame, 1994, Lifetime Achievement award, nat. Black Nurses Assn., 2000—. Fellow A.K. Rice Inst., Am. Coll. Mental Health Adminstrs. (founding), Am. Acad. Nursing (charter, pres. 1987-89); mem. Inst. Medicine NAS, Am. Nurses Assn., Nat. Black Nurses Assn., Am. Assn. Colls. Nursing (govtl. affairs com. 1990-93), Am. Pub. Health Assn., Nat. League Nursing (pres. 1997-99), Nat. Bioethics Adv. Commn., Sigma Theta Tau Internat. (mentor award 1989), Delta Sigma Theta. Office: U Mich 400 N Ingalls St Rm 4320 Ann Arbor MI 48109-2003

DUMAS, TYRONE PIERRE, architect, construction manager, consultant; b. Milw., July 11, 1952; s. Augustus Elerby and Darlene (Elerby) Ingram; m. Ceciel Harrell Dumas, Aug. 18, 1973; children: Maurice A., Danielle S.; foster children: Latrice Harrell, Stonia Harrell. AArch, Milw. Area Tech. Coll., 1975; BArch, U.Wis., Milw., 1977. Construction bldg. inspection dept. City Milw., 1977-79; corporate engr. Miller Brewing Co., Milw., 1979-86; constrn. mgr. Heike/Design Assn. Inc., Brookfield, Wis., 1986; with Dumas Cons. Specialties, Milw., 1986—. Vol., speaker United Way, Milw., 1984-86; vol. speaker Milw. Pub. Schs., 1984-86; asst. basketball coach Bethlehem Luth. Sch.; trustee Bethlehem Luth. Ch., steward various coms. Recipient Merit award State of Wis., 1973, Role Model of Yr. award Milw. Pub. Sch., 1983-84, Community Service award Miller Brewing Co., 1985. Mem. AIA (assoc.), Wis. Soc. Architects (assoc.), Project Mgmt. Inst., U.S. Brewers Acad., Constrn. Specifications Inst. (assoc.), U.W. Milw. Alumni Assn. Lutheran. Avocations: stand-up comedy, motivational speaking. Home and Office: 5963 N 78th St Milwaukee WI 53218-1712

DUMESIC, JAMES A. chemical engineer; BS, U. Wis., Madison; MS, PhD, Stanford U. Steenbock prof. dept. chem. engring. U. Wis., Madison. Contbr. articles to profl. jours. Recipient Emmeett award N.Am. Catalysis Soc., 1989, award N.Y. Catalysis Soc. award, 1994, Parravano award Mich. Catalysis Soc., 1999. Mem. AIChE (Colburn award 1983, Wilhelm award 1997), NAE. Achievements include research in kinetics and catalysis, surface adn solid-state chemistry, in situ catalyst studies. Office: U Wis 3014 Engineering Hall 1415 Engineering Dr Madison WI 53706 E-mail: dumesic@engr.wisc.edu.

DUMOVICH, LORETTA, real estate and transportation company executive; b. Kansas City, Kans., Sept. 29, 1930; d. Michael Nicholas and Frances Barbara (Horvat) D. Student public schs., Kansas City. Lic. real estate broker, Kans., Mo. Corp. sec., dir. Riss Internat. Corp., 1950-86, Riss Intermodal Corp., 1969-86, World Leasing Corp., 1969-86; pres., dir. Columbia Properties, Inc., 1969-86; v.p., dir. Republic Industries, 1969-86; corp. sec., dir. Comml. Equipment Co. Inc., Charlotte, N.C., 1980-93; v.p., corp. sec. Commonwealth Gen. Ins. Co., Kansas City, Mo., 1986-93, Heart of Am. Fire & Casualty Co., Kansas City, 1986-93. Mem. Kansas City (Mo.) Real Estate Bd., Bldg. Owners and Mgrs. Assn. of Kansas City (Mo.), Terminal Properties Exchange (founding mem.), Am. Royal Assn. (gov.) Office: 215 W Pershing Rd Kansas City MO 64108-4317

DUNASKISS, MAT J. state legislator; b. Pontiac, Mich., Sept. 21, 1951; s. Frank and Aldona (Suvesdis) D.; m. Diane L. Tench, 1978; three children. AA, Oakland C.C., 1971; BA, U. Mich., 1973, MA, 1976. Tchr. Lake Orion (Mich.) Cmty. Sch., 1974-78; commr. Oakland County, Mich., 1979-80; rep. Mich. Dist. 61, 1980-90; mem. Mich. Senate from dist. 16, Lansing, 1991—. Chmn. tech. & energy com. Mich. State Sen., vice chmn. natural resources & environ. affairs com., local, urban & state affairs com. Recipient cmty. svc. award Lake Orion Area Jaycees, 1981. Mem. Oakland County C. of C., Optimists, K. of C., Lake Orion Lake Assn., St. Joseph Catholic Ch. Usher's Club. Address: S-8 Capitol Bldg PO Box 30036 Lansing MI 48909-7536

DUNBAR, MARY ASMUNDSON, communications executive, investor and public relations consultant; b. Sacramento, Feb. 6, 1942; d. Vigfus Samundur and Aline Mary (McGrath) Asmundson; m. Robert Copeland Dunbar, June 21, 1969; children: Geoffrey Townsend, William Asmundson. BA in English Lit., Smith Coll., 1964; MA in Communications, Stanford, 1967; MBA in Fin., Case Western Res. U., 1985. Cert. pub. rels. profl. Tchr. Peace Corps, Cameroun, Africa, 1964-66; writer, editor Ednl. Devel. Corp., Palo Alto, Calif., 1967-68, Addison-Wesley, Menlo Park, 1969-70; free lance writer, editor various, Cleve., 1970-85; account exec. Edward Howard & Co., 1985-87, Dix & Eaton, Inc., Cleve., 1987-89, sr. account exec., 1990-92, v.p., 1992-96, sr. v.p., 1997—. Author publs. in field. Trustee Cleve. Coun. World Affairs, 1994—99. Smith Coll. scholar, Northampton, Mass., 1960-64; fellowship Stanford Univ., Palo Alto, Calif., 1967; recipient Internat. Assn. Bus. Comm. award, 1987, Women in Comm. award, 1987, Arthur Page award, 1990. Mem. Smith Coll. Club Cleve., Pub. Rels. Soc. Am. (Silver Anvil award 1997), Nat. Investor Rels. Inst. (past pres. Cleve.-No. Ohio chpt., elected to nat. bd. dirs. 2002), Cleve. Soc. Security Analysts. Republican. Episcopalian. Avocations: jogging, music. Home: 2880 Fairfax Rd Cleveland OH 44118-4014 Office: Dix & Eaton Inc 1301 E 9th St Ste 1300 Cleveland OH 44114-1820 E-mail: mdunbar@dix-eaton.com.

DUNCAN, CLEO, state legislator; m. John Duncan. BS, Ball State U.; MS, Purdue U. Sales rep. Gray & Gray Specialties; mem. Ind. State Ho. of Reps. Dist. 67, mem. edn., pub. policy, ethics and vet. affairs com., mem. roads and transp. com., vice-chmn. environ. affairs com. Councilman Greensburg, Ind.; pres. Decatur County Solid Waste Bd.; mem. Greensburg City Planning Commn., Decatur County Coun. Youth; founder Project HELP. Mem. Greensburg C. of C., Decatur County Found.

DUNCAN, DALE A. publishing executive; BA in Journalism, Cen. Mich. U., 1976; student, Am. Press Inst., 1980, 83, 86, Northwestern U., 1996. Reporter Belleville (Ill.) News-Dem. and Oakland Press, Pontiac, Mich., 1976-80; exec. editor, city editor Times Leader, Wilkes-Barre, Pa., 1980-86, pres., pub., 1986-94, Oakland Press, Pontiac, 1995-97; v.p. ABC Pub. Group, 1995-97; pres., gen. mgr. Indpls. Newspapers, Inc., 1998-99, pres., pub., 1999—. Bd. chmn. Salvation Army; dir. F. M. Kirby Ctr. for Performing Arts; bd. dirs. United Way Oakland County; adv. bd. Clinton Valley coun. Boy Scouts Am.; mem. ch. and soc. task force St. Paul's United Meth. Ch.; co-chair minority journalism fundraising com. Cen. Mich. U. Recipient 3 nat. journalism awards Scripps-Howard, 4 Pa. state awards for editl. writing, Disting. Citizen award Penn Mountains coun. Boy Scouts Am., 1995. Mem. Pa. Newspaper Pub.'s Assn. (bd. dirs., chmn. diversity com.), C. of C. Office: Indpls Newspapers Inc 307 N Pennsylvania St Indianapolis IN 46204-1819 Fax: 317-633-9331.

DUNCAN, DICK, state agency administrator; s. Charles Arthur and Vera (Glidden) D.; m. Grace Duncan, Aug. 17, 1998; children: Sally, Sandra, Douglas, Lisa. LLB, S.D. U., 1962. Asst. atty. gen. State S.D., Pierre, 1962-65; pvt. practice law Duncan Olinger Sistka Law Office, 1965-86; dir. banking State S.D., 1986—. With USMC, 1951-54. Republican. Avocation: sailing. Office: Commerce and Regulations Dept 118 W Capitol Ave Pierre SD 57501-2000

DUNCAN, ED EUGENE, lawyer; b. Gary, Ind., Dec. 10, 1948; s. Attwood and Freddie Leon (Ballard) D.; m. Patricia Louise Revado, Sept. 8, 1973 (div.); children: Kristin, Anika, Gregory. BA, Oberlin Coll., 1970; JD, Northwestern U., 1974. Bar: Ohio 1974, U.S. Dist. Ct. (no. dist.) Ohio 1977, U.S. Supreme Ct. 1977. Assoc. Arter & Hadden, Cleve., 1974-82, ptnr., 1982—. Bd. mem. Glenville br. YMCA, Cleve., 1979—, Ohio Bd. of Bldg. Standards, Columbus, 1986-89; trustee Legal Aid Soc., Cleve., 1990-91. Mem.: Cleve. Bar Assn., Ohio Bar Assn. Avocations: writing, reading. Home: 935 Roland Rd Cleveland OH 44124-1033 Office: Arter & Hadden 925 Euclid Ave Ste 1100 Cleveland OH 44115-1475 E-mail: eduncan1@arterhadden.com.

DUNCAN, FRED A. food products company executive; Various acctg. and planning positions J.M. Smucker Co., Orrville, Ohio, 1977-88, treas., 1988, v.p. procurement and tech. svcs., v.p., gen. mgr., 1995—. Mng. dir. Australian subs. Henry Jones Foods Pty. Ltd. Office: J M Smucker Co 1 Strawberry Ln Orrville OH 44667-1241

DUNCAN, JOHN PATRICK CAVANAUGH, lawyer; b. Kalamazoo, Jan. 25, 1949; s. James H. and Colleen Patricia (Cloney) D.; children: Sarah Ellen, James Patrick Cloney. BA cum laude, Yale U., 1971; JD, U. Chgo., 1974. Bar: Ill. 1974, U.S. Dist. Ct. (no. dist.) Ill. 1974, U.S. Ct. Appeals (7th cir.) 1975, U.S. Supreme Ct. 1979. Assoc. firm Holleb & Coff, Chgo., 1974-79; mem., 1979-87; ptnr. Jones, Day, Reavis & Pogue, Chgo., 1987-99; leader banking and investment practice area, 1996-99; prin. Duncan Assocs., LLC, 2000—. Adj. prof. IIT Chgo.-Kent Coll. Law Fin. Svcs. LLM Program, 1988—; mem. Fulbright Vis. Scholar Adv. Bd., 1995—98; mem. Chgo. com. Chgo. Coun. on Fgn. Rels., 1998—2000. Contbr. articles to profl. jours. Fellow NSF, 1970. Fellow: Ill. Bar Found.; mem.: ABA (chmn. securities activities banks subcom. 1995—98, privacy task force 1998—2001, banking com.), Ill. Bankers Assn. (legal affairs com. 1986—87), Chgo. Bar Assn. (chmn. fin. insts. com. 1985—86), Met. Club (Chgo.), Yale Club (Chgo., N.Y.). Home: 3814 N Paulina St Chicago IL 60613-2716 Office: Duncan Assocs LLC 180 N LaSalle Ste 2410 Chicago IL 60601-2704 E-mail: jpcd@jpcdlaw.com.

DUNCAN, R. FOSTER, utilities company executive; V.p., corp. treas. Freeport-McMoRan Inc., Freeport-McMoRan Cooper & Gold; v.p. planning and devel. LG&E Energy Corp., Louisville, 1998-99, exec. v.p., CFO, 1999-2001; CFO Cinergy Corp., Cin., 2001—. Office: 139 E 4th St Cincinnati OH 45202-4003

DUNCAN, ROBERT BANNERMAN, strategy and organizations educator; b. Milw., July 4, 1942; s. Robert Lynn and Irene (Hoenig) D.; m. Susan Jean Phillips, June 12, 1965; children: Stephanie Olcott, Christopher Robert. BA, Ind. U., 1964, MA, 1966; PhD, Yale U., 1971. Asst. prof. Northwestern U. Kellogg Grad. Sch. Mgmt., Evanston, Ill., 1970-73, assoc. prof. orgn. behavior, 1973-76, prof., 1976, Earl Dean Howard prof. orgn. behavior, 1980-83, J.L. Kellogg disting. prof. strategy and orgns., 1983-86, 92—, J. Allen disting. prof. strategy and orgns., 1986-89; Richard L. Thomas prof. leadership orgnl. change Northwestern U., 1996—2002; assoc. dean acad. affairs Northwestern U. Kellogg Grad. Sch. Mgmt., Ill., 1975-76, 80-82, 84-86; provost, chief acad. affairs Northwestern U., 1987-92; Eli and Edythe L. Broad dean Eli Broad Coll. Bus. Mich. State U., East Lansing, 2002—. Co-author: Innovations and Organizations, 1973, Strategies for Planned Change, 1977; also numerous articles in profl. jours. Fellow Acad. Mgmt. (chair nat. program 1980-81, pres. 1983-84). Avocation: sailing.

DUNCAN, ROYAL ROBERT, publisher; b. Bloomington, Ill., May 6, 1952; s. Robert E. and Audrey L. Gresham (Mossberger) D. AA, Rock Valley Coll., Rockford, Ill., 1972; BS, Bradley U., 1974. Sales mgr. Sports Svcs., Peoria, Ill., 1975-77, 4-B Advt., East Peoria, 1977-78; pres. Royal Pub., Peoria, 1978—. Home: 4408 W Collingwood Cir Peoria IL 61614-2069 Office: 7620 Harker Dr Peoria IL 61615-1849

DUNCANSON, DONALD GEORGE, retired encyclopedia editor; b. L.A., Feb. 26, 1928; s. George H. and Addie (Biddison) D. BA, U. So. Calif., L.A., 1953; MA, Harvard U., 1954; postgrad., U. Chgo., 1954-56. Lexicographer Funk & Wagnalls Inc., N.Y.C., 1956-57; assoc. editor Scott, Foresman & Co., Chgo., 1958-64, Sci. Rsch. Assocs., Inc., Chgo., 1964-67; editor Ency. Britannica, Inc., 1967-73, 77-93. With USN, 1946-49. Democrat. Avocations: reading, travel. Home: 3605 Sarah St Franklin Park IL 60131-1632 E-mail: 28492@attbi.com.

DUNEA, GEORGE, nephrologist, educator; b. Craiova, Rumania, June 1, 1933; came to U.S., 1964; s. Charles L. and Gerda (Low) D.; 1 dau., Melanie. M.D., U. Sydney, Australia, 1957. Diplomate Am. Bd. Internal Medicine, Am. Bd. Nephrology. Intern Royal North Shore Hosp., Sydney, 1958-59; resident in internal medicine Australia and Eng., 1959-63; fellow in nephrology Cleve. Clinic, Presbyn.-St. Luke's Hosp., Chgo., 1964-66; practice internal medicine specializing in nephrology, 1972—; attending physician Cook County Hosp., 1966—, dir. dept. nephrology-hypertension, 1969—; prof. medicine U. Ill., 1986—; exec. dir. Hektuen Inst. of Med. Rsch., 1991—. Vis. prof. medicine Rush Med. Sch., Chgo., 1976—. Contbr. chpts. to books, articles to profl. publs. Fellow A.C.P., Royal Coll. Physicians (London, Edinburgh); mem. AMA, Am. Soc. Nephrology, Brit. Med. Assn., Soc. Med. History. Home: 222 E Chestnut St Chicago IL 60611-2360 Office: 1835 W Harrison St Chicago IL 60612-3701 E-mail: geodunea@aol.com.

DUNGAN, JOHN RUSSELL, JR. (TITULAR VISCOUNT DUNGAN OF CLANE AND HEREDITARY CHIEF OF THE NAME; PRINCE OF FERMOY AND ARRA), anesthesiologist; b. Boston, Dec. 12, 1953; s. John Russell and Nancy Pauline (Beaton) D.; m. Nancy Elizabeth Perkins, July 12, 1986 (div. 1997); children: Elizabeth Adelaide, Thayer Warren, Eleanor Grace Appleton. AB magna cum laude, Harvard U., 1977, EdM, 1978; DDS, Baylor U., 1984; MD cum laude, Creighton U., 1989. Diplomate Nat. Bd. Anesthesiology (dir. 1989-92, 97—, v.p. 1997—), Am. Acad. Pain Mgmt. Instr. anesthesiology Boston U. Sch. Medicine, 1986-89; attending staff anesthesiologist, residency instr. Boston City Hosp., 1986-89; anesthesiologist, chief Tobey Hosp., Wareham, Mass., 1989-91; chief of anesthesia Mary Lanning Hosp., Hastings, Nebr., 1991—, chief of surgery, 1995, 2001; pres. Hastings Anesthesiology Assocs., 1992—. Chmn. pharmacy and therapeutics, 1993-94, 96—. Author: The Kings of the Picts and Dál Riads, 1976, The Beatons, 1976, Angus Macdonald, 1977; contbr. articles to profl. jours. Rschr. nat. trust Restoration of Celbridge Chapel and Cemetery, Kildare, Ireland, 1995. John Eliot scholar, 1967, Nat. Merit scholar, 1971; Internat. fellow English-Speaking Union, 1971-72; Harvard Coll. scholar, 1975-77, John Harvard scholar, 1976; head and comdr. Mil. Order Knights of Leinster; named to Honorable Order of Ky. Cols. Mem. Am. Soc. Anesthesiologists, English-Speaking Union U.S., Nebr. Soc. Anesthesiologists, Adams County Med. Soc. (pres. 2001), N.Y. Biog. and Geneal. Soc., N.Y. Irish History Roundtable, N.Eng. Historic Geneal. Soc., United Empire Loyalists Assn. (Can.), Phi Beta Kappa, Cum Laude Soc. (Tabor chpt.), Hasty Pudding Inst. 1770, Harvard Club of Nebr., Old Tonbridgian Soc., The Wild Geese, Clan Dungan (acting chief and pres. 1998—). Republican. Episcopalian. Avocations: Medieval and Jacobean British history research, family history. Home: Heartwell Park 923 N Elm Ave Hastings NE 68901-4021 Office: Hastings Anesthesiology Ste 101 420 W 5th St Hastings NE 68901-7551

DUNGY, TONY, professional football coach; b. Jackson, Mich., Oct. 6, 1955; Def. asst. Pitts. Steelers, 1981-83, def. back coach, 1982-83, def. coord., 1984-88; def. backs coach Kansas City Chiefs, 1989-91; def. coord. Minn. Vikings, 1992-95; head coach Tampa Bay (Fla.) Buccaneers, 1996—. Mem. Super Bowl Championship Team, 1978. Office: Indianapolis Colts 7001 West 56th Street Indianapolis IN 46254

DUNHAM, JOHN L. retail company executive; m. M. Jane Beadles. BA in Engring., U.S. air Force Acad., 1968. Divisional v.p. merchandise processing Ohio divsn. May dept. Stores, 1976-78, v.p. ops. D&F divsn., 1978-83, sr. v.p. ops. Calif. divsn., 1983-87, chmn. Sibley's divsn., 1987-89, chmn. G. Fox divsn., 1989-93, chmn. mechandising co., 1993-96, exec. v.p., CFO, 1996—, also bd. dirs. Bd. dirs. YMCA of Greater St. Louis. Office: May Department Stores Co 611 Olive St Saint Louis MO 63101-1721

DUNHAM, KATHERINE, choreographer, dancer, anthropologist; b. Glen Ellyn, Ill., June 22, 1909; d. Albert Millard and Fanny June (Taylor) D.; m. Jordis McCoo, 1931 (div.); m. John Thomas Pratt, July 10, 1941 (dec. 1986); 1 child, Marie Christine. BA in Anthropology, U. Chgo., 1936, MS; PhD, Northwestern U.; LhD (hon.), MacMurray Coll., 1972. Dir., tchr. of own schs. of dance, theatre and cultural arts, Chgo., N.Y.C., Haiti, Stockholm and Paris, from 1931; profl. dancer, from 1934; choreographer for theatre, opera, motion pictures and TV; mem. Chgo. Opera Co., 1935-36; supv. Chgo. City Theatre Project on cultural studies, 1939; dance dir. Labor Stage, 1939-40; prodr., dir. Katherine Dunham Dance Co., from 1945; established dance sch. Port-au-Prince, Haiti, 1961; advisor to First World Festival on Negro Art U.S. Dept. State, 1966; artistic and tech. advisor to Pres. of Senegal, 1966-67; cultural counselor and dir. Performing Arts Tng. Ctr., So. Ill. U., East St. Louis, from 1967; prof. So. Ill. U., Edwardsville, from 1968. Choreographed works include: (concerts) Tropics, 1937, Schulhoff Tango, 1937, Madame Christoff, 1937, Primitive Rhythms, 1937, Biguine-Beguine, 1937, Florida Swamp Shimmy, 1937, Lotus Eaters, 1937, Haitian Suite, 1937, Peruvienne, 1938, Le Jazz Hot (Boogie-Woogie), 1938, Saludade da Brazil, 1938, Spanish Earth Suite, 1938, Island Songs, 1938, Mexican Rhumba, 1938, L'Ag'Ya, 1938, A Las Montanas, 1938, Bre'r Rabbit an' de Tah Baby, 1938, Bahiana, 1939, Cuidad Maravillosa, 1939, Concert Rhumba, 1939, Cumbancha, 1939, Plantation Dances, 1940, Babalu, 1941, Haitian Suite II, 1941, Honky-Tonk Train (added to Le Hot Jazz), 1941, Rites de Passage, 1941, Tropical Revue, 1943, Callaco, 1944, Choros Nos. 1-5, 1944, Flaming Youth 1927, 1944, Para Que Tu Veas, 1944, Havana 1910/1919, 1944, Carib Song, 1945, Bal Negre, 1946, Motivos, 1946, Haitian Roadside, 1946, Nostalgia (Ragtime), 1946, Batacada, 1947, Bolero, 1947, C'Est Lui, 1947, Rhumba Trio, 1947, Floor Exercises, 1947, La Valise, 1947, Octaroon Ball, 1947, Angelique, 1948, Blues Trio, 1948, Macumba, 1948, Missouri Waltz, 1948, Street Scene, 1948, Veracruzana, 1948, Adeus Terras, 1949, Afrique, 1949, Jazz in Five Movements, 1949, Brazilian Suite, 1950, Los Indios, 1950, Frevo, 1951, Rhumba Jive, 1951, Rhumba Suite, 1951, Spirituals, 1951, Caymmi, 1952, Ramona, 1952, La Blanchisseuse, 1952, Southland, 1952, Afrique du Nord, 1953, Samba, 1953, Cumbia, 1953, Dora, 1953, Honey in the Honeycomb, 1953, Incantation, 1953, Carnaval, 1955, Floy'd Guitar Blues, 1955, Jazz Finale, 1955, Just Wild About Harry, 1955, New Love, 1955, Banana Boat, 1957, Plating Rice, 1957, Sister Kate, 1957, Ti'Cocomaque, 1957, A Touch Of Innocence, 1959, Bamboche, 1962, Diamond Thief, 1962, Anabacoa, 1963; (theatre works) The Emperor Jones, 1939, Cabin in the Sky (co-choreographed with George Balanchine), 1940, Pins and Needles, 1940, Tropical Pinafore, 1939, Les Deux Anges, 1965; (film) Carnaval of Rhythum, 1939, Pardon My Sarong, 1942, Star Spangled Rhythum, 1942, Stormy Weather, 1943, Casbah, 1948, Boote e Risposta, 1950, Mambo, 1954, Green Mansions, 1958, The Bible, 1966; (opera) Aida, 1963; author: Katherine Dunham's Journey to Accompong, 1946, rev. edit., 1972, (autobiography) A Touch of Innocence, 1959, rev. edit., 1980, Island Possessed, 1969, Kasamance: A Fantasy, 1974; co-author (play) Ode to Taylor Jones, 1967-68; author of TV scripts, produced in Mexico, Australia, France, Eng. and Italy; contbr. short stories, somtimes under psedonym Kaye Dunn to mags.; consulting editor: Dance Scope. Pres. Dunham Fund for Rsch. and Devel. Cultural Arts, Inc.; founder Found. Study of Arts and Scis. of Vodun; v.p. Found. Devel. and Preservation Cultural Arts, Inc.; bd. dirs. Nat. Inst. Aging, Ill. Arts Coun.; mem. Ill. com. JFK Ctr. Alliance Arts Edn., Am. Coun. Arts in Edn., Arts Worth/Intercultural Com.; cons. Interamerican Inst. Ethnomusicology and Folklore, Caracas, Venezuela, NEH; mem. rev. com. OAS; mem. adv. bd. Modern Orgn. Dance Evolvement. Decorated Legion of Honor (Haiti), Merit Chevalier (Haiti), Cmdr. (Haiti), Grand Officer (Haiti); Julius Rosenfeld Travel fellow, 1936-37, Fulbright fellow State Dept. Internat. Edn.; Mather scholar Case Western Res. U., 1973; recipient Dance Mag. award, 1968, Eight Lively Arts award, 1969, Disting. Svc. award So. Ill. U., 1970, East St. Louis. Monitor award, 1970, Dance Divsn. Heritage award Am. Assn. Health, Physical Edn. and Recreation, 1972, Nat. Ctr. Afro-Am. Artists award, 1972, Black Merit Acad. award, 1972, Am. Dance Guild award, 1975, 6th Kennedy Ctr. Honors award, 1983, Profl. Achievement award U. Chgo., Samuel M. Scripps/Am. Dance Festival award, 1986, Nat. Medal Arts, 1989, Capezio Dance award, 1991; given key to city East St. Louis, Ill., 1968; named hon. citizen Port-au-Prince, Haiti, 1957. Mem. ASCAP, SAG, AEA, Am. Guild Variety Artists, Am. Guild Music Artists (bd. govs. 1943-49), Am. Fedn. Radio Artists, Writers Guild, Black Acad. Arts and Scis., Inst. Black World (bd. dirs.), Negro Actors Guild, Royal Anthrop. Soc., Lincoln Acad., Sigma Epsilon. Avocations: steam baths, horseback riding, cooking, painting, reading, walking after midnight. Office: Katherine Dunham Mus 532 N 10th St East Saint Louis IL 62201-1946

DUNIPHAN, J. P. state legislator, small business owner; b. Aug. 31, 1946; Mem. S.D. Ho. of Reps., Pierre, 1995—, mem. commerce com., judiciary com., chair local govt. com. Republican. Fax: 605 342 6399.

DUNKLAU, RUPERT LOUIS, personal investments consultant; b. Arlington, Nebr., May 19, 1927; s. Louis Z. and Amelia S. (Gnuse) Dunklau; m. Ruth Eggert, June 4, 1950 (dec. Nov. 1998); children: Paul, Janet; m. Ruth King, Sept. 3, 2000. B.S., U. Nebr., 1950; Litt.D. (hon.), Concordia Coll., St. Paul, 1982; LL.D. (hon.), Midland Luth. Coll., Fremont, Nebr., 1985. Exec. v.p. Valmont Industries, Inc., Valley, Nebr., 1950-73; dir. Fremont Nat. Bank, 1968-2000. Bd. dirs. Midland Luth. Coll., Cmty. Chest Fremont; bd. dirs. Concordia Pub. House Valparaiso (Ind.) U.; chmn. bd. dirs. Meml. Hosp. Dodge County; bd. dirs. Luth. Ch.-Mo. Synod, St. Louis. With USNR, 1945. Mem.: Rotary Club. Republican. Home: 2146 Phelps Ave Fremont NE 68025-4522 Office: PO Box 1558 Fremont NE 68026-1558

DUNLAP, CONNIE SUE ZIMMERMAN, real estate professional; b. Defiance, Ohio, Mar. 3, 1952; d. John Eldon and Loisann (May) Zimmerman; m. Joseph Richard Dunlap, Dec. 20, 1972; children: Brad, Todd, Eric. Student, MacMurray Coll., 1970-71, Ohio State U., 1973; BA, Wayne State U., 1989. Grad. Realtor Inst.; cert. residential specialist, 1991. Dental hygienist Dr. A. Lamar Byrd, San Diego, 1973-75; realtor, assoc. broker Champion & Baer, Inc., Grosse Pointe, Mich., 1986-95, Bolton-Johnston Assocs., Grosse Pointe Farms, 1995—. Mem. Grosse Pointe Bd. Realtors, Macomb Bd. Realtors. Mem. Jr. League of Detroit., 1981—. Nat. Merit scholar Mature and Returning Women Wayne State U., Detroit, 1985-89. Mem. Phi Beta Kappa, Kappa Alpha Theta. Republican. Presbyterian. Home: 544 University Pl Grosse Pointe MI 48230-1640 Office: Bolton-Johnston Assocs 18332 Mack Ave Grosse Pointe Farms MI 48236-3219

DUNLAP, DAVID HOUSTON, judge; b. Columbia, Mo., Apr. 24, 1947; s. James Vardeman and Cynthia May (Roby) D.; m. Dana Sue Coburn, Apr. 23, 1982. BA, Southwest Mo. State U., 1969, MA, 1971; JD, U. Mo., 1975. Assoc. Campbell, Morgan & G, Kansas City, Mo., 1975-82; editor Mo. Law Tape, Inc., 1982-86; judge Howell County Cir. Ct. (37th cir.), West Plains, Mo., 1986—. Cons. appellate law, Mo., 1982-86; profl. judge USA Nat. Debate tournament, 1972, 73. Author, editor: (audio tapes) Legal Ednl., 1974-86; author: The Adult Abuse Act: Theory vs. Practice, 1996; contbr. articles to profl. publs. Speaker Mo. Right-to-Work Com., Kansas City, 1978; bd. dirs. St. Francis' Farm, West Plains, Mo., 1986-90; mem. Mo. Task Force on Gender and Justice, 1990-93. Am. Forensic Assn. grantee, 1971. Mem. Mo. Bar Assn., Mo. Judicial Conf., Ozark Gastronomic Soc. (bd. dirs. 1983—). Avocations: gastronomy, horticulture. Home: 1611 Luna Dr West Plains MO 65775-4220 Office: Howell County Cir Ct Assoc Div Howell County Courthouse West Plains MO 65775

DUNLAP, WILLIAM DEWAYNE, JR. advertising agency executive; b. Austin, Minn., Apr. 8, 1938; s. William D. and Evelyn (Hummel) D.; m. Lois Mary Apple, Sept. 23, 1961; children: Kristin, Leslie, Brenda. B.A., Carleton Coll., 1960. Brand mgr. soap Procter & Gamble, Cin., 1960-69; asst. postmaster gen. U.S. Postal Svc., Washington, 1970-75, chmn. postmaster gen.'s customer coun., 1971-75, chmn. stamp adv. coun., 1972-75; pres. MCA Advt., Westport, Conn., 1976-81; chmn. Campbell-Mithun Esty, Mpls., 1981—. Bd. dirs. Operation Smile Internat. Lutheran. Office: Campbell-Mithun-ESTY 222 S 9th St Ste 2100 Minneapolis MN 55402-3803

DUNLOP, MICHAEL, broadcast executive; b. Pontiac, Mich., Nov. 11, 1946; Student, Wayne State U. Gen. mgr. Sta WKBD-TV, Southfield, Mich., 1996—. Office: Sta WKBD-TV 26905 W 11 Mile Rd Southfield MI 48034-2292

DUNN, EDWIN RYDELL, lawyer; b. Boston, July 24, 1942; s. Richard Joseph and Clara Hudson (Rydell) D.; m. Kathleen Lynch, July 23, 1966; children— Jeanne, Kathleen, Anne, Daniel. B.A., U. Notre Dame, 1964; J.D. cum laude, Northwestern U., Chgo., 1967. Bar: Ill. 1967. Assoc., Baker & McKenzie, Chgo., 1967-73, ptnr., 1973— . Mem. ABA, Ill. Bar Assn., Chgo. Bar Assn. Office: Baker & McKenzie 1 Prudential Pla 130 E Randolph St Ste 3700 Chicago IL 60601-6342

DUNN, FLOYD, biophysicist, bioengineer, educator; b. Kansas City, Mo., Apr. 14, 1924; s. Louis and Ida (Leibtag) D.; m. Elsa Tanya Levine, June 11, 1950; children: Andrea Susan, Louis Brook. Student, Kansas City Jr. Coll., 1941-42, Tex. A&M U., 1943; BS, U. Ill., Urbana, 1949, MS, 1951, PhD, 1956. Rsch. assoc. elec. engring. U. Ill., Urbana, 1954-57, rsch. asst. prof. elec. engring., 1957-61, assoc. prof. elec. engring. and biophysics, 1961-65, prof., 1965—, prof. elec. engring., biophysics and bioengring., 1972-95; faculty mem. Beckman Inst. for Advanced Sci. and Tech., prof. emeritus, 1995—; dir. bioacoustics rsch. lab. U. Ill., 1976-95, chmn. bioengring. faculty, 1978-82; vis. prof. dept. microbiology U. Coll., Cardiff, Wales, 1968-69; vis. sr. scientist Inst. Cancer Research, Sutton, Surrey, Eng., 1975-76, 82-83, 90; vis. prof. Inst. Chest Diseases and Cancer, Tohoku U., Sendai, Japan, 1982, 89-90, U. Nanjing, Nanjing, People's Republic of China, 1983; mem. radiation study sect. NIH, 1976-81; adj. prof. radiation oncology U. Ariz., Tucson, 1996—. Steering com. NSF Workshop on Interaction of Ultrasound and Biol. Tissues , 1971—72; chmn. WHO working group on health aspects of exposure to ultrasound radiation , London, 1976; mem. FDA tech.-elec. products radiation stds. com. , 1974-76, NIH bioengring., radiation and diagnostic radiology study sects., 1970-81 ; faculty mem. Beckman Inst. Advanced Sci. and Tech. , 1991—; adj. prof. radiation oncology U. Ariz., Tucson, 1996—. Mem. editl. bd. Jour. Acoustical Soc. Am., 1968—, Ultrasound in Medicine and Biology, Ultrasonics, Handbook of Acoustics, and Encyclopedia of Applied Physics, 1981—, Am. Inst. of Physics Series in Modern Acoustics and Signal Processing, 1990-97; contbr. articles on biophys. acoustics to profl. jours. Trustee Hensley Twp., Ill., 1980-81. With AUS, 1943-46. NIH Spl. Rsch. fellow, 1968-69, Am. Cancer Soc.-Eleanor Roosevelt-Internat. Cancer fellow, 1975-76, 82-83, Fulbright fellow, 1982-83, Japan Soc. for Promotion of Sci. fellow, 1982, 1996, Fogarty Internat. fellow, 1990; recipient U. Ill. Sr. Scholar award, 1988, medal Spl. Merit Acoustical Soc. Japan, 1988, AIUM/WFUMB History Med. Ultrasound Pioneer award, 1988. Fellow: AAAS, IEEE (life Engring. Medicine and Biology Soc. Career Achievement award 1995, Edison medal 1996), Inst. Acoustics (U.K.), Am. Inst. Ultrasound in Medicine (William J. Fry meml. award 1984, Joseph H. Holmes Basic Sci. Pioneer award 1990), Am. Inst. Med. Biol. Engring. (assoc. editor Jour. 1968-, exec. coun. 1977-80, v.p. 1980-81 , pres. 1985-86, chmn. pub. policy com. 1994-), Acoustical Soc. Am. (Silver medal 1989, Gold medal 1998), Internat. Acad. Med. Biol. Engring.; mem.: NAE, NAS, Nat. Coun. Radiation Protection and Measurement, Biophys. Soc., Rochester Soc. Biomed. Ultrasound (hon.), Japan Soc. Ultrasound in Medicine (hon.), Am. Inst. Physics (mem. editl. bd. series in modern acoustics and signal processing 1990—97, publs. policy com. 1992—), Phi Sigma Phi, Phi Sigma, Pi Mu Epsilon, Tau Beta Pi, Eta Kappa Nu, Sigma Tau, Sigma Xi. Home: 2631 E Avenida De Maria Tucson AZ 85718-3081 Office: U Ill Bioacoustics Rsch Lab Beckman Institute Urbana IL 61801-2918

DUNN, HORTON, JR. organic chemist; b. Coleman, Tex., Sept. 3, 1929; s. Horton and Lora Dean (Bryant) D. BA summa cum laude, Hardin-Simmons U., 1951; MS, Case Western Res. U., 1975, PhD, 1979. Instr. chemistry Hardin-Simmons U., 1951; ONR fellow Ohio State U., Columbus, 1951-52; teaching fellow in chemistry Purdue U., Lafayette, Ind., 1952-53; rsch. chemist Lubrizol Corp., Cleve., 1953-70, dir. tech. info. ctr., 1970-79, supr. rsch. divsn., 1980-98, cons. in chemistry, 1998—. Chmn. bd., bus. mgr. Isotopics, Cleve., 1964-67, editor, 1961-63, supr. rsch. divsn., 1989-97, cons. in chemistry, 1998—. Contbr. articles to profl. jours.; patentee in field. Treas. Cleve. Cir. Decorative Arts Trust, 1990-91, 93—, v.p., 1992-93; bd. mgrs. One Bratenahl Place, 2001—; active Cleve. Art Assn., Cleve. Mus. of Art, Rock and Roll Hall of Fame, Mus. Founders Club.; mem., vol. Great Lakes Sci. Ctr., Cleve. Mus. Natural History; mem. Cleve. Bot. Garden. Fellow Am. Inst. Chemists; mem. AAAS, SAR (life), Am. Chem. Soc. (treas. Cleve. chpt. 1968-70, chmn. 1987, bd. dirs. 1990—), Am. Soc. for Info. Sci. (chpt. pres. 1973-74), Royal Soc. Chemistry (life), Soc. Tribologists and Lubrication Engrs., Nat. Coun. Met. Opera, Royal Oak Soc. (life), Cleve. Tech. Soc. Coun. (treas. 1987), Cleve. Art Assn., Univ. Club, Cleve. Club, Cleve. Play House Club, Rock and Roll Hall of Fam Mus. Founders Club (charter). Home and Office: 1 Bratenahl Pl Apt 103 Bratenahl OH 44108-1152 Office: Lubrizol Corp 29400 Lakeland Blvd Wickliffe OH 44092-2298 Fax: 216-541-6431.

DUNN, JAMES BERNARD, mining company executive, state legislator; b. Lead, S.D, June 27, 1927; s. William Bernard and Lucy Marie (Mullen) D.; m. Elizabeth Ann Lanham, Sept. 5, 1955; children: Susan, Thomas, Mary Elizabeth, Kathleen. BS in Bus. Adminstrn. and Econ., Black Hills State U., 1962. Heavy equipment mechanic Homestake Mining Co., Lead, 1945-62, asst. dir. pub. relations, 1962-78, dir. pub. affairs, 1978-85; mem. S.D. Ho. Reps., Pierre, 1971-72, S.D. State Senate, Pierre, 1973-2000, asst. majority leader, 1989-92, asst. minority leader, 1993-94, sr. asst. majority leader, 1995-2000. Exec. com. Nat. Conf. State Legislatures, 1979-81, 93-95, Coun. State Govt., 1983—; chmn. Midwestern Conf. Coun. of State Govts., 1984; bd. dirs. S.D. Blue Shield, S.D. Automobile Assn. Editor: Homestake Gold Mine 1876-1976, 1976, Bulldog Mountain Silver Mine, 1978. Bd. dirs. S.D. State Hist. Soc., Pierre,. 1971—; chmn. bd. trustees Adams Mus., Deadwood, S.D., 1962—. With U.S. Army, 1945-47. Republican. Roman Catholic. Avocations: hunting, fishing, hiking, historical research. Home: 619 Ridge Rd Lead SD 57754-1144 Office: State Senate State Capitol Pierre SD 57501

DUNN, JOHN FRANCIS, lawyer, state representative; b. Logansport, Ind., Dec. 24, 1936; s. John Francis and Bertha (Newman) D.; m. Barbara Burke, Feb. 10, 1962; children: John F. III, Robert E., William M., Nancy L. BS in Chem. Engring., U. Notre Dame, 1958, JD, 1961. Bar: Ill. 1961, Ind. 1961, U.S. Dist. Ct. (so. dist.) Ill. 1961, U.S. Ct. Appeals (4th cir.) 1962. Atty. Standard Oil Ind. (now Amoco), Chgo., 1961-64; assoc. Morey and Dunn, Attys., Decatur, Ill., 1964-74; ptnr. Dunn and Fichter, Attys., 1975-85; pvt. practice, 1986—. State rep. Ill. Gen. Assembly, Springfield, 1974-94, asst. majority leader; city councilman City of Decatur, 1971-74. Democrat. Roman Catholic. Avocations: bicycling, jogging. Office: 330 Millikin Ct Decatur IL 62523-1399

DUNN, JON MICHAEL, informatics educator, dean; b. Ft. Wayne, Ind., June 19, 1941; s. Jon Hardin and Philomena Elizabeth (Lauer) D.; m. Sarah Jane Hutchison, Aug. 8, 1964; children— Jon William, Jennifer Anne A.B., Oberlin Coll., 1963; Ph.D., U. Pitts., 1966. Asst. prof. philosophy Wayne State U., Detroit, 1966-69; vis. asst. prof. philosophy Yale U., New Haven, 1968-69; assoc. prof. philosophy Ind. U., Bloomington, 1969-76, prof., 1976—, Oscar Ewing prof. philosophy, 1989—, chmn. dept. philosophy, 1980-84, 94-97, adj. prof. computer sci., 1987-89, prof., 1989—, assoc. dean Coll. Arts and Scis., 1988-91, exec. assoc. dean, 1991-93, dir., dean Sch. Informatics, 1999—. Vis. fellow Inst. Advanced Studies, Australian Nat. U., Canberra, 1975-76; sr. visitor Math. Inst., U. Oxford, Eng., 1978; faculties vis. scholar U. Melbourne, Australia, 1983; fellow Ind. U. Inst. for Advanced Study, 1984; sr. visitor Ctr. for Philosophy of Sci., U. Pitts., Nov. 1984; adj. prof. U. Mass., Amherst, spring 1985. Author: (with G. Hardegree) Algebraic Methods in Philosophical Logic, 2001; contbg. author: Entailment, Vol. I, 1975, co-author Vol. II, 1992; editor: (with A. Gupta) Truth of Consequences: Essays in Honor of Nuel Belnap, 1990, (with G. Epstein) Modern Uses of Multiple-Valued Logic, 1975, (with G. Hardegree) Algebraic Methods in Philosophical Logic, 2001; editor Jour. Symbolic Logic, 1982-87; chief editor Jour. Philos. Logic, 1987-95; mem. editl. bds. Jour. Philos. Logic, 1979-87, Nous, 1968—, Studia Logica, 1978—, Jour. Non-Classical Logic, 1985-91. Am. Council Learned Socs. fellow, 1984-85; NSF prin. investigator, 1969-74; Fulbright-Hays research sr. scholar, 1974 Mem. Assn. Symbolic Logic (exec. com. 1978-81, council

1982—), Soc. Exact Philosophy (treas. 1982-84, v.p. 1986-88, pres. 1988-90), Am. Philos. Assn. (com. research and publs. 1985-88). Office: Ind U Sch Informatics Sycamore Hall 339 Bloomington IN 47405

DUNN, M. CATHERINE, college administrator, educator; b. Chgo., Mar. 26, 1934; d. John and Catherine (Donovan) Dunn BA, Ariz. State U., 1968, MA, 1970, PhD, 1977. Cert. tchr., Iowa, Ariz. Tchr. St. Mathew Sch., Phoenix, 1956-60; tchr. St. Vincent Sch., Chg., 1960-68; asst. prin. Carroll Sch., Lincoln, Ill., 1970-73; mem. faculty Clarke Coll., Dubuque, Iowa, 1973-79, v.p. devel., 1979-84, pres., 1984—. Bd. dirs. Am. Trust Bank, Dubuque, 1989—; cons. in field. Bd. dirs. Internat. Student Leadership, Notre Dame, Ind., 1975— , Med. Assocs. HMO, Dubuque, 1980— , Jr. Achievement, 1982—; mem. Iowa Dept. Transp. Commn., Ames, 1989—. Named One of Ten Outstanding Leaders in Dubuque Telegraph Herald newspaper, 1987, 88, 89. Mem. Am. Coun. Edn., Coun. Ind. Colls. (bd. dirs.), Am. Assn. Cath. Colls., Iowa Assn. Coll. Pres. (bd. dirs. 1984—), Ariz. State Alumni Assn., Dubuque C. of C. (mem. coun. 1973—, bd. dirs. 1986—, Outstanding Civic Leader award 1974, Civic Svc. award 1993), Coun. Advancement and Support Edn. (bd. dirs.), Phi Delta Kappa, Pi Lambda Theta. Avocations: cooking; music; walking; traveling. Home: 2350 Clarke Crest Dr Dubuque IA 52001-3125 Office: Clarke Coll 1550 Clarke Dr Dubuque IA 52001-3117

DUNN, MARGARET M. general surgeon, educator, university official; b. Freeport, N.Y., Sept. 8, 1954; d. Howard James and Evelyn Ann (Madden) D.; m. William Anthony Spohn, July 4, 1982; children: Christopher, Marie. BS, Pa. State U., 1974; MD, Jefferson Med. Coll., 1977. Diplomate Am. Bd. Surgery. Resident in surgery Montefiore Hosp., Bronx, N.Y., 1977-82; prof. surgery Wright Sch. Medicine, Dayton, Ohio, 1982—, assoc. dean for faculty and clin. affairs, 1999—. Fellow ACS; mem. Assn. Women Surgeons, Am. Med. Women's Assn., Ctrl. Surg. Assn., Soc. Surgery Alimentary Tract. Office: Wright State U Sch Medicine 3640 Col Glenn Hwy Dayton OH 45435

DUNN, MARVIN IRVIN, physician; b. Topeka, Dec. 21, 1927; s. Louis and Ida (Leibtag) D.; m. Maureen Cohen, Mar. 10, 1956 (dec. Nov. 1988); children: Jonathan Louis, Marilyn Paulette. B.A., U. Kans., 1950, M.D., 1954. Intern USPHS, San Francisco, 1954-55; resident U. Kans., 1955-58, fellow, 1958-59, instr. medicine, 1958-60, assoc. in medicine, 1960-62, asst. prof. medicine, 1962-65, assoc. prof., 1965-70, prof., 1970-2000, prof. emeritus, 2001—, Franklin E. Murphy Disting. prof., 1978-2000, dir. Cardiovascular Lab., head sect. Cardiovascular Disease Med. Center, 1963-92, dean Sch. of Medicine, 1979-84. Cons. USAF, 1971-95; spl. cons. to fed. air surgeon of FAA, 1990—. Author: Home Study Course: Difficult EKG Diagnosis, 1969, Translator Deductive and Polyparametric Electrocardiography, 1970; (with others) Clinical Vectorcardiography and Electrocardiography, 2d edit., 1977, Clinical Electrocardiography, 8th edit., 1989; editor in chief Cardiovascular Perspectives, 1985-89; mem. editl. bd. Am. Jour. Cardiology, 1970-75, Catheterization and Cardiovascular Diagnosis, 1980-87, AMA Archives Internal Medicine, 1984-94, Jour. Am. Coll. Cardiology, 1983-89, Biomedicine and Pharmacotherapy, 1985-90, Am. Jour. Noninvasive Cardiology, 1985-89, Chest, 1984-89, 94-98, Practical Cardiology, 1980-88, Heart and Lung, 1986-88, Bd.-Advanced in Therapy, 1992, Slovak Jour. Noninvasive Cardiology, 1993, Griffith Resource Libr., 1980-90, Am. Heart Jour., Jour. Acoustical Soc. Bd. dirs. Hebrew Acad. Jewish Geriatric and Convalescent Center, Beth Shalom Synagogue. Served with AUS, 1946-47. Recipient Alumnus of Yr. award U. Kansas Sch. Medicine, 1987, silver medal U. Socrates, Thessaloniki, Greece, 1992. Master Am. Coll. Chest Physicians (mem. bd. regents, pres. 1988-89, gov. State of Kans.); fellow ACP (Laureate award 1990), Am. Coll. Cardiology (trustee), Am. Heart Assn., Royal Acad. Medicine (Ireland), Royal Coll. Physicians (Valencia, Spain); mem. Am. Physicians Fellowship (dir.), Univ. Cardiologists, Alpha Omega Alpha, Phi Chi. Home: 3205 Tomahawk Rd Mission Hills KS 66208-1861 Office: U Kans Hosp 3901 Rainbow Blvd Kansas City KS 66160-0001

DUNN, MICHAEL J. dean; Dean Med. Coll. Wis., Milw. Office: Med Coll Wis Office of the Dean 8701 W Watertown Plank Rd Milwaukee WI 53226-3548

DUNN, REBECCA JO, state legislator; d. Francis G. and Eldred (Wagner) D. BA, U. S.D., 1967; MA, U. Hawaii, 1972. Senator S.D. State Senate Dist. 15, 1993—2001. Asst. minority leader, mem. legis. exec. bd., corrections com., S.D. State Senate Dist. 15; motivational spkr. Author: The Pearl of Potentiality, Co-A, 1979. Bd. dirs. S.D. Humanities Found. Mem. PEO, Downtown Rotary, Hawaii Yacht Club, Kappa Alpha Theta. Home: 320 N Summit Ave Sioux Falls SD 57104-2933

DUNN, ROBERT SIGLER, engineering executive; b. Cin., Aug. 13, 1926; s. John W. and Mirian S. (Sigler) D.; m. Barbara A. Rigdon, June 26, 1949; children: Anne Dunn Stockman, John R., Mark A. BSME, BSEE, Purdue U., 1949. With Collins Radio Co., Cedar Rapids, Iowa, 1949-72, regional v.p., gen. mgr.; v.p. ops. King Radio Corp., Olathe, Kans., 1973-91, also bd. dirs.; pvt. cons., 1991—. Mem. Iowa State Bd. Engring. Examiners, 1969-72. Bd. dirs., v.p. Olathe Comm. Hosp., 1982-90; mem. bd. trustees, past chmn. Olathe Health Sys.; chmn. bd. trustees Miami County Med. Ctr.; mem. bd. advisors Kans. U. Sch. Engring., 1979—. Mem. IEEE, NSPE, Am Soc. Quality, Rotary, Pi Tau Sigma, Eta Kappa Nu, Tau Beta Pi. Home and Office: 15320 Melrose Pl Overland Park KS 66221-9556

DUNN, STEVEN M. construction executive; Exec. v.p. ops. Crossman Cmtys., Indpls., 1998—. Office: Crossman Communities 9202 N Meridian St Ste 300 Indianapolis IN 46260-1833

DUNNIGAN, BRIAN LEIGH, military historian, curator; b. Detroit, July 11, 1949; s. James Patrick and Dorothy Jane (McKay) D.; m. Carol Lynn Fredriksen, Sept. 21, 1974 (div. Oct. 1988); m. Candice Maria Cain, Apr. 22, 1989; children: James Cain, Claire Beausom. BA in History, U. Mich., 1971, MA in History, 1973; MA in History and Museum Studies, Cooperstown Grad. Programs, 1979. Curator Mackinac Island (Mich.) State Park Commn., 1971-74; mng. dir. Historic Fort Wayne, Ind., 1974-79; exec. dir. Old Fort Niagara Assn., Youngstown, N.Y., 1979-96; curator of maps William L. Clements Libr. U. Mich., Ann Arbor, 1996—. Author: History and Guide to Old Fort Niagara, 1985, Siege-1759, 1986, rev. edit., 1996, Glorious Old Relic, 1987, Forts Within A Fort, 1989, Old Fort Niagara in Four Centuries, 1991; editor: Pouchot's Memoirs on the Late War in North America, 1994, Niagara, 1796, 1996, Frontier Metropolis, 2001. Fellow Co. Mil. Historians. Home: 4531 Maute Rd Grass Lake MI 49240 Office: William L Clements Libr 909 S University Ave Ann Arbor MI 48109-1190

DUNSTON, SHAWON DONNELL, professional baseball player; b. Bklyn., Mar. 21, 1963; Grad. high sch., N.Y.C. Shortstop Chgo. Cubs, 1985-97, Pitts. Pirates, 1997, Cleve. Indians, 1998-99; outfield St. Louis Cardinals, 1999—. Named to Nat. League All-Star Team, 1988, 90, "The Sporting News" Nat. League All-Star Team, 1989. Achievements include Nat. League East Divsn. Champions, 1989. Office: St Louis Cardinals Busch Stadium 250 Stadium Plz Saint Louis MO 63102-1722

DUPONT, TODD F. mathematics and computer science educator; b. Houston, Aug. 29, 1942; s. T.F. and Nan G. D.; m. Judy Smith, Aug. 20, 1964; children: Michelle, Todd K. BA, Rice U., 1963, PhD, 1968. Research mathematician Esso Prodn. Research, Houston, 1968; instr. U. Chgo., 1968-69, asst. prof., 1969-72, assoc. prof., 1972-75, prof. math., 1975—, prof. computer sci., 1985—, chmn. computer sci., 1994-97. Prin., officer, past bd. dirs. DREM (formerly Dupont-Rachford Engring. Math. Co.), Houston, 1969-92; prin. tech. adv. Stoner Assocs., Inc., 1992—. Editor: Math. of Computation, SIAM Jour. Home: 1335 E Park Pl Chicago IL 60637-1767 Office: Univ Chgo Dept Computer Sci 1100 E 58th St Chicago IL 60637-1588

DUQUETTE, DONALD NORMAN, law educator; b. Manistique, Mich., Apr. 3, 1947; s. Donald Francis and Martha Adeline (Rice) D.; m. Kathy Jo Loudenbeck, June 17, 1967; 1 child, Gail Jean. BA, Mich. State U., 1969; JD, U. Mich., 1974. Bar: Mich. 1975. Children's caseworker Mich. Dept. Social Svcs., Muskegon, 1969-72; asst. prof. pediatrics and human devel. Mich. State U. Coll. Human Medicine, East Lansing, 1975-76; clin. prof., dir. child advocacy law clinic U. Mich., Ann Arbor, 1976—, co-dir. interdisciplinary project on child abuse and neglect, 1979-89, dir. permanency planning legal svcs., 1984—, dir. interdisciplinary grad. edn. in child abuse-neglect, 1986-92, dir. Kellogg child welfare law program, 1995-98. Bd. visitors U. Ariz. Sch. of Law, 1995-99; legal cons. U.S. Children's Bur., Pres. Clinton's Initiative on Adoption and Foster Care, 1997-98; bd. dirs. Nat. Assn. Counsel for Children, 1999—. Author: (non-fiction) Advocating for the Child, 1990, Michigan Child Welfare Law, 1990, Michigan Child Welfare Law, rev. edit., 2000; editor (mem. editl. bd.): (jour.) Child Abuse and Neglect Internat. Jour., 1985—90; contbr.: articles to profl. jours. Commr. Washtenaw County Bd. Commrs., 1981-88; bd. dirs. Children's Trust Fund for Prevention of Child Abuse, 1983-85; mem. Permanency Planning Com. Mich. Supreme Ct., 1982-85, Probate Ct. Task Force, 1986-87, Govs. Task Force on Children's Justice, 1992—. Named Citizen of Yr. Huron Valley NASW, Ann Arbor, 1985; recipient Rsch. in Advocacy award Nat. Ct. Apptd. Spl. Advocate Assn., Seattle, 1985, Outstanding Legal Advocacy award Nat. Assn. of Counsel for Children, 1996, Hicks Child Welfare Leadership award Mich. Fedn. Children's Agys., 1998. Mem. Am. Profl. Soc. on Abuse of Children, Mich. State Bar (co-chair Children's Task Force 1993-95). Democrat. Unitarian. Avocations: piano, sailing. Home: 1510 Linwood Ave Ann Arbor MI 48103-3659 Office: U Mich Sch Law Child Advocacy Law Clinic 625 S State St Ann Arbor MI 48109-1215 E-mail: duquette@umich.edu.

DURBIN, RICHARD JOSEPH, senator; b. East St. Louis, Ill., Nov. 21, 1944; s. William and Ann D.; m. Loretta Schaefer, June 24, 1967; children: Christine, Paul, Jennifer. B.S. in Econs., Georgetown U., 1966, J.D., 1969. Bar: Ill. 1969. Chief legal counsel Lt. Gov. Paul Simon of Ill., 1969; mem. staff minority leader Ill. Senate, 1972-77, parliamentarian, 1969-77; practice law, 1969—; assoc. prof. med. humanities So. Ill. U., 1978—; mem. 98th-104th Congresses from 20th Dist. Ill., 1983-97; U.S. senator from Ill., 1997—; mem. judiciary com., govtl. affairs com., budget com. Mem. appropriations com., subcoms. on agriculture, rural devel. and related agys., def., legis. br., and D.C. (ranking mem.), 1999—; mem. budget com.; mem. govt. affairs com. subcom. on oversignt of govt. mgmt., restructuring and the D.C., 1999—, and permanent subcom. on investigations, 1997—; mem. select com. on ethics, 1999—; asst. Dem. fl. leader. Campaign worker Sen. Paul Douglas of Ill., 1966; staff Office Ill. Dept. Bus. and Econ. Devel., Washington; candidate for Ill. Lt. Gov., 1978; staff alt. Pres.'s State Planning Council, 1980; advisor Am. Council Young Polit. Leaders, 1981; mem. YMCA Ann. Membership Roundup, YMCA Bldg. Drive, Pony World Series; bd. dirs. Cath. Charities, United Way of Springfield, Old Capitol Art Fair, Springfield Youth Soccer; mem. Sch. Dist. 1986 Referendum Com., Springfield NAACP. Democrat. Roman Catholic. Office: US Senate 332 Dirksen Sen Office Bldg Washington DC 20510-0001*

DURCHSLAG, STEPHEN P. lawyer; b. Chgo., May 20, 1940; s. Milton Lewis and Elizabeth (Potovsky) D.; m. Ruth Florence Mayer, Nov. 21, 1976; children: Rachel Beth, Danielle Leah. BS, U. Wis., 1963; LLB, Harvard U., 1966. Bar: Ill. 1966. Assoc. Sidley & Austin, Chgo., 1966-72, ptnr., 1972-89, Winston & Strawn, Chgo., 1989—. Contbr. articles to profl. jours. Pres. Anshe Emet, Chgo., 1983—; bd. trustee Nathan Cummings Found., 1996—. Mem. ABA (AAF legal com.), Promotion Mktg. Assn. (bd. dirs.), Am. Standard Club, East Bank Club. Jewish. Avocations: skiing, running, tennis, rare books. Office: Winston & Strawn 35 W Wacker Dr Ste 3600 Chicago IL 60601-1695 E-mail: sdurchsl@winston.com.

DURHAM, CHARLES WILLIAM, civil engineer; b. Chgo., Sept. 28, 1917; s. John Barnett and Monica (O'Dea) D.; B.S. in Gen. Engring., Iowa State U., 1939, B.S. in Civil Engring., 1940, C.E., 1940; m. Margre Ann Henningson, Oct. 12, 1940; children— Steven, Mary Helen, Lynn Barnett, Debra Ann. Civil engr. Henningson Engring. Co., Omaha, 1939-46, partner, 1946-50; pres., chief exec. officer Henningson, Durham & Richardson, Omaha, 1950-76, chmn. bd., chief exec. officer, 1976— ; chmn. bd. Gt. Plains Natural Gas Co.; dir. Omaha Nat. Bank, ONB Realbanc, Minn. Enterprises Inc. (MEI), Bd. dirs. Iowa State U. Found.; mem. engring. advisory council U. Nebr.; mem. adv. com. SAC. Registered profl. engr., 30 states and D.C. Diplomate Am. Acad. Environ. Engrs. Fellow ASCE, Cons. Engrs. Council; mem. Am. Pub. Works Assn., Soc. Am. Mil. Engrs., Nat., Nebr. (past pres., nat. dir.) socs. profl. engrs., Water Pollution Control Fedn., Beavers, Chief Execs. Forum (past pres.), U.S. C. of C. (dir.), Omaha C. of C. (past pres., past dir.), Knights of Ak-Sar-Ben (gov.). Clubs: Masons, Shriners, Jesters. Office: Durham Resources Inc 8401 W Dodge Rd Ste 100 Omaha NE 68114-3438

DURHAM, RAY, professional baseball player; b. Charlotte, N.C., Nov. 30, 1971; Baseball player Chgo. White Sox, 1995—. Named to Am. League All Star Game, 1998. Office: Chgo White Sox 333 W 35th St Chicago IL 60616*

DURIG, JAMES ROBERT, college dean; b. Washington, Apr. 30, 1935; s. and Roberta Wilda Mounts; m. Kathryn Marlene Sprowls, Sept. 1, 1955; children: Douglas Tybor, Bryan Robert, Stacey Ann. B.A., Washington and Jefferson Coll., 1958, D.Sc. (hon.), 1979; Ph.D., M.I.T., 1962. Asst. prof. chemistry U. S.C., Columbia, 1962-65, asso. prof., 1965-68, prof., 1968-93, Ednl. Found. prof. chemistry, 1970-73, dean Coll. Sci. and Math., 1973-93; dean Coll. Arts & Scis. U. Mo., Kans. City, 1993—2000, prof. chemistry & geosci., 1993—. Editor: Vibrational Spectra and Structure, 22 vols., 1972—, Jour. Raman Spectroscopy, 1979-94; mem. editl. bd. Jour. Molecular Structure, 1972—; contbr. articles to profl. jours. Served with Chem. Corps U.S. Army, 1963-64. Recipient Russell award U.S.C., 1968; Alexander von Humboldt Sr. Scientist award W. Ger., 1976; award Spectroscopy Soc. of Pitts., 1981; U. S.C. Ednl. Found. award, 1984 Mem. Am. Chem. Soc. (So. Chemist award Memphis sect. 1976, Charles A. Stone award S.E. Piedmont sect. 1975), Am. Phys. Soc., Soc. for Applied Spectroscopy (Pitts. sect. award 1981), Coblentz Soc. (mem. governing bd. 1972-76, pres. 1974-76, award for outstanding research in molecular spectroscopy 1970), Internat. Union Pure and Applied Chemistry (chmn. sub-commn. on infrared and Raman spectroscopy 1975-95 , mem. commn. molecular spectra and structure 1978-89 , sec. 1981-83 , chmn. 1983-89, editor Spectrochimica Acta 1999—), Blue Key Soc., Phi Beta Kappa (pres. Alpha chpt. S.C. 1970), Sigma Xi, Phi Lambda Upsilon. Presbyterian. Home: 1213 W 64th Ter Kansas City MO 64113-1516 Office: Univ Mo 410 RHFH Kansas City MO 64110

DURKIN, JAMES B. state legislator; BS, Ill. State U.; JD, John Marshall U. Former asst. state atty. Cook County; former asst. atty. gen. Ill.; pres. Proviso Twp. Rep. Orgn.; Ill. state rep. Dist. 44, 1995—. Mem. Elec. and State Govt., Higher Edn., Judiciary and Criminal and Pers. and Pensions Coms., 1995—, Ill. Ho. of Reps. Vice-chmn., bd. trustees Triton Coll. Mem. Chgo. Bar Assn., Fenwick Bar Assn. (bd. dirs.). Office: 10544 W Cermak Rd Westchester IL 60154-5202

DURNELL, EARL, rancher; b. Cabool, Mo., Dec. 4, 1935; m. Emily Gay Spencer; 6 children. Student, Southwest Mo. State U., 1954-56. Rep. candidate for U.S. House, 1992, 96. Baptist.

DURYEE, HAROLD TAYLOR, insurance consultant; b. Willoughby, Ohio, Feb. 11, 1930; s. Gerald Fancher and Margaret Grace (Taylor) D.; m. Phyllis Annette Painter, June 18, 1966. AB, Kenyon Coll., 1951. Field rep. Mahoning Valley Coun., Boy Scouts Am., Youngstown, Ohio, 1951-56; mgr. claims svcs. Nationwide Ins. Cos., Canton, 1956-65; legis. and field dir. Ohio Rep. Party, Columbus, 1965-70, exec. dir., 1970-77, cons., 1980-81; dep. adminstr. Ohio Bur. Workers' Compensation, 1977-84; exec. dep. adminstr. Fed. Ins. Adminstrn., Washington, 1984-86; adminstr. fed. ins. Fed. Emergency Mgmt. Agy., 1986-90; dir. Ohio Dept. Ins., 1991-99; sr. advisor Internat. Ins. Found., 1999—. Trustee, exec. com. Griffith Found. for Ins. Edn.; mem. Ohio Elections Commn., 1980-84. Vice chmn. North Canton City Planning Commn., 1958-67; precinct committeeman Stark County Cen. Com., 1958-72; organizer North Canton Rep. Com., 1958, chmn., 1960-72; sec. North Canton Area Devel. Com., 1959-64; chmn. North Canton City Charter Commn., 1960; campaign mgr. U.S. Rep. Frank T. Bow, 1962, Oliver P. Bolton for U.S. Congress, 1964, Clarence J. Brown, Jr. for U.S. Congress, 1965; state chmn. Ohio League Young Rep. Clubs, 1962-63; nat. vice chmn. Young Rep. Nat. Fedn., 1963-65; former chmn. bd. trustees Nat. Assn. Ins. Commrs. Edn. and Rsch. Found.; former trustee ASFPM Edn. and Rsch. Found. Recipient Disting. Svc. award Jaycees, 1961, Civic Affairs award Rotary, 1964, Meritorious Svc. award Fed. Emergency Mgmt. Agy., 1989, Disting. Civilian Svc. medal, Fed. Emergency Mgmt. Agy., 1990. Mem. Nat. Assn. Ins. Commrs. (mem. exec. com. 1993-96, 98), Acad. Polit. Sci. Episcopalian. Avocation: genealogy. Home: 925 City Park Ave Columbus OH 43206-2511 E-mail: hduryee@columbus.rr.com.

DUSANIC, DONALD GABRIEL, parasitology educator, microbiologist; b. Chgo., Dec. 15, 1934; s. Gabriel John and Harriet (Rojewski) D.; m. Roberta Leona Drost (dec. Feb. 1970); children: Donald, Robert; m. Jane Mitchell Haw, June 11, 1971; children: Belinda Conrad, Karla Conrad, Allan Conrad. BS, U. Chgo., 1957, MS, 1959, PhD, 1963. Instr. U. Chgo., 1963-64; asst. prof. U. Kans., Lawrence, 1964-68, assoc. prof., 1968-71, prof., 1971-72; prof. parasitology Ind. State U., Terre Haute, 1972-95, dir. Interdisciplinary Ctr. for Cell Products and Techs., 1987-95; prof. emeritus, 1995—. Vis. prof. U. Philippines Sch. Medicine, Manila, 1964, Nat. Taiwan U. Sch. Medicine, Taipei, 1971, Nat. Sun Yat-sen U., Kaohsiung, Taiwan, 1991; adj. prof. Ind. U. Sch. Medicine, Terre Haute, 1982-95. Contbr. numerous articles on biochemistry and immunology of schistosomes, nematodes, amebae, and trypanosomes to sci. jours., chpts. to books. Recipient rsch. and creativity award Ind. State, 1982, Coll. Arts and Scis. Disting. Prof. award, 1990; rsch. grantee NIH, NSF, Office Naval Rsch. Mem. Am. Soc. Parasitologists, Am. Soc. Tropical Medicine and Hygiene, Am. Soc. Protozoologists, Am. Assn. Immunologists, N.Y. Acad. Scis., Sigma Xi. Home: 5726 E Cougar Dr Terre Haute IN 47802-8533 Office: Ind State U Dept Life Scis Terre Haute IN 47809-0001 E-mail: dusanic@mama.indistate.edu.

DU SHANE, JAMES WILLIAM, physician, educator; b. Madison, Ind., Apr. 17, 1912; s. Donald and Harriette Graham (McLell) DuS.; m. Mary Margaret Hill, May 7, 1939; children: Mary Margaret, James Anderson. A.B., DePauw U., 1933; M.D., Yale U., 1937. Diplomate Am. Bd. Pediatrics (chmn. sub-bd. cardiology 1961-66). Intern Yale-New Haven Hosp., 1937-38, resident in pediatrics, 1938-39; resident Children's Meml. Hosp., Chgo., 1939-42; pvt. practice pediatrics Evanston, Ill., 1942-44; instr. Northwestern U. Med. Sch., 1942-44; mem. staff Mayo Clinic, Rochester, Minn., 1946—, head sect. pediatrics, 1957-69, mem. bd. govs., 1961-73; prof. pediatrics Mayo Found., U. Minn., 1960—. Contbr. articles to med. jours. Trustee Mayo Found., 1967-73. Served to lt. USNR, 1944-46. Mem. AMA, Am. Acad. Pediatrics (founding chmn. cardiology sect. 1958), Am. Coll. Chest Physicians, Am. Pediatric Soc., Am. Heart Assn. (chmn. council rheumatic fever and congenital heart disease 1960-62), Alpha Omega Alpha, Phi Kappa Psi. Home: 211 2nd St NW Rochester MN 55901-2807 Office: Mayo Clinic Rochester MN 55905-0001

DUSK, BROOKE, meteorologist; BS in Meteorology, Iowa State U., 2000. Weekend meteorologist NewsCenter 13 WEAU-TV, Eau Claire, Wis., 2001—. Avocation: golf. Office: WEAU-TV Po Box 47 Eau Claire WI 54702

DUTCHER, JUDI, state auditor; b. MI, Nov. 27, 1962; married; two children. BA, U. of MN, 1984, JD, 1987. Asst. atty. City of Minneapolis, MN, 1987-88; atty. Lang, Pauly & Gregerson, Ltd, Minneapolis, 1988-94; state auditor Minn. State, Saint Paul, 1995—. Bd. dirs. State Bd. of Investment, State Exec. Coun., Land Exch. Bd., Pub. Employees Retirement Assoc. Bd., MN Housing Fin. Agy., Rural Fin. Adminstrn. Bd., Bd. of Govt. Innovation and Cooperation. Office: Minn State Auditor Off 525 Park St Ste 300 Saint Paul MN 55103-2197 Fax: 651-206-4755. E-mail: stateduditor@osa.state.mn.us.

DUTILE, FERNAND NEVILLE, law educator; b. Lewiston, Maine, Feb. 15, 1940; s. Wilfred Joseph and Lauretta Blanche (Cote) D.; m. Brigid Dooley, Apr. 4, 1964; children: Daniel, Patricia. AB, Assumption Coll., 1962; JD, U. Notre Dame, 1965. Bar: Maine 1965. Atty. U.S. Dept. Justice, Washington, 1965-66; prof. law Cath. U. Am., 1966-71, U. Notre Dame Law Sch., Ind., 1971—. Bd. dirs. Ind. Lawyers Commn., Indpls., 1975-85, Legal Svcs. No. Ind., South Bend, 1975-83; dir. South Bend Work Release Ctr., 1973-75, Ind. Criminal Law Study Commn., 1991-99. Editor: Legal Education and Lawyer Competency, 1981; author: Sex, Schools and the Law, 1986; co-editor: Early Childhood Interventiion and Juvenile Delinquency, 1982, The Prediction of Criminal Violence, 1987; co-author: State and Campus, 1984. Democrat. Roman Catholic.

DUTILE, ROBERT ARTHUR, financial services executvie; b. Stoneham, Mass., Dec. 26, 1959; s. Robert Arthur and Mary-Helene (Revane) D.; m. Ellen R. Ahearn, June 9, 1995. BS, Boston Coll., 1981. Cons. Monchik-Weber, Boston, 1981-83, Gately, Glew & Co., Wellesley, Mass., 1983-84; dir. MIS Reebok Internat., Ltd., Stoughton, 1984-91; sr. cons. Grant Thornton, LLP, Boston, 1992, mgr., 1992-95, sr. mgr., 1995-97, prin., 1997-99; exec. Key Corp., Cleve., 1999—. Author: The Benchmarking Course, 1993. Mem. Am. Soc. Quality Control, Am. Mgmt. Assn., Am. Prodn. & Inventory Control Soc., Am. Mountain Guides Assn., Am. Alpine Club (life), Two/Ten Found, (life.). Avocations: writing, rock climbing, mountaineering, golf. Office: Key Corp 2025 Ontario St Cleveland OH 44115 E-mail: robert_dutile@keybank.com.

DUTTA, RONO J. air transportation executive; b. Calcutta, India; married; 3 children. BS in Mech. Engring., Indian Inst. Tech., Kharagpur; MBA, Harvard U. Mgr. planning Bell & Howell, Chgo.; mgmt. cons. Booz, Allen and Hamilton; v.p. fin. planning and analysis United Airlines, Chgo., 1985, v.p. base ops., sr. v.p. maint. ops. Maint. Ops. Ctr. San Francisco, v.p. mgmt. info. sys., v.p. Shuttle-by-United Devel., v.p. cargo, sr. v.p. planning, pres., 1999—. Office: UAL & United Airlines World Hqrs United Airlines PO Box 66100 Chicago IL 60666-0100

DUTTON, STEPHEN JAMES, lawyer; b. Chgo., Sept. 20, 1942; S. James H. and Marjorie C. (Smith) D.; m. Ellen W. Lee; children: Patrick, Mark. BS, Ill. Inst. Tech., 1965; JD, Ind. U., 1969. Bar: Ind. 1969, U.S. Dist. Ct. (so. dist.) Ind. 1969, U.S. Ct. Appeals (7th cir.) 1972, U.S. Ct. Appeals (D.C. cir.) 1980, U.S. Supreme Ct. 1978. With McHale, Cook & Welch, P.C., Indpls., 1969-86, Dutton & Overman, P.C., 1986-91, Dutton &

Bailey, P.C., 1991-94, Locke, Reynolds, Boyd & Weisell, 1994-99, Leagre Chandler & Millard LLP, Indpls., 1999—. Mem. Com. on Law of Cyberspace Bus. Law Sect. Mem. ABA. Home: 3705 Spring Hollow Rd Indianapolis IN 46208-4169 Address: 135 N Pennsylvania St Ste 1400 Indianapolis IN 46204-2489 E-mail: sdutton@lcmlaw.com.

DUVAL, DANIEL WEBSTER, manufacturing company executive; b. Cin., May 27, 1936; s. Harry A. and Wilda (Webster) V.; m. Sue Ann Howard, July 20, 1962; children: Laurie Ann, Paula Lee, Christopher Webster. BA, U. Cin., 1960. V.p. staff elec. products div. Midland-Ross, Cleve., 1976-78, group v.p., 1979-81, exec. v.p., 1981-83, pres., chief operating officer, 1983-86; pres., chief exec. officer Robbins & Myers Inc., Dayton, Ohio, 1986-98, also bd. dirs., ret. vice chmn., bd. dirs., 1999. Bd. dirs. Arrow Electronics, Nat. City Bank, Cleve., Gosiger, Inc., Dayton, The Manitowac Co., WI. Patentee container coupling mechanism. Bd. trustees Wright State U., 1991-2000, Wright State U. Found.; pres. Civitan Found., Ariz., 1973-74, Dayton Ballet Assn., 1990-93; participant Leadership Cleve.; bd. dirs. U.S. Air and Trade Show. Mem. Dayton Racquet Club. Republican. Roman Catholic. Home: 1160 Ridgeway Rd Dayton OH 45419-3031 Office: 1480 Kettering Tower Dayton OH 45423-1001

DUVICK, DONALD NELSON, plant breeder; b. Sandwich, Ill., Dec. 18, 1924; s. Nelson Daniel and Florence Henrietta (Appel) D.; m. Selma Elizabeth Nelson, Sept. 10, 1950; children: Daniel, Jonathan, Randa. BS, U. Ill., 1948; PhD, Washington U., St. Louis, 1951. With Pioneer Hi-Bred Internat., Inc., Johnston, Iowa, 1951-90, corn breeding coordinator Ea. and So. div., 1965-71, dir. corn breeding dept., 1971-75, dir. plant breeding div., 1975-85, v.p. research, 1985-86, sr. v.p. research, 1986-90, co. dir., 1982-90; affiliate prof. Iowa State U., 1990—. Chmn. nat. plant genetic resources bd. USDA, 1990-91, vice-chmn. nat. genetic resources adv. com., 1992-93; trustee Internat. Ctr. for Maize and Wheat Improvement, 1988-94, trustee Internat. Rice Rsch. Inst., 1996-98; lectr. in field. Assoc. editor: Plant Physiology Jour., 1977-78; contbr. articles on genetics and plant breeding, devel. anatomy and cytology, cytoplasmic inheritance, quantititive genetics and biodeversity. Pres. Johnston Consol. Sch. Bd., 1965-67. Served with AUS, 1943-46. Pioneer Hi-Bred fellow U. London, 1968; Disting. fellow Iowa Acad. Sci. Fellow AAAS, Crop Sci. Soc. Am. (pres. 1986), Am. Soc. Agronomy (pres. 1992), Iowa Acad. Sci.; mem. NAS, N.Y. Acad. Sci., Coun. Agrl. Sci. and Tech. (bd. dirs. 1987-90), The Nature COnservancy (chair bd. trustees Iowa chpt. 1994). Democrat. Mem. United Ch. Christ. Achievements include identification of intra cellular site of zein storage in maize endosperm; research in maize cytoplasmic male sterility, in plant breeding's effects on crop plant genetic diversity, in changes in productivity of hybrid maize since 1930. Office: 6837 NW Beaver Dr Johnston IA 50131-1245 E-mail: dnd307@aol.com.

DUVIN, ROBERT PHILLIP, lawyer; b. Evansville, Ind., May 18, 1937; s. Louis and Henrietta (Hamburg) D.; m. Darlene Chmiel, Aug. 23, 1961; children: Scott A., Marc A., Louis A. BA with honors, Ind. U., 1958, JD with highest honors, 1961; LLM with highest honors, Columbia U., 1963. Bar: Ohio 1964. Since practiced in, Cleve.; pres. Duvin, Cahn & Hutton, 1972—. Lectr. law schs.; labor adviser corps., cities and hosps. Contbr. to books and legal jours.; bd. editors: Ind. Law Jour., 1961, Columbia Law Rev., 1963. Served with AUS, 1961-62. Mem. ABA, FBA, Ohio Bar Assn., Cleve. Bar Assn., Cleve. Racquet Club, Beechmont Country Club, Soc. Club, Canterbury Golf Club, Sanctuary Golf Club. Jewish. Home: 2775 S Park Blvd Cleveland OH 44120-1669 Office: Duvin Cahn & Hutton Erieview Tower 1301 E 9th St Ste 2000 Cleveland OH 44114-1886 E-mail: rduvin@duvin.com.

DUXBURY, ROBERT NEIL, state legislator; b. Mar. 14, 1933; s. Joy Chase and Lois Mae (McNeil) Duxbury; m. Rose Ann Radcliffe, 1953; children: Robert Neil Jr., Kathryn Ann Duxbury Meyer, Dale Lynn, Dean Douglas, Brian Richard. BS, S.D. State U., 1956. Sec. of Agrl., S.D., 1975-79; mem. S.D. Ho. of Reps. from 5th dist., Pierre, 1984-98, S.D. Senate from 22nd dist., Pierre, 1998—. Former minority leader, former mem. legis. procedure com. Dist. 22; currently mem. appropriations com. S.D. Ho. Reps.; farmer, rancher. Mem. Farmers Union, Hand County Livestock Improvement Assn. Home: 21030 373rd Ave Wessington SD 57381-6911

DVORAK, ALLEN DALE, radiologist; b. Dodge, Nebr., Mar. 13, 1943; s. Rudolph Charles and Mildred B. (Misek) D.; m. Carol Ann Cockson, July 22, 1967; children: Kristin Ann, Andrea Marie, Ryan Allen. Grad., Creighton Coll. Arts and Scis., Omaha, Nebr., 1961-64; MD, Creighton Sch. Medicine, Omaha, Nebr., 1969. Intern Creighton Meml. St. Joseph Hosp., Omaha, 1969-70; resident Ind. U. Med. Ctr., Indpls., 1970-73; asst. prof. radiology Creighton U. Sch. Medicine, Omaha, 1973-83; diagnostic radiologist Nebr.-Iowa Radiology Cons., Papillion, Nebr., 1983—, mng. ptnr., 1987—. Staff radiologist Alegent Midlands Cmty. Hosp., Papillion, 1983—, med. staff exec. bd., 1996—, pres. med. staff, 2000-02 med. staff exec. bd. Nebr. Bd. Health, 1995-2000; bd. dirs. Blue Cross Blue Shield Nebr. Author: (chpt.) Ultrasound, 1981; contbr. articles to profl. jours. Chmn. Midlands Area Health Adv. cuon., State of Nebr., 1982-86; trustee Duchesne Acad., 1988-91, Boys Town Nat. Coun. Friends, 1989—; bd. dirs. Safety and health Coun. of Greater Omaha, 1990-91; mem. Gov.'s Blue Ribbon Coalition to Study Health Care in Nebr., 1991-98; mem. Creighton Med. Sch. Alumni Adv. Bd., 1993—, pres., 1998-2000. Fellow Am Coll. Radiology; mem. AMA (alt. del. 1992-98, del. 1999-2000), Nebr. Radiol. Soc. (pres. 1980-81), Omaha Midwest Clin. Soc. (pres. 1982), Nebr. Assn. Nuclear Physicians (pres. 1976-78, del. 1984—), Met. Omaha Med. Soc. (exec. com. 1980—, pres. 1990), Nebr. Med. Assn. (del. 1986—, pres. 1997-98), Regency Lake and Tennis Club (bd. dirs. 1981-85, chmn. bd. 1983-85), Happy Hollow Country Club. Avocations: tennis, boating. Home: 9733 Brentwood Rd Omaha NE 68114-4970 Office: Nebr-Iowa Radiology Cons Mng Ptnr 401 E Gold Coast Rd Ste 102 Papillion NE 68046-4194

DVORAK, KATHLEEN S. business products company executive; married; 2 children. BS in Edn., No. Ill. U., 1978; MBA in Fin., DePaul U., 1988. Tchr. math. Conrady Jr. H.S., 1977-82; dir. investor rels./corp. comms. United Stationers Inc., Des Plaines, Ill., 1982-97, v.p. investor rels., 1997-2000, v.p. investor rels. and fin. adminstrn., 2000—. Recipient Howard Beasley Managerial Excellence award. Mem. Nat. Investor Rels. Inst. Home: 1032 Oakwood Dr Westmont IL 60559-1040 Office: United Stationers Inc 2200 E Golf Rd Des Plaines IL 60016-1257

DVORAK, MICHAEL A. state legislator; b. South Bend, Ind., Oct. 24, 1948; s. William E. and Marilyn J. (Radican) D.; m. Kathleen Braunsdorf, 1970; children: Ryan, Todd, Sean, Brett, Carrie, Brady, Casey, Tyler. BA, Loyola U., Chgo., 1970; JD, Western State U., San Diego, 1975. Ptnr. Dvorak & Dvorak, South Bend, 1977—; dep. pros. atty. Santislaus County, Modesto, Calif., 1975-77; rep. Dist. 8 Ind. Ho. of Rep., 1986—, chmn. cts. and criminal code com., mem. families, children and human affairs com. Mem. Ind. State Bar Assn., St. Joseph County Bar Assn. Home: 218 W Washington St Ste 1000 South Bend IN 46601-1829

DVORSKY, ROBERT E. state senator; b. Burlington, Iowa, Aug. 18, 1948; m. Susan M. Mandernach; 2 children. BS, U. Iowa, 1972, MPA, 1984. Former mgr. small bus.; with Mason City Supt. Recreation, 1973-79; mem. Coralville City Coun., 1980-86, Iowa Ho. of Reps., 1986-94; with E. Ctrl. Iowa Employment and Tng. Consortium, Cedar Rapids, 1993—; mem. Iowa Senate from 25th dist., 1982—. Former bd. dirs. Iowa City Area Devel. Group; mem. Iowa City/Coralville Conv. and Visitors Bur., Johnson County Coun. Govts., Johnson County Dem. Ctrl. Com. and Exec. Com. Mem. Johnson County Hist. Soc., Friends of Coralville Pub. Libr. Democrat. Roman Catholic. Home: 412 6th St Coralville IA 52241-2511 Office: State Capitol Dist 25 3 9th And Grand Des Moines IA 50319-0001 E-mail: robert_dvorsky@legis.state.ia.us.

DWELLE, TERRY, state agency administrator; b. Garrison, N.D. MD cum laude, St. Louis U.; MPH Tropical Medicine, Tulane U. With U. N.D. Sch. Medicine, Ctrs. for Disease Control Prevention and the Indian Health Svc.; pediatrician Bismarck, ND; chief med officer N.D. Dept. Health, state health officer, 2001—. Office: ND Dept Health 600 E Blvd Ave Bismarck ND 58505-0200*

DWORKIN, HOWARD JERRY, nuclear medicine physician, educator; b. Bklyn., Oct. 29, 1932; s. Joseph Henry and Mollie M. (Hodas) Dworkin; m. Gina Gora; children: Rhonda Fran, Steven Irving, Paul J., Edward Joshua, Joseph Jacob. BSChemE, Worcester Poly. Inst., 1955; MD, Albany Med. Coll., 1959; MS in Radiation Biology, U. Mich., 1965. Diplomate Am. Bd. Internal Medicine, Am. Bd. Nuclear Medicine. Intern Albany Hosp., NY, 1959-60; resident Rochester (N.Y.) Gen. Hosp., 1960-62, U. Mich. Hosps., 1962-65, asst. coord. nuclear medicine unit, 1963-66, instr., 1965-66; asst. prof. medicine U. Toronto, Canada, 1966, assoc. prof. Canada, 1967; head dept. nuclear medicine Princess Margaret Hosp., Toronto, 1967; head nuclear medicine sect., radiology Nat. Naval Med. Ctr., Bethesda, Md., 1967-69; dir. sch. nuclear medicine tech. William Beaumont Hosp., Royal Oak, Mich., 1969—, chief dept. nuclear medicine, 1969—, dir. nuclear medicine resident tng. program, 1970—, chmn. CME com., 1993—. Clin. asst. prof. dept. medicine Wayne State U. Med. Sch., Detroit, 1970—; clin. assoc. prof. dept. radiology Mich. State U., East Lansing, 1976—; clin. prof. med. physics Ctr. Health Scis. Oakland U., Rochester, Mich., 1977—. Author (with N. Aspin and R. G. Baker): (book) Use of Isotopes in the Physics of Radiology, 1969, Part Two, Clinical Procedures in Radioisotope Laboratory Procedures, 1969; contbr. articles and chpts. to med. jours. and texts. With USN, 1967—69. Mem.: AMA, Am. Coll. Nuc. Physicians (sec. 1974—75, pres. 1978—79), Endocrine Soc., Am. Thyroid Assn., Soc. Nuc. Medicine (trustee 1973—81, v.p. 1982, pres. 1986—87), Am. Bd. Nuc. Medicine (treas. 1982—84), Accrediation Coun. Continuing Med. Edn. (chmn. 1998). Achievements include patents for in radioactive labeled protein material process and apparatus. Office: William Beaumont Hosp Dept Nuclear Medicine Royal Oak MI 48073 E-mail: hdworkin@beaumont.edu.

DWORKIN, MARTIN, microbiologist, educator; b. N.Y.C., Dec. 3, 1927; s. Hyman Bernard and Pauline (Herstein) D.; m. Nomi Rees Buda, Feb. 2, 1957; children: Jessica Sarah, Hanna Beth. B.A., Ind. U., 1951; Ph.D. (NSF predoctoral fellow), U. Tex., Austin, 1955. NIH research fellow U. Calif., Berkeley, 1955-57, vis. prof., summers 1958-60; asst. prof. microbiology Ind. U. Med. Sch., 1957-61, assoc. prof., 1961-62, U. Minn., 1962-69, dir. MD/PhD tng. program, 1990-97, prof., 1969—. Vis. prof. U. Wash., summer 1965, Stanford U., 1978-79; vis. scholar Oxford (Eng.) U., 1970-71; Found. for Microbiology lectr., 1973-74, 76-77, 81-82; Sackler scholar Tel Aviv U., 1992. Author: Developmental Biology of the Bacteria, 1985, Microbial Cell-Cell Interactions, 1991; contbr. numerous articles, revs. to profl. publs.; mem. editorial bd. Jour. Bacteriology, 1967-74, 86-88, Ann. Revs. Microbiology, 1975-79, The Prokaryotes, 2d edit., editor-in-chief 3d edit. Alt. del. Democratic Nat. Conv., 1968; mem. Minn. Dem. Farm Labor Central Com., 1969-70. Served with U.S. Army, 1946-48. Recipient Career Devel. award NIH, 1963-68, 68-73; John Simon Guggenheim fellow, 1978-79 Fellow Am. Acad. Arts and Scis. (chmn. Midwest coun., v.p.); mem. Am. Soc. Microbiology (vice chmn. div. gen. microbiology 1977-78, chmn. 1978-79, div. councillor 1980-82), Soc. Gen. Microbiology (Eng.). Home: 2123 Hoyt Ave W Saint Paul MN 55108-1314 Office: U Minn Dept Microbiology Minneapolis MN 55455

DWYER, JOHN WILLIAM, JR. accountant; b. Chgo., Aug. 21, 1952; s. John William and Margaret Josephine (Cain) D.; m. Joan Mary Gillespie, Oct. 28, 1978. BS, DePaul U., 1974. CPA, Ill. Various positions Arthur Young, Chgo., 1974-86, ptnr., 1986—, Ernst & Young, Chgo.; corp. controller Bally Mfg. Corp, 1992—; v.p. & CFO Bally's Health & Tennis Corp., 1994—; sr. v.p., CFO & treas. Bally Total Fitness Holdings Corp. Adv. bd. Bus. Adminstrn. Program DePaul U., 1986-87; mem. fin. com. St. Alexander's Ch., Villa Park, Ill., 1984-87; mem. com. United Way of Met. Chgo. Venture Grants, 1988—. Mem. Am. Inst. CPA's, Ill. CPA Soc. (mem. not-for-profit com. 1986). Roman Catholic. Clubs: DePaul Ledger & Quill, Chgo. Soc. of Clubs. Avocations: golf, racketball, tennis, spectator sports, music. Office: Bally Total Fitness Holdings 8700 W. Bryn Mawr Ave Chicago IL 60631

DYBEK, STUART, English educator, writer; b. Chgo., Apr. 10, 1942; s. Stanley and Adeline (Sala) S.; m. Caren Bassett, Feb. 7, 1967; children: Anne, Nicholas. BS, Loyola U., Chgo., 1964, MA, 1967; MFA, U. Iowa, 1973. Tchr. U.S. V.I. Sch., St. Thomas, 1968-70, U. Iowa, Iowa City, 1970-73; prof. English Western Mich. U., Kalamazoo, 1973—. Vis. prof. creative writing Princeton (N.J.) U., 1991, U. Calif., Irvine, 1995, U. Iowa, 1998, Northwestern U., 2001. Author: (poetry) Brass Knuckles, 1979; (fiction) Childhood and Other Neighborhoods, 1980, The Coast of Chicago, 1990. Guggenheim fellow, 1982; recipient Whiting Writers award, 1985, O. Henry first prize, 1985, Acad. award in fiction Am. Acad. Arts and Letters, 1994, PEN/Malamud award, 1995, Lannan Lit. prize, 1998. Mem. PEN. Home: 320 Monroe St Kalamazoo MI 49006-4436 Office: Western Michigan U Dept English Kalamazoo MI 49008 also: care Amanda Urban Intl Creative Mgt 40 W 57th St New York NY 10019-4001 E-mail: dybek@wmich.edu.

DYE, JAMES LOUIS, chemistry educator; b. Soudan, Minn., July 18, 1927; s. Ray Ashley and Hildur Ameda Dye; m. Angeline Rosalie Medure, June 10, 1948; children: Roberta Rae, Thomas Anthony, Brenda Lee. AA, Virginia (Minn.) Jr. Coll., 1948; BA, Gustavus Adolphus Coll., 1949; PhD, Iowa State U., 1953; DSc (hon.), No. Mich. U., 1992. Rsch. assoc. Iowa State U., Ames, 1953; asst. prof. chemistry Mich. State U., East Lansing, 1953-60, assoc. prof., 1960-63, prof., 1963-94, chmn. dept. chemistry, 1986-90, prof. emeritus, 1994—. Vis. scientist Ohio State U., Columbus, 1968-69; cons. AT&T Bell Labs., Murray Hill, N.J., 1982-83. Author: Thermodynamics and Equilibrium, 1978; contbr. over 200 articles to profl. jours. With U.S. Army, 1945-46. NSF fellow, 1961-62, Guggenheim fellow, 1975-76, 90-91, Fulbright scholar, 1975-76; recipient Disting. Alumni award Gustavus Adolphus Coll., 1969. Fellow AAAS; mem. NAS, Am. Acad. Arts and Scis., Am. Chem. Soc. (Inorganic Chemistry award 1997), Am. Inst. Chemists (Chem. Pioneer award 1990), Am. Phys. Soc., Materials Rsch. Soc., Phi Kappa Phi, Sigma Xi (rsch. awards 1968, 87), Golden Key (teaching award 1986). Lutheran. Avocations: fishing, golf. Home: 2698 Roseland Ave East Lansing MI 48823-3847 Office: Mich State Univ Dept Of Chemistry East Lansing MI 48824 E-mail: dye@msu.edu.

DYE, JERMAINE, professional baseball player; b. Overland, Kansas, Jan. 28, 1974; Student, Cosumnes River C.C. With Atlanta Braves, 1996-97; outfielder Kansas City Royals Maj. League Baseball, 1997—. Office: c/o Kansas City Royals PO Box 419969 Kansas City MO 64141-6969*

DYE, NANCY SCHROM, academic administrator, history educator; b. Columbia, Mo., Mar. 11, 1947; d. Ned Stuart and Florence Andrea Elizabeth (Ahrens) Schrom; m. Griffith R. Dye, Aug. 21, 1972; children: Molly, Michael. AB, Vassar Coll., 1969; MA, U. Wis., 1971, PhD, 1974. Asst. prof. U. Ky., Lexington, 1974-80, assoc. prof., 1980-88, prof., 1988, assoc. dean arts and scis., 1984-88; dean faculty Vassar Coll., Poughkeepsie, N.Y., 1988-92, acting pres., 1992-94; pres. Oberlin Coll., Oberlin, Ohio, 1994—. Author: As Equals And As Sisters, 1981; contbr. articles to profl. jours. Mem. Coun. of Colls. of Arts and Scis. (bd. dirs. 1989—). Office: Oberlin Coll 70 N Professor St Oberlin OH 44074-1019

DYER, WILLIAM EARL, JR. retired newspaper editor; b. Kearney, Nebr., May 15, 1927; s. William Earl and Hazel Maud (Hosfelt) D.; m. Betty M. Meisinger, June 26, 1967; children: Lee Michael, Scott William. BA, U. Nebr., 1949. Reporter Nebr. City Daily News Press, 1943-44; reporter, copy editor The Lincoln Star, Nebr., 1948-50, city editor, 1951-60, exec. editor, 1960-92. Pres. Nebr. AP Editors, 1964. Author: Headline: Starkweather, 1993. Pres. Lincoln Unitarian Ch., 1962-63; state chmn. Nebr. We Shake Hands Indian Project, 1958-60; mem. Nebr. Adv. Com. on Indian Law Enforcement, 1960-62; mem. STate Adv. Com. to Welfare Dept., 1970-73, 80-84. With AUS, 1945-46. Named hon. mem. Omaha Indian Tribe. Mem. Open Forum Club, Phi Beta Kappa, Sigma Delta Chi. Democrat. Home: 1115 Fall Creek Rd Lincoln NE 68510-4947 Office: Jour-Star Printing Co PO Box 81609 926 P St Lincoln NE 68508-3615

DYKEN, MARK LEWIS, JR. neurologist, educator; b. Laramie, Wyo., Aug. 26, 1928; s. Mark L. and Thelma Violet (Achenbach) D.; m. Beverly All, June 8, 1951; children: Betsy Lynn, Mark Eric, Julie Suzanne, Amy Luise, Andrew Christopher, Gregory Allen. BS in Anatomy and Physiology, Ind. U., 1951, MD, 1954. Diplomate Am. Bd. Psychiatry and Neurology. Intern Indpls. Gen. Hosp., 1954-55; resident in neurology Ind. U. Med. Ctr., 1955-58; clin. dir., dir. rsch. New Castle (Ind.) State Hosp., 1958-61; asst. dept. neurology Ind. U., 1958-61, assoc. prof. neurology, 1964-69, prof., 1969—, chmn. dept. neurology, 1971-94, prof. emeritus, 1994—, dir. Cerebrovascular Disease Ctr., 1966—. Chmn. profl. adv. coun. Nat. Easter Seal Soc., 1974-82; cons., chmn. panel on rev. neurol. devices subcom. FDA, 1979-83. Editor-in-chief Stroke, 1992—; contbr. numerous articles on topics including cerebral vascular disease, blood flow, epilepsy, electroencephalography, muscle disease, to profl. jours. With U.S. Army, 1946-48. Recipient numerous grants in cerebrovascular disease. Fellow ACP; mem. AMA, Am. Assn. Univ. Profs. Neurology (pres. 1986-88), Epilepsy Found. Am., Am. Heart Assn (chmn. stroke coun. 1984-86, v.p. for sci. couns. 1988-89), Ind. Neurol. Assn. (charter pres. 1966-68), Am. Acad. Neurology, Am. Neurol. Assn., Sigma Xi, Alpha Omega Alpha. Home: 7406 W 92nd St Zionsville IN 46077-9103 Office: Ind U Med Ctr Neurol Dept Wishard BA 402 1001 W 10th St Indianapolis IN 46202-2859

DYKSTRA, DENNIS DALE, physiatrist; b. Lakewood, Ohio, Feb. 21, 1950; s. Gerald and Grace Maire (Thomas) D.; m. Mary Louise Kerker, May 16, 1992; children: Dorothy, Perry, Caitlin, Patrick. AB in Zoology summa cum laude, Ohio U., 1972; MD, U. Cin., 1976; PhD, U. Minn., 1988, M in Health Adminstrn., 1999. Diplomate Am. Bd. Pediatrics, Am. Bd. Phys. Medicine and Rehab. Intern/resident Cin. Children's Hosp., 1976-81; instr. U. Minn., Mpls., 1981-88, asst. prof., 1988-92, assoc. prof. phys. medicine/rehab./pediatrics/urol. surgery, 1992—, head dept. phys. medicine/rehab., 1992—; assoc. chief staff for rehab. VA Med. Ctr., 1994-97. Author: Krusen's Handbook of Phys. Medicine and Rehabilitation, 1991; contbr. articles to profl. jours. Med. advisor Minn. Spasmodic Torticolits Soc., Duluth, Minn., 1991—. Recipient Phys. Med. and Rehab. Investigator award Phys. Med. and Rehab. Rsch. Found., 1984, 85; Spinal Cord Soc. grantee, 1990. Fellow Am. Acad. Phys. Med. and Rehab. (chair edn. com. 1994—), Am. Acad. Pediatrics, Am. Assn. Electrodiagnostic Medicine. Achievements include 2 patents on method of apparatus for mechanical stimulation of nerves, method and device for pharmacological control of spascitity. Avocations: Karate (2d degree Black Belt), classical music. Office: Univ of Minn 420 Delaware St SE Box 297 Mayor Bldg Minneapolis MN 55455

DYKSTRA, PAUL HOPKINS, lawyer; b. Chgo., July 13, 1943; s. Paul C. and Frances Marie (Hopkins) D. Student, Exeter Coll. Oxford U., Eng., 1964; AB, Princeton U., 1965; LLB, Yale U., 1968. Bar: Ill. 1968, D.C. 1977. Assoc. Gardner, Carton & Douglas, Chgo., 1968-74, ptnr., 1975—, ptnr. Washington office, 1977-79, fin. ptnr., 1985-89, chmn., 1989-95. Adj. prof. law Northwestern U. Sch. Law, 2001—. Contbr. articles to profl. jours. Trustee Chgo. Theatre Group, Inc. (Goodman Theatre), 1975—, pres., 1983-85, vice chmn., 1988-92, pres., 1992-97; mem. aux. bd. Art Inst. Chgo., 1973-77, 79-88, exec. com., 1976-77, 82-87; chmn. Orange and Black Club of Princeton Club of Chgo., 1987-90; chmn. maj. gifts Princeton U. Class of 1965, 1982-85; mem. cultural affairs adv. bd. City of Chgo., 1990—, Blue Skies for Kids, Chgo. Cmty. Trust, Chgo. Pub. Libr. Bd., 1991-97, chmn. adminstrn. and fin. com., 1996—; trustee Chgo. Pub. Libr. Found., 1999—. Mem. ABA (fed. and regulation of securities com.), Chgo. Bar Assn. (sec. 1976-77), Chgo. Hist. Soc. (trustee 1999—, mem. Making History awards com. 1994—, chmn. 2000—), Econ. Club of Chgo. (reception com. 1982-85), Legal Club of Chgo., Law Club Chgo., Racquet Club of Chgo. (bd. govs., vice chmn. membership com. 1980-83), Chgo. Club (bd. dirs., sec. 1996-2000), Shoreacres, Chgo. Commonwealth Club, The Comml. Club of Chgo. (sec., mem. exec. com. 2001—), Chgo. Coun. Fgn. Rels. (Chgo. com.). Episcopalian. Avocations: travel, golf, bicycling. Office: Gardner Carton & Douglas 321 N Clark St Ste 3300 Chicago IL 60610-4720 E-mail: pdykstra@gcd.com.

DYKSTRA, ROBERT, retired education educator; b. Vesper, Wis., Feb. 26, 1930; s. John and Anna (Holstein) D.; m. Lou Ann Conselman, Oct. 6, 1956; children: S. Kim, Paul, Randall. BS in Elem. Edn., U. Wis., River Falls, 1957; MA in Ednl. Psychology, U. Minn., 1959, PhD in Ednl. Psychology, 1962. Cert. elem. edn. Elem. tchr. Cedar Grove (Wis.) Pub. Sch., 1954-55; asst. prof. U. Minn., Mpls., 1962-64, assoc. prof., 1965-69, prof., 1970-73, chair dept. curriculum and instrn., 1974-85, prof., 1986-93, ret., 1993. Co-author: Teaching Reading, 1974, Language Arts: Teaching and Learning Effective Use of Language, 1988; contbr. articles to profl. jours. With U.S. Army, 1952-54. Recipient Disting. Alumnus award U. Wis./River Falls, 1998; elected to Reading Hall of Fame, 1996; U.S. Office Edn. rsch. grantee, 1963, 65. Mem. Nat. Coun. Tchrs. of English (mem. exec. com. 1969-71), Nat. Conf. on Rsch. in English (pres. 1984-85), Twin City Area Reading Coun. (pres. 1990-91), Internat. Reading Assn. (mem. pub. com. 1975-77), Nat. Reading Conf. (mem. pub. com. 1978-80). Lutheran. Avocations: barbershop quartet singing, reading, golf. Home: 1998 16th St NW Saint Paul MN 55112-5555 E-mail: bobdykstra@prodigy.net.

DYNEK, SIGRID, corporate lawyer, retail executive; b. 1949; BS, JD, Marquette U. Bar: Wis. 1973. V.p., gen. counsel Kohl's Dept. Stores, Inc., Menomonee Falls, Wis. Office: Kohl's Dept Stores Inc N56w17000 Ridgewood Dr Menomonee Falls WI 53051-5660

DYRKACZ, GARY R. chemist, researcher; Rsch. chemist Argonne (Ill.) Nat. Lab. Recipient Henry H. Storch award in Fuel Chemistry Am. Chem. Soc., 1994. Office: Argonne Nat Lab 9700 Cass Ave Argonne IL 60439-4803

DYRSTAD, JOANELL M. former lieutenant governor, consultant; b. St. James, Minn., Oct. 15, 1942; d. Arnold A. and Ruth (Berlin) Sletta; m. Marvin Dyrstad, 1965; children: Troy, Anika. BA, Gustavus Adolphus Coll., St. Peter, Minn., 1964; MA, Hamline U., 1996. Mayor City of Red Wing, Minn., 1985-90; lt. gov. State of Minn., 1991-94; now independent bus. and govt. cons. Ptnr. Corner Drugstore, Red Wing, 1968—; v.p. League Minn. Cities, 1990-91, Minn. Mayors Assn., 1989-90; mem. Nat. Conf. Lt. Gov.'s, 1991-94, chair, 1993-94. Trustee Gustavus Adolphus Coll., 1989-98, U. Minn. Found., 1993-99; dir. corp. bd. Fairview Health Sys., vice chair, 1997—. Mem. AAUW (Citizen of yr. award 1985), LWV.

DYSON, MARV, broadcast executive; Pres. Sta. WGCI-AM, Chgo. Office: WGCI Radio 332 S Michigan Ave Ste 600 Chicago IL 60604-4392

DZIADYK, BOHDAN, botany and ecology educator; b. Aschaffenburg, Germany, Mar. 26, 1948; came to U.S., 1950; s. Iwan and Maria (Jaroszuk) D.; m. Marietta Jay Johnston, Mar. 23, 1974; children: Jennifer Maria, Joseph Walter. BA, Southern Ill. U., 1970, MS, 1980; PhD, N.D. State U., 1982. From instr. to assoc. prof. botany and ecology Augustana Coll., Rock Island, Ill., 1980-96, prof., 1996—, co-dir. environ. studies program, 1991—, dir. coll. field stas., 1991—; chmn. biology dept., 1992-95. Bd. dirs. Quad Cities Bot. Ctr. Contbr. articles to profl. jours. Sgt. AUS, 1970-73. Pew Sci. Program researcher and grantee, 1988-94. Mem. Ecol. Soc. Am., Ill. Native Plant Soc., Ctr. for Plant Conservation, Ill. State Acad. Sci. (pres. 1993-95), Alpha Phi Omega (adv. and scouting coord. 1981—), Sigma Xi (pres. John Deere chpt. 1987-88). Office: Augustana Coll Dept Biology 639 38th St Rock Island IL 61201-2210 E-mail: bidziadyk@augustana.edu.

DZIUK, PHILIP JOHN, animal scientist educator; b. Foley, Minn., Mar. 24, 1926; s. Edmund William and Ellen Catherine (Carlin) D.; m. Patricia Rosemary Weber, Sept. 29, 1951; children: Corinne, Constance, Rita, Catherine, Kenneth, Ronald, Carl. BS, U. Minn., 1950, MS, 1952, PhD, 1955. From rsch. asst. to rsch. assoc. U. Minn., Mpls., 1950-55; from asst. prof. to prof. U. Ill., Urbana, 1955-88, prof. emeritus, 1988—. Cons. Upjohn, Abbott, Eli Lilly, Am. Cynamid, Schering, Batelle; reviewer of grants NIH, Bethesda, Md., 1982-86, USDA, Beltsville, Md., 1983-89. Contbr. peer reviewed publs. in sci. and profl. jours. With USN, 1945-46. Fellow Lalor Found., 1958, 61, Pig Industry Devel. Authority, Eng., 1961; recipient Achievement in Rsch. award Am. Fertility Soc., 1970, Sr. Scientist award Alexander von Humboldt Found., 1981, Pioneer award Internat. Embryo Transfer Soc., 2001, Outstanding Achievement award U. Minn., 2002. Mem. AAAS, KC, Am. Assn. Anatomist, Am. Soc. Animal Scis. (fellow 1987, Rsch. in Physiology award 1971), Soc. Study of Fertility, Soc. Study of Reproduction (dir., pres. 1987-88, Disting. Svc. award 1989), Lions Internat. (pres., sec. 1992-94), Farm House, Sigma Xi, Gamma Alpha, Phi Kappa Phi, Phi Zeta, Gamma Sigma Delta, Alpha Zeta. Avocations: woodworking, gardening, racquetball. Office: U Ill Dept Animal Scis 1207 W Gregory Dr Urbana IL 61801-4733

EADIE, JOHN WILLIAM, history educator; b. Ft. Smith, Ark., Dec. 18, 1935; s. William Robert and Helen (Montgomery) B.; m. Joan Holt, Aug. 18, 1957; children: Robin, Christopher. B.A. with honors, U. Ark., 1957; M.A., U. Chgo., 1959; Ph.D., Univ. Coll., London, 1962. Asst. prof. Ripon Coll., Wis., 1962-63; asst. prof. history U. Mich., Ann Arbor, 1963-67, assoc. prof., 1967-73, prof., 1973-86, assoc. chmn. dept. history, 1970-71, humanities-arts advisor Office V.p. for Research, 1974-86, assoc. dean Rackham Sch. Grad. Studies, 1984-86; prof. history, dean Coll. Arts and Letters Mich. St. U., East Lansing, 1986-97, sr. advisor to Provost, 1997—. Dir. Consortium for Inter-Instnl. Collaboration in African and L.Am. Studies, 1989—, chmn. liberal arts and scis. dean Consortium for Instnl. Collaboration, 1991-94. Author: The Breviarium of Festus: A critical-Edition with Historical Commentary, 1967, The Conversion of Constantine, 1971, (with others) Western Civilization, 1975; editor: Classical traditions in Early America, 1976; co-editor The Craft of the Ancient Historian, 1985, Urban Centers and Rural Contexts in Late Antiquity, 2001. Chmn. Mich. Council for Humanities, E. Lansing, Mich., 1977-80, Mich. Alliance for Conservation Cultural Heritage, 1988-90. Marshall scholar Brit. Marshall Commn. Univ. Coll., London, 1960-62; recipient Disting. Service award Mich. Council Humanities, 1980, Ralph Smucker award for advancing internat. programs, 2001. Mem. Am. Hist. Assn., Assn. Ancient Historians, Soc. Promotion Roman Studies, Archaeol Inst. Am. Democrat. Presbyterian. Office: Mich State U 752 Wells Hall East Lansing MI 48824-1027

EARL, ANTHONY SCULLY, former governor of Wisconsin, lawyer; b. Lansing, Mich., Apr. 12, 1936; s. Russell K. and Ethlynne Julia (Scully) E.; children: Julia, Anne, Mary, Catherine. B.S., Mich. State U.; J.D., U. Chgo. Bar: Wis., Minn. Asst. dist. atty. Marathon County, Wausau, Wis., 1965-66; city atty. City of Wausau, 1966-69; mem. Wis. Assembly, Madison, 1969-74; mem. firm Crooks, Low & Earl, 1969-74; sec. Wis. Dept. Adminstrn., Madison, 1974-75, Dept. Nat. Resources, Madison, 1975-80; v.p. firm Foley & Lardner, 1980-82; gov. State of Wis., 1983-87; ptnr. Quarles and Brady, 1987—. Served as lt. USN, 1962-65. Democrat. Roman Catholic. Office: Quarles & Brady 1 S Pinckney St PO Box 2113 Madison WI 53701-2113

EARLE, TIMOTHY KEESE, anthropology educator; b. New Bedford, Mass., Aug. 10, 1946; s. Osborne and Eleanor (Clark) E.; m. Eliza Howe, June 14, 1969; children: Caroline, Hester. BA summa cum laude, Harvard U., 1969; MA, U. Mich., 1971, PhD, 1973. Rsch. archaeologist Bishop Mus., Honolulu, 1971-72; prof. anthropology UCLA, 1973-95, dir. Inst. of Archaeology, 1987-92; prof. anthropology Northwestern U., Evanston, Ill., 1995—, chair dept., 1995-2000. Author: Bronze Age Economics, 2002 How Chiefs Come to Power, 1997; co-author: Evolution of Human Society, 1987, 2nd edit., 2000, Bronze Age Economics, 2002; editor: Exchange Systems in Prehistory, 1977, Contexts for Prehistoric Exchange, 1982, Chiefdoms, 1991. Mem.: Soc. Econ. Anthrop., Soc. Am. Archaeology, Am. Anthrop. Assn. (pres. archaeology divsn. 1995—97; exec. bd. 1999—2002), Phi Beta Kappa. E-mail: tke299@northwestern.edu.

EARLEY, ANTHONY F., JR. utilities executive; BS in Physics, MS in Engring, JD, U. Notre Dame. Ptnr. Hunton & Williams; exec. v.p., gen. counsel L.I. Lighting Co., 1985—89, pres., COO, 1989—94, Detroit Edison (now DTE Energy), Detroit, 1994—2000, chmn., CEO, 2001—. Bd. dirs. Mut. Am. Capital Mgmt. Corp., Comerica Bank, Henry Ford Health Sys. Mem. adv. coun. Coll. Engring. U. Notre Dame; mem. bd. coun. Loyola H.S.; exec. bd. Cornerstone Schs.; bd. dirs. Detroit Renaissance, New Detroit, United Way Cmty. Svcs. Officer USN. Office: 2000 2d Ave Detroit MI 48226-1279

EARLEY, ANTHONY FRANCIS, JR. utilities company executive, lawyer; b. Jamaica, N.Y., July 29, 1949; s. Anthony Francis and Jean Ann (Draffen) E.; m. Sarah Margaret Belanger, Oct. 14, 1972; children: Michael Patrick, Anthony Matthew, Daniel Cartwright, Matthew Sean. BS in Physics, U. Notre Dame, 1971, MS in Engring., JD, U. Notre Dame, 1979. Bar: Va. 1980, N.Y. 1985, U.S. Ct. Appeals (6th cir.) 1981. Assoc. Hunton & Williams, Richmond, Va., 1979-85, ptnr., 1985; gen. counsel L.I. Lighting Co., Hicksville, N.Y., 1985-89, exec. v.p., 1988-89, pres., COO, 1989-94, also bd. dirs.; pres., COO The Detroit Edison Co. (now DTE Energy Co.), 1994—, also bd. dirs., chmn., CEO. Bd. dirs. Mutual Am. Contbr. articles to profl. jours. Mem. adv. coun. Coll. Engring., U. Notre Dame. Served to lt. USN, 1971-76. Mem. ABA. Roman Catholic. Avocations: tennis, skiing, furniture restoration. Office: DTE Energy Co 2000 2ND Ave Detroit MI 48226

EARLY, BERT HYLTON, lawyer, consultant; b. Kimball, W.Va., July 17, 1922; s. Robert Terry and Sue Keister (Hylton) E.; m. Elizabeth Henry, June 24, 1950; children— Bert Hylton, Robert Christian, Mark Randolph, Philip Henry, Peter St. Clair Student, Marshall U., 1940-42; A.B., Duke U., 1946; J.D., Harvard U., 1949. Bar: W.Va. 1949, Ill. 1963, Fla. 1981. Assoc. Fitzpatrick, Marshall, Huddleston & Bolen, Huntington, W.Va., 1949-57; asst. counsel Island Creek Coal Co., 1957-60, assoc. gen. counsel, 1960-62; dep. exec. dir. ABA, Chgo., 1962-64, exec. dir., 1964-81; sr. v.p. Wells Internat., 1981-83, pres., 1983-85, Bert H. Early Assocs. Inc., Chgo., 1985-94, Early Cochran & Olson, Chgo., 1994-98, of counsel, 1999—. Dir. Am. Bar Found., Chgo., 1993-95; instr. Marshall U., Huntington, W.Va., 1950-53; legal search cons. and lectr. in field. Bd. dirs. Morris Meml. Hosp. for Crippled Children, 1954-60, Huntington Pub. Libr., 1951-60, W.Va. Tax Inst., 1961-62, Huntington Mus. Art, 1961-62; mem. W.Va. Jud. Coun., 1960-62, Huntington City Coun., 1961-62; bd. dirs. Cmty. Renewal Soc., Chgo., 1965-76, United Charities Chgo., 1972-80, Hinsdale (Ill.) Hosp. Found., 1987-93, Internat. Bar Assn. Found., 1987-89; bd. dirs. Am. Bar Endowment, 1983-95, sec., 1987-89, treas., 1989-91, v.p., 1991-93, pres., 1993-95, dir. emeritus, 1995-2000; mem. vis. com. U. Chgo. Law Sch., 1975-78; trustee Davis and Elkins Coll., 1960-63; mem. Hinsdale Plan Commn., 1982-85. 1st lt. AC, U.S. Army, 1943-45. Fellow Am. Bar Found., Ill. Bar Found. (charter); mem. ABA (ho. of dels. 1958-59, 84-93, chmn. young lawyers divsn. 1957-58, Disting. Svc. award young lawyers divsn. 1983), Am. Law Inst. (life), Internat. Bar Assn. (asst. sec. gen. 1967-82), Nat. Legal Aid and Defender Assn., Legal Aid Soc. Chgo., Am. Judicature Soc. (bd. dirs. 1981-84), Fla. Bar, W.Va. Bar Assn., Chgo. Bar Assn. Presbyterian. Office: Early Cochran & Olson LLC 401 N Michigan Ave Ste 2010 Chicago IL 46061-4206

EARLY, JACK JONES, foundation executive; b. Corbin, Ky., Apr. 12, 1925; s. Joseph M. and Lela (Jones) E.; m. Nancye Bruce Whaley, June 1, 1952; children: Lela Katherine, Judith Ann, Laura Hattie. A.B., Union Coll., Barbourville, Ky., 1948; M.A., U. Ky., 1953, Ed.D. (So. scholar 1955-56), 1956; B.D., Coll. of Bible, Lexington, Ky., 1956; D.D., Wesley Coll., Grand Forks, N.D., 1961; LL.D., Parsons Coll., 1962, Iowa Wesleyan Coll., 1972; Litt.D., Dakota Wesleyan U., 1969; L.H.D., Union Coll., Barbourville, Ky., 1979; D.Adminstrn., Cumberland Coll., 1981. Ordained to ministry Methodist Ch., 1954; pastor Rockhold Circuit, Ky., 1943-44, Craig's Chapel and Laurel Circuit, London, 1944-47, Trinity Ch., Oak Ridge, summer 1945, Hindman Ch., Ky., 1947-52; dean of men Hindman Settlement Sch., 1948-51; assoc. pastor Park Ch., Lexington, Ky., 1952-54; asst. to pres., dean Athens Coll., Ala., 1954- 55; v.p., dean of coll. Iowa Wesleyan Coll., Mount Pleasant, 1956-58; pres. Dakota Wesleyan U., 1958-69, Pfeiffer Coll., Misenheimer, N.C., 1969-71; exec. dir. Am. Bankers Assn., Washington, 1971-73; pres. Limestone Coll., Gaffney, S.C., 1973-79; exec. dir. edn. Combined Ins. Co. Am., Chgo., 1979-82, v.p., exec. dir. edn. and communications, 1982-84; pres. Ky. Ind. Coll. Fund, Louisville, 1984-93, pres. emeritus, 1993—; dir. edn., con. Napoleon Hill Found., Northbrook, Ill., 1997—. Pres. W. Clement Stone PMA Communications, Inc., Chgo., 1987—. Active Boy Scouts Am.; mem. pres. adv. coun. North Pk. Coll.; mem. Felician adv. bd. Felician Coll.; mem. Ky. Ho. of Reps., 1952-54; bd. dirs. S.D. Found. Pvt. Colls., S.D. Meth. Found., Nat. Coun. on Youth Leadership, Ctr. for Citizenship Edn., YMCA, Motivational Inst., Mid-Am. chpt. ARC, 1980—, W. Clement and Jessie V. Stone Found., Northbrook Symphony Orch., Ky. Mountain Laurel Festival, 1990—, Internat. Coun. on Edn. for Teaching, 1990—; chmn. bd. Religious Heritage Am., 1989-92, Internat. Leadership Network, 1991—; Rep. nominee for Metro Mayor, Louisville, 2002. Recipient Spoke award Mitchell Jr. C. of C., 1959, Disting. Svc. award, 1960, Disting. Svc. award S.D. Jr. C. of C., 1960, Gaffney Jaycees, 1979, Chief Iron Eyes Cody medal of Peace, 1987, Outstanding Kentuckian award O'Tucks, 1990; named Outstanding Former Kentuckian, 1963; hon. fellow Wroxton Coll., Oxfordshire, Eng.; named to Disting. Alumni Hall of Fame, U. Ky., 1965. Mem. Am. Soc. Assn. Execs., Louisville C. of C., Blue Key, Masons (33d degree, chaplain Valley of Louisville chpt. 1990—), Rotary (pres. Louisville 1992-93, dist. 6710 gov. 1996—), Ky. Soc. Sons of the Am. Revolution (pres. 1998—), Soc. War of 1812 in the Commonwealth of Ky. (pres. 1997—), Huguenot Soc. of Ky. (pres. 1999—), Huguenot Soc.-Soc. of Manakin (Ky. br. pres. 1999—), Gen. for Pub. Rels.-Gen. Soc. of the War of 1812 (v.p. 1998—), Del. State Soc. of Cin., Nat. Sojourners Camp #134, Heroes of '76 (E.B. Jones Camp), Kappa Delta Pi, Phi Delta Kappa (bd. dirs. Northwestern U. chpt. 1980—), Kappa Phi Kappa, Alpha Psi Omega, Theta Phi, Pi Tau Chi. Republican. Home: 9002 Hurstwood Ct Louisville KY 40222-5716

EARLY, JUDITH K. social services director; b. Evansville, Ind., 1954; d. Forrest M. and Dorothea E. Early. BA, Brescia Coll., 1976; MS, So. Ill. U., 1985, RhD, 1991. Cert. vocat. evaluator; cert. family devel. specialist. Work activity supr. So. Ind. Rehab. Svcs., Inc., Boonville, 1976-78; vocat. evaluator Evansville Assn. for Retarded Citizens, 1978-85; vocat. evaluator Evaluation and Developmental Ctr., Carbondale, Ill., 1985-88; grad. asst., program evaluator So. Ill. U., 1988-90, rsch. and teaching asst., 1990-91; exec. dir. Albion Fellow Bacon Ctr., Evansville, Ind., 1991-93; family svcs. dir. Goodwill Family Ctr., 1993-95, program evaluation dir., 1995-96, dir., 1996-2000; cmty. rels. dir. Evansville Goodwill Industries, Inc., 2000—. Contbr. articles to profl. publs. Bd. dirs. So. Ill. Ctr. for Ind. Living, Carbondale, 1990-91, Vanderburgh County Coun. Aging, 2000—; bd. dirs., youth worker 1st United Meth. Ch., Carbondale, 1989-91; v.p. Altrusa of Evansville, 1993-94; mem. leadership Evansville Asbury United Meth. Ch., 1993—, treas., 1998—; bd. dirs. Youth as Resources, 1995-98, Transitional Svcs., Inc., Human Rights Com., 1992-99; bd. dirs. Family Resource Ctr., 1997—, v.p., 2000—; bd. dirs. Leadership Evansville, 1999—; bd. dirs. Family Resource Ctr., 1995—, v.p., 2000—. Mem. AAUW, Vocat. Evaluation and Work Adjustment Assn. (chmn. student affairs com. 1988-90, Student Lit. award 1987), Ill. Rehab. Assn. (bd. dirs. 1989-91), Ill. Vocat. Evaluation and Work Adjustment Assn. (chmn. mem. 1989-91, pres. 1991—, Disting. Svc. award 1989), Assn. Retarded Citizens, Altrusa Internat. of Evansville. Avocations: needlepoint, gardening, photography, cooking. Office: Evansville Goodwill Industries Inc Goodwill Family Ctr 500 S Green River Rd Ste 2 Evansville IN 47715-7392

EARLY, PATRICK JOSEPH, retired oil and gas company executive; b. Lincoln, Nebr., Feb. 4, 1933; s. John Joseph and Irene Cecelia (McManus) E.; m. Evelyn Louise Wiese, Aug. 30, 1955; children: Timothy, Christopher, Pamela, Kathleen, William, Andrew. BS in Engring., Colo. Sch. Mines, 1955; grad. mgmt. tng. program, U. Western Ont., Can., 1971; grad. advanced mgmt. program, Harvard U., 1980. Various operating and engring. positions Amoco Prodn. Co., Wyo., Tex. and La., 1955-75, regional prodn. mgr., 1975-76, sr. v.p. prodn., exec. v.p. Chgo., 1976-87, pres., 1987-92; vice-chmn. Amoco Corp., 1992-95. Trustee Chgo. Mus. Sci. and Industry; bd. advisors Chgo. Cath. Charities. With USAF, 1957, bd. dirs. Questar Corp. Mem. Am. Petroleum Inst., Soc. Petroleum Engrs., Naperville Country Club. Republican. Roman Catholic. Avocations: golf, bird hunting.

EASTABROOK, DIANNE, news correspondent; Grad., Northwestern U., 1982. Weekend prodr., anchor Sta. WSAN-TV, Wausau, Wis.; contbr. consumer news Sta. WEEK-TV, Peoria, Ill.; money editor Sta. WNYT-TV, Albany, N.Y.; Midwest corr., bur. chief Nightly Bus. Report, Chgo. Office: NBR 100 S Sangamon St Chicago IL 60607-2614

EASTER, STEPHEN SHERMAN, JR. biology educator; b. New Orleans, Feb. 12, 1938; s. Stephen Sherman and Myrtle Olivia (Bekkedahl) E.; m. Janine Eliane Piot, June 4, 1963; children: Michele, Kim BS, Yale U., 1960; postgrad., Harvard U., 1961; PhD, Johns Hopkins U., 1966. Postdoctoral fellow Cambridge U., Eng., 1967; postdoctoral U. Calif., Berkeley, 1968-69; asst. prof. biology U. Mich., Ann Arbor, 1970-74, assoc. prof., 1974-78, prof., 1978—, assoc. chmn., 1992-93, mem. Coll. Lit., Sci. and the Arts exec. com., 1993-96, dir. neurosci. program, 1984-88, Mathew Alpern Collegiate prof., 1998—. Vis. prof. U. Murcia, Spain, 1997, Ecole Normale Supérieure, Paris, 1997. Editor Vision Rsch., 1978-85, Jour. Neurosci., 1989-95, Visual Neurosci., 1990-92, Investigative Ophthalmology and Visual Sci., 1992-97, Jour. Comparative Neurology, 1994-99. Recipient Sokol award, 1998. Mem. Soc. Neurosci., Assn. Rsch. in Vision and Ophthalmology, Internat. Brain Rsch. Orgn., Soc. for Devel. Biology. Office: U Mich Dept Biology 3113 Natural Sci Bldg Ann Arbor MI 48109-1048 E-mail: sseaster@umich.edu.

EASTERBROOK, FRANK HOOVER, federal judge; b. Buffalo, Sept. 3, 1948; s. George Edmund and Vimy (Hoover) E. B.A., Swarthmore Coll., 1970; J.D., U. Chgo., 1973. Bar: D.C. Law clk. to judge U.S. Ct. Appeals, Boston, 1973-74; asst. to solicitor gen. U.S. Dept. Justice, Washington, 1974-77, dep. solicitor gen. of U.S., 1978-79; asst. prof. law U. Chgo., 1978-81, prof. law, 1981-84, Lee & Brena Freeman prof., 1984-85; prin. employee Lexecon Inc., Chgo., 1980-85; sr. lectr. U. Chgo., 1985—; judge U.S. Ct. Appeals (7th cir.), Chgo., 1985—. Mem. adv. com. on tender offers SEC, Washington, 1983 Author: (with Richard A. Posner) Antitrust, 1981, (with Daniel R. Fischel) The Economic Structure of Corporate Law, 1991; editor Jour. Law and Econs., Chgo., 1982-91; contbr. articles to profl. jours. Trustee James Madison Meml. Fellowship Found., 1988—. Recipient Prize for Disting. scholarship Emory U., Atlanta, 1981 Mem. AAAS, Am. Law Inst., Mont Pelerin Soc., Order of Coif, Phi Beta Kappa. Office: US Ct Appeals Everett McKinley Dirksen Fed Bldg 219 S Dearborn St Ste 2746 Chicago IL 60604-1803

EASTERDAY, BERNARD CARLYLE, veterinary medicine educator; b. Hillsdale, Mich., Sept. 16, 1929; s. Harley B. and Alberta M. Easterday D.V.M., Mich. State U., 1952; M.S., U. Wis., 1958, Ph.D., 1961. Diplomate Am. Coll. Veterinary Microbiologists. Pvt. practice veterinary medicine, Hillsdale, Mich., 1952; veterinarian U.S. Dept. Def., Frederick, Md., 1955-61; assoc. prof., then prof. veterinary sci. U. Wis., Madison, 1961-94, prof. emeritus, 1994—, dean Sch. Vet. Medicine, 1979-94, dean emeritus, prof emeritus Sch. Vet. Medicine, 1994—. Mem., chmn. com. animal health Nat. Acad. Sci.-NRC, Washington, 1980-83, mem. com. on sci. basis meat and poultry inspection program, 1984-85; mem. tech. adv. com. Binat. Agrl. Research and Devel., Bet-Degan, Israel, 1982-84; mem. expert adv. panel on zoonoses WHO, Geneva, 1978-94; mem. tech. adv. com. on avian influenza USDA, 1983-85; mem. sec. USDA adv. com. on fgn. animal and poultry diseases, 1991-96. 1st lt. V.C., U.S. Army, 1952-54. Recipient Disting. Alumnus award Coll. Vet. Medicine, Mich. State U., 1975; named Wis. Veterinarian of Yr., Wis. Vet. Med. Assn., 1979, Disting. Alumni award Mich. State U., 1999. Mem. AVMA, Am. Assn. Vet. Med. Colls. (pres. 1975), Am. Assn. Avian Pathologists Office: U Wisconsin-Madison Sch Vet Medicine 2015 Linden Dr W Madison WI 53706-1100

EASTHAM, DENNIS MICHAEL, advertising executive; b. Jacksonville, Ill., Dec. 18, 1946; s. Glenn R. and Ona M. (Camerer) E.; m. Dianne C. L. Watts; children: Susie, Brian, Brad. BA in Fin., U. Ill., 1968; MBA, U. Santa Clara, 1972. Asst. v.p. Crocker Bank, San Francisco, 1976-79; v.p. T & E Card div. Citicorp, L.A., 1979-81; exec. v.p. Barry Blau and Ptnrs. Inc., L.A., N.Y.C. and Chgo., 1981-87; pres. Barry Blau Worldwide, Deerfield, Ill., 1987—. Bd. dirs. Barry Blau and Ptnrs. Inc., Fairfield, Conn., 1985—. Mem. Direct Mktg. Assn. Home: 21835 Vernon Ridge Dr Mundelein IL 60060-5316 Office: BrannWorldwide 540 Lake Cook Rd Deerfield IL 60015-5289

EASTMAN, DEAN ERIC, physicist, educator; b. Oxford, Wis., Jan. 20, 1940; m. Ella Mae Staley. BSEE, MIT, 1962, MSEE, 1963, PhDEE, 1965. Rsch. staff IBM T.J. Watson Rsch. Ctr., Yorktown Heights, N.Y., 1963-71, mgr. photoemission and surface physics group, 1971-81, mgr. lithography packaging and compound semicondr. tech., 1981-82, dir. Advanced Packaging Tech. Lab., 1983-85, rsch. v.p. system tech. and sci., 1986-94; dir. product devel. IBM Systems Tech. Div., Danbury, Conn., 1985-86; dir. hardware devel. reengring. IBM Corp., Armonk, N.Y., 1994-96; dir. Argonne Nat. Lab., 1996-98; prof. physics U. Chgo., 1998—. Prof. physics U. Chgo., 1998—. Contbr. over 180 articles to profl. jours. Recipient Oliver E. Buckley prize, 1980; IBM Corp. fellow, 1974. Fellow Am. Phys. Soc.; mem. NAS, NAE, Am. Acad. Arts and Scis. Office: University of Chicago JFI Box 15 RI 231 5640 S Ellis Ave Chicago IL 60637-1433

EASTON, LORY BARSDATE, lawyer; BA in Linguistics summa cum laude, Yale U., 1983, JD, 1988. Bar: Pa. 1990, Conn. 1990, Ill. 1991. Clk. to Jose A. Cabranes, U.S. Dist. Ct. for Conn., 1988-89; clk. to Hon. Ralph K. Winter, U.S. Ct. Appeals for 2d Cir., 1989-90; assoc. Sidley & Austin, Chgo., 1990-96, ptnr., 1996—. Mng. editor Yale Law Jour., 1987-88. Office: Sidley & Austin Bank One Plz 425 W Surf St Apt 605 Chicago IL 60657-6139 Fax: 312-853-7036. E-mail: leaston@sidley.com.

EATON, HENRY FELIX, public relations executive; b. Cleve., Nov. 30, 1925; s. Henry F. and Stella (Simon) E.; m. Barbara Feder, Aug. 28, 1950; children: Deborah, Richard, David, Susan. B.A., U. Chgo., 1947. Asst. advt. mgr. Kromex Corp., Cleve., 1947-48; editor Material Handling mag., 1948-52; chmn. Dix & Eaton Inc., 1952-2000, The Eaton Group, Cleve., 2000—. Vice chmn. bd. trustees Playhouse Sq. Found., Mus. Arts Assn., Cleve. With AUS, 1944-46. Mem. Pub. Rels. Soc. Am. (counselors sect.), Nat. Investor Rels. Inst., Union Club, Pepper Pike Club, Cleve. Racquet Club, Oakwood Country Club. Home: 23690 Letchworth Rd Cleveland OH 44122-4110 Office: The Eaton Group 1301 E 9th St Ste 2700 Cleveland OH 44114-1882

EATON, JAY, lawyer; b. Waterloo, Iowa, Feb. 24, 1946; BBA, U. Iowa, 1968, JD with honors, 1971. Bar: Iowa 1971, Ohio 1972, Wis. 1977. Assoc. Nyemaster, Goode, Voigts, West, Hansell & O'Brien, Des Moines. Mem. ABA, Iowa State Bar Assn. (v.p. 1997-98, pres. 1998—), Polk County Bar Assn. (bd. dirs. 1989-97, pres. 1992-93). Office: Nyemaster Goode Voigts West Hansell & O'Brien PC 700 Walnut St Ste 1600 Des Moines IA 50309-3800 E-mail: je@nyemaster.com.

EATON, JOHN C. composer, educator; b. Bryn Mawr, Pa., Mar. 30, 1935; s. Harold C. and Fannie E. (Geer) E.; m. Nelda E. Nelson, May 31, 1973; children: Elizabeth Estela, Julian R.P. AB, Princeton U., N.J., 1957, MFA, 1959. Performing artist Columbia Artists, N.Y.C., 1961-65; prof. music Ind. U., Bloomington, 1970—, U. Chgo., 1991—. Composer-in-residence Am. Acad., Rome, Italy, 1975-76; lectr. Salzburg Seminar in Am. Studies, Austria, 1976; honored guest Soviet Composers Soc., 1977 Composer numerous operas, most recently: Myshkin, 1972 (Peabody award 1972), Danton and Robespierre, 1978, The Cry of Clytaemnestra, 1980, The Tempest, 1985 (Santa Fe Commn.), The Reverend Jim Jones, 1988, Peer Gynt, 1989, Let's Get This Show on the Road, 1993, Don Quixote, 1994, Golk, 1995, Travelling with Gulliver, 1997, Antigone, 1999, numerous chamber orchs. and elec. comps.; featured in numerous articles in profl. jours. Recipient Prix de Rome, Am. Acad., Rome, 1959-62; citation Am. Inst. Arts and Letters, 1972; plaque Ind. Arts Council, 1975; MacArthur award, 1990; Guggenheim fellow, 1962, 65 Achievements include being called the most interesting opera composer writing in America today. Office: U Chgo Dept Music Chicago IL 60637 E-mail: eat2@midway.uchicago.edu.

EATON, LARRY RALPH, lawyer; b. Quincy, Ill., Aug. 18, 1944; s. Roscoe Ralph and Velma Marie (Beckett) E.; m. Janet Claire Rosen, Oct. 28, 1978. BA, Western Ill. U., 1965; JD, U. Mich., 1968. Bar: Ill. 1968, U.S. Dist. Ct. (no. dist.) Ill. 1978, U.S. Ct. Appeals (D.C. cir.) 1984, U.S. Ct. Appeals (7th cir.) 1989, N.Y. 1997. Vol., instr. law U. Liberia Sch. Law, U.S. Peace Corps, Monrovia, 1968-70; lawyer Forest Park Found., Peoria Heights, Ill., 1970-71; asst. atty. gen. State of Ill., Springfield, 1971-75; ptnr. Peterson & Ross and predecessors, Chgo., 1975-94; founder Blatt, Hammesfahr & Eaton, 1994-2000; sr. mem. Cozen O'Connor, 2000—. Instr. environ. law Quincy Coll., Ill., 1973-75. Mem. Young Men's Jewish Coun., Chgo., 1974—84; trustee Edgewater Cmty. Coun., 2000—; pres.

Lakewood Balmoral Residents' Coun., 2000—02; bd. dirs. Near North Montessori Sch., 1989—95, vice chmn., 1992—95; bd. dirs. Edgewater Devel. Corp., 0200—. Contbg. writer Chgo. Daily Law Bull., 1975-77; field editor Pollution Engring., 1976. Fellow: Ill. Bar Found. (charter); mem.: ABA (environ. ins. litig. task force 1990—), Bar Assn. for 7th Jud. Cir., Chgo. Bar Assn., Ill. Bar Assn. (chmn. environ. control law sect. 1976—77, coun. 1973—77, 1990—94, editor sect. newsletter 1972—77, assembly 1980—86, 1989—92, coun. jud. evaluation Cook County 2000—), Atticus Finch Inn of Ct., Lawyers Club Chgo., Law Club Chgo.

EATON, MERRILL THOMAS, psychiatrist, educator; b. Howard County, Ind., June 25, 1920; s. Merrill Thomas and Dorothy (Whiteman) E.; m. Louise Foster, Dec. 23, 1942; children: Deirdre Ann, Thomas Anthony, David Foster. AB, Ind. U., Bloomington, 1941, MD, 1944. Diplomate: Am. Bd. Psychiatry. Intern St. Elizabeth's Hosp., Washington, 1944-45; resident Sheppard and Enoch Pratt Hosp., Towson, Md., 1948-49; pvt. practice medicine specializing in psychiatry Kansas City, Kans., 1949-60, Omaha, 1960-2000; dir. Nebr. Psychiat. Inst., 1968-85; assoc. in psychiatry Kans. U. Sch. Medicine, 1949-50, asst. prof., 1951-54, assoc. prof., 1954-60; assoc. prof. psychiatry U. Nebr. Coll. Medicine, 1960-63, prof., 1963-88, prof. emeritus, 1989—, chmn. dept. psychiatry, 1968-85; psychiatrist Immanuel Mental Health Ctr., 1986-88; pvt. practice cons. Omaha, 1989-2000. Author: Psychiatry, 1967, 5th edit., 1985, (with David Kentsmith) Treating Sexual Problems in Medical Practice, 1979. Served to capt. U.S. Army, 1945-47. Fellow ACP, Am. Psychiat. Assn.; mem. Group for Advancement Psychiatry (chmn. com. on mental health services 1970-73, chmn. publ. bd. 1976-83, cons. pub. bd. 1983—, bd. dirs. 1984-86), Nebr. Med. Assn., Nebr. Psychiat. Soc. (pres. 1973-75). E-mail: mteaton1@cox.net.

EATON, ROBERT JAMES, retired automotive executive; b. Buena Vista, Colo., Feb. 13, 1940; s. Eugene Hiram and Mildred Inez (Stokes) E.; m. Cornelia Cae Drake, June 28, 1964; children: Scott C., Matthew D. BSME, U. Kans., 1963. Exec. engr. engring. staff GM, Warren, Mich., 1974-75, chief engr. small family car project Chevrolet div., 1975-76, chief engr. corp. car programs engring. staff, 1976-79, asst. chief Oldsmobile div. Lansing, 1979-82, dir. reliability, 1982, v.p. advanced product and mfg. engring. staff Detroit, 1982-86, v.p. and group exec. Tech. Staffs Group, 1986-88; pres. GM Europe, Zurich, Switzerland, 1988-92; vice chmn., COO, Chrysler Corp., Auburn Hills, Mich., 1992-93, chmn., CEO, pres., from 1993; chmn. Daimler Chrysler Corp., until 2000. Chmn. bd. dirs. SAAB Automobile; bd. dirs. Internat. Paper Co. Mem. indsl. adv. coun. Coll. Engring., Stanford U., 1986—, U. Mich.; chmn. indsl. adv. group Stanford Inst. for Mfg. and Automation, 1984-86; bd. chmn. Met. Ctr. for High Tech., 1982-88; chmn. Detroit Renaissance; dir. United Way of Southeastern Mich., Econ. Alliance for Mich., Detroit Symphony Orch., Mich. Leaders Health Care Group. Chevalier du Tastevin, 1989—. Fellow Soc. Automotive Engrs. (chmn. tech. bd. 1986-87, fin. com. 1985—, chmn. Engring. Expo), Engring. Soc. Detroit (co-chmn. membership com. 1986-87, bd. dirs.); mem. NAE, Am. Automobile Mfrs. Assn. (chmn., dir.), Indsl. Tech. Inst. (bd. dirs. 1982-85), Electronic Data Systems (bd. dirs. 1984-89), Group Lotus (bd. dirs.), Bus. Coun., Bus. Roundtable, U.S./Japan Bus. Coun., Pres.'s Adv. Com. on Trade Policy & Negotiations. Office: Daimler Chrysler Corp 1000 Chrysler Dr Auburn Hills MI 48326-2766

EBBEN, JAMES ADRIAN, college president; V.p. planning/resource allocation Siena Heights Coll., Adrian, Mich., 1986-87; pres. Edgewood Coll., Madison, Wis., 1987—. Office: Edgewood Coll Office of Pres 1000 Edgewood College Dr Madison WI 53711-1958

EBBERS, LARRY HAROLD, education educator; b. Rockwell, Iowa, June 17, 1941; s. Harold Theodore and Gertrude Elanor (Robeoltmann) E.; m. Barbara Ellen Smith, June 17, 1962; children: Lori Ann, Kimberly Jo. BS, Iowa State U., 1962, MS, 1968, PhD, 1971. Vocat. agrl. instr. Iowa Falls (Iowa) Sch., 1962-63, Spencer (Iowa) Schs., 1963-65; asst. dir. residences Iowa State U., Ames, 1965-72, asst. prof., 1972-75, assoc. prof., 1975-80, prof. edn., 1981—, dept. chair, prof. studies in edn., 1983-93, asst. to dean Coll. Edn., 1972-76, asst. dean Coll. Edn., 1976-83, assoc. dean, 1996-2000. Contbr. articles to profl. jours. Bd. dirs. Ames Parks and Recreation Commn., 1983-86, Iowa State U. Meml. Union, 1989-94; pres. Ctrl. Iowa Regional Substance Abuse Ctr., Ames, 1984-85, Meeker Sch. PTO, Ames, 1975-76; mem. task force on campus ministry Am. Luth. Ch., Des Moines, 1979-84; bd. regents Waldorf Coll., Iowa, 1999—. Recipient Outstanding Young Alumnus award, 1976, Outstanding Acad. Adv. award, 1977, Human Rels. award Human Rels. Commn., 1984, Human rels. award Student Affairs Divsn., 1985, Outstanding Faculty Citation award, 1991, Cardinal Key Leadership Hon., 1995, Golden Key Honor Soc., 1996, Pres.'s Disting. Svc. award, 1999, Regents award for faculty excellence, 2001, all from Iowa State U.; Rotary Found. fellow, Brazil, 1977; Fulbright scholar, Germany, 2000. Mem. Nat. Assn. Student Pers. Adminstrs. (dir. rsch. and program devel. 1979-81, chmn. Am. Coun. on Edn. Inst. 1984-86, editor jour. 1981-84, pres. 1987-88, v.p. Found. 1989-92, Disting. Svc. award 1990, Fred Turner award 1991, nat. conf. program chair 1992, chair Acad. Leadership & Exec. Effectivness, dir. acad. leadership & exec. effectiveness, 2002-, Robert Shaffer award for academic excellence as a grad. faculty mem. 1996), Kiwanis (Ames pres. 1977-78), Phi Delta Kappa, Phi Kappa Phi (pres. 1977-79, centennial medalist 1997). Lutheran. Avocations: athletics, spectator sports, jogging, mng. family farm. Home: 220 24th St Ames IA 50010-4832 Office: Iowa State U N226 N Lagomarcino Hl Ames IA 50011-0001

EBERHARD, WILLIAM THOMAS, architect; b. St. Louis, Apr. 11, 1952; s. George Walter and Bettie Alma (Seilkop) E.; m. Cynthia Ann Hardy, Aug. 20, 1977 (div. 1981); m. Linda W. Bayer, Dec. 5, 1986; children: Elena Lynn, Alysse Marie. BArch, U. Cin., 1976; postgrad., Archtl. Assn., London, 1974. Registered arch. Ohio, Mich., Pa., Fla., D.C., Ill., Mo. V.p. Visnapuu & Assocs., Inc., Cleve., 1972-82; prin.-in-charge Oliver Design Group, 1983—. V.p., prin.-in-charge Grubb & Ellis, Cleve., Detroit, Pitts., 1989-90, Grubb & Ellis Nat. Accounts Team, 1987-90. Author: Public Interiors, 1986, 2d edit., 1996, Professional Office Design, 1988, Docket, 1988, Facility Design & Management, 1990, 91, Interior Design, 1992, Contract Design, 1995, Architecture Record Lighting, 1996, Facility Management Journal, 1996; contbr. articles to profl. jours. Profl. team leader Inst. Urban Design, Cleve., 1983; mem. evangelism com. First Bapt. Ch. of Greater Cleve., 1990—. Recipient Best Comml. Interior Design Project award NAIOP, 1991-96, 2000, Best Office Interior Design Project award, 1992, Best Renovation Project, 1995, Design award Nat. Inst. Bus., 1992, 93, Best Comml. Space, 1993, NAIOP Design award Best Pub. Space, 1993, Best Comml. Interior Design, 1994, 95, 96, 97, 2000, Best Renovation Project, 1995, 1st Pl. award Build Ohio Competition, 1992, AIA, 1993, Cleve. Chpt. Design award AIA, 1993, 94, 99, Ohio Area Design awards AIA, 1994-95, Internat. Int. Design awards, 1992, 94, 95, Best of Show, First Place Large Corp. Category, Details Category, Award of Merit Details Category, Award of Merit Retail Category IIDA Regional Design Awards Program, 1998. Mem. AIA (chpt. sec. 1982-84, 2 Design awards 1993, 1 Design award 1994), Internat. Facility Mgrs. Assn., Cleve. Art Assn., Nat. Trust for Hist. Preservation, Inst. Urban Design, Am. Soc. Interior Designers (assoc.), Seminotic Soc. Am. (founding), Design Forum of Cleve. (founding 1990—, pres. 1991—), Club Soc. Ctr. (founding), Cleve. Design Task Force (founding pres. 1996—), Shaker Heights Country Club (house com., design com.), Union Club of Cleve. Avocations: drawing, photography, tennis, snowmobiling, golf. Home: 2867 Torrington Rd Shaker Heights OH 44122-2555 Office: Oliver Design Group One Park Pla 1111 Chester Ave Cleveland OH 44114-3516 E-mail: wte@odgarch.com.

EBERLE, TERRY R. editor, newspaper executive; With Chronicle-Tribune, Marion, Ind., mng. editor; with The Herald-Dispatch, Huntington, W.Va., 1971—75; editor The Times in Shreveport, 1990—92, N Hills News-Record, Valley News Dispatch, 1992—95; exec. editor The News-Press; v.p., editor The Indianapolis Star, 2001—. Address: PO Box 145 Indianapolis IN 46206-0145 Office: Indianapolis Star 307 N Pennsylvania St Indianapolis IN 46204*

EBERLEY, HELEN-KAY, opera singer, classical record company executive, poet; b. Sterling, Ill., Aug. 3, 1947; d. William Elliott and P. (Conneely) E. MusB, Northwestern U., 1970, MusM, 1971. Chmn., pres., artistic coord. Eberley Inc., Evanston, Ill., 1973-92; founder H.K.E. Enterprises, 1993—, pres., 1993—; circulation libr. Evanston Pub. Libr., 1995-98. Founder EB-SKO Prodns., 1976-92, tchr., coach, 1976—; exec. dir., performance cons. E-S Mgmt., 1985-92; featured artist Honors Concert, Northwestern U., 1970, Alumni Concert, 1999, Master Class and guest lectr. various colls. and univs.; host Poetry in Process monthly seminar Barnes & Noble; music lectr. rep. Harvard Club, Chgo.; numerous TV and radio talk show appearances and interviews. Operatic debut in Peter Grimes, Lyric Opera, Chgo., 1974; starred in: Cosi Fan Tutte, Le Nozze Di Figaro, Dido and Aeneas, La Boheme, Faust, Tosca, La Traviata, Falstaff, Don Giovanni, Brigadoon, others; jazz appearances with Duke Ellington, Dave Brubeck and Robert Shaw; performing artist Oglebay Opera Inst., Wheeling, W.Va., 1968, WTTW TV/PBS, Chgo., 1968; solo star in: Continental Bank Concerts, 1981-89, United Airlines-Schubert, Schumann, Brahms, Mendelssohn, Faure, Mozart, Duparc/Wolf, Supersta. WFMT Radio, Chgo., 1982-90; featured artist with North Shore Concert Band, 1989; starring artist South Bend Symphony, 1990, Mo. Symphony Soc., 1990, Milw. Symphony, 1990; spl. guest artist New Studios Gala Sta. WFMT, 1995, West Valley Fine Arts Concert Series, Phoenix, 1999; prodr.-annotator Gentlemen Gypsy, 1978, Strauss and Szymanowski, 1979, One Sonata Each: Franck and Szymanowski, 1982; starring artist-exec. prodr. Separate But Equal, 1976, All Brahms, 1977, Opera Lady, 1978, Eberley Sings Strauss, 1980, Helen-Kay Eberley: American Girl, 1983, Helen-Kay Eberley: Opera Lady II, 1984; performed Am. and Can. nat. anthems for Chgo. Cubs Baseball Team, 1977-83, Chgo. Bears Football, 1977; also starred in numerous concert recital and symphony appearances, Europe, Can., U.S.; author: Angel's Song, 1994, The Magdaleva Poems, 1995, ChapelHeart, 1996, Desert Dancing, 1997, Canyon Ridge, 2000, Rivervoice, 2002. Docent, new mem. tour guide Art Inst. Chgo.; spl. events hotline vol. Art Inst. Chgo., Chgo. Christian Indsl. League, St. Joseph's Table of St. Peter's in the Loop, Chgo.; vol., facilitator City Yr. Chgo.-Urban Peace Corps; Chgo. Humanities Festival VIII of Ill. Humanities Coun., Evanston Shelter for Battered Women, Rape Victim Adv., Habitat for Humanity; Midwest Vol. Facilitator 1st Indsl. Realty Trust; mem. Mayor's founding com. Evanston Arts Coun., 1974-75; judge Ice-Skating Competition, Wilmette (Ill.) Park Dist., 1974-77, bd. dirs., 1973-77; bd. dirs. Ctr. for Voice, Chgo., 1994-96; vol. Saints-Usher Corps of Chgo., 1998-99. Recipient Creative and Performing Arts award Ind. Jr. Miss. and South Bend Jr. Miss, 1965, Milton J. Cross award Met. Opera Guild, 1968; prize winner Met. Opera. Nat. Auditions, 1968, 1st pl. prize for The Pond, Chicagoland Poetry Contest, 1997, 1st pl. prize and Best of the Best award for The Rose Garden, 1999; F.K. Weyerhauser scholar Met. Opera, 1967. Mem. People for Ethical Treatment of Animals, Am. Soc. for Prevention of Cruelty to Animals, Assisi Animal Found., Am. Guild Mus. Artists, Internat. Platform Assn., Whale Adoption Project, Amnesty Internat., Environ. Def. Fund, Doris Day Animal Found., Poets and Patrons, Humane Soc., Greenpeace, Physicians Com. for Responsible Medicine, St. Mary's Acad. Alumnae Assn., Delta Gamma. Office: HKE Enterprises 1726 Sherman Ave Evanston IL 60201-5619

EBERT, DOROTHY ELIZABETH, county clerk; b. Beaver Dam, Wis., Apr. 16, 1941; d. Merlin Herman and Gertrude Elizabeth (Hupke) E. Grad. high sch., Beaver Dam. Sec., receptionist Household Fin. Corp., Beaver Dam, 1958-67; dep. county clk. Dodge County, Juneau, Wis., 1967-82, county clk., 1983—. Past bd. dirs. Dodge County chpt. Am. Cancer Soc. Mem. Wis. County Clks. Assn. (historian 1994-95, treas. 1995-96, sec. 1996-97, v.p. 1997-98, pres. 1998-99). Republican. Lutheran. Avocations: bowling, golf, calligraphy, singing, bell choir. Office: County Clk Office 127 E Oak St Juneau WI 53039-1329

EBERT, DOUGLAS EDMUND, banker; b. Washington, Oct. 21, 1945; s. Edmund Francis and Lathelia Marie (Keesey) E.; m. Linda Sue Weick, June 24, 1994; children: Elizabeth Anne, Leslie Anne, Kevin Edward, Ashley Edward. B.A., Williams Coll., 1968. Asst. sec. Mfrs. Hanover Trust Corp., N.Y.C., 1969-72, asst. v.p., 1972-73, v.p., 1973-76, sr. v.p., dep. gen. mgr., 1976-82, exec. v.p., 1982-85, sr. exec. v.p. investment banking sector, 1985-90; pres., CEO S.E. Bank N.A., Miami, 1990-91, also chmn. bd. dirs., 1990-91; with Lincoln Fin. Corp., Fort Wayne, Ind., 1992-93; pres., COO Mich. Nat. Bank, Farmington Hills, 1993-95; CEO Mich. Nat. Bank, Mich. Nat. Corp., 1995—. Pres., chief exec. officer, S.E. Banking Corp., 1990-91, Miami, also bd. dirs.; bd. dirs. HomeSide Internat., Inc., Ind. One Capital Mgmt., Independence One Mortgage Corp., Detroit Renaissance, Detroit Symphony Hall, Detroit Regional C. of C., Detroit Econ. Club; trustee Cranbrook Inst. Sci. Bd. dirs. Cancer Research Ctr. Mem. Com. Econ. Devel., Bankers Assn. Fgn. Trade, U.S. Bus. Council, Bank Adminstrn. Inst., Assn. Res. City Bankers. Avocations: tennis, golf, bicycling, carpentry, reading. Office: Mich Nat Bank 27777 Inkster Rd Farmington Hills MI 48334-5326

EBERT, ROGER JOSEPH, film critic; b. Urbana, Ill., June 18, 1942; s. Walter H. and Annabel (Stumm) E.; m. Chaz Hammelsmith, July 18, 1992. BS, U. Ill., 1964; postgrad., U. Cape Town, South Africa, 1965, U. Chgo., 1966-67; LHD (hon.), U. Colo., 1993. Editor Daily Illini, 1963-64; pres. U.S. Student Press Assn., 1963-64; staff writer News-Gazette, Champaign-Urbana, Ill., 1958-66; film critic Chgo. Sun-Times, 1967—, US mag., 1978-79, NBC-TV News, Chgo., 1980-83, ABC-TV News, Chgo., 1984—, N.Y. Post, N.Y.C., 1986-88, N.Y. Daily News, 1988-92, Compu Serve, 1991—; pres. Ebert Co., Ltd., 1981—; Microsoft Cinemania, 1994-97; columnist Yahoo Internet Life mag., 1997—. Instr. English Chgo. City Coll., 1967-68; lectr. film criticism, fine arts program U. Chgo., 1969— ; Kluge fellow U. Va., 1995-96, adj. prof. U. Ill., 2000—; lectr. film Columbia Coll., Chgo., 1973-74, 77-80; cons. Nat. Endowments for Arts and Humanities, 1972-77; juror film festivals. Co-host (TV shows) Sneak Previews, PBS, 1976-82, At the Movies, syndicated, 1982-86, Siskel & Ebert, syndicated, 1986—; broadcaster: Movie News, ABC Radio, 1982-85; author: An Illini Century, 1967, (screenplay) Beyond the Valley of the Dolls, 1970, Beyond Narrative: The Future of the Feature Film, 1978, A Kiss Is Still a Kiss, 1984, Roger Ebert's Movie Home Companion, 1986-93, Roger Ebert's Video Companion, 1994-98, (with Daniel Curley) The Perfect London Walk, 1986, Two Weeks in the Midday Sun, 1987, Behind the Phantom's Mask, 1993, Ebert's Little Movie Glossary, 1994, Roger Ebert's Book of Film, 1996, Questions for the Movie Answer Man, 1997, Roger Ebert's Movie Yearbook, 1998—, Ebert's Bigger Little Movie Glossary, 1999, I Hated, Hated, Hated This Movie, 2000; co-author: The Future of the Movies, The Computer Insectiary, 1994. Recipient Overseas Press club, 1963, award Chgo. Headline Club, 1963, award Chgo. Newspaper Guild, 1973, Pulitzer prize, 1975, Emmy award, 1979, Peter Lisagor award, 1998, Online Film Critics Soc. Best Movie Website award, 1999; inducted into Chgo. Journalism Hall of Fame, 1997; Rotary fellow, 1965, Kluge fellow in film studies U. Va., 1995-96. Mem. Newspaper Guild, Writers Guild Am. West, Nat. Soc. Film Critics, Acad. TV Arts and Scis., Arts Club of Chgo., Cliff Dwellers, Acad. Club (London), Sigma Delta Chi, Phi Delta Theta. Avocations: drawing, painting, art collecting. Office: Chgo Sun-Times Inc 401 N Wabash Ave Rm 110 Chicago IL 60611-5642

EBNER, KURT EWALD, biochemistry educator; b. New Westminster, B.C., Can., Mar. 30, 1931; s. Sebastian Alois and Martha (Gmundner) E.; m. Dorothy Colleen Reader, May 4, 1957; children: Roger, Michael, Colleen, Paul. B.S.A., U. B.C., 1955, M.S.A., 1957; Ph.D., U. Ill., 1960; postdoctoral, U. Reading, Eng., 1960-61, U. Minn., 1961-62. Diplomate Nat. Bd. Med. Examiners. Mem. faculty Okla. State U., Stillwater, 1962-74, prof. biochemistry, 1969-71, Regents prof., 1971-74; chmn. dept. biochemistry U. Kans. Med. Ctr., Kansas City, 1974-94, prof., 1994-98, prof. emeritus, 1998—. Can. Overseas Postdoctoral fellow, 1960; recipient NIH Career Devel. award, 1969, Borden award Am. Chem. Soc., 1969; Okla. State U. Sigma Xi lectr., 1970 Mem. AAAS, Am. Soc. Biol. Chemistry, Coun. Acad. Socs., Sigma Xi, Phi Kappa Phi, Gamma Sigma Delta. Presbyterian (elder). Office: U Kans Med Ctr Dept Biochem Kansas City KS 66103-7421

EBY, MARTIN KELLER, JR. construction company executive; b. Wichita Falls, Tex., Apr. 19, 1934; s. Martin and A. Pauline (Kimbell) E.; m. Melodee Stanley, Aug. 20, 1955; children: Stanley, Suzanna, David. B.S. in Civil Engring, Kans. State U., 1956. Registered profl. engr., Kan. With Martin K. Eby Constrn. Co., Inc., Wichita, Kan., 1956—, engr., project mgr., v.p., 1956-67, pres., 1967-92, chmn., 1979—. Bd. dirs. Intrust Bank in Wichita, Intrust Fin. Corp., SBC Comms. Inc.; mem. engring. adv. coun. Kans. State U., Manhattan, 1970—. Bd. dirs. Kans. Pub. Policy Inst., chmn.; mem. Kans. State U. Coll. of Engring. Hall of Fame, 1989—; chmn. Constrn. Industry Polit. Action Com. of Kans., Topeka, 1978. Mem. ASCE, NSPE, Kans. Engring. Soc., Wichita Profl. Engring. Soc., Chief Execs. Orgn., Beavers (bd. dirs., pres. 1996-97), Moles (hon.). Congregationalist. Home: 624 N Longford Ln Wichita KS 67206-1818 Office: Martin Eby Constrn Co Inc PO Box 1679 610 N Main St Wichita KS 67203-3601

ECCARIUS, SCOTT, state official, eye surgeon; m. Alison Eccarius. Degree, U. S.D. Majority whip S.D. Ho. Reps., spkr. pro tempore, Spkr. of Ho. Dist. 34, 2001—. Mem.: State Affairs Com., Edn. Com. (chmn.), Taxation Com. (chmn.), Ho. Edn. Com. (past chmn.), Edn. and Legis. Procedures Com. (chmn.). Republican. Home: 4780 Carriage Hills Dr Rapid City SD 57702 Business E-Mail: NemoSD@aol.com.*

ECHOLS, M(ARY) EVELYN, travel consultant; b. LaSalle, Ill., Apr. 5, 1915; d. Francis Ira and Mary Irene (Coleman) Bassett; m. David H. Echols, Aug. 31, 1951 (dec.); children: Susan Echols O'Donnell, William. Grad. high. sch., Chgo. Founder Internat. Travel Tng. Courses, Inc., Chgo., 1962—; pres. Evelyn Echols Cons. Ltd., 1998. Bd. dirs. Conv. and Tourism Bur.; past pres. Pres. Reagan's Adv. Com. for Women's Bus. Ownership; v.p. United Cerebral Palsy Assn., Ptnrs. in Home Care; mem. Women's Internat. Forum. Named Entrepreneur of Yr. Women Bus. Owners N.Y., 1985, Bus. Woman of Yr. Nat. Assn. Women Bus. Owners, 1985, Crain's Chgo. Bus., 1993; named to Chgo.'s Hall of Fame, 1992. Mem.: Soc. Am. Travel Agts., Acad. TV Arts and Scis., Chgo. Execs. Club. Home and Office: # 403 155 N Harbor Dr Chicago IL 60601

ECK, GEORGE GREGORY, lawyer; b. Evanston, Ill., Sept. 3, 1950; s. George F. and Dorothy E. (Frake) E.; m. Margaret K. Gorman, Sept. 1, 1973; children: Jessica Elizabeth, Michelle Margaret. BS, No. Ill. U., 1972; JD cum laude, U. Minn., 1977. Bar: Minn. 1977, U.S. Dist. Ct. Minn. 1977, U.S. Ct. Appeals (8th cir.) 1977. Assoc. Dorsey & Whitney, Mpls., 1977-83, ptnr., 1983—. Mem. editorial bd. U. Minn. Law Rev., 1977. With U.S. Army, 1972—74. Home: 6413 Mendelssohn Ln Hopkins MN 55343-8424 Office: Dorsey & Whitney 220 S 6th St Ste 2200 Minneapolis MN 55402-1498

ECKERT, ERNST R. G. mechanical engineering educator; b. Prague, Czech Republic, Sept. 13, 1904; came to U.S., 1945, naturalized, 1955; s. Georg and Margarete (Pfrogner) E.; m. Josefine Binder, Jan. 30, 1931; children: Rosemarie Christa Eckert Kohler, Elke, Karin Eckert Winter, Dieter. Diploma Ing., German Inst. Tech., Prague, 1927, Dr.Ing., 1931; Dr. habil., Inst. Technology, Danzig, 1938; Dozent, Inst. of Technol., Braunschweig, Germany, 1940; hon. doctorates, Inst. Tech., Munich, 1968, Purdue U., 1968, U. Manchester, Eng., 1968, U. Notre Dame, 1970, Poly. Inst. Romania, Jassy, 1973, U. Minn., 1995, Czech Republic, 1999. Chief engr., lectr. Inst. Technology, Danzig, 1934-38; sect. chief thermodynamics Aero. Research Inst., Braunschweig, 1938-45; prof., dir. Inst. Technology, Prague, 1943-45; cons. USAF, 1945-49, Lewis Flight Propulsion Lab., NASA, 1949-51; prof. mech. engring. dept. U. Minn., 1951-73, dir. thermodynamics and heat transfer and of heat transfer lab., 1955-73, Regents' prof. emeritus mech. engring., 1973—. Former vis. prof. Purdue U.; former cons. Gen. Electric Co., Trane Co.; U.S. rep. aerodynamics panel Internat. Com. Flame Radiation Author: (with Drake) Introduction to the Transfer of Heat and Mass, 1950, 2d edit., 1959, Heat and Mass Transfer, (translated by J.F. Gross), 1963; others in German, Russian, and Chinese, (with Goldstein) Measurement Techniques in Heat Transfer, 1970, 2d edit., 1976, (with Drake) Analysis of Heat and Mass Transfer, 1972; Chmn. hon. editorial adv. bd. Internat. Jour. Heat and Mass Transfer; former editor: Thermal Scis. series, Wadsworth Pub. Co., Belmont, Cal.; editor: Thermo and Fluid Dynamics; co-chmn. adv. editorial bd.: Heat Transfer-Japanese Research; co-editor: Energy Developments in Japan; chmn. hon. editorial adv. bd.: Letters in Heat and Mass Transfer; editorial adv. bd.: Numerical Heat Transfer; contbr. articles to sci. mags. Mem. Nat. Commn. Fire Prevention and Control, 1970-73. Recipient Max Jacob Meml. award, 1961, Disting. Teaching award U. Minn., 1965, award Western Electric Fund, 1965, gold medal French Inst. Energy and Fuel, 1967, Vincent Bendix award, 1972, Alexander von Humboldt U.S. sr. scientist award, 1980, A.V. Luikov medal, 1979, Aircraft Gas Turbine Tech. award, 1994, gold medal Czech Acad. Sci., 1994, Founders award Nat. Acad. of Engring., 1995; rsch. fellow Japan Soc. Promotion Sci., 1982. Fellow N.Y. Acad. Scis., AIAA; mem. ASME (hon.), NAE (Gold medal and Founders award 1995), Wissenschaftliche Gesellschaft für Luft und Raumfahrt, Sigma Xi, Pi Tau Sigma, Tau Beta Pi. Home: 60 W Wentworth Ave West Saint Paul MN 55118-3881 Office: Mech Engring Dept U Minn Minneapolis MN 55455

ECKERT, RALPH JOHN, insurance company executive; b. Milw., Mar. 12, 1929; s. John C. and Vlasta (Stauber) E.; m. Greta M. Allen, July 11, 1953; children: Maura Eckert Benseler, Peter, Thomas, Karen Eckert Schmidt, Edward. BS, U. Wis., 1951. With Trustmark Life Ins. Co., Lake Forest, Ill., 1954—; chmn. bd., chief exec. officer Benefit Trust Life Ins. Co., Chgo., 1971-91; chmn. bd. of pensions Evang. Luth. Ch. Am., Mpls., 1991-97; chmn. bd. Trustmark Life Ins. Co., Lake Forest, Ill., 1991-97, chmn. emeritus, 1997—. Bd. dirs. Prin. Preservation Mutual Funds, 1996—. With AUS, 1951-53. Fellow Soc. Actuaries; mem. Am. Acad. Actuaries, Ill. Life Ins. Coun. (chmn. 1978-79), Ill. Life & Health Ins. Guaranty Assn. (chmn. 1980-81), Health Ins. Assn. Am. (bd. dirs., chmn. 1984-85), Am. Coun. Life Ins. (bd. dirs. 1986-88), Masons. Lutheran. Office: Trustmark Life Ins Co 400 N Field Dr Lake Forest IL 60045-4809

ECKERT, ROGER E(ARL), chemical engineering educator; b. Lakewood, Ohio, Aug. 8, 1926; s. Elmer George and Elsie V. (Schwede) E.; children: Roger Earl, Rhonda Carol, Robyn Claire. B.S., Princeton U., 1948; M.S., U. Ill., 1949, Ph.D., 1951. Process devel. engr., indsl. and biochems. dept. E.I. duPont de Nemours & Co., Inc., Wilmington, Del., 1951-64, math. cons., 1956-60, sr. research engr., engring. research lab. and elastomers chems. dept., 1960-64; assoc. prof. Purdue U., West Lafayette, Ind., 1964-73; asst. head Sch. Chem. Engring., 1970-75, prof. chem. engring., 1973—. Vis. prof. U. Colo., 1971, U. Wis., 1981; Am. Soc. Engring. Edn.-NASA faculty fellow Case Western Res. U. and Lewis Research Center, 1966-67 Contbr. tech. articles to profl. jours. Served with U.S. Army, 1946-47. Mem. Am. Inst. Chem. Engrs., Phi Beta Kappa,

Sigma Xi, Phi Lambda Upsilon, Pi Mu Epsilon, Alpha Chi Sigma. Presbyterian. Home: 153 Indian Rock Dr West Lafayette IN 47906-1255 Office: Sch Chem Engring Purdue U West Lafayette IN 47906

ECKSTEIN, JOHN WILLIAM, physician, educator; b. Central City, Iowa, Nov. 23, 1923; s. John William and Alice (Ellsworth) Eckstein; m. Imogene O'Brien, June 16, 1947; children: John Alan, Charles William, Margaret Ann, Thomas Cody, Steven Gregory. BS, Loras Coll., 1946; MD, U. Iowa, 1950; DSc (hon.) , Ind. U., 1995. Asst. prof. internal medicine U. Iowa, Iowa City, 1956—60, assoc. prof., 1960—65, prof., 1965—92, prof. emeritus, 1993; assoc. dean VA Hosp. affairs, 1969—70, dean coll. medicine, 1970-91, dean emeritus, 1993. Chmn. cardiovasc. study sect. NIH, 1970—72, Nat. Heart, Lung and Blood Adv. Coun., 1974—78; mem. adv. com. to dir. NIH, 1990—95. Author papers and abstracts. Mem. VA Manpower Study Group, 1988—92. Served with USAAF, 1943—45. Named established investigator, Am. Heart Assn., 1958—63, in his honor, Eckstein Med. Rsch. Bldg., U. Iowa, 1988; recipient Rsch. Career award, USPHS, 1963—70, Dist. Alumni Svc. award, U. Iowa, 1994, Disting. Physicians, Dept. Vets. Affairs, 1995—98; fellow postdoctoral, Rockefeller Found., 1953—54, Am. Heart Assn. Rsch., 1954—55, spl. rsch., Nat. Heart Inst., 1955—56. Mem.: Assn. Acad. Health Ctrs. (mem. sci. policy study group 1988—93), Inst. Medicine, Assn. Am. Med. Colls. (exec. coun. 1981—82, adminstrv. bd. 1980—82, 1985—86), Assn. Am. Physicians, Am. Clin. and Climatol. Assn., Am. Soc. Clin. Investigation, Ctrl. Soc. Clin. Rsch. (sec.-treas. 1965—70, pres. 1973—74), Am. Fedn. Clin. Rsch. (chmn. Midwestern sect. 1965), AMA (mem. health policy agenda panel 1982—86, mem. study sect. faculty and resh. 1985—86, governing. coun. sect. on med. schs. 1985—95, alt. del. Ho. of Dels. 1986—90, del. 1990—92, Disting. Svc. award 1992), Am. Heart Assn. (v.p. 1969, chmn. coun. on circulation 1969—71, pres. 1978—79). Home: 1415 William White Blvd Iowa City IA 52245-4443 Office: U Iowa Hosps & Clinics Iowa City IA 52242-1101 E-mail: john-eckstein@uiowa.edu.

ECONOMUS, PETER CONSTANTINE, judge; s. Constantine G. Economus; m. Marie Misko, June 29, 1968; children: Paula, Kristine, Jennifer. BA, Youngstown (Ohio) State U., 1967; JD, Akron U., 1970. Bar: Ohio, 1971. Ptnr. Economus, Economus & Economus; judge Ct. Common Pleas, Mahoning County, Ohio, 1982-95; U.S. dist. judge No. Dist. Ohio, Youngstown, 1995—. Apptd. mentor new judges, vis. judge various Ohio Ct. Appeals Chmn. Cmty. Corrections Planning Bd., 1987-91; former trustee Ohio Common Please Judges Assn., legis. com.; trustee U. Akron Sch. Law Alumni Assn, 1989-95; mem. com. celebrate bi-centennial U.S. Constn. Youngstown State U.; mem. adv. bd. State Victims, 1986-95; trustee Butler Inst. Am. Art, 2000. Recipient Outstanding Citizen's award Buckeye Elks Lodge #73, 1988, Pub. Svc. award Cmty. Corrections Assn., 1989, Office Holder of Yr. Truman Johnson Women's Dem. Club, 1990, Gt. Communicator award cmty. svc. Youngstown Hearing & Speech Ctr., 1995, Outstanding Alumni award U. Akron Law Alumni Assn., 1996, Ellis Island medal of honor, 1999, Outstanding Alumni award Youngstown State U., 2000. Mem. Am. Judges Assn. Office: US Courthouse 125 Market St Youngstown OH 44503-1780

EDDIE, RUSSELL JAMES, state legislator, sales executive; b. Wayne, Nebr., June 9, 1938; s. Robert Alex and Myrtle (Kruse) E.; m. Gladys Ann Pederson, Aug. 6, 1960; children: Julie, Thomas, Robert, Steven. BA, Buena Vista Coll., 1960. Tchr. Clayton Pentral Cmty. Sch., Royal, Iowa, 1961-66; farmer Storm Lake, 1966-89; mem. Iowa Ho. of Reps., 1989—; sales exec. E-D Assocs., Storm Lake, 1991—. Mem. BU County Hist. Soc., Pork Prodrs. Assn., Farm Bur., Kiwanis Internat. Republican. Lutheran. Avocations: little league coaching, sports, reading, collecting farm toys. Home: 1101 Pierce Dr Storm Lake IA 50588-2744

EDDY, CHARLES ALAN, chiropractor; b. Kansas City, Mo., Feb. 20, 1948; s. Sam Albert and Ella Louise (Gani) E.; m. Donna Darlene Perry, Oct. 23, 1971. Student, U. Mo., Kansas City, 1967; D in Chiropractic, Cleveland Chiropractic, Kansas City, 1970. Diplomate Nat. Bd. Chiropractic Examiners. Pvt. practice, Kansas City, 1970—. Peer rev. bd. Blue Cross and Blue Shield, Kansas City, 1972; pres. hon. bd. govs. Bapt. Hosp., Kansas City, 1993-94; cons. Quality Corp., Overland Park, Kans., 1988. Leader, profl. musician Chuck Eddy Band, Kansas City, 1964—; res. officer Kansas City Police Dept., 1970-77, sgt., 1977-82, capt., 1982-94; vice chmn. Citizens Assn., 1995-98, candidate for City Coun., Kansas City, 1995; mem. pub. improvement adv. com. City of Kansas City, 1997-98; city councilperson 6th Dist., bd. mem. mid am. reg. coun., Kansas City, Mo., 1 v.p., 2001—; bd. dirs. Econ. Devel. Coun., 1999—, 1st v.p., 2001—; bd. dirs. Mid Am. Regional Coun., 1999—. Mem. Am. Chiropractic Assn., Mo. State Chriopractic Assn., Mo. Dist. II Chiropractic Assn. (bd. dirs., v.p. 1998—), Cleve. Chiropractic Coll. (trustee 1990, vice chmn. 1992—), Cleve. Chiropractic Alumni Assn. (v.p. 1995-97, pres. 1997-99, bd. dirs. 1990—, amb.'s soc. 1983—, chmn. 1990-96, bd. mem. Truman Med. Ctr.), Optimist Club of Landing (pres. 1980, lt. gov. Mo. dist. 1982), South Kansas City C. of C. (Sml. Bus. of Yr. award 1998), Am. Lebanon Syrian Men's Club (pres. 1988-91, chmn. bd. 1992), St. Andrews Soc. (drummer in pipe band), DeMolay Legion Hon. (sec. 1988, treas. 1990, vice-dean 1991, dean 1992), Pipes and Drums of Ararat (treas. 1977-90, pres. 1985, dir. 1989, 90), Elks, Shriners (Potentate of Ararat shrine temple 1999, publicity chmn. 1991-92), Royal Order Jesters, Order Quetzalcoatl. Episcopalian. Avocations: photography, guns, stereo and video entertainment. Home: 406 W 109th St Kansas City MO 64114-4910 Office: 8301 State Line Rd Ste 108 Kansas City MO 64114-2019

EDDY, DAVID LATIMER, banker; b. Simsbury, Conn., July 3, 1936; s. Edward McChesney and Alberta (Messenger) E.; m. Doris Janeczek, Jan. 7, 1958 (div.); children: Craig, Carol, Dianne, Linda, Elizabeth; m. Gaye Margaret Peterson, May 15, 1976; children: Breese, Taryn, Daniel. BS, U. Conn., 1958; MBA, Harvard U., 1960. Asst. mgr. No. Trust Co., Chgo., 1964-68, 2d v.p., 1968-72, v.p., 1972-85, sr. v.p., 1986—; sr. v.p., treas. No. Trust Corp., 1986—. Mem. Planning Forum, Fin. Execs. Inst. Congregationalist. Clubs: Harvard (Chgo.), Harvard Grad. Bus. Sch. Office: No Trust Corp 50 S La Salle St Chicago IL 60603-1006

EDELMAN, ALVIN, lawyer; b. Chgo., Dec. 12, 1916; m. Rose Marie Slossy, Sept. 22, 1940; children: Marilyn Frances Edelman Snyder, Stephen D., Leon F. BS in Law, Northwestern U., 1938, JD, 1940. Bar: Ill. 1940. Practiced in Chgo., 1940—; pres. Edelman & Edelman, Chartered and predecessors, 1973—; gen. counsel Internat. Coll. Surgeons. Lectr. Internat. Mus. Surg. Sci. and Hall of Fame; chmn. wills and gifts com. Medinah Temple of Masonic Shrine, Chgo., 1975-79; pres. Lawyers Shrine Club of Medinah Temple, 1971-73. Contbr. articles to profl. jours. Fellow Am. Coll. Trust and Estate Counsel; mem. ABA, Ill. Bar Assn., Chgo. Bar Assn. (chmn. grievance com. 1971-72), Phi Beta Kappa (pres. Chgo. area assn. 1975-85), Phi Beta Kappa Fellows (bd. dirs. 1985—, nat. v.p. 1986-95, nat. pres. 1996-2001), Elks (past exalted ruler). Office: 100 W Monroe St Chicago IL 60603-1967

EDELSBERG, SALLY COMINS, physical therapy educator and administrator; b. Rowno, Poland, Aug. 6, 1937; came to U.S., 1949; d. Joseph Luria and and Chana (Bebczuk) Comins; m. Warde C. Pierson, Oct. 8, 1968 (div. 1978); m. Paul Edelsberg, Feb. 2, 1979; 1 child, Tema. BS in Phys. Medicine, U. Wis., 1963; MS, Northwestern U., 1972. Lic. phys. therapist. Staff and supervisory phys. therapist Hines VA Hosp., Maywood, Ill., 1963-67; program dir. Health Careers Council of Ill., Chgo., 1967-70; instr., clin. edn. coordinator Programs in Phys. Therapy, Northwestern U. Med. Sch., 1970-73, dir., assoc. prof., 1973—, dir. devel. and alumni rels., 1999—. Pres. Phys. Therapy Ltd., Chgo., 1986-95; v.p. World Confedn. Phys. Therapy, 1995-99, exec. com., 1991-95. Office: Northwestern U Med Sch Dept of Phys Therapy 645 N Michigan Ave Ste 1100 Chicago IL 60611-2877 E-mail: s-edelsberg@northwestern.edu.

EDELSON, IRA J. venture banker, trade finance executive; b. Chgo., Dec. 30, 1946; s. Alvin L. and Naomi Edelson; m. Starr Gramaila, Feb. 11, 1973; children: Jason Avrum, Megan Anne. BS, DePaul U., 1968. Spl. advisor to chmn. Chgo. Housing Authority, 1983; acting dir. revenue City of Chgo., 1984; ptnr.-in-charge bus. svcs. dept. Deloitte, Haskins & Sells, Chgo., 1979-87; ptnr.-in-charge corp. fin. Deloitte & Touche-U.S. Partnership, 1987-91; pres. Transcap Assocs. Inc., Northbrook, Ill., 1991—. Fin. and policy advisor to mayor City of Chgo., 1984-85; former instr. Northwestern U. Kellogg Sch. Mgmt.; cons., speaker in field. Co-chmn. Chgo. Sports Stadium Commn., 1985. Mem. AICPA, Ill. Soc. CPA's, Nat. Assn. Securities Profls., Nat. Assn. Realtors, Comml. Fin. Assn., Nat. Contract Mgmt. Assn. Office: Transcap Assocs Inc 900 Skokie Blvd Ste 210 Northbrook IL 60062-4031

EDELSTEIN, TERI J. art history educator, art administrator; b. Johnstown, Pa., June 23, 1951; d. Robert Morten and Hulda Lois (Friedhoff) E. BA, U. Pa., 1972, MA, 1977, PhD, 1979; cert., NYU, 1984. Lectr. U. Guelph, Ont., 1977-79; asst. dir. for acad. programs Yale Ctr. Brit. Art, New Haven, 1979-83; dir. Mt. Holyoke Coll. Art Mus., South Hadley, Mass., 1983-90, Skinner Mus., 1983-90, mem. faculty dept. art., 1983-90; dir. Smart Mus. Art U. Chgo., 1990-92, sr. lectr. dept. art, 1990-2000. Dep. dir. Art Inst. Chgo., 1992—99, mus. con., 1999—; mem. adv. bd. Sculpture Chgo., 1991—96, Mus. Loan Network, Knight and Pew Founds., 1994—96. Office: 1648 E 50th St # 6B Chicago IL 60615-3166 Fax: 773-241-9992.

EDELSTEIN, TILDEN GERALD, university official, history educator; b. N.Y.C., June 11, 1931; s. Theodore and Nettie (Strusser) E.; m. Rose Ann Stargardter, Nov. 1, 1970; children: Jordan, Russell. BS, U. Wis., 1953; PhD, Johns Hopkins U., 1961. From instr. to assoc. prof. Simmons Coll., Boston, 1957-67; from adj. assoc. prof. to prof. history Rutgers U., New Brunswick, N.J., 1967-89, chmn. history dept., grad. dir., 1974-81, assoc. dean social sci. and humanities, faculty personnel, 1981-84, dean faculty arts and scis., 1984-89; prof. history, provost, acad. v.p. SUNY, Stony Brook, 1989-93, prof. history, provost, exec. v.p. for academic affairs, 1992-94; v.p. for acad. affairs Wayne State U., Detroit, 1995-98, prof. history, 1998—. Hist. cons. Columbia Pictures, Hollywood, Calif., 1978-80, NBC, N.Y.C., 1980-89; chair Sponsors Bd. The Thomas A. Edison Papers Project, 1980-89. Author: Strange Enthusiasm, 1968, 2d edit., 1970; co-editor: The Black Americans, 1975. Commr. Housing Authority, Highland Park, N.J., 1977-89; Einstein Archives Adv. Com. Hebrew U., 1993-94. Mem. Orgn. Am. Historians, Prismatic Club Detroit. Office: Wayne State U Coll Liberal Arts Dept of History Detroit MI 48202 E-mail: aa1768@wayne.edu.

EDEN, BARBARA JANIECE, commercial and residential interior designer; b. Inpls., Oct. 14, 1951; d. Justin January and Marjorie May (Miller) E.; m. Stephen A. Bowman, Oct. 25, 1975; children: Christopher Eden Bowman, Jessica Eden Bowman. BA, Purdue U., 1973. Interior design dir. Bohlen, Meyer, Gibson & Assoc., Indpls., 1973-78; interior designer, sole propr. Barbara Eden Design, 1978-85; pres., prin. designer Eden Design Assocs., Inc., Carmel, Ind., 1985-97, Carson Design Assocs. Design/Project Mgmt./ Mktg., Carmel, 1997—. Past mem. accreditation team Found. for Interior Design Edn. Rsch. (FIDER); past mem. adv. bd. Purdue U. Interior Design Dept. Prin. projects include wheelchair accessible bathroom Kohler (Wis.) Design Ctr., United Airlines, Indpls. Maintenance Ctr., N.Am. hdqrs. Brightpoint, Inc., Plainfield, Ind., Huntington (Ind.) Coll. Libr. & Fine Arts Ctr., Oakwood Inn, Syracuse, Ind., Resort Condominiums, Internat., Carmel, Ind., Merchants' Pointe, Carmel, restaurant, retail & office devel., arch., interior design; also corp., healthcare, schs., univs., librs., sr. living and residential interior design, space planning and project mgmt. Mem. AIA (assoc.), Internat. Facility Mgrs. Assn., Internat. Interior Design Assn., Illuminating Engring. Soc., Carmel Clay C. of C. (mem. exec. bd., chair edn. com., Small Bus. Person of Yr. 1993). Avocations: hiking, horseback riding, traveling. Office: Carson Design Assocs 11590 N Meridian St Ste 104 Carmel IN 46032-6955 E-mail: edenbj@carsondesign.com.

EDEN, JAMES GARY, electrical engineer, educator, physicist, researcher; b. Washington, Oct. 11, 1950; s. Robert Otis and Joyce (West) Eden; m. Carolyn Sue Thomas, June 10, 1972; children: Robert Douglas, Laura Ann, Katherine Joy. BS, U. Md., 1972; MS, U. Ill., 1973, PhD, 1976. Teaching asst. elec. engring. dept. U. Ill., Urbana, Jan.-June 1972, rsch. asst., 1972-75, asst. prof. elec. engring. dept., 1979-81, assoc. prof., 1981-83, prof. elec. engring. dept. and rsch. prof. Coordinated Sci. Lab, 1983—, dir. Lab. for Optical Physics and Engring., 1995—, assoc. vice-chancellor for rsch., 2000—, assoc. dean Grad. Coll., 1994-96, rsch. prof. Microelectronics Lab., 2000—, mem. physics grad. rsch. faculty, asst. dean Coll. Engring., 1992-93; postdoctoral rsch. assoc. NRC, Washington, 1975-76; rsch. physicist U.S. Naval Rsch. Lab., 1976-79. Mem. tech. adv. bd. Anvik Corp., Hawthorne, NY; mem. tech. adv. bd. Caviton, Inc., Urbana; assoc. mem. Ctr. Advanced Study U. Ill., 1987—88; mem. program com. Conf. Lasers and Electro-Optics, 1982, 83, 88, 89, 1Conf. Lasers and Electro-Optics, 1994—97; chmn. Engring. Found. Conf. Ultraviolet Lasers, 1987, co-chair, 90, 94; program chair ann. meeting IEEE Lasers and Electro-Optics Soc., 1990, conf. chair, 92; program vice chmn. Interdisciplinary Laser Sci. Conf. V, 1989; program chair ILS V, 1990; conf. chair ILS VII, 1992; mem. adv. bd. Chem. Vapor Deposition, 1995—, CRC Handbook Series Laser Sci. and Tech., 1996—; cons. Wilson, Sonsini, Goodrich and Rosati, Palo Alto, Calif., 1996—, Morrison & Foerster, 1998—2000, Smart and Biggar, Ottawa, Canada, 1999—2000. Author: (book) Photochemical Vapor Deposition, 1992, Gas Laser Technology, 2000; editor: IEEE Jour. Quantum Electronics, 1996—; assoc. editor: Photonics Tech. Letters, 1988—94; contbr. chapters to books, more than 160 articles to profl. jours. Recipient Rsch. Publ. award, Naval Rsch. Lab., 1978, Beckman Rsch. award, U. Ill., 1988, IBM Rsch. award, 1994, Faculty Outstanding Tchg. award, Dept. Elec. and Computer Engring., U. Ill., 2000; scholar James F. Towey Univ., U. Ill., 1996—99. Fellow: IEEE (3d Millennium medal 2000), Am. Phys. Soc., Optical Soc. Am.; mem.: IEEE Lasers and Electro-Optic Soc. (bd. govs. 1991—93, v.p. tech. affairs 1993—95, pres. 1998, Disting. Svc. award 1996), Phi Kappa Phi, Eta Kappa Nu, Tau Beta Pi, Sigma Xi. Achievements include patents for for 15 inventions. Home: 314 County Rd 2650 N Mahomet IL 61853-9579 Office: U Ill Everitt Lab 1406 W Green St Urbana IL 61801-2918 E-mail: jgeden@uiuc.edu.

EDGAR, JIM, former governor; b. Vinita, Okla., July 22, 1946; m. Brenda Smith; children: Brad, Elizabeth. Grad., Eastern Ill. U., 1968; postgrad., U. Ill., Sangamon State U., 1971-74. Legis. intern pres. pro tem Ill. Senate, 1968; key asst. to speaker ho. Ill. Ho. of Reps., 1972-73; aide to pres. Ill. Senate, 1974, to Ho. minority leader, 1976; mem. Ill. Ho. of Reps., 1977-79; dir. legis. affairs Ill. Gov., 1979-80; sec. state State of Ill., 1981-91; gov. State of Ill., 1991-98; disting. fellow Inst. Govt. and Publs. U. Ill., Urbana, 1999—. Co-lead gov. Nat. Gov.'s Assn. Transp. Com., 1995-96; chair Edn. Commn. of States, 1993-94; chair Nat. Gov.'s Assn. Com. on Econ. Devel. and Commerce, 1992-93; pres. Coun. State Govts., 1992-93; chair Gov.'s Ethanol Coalition, 1992-93; chair Nat. Gov.'s Assn. Com. on Econ. Devel. and Tech. Innovation, 1991-92. Precinct committeeman, treas. Coles County Rep. Com., 1974; dir. state svc. Nat. Conf. State Legislatures, 1975, 76; mem. campaign com. Ill. Ho. of Reps.; pres. Nat. Assn. Secs. of State, 1988; exec. com. Coun. State Govts., 1988, v.p. exec. com., 1991, pres., 1992-93; bd. dirs. Nat. Commn. Against Drunk Driving, 1989; chmn. Ill. Literacy Coun., 1989; chmn. Edn. Commn. of the States, 1993-94; chmn. Gov.'s Ethanol Coalition, 1992-93; pres. Bd. Coun. State Govts. Mem. Nat. Govs. Assn. (chmn. econ. devel. and commerce com. 1992-93, strategic planning rev. task force 1991—, past chmn. task force on edn., mem. edn. goals panel, chair com. econ. devel. and technol. innovation 1991-92, edn. commn. of states 1993-94, co-lead gov. transp. com. 1995-96), Coles County Hist. Soc. (pres. 1976-79). Baptist. Office: U Ill Inst Govt and Pub Affairs 1007 W Nevada St # MC-037 Urbana IL 61801-3812

EDGAR, JOHN M. lawyer; b. Tex., 1943; BS, U. Kans., 1965; JD with distinction, U. Mo., Kans. City, 1968. Bar: Mo. 1968. Resident mng. ptnr. Bryan Cave LLP, Kans. City, Mo., lead resident ptnr., 1999—. Mem. Lawyers Assn. Kansas City, Phi Alpha Delta, Order of Bench and Robe. Office: Bryan Cave LLP 3500 1 Kansas City Pl Kansas City MO 64105

EDGERTON, WILLIAM B. foreign language educator; b. Winston-Salem, N.C., Mar. 11, 1914; s. Paul Clifton and Annie Maude (Benbow) E.; m. Jewell Mock Conrad, June 6, 1935 (dec. Dec. 1993); children: Susan, David. B.A., Guilford Coll., 1934; M.A., Haverford Coll., 1935; Ph.D., Columbia U., 1954. Tchr. French. German, Spanish, English in secondary schs., U.S. and France, 1935-39; faculty French and Spanish Guilford Coll., 1939-47; faculty Russian lit. Pa. State U., University Park, 1950-56, U. Mich., Ann Arbor, 1954-55, Columbia U., N.Y.C., 1956-58; prof. Slavic langs. and lits. Ind. U., Bloomington, 1958-83, prof. emeritus, 1983—, chmn. Slavic dept., 1958-65, 69-73, acting dir. Russian and East European Inst., 1981-82. Cons. Ford Found., 1952-61; mem. joint com. on Slavic studies Am. Coun. Learned Socs., 1951-62, chmn. 1958-61; vis. rsch. scholar USSR Acad. of Sci., 1963-64, 78, 87, 88, 89, 90, Bulgarian Acad. Scis., 1986, 88. Editor, co-author: Quaker Profiles, 1995; gen. editor: Columbia Dictionary of Modern European Literature, 1980; translator, editor: Satirical Stories of Nikolai Leskov, 1969, Memoirs of Peasant Tolstoyans in Soviet Russia, 1993; editor: Ind. Slavic Studies, III, 1963, Ind. Slavic Studies, IV, 1967, Am. Contributions to the Fifth Internat. Congress of Slavists, 1963; contbr. articles to profl. internat. jours. Bd. dirs. Am. Friends Svc. Com., 1956-59; trustee Guilford Coll., 1969-86; mem. vis. com. for Slavic Studies Harvard U., 1967-77; mem. adv. com. Nat. Humanities Ctr., 1978—; war relief work Am. Friends Svc. Com. Yugoslav refugee camp, Egypt, 1944-45, dir., lectr. internat. student seminars U.S., 1948, 51, Geneva, 1949, Vienna, 1956, Leningrad, 1960; organizing search fgn. child victims Nazis, Germany, 1945-46, Quaker relief work, Poland, 1946, internat. missions Yugoslavia, Greece, 1950, USSR, 1955, Poland, 1957. Recipient Josef Dobrovsky medal Czechoslovak Acad. Sci., 1968; Am. Council Learned Socs. fellow, 1948-50; Guggenheim fellow, 1963-64 Mem. MLA (exec. council 1962-65), Am. Assn. Advancement Slavic Studies (pres. 1961), Am. Com. Slavists (chmn. 1958-78), Internat. Com. Slavists (Am. rep., 1958-78, hon. mem 1978—). Quaker. Home: 1801 E Maxwell Ln Bloomington IN 47401-5208 Office: Ind U 502 Ballantine Rd Bloomington IN 47401-5018

EDGERTON, WINFIELD DOW, retired gynecologist; b. Caruthersville, Mo., Nov. 8, 1924; s. Winfield Dow and Anna Kathryn (Hale) E.; m. Rose Marie Cahill, June 24, 1945; 1 child, Winfield Dow Student, Central Coll., Fayette, Mo., 1942-44; MD, Washington U., St. Louis, 1947. Intern St. Luke's Hosp., St. Louis, 1947-48; resident Chgo. Lying-In Hosp., 1948-49, Free Hosp. for Women, Brookline, Mass., 1951, U.S. Naval Hosp., Chelsea, 1951-53; practice medicine specializing in obstetrics and gynecology Davenport, Iowa, 1955-87; clin. asst. prof. obstetrics and gynecology U. Iowa Coll. Medicine, 1971-78, clin. assoc. prof., 1979-82, clin. prof., 1982—; ret., 2000. Mem. staff, med. dir. Maternal Health Ctr. St. Luke's Hosp. (name changed to Edgerton Women's Health Ctr.), 1972-2000. Contbr. articles to med. jours. and texts Served to lt. M.C., USN, 1949-55 Fellow Am. Coll. Obstetricians and Gynecologists (past chmn. Iowa sect.), Royal Soc. Medicine; mem. Central Assn. Obstetricians and Gynecologists, Am. Fertility Soc., Am. Assn. Gynecologic Laparoscopists (past trustee), Gynecologic Laser Soc., AMA, Iowa Med. Soc., Scott County Med. Soc. (past pres.) Republican. Congregationalist. Home: 4 Lombard Ct Davenport IA 52803-2348

EDIGER, MARK D. chemistry educator; b. Newton, Kans., July 26, 1957; BA in Chemistry and Math., Bethel Coll., 1979; PhD in Phys. Chemistry, Stanford U., 1984. Asst. prof. dept. chemistry U. Wis., Madison, 1984-90, assoc. prof., 1990-94, prof. dept. chemistry, 1994—. Grantee Polymers Program, NSF, 1998—, Chemistry Program, 2000—, Am. Chem. Soc., 2000—. Fellow Am. Phys. Soc.; mem. Am. Chem. Soc. Office: Univ Wis Dept Chemistry 1101 University Ave Madison WI 53706-1322

EDISON, BERNARD ALAN, retired retail apparel company executive; b. Atlanta, 1928; s. Irving and Beatrice (Chanin) Edison; m. Marilyn S Wewers, Apr. 26, 1975. B.A., Harvard U., 1949, M.B.A., 1951. With Edison Bros. Stores Inc., St. Louis, 1951—, asst. v.p., 1957-58, v.p. leased depts., 1958-67, v.p., asst. treas., 1967-68, pres., 1968-87, chmn. fin. com., 1987-89, dir. emeritus, 1989-96. Bd dirs Anheuser-Busch Cos, Inc. Office: Edison Founds 220 N Fourth St Ste A Saint Louis MO 63102

EDMONDS, JAMES PATRICK (JIM EDMONDS), professional baseball player; b. Fullerton, Calif., June 27, 1970; Grad. H.S., Calif. Outfielder Calif. Angels (now Anaheim Angels), 1993-99, St. Louis Cardinals, 1999—. Selected to Am. League All-Star Team, 1995. Office: St Louis Cardinals 250 Stadium Plz Saint Louis MO 63102-1722*

EDMONDS, JOHN, state legislator; m. Marta Edmonds. Pub. acct.; mem. for dist. 112 Kans. State Ho. of Reps., 1994—. Address: PO Box 1805 Great Bend KS 67530-1805

EDMONDS, WILLIAM L. federal judge; b. 1944; BA, U. Mo., 1966, MA, 1969; JD, U. Iowa, 1978. Bar: Iowa 1978. Ptnr. Carter, Sar, Edmonds & Green, 1978-87; bankruptcy judge U.S. Bankruptcy Ct. (no. dist.) Iowa, Sioux City, 1987—, chief bankruptcy judge, 1992-99. Mem. Order of Coif. Office: Fed Bldg and US Courthouse 320 6th St Ste 114 Sioux City IA 51101-1244

EDMONDSON, FRANK KELLEY, retired astronomer; b. Milw., Aug. 1, 1912; s. Clarence Edward and Marie (Kelley) E.; m. Margaret Russell, Nov. 24, 1934 (dec. Jan. 1999); children: Margaret Jean Olson, Frank K. Jr. A.B., Ind. U., 1933, A.M., 1934; Ph.D., Harvard U., 1937. Lawrence fellow Lowell Obs., 1933-34, research asst., 1934-35; Agassiz fellow Harvard Obs., 1935-36, asst., 1936-37; instr. astronomy Ind. U., Bloomington, 1937-4O, asst. prof., 1940-45, assoc. prof., 1945-48, prof., 1949-83, prof. emeritus, 1983—, dir. Kirkwood Obs., 1945-78; dir. Goethe Link Obs., 1948-78, chmn. astronomy dept., 1944-78; research asso. McDonald Obs., 1944-83. Observations of asteroids in cooperation with Internat. Astron. Union's Minor Planet Center; statistical adviser to Prof. Alfred Kinsey for gall wasp and human sex behaviour rsch., 1939-56; program dir. for astronomy NSF, 1956-57; acting dir. Cerro Tololo Inter-Am. Obs., 1966; lectr. astron. socs.; mem. adv. bd. Lowell Obs., 1988-2000. Author: AURA and its US National Observatories, 1997; contbr. numerous papers to Am., Brit., German astron. jours. Decorated Order of Merit Chile, 1964; recipient Meritorious Pub. Service award NSF, 1983, Disting. Alumni Svc. award Ind. U., 1997; honored with Daniel Kirkwood (1814-95) in Ho. Resolution No. 58 adopted by Ind. 109th Gen. Assembly, First Session, 1995. Fellow AAAS (chmn. sect. D, v.p. 1962); mem. Assn. Univs. Research in Astronomy (v.p. 1957-61, pres. 1962-65, dir. 1957-83, cons./historian 1983—), Can. Astron. Soc., Am. Astron. Soc. (treas. 1954-75, 70 yr. attendance award 2001), Astron. Soc. Pacific, Internat.

Astron. Union (chmn. U.S. nat. com. 1963-64, v.p. commn. minor planets, comets and satellites 1967-70, pres. 1970-73), Ind. Acad. Science, Am. Mus. Natural History (corr. mem.), Explorers Club, Phi Beta Kappa, Sigma Xi. Home: 716 S Woodlawn Ave Bloomington IN 47401-4936 Office: Ind U Dept Astronomy 319 Swain Hall West 727 E 3rd St Bloomington IN 47405-7105

EDMONDSON, KEITH HENRY, chemical company executive, retired; b. Wheaton, Ill., May 16, 1924; s. Edwin Ray and Mildred Lorraine (Henry) E.; m. Peggy Eleanor Wood, Sept. 22, 1945; children— Robert Earl, Kris E., John David, Keith Clark. B.S., Purdue U., 1948, M.S., 1949. With Upjohn Co., Kalamazoo, 1949-86, exec. v.p. internat. div., 1962-67, v.p., gen. mgr. chem. div., 1967-86; exec. dir. Stryker Ctr., 1986-90; prof. Kalamazoo Coll., 1986-90; dir. Career Devel. Ctr., Kalamazoo Coll., 1990-94; retired, 1994—. Mem. Kalamazoo Bd. Edn., 1958-62, pres., 1962. Served to 1st lt. USAAF, 1942-45. Decorated D.F.C. with oak leaf cluster, Air medal with 6 oak leaf clusters. Mem. Internat. Isocyanate Inst. (pres. 1976), Kalamazoo C. of C. (v.p. 1973), Kalamazoo Mgmt. Assn. (pres. 1957), Am. Inst. Chem. Engrs., Am. Chem. Soc., Tau Beta Pi, Sigma Xi, Phi Lambda Upsilon. Republican. Methodist. Home: 8565 W H Ave Kalamazoo MI 49009-7516 Office: Kalamazoo Coll 1200 Academy St Kalamazoo MI 49006-3268 E-mail: edmond@iserv.net.

EDMUNDS, JANE CLARA, communications consultant; b. Chgo., Mar. 16, 1922; d. John Carson and Clara (Kummerow) Carrigan; m. William T. Dean, Aug. 30, 1947 (div. 1953; dec. July 1984); 1 son, John Charles; Edmund S. Kopacz, Sept. 24, 1955 (div. 1973); children: Christine Ellen, Jan Carson. Student in chemistry and math., Northwestern U. Chemist Mars Inc., Oak Park, Ill., 1942-47; with Cons. Engr. Mag., Maujer Pub. Co., St. Joseph, Mich., 1953-58, 69-74; sr. editor Cons. Engr. Mag. Tech. Pub. Co., Barrington, Ill., 1975-77, exec. editor, 1977-82, editorial dir., 1983-86; asst. editor women's pages rewrite desk News-Palladium, Benton Harbor, Mich., 1967-68; freelance journalist St. Joseph, 1959-68; communications cons. Schaumburg, Ill., 1987—. Chmn. Berrien County (Mich.) Nat. Found. March of Dimes, 1968; mem. campaign com. Rep. Party, 1954. Recipient award Bausch & Lomb, 1940, award Nat. Found. Service, 1969, Silver Hat award Constrn. Writers Assn., 1986, honor mem. 2000, Chmn.'s award Profl. Engrs. in Pvt. Practice div. NSPE, 1987; grantee AID, 1979 Assoc. fellow Soc. Tech. Communication (chmn. St. Joseph chpt. 1972 Disting. Tech. Communication awards); mem. Am. Soc. Bus. Press Editors (past bd. mem.), Constrn. Writers Assn., Smithsonian Instn., Chgo. Art Inst. Assocs., Field Mus. Assocs. Republican. Episcopalian.

EDMUNDS, NANCY GARLOCK, federal judge; b. Detroit, July 10, 1947; m. William C. Edmunds, 1977. BA cum laude, Cornell U., 1969; MA in Teaching, U. Chgo., 1971; JD summa cum laude, Wayne U., 1976. Bar: Mich. 1976. With Plymouth Canton Public Schools, 1971-73; law clk. to Barris, Sott, Denn & Driker, 1973-75; law clk. to Hon. Ralph Freeman U.S. Dist. Ct. (ea. dist.) Mich., 1976-78; with Dykema Gossett, Detroit, 1978-84, ptnr. litigation sect., 1984-92; apptd. judge U.S. Dist. Ct. (ea. dist.) Mich., 1992—. Commr. 21st Century Commn. on Cts., 1990; mem. faculty, bd. mem. Fed. Advocacy Inst., 1983-91. Editor in chief Wayne Law Review. Mem. com. of visitors Wayne Law Sch., Detroit; mem. com. on defender svcs. Nat. Jud. Conf.; mem. Nat. Coun. Jewish Women; bd. gov.'s Cranbrook Schs.; bd. dirs. Mich. Mems. of Stratford Festival; bd. trustees Stratford Shakespearean Festival of Am., Temple Beth El, 1990-97, Hist. Soc. U.S. Dist. Ct. (ea. dist.) Mich., 1993-98. Mem. ABA, Fed. Bar Assn. (exec. bd. dirs. 1989-92), Am. Judicature Soc., Fed. Judges Assn., State Bar Mich. (chair U.S. cts. com. 1990-91). Avocations: skiing, reading. Office: US Dist Ct US Courthouse #211 231 W Lafayette Blvd Detroit MI 48226-2700 E-mail: khillebrand@ckb.uscourts.gov.

EDWARDS, BENJAMIN FRANKLIN, III, investment banker; b. St. Louis, Oct. 26, 1931; s. Presley William and Virginia (Barker) E.; m. Joan Moberly, June 13, 1953; children: Scott P., Benjamin Franklin IV, Pamela M. Edwards Bunn, Susan B. B.A., Princeton U., 1953. With A.G. Edwards & Sons, Inc., St. Louis, 1956—, pres., 1967—, chmn., 1983—, also CEO, 1983—. Bd. dirs. Jefferson Bank and Trust Co., Psychol. Assocs., Helig-Meyers, Inc., N.Y. Stock Exch., Washington U., St. Louis Art Mus., Barnes Hosp. Mem. U. Mo., St. Louis, Civic Progress, Arts and Edn. Coun. With USNR, 1953-56. Mem. Investment Bankers Assn. (gov. 1968—), Securities Industry Assn. (gov. 1974-81, chmn. 1980—). Presbyterian. Clubs: Old Warson Country (St. Louis); Bogey. Office: A G Edwards & Sons Inc 1 N Jefferson Ave Saint Louis MO 63103-2205

EDWARDS, CHARLES RICHARD, entomology and pest management educator; b. Lubbock, Tex., Jan. 22, 1945; s. Troy B. and Jeanette E. E.; m. Claudia Frances Henderson, Dec. 21, 1966; children: Cecily Elizabeth, Celeste Elaine. BS, Tex. Tech. U., 1968; MS, Iowa State U., 1970, PhD, 1972. Bd. cert. entomoloist. Prof. Entomology Purdue U., West Lafayette, Ind., 1972—. Cons. Consortium for Internat. Crop Protection, Corvallis, Oreg., 1985—, Food and Agr. Orgn. UN, 1995—; USAID Integrated Pest Mgmt. Collaborative Rsch. Support Program, 1993—. Contbr. articles to profl. jours. Mem. Entomol. Soc. Am. (Ext. Achievement award 1984, award of merit 1985), Royal Entomol. Soc. London, Sigma Xi, Alpha Zeta, Gamma Sigma Delta. Avocations: running, woodworking. Office: Purdue U 1158 Smith Hall West Lafayette IN 47907-1158 E-mail: rich_edwards@entm.purdue.edu.

EDWARDS, CLIFFORD HENRY COAD, law educator; b. Jamalpur, Bihar, India, Nov. 8, 1924; s. George Henry Probyn and Constance Ivy (Coad) E.; m. Kathleen Mary Faber, Jan. 6, 1951; children: Jeanette Marie, John Philip, Michael Hugh, Margaret Susan. LLB with 1st class honors, U. London, 1945. Sr. lectr. Kumasi Coll., Chana, 1956-58; assoc. prof. law U. Man., Winnipeg, 1958-64, prof., dean Sch. Law, 1964-79, dean emeritus, 1986—; pres. Man. Law Reform Commn., 1979—. Queen's coun., 1980. Recipient Stanton Tchg. Award for Excellence, U. Man., 1994. Mem. Soc. Internat. Ministries (chmn. 1984-90), Can. Bar Assn., Man. Bar Assn. (Disting. Svc. award 1995). Baptist. Office: Univ of Manitoba Fort Garry Campus Robson Hall Winnipeg MB Canada R3T 2N2

EDWARDS, DONALD MERVIN, biological systems engineering educator, university dean; b. Tracy, Minn., Apr. 16, 1938; s. Mervin B. and Helen L. (Halstenrud) E.; m. Judith Lee Wilson, Aug. 8, 1964; children: John, Joel, Jeffrey, Mary. B.S., S.D. State U., 1960, M.S., 1961; Ph.D. in Agrl. Engring, Purdue U., 1966. Registered profl. engr. With soil conservation svc. U.S. Dept. Agr., Marshall, Minn., 1957-62; teaching, rsch. asst. S.D. State U. and Purdue U., 1960-66; assoc. prof. agrl. engring. U. Nebr., Lincoln, 1966-71, prof., 1971-80, asst. dean Coll. Engring and Architecture, 1970-73, assoc. dean, dir. Engring Rsch. Ctr., Coll. Engring and Tech., 1973-80, dir. Energy Rsch and Devel. Ctr., 1976-80; prof. and chmn. dept. agrl. engring Mich. State U., East Lansing, 1980-89; prof. biol. systems engring., dean Coll. Agrl. Scis. and Natural Resources U. Nebr., Lincoln, 1989-00, spl. projects, 2000-01, emeritus prof. biol. sys. engring., 2001—, emeritus dean Coll. Agrl. Scis. and Natural Resources, 2001—. Mem. Engring. Accreditation Bd. Engring. and Tech.; collaborator, cons. to numerous industries and agys., 1966—. Contbr. numerous articles on irrigation, water pollution, remote sensing, energy, agrl., natural resources and engring. edn. to profl. jours. Active Boy Scouts Am., Am. Field Svc., 4-H; past bd. dirs. Nat. Safety Coun.; past chmn. bd. dirs. Lincoln Transp. System. Recipient Massey-Furguson award Am. Soc of Agriculture Engineers, 1994, Outstanding Tchr. award U. Nebr. Fellow Am. Soc. Engring. Edn., Am. Soc. Agrl. Engrs.; mem. AAAS, NSPE (nat. bd. dirs., nat. v.p.), Profl. Engrs. Nebr., Mich. Soc. Profl. Engrs., Coun. for Agrl. Sci. and Tech., Farmhouse Club, Sigma Xi, Alpha Gamma Rho, Triangle. Home: 11420 Wenzel Dr Lincoln NE 68527-9484 E-mail: dedwards1@unl.edu.

EDWARDS, GERALD, plastics company executive; b. Chgo., July 13; m. Jada; children: Charlene, Candice Rae, Gerald II. Student, Heidelberg Coll. With Ford Motor Co.; asst. plant mgr., then plant mgr. Detroit Plastic Molding; pres., CEO Engineered Plastic Products, 1987—. Office: Engineered Plastic Products Inc 699 James L Hart Pkwy Ypsilanti MI 48197-9791

EDWARDS, HORACE BURTON, former state official, former oil pipeline company executive, management consultant; b. Tuscaloosa, Ala., May 20, 1925; children: Adrienne, Paul, David, Michael; m. Fran M. Allerheiligen, Sept. 3, 1994. BS in Naval Sci., Marquette U., 1947, BSME, 1948; MBA in Fin. Mgmt., Iona Coll., 1972; LDH (hon.), Tex. So. U., 1982; LLD, Stillman Coll., 1984. Registered profl. engr., Wis., Kans. Various engring. positions Allis Chalmers, 1948-52, GM, 1952-56, Conrac, 1956-63, Northrop, 1963-71; with Atlantic Richfield Co., 1967-80, mgr. planning, evaluation, 1976-79, v.p. planning, control L.A., 1979-80; pres., CEO, chmn. bd. dirs. ARCO Pipe Line Co., Independence, Kans., 1980-86; sec. transp. State of Kans., 1987-91; pres. Edwards and Assocs. Inc., Topeka, 1991—. Mem. adv. bd. Energy Bur., Strategic Hwy. Rsch. Program Res. Mississippi Valley Conf. State Hwy. and Transp. Ofcls., 1989-90; trustee Kans. Coun. Econ. Edn., Topeka, 1981—, Leadership Independence, 1984-86, Kans. Ind. Coll. Fund, 1985-91, Stillman Coll., Tuscaloosa, Ala., 1985—, Ins. Logopedics, Wichita, Kans., 1985-91. Recipient Marquette U. Dist. Engring. Alumnus award, 1984 Mem. Am. Petroleum Inst., Assn. Oil Pipelines (mem. adv. com.), Am. Assn. Blacks in Energy (bd. dirs.), Kans. C. of C. and Industry (trustee Leadership Kans. 1983, bd. dirs. 1983-91), Kans. Contractors Assn., Assn. Gen. Contractors (assoc.). Office: Edwards & Assocs Inc 106 E 11th St Ste 1450 Kansas City MO 64106-2120 also: Edwards & Assocs Inc 1805 N Dr Martin Luther King D Milwaukee WI 53212-3639

EDWARDS, JAY, radio personality; b. Ft. Smith, Ark., Oct. 20; Radio host WDAF, Westwood, Kans., 1996—. Avocations: movies, cooking. Office: WDAF 4935 Belinder Rd Westwood KS 66205*

EDWARDS, JESSE EFREM, physician, educator; b. Hyde Park, Mass., July 14, 1911; s. Max and Nellie (Gordon) E.; m. Marjorie Helen Brooks, Nov. 12, 1952; children— Ellen Ann Villa, Brooks Sayre. BS, Tufts Coll., 1932, MD, 1935; DSc (hon.), Georgetown U., 1990. Diplomate Am. Bd. Med. Examiners, Am. Bd. Pathology. Resident Mallory Inst. Pathology, Boston, 1935-36, asst., 1937-40; intern Albany (N.Y.) Hosp., 1936-37; instr. pathology Boston U., 1938; instr. pathology, bacteriology, surgery Tufts Med. Coll., 1939-40; research fellow Nat. Cancer Inst. USPHS, 1940-42; cons. sect. pathologic anatomy Mayo Clinic, 1946-60; asst. prof. grad. sch. U. Minn., Mpls., 1946-51, asso. prof., 1951-54, prof. pathologic anatomy 1954-60, clin. prof. med. sch., prof. pathology grad. sch., 1960—; chief pathologist United Hosp. (formerly Chas. T. Miller Hosp.), St. Paul, 1960-80; cons. pathologist Hennepin County Hosp., Mpls., 1964—; cons. dept. pathology Mpls. Vets. Hosp., 1966—; cons. pathologist St. Paul Ramsey Hosp., 1967-80; dir. registry of cardiovascular disease United Hosp., St. Paul, 1980-87, sr. cons. registry of cardiovascular disease, 1987—, also sr. cons. Jesse E. Edwards Registry of Cardiovascular Disease, 1987—. Pres. World Congress Pediatric Cardiology, 1980; mem. pathology study sect. USPHS, 1957-62; civilian cons. surgeon gen. AUS, 1947-69 Author: Atlas Acquired Diseases of Heart and Great Vessels, 1961, (with T.J. Dry and others) Congenital Anomalies of the Heart and Great Vessels, 1948, (with others) An Atlas of Congenital Anomalies of the Heart and Great Vessels, 1954, (with R.S. Fontana) Congenital Cardiac Disease, 1962, (with J.R. Stewart, O. Kincaid) An Atlas of Vascular Rings and Related Malformations of the Aortic System, 1963, (with C.A. Wagenvoort, D. Heath) Pathology of Pulmonary Vasculature, 1963, (with others) Correlation of Pathologic Anatomy and Angiocardiography, 1965, Coronary Arterial Variations in the Normal Heart and in Congenital Heart Disease, 1975, Coronary Heart Disease, 1976, (with Brooks S. Edwards) Jesse E. Edwards Synopsis of Congenital Heart Disease, 2000; Editor: (with others) Circulation; Contbr. (with others) articles to profl. jours. Served from capt. to lt. col. M.C. AUS, 1942-46. Recipient Distinguished Tchr. award Minn. Med. Found., 1974; Gold Heart award Am. Heart Assn., 1970; Gifted Tchr. award Am. Coll. Cardiology, 1977 Mem. AMA, Minn. Med. Assn., Soc. Exptl. Biology and Medicine, Am. Heart Assn. (pres. 1967-68), Minn. Heart Assn. (pres. 1962-63), Internat. Acad. Pathology (pres. 1955-56), Am. Assn. Pathologists and Bacteriologists, World Congress Pediat. Cardiology, Coll. Am. Pathologists, Am. Soc. Exptl. Pathology, Sigma Xi, Alpha Omega Alpha. Home: 1565 Edgcumbe Rd Saint Paul MN 55116-2304 Office: United Hosp Saint Paul MN 55102

EDWARDS, JOHN DUNCAN, law educator, librarian; b. Louisiana, Mo., Sept. 15, 1953; s. Harold Wenkle and Mary Elizabeth (Duncan) E.; m. Beth Ann Rahm, May 21, 1977; children: Craig, Martha, Brooks. BA, Southeast Mo. State U., 1975; JD, U. Mo., Kansas City, 1977; MALS, U. Mo., Columbia, 1979. Bar: Mo. 1978, U.S. Dist. Ct. (we. dist.) Mo. 1978. Instr. legal research and writing U. Mo., Columbia, 1978, dir. legal research and writing, librarian, 1979-80; pub. svcs. librarian Law Sch., U. Okla., Norman, 1980-81, assoc. librarian, 1981-84, adj. instr. sch. library sci., 1983-84; prof. law, dir. law library law sch. Drake U., Des Moines, 1984—. Adj. instr. Cleveland Coll., 1979-80; cons. Cleveland County Bar Assn., 1984. Contbr. articles to profl. jours. Cons. Friends Drake U. Libr., 1985—; coach, mgr. Westminster Softball Team. Des Moines, 1987-94; pres. Crestview Parent-Tchr. Coun., Des Moines, 1988-90; trustee Westminster Presbyn. Ch., Des Moines, 1988-89, treas., 1990, pres., 1991; mem. Clive City Coun., 1995—, mayor pro tem, 1998—; trustee Des Moines Metro Transit Authority, 1996—, chmn. bd. dirs., 1997-98, sec.-treas., 1996, 2001. Recipient Presdl. award Drake U. Student Bar Assn., 1987; named Outstanding Vol., Crestview Elem. Sch., 1989-90. Mem. Am. Assn. Law Librs. (chmn. awards com. 1987-88, chmn. grants com. 1996-97, chmn. scholarship com. 1998-99), Mid-Am. Assn. Law Librs. (chmn. resource sharing 1986-93, v.p. 1994-95, pres. 1995-96), Mid-Am. Law Sch. Librs. Consortium (pres. 1986-88), Delta Theta Phi, Beta Phi Mu. Avocations: softball, tennis. Office: Drake U Libr Law Sch 27th & Carpenter Sts Des Moines IA 50311

EDWARDS, JUDITH ELIZABETH, retired advertising executive; b. St. Louis, May 22, 1933; d. Archie Earl and Ivy Elizabeth (Jones) Hector; m. George N. LaMont Jr., Jan. 9, 1960 (div. Oct. 1965); m. Gary W. Edwards, Nov. 25, 1966 (dec. Feb. 14, 2001); stepchildren: Michael Brent, David Reed. Grad. high sch., St. Louis, 1951; student, Brown's Bus. Coll., St. Louis. Exec. sec., asst. to chmn. Rep. Nat. Com., Washington, 1958-60; dep. to county clk. Vanderburgh County, Evansville, Ind., 1972-76; sec.-treas. Edwards Outdoor Advtg., Carmi, Ill., 1979-2000, ret., 2000. Mem. Evansville Health Planning Coun., 1974-76. Pres. White County Rep. Women's Club, Carmi, 1989—, White County Hosp. Aux. Named Ky. Col. Mem. Carmi Bus. and Profl. Women's Club (past pres.), Carmi C. of C., Kiwanis, Order Ea. Star, Sigma Alpha. Methodist. Avocation: music (vocalist for ch., civic and fraternal groups). Home: PO Box 260214 Saint Louis MO 63126-8214

EDWARDS, MARK U., JR. college president, history educator, author; b. Oakland, Calif., June 2, 1946; s. Mark U. and Margaret Edwards; m. Linda Johnson, Mar. 1968; 1 child, Teon. BA in Psychology, Stanford U., 1968, MA in History, 1969, PhD in History, 1974. Jr. fellow U. Mich., 1971-74; asst. prof. history Wellesley (Mass.) Coll., 1974-80; asst. prof. Purdue U., West Lafayette, Ind., 1980-83, assoc. prof., 1983-86, prof. history, 1986-87; prof. christianity Harvard U., Cambridge, Mass., 1987-94; pres. St. Olaf Coll., Northfield, Minn., 1994—. Founder, v.p. ELK Software Devel. Corp., 1985—; pres. Sixteenth Century Studies Conf., 1987-88; chair continuing com. Internat. Congress for Luther Rsch., 1988-94; bd. dirs. Wittenberg U., 1985—. Author: Luther and the False Brethren, 1975, Luther's Last Battles, 1983, Printing, Propaganda and Martin Luther, 1994; co-author: Luther, A Reformer for Churches, 1983; mem. editl. bd. The Ency. of the Reformation, 1989—. Bd. dirs. Holden Village, 1993-94, 96—. Mem. Am. Norwegian Hist. Assn. Office: St Olaf Coll 1520 Saint Olaf Ave Northfield MN 55057-1574

EDWARDS, MICHELLE DENISE, professional basketball player; b. Mar. 6, 1966; Degree in gen. studies, Iowa State U., 1988. Basketball player, Faenza, Italy, 1989-90, Pistoia, Italy, 1990-93, Ferrara, Italy, 1993-95, Pavia, Italy, 1995-97; basketball player Cleveland Rockers Women's NBA, Cleve., 1997—. Mem. Olympic Festival Team, 1985; recipient Bronze medal Pan Am. Games, 1991; named MVP Italian League All-Star team, 1997. Office: Cleveland Rockers Gund Arena One Center Ct Cleveland OH 44115

EDWARDS, WALLACE WINFIELD, retired automotive company executive; b. Pontiac, Mich., May 9, 1922; s. David W. and Ruby M. (Nutting) E.; m. Jean Austin Wolfe, Aug. 24, 1944; children: Ronald W., Gary R., Ann E. B.S. in Mech. Engring, Gen. Motors Inst., 1949; M.B.A., Mich. State U., 1966. With GMC Truck & Coach div. Gen. Motors Corp., Pontiac, Mich., 1940-78, truck service mgr., 1961-62, head engine design, 1962-64, dir. reliability, 1964-66, dir. prodn. control and purchasing, 1966-70, dir. engring., 1970-78; dir. Worldwide Truck Project Center, Warren, Mich., 1978-80; gen. dir. Worldwide Truck and Transp. Sys. Center, 1980-81; v.p. G.M.O.D.C., 1980-81; group mgr. small and light truck and van ops. Truck and Bus. Group, Gen. Motors Corp., 1981-82, mgr. internat. staff, 1982-84, gen. dir. mil. vehicle ops. Power Products and Def. Group, 1984-86. Bd. dirs. Crystal Mountain Resort, Thompsonville, Mich., 1991—. Past pres., mem. exec. com. Clinton Valley coun. Boy Scouts Am.; dir. Grand Traverse Regional Land Conservancy, 1991—, chmn. 1996-98; regent Nat. Eagle Scout Assn. (life). Served with USNR, 1944-46. Mem. Soc. Automotive Engrs., Def. Preparedness Assn., Am. Security Council, U.S. Navy League, Tau Beta Pi, Beta Gamma Sigma. Office: 5089 Crystal Dr Beulah MI 49617-9617

EDWARDSON, SANDRA, dean, nursing educator; Dean Sch. Nursing, U. Minn., Mpls. Office: U Minn Twin Cities Sch Nursing 6-101 Weaver-Densford Hall 308 Harvard St SE Minneapolis MN 55455-0353

EFRON, BRUCE, radio personality; b. Mpls., Oct. 12; m. Betsy Efron; children: Joshua, Erica. Radio host WDAF, Westwood, Kans., 1990—. Avocations: acting, singing. Office: WDAF 4935 Belinder Rd Westwood KS 66205*

EGAN, CHARLES JOSEPH, JR. lawyer, greeting card company executive; b. Cambridge, Mass., Aug. 11, 1932; s. Charles Joseph and Alice Claire (Ball) E.; m. Mary Bowersox, Aug. 6, 1955; children: Timothy, Sean, Peter, James. AB, Harvard U., 1954; LLB, Columbia U., 1959. Bar: N.Y. 1960, Mo. 1973. Assoc. Donovan, Leisure, Newton & Irvine, N.Y.C., 1959-62; ptnr. Hall, McNicol, Marett & Hamilton, 1962-68; v.p., gen. counsel Thomson & McKinnon Securities, 1969-70, Hallmark Cards, Inc., Kansas City, Mo., 1972—. Bd. dirs. Am. Multi Cinema, Inc., Kansas City, Mo. Trustee Notre Dame de Sion Sch., Kansas City, 1973-77, Pembroke Country Day Sch., Kansas City, 1976-82, Kansas City Art Inst., 1995—; bd. dirs. Kansas City YMCA, 1976-80; mem. dean's coun. Columbia Law Sch., 1991—; vice chmn. Harvard Coll. Fund, 1994-99, co-chmn., 2000—. Served to 1st lt. USMC, 1954-56. Mem. Mo. Bar Assn., Kansas City Lawyers Assn., Harvard Alumni Assn. (pres. 1989-90, exec. com. 1987—), Century Assn., Somerset Club, Harvard Club of N.Y., Harvard Club of Kansas City (pres. 1985-87). Roman Catholic. Office: Hallmark Cards Inc 2501 Mcgee St Kansas City MO 64108-2600

EGAN, KEVIN JAMES, lawyer; b. Chgo., June 24, 1950; s. Raymond Basil and Harriet Olene (Landbo) E.; children: Ryan, Daniel. BA, U. Ill., 1972; JD, Northwestern U., 1975. Bar: Ill. 1975, U.S. Dist. Ct. (no. dist.) Ill. 1975, U.S. Ct. Appeals (7th cir.) 1976, U.S. Ct. of Customs and Patent Appeals 1978. Law clk. to judge U.S. Dist. Ct. (no. dist.) Ill., Chgo., 1975-77; assoc. Pattishall, McAuliffe & Hofstetter, 1977-78; asst. U.S. atty. No. Dist. of Ill., 1978-82; assoc. Winston & Strawn, Chgo., 1982-84, ptnr., 1984-93, Sonnenschein, Nath & Rosenthal, Chgo., 1993-98, Foley & Lardner, Chgo., 1998—. Article editor Jour. Criminal Law and Criminology, 1974-75. Bd. trustees Village of Frankfort, 1991—. Mem. ABA, Chgo. Bar Assn. (com. mem.), Bar Assn. of 7th Cir., Prestwick Country Club (Frankfort, Ill.). Roman Catholic. Avocation: hockey. Home: 904 Huntsmoor Dr Frankfort IL 60423-8747 Office: Foley & Lardner 330 N Wabash Ave Ste 3300 Chicago IL 60611-3603

EGBERT, ROBERT IMAN, electrical engineering educator, academic administrator; b. May 25, 1950; BSEE, U. Mo., Rolla, 1972, MSEE, 1973, PhD, 1976. Registered profl. engr., Mo., Kans. Grad. teaching asst. U. Mo., Rolla, 1972-75, grad. instr., 1975-76; systems engr. power div. Black & Veatch Cons. Engrs., Kansas City, Mo., 1976-80; asst. prof. elec. engring. Wichita (Kans.) State U., 1980-86, assoc. prof., 1986-95, prof., 1995—, dir. Ctr. for Energy Studies, 1987—. Contbr. articles to profl. jours. Mem. IEEE (sr.), NSPE, Am. Soc. Engring. Edn. (Dow Outstanding Young Faculty award 1982-83), Eta Kappa Nu (nat. bd. dirs. 1993-95, v.p. 1995-96, pres. 1996-97), Phi Kappa Phi, Tau Beta Pi, Sigma Xi. Office: Wichita State U Ctr Energy Studies Wichita KS 67260-0001

EGGE, JOEL, clergy member, academic administrator; Pres. Lutheran Brethren Schools of the Church of the Lutheran Brethren of America, Fergus Falls, Minn., Luth. Brethren Schs., Fergus Falls. Office: Lutheran Brethren Schools Ch of Lutheran Brethren of Am 815 W Vernon Ave Fergus Falls MN 56537-2699

EGGER, TERRANCE C.Z. V.p. adv. Tucson Newspapers; gen. mgr. Post-Dispatch, 1996; pub. St. Louis Post-Dispatch, LLC , 1999—, pres., 2000—. Holder mktg. positions, adv. positions Copley Newspapers; tchr. coll. comm. courses, Calif. Office: St Louis Post Dispatch 900 N Tucker Blvd Saint Louis MO 63101 Business E-mail: tegger@post-dispatch.com.*

EGGERS, GEORGE WILLIAM NORDHOLTZ, JR. anesthesiologist, educator; b. Galveston, Tex., Feb. 22, 1929; s. George William Nordholtz and Edith (Sykes) E.; m. Mary Futrell, Dec. 30, 1955; children: Carol Ann, George William Nordholtz III. BA, Rice U., 1949; MD, U. Tex., 1953. Diplomate Am. Bd. Anesthesiology. Instr. dept. anesthesiology, U. Tex., Galveston, 1956-59, asst. prof., 1959-61; assoc. prof. dept. anesthesiology, U. Mo., Columbia, 1961-67; prof. dept anesthesiology U. Mo., 1967—94, acting chmn. dept. anesthesiology, 1969, chmn. dept. anesthesiology, 1970-94, prof. emeritus, 1994—2001. Vis. instr. USAF Hosp., Lackland AFB, San Antonio, 1956-61; vis. research prof. dept. anesthesiology Northwestern U. Med. Sch., Chgo., 1968-69; research assoc. Space Sci. Research Ctr., Columbia, 1965-66. Contbr. over 50 articles to profl. jours. Recipient Ashbel Smith Disting. Alumnus award U. Tex., 1993. Mem. Am. Soc. Anesthesiology (bd. dirs. 1979-86, v.p. 1986-88, 1st v.p. 1989, pres.-elect 1990, pres. 1991), Am. Coll. Anesthesiology (bd. govs. 1965-74, chmn. bd. govs. 1973), Soc. Acad. Anesthesiology Chmn. (pres. 1971), Assn. Am. Med. Colls. (adminstrv. bd. council acad. socs. 1976-79), Mo. Soc. Anesthesiologists (pres. 1970, Disting. Svc. award 2001), Tex. Gulf Coast Anesthesiology Soc. (v.p. 1960), Boone County Med. Soc. (pres. 1988), Am. Bd. Anesthesiology (assoc. examiner 1968, joint council with Am. Soc. Anesthesiology on in-tng. exams.), Acad. Anesthesiology (pres. 1994, Citation of Merit 1997), Accreditation Council Grad. Med. Edn.

(mem. residency rev. com. for anesthesiology 1989-94), Anesthesia Found. (trustee 1993—), Alpha Omega Alpha, Mu Delta, Sigma Xi. Republican. Roman Catholic. Avocations: shooting, hunting, astronomy, magic, photography. Home: 1509 Woodrail Ave Columbia MO 65203-0931 Office: Univ Mo Dept Anesthesiology 1 Hospital Dr Dept Columbia MO 65201-5276

EGGERS, JAMES WESLEY, executive search consultant; b. Des Moines, Feb. 7, 1925; s. Paul William and Opal Imo (Cardiff) E.; m. Marjorie Mardell Freel, Aug. 2, 1947; children: James S., Barbara Bucher, Mark D. Grad., Knoxville High Sch., 1943. Farmer, Knoxville, Iowa, 1948-55; sales rep. Iowa Power & Light Co., Des Moines, 1953-60, Cedar Rapids, Iowa, 1960-62; sales exec. Thomas D. Murphy Co., Red Oak, 1962-67; pres., owner Eggers Cos., Omaha, 1967—. Bd. dirs. Nebr. State Bank, Omaha; owner, mgr. Exec. Realty and Mgmt. Co., Omaha, 1979—. Bd. dirs. local Meth. Ch., Nebr. Meth. Hosp. Found.; chmn. local dist. George Bush for Pres. campaign, Nebr., 1988; chmn. State of Nebr. Merit Coun., Lincoln, 1979-83; mem. nat. adv. cabinet Guideposts, Pawling, N.Y.; chmn. and mem. various civic bds. Mem. Nebr. Assn. Pers. Cons. (pres. 1974-75), Nat. Assn. Pers. Cons. (mem. nat. com. 1979-83, cert.), Omaha C. of C. (bd. dirs. 1980-83), Rotary (bd. dirs. Omaha chpt. 1983—, sgt.-at-arms 1986-90), Masons, Shriners. Republican. Avocations: reading, travel, religious study, walking. Office: Eggers Cons Co Inc Eggers Plz 11272 Elm St Omaha NE 68144-4788 E-mail: admin@eggersconsulting.com.

EGGERT, GLENN J. manufacturing executive; BS, ME, U. Wis. Various positions Meritor, Troy, Mich., 1978-98, sr. v.p. ops., 1998—. Mem. ASME, Soc. Mfg. Engrs., Assn. Mfg. Excellence. Office: Meritor Automotive Inc. 2135 W Maple Rd Troy MI 48084-7121

EGGERT, RUSSELL RAYMOND, lawyer; b. Chgo., July 28, 1948; s. Ralph A. and Alice M. (Nischwitz) E.; m. Patricia Anne Alegre, 1998. AB, U. Ill., 1970, JD, 1973; postgrad., Hague Acad. Internat. Law, The Netherlands, 1972. Bar: Ill. 1973, U.S. Supreme Ct. 1979. Assoc. U. Ill., Champaign, 1973-74; asst. atty. gen. State of Ill., Chgo., 1974-79; assoc. O'Conor, Karaganis & Gail, 1979-83; legal counsel to Ill. atty. gen., 1983-87; ptnr. Mayer, Brown, Rowe & Maw, 1987—. Contbr. articles to profl. jours. Mem. ABA. Democrat. Office: Mayer Brown Rowe & Maw 190 S La Salle St Ste 3100 Chicago IL 60603-3441 E-mail: reggert@mayerbrownrowe.com.

EGGERTSEN, JOHN HALE, lawyer; b. Ann Arbor, Mich., Jan. 7, 1947; s. Claude Andrew and Nita (Wakefield) E.; m. Claire Chenoweth, July 19, 1969 (div. 1987); children: Melissa Anne, Helen Emma; m. Sharon Ingram, June 13, 1987 (div. 1994); children: Alexandria, Andrea; m. Robin Rich, Sept. 23, 1995; 1 child, Brendon Hale. BA, U. Mich., 1968; JD cum laude, U. Toledo, 1974; LLM in Taxation, NYU, 1975. Bar: Ohio 1974, Mich. 1975. Instr. Highland Park (Mich.) Sch. Dist., 1968; claims adjuster State Farm Mutual Ins. Co., Ann Arbor, Mich., 1968-70; ptnr. Honigman Miller Schwartz and Cohn, Detroit, 1975-2000. Adj. prof. Wayne State U. Law Sch., Detroit, 1980-94; active Mich. Employee Benefits Conf., Detroit, 1980—. Contbr. articles to profl. jours. Bd. dirs. Neighborhood Svcs. Orgn., Detroit, 1992-2000, pres., 1994-97. Rsch. grantee NYU, 1974-75; Gerald Wallace scholar NYU, 1974-75. Mem. ABA (taxation sect., employee benefits com.), State Bar Ohio, State Bar Mich. Democrat. Mem. LDS Ch. Avocations: softball, bowling, reading. Home: 6369 Munger Ypsilanti MI 48197 Office: Eggertsen & Assocs PC Ste 107 5340 Plymouth Rd Ann Arbor MI 48105 Office Fax: 734-794-7104. Business E-Mail: john@jhelaw.com.

EGGLESTON, HARRY, optometrist; b. Dec. 31, 1941; m. Julie Kassebaum; 1 child. Student, Benedictine Coll., 1959-61; BA, St. Louis U., 1962; BA, MA, Creighton U., 1966; MD, U. Cin., 1972. Rep. candidate for U.S. House 9th Dist., Mo., 1996. With USAF, 1967-69. Roman Catholic. Address: Harry Eggleston For Congress 4141 S Old Highway 94 Saint Charles MO 63304-2846

EGLOFF, FRED ROBERT, manufacturers representative, writer, historian; b. Evanston, Ill., Nov. 30, 1934; s. Edward Gottfried and Pearl Elizabeth (Fischrupp) E.; m. Sharon Lee Geyer, June 30, 1962. BS in Commerce, Loyola U., 1956. Asst. adv. mgr. The Englander Co., Chgo., 1956-57; indsl. film svc. Accurate Cinema Svc., 1960-62; indsl. sales The EMF Co., 1962-69, Avery Internat., Azusa, Calif., 1969-77, The Stanley Works, Hartford, Conn., 1977-78; mfg. rep. ARTCO, Chgo., 1979-99. V.p., bd. dirs. Westerners Internat., Oklahoma City, 1982—, pres. 1997-99; cons. ALA, Chgo., 1982—; tchr. New Trier Extension, Wilmette, Ill., 1985—; adv. bd. Western Outlaw-Lawman History Assn., 1999—. Author: El Paso Lawman, 1982; editor Westerners Brand Book, 1986-96. Bd. dirs. Wilmette Hist. Soc., 1973-77; hist. cons. Wilmette Hist. Mus., 1978; com. mem. Save the Depot Preservation, Wilmette, 1974; sec. Wilmette Sailing Assn., 1974; vis. com. D'Arcy McNickle Ctr. for Am. Indian History, Newberry Libr., 1999-02. Recipient Don Russell Meml. award, 1998, Wola award for most outstanding contbns. to western history, 1999. Mem. Western History Assn., Western Writers Am., Soc. Midland Authors, Chgo. Corral the Westerners (sheriff 1978-80, sidewinder 1984), Windy City BMW Car Club Am. (pres. 1976, Big Wheel 1972, Founders Recognition award 1997), Vintage Sportscar Club (sec. 1972-80, top competitor award 1970, 97), Nat. Cowboy Hall Fame, Soc. of Automotive Historians, Am. Legion. Republican. Roman Catholic. Avocations: vintage sports cars, photography, skiing, horseback riding, books. Office: ARTCO 2035 Greenwood Ave Wilmette IL 60091-1439

EHLERS, VERNON JAMES, congressman; b. Pipestone, Minn., Feb. 6, 1934; m. Johanna Meulink, 1958; children: Heidi, Brian, Marla, Todd. Student, Calvin Coll.; AB, U. Calif., Berkeley, 1956, PhD in Physics, 1960. Tchg. asst. U. Calif., Berkeley, 1956-57, rsch. asst., 1957-60, lectr. in physics, 1960-66; prof. physics Calvin Coll., 1966-83; mem. Mich. State Ho. of Reps., 1983-85, Mich. State Senate, 1985-94, pres. pro tem, 1991-94; mem. U.S. Congress from 3d Mich. dist., 1994—; mem. transp. and infrastructure com., sci. com., edn. and workforce com., house adminstrn. com. Mem. Gov. Milliken's Task Force on Environ. Problems, 1977, Kent County Rep. Exec. Com., Kent County Bd. Commrs., 1975-83, chmn., 1979-82, Mich. Toxic Substance Control Commn., 1982; asst. floor leader Mich. State Ho. of Reps., 1983-85 Contbr. articles to profl. jours. NATO Rsch. fellow U. Heidelberg, Germany, 1961-62, Sci. Faculty fellow NSF, Joint Insts. for Lab. Astrophysics, U. Colo. 1971-72, fellow Calvin Coll. Ctr. for Christian Scholar, 1977-78. Mem. AAAS, Am. Phys. Soc., Am. Assn. Phys. Tchrs. Mem. Christian Reformed Ch. Home: 1848 Morningside Dr SE Grand Rapids MI 49506-5121 Office: 1714 Longworth House Ofc Bldg Washington DC 20515-2203 also: Federal Bldg 110 Michigan St Grand Rapids MI 49503-2313

EHLKE, NANCY JO, agronomist; Assoc. prof. U. Minn., St. Paul, 1986—. Recipient CIBA GEIGY award in Agronomy Am. Soc. of Agronomy, 1995. Office: U Min Dept of Agronomy and Plant Genetics 411 Borleug Hall 1991 Buford Ave Saint Paul MN 55108-1013

EHLMANN, STEVEN E. state legislator; b. St. Charles, Mo., Dec. 6, 1950; m. Jean Poggmeier, 1988. BA, Furman U., 1973; MA, U. Mo., 1975; JD, Washington U., 1985. Former tchr.; ptnr. law firm. State rep. dist. 19 Mo. Ho. of Reps., mem. higher edn. and judiciary coms., tourism, recreational and cultural affairs, St. Charles Citizens Participatory Adv. Com.; state senator dist. 23, 1993—. Mem. Salvation Army, Boys Club Am. Home: 415 N 2d St Saint Charles MO 63301-3306

EHRENBERG, MAUREEN, management consultant; Pres. Grubb & Ellis Mgmt. Svcs., Inc., Northbrook, Ill., 1999—. Office: Grubb & Ellis Mgmt Svcs Inc 2215 Sanders Rd Ste 400 Northbrook IL 60062-6114

EHRLICH, AVA, television executive; b. St. Louis, Aug. 14, 1950; d. Norman and Lillian (Gellman) Ehrlich; m. Barry K. Freedman, Mar. 31, 1979; children: Alexander Zev, Maxwell Samuel. BJ, Northwestern U., 1972, MJ, 1973; MA, Occidental Coll., 1976. Reporter, asst. mng. editor Lerner Newspapers, Chgo., 1974-75; reporter, news editor Sta. KMOX, St. Louis, 1976-79; producer Sta. WXYZ, Detroit, 1979-85; exec. producer Sta. KSDK-TV, St. Louis, 1985—. Guest editor Mademoiselle mag., N.Y.C., 1971; freelance writer, coll. prof. Detroit, Chgo., St. Louis, 1987; adj. faculty mem. Washington U., St. Louis, 1994—. Trustee CORO Found., St. Louis, 1976-77, 86—, St. Louis Jewish Light, 1999—, Crown Ctr., 2000; bd. dirs. Nat. Kidney Found., St. Louis, 1987, St. Louis Jewish Light, 2000—, Crowne Ctr., 2000—. Named Outstanding Woman in Broadcasting, Am. Women in Radio & TV, 1983, Among 18 Most Influential Women in the Region St. Louis Dispatch, 2000; recipient Journalism award Am. Chiropractic Assn., 1989, AP award Ill. UPI, 1989, Illuminator award AMC Cancer Rsch., 1994, Women in Comms. Nat. award, 1988, Emmy award, 1995, Virginia Betts award for Contbns. in Journalism, 1999; CORO Found. fellow in pub. affairs, 1975-76. Mem. NATAS (com. mem. 1986—, bd. dirs. 1994—, 18 local Emmy awards 1986—), Women in Comms., Inc. (sec. 1978-79, Clarion award 1989, Best in Midwest Feature award 1989), Soc. Profl. Journalists. Democrat. Jewish. Home: 8002 Walinca Ter Saint Louis MO 63105-2565 Office: Sta KSDK-TV 1000 Market St Saint Louis MO 63101-2011 E-mail: aehrlich@ksdk.gannett.com.

EHRLICH, GERT, science educator, researcher; b. Vienna, Austria, June 22, 1926; came to U.S., 1939; s. Leopold and Paula Maria (Kucera) E.; m. Anne Vogdes Alger, Apr. 27, 1957. AB with honors in Chemistry, Columbia U., 1948; AM, Harvard U., 1950, PhD, 1952. NIH postdoctoral fellow Harvard U., Cambridge, Mass., 1951-52; research assoc., Dept. Physics U. Mich., Ann Arbor, 1952-53; mem. research staff GE Rsch. Lab., Schenectady, N.Y., 1953-68; prof. materials sci. Coordinated Sci. Lab. U. Ill., Urbana-Champaign, 1968—. Former mem. editorial adv. bd. Chem. Physics Letters, Jour. Chem. Physics, Jour. Vacuum Sci. & Tech., Surface & Colloid Sci., Progress in Surface & Membrane Sci.; contbr. numerous articles on molecular behavior at crystal surfaces and on properties of individual atoms and atom clusters. Served to cpl. U.S. Army, 1945-47, ETO. Guggenheim fellow, 1985. Fellow Am. Phys. Soc., N.Y. Acad. Scis.; mem. Nat. Acad. Scis., Am. Chem. Soc. (Kendall award 1982), Am. Vacuum Soc. (Medard W. Welch award 1979), Alexander von Humboldt Found. (Humboldt-Preis 1992), Sigma Xi, Phi Beta Kappa. Office: U Ill Materials Rsch Lab 104 S Goodwin Ave Urbana IL 61801-2902

EIBEN, ROBERT MICHAEL, pediatric neurologist, educator; b. Cleve., July 12, 1922; s. Michael Albert and Frances Carlysle (Gedeon) E.; m. Anne F. Eiben; children: Daniel F., Christopher J., Thomas M., Mary, Charles G., Elizabeth A. BS, Western Res. U., 1944, MD, 1946. Diplomate Am. Bd. Pediatrics. Intern medicine Univ. Hosp., Cleve., 1946-47; asst. resident pediatrics and contagious diseases City Hosp., 1947, asst. med. dir. div. contagious diseases, 1949-50, visitant in pediatrics, 1949-50, acting dir. dept. pediatrics and contagious diseases, 1950-52; asst. resident pediatrics Babies and Children's Hosp., Cleve., 1948, clin. fellow pediatrics, 1948-49; practice medicine specializing in pediatrics Cleve., 1949-90; asst. dir. dept. pediatrics and contagious diseases Cleve. Met. Gen. Hosp., 1952-60; med. dir. Respiratory Care and Rehab. Center, 1954-60, pres. med. staff, 1958-60, pediatric neurologist, 1963-90, acting med. dir. comprehensive care program, 1966-67, med. dir., 1968-73, mem. med. exec. com., 1974-76, acting dir. dept. pediatrics, 1979-80; USPHS fellow in neurology U. Wash., 1960-63; acting chief, sect. on clin. investigations and therapeutics Developmental and Metabolic Neurology br. Nat. Inst. Neurol. and Communicative Disorders and Strokes, NIH, Bethesda, Md., 1976-77; clin. instr. pediatrics Western Res. U., 1949-50, instr. pediatrics, 1950-51, asst. clin. prof., 1951-54, asst. prof., 1954-65, asst. prof. neurology, 1964-72, assoc. prof. pediatrics, 1965-75, assoc. prof. neurology, 1972-85, prof. pediatrics, 1975-90, prof. neurology, 1985-90, prof. emeritus pediatric neurology, 1991—. Cons., project site visitor Nat. Found. Birth Defects Center Programs, 1961-66; mem. adv. com. on grants to train dentists to care for handicapped Robert Wood Johnson Found., 1975-80; marshall emeriti faculty Case Western Reserve U., 1994—. Mem. coun. Bratenahl Village-County of Cuyahoga, 1982-98. Recipient Presdl. award Internat. Poliomyelitis Congress, Geneva, 1957, Clifford J. Vogt Alumni Svc. award Case Western Res. U., Cleve., 1985; established Annual Robert M. Eiben, M.D. vis. professorship in child neurology MetroHealth Med. Ctr. Dept. Pediat., 1991. Mem.: Child Neurology Soc. (chmn. tng. program com. 1976—77, sec.-treas. 1978—81, pres. 1983—85), Innominatum Soc., No. Ohio Pediat. Soc., Am. Epilepsy Soc., Am. Pediat. Soc., Am. Soc. Human Genetics, Am. Acad. Neurology (chmn. residence exam. com. 1989—93), Am. Acad. Pediat., Case Western Res. U. Med. Alumni Assn. (pres. 1979), Pasteur Club. Home: 2 Oakshore Dr Bratenahl OH 44108-1118 Office: MetroHealth Med Ctr 2500 Metrohealth Dr Cleveland OH 44109-1900

EIBENSTEINER, RON, venture capitalist; Co-founder, CFO Arden Med. Sys., 1983-87; pres., CEO, chmn. Mirror Techs., Inc., 1988-92, 94—, chmn., 1992-94; pres. Wyncrest Captial. Chmn. Minn. Reps., 1999—. Office: Rep Party Minn 480 Cedar St Ste 560 Saint Paul MN 55101-2240

EIBL, CLEMENT, management consulting firm executive; CFO Arthur Anderson, Chgo. Office: Arthur Anderson 33 W Monroe St Ste 1000 Chicago IL 60603-5386

EICH, SUSAN, public relations executive; Dir. corp. pub. rels. Target Corp. (formerly Dayton Hudson Corp.), Mpls., 1995—. Office: Target Corp 33 S 6th PO Box 1392 Minneapolis MN 55440-1392

EICHHOLZ, DENNIS R. controller, treasurer; Contr., treas. Clark USA, Inc., St. Louis, 1994—. Office: Clark USA Inc 8182 Maryland Ave Saint Louis MO 63105-3786

EICHHORN, ARTHUR DAVID, music director; b. St. Louis, Oct. 13, 1953; s. Arthur Louis and Adele (Stankunas) E. BA, Concordia U., River Forest, Ill., 1975, MA, 1976, Webster U., 1986; EdD, Calif. Coast U., 1997. Cert. elem. tchr., Mo. Dir. music St. John Luth. Ch., Mt. Prospect, Ill., 1974-76, Our Savior Luth. Ch., Springfield, 1976-81, Holy Cross Luth. Ch., St. Louis, 1981-91, Timothy Luth. Ch., St. Louis, 1991—. Part-time instr., dir. St. Louis extension site Concordia U., Wis. Mem.: Assn. Luth. Ch. Musicians, Am. Guild Organists, Choristers Guild (pres. local chpt. 1990—92). Republican. Home: 7116 Mardel Ave Saint Louis MO 63109-1123 Office: Timothy Luth Ch 6704 Fyler Ave Saint Louis MO 63139-2239 E-mail: timothy@birch.net., aeich53024@aol.com.

EICKHOFF, JOHN R. (JACK), business executive; BA in Bus. Adminstrn. and Acctg., St. Cloud State U. Various acctg. and fin. planning positions Ceridian Corp., Mpls., 1963-82, v.p. corp. svcs., 1983, v.p., contr. fin. plans and controls, comml. credit, 1983, v.p., contr. fin. plans and controls, fin. and bus. svcs., 1985, v.p., contr. fin. plans and controls, computer sys. group, 1986, v.p., contr. fin. plans and controls computer products group, 1988, v.p., corp. contr., 1989, exec. v.p., CFO, 1995—. Mem. retirement com. Ceridian Corp.; bd. dirs. Norstan Inc. Trustee Boys and Girls Club Mpls. Mem. Fin. Execs. Inst., Fin. Execs. Inst. (Twin Cities chpt.). Office: Ceridian Corp 3311 E Old Shakopee Rd Minneapolis MN 55425-1640

EIGEN, HOWARD, pediatrician, educator; b. N.Y.C., Sept. 8, 1942; s. Jay and Libbie (Kantrowitz) E.; m. Linda Hazzard; children: Sarah Elizabeth, Lauren Michelle B.S., Queens Coll., 1964; M.D., Upstate N.Y. Med. Ctr., Syracuse, 1968. Diplomate Am. Bd. Pediatrics, Am. Bd. Pediatric Pulmonology, Am. Bd. Critical Care Medicine, Nat. Bd. Med. Examiners (mem. pediatric test com. 1986-90). Resident in pediatrics Upstate Med. Ctr., Syracuse, 1968-71; fellow in pediatric pulmonology Tulane U., New Orleans, 1973-76; asst. prof. pediatrics Ind. U., Indpls., 1976-84, prof., 1984-96, Billie Lou Wood Prof. pediatrics, 1996—. Assoc. chmn. of pediatrics for Clin. Affairs, dir. pediatric intensive care, pulmonology sect. Riley Hosp. for Children, med. dir. ambulatory care, 1989— Co-editor: Respiratory Disease in Children: Diagnosis and Management; assoc. editor Pediatric Pulmonology, 1984-91; contbr. articles to profl. jours. Served to maj. U.S. Army, 1971-73. Fellow Am. Acad. Pediatrics (pres. chest sect. 1983-85, pulmonology 1986—), Am. Thoracic Soc., Am. Bd. Pediatrics, Am. Lung Assn. (pres. Ind. 1984-85). Avocation: tennis. Office: Ind U Dept Pediatrics 702 Barnhill Dr Rm 2750 Indianapolis IN 46202-5128

EIKEN, DOUG K. state agency administrator; With N.D. Pks. and Recreation Dept., Bismarck; dir. Mo. State Pk. Divsn., Jefferson City, 1994—. Office: Mo State Pk Divsn PO Box 176 1659 E Elm St Jefferson City MO 65101-4124 Fax: 373-526-7716.

EIMER, NATHAN PHILIP, lawyer; b. Chgo., June 26, 1949; s. Irving A. and Charlotte Eimer; m. Kathleen L. Roach; children: Micah Jacob, Noah Joseph, Daniel Jordan, Anna Beatrice. AB in Econs. magna cum laude, U. Ill., 1970; JD cum laude, Northwestern U., 1973. Bar: Ill. 1973, U.S. Supreme Ct. 1978, N.Y. 1985, Tex. 1998. Assoc. Sidley & Austin, Chgo., 1973-80, ptnr., mem. exec. com., 1980—2000; founding ptnr. Eimer Stahl Klevorn & Solberg, 2000—. Adj. prof. Law Sch., Northwestern U., Chgo., 1989-96. Note and comment editor Northwestern U. Law Rev., 1972-73. Bd. dirs. Chgo. Lawyers Com. for Civil Rights, 1991—, pres., 1993-94; bd. dirs. UNICEF, 1992-93, Infant Welfare Soc., Chgo., exec. v.p., 1992-96, pres., 1996-98; mem. adv. bd. Children & Family Justice Ctr., Northwestern U. Legal Clinic, 1996—. Mem. ABA, Univ. Club. Office: Eimer Stahl Klevorn & Solberg 122 S Michigan Ave Ste 1776 Chicago IL 60603 E-mail: neimer@eimerstahl.com.

EINHORN, EDWARD MARTIN (EDDIE EINHORN), professional baseball team executive; b. Paterson, N.J., Jan. 3, 1936; s. Harold Benjamin and Mae (Lippman) E.; m. Ann Magdelene Pelachik, Apr. 24, 1962; children: Jennifer, Jeffrey. AB, U. Pa., 1957; JD, Northwestern U., 1960. Radio sports announcer Sta.-WXPN, Phila., 1954-57; founder, pres. Midwestern Sports Network, Chgo., 1957-61, TV sports Inc. (name changed to TVS 1968, became subs. Corinthian Broadcasting Corp. 1973), N.Y.C., 1961-65, pres., chief exec. officer, 1965-78; exec. producer CBS Sports Spectacular, 1978—; pres. Chgo. White Sox, 1981-93, vice chmn., 1993—; founder Sports Vision Chgo., 1982. Dir. Corinthian Broadcasting Corp., 1973-77; format com. mem. Major League Baseball; co-architect Baseball Network; TV cons. U.S. Olympic Com.; initiator 200 hour Olympic TV package, 1990; TV cons. U.S. Figure Skating Assn., Internat. Skating Union. bd. dirs. Chgo. Bulls. Editor-in-chief Jour. Air Law and Sci., 1959-60, Northwestern Jour. Criminal Law Sci., 1958-60; producer (TV spl.) Gossamer Albatross, Flight of Imagination (Emmy award 1980). Recipient Honor award Naismith Basketball Hall of Fame, 1973, Merit award Nat. Basketball Coaches, 1973, Victor award City of Hope, 1974. Mem. Nat. Acad. Radio, TV Arts and Scis., Internat. Radio, TV Soc., Nat. Assn. TV Program Execs., Nat. Assn. Coll. Dirs., Nat. Assn. Basketball Coaches (TV negotiation com.) Profl. Baseball Assn. (TV com. mem. 1992-95, sr. Am. League rep. on player devel. negotiating com.). Office: Chgo White Sox 333 W 35th St Chicago IL 60616-3651

EISENBERG, HOWARD BRUCE, law educator; b. Chgo., Dec. 9, 1946; s. Herman Levy and Margie M. (Meyers) E.; m. Phyllis Terry Borenstein, Aug. 25, 1968; children: Nathan, Adam, Leah. BA, Northwestern U., 1968; JD, U. Wis., 1971. Bar: Wis. 1971, D.C. 1980, Ill. 1983, U.S. Dist. Ct. (ea. and we. dists.) Wis. 1971, U.S. Ct. Appeals (8th cir.) 1983, U.S. Supreme Ct. 1974, U.S. Ct. Appeals (D.C. cir.) 1978, U.S. Dist. Ct. (ea. and we. dists.) Ark. 1991. Mem. staff Wis. Judicare Legal Svcs. Agy. OEO, Madison, 1968-71; law clk. to justice Wis. Supreme Ct., 1971-72; asst. state pub. defender State of Wis., 1972, state pub. defender, 1972-78; dir. defender divsn. Nat. Legal Aid and Defender Assn., Washington, 1978-79, exec. dir., 1979-83; assoc. prof. law, dir. clin. edn. So. Ill. U., Carbondale, 1983-91, assoc. prof., 1983-87, prof., 1987-91; dean Sch. Law, prof. law U. Ark., Little Rock, 1991-95; dean, prof. law Law Sch. Marquette U., 1995—. Mem. Wis. Bd. Bar Examiners, 1996—, chmn., 2001; bd. dirs. appellate practice sect. Bar of Wis., 1999—, chmn., 2001—; dir. Coalition for Legal Assn., 1981—82, Ill. Guardianship and Protective Svcs. Assn., 1990—91, Ark. CLE Bd., 1991—95, Pulaski County Bar Assn., 1991—95, Ark. Inst. CLE, Assn. Religiously Affiliated Law Schs.; chair Fed. Jud. Nominating Commn., Ea. Dist., Wis., 1995—. Contbr. articles to profl. jours. Bd. dirs. Hospice So. Ill., 1988-91, Milw. Legal Aid Soc., 1997—. Ill. State scholar, 1964-68; NDEA grantee, 1967. Mem. ABA, Am. Acad. Appellate Lawyers, Nat. Acad. Elder Law Attys., State Bar Wis., Wis. Assn. Criminal Attys., Ark. State Bar Assn., 7th Cir. Bar Assn., Ill. State Bar Assn., Milw. Bar Assn., Milw. Bar Assn. Found. (bd. 1997—), Equal Justice Coalition (bd. mem. 1998—), Nat. Assn. Criminal Def. Lawyers, Northwestern U. Alumni Assn., Wis. U. Alumni Assn., Phi Beta Kappa. Democrat. Jewish. Office: Marquette U Sch of Law PO Box 1881 Milwaukee WI 53201-1881

EISENBERG, LEE B. communications executive, author; b. Phila., July 22, 1946; s. George M. and Eve (Blonsky) E.; m. Linda Reville, June 7, 1986; children: Edmund George, Katherine Eve. AB, U. Pa., 1968; MA, Annenberg Sch. Communications, 1970. Assoc. editor Esquire Mag., N.Y.C., 1970-72, sr. editor, 1972-74, mng. editor, 1974-75, editor, 1976-77, v.p. devel., 1980-84, editor-in-chief, 1987-90; founding editor-in-chief Esquire, U.K., London, 1990-91; founding ptnr. The Edison Project, Knoxville, Tenn., 1992-95; editor creative devel. Time Mag., N.Y.C., 1995-99; exec. v.p., creative dir. Lands' End, Dodgeville, Wis., 1999—. Cons. N.Y. Times Co., 1977-78, Warner Bros., Los Angeles, 1978-79; founder Eisenberg, McCall & Okrent, N.Y.C., 1978-81. Author: Sneaky Feats, 1974, Atlantic City, 1978, Ultimate Fishing Book, 1981, Breaking Eighty, 1997. Founder Rotisserie League Baseball, N.Y.C., 1980—. Recipient One Show award Art Dirs. Club, 1976, Gold Cindy award Assn. Visual Comms., 1984, various nat. mag. awards, 1984-90. Office: Lands' End 1 Lands End Ln Dodgeville WI 53595-0001

EISENBERG, MARVIN JULIUS, art history educator; b. Phila., Aug. 19, 1922; s. Frank and Rosalie (Julius) E. B.A., U. Pa., 1943; M.F.A., Princeton, 1949, Ph.D., 1954. Mem. faculty U. Mich., Ann Arbor, 1949-89, prof. art history, chmn. dept., 1960-69, Collegiate prof., 1974-75, prof. emeritus, 1989—; mem. Inst. for Advanced Study, Princeton, N.J., 1970. Vis. prof. Stanford U., 1973; mem. adv. com. Center for Advanced Study in Visual Arts, Nat. Gallery, Washington, 1981-84; mem. vis. com. dept. fine arts, Harvard U., 1975-81, Freer Gallery Art, Washington, 1970-96, Commn. on Preservation and Access, Washington, 1991-94, Ga. Mus. Art, 1997—; disting. Berg prof. Colo. Coll., 1990, 93, 95, 97, 2000, 2002; Hooker disting. vis. prof. McMaster U., 1993; Saunders lectr. St. Andrews U., 1998. Author: Lorenzo Monaco, 1989; co-author: The Confraternity Altarpiece by Mariotto di Nardo, 1998; contbr. articles on early Italian painting to profl. jours. Served with AUS, 1943-46. Recipient Star of Solidarity II Italy, 1966; Coll. Art Assn. Disting. Teaching of Art History award, 1987; Guggenheim fellow, 1959. Fellow Japan Soc. for Promotion of Sci.; mem. Coll. Art Assn. Am. (dir. 1965-70, v.p. 1966-67, pres. 1968-69), Royal Soc. Arts (Benjamin Franklin fellow 1969), Phi Beta Kappa, Phi Kappa Phi. Home: 2200 Fuller Ct Apt 1201 Ann Arbor MI 48105-2307

EISENBERG, PAUL RICHARD, cardiologist, consultant, educator; b. Rome, Mar. 9, 1955; came to U.S., 1956; s. David Marvin and Sonia Maria (Benesdetti) E.; m. Patricia Lynn Goodman, Apr. 25, 1982; 1 child, Jamie. BS, Tulane U., 1975, MPH, 1980; MD, N.Y. Med. Coll., Valhalla, 1980. Diplomate Am. Bd. Internal Medicine, Am. Bd. Cardiology. Intern in internal medicine Barnes Hosp., St. Louis, 1980-83, fellow in cardiology, pulmonary medicine, 1983-85, asst. dir. CCU, 1986-91, dir. CCU, 1991-98; asst. prof. Washington U., 1985-91, assoc. prof., 1991-97, prof., 1997-98; med. dir. cardiovasc. therapeutics Eli Lilly & Co., Indpls., 1998-2000, exec. dir. cardiovasc. discovery, 2000—01, v.p. med., 2001—, 2001. Asst. editor: Medical Management of Heart Disease; contbr. over 100 articles to profl. jours. Fellow Am. Heart Assn. (clin. cardiology), Am. Coll. Chest Physicians, Am. Coll. Cardiology; mem. Am. Fedn. Clin. Rsch., Internat. Soc. Thrombosis and Haemostasis. Office: Lilly Rsch Labs Lily Corp Ctr Drop Code 0520 Ctr Indianapolis IN 46285-0001

EISENBERG, RICHARD MARTIN, pharmacology educator; b. Weehawken, N.J., May 15, 1942; s. Herbert and Evelyn (Stecker) E.; m. Marsha Eisenberg, July 3, 1966; children: Marla, Aaron, Shana. BA, UCLA, 1963, MS, 1967, PhD, 1970; postdoc., U. Rochester, 1970-71. Asst. prof. pharmacology U. Minn., Duluth, 1971-76, assoc. prof., 1976-77, assoc. prof., acting dept. head, 1977-80, assoc. prof., dept. head, 1980-85, prof., dept. head, 1985—. Author-developer: (computer software) Mac Pharmacology, Mac MedVirology, Mac BrainLesion; presenter in field; contbr. articles to profl. jours. Recipient numerous rsch. grants Nat. Inst. Drug Abuse, 1978—, other instns., 1975—. Mem. Am. Soc. Pharmacology and Exptl. Therapeutics, Assn. Med. Sch. Pharmacology (treas. 1994-98, pres. 1998-2000), Endocrine Soc., Western Pharmacology Soc., Coll. on Problems of Drug Dependence. Avocations: cabinet making, microcomputers, photography. Office: U Minn Duluth Sch Medicine Dept Pharmacology 10 University Dr Duluth MN 55812-2403

EISENSTARK, ABRAHAM, research director, microbiologist; b. Warsaw, Poland, Sept. 5, 1919; came to U.S., 1922; s. Isadore and Sarah (Becker) E.; m. Roma Gould, Jan. 18, 1948 (dec. July 1984); children: Romalyn, David Allen, Douglas Darwin; m. Joan Weatherly, Apr. 6, 1991. BA, U. Ill., 1941, MA, 1942, PhD, 1948. Program dir., acting sect. head Molecular Biology Sect. NSF, Washington, 1969-70; assoc. prof. Okla. State U., Stillwater, 1948-51; prof. Kans. State U., Manhattan, 1951-71; prof., dir. divsn. biol. scis. U. Mo., Columbia, 1971-80, prof., 1980-90, prof. emeritus, 1990—; dir. Cancer Rsch. Ctr., 1990—; sr. scientist Lab. and Environ. Tech., Inc., 1990—. Contbr. over 100 articles to profl. jours. With U.S. Army, 1942-46. Fellow John Simon Guggenheim Found., 1958-59, USPHS, 1959; sr. postdoctoral fellow NSF, 1966-67; recipient Sigma Xi Rsch. award Kans. State U., 1954, Thomas Jefferson Faculty Excellence award U. Mo., 1986, Most Disting. Scientist award Mo. Acad. Sci., 1989; Byler Disting. Prof., 1990. Mem. AAAS, Am. Soc. Microbiology. Office: Cancer Research Center 3501 Berrywood Dr Columbia MO 65201-6570 E-mail: eisenstarka@missouri.edu.

EISENSTEIN, ELIZABETH LEWISOHN, historian, educator; b. N.Y.C., Oct. 11, 1923; d. Sam A. and Margaret V. (Seligman) Lewisohn; m. Julian Calvert Eisenstein, May 30, 1948; children: Margaret, John (dec.), Edward. A.B., Vassar Coll., 1944; M.A., Radcliffe Coll., 1947, Ph.D., 1953; Litt. D. (hon.), Mt. Holyoke Coll., 1979. From lectr. to adj. prof history Am. U., Washington, 1959-74; Alice Freeman Palmer prof. history U. Mich., Ann Arbor, 1975-88, prof. emerita, 1988—. Scholar-in-residence Rockefeller Found. Center, Bellagio, Italy, June 1977; mem. vis. com. dept. history Harvard U., 1975-81, vice-chmn., 1979-81; dir. Ecole des Hautes Etudes en Sciences Sociales, Paris, 1982; guest speaker, participant confs. and seminars; I. Beam vis. prof. U. Iowa, 1980; Mead-Swing lectr. Oberlin Coll., 1980; Stone lectr. U. Glasgow, 1984; Van Leer lectr. Van Leer Fedn., Jerusalem, 1984; Hanes lectr. U. N.C., Chapel Hill, 1985 first resident cons. Center for the Book, Library of Congress, Washington, 1979; mem. Coun. Scholars, 1980-88; pres.'s disting. visitor Vassar Coll., 1988; Pforzheimer lectr. N.Y. Pub. Libr., 1989, Lyell lectr. Bodleian Libr., Oxford, 1990, Merle Curti lectr. U. Wis., Madison, 1992, Jantz lectr. Oberlin Coll., 1995, Clifford lectr. Austin, Tex., 1996; vis. fellow Wolfson Coll., Oxford, 1990; sem. dir. Folger Inst., 1999. Author: The First Professional Revolutionist: F. M. Buonarroti, 1959, The Printing Press as an Agent of Change, 1979 , 2 vols. paperback edit., 1980 (Phi Beta Kappa Ralph Waldo Emerson prize 1980), The Printing Revolution in Early Modern Europe, 1983 (reissued as Canto Book, 1993), Grub Street Abroad, 1992; mem. editorial bd. Jour. Modern History, 1973-76, 83-86, Revs. in European History, 1973-86, Jour. Library History, 1979-82, Eighteenth Century Studies, 1981-84; contbr. articles to profl. jours., chpts. to books. Bd. dirs. Folger Shakespeare Libr., 2000—. Belle Skinner fellow Vassar Coll., NEH fellow, 1977, Guggenheim fellow, 1982, fellow Ctr. Advanced Studies in Behavioral Scis., 1982-83, 92-93, Humanities Rsch. Ctr. fellow Australian Nat. U., 1988. Fellow Am. Acad. Arts and Scis., Royal Hist. Soc.; mem. Soc. French Hist. Studies (v.p. 1970, mem. program com. 1974), Am. Soc. 18th Century Studies (nominating com. 1971), Soc. 16th Century Studies, Am. Hist. Assn. (com. on coms. 1970-72, chmn. Modern European sect. 1981, council 1982-85), Renaissance Soc. Am. (council 1973-76, pres. 1986), Am. Antiquarian Soc. (exec. com., adv. bd. 1984-87), Phi Beta Kappa. Office: U Mich Dept History Ann Arbor MI 48109 E-mail: eisenst@mindspring.com.

EISLER, MILLARD MARCUS, financial executive; b. Toledo, Mar. 31, 1950; s. Joseph R. and Marilynn (Gross) E. BS, Ind. U., 1972; MBA, Cornell U., 1977. CPA, Ill., Mass., N.H. Auditor Arthur Andersen & Co., Boston, 1977-79; mgr. internat. acctg. Wheelabrator-Frye, Inc., Hampton, N.H., 1979-81; mgr. ops. analysis and audit GCA Corp., Bedford, Mass., 1981-85; mgr. cost acctg. and fin. analysis Precision Sci., Inc., Chgo., 1985-86, contr., chief fin. officer, 1986-89; tax preparer H&R Block, Inc., 1989-92, Lincoln, Nebr., 1993, quality control mgr., 1994, franchise dir., dist. mgr. Madison, Wis., 1994-98; tax preparer H.R. Block, 1999—; fin. mgmt. cons. CUNA Mutual Group, 1998—. Bd. dirs. Franklin Software Co., Arvada, Colo.; lectr. Northeastern Ill. U., Chgo., 1986-88. Mem. Ind. U. Alumni Assn., Cornell U. Alumni Assn. of Wis. Democrat. Jewish. Home: 834 S Gammon Rd Madison WI 53719-1381 Office: CUNA Mutual Group 5910 Mineral Point Rd Madison WI 53705-4498

EITRHEIM, NORMAN DUANE, bishop; b. Baltic, S.D., Jan. 14, 1929; s. Daniel Tormod and Selma (Thompson) E.; m. Clarice Yvonne Pederson, Aug. 23, 1952; children: Daniel, David, John, Marie. BA, Augustana Coll., 1951; BTh, Luther Sem., St. Paul, 1956; LHD (hon.), Augustana Coll., 1988. Pastor 1st English Luth. Ch., Tyler, Minn., 1956-63, St. Philips Luth. Ch., Fridley, 1963-76; asst. to pres. Luther Northwestern Sem., St. Paul, 1976-80; bishop S.D. dist. Am. Luth. Ch., Sioux Falls, 1981-87; bishop S.D. Synod Evang. Luth. Ch. in Am., 1988-95. Staff sgt. USAF, 1951-52.

EK, ALAN RYAN, forestry educator; b. Mpls., Sept. 5, 1942; cons. in field in U.S. and world; mem. forestry rsch. adv. coun. USDA. BS in Forestry, U. Minn., St. Paul, 1964, MS, 1965; PhD, Oreg. State U., Corvallis, 1969. Rsch. officer Can. Dept. Forestry and Rural Devel., Sault Ste Marie, Ont., Can., 1966-69; asst. prof., then assoc. prof. forestry U. Wis., Madison, 1969-77; assoc. prof., then prof. forestry U. Minn., St. Paul, 1977—, head dept. forest resources, 1984—. Mem. USDA Forestry Rsch. Adv. Coun., 1994-96, 98-99, chair, 1998-99; cons. in field in U.S. and world. Contbr. chpts. to books, articles to profl. jours. Fulbright scholar to Finland, 1997. Fellow Soc. Am. Foresters (various coms., chmn. forest sci. and tech. bd. 1989-90); mem. AAAS, Nat. Assn. Profl. Forestry Schs. and Colls. (chmn. rsch. com. 1993-95, 99-2000), Am. Statis. Assn., Am. Soc. Photogrammetry and Remote Sensing, Sigma Xi, Xi Sigma Pi, Gamma Sigma Delta. Avocations: reading, sports. Home: 4744 Kevin Ln Saint Paul MN 55126-5849 Office: U Minn Dept Forest Resources Saint Paul MN 55108

EKDAHL, JON NELS, lawyer, retired corporate secretary; b. Topeka, Nov. 15, 1942; s. Oscar S. and Dorothy O. (Ekdahl) M.; m. Marcia Opp, May 24, 1975; children: Kirsten, Erika, Kristofer. AB magna cum laude, Harvard U., 1964, LLB, 1968; MS in Econs., London Sch. Econs., 1965. Bar: Ill. 1969, U.S. Ct. Appeals (7th cir.) 1981, U.S. Supreme Ct. 1981. Assoc. Sidley & Austin, Chgo., 1968-75, ptnr., 1973-75; mng. ptnr., gen. counsel Andersen Worldwide SC, 1975-2000. With USAR, 1968-74. Mem. ABA, Chgo. Bar Assn., Mid-Am. Club, Chgo. Club. Office: 33 W Monroe St Fl 18 Chicago IL 60603-5662 E-mail: jon.n.ekdahl@awo.com., ekdahl42@aol.com.

ELAM, JOHN CARLTON, lawyer; b. Ft. Wayne, Ind., Mar. 6, 1924; s. Bernard C. and Eunice (Gawthrop) E.; m. Virginia Mayberry, July 14, 1945; children: Nancy Lee, Patricia Scott, Mary Jane, John William. B.A., U. Mich., 1948, J.D. with distinction, 1949. Bar: Mich. 1949, Ohio 1950. Assoc. Vorys, Sater, Seymour & Pease, Columbus, Ohio, 1949-54, ptnr., 1954—, presiding ptnr., 1964-94, of counsel, 1995—. Trustee Columbus Coll. Art and Design, 1981-88. Fellow Am. Coll. Trial Lawyers (pres. 1980-81); mem. ABA (standing com. on fed. judiciary and ho. of dels.), Ohio Bar Assn., Columbus Bar Assn. (pres. 1964), 6th Cir. Jud. Conf. Home: 5000 Squirrel Bnd Columbus OH 43220-2278 Office: Vorys Sater Seymour & Pease 52 E Gay St Columbus OH 43215-3161

ELBAZ, SOHAIR WASTAWY, library dean, consultant; b. Cairo, Nov. 7, 1954; came to U.S., 1981; s. Fahmy Elsayed Wastawy and Alia Ahmed Shaffie; m. Nabil Gamal, July 28, 1987; children: Kareim, Tahany. BA, Cairo U., 1975, MA, 1978; MLS, Cath. U., 1983; PhD, Simmons Coll., 1987. Micrographics specialist Cairo U., 1975-83; asst. prof. Inst. Pub. Administrn., Riyadh, Saudi Arabia, 1984-85; info. specialist, mktg. dir. Data Processing Services, Cairo, 1983-87; info. researcher Ill. Inst. Tech., Chgo., 1988-91, dir. libr., 1991—. Cons. UN, 1989—. Mem. Egyptian Soc. Info. Sci., Ill. Libr. Assn. Republican. Office: Illinois Inst of Tech Paul V Galvin Libr 35 W 33rd St Chicago IL 60616-3739

ELBERGER, RONALD EDWARD, lawyer; b. Newark, Mar. 13, 1945; s. Morris and Clara (Denes) Elberger; m. Rena Ann Brodey, Feb. 15, 1975; children: Seth, Rebecca. AA, George Washington U., 1964, BA, 1966; JD, Am. U., 1969. Bar: Md. 1969, D.C. 1970, Ind. 1971, U.S. Ct. Appeals (7th cir.) 1971, U.S. Supreme Ct. 1973. Atty. Balt. Legal Aid Bur., 1969-70; chief counsel Legal Services Orgn., Indpls., 1970-72; ptnr. Elberger & Stanton, 1974-76; assoc. Bose, McKinney & Evans, LLP, 1972—74, ptnr., 1976—. V.p. Worldwide Slacks, Inc., 1984—, Cardboard Shoe Prodns., Inc., 1989—; asst. sec., v.p., litig. counsel Emmis Comm. Corp., 1986—. Mem., v.p. Med. Licensing Bd., Ind., 1982—98; pres., chmn. bd. dirs. Ind. Civil Liberties Union, Indpls., 1972—77, bd. dirs., 1972, 1980—82; mem. nat. coun. media and pub. affairs George Washington U., 2000—; bd. dirs. Jewish Cmty. Rels. Coun., 1997—2000, ACLU, N.Y.C., 1972—77; trustee Children's Mus. Indpls., 1994—; bd. dirs. Flanner Ho. Indpls., Inc., 1999—. Fellow Reginald Heber Smith, U. Pa., 1969—71. Fellow: Indpls. Bar Found.; mem.: ABA, Ind. Bar Assn. Democrat. Jewish. Avocations: fishing, music, gardening. Office: Bose McKinney & Evans LLP 2700 First Indiana Pla 135 N Pennsylvania St Indianapolis IN 46204-2400

ELBIN, JOHN C. food company executive; b. Columbus, Ohio, Dec. 24, 1952; s. John William and Beatrice A. (Behmer) E.; m. Mary Paulette O'Brien, June 28, 1986; children: John William, Julie Christina. BS in Acctg. cum laude, Fla. State U., 1975. Sr. acct. Price Waterhouse, Columbus & Ft. Lauderdale, Fla., 1975-79; acctg. mgr. specialty projects Pet Inc., St. Louis, 1979, v.p., contr. grocery group, 1980-83, v.p. ops. analysis, 1984, v.p. corp. planning and devel., 1985-90, v.p. specialty ops., 1988-90, sr. v.p., CFO, treas., 1990—. Chmn. Better Bus. Bur., St. Louis, 1989-90. Mem. AICPA, Fin. Execs. Inst. Avocations: golf. Office: Pet Inc 400 S 4th St Saint Louis MO 63102-1815 ALSO: LILLY INDUSTRIES 546 Abbott St Indianapolis IN 46225-1225

ELDEN, GARY MICHAEL, lawyer; b. Chgo., Dec. 11, 1944; s. E. Harold and Sylvia Arlene (Diamond) E.; m. Phyllis Deborah Mandler, Apr. 20, 1975; children: Roxanna Mandler, Erica Mandler. BA, U. Ill., 1966; JD, Harvard U., 1969. Bar: Ill. 1969, U.S. Dist. Ct. (no. dist.) Ill. 1969, U.S. Ct. Appeals (7th cir.) 1973, U.S. Supreme Ct. 1973, U.S. Dist. Ct. (ea. dist.) Mich. 1985, U.S. Ct. Appeals (8th cir.) 1988, U.S. Ct. Appeals (6th and 10th cirs.) 1990, U.S. Dist. Ct. (ea. dist.) Wis. 1992. Ptnr. Kirkland & Ellis, Chgo., 1969-78, Reuben & Proctor, Chgo., 1978-86, Isham, Lincoln & Beale, Chgo., 1986-88, Grippo & Elden, Chgo., 1988—. Contbr. articles to profl. jours. Fellow Am. Coll. Trial Lawyers; mem. ABA, Chgo. Bar Assn. (sec. com. appellate procedures 1975-77), Chgo. Coun. Lawyers, Appellate Lawyers Assn. (bd. dirs. 1975-77), Met. Club. Home: 3750 N Lake Shore Dr Chicago IL 60613-4238 Office: Grippo & Elden 227 W Monroe St Ste 3600 Chicago IL 60606-5098

ELDER, IRMA, automotive company executive; Pres. Troy (Mich.) Motors. Office: Troy Motors 777 John R Rd Troy MI 48083-4302

ELDREDGE, CHARLES CHILD, III, art history educator; b. Boston, Apr. 12, 1944; s. Henry and Priscilla Marion (Bateson) E.; m. Jane Allen MacDougal, June 11, 1966; children: Henry Gifford, Janann Bateson. BA, Amherst Coll., 1966; PhD, U. Minn., 1971. Curator asst. Minn. Hist. Soc., St. Paul, 1966-68; mem. edn. dept. Mpls. Inst. Arts, 1967-69; teaching assoc. art history U. Minn., 1968-70; asst. prof. art history, curator collections Spencer Mus. Art, U. Kans., Lawrence, 1970-71, dir. mus., 1971-82, assoc. prof., 1974-80, prof., 1980-82; dir. Nat. Mus. Am. Art, Washington, 1982-88; Hall disting. prof. of Am. art and culture U. Kans., Lawrence, 1988—. C.H. Hynson vis. prof. U. Tex., Austin, 1985; trustee Watkins Cmty. Mus., Lawrence, 1972-76, Assn. Art Mus. Dirs., 1982, 87, Reynolda House Mus. Am. Art, 1986-88, Amherst Coll., 1987-93, trustee emeritus, 1993—; trustee Georgia O'Keeffe Found., 1989-95; rsch. assoc. Smithsonian Instn., 1988—; founder Smithsonian Studies in Am. Art, 1987. Author: Marsden Hartley: Lithographs and Related Works, 1972, Ward Lockwood, 1894-1963, 1974, American Imagination and Symbolist Painting, 1979, Charles Walter Stetson, Color and Fantasy, 1982, Pacific Parallels: Artists and the Landscape in New Zealand, 1991, Georgia O'Keeffe, 1991, Georgia O'Keeffe: American and Modern, 1992, The College on the Hill, 1996, Reflections on Nature: Small Paintings by Arthur Dove, 1997, The Floor of the Sky: Artists and the North American Prairie, 2000; co-author: The Arcadian Landscape: 19th Century American Painters in Italy, 1972, Art in New Mexico, 1900-1945, 1986, American Originals: Selections from Reynolda House, Mus. of American Art, 1990, Life Cycles: The Charles E. Burchfield Collection, 1996, John Steuart Curry: Inventing the Middle West, 1997, The Regionalist Vision of William Dickerson, 1997, Georgia O'Keeffe and The Calla Lily in American Art, 2002; gen. editor: The Register of Mus. Art, 1971—82; mem. editl. bd. Am. Studies, 1974—77, Am. Art, 1996—. Smithsonian Instn. fellow Nat. Collection Fine Arts, 1979; Fulbright scholar N.Z., 1983; Found. Visitor fellow U. Auckland, 1993, Smithsonian fellowship Nat. Mus. of Am. Art, 1995; recipient Outstanding Alumnus award U. Minn., 1986, Ctr. for Tchg. Excellence award U. Kans., 2000. Mem. Coll. Art Assn. Am., Am. Studies Assn., Am. Assn. Mus., Assn. Art Mus. Dirs Office: U Kans Dept Art History 209 Spencer Mus Art 1301 Mississippi St Lawrence KS 66045-0001 E-mail: cce@ku.edu.

ELDRIDGE, JAMES FRANCIS, insurance executive; b. Appleton, Wis., Nov. 6, 1946; s. C.H. and Florence M. (Dorschel) E.; m. Mary E. Evenson; children: Stacy M., Thomas J., Michael P., Kevin J. BA, Dartmouth Coll., 1968; JD, Marquette U., 1971. Bar: Wis. Assoc. counsel Kivett and Kasdorf, Milw., 1971-74; claim counsel Am. Family Mut. Ins. Co., 1974-81, regional claim counsel Madison, Wis., 1981-84, regional claim mgr., 1984-85, v.p., claims, 1985-90, exec. v.p. corp. legal, sec., 1990—. Mem. Civil Trial Counsel of Wis., Wis. Acad. Trial Lawyers, Dane County Bar Assn., Am. Arbitration Assn., Nat. Assn. Ind. Insurers (laws com.). Republican. Roman Catholic. Avocations: golf, tennis, racquetball, softball, tropical fish. Home: 1830 Cobblestone Ct Sun Prairie WI 53590-3520 Office: Am Family Ins Group 6000 American Pky Madison WI 53783-0001

ELDRIDGE, TRUMAN KERMIT, JR. lawyer; b. Kansas City, Mo., July 27, 1944; s. Truman Kermit and Nell Marie (Dennis) E.; m. Joan Ellen Jurgeson, Feb. 9, 1965; children: Christina Joanne, Gregory Truman. AB, Rockhurst Coll., 1966; JD, U. Mo., Kansas City, 1969. Bar: Mo. 1969, U.S. Dist. Ct. (we. dist.) Mo. 1969, U.S. Ct. Appeals (8th cir.) 1977, (10th cir.) 1995, U.S. S. Ct., 1992, U.S. Dist. Ct. Kans. 1998. Assoc. Morris, Foust, Moudy & Beckett, Kansas City, 1969-70, Dietrich, Davis, Dicus, Rowlands & Schmitt, Kansas City, 1971-74, ptnr., 1975, Armstrong, Teasdale, LLP, Kansas City, 1989-2000; sr. counsel Schlee, Huber McMullen & Krause, 2001—. Author: (with othrs) Missouri Environmental Law Handbook, 1990, 2d edit., 1993, 3d edit., 1997; contbr. articles to profl. jours. Chmn. bd. dirs. Loretto Sch., Kansas City, 1981-83; mem. Friends of Art, Nelson Atkins Gallery, Kansas City, 1980-2000; mem. Energy and Environ. Commn. City of Kansas City, 1990-91, 1994, bd. dirs. Sheffield Pl., 1997—, vice chair, 1998-99, chair, 1999-2000. Master Ross T. Roberts Inn of Ct.; mem. ABA, Def. Rsch. Inst., Mo. Bar Assn., Kansas City Met. Bar Assn. (fed. ct. com., vice chair 1989-90, chair 1990-91), Mo. Orgn. Def. Lawyers, Internat. Trademark Assn., Greater Kansas City C. of C. (mem. environ. com. 1989-2000), Kansas City Club (athletic com. 1990—2001, chair 1995—2001, house com. 1993-96, 98-99, long range planning com. 1993-97, bd. dirs. 1997—2001). Roman Catholic. Avocations: sailing, reading, photography, raquetball. Home: 448 W 68th Ter Kansas City MO 64113-1933 Office: PO Box 32430 4050 Pennsylvania Ste 300 Kansas City MO 64171-5430 E-mail: truman_eldridge@hotmail.com., teldridge@schleehuber.com.

ELFSTRAND, MARK, radio personality; b. Fergus Falls, Minn., Oct. 22; m. Rhonda Elfstrand; children: Marshall, Adam, Ingrid. Morning program host Sta. WMBI Radio, Chgo. Avocations: golf, travel. Office: WMBI 820 N LaSalle Blvd Chicago IL 60610*

ELGER, WILLIAM ROBERT, JR. accountant; b. Chgo., Mar. 20, 1950; s. William Robert and Grace G. (LaVaque) E.; m. Kathryn Michele Johnson, July 10, 1971; children: Kimberly, William, Kristin, Joseph. AS in Applied Sci., Coll. of DuPage, Glen Ellyn, Ill., 1970; BS magna cum laude, U. Ill.-Chgo., 1972. CPA, Ill. Staff acct. Ernst & Whinney, Chgo., 1973, in-charge acct., 1973-74, sr. acct., 1974-78, mgr., 1978-82, sr. mgr., 1982-88; chief fin. officer U. Ill. Eye and Ear Infirmary, 1988-89; CFO U. Mich. Med. Sch., Ann Arbor, 1989-99, exec. dir. adminstrn., CFO, 2000—. Chair fin. controls frame work task force U. Mich.; presenter various confs. in field. Author, developer: (tng. course) Auditing Third Party Reimbursement, 1986, 87. Active Union League Civic and Arts Found., Chgo., 1982-89, Union League Found. for Boys and Girls Clubs, Chgo., 1982-89; treas. Newport Assn., Carol Stream, Ill., 1982-83; coach Tri-City Soccer Assn., St. Charles, Ill., 1984, 87, Saline Soccer Assn., 1990, 91, 93, 94, 95, Saline H.S. Soccer Club, 1996, 97. Mem. AICPA, Healthcare Fin. Mgmt. Assn. (advanced mem., acctg. and reimbursement com. 1982-87, chpt. task force com. 1986, 87, auditing com. 1986, 87, Spl. Recognition award 1986, Follmer Bronze Merit award 1999), Ill. Soc. CPAs (mem. long term healthcare com. 1983, hosps. com. 1988-89), Nat. Coun. Univ. Rsch. Adminstrs., Assn. of Univ. Technology Mgrs., Med. Group Mgmt. Assn., Assn. Am. Med. Colls. Group on Bus. Affairs. Methodist. Avocation: golf. Office: 1301 Catherine St PO Box 624 Ann Arbor MI 48106-0624

ELIAS, PAUL S. marketing executive; b. Chgo., July 5, 1926; s. Maurice I. and Ethel (Tieger) E.; m. Jennie Lee Feldschreiber, June 28, 1953; children— Eric David, Stephen Mark, Daniel Avrum. B.S., Northwestern U. Sch. Bus., 1950; hon. degree, N.Y. U. Sch. Continuing Edn., 1972. Buyer Mandel Bros., Chgo., 1950-53; salesman Internat. Latex Corp., 1953-56; v.p. Hy Zeiger & Co., Milw., 1957-59; exec. v.p. K-Promotions, Inc., 1960-78, pres., 1979-80; chief exec. officer, pres. consumer promotions Carlson Mktg. Group, Mpls., 1981-84, chief exec. officer promotions div. Milw., 1985-86; pres. K-Promotions Div. Carlson Promotion Group, 1987-88, Giftmaster Div. Carlson Promotion Group, 1989—, Elias Mktg., Inc., 1989—. Officer, dir. Milw. Jewish Community Center; pres. regional bd. Anti-Defamation League; pres. Regional Bd. Jewish Nat. Fund, 1993-96. Served with USAAF, 1945-46. Mem. Am. Jewish. Achievements include developing inflight mail order mktg. programs for airlines. Office: Elias Mktg Inc PO Box 170107 Milwaukee WI 53217-8016

ELIAS, SAMY E. G. engineering executive; b. Cairo, June 28, 1930; came to U.S., 1956, naturalized, 1964; s. Elias Girgis and Tahia N. (Kassabgy) E.; m. Janice Lee Craig, Aug. 21, 1960; children: Mona Lee, Tresa Jean, Cecilia Ruth. BS in Aero. Engring., Cairo U., 1955; MS in Aero. Engring., Tex. A&M U., 1958; PhD in Indsl. Engring. and Mgmt., Okla. State U., 1960. Grad. asst. Tex. A&M U., College Station, 1957-58; grad. asst. Okla. State U., Stillwater, 1958-60; asst. prof., indsl. engring. Kans. State U., Manhattan, 1960-61; exec. asst. to chmn. bd. Orgn. of Mil. Factories, Egypt, 1961-62; asso. prof. indsl. engring. Kans. State U., 1962-65; assoc. prof. indsl. engring. W.Va. U., Morgantown, 1965-67, prof., 1967-79, chmn. dept. indsl. engring., 1969-76, spl. asst. to univ. pres. for personal rapid transit, 1970-77, Claude Worthington Benedum prof. transp., 1976-82; dir. Harley O. Staggers Nat. Transp. Ctr., 1980-82; dir. transit engring. and safety Washington Met. Area Transit Authority, 1982-84; v.p. Transp. and Distbn. Assocs., Inc. subs. Day & Zimmermann, Phila., 1984-87; prin. FAI Assocs., Inc., McLean, Va., 1987—; assoc. dean engring. rsch. U. Nebr., Lincoln, 1988—. Cons. Kansas City Transit, N.Y. Transit Authority, N.Y. Transit Authority Police Dept., Omaha Transit Co., Cin. Transit Co., W.C. Gilman & Co., Inc., Brown Engring., Transp. and Distbn. Assocs., PRC Harris, Arab Petroleum Cons., Urban Transp. Devel. Corp., World Bank, also others. Contbr. over numerous publs. to profl. jours. Recipient Americanism medal DAR, 1977 Fellow Chartered Inst. Transp., Inst. Indsl. Engrs. (Transp. and Distbn. award 1979); mem. Soc. Am. Value Engrs., Am. Soc. Engring. Edn. (chmn. indsl. engring. divsn. 1972-73), Soc. for Computer Simulation, Nat. Soc. Propl. Engrs., Accreditation Bd. Engring. Tech. (engring. accreditation com. 1987-92, W.Va. Soc. Profl. Engrs. Coptic Orthodox. Home: 8111 Dorset Dr Lincoln NE 68510-5209 Office: U Nebr Engring Rsch Ctrs 150 W Nebraska Hall Lincoln NE 68588

ELKINS, KEN JOE, retired broadcasting executive; b. Prenter, W.Va., Oct. 12, 1937; s. Ernest Eugene Elkins and Gay (Avis) Dodrill; married; children: James, Diana. Student, Nebr. U., 1966-69. Engr. Sta. KETV-TV, Omaha, 1960-67, asst. chief engr., 1967-70, ops. mgr., nat. sales, gen. sales mgr., 1972-75, gen. mgr., 1975-80; chief engr. Sta. KOUB-TV, Dubuque, Iowa, 1970-71, gen. mgr., 1971-72, Sta. KSDK-TV, St. Louis, 1980-81; v.p., CEO Pulitzer Broadcasting Co., 1981-84, pres., CEO, 1984-99; ret., 1999. Bd. dirs. Commerce Bank St. Louis, Maximum Svc. Telecasters,

Washington; chmn. BMI; pres. Nebr. Broadcasters, Omaha, 1979-80; chmn. NBC Affiliate Bd. Govs. Bd. dirs. BJC Health Sys. With USAF, 1957-61. Inducted into Nebr. Broadcasters Hall of Fame, 1990. Mem. Nat. Assn. Broadcasters (1st amendment com. Washington chpt. 1986-91, 1st amendment com. 1986, bd. dirs.), Found. Broadcasters Hall of Fame (bd. dirs., trustee 1990), TV Operators Caucus, Algonquin Club. Avocations: golf, water sports. Home: 720 Twin Fawns Dr Saint Louis MO 63131-4722 E-mail: kelkins@stlnet.com.

ELLEMAN, BARBARA, editor; b. Coloma, Wis., Oct. 20, 1934; d. Donald and Evelyn (Kissinger) Koplein; m. Don W. Elleman, Nov. 14, 1970. BS in Edn., Wis. State U., 1956; MA in Librarianship, U. Denver, 1964. Sch. libr. media specialist Port Washington (Wis.) High Sch., 1956-59, Homestead High Sch., Thiensville-Mequon, Wis., 1959-64; children's libr. Denver Pub. Libr., 1964-65; sch. libr. media specialist Cherry Creek Schs., Denver, 1965-70, Henry Clay Sch., Whitefish Bay, Wis., 1971-75; children's reviewer ALA, Chgo., 1975-82, children's editor, 1982-90, editor Book Links, 1990-96. Vis. lectr. U. Wis., 1974-75, 81-82, U. Ill., Circle Campus, 1983-85; Disting. scholar children's lit., Marquette U., 1996—; cons. H.W. Wilson Co., 1969-75; mem. Libr. Congress Adv. Com. on selection for children's books for blind and physically handicapped, 1980-88, Caldecott Calendar Com., 1986; judge The Am. Book Awards, 1982, Golden Kite, 1987, Boston Globe/Horn Book, 1990; mem. faculty Highlights for Children Writers Conf., 1985-90; mem. orgn. com. MidWest Conf. Soc. Children's Books Writers, 1974-76; chair Hans Christian Andersen Com., 1987-88; advisor Reading Rainbow, 1986-96, Ind. R.E.A.P. project, 1987-93; jury mem. VI Catalonia Premi Children's Book Exbhn., Barcelona, Spain, 1994; adv. bd. Parent's Choice, Cobblestone Publ., Georgia Pub. TV's 2000, The New Advocate mag., 20th Century Children's Writers, Encyclopedia of Children's Literature, Cooperative Children's Book Ctr., U. Wis., Madison, Riverbank Rev., 1998—, Ency. of Children's Lit., 1998—; lang. arts com. NCTE Notable Books, 1997—; spkr. in field. Author: Reading in a Media Age, 1975, 20th Century Children's Writers, 1979, rev. edit., 1984, What Else Can You Do With a Library Degree?, 1980, Popular Reading for Children, 1981, Popular Reading II, 1986, Children's Books of International Interest, 1984, Tomie dePaola, His Art and His Stories, 1999, Virginia Lee Burton: A Life in Art, 2002; contbr. articles to profl. jours. Publicity chair Internat. Bd. Books for Young People Congress, Williamsburg, Va., 1990. Recipient Jeremiah Ludington award Ednl. Paperback Assn., 1996, Hope S. Dean award Found. Children's Lit., 1996. Mem. ALA (2000 Caldecott Com. 1999—), Soc. Children's Book Writers (mem. orgn. com. MidWest Conf. 1974-76), Internat. Bd. Books for Young People (U.S. assoc. editor Bookbird 1978-86, chair nominating com., 1985, bd. dirs. 1990-92), Children's Reading Round Table Chgo. (award 1987), Nat. Coun. Tchrs. English (bd. dirs. children's lit. assembly 1986-88, mem. editl. adv. bd. CLA bull. 1989-91, mem. using nonfiction in classroom com. 1990-96, 2000 Caldecott com., Laura I. Wilden com. 2001--). Office: 1884 Somerset Ln Northbrook IL 60062-6066

ELLENBERGER, RICHARD G. telecommunications executive; Grad., Old Dominion. CEO XL/Connect, Phila., Entrad Corp., Louisville; v.p. S.E. region MCI, sr. v.p. br. ops., sr. v.p. worldwide sales, pres. Bus. Svcs.; pres., COO Cin. Bell, Inc.; pres & CEO Broadwing Inc., Cincinnati, 2000—. Mem. Family Svcs. Bd. Greater Cin. Mem. Cin. C. of c. (bd. dirs.), Ohio Bus. Roundtable. Office: Broadwing Inc 201 E 4th St PO Box 2301 Cincinnati OH 45201-2301

ELLENS, J(AY) HAROLD, philosopher, educator, psychotherapist, pastor; b. McBain, Mich., July 16, 1932; s. John S. and Grace (Kortmann) E.; m. Mary Jo Lewis, Sept. 7, 1954; children: Deborah, Jackie, Dan, Beckie, Rocky, Brenda. AB, Calvin Coll., 1953; BD, Calvin Sem., 1956; ThM, Princeton Sem., 1965; PhD, Wayne State U., 1970; M in Divinity, Calvin Seminary, 1986; MA, U. Mich., 2000, PhD, 2002. Ordained to ministry Christian Reformed Ch., 1956; ordained theologian and pastor Presbyn. Ch., 1978. Pastor Newton (N.J.) Christian Reformed Ch., 1961-65, North Hills Ch., Troy, Mich., 1965-68, Univ. Hills Ch., Farmington Hills, 1968-78, Westminster Presbyn. Ch., 1980-84, Erin Presbyn. Ch., 1986-88, Cherry Hill Presbyn. Ch., 1994-96, White Lake Presbyn. Ch., 1998-2000, Troy Presbyn. Ch., 2000—01, Mt. Clemens 1st Presbyn. Ch., 2001—02; pvt. practice psychotherapy Farmington Hills, 1967—. Religious broadcaster TV, weekly, 1970-74, periodically to date; lectr. humanities and classics Wayne State U., John Wesley Coll., 1970—, Oakland U., 1970-90, Wayne C.C., Oakland C.C., Calvin Sem.; vis. lectr. Princeton Theol. Seminary, 1977-79; with Inst. for Antiquity and Christianity, Claremont U.; lectr. U.S. and abroad. Author: Program Format in Religious Television, 1970, Models of Religious Broadcasting, 1974, Chaplain (Major General) Gerhart W. Hyatt: An Oral History, 1977, (with others) Internat. Standard Bible Encyclopedia, 1979-89, Eternal Vigilance, 1980, God's Grace and Human Health, 1982, Life and Laughter, 1983, Psychology in Worship, 1984, (with others) Baker's Encyclopedia of Psychology, 1984, 1995, Psychotheology: Key Issues, 1986, (with others) Psychotherapy in Christian Perspective, 1987, (with others) Christian Counseling and Psychotherapy, 1987, Love, Life and Laughter, 1988, (with others) Psychology and Religion, 1988, (with others) The Church and Pastoral Care, 1988, (with others) Moral Obligation and the Military, 1988, (with others) God se genade is genoeg, 1989, (with others) Counseling and the Human Predicament, 1989, (with others) Turning Points in Pastoral Care, (with others) Christian Perspectives on Human Development, 1992, The Ancient Library of Alexandria and Early Christian Theological Development, 1993, 95, Alexander The Great and Hellenistic Culture, 1997, Human Disfunction, 1998, (with others) Humanistic Psychology, 1998, (with others) Dictionary of Pastoral Care and Counseling, 1990, (with others) The Interpretation of the Bible, 1998, three books in Portuguese and one in Spanish; editor: CAPS Internat. Directory vols. II-V, 1976-87, Ethical Reflections, 1977, The Beauty of Holiness, 2d edit., 1985, God's Grace in Free Verse, 1987, (with others) Eerdmans Dictionary of the Bible, 2000, with others; editor in chief Jour. Psychology and Christianity, 1975-88; contbr. 150 articles to profl. jours. Served to col. AUS, 1956-61, ret., 1992. Created knight, Queen Juliana, The Netherlands, 1974. Mem. Christian Assn. Psychol. Studies (now exec. dir. emeritus), Soc. Bibl. Lit., Mil. Chaplain Assn., Ret. Officers Assn., Archeol. Inst. Am., Mil. Order World Wars. Home and Office: 26705 Farmington Rd Farmington MI 48334-4329 Office: 1150 Delaney Ave Orlando FL 32806-1264 E-mail: jharoldellens@juno.com.

ELLERBROOK, NIEL COCHRAN, gas company executive; b. Rensselaer, Ind., Dec. 26, 1948; s. James Harry and Margaret (Cochran) E.; children: Jennifer, Jeffrey, Jayma. BS, Ball State U., 1970. CPA, Ind. Staff acct. audit Arthur Andersen & Co., Indpls., 1970-72, audit sr., 1972-75, audit mgr., 1975-80; asst. to sr. v.p. adminstrn. and fin. Ind. Gas Co., Inc., 1980-81, v.p. fin., 1981-84, v.p. fin., chief fin. officer, 1984-87, sr. v.p., CFO, 1987—; v.p., treas., CFO Ind. Energy, Inc., 1986—, also bd. dirs. Bd. dirs. Ind. Gas Co., Ind. Energy, Inc. 5th 3d Bank of Ctrl. Ind Bd. dirs. Crossroads of Am. Coun. Boy Scouta Am., Indpls. Civic Theatre. Mem. AICPA, Ind. CPA Soc. (bd. dirs. Indpls. chpt., past pres. 1977-83, state bd. dirs. 1984-87), Fin. Exec. Inst., Ind. Fiscal Policy Inst. (bd. dirs. 1985—, vice chmn. 1988-91, chmn. 1991-94), Ind. C. of C. (taxation com. 1982-94, chmn. 1987-94), Ind. Gas Assn. (treas., asst. sec. 1988—). Office: Ind Gas Co Inc 1630 N Meridian St Indianapolis IN 46202-1496

ELLINGTON, DONALD E. transportation company executive; CFO Unigroup, Inc., Fenton, Mo. Office: Unigroup Inc One United Dr Fenton MO 63026

ELLINGTON, HOWARD WESLEY, architect; b. Anthony, Kans., Mar. 2, 1938; s. John Wesley and Cressie May (Wilson) E.; m. Nelda Lee Newlin, Sept. 5, 1959; children: Howard Wesley II, Eric John, Craig Alan, Amy Lee. BArch, U. Kans., 1961. Registered architect, Kans., N.Mex., Mo., Ohio. Prin. Howard W. Ellington, AIA, Architect, Wichita, Kans., 1979—; co-owner Gallery Ellington, 1978-97. Founding trustee Kans. Cultural Trust, Wichita, 1985—; mem. bldg. and grounds com. Wichita Ctr. for Arts, trustee, 1995-97, treas., 1997, acting exec. dir., 1997-98, exec. dir. 1998—; bd. dirs. arts com. Ulrich Mus., Wichita, 1992-97; founding trustee, exec. dir. Allen-Lambe House Found., Wichita, 1990—; mem. Wichita Wayfinding Design Adv. Group, 1997. Editor: The Prairie Print Makers, 1984. Mem. aesthetic rev. team Wichita City Mgrs., 1992-99; trustee Wichita Ctr. for the Arts, 1995-97; bd. dirs. Wichita-Sedgwick County Arts & Humanities Coun., 1996—, Wichita Pub. Arts Adv. Bd., 1996-99, Wichita Art and Design Bd., 1999—. Recipient Kans. Preservation award, 1993, Pedestal award Wichita Hist. Preservation Bd., 1996. Mem. Friends of Wichita Art Mus., Western Penn. Conservation, Nat. Trust for Hist. Preservation, Chgo. Archtl. Found., Frank Lloyd Wright Home and Studio Found., Birger Sandzen Meml. Gallery. Republican. Episcopalian. Avocation: art collecting. Office: 255 N Roosevelt St Wichita KS 67208-3720

ELLIOT, BILL, radio personality; b. St. Louis; Student, U. Ill., Southeast Mo. State U., Wash. U., Webster U. Radio host Classic 99, St. Louis. Avocations: photography, movies, music, electronics. Office: Classic 99 85 Founders Ln Saint Louis MO 63105

ELLIOT, DAVID HAWKSLEY, geologist, educator; b. Chilwell, Eng., May 22, 1936; came to U.S., 1966; m. Ann Elliot, 1963. B.A., Cambridge U., Eng., 1959; Ph.D., Birmingham U., 1965. Mem. faculty Ohio State U., Columbus, 1969—, prof. dept. geol. scis., 1979—, dir. Byrd Polar Reseach Ctr. (formerly Inst. Polar Studies), 1973-89. Mem. Geol. Soc. Am., Geol. Soc. London, Ohio Acad. Sci., Am. Geophys. Union, Sigma Xi. Office: Ohio State Univ Dept Geol Scis Columbus OH 43210 E-mail: elliot.1@osu.edu.

ELLIOT, TAMMY, newscaster; B Comms., U. Wis., 1991. Anchor WFRV-TV, Green Bay, Wis.; morning co-host Murphy in the Morning WIXX; news anchor WISN, Milw. Office: WISN PO Box 402 Milwaukee WI 53201-0402

ELLIOTT, BARBARA JEAN, librarian; b. Bluffton, Ind., Oct. 2, 1927; d. Dale A. and Gwendolyn I. (Long) E.; m. Robert J. Elliott, June 13, 1949; 1 son, Michael Roger. BS with honors, Ind. U., 1949, MLS, 1979. Dir. tech. info. svcs. uranium divsn. Mallinckrodt Chrms., St. Louis, 1949-59; rsch. libr. Petrolite Corp., Webster Groves, Mo., 1961-63; head tech. svcs. St. Frances Coll., Ft. Wayne, Ind., 1974-76; dir. Bluffton-Wells County Pub. Libr., 1976-95, ret., 1995. Pres. Wells County Found., 1995; pres. Ch. Women United of Wells County, Family Centered Svcs., 1999—. Mem. ALA, LWV of Ind. (state sec. 1981-83, chmn. health care 1983-89, 3d v.p. 1985-86), Ind. Libr. Assn. (fed. legis. coord.), Ind. Bus. and Profl. Women (pres. 1987-88, dist. dir. 1988-93), Wells County Hist. Soc. (pres. 1997-2000), Bluffton Garden Club (pres.), Wells County Coun. on Aging (sec. 1996-2001). Home: 6831 SE State Rd 116 Bluffton IN 46714-9420 E-mail: belliott@parloscity.com.

ELLIOTT, EDDIE MAYES, academic administrator; b. Grain Valley, Mo., Sept. 12, 1938; s. Franklin E. and Edna Mae (Rowe) E.; m. Sandra Temple, Nov. 23, 1960; children: Glenn, Gregg, Grant. AB, William Jewell Coll., 1960; MA, Columbia U., 1964; EdD, U. No. Colo., 1969. Tchr. Harrisonville (Mo.) High Sch., 1960-61, Excelsior Springs (Mo.) Pub. Schs., 1961-63, The Trinity Sch., N.Y.C., 1963-64; mem. faculty dept. phys. edn. CUNY, 1964-65; chmn. athletics, coach Mo. Valley Coll., Marshall, 1965-71; dir. grad. studies Wayne (Nebr.) State Coll., 1971-73, dean spl. studies, 1973-75, v.p., 1975-82, pres., 1982-85, Cen. Mo. State U., Warrensburg, 1985-99, pres. emeritus, 1999—. Assoc. Ctr. for Planned Change, 1975-82; mem. adv. bd., bd. dirs. Nebr. Coun. on Econ. Edn., 1977-83; bd. incorporators Higher Edn. Strategic Planning Inst., 1981—; mem. Coun. Pub. Higher Edn. Mo.; bd. advisors Apple Restaurants Europe. Mem. land-grant mission adv. com. U. Mo. Named outstanding faculty mem. Wayne State Coll., 1973, to U. No. Colo. Alumni Hall of Fame, 1989; recipient Disting. Svc. award Wayne State Coll., 1986, Cecil R. Martin award William Jewell Coll., 1960, citation for achievement, 1986, Disting. Alumni award, 1986, James C. Kirkpatrick Excellence in Givernance Awd., 1999. Mem. AAUP, AAHPERD, Am. Assn. State Colls. and Univs. (task force on emerging issues, bd. dirs., past chair, chair pres.'s commn. tchr. edn. 1993-94), Assn. Governing Bds. (adv. com. on strengthening governance of pub. univs.), Am. Assn. Higher Edn., Am. Coll. Sports Medicine, North Cen. Assn. Evaluation Teams, Nat. Coun. Accreditation of Tchrs., Mo. Corp. for Sci. and Tech., Warrensburg C. of C., Phi Kappa Phi.

ELLIOTT, MARK T. state legislator; b. Carthage, Mo., July 18, 1956; m. Denise Ann Severn, 1976; children: Rhett Thomas, Haley Dawn, Hillery Ann. Student, Drake U., Mo. So. State Coll. Current state rep. dist. 127 Mo. Ho. of Reps., former state rep. dist. 126, asst. minority whip, mem. agrl. bus. com., appropriations natural and econ. resource, ethics coms., human rights and resources com. Mem. Farm Bur. Home: 2 S Main St Webb City MO 64870-2326

ELLIOTT, PETER R. retired athletic organization executive; b. Bloomington, Ill., Sept. 29, 1926; s. Joseph Norman and Alice (Marquis) E.; m. s. Joan Connaught Slater, June 14, 1949; children: Bruce Norman, David Lawrence. B.A., U. Mich., 1949. Asst. football coach Oreg. State U., 1949-50, U. Okla., 1951-55; head football coach Nebr. U., 1956, U. Calif., Berkeley, 1957-59, U. Ill., 1960-66, U. Miami, Fla., 1973-74, dir. athletics, 1974-78; asst. football coach St. Louis Cardinals, 1978; exec. dir. Pro Football Hall of Fame, Canton, Ohio, 1979-96, ret., 1996. Served with USNR, 1944-45. Named to Mich. Sports Hall of Fame, 1983, Coll. Football Hall of Fame, 1994. Mem. Am. Football Coaches Assn. (Region 8 Coach of Yr. 1958, Region 5 Coach of Yr. 1963). Presbyterian. Home: 3003 Dunbarton Ave NW Canton OH 44708-1818

ELLIS, ARTHUR BARON, chemist, educator; b. Lakewood, Ohio, Apr. 4, 1951; s. Nathan and Carolyn Joan (Agulnick) E.; m. Susan Harriet Trebach, Nov. 9, 1975; children: Joshua, Margot. BS, Calif. Inst. Tech., 1973; PhD, MIT, 1977. Asst. prof. chemistry U. Wis., Madison, 1977-82, assoc. prof., 1982-84, prof., 1984-86, Meloche-Bascom prof., 1986—. Editor: Chemistry and Structure at Interfaces, 1986; patentee in field; contbr. articles to profl. jours. Fellow A.P. Sloan Found., 1981, H.I. Romnes fellow U. Wis., 1985, Guggenheim fellow, 1989; recipient Nat. Catalyst Tchg. award Chem. Mfrs. Assn., 1994. Mem. Am. Chem. Soc. (Exxon fellow 1980, chmn. edn., Pimentel award 1997). Jewish. Achievements include creating 1-2-3 levitation kit based on high-temperature superconductors. Office: U Wis Dept Chemistry 1101 University Ave Madison WI 53706-1322

ELLIS, DORSEY DANIEL, JR. lawyer, educator; b. Cape Girardeau, Mo., May 18, 1938; s. Dorsey D. and Anne (Stanaland) E.; m. Sondra Wagner, Dec. 27, 1962; children: Laura Elizabeth, Geoffrey Earl. BA, Maryville Coll., 1960; JD, U. Chgo., 1963; LLD, Maryville Coll., 1998. Bar: N.Y. 1967, U.S. Ct. Appeals (2d cir.) 1967, Iowa 1976, U.S. Ct. Appeals (8th cir.) 1976. Assoc. Cravath, Swaine & Moore, N.Y.C., 1963-68; assoc. prof. U. Iowa, Iowa City, 1968-71, prof., 1971-87, v.p. fin. and univ. svcs., 1984-87, spl. asst. to pres., 1974-75; dean Washington U. Sch. Law, St. Louis, 1987-98, prof. law, 1998-99; disting. prof. law, 1999—. Vis. mem. sr. common room Mansfield Coll., Oxford U., Eng., 1972-73, 75; vis. prof. law Emory U., Atlanta, 1981-82, Victoria U., New Zealand, 1999; vis. sr. rsch. fellow Jesus Coll. Oxford U., Eng., 1998; bd. dirs. Maryville Coll., 1989-98, 99—. Contbr. articles to profl. jours. Trustee Mo. Hist. Soc., St. Louis, 1995-2000. Nat. Honor scholar U. Chgo., 1960-63; recipient Joseph Henry Beale prize, 1961, Alumni award Maryville Coll., 1988. Mem. ABA, Am. Law Inst., Bar Assn. Metro St. Louis, Mound City Bar Assn., Iowa Bar Assn., AALS Acad. Resource Corps., Order of Coif. Home: 1 Brookings Dr Saint Louis MO 63130-4862 E-mail: ellis@wulaw.wustl.edu.

ELLIS, JEFFREY ORVILLE, lawyer; b. Parsons, Kans., Mar. 9, 1944; s. Orman Carl Ellis and Esther Jane (Landreth) Ellis-Hett; m. Carol Lynne Byington, Aug. 6, 1966; children: Robert James, Jeffrey Todd. BS, U. Kans., 1966; JD, Washburn U., 1977. Bar: Kans. 1977, U.S. Dist. Ct. Kans. 1977, Mo. 1993. Tchr. Shawnee Mission (Kans.) Dist. Schs., 1966-68; atty., ptnr. Holbrook, Ellis & Heaven, Shawnee Mission, 1977-91, Lathrop & Gage, L.C., Kansas City, Mo., 1991—. Bd. dirs. United Cmty. Svcs., Johnson County, Johnson County Health Partnership, Mid-Am. chpt. MS Soc., United Way of Johnson County; spkr. in field. Author, editor: Handbook for Peer Review, 1992. Chmn. task force Gov.'s Commn. on Health Care, Topeka, 1989-90; mem. Legis.'s Commn. on Health Care Svcs., Topeka, 1987-90; chmn. Kans. Rep. Party, 3d Congl. Dist., 1990-92. Capt. U.S. Army, 1968-74, Vietnam. Mem. Am. Health Lawyers Assn., Kans. Assn. Hosp. Attys. (bd. dirs. 1987-90, pres. 1992-93), Kansas Head Injury Assn. (bd. dirs. 1987-91), Greater Kansas City C. of C. (chmn. task force 1991-93), Rotary (pres. Overland Park 1992). Republican. Episcopalian. Avocations: golf, bicycling. Home: 183 Hillcrest Rd W Shawnee Mission KS 66217-8731 Office: Lathrop & Gage LC 1050 Corporate Woods Overland Park KS 66210-2019

ELLIS, LLOYD H., JR. emergency physician; b. Denver, Apr. 7, 1936; s. Lloyd Harris and Lura Lou (Wallace) E.; m. Nancy Kay Greenamyre, June 4, 1962 (div. June 1979); children: Peter, Amanda Hunt; m. Eva Marie Bevan, Sept. 1, 1984; children: Gwendolyn Ruth, David Bevan. BA, Yale U., New Haven, Conn., 1960, MA, 1961; MD, Case Western Reserve U., Cleve., 1970; MA, Case Western Reserve U., 1990. Diplomate Am. Bd. Emergency Medicine. Farm mgr., Hastings, Nebr., 1961-62; vice consul Dept. of State, Lourenco Marques, Mozambique, 1963-64, intelligence analyst Washington, 1965-66; dir. emergency dept. Univ. Hosps., Cleve., 1976-84, emergency physician, 1985-94, Emergency Profl. Svcs., Wooster, Ohio, 1995-96, Chardon, 1997, Warren, 1998. Instr. in surgery Case Western Reserve U., Cleve., 1976-78, asst. prof. surgery, 1979-94. Med. dir. Cleve. Emergency Svc., 1976-94; pres. Jeffrey Wallace Ellis Found., Hastings, 1993—; sr. warden Good Shepard, Lyndhurst, Ohio, 1985-86; jr. warden St. Christopher's, Gates Mills, 1998, sr. warden, 1999, Diocesan Coun., 1999—. 1st Lt. Armor, 1956-59. Recipient Ford scholar Ford Found., New Haven, 1952-55. Mem. Am. Coll. Emergency Physicians, Am. Acad. Emergency Medicine. Republican. Episcopalian. Avocation: art history. Home and Office: 32250 Woodsdale Ln Cleveland OH 44139-1335

ELLIS, MARY LOUISE HELGESON, retired insurance company executive, other: health services, consultant; b. Albert Lea, Minn., May 29, 1943; d. Stanley Orville and Neoma Lois (Guthier) Helgeson; m. David Readinger, Nov. 5, 1994; children from previous marriage: Christopher, Tracy. BS in Pharmacy, U. Iowa, 1966; MA in Pub. Adminstrn., Iowa State U., 1982, postgrad., 1982—83. Faculty Duquesne U. , Pitts., 1977; cons. in pharmacy Colville, Wash., 1978—79; dir. pharmacy Mt. Carmel Hosp., 1978—79; clin. pharmacist Iowa Vets. Home, Marshalltown, Iowa, 1980—81; instr. Iowa Valley C.C., 1981—83; dir. Iowa Dept. Substance Abuse, Des Moines, 1983—86, State of Iowa Pub. Health; dir. Iowa Dept. Pub. Health, Des Moines, 1986—90; spl. cons. health affairs Blue Cross/Blue Shield of Iowa, 1990—91; v.p. Blue Cross/Blue Shield of Iowa and S.D., 1991—2000; ret., 2000; bus. cons., 2001—. Chair Iowa Health Data Commn., Des Moines, 1986—90; bd. dirs. Health Policy Corp. Iowa, 1986—90; adj. asst. prof. U. Iowa, Iowa City, 1984—; commd. officer U.S. FDA, 1989—90; mem. alumnae bd. dirs. U. Iowa Coll. of Pharmacy, 1989—; chair Nat. Commn. Accreditation of Ambulance Svcs., 1992—. Mem. Iowa State Bd. Health, 1981—83, v.p., 1982—83; mem. adv. coun. Iowa Valley C.C., 1983—85. Recipient Woman of Achievement award, Des Moines YWCA, 1988. Mem.: APHA, Iowa Pub. Health Assn. (bd. dirs., Henry Albert award 1990), Iowa Pharmacists Assn., Pi Sigma Alpha, Phi Kappa Phi, Alpha Xi Delta. Republican. Home: 2912 Caulder Ave Des Moines IA 50321-2637

ELLIS, MICHAEL EUGENE, documentary film producer, writer, director, marketing executive; b. Murphysboro, Ill., Aug. 1, 1946; s. Robert Eugene and Lula May (Williams) E. BS, So. Ill. U., Carbondale, 1971. Asst. to pres. So. Ill. U., 1970; asst. dir. Ill. Info. Svc., Springfield, 1971-72; mgr. press rels. Ill. Ho. of Reps., 1973-77; dep. dir. com. Rep. Nat. Com., Washington, 1977; pres. Lincana Corp., Springfield, 1978-80; mgr. mktg. presentations Ill. Dept. Commerce, 1980-91; dir. devel. and comms. Sparc Inc., 1993—. Co-author: Work and the College Student, 1975; author: Elements of Political Public Relations, 1977; editor: Springfield Eats, 1996; author film scripts, 1983—. Dir. comm. Pres. Ford Com. in Ill., Chgo., 1976; mem. Ill. Rep. Com., Springfield, Rep. Presdl. Task Force, Washington, Sangamon Rep. Found., Springfield. Recipient Gold Award Advt. Assn., Springfield, Ill., 1987-89. Mem. Internat. Communications Industry Assn., Am. Film Inst., Assn. for Multi Image Internat., World Affairs Coun., Nat. Soc. Fund Raising Execs. (bd. dirs. 1998-2001), Ill. Soc. Assn. Execs. (bd. dirs. 1998-2000, Excellence in Comms. award 1998, 2000). Avocations: writing, gardening, photography. Home: 627 Witherspoon Dr Springfield IL 62704-1424 Office: Sparc Inc 1 Sparc Ctr Plz 232 N Bruns Ln Springfield IL 62702-4613 E-mail: Development@spfldsparc.org., Club627@aol.com.

ELLIS, MICHAEL G. state legislator; b. Neenah, Wis., Feb. 21, 1941; married. BS, U. Wis., Oshkosh, 1965. Horse breeder, farmer; mem. Wis. Assembly, Madison, 1970-82; mem. from dist. 19 Wis. Senate, 1982—, minority leader, 1996-98,99-2000, majority leader, 1993-96, 98-99. Alderman City of Neenah. Office: 1752 County Road Gg Neenah WI 54956-9762 also: State Senate State Capitol Madison WI 53702-0001

ELLISON, EDWIN CHRISTOPHER, physician, surgeon; b. Columbus, Ohio, Jan. 10, 1950; s. Edwin Homer and Molly (Scheeler) E.; m. Mary Pat Borgess, Dec. 23, 1978; children: Jonathan Scott, Eric Christopher. BS, U. Wis., 1972; MD, Med. Coll. Wis., 1976. Diplomate Am. Bd. Surgery. Resident surgery Ohio State U., Columbus, 1976—83, asst. prof. surgery, 1983—93, assoc. prof., 1993—99, prof., 1999—; chief divsn. gen. surgery, bd. dirs. Ohio Digestive Disease Inst., 1987—93; chief of staff Ohio State U. Med. Ctr., 1999—2000, vice chmn. dept. surgery, 1996—99, 1interim chair surgery, 0999—2000, chmn. surgery, 2000—, assoc. v.p. health sci., 2002—, vice dean clin. affairs, 2002—. Fellow ACS. Office: 327 Means Hall 1654 Upham Dr Columbus OH 43210-1240

ELLMANN, SHEILA FRENKEL, investment company executive; b. Detroit, June 8, 1931; d. Joseph and Rose (Neback) Frenkel; m. William M. Ellmann, Nov. 1, 1953; children: Douglas Stanley, Carol Elizabeth, Robert Lawrence. BA in English, U. Mich., 1953. Dir. Advance Glove Mfg. Co., Detroit, 1954-78; v.p. Frome Investment Co., 1980-96, pres., 1996—. Mem. U. Mich. Alumni Assn., Nat. Trust Hist. Preservation. Home: 28000 Weymouth Dr Farmington Hills MI 48334

ELLWOOD, SCOTT, lawyer; b. Boston, July 8, 1936; s. William Prescott and Doris (Cook) E.; m. Suzanne M. Timble; children: Victoria, William Prescott II, Marjorie. Student, Williams Coll., 1954-56; AB, Eastern Mich. U., 1958; LLB, Harvard U., 1961. Bar: Iowa 1961, Ill. 1961, U.S. Dist. Ct. (no. dist.) Ill., 1961. Assoc. McBride & Baker, Chgo., 1961-67, ptnr., 1968-84, McDermott, Will & Emery, Chgo., 1984-99. Pres. Miller Investment Co., 1973-93, bd. dirs.; pres. SMI Investment Corp., 1978—. Pres., bd. dirs. 110 N Wacker Dr Found., 1974-84, Northfield Found., 1978-84, Leadership Found., 1979-84, Woodbine Found., 1980-84, The Cannon River Found., 1982-84, L.M. McBride Found., 1982-84, Bellarmine Found., 1982-84, Mark Morton Meml. Fund, 1982—. Mem. Iowa Bar Assn., Ill. State Bar Assn., Harvard Law Soc. Ill. (bd. dirs. 1983-98, treas. 1987-88, sec. 1988-89, v.p. 1989-93, pres. 1993-95), Harvard Club Chgo. (bd. dirs. 1993-95), Monroe Club (bd. dirs. 1988-98), Skokie Country Club (Glencoe, Ill.). Republican. Episcopalian. Home: 1296 Hackberry Ln Winnetka IL 60093-1606 Office: McDermott Will & Emery 227 W Monroe St Ste 3100 Chicago IL 60606-5096

ELROD, LINDA DIANE HENRY, lawyer, educator; b. Topeka, Mar. 6, 1947; d. Lyndus Arthur Henry and Marjorie Jane (Hammel) Allen; divorced; children: Carson Douglas, Bree Elizabeth. BA in English with honors, Washburn U., 1969, JD cum laude, 1971. Bar: Kans. 1972. Instr. U. S.D., Topeka, 1970-71; research atty. Kans. Jud. Council, 1972-74; asst. prof. Washburn U., 1974-78, assoc. prof., 1978-82, prof. law, 1982-93; disting. prof., 1993—. Vis. prof. law U. San Diego, Paris Summer Inst., 1988, 90, Washington U. Sch. Law, St. Louis, 1990, 98, summer 1991, 93, Fla. State U. Law Sch., spring, 2000. Author: Kansas Family Law Handbook, 1983, rev. edit., 1990, supplement, 1993, Child Custody Practice and Procedure, 1993, supplements, 1994-97, 99, 2000, 2001; co-author: Principles of Family Law, 1999, supplement, 2000, Kansas Family Law Guide, 1999, supplement, 2000, 2001; editor Family Law Quar., 1992—; contbr. articles to profl. jours. Pres. YWCA, Topeka, 1982-83; vice-chair Kans. Commn. on Child Support, 1984-87, Supreme Ct. Com. on Child Support, 1989—; chair Kans. Cmty. Svc. Orgn., 1986-87; adv. bd. CASA, 1997—; bd. dirs. Appleseed, 2000—. Recipient Disting. Service award Washburn Law Sch. Assn., 1986; named YMCA Woman of Distinction, 1997. Mem. ABA (coun. family law sect. 1988-92, sec. 1998, vice-chair, 1999, chair-elect 1999-2000, chair 2000-01, chair Schwab Meml. Grant Implementation 1984-87, co-chair Amicus Curiae com. 1987-92), Topeka Bar Assn. (sec. 1981-85, v.p. 1985-86, pres. 1986-87), Kans. Child Support Enforcement Assn. (bd. dirs. 1988—, Child Support Hall of Fame 1990), Kans. Bar Assn. (sec.-treas. 1988-89, com. ops. and fin. 1988, pres. family law sect. 1984-86, Disting. Svc. award 1985), NONOSO, Phi Kappa Phi, Phi Alpha Delta Alumni Assn. (justice 1976-77), Phi Beta Delta, Kappa Alpha Theta (pres. alumnae chpt. 1995-97). Presbyterian. Avocations: bridge, reading, quilting. Office: Washburn U Law Sch 17th and College Topeka KS 66621 E-mail: zzelro@washburn.edu.

ELSMAN, JAMES LEONARD, JR. lawyer; b. Kalamazoo, Sept. 10, 1936; s. James Leonard and Dorothy Isabell (Pierce) E.; m. Janice Marie Wilczewski, Aug. 6, 1960; children— Stephanie, James Leonard III. B.A., U. Mich., 1958, J.D., 1962; postgrad., Harvard Div. Sch., 1958-59. Bar: Mich. 1963. Clk. Mich. Atty. Gen.'s Office, Lansing, 1961; atty. legal dept. Chrysler Corp., Detroit, 1962-64; founding ptnr. Elsman, Young, O'Rourke, Bruno & Bunn, Birmingham, Mich., 1964-72; pvt. practice Elsman Law Firm, 1972—. Owner Radio Sta. WOLY, Battle Creek, Mich. Author: The Seekers, 1962; screenplay, 1976, 200 Candles to Whom?, 1973; contbr. articles to profl. jours.; Composer, 1974, 76; talk show host Citizen's Court, TV-48, Detroit. Mem. Regional Export Expansion Coun., 1966-73, Mich. Ptnrs. for Alliance for Progress, 1969-80; cand. U.S. Senate, 1966, 76, 94, 96, U.S. Ho. of Reps., 1970. Rockefeller Bros. Found. fellow Harvard Div. Sch., 1959. Mem. ABA, Am. Soc. Internat. Law, Econ. Club Detroit, World Peace Through Law Center, Full Gospel Businessmen, Bloomfield Open Hunt Club, Pres. Club (U. Mich.), Circumnavigators Club, Naples Bath and Tennis, Rotary. Republican. Mem. Christian Ch. Home: 4811 Burnley Dr Bloomfield Hills MI 48304-3781 Office: 635 Elm St Birmingham MI 48009-6768

ELSTON, ROBERT C. medical educator; BA with honors, Cambridge (Eng.) U., 1955, diploma in agr., 1956, MA, 1957; PhD, Cornell U., 1959; postgrad., U. N.C., 1960. Asst. prof. U. N.C., Chapel Hill, 1960-62, assoc. prof., 1964-69, prof., dir. genetics lab. Sch. Pub. Health, 1969-79; sr. rsch. fellow biometric medicine U. Aberdeen, 1962-64; prof., head dept. biometry & genetics La. State U. Med. Ctr., New Orleans, 1979-95; prof. dept. epidemiology & biostats. Case Western Res. U., Cleve., 1995—. Vis. prof. Yale U., 1965-66, London U., 1967, Cambridge U., 1970, Fourth Mil. Med. Coll. Xian, China, 1987, U. Calif., Irvine, 1988-89; dir. Ctr. Molecular & Human Genetics La. State U. Med. Ctr., 1991-95; mem. internat. adv. bd. Genetics Selection Evolution, 1992-97; exec. com. mem. teaching of stats. in health scis. sect. Am. Stats. Assn., 1992-94, chair, 1993; pres. Internat. Genetic Epidemiology Soc., 1997. Assoc. editor Biometrics, 1967-71, 1984-88, Am. Jour. Human Genetics, 1974-82, Stats. in Medicine, 1997—; editl. bd. Thrombosis Rsch., 1972-76, Neuropsychobiology, 1974-79, Am. Jour. Med. Genetics, 1977-99, Genetic Epidemiology, 1984-96, T. Human Genetics, 2000; contbr. articles to profl. jours. Recipient Career Devel. award NIH, 1966-76, Rsch. Scientist award, NIMH, 1977-79, Hoch award Am. Psychopath. Assn., 1992, Wick R. Williams Meml. award Fox Chase Cancer Ctr., 1994, Leadership award Internat. Genetic Epidemiology Soc., 1995, William Allan Meml. award Am. Soc. Human Genetics, 1996, Merit award NIH, 1998; King George VI Meml. fellow, 1956-57, John Simon Guggenheim Meml. fellow, 1973-74; Coulthurst scholar, 1955-56, Cornell scholar, 1956-59. Fellow Am. Stats. Assn. Office: Case Western Res U Dept Epidemiology & Biostats 2500 Metrohealth Dr Rm R-258 Cleveland OH 44109-1900 E-mail: rce@darwin.cwru.edu.

ELY, LAWRENCE ORLO, retired surgeon; b. Guthrie Center, Iowa, Dec. 13, 1919; s. John Ermerson and Luella Mabel (Knapp) E.; m. Dorothy Maxine Jenkins, Aug. 23, 1942; children: Patricia Anne, Lawrence Orlo, Stephen Craig, Bennett Knapp, Carolyn Elizabeth. BA, State U. Iowa, 1942, MD, 1943, MS, 1948, PhD, 1950. Diplomate Am. Bd. Gen. Surgery. Intern Mt. Carmel Mercy Hosp., Detroit, 1943-44; instr. dept. physiology Med. Sch., State U. Iowa, Iowa City, 1946-48, resident, instr. dept. surgery, 1948-52; pvt. practice gen. surgery Des Moines, 1952-85. Mem. staff Iowa Luth. Hosp., Des Moines, 1952-85, Mercy Med. Ctr., Des Moines, 1952-85, Iowa Meth. Med. Ctr., Des Moines, 1952-86; cons. Iowa Blue Cross-Blue Shield, 1985-86, Iowa Found. for Med. Care, 1985-86. Sect. head United Campaign, Des Moines, 1958-60; mem. Des Moines Opera Bd., 1973—, pres., 1973-78; mem. Health Planning Coun. of Iowa Med. Corp., 1970-78; bd. dirs., pres. Ramsey Home, 1988-94; bd. dirs. Civic Music Assn. Des Moines, 1984-98; mem. steering com. Friends of the Arts, Drake U., Des Moines. Capt. M.C., U.S. Army, 1944-46. Fellow ACS; mem. AMA, Iowa Med. Soc., Polk County Med. Soc. Republican. Mem. Disciples of Christ Ch. Avocation: singing. Home: 3500 Fleur Dr Des Moines IA 50321-2650

ELZAY, RICHARD PAUL, retired dental school administrator; b. Lima, Ohio, Dec. 6, 1931; s. Paul William and Edna Virginia (Moyer) E.; 1 child, Mark S. BS, Ind. U., Indpls., 1957, DDS with honors, 1960, MS in Dental Surgery, 1962. Diplomate Am. Bd. Oral Maxillofacial Pathology. Gen. practice dentistry, Brownsburg, Ind., 1960-62; instr. dept. oral pathology Med. Coll. Va. Sch. Dentistry, Richmond, 1962-64; asst. prof. Sch. Dentistry Med. Coll. Va., 1964-66, assoc. prof., 1966-69, prof., chmn. dept. oral pathology, 1969-86, asst. dean acad. affairs, 1970-74; prof., dep. v.p. for health scis., dean Sch. Dentistry U. Minn., Mpls., 1986-96.

EMERSON, JO ANN, congresswoman; b. Sept. 16, 1950; d. Ab and Sylvia Hermann; m. Bill Emerson, 1975 (dec.); children: Victoria, Katharine; m. Ron Gladney, 2000; stepchildren: Elizabeth, Abigail, Alison, Jessica, Stephanie, Sam. BA in Polit. Sci., Ohio Wesleyan U., 1972; DHL (hon.), Westminster Coll., Fulton, Mo. Mem. 105th-106th Congress from 8th Mo. dist., 1997—; mem. agr. com. 105th Congress from 8th Mo. dist., mem. small bus. com., mem. transp. and infrastructure com.; appropriations com. 106th Congress, 1998—. Sr. v.p. Am. Ins. Assn.; dir. state rels. and grassroots programs Nat. Restaurant Assn.; dep. dir. comm. Nat. Rep. Congl. Com. Mem. PEO Womens's Svc. Group (FY chpt.), Cape Girardeau; mem. adv. com. Children's Inn, NIH; mem. adv. bd. Arneson Inst. Practical Politics and Pub. Affairs, Ohio Wesleyan U.; mem. bd. trustees Harry Truman Scholarship Found.; bd. trustees, hon. and life trustee Westminster Coll. Mem. Copper Dome Soc. Presbyterian. Office: 8th Congl Dist Mo 326 Cannon Bldg Washington DC 20515-2508*

EMERSON, ROBERT, state legislator; b. Alpena, Mich., Mar. 23, 1948; s. Melvin Frances and Elaine (Larmer) E.; m. Judy Samelson, 1981; children: Melanie Erica, Phillip James, Erin Samelson. Student, Wayne State U., 1969-69, U. Mich., 1970-71. Legal aide Mich. Ho. Reps., Lansing, 1978-79; mem. Mich. Ho. of Reps. from 81st dist., 1980-94, Mich. Ho. of Reps. from 49th dist., Lansing, 1995-98, Mich. Senate from 29th dist., 1998—; mem. appropriations com. Address: PO Box 30036 220 Farnum Bldg Lansing MI 48909 also: PO Box 30036 Lansing MI 48909-7536

EMERT, TIMOTHY RAY, lawyer; b. Independence, Kans., Jan. 29, 1940; s. Walter Glen and Fern LaVon (Braschler) E.; m. BarbaraA. Meitner, Aug. 22, 1964; children: Kate, Jennifer, Babs. BS in Journalism, JD, U. Kans. Bar: Kans. 1965. Ptnr. Scovel, Emert, Heasty and Chubb, Independence. Senator 15th dist. State of Kans.; bd. dirs. Independence C. C. Found., Class LTD; commr. Uniform Laws Conf.; mem. Kans. Judicial Coun.; former bd. dirs. Independence Bd. Edn., Independence Pub. Libr., Kans. State Bd. Edn., Kans. State H.S. Activities Assn., Kans. Commn. on Pub. Broadcasting, William Inge Festival Found., Kans. Commn. on Edn. Restructuring and Accountability Corp. for Change, Kans.; vol. Kans. Advocacy and Protective Svcs.; mem. adv. bd. Manor Nursing Home, Independence. Mem. S.E. Kans. Bar Assn., Kans. Bar Assn., Independence C. of C., Rotary. Republican. Roman Catholic.

EMISON, EWING RABB, JR. lawyer; b. Vincennes, Ind., Feb. 3, 1925; s. Ewing and Tuley (Sheperd) E.; m. Kathleen M. Crowley, Nov. 28, 1952; children: Susan, Anne Emison Wishard. AB, DePauw U., 1947; LLB, Ind. U., 1950. Bar: Ind. 1950. Ptnr. Emison Doolittle Kolb & Roellgen, Vincennes; dep. atty. gen. State of Ind., 1968-69. Lectr. CLE seminars. Contbg. columnist Res Gestae, Ind. State Bar mag. Mem. Wabash Valley Interstate Commn., 1959-62, Ind. Flood Control and Water Resources Commn., 1961-65; mem. bd. visitors Ind. Univ. Sch. Law, 1984-87. With USN, 1943-46, 52-53. Mem. ABA (sects. on litigation, econs. of law practice), Ind. State Bar Assn. (bd. of mgrs. 1975-77, chmn. ho. of dels. 1979, pres. 1986-87), Internat. Assn. Def. Counsel, Columbia Club, Phi Delta Phi, Phi Kappa Psi. Republican. Presbyterian. Avocations: golf, assistance to minority law students, military history. Office: Emison Doolittle Kolb & Roellgen PO Box 215 8th and Busseron Sts Vincennes IN 47591

EMISON, JAMES WADE, petroleum company executive; b. Indpls., Sept. 21, 1930; s. John Rabb and Catherine (Stanbrough) E.; divorced; children: Catherine Emison Stoick, Elizabeth Ann, Thomas Weston, William Ash; m. Jane Bale Larson, Feb. 14, 1983. BA, DePauw U., 1952. Gen. mgr. C&C Oil Co. Inc., Huntington, Ind., 1954-59; pres. May Petroleum Co. Inc., Lima, Ohio, 1959-61; sales mgr. Oskey Bros. Petroleum Corp., St. Paul, 1961-66; v.p. mktg. Nfld. Refining Co. Ltd., N.Y.C., 1965—69; v.p. Oskey Gasoline & Oil Co., Mpls., 1969-76; pres. Western Petroleum Co. (successor to Oskey Gasoline & Oil Co.), 1977—. Pres. Western Internat. Trading Co., Eden Prairie, Minn., 1981—; bd. dirs. Hydrocarbon Trading & Transport Co., Houston, Community Bank Group, Inc., Eden Prairie, Minn.; ptnr. Bellwood Ptnrs., City Ctr. East and Riverview Bus. Pl. Trustee DePauw U., Greencastle, Ind., 1981—, former vice chair bd. trustees, co-founder Ctr. for Mgmt. and Entrepreneurship; trustee USMC Marine Corps U. Fund Inc., Quantico, Va., 1984—95; past chair bd. trustees Phi Kappa Psi Endowment Found. Capt. USMC, 1952—54. Recipient Old Gold Goblet, DePauw U., 1987. Mem.: Ind. Acad., Nat. Assn. Scholars, Nat. Petroleum Coun., Assn. Governing Bds. of Univs. and Colls. (bd. dirs. 1993), Marine Corps Assn. (bd. govs. 1981—84), Minn. Petroleum Assn., Am. Petroleum Inst., Nat. Soc. Sons of Am. Revolution, DePauw U. Alumni Assn. (bd. dirs. 1975—81, pres. 1979—81), Army and Navy Club (Washington), Woodhill Country Club (Orono), Spring Hill Country Club (Orono, Minn.), Tralee Golf Club, Ballybunion Golf Club, Monterey Peninsula Country Club, The Minikahda Club (Mpls.), Am. Legion. Republican. Avocations: golf, fly fishing. Home: 3340 Hill Ln Wayzata MN 55391-2602 Office: Western Petroleum Co 9531 W 78th St Ste 102 Eden Prairie MN 55344-3897

EMLER, JAY SCOTT, senator; b. Denver, May 25, 1949; s. Joseph Frederick and Lois Justine (Scott) E.; m. Lorraine Kristine Pearson, May 30, 1970. BA, Bethany Coll., Kans., 1971; JD, U. Denver, 1976; emergency med. technician degree, Hutchinson Community Coll., Kans., 1979. Bar: Colo. 1977, Kans. 1977. Pvt. practice, Lindsborg, Kans., 1977-90; corp. counsel Kans. Ind. Networks, Inc., Salina, 1990-92, gen. counsel, 1993-96, v.p., gen. counsel, 1996—99; pvt. practice, 2000—; judge Lindsborg Mcpl. Ct., 1978-90; mem. Kans. Senate from dist. 35, Topeka, 2001—. Instr. Barton County (Kans.) Community Coll., 1979; bd. dirs. Falun (Kans.) State Bank, 1983-87, sec., 1986-87; mem. Kans. Supreme Ct. Mcpl. Ct. Judges Testing and Edn. Com., 1989—. Adminstr. Lindsborg Vol. Ambulance Corps., 1979-85; chmn. Lindsborg chpt. McPherson County March of Dimes, 1979-86; mem. Kans. Emergency Med. Svcs. Coun., 1985-88, chmn., 1987-88; bd. dirs. Lindsborg Community Hosp., 1981-93, v.p., 1987-91, pres., 1992-93. Mem. ABA, Kans. Bar Assn., McPherson County Bar Assn. (chmn. law day com. 1978, sec.-treas. 1985-86, pres. 1994-95), Kans. Mcpl. Judges Assn. (bd. dirs. 1981-88, pres. 1985-87, chmn. legis. action com. 1983-85), Kans. Supreme Ct. Mcpl. Judges Adv. Com., Kans. Judicial Coun. (mcpl. ct. manual rev. com. 1981-, chmn. 1995-), Kans. Assn. Emergency Med. Svcs. Adminstrs. (sec. 1980-85). Office: 1233 N Main Mcpherson KS 67460

EMMA, EDWARD C. apparel executive; b. 1955; m. Penny Emma; 3 children. BA cum laude, Harvard U. Dir. menswear Jockey Internat., Kenosha, Wis., 1990-93, sr. v.p. retail ops., 1993-95, mng. dir., COO, 1995—. Office: Jockey Internat PO Box 1417 2300 60th St Kenosha WI 53141 Fax: 414-658-3074.

EMMANUEL, RAHM, former federal official, investment banker; Asst. to Pres., polit. affairs div., dep. dir. comms. Polit. Affairs Office, Washington, 1993-99; mng. dir. Wasserstein & Perella, Chgo., 1999—. Office: Wasserstein & Perella Ste 5700 3 1st National Plaza Chicago IL 60602

EMMERICH, KAROL DENISE, foundation executive, daylily hybridizer, former retail executive; b. St. Louis, Nov. 21, 1948; d. George Robert and Dorothy (May) Van Houten; m. Richard James, Oct. 18, 1969; 1 son, James Andrew. BA, Northwestern U., 1969; MBA, Stanford U., 1971. Nat. divsn. account officer Bank of Am., San Francisco, 1971-72; fin. analyst Dayton Hudson Corp., Mpls., 1972-73, sr. fin. analyst, 1973-74, mgr. short term financing, 1974-76, asst. treas., 1976-79, treas., 1979—, v.p., 1980-93; exec. fellow U. St. Thomas Grad. Sch. Bus., 1993—; pres. Emmerich Found., Edina, Minn., 1993—. Bd. dirs. Slumberland. Bd. dirs. Hemerocallis Soc. Minn., Royal Treasure. Mem. Minn. Women's Econ. Roundtable. Home and Office: 7302 Claredon Dr Edina MN 55439-1722

EMMERT, GILBERT ARTHUR, engineer, educator; b. Merced, Calif., June 2, 1938; s. Allan Valentine and Mildred (Vanderbilt) E.; m. Nancy Sue Johnson, June 12, 1964; children: David Allan, Daniel Andrew. BS, U. Calif., Berkeley, 1961; MS, Rensselaer Poly. Inst., Troy, N.Y., 1964; PhD, Stevens Inst. Tech., Hoboken, N.J., 1968. Analytical engr. United Tech. Corp., East Hartford, Conn., 1961-64; asst. prof. U. Wis., Madison, 1968-72, assoc. prof., 1972-79, prof., 1979—, dept. chair, 1992-01. Contbr. articles to profl. jours. Mem. AIAA, Am. Physical Soc., Am. Nuclear Soc. Office: U Wis Dept Engring Physics 1500 Engineering Dr Madison WI 53706-1609 E-mail: emmert@engr.wisc.edu.

EMMETT, JOHN COLIN, retired inventor, consultant; b. Bradford, Yorkshire, Eng., Apr. 27, 1939; BS, PhD, London U. Former rsch. team leader SmithKline Beecham Corp.; cons. Euromedica Ltd. Co-inventor over 100 patents in field. Office: Nat Inventors Hall of Fame 221 S Broadway St Akron OH 44308-1505

EMMONS, JOANNE, state legislator; b. Big Rapids, Mich., Feb. 8, 1934; d. Ray J. and Emma M. (Von Glahn) Gregory; m. John Francis Emmons, June 9, 1956; children: Sarah, Dorothy. BS, Mich. State U., 1956; degree in pub. svc. (hon.), Ferris State U., 1992. Tchr. Mecosta (Mich.) High Sch., 1956-58; treas. Big Rapids Twp., 1976-86; state rep. State of Mich., Lansing, 1987-91; mem. Mich. Senate from 23rd dist., 1991—. Chair Mecosta County Rep. Com., 1976-80; vice chair 10th dist. Rep. Com., 1984-86; bd. dirs. Luth. Child and Family Svcs., 1990-96; chair Senate fin. nat. conf. of state legis. exec. com., 1993—. Named Nat. Rep. Legislator of Yr., Nat. Assn. State Legislators, 1993, Legislator of Yr., Mich. Twp. Assn., 1993. Mem. Am. Legion Aux., Mich. Farm Bur. (legis. com. 1970-96), Milk Haulers Assn. (Legislator of Yr. 1995), Omicron Delta Kappa. Avocations: reading, sewing. Home: PO Box 30036 Lansing MI 48909-7536 Office: Mich State Senate State Capitol Lansing MI 48909

EMPSON, JON R. utilities executive; BA in Econs., Carleton Coll.; MBA in Econs., U. Nebr. With mgmt. Omaha (Nebr.) C. of C., 1972-78; mgr. pub. affairs No. Natural Gas Co., 1978-80; v.p. adminstrn. No. Plains Natural Gas, 1980-83, Enron Liquid Fuels, 1983-86; v.p. regualtion, fin., adminstrn. Peoples Natural Gas, 1986-87, sr. v.p. adminstr., 1988-93; sr. v.p. gas supply and regulatory svcs. UtiliCorp United, Inc., Kansas City, 1993-96, sr. v.p. regulatory, legis., environ. svcs., 1996—. Office: UtiliCorp United 20 W 9th St Kansas City MO 64105-1704

EMRICK, DONALD DAY, chemist, consultant; b. Waynesfield, Ohio, Apr. 3, 1929; s. Ernest Harold and Nellie (Day) E.; B.S. cum laude, Miami U., Oxford, Ohio, 1951; M.S., Purdue U., 1954, Ph.D., 1956 Grad. teaching asst. Purdue U., Lafayette, Ind., 1951-55; with chem. and phys. research div. Standard Oil Co. Ohio, 1955-64, research asso., 1961-64; cons., sr. research chemist research dept. Nat. Cash Register Co., Dayton, Ohio, 1965-72, chem. cons., 1972— . Mem. AAAS, Am. Chem. Soc., Phi Beta Kappa, Sigma Xi. Patentee in Field. Contbr. articles to profl. jours. Home: 4240 Lesher Dr Dayton OH 45429-3042

ENDRESS, ANTON G. horticulturist, educator; b. Boise, Idaho, Aug. 19, 1945; s. Rudolph George and Ruth Marie (Wallace) E.; m. Nancy C. Statius-Muller; children: Gregory Anton, Bryan Anton. BS in Biology, Duquesne U., 1967; MS in Botany, U. Iowa, 1970, PhD in Botany, 1974. Instr. dept. biology U. Dubuque, Iowa, 1972; postgrad. rsch. biologist I-IV Dept. Biology U. Calif., Riverside, 1974-77, asst. rsch. biologist I-III Statewide Ari Pollution Rsch. Ctr., 1977-80, instr. dept. biology, 1978, 80; assoc. botanist Sect. Botany and Plant Pathology Ill. Natural History Survey, 1980-85, head Sect. Botany and Plant Pathology, 1985-89, asst. chief. for planning, 1989-90, affiliate profl. scientist Ctr. for Biodiversity, 1990—; affiliate prof. dept. agronomy U. Ill., 1986-90, prof., head dept. horticulture, 1990-96, prof. dept. natural resources and environ. scis., 1996—. Mem. numerous coms. Ill. Natural History Survey, 1980-89, U. Ill., 1988—; participant numerous symposiums, confs. and workshops; lectr. in field. Contbr. articles to profl. jours., chpts. to books. Sci. Fair Judge, Champaign Schs., 1985-86, Ill. Jr. Acad. Sci., 1994; mem. Sci. Curriculum Revision Project, Unit 4 (Champaign) Sch. Dist., 1989-90; bd. mem., sec., v.p., coach Champaign Park Dist. Soccer League, 1980-85; founder, bd. mem., coach Little Illini Soccer Club, 1981-90; v.p., bd. dirs. Ctrl. Ill. Soccer League, 1986-90. Grantee USAF Office Sci. Rsch., 1977-80, U. Ill. Campus Rsch. Bd., 1980, Abandoned Mine Land Reclamation Coun., 1982, Ill. Dept. Energy and Natural Resources, 1982, 83, Nat. Arborist Assn., 1989-92, Environ. Protection Trust Fund Commn., 1990, UIUC Campus Rsch. Bd., 1994-95; recipient Amah-LO Nation Y-Indian Guides Achievement award Riverside (Calif.) YMCA, 1979, Disting. Svc. award, 1979, Vol. Svc. award Champaign Park Dist., 1983, Appreciation award Ill. Vegetable Growers Assn., 1995. Mem. AAAS, Am. Inst. Biol. Scis., Am. Soc. Agronomy, Am. Soc. Horticultural Sci., Crop Sci. Soc. Am. (Fred V. Grau Turfgrass Sci. Award Com. 1992—), Minorities in Agriculture and Natural Resources Assn., Soc. Ecological Restoration, Pi Alpha Xi, Gamma Sigma Delta. Office: U Ill 36 Environ and Agr Bldg 36 EASB Madigan Lab MC-637 Urbana IL 61801

ENENBACH, MARK HENRY, community action agency executive, educator; b. Chgo., July 28, 1949; s. Joseph Henry and Antonette Regina (Kasko) E.; children: Joy Elizabeth, Erin Regina; m. Kai Lindquist Bergin, Sept. 28, 1985; 1 child, Faith Marie. BA in Polit. Sci. with honors, Loyola U., Chgo., 1971, MA in Urban Studies with honors, 1973. Cmty. resource specialist Model Cities, Chgo., 1974-79; grad. prof. Govs. State U., Park Forest South, Ill., 1977-89; dir. energy program City of Chgo., 1980-83; prof. St. Augustine's Coll., Chgo., 1981-82; coord. cmty. svcs. Dept. Human Svcs., 1984-91; prof. urban planning and pub. adminstrn. DePaul U., 1987—; dir. cmty. svcs. block grant programs Cmty. and Econ. Devel. Assn. Cook County, Inc., 1992-96, v.p./COO, 1997—; CEO CEDA Neighborhood Devel. Corp., 2000—. Mem. adv. bd. City Colls. Chgo., 1984-88; spkr. Nat. Headstart Assn., Washington, 1995; mem. task force Ill. Dept. Commerce and Cmty. Affairs, Springfield, 1996—; spkr. Nat. Assn. Cmty. Action Agys., 1996-2000, Nat. Assn. State Cmty. Svcs. Programs, 2000. Pres. Lincoln Park Interagy. Coun., Chgo., 1986-91; mem. adv. bd. Salvation Army, Chgo., 1987-91. Grad. rsch. fellow Loyola U., 1972-73. Mem. Nat. Assn. Cmty. Action Agys., Ill. Assn. Cmty. Action Agys. Avocations: urban research, writing and travel in over 30 countries. Office: Cmty and Econ Devel Assn 208 S Lasalle St Ste 1900 Chicago IL 60604-1119 E-mail: menebach@cedaorg.net.

ENGEL, ALBERT JOSEPH, judge; b. Lake City, Mich., Mar. 21, 1924; s. Albert Joseph and Bertha (Bielby) Engel; m. Eloise Ruth Bull, Oct. 18, 1952; children: Albert Joseph III, Katherine Ann, James Robert, Mary Elizabeth. Student, U. Md., 1941—42; AB, U. Mich., 1948, LLB, 1950. Bar: Mich. 1951. Ptnr. firm Engle & Engel, Muskegon, Mich., 1952—67; judge Mich. Circuit Ct., 1967—71; judge U.S. Dist. Ct. Western Dist. Mich., 1971—74; circuit judge U.S. Ct. Appeals, 6th Circuit, Grand Rapids, Mich., 1974—88, chief judge, 1988—89, sr. judge, 1989—. With U.S. Army, 1943—46, ETO. Fellow: Am. Bar Found.; mem.: FBA, ABA, Am. Judicature Soc., Grand Rapids Bar Assn., Cin. Bar Assn., Mich. Bar Assn., Grand Rapids Torch Club, Am. Legion, Phi Delta Phi, Phi Sigma Kappa. Episcopalian. Home: 5497 Forest Bend Dr SE Ada MI 49301-9079 Office: US Ct Appeals 100 E 5th St Ste 418 Cincinnati OH 45202-3911 also: 640 Federal Bldg 110 Michigan St NW Grand Rapids MI 49503-2313

ENGEL, ANDREW GEORGE, neurologist; b. Budapest, Hungary, July 12, 1930; s. Alexander and Alice Julia (Gluck) E.; m. Nancy Jean Brombacher, Aug. 15, 1958; children: Lloyd William, Andrew George. BSc, McGill U., 1953, MD, 1955. Diplomate: Am. Bd. Internal Medicine, Am. Bd. Psychiatry and Neurology. Intern Phila. Gen. Hosp., 1955-56; sr. asst. surgeon, clin. asso. USPHS, NIH, Bethesda, Md., 1958-59; fellow in neuropathology Columbia U., N.Y.C., 1962-64; with Mayo Clinic, Rochester, Minn., 1956-57, 60-62; cons., 1965—; prof. neurology Mayo Med. Sch., 1973—, William L. McKnight-3M prof. neurosci., 1984—; disting. investigator Mayo Clinic, 1995—. Mem. sci. adv. com. Muscular Dystrophy Assn., 1973-99; mem. rev. com. NIH, 1977-81. Mem. editl. bd. Neurology, 1973-77, Annals Neurology, 1978-84, 90-95, Muscle and Nerve, 1978-97, 2000—, Jour. Neuropathology, 1981-83, 1996-2000, European Neurology, 1989—, Jour. Neuroimmunology, 1991-98, Molecular Neurobiology, 1997—; contbr. over 300 articles to med. jours. Served with USPHS, 1957-59. Mem. Am. Acad. Neurology, Am. Neurol. Assn., Am. Assn. Neuropathologists, Am. Soc. Cell Biology, Soc. Neuroscis., AAAS. Home: 2027 Lenwood Dr SW Rochester MN 55902-1051 Office: Mayo Clinic 200 1st St SW Rochester MN 55905-0002

ENGEL, CHARLES T. lawyer; BBA, B Journalism, Kans. State U.; JD, U. Kans. Ptnr. Cosgrove, Webb & Oman, Topeka. Mem. bd. regents Washburn U., 1997—. Mem.: Washburn Endowment Assn. (trustee), Washburn Alumni Assn. (former pres.). Office: Cosgrove Webb & Oman 1100 Nations Bank Tower 534 S Kansas Ave Topeka KS 66603 Home: 2824 SW Plass Ave Topeka KS 66611

ENGEL, LEO PATRICK, state legislator; b. South Sioux City, Nebr., May 18, 1932; m. Dee Smith, 1952; children: Kathie, Kim, Jeff, Julie, Michael. Student, U. Nebr. Ins. agt. State Farm Ins., South Sioux City, Nebr.; commr. Dakota County; mem. Nebr. Legislature from 17th dist., Lincoln, 1994—. Mem. appropriations com., exec. bd. Nebr. Senate. Mem. South Sioux City Sch. Bd., fin. com. St. Michael's Ch., South Sioux City Comty. Sch. Cardinal Found. Mem. KC (past grand knight, dist. dep.), Mended Hearts (chpt. 41), Sertoma, Toastmasters. Office: Nebr State Senate State Capitol Rm 2011 Lincoln NE 68509

ENGEL, PHILIP L. retired insurance company executive; BA, U. Chgo., 1961, MBA, 1980. With CNA, Chgo., 1961, asst. v.p. corp. planning and control divsn., 1972-76, v.p., 1976-78, v.p. mktg., 1978-90, v.p. sys. and svcs., 1990, exec. v.p. claims, mktg., svcs., sys., underwriting, 1990-92; pres. CNA Ins. Cos., 1992-99. Bd. dirs. CNA Fin. Corp., Agy. Mgmt. Svcs., Inc. Vice chmn. bd. trustees Pacific Garden Mission, Chgo.; pres., bd. dirs. Shakespeare Repertory Theater, Chgo. Fellow Soc. Actuaries, Casualty Actuarial Soc.; mem. Am. Acad. Actuaries, Quality Ins. Congress (chmn. bd. dirs.). Office: CNA Cna Plz Chicago IL 60685-0001

ENGEL, SUSAN E. retail executive; Degree Indsl. and Labor Rels., Cornell U., 1968; MBA, Harvard U., 1976. With mgmt. and mktg. dept. J.C. Penney, N.Y.C., 1968-77; v.p. Booz, Allen and Hamilton, 1977-91; pres., CEO Champion Products, Inc., 1991-94; pres., COO Dept. 56, Inc., Eden Prairie, Minn., 1994-96, CEO, 1996—, also bd. dirs. Bd. dirs. Wells Fargo & Co., SuperValu Inc. Mem. pres. coun. Cornell Women, Cornell U.; bd. overseers Carlson Sch. Mgmt.; bd. dirs. Mpls. Guthrie Theater. Mem. Mpls. LWV. Avocations: sailing, tennis, collecting antiques, classical music and theater. Office: Dept 56 Inc One Village Pl 6436 City West Pkwy Eden Prairie MN 55344-7728

ENGELBREIT, MARY, art licensing entrepreneur; b. St. Louis, 1952; Freelance illustrator greeting card cos., 1983; founder, head Mary Engelbreit Art Licensing, Retail and PUb. Cos., St. Louis, 1983—. Office: Mary Engelbreit Studios 6900 Delmar Blvd Saint Louis MO 63130-4316

ENGELHARDT, IRL F. coal company executive; b. Oct. 19, 1946; m. Suzanne C.; children: Joel, Erin, Evan. BS in Acctg., U. Ill., 1968; MBA, So. Ill. U., 1971. From mem. staff to pres., CEO Peabody Energy, St. Louis, 1979-90, pres., CEO, 1990—, now chmn., CEO. Bd. dirs. U.S. Bank N.A., St. Louis. Mem. Nat. Mining Assn. (bd. dirs., chmn. 1995-96), Nat. Coal Assn. (chmn. 1995-96), Internat. Energy Agy. (coal industry adv. bd., chmn., special com. mem.), Nat. Assn. Mfrs. (bd. dirs.), Coal Utilization Rsch Group (co-chmn.), Coal Based Stockholders Group (co-chmn.), St. Louis Arts and Edn. Council, St. Louis Area Council (exec. bd.), Boy Scouts of Am. Office: Peabody Energy 701 Market St Saint Louis MO 63101 Fax: 314-342-7797. E-mail: lengelhardt@peabodyenergy.com.

ENGELHARDT, THOMAS ALEXANDER, editorial cartoonist; b. St. Louis, Dec. 29, 1930; s. Alexander Frederick and Gertrude Dolores (Derby) E.; m. Katherine Agnes McCue, June 25, 1960; children—Marybeth, Carol Marie, Christine Leigh, Mark Thomas. Student, Denver U., 1950-51, Ruskin Sch. Fine Arts, Oxford (Eng.) U., 1954-56, Sch. Visual Arts, N.Y.C., 1957. Free-lance cartoonist, comml. artist, N.Y.C., 1957-60, Cleve., 1961-62, asst. editorial cartoonist, Newspaper Enterprise Assn., Cleve., 1960-61; editorial cartoonist St. Louis Post-Dispatch, 1962-97; freelance cartoonist, 1998—; one-man exhbns. of cartoons at Fontbonne Coll. Art Gallery, St. Louis, 1972, Old Courthouse (Jefferson Nat. Meml.), St. Louis, 1981, Mark Twain Bank, Frontenac, Mo., 1989; group exhbns. Washington U., St. Louis, 2000, Nat. Press Club, Washington, 2001, St. Louis Artists Guild, 2001. Served with USAF, 1951-53. Recipient Ethical Humanist of Yr. award St. Louis Ethical Soc., 1986, Kay and Leo Drey Environ. Leadership award Mo. Coalition for Environment, 1999. Roman Catholic. Office: 7830 Lafon Pl Saint Louis MO 63130-3805

ENGELS, THOMAS JOSEPH, sales executive; b. New Orleans, May 24, 1958; s. Ronald Henry and Sally (Jacobsen) E.; m. Tamara Lewis Engels, May 29, 1982; children: Kristen, Danielle. BS in Gen. Mgmt., Purdue U., 1980. Sales rep. Johnson & Johnson, New Brunswick, N.J., 1980-82, mgr., 1982-83; dist. sales mgr. Pepsi Cola U.S.A., Somers, N.Y., 1983-87; regional sales mgr. Rich Sea Pak Corp., St. Simons Island, Ga., 1988-89; cen. regional mgr. food svc. div. Sara Lee Bakery, Chgo., 1990-93; area mgr. Ctrl. Zone Sara Lee Bakery Food Svc., 1993-94, divsn. promotion mgr. East, 1995-96; no. zone mgr. food svc. Land O'Lakes, Inc., 1996-2000, dir. sales No. U.S.; v.p. sales, food svc. Aurora Foods Co., St. Louis, 2000—. Roman Catholic. Avocations: tri-athlons, golf, basketball, coaching soccer. E-mail: engs3x5@aol.com.

ENGLAND, ANTHONY WAYNE, electrical engineering and computer science educator, astronaut, geophysicist; b. Indpls., May 15, 1942; s. Herman U. and Betty (Steel) E.; m. Kathleen Ann Kreutz, Aug. 31, 1962. SB, MIT, 1965, PhD, 1970, SM, 1965. With Texaco Co., 1962; field geologist Ind. U., 1963; scientist-astronaut NASA, 1967-72, 79-88; with U.S. Geol. Survey, 1972-79; crewmember on Spacelab 2, July, 1985; adj. prof. Rice U., Houston, 1987-88; prof. elec. engring. and computer sci. U. Mich., Ann Arbor, 1988—, prof. atmospheric, oceanic and space sci., 1989—, assoc. dean Rackham Grad. Sch., 1995-98. Mem. space studies bd. NRC, 1992-98. Assoc. editor Jour. Geophys. Rsch. Recipient Antarctic medal, Spaceflight medal NASA, Spaceflight award Am. Astron. Soc., Outstanding Scientific Achievement medal NASA. Fellow IEEE; mem. Am. Geophys. Union. Home: 7949 Ridgeway Ct Dexter MI 48130-9700 Office: U Mich Dept Elec Engring-Comp Sci Ann Arbor MI 48109-2122

ENGLAND, JOSEPH WALKER, heavy equipment manufacturing company executive; b. Moline, Ill., June 21, 1940; s. Stanley B. and Mary (Walker) E.; m. Mary Jo Richter, Oct. 26, 1963; children: Kathleen, Amy, Sarah. B.S., U. Ill., 1962. With Deere & Co., Moline, 1963—, sr. v.p. worldwide parts and corp. adminstrn., 1994—. Bd. dirs. 1st Midwest Bank Corp.; chmn. Moline Found., 1987—. Bd. dirs. United Way, 1978-82, pres., 1980, 81. Served with AUS, 1963. Mem. AICPA, Ill. Soc. CPAs, Nat. Assn. Accountants, U. Ill. Alumni Assn. (dir. 1977), Nat. Assn. Mfrs. (bd. dirs. 1991—). Club: Short Hills Country. Home: 1105 24th Ave Moline IL 61265-4721 Office: Deere & Co John Deere Rd Moline IL 61265-8098

ENGLE, DONALD EDWARD, retired railway executive, lawyer; b. St. Paul, Mar. 5, 1927; s. Merlin Edward and Edna May (Berger) E.; m. Nancy Ruth Frank, Mar. 18, 1950; children: David Edward, Daniel Thomas, Nancy Ann. B.A., Macalester Coll., St. Paul, 1948; J.D., U. Minn., 1952, B.S.L., 1950. Bar: Minn. 1952, Mo. 1972. Law clk., spl. atty. Atty. Gen.'s Office Minn., 1951-52; atty., asst. gen. solicitor, asst. gen. counsel G.N. Ry., St. Paul, 1953-70; asso. gen. counsel Burlington No., Inc., 1970-72; v.p., gen. counsel S.L.-S.F. Ry., St. Louis, 1972-80, v.p. law, sec., 1979-80; v.p. law Burlington No., Inc., St. Paul, 1980-81, Burlington No. Ry., St. Paul, 1981-83, sr. v.p. law and govt. affairs, sec., 1983-86, also dir.; ptnr., chmn., chief exec. officer Oppenheimer, Wolff & Donnelly, 1986-93, chmn., chief exec. officer, 1991-93, of counsel, 1993—. Continuing edn. lectr. U. Minn.; bd. dirs. Regions Hosp. Found., 2001—. Bd. dirs. YMCA, St. Paul, 1981-84, ARC, 1981-84; bd. dirs. Boy Scouts Am., 1991—. Mem. ABA, Mo. Bar Assn., Minn. Bar Assn., Ramsey County Bar Assn., St. Louis Bar Assn., St. Paul C. of C. (bd. dirs. 1994-97), North Oaks Golf Club, Phi Delta Phi. Republican. Lutheran. Home: 9 W Bay Ln Saint Paul MN 55127-2601

ENGLEHART, HUD, communications company executive; Grad., U. Mich., 1969. V.p. corp. comms. Lockheed Corp., 1988-90; various positions Hill and Knowlton, Pitts., 1982-96, former creative dir., global account mgr. Kraft Gen. Foods Chgo., former exec. mng. dir.; pres., COO KemperLesnik Comms. Pres. bd. trustees Chgo. Victory Gardens Theater; bd. dirs. Chgo. Internat. Film Festival; mem. devel. bd. U. Mich. Bus. Sch. Mem. PRSA, Arthur Page Soc. Office: KemperLesnik Comms 455 N Cityfront Pl Dr #1500 Chicago IL 60611

ENGLER, JOHN, governor; b. Mt. Pleasant, Mich., Oct. 12, 1948; s. Mathias John and Agnes Marie (Neyer) E.; m. Michele; children: Margaret Rose, Hannah Michelle, Madeleine Jenny; B.S. in Agrl. Econs., Mich. State U., 1971; J.D., Thomas M. Cooley Law Sch., 1981. Mem. Mich. Ho. of Reps., 1971-78; mem. Mich. Senate, 1979-90, Republican leader, 1983, majority leader, 1984-90; ; state senator, 1979-90; gov., 1990—. Del. White House Conf. on Youth, 1972; U.S. Trade Reps.' Intergovernmental Policy Adv. com., 1988, Intergovernmental Adv. Coun. on Edn., 1988. Bd. dirs. Mich. Spl. Olympics; chmn. Presdl. Scholars, 1991-92. Recipient Disting. Service to Agr. award Mich. Agr. Conf., 1974; named Legislator of Yr., Police Officers Assn. Mich., 1981; One of 5 Outstanding Young Men of Mich., Mich. Jaycees, 1983. Fellow State Bar Mich.; mem. Nat. Gov.'s Assn. (welfare reform task force 1993—, edn. goals panel 1993—). Republican. Roman Catholic. Club: Detroit Economic. *

ENGLES, GREGG L. food company executive; b. ; Chmn. bd., CEO various predecessors Suiza Foods, Dallas, 0chmn. bd., CEO, 1994—. Bd. dirs. Evercom, Inc., Tex. Capital Bankshares. Office: Suiza Foods 2515 Mckinney Ave Ste 1200 Dallas TX 75201-1945

ENGLISH, FLOYD LEROY, telecommunications company executive; b. Nicholas, Calif., June 10, 1934; s. Elvan L. and Louise (Corliss) E.; children from previous marriage: children: Roxane, Darryl; m. Elaine Ewell, July 3, 1981; 1 child, Christine. AB in Physics, Calif. State U., Chico, 1959; MS in Physics, Ariz. State U., 1962, PhD in Physics, 1965. Divsn. supr. Sandia Labs., Albuquerque, 1965-73; gen. mgr. Rockwell Internat.-Collins, Newport Beach, Calif., 1973-75; pres. Darcom, Albuquerque, 1975-79; cons in energy mgmt. and acquisitions, 1980-81; v.p. U.S. ops. Andrew Corp., Orland Park, Ill., 1981-82, pres., 1981-82, COO, 1981-82, CEO, 1983-92, also bd. dirs., 1982—, chmn. bd. dirs., pres., CEO, 1992-2000, 2000—, chmn., bd. dirs., 1982—. Bd. dirs. Internat. Engring. Consortium. Contbr. articles to profl. jours. Bd. dirs. Ill. Math. and Sci. Acad. Fund for Advancement of Edn. 1st lt. U.S. Army, 1954-57; capt. Res., 1957-69. Mem. IEEE, Execs. Club of Chgo. (bd. dirs.). Republican. Presbyterian. Office: Andrew Corp 10500 W 153rd St Orland Park IL 60462-3071

ENGLISH, JOHN DWIGHT, lawyer; b. Evanston, Ill., Mar. 28, 1949; s. John Francis English and Mary Faye (Taylor) Butler; m. Claranne Kay Lundeen, Apr. 22, 1972; children: Jennifer A., Katharine V., Margaret E. BA, Drake U., 1971; JD, Loyola U., 1976. Bar: Ill. 1976, U.S. Dist. Ct. (no. dist.) Ill. 1976, U.S. Tax Ct. 1977. Assoc. Bentley DuCanto Silvestri & Forkins, Chgo., 1976-79; ptnr. Silvestri Mahoney English & Zdeb, 1979-81; assoc. Cuffield Ungaretti Harris & Slavin, 1981-83; ptnr. Coffield Ungaretti & Harris, 1983—. Instr. estate planning Loyola U., Chgo., 1982-87; instr. Ill. Inst. Continuing Edn. Estate Planning Short Course, 1998, 2001. Bd. dirs. Prince of Peace Luth. Sch., Chgo., 1977-83, Bethesda Home for the Aged, Chgo., 1981-89, 2000—, Luth. Family Mission, Chgo., 1985-91; alderman Park Ridge (Ill.) City Coun., 1991-95. Mem.: Chgo. Bar Assn. (former chmn. divsn. II probate practice com.), Ill. State Bar Assn., Phi Beta Kappa. Lutheran. Home: 631 Wisner St Park Ridge IL 60068-3428 Office: Ungaretti & Harris 3500 Three 1st Nat Bank Plz Chicago IL 60602

ENGLISH, RAY, library administrator; b. Brevard, N.C., Dec. 11, 1946; s. Daniel Leon and Lois (Dorsett) E.; m. Allison Scott Ricker, Oct. 19, 1985; children: John, Michael. AB with honors in German, Davidson Coll., 1969; MA in German Lit., U. N.C., 1971, MSLS, 1977, PhD, 1978. Teaching asst. German dept. U. N.C., Chapel Hill, 1970-73, 74-75, rsch. asst., 1976; reference libr. Alderman Libr. U.Va., Charlottesville, Va., 1977-79; head reference libr. Oberlin (Ohio) Coll. Libr., 1979-89, assoc. dir., 1986-90; dir. libr. Oberlin (Ohio) Coll., 1990—. !cad. advisor Oberlin Coll., 1980—, lectr. in German, 1986—; vis. lectr. Sch. Libr. Sci., U. N.C., Chapel Hill, 1981; spkr. in field; mem. steering com. Scholarly Pub. and Acad. Resources Coalition, 1999—. Contbr. articles to profl. jours. German Acad. Exchange Svc. fellow, 1973-74. Mem. ALA, Assn. Coll. and Rsch. Librs. (bd. dirs., exec. com. 1996-98), Libr. Adminstrn. and Mgmt. Assn., Acad. Libr. Assn. Ohio. Home: 83 S Cedar St Oberlin OH 44074-1559 Office: Oberlin Coll Library 148 W College St Oberlin OH 44074-1575 E-mail: ray.english@oberlin.edu.

ENGLISH, R(OBERT) BRADFORD, marshal; b. Jefferson City, Mo. BS in Criminal Justice, Lincoln U., 1982; MPA, U. Mo., 1984. Residential juvenile counselor Cole County Juvenile Ctr., Jefferson City, Mo., 1972-74; patrolman Jefferson City Police Dept., 1975-76, detective, 1976-78; comdr. Mo. Capitol Police, Jefferson City, 1978-79, police chief, 1979-94; marshal U.S. Marshal Svc., Kansas City, Mo., 1994—. Chmn. ct. security com. U.S. Dist. Ct. (we. dist.) Mo., Kansas City, 1995—; mem. dirs. adv. and leadership coun. U.S. Marshall Svc., 1996—. Chmn. bd. dirs. Capitol Area Cmty. Svc. Agy., Jefferson City, 1994. Named Statesman of Month, News Tribune Co., 1994. Mem. Internat. Assn. Chiefs of Police (life), Masons. Democrat. Avocations: golf, scuba diving, walking, weight lifting. Office: US Marshal Svc 400 E 9th St Ste 3740 Kansas City MO 64106-2635

ENK, SCOTT, editor; b. Milw., Apr. 9, 1958; s. Kenneth and Audrey (Szymanowski) E. BA in Mass Comm. and Econs. with distinction, U. Wis., Milw., 1981. Pers. asst. Fleet Mortgage Corp., Milw., 1982, foreclosure asst., 1983, publs. designer, editor, writer, 1983-87; documentation editor, writer, tester Aardvark/McGraw-Hill, 1987-88; rsch./quality assurance editor Gareth Stevens, Inc., 1988-91; sr. editor Southea. Wis. Regional Planning Commn., Waukesha, 1992—. Guest lectr. silent film history and women's roles in silent film Alverno Coll., Milw., 1991-93, 96, 2000, Pewaukee Area (Wis.) Hist. Soc., 1997; spkr., presenter on radio, TV shows. Editor, writer, rschr. reports, newsletters, manuals, children's books; contbr. articles, essays and editls. to various publs. Founder, pres. Greater Milw. chpt. Hear My Voice/Protecting Our Nation's Children, 1993—; mem. Milwaukee County Hist. Soc., 1984—, ACLU, 1987—; officer Wis. Phi Beta Kappa Found., Inc.; sec. West Suburban Milw. chpt. NOW, 1984-89, pres., 1987—, chair fundraising com., 1983-84. Recipient awards in recognition of children's rights work United Foster Parents Assn. Greater Milw., 1995, Hear My Voice/Protecting Our Nation's Children, 1998; journalism scholar Milw. profl. chpt. Soc. Profl. Journalists, 1979, Harry J. Grant Found., Milw., 1979-81. Mem. NOW (chpt. rep. to state coun.), U. Wis. Milw. Alumni Assn. (Coll. Letters and Sci. scholar 1979), Mensa, Milw. 9 to 5, Nat. Model R.R. Assn., Phi Beta Kappa (bd. dirs. Greater Milw. assn. 1984—, sec. 1985-90, pres. 1990—, del. to nat. triennial coun. 1988, 91, 94, 97, 2000), Phi Kappa Phi, Phi Alpha Theta, Sigma Epsilon Sigma, Phi Eta Sigma. Avocations: computers/Internet, silent films and other media, political and social history, chess, architecture. Home: 3163 S 10th St Milwaukee WI 53215-4729 E-mail: senk@execpc.com.

ENLOW, DONALD HUGH, anatomist, educator, university dean; b. Mosquero, N.Mex., Jan. 22, 1927; s. Donald Carter and Martie Blairene (Albertson) E.; m. Martha Ruth McKnight, Sept. 3, 1945; 1 child, Sharon Lynn. B.S., U. Houston, 1949, M.S., 1951; Ph.D., Tex. A&M U., 1955. Instr. biology U. Houston, 1949-51; asst. prof. biology West Tex. State U., 1955-56; instr. anatomy Med. Coll. S.C., 1956-57; asst. prof. U. Mich. Med. Sch., Ann Arbor, 1957-62, assoc. prof., 1962-67, prof. anatomy, 1969-72; dir. phys. growth program Center for Human Growth and Devel., 1966-72; prof., chmn. dept. anatomy W.Va. U. Sch. Medicine, Morgantown, 1972-77; Thomas Hill disting. prof., chmn. dept. orthodontics Case Western Res. Sch. Dentistry, Cleve., 1977-89, prof. emeritus, 1989—, asst. dean for rsch. and grad. studies, 1977-85, acting dean, 1983-86. Adj. prof. U. N.C., 1992—; guest lectr. 29 fgn. countries, 1963—. Author: Principles of Bone Remodeling, 1963, The Human Face, 1968, Handbook of Facial Growth, 1975, 3d edit., 1990, Essentials of Facial Growth, 1996; contbr. chpts. to 30 books, numerous articles to profl. jours. Served with USCGR, 1945-46. Recipient Outstanding Research award Tex. Acad. Sci., 1952 Fellow Royal Soc. Medicine, Am. Assn. Anatomists, Internat. Assn. Dental Research; hon. mem. Am. Assn. Orthodontists (Mershon Meml. lectr. 1968, Spl. Merit award 1969, award for outstanding contbns. to orthodontia, 1984), Gt. Lakes Orthodontic Soc., Cleve. Dental Soc., Cleve. Orthodontic Soc., Omicron Kappa Upsilon. Republican. Methodist. Home: 5 Arbutus Ln Whispering Pines NC 28327-9465 E-mail: donnlo@pinehurst.net.

ENNEST, JOHN WILLIAM, bank executive; b. Bad Axe, Mich., Oct. 14, 1942; s. William J. and Margaret J. (Kritzman) E.; m. Mary Ellen Sweeney, Jan. 27, 1968 (dec. 1995); children: John W., James G., Anne M.; m. Cheryll Ann Pease, Dec. 1997. BS, U. Detroit, 1964; MBA, Mich. State U., 1965. Pres.'s exec. Exch. Program, Washington, 1979-80; v.p. Nat. Bank Detroit, 1973-81, NBD Bank Corp., Detroit, 1981-83; exec. v.p., chief fin. officer Citizens Bank, Flint, Mich., 1983-85; chief fin. officer, treas. Citizens Banking Corp., 1985-87; sr. exec. v.p., chief oper. officer Citizens Bank, 1985-87, pres., chief exec. officer, 1987-91; vice chmn., chief oper. officer Citizens Banking Corp., 1991—; chmn. bd., CEO Comml. Nat. Bank of Berwyn, Ill., 1992—; also bd. dirs. Citizens Bank, Citizens Banking Corp., Flint, Mich. Bd. dirs. Citizens Bank, 1987-91, Citizens Banking Corp., 1991, Second Nat. Bank, Saginaw, 1991, Comml. Nat. Bank, Berwyn, Ill., 1991. Author: (with others) Changing World of Banking, 1974. Chmn. bd. United Way, Flint, 1989, C. of C., Flint, 1991; dir. Baker Coll. Recipient cert. of merit USDA, 1980. Mem. Fin. Execs. Inst., Detroit Athletic Club, Warwick Hills Club. Republican. Roman Catholic.

ENO, WOODROW E. lawyer; b. Nebr. m. Ann Eno; 3 children. BA in History/Econs., Pittsburg (Kans.) State U., 1968; JD, U. Nebr., 1971; LLM, Judge Advocate Gen. Sch., Charlottesville, Va. Trial atty., regional counsel criminal investigation command U.S. Army; dir. law dept. market support div. CNA Ins. Co.; with legal/state affairs dept. Health Ins. Assn. Am., Appleton, Wis., 1975, v.p., gen. counsel, dir. state affairs, 1975—. Developer model laws and regulators on timely issues Nat. Assn. Ins. Commrs. Contbr. articles to profl. jours. Fundraiser several Washington area charities. Lt. col. JAGC U.S. Army. Mem. Nat. Health Lawyers Assn. (bd. dirs. 1992). Methodist. Office: Aid Association for Lutherans 4321 N Ballard Rd Appleton WI 54919-0001

ENOS, PAUL, geologist, educator; b. Topeka, July 25, 1934; s. Allen Mason and Marjorie V. (Newell) E.; m. Carol Rae Curt, July 5, 1958; children: Curt Alan, Mischa Enos Martin, Kevin Christopher, Heather Lynne BS, U. Kans., 1956; postgrad., U. Tübingen, W.Ger., 1956-57; MS, Stanford U., 1961; PhD, Yale U., 1965. Geologist Shell Devel. Co., Coral Gables, Fla., 1964-68, research geologist Houston, 1968-70; from assoc. prof. to prof. geology SUNY, Binghamton, 1970-82; Haas Disting. prof. geology U. Kans., Lawrence, 1982-2000, prof., 2001—. Cons. to industry; sedimentologist Ocean Drilling, 1975, 92; rsch. vis. Oxford U., 1989, U. Erlangen, Germany, 1995-96; fgn. scientist Ministry Geology, People's Republic China, 1988; with Global Sedimentary Geology Project, 1988—, co-convener Working Group 4, 1992-2000. Co-author: Quaternary Sedimentation of South Florida, 1977, Mid-Cretaceous, Mexico, 1983; editor: Field Trips: South-Central New York, 1981, Deep-Water Carbonates, 1977; contbr. articles to sci. jours. Served to 1st lt. C.E., U.S. Army, 1957-59 Recipient Pettijohn medal Sedimentology, 2001; U. Liverpool fellow, 1976-77; NSF fellow, 1959-62; Fulbright fellow, 1956-57; Summerfield scholar, 1954-56 Mem. Soc. Econ. Paleontologists and Mineralogists (assoc. editor 1976-80, 83-87, Best Paper award 1969), Internat. Assn. Sedimentologists (assoc. editor 1983-87), Am. Assn. Petroleum Geologists, AAAS, Sigma Xi, Omicron Delta Kappa. Avocations: photography, diving, cycling, history. Home: 2032 Quail Creek Dr Lawrence KS 66047-2139 Office: U Kans Dept Geology Lawrence KS 66045-0001

ENROTH-CUGELL, CHRISTINA ALMA ELISABETH, neurophysiologist, educator; b. Helsingfors, Finland, Aug. 27, 1919; came to U.S., 1956, naturalized, 1962; d. Emil and Maja (Syren) E.; m. David W. Cugell, Sept. 5, 1955. MD, Karolinska Inst., 1948, PhD, 1952; Hon. Doctors Degree, U. Helsinki, Finland, 1994. Resident Karolinska Sjukhuset, 1949-52; intern Passavant Meml. Hosp., 1956-57; with Northwestern U., Evanston, Ill., 1959-91, prof. emeritus, 1991—, prof. dept. neurobiology and physiology and dept. biomed. engring., 1974—; mem. vision research program com. Nat. Eye Inst., 1974-78, mem. nat. adv. eye council, 1980-84. Contbr. articles to profl. jours. Recipient Ludwig von Sallman award Internat. Assn. Rsch. in Vision and Ophthalmology, 1982. Fellow Am. Inst. Med. and Biol. Engring., Am. Acad. Arts and Scis.; mem. Am. Assn. Rsch. in Vision and Ophthalmology (co-recipient Friedenwald award 1983, recipient W.H. Helmerich III award 1992), Soc. Neuroscis., Am. Physiol. Soc., Physiol. Soc. (U.K.) Office: Northwestern U McCormick Sch Engring Technl Inst 2145 Sheridan Rd Evanston IL 60208-0834 E-mail: enroth@northwestern.edu.

ENSIGN, JERALD C. bacteriology educator; Prof. dept. bacteriology U. Wis., Madison, 1990—. Recipient Disting. Tchr. award Carski Found., 1992. Office: Univ Wis Dept Bacteriology 114 E Fred Hall 1550 Linden Dr Madison WI 53706-1521

ENSLEN, RICHARD ALAN, federal judge; b. Kalamazoo, May 28, 1931; s. Ehrman Thrasher and Pauline Mabel (Dragoo) E.; m. Pamela Gayle Chapman, Nov. 2, 1985; children— David, Susan, Sandra, Thomas,

Janet, Joseph, Gennady. Student, Kalamazoo Coll., 1949-51, Western Mich. U., 1955; LL.B., Wayne State U., 1958; LL.M., U. Va., 1986. Bar: Mich. 1958, U.S. Dist. Ct. (we. dist.) Mich. 1960, U.S. Ct. Appeals (6th cir.) 1971, U.S. Ct. Appeals (4th cir.) 1975, U.S. Supreme Ct 1975. Mem. firm Stratton, Wise, Early & Starbuck, Kalamazoo, 1958-60, Bauckham & Enslen, Kalamazoo, 1960-64, Howard & Howard, Kalamazoo, 1970-76, Enslen & Schma, Kalamazoo, 1977-79; dir. Peace Corps, Costa Rica, 1965-67; judge Mich. Dist. Ct., 1968-70; U.S. dist. judge Kalamazoo, 1979—; chief judge, 1995-2001. Mem. faculty Western Mich. U., 1961-62, Nazareth Coll., 1974-75; adj. prof. polit. sci. Western Mich. U., 1982— Co-author: The Constitution Law Dictionary: Volume One, Individual Rights, 1985; Volume Two, Governmental Powers, 1987, Constitutional Deskbook: Individual Rights, 1987, (with Mary Bedikian and Pamela Enslen) Michigan Practice, Alternative Dispute Resolution, 1998. Served with USAF, 1951-54. Named Person of the Century-Law and Courts, The Kalamazoo Gazette, 1999; recipient Disting. Alumni award, Wayne State Law Sch., 1980, Western Mich. U., 1982, Outstanding Practical Achievement award, Ctr. Pub. Resources, 1984, award for Excellence and Innovation in Alternative Dispute Resolution and Dispute Mgmt., Legal Program; scholar, Jewel Corp., 1956—57, Lampson McElhorne, 1957. Mem. ABA (standing com. on dispute resolution 1983-90), Mich. Bar Assn., Am. Judicature Soc. (bd. dirs. 1983-85), Sixth Cir. Jud. Coun. Office: US Dist Ct 410 W Michigan Ave Kalamazoo MI 49007-3757

ENSLIN, JON S. bishop; b. Apr. 4, 1938; m. Crystal Enslin; children: Jonathan, Joshua. Piano teaching cert., Wis. Conservatory Music; BA magna cum laude, Carroll Coll., Waukesha, Wis.; MDiv, Northwestern Luth. Theol. Sem., Mpls. Mission devel., then pastor Christ the Servant Luth. Ch., Waukesha, Wis., 1964-75; sr. pastor St. Stephen's Luth. Ch., Monona, 1975-87; asst. to bishop, adminstrv. dean South-Ctrl. Synod, 1988-91, bishop, 1991—. Trainer Clergy in Transition Growth in Excellence in Ministry Program, ELCA; mem. transition team South-Ctrl. Synod Wis. ELCA; mem. exec. bd. Wis.-Upper Mich. Synod of LCA, chmn. adminstrn. and fin. sect. exec. bd. Office: Evangelical Lutheran Church 2909 Landmark Pl Ste 202 Madison WI 53713-4200

ENTENZA, MATT, state legislator; b. Oct. 4, 1961; m. Lois Quam; 3 children. BA, Macalester Coll.; postgrad., Oxford (Eng.) U.; JD, U. Minn. Pvt. practice; rep. Dist. 64A Minn. Ho. of Reps., 1994—.

ENTRIKEN, ROBERT KERSEY, JR. motorsport writer, retired newspaper editor; b. Houston, Feb. 13, 1941; s. Robert and Jean (Finch) (stepmother) E.; married 1972 (div. 1982); 1 child, Jean Louise; m. Sandra Jo Miller, Mar. 4, 1989; children: Caitlyn Miller, Matthew Kersey; 1 adopted child, Stephanie Lynn; 1 stepchild, Jared Ray Adamson. Student, Sch. Journalism, U. Kans., 1961-69. Gen. assignment reporter Salina Jour., Kans., 1969-71, motorsport columnist, 1970-83, courts reporter, 1971-82, Sunday editor, 1972-75, spl. sects. editor, 1975-94, neighbors editor, 1982-95, TV editor, 1994-95. Contbg. editor Sports Car Mag., Tustin, Calif., 1972—; motorsport columnist Motorsports Monthly, Tulsa, Okla., 1983-85, Nat. Speed Sport News, 1996—; operator Ikke sa Hurtig Racing. Contbr. Performance Racing Industry mag., Sports Car World mag., Car Collector mag., Parts & People mag., Kansas! mag., Jox mag., Speedvision.com mag.; editor Kansas Motor Sports Ann., 1996. With USN, 1969-71, Guam. Mem.: Soc. of Profl. Journalists, Ea. Motorsports Press Assn., Am. Auto Racing Writers and Broadcasters Assn. (gen. v.p. 1982—86, Midwest v.p. 1980—82, chmn. All-Am. Team selections 1983—, chmn. Legends in Racing selections hall of fame 1989—), Sports Car Club Am. (regional exec. Kans. region 1974, founding mem. Salina region 1990, pointskeeper 1974—, 1995—2000, Best Story award 1972, 1973, 1976—78, 1983—87, 1989, 1992, inaugural recipient Vern Jaques Sports Car Contbr. of Yr. nat. award 1999, Solo Cup nat. award 1981, England-Stipe award 1989, Nat. Solo I champion 1986, Road Racing Driver of the Yr. Salina Region 1995, Solo Driver of Yr. Wichita Region 1976, 1982, Solo II Champion Kans. 1978, 1984, Midwest divsn. Mid-Am. nat.), Sigma Delta Chi. Avocations: sports car racing, autocrossing, skiing. Home and Office: 2731 Scott Ave Salina KS 67401-7858 E-mail: rocky@tri.net.

ENYEDY, GUSTAV, JR. chemical engineer; b. Cleve., Aug. 23, 1924; s. Gustav and Mary (Silay) E.; m. Zoe Agnes Zachlin, Aug. 25, 1956 (div.); children: Louise Elaine, Roseann Marie, Arthur Gustav, Lillian Alice, Edward Anthony; m. Barbara Martha Ludwig Holley, May 9, 1987. B.S. in Chem. Engring., Case Inst. Tech., 1950, M.S., 1955. Registered profl. engr., Ohio. Engr., Rayon Tech. div. E.I. duPont, Richmond, Va., 1950-51; project engr. Grasselli Chem. Div., Cleve., 1951-54; devel. engr. Diamond Alkali (Soda Products), Painesville, Ohio, 1954-60; process engr. Central Engring., Cleve., 1960-61, staff engr. research dept. Painesville, 1961-65, supr. computer services, 1965-68; mgr. Diamond Shamrock Corp., Painesville, 1968-73; engring. cons., 1973-85; pres. PDQS, Inc., 1975—. Lectr. chem. engring. Fenn Coll., Cleve., 1957-61, Cleve. State U., 1975-76 Contbr. articles to tech. jours., textbooks. Treas., cubmaster, chmn. Gates Mills Cub Scout Pack, 1970-71, 75-78. Served with AUS, 1943-46. Decorated Bronze Star medal, Combat Inf. badge. Fellow Am. Inst. Chem. Engrs., Am. Assn. Cost Engrs. (tech. v.p. 1966-68, pres. 1969-70, speakers' bur. program 1971-89, O.T. Zimmerman Founder's award and hon. life mem., 1992); mem. Hungarian Geneal. Soc. of Greater Cleve. (founder 1996), Tau Beta Pi, Pi Delta Epsilon. Home and Office: 7830 Sugarbush Ln Gates Mills OH 44040-9317

ENZ, CATHERINE S. state legislator; Mem. Mo. Ho. of Reps., Jefferson City, 1994—. Republican.

EPNER, STEVEN ARTHUR, computer consultant; b. Buffalo; s. Robert and Rosann (Krohn) E.; m. Louise Berke, June 20, 1970; children: Aaron J., Brian D. BS, Purdue U., 1970. Computer operator/programmer Union Carbide, Chgo. and London, 1966-68; system analyst process design III, Chgo., 1969; analyst, sr. systems analyst Monsanto Co., St. Louis, 1970-74; lead analyst Citicorp., 1974-76; cons., pres. The User Group, Inc. (name changed to BSW Consulting, Inc. 1995), 1976—. Lectr. U. Mo., St. Louis Bus. Program, AICPA, Mo., 1983-93; SBA Task Force on Small Bus.; dir. Programming and Systems Cons., Inc. Editor: The Independent, 1977-84; contbg. editor St. Louis Bus. Jour., St. Louis Computing; contbr. articles to profl. jours. Trustee Steven A. Epner/ICAA Scholarship fund; mem. tech. com., founding rep. EDI Coalition of Assns. Mem. Ind. Computer Cons. Assn. (dir., pres. chpt., nat. pres.), Nat. Cons. Council, Nat. Spkrs. Assn., Internat. Brotherhood Magicians. Office: BSW Cons Inc 1050 N Lindbergh Blvd Saint Louis MO 63132-2912

EPPEN, GARY DEAN, business educator; b. Austin, Minn., Apr. 28, 1936; s. Marldene Fredrick and Elsie Alma (Wendorf) E.; m. Ann Marie Sathre, June 14, 1958; children: Gregory, Peter, Paul, Amy. AA, Austin Jr. Coll., 1956; BS, U. Minn., 1958, MSIE, 1960; PhD, Cornell U., 1964; Hon. Doctorate, Stockholm Sch. Econs., 1998. Prof. mgmt. European Inst. Advanced Studies, Brussels, 1972-73; assoc. dean Grad. Sch. Bus., U. Chgo., 1969-75, prof. indsl. adminstrn., 1970—, assoc. dean Ph.D. studies, 1978-85, dir. internat. bus. exchange program, 1977-92, dir. Life Officers Investment Seminar, 1975-88, dir. Fin. Analysts Seminar, 1982-88, Robert Law prof., 1989-97, dir. exec. program, 1989-94, Keller Disting. Svc. prof., 1997-2001, dep. dean part-time programs, 1998-2001, dean emeritus, 2001—, Keller Disting. Svc. prof. emeritus, 2001—. Francqui prof. Cath. U. Leuven, Belgium, 1979; Urwitz vis. prof. Stockholm Sch. Econs., 1994; external examiner U. W.I., 1979-82; dir. Landauer, Inc., Hub Group, Inc., ROZ Trading Ltd., Hornet Capital, LLC. Author: (with F.J. Gould) Quantitative Concepts for Management, 1979, (with Metcalfe and Walters) The MBA Degree, 1979, (with F.J. Gould and C.P. Schmidt) Introductory Management Science, 1984; editor: Energy the Policy Issues, 1975; contbr. articles to profl. jours. FMC Faculty Rsch. scholar, 1986-89. Mem. Ops. Rsch. Soc. Am., Inst. Mgmt. Sci. Home: 3107 N Snead Dr Goodyear AZ 85338 E-mail: gary.eppen@gsb.uchicago.edu.

EPSTEIN, RAYMOND, engineering and architectural executive; b. Chgo., Jan. 12, 1918; s. Abraham and Janet (Rabinowitz) E.; m. Betty Jadwin, Apr. 7, 1940; children: Gail, David, Norman, Harriet. Student, MIT, 1934-36; B.S., U. Ill., 1938. Registered architect registered profl. engr. With A. Epstein & Sons Internat., Inc., Chgo., 1938—, chmn. bd., 1961-83, chmn. exec. com., 1983—. Bd. dirs., life trustee United Israel Appeal; past sec., hon. dir. Am. Jewish Joint Distbn. Com.; mem. exec. com. Nat. Jewish Cmty. Rels. Adv. Coun.; v.p. nat. bd. Jewish Telegraphic Agy.; mem. citizens bd. Loyola U.; past pres. Coun. Jewish Fedns., Welfare Funds, Inc., Jewish Welfare Fund Met. Chgo., Jewish United Fund, Young Men's Jewish Coun.; past sec. Jewish Fed. Met. Chgo.; past chmn. budget com., bd. govs. Jewish Agy.; past trustee Chgo. Med. Sch; past bd. dirs. United Jewish Appeal; past exec. com. Meml. Found. Jewish Culture; past chmn. pub. affairs com., past chmn. campaign Jewish United Fund Met. Chgo.; past. sec. Welfare Coun. Met. Chgo.; past bd. dirs. Chgo. Bldg. Congress; life dir. Mt. Sinai Med. Rsch. Found.; trustee, past dir. Ampal-Am. Israel Corp. Decorated comdr. Legion of Honor Ivory Coast, 1982; recipient Disting. Alumnus award U. Ill., 1974, Julius Rosenwald Meml. award Jewish Fedn. Chgo., 1974, Citation Brandeis U., 1992; named to City of Chgo. Sr. Citizens Hall of Fame, 1991. Fellow Soc. Civil Engr. France, Soc. Am. Registered Architects; mem. NSPE , ASCE, Am. Concrete Inst., Western Soc. Engrs., Assn. Engrs. and Architects in Israel, French Engrs. in the U.S., Inc., Pi Lambda Phi. Clubs: Standard (past trustee), Illini, MIT, Caxton (Chgo.). Home: 4950 S Chicago Beach Dr Chicago IL 60615-3207 Office: 600 W Fulton St Chicago IL 60661-1100 E-mail: raye@thepowhatan.com.

EPSTEIN, RICHARD A. law educator; b. 1943; AB, Columbia U., 1964; BA, Oxford U., 1966; LLB, Yale U., 1968. Bar: Calif. 1969. Asst. prof. Sch. Law U. So. Calif., L.A., 1969-70, assoc. prof., 1968-69; prof. Law Sch. U. Chgo., 1973-82; James Parker hall prof. law, 1982-88; James Parker Hall Disting. Svc. prof., 1988—. Vis. assoc. prof. Law Sch. Chgo. U., 1972-73. Author: Cases and Materials in Torts, 6th dit., 1995, Takings: Private property and the Power of Eminent Domain, 1985, Simple Rules for a Complex World, 1995, Mortal Peril: Our Inalienable Right to Health Care, 1997, Principles for a Free Society: Reconciling Individual Liberty with the Common Good, 1998; editor: Jour. Legal Studies, 1981-91, Jour. Law and Econs., 1991—; mem. editl. bd. Yale Law Jour. Mem. Am. Acad. Arts and Scis., Order of Coif. Office: U Chgo Law Sch 1111 E 60th St Chicago IL 60637-2776

EPSTEIN, SIDNEY, architect, engineer; b. Chgo., 1923; m. Sondra Berman, Sept. 4, 1987; children from previous marriage: Donna Epstein Barrows, Laurie Epstein Lawton. BS in Civil Engring. with high honors, U. Ill., 1943. Various positions A. Epstein & Sons Internat.; chmn. bd. dirs. A. Epstein & Sons Internat., Inc., Chgo. Dir. Amal. Trust & Savs. Bank, Polk Bros. Found., Michael Reese Found.; trustee emeritus Northwestern Mut. LIfe Ins. Co. Founder, bd. dirs., past chmn. Chgo. Youth Ctrs.; past chmn. bd. trustees Michael Reese Hosp. and Med. Ctr.; bd. govs., life mem. U. Chgo. Hosps. and Clinics; life trustee Orchestral Assn. Chgo. Mem.: Standard Club (life; past pres.), Chi Epsilon, Phi Eta Sigma, Phi Kappa Phi, Sigma Tau, Tau Beta Pi, Sigma Xi. Home: 1430 N Lake Shore Dr Chicago IL 60610-6682 Office: A Epstein & Sons Internat Inc 600 W Fulton St Chicago IL 60661-1100 E-mail: sidneyepstein@epstein-isi.com.

EPSTEIN, WOLFGANG, retired biochemist, educator; b. Breslau, Germany, May 7, 1931; came to U.S., 1936, naturalized, 1943; s. Stephan and Elsbeth (Lauinger) E.; m. Edna Selan, June 12, 1961; children: Matthew, Ezra, Tanya. B.A. with high honors, Swarthmore Coll., 1951; M.D., U. Minn., 1955. Postdoctoral fellow in physiology U. Minn., Mpls., 1959-60; postdoctoral fellow Pasteur Inst., Paris., 1963-65; postdoctoral fellow in biophysics Harvard Med. Sch., 1961-63, research asso., then asso. in biophysics, 1965-67; asst. prof. biochemistry U. Chgo., 1967-73, asso. prof., 1973-79, prof., 1979-84, prof. dept. molecular genetics and cell biology, 1984—; ret., 1999. Served with M.C. U.S. Army, 1957-59. Mem. AAAS, Am. Soc. for Biochemistry and Molecular Biology, Am. Soc. for Microbiology. Home: 1120 E 50th St Chicago IL 60615-2804 Office: 920 E 58th St Chicago IL 60637-5415

EPTING, C. CHRISTOPHER, bishop; b. Greenville, S.C. m. Pam Flagg; children: Michael, Amanda. Grad., U. Fla., Seabury-Western Theol. Sem., Evanston, Ill., 1952; STM, Gen. Theol. Sem., N.Y.C., 1984. Formerly curate Holy Trinity Ch., Melbourne; vicar Ch. of St. Luke the Evangelist, Mulberry, Fla., 1974-78; founding vicar St. Stephen's Ch., Lakeland; canon residentiary St. John's Cathedral, from 1978; rector St. Mark's Episc. Ch. and Sch., Cocoa, Fla.; bishop coadjutor, then bishop Episc. Diocese of Iowa, Des Moines, 1988—. Formerly dean Inst. Christian Studies, St. Luke's Cathedral, Orlando, Fla. Office: Episc Diocese of Iowa 225 37th St Des Moines IA 50312-4399

ERBELE, ROBERT S. state legislator; m. Susan Erbele; 4 children. Student, U. Sioux Falls, North Dakota State U. Rancher Bison; EMT-B; choral music dir., 1999—2000; mem. N.D. Senate from 28th dist., Bismark, 2001—; vice chair Senate AG Committee; senate Human Svcs. Com. Dir. Logan County Hist. Soc. Mem. N.D. Buffalo Assn. (v.p.). Republican. Office: 6512 51st St Ave SE Lehr ND 58460 E-mail: rerbele@state.nd.us.

ERBER, THOMAS, physics educator; b. Vienna, Austria, Dec. 6, 1930; m. Audrey Burns. B.Sc., MIT, 1951; M.S., U. Chgo., 1953, Ph.D. in Physics, 1957. Asst. prof. physics Ill. Inst. Tech., Chgo., 1957-62, assoc. prof., 1962-69, prof., 1969—, prof. math., 1986—, disting. prof., 1999—. Vis. scientist Stanford Linear Accelerator Ctr., 1970; prof. physics U. Graz, 1971, 82, hon prof., 1971—; prof. physics UCLA, 1978-79, 84-85, 87—, U. Grenoble, 1982; prof. physics U. Chgo., 1998-99; adv. bd. rsch. corp. Mem. editl. bd. Acta Physica Austriaca. Rsch. fellow, Brussels, Belgium, 1963-64. Fellow: Inst. Physics (U.K.), Am. Math. Soc., Am. Phys. Soc.; mem.: IEEE (life sr.), Nuclear, Plasma & Magnetics Soc., Am. Acad. Mechanics, Am. Radio Relay League, N.Y. Acad. Sci., Magnetics Soc., Oesterreichische Physikalische Gesellschaft, European Phys. Soc. Office: Ill Inst Tech Dept Physics Chicago IL 60616

ERDMAN, PHILIP, state legislator, farmer; b. Scottsbluff, Nebr., Apr. 7, 1977; BS in Agrl. Scis., U. Nebr., 2000. Mem. Nebr. Legis. from 47th dist., Lincoln, 2001—. Cons. strategic planning Farmland Industries, Inc.; football recruiter U. Nebr., Lincoln. Mem. adv. bd., mem. curriculum com. Coll. Agrl. Scis. and Natural Resources, 1999-2000; del. Nebr. State Rep. Conv., 2000, Morrill County Rep. Conv., 2000. Mem. Fellowship Christian Athletes, Nat. FFA Alumni, Nebr. FFA Alumni (state pres. 1996-97), Rock Jaycees, Bayard FFA Alumni, Cheyenne County C. of C., Alpha Zeta, Gamma Sigma Delta. Home: Rural Rt 1, Box 314 Bayard NE 69334 Office: Rm 1101 State Capitol Lincoln NE 68509

ERDÖS, ERVIN GEORGE, pharmacology and biochemistry educator; b. Budapest, Hungary; came to U.S., 1954; naturalized, 1959; s. Andor and Aranka (Breuer) E; m. Sara F. Rabito, May 30, 1986; children from previous marriage: Martin, Peter, Philip. Grad., U. Budapest Sch. Medicine, 1950; MD, U. Munich, 1950. With hosp., Munich, 1951; rsch. assoc. in biochem. rsch. lab. U. Munich, 1952-54; rsch. assoc. Mercy Hosp., Pitts., 1955-58; fellow in biochemistry, ind. rsch. Mellon Inst., 1958-63; asst. prof. pharmacology U. Pitts., 1958-61, assoc. prof., 1961-63; prof. pharmacology U. Okla. Sch. Medicine, Oklahoma City, 1963-73, George Lynn Cross rsch. prof., 1970-73; prof. pharmacology, internal medicine U. Tex., Southwestern Med. Sch., Dallas, 1973-85; prof. pharmacology and anesthesiology, dir. Peptide Rsch. Lab. U. Ill. Coll. Medicine, Chgo., 1985—. Vis. prof. Tulane U., 1963; Disting. Fulbright prof., 1975; vis. scientist U.S.-Japan Coop. Sci. Program, NSF, 1966; vis. prof. dept. pharmacology Rush Med. Coll., Chgo., 1993—; cons. in field; mem. coms. Nat. Heart and Lung Inst. Editor books; mem. editorial bd. jours. Recipient gold medal Frey-Werle Found., Munich, 1988, Disting. Faculty award U. Ill. Coll. Medicine, 1992; Deutsche Forschungsgemeinschaft fellow, 1954; Wellcome Rsch. travel grantee, 1964; Univ. scholar U. Ill., 1990. Fellow: Am. Heart Assn. (mem. adv. bd. Coun. for High Blood Pressure Rsch. 1972—, Ciba award for hypertension rsch. 1994, Rsch. Achievement award 1995); mem.: Am. Soc. Biochemistry and Molecular Biology, Hungarian Acad. Sci. (fgn.) (hon.), Am. Soc. Pharmacology and Exptl. Therapeutics. Office: U Ill Coll Medicine Dept Pharmacology MC 868 835 S Wolcott Ave Chicago IL 60612-7340 E-mail: egerdos@uic.edu.

ERENS, JAY ALLAN, lawyer; b. Chgo., Oct. 18, 1935; s. Miller S. and Annette (Goodman) R.; m. Patricia F. Brett, Aug. 21, 1960 (div. May 1985); children: Pamela B., Bradley B.; m. Patrice K. Franklin, June 15, 1985; 1 child, Cameron Jay. BA, Yale U., 1956; LLB, Harvard U., 1959. Bar: Ill. 1960. Law clk. to Justice John M. Harlan U.S. Supreme Ct., Washington, 1959-60; pvt. practice Chgo., 1960-64; founding and sr. ptnr. Levy and Erens (name changed to Erens and Miller 1985), 1964-86; sr. ptnr. Hopkins & Sutter, 1986-2001; with Foley & Lardner, 2001—. Lectr. law Northwestern U., Chgo., 1961-63; spl. asst. atty. gen. State Ill., Chgo., 1964-70. Trustee Latin Sch. Chgo., 1975-80. Mem. ABA, Chgo. Bar Assn. Office: Foley & Lardner 3 First National Plz Chicago IL 60602 E-mail: jerens@foleylaw.com.

ERHARDT, RON, state legislator; m. Jacquelyn. BBA, U. Minn., 1958, BA, 1959. State rep. Minn. Ho. Reps., Dist. 42A, 1991—. Mem. govt. oper. com., com. & econ. devel.-internat. trade, tech. & econ. devel. divsn., regulated indsl. & energy & taxes coms., Minn. Ho. Reps. Home: 4214 Sunnyside Rd Edina MN 55424-1114 Office: 100 Constitution Ave Saint Paul MN 55155-1232

ERICKSON, GERALD MEYER, classical studies educator; b. Amery, Wis., Sept. 23, 1927; s. Oscar Meyer and Ellen Claire (Hanson) E.; m. Loretta Irene Eder, Feb. 11, 1951; children: Rachel, Viki, Kari BS, U. Minn., 1954, MA, 1956, PhD, 1968. Cert. secondary sch. tchr., Minn. Tchr. Edina-Morningside Pub. Sch., Minn., 1956-65, 66-67; vis. lectr. U. Minn., Mpls., 1965-66, asst. prof., 1968-71, assoc. prof., 1971-83, prof. classical studies, 1983-95, prof. emeritus, 1995—. Exchange prof. Moscow State U., 1980, 86; vis. prof. U. Ill., 1967, 68, Coll. of William and Mary, 1984; bd. regents La. Univ. System, 1981, chmn. evaluation team for classics programs; reader Coll. Bds. Advanced Placement Program, 1975-77, chief reader, 1978-81; cons., lectr. in field Assoc. editor, mem. editorial staff Nature, Society and Thought, 1987—; author, lectr. various TV and radio courses Served with U.S. Mcht. Marine, 1945-46, U.S. Army, 1946-47, PTO; served to capt. USAF, 1951-53 NEH grantee, 1977-79; recipient award Horace T. Morse Amoco Found., 1984 Mem. Minn. Classical Conf. (pres. 1971-74), Minn. Humanities Conf. (pres. 1974-75), Classical Assn. Midwest/South (Ovatio award 1971). Avocations: short-wave radio listening; bicycling. Home: 121 E 51st St Minneapolis MN 55419-2605 Office: 305 Folwell Hall 9 Pleasant St SE Minneapolis MN 55455-0194

ERICKSON, HOWARD HUGH, veterinarian, physiology educator; b. Wahoo, Nebr., Mar. 16, 1936; s. Conrad and Laurene (Swanson) E.; m. Ann E. Nicolay, June 6, 1959; children: James, David. BS, DVM, Kans. State U., 1959; PhD, Iowa State U., 1966. Commd. 1st lt. U.S. Air Force, 1959, advanced through grades to col., 1979; veterinarian U.K., 1960-63; vet. scientist Sch. Aerospace Medicine, Brooks AFB, Tex., 1966-75; dir. rsch. and devel. aerospace med. divsn., 1975-81; prof. physiology Kans. State U., Manhattan, 1981—, acting head dept. anatomy and physiology, 1989—90, Roy W. Upham prof. vet. medicine, 2001—. Sci. adv. bd. Morris Animal Found., Englewood, Colo., 1990-93; cons. Tex. Higher Edn. Coordination Bd., Austin, 1990-91; clin. asst. prof. U. Tex. Health Sci. Ctr., San Antonio, 1972-81; vis. mem. grad. faculty Tex. A&M U., College Station, 1967-81; affiliate prof. Colo. State U., Fort Collins, 1970-75. Editor: Animal Pain, 1983; contbr. articles to profl. jours. Recipient Alumni Achievement award Midland Luth. Coll., Fremont, Nebr., 1977, Merck award for Creativity, 1993, Bayer Excellence in Equine Rsch. award Am. Vet. Med. Assn. Coun. on Rsch., 2000. Fellow AAAS, Royal Soc. Health, Aerospace Med. Assn. (assoc.); mem. Am. Vet. Med. Assn. (chmn. coun. on rsch. 1984), Am. Physiol. Soc., Optimists Club (Manhattan). Republican. Lutheran. Home: 1700 Kings Rd Manhattan KS 66503-7550 Office: Kans State U Coll Vet Medicine Dept Anatomy and Physiology Manhattan KS 66506 E-mail: erickson@vet.ksu.edu.

ERICKSON, JOHN DUFF, retired educational association administrator; b. Crawford, Nebr., Apr. 1, 1933; s. Harold Edward and Ruth Isabel (Duff) E.; m. Janet Eileen Lind, Dec. 28, 1955 (dec. Mar. 1992); children: Gregory Duff, Sheryl Ann; m. Bettie M. Hankins, July 7, 1994. BS in Mining Engring., S.D. Sch. Mines and Tech., 1955; MS in Indsl. Mgmt., MIT, 1965. Mine planning engr. Kennecott Copper Corp., Salt Lake City, 1965-67, truck ops. supt., 1968-69; mine mgr. Bougainville (New Guinea) Copper Ltd., Bougainville, Papua, New Guinea, 1970-72, exec. mgr. tech. services New Guinea, 1973-75, asst. gen. mgr. New Guinea, 1976-77; head dept. mining engring. S.D. Sch. Mines and Tech., Rapid City, S.D., 1978-94; exec. dir. S.D. Sch. of Mines and Tech. Alumni Assn., 1984-98, prof. emeritus, 1998—. Mining cons. Bechtel Civil and Minerals, San Francisco, 1979—, Fluor Daniel Engrs., Redwood City, Calif., 1983—, Davy McKee, San Ramon, Calif., Mineral Resources Devel., San Mateo, Calif.; bd. dirs. South Hills Mining Co., Rapid City. Bd. dirs. Nat. Mining Hall of Fame and Mus. Capt. U.S. Army, 1961-62. Sloan fellow MIT, 1964-65. Mem. SME/AIME (chmn. Black Hills sect. 1983), S.D. Mining Assn. (bd. dirs.), Arrowhead Country Club, Elks. Republican. Home: 2958 Tomahawk Dr Rapid City SD 57702-4276 Office: SD Sch Mines and Tech 501 E Saint Joseph St Rapid City SD 57701-3901 E-mail: duffe@gwtc.net.

ERICKSON, KIM, consumer products company executive; Sr. v.p. fin. SuperValu Inc., Eden Prairie, Minn., sr. v.p. strategic planning, treas., 1998—. Office: SuperValu Inc 11840 Valley View Rd Eden Prairie MN 55344-3691

ERICKSON, RONALD A. retail executive; CEO Holiday Cos., Mpls. Office: Holiday Companies PO Box 1224 Minneapolis MN 55440-1224

ERICKSON, W(ALTER) BRUCE, business and economics educator, entrepreneur; b. Chgo., Mar. 4, 1938; s. Clifford Eric and Mildred B. (Brinkmeier) E. BA, Mich. State U., 1959, MA, 1960, PhD in Econs., 1965. Rsch. assoc. subcom. on antitrust and monopoly U.S. Senate, 1960-61; asst. prof. econs. Bowling Green (Ohio) U., 1964-66; asst. prof. bus. and govt. Coll. Bus. Adminstrn., U. Minn., Mpls., 1966-70, assoc. prof., 1971-75, prof. dept. mgmt., 1975—, prof., chmn. dept. mgmt., 1977-80, co-chmn., then chmn., 1988-92. Bd. dirs. various bus., non-profit and venture capital orgns.; cons. rock salt antitrust cases for atty. gens. Mich., cons. rock salt antitrust cases for atty. gens. Calif., Ill., Wis., Minn.; cons. U.S. Justice Dept. Author: An Introduction to Contemporary Business, 4th edit., 1985, Government and Business, 1980, 2d edit., 1984, International Business, 1998; co-author: International Business, 1998; bd. editors Antitrust Law and Econs. Rev., Jour. Indsl. Orgn.; contbr. articles to profl. jours. Bd. dirs. Found. for Constl. Edn. and the Citizens League, 1991-92; mem. ethics com. Ebenezer System, Minn. Mem. Am. Econ. Assn., Royal Econ. Soc. E-mail: berickson@cs&m.comm.edu. Office: Carlson Sch Mgmt 321 19th Ave S Minneapolis MN 55455-0438

ERICSON, JAMES DONALD, lawyer, insurance executive; b. Hawarden, Iowa, Oct. 12, 1935; s. Elmer H. and Martha (Sydness) E.; children: Linda Jean, James Robert. B.A. in History, State U. Iowa, 1958, J.D., 1962. Bar: Wis. 1965. Assoc. Fitzgerald, Brown, Leahy, McGill & Strom, Omaha, 1962-65; with Northwestern Mut. Life Ins. Co., Milw., 1965—, asst. to pres., 1972-75, dir. policy benefits, 1975-76, v.p., gen. counsel, sec., 1976-80, sr. v.p., 1980, exec. v.p., 1987, pres., 1990, chief operating officer, 1991-93, pres., CEO, 1993-2000, chmn., CEO, 2000-2001. Dir. MGIC Investment Corp., Green Bay Packaging Inc., Kohl's Corp., Marcus Corp., Northwestern Mut. Investment Svcs., Frank Russell Co.; immediate past chmn. Am. Coun. Life Ins. Bd. dirs. Wis. Taxpayers Alliance, Competitive Wis., Inc., Greater Milw. Com., Milw. Redevel. Com., United Way, Met. Milw. Assn. Commerce, Med. Coll. Wis., Milw. Sch. Engring.; trustee Lawrence U., Com. for Econ. Devel., Boys and Girls Club Greater Milw., Lyric Opera Chgo. Mem. ABA, Assn. Life Ins. Counsel (hon.), Wis. Bar Assn., Milw. Club (bd. dirs.), Phi Beta Kappa. Republican. Presbyterian. Office: Northwestern Mut 777 E Wisconsin Ave Ste 3010 Milwaukee WI 53202-4703

ERICSSON, RICHARD L. lawyer; b. 1948; BA, JD, U. S.D. Bar: S.D. 1974. Ptnr. Ericsson Ericsson & Leibel, Madison, S.D. Mem. State Bar S.D. (pres.-elect). Office: Ericsson Ericsson & Leibel 100 N Egan Ave Madison SD 57042-2909

ERIKSEN, CHARLES WALTER, psychologist, educator; b. Omaha, Feb. 4, 1923; s. Charles Hans and Luella (Carlson) E.; m. Garnita Tharp, July 22, 1945 (div. Jan. 1971); children: Michael John, Kathy Ann; m. Barbara Becker, Apr. 1971. BA summa cum laude, U. Omaha, 1943; PhD, Stanford, 1950. Asst. prof. Johns Hopkins U., Balt., 1949-53, research scientist, 1954-55; lectr. Harvard U., Cambridge, Mass., 1953-54; mem. faculty U. Ill., Urbana, 1956—, prof., 1959-93, prof. emeritus, 1993—. Rsch. cons. VA, 1960-80; mem. psycho-biology panel NSF, 1963; mem. exptl. psychology study sect. NIH, 1958-62, 66-70; Pillsbury Meml. lectr. Cornell U., 1966; keynote address 1st Internat. Congress on Visual Search, U. Durham, U.K., 1988, European Congress for Cognitive Psychology, Elsinore, Denmark, 1993; invited lectr. Max Plank Inst., Munich, 1993, Universidad Autonoma de Madrid, 1993, U. of Salamanca, Spain, 1993. Author: Behavior and Awareness, 1962; editor Am. Jour. Psychology, 1968; prin. editor Perception and Psychophysics, 1971-93; cons. editor Jour. Exptl. Psychology, 1965-71, Jour. Gerontology, 1980—; contbr. articles to profl. jours. Recipient Stratton award Am. Psychopath. Assn., 1964, NIMH Research Career award, 1964 Fellow AAAS; mem. Am. Psychol. Soc., Psychonomic Soc., Soc. Exptl. Psychologists, Midwestern Psychol. Assn., Sigma Xi. Home: 22485 State Highway 133 Oakland IL 61943-6822 Office: U Ill Psychol Bldg 603 E Daniel St Champaign IL 61820-6232 E-mail: eriksen@advant.com., eriksen@Gulftel.com.

ERKONEN, WILLIAM E. radiologist, medical educator; BS, U. Iowa, 1955, MD, 1958. Diplomate Am. Bd. Radiology. Intern U. Oreg., Portland, 1959; pvt. practice; resident in radiology U. Iowa Coll. Medicine, Iowa City, 1968-71; pvt. practice, 1971-87; faculty U. Iowa Coll. Medicine, 1988-94, asst. prof. radiology, 1994-98, assoc. prof., 1995-98, co-dir. Electric Differential Multimedia Lab., 1993—, assoc. prof. emeritus, 1998—. Rschr. in med. informatics and med. student instrn. and edn. Editor: (textbook) Radiology 101; contbr. articles to profl. jours.; developer electronic med. textbooks. Recipient numerous certs. of merit Radiology Soc. N.Am.; named Tchr. of Yr., U. Iowa Coll. Med., 1990, 93, 96; recipient Disting. Tchr. award for jr. faculty in clin. scis. Alpha Omega Alpha. Fellow Am. Coll. Radiology. Office: Univ Iowa Coll Medicine Dept Radiology Iowa City IA 52240

ERLANDSON, MIKE, legislative staff member; b. Apr. 14, 1964; m. Dawn Erlandson. B, St. Johns U., 1986. Aid Rep. Martin Sabo, St. Paul, 1985-93, chief staff, 1993—. Chmn. Minn. Dems., 1999—. Office: Minn DFL Party 352 Wacouta St Saint Paul MN 55101-1952*

ERLANDSON, PATRICK J. medical association administrator; Joined UnitedHealth Group, Minnetonka, Minn., 1997-2000, CFO, 2000—. Office: UnitedHealth Group 9900 Bren Rd E Minnetonka MN 55343

ERLEBACHER, ALBERT, history educator; b. Ulm, Württemburg, Fed. Republic of Germany, Sept. 28, 1932; came to U.S., 1937; s. Alfred Samuel and Rosa (Wertheimer) E.; m. Dolores Adler, Aug. 20, 1961; children: Seth Allen, Steven John, Ross Maier. BA, Marquette U., 1954, MA, 1956; PhD, U. Wis., 1965. Cert. prin., Wis. Tchr. Independence (Wis.) H.S., 1954-55, Cen. H.S., Sheboygan, Wis., 1956-59; prin. Lone Rock (Wis.) H.S., 1960-62; asst. prof. U. Wis., Oshkosh, 1962-65; prof. DePaul U., Chgo., 1965—, chmn. history dept., 1982-88. Dist. 69 Sch. Bd., Skokie, Ill., 1978-81; faculty adv. com. State Bd. Higher Edn., Champaign, Ill., 1974-80, 92-97. Mem. Temple Judea-Mizpah. Mem. AAUP, Am. Hist. Assn., State His. Soc. Wis. Home: 8232 Kilbourn Ave Skokie IL 60076-2614 Office: DePaul U 2320 N Kenmore Ave Chicago IL 60614-3210 E-mail: aerlebac@condor.depaul.edu.

ERLEBACHER, ARLENE CERNIK, retired lawyer; b. Chgo., Oct. 3, 1946; d. Laddie J. and Gertrude V. (Kurdys) Cernik; m. Albert Erlebacher, June 14, 1968; children: Annette Doherty, Jacqueline. BA, Northwestern U., 1967, JD, 1973. Bar: Ill. 1974, U.S. Dist. Ct. (no. dist.) Ill. 1974, U.S. Ct. Appeals (7th cir.) 1974, Fed. Trial Bar 1983, U.S. Supreme Ct. 1985. Assoc. Sidley & Austin, Chgo., 1974-80, ptnr., 1980-95, ret., 1996. Fellow Am. Bar Found.; mem. Order of Coif. E-mail: Erlebacher@attbi.com.

ERNEST, J. TERRY, ocular physiologist, educator; b. Sycamore, Ill., June 26, 1935; married, 1965; 2 children. BA, Northwestern U., 1957; MD, U. Chgo., 1961, PhD in Visual Sci., 1967. Prof. ophthalmology U. Wis., 1977-79; prof., chmn. ophthalmology Ind. U., 1980-81; prof. ophthalmology U. Ill., 1981-85; prof., chmn. ophthalmology U. Chgo., 1985—. Mem visual sci. A study sect., NIH, 1975-78, chmn. 1978-79, chmn. visual disorders study sect., 1979-80; rsch. prof. Rsch. to Prevent Blindness, Ind., 1981-84; mem. Vision Rsch. Program Com., 1982-84. Founding editor, Key, 1986-88; editor, Year Book of Ophthamology, 1982-88, Investigative Ophthalmology and Visual Sci., 1988-92. Recipient Rsch. Career Devel. award NIH, 1972. Mem. AASS, Am. Ophthalmol. Soc., Am. Acad. Ophthalmology (Honor award 1982), Assn. Rsch. Vision and Ophthalmology. Achievements include research in ocular circulation with special emphasis on glaucoma and diabetic retinopathy using various methods of in vivo blood flow measurements. Office: U Chgo Visual Sciences Ctr 5841 S Maryland Ave MC2114 Chicago IL 60637-1454

ERNST, MARK A. diversified financial services company executive; m. Annette Ernst; two children. Degree in Acctg. & Fin. summa cum laude, Drake U.; MBA, U. Chgo. With tax, investment and corp. adv. svcs. dept. Coopers & Lybrand; v.p., gen. mgr. tax and bus. svcs. divsn. Am. Express Co., Mpls., sr. v.p. workplace fin. svcs., sr. v.p.; exec. v.p., COO H&R Block, Inc., 1998-99, pres., COO, 1999—, also bd. dirs. Office: H&R Block 4400 Main St Kansas City MO 64111-1812

ERNSTBERGER, ERIC, landplanning architectural company executive; Prin. Rundell Ernstberger & Assocs., Muncie, Ind. Office: Rundell Ernstberger 315 S Jefferson St Muncie IN 47305-2470 E-mail: eernstberger@reasite.com.

ERON, LEONARD DAVID, psychology educator; b. Newark, Apr. 22, 1920; s. Joseph I. and Sarah (Hilfman) E.; m. Madeline Marcus, Mar. 21, 1950; children: Joan Hobson, Don, Barbara. B.S., CCNY, 1941; M.A., Columbia U., 1946; Ph.D., U. Wis., 1949. Diplomate Am. Bd. Profl. Psychology. Asst. prof. psychology and psychiatry Yale U., New Haven, 1948-55; dir. research Rip Van Winkle Found., 1955-62; prof. psychology U. Iowa, Iowa City, 1962-69; research prof. U. Ill.-Chgo., 1969-89; emeritus rsch. prof. of the social sci. in psychology, 1989—; rsch. scientist, prof. psychology Inst. for Social Rsch., U. Mich., Ann Arbor, 1992—. Author 8 books; editor Jour. Abnormal Psychology, 1973-80; assoc. editor Am. Psychologist, 1986-90; contbr. numerous articles to profl. jours. Served to 1st lt. AUS, 1942-45 Fulbright lectr., Free U. Amsterdam, 1967-68; recipient Fulbright Sr. Scholar award, Queensland U., Australia, 1976-77, James McKeen Cattell Sabbatical award, U. Rome, 1984-85. Fellow AAAS, Am. Psychol. Assn. (chair commn. violence and youth 1991-93, Disting. Contbns. to Knowledge award 1980, Gold medal award for Life Contbn. to Psychology in the Pub. Interest 1995), Am. Orthopsychiat. Assn.; mem. Midwestern Psychol. Assn. (pres. 1985-86), Internat. Soc. for Rsch. in Aggression (pres. 1989-90). Office: U Mich Inst for Social Rsch 426 Thompson St Ann Arbor MI 48104-2321 E-mail: lderon@umich.edu.

ERPENBACH, JON, state legislator; b. Madison, Wis., Jan. 28, 1961; m. Katherine Erpenbach; children: Joseph, Amy. Student, U. Wis., Oshkosh. Mem. dist. 27 Wis. Senate, Madison, 1998—. Democrat. Office: PO Box 7882 Madison WI 53707-7882

ERTL, WOLFGANG, German language and literature educator; b. Sangerhausen, Germany, May 27, 1946; came to U.S., 1969; m. Mary R. Clough, Aug. 30, 1969. BA in German and English, Philipps U., Marburg, Germany, 1969; MA in German, U. N.H., 1970; PhD in Germanic Langs. and Lits., U. Pa., 1975. Lectr. German U. Pa., Phila., 1974-76; asst. prof. German Swarthmore (Pa.) Coll., 1976-77, U. Iowa, 1977-82, assoc. prof., 1982-88, prof., 1988—, chmn. dept. German, 1988-96. Author: Stephan Hermlin and Tradition, 1977, Nature and Landscape in the Poetry of the GDR: Walter Werner, Wulf Kirsten, and Uwe Gressmann, 1982, (with Christine Cosentino) On Volker Braun's Lyric Poetry, 1984; co-editor: GDR Poetry in Context, 1988; co-editor Glossen: An Internat. Bi-Lingual Scholarly Jour. on Lit., Film, and Art in the German Speaking Countries After 1945; co-editor (with C. Cosentino and W. Muller) Taking Stock--German Literature after Unification: Contributions to the 1st Carlisle Symposium on Modern German Literature, glossen: 10, 2000, Crosscurrents--German Literature(s) and the Search for Identity, 2002; contbr. chpts. to books, revs. and articles to profl. jours. May Brodbeck Humanities fellow, 1987. Mem. MLA, N.E. MLA, Am. Assn. Tchrs. German, German Studies Assn. Office: U Iowa Dept German 526 Phillips Hall Iowa City IA 52242-1323

ERWIN, JUDY, state legislator; b. Detroit, 1950; BS, U. Wis.; MA, Nat. Coll. Edn., Evanston, Ill.; postgrad., Kennedy Sch. Govt., 1987. Formerly tchr. pub. schs.; mgmt. cons. Grant Thornton LPP; formerly dir. comms. staff Senate Dem. Staff; mem. from 11th dist. Ill. Ho. of Reps. Former del. Dem. Convs.; mem. Gov.'s Human Resource Task Force. Home: 1545 N Wells Chicago IL 60610-1307 Office: Ill Ho of Reps State Capitol Springfield IL 62706-0001

ESHBAUGH, W(ILLIAM) HARDY, botanist, educator; b. Glen Ridge, N.J., May 1, 1936; -; s. William Hardy Eshbaugh Jr. and Elizabeth (Wakeman) Henderson; m. Barbara Keller, Sept. 6, 1958; children: David Charles, Stephen Hardy, Elizabeth Wendy, Jeffrey Raymond. BA, Cornell U., 1959; MA, Ind. U., 1961, PhD, 1964. Lectr. in botany Ind. U., Bloomington, 1962; spl. asst. to chief ecology and epidemiology br. Dugway (Utah) Proving Ground, 1964-65; asst. prof., curator botany So. Ill. U., Carbondale, 1965-67; asst. prof. Miami U., Oxford, Ohio, 1967-71, assoc. prof., 1971-77, prof. botany, 1977-98, chmn. dept. botany, 1983-88, prof. emeritus, 1998. Cur., Willard Sherman Turrell Herbarium, Miami U., 1967-82; assoc. program dir. NSF, Washington, 1982-83; co-chmn. steering com. Systematics Agenda 2000-Charting the Biosphere; adv. bd. Am. Bot. Coun., 1996—; instr. Internat. Rainforest Workshops, 1991-99. Co-author: (Book) The Vascular Flora of Andros Island, Bahamas, 1988; contbr. articles to profl. jours. Bd. dirs. Childrens Environ. Trust Found., 1992-94; troop com. Oxford area Boy Scouts Am., 1986-90; pres. Elizabeth Wakeman Henderson Charitable Found., 1997—. Capt. U.S. Army, 1964-65. Fellow: AAAS, Inst. Environ. Scis., Ohio Acad. Sci.; mem.: Internat. Field Studies (trustee 1989—95), Internat. Orgn. Plant Biosystematists (coun. 1987—89, ad hoc com. 1989—92, N. Am. treas. 1992—95), Assn. Systemic Collections (bd. dirs. 1981—84, rep.-at-large), Nature Conservancy (vice chmn. Ohio chpt. 1970—75, trustee 1970—77), Atlantic Salmon Confed. (bd. dirs. 2002—05), Bot. Soc. Am. (pres. 1988—89, Merit award 1992), Soc. Econ. Botany (v.p. 1982—83, pres. 1983—84), Am. Soc. Plant Taxonomists 1991—92, Am. Inst. Biol. Scis. 1995, Nat. Audubon Soc. (bd. dirs. 1983—). Methodist. Avocations: camping, fly fishing, photography, sailing, swimming. Home: 209 Mckee Ave Oxford OH 45056-9059 Office: Miami U Dept Botany Oxford OH 45056 E-mail: eshbauwh@muohio.edu.

ESKOLA, ERIC, radio personality; Grad., U. Minn., 1975. Radio host, polit. news anchor Sta. WCCO Radio, Mpls. Recipient awards, AP. Office: WCCO 625 2nd Ave S Minneapolis MN 55402*

ESPEGARD, DUAINE C. state legislator; m. Phyllis Espegard; 3 children. BBA, Aakers Bus. Coll. Pres., CEO Bremer Bank; mem. N.D. Senate from 43d dist., Bismark, 2001—. Mem. NDAK Commn. Econ. Devel. Republican. Office: 3649 Lynwood Cir Grand Forks ND 58201 E-mail: despegar@state.nd.us.

ESPESETH, ROBERT D. park and recreation planning educator; b. Cameron, Wis., July 11, 1930; s. Robert I. and Mary (Willemssen) E.; m. Mary Ann Krepps, Dec. 30, 1952; children: Robert D. Jr., Steven R., Michael W., Karen S. BS in Landscape Architecture, U. Wis., 1952, MS in Landscape Arch./Regional Planning, 1956. Registered landscape architect, Ill., Neb. Park planner div. state forest and parks Wis. Conservation Dept., Madison, 1955-56; chief park planning bureau state parks and recreation Wis. Dept. Natural Resources, 1956-67; with Genesee County Park and Recreation Commn., Flint, Mich., 1967-73; asst. prof. dept. leisure studies U. Ill., Champaign, 1973-79, assoc. prof., 1979-95; ret., 1995. Expert witness, Champaign, Ill., 1974—. Author monographs, Site Planning of Park Areas, 1987, Developing a Bed and Breakfast Business Plan, 1988, Use of Conservation Easements, 1990, Community Park and Recreation Planning, 1994. Commr. Champaign County Forest Preserve Dist., Mahomet, Ill., 1974-86; bd. dirs. Green Meadows coun. Girl Scouts USA, 1975-83. With USN, 1952-54, capt. USNR, ret. Recipient Disting. Svc. award Am. Inst. Park Execs., 1965, Scroll Honor award Navy League U.S., 1973. Fellow Ill. Park and Recreation Assn. (bd. dirs. 1977); mem. Nat. Soc. Park Resources (Meritorious Svc. award 1985), Nat. Recreation and Park Assn. (trustee 1989-95, Park Profl. of Yr. award 1992), Univ. Club (past pres. U. Ill.). Avocations: golf, gardening, fishing, biking. Office: U Ill 1206 S 4th St Ste 104 Champaign IL 61820-6920 E-mail: respeset@uiuc.edu.

ESPICH, JEFFREY K. state legislator; m. Sharon Espich; 2 children. BS, Ind. U. With Kozy Kourt Inc.; rep. Dist. 32 Ind. Ho. of Reps., 1972-91, rep. Dist. 82, 1991—, minority whip, asst. minority floor leader, mem. elec. and appropriations coms., ins. and corps. com., rds. and transp. com., ways and means com., mem. cts. and criminal code, ins. and corp., small bus. coms. Bd. dirs. Old First Bank. Mem. Farm Bur., Bluffton C. of C. Home: PO Box 158 1250 W Hancock St Uniondale IN 46791

ESPY, BEN, state legislator, lawyer; m. Kathy Espy; children: Elizabeth, Amy, Laura, Lynette. BA, Ohio State U.; JD, Howard U. Bar: Ohio. Pvt. practice, Columbus, Ohio; mem. Ohio Senate, 1993—. Councilman City of Columbus, 1982-92; mem. adv. bd. Cath. Diocese Found.; mem. Big Ten Adv. Bd. Commn. Named Outstanding Legislator of Yr., Franklin County Trial Lawyers Assn.; recipient Young Black Dem. recognition, Columbus Man of Yr. award Frank Loris Peterson Soc. Adventist Men, vol. svc. award Neighborhood House; named to Sandusky H.S. Athletic Hall of Fame, Carter G. Woodson Hall of Fame. Mem. ABA, Ohio Bar Assn., Columbus Bar Assn., Urban Christian Leadership Assn., Kappa Alpha Psi, Sigma Delta Tau. Democrat. Home: 1350 Brookwood Pl Columbus OH 43209-2813 Office: 4300 Hamilton Ct Columbus OH 43232

ESREY, WILLIAM TODD, telecommunications company executive; b. Phila., Jan. 17, 1940; s. Alexander J. and Dorothy (B.) E.; m. Julie L. Campbell, June 13, 1964; children: William Todd, John Campbell. BA, Denison U., Granville, Ohio, 1961; MBA, Harvard U., 1964. With Am. Tel & Tel. Co., also N.Y. Tel. Co., 1964-69; pres. Empire City Subway Ltd., N.Y.C., 1969-70; mng. dir. Dillon, Read & Co. Inc., 1970-80; exec. v.p. corp. planning United Telecommunications, Inc. (now Sprint), Westwood, Kans., 1980-81, exec. v.p., CFO, 1981-82, 84-85, pres., CEO, 1985—; pres. United Telecom Communications, Inc. (now Sprint), Kansas City, Mo., 1982-85; chmn., CEO Sprint Corp., Westwood, Kans., 1990—. Bd. dirs. Earthlink Network, Inc., Exxon Corp., Duke Energy Corp., Gen. Mills, Inc., Everen Capital Corp. Bd. dirs. Midwest Rsch. Com. for Econ. Devel. Mem. Mission Hills Country Club, River Club, Links Club, Kans. City Country Club, Phi Beta Kappa. Office: Sprint 2330 Shawnee Mission Pkwy Westwood KS 66205-2090

ESRICK, JERALD PAUL, lawyer; b. Moline, Ill., Oct. 1, 1941; s. Reuben and Nancy (Parson) E.; m. Ellen Feinstein, June 18, 1966; children: Sara Elizabeth, Daniel Michael. BA, Northwestern U., 1963; JD, Harvard U., 1966. Bar: Ill. 1966, U.S. Dist. Ct. (no. dist.) Ill. 1967, U.S. Supreme Ct. 1974, U.S. Ct. Appeals (9th cir.) 1985, U.S. Ct. Appeals (7th cir.) 1967. Law clk. U.S. Dist. Ct. (no. dist.) Ill., 1966-68; assoc. Wildman, Harrold, Allen & Dixon, Chgo., 1968-73, ptnr., 1973—, also chmn. firm mgmt. com., 1987-90. Lectr. Northwestern U., 1984-93, Coll. Arts and Scis. bd. advs., 1993—, Nat. Panel Comml. Arbitrators, Am. Arbitration Assn. Pres. bd. trustees Nat. Lekotek Ctr., Evanston, Ill., 1989-93, U.S. Toy Libr. Assn., 1987-88; bd. dirs. Evanston Mental Health Assn., 1984-86, Fund for Justice, 1969-95, Lawyers' Com. for Civil Rights, 1974-84. Fellow Am. Coll. Trial Lawyers; mem. ABA, Ill. State Bar Assn., Chgo. Coun. Lawyers (bd. dirs., sec., founding mem.), Chgo. Bar Assn., Lawyers Club Chgo. Avocations: running, skiing, sailing, windsurfing, classical music. Home: 1326 Judson Ave Evanston IL 60201-4720 Office: Wildman Harrold Allen & Dixon 225 W Wacker Dr Ste 3000 Chicago IL 60606-1229 E-mail: esrick@wildmanharrold.com.

ESSEX, JOSEPH MICHAEL, visual communication planner; b. Santa Barbara, Calif., May 27, 1947; Student, Montgomery Coll., Rockville, Md., Va. Commonwealth U., Richmond. Art dir. Met. Pitts. Pub. Broadcasting, 1970-73; sr. designer Ctr. for Comm. Planning, 1973-76; assoc. creative dir. Jim Johnston Advt., 1976; design dir. Burson-Marsteller Design Group, Chgo., 1976-86, v.p., dir. visual comm. planning Americas, 1980-88; prin. Design By Objectives, 1986-88; ptnr. Essex Partnership, 1988-89, Essex Two Inc., Chgo., 1989—. One man poster exhbn. Chgo., 1979; exhibited in group shows: Japan, 1976, Ireland, 1977, Cooper-Hewitt Mus., N.Y.C., 1981. Recipient Silver medals, Merit award Art Directors Club, N.Y.C., 1979, 80, over 300 other awards from design and advt. orgns. Office: Essex Two Inc 2210 W North Ave Chicago IL 60647-5430

ESSEY, BASIL, bishop; b. North Charleroi, Pa., Nov. 26, 1948; s. William Frederick and Genevieve Alberta (Lhota) E. BA, California U. of Pa., 1970; MDiv, St. Vladimir's Sem., Crestwood, N.Y., 1973. Tonsured reader Antiochian Orthodox Ch., Monessen, Pa., 1964, ordained subdeacon, then deacon Ligonier, 1979, ordained priest Bergenfield, N.J., 1980, elevated to archimandrite Wichita, Kans., 1987; consecrated bishop Antiochian Orthodox Christian Archdiocese of N.Am., 1992—. Translator, editor: The Liturgikon, 1989. Recipient Jackman award for disting. alumnus California Univ. of Pa., 1993. Office: Antiochian Orthod Chancery 1559 N Woodlawn Blvd Wichita KS 67208-2429

ESSMAN, ALYN V. photographic studios company executive; b. St. Louis, May 3, 1932; BBA, Washington U., St. Louis, 1953. Chmn. & CEO CPI Corp., St. Louis. Office: CPI Corp 1706 Washington Ave Fl 8 Saint Louis MO 63103-1717

ESTENSON, NOEL K. refining and fertilizer company executive; b. 1938; BS, N.D. U. Pres., CEO Cenex, Inc., St. Paul, 1987-98, CEO, 1998—. Office: Cenex Harvest States Cooperative PO Box 64089 Saint Paul MN 55164-0089

ESTEP, MICHAEL R. church administrator; Dir. comm. divsn. Ch. of the Nazarene, Kansas City, Mo., 1994—; exec. dir. Beacon Hill Press, 1994; dir. Nazarene Comm. Network, 1995. Office: Church of Nazarene 6401 Paseo Blvd Kansas City MO 64131-1213 E-mail: mrestep@aol.com.

ESTERLY, NANCY BURTON, physician; b. N.Y.C., Apr. 14, 1935; d. Paul R. and Tanya (Pasahow) Burton; m. John R. Esterly, June 16, 1957; children: Sarah Burton, Anne Beidler, John Snyder, II, Henry Clark, II. AB, Smith Coll., 1956; MD, Johns Hopkins U., 1960. Intern, then resident in pediatrics Johns Hopkins Hosp., 1960-63, resident in dermatology, 1964-67; instr. pediatrics Johns Hopkins U. Med. Sch., 1967-68; instr., trainee La Rabida U. Chgo. Inst.; also dept. pediatrics U. Chgo. Med. Sch., 1968-69; asst. prof. Pritzker Sch. Medicine, U. Chgo., 1969-70, assoc. prof., 1973-78; asst. prof. dermatology Abraham Lincoln Sch. Medicine, U. Ill., 1970-72, assoc. prof. dermatology and pediatrics, 1972-73; dir. div. dermatology, dept. pediatrics Michael Reese Hosp. and Med. Ctr., Chgo., 1973-78; prof. pediatrics and dermatology Northwestern U. Med. Sch., 1978; head div. dermatology, dept. pediatrics Children's Meml. Hosp., Chgo., 1978-87; prof. pediatrics and dermatology Med. Coll. Wis., Milw., 1987—; head div. dermatology, dept. pediatrics Children's Hosp. Wis., 1987—. Editor: Pediatric Dermatology, 1983—; contbr. numberous articles to profl. jours. Recipient David Martic Carter award, Am. Skin Assn., 2002, Lifetime Career Educator award, Dermatology Found., 2002. Mem.: Wis. Pediat. Soc., Women's Dermatol. Soc., Soc. Pediat. Dermatology (1st Lifetime Achievement award 1998), Soc. Pediat. Rsch., Am. Acad. Pediatrics, Soc. Investigative Dermatology, Wis. Dermatol. Soc., Am. Dermatol. Assn., Am. Acad. Dermatology, Internat. Soc. Pediat. Dermatology, Sigma Xi. Office: 9200 W Wisconsin Ave Milwaukee WI 53226-3522

ESTES, ELAINE ROSE GRAHAM, retired librarian; b. Springfield, Mo., Nov. 24, 1931; d. James McKinley and Zelma Mae (Smith) Graham; m. John Melvin Estes, Dec. 29, 1953. BSBA, Drake U., 1953, tchg. cert., 1956; MSLS, U. Ill., 1960. With Pub. Libr. Des Moines, 1956-95, coord. extension svcs., 1977-78, dir., 1978-95, ret., 1995. Lectr. antiques, hist.

architecture, libraries; mem. conservation planning com. for disaster preparedness for libraries. Author bibliographies of books on antiques; contbr. articles to profl. jours. Mem. State of Iowa Cultural Affairs Adv. Coun., 1986—94; mem. Nat. Commn. on Future of Drake U., 1987—88; chmn. Des Moines Mayor's Hist. Dist. Commn.; mem. nominations review com. Iowa Iowa State Nat. Hist. Register, 1983—89; chmn. hist. subcom. Des Moines Sesquecentennial Com., 1993, Iowa Sister State Commn., 1993—95; mem. com. 40th Anniversary Drake U. Alumni Weekend; mem. July 4 com. Iowa Sesquecentennial; nat. exch. dir. Friendship Force, 1997; mem. nat. adv. bd. Cowles Libr., 1998—; mem. Gov.'s Iowa Centennial Meml. Found., 1998—; mem. acquisition com. Salisbury House; mem. cultural ctr. task force African Am. Hist. Mus., 1999; mem. Iowa author com. Pub. Libr. Des Moines Found., 2001; mem. Terrace Hill Commn., 2001—; bd. dirs. Des Moines Art Ctr., 1972—83, hon. mem., 1983—; bd. dirs. Friends of Libr. USA, 1986—92, Henry Wallace House Found., Iowa Libr. Centennial Com., 1990—91. Recipient recognition for outstanding working women - leadership in econs. and civic life of Greater Des Moines, YWCA, 1975, Disting. Alumni award Drake U., 1979, Woman of Achievement award YWCA, 1989, City of Des Moines Excellence in Hist. Preservation award, 1994, Connect Found. Contribution to Cmty. award, 1995. Mem.: ALA (30th Anniversary Honor Roll for Intellectual Freedom 1999), Iowa Soc. Preservation Hist. Landmarks (bd. dirs. 1969—97), Libr. Assn. Greater Des Moines Metro Area (pres., chmn. 1992), Iowa Urban Pub. Libr. Assn., Iowa Libr. Assn. (life; pres. 1978—79), Iowa Antique Assn., Terrace (Gov.'s Mansion) Soc. (v.p. 1991—93, pres. 1993—96), Links Inc. (40th ann. com. 1997), Questers Inc. Club (pres. 1982, 1997, 2001, state 2d v.p. 1984—86, 1st v.p. 1990—2000), Rotary (history com. 2001), Proteus.

ESTES, JAMES RUSSELL, botanist; b. Burkburnett, Tex., Aug. 28, 1937; s. Dow Worley and Bessie (Seidlitz) E.; B.S. in Biology, Midwestern State U., 1959; Ph.D. in Systematic Botany, Oreg. State U., 1967; m. Nancy Elizabeth Arnold, Dec. 21, 1962; children: Jennifer Lynn Estes Varma, Susan Elizabeth Estes Honaker. Mem. faculty U. Okla., Norman, 1967— , asst. prof., 1967-70, assoc. prof., 1970-82, prof. botany, 1982—, dir. Okla. Natural Heritage Program, 1981-82, curator Bebb Herbarium, 1979—; assoc. program dir. NSF, 1990-92, program dir., 1993—, mem. systematic biology adv. panel, 1986-89; mem. ecology adv. panel U.S. Agy. per Internat. Devel., 1991; mem. adv. panel Internat. Biodiversity Conservation Group NIH, 1993; mem. adv. panel Biotic Surveys and Inventories NSF, 1993; cons. in environ. work, 1979—; expert witness in environ. work, 1983—. Bd. govs. United Campus Christian Found., 1976-80; mem. adv. bd. Sutton Urban Wilderness Park, 1980—; mem. editorial bd. Systematic Botany Monographs, 1985-89, Flora N.Am., 1986—; asst. editor Flora Okla. Project, 1984—; mem. steering com., trustee Flora Okla., Inc., 1985-92. With U.S. Army, 1960-63. Grantee NSF, 1968-70, 81-87; NSF fellow, 1963, 65-67; Ortenburger award Phi Sigma, 1975; Baldwin Study Travel award Okla. U. Alumni Found., 1976; named Outstanding Undergraduate Instr. Mortar Bd., 1990. Mem. Am. Soc. Plant Taxonomists (past pres. 1987-88, sec. 1980-83; program chmn. 1980-83, pres. elect 1984-85, pres. 1985-86), Bot. Soc. Am., Southwestern Assn. Naturalists (bd. govs. 1980-83, assoc. editor 1980-82, trustee 1986-93), Okla. Acad. Sci. (pres. 1992-93, sec. 1968-69). Democrat. Presbyterian. Co-editor: Grasses and Grasslands: Systematics and Ecology, 1981; contbr. articles to sci. books and jours. Home: 4930 Larkwood Rd Lincoln NE 68516-3360 Office: U Nebraska State Museum 307 Morrill Hall Lincoln NE 68588

ESTES, ROYCE JOE, lawyer; b. Topeka, Kans., Mar. 30, 1944; s. Joseph Sumner and Mildred Eve (Lunday) E.; m. Marla Ann Hampton, June 13, 1964; children— Gina Christine, Darin Wesley, Erika Alynn. B.A., Kans. State U., 1968; J.D., U. Mo., 1972, LL.M., 1975. Bar: Mo. 1972, Ill. 1976. Ptnr. firm Linde, Thomson, Fairchild, Langworthy & Kohn, Kansas City, Mo., 1972-75; asst. gen. counsel A.E. Staley Mfg. Co., Decatur, Ill., 1975-79; assoc. gen. counsel Anheuser-Busch Cos., Inc., St. Louis, 1979-82, sr. assoc. gen. counsel, 1983, dep. gen. counsel, 1983-90, v.p., dep. gen. counsel, 1992-95, v.p. corp. law antitrust, mktg. & distbn., 1995—; dir. Metal Container Corp., Sunset Hills. Staff mem. U. Mo. Law Rev., 1970-71. Served with USN, 1969-70. Law Found. scholar U. Mo., 1967-68. Mem. ABA, Mo. Bar Assn., Ill. State Bar Assn. Home: 628 Wood Fern Dr Ballwin MO 63021-5865 Office: Anheuser Busch Cos Inc One Busch Pl Saint Louis MO 63118

ESTES, STEPHEN ARTHUR, dermatologist; b. Rochester, N.Y., July 7, 1947; s. Cameron and Ruth (Madden) E.; m. Barbara Jane Carbary, May 29, 1977; children: Cameron, Jessica. BS, Purdue U., 1969; MD, U. Rochester, 1973. Diplomate Am. Bd. Dermatology. Intern Tucson Hosp., 1973-74; resident Johns Hopkins Hosp., Balt., 1974-77; instr. dermatology U. Ariz. Med. Ctr., Tucson, 1977-78; assoc. prof. U. Cin., 1978-85; pvt. practice Cin., 1985—. Contbr. more than 50 articles to profl. jours. Mem. Cin. Dermatol. Assn. (sec.-treas. 1994-96, pres. 1997-98), Ohio Dermatology Assn. (trustee 1993-96). Home: 1227 Ridgecliff Dr Cincinnati OH 45215-2031 Office: 800 Compton Rd Unit 28 Cincinnati OH 45231-3850

ESTES, WILLIAM KAYE, psychologist, educator; b. Mpls., June 17, 1919; s. George D. and Mona Estes; m. Katherine Walker, Sept. 26, 1942; children: George E., Gregory W. Mem. faculty Ind. U., 1946—62, prof. psychology, 1955—60, research prof. psychology, 1960—62; faculty research fellow Social Sci. Research Council, 1952—55; lectr. psychology U. Wis., 1949; vis. prof. Northwestern U., 1959; fellow Center Advanced Study Behavioral Scis., 1955—56; spl. univ. lectr. U. London, 1961; prof. psychology, mem. Inst. Math. Studies Social Scis., Stanford, 1962—68; prof. Rockefeller U., 1968—79, Harvard U., 1978—89, prof. emeritus, 1989—; prof. Ind. U., 1999—. Chmn. Office Sci. and Engring. Personnel NRC, 1982—85, chmn. com. on prevention of nuclear war, 1984—89. Author: An Experimental Study of Punishment, 1944, Learning Theory and Mental Development, 1970, Models of Learning, Mempry and Choice, 1982, Statistical Models in Behavioral Research, 1991, Classification and Cognition, 1994; co-author: Modern Learning Theory, 1954; contbr. articles to profl. jours.; editor: Handbook of Learning and Cognitive Processes, 1962—68, Psychol. Rev., 1977—82, Psychol. Sci., 1990—94; : assoc. editor Jour. Exptl. Psychology, 1958—62. Recipient U.S. Nat. medal of Sci., 1997. Fellow: AAAS, APA (pres. divsn. exptl. psychology 1958—59, Disting. Sci. Contbn. award 1962, gold medal for lifetime achievement in psychol. sci. 1992), Am. Acad. Arts and Scis.; mem.: NAS, Fedn. Behavioral Psychol. and Cognitive Scis. (v.p. 1988—91), Midwestern Psychol. Assn., N.Y. Acad. Scis. (life), N.Y. Acad. Scis. (hon.), Soc. Exptl. Psychologists (Warren medal 1963). Home: 2714 E Pine Ln Bloomington IN 47401-4423 Office: Ind U Psychology Bldg Bloomington IN 47405 E-mail: wkestes@indiana.edu.

ETGES, FRANK JOSEPH, parasitology educator; b. Chgo., June 18, 1924; s. Joseph Peter and Anna Marie (Foss) E.; m. Ruth Camille Storkan, Sept. 20, 1948 (div. June 1984); children: Robert J., William J., Anne C., David J., Thomas J.; m. Lesta Judith Cooper-Freytag, July 6, 1985. AB, U. Ill., 1948, MS, 1949; PhD, NYU, 1953. Asst. prof. U. Ark., Fayetteville, 1953-54, U. Cin., 1954-59, assoc. prof., 1959-66, prof. parasitology, 1966-95; prof. emeritus, 1995—. Rsch. assoc. U.S. Army Tropical Rsch. Med. Lab., San Juan, P.R., 1961-62; guest investigator London Sch. Tropical Medicine and Hygiene, 1971-72. Sgt. U.S. Army, 1943-46, ETO, PTO. NSF rsch. grantee, 1959-65; La. State U. Med. Sch. rsch. fellow, Santo Domingo, P.R., 1961-62, 64, 65, 67, 69; postdoctoral fellow NIH, London, 1971-72, WHO, Egypt, Sudan, Rhodesia, 1975. Mem. Am. Soc. Parasitologists (editorial com.), Am. Soc. Tropical Medicine and Hygiene, Am. Microscopical Soc. (v.p. 1970), Royal Soc. Tropical Medicine and Hygiene, Australian Soc. Parasitology, Soc. Protozoologists, Midwestern Parastiologists (pres. 1969), Helminthol. Soc. Washington, Sigma Xi. Avocations: travel, golf. Home: 8284 Sunfish Ln Maineville OH 45039-8978 Office: U Cin Dept Biol Scis Cincinnati OH 45221-0006 E-mail: cooperlj@ucfwcu.rwc.uc.edu.

ETHEREDGE, FOREST DEROYCE, former state senator, former university administrator; b. Dallas, Oct. 21, 1929; s. Gilbert Wybert and Theta Erlene (Tate) E.; m. Joan Mary Horan, Apr. 30, 1955; children: Forest William, John Bede, Mary Faith, Brian Thomas, Regina Ann. BS, Va. Poly. Inst. and State U., 1951; MS, U. Ill., 1953; postgrad., Northwestern U., 1953-55; PhD, Loyola U., Chgo., 1968. Mem. faculty City Colls. Chgo., 1955-65, chmn. phys. sci. dept., 1963-65; dean instrn. Rock Valley Coll., 1965-67, v.p., 1966-67; pres. McHenry County Coll., 1967-70, Waubonsee Community Coll., 1970-81; Ill. state senator Ill. State Senate, 1981-93, higher edn. com., 1981-91, mem. intergovtl. coop. commn., 1982-91, co-chmn. legis. info. system, 1983-93, minority spokesman appropriations I com., 1986-93; prof. pub. adminstrn. Aurora (Ill.) U., 1991-2001, dean Sch. of Bus. and Profl. Studies, 1994-99, dean emeritus, 1999—. Author: School Boards and the Ballot Box, 1989. Bd. dirs. Ill. Math. and Sci. Acad. Republican. Roman Catholic. Lodge: Rotary (pres. Aurora chpt. 1978-79). Home: 843 Hardin Ave Aurora IL 60506-4936 E-mail: fethered@aurora.edu., fethered@prodigy.net.

ETHINGTON, RAYMOND LINDSAY, geology educator, researcher; b. State Center, Iowa, Aug. 28, 1929; s. Lindsay E. and Hilda Ruby (Weuve) E.; m. Leslie Ann Nielsen, June 15, 1955; children: Elaine Marie, Mary Frances. BS, Iowa State U., 1951, MS, 1955; PhD, U. Iowa, 1958. Asst. prof. geology Ariz. State U., Tempe, 1958-62; asst. prof. U. Mo., Columbia, 1962-65, assoc. prof., 1965-68, prof., 1968-2000, prof. emeritus, 2000—. With U.S. Army, 1951-53. NSF grantee, 1966, 87. Fellow Geol. Soc. Am.; mem. Soc. Econ. Paleontologists and Mineralogists (editor Jour. Paleontology 1979-83, spl. publs. editor 1980-83, chmn. publs. com. 1974-76, pres. 1989-90), Pander Soc. (chief panderer 1990-98), Am. Assn. Petroleum Geologists, Palaeontol. Assn. G.B., Paleontol. Soc. Mem. LDS Ch. Home: 1012 Pheasant Run Columbia MO 65201-6252 Office: U Mo Dept Geol Sci Columbia MO 65211-0001 E-mail: EthingtonR@missouri.edu.

ETZEL, TIMOTHY, manufacturing executive; BBA, Washburn U., 1964. Pres., CEO Jetz Svc. Co., Inc., Topeka. Mem. bd. regents Washburn U.; trustee Washburn Endowment Assn., 1993—, former vice chmn. endowment bd. Office: Jetz Svc Co Inc 901 NE River Rd Topeka KS 66616

ETZKORN, K. PETER, sociology educator, administrator, consultant, writer; b. Karlsruhe, Germany; naturalized, 1958; s. Johannes and Luise (Schlick) E.; m. Hildegard Elizabeth Garve; children: Kyle Peter, Lars Peter. A.B., Ohio State U.; student, Ind. U.; A.M., Ph.D., Princeton. Asst. prof. U. Calif., Santa Barbara; assoc. prof. Am. U. Beirut, Lebanon; dir. Office Instl. Research; chmn. dept. sociology and anthropology U. Nev.; prof., chmn. faculty sociology and anthropology U. West Fla., 1967-68; prof. sociology San Fernando Valley State Coll., 1968-69, U. Mo., St. Louis, 1969-99, asso. dean Grad. Sch., 1978-87, dir. Office Rsch., 1979-87. Vis. prof. U. Münster, Germany, 1975-76, U. Vienna, Austria, 1987-88; cons. in field; prof. tng. adv. panel music divsn. NEA, 1994-97. Author: The Conflict in Modern Culture, 1968, Music and Society, 1973, Sociologists and Music, 1989; editor Jour. Ethnomusicology, 1984-87, Current Studies in the Sociology of Arts and Music, 1988—; contbr. articles to profl. jours. Mem. Gov. Nev. Com. on Dept. Correction, 1966; Mo. Gov. liaison German-Am. Tricentennial Task Force, 1983; mem. Mo. Adv. Com. on Humanities; chmn. Univ. Symposia Com. Bicentennial Horizons Am. Music; mem. St. Louis-Stuttgart Sister City Com.; Mo. state rep. Sister Cities Internat., 1976-81; cons. Nat. Endowment Arts, NSF; pres. St. Louis New Music Circle; bd. dirs. Am. Kantorei, MEDIACULT, Vienna; v.p. Internat. Inst. Met. St. Louis, 1982-86; pres. MEDIACULT, 1995—; exec. com. Coun. on Fgn. Rels. St. Louis Com., 1996—; bd. dirs. St. Louis Soc. for Blind and Visually Impaired, 1996, v.p., 2000—; chmn. Sister Cities 2003. Fulbright scholar, Vienna, Austria, 1987. Fellow Am. Sociol. Assn., Am. Anthrop. Assn.; mem. Soc. Ethnomusicology (coun. 1963-71, 76-79, 81-86, editor spl. publs.), Inst. Internat. Sociologie (mem. bur.), Internam. Orgn. Higher Edn. (dep. coun. 1980-87), Town Affiliation Assn. U.S. (bd. dirs. 1981-93, v.p. 1987-90, sec. 1990-93), St. Louis Coun. Sister Cities (chmn. 1981-86), Internat. Soc. for Music Edn. (chmn. commn. on media, culture and pub. policy 1990-96), St. Louis Princeton Club (bd. dirs. 1987—). Home: 21 Ladue Ridge Rd Saint Louis MO 63124-1449 E-mail: socetz@alumni.princeton.edu.

EUANS, ROBERT EARL, architect; b. Columbus, Ohio, July 6, 1941; s. William Weldon Euans and Hilda Aurelia (Daugherty) Roberts; m. Carol May Chamberlain, Dec. 18, 1964; children: Bradley James, Lori Ellen, Bryant Scott, Bruce Allen. BArch, Ohio State U., 1967. Registered architect, Ohio, Mich., Pa., Ind., Ill., Minn, Mo., Ky., Fla. Draftsman Blaw-Knox Corp., Pitts., 1967-68; chief draftsman Schofield & Assocs., Columbus, Ohio, 1968-70; project architect Karlsberger & Assocs., 1970-74, dir. tech., 1974-77; pvt. practice architecture, 1977—. Mem. AIA (bd. dirs. Columbus chpt. 1984-86), Architects Soc. Ohio, Constrn. specification Inst. Lutheran. Avocations: camping, sports, swimming.

EUBANKS, EUGENE EMERSON, education educator, consultant; b. Meadville, Pa., June 6, 1939; s. Nelson Eubanks and Emily (Princes) Jackson; m. Audrey Hunter, Aug. 4, 1962; children: Brian, Regina. BS, Edinboro (Pa.) State U., 1963; PhD, Mich. State U., 1972. Tchr. Cleve. Pub. Schs., 1963-68, unit prin., 1968-70; asst. prof. U. Del., Newark, 1972-74; asst. dean U. Mo., Kansas City, 1974-79, dean, 1979-88, prof. edn. and urban affairs, 1988—; dept. supt. Kansas City Pub. Schs., 1984-85. Contbr. articles to profl. jours. Cons. Urban League, 1978—, legal def. fund NAACP, 1978, Cleve. Found., 1978, U. Wis., 1988; bd. dirs. Operation PUSH, 1982-87, Mid-Continent Girl Scouts, Kansas City, 1983—, Genesis Sch., 1984—; chair Desegration Monitoring Com., 1985—. Mem. Am. Assn. Coll. Tchr. Edn. (pres. 1988-89), Nat. Alliance Found. (chmn. 1984-85), Black Sch. Educators (edn. commn.). Home: 12737 Oakmont Dr Kansas City MO 64145-1140 Office: U Mo Sch Edn 5100 Rockhill Rd Kansas City MO 64110-2481 E-mail: EubanksE@UMKC.edu.

EUBANKS-POPE, SHARON G. real estate company executive, entrepreneur; b. Chgo., Aug. 26, 1943; d. Walter Franklyn and Thelma Octavia (Watkins) Gibson; m. Larry Hudson Eubanks, Dec. 20, 1970 (dec. Jan. 1976); children: Rebekah, Aimée; m. Otis Eliot Pope, June 7, 1977; children: O. Eliot Jr., Adrienne. BS in Edn., Chgo. Tchrs. Coll., 1965; postgrad., Ill. Inst. Tech., 1967, John Marshall Law Sch., 1970, Governor's State U., 1975-76. Educator, parent coord. Chgo. Bd. Edn., 1965-77; owner, ptnr. Redel Rentals, Chgo., 1977—. Bd. dirs. Jack and Jill of Am. Found. Adminstrv. bd. St. Mark United Meth. Ch., Chgo., 1967, bd. trustees, 1988; com. chair Englewood Urban Progress Ctr., Chgo., 1973; coord., educator LWV, 1975-76; chair comms. Marian Cath. H.S., 1999—, adv. bd.. Named Outstanding Sch. Parent Vol., Chgo. Bd. Edn., 1977; recipient Outstanding Cmty. Law Class award LWV, 1975-76, Christian Leadership award United Meth. Women, Chgo., 1985. Mem.: NAACP, NAFE, Nat. Assn. Realtors, Am. Soc. Profl. and Exec. Women, St. Mark Cmty. Devel. Corp., Jack and Jill Am., Inc. (Chgo. chpt. journalist 1989—91, Midwestern region sec./treas. 1993—95, nat. treas. 1998—2000, founder Parents for Parity in Edn. 1992, pres. Eubanks-Pope Devel. Co., Inc. 1993, parliamentarian of Parity 1991), Jack & Jill of Am. Found. (bd. dirs. 1995—2000), Links, Inc., Alpha Beta Gamma (female exec. del. to China People to People Amb. program 1998). Office: Redel Rentals 4338 S Drexel Blvd Chicago IL 60653-3536

EVANS, BRENT, state legislator; Rep. dist. 92 Mo. Ho. of Reps., Jefferson City, 1994-2000. Republican.

EVANS, CHARLES H. federal judge; b. 1922; BA, U. Ill., 1947, JD, 1948. Pvt. law practice, 1957-62; atty. gen. State of Ill., 1962-76; magistrate judge Ill. Ctrl., Springfield, 1977—. Served with U.S. Army, 1942-45. Office: 110 US Courthouse 600 E Monroe St Springfield IL 62701-1626

EVANS, DANIEL E. sausage manufacturing and restaurant chain company executive; b. Gallipolis, Ohio, Aug. 24, 1936; With Bob Evans Farms Inc., Columbus, Ohio, 1957—; chmn. bd., sec., CEO, dir., 1971—. Office: Bob Evans Farms Inc 3776 S High St Columbus OH 43207-4000

EVANS, DANIEL FRALEY, JR. lawyer; b. Indpls., Apr. 19, 1949; s. Daniel Fraley and Julie (Sloan) E.; m. Marilyn Schultz, Aug. 11, 1973; children: Meredith, Benjamin, Suzannah, Theodore. BA, Ind. U., 1971, JD, 1976. Bar: Ind. 1976, U.S. Dist. Ct. (so. dist.) Ind. 1976, U.S. Ct. Appeals (7th cir.) 1983, U.S. Supreme Ct. 1983. Assoc. Sparrenberger, Duvall, Tabbert, Lalley & Newton, Indpls., 1976-77; ptnr. Duvall, Tabbert, Lalley & Newton, 1977-81, Bayh, Tabbert & Capehart, Indpls., 1981-85, Baker & Daniels, Indpls., 1985—. Chmn. Ind. Bd. Correction, Indpls., 1976-88, Qyaule for Senate Com., 1980, 86, Quayle for v.p. com.; mem. Fed. Jud. Merit Sel. Com., Indpls., 1981-88, Adminstrv. Conf. U.S., 1983-88; chmn. Indpls. Dist. Fed. Home Loan Bank Bd., 1987-90, Fed. Housing Fin. Bd., 1990-93; vice chmn. Methodist Health Group, Inc., 1996—, Cir. Investors, Inc., 1997—; vice chmn. Hudson Inst., Inc., 1996—, Cir. Investors, 1994-99; chancellor South Ind. Conf. United Meth. Ch., 1998—; gen. coun. Citizens Gas Utility, 1999—; bd. dirs. Clarian Health Ptnrs., Inc., Indpls., Downtown, Inc., 1992-96, Meth. Hosp. Ind. Mem. Ind. Bar Assn., Indpls. Bar Assn., Woodstock Club, Indpls. Club. Republican. Methodist. Office: Baker & Daniels 300 N Meridian St Ste 2700 Indianapolis IN 46204-1782

EVANS, DOUGLAS MCCULLOUGH, surgeon, educator; b. Vandergrift, Pa., July 31, 1925; s. Archibald Davis and Helen Irene (McCullough) E.; m. Thelmajean Volkers, Aug. 1, 1959; children: Matthew Kirk, Daniel Scott. MD, Western Res. U., 1952; postgrad., U. Mich., 1956-58; PhD, Ohio State U., 1993. Diplomate: Am. Bd. Surgery. Resident in surgery Henry Ford Hosp., 1952-57, chief resident in surgery, 1957-58, mem. surgery staff, 1959-60, Akron (Ohio) Gen. Hosp., 1960-70; chmn. dept. surgery Akron Gen. Med. Ctr., 1971-90, rsch. cons.; prof. and chmn. surgery emeritus Northeastern Ohio U. Coll. Medicine. Served with AUS, 1943-46. Fellow: ACS; mem.: AAAS, AMA, N.Y. Acad. Scis., Ohio Med. Assn., Midwest Surg. Soc., Soc. Critical Care Medicine, Metastasis Rsch. Soc., Am. Assn. Cancer Rsch. Republican. Presbyterian. Office: 400 Wabash Ave Akron OH 44307-2433

EVANS, FRANCIS COPE, retired ecologist; b. Phila., Dec. 2, 1914; s. Edward Wyatt and Jacqueline Pascal (Morris) E.; m. Rachel Worthington Brooks, June 12, 1942; children— Kenneth Richardson, Katharine Cope, Edward Wyatt II, Rachel Howe. B.S., Haverford Coll., 1936; D.Phil. (Rhodes scholar), Oxford U., 1939; Claypole fellow, U. Calif., Berkeley, 1939-40. Research asst. Hooper Found., San Francisco, 1939-41; jr. zoologist U. Calif., Davis, 1941-43; instr., asst. prof. Haverford (Pa.) Coll., 1943-48, acting dean, 1944; asst. prof., assoc. prof. U. Mich., Ann Arbor, 1948-59, prof., assoc. dir. E.S. George Res., 1959-82, prof. emeritus, 1982—. Editor publs.: Mus. Zoology, Ann Arbor, 1968-78; Contbr. sci. articles to profl. jours. Recipient Painton award Cooper Ornithol. Soc., 1963; Guggenheim fellow, 1962-63; Erskine fellow U. Canterbury, Christchurch, N.Z., 1976-77 Fellow AAAS; mem. Ecol. Soc. Am. (pres. 1983, Disting. Service award 1987), Brit. Ecol. Soc., Am. Soc. Naturalists, Soc. for Study Evolution. Mem. Soc. of Friends. Home: Glacier Hills 1200 Earhart Rd Apt 253D Ann Arbor MI 48105-2768

EVANS, GORTON M. paper products executive; Exec. v.p. Consolidated Papers, Inc., Wisconsin Rapids, Wis., 1996, pres., CEO, 1997—. Mem. Nat. Assn. Mfrs. (dir.), Am. Forest and Paper Assn. (past chmn. printing and writing div.). Office: Consolidated Papers Inc 231 1st Ave North Wisconsin Rapids WI 54495

EVANS, IVOR J. (IKE), railroad executive; Diploma, Kans. State U.; postgrad., Harvard U., Emory U. Exec. GM Corp., 1973-85, gen. mgf. mgr. Harrison Radiator divsn.; pres. Blackstone N.Am. Co., Jamestown, N.Y., 1985-87; exec. v.p. Armtek, New Haven, 1987; sr. v.p. Emerson Electric Co., St. Louis; pres., COO Union Pacific RR, Omaha, 1998—. Office: Union Pacific Corp 1416 Dodge St Rm 1230 Omaha NE 68179

EVANS, JAMES E. lawyer; b. 1946; BA, Mich. State U., 1968; JD, Ohio State U., 1970. Bar: Ohio 1971. Assoc. Keating, Muething & Klekamp, 1971-76; v.p., gen. counsel Am. Fin. Corp., Cin., 1976—, now sr. v.p., dir. Office: Am Fin Corp 1 E 4th St Cincinnati OH 45202-3717

EVANS, KENNETH M. company executive; Student, Villanova U.; grad., Stanford Bus. Sch. Various mgmt. positions The Sherwin Williams Co., Evans Paints, Inc., Thompson & Formby, Inc., Kodak, Homecare Products Group; pres., CEO, dir. Armor All Products Corp., 1997, Clorox, 1997; exec. v.p. RPM, Inc., 1998-99, pres. consumer group, 1999—. Office: 2628 Pearl Rd Medina OH 44256-7623

EVANS, LANE, congressman; b. Rock Island, Ill., Aug. 4, 1951; s. Lee Herbert and Joycelene (Saylor) E. B.A., Augustana Coll., 1974; J.D., Georgetown U., 1978. Bar: Ill. 1978. Mng. atty. Western Ill. Legal Assistance Found., Rock Island, 1978-79; mem. nat. staff Kennedy for Pres., Washington, 1978-80; atty., ptnr. Community Legal Clinic, Rock Island, Ill., 1981-82; mem. 98th-107th Congresses from 17th Ill. Dist., 1983—; mem. nat. security com., ranking mem. vets. affairs com., armed svcs. com. Served with USMC, 1969-71. Mem. AmVets, Am. Legion, Marine Corps League, Vietnam Vets Ill. Democrat. Roman Catholic. Office: US Ho of Reps 2211 Rayburn HOB Washington DC 20515-0001*

EVANS, MARIWYN, periodical editor; Exec. editor Jour. Property Mgmt., Chgo. Office: Jour Property Mgmt 430 N Michigan Ave Chicago IL 60611-4011

EVANS, ROBERT E. banking executive; b. 1940; BS, Ohio No. U., 1962; JD, Capital U., 1967. Bar: Ohio 1967. Pres., CEO People's Bancorp Inc., Marietta, Ohio, 1980—. Bd. dirs. McDonough Corp.; trustee Marietta Coll., Found. for Appalachian Ohio. Mem. ABA. Office: Peoples Bancorp Inc 138 Putnam St Marietta OH 45750-2923

EVANS, ROGER LYNWOOD, scientist, patent liaison; b. Ipswich, Suffolk, Eng., June 25, 1928; came to U.S., 1953; s. Evelyn Jesse and Ethel Jane (Woods) E.; m. Jane Adelaide Baird, Nov. 24, 1954 (div. 1976); children: Robert Malcolm Baird, Roderick Lawrence Woods, Alison Clare; m. Wendy Dorothy Grove, Apr. 11, 1977. BA in Natural Sci., Oxford (Eng.) U., 1953, MA, 1955, DPhil in Natural Sci., 1958; MS in Inorganic Chemistry, U. Minn., 1955. With chem. and radiopharm. R & D dept. 3M Co., St. Paul., 1958-77, patent liaison, 1977-91; developer intellectual property initiative, tech. devel. dept., 1992-93; cons. 3M, 1993-99. Originator 3M Richard G. Drew Creativity Award, 1970, program cons., 1995—. Founder, editor Newsletter of the Tech. Forum, 1971-93; inventor, writer, producer series of videos on intellectual property topics. Mem., chmn. Mendota Heights Planning Commn., 1962-68, Sunfish Lake Planning Commn., 1968-84, Dakota County Planning Commn., Minn., 1965-

72. 2d lt. Brit. Army, 1946-49, Eng. Anglican. Avocations: photography, amateur opera singer, travel, writing. Home and Office: 9965 Rich Valley Blvd Inver Grove Heights MN 55077-4529

EVANS, TERENCE THOMAS, judge; b. Milwaukee, Wisc., Mar. 25, 1940; s. Robert Hansen and Jeanette (Walters) Evans; m. Joan Marie Witte, July 24, 1965; children: Kelly Elizabeth, Christine Marie, David Rourke. BA, Marquette U., 1962, JD, 1967. Bar: Wis. 1967. Law clk. to justice Wis. Supreme Ct., 1967—68; dist. atty. Milw. County, 1968—70; pvt. practice law Milw., 1970—74; cir. judge State of Wis., 1974—80; judge U.S. Dist. Ct. (ea. dist) Wis., Milw., 1980—95, U.S. Ct. Appeals (7th cir.), 1995—. Mem.: ABA, Milw. Bar Assn., State Bar Wis. Roman Catholic. Office: US Courthouse & Federal Bldg 517 E Wisconsin Ave Rm 721 Milwaukee WI 53202-4504

EVANS, THOMAS E. autoparts company executive; BSME, Pa. State U.; MSME, MBA, U. Mich. Various positions Rockwell Internat., 1973-89; gen. mgr. worldwide sealing and ball bearing products Fed. Mogul; various positions Case Corp.; pres. Tenneco Automotive; CEO, chmn. Collins & Aikman, Troy, Mich., 1999—. Bd. dirs. Wis. Ctrl. Transp. Corp.; trustee Inst. Textile Tech. Mem. Nat. Assn. Mfrs. (bd. dirs.). Office: Collins and Aikman 5755 New King Ct Troy MI 48098-2396

EVANSON, BARBARA JEAN, middle school education educator; b. Grand Forks, N.D., Aug. 15, 1944; d. Robert John and Jean Elizabeth (Lommen) Gibbons; m. Bruce Carlyle Evanson, Dec. 27, 1965; children: Tracey, John, Kelly. AA, Bismarck State Coll., 1964; BS in Spl. and Elem. Edn., U. N.D., 1966. Tchr. spl. edn. Winship Sch., Grand Forks, 1966-67, Simle Jr. High, Bismarck, 1967-70; tchr. Northridge Elem. Sch., 1980-86, Wachter Middle Sch., Bismarck, 1986—. Cons. Dept. Pub. Instrn., Bismark, 1988—, Chpt. I, Bismark, 1989—, McRel for Drug Free Schs., Denver, 1990-95. Co-founder The Big People, Bismarck, 1978-95; mem. task force Children's Trust Fund, N.D., 1984; senator N.D. Legislature, Bismarck, 1989-94; mem. N.D. Bridges Adv. Bd., 1991-97, DPI English Adv. Com., 1993—; co-facilitator Lead Mid. Sch. for Carnegie, 1994-97, N.D. Health Adv. Coun., 1993-94, N.D. Tchr.'s Fund for Retirement, State Investment Bd. 1996—; co-founder, bd. dirs. Neighbors Network, 1983—. Recipient Gold Award Bismark Norwest Bank, 1985; named Tchr. of Yr. , N.D. Dept. Pub. Instrn., 1989, Legislator of Yr., Children's Caucus, 1991, Outstanding Alumnae, Bismarck State Coll., 1991, Milken Nat. Tchr. of Yr., 1995-96, KX Golden Apple award, 1999. Mem. N.D. Reading Assn., N.D. Coun. of Tchrs. of English., NEA, N.D. Edn. Assn., Bismarck Edn. Assn. Avocations: clown, walking, reading, travel, remodeling. Office: Wachter Middle Sch 1107 S 7th St Bismarck ND 58504-6533

EVEN, FRANCIS ALPHONSE, lawyer; b. Chgo., Sept. 8, 1920; s. George Martin and Cecilia (Neuman) E.; m. Margaret Hope Herrick, Oct. 16, 1945; children: Janet Beth, Dorothy Elizabeth. B.S. in Mech. Engring, U. Ill., 1942; J.D., George Washington U., 1949. Bar: D.C. bar 1949, Ill. bar 1950. Engr. GE, 1945-49; ptnr. Fitch, Even, Tabin & Flannery (patent and trademark law), Chgo., 1952—. Mem. bd. edn., River Forest, Ill., 1963-69; trustee West Suburban Hosp., Oak Park, Ill., 1974-77; mem. bd. Ill. State Hist. Soc., 2000—. With combat engrs. AUS, 1942-45. Fellow Am. Coll. Trial Lawyers (emeritus); mem. ABA, Am. Intellectual Property Law Assn. (bd. mgrs. 1963-66), Ill. Bar Assn., Chgo. Bar Assn., Intellectual Property Law Assn. Chgo. (bd. mgrs. 1972-73, pres. 1984), No. Ill. Ct. Hist. Assn. (pres.), Union League Club (Chgo.), Oak Park (Ill.) Country Club, Chgo. Literary Club. Republican. Home: 1018 Park Ave River Forest IL 60305-1308 Office: 120 S La Salle St Chicago IL 60603-3403

EVENS, RONALD GENE, radiologist, medical center administrator; b. St. Louis, Sept. 24, 1939; s. Robert and Dorothy (Lupkey) E.; m. Hanna Blunk, Sept. 3, 1960; children: Ronald Jr., Christine, Amanda. BA, Washington U., 1960, MD, 1964, postgrad. in bus. and edn., 1970-71. Intern Barnes Hosp., St. Louis, 1964-65; resident Mallinckrodt Inst. Radiology, 1965-66, 68-70; rsch. assoc. Nat. Heart Inst., 1966-68; asst. prof. radiology, v.p. Washington U. Med. Sch., 1970-71, prof., head dept. radiology, dir., 1971-72, Elizabeth Mallinckrodt prof., head radiology dept., 1972-99, prof. med. econs., 1988—; pres., sr. exec. ofcr. Barnes-Jewish Hosp., St. Louis, 1999—. Radiologist-in-chief Barnes Hosp., St. Louis, 1971-99; radiologist-in-chief Children's Hosp., 1971-99, pres., chief exec. officer, 1985-88; vice chancellor fin. Washington U., St. Louis, 1988-91; mem. adv. com. on splty. and geog. distbn. of physicians Inst. Medicine, Nat. Acad. Scis., 1974-76, Hickey lectr., 1976, Carmen lectr. Calif. U., 1985, Kiewit lectr. Eisenhower Med. Ctr., 1986; Hornick lectr. U. Pitts., 1986; ann. orator Can. Radiol. Soc., 1984; Hodes lectr. Jefferson U., 1991—; Smith lectr. Royal Coll. Physicians, Edinburgh, 1992; Seaman lectr. Columbia Presbyn., 1992; dir. Boatmens Bank Inc., Mallinckrodt Group Inc., Right Choice Inc., Blue Choice, Inc.; chmn. bd. Med. Care Group St. Louis, 1980-86. Contbr. over 210 articles to profl. jours. Active Boy Scouts Am., 1975—; elder Glendale Presbyn. Ch., 1971-74, Kirkwood Presbyn. Ch., 1983-86. Served with USPHS, 1966-68. Advance Acad. fellow James Picker Found, 1970; recipient Disting. Svc. award. St. Louis C. of C., 1972; named Disting. Eagle Scout Nat. Coun., 1983. Fellow Am. Coll. Radiology (chair elect 1995, chair bd. chancellors 1996—); mem. AMA (editl. bd. JAMA), Mo. Radiol. Soc. (pres. 1977-78), Soc. Nuclear Medicine (trustee 1971-75), St. Louis Med. Soc., Mo. State Med. Assn., Soc. Chmn. Acad. Radiology Depts. (pres. 1979), Radiol. Soc. N.Am., Assn. Univ. Radiologists (pres. 1988), Am. Roentgen Ray Soc. (pres. 1989), Phi Beta Kappa, Alpha Omega Alpha (Sheard-Sanford award). Office: Barnes Jewish Hosp Mallinckrodt Inst Radiology Barnes Jewish Plz Saint Louis MO 63110-1016 Address: Barnes-Jewish Hosp One Barnes-Jewish Hospital Plz Saint Louis MO 63110

EVENSON, MERLE ARMIN, chemist, educator; b. LaCrosse, Wis., July 27, 1934; s. Ansel Bernard and Gladys Mabel (Nelson) E.; m. Peggy L. Kovats, Oct. 5, 1957; children— David A., Donna L. BS in Chem. Physics and Math., U. Wis., LaCrosse, 1956; MS in Guidance, MS in Sci. Edn., Madison, 1960, PhD in Analytical Chemistry, 1966. Diplomate Am. Bd. Clin. Chemists, v.p., 1978-81. Tchr. math. and physics St. Croix Falls (Wis.) High Sch., 1956-57; tchr. chemistry Central High Sch., LaCrosse, 1957-59; instr. dept. medicine U. Wis., Madison, 1965-66, asst. prof., 1966-69, asso. prof., 1971-75, prof., 1975—, prof. dept. pathology, 1979—; asst. dir. clin. lab. Univ. Hosps., 1965-66, dir. clin. chemistry lab., 1966-69, dir. toxicology lab., 1971-87. Chmn. Gordon Rsch. Conf. on Analytical Chemistry, 1978; vis. lectr. Harvard Med. Sch., 1969-71; mem. staff Peter Bent Brigham Hosp., Boston, 1969-71; cons. on analytical and clin. chemistry to AEC, 1968-93, Am. Chem. Soc., Nat. Bur. Standards, FDA, NIH, study sect. mem. 1968-72, ad hoc memberships, 1973-87. Bd. editors: Chemical Instrumentation, 1973-87, Analytical Chemistry, 1974-77, Jour. Analytical Toxicology, 1976-79, Selected Methods in Clin. Chemistry, 1977-81; editor: Contemporary Topics in Analytical and Clincal Chemistry, 1974-83; contbr. numerous chpts. to books, articles to profl. jours.; patentee continuous oil hemoperfusion unit. NIH fellow, 1970-71, NSF, 1959-62; recipient Maurice O. Graff Disting. Alumni award U. Wis., LaCrosse, 1981 Mem. AAAS, Acad. Clin. Lab. Physicians and Scientists, Am. Assn. Clin. Chemists (bd. editors Clin. Chemistry 1970-80, nat. chair pub. rels. com. 1973-78, diplomat 1974, v.p. 1978-81), Am. Chem. Soc. (com. on clin. chemistry 1973-93), Sigma Xi, Kappa Delta Pi. Office: U Wis 1300 University Ave Madison WI 53706-1510

EVERETT, KAREN JOAN, retired librarian, genealogy educator; b. Cin., Dec. 12, 1926; d. Leonard Kelly and Kletis V. (Wade) Wheatley; m. Wilbur Mason Everett, Sept. 25, 1950; children: Karen, Jan, Jeffrey, Jon, Kathleen, Kerry, Kelly, Shannon. BS in Edn. magna cum laude, U. Cin., 1976, postgrad., 1982-85, Coll. Mt. St. Joseph, 1981-86, Xavier U., Cin., 1985-87, U. Cin., 1982-85, Miami U., 1987. Libr. S.W. Local Schs., Harrison, Ohio, 1967-97, dist. media coord., 1980-97, dist. vol. dir., 1980-97, ret., 1997; instr. genealogy U. Cin., 1998—. Tchr. genealogy U. Cin., 1997—; cons. in field; bd. dirs. U. Cin. ILR; lectr. in field. Contbr. articles to profl. jours. Pres. Citizens Adv. Coun., Harrison, Ohio, 1981-84, 88—, Citizens Adv. Coun., 1989; state chmn. supervisory div. Ohio Ednl. Libr./Media Assn.; mem. Ohio Ambulance Licensing Bd., 1991—. Named Woman of the Yr., Cin. Enquirer, 1978, Xi Eta Iota, 1979; named PTA Educator of the Yr., 1981, others. Mem. NEA, Ohio Ednl. Libr./Media Assn. (chair supervisory div. 1990—, bd. dirs. 1993-94), Ohio Edn. Assn., S.W. Local Classroom Tchrs. Assn., Hamilton County Geneal. Soc. (bd. dirs. 1992—). Avocations: flying, travel, genealogy. Office: U Cin PO Box 210146 Cincinnati OH 45221-0146

EVERHART, BRUCE, radio station executive; Sta. mgr. WMBI-AM/FM, Chgo. Home: WMBI-FM 820 N LaSalle St Chicago IL 60610

EVERHART, ROBERT PHILLIP (BOBBY WILLIAMS), entertainer, songwriter, recording artist; b. St. Edward, Nebr., June 16, 1936; s. Phillip McClelland and Martha Matilda (Meyer) E.; m. Sheila Dawn Armstrong, Feb. 14, 1992; 1 child, Bobbie Lhea. Student, U. Nebr., 1959-62; Assoc. in Radio-TV, Iowa Western Coll., 1971, Assoc. in Graphic Arts, 1974; diploma in Journalism, London Sch. Journalism, 1983; spl. studies Mex. Indian culture, U. Okla., 1990—. Disc jockey various stas., Omaha and Juneau, Alaska, 1959-63; songwriter Royal Flair Music, BMI Pub., Walnut, Iowa, 1964—. Prodr. Bus Stop radio program, 2000—. Host prodr. (TV series) Old Time Country Music, (radio show) Old-Time Music Hour; prodr. The Great Plains and Prairie music Tour, World Music Events, American Traditional Music and Dance Festival, 1998, 2000; rec. artist Folkway Records, N.Y.C., 1970—, Smithsonian Inst., Westwood Records, Wales, 1981, Folk Variety Records, Europe, 1980—, Allied Records, The Philippines, OGA Records, Austria, Otro Records, Poland, Prairie Music Records, Unltd. Prodns., internat. concert artist performing traditional Am. country and folk music; curator, owner Pioneer Music Instrument Mus., Am. Country Music Hall of Fame, Am. Old Time Fiddlers Hall of Fame, Capt.'s Quarters Bed & Breakfast, all located in Walnut, Iowa, and Vera Cruz, Mex., Oaktree Opry, Anita, Iowa; festival promoter Nat. Old-Time Country Music Contest and Pioneer Exposition, 1976—, Am. Traditional Music and Dance Festival, Nat. Traditional Music Performer Awards, 1991—; pres. Nat. Traditional Country Music Assn., Inc., 1982—; regular performer La. Hayride, 1985—; editor: Tradition Country Music Mag., 1980—; author: Clara Bell, 1976, Hart's Bluff, 1977, Listen to the Mockingbird, 1995; (poetry) Silver Bullets, 1979, Savage Trumpet, 1980, Prairie Sunrise, 1982, Snoopy Goes to Mexico, 1983; (TV scripts) The Life of Jimmie Rodgers, 1984, Matecombe Treasure, 1984, The Ghost of Carl Herrmann, 1993, Listen to the Mockingbird, 1998; recs. include: Let's Go, Dream Angel, She Sings Sad Songs, Love to Make Love, Bad Woman Blues, Fishpole John, Time After Time, Street Sleepers, No One Comes Near, Berlin Folksinger My Sweet Love Aint Around Compact Disc release on Otro Records, Dear Grand Ole Opry, 2001; host (TV) Old Time Country Music, 1990-97. With USN, 1954-59. Named to Profl. Musicians and Entertainers Club Iowa Hall of Fame, 1994, Country Music Showcase Internat. Hall of Fame, 1995, Am.'s Old Time Country Music Hall of Fame; Ky. col., 1995; recipient Lifetime Achievement award World Music Events, Vienna, 1998, Kitty Wells/Johnny Wright Country Music Leadership award, 2000; honored as Tenn. Amb. of Goodwill by Gov. Don Sundquist, 2000; honored by Iowa State Legis., 2001. Mem. Internat. Coun. Festivals Fedn., Great Plains Old Time Music Assn., Acad. Country Music, Nat. Bluegrass Assn., Ill. Traditional Country Music Assn., Tri-State Bluegrass Assn., Ky. Cols., Internat. Bluegrass Music Assn., Profl. Musicians Club of Iowa, Midwest Prodrs. Assn. (chmn.), Carribean Club. Democrat. Lutheran. Avocations: scuba diving, traveling. Office: Country Opera House PO Box 492 Anita IA 50020-0492 also: Nat Traditional Country Music Assn PO Box 492 Anita IA 50020-0492 E-mail: bobeverhart@yahoo.com.

EVERIST, BARBARA, state legislator; b. Sioux Falls, S.D., July 6, 1949; d. F. M. and H. M. (Kobb) McBride; m. Thomas Stephen Everist Jr., 1968; children: Thomas Stephen III, Michael Clayton, Lacey Elizabeth. BA, U. Santa Clara, 1971; JD, U. S.D., 1990. Bar: S.D. 1990, U.S. Dist. Ct. S.D. 1990. Law clk. S.D. 2d Cir., 1990-91; state rep. S.D. Ho. Reps. Dist. 14, 1993-94; mem. S.D. Senate Dist. 14, 1995—; mem. state affairs and judiciary coms. S.D. State Senate Dist. 14, chmn. edn. com. Mem. Commerce, Judiciary and Taxation Coms.; atty., Sioux Falls, 1990—. Mem. S.D. State Bar Assn., Assn. Gifted and Talented (pres. 1985), Jr. League Sioux Falls (pres. 1980-81), Phi Alpha Delta, Pi Beta Phi. Home: 709 E Tomar Rd Sioux Falls SD 57105-7053 Office: SD Senate 500 E Capitol Ave Pierre SD 57501-5070

EVERSON, CURT, commissioner, state; Commr. S.D. State Fin. and Mgmt. Bur., Pierre. Office: SD State Fin and Mgmt Bur 500 E Capitol Ave Pierre SD 57501-5070

EVERSON, DIANE LOUISE, publishing executive; b. Edgerton, Wis., Mar. 27, 1953; d. Harland Everett and Helen Viola (Oliver) E. BS, Carroll Coll., 1975. Co-pub. Edgerton (Wis.) Reporter, 1976—; v.p. Silk Screen Creations, 1981—. Bd. dirs. Inland Press. Pub. Career Directors newspaper, 1981—, Directions mag., 1981—, Career Waves Newsletter, 1989—, Coll. and Univs. Directories. Trustee Carroll Coll., 1987—; active ARC, bd. dirs. Badger chpt., pres. local bd., 1997—. Mem. Nat. Newspaper Assn. (regional bd. dirs., pres.-elect), Inland Press Assn. (bd. dirs. 1993—), Madison TEMPO (pres. 1998—). Democrat. Lutheran. Home: 114 Kellog Rd Edgerton WI 53534-9352 Office: Directions Pub 21 N Henry St Edgerton WI 53534-1821

EVERT, RAY FRANKLIN, botany educator; b. Mt. Carmel, Pa., Feb. 20, 1931; s. Milner Ray and Elsie (Hoffa) I.; m. Mary Margaret Maloney, Jan. 2, 1960; children: Patricia Ann, Paul Franklin. B.S., Pa. State U., 1952, M.S., 1954; Ph.D., U. Calif. at Davis, 1958. Mem. faculty Mont. State U., 1958-60; mem. faculty U. Wis.-Madison, 1960—, prof. botany, 1966-77, prof. botany and plant pathology, 1977-88, Katherine Esau prof. botany and plant pathology, 1988-2001, emeritus prof. botany and plant pathology, 2001—, chmn. dept. botany, 73-74, 77-79, 1994-98. Vis. prof. U. Natal, Pietermaritzburg, S. Africa, winter, spring 1971, U. Göttingen, W.Ger., summer 1971, 74-75, summer 1988; mem. gen. biology and genetics fellowship rev. panel NIH, 1964-68, NSF Adv. Com. for Biol. Research Ctrs. Program, 1987-88; forensic plant anatomy cons. Co-author: Biology of Plants; sci. editor Physiol. Plantarum, 1983-98; mem. editl. bd. Trees, 1991-2000, Internat. Jour. Plant Scis., 1991-98; contbr. articles on food conducting tissue in higher plants and leaf structure-function relationships. Recipient Alexander von Humboldt award, 1974-75, Emil H. Steiger award for excellence in tchg. U. Wis., 1981, Bessey Lectr. award Iowa State U., Ames, 1984, Benjamin Minge Duggar lectureship award Auburn U., 1985, Disting. Svc. citation Wis. Acad. Scis., Arts and Letters, 1985, Hilldale award in biol. sci., 1998; Guggenheim fellow, 1965-66 Fellow Am. Acad. Arts and Scis., AAAS; mem. Bot. Soc. Am. (pres. 1986-87, Merit award 1982), Am. Inst. Biol. Scis., Wis. Acad. Scis., Arts and Letters, Am. Soc. Plant Physiol., Internat. Assn. Wood Anatomists, Deutschen Botanischen Gesellschaft, Golden Key Nat. Honor Soc., Sigma Xi, Phi Kappa Phi, Phi Sigma, Phi Epsilon Phi., Pi Alpha Xi. Home: 810 Woodward Dr Madison WI 53704-2238

EVERY, MICHAEL A. state legislator; m. Laura Every; 4 children. Student, Milton Coll., 1981. Sales mgr. Double Z Broadcasting; mayor City of Minnewauken, N.D.; mem. N.D. Senate from 12th dist., Bismark, 2001—. Coun. pres. City of Minnewauken. Democrat. Office: PO Box 56 Minnewaukan ND 58351-0056 E-mail: mevery@state.nd.us.

EWALD, ROBERT FREDERICK, insurance association executive; b. Newark, May 5, 1924; s. Frederick J. and Florence M. (Reiley) E.; m. Jeanine Martinez, Jan. 3, 1976; children: Robert, Steven; children by a previous marriage: William F., John C., George E. BS in Bus. Adminstrn. with spl. honors in Econs., Rutgers U., 1948. Asst. corp. auditor Prudential Ins. Co., Newark, Houston, Chgo., 1948-61; audit mgr. N.Y. Life Ins. Co., N.Y.C., 1962-64; treas. Mass. Gen. Life Ins. Co., Boston, 1965-68; adminstrv. v.p., controller Res. Life Ins. Co., Dallas, 1969-70; pres. Nat. Ben Franklin Life, Chgo., 1971-77; trustee, pres. Rockford (Ill.) Blue Cross Plan, North Cmties. Health Plan, Inc., 1979-82; dir., chmn. audit com. Guaranty Reasurance Corp., 1993-95; exec. dir. Guaranty Sys. Cons. LTD, Guaranty Assn., Chgo. Served with U.S. Army, 1943-46. Fellow Life Mgmt. Inst.; mem. Fin. Execs. Inst., Am. Arbitration Assn., Adminstrv. Mgmt. Soc., Mensa, Nat. Orgn. Life and Health Ins. Guaranty Assn. (emeritus dir., chmn. mems. coun. 1992-95, chmn. exec. com.), VFW. Home: 12 Wisner St Park Ridge IL 60068-3546 E-mail: bobewald@attbi.com.

EWICK, CHARLES RAY, librarian; b. Shelbyville, Ind., Sept. 13, 1937; s. Laurel R. and Loraine Pearl (Tufts) E.; m. Joann Hotchkiss, June 14, 1958; children— David Lee, Jeffrey Allen. B.A., Wabash Coll., 1962; M.A., Ind. U., 1966. Cons. Ind. State Library, Indpls., 1966-68, asst. dir., 1968-72, dir., 1978—. Dir. Rolling Prairie Libraries, Decatur, Ill., 1972-78 Mem. ALA, Ind. Library Assn., Phi Beta Mu. Office: Ind State Library 140 N Senate Ave Indianapolis IN 46204-2296

EWING, BERNIE EDWARD, manufacturing company executive; b. Indpls., Sept. 17, 1944; s. Bernie Howard and Wanda Gertrude (Painter) E.; m. Jean Marie McIntosh; children: Chris, Tony, Erin. Student, U. Md., 1963; cert. in bus., Harvard U., 1984. Staff drafting design Kimball Pianos, Jasper, Ind., 1961-62; from detailed draftsman to design engr. engine, body, chassis and electrical groups Internat. Harvester Truck, Ft. Wayne, 1967-72; supr., gen. foreman material scheduling and expediting Internat. Harvester, 1972-75, mgr. scheduling expediting and procurement, 1976-77, gen. supr. prodn. control Springfield, Ohio, 1975-76, mgr. material truck group, 1977-79, mgr. supply and inventory, v.p. medium duty truck group, 1979-81; asst. to v.p. prodn. Gen. Dynamics, Ft. Worth div., 1981, dir. prodn. planning and control, 1981-82; v.p. mfg. Gen. Dynamics Land Systems div., Troy, Mich., 1982-85, v.p., program dir. M1 tank, 1985-86; corp. v.p. ops. and prodn. engring. Gen. Dynamics, St. Louis, 1986—. Served with USAF, 1962-66. Avocations: sports, cars, real estate. Office: Gen Dynamics Corp Pierre Laclede Ctr Saint Louis MO 63105

EWING, LYNN MOORE, JR. lawyer; b. Nevada, Mo., Nov. 14, 1930; s. Lynn Moore and Margaret Ray (Blair) E.; m. Peggy Patton Adams, July 10, 1954; children: Margaret Grace, Melissa Lee, Lynn Moore. AB, U. Mo., Columbia, 1952, JD, 1954. Bar: Mo. 1954. Ptnr. Ewing & Hoberock, Nevada, Mo., 1958—. Mem. Mo. Ho. of Reps., 1959-64; mem. Nevada City Coun., 1967-73, mayor, 1969-70, 72-73; mem., Mo. Land Reclamation Commn., 1971-75, Nevada Charter Comm., 1978-79, devel. coun. U. Mo., Columbia, Mo. Acad. of Squires, 1994—; mem. Mo. coord. bd. Higher Edn., 1997—, chmn., 2000—. Bd. dirs. Nevada Hosp., 1974-83; bd. dirs., pres. Nev. Area Econ. Devel. Commn., 1985-88; vestryman, sr. warden All Saints Episcopal Ch. Served to 1st lt. USAF, 1954-56. Recipient Legis. award St. Louis Globe-Democrat, 1960, 62; named Citizen of Year, Nevada Rotary Club, 1975 Fellow Am. Bar Found. (life); mem. ABA, Mo. Bar Found. (life), Am. Coll. Trust and Estate Counsel, Am. Coll. Mortgage Attys., Am. Judicature Soc., U.S. League Savs. Assn. (chmn. attys. com. 1977-79), Mo. Bar (adv. com. 1975-84, bd. govs. 1974-78), Vernon County Bar Assn., Jefferson Club (trustee), Nevada Rotary (pres. 1969-70), Nevada Country Club. Democrat. Episcopalian. Office: 223 W Cherry St Nevada MO 64772-3361 Home: 307 West Blvd S Columbia MO 65203-2750

EWING, STEPHEN E. natural gas company executive; b. 1944; married. B.A., DePauw U., 1965; M.B.A., Mich. State U., 1971, Harvard U., 1982. With Gen. Electric Co., 1965-66; with Mich. Consolidated Gas. Co., 1971—, coordinator mgmt. orgn. devel., 1972-73, mgr. adminstr. planning devel. services, 1973, dir. customer service, 1973-75, v.p. personnel, 1975-79, v.p. personnel and adminstrn., 1979-81, v.p. customer service, 1981-84, exec. v.p., 1984—, chief operating officer, pres., pres., 1985—. Served with USAF, 1966-70. Office: DTE Energy 2000 Second Ave. Detroit MI 48226-1279

EWING, SUSAN R. artist, educator; b. Lawrenceville, Ill., 1955; AA in Music, Stephens Coll., 1974; BA in Jewelry, Metalsmithing, Ind. U., 1976, MFA in Jewelry, Metalsmithing, 1980. Head metals program Miami (Ohio) U., 1981—. One-person shows include Hans Hansen Sølv, Copenhagen, Denmark, Nat. Tech. Mus., Prague, Czech Republic, Phoenix Mus. Art, Ohio Craft Mus., Columbus, Ork. Art Ctr., Little Rock; group shows include Aspects Gallery, London, Park Ryu Sook Gallery, Seoul, Korea, Schweizerisches Landesmuseum, Zurich, Switzerland, Cercle Mcpl. Galerie Oféo, Luxembourg, Mus. Kunsthandwerk, Frankfurt, Germany, Deutsches Klingenmuseum, Solingen, Germany, Schmuckmuseum, Pforzheim, Germany, Galerie Matter, Cologne, Germany, Galerie Ende, Cologne, Mathildenhohe Mus., Darmstadt, Germany, Galerie Spectrum, Munich, Germany, Galerie Ventil, Munich, Fortunoff's N.Y.C., Urban BobKat Gallery, N.Y.C., Lever House, N.Y.C., Seventh Regiment Armory, N.Y.C., Am. Craft Mus., N.Y.C.; represented in permanent collections White House. Recipient Dolibois Faculty Devel. award, disting. Lifetime Achievement award Ohio Designer Craftsmen; Summer Rsch. fellow Miami U., Ohio Arts Coun. Individual Artist fellow, 1987, 89, 91, Fulbright grantee, 1997, 98; Rsch. Challenge grantee Ohio State Bd. Regents. Office: Sch Art Fine Arts Dept Miami U Oxford OH 45056

EWING, THOMAS WILLIAM, former congressman, lawyer; b. Atlanta, Sept. 19, 1935; m. Connie Lupo, 1981; children: Jane, Kathryn, Sam, Christine Lupo, John Lupo, Stephanie Lupo. BS, Millikin U., 1957; JD, John Marshall Law Sch., Chgo., 1968. Asst. state atty. Livingston County, 1968-73; ptnr. Satter Ewing Beyer & Spires, Pontiac, Ill., 1969-91; mem. Ill. Ho. of Reps., 1974-91, U.S. Congress from 15th Ill. Dist., 1991-2001; mem. sci. com., agr. subcom., transp. and infrastructure coms., house adminstrn. com. Mem. agr. com. Ill. Ho. Reps., chmn. subcom. on risk mgmt. and specialty crops, subcom. on dept. ops., nutrition and fgn. agr., transp. and infrastructure com., aviation subcom., water resources and environment subcom., joint econ. com., former dep. minority leader, chmn. policy com., house revenue com., 1980, co-chmn. Ill. Econ. and Fiscal Commn., co-chmn. Legis. Space Needs Commn. Rep. precinct committeeman; del. Rep. Nat. Conv., 1980, 84, 88; committeeman 15th Congl. Dist., 1986-93. With U.S. Army, 1958, USAR, 1957-63. Recipient Best Legislator award Nat. Rep. Legislator of the Yr. award, 1982, Ill. Small Businessmen Assn., 1983, 85, 87, Friend of Agr. award Ill. Agrl. Assn., 1985, 87, 89, 91, Legislator of Yr. award Ill. Assn. Homes for the Aging, 1986. Mem. Livingston County Bar Assn., Pontiac C. of C. (past exec. dir., past pres.), Livingston County Farm Bur., Elks, Moose, Masons. Methodist.

EXON, J(OHN) JAMES, former senator; b. Lake Andes, S.D., Aug. 9, 1921; s. John James and Luella (Johns) E.; m. Patricia Ann Pros, Sept. 18, 1943; children: Stephen, Pamela, Candace. Student, U. Omaha, 1939-41; LLD (hon.), Creighton U., 1991, Doane Coll., 1995; LittD (hon.), U. Nebr., 1997. Mgr. Universal Finance Corp., Nebr., 1946-53; pres. Exon's, Inc., Lincoln, 1954-71; gov. State of Nebr., 1971-79; mem. U.S. Senate, Nebr., 1979-96. Mem. Armed Svcs. Com., ranking Min. mem. of budget com., ranking Min. mem. commerce, sci. and transp. subcom. of consumer affairs, fgn. commerce and tourism. Active state, local, nat. Democratic coms., 1952— ; del. Dem. Nat. Conv., 1964, 72, 74, 76, 88, 92; former Dem. nat. committeeman. Served with Signal Corps AUS, 1942-45. Mem. Am. Legion, VFW, Masons (33rd degree), Shriners, Elks, Eagles, Optimist Internat. Home: 1615 Brent Blvd Lincoln NE 68506-1867

EYMAN, EARL DUANE, electrical science educator, consultant; b. Canton, Ill., Sept. 24, 1925; s. Arthur Earl and Florence Mabel (Hardin) E.; m. Ruth Margaret Morgan, Apr. 20, 1951; children: Joseph Earl, David James. B.S. in Engring. Physics, U. Ill., 1949, M.S. in Math, 1950, postgrad., 1951-64, U. Bradley, 1952-58; Ph.D. in Elec. Engring., U. Colo., 1966. Registered profl. engr., Ill. Scientist Westinghouse Atomic Power Div., Pitts., 1950-51; research engr. Caterpillar Tractor Co., Peoria, Ill., 1951-58, project engr., 1958-66; mem. faculty Bradley U., 1952-64; prof. elec. engring. U. Iowa, Iowa City, 1966-92, chmn. elec. engring., 1969-76. Cons. Sundstrand Aviation, Denver, 1966, Gould Simulation Systems Div., Melville, N.Y., 1978-81, U.S. Dept. Commerce, Boulder, 1978-92. Author: Modeling Simulation and Control, 1988; contbr. articles to profl. jours. Chmn., mem. Electricians Examining Bd., Iowa City, 1969-74. Served with USNR, 1944-46 Mem. Eta Kappa Nu (mem., pres. internat. bd. 1972-77), Tau Beta Pi, Theta Tau Avocations: skiing; mountain climbing and hiking. Home: PO Box 3282 Estes Park CO 80517-3282 Office: U Iowa 4400 EB Iowa City IA 52242

FABEL, THOMAS LINCOLN, lawyer; b. St. Paul, Feb. 12, 1946; s. George Forest and Beatrice Evelyn (Ostrom) F.; m. Jean Marquerite Hoisser, Nov. 21, 1946; children: Jessica, Anne, Leah, Theodore. BA, Carleton Coll., 1968; JD, U. Chgo., 1971; LLD (Hon.), William Mitchell Coll. Law, 1988. Bar: Minn. 1971; U.S. Dist. Ct. Minn. 1972; U.S. Ct. Appeals (8th cir.) 1974; U.S. Supreme Ct. 1976. Special asst. atty. gen. Minn. Atty. Gen., St. Paul, 1971-73, deputy atty. gen., 1973-87; ptnr. Lindquist & Vennum, Mpls., 1987-97, 99—; dep. mayor City of St. Paul, 1998. Adj. faculty William Mitchell Coll. Law, St. Paul, 1982—. Mem. Minn. Bar Assn., Ramsey County Bar Assn., Rotary. Home: 1550 Edgewater Ave Saint Paul MN 55112-3630 Office: Lindquist & Vennum 444 Cedar St Saint Paul MN 55101-2179

FABENS, ANDREW LAWRIE, III, lawyer; b. Washington, Apr. 8, 1942; s. Andrew Lawrie Jr. and Alicia Gordon (Hail) F.; m. Martha Leigh Leingang, June 24, 1966; children: Andrew Lawrie IV, Jennie Leigh. AB, Yale U., 1964; JD, U. Chgo., 1967. Bar: Ohio 1967. Assoc. Thompson, Hine and Flory, Cleve., 1967-74; ptnr. Thompson Hine LLP (formerly Thompson, Hine and Flory), 1974—, chmn. estate planning and probate area, 1988-94. Contbr. articles on estate planning and related topics to profl. publs. Pres. Family Health Assn., Cleve., 1978-80, 83-84; trustee A.M. McGregor Home, East Cleveland, Ohio, 1991—, chmn., 2001—; trustee Bascom Little Fund, Cleve., 1985—, Great Lakes Basin Conservancy, 1999—; vestryman Christ Episcopal Ch., Shaker Heights, Ohio, 1972-77. Fellow Am. Coll. Trust and Estate Counsel, The Rowfant Club (adv. 1998-2000); mem. Ohio State Bar Assn. (bd. govs. probate and trust law sect. 1983—, treas. 1997-99, sec. 1999-2001, vice-chmn. 2001—), Probate Law Jour. Ohio (adv. bd.), Cleve. Bar Assn. (speaker, com. mem. 1976—), Cleve. Skating Club, The Novel Club (sec. 1986-88, pres. 1995-97), The Union Club. Home: 2280 Woodmere Dr Cleveland OH 44106-3604 Office: Thompson Hine LLP 3900 Key Ctr 127 Public Square Cleveland OH 44114-1216

FABRIS, JAMES A. journalist; b. Cleve., Aug. 6, 1938; s. Andrew and Geraldine (Foretic) F.; m. Donna Wilker, Dec. 26, 1960; children— Julia, John, James F., Gerald, Andrew, Fredric Student, Case Western Res. U., Cleve., 1956-58. Reporter Bklyn.-Parma News, Parma, Ohio, 1954-58; editorial staff Lake County News-Herald, Willoughby, 1958-67, Chgo. Daily News, 1967-77, Chgo. Sun-Times, 1977-84, dep. mng. editor, 1984-86; mng. editor N.Y. Post, N.Y.C., 1986-89; editorial staff New York Daily News, 1990-92; deputy mng. editor Cleve. Plain Dealer, 1992—. Recipient Marshall Field award Field Enterprises, 1974; Soc. of Publ. Designers award, 1978 Roman Catholic Home: 20791 Lake Rd Rocky River OH 44116-1335 Office: Cleve Plain Dealer 1801 Superior Ave Cleveland OH 44114-2107

FAETH, GERARD MICHAEL, aerospace and mechanical engineering educator, researcher; b. N.Y.C., July 5, 1936; s. Joseph and Helen (Wagner) F.; m. Mary Ann Kordich, Dec. 27, 1959; children: Christine Louise, Lorraine Vera, Elinor Jean. BME, Union Coll., 1958; MS, Pa. State U., 1961, PhD, 1964. Instr. mech. engring. Pa. State U., University Park, 1958-59, research asst., 1959-64, asst. prof., 1964-68, assoc. prof., 1968-74, prof., 1974-85, prof. emeritus, 1985—; Modine prof., head gas dynamics labs. U. Mich., Ann Arbor, 1985—. Vis. prof. Air Force Office Sci. Rsch., Washington, 1983-84; cons. GM, Warren, Mich., 1977-1992, Applied Rsch. Lab., Pa. State U., 1964-85; prof.-in-residence GM Inst., Detroit, 1983. Mem. editorial bd. Combustion Sci. and Tech., 1979-99, Ann. Rev. Numerical Fluid M echanics and Heat Transfer, 1985—, Atomization and Sprays, 1989—, Progress in Energy and Combustion Sci., 1991—, Internat. Jour. Multiphase Flow, 1997—; contbr. numerous articles to profl. jours. Rep. Precinct Cmm. Centre County, Pa., 1977-84; bd. dirs. Eagles Mere (Pa.) Assn., 1982-88, Eagles Mere Park Assn., 1978-85. Recipient Oustanding Engr. Alumnus award Pa. State Univ. Alumni Assn., 1990, Pub. Svc. medal NASA, 1999; Highly-Cited Rschr. cert., Inst. of Scientific Info., 2000, Appreciation award, Holwen U., Cairo, 2002. Fellow ASME (tech. editor 1981-84, sr. tech. editor 1985-90, Meml. award heat transfer divsn. 1988), AIAA (Propellants and Combustion award 1993, editor-in-chief 1997—2002), AAAS; mem. NAE, Combustion Inst. (dep. editor 1984-90, tech. editor 1990-96, bd. dirs. 1990-96), Am. Phys. Soc., Sigma Xi, Pi Tau Sigma, Phi Kappa Phi. Episcopalian. Office: U Mich 3000 FXB Bldg Ann Arbor MI 48109-2140 Home: PO Box 1468 Ann Arbor MI 48106-1468 E-mail: gmfaeth@umich.edu.

FAGG, GEORGE GARDNER, federal judge; b. Eldora, Iowa, Apr. 30, 1934; s. Ned and Arleene (Gardner) Fagg; m. Jane E. Wood, Aug. 19, 1956; children: Martha, Thomas, Ned, Susan, George, Sarah. BSBA, Drake U., 1965, JD, 1956. Bar: Iowa 1958. Ptnr. Cartwright, Druker, Ryden & Fagg, Marshalltown, Iowa, 1958—72; judge Iowa Dist. Ct., 1972—82, U.S. Ct. Appeals (8th cir.), 1982—99, sr. judge, 1999—. Faculty Nat. Jud. Coll., 1979. Mem.: ABA, Iowa Bar Assn., Order of Coif. Office: US Ct Appeals US Courthouse Annex 110 E Court Ave Ste 455 Des Moines IA 50309-2044

FAHEY, MIKE, mayor; b. Kansas City, Kansas ; 4 children. Postgrad, Creighton Univ., 1973. Mayor City of Omaha, 2001—; ret. CEO Am. Land Title Co., former owner. Bd. Holy Name Housing, Am. Red Cross Heartland Chpt., Creighton Prep H.S.; chmn. Omaha Planning Bd., 1981. Office: 1819 Farnam St Ste 300 Omaha NE 68183*

FAHEY, RICHARD PAUL, lawyer; b. Oakland, Calif., Nov. 2, 1944; s. John Joseph and Helene Goldie (Whetstone) F.; m. Suzanne Dawson, June 8, 1968; children: Eamon, Aaron Chad. AA, Meritt Coll., 1964; BA, San Francisco State Univ., 1966; JD, Northwestern U., 1971. Bar: N. Mex., 1971, U.S. Dist. Ct., N. Mex., 1972, U.S. Ct. Appeals (10th cir.) 1972, Ohio 1973, U.S. Dist. Ct. (no. and so. dists.), U.S. Supreme Ct. 1975. Atty. in charge Dinebeiina Nahiilna Be Agaditahe, Shiprock, New Mexico, 1971-73; asst. atty. genl. State of Ohio, Columbus, OH, 1973-76; ptnr. Fahey & Schraff, 1976-80; atty. Sanford, Fisher, Fahey, Boyland & Schwarzwalder, 1980-84; of counsel Knepper, White, Arter & Hadden, 1984-85; ptnr. Arter & Hadden, 1985-99; of counsel Vorys Sater Seymour and Pease LLP, 2000—; adj. prof.law Capital U., 1976-86; adj. prof. law Ohio State Univ., 1986-87; chmn. Ohio Oil and Gas Regulatory Rev. Commn., 1986-87. Author: Underground Storage Tanks A Primer of the Federal Regulatory Program, 2nd edit., 1995; contbr. articles to profl. jours. Vol. Peace Corps., Liberia, 1966—68; active Columbus Pub. Schs. Bd. Edn., 1986—93, pres., 1989; trustee Godman Guild Settlement House, 1976—82, Ohio Environ. Coun., 1981—83; adv. bd. WCBE Pub. Radio; Charter rev. com. Columbus City, 1998—99; exec. com. Dem. Party, 1996—; trustee Downtown Columbus, Inc., 1989, Pilot Dogs, Inc., 1993—, pres., 2001, Audubon Ohio, 1999—, Cmty. in Sch., 2000—. Grantee, Russell Sage Found., 1969. Mem. ABA (vice chair Sonreel water quality com. 1993-97), Ohio Bar Assn., N. Mex. Bar Assn., Columbus Bar Assn., Columbus Bar Found. Democrat. Unitarian. Avocations: travel, fishing, reading, jogging, skiing. Home: 449 E Dominion Blvd Columbus OH 43214-2216 Office: Vorys Sater Seymour and Pease LLP 52 E Gay St Columbus OH 43215

FAHIEN, LEONARD AUGUST, physician, educator; b. St. Louis, July 26, 1934; s. John Henry and Alice Katherine (Schubkegel) F.; m. Rose Marian Burmeister, June 21, 1958; children: Catherine Fahien Reuter, Lisa Fahien Uldrich, James. A.B., Washington U., St Louis, 1956; M.D., Washington U., 1960. Intern U. Wis., Madison, 1960-61; surgeon NIH, Bethesda, Md., 1964-66; asst. prof. dept. pharmacology U. Wis. Med. Sch., Madison, 1966-69, asso. prof., 1969-74, prof., 1974—, asso. dean, 1979-83; vis. prof. Inst. Protein Rsch. Osaka U., Japan, 1991; prof. El Julios U. Barcelona (Spain), 1997. Contbr. chpts. to books; contbr. articles to profl. jours. Served with USPHS, 1964-66. Numerous NIH grants, 1966— Mem. Phi Beta Kappa, Sigma Xi. Lutheran. Home: 3212 Topping Rd Madison WI 53705-1435 Office: 426 S Charter St Madison WI 53715-1626 E-mail: lafahien@facstaff.wisc.edu.

FAHNER, TYRONE C. lawyer, former state attorney general; b. Detroit, Nov. 18, 1942; s. Warren George and Alma Fahner; BA, U. Mich., 1965; JD, Wayne State U., 1968; LLM, Northwestern U., 1971; m. Anne Beauchamp, July 2, 1966; children— Margaret, Daniel, Molly. Bar: Mich. 1968, Ill. 1969, Tex. 1984, U.S. Dist. Ct. (ea. dist.) Mich. 1968, U.S. Dist. Ct. (no. dist.) Ill. 1969, U.S. Ct. Appeals (7th cir.) 1969, U.S. Ct. Appeals (5th cir.) 1981. asst. U.S. atty. for No. Dist. Ill., Chgo., 1971-75, dep. chief consumer fraud and civil rights, 1973-74, chief ofcl. corruption, 1974-75; ptnr. Freeman, Rothe, Freeman & Salzman, Chgo., 1975-77; dir. Ill. Dept. Law Enforcement, Springfield, 1977-79; ptnr. Mayer, Brown & Platt, Chgo., 1979-80, 83—; Co-chmn of managmnt comm., Mayer, Brown & Platt, 1998—; atty. gen. State of Ill., Springfield, 1980-83; instr. John Marshall Law Sch., 1973-76, 78-84; pvt. sector rep. UNCTAD; former chmn. Coun. Great Lakes Govs.; chmn. Govs. Adv. Bd. Law Enforcement, 1980-83, Ill. Jud. Inquiry Bd, 1988-92, Chgo., Com. Honest Elections, 1984-92, Com. Internat. Trade and Tourism, Chgo. com. Chgo. Coun. Fgn. Rels. Mem. Toronto sister city com. Chgo. Sister Cities Internat. Program; bd. dirs. Mex.-Am. Legal Defense and Ednl. Fund; mem. corp. adv. com. U. Mich. Coll. Lit., Sci. & The Arts, mem. major gifts com.; Mex.-Am. Legal Def. and Ednl. Fund; mem. William J. Fulbright bd. fgn. scholarships USIA, 1988-93; active Law Sch.'s Com. Visitors Wayne State U., U.S. Info. Agy., Ill. Racing Bd., 1979-80, United Cerbral Palsy, Chgo., 1981-84, Epilepsy Found. Greater Chgo., Evanston Hist. Soc., Bureau Ednl. and Cultural Affairs, 1988-93. Mem. ABA, Am. Coll. Trial Lawyers, Internat. Assn. Gaming Attys., Mich. Bar Assn., Tex. Bar Assn., Chgo. Bar Assn., Law Club Chgo., Am. Inns of Ct. (Chgo. chpt.), Ill. Ambs. (bd. dirs., past pres.), Northwestern U. Sch. Law Alumni Assn. (bd. dirs. 1990-95, chmn. Class 1967 James B. Haddad professorship fundraising com.), Econ. Club of Chgo., Chgo. Club, Chgo. Commonwealth Club, Legal Club Chgo., Am. Effective Law Enforcement (com. cts. and justice), Commercial Club Chgo., U. Mich. Major Gifts com., Just The Beginning Found. Republican. Lutheran. Office: Mayer Brown & Platt 190 S La Salle St Chicago IL 60603-3441

FAHRNBRUCH, DALE E. retired state supreme court justice; b. Lincoln, Nebr., Sept. 13, 1924; s. Henry and Bessie M. (Osborne) F.; m. Margaret L. Hunt, July 4, 1952; children: Rebecca Kay Fahrnbruch Braymen, Daniel D. (dec.). AD in Journalism, U. Nebr., 1948, BS in Law, 1950; JD, Creighton U., 1951; LLM, U. Va., 1986. Bar: Nebr. 1951, U.S. Ct. Appeals (8th cir.) 1969. City editor Jour. Newspaper, Lincoln, 1951-52; asst., then dep. county atty. Lancaster County, Nebr., 1952-55, chief dep. county atty., 1955-59; ptnr. Beynon, Hecht & Fahrnbruch, 1959-73; dist. judge Nebr., 1973-87; justice Nebr. Supreme Ct., 1987-97.

FAIR, HUDSON RANDOLPH, recording company executive; b. Evanston, Ill., Aug. 15, 1953; s. Harry Joel Jr. and Virginia (Gauntlett F. BS in Speech, Northwestern U., 1976, MA in Speech, 1979. Mktg. rep. Calumet Refining Co., Chgo., 1975-78, Calumet Petro-Chems., Inc., Houston, 1977-78, Stellavox, S.A., Schaumburg, Ill., 1986-87, Nagra Magnetic Recorders, Inc., N.Y.C., 1987-91; pres. Ealing Mobile Recording, Ltd., Chgo., 1981—. Music prodr. WFMT Radio, Chgo., 1992—, Ravinia Festival, 1997—; cons. in field. Prodr. more than 125 classical albums, 1981—. Speech writer Rep. George Bush Presdl. Campaign, Chgo., 1979-80. Recipient Chorus award for best choral rec., 1989, Deutsche Schallplatten-preis for best chamber music record Juilliard String Quartet, 1998; grantee Ill. Arts Coun., 1982-86, Nat. Endowment for Arts, 1986. Mem. NARAS (bd. govs. 1991-95, 96-2000, nat. trustee 1993-95), Audio Engring. Soc., Engring. and Rec. Soc. (bd. dirs. 1987—, chmn. 1991-92). Republican. Episcopalian. Avocations: travel, motorcycles, skiing. Office: Ealing Mobile Rec Ltd 4906 N Talman Ave Chicago IL 60625-2722 E-mail: ffrr1@msn.com.

FAIRCHILD, THOMAS E. judge; b. Milw., Dec. 25, 1912; s. Edward Thomas and Helen (Edwards) Fairchild; m. Eleanor E. Dahl, July 24, 1937; children: Edward, Susan, Jennifer, Andrew. Student, Princeton, 1931—33; AB, Cornell U., 1934; LLB, U. Wis., 1938. Bar: Wis. 1938. Practiced, Portage, Wis., 1938—41, Milw., 1945—48, 1953—56; atty. OPA, Chgo., Milw., 1941—45; hearing commr. Chgo. Region, 1945; atty. gen. Wis., 1948—51; U.S. atty. for Western Dist. Wis., 1951—52; justice Supreme Ct. Wis., 1957—66, U.S. Ct. Appeals for 7th Circuit, 1966—. Dem. candidate Senator from Wis., 1950, 1952. Mem.: KP, FBA, ABA, Am. Law Inst., Am. Judicature Soc., Dane County Bar Assn., 7th Cir. Bar Assn., Milw. Bar Assn., Wis. Bar Assn., Phi Delta Phi. Democrat. Mem. United Church Of Christ. Office: US Courthouse Rm 2764 219 S Dearborn St Chicago IL 60604-1702

FAIRFIELD, BILL L. company executive; BS in Engring., Bradley U.; MBA in Bus. Admistrn., Harvard U. Sr. exec. Eastman Kodak, 1969-73; sr. v.p. Lindsay Mfg. Co., 1975-79; pres. mktg. domestic irrigation divsn. Valmont Industries Inc., 1979-81, pres., gen. mgr. irrigation divsn., 1981-82; pres., CEO, Inacom Corp., Omaha, 1982-99, also bd. dirs.; chmn. Dreamfield Ptnrs. Inc., Dreamfield Capital Ventures, 2000—. Bd. dirs. Fed. Res. Bank Kansas City, Omaha, Sitel Corp., others. Trustee U. Nebr., Lincoln; bd. trustees Boy Scouts Am.; mem. Chancellor's Adv. Coun., U. Nebr., Omaha. Office: Inacom Corp 1004 Farnam St Ste 204 Omaha NE 68102

FAIRHURST, CHARLES, civil and mining engineering educator; b. Widnes, Lancashire, Eng., Aug. 5, 1929; came to U.S., 1956, naturalized, 1967; s. Richard Lowe and Josephine (Starkey) F.; m. Margaret Ann Lloyd, Sept. 7, 1957; children: Anne Elizabeth Charlet, David Lloyd, Charles Edward, Catherine Mary Kotz, Hugh Richard, John Peter, Margaret Mary Evans. BEng with honors, U. Sheffield, Eng., 1952, PhD, 1955; DSc, U. Sheffield, 1998; D in Engring. (hon.), St. Petersburg Mining Inst., Russia, 1995, Inst. Nat. Poly de Lorraine, France, 1996; DSc (hon.), U. Minn., 2000. Mining engr. trainee Nat. Coal Bd., St. Helens, Eng., 1949-56; research assoc. prof. U. Minn., Mpls., 1956-67, head Sch. Mineral and Metall. Engring., 1967-70, prof. dept. civil and mineral engring., 1970-94, prof. dept. civil engring., 1994-97, head dept., 1972-87, T.W. Bennett Prof. mining engring. and rock mechanics, 1983-97, prof. emeritus, 1997—. Sr. cons. Itasca Group Inc., Mpls.; cons. Petrobras, Brazil, Spie. Batignolles, France, Charbonnages de France; chmn. U.S. Com. Rock Mechanics, 1971-74, Waste Isolation Pilot Plant Panel NAS/NRC, Carlsbad, N.Mex., 1989-96; chmn. study underground nuclear testing in French Polynesia, Internat. Geomechanics Commn., 1995-98; mem. bd. radioactive waste mgmt. NAS/NRC, 1987-94, vice chmn., 1989-94; adv. prof. Tongji U., Shanghai, 1994. Mem. Conseil Sci. ANDRA (France), 1994—, Mon. Geol. Rep. Consulting Bd., Yucca Mountain, 1999-2001. Mem. AIME, ASCE (chmn. rock mechanics com. 1978-80), Internat. Soc. Rock Mechanics (pres. 1991-95), Am. Rock Mechanics Assn. (pres. 1995-97), Am. Underground Constrn. Assn. (pres. 1976-77), Royal Swedish Acad. Engring. Scis. (fgn.), U.S. Nat. Acad. Engring., Sigma Xi. Roman Catholic. Home: 417 5th Ave N South Saint Paul MN 55075-2035 Office: 417 Fifth Ave N South Saint Paul MN 55075-2035 E-mail: fairh001@tc.umn.edu.

FAISON, W. MACK, lawyer; b. Roanoke Rapids, N.C., Oct. 25, 1945; BA, N.C. Ctrl. U., 1966; JD, Harvard U., 1969. Bar: N.Y. 1970, Mich. 1972. Mem. Miller, Canfield, Paddock and Stone, Detroit. Mem. local rules adv. com. Ea. Dist. Mich., U.S. Dist. Ct., civil justice reform act adv. com. Mem. ABA, State Bar Mich., Nat. Bar Assn., Detroit Bar Assn., Wolverine Bar Assn., Am. Coll. of Trial Lawyers. Office: Miller Canfield Paddock & Stone 150 W Jefferson Ave Ste 2500 Detroit MI 48226-4416

FAITH, MARSHALL E. grain company executive; Chmn. The Scoular Co., Omaha. Office: The Scoular Co Scoular Bldg 2027 Dodge St Ste 300 Omaha NE 68102-1229

FAJANS, STEFAN STANISLAUS, retired internist, internist, educator; b. Munich, Mar. 15, 1918; arrived in U.S., 1936, naturalized, 1942; s. Kasimir M. and Salomea (Kaplan) Fajans; m. Ruth Stine, Sept. 6, 1947; children: Peter S., John S. BS, U. Mich., Ann Arbor, 1938, MD, 1942. Intern Mount Sinai Hosp., N.Y.C., 1942—43; research fellow U. Mich., 1946—47, rsch. fellow, 1949—51, resident, 1947—49; mem. faculty U. Mich. Med. Sch., 1950—, prof., 1961—88, prof. emeritus, 1988—. Mem. endocrinology study sect. NIH, 1958—62, mem. diabetes and metabolism tng. grants com., 1966—70, mem. nat. diabetes adv. bd., 1987—91; chief divsn. endocrinology and metabolism Mich. Diabetes Rsch. and Tng. Ctr., 1973—87, dir., 1977—86; chmn. Am. zone internat. sci. adv. com. Congresses Internat. Diabetes Fedn., 1977—79; Banting meml. lectr., 1978. Contbr. articles med. publs. Mem. career devel. com. VA Med. Rsch. Svcs., 1987—91. Officer M.C. U.S. Army, 1943—46. Fellow rsch. fellow in medicine, ACP, 1949—50, Life Ins. Med. Inst., 1950—51. Master: ACP; mem.: NAS (sr. mem. inst. med.), Ctrl. Soc. Clin. Rsch., Assn. Am. Physicians, Am. Soc. Clin. Investigation, Am. Fedn. Clin. Rsch., Endocrine Soc. (v.p. 1970—71, coun. 1967—71, 1978—81), Am. Diabetes Assn. (pres. 1971—72, Banting medal 1972, Banting Meml. award 1978), Alpha Omega Alpha, Sigma Xi. Home: 827 Asa Gray Dr # 360 Ann Arbor MI 48105-2566 Office: PO Box 354 Ann Arbor MI 48106-0354 E-mail: sfajans@umich.edu.

FALCONE, FRANK S. academic administrator; b. Kenosha, Wis., Sept. 26, 1940; s. Frank R. and Theresa (Barca) F.; m. Judith Herbert, Aug. 17, 1963; children: Jennifer, F. Jeffrey. BS, U. WIs., 1963; MA, U. Denver, 1965; PhD, U. Mass., 1973. Prof., provost Ithaca (N.Y.) Coll., 1969-80; v.p., dean Pace U., White Plains, N.Y., 1980-82, exec. v.p. Pleasantville, 1982-85; pres. Springfield (Mass.) Coll., 1985-93, Carroll Coll., Waukesha, Wis., 1993—. Bd. dirs. Springfield YMCA, 1990-92, Basketball Hall of Fame; bd. visitors Air U., Maxwell AFB, Ala., 1989-90; exec. com. Boy Scouts, 1994—, United Way Exec. Comm., 1994. Mem. Assn. Ind. Colls. and Univs. in Mass. (exec. com. 1987-89, chmn. 1990-91), Assn. Ind. Colls. Mass. (pres. 1990-91), Greater Springfield C. of C. (bd. dirs. 1987-92), Waukesha C. of C. (bd. dirs. 1994-98, exec. com. 1995—, v.p. 1995), Wis. Found. for Ind. Colls. (treas. 1995-99). Home: 115 S East Ave Waukesha WI 53186-6207 Office: Carroll Coll Office of Pres 100 N East Ave Waukesha WI 53186-3103 E-mail: ffalcone@carroll1.cc.edu.

FALK, JULIA S. linguist, educator; b. Englewood, N.J., Sept. 21, 1941; d. Charles Joseph and Stella Sableski; m. Thomas Heinrich, Jan. 20, 1967; 1 child, Tatiana Prentice. BS, Georgetown U., 1963; MA, U. Wash., 1964, PhD, 1968. Instr. linguistics Mich. State U., East Lansing, 1966-68, asst. prof., 1968-71, assoc. prof., 1971-78, prof., 1978-2001, asst. dean coll. of Arts and Letters, 1979-81, assoc. dean Coll. Arts and Letters, 1981-86, prof. emerita, 2001—. Vis. scholar U. Calif., San Diego, 2000—; cons. on lang. and law, lang. and gender, bias-free communication. Author: Linguistics and Language, 1973, 2d revised edit., 1978, Women, Language and Linguistics, 1999; contbr. articles on history of linguistics to profl. jours. Fellow Woodrow Wilson Found., 1963, NDEA Title IV, 1963-66, NSF, 1965; recipient Paul Varg Alumni award for Teaching, 1993, Faculty Profl. Women's Assn. Outstanding U. Woman Faculty award, 1999. Mem.: N.Am. Assn. History of Lang. Scis. (pres. 2000), Linguistic Soc. Am. Home: 8939 Caminito Verano La Jolla CA 92037-1606

FALK, WILLIAM JAMES, lawyer; b. Kew Gardens, N.Y., Aug. 15, 1952; s. Sam and Bertha (Schwartzwald) F.; m. Laurie Jean Dombrowski, June 24, 1973; children: Douglas Charles, Andrew Stephen, Edward Allaire. BS, Ill. Inst. Tech., 1973; JD cum laude, Suffolk U., 1977; LLM in Taxation, Washington U., St. Louis, 1982. Bar: Mass. 1977, Mo. 1981. Trial atty. IRS Office of Dist. Counsel, St. Louis, 1977—81; assoc. Thompson & Mitchell, 1982—83, ptnr., 1984—96, Thompson Coburn LLP, St. Louis, 1996—99; mem. Lewis, Rice & Fingersh, L.C., 1999—. Contbg. author: Missouri Taxation Law and Practice, 1987, 96; contbr. articles to legal jours. Mem. ABA, Mo. Bar Assn., Bar Assn. Met. St. Louis (chmn. taxation sect. 1992-93, mem. exec. com. 1992-93). Avocations: camping, music. Office: Lewis Rice & Fingersh LC 500 N Broadway Ste 2000 Saint Louis MO 63102-2147 E-mail: wfalk@lewisrice.com.

FALKER, JOHN RICHARD, investment advisor; b. Detroit, July 15, 1940; s. John Jacob and Helen Katherine (Loeffler) F.; m. Mary Eileen Jacobsen, Nov. 10, 1964; children: Mary Anne, John R. Jr., Peter J. B.A. in English, U. Mich., 1962; M.B.A. in Fin., U. Detroit, 1980. With Chrysler Corp., Detroit, 1964-77; v.p., treas. Chrysler Fin. Corp., 1974-77; treas. Internat. Multifoods Corp., Mpls., 1977-87; founder, co-owner Swenson/Falker Assocs. Inc., 1987-95; owner FalkerInvestments, Inc., 1997—. Adj. prof. fin. U. St. Thomas, 1987-99. Served to lt. (j.g.) USNR, 1962-64. Mem. Am. Radio Relay League (life) Republican. Roman Catholic. Office: FalkerInvestments Inc TCF Tower 121 S 8th St Minneapolis MN 55402 E-mail: jack@falkerinvestments.com.

FALLER, SUSAN GROGAN, lawyer; b. Cin., Mar. 1, 1950; d. William M. and Jane (Eagen) Grogan; m. Kenneth R. Faller, June 8, 1973; children: Susan Elisabeth, Maura Christine, Julie Kathleen. BA, U. Cin., 1972; JD, U. Mich., 1975. Bar: Ohio 1975, Ky. 1989, U.S. Dist. Ct. (so. dist.) Ohio 1975, U.S. Ct. Claims 1982, U.S. Ct. Appeals (6th cir.) 1982, U.S. Supreme Ct. 1982, U.S. Tax Ct. 1984, U.S. Dist. Ct. (ea. dist.) Ky., 1991. Assoc.

Frost & Jacobs, Cin., 1975-82; ptnr. Frost & Jacobs LLP, 1982-2000; mem. Frost Brown Todd LLC, 2000—. Assoc. editor Mich. Law Rev., 1974-75; contbg. author: LDRC 50-State Survey of Media Libel and Privacy Law, 1982-93, LDRC 50-State Survey of Media Libel Law, 1999-, LDRC State Survey of Employment Libel and Privacy Law, 1999-. Bd. dirs. Summit Alumni Coun., Cin., 1983-85; trustee Newman Found., Cin., 1980-86, Cath. Social Svc., Cin., 1984-93, nominating com., 1985-88, sec., 1990; mem. Class XVII Leadership Cin., 1993-94; pres. emeritus, mem. exec. com., def. counsel sect. Libel Def. Resource Ctr., 2001; parish coun. St. Monica-St. George Ch., 1996-2000. Recipient Career Women of Achievement award YWCA, 1990. Mem. ABA (co-editor newsletter media litigation 1993-97), FBA, Ky. Bar Assn., No. Ky. Bar Assn., No. Ky. Women's Bar Assn., Ohio Bar Assn. (chair media law com.), Cin. Bar Assn. (com. mem.), Potter Stewart Inn of Ct., U. Cin. Alumni Assn., Arts & Scis. Alumni Assn. (bd. govs. U. Cin. Coll. 1988—), U. Mich. Alumni Assn., Mortar Bd., Leland Yacht Club, Lawyers Club, Coll. Club, Clifton Meadows Club, Phi Beta Kappa, Theta Phi Alpha. Roman Catholic. Home: 5 Belsaw Pl Cincinnati OH 45220-1104 Office: Frost Jacobs Todd LLC 2200 PNC Ctr 201 E 5th St Cincinnati OH 45202-4182

FALLON, PATRICK R. advertising executive; b. 1946; With Leo Burnett, Chgo., 1967-69, Stevson & Assocs., Mpls., 1969-76, v.p.; with Martin/Williams Advt., 1976-81, v.p.; chmn. bd. dirs. Fallon McElligott, Inc., 1981—. Office: Fallon-McElligott Inc Ste 2800 50 S 6th St Minneapolis MN 55402-1550

FALLS, JOSEPH FRANCIS, sportswriter, editor; b. N.Y.C., May 2, 1928; s. Edward and Anna (Zincak) F.; m. Mary Jane Erdei, Oct. 10, 1975; children by previous marriage: Robert, Kathleen, Susan, Janet, Michael. Grad. high sch. Reporter AP, N.Y.C., 1946-56; sports writer Detroit Times, 1956-60; sports editor, sports writer Detroit Free Press, 1960-78; sports writer Detroit News, 1978—. Author: Man in Motion, 1973, The Detroit Tigers, 1975, The Boston Marathon, 1977, So You Think You're A Die-Hard Tiger Fan, 1986, An Illustrated History, The Detroit Tigers, 1989, Daly Life, 1990, So You ove Tiger Stadium*Do Give It a Hug, Glory of Their Game; compact disc recs. include Echoes of Tiger Stadium, Echoes of Detroit Hockey Legents Tom 1220, Celebrating Michigan State's National Basketball Championship...In His Own Work. Elected to Mich. Hall of Fame, 2000; honored by Mich. Jewish Sports Hall of Fame, 2000. Mem. Baseball Writers Assn. Am. Office: Detroit News 615 W Lafayette Blvd Detroit MI 48226-3197

FALSGRAF, WILLIAM WENDELL, lawyer; b. Cleve., Nov. 10, 1933; s. Wendell A. and Catherine J. F.; children: Carl Douglas, Jeffrey Price, Catherine Louise. AB cum laude, Amherst Coll., 1955, LLD (hon.), 1986; JD, Case Western Res. U., 1958. Bar: Ohio 1958, U.S. Supreme Ct. 1972. Ptnr. Baker & Hostetler, Cleve., 1971—; ret. Chmn. vis. com. Case Western Res. U. Law Sch., 1973-76; trustee Case Western Reserve U., 1978-90, chmn. bd. overseers, 1977-78; trustee Cleve. Health Mus., 1975-90, Hirom Coll., 1989—; chmn. bd. trustees Hiram Coll., 1990-99. Recipient Disting. Service award; named Outstanding Young Man of Year Cleve. Jr. C. of C., 1962. Fellow Am. Bar Found., Ohio Bar Found.; mem. ABA (chmn. young lawyers sect. 1966-67, mem. ho. of dels. 1967-68, 70—, bd. govs. 1971-75, pres. 1985-86, bd. dirs. Am. Bar Endowment 1974-84, 87-97), Am. Bar Ins. Plans Cons. (pres. 1991—), Ohio Bar Assn. (mem. coun. of dels. 1968-70), Cleve. Bar Assn. (trustee 1979-82), Amherst Alumni Assn. (pres. N.E. Ohio 1964), The Country Club, LaPaloma Country Club. Home: 616 North St Chagrin Falls OH 44022-2514 Office: Baker & Hostetler LLP 3200 National City Ctr Cleveland OH 44114-3485 E-mail: wfalsgraf@bakerlaw.com.

FAN, LIANG-SHIH, chemical engineering educator; Chmn., disting. univ. prof. dept. chem. engring. Ohio State U., Columbus. Recipient Thomas Baron award in fluid-particle sys. AIChE, 1994, Alpha Chi Sigma award AIChE, 1996, Union Carbide Lectureship award Chem. Engring. Divsn. ASEE, 1999. Mem. Nat. Acad. Engring. Office: Ohio State U Dept Chem Engring 140 W 19th Ave Columbus OH 43210-1110

FANCHER, ROBERT BURNEY, electric utility executive, entrepreneur; b. Wharton, Ark., Dec. 13, 1940; s. Robert Burney and Lillian Olga (Steele) F.; m. Patricia Elizabeth Donahae, Mar. 25, 1967; children: Terri Michele, John Robert, Samuel Joseph. BSEE, Okla. State U., 1966; MSEE, U. Ark., 1971. Registered profl. engr., Mo. Enlisted as airman USAF, 1960, commd. 2d lt., 1966, advanced through grades to capt., 1969, electronics officer Md., 1967-70, resigned, 1970; engr. Empire Dist. Electric Co., Joplin, Mo., 1972-75, rate engr., 1975-76, dir. computer services, 1976-77, dir. corp. services, 1977-84, v.p. corp. services, 1984-95; v.p. fin., 1995—. Deacon Villa Heights Christian Ch., Joplin, 1975-86, elder, 1987—. Named Young Engr. of Yr., Southwest Chpt. Mo. Soc. Profl. Engrs., 1976. Mem. Soc. Profl. Engrs. (S.W. Mo. chpt. pres. 1978-79), Ark. Acad. Elec. Engring. (pres. 1989), Edison Electric Inst. (rate com., strategic planning com., fin. com.), Mo. Valley Electric Assn., Rotary (bd. dirs. 1992—, sec.-treas. 1993-94, pres.-elect 1994-95, pres. 1995-96). Republican. Avocations: photography, golf. Home: 2519 S Kingsdale St Joplin MO 64804-1342 Office: Empire Dist Electric Co PO Box 127 Joplin MO 64802-0127

FANNING, EDWARD J. bank executive; BS in Acctg. and Fin., No. Ill. U., 1980; MBA in Fin. and Managerial Econ., Northwestern U. CPA, CMA. With McGladrey, Hendrickson and Co., CPA's, Sundstrand Corp., Harris Trust and Savings Bank, PaineWebber, Inc., Delta Mgmt. Group, LP; founder, pres. Strategic Fin. Assocs.; prin. Franklin St. Equity Partners, Inc.; sr. v.p., group head corp. fin. group Provident Capital Corp., 1997—.

FANNING, RONALD HEATH, architect, engineer; b. Evanston, Ill., Oct. 5, 1935; s. Ralph Richard and Leone Agatha (Heath) F.; m. Jenine Vivian Schnelle, Jan. 9, 1960; children: Anthony Lee, Traycee Anne. BArch, Miami U., Oxford, Ohio, 1959. Registered architect in 24 states; registered profl. engr. in 13 states Nat. Coun. of Archtl. Registration Bds., Nat. Coun. of Engring. Examiners. Chmn. bd. Fanning/Howey Assocs., Inc., Celina, Ohio, 1959—. Mng. ptnr. Manning Partnership, Celina 1978—, F/H Bldg. Partnership, 1986—. Chmn. Mercer County Young Reps., Celina, 1962-65. Recipient Fred B. Joyner Profl. Achievement award Delta Gamma chpt. Pi Kappa Alpha, 1997. Mem. NSPE, Am. Inst. Architects, Coun. Ednl. Facility Planners Internat. (Great Lakes Midwest regional membership chmn. 1992-97, pres. Great Lakes Midwest region coun. ednl. facility planners internat. 1997-98), Ohio Soc. Profl. Engrs., Ohio Soc. Architects, Soc. Mktg. Profl. Svcs., Fla. Ednl. Facilities Planners Assn., Buckeye Assn. Sch. Adminstrs., Coun. Ednl. Faculty Planners Internat. (membership chmn. 1994-96, dir., 1997—, cert.). Methodist. Avocations: tennis, bowling, golf. Home: 422 Magnolia St Celina OH 45822-1254 Office: Fanning Howey Assoc Inc PO Box 71 Celina OH 45822-0071 E-mail: rfanning@fhai.com.

FANTA, PAUL EDWARD, chemist, educator; b. Chgo., July 24, 1921; s. Joseph and Marie (Zitnik) F.; m. LaVergne Danek, Sept. 3, 1949; children— David, John. B.S., U. Ill., 1942; Ph.D., U. Rochester, 1946. Postdoctoral research fellow U. Rochester, 1946-47; instr. Harvard, 1947-48; mem. faculty Ill. Inst. Tech., 1948—, prof. chemistry, 1961-84, prof. emeritus, 1984—. Exchange scholar Czechoslovak Acad. Sci., Prague, 1963-64, Soviet Acad. Sci., Moscow, 1970-71 Contbr. articles to profl. jours. NSF fellow Imperial Coll., London, Eng., 1956-57 Mem. Am. Chem. Soc., Sigma Xi, Phi Lambda Upsilon. Home: 947 Clinton Ave Oak Park IL 60304-1821

FANTIN, ARLINE MARIE, state legislator; b. Hammond, Ind., Sept. 26, 1937; Ill. state rep. Dist. 29, 1995-99; twp. assessor Thornton Twp., South Holland, Ill., 1994—. Address: Fantin State Rep 109 Foresdale Park Calumet City IL 60409-5309

FARAH, CAESAR ELIE, Middle Eastern and Islamic studies educator; b. Portland, Oreg., Mar. 13, 1929; s. Sam Khalil and Lawrice Farah; m. Irmgard Tenkamp, Dec. 13, 1987; 1 child Elizabeth ;children from previous marriage: Ronald, Christopher, Ramsey, Laurence, Raymond, Alexandra. Student, Internat. Coll. Am. U. Beirut, 1941-46; B.A., Stanford U., 1952; M.A., Princeton U., 1955, Ph.D., 1957. Pub. affairs asst., cultural affairs officer ednl. exchanges USIS, New Delhi, 1957-58, Karachi, Pakistan, 1958; asst. to chief Bur. Cultural Affairs, Washington, 1959; asst. prof. history and Semitic langs. Portland State U., 1959-63; asst. prof. history Calif. State U.-Los Angeles, 1963-64; assoc. prof. Near Eastern studies Ind. U., Bloomington, 1964-69; prof. Middle Eastern and Islamic history U. Minn., Mpls., 1969—, chmn. South Asian and Middle Eastern studies, 1988-91. Guest lectr. Fgn. Ministry, Spain, Iraq, Iran, Ministry Higher Edn., Saudi Arabia, Yemen, Turkey, Kuwait, Qatar, Tunisia, Morocco, Syrian Acad. Scis., Acad. Scis., Beijing; vis. scholar Cambridge U., 1974; resource person on Middle East media and svc. group, Minn., 1977—; bd. dirs., chmn. Upper Midwest Consortium for Middle East Outreach, 1980—; vis. prof. Harvard U., 1964, 65, Sanaa U., Yemen, 1984, Karl-Franzens U. Austria, 1990, 91, 1997—98, Ludwig-Maximilian U., Munich, 1992—93; vis. Fulbright-Hays scholar U. Damascus, 1994; vis. lectr. Am. U. Beirut, 2001; exec. sec., editor Am. inst. Yemeni Studies, 1982—86; sec.-gen., exec. bd. dirs. Internat. Com. for Pre-Ottoman & Ottoman Studies, 1988—2000, v.p., 2000—; fellow Rsch. Ctr. Islamic History, Istanbul, 1993, Ctr. Lebanese Studies & St. Anthony Coll., Oxford, England, 1994; vis. cons. Sultan Qaboos U., Oman, 2000. Author: (book) The Addendum in Medieval Arabic Historiography, 1968, Islam: Beliefs and Observances, 5th edit., 1994, Islam: Beliefs and Observances, 6th edit., 2000, Eternal Message of Muhammad, 1964, Eternal Message of Muhammad, 3d edit., 1981, Tarikh Baghdad li-Ibn-al-Najjar, 3 vols., 1980—83, Tarikh Baghdad li-Ibn-al-Najjar, 2d edit., 1986, al-Ghazali on Abstinence in Islam, 1992, Decision Making in the Ottoman Empire, 1992, The Road to Intervention: Fiscal Policies in Ottoman Mount Lebanon, 1992, The Politics of Interventionism in Ottoman Lebanon, 2000, The Sultan's Yemen, 2002; contbr. articles to profl. jours.; mem. editl. bd.: Digest of Middle East Studies. Mem. Oreg. Rep. Committeeman, 1960—64. Named Fulbright-Hayes lectr., 1993—94; recipient cert. of merit, Syrian Minstiry Higher Edn.; fellow, Am. Coun. Learned Socs., 1953, Am. Rsch. Ctr. Egypt, 1966—67, Fulbright Tgn. and Rsch., Germany, 1992—93, Ford Found., 1966, Am. Philos. Soc., 1970—71; grantee Participants Program, Dept. State Am., 1981, 1984, 1984, 1993, Minn. Humanities Commn., 1981, 1985, 1989, 1995, 1998, 2001, Am. Inst. Yemeni Studies, 1999, Coun. Am. Overseas Rsch. Ctrs., 2000, Travel to Collection, NEH, 1989, others; scholar Fulbright Rsch., 1966—67, 1985—86. Mem.: Turkish Studies Assn., Am. Assn. Tchrs. Arabic (exec. bd.), Mid. East Studies Assn. N.Am., Am. Hist. Assn., Royal Asiatic Soc. Gt. Britain, Am. Oriental Soc., Stanford U. Alumni Assn. (Leadership Recognition award), Princeton Club, Stanford Club Minn. (dir., pres. 1979), Phi Alpha Theta, Pi Sigma Alpha. Greek Orthodox. Home: 5125 Blake Rd S Edina MN 55436-1125 Office: Univ Minn 839 Soc Sci Towers Minneapolis MN 55455 Fax: 612-624-9383. E-mail: farah001@tc.umn.edu.

FARBER, BERNARD JOHN, lawyer; b. London, Feb. 27, 1948; came to U.S., 1949; s. Solomon and Regina (Wachter) F.; m. Mary Lee Mueller, Feb. 14, 1987; children: Zachary, Anne. BS, U. of State of N.Y., Albany, 1978; JD, Ill. Inst. Tech., 1983. Bar: Ill. 1983, U.S. Dist. Ct. (no. dist.) Ill. 1983, U.S. Ct. Appeals (7th cir.) 1985, U.S. Tax Ct. 1986, U.S. Ct. Mil. Appeals 1986, U.S. Supreme Ct. 1987, U.S. Ct. Appeals (6th cir.) 1988, U.S. Ct. Appeals (4th cir.) 1989, U.S. Ct. Appeals (11th cir.) 1990. Instr. legal writing Chgo.-Kent Law Sch. Ill. Inst. Tech., 1983-85, computer rsch. atty., 1985-86, adj. prof. law, 1987—; legal editor Longman Fin. Svcs., Chgo., 1986-87; rsch. counsel publs. Ams. for Effective Law Enforcement, 1987—. Instr. Law Scholastic Aptitude Test; preparation course BAR/BRI, Chgo., 1984-88; v.p. Brickton Montessori Sch., Chgo., 1992-93; sec. bd. dirs., 1993-95. Mng. editor: Chgo.-Kent Law Rev., 1981-82, editor-in-chief, 1982-83; co-author: Protective Security Law, 1996; editor: (with others) Dow Jones-Irwin Handbook of Micro Computer Applications in Law, 1987, Illinois Law of Criminal Investigation, 1986; contbr. articles to profl. jours. Elected mem. Local Sch. Coun., Agassiz Elem. Sch., Chgo., 1996—, chmn., 1999—. Mem. ABA, Ill. State Bar Assn., Chgo. Bar Assn., Sci. Fiction Rsch. Assn., Mensa. Avocations: history, computers, science fiction. Home and Office: 1126 W Wolfram St Rear Chicago IL 60657-4330 E-mail: bernfarber@aol.com., bernardjfarber@voyager.net.

FARICY, RICHARD THOMAS, architect; b. St. Paul, June 1, 1928; s. Roland J. and Clare (Sullivan) F.; m. Carole Murphy, June 24, 1961; children: Althea, Bridget. Registered architect, Minn., Wis., N.D., Colo., N.Mex., Fla., Tex., Okla., Ohio. V.p. The Cerny Assocs., Mpls., 1961-71; exec. v.p. Winsor/Faricy Architects, Inc., St. Paul, 1971-96; founding prin. Symmes Maini McKee Assoc./Winsor Faricy, 1996—. Pres. Minn. Archtl. Found., 1986; trustee Am. Mus. Asmat Art, 1995—. Prin. works include: Raughurst Libr., Jamestown, N.C., Warren E. Burger Libr. at William Mitchell Coll. Law, St. Paul, Collier County Courthouse, Naples, Fla., Bandana Sq., St. Paul, Como Park Conservatory Restoration, St. Paul, Earl Brown Heritage Ctr., Brooklyn Center, Minn. Pres. Merrick Community Ctr., St. Paul, 1969; pres. Ramsey County Hist. Soc., 1981-82; chmn. Blue Cross Blue Shield Minn., 1974-77, HMO Minn., 1974-76; bd. dirs. Minn. State Arts Bd., 1988-94, HealthEast Found., 1987-99, James J. Hill Reference Libr., 1996-99; bd. dirs. Friends St. Paul Pub. Libr., 19862000, pres., 1992-95; trustee Minn. Mus. Art, 1980-86; commr. St. Paul Heritage Preservation Commn., 1986-87; bd. zoning appeals, St. Paul, 2001-; vice chmn. Mounds Midway Found., 1987-91; bd. dirs. sponsor bd. Bapt. Hosp. Fund, 1991—. 1st lt. USAR, 1952-57. Fellow AIA (nat. housing com. 1984-92, trustee AIA Benefit Ins. Trust 1986-89); mem. Minn. Soc. Architects (dir. 1973-77, chair Ins. Trust 1984-86), St. Paul AIA (pres. 1974), St. Paul Athletic Club (pres. 1980), Minn. Club (St. Paul). Home: 2211 St Clair Ave Saint Paul MN 55105-1136 Office: Collaborative Design Group Inc Ste 300 1501 Washington Ave South Minneapolis MN 55454 E-mail: rfaricy@collaborativedesigngroup.com.

FARLEY, JERRY B. academic administrator; m. Susan Farley. BS in Fin. and Acctg., U. Okla., 1968; MBA, Okla. U., 1972. V.p. bus. and fin. Okla. State U., 1986; CFO Okla. U., Oklahoma City, v.p. adminstrn. and fin., 1994; pres. Washburn U., Topeka, 1997—. Named No. 4 most powerful Topekan, Topeka Capital-Jour., 2000. Office: Washburn U Office of Pres 1700 SW College Ave MO 202 Topeka KS 66621

FARMAKIS, GEORGE LEONARD, education educator; b. Clarksburg, W.Va., June 30, 1925; s. Michael and Pipitsa (Roussopoulos) F. BA, Wayne State U., 1949, MEd, 1950, MA, 1966, PhD, 1971; MA, U. Mich., 1978; postgrad., Columbia U., Yale U., Queens Coll. Tchr. audio-visual aids dir. Roseville (Mich.) Pub. Schs., 1951-57; tchr. Birmingham (Mich.) Pub. Schs., 1957-61, Highland Park (Mich.) Pub. Schs., 1961-90; substitute tchr. Grosse Pointe Pub. Schs., 1990—. Lectr. Oakland County C.C., 1990-92, Lawrence U., 1990-98, Oakland U., 2000—; instr. Highland Park C.C., 1966-68, Wayne County C.C., 1969-70; assoc. mem. grad. faculty Coll. Edn. Wayne State U., 1988-89; founder Ford Sch. Math. High Intensity Tutoring Program, 1971; chairperson Highland Park Sch. Dist. Curriculum Coun. and Profl. Staff Devel. Governing Bd., 1979-82; pres. Mich. Coun. Social Studies, 1985-86; founder, dir. Mich. Social Studies Olympiad, 1987; founder, editor Mich. Social Studies Jour., 1986; participant ESEA Title I/Nat. Diffusion Network. Author, translator: Letters of Nicholas Gysis, 1842-1901; co-author: Michigan School Finance Curriculum Guide; contbr. poems to books of poetry, articles to Focus jour. Cpl. USNG, 1948-51. Recipient spl. commendation Office of Edn., 1978, Outstanding Svc. award Nat. Coun. Social Studies, 1987, Presdl. award Mich. Coun. Social Studies, 1988, 96. Mem. ASCD (bd. dirs. Mich. chpt. 1983-86), Internat. Reading Assn., Am. History Assn., Nat. Coun. Social Studies (pres. SIG-CASE 1987-88, pres. JESIG 1988-89), Am. Philol. Assn., U. Mich. Alumni Assn., Wayne State U. Coll. Edn. Alumni Assn. (bd. dirs. 1985-86), Mich. Reading Assn., Masons (32 degree), Shriners, Ancient Accepted Scottish Rite, Phi Delta Kappa (Outstanding Educators award 1988). Greek Orthodox. Home: 15215 Windmill Dr Macomb MI 48044-4929

FARMER, MIKE, state legislator; m. Jean Farmer. Sys. analyst, 1980-2000; mem. Kans. State Ho. of Reps. Dist. 87, 1993-2000; exec. dir. Kans. Cath. Conf., 2000—.

FARMER, NANCY, state official; b. Jacksonville, Ill. Student, Ill. Coll., 1979—. Exec. dir. Skinker-DeBaliviere Cmty. Coun.; state rep. dist. 64 Mo. Ho. of Reps., 1993—2001; treas. State of Mo., 2001—. Mem. Woman's Polit. Caucus Mo. Ho. of Reps. Active Woman's Com. Forest Park, Rosedale Neighborhood Assn., mem. exec. com.; active West End Arts Coun.; card. for treas. State of Mo., 2000. Mem. Ctrl. West End Assn., Women Legislators Mo. Office: PO Box 210 Jefferson City MO 65102

FARMER, RICHARD T. uniform rental and sales executive; b. Dayton, Ky., Nov. 22, 1934; BBA, Miami U., Ohio, 1956. Chmn. bd. Cintas Corp., Cin. Office: Cintas Corp 6800 Cintas Blvd PO Box 625737 Cincinnati OH 45262-5737

FARMER, SCOTT D. apparel executive; BA, Miami U., 1981. V.p. mktg. & merchandising Cintas Sales Corp., Cin., v.p. nat. account divsn., pres., 1992-94, CEO, 1994—, also chmn. bd. dirs. Office: Cintas Sales Corp 6800 Cintas Blvd Cincinnati OH 45262

FARR, LEONARD ALFRED, hospital administrator; b. Pleasant Hill, La., Mar. 19, 1947; BA, La. State U., 1969; MA, Washington U., 1974. Adminstr. resident HCA Wesley Med. Ctr., Wichita, Kans., 1973-74, night adminstr., 1974-75; asst. adminstr. Physicians & Surgeons Hosp., Shreveport, La., 1975, exec. v.p., 1975-76; adminstr. Colo. Springs. (Colo.) Community Hosp., 1976-78; pres., CEO St. Francis Hosp. Systems, Colo. Springs, Colo., 1978-87; COO Penrose-St. Francis Hosp., 1987-91, pres., CEO, 1991—; s.r. v.p. United HealthCare, Mpls., 1997; COO ret. and sr. svcs. Ovations, a UnitedHealth Group Co., 1997—; pres. Small Bus. Group United Healthcare, 1999—. Mem. Am. Hosp. Assn. (alternate del., del.), Colo. Hosp. Assn. (chmn. bd.). Office: United Health Group Mail Stop MN008 W319 PO Box 1459 Minneapolis MN 55440-1459

FARR, MEL, automotive sales executive, former professional football player; b. Beaumont, Tex., Nov. 2, 1944; BS, UCLA. CEO Mel Farr Automotive Group, Mich., Ohio, Tex. and Md.; prin. Triple M Fin. Co. With Detroit Lions, 1967-73; mem. NFL Players Adv. Bd., 1990-92. Named to UCLA Sports Hall of Fame, 1988, NFL Rookie of Yr., Most Valuable Offensive Player, 1967, Most Valuable Offensive Player, 1968.

FARRAKHAN, LOUIS, religious leader; b. N.Y.C., May 11, 1933; changed name from Louis Eugene Wolcott to Louis X, then to Louis Farrakhan; m. Betsy Wolcott; 9 children. Student, Winston-Salem (N.C.) Tchrs. Coll. Formerly leader of Harlem mosque Nation of Islam, N.Y.C., nat. spokesman, founder reorganized orgn., 1977. Office: Nation of Islam 7351 S Stony Island Ave Chicago IL 60649-3106

FARRAND, WILLIAM RICHARD, geology educator; b. Columbus, Ohio, Apr. 27, 1931; s. Harvey Ashley and Esther Evelyn (Bowman) F.; m. Claudine Brickmann, Aug. 17, 1962 (div. 1983); children: Frederic Hervé, Anne Marie; m. Carola Hill Stearns, Dec. 6, 1988; 1 child, Michelle Diane. BS in Geology, Ohio State U., 1955, MS in Geology, 1956; PhD, U. Mich., 1960. Rsch. assoc. Lamont Geol. Obs. Columbia U., N.Y., 1960-61, asst. prof., 1961-64; rsch. assoc. in geology U. Mich., Ann Arbor, 1962; postdoctoral rsch. fellow NAS/NRC, Strasbourg, France, 1963-64; asst. prof. geol. scis. U. Mich., Ann Arbor, 1965-67, assoc. prof. geol scis., 1967-74, prof., 1974-2000, prof. emeritus, 2000—, curator analytical collections Mus. Anthropology, 1975-2000, dir. Exhibit Mus., 1993-2000. Vis. prof. U. Strasbourg, France, 1964-65, Hebrew U., Jerusalem, 1971-72, U. Colo., Boulder, 1983, U. Tex., Austin, 1986; fellow Inst. for Advanced Study, Ind. U., 1985; mem. archaeometry panel NSF, 1989-91; apptd. mem. U.S. Nat. com. Internat. Quaternary Assn., 1989-99, chair, 1995-99; sr. fellow Inst. for Study Earth and Man, So. Meth. U., Dallas, 1991—. Mem. editorial bd. Quaternary Sci. Review, Paleorient, Jour. Archaeological Sci., Review Archaeology, Stratigraphica Archaeologica; contbr. articles and maps to profl jours. With U.S. Army, 1951-53. Fellow AAAS, Geol. Soc. Am. (mem. panel quaternary geology and geomorphology divsn. 1978, vice chmn. archaeological geology divsn, 1979, chmn, 1980, Archaeological Geology award 1986), Ohio Acad. Sci., 1994-96; mem. Am. Quaternary Assn. (sec. 1978-90, program chmn. biennial meeting 1980, pres. 1994-96), Mich. Acad. Sci., Arts and Letters, Internat. Union for Quaternary Rsch. (chmn. working group on Southwest Asia commn. paleoecology early man 1975-83), L'Assn. Francaise pour l'Etude de Quaternaire, Sigma Xi, Phi Beta Kappa. Office: U Mich Mus Anthropology 4016 Ruthven Mus Ann Arbor MI 48109-1079 E-mail: wfarrand@umich.edu.

FARRAR, STEPHEN PRESCOTT, glass products manufacturing executive; b. Concord, N.H., Jan. 27, 1944; s. Prescott Samuel and Katherine (Hitchcock) F.; m. Kathleen D. Clark, Dec. 28, 1968 (dec.); children: Sheila E. Bermudez, Stephen Prescott Jr.; m. Rose Marie Bucar, July 4, 1998. BA, Bowdoin Coll., 1965; MSFS, Georgetown U., 1967. Internat. economist U.S. Dept. Commerce, Washington, 1966-72, Office of Mngt. and Budget, Washington, 1972-80, chief econ. affairs br. IAD, 1980-86; dir. internat. econ. affairs NSC, 1986-88, spl. asst. to Pres. and sr. dir. internat. econ. affairs, 1988-89; dep. exec. sec. Econ. Policy Coun., The White House, 1989-92; spl. asst. to Pres. for Policy Devel. Office of Policy Devel., the White House, 1989-92; chief of staff Office of the U.S. Trade Rep., 1992-93; dir. internat. bus. Guardian Industries Corp., Auburn Hills, Mich., 1993—. Mem. Coun. on Fgn. Rels. Republican. Avocations: tennis, running. Office: Guardian Industries Corp 2300 Harmon Rd Auburn Hills MI 48326-1714 E-mail: steve_farrar@guardian.com.

FARRAR, THOMAS C. chemist, educator; b. Independence, Kans., Jan. 14, 1933; s. Otis C. and Agnes K. F.; m. Friedemarie L. Farrar, June 22, 1963; children: Michael, Christian, Gisela. BS in Math., Chemistry, Wichita State U., 1954; PhD in Chemistry, U. Ill., 1959. NSF fellow Cambridge U., Eng., 1959-61; prof. chemistry U. Oregon, Eugene, 1961-63; chief, magnetism sect. Nat. Bur. Standards, Washington, 1963-71; dir. R & D Japan Electron Optics Lab., Cranford, N.J., 1971-75; dir. instr. NSF, Washington, 1975-79; prof. chemistry U. Wis., Madison, 1979—. Chmn. adv. com. MIT Nat. Magnetics Lab., Cambridge, Mass., 1979-84. Author: Introduction to Pulse NMR Spectros, 1989, Density Matrix Theory, 1995; contbr. over 120 articles to profl. jours. Recipient Silver medal Dept. Commerce, Washington, 1971, Silver medal Nat. Science Found., Washington, 1979. Fellow Wash. Acad. Science; mem. Am. Chem. Soc. (sec.-treas. Wis. sect. 1986-89), Am. Physical Soc. Office: Univ Wis Dept Chemistry 1101 University Ave Madison WI 53706-1322 E-mail: tfarrar@chem.wisc.edu.

FARRELL, DAVID COAKLEY, former department store executive; b. Chgo., June 14, 1933; s. Daniel A. and Anne D. (O'Malley) F.; m. Betty J. Ross, July 9, 1955; children: Mark, Lisa, David. B.A., Antioch Coll., Yellow Springs, Ohio, 1956. Asst. buyer, buyer, br. store gen. mgr., mdse. mgr. Kaufmann's, Pitts., 1956-66, v.p., gen. mdse. mgr., 1966-69, pres., 1969-74; v.p. May Dept. Stores Co., St. Louis, 1969-75, dir., 1974-98, chief operating officer, 1975-79, pres., 1975-85, chief exec. officer, 1979-98, chmn., 1985-98, ret., 1998. Bd. dirs. Emerson Elec. Co., Ralston Purina Co., St. Louis. Bd. dirs. St. Louis Symphony Soc., St. Louis Area Coun. Boy Scouts Am.; bd. govs. Lauder Inst. of Mgmt. and Internat. Studies, The Wharton Sch. U. Pa., Washington U., St. Louis; mem. Bus. Com. for Arts, Civic Progress. Mem. Links Club, Penn Club, Sky Club, Univ. Club (N.Y.C.), Bogey Club, Noonday Club, Racquet Club (St. Louis), St. Louis Country Club. Roman Catholic.

FARRELL, PHILIP M. physician, educator, researcher; b. St. Louis, Nov. 26, 1943; m. Alice Yeakle; children: Michael Henry, David Sean, Bridget Mary A.B., St. Louis U., 1964, M.D., Ph.D., St. Louis U., 1970. Diplomate Am. Bd. Pediatrics. Asst. prof. dept. child health Washington U., Washington, 1975; asst. prof. dept. pediatrics U. Wis., Madison, 1977-78, assoc. prof. pediatrics, 1978-82, prof. pediatrics, 1982—, chmn. dept. pediatrics, 1985-95, affiliate scientist Wis. Regional Primate Research Ctr., 1978, affiliate faculty dept. nutrition scis., 1978, dir. Pediatric Pulmonary Specialized Ctr. of Research, 1981-85, co-dir. Cystic Fibrosis Ctr., 1983-85, dean Med. Sch., 1995—. Sr. investigator pediatric metabolism br. Nat. Inst. Arthritis, Metabolism and Digestive Diseases NIH, Bethesda, Md., 1974-75, chief sect. on devel. biology and clin. nutrition Neonatal and Pediatric Medicine br. Nat. Inst. Child Health and Human Devel., 1975, chief Neonatal and Pediatric Medicine br., 1975 Editor: Lung Development: Biological and Clinical Perspectives, 1982 Avalon Found. scholar, 1965-67, Thurston Meml. scholar, 1966-70; Fogarty Internat. fellow, 1985 Mem. Am. Chem. Soc., Am. Acad. Pediatrics, Soc. Pediatric Research, Am. Thoracic Soc., Soc. Exptl. Biology and Medicine, Am. Inst. Nutrition, Am. Soc. Clin. Nutrition, Wis. Assn. Perinatal Care, Sigma XI, Phi Beta Kappa, Alpha Omega Alpha. Office: Univ Wis Office of Dean 1300 University Ave Rm 1217 Madison WI 53706-1510

FARRELL, W. JAMES, metal products manufacturing company executive; b. N.Y.C., 1942; BA, U. Detroit, 1965. Salesman Ill. Tool Wks., Inc., Glenview, Ill., exec. v.p., pres., chmn. bd., chmn. bd., CEO, 1996—. Office: Illinois Tool Wks Inc 3600 W Lake Ave Glenview IL 60025-5811

FARRIS, CLYDE C. lawyer; b. Houston, May 24, 1943; BA, Tex. Tech U., 1966; JD, Washington U., 1973. Bar: Mo. 1973, U.S. Dist. Ct. (ea. dist.) Mo. 1974, U.S. Ct. Appeals (8th cir.) 1976, Ind. 1987, U.S. Supreme Ct. Mem. Copeland Thompson & Farris, PC, St. Louis. Instr. St. Louis U., 1976-77; mem. civil rules com. of the Mo. Supreme Ct., 1989—. Mem. St. Louis Commn. on Crime and Law Enforcement, 1975-77, Kirkwood Rotary Club, City of Kirkwood Tax Increment Financing Commn. Mem. ABA, ATLA, Mo. Bar, Mo. Assn. Trial Attys., Bar Assn. Met. St. Louis, Rotary. Office: Copeland Thompson & Farris PC 231 S Bemiston Ave Ste 1220 Saint Louis MO 63105-1914

FARRIS, PAUL LEONARD, agricultural economist; b. Vincennes, Ind., Nov. 10, 1919; s. James David and Fairy Julia (Kahre) F.; m. Rachel Joyce Rutherford, Aug. 16, 1953; children: Nancy, Paul, John, Carl. B.S., Purdue U., 1949; M.S., U. Ill., 1950; Ph.D., Harvard U., 1954. Asst. prof. agrl. econs. Purdue U., West Lafayette, Ind., 1952-56, assoc. prof., 1956-59, prof., 1959-90, prof. emeritus, 1990—, head dept. agrl. econs., 1973-82; agrl. economist Dept. Agr., Washington, 1962; project leader for meat and poultry Nat. Commn. Food Mktg., 1965-66. Editor: Market Structure Research, 1964, Future Frontiers in Agricultural Marketing Research, 1983; contbr. articles to profl. jours. Served with AUS and USAAF, 1941-46. Fellow Am. Agrl. Econs. Assn.; mem. Am. Econ. Assn. Home: 1510 Woodland Ave West Lafayette IN 47906-2376 Office: Purdue U Dept Agrl Econs West Lafayette IN 47907

FARRIS, THOMAS N. engineering educator, researcher; b. Daisetta, Tex., Sept. 29, 1959; s. Robert Quentin and Kathleen Ruth (Kelling) F.; m. Bernadette Paulson, May 9, 1982; children: Joanna K., John T., Steven Q., Andrew B., Daniel J. BSME cum laude, Rice U., 1982; MS in Theoretical And Applied Mechanics, Northwestern U., 1984, PhD, 1986. Asst. prof. aeronautics and astronautics Purdue U., West Lafayette, Ind., 1986-91, assoc. prof., 1991-94, prof., 1994—, head, 1998—. Reviewer in field. Contbr. articles to profl. jours. Roy scholar Rice U., 1981; Cabell fellow Northwestern U., 1982; NSF Presdl. Young Investigator, 1990; Japan Soc. for Promotion of Sci. fellow, 1991, ASME Newkirk award, 1992, Structures and Materials award ASME/Boeing, 1998. Mem. ASME (assoc. editor Jour. Tribology 1994-2000), AIAA (advisor 1988-93, assoc. editor Jour. Aircraft 1992-98), Soc. Tribologists and Lubrication (chmn. lubrication fund com. 1993-94), Inst. Mech. Engrs. (editl. bd. Jour. Strain Analysis 1998—). Avocations: basketball, running, reading, family. Home: 701 Crestview Pl West Lafayette IN 47906-2313 Office: Purdue U Sch Aeronautics & Astronautics 1282 Grisson Hall West Lafayette IN 47907-1282

FARRIS, TRUEMAN EARL, JR. retired newspaper editor; b. Sedalia, Mo., June 2, 1926; PhB in Journalism, Marquette U., Milw., 1948; MA in Polit. Sci., U. Wis.-Milw., 1989. Reporter Milw. Sentinel, 1945-62, asst. city editor, 1962-75, city editor, 1975-77, mng. editor, 1977-89. Juror Pulitzer Prizes, 1985-86; mem. dean's coun. Student Publs. Bd., Coll. of Comm., Journalism and Performing Arts, Marquette U., 1987-92; mem. bd. visitors U. Wis., Milw., 1991-2000; mem. commitment adv. panel, U. Wis., Milw., 2000; bd. dirs. Wis. Masonic Jour., Newspaper of State Grand Lodge, 1993—. Author series of stories: Japan, 1980. Served with U.S. Army, 1955 Recipient By-Line award Marquette U., 1987; named to Milw. Press Club Media Hall of Fame, 1989. Mem. AP Mng. Editors Assn. (dir. 1980-87, editor ann. reports 1979-85), Milw. Soc. Profl. Journalists (pres. 1982-83), Milw. Press Club (pres. 1968, several reporting awards, editorial writing award 1957, included Media Hall of Fame 1989), Civil War Round Table (sec.), Mil. Order Loyal Legion of U.S. (recorder). Methodist. Avocations: reading, genealogy, Civil War History. Home: 3192 S 80th St Milwaukee WI 53219-3501 Office: Milwaukee Sentinel PO Box 371 Milwaukee WI 53201-0371

FARROW, MARGARET ANN, state official; b. Kenosha, Wis., Nov. 28, 1934; d. William Charles and Margaret Ann (Horan) Nemitz; m. John Harvey Farrow, Dec. 29, 1956; children: John, William, Peter, Paul, Mark. Student, Rosary Coll., 1952-53; BS in Polit. Sci. and Edn., Marquette U., 1956, postgrad., 1975-77. Tchr. Archdiocese of Milw., 1956-57; trustee Elm Grove Village, Wis., 1976-81, pres., 1981-86; mem. Wis. Assembly, Madison, 1986-89, Wis. Senate from 33rd dist., Madison, 1989—2001; lt. gov. State of Wis., 2001—. Chair govt. effectiveness, 1998—, asst. majority leader, 1998; mem. joint com. on audit, 1993-97, mem. joint survey com. on tax exemptions, 1993-97, chair Wis. women's coun., 1991—, Rep. caucus chair, 1996, 99, mem. coun. on workforce excellence, 1995—, mem. Wis. glass ceiling commn., 1993—; mem. Senate Com. on edn., 1999, Senate com. on labor, 1999. Home: W 262 # 2402 Deer Haven Dr Pewaukee WI 53072-4572 Office: Wis State Capitol Rm 106 S PO Box 7882 Madison WI 53707-7882*

FARWELL, WALTER MAURICE, vocalist, educator; b. Sidney, Iowa, Mar. 29, 1928; s. Clyde Ross and Erma Leona (Liggett) F. B.Mus.Edn., U. Mo., Kansas City, 1950; MA, U. Iowa, 1953. Vocal music tchr. pub. schs., Fayette, Iowa, 1953-59; head voice tchr. Wartburg Coll., Waverly, 1960-61; vocal music tchr. pub. schs., Tipton, 1961-67, music educator Davenport, 1967-90. Choir dir. Meth. Ch., Fayette, Tipton, 1953—; vocal soloist, 1953—; organist Replacement Tng. Ctr., Ft. Bragg, N.C., 1951-52. Author: (4 vols.) History of Fremont County, Iowa, 1968-91; contbr.: Bells of Stony Creek, 1994; editor: Court Records Atchison County, Mo. (pamphlet), 1985; cons. (county history) Thumbprints in time, 1996; contbr. historical articles to profl. pubs. Cpl. U.S. Army, 1950-52. Recipient Am. Legion award, 1941. Mem. NEA, Davenport Area Ret. Tchrs. Assn., Fremont County Hist. Soc. (charter). Methodist. Avocation: historical and genealogical research. Home: 549 E 4th St Tipton IA 52772-1933 E-mail: farwellwalter@hotmail.com.

FASS, ROBERT J. epidemiologist, academic administrator; b. N.Y.C., Feb. 23, 1939; BS in Chemistry, Biology, Tufts U., 1960, MD, 1964; MS in Med. Microbiology, Ohio State U., 1971. Diplomate Am. Bd. Internal Medicine; licensed physician, Ohio, N.Y., Pa. Intern in mixed medicine Montefiore Hosp., N.Y.C., 1964-65, resident in medicine, 1965-66, Ohio State U., Columbus, 1968-69, fellow in infectious diseases, rsch. asst. in med. microbiology, 1969-71, clin. instr. medicine, 1970-71, asst. prof. medicine, 1971-75, asst. prof. med, microbiology, 1971-76, assoc. prof. medicine, 1975-80, assoc. prof. med. microbiology, 1976-80, prof. internal medicine, medical microbiology and immunology, 1980—, Samuel Saslaw prof. infectious diseases, 1991—, dir. divsn. infectious diseases, 1987—. Dir. infectious diseases fellowship tng. program Ohio State U., 1987-93, mem. task force on program evaluation Coll Medicine, 1973-75, search com. chmn. dept. med. microbiology, 1973-76, clin. curriculum devel. project, 1875-77, profl. adv. com. to med. illustations, 1975-85, vice chmn. practice plan com., 1979-85, trustee Med. Rsch. and Devel. Found., 1979-86, treas., 1979-85, assocs. medicine exec. com. dept. medicine, 1973-76, chmn., 1974-75, chmn. libr. com., 1973-78, bd. dirs. Dept. Medicine Found., 1987—, finance com., 1979-86, 91—, chmn., 1981-86, phase III module com. Med. Microbiology and Immunology divsn., 1973, 75, 76, 81, dir., 1976, 81, mem. infection control com. Univ. Hosp., 1972-77, exec. com., 1976-77, pharmacy and therapeutics com., 1981—, chmn. pharmacy and therapeutics antimicrobial com., 1984—, exec. com., 1984—; mem. infectious disease conf. Riverside Meth. Hosp., 1971-76; prin. investigator for Ohio State U. NIH AIDS Clin. Trials Group, 1987—, opportunistic info. com., 1987—, instl. evaluation com., 1989—; mem. internat. adv. bd. Bayer AG Auinolone Bd., 1985-93, Miles Inc. External Adv. Bd., 1988-93. Mem. editorial bd. Antimicrobial Agents and Chemotherapy, 1982-91, Quinolene Bulletin, 1989—; reviewer Am. Jour. Medicine, Am. Soc. Hosp. Pharmacists Drug Info., Antimicrobial Agents and Chemotherapy, Annals of Internal Medicine, Archives of Internal Medicine, Chest, Clin. Microbiology Revs., Jour. Infectious Diseases, Infectious Diseases in Clin. Practice, N.Y. State Jour. Medicine, Revs. Infectious Diseases, New England Jour. Medicine. Med. officer USAF, 1966-68. Fellow ACP, Infectious Diseases Soc. Am.; mem. AMA (reviewer AMA Drug Evaluations, Jour. AMA), Am. Fedn. Clin. Rsch., Am. Soc. for Microbiology, Am. Thoracic Soc., Ctrl. Soc. for Clin. Rsch., Inter-Am. Soc. for Chemotherapy, Brit. Soc. Antimicrobial Chemotherapy, Columbus Soc. Internal Medicine (sec.-treas. 1979, pres. 1980). Achievements include research in laboratory predictors of antimicrobial efficacy, pathogenesis of anaerobic and mixed bacterial infections, antibiotic susceptibility testing and resistance, antimicrobial agents in clinical, pharmacological and laboratory studies, biology and significance of cell-wall defective bacteria, infective endocarditis, AIDS. Office: Ohio State U Med Ctr 4715 Univ Hosp Clinic 456 W 10th Ave Columbus OH 43210-1240

FAST, DARRELL WAYNE, minister; b. Mountain Lake, Minn., Sept. 5, 1939; s. Henry L. and Anna R. (Rempel) F.; m. Loretta J. Janzen, Aug. 20, 1966; children: Douglas Henry, Larissa Ann. BA, U. Nebr., 1963; BD, Mennonite Biblical Sem., 1966; MTh, Emmanuel Coll., 1977, DMin, 1986. Ordained minister Mennonite Ch., 1970. Mem. conf. staff Gen. Conf. Offices Mennonite Ch., Newton, Kans., 1966-70; pastor Toronto (Ont., Can.) United Mennonite Ch., 1970-86, Bethel Coll. Mennonite Ch., North Newton, Kans., 1986—. Moderator Gen. Conf. Mennonite Ch., Newton, 1992—; sec. United Mennonite Chs. of Ont., Toronto, 1972-78. Mem. Leadership Newton, Newton C. of C., 1989; pres. Ministerial Alliance, Newton, 1989-90; mem. exec. com. Man to Man Ont., Toronto, 1972-82; trustee Mennonite Biblican Sem., Elkhart, Ind., 1980-92. Mem. Rotary. Avocations: tennis, chorale singing. Office: Bethel Coll Mennonite Ch 2600 College Ave PO Box 364 North Newton KS 67117-0364

FAUGHT, HAROLD FRANKLIN, electrical equipment manufacturing company executive; b. Washington, Oct. 16, 1924; s. Robert A.N. and Bessie I. (Towns) F.; m. Kathleen M. Quinn, June 21, 1947; 1 son, Richard H. B.M.E., Cornell U., 1945; M.M.E., U. Pa., 1951; grad. Advanced Mgmt. Program, Harvard U., 1961. Registered profl. engr., Pa. Div. gen. mgr. Westinghouse Electric Corp., 1946-69; sr. asst. postmaster gen. U.S. Postal Service, 1969-73; sr. v.p., cons. Emerson Electric Co., St. Louis, 1973—. Served with USNR, 1943-46. Mem. AIAA. Club: Old Warson Country (St. Louis). Home: 1527 Candish Ln Chesterfield MO 63017-5612 Office: Emerson Electric Co 8100 W Florissant Ave Saint Louis MO 63136-1494

FAULK, MARSHALL WILLIAM, professional football player; b. New Orleans, Feb. 26, 1973; Student, San Diego State U. Running back Indpls. Colts., 1994-99, St. Louis Rams, 1999—. Named to Sporting News Coll. All-Am. 1st Team, 1991-93, NFL Rookie of Year 1994; selected to Pro Bowl, 1994, named outstanding player, 1994. Office: c/o St Louis Rams One Rams Way Bridgeton MO 63045

FAULKNER, JOHN ARTHUR, physiologist, educator; b. Kingston, Ont., Can., Dec. 12, 1923; s. Jack and Winifred (Esdaile) F.; m. Margaret Isabelle Rowntree, Apr. 9, 1955; children: Laura Megan, Melanie Anne. B.A., Queen's U., 1949, B.P.H.E., 1950; M.S., U. Mich., 1956, Ph.D., 1962. Tchr. sci. Glebe Collegiate Inst., Ottawa, Ont., Can., 1952-56; asst. prof. phys. edn. U. Western Ont., 1956-60; asst. prof. edn. U. Mich., 1962-64, assoc. prof. edn., 1964-66, assoc. prof. physiology, 1966-71, prof. physiology, 1971—; rsch. scientist U. Mich. Inst. Gerontology, 1986—, acting dir., 1988-89, assoc. dir. biol. rsch. Inst. Gerontology, 1990—, interim dir., 1997-98. Assoc. editor Jour. Applied Physiology, 1991-93, Basic and Applied Myology, 1990—; contbr. articles on altitude acclimatization, cardiovascular response to swimming and running, skeletal muscles adaptation, mechanism of contraction-induced injury, regeneration of skeletal muscles following transplantation, injury and repair of muscle fibers following pliometric contractions, and contractile properties of muscles in aged rodents, mdx mice, and transgenic mdx mice, to profl. jours. Dir. Nathan Shock Ctr. for Basic Biology of Aging. Served as pilot RCAF, 1942-45, ETO. Burke Aaron Hinsdale scholar, 1962; recipient Glenn Edmonson award U. Mich., Established Investigators award Am. Physiol. Soc., EEP sect., 1998. Mem. Biol. Engring. (founding fellow), Gerontol. Soc. Am., Am. Coll. Sports Medicine (pres. 1971-72, Citation award 1978, Honor award 1992); mem. Biophys. Soc., Nat. Inst. Health (mem. respiration and applied physiology study sect. 1980-84, reviewers res. 1989—). Home: 2200 Navarre Cir Ann Arbor MI 48104-2759 Office: University of Michigan Institute of Gerontology 300 N Ingalls St Ann Arbor MI 48109-2007

FAURE, GUNTER, geology educator; b. Tallinn, Estonia, May 11, 1934; s. Arnulf and Stella (von Harpe) F.; m. Barbara L.L. Goodell, Sept. 5, 1959 (div. Feb. 1985); children: Mary Jennifer, John Eric, Pamela Anne, David Christopher; m. Teresa M. Mensing, June 4, 1988. B.Sc., U. Western Ont., 1957; Ph.D., MIT, 1961; fellow, Sch. Advanced Studies, 1961-62. Asst. prof. geology Ohio State U., 1962-65, assoc. prof., 1965-68, prof., 1968—2002, prof. emeritus, 2002—; field work Antarctica. Author: (with J.L. Powell) Strontium Isotope Geology, 1972, Principles of Isotope Geology, 1977, 2d edit., 1986, Principles and Applications of Geochemistry, 1991, 2d edit., 1998, Origin of Igneous Rocks, 2001; editor-in-chief Jour. Isotope Geoscience, 1983-88; exec. editor Geochimica et Cosmochimica Acta, 1989-97; assoc. editor Geochimica et Cosmochimica Acta, 1989-99; contbr. articles to profl. jours. Recipient univ. gold medal in honours geology U. Western Ont., 1957, disting. teaching award Ohio State U., 1970, 83, 99, Antarctic Service medal, 1976 Fellow Geol. Soc. Am., Geochem. Soc., European Assn. Geochemistry; mem. Planetary Soc., Meteoritical Soc., Internat. Assn. Geochemistry and Cosmochemistry (v.p. 1992-96, pres. 1996-2000, newsletter editor 1999—). Office: 125 S Oval Mall Columbus OH 43210-1308 E-mail: faure.1@osu.edu.

FAUTH, JOHN J. venture capitalist; Chmn., dir., pres., CEO Churchill Capital, Inc., Mpls. Office: Churchill Capital Inc 333 S 7th St Ste 2400 Minneapolis MN 55402-2435

FAVRE, BRETT LORENZO, professional football player; b. Pass Christian (Gulfport), Miss., Oct. 10, 1969; m. Deanna Tynes, July, 1996; 1 child, Brittany. Student, So. Miss. U., 1991. Quarterback Atlanta Falcons, 1991-92, Green Bay Packers, 1992—; first team all-pro Assoc. Press, 1995. MVP, East-West Shrine Game, All-American Bowl. Named to Pro Bowl Team, 1992, 93, 95, 96; named NFL MVP 1995. Office: Green Bay Packers PO Box 10628 Green Bay WI 54307-0628

FAW, MELVIN LEE, retired physician; b. Kansas City, Mo., Dec. 4, 1925; s. Floyd Butler and Ivalee Muriel (Harvey) F.; m. Anna Margaret Rose, July 17, 1948; children— Linda, Gary, David, Nancy; m. Rosemary Amelia Schoppert, Aug. 17, 2001. Student, U. Kans., 1943-44, Baylor U., 1945; BS magna cum laude, Washburn U., 1948; MD, Washington U., St. Louis, 1951. Diplomate Am. Bd. Internal Medicine. Intern Washington U. Service St. Louis City Hosp., 1951-52; asst. in medicine Washington U. Sch. Medicine, St. Louis, 1951-54; resident in internal medicine Washington U. Service St. Louis City Hosp., 1952-54, U. Kans. Hosp., Kansas City, 1954-55; practice medicine specializing in internal medicine and cardiology Welborn Clinic, Evansville, Ind., 1955-87, mng. ptnr., 1965-78. Pres. med. staff Welborn Hosp., 1980, chief medicine, 1958-64, dir. cardiovascular services, 1981-87; mem. So. Ind. Health Service Agy., 1976-80. Served with Inf. AUS, 1944-45 Decorated Bronze Star medal with V device oak leaf cluster, Purple Heart, Combat Infantryman Badge; recipient Disting. Service award U. Evansville, 1980 Fellow Am. Coll. Chest Physicians; mem. ACP, Am. Soc. Internal Medicine, AMA, Ind. Med. Assn., Vanderburgh County Med. Soc., Phi Kappa Phi Methodist. Home: 2400 E Chandler Ave Evansville IN 47714-2421 Office: Welborn Clinic 421 Chestnut St Evansville IN 47713-1297 E-mail: melfaw@aol.com.

FAWCETT, JOY LYNN, soccer player; b. Inglewood, Calif., Feb. 8, 1968; m. Walter Fawcett; children: Katelyn Rose, Carli. Degree in phys. edn., U. Calif., Berkeley, 1990. Women's soccer coach UCLA, 1993-97. Mem. U.S. Nat. Women's Soccer Team, 1987—, including 1991 World Cup, China, 1995 FIFA World Cup, Sweden, 1994 CONCACAF Qualifying Championship, Montreal, U.S. Olympic Festival, Denver, 1995, FIFA Women's World Cup, Sweden, 1995, gold medal U.S. Olympic team, 1996; mem. Ajax of Manhattan Beach Club Soccer Team (champions U.S. Women's Amateur Nat. Cup 1992, 93). Named to U. Calif. Berkeley Hall of Fame, 1997; 3-time All-Am., 1987-89; selected Most Valuable Player So. Calif., L.A. Times, 1987. Office: US Soccer Fedn 1801-1811 S Prairie Ave Chicago IL 60616

FAWCETT, SHERWOOD LUTHER, research laboratory executive; b. Youngstown, Ohio, Dec. 25, 1919; s. Luther T. and Clara (Sherwood) F.; m. Martha L. Simcox, Feb. 28, 1953; children: Paul, Judith, Tom. BS, Ohio State U., 1941; MS, Case Inst. Tech., 1948, PhD, 1950, Ohio State U., Gonzaga U., Whitman Coll., Otterbein Coll., Detroit Inst. Tech., Ohio Dominican Coll. Registered profl. engr., Ohio. Mem. staff Columbus Labs. Battelle Meml. Inst., 1950-64, mgr. physics dept., 1959-64; dir. Pacific Northwest Labs., Richland, Wash., 1964-67; trustee Battelle Meml. Inst., Columbus, Ohio, 1968-92, exec. v.p., 1967-68, CEO, 1968-84, pres., 1968-80, chmn., 1981-84, chmn. bd. trustees, 1985-87; assoc. trustee, 1987-94. Chmn. bd. dirs. Transmet Corp. With USNR, 1941-46. Decorated Bronze Star; recipient Washington award Western Soc. Engrs., 1989. Mem. AIME, NSPE, Am. Phys. Soc., Am. Nuclear Soc., Am. Phys. Soc., Sigma Xi, Tau Beta Pi, Delta Chi, Sigma Pi Sigma. Home: 1852A Riverside Dr Columbus OH 43212-1875 Office: Transmet Corp 4290 Perimeter Dr Columbus OH 43228-1036

FAWELL, HARRIS W. lawyer, former congressman; b. West Chicago, Ill., Mar. 25, 1929; m. Ruth Johnson, 1954; children: Richard, Jane, John. Student, Naperville North Ctrl. Coll., 1949; LLD, Chgo. Kent Coll. Law, 1952. Ptnr. Fawell, James & Brooks, Naperville, Ill., 1954—84; mem. Ill. Senate, Springfield, 1963—77; gen. counsel Ill. Assn. Park Dists., 1977—84; mem. 99th-105th Congresses from 13th Ill. dist., 1985—98; of counsel James, Gustafson & Thompson, 1999—. Mem. Edn. and the Workforce Com., chmn. subcom. on employer-employee rels.; mem. House Sci. Com. Office: 1001 E Chicago Ave Ste 103 Naperville IL 60540-5500

FAY, SISTER MAUREEN A. university president; BA in English magna cum laude, Siena Heights Coll., 1960; MA in English, U. Detroit, 1966; PhD, U. Chgo., 1976. Tchr. English, speech, moderator student newspaper, student council St. Paul High Sch., Grosse Pointe, Mich., 1960-64; chairperson English dept., dir. student dramatics, moderator student publs. Dominican High Sch., Detroit, 1964-69; co-dir. Cath. student ctr. Adrian (Mich.) Coll., 1969-71; instr. English Siena Heights Coll., Adrian, 1969-71; evaluators inst. criminal justice execs. U. Chgo., 1971-73; instr. English U. Ill., Chgo., 1971-74; dir. evaluation sch. new learning DePaul U., 1974-75; fellow in acad. adminstrn. Saint Xavier Coll., 1975-76, dean. grad. studies, 1979-83, dean continuing edn., 1976-83; asst. prof. No. Ill. U., Dekalb, 1980-83; pres. Mercy Coll. Detroit, 1983-90, U. Detroit Mercy, 1990—. V.p. VAUT Corp, bd. dirs. four inner city high schs., Archdiocese Chgo.; mem. exec. com. Assn. Mercy Colls.; adv. com. Adult Learning Svcs., The Coll. Bd., Met. Affairs Corp. of Detroit and S.E. Mich., cons. Nat. Assn. for Religious Women, 1974-75, North Cen. Assn. Colls. and Schs., evaluator commn. on higher edn.; trustee Rosary Coll., River Forest, Ill., New Detroit, Inc., 1993; emeritus mem. div. bd. Mercy Hosps. and Health Svcs. of Detroit; bd. dirs. Nat. Bank of Detroit., Detroit Econ. Growth Corp., 1992; mem. Nat. Commn. Ind. Higher Edn.; commr. North Centrl Assocs., Commn. on Instns. of Higher Edn., 1993. Asst. editor: (book rev.): Adult Education, A Journal of Research and Theory, 1971-74. Bd. dirs. United Way SE Mich., 1991, Assn. Catholic Colls. and Univs., 1992; Steering com. Metro Detroit GIVES; exec. com., edn. task force Detroit Strategic Planning com., 1987; trustee Mich. Opera Theatre; bd. dirs. Greater Detroit Interfaith Round Table Nat. Conf. Christians and Jews, Inc., The Detroit Symphony; mem. Nat. Bipartisan Commn. on Ind. Higher Edn. in U.S., 1993. Mem. Am. Assn. Higher Edn., North Cen. Assn. (cons., evaluator commn. on higher edn.), Nat. Assn. Ind. Colls. and Univs. (bd. dirs.), Assn. Ind. Colls. and Univs. of Mich. (exec. com., chairperson), Am. Assn. Cath. Colls. and Univs., AAUW, Pi Lambda Theta. Office: U Detroit Mercy Office Pres PO Box 19900 4001 W McNichols Rd Detroit MI 48219-0900

FAY, REGAN JOSEPH, lawyer; b. Cleve., Sept. 19, 1948; s. Robert J. and Loretta Ann (Regan) F.; married; children: John, Mary, Matthew, Jessica, Samantha. BS in Chem. Engring., MIT, 1970; JD with honors, George Washington U., 1974. Bar: Ohio 1974, U.S. Dist. Ct. (no. dist.) Ohio 1974, U.S. Patent Office 1973, U.S. Ct. Appeals (fed. cir.) 1974, U.S. Ct. Appeals (9th cir.) 1975, U.S. Dist. Ct. (ea. dist.) Wis. 1976, U.S. Dist.

Ct. (no. dist.) Tex. 1986, U.S. Supreme Ct. 1988. Patent examiner U.S. Patent and Trademark Office, Washington, 1970-72; law clk. to presiding justice U.S. Ct. Customs and Patent Appeals, 1973-75; assoc. Yount & Tarolli, Cleve., 1975-79; assoc., then ptnr. Jones, Day, Reavis & Pogue, 1979—. Lectr. patent and trademark law Case Western Res. U., Cleve., 1976-86. Mem. Cleve. Intellectual Property Law Assn (pres. 1996-97). Republican. Roman Catholic. Avocation: skiing. Office: Jones Day Reavis & Pogue 901 Lakeside Ave E Cleveland OH 44114-1190 E-mail: rjfay@jonesday.com.

FAY, TERRENCE MICHAEL, lawyer; b. Cleve., Feb. 25, 1953; s. J. Francis and Alice Wilsona (Porter) F.; m. Beverly Ann Luciow, Feb. 25, 1983; children: Robert Michael, Katherine Elizabeth. BA cum laude, Baldwin Wallace Coll., 1974, BS cum laude, 1975; JD, Ohio State U., 1978. Bar: Ohio 1978, U.S. Dist. Ct. (no. dist.) Ohio 1983, U.S. Dist. Ct. (so. dist.) Ohio 1987, U.S. Ct. Appeals (6th cir.) 1987, U.S. Dist. Ct. (no. dist.) Ind. 1992, U.S. Dist. Ct. (ea. dist.) Mich. 1993. Law clk. for chief adminstrv. law judge Ohio Power Siting Commn., Columbus, 1977-78; asst. atty. gen. environ. sect. Ohio Atty. Gen.'s Office, 1978-87, chief civil atty., 1987-88; sr. assoc. Smith & Schnacke, L.P.A., 1988-89, Benesch, Friedlander, Coplan & Aronoff, Columbus, 1989-90, ptnr., 1992—2001, chair hiring com., 1995—97; of counsel Frost, Brown Todd LLC, 2002—. Bd. dirs. Hucksters, Inc., Columbus, 1990. Abrahms scholar, 1975; recipient Book award Lawyers Coop., Inc., 1978, Ohio Gov.'s Spl. Recognition award, 1988. Mem. Phi Alpha Theta, Omicron Delta Kappa, Pi Kappa Delta, Psi Chi. Office: Frost Brown Todd LLC One Columbus Ste 1000 10 W Broad St Columbus OH 43215-3467 E-mail: tfay@ftblaw.com.

FAYNE, HENRY W. electric power industry executive; BS in Econs., Columbia Coll.; MBA, Columbia U. Asst. to commr. N.Y.C. Dept. Air Resources; asst. forecast analyst in contr.'s dept., contr., sr. v.p. corp. planning and budgeting, exec. v.p. fin. svcs. Am. Elec. Power, Inc., Columbus, Ohio, 1974-98, exec. v.p. fin. & analysis, CFO, 1998—. Bd. dirs. Am. Elec. Power, Inc. Office: Am Elec Power Inc 1 Riverside Plz Columbus OH 43215-2373

FAZIO, PETER VICTOR, JR. lawyer; b. Chgo., Jan. 22, 1940; s. Peter Victor and Marie Rose (LaMantia) F.; m. Patti Ann Campbell, Jan. 3, 1966; children: Patti-Marie, Catherine, Peter. AB, Coll. of Holy Cross, Worcester, Mass., 1961; JD, U. Mich., 1964. Bar: Ill. 1964, U.S. Dist. Ct. (no. dist.) Ill. 1965, U.S. Ct. Appeals (7th cir.) 1972, U.S. Supreme Ct. 1977, D.C. 1981, U.S. Ct. Appeals (D.C. cir.) 1988, Ind. 1993. Assoc. Schiff, Hardin & Waite, Chgo., 1964-70, ptnr., 1970-82, 84-95, mng. ptnr., 1995—2000; exec. v.p. Internat. Capital Equipment, 1982-83, also bd. dirs., 1982-85, sec., 1982-87; exec. v.p., gen. counsel NiSource Inc., 2000—. Bd. dirs. Planmetrics Inc., Chgo., 1984-92, Chgo. Lawyers Commn. for Civil Rights Under Law, 1976-82, co-chmn., 1978-80; bd. dirs. Seton Health Corp. No. Ill., Chgo 1987-90, vice chmn., 1989-90. Trustee Barat Coll., Lake Forest, Ill., 1977-82; bd. dirs. St. Joseph Hosp., Chgo., 1990-95, mem. exec. adv. bd., 1984-89, chmn., 1986-89; vice chmn. bd. dirs. Cath. Health Ptnrs., 1995-99, chmn., 1999—; dir. exec. com. Ill. Coalition, 1994—, N.W. Ind. Forum, 1994-98. Mem. ABA (coun. 1991-94, chmn. sect. pub. utility, transp. and comm. law 2000-01), FBA, Ill. Bar Assn., Chgo. Bar Assn., Fed. Energy Bar Assn., Edison Electric Inst. (chmn. legal com. 1999-2001), Am. Gas Assn. (legal com.), Am. Soc. Corp. Secs., Met. Club, Econ. Club Chgo., Comml. Club Chgo. Office: Schiff Hardin & Waite 6600 Sears Tower 233 S Wacker Dr Chicago IL 60606-6473

FAZIO, VICTOR WARREN, physician, colon and rectal surgeon; b. Sydney, Australia, Feb. 2, 1940; came to U.S., 1971; s. Victor Warren and Kathleen Eleanor (Hills) F.; m. Carolyn Kisandra Sawyer, Dec. 2, 1961; children: Victor, Jane, David. MB, BChir, U. Sydney, 1965, MS (hon.), 1997. Diplomate Am. Bd. Colon and Rectal Surgery (pres. 1991-92). Intern and resident St. Vincent's Hosp., Sydney, 1965-67, surgical registrar, 1969-71; lectr. anatomy U. NSW Med. Sch., 1967; surg. registrar Repatriation Gen. Hosp., Concord, Australia, 1968; gen. surgeon Australian Surg. Team, Bien Hoa, Vietnam, 1971; fellow gen. surgery Lahey Clinic, Boston, 1972; fellow colorectal surgery Cleve. Clinic, 1973, staff surgeon colorectal surgery, 1974, chmn. dept. colon and rectal surgery, vice chmn. divsn. surgery, 1975—. Bd. govs. Cleve. Clinic Found., 1990-95, 98-99, exec. mem. bd. trustees, 1994-95. Author 320 manuscripts and book chpts.; editor: Current Therapy in Colon and Rectal Surgery, 1989; editor-in-chief Diseases of Colon and Rectum, 1997—. Fellow ACS, Royal Australian Coll. Surgeons (hon.), Royal Australasian Coll. Surgeons, Am. Soc. Colon and Rectal Surgery (pres. 1995-96); mem. Soc. Pelvic Surgeons (exec. com. 1980), Soc. for Surgery Alimentary Tract, Ctrl. Surg. Assn., James IV Assn. Surgeons, Ohio Valley Soc. Colon and Rectal Surgeons (past pres.). Roman Catholic. Avocations: naval history, sailing. Office: Cleve Clinic Desk A-111 9500 Euclid Ave Cleveland OH 44195-0001

FEALY, ROBERT S. manufacturing executive; CFO Duchossois Industries, Elmhurst, Ill. Office: Duchossois Industries Inc 845 N Larch Ave Elmhurst IL 60126

FEATHER, WILLIAM L. corporate lawyer; BA, U Tex. Austin, 1969, JD, 1972. Bar: Tex. 1972, D.C. 1975, Ill. 1977. Gen. coun. Continental Can. Co., 1978-81; sr. coun. Wickes Co., Inc., 1981-82; sr. staff coun. Household Internat., Inc., 1982-86; sr. coun. Baxter Internat., Inc., 1986-95; asst. gen. counsel, 1995-96; assoc. gen. counsel; sr. v.p., sec., gen. counsel Allegiance Corp., McGaw Pk., Ill., 1996—. Office: Allegiance Corp 1430 Waukegan Rd Mc Gaw Park IL 60085-6726

FECK, LUKE MATTHEW, retired utility executive; b. Cin., Aug. 15, 1935; s. John Franz and Mercedes Caroline (Rielag) F.; m. Gail Ann Schutte, Aug. 12, 1961; children: Lisa, Mara, Paul. BA, U. Cin., 1957. Copyboy Cin. Enquirer, 1956, reporter, TV editor, columnist, 1957-64, asst. features editor, 1969-70, mag. editor, 1970, news editor, 1971-73, mng. editor, 1974-75, exec. editor, 1975, editor, 1976-80, Columbus Dispatch, 1980-89; sr. v.p. corp. comms. Am. Electric Power, Columbus, 1990-2000; ret. Pres. Ackerman and Feck Press, Inc., 1964-69, Feicke Web, Inc., 1974-75 Bd. dirs. Thurber House. 1st lt. AUS, 1957-59. Mem. Pub. Rels. Soc. Am., Edison Electric Inst., Lit. Club Cin., Capital Club, Lakes Golf and Country Club, Torch Club of Columbus, Sigma Delta Chi (pres. chpt.), Phi Kappa Theta. Home: 6880 Worthington Rd Westerville OH 43082-9491

FEDER, ROBERT, television and radio columnist; b. Chgo., May 17, 1956; s. Harold J. and Selma (Reisberg) F.; m. Janet Gail Elkins, June 16, 1985; 1 child, Emily Jacklyn. BS in Journalism, Northwestern U., 1978. Reporter, news editor Lerner Newspapers, Chgo., 1974-78, mng. editor, 1978-80; reporter Chgo. Sun-Times, 1980-83, TV/radio columnist, 1983—. Project cons. (TV documentary) Radio Faces, 1989; contbr. (spl. report) Ency. Brittanica, 1983, World Book Ency., 1996. Recipient Page One award Chgo. Newspaper Guild, 1976; named Best Daily Newspaper Columnist, New City, 1997. Mem. Soc. Profl. Journalists, Chgo. Headline Club, Chgo. Newspaper Guild, Northwestern Club of Chgo., Skokie Hist. Soc. Office: Chgo Sun-Times 401 N Wabash Ave Chicago IL 60611-5642

FEDERMAN, ARTHUR, federal judge; b. 1951; Bankruptcy judge U.S. Bankruptcy Ct. (we. dist.) Mo., Kansas City, 1989—. Adj. instr. U. Mo., Kansas City. Office: US Courthouse 400 E 9th St Ste 6552 Kansas City MO 64106-2615

FEDOROV, SERGEI, hockey player; b. Pskov, Russia, Dec. 13, 1969; Forward Detroit Red Wings, 1990—, 1998—. Founder Sergei Fedorov Found., 1998—. Recipient Hart Trophy, 1994, Selke Trophy, 1994, Lester B. Pearson award, 1994, Player of Yr. award Hockey News, 1994, Sporting News, 1994, Hockey Digest, 1994, ice hockey Silver medal Olympic Games, Nagano, Japan, 1998. Avocations: golfing, boating, travel. Office: Detroit Red Wings 600 Civic Center Dr Detroit MI 48226-4419

FEHLNER, THOMAS PATRICK, chemistry educator; b. Dolgeville, N.Y., May 28, 1937; s. Herman Joseph and Mary (Considine) F.; m. Nancy Lou Clement, July 28, 1962; children: Thomas P., Anne Marie. BS, Siena Coll., Loudonville, N.Y., 1959; PhD, Johns Hopkins U., 1963. Rsch. assoc. Johns Hopkins U., Balt., 1963-64; asst. prof. U. Notre Dame, South Bend, Ind., 1964-67, assoc. prof., 1967-75, prof., 1975-87, prof. chemistry, Grace Rupley chair chemistry, 1988, chmn. dept. chemistry, 1982-88. Author: (with others) Inorganic Chemistry; contbr. articles to profl. jours. Guggenheim fellow, 1988-89. Fellow AAAS; mem. Am. Chem. Soc., Materials Rsch. Soc., Internat. Union Pure & Applied Chemistry. Democrat. Roman Catholic. Office: U Notre Dame Dept Chemistry Notre Dame IN 46556

FEHR, KENNETH MANBECK, retired computer systems company executive; b. Schuylkill Haven, Pa., Feb. 21, 1928; s. Theodore E. and Eva (Manbeck) F.; m. Jean Alice Greenawalt, June 28, 1952; children: K. Craig, Karen Jean, K. Todd. BS, Pa. State U., 1951; MBA, U. Pitts., 1953. With U.S. Steel Corp., 1951-62, div. controller, 1962; controller Interlake Steel Corp., Chgo., 1962-68; v.p. fin. Hallicrafters Co., 1968-71, E.W. Bliss Co., Salem, Ohio, 1971-74; treas. Alliance Machine Co., 1974-86; pres. I.M.S. Corp., Hudson, 1986-90, Fehr & Greenawalt Investments, Salem, 1990—, Salem Security Storage, LLB, Salem, 2002—. Bd. dirs. Fegreen Inc.; pres. Salem Security Storage LLP; night sch. tchr. U. Pitts., 1956—57. Trustee Save Our Salem, Inc.; treas. Salem Renaissance. With USNR, 1945—46. Mem.: Nat. Assn. Accts., Fin. Execs. Inst., Salem Hist. Soc., Salem Preservation Soc., Salem-Golf Club, Kiwanis (chpt. pres.), Masons. Home and Office: 725 S Lincoln Ave Salem OH 44460-3709

FEHR, WALTER RONALD, agronomist, researcher, educator; b. East Grand Forks, Minn., Dec. 4, 1939; m. Elinor Lee Otis, July 1, 1961; children: Susan, Steven, Kevin. B.S., U. Minn.-St. Paul, 1961, M.S., 1962; Ph.D., Iowa State U., 1967. Grad. asst. U. Minn., St. Paul, 1961-62; instr. Congo Poly Inst., Zaire, 1962-64; research assoc. Iowa State U., Ames, 1964-67, prof. dept. agronomy, biotech. dir., 1967—, disting. prof. agronomy. Author: Applied Plant Breeding, 1982, Principles of Cultivar Development: Theory and Technique, 1987; editor: Hybridization of Crop Plants, 1980, Principles of Cultivar Devel.: Crop Species, 1987; contbr. writings to book chpts. and profl. articles. Recipient, Agronomic Acheivement Awd.- Crops, American Society of Agronomy, 1994 Fellow Am. Soc. Agronomy, Crop Sci. Soc. Am. Office: Iowa State Univ Dept Agronomy 1212 Agronomy Hl Ames IA 50011-0001

FEIGENHOLTZ, SARA, state legislator; b. Chgo., Dec. 11, 1956; d. Bernard and Florence (Buky) F. Student, Northeastern Ill. U. Ill. state rep. Dist. 12, 1995—. Chmn. human svcs. com. Ill. Ho. of Reps., co-chair tobacco settlement proceeds distribution, vice-chair health care availabity com., mem. state govt. adminstrn. and appropriations human svcs. coms.; exec. dir. Cen. Lakeview Merchants Assn., 1993-94; former cons., Chgo. Mem. NOW, Nat. Coun. Jewish Women, Am. Jewish Coun. (gov. coun. 1994-95), Conf. Women Legislators, Phi Theta Kappa. Office: 1051 W Belmont Ave Chicago IL 60657-3327

FEIGL, DOROTHY MARIE, chemistry educator, university official; b. Evanston, Ill., Feb. 25, 1938; d. Francis Philip and Marie Agnes (Jacques) F. B.S., Loyola U., Chgo., 1961; Ph.D., Stanford U., 1966; postdoctoral fellow, N.C. State U., 1965-66. Asst. prof. chemistry St. Mary's Coll., Notre Dame, Ind., 1966-69, assoc. prof., 1969-75, prof., 1975—, chmn. dept. chemistry and physics, 1977-85, bd. regents, 1976-82, acting v.p., dean faculty, 1985-87, v.p., dean faculty, 1987-99. Author: (with John Hill and Erwin Boschmann) General Organic and Biological Chemistry, 1991, (with John Hill and Stuart Baum) Chemistry and Life, 1997; contbr. articles to chem. jours., chpts. to texts. Recipient Spes Unica award St. Mary's Coll., 1973, Maria Pieta award, 1977 Mem. Am. Chem. Soc., Royal Soc. Chemistry, Internat. Union Pure and Applied Chemistry, Sigma Xi, Iota Sigma Pi. Democrat. Roman Catholic. Office: Dept Chemistry Saint Mary's College Notre Dame IN 46556

FEIKENS, JOHN, federal judge; b. Clifton, N.J., Dec. 3, 1917; s. Sipke and Corine (Wisse) F.; m. Henriette Dorothy Schulthouse, Nov. 4, 1939; children: Jon, Susan Corine, Barbara Edith, Julie Anne, Robert H. A.B., Calvin Coll., Grand Rapids, Mich., 1938; J.D., U. Mich., 1941; LL.D., U. Detroit, 1979, Detroit Coll. Law, 1981. Bar: Mich. 1942. Gen. practice law, Detroit; dist. judge Ea. Dist. Mich., 1960-61, 70-79, chief judge, 1979-86, sr. judge, 1986—. Past co-chmn. Mich. Civil Rights Commn.; past chmn. Rep. State Central Com.; past mem. Rep. Nat. Com.; mem. com. visitors U. Mich. Law Sch. Past bd. trustees Calvin Coll. Fellow Am. Coll. Trial Lawyers; mem. ABA, Detroit Bar Assn. (dir. 1962, past pres.), State Bar Mich. (commr. 1965-71), U. Mich. Club (com. visitors). Office: US Dist Ct 851 Theodore Levin US Ct 231 W Lafayette Blvd Detroit MI 48226-2700

FEIN, ROGER GARY, lawyer; b. St. Louis, Mar. 12, 1940; s. Albert and Fanny (Levinson) F.; m. Susanne M. Cohen, Dec. 18, 1965; children: David I., Lisa J. Student, Washington U., St. Louis, 1959, NYU, 1960; BS, UCLA, 1962; JD, Northwestern U., 1965; MBA, Am. U., 1967. Bar: Ill. 1965, U.S. Dist. Ct. (no. dist.) Ill. 1968, U.S. Ct. Appeals (7th cir.) 1968, U.S. Supreme Ct. 1970. Atty. divsn. corp. fin. SEC, Washington, 1965—67; ptnr. Arvey, Hodes, Costello & Burman, Chgo., 1967—91; ptnr., chmn. adminstrn. and dissolution com. Wildman, Harrold, Allen and Dixon, 1992—. Co-chair Corp., Securities and Tax Practice Group, 1992-99; mem. Securities Adv. Com. to Sec. State Ill., 1973—, chmn., 1973-79, 87-93, vice-chmn., 1983-87, chmn. emeritus, 1994—; spl. asst. atty. gen. State of Ill., 1974-83, 85-99; spl. asst. state's atty. Cook County, Ill., 1989-90; mem. Appeal Bd., Ill. Law Enforcement Commn., 1980-83; mem. lawyer's adv. bd. So. Ill. Law Jour., 1980-83; mem. adv. bd. securities regulation and law report Bur. Nat. Affairs Inc., 1985—; lectr., author on land trust financing, consumer credit and securities law. Mem. Bd. Edn., Sch. Dist. No. 29, Northfield, Ill., 1977-83, pres., 1981-83; mem. Pub. Vehicle Ops. Citizens Adv. coun. City Chgo., 1985-86; mem. Anti-Defamation League Greater Chgo./Upper Midwest Region, Chgo. regional bd., 1975-91, vice chmn., 1980-88, mem. exec. com., 1996—, co-chair pub. affairs com., 1999--, assoc. nat. commr., 2000—; chmn. lawyers' com. for ann. telethon Muscular Dystrophy Assn., 1983; past bd. dirs. Jewish Nat. Fund, Am. Friends Hebrew U., Northfield Comty. Fund. Recipient Sec. State Ill. Pub. Svc. award, 1976, Citation of Merit, WAIT Radio, 1976, Sunset Ridge Sch. Comty. Svc. award, 1984, City of Chgo. Citizen's award, 1986; named one of Leading Ill. Attys., Am. Rsch. Corp., 1997. Fellow Am. Bar Found., Ill. Bar Found. (bd. dirs. 1978-88, v.p. 1982-84, pres. 1984-86, chmn. Fellows 1983-84, chmn., past pres. adv. com. 1988-90, Cert. of Appreciation 1985, 86, Stalwart fellow 1997), Chgo. Bar Found; mem. ABA (ho. of dels. 1981-85, state regulation of securities com. 1982—, Ill. liaison of com., chmn. subcom. liaison with securities adminstrs. and NASD 1998—), Ill. State Bar Assn. (bd. govs. 1976-80, del. assembly 1976-88, sec. 1977-78, cert. of appreciation 1980, 88, chmn. Bench and Bar com. 1982-83, chmn. Bench and Bar sect. coun., 1983-84, chmn. bar elections supervision com. 1986-87, chmn. assembly com. on hearings 1987-88, mem. com. on jud. appointments 1987-90), Chgo. Bar Assn. (mem. task force delivery legal svcs. 1978-80, cert. of appreciation 1976, chmn. land trusts com. 1978-79, chmn. consumer credit com. 1977-78, chmn. state securities law subcom. 1977-79), Decalogue Soc. Lawyers, Northwestern U. Sch. of Law Alumni Assn. (dir.), Standard Club, The Law Club of the City of Chgo., Tau Epsilon Phi, Alpha Kappa Psi, Phi Delta Phi. Office: Wildman Harrold Allen & Dixon 225 W Wacker Dr Ste 2800 Chicago IL 60606-1224 E-mail: fein@wildmanharrold.com.

FEINBERG, DAVID ERWIN, publishing company executive; b. Mpls., 1922; Grad., U. Minn., 1948. Chmn., chief exec. officer EMC Corp., St. Paul. Sec. bd. dirs., v.p. Paradigm Pub., Inc. Home: 111 Kellogg Blvd E Saint Paul MN 55101-1237 Office: EMC Corp 875 Montreal Way Saint Paul MN 55102-4245 E-mail: defein@emcp.com.

FEINBERG, HENRY J. publishing executive; BS in Chemistry magna cum laude, Rutgers U., 1973. Gen. mgr. internat. ops. and bus. devel. Covia Partnership; pres. Rand McNally Pub. Group, Skokie, Ill., 1991—. Chmn. DeAgoistini-Rand McNally, Europe. Office: Rand McNally & Co 8233 Central Park Ave Skokie IL 60076-2908

FEINBERG, MARTIN ROBERT, chemical engineering educator; b. N.Y.C., Apr. 2, 1942; s. Max and Lillian (Ziegler) F.; m. Gail Lynn Bobkier, Aug. 26, 1965; children: Donna, Sarah B.Ch.E., Cooper Union, 1962; M.S., Purdue U., 1963; Ph.D., Princeton U., 1968. Asst. prof. U. Rochester, N.Y., 1967-73, assoc. prof., 1973-80, prof., 1980-97; Morrow prof. chem. engring., prof. math. Ohio State U., Columbus, 1997—. Mem. editorial bd. Archive for Rational Mechanics and Analysis, 1978-91; contbr. articles to profl. jours. Named Dreyfus Tchr.-Scholar Camille and Henry Dreyfus Found., N.Y.C., 1973, Edward Peck Curtis award, 1994, John von Neumann Lectr. in Theoretical Biology, Inst. for Advanced Study, 1997. Mem. Am. Inst. Chem. Engrs. (Richard Wilhelm award 1996), Soc. Natural Philosophy (sec. 1982-84), Soc. Indsl. and Applied Math. Office: Ohio State University Dept Chem Engring Columbus OH 43210-1180

FEINBERG, PAUL H. lawyer; b. Yonkers, N.Y., Nov. 24, 1938; AB, U. Pa., 1960; LLB cum laude, Harvard U., 1963; LLM, NYU, 1970. Bar: N.Y. 1965, Ohio 1979. Asst. gen. counsel The Ford Found., 1971-77; ptnr. Baker & Hostetler LLP, Cleve. Speaker in field. Contbr. articles to profl. jours. Mem. ABA (mem. sect. taxation, mem. tax exempt orgns. com., co-chair subcom. non C3 organs. 1993-94, co-chair subcom. pvt. founds. 1995—), N.Y. State Bar Assn., Ohio State Bar Assn., Cleve. Bar Assn. (treas. 1996-99). Office: Baker & Hostetler LLP 3200 Nat City Ctr 1900 E 9th St Cleveland OH 44114-3475

FEINBERG, RICHARD, anthropologist, educator; b. Norfolk, Va., Nov. 4, 1947; s. Isadore and Rose Selma (Hartmann) F.; m. Nancy Ellen Grim, Apr. 15, 1978; children: Joseph Grim-Feinberg, Kate Grim-Feinberg. AB, U. Calif., Berkeley, 1969; MA, U. Chgo., 1971, PhD, 1974. Asst. prof. anthropology Kent (Ohio) State U., 1974-80, assoc. prof., 1980-86, prof., 1986—. Mem. editorial bd. Kent State U. Press, 1990-93; chair Kent State U. Faculty Senate, 1997-98; pres. Kent Rsch. Group, 1997-98. Author: Anuta: Social Structure of a Polynesian Island, 1981, Polynesian Seafaring and Navigation, 1988; editor: Politics of Culture in the Pacific Islands, 1995, Seafaring in the Contemporary Pacific Islands, 1995, Leadership and Change in the Western Pacific, 1996, Oral Traditions of Anuta, 1998, The Cultural Analysis of Kinship: The Legacy of David M. Schneider, 2001. Kent State Rsch. Coun. grantee, 1983, 88, 00; Wenner-Gren Found. grantee, 1991. Fellow: Assn. for Social Anthropology in Oceania (newsletter editor 1986—90, program coord. 2000—), Am. Anthrop. Assn.; mem.: Ctrl. States Anthrop. Soc. (bull. editor 1994—98, 2d v.p. 2002—), Am. Ethnological Soc., Polynesian Soc. Avocations: camping, white water kayaking, scuba diving, folk music. Office: Kent State U Dept Anthropology Kent OH 44242-0001

FEINGOLD, RUSSELL DANA, U.S. senator, lawyer; b. Janesville, Wis., Mar. 2, 1953; s. Leon and Sylvia (Binstock) F.; m. Susan Levine, Aug. 21, 1977; children: Jessica, Ellen; m. Mary Speerschneider, Jan. 20, 1991; stepchildren: Sam, Ted. B.A. with honors, U. Wis.-Madison, 1975; postgrad. Magdalen Coll., Oxford U., 1975-77; J.D. with honors, Harvard U., 1979. Bar: Wis. 1979. Assoc., Foley & Lardner, Madison, 1979-82, LaFollette, Sinykin, Anderson & Munson, Madison, 1983-85, Goldman & Feingold, 1985-88; mem. Wis. Senate, 1983-92, U.S. senator from Wis., 1993—, mem. aging com., budget com., fgn. rels. com., judiciary com., senate Dem. policy com. Wis. Honors scholar, 1971; Rhodes scholar, 1975. Mem. Phi Beta Kappa. Democrat. Jewish. Office: US Senate 506 Hart Senate Office Bldg Washington DC 20510-0001 also: US Senators Office 8383 Greenway Blvd Middleton WI 53562-4626

FEINSTEIN, FRED IRA, lawyer; b. Chgo., Apr. 6, 1945; s. Bernard and Beatrice (Mines) F.; m. Judy Cutler, Aug. 25, 1968; children: Karen, Donald. BSC, DePaul U., 1967, JD, 1970. Bar: Ill. 1970, U.S. Supreme Ct. 1977. Ptnr. McDermott, Will & Emery, Chgo., 1976—; lectr. in field. Pres., Skokie/Evanston (Ill.) Action Council, 1981-84; bd. dirs. Temple Judea Mizpah, Skokie, 1982-84, 2000—, Deborah Goldfine Meml. Cancer Research, 1968—, YMCA of Chgo., 1985—. Mem. Ill. Bar Assn., Am. Coll. Real Estate Lawyers, Union League, Blue Key, Beta Gamma Sigma, Beta Alpha Psi, Pi Gamma Mu, Lambda Alpha. Contbr. articles to profl. jours. Office: McDermott Will & Emery 227 W Monroe St Ste 3100 Chicago IL 60606-5096

FEKETY, ROBERT, physician, educator; b. Pitts., June 29, 1929; s. Francis Robert and Grace (McShaffery) F.; m. Nancy Jane Baker, June 24, 1954; children: Susan Elizabeth, Sally Jane. AB, Wesleyan U., 1951; MD, Yale U., 1955. Instr. dept. medicine Johns Hopkins U., Balt., 1960-64, asst. prof., 1964-67; assoc. prof. medicine U. Mich., Ann Arbor, 1967-71, chief div. infectious diseases, 1967-95, prof. medicine, 1971-95, prof. medicine emeritus, 1995—; prof. epidemiology, 1987-95; active emeritus prof. medicine U. Mich., Ann Arbor, 1995—. Sr. asst. surgeon USPHS, 1956-58. Fellow ACP, Infectious Diseases Soc. Am. (councillor). Roman Catholic. Home: 812 Berkshire Rd Ann Arbor MI 48104-2631 Office: Univ Mich Hosp 3116 Taubman Ctr Ann Arbor MI 48109 Fax: 734-747-9965. E-mail: rfekety@umich.edu.

FELD, THOMAS ROBERT, religious organization administrator; b. Carroll, Iowa, Sept. 30, 1944; s. Edward Martin and Elaine (Wirtz) F.; m. Donna Jean Jorstad, June 1, 1968; children: Jacqueline Joan, William Jay. BA, Loras Coll., 1966; MA, No. Ill. U., 1969; PhD, Purdue U., 1972. Instr. Loras Coll., Dubuque, Iowa, 1966-70; v.p. Lea Coll., Albert Lea, Minn., 1972-73, Cen. Meth. Coll., Fayette, Mo., 1973-76, acting pres., 1976-77; pres. Mt. Mercy Coll., Cedar Rapids, Iowa, 1977-99; exec. dir. Iowa Cath. Conf., Des Moines, 1999—. Bd. dirs. Assn. Mercy Colls., Washington, D.C., Norwest Bank. Bd. dirs. Iowa Coll. Found., Des Moines, 1977—, chmn., 1988-89; bd. dirs. Assn. Retarded Citizens, Cedar Rapids, 1979-85. Recipient Poetry award Am. mag., 1966, Teaching award Purdue U., 1971, Outstanding Fundraiser award Nat. Soc. Fundraising Execs., 1996; named Outstanding Young Dem. of Iowa, State Dems., 1965, knight Order Holy Sepulchre, 1992, Knight Comdr., 1996. Mem. CMC Colls. Assn. (bd. dirs., pres. 1979-80, 84-85, 88-89), Iowa Coordinating Coun. Postsecondary Edn. (chmn. bd. dirs. 1985-86), Assn. Mercy Colls. (exec. com. 1985—, bd. dirs.), Nat. Assn. Intercollegiate Athletics (chmn. bd. dirs. 1986-89, 94—, Hall of Fame 1996), Iowa Assn. Ind. Colls. and Univs. (chmn. bd. dirs. 1984-85), Nat. Assn. Ind. Colls. and Univs. (bd. dirs. 1990-93), Rotary (bd. dirs. 1993-97, pres. 1995—). Democrat. Roman Catholic. Avocations: golfing, fishing, poetry. Home: 4404 Hickory Wind Ln Marion IA 52302-9600 Office: Iowa Cath Conf Ste 818 505 5th Ave Des Moines IA 50309

FELDHOUSE, LYNN, automotive company executive; m. Bob Feldhouse; 1 child, Katherine. Grad., Wayne State U.; postgrad., Oakland U. V.p., sec. Chrysler Corp. Fund, 1982—. Immediate past chair Nat. Contbns. Coun., The Conf. Bd., N.Y.C., bd. trustee Coun. Mich. Founds., Grand Haven, Citizens' Scholarship Found. of Am., St. Peter, Minn.; bd. trustees, treas. Mich. Womens' Found., Lansing; mem. nat. corp. com. Philanthropic Adv. Svc., Coun. of BBBs, Washington; mem. exec. com. Detroit Funders' Collaborative. Active vol. United Way Comty. Svcs. Southeastern Mich., Mich. Corp. Vol. Coun., Wayne State Alumni Assn. Office: Chrysler Fund Detroit MI 48231

FELDMAN, EVA LUCILLE, neurology educator; b. N.Y.C., Mar. 30, 1952; d. George Franklin and Margherita Enriceta (Cafiero) F.; children: Laurel, Scott, John Jr. BA in Biology and Chemistry, Earlham Coll., 1973; MS in Zoology, U. Notre Dame, 1975; PhD in Neurosci., U. Mich., 1979, MD, 1983. Diplomate Am. Bd. Neurology; lic. med. practitioner, Mich. Instr. dept. neurology U. Mich., Ann Arbor, 1987-88, asst. prof. neurology, 1988-94, mem. faculty Cancer Ctr., 1992-2000, assoc. prof. neurology, 1994-2000, prof., 2000. Mem. faculty neurosci. program U. Mich., Mich. Diabetes Rsch. and Tng., Ann Arbor, 1988—; dir. JDRF Ctr. for the Study of Complications in Diabetes. Author (book chpts.) Diabetes in the New Millenium, 1999, Cecil's Textbook of Medicine, 2000; contbr. articles to profl. jours. Grantee, NIH, 1989, 1994, 1997, 1998, 2001, Juvenile Diabetes Inst., 1994, 1997, 1999, 2001. Avocation: research on the elucidation of the role of growth factors in the pathogenesis of human disease. Office: Dept Neurology U Mich 200 Zina Pitcher Pl Rm 4144 Ann Arbor MI 48109-2205

FELDMAN, NANCY JANE, health organization executive; b. Green Bay, Wis., July 6, 1946; d. Benjamin J. and Ellen M. Naze; m. Robert P. Feldman, Aug. 24, 1968; 1 child, Sara J. BA, U. Wis., 1969, MS, 1974. Supr. EPSDT program Minn. Dept. Human Svcs., St. Paul, 1974-80, supr. healthcare programs, 1980-84; team leader human resources budget Minn. Dept. Fin., 1984-87; asst. commr. Minn. Dept. Health, 1987-91; team leader CORE program Minn. Dept. Adminstrn., 1991-93; dir. state pub. programs Medica, Allina Health Sys., Mpls., 1993-95; CEO UCare Minn., St. Paul, 1995—. Mem. Minn. Coun. Health Plans, Mpls., 1995—; bd. dirs. Stratis Health. Bd. dirs. Vols. Am. Health Svcs., 1994—, chair, 1999—; vice chair bd. dirs. Ctr. for Victims of Torture, 1997—. Mem. Women's Health Leadership Trust. Avocations: distance swimming, bicycling, travel. Home: 4124 Burton Ln Minneapolis MN 55406-3638 Office: UCare Minn PO Box 52 Minneapolis MN 55440-0052 E-mail: nfeldman@ncare.org.

FELDMAN, RICHARD DAVID, health commissioner; BA in Psychology phi beta kappa, Ind. U., 1972, MD, 1977. Diplomate Am. Bd. Family Practice; Lic. physician, Indiana. Resident Ind. U. Sch. Med., Indpls., 1977, St. Francis Hosp., Beech Grove, Ind., 1977-80, pvt. practice, 1981—, Family Physicians of Carmel, 1980-81. Asst. prof. Family Med., Ind. U., 1981—; cons. in field; lectr. in field. Contbr. articles to profl. jours. Pres. Golden Hill Neighborhood Assn., 1988-90, 1995-97; founder Indpls. Totem Pole Reconstruction Project Eiteljorg Mus., 1990-96; mem. O'Bannon Ind. Gubinatorial Campaign (health care policy com. 1996); bd. dirs. Ind. State Med. Assn. Political Action Com., 1996, Golden Hill Neighborhood Assn., 1986—, United Northwest Neighborhood Day Care Ctr., Indpls.; pres. Ethnographic Art Soc. Indpls., 1983—. Rsch. grantee Mead-Johnson Nutritional Div., 1982, St. Joseph County Cancer Soc., 1982. Fellow Am. Acad. Family Physicians (Ind. chpt. Rsch. award 1980, A. Alan Fischer award 1994, Pres. award 1995, Distinguished Pub. Svc. award 1997); mem. AMA, Nat. Assn. Family Practice Residency Dirs., Soc. Tchrs. Family Med., Ind. State Med. Assn., Marion County Med. Soc., Assn. Ind. Dirs. Med. Edn. Office: Indiana State Dept Health 2 N Meridian St Indianapolis IN 46204-3003 also: St Francis Family Practice Residency 1500 Albany St Ste 807 Beech Grove IN 46107-1563

FELDMAN, SCOTT MILTON, lawyer; b. N.Y.C., July 31, 1942; s. Abe and Lilian F.; m. Susan Lauer, July 13, 1968; children: James W., Mark A. BA, Amherst Coll., 1964; JD, Harvard U., 1967. Bar: NY 1968, Ill. 1978. Instr. UCLA Law Sch, 1967-68; lt. Judge Advocate Gen's. Corp. U.S. Navy, Washington, 1968-71; assoc. Sullivan & Cromwell, N.Y.C., 1971-77; ptnr. Winston & Strawn, Chgo., 1978-2001; assoc. gen. counsel Bank of Am. N.A., 2001—. Trustee Village of Glencoe, Ill., 1983-91. Mem. ABA, Chgo. Bar Assn., Assn. Bar City N.Y., Amherst Alumni Assn. Office: Bank of America NA Mail Code ILI-231-07-17 231 S LaSalle St 7th Fl Chicago IL 60697 E-mail: scott.m.feldman@bankofamerica.com.

FELDT, LEONARD SAMUEL, university educator and administrator; b. Long Branch, N.J., Nov. 2, 1925; s. Harry and Bessie (Doris) F.; m. Natalie Ruth Fischer, Aug. 29, 1954; children: Sarah Feldt Roach, Daniel C. BS in Edn., Rutgers U., 1950, MEd, 1951; PhD, U. Iowa, 1954. From asst. prof. to prof. U. Iowa, Iowa City, 1954-94; prof. emeritus, 1994; dir. testing programs U. Iowa, Iowa City, 1981-94, Lindquist prof. ednl. measurement, 1981-94. Pres. Iowa Measurment Rsch. Found., Iowa City, 1978—; editor standardized tests Iowa Tests Ednl. Devel., 1960—. With U.S. Army, 1943-46. Recipient Disting. Svc. award Rutgers U., 1999, Disting. Achievement award Nat. Ctr. for Rsch. on Evaluation, Stds. and Student Testing, 1999. Mem.: Psychometric Soc., Inst. Math. Stats., Am. Statis. Assn., Nat. Coun. on Measurement in Edn. (Career Contbns. award 1994), Am. Ednl. Rsch. Assn. (E.F. Lindquist award 1995), Sigma Xi, Phi Beta Kappa. Avocation: golf. Home: 810 Willow St Iowa City IA 52245-5438 Office: Univ Iowa Lindquist Ctr Iowa City IA 52242 E-mail: leonard-feldt@uiowa.edu.

FELDT, ROBERT HEWITT, pediatric cardiologist, educator; b. Chgo., Aug. 3, 1934; s. Robert Hewitt and Frances (Swanson) F.; m. Barbara Ann Fritz, Aug. 17, 1957; children: Christine, Susan, Kathryn. B.S., U. Wis., 1956; M.D., Marquette U., 1960; M.S., U. Minn., 1965. Diplomate: Am. Bd. Pediatrics, Am. Bd. Pediatric Cardiology. Intern Miller Hosp., St. Paul, 1960-61; resident in pediatrics cardiology Mayo Found., Rochester, Minn., 1961-65; cons. pediatrics Mayo Clinic, 1966—, chmn. dept. pediatrics, 1980-85, prof. pediatrics. Mem. Am. Bd. Pediatrics; chmn. sci. coun. Am. Heart Assn. Author numerous sci. articles, book chpts., monographs. Fellow Am. Acad. Pediatrics, Am. Cardiology Coll.; mem. Minn. Heart Assn. (pres. 1982), Midwest Soc. Pediatric Research, Am. Pediatric Soc. Congregationalist. Home: 1804 Walden Ln SW Rochester MN 55902-0903 Office: Mayo Clinic Dept Pediatrics 200 1st St SW Rochester MN 55905-0002

FELECIANO, PAUL, JR. state legislator; b. N.Y.C., Mar. 27, 1942; m. V. Arlene Williams, 1966; children: Treven, Eric, Heather. AAS, N.Y.C. C.C., 1961. Mem.. state rep. Kans. Ho. of Reps., 1972-76; rep. for dist. 28 Kans. State Senate, 1998—; minority whip, former asst. senate Dem. leader; former ranking minority mem. com. and jud. com.; former assessment and taxation com.; mem. comm. com. State-Fed. Assembly Nat. Conf. State Legisatures; mem. joint com. arts and cultural resources, investments pensions and benefits com.; mem. children and youth adv. com. Women's Correctional Task Force; mem. Kans. Coun. Employment and Tng.; mem. Gov.'s Task Force on Housing and Homeless, Washington; mem. force and policy alt. leader Ctr. Policy Alternatives. Sec. Aircap Truck Plz., Inc.; v.p. Air Cap Motel, Inc.; pres. polit. affairs Nat. Telecom. Cons. Mem. Riverside Dem. Club. Mem. Am. Legion (Post 401, Wichita). Office: 815 Barbara St Wichita KS 67217-3115 also: State Senate State Capitol Topeka KS 66612

FELICETTI, DANIEL A. academic administrator, educator; b. N.Y.C., Apr. 25, 1942; s. Ernest and Rose (DiAdamo) F.; m. Barbara D'Antonio, July 13, 1969. BA in Polit. Sci., Hunter Coll., 1963; MA in Polit. Sci., NYU, 1966, PhD in Polit. Sci., 1971. From asst. to assoc. prof. Fairfield (Conn.) U., 1967-77, chmn. dept. politics, 1973-76, spl. asst. to pres., 1977; acad. v.p., acad. dean Wheeling (W.Va.) Coll., 1977-80; sr. v.p. for acad. affairs Coll. New Rochelle, N.Y., 1980-81, Southeastern U., Washington, 1982-84; v.p. acad. affairs U. Detroit, 1984-89; pres. Marian Coll., Indpls., 1989-99, Capital U., Columbus, Ohio, 1999-2001. Participant Am. Coun. on Edn., Washington, 1976-77, vis. assoc., 1984-85; intern Inst. for Ednl. Mgmt. program Harvard U., 1981; cons. Coun. for Ind. Colls., Washington, 1986. Trustee Am. Heart Assn., Mich.; bd. dirs. Am. Heart Assn., Ind., Mental Health Assn. Marion County, Econ. Club Indpls., Coun. Ind. Colls.; mem. health and substance abuse com. New Detroit, Inc., 1986-89; mem. Greater Indpls. Progress Com.; mem. Pub. Safety Task Force Ind.; mem. Colls. Ind. Found.; mem. Indpls. delegation to Pres.'s Summit for Am.'s Future, 1997. Trustee Am. Heart Assn., Mich.; bd. dirs. Am. Heart Assn., Ind., Mental Health Assn. Marion County, Econ. Club Indpls., Coun. Ind. Colls.; mem. health and substance abuse com. New Detroit, Inc., 1986-89; mem. Greater Indpls. Progress Coml; mem. Pub. Safety Task Force Ind.; mem. Colls. Ind. Found.; mem. safety vision coun. United Way Columbus. Named to Hunter Coll. Hall of Fame, Hunter Coll. Alumni Assn., 1986; recipient Cert. of Recognition Sen. Lugar, 1994; Lilly Found. vis. faculty fellow Yale U., 1975; named Sagamore of the Wabash Gov. of Ind., 1990. Mem. Indpls. Athletic Club, Columbus C. of C. (pub. rels. com.), Rotary, Alpha Sigma Nu (hon.), Beta Gamma Sigma (hon.). Democrat. Roman Catholic. Avocations: baseball, reading, antiques. Office: Capital Univ 2199 E Main St Columbus OH 43209-2394

FELKER, HARRY L. mayor; m. Bette Felker; 3 children. BA in Polit. Sci., Washburn U., 1967, JD, 1972. Mem. staff Kans. Revisor of Statutes Office, 1972—75; commr. City of Topeka Parks Commn., 1975—85; dir. econ. devel. Topeka C. of C., 1985—89; mayor City of Topeka, 1989—97, 2001—; CEO Topeka Youth Project, 1997—2001. Mem. bd. regents Washburn U. With USNR, 1967—72. Avocations: sports, gardening, reading, music. Office: City Hall Bldg 215 E 7th St Rm 352 Topeka KS 66603

FELKNOR, BRUCE LESTER, editorial consultant, writer; b. Oak Park, Ill., Aug. 18, 1921; s. Audley Rhea and Harriet (Lester) F.; m. Joanne Sweeney, Feb. 8, 1942 (div. Jan. 1952); 1 child, Susan Harriet Felknor Pickard; m. Edith G. Johnson, Mar. 1, 1952; children: Sarah Anne, Bruce Lester II. Student, U. Wis., 1939-41. Reporter Dunn County News, Menomonie, Wis., 1937-39; freight brakeman Pa. R.R., N.Y.C., 1941, asst. yardmaster, 1942; prodn. coordinator Hwy. Trailer Co., Edgerton, Wis., 1943; radio officer U.S. Maritime Service, 1944-45; flight radio officer Air Transport Command, 1945; mem. pub. relations dept. Am. Airlines, 1945; writer pub. relations dept. ITT, 1946; Southeast regional pub. relations dir. Ford Motor Co., Chester, Pa., 1946-48; free lance pub. relations N.Y.C., 1948-49; pub. relations exec. Foote, Cone & Belding, Inc., 1950-53; v.p. Market Relations Network, 1954-55; exec. dir. Fair Campaign Practices Com., Inc., 1956-66; asst. to William Benton (chmn. and pub. Ency. Brit.), 1966-70; dir. mktg. info. internat. div. (Ency. Brit.), 1970-73, dir. advt. and promotion, 1973, dir. pub. info., 1974-76, exec. editor, 1977-83; dir. yearbooks Ency. Brit., 1983-85; editorial cons., 1985—. Vis. lectr. Hamilton Coll., 1966, 75, 82; history editor Mcht. Marine internet web site www.usmm.org, 1999—. Author: Fair Play in Politics, 1960, State-by-State Smear Study, 1956, You Are They, 1964, (with C.P. Taft) Prejudice & Politics, 1960, Dirty Politics, 1966, reprinted, 1975, 2001, (with Frank Jonas et al) Political Dynamiting, 1970, How to Look Things Up and Find Things Out, 1988, Political Mischief: Smear, Sabotage, and Reform in U.S. Elections, 1992, The Highland Park Presbyterian Church: A History 1871-1996, 1996 (Robert Lee Stowe award 1997), The U.S. Merchant Marine at War 1775-1945, 1998, The Great Witch Hunt of the Presbyterian Left, 2001; editor: The U.S. Government: How and Why it Works, 1978; also various newspaper, jour. and yearbook articles on politics; contbg. editor (with Clifton Fadiman) The Treasury of the Encyclopaedia Britannica, 1992; contbr. Encyclopedia of the American Presidency, 1993. Chmn. Citizens Com. for Sch. Centralization in Armonk, N.Y., 1957-61; ruling elder, chmn. com. religion and race Presbytery Hudson River, 1963-67, mem. nat. coun. on ch. and soc., 1966-72; bd. dirs., mem. exec. com. Fair Campaign Practices Com.; mem. nat. adv. bd. Amigos de las Americas, 1982-89, Am. U., Washington, 1982—; mem. Ill. Literacy Coun., 1984-86; mem. bd. advisors, acad. adv. coun. Nat. Strategy Forum, 1987—; mem. bd. edn. Lake Forest (Ill.) H.S. Dist., 1989-93. Mem. Am. Legion, Am. Mcht. Marine Vets., Navy League, Am. Polit. Sci. Assn., Authors League Am., Authors Guild, Soc. Midland Authors, Tavern Club (Chgo., Bonifex Maximus award 1995), Dutch Treat Club (N.Y.C.). Republican. Presbyterian. Home and Office: 509 Trinity Ct Evanston IL 60201-1908 E-mail: brucefelk@cs.com.

FELLER, ROBERT WILLIAM ANDREW, baseball team public relations executive, retired baseball player; b. Van Meter, Iowa, Nov. 3, 1918; s. William and Lena (Forrett) F.; m. Anne Morris Gilliland, Oct. 1, 1974. Pub. rels. exec. Cleveland Indians Baseball Team, 1936-56. Played first major league game Cleve. vs. St. Louis Browns, 1936; pitched 3 no-hitters Cleve. vs. Chgo., 1940, Cleve. vs. N.Y., 1946, Cleve. vs. Detroit, 1951; member 9 all-star teams. Author: Strikeout Story, 1947, How to Pitch, 1948, Now Pitching Bob Feller, 1990, Bob Feller's Little Black Book of Baseball Wisdom, 2000. CPO USNavy, 1941-45, PTO. Inducted to Baseball Hall of Fame, Cooperstown, N.Y., 1962; named Greatest Living Right-Hand Pitcher Profl. Baseball Centennial Celebration, 1969. Mem. Green Berets (hon.). Republican. Episcopalian. Avocation: restoring Caterpiller tractors. Fax: 440-423-3248.

FELLER, STEVEN ALLEN, physics educator; BS in Physics, Clarkson Coll. of Tech., 1973; MSc in Physics, Brown U., 1975, PhD in Physics, 1979. Asst. prof. Coe Coll., Cedar Rapids, Iowa, 1979-85, assoc. prof., 1985-91, B.D. Silliman prof. of physics, chair, 1991—. Editor Internat. Bank Note Soc. Jour., 1990. Recipient Bendix award Am. Inst. Physics, 1981-82, Fulbright award to U.K., 1996; grantee Rsch. Corp., 1983, 86-87, Iowa Acad. of Sci., 1986-87, Tex. Nat. Rsch. Lab. Commn., 1991-93, NSF, 1986-88, 88-90, 90-93, 91, 93-96, 96—; named Iowa Prof. of Yr. Carnegie Found., 1995. Mem. Am. Ceramic Soc., Am. Numismatic Assn., Internat. Bank Note Soc., Iowa Acad. Sci. Achievements include research in materials physics and physics education and numismatics. Office: Coe Coll Dept Physics Cedar Rapids IA 52402

FELLINGHAM, WARREN LUTHER, JR. retired banker; b. Chgo., Dec. 28, 1934; s. Warren Luther and Dorothy Eaton (Park) F.; m. Judith Cutler, Sept. 14, 1962; children: Warren III, Margo, Victoria. AB, Dartmouth Coll., 1956; MBA, Northwestern U., 1968. Cert. bank compliance officer. Auditing asst. The Northern Trust Co., Chgo., 1956-61, asst. cashier, 1962-71, 2d v.p., 1972-77, v.p., 1978-96, consumer compliance officer, 1988-96. Pres. Chicagoland Compliance Assn., 1988-96. Village pres., mayor Village of Golf, Ill., 1981-85, village trustee, clk., 1973-81; bd. dirs. United Way of Glenview-Golf, 1983-92; unit commr. N.E. Ill. coun. Boy Scouts Am., 1996—; treas. Glenview Area Hist. Soc., 1998—. Recipient Dist. award of Merit, 1989, N.E. Ill. Coun. Boy Scouts of Am., 1989, William H. Spurgeon III award, 1998, Silver Beaver award, Vigil Honor, Order of Arrow, Boy Scouts Am., 2001. Mem. Glenview Area Hist. Soc. (treas. 1998—), Dartmouth Club Chgo., Order of Arrow. Avocation: bicycling. Home: 37 Overlook Dr Golf IL 60029

FELLOWES, JAMES, manufacturing company executive; BA, Denison U. CEO Fellowes Mfg., Itasca, Ill. Named Entrepreneur of Y., Ernst & Young, 1997. Office: Fellowes Manufacturing 1789 Norwood Ave Itasca IL 60143-1095

FELLOWS, JERRY KENNETH, lawyer; b. Madison, Wis., Mar. 19, 1946; s. Forrest Garner and Virginia (Witte) F.; m. Patricia Lynn Graves, June 28, 1970; children: Jonathon, Aaron, Daniel. BA in Econs., U. Wis., 1968; JD, U. Minn., 1971. Bar: U.S. Dist. Ct. (no. dist.) Ill. 1971. Ptnr. McDermott, Will & Emery, Chgo., 1971—2002; with Bell, Boyd & Lloyd LLC, 2002—. Speaker Bur. Nat. Affairs, Washington, 1985—. Contbr. articles to profl. jours. Bd. dirs. Midwest Benefits Coun., 1998. Mem. U. Minn. Law Alumni Assn. (bd. visitors), Gamma Eta Gamma. Avocations: coaching track, basketball, baseball. Home: 4541 Middaugh Ave Downers Grove IL 60515-2761 Office: Bell Boyd & Lloyd LLC 70 West Madison St Ste 3100 Chicago IL 60602-4207 E-mail: jfellows@bellboyd.com., jpfellows@msn.com.

FELLOWS, ROBERT ELLIS, medical educator, medical scientist; b. Syracuse, N.Y., Aug. 4, 1933; s. Robert Ellis and Clara (Talmadge) F.; m. Karlen Kiger, July 2, 1983; children: Kara, Ari. AB, Hamilton Coll., 1955; MD, CM, McGill U., 1959; PhD, Duke U., 1969. Intern N.Y. Hosp., N.Y.C., 1959-60, asst. resident, 1960-61, Royal Victoria Hosp., Montreal, Que., Can., 1961-62; asst. prof. dept. medicine Duke U., Durham, N.C., 1966-76, asst. prof. dept. physiology and pharmacology, 1966-70, assoc. prof. dept. physiology and pharmacology, asso. dir. med. scientist tng. program, 1970-76; prof., chmn. dept. physiology and biophysics U. Iowa Coll. Medicine, 1976—, dir. med. sci. tng. program, 1976-97, dir. physician sci. program, 1984-88, dir. neurosci. program, 1984-88. Mem. Nat. Pituitary Agy. Adv. Bd.; mem. NIH Population Rsch. Com., 1981-86, VA Career Devel. Rev. Com., 1985-88; cons. NIH, NSF March of Dimes. Mem. editorial bd.: Endocrinology, Am. Jour. Physiology. Mem. AAAS, Am. Chem. Soc., Am. Fedn. Clin. Research, Am. Physiol. Soc., Am. Soc. Biol. Chemists, Am. Soc. Cell Biology, Assn. Chairmen Depts. Physiology, Biochem. Soc., Biophys. Soc., Endocrine Soc., Internat. Soc. Neuroendocrinology, N.Y. Acad. Scis., Soc. for Neurosci., Assn. Neuroscience Depts. and Programs (pres. 1995-96), Sigma Xi, Alpha Omega Alpha. Home: 135 Pentire Cir Iowa City IA 52245-1575 Office: 5-660 Bowen Sci Bldg Iowa City IA 52242 E-mail: robert-fellows@uiowa.edu.

FELTON, CYNTHIA, educational administrator; b. Chgo., Apr. 1, 1950; d. Robert Lee Felton Sr. and Julia Mae (Cheton) Felton-Phillips. BA, Northeastern, 1970; MEd, National Coll., 1984; MA, DePaul U., 1988; PhD, Loyola U., Chgo., 1992. Cert. tchr, adminstrv., Ill. Tchr. Chgo. Pub. Schs., 1971-86, adminstr., 1986-89, asst. prin., 1989-92, prin., 1992-97; dir. Chgo. Acad. for Sch. Leadership, 1997—. Mem. ASCD, Nat. Staff Devel. Coun., Nat. Coun. Tchrs. Math, Nat. Coun. Suprs. Math, Ill. Coun. Tchrs. Math (bd. dirs. 1992-95). Office: Chgo Acad Sch Leadership 221 N Lasalle St Chicago IL 60601-1206

FENECH, JOSEPH CHARLES, lawyer; b. London, May 28, 1950; came to U.S., 1953; s. Carmel John and Elizabeth Frances (Borg) F.; m. Cynthia A. Rennie, June 14, 1980 (div. 1998); children: Paul C., Peter J., Elizabeth F. BA with honors, Mich. State U., 1972; JD, U. Mich., 1975. Bar: Mich. 1975, U.S. Dist. Ct. (ea. dist.) Mich. 1975, U.S. Ct. Appeals (6th cir.) 1977, Ill. 1980, U.S. Dist. Ct. (no. dist.) Ill. 1980, U.S. Dist. Ct. (ctrl. dist.) Ill. 1993, U.S. Dist. Ct. (ea. dist.) Wis. 1993, U.S. Ct. Appeals (7th cir.) 1980, U.S. Supreme Ct. 1993, U.S. Tax Ct. 1993. Law clk. Washtenaw Cir. Ct., Ann Arbor, Mich., 1975-76; asst. atty. gen. State of Mich., Detroit, 1976-80; labor rels. counsel McDonald's Corp., Oak Brook, Ill., 1980-82, sr. internat. atty., 1982-84; sr. mem. Fenech & Assoc., 1985—. Contbr. articles to profl. jours. Bd. dirs. Cath. Charities Diocese of Joliet, Ill.; active Family Focus, Mich., 1979-80, Internat. Found. Employee Benefit Plans, Brookfield, Wis., 1980-83, Chmns. Club Ctrl.; mem. bd. govs. DuPage Hosp., Ctrl. DuPage Hosp. Tree Life, Ctrl., Glen Oaks Med. Ctr., Tree of Life, Rep. Campaign Coun., 1995; supt. adv. com. Naperville Cmty. Sch. Dist. 203; improvement com. Mill St. Sch., Naperville; charter mem. Marklund Children's Home Endowment; bd. govs. Ctrl. DuPage Hosp. Named Regents scholar U. Mich., 1973, 74, 75, Trustees scholar Mich. State U., 1969-72. Mem. ABA, Ill. State Bar Assn., Mich. Bar assn., DuPage Estate Planning Coun., U. Mich. Lawyers Club, Ill. Bankers Assn., Ill. Mortgage Bankers Assn., Internat. Platform Assn. Am. Hosp. Assn. (sr. mem.), Am. Acad. Healthcare Attys. (sr. mem.). Office: Fenech & Pachulski PC PO Box 5996 Naperville IL 60567

FENG, MILTON, engineering educator; b. Taiwan, July 21, 1950; BSEE, Columbia U., 1973; MSEE, U. Ill., 1976, PhD in Elec. Engring., 1979. Sect. head material and device group Torrance (Calif.) Rsch. Ctr., Hughes Aircraft Co., 1979-83; mgr. advanced digital integrated ciruit devel. program, dir. advanced devel. & fabrication digital & microwave/millimeter-wave devel. programs Ford Microelectronics, Inc., Colorado Springs, Colo., 1984-91; prof. elec. and computer engring., mem. faculty Ctr. Compound Semiconductor Microelectronics and Material Rsch. Lab. U. Ill., Urbana, 1991—. Fellow IEEE (Beckman Rsch. award 1994, David Sarnoff award 1997). Achievements include research in ion-implantation technology in III-V technology, optoelectronics IC's, ultra-high-speed analog-digital HBT IC's, and RF, microwave and millimeter-wave IC's. Office: U Ill 325 Microelectronics Lab 208 N Wright St Urbana IL 61801-2355

FENN, WADE R. retail executive; Exec. v.p. mktg. Best Buy Co., Eden Prairie, Minn., 1995—. Office: Best Buy Co 7075 Flying Cloud Dr Eden Prairie MN 55344-3538

FENNELL, CHRISTINE ELIZABETH, healthcare system executive; b. Providence, July 14, 1948; d. Edmond John and Geraldine Mary (Goodenough) F. BS cum laude, Nat. Coll, Denver, 1983. Activity dir. Turtle Creek Convalescent Centre, Ft. Wayne, Ind., 1974-76; co-owner, operator Trail Ridge Welding, Estes Park, Colo., 1976-77; accounts mgr. Mayfair Women's Clinic, Denver, 1977-80; asst. adminstr. Ob-Gyn. Assocs., Aurora, Colo., 1980-82; admissions supr. St. Anthony Hosp. Sys., Denver, 1982-86; adminstr. Parkside Lodge of Colo., Thornton, 1986-89; ops./fin. mgr. Colo. Biodyne, Inc., Denver, 1989-90; adminstr. Kimberly Quality Care, 1990-93; br. mgr. Preferred Home Health Care, Inc., Lafayette, Ind., 1993-95; regional v.p. Arcadia Health Svcs., Inc., Southfield, 1995—. Part-time instr. Nat. Coll., Denver, 1983-84. Contbr. articles to profl. jours. Bd. dirs. S.W. Denver Community Mental Health Svcs., 1986. Mem. Denver Bus. Women's Network (pres. 1986-87), Colo. Coun. Hosp. Admitting Mgrs. (v.p. 1985-86), Rotary Club. Avocations: target shooting, horseback riding, tennis. Office: Arcadia Health Svcs Inc 26777 Central Park Blvd Southfield MI 48076-4162 E-mail: cefinc@aol.com.

FENNEMA, OWEN RICHARD, food chemistry educator; b. Hinsdale, Ill., Jan. 23, 1929; s. Nick and Fern Alma (First) F.; m. Ann Elizabeth Hammer, Aug. 22, 1948; children: Linda Gail, Karen Elizabeth, Peter Scott. BS, Kans. State U., 1950; MS, U. Wis., 1951, PhD, 1960; PhD of Agrl. and Environ. Scis. (hon.), Wageningen Agrl. U., The Netherlands, 1993. Project leader for R&D, Pillsbury Co., Mpls., 1953-57; asst. prof. food sci. dept. U. Wis., Madison, 1960-64, assoc. prof., 1964-69, prof., 1969-96, chmn. dept., 1977-81, interim chmn. dept. landscape architecture, 1994-96, prof. emeritus, 1996—. Cons. Grand Metropolitan, Mpls., 1979-99; pub. mem. Internat. Life Scis. Inst.-Nutrition Found., 1987-90; mem. food adv. com. U.S. FDA, 1995-99, mem. sci. bd., 2000-02. Author: Low Temperature Preservation of Foods, 1973; editor: Principles of Food Science, 2 vols., 1976, Proteins at Low Temperatures, 1979, Food

Chemistry, 3d edit., 1996; mem. editl. bd. Cryobiology, 1966-82, Internat. Jour. Food Sci. and Nutrition, Jour. Food Sci., 1975-77, Jour. Food Processing Preservation, 1977—, Jour. Food Biochemistry, 1977-80, Nutrition Rsch. Newsletter, 1983-98, Acta Alimentaria (Budapest, Hungary), 1990-98, South African Jour. Food Sci. and Nutrition, 1991—; editor-in-chief Jour. Food Sci., 1999—. Served to 2d lt. U.S. Army, 1951-53. Recipient Excellence in Tchg. award U. Wis., Madison, 1977, Dir.'s Spl. Citation award Ctr. Food Safety and Nutrition, FDA; Fulbright disting. lectr., Spain, 1992. Fellow Am. Chem. Soc. (Agrl. and Food Chemistry Divsn. award 1995), Inst. Food Technologists (pres. 1982-83, treas. 1994-99, Excellence in Tchg. award 1978, Carl R. Fellers award 1988, Nicholas Appert award 1988), Inst. Food Sci. and Tech.; mem. Am. Soc. Nutritional Sci., Am. Soc. Landscape Archts. (Wis. chpt. award Merit), Internat. Union Food Sci. and Tech. (del. 1983-88, exec. com. 1988-99, v.p. 1992-95, founding fellow Internat. Acad. Food Sci. and Tech. 1997, chair 1999-2001. Home: 5010 Lake Mendota Dr Madison WI 53705-1305 Office: U Wis 1605 Linden Dr Madison WI 53706-1519 Fax: 608-262-6872. E-mail: ofennema@facstaff.wisc.edu.

FENNESSY, JOHN JAMES, radiologist, educator; b. Clonmel, Ireland, Mar. 8, 1933; s. John and Ann (McCarthy) F.; m. Ann M. O'Sullivan, Aug. 20, 1960; children— Deirdre, Conor, Sean, Emer, Rona, Nial, Ruairi M.B., B.Ch., BAO, Univ. Coll., Dublin, Ireland, 1958. Assoc. prof. U. Chgo., 1971-74, prof., 1974—, chief chest and gastrointestinal radiology, 1971-73, acting chief diagnostic radiology, 1973-74, chmn. dept. radiology, 1974-84, assoc. chair edn., 1990—. Fellow Royal Coll. Surgeons Ireland (hon.), Am. Coll. Radiology; mem. Am. Assn. Univ. Radiologists, Chgo. Radiol. Soc., Thoracic Radiology Soc., Radiology Soc. N.Am., Am. Gastroent. Soc., Fleischner Soc., Irish Am. Cultural Inst., County Tipperary Hist. Soc., Sigma Xi, Alpha Omega Alpha Republican. Roman Catholic. Office: U Chgo Dept Radiology 5841 S Maryland Ave Chicago IL 60637-1463

FENOGLIO-PREISER, CECILIA METTLER, pathologist, educator; b. N.Y.C., Nov. 28, 1943; d. Frederick Albert and Cecilia Charlotte (Asper) Mettler; m. John Fenoglio Jr., May 27, 1967 (div. 1977); 1 child, Timothy; stepchildren: Johanna, Andreas, Nicholas; m. Wolfgang F.E. Preiser, Feb. 16, 1985. Ach, Coll. St. Elizabeth, 1965; MD, Georgetown U., 1969. Diplomate Am. Bd. Pathology. Intern Presbyn. Hosp., N.Y.C., 1969-70; dir. Central Tissue Facility Columbia-Presbyn. Med. Ctr., 1976-83; co-dir. div. surg. pathology Presbyn. Hosp., 1978-82, div. div. surg. pathology, 1982-83; dir. Electron Microscop. Lab. Internat. Inst. Human Reprodn., 1978-85; assoc. prof. pathology Coll. Physicians and Surgeons, Columbia U., 1981-82, prof., 1982-83, attending pathologist, 1982-83; dir. lab. services Albuquerque VA Med. Ctr., 1983-90; prof. pathology U. N.Mex. Sch. Medicine, Albuquerque, 1983-90, also vice-chmn. dept. pathology; MacKenzie prof., chmn. dept. pathology and lab. medicine U. Cin. Sch. Medicine, 1990—, dir. cancer programs, 2001—. Mem. com. gastrointestine cancer WHO. Author: General Pathology, 1983, Gastrointestinal Pathology, An Atlas and Text, 1999, 2nd edit., 1999, Tumors of the Large and Small Intestine, 1990; editor: Advances in Pathobiology Cell Membranes, 1988-92, Advances in Pathobiology: Aging and Neoplasia, 1976, Progress in Surgical Pathology, vols. I-XIV, 1980-87, Advances in Pathology, vols. I-V, 1988-89. Grantee NIH, 1973, 79-82, 84-87, 85-2001, Cancer Rsch. Ctr., 1975-83, Population Coun., 1977-83, Nat. Ileitis and Colitis Found., 1979-80, Am. Cancer Soc., 1987-94. Mem. AAAS (life), U.S. and Can. Acad. Pathology (edn. com. 1980-85, coun. 1984-87, exec. com. 1987-91, v.p. 1987, pres.-elect 1988, pres. 1989, fin. com. 1998—), Internat. Acad. Pathology (N.Am. v.p. 1990-94, pres. 1996-98, exec. com. 1990-2000, edn. com. 1998—), Nat. Surg. Adj. Breast Project (sci. adv. bd.), Am. Assn. Pathologists, Armed Forces Inst. Pathology (sci. adv. bd. 1990—), N.Y. Acad. Sci., N.Y. Acad. Medicine, Fedn. Am. Scientists for Exptl. Biology, Gastrointestinal Pathologist Group (founding mem. edn. com. 1983-85, sec.-treas. 1993-96, pres.-elect 1996, pres. 1997), S.W. Oncology Group (chmn. GI tumor biology com., chmn. pathology com.), Arthur Purdy Stout Soc. (coun. 1987-90). Office: U Cin Sch Medicine 231 Bethesda Ave Cincinnati OH 45229-2827 E-mail: cecilia.fenogliopreiser@uc.edu.

FENSIN, DANIEL, diversified financial service company executive; b. 1943; BS in Acctg., DePaul U., 1965. Ptnr. Topel, Forman & Co., 1965-74; ceo, mng. ptnr. Blackman Kallick Bartelstein, L.L.P., Chgo., 1974—. Office: Blackman Kallick Bartelstein 300 S Riverside Plz Ste 660 Chicago IL 60606-6613

FENTON, CLIFTON LUCIEN, investment banker; b. Bryan, Ohio, May 11, 1943; s. Gibson Lucien and Elizabeth (Newcomer) F.; m. Judith Todd Wallis, June 23, 1973; children: Gregory, Eric, Alyssa. AB, Princeton U., 1965; JD, Ohio State U., 1968; MBA, Columbia U., 1970; grad., Kellog Grad. Sch. Mgmt., 2001. Bar: Ohio 1968. Assoc. Bank N.Y., N.Y.C., 1970-72, Morgan Guaranty Trust Co., N.Y.C., 1972; v.p. Kidder, Peabody, 1972-84; mng. dir. Prudential-Bache Securities, 1984-89; v.p., nat. mgr. John Nuveen & Co., Chgo., 1989-95, v.p. and mgr. Investment Banking Divsn., 1995-99; mng. dir. and co-head pub. fin. U.S. Bancorp Piper Jaffray, 1999-2000. Trustee Ravinnia Festival, Associated Colls. Ill., Associated Colls. of Ill. Mem. Met. Club (N.Y.C.), Univ. Club Chgo. Avocations: water and snow skiing, sailing, piano. Home: 808 Sunset Rd Winnetka IL 60093-3850 E-mail: cliffenton@attbi.com.

FENTON, LAWRENCE JULES, pediatric educator; b. Chgo., June 1, 1940; s. Arthur S. Fenton and Dorothy (Schochet) Wade; m. Gayle Ann Yeager, Apr. 10, 1965; children: Lori Ann, Scott L. BS, U. Mich., 1962; MD, U. Cin., 1966. Diplomate Am. Bd. Pediatrics, Sub-bd. Neonatal and Perinatal Medicine. Intern U. Cin. Med. Ctr., 1966-67, jr. and sr. resident, 1967-69, chief pediatric resident, 1969-70, fellow neonatal, perinatal medicine, 1972-74; asst. prof. pediatrics U. Ariz. Health Scis. Ctr., Tucson, 1974-78; assoc. prof. pediatrics U. S.D. Sch. Medicine, Sioux Falls, 1978-84, head sect. of neonatal, perinatal medicine, 1979-88, prof. pediatrics, 1984—, chmn. dept. pediatrics, 1988—. Dir. newborn intensive care unit Sioux Valley Hosp., 1980-88; chmn. pharmacy and therapeutics com. Sioux Valley Hosp., 1982-97, bd. dirs., 1997—; v.p. children's med. svcs. Sioux Valley Hosp. and U. S.D. Med. Ctr., 2000—. Contbr. articles to med. jours.; author: (with others) Current Therapy in Neonatal and Perinatal Medicine, 1989, Conn's Current Therapy, 1989, 90. Chmn. rsch. funding group Am. Heart Assn., Dakota Affiliate, 1986-88; mem. allocations com. Childrn's Miracle Network Telethon, Sioux Falls, 1986-87; bd. dirs. Childrens Miracle Network, 1996-99; chmn. Health Svcs. Adv. Com., State of S.D., 1991-93. Maj. U.S. Army, 1970-72. Rsch. grantee Nat. Inst. Child Health and Human Devel., Tucson, Sioux Falls, 1976-79, Am. Heart Assn., Sioux Falls, 1984; recipient Army Commendation medal, 1991-93, Pioneer award S.D. Perinatal Assn., 1993; inductee Hall of Honor Children's Hosp. U. Cin. MEd. Ctr., 1993. Fellow Am. Acad. Pediatrics; mem. Society for Pediatric Rsch., Midwest Soc. for Pediatric Rsch., Assn. Med. Sch. Pediatric Dept. Chmn., S.D. States Med. Assn. Avocations: water skiing, boating, hiking, cross country skiing, classical music. Office: 1100 S Euclid Ave Sioux Falls SD 57105-0411

FENTON, ROBERT EARL, electrical engineering educator; b. Bklyn., Sept. 30, 1933; s. Theodore Andrew and Evelyn Virginia (Brent) F.; m. Alice Earlyn Gray, Dec. 13, 1934; children: Douglas Earl, Andrea Leigh. BEE, Ohio State U., 1957, MEE, 1960, PhD in Electrical Engring., 1965. Registered profl. engr., Ohio. Engr. rsch. N. Am. Aviation, Columbus, Ohio, 1957; instr. electric engring. Ohio State U., 1960-65, prof., 1965-95, prof. emeritus, 1995—. Cons. transp. sys. divsn. GM, Warren, Mich., 1974-80, Battelle Meml. Inst., Columbus, Ohio, 1991-93. Inventor kinesthetic-tactile display; contbr. articles to profl. jours. Capt. USAF, 1957-60. Recipient Outstanding Tchr. award Eta Kappa Nu, 1963, Neil Armstrong award Ohio Soc. Profl. Engrs., 1971, Pioneering Rsch. award Nat. Automated Hwy. Systems Consortium, 1997, Significant Achievement award Intelligent Vehicle Hwy. Sys. Ohio, 1993. Fellow IEEE (IEEE Millennium medal 2000), Radio Club Am., IEEE Vehicular Tech. Soc. (pres. 1985-87, v.p. 1983-85, treas. 1981-83, prize paper 1980, Stuart F. Meyer Meml. award 1998); mem. Sigma Xi. Avocations: bicycling, swimming, classical music. Home: 2177 Oakmount Rd Columbus OH 43221-1229 Office: Ohio State Univ Dept Elec Engring 2015 Neil Ave Dept Elec Columbus OH 43210-1210 E-mail: fenton.2@osu.edu.

FENTON, ROBERT LEONARD, lawyer, literary agent, movie producer, writer; b. Detroit, Sept. 14, 1929; s. Ben B. and Stella Frances (Saffir) F.; children: Robert L. Jr., Cynthia R. AB, Syracuse U., 1952; LLB, U. Mich., 1955. Bar: Mich. 1955. Asso. Marks, Levi, Thill & Wiseman, Detroit, 1955-60; ptnr. Fenton, Nederlander, Tracy & Dodge, 1960-85; pvt. practice, 1985—. Adj. prof. U. Mich. Law Sch., Marygrove Coll., Detroit; lectr. Flint and Lansing Real Estate Bds., 1966-68; spl. counsel Detroit Fire Dept., 1975—, Mich. Motion Picture and TV Commn., 1978-82; producer Universal Studios, Calif., 1983-86, 20th Century Fox, 1986-87; guest lectr. U. Mich. Law Sch., 1998; presenter entertainment law seminar, U. Mich., Apr. 1998, writer's workshop Holland Am. Cruise Lines, Feb. 1999; conductor writer's workshops. Author: (novels) Black Tie Only, 1990, Blue Orchids, 1992, Royal Invitation, 1995; producer NBC movie of week Double Standard, 1988, Woman on the Ledge, 1993. Treas. Oakland County Dem. Com., 1960-64; mem. Dem. State Fin. Com., 1966-69, Nat. Fin. Com., 1962-74, Dem. Pres.'s Club, 1962-74; fin. adviser to Mayor Roman S. Gribbs, 1969-73, Mayor Coleman A. Young, 1974-94; chmn. State of Mich. Film and TV Commn.; bd. dirs. Detroit Bicentennial Commn., Rivers and Harbour Congress of U.S.; mem. adv. bd. NAACP, U. Mich. Pres.'s Club. Served with USAF, 1950-52. Recipient Distinguished Pub. Service medal City of Detroit, 1973, Letter of Commendation USAF, 1953; named Man of the 60's City of Detroit, 1964; decorated Order of St. Johns of Jerusalem, 1980. Mem. ABA, Mich., Detroit bar assns., Econs. Club, Acad. Magical Arts, Soc. Preservation Variety Arts, Franklin Hills Country Club, Variety Club of Detroit (bd. dirs.), Variety Clubs Internat., Recess Club (Detroit), St. James Club (L.A., N.Y.C., London, Paris), Mt. Kenya Safari Club (Nairobi), Masons, Shriners. Office: Village Park Bldg 31800 Northwestern Hwy Ste 390 Farmington Hills MI 48334-1604 E-mail: fenent@msn.com.

FERDERBER, JUNE H. state legislator; children: Deven Armeni, Adrien. Student, Youngstown State U. Mem. Ohio Ho. of Reps., 1986—, mem. energy and environment, judiciary and criminal justice coms. Mem. adv. com. ohio child support guidelines, women's policy and rsch. Com.; ranking minority mem. family svcs. com. Contbr. articles to Warren Tribune Chronicle. Active Animal Welfare League. Named Woman of Yr., Coalition Labor Union Women, YWCA, 1988. Mem. NOW (Trumbull County chpt.), LWV, Ohio Bus. and Profl. Women, Ohio Farm Bur., Mosquito Creek Devel. Assn., Farmer's Union, Sierra Club. Democrat. Home: 1435 Locust St Mineral Ridge OH 44440-9721 Office: Ohio House of Reps Office of House Mems Columbus OH 43215

FERENCZ, ROBERT ARNOLD, lawyer; b. Chgo., Sept. 10, 1946; s. Albert and Frances (Reiss) F.; m. Marla J. Miller, May 20, 1973; children: Joseph, Ira. BS in Acctg., U. Ill., 1968; JD magna cum laude, U. Mich., 1973. Bar: Ill. 1973. From assoc. to ptnr. Sidley, Austin, Brown & Wood, Chgo., 1973—. Mem. ABA, Ill. Bar Assn., Chgo. Bar Assn. Office: Sidley Austin Brown & Wood Bank One Plz 10 S Dearborn St Chicago IL 60603-2000

FERGER, LAWRENCE A. gas distribution utility executive; b. Des Moines, May 3, 1934; s. Cleon A. and Helen K. (Jacobs) F.; m. LaVon Stark, Oct. 20, 1957; children: Kirsten A., Jane S. B.S. in Bus. Adminstrn., Simpson Coll., Indianola, Iowa, 1956. Auditor Arthur Andersen & Co., Chgo., 1956-64; dir. data processing Ind. Gas Co., Inc., Indpls., 1964-74, v.p. planning, 1974-79, v.p., treas., 1979-80, sr. v.p. fin., 1980-81, exec. v.p., 1981-84, pres., 1984—, also bd. dirs. bd. dirs. Ind. energy Inc., Ind. Gas Co., Inc., Community Hosp. of Indpls., Nat. City Bank of Ind. Served with U.S. Army, 1957-59. Mem. Am. Gas Assn., Ind. Gas Assn. (treas. 1966-80, sec. 1966-70, dir. 1980—), Ind. State C. of C. Office: Ind Gas Co Inc 1630 N Meridian St Indianapolis IN 46202-1496

FERGUSON, BRADFORD LEE, lawyer; b. Ottumwa, Iowa, May 29, 1947; s. G. Wendell and Virginia Sue (Baker) Ferguson. BA, Drake U., 1969; JD, Harvard U., 1972. Bar: Minn. 1972, Ill. 1980. Assoc. Dorsey, Marquart, Windhorst, West & Halladay, Mpls., 1972-75; legis. asst. Senator Walter F. Mondale, Washington, 1975-77; spl. asst. to asst. sec. tax policy U.S. Treasury Dept., 1977-78, assoc. tax legis. counsel, 1978-80; ptnr. Hopkins & Sutter, Chgo., 1980-96, Sidley & Austin, Chgo., 1996-2001. Fellow Am. Coll. Tax Counsel; mem. ABA (taxation sect., chair com. formation tax policy 1991-93, mem. coun. 1994-97), Chgo. Bar Assn., Nat. Tax Assn. (bd. dirs. 1994-97).

FERGUSON, DANIEL C. diversified company executive; b. 1927; married. BA, Hamilton Coll.; MBA, Stanford U., 1950. With Newell Co., Freeport, Ill., 1950—, pres., CEO, 1965-92, chmn., 1992—, also bd. dirs. With USN. Office: Newell Co Newell Ctr 29 E Stephenson St Freeport IL 61032-4251 also: 1300 3rd St S Ste 300 Naples FL 34102-7239

FERGUSON, DONALD JOHN, surgeon, educator; b. Mpls., Nov. 19, 1916; s. Donald Nivison and Arline (Folsom) F.; m. Lillian Elizabeth Mack, June 26, 1943; children: Anne Elizabeth, Donald John, Merrill James. B.S., Yale, 1939; M.D., U. Minn., 1943, M.S. in Physiology, Ph. D. in Surgery, U. Minn., 1951. Intern, then resident U. Minn. Hosp., 1947-52; asst. prof. surgery U. Minn., 1952-54, assoc. prof., 1954-56, prof., 1956-60; prof. surgery U. Chgo., 1960-87, prof. emeritus, 1987—. Contbr. articles in field. Served to capt. M.C. AUS, 1943-46. Mem. ACS, Am. Surg. Assn., Soc. U. Surgeons. Home: The Mather 1615 Hinman Ave Evanston IL 60201-4509 Office: U Chgo Med Ctr 5841 S Maryland Ave Chicago IL 60637-1463

FERGUSON, JAMES PETER, distilling company executive; b. Landis, Sask., Can., Aug. 12, 1937; s. James and Gertrude (Schmit) F.; m. Patricia Woodruff, Aug. 27, 1960; children— James, Carolyn Chartered Acct., McGill U., 1971. Mgr. Clarkson Gordon, Montreal, Que., Can., 1965-73; lectr. McGill U., Can., 1970-72; contr. CI Power Ltd., Can., 1973-74; mgr. taxation Hiram Walker-Gooderham & Worts Ltd., Windsor, Ont., Can., 1974-79, treas., v.p., chief fin. officer Can., 1979-82, sr. v.p., treas., chief fin. officer Can., 1982-88; exec. v.p., corp. devel. dir. Hiram Walker-Allied Vintners, 1988-90, exec. v.p., chmn. Latin Am. and So. Europe sector, 1990-92; pres. Latin Am., corp. devel. dir. Allied Domecq Spirits and Wine (The Hiram Walker Group), 1992-95, corp. strategy dir., 1995-97; ret., 1998. Bd. dirs. Pedro Demecq S.A., Spain, Corby Distilleries Ltd., Montreal. Chmn. Met. Gen. Hosp., Windsor, Ont., 1979-80. Capt. Can. Air Force, 1956-65. Mem. Inst. Chartered Accts., Order Chartered Accts. Que., Essex Golf Club. Home: 6470 Riverside Dr E Windsor ON Canada N8S 1B9 Office: Allied Domecq Spirits/Wine PO Box 33006 Detroit MI 48232-5006

FERGUSON, JOHN WAYNE, SR. librarian; b. Ash Grove, Mo., Nov. 4, 1936; s. John William and Eula Marie (Rogers) F.; m. Nancy Carolyn Southerland, Apr. 4, 1958; children: John Wayne Jr., Mark Warren, Steven Ward. BS, S.W. Mo. State Coll., 1958; MS, U. Okla., 1961. Libr. Springfield (Mo.) Pub. Libr., 1952-64; asst. dir. Jackson County Pub. Libr., 1964-65; dir. Mid-Continent Pub. Libr., 1965-81, 1981—, libr. Mo. Bd. dirs. YMCA, Independence, 1969-89, Independence Regional Health Ctr., 1981-90, S.E. Enterprises Sheltered Workshop, 1996—. Capt. U.S. Army, 1959-65. Named Libr. of Yr. Libr. Jour. mag., 1993. Mem. Rotary (dist. govt. Independence chpt. 1986-87, pres. 1981-82). Avocation: amateur radio. Home: 14504 E 43rd St S Independence MO 64055-4840 Office: Mid-Continent Pub Libr 15616 E 24 Hwy Independence MO 64050-2057

FERGUSON, LARRY, food products executive; Pres., CEO Schrieber Foods Inc., Green Bay, Wis. Office: Schreiber Foods Inc PO Box 19010 Green Bay WI 54307 Office Fax: (920) 437-1617.

FERGUSON, PAMELA ANDERSON, mathematics educator, educational administrator; b. Berwyn, Ill., May 5, 1943; d. Clarence Oscar and Ruth Anne (Stroner) Anderson; m. Donald Roger Ferguson, Dec. 18, 1965; children: Keith, Amanda. BA, Wellesley Coll., 1965; MS, U. Chgo., 1966, PhD, 1969. Asst. prof. Northwestern U., Evanston, Ill., 1969—70, U. Miami, Coral Gables, Fla., 1972—77, assoc. prof., 1978—81, prof. math., 1981—91, dir. honors program, 1985—87, assoc. provost, dean Grad. Sch., 1987—91; pres. Grinnell Coll., Iowa, 1991—97, prof. math., 1991—. Mem. Nat. Sci. Bd., 1998—2004. Contbr. articles to refereed jours. Mem. Iowa Rsch. Coun., 1993—97. Grantee NSF grantee. Mem.: Am. Women in Math., Am. Math. Soc., Wellesley Club, Phi Beta Kappa, Omicron Delta Chi, Sigma Xi. Lutheran. Avocations: hiking, reading, skiing. Office: Grinnell Coll Dept Math PO Box 805 Grinnell IA 50112-0805

FERGUSON, RENEE, news correspondent, reporter; m. Ken Smikle; 1 child Jason. B Journalism, Ind. U. With Sta. WLWI-TV, Indpls.; reporter Sta. WBBM-TV, Chgo., 1977—81; news corr. CBS Network, N.Y.C., Atlanta; gen. assignment reporter Sta. WMAQ-TV, Chgo., 1987—, investigative reporter, 1997—. Recipient 6 Chgo. emmys, AWRT Gracie Allen award, Columbia-duPont award; fellow Benton fellowship in Journalism, U. Chgo., 1991. Office: NBC 454 N Columbus Dr Chicago IL 60611*

FERGUSON, RICHARD L. educational administrator; Pres. Am. Coll. Testing Program, Iowa City. Office: Am Coll Testing Program Instl Srvcs 2201 N Dodge St Iowa City IA 52243-0001

FERGUSON, ROBERT BURY, mineralogy educator; b. Cambridge, Ont., Can., Feb. 5, 1920; s. Alexander Galt and Harriet Henrietta (Bury) F.; m. Margaret Irene Warren, Dec. 29, 1948; children: Evelyn Bury, Robert Warren, Marion Galt. B.A., U. Toronto, 1942, M.A., 1943, Ph.D., 1948. Asst. prof. mineralogy U. Man. (Can.), Winnipeg, 1947-50; assoc. prof. U. Man, Can., 1951-59; prof. U. Man.(Can.), 1959-85, disting. prof., 1983, prof. emeritus, 1985—. Fellow Royal Soc. Can., Mineral Soc. Am.; mem. Mineral Soc. Great Britain, Mineral Assn. Can. (Hawley award 1981). New Democratic Party. Unitarian. Home: 184 Wildwood Park Winnipeg MB Canada R3T 0E2 Office: U Man Dept Geol Scis Winnipeg MB Canada R3T 2N2 E-mail: ferguson@ms.umanitoba.ca.

FERGUSON, RONALD MORRIS, surgeon, educator; b. Milaca, Minn., Nov. 12, 1945; children: Melissa, Jason, Meredith. BS, Augsburg Coll., 1967; MD, Washington U., St. Louis, 1971; PhD, U. Minn., 1982. Diplomate Am. Bd. Surgery. Dir. transplantation VA Med. Ctr., Mpls., 1980-82; assoc. prof. surgery Ohio State U., Columbus, 1982-88, prof. surgery, 1988—, chmn. dept. surgery, transplant, 1993-99, chief divsn. transplant, 1999—. Asst. prof. surgery U. Minn. Health Sci. Ctr., Mpls., 1980-82; med. dir. Lifeline of Ohio Organ Procurement, Columbus, 1985—. Mem. Am. Coll. Surgeons, Am. Soc. Transplant Surgeons, Soc. Univ. Surgeons (pres. 1988), Transplantation Soc. (v.p. 1992—). Office: Ohio State U 363 Means Hall 1654 Upham Dr Columbus OH 43210-1250

FERGUSON, TAMARA, clinical sociologist; b. The Hague, Netherlands; came to U.S., 1955; d. Simon and Sonia (Pokrowska) Van den Bergh; m. John D.A. Ferguson, Sept. 12, 1958. MA in Sociology, Columbia U., 1962, PhD, 1970. Asst. prof. U. Detroit, 1960-71; from asst. prof. to assoc. prof. U. Windsor, Ont., Can., 1971-78; adj. assoc. prof. sociology Wayne State U. Med. Sch., Detroit, 1978-99; assoc. med. staff dept. psychiatry Harper Hosp., 1982-99. Co-author: The Young Widow: Conflict and Guidelines, 1981; contbg. author: Clinical Sociology in Mental Health Setting, 1991, Qualitative Analysis in Human Sciences: New Perspectives in Methodology, 1996. 2d lt. Free French armed forces, 1944-45, ETO. Mem. Am. Sociol. Assn., Found. Thanatology, Sociol. Practice Assn. (bd. dirs. 1990-96). Avocations: reading, music, swimming. Office: UPC Jefferson 2751 E Jefferson Ave Detroit MI 48207-4166

FERGUSON, THOMAS JOSEPH, lawyer; b. Waterloo, Iowa, Feb. 27, 1956; s. Thomas Raymond and Elizabeth Ann (Callahan) F.; m. Kathleen Ann Flynn, Oct. 9, 1981; 1 child, Christopher. BSBA, Creighton U., 1978, JD, 1980. Bar: Iowa 1980, U.S. Dist. Ct. (no. dist.) Iowa 1981, U.S. Ct. Appeals (8th cir.) 1980. Assoc. Cutler and Rausch, Waterloo, 1980-82; ptnr. Rausch and Ferguson, 1983-85; 1st asst. Black Hawk County Atty.'s Office, 1985-90, county atty., 1990—. Mem. Black Hawk County Bar Assn., Nat. Dist. Atty.'s Assn., Iowa County Atty.'s Assn. Democrat. Roman Catholic. Avocations: hunting, sports. Office: Black Hawk County Courthouse 316 E 5th St Waterloo IA 50703-4712

FERKENHOFF, ROBERT J. retail executive; b. Kansas City, Mo., Aug. 17, 1942; s. John Michael and Eileen Marie (Owens) F.; m. Patricia Lee Venneman, Oct. 1, 1966; children: Jennifer, Deborah, Carrie. BA, Benedictine Coll., Atchison, Kans., 1964. Staff asst. Sears Mdse. Group, Chgo., 1972-73, nat. mgr. retail inventory mgmt., 1973-74, group mgr. retail systems, 1974-77, group retail mdse. mgr., 1977-79, nat. retail mktg. mgr., 1979-81, asst. dir. strategic planning, 1981-84, nat. mgr. bus. planning, 1984-88; v.p. data processing and info. svcs. Sears Canada, Toronto, 1988-89; v.p. info. svcs. Sears Mdse. Group, Chgo., 1989-93; v.p. CIO SPS Payment Systems, RIverwoods, Ill., 1993-98; I/T Cons., 1998—. Judge Retail Innovation Tech. Award, 1991-92; bd. dirs. Voluntary Interindustry Coun. Standards, 1989-93, Nat. Retail Fed. Info. Svcs., N.Y.C., 1989-93, Chgo. Rsch. and Planning Group, 1991—. Chmn. Sears United Fund, Chgo., 1991. Recipient Retail Innovation Tech. award Chain Store Age and DEC, 1990. Republican. Roman Catholic. Avocations: gardening, golf, biking. Office: SPS Payment Systems 4 Parkway N Deerfield IL 60015-2502

FERLIC, RANDOLPH, medical educator; b. Omaha, July 17, 1936; m. Teresa L. Kolars, June 20, 1959; 4 children. BS, MD, Creighton U., 1958; postgrad., U. Minn., 1965—66. Intern, fellow, resident in gen. thoracic and cardiovascular surgery U. Minn., Mpls., 1961—67; instr., resident surgeon NY Hosp./Cornell Med. Ctr., N.Y.C., 1967—68; founder, mgr. Thoracic & Cardiovascular Surgery P.C. (later Surg. Svcs. of the Great Plains), 1974—91; assoc. prof., then clin. assoc. prof. surgery U. Nebr. Med. Ctr., Omaha, 1970—. Contbr. more than 50 articles to profl. publs. Mem. bd. regents U. Nebr., 2000—, vice chmn. bd. regents, 2002—; mem. Commn. for Postsecondary Edn., 1991—2001, chmn., 1994—96; mem. Midwest Higher Edn. Commn., 1991—, treas., 1997—; founding dir., treas. Distributed Learning Workshop, 1999—. Named Man of Yr., Notre Dame Club of Omaha, 1988; recipient award for contbn. to med. sci., Omaha Bar Assn., 1986. Fellow: Am. Coll. Chest Physicians, Am. Coll. Cardiology, ACS; mem.: AMA, Lillehei Surg. Soc., Midwest Clin. Soc. (award for individual investigation exhibit 1970, Premier award 1971, award for rsch. sci. exhibit 1977), Omaha Douglas County Med. Soc., Nebr. Med. Assn., Am. Bronch-Esophagological Assn., Acad. Surgeons, Soc. Thoracic Surgeons, Rotary Club (hon. personal honors 1986, merit award 1986, Paul Harris fellow). Mailing: 2254 S 8th Ave Omaha NE 68124-2136

FERLINZ, JACK, cardiologist, medical educator; b. Marburg, Austria, Feb. 18, 1942; came to U.S., 1957. s. Anthony and Maria (Nachtigall) F. AB, Harvard U.; MBA, Northeastern U., 1965; MD, Boston U., 1969; doctorate (hon.), U. Maribor, Slovenia, 1990. Diplomate Am. Bd. Internal Medicine, Am. Bd. Cardiovascular Diseases. Intern. U. Hosp. Boston U., 1969-70; jr. resident M. Hitchcock Hosp. Dartmouth Med. Sch., Hanover, N.H., 1970-71; sr. resident Jackson Meml. Hosp., U. Miami, 1971-72; NIH rsch. fellow cardiology P.B. Brigham Hosp., Harvard U., Boston, 1972-74; dir. cardiac cath. lab., asst. chief cardiology V.A.M.C., Long Beach, Calif., 1974-82; asst. prof. medicine U. Calif., Irvine, 1975-81, assoc. prof. medicine, 1981-82; chmn. adult cardiology Cook County Hosp., Chgo., 1982-88; prof. medicine Chgo. Med. Sch., North Chicago, Ill., 1984-88; chmn. dept. of internal medicine Providence Hosp., Southfield, Mich., 1988-92; clin. prof. medicine Wayne State U. Sch. Medicine, Detroit, 1989-92; dir. med. edn. & rsch., prof. medicine & cardiology Hamad Med. Ctr., Doha, Qatar, 1992-94; chief dept. medicine Aleda E. Lutz VA Med. Ctr., Saginaw, Mich., 1994—; clin. prof. medicine Mich. State U. Coll. Human Medicine, 1994—. Vis. prof. numerous U.S., Canadian and European med. schs., 1980—. Mem. editl. bds. Am. Jour. Cardiology, 1989—, Am. Jour. Noninvas Cardiology, 1987—, Jour. Am. Coll. Cardiology, 1984-88, 89-93; contbr. over 300 book chpts. and sci. papers. Named to Begg's Soc. Boston U. Sch. Medicine, 1969. Fellow Am. Coll. Cardiology, Am. Coll. Chest Physicians (chmn. coronary sect. 1983-85), Am. Heart Assn., Am. Coll. Physicians, Am. Coll. Angiology; mem. Am. Fedn. Clin. Rsch., Am. Soc. Clin. Pharm. Therapy. Avocations: mountain climbing, skiing, tennis, scuba diving. Office: VA Med Ctr 1500 Weiss St Saginaw MI 48602-5251 E-mail: jack.ferlinz@med.va.gov.

FERNANDEZ, KATHLEEN M. cultural organization administrator; b. Dayton, Ohio, Oct. 8, 1949; d. Norbert Katzen and Yenema Vermeda (Bermingham) F.; m. James Robert Hillibish, Oct. 1, 1977. BA, Otterbein Coll., 1971. Edn. asst. Ohio Hist. Soc., Columbus, 1971, vol. coord., 1971-74, interpretive specialist Zoar, 1975-88, site mgr., 1988—. Bd. dirs., newsletter editor Ohio & Erie Canal Corridor Coalition, Akron, 1989—. Mem. Am. Assn. State and Local History, Nat. Trust Hist. Preservation, Zoar Cmty. Assn., Communal Studies Assn. (pres. 1981, editor newsletter 1981-86, 97—, bd. dirs. 1995—), Am. Assn. Mus. (surveyor mus. assistance program 1999—). Office: Zoar Village State Meml PO Box 404 221 W 3d St Zoar OH 44697

FERNER, DAVID CHARLES, non-profit management and development consultant; b. Rochester, N.Y., Mar. 14, 1933; s. John Theodore and Dorothy Flora (Seel) F.; m. Ursula Milda Thieme, Sept. 6, 1958. BA, Amherst Coll., 1955; MEd, U. Rochester, 1957; postgrad., Columbia U., 1961. Dir. student activities U. Rochester, N.Y., 1956-58; asst. to provost Tchrs. Coll. Columbia U., N.Y.C., 1959-60; asst. dir. devel. St. Lawrence U., Canton, N.Y., 1961-62; dir. devel. Sarah Lawrence Coll., Bronxville, 1962-66; cons., v.p. Frantzreb & Pray Assocs., Inc., N.Y.C., 1966-72, v.p., sec. Arlington, Va., 1972-75; pres. Frantzreb, Pray, Ferner & Thompson, Inc., 1975-77, David C. Ferner & Assocs., Annandale, Va., 1977-80; v.p., dir. devel. Minn. Orchestral Assn., Mpls., 1980-87; mng. ptnr. Currie, Ferner, Scarpetta & DeVries, 1987-99, founding ptnr., cons., 2000—. Contbr. articles to profl. publs. Bd. dirs. Madeline Island Mus. Camp. Amherst Coll. scholar, 1951-55. Mem. Nat. Soc. Fundraising Execs. (bd. dirs. Minn. chpt. 1995-97), Assn. Fundraising Profls., Nat. Com. Planned Giving, Coun. for Advancement and Support of Edn., Am. Symphony Orch. League, Opera Am. Home: 245 Wekiva Cv Destin FL 32541-4763

FERRALL, VICTOR EUGENE, JR. college administrator, lawyer; b. Urbana, Ill., July 31, 1936; s. Victor Eugene and Lucile Elizabeth (Hill) F.; m. Suzanne Elizabeth Lilly (div. 1985); children: Christopher Key, David Hill, Katherine Elizabeth; m. Linda K. Smith, 1987. AB, Oberlin Coll, 1956; student law, Harvard U., 1956-57; MA in Econs., Yale U., 1958, LLB, 1960. Bar: D.C. 1961, U.S. Supreme Ct. 1981. Atty. U.S. Dept. Justice, Washington, 1960-61; asst. to staff dir. antitrust and monopoly subcom. U.S. Senate, 1961-63; assoc. then ptnr. Koteen & Burt, 1963-75; ptnr. Jones, Day, Reavis & Pogue, 1975-79, Crowell & Moring, Washington, 1979-91; pres. Beloit (Wis.) Coll., 1991-2000; ret., 2000. Contbr. articles to profl. jours.; editor: Yearbook of Broadcasting Articles (anthology edition), 1980. Trustee Olivet (Mich.) Coll., 1979-81. Mem. ABA, D.C. Bar Assn., Wis. Bar Assn., Nat. Assn. Ind. Colls. and Univs. (bd. dirs. 1993—). Democrat. Episcopalian. Home: 709 College St Beloit WI 53511-5571 Office: Beloit Coll 700 College St Beloit WI 53511-5509

FERRARI, GIANNANTONIO, electronics executive; Diploma in acctg., U. Milan. With Gavazzi SpA, 1960, Honeywell Italia, 1965; gen. mgr. Honeywell Iran, Honeywell Greece; dir. fin., administrn., and human resources Honeywell Mid. E.; controller Honeywell Europe, 1981-85, v.p. fin. and adminstrn., 1985-88, pres., 1992-97; v.p. Western Europe, Mid. E., Africa Honeywell, Inc., Italy, 1988-92, pres., COO, 1997—. Bd. dirs. No. State Power Co., Nat. Assn. Mfrs.; bd. govs. Nat. Elec. Mfrs. Assn. Office: Honewell Inc Honeywell Plz Minneapolis MN 55408

FERREE, DAVID CURTIS, horticultural researcher; b. Lock Haven, Pa., Feb. 9, 1943; s. George H. and Ruth O. (McClain) F.; m. Sandra J. Corman, Aug. 31, 1968; children: Curtis P., Thomas A. BS, Pa. State U., 1965; MS, U. Md., 1968, PhD, 1969. From asst. to assoc. prof. Ohio State U., Wooster, 1971-81, prof., 1981—. Contbr. numerous articles to profl. jours. Capt. U.S. Army, 1969-71. Recipient sr. scientist disting. rsch. award Ohio Agrl. Rsch. and Devel. Ctr., 1997, Disting. Svc. award Ohio Fruit Growers Soc., 1998. Fellow Am. Soc. Hort. Sci. (assoc. editor 1983-86, v.p. 1988-89, J.H. Gourley award 1982, Stark award 1983), Am. Pomological Soc. (editor), Internat. Dwarf Fruit Tree Assn. (Disting. Rschr. award 1989), Gamma Sigma Delta (Rsch. award 1981). Lutheran. Office: Ohio Agrl R & D Ctr Dept Horticulture Crop Sci Wooster OH 44691 E-mail: ferree.1@osu.edu.

FERRELL, JAMES EDWIN, energy company executive; b. Atchison, Kans., Oct. 17, 1939; s. Alfred C. and Mabel A. (Samson) F.; m. Elizabeth J. Gillespie, May 10, 1959; children: Kathryn E., Sarah A. B.S. in Bus. Adminstrn., U. Kans., 1963. Pres. Ferrell Cos., Inc., Liberty, Mo., 1965—; chmn., chief exec. officer Gas Service Co., Kansas City, 1983-85. Bd. dirs. United Mo. Bancshares, Kansas City, Ferrell Cos., Inc. Bd. dirs. Coun. Ind. Colls., 1988-91; trustee Kansas City Symphony, 1987—. Served to 1st lt. U.S. Army, 1963-65. Republican. Lutheran. Office: Ferrell Cos Inc 1 Liberty Plz Liberty MO 64068-2970

FERRELL, ROBERT HUGH, historian, educator; b. Cleve., May 8, 1921; s. Ernest Henry and Edna Lulu (Rentsch) F.; m. Lila Esther Sprout, Sept. 8, 1956 (dec. Jan. 2002); 1 dau., Carolyn Irene. BS in Edn., Bowling Green State U., 1946, BA, 1947, LLD (hon.), 1971; MA, Yale U., 1948, PhD, 1951. Intelligence analyst U.S. Air Force, 1951-52; lectr. in history Mich. State U., 1952-53; asst. prof. history Ind. U., 1953-58, asso. prof., 1958-61, prof., 1961-74, Disting. prof., 1974-88, emeritus, 1988—. Vis. prof. Yale U., 1955-56, Am. U. at Cairo, 1958-59, U. Conn., 1964-65, Cath. U. Louvain, Belgium, 1969-70, Naval War Coll., 1974-75, U.S. Mil. Acad., 1987-88. Author: Peace in Their Time, 1952, American Diplomacy in the Great Depression, 1957, American Diplomacy: A History, 1959, 4th edit., 1987, Frank B. Kellogg and Henry L. Stimson, 1963, (with M.G. Baxter and J.E. Wiltz) Teaching of American History in High Schools, 1964, George C. Marshall, 1966, (with R.B. Morris and W. Greenleaf) America: A History of the People, 1971, (with others) Unfinished Century, 1973, Harry S. Truman and the Modern American Presidency, 1983, Truman: A Centenary Remembrance, 1984, Woodrow Wilson and World War I, 1985, Harry S. Truman: His Life on the Family Farms, 1991, Ill-Advised, 1992, Choosing Truman: The Democratic Convention of 1944, 1994, Harry S. Truman: A Life, 1994, The Strange Deaths of President Harding, 1996, The Dying President: Franklin D. Roosevelt, 1998, The Presidency of Calvin Coolidge, 1998, Truman and Pendergast, 1999; editor: Off the Record: The Private Papers of Harry S Truman, 1980, The Autobiography of Harry S. Truman, 1980, The Eisenhower Diaries, 1981, Dear Bess: The Letters from Harry to Bess Truman, 1983, (with Samuel Flagg Bemis) American Secretaries of State and Their Diplomacy, 10 vols., 1963-85, Banners in the Air: The Eighth Ohio Volunteers and the Spanish-American War, 1988, Monterrey is Ours!, 1990; Truman in the White House: The Diary of Eben Ayers, 1991, (with L.E. Wikander) Grace Coolidge: An Autobiography, 1992, Holding the Line: The Third Tennessee Infantry 1861-64, 1994; Truman and the Bomb, 1996, (with Joan Hoff) Dictionary of American History Supplement, 2 vols., 1996, FDR's Quiet Confidant: The Autobiography of Frank C. Walker, 1997, The Kansas City Investigation, 1999, A Youth in the Meuse-Argonne: A Memoir of World War I, 1917-1918, 2000, A Colonel in the Armored Divisions: A Memoir (1941-1945), 2001, In the Philippines and Okinawa: A Memoir (1945-1948), 2001. Served with USAAF, 1942-45. Mem. Soc. Historians Am. Fgn. Relations, Am. Hist. Assn. Home: 512 S Hawthorne Dr Bloomington IN 47401-5024 Office: Dept History Ind U Bloomington IN 47405

FERRILLO, PATRICK J., JR. academic dean, endodontist; b. St. Louis, Mar. 4, 1941; s. Patrick J. Ferrillo Sr. BS, Georgetown U., 1973; DDS, Baylor U., 1976, cert., 1978. Instr. Baylor Coll. of Dentistry, Dallas, 1976-78; clin. asst. prof. Sch. Dental Medicine So. Ill. U., Alton, 1978-79, asst. prof. Sch. Dental Medicine, 1979-84, sect. head Sch. Dental Medicine, 1979-87, dir. current affairs Sch. Dental Medicine, 1982-87, acting chmn. Sch. Dental Medicine, 1984-85, chairperson Sch. Dental Medicine, 1985-87, acting dean Sch. Dental Medicine, 1986-87, dean Sch. Dental Medicine, assoc. prof., 1987—; pres. Am. Assoc. Dental Schs., Washington. Fellow Am. Coll. Dentists, Internat. Coll. Dentists; mem. Omicron Kappa Upsilon (v.p. 1988-89, pres. 1989-91), Phi Kappa Phi. Office: So Ill U Sch Dental Med Office of the Dean 2800 College Ave Alton IL 62002-4742

FERRINI, JAMES THOMAS, lawyer; b. Chgo., Jan. 14, 1938; s. John B. and Julia (Marre) F.; m. Jeanne Marie Fontana, June 8, 1963; children: Anthony, Mary Caren, Emily, Joseph, Danielle. JD, Loyola U., 1963. Bar: U.S. Supreme Ct. 1963, U.S. Ct. Appeals (7th cir.) 1967, U.S. Ct. Appeals (8th cir.) 1969, U.S. Ct. Appeals (3d cir.) 1975, U.S. Ct. Appeals (6th cir.) 1982, U.S. Ct. Appeals (10th cir.) 1984, U.S. Ct. Appeals (4th cir.) 1987, U.S. Ct. Appeals (9th cir.) 1989. Sr. ptnr. Clausen Miller Gorman Caffrey & Witous, P.C., Chgo., 1963—. Mem. pattern jury instructions Ill. Supreme Ct. Commn., Chgo., 1978-94. Contbr. articles to profl. jours. Mem. Mary Seat of Wisdom Parish, Park Ridge. Fellow Am. Acad. Appellate Lawyers; mem. ABA, Ill. Bar Assn., Chgo. Bar Assn. (chmn. civil practice com.), Ill. Assn. Def. Trial Counsel, Appellate Lawyers Assn. (pres. Chgo. chpt. 1978, 79), Justinian Soc. Roman Catholic. Avocations: handball, sailing, skiing, cooking. Office: Clausen Miller PC 10 S La Salle St Ste 1600 Chicago IL 60603-1098

FERRY, JAMES ALLEN, physicist, electrostatics company executive; b. Sept. 9, 1937; s. Darwin J. and Eleanor J. (Irwin) F.; m. Karen A. Greenwood, Feb. 8, 1964; children: Thomas E., Jennifer J. BS in Physics, U. Wis., 1959, MS in Physics, 1962, PhD in Physics, 1965. Rsch. assoc. U. Wis., Madison, 1965-66; exec. v.p., COO Nat. Electrostatics Corp., Middleton, Wis., 1967-95, pres., CEO, chmn. bd., 1995—. Patentee in field. Mem. Am. Phys. Soc. Home: 4105 Teal Ct Middleton WI 53562-5266 Office: Nat Electrostatics Corp Graber Rd PO Box 620310 Middleton WI 53562-0310 E-mail: nec@pelletron.com.

FESTA, ROGER REGINALD, chemist, educator; b. Norwalk, Conn., Sept. 6, 1950; s. Reginald and Rosemary (Chappa) F. BA in Biology and Chemistry magna cum laude, St. Michael's Coll., 1972; MA in Agr., U. Vt., 1979; cert. in Adminstrn., Fairfield U., 1981; PhD in Edn., U. Conn., 1982. Tchr. Cen. Cath. High Sch., Norwalk, 1975-79, Brien McMahon High Sch., Norwalk, 1979-82; asst. prof. chemistry Truman State U. (formerly N.E. Mo. State U.), Kirksville, 1983-89, dir. Chem. Comm. Devel. Ctr., 1983-90, assoc. prof., 1989-97, prof., 1997—, coach men's volleyball, 1991-2000, dean frats., 1991-92. Adj. prof. U. Conn., 1983. Author: National Curriculum Development Programming for Teachers of High School Chemistry, 1981, Fairfield County High School Chemistry Curriculum Handbook, 1982. Sec. Diocese Bridgeport (Conn.) Edn. Assn., 1978-79, sci. cons. schs. office, 1979, exec. adminstr., 1979; bd. dirs. Norwalk Community Services Agy., 1980-81. Named one of Ten Outstanding Young Men of Mo., Mo. Jaycees, 1986. Fellow Am. Inst. Chemists (pub. edn. com. 1980-83, edn. editor The Chemist Jour. 1981-95, mem. editl. bd. The Chemist 1986-91, bd. dirs. 1982-99, chmn. nat. meetings com. 1982-91, 94-95, history com. 1982—, archivist 1983—, sec. 1991-93, pres.-elect 1994-95, pres. 1996-97); mem. Am. Chem. Soc. (founding editor The Fairfield Chemist 1978-79, assoc. editor Jour. Chem. Edn. 1980-89, vice chmn. edn. com. Western Conn. sect. 1979-81, chmn. elect Mark Twain sect. 1985, chmn. 1986, exec. bd. 1984-95, program chair 1984-95), St. Louis Inst. Chemists (founder 1984, pres. 1985-87, sec.-treas. 1987—), Acad. Sci. St. Louis, Assn. Frat. Advisors, Coll. Frat. Editors' Assn., Kirksville Jaycees (bd. dirs. 1983-86, sec. 1984-85, chair ret. sr. vols. com. 1985-87), Order of Omega, Delta Epsilon Sigma, Alpha Chi Sigma (assoc. editor The Hexagon 1984-99), Sigma Phi Epsilon (bd. govs. 1994—, advisor Truman State U. chpt. 1991—). Democrat. Roman Catholic. Home: 114 E Mcpherson St Kirksville MO 63501-3570 Office: Truman State U 100 E Normal Ave MG 202 Kirksville MO 63501-4200

FETLER, PAUL, composer, educator; b. Phila., Feb. 17, 1920; s. William Basil and Barbara (Kovalevski) Fetler-Malof; m. Ruth Regina Pahl, Aug. 13, 1947; children: Sylvia, Daniel, Beatrix. MusB, Northwestern U., 1943; MusM, Yale U., 1948; PhD, U. Minn., 1956. From instr. to prof. music theory and composition U. Minn., Mpls., 1948—. Vis. composer, condr. and lectr. various colls. and univs. Composer: Symphonie Fantasia, 1941, Passacaglia for orch., 1942, Dramatic Overture, 1943, Prelude for orch., 1946, Contrasts for orch., 1958, Soundings for orch., 1962, Jubilate Deo for voices and brass, 1963, Te Deum for mixed voices, 1963, Four Symphonies, 1948-67, Cantus Tristis for orch., 1964; opera Sturge Maclean, 1965, A Contemporary Psalm for chorus, organ and percussion, 1968, Cycles for percussion and piano, 1970, The Words From the Cross for mixed voices, 1971, First Violin Concerto, 1971, Dialogue for flute and guitar, 1973, Lamentations for chorus, narrator, percussion and flute, 1974, Three Venetian Scenes for guitar, 1974, Dream of Shalom for mixed voices, 1975, Songs of the Night for voices, narrator and flute, 1976, Three Poems by Walt Whitman for narrator and orch., 1975, Pastoral Suite for piano trio, 1976, Celebration for orch., 1976, Three Impressions for guitar and orch., 1977, Five Piano Games, 1977, Sing Alleluia, 1978, Song of the Forest Bird for voices and chamber orch., 1978, Six Songs of Autumn for guitar, 1979, Second Violin Concerto, 1980, Missa de Angelis for three choirs, orch., organ and handbells, 1980, Serenade for chamber orch., 1981, Rhapsody for violin and piano, 1982; song cycle The Garden of Love for voice and orch., 1983, Piano Concerto, 1984; Capriccio for chamber orch., 1985; Frolic for Flute, Winds and Strings, 1986, Three Excursions, A Concerto for Percussion, Piano and Orchestra, 1987, String Quartet, 1989, Toccata for Organ, 1990, numerous sacred and secular choral works, 1949-93, Twelve Sacred Hymn Settings, 1993, Divertimento for Flute and Strings, 1994, December Stillness for Flute, Harp and Voices, 1994, Suite for Woodwind Trio, 1995, Up the Dome of Heaven, Three Pieces for Mixed Voices and Flute, 1996; The Raven for basso, clarinet, percussion and string, 1998, Saraband variations for guitar, 1999. Served with AUS, 1943-45. Recipient Guggenheim awards, 1953, 60, Soc. for Publ. Am. Music award, 1953, Yale U. Alumni Assn. cert. of merit, 1975, NEA award, 1975, 77, 87; Ford Found. grantee, 1958. Mem. ASCAP (ann. award 1962—), Sigma Alpha Iota (nat. arts assoc.) Home: 174 Golden Gate Pt Apt 32 Sarasota FL 34236-6602 Office: U Minn 100 Ferguson Hall Minneapolis MN 55455 E-mail: pf-tonus8@webtv.net.

FETTIG, JEFF M. manufacturing executive; BA in Fin., MBA, Ind. U. Mem. fin. ops. Whirlpool Corp., 1981, various, 1981-89, v.p. mktg. KitchenAid, 1989-90; v.p. mktg. appliance group Whirlpool Europe, 1994-99, pres., COO, 1999—; also bd. dirs. Whirlpool Corp. Office: Whirlpool Corp 2000 N M 63 Benton Harbor MI 49022-2692

FEUER, HENRY, chemist, educator; b. Stanislau, Austria, Apr. 4, 1912; came to U.S., 1941, naturalized, 1946; s. Jacob and Julia (Tindel) F.; m. Paula Berger, Jan. 19, 1946. M.S., U. Vienna, Austria, 1934, Ph.D., 1936. Postdoctoral fellow U. Paris, France, 1939; with dept. chemistry Purdue U., Lafayette, Ind., 1943-79, prof. chemistry, 1961-79, prof. emeritus, 1979—. Vis. prof. Hebrew U., Jerusalem, Israel, 1964, Indian Inst. Tech., Kanpur, India, 1971, Peking (China) Inst. Tech., 1979 Pres., contbr. Organic Electronic Spectral Data, Inc., 1962-89; mng. editor Organic Nitro Chemistry Series, 1982—; mem. adv. bd. Turkish Jour. Chemistry; mem. editl. bd. Chimica Acta Turcica. Fellow AAAS; mem. Am. Chem. Soc., Chem. Soc., Sigma Xi, Phi Lambda Upsilon. Achievements include research, publs. in organic nitrogen compounds; discovered new methods for syntheses nitro compounds, cyclic hydrazides; research on mechanism of these reactions. Home: 726 Princess Dr West Lafayette IN 47906-2036 Office: Purdue U Dept Chemistry Lafayette IN 47907

FEUER, MICHAEL, office products superstore executive; Chmn., CEO OfficeMax, Shaker Heights, Ohio. Office: OfficeMax 3605 Warrensville Center Rd Shaker Heights OH 44122-5203

FEUERBORN, BILL, state legislator; m. Linda Feuerborn. Mem. Kans. State Ho. of Reps. Dist. 5, 1994—; mem. agrl. and appropriations coms.

FEUERWERKER, ALBERT, history educator; b. Cleve., Nov. 6, 1927; s. Martin and Gizella (Feuerwerker) F.; m. Yi-tsi Mei, June 11, 1955; children: Alison, Paul. AB, Harvard U., 1950, PhD, 1957. Lectr. history U. Toronto, Ont., Can., 1955-58; rsch. fellow Harvard U., Cambridge, Mass., 1958-60; assoc. prof. history U. Mich., Ann Arbor, 1960-63, prof., 1963-96, chmn. dept., 1984-87; dir. U. Mich. Ctr. for Chinese Studies, 1961-67, 72-83; A.M. and H.P. Bentley prof. of history U. Mich., 1986-96, prof. emeritus, 1996—; dir. d'études École des Hautes Etudes en Scis. Sociales, Paris, 1981; vis. scholar Acad. Social Scis., Shanghai, China, 1981, 88, Sichuan U., Chengdu, China, 1988. Joint com. on contemporary China, Social Sci. Research Council-Am. Council Learned Socs., 1966-78, 80-83, chmn., 1970-75; mem. com. on scholarly comm. with the People's Republic of China, Nat. Acad. Scis.-Social Sci. Rsch. Coun.-Am. Council Learned Socs., 1971-78, 81-83, vice-chmn., 1975-78 Author: China's Early Industrialization, 1958, History in Communist China, 1968, The Chinese Economy 1870-1911, 1969, Rebellion in 19th Century China, 1975, The Foreign Establishment in China, 1976, Economic Trends in the Republic of China, 1977, Chinese Social and Economic History from the Song to 1900, 1982, Studies in the Economic History of Late Imperial China, 1996, The Chinese Economy, 1870-1949, 1996; co-editor: Cambridge History of China, vol. 13, 1986; mem. editl. bd. Am. Hist. Rev., 1970-75, The China Quar., 1967-91, Comparative Studies in Soc. and History, 1964-2001. Served with AUS, 1946-47. Fellow NEH, 1971-72, Social Sci. Research Council-Am. Council of Learned Socs., 1962-63, Guggenheim Found., 1987-88. Fellow AAAS; mem. Assn. for Asian Studies (v.p. 1990, pres. 1991), Nat. Com. on U.S.-China Rels. Home: 827 Asa Gray Dr Apt 356 Ann Arbor MI 48105 Office: U Mich Ctr for Chinese Studies 1080 S University Ave Ste 3668 Ann Arbor MI 48109-1106 E-mail: afeuer@umich.edu.

FEUSS, LINDA ANNE UPSALL, lawyer; b. White Plains, N.Y., Dec. 9, 1956; d. Herbert Charles and Edna May (Hart) Upsall; m. Charles E. Feuss, Aug. 16, 1980; children: Charles Herbert, Anne Hart. BA, Colgate U., 1978; JD, Emory U., 1981. Bar: Ga. 1981, S.C. 1981, Minn. 2000. Assoc. Rainey, Britton, Gibbes & Clarkson, Greenville, S.C., 1981-83; counsel Siemens Energy & Automation, Atlanta, 1983-91, Siemens Corp., Atlanta, 1991-93, sr. counsel, 1993-94, assoc. gen. counsel, 1994-98; v.p., gen. counsel Pillsbury Co., 1998-2000, Demstar Inc., 2001—. Rep. law coun. II Mfr.'s Alliance, Washington, 1995-98; rep. law com. Nat. Elec. Mfr.'s Assn., Washington, 1995-98. Bd. dirs. Am. Heart Assn., Greenville, 1981-83, Success with Children, 1999, CityLights, 1999; mem. leadership com. Woodruff Arts Ctr. Campaign, Atlanta, 1985-90; vol. High Mus. Art, Atlanta, 1993-99, Ga. 100 Mentor Exch., 1998. Mem. ABA, Am. Corp. Coun. Assn. (dir. Ga. chpt. 1995-98, v.p. Ga. chpt. 1996, pres. 1997), State Bar Ga., S.C. Bar, Minn. Bar Assn., Colgate Club Atlanta (pres. 1986-88, bd. dirs. 1989-98). Office: Pillsbury Co MS 19F3 200 S 6th St Ste 200 Minneapolis MN 55402-6005 E-mail: linda.Feuss@pemstar.com.

FEZZEY, MIKE, radio station executive; Pres., gen. mgr. WJR-AM, Detroit, 1994—. Office: WJR-AM 2100 Fisher Bldg Detroit MI 48202

FICK, ROBERT, baseball player; b. Torrance, Calif., Mar. 15, 1974; Right fielder Detroit Tigers, 1998—. Played Team USA, 1996, Hawaii Winter League, 1997, Ariz. Fall League, 1998, 99. Office: Detroit Tigers 2100 Woodward Ave Detroit MI 48201*

FIEDLER, JOHN F. automotive executive; b. 1938; B in Chemistry, Kent State U., 1960; M in Bus., MIT, 1979. Joined The Goodyear Tire & Rubber Co., Akron, Ohio, 1964, various positions including pres. Retread Sys. Co. divsn., pres. Kelly Springfield Tire Co. divsn., exec. v.p. N.Am. tire divsn.; pres., COO Borg-Warner Automotive, Inc., Chgo., 1994—, also bd. dirs. Office: Borg Warner 200 S Michigan Ave Chicago IL 60604

FIEGEN, KRISTIE K. state legislator; State rep. S.D. Dist. 11, 1992-2000. Mem. Health and Human Svc. and Local Govt. Coms., S.D. Ho. Reps. Home: 6832 W Westminster Dr Sioux Falls SD 57106-3234 Office: SD House of Reps State Capitol Pierre SD 57501

FIEGEN, THOMAS L. state legislator, lawyer, economics educator; b. Mitchell, S.D., Oct. 2, 1958; s. Clarence L. and Phyllis Jean Fiegen; m. Sandra Lynn Cutler, Oct. 31, 1981; children: Maureen Sarah, Kathryn Ann, Paul Lewis, Theresa Jean. BS in Agrl. Econ., BS in Speech, Kans. State U., 1984; MA in Econ., JD, U. Iowa, 1988. Bar: S.D. 1988, Iowa 1988, Minn. 1991, U.S. Dist. Ct. S.D. 1989, U.S. Dist. Ct. (no. and so. dists.) Iowa 1990, U.S. Ct. Appeals (8th cir.) 1990. Assoc. McCann, Martin & McCann, Brookings, S.D., 1988-90, Childers & Vestle, P.C., Cedar Rapids, Iowa, 1990-93; ptnr. Childers & Fiegen, P.C., 1993—; mem. Iowa Senate from 20th dist., 2001—. Student rsch. asst. Konza Prairie Tallgrass Preserve, divsn. biology Kans. State U., Manhattan, 1982-84; tchg. asst. dept. econ. U. Iowa, Iowa City, 1985-87, instr., 1987-88; adj. faculty Kirkwood C.C., Cedar Rapids, 1992—. State conv. del. Iowa Dem. Party, Des Moines, 1992. Mem. ABA, Am. Bankruptcy Inst., Iowa Bar Assn., S.D. Bar Assn., Minn. Bar Assn., Phi Kappa Phi. Roman Catholic. Home: 93 Lombard St Clarence IA 52216-9334 Office: Childers & Fiegen PC 425 2nd St SE Ste 350 Cedar Rapids IA 52401-1819

FIEGER, GEOFFREY NELS, lawyer; b. Detroit, Dec. 23, 1950; s. Bernard Julian and June Beth (Oberer) F.; m. Kathleen Janice Podwoiski, June 25, 1983. BA, U. Mich., 1974, MA, 1976; JD, Detroit Coll. Law, 1979. Bar: Mich. 1979, U.S. Dist. Ct. (ea. dist.) Mich. 1979, Fla. 1980, U.S. Dist. Ct. (mid. dist.) Fla. 1980, Ariz. 1980. Ptnr. Fieger Fieger Kenney & Johnson, P.C., Southfield, Mich., 1979—. V.p. Orgn. United to Save Twp.,

West Bloomfield, Mich., 1987; dem. nominee for gov. of Mich., 1998. Mem. ABA, Detroit Bar Assn., Assn. Trial Lawyers Am. Unitarian. Avocations: running, swimming. Office: Fieger Fieger Kenney & Johnson PC 19390 W 10 Mile Rd Southfield MI 48075-2463

FIELD, BENJAMIN R., III, packaging manufacturing executive; Sr. v.p., CFO, treas. Bemis Co., Inc., Mpls. Office: Bemis Co Inc Ste 2300 222 S 9th St Minneapolis MN 55402-4099

FIELD, HENRY AUGUSTUS, JR. lawyer; b. Wisconsin Dells, Wis., July 8, 1928; s. Henry A. and Georgia (Coakley) F.; m. Patricia Ann Young, Nov. 30, 1957 (dec. 1980); children: Mary Patricia (dec. 1992), Thomas Gerard, Susan Therese (Mrs. Thomas Hempel); m. Molly Kelly Martin, Apr. 13, 1985. Student, Western Mich. Coll., 1946-47; PhD, Marquette U., 1950; LLB (cum laude), U. Wis., 1952. Bar: Wis. 1952, U.S. Dist. Ct. (we. and ea. dists.) Wis. 1952, U.S. Ct. Appeals (7th cir.) 1957, U.S. Supreme Ct. 1980. Asst. U.S. atty. Western Dist. of Wis., 1956-57; assoc. Roberts, Boardman, Suhr, Bjork & Curry, 1957-62; jr. ptnr. Roberts, Boardman, Suhr & Curry, 1962-70; ptnr. Boardman, Suhr, Curry & Field, Madison, Wis., 1970—, chmn. exec. com., 1985-95; mem. Wis. Jud. Council, 1974-79. Dir. Family Service Soc., 1969-75, treas., 1971-72, pres., 1973-74; trustee Dane County Bar Pro Bono Trust Found., 1995-99. Served with C.I.C., AUS, 1952-55. Fellow: Wis. Bar Found. (chmn. litigation sect. 1971—72), Am. Bar. Found., Am. Coll. Trial Lawyers (state chmn. 1982—83); mem.: ABA (Wis. chmn. legis. com. 1975—76), Milw. and Dane County Bar Assn. (pres. 1971—72), 7th Fed. Cir. Bar Assn., Order of Coif, Sigma Tau Delta, Phi Delta Phi. Republican. Roman Catholic. Club: Madison. Home: 3310 Valley Creek Cir Middleton WI 53562-1988 Office: Boardman Suhr Curry & Field 1 S Pinckney St Madison WI 53703-2892

FIELD, MARSHALL, business executive; b. Charlottesville, Va., May 13, 1941; s. Marshall IV and Joanne (Bass) F.; m. Joan Best Connelly, Sept. 5, 1964 (div. 1969); 1 child, Marshall; m. Jamee Beckwith Jacobs, Aug. 19, 1972; children: Jamee Christine, Stephanie Caroline, Abigail Beckwith. BA, Harvard Coll., 1963. With N.Y. Herald Tribune, 1964-65; pub. Chgo. Sun-Times, 1969-80, Chgo. Daily News, 1969-78; dir. Field Enterprises, Inc., Chgo., 1965-84, dir., mem. exec. com., 1965-84, chmn. bd., 1972-84, The Field Corp., 1984—, Cabot, Cabot & Forbes, 1984—, chmn. exec. com., 1985-89, sr. dir., chief exec. officer, 1989—; pub. World Book-Childcraft Internat. Inc., 1973-78, dir., 1965-80. Bd. trustees Art Inst. Chgo., Chgo. Pub. Libr. Found., Rush-Presbyn.-St. Lukes Med. Ctr., Chgo. Cmty. Trust; vice-chmn. bd. trustees Field Mus. Natural History; chmn. bd. Terra Mus. Am. Art; adv. bd. Brookfield Zoo; mem. charitable adv. coun. Office of Atty. Gen. of State of Ill.; active Chgo. Orchestral Assn.; mem. bd. visitors, vice chair Nicholas Sch. of the Environment, Duke U.; bd. dirs. First Nat. Bank Chgo., 1970—85, Field Found. Ill., Lincoln Park Zool. Soc., World Wildlife Fund, Atlantic Salmon Fedn. Mem. Nature Conservancy, River Club, Chgo. Club, Comml. Club, Harvard Club, Racquet Club, Onwentsia Club, Jupiter Island Club, Shore Acres Club. Office: 225 W Wacker Dr Ste 1500 Chicago IL 60606-1235

FIELD, ROBERT EDWARD, lawyer; b. Chgo., Aug. 21, 1945; s. Robert Edward and Florence Elizabeth (Aiken) F.; m. Jenny Lee Hill, Aug. 5, 1967; children: Jennifer Kay, Kimberly Anne, Amanda Brooke. BA, Ill. Wesleyan U., 1967; MA, Northwestern U., 1969, JD, 1973. Bar: Ill. 1973, U.S. Dist. Ct. (no. dist.) Ill. 1974, U.S. Supreme Ct. 1979. Exec. dir. Winnetka (Ill.) Youth Orgn., 1969-73; assoc. Seyfarth, Shaw, Fairweather & Geraldson, Chgo., 1973-79, ptnr., 1979-93, Field & Golan, Chgo., 1993—. Bd. dirs. Gt. Lakes Fin. Resources, Matteson, Ill., 1983—, vice chmn., 1988-91, chmn. 1991—; bd. dirs. Chgo. chpt. Ill. Wesleyan U. Assocs.; chmn. bd. dirs. 1st Nat. Bank of Blue Island, 1989-2001, Great Lake Bank, 2001—, Bank of Homewood, 1988-2001; bd. dirs. Winchester Mfg. Co., Wood Dale, Ill., Ludell Mfg. Co., Milw., Comml. Resources Corp., Naperville, Ill., 1984-93; dir., sec. Ellis Corp., Itasca, Ill., 1980—; chmn. bd. dirs. Cmty. Bank of Homewood-Flossmoor, Ill., 1983-92, Bank of Matteson, Ill., 1992-99; mem. State Banking Bd. Ill., 1993-97. Bd. dirs. Ctr. for New Beginnings, 1997—, Svcs. Exch., 1998—, Family Svc. Ctrs. Cook County, Matteson, 1979—, treas., 1981-82, pres., 1986-88, chmn., 1988-93; pres. Lakes of Olympia Condominium Assn., 1987-89; trustee Village of Olympia Fields, Ill., 1981-89, pres., 1991-97; trustee Ill. Wesleyan U., 1990—, treas., 1994—; bd. dirs. Northwestern U. Sch. Law Alumni Assn., 1990-94. Mem. ABA, Ill. Bar Assn., Am. Bankers Assn., Ill. Bankers Assn., United Meth. Bar Assn. (v.p. Chgo. chpt. 1989), Chgo. Bar Assn., Bankers Club Chgo., Union League Club Chgo., Calumet Country Club. Home: 3424 Parthenon Way Olympia Fields IL 60461-1321 Office: Field & Golan 3 1st National Plz Ste 1500 Chicago IL 60602 E-mail: refield@fieldgolan.com.

FIELDING, RONALD, food products executive; Group v.p. meat products Hormel Foods Corp., Austin, Minn., 1999—. Office: Hormel Foods Corp One Hormel Pl Austin MN 55912-3680

FIELDS, ALLEN, artistic director; b. Pinehurst, N.C. Student, N.C. Sch. Arts, Am. Ballet Theatre Sch., N.Y.; studied with Patricia Wilde, Wilhelm Burman, David Howard, Ivan Nagy, Melissa Hayden. Performer with Cynthia Gregory, Gwen Verdon, Samuel Ramie, Madonna, Geena Davis; guest appearances in South Am., Europe, Can., Mex.; dancer with Ohio Ballet, Eglevsky Ballet, Ballet du Nord, France, Atlanta Ballet, Newport News Ballet, Phoenix Ballet, Hubbard St. Dance Co.; prin. dancer Cleve. San Jose Ballet; artistic dir. Minn. Ballet, 1992—. Office: Minn Ballet Ste 800 301 W 1st St Duluth MN 55802

FIELDS, HENRY WILLIAM, college dean; b. Cedar Rapids, Iowa, Sept. 25, 1946; m. Anne M. Fields; children: Benjamin Widdicomb, Justin Riley. AB in Psychology, Dartmouth, Hanover, N.H., 1969; DDS in Dentistry, Univ. Iowa, Iowa City, 1973, MS in Pedodontics, 1975; MSD in Orthodontics, Univ. Wash., Seattle, 1977. Cert. dentistry Iowa 1973, N.C. 1978, Ohio 1991. Staff, Dept. Hosp. Dentistry Univ. Iowa Hosps., Iowa City, 1973; grad. supr. Muscatine (Iowa) Migrant Program, 1974; grad. instr., Undergrad. Pedodontic Clinic and Lab. Univ. Iowa, 1974-75; AFDH tchr. tng. fellow, Dept. Orthodontics Univ. Wash., 1975-77, clin. asst., Undergrad. Pediatric Dentistry Clinic and Seminars, 1977; active participant Dental Faculty Practice, Sch. Dentistry Univ. N.C., Chapel Hill, 1977-91, asst. prof., Depts. of Pediatric Dentistry and Orthodontics, 1977-82; with N.C. Meml. Hosp., 1978-91; assoc. prof., Depts. of Pediatric Dentistry and Orthodontics Univ. N.C., 1982-87, grad. program dir., Dept. Pediatric Dentistry, 1984-89, prof., Dept. Pediatric Dentistry and Orthodontics, 1987-91, acting dir. grad. studies, Sch. Dentistry, 1989, asst. dean acad. affairs, Sch. Dentistry, 1990-91; chair, Dept. Dentistry OSU Hosps., Columbus, Ohio, 1991—, adj. prof. of Orthodontics, Sch. Dentistry, 1992—; participant, Faculty Practice OSU Coll. of Dentistry, Ohio, 1991—, prof. Dept. Orthodontics, 1991—, dean, 1991—; staff Columbus Children's Hosp., 1992—. Mem. human subjects com. Sch. Dentistry, Univ. N.C., 1989-91, chmn. curriculum com., 1990-91, chmn. dirs. com. adv. edn. program, 1989-91, health promotion disease prevention task force, 1990-91; deans coun. computerization com. The Ohio State Univ., 1991—; bd. dirs. IADR-AADR Craniofacial Biology Group, 1988-90; cons. to com. to review grad. Pediatric Dentistry Univ. Pitts., 1991; co-chair cont. edn. com. Am. Acad. Pediatric Dentistry/ Am. Assoc. of Orthodontic, 1991—; cons. Callahan award commn., 1992; external examiner BDS and MDS programs Dept. Pediatric Dentistry and Orthodontics Univ. Hong Kong, 1991-93; course dir. and coord. for numerous grad. and undergrad. programs. Contbr. chpts. to books, articles to profl. jours. Recipient NIDR grantee, 1980-83, NIDR Inst. grantee, 1985-86, 1988-93. Home: 4066 Fenwick Rd Columbus OH 43220-4870 Office: Ohio State U Coll Dentistry 1159 Postle Hall Columbus OH 43210-1241

FIELDS, SARA A. travel company executive; Sr. v.p. onboard svc. UAL Corp., Elk Grove Village, Ill. Office: UAL Corp 1200 E Algonquin Rd Arlington Heights IL 60005-4712 also: PO Box 66100 Chicago IL 60666-0100 Fax: 847-700-4899.

FIELDS, WILLIAM ALBERT, lawyer; b. Parkersburg, W.Va., Mar. 30, 1939; s. Jack Lyons and Grace (Kelley) F.; m. Prudence Brandt Adams, June 26, 1964. B.S. magna cum laude, Ohio State U., 1961; postgrad., Harvard Law Sch., 1961-64. Bar: Ohio bar 1964. Since practiced in, Marietta; city prosecutor, 1964-65; acting Judge Marietta Mcpl. Ct.; dir. elections Washington County, 1967-74; profl. bass-baritone soloist. Bd. dirs. Bank One, Marietta, N.A.; lectr. on estate planning and probate matters. Mem. editl. bd. Probate Law Jour. of Ohio. Chmn. Washington County Heart Assn., 1965-67; county chmn. Am. Cancer Soc., 1967; mem. dist. exec. com. Boy Scouts Am., 1967-74; Treas. County Republican Exec. Com., 1966—; trustee YMCA, Salvation Army; pres. bd. trustees Washington State Community Coll., Marietta; exec. com., trustee Coll. Adminstrv. Scis., Ohio State U.; trustee Appalachian Bible Coll., Bradley, W.Va., 1974-77, Marietta Meml. Hosp., also treas. Recipient Wall St. Jour. award, 1961; named Outstanding Young Man of Marietta, 1968, Outstanding Citizen of Marietta, 1992; named to Ohio Valley Sports Hall of Fame, 2001. Fellow Am. Coll. Trust and Estate Counsel; mem. Ohio Bar Assn. (chmn., bd. govs., probate and trust law sect.), Washington County Bar Assn., Marietta Area C. of C. (v.p., trustee), Am. Mensa, Nat. Soc. of Arts and Letters (bd. trustees), Sigma Chi, Beta Gamma Sigma. Clubs: Rotarian (pres. 1970-71), Marietta Country (trustee). Home: 129 Hillcrest Dr Marietta OH 45750-9321 Office: 217 2nd St Marietta OH 45750-2916 E-mail: WAF125@wirefire.com.

FIES, JAMES DAVID, elementary education educator; b. Chgo., May 19, 1950; s. Arthur Herbert Sr. and Ruth Paulina (Rehm) F.; m. Ruth Elaine Carlson, June 24, 1972; children: Samuel Jacob, Sarah Rae. BA, Purdue U., 1972, MS, 1975. Cert. elem. edn. tchr., Ind. Tchr. math. Morton Elem./Mid. Sch., Hammond, Ind., 1972-82, Eggers Elem./Mid. Sch., Hammond, 1982-88, Gavit Jr./Sr. High Sch., Hammond, 1988—, interim asst. prin., 1992. Dept. chair Eggers Mid. Sch., 1983-86. Bldg. union rep. Hammond Tchrs. Fedn. Local 394, 1981-87; trustee Trinity Luth. Ch., Hammond, 1976-82, 86-87, bd. fin., 1993—. Mem. Nat. Coun. Tchrs. of Maths., Hammond Tchrs. Fedn., Am. Fedn. of Tchrs. Avocations: traveling, fishing, family activities. Home: 544 Hickory Ln Munster IN 46321-2409

FIFE, WILMER KRAFFT, chemistry educator; b. Wellsville, Ohio, Oct. 19, 1933; s. Wilmer George and Lourene Elizabeth (Krafft) F.; m. Betsy Louise Jones, Dec. 26, 1959; children: Kimberly, Julia, Steven. B.Sc. in Chemistry, Case Inst. Tech., 1955; Ph.D. in Organic Chemistry, Ohio State U., 1960. Applications chemist Monsanto Chem. Co., Dayton, Ohio, summers 1955, 57; instr. Muskingum (Ohio) Coll., 1959-60, asst. prof., 1960-64, asso. prof., 1964-70, prof., 1970-71, chmn. dept. chemistry, 1966-71; prof. chemistry Ind. U.-Purdue U. at Indpls., 1971—, chmn. dept., 1971-80. NIH postdoctoral fellow Harvard U., 1965-66; NIH postdoctoral fellow Columbia U., 1968-69; NSF fellow, 1955-56; Sinclair Oil Co. fellow, 1958-59; DuPont fellow, 1960; Danforth assoc., 1969—; others; vis. scholar in chemistry Louis Pasteur U., Strasbourg, France, 1994, U. San Francisco, 1999; named Outstanding Rschr. in Sci. Ind. U.-Purdue U., Indpls. Mem. Am. Chem. Soc., AAAS, Sigma Xi, Tau Beta Pi, Phi Lambda Upsilon. Home: 7102 Dean Rd Indianapolis IN 46240-3626 Office: IUPUI Chemistry 402 N Blackford St Indianapolis IN 46202-3217 E-mail: fife@chem.iupui.edu.

FIJALKOWSKI, ISABELLE, professional basketball player; b. May 23, 1972; d. Tadeusz and Leokadia Fijalkowski. Student, U. Colo., 1995, U. d'Orleans, 1997—. Basketball player Euroleague, 1996-97; forward Cleveland Rockers, (WNBA), 1997—. Office: Cleveland Rockers Gund Arena One Center Ct Cleveland OH 44115

FILIPPINE, EDWARD LOUIS, federal judge; b. 1930; A.B., St. Louis U., 1951, J.D., 1957. Bar: Mo. 1957. Pvt. practice law, St. Louis, 1957-77; spl. asst. atty. gen. State of Mo., 1963-64; chief judge U.S. Dist. Ct. (ea. dist.) Mo., St. Louis, 1977-95, sr. judge, 1995—; U.S. sr. dist. judge U.S. Dist. Ct. for Ea. Dist. Mo., 1995—. Served with USAF, 1951-53 Mem. ABA, Mo. Bar Assn., Bar Assn. Met. St. Louis, St. Louis County Bar Assn., Lawyers Assn. of St. Louis. Office: US Dist Ct 1114 Market St Rm 329 Saint Louis MO 63101-2038

FILISKO, FRANK EDWARD, physicist, educator; b. Lorain, Ohio, Jan. 29, 1942; s. Joseph John and Mary Magdalene (Cherven) F.; m. Doris Faye Call, Aug. 8, 1970; children: Theresa Marie, Andrew William, Edward Anthony. BA, Colgate U., 1964; MS, Purdue U., 1966; PhD, Case Western Res. U., 1969. Post doctoral fellow Case Western Res. U., Cleve., 1968-70; prof. materials sci. engring. and macromolecular sci. U. Mich., Ann Arbor, 1970—, acting dir. macromolecular sci. and engring., 1987-96. Dir. Polymer Lab., U. Mich. Editor: Progress in Electrorheology, 1995; contbr. more than 125 articles to profl. jours. Mem. Am. Phys. Soc., Am. Chem. Soc., KC, Soc. of Rheology. Roman Catholic. Achievements include patents for Electric field dependent fluids and Electric dependent fluids-CIP. Office: U Mich Materials Sci & Engring Ann Arbor MI 48109 E-mail: fef@engin.umich.edu.

FILLOON, KAREN, radio personality; BS Meteorology, Fla. State U. With Nat. Weather Svc.; on-air meteorologist TV Tallahassee; meterologist Sta. KSTP-TV, Sta. KSTP-FM; staff meteorologist Sta. WCCO Radio, Mpls., 1989—. Instr. meteorology U. St. Thomas. Co-chair ann. golf tournament Am. Heart Assn. Mem.: Minn. Multiple Sclerosis Soc. (mem. strategic bd. devel. com., bd. trustees). Office: WCCO 625 2nd Ave S Minneapolis MN 55402*

FILMON, GARY ALBERT, Canadian provincial premier, civil engineer; b. Winnipeg, Man., Can., Aug. 24, 1942; s. Albert and Anastasia (Doskcoz) F.; m. Janice Clare Wainwright, 1963; children: Allison, David, Gregg, Susanna. BSc in Civil Engring., U. Man., 1964, MSc, 1967. Registered profl. engr. Mcpl. design engr. Underwood McLellan and Assocs., Winnipeg, 1964-67, br. mgr. Brandon, Man., 1967-69; v.p. Success Bus. Coll., Winnipeg, 1969-71, pres., 1971-81. City councillor Queenston Ward, City of Winnipeg, 1975-77, Crescent Heights Ward, City of Winnipeg, 1977-79; mem. legis. assembly River Heights Constituency, Man., 1979-81, Tuxedo Constituency, Man., 1981— , minister consumer and corp. affairs and environment Man. Govt., 1981, leader of the opposition, 1983-88, 99—premier of Manitoba, 1988-99; chmn. com. of works and ops. City of Winnipeg, 1977-79. Recipient award of merit B'nai B'rith Can., 1991; honored for may yrs. of svc. to Jewish Cmty., Man.-Sask. region Jewish United Fund Can., 1996. Mem. Assn. Profl. Engrs. Province of Man., Assn. Can. Career Colls. (pres. 1974-75), U. Man. Alumni Assn. (pres. 1974-75). Mem. Conservative Party. Anglican. Office: Man Legis Assembly Legislature Bldg Rm 204 Winnipeg MB Canada R3C OV8

FINAN, RICHARD H. state legislator, lawyer; b. Cin., Aug. 16, 1934; m. Joan L. Finan, 1956; children: Patrick, Nancy, Julie, Michael. BS, U. Dayton; LLB, U. Cin. Bar: Ohio. Pvt. practice, Sharonville, Ohio; mem. Ohio Senate from 7th dist., Columbus, 1978—; pres. Ohio Senate, 1997—. Asst. pro tem, chmn. ways and means com., Senate legis. ethics com., fin. com., commerce and labor com., rules com., reference and oversight com., joint legis. com. on fed. funds, welfare oversight com., taxation rev. com., mem. Rep. campaign com.; chmn. fed. budget and taxation com. Nat. Conf. State Legislators; bd. dirs. Franklin Savs. & Loan; arbitrator Hamilton County Ct. Common Pleas, Am. Arbitration Assn. Councilman Evendale Villae, Ohio, 1963-69, mayor, 1969-73; mem. Ohio Ho. of Reps., Columbus, 1973-78; exec. dir. Hamilton County Reagan-Bush Campaign, 1984; dir. Dole for Pres. Campaign, 1988; trustee U. Dayton; past trustee St. Rita's Sch. for Deaf; bd. dirs. Cath. Social Svcs. Southwestern Ohio, Carillon Funds, Rest Haven. Named Legislator of Yr., Ohio Trial Lawyers Assn., 1975, Twp. Clks. and Trustees Assn., 1976, Disting. Alumnus award U. Dayton, Andrew Carnegie award Oho Libr. Assn., 1993, Outstanding Merit award for statehouse preservation Ohio Hist. Soc. Mem. Ohio Bar Assn., Cin. Bar Assn., Sharonville Bus. Assn., U. Dayton Alumni Assn. (past pres. Cin. chpt.), U. Dayton Nat. Alumni Assn. (past pres.). Office: 3068 Stanwin Pl Cincinnati OH 45241-3360 also: State House 11137 Main St Cincinnati OH 45241-2614 also: 3457 Sherbrooke Dr Cincinnati OH 45241-3282 Office: State House Rm 201 2nd Fl Columbus OH 43215

FINDLEY, PAUL, former congressman, author, educator; b. Jacksonville, Ill., June 23, 1921; s. Joseph S. and Florence Mary (Nichols) F.; m. Lucille Gemme; children: Craig Jon, Diane Lillian. AB, Ill. Coll., 1943, LLD, 1972; LHD (hon.), Lindenwood Coll., 1969, Lincoln U., 1988, MacMurray Coll., 1997; LLD, Sana'a U., Yemen, 1997. Mem. 87th-97th Congresses from 20th Ill. dist., mem. Fgn. Affairs com., mem. Agr. com.; chmn. factfinding mission to Paris, 1965; chmn. Rep. NATO Task Force, 1965-68; chmn. com. to investigate internat. problems caused by agrl. support policies Ditchley (Eng.) Conf., 1973; del. N. Atlantic Assembly, 1965-70, 72-79, Munich Conf. German Rels., 1969-71; Ditchley Conf. Atlantic Trade, 1967; European Parliament, 1974-76; mem. 7th Congl. Del. to People's Republic China, 1975; chmn. Ill. Trade Mission to, USSR, 1972, People's Republic of China, 1978. Mem. internat. food and agrl. devel. bd. AID, 1983-94; vis. prof. MacMurray Coll., 1994-96. Author: Abraham Lincoln: The Crucible of Congress, The Federal Farm Fable, They Dare to Speak Out: People and Institutions Confront Israel's Lobby, Deliberate Deceptions: Facing the Facts About the U.S.-Israel Relationships, Silent No More: Confronting America's False Images of Islam; contbr. numerous articles on fgn. policy and agr. to periodicals. Trustee emeritus Ill. Coll.; lectr. leadership program UN Leadership Acad., Amman, Jordan, 1987-88; chmn. Coun. for the Nat. Interest, 1989-2000. Served to lt. (j.g.) USNR, WWII. Named laureate Lincoln Acad., 1980; decorated Grand Cross Order of Merit Fed. Republic of Ger.; recipient Outstanding Svc. to Agr. citation So. Ill. U., Kefauver award for promoting Fedn. of Atlantic Nations; Hon. Am. Farmer degree FFA, Outstanding Achievmeent award FFA Alumni Assn., citation Nat. Assn. State Univs. and Land-Grant Colls., EAFORD Humanitarian award, 1986, Alex Odeh Human Rights award Am. Arab Anti-Discrimination Com., 1992, Disting. Svc. award Assn. for Internat. Agr. and Rural Development, 1995; Malcolm X award Muslim Assn., 2000. Mem. Assn. to Unite Democracies (bd. dirs.), Am. Legion, Phi Beta Kappa. Republican. Presbyterian. Home and Office: 1040 W College Ave Jacksonville IL 62650-2306

FINDLEY, TROY RAY, state legislator; B in Polit. Sci., U. Kans., 1990. With grocery/retail industry, 1982-92; county desk dir. Kans. Dem. Party, 1992-94; mem. Kans. State Ho. of Reps. Dist. 46, 1995—, mem. banking com. Office: Kansas State Capitol Rm 272 West Topeka KS 66612

FINE, ARTHUR I. philosopher, educator; b. Lowell, Mass., Nov. 11, 1937; s. David Fine and Rae (Silverberg) Mintz; m. Helene S. Feldberg, June 16, 1957 (div. May 1980); children: Dana S., Sharon D.; m. Micky Forbes, July 11, 1980. Student, Harvard U., 1955-56; BS, U. Chgo., 1958; MS, Ill. Inst. Tech., 1960; PhD, U. Chgo., 1963. Asst. prof. math and philosophy Ill. Inst. Tech., Chgo., 1961—63; asst. prof. philosophy U. Ill., Urbana, 1963—65; assoc. prof. philosophy Cornell U., Ithaca, NY, 1967—71, prof. philosophy, 1971—72, U. Ill., Chgo., 1972—82, Northwestern U., Evanston, 1982—85, John Evans prof. philosophy, 1985—2001; prof. philosophy U. Wash., Seattle, 2001—. Mem. nat. com. Internat. Union History and Philosophy of Sci. Nat. Acad. Sci., 1973-77; mem. adv. panel History and Philosophy of Sci. Nat. Sci. Found., 1975-77, 87-88, 92-93. Author: The Shaky Game, 1986, 2d edit., 1996; co-editor: Philosophical Review, 1969-71; editor: (with others) PSA: 1986, 88, 90, vols. I and II; subject editor: Philosophy of Science Routledge Encyclopedia of Philosophy, 1993-98; contbr. articles to profl. jours. NSF fellow, 1966-67; NSF grantee 1968, 73, 78, 80, 89; sr. fellow NEH, 1974-75; Guggenheim fellow, 1982-83; fellow Ctr. Advanced Study in Behavioral Scis. Stanford, 1985-86; vis. fellow Dibner Inst., MIT, 1996. Mem. Philosophy of Sci. Assn. (pres. 1986-88), Am. Philos. Assn. (ctrl. divsn. pres. 1997-98). Office: U Wash Philosophy Dept Box 353350 Seattle WA 98195-3550

FINE, MORRIS EUGENE, materials engineer, educator; b. Jamestown, N.D., Apr. 12, 1918; s. Louis and Sophie (Berrington) F.; m. Mildred Eleanor Glazer, Aug. 13, 1950; children: Susan Elaine, Amy Lynn. B.Metall. Engring. with distinction, U. Minn., 1940, M.S., 1942, Ph.D., 1943. Instr. U. Minn., 1942-43; mem. tech. staff Bell Telephone Labs., Murray Hill, N.J., 1946-54; prof. emeritus Northwestern U., Evanston, Ill., 1954—, prof., chmn. dept. metallurgy Tech. Inst., 1955-57, chmn. dept. materials sci., 1958-60, prof. and chmn. materials research center, 1960-64, Walter P. Murphy prof. materials sci., 1963-89, tech. inst. prof., 1985-89, dir. Am. Iron and Steel Inst. steel resource ctr., 1986-93, assoc. dean grad. studies and research Tech. Inst., 1973-85, prof. emeritus, 1989, mem. grad. faculty, 1989—. Vis. prof. dept. materials sci. Stanford U., 1967-68; JSPS vis. scholar, Japan, 1979; chmn., vis. prof. materials sci. and engring. U. Tex., Austin, 1984-95; assoc. engr. Manhattan Project, U. Chgo. and Los Alamos, N.Mex., WWII; mem. materials adv. bd. NAS, 1963-68; mem. com. geol. and materials scis. NRC, 1979-82; chmn. adv. bd. program on modular methods for tchg. materials Pa. State U., 1973-77; chmn. vis. com. metallurgy and materials Sci. and Materials Rsch. Ctr., Lehigh U., 1965-75; mem. vis. com. Lawrence Berkeley Lab., 1978-81, chmn., 1981, mem. vis. com. Ames Dept. Energy Lab., 1976-80, Materials Rsch. Ctr., Pa. State U., 1988-91, Colo. Sch. Mines, 1991-96; chmn., organizer numerous confs. in field. Author numerous tech. and sci. articles on mech. properties of metals and ceramics, fatigue of metals, phase transformations, high temperature alloys, and other subjects.; author: Introduction to Phase Transformation in Condensed Systems. Recipient Gilbert Speich award Iron and Steel Soc., 1993; named Chicagoan of Year in Sci., 1961 Fellow Am. Phys. Soc., Japan Soc. Metals (hon.), Am. Soc. Metals (chpt. chmn. 1963, Campbell lectr. 1979, chmn. seminar com. 1979, hon. mem. com. 1993-96, gold medal 1986), Metall Soc. of AIME (chmn. inst. metals div. 1966-68, bd. dirs. 1968-71, bd. dirs. inst. 1972-75, mem. Bardeen gold medals com. 1992-96, chmn. 1995-96, Methewson gold medal for rsch. 1981, James Douglas gold medal 1982, Educator award 1993, hon. mem.), Am. Ceramic Soc. (keynote lectr. electronic materials div. 1972); mem. NAE (astronautics space engring. bd. 1973-77, membership com. 1974-79, chmn. 1977-78, mem. membership adv. com. 1991-94), Scripta Met et Mat (Outstanding Paper award 1991), The Metals, Materials, Minerals Soc. (inst. metals lecture and R.F. Mehl gold medal 1996), Sigma Xi, Tau Beta Pi, Alpha Sigma Mu, Sigma Alpha Sigma. Home: 1101 Manor Dr Wilmette IL 60091-1026 Office: Dept Materials Sci and Engring Northwestern U Evanston IL 60208-3108 E-mail: m-fine@northwestern.edu.

FINE, PAM, newspaper editor; Mng. editor Mpls. Star Tribune. Office: Star Tribune 425 Portland Ave Minneapolis MN 55488-0002

FINGERHUT, ERIC D. state legislator, former congressman, lawyer; b. University Hts., Ohio, May 6, 1959; BS summa cum laude, Northwestern U., 1981; JD, Stanford U., 1984. Staff atty. older persons law office Legal Aid Soc., Cleve., 1984-85; assoc. dir. Cleveland Works, 1987-89; atty. Hahn Loeser & Parks; campaign mgr., transition dir., spl. asst. to Mayor Mike White, 1989; mem. Ohio Senate from 25th Dist., Columbus, 1991-93, 103rd Congress from 19th Ohio dist., Washington, 1993-94, Ohio

Senate from 25th dist., Columbus, 1999—. Mem. Energy, Nat. Resources and Environ. com., Fin. com., Health and Human Svcs. com., Child Support Guidelines Adv. com., Ohio Adv. Coun. for Aging com., Task Force on Campaign Fin. reform com., Welfare Oversight Commission com., House Banking, Fin. and Urban Affairs com., Sci., Space and Tech. com., Fgn. Affairs Com. Bd. trustees Cleve. Zelma George Shelter; pres. Common Cause/Ohio, 1986-88; leader FITE; tchr. Sunday Sch. Synagogue Beth-Am. Recipient Future of Cleve. Jewry award, Stanford Law Review award; named to Cleve. Heights High Sch. Hall of Fame. Mem. Ohio Bar Assn., Cleve. Bar Assn. Democrat. Jewish. Home: 22675 Fairmont Blvd Cleveland OH 44118 Office: Ohio Senate Rm 049 Senate Bldg Columbus OH 43215 Address: 2550 Som Center Rd Ste 385 Willoughby OH 44094-9655

FINK, BILL A. state legislator; b. Ringsted, Iowa, May 5, 1955; m. Donna; 2 children. BS, Iowa State U., 1977; MS in Edn., Drake U., 1984. Tchr. govt., econ., social studies Carlisle (Iowa) H.S.; mem. Warren County Dem. Ctrl. Com., Iowa Senate from 45th dist., 1990—. Mem. Redeemer Luth. Ch., Polk Suburban Uniserve Unit. Mem. NEA, Iowa State Edn. Assn., Iowa State Univ. Alumni Assn., Carlisle Cmty. Edn. Assn., Ducks Unltd. Democrat. Home: 379 S23 Hwy Carlisle IA 50047-9413 Office: State Capitol Dist 45 3 9th And Grand Des Moines IA 50319-0001 E-mail: bill_fink@legis.state.ia.us.

FINK, JEROLD ALBERT, lawyer; b. Dayton, Ohio, July 16, 1941; s. Albert Otto and Marjorie Carolyn (Scheidt) F.; m. Mary Jo McHone, Dec. 31, 1961 (div. July 1978); children: Marjorie, Kathryn, Erick; m. 2d, Deborah Lynn Bailey, Dec. 25, 1980 (div. Oct. 1986); 1 child, Justin. AB, Duke U., 1963, LLB, 1966. Bar: Ohio 1966. Assoc. Taft, Stettinius & Hollister, Cin., 1966-73, ptnr., 1973—. Bd. dirs. The Wm. Powell Co., Cin., 1974—, Great Trails Broadcasting Co., Cin., 1974-79. Co-author: (with Judy Cohn) Power Defensive Carding, 1988, (with Joe Lutz) The American Forcing Minor Bidding System, 1995, (with Joe Lutz) Defensive Carding in the 21st Century, 2001. Pres. Cin. Musical Festival Assn., 1978-79; trustee Cin. Playhouse, 1976-95, New Life Youth Svcs., Cin., 1971—. Republican. Presbyterian. Office: 1800 Firstar Tower 425 Walnut St Cincinnati OH 45202-3923 E-mail: fink@taftlaw.com.

FINK, JOSEPH ALLEN, lawyer; b. Lexington, Ky., Oct. 4, 1942; s. Allen Medford and Margaret Ruth (Draper) F.; m. Marcia L. Horton; children: Alexander Mentzer, Justin McGranahan. Student, Wayne State U., 1960-61; BA, Oberlin Coll., 1964; JD, Duke U., 1967. Bar: Mich. 1968, U.S. Dist. Ct. (ea. dist.) Mich. 1968, U.S. Dist. Ct. (we. dist.) Mich. 1974, U.S. Ct. Appeals (6th cir.) 1987, U.S. Supreme Ct. 1998. Assoc. Dickinson, Wright, McKean & Cudlip, Detroit, 1972-75, Lansing, Mich., 1968-75; ptnr. Dickinson Wright PLLC, 1976—. Instr. U.S. Internat. U. Grad. Sch. Bus., San Diego, 1971; adj. prof. trial advocacy Thomas M. Cooley Law Sch., Lansing, 1984-85; mem. com. on local rules U.S. Dist. Cts., 1985; chmn. trial experience subcom. U.S. Dist. Ct. (we. dist.) Mich., 1981. Contbg. author: Construction Litigation, 1979, Legal Considerations in Managing Problem Employees, 1988, Michigan Civil Procedure During Trial, 2d edit., 1989; contbr. articles to profl. jours. Bd. dirs. Lansing 2000 Inc., 1985-92; bd. trustees Olivet (Mich.) Coll., 1985-94; mem. bd. advisors Mich. State U. Press, 1993-96. Lt. JAGC, USNR, 1968-72. Fellow Mich. State Bar Found.; mem. Fed. Bar Assn., State Bar of Mich. (chmn. local disciplinary com. 1983—, mem. com. for U.S. Cts. 1984). Episcopalian. Avocations: writing, reading, golf. Home: 6302 W Lake Dr Haslett MI 48840-8930 Office: Dickinson Wright PLLC 215 S Washington Sq Ste 200 Lansing MI 48933-1816

FINK, RICHARD, uniform company executive; b. Mpls., 1930; Grad., U. Minn., 1952, Harvard U., 1961. Chmn. bd. dirs. G & K Svcs., Inc., Minnetonka, Minn. Office: G & K Svcs Inc 5995 Opus Pky Ste 500 Minnetonka MN 55343 Fax: (612) 912-5999.

FINKBEINER, CARLTON S. (CARTY FINKBEINER), mayor; b. Toledo, 1939; BA, Dennison U. Tchr., football coach Maumee Valley Country Day Sch., St. Francis De Sales H.S., U. Toledo; city councilman City of Toledo, vice-mayor, mayor, 1994—; founder Toledo's Cmty.-Oriented Drug Enforcement program; co-sponsor City-wide Curfew; chair Coun.'s Housing, Neighborhood Revitalization and Natural Resources Com., Toledo. Mem. Econ. Opportunity Planning Assn. of Greater Toledo, Presidential Scholars Commn., U.S. Small Bus. Adminstrn. Adv. Commn. Northeastern and Northwestern Ohio, Internat. Gt. Lakes St. Lawrence Mayors Conf. Achievements include being appointed to the Presidential Scholars Commission by President Gerald Ford, 1975. Office: Office of the Mayor/City Coun One Goverment Ctr Ste 2200 Toledo OH 43604

FINKE, ROBERT FORGE, lawyer; b. Chgo., Mar. 11, 1941; s. Robert Frank and Helen Theodora (Forge) Finke. AB, U. Mich., 1963; JD, Harvard U., 1966. Bar: Ill. 1966, U.S. Dist. Ct. (no. dist.) Ill. 1966, U.S. Ct. Appeals (7th cir.) 1966, U.S. Supreme Ct. 1970, U.S. Ct. Appeals (9th cir.) 1980, U.S. Ct. Appeals (4th and 6th cirs.) 1982. Law clk., 1966—67; assoc. Mayer, Brown Rowe & Maw, Chgo., 1967—71, ptnr., 1972—. Bd. dirs. Lyric Opera Guild; trustee Rush Presbyn. St. Luke's Med. Ctr. Mem. ABA (sects. litigation, bus., antitrust, legal edn. and admissions to the bar, vice chmn. 1974-75), Lawyers Club Chgo., Univ. Club, Econ. Club. Office: Mayer Brown Rowe & Maw 190 S La Salle St Ste 3100 Chicago IL 60603-3441

FINKEL, BERNARD, public relations, communications and association management consultant, radio host; b. Chgo., Nov. 12, 1926; s. Isadore and Sarah (Goldzweig) F.; m. Muriel Horwitz, Dec. 23, 1951; children: Phillip Stuart, Calvin Mandel, Norman Terry. Student, Hebrew Theol. Coll., Chgo., 1939-44, Ill. Inst. Tech., 1944-45, U. Ill., 1947-48; BS in Journalism, U. Ill., 1951. Reporter, rewriter Peacock Newspapers, Chgo., 1949, Defender Newspapers, Chgo., 1951, Chgo. North Side Newspapers, 1952; asst. dir. pub. rels. Combined Jewish Appeal-Jewish Fedn. Met. Chgo., 1953; mng. editor Electric Appliance Svc. News, Chgo., 1954-57; asst. account exec. Burlingame-Grossman Advt., 1957; account exec. Glassner & Assocs., Pub. Rels., 1958-61; pub. rels. cons. Bernard Finkel Comm., 1961—. Dir. devel. and pub. rels. Jewish Am. Svc. Com., 1981-89; nat. dir. comm. and donor rels. Little Bros.-Friends of the Elderly, Chgo., 1989-90; owner, prodr., host weekly radio show Jewish Cmty. Hour, Sta. WONX-AM, Evanston, Ill. Author: Life and the World, 1947. Mem. pub. rels. and youth commns. Village of Skokie, 1964-65; v.p., coach Boys Baseball, Skokie, 1963-67; mem. adv. bd., chmn. pub. rels. Chgo. Area Career Conf., 1961-62; pres. Acad. Assocs. of Ida Crown Jewish Acad., Chgo., 1973-75; v.p. Hillel Torah North Suburban Day Sch., 1965-66, Congregation Or Torah, Skokie, 1970-71; bd. dirs. Skokie Valley Traditional Synagogue, 1987—. With U.S. Army, 1945-46. Recipient award for pub. svc. Jewish Cmty. Hour, 1978, Chgo. Rabbinical Coun., Chgo. Bd. Rabbis, Coun. Traditional and Orthodox Synagogues of Greater Chgo., Midwest Region of Nat. Fedn. Jewish Men's Clubs, Israel Aliyah Ctr. of World Zionist Orgn., Religious Zionists of Chgo., B'nai B'rith Lodge of Survivors of Nazi Holocaust, others. Mem. Nat. Soc. Fund-Raising Execs., Pub. Rels. Soc. Am., Social Svc. Communicators, Publicity Club Chgo. (profl. achievement awards). Home and Office: 3300 Capitol St Skokie IL 60076-2402

FINKELSTEIN, RICHARD ALAN, retired microbiology educator, consultant; b. N.Y.C., Mar. 5, 1930; s. Frank and Sylvia (Lemkin) F.; m. Helen Rosenberg, Nov. 30, 1952; children: Sheri, Mark, Laurie; m. Mary Boesman, June 20, 1976; 1 dau., Sarina Nicole. B.S., U. Okla., 1950; M.A., U. Tex., Austin, 1952, Ph.D., 1955. Teaching fellow, research scientist U. Tex., Austin, Austin, 1950-55; fellow, instr. U. Tex. Southwestern Med. Sch., Dallas, 1955-58; chief bioassay sect. Walter Reed Army Inst. Research, Washington, 1958-64; dep. chief, chief dept. bacteriology and mycology U.S. Army Med. Component, SEATO Med. Research Lab., Bangkok, Thailand, 1964-67; assoc. prof. dept. microbiology U. Tex. Southwestern Med. Sch., Dallas, 1967-73, prof., 1973-79; prof., chmn. dept. microbiology Sch. Medicine U. Mo., Columbia, 1979-93, Curators' prof., 1990-2000, Millsap Disting. Prof., 1985-2000, prof. emeritus, 2000—. Mem. Nat. Com. for Coordination Cholera Rsch., Ministry for Pub. Health, Bangkok, 1965-67; cons. WHO, 1970—, commdg. gen. U.S. Army Med. R&D Command, 1975-79, Schwarz-Mann Labs., 1974-79, ICN Biomeds., 1979—, Wyeth-Ayerst, 1992—, Amgen, 1992, Molecular Pharms., 1993—; Microbiolog. and Infectious Diseases Rsch. Com. Nat. Inst. Allergy and Infectious Diseases, NIH, 1994-98; vis. assoc. prof. U. Med. Scis., Bangkok, 1965-67; vis. prof. U. Chgo., Med. Sch., 1977; vis. scientist Japanese Sci. Coun., 1976, Ciba-Geigy lectr. Waksman Inst., Rutgers U., 1975; vis. lectr. Nat. Sci. Coun., Taipei, Taiwan, 1995, others. Contbr. articles on cholera, enterotoxins, gonorrhea, and role of iron in host-parasite interactions to profl. jours. Recipient Robert Koch prize Bonn, Fed. Republic Germany, 1976; Chancellor's award for outstanding faculty rsch. in biol. scis. U. Mo.-Columbia, 1985, Sigma Xi Rsch. award U. Mo.-Columbia, 1986. Fellow Am Acad. Microbiology (bd. govs. 1990-93), Am. Soc. for Microbiology (pres. Tex. br. 1974-75, hon. Tex. br. divsn. councilor, chmn. program com. 1979-82, sec.-treas. Mo. br. 1985-87, v.p. 1987-89, pres. 1989-91, councillor, 1991-92, coun. policy com. 1992-95, Disting. Svc. award 1998), Am. Assn. Immunologists, Infectious Diseases Soc. of Am., Soc. Gen. Microbiology, Pathol. Soc. Gt. Britain and Ireland, Sigma Xi. Achievements include first purification of cholera enterotoxin; first purification of heat-labile enterotoxin from Escherichia coli; patent for living attenuated candidate cholera vaccine. Home: 3861 S Forest Acres Dr Columbia MO 65203-8608 Office: U Mo Sch Medicine Dept Molecular Microbiol Columbia MO 65212-0001

FINLAY, TIMOTHY, agricultural products supplier; BS, U. Ill., 1983; MBA, Quincy U., 1989. CPA. Gen. dir. fin. and adminstrn. ADM Alliance Nutrition, Inc., Quincy, Ill., 2000. Office: Moormans Inc 1000 N 30th St Quincy IL 62301-3400 E-mail: tim-findlay@admworld.com.

FINLEY, CHUCK (CHARLES EDWARD FINLEY), baseball player; b. Monroe, La., Nov. 26, 1962; Student, N.E. La. U., Monroe. Pitcher Anaheim Angels (formerly Calif. Angels), 1986-99, Cleve. Indians, 1999—. Mem. Calif. Angels Am. League West Divsn. Champions, 1986; selected to Am. League All Star Team, 1989-90, 95-96; named to The Sporting News All-Star Team, 1989-90. Office: Cleve Indians 2401 Ontario St Cleveland OH 44115-4003

FINLEY, KATHERINE MANDUSIC, professional society administrator; b. Mansfield, Ohio, Nov. 8, 1954; d. Sam and Ann Julia (Konves) Mandusic; m. Edwin D. McDonell, Aug. 18, 1979 (div. Dec. 1994); m. Jeffrey A. Finley, June 12, 1999. BA, Ohio Wesleyan U.; MA in History and Mus. Studies, Case Western Res.; MBA, Ind. U. Rschr. Conner Prairie Mus., Fishers, Ind., 1978-82; exec. dir./rsch. historian Ind. Med. History Mus./Ind. Hist. Soc., Indpls., 1982-91; asst. dir. for comm. and mktg. Ind. U. Ctr. on Philanthropy, 1991-93; exec. dir. Roller Skating Assn. Internat., Indpls., 1993-2000, Assn. for Rsch. on Nonprofit Orgns. and Voluntary Action, 2000—; mem. faculty philanthropic studies Ind. U.-Purdue U., Indpls., 2001—. Author: (book) The Journals of William A. Lindsay, 1989; contbg. editor: The Encyclopedia of Indianapolis, 1994; contbr. articles to profl. jours. Pres. Altrusa Internat. Indpls., 1995—97, treas., 1998—99, chmn. svc. com., 1999—2000; pres. Altrusa Found. Indpls.; bd. dirs. Nat. Mus. Roller Skating, Lincoln, 1994—2000. Mem.: Ind. Soc. Assn. Execs. (chair edn. com. 1997—98, bd. dirs. 1999—2001, chair conv. com. 1999—2000, chair found. 2000), Nat. Soc. Fund Raising Execs. (cert.), Am. Soc. Assn. Execs. (cert.), Toastmasters (v.p. edn. 1998—99, 2000—02, v.p. pub. rels. 2000, gov. area 18 2001—02), Phi Beta Kappa, Sigma Iota Epsilon, Beta Gamma Sigma. Avocations: reading, walking, gourmet cooking. Office: Arnova 550 W North St Ste 301 Indianapolis IN 46202 E-mail: kmfinley@iupui.edu.

FINLEY, PHILIP BRUCE, retired state adjutant general; b. White City, Kans., Mar. 25, 1930; s. Marshall Arthur and Zelma Rena (Krenkle) F.; m. Jacqueline Lou Thomas, May 23, 1952; children: Jeffrey Allen, Robin Lyn. BS, Kans. State U., 1951, MS, 1954. Commd. U.S. Army, 1951, advanced through grades to maj. gen., 1988; served in Kans. N.G., 1967-84; served with Res. Norton, Kans., 1954-67; high sch. tchr. Bird City, 1954-55, Norton, 1955-67; extension agt. Decatur County Agr. Extension Council, Oberlin, 1967-72; rural devel. specialist Kans. State U. Area Office, Colby, 1972-74; N.W. Area dir. Kansas State U. Agrl. Extension, 1974-86, assoc. head, 1986—; adjutant-gen. State of Kans., Topeka, 1987-90; retired, 1990. Mem. N.W. Kans. Planning and Devel. Group, Hill City, 1972-74, "Future Kans." Planning Commn., Topeka, 1985-86. Mem. 7th Div. Assn., VFW, Am. Legion, Phi Delta Kappa, Epsilon Sigma Phi. Republican. Methodist. Avocations: game bird hunting, horsemanship, beekeeping, automobile mechanics. Home: 685 S Court Ave Colby KS 67701-3411

FINNEY, WILLIAM K. police chief; b. St. Paul, Nov. 28, 1948; BA, Mankato State U., 1970. Patrolman through granks to chief of police St. Paul Police Dept., 1971-92, chief of police, 1992—. Office: St Paul Police Dept 100 11th St E Fl 3 Saint Paul MN 55101-2227

FINNO, RICHARD J. engineering educator; Assoc. prof. Northwestern U., Evanston, 1989—, James N. and Margie M. prof. dept. civil engring. Ill., 1993-96. Recipient Walter L. Huber Civil Engring. Rsch. prize ASCE. Office: Northwestern U Dept Civil Engring 2145 Sheridan Rd Dept Civil Evanston IL 60208-0834

FINSETH, TIM, state legislator; b. Jan. 7, 1964; m. Ruth Finseth; 1 child. AA, Northland C.C.; BA, Moorhead State U. Mgr. Marshall County Soil and Water Conservation Dist.; rep. Dist. 1B Minn. Ho. of Reps., 1993—.

FINZEN, BRUCE ARTHUR, lawyer; b. Mpls., Mar. 11, 1947; s. Floyd Arthur and Lorraine Jeannette (Offerdahl) F.; children: Margaret, Sara, Stephanie. BA, U. Minn., 1970; JD, U. Kans., 1973. Bar: Minn. 1973, U.S. Dist. Ct. Minn. 1973, Calif. 1988, U.S. Ct. Appeals (8th cir.) 1973, U.S. Ct. Appeals (7th cir.) 1983, U.S. Ct. Appeals (2d cir.) 1986, U.S. Ct. Appeals (4th cir.) 1994, U.S. Ct. Appeals (9th cir.) 1994, U.S. Supreme Ct. 1996. Law clk. to presiding justice Minn. Supreme Ct., St. Paul, 1973-74; assoc. Robins, Kaplan, Miller & Ciresi, Mpls., 1974-79; ptnr. Robins, Kaplan, Miller & Ciresi LLP, 1979—. Bd. adv. Ctr. Pub. Integrity , Washington, 2001—. Mem. adv. bd. Ctr. for Pub. Integrity, 2001—; trustee Ho. of Hope Presbyn. Ch., 1988—94; bd. dirs. Union Gospel Mission, St. Paul, 1983—89; sec. bd. dirs. Boys and Girls Clubs St. Paul, 1984—91. Mem. ABA, Minn. Bar Assn., Assn. Trial Lawyers Am., Minn. Trial Lawyers Assn., Consumer Attys. Calif., Assn. Pers. Injury Lawyers, Internat. Bar Assn. Avocations: hunting, fishing. Office: Robins Kaplan Miller & Ciresi LLP 2800 LaSalle Plz 800 Lasalle Ave Ste 2800 Minneapolis MN 55402-2015

FIRCHOW, EVELYN SCHERABON, German language and literature educator, writer; b. Vienna, Austria; came to U.S., 1951, naturalized, 1964; d. Raimund and Hildegard (Nickl) Scherabon; m. Peter E. Firchow, 1969; children: Felicity (dec. 1988), Pamina. BA, U. Tex., 1956; MA, U. Man., 1957; PhD, Harvard U., 1963. Instr. coll. math. Balmoral Hall Sch., Winnipeg, Man., Can., 1953-55; tchg. fellow in German Harvard U., Cambridge, Mass., 1957-58, 61-62; lectr. German U. Md. in Munich, 1961; instr. German U. Wis., Madison, 1962-63, asst. prof., 1963-65; assoc. prof. German U. Minn., Mpls., 1965-69, prof. German and Germanic philology, 1969—; vis. prof. U. Fla., Gainesville, 1973; Fulbright research prof. Iceland, 1966-67, 80, 94; vis. rsch. prof. Nat. Cheng Kung U., Tainan, Taiwan, 1982-83; permanent vis. prof. Jilin U., Changchun, People's Republic of China, 1987—. Vis. prof. U. Graz, Austria, 1989, 91, 2002, U. Vienna, Austria, 1995, U. Bonn, 1996, Nat. U. Costa Rica, 2000. Editor and author: (under name E.S. Coleman) Taylor Starck-Festschrift, 1964, Stimmen aus dem Stundenglas, 1968, (under name E.S. Firchow) Studies by Einar Haugen, 1972, Studies for Einar Haugen, 1972, Was Deutsche lesen, 1973, Deutung und Bedeutung, 1973, Elucidarius in Old Norse Translation, 1989, The Old Norse Elucidarius: Original Text and English Translation, 1992, Notker der Deutsche von St. Gallen: De interpretatione, 1995, Categoriae, 2 Vols., 1996, De nuptiis Philologiae et Mercurii, 2 Vols., 1999, Notker der Deutsche von St. Gallen (950-1022): Ausführliche Bibliographie, 2000, De consolatione Philosophial, 2002, Reluctant Modernists, Festschrift Peter Firchow, 2002; translator: Einhard: Vita Caroli Magni, Das Leben Karls des Grossen, 1968, 84, 95, Einhard: Vita Caroli Magni, The Life of Charlemagne, 1972, 85, Icelandic Short Stories, 1974, 87, (with P.E. Firchow) East German Short Stories, 1979, (with P.E. Firchow) Alois Brandstetter, The Abbey, 1998; dir., editor Computer Clearing-House Project for German and Medieval Scandinavian; assoc. editor Germanic Notes and Revs., Am. Jour. Linguistics and Lit.; contbr. articles and book revs. to profl. jours. Fulbright scholar Tex., 1951-52; fellow Alexander von Humboldt-Stiftung, Munich, 1960-61, Tuebingen, 1974, Marburg, 1981, Goettingen, 1985, Tokyo, 1991, Marburg and Berlin, 1993, Bonn, 2001, Fulbright Found., Iceland, 1967-68, 80, 94, Austrian Govt., 1977, NEH, 1980-81, Am. Inst. Indian Studies, 1988, BUSH fellow, 1989, Thor Thors fellow, 1994, Mc Knight summer fellow, 1995, 96, 99, Deutscher Akademischer Austausdienst (DAAD) rsch. fellow, 2000; elected hon. mem. Multilingual Rsch. Ctr., Brussels, 1986. Mem. AAUP, MLA (chmn. div. German lit. to 1700 1979-80, 93-96, vice chmn. pedagogical seminar for Germanic philology 1979-86, 91-93, chair 1994), Medieval Acad. Am., Soc. German-Am. Studies (chair Linguistics I 1992), Internat. Comparative Lit. Assn., Soc. for Advancement Scandinavian Studies (chmn. Germanic philology 1979, text editing 1980, linguistics 1984, computers and Old Norse 1985), Assn. for Lang. and Linguistic Computing (founding mem.), Am. Comparative Lit. Assn., Midwest Modern Lang. Assn. (chmn. German I 1965-66, chmn. Scandinavian 1979), Internationale Vereinigung der Germanisten, Am. Assn. Tchrs. German, Modern Humanities Rsch. Assn., Mediävisten Verband, Soc. for Germanic Philology, Österreichische Germanisten-Gesellschaft. Office: U Minn Dept German Minneapolis MN 55455 E-mail: firch001@umn.edu.

FIRCHOW, PETER EDGERLY, language professional, educator, author; b. Needham, Mass., Dec. 16, 1937; s. Paul Karl August and Marta Loria (Montenegro) F.; m. Evelyn Maria Scherabon Coleman, Sept. 18, 1969; 1 dau., Pamina Maria Scherabon. B.A., Harvard Coll., 1959; postgrad., U. Vienna, Austria, 1959-60; M.A., Harvard U., 1961; Ph.D., U. Wis., 1965. Asst. prof. English U. Mich., 1965-67; asst. prof. English and comparative lit. U. Minn., Mpls., 1967-69, assoc. prof., 1969-73, prof., 1973—, chmn. Comparative Lit. Program, 1972-78. Disting. vis. prof. Nat. Cheng Kung U., Taiwan, 1982-83, Jilin U., Peoples Republic China, 1987, U. Munich, Germany, 1988, U. Graz, Austria, 1989; Fulbright prof. U. Bonn, Germany, 1995-96, Nat. U. Costa Rica, 2000. Author: Friedrich Schlegel's Lucinde and the Fragments, 1971, Aldous Huxley, Satirist and Novelist, 1972, The Writer's Place: Interviews on the Literary Situation in Contemporary Britain, 1974; (with E.S. Firchow) East German Short Stories: An Introductory Anthology, 1979; The End of Utopia: A Study of Huxley's Brave New World, 1984; The Death of the German Cousin: Variations on a Literary Stereotype, 1986; translator (with E.S. Firchow) The Abbey (Alois Brandstetter), 1998, Envisioning Africa: Racism and Imperialism in Conrad's "Heart of Darkness", 2000, W.H. Auden: Contexts for Poetry, 2002; contbr. articles on modern lit. subjects to profl. jours. Fellow Inst. Advanced Studies in Humanities, Edinburgh, 1977. Mem. Midwest Modern Lang. Assn. (v.p. 1977, pres. 1978), Am. Comparative Lit. Assn., Assn. Lit. Scholars and Critics, Internat. Aldous Huxley Soc. Home: 135 Birnamwood Dr Burnsville MN 55337-6814 Office: U Minn Dept English 310D Lind Hall 207 Church St SE Minneapolis MN 55455-0134 E-mail: pef@tc.umn.edu.

FIRMIN, MICHAEL WAYNE, counselor educator; b. New Orleans, July 28, 1961; s. Lloyd John and Betty L. (Shepherd) F.; m. Karen Sue Tuttle, Aug. 4, 1984; children: Ruth, Sarah. BA, Calvary Bible Coll., 1983; MA, Calvary Theol. Sem., 1985; MS, Bob Jones U., 1987, PhD, 1988; MA, Marywood U., 1992; PhD, Syracuse U. Nat. cert. counselor. Dir. counseling svcs. Bapt. Bible Coll. of Pa., Clarks Summit, 1988-98, assoc. prof., 1988-98, chmn. divsn. grad. studies, 1995-97; assoc. prof. psychology Cedarville (Ohio) U., 1998—; resident in psychology TCN: Behavioral Health Svcs., 2000—01; chmn. dept. psychology Cedarville U., 2000—. Cons. for psychol. svcs. Assn. Bapts. for World Evangelism, Harrisburg, Pa., 1991—94, 1999—; clin. assessment cons. Keystone City Residence, 1994—2000. Pastor Faith Fellowship Bapt. Ch., Danbury, Conn., 1991-94. Mem. Psi Chi. Republican. Home: 84 E Elm St Cedarville OH 45314-8513 Office: Cedarville Univ 251 N Main St Cedarville OH 45314-0601

FISCH, CHARLES, physician, educator; b. Nesterov (Zolkiew), Poland, May 11, 1921; s. Leon and Janette (Deutscher) F.; m. June Spiegal, May 23, 1943; children: Jonathan, Gary, Bruce. AB, Ind. U., 1942, MD, 1944; MD (hon.), U. Utrecht, The Netherlands, 1983. Diplomate Am. Bd. Internal Medicine, Am. Bd. Cardiovasc. Medicine (mem. 1977-82). Intern St. Vincent's Hosp., Indpls., 1945; resident in internal medicine VA Hosp., 1948-50; fellow gastroenterology Marion County Gen. Hosp., 1950-51, fellow in cardiology, 1951-53; asst. prof. medicine Ind. U. Med. Sch., 1953-59, assoc. prof., 1959-63, prof., 1963—, disting. prof., 1975, dir. cardiovasc. divsn., 1963-90, disting. prof. emeritus, 1990—; dir. Krannert Inst. Cardiology, 1953-90. Mem. cardio-renal adv. com. HEW-FDA, 1973-77, 79—; Connor lectr. Am. Heart Assn., 1980; chmn. manpower rev. com. Nat. Heart, Lung and Blood Inst., 1985-89; Charles Fisch chair in cardiology Ind. U. Author: Electrocardiography of Arrythmias, 1989; co-editor Digitalis, 1969, Cardiac Electrophysiology and Arrythmias, 1991, Electrophysiology of Clinical Arrythmias, 2000; contbr. articles to med. jours.; mem. editorial bd. Am. Heart Jour., 1967—, Am. Jour. Electrocardiology, 1967—, Coeur et Medicine Interne, 1970—, Am. Jour. Medicine, 1973—, Circulation, 1977—, Am. Jour. Cardiology, 1967—; assoc. editor Am. Jour. Cardiology, 1977—. Capt. M.C. AUS, 1946-48. Recipient James Herrick award Am. Heart Assn. Fellow ACP, Am. Coll. Cardiology (pres. 1975-77, dir., chmn. publ. com. 1988-94, Gifted Tchr. award 1993), World Congress Cardiology (v.p. 1986); mem. Am. Fedn. Clin. Rsch., Ctrl. Soc. Clin. Rsch., Am. Physiol. Soc., Assn. Univ. Cardiologists, Assn. Am. Physicians, N.Am. Soc. for Pacing and Electrophysiology (Dist. Tchr. award 1994). Home: 7901 Morningside Dr Indianapolis IN 46240-2526 Office: Ind U Med Ctr Krannert Inst Card 1111 W 10th St Indianapolis IN 46202-4800

FISCH, ROBERT OTTO, medical educator; b. Budapest, Hungary, June 12, 1925; came to U.S., 1957. s. Zoltan and Irene (Manheim) F.; divorced; 1 dau., Rebecca A. Med. diploma, U. Budapest, 1951; study art, Acad. Fine Arts, Budapest, 1943, Mpls. Coll. Arts and Design, 1970-76. Gen. practice medicine, Hungary, 1951-55; pub. health officer Hungary, 1955; pediatrician Hosp. for Premature Children, Budapest, 1956; intern Christ Hosp., Jersey City, 1957-58; intern pediatrics U. Minn. Hosps., 1958-59, researcher, 1959-60, research fellow, 1961; instr. U. Minn. Sch. Medicine, 1961-63, asst. prof., 1963-72, assoc. prof., 1972-79, prof., 1979—, dir. phenylketonuric clinic, 1961-97. Author: Respiratory Diseases; PKU, Child Development (Best Cover Minn. Med. 1975), Light from the Yellow

Star: A Lesson of Love from the Holocaust, 1994, The Metamorphosis to Freedom, 2000; contbr. articles to profl. jours.; exhibited art works in various one-man and group shows. Mem. Soc. Pediatric Rsch., Am. Physician Art Assn. (1st prize 1990, numerous others). Office: U Minn Mayo Hosp MMC 384 Minneapolis MN 55455 E-mail: fisch001@umn.edu.

FISCH, WILLIAM BALES, lawyer, educator; b. Cleve., May 11, 1936; s. Max Harold and Ruth Alice (Bales) F.; m. Janice Heston McPherson, Sept. 2, 1961 (dec. 1987); m. Suzanne Fischer Good, June 19, 1993 (dec. 1998); children: Katherine Emily, Stephen McPherson. AB, Harvard Coll., 1957; LLB, U. Ill., 1960; M.Comparative Law (univ. fgn. law fellow), U. Chgo., 1962; JUD, U. Freiburg, Germany, 1972. Bar: Ill. 1961, Mo. 1982. Assoc. firm Kirkland & Ellis, Chgo., 1962-65; asst. prof. law U. N.D., 1965-68, assoc. prof., 1968-70, U. Mo., Columbia, 1970-74, prof., 1974—, Isador Loeb prof. law, 1977—. Author: Die Vorteilsausgleichung im amerikanischen und deutschen Recht, 1974; co-author: Problems, Cases and Materials on Professional Responsibility, 1985, 2d edit., 1995; bd. editors: Am. Jour. Comparative Law; contbr. articles, revs. to law jours. Alexander von Humboldt-Stiftung Rsch. fellow, 1968-69, 89-90; Fulbright-Hays Rsch. scholar Hamburg, Germany, 1980-81, 89-90; Max Planck Soc. Rsch. fellow, Hamburg, 1992. Mem. ABA, AAUP, Am. Law Inst. Office: U Mo Law Sch Columbia MO 65211-0001

FISCHBACH, MICHELLE L. state legislator; b. Nov. 3, 1965; m. Scott Fischbach; 2 children. BA, St. Cloud State U. Mem. Minn. Senate from 14th dist., St. Paul, 1996—. Home: 416 Burr St Paynesville MN 56362-1110 Office: 149 State Office Bldg 100 Constitution Ave Saint Paul MN 55155-1232

FISCHER, A(LBERT) ALAN, family physician; b. Indpls., June 30, 1928; 4 children. MD, Ind. U., 1952. Diplomate Am. Bd. Family Practice. Intern St. Vincent Hosp., Indpls., 1952—53; pvt. practice, 1953—70; dir. family practice residency program St. Vincent Hosp., Indpls., 1969—75; prof. family medicine, chmn. dept. Ind. U., 1974—90; med. dir. Lakeview Manor, 1970—. Pvt. practice family medicine, 1953—. Mem.: AMA, Am. Acad. Family Physicians (v.p. 1971—72), Inst. Medicine-NAS (mem. nat. joint practicing commn.).

FISCHER, LAWRENCE JOSEPH, toxicologist, educator; b. Chgo., Sept. 2, 1937; s. Lawrence J. and Virginia H. (Dieker) F.; m. Elizabeth Ann Dunphy, Oct. 24, 1964; children— Julie Ann, Pamela Jean, Karen Sue B.Sc., U. Ill.-Chgo., 1959, M.S., 1961; Ph.D., U. Calif.-San Francisco, 1965. NIH postdoctoral fellow St. Mary's Hosp. Med. Sch., London, 1965-66; sr. research pharmacologist Merck Sharp and Dohme, West Point, Pa., 1966-68; asst. prof. pharmacology U. Iowa, Iowa City, 1969-73, assoc. prof., 1974-76, prof., 1976-85; prof., dir. Inst. for Environ. Toxicology Mich. State U., East Lansing, Mich., 1985—. Cons. FDA Bur. Vet. Medicine, 1974-77; mem. bd. scientific counselors div. of cancer Etiology Nat. Cancer Inst., 1986-92. Mem. editorial adv. bd. Jour. Pharmacology and Exptl. Therapeutics, Toxicology and Applied Pharmacology, Drug Metabolism Revs. Recipient Faculty Scholar award Josiah Macy Found., U. Geneva, 1976 Mem. Am. Soc. for Pharmacology and Exptl. Therapeutics, Soc. Toxicology, AAAS, Soc. for Environ. Toxicology and Chemistry. Avocations: hunting upland birds, tennis. Home: 11630 Center Rd Bath MI 48808-9431 Office: Mich State U Inst for Environ Toxicology C231 Holden Hall East Lansing MI 48824

FISCHER, TOM, state legislator; , St. Thomas U. Owner A.I.O. Syss., Inc.; mem. N.D. Senator, Bismark, 1997—. Recipient Fed. Emerg. Mgmt. Agency Outstanding Pub. Svc. award, 1991. Office: 2823 64th Ave S Fargo ND 58104-7407 E-mail: tfischer@state.nd.us.

FISCHLER, BARBARA BRAND, librarian; b. Pitts., May 24, 1930; d. Carl Frederick and Emma Georgia (Piltz) Brand; m. Drake Anthony Fischler, June 3, 1961 (div., Oct. 1995); 1 child, Owen Wesley. AB cum laude, Wilson Coll., Chambersburg, Pa., 1952; MM with distinction, Ind. U., 1954, AMLS, 1964. Asst. reference librarian Ind. U., Bloomington, 1958-61, asst. librarian undergrad. library, 1961-63, acting librarian, 1963; circulation librarian Ind. U.-Purdue U., Indpls., 1970-76, pub. services librarian Univ. Library, sci., engrng. and tech. unit, 1976-81, acting dir. univ. libraries, 1981-82, dir. univ. libraries, 1982-95; retired, 1995; dir. Sch. Libr. and Info. Sci. Ind. U.-Purdue U., Indpls., 1995—. Vis. and assoc. prof. (part-time) Sch. Libr. and Info. Sci. Ind. U., Bloomington, 1972-95, counselor-coord., Indpls., 1974-82, dir. sch. libr. and info. sci. campus Ind. U.-Purdue U., Indpls., 1995—; resource aide adv. com. Ind. Voc. Tech. Coll., Indpls., 1974-86; adv. com. Area Libr. Svcs. Authority, Indpls., 1976-79; mem. core com., chmn. program com. Ind. Gov.'s Conf. on Librs. and Info. Svcs., Indpls., 1976-78, mem. governance com., del. to conf., 1990; mem. Ind. State Libr. Adv. Coun., 1985-91; cons. in field. Contbr. articles to profl. jours. Fund-raiser Indpls. Mus. Art, 1971, Am. Cancer Soc., Indpls., 1975; vol. tchr. St. Thomas Aquinas Sch., Indpls., 1974-75; fund-raiser Am. Heart Assn., Indpls., 1985; bd. dirs., treas. Historic Amusement Found., Inc., Indpls., 1984-91; bd. advisors N.Am. Wildlife Park Found., Inc., Battle Ground, Ind., 1985-91, bd. dirs., 1991—; mem. adv. bd. Ind. U. Ctr. on Philanthropy, 1987-90. Recipient Outstanding Svc. award Ctrl. Ind. Area Libr. Svc. Authority, 1979, Outstanding Libr. award Ind. Libr.-Ind. Libr. Trustee Assn., 1988, Louise Maxwell award for Outstanding Achievement, 1989, William Jenkins award for Outstanding Svc. to Ind. U. Libr. and the Libr. Profession, 1996. Mem. ALA, Libr. Adminstrn. and Mgmt. Assn. (vice chair and chair elect fund raising and fin. devel. sect. 1991-92), Ind. State Libr. Adv. Coun., Midwest Fedn. Libr. Assns. (chmn. local arrangements for conf. 1986-87, sec. 1987—, bd. dirs. 1987-91), Ind. Libr. Assn. (chmn. coll. and univ. div. 1977-78, chmn. libr. edn. div. 1981-82, treas. 1984-86), German Shepherd Dog Club of Cen. Ind. (pres. 1978-79, treas. 1988-89, v.p. 1989-90, pres. 1990-93, bd. dirs. 1993—), Wabash Valley German Shepherd Dog Club (pres. 1982-83), Cen. Ind. Kennel Club (bd. dirs. 1984-86), Pi Kappa Lambda, Beta Phi Mu. Republican. Presbyterian. Avocations: ethology, exhibiting American Saddlebred horses. Home: 735 Lexington Ave Apt 3 Indianapolis IN 46203-1000 Office: Ind-Purdue U 755 W Michigan St Indianapolis IN 46202-5195

FISH, STANLEY EUGENE, university dean, English educator; b. Providence, Apr. 19, 1938; s. Max and Ida Dorothy (Weinberg) F.; m. Adrienne A. Aaron, Aug. 23, 1959 (div. 1980); 1 dau., Susan.; m. Jane Parry Tompkins, Aug. 7, 1982. B.A., U. Pa., 1959; M.A., Yale U., 1960, Ph.D., 1962. Instr. U. Calif., Berkeley, 1962-63, asst. prof., 1963-67, assoc. prof., 1967-69, prof., 1969-74; Kenan prof. English and Humanities Johns Hopkins U., Balt., 1978-85, chmn. dept., 1983-85; Arts and Sci. Disting. prof. English and prof. law Duke U., Durham, N.C., 1985-98, chmn. dept., 1986-92; exec. dir. Duke U. Press, 1994-98; dean U. Ill. Coll. Liberal Arts and Scis., Chgo., 1999—. Author: John Skelton's Poetry, 1965, Surprised by Sin: The Reader in Paradise Lost, 1967, 97 (Hanford Book award 1998), Seventeenth Century Prose: Modern Essays in Criticism, 1971, Self-Consuming Artifacts, 1972, The Living Temple: George Herbert and Catechizing, 1978, Is There a Text in This Class?, 1980, Doing What Comes Naturally, 1989, There's No Such Thing as Free Speech...And It's a Good Thing Too, 1994 (PEN/Spielvogel-Diamonstein award 1994), Professional Correctness: Literary Studies and Political Change, 1995, The Trouble with Principle, 1999, How Milton Works, 2001; mem. editl. bd. Milton Studies, Milton Quar. Recipient 2d place, Explicator prize, 1968; Am. Council Learned Socs. fellow, 1966; Guggenheim fellow, 1969 Mem. MLA, Am. Acad. Arts and Scis., Milton Soc. (hon. scholar 1991), Spenser Soc. Office: U Ill Chgo LAS Dean's Office M/C 228 601 S Morgan St Chicago IL 60607-7100

FISHBUNE, ROBERT, food products executive; CFO Specialty Foods Corp., Deerfield, Ill. Office: Specialty Foods Corp PO Box 3400 Saint Charles IL 60174-9093

FISHER, ALAN WASHBURN, historian, educator; b. Columbus, Ohio, Nov. 23, 1939; s. Sydney Nettleton and Elizabeth E. (Scipio) F.; m. Carol L. Garrett, Aug. 24, 1963; children: Elizabeth, Ann Christy, Garrett. BA, DePauw U., 1961; MA, Columbia U., 1964, PhD, 1967. Instr. history Mich. State U., East Lansing, 1966-67, asst. prof., 1967-70, assoc. prof., 1970-78, prof. Russian and Turkish history, 1978—, assoc. dean grad. studies and research, Coll. Arts and Letters, 1987-89, dir. Ctr. for Integrative Studies in Arts and Humanities, 1989-97. Author: Russian Annexation of the Crimea, 1772-1783, 1970, The Crimean Tatars, 1978, revised edit., 1987, Ottoman Studies Directory, I, 1979, II, 1981, III, 1983, Between Russians, Ottomans, and Turks: Crimea and Crimean Tatars, 1998, A Precarious Balance: Conflict, Trade and Diplomacy on the Russian-Ottoman Frontier, 1999. Am. Rsch. Inst. in Turkey fellow, 1969, 73, 76; Am. Coun. Learned Socs. grantee, 1976-77 Fellow Royal Hist. Soc., Turkish Hist. Assn. (corr.), Am. Rsch. Inst. Turkey (mem. bd. dels. 1990-99, v.p. 1995-99), Mid. East Studies Assn., Turkish Studies Assn. (pres. 1982-84, editor bull. 1984-87), Inst. Turkish Studies (dir. 1995-97, chmn. 1997-99). Office: Mich State U Dept History 301 Morrill Hall East Lansing MI 48824-1036 E-mail: fishera@msu.edu.

FISHER, CALVIN DAVID, food manufacturing company executive; b. Nerstrand, Minn., June 10, 1926; s. Edward and Sadie (Wolf) F.; m. Patricia Vivian Capriotti, July 28, 1950; children: Cynthia, Nancy Joann, Michael. BS, U. Minn., 1950. Dairy specialist U.S. Dept. Agr., Mpls., 1950-54, chemist and dairy specialist Omaha, 1954-58; with Roberts Dairy Co., 1958-80, sr. v.p., chief operating officer, 1967-70, pres., chief exec. officer, 1970-80, owner, chief exec. officer, 1975-80, Fisher Foods Ltd., Lincoln, Nebr., 1980—; pres., dir. Master Dairies, Indpls., 1968-80; bd. dirs. Internat. Assn. Ice Cream Mfrs. Milk Industry Found., 1973-80. Patentee spray-dried ice cream mix, pasteurized egg products. Bd. dirs., v.p. Omaha Safety Council, 1981; bd. dirs. Arthritis Found., 1972-81; mem. adv. council SBA; bd. dirs. Nebr. State Patrol Found., 1990—. With USN, 1944-47. Mem. Omaha C. of C. (pres.'s coun. 1976, 78), Internat. Food Scientists Assn., Inst. Food Tech., Nat. Ind. Dairies Assn., Rotary, Univ. Club (Lincoln), Firethorn Country Club. Republican. Methodist. Home: University Towers 128 N 13th St Ste 1001 Lincoln NE 68508-1501 Office: Fisher Foods Ltd 220 S 20th St Lincoln NE 68510-1007

FISHER, JAMES LEE, lawyer; b. Akron, Ohio, Apr. 10, 1944; s. James Lee and Maxine (Sumner) F.; m. Nancy Lorenz, Dec. 20, 1980. BSCE, U. Akron, 1968, JD, 1971. Bar: Ohio 1971. Staff atty. Brunswick Mgmt. Co., Akron, 1972-77; prin. James L. Fisher Co., L.P.A., 1977-88, Buckingham, Doolittle & Burroughs, Akron, 1988—. City planner City of Akron, 1968-71, community devel. atty., 1971-73; mem. Metro Regional Transit Authority Bd., 1992—; sec.-treas. Summit County Planning Commn., 1978-99. Mem. ABA, Ohio Bar Assn., Akron Bar Assn., Home Builders Assn., Am. Planning Assn., Ohio Planning Conf., Copley Lions (pres. 1982). Republican. Mem. United Ch. of Christ. Home: 1135 Forest Pool Rd Akron OH 44333-1509 Office: Buckingham Doolittle & Burroughs PO Box 1500 Akron OH 44309-1500

FISHER, JAMES R. lawyer; b. South Bend, Ind., Apr. 15, 1947; s. Russell Humphries and Virginia Opal (Maple) F.; m. Cynthia Ann Winters, Aug. 14, 1971; children: Gabriel Christopher, Cory Andrew. AB in Psychology, Ind. U., 1969, JD summa cum laude, 1972. Bar: Ind. 1972, U.S. Dist. Ct. (so. dist.) Ind. 1972. Ptnr. Ice Miller, Indpls., 1971—. Co-author: Personal Injury Law and Practicesol. 23 of Indiana Practico series; contbr. articles to legal publs. Mem. ABA, Am. Trial Lawyers Assn., Am. Bd. Trial Advs., Ind. Bar Assn., Ind. Trial Lawyers Assn., Indpls. Bar Assn., Order of Coif. Office: Ice Miller 1 Am Sq PO Box 82001 Indianapolis IN 46282

FISHER, JOHN JAMES, advertising executive; b. St. Louis, Mar. 23, 1941; s. Benjamin Edwards Fisher and Beulah Fay (Tucker) Hughes; m. Beverly Firth Brown, June 7, 1962; children: John J. Jr., Jennifer Leigh. BBA in Mktg., Memphis State U., 1964. Sales rep. Pfizer Labs., Memphis, 1965-69, product mgr. N.Y.C., 1969-71; account exec. L.W. Froelich Inc., 1971-72; account supr. Lavey/Wolff/Swift Inc., 1972-74, v.p., account supr., 1974-76, sr. v.p., dir. client svcs., 1976-78; exec. v.p. Frank J. Corbett Inc., Chgo., 1978-80, pres., 1980-91, chmn., chief exec. officer, 1991—. Exec. v.p. Health and Med. Com., N.Y.C., 1986-92, chmn., CEO, 1993—. Contbr. articles to profl. jours. Chmn. Rep. Com., Weston, Conn., 1970-78; mgr. campaign state rep. and senator, Weston, 1974, congl. dist., Weston, 1977. Mem. Med. Mktg. Assn., Biomed. Mktg. Assn., Pharm. Advt. Coun., Midwest Pharm. Advt. Coun. (pres. 1984-85, Sweeny award 1985), Biltmore Country Club (Barrington, Ill.), N.Y. Athletic Club. Avocation: golf. Office: Frank J Corbett Inc 211 E Chicago Ave Ste 1600 Chicago IL 60611-2660

FISHER, JOHN WESLEY, manufacturing company executive; b. Walland, Tenn., July 15, 1915; s. Arthur Justin and Rachel (Malott) F.; m. Janice Kelsey Ball, Aug. 10, 1940; children: Joan Fisher Woods, Michael J., James A., Jeffrey E., Judith Fisher Oetinger, John Wesley III, Jerrold M. BS, U. Tenn., 1938; MBA, Harvard U., 1942; LLD (hon.), Ball State U., 1972, Butler U., 1977, DePauw U., 1981, Ind. U., 1985. Field sec. Delta Tau Delta Frat., Indpls., 1938-40; trainee, various mfg., sales and adminstrv. positions Ball Corp., Muncie, Ind., 1941-70, pres., chief exec. officer, 1970-78, chmn. bd., chief exec. officer, 1978-81, chmn. bd., 1981-86, also dir., chmn. emeritus, 1986—. Bd. dirs. Kindel Furniture Co., Grand Rapids, Mich.; ptnr. Blackwood & Nichols Corp., Oklahoma City; chmn. CID Equity Ptnrs., Indpls., Nat. Trust and Investment Mgmt. Co., Muncie; pres. Nature's Catch, Inc., Clarksdale, Miss., Fisher Properties of Ind., Inc. State del. Rep. Party, Ind., 1950-70; mem. Rep. State Fin. Com., 1952-56, del. nat. conv., 1952, 54, 64, 68; chmn. bd. dirs. Ball Meml. Hosp.; pres. Cardinal Health Sys. Mem. NAM (chmn. 1979-80, bd. dirs.), Glass Packaging Inst. (trustee 1962-68, pres. 1965-67), Grocery Mfrs. Assn. (bd. dirs.), Ind. C. of C. (dir. 1959—, pres. 1966-68), Muncie C. of C. (past pres.), Conf. Bd., Ind. Acad., Delaware Country Club, Indpls. Athletic Club, Columbia Club (Indpls.), Royal Poinciana Country Club, Naples (Fla.) Yacht Club, Rotary, Naples Nat. Golf Club, Delta Tau Delta. Republican. United Methodist. Home: PO Box 832 Muncie IN 47308-0832 Office: Ball Assocs PO Box 1408 Muncie IN 47308-1408

FISHER, LAWRENCE L. lawyer; b. Mt. Sterling, Ohio, Jan. 4, 1941; BS, Ohio State U., 1964; postgrad., U. Bonn, Germany; JD, Harvard U., 1967. Bar: Ohio 1967. Mem. Vorys, Sater, Seymour & Pease, Columbus, Ohio. Fellow Am. Coll. Trust and Estate Counsel; mem. ABA, Ohio State Bar Assn. (chmn. probate and trust law sect. 1979-80), Columbus Bar Assn. (Community Svc. award 1976-77), Phi Eta Sigma. Office: Vorys Sater Seymour & Pease PO Box 1008 52 E Gay St Columbus OH 43216

FISHER, LESTER EMIL, zoo administrator; b. Chgo., Feb. 24, 1921; s. Louis and Elizabeth (Vodicka) F.; m. Wendy Fisher, Jan. 23, 1981; children: Jane Serrita, Katherine Clark. MDV, Iowa State U., 1943. Supr. animal care program Northwestern U. Med. Sch., 1946-47; attending veterinarian Lincoln Park Zoo, Chgo., 1947-62, zoo dir., 1962-92, dir. emeritus, 1992—; owner, dir. Berwyn (Ill.) Animal Hosp., 1947-68. Producer, moderator ednl. closed circuit TV for nat. vet. meetings, 1949-66; asso. prof. dept. biology DePaul U., 1968-98; adj. prof. zoology U. Ill., from 1972 Editor: Brit. Small Animal Jour. and Small Animal Clinician, 1958-72. Mem. citizens com. U. Ill.; chmn. zoo and wildlife div. Morris Animal Found. Served to maj., Vet. Corps AUS, 1943-46. Recipient Alumni Merit award Iowa State U., 1968, Stange award Iowa State U., 1988, Chgo. Superior Pub. Svc. award Chgo. Park Dist., 1973, 92, Laureate Ill. Lincoln Acad., 1993. Mem. Am. Animal Hosp. Assn. (regional dir., outstanding Service award 1969), Am. Vet. Med. Assn., Nat. Recreation and Park Assn., Internat. Union Dirs. Zool. Gardens (v.p. 1980-83, pres. 1983-86), Am. Assn. Zoo Veterinarians (pres. 1966-69), Am. Assn. Zool. Parks and Aquariums (pres. 1972-73, chmn. gorilla species survival plan 1982-92), Chgo. Geographic Soc. (v.p.), Econ. Club Chgo., Theta Xi. Clubs: Adventures (pres. 1971-72), Execs. of Chgo. (bd. dirs. 1968-71), Arts. Assoc., Chgo. Econs. (membership com.) (Chgo.). Home and Office: PO Box 656 Alexandria Bay NY 13607-0656

FISHER, LLOYD EDISON, JR. lawyer; b. Medina, Ohio, Oct. 23, 1923; s. Lloyd Edison and Wanda (White) F.; m. Twylla Dawn Peterson, Sept. 11, 1949 (dec. Apr. 1996); children: Karen S., Kirk P. BS, Ohio State U., 1947, JD, 1949. Bar: Ohio 1950. Mem. gen. hearing bd. Ohio Dept. Taxation, 1950-53; trust officer Huntington Nat. Bank, Columbus, 1953-62; ptnr. Porter, Wright, Morris & Arthur and predecessor firm, 1962—. Adj. prof. law Ohio State U., Columbus, 1967-69, 84-91. Bd. dirs Wesley Glen Retirement Ctr., 1974-80, 88-95; bd. dirs. Grant/Riverside Hospice, 1997—. Served with AUS, 1943-45. Fellow Am. Coll. Trust and Estate Counsel; mem. ABA, Ohio Bar Assn., Columbus Bar Assn., Order of Coif. Home: 6478 Strathaven Ct E Worthington OH 43085-2985 Office: 41 S High St Columbus OH 43215-6101 E-mail: lfisher@porterwright.com.

FISHER, NEAL FLOYD, religious organization administrator; b. Washington, Apr. 4, 1936; s. Floyd Russell and Florence Alice (Williams) F.; m. Ila Alexander, Aug. 18, 1957; children: Edwin Kirk, Julia Bryn. AB, DePauw U., 1957, LHD (hon.), 1982; MDiv, Boston U., 1960, PhD, 1966; STD, MacMurray Coll., Jacksonville, Ill., 1991; DD, Coe Coll., 1994. Ordained to ministry United Meth. Ch., 1958; pastor 1st United Meth. Ch., Revere, Mass., 1960-63, North Andover, 1963-68; planning assoc. United Meth. Bd. Global Ministries, N.Y.C., 1968-73, dir. planning, 1973-77; assoc. dean, asst. prof. theology and society Boston U. Sch. Theology, 1977-80; pres., prof. theology and society Garrett-Evang. Theol. Sem., Evanston, Ill., 1980-2001, pres. emeritus, sr. scholar, 2001—. Mendenhall lectr. DePauw U., Greencastle, Ind., 1982, Willson lectr., Nashville, 1983, Voigt lectr. McKendree Coll., 1984, McKendree Blair lectr. MacMurray Coll., 1986, Henry Martin Loud lectr. U. Mich., Ann Arbor, 1987; Wright lectr. Morningside Coll., 1991, Bransford lectr., 1999; chaplain, preacher, Chautauqua, N.Y., 1984, 88, Lakeside, Ohio, 1996; mem. theol. edn. commn. United Meth. Ch., 1992-2000, former mem. univ. senate; mem. bd. No. Ill. Conf. United Meth. Ch.; chmn. com. on acad. affairs DePauw U. Bd. Trustees. Author: Parables of Jesus: Glimpses of the New Age, 1979, rev. edit., 1990, Context for Discovery, 1980, Parables of Jesus: Glimpses of God's Reign, 1990; contbg. editor: Truth and Tradition: A Conversation about the Future of United Methodist Theological Education, 1995. Trustee DePauw U., Greencastle, Ind., 1996-2000. Recipient Disting. Alumnus award Boston U. Sch. Theology, 1985, Disting. Alumni citation DePauw U., 1993; Jacob Sleeper fellow, 1960-61. Mem. Assn. United Meth. Scis., Assn. Chgo. Theol. Schs. (pres. 1985-87, 95-97). Home: 2008 Elmore Pond Road Wolcott VT 05680 E-mail: nfisher@nwu.edu.

FISHER, PIERRE JAMES, JR. physician; b. Chgo., Oct. 29, 1931; s. Pierre James and Evelyn (Trevithick) F.; m. Carol Ann Walton, Mar. 16, 1951; children: James Walton, David Alan, Steven Edward, Teresa Ann. Student, Taylor U., 1949-51, Ball State U., 1951-52; M.D., Ind. U., 1956. Diplomate Am. Bd. Surgery. Intern U.S. Naval Hosp., San Diego, 1956-57, resident in surgery, 1957-61; pvt. practice specializing in surgery Surgeons Inc., Marion, Ind., 1965—, pres., 1977—; mem. staff Marion Gen. Hosp., chief staff, 1970. Trustee Meth. Hosp., Indpls., 1972-94. Served with USN, 1956-65. Recipient Physicians Recognition award AMA, 1974, 77, 80, 83, 89; commd. Ky. Col., Gov. Ky., 1997. Fellow ACS; mem. AMA, Grant County Med. Soc. (pres. 1980), Marion Area C. of C. (v.p. 1979-81), N.Am. Med. Golf Assn. (v.p. 1989-90, pres. 1991-93), Rotary (pres. Marion 1983-84, Dist. 656 Disting. Svc. award 1989), Kingsway Country Club (bd. dirs., pres. 1997-99). Methodist. Home: 11250 SW Essex Dr Lake Suzy FL 34269-9162 Office: Surgeons Inc 330 N Wabash Ave Ste 450 Marion IN 46952-2600

FISHER, RONALD C. economics educator; b. Schenectady, Feb. 26, 1950; s. William K. and Agnes M. (McNulty) F.; children: Michael, Charles. BA in Chemistry, Mich. State U., 1972; MA in Econs., Brown U., 1974, PhD in Econs., 1977. Research economist U.S. Adv. Commn. on Interngovtl. Relations, Washington, 1975-76; prof. econs. Mich. State U., East Lansing, 1976—, prof. econs., chmn. dept. econs., 1988-92, dir. Honors Coll., 1996—; dep. state treas. Mich. Dept. Treasury, Lansing, 1983-85. Bd. dirs. Ind. Bus. Rsch. Office of Mich., Detroit, 1988-92; vis. fellow Australian Nat. U., 1992; cons. to the U.S. Adv. Commn. on Intergovtl. Rels., U.S. Dept. HUD, U.S. Dept. Treasury, States of Ariz., Conn., Maine, Mich., Minn., N.J., W.Va., and D.C. Author: State and Local Public Finance, 1989, 96; contbr. articles to profl. jours. Exec. dir. Gov.'s Study Group on Govt. Expenditures, Hartford, 1978-79. NSF grantee, 1980. Mem. AAUP, Am. Econ. Assn., Nat. Tax Assn., Assn. for Pub. Policy Analysis and Mgmt., Midwest Econ. Assn. Office: Mich State U Honors Coll East Lansing MI 48824

FISHER, THOMAS GEORGE, lawyer, retired media company executive; b. Debrecen, Hungary, Oct. 2, 1931; came to U.S., 1951; s. Eugene J. and Viola Elizabeth (Rittersporn) F.; m. Rita Knisley, Feb. 14, 1960; children: Thomas G. Jr., Katherine F. Vaaler. B.S., Am. U., 1957, J.D., 1959; postgrad., Harvard U., 1956. Bar: D.C. 1959, Iowa 1977. Atty. FCC, Washington, 1959-61, 65-66; pvt. law practice, 1961-65, 66-69; asst. counsel Meredith Corp., N.Y.C., 1969-72, assoc. gen. counsel Des Moines, 1972-76, gen. counsel, 1976-80, v.p. gen. counsel, 1980-94, corp. sec., 1988-94. Comml. law liaison ABA Ctr. and East European Law Initiative, Krakow, Poland, 1994-95; atty. Legal Aid Soc. Polk County, 1996—. Contbr. articles to profl. jours. Bd. dirs. Des Moines Met. Opera Co., Indianola, 1980-94, pres., 1990-91; bd. dirs. Civic Music Assn., Des Moines, 1982-92, pres., 1987-88; chmn. legis. com. Greater Des Moines C. of C., 1976-77; bd. dirs. Legal Aid Soc. Polk County, 1986-93, pres., 1993; bd. dirs., sec., treas. Friends of Benedictine Edn. in Hungary Found., 1999—. With U.S. Army, 1952-54. Mem. ABA, Iowa State Bar Assn. (chmn. corp. counsel subcom. 1979-82), Polk County Bar Assn., Embassy Club. Office: Legal Aid Assn Polk County 1111 9th St Ste 380 Des Moines IA 50314-2527

FISHER, THOMAS GEORGE, JR. lawyer; b. Washington, June 1, 1961; s. Thomas George and Rita (Knisley) F.; m. Susan Jane Koenig, June 23, 1990. BA, Iowa State U., 1983; JD with high distinction, U. Iowa, 1986. Bar: Iowa 1986, U.S. Dist. Ct. (so. dist.) Iowa 1987, U.S. Ct. Appeals (8th cir.) 1987, U.S. Dist. Ct. (no. dist.) Iowa 1993. Jud. clk. Iowa Supreme Ct., Davenport, 1986-87; assoc. Duncan, Jones, Riley & Finley, P.C., Des Moines, 1987-91; asst. atty. gen. State of Iowa, Justice Dept., 1991-95; counsel Am. Mut. Life Ins. Co., 1995-96; ptnr. Hogan & Fisher, PLC, 1997—. Precinct chair Polk County Dem. Party, Des Moines, 1988-90, 94-96, 98-2000, 02--; candidate Iowa Ho. of Reps. Dists. 73, 1994; mem. Des Moines Leadership Inst., 1998-99; bd. dirs. Anawim Housing; bd. dirs., mem. exec. com. Metro Arts Alliance of Greater Des Moines. Mem. Blackstone Inn of Ct. Democrat. Roman Catholic. Office: Hogan & Fisher PLC 3101 Ingersoll Ave Des Moines IA 50312-3918 E-mail: Tom@Hogan-Fisher.com.

FISHER, WILL STRATTON, illumination consultant; b. Nashville, June 27, 1922; s. Will Stratton and Estelle (Carr) R.; m. Patricia A. Fesco, Nov.

10, 1945; children: Patricia Jo, Will Stratton, Robert J. B.S.E.E., Vanderbilt U., 1947. Registered profl. engr., Ohio. With Lighting Bus. Group, Gen. Elec. Co., Cleve., 1947-87, mgr. advanced application engring., 1971-84, mgr. lighting edn., 1985-87; cons. lighting Moreland Hills, Ohio, 1987—. Cons. Lighting Research Inst. Contbr. articles, papers to profl. jours., symposia and internat. profl. meetings. Patentee parabolic wedge louver; developer concepts for utilizing heat from lighting systems to heat bldgs.; designer calorimeter; developer procedure for calculation contbn. of lighting to heating of bldgs. Served to 1st lt. C.E., AUS, 1943-46, Manhattan Project. Fellow Illuminating Engring. Soc. North Am. (pres. 1978-79, Disting. Service award 1980, Louis B. Marks award for exceptional service 1988); mem. SAR, Internat. Commn. Illumination (U.S. expert on tech. com., U.S. rep. to div. 3, interior lighting), ASHRAE, IEEE. Methodist. Lodge: Kiwanis (pres. 1990-91). Home and Office: 120 Meadowhill Ln Moreland Hills OH 44022-1337

FISK, LENNARD AYRES, physicist, educator; b. Elizabeth, N.J., July 7, 1943; s. Lennard Ayres and Elinor (Fischer) F.; m. Patricia Elizabeth Leuba, Dec. 28, 1966; children: Ian, Justin, Nathan. AB, Cornell U., 1965; PhD, U. Calif., San Diego, 1969. Postdoctoral fellow NASA/Goddard Space Flight Ctr., Greenbelt, MD., 1969-71, astrophysicist, 1971-77; assoc. prof. U. N.H., Durham, 1977-81, prof., 1981-87, dir. rsch., 1982-83, interim v.p./fin. affairs, 1983-84, v.p. rsch. and fin., 1984-87; assoc. administr. space sci. and applications NASA Hdqrs., Washington, 1987-93; prof. U. Mich., 1993—. Advisor NAS, NASA, 1980-87. Contbr. more than 120 articles to profl. jours. Recipient Space Science award Am. Inst. Aeronautics and Astronautics, 1994. Fellow Am. Geophys. Union; mem. Internat. Acad. Astronautics, Academia Europaea (fgn. mem.). Office: Univ of Michigan Atmos Oceanic & Space Scis 2455 Hayward St Ann Arbor MI 48109-2143

FISK, MARTIN H. lawyer; b. St. Paul, Apr. 11, 1947; BA, U. Minn., 1969; JD, Harvard U., 1976. Bar: Minn. 1976. Mem. Briggs and Morgan P.A., St. Paul. Mem. ABA, Phi Beta Kappa. Office: Briggs and Morgan PA 2200 1st Nat Bank Bldg Saint Paul MN 55101-3210

FITCH, COY DEAN, physician, educator; b. Marthaville, La., Oct. 5, 1934; s. Raymond E. and Joey (Youngblood) F.; m. Rachel Farr, Mar. 31, 1956; children: Julia Anne, Jaquelyn Kay. BS, U. Ark., 1956, MS, MD, U. Ark., 1958. Diplomate Am. Bd. Internal Medicine and Endocrinology. Intern U. Ark. Sch. Medicine, 1958-59, resident, 1959-62, instr. biochemistry, 1959-62, asst. prof. medicine and biochemistry, 1962-66, asso. prof., 1966-67; dir. U. Ark. Sch. Medicine (Honors Med. Student Research Program), 1965-67; asso. prof. internal medicine and biochemistry St. Louis U. Sch. Medicine, 1967-73, prof. internal medicine, 1973—, prof. biochemistry, 1976—, head sect. metabolism, 1969-76, dir. div. endocrinology and metabolism, 1977-85; chief med. service St. Louis U. Hosps., 1976-77, vice-chmn. dept. internal medicine, 1983-85, acting chmn. dept. internal medicine, 1985-88, chmn. dept., 1988-2000; practice medicine, specializing in internal medicine Little Rock, 1962-67, St. Louis, 1969—. Dir. Diabetic Clinic, U. Ark. Med. Ctr., 1962-67, head sect. metabolism and endocrinology, 1966-67; mem. nutrition study sect. div. research grants NIH, 1967-71 Assoc. editor: Nutrition Revs., 1964; contbr. articles to profl. jours. Served from capt. to lt. col., M.C. AUS, 1967-69. Recipient Lederle Med. Faculty award, 1966-67; Russell M. Wilder-Nat. Vitamin Found. fellow, 1959-62 Master ACP (gov. Mo. chpt. 1995-99); mem. Am. Inst. Nutrition, Am., So. Socs. Clin. Investigation, Am. Soc. Biol. Chemists, Ctrl. Soc. Clin. rsch., Phi Beta Kappa, Sigma Xi. Office: 1402 S Grand Blvd Saint Louis MO 63104-1004 E-mail: fitchcd@slu.edu.

FITCH, FRANK WESLEY, pathologist educator, immunologist, educator, administrator; b. Bushnell, Ill., May 30, 1929; s. Harold Wayne and Mary Gladys (Frank) F.; m. Shirley Dobbins, Dec. 23, 1951; children—Mary Margaret, Mark Howard. M.D., U. Chgo., 1953, S.M., 1957, Ph.D., 1960; M.D. (hon.), U. Lausanne, Switzerland, 1990. Postdoctoral research fellow USPHS, 1954-55, 57-58; faculty U. Chgo., 1957—, prof. pathology, 1967—, Albert D. Lasker prof. med. sci., 1976—, emeritus prof., 1996, assoc. dean med. and grad. edn. div. biol. scis., 1976-85, dean acad. affairs, 1985-86, dir. Ben May Inst., 1986-95. Vis. prof. Swiss Inst. Exptl. Cancer Research, Lausanne, Switzerland, 1974-75. Editor-in-chief The Jour. of Immunology, 1997-2002; contbr. chpts. to books, articles to profl. jours. Recipient Borden Undergrad. Research award, 1953, Lederle Med. Faculty award, 1958-61; Markle Found. scholar, 1961-66; Commonwealth Fund fellow U. Lausanne (Switzerland) Institut de Biochimie, 1965-66; Guggenheim fellow, 1974-75 Mem. Fedn. Am. Socs. for Exptl. Biology (pres. 1993-94), Am. Assn. Immunologists (pres. 1992-93), Am. Soc. for Investigative Pathology, Am. Assn. for Cancer Rsch., Chgo. Path. Soc., Transplantation Soc., Sigma Xi, Alpha Omega Alpha. Home: 5449 S Kenwood Ave Chicago IL 60615-5312 E-mail: ffitch@uchicago.edu.

FITCH, MORGAN LEWIS, JR. intellectual property lawyer; b. Chgo., Nov. 21, 1922; s. Morgan Lewis and Marian (Ringer) F.; m. Helen Shearer, June 9, 1945; children: Ruth F. White, Mary F. White, Morgan Lewis, Frederick Shearer. B.S. in Chem. Engring., Ill. Inst. Tech., 1943; student, Princeton U., 1943, MIT, 1943-44; J.D., U. Mich., 1948. Bar: Ill. 1948. Since practiced in Chgo.; partner Fitch, Even, Tabin, & Flannery, 1953—. Bd. dirs. Advance Bank, Advance Bancorp. Trustee emeritus Tri-State Coll., Angola, Ind.; trustee YMCA, Chgo.; bd. dirs. YMCA Found. Lt. USNR, 1943-46. Recipient Disting. Pub. Service award Sec. Navy, 1960, 65 Mem. ABA, Ill. Bar Assn., Chgo. Bar Assn., Intellectual Property Law Assn. of Chgo., Lawyers Club Chgo., Navy League U.S. (pres. 1965-67), U.S. Naval Sea Cadet Corps (pres. 1963-65), Naval Commandery, Naval Res. Assn., Soc. Mayflower Descs.. Home: 4640 Clausen Ave Western Springs IL 60558-1640 Office: 120 S La Salle St Chicago IL 60603-3403 E-mail: hsfmlf@aol.com.

FITES, DONALD VESTER, retired tractor company executive; b. Tippecanoe, Ind., Jan. 20, 1934; s. Rex E. and Mary Irene (Sackville) F.; m. Sylvia Dempsey, June 25, 1960; children: Linda Marie. BS in Civil Engring., Valparaiso U., 1956; MS, MIT, 1971. With Caterpillar Overseas S.A., Peoria, Ill., 1956-66, dir. internat. customer divsn. Geneva, 1966-67; asst. mgr. market devel. Caterpillar Tractor Co., Peoria, 1967-70; dir. Caterpillar Mitsubishi Ltd., Tokyo, 1971-75; dir. engine capacity expansion program Caterpillar Tractor Co., Peoria, 1975-76, mgr. products control dept., 1976-79; pres. Caterpillar Brasil S.A., 1979-81; v.p. products Caterpillar Tractor Co., Peoria, 1981-85, exec. v.p., 1985-89; pres., chief opd. officer Caterpillar Inc., 1989-90, pres., COO, 1989-90, chmn., CEO, 1990-99, also bd. dirs.; mem. bd. dirs. Oshkosh Truck Corp., 2000—. Bd. dirs. Caterpillar Inc., Wolverine Worldwide, Mobil Corp., AT&T, Ga.-Pacific Corp.; past chmn. Equip. Mfg. Inst. Trustee Farm Found., 1985—, Meth. Med. Ctr., 1985—, Knox Coll., 1986—; chmn., nat. adv. bd. Salvation Army, 1985—, adminstrv. bd. 1st United Meth. Ch., 1986—; bd. dirs. Valparaiso U., Keep Am. Beautiful; past chmn. U.S.-Japan Bus. Coun. Mem. Agrl. Roundtable (chmn. 1985-87), SAE, ACTPN, Bus. Coun., Bus. Roundtable (past chmn.)., Nat. Assn. Mfrs. and Bus. Coun., Nat. Fgn. Trade Coun., Mt. Hawley Country Club, Creve Coeur Club, Country Club of Peoria. Republican. Office: Oshkosh Truck Corp 2307 Oregon Street Oshkosh WI 54902

FITZ, BROTHER RAYMOND L. university president; b. Akron, Ohio, Aug. 12, 1941; s. Raymond L. and Mary Lou (Smith) F. B.S. in Elec. Engring., U. Dayton, Ohio, 1964; M.S., Poly. Inst. Bklyn., 1967, Ph.D., 1969. Joined Soc. of Mary, Roman Catholic Ch., 1960; mem. faculty U. Dayton, 1968—, prof. elec. engring. and engring. mgmt., 1975—, exec. dir. Center Christian Renewal, 1974-79, univ. pres., 1979—. Author numerous papers, reports in field. Bd. dirs. various civic organs. Recipient Disting. Alumnus award Poly. Inst. Bklyn., 1980 Office: U Dayton 300 College Park Ave Rm 207 Dayton OH 45469-0001

FITZGERALD, CAROL E. state legislator; Mem. S.D. Ho. of Reps., until 2000, mem. agr. and natural resources and judiciary coms.; rental mgr., until 2000. Home: 5625 Cleghorn Canyon Rd Rapid City SD 57702-9417

FITZGERALD, GERALD FRANCIS, retired banker; b. Chgo., July 6, 1925; s. John J. and Olivia (Trader) F.; m. Marjorie Webb Gosselin, Sept. 10, 1949; children: Gerald Francis Jr., James Gosselin, Thomas Gosselin, Julie Ann Fitzgerald Schauer, Peter Gosselin. BS in Commerce, Northwestern U., 1949. Salesman Premier Printing Co., 1949-53; founder, ptnr. Fitzgerald & Cooke (now Hill and Knowlton, Inc. div. J. Walter Thompson), 1953-60, v.p., 1960-64; chmn. Lake Villa Trust & Savs. Bank, 1961-69, Palatine Nat. Bank, 1961-87, Suburban Nat. Bank of Palatine, Suburban Bank of Hoffman-Schaumburg, Suburban Bank of Cary-Grove, Suburban Bank of Rolling Meadows, Suburban Bank of Barrington, Suburban Bank of Bartlett, 1964-90; pres. Suburban Bancorp, Inc., Palatine, 1982-90, chmn., 1982-94, So. Colo. Bank Holding Co., 1991—, Citizens Bank of Pagosa Springs, 1991-94. Cons. Am. Del. to NATO CCMS, Brussels, 1976; former chmn. Suburban Computer Svcs. Corp., Palatine; lectr. in banking field. Contbr. articles to profl. jours. Bd. dirs., past pres. Inverness Assn.; former mem. Govs. Adv. Coun. of Ill.; past mem. Ill. Racing Bd.; mem. Chgo. Coun. of Fgn. Rels.; cons. Portsmouth, R.I. Abbey Sch., 1978-80; life trustee Newberry Libr.; mem. John Evans Club, Northwestern U. Sgt. U.S. Army, 1944-46, ETO. Mem. Ill. Thoroughbred Owners and Breeders Found., Nat. Assn. of State Racing Commrs., Newcomen Soc., Max McGraw's Wildlife Found., Chgo. Athletic Assn., Inverness Golf Club, Safari Internat. Club, Caxton Club, Delta Upsilon. Avocations: world travel, opera, rare books, photography, big game hunting and fishing. Home: 19 Creekside Ln Barrington IL 60010-9343 Office: 50 N Brockway St Palatine IL 60067-5076

FITZGERALD, JAMES FRANCIS, cable television executive; b. Janesville, Wis., Mar. 27, 1926; s. Michael Henry and Chloris Helen (Beiter) F.; m. Marilyn Field Cullen, Aug. 1, 1950; children: Michael Dennis, Brian Nicholas, Marcia O'Loughlin, James Francis, Carolyn Jane, Ellen Putnam. B.S., Notre Dame U., 1947. With Standard Oil Co. (Ind.), Milw., 1947-48; pres. F.-W. Oil Co., Janesville, 1950—, Total TV, Inc. (cable TV Systems), Wis., 1965-86. Bd. dirs. Milw. Ins. Co., Bank One, Janesville N.A.; chmn. bd. Golden State Warriors, Oakland, Calif., 1986-95, Total TV Calif., 1987-96. Bd. govs., chmn. TV com. NBA; chmn. bd., pres. S.P.A.C.E. Inc. subs. Milw. Bucks NBA team, 1976-85; chmn. Greater Milw. Open (PGA Tournament), 1985, Notre Dame Bus. Adv. Coun., 1989—. Served to lt. (j.g.) USNR, 1944-46, 51-53. Mem. Chief Execs. Forum, World Bus. Coun., Wis. Petroleum Assn. (pres. 1961-62), Janesville Country Club, Castles Pines Golf Club, Vintage Club (pres. 1989-91), San Francisco Golf Club, El Dorado Country Club. Roman Catholic. Home and Office: PO Box 348 Janesville WI 53547-0348

FITZGERALD, JAMES PATRICK, lawyer; b. Omaha, Nov. 30, 1946; s. James Joseph and Lorraine (Hickey) F.; m. Dianne Fager, Dec. 27, 1968; 1 child, James Timothy. BA, U. Nebr., 1968; JD, Creighton U., 1974. Bar: Nebr. 1974, U.S. Dist. Ct. Nebr. 1974, U.S. Ct. Appeals (8th cir.) 1974. Law clk. U.S. Dist. Ct. Nebr., Omaha, 1974-76; atty. McGrath, North, Mullin & Kratz, P.C., 1976—. Sgt. U.S. Army, 1968-71. Mem. ABA, Nebr. Bar Assn., Assn. Trial Lawyers Am., Nebr. Assn. Trial Attys., Def. Rsch. Inst. Home: 16728 Jones Cir Omaha NE 68118-2711 Office: McGrath North Mullin & Kratz 1 Central Park Plz Ste 1400 Omaha NE 68102-1638

FITZGERALD, JAMES T. architect; BA in Philosophy, Josephinum Coll.; BArch, U. Notre Dame. Cert. Nat. Coun. Archtl. Registration Bd.; registered architect 31 states. Chmn., CEO FRCH Design Worldwide (previously Space Design Internat.), 1968—. Spkr. in field; tchr. U. Cin. Coll. of Design, Architecture, Art and Planning; bd. advisors Kirk & Blum Co. Former chmn. steering com. for downtown retail devel. strategy City of Cin.; v.p., trustee Contemporary Arts Ctr., Cin.; bd. dirs. Archtl. Found., Cin.; trustee Cin. Opera. Fellow AIA (former pres. Cin. chpt., former nat. chmn. interiors com., vice chmn. internat. com.), Internat. Coun. Shopping Ctrs., Urban Land Inst., Am. Arbitration Assn., Nat. Retail Fedn. Office: FRCH Design Worldwide 311 Elm St Ste 600 Cincinnati OH 45202-2737

FITZGERALD, JEREMIAH MICHAEL, lawyer; BSBA, Xavier U., 1975; JD, U. Chgo., 1978. Bar: Ill. 1978. Asst. sec., asst. gen. counsel Comdisco Inc., Rosemont, Ill., v.p., asst. sec., gen. counsel, 1989—. Office: Comdisco Inc Legal Dept 6111 N River Rd Rosemont IL 60018-5158

FITZGERALD, JOHN WARNER, law educator; b. Grand Ledge, Mich., Nov. 14, 1924; s. Frank Dwight and Queena Maud (Warner) F.; m. Lorabeth Moore, June 6, 1953; children: Frank Moore, Eric Stiles, Adam Warner. B.S., Mich. State U., 1947; J.D., U. Mich., 1954. Bar: Mich. 1954. Practiced in Grand Ledge, 1955-64; chief judge pro tem Mich. Ct. Appeals, 1965-73; justice Mich. Supreme Ct., 1974-83, dep. chief justice, 1975-82, chief justice, 1982; prof. law Thomas M. Cooley Law Sch., Lansing, Mich., 1982—. Mem. Mich. Senate from 15th Dist., 1958-64 Served with AUS, 1943-44. Mem. ABA, State Bar Mich. (bd. commrs. 1985-90), Am. Judicature Soc. Office: Thomas M Cooley Law Sch PO Box 13038 Lansing MI 48901-3038

FITZGERALD, MICHAEL LEE, state official; b. Marshalltown, Iowa, Nov. 29, 1951; s. James Martin and Clara Francis (Dankbar) F.; m. Janet Roewe; children: Ryan, Chris, Erin, Bridie. B.B.A., U. Iowa, 1974. Campaign mgr. Fitzgerald for Treas., Colo., Iowa, 1974; market analyst Massey Ferguson, Inc., Des Moines, 1975-83; treas. State of Iowa, 1983—. Democrat. Roman Catholic. Office: Office of State Treas Capitol Bldg Rm 114 Des Moines IA 50319-0001

FITZGERALD, PETER GOSSELIN, senator, lawyer; b. Elgin, Ill., Oct. 20, 1960; s. Gerald Francis and Marjorie (Gosselin) F.; m. C. Nina Kerstiens, July 25, 1987; 1 child, Jake Buchanan. AB, Dartmouth Coll., 1982; cert. of attendance, Aristotelian U., Salonica, Greece, 1983; JD, U. Mich., 1986. Bar: Ill. 1986, U.S. Dist. Ct. (no. dist.) Ill. 1986. Assoc. Isham, Lincoln & Beale, Chgo., 1986-88; ptnr. Riordan, Larson, Bruckert & Moore, 1988-92; mem. Ill. Senate, 1993-98, chmn. state govt. ops. com., 1997-98; U.S. senator from Ill., 1999-. Counsel Harris Bankmont, Inc., 1992-96. Rotary Found. internat. grad. scholar, 1982-83. Mem. Econ. Club Chgo., Inverness Golf Club, Union League Club. Roman Catholic. Office: US Senate 555 Dirksen Bldg Washington DC 20510-0001 E-mail: senator_fitzgerald@fitzgerald.senate.gov.

FITZGERALD, ROBERT MAURICE, financial executive; b. Chgo., Jan. 8, 1942; s. James Patrick and Catherine (McNulty) Fitzgerald; children: Stephen, Peter, Susan, Martin. BS, Loyola U., Chgo., 1971; postgrad., U. Wis., 1974-76, Northwestern U., 1980. Sr. v.p. Fed. Reserve Bank, Chgo., 1979-85; pres. Chgo. Clearing House Assn., 1985—. Cons. Currency Bd., Abu Dhabi, United Arab Emirates, 1979; past bd. dirs. Nat. Automated Clearing House Assn., Washington; advisor U.S. Coun. on Internat. Banking, N.Y.C. Pres. Coun. on Alcoholism, Ann Arbor, Mich., 1978, Diocesan Bd. Edn., Joliet, Ill., 1981—84; bd. dirs. Frances Xavier Warde Sch.; vice chair. Chgo. Crime Commn.; trustee Union League Boys and Girls Clubs; sec. Civic and Arts Found.; former mem. adv. bd. St. Mary of Nazereth Hosp.; past pres., bd. dirs., vice chmn. exec. com. LaLalle St Coun.; chair, bd. trustees Old St. Patrick's Ch., Chgo.; bd. dirs. Concern Worldwide (U.S.), Inc. Mem.: Bankers Club Chgo. (sec., treas., exec. com.), Union League Club Chgo. (past pres.), Econ. Club Chgo., Execs. Club of Chgo. (bd. dirs., treas.). Democrat. Roman Catholic. Office: Chgo Clearing House Assn 230 S La Salle St Ste 700 Chicago IL 60604-1410 E-mail: fitz@chgo.org.

FITZGERALD, SCOTT, state legislator; b. Nov. 16, 1963; m. Lisa Fitzgerald; children: Scott William, Brennan, Connor. BS in Journalism, U. Wis., 1985. Mem. Wis. Senate from 13th dist., Madison, 1994—. Mem. com. on econ. devel., housing and govt. ops., com. on health, human svcs., aging, corrections, vets. and mil. affairs, spl. legis. coun. com. on recodification of fish and game laws, rural econ. devel. com. Wis. State Senate; owner Dodge County Ind. News, 1990—. Chmn. Dodge County (Wis.) Rep. Com.; planning com. City of Juneau, Wis.; former mem. Juneau Planning Commn. Major U.S. Army Res., 1981—. Mem. Juneau Area C. of C., Wis. Newspaper Assn. Address: N4692 Maple Rd Juneau WI 53039-9514

FITZGERALD, THOMAS JOE, psychologist; b. Wichita, Kans., July 8, 1941; s. Thomas Michael and Pauline Gladys (Zink) F.; B.A., San Francisco State U., 1965; M.A., U. Utah, 1969, Ph.D., 1971. Dir. behavioral services programs VA Hosp., Topeka, 1971-73; pvt. practice as psychologist, Topeka, 1973-74, Prairie Village, Kans., 1974—; clin. instr. Menninger Sch. Psychiatry, Topeka, 1972-74; v.p. Preferred Mental Health Care Mgmt., Inc., 1986-90, pres., Preferred Mental Health, Inc., 1990—; sec.-treas. Kans. Bd. Psychologist Examiners, 1976-79, 79-80, chmn., 1980—, chmn. psychology examining com.; mem. Behavioral Scis. Regulatory Bd., 1980-82; pres. Psychol. Services Corp., Prairie Village, 1974—. Mem. Gov.'s Commn. on Criminal Adminstrn., 1974-76; vice-chmn. Gov.'s Com. on Med. Assistance, 1978-80; mem. Mid-Am. Health Systems Agy., 1979-82; mem. com. on utilization review orgns. Kansas Ins. Commr. Adv. Com., 1994—. Served with USMC, 1958-61. Mem. Kans. Psychol. Assn. (pres. 1980-81), Kans. Assn. Profl. Psychologists (pres. 1981-82, Outstanding Psychologist award 1979, 80, 81, 82), Greater Kansas City Soc. Clin. Hypnosis (pres. 1978-85). Office: Preferred Mental Health Inc PO Box 4404 Overland Park KS 66204-0404

FITZGERALD, THOMAS ROBERT, judge; b. Chgo., July 10, 1941; s. Thomas Henry and Kathryn (Touhy) F.; m. Gayle Ann Aubry, July 1, 1967; children: Maura, Kathryn, Jean, Thomas., Ann. Student Loyola U., Chgo., 1959-63; J.D., John Marshall Law Sch., Chgo., 1968. Bar: Ill. 1968, U.S. Dist. Ct. (no. dist.) Ill. 1968. Asst. state's atty. State's Atty. Cook County, Chgo., 1968-76, trial asst., 1968-72, felony trial supr., 1973-76; judge criminal div. Circuit Ct. Cook County, 1976—2000, justice Ill. State Supreme Ct., 2000-; adj. prof. law Chgo., Kent Coll. Law, 1977— , asst. coor. trial ad program, 1989-96, instr. Einstein Inst. for Sci., Health and Cts.; mem. faculty Nat. Inst. Trial Advs., Boulder, Colo., 1982, Ill. Jud. Conf., Chgo., 1982— . Pres. Sch. Bd. Queen of Universe Parish, Chgo., 1974-75. Served with USN. Recipient Outstanding Jud. Performance award Chgo. Crime Commn., Herman Kogan Media award for excellence in broadcast jour.; named Celtic Man of Yr. Celtic Legal Soc. Fellow Ill. Bar Found.; mem. Chgo. Bar Assn., Ill. Bar Assn., Ill. Judges Assn. (bd. dirs. 1981-84, treas. 1985, sec. 1986, 3d v.p. 1987, pres.). Office: 160 N LaSalle St Rm N-2013 Chicago IL 60601 Fax: 312-793-4579.*

FITZGERALD, WILLIAM ALLINGHAM, savings and loan association executive, director; b. Omaha, Nov. 18, 1937; s. William Frances and Mary (Allingham) F.; m. Barbara Ann Miskell, Aug. 20, 1960; children—Mary Colleen, Katherine Kara, William Tate. B.S.B.A. in Fin., Creighton U., 1959; grad. Savs. and Loan League exec. tng. program, U. Ga., 1962, U. Ind., 1969. With Comml. Fed. Savs. & Loan Assn., Omaha, 1959—, v.p., asst. sec., 1963-68, exec. v.p., 1968-73, pres., 1974-82, CEO, 1983—, chmn., CEO NE, 1994—. Trustee Ind. Coll. Found.; vice chmn. bd. dirs. Creighton U.; bd. dirs. Coll. of St. Mary, United Way of Midlands; trustee Archbishop's com. for ednl. devel. Roman Catholic Ch. Served to lt. Fin. Corps, U.S. Army. Chmn. Am. Cmty. Bankers, 1998—. Clubs: Omaha Country, Kiewit Plaza. Lodge: Knights of Ak-Sar-Ben (gov.). Office: Comml Fed Bank FSB 2120 S 72nd St Omaha NE 68124

FITZGIBBON, DANIEL HARVEY, lawyer; b. Columbus, Ind., July 7, 1942; s. Joseph Bales and Margaret Lenore (Harvey) FitzG.; m. Joan Helen Meltzer, Aug. 12, 1973; children: Katherine Lenore, Thomas Bernard. BS in Engring., U.S. Mil. Acad., 1964; JD cum laude, Harvard U., 1972. Bar: Ind. 1972; U.S. Dist. Ct. (so. dist.) Ind. 1972, U.S. Tax Ct. 1977. Commd. 2d lt. U.S. Army, 1964, advanced through grades to capt., 1967, served with inf. Vietnam, resigned, 1969; assoc. Barnes & Thornburg, Indpls., 1972-79, ptnr., 1979-99, mem. mgmt. com., 1983-95, of counsel, 2000—. Speaker various insts; comml. law liaison, ABA-CEELI, Moscow, 1998-99. Mem. Sch. Bd. Met. Sch. Dist. Lawrence Twp., 1988-96, pres., 1990-91, 94-95; bd. advs. Eiteljorg Mus. Am. Indian and Western Art. Capt. U.S. Army, 1964-69, Vietnam. Fellow Am. Coll. Tax Counsel, Am. Bar Found.; mem. ABA (internat. law sect.), Am. Law Inst., Ind. State Bar Assn. (tax sect.), Indpls. Bar Assn. (chmn. tax sect. 1982-83, coun. 1982-86), Indpls. Athletic Club, Lawyers Club, Woodstock Club. Home: 6460 Lawrence Dr Indianapolis IN 46226-1035 Office: Barnes & Thornburg 1313 Merchants Bank Bldg Indianapolis IN 46204-3506

FITZPATRICK, CHRISTINE MORRIS, legal administrator, former television executive; b. Steubenville, Ohio, June 10, 1920; d. Roy Elwood and Ruby Lorena (Mason) Morris; student U. Chgo., 1943-44, U. Ga., 1945-46; m. T. Mallary Fitzpatrick, Jr., Dec. 19, 1942; 1 child, Thomas Mallary III. BA, Roosevelt U., 1947; postgrad. Trinity Coll., Hartford, Conn., 1970. Assoc. dir. Joint Human Rels. Project, City of Chgo., 1965-66; tchr. English, Austin Sch. for Girls, Hartford, 1966-70; promotion coord. Conn. Pub. TV, Hartford, 1971-72, dir. community rels., 1972-73, v.p., 1973-77; pub. rels./pub. affairs cons. Commonwealth Edison Co., Chgo., 1977-79; dir. spl. events Chgo. Public TV, 1979-84; v.p. Fitzpatrick Group, Inc., Chgo., 1986-88; adminstrv. dir. Fitzpatrick Law Offices, 1988-94, Fitzpatrick Eilenberg & Zivian, 1994-96; adminstrv. dir. Fitzpatrick Law Offices, Chgo., 1997-99, 2200 Ventures LLC, Chgo., 1999—; v.p. Pub. Rels. Clinic Chgo., 1980-81. Bd. advisers Greater Hartford Mag., 1975-77; bd. dirs. World Affairs Ctr., Hartford, 1975-77; mem. adv. coun. Am. Revolution Bicentennial Commn. Conn., 1975-77. Mem. Pub. Rels. Soc. Am. (dir. Conn. Valley chpt. 1976-77), Am. Women in Radio and TV (New Eng. chpt. pres. 1976-77), LWV (Chgo. chpt. pres. 1962-64, Hartford chpt. v.p. 1971-73). Home: 5518 S Harper Ave Chicago IL 60637-1830

FITZPATRICK, JOYCE J. nursing educator, former dean; BSN, Georgetown U., LHD (hon.), 1990; MS in Psychiatric-Mental Health Nursing, Ohio State U.; PhD in Nursing, NYU; MBA, Case Western Reserve U., 1992. Dean Frances Payne Bolton Sch. Nursing Case Western Reserve U., Cleve., 1982—97, Elizabeth Brooks Ford prof. nursing, 1998—. Dir. WHO Collaborating Ctr. for Nursing, Bolton Sch. Editor: Applied Nursing Rsch.; co-editor: Annual Rev. Nursing Rsch.; contbr. articles. Recipient Book of Yr. awards, Am. Jour. Nursing, Disting.Contbn. to Nursing Rsch. award, Midwest Nursing Rsch. Soc.; fellow USPHS Primary Care Policy fellow, 1995; scholar Inst. Medicine/Am. Acad. Nursing/Am. Nurses Found. scholar, 1994—95. Fellow: Am. Acad. Nursing; mem.: N.Am. Nursing Diagnosis Assn. (chair taxonomy com.). Office: Case Western Res U F P Bolton Sch Nursing 2121 Abington Rd Cleveland OH 44106-4904

FITZPATRICK, SUSAN, biochemist, neurologist, foundation executive; married. Grad., St. John's U.; PhD in Biochemistry and Neurology, Cornell U. Postdoctoral tng. Yale U., New Haven; dir. edn. Miami Project To Cure

Paralysis, Miami, Fla., assoc. exec. dir.; adminstr. grants program Brain Trauma Found.; program dir. James S. McConnell Found., St. Louis. Office: James S McDonnell Found Ste 1850 1304 S Brentwood Blvd Saint Louis MO 63117

FITZWATER, RODGER L. state legislator; Mem. Mo. Ho. of Reps., Jefferson City. Democrat.

FIZDALE, RICHARD, advertising agency executive; b. Aug. 4, 1939; BA, U of Texas, Arlington. Copywriter BBDO Advt., 1967-68, Leo Burnett Co., Inc., Chgo., 1969-70, copy supr., 1970-72, assoc. creative dir., 1972-73, creative dir., 1973-74, v.p., 1974-78, v.p., exec. creative dir., 1978-79, sr. v.p., exec. creative dir., 1979, sr. v.p., mgr. creative ops., 1979-82, exec. v.p., dep. dir. creative svcs., 1982-85, pres., chief creative officer, bd. dirs., 1985-86, exec. com., 1986-87, pres., chief creative officer, 1987-92, chmn., CEO, chief creative officer, 1992-93, chmn., chief creative officer, 1993-97, chmn., CEO, 1997-2000; chmn. Leo Burnett Co., Inc. (The Leo Group), 2000—; vice chmn. BDM Inc. (merger Leo Group & MacManus Group), 2000—. Office: Leo Burnett USA 35 W Wacker Dr Ste 2220 Chicago IL 60601-1614

FJELL, MICK, principal; Prin. Millard Ctrl. Mid. Sch., 1978—. Recipient Blue Ribbon Sch. award 1990-91. Office: Millard Central Mid Sch 12801 L St Omaha NE 68137-2020

FLAGG, MICHAEL JAMES, communications and graphics company executive; b. N.Y.C., Aug. 14, 1958; s. Wilbor Thomas and Sylvia (Kobitz) F. BA with highest distinction, U. Va., 1980. Intern, internat. economist U.S. Customs, Washington, 1979; mgmt. assoc. First Nat. Bank Atlanta, 1980-81, cash mgmt. officer, 1981-83, asst. v.p., group mktg. mgr., 1983-84; treasury mgr., asst. to chief exec. officer Contel Corp., Atlanta, 1984-89; v.p. fin. Contel Office Communications, Inc., St. Louis, 1989-91; v.p., treas. Am. Internat., Inc., Chgo., 1991-94; v.p. fin. Alliance Capital, N.Y.C., 1994; sr. v.p. corp. bus. devel. USL Capital, San Francisco, 1995; CFO InterCall, Chgo., 1995, COO, 1996-97; cons. Heidrich & Struggles, Inc., 1997—2000, ptnr., 1999—2000, ptnr.-in-charge, 2000—. Instr. Am. Inst. Banking, 1982-83; chmn. Contel Profl. Devel. Assn., Atlanta, 1986. Assoc. editor Cash Mgmt. Forum, 1982-84; co-founder, co-editor First Word newsletter, 1983-84. Chmn. fundraising unit United Way, Atlanta, 1985—88, Atlanta unit Am. Cancer Soc., 1985—88, Atlanta Coll. Arts, 1985—88; governing mem. Brookfield Zoo, Chgo., 1992—99. Mem. Nat. Corp. Cash Mgmt. Assn. (bd. dirs. 1987-91, exec. com. 1988-91), Fin. Execs. Inst., Treasury Mgmt. Assn. Chgo., St. Louis Zoo Friends Assn. (bd. dirs. 1990-91). Avocations: sports, art, travel. Office: 1750 Tysons Blvd Ste 300 Mc Lean VA 22102 E-mail: MJF@H-S.com.

FLAHERTY, EMALEE GOTTBRATH, pediatrician; b. LaGrange, Ky., May 24, 1944; d. Frank Herman and Katherine Lee (Carothers) Gottbrath; m. Joseph Flaherty, Apr. 28, 1973 (div.); children: Joshua, Megan. BS, Purdue U., W. Lafayette, Ind., 1966; MD, Ind. U., Indpls., 1970. Resident, pediatrics U. Ill. Hosp., 1970-72, Columbus Hosp., 1972-73, med. dir. outpatient dept., 1984-96; med. dir. Columbus-Maryville Reception Ctr., 1986-95; dir. ambulator pediatrics Columbus Hosp., 1979-96, project dir. pediatric primary care tng. grant, 1989-95; med. dir. protective svcs. team Children's Meml. Hosp., 1996—; asst. prof. pediatrics Northwestern U. Sch. Medicine, 1997—. Mem. Am. Acad. Pediat. (chpt. treas.), Pediatric Primary Care Rsch. Grp. (steering com.), Pediatric Rsch. Office Setting (dist. coord.), Columbus Hosp. Woman's Bd. (exec. bd. 1988-96). Office: Children's Hosp 2300 N Childrens Plz # 16 Chicago IL 60614-3363

FLAHERTY, JOHN JOSEPH, quality assurance company executive; b. Chgo., July 24, 1932; s. Patrick J. and Mary B. Flaherty; m. Norrine Grow, Nov. 20, 1954 (dec. Sept. 1995); children: John, Bridgette, George, Eileen, Daniel, Mary, Michael, Amy; m. Rosemarie Clausen, Dec. 27, 2001. BEE U. Ill., 1959. Design engr. Admiral Corp., Chgo., 1959—60; project engr. Magnaflux Corp., 1960—79, v.p., mgr. rsch. and engring., 1979—84, v.p., mgr. mktg. and sales, 1984—86, v.p., gen. mgr. electronic products, 1986—88; pres. Flare Tech., 1988—. Fellow: Am. Soc. Non-Destructive Testing; mem.: IEEE, Am. Soc. Metals. Roman Catholic. Achievements include patents and publications on nondestructive testing, including medical ultrasonic; laser scanning. Home: 671 Grosvener Ln Elk Grove Village IL 60007-4203 Office: 2869 Old Higgins Rd Elk Grove Village IL 60007-6416

FLAHERTY, TIMOTHY THOMAS, radiologist; b. Fond du Lac, Wis., 1933; m. Joan Flaherty; 4 children. MD, Marquette U., 1959. Diplomate Am. Bd. Radiology. Intern St. Marys Hosp., Milw., 1959-60; resident in radiology, chief resident U. Wis., Madison, 1963—66; fellowship U. Wis. Hosps., 1964-65; pvt. practice. Bd. dirs., sec. Nat. Patient Safety Found.; founding dir. Physicians Ins. Co.-Wis., exec. com. and underwriting com., chair investment com., chmn. bd. dirs.; mem. Govs. task force on health reform, Wis.; founding dir. SMS Svcs., Inc.; bd. dirs. Bank One of Appleton, N.A.; chair Profl. Svcs. Network, Inc.; trustee Novus Health Group Inc., Appleton, Wis., 1988-94; mem. med. exec. com., bd. trustees dept. radiology Theda Clark Regional Med. Ctr., Neenah, Wis., chmn. dept. radiology, 1980-95; clin. prof. dept. radiology U. Wis. Ctr. for Health Scis., Madison, Med. Coll. of Wis., Milw. Maj. gen. USAF, ret. Fellow Am. Coll. Radiology (councilor); mem. AMA (exec. com. 1995—, chair fin. com., chair com. on membership 1996-97, chair com. on orgn. and operation, mem. compensation com., commr. to joint commn. on accreditation of healthcare orgns. 1994, dir. Commn. on Office Lab. Assessment, 1996—, bd. trustees 1994—, chair bd. trustees, 2001-02, sec.-treas. exec. com.), AMPAC (bd. dirs.), State Med. Soc. of Wis. (vice chair bd. dirs., commn. chair), Wis. Radiol. Soc. (past pres.), Radiol. Soc. of N.Am. (counselor 1991-97), Soc. of Med. Cons. of the Armed Forces, Aerospace Med. Assn., Assn. of Mil. Surgeons, Soc. of Air Force Flight Surgeons. Office: AMA 515 N State St Chicago IL 60610-4325 Address: Radiology Assoc Fox Valley 325 N Commercial St Neenah WI 54956-2665

FLAKOLL, TIMOTHY JOHN, state legislator, animal scientist; b. Ellendale, N.D., Oct. 8, 1959; s. Alden James and Wilma Jean (Wolff) F., m. Beverly Flakoll. BS, N.D. State U., 1981, MS, 1984; PhD, Somerset U., Eng., 1988. Cert. Internat. Soc. Livestock Appraisers. Cons./foreman Flakoll Enterprises, Forbes, N.D., 1970—; grad. asst. to resident asst. N.D. State U., Fargo, 1981-84; internat. cons. Cattleana Corp., Wheatland, N.D., 1982—; lectr./asst. animal scientist N.D. State U., Fargo, 1984—; mem. N.D. Senate from 44th dist., Bismark, 1998-. Advisor, Blue Key Nat. Honor Frat., Fargo, 1986—, Mortar Bd. Nat. Honor Frat., Fargo, 1986-92, Alpha Zeta Nat. Agrl. Frat., Fargo, 1990-93; com. mem. Beef Rsch./Mgmt. Com., Fargo, 1984—. Author: (books) Supplemental Niacin in Feeder Lamb Rations, 1984, Environmental Effectuation for Enhanced Productivity, 1988, Beef Showman's Guide, 1991; contbr. numerous articles to profl. jours. Clay county bd. Am. Cancer Soc., 1993—. Recipient Bursary award Somerset U., Eng., 1987, Blue Key Nat. Honor Frat. Membership Honor, 1983, Alpha Zeta Nat. Honor Agrl. Frat. Membership Honor, 1984, 10th degree Leadership award U.S. Jr. C. of C., 1992, Project of the Yr. N.D. Jaycees, 1992, 93, Outstanding Young Fargoan, 1990, N.D.S.U. Preferred Prof. award, 1987, 89. Mem. Am. Quarter Horse Assn., Continental Cattle Assn. (nat. sect. 1985—), N.D. Shorthorn Assn. (pres. 1989-91, Man of Yr. 1991), N.D. Winter Show (dir. 1988—), N.D. Purebred Coun. (dir. 1990-93), N.D. Stockman's Assn., Fargo Jr. C. of C. (dir. 1990-91, pres. 1991-92, historian 1992-93, parliamentarian 1992-94, v.p. community devel. 1993—). Lutheran. Avocations: softball, volley ball, golf, horseback riding, antique collecting. Home: 1350 2nd St N Fargo ND 58102-2725 Office: PO Box 5727 Fargo ND 58105-5727

FLANAGAN, BARBARA, journalist; b. Des Moines; d. John Merrill and Marie (Barnes) F.; m. Earl S. Sanford, 1966. Student, Drake U., 1942-43. With promotion dept. Mpls. Times, 1945-47; reporter Mpls. Tribune, 1947-58; women's editor, spl. writer Mpls. Star and Tribune, 1958-65; columnist Mpls. Star, 1965—. Author: Ovation, Minneapolis. Active Junior League Mpls., Womans Club Mpls.; bd. dirs. Minn. Opera., Friends of Mpls. Pub. Libr. Mem. Mpls. Soc. Fine Arts (life), Mpls. Inst. Arts (founding mem. Minn. Arts Forum), Kappa Alpha Theta, Sigma Delta Chi. Episcopalian. Home: 3200 W Calhoun Pky Apt 301 Minneapolis MN 55416-4650 Office: Mpls Star Tribune 5th And Portland Sts Minneapolis MN 55488-0001

FLANAGAN, JOHN ANTHONY, lawyer, educator; b. Sioux City, Iowa, Nov. 29, 1942; s. J. Maurice and Lorna K. (Fowler) F.; m. Martha Lang, May 8, 1982; children: Sean, Kathryn, Molly. BA, State U. of Iowa, 1964; JD, Georgetown U., 1968. Bar: Iowa 1968, D.C. 1975, Ohio 1977. Law clk. to judge U.S. Tax Ct., Washington, 1968-70; trial atty. U.S. Dept. Justice, 1970-74; prof. law U. Cin., 1974-78; sr. tax ptnr. Graydon, Head & Ritchey, Cin., 1978—. Adj. prof. U. Cin., 1978—. Contbr. articles to profl. jours. Corp. mgr. United Way, Cin., 1988; head lawyers' div. Fine Arts Fund, Cin., 1987-88; mem. Downtown Cin. Inc., 1995-2000. Mem. D.C. Bar Assn., Cin. Bar Assn., Order of Coif. Roman Catholic. Avocations: gardening, golf, fly fishing. Home: 5 Walsh Ln Cincinnati OH 45208-3435 Office: Graydon Head & Ritchey 1900 Fifth-Third Ctr PO Box 6464 Cincinnati OH 45202

FLANAGAN, JOHN F. publishing executive; b. Chgo., Feb. 24, 1944; AB, Wabash Univ., 1966; MBA, Univ. Mich., 1968. Pres., CEO Goodheart Willcox Publ., Tinley Park, Ill., 1980—. Office: Goodheart Willcox Publ 18604 W Creek Dr Tinley Park IL 60477-6243

FLANAGAN, SYLVIA, editor; b. Chgo., June 26, 1952; BA in Journalism, Chgo. State U.; MS in Journalism, Roosevelt U. Various to sr. editor Jet newsmag. Johnson Pub. Co., Chgo., 1972-85. Mem. The Chgo. Bd. Rossevelt Univ., 2000. Former bd. govs. Roosevelt U.; bd. trustees LaRabida Children's Hosp. and Rsch. Ctr., Chgo. Mem. Nat. Assn. Black Journalists, Chgo. Assn. of Black Journalists. Office: Johnson Pub Co 820 S Michigan Ave Chicago IL 60605-2103

FLANAGIN, NEIL, lawyer; b. Chgo., Dec. 2, 1930; s. Norris Cornelius and Virginia (Riddell) F.; m. Mary Mead, Nov. 19, 1960; children: John Mead, Margot, Nancy, Jill. B.A., Yale U., 1953; J.D., U. Mich., 1956. Bar: Ill. 1956. Assoc. Leibman, Williams, Bennett, Baird & Minow, Chgo., 1960-66, ptnr., 1966-72, Sidley & Austin, Chgo., 1972-95, sr. counsel, 1996—. Bd. dirs. Dr. Scholl Found., Chgo., 1973—. Served to 1st lt. AUS, 1956-59. Fellow Am. Coll. Investment Counsel (emeritus); mem. Univ. Club, Indian Hill Club (Winnetka). Home: 1010 Mt Pleasant Rd Winnetka IL 60093-3615 Office: Sidley & Austin Bank One Plz 425 W Surf St Apt 605 Chicago IL 60657-6139

FLATEN, ALFRED N. retired food and consumer products executive; b. 1935; With Nash-Finch Co., Mpls., 1861-98, mgr. Iowa divsn., 1983-86, v.p. S.E. divsn., 1986-89, v.p. retail ops., 1989-91, past exec. v.p., past pres., CEO, COO, also bd. dirs.

FLAUM, JOEL MARTIN, judge; b. Hudson, N.Y., Nov. 26, 1936; s. Louis and Sally (Berger) Flaum; m. Delilah Brummet, June 4, 1989. BA, Union Coll., Schenectady, 1958; JD, Northwestern U., 1963, LLM, 1964; LLD, John Marshall Law Sch., 2002. Bar: Ill. 1963. Asst. state's atty. Cook County, Ill., 1965—69, 1st asst. atty. gen. Ill., 1969—72; 1st asst. U.S. atty. Chgo., 1972—75; judge U.S. Dist. Ct. (no. dist.) Ill., 1975—83, U.S. Ct. Appeals (7th cir.), 1983—. Mem. Ill. Law Enforcement Commn., 1970—72; cons. U.S. Dept. Justice, Law Enforcement Assistance Adminstrn., 1970—71; lectr. DePaul U. Coll. Law, 1987—88; adj. prof. Northwestern U. Sch. Law, 1993—2000. Mem.: Northwestern U. Law Rev., 1962—63; contbr. articles to legal jours. Mem. vis. com. U. Chgo. Law Sch., 1983—86, Northwestern U. Sch. Law, 1983—; mem. adv. com. USCG Acad., 1990—93. Lt. comdr. JACG USNR, 1981—92. Fellow Ford Found. fellow, 1963—64. Fellow: Am. Bar Found. (licentiate); mem.: FBA, ABA, Am. Judicature Soc., Navy-Marine Corps Ret. Judges Advs. Assn., Maritime Law Assn., Chgo. Bar Assn., Chgo. Inn of Ct., 7th Cir. Bar Assn., Ill. Bar Assn., Chgo. Bar Found. (licentiate), Naval Res. Assn., Lawyers Club Chgo., Legal Club Chgo. Jewish. Office: US Ct Appeals 7th Ct 219 S Dearborn St Chicago IL 60604-1702

FLAUM, RUSSELL M. tool manufacturing company executive; With Signode Packaging Sys. divsn. Ill. Tool Works Inc., Glenview, 1975—, dir. mktg. Signode Packaging Sys., 1984-86, v.p. Signode Packaging Sys., 1986-90, pres. Signode Packaging Sys. divsn., 1990-92, exec. v.p., 1993—. Bd. dirs. Quanex Corp. Bd. dirs. Evanston (Ill.) Hosp. Corp., 1993—, Lake Forest Grad. Sch. Mgmt. Mem. Am. Mktg. Assn., Am. Mgmt. Assn. (mem. conf. bd.). Office: Ill Tool Works Inc 3600 W Lake Ave Glenview IL 60025-5811

FLECK, ALBERT HENRY, JR. retired insurance agency executive; b. Jasper, Ind., Aug. 4, 1929; s. Albert J. and Emily M. (Hopf) F.; m. LaVern C. Sermersheim, Oct. 8, 1953 (dec. 1980); children: Steven L., Jeffery E., Patrick J., Gregory K., Lisa A., Christopher A., Douglas G. Grad. high sch., Jasper. With Jasper Turning Co., 1952-56; pres. A.H. Fleck Agy., Inc., Jasper, 1956-98; retired. Clk. cir. ct. Dubois County, Jasper, 1971-78; councilman County of Dubois, Jasper, 1982-94. With U.S. Army, 1948-52, Korea. Mem. K.C., Jasper Civitan (pres. 1972-74), Am. Legion, Ind. Guard Res. (capt. 1987—). Democrat. Roman Catholic. Home and Office: AH Fleck Agy Inc 309 E State Road 164 Jasper IN 47546-9305

FLEEZANIS, JORJA KAY, violinist, educator; b. Detroit, Mar. 19, 1952; d. Parios Nicholas and Kaliope (Karageorge) F.; m. Michael Steinberg, July 3, 1983. Student, Cleve. Inst. Music, 1969-72, Cin. Coll.-Conservatory Music, 1972-75. Violinist Chgo. Symphony Orch., 1975-76; concertmaster Cin. Chamber Orch., 1976-80; violinist Trio D'Accordo, Cin., 1976-80; asst. prin. 2d violinist San Francisco Symphony Orch., 1980-81; assoc. concertmaster San Francisco Sympony Orch., 1980-89; acting concertmaster Minn. Orch., Mpls., 1988-89, concertmaster, 1989—; violinist Fleezanis-Ohlsson-Grebanier Piano Trio, San Francisco, 1984—; faculty mem. San Francisco Conservatory of Music, 1983-89, U. Minn., 1989—. Founder Chamber Music Sundaes, San Francisco, 1980-89, The Am. String Project, 2002; artist-in-residence U. Calif., Davis, 1995—; radio host St. Paul Sunday Show, Minn. Pub. Radio, 1998-2000; guest concertmaster, London Classical Players, L.A. Philharmonic, Sydney Symphony, Balt. Symphony. Performer World Premiere John Adams Violin Concerto with Minn. Orch., 1994 and Nicholas Maw, Sonata for Solo Violin, commd. by Minn. Pub. Radio, 1997; commd. by Pub. Radio Internat. and Minn. Pub. Radio for world premiere of Nicholas Maw Sonata for Solo Violin, 1998; soloist Am. premier Benjamin Britten Double Concerto, 1998; rec. artist CRI and Koch Classical Records. Democrat. Avocations: photography, cooking. Office: Minn Orch 1111 Nicollet Mall Minneapolis MN 55403-2406

FLEISCHAUER, JOHN FREDERICK, retired English language educator, administrator; b. Dayton, Ohio, Apr. 29, 1939; s. Paul J. and Ruth (Hedgecock) F.; m. Janet Elaine Patterson, June 17, 1961; children: John Eric, Marc Lawrence, Scott Christopher. BA, Cornell U., 1961; MA, Ohio State U., 1966; PhD, 1970. Tchg. fellow Denison U., 1968-69; asst. prof. English Ohio U., Athens, 1970-74; dir. 100-level English, 1973-74; div. chmn., prof. English Columbus (Ga.) State U., 1974-81; dean coll. Coll. Mt. Union Coll., 1981-87; dean liberal arts Edinboro U., Pa., 1987-88; provost, v.p. acad. affairs, 1989-95; acting pres., 1990-91; provost, v.p. acad. and student affairs, 1995; provost Wright State U., 1995-98; spl. asst. to pres., 1998-99; ret., 1999. Cons., lectr. bus. communications, humanities, acad. adminstrn., strategic planning, academic standards, 1975—; moderator Northwest Pa. Health Care Cost Summit, 1993—; co-writer academic grants, 1981—; chair Nat. Aerospace Conf., 1997-98. Author: Writing Skills, 1978; contbr. articles to profl. jours. Served with USN, 1961-65. Rsch. grantee Ohio U., 1973, grantee NEH, 1978. Mem. SOCHE (chair trustees), Am. Assn. State Colls. and Univs., Middle States Assn. (evaluator), Dayton Art Inst. (trustee), Alliance for Edn. (trustee), Ohio Humanities Coun. (scholar), Kiwanis Internat. (dir.). Methodist. Avocations: choral music, canoeing, art.

FLEISCHER, CORNELL HUGH, history educator; b. Berkeley, Calif., Oct. 23, 1950; s. Hugh Warren and Florence Robie Fleischer. Student, Brown U., 1968-70; AB, Princeton U., 1972, AM, 1976, PhD, 1982. Instr. Persian and Turkish langs. and lit. Ohio State U., Columbus, 1979-82; asst. prof. Islamic history Washington U., St. Louis, 1982-85, assoc. prof., 1985-89, prof., 1989-93; prof. Ottoman history U. Chgo., 1993-98; Kanuni Süleyman prof. Ottoman and Modern Turkish Studies Univ. Chgo., 1998—. Dir. Ctr. for Study Islamic Socs. and Civilizations, St. Louis, 1986-91; dir. Ctr. for Mid. Eastern Studies, U. Chgo., 1996-98; lectr. Phi Beta Kappa 1999-2000. Author: Bureaucrat and Intellectual in the Ottoman Empire, 1986 (book prize N.W. Assn. Grad. Schs. 1987); assoc. editor Cambridge History of Turkey, 1990—; mem. editorial bd. Internat. Jour. Mid. Ea. Studies, 1994-99; contbr. articles to profl. jours. Fulbright-Hays rsch. fellow, 1976-78, MacArthur fellow, 1988-93; rsch. grantee Social Sci. Rsch. Coun., 1984, 86, Fulbright Islamic Civilization grantee, 1986-87; resident Bellagio Ctr., 1991. Mem. Am. Acad. Arts Scis., Am. Hist. Assn., Mid East Studies Assn., Soc. for Iranian Studies, Turkish Studies Assn. (bd. dirs. 1986-88, pres., 1996-98). Office: Ctr Mid Ea Studies U Chgo Chicago IL 60637

FLEISCHMAN, STEPHEN, art center director; b. Newton, Mass., July 7, 1954; s. David and Dorothy (Myers) F.; m. Barbara Jane Katz, May 18, 1986; children: Daniel Katz Fleischman, Benjamin Katz Fleischman, Jacob Katz Fleischman. BS in Fine Arts, U. Wis., 1977, MA in Bus. Adminstrn., 1983. Gallery owner, studio potter, Seattle, 1977-81; devel. asst. Madison (Wis.) Art Ctr., 1981-83; spl. asst. to dir. Walker Art Ctr., Mpls., 1983-86, dir. program planning, 1986-90; dir. Madison Art Ctr., 1991—. Bd. dirs. So. Theater, Mpls., 1988-90, Minn. Citizens for the Arts, Mpls., 1985-90, Cable Arts Consortium, Mpls., 1986-88, Madison CitiArts, 1991-97, Greater Madison Conv. and Visitors Bur., 2000—; pres. adv. bd. Bolz Ctr. for Arts Adminstrn., U. Wis., 1995-97. Mem. Rotary Internat. Office: Madison Art Ctr 211 State St Madison WI 53703-2214

FLEMING, CECIL, business executive; Exec. ptnr. BDO Dunwoody, Ward, Mallette, Toronto, Ont., Can., 1991-95; sr. ptnr. BDO Seidman, N.Y.C., 1995-97, CEO, pres., 1997—. Office: BDO Seidman Ste 4300 2 Prudential Plz Chicago IL 60601

FLEMING, JAMES RICHARD, lawyer; b. Kokomo, Ind., Mar. 12, 1944; s. Richard V. and Evelyn (Daily) F.; m. Cynthia Bryant, Nov. 29, 1969; children: Amy, Nicklaus, Sara. BS, Ind. U., 1967; JD, U. S.C., 1970. Bar: Ind. 1970, U.S. Dist. Ct. (so. dist.) Ind. 1970. Ptnr. O'Mahoney, Mahoney, Simmons & Fleming, Kokomo, 1970-74, Simmons & Fleming, Kokomo, 1974%. Pub. defender Howard County Pub. Defender, Kokomo, 1973—. Bd. dirs. Kokomo Humane Soc. Mem. KC, Ind. State Bar Assn., Howard County Bar Assn. (pres. 1990), Ind. Assn. Criminal Def. Attys. (bd. dirs.), Benevolent Protective Order Elks, Kokomo Country Club (bd. dirs.), Columbian Club Kokomo (bd. dirs.). Avocations: gardening, fishing, golf. Office: PO Box 626 Kokomo IN 46903-0626

FLEMING, MAC ARTHUR, labor union administrator; b. Walnut Grove, Miss., Sept. 22, 1945; s. Austin J. and Dorothy (Downey) F.; m. Phyllis Jean Tatro, May 18, 1984; children: Vaughn L. Voth, Denise. AA, Jones County Jr. Coll., Laurel, Miss., 1967; student, So. Colo. State Coll., Pueblo, 1967-68; student in trade union program, Harvard U., 1979. System organizer Atchison, Topeka & Santa Fe System Fedn., Pueblo, 1972, asst. gen. chmn. San Bernardino, Calif., 1972-73, asst. chmn., sec.-treas. Newton, Kans., 1974-75, vice chmn., 1975-80, gen. chmn., 1980-86; grand lodge sec.-treas. Brotherhood Maintenance Ways Employees, Detroit, 1986-90; pres. Brotherhood Maintenance of Way Employees, 1990—; v.p. AFL-CIO, 1995—. Democrat. Avocations: tennis, golf,. Home: 38271 Long St Harrison Township MI 48045-3585 Office: Brotherhood Maintenance Way Employees 26555 Evergreen Rd Ste 200 Southfield MI 48076-4225

FLEMING, MARCELLA, journalist; b. Paoli, Ind., Oct. 14, 1955; d. Kenneth Gale and Neva Louise (Thomas) F.; m. Brian D. Smith. AB in Journalism and English, Ind. U., 1978. Cert. tchr. Reporter Wabash Plain Dealer, 1978-80, Marion Chronicle-Tribune, 1980-83, city editor, 1990-91; city reporter, feature writer, copy editor, Sunday editor Ft. Wayne (Ind.) Jour.-Gazette, 1983-88; editor pubs. Children's Mus. Indpls., 1988-90; freelance writer Indpls. Monthly, 1989-91; nat. editor Indpls. CEO, Columbus (Ohio) CEO mags., 1991-92; writer state desk Indpls. Star & News, 1992—. Judge Thomas R. Keating Writing Competition, 1990. Recipient award of Excellence Nat. Down Syndrome Congress, 1988, Best Newsletter, Best Feature Story and Best News Story awards Editor's Forum, 1990, Best Ann. Report award Internat. Assn. Bus. Communicators, 1990. Mem. Ednl. Press Assn. (Breaking News Story Disting. Achievement award 1994). Office: Indpls Star 307 N Pennsylvania St Indianapolis IN 46204-1819

FLEMING, RICHARD H. finance executive; b. Milw., July 22, 1947; s. David M. and Mildred (Codere) F.; m. Diana Loane, Mar. 21, 1970; children: Douglas Codere, Petria Anne. BA, U. Pacific, 1969; MBA, Dartmouth, 1971. Fin. analyst Graco, Inc., Mpls., 1971-72, mgr. banking and fgn. exchange, 1972-73; fin. analyst Masonite Corp., Chgo., 1973-74, mgr. capital investment, 1974-77, asst. treas., 1977-82, treas., 1982-84, v.p. fin., chief fin. officer, 1985-89; dir. corp. fin. and asst. treas. USG Corp., 1989-90, v.p., treas., 1991-94, v.p., CFO, 1994-95, sr. v.p., CFO, 1995-99, exec. v.p., CFO, 1999—. Trustee USG Found., 1989—; bd. dirs. Columbus McKinnon Corp. Bd. dirs. Family Care Services Met. Chgo., 1977—, pres. 1983-86; bd. dirs. Child Welfare League Am., Washington, 1987—, pres. 1999-2000. Alumni fellow U. Pacific Sch. Bus. Adminstrn. and Pub. Policy, 1990. Office: USG Corp PO Box 6721 125 S Franklin St Chicago IL 60680-6721 Home: Apt 2802 195 N Harbor Dr Chicago IL 60601-7532

FLEMING, SUZANNE MARIE, university official, chemistry educator; b. Detroit, Feb. 4, 1927; d. Albert T. and Rose E. (Smiley) F. BS, Marygrove Coll., 1957; MS, U. Mich., 1960, PhD, 1963. Joined Congregation of Sisters Servants of Immaculate Heart of Mary, Roman Catholic Commn. for Cmty., 1945. Chmn. natural sci. div. Marygrove Coll., Detroit, 1970-75, v.p., dean, 1975-78, acad. v.p., 1978-80; asst. v.p. acad. affairs Eastern Mich. U., Ypsilanti, 1980-82, acting assoc. v.p. acad. affairs, 1982-83; provost, acad. v.p. Western Ill. U., Macomb, 1983-86; vice chancellor U. Wis., Eau Claire, 1986-89; freelance writer, 1989—. Vis. scholar U. Mich., 1989-2000; pres. Mich. Coll. Chemistry Tchrs. Assn., 1975; councilor Mich. Inst. Chemists, 1973-77; bd. dirs. Nat. Ctr. for Rsch. to Improve Postsecondary Teaching and Learning, 1988-90. Contbr. articles to profl. publs. NIH research grantee, 1966-69 Home and Office: 2888 Cascade Dr Ann Arbor MI 48104-6659

FLEMING, THOMAS A. former special education educator; Spl. asst. to the provost Ea. Mich. U., Ypsilanti, Mich. Named Tchr. of Yr. Mich., 1991, Nat. Tchr. of Yr., 1992. Office: Ea Mich U 106 Welch Hall Ypsilanti MI 48197-2214

FLEMING, THOMAS J. editor, publishing executive; b. Superior, Wis., 1945; BA in Greek, Charleston Coll., 1967; PhD in Classics, U. N.C., 1973. Prof. classics Miami U., Charleston (S.C.) Coll., Shaw U., Raleigh, N.C. Founding editor The Southern Partisan, 1979-83; mng. editor Chronicles, Rockford, Ill., 1984-85, editor, 1985—, pres., 1997—. Author: The Politics of Human Nature, 1987. Office: The Rockford Inst Chronicles 928 N Main St Rockford IL 61103-7061 E-mail: tri@rockfordinstitute.org.

FLETCHER, JAMES WARREN, physician; b. Belleville, Ill., Oct. 6, 1943; m. Mary Bernadette Gatson; children: Michelle Marie, James W., Rebecca Lynn. MD, St. Louis U., 1968. Diplomate Am. Bd. Nuclear Medicine, lic. physician Mo. Intern in internal medicine St. Louis U. Hosp., 1968—69, asst. resident in internal medicine, 1969—70, resident in nuclear medicine, 1970—71; clin. fellow in radiology Harvard Med. Sch., Boston, 1971—72; sr. resident in nuclear medicine Peter Bent Brigham and Children's Hosp. Med. Ctr., 1971—72; asst. prof. medicine dept. internal medicine St. Louis U., 1972—75, assoc. prof. medicine dept. internal medicine, 1976—83, assoc. prof. radiology dept. radiology, 1977—84, assoc. dir. divsn. nuclear medicine, 1978—85, prof. medicine dept. internal medicine, 1983—, prof. radiology, 1984—, acting dir. divsn. nuclear medicine, 1985—88, dir. divsn. nuclear medicine, 1988—; staff physician nuclear medicine svc. VA Med. Ctr., St. Louis, 1972—76, med. dir. nuclear medicine network, 1972—79, asst. chief nuclear medicine svc., 1976—79, chief, 1979—, med. dir. AMA nuclear medicine technologist tng. program, 1983—, dir. opers. NMR program project, 1983—88; staff physician St. Louis U. Hosps., 1972—, dir. nuclear medicine dept., 1988—, dir. PET imaging ctr., 1991—; dir., program official nuclear medicine svc., dept. medicine and surgery VA Adminstrn. Ctrl. Office, Washington, 1986—89; dir. diagnostics svc. St. Louis VA Med. Ctr., 1997—99. Mem. tech. adv. com. to dir. nuclear medicine svc. VA Ctrl. Office, Washington, 1979—86, chmn. spl. interest user groups computer applications in nuclear medicine, 1984—85; spl. soc. liaison rep. Inst. Medicine Com. on Clin. Practice Guidelines, 1990—91; mem. residency rev. com. nuclear medicine Accreditation Coun. Grad. Med. Edn., 1992—97; interagy. NMR rask force Office Health Tech. Assessment, 1982; mem. Dept. Vet. Affairs Nat. Task Force on Tech. Assessment, 1992—97. Contbr. articles. 2d v.p. sch. bd. een of Peace Elem. Sch., Webster Groves, Mo., 1981, treas., 1982. Lt. comdr. USNR, 1966—77. Recipient Spl. Commendation award, Dept. Vets. Affairs, 1990. Mem.: AMA, Inst. for Clin. Positron Emission Tomography (bd. dirs. 1999—), Soc. Nuclear Medicine (bd. trustees 1988—92, chmn. health care policy com. 1991—92, vice chmn. commn. health care policy 1996—97, chmn. commn. health care policy 1997—98, pres., bd. dirs. 1998—99), Radiol. Soc. N.Am., Am. Bd. Nuclear Medicine (bd. dirs. 1990—93, vice chmn. 1992—93, chmn. 1994—95), Am. Coll. Radiology, Alpha Omega Alpha. Office: St Louis U Med Ctr PO Box 15250 3635 Vista Ave at Grand Blvd Saint Louis MO 63110-0250

FLETCHER, WINONA LEE, theater educator emeritus; b. Nov. 25, 1926; m. Joseph Grant; 1 child, Betty. BA, Johnson C. Smith U., 1947; MA, U. Iowa, 1951; PhD, Ind. U., 1968. Prof. speech and theatre Ky. State U., Frankfort, 1951-78; prof. theatre and afro-Am. studies Ind. U., Bloomington, 1978-94, prof. emeritus, 1994; assoc. dean COAS, 1981-84. Costumer, dir. summer theatre, U. Mo., Lincoln, 1952-60, 69. Recipient Lifetime Achievement award, 1993; Am. Theatre fellow, 1979. Mem. Am. Theatre for Higher Edn., Black Theatre Network, Nat. Assn. Dramatic and Speech Arts, Nat. Theatre Conf., Alpha Kappa Alpha. Home: 317 Cold Harbor Dr Frankfort KY 40601-3011

FLICK, THOMAS MICHAEL, mathematics educator, educational administrator; b. Covington, Ky., July 14, 1954; s. Thomas Lawrence and Crystel (Moore) F.; m. Jeanine M. Moran, Nov. 23, 1991. BS, No. Ky. U., 1976, MA, 1981; MEd, Xavier U., 1977; PhD, Southeastern U., 1979; EdD, U. Sarasota, 1989. Cert. secondary tchr., Ohio, Ky. Assoc. vice prin., dean, chmn. math., prin. summer sch. Purcell Marian High Sch., Cin., 1977-89; asst. prof. Xavier U., 1989-95, assoc. prof., 1995—. Lectr. astronomy Wilmington Coll., Ohio, 1977-78, engring. and nat. sci., U. Cin., 1979—. Author: Guidelines for Astronomy Courses, 1976, 78, (with J. Ventre & J. Boothe) Astronomy Teaching Handbook, 1992, Introduction to the Universe, 1991, 93, Eclipses: Presentations for Educators, 1999; contbr. articles to profl. jours. Guest lectr. Cin. Nature Ctr., Milford, 1976—; chmn. edn. Astron. League, Washington; tchr. Super Saturday Program for Gifted and Talented., Cin., 1983; commn. mem. Archdiocese Cin., 1986. Recipient Ohio NSF Presdl. Award for Excellence in Math. Edn., 1986, Greater Cin. Found./GE grantee, 1987. Mem. Ohio Coun. Tchrs. Math. (contest coord. 1983—, Outstanding Math. Tchr. award 1982), Nat. Astron. League (v.p. 1980-82, chmn. edn. 1975—), Nat. Coun. Tchrs. Math., Math. Assn. Am., Ohio Acad. Sci. (Jerry Acker Outstanding Math. Tchr. award 1986-87), Sigma Xi (Outstanding Math. Tchr. award 1985), Pi Mu Epsilon. Roman Catholic. Club: Midwestern Astronomers. Avocations: golf, piano, bicycling, model railroading. Office: Xavier U Dept Edn 3800 Victory Pkwy Dept Edn Cincinnati OH 45207-1035

FLICKINGER, THOMAS LESLIE, hospital alliance executive; b. Carroll, Iowa, Apr. 22, 1939; s. Leslie Winfred and Evelyn (Hanson) F.; m. Marjorie Ellen Madison, Apr. 19, 1970; children: Benjamin, Samuel. BBA, U. Iowa, 1961, MA, 1963. Adminstrv. asst. Presbyn.-St. Luke's Hosp., Chgo., 1963-64; asst. adminstr. 1 Creighton Meml. St. Joseph Hosp., Omaha, 1964-66, assoc. dir., 1966-68, adminstr., 1968-73; exec. dir. Creighton Omaha Regional Health Care Corp., 1973-75; assoc. dir. Vanderbilt U. Hosp., 1975-77; adminstr. Routt Meml. Hosp., Steamboat Springs, Colo., 1977-85; pres. VHA (Vol. Hosps. Am.) Midlands, Omaha, 1986-97; sr. exec. VHA Mid-Am., 1998; retired. Mem. Omaha Hosp. Assn. (pres. 1971), Am. Coll. Hosp. Adminstrs., Colo. Hosp. Assn. (chmn. 1982), Phi Kappa Psi. Home: 3421 N 128th Cir Omaha NE 68164-4237

FLINT, H. HOWARD, II, printing company executive; b. Apr. 17, 1939; MBA, U of Penn Wharton Sch. With Flint Ink Corp., Detroit, 1960—, pres., 1985-92, chmn. bd., ceo, 1992—. Office: Flint Ink Corp 4600 Arrowhead Dr Ann Arbor MI 48105-2773

FLISS, RAPHAEL M. bishop; b. Milw., Oct. 25, 1930; Student, St. Francis Sem., Houston, Cath. U., Washington. Ordained priest, Roman Cath. Ch., 1956. Bishop, Superior, Wis., 1985—. Office: Chancery Office 1201 Hughitt Ave PO Box 969 Superior WI 54880-0017

FLOCK, JEFFREY CHARLES, news bureau chief; b. Lakewood, N.J., Mar. 16, 1958; s. Byron Harry and Vicki Ruth (Macaulay) F.; m. Elizabeth Brack, Sept. 19, 1998; children: Elizabeth Kathryn, Emily Macaulay. BS in Broadcast Journalism, Boston U., 1980. Writer, producer Cable News Network, Atlanta, 1980-81, corr. Chgo., 1981-84, bur. chief, 1985—. Methodist. Avocations: running, antiques. Office: Cable News Network 435 N Michigan Ave Ste 715 Chicago IL 60611-4008

FLOM, GERALD TROSSEN, lawyer; b. Neenah, Wis., Feb. 6, 1930; s. Russell Craig and Lois Eva (Trossen) F.; m. Martha Herrington Benton, Aug. 21, 1954 (div. June 25, 1980); children— Katherine Simmons, Sarah Elizabeth Kiecker, Russell Craig BA magna cum laude, Lawrence U., 1952; JD, Yale U., 1957. Bar: Minn. 1957, U.S. Dist. Ct. Minn. 1957. Assoc. Faegre & Benson LLP, Mpls., 1957-64, ptnr., 1964-95; retired, 1995. Adj. asst. prof. Law Sch., U. Minn., Mpls., 1966, bd. dirs., Old Republic Natl. Title Holding Co. and Old Republic Natl. Title Ins. Co., 1977-99. Mem. editorial bd. Yale Law Jour. Trustee Mpls. Soc. Fine Arts, 1970-76, Lawrence U., 1974-81, Plymouth Congl. Ch., 1978-81, William Mitchell Coll. Law, St. Paul, 1983-89; bd. dirs. Met. Med. Ctr. Research Found., Mpls., 1975-85. Served with U.S. Army, 1952-54 Mem. ABA, Minn. State Bar Assn., Hennepin County Bar Assn., Assn. Bar City of N.Y., Phi Beta Kappa, Phi Delta Theta, Phi Alpha Delta Congregationalist. Clubs: Mace; Minneapolis; Interlachen Country (Edina, Minn.). Home: 3434 Zenith Ave S Minneapolis MN 55416-4663 Office: Faegre & Benson LLP 2200 Wells Fargo Ctr 90 S 7th St Minneapolis MN 55402-3901

FLORA, CORNELIA BUTLER, sociologist, educator; b. Santa Monica, Calif., Aug. 5, 1943; d. Carroll Woodward and May Fleming (Darnall) Butler; m. Jan Leighton Flora, Aug. 22, 1967; children: Gabriela Catalina, Natasha Pilar. BA, U. Calif., Berkeley, 1965; MS, Cornell U., 1966, PhD, 1970. Asst. to full prof. Kans. State U., Manhattan, 1970-89, dir. population rsch. lab., 1970-78, univ. disting. prof., 1988-89; program adviser Ford Found., Bogota, Colombia, 1978-80; prof., head dept. sociology Va. Poly. Inst. and State U., Blacksburg, 1989-94, univ. disting. prof., 2001—; dir. north ctrl. regional ctr. for rural devel. Iowa State U., Ames, 1994—2001, prof. agr., 2001—. Bd. dirs. Winfock Internat.; cons. USAID, 1981-91, Inter Am. Devel. Bank, 1992, UN, 1992. Author: Interactions between Agroecosystems and Rural Communities, Rural Communities: Legacy and Change; editor: Sustainable Agriculture, 1990, Rural Policy for the 1990s; contbr. articles to sociol. publs. Bd. dirs. N.W. Area Found., 1998—, Agrl. Nat. Rsch. Coun., 1996-98, Agrl. and Natural Resouces, NRC, NAS, Heartland Ctr. for Leadership Devel. Nat. Ctr. for Small Cmtys.; bd. dirs. Henry A. Wallace Inst. for Alt. Agr., 1994-99, pres., 1997-99. Recipient Outstanding Alumni award Coll. Agrl. and Life Scis., Cornell U., 1994; sr. fellow U. Minn. Sch. Agr. Endowed Chair in Agrl. Sys. Mem. Rural Sociol. Soc. (pres. 1988-89, Outstanding Rsch. award 1987), Latin Am. Studies Assn. (bd. dirs. 1982-84, pres. Midwest sect. 1989-90), Am. Sociol. Assn., Agr., Food and Human Values Soc. (pres. elect 2001—), Cmty. Devel. Soc. (v.p. 2001—). Mem. United Ch. of Christ. Office: Iowa State U N Ctrl Regional Ctr Rural Devels 107 N Curtiss Hl Ames IA 50011-0001 E-mail: cflora@iastate.edu.

FLORA, JAIRUS DALE, JR. statistician; b. Northfield, Minn., Mar. 27, 1944; s. Jairus Dale and Betty Ruth (Garvin) F.; m. Sharyl Ann Hughes, Aug. 18, 1967; 1 child, Edward Hughes BS magna cum laude, Midland Luth. Coll., 1965; postgrad., Tech. U. Karlsruhe, Fed. Republic Germany, 1965-66; MS, Fla. State U., 1968, PhD, 1971. Asst. prof. biostats Sch. Pub. Health U. Mich., Ann Arbor, 1971-73, asst. prof., asst. rsch. scientist Hwy. Safety Rsch. Inst., 1973-76, assoc. rsch. scientist Hwy. Safety Rsch. Inst., 1976-81, assoc. prof. biostats. Sch. Pub. Health, 1976-81, prof. biostats. Sch. Pub. Health, rsch. scientist Transp. Rsch. Inst., 1981-84; prin. statistician Midwest Rsch. Inst, Kansas City, Mo., 1984-90; sr. advisor for stats. Midwest Rsch. Inst., 1991-99, pres. coun. prin. scientists, 1986; clin. prof. biostats. Sch. Medicine U. Mo., Kansas City, 1984—; prin. statistician Ken Wilcox Assocs., Inc., Grain Valley, Mo., 1999, statis. cons., 1999—. Cons. statistician Nat. Burn Info. Exchange, 1971-76 Editorial collaborator Annals of Thoracic Surgery, Mathematical Bioscis., Biometrics, Accident Analysis and Prevention, 1979-90; contbr. articles to profl. jours.; patentee in field. Mem. adminstrn. bd. Valley View U. Meth. Ch., 1989-92; vol. leader Boy Scouts Am. Recipient CPS Enterprise award, 1985, Dir.'s award, 1987; German Acad. Exch. Svc. fellow, 1965-66; NASA trainee, 1966-69; NIH trainee, 1969-71; Nat Hwy. Traffic Safety Adminstrn. rsch. grantee, 1974-81. Mem. Am. Statis. Assn., Biometric Soc., Inst. Math. Stats., Masons, Blue Key, Sigma Xi (pres. Kansas City chpt. 1990-91, v.p. 1994-96). Republican. Home: 9921 Foster St Shawnee Mission KS 66212-2452 E-mail: jdflora@swbell.net.

FLORA, VAUGHN LEONARD, state legislator; b. Quinter, Kans., Jan. 17, 1945; s. Leonard Henry and Billie Hazel (Leighton) F.; m. Rose Mary Owens, 1963; children: Troy Vaughn, Trent Leighton, Trina Rose. BS, Kans. State U., 1968; postgrad., Lincoln Grad. Sch., 1989. Pres. Topeka City Homes, 1993-94; mem. Kans. State Ho. of Reps. Dist. 57, 1995—. Precinct committeeman Ward 2 Precinct 6, 1988—; mem. Govs. Commn. on Housing, 1994—.

FLOREN, DAVID D. advertising executive; BA in Journalism, U. Minn. Copywriter, account svc. rep. GE; with Martin/Williams Advt., Mpls., chmn., CEO, 1998—. Recipient Silver Medal award Am. Advt. Fedn., 1990. Mem. Am. Assn. Advt. Agys. (ctrl. region bd., nat. bd.). Office: Martin Williams Advt Inc 60 S 6th St Ste 2800 Minneapolis MN 55402-4444

FLORIAN, MARIANNA BOLOGNESI, civic leader; b. Chgo.; d. Giulio and Rose (Garibaldi) Bolognesi; BA cum laude, Barat Coll., 1940; postgrad. Moser Bus. Sch., 1941-42; m. Paul A. Florian III, June 4, 1949; children: Paul, Marina, Peter, Mark. Asst. credit mgr. Stella Cheese Co., Chgo., 1942-45; With ARC ETO Clubmobile Unit, 1945-47; mgr. Passavant Hosp. Gift Shop, 1947-49; pres., Jr. League Chgo., Inc., 1957-59; pres. woman's bd. Passavant Hosp., 1966-68; bd. dirs. Northwestern Meml. Hosp., 1974-81, mem. exec. com., 1974-79; pres. Women's Assn., Chgo. Symphony Orch., 1974-77, founder WFMT/CSO Radiothon, 1976; chmn. Guild Chgo. Hist. Soc., 1981-84, trustee Chgo. Hist. Soc., 1981-84; life trustee Orchestral Assn., v.p. 1978-82, vice chmn. 1982-86, mem. exec. com. 1978-87; mem. women's bd. U. Chgo.; mem. vis. com. dept. music U. Chgo., 1980-90; pres. bd. dirs. Antiquarian Soc. of Art Inst., 1989-91. Recipient Citizen Fellowship, Inst. Medicine Chgo., 1975, Presdl. Commendation for leadership and svc. Barat Coll., 1990. Clubs: Friday (pres. 1972-74), Contemporary; Winnetka Garden.

FLORSHEIM, RICHARD STEVEN, lawyer; b. Milw., Apr. 2, 1949; s. Ernst Frederick and Ingeborg Miriam Florsheim; m. Neena B. Florsheim; children: Ali Brynn, David Ira, Rebecca Lynn. BS, MIT, 1971; JD magna cum laude, Marquette U., 1974. Bar: Wis. 1974, Fla. 1983. Assoc. Foley & Lardner, Milw., 1974-81, ptnr., 1981—, leader intellectual property litigation group, 1987-97, chair intellectual property dept., 1997—. Co-author: Biotechnology Patent Practice, 1994, Inside the Minds: Leading Intellectual Property Lawyers, 2001. Pres. North Shore Libr., Milw., 1985-87, Jewish Found. Econ. Opportunity, Milw., 1992-96; bd. dirs. Milw. Jewish Fedn., 1987-93, 96—, NCCJ Wis. region, 1990—. Mem. ABA, Am. Intellectual Property Law Assn. (subcom. chmn. 1992-97), Fed. Cir. Bar Assn., Wis. Bar Assn., Milw. Bar Assn., Marquette Law Alumni Assn. (pres. 1985-86). Office: Foley & Lardner 777 E Wisconsin Ave Ste 3800 Milwaukee WI 53202-5367 Business E-Mail: rflorsheim@foleylaw.com.

FLOSKI, DOUG, lawyer; b. Paris, Nov. 15, 1956; s. Frank Jr. and Mary Floski; m. Betsy Burkhard; 3 children. BA in Polit. Sci. and Econs. cum laude, Knox Coll., 1978; JD, U. Ill., 1981. Asst. state's atty. Ogle County State's Atty.'s Office, 1981-84; assoc. Bikakis, Huebaum, Titus, Vohs & Storm, Sioux City, Iowa, 1984-86; 1st asst. Ogle County State's Atty.'s Office, 1986-90; pvt. practice Byron, Ill., 1990-92; state's atty. Ogle County, 1992—. Chairperson Human Rights Commn. of Village of Progress; bd. dirs. H.O.P.E. Nat. Merit scholar. Mem. Nat. Dist. Attys. Assn., Ill. State Bar Assn., Ogle County Bar Assn. Office: Ogle County State's Atty County Courthouse 110 S 4th St Oregon IL 61061-1610

FLOWER, JOANN, state legislator; b. May 6, 1935; m. Paul Flower. BS, Johns Hopkins U. Kans. state rep. Dist. 47, 1996—; nurse, 1996—. Home: PO Box 97 Oskaloosa KS 66066-0097 Office: Kans State Ho of Reps State Capital Topeka KS 66612

FLOWERS, CHARLES EDWARD, state legislator; m. Aleta Flowers; 3 children. Student, Huron Coll., 1958. Mem. S.D. State Senate, 1989—, mem. taxation, edn., local govt., transp. coms., mem. agr. and natural resources coms. Home: PO Box 156 Iroquois SD 57353-0156

FLOWERS, DAMON BRYANT, architect, facility planner; b. Detroit, May 16, 1952; s. Marrell Curtis and Mattie (Rice) F.; m. Adria Faye Burrows, July 28, 1979; children: Lee, Dadria, Damon Bryant II. BS in Architecture, Lawrence Inst. Tech., 1974; BA in Liberal Arts, Cen. Mich. U., 1982; MS in Fin., Ctrl. Mich. U., 1984; JD, Detroit Coll. Law, 1990. Bar: Mich. 1990; registered arch., Mich., Ill., Wis., Ohio, Fla., N.Y. Architect Wayne State U., 1983-85; construction project mgmt. dir. St. Joseph Hosp. and Health Ctrs., 1985-91; v.p. ops. Argus & Assocs., 1991-94; assoc. v.p. facilities devel. and ops. Washtenaw C.C., 1994—. Mem. AIA, APPA, BOCA, Constrn. Spec. Inst., NFPA. Mem. African Methodist Episcopal Ch. Avocation: photography. Home: 1706 Mountain Ash Dr West Bloomfield MI 48324-4003 Office: Washtenaw CC Ann Arbor MI 48106 E-mail: dflowers@wccnet.org.

FLOWERS, MARY E. state legislator; b. July 31, 1951; married. Ed., Kennedy-King C.C., U. Ill. Mem. from 21st dist. Ill. Ho. of Reps., 1985—, now asst. majority leader, mem. appropriations and pub. utilities coms. Co-chmn. Il. Conf. Women Legis.; spokesperson Com. on Ins.; mem. Healthcare and Human Svcs. Com., Fin. Instns. Com., Consumer Protection Com. Recipient Black Rose award League of Black Women, 1988, Kizzy award Black Women Hall of Fame Found., 1990, Friend of Labor award AFL-CIO, 1990. Home: 2539 W 79th St Chicago IL 60652-1729 Office: Ill Ho of Reps State Capitol 2048-j Stratton Bldg Springfield IL 62706-0001

FLOWERS, ROBERT B. military career officer; b. Pa., July 9, 1947; m. Lynda F.; 4 sons. Grad., Va. Mil. Inst., 1969; M in Civil Engring., U. Va., 1976; grad., Command & Gen. Staff Coll., Nat. War Coll. Registered profl. engr., Va. Commd. 2nd lt. U.S. Army, 1969, advanced through grades to maj. gen., 1997, various positions, 1969-85, comdr. 307th Engr. Battalion, 1985-87, joint staff Nat. Mil. Command Ctr./Counternarcotics Divsn., 1987-90, comdr. 20th Engr. Brigade (Combat) (Airborne Corps) Ft. Bragg, N.C., 1990-92; dep. asst. commandant U.S. Army Engr. Sch., 1992-93, asst. commandant, 1993-95; dep. commdg. gen. U.S. Army Engring. Ctr., 1993-95; asst. divsn. comdr. 2nd Inf. Divsn. (Mechanized) Eighth U.S. Army; dep. chief staff engring. U.S. Army Europe, 1996; pres. Miss. River Commn. U.S. Army, comdr. Miss. Valley Divsn.; commandant U.S. Army Engr. Sch.; commdg. gen. U.S. Army Engr. Ctr. and Ft. Leonard Wood, 1997—. Joint task force engr. Joint Task Force, Somalia. Office: US Army Engr Ctr Fort Leonard Wood MO 65473

FLOYD, ALTON DAVID, cell biologist, consultant; b. Henderson, Ky., July 17, 1941; s. Frank and Queen Tina (Melton) F.; m. Barbara Wilson, Aug. 18, 1962; children: Fara Alison, Heather Lynn. BS, U. Ky., 1963; PhD, U. Louisville, 1968. From lectr. to asst. prof. U. Mich., Ann Arbor, 1967-72; from asst. to assoc. prof. Sch. of Medicine Ind. U., Bloomington, 1972-83, assoc. prof. Sch. of Medicine Indpls., 1983-84; sect. head cell biology Miles Sci., Inc., Naperville, Ill., 1984-85; sr. staff scientist Miles, Inc., Elkhart, Ind., 1985-89; pvt. practice cons. Edwardsburg, Mich., 1989—; assoc. dir. Ctr. Light Microscope Inaging and Biotech. Carnegie Mellon U., Pitts., 1991. Bd. dirs. Endotech Corp., Indpls.; mem. subcom. immunohistochem. stains NCCLS, 1995-96; industry rep. adv. panel hematology and pathology devices FDA, 1996-99; trustee Biol. Stain Commn., 1997—. Mem. Am. Assn. Anatomists, Tissue Culture Assn., Soc. Analytical Cytology, Histochem. Soc., Soc. Quantitative Morphology, Soc. Histotech. Avocations: sailing, reading, wood and metal shopwork, computing. Home and Office: 23126 S Shore Dr Edwardsburg MI 49112-8502

FLOYD, GARY LEON, plant cell biologist; b. Moline, Ill., Dec. 23, 1940; s. Leland L. and Zenta (Henderson) F.; m. Myrna A. Floyd, Aug. 18, 1963. BA, U. No. Iowa, 1962; MS, U. Okla., 1966; PhD, Miami U., Oxford, Ohio, 1971. Sci. tchr. Grinnell (Iowa) Jr. High Sch., 1962-65; instr. Miami U., 1966-68; asst. prof. Rutgers U., New Brunswick, N.J., 1971-75; asst. prof. plant biology Ohio State U., Columbus, 1975-78, assoc. prof., 1978-83, prof., 1983-96, assoc. dean biol. scis., 1986-88, dean, 1989-96, prof. and dean emeritus, 1996—. Dir. TEM facility plant biology dept. Ohio State U., Columbus, 1978-86. Contbr. articles to profl. jours. NSF scholar, 1965-66; recipient Alumni Teaching award Ohio State U., 1980, Disting. Rsch. award, 1982, Darbaker prize Bot. Soc. Am., 1993; Phycological Soc. Am. nat. lectr., 1983-85. Avocation: golf. Home: 936 Kendale Rd S Columbus OH 43220-4148

FLOYD, TIM, professional basketball coach, former collegiate basketball coach; b. Hattiesburg, Miss. m. Beverly Floyd; 1 child, Shannon. BS, La. Tech. Univ., 1977. Coach Univ. El Paso, 1977-86, Idaho Univ., 1986-88, Iowa State Univ., 1994-98; head coach Chgo. Bulls, 1998—. Named Coach of Yr.. Office: Chicago Bulls 1901 W Madison St Chicago IL 60612-2459

FLUCK, MICHELE M(ARGUERITE), biology educator; b. Geneva, Aug. 5, 1940; came to U.S., 1972; d. Wilhelm and Henriette Alice (Delaloye) F. MS, U. Geneva, 1964, 66, PhD, 1972. Rsch. assoc. N.Y. Pub. Health Rsch. Inst., N.Y.C., 1972-73; instr. Harvard Med. Sch., Boston, 1973-78, asst. prof., 1978-79; assoc. prof. Mich. State U., East Lansing, 1979-86, prof., 1986-90, disting. prof., 1990—. Contbr. articles to profl. jours. Recipient Young Investigator's award, Nat. Cancer Inst.; grantee Nat. Cancer Inst., 1979—, Am. Cancer Soc. grantee, 1987—. Fellow Leukemia Soc. Am. (scholar 1979-85); mem. AAAS, Am. Assn. virologists. Avocations: music, feminism, social issues. Office: Mich State U Microbiology Dept Giltner Hall East Lansing MI 48824-1101

FLUNO, JERE DAVID, business executive; b. Wisconsin Rapids, Wis., June 3, 1941; s. Rexford Hollis and Irma Dell (Wells) F.; m. Anne Marie Derezinski, Aug. 10, 1963; children: Debra, Julie, Mary Beth, Brian. BBA, U. Wis., 1963. CPA, Ill. Audit supr. Grant Thornton, Chgo., 1963-69; controller W.W. Grainger, Inc., Skokie, Ill., 1969-74, v.p., controller, 1974-75, v.p. fin., 1975-81, sr. v.p., CFO, 1981-84, vice chmn., 1984—, dir., 1975—. Bd. dirs. W.W. Grainger, Inc., Skokie, Ill., Grainger FSC, Inc., Dayton Elec. Mfg. Co., Chgo., Midwest Clearing Corp., Midwest Securities Trust Co., Securities Trust Co. of N.J., Andrew Corp., Chgo. Trustee Mus. Sci. and Industry, Chgo., 1994; bd. govs. Chgo. Stock Exch., 1989, bd. dirs. Lake Forest Symphony, 1995—; adv. coun. Divsn. Intercollegiate Athletics U. Wis.-Madison, 1993—, dir. dean's adv. bd. Wis. Sch. Bus., 1993—, U. Wis.-Madison Found., 1985—; mem. Chgo. com. Chgo. Coun. Fgn. Rels. Mem. AICPA, Fin. Execs. Inst., Ill. CPA Soc., Econ. Club Chgo. (bd. dirs. 1979—), The Hundred Club of Lake County (bd. dirs.), U. Wis. Alumni Assn. (bd. dirs.), Comml. Club Chgo. Republican. Roman Catholic. Clubs: Knollwood (gov., Lake Forest, Ill.); U. Wis. (Chgo.); Island Country (Marco Island, Fla.). Office: W W Grainger Inc 100 Grainger Pkwy Lake Forest IL 60045-5201

FLYE, M. WAYNE, surgeon, immunologist, educator, writer; b. Tarboro, N.C., June 23, 1942; s. Charlie A. and Martha E. (Bullock) F.; m. Phyllis Webb, June 7, 1964; children: Christopher Warren, Brandon Reid. BS, U. N.C., 1964, MD, 1967; MA in Immunology, Duke U., 1972, PhD in Immunology, 1980; MA (hon.), Yale U., 1985. Diplomate Am. Bd. Surgery, Am. Bd. Thoracic Surgery, Am. Bd. Vascular Surgery. Intern. surg. Case-We. Res. U., Cleve., 1967-68, res. gen. and cardio-thoracic surgery, 1968-75; instr., teaching scholar, vascular and transplantation surgery Duke U. Med. Ctr., Durham, N.C., 1975-76; sr. investigator , chief thoracic surg. svc. NIH, Bethesda, Md., 1977-79; chief vascular surgery U. Tex. Med. Br.,

Galveston, 1979-82, assoc. prof. surgery and microbiology, 1980-82; dir. div. organ transplantation and immunology, prof. transplantation, dir. sect. gen. surgery Yale U. Sch. Medicine, New Haven, 1983-85; prof. surgery, molecular microbiology and immunology Washington U. Med. Sch., St. Louis, 1985—, prof. radiology, 2000—, mem. admissions com., 2000—. Trustee New Eng. Organ Bank, Boston, 1984-85; com. mem. United Network Orgn. Sharing, Richmond, Va., 1986-89; mem. anesthesiology and trauma study sect. NIH Surgery, 1991-95; merit rev. com. for surgery VA, 1994-96, chmn., 1996—; merit rev. com. Am. Heart Assn. study sect., 2001-; chief of surgery St. Louis Regional Hosp., 1996; chief thoracic surgery St. Louis VA Hosp., 1996—. Editor: Principles of Organ Transplantation, 1989, The Thymus: Regulator of Cellular Immunity, 1993, Atlas of Organ Transplantation, 1994; mem. editl. bd. Clin. Transplantation, 1986—, Prospectives in Gen. Surgery, 1988-94, Transplantation, 1989—, Xanthus Intelligence Unit Reports, 1990—, Shock: Molecular, Cellular and Systemic Pathobiology of Injury, 1993—, Transplantation Sci., 1993—, Jour. Surg. Rsch., 1995—, Surgery, 1997—, Graft, Jour. Organ and Cellular Transplantation, 1998—, New Surgery, 2000—; assoc. editor Jour. Immunology, 1996—. Lt. col. U.S. Army, 1976-78. Recipient James W. McLaughlin medal U. Tex.-Galveston, 1982. Fellow ACP, So. Thoracic Surg. Assn. (Best Sci. Paper award 1980); mem. Am. Assn. Immunologists, Internat. Cardiovascular Soc., N.Y. Acad. Sci., Soc. Thoracic Surgeons, Am. Soc. Transplant Physicians, Am. Soc. Transplant Surgeons (program com. 1984-86, Ethics Com. 1994-95), Brit. Soc. Immunology, Transplantation Soc., Mid-Am. Transplant Assn. (bd. dirs. 1986-89), Am. Fedn. Clin. Rsch., Royal Soc. Medicine, AAAS, Surg. Infection Soc. (edn. and fellowship com. 1998—), Reticuloendothelial Soc., Soc. Univ. Surgeons, Soc. Clin. Vascular Surgery, Brit. Transplantation Soc., So. Assn. Vascular Surgery, Am. Coll. Chest Physicians, Soc. Surg. Oncology, Am. Assn. Thoracic Surgery, Surg. Biology Club I, Am. Assn. Study Liver Diseases, Am. Surg. Assn., So. Surg. Assn., Cen. Surg. Assn., Soc. Internat. de Chirurgie, Midwestern Vascular Surg. Soc., Soc. Vascular Surg., World Ann. Hepato-Pancreato-Bilary Surg., Soc. Surgery of Alimentary Tract, Shock Soc., Gen. Thoracic Surgery Club, Soc. Thoracic Surg., Sigma Xi, Alpha Omega Alpha., Chi Psi, Young Republicans N.C. Episcopalian. Avocations: sports, geneology, medical history. Home: 585 Coeur De Royale Dr Apt 402 Saint Louis MO 63141-6915 E-mail: flyew@msnotes.wustl.edu.

FLYNN, CAROL, state legislator; b. Aug. 7, 1933; m. Richard L. Flynn; 2 children. Mem. Minn. State Senate, 1990—. Mem. Democratic Farm Labor Party. Office: Minn Senate 120 State Capitol 75 Constitution Ave Saint Paul MN 55155-1606

FLYNN, JOHN J. museum curator; b. Wilkes-Barre, Pa., Aug. 10, 1955; s. John J. and Phyllis B. (Allen) F.; m. Alison L. Gold; children: Rachel S., Peter J. BS cum laude, Yale U., 1977; MA, Columbia U., 1979, MPhil, 1980, PhD, 1983. Lectr. dept. geology and geophysics Yale U., New Haven, 1982; asst. prof. geol. scis. Rutgers U., New Brunswick, N.J., 1982-88; assoc. curator dept. geology Field Mus. Natural History, Chgo., 1988-92, curator dept. geology, 1992—, chmn. dept. geology, 1993-2000, MacArthur curator dept. geology, 1995—. Rsch. assoc. Am. Mus. Natural History, N.Y.C., 1984—; co-chair Earth History and Global Change com. Systematics Agenda 2000, 1991-96; lectr. Com. on Evolutionary Biology, U. Chgo., 1990—, assoc. chair, 1995—; adj. prof. dept. biol. scis. U. Ill., Chgo., 1994—. Co-editor: Vertebrate Paleontology in the Neotropics: The Miocene Fauna of La Venta, Colombia, 1997, Mesozoic/Cenozoic Vertebrate Paleontology: Classic Localities, Contemporary Approaches, 1989; assoc. editor Jour. Vertebrate Paleontology, 1988-91; contbr. articles to profl. jours. Grantee in field; recipient William R. Belknap prize, 1977, Best Mus. Curator award Chgo. Mag., 1995. Mem. Soc. Vertebrate Paleontology (chair affiliated soc. liaison 1986-93, mem. devel. com. 1987-89, chair collections computerization com. 1990-93, sec. 1993-96, v.p. 1996-98, pres. 1998-2000, past pres. 2000-02, Alfred Sherwood Romer prize 1982), Geol. Soc. Am., The Paleontological Soc., Soc. Systematic Biologists. Achievements include discovery of oldest S.Am. rodent, oldest well-preserved S.Am. monkey skull, oldest dinosaurs, work on geologic time scales. Office: Field Mus Natural History Dept Geology Roosevelt Rd at Lake Shore Dr Chicago IL 60605

FLYNN, THOMAS L. (TOM FLYNN), state legislator; b. Dubuque, Iowa, June 11, 1955; m. Jane. BA in Acctg. and Fin., Loras Coll., 1977; MBA, U. Dubuque, 1985. Owner small bus.; mem. faculty dept. bus. Clark Coll.; mem. Iowa Senate from 17th dist., 1994—. Past pres. N.E. Iowa Coun. Boy Scouts Am.; trustee United Way Dubuque. Mem. Nat. Ready-Mix Concrete Assn. (bd. dirs.), Nat. Aggregates Assn. (bd. dirs.), Dubuque Area C. of C. (bd. dirs.). Democrat. Home: 21367 Girl Scout Rd Epworth IA 52045-9698 Office: State Capitol Dist 17 3 9th And Grand Des Moines IA 50319-0001 E-mail: tom_flynn@legis.state.ia.us.

FODREA, CAROLYN WROBEL, educational researcher, publisher, consultant; b. Hammond, Ind., Feb. 1, 1943; d. Stanley Jacob and Margaret Caroline (Stupeck) Wrobel; m. Howard Frederick Fodrea, June 17, 1967 (div. Jan. 1987); children: Gregory Kirk, Lynn Renee. BA in Elem. Edn., Purdue U., 1966; MA in Reading and Lang. Devel., U. Chgo., 1973; postgrad., U. Colo., Denver, 1986-87. Cert. elem. tchr., Ind., Ill. Tchr. various schs., Ind., Colo., 1966-87; founder, supr., clinician Reading Clinic, Children's Hosp., Denver, 1969-73; pvt. practice in reading and lang. rsch. clinic, 1973-87; pvt. practice in reading rsch. ctr. Deerfield, Ill., 1973—; creator of pilot presch.-kindergarten lang. devel. program Gary, Ind. Diocese Schs., 1987—, therapist lang. and reading disabilities, 1987—; pres. Reading Rsch. Ctr., Arlington Heights, Ill., 2000—. Conducted Lang. Devel. Workshop, Gary, Ind. 1988; tchr. adult basic edn. Dawson Tech. Sch., 1990, Coll. Lake County, 1991, Prairie State Coll., 1991—, Chgo. City Colls., 1991, R.J. Daley Coll., 1991, Coll. DuPage, 1991—; condr. adult basic edn. workshops for Coll. of DuPage, R.J. Daley Coll., 1992, Ill. Lang. Devel. Literacy Program; tchr. Korean English Lang. Inst., Chgo., 1996, Lang. Devel. Program for Minorities, 2000; dir. pilot study Cabrini Green Tutoring Ctr., Chgo., 2000. Author: Language Development Program, 1985, Presch. Kindergarten Lang. Devel. Program, 1988, A Multi-Sensory Stimulation Program for the Premature Baby in Its Incubator to Reduce Medical Costs and Academic Failure, 1986, Predicting At-Risk Babies for First Grade Reading Failure Before Birth A 15 Year Study, A Language Development Program, Grades 1 to Adult, 1988, 92; editor, pub.: ESL For Native Spanish Speakers, 1996, ESL for Native Korean Speakers, 1996. Active Graland Country Day Sch., Denver, 1981-83, N.W. Ind. Children's Chorale, 1988—; Ill. state chair Babies and You com. March of Dimes, 1999—. Mem. NEA, Am. Ednl. Rsch. Assn., Internat. Reading Assn., Am. Coun. for Children with Learning Disabilities, Assn. for Childhood Edn. Internat., Colo. Assn. for Edn. of Young Children, Infant Stimulation Edn. Assn., Art Inst. Chgo., U. Chgo. Alumni Club (Denver area ann. fund, Pres. fund com. 1988—, numerous positions Denver area chpt. 1974-87). Roman Catholic. Avocations: sports, health and nutrition, literary and cultural activities, sewing. E-mail: cfodrea1@aol.com.

FOGARTY, ROBERT STEPHEN, historian, educator, editor; b. Bklyn., Aug. 30, 1938; s. Michael Joseph and Marguerita (Carmody) F.; m. Geraldine Wolpman, Dec. 30, 1961 (div. Apr. 1984); children: David, Suzanne. B.S., Fordham U., 1960; Ph.D., U. Denver, 1968. Instr. Mich. State U., 1963-67; asst. prof. Antioch Coll., Yellow Springs, Ohio, 1968-73, chmn. humanities area, 1973-74, 78-79, assoc. prof., 1974-80, prof. history, 1980—; prof. Advanced Internat. Studies, Ctr. for Chinese-Am. Johns Hopkins U., 1986-87; editor Antioch Rev., 1977—; dir. Associated Colls. Midwest/Gt. Lakes Coll. Assn., Program in Humanities, Newberry Library, 1978-79; cons. Nat. Endowment for Arts, 1975-81, U. Waterloo, Ont., Can., 1981. Vis. fellow NYU Inst. for Humanities, 1992—93; Darwin lectr. human biology Galton Inst., London, 1994. Author: Dictionary of American Communal and Utopian History, 1980, The Righteous Remnant-The House of David, 1981, All Things New: Communes and Utopian Movements, 1860-1914, 1990, Special Love/Special Sex, 1994, Desire and Duty at Oneida: Tirzah Miller's Intimate Memoir, 2000; editor Antioch Rev., 1977—; contbr.: American Encyclopeida of American Culture, 2001; contbr. essays to The Nation, TLS, Mo. Rev. Recipient Martha K. Cooper award for editl. achievement, 1981; grantee Am. Philos. Soc., 1976, Am. Coun. Learned Socs.; fellow NEH, 1980, All Souls Coll., Oxford U., 1988, Lloyd Lewis fellow Newberry Libr., 1995, Galton Inst. fellow, 1995; Fulbright Disting. Lectr. to Korea, 2000, Gilder Lehrman fellow 2001. Mem.: Orgn. Am. Historians, Nat. Hist. Communal Sites Assn. (exec. com. 1975—2002), Am. Studies Assn. (bibliography com. 1981—). Office: Antioch Rev Inc PO Box 148 Yellow Springs OH 45387-0148

FOGEL, HENRY, orchestra administrator; b. N.Y.C., Sept. 23, 1942; s. Julius and Dorothy (Levine) F.; m. Frances Sylvia Polner, June 12, 1945; children— Karl Franz, Holly Dana Student, Syracuse U., 1960-63. Program dir., v.p. Sta. WONO, Syracuse, N.Y., 1963-78; orch. mgr. N.Y. Philharm., N.Y.C., 1978-81; exec. dir. Nat. Symphony Orch., Washington, 1981-85; pres. Chgo. Symphony Orch. Assn., 1985—. Record reviewer Fanfare Mag., 1979—; contbr. to Contemporary Composers. Mem. music panel NEA, 1986-90; past pres. U. Ill. Arts Alliance, 1988-94. Mem. NARAS, Am. Symphony Orch. League (bd. dirs. 1988—), Assn. Recorded Sound Collections (record reviewer jour. 1978). Office: Chgo Symphony Orch 220 S Michigan Ave Chicago IL 60604-2596

FOGEL, ROBERT WILLIAM, economist, educator, historian; b. N.Y.C., July 1, 1926; s. Harry Gregory and Elizabeth (Mitnik) Fogel; m. Enid Cassandra Morgan, Apr. 2, 1949; children: Michael Paul, Steven Dennis. AB, Cornell U., 1948; AM, Columbia U., 1960; PhD, Johns Hopkins U., 1963; MA, U. Cambridge, Eng., 1975, Harvard U., 1976; DSc, U. Rochester, 1987, U. de Palermo, Argentina, 1994, Brigham Young U., 1995. Instr. Johns Hopkins U., 1958—59; asst. prof. U. Rochester, 1960—64; Ford Found. vis. research prof. U. Chgo., 1963—64, asso. prof., 1964—65, prof. econs., 1965—69, prof. econs. and history, 1970—75; prof. econs. U. Rochester, 1968—71, prof. econs. and history, 1972—75; Taussig research prof. Harvard U., Cambridge, Mass., 1973—74, Harold Hitchings Burbank prof. polit. economy, prof. history, 1975—81; Charles R. Walgreen Disting. Svc. prof. Am. instns. U. Chgo., 1981—. Pitt prof. Am. history and insts. U. Cambridge, 1975—76; chmn. com. math. and statis. methods in history Math. Social Sci. Bd., 1965—72; rsch. assoc. Nat. Bur. Econ. Rsch., 1978—; dir. DAE program, 1978—91; dir. Ctr. for Population Econ., Chgo. Author: The Union Pacific Railroad: A Case in Premature Enterprise, 1960, Railroads and American Economic Growth: Essays in Econometric History, 1964; author: (with others) The Reinterpretation of American Economic History, 1971, Dimensions of Quantitative Research in History, 1972; author: (with S.L. Engerman) Time on the Cross: The Economics of American Negro Slavery, 1974; author: Ten Lectures on the New Economic History, 1977; author: (with G.R. Elton) Which Road to the Past? Two Views of History, 1983; author: Without Consent of Contract: The Rise and Fall of American Slavery, Vol. 1, 1989; author: (with others) Without Consent of Contract: The Rise and Fall of American Slavery, Vols. 2-4, 1992; author: The Fourth Great Awakening and the Future of Egalitarianism, 2000. Co-recipient The Bancroft prize, 1975, Gustavus Myers prize, 1990, Nobel Prize in Econ. Sci., Nobel Found., 1993; recipient Arthur H. Cole prize, 1968, Schumpter prize, 1971, Disting. Alumnus award, Johns Hopkins U., 2000; fellow, Gilman, 1957—60, Social Sci. Rsch. Coun., 1960, Ford Found. Faculty Rsch., 1970; grantee Faculty Rsch., 1966, NSF, 1967, 1970, 1972, 1975, 1976, 1978, 1992, 1993, 1994, 1995, 1996, Fulbright, 1968, NIH, 1991—. Fellow: AAAS, Royal Hist. Soc., Econometric Soc., Brit. Acad. (corr.); mem.: NAS, Internat. Union for Sci. Study of Population, Population Assn. Am., Am. Acad. Arts and Scis., Agrl. History Soc., Social Sci. History Assn. (pres. 1980—81), Assn. Am. Historians, Am. Hist. Assn., Econ. History Soc., Econ. History Assn. (trustee 1972—81, pres. 1977—78), Royal Econ. Soc., Am. Econ. Soc. (pres.-elect 1997), European Acad. Arts, Scis. and Humanities, Phi Beta Kappa. Office: U Chgo Grad Sch Bus Ctr for Population Econ 1101 E 58th St Chicago IL 60637-1511

FOIAS, CIPRIAN ILIE, mathematics educator; Prof. math. Ind. U., disting. prof. math., 1983—. Recipient Norbert Wiener award in Applied Mathematics, American Math. Soc., 1995. Office: Ind Univ Dept of Math Bloomington IN 47405

FOK, THOMAS DSO YUN, civil engineer; b. Canton, China, July 1, 1921; came to U.S., 1947, naturalized, 1956; s D. H. and C. (Tse) F.; m. Maria M.L. Liang, Sept. 18, 1949. B.Eng., Nat. Tung-Chi U., Szechuan, China, 1945; M.S., U. Ill., 1948; M.B.A. Dr. Nadler Money Marketeer scholar, NYU, 1950; Ph.D., Carnegie-Mellon U., 1956. Registered profl. engr., N.Y., Pa., Ohio, Ill., Ky., W.Va., Ind., Md., Fla. Structural designer Lummus Co., N.Y.C., 1951-53; design engr. Richardson, Gordon & Assocs., cons. engrs., Pitts., 1956-58; assoc. prof. engring. Youngstown U., Ohio, 1958-67, dir. computing ctr., 1963-67; ptnr. Cernica, Fok & Assocs., cons. engrs., Youngstown, 1958-64; prin. Thomas Fok & Assocs., cons. engrs., 1964-65; ptnr. Mosure-Fok & Syrakis Co., Ltd., cons. Engrs., 1965-76; cons. engr. to Mahoning County Engr., 1960-65; pres. Computing Systems & Tech., Youngstown, 1967-72; chmn. Thomas Fok and Assocs., Ltd., cons. engrs., 1977—. Contbr. articles to profl. jours. Trustee Pub. Libr. of Youngstown and Mahoning County, 1973—; trustee Youngstown State U., 1975-84, chmn., 1981-83; mem. Ohio State Bd. Registration for Profl. Engrs. and Surveyors, 1992-96. Recipient Walter E. and Caroline H. Watson Found. Disting. Prof.'s award Youngstown U., 1966, Outstanding Person award Mahoning Valley Tech. Socs. Council, 1987. Fellow ASCE; mem. Am. Concrete Inst., Internat. Assn. for Bridge and Structural Engring., Am. Soc. Engring. Edn., Nat. Soc. Profl. Engrs., AAAS, Soc. Am. Mil. Engrs., Ohio Acad. Sci., N.Y. Acad. Sci., Sigma Xi, Beta Gamma Sigma, Sigma Tau, Delta Pi Sigma Lodge: Rotary. Achievements include development of a design method by computer for a solid-ribbed tied, through arch Ft. Duquesne Bridge; development of Analysis of Continuous Truss by Digital Computer. Home: 325 S Canfield Niles Rd Youngstown OH 44515-4020 Office: 3896 Mahoning Ave Youngstown OH 44515-3022

FOLAND, KENNETH A. geological sciences educator; b. Frederick, Md., May 25, 1945; s. Austin Franklin and P. Lillian (Wachter) F.; m. Ellen Lee Spero, June 18, 1968. BS, Bucknell U., 1967; MSc, Brown U., 1969, PhD, 1972. Postdoctoral fellow U. Pa., Phila., 1972-73, from asst. prof. to assoc. prof., 1973-80; assoc. prof. Ohio State U., Columbus, 1980-87, prof. geological scis., 1987—. Cons. divsn. nuclear chemistry Lawrence Livermore Nat. Lab., 1982-86, adv. com. nuclear waste U.S. Nuclear Regulatory Commn., 1990-99; mem. indoor radon panel Am. Lung Assn. Ohio, mem. steering and rev. com. Columbus and Franklin County Radon Study, Columbus Health Dept. Assoc. editor Isotope Geosci., 1982-99, Jour. Geophys. Rsch., Solid Earth, 1992-98; adv. editor Jour. Geol. Soc.; reviewer rsch. papers, rsch. proposals; author, co-author numerous rsch. papers, abstracts, revs. Recipient numerous grants NSF, NIH, DAAD and NATO. Fellow Geol. Soc. Am.; mem. Am. Geophys. Union, Geochem. Soc., Sigma Xi. Home: 4090 Fenwick Rd Columbus OH 43220-4870 Office: Ohio State U 125 South Oval Mall 379 Mendenhall Lab Columbus OH 43210

FOLEY, CHERYL M. company executive; V.p., gen. counsel PSI Energy, Inc., Ind., 1989-91; v.p., gen. counsel, corp. sec. PSI Energy, Inc. and PSI Resources Inc., 1991-94; v.p., sec., gen. counsel Cinergy Corp., Cin., 1994-99, v.p., sec., 1999—; pres. Cinergy Global Resources subs. Cinergy Corp., Cin. Office: Cinergy Corp 221 E 4th St # 30 Cincinnati OH 45202-4124

FOLEY, DANIEL RONALD, personnel director, lawyer; b. Chgo., Dec. 13, 1941; s. Daniel Edward and Louise Jean (Connolly) Foley; m. Mae Geraldine Muscarello, Jan. 30, 1965; children: Louise Ann, Sarah Elizabeth. AB in Psychology, Marquette U., 1965; JD, Depaul U., 1971. Bar: Ill. 1971, U.S. Dist. Ct. (no. dist.) Ill. 1971, U.S. Supreme Ct. 1975, Mich. 1989. Pers. recruiter Civil Svc. Commn. City of Chgo., 1965-66; pers. adminstr. Alberto Culver Co., Melrose Park, 1966-67; pers. dir. Litton Industries, Des Plaines, 1967-68; equal opportunity coord., mgr. labor rels. Canteen Corp., Chgo., 1968-71; mgr. labor rels. Internat. Telephone and Telegraph World Hdqs., N.Y.C., 1971-79, dir. employee rels., 1979-81, 1981-85; dir. employee rels., environ. health and safety, group v.p. human resources IBP, Dakota City, Nebr., 1985-88; v.p. adminstrn., gen. counsel Domino's Pizza Inc., Ann Arbor, Mich., 1988-93; pres. Exec. Bus. Ptnrs., Inc., 1993-94; v.p. human resources MascoTech, Inc., 1994-96, Masco Corp., Taylor, Mich., 1996—. Spkr. labor law and bus. seminars Wharton Sch., U. Pa., St. Mary's Coll., U. Mich., LEGATUS. Mem.: Knights of Holy Sepulchre, Knights of Malta. Roman Catholic. Avocation: photography. Home: 3399 Robinwood Dr Ann Arbor MI 48103-1748 E-mail: dcn@aol.com., daniel_foley@mascohq.com.

FOLEY, JAMES M. state legislator; State rep. dist. 81 Mo. Ho. of Reps. Home: 3274 Adie Rd Saint Ann MO 63074-3402

FOLEY, JOSEPH LAWRENCE, sales executive; b. Albuquerque, June 14, 1953; s. Joseph Bernard and Joan Marie (Johnston) F.; m. Michelle Troglia, Jan., 1992; children: Joseph Louis, Kyle Benjamin. BS in Polit. Sci. & Mktg., Niagara U., 1975. Asst. retail buyer Lord & Taylor, N.Y.C., 1975, E.J. Korvette Co., N.Y.C., 1976-78, retail buyer, 1978-80, retail msde. mgr., 1980; import sales coord. Block Industries, 1980-81; v.p. sales Sutton Shirt Co., 1981-83; exec. v.p. V.I.P. Imports, 1984-97; prin. Long-Term Care Cons., 1998—. Mem.: Chi Are Racing Assn. Republican. Roman Catholic. Avocations: marathon running, baseball, tennis, skiing, golf. Home and Office: 225 Sunset Ridge Rd Hinsdale IL 60521-8406

FOLEY, LEO THOMAS, state legislator, lawyer; b. Anoka, Minn., Oct. 25, 1928; s. John Edward and Anna Mathilda (Leubrecht) F.; m. Sally Lynn Werner, July 6, 1954 (dec. Aug. 1990); children: Jane Anne Foley Doyle, Nancy Lee Foley Nelson; m. Kathryn Marlys Nutter, Aug. 23, 1997. BA, U. Minn., 1974; MA, Mankato State U., 1979; JD, William Mitchell Coll. Law, 1994. Cert. insdsl. security mgr. Security officer Fed. Cartridge Corp., New Brighton, Minn., 1952-54; maj. Minn. State Patrol, St. Paul, 1954-87; security mgr. Unisys, 1987-91; asst. Anoka County (Minn.) atty. pub. law sect., 1994—; mem. Minn. Senate from 49th dist., St. Paul, 1997—. Bd. dirs. Citizens League, Mpls., 1972-76; mem., chmn. Planning Commn., Anoka, 1972—; mem., treas. Minn. Bicentennial Com. of U.S. Constn., St. Paul, 1984-91. With USN, 1947-52. Mem. ABA, ACLU, LWV, Minn. Bar Assn., Hennepin County Bar Assn., Minn. Justice Found., Am. Soc. for Indsl. Security, Wilderness Soc., Audubon Soc., Minn. Police and Peace Officers Assn. (life), Am. Legion, Common Cause, U. Minn. Alumni Assn., Sierra Club. Democrat. Mem. United Ch. of Christ. Avocations: photography, fishing, computer programming, gardening. Address: 12275 Hummingbird St NW Coon Rapids MN 55448-1936

FOLEY, MIKE, state legislator; b. Rochester, N.Y., Apr. 5, 1954; m. Susan Foley; children: Laura, Matthew, Marie, Elizabeth, Peter. BS, SUNY, Brockport, 1976; MBA, Mich. State U., 1978. Cons. Kirschner Assn., 1978-79; dir. fin. analysis Nat. Assn. Regulatory Utility Commrs., 1979-97; corp. planning analyst Nebr. Pub. Power Dist., 1997—; mem. Nebr. Legislature from 29th dist., Lincoln, 2001—. Adv. neighborhood commr., Washington, 1984. Home: 6410 S 41st St Ct Lincoln NE 68516 Office: Rm 1101 State Capitol Lincoln NE 68509

FOLK, FRANK ANTON, surgeon, educator; b. Chgo., Dec. 15, 1925; s. Frank A. and Anna (Pilisauer) F.; m. Lorna C. Hill, June 18, 1949; children: Laura, Lawrence, Patricia, Elizabeth, Thomas, James, Mary, Tracy Ann, William. BS, Northwestern U., 1945; postgrad., U. Wis., 1945-46; MD, U. Ill., 1949. Diplomate Am. Bd. Surgery, Nat. Bd. Med. Examiners; lic. Ill., Wis. Rotating intern Cook County Hosp., Chgo., 1949-51; resident in gen. surgery Cook County/Columbus Hosp., 1951, Cook County Hosp., Chgo., 1954-57, surgeon, 1958-69, dir. of surgery, 1969-72; mem. faculty Stritch Sch. Medicine Loyola U., Maywood, Ill., 1958—, prof. surgery Stritch Sch. Medicine, 1972-96; prof. emeritus, 1997—; rsch. fellow Hektoen Inst., Chgo., 1959-64; asst. chief surgery VA Hosp., Hines, Ill., 1972-95, chief surg. svc., 1995-96. Mem. editl. bd.: The Am. Surgeon, 1984-92; contbr. articles to med. jours. including Am. Jour. Physiology, Jour. Occupl. Medicine, Annals of Surgery, Archives of Surgery, Jour. Trauma, Surg. Clinics of N.Am. Unit pres., exec. bd. Am. Cancer Soc., Chgo., 1972-89; mem. pres.'s adv. com. Benedictine U., Lisle, Ill., 1965-90. Lt. USN, 1951-53, Korea. Decorated Bronze Star, 1953. Fellow ACS (gov., chmn. gen. surgery Chgo. com. on trauma 1975-83, pres. met. chpt. 1977-78, mem. SESAP com. II and III, instr. ACS advanced trauma life support course 1980-87); mem. Am. Surg. Assn., Am. Assn. for Surgery of Trauma, Assn. Mil. Surgeons of U.S., Assn. for Acad. Surgery, Soc. for Surgery of Alimentary Tract, Assn. VA Surgeons, Collegium Internat. Chirurgiae Digestivae, Cen. Surg. Assn., Midwest Surg. Assn. (pres. 1974-75), Western Surg. Assn., Ill. Surg. Soc. (pres. 1971-72), Chgo. Surg. Soc. (pres. 1989-90), Inst. Medicine of Chgo. Roman Catholic. Avocations: medical history, Civil War history, Central American civilizations. Office: VA Hosp Surg Svc PO Box 5000 Hines IL 60141-1489 Fax: (708) 202-2180.

FOLLAS, WILLIAM DANIEL, management; b. Lima, Oct. 30, 1951; s. William Isaac and Carol Sue (Maxson) F.; m. Kathy Jo Roberts, Dec. 28, 1974; children: David Clay, Emily Jane, Jonathan Daniel. BS in Biology, Chem., Manchester Coll., 1974; MS in Med. Chem. Pharmaco, Purdue U., 1977. Research assoc. Ind. U. Med. Ctr., Indpls., 1977-79; pres. Follas Labs. Inc., 1979--. Co-founder Follas Lab. Inc., Indpls. 1979--. Tchr. Chapel Rock Christian Ch., Indpls. 1979—, evaluate lab. needs Lifeline, Columbus 1986. Mem. Am. Assn. for Clinical Chem., Ohio Valley Section, Clin. Lab. Mgmt. Assn., Cen. Ind. Biochem. Forum. Republican. Avocations: golf, gardening. Home: 4909 Cherryhill Ct Indianapolis IN 46254-9549 Office: Follas Labs Inc 7750 Zionsville Rd Ste 450 Indianapolis IN 46268-4189

FOLSOM, LOWELL EDWIN, language educator; b. Pitts., Sept. 30, 1947; s. Lowell Edwin and Helen Magdalene (Roeper) Folsom; m. Patricia Ann Jackson, Aug. 30, 1969; 1 child Benjamin Bradford. BA, Ohio Wesleyan U., 1969; MA, U. Rochester, 1972, PhD, 1976. Chmn. English dept. Lancaster (Ohio) H.S., 1969-70, 71-72; instr. Eastman Sch. Music, Rochester, NY, 1974-75; vis. asst. prof. SUNY, Geneseo, 1975-76; asst. prof. U. Iowa, Iowa City, 1976-82, assoc. prof., 1982-87, prof., 1987—, chair English dept., 1991-95, F. Wendell Miller disting. prof., 1997—. Cons. Am. Coll. Testing Co., Iowa City, 1980—, Nat. Assessment Ednl. Progress, Denver, 1980—84; dir. Walt Whitman Centennial Conf., Iowa City, 1992, Walt Whitman Conf., Beijing, 2000; Fulbright sr. prof. U. Dortmund, Germany, 1996. Author: Walt Whitman's Native Representations, 1994 (Choice Best Acad. Book, 1995); editor: Walt Whitman: The Centennial Essays, 1994, Walt Whitman: The Measure of His Song, 1981 (Choice Best Acad. Book, 1982), rev. edit., 1998 (Ind. Publisher Book award, 1999), Walt Whitman and the World, 1995, (CD-ROM) Walt Whitman, 1997 (choice Best Acad. Book, 1998), Whitman East and West, 2002, Walt Whitman Quar. Rev., 1983—; co-dir.: Walt Whitman Hypertext Archive, 1997—; editl. bd. Walt Whitman Encyclopedia, 1994—98, PMLA, 1999—2002, Profession, 2002—. Recipient Rsch. award, NEH, 1991—94, Collaborative Rsch. award, 2000—, Faculty Excellence award, Iowa Bd. Regents, 1996; scholar Disting., U. Rochester, 1995. Mem.: MLA, Whitman Scholars Assn. (dir. 1992—), Am. Studies Assn., Am. Lit. Assn. Home: 739 Clark St Iowa City IA 52240-5640 Office: Univ Iowa Dept English 308 EPB Iowa City IA 52242 E-mail: ed-folsom@uiowa.edu.

FOLZ, CAROL ANN, financial analyst; b. Cedar Rapids, Iowa, Dec. 28, 1951; D. Glenn Frederick and Ruth Frances (McIntosh) Rullman; m. Donald Harold McElderry, Oct. 3, 1970 (div. 1981); m. David Charles Folz, Mar. 19, 1983. AA, AS in Library Svcs., St. Louis Community Coll., 1973; BSBA, U. Mo., St. Louis, 1980. Library asst. Bloomfield (Iowa) Pub. Library, 1968-70, Ferguson (Mo.) Pub. Library, 1972-77; payroll clk. U. Mo., St. Louis, 1977-79, sr. sec., 1979-80, acct., 1980-82, sr. acct., 1982, sr. fiscal analyst, 1982-1989; payroll analyst Blue Cross and Blue Shield of Mo., 1990-91, sr. payroll acct., 1991; acct. Harris-Stowe State Coll., 1996-98, Accoutemps, St. Louis, 1998-2000; benefits specialist May Dept. Stores Co., 2000—. Methodist. Avocations: genealogy, music, reading, sports, needlework, crafts. Office: 611 Olive St Saint Louis MO 63101-1721 E-mail: cfolz21464@aol.com., carol.folz@may-co.com.

FONDAW, RONALD EDWARD, artist, educator; b. Paducah, Ky., Apr. 25, 1954; s. Lex Alan and Rose Mary (Holley) Kilgore; m. Lynn S. Shepard, Oct. 7, 1987; children: Andrea Rose, Wyler S. BFA, Memphis Coll. Art, 1976; MFA, U. Ill., 1978. Instr. Ohio U., Athens, 1978; assoc. prof. art U. Miami, Coral Gables, Fla., 1978-95, prof., 1997—; prof. art Washington U., St. Louis, 1995—. Lectr., presenter workshops Ohio State U., Chgo. Art Inst., Tokyo U. Fine Art, Chautauqua Sch. Art. Exhbns. nat. and internat.; several public art commissions. Ford Found. fellow, 1977, Gla. Arts Coun. fellow, 1981, Guggenheim fellow, 1985, Pollack/Krasner fellow, 1997-98; grantee NEA, 1988; Kransberg award St. Louis Art Mus., 1998. Home: 7345 Elm Ave Saint Louis MO 63143-3216 Office: Wash U 721 Kingsland Ave Saint Louis MO 63130-3107 E-mail: refondaw@art.wustl.edu.

FONTANAROSA, PHIL BERNARD, emergency physician; b. Youngstown, Ohio, 1954; m. Kristine Fontanarosa, Aug. 1977; children: Jennifer, Joel, Beth, Julie. Youngstown State U., 1975; MD, Med. Coll. Ohio, 1978; postgrad., Kent St. U., 1992-93. Diplomate Am. Bd. Emergency Medicine. Intern Akron (Ohio) City Hosp., 1978-79, resident in emergency medicine, 1979-81; assoc. prof., rsch. dir. emergency medicine Northeastern Ohio Universities Coll. Medicine, 1983-93; adj. prof. medicine Northwestern Med. Sch., Chgo. Dep. editor, dir. editl. affairs Jour. AMA; editor-in-chief text: Physicians' Evaluation and Educational Review in Emergency Medicine, 1996, Alternative Medicine: An Objective Assessment, 2000. Mem. Am. Coll. Emergency Physicians. Office: AMA 515 N State St Chicago IL 60610-4325

FORD, ALLYN, manufacturing company executive; CEO Roseburg (Ohio) Forest Products. Bd. dirs. South Umpqua Bank. Office: Roseburg Forest Products PO Box 1088 Roseburg OR 97470

FORD, ANDREW THOMAS, academic administrator; b. Cambridge, Mass., May 22, 1944; s. Francis Lawler and Eleanor (Vahey) F.; m. Anne M. Monahan, July 2, 1966; 1 dau., Lauren Elizabeth. B.A., Seton Hall U., 1966; M.A., U. WIs., 1968; Ph.D., U. Wis., 1971. Asst. prof. history Stockton State Coll., Pomona, N.J., 1971-72, asst. to v.p. for acad. affairs, 1972-74; acting dir. Nat. Materials Devel. Ctr. for French and Portuquese, Bedford, N.H., 1976-77; acad. programs coordinator N.H. Coll. and Univ. Council, Manchester, 1975-78; v.p. acad. affairs R.I. Sch. Design, Providence, 1978-81; dean Allegheny Coll., Meadville, Pa., 1981-93, provost, 1983-93; pres. Wabash Coll., Crawfordsville, Ind., 1993—. Mem. adv. bd. Marine Bank, 1987-93; founding mem. Commonwealth Partnership. Author: (with R. Chait) Beyond Traditional Tenure, 1982. Bd. dirs. Vis. Nurse Assn., Providence, 1979-81, Allegheny Summer Music Festival, Meadville, 1981-89, Meadville Med. Ctr., 1985-87; bd. incorporators Spencer Hosp., 1981-85; mem. Nat. Com. on U.S.-China Rels., 1986—. Democrat. Home: 400 E Pike St Crawfordsville IN 47933-2520 Office: Wabash Coll Office of Pres Crawfordsville IN 47933

FORD, BARBARA JEAN, library studies educator; b. Dixon, Ill., Dec. 5, 1946; BA magna cum laude with honors, Ill. Wesleyan U., 1968; MA in Internat. Rels., Tufts U., 1969; MS in Libr. Sci., U. Ill., 1973. Dir. Soybean Insect Rsch. Info. Ctr. Ill. Natural History Survey, Urbana, 1973-75; from asst. to assoc. prof. U. Ill., Chgo., 1975-84, asst. documents libr., 1975-79, documents libr., dept. head, 1979-84, acting audiovisual libr., 1983-84; asst. dir. pub. svcs. Trinity U., San Antonio, 1984-86, assoc. prof., assoc. dir., 1986-91, acting dir. librs., 1989, 91; prof., dir. univ. libr. svcs. Va. Commonwealth U., Richmond, 1991-98; asst. commr. Chgo. Pub. Libr., 1998—. Mem. women's re-entry adv. bd. U. Ill., Chgo., 1980-82, student affairs com., 1978-80, student admissions, records, coll. rels. com., 1981-84, univ. senate, 1976-78, 82-84, chancellor's libr. coun. svcs. com. 1984, campus lectrs. com. 1982-83; admissions interviewer for prospective students Trinity U., 1987-91, reader for internat. affairs theses, 1985-91, libr. self-study com., 1985-86, internat. affairs com., 1986-91, inter-Am. studies com., 1986-91, faculty senate, 1987-90; with libr. working group U.S./Mex. Commn. Cultural Coop., 1990. Contbr. articles to profl. publs., papers to presentations. Bd. dirs. Friends of San Antonio Pub. Libr., 1989-91; adv. com. chair Office for Libr. Pers. Resources, 1994-95; mem. steering com. Virtual Libr. Va., 1994-98, chair user svcs. com., 1995-96. Celia M. Howard fellow Tufts U., 1969; sr. fellow UCLA Grad. Sch. Libr. and Info. Sci., 1993. Mem. ALA (conf. program com. 1985-91, libr. edn. assembly 1983-84, membership com. 1978-79, status of women in librarianship com. 1983-85, exec bd., 1996-99, Lippincott Award Jury 1979-80, Shirley Olofson Meml. award 1977), ALA Coun. (at-large councilor 1985-89, chpt. councilor Ill. Libr. Assn. 1980-84, com. on coms. 1987-88, spl. coun. orientation com. 1982-83, ALA exec. bd., 1996-99, pres.- elect 1996-97, pres. 1997-98), Assn. Coll. and Rsch. Librs. (bd. dirs. 1989-92, pres.-elect 1989-90, pres. 1990-91, publs. com. 1990-91, conf. program planning 1990-91), Nat. Assn. State Univs. and Land Grant Colls. (commn. info. tech. 1992-94), Internat. Fedn. Libr. Assns. and Instns. (sec. official pubs. sect., gen. info. com. 1985 conf., moderator Latin Am. seminar on official pubs. 1991), Med. Libr. Assn., Mid. Atlantic Libr. Assn., Spl. Librs. Assn. (program com. 1976-77, 80-82, publicity com. 1977-79, chair 1978-79, chair spl. projects com. 1981-82, sec./treas. divsn. social sci. internat. affairs sect. 1984-86), Assn. Libr. Info. Sci. Edn. (chair local arrangements conf. planning com. 1988, 92), Ill. Libr. Assn. (chair election com. 1976-77, exec. bd. 1978-79, 80-84, bd. govt. documents round table 1976-79, chair 1978-79, long range planning com. 1980-84), Tex. Libr. Assn. (pubs. com. 1985-87, legis. com. 1986-87, judge best of exhibits award 1987, task force Amigos Fellowship 1990, del. conf. on librs. and info. svcs., 1991, Va. Libr. Assn. (ad hoc. com. distance learning 1992), Va. State Libr. and Archives (Va. libr. and info. svcs. task force 1991-93, steering com. Arbuthnot lecture 1992-93, coop. continuing edn. adv. com. 1992-94), VIVA (steering com. 1994-98), Chgo. Libr. Club (2d v.p. 1983-84), Richmond Acad. Libr. Consortium (v.p. 1991-92, pres. 1992-93), Beta Phi Mu, Phi Kappa Phi, Phi Alpha Theta, Kappa Delta Pi. Office: Chicago Pub Libr Box 2033 400 S State St Chicago IL 60605-1216

FORD, CHARLES NATHANIEL, otolaryngologist, educator; b. N.Y.C., June 25, 1940; s. Charles Nathaniel and Marie (Casa) F.; children: C. David, Brian C.; m. Sharon L. James, Feb. 3, 1990; stepchildren: Scott James, Julie James. BA, SUNY, Binghamton, 1961; MD, U. Louisville, 1965. Intern and resident Henry Ford Hosp., Detroit, 1965-70, staff, 1970-71; with Gundersen Clinic, LaCrosse, Wis., 1973-81; chief otolaryngology Middleton VA Hosp., Madison, 1982-94; prof. otolaryngol. divsn. dept. surgery U. Wis., 1981-93, chmn. otolaryngol. divsn. dept. surgery, 1993—. Mem.-at-large med. bd. U. Wis. Ctr. for Health Scis., 1989-91, sec., 1992-93, v.p., 1994-95, pres. med. staff, chair med. bd. 1996-98; DeWeese lectr. U. Oreg., 1994; Manion Meml. lectr. Ind. U., 1995; Hough lectr. U. Okla., 1996; Sartian lectr. U. Tex., 1998; keynote lectr. Brit. Voice Assn., 2000. Author, editor: Phonosurgery: Assessment and Surgical Management of Voice Disorders, 1991; mem. editl. bd.: Jour. Voice, Laryngoscope, Microsurgery; author editor numerous sci. papers, chpts. and abstracts. Maj. USAF, 1971-73. Avalon Found. scholar, 1962-63; named to Best Drs. in Am., Woodward/White, Inc., 1991—. Fellow ACS, Am. Laryngol., Rhinol. and Otolog. Soc., Am. Bronchoesophical Assn. (pres.-elect), Am. Laryngol. Assn., Am. Soc. for Head and Neck Surgery, Am. Acad. Otolaryngology, Head and Neck Surgery (honor award 1992); mem. AMA, Soc. Univ. Otolaryngologists-Head and Neck Surgeons (pres.), Internat. Assn. Phonosurgeons, Am. Speech-Lang.-Hearing Assn. Democrat. Unitarian Universalist. Avocations: tennis, golf, theater, art, music. Office: U Wis Ctr Health Sci 600 Highland Ave Madison WI 53792-0001

FORD, DAVID CLAYTON, state senator, lawyer; b. Hartford City, Ind., Mar. 3, 1949; s. Clayton I. and Barbara J. (McVicker) F.; m. Joyce Ann Bonjour, Aug. 22, 1970; children: Jeff, Matthew, Kelly, Andrew. BA in Polit. Sci., Ind. U., 1973, JD, 1976; MBA in Internat. Trade, Ball State U., 1988. Bar: Ind. 1975, U.S. Dist. Ct. (so. dist.) Ind. 1976, U.S. Dist. Ct. (no. dist.) Ind. 1977, U.S. Tax Ct. 1988, U.S. Supreme Ct. 1983. City atty. City of Montpelier, Ind., 1977-79; town atty. Town of Shamrock Lakes, 1977—; mem. Ind. Senate from 19th dist., 1994—. Gen. counsel, internat. trade dir. Ind. Farm Bur. Inc., 1988—; chief dep. prosecutor, Blackford County, 1979; pros. atty. 71st Jud. Cir., Blackford County, Hartford City, Ind., 1983-86; mem. com. on character and fitness State Bd. of Law Examiners. Mem. Ind. Agrl. Leadership Program, 1990-91; bd. dirs. Blackford County Young Reps., 1977-82, pres., 1977-78; chmn. Town of Shamrock Lakes Rep. Com., 1983, Ind. Lawyers for Bush and Quayle, 1988; vice chmn. Blackford County Rep. Ctrl. Com., 1978-82, chmn., 1993-2001; precinct committeeman Blackford County, Licking 7, 1980-93; mem. Ind. 10th Congl. Dist. Rep. Caucus, 1978-82, U.S. Edn. Appeals Bd., U.S. Dept. Edn., 1982-90, Nat. Def. Execs. Res., 1983-99; former mem. bus. adv. com. to Congressman Dan Burton; chmn. bus., industries and devel. com. Ptnrs. of Ams., Ind. chpt., 1983-84; mem. Blackford County Bd. Aviation Commrs., 1977-83, pres., 1979-83; bd. dirs. Dollars for Scholars, Blackford County, 1977-95, v.p., 1977-95; mem. St. John's-Riedman Meml. Sch. Bd., 1978-82, pres., 1978-82; mem. Blackford County Sheriff's Merit Bd., 1981-82. Named Man of Yr. Hartford City C. of C., 1978, Sagamore of the Wabash, Gov. Otis Bowen, 1978, Hon. Sec. of State Edwin J. Simcox, 1981; participant Rotary group study exch. to São Paulo, Brazil, 1981; named Outstanding Young Man of Am., U.S. Jaycees, 1982. Mem. ABA, ATLA, Ind. State Bar Assn., Blackford County Bar Assn., World Trade Club Ind., Mensa, Sigma Iota Epsilon. Home: 1023 N Walnut St Hartford City IN 47348-1553 Office: 210 W Main St Hartford City IN 47348-2209 E-mail: s19@in.gov.

FORD, EMORY A. chemist, researcher; b. South New Berlin, N.Y., Oct. 17, 1940; s. Merritt L. and Verda M. (Manwaring) F.; m. Susan Dorothy Rogers, Sept. 14, 1963; children: Kelly Diane, Kendra Lee. BA, Hartwick Coll., 1962; PhD, Syracuse U., 1966. Sr. rsch. chemist Monsanto Co., Springfield, Mass., 1966-72, rsch. group leader, 1972-76, sr. rsch. group leader, 1976-78, tech. mgr. Pensacola, Fla., 1978-81; rsch. mgr. No. Petrochem. Co., Morris, Ill., 1981-84; dir. basic rsch. Enron Chem. Co., Rolling Meadows, 1984-86, Quantum Chem. Co., Cin., 1987-97; chief scientist Equistar, 1997—. Mem. AAAS, Am. Chem. Soc., N.Y. Acad. Sci., Chemists Club of Chgo., Internat. Union Pure and Applied Chemistry, Sigma Xi. Unitarian. Avocations: reading, running, traveling. Office: Equistar 11530 Northlake Dr Cincinnati OH 45249-1642

FORD, FREDERICK ROSS, retired university official; b. Kentland, Ind., Mar. 25, 1936; s. Merl Jackson and Marie Jeanne (Ross) F.; m. Mary A. Harrison, May 31, 1959; children: Lynne Elizabeth, Steven Harrison, Katherine Jeannette. BS in Mech. Engring., Purdue U., 1958, MS, 1959, PhD, 1963. Asst. to bus. mgr. Purdue U., West Lafayette, Ind., 1959-61, asst. to v.p., treas., 1961-65, asst. bus. mgr., 1965-69, bus. mgr., asst. treas., 1969-74, exec. v.p., treas., 1974-98; ret., 1998. Trustee Tchrs. Ins. and Annuity Assn., N.Y.C., 1982-2002. Treas. capital funds found. United Way, Lafayette, 1984-85. Mem. Coun. on Govtl. Rels. (bd. mgmt. 1984-90), Nat. Assn. Coll. and Univ. Bus. Officers (bd. dirs. 1980-83, sec. 1982-83, Disting. Bus. Officer award 1989), Ctrl. Assn. Coll. and Univ. Bus. Officers (exec. com. 1976-81, pres. 1979-80), Lafayette C. of C. (pres. 1978-79, chmn. edn. rels. com. 1984-85), Rotary, Delta Upsilon. Republican. Presbyterian. Avocations: sailing, fishing. Home: 160 Creighton Rd West Lafayette IN 47906-2102

FORD, GEORGE BURT, lawyer; b. South Bend, Ind., Oct. 1, 1923; s. George W. and Florence (Burt) F.; m. Charlotte Ann Kupferer, June 12, 1948; children: John, Victoria, George, Charlotte. BS in Engring. Law, Purdue U., 1946; LLB, Ind. U., 1949. Bar: Ind. 1949, U.S. Dist. Ct. (no. dist.) Ind. 1949. Assoc. Jones, Obenchain & Butler, South Bend, Ind., 1949-52; ptnr. Jones, Obenchain, Ford, Pankow & Lewis, 1953-93, of counsel, 1994—. Co-author: Forms for Indiana Corporations, 1967, 2nd edit. 1977. With U.S. Army, 1943-45, ETO. Fellow Am. Coll. of Trust and Estate Counsel; mem. ABA, Ind. Bar Assn., St. Joseph County Bar Assn. (pres. 1976-77), Phi Gamma Delta, Phi Delta Phi. Presbyterian (trustee 1966-68, elder 1967-70). Office: Jones Obenchain LLP 600 Key Bank Bldg 202 S Michigan St Box 4577 South Bend IN 46634-4577

FORD, GORDON BUELL, JR. English language, linguistics, and medieval studies educator, author, retired hospital industry accounting financial management executive; b. Louisville, Sept. 22, 1937; s. Gordon Buell Sr. and Rubye (Allen) F. AB summa cum laude in Classics, Medieval Latin, and Sanskrit, Princeton U., 1959; AM in Classical Philology and Linguistics, Harvard U., 1962, PhD in Linguistics, Slavic and Baltic Langs. and Lits., 1965; postgrad., U. Oslo, 1962-64, U. Sofia, Bulgaria, 1963, U. Uppsala, Sweden, 1963-64, U. Stockholm, 1963-64, U. Madrid, 1963. CPA. Yeager, Ford, and Warren Found. Disting. prof. Indo-European, Classical, Slavic, and Baltic linguistics, Sanskrit, and Medieval Latin Northwestern U., Evanston, Ill., 1965—; Lybrand, Ross Bros., and Montgomery Found. Disting. prof. English and linguistics U. No. Iowa, Cedar Falls, 1972—; sr. exec. v.p. for real estate acctg. fin. mgmt., bd. dirs. The Southeastern Real Estate Co., Inc., Louisville, 1976-93; sr. exec. v.p. reimbursement and rates acctg. fin. mgmt., hosp. acctg. divsn. Humana Inc., The Hosp. Co., 1976-93; ret., 1993; bd. dirs. Southeastern Investment Trust, Inc., Louisville, 1976-93; ret., 1993; rsch. prof. The Southeastern Investment Trust, Inc. Rsch. Found., Louisville, 1976—. Vis. prof. Medieval Latin, U. Chgo., 1966—; vis. prof. linguistics U. Chgo., Downtown Ctr., 1966—; prof. English evening divs. Northwestern U., Chgo., 1968-69, prof. anthropology, 1971-72. Author: The Ruodlieb: The First Medieval Epic of Chivalry from Eleventh-Century Germany, 1965, The Ruodlieb: Linguistic Introduction, Latin Text with a Critical Apparatus, and Glossary, 1966, The Ruodlieb: Facsimile Edition, 1965, 3d edit. 1968, Old Lithuanian Texts of the Sixteenth and Seventeenth Centuries with a Glossary, 1969, The Old Lithuanian Catechism of Baltramiejus Vilentas (1579): A Phonological, Morphological, and Syntactical Investigation, 1969, Isidore of Seville's History of the Goths, Vandals, and Suevi, 1966, 2d edit. 1970, The Letters of Saint Isidore of Seville, 1966, 2d edit. 1970, The Old Lithuanian Catechism of Martynas Mazvydas (1547), 1971, others; translator: A Concise Elementary Grammar of the Sanskrit Language with Exercises, Reading Selections, and a Glossary (Jan Gonda), 1966, The Comparative Method in Historical Linguistics (Antoine Meillet), 1967, A Sanskrit Grammar (Manfred Mayrhofer), 1972; contbr. numerous articles to many scholarly jours. Appointed to Hon. Order Ky. Cols. (life). Mem. Linguistic Soc. Am. (life, Sapir life patron), Internat. Linguistic Assn. (life), Societas Linguistica Europaea (charter, life), Am. Philol. Assn. (life), Classical Assn. of the Atlantic States (life), Classical Assn. of the Middle West and South (life), Classical Assn. of N.Eng. (life), Medieval Acad. of Am. (life), Renaissance Soc. of Am. (life), MLA (life), Am. Assn. Tchrs. Slavic and East European Langs. (life), Am. Assn. Advancement Slavic Studies (life), Am. Coun. Tchrs. Russian (life), Assn. for Advancement Baltic Studies (life), Inst. Lithuanian Studies (life), Tchrs. of English to Speakers of Other Langs. (charter, life), SAR (life), Princeton Club (N.Y.C., Chgo.), Princeton Alumni Assn. (Louisville), Harvard Club (N.Y.C., Chgo., Louisville, Lexington, Ky.), Pres.'s Soc. Bellarmine Coll. (life), Louisville Country Club, KC (life), Phi Beta Kappa (life). Baptist. Home: 3619 Brownsboro Road Louisville KY 40207-1863 also: PO Box 2693 Clarksville Br Jeffersonville IN 47131-2693

FORD, JACK, state legislator; m. to Cynthia Ford; children: Ryan, Jessica, Jacqueline. BA, Ohio State U.; MPA, Univ. Toledo. Mem. Ho. of Reps., Columbus, Ohio, 1994—. Past city councilman City of Toledo, former pres. Toledo coun.; instr. U. Tpoledo. Former mem. citizens' adv. bd. Toledo Mental Health Ctr.; chmn. bd. Cordelia Martin Mental Health Home, former pres. Mental Health Agy. Ins. Trust, pres. and founder Substance Abuse Svc.; current mem. Toledo Symphony Bd.

FORD, JEAN ELIZABETH, former English language educator; b. Branson, Mo., Oct. 5, 1923; d. Mitchell Melton and Annie Estella (Wyer) F.; m. J.C. Wingo, 1942 (div. 1946; m. E. Syd Vineyard, 1952 (div. 1956); m. Vincent Michel Wessling, Feb. 14, 1983 (div. Dec. 1989). AA in English, L.A. City Coll., 1957; BA in English, Calif. State U., 1959; MA in Higher Edn., U. Mo., 1965; postgrad., UCLA, 1959-60, U. Wis., 1966, U. Mo. Law Sch., 1968-69. Cert. English tchr., real estate broker, Mo. Dance instr. Arthur Murray Studios, L.A., 1948-51; office mgr. Western Globe Products, 1951-55; pvt. dance tchr., various office jobs, 1955-59; social dir. S.S. Matsonia, 1959; social worker L.A. County, 1959-61; 7th grade instr. Carmenita Sch. Dist., Norwalk, Calif., 1961-62; English instr. Leadwood (Mo.) High Sch., 1962-63; dance instr. U. Mo., 1963-66, SW Mo. State U., 1966-68, NW Mo. State U., 1970-76, Johnson County Community Coll., 1976-77; tax examiner IRS, Kansas City, Mo., 1978-80; tax acct. Baird, Kurtz & Dobson, 1981; dance tchr. Singles Program Village, Presbyn. Ch., Kans., 1981-96. Substitute tchr. various sch. dists., 1976-85; dance chmn. Mo. Assn. Health, Phys. Edn. and Recreation, 1965-66, 68-69, dance chmn. ctrl. dist. AAHPER, 1972-73; vis. author Young Author's Conf., Ctrl. Mo. State U., 1987, 88, 89; speaker Am. Reading Assn., Grandview, Mo., 1990; real estate sales agt., Kansas City, 1980-84; real estate sales broker, Mo., 1990—, Kans., 1990-2000; pvt. practice tax acct., dance tchr., 1984—. Author, pub.: Fish Tails and Scales, 1982, 3d edit., 2000; speaker at libraries. Mem. Village Presbyn. Ch., Prairie Village, Kans. Mem. Am. Contract Bridge League, Kansas City Ski Club, U.S. Amateur Ballroom Dancers Assn., Inc. (assoc.), U.S. Tennis Assn. Democrat. Presbyterian. Avocations: tennis, swimming, skiing, sailing, bridge. Home and Office: 142 Grandview Dr Bldg 4 #7 Branson MO 65616

FORD, LOUIS H. state legislator; b. Miss., Mar. 12, 1935; Mgr. Pest Control Co. State rep. dist. 58 Mo. Ho. of Reps., 1983—. Home: 3229 N 20th St Saint Louis MO 63107-3538

FORD, LUCILLE GARBER, economist, educator; b. Ashland, Ohio, Dec. 31, 1921; d. Ora Myers and Edna Lucille (Armstrong) Garber; m. Laurence Wesley Ford, Sept. 1, 1946; children: Karen Elizabeth, JoAnn Christine. AA, Stephens Coll., 1942; BS in Commerce, Northwestern U., 1944, MBA, 1945; PhD in Econs., Case Western Res. U., 1967; PhD (hon.), Tarkio Coll., 1991, Ashland U., 1995. Cert. fin. planner. Instr. Allegheny Coll., Meadville, Pa., 1945-46, U. Ala., Tuscaloosa, 1946-47; personnel dir., asst. sec. A.L. Garber Co., Ashland, Ohio, 1947-67; prof. econs. Ashland U., 1967-95, chmn. dept. econs., 1970-75; dir. Gill Ctr. for Econ. Edn. Ashland Coll., 1975-86, v.p., dean Sch. Bus., Adminstrn. and Econs., 1980-86, v.p. acad. affairs, 1986-90, provost, 1990-92; exec. asst. to pres., 1993-95; pres. Ashland Comm. Found., 1995—. Bd. dirs. Peco II, Inc., Western Res. Econ. Devel. Coun., Morgan Freeport Corp., Ohio Coun. Econ. Edn.; lectr. in field; mem. govs. adv. com. on econ. devel. Author: University Economics-Guide for Education Majors, 1979, Economics: Learning and Instruction, 1981, 91; contbr. articles to profl. jours. Mem. Ohio Gov.'s Commn. on Ednl. Choice, 1992; candidate for lt. gov. of Ohio, 1978; trustee Stephens Coll., 1977-80, Ashland U., 1995—, North Cen. State Coll., 1998—; elder Presbyn. Ch.; bd. dirs. Presbyn. Found., 1982-88; chair, trustee Synod-Presbyn. Ch., 1994-2000; active ARC. Named to Ohio Women's Hall of Fame, 2001; recipient Outstanding Alumnus award, Stephens Coll., 1977, Outstanding Profl. award, Ashland U., 1971, 1975, Roman F. Warmke award, 1981, Women of Achievement award, 1998. Mem. Am. Econs. Assn., Nat. Indsl. Research Soc., Am. Arbitration Assn. (profl. arbitrator), Assn. Pvt. Enterprise Edn. (pres. 1983-84), North Ctrl. Assn. Colls. & Schs. (commr.), Omicron Delta Epsilon, Alpha Delta Kappa. Republican. Office: Ashland Comm Found PO Box 733 Ashland OH 44805-0733

FORD, PHILLIP J. career officer; BSBA, U. Tex., 1965; Diploma, Squadron Officer Sch., 1973; MS in Counseling/Human Devel., Troy State U., 1978; Diploma, Air Command and Staff Coll., 1978, Nat. War Coll., 1984; postgrad., Harvard U., 1993. Commd. 2d lt. USAF, 1967, advanced through ranks to lt. gen., 1996; various assignments to dir. for opers. and logistics Hdqtrs. U.S. Strategic Comman, Offutt AFB, Nebr., 1994-96; comdr. 8th Air Force, Barksdale AFB, La., 1996-98; dep. comdr.-in-chief U.S. Strategic Command, Offutt AFB, 1998—. Decorated Disting. Svc. medal, Def. Superior Svc. medal, Legion of Merit with oak leaf cluster, Meritorious Svc. medal with two oak leaf clusters, Air medal with oak leaf cluster, Aerial Achievement medal, Joint Svc. Commendation medal, Air Force Commendation medal with oak leaf cluster. Office: Dep USCINCSTRAT 901 Sac Blvd Ste 2A Offutt A F B NE 68113-5455

FORD, WILLIAM CLAY, automotive company executive, professional sports team executive; b. Detroit, Mar. 14, 1925; s. Edsel Bryant and Eleanor (Clay) F.; m. Martha Firestone, June 21, 1947; children: Martha, Sheila, William Clay, Elizabeth. BS, Yale U., 1949. Sales and advt. staff Ford Motor Co., 1949; indsl. relations, labor negotiations with UAW, 1949; quality control mgr. gas turbine engines Lincoln-Mercury Div., Dearborn, Mich., 1951, mgr. spl. product ops., 1952, v.p., 1953, gen. mgr. Continental Div., 1954, group v.p. Lincoln and Continental Divs, 1955, v.p. product design, 1956-80; dir., 1948—; vice chmn. bd., 1980-89; mem. fin. com. Ford Motor Co., 1987—; owner, chair Detroit Lions, 1964—. Chmn. emeritus Edison Inst.; hon. life trustee Eisenhower Med. Ctr. Mem. Soc. Automotive Engrs. (asso.), Automobile Old Timers, Econ. Club Detroit, Masons, K.T., Phelps Assn., Psi Upsilon. Office: Ford Motor Co Design Ctr PO Box 6012 Dearborn MI 48121-6012 also: The Detroit Lions Inc 222 Republic Dr Allen Park MI 48101

FORD, WILLIAM CLAY, JR. automotive executive; b. May 3, 1957; married. BA, Princeton U., 1979; MBA in Mgmt., MIT, 1984. Prodn. planning analyst, advisor vehicle devel. design ctr., mfg. engr. auto assembly divsn., mgr. Ford Motor Co., N.Y., 1979-82, mem. nat. bargaining team Ford/UAW labor talks, mktg. strategy analyst No. Am. Auto

Opns., advt. specialist, 1982-83, internat. fin. specialist, mem. fin. staff, 1984-85, planning mgr. car prodn. devel., 1985-86, dir. com. vehicle mktg. Europe divsn., 1986-87, chmn., mng. dir. Switzerland divsn., 1987-89, mgr. heavy truck engr. and mfg. Ford Truck Opns., 1989-90, dir. bus. strategy Ford Auto Group, 1990-91, exec. dir. bus. strategy Ford Auto Group, 1991-92, gen. mgr. climate control divsn., 1992-94, v.p. com. tracking vehicle ctr. Ford Auto Opns., 1994-95, chmn. fin. com., 1995-99, chmn. bd., 1998—, CEO, 2001—. Vice chmn. Detroit Lions; mem. fin. com., properties com. NFL. Chmn. bd. trustees Henry Ford Mus., Greenfield Village; trustee Henry Ford Health Sys., Detroit Renaissance, Conservation Internat.; mem. World Econ. Forum's Global Leaders for Tomorrow; vice-chmn., bd. dirs. Greater Downtown Partnership Inc., Detroit. Alfred P. Sloan fellow MIT, 1983-84. Office: Ford Motor Co 1 American Rd Dearborn MI 48126-2798*

FORDYCE, JAMES GEORGE, physician; b. Detroit, Jan. 9, 1945; s. James Alexander and Stella Marie (Pakron) F.; m. Kathleen Marie Ray, June 17, 1967; children: James A., Jonathan A., Jared A. BS, Mich. State U., 1966, DVM, 1968; MD, Wayne State U., 1974. Diplomate Am. Bd. Pediats., Am. Bd. Allergy and Immunology. Intern, resident Children's Hosp. Mich., Detroit, 1973-76; fellow allergy and clin. immunology Henry Ford Hosp., 1976-78; physician Dearborn (Mich.) Allergy and Asthma Clinic, PC, 1978—. Cons. Metro Med. Group, Detroit, 1979-95. Author: Asthma in Clinical Pulmonary Medicine, 1992. Bd. trustees Oakwood Healthcare, Inc., 1996-2000. Fellow Am. Acad. Pediats., Am. Acad. Allergy, Asthma and Clin. Immunology; mem. Mich. Allergy and Asthma Soc. (pres. 1991-92). Avocations: fishing, flying, sailing. Office: Dearborn Allergy & Asthma Clinic PC 20200 Outer Dr Dearborn MI 48124-2634

FORDYCE, JAMES STUART, non-profit organization executive; b. London, Dec. 10, 1931; came to U.S., 1947; s. James Wilfred and Doris Vera (Macrae) F.; m. Beverly Ann Arnold, June 12, 1954; children: Cameron James, Jean Margaret. AB, Dartmouth Coll., 1953; PhD in Phys. Chemistry, MIT, 1959. Rsch. scientist Parma (Ohio) rsch. lab. Union Carbide Corp., 1959-66; rsch. scientist Lewis rsch. ctr. NASA, Cleve., 1966-68, head electrochemical fundamentals, 1968-73, mgr. environ. monitoring office, 1973-76, chief electrochemistry br., 1976-80, dep. chief space power tech. divsn., 1980-81, chief, 1981-84, dep. dir. aerospace tech., 1984-85, dir., 1985-91, dep. ctr. dir., 1991-94; v.p., chief scientist Ohio Aerospace Inst., 1995-2000, sr. cons., 2000—. Spl. lectr. Internat. Space U.; disting. space tech. lectr. Columbia U., 1988; bd. trustees Edison Polymer Innovation Corp., Akron, Ohio, 1991—. Author: (with others) Solar Power Satellites, 1993; contbr. articles to profl. jours. Mem. spl. com. Mus. Natural History, Cleve., 1991-96, 2000—; active Leadership Cleve., 1992—; internat. mem. program adv. bd. Ctr. for Rsch. in Earth and Space Tech., Toronto. Fellow AIAA (assoc.); mem. AAAS, Am. Chem. Soc., Fedn. Am. Scientists, Electrochem. Soc. (lectr. 106th mtg. 1985), Sigma Xi. Democrat. Unitarian. Home: 21295 Cromwell Ave Fairview Park OH 44126-2714 Business E-Mail: stfordyce@cox.net.

FOREHAND, JOSEPH W. finance company executive; b. Alexander City, Ala. m. Gayle Forehand; 2 children. BS in Indsl. Engring., Auburn U.; MS in Indsl. Adminstrn., Purdue U. With Anderson Cons., 1972—, various positions with product group, regional dir. products industry, office mng. ptrn. Dallas, head Ams. products group, mng. ptrn. products, 1997-98, mng. ptnr. global comms. and high tech market unit; mng. ptrn., CEO Accenture(formerly Anderson), 2001—. Spkr. in field. Office: Accentire 100 S Wacker Dr Ste 1059 Chicago IL 60606 also: 100 S Wacker Dr Ste 1059 Chicago IL 60606-4006

FOREMAN, JAMES LOUIS, retired judge; b. Metropolis, Ill., May 12, 1927; s. James C. and Anna Elizabeth (Henne) F.; m. Mabel Inez Dunn, June 16, 1948; children: Beth Foreman Banks, Rhonda Foreman Wittig, Nanette Foreman Love. BS in Commerce and Law, U. Ill., 1950, JD, 1952. Bar: Ill. Ind. practice law, Metropolis, Ill.; ptnr. Chase and Foreman, until 1972; state's atty. State of Ill., Massac County, asst. atty. gen.; chief judge U.S. Dist. Ct. (so. dist.) Ill., Benton, 1979-92, sr. status, 1992—. Pres. Bd. of Edn., Metropolis. With USN, 1945-46. Mem. Ill. State Bar Assn., Metropolic C. of C. (past pres.). Republican. Home: 38 Hilanoa-East Dr Metropolis IL 62960-2533 Office: US Dist Ct 301 W Main St Benton IL 62812-1362

FORESMAN, JAMES BUCKEY, geologist, geochemist, industrial hygienist; b. Neosho, Mo., Apr. 8, 1935; s. Frank James and Helen Blackburn (Buckey) F.; m. Barbara Ellen Runkle, Aug. 13, 196l; children: James Runkle, Robert Buckey. BSBA, BS, Kans. State U., 1962; MS, U. Tulsa, 1970. Cert. insp., mgmt. planner, contractor. From geologist, geochemist to staff dir. geology N.Am.-S.Am. Phillips Petroleum Co., Denver, Midland, Tex., Bartlesville, Okla., 1962-83; petroleum cons., 1983-84; v.p. Mopro, Inc., Lyons, Mich., l985-87; indsl. hygienist, asst. dir. phys. plant Pittsburg (Kans.) State U., l987—. Geochemistry advisor Joint Oceanographic Instsn. for Deep Earth Sampling, 1974-75; ocean drilling advisor NSF, Washington, 1974-75; indsl. rep. for joint ventures with USSR, 1978; rep. Univ.-Indsl. Assoc. Programs, N.Y., Tex., Ariz., Mass., Calif., Cambridge (Eng.), 1981-83; citizen amb. programs Environ. Del. to Russia, Latvia, and Estonia, 1992. Contbr. articles to periodicals, jours., chpts. to books. Com. mem. Boy Scouts Am., Bartlesville, 1975-82; mem. Pitts. Planning and Zoning Commn., 1997-2000; bd. dirs. U.S. Little League, Bartlesville, 1975; smoke jumper Forest Svc., USDA. Sgt. USMC, 1954-57, Korea. Recipient Disting. Svc. award City of Bartlesville, 1977. Mem. Assn. Higher Edn. Facilities Officers, Kiwanis (past pres.), Kans. Kiwanis Found. (life). Republican. Presbyterian. Avocations: reading, collecting rare and antique books, YMCA activities. Home: 1506 Woodland Ter Pittsburg KS 66762-5551

FORET, MICKEY PHILLIP, air transportation company executive; b. McComb, Miss., Oct. 23, 1945; s. Fadias Phillip and Christine (Brown) F.; m. Mary Ann Tramonte, Aug. 12, 1966; 1 child, Keri. BS in Fin., MBA in Fin., La. State U., 1971. Dir. credit/interim dir. internal audit Tex. (Houston) Internat. Airlines, 1975-77, dir. cash mgmt., 1977-78, asst. treas., 1978-81, v.p. fin. svcs., 1981-82; v.p., treas. Continental Airlines, L.A., 1982-84, v.p., chief fin. officer, 1984-86, also bd. dirs.; sr. v.p. fin. and internat. Eastern Airlines, Miami, Fla., 1987-88, v.p., chief fin. officer, 1986—, also bd. dirs.; sr. v.p. Tex. (Houston) Air Corp., 1988—; exec. v.p. fin. and planning Continental Airlines, Houston, 1988-89, pres., 1989-90; exec. v.p., CFO Northwest Airlines, 1992-96; pres. Atlas Air, Inc., 1996-1997; spec. projects offcr. Northwest Airlines, 1998—, CFO, exec. v.p., 1998—. Chmn. bd. dirs., chief exec. officer Chelsea Catering Co., Houston. Pres. Clear Wood Improvement Assn., Houston, 1975-78; coach Friendswood (Tex.) Girls Softball Team, 1981. Served with USAF, 1966-69, Vietnam. Mem. Phi Kappa Phi, Beta Gamma Sigma. Republican. Baptist. Avocations: boating, water skiing, biking. Home: 7001 Valley View Rd Edina MN 55439-1652

FORMELLER, DANIEL RICHARD, lawyer; b. Chgo., Aug. 15, 1949; s. Vernon Richard and Shirley Mae (Gruber) F.; m. Ann M. Paa, Aug. 17, 1974; children: Matthew Daniel, Kathryn Ann, Christina Marie. BA with honors, U. Ill., 1970; JD cum laude, DePaul U., 1976. Bar: (Ill.) 1976, (U.S. Dist. Ct. (no. and ctrl. dist.) Ill.) 1976, (U.S. Ct. Appeals (7th and 9th cirs.)) 1976, (U.S. Ct. Appeals (D.C. cir.)) 1995. Assoc. McKenna, Storer, Rowe, White & Farrug, Chgo., 1976-82, ptnr., 1982-86, Tressler, Soderstrom, Maloney & Priess, Chgo., 1986—. Editor: DePaul U. Law Rev., 1975—76. With USN, 1970—72, Vietnam. Mem. ABA, Ill. Bar Assn., Ill. Assn. Def. Trial Counsel (pres. 1994-95), Chgo. Bar Assn., Assn. Def. Trial Attys. Office: Tressler Soderstrom et al 233 S Wacker Dr Chicago IL 60606-6306 E-mail: dformeller@mail.tsmp.com.

FORNERIS, JEANNE M. lawyer; b. Duluth, Minn., May 23, 1953; d. John Domenic and Elva Lorraine (McDonald) F.; m. Michael Scott Margulies, Feb. 6, 1982. AB, Macalester Coll., 1975; JD, U. Minn., 1978. Bar: Minn. 1978. Assoc. Halverson, Watters, Bye, Downs & Maki, Ltd., Duluth, 1978-81, Briggs & Morgan, P.A., Mpls., St. Paul, 1981-83; ptnr. Hart & Bruner, P.A., Mpls., 1983-86; assoc. gen. counsel M.A. Mortenson Co., 1986-90, v.p., gen. counsel, 1990-96; with Gen. Counsel, Ltd., 1997-98; v.p., sr. counsel Medtronic, Inc., 1999—. Instr. women's studies dept. U. Minn., Mpls., 1977-79. Author profl. edn. seminars; contbr. articles to profl. jours. Bd. dirs. Good Will Indusries Vocat. Enterprises, Inc., 1979-81; chmn. bd. trustees Duluth Bar Libr., 1981; mem. United Way Family and Individual Svcs. Task Force, Duluth, 1981. Nat. Merit Assn. scholar, 1971. Fellow Am. Coll. Constrn. Lawyers (bd. dirs.); mem. AMA, Am. Arbitration Assn. (mem. large complex case panel), Minn. State Bar Assn., Minn. Women Lawyers (bd. dirs.), U.S. Dist. Ct. Hist. Soc. (pres.). Democrat. Roman Catholic. Office: Medtronic Inc 7000 Central Ave NE Minneapolis MN 55432-3576

FORRESTER, W. THOMAS, II, insurance company executive; With The Progressive Corp., Mayfield, Ohio, 1984—, CFO, treas., 1998—. Office: The Progressive Corp 6300 Wilson Mills Rd Mayfield OH 44143

FORST, MARION FRANCIS, bishop; b. St. Louis, Sept. 3, 1910; s. Frank A.J. and Bertha T. (Gulath) F. Grad., Kenrick Sem., Webster Groves, Mo., 1934. Ordained priest Roman Catholic Ch., 1934; pastor St. Mary's Cathedral, Cape Girardeau, Mo., 1949-60; vicar gen. Diocese of Springfield-Cape Girardeau, 1956-60; bishop Dodge City, Kans., 1960-76; aux. bishop Archdiocese of Kansas City, 1976-86; ret., 1986. Kan. chaplain K.C., 1964— Served with Chaplains Corps USNR, World War II.

FORSTER, FRANCIS MICHAEL, physician, educator; b. Cin., Feb. 14, 1912; s. Michael Joseph and Louise Barbara (Schmid) F.; m. Helen Dorothy Kiley, June 15, 1937; children— Denis, Susan, Kathleen, Mark, Gabrielle. Student, Xavier U., Cin., 1930-32, LL.D., 1955; B.S., U. Cin., 1935, B.M., 1936, M.D., 1937; D.Sc. hon., Georgetown U., 1982. Diplomate: Am. Bd. Psychiatry and Neurology (dir.). Rotating intern Good Samaritan Hosp., Cin., 1936-37; house officer neurology and neurosurgery Boston City Hosp., 1937-38, resident neurology, 1939-40; fellow psychiatry Pa. Hosp., Phila., 1938-39; asst. neurology Harvard Med. Sch., 1939-40; Rockefeller Found. research fellow physiology Yale Sch. Medicine, 1940-41; instr. neurology Boston U. Sch. Medicine, 1941-43; asst. prof. neurology Jefferson Med. Sch., 1943-47, assoc. prof. neurology, 1947-50; prof. neurology, dir. dept. Georgetown U. Sch. Medicine, 1950-58, dean Sch. Medicine, 1953-58; prof., chmn. dept. neurology U. Wis. Sch. Medicine, 1958-78; emeritus, 1978—; dir. Epilepsy Center, VA Hosp., Madison, Wis., 1977-82. Cons. neurology. Author: Synopsis of Neurology, 1962, 66, 73, 78, Reflex Epilepsy, Behavioral Therapy and Conditional Reflexes, 1977; editor: Modern Therapy in Neurology, 1957, Evaluation of Drug Therapy, 1961. Mem. AMA (chmn. nervous and mental diseases sect. 1952-53), AAAS, D.C. Med. Soc. (chmn. sect. neurology and psychiatry 1955-56, pres. 1958), Am. Acad. Neurology (chmn. survey com. 1948-51, pres. 1957-59), Am. Neurol. Assn. (chmn. com. internat. collaboration 1954-55), Am. Epilepsy League (pres. 1951-52), Assn. Rsch. Nervous and Mental Diseases, Am. Physiol. Soc., Am. Assn. Electroencephalographers, Med. Soc. Wis., Cosmos Club (Washington), Sigma Xi, Alpha Omega. Club: Cosmos (Washington). Home: 21 Fallen Br Cincinnati OH 45241-3242 Office: U Wis Med Sch 600 Dept Neurology Madison WI 53792-0001 E-mail: fmforster@worldnet.att.net.

FORSTER, PETER HANS, utility company executive; b. Berlin, Germany, May 28, 1942; s. Jerome and Margaret Hanson; m. Susan E. Forster. B.S., U. Wis., 1964; postgrad., Bklyn. Law Sch., Columbia U., 1972. Engr. trainee Wis. Electric Power Co., 1960-64; head regional planning Am. Electric Power Service Corp., 1964-73; atty. Dayton Power & Light Co., Ohio, from 1973, v.p. adminstrn., treas., 1977, v.p. fin. and adminstrn., 1977-78, v.p. energy resources, 1978-79, exec. v.p., 1980-81, exec. v.p., chief operating officer, 1981-82, pres., chief operating officer, 1982-84, pres., chief exec. officer, 1984-88, chmn., 1988—. Chmn. Miami Valley Rsch. Found.; bd. dirs. Bank One, Dayton, Ohio. Bd. dirs. Amcast, Comair; trustee Med Am. Health Systems, F.M. Tait Found., Dayton Bus. Com., Arts Ctr. Found. Mem. Am. Bar Assn., Ohio Bar Assn., Dayton Bar Assn. Office: DPL Inc PO Box 1247 Dayton OH 45401

FORSYTH, ILENE HAERING, art historian; b. Detroit, Aug. 21, 1928; d. Austin Frederick and Eleanor Marie (Middleton) H.; m. George H. Forsyth, Jr., June 4, 1960. AB, U. Mich., 1950; AM (univ. fellow), Columbia U., 1955, Ph.D. (Fulbright, AAUW, Fels Found. fellow), 1960. Lectr. Barnard Coll., 1955-58; instr. Columbia U., 1959-61; mem. faculty U. Mich., Ann Arbor, 1961—, prof. history of art, 1974-97, prof. emerita, 1998—, Arthur F. Thurnau prof., 1984—; vis. prof. Harvard U., 1980; Mellon vis. prof. U. Pitts., 1981; vis. prof. U. Calif., Berkeley, 1996. Mem. Nat. Com. History Art, 1975-97; bd. dirs. Internat. Ctr. Medieval Art, 1970-95, v.p., 1981-85; mem. supervisory com. Woodrow Wilson Found., 1985-88; Rome prize juror Am. Acad. in Rome, 1986-88; bd. advisors Ctr. Advanced Study in the Visual Arts, Nat. Gallery Art, 1985-88; mem. vis. com. medieval dept. Met. Mus. Art, N.Y.C., 1990-95; Samuel H. Kress prof. Ctr. Advanced Study in the Visual Arts, Nat. Gallery Art, 1998-99, bd. advisors, 1999-2000. Author: The Throne of Wisdom, 1972 (Charles Rufus Morey Book award 1974), The Uses of Art: Medieval Metaphor in The Michigan Law Quadrangle, 1993 (Annie award for non-fiction 1994); co-editor: Current Studies on Cluny, 1988; contbr. articles to profl. jours. Rackham research grantee and fellow, 1965-66, 75-76; grantee Am. Council Learned Socs., 1972-73; mem. Inst. Advanced Study Princeton, 1977 Mem. Coll. Art Assn. (dir. 1980-84), Archaeol. Inst. Am., Medieval Acad. Am. (bd. advs. 1985-86, editorial bd. 1986-90), Medieval Club N.Y., Soc. francaise d'archéologie, Soc. Archtl. Historians, Acad. Arts, Scis. et Belles Lettres Dijon (France), Centre de recherches et d'études préromanes et romanes. Home: 5 Geddes Hts Ann Arbor MI 48104-1724 Office: U Mich Dept Art History Ann Arbor MI 48109

FORSYTHE, ROBERT ELLIOTT, economics educator; b. Pitts., Oct. 25, 1949; s. Robert Elliott and Dolores Jean (Davis) F.; m. Lynn Maureen Zollweg, June 17, 1970 (div. June 1978); m. Patricia Ann Hays, June 20, 1981; 1 child, Nathaniel Ryan. BS, Pa. State U., 1970; MS, Carnegie-Mellon U., Pitts., 1972, MS, 1974, PhD, 1975. Ops. rsch. analyst PPG Industries Inc., Pitts., 1970-72; instr. Carnegie-Mellon U., 1974-75; asst. prof. Calif. Inst. Tech., Pasadena, 1975-81; assoc. prof. U. Iowa, Iowa City, 1981-86, prof. econ., 1986-90, chmn. dept. econ., 1990-94, sr. assoc. dean Coll. Bus., 1994—, Cedar Rapids Area Bus. Chair, 1992-2000, Leonard A. Hadley Chair in Leadership, 2000—. Founder Iowa Polit. Stock Market; pres. Iowa Market Systems, Inc., 1993-2000. Author: Forecasting Presidential Elections: Polls, Markets, Models; assoc. editor Jour. Econ. Behavior and Orgn., Jour. Exptl. Econs., 1997—. Univ. faculty scholar U. Iowa, 1985-88. Mem. Econometric Soc., Am. Econ. Assn., Econ. Sci. Assn. (sect. head 1989-92, pres.-elect 1992-93, pres. 1993-95). Congregationalist. Home: 1806 E Court St Iowa City IA 52245-4643 Office: U Iowa Tippie Coll Bus 108 Pappajohn Bus Bldg Iowa City IA 52242-1000 E-mail: robert-forsythe@uiowa.edu.

FORT, JEFFREY C. lawyer; b. Burlington, Iowa, Oct. 10, 1950; s. Lyman R. and Lucille (Gibb) F.; m. Diane Locandro; children: Christopher Glen, Elizabeth Anne. BA, Monmouth, 1972; JD, Northwestern U., 1975. Bar: Ill. 1975, U.S. Dist. Ct. (no. dist.) Ill. 1976, U.S. Ct. Appeals (7th cir.) 1977, U.S. Ct. Appeals (D.C. cir.) 1985, U.S. Supreme Ct. 1980. Law clk. to John M. Karns, Jr. Appellate Ct., Belleville, Ill., 1975-76; assoc. Martin Craig Chester, et al, Chgo., 1976-83, ptnr., 1983-88, Gardner Carton & Douglas, Chgo., 1988-90, Sonnenschein Nath & Rosenthal, Chgo., 1990—. Adj. prof. Northwestern U. Sch. Law, Chgo., 1990-92; presenter in field. Author: Establishing an Effective Environmental Law Compliance Program, 1993—; editl. bd. Environmental Law for the Transactional Lawyer, 1991, rev. edit., 1994, 2001, Illinois Environmental Law, 1993, 2000; contbr. articles to profl. jours. Chair Lake Mich. States sect. Air and Waste Mgmt. Assn., Chgo., 1988-89; elder 1st Presbyn. Ch. Wilmette, Ill., 1990-93, 2001—. Mem. ABA, Chgo. Bar Assn. (chair environ. law com. 1987-88), Met. Club. Office: Sonnenschein Nath & Rosenthal 8000 Sears Tower Chicago IL 60606

FORTIER, MARDELLE LADONNA, English educator; b. Brookings, S.D., Sept. 15, 1947; d. Leon Doneval and Edna Pearl (Rosenstock) Eide; m. Robert Frederic Fortier, July 27, 1974. BA, U. Minn., 1970; MA, U. Ill., 1971, PhD, 1978. Instr. Berlitz, Hinsdale, Ill., 1983-84, North Ctrl. Coll., Naperville, 1985; sr. lectr. Loyola U., Chgo., 1984-95; instr. Coll. DuPage, Glen Ellyn, Ill., 1985—; English instr. Benedictine U., Lisle, 1985, 95—. Cons. in field. Author: The Utopian Thought of St. Thomas More, 1994; author numerous poems. Mem. Ill. State Poetry Soc., Poets and Patrons, Inc. (1st prize 1992, 2d prize 1995), Poets Club Chgo. Roman Catholic. Avocations: music, travel. Home: 5515 E Lake Dr Apt A Lisle IL 60532-2664

FORTUNA, WILLIAM FRANK, architectural engineer, architect; b. Paris, Apr. 3, 1948; s. William F. Sr. and Mary O. (Komatz) F. BArch, U. Ill., 1972, MS in Archtl. Engring., 1973. Lic. arch., Ill., Wis., Iowa, lic. structural engr., Ill., lic. profl. engr., Wis., lic. archtl. engr. specializing in crisis mgmt., Nat. Coun. Examiners for Engring. and Surveying, Nat. Coun. Archtl. Registration Bds. Designer Unteed Assocs. Ltd., Champaign, Ill., 1973-76; structural engr. Consoer Townsend, Chgo., 1976-79, Schmidt, Garden & Erikson, Chgo., 1979-83; sr. project structural engr. Skidmore Owings & Merrill, 1983-87; pres. W.F. Fortuna Ltd., Archtl. Engring., Highland Park, 1987—. Project engr. World Trade Ctr., Cairo; structural engr. exhbn. ctr. McCormick Place Annex, Chgo., United Airlines terminal O'Hare Airport, Bishop's Gate, London; contract adminstr. One and Two Prudential Plaza, Chgo. (SEAOI Best Structure award and tallest concrete bldg. in the world). Active mem. Illinois Emergency Mgmt. Agency. Mem. AIA, NCARB, Structural Engrs. Assn. Ill., Nat. Coun. Examiners for Engring. and Surveying, Am. Concrete Inst., Am. Inst. Steel Constrn., Chgo. Hist. Soc., Nat. Trust His. Preservation. Home: WF Fortuna Ltd Archtl Engr 1420 Ridge Rd Highland Park IL 60035-2734 Office: Two Prudential Plz Chicago IL 60601 E-mail: bill42na@aol.com.

FOSS, JOHN FRANK, mechanical engineering educator; b. Washington, Mar. 24, 1938; s. Maurice Felker and C. Catharine (Reynard) F.; m. Jacqueline Kay Voss, July 24, 1960; children: Judith Kathleen, Janette Diane. Student, Wilmington Coll., 1956-58; B.S., Purdue U., 1961, M.S., 1962, Ph.D., 1965. Mem. faculty Mich. State U., East Lansing, 1964—, asso. prof. mech. engring., 1968-75, prof., 1975—. Dir. fluid dynamics & hydraulics program NSF, 1998-2000; cons. McDonnel Douglas Helicopter Co., Ford Motor Co., Bd. Water and Light, Lansing, Tranter Corp., United Techs. Rsch. Ctr., East Hartford, Conn. Author: (with M.C. Potter) Fluid Mechanics, 1975. Mem. Oaks Recreation Program staff, 1976-78; moderator Edgewood United Ch., 1975-77. Sloan fellow John Hopkins U., Balt., 1970-71; Alexander von Humboldt fellow U. Karlsruhe, Fed. Republic Germany, 1978-79, U. Erlangen, Fed. Republic Germany, 1985-86, rsch. fellow U. Melbourne, Australia, 1995. Fellow ASME; mem. AIAA, AAAS, AAUP, Am. Soc. Engring. Edn., Am. Phys. Soc., Soc. Scholars Johns Hopkins U., Sigma Xi, Tau Beta Pi, Pi Tau Sigma. Mem. United Ch. of Christ. Home: 2353 Sapphire Lane East Lansing MI 48823 Office: Mich State U Dept Mech Engring East Lansing MI 48824 E-mail: foss@egr.msu.edn.

FOSS, RICHARD JOHN, bishop; b. Wauwatosa, Wis., Dec. 27, 1944; s. Harlan Funston and Beatrice Naomi (Lindaas) F.; m. Nancy Elizabeth Martin, June 21, 1969; children: Susan, Naomi Foss Welsh, Elizabeth, Peter, Andrew. BA, St. Olaf Coll., 1966; MDiv, Luther Theol. Seminary, 1971; ThM, Luther N.W. Theol. Seminary, 1984. Ordained to ministry Luth. Ch., 1971. Pastor St. Andrews Ch. and Ch. of Christ the Redeemer, Mpls., 1971-77; assoc. pastor First Luth., Fargo, N.D., 1977-79; sr. pastor Prince of Peace Luth., Seattle, 1979-86, Trinity Luth., Moorhead, Minn., 1986-92; bishop Ea. N.D. Synod, Fargo, 1992—. Soloist F-M Opera Co., Fargo, 1979; coach St. James Girls' Basketball Team, Seattle, 1982-84; vol. Wash. State Patrol Crisis Chaplaincy, Seattle, 1983-86; bd. dirs. Discovery, Inc., Mpls., 1972-77, Highline Boys' and Girls' Club, Burien, Wash., 1980-81, Luth. Compass Ctr., Seattle, 1983-86, v.p., 1985-86; mem. Master Chorale, 1987-99; bd. regents Concordia Coll., 1993—; bd. dirs. Daily Bread, 1991-2000, Luth. Social Svcs. of N.D., 1992—, Oak Grove Luth. H.S., 1990—, Luth. Resources Network, 1994-97, Healthy Congregations Adv. Bd., 1997—, N.D. Conf. Chs., 1993—.United Way Cmty. Bd., 2001. Avocations: racquetball, golf, reading, travel, vocal performance. Home: 1510 2nd St S Moorhead MN 56560-4014 Office: Ea ND Synod 1703 32nd Ave S Fargo ND 58103-5936 E-mail: rick.foss@ecunet.org.

FOSSUM, ROBERT MERLE, mathematician, educator; b. Northfield, Minn., May 1, 1938; s. Inge Martin and Tina Otelia (Gaudland) F.; m. Cynthia Carol Foss, Jan. 30, 1960 (div. 1979); children: Karen Jean, Kristin Ann; m. Barbara Joel Mason, Aug. 4, 1979 (div. 1993); children: Jonathan Robert, Erik Anton; m. Robin Karyl Goodman, Aug. 10, 1997. BA, St. Olaf Coll., 1959; AM, U.Mich., 1961, PhD, 1965. Instr. U. Ill., Urbana, 1964-66, asst. prof., 1966-68, assoc. prof., 1968-72, prof. math., 1972—, chair Senate Coun., 2001—; affiliate Beckman Inst., 2000—. Lectr. Aarhus U., Denmark, 1971-73, Copenhagen U., Denmark, 1976-77; vis. prof. Université de Paris VI, 1978-79, Oslo U., 1968-69. Contbr. numerous articles to profl. jours. Recipient Disting. Alumni award Northfield H.S.; Fulbright grantee Oslos U., 1967-68. Fellow: AAAS; mem.: Det Kongelig Norske Videnskabers Selskab (elected natural scis. sect.), Inst. Algebraic Meditation (sec.), Am. Math. Soc. (assoc. sec. cen. sect. 1983—87, sec. 1989—99), Soc. for Indsl. and Applied Math., Internat. Assn. Math. Physics, IEEE, Assn. Computing Machinery, Sigma Xi, Phi Beta Kappa. Democrat. Lutheran. Club: Heimskringla (Urbana) Office: U Ill Dept Math 1409 W Green St Urbana IL 61801-2943 E-mail: r-fossum@uiuc.edu.

FOSTER, BILL I. state legislator; b. Piggot, AK, Dec. 23, 1946; m. Karen; i child, Karmen. City councilman Poplar Bluff, 1977-78, mayor pro tem, 1978-79, mayor, 1979-80; mem. Mo. Ho. of Reps. from 156th dist., Jefferson City, 1993-2000, Mo. Senate from 25th dist., Jefferson City, 2001—. Mem. appropriations-nat. and econ. resources com., budget com., labor com., retirement com., state parks, natural resources & mining com., workers compensation and employment security com. Republican.

FOSTER, JOE C., JR. lawyer; b. Lansing, Mich., Feb. 5, 1925; s. Joe C. and Grace E. (McComb) F.; m. Janet C. Shanks, July 6, 1946; children: Cathy Foster Young, Susan Foster Ambrose, Thomas, John, Amy Foster Trenz. Student, Wabash Coll., Ind., 1943-44; JD, U. Mich., 1949. Bar: Mich. 1949, Fla. 1986. Assoc. Fraser, Trebilcock, Davis & Foster, and predecessors, Lansing, Mich., 1949-53, ptnr. and shareholder, 1954-2000; shareholder Foster Zack & Lowe, P.C., 2001—. Co-author: Independent Probate Administration, 1980, 3d edit., 1995, Informal Estat Procs. in Mich., 2000. Trustee, sec. Renaud Found., Lansing, 1960-87; bd. dirs., sec. Abrams Found., Lansing, 1960—; bd. dirs., officer ACTEC Found., L.A., 1983-87, 98—; trustee Jr. League Endowment Found., Lansing, 1984-90; trustee, chmn. Sparrow Hosp., Lansing, 1970-84; trustee, pres. Okemos Bd. Edn., Mich., 1962-66; bd. dirs., pres. county unit Am. Cancer Soc., 1950-60; bd. dirs., pres. Community Nursing Bur., Lansing, 1956-57. Lt. USNR, 1943-46, PTO. Fellow Am. Coll. Trust and Estate Counsel (pres.

1985-86), Am. Coll. Tax Counsel, Am. Bar Found., Mich. Bar Found.; mem. ABA, Fla. Bar Assn., Mich. Bar Assn. (chmn. probate and estate planning sect. 1977-78), Internat. Acad. Estate and Trust Law (exec. coun. 1990-94), Joint Editl. Bd. for Uniform Probate Code 1991-2000, Rotary (bd. dirs. Lansing 1968-70), Phi Beta Kappa, Phi Gamma Delta. Avocations: sailing; running; tennis. Home: 1965 Yuma Trl Okemos MI 48864-2746 Office: Foster Zack and Lowe PC PO Box 27337 Lansing MI 48909-7337 E-mail: joe.foster@fosterzacklowe.com.

FOSTER, KENNARD P. magistrate judge; b. 1944; Student, Purdue U., 1962-64; BS, Ball State U., 1966; JD, Ind. U., 1970. Bar: Ind. Spl. agt. FBI, 1970-71; atty. Jones, Foster & Loveall, 1971-76; asst. U.S. Atty., 1976-86; magistrate judge U.S. Dist. Ct. (so. dist.) Ind., Indpls., 1986—. Mem. Fed. Bar Assn., Johnson County Bar Assn., Fed. Magistrate Judges Assn. Office: US Courthouse Rm 277 46 E Ohio St Indianapolis IN 46204-1903

FOSTER, MARK STEPHEN, lawyer; b. Edgerton, Mo., Feb. 6, 1948; s. George Elliott and Annabel Lee (Bradshaw) F.; m. Camille Pepper, June 27, 1970; children: Natalie Ashley, Stephanie Ann. BS, U. Mo., 1970; JD, Duke U., 1973. Bar: Mo. 1973, U.S. Ct. Mil. Appeals 1974, Hawaii 1975, U.S. Dist. Ct. Hawaii 1975, U.S. Dist. Ct. (we. dist.) Mo. 1977, U.S. Ct. Appeals (8th cir.) 1986, U.S. Supreme Ct. 1994. Assoc. Stinson, Mag & Fizzell, Kansas City, 1977-80, ptnr., 1980—, mng. ptnr., 1987-90, also bd. dirs., 1991—, chmn. bd. dirs., 1998—. Arbitration panelist Nat. Assn. Securities Dealers, N.Y.C., 1985—, Pvt. Adjudication Found., Durham, N.C., 1988—. Active Citizens Assn., Kansas City, 1982-92; pres. Spelman Med. Found., Smithville, Mo., 1984-88; bd. dirs. Alzheimers Assn. Metro. Kansas City, 1997—, 1st v.p., 1998, pres., 1999. Lt. comdr. USNR, ret. Mem. ABA, Hawaii Bar Assn., Mo. Bar Assn., Kansas City Met. Bar Assn., Am. Arbitration Assn. (panelist 1990—, large complex case adv. com. 1993—), Carriage Club (bd. dirs. 2000—, 2d v.p. 2001, 1st v.p. 2002), Lawyers Edn. Assistance Program (bd. dirs. 2000—), Masons. Home: 1035 W 65th St Kansas City MO 64113-1813 Office: Stinson Mag & Fizzell PC PO Box 419251 1201 Walnut St Ste 2800 Kansas City MO 64106-2117

FOSTER, MICHAEL, agricultural products supplier; CEO Moorman's Inc., Quincy, Ill. Office: Moormans Inc 1000 N 30th St Quincy IL 62301-3400

FOSTER, RICHARD, journalist; b. Chgo., Oct. 16, 1938; s. James Edward and Mary (Sebat) Foster; m. Susanne Elisabeth Hill, Sept. 28, 1996; children: Katherine Elisabeth, Arthur Edward. B.A., Lawrence Coll., 1963. Reporter City News Bur., Chgo., 1963-64; reporter Chgo. Sun-Times, 1964-72, editorial writer, mem. editorial bd., 1972-78; editorial writer Des Moines Register & Tribune, 1978-82, Milw. Journal Sentinel, 1983—. Journalist-in-residence Colo. State U., spring 1982 Served with AUS, 1958-61. Recipient 1st place award, UPI, 1984, Inter-Am. Press Assn. award, 1988, 1st award (Group A), Wis. Newspaper Assn., 2000; fellow NEH Profl. Journalism, Stanford U., 1976—77. Mem. Nat. Conf. Editorial Writers, Nat. Press Club. Home: 4645 N Murray Ave Whitefish Bay WI 53211-1259 Office: 333 W State St Milwaukee WI 53203-1305 E-mail: rFoster@onwis.com.

FOSTER, SCARLETT LEE, investor relations executive; b. Charleston, W.Va., Dec. 14, 1956; d. William Christoph Foster, Jr. and Anne (Howes) Conway. B in Comm., Bethany Coll., 1979; MBA, Washington, 2000. Dir. pub. rels. Allergy Rehab. Found., Charleston, 1979-80; dir. pubs. Contractors Assn. W.Va., 1980-82; comm. rep. Monsanto Co., Nitro, W.Va., 1982-84, 1984-87, mgr. environ. and community rels. St. Louis, 1987-89, mgr. pub. rels., 1989-91, mgr. fin. pub. rels., 1991-93, dir. pub. rels., 1993-94, dir. pub. affairs, 1994-2001, dir. investor rels., 2001—. Trustee Bethany (W.Va.) Coll., 1994—. Named Outstanding Alumni of Achievement Bethany Coll., 1990. Mem. Nat. Investor Rels. Inst. Episcopalian. Avocations: biking, reading, cooking, gardening. Office: Monsanto Co A2SP 800 N Lindbergh Blvd # A2sp Saint Louis MO 63167-0001 E-mail: scarlett.l.foster@monsanto.com.

FOSTER, TEREE E. law educator, dean; BA in English Lit., U. Ill., Chgo., 1968; JD, Loyola U., Chgo., 1976. Bar: Ill. 1976, U.S. Dist. Ct. (no. dist.) Ill. 1976, U.S. Dist. Ct. (we. dist.) Okla. 1976, U.S. Ct. Appeals 7th and 10th cirs.) 1983, Okla. 1984. Admissions officer U. Ill., Chgo., 1968-69; co-dir. Dept. Def., Hanau, Germany, 1969-72; intern Office of State Appellate Defender, Springfield, Ill., 1974; law clk. Philip H. Corboy and Assocs., Chgo., 1974-76; instr., teaching asst. Loyola U., 1975-77; jud. law clk. U.S Ct. Appeals, 1976-77; of counsel Hastie & Kirschner, Oklahoma City, 1984-90; from asst. prof. to assoc. prof. U. Okla., Norman, 1980-83, prof., 1983-93, assoc. dean, 1990-92; dean, prof. law U. W.Va., Morgantown, 1993-97, mem. bd. advisors, 1994-96, facilitator social justic common ground forum, 1994-97; dean, prof. law DePaul U., Chgo., 1997—. Vis. prof. U. Denver, 1992-93, U. Fla., 1988-89, Ohio State U., 1987-88; mem. Chgo. com. Chgo. Coun. on Fgn. Rels., 1997—; mem. Chgo. Lawyers Com. for Civil Rights under Law, 1997—. Contbr. articles to profl. jours. Host Perspectives, 1986-87, The Law in Your Life, 1995-97, Legal Lines, 1996-97; co-host Encounter, 1983-85; gov. bd. W.Va. Rape and Domestic Violence Info. Ctr., 1993-97, W.Va. Women's Alliance, 1993-97, Okla. Com. Prevention Child Abuse, 1990-93; instr. Rite Christian Initiation Adults St. Thomas More U., 1983-87; exec. com. Southwest Ctr. Human Rels. Studies, 1983-86, directorship search com., 1984-85; task force Quality of Okla. Life, 1983-84; mem. Chgo. com. Chgo. Coun. on Fgn. Rels., 1997—; mem. Chgo. Com. for Civil Rights Under Law, 1997—. Mem. ABA, Ill. Bar Assn., Soc. Am. Law Tchrs., Assn. Am. Law Schs., Am. Judicature Soc. Home: 851 W Roscoe St Chicago IL 60657-2303 Office: DePaul U Office of Dean College of Law 25 E Jackson Blvd Chicago IL 60604-2289

FOTA, FRANK GEORGE, artist; b. Northampton, Pa., Feb. 20, 1921; s. Frank Michael and Elizabeth Rose (Simko)F.; m. Christine June Ringwald, Oct. 18, 1947. Student, Chgo. Acad. of Fine Art, 1951-53. Artist Studio Maintained in Residence, S. Holland, Ill.; comml. artist, designer Triangle Outdoor Advt. Co., Chgo., 1956-61, Gen. Outdoor Advt. Co., Chgo., 1961-63; art dir. Triangle Outdoor Advt. Co., 1963-83. Artist: (paintings) The Juniper Tree, 1971, Moab, Utah, 1974, Give Us This Day, Crete, Ill., 1972; exhibits include Wally Findlay Gallery, Chgo., 1953, 54, 55, Richard H. Love Gallery, Steger, Ill., Olympia Fields, Ill., Chgo., 1973, 74, 75, others. Mem., photographer Dolton (Ill.) Civic Assn., 1983-85 Roman Catholic. Clubs: Veteran of Foreign Wars, Dolton, Ill. (Trustee), Am. Legion, Riverdale, Ill. (Photog.). Avocations: photography, music. Home: 16748 Clyde Ave South Holland IL 60473-2611

FOTI, STEVEN M. state legislator; b. Oconomowoc, Wis., Dec. 3, 1958; married; 3 children. Student, U. Wis., Whitewater, 1978-81. Real estate sales agt., Oconomowoc; aide to Rep. James Sensenbrenner U.S. Ho. of Reps., Washington; mem. from dist. 33 Wis. State Assembly, Madison, 1982-92, mem. from dist. 38, 1993—. Bd. dirs. Watertown Meml. Hosp.; mem. Oconomowoc C. of C. Mem. Jaycees, Lions, Elks, KC. Republican. Home: 1117 Dickens Dr Oconomowoc WI 53066-4316

FOTOPOULOS, DANIELLE, former soccer player; b. Camp Hill, Pa., Mar. 24, 1976; Student, U. Fla. Mem. U.S. Nat. Women's Soccer Team, 1996—. Recipient Southeastern Conf. Player of Yr. award 1996; appeared twice in Faces in the Crowd, Sports Illustrated. Office: US Soccer Fedn 1801-1811 S Prairie Ave Chicago IL 60616

FOUDREE, BRUCE WILLIAM, lawyer; b. Des Moines, Mar. 27, 1947; s. Shie Wilbur and Dorothy Mable (Lynde) F.; m. Suzanne Joan Floss Reade, May 31, 1986; children: Andrew A., Grant R. BA, Drake U., 1969; student, U. Geneva, Switzerland, 1968, U. Vienna, Austria, 1968; JD, Drake U., 1972; LLM, U. Pa., 1975. Bar: Iowa 1972, U.S. Ct. Appeals (8th cir.) 1976, U.S. Supreme Ct. 1977, Ill. 1986. Asst. atty. gen. Iowa Dept. Justice, Des Moines, 1976-80; ins. commnr. Iowa Ins. Dept., 1980-86; of counsel Mitchell, Williams, Selig and Tucker, Little Rock, 1986-88; shareholder Keck, Mahin & Cate, Chgo., 1988-96; of counsel Lord, Bissell & Brook, 1996—. Commr., chmn. Iowa Ins. Dept., 1980-86; commr. Iowa Health Data Commn., 1983-86, chmn. 1985. Assoc. editor Drake Law Rev., 1971-72; dir. Jour. Ins. Regulation, 1982-89. Mem. ABA (TIPS scope and correlation com. 1991-94, chmn. fin. svcs. com. 1990-91, professionalism com. 1994-96), Nat. Assn. Ins. Commrs. (chmn. 1984, pres. 1985), Ins. Regulatory Examiners Soc. Found. (bd. dirs. 1991—, chmn. 1999-2000), Iowa State Bar Assn., Union League Club of Chgo. (chmn. ins. group 1989-92), The Chicago Lighthouse (bd. dirs. 1995—, sec. 1998). Avocations: travel, history, literature, music. Office: Lord Bissell & Brook 115 S La Salle St Fl 3600 Chicago IL 60603-3902 E-mail: bfoudree@lordbissell.com.

FOUDY, JULIA MAURINE, soccer player; b. San Diego, Jan. 23, 1971; m. Ian Sawyers, July 1995. BSW in Biology, Stanford U., 1993. Mem. U.S. Women's Nat. Soccer Team. Color commentator Men's World Cup, ESPN, 1998. Mem. Tyresco Football Club, Sweden, 1994. Appeared on cover Women's Soccer World mag., 1997; recipient Gold medal Centennial Olympic Games, 1996; mem. championship team World Championships, Sweden, 1995, CONCACAF, Montreal, 1994. Office: c/o US Soccer Fedn 1801 S Prairie Ave # 1811 Chicago IL 60616-1319

FOULSTON, NOLA TEDESCO, lawyer; b. Mt. Vernon, N.Y., Dec. 14, 1940; d. Dominick J. and Theresa M. (Pellino) Tedesco; m. Steven L. Foulston, Jan. 2, 1983; 1 child, Andrew. BA, Ft. Hays State U., 1972; postgrad., U. Kans., 1972-73; JD, Washburn U., 1976. Bar: Kans. 1977, U.S. Dist. Ct. Kans., U.S. Ct. Appeals (10th cir.). Asst. dist. atty. 18th Jud. Dist., Dist. Atty.'s Office, Wichita, Kans., 1977-81; assoc. Foulston, Siefkin, Powers & Eberhardt, 1981-86; ptnr. Foulston & Foulston, 1986-89; dist. atty. Office of Dist. Atty. Eighteenth Jud. Dist. Sedgwick County Courthouse, 1989—. Bd. dirs., legal counsel YWCA, Wichita, 1978-83, pres. 1980-81; active YWCA's Women's Crisis Ctr., Wichtia Area Sexual Assault Ctr.; bd. dirs. Exploited and Missing Children's Unit, Project Freedom, Community Corrections, County-Wide Substance Abuse Task Force, State of Kans. Law Enforcement Coordinating Com., Community Rels. Task Force, Inter-Agy. Truancy Adv. Com., Women's Rsch. Inst., Crime Stoppers of Wichita Adv. Bd.; apptd. by Gov. Hayden of Kans. to the Weigand Commn. on State Expenditures. Named one of Outstanding Young Women of Am., Outstanding Young Wichitan, Wichita Jaycees, 1990; recipient Alumni Achievement award Ft. Hays State U., 1992, Law Enforcement Commendation medal SAR, 1992. Mem. ABA, Kans. Bar Assn., Wichita Bar Assn. (Outstanding Atty. of Achievement 1992), Nat. County and Dist. Attys. Assn., Kansas County and Dist. Attys. Assn., Golden Key (hon.). Democrat. Roman Catholic. Office: 535 N Main Wichita KS 67203-3702

FOUNTAIN, RONALD GLENN, management consultant, finance/marketing executive, finance educator; b. Mason City, Wash., Feb. 12, 1939; s. Aldine Shirah and Ella Maude (Fordham) F.; m. Ethel Joan Hightower, Aug. 22, 1968; children: John Hightower, Dana Leigh. AS, Ga. Southwestern Coll., 1959; BS, Valdosta State U., 1965; MBA, Case Western Res. U., 1983, ExecDrMgmt, 1999. V.p. nat. accounts Ctrl. Bancshares, Birmingham, Ala., 1973-74; cash control mgr. White Consol., Cleve., 1974-76, asst. treas., 1976-79, treas., dir. investor rels., 1979-82, v.p., treas., 1982-83, v.p. fin., treas., 1983-86; pres. Dix & Eaton, 1986-88; v.p. fin., CFO M.A. Hanna Co., Cleve., 1988-93; mng. prin. The Commonwealth Group, 1993-04; sr. exec. v.p. Roulston & Co., 1994-96; adv. dir. InfoSource, Harris Co., 1995-98; ptnr. The Parkland Group, 1996—; pres., CEO United Truck Fin. & Mktg., 1998—2001. Adj. faculty Weatherhead Sch. Mgmt., exec. dir. profl. fellow program, 2000—; bd. dirs. Epilogue Coun. Issues Mgmt.; bd. dirs. Dise & Co., Delta Sys. Inc. Trustee Notre Dame Coll., Cleve., 1984-90, Laurel Sch., 1986-90, Pub. Radio Sta. WCPN, 1990-93, MetroHealth Sys., Ctr. Families and Children; chmn. N.E. Hospice Study Com., 1989-93; bd. dirs. Jr. Achievement Cleve., 1982, Nat. Adoption Exch., Phila., 1983, Cleve. Edn. Fund, 1983-87. Mem.: Planning Forum (pres. 1992—94), Nat. Investor Rels. Inst. 1978—79, Assn. Corp. Growth, Fin. Execs. Inst. (membership chmn. 1983—84), Alumni Assn. Weatherhead Sch. Mgmt. (pres. 1985—88), Country Club, Union Club, Rowfant Club. Home: 2908 Paxton Rd Cleveland OH 44120-1824

FOURER, ROBERT HAROLD, industrial engineering educator, consultant; b. Phila., Sept. 2, 1950; s. Herbert S. and Priscilla (Silver) F. BS in Math., MIT, 1972; MS in Ops. Rsch., MS in Stats., Stanford U., 1979, PhD in Ops. Rsch., 1980. Rsch. analyst Nat. Bur. Econ. Rsch., Cambridge, Mass., 1974-77; asst. prof. dept. indsl. engring. and mgmt. scis. Northwestern U., Evanston, Ill., 1979-85, assoc. prof., 1985-93, dept. chair, 1989-95, prof., 1993—. Vis. mem. tech. staff AT&T Bell Labs., Murray Hill, N.J., 1985-86, 95-96; cons. AT&T, Exxon, Goldman Sachs & Co., Keebler Co., Kraft Foods, Sears Roebuck & Co. Co-author: AMPL: A Modeling Language for Mathematical Programming, 1993; assoc. editor Mgmt. Sci., 1983—, Ops. Rsch., 1986—; contbr. articles to profl. jours. Grantee NSF; recipient Computer Sci. Tech. Sect. prize, Ops. Rsch. Soc. Am., 1993. Mem. Inst. Indsl. Engrs., Soc. Indsl. and Applied Math, Inst. Ops. Rsch. and Mgmt. Scis. (chair Computer Sci. Tech. sect., 1996-97), Math. Programming Soc. (mem.-at-large, coun. 1994-97). Achievements include AMPL modeling lang. Office: Northwestern Univ Dept Ind Eng and Mgmt Scis 2145 Sheridan Rd Evanston IL 60208-3119 E-mail: 4er@iems.northwestern.edu.

FOURNELLE, RAYMOND ALBERT, engineering educator; b. St. Louis, Dec. 9, 1941; s. August Carl and Adella Emma (Fleer) F. BS in Metall. Engring., U. Mo., 1964, MS in Metall. Engring., 1968, PhD in Metall. Engring., 1971. Registered profl. engr., Wis. Rsch. engr. Shell Oil Co., Wood River, Ill., 1964-66; rsch. assoc. Northwestern U., Evanston, 1971-72; asst. prof. Marquette U., Milw., 1972-78, assoc. prof., 1978-86, prof., 1986—; interim chairperson Dept. of Mech. and Indsl. Engring., 1998—2001. Contbr. articles to profl. jours. 1st lt. U.S. Army, 1964-66, Fed. Republic Germany. Rsch. grantee NSF, 1975, 79, 86; Fulbright fellow U. Stuttgart (Germany), 1983-84, 90-91, Alexander von Humboldt fellow, 1985-88, Mac-Planck-Forschungspreis, 1994, ASM Internat. fellow, 1996. Mem. ASME, ASTM, AAUP, ASM Internat. (bd. rev. 1981—), Minerals, Metals and Materials Soc. (com. mem.), Am. Ceramic Soc., Am. Soc. Engring. Edn. Achievements include development of theories and models for various solid state reactions in metals and alloys, including discontinuous precipitation, coarsening, and dissolution, diffusion induced grain boundary and liquid film migration. Home: 1129 N Jackson St Apt 1207 Milwaukee WI 53202-3290 Office: Marquette U Dept Mech/Indsl Engring PO Box 1881 Milwaukee WI 53201-1881 E-mail: raymond.fournelle@marquette.edu.

FOURNIE, RAYMOND RICHARD, lawyer; b. Belleville, Ill., Jan. 3, 1951; s. Raymond Victor and Gladys M. (Muskopf) F.; m. Mary Lindeman, Sept. 2, 1978; children: Sarah Dozier, John David, Anne Gerard, David Raymond. BS, U. Ill., 1973; JD, St. Louis U., 1979. Bar: Mo. 1979, Ill. 1980. Assoc. Moser, Marsalek, et al., St. Louis, 1979-80, Brown, James & Rabbitt, P.C., St. Louis, 1981-82, Shepherd, Sandberg & Phoenix, P.C., St. Louis, 1982-86; shareholder Shepherd, Sandberg & Phoenix, 1986-88; ptnr. Armstrong Teasdale LLP, 1988—. U. Ill. fellow, 1974. Mem. Mo. Bar Assn., Ill. Bar Assn., St. Louis Bar Assn. (sec. trial sect.), Lawyers Assn. (v.p. 1987-88, pres. 1990-91), Actors Equity Assn. Roman Catholic. Avocations: professional singer and actor, baseball, golf. Home: 4 Ridgetop St Saint Louis MO 63117-1021 Office: Armstrong Teasdale LLP One Metropolitan Sq Ste 2600 Saint Louis MO 63102-2740

FOUST, CHARLES WILLIAM, judge; b. Bethlehem, Pa., May 27, 1952; s. Alan Shivers and Helen Elizabeth (Aigler) F.; m. Melissa A. Cherney, July 31, 1982; children: Kyle Cherney, James Terrell. BA, U. Wis., 1974, JD, 1978. Bar: Wis. Bar, U.S. Dist. Ct. (we. dist.) Wis. 1978. Asst. dist. atty. Dane County Dist. Atty.'s Office, Madison, 1979-82; asst. pub. defender State Pub. Defender's Office, Milw., 1982-83; assoc. Smoler & Albert SC, Madison, 1983-88; dist. atty. Dane County, 1988-97; judge Dane County Circuit Ct., 1997—, presiding judge criminal divsn., 2001—. Mem. govs. adv. bd., Dane County adv. bd. Treatment Alternatives Program; chair coordinated commun. response task force on domestic violence Dane County Commn. on Sensitive Crimes; mem. Dane County Jail/Space Needs, Dane County Long Range Jud. Planning; mem. Dane County Jury Selection, Wis. Jud. Coun. Commn. on Criminal Procedure; mem. Wis. Working Group on Sentencing and Corrections. Mem. State Bar Wis., Dane County Bar Assn. (bd. dirs. criminal law sect. 1985-89, chmn. 1985-89), Wis. Dist. Attys. Assn. (exec. bd., 1st v.p., com. on DNA evidence, dir. state cts. criminal benchbook com. 2000—). Home: 2105 Madison St Madison WI 53711-2131 Office: Dane County Circuit Ct Br 14 210 Martin Luther King Jr Blvd Madison WI 53703 E-mail: william.foust@dane.courts.state.wi.us.

FOWLER, BARBARA HUGHES, classics educator; b. Lake Forest, Ill., Aug. 23, 1926; d. Fay Orville and Clara (Reber) Hughes; m. Alexander Murray Fowler, July 14, 1956; children: Jane Alexandra, Emily Hughes. BA, U. Wis., 1949; MA, Bryn Mawr Coll., 1950, PhD, 1955. Instr. classics Middlebury (Vt.) Coll., 1954-56; asst. prof. Latin Edgewood Coll., Madison, Wis., 1961-63; mem. faculty U. Wis., 1963—, prof. classics, 1976—, John Bascom prof., 1980—, prof. emeritus, 1991—. Author: The Hellenistic Aesthetic, 1989, The Seeds Inside a Green Pepper, 1989, Hellenistic Poetry, 1990, Archaic Greek Poetry, 1992, Love Lyrics of Ancient Egypt, 1994, Songs of a Friend, 1996, Vergil's Eclogues, 1997; also articles. Fulbright scholar Greece, 1951-52; Fanny Bullock Workman travelling fellow, 1951-52 Mem. Am. Philol. Assn., Archaeol. Inst. Am. Office: U Wis 910 Van Hise Hall Madison WI 53706 Home: N8194 Springer Rd Lake Mills WI 53551-9634

FOWLER, CHUCK, state legislator; b. Dec. 21, 1939; m. Debra Fowler; 2 children. Grad. H.S. Product mgr. 3M Co.; mem. Minn. State Senate, 2000—, vice chair taxes com., mem. edn. com., mem. agr., gen. legislation and vets. affairs com., mem. higher edn. budget divsn. com., mem. income and sales tax budget divsn. com., state and local govt. ops. com. Home: 710 N State St Fairmont MN 56031 Office: 710 N State St Fairmont MN 56031-3851 also: G-9 Capitol 75 Constitution Ave Saint Paul MN 55155-1206 E-mail: sen.chuck.fowler@senate.leg.state.mn.us.

FOWLER, JOHN, printing company executive; CFO, v.p. fin. Quad/Graphics, Hartford, Wis. Office: Quad/Graphics 1900 W Sumner St Hartford WI 53027

FOWLER, NOBLE OWEN, physician, university administrator; b. Vicksburg, Miss., July 14, 1919; s. Noble Owen and Annie Lou (Robertson) F.; m. Charlotte Ruth Walters, June 13, 1942; children: Joann, Michael, Anne Stewart. Student, Memphis State U., 1936-38; MD, U. Tenn., 1941. Diplomate Am. Bd. Internal Medicine (examining bd. 1970-72, cardiovascular subspecialty examining bd. 1966-72, chmn. cardiovascular subspecialty bd. 1970-72). Intern Cin. Gen. Hosp., 1942-43, resident in internal medicine, 1945, 47-48, fellow in cardiology, 1948-52; resident in internal medicine Peter Bent Brigham Hosp., Boston, 1946; instr. U. Cin., 1950-51, asst. prof. medicine, 1951-52, assoc. prof., 1957-64, prof., 1964—, prof. pharmacology and cell biophysics, 1980-84, prof. emeritus, 1984—, assoc. dir. dept. medicine, 1970-79, dir. divsn. cardiology, 1970-86. Asst. prof. SUNY, 1952-54; chmn. cardiovascular research Emory U., 1954-57; mem. adv. com. on cardiovascular and renal drugs FDA, 1970-78, chmn., 1974-78; sci. adv. com. Nat. Inst. Aging, NIH, Balt., 1983-86. Author: Cardiac Diagnosis and Treatment, 3d edit., 1980, Myocardial Diseases, 1973, Cardiac Arrhythmias; Diagnosis and Treatment, 1977, Pericardium in Health and Disease, 1985, Diagnosis of Heart Disease, 1991, Diagnosis in Color: Physical Signs in Cardiology, 1998, Clinical Electrocardiographic Diagnosis, 2000. Capt. M.C., AUS, 1943-44. Recipient award for contbns. to cardiology Georgetown U., 1978; Nat. Heart and Lung Inst. grant, 1961-73. Fellow ACP, Am. Coll. Cardiology (Master Tchr. award 1974), Am. Heart Assn. Coun. on Clin. Cardiology; mem. Am. Clin. and Climatol. Assn., Am. Physiol. Soc., Cttrl. Soc. Clin. Rsch., Am. Fedn. Clin. Rsch., Assn. Univ. Cardiologists (founding mem., pres. 1976), Am. Heart Assn. (local chpt. trustee, exec. com., pres. 1979—, Samuel Kaplan Rsch. award 1994, Spl. Recognition award Laennec Soc. 1994), U. Tenn. Coll. Medicine (Disting. Alumnus award 1992), Sigma Xi, Alpha Omega Alpha, Phi Chi. Presbyterian. Home: 3533 Deepwoods Ln Cincinnati OH 45208-2530 E-mail: nfowler@spspnet.

FOWLER, ROBERT EDWARD, JR. former agricultural products company executive; b. Camden, Tenn., Oct. 7, 1935; s. Robert Edward and Rebecca (Watson) F.; m. Margaret Caroline Armstrong, Dec. 28, 1957; children: Robert, William, Margaret B.Engring., Vanderbilt U., 1957. With GE, Louisville, 1957-78, v.p., 1978-81; pres., COO, Rubbermaid, Inc., Wooster, Ohio, 1981-87, bd. dirs., 1981-87; chmn., CEO, pres. Josephson Office Products, Chgo., 1987-90; pres., CEO, BCC Indsl. Svcs., 1991-93; pres., COO, The Vigaro Corp., 1993-94, pres., CEO, 1994-96; pres., COO, IMC Global (merged with The Vigoro Corp. 1996), Northbrook, Ill., 1996-97; CEO, pres., chmn. IMC Global, 1997-99. Bd. dirs. Alltrista Corp., Anixter Internat. Mem. Chgo. Christian Indsl. League (bd. dirs.) Office: IMC Global 100 Saunders Rd # 300 Lake Forest IL 60045-2561

FOX, CARL ALAN, research executive; b. Waukesha, Wis., Nov. 24, 1950; s. Frank Edwin and Margaret Alvilda (Rasmussen) F.; m. Susan Jane Smith, June 18, 1977; children: Thomas Gordon, James David, Joseph Carl. BS, U. Wis., River Falls, 1973; MS, U. Minn., 1975; PhD, Ariz. State U., 1980; postgrad., Stanford U., 1993. Lab. asst. dept. biology U. Wis., River Falls, 1971-73; rsch. asst. dept. agronomy and plant genetics U. Minn., St. Paul, 1973-75; tchr. high sch. Le Center (Minn.) Pub. Schs., 1975-76; rsch. fellow dept. botany Ariz. State U., Tempe, 1976-79; rsch. asst. Lab. Tree-Ring Rsch. U. Ariz., Tucson, 1978-79; rsch. scientist, then sr. rsch. scientist So. Calif. Edison Co., Rosemead, 1979-87; rsch. assoc. agrl. experiment sta. U. Calif., Riverside, 1986-87; exec. dir. Desert Rsch. Inst., Reno, 1987-96, assoc. v.p. rsch., 1994-95; dir. Office of Rsch. and Program Devel. U. N.D., Grand Forks, 1996—, assoc. dean grad. sch., rsch. prof. dept. tchg. and learning and biology, interim dean grad. sch., 2000—. Rsch. adviser Electric Power Rsch. Inst., Palo Alto, Calif., 1983-87; liaison Utility Air Regulatory Group, Washington, 1983-87, cons., 1989-91; mem. peer rev. panel EPA, 1986, 97, 98, 99; invited reviewer air quality rsch. div. Nat. Park Svc., Denver, 1989; peer rev. panel Minn. Legis. Commn. on Resources, 1998. Contbr. numerous papers to profl. publs. Asst. troop leader Newport Beach (Calif.) area Boy Scouts Am., 1981-82, cub scout leader Reno area, 1990-91; bd. dirs. World Rainforest Found., Reno, 1989-92, Internat. Visitors Coun. No. Nev., Reno, 1991-96; coach YMCA, Reno, 1989-95, Grand Forks, N.D., 1996—; deacon Covenant Presbyn. Ch., 1989-92; judge State of Nev. Odyssey of the Mind. NSF fellow, 1976-79; grantee EPA, 1978-79, 83-85, 89-95, 99, NSF, 1987-95, 98—, Dept. of Def. and Energy, 1987. Mem. AAAS, Air

Pollution Control Assn., Ecol. Soc. Am., Am. Soc. Agronomy, Greentree Gators Swim Team (pres. 1986-87), N.D. Acad. of Scis., Nat. Coun. of Univ. Rsch. Adminstrs., Soc. of Rsch. Adminstrn., Sigma Xi, Beta Beta Beta. Republican. Presbyterian. Avocations: camping, canoeing, tennis, gardening, basketball. Office: U ND Office Rsch/Program Devel PO Box 7134 Grand Forks ND 58202-7134

FOX, DAVID ALAN, rheumatologist, immunologist; b. Montreal, July 5, 1953; s. Lester L. and Zelda L. (Rothbart) F.; m. Paula L. Bockenstedt, July 10, 1977; children: Sharon Elizabeth, Michelle Caroline, Jonathan William. BS, MIT, 1974; MD, Harvard U., 1978. Diplomate Am. Bd. Internal Medicine, Am. Bd. Rheumatology. Intern, then resident Brigham and Women's Hosp., Boston, 1978-81; fellow in rheumatology and immunology Harvard U. Med. Sch., 1981-85; asst. prof. U. Mich., Ann Arbor, 1985-90, assoc. prof., 1990-95, prof., 1995—, acting chief divsn. rheumatology, 1990-91, chief divsn., 1991—. Dir. U. Mich. Multipurpose Arthritis Ctr., Ann Arbor, 1990—2001, U. Mich. Rheumatic Disease Care Ctr., 2001—; trustee Arthritis Found., 1992—. Assoc. editor Jour. Clin. Investigation, 1997-2002; contbr. chpts. to books, articles to profl. jours. Mem.: Assn. Am. Physicians, Am. Soc. Clin. Investigation, Am. Assn. Immunologists, Am. Coll. Rheumatology. Achievements include discovery of T lymphocyte surface molecules and development of various monoclonal antibodies. Office: U MichMed Ctr Rackham Arthritis Rsch Unit 3918 Taubman Ctr Ann Arbor MI 48109

FOX, ELAINE SAPHIER, lawyer; b. Chgo., Nov. 18, 1934; d. Nathan Abraham and Rhoda M. (Schneidman) Saphier; m. Alan A. Fox, Apr. 25, 1954; children: Susan Fox Lorge, Wendy Fox Schneider, Mimi. BS, Northwestern U., 1955; JD, Ill. Inst. Tech., 1975. Bar: Ill., 1975, U.S. Dist. Ct. (no. dist.) Ill., 1975, U.S. Ct. Appeals (7th cir.) 1975, U.S. Ct. Appeals (fed. cir.) 1985. Trial atty. NLRB, Chgo., 1975-80; assoc. Hirsh & Schwartzman, 1980-81, Gottlieb & Schwartz, Chgo., 1981-84, ptnr., 1984-90, D'Ancona & Pflaum, Chgo., 1990—. Co-editor in chief How to Take a Case to the NLRB, 7th edit.; contbr. articles to profl. jours. and mags. Bd. dirs., exec. com. Am. Cancer Soc., Chgo., 1993—; mem. nat. and local governing coun. Am. Jewish Congress, Chgo., 1991—; bd. dirs. Jewish Vocat. Svc. Mem. ABA (subcom. NLRB practice and procedures, employment and labor rels. law, labor and employment law com., Women Rainmakers, midwest regional mgmt. chair NLRB practice and procedure com.), Women's Bar Assn., Chgo. Bar Assn. (labor and employment rels. vice chmn. 1989-90, chmn. 1990-91, co-chmn. Alliance for Women 1994-95, co-chair bd. mgrs. 1996-98), Decalogue Assn. Avocations: swimming, walking, reading, theater, art. Office: Dancona and Pflaum 11 E Wacker Dr Ste 2800 Chicago IL 60601-2101 E-mail: efox@dancona.com.

FOX, KARL AUGUST, economist, eco-behavioral scientist; b. Salt Lake City, July 14, 1917; s. Feramorz Young and Anna Teresa (Wilcken) F.; m. Sylvia Olive Cate, July 29, 1940; children: Karl Richard, Karen Frances Anne. BA, U. Utah, 1937, MA, 1938; PhD, U. Calif., 1954. Economist USDA, 1942-54; head divsn. statis. and hist. rsch. Bur. Agrl. Econs., 1951-54; economist Coun. Econ. Advisers, Washington, 1954-55; head dept. econs. and sociology Iowa State U., Ames, 1955-66, head dept. econs., 1966-72, disting. prof. scis. and humanities, 1968-87, prof. emeritus, 1987—. Vis. prof. Harvard, 1960-61, U. Calif., Santa Barbara, 1971-72, 78, vis. scholar, Berkeley, 1972-73; William Evans vis. prof. U. Otago, N.Z., 1981; Bd. dirs. Social Sci. Rsch. Coun., 1963-67, mem. com. econ. stability, 1963-66, chmn. com. areas for social and econ. statistics, 1964-67; mem. Com. Reg. Accounts, 1963-68 Author: Econometric Analysis for Public Policy, 1958, (with M. Ezekiel) Methods of Correlation and Regression Analysis, 1959, (with others) The Theory of Quantitative Economic Policy, 1966, rev. edit., 1973, Intermediate Economic Statistics, 1968, rev. edit, (with T.K. Kaul), 1980, (with J. K. Sengupta) Economic Analysis and Operations Research, 1969, (with W.C. Merrill) Introduction to Economic Statistics, 1970, Social Indicators and Social Theory, 1974, Social System Accounts, 1985, The Eco-Behavioral Approach To Surveys and Social Accounts for Rural Communities, 1990, repub., 1994, Demand Analysis, Econometrics and Policy Models, 1992, Urban-Regional Economics, Social System Accounts and Eco-Behavioral Science, 1994; author-editor: Economic Analysis for Educational Planning, 1972; co-editor: Readings in the Economics of Agriculture, 1969, Economic Models, Estimation and Risk Programming (essays in honor of Gerhard Tintner), 1969, Systems Economics, 1987; contbr. articles to profl. jours. Recipient superior service medal USDA, 1948, award for outstanding pub. research Am. Agrl. Econs. Assn., 1952, 54, 57, for outstanding doctoral dissertation, 1953 Fellow Econometric Soc., Am. Statis. Assn. (Census Research fellow 1980-81), Am. Agrl. Econs. Assn. (v.p. 1955-56, award for publ. of enduring quality 1977), AAAS; mem. Am. Econs. Assn. (research and publs. com. 1963-67), Regional Sci. Assn., Ops. Research Soc. Am., Am. Ednl. Research Assn., Phi Beta Kappa, Phi Kappa Phi. Home: 1801 20th St Apt J-31 Ames IA 50010-5166 Office: Iowa State U Econs Dept Ames IA 50011-0001 E-mail: fox328L@aol.com.

FOX, MICHAEL, former state legislator, underwriting consultant; b. Hamilton, Ohio, Dec. 15, 1948; m. Mary Ann Fox; children: Ryan, Ashley. BS in Edn. in Polit. Sci., Miami U., Oxford, Ohio, 1971. Asst. to sec. of agr. USDA, Washington, 1973; spl. asst. to Senator Robert Taft, Jr. of Ohio, U.S. Senate, 1973-74; mem. Ohio Ho. of Reps., Columbus, 1975-97; underwriting cons., Hamilton. Mem. Butler County Youth Svc. Bur. Named Legislator of Yr., Ohio Vocat. Edn. Assn., 1988; recipient leadership award Middletown Sch. Dist., 1989, President's award, Ohio. Mem. Butler County trustees Assn., Fraternal Order Police, Hamilton O'Tucks, Ky. Cols., Elks, Delta Tau Delta. Republican. Home: 6109 Creekside Way Hamilton OH 45011-7884

FOX, MICHAEL VASS, Hebrew educator; b. Detroit, Dec. 9, 1940; s. Leonard W. and Mildred (Vass) F.; m. Jane Schulzinger, Sept. 4, 1961; children: Joshua, Ariel BA, U. Mich., 1962, MA, 1963; PhD, Hebrew U., Jerusalem, 1972. Ordained rabbi, 1968. Lectr. Haifa U., Israel, 1971-74, Hebrew U., Jerusalem, 1975-77; prof. Hebrew U. Wis., Madison, 1977—, chmn. dept., 1982-88, 92-99, Weinstein-Bascom prof. in Jewish studies, 1990—, Halls-Bascom prof., 1999—. Fellow Am. Acad. Jewish Rsch., 2000—. Author: The Song of Songs and the Ancient Egyptian Love Songs, 1985, Shirey Dodim Mimitzrayim Ha'atiqa, 1985, Qohelet and his Contradictions, 1988, The Redaction of the Books of Esther, 1991, Character and Ideology in the Book of Esther, 1991, 2001; editor: A Time to Tear Down and a Time to Build Up: A Rereading of Ecclesiastes, 1999, Anchor Bible: Proverbs, vol. I, 2000; contbr. articles to profl. jours. Named Vilas assoc., 1988—90; recipient Wahrburg prize, Hebrew U., 1971—72, Kellett Mid-Career award, 1999, Leverhulme fellow, U. Liverpool, Eng., 1974—75; fellow, Brit. Friends of Hebrew U., Liverpool, 1974—75, NEH, 1992, Am. Coun. Learned Studies, 2001—. Mem. Soc. for Bibl. Lit. (editor SBL Dissertation Series 1994-99, editl. bd. Jour. Bibl. Lit. 1991-95; pres. midwest region 1998-2000), Nat. Assn. Profs. Hebrew (editor Hebrew Studies 1985-93, v.p. 2000—). Home: 2815 Chamberlain Ave Madison WI 53705-3607 Office: U Wis Dept Hebrew 1220 Linden Dr Rm 1338 Madison WI 53706-1525

FOX, PAUL T. lawyer; b. N.Y.C., Jan. 17, 1953; BA, Northwestern U., 1975, JD cum laude, 1978. Bar: Ill. 1978, U.S. Dist. Ct. (no. dist. trial bar) Ill. 1979, U.S. Ct. Appeals (7th cir.) 1979, U.S. Supreme Ct. 1986, U.S. Ct. Appeals (fed. cir.) 1987, Wis. 1989. Mng. shareholder Greenberg Traurig, Chgo. Faculty mem. Nat. Inst. for Trial Advocacy; adj. prof. Northwestern U. Sch. Law. Mem. ABA (mem. litigation sect.), State Bar Wis., Chgo. Bar Assn., Order of Coif. Office: Greenberg Traurig 77 W Wacker Drive Ste 2500 Chicago IL 60601

FOX, ROBERT WILLIAM, mechanical engineering educator; b. Montreal, Que., Can., July 1, 1934; s. Kenneth and Jessie (Glass) F.; m. Beryl Williams, Dec. 15, 1962; children— David, Lisa. B.S. in Mech. Engring, Rensselaer Poly. Inst., 1955; M.S., U. Colo., 1957; Ph.D., Stanford U., 1961. Instr. mech. engring. U. Colo., Boulder, 1955-57; research asst. Stanford (Calif.) U., 1957-60; mem. faculty Purdue U., Lafayette, Ind., 1960-99, assoc. prof., 1963-66, prof., 1966-99, asst. head mech. engring., 1971-72, asst. dean engring. for instrn., 1972-76; acting head Purdue U. (Sch. Mech. Engring.), 1975-76, asso. head, 1976-98, chmn. univ. senate, 1971-72, prof. emeritus, 1999. Cons. Owens-Corning Fiberglass Co., Edn. Services Inc., Nelson Mfg. Co., Peoria, Ill., B. Offen Co., Chgo., Agard Co., Johns-Marsville Co., Richmond, Ind., Babcox & Wilcox, Alliance, Ohio. Named Standard Oil Outstanding Tchr. Purdue U., 1967; recipient Harry L. Solberg Outstanding Tchr. award, 1978, 83, Donald E. Marlowe awd., Am. Soc. for Engineering Education, 1992. Fellow ASME, Am. Soc. for Engring. Edn.; mem. Sigma Xi, Pi Tau Sigma, Tau beta Pi, Delta Tau Delta. Home: 3627 Chancellor Way Lafayette IN 47906-8809 Office: Purdue U Sch Mech Engring Lafayette IN 47907

FOXWORTHY, JAMES C. manufacturing executive; BSBA, U. Tenn., 1973. Various Union Camp Corp., 1973-92; exec. v.p. pres. paperboard group Inland Paperboard & Packaging, Inc. subs. Temple-Inland Inc., 1992-00; group v.p. paperboard Temple-Inland Inc., Indpls., 2000—. Office: Temple Inland Inc 4030 Vincennes Rd Indianapolis IN 46268-3007

FOYE, THOMAS HAROLD, lawyer; b. Rapid City, S.D., Nov. 23, 1930; s. Harold Herbert and Jean Winifred (McCormick) F.; m. Laurene Fowler, Aug. 7, 1972; children: David Snyder, Stewart Snyder BS in Commerce, Creighton U., 1952; LLB, Georgetown U., 1955. Bar: S.D. 1955, D.C. 1955, U.S. Supreme Ct. 1968. Trial atty. tax div. U.S. Dept. Justice, Washington, 1955-58; assoc. Bangs, McCullen, Butler, Foye & Simmons, predecessor firms, Rapid City, 1958-60, ptnr., 1960—. Lectr. in field Fellow Am. Coll. Trust and Estate Counsel, Am. Bar Found.; mem. ABA, State Bar S.D. (pres. 1982-83), Pennington County Bar Assn. (pres. 1962), Am. Coll. Real Estate Lawyers, Internat. Acad. Estate and Trust Law., Am. Coll. Tax Counsel. Democrat. Roman Catholic. Club: Arrowhead Country (Rapid City). Avocations: snow skiing, water skiing, hiking. Office: Bangs McCullen Butler Foye & Simmons PO Box 2670 Rapid City SD 57709-2670

FRADE, PETER DANIEL, chemist, educator; b. Highland Park, Mich., Sept. 3, 1946; s. Peter Nunes and Dorathea Grace (Gehrke) F.; m. Karen L. Kovich, Mar. 14, 1992. BS in Chemistry, Wayne State U., 1968, MS, 1971, PhD, 1978. Chemist Henry Ford Hosp., Detroit, 1968-75, analytical chemist, toxicologist dept. pathology, divsn. pharmacology and toxicology, 1975-86, sr. clin. lab. scientist dept. pathology divsn. clin. chemistry and pharmacology, 1987-96; assoc. prof. Eugene Applebaum Coll. of Pharmacy and Allied Health Sci. Wayne State U., 1996—, interim chair dept. mortuary sci., 2000—. Rsch. assoc. in chemistry Wayne State U., Detroit, 1978—79; vis. scholar U. Mich., Ann Arbor, 1980—90; vis. scientist dept. hypertension rsch. Henry Ford Hosp., Detroit, 1986—88; adj. prof. Eugene Applebaum Coll. of Pharmacy and Health Scis. Wayne State U., 1991—96; dir. Anatomic Pathologists' Assts. Program. Contbr. sci. articles to profl. jours.; peer reviewer for profl. jours., 1988—. Mem. Rep. Presdl. Task Force, 1984-88; organist St. John's Episcopal Ch., Royal Oak, Mich., 1995-97. Recipient David F. Boltz Meml. award, Wayne State U., 1977, Teaching Excellence award. Fellow Am. Inst. Chemists, Nat. Acad. Clin. Biochemistry, Assn. Clin. Scientists; mem. Am. Coll. Forensic Examiners, Am. Chem. Soc., Am. Assn. Clin. Chemistry, Am. Guild Organists, Assn. Analytical Chemists, Mich. Inst. Chemists (treas. 1994—), N.Y. Acad. Scis., Am. Coll. Toxicology, Royal Soc. Chemistry (London), Titanic Hist. Soc., Virgil Fox Sox., Sigma Xi, Phi Lambda Upsilon, Alpha Chi Sigma. Episcopalian. Home: 20200 Orleans St Detroit MI 48203-1356 Office: Wayne State U 5439 Woodward Ave Detroit MI 48202-4009

FRAEDRICH, ROYAL LOUIS, magazine editor, publisher; b. Weyauwega, Wis., Apr. 23, 1931; s. Clarence Otto and Libbie Clara (Trojan) F.; m. Phyllis Bohren, June 26, 1955; children— Lynn, Craig, Ann, Sarah, Paul. B.S., U. Wis., 1955. With Doane Agrl. Service, St. Louis, 1955-57; info. specialist Mich. State U., East Lansing, 1957-59; mng. editor Agrl. Pubs., Inc., Milw., 1959-64; editor Big Farmer mag., 1964-69, Frankfort, Ill., 1969-73, Farm Futures mag., Milw., 1973-81, pub., 1981-85; exec. v.p. Top Farmers Am. Assn., Milw., 1973-81; pub. print services AgriData Resources, Inc., 1981-85, v.p. editorial and adminstrn., 1986-89, v.p., sr. editorial dir., 1990-92; sr. editorial dir. ARI Network Svcs. Inc., 1992-94; sr. editor AgEd Network Stewart-Peterson Group, West Bend, Wis., 1994-96, cons. editor, 1996—. V.p., dir. Big Farmer Inc., 1969-73; v.p. Market Communications Inc., Milw., 1973-78 Vice pres. Grace Lutheran Ch., Menomonee Falls, Wis., 1963, mem. stewardship com., 1965-67, sec. bd. elders, 1974-77, mem. bd. elders, 1987-89. Mem. Am. Agrl. Editors Assn. Home: N95w16529 Richmond Dr Menomonee Falls WI 53051-1452 Office: 137 S Main St West Bend WI 53095-3321

FRAENKEL, STEPHEN JOSEPH, engineering and research executive; b. Berlin, Germany, Nov. 28, 1917; came to U.S., 1938, naturalized, 1943; s. Max S. and Martha (Plessner) F.; m. Josephine Rubnitz, June 28, 1941; children: Richard Mark, Charles Matthew, Martha Ann. B.S. in Civil Engring. with distinction, U. Nebr., 1940, M.S. in Civil Engring, 1941; Ph.D., Ill. Inst. Tech., 1951. Registered profl. engr., Ill., registered structural engr., Ill. Engr. Pitts.-Des Moines Steel Co., 1941-44, Link Belt Co., 1944-46; with Ill. Inst. Tech. Research Inst., successively research engr., supr., dept. mgr., head dept. propulsion and structural research, 1946-55; dir. research and devel. Stanray Corp., Chgo., 1955-62; dir. research engring. Continental Can Co., 1962-64; gen. mgr. research and devel. Container Corp. Am., Chgo., 1964-75, dir. research and devel., 1975-82; pres., dir. Tech. Services, Inc., Chgo., 1982—; dir. Tech. Commercialization Ctr., Ill. Inst. Tech., 1986-89. Arbitrator Am. Arbitration Assn., 1983—; adviser effects nuclear weapons Dept. Def., 1950—; cons. space flight programs ABC. Mem. bd. editors Research Mgmt., 1976-82; contbr. articles to profl. jours. Ency. Chem. Tech. Bd. dirs. Alsip Paper Condominium Assn., 1989—. Recipient certificate of achievement for atomic test Greenhouse, U.S. Joint Task Force Three. Mem. TAPPI (chmn. Chgo. sect. 1968-69, dir. 1969— , chmn. acad. adv. group 1971-73, chmn. acad. rels. div. 1973-76), AIAA (pres. Chgo. sect. 1958-59, dir. 1959—), Soc. Exptl. Stress Analysis, Navy League, Sigma Xi, Sigma Tau, Tau Beta Pi, Chi Epsilon. Home and Office: 1252 Spruce St Winnetka IL 60093-2148 E-mail: stjo1wntka@aol.com.

FRAHM, SHEILA, association executive, former government official, academic administrator; b. Colby, Kans., Mar. 22, 1945; m. Kenneth Frahm; children: Amy, Pam, Chrissie. BS, Ft. Hays State U., 1967. Mem. bd. edn. State of Kans., 1985-88; mem. Kans. Senate, Topeka, 1988-94, senate majority leader, 1993-94; lt. gov. State of Kans., 1995-96; mem. from Kans., U.S. Senate, Washington, 1996; exec. dir. Kans. Assn. C.C. Trustees, Topeka, 1996—. Mem. AAUW (Outstanding Br. Mem. 1985), Thomas County Day Care Assn., Shakespeare Fedn. Women's Clubs, Farm Bur., Kans. Corn Growers, Kans. Livestock Assn., Rotary (Paul Harris fellow 1988). Republican. Home: 410 N Grant Colby KS 67701-2036 Office: 700 SW Jackson St Ste 401 Topeka KS 66603-3757 E-mail: sfrahm@colbyweb.com.

FRAISE, EUGENE S. state legislator; b. West Point, Iowa, May 7, 1932; m. Faye Pumphrey. Farmer; mem. Iowa Senate from 50th dist., 1986—. Chair Lee County Bd. Suprs., 1985. Mem. St. Mary's Ch., Augusta, Iowa. Mem. Iowa Corn Growers Assn., Lee County Pork Prodrs., KC. Democrat. Home: 1699 280th Ave Fort Madison IA 52627-9557 Office: State Capitol 50th Dist 3 9th And Grand Des Moines IA 50319-0001 E-mail: eugene_fraise@legis.state.ia.us.

FRAKES, JAMES TERRY, physician, gastroenterologist, educator; b. Burlington, Iowa, Feb. 22, 1946; s. Harold Decatur and Marjorie Marie (Kinnison) F.; m. Nancy Jean French, June 15, 1968; children: Sarah Jane Frakes, David Harold Frakes. BS, U. Ill., Urbana, 1968, MS, 1972; MD, U. Ill., Chgo., 1976. Diplomate Am. Bd. Internal Medicine and Gastroenterology, Nat. Bd. Med. Examiners; lic. Ill. Staff engr. Westinghouse Astronuc. Lab., Pitts., 1968-69; staff scientist Los Alamos (NMex.) Sci. Lab., 1970-71; intern, resident in internal medicine U. Mo. Med. Ctr., Columbia, 1976-78; fellow in gastroenterology U. N. Carolina Sch. Medicine, Chapel Hill, 1978-80; physician, gastroenterologist Rockford (Ill.) GE Assoc., Ltd., 1980—. Clin. prof. medicine U. Ill. Coll. Medicine, Rockford, 1981—; dir. digestive disease unit Saint Anthony Med. Ctr., Rockford, 1983—; course dir. AGA/ASGE, 1991—; med. lectr., 1987—. Bd. dirs. U. Ill. Alumni Assn., 1991-96; mem. U. Ill. Found., Urbana, 1991—, mem. pres.'s coun., 1994—. Recipient Faculty Disting. Tchg. award U. Ill. Coll. Medicine, Rockford, 1990, Faculty Disting. Svc. award, 1997, Disting. Alumnus award, 1999. Fellow ACP, Am. Coll. Gastroenterology; mem. AMA, Am. Gastroenterol. Assn. (numerous coms.) Am. Soc. Gastroinestinal Endoscopy (treas. 1995-98, pres.-elect 1998-99, pres. 1999-00). Republican. Avocations: gardening, wine collecting, college sports. Office: Rockford Gastroenterology Assocs Ltd 401 Roxbury Rd Rockford IL 61107-5078

FRALEY, ROBERT T. biotechnologist; b. Danville, Ill. m. Laura Fraley; children: Steven, Devin, Katherine. BS in Biology, U. Ill., 1974, PhD in Microbiology/Biochemistry, 1978; postgrad., Northwestern U., 1991. Postdoctoral fellow U. Calif., San Francisco, 1979—80; co-pres. agrl. sector Monsanto Co., St. Louis, 1980—2000, chief tech. officer, 2000—, co-pres. agrl. sector, 1980—2000, chief tech. officer St Louis, 2000—. Recipient Nat. Medal Tech., 1998. Achievements include development of part of the team that developed the world's first practical system to introduce foreign genes into crop plants and development of insect-and-herbicide-resistant plants. Office: Monsanto Co 800 N Lindbergh Blvd Saint Louis MO 63167-0001

FRANANO, SUSAN MARGARET KETTEMAN, arts consultant and administrator, musician; b. Kansas City, Mo., Sept. 30, 1946; d. Charley Gilbert and Mary Elizabeth (Bredehoeft) Ketteman; m. Frank Salvatore Franano, Dec. 20, 1969; 1 child, Domenico Frank. AA, Stephens Coll., Columbia, Mo., 1966, BFA, 1967; postgrad., U. Mo., Kansas City, 1967-68, So. Ill. U., Edwardsville, 1968-69. Mgr. Lyric Opera Group, Kansas City, 1976-82; tour coordinator Lyric Opera Kansas City, 1978-85; dir. outreach Kansas City Symphony, 1982-84, asst. mgr., 1984-85, ops. mgr., 1985-86, gen. mgr., 1986-95; exec. dir. Columbus (Ohio) Symphony Orch., 1995-97, Ohio Citizens for Arts, Columbus, 1998—. Guest lectr. Ohio State U., 1999. Regional liaison Mo. Citizens for Arts, Kansas City, 1984-86; regional rep. Am. Guild Mus. Artists, Kansas City, 1977-81; regional ammenities task force mem. Mid-Am. Regional Coun., 1989-95; panelist Nat. Endowment for Arts, 1991-2000, site visitor, 1998—; chmn. group 2 orchs. Am. Symphony Orch. League, 1992-94; site visitor Fla. Dept. Cultural Affairs, 1998—; mem. bd. Statewide Arts Advocacy League Am., Ohio Alliance for Art Edn. Mem. Mo. Citizens for Arts, Ohio Citizens for the Arts, Actors Equity, New Albany Arts Coun., Columbus Mus. Art. Democrat. Roman Catholic. Avocations: tennis, cooking, travel. Office: Ohio Citizens for the Arts 77 S High St Columbus OH 43215-6108

FRANCH, RICHARD THOMAS, lawyer; b. Melrose Park, Ill., Sept. 23, 1942; s. Robert and Julia (Martino) F.; m. Patricia Staufenberg, Apr. 18, 1971 (dec. Apr. 1994); children: Richard T. Jr., Katherine J.; m. Susan L. Rice, Sept. 1, 1995. B.A. cum laude, U. Notre Dame, 1964; J.D., U. Chgo., 1967. Bar: Ill. 1967, U.S. Dist. Ct. (no. dist.) Ill. 1967, U.S. Supreme Ct. 1980, U.S. Ct. Appeals (2d cir.) 1984, U.S. Ct. Appeals (3d cir.) 1981, U.S. Ct. Appeals (6th cir.) 1991, U.S. Ct. Appeals (7th cir.) 1971, U.S. Ct. Appeals (8th cir.) 1981, U.S. Ct. Appeals (9th cir.) 1997, U.S. Dist. Ct. (no. dist.) Wis. 1989, U.S. Tax Ct. 1994. Assoc. Jenner & Block, Chgo., 1967-68, 70-74, ptnr., 1975—. Former mem. Ill. Supreme Ct. Rules Com. Served to capt. U.S. Army, 1968-70 Decorated Bronze star, Army Commendation medal. Fellow Am. Coll. Trial Lawyers; mem. Am. Law Inst. Office: Jenner & Block Ste 4700 One IBM Plz Chicago IL 60611 E-mail: dickfranch@aol.com., rfranch@jenner.com.

FRANCIS, CHARLES ANDREW, agronomy educator, consultant; b. Monterey, Calif., Apr. 12, 1940; s. James Frederick and G. Louise (Epperson) F.; m. Barbara Louise Hanson, June 23, 1962; children: Todd (dec.), Kevin, Andrea, Karen. BS, U. Calif., Davis, 1961; MS, Cornell U., 1967, PhD, 1970; DSc honoris causa, Helsinki U., 1999. Dir., maize breeder Internat. Ctr. for Tropical Agr., Cali, Colombia, 1970-72, dir., bean agronomist Colombia, 1973, dir. small farm systems Colombia, 1974-75, rsch. agronomist Colombia, 1976-77; prof. U. Nebr., Lincoln, 1977—, dir. Morocco project, 1982-84; dir. internat. program Rodale Inst., Emmaus, Pa., 1984-85. Agronomist U.S. AID, Botswana, Liberia, Uganda, Malawi, Morocco, Senegal, Tanzania, 1978-94, World Bank, Colombia, S.Am., 1980; dir. Ctr. Sustainable Agr. Sys., 1990—; bd. dirs., sec. The Land Inst., Salina, Kans., 1990—; cons. OTA, Rockefeller Found., FAO/UN, 1978—. Editor: Multiple Cropping Systems, 1986; co-editor: Sustainable Agriculture, 1990, Crop Improvement for Sustainable Systems, 1993; contbr. chpts. to books and numerous articles to profl. jours. Cubmaster Cub Scout Pack 20, Lincoln, 1978-81; mem. ch. bd. Unitarian Universalist Ch., Lincoln, 1987-89; bd. dirs., v.p. sch. bd. Colegio Bolivar, Cali, 1973-77. 1st lt. U.S. Army, 1961-63. Recipient Agr. Stewardship award, Sustainable Agr. Soc., 1997, 7th Generation Rsch. award, Ctr. for Rural Affairs and CSARE, 2000. Fellow Am. Soc. Agronomy (divsn. chair 1968-70, Robert E. Wagner award for Efficient Agr. 1992), Crop Sci. Soc. Am.; mem. Phi Kappa Phi, Phi Beta Delta, Gamma Sigma Delta, Alpha Zeta. Democrat. Avocations: bicycling, camping, jogging, reading, travel. Office: U Nebr 225 Keim Hall Lincoln NE 68583-0910

FRANCIS, EDWARD D. architect; b. Cleve., Aug. 15, 1934; s. Michael and Anna (Buchinsky) F.; m. Betty-Lee Seydler, Aug. 25, 1956 (div. 1982); children— Tameron, Theron; m. Lynne Marie Merrill, Sept. 6, 1984. B.Arch, Miami U., 1957. Draftsman, designer David Maxfield, Oxford, Ohio, 1953-59; draftsman Austin Co., Cleve., summers 1954, 56; designer Meathe, Kessler & Assoc., Grosse Pointe, Mich., 1959-68; prin. William Kessler & Assoc., Detroit, 1968—, pres., 1985-95, Kessler Assoc. Inc., 1995-99; CEO Kessler/Francis/Cordoza Architects, 1999—. Mem. archtl. adv. com. Ferris State U., Big Rapids, Mich. Chmn. Franklin Village Hist. Commn., Mich., 1971-79; pres. Friends of Capitol, Lansing, 1984-85, State Hist. Preservation Rev. Bd., 1984-94. Fellow AIA (Gold medal Detroit and Mich. chpts.); mem. Frank Lloyd Wright Assn., Frank Lloyd Wright Preservation Trust, Nat. Trust for Hist. Preservation, Mich. Hist. Preservation Network (Lifetime Achievement award 2001), Gabriel Richard Hist. Soc. (bd. dirs.). Office: Kessler/Francis/Cardoza 300 River Pl Ste 1650 Detroit MI 48207 E-mail: kessler@ameritech.net.

FRANCIS, MARION DAVID, consulting chemist; b. Campbell River, B.C., Can., May 9, 1923; came to U.S., 1949; s. George Henry and Marian (Flanagan) F.; m. Emily Liane Williams, Aug. 27, 1949 (dec. 1995); children: William Randall, Patricia Ann; m. Jacqueline S. Lohman, June 14, 1997. BA, U. B.C., Vancouver, 1946, MA, 1949; PhD, U. Iowa, 1953. Instr. U. B.C., Vancouver, Can., 1946-49; chemist Can. Fishing Co., Can., 1946; research asst. U. Iowa, Iowa City, 1949-51; research chemist Procter

& Gamble Co., Cin., 1952-76, sr. scientist, 1976-85, Norwich Eaton Pharms., Inc., Norwich, N.Y., 1985-89; rsch. fellow Victor Mills Soc., Cin., 1990-93; cons., 1993—. Chmn. Gordon Rsch. Conf., N.H., 1968, 79, session chmn., 1985; invited speaker, panel discussion mem. 1st Internat. Conf. on Crystal Deposition and Dissolution in Tissues, Evion, France, 1985; invited speaker Internat. Workshop on Flouride in Bone, 1988, Bisphosphonates: Current Status and Future Prospects, London, 1990; invited speaker for Tng. for Pharm. Industry, London, 1992, 24th Internat. Sun Valley Workshop on Hard Tissue Biology, 1993, Internat. Bone Disease Symposium, Chantilly, Va., 1996; session chmn. workshop, Sienna, Italy, 1992; invited symposium speaker Japanese Bone & Mineral Soc., Yokahoma, 1993; invited speaker, co-chmn. "Bisphosphonate Therapies for Osteoporosis: Today and Tomorrow" Symposium, Davos, Switzerland, 1996, spkr./chmn. XIV Internat. Conf. on Phosphorus Chemistry, Cin., 1998, others; lectr. numerous univs., U.S., Can., Europe and China, 1965-90; spkr. in field; session chmn. 26th Internat. Congress on Arts and Comms., Lisbon, Portugal, 1999, 27th Internat. Congress on Arts and Comms., Washington, 2000, chmn., chmn. 28th congress, Cambridge, Eng., 2001. Contbr. articles to sci. jours.; patentee in field. Dist. chmn. Cin. United Appeal, 1956-60. Recipient Profl. Accomplishment award Tech. and Sci. Socs. Cin., 1979, Tech. Innovation award Victor Mills Soc., 1990, Perkin medal Soc. of Chem. Industry, 1996; U.S. Pub. Health predoctoral fellow, 1951-52. Fellow Am. Soc. Bone and Mineral Rsch., Am. Chem. Soc. (program chmn. cen. regional meeting 1983, invited symposium spkr. nat. meeting 1987, 92, invited awards symposium spkr. 1994, Cin. Chemist of Yr. award 1977, Nat. Indsl. Chemist award 1994, Morley medal 1996, Heros of Chemistry award 2000), Am. Coll. Rheumatologists, Dance Club (pres. 1972-73), Wyo. (Ohio) Sunday Supper Club (pres. 1998-99). Republican. Roman Catholic. Home and Office: 23 Diplomat Dr Cincinnati OH 45215-2074 E-mail: dinbug4me@compuserve.com.

FRANCIS, PHILIP HAMILTON, management consultant; b. San Diego, Apr. 13, 1938; s. William Samuel and Ruth Kathryn (Allison) F.; m. Regina Elizabeth Kirk, June 10, 1961 (div. May 1971); m. Diana Maria Villarreal, July 15, 1972; children: Philip Scott, Edward Philip, Mary Allison, Kenneth Joseph. BSME, Calif. Poly. State U., 1959; MSME, U. Iowa, 1960, PhD in Engring. Mechanics, 1965; MBA in Mgmt., St. Mary's U., San Antonio, 1972. Registered profl. engr., Tex. With Douglas Aircraft Co., Santa Monica, Calif., 1960-62, S.W. Rsch. Inst., San Antonio, 1965-79; prof., chmn. dept. mech. and aerospace engring. Ill. Inst. Tech., Chgo., 1979-84; with Indsl. Tech. Inst., Ann Arbor, Mich., 1984-86; dir. advanced mfg. tech. Motorola Inc., Schaumburg, Ill., 1986-88; corp. v.p. Square D Co. (Schneider-N.Am.), Palatine, 1988-94; client ptnr. AT&T Solutions, AT&T, Chgo., 1995-96; mng. ptnr. Mascon Global, Ltd., Schaumburg, 1996—2002; pres. Group Fin., LLC, Georgetown, Tex., 2001—, Group Francis, LLC., 2002—. Mem. various indsl. and acad. adv. bds. Recipient Gustas Larson award ASME and Pi Tau Sigma, 1978 Fellow ASME, Ill. Math. and Sci. Acad. (pres. fund bd. dirs.); mem. Soc. Mfg. Engrs., Sigma Xi, Tau Beta Pi, Pi Tau Sigma. Roman Catholic. Avocation: writing mgmt. books. E-mail: phil@groupfrancis.com.

FRANCK, ARDATH AMOND, psychologist; b. Wehrum, Pa., May 5, 1925; d. Arthur and Helen Lucille (Sharp) Amond; m. Frederick M. Franck, Mar. 18, 1945; children: Sheldon, Candace. B.S. in Edn., Kent State U., 1946, M.A., 1947; Ph.D., Western Res. U., 1956. Cert. high sch. tchr., elem. supr., sch. psychologist, speech and hearing therapist. Instr., Western Res. U., Cleve., summer 1953, U. Akron, 1947-50; sch. psychologist Summit County Schs., Ohio, 1950-60; cons. psychologist Wadsworth Pub. Schs., Ohio, 1946-86; dir. Akron Speech & Reading Ctr., Ohio, 1950—; pres. Twirling Unlimited; cons., dir. Hobbitts Pre-Sch., 1973-88. Author: Your Child Learns, 1976. Pres. Twirling Unltd., 1982—. Mem. Am. Speech and Hearing Assn., Internat. Reading Assn., Ohio Psychol. Assn., Mensa, Soroptomist (Akron). Home: 631 Ghent Rd Akron OH 44333-2629 Office: Akron Speech & Reading Ctr 700 Ghent Rd Akron OH 44333-2698

FRANCO, CARLO DIAZ, surgeon, anatomist, anesthesiologist; b. Valparaiso, Chile, Nov. 9, 1956; came to U.S., 1985; s. Ismael Segundo and Aida Rosa (Franco-Huerta) Diaz-Labarca; m. Jennifer Ann Leepard, Mar. 31, 1989 (div. May 1993). MD, U. Valparaiso, Chile, 1981. Instr. anatomy Sch. of Medicine Univ. Valparaiso, Chile, 1982; surgery resident U. Valparaiso, Chile, 1982-85; asst. prof. anatomy, surgery Univ. Valparaiso, Chile, 1983-89; vis. prof. anatomy Med. Coll. of Ohio, Toledo, 1985-86, 88-89; surgeon, pvt. practice Valparaiso U. Hosp., Chile, 1986-89; surgery resident Sinai Hosp., Detroit, 1990-91, anesthesiology resident, 1991-94; chmn. orthopedic anesthesia Cook County Hosp., Chgo., 1994—; asst. prof. anesthesiology Rush Med. Coll. Asst. prof. anesthesiology Rush Med. Coll., Chgo. Contbr. articles to profl. jours. Grantee WHO, 1985-86, Ednl. Commn. for Foreign Med. Grads., 1988-89. Fellow AMA, Am. Soc. Anesthesiologists, Latin Am. Soc. Regional Anesthesia. Roman Catholic. Avocations: reading, writing, traveling, tennis, ice skating. Home: 419 W Grand Ave # J Chicago IL 60610-4265 Office: Cook Co Hosp Dept Anesthesia 1835 W Harrison St Dept Chicago IL 60612-3785

FRANCOIS, WILLIAM ARMAND, lawyer; b. Chgo., May 31, 1942; s. George Albert and Evelyn Marie (Smith) F.; m. Barbara Ann Sala, Aug. 21, 1965; children: Nicole Suzanne, Robert William. B.A., DePaul U., 1964, J.D., 1967. Bar: Ill. 1967. Pvt. practice, Lyons, Ill., 1967-68; with Am. Nat. Can Group, Inc., Chgo., 1970-74, sec., 1974, v.p., 1978, sr. v.p., gen. counsel, sec., 1999-2000; dep. gen. counsel N.Am. Pechiney Group, 1996-99; pvt. practice Lake Forest, Ill., 2000—. Served to capt. U.S. Army, 1968—70. Mem. ABA, Ill. Bar Assn., Chgo. Bar Assn., Am. Soc. Corp. Secs., Am. Corp. Counsel Assn. Office: 642 Balmoral Ct Lake Forest IL 60045-4842 E-mail: chgowaf@aol.com.

FRANK, JAMES S. automotive executive; b. 1942; BS, Dartmouth Coll.; MBA, Stanford U. With ZF, Inc., 1965, Wheels, Inc., Des Plaines, Ill., 1965; pres. Four Wheels, Inc., 1965; pres., CEO Frank Consol Enterprises, Wheels, IL, 1974—. Office: Frank Consol Enterprises 666 Garland Pl Des Plaines IL 60016-4725

FRANK, RICHARD CALHOUN, architect; b. Louisville, May 17, 1930; s. William George and Helen (Calhoun) F.; m. Janet Nickerson, Feb. 12, 1966; children: Richard, Scott, Elizabeth, William, Jennifer, Philip. BArch, U. Mich., 1953. Assoc. archtl. firms, Lansing, Mich., 1953-61; pres. Frank & Stein Assocs., Inc., 1961-70; prin. Johnson, Johnson & Roy, Ann Arbor, 1971-75; pres. Preservation/Urban Design/Inc., Ann Arbor and Washington, 1975-84; pvt. practice Saline and Gregory, Mich., 1985—; hist. preservation counsel SmithGroup Historic Preservation Practice, Ann Arbor, 1997—. Ind. contractor C.S. Mott Found., 1999-2000. Life trustee Hist. Soc. Mich. Fellow AIA (gold medal Mich. 1992); mem. Nat. Trust for Historic Preservation (trustee emeritus), Victorian Soc. Am. (v.p.). Home and Office: 7172 Glencoe Dr Gregory MI 48137-9657 E-mail: rfrankfaia@aol.com.

FRANK, STUART, cardiologist; b. N.Y.C., Dec. 25, 1934; s. Henry and Kitty (Sternberg) F.; m. Nanchen O'Brien, Aug. 1976 (div. Feb. 1980); children: Rachel Arthur, Sebastian Noah; m. Amber Barnhart, June 22, 1982; children: Amelia Elizabeth, Abigail Kitty, Jessica Cole. BS in Chemistry, MIT, 1956; MD, NYU, 1960. Diplomate Am. Bd. Internal Medicine, Am. Bd. Cardiovascular Disease. Intern and resident in internal medicine Yale U. New Haven Hosp., 1960-64; postdoctoral fellow Inst. Cardiology, London, 1964-65, Nat. Heart Inst., Bethesda, Md., 1965-67; chief cardiology Kaiser Permanente Med. Ctr., San Francisco, 1967-77; assoc. prof. dept. medicine So. Ill. U., Springfield, 1977-86, chief div. cardiology, 1977-90, asst. chmn. dept. medicine, 1981-88, prof. dept. medicine, 1986—, dean of students, 1990-95. Author: The People's Handbook of Medical Care, 1972; contbr. numerous articles to profl. jours. Recipient Nellie Westerman prize Am. Fedn. Clin. Research, 1986. Fellow ACP, Am. Coll. Cardiology, Am. Coll. Chest Physicians, Am. Heart Assn. (council clin. cardiology), Laennec Soc. Office: So Ill Univ Medicine Dept Cardiology PO Box 19636 Springfield IL 62794-9636

FRANKE, RICHARD JAMES, arts advocate, former investment banker; b. Springfield, Ill., June 23, 1931; s. William George and Frances Marie (Brennan) F. BA, Yale U., 1953; MBA, Harvard U., 1957. With John Nuveen & Co., Chgo., 1957-96, v.p., 1965-69, exec. v.p., 1969-74, chief adminstrv. officer, 1970-74, pres., 1974-89, CEO, 1974-96, chmn., 1988-96, also dir., chmn., CEO emeritus, 1996—. Vice chmn. Yale Corp., 1987-94, chmn., 1994—. Chmn. investment com. Yale U.; mem. Pres.'s Com. on the Arts and Humanities; trustee Chgo. Symphony Orch.; trustee U. Chgo.; bd. dirs. Lyric Opera, Newberry Libr. 1st lt. U.S. Army, 1953-55. Office: 400 N Michigan Ave Ste 300 Chicago IL 60611-4130

FRANKEL, BERNARD, advertising executive; b. 1929; B in Mktg., U. Buffalo, 1951. Sales rep. Rugby Knitting Mi, Chgo., 1951-54; midwest rep. E.O. Hirsch & Assocs., 1954-57; dir. sales promotion Kling Studios, 1957-59; account exec., account supr., v.p. Knipschild-Robinson, Inc. (now William A. Robinson and Co.), 1959-62; CEO Frankel & Co., Chgo., 1962—, also chmn. bd. dirs. Media rep., advt. sales mgr., advertising and promotion mgr. Concrete Pub. Co., Chgo., 1955-57. Office: Frankel & Co 111 E Wacker Dr Chicago IL 60601-3713

FRANKLIN, AL, artistic director; b. Oceanside, Calif., Mar. 3, 1951; m. Elizabeth Amey Sanchez, June 22, 1985; children: Jacob Sanchez, Caleb Alexander. Freelance stage mgr., tour mgr., line prodr., various locations, 1979-86; prodn. mgr. Walnut St. Theatre, Phila., 1987-91; producing artistic dir. Gretna Theatre, Mt. Gretna, Pa., 1991-94; exec. dir. Theatre Assn. of Pa., 1995-96; artistic dir. Fort Wayne Civic Theatre, Ind., 1996—. Founder, chmn. C-PATH, Lancaster, 1992-96. Prodr., dir. large and small musicals, new plays, Shakespeare and other classic plays, contemporary dramas and comedies, children's plays, workshops, play readings, spl. projects and fundraising events. Bd. dirs. Fort Wayne Civic Theatre, 1996—, Leadership Lebanon (Pa.) Valley, 1993-95, Friends of Colonial, Lebanon, 1992-94. With USAF, 1969-73, The Netherlands. Avocations: writing, martial arts, painting, clay sculpting. Home: 4811 Old Mill Rd Fort Wayne IN 46807-2927 Office: Ft Wayne Civic Theatre 303 E Main St Fort Wayne IN 46802-1907

FRANKLIN, DOUGLAS E. publishing executive; b. 1957; Grad., U. Dayton, 1979. Staff acct. Dayton (Ohio) Newspapers, 1979, asst. contr., 1980, 1986-90; with Springfield (Ohio) Newspaper, 1981-83; bus. mgr. Longview Newspaper, Tex., 1983-86; with Dayton (Ohio) Daily News, 1990—, exec. v.p., gen. mgr. Office: Dayton Daily News 45 S Ludlow St Dayton OH 45402-1858

FRANKLIN, J. RICHARD, state representative; b. Milan, July 15, 1934; m. Joyce Ann Fishback; children: James, Elizabeth. BS, Truman State U., 1956; MA, U. Mo., 1963; postgrad., Ctrl. Mo. State U., 1972—. Prin. Ft. Osage High Sch., Independence, Mo. State rep. dist. 53 Mo. Ho. of Reps., mem. edn. com., retirement com., banking com.; chmn. budget com. Mem. Masons, Shriners. Home and Office: 18005 Cheyenne Dr Independence MO 64056-1981

FRANKLIN, LYNNE, business communications consultant, writer; b. St. Paul, Aug. 24, 1957; d. Lyle John Franklin and Lois Ann (Cain) Kindseth; stepdau. Thomas John Kindseth; m. Lawrence Anton Pecorella, Sept. 2, 1989; 1 stepchild, Lauren. BA in Psychology and English, Coll. St. Catherine, 1979; MA, Hamline U., 1989. Residential treatment counselor St. Joseph's Home, Mpls., 1979-80; staff writer Comml. West Mag., 1980-81; acct. exec. Edwin Neuger & Assocs., 1981-83, Hill and Knowlton, Mpls., 1983-84; mgr. pub. rels. Gelco Corp., Eden Prarie, Minn., 1984-86; dir. financial rels. Dunstan & Assocs., Mpls., 1986; cons. MC Assocs., Chgo., 1986-87; v.p. Fin. Rels. Bd., 1987—; prin. Wordsmith, Glenview, Ill., 1993—. Trustee Lawrence Hall Youth Svcs.; judge achievement awards Internat. Assn. of Bus. Communicators, Mpls., 1986, presenter fin. rels., 1990; judge achievement awards Publicity Club of Chgo., 1992-94; presenter annual report seminar Nat. Investor Rels. Inst., Chgo., 1992. Author: (novel) Second Sight, 1989. Tchr. Great Books Program, St. Paul, 1976-79, Minn. Literacy Coun., 1985-87. Recipient Ann. Report Excellence award, Fin. World Mag., 1991—98, award, MerComm-ARC Competition, 1992—2001, Nat. Assn. Investors Corp., 1994—2001, Equities Mag., 1999—2001. Office: Wordsmith 2019 Glenview Rd Glenview IL 60025-2849

FRANKLIN, RICHARD MARK, lawyer; b. Chgo., Dec. 13, 1947; s. Henry W. and Gertrude (Gross) F.; m. Marguerite June Wesle, Sept. 2, 1973; children: Justin Wesley, Elizabeth Cecilia, Catherine Helena, Caroline Lucinda. BA, U. Wis., 1970; postgrad., U. Freiburg, Fed. Republic Germany, 1968-69; JD, Columbia U., 1973. Bar: Ill. 1973, U.S. Dist. Ct. (no. dist.) Ill. 1973, U.S. Ct. Appeals (7th cir.) 1973. Assoc. Baker & McKenzie, Chgo., 1973-79, Frankfurt, Fed. Republic Germany, 1979-80, ptnr. Chgo., 1980—. Mem. ABA, Ill. Bar Assn., Chgo. Bar Assn. Mem. United Ch. Christ. Avocations: music, literature, theatre, outdoor activities. Home: 1161 Oakley Ave Winnetka IL 60093-1437 Office: Baker & McKenzie 1 Prudential Plz 130 E Randolph St Ste 3700 Chicago IL 60601-6342 E-mail: rmfwim@aol.com., richard.m.franklin@bakenet.com.

FRANKLIN, WILLIAM EDWIN, bishop; b. Parnell, Iowa, May 3, 1930; Attended, Loras Coll., Mt. St. Bernard Sem., Dubuque, Iowa. Ordained priest Roman Cath. Ch., 1956. Priest Roman Cath. Ch., Dubuque, titular bishop Surista aux. bishop, 1987-93; bishop Davenport, Iowa, 1994—. Office: Diocese of Davenport St Vincent Ctr 2706 N Gaines St Davenport IA 52804-1998

FRANKS, DAVID BRYAN, internist, emergency physician; b. Washington, Nov. 18, 1956; s. David Ardell and Erta Mae (Williford) F.; m. Deborah Ann Hayek, Jan. 31, 1987; children: Ariel Ann, David Henry, Theodore Gabriel. BS, U. Md., 1978, MD, 1980. Diplomate Am. Bd. Internal Medicine, Am. Bd. Emergency Medicine. Resident Thomas Jefferson U. Hosp., Phila., 1980-83; physician Temple U. Hosp., 1983-85, St. Joseph Health Ctr., St. Charles, Mo., 1985-87, Belleville (Ill.) Meml. Hosp., 1987—. Fellow Am. Coll. Emergency Physicians. Office: 4500 Memorial Dr Belleville IL 62226-5360

FRANKS, HERBERT HOOVER, lawyer; b. Joliet, Ill., Jan. 25, 1934; s. Carol and Lottie (Dermer) F.; m. Eileen Pepper, June 22, 1957; children: David, Jack, Eli. BS, Roosevelt U., 1954; postgrad., Am. U., 1960. Bar: Ill. 1961, U.S. Dist. Ct. (no. dist.) Ill. 1961, U.S. Supreme Ct. 1967. Ptnr. Franks, Gerkin & McKenna, 1985—. Chmn. Wonder Lake State Bank, Ill., 1979—, First Nat. Bank, Marengo, Ill., 1976-84, mem. exec. com., 1976—; vice-chmn. hotel mgmt. orgn. Bricton Group, Park Ridge, Ill., 1992-98. Bus. editor Am. U. Law Rev., 1959, 60. State pres. Young Dems. of Ill., 1970-72; trustee Hebrew Theol. Coll., Skokie, Ill., 1974—; trustee, sec. Forest Inst. Profl. Psychology, Springfield, Mo., 1979-91; chmn. Forest Hosp., Des Plaines, 1980-88. With U.S. Army, 1956-58. Mem.: Ill. Trial Lawyers (mng. bd. 1975—92, treas. 1985—87), Ill. State Bar Assn. (bd. govs. 1994—97, treas. 1996—97, 3d v.p. 1997—98, 2d v.p. 1998—99, pres.-elect 1999—2000, pres. 2000—01), Shriners, Masons (33 deg.), Sigma Nu Phi (pres. 1980—82). Home: 19324 E Grant Hwy Marengo IL 60152-9438 Office: Franks Gerkin & McKenna 19333 E Grant Hwy Marengo IL 60152-8234 E-mail: franklaw@mc.net.

FRANKSON-KENDRICK, SARAH JANE, publisher; b. Bradford, Pa., Sept. 24, 1949; d. Sophronus Ahimus and Elizabeth Jane (Sears) McCutcheon; m. James Michael Kendrick, Jr., May 22, 1982. Customer svc. rep. Laros Printing/Osceola Graphics, Bethlehem, Pa., 1972-73; assoc. editor Babcox Publs., Akron, Ohio, 1973-74, Bill Comms., Akron, 1974-75, sr. editor, 1975-77, editor-in-chief, 1977-81; assoc. pub. Chilton Co./ABC Pub., Chgo., 1981-83, pub., 1983-89, group pub. Radnor, Pa., 1989-93; group v.p. Cahners Bus. Info. (formerly Chilton Co.), 1993-98; divsn. v.p. Primedia Intertec, Chgo., 1999—2001. Exec. MBA prof. Northwood U., mem. adv. coun. Mem. oper. com. Primedia Intertec. Recipient Automotive Replacement Edn. award Northwood Inst., 1983, award for young leadership and excellence Automotive Hall of Fame, 1984; bd. dirs. Automotive Hall of Fame. Mem. Automotive Found. for Aftermarket (trustee), Automotive Parts and Accessories Assn. (bd. dirs., exec. com., sec., treas., strategic planning com., edn. com., Disting Svc. award 1993), Automotive Svc. Industry Assn. (bd. dirs. automotive divsn. com.), Automotive Svc. Assn. Mgmt. Inst. (trustee, exec. com.), Palm Beach (Fla.) Polo and Country Club, Winged Foot (Mamaroneck, N.Y.). Republican.

FRANK-STROMBORG, MARILYN LAURA, nursing educator; b. Chgo., Jan. 20, 1942; d. Irving and Roseann (Krcek) Frank; m. Paul Stromborg, 1966; children: Nels, Danny. BS, No. Ill. U., 1964, MS, cert. in nursing, No. Ill. U., 1966, EdD, 1974, JD, 1994. RN. Mem. faculty Sch. Nursing U. Ill., Chgo., 1970-71, No. Ill. U., DeKalb, 1976—; acting chair, 1995-96. Part-time mem. nursing faculty U. Loyola U., Chgo., 1974-76, Rush U., Chgo., 1974-76. Author: Primary Care Assessment and Management Skills for Nurses, 1979; editor Instruments for clinical Nursing Research, 1989 (AJN award 1989), Cancer Prevention and Early Detection in Minorities: Culturial Implications, 1993. Founder, vol. trainer De Kalb County Hospice, 1977—; v.p. Am. Cancer Soc., 1977. Capt. USAF, 1966-70. Named Researcher of Yr., Pace U., 1990; grantee Nat. Cancer Inst., NIH, 1984—; Ctr. for Nursing Rsch., 1985-90, Div. Nursing, 1990—. Fellow Am. Acad. Nursing; mem. Midwest Nursing Rsch. Soc. (treas. 1989-91), Oncology Nursing Soc. (chair rsch. com. 1985-87, sec. 1987-89, excellence in cancer nursing edn. award 1991). Avocations: gardening, skiing. Home: 215 Dunkery Dr Sycamore IL 60178-1017 Office: No Ill U Dept Nursing Dekalb IL 60115

FRANTZ, DEAN LESLIE, psychotherapist; b. Beatrice, Nebr., Mar. 27, 1919; s. Oscar C. and Flora Mae (Gish) F.; m. Marie Flory, Aug. 31, 1940; children: Marilyn, Shirley, Paul. BA, Manchester (Ind.) Coll., 1942; MDiv, Bethany Theol. Sem., Oak Brook, Ill., 1945; diploma, C.G. Jung Inst. Zurich, 1977. Assoc. prof. Bethany Theol. Sem., 1957-64; dir. ch. rels. Manchester Coll., North Manchester, Ind., 1964-72; pvt. practice Ft. Wayne, 1977—. Author: Meaning for Modern Man in the Paintings of Peter Birkhauser, 1977; editor: Barbara Hannah: The Cat, Dog, and Horse Lectures, and the Beyond, 1992, Barbara Hannah: The Inner Journey, 1999. Mem. Internat. Assn. Analytical Psychology, Assn. Grad Analytical Psychologists. Home: Apt 24C 3143 Golden Years Homestead Dr 24C New Haven IN 46774-3002

FRANTZ, MARTIN H. prosecutor; b. Akron, Ohio, July 24, 1952; s. Harry W. and Jayne M. (Harvey) F.; m. Mary Ann Rittman, Sept. 9, 1978; children: Laine Elizabeth, Rachel Elaine, Michael Andrew. BA cum laude, Ohio State U., 1974, JD, 1978. Bar: Ohio 1978, U.S. Dist. Ct. (no. dist.) Ohio 1979, U.S. Supreme Ct. 1986; cert. trial advocate. Asst. prosecutor Wayne County, Wooster, OH, 1979-97, pros. atty., 1997—. Mem. adv. bd. Wayne County Schs. Career Ctr., Smithville, Ohio, 1996—. Author newsletter Crime and Punishment, 1995—. Chmn. Wayne County Rep. Ctrl. Com., 1984-96. Mem. Wooster Evening Lions Club (pres. 1986-87). Roman Catholic. Office: Wayne County Prosecutor 132 S Market St Wooster OH 44691-4765

FRANZ, DANIEL THOMAS, financial planner; b. Dayton, Ohio, Jan. 30, 1949; s. Albin Benedict and Monica Elizabeth (Moeller) F.; m. Sally Ann Stickley, Oct. 11, 1968; children: Amanda Marie, Stephanie Ann. BS, Charleston So. U., 1971, postgrad., 1975, S.C. State U., 1974. Cert. fin. aid adminstr., fin. planner. Coach, admissions officer Bapt. Coll., Charleston (S.C.) So. U., 1971-72; dir. fin. aid Bapt. Coll., Charleston, S.C., 1972-76; pvt. practice fin. planning Greenville, Ohio, 1977—. Cons. S.C. Bapt. Conv., Columbia, 1974-76, U.S. Office Edn., Atlanta, 1974-76, Corning Glass Works, Greenville, 1984—, Franklin-Monroe High Sch., Pitsburg, Ohio, 1985—, United Telephone Co., Bellefontaine, Ohio, 1986—. Bd. dirs. Darke County Supts. Roundtable, Greenville, 1983—, Darke County Widows Assn., 1984-86; mem., chmn. bd. dirs. S.C. Com. Higher Edn., Columbia, 1974-76, Darke County Mental Health Clinic, 1984-90; bd. dirs. Coun. on Rural Svcs. Programs, 1991—; chmn. bd. dirs. Ch. of the Transfiguration Cath. Ch., West Milton, Ohio, 1978-82. Mem. Inst. Cert. Fin. Planners, Internat. Assn. Fin. Planners, Nat. Assn. Life Underwriters, Miami Valley Assn. Life Underwriters, S.C. Assn. Student Fin. Aid Adminstrs. (bd. dirs. 1971—), Darke County C. of C. (bd. dirs. 1993—), Lions. Republican. Avocation: sports. Office: Fin Achievement Svcs PO Box 657 5116 Childrens Hm Bradford Rd Greenville OH 45331-9327

FRASER, DONALD MACKAY, former mayor, former congressman, educator; b. Mpls., Feb. 20, 1924; s. Everett and Lois (MacKay) F.; m. Arvonne Skelton, June 30, 1950; children: Thomas Skelton, Mary MacKay, John DuFrene, Lois MacKay (dec.), Anne T. (dec.), Jean Skelton. BA cum laude, U. Minn., 1944, LLB, 1948. Bar: Minn. 1948. Ptnr. Lindquist, Fraser & Magnuson (and predecessors), 1948-62; Minn. State senator, 1954-62; sec. Senate Liberal Caucus, 1955-62; mem. 88th-95th Congresses from 5th Dist. Minn., mem. fgn. affairs com., chmn. subcom. on internat. orgn., mem. budget com.; mayor City of Mpls., 1980-93; mem. study and rev. com. Dem. Caucus; mem. Commn. on Role and Future Presdl. Primaries, 1976; adj. prof. law and pub. affairs U. Minn., Mpls. Vice chmn., dir. Mpls. Citizens Com. on Pub. Edn., 1950-54; Sec. Minn. del. Democratic Nat. Conv., 1960; chmn. Minn. Citizens for Kennedy, 1960; mem. platform com. Dem. Nat. Conv., 1964, mem. rules com., 1972, 76; vice chmn. Com. Dem. Selection Presdl. Nominees, 1968; chmn. Democratic Study Group Congress, 1969-71, Commn. on Party Structure and Del. Selection Dem. Party, 1971-72; 1st Am. co-chmn. Anglo-Am. Parliamentary Conf. on Africa, 1964; mem. U.S. del. 7th spl. session and 30th session UN Gen. Assembly, 1975; Congl. adviser to U.S. del. to UN Conf. on Disarmament, 1967-73, to U.S. del. to 3d Law of Sea Conf., 1972, to UN Commn. on Human Rights, 1974; cons. on families HUD, 1994. Chair health com. U.S. Conf. Mayors; bd. dirs. Mpls. United Way, 1986-93, Twin Cities Rise!, 1994—, Connect/U.S.-Russia, 1994—, Greater Mpls. Coun. Chs., 2000—; co-chair Ctr. for Internat. Policy, 1976-94, Early Care and Edn. Fin. Commn., 1999—; co-founder, pres. Dem. Farmer-Labor Edn. Found.; initiated numerous youth programs such as Transitional Work Internship Program, Youth Work Internship Program, Neighborhood Early Learning Ctrs., Youth Coordinating Bd., Youth Trust. Lt. (J.G.) USNR, 1944-46. Recipient 1st Minn. Internat. Human Rights award, 1985, Disting. Svc. award Mpls. United Way, 1992; fellow Kennedy Sch., spring 1994. Mem. Mpls. Fgn. Policy Assn. (pres. 1952-53), Citizens League Greater Mpls. (sec. 1951-54), Minn. Bar Assn., Hennepin County Bar Assn., Ams. for Dem. Action (nat. chmn. 1973-76), Dem. Conf. (nat. chmn. 1976-78), U. Minn. Law Alumni Assn. (dir. 1958-61), Univ. Dist. Improvement Assn. (pres. 1950-52), Nat. League of Cities (2d v.p. 1991, 1st v.p. 1992, pres. 1993), Minn. Advocates for Human Rights (co-founder, bd. dirs. 1983-92, 2000—), League of Minn. Cities (bd. dirs. 1991-93).—.

FRASER, JOHN FOSTER, management company executive; b. Saskatoon, Sask., Sept. 19, 1930; s. John Black and Florence May (Foster) F.; m. Valerie Georgina Ryder, June 21, 1952; children: John Foster Jr., Lisa Ann. B of Commerce, U. Sask., 1952; LLD (hon.), U. Winnipeg, 1993. Pres.

Empire Freightways Ltd., Saskatoon, Sask., 1953-60, Empire Oil Ltd., Saskatoon, 1960-62, Hanford Drewitt Ltd., Winnipeg, 1962-68, Norcom Homes Ltd., Mississauga, Ont., 1969-78; pres., chief exec. officer Fed. Industries Ltd., Winnipeg, 1978-91, chmn., chief exec. officer, 1991-92, chmn. bd., 1992-95; vice chmn. Russel Metals, 1995-97; chmn. bd. Air Canada, 1996—. Bd. dirs. Internat. Comfort Products Corp., Bank of Montreal, Air Can., Investors Group, Inc., Can. Devel. Investment Corp., Shell Can. Ltd., The Thomson Corp., Ford Motor Co. Can. Ltd., Man. Telecom Svcs. Inc., Centra Gas Man. Inc., Coca-Cola Beverages Ltd., Inter-City Products Corp., Continental Airlines, Inc., Am. West Airlines; past chmn. Coun. for Bus. and Arts in Can. Bd. dirs., founding chmn. Assocs. Faculty of Mgmt. Studies U. Man.; past pres. Man. Theatre Centre; past bd. govs. St. John's Ravenscourt Sch., Winnipeg; mem. cultural rev. policy com. Province of Man., 1979; past pres. Royal Winnipeg Ballet, 1992-93. Decorated officer Order of Can., 1990; recipient Peter D. Curry award U. Man., 1984, Outstanding Bus. Achievement award as Citizen of Yr. Man. C. of C., 1984; named Transp. Person of Yr. Nat. Transp. Week, 1990. Mem. Am. Mgmt. Assn. (pres.'s assn.), Royal Lake of the Woods Yacht Club, Toronto Club. Progressive Conservative. Presbyterian. Avocations: boating, reading. Office: 201 Portage Ave Ste 3100 Winnipeg MB Canada R3B 3L7

FRASIER, RALPH KENNEDY, lawyer, banker; b. Winston-Salem, N.C., Sept. 16, 1938; s. LeRoy Benjamin and Kathryn O. (Kennedy) F.; m. Jeannine Quick, Aug. 1981; children: Karen D. Frasier Alston, Gail S. Frasier Cox, Ralph Kennedy Jr., Keith Lowery, Marie Kennedy, Rochelle Doar. BS, N.C. Cen. U., Durham, 1963, JD, 1965. Bar: N.C. 1965, Ohio 1976. With Wachovia Bank and Trust Co., N.A., Winston-Salem, N.C., 1965-70, v.p., counsel, 1969-70; asst. counsel, v.p. parent co. Wachovia Corp., 1970-75; v.p., gen. counsel Huntington Nat. Bank, Columbus, Ohio, 1975-76, sr. v.p., 1976-83, sec., 1981-98, exec. v.p., 1983-98, cashier, 1983-98. V.p. Huntington Bancshares Inc., 1976-86, gen. counsel, 1976-98, sec., 1981-98; sec., dir. Huntington Mortgage Co., Huntington State Bank, Huntington Leasing Co., Huntington Bancshares Fin. Corp., Huntington Investment Mgmt. Co., Huntington Nat. Life Ins. Co., Huntington Co., 1976-88; v.p., asst. sec. Huntington Bank N.E. Ohio, 1982-84; asst. sec. Huntington Bancshares Ky., 1985-97; sec. Huntington Trust Co., N.A., 1987-97, Huntington Bancshares Ind., Inc., 1986-97, Huntington Fin. Services Co., 1987-98; dir. The Huntington Nat. Bank, Columbus, Ohio, 1998—; of counsel Porter Wright Morris & Arthur LLP, Columbus, 1998—; trustee OCLC Online Computer Libr. Ctr., Inc., Dublin, Ohio, 1999—, mem. fin. com., 2000—, mem. audit com., 2000—; dir. ADATOM.COM, Inc., Milpitas, Calif., 1999-2001, mem. compensation com., 1999-2001, chair audit com., 1999-2001. Bd. dirs. Family Svcs. Winston-Salem, 1966-74, sec., 1966-71, 74, v.p., 1974; chmn. Winston-Salem Transit Authority, 1974-75; bd. dirs. Rsch. for Advancement of Personalities, 1968-71, Winston-Salem Citizens for Fair Housing, 1970-74, N.C. United Community Svcs., 1970-74; treas. Forsyth County (N.C.) Citizens Com. Adequate Justice Bldg., 1968; trustee Appalachian State U., Boone, N.C., 1973-83, endowment fund, 1973-83, Columbus Drug Edn. and Prevention Fund, Inc., 1989-92; trustee, vice chmn. employment and Edn. Commn. Franklin County, 1982-85; mem. Winston-Salem Forsyth County Sch. Bd. Adv. Coun., 1973-74, Atty. Gen's Ohio Task Force Minorities in Bus., 1977-78; bd. dirs. Inroads Columbus, Inc., 1986-95, Greater Columbus Arts Coun., 1986-94, Columbus Urban League Inc., 1987-94, vice chmn., 1990-94; trustee Riverside Meth. Hosp. Found., 1989-90, Grant Med. Ctr., 1990-95, Grant/Riverside Meth. Hosps., 1995-97; trustee Ohio Health Corp., 1997—, treas., chair Fin./Audit Com., 2001—; dir. Cmty. Mutual Ins. Co., 1989-92, mem. audit com., 1989-92; trustee N.C. Ctrl. U., Durham, N.C., 1993-2001, vice-chmn., 1993-94, chmn. 1995, chair ednl. planning and acad. affairs com., 1995-98, audit, devel. and personnel coms., 1998-2001, chair audit com., 1999-2001; mem. Ohio Bd. Regents, 1987-96, vice-chmn., 1993-95, chmn., 1995-96; trustee Nat. Jud. Coll., Reno, Nevada, 1996-02, fin. and audit com., 1997—02 treas., chair, 1999—, Columbus Bar Found., 1998— (fellows com. 1998—, grants com., 1998—); AEFC Pension Adminstrn. Com. defined benefit plan of the ABA, Am. Bar Endowment, Am. Bar Found., and Nat. Jud. Coll., Chgo, Ill., 1998-02. With AUS, 1958-64. Mem. ABA, Nat. Bar Assn., Ohio Bar Assn., Columbus Bar Assn. Office: Porter Wright Morris & Arthur LLP 41 S High St Ste 3100 Columbus OH 43215-6194 E-mail: rfrasier@porterwright.com., rfrasier@columbus.rr.com.

FRAUMANN, WILLARD GEORGE, lawyer; b. San Francisco, July 21, 1948; m. Anne C. Derleth, Dec. 18, 1971; children: Ellen, Robert, Sarah. AB, U. Mich., 1970; JD, Harvard U., 1973. Bar: Ill., U.S. Dist. Ct. (no. dist.) Ill. Ptnr. Kirkland & Ellis, Chgo., 1977—. Served to lt. USNR, 1973-77. Office: Kirkland & Ellis 200 E Randolph St Fl 54 Chicago IL 60601-6636

FRAUTSCHI, TIMOTHY CLARK, lawyer; b. Madison, Wis., Apr. 8, 1937; s. Lowell E. and Grace C. (Clark) F.; m. Pamela H. Hendricks, June 23, 1964; children: Schuyler, Jason; m. Susan B. Brumm, June 13, 1981; 1 child, Jacob. B.A., U. Wis., 1959; LL.B., London Sch. Econs., U. Wis., 1963. Bar: Wis. 1963, U.S. Ct. Claims 1976, U.S. Tax Ct., 1976. Assoc. firm Foley & Lardner, Milw., 1963-70, ptnr., 1970—. Editor Wis. Law Rev. Co-founder Milw. Forum; pres. Lakeside Cmty. Coun., Present Music, Inc., 1991—98, Skylight Comic Opera, Ltd., 1980—85, Next Act Theatre, 2001—; bd. dirs. Am. Players Theater, Milw., Repertory Theater, Northcott Neighborhood House, United performing Arts Fund, Inc., Milw., Children's Svc. Soc., Wis. Theatre Tesseract; pres. Next Act Theatre, 1986—89, Watertower Landmark Trust, 1986—89; v.p. Frank Lloyd Wright Wis. Conservancy, 2001—. Mem. Milw. Jr. Bar Assn. (pres. 1969-70), Milw. Bar Assn. (dir. 1971-74), Order of Coif, Phi Beta Kappa (pres. Milw. chpt. 1968-70), Phi Kappa Phi, Phi Eta Sigma Office: Foley & Lardner First Wis Ctr 777 E Wisconsin Ave Ste 3800 Milwaukee WI 53202-5367

FRAZIER, JOHN W. retired physiologist, researcher; b. Wilmington, Ohio; With, Wright-Patterson AFB, 1956—; rsch. physiologist. Recipient Eric Liljencrantz award, 1996. Fellow Aerospace Med. Assn.; mem. SAFE (Sr. Scientist award, Pres. award), Aerospace Physiology Soc. (space medicine br., Paul Bert award), Aerospace Human Factors Assn. (life scis. & biomed. engrng. br.). Office: AFRL/HESA 2245 Monahan Way Bldg 33 Wright Patterson AFB OH 45433-7008

FRAZZETTA, THOMAS HENRY, evolutionary biologist, functional morphologist, educator; b. Rochester, N.Y., May 13, 1934; s. Joseph H. and Louise V. (Cross) F. B.S., Cornell U., 1957; Ph.D., U. Wash., 1964. Instr. in zoology U. Wash., Seattle, 1963-64; assoc. in herpetology Harvard U., Cambridge, Mass., 1964-65; asst. prof. U. Ill., Urbana, 1965-71, assoc. prof., 1971-76, prof. dept. ecology, ethology, evolution, 1976—. Author: Complex Adaptations in Evolving Populations, 1975; contbr. articles to jours. Active ACLU, World Wildlife Fedn., Planned Parenthood Fedn. Am., Zero Population Growth, Amnesty Internat. NIH postdoctoral fellow, 1964; NSF research grantee, 1969, 77, 86. Mem. AAAS, Am. Soc. Naturalists, Soc. Study of Evolution, Am. Soc. Ichthyologists and Herpetologists, Am. Elasmobranch Soc., Soc. for Integrative and Comparative Biology. Democrat Office: Univ Ill Dept Animal Biology 515 Morrill Hall Urbana IL 61801 E-mail: tomfrazz@life.uiuc.edu.

FREBORG, LAYTON W. state legislator; b. Underwood, N.D., May 13, 1933; m. Delilah Freborg; 4 children. Gen. contractor; mem. N.D. Ho. of Reps., Bismark, 1973-81, N.D. Senate from 8th dist., Bismark, 1985—. Chmn. edn. and natural resources com. N.D. State Senate. Chmn. N.D. State Rep. Com. (mem. edn. and agr. com.); mem. Underwood Sch. Bd. (pres. 14 yrs.). Mem. Farm Bur., Turtle Lake Civic Club, Underwood Civic Club, Underwood C. of C. Republican. Address: PO Box 677 Underwood ND 58576-0677

FRECHETTE, PETER LOREN, dental products executive; b. Janesville, Wis., Aug. 15, 1937; s. Francis Michael and Gladys Jean F.; m. Patricia Jean O'Brien, June 24, 1961; children: Kathleen and Kristen (twins). B.S. in Econs., U. Wis., 1960; M.B.A., Northwestern U. 1980. Pres. Sci. Products, McGaw Park, Ill., 1975-82; pres., CEO Patterson Dental Co., Mpls., 1982—. Served with U.S. Army, 1961-63. Mem. Am. Dental Trade Assn. Office: Patterson Dental Co 1031 Mendota Heights Rd Mendota Heights MN 55120-1401

FREDEN, SHARON ELSIE CHRISTMAN, state education official; b. Watertown, S.D., Jan. 11, 1941; d. Harlon Arthur and Mildred Lillian (Jensen) Christman; m. Noble Everett Freden, July 3, 1973; 1 child, Anne Victoria. BS, No. State Coll., Aberdeen, S.D., 1962; MA, U. Iowa, 1966; EdD, U. Colo., 1973. Tchr. Manitowoc (Wis.) Pub. Schs., 1962-64, Boulder Valley Pub. Schs., Colo., 1966-70, K-12 lang. arts cons., 1970-72; cons. Colo. Dept. Edn., Denver, 1973-76, 77-80; ITV insvc. coord. Sta. KCPT-TV, Kansas City, Mo., 1980-81; dir. Kans. Dept. Edn., Topeka, 1981-84, asst. commr., team leader, 1984—2001, 2001—. Editor: Basic Skills: Promising Practices in Colorado, 1979, (with others) Pupil Progress in Colorado, 1978; contbr. chpts. to books. Chmn. precinct com. Broomfield (Colo) Dem. Com., 1978. Recipient leadership award YWCA, 1990; Hildegard Sweet Meml. scholar, 1972. Mem. ASCD, Kans. ASCD, United Sch. Adminstrs., Phi Delta Kappa. Home: 3711 SW 31st St Topeka KS 66614-2809 Office: Kans Dept Edn 120 E 10th Topeka KS 66612

FREDERICK, EDWARD CHARLES, university official; b. Mankato, Minn., Nov. 17, 1930; s. William H. and Wanda (MacNamara) F.; m. Shirley Lunkenheimer, Aug. 16, 1951; children: Bonita Frederick Treangen (dec.), Diane Frederick Fox, Donald, Kenneth, Karen Frederick Swenson. B.S. in Agrl. Edn, U. Minn., 1954, M.S. in Dairy Husbandry, 1955, Ph.D. in Anatomy and Physiology, 1957. Animal scientist, instr. N.W. Sch. and Expt. Sta. U. Minn., Crookston, 1958-64, supt. So. Sch. and Expt. Sta. Waseca, 1964-69, provost Tech. Coll., 1969-85, chancellor Tech. Coll., 1985-90; sr. fellow Hubert H. Humphrey Inst. Pub. Affairs, 1990-91, U. Minn. Coll. of Agr., Food and Environ. Sci., 1991—. Mem. Tech. Agrl. Edn. Study Team to Morocco, 1977. Contbr. articles on dairy physiology, mgmt., agrl. edn. and adminstrn. to tech. jours. and popular publs. Bd. dirs. Bob Hodgson Student Loan Fund, 1971-90, Minn. Agrl. Interpretive Ctr., 1978—, chair, 1994—; bd. dirs. Minn. Agri-Growth Coun., 1980—, pres. 1992—; bd. dirs. Southeastern Minn. Initiative Fund, 1986-92, v.p., 1991-92; bd. dirs. Waseca area United Way, 1988-94, pres., 1992; bd. dirs. Minn. Agriculture in the Classroom, 1993-99, pres., 1995-96. Recipient Alumni award 4-H, 1972, Good Neighbor award, WCCO, 1990, Ed Frederick Day award State of Minn., 1990, Award of Merit Gamma Sigma Delta, 1994, Waseca Cmty. Svc. Above Self award, 2002. Mem. Am. Dairy Assn., Am. Soc. Animal Prodn., AAAS, Nat. Assn. Colls. and Tchrs. Agr. (pres. 1976-77), Am. Assn. Community and Jr. Colls. (pres. Council of Two Yr. Colls. of Four Yr. Instns. 1988-90), Minn. FFA Alumni Assn. (pres. 1998-00), South Central Edn. Assn. (Disting. Service award 1971), Waseca Area C. of C. (dir. 1979), Phi Kappa Phi. Roman Catholic. Club: Foresters. Lodges: Rotary (gov. dist. 596 1982-83); K.C. Home: 39031 State Highway 13 Waseca MN 56093-4212 Office: U Minn Coll Agrl Food and Env Sci Waseca MN 56093 E-mail: frede010@umn.edu.

FREDERICK, RANDALL DAVIS, state legislator; m. Cindy Abraham; 3 children. Student, S.D. State U., 1974-76. Mem. S.D. Ho. of Reps., 1989-92, mem. appropriations com., 1992-93, mem. taxation and transp. coms., 1992—, chmn. appropriations com., 1994—, co-chmn. joint appropriations com., 1994—; senator S.D. State Senate, 1993—, co-chair appropriations com., 1993—. Farmer, Hayti, S.D., 1976—. Home: RR 1 Box 106 Hayti SD 57241-9629

FREDERICK, VIRGINIA FIESTER, state legislator; b. Rock Island, Ill., Dec. 24, 1916; d. John Henry and Myrtle (Montgomery) Heise; m. C. Donnan Fiester (dec. 1975); children: Sheryl Fiester Ross, Alan R., James D.; m. Kenneth Jacob Frederick, 1978. BA, U. Iowa, 1938; postgrad., Lake Forest Coll., 1942-43, LLD, 1994, MLS, 1999. Freelance fashion designer, Lake Forest, Ill., 1952-78; pres. Mid Am. China Exch., Kenilworth, 1978-81; mem. Ill. Ho. of Reps., Springfield, 1979-95, asst. minority leader, 1990-95. Alderman first ward, Lake Forest, 1974-78; del. World Food Conf., Rome, 1974; subcom. pensions and employment Ill. Commn. on Status of Women, 1976-79; co-chair Conf. Women Legislators, 1982-85; bd. dirs. Lake Forest Coll., 1995-98, Lake Forest Symphony Guild, 1998—; city supr. City of Lake Forest, 1995-98. Named Chgo. Area Women of Achievement, Internat. Orgn. Women Execs., 1978; recipient Lottie Holman O'Neal award, 1980, Jane Addams award, 1982, Outstanding Legislator award Ill. Hosp. Assn., 1986, VFW Svc. award, 1988, Joyce Fitzgerald Meml. award, 1988, Susan B. Anthony Legislator of Yr. award, 1989, Delta Kappa Gamma award, 1991, Outstanding Legislator award, 1995, Svcs. for Srs. award, Ill. Dept. Aging, 1991, Ethics in Politics award, Rep. Womens's Club, 1992, Woman of Achievement award YWCA North Eastern Ill., 1994, Ill. Women in Govt. award, 1994, Lifetime Achievement award Equip for Equality, 1999. Mem. LWV (local pres. 1958-60, state dir. 1969-75, nat. com. 1975-76), AAUW (local pres. 1968-70, state pres. 1975-77, state dir. 1963-69, nat. com. 1967-69, Legislator of Yr. 1993), UN Assn. (bd. dirs.), Chgo. Assn. Commerce and Industry (bd. dirs.). Home: 1290 N Western Ave Lake Forest IL 60045-1258 E-mail: k16v13@aol.com.

FREDERICKSON, DENNIS RUSSEL, state legislator, farmer; b. Morgan, Minn., July 27, 1939; s. Louis Bernard and Mary (Kragh) F.; m. Marjorie Davidson, July 15, 1961; children: Kari, Karl, Disa. BS, U. Minn., 1961. Farmer, Morgan, 1967—; commr. Redwood County, Minn., 1973-80; mem. Minn. Senate, St. Paul, 1981—. Past bd. dirs. Redwood Electric Coop. Author: (with others) The Fairy Tale Grim of Prince Perp, 1986. Served to lt. comdr. USN, 1962-67. Mem. S.W. Farm Mgmt. Assn. Republican. Lutheran. Avocation: running. Home: 4 Sunrise Dr New Ulm MN 56073-3615 Office: Minn Senate State Office Bldg Rm 143 Saint Paul MN 55155-0001

FREDERICKSON, HORACE GEORGE, former college president, public administration educator; b. Twin Falls, Idaho, July 17, 1937; s. John C. and Zelpha (Richins) F.; m. Mary Williams, Mar. 14, 1958; children—Thomas, Christian, Lynne, David. B.A., Brigham Young U., 1959; M.P.A., UCLA, 1961; Ph.D., U. So. Calif., 1967; LL.D. (hon.), Dongguk U., Korea. Intern Los Angeles County, 1960; research asst. Bur. Govtl. Research, U. Calif., Los Angeles, 1960-61; lectr. pub. adminstrn. U. So. Calif., 1962-64; lectr. govt. and politics U. Md., 1964-66; asst. prof. polit. sci. Maxwell Sch., Syracuse U., 1967-71; assoc. dir. Met. Studies Program, 1970-72, assoc. prof. polit. sci., 1971-72; fellow in higher edn. fin. adminstrn. U. N.C. System, 1972; chmn. Grad. Program, Sch. Pub. and Environ. Affairs, Ind. U., 1972-74, assoc. dean for policy and adminstrv. studies, 1973-74; dean Coll. Pub. and Community Services, prof. regional and community affairs U. Mo., Columbia, 1974-76; pres. Eastern Wash. U., Cheney, 1976-87; Edwin O. Stene Disting. prof. pub. adminstrn. U. Kans., Lawrence, 1987—. Author: New Public Administration, 1980, The Spirit of Public Administration, 1997; editor: Ethics and Public Administration, 1993, Public Policy and the Two States of Kansas, 1994, Ideal and Practice in Council-Manager Government, 2nd edit., 1994; editor in chief Jour. Pub. Adminstrn. Rsch. and Theory, 1991—. Haynes Found. fellow U. So. Calif., 1963-64 Mem. Am. Soc. Pub. Adminstrn. (pres.), Nat. Acad. Pub. Adminstrn. Home: 3420 Doral Ct Lawrence KS 66047-2131 Office: U Kans 318 Blake Hall Lawrence KS 66045-7508

FREDERIKSEN, MARILYNN ELIZABETH CONNERS, physician, researcher; b. Chgo., Sept. 12, 1949; d. Paul H. and Susanne (Ostergren) Conners; m. James W. Frederiksen, July 11, 1971; children: John Karl, Paul S., Britt L. BA, Cornell Coll., 1970; MD, Boston U., 1974; grad. Exec. Leadership in Acad. Medicine, Allegheny U. Health Scis., 1998. Diplomate Am. Bd. Ob-Gyn., Am. Bd. Maternal-Fetal Medicine, Am. Bd. Clin. Pharmacology. Pediat. intern U. Md. Hosp., 1974-75, resident in pediat., 1975-76; resident in ob-gyn. Boston Hosp. for women, 1976-79; fellow in maternal fetal medicine Northwestern U., 1979-81, fellow clin. pharmacology, 1981-83, instr. ob-gyn., 1981-83, asst. prof. ob-gyn., assoc. clin. pharmacology, 1983-91, assoc. prof. ob-gyn., assoc. in clin. pharmacology, 1991—, sect. chief gen. ob-gyn., 1993—2001. Mem. gen. faculty com. Northwestern U., Chgo., 1994—97, mem. ob-gyn. adv. panel, 1985—2000, chair ob-gyn. adv. panel, 2000—; mem. U.S. Pharm. Com. Revision, Rockville, Md., 1986—; del. U.S. Pharm. conv. Northwestern U. Med. Sch., 1990, 95, 2000; mem. gen. clinic rsch. ctr. com. NIH, 1989—93, chairperson, 1992—93; mem. Task Force Writing Group on Asthma in Pregnancy, Nat. Heart, Lung and Blood Inst., 1991—92; examiner Am. Bd. Ob-Gyn., 1997—; mem. Task Force Working Group, Nat. Bd. Med. Examiners, 1997—98, mem. acute care com., 1999—2001. Mem. editorial bd. Clin. Pharmacology & Therapeutics, 1993; contbr. numerous articles to profl. jours. Bd. dirs. Cornell Coll. Alumni Assn., Mt. Vernon, Iowa, 1986—90, PRCH, 1997—, Planned Parenthood of Chgo. Area, 1999—, Northwestern Med. Faculty Found., 1995—98. Recipient Pharm. Mfrs. Assn. Found. Faculty Devel. award, 1984-86, Civil Liberties award ACLU, 1991. Fellow Am. Coll. Ob-Gyn.; mem. Soc. Maternal Fetal Medicine, Ctrl. Assn. Obstetricians and Gynecologists (bd. dirs. 1997-99), Am. Soc. Clin. Pharmacology and Therapeutics (bd. dirs. 1994-97), Chgo. Gynecologic Soc. (treas. 1994-97), Phi Beta Kappa. Episcopalian. Avocations: gardening, needlework. Office: Northwestern Perinatal Assocs Ste 1230 680 N Lake Shore Dr Chicago IL 60611 E-mail: mcf810@northwestern.edu.

FREDRICKSON, JOHN MURRAY, otolaryngologist; b. Winnipeg, Man., Can., Mar. 24, 1931; s. Frank S. and Beatrice (Rannveig) F.; m. Alix Gordon, June 8, 1956; children: Kristin, Lisa, Erik. BA, U. B.C., Vancouver, 1953, MD, 1956. Intern Vancouver Genl Hosp., 1957-58, resident in pathology, 1959-60; resident in gen. surgery Shaughnessy Gen. Hosp., Vancouver, 1958-59; resident in otolaryngology U. Chgo., 1960-63, instr. in otolaryngologic surgery, 1963-65; asst. prof. surgery Stanford U., Calif., 1965-68; assoc. prof. otolaryngology U. Toronto, 1968-77, asst. prof. physiology, 1969-82, prof. otolaryngology, 1977-82; Lindburg prof. Sch. Medicine Washington U., St. Louis, 1982—, head dept. otolaryngology, 1982-98. Bd. dirs. Am. Bd. Otolaryngology, 1985-97. Co-editor: Advances in Oto-Rhino-Laryngology, 1973, Otolaryngology-Head and Neck surgery, 1983; editor Am. Jour. Otolaryngology, 1987-92; patentee implantable hearing aid, 1973, implantable voice box, 1981. Lt. RCAF, 1946-59. Mem. Am. Acad. Otolaryngology, Head and Neck Surgery, Soc. Univ. Otolaryngologists, Collegium Othrhinolaryngolica, Am. Laryngological Assn. (pres. 1992-93), Am. Otological Soc. Avocations: sports, music. Office: Washington U Med Sch Campus Box 8115 517 S Euclid Ave Saint Louis MO 63110-1007

FREE, HELEN MAE, chemist, consultant; b. Pitts., Feb. 20, 1923; d. James Summerville and Daisy (Piper) Murray; m. Alfred H. Free, Oct. 18, 1947; children: Eric, Penny, Kurt, Jake, Bonnie, Nina. BA in Chemistry, Coll. of Wooster, Ohio, 1944, DSc (hon.), 1992; MA in Clin. Lab. Mgmt., Ctrl. Mich. U., 1978, DSc (hon.), 1993. Cert. clin. chemist Nat. Registry Cert. Chemists. Chemist Miles Labs., Elkhart, Ind., 1944—78, dir. mktg. svcs. rsch. products divsn., 1978-82; chemist, mgr., cons. diagnostics divsn. Bayer Corp., 1982—. Mem. adj. faculty Ind. U., South Bend, 1975-96. Author: (with others) Urodynamics and Urinalysis in Clinical Laboratory Practice, 1972, 76; contbr. articles to profl. jours.; patentee in field. Women's chmn. Centennial of Elkhart, 1958. Named Woman of Yr., YWCA, 1993, Kilby Found. laureate, 1996; named to Hall of Excellence, Ohio Found. Ind. Colls., 1992, Nat. Inventors Hall of Fame, 2000, Engring. and Sci. Hall of Fame, 1996; recipient Disting. Alumni award, Coll. of Wooster, 1980, award, Medi Econ. Press, 1986, Nat. Leadership award, Lab. Pub. Svc., 1994. Fellow AAAS, Am. Inst. Chemists (co-recipient Chgo. award 1967), Royal Soc. Chemistry; mem. Am. Chem. Soc. (pres. 1993, bd. dirs., chmn. Chemistry Week task force, bd. com. pub. affairs and pub. rels., chmn. women chemists com. internat. activities com., grants and awards com., profl. and mem. rels. com., nominating com., coun. policy pub. affairs and budget, svc. award local chpt. 1981, councilor; Garvan medal 1980, co-recipient Mosher award 1983, 1st recipient Helen M. Free Pub. Outreach award 1995, Helen M. Free award named in her honor 1995), Am. Assn. for Clin. Chemistry (coun., bd. dirs., nominating com. and pub. rels. com., nat. membership chmn., coord. profl. affairs, pres.), Assn. Clin. Scientists (diploma of honor 1992), Am. Soc. Clin. Lab. Sci. (chmn. assembly, achievement award 1976), Nat. Com. Clin. Lab. Stds. (bd. dirs.), Soc. Chem. Industry (hon.), Altrusa (pres. 1982-83, bd. dirs.), Iota Sigma Pi (hon.), Sigma Delta Epsilon (hon.). Presbyterian. Home: 3752 E Jackson Blvd Elkhart IN 46516-5205 Office: Bayer Corp Diagnostics Divsn 1884 Miles Ave Elkhart IN 46514-2291 E-mail: Hmfree23@aol.com., helen.free.b@bayer.com.

FREEARK, ROBERT JAMES, surgeon, educator, administrator; b. Chgo., May 14, 1927; s. Ray H. and Lizette (Stauffer) F.; m. Ruth Nelson, June 24, 1950; children: Kris, Kim. BS, Northwestern U., 1949, MD magna cum laude, 1952; grad., Oak Ridge Inst. Nuclear Studies, 1953. Diplomate Am. Bd. Surgery (dir. 1980-86), Nat. Bd. Med. Examiners. Rotating intern, then resident in gen. surgery Cook County Hosp., Chgo., 1952-58, dir. surgery, 1958-68, attending physician, 1960-70, hosp. dir., 1968-70; research fellow Jerome D. Solomon Found. Chgo., 1953-54; mem. faculty Northwestern U. Med. Sch., 1960-70, prof. surgery, 1968-70; prof. surgery, chmn. dept. Loyola U.-Stritch Sch. Medicine, Maywood, Ill., 1970-95. Surgeon-in-chief Loyola U.-Foster G. McGaw Hosp., 1970-95, prof. emeritus, 1995—; asst. to pres. Loyola U. Health Sys., 1995-2002. Served with USMCR, 1945-46. Recipient Outstanding Clin. Prof. award Stritch Sch. Medicine, 1973, Alumni medal Northwestern U., 1980, Stritch medal Loyola U., 1981; named to Navy Pier Hall of Fame, Alumni Assn./U. Ill., Chgo, 1991. Fellow ACS (Surgeons award Nat. Safety Council 1987); mem. Am. Assn. Surgery Trauma (pres. 1982), Am. Surg. Assn. (v.p. 1995), AMA, Am. Trauma Soc. (pres. 1982), Central Surg. Assn. (pres. 1980-81), Soc. Internat. de Chirurgie, Soc. Surgery Alimentary Tract, Soc. Surg. Chmn., Soc. U. Surgeons, Western Surg. Assn., Ill. Surg. Soc. (pres. 1983-84), Ill. Med. Soc., Midwest Surg. Soc. (pres. 1970), Chgo. Med. Soc., Inst. Medicine Chgo., Chgo. Surg. Soc. (pres. 1984), Alpha Omega Alpha, Omega Beta Pi. Congregationalist. Office: 2160 S 1st Ave Maywood IL 60153-3304

FREEBORN, JOANN LEE, state legislator, farmer, former educator; m. Warren S. Freeborn Jr. BA, Kans. State U., 1966. Mem. from Dist. 107, Kans. State Ho. of Reps., 1992—, vice chmn. environ. com., mem. agr. com.; farmer, Concordia, Kans., 1996—. Home: RR 3 Box 307 Concordia KS 66901-9105

FREEBURG, RICHARD L. primary education educator; Elem. tchr. Nicollet Jr. High Sch., tchr. tech. edn. Recipient Tchr. Excellence award Internat. Tech. Edn. Assn., 1992. Office: Nicollet Jr High Sch 400 E 134th St Burnsville MN 55337-4010

FREED, DEBOW, college president; b. Hendersonville, Tenn., Aug. 26, 1925; s. John Walter and Ella Lee (DeBow) F.; m. Catherine Carol Moore, Sept. 10, 1949; 1 child, Debow II. BS, U.S. Mil. Acad., 1946; grad., U.S. Inf. Sch., 1953, U.S. Army Command and Gen. Staff Coll., 1959; MS, U. Kans., 1961; PhD, U. N.Mex., 1966; grad., U.S. Air War Coll., 1966; LLD, Monmouth (Ill.) Coll., 1987; DLitt (hon.), Ohio No. U., 1999. Comdg. officer U.S. Army, 1946; comdr. 35th Inf. Japan, 1947-48; asst. to cmdr. 17th Airborne Div., 1948-49; comdr. 26th Inf., Federal Republic of Germany, 1949-51; asst. to chief U.S. Mission, Iran, and chief Middle Ea. Affairs, 1951-53; instr. The Inf. Sch., 1953-56; comdr. 32d Inf., Korea, 1956-57; instr. Command and Gen. Staff Coll., 1957-58; chief nuclear br. U.S. Atomic Energy Agy., 1961-65; chief Plans Div. Vietnam, 1966-67; prof. physics dept. U.S. Mil. Acad., 1967-69, ret., 1969; dean Mt. Union Coll., 1969-74; pres. Monmouth Coll., 1974-79, Ohio No. U., Ada, 1979-99, pres. emeritus, 1999—. Chmn. Assoc. Colls. of Midwest, 1977-79, also officer other consortia of colls. and univs. Author: Using Nuclear Capabilities, 1959, Pulsed Neutron Techniques, 1965; contbr. articles, revs. to profl. publs.; editor: Atomic Development Report, 1962-64. Bd. dirs. Presbyn. Coll. Union, 1974-79; trustee Ctr. Sci. and Industry, 1982—, Toledo Symphony, 1994—, Blanchard Valley Health Assn., 1999—; v.p., dir. Buckeye coun. Boy Scouts Am., 1972-74, dir. Prairie coun., 1974-78. Decorated Bronze Star, (2) Legion of Merit, Legion of Honor Iran, Army Commendation medal, Air medal, Joint Svcs. Commendation medal, others; recipient various civic awards; Associated Western Univs. fellow, 1963-65; AEC fellow, 1963-65; Fgn. Policy Rsch. Inst. fellow, 1966; named Ohio Commodore, 1990. Mem. Assn. Meth. Colls. and Univs. (bd. dirs. 1979-99), Ohio Coll. Assn. (bd. dirs. 1980-84, 85-88, pres. 89-90), Ohio Found. Independent Colls. (bd. dirs. 1979-99), Am. Assn. Pres. of Colls. and Univs. (bd. dirs. 1988-99, treas. 1997-98, v.p. 1998-99), Ohio Commodores, Sixma Xi, Phi Kappa Phi, Phi Eta Sigma, Delta Theta Phi, Omicron Delta Kappa. Home: 205 W Lima Ave Ada OH 45810-1635 Office: Ohio No U Office of Pres Emeritus Ada OH 45810 E-mail: d-freed@onu.edu.

FREED, KARL FREDERICK, chemistry educator; b. Bklyn., Sept. 25, 1942; s. Nathan and Pauline Freed; m. Gina P. Goldstein, June 14, 1964; children: Nicole Yvette, Michele Suzanne. B.S., Columbia U., 1963; A.M., Harvard U., 1965, Ph.D., 1967. NATO postdoctoral fellow U. Manchester (Eng.), 1967-68; asst. prof. U. Chgo., 1968-73, assoc. prof., 1973-76, prof. chemistry, 1976—, dir. James Frank Inst., 1983-86. Author: Renormalization Group Theory of Macromolecules, 1987; editl. bd. Jour. Statis. Physics, 1976-78, Advances in Chem. Physics, 1985—, Computational Theoretical Polymer Sci., 1996—; adv. editor Chem. Physics, 1979-92, Chem. Revs., 1981-83, Internat. Jour. Quantum Chemistry, 1995-99; assoc. editor Jour. Chem. Physics, 1982-84; contbr. articles to profl. jours. Recipient Marlow medal Faraday div. Chem. Soc. London, 1973; recipient Pure Chemistry award Am. Chem. Soc., 1976; fellow Sloan Found., 1969-71; Guggenheim fellow, 1972-73; fellow Dreyfus Found., 1972-77 Fellow Am. Phys. Soc.; mem. Royal Soc. Chemistry (London), Am. Chem. Soc. Office: U Chgo 5640 S Ellis Ave Chicago IL 60637-1433 E-mail: k-freed@uchicago.edu.

FREED, MAYER GOODMAN, law educator; b. Phila., Oct. 26, 1945; s. Abraham H. and Fannie (Rothenberg) F.; m. Paulette Kleinhaus, Aug. 23, 1970; children: Daniel, Joshua. A.B. cum laude, Columbia Coll., 1967, JD, 1970. Bar: N.Y. 1971, Ill. 1975, U.S. Dist. Ct. (so. and ea. dists.) N.Y. 1972, U.S. Ct. Appeals (2d cir.) 1972, U.S. Supreme Ct. 1974. Assoc. Proskauer Rose Goetz & Mendelsohn, N.Y.C., 1970-71; staff atty. Nat. Employment Law Project, 1971-73, sr. staff atty., 1973-74; asst. prof. law Northwestern U., 1974-77, assoc. prof., 1977-79, prof., 1979—, assoc. dean acad. affairs, 1986—. Contbr. articles to legal publs.; bd. editors Columbia Law Rev., 1969-70. Bd. dirs. Legal Assistance Found. Chgo., 1980-82. Stone scholar, 1968-69. Mem. ABA. Office: Northwestern U Sch Law 357 E Chicago Ave Chicago IL 60611-3059 E-mail: mfreed@law.northwestern.edu.

FREEDMAN, ERIC, journalist, educator, writer; b. Brookline, Mass., Nov. 6, 1949; s. Morris and Charlotte (Nadler) F.; m. Mary Ann Sipher, May 24, 1974; children: Ian Sipher, Cara Sipher. BA, Cornell U., 1971; JD, NYU, 1975. Bar: N.Y. 1976, Mich. 1985. Congl. aide U.S. Rep. Charles Rangel, Washington and N.Y.C., 1971-76; reporter Knickerbocker News, Albany, N.Y., 1976-84, Detroit News, Lansing, Mich., 1984-95. Asst. prof. journalism Mich. State U., 1996—. Author: Pioneering Michigan, 1992, On the Water, Michigan, 1992, Michigan Free, 1993, Great Lakes, Great National Forests, 1995; co-author: What to Study, 1997; contbr. numerous articles to profl. jours. Recipient Merit citation Am. Judicature Soc., Journalism awards AP, Pulitzer prize for beat reporting, 1994. Mem. Am. Soc. Writers on Legal Subjects, Investigative Reporters and Editors, State Bar Mich. (journalism award), N.Y. State Bar Assn. (journalism awards), Ingham Country Bar Assn. Avocations: bicycling, travel, writing. Home and Office: 2698 Linden Dr East Lansing MI 48823-3814 E-mail: freedma5@msu.edu.

FREEDMAN, WILLIAM MARK, lawyer, educator; b. Washington, Dec. 8, 1946; s. Henry E. and Dorothy (Markowitz) F.; m. Harriet Arnold, Mar. 9, 1980; children: Alex, Emily. BA, Carleton Coll., 1968; JD, Harvard U., 1973. Bar: Ohio 1973, U.S. Dist. Ct. (so. dist.) Ohio 1973, U.S. Tax Ct. 1974. Assoc. Dinsmore & Shohl, Cin., 1973-80, ptnr., 1980—. Adj. prof. grad. dept. health svcs. adminstrn. Xavier U., Cin. Contbr. articles to profl. jours. Trustee Jewish Fedn. Cin., 1983-94, Yavneh Day Sch., Cin., 1988—, Norther Hills Synagogue, 1988-2001, Cin. Symphony Orch., 1990-94; v.p. No. Hills Synagogue, Cin., 1992-94, pres., 1994-96; chair Jewish Fedn. Cin. Endoment Fund Profl. Advisers Roundtable. With U.S. Army, 1968-70. Mem. ABA, Ohio State Bar Assn., Cin. Bar Assn., Am. Health Lawyers Assn., Soc. Ohio Hosp. Attys. Home: 10405 Stablehand Dr Cincinnati OH 45242-4652 Office: Dinsmore & Shohl LLP 1900 Chemed Ctr 255 E 5th St Cincinnati OH 45202-4700 Fax: 513-977-8141. E-mail: freedman@dinslaw.com.

FREEHLING, STANLEY MAXWELL, investment banker; b. Chgo., July 2, 1924; s. Julius and Juliette (Stricker) F.; m. Joan Steif, Jan. 26, 1947; children: Elizabeth, Robert Stanley, Margaret J. Student, U. Chgo., 1942-43, Ind. U., 1943-44, U. Stockholm, Sweden, 1946-47. With 1st Nat. Bank Chgo., 1947—52; ptnr. Freehling Bros., Chgo., 1948—, Freehling & Co., Chgo., 1960—87; spl. ltd. ptnr. Cowen & Co., 1987—2000; v.p. Lehman Bros., 2000—. Bd. dirs. Chgo. Sun Times Cos. Mem. Ill. Pub. Employees Pension Laws Commn., 1962-66; chmn. Ravinia Festival Assn., 1967-71; pres. men's coun. Art Inst. Chgo., 1962-65, trustee, 1970—, now life trustee; trustee Glenwood (Ill.) Sch. for Boys, 1967-80, Lake Forest Coll., 1972-83, Shedd Aquarium, U. Chgo., 1983—, Cradle Soc.; hon. mem. The Court Theatre; chmn. bd. Ill. Arts Coun., 1971-72; hon. chmn. Chgo. Theatre Group; bd. dirs. Northwestern Meml. Hosp., Chgo., Chgo. Pub. Libr. Found.; hon. chmn. bd. Goodman Theatre; chmn. Pub. Arts Adv. Com., 1978-90; mem. Pres.'s Com. on Arts and Humanities, Washington, 1984-88; bd. govs. Smart Mus. Art. Mem. Northwestern U. Assocs., Arts Club, Bond Club, Commercial Club (Chgo.), Lake Shore Country Club (Glencoe, Ill.), Old Elm Country Club (Highland Park, Ill.), Mid-Day. Clubs: Arts, Bond, Commercial (Chgo.); Lake Shore Country (Glencoe, Ill.); Mid-Day. Home: 121 Belle Ave Highland Park IL 60035-2503 Office: 190 S La Salle St Chicago IL 60603-3410

FREEMAN, ALBERT E. agricultural science educator; b. Lewisburg, W.Va., Mar. 16, 1931; s. James A. and Grace Vivian (Neal) F.; m. Christine Ellen Lewis, Dec. 23, 1950; children: Patricia Ellen, Lynn Elizabeth, Ann Marie BS, W.Va. U., Morgantown, 1952, MS, 1954; PhD, Cornell U., 1957. Grad. asst. W.Va. U., Morgantown, 1952-54; grad. asst. Cornell U., Ithaca, N.Y., 1955-57; asst. prof animal sci Iowa State U., Ames, 1957-61, assoc. prof. animal sci., 1961-65, prof. animal sci., 1965-78, Charles F. Curtiss Disting. prof. agriculture, 1978—. Contbr. numerous articles to profl. jours. Active Collegiate Presbyterian Ch., Ames Recipient 1975, Sr. Fulbright-Hays award, 1975, First Miss. Corp. award, 1979, award of appreciation for contbns. to Dairy Cattle Breeding 21st Century Genetics, 1984, Disting. Alumni award W.Va. U., 1985, faculty citation Iowa State U., 1987; named Charles F. Curtiss Disting. Prof. Agr., 1978. Fellow Am. Soc. Animal Sci. (Rockefeller Prentice Meml. award 1979, award of Honor 1987), Am. Dairy Sci. Assn. (bd. dirs. 1981-83, Nat. Assn. Animal Breeders Research award 1975, Borden award, 1982, J.L. Lush award 1984, Disting. Svc. award); mem. Biometrics Soc., First Acad. Disting. Alumni W.Va. U., Gamma Sigma Delta (award of Merit). Office: Iowa State Univ 239 Kildee Hall Ames IA 50010

FREEMAN, ANTONIO MICHAEL, professional football player; b. Balt., May 27, 1972; Student, Va. Poly. U. Wide receiver Green Bay (Wis.) Packers, 1995—; mem. Superbowl 31 championship team, 1996; lost Superbowl 32 to New Eng. Patriots, 1997. Holder Super Bowl record for longest pass reception, 1997; shares NFL postseason record for most touchdowns by punt return. Office: c/o Green Bay Packers PO Box 10628 Green Bay WI 54307-0628

FREEMAN, ARTHUR, veterinarian, retired association administrator; b. Youngstown, Ohio, Jan. 12, 1925; Student, Stanford U., 1949-50; D.V.M., Ohio State U., 1955. Pvt. practice Bellingham (Wa.) Vet. Hosp., 1955-56; dir. profl. rels. Jensen Salsbery Labs., Kansas City, Mo., 1956-59; editor Am. Vet. Med. Assn., Chgo., 1959-72, asst. exec. v.p. Schaumburg, Ill., 1977-84, editor-in-chief, 1972-84, exec. v.p., 1985-89. Dir. Coun. of Sci. Editors, Chgo., 1982-85, pres., 1985-86; adj. asst. prof. vet. med. Purdue U., 1997-2000. Contbr. articles to profl. publs. Mem. Indpls. Mus. Art, Indpls. Symphony Orch. 1st lt. USAF, 1942-60. Recipient Disting. Alumnus award Ohio State U., 1976, Ind. Vet. of the Yr. award, 1995. Mem. AVMA, Ohio Vet. Med. Assn. (Meritorious Svc. award 1989), Ind. State Vet. Med. Assn. (hon.), Ill. Vet. Med. Assn. (hon.), Mich. Vet. Med. Assn. (hon.), Indpls. Exec. Svc. Corps (Frederic M. Hadley Svc. award 1995), Ind. Hist. Soc., Indpls. Aero. Club. E-mail: freemanart@webtv.net.

FREEMAN, ARTHUR J. physics educator; b. Lublin, Poland, Feb. 6, 1930; s. Louis and Pearl (Mandelbaum) F.; m. Rhea B. Landin, June 21, 1952 (div. 1990); children: Jonathan (dec.), Seth, Claudia, Sarah; m. Doris Caro, Mar. 1991. B.S. in Physics, Mass. Inst. Tech., 1952, Ph.D., 1956. Instr. Brandeis U., 1955-56; solid state physicist Army Materials Research Agy., Watertown, Mass., 1956-62; instr. Northeastern U., 1957-59; assoc. lab. dir., leader theory group Francis Bitter Nat. Magnet Lab., Mass. Inst. Tech., 1962-67; prof. physics Northwestern U., Evanston, Ill., 1967-83, Morrison prof. physics, 1983—, chmn. dept. physics, 1967-71. Cons. Argonne Nat. Lab., Los Alamos Nat. Lab. Editor: Hyperfine Interactions, 1967, The Actinides: Electronic and Related Properties, Handbook on the Physics and Chemistry of the Actinides, Internat. Jour. Magnetism, 1970-75, Jour. Magnetism and Magnetic Materials, 1975—; mem. editl. adv. bd. Computational Materials Sci., 1992, Jour. Computer-Aided Materials Design, 1993; contbr. numerous articles to tech. lit. Guggenheim fellow, 1970-71; Fulbright-Hays fellow, 1970-71; Alexander von Humboldt Stiftung fellow 1977-78; 1st recipient medal Materials Rsch. Soc., 1990, award in magnetism Internat. Union Pure and Applied Physics, 1991. Fellow Am. Phys. Soc.; fgn. mem. Acad. Natural Scis. Russia, Russian Acad. Scis., Polish Acad. Scis. Home: 2739 Ridge Ave Evanston IL 60201-1719 Office: Northwestern Univ Dept Of Physics Evanston IL 60208-0001

FREEMAN, CHARLES E. state supreme court justice; b. Richmond, Va., Dec. 12, 1933; m. Marylee Voelker; 1 child Kevin. BA in Liberal Arts, Va. Union U., 1954; JD, John Marshall Law Sch., 1962, LLD (hon.) , 1992. Bar: Ill. 1962. Pvt. practice, 1962—76; pvt. practice, Cook County, Chgo., 1962—76, asst. state's atty., 1964; asst. atty. Bd. Election Commrs., Chgo., 1964—65; mem. Ill. Indsl. Commn., 1965—73, Ill. Commerce Commn., Chgo., 1973—76; judge law and chancery divsns. Cook County Cir. Ct., 1976—86; judge Appellate Ct. Ill., 1986—90; justice Ill. Supreme Ct., 1990—, chief justice, 1997—2000. Recipient Cert. Achievement, Internat. Christian Fellowship Missions, Earl B. Dickerson award, Chgo. Bar Assn., Merit award, Habilitative Sys., Statesmanship award, Monarch Awards Found. of Alpha Kappa Alpha, Freedom award, John Marshall Law Sch. Mem.: ABA (task force opportunities minorities in jud. adminstrn. divsn., coms. opportunities minorities in profession, cert. Recognition), DuPage County Bar Assn., Cook County Bar Assn. (Kenneth E. Wilson award, Cert. Merit, Ida Platt award, Presdl. award, Jud. award), Ill. Judges' Assn., Ill. Jud. Coun. (Kenneth Wilson Meml. award, Meritorious Svc. award), Ill. State Bar Assn., Am. Judicature Soc., Am. Judges' Assn. Achievements include being first African-American to swear in a Mayor, City of Chicago, to serve on Illinois Supreme Court, 1990;being leader in case disposition by published opinion, 1988, 89.*

FREEMAN, JEFFREY VAUGHN (JEFF FREEMAN), art educator, artist; b. Bismarck, N.D., Oct. 19, 1946; s. Dorrance Samuel Evan and Ethel Beatrice (Peterson) F. BS, Moorhead State U., 1970; MA, U. N.D., 1972; MFA, U. Wis., 1980. Grad. teaching asst. U. N.D., Grand Forks, 1970-72, U. Wis., Madison, 1978-80; prof. art U. S.D., Vermillion, 1980—. Subst. tchr. Moorhead (Minn.) Pub. Schs., 1973; mem. faculty adult edn. Ctrl. Cass Pub. Schs., 1973-74; adj. prof. Moorhead State U., 1973-75; coord. S.D. Coll. Art Assn. Painting Conf., U. S.D., Vermillion, 1981; cons., W.H. Over Mus., Vermillion, 1985; lectr. in field. One man shows include Jamestown (N.D.) Coll., 1973, Bison Gallery, Fargo, N.D., 1975, Plains Art Mus., Moorhead, 1979, U. Wis., Madison, 1980, Ritz Gallery, S.D. State U, Brookings, 1982, No. State Coll, Lincoln Hall Gallery, Aberdeen, S.D., 1984, Buena Vista Coll., Storm Lake, Iowa, 1985, S.D. Meml. Art Ctr., Brookings, 1985, Gallery 306, Sioux Falls, S.D., 1987, Gallery 72, Omaha, 1988, Ruddell Gallery, Black Hills State Coll., Spearfish, S.D., 1988, LeMars (Iowa) Civic Fine Arts Ctr., 1989, Nobles County Art Ctr., Worthington, Minn., 1990, U. S.D. Art Galleries, Vermillion, 1990, Olivet Nazarene U., Bourbonnais, Ill., 1990, Mount Vernon (Ohio) Nazarene Coll., 1990, Coffee Shop Gallery, Vermillion, 1991, U. Ark., 1992, DuPont Gallery, Lexington, Va., 1992, Nordstrand Gallery, Wayne, Nebr., 1993, The New Gallery, Rapid City, S.D., 1993, Bede Art Gallery, Yankton, S.D., 1993, 99, Gus Lucky Gallery, Minn., 1998, Pegasus Gall. Dorot Coll. Siouz Ctr. IA, 1999, others; exhibited in group shows at Minn. Mus. Art, St. Paul, 1975, Moorhead State U., 1975, 76, U. Minn., Morris, 1975, Thief River Falls C.C., Minn., 1976, 1st Nat. Bank, Moorhead, 1976, U. Wis., 1978, Plains Art Mus., Moorhead, 1978, 79, 93, U. S.D., 1981, 82, 83, 84, 85, 87, 88, 90, 92, 94, 96, 98, Rourke Art Gallery, Moorhead, Minn., 1982, 83, 84, 85, 86, 89, 90, 97, 98, No. State Coll., Student Union Gallery, 1981, Sioux City Art Ctr., 1983, 88, 90, 92, 98, 99, N.D. State U. Art Gallery, Fargo, 1984, N.D. Mus. Art, Grand Forks, 1984, Sioux Falls (S.D.) Civic Fine Arts Ctr., 1987, Gallery 72, Omaha, 1988, 90, 2001, Dahl Fine Arts Ctr., Rapid City, S.D., 1988, Joslyn Art Mus., Omaha, 1990, S.D. Art Mus., Brookings, 1991, 93, 95, 97, Sheldon Meml. Art Gallery, Lincoln, Nebr., 1991, The New Gallery, Rapid City, 1992, 94, 96, Thimmesh Gallery, Mpls., 1992, 93, 94, Chgo. Art Expo, 1993, Jamestown (N.D.) Art Ctr., 1993, Mus. Der Stadt Ratingen, Germany, 1997, others; represented in permanent collections Joslyn Art Mus., Donaghey Found., Little Rock, U. Ark., Little Rock, Sheldon Meml. Art Gallery, Lincoln, Nebr., Legrand and Co., Sioux City, Sioux City Art Ctr., Sioux Falls Civic Fine Arts Ctr., Klinger Corp., Sioux City, S.D. Art Mus., Brookings, Plains Art Mus., Moorhead, N.D. Mus. of Art, Grand Forks, Madison Art Ctr., Comstock Meml. Union, Moorhead State U., U. S.D., Vermillion, Norwest Bank, Moorhead, Grafton, N.D. and various pvt. collections in N.D., S.D., Minn., Nebr., Iowa, Ohio, Ill., Alaska, Wis., La., Mass, Calif., N.Y., Ariz., N.C., Tex., Wash., Oreg. and N.J. Rsch. grantee S.D. Rsch. Inst., U. S.D., 1982, 86, Bush Found. grantee, 1988; Visual Artist grantee S.D. Arts Coun., 1988-89; Painting fellow Arts Midwest/Nat. Endowment for the Arts, 1990-91, Nat. Endowment for the Arts, 1991-92; recipient 1st Place and Purchase award Plains Art Mus., Moorhead, 1978, Jury Purchase award Madison Art Ctr., 1978, Best Painting award Sioux City Fall Biennial, 1983, Merit award ARTQUEST, 1985. Home: 900 W Main St Vermillion SD 57069-2915 Office: U SD Art Dept 414 E Clark St Vermillion SD 57069-2307

FREEMAN, LEE ALLEN, JR. lawyer; b. Chgo., July 31, 1940; s. Lee Allen and Brena (Dietz) F.; m. Glynna Gene Weger, June 8, 1968; children: Crispin McDougal, Clark Dietz, Cassidy Bree. A.B. magna cum laude, Harvard U., 1962, J.D. magna cum laude, 1965. Bar: Ill. 1966, D.C. 1966, Mont. 1986, U.S. Supreme Ct. 1969. Practiced in, Washington, 1965-68, Chgo., 1968—; law clk. to Justice Tom C. Clark, Washington, 1965-66; asst. U.S. atty., 1966-68; v.p. Freeman, Freeman & Salzman, P.C., 1970—; spl. asst. atty. gen. Ill., W.Va., 1969-82, Mich., Wis., Minn., Colo., Ky., N.D., 1973-79; spl. dep. atty. gen. Pa., 1971-82; spl. asst. corp. counsel Chgo., 1971-76. Pres. Chgo. Lyric Opera Guild; pres. Fine Arts Music Found.; dir. Chgo. Lyric Opera, 1995—; mem. Middlebury Coll. Arts Coun. Named Outstanding Young Citizen Chgo. Jaycees, 1976 Fellow: ABA Found.; mem.: ABA (coun. mem. antitrust sect. 1985—87), Am. Coll. Trial Lawyers, Chgo. Inn of Ct., Std. Club. Home: 232 E Walton St Chicago IL 60611-1507 also: 22 Bright Ln Wilsall MT 59086-9432 Office: 401 N Michigan Ave Chicago IL 60611-4255 E-mail: lfreemanjr@ffspc.com.

FREEMAN, LESLIE GORDON, anthropologist, educator; b. Warsaw, Sept. 9, 1935; s. Leslie Gordon and Theresa Rosalie (Stanbro) F.; m. Susan Tax, Mar. 20, 1964; 1 child, Sarah Elisabeth. AB, U. Chgo., 1954, AM, 1961, PhD, 1964. Asst. prof. anthropology Tulane U., 1964-65; asst. prof. U. Chgo., 1965-70, assoc. prof., 1970-76, prof., 1976-2000, prof. emeritus, 2000—; pres. Inst. Prehistoric Investigations, Chgo., 1983—2001. Author: (with J. Gonzalez) Cueva Morin, 2 vols., 1971, 73, Vida y Muerte en Cueva Morin, 1978, Le Paleolithique Inferieur et Moyen en Espagne, 1998, La Grotte d'Altamira, 2001; editor: Views of the Past, 1978, (with Sol Tax) Horizons of Anthropology, 1976, (with others) Altamira Revisited, 1987, Beato de Liebana, 1995. Corporator Internat. Inst. Spain. With U.S. Army, 1957-59. Recipient Silver Plaque Provincial Deputation of Santander, Spain, 1973 Fellow AAAS, Am. Anthropol. Assn., Royal Anthropol. Inst.; mem. Reial Academia Catalana de Belles Arts de Sant Jordi Barcelona (corr.), Reial Academia Catalana de Bones Lletres Barcelona (corr.), Chgo. Acad. Scis. (trustee, 2d v.p. 1981-83). Home: Apt 507 1700 E 56th St Chicago IL 60637 Office: U Chgo Dept Anthropology Haskell Hall M-306 Chicago IL 60637

FREEMAN, LOUIS S. lawyer; b. Cin., Apr. 21, 1940; s. Emanuel and Sadye (Harris) F.; m. Diane Ruth Edson, Jan. 28, 1967; children: Matthew E., James H., Jill E. BBA, U. Cin., 1963; JD, Harvard U., 1966; LLM in Taxation, NYU, 1972. Bar: Ohio 1966, N.Y. 1968, Ill. 1975. CPA. Mem. staff Coopers & Lybrand, N.Y.C., 1966-68; assoc. Mudge, Rose, Guthrie & Alexander, 1968-74, Sonnenschein Nath & Rosenthal, Chgo., 1974-76, ptnr., 1976-97, Skadden, Arps, Slate, Meagher & Flom, Chgo., 1997—. Adj. prof. of taxation Ill. Inst. Tech., Chgo.-Kent Coll. of Law Grads. Program in Taxation, 1985-89 Mem. bds. of contbg. editors Jour. Corp. Taxation, Jour. Real Estate Taxation, Jour. Taxation of Investments; bd. advisors the M&A Tax Report, Jour. Corp. Taxation; also author articles. Fellow Am. Coll. Tax Counsel; mem. ABA (tax sect. com. on corp. tax), Chgo. Bar Assn., (chmn. exec. com. of fed. tax com. 1986-87), N.Y. Sate Bar Assn. (tax sect. exec. com. 1990-92), Am. Law Inst. (tax adv. group subchpt. C. Fed. Income Tax Project), Met. Club of Chgo. Office: Skadden Arps Slate Meagher & Flom 333 W Wacker Dr Chicago IL 60606-1220 E-mail: LFreeman@skadden.com.

FREEMAN, MARY LOUISE, state legislator; b. Willmar, Minn., Oct. 21, 1941; d. James Martin and Luella Anna (Backlund) Hawkinson; children: Mark D., Sara L., Cary D., Maret S. BA, Gustavus Adolphus Coll., 1963. Substitute tchr. Arrowhead Edn. Assn., Storm Lake, Iowa, 1982-93; tchr., cons. Midwest Power, Des Moines, 1991-94; mem. Iowa Senate from 5th dist., 1994—. Mem. Iowa State Bd. Health, 1988-94; mem. early childhood intervention com., 1994—, mem. disaster prevention svcs. com., 1994—. Del. alt. Rep. Nat. Conv., Kansas City, 1976; active Midwest-Can. Relations Co., 1994—. Mem. Am. Legis. Exch. Coun., Nat. Coun. State Govts., Buena Vista County Farm Bur., Storm Lake C. of C., Delta Kappa Gamma. Lutheran. Home: 203 Lake St Alta IA 51002-1228 Office: Iowa State Senate State Capitol Des Moines IA 50319-0001

FREEMAN, MICHAEL O. lawyer; m. Terry Mathison; children: Katie, Beth, Matthew. BA, Rutgers Coll., 1970; JD, U. Minn., 1974; grad. exec. leadership program, Harvard U., 1995. Bar: Minn. 1974, U.S. Ct. Appeals (8th cir.) 1974, U.S. Supreme Ct. 1992. Law clk. to Judge Earl Larson U.S. Dist. Ct. Minn., 1974-75; law clk. to Judge Gerald W. Heaney U.S. Ct. Appeals (8th cir.), 1975-76; trial atty. Popham, Haik, Mpls., 1979-91; atty. Hennepin County, 1991, 95—. Minn. state campaign mgr. Carter/Mondale Presdl. Campaign, 1976; cand. 3d Congl. Dist., U.S. Congress, 1978; chair 3d Congl. Dist. DFL Party, 1980; chair conf. com. Senate Capital Bonding Bill, 1987, 89, 90; chair Hennepin County Legis. Del., 1989-90; vice-chair Senate Econ. Devel. and Commerce Com., 1983-89, Senate Fin. Com., 1987-91. Commr. Richfield Housing and Redevel. Authority, 1979-82; treas. Minn. Found. for Improvement of Elem. Edn., 1986-92; chair Hennepin County Criminal Justice Coordinating Com., 1992-96; bd. dirs. CornerHouse, 1991—, treas., 1994-96; bd. dirs. Summit Acad. OIC; mem. Citizens League, Richfield Am. Legion; coach Richfield Girls Basketball, 1990-96, Richfield Boys Football, 1992-96; Sunday sch. tchr. St. Richard's Cath. Ch., 1989-93. Mem. Minn. State Bar Assn. (designated civil trial specialist). Office: Office of Hennepin County Atty 2000 Government Ctr Minneapolis MN 55487-0001

FREEMAN, SUSAN TAX, anthropologist, educator, culinary historian; b. Chgo., May 24, 1938; d. Sol and Gertrude Tax.; m. Leslie G. Freeman, Jr., Mar. 20, 1964; 1 dau., Sarah Elisabeth. BA, U. Chgo., 1958; MA, Harvard U., 1959, PhD, 1965. Asst. prof. anthropology U. Ill., Chgo., 1965-70, assoc. prof., 1970-78, prof., 1978—, prof. emerita, 1999—, chmn., 1979-82. Rsch. assoc. dept. sociology and anthropology Mont. State U., Bozeman, 1992—; panelist NEH, Council for Internat. Exchange of Scholars; mem. anthropology screening com. Fulbright-Hays Research Awards, 1975-78; mem. ad hoc com. on research in Spain Spain-U.S.A. Friendship Agreement, various yrs., 1977-84; field researcher Mex., 1959, Spain, 1962—, Japan, 1983; instr. Radcliffe Coll. Seminars on Food in History and Culture, 1998. Author: Neighbors: The Social Contract in a Castilian Hamlet, 1970, The Pasiegos-Spaniards in No Man's Land, 1979; assoc. editor: Am. Anthropologist, 1971-73, Am. Ethnologist, 1974-76; editl. bd. Gastronomica, 2000—. Named to Inst. for the Humanities, U. Ill. Chgo., 1987-88; Wenner-Gren Found. for Anthrop. Research grantee, 1966, 83; NIMH grantee, 1967, 68-71; NEH fellowships , 1978-79, 89-90. Fellow Am. Anthrop. Assn. (nominating com. 1981-82, Centennial Adv. Commn. 1999—), Royal Anthrop. Inst. Gt. Britain and Ireland; mem. Soc. for Anthropology of Europe (exec. com. 1987-88), Soc. Spanish and Portuguese Hist. Studies (exec. com. 1990-92), Coun. European Studies (steering com. 1980-83), Internat. Inst. Spain (corporator, bd. dirs. 1982-87, 2000—), Centro Estudios Sorianos (hon.), Assn. Anthropologia Castilla y Leon (hon.). Home: 1700 E 56th St Apt 507 Chicago IL 60637 Office: U Ill Dept Anthro M/C 027 1007 W Harrison St Chicago IL 60607-7135

FREEMAN, TODD IRA, lawyer; b. Mpls., Nov. 24, 1953; s. Earl Stanley and Gretta Lois (Rudick) F.; m. Judy Lynn Sigel, June 15, 1975; children: Jennifer, Katie, Zachary. BS in Mktg., U. Colo., 1974; JD, U. Minn., 1978. Bar: Minn. 1978, U.S. Dist. Ct. Minn. 1978, U.S. Tax Ct. 1980; CPA, Minn. Acct. Coopers & Lybrand, Mpls., 1978-80; shareholder Larkin, Hoffman, Daly & Lindgren, 1980—, treas., 1990—, also bd. dirs., 1990-93. Mem. ABA (tax sect., past chmn. personal svc. orgns.), Minn. Soc. CPAs, Minn. State Bar Assn., Hennepin County Bar Assn. Avocations: tennis, golf. Office: Larkin Hoffman Daly & Lindgren 7900 Xerxes Ave S Ste 1500 Minneapolis MN 55431-1128

FREEMAN-WILSON, KAREN, former attorney general, prosecutor, educational association administrator; m. Carmen Wilson; 1 child Jordan ;3 stepchildren. BA cum laude in Econs. and Afro-Am. studies, Harvard Coll., 1982, JD, 1985. Pub. defender Lake County; ptnr. Freeman-Wilson and Lewis; dir. Ind. Office Drug Control Policy; atty. gen., chief legal officer State of Ind., judge drug ct.; pub. defender, exec. dir. Ind. Civil Rights Commn.; dep. prosecutor Lake County, 1985—88; exec. dir. Ind. Civil Rights commn., 1989—92; judge Gary City Ct., 1994—2000; atty. gen. State Ind., Indpls., 2000—01; exec. dir. Nat. Drug Ct. Inst., 2002—; CEO Nat. Assn. Drug Ct. Profls., 2002—. Instr. Valparaiso U. Law Sch., Ind. U. Sch. Law; bd. dirs. Conf. for Legal Edn. and Opportunity, Ind. Supreme Ct. Trainer rape awareness Gary Commn. for Women; active Harbor House; bd. dirs. Rainbow Shelter. Address: 4900 Seminary Rd Ste 320 Alexandria VA 22311 Business E-Mail: kfwilson@nadcp.org.*

FREESE, STEPHEN J. state legislator; b. Dubuque, Iowa, Mar. 16, 1960; s. Joseph and Rowetta (Johnson) F.; m. Dawn Freshe; 1 child, Marie. BS, U. Wis., Platteville, 1982. Asst. to chmn. 3d Dist. Rep. Com., Wis., 1981-82; sales rep. Tegler's Inc., 1982-91; mem. from dist. 51 Wis. State Assembly, Madison, 1990—, vice chmn. Rep. caucus, 1993-94, spkr. pro tempore, 1995—. Supr. Town of Jamestown, Wis., 1980-94; mem. Grant County Bd. Suprs., 1982-92; mem. Wis. Fedn. Young Reps.; mem. Wis. State Rep. Com.; chmn. Grant County Rep. Com., 1983—.

FREESE, UWE ERNEST, physician, educator; b. Bordesholm, Germany, May 11, 1925; s. Heinrich and Frida (Lessau) F.; m. Gabriela Friederici, Oct. 11, 1961; children: Axel, Pamela. M.D., U. Kiel, W.Ger., 1951. Diplomate: Am. Bd. Obstetrics and Gynecology. Resident U. Kiel, 1954-56, U. Chgo. Lying-in Hosp., 1956-59, prof. ob-gyn., 1971-75; prof., chmn. dept. Chgo. Med. Sch., 1975-95; prof. emeritus, 1995; chmn. dept. ob-gyn. Cook County Hosp., 1976-95, chmn. emeritus, 1995—; prof., chair emeritus ob/gyn The Chgo. Med. Sch., 1995—. Patentee cervical cap. Mem. Soc. Gynecol. Investigation, Perinatal Research Soc. (founding mem.), Central Assn. Obstetrics and Gynecology (cert. of merit 1967), Perinatal Soc. Ill. East (chmn.), N.Y. Acad. Scis., Sigma Xi Lutheran. Home: 238 Forest Ave Oak Park IL 60302-1908 Office: U Health Scis Chicago Med Sch 3333 Green Bay Rd North Chicago IL 60064-3037

FREIBAUM, BERNARD, real estate development company executive; b. 1953; V.p. fin. Stein & Co., sr. v.p. fin., CFO, 1988-93; CFO, contr. Gen. Growth Properties, Inc., Des Moines, 1993—. Office: Gen Growth Properties Inc 110 N Wacker Dr Chicago IL 60606-1511

FREIER, TOM D. state legislator; m. Melinda Freier; 2 children. Student, Valley City (N.D.) State Coll. Owner restaurant, Linton, N.D.; fin. planner; state rep. dist. 28 State of N.D., 1991—; dir. N.D. Dept. Transp. Mem. appropriations com., edn. and environ. com., asst. majority leader N.D. Ho. Reps. Bd. dirs. Linton Indsl. Devel. Corp., N.D. Credit Union; former pres. Linton City Coun. Mem. N.D. Hosp. Assn., Linton C. of C., Lions, Elks. Republican. Home: 2624 E Divide Ave Bismarck ND 58501-2559

FRENCH, CATHERINE E. WOLFGRAM, engineering educator, researcher; b. Dec. 17, 1957; BS in Civil Engring., U. Minn., 1979; MS in Civil Engring., U. Ill., 1980, PhD in Civil Engring., 1984. Rsch. and tchg. asst. dept. civil engring. U. Ill., Urbana-Champaign, 1979-83; asst. prof. dept. civil engring. U. Minn., Mpls., 1984-90, assoc. prof. dept. civil engring., 1990-97, prof., assoc. head dept. civil engring., 1997-2000. Mem. external adv. com. FEMA external adv. com. Earthquake Engring. Simulation Facility U. Nev., Reno, 1994-97. Erskine fellow U. Canterbury, New Zealand, 1995, Fulbright Travel fellow New Zealand, 1995; recipient Presdl. Young Investigator award NSF, 1985, R.J. Boase award for contbns. to prestressed concrete rsch. Reinforced Concrete Rsch. Coun., Young Civil Engrs. Achievement award U. Ill. Civil Engring. Alumni Assn., 1987, Minn. Young Civil Engr. of Yr. Minn. Soc. Profl. Engrs., 1989, Faculty Award for Women, 1991-96, Bonestroo, Rosene, Anderlik and Assoc. Undergrad. Faculty award, 1994. Fellow Am. Concrete Inst. Inst. (chair com. joint ASCE-ACI com. 445 shear and torsion, com. 318 std. bldg. code 1996—, bd. dirs. Iowa-Minn. chpt. 1987-91, pres. 1991, Outstanding Chpt. award 1991, bd. dirs. 1996-91); mem. ASCE (award for Outstanding Svc. as Faculty Adv. to student chpt. 1986-90, 1986, Edmund Friedman Young Engr. award for Profl. Achievement 1989, U. Minn. Gordon L. Starr award Outstanding Faculty Contbn. to student chpt. 1990, Raymond C. Reese Rsch. prize 1990, mem. structures com. Minn. 1986-90, pres. Minn. chpt. 1996-97), Earthquake Engring. Rsch. Inst. (Travel grant 1988, 2000), Precast/Prestressed Concrete Inst. (seismic com., high strength concrete com.), Transportation Rsch. Bd. (concrete bridges com.), Minn. Surveyors and Engrs. Soc. Achievements include research in behavior of reinforced concrete and prestressed concrete structures subjected to lateral loads, extra spaces, bond strength and durability of reinforcement in concrete, investigation of causes and methods to eliminate end cracking in the fabrication of prestressed bridge girders, application of high strength concrete to prestressed systems, investigation of mechanical properties of high strength concrete and structural behavior of prestressed bridge girders fabricated with high strength concrete, development of testing method "effective force testing" for real-time earthquake simulation. Office: U Minn Dept Civil Engring 122 Civil Engring Bldg 500 Pillsbury Dr SE Minneapolis MN 55455-0233

FRENCH, JOHN DWYER, lawyer; b. Berkeley, Calif., June 26, 1933; s. Horton Irving and Gertrude Margery (Ritzen) F.; m. Annette Richard, 1955; m. Berna Jo Mahling, 1986. BA summa cum laude, U. Minn., 1955; postgrad, Oxford U., Eng., 1955-56; LLB magna cum laude, Harvard U., 1960. Bar: D.C. 1960, Minn. 1963. Law clk. Justice Felix Frankfurter, U.S. Supreme Ct., 1960-61; legal asst. to commr. FTC, 1961-62; assoc. Ropes & Gray, Boston, 1962-63, Faegre & Benson, Mpls., 1963-66, ptnr., 1967-75, mng. ptnr., 1975-94, chmn. mgmt. com., 1989-94. Mem. adj. faculty Law Sch. U. Minn., 1965-70, mem. search com. for dean of Coll. of Liberal Arts, 1996; mem. exec. com. Lawyers Com. for Civil Rights Under Law, 1978—; co-chmn. U.S. Dist. Judge Nominating Commn., 1979; vice chmn. adv. com., mem. dir. search com., chmn. devel. office search com. Hubert Humphrey Inst., 1979-87. Contbr. numerous articles and revs. to legal jours. Chmn. or co-chmn. Minn. State Dem. Farm Labor Party Conv., 1970-90, 94, chmn. Mondale Vol. Com., 1972, treas., 1974; assoc. chmn. Minn. Dem.-Farmer-Labor Party, 1985-86; mem. Dem. Nat. Com., 1985-86; mem. Dem. Nat. Conv., 1976, 78, 80, 84, 88; trustee Twin Cities Public TV, Inc., 1980-86, mem. overseers com. to visit Harvard U. Law Sch., 1970-75, 77-82; chmn. Minn. steering com. Dukakis for Pres., 1987-88; mem. Sec. of State's Commn. on Electoral Reform, Minn., 1994; mem. Mayor's Commn. on Regulatory Reform, Mpls., 1995. With U.S. Army, 1955-56. Rotary Found. fellow, 1955-56 Mem. ABA (editorial bd. jour. 1976-79, commn. to study fed. trade 1969—), Minn. Bar Assn., Hennepin County Bar Assn., Jud. Coun. Minn., Lawyers Alliance for Nuclear Arms Control (nat. bd. dirs. 1982-84), U. Minn. Alumni Assn. (exec. com. 1985-87, v.p. 1989-91, pres. 1991-92, Vol. of Yr. award 1988), Phi Beta Kappa. Episcopalian. Office: Faegre & Benson 2200 Wells Fargo Ctr 90 S 7th St Ste 2200 Minneapolis MN 55402-3901

FRERICHS, DONALD L. retired state legislator; b. Ocheyedan, Iowa, Jan. 3, 1931; m. Dianne R. Rickbeil, 1951; children: Craig D., Scott R., Krista B. BA, Mankato State U., 1954. Supr. Rochester Twp., 1968-81; state rep. Minn. Ho. Reps., Dist. 31A, 1981-96, ret., 1996. Mem. econ. devel. infrastructure and regulation fin., transp. and transit, transp. fin. and ways and means coms.; pres. Bio-Conversion Inc.; advisor to commr. Minn. Dept. Commerce. Home: 644 Southern Woods Cir SW Rochester MN 55902-1836 E-mail: dlfrerichs@msn.com.

FREY, DONALD NELSON, b. St. Louis, Mar. 13, 1923; s. Muir Luken and Margaret Bryden (Nelson) Frey; m. Bonnie A. Gore, May 28, 1989; children from previous marriage: Donald Nelson, Judith Kingsley(dec.) , Margaret Bente, Catherine, Christopher, Elizabeth. Student, Mich. State Coll., 1940—42; BS, U. Mich., 1947, MS, 1949, PhD, 1950, DSc (hon.) , 1965; DSc, U. Mo., Rolla, 1966. Instr. metall. engring. U. Mich., 1949—50, asst. prof. chem. and metall. engring., 1950—51; rsch. engr. Babcock & Wilcox Tube Co., Beaver Falls, Pa., 1951; various rsch. positions Ford Motor Co. (Ford div.), 1951—57, various engring. positions, 1958—61, product planning mgr., 1961—62, asst. gen. mgr., 1962—65, gen. mgr., 1965—68, co. v.p. for product devel., 1965—67; pres. Gen. Cable Corp., N.Y.C., 1968—71, Bell & Howell Co., Chgo., 1973—81, chmn., CEO, 1971—88, also bd. dirs.; prof. of indsl. engring. and mgmt. sci. Northwestern U., Evanston, 1988—. Bd. dirs. Cin. Milacron, Clark Equipment Co., Packer Engring., My Own Meals, Hyatt Corp., Springs Industries, Quintar, 20th Century Fox Corp.; co-chair Japan study multinats. NRC, 1992—94; surveyor World Book, Poland, 1990. Co-chmn. Gov.'s Commn. of Sci. and Industry, Ill., 1988—. With U.S. Army, 1942—46. Named Young Engr. of Yr., Engring. Soc. Detroit, 1953, Outstanding Alumni, U. Mich. Coll. Engring., 1957, Outstanding Young Man of the Yr., Detroit Jr. Bd. of Commerce, 1958, Man of the Yr., Weissmann Inst., 1988; recipient Nat. medal for tech., 1990. Fellow: AAAS; mem.: ASME, Coun. on Fgn. Rels., Detroit Engring. Soc. (pres., bd. dirs. 1962—65), Soc. Automotive Engrs. (vice chmn. Detroit 1958, Russell Springer award 1956), Nat. Acad. Engring. (mem. coun. 1972), Am. Soc. Metals, Am. Inst. Mining and Metall. Engrs. (chmn. Detroit chpt. 1954, chmn., editor Nat. Symposium on Sheet Steels 1956), Econ. Club, Saddle and Cycle Club, Chgo. Club, Hundred Club Cook County, Chgo. Commonwealth Club, Phi Delta Theta, Tau Beta Pi, Phi Kappa Phi, Sigma Xi. Home: 2758 Sheridan Rd Evanston IL 60201-1728 Office: Northwestern U 2145 Sheridan Rd Rm M237 Evanston IL 60208-0834

FREY, HARLEY HARRISON, JR. anesthesiologist; b. Toledo, Feb. 22, 1920; s. Harley Harrison and Mina Rosina (Wiedemann) F.; m. Jane Luceia Murray, Aug. 28, 1944 (dec. 1964); children: Richard E., Martha J., Thomas C.; m. Emma Jean Hamilton, Apr. 15, 1966; 1 stepchild, Rick A. Gregory. BS, U. Toledo, 1942; MD, U. Cin., 1945. Diplomate Am. Bd. Anesthesiology. Intern Akron City Hosp., Ohio, 1946—47; fellow anesthesia U. Minn., Mpls., 1950; hon. mem. staff St. Elizabeth Hosp. Med. Ctr., Lafayette, Ind., 1950—, Lafayette Home Hosp., 1950—. Bd. dirs. Lafayette Symphony Orch., 1952-54; counselor, committeeman Lafayette coun. Boy Scouts Am., 1955-63; ruling elder Presbyn. Ch., 1964-67, active deacon, 1991-94; bd. dirs. Lafayette Citizens Band, 1997-2000. Capt. U.S. Army, 1947—49. Fellow Am. Coll. Anesthesiology; mem. Am. Soc. Anesthesiology (bd. dirs. 1965-74), Ind. Soc. Anesthesiology (pres., bd. dirs. 1961-74, Disting Svc. award 1992), Ind. State Med. Soc. (Cert. Distinction 1995), Tippecanoe County Med. soc. (pres. 1961), Rotary (bd. dirs. 1992-95) Lafayette Country Club (bd. dirs. 1963-65). Avocations: music, painting. Home and Office: 3513 Creek Ridge Lafayette IN 47905-5619

FREYTAG, DONALD ASHE, management consultant; b. Chgo., Apr. 17, 1937; s. Elmer Walter and Mary Louise (Mayo) F.; m. Elizabeth Ritchie Robertson, Dec. 19, 1964; children: Donald C., Gavin K., Alexander M. BA, Yale U., 1959; MBA, Harvard U., 1963. Pres. Mgmts. West, LaJolla, Calif., 1963-65; mktg. asst. Norton Simon, Inc., Fullerton, 1965-67; product mgr. Warner-Lambert, Inc., Morristown, N.J., 1967-70; group mgr. mktg.-planning dir. advt. Pepsi-Cola Co., Purchase, N.Y., 1970-72; from v.p. mktg. to exec. v.p. Beverage Mgmt., Inc., Columbus, Ohio, 1972-76, pres., 1976-79, vice-chmn., 1979-80; pres. Freytag Mgmt. Co., 1980-82, 84—, G.D. Ritzy's, Inc., Columbus, 1982-84. Bd. dirs. Antolino & Assoc., Atlas-Butler, Barney Corp., Century Resources, Contract Sweepers, Contrack Corp., Inc., Columbus Showcase Co., Columbus Paper and Copy Supply Co., Eastway Supplies, Inc., Greencrest Mktg., Ohio Full Ct. Press, Inc., Reitter Stucco, Inc., Profitworks Ltd., Paul Werth & Assoc., Coughlin Automotive Group, Newark, Hugo Bosca Co., Springfield, Ohio, Fenton Art Glass Co., Inc., Williamstown, W.Va., Scioto Properties, LLC, Columbus; ctrl. region dir. Ohio Com. for Employer Support of the Guard and Res., 1992—95. Pres. Cen. Ohio Ctr. for Econ. Edn., 1978-80, 81-87; bd. dirs. Columbus Acad., 1982-84. Capt. U.S. Army, 1959-61. Recipient Roman F. Warmke award, Ohio Coun. on Econ. Edn., 1991. Mem. Nat. Assn. Corp. Dirs., HBS Club Columbus, Yale Club. Avocations: jogging, bicycling, scuba diving, golf, reading. Office: 7955 Riverside Dr Dublin OH 43016-8234 E-mail: dafreytag@cs.com.

FRIAS, RAFAEL, city official; BA, U. Ill., Chgo. Police officer Chgo. Police Dept.; mem. from 1st dist. U.S. Ho. of Reps.; alderman City of Chgo. Founder United Neighbors Improving the Environment. Home: 3637 S Maplewood Ave Chicago IL 60632-1022 Office: 121 N LaSalle St Rm 209 Office 21 Chicago IL 60602

FRIED, SAMUEL, lawyer; b. Bklyn., Aug. 16, 1951; s. Zoltan and Helen (Katina) F.; m. Gigi Panush, Dec. 27, 1981; children: Eva M., Orly Z., Jacob J., Molly R., Susanna R. AB, Washington U., St. Louis, 1971; JD, Boston U., 1974, LLM, 1997. Bar: Mass. 1974, Ill. 1983, Mich. 1989; ordained rabbi, 1971. Assoc. Warner & Stackpole, Boston, 1974-77; staff atty. The Bendix Corp., Southfield, Mich., 1977-79, sr. atty., 1979-80, asst. treas., 1980-81; v.p., corp. counsel Clevite Industries, Inc., Glenview, Ill., 1981-83, v.p., sec., gen. counsel, 1983-87; v.p., sec. gen. counsel Exide Corp., Troy, Mich., 1987-91; v.p., gen. counsel The Limited Inc., 1991-99, sr. v.p., gen. counsel, sec., 1999—. Editor: Psychosurgery, 1974. Mem. ABA, Am. Corp. Counsel Assn., Mich. Gen. Counsels Assn., Phi Beta Kappa. Jewish. Avocations: music, reading. Office: The Limited Inc PO Box 16000 3 Limited Pkwy Columbus OH 43230-1467

FRIEDLAENDER, FRITZ JOSEF, electrical engineering educator; b. Freiburg/Breisgau, Germany, May 7, 1925; came to U.S., 1947, naturalized, 1953; s. Ludwig and Frieda (Murzynski) F.; m. Gisela Triebe, Aug. 7, 1969; 2 children. BS, Carnegie Mellon U., 1951, MS, 1952, PhD, 1955; Dr.-Ing. (E.h.), Ruhr-Universität Bochum, Germany, 1992. Asst. prof. Columbia, 1954-55, Purdue U., West Lafayette, Ind., 1955-59, assoc. prof., 1959-62, prof. elec. and computer engring., 1962-2000; guest prof. Max-Planck Institut Metallforschung, Tech. U. Stuttgart, Fed. Republic Germany, 1964-65; Humboldt award and guest prof. Institut für Werkstoffe der Elektrotechnik, Ruhr-Universität, Bochum, West Germany, 1972-73; Japan Soc. for Promotion Sci. fellow and guest prof. Nagoya U., summer 1980; guest prof. U. Regensburg (Fed. Republic Germany), 1981-82; Meyerhoff vis. prof. Weizmann Inst. Sci., Rehovot, Israel, Jan.-June 1990; prof. emeritus, 2001—. Cons. Gen. Electric Corp., Ft. Wayne, Ind., 1956-58, Components Corp., Chgo., 1959-61, Lawrence Radiation Lab., U. Calif. at Livermore, 1967-69, P.R. Mallory & Co., 1974-78, Oakridge Nat. Lab., 1979-82 Adv. editor Jour. Magnetism and Magnetic Materials, 1975—; co-editor Magnetic Separation News, 1983-91, Magnetic and Electrical Separation, 1991—; mem. editorial bd. Proc. IEEE, 1975-78; contbr. articles to profl. jours. Recipient Millennium medal IEEE, 2000, Carnegie Mellon U. Alumni Merit award, 2001. Fellow IEEE (revs. editor trans. Magnetics 1965-67, editorial bd. jour. 1968— , chmn. awards Magnetics Soc. 1966-74, 85—, achievement award Magnetics Soc. 1986, chmn. Intermag 1975, London, program co-chmn. Intermag 1978, Florence, Italy, v.p. Magnetics Soc. 1975-76, pres. 1977-78, chmn. Central Ind. sect. 1979-80, J. Fred Peoples award 1989, disting. lectr. 1991-93, IEEE Magnetics Soc., 3d Millennium medal 2000, 8th Internat. Conf. on Ferrites Spl. award 2000, Spl. Recognition award Magnetics Soc. 2001), Am. Phys. Soc.; mem. Am. Soc. Engring. Edn., Magnetics Soc. of Japan (hon.), Arbeitsgemeinschaft Magnetismus, Sigma Xi, Phi Kappa Phi, Tau Beta Pi, Eta Kappa Nu, Beta Sigma Rho. Achievements include research in magnetics, magnetic devices and memories, high gradient magnetic separation, magnetic bubble dynamics, Vertical Bloch Lines, microwave ferrites, Ni-Fe tape magnetization processes. Home: 150 Colony Rd West Lafayette IN 47906-1209 Office: Purdue U Sch Elec and Computer Engrn 1285 Electrical Engineering West Lafayette IN 47907-1285 E-mail: fritz@ecn.purdue.edu.

FRIEDLANDER, MICHAEL WULF, physicist, educator; b. Cape Town, South Africa, Nov. 15, 1928; came to U.S., 1956; m. Jessica R. Friedlander; 2 children. BS in Physics, U. Cape Town, 1948, MS with 1st class honors, 1950; PhD in Physics, U. Bristol (Eng.), 1955. Jr. lectr. U. Cape Town, 1950-52; rsch. assoc. U. Bristol, 1954-56; asst. prof. physics Washington U., St. Louis, 1956-61, assoc. prof., 1961-67, prof., 1967—. Author: The Conduct of Science, 1972, Astronomy: From Stonehenge to Quasars, 1985, Cosmic Rays, 1989, At the Fringes of Science, 1995, A Thin Cosmic Rain, 2000; contbr. articles to Ency. Brit. and profl. jours. Guggenheim Found. fellow, vis. prof. Imperial Coll., London, 1962-63. Mem. AAUP (2d v.p. 1978-80, mem. nat. coun. 1975-78, 86-89), AAAS, Am. Phys. Soc., Am. Astron. Soc., History of Sci. Soc. Achievements include research in elementary particles, cosmic rays, infrared astronomy, and gamma ray astronomy. Office: Washington U Dept Physics One Brookings Dr Saint Louis MO 63130

FRIEDMAN, AVNER, mathematician, educator; b. Petah-Tikva, Israel, Nov. 19, 1932; arrived in U.S., 1956; s. Moshe and Hanna (Rosenthal) Friedman; m. Lillia Lynn, June 7, 1959; children: Alissa, Joel, Naomi, Tamara. MSc, Hebrew U., Jerusalem, 1954, PhD, 1956. Prof. math. Northwestern U., Evanston, Ill., 1962-86; prof. Purdue U., West Lafayette, Ind., 1984-87, dir. Ctr. Applied Math., 1984-87; prof. math., dir. Inst. Math. and Its Applications U. Minn., Mpls., 1987-97, dir. Minn. Ctr. for Indsl. Math., 1994—2002; prof. Ohio State U., Columbus, 2002—. Author: (book) Generalized Functions and Partial Differential Equations, 1963, Partial Differential Equations of Parabolic Type, 1964, Partial Differential Equations, 1969, Foundations of Modern Analysis, 1970, Advanced Calculus, 1971, Differential Games, 1971, Stochastic Differential Equations and Applications, Vol. 1, 1975, Stochastic Differential Equations and Applications, Vol. 2, 1976, Variational Principle's and Free Boundary Problems, 1983, Mathematics in Industrial Problems, 10 vols., 1988—98; contbr. articles to profl. jours. Recipient Creativity award, NSF, 1983—85, 1990—92; fellow, Sloan Found., 1962—65, Guggenheim, 1966—67. Mem.: NAS, AAAS, Soc. Indsl. Applied Math. (pres. 1993, 1994, chair bd. math. scis. 1994—97), Am. Math. Soc. Office: Ohio State U Math Dept 231 18th Ave Columbus OH 43210 Business E-Mail: afriedman@mbi.osu.edu.

FRIEDMAN, BARTON ROBERT, English educator; b. Bklyn., Feb. 5, 1935; s. Abraham Isaac and Mazie Diana (Cooper) F.; m. Sheila Lynn Siegel, June 22, 1958; children— Arnold, Jonathan, Daniel, Esther. B.A., Cornell U., 1956, Ph.D. (univ. dissertation fellow), 1964; M.A., U. Conn., 1958. Instr. Bowdoin Coll., Brunswick, Maine, 1961-63; from instr. to prof. English lit. U. Wis., Madison, 1963-78; prof. English lit. Cleve. State U., 1978-97, chmn. dept. English, 1978-87, prof. emeritus, 1997—. Visitor Psychoanalytic Inst. Cleve. Author: Adventures in the Deeps of the Mind: The Cuchulain Cycle of W.B. Yeats, 1977, You Can't Tell the Players, 1979, Fabricating History: English Writers on the French Revolution, 1988 (Nancy Dasher award for best scholarly book by mem. Coll. English Assn. Ohio 1989); mem. editl. bd. Irish Renaissance Ann., 1980-84, Lit. Monographs, 1970-76. Recipient William Kiekhofer Teaching Excellence award U. Wis., 1967, Disting. Scholar award Cleve. State U., 1990. Mem. MLA, Am. Com. Irish Studies, Coll. English Assn. Ohio (bd. govs. 1980-81), Soc. Lit. and Sci. (bibliographer Bibliography of Lit. and Sci. in Configurations 1996-98), Phi Kappa Phi. Jewish. Home: 2916 E Overlook Rd Cleveland OH 44118-2434 Office: Cleve State Univ Dept English Dept English Cleveland OH 44115 E-mail: sheilaf@stratos.net.

FRIEDMAN, BERNARD ALVIN, federal judge; b. Detroit, Sept. 23, 1943; s. David and Rae (Garber) F.; m. Rozanne Golston, Aug. 16, 1970; children: Matthew, Megan. Student, Detroit Inst. Tech., 1962-65; JD, Detroit Coll. Law, 1968. Bar: Mich. 1968, Fla. 1968, U.S. Dist. Ct. (ea. dist.) Mich. 1968, U.S. Ct. Mil. Appeals 1972. Asst. prosecutor Wayne County, Detroit, 1968-71; ptnr. Harrison & Friedman, Southfield, Mich., 1971-78, Lippitt, Harrison, Friedman & Whitefield, Southfield, 1978-82; judge Mich. Dist. Ct. 48th dist., Bloomfield Hills, 1982-88; U.S. dist. judge Ea. Dist. Mich., Detroit, 1988—. Lt. U.S. Army, 1967-74. Recipient Disting. Service award Oakland County Bar Assn., 1986. Avocation: running. Office: US Dist Ct US Courthouse Rm 238 231 W Lafayette Blvd Detroit MI 48226-2700

FRIEDMAN, HANS ADOLF, architect; b. Hamburg, Germany, June 10, 1921; came to U.S., 1939, naturalized, 1942; s. Sally and Erna (Samson) F.; m. Maxine Oppenheimer, May 31, 1952; children: Eric, Katy, John, Paul. B.Arch., Ill. Inst. Tech., 1950. Chief architect DeLeuw, Cather & Co., Chgo., 1951-61; sr. partner Friedman, Omarzu, Zion & Lundgoot, 1961; pres. A.M. Kinney Assocs., Inc., 1961-87, vice chmn., 1988-92; partner A.M. Kinney Assocs., Cin., 1961-93; cons., pvt. practice Evanston, Ill., 1992—. V.p. Kintech Svcs., Inc., 1975-93; lectr. So. Ill. U., 1959. Editor: Inland Architect, 1958-64. Mem. Evanston (Ill.) Preservation Commn., 1978-85, chmn., 1981-82; mem. Evanston Site Plan and Appearance Rev. Com., 1996—. Recipient Distinguished Bldg. awards Chemplex Co., Rolling Meadows, Ill., 1969, Distinguished Bldg. awards S.C. Johnson & Sons, Wind Point, Wis., 1969, Distinguished Bldg. awards Quaker Oats Co., Jackson, Tenn., 1973, Disting. Bldg. awards Moore Bus. Forms, Inc., Glenview, Ill., 1973; Lab. of Yr. award Am. Critical Care, 1980; Disting. Pub. Service award City of Evanston, 1985 Fellow AIA (emeritus); mem. Nat. Trust for Historic Preservation, Landmarks Preservation Council of Ill. Home and Office: 1501 Hinman Ave Evanston IL 60201 E-mail: hafriedman@attbi.com.

FRIEDMAN, HAROLD EDWARD, lawyer; b. Cleve., Apr. 7, 1934; s. Joseph and Mary (Schreibman) F.; m. Nancy Schweid, Aug. 20, 1961; children: Deborah, Jay, Susan. B.S., Ohio State U., 1956; LL.B., Case Western Res U., 1959. Bar: Ohio 1960. Practiced in, Cleve., since 1960; ptnr. Simon, Haiman, Gutfeld, Friedman & Jacobs, 1967-80, Ulmer & Berne, 1981—; chair real property practice group. Sec., trustee Harry K. and Emma R. Fox Charitable Found.; pres. Jewish Vocat. Svcs., Cleve.; pres. Internat. Assn. Jewish Vocat. Svcs.; pres. Cleve. Hillel Found.; vice chmn. endowment fund Jewish Cmty. Fedn. Cleve., bd. dirs.; pres. Metro Health Found.; bd. dirs. Bur. Jewish Edn., Jewish Convalescence and Rehab. Ctr., Big Bros. Greater Cleve., Jewish Cmty. Fedn. Cleve., Jewish Family Svc. Assn., YES, Inc., Bellefaire/Jewish Children's Bur. Recipient Kane Leadership award Jewish Community Fedn. Cleve., 1974 Mem.

ABA, Ohio Bar Assn., Cleve. Bar Assn., Oakwood Country Club. Home: 23149 Laureldale Rd Cleveland OH 44122-2101 Office: 900 Bond Ct Bldg Cleveland OH 44114 E-mail: hfriedman@ulmer.com., hedwfried@aol.com.

FRIEDMAN, JAMES DENNIS, lawyer; b. Dubuque, Iowa, Jan. 11, 1947; s. Elmer J. and Rosemary Catherine (Stillmunks) F.; m. Kathleen Marie Maersch, Aug. 16, 1969; children: Scott, Ryan, Andrea, Sean. AB in Polit. Sci., Marquette U., 1969; JD, U. Notre Dame, 1972. Bar: Wis. 1972, U.S. Ct. Appeals (D.C. cir.) 1973, U.S. Ct. Appeals (7th cir.) 1976, U.S. Supreme Ct. 1978, U.S. Ct. Appeals (6th cir.) 1989, Ill. 1996, U.S. Tax Ct. 1997. Pvt. practice, Milw., 1972-81; ptnr. Quarles & Brady, 1981—. Presenter in field; mem. legis. coun. spl. study com. on regulation of fin. instns. State of Wis., 1986-87; bd. dirs. Concours Motors, Inc., Equal Justice Coalition, Inc.; mem. dept. fin. instns. task force on fin. competitiveness 2005, State of Wis., 2000; mem., vice chair State of Wis. Supreme Ct., Office of Lawyer Regulation Preliminary Rev. Com., 2000—; mem. Gov.'s Adv. Coun. on Jud. Selection of the State of Wis., 2002. Mng. editor: Notre Dame Law Rev., 1971—72; contbr. articles to profl. jours. Alderman 4th and 7th dists. Mequon, Wis., 1979-85, pres. common coun., 1980-82, bd. ethics 1996-98, 2000—, chair blue ribbon visioning com. 1998-99; bd. dirs. Weyenrg, Pub. Libr. Found. Inc., 1983—, pres., 1984—; bd. dirs. Ptnrs. Advancing Values in Edn. Inc., 1987—, Wis. Law Found., 1998—; bd. visitors Marquette U. Ctr. for Study of Entrepreneurship, Milw., 1987-95; bd. dirs. Ozaukee Family Svcs., 1983-99, sec., 1993-98; bd. dirs. Notre Dame Club of Milw., 1984-88, sec., 1978, v.p., 1986-88; bd. dirs. Marquette Club of Milw., 1987-88; chair attys. unit United Way Fund Dr. Greater Milw., 1987; mem. St. James Ch., Mequon. Named Outstanding Sr., Coll. of Liberal Arts, Marquette U., 1969. Fellow Wis. Law Found., ABA (banking law com. sect. bus. law); mem. State Bar Wis. (chair bd. govs. 1999-2000, chair exec. com. 1999-2000, fin. com. 1997-98, strategic planning task force 1997-98, bd. govs. 1996-2000, exec. com. 1998-2000, internat. transactions sect. bd. dirs. 1984-99, sec. and chair-elect 1988-89, chair 1989-90, del. to ABA Ho. of Dels. 1980-82, standing com. on adminstrn. justice and judiciary 1979-81, legal edn. and bar admissions com. 1984-89, com. on minority lawyers 1992-99, chmn. 1997-1999, bd. dirs. young lawyers divsn. 1978-82, chmn. bar admission stds. and requirements com. 1979, So. Regional chair capital fund campaign 1998-99), Milw. Bar Assn., Wis. Acad. Trial Lawyers (bd. dirs. 1980-82), Wis. Bankers Assn., Milw. Country Club, Sigma Phi Epsilon. Roman Catholic. Avocations: tennis, golf. Office: Quarles & Brady LLP 411 E Wisconsin Ave Ste 2040 Milwaukee WI 53202-4497 E-mail: jdf@quarles.com.

FRIEDMAN, JAMES MOSS, lawyer; b. Cleve., Aug. 1, 1941; s. Senor I. and Rose L. (Moskowitz) F.; m. Ruth E. Aidlin, Aug. 2, 1964; children: Laura M., Seth M. AB, Dartmouth Coll., 1963; JD, Harvard U., 1966. Bar: Ohio 1966, U.S. Ct. Appeals (6th cir.) 1966, U.S. Dist. Ct. (no. dist.) Ohio 1967. Law clk. U.S. Ct. Appeals, 6th Cir., 1966-67; assoc. Gottfried, Ginsberg, Guren & Merritt, Cleve., 1967-71; chief staff Ohio Gov. John J. Gilligan, Columbus, 1971-72; ptnr. Guren, Merritt, Feibel, Sogg & Cohen, Cleve., 1972-84, Benesch, Friedlander, Coplan & Aronoff, Cleve., 1984—. Chmn. Ohio Civil Rights Commn., 1972-74; dir. Overseas Pvt. Investment Corp., Washington, 1978-82; spl. counsel Ohio Atty. Gen., Cleve., 1983-94. Co-author: The Silent Alliance, 1984. Vice chmn. nat. fin. coun. Dem. Nat. Com., 1975-85; pres. Fedn. for Cmty. Planning, Cleve., 1989-92; bd. dirs. United Way Svcs., Cleve., 1989-92, Cuyahoga C.C. Found., 1989-95; bd. dirs. Citizens League Greater Cleve., 1989-95, v.p., 1993-95; pres. Fairmount Temple, 1993-96; mem. Am. Jewish Com., 1981—, pres. Cleve. chpt., 1991-93; mem. nat. bd. trustees Union Am. Hebrew Congregation, 1991—, mem. exec. com., 1997—. Jewish. Office: Benesch Friedlander 2300 BP Town Bldg 200 Public Sq Ste 2300 Cleveland OH 44114-2378

FRIEDMAN, JEFFREY I. real estate company executive; CEO Associated Estates Realty Corp., Richmond Heights, Ohio, 1993—. Office: Associated Estate Realty Corp 5025 Swetland Ct Richmond Heights OH 44143-1467 Fax: 216-289-6400.

FRIEDMAN, JOAN M. accounting educator; b. N.Y.C., Nov. 30, 1949; d. Alvin E. and Pesselle Gail (Rothenberg) F.; m. Charles E. Blair III, Sept. 20, 1992. AB magna cum laude, Harvard U., 1971; MA, Courtauld Inst., U. London, 1973; MS with honors, Columbia U., 1974; MAS, U. Ill., 1993. CPA, Ill. Asst. research librarian Beinecke Library, New Haven, 1974-75; asst. research librarian Yale Ctr. for Brit. Art, 1975-76, curator of rare books, 1976-90; computer cons., teaching asst. dept. accountancy U. Ill., Champaign, 1990-95; vis. asst. prof. acctg. Ill. Wesleyan U., Bloomington, Ill., 1995-99, asst. prof. acctg. IL, 1999—. Cons. Johns Hopkins U., Balt., 1983; tchr. Sch. Library Service Columbia U., 1983-88, Sysop WordPerfect Users Forum on CompuServe, 1987-2000, Sysop, Tapcis Forum on CompuServe, 1988-95. Author: Color Printing in England, 1978; contbr. articles in field Recipient student achievement award Fedn. Schs. Accountancy, 1993; Nat. Merit scholar Harvard U., 1967; Moss Accountancy fellow U. Ill. 1990. Mem. ALA (chmn. rare books and manuscripts sect. 1982-83), Bibliog. Soc. Am. (coun. 1982-86, sec. 1986-88), Am. Printing History Assn., Phi Beta Kappa, Beta Phi Mu. Jewish. Clubs: Grolier (N.Y.C.); Elizabethan (New Haven) Avocations: microcomputers, bicycling. Office: Ill Wesleyan U Divsn Bus & Econs PO Box 2900 Bloomington IL 61702-2900 E-mail: jfriedma@titan.iwu.edu.

FRIEDMAN, LAWRENCE MILTON, lawyer; b. Chgo., Apr. 2, 1945; s. Armin C. and Mildred T. Friedman; m. Linda M. Friedman, June 25, 1967; children: Benjamin J., David K. BA, U. Ill., 1966; JD, Ohio State U., 1969. Bar: Ill. 1970, U.S. Tax Ct. 1970; CPA, Md., Ill. Ptnr. Coopers & Lybrand, Chgo., 1969-85, Lord, Bissell & Brook, Chgo., 1985—. Adj. prof. law IIT Chgo. Kent Coll. Law, Chgo., 1990—; mem. adv. bd. Hartford Inst. Ins. Tax, 1995-2000; spkr. on mergers, aquisitions and taxation. Mem. adv. bd. Ins. Tax Rev., 1987—; contbr. articles to law jours. Sec.-treas., dir. North Shore Performing Arts Ctr. Found. in Skokie, Ill., 1993-97; vice chmn., dir. Jewish Fedn. Met. Chgo., 1992-99. Mem. ABA, AICPA, Chgo. Fed. Tax Forum. Office: Lord Bissell & Brook 115 S La Salle St Ste 3200 Chicago IL 60603-3902

FRIEDMAN, ROSELYN L. lawyer; b. Cleve., Dec. 9, 1942; d. Charles and Lillian Edith (Zalzneck) F. BS, U. Pitts., 1964; MA, Case Western Res. U., 1967; JD cum laude, Loyola U., Chgo., 1977. Bar: Ill. 1977, U.S. Dist. Ct. (no. dist.) Ill. 1977. Mem. legal dept. No. Trust Co., Chgo., 1977-79; assoc. Rudnick & Wolfe, 1979-84, ptnr., 1984-95, Sachnoff & Weaver, Ltd., Chgo., 1995—. Mem. Loyola U., Chgo. law rev.; mem. profl. adv. com. Chgo. Jewish Fedn., chmn., 1999-2001; mem. profl. adv. com. Chgo. Cmty. Trust, 2001--. Trustee Jewish Women's Found., 1997—2001; mediator Ctr. for Conflict Resolution, 2000—. Fellow Am. Coll. Trust and Estate Counsel; mem. ABA, Am. Jewish Congress (gov. coun. Midwest region 1995-97), Chgo. Bar Assn. (cert. appreciation continuing legal edn. program 1984, chmn. trust law com. 1989-90), Chgo. Estate Planning Coun. (program com. 1992-94, 98-2000, membership com. 1997-98, bd. dirs. 2001—), Chgo. Fin. Exch. (bd. dirs. 1995-97, sec. 1996-97). Office: Sachnoff & Weaver Ltd 30 S Wacker Dr Ste 2900 Chicago IL 60606-7413 E-mail: rfriedman@sachnoff.com.

FRIEDMAN, STANLEY, insect physiologist, educator; b. N.Y.C., Dec. 11, 1925; s. Nathan and Eva (Rothstein) F.; m. Frances Ray Shapiro, May 21, 1955; children: David, Douglas, Catherine, Matthew. Student, CCNY, 1941-43; BA, U. Ill., 1948; PhD, Johns Hopkins U., 1952. Rsch. assoc. U. Ill., 1953-56; biochemist NIH, 1956-58; asst. prof. entomology Purdue U., 1958-62; rsch. fellow London Sch. Hygiene and Tropical Medicine, 1962-63; assoc. prof. entomology Purdue U., 1963-64, U. Ill., Urbana, 1964-68, prof., 1968-92, prof. emeritus, 1992—, head dept., 1976-92, assoc. dir. Sch. Life Scis., 1989-92. With USN, 1943-46. Fellow AAAS; mem. Am. Soc. Zoology, Am. Soc. Biol. Chemists, Entomol. Soc. Am., Federated Socs. Exptl. Biology and Medicine, Sigma Xi. Office: 320 Morrill Hall 505 S Goodwin Ave Urbana IL 61801-3707

FRIEDMAN, WILLIAM HERSH, otolaryngologist, educator; b. Granite City, Ill., Aug. 14, 1938; s. Joseph and Lily May (Brody) F.; m. Hillary Lee, Aug. 9, 1974; children: Joseph Morgan, Alexander Lawrence. AB, Washington U., St. Louis, 1960, MD, 1964. Diplomate: Am. Bd. Otolaryngology. Intern Jackson Meml. Hosp., Miami, Fla., 1964-65; resident in surgery and otolaryngology Mt. Sinai Hosp., N.Y.C., 1965-70, NIH fellow, 1966-67; assoc. prof. otolaryngology Mt. Sinai Sch. Medicine, 1974-76, assoc. attending physician, 1973-76; dir. otolaryngology City Hosp. Center, Elmhurst, N.Y., 1971-76; practice medicine specializing in otolaryngology Beverly Hills, Calif., 1976, Boston, 1977; prof. otolaryngology, chmn. dept. St. Louis U. Sch. Medicine, 1977-87; chief otolaryngology Firmin Desloge Hosp., Cardinal Glennon Meml. Hosp. for Children, 1977-87; dir. Park Cen. Inst., 1987—; prof. otolaryngology Columbia U., N.Y.C., 1987-90. Dir. dept. otolaryngology St. Luke's/Roosevelt Hosp. 1987-90; chief dept. otolaryngology, head neck surgery Deaconess Hosp., 1988-98; pres. Friedman & Assocs., Inc. Contbr. articles to books and profl. jours. Fellow ACS, Am. Acad. Otolaryngology, Am. Acad. Facial Plastic and Reconstructive Surgery (chmn. forum for surg. excellence, credentials com., Ira J. Tresley Meml. award 1978), Am. Soc. Head and Neck Surgery, Am. Laryngol., Rhinol. and Otol. Soc.; mem. AMA (Hektoen gold medal 1978), Med. Soc. County New York, Soc. Univ. Otolaryngologists, Centurion Club of Deafness Rsch. Found., N.Y. State Soc. Surgeons, Assn. Acad. Depts. Otolaryngology, Mo. Ear, Nose and Throat Club (pres. 1987-88), Westwood Country Club, Mission Hills Country Club, Boothbay Harbor Yacht Club, Phi Beta Kappa, Sigma Alpha Mu. Achievements include inventor surg. instruments, including facial plastic instrumentarium. Home: 15 Lake Forest Saint Louis MO 63117-1356 Office: Park Cen Inst 6125 Clayton Ave Saint Louis MO 63139-3265

FRIEDMAN, WILLIAM JOHN, psychology educator; b. May 22, 1950; BA in Psychology with honors, Oberlin Coll., 1972; PhD in Psychology, U Rochester, 1977. Asst. instr. grad. stats. U. Rochester, 1973-74, instr. devel. psychology, 1975-76; trainee in devel. psychology U.S. Dept. Pub. Health, 1972-76; asst. prof. psychology Oberlin (Ohio) Coll., 1976-84, assoc. prof. psychology, 1984-91, prof., 1991—, chair dept. psychology, 1992-2000. Vis. scientist Applied Psychology Unit, Med. Rsch. Coun., Cambridge, Eng., 1983; vis. scientist lab. exptl. psychology U. Grenoble II, 1988-89; vis. scientist U. Canterbury, 1994; U. Otago, 2000-2001. Author (book) About Time: Inventing the Fourth Dimension, 1990; editor (book) The Developmental Psychology of Time, 1982; co-editor (book) Time, Action & Cognition, 1992; contbr. articles to profl. jours. Mem. Soc. for Rsch. in Child Devel., Cognitive Devel. Soc. Office: Oberlin Coll Dept Psychology Oberlin OH 44074

FRIEDMANN, PERETZ PETER, aerospace engineer, educator; b. Timisoara, Romania, Nov. 18, 1938; came to U.S., 1969; s. Mauritius and Elisabeth Friedmann; m. Esther Sarfati, Dec. 8, 1964. DSc, MIT, 1972. Engring. officer Israel Def. Force, 1961-65; sr. engr. Israel Aircraft Industries, Ben Gurion Airport, Israel, 1965-69; research asst. dept. aeronautics and astronautics MIT, Cambridge, 1969-72; asst. prof. mech. and aerospace engring. dept. UCLA, 1972-77, assoc. prof., 1977-80, prof., 1980-98, chmn. dept. mech. and aerospace engring., 1988-91; François-Xavier Bagnoud prof. aerospace engring. dept. U. Mich., Ann Arbor, 1999—. Editor in chief Vertica-Internat. Jour. Rotocraft and Powered Lift Aircraft, 1980-90; contbr. numerous articles to profl. jours. Grantee NASA, Air Force Office Sci. Rsch., U.S. Army Rsch. Office, NSF. Fellow AIAA (recipient Structures, Structural Dynamics and Materials award 1996, Structures, Structural Dynamics and Materials Lectr. award 97); mem. ASME (Structures and Materials award 1984), Am. Helicopter Soc., Sigma Xi. Jewish. Office: U Mich Aerospace Engring Dept 3001 FXB Bldg Ann Arbor MI 48109-2140 E-mail: peretzf@umich.edu.

FRIEDRICH, PAUL, linguist, poet; b. Cambridge, Mass., Oct. 22, 1927; s. Carl Joachim and Lenore Louise (Pelham) F.; m. Lore Bucher, Jan. 6, 1950 (div. Jan. 1966); children: Maria Elizabeth, Susan Guadalupe, Peter Roland; m. Margaret Hardin, Feb. 26, 1966 (div. June 1974); m. Deborah Joanna Gordon, Aug. 9, 1975 (div. Nov. 1996); children: Katherine Ann, Joan Lenore; m. Domnica Radulescu, Nov. 10, 1996; 1 child, Nicholas Anton. BA, Harvard Coll., 1950; MA, Harvard U., 1951; PhD, Yale U., 1957. Instr. U. Conn., Storrs, 1956-57; asst. prof. Harvard U., Cambridge, Mass., 1957-58; jr. linguistic scholar Deccan Coll., Poona, India, 1958-59; asst. prof. anthropology U. Pa., Phila., 1959-62; assoc. prof. anthropology U. Chgo., 1962-67, prof. anthropology, linguistics and soc. thought, 1967-96, prof. emeritus (active), 1996—. Vis. prof. linguistics Georgetown U., winter, 1998-2001, U. Va., 2002. Author: Proto-Indo-European Trees, 1970, Agrarian Revolt in a Mexican Village, 1970, The Meaning of Aphrodite, 1978, Bastard Moons, 1979, Language, Context and Imagination, 1979, The Language Parallax, 1986, The Princes of Naranja, 1987; co-editor: Russia and Eurasia-China, 1994, Music in Russian Poetry, 1998. Served to pfc. U.S. Army, 1946-47, Germany. Grantee Wenner-Gren Found., 1955; grantee NIMH, summers 1961-62; fellow Social Sci. Research Council, 1966-67; Guggenheim fellow, 1982-83 Mem. Linguistic Soc. Am. (chmn. program com. 1972, chmn. nominating com. 1975, mem. exec. com. 1981-83), Am. Acad. Arts and Scis. Home: 5500 S South Shore Dr Apt 1609 Chicago IL 60637-1986 Office: U Chgo Dept Anthropology 1126 E 59th St Chicago IL 60637-1580

FRIEND, HELEN MARGARET, chemist; b. Lyndon, Ohio, Jan. 30, 1931; d. Maurice Chapmàn and Margaret (Beath) Mossbarger; m. William Warren Friend, Oct. 9, l982. BA in Chemistry, Coll. of Wooster, l953. Rsch. chemist Union Carbide Co., Cleve., 1953-56, asst. patent coord. battery products div., 1956-59, patent coord., 1959-86, Eveready Battery Co., Westlake, Ohio, 1986-90, tech. patent assoc., 1990-95; ret., 1995. Mng. editor JEC Press-Internat. Battery Materials Assn., Cleve., 1978-97. Mng. editor Progress in Batteries and Battery Materials, 1978-98, JEC Battery Newsletter, 1987-98, ITE Battery Newsletter; tech. editor Electrochem. Soc. Japan, U.S. br., 1975-96; editor-in-chief tech. English divsn. Internat. Tech. Exch. Soc., 1998—. Mem. Am. Chem. Soc., Electrochem. Soc., Phi Beta Kappa. Presbyterian. Avocations: little theater, reading, choral singing. Home: 576 Buckeye Dr Lorain OH 44054-1615

FRIEND, WILLIAM C. state legislator; m. Ann friend. BA, U. Indpls. Auditor; rep. Dist. 23 Ind. Ho. of Reps., 1992—, mem. agr. and rural devel., county and twp. coms., mem. family and children, ways and means coms. Owner/farmer Friend Farms. Trustee Allen Twp.; mem. coun.-at-large Miami County; contr. Miami County Solid Waste Dist.; mem. Farm Bur., Grissom Cmty. Redevel. Authority. Mem. Ind. Auditors Assn., Miami County Pork Prodrs., Peru C. of C., Scottish Rite. Home: RR 2 Box 314 Macy IN 46951-9582

FRIER, BRUCE W. law educator; b. 1943; BA, Trinity Coll., 1964; PhD, Princeton U., 1970. Prof. classics and law U. Mich., 1969—. Lectr. Bryn Mawr Coll., Pa., 1968-69. Recipient Goodwin award of merit, 1983. Fellow Am. Acad. of Arts and Scis.; mem. Am. Soc. for Legal Hist., Am. Philol. Assn. Office: U Mich Law Sch 625 S State St Ann Arbor MI 48109-1215

FRIER, CHUCK, radio personality; b. St. Louis; BS Radio-TV, So. Ill. U., Carbondale. Radio host Classic 99, St. Louis. Avocation: bicycling. Office: Classic 99 85 Founders Ln Saint Louis MO 63105

FRIESEN, HENRY GEORGE, endocrinologist, educator; b. Morden, Man., Can., July 31, 1934; s. Frank Henry and Agnes (Unger) F.; m. Joyce Marylin Mackinnon, Oct. 12, 1967; children: Mark Henry, Janet Elizabeth. BSc, MD, U. Man., 1958. Diplomate: Am. Bd. Internal Medicine. Intern Winnipeg (Man.) Gen. Hosp., 1958-60; resident Royal Victoria Hosp., Montreal, Que., 1961-62; rsch. assoc. New Eng. Centre Hosp., Boston, 1962-65; prof. exptl. medicine McGill U., Montreal, 1965-73; prof. physiology and medicine U. Man., 1973-92, head dept. physiology, 1973-92; pres. Med. Rsch. Coun. Can., 1991-2000; chmn. Genome Can., Winnipeg. Chmn. exec. com. Med. Rsch. Coun. Can., mem. exec. com., 1981-87; pres. Nat. Cancer Inst. Can., 1990-92. Contbr. numerous articles to profl. jours. Decorated Companion Order of Can.; named to, Can. Med. Hall of Fame, 2001; recipient Gairdner award, Gairdner Found., 1977, Wightman award, 2001. Fellow Royal Soc. Can. (McLaughlin medal 1987), Royal Coll. Physicians and Surgeons; mem. AAAS, Am. Physiol. Soc., Endocrine Soc. (Koch award 1987), Can. Soc. Clin. Investigation (pres. 1974, G. Malcolm Meml. award 1982, Disting. Sci. award 1987), Nat. Acad. Scis. (fgn. assoc.), Can. Physiol. Soc., Am. Fedn. Clin. Research, Am. Soc. Clin. Investigation, Can. Soc. Endocrinology and Metabolism (past pres.), Internat. Soc. Neuroendocrinology, U.S. Nat. Acad. Sci. (fgn. assoc.). Mennonite. Office: Ctr Advancement Medicine 753 McDermot Ave Winnipeg MB Canada R3E 0WE Fax: (204) 789-3979. E-mail: Henry_Friesen@umanitoba.ca.

FRIGGENS, THOMAS GEORGE, state official, historian; b. Pontiac, Mich., July 12, 1949; s. Francis G. and Jane E. (Pettit) F.; m. Mary T. Bahra; children: Christopher P., Michael C. BA, Albion Coll., 1971; MA, Wayne State U., 1973. Contract historian Mich. Dept. Natural Resources, Fayette, 1973; site historian 07 Mich. Dept. State, History Div., Fort Wilkins Hist. Complex, Copper Harbor, 1974-75, site historian 09, 1975-76, site historian 11, 1976-80, site historian VII, 1980-85, Dept. State, Bur. History, Mich. Iron Industry Mus., Negaunee, 1985-87, regional historian VII, 1987-92, regional historian VII supr., 1992-96, historian mgr. XII, 1996-98, history mgr. 13, 1998—2001; history mgr. 13 dept. history, arts and librs. Mich. Histl. Ctr., 2001. Cons. St. Louis County Hist. Soc., Duluth, Minn., 1985, 86. Contbr. articles to jours. in field. Active Hist. Soc. Mich., bd. dirs., 1984-90; active Copper County Heritage Coun., pres., 1982-83; bd. dirs. Marquette County Hist. Soc., 1992-97; mem. Mich. Hist. Preservation Network. Recipient Roy W. Drier award Houghton County (Mich.) Hist. Soc., 1987, Merit award Hist. Soc. Mich., 1983, Disting. Svc. award, 1983, Dwight B. Waldo award No. Mich. U. Dept. History, 1999. Mem. Am. Assn. State and Local History, Nat. Trust for Hist. Preservation, Mich. Mus. Assn., Phi Alpha Theta. Office: Mich Iron Industry Mus 73 Forge Rd Negaunee MI 49866-9532

FRINK, BRIAN LEE, artist, educator; b. Ft. Lee, Va., Sept. 22, 1956; s. Joseph Lee and Darlene Jean (Ratcliff) F.; m. Denise Ellen Neushwander; children: Blake, Annakeiko. BFA, Ill. State U., 1979; MFA, U. Wis., 1988. Assoc. prof. art Mankato (Minn.) State U., 1989—. Vis. lectr. U. Wis., Madison, 1989. One-man show Rochester (Minn.) Art Ctr., 1997; exhibited in group shows Mpls. Inst. Art, Mpls. Coll. Art and Design, Morgan Gallery, Kansas City, Mo. Individual fellow Nat. Endowment for Arts, 1993, Minn. Arts Bd., 1993, 95, McKnight fellow McKnight Corp., 1992. Home: RR 6 Box 252 Mankato MN 56001-9223 Office: Mankato State U PO Box 42 Mankato MN 56002-0042

FRISON, RICK, agricultural company executive; b. Worland, Wyo., Aug. 22, 1949; s. David T. and Maureen M. (Nelson) F.; m. Nadine M. Van Overbeke; children: Cara M., Jennifer M. BS, Mont. State U., 1977. Salesman ConAgra Mont., Inc., Great Falls, 1977-81, mktg. mgr., 1981-83; div. mgr. ConAgra Fertilizer Co., Billings, Mont., 1983-86, div. mgr. no. region Knoxville, Tenn., 1986-89, v.p., gen. mgr. no. region, 1989-91, retail v.p., 1991-92, pres. Pekin, Ill., 1994—, Cropmate Co., Pekin, 1992—, United Agri Products, Greeley, Colo., 1993—. Mem. editl. adv. bd. Dealer Progress mag., Ballwin, Mo., 1992—; field editor Crop Protection mag., Eugene, Oreg., 1992—. Mem. Fertilizer Inst. (retail coun. 1992—). Office: Cropmate Co PO Box 977 Pekin IL 61555-0977

FRISWOLD, FRED RAVNDAHL, manufacturing executive; b. Mpls., Jan. 21, 1937; s. Ingolf Oliver and Derrice Ernestine (Anderson) F.; m. C. Marie Martin, Sept. 14, 1957; children— Cynthia, Steven, Barry, Michelle (dec.), Benjamin. BBA with distinction in Fin, U. Minn., 1958. Chartered fin. analyst. With J.M. Dain & Co. (now Dain, Rauscher, Inc.), Mpls., 1958—; exec. v.p. Dain, Bosworth, Inc., 1976-82, pres., CEO, 1982-90, cons., 1990-92; CEO Tonka Equipment Co., Plymouth, Minn., 1992—. Bd. chair, Mpls. Rotary Found., U. Gateway Corp., UMF Investment Advisors. Trustee Metro YMCA, U. Minn. Found.; trustee Univ. Children's Found.; mem. bd. advisors Otologics L.L.C. Mem. Twin City Soc. Security Analysts, Wildwood Lodge, Mpls. Rotary (pres. 1997-98). Methodist. Home: 7033 Comanche Ct Minneapolis MN 55439-1004 Office: Tonka Equipment Co 13305 Water Tower Cir Plymouth MN 55441-3803

FRITZ, CECIL MORGAN, investment company executive; b. Modoc, Ind., July 30, 1921; s. Kenneth M. and Ruby (Howell) F.; m. Lucile Johnson, June 9, 1946; children: John, Susan, Marcia. BS, Ind. U., 1948, MBA, 1949. With City Securities Corp., Indpls., 1949—, pres., 1980-92, ret., 1994, now dir. Capt. USAAF, 1940-46. Recipient Sagamore of the Wabash-Indiana award. Mem. Masons (32 degree). Republican. Methodist. Office: City Securities Corp 135 N Pennsylvania St Ste 2200 Indianapolis IN 46204-2462

FRITZ, JAMES SHERWOOD, chemist, educator; b. Decatur, Ill., July 20, 1924; s. William Lawrence and Leora Mae (Troster) F.; m. Helen Joan Houck, Apr. 26, 1949 (dec. Oct. 1987); children— Barbara Lisa, Julie Ann, Laurel Joan, Margaret Ellen; m. Miriam Simons Reeves, July 15, 1989. B.S., James Millikin U., 1945; M.S., U. Ill., 1946, Ph.D., 1948. Asst. prof. chemistry Wayne State U., Detroit, 1948-51; asst. prof. Iowa State U., Ames, 1951-55, assoc. prof., 1955-60, prof., 1960-90, disting. prof., 1990—. Author: Acid Base Titrations in Nonaqueous Solvents, 1973, An Analytical Solid-Phase Extraction, 1999; co-author: Quantitative Analytical Chemistry, Ion Chromatography, 1982, 3d edit., 2000, Solid Phase Extraction, 1999; contbr. articles to profl. jours. Recipient Minn. Chromatography Forum award, 1987, Dal Nogare award in chromatography, 1991. Mem. Am. Chem. Soc. (award in chromatography 1976, award in analytical chemistry 1985) Methodist Avocations: tennis; collecting wall hangings. Home: 2018 Greenbriar Cir Ames IA 50014-7820 Office: Iowa State U 322 Wilhelm Ames IA 50011-0001 E-mail: kniss@ameslab.gov.

FRITZ, KRISTINE RAE, secondary education educator; b. Monroe, Wis. BS in Phys. Edn., U. Wis., LaCrosse, 1970; MS in Phys. Edn., U. N.C., Greensboro, 1978. Softball and fencing program coord. Mequon (Wis.) Recreation Dept., 1970; phys. edn., health and English tchr. Horace Jr. H.S., 1970—81; phys. edn. and health tchr. Sheboygan (Wis.) South H.S., 1982—; basketball and volleyball coach, 1972—89; girls track coach, 1972—. Mem. dist. wide curriculum and evaluation coms., 1978—; mem. sch. effectiveness team, 1991—94; sch. evaluation consortium evaluator, 1988—; inbound/outbound coach Sport for Understanding, 1991—96. Contbr. articles to profl. jours. Active Sheboygan (Wis.) Spkrs. Bur., 1987—95, Women Reaching Women. Recipient Nat. H.S. Coaches award for girls track, 1987. Mem.: AAHPERD (Midwest dist. Tchr. of Yr. 1995,

Pathfinder award 1997), NEA, Sheboygan Edn. Assn., Wis. Assn. Health, Phys. Edn., Recreation and Dance (pres.-elect 1998—99, pres. 1999—2000, Phys. Edn. Tchr. Yr. 1993), Phi Delta Kappa. Home: 1841 N 26th St Sheboygan WI 53081-2008

FRITZ, ROGER JAY, management consultant; b. Browntown, Wis., July 18, 1928; s. Delmar M. and Ruth M. (Sandley) F.; m. Kathryn Louise Goddard, Oct. 13, 1951; children: Nancy Goddard, Susan Marie. BA in Polit. Sci, Monmouth (Ill.) Coll., 1950; MS in Speech, U. Wis., 1952, PhD in Ednl. Counseling, 1956. Asst. dean men, asst. prof. Purdue U., 1953-56; mgr. pub. relations Cummins Engine Co.; also sec. Cummins Engine Found., 1956-59; sec. John Deere Found.; also mem. pub. relations staff Deere & Co., 1959-65, dir. mgmt. devel. and personnel research; also dir. John Deere Found., 1965-69; pres. Willamette U., 1969-72, Orgn. Devel. Cons., Naperville, Ill., 1972—. Bd. dirs. Intelligent Electronics, Inc., List Processing Co., Todays Computers Bus. Ctrs., Entre Computer Ctrs., Inc., Natural Golf, Inc., Quote Me, Optionize, Envisionworks, Inc. Author: A Handbook for Resident Counselors, 1952, The Argumentation of William Jennings Bryan and Clarence Darrow in the Tennesee Evolution Trial, 1952, How Freshmen Change, 1956, The Power of Professional Purpose, 1974, MBO Goes to College, 1975, Practical Management by Objectives, 1976, What Managers Need to Know-A Practical Guide for Management Development, 1978, Performance Based Management, 1980, Productivity and Results, 1981, People Compatibility System, 1983, Rate Yourself as a Manager, 1985, You're in Charge, 1986, Personal Performance Contracts: The Key to Job Success, 1986, Nobody Gets Rich Working for Somebody Else, 1987, Rate Your Executive Potential, 1987, The Inside Advantage, 1987, If They Can-You Can, 1988, Be Your Own Boss, 1988, Managing a Successful Team, 1989, Management Ideas That Work, 1989, Developing A Positive Attitude, 1990, The Entrepreneurial Family, 1991, Think Like a Manager, 1991, How to Export, 1992, How to Get Rich Working for Yourself, 1992, Sleep Disorders-America's Hidden Nightmare, 1993, The Sales Manager's High Performance Guide, 1993, How to Manage Your Boss, 1994, A Team of Eagles, 1994, The Small Business Troubleshooter, 1995, The Field Guide for Boss Types...And How to Deal With Them, 1996, An Idea-A-Day For Promotable People, 1996, Crime Crisis: Bold New Ideas to Fit Punishment with Crimes, 1997, Wars of Succession, 1997, One Step Ahead: The Unused Keys to Success, 1998, Bounce Back and Win, 1999, Fast Track-How to Gain Momentum and Keep It, 1999, Attitude Makes The Difference, 2000, Beyond Commitment: The Skills All Leaders Need, 2000, Family Ties and Business Binds, 2000, Magnet People: Their Secrets and How To Learn From Them, 2001, Little Things-Big Results, 2002, How To Make Your Boss Your Ally and Advocate, 2002; also articles, papers; columnmist Entrepreneur mag., New Bus. Opportunity mag., 1989, Benefits and Compensation Solutions Mag., Bus. Start Ups Mag.; mgmt. editor Communication Briefings Newsletter, 1989. Mem. com. preparation coll. tchrs. Ill. Bd. Higher Edn., 1965-67, mem. com. med. edn., 1967-68; edn. com. N.A.M., 1967-69; mem. Iowa-Ill. Indsl. Devel. Group, 1964-69; council contbr. Nat. Indsl. Conf. Bd., 1960-65, council devel., edn. and tng., 1966-69; adv. com. solicitations Nat. Better Bus. Bur., 1964-69; v.p. Oreg. Ind. Colls. Assn., 1969-72; mem. Pres. Johnson's Citizens Adv. Bd. on Youth Opportunity, 1968-69, Gov.'s Personnel Grievance Panel, Ill., 1974-77; trustee Monmouth Coll., 1967-79, chmn., 1961-69; trustee Oreg. Colls. Found., 1969-72, Ind. Coll. Funds Am., N.Y.C., 1972, Internat. Coll. Commerce and Econs., Tokyo, 1970-72, U. Chgo. Cancer Research Found., 1973-78. Mem. Phi Eta Sigma, Omicron Delta Kappa, Tau Kappa Epsilon, Phi Alpha Theta, Sigma Tau Delta, Pi Kappa Delta. Republican. Methodist. Club: Naperville (Ill.) Country. Home: 1113 N Loomis St Naperville IL 60563-2745 Office: 1240 Iroquois Dr Naperville IL 60563-8536 Fax: 630-420-7835. E-mail: R.Fritz3800@aol.com.

FRITZSCHE, HELLMUT, physics educator; b. Berlin, Feb. 20, 1927; came to U.S., 1952; s. Carl Hellmut and Anna (Jordan) F.; m. Sybille Charlotte Lauffer, July 5, 1952; children: Peter Andreas, Thomas Alexander, Susanne Charlotte, Katharina Sabine. Diploma in Physics, U. Göttingen, Fed. Republic Germany, 1952; PhD in Physics, Purdue U., 1954, DSc (hon.), 1988. Instr. physics Purdue U., Lafayette, Ind., 1954-55, asst. prof., 1955-56, U. Chgo., 1957-61, assoc. prof., 1961-63, prof., 1963-96, dir. Materials Rsch. Lab., 1973-77, chmn. dept., 1977-86, Louis Block prof. physics, 1989-96. V.p., bd. dirs. Energy Conversion Devices, Inc., Troy, Mich., United Solar Systems Corp.; mem. adv. com. Encyclopaedia Britannica, 1969-96. Editor: 10 sci. books; assoc. editor Jour. Applied Physics, 1975-80; regional editor Jour. Non-Crystalline Solids, 1987-96; contbr. 270 articles to profl. jours.; patentee in field. Named hon. prof. Shanghai Inst. Ceramics, 1985, Nanjing U., 1987, Beijing U. Astronautics, 1988. Fellow AAAS, Am. Physical Soc. (Oliver Buckley Condensed Matter Physics prize 1989), N.Y. Acad. Scis. (chmn. divsn. condensed matter physics 1979-80). Avocations: the violin, sailing, skiing. Home: 3140 E Camino Juan Paisano Tucson AZ 85718-4206 Office: Energy Conversion Devices Inc 2956 Waterview Dr Rochester Hills MI 48309 E-mail: hellmutf@aol.com.

FRIZZELL, DAVID NASON, state legislator; m. Valda Frizzell. BA, Loyola U.; postgrad., Ind. Christian U. Cert. fundraising exec. Fundraising exec.; rep. dist. 93 Ind. Ho. of Reps., 1992—, mem. election and apportionment, family and children coms., mem. ways and means, urban affairs coms., chmn. commerce and econ. devel. Pres. Greater Indpls. Rep. Fin. Com.; mem. variance bd. City of Indpls.; bd. dirs. Ind. Opera Theatre, Inc., ARC, Johnson County, Ind.; past pres. Nat. Kidney Found. of Ind.; past chmn. devel. Alzheimer's Assn. Ind. Mem. Nat. Soc. Fundraising Execs. Home: 8310 Hill Gail Dr Indianapolis IN 46217-4813

FROBENIUS, JOHN RENAN, hospital administrator; b. Muscatine, Iowa, Jan. 25, 1942; s. Reno Reinhold and Ann Sylvia (Kolar) F.; m. Nancy Frobenius; children: Erin, Chris, Anne, Kai. BA, U. Nebbr., 1963; MHA, U. Minn., 1969. Bus. office mgr. Northwestern Bell Telephone, Omaha/North Platte, Nebr., 1963-67; adminstrv. resident The Charles T. Miller Hosp., St. Paul, 1968-69; assoc. adminstr. Stormont-Vail Hosp., Topeka, 1969-73, St. Luke's Reg. Med. Ctr., Boise, 1973-80, exec. v.p., 1980-85; pres., chief exec. officer St. Cloud (Minn.) Hosp., 1985—. Bd. dirs. United Way of St. Cloud Area, 1988—. Mem. Am. Coll. Healthcare Execs., Vol. Hosps. of Am. (bd. dirs. 1982-85, chmn. bd. 1991—), Minn. Hosp. Assn. (bd. dirs. 1988—, chmn. bd. 1991-93), Minn. Conf. Cath. Health Facilities, Rotary. Republican. Lutheran. Avocations: skiing, running, fishing, backpacking, camping, carpentry. Office: St Cloud Hosp 1406 6th Ave N Saint Cloud MN 56303-1901

FROBOM, LEANN LARSON, lawyer; b. Ramona, S.D., May 31, 1953; d. Floyd Burdette and Janice Anne (Quist) L.; m. Richard Curtis Finke, May 19, 1973 (div. Jan. 1978); 1 child, Timothy; m. Dwayne Jeffery LaFave, May 31, 1981 (div. 1992); children: Jeffrey, Allison; m. Jerome B. Frobom, Aug. 21, 1999. BS, U. S.D., 1974, JD with honors, 1977. Bar: S.D. 1977, U.S. Dist. Ct. S.D. 1977, U.S. Ct. Appeals (8th cir.) 1977, N.D. 1978, U.S. Dist. Ct. N.D. 1978, Iowa 1998, Nebr. 2001. Asst. atty. gen. State of S.D., Pierre, 1977-78, 79-81; assoc. Bjella, Neff, Rathert & Wahl, Williston, N.D., 1978-79, Tobin Law Offices, P.C., Winner, S.D., 1981-83; assoc. dean, asst. prof. U. S.D. Sch. Law, Vermillion, 1983-86, dir. continuing legal edn., 1983-89, assoc. prof. law, 1986-89; ptnr. Aho & LaFave, Brookings, S.D., 1990-91; pvt. practice, 1991-92; asst. U.S. atty. U.S. Dist. Ct. S.D., 1992-97; gen. counsel S.D. Auto Group, Inc., Sioux Falls, 1997-98; atty. Hughes Law Offices, 1998-99, Cline Williams Wright Johnson & Oldfather, Lincoln, Nebr., 1999—; seasonal tax preparer H&R Block Co., 1999—. Mem. S.D. Bd. Pardons and Paroles, 1987-90, chmn., 1989-90; comml. arbitrator Am. Arbitration Assn., 1985-92; prof. Kilian C.C. Contbr. articles to profl. jours. Mem. planning coun. Nat. Identification Program for Advancement Women in Higher Edn. Adminstrn., Am. Coun. on Edn., S.D., 1984-90; bd. dirs. Mo. Shores Women's Resource Ctr., Pierre, 1980, W.H. Over Mus., Vermillion, 1986-87, S.D. Vol. Lawyers for Arts, 1987-92, Brookings Interagy. Coun., 1990-91, Brookings Women's Ctr., 1990-94; sec. Mediation Ctr., Inc. Named S.D. Woman Atty. of Yr. Women in Law U. S.D., 1985. Mem. Epsilon Sigma Alpha (S.D. coun. sect. 1985-86). Republican. Episcopalian. Avocation: reading. Home: 4911 High St Lincoln NE 68506-3970 Office: 1900 US Bank Bldg 233 S 13th St Lincoln NE 68508

FROEHLICH, HAROLD VERNON, judge, former congressman; b. Appleton, Wis., May 12, 1932; s. Vernon W. and Lillian F.; m. Sharon F. Ross, Nov. 20, 1970; children: Jeffrey Scott, Michael Ross. BBA, U. Wis., 1959, LLB, 1962. Bar: Wis. 1962. Staff acct. Ruschlien & Stortreon, CPAs, Madison, Wis., 1958-62; practiced in Appleton, 1962-81; judge Circuit Ct., 1981—; dep. chief judge 8th Jud. Dist. Wis., 1983-85, spl. dep. chief judge, 1985-88, chief judge, 1988-94; sec. Wis. Judicial Conf., 1991-97; mem. Wis. Ho. of Reps., 1963-73, speaker, 1967-71, minority floor leader, 1971-73; mem. 93d Congress from 8th Dist., Wis.; v.p. Black Creek Improvement Corp., Outagamie County Family Ct. Commn., 1975-78. Chmn. Com. Chief Judges, 1992—94; chief adminstrn. judge Outagamie County, 1983—88, 1994—. Rep. precinct committeeman 19th ward, Appleton, 1956-62; chmn. Outagamie County Rep. Statutory Com., 1958-62; sec. Assembly Rep. Caucus, 1965-66; bd. regents Fox Valley Luth. H.S., Appleton, 1990-93. With USN, 1951-55. Mem. ABA, Am. Judges Assn. (bd. govs. 1997-99, asst. treas. 1998-99, treas. 1999—), Wis. Bar Assn., Outagamie County Bar Assns., Wis. Assn. Trial Judges (pres. 1991-2000), Am. Legion, VFW (judge adv. 1963-75, 82-99), Assn. Trial Judges in Wis. (sec. 1984-91), Midwest Coun. State Govts. (vice chmn. 1968-69, chmn. 1969-70), Coun. State Govts. (nat. exec. com. 1970-72), Phi Alpha Delta. Office: 410 S Walnut St Appleton WI 54911-5920 E-mail: harold.froehlich@outagamie.courts.state.wi.us.

FROELKER, JIM, state legislator; b. Gerald, Mo., Aug. 9, 1949; m. Terry S. Hempelmann, 1974; children: Chad, Becky. Grad., United Electronic Inst., Louisville. Quality control inspector. Rep. com. mem. Boone Twp.; state rep. dist. 111 Mo. Ho. Reps., mem. agrl. bus., elec. com., local govt. com. Mem. Mo. State Sch. Bd. Assn., Cattleman's Assn., C. of C. Home: RR 2 Box 262ab Gerald MO 63037-9652 Office: 7437 Highway H Gerald MO 63037-2824

FROHMAN, LAWRENCE ASHER, endocrinology educator, scientist; b. Detroit, Jan. 26, 1935; s. Dan and Rebecca (Katzman) F.; m. Barbara Hecht, June 9, 1957; children: Michael, Marc, Erica, Rena. M.D., U. Mich., 1958. Diplomate: Am. Bd. Internal Medicine. Intern Yale-New Haven Med. Ctr., 1958—59, resident in internal medicine, 1959—61; asst. prof. medicine SUNY, Buffalo, 1965—69, assoc. prof., 1969—73; prof. medicine U. Chgo., 1973—81; dir. endocrinology Michael Reese Hosp., Chgo., 1973—81; prof., dir. div. endocrinology and metabolism U. Cin., 1981—92; prof. medicine U. Ill., Chgo., 1992—, chmn. Dept. Medicine, 1992—2001; dir. Med. Svcs. U. Ill. Hosp., 1992—2001. Dir. Gen. Clin. Rsch. Ctr., 1986-90; mem. sci. rev. com. NIH, Bethesda, Md., 1972-76; mem. sci. rev. bd. VA, Washington, 1979-82; mem. endocrine adv. bd. FDA, Washington, 1982-86; mem. adv. com. Nat. Inst. Diabetes, Digestive and Kidney Diseases, NIH, 1983-94, chmn., 1991-93; mem. sci. adv. bd. Edison Biotech. Inst., Ohio U. Editor: (with others) Endocrinology and Metabolism, 2001; editl. bd. 7 med. and sci. jours., 1970—; contbr. articles to profl. jours. NIH research grantee, 1967-98, Endocrine Soc. Rorer Clin. Investigator award, 1991. Mem.: ACP, Am. Clin. Climatological Assn., Pituitary Soc., Assn. Profs. Medicine, Inernat. Soc. Neuroendocrinology, Am. Diabetes Assn., Am. Soc. Clin. Investigation, Assn. Am. Physicians, Endocrine Soc. Office: U Ill at Chgo Section Endocrinology M/C 640 1819 W Polk St Chicago IL 60612-7333 E-mail: frohman@uic.edu.

FROMM, DAVID, surgeon; b. N.Y.C., Jan. 21, 1939; s. Alfred and Hanna F.; m. Barbara Solter, June 13, 1961; children— Marc, Kenneth, Kathleen. BS, U. Calif., Berkeley, 1960, MD, 1964. Diplomate Am. Bd. Surgery. Intern U. Calif. Hosp., San Francisco, 1964-65; resident in surgery U. Calif., 1965-71; asst. prof. surgery Harvard Med. Sch., Boston, 1973-77, asso. prof., 1977-78; prof. chmn. dept. surgery SUNY-Upstate Med. Center, Syracuse, 1978-88; Penberthy prof., chmn. dept. surgery Wayne State U., 1988—; surgeon-in-chief Detroit Med. Ctr., 1988—; chief surgery Harper Hosp., Detroit, 1988. Dir. Am. Bd. Surgery, 1996-2001. Author: Complications of Gastric Surgery, 1977; editor Gastrointestinal Surgery, 1985; contbr. articles to profl. jours. Trustee Karmanos Cancer Inst. With M.C., U.S. Army, 1971-73. NIH career devel. awardee, 1976-79; grantee, 1974— Fellow: ACS (gov. 1977—83); mem.: Detroit Acad. Medicine, Detroit Acad. Surgery, Soc. Surgery Alimentary Tract (sec. 1994—97, pres. 1998, chmn. bd. trustees 1999—2000), Halsted Soc., Am. Surg. Assn., Am. Physiol. Soc., Assn. Acad. Surgery, Soc. Clin. Surgery, Am. Gastroent. Assn., Soc. Univ. Surgeons. Office: Wayne State U 6C Univ Health Ctr 4201 St Antoine St Detroit MI 48201-2153 E-mail: dfsurg@aol.com.

FROMM, ERIKA (MRS. PAUL FROMM), clinical psychologist; b. Frankfurt, Germany, Dec. 23, 1910; came to U.S., 1938, naturalized, 1944; d. Siegfried and Clementine (Stern) Oppenheimer; m. Paul Fromm, July 20, 1938; 1 child, Joan (Mrs. Greenstone). PhD magna cum laude, U. Frankfurt, 1933; postgrad. child care program, Chgo. Inst. for Psychoanalysis, 1949-51. Diplomate: Am. Bd. Examiners in Profl. Psychology, Am. Bd. Examiners Clin. Hypnosis. Rsch. assoc. dept. psychiatry U. Amsterdam, Holland, 1934-35; chief psychologist Apeldoorn State Hosp., Holland, 1935-38, Francis W. Parker Sch., Chgo., 1944-51; supervising psychologist Inst. for Juvenile Rsch., 1951-53; asst. prof. to assoc. prof. med. sch. Northwestern U., 1954-60; prof. U. Chgo., 1960-76, prof. emeritus, 1976—. Author: (with L.D. Hartman) Intelligence - A Dynamic Approach, 1955; (with Thomas M. French) Dream Interpretation: A New Approach, 1964 2d edit., 1986; (with Ronald E. Shor) Hypnosis: Developments in Research and New Perspectives, 1972, 2d. edit., 1979; (with Daniel P. Brown) Hypnotherapy and Hypnoanalysis, 1986; (with Daniel P. Brown) Hypnosis and Behavioral Medicine, 1987; (with Stephen Kahn) Selfhypnosis: The Chicago Paradigm, 1990; (with Michael R. Nash) Contemporary Hypnosis Research, 1992; (with Michael R. Nash) Psychoanalysis and Hypnosis, 1997; also numerous articles in profl. jours.; mem. editl. bd. Jour. Clin. and Exptl. Psychopathology, 1951-59; clin. editor: Internat. Jour. Clin. and Exptl. Hypnosis 1968-97, editl. cons., 1998—; assoc. editor Bull. Brit. Soc. Exptl. and Clin. Hypnosis, 1982-90; mem. bd. cons. editors Psychoanalytic Psychology, 1982-88; mem. adv. bd. editors Imagination, Cognition and Personality: Sci. Study of COnsciousness, 1982—; assoc. editor Hypnos: European Jour. Hypnosis, 1996—. Fellow AAAS, APA (pres. divsn. 30 1972-73, Psychoanalysis award 1985, 97, Hypnosis award for Eminent Enduring Contbns. to Advancement of Profl. Hypnosis 1994); mem. Am. Orthopsychiat. Assn. (dir. 1961-63), Soc. Clin. Exptl. Hypnosis (Best Rsch. Paper award 1965, sec. 1965-67, v.p. 1971-75, pres. 1975-77, Arthur Shapiro award 1973, Best Clin. Paper award 1986, Best Book pub. in Field of Hypnosis award 1987, 91, 93), The Netherlands Soc. for Hypnosis (hon.), Am. Bd. Psychol. Hypnosis (pres. 1971-74, Rollo May award Saybrook Inst. 1997), Ill. Psychol. Assn. (coun. 1951-53, 55-57, bd. examiners 1959-62, v.p. bd. examiners 1960-61), Soc. Projective Techniques, Am. Bd. Examiners in Psychol. Hypnosis (Morton Prince award 1970), Nat. Acad. Practice Psychology (Disting. Practioner in Psychology award 1982), Am. Soc. Clin. Hypnosis (award 1997, 99), Sigma Xi. Home: 5715 S Kenwood Ave Chicago IL 60637-1742 Office: U Chgo Dept Psychology Chicago IL 60637

FROMM, PAUL OLIVER, physiology educator; b. Ramsey, Ill., Dec. 2, 1923; s. August Moltke and Edith Marie (Wollerman) F.; m. Mary Magdalene Shaw, June 15, 1947; children: David, Emily. B.S., U. Ill., 1949, M.S., 1951, Ph.D., 1954. Instr. dept. physiology Mich. State U., East Lansing, 1954-58, asst. prof., 1958-62, assoc. prof., 1962-65, prof., 1965-87, prof. emeritus, 1987—. Cons. U.S.-Can. Great Lakes Commn., Windsor, Ont., Can., 1981, Nat. Research Council Can., 1983 Contbr. articles to profl. jours. Served with USMC, 1943-46 Fulbright rsch. scholar Musée Oceanographique Monaco, 1963-64. Mem. N.Am. Benthological Soc. (pres. 1958), Am. Soc. Zoologists, Am. Physiol. Soc., Soc. Exptl. Biology and Medicine Home: 6741 S Lake RR 1 Pentwater MI 49449-9801 Office: Mich State U Dept Physiology East Lansing MI 48824

FROMM, RONALD A. apparel executive; m. Cheryl Fromm; children: Dawn, Dana. BS in Acctg., MBA, U. Wis. Former v.p. Heath Corp.; dir. fin. Famous Footwear divsn. Brown Group, Madison, Wis., 1986-88, v.p., 1988-90, v.p., CFO, 1990-92, exec. v.p., then pres. Brown Shoe Co. divsn., 1992-99, pres., CEO, chmn. bd. dirs. St. Louis, 1999—. Bd. dirs. Footwear Distributors and Retailers of Am., Fashion Footwear Assn. N.Y., Two/Ten Footwear Industry charitable found. Office: Brown Shoe 8300 Maryland Ave Saint Louis MO 63105

FROMSTEIN, MITCHELL S. retired office services company executive; b. 1928; Grad., U. Wis., 1947. With Krueger Homes Inc., 1948-49; account exec. Mautner Advt. Agy., 1949-53; former pres. TV Parts Inc.; ptnr. Fromstein Assocs.; pres., chief exec. officer, dir. The Parker Pen Co., Janesville, Wis., 1985-86; chmn., pres., chief exec. officer Manpower, Inc., Milw., 1976-99. Office: Manpower Inc Box 2053 5301 N Ironwood Ln Milwaukee WI 53217-4982

FRONTIERE, GEORGIA, professional football team executive; m. Carroll Rosenblum, July 7, 1966 (dec.); children: Dale Carroll, Lucia; m. Dominic Frontiere. Pres., owner L.A. Rams, NFL, 1979—; now mng. ptnr. St. Louis Rams. Bd. dirs. L.A. Boys and Girls Club, L.A. Orphanage Guild, L.A. Blind Youth Found. Named Headliner of Yr., L.A. Press Club, 1981. Office: St Louis Rams 1 Rams Way Earth City MO 63045-1525 also: Transworld Dome 701 Convention Plz Saint Louis MO 63101

FROSETH, GLEN, state legislator; m. Donna Froseth; 4 children. Newspaper pub.; state rep. dist. 6, 1993—. Mem. industry, bus. and labor com., polit. subdivsns. com. N.D. Ho. Reps. Mem. N. Dak. Newspaper Assn. (past pres.), Lions, Eagles. Home: PO Box 894 Kenmare ND 58746-0894

FROSS, ROGER RAYMOND, lawyer; b. Rockford, Ill., Mar. 8, 1940; s. Hollis H. and Dorothy (George) F.; m. Madelon R. Rose, Feb. 14, 1970; 1 child, Oliver. AB, DePauw U., 1962; JD, U. Chgo., 1965. Bar: Ill. 1965. Assoc. Norman and Billick, Chgo., 1965-70; ptnr. Lord, Bissell & Brook, 1970—, mng. pntr., 1982-87. Bd. dirs. Hyde Park Bank and Trust Co., Chgo., 1975—; pres. Hyde-Park-Kenwood Devel. Corp., 1998—. Bd. dirs. Hyde Park Neighborhood Club, Chgo., 1970—, pres. 1972-73; bd. dirs., mem. exec. com. South East Chgo. Commn., 1978—; mem. Community Conservation Council, Chgo., 1980-99; bd. dirs., sec. Chgo. Metro History Fair, 1991—; bd. dirs. The Joyce Found., 1991—, Lab. Sch. U. Chgo., 1991-94, Citizens Com. of the Juvenile Ct., 1973-96. Rector schlor DePauw U., Greencastle, Ind., 1958-62. Mem. ABA, Ill. Bar Assn., Chgo. Bar Assn. (chmn. com. juvenile delinquents 1972). Office: Lord Bissell & Brook Harris Bank Bldg 115 S La Salle St Ste 3500 Chicago IL 60603-3801

FRUCHTENBAUM, EDWARD, greeting card company executive; b. 1948; BA, Calif. State U., Northridge, 1971. Sales rep. Am. Greetings, Calif., 1973-82, regional mgr., 1982-86, v.p. mktg., 1986-87, group v.p., 1987-88, sr. v.p. mktg., 1988-90, pres. U.S. greeting card div., 1990—, pres., COO, also bd. dirs., 1992—. Mem. alumni Leadership Cleve., 1989—; mem. Chagrin Hist. Soc., Chagrin Falls, Ohio, Stan Hywett Hall Found., Akron, Ohio. Mem. Am. Mktg. Assn. Office: Am Greetings One American Rd Cleveland OH 44144-2301

FRUEH, BARTLEY RICHARD, surgeon; b. Cleve., Sept. 1, 1937; s. Lloyd Walter and Elizabeth Virginia (Scott) F.; m. Frances Olive Beach, June 10, 1961 (div. Dec. 1976); children: Bartley Christopher, Dylan Beach (dec.), Walter Terry; m. Frances Mallet-Prevost Gaston Sargent, Dec. 31, 1976 (div. Oct. 1997); stepchildren: Eric Winslow Sargent, Laura Elizabeth Sargent. BChemE, Cornell U., 1960; MD, Columbia Coll. Phys./Surgeons, 1964; MS Ophthalmology, U. Mich., 1970. Diplomate Am. Bd. Ophthalmology. Surg. intern N.C. Meml. Hosp., Chapel Hill, N.C., 1964-65; resident in ophthalmology U. Mich., Ann Arbor, 1967-70; fellow eye plastic surgery Alston Callahan, Birmingham, Ala., 1970; asst. prof. ophthalmology, eye plastic surgery U. Mo., Columbia, 1971-72, asst. clin. prof. ophthalmology eye plastic surgery, 1972-76, assoc. clin. prof. ophthalmology eye plastic surgery, 1976-79; pvt. practice, ophthalmology, 1972-79; assoc. prof. ophthalmology, eye plastic and orbital surgery U. Mich., Ann Arbor, 1979-86, prof. ophthalmology, 1986—. Cons. med. staff U. Mo. Med. Ctr., Columbia, 1971-79, Meml. Hosp., Jefferson City, 1971-73, Boone County Hosp., Columbia, 1972-79, Harry S. Truman Meml. Vet.'s Hosp., Columbia, 1971-79; med. staff Columbia Regional Hosp., Columbia, 1974-79, U. Mich. Med. Ctr., 1979—, VA Med. Ctr., 1979—; hon. guest spkr. Royal Australian Coll. Ophthalmology, 1995, Peter Rogers lectr., 1999; lectr. in field. Author: Transactions, American Ophthalmological Society, 1984; editor/author: Surgery of the Eye, 1988; editl. bd.: Ophthalmic Surgery, 1980-87, Am. Acad. Ophthalmology Clin. Modules, 1983-86, Ophthalmic Plastic and Reconstructive Surgery, 1984-98, Orbit; contbr. articles to profl. jours./publs., books in field. Capt. USAF, 1965-67, Taiwan. Grantee in field. Fellow Am. Acad. Ophthalmology (Wendell Hughes lectr. 1993, Sr. Honor award 1990); mem. Am. Soc. Ophthal. Plastic and Reconstructive Surgery (sec. 1973-74, pres. 1976), Am. Ophthalmol. Soc., Orbital Soc., Ptosis Rsch. Soc., Australasian Soc. Ophthalmic Plastic Surgeons (hon.), European Soc. Ophthal. Plastic and Reconstructive Surgeons (hon.). Avocations: pocket billiards, Model T Fords and old Morgans, wine, violin. Office: WK Kellogg Eye Ctr U Mich 1000 Wall St Ann Arbor MI 48105-1986

FRUEHLING, ROSEMARY THERESE, publishing executive, author; b. Gilbert, Minn., Jan. 23, 1933; d. Tony and Mary (Scalise) Leoni; 1 child, Shirley Adzick. BS, U. Minn., 1954, MA, 1968, PhD, 1980. Cert. vocat. tech. inst. dir.; cert. in bus. edn. Mgr. instructional svcs. State Bd. Voc-Tech. Edn., St. Paul; dir. Minn. Software Office State of Minn.; mgr. office tech. Gregg, McGraw Hill, Mpls.; pres. EMC/Paradigm Pub. Inc. (Coll. Divsn.), St. Paul. Nat. cons. editor SRA. Author: (textbooks) Communicating for Results: Write to The Point, Office Systems: People, Procedures and Technology, Business Communications: A Case Method Approach, Business Writing: Integrating Process and Purpose, Psychology: Realizing Human Potential, Working at Human Relations, Your Attitude Counts, Communicating for Results, Working in Teams. Mem. Am. Vocat. Assn., Minn. Vocat. Assn., Nat. Bus. Edn. Assn., Delta Pi Epsilon. Office: EMC Corp 875 Montreal Way Saint Paul MN 55102-4245

FRUEHWALD, KRISTIN G. lawyer; b. Sidney, Nebr., May 15, 1946; d. Chris U. and Mary E. (Boles) Bitner; m. Michael R. Fruehwald, Feb. 23, 1980; children: Laurel Elizabeth, Amy Marie. BS with highest distinction in History, U. Nebr., 1968; JD summa cum laude, Ind. U., 1975. Bar: Ind. 1975, U.S. Dist. Ct. (so. dist.) Ind. 1975. Assoc. Barnes & Thornburg, Indpls., 1975-81, ptnr., 1982—. Spkr. in field. Contbr. articles to profl. jours. Trustee The Orchard Sch., 1993—, chmn., 1997—98; bd. dirs.

Indpls. Parks Found., 1995—2000, Arts Ind., 1994—98, Ind. Continuing Legal Edn. Forum, 1993—2001, pres., 2000—01; bd. dirs. Indpls. Bar Found., 1992—, chmn., 1997—99; bd. dirs. James Whitcomb Riley Meml. Assn., 1995—, treas., 2000—; bd. dirs. Planned Giving Group Ind., Fedn. Cmty. Defenders, Inc., 1993—99, pres., 1999—2001; bd. dirs . Ind. affiliate Am. Heart Assn., 1977—81, vice chmn. Marion County chpt., 1981. Fellow: ABA (chmn. distributable net income subcom 1985—91, sect. taxation, mem. real property, probate and trust sect.), Ind. State Bar Assn. (bd. mgrs. 1989—90, pres. 2001—02, chmn. probate, trust and real property sects. 1987—88, mem. sect. taxation, mem. ho. of dels. 1987—, treas. 1996—97, chair ho. of dels. 1998—99), Ind. Bar Found., Am. Coll. Trust and Estate Counsel (chmn. Ind. state laws com. 1992—95); mem.: Ind. Code Study Commn., Internat. Assn. Fin. Planners, Indpls. Estate Planning Coun., Indpls. Bar Assn. (pres. 1993, chmn. estate planning and adminstrn. sect. 1982—83, chmn. long range fin. planning com. 1988—89). Office: Barnes & Thornburg 11 S Meridian St Indianapolis IN 46204-3535 E-mail: kris.fruewald@btlaw.com.

FRUSTI, DOREEN KAYE, nursing administrator; BSN summa cum laude, Augustana Coll., 1970; MS in Ednl. Psychology and Counseling, Winona State U., 1979, postgrad., 1988—. RN, Minn. Developer, implementor group therapy program acute psychiat. unit McKennan Hosp., Sioux Falls, S.D., 1970; asst. head nurse gen. surgery Rochester (Minn.) Meth. Hosp., 1970-73, head nurse nephrology and renal transplant, 1973-78, instr. electrocardiology, 1975, asst. DON, 1978-83, mem. facility and program devel. chem. dependence svcs., 1981-83, mem. adminstrv. com., 1983-85, mem. lab. medicine study, 1978, mem. weekened phys. medicine feasibility study, 1978-79, mem. liason com., 1978-80, mem. hospice feasibility study, 1978-82, clin. DIN, 1978-91, mem. mgmt. coun., 1987—, mem. clean air task force com., 1986-87, mem. tornado and disaster coms., 1986-88, mem. nursing info. system steering com., 1987-91, joint head nurse planning com., 1988-91, chair dept. nursing, 1991—; grad. intern supr. Winona (Minn.) State U., 1983-88; co-instr. chem. dependence course Rochester Community Coll., 1985; cons. Meth. Hosp. Indpls., 1989. Adj. asst. prof. St. Mary's Coll., Winona, 1986—; mem. cons. com. on alcoholism and drug dependence unit Mayo Clinic, 1980-91, adminstrv. mgmt. com., 1983-88, adolescent chem. dependence unit, 1984-88, mgmt. forum, 1988—, coordinating com., 1988-90, smoking cessation program com. Mayo Med. Ctr., 1985-89, smoke free implementation task force, 1987; cons. Genesee Hosp., Rochester, N.Y., 1989. Mem. hypertension screening program Bethel Luth. Ch., 1976, stewardship com., 1976-78, usher, 1985—, group discussion facilitator, 1985-90, chair, 1986-89, chair pers. and exec. coms., 1987-89, capt., 1988—, lead usher, 1991—; del. dist. conv. Am. Luth. Ch., 1987; del. synodical conv. Evang. Luth. Ch. Am., 1988; chair Outpatient Observation Task Force, 1990-91, steering com. Nursing Ops. Assessment, 1990-91, Incident Report Task Force, 1990-91, Allied Health, 1992—; mem. Bread of the World, 1989—; mem. ops. bd. dirs. Probation Offenders Rehab. and Tng., 1987-90, chair pers. com., 1988-90; supr. Roundtable, 1992—. Mem. Dist. F Orgn. Nurse Execs., Am. Orgn. Nurse Execs., Minn. Orgn. Nurse Execs., Minn. Nurses Assn. (del. 1971, 77, 81, 83, program com. 6th dist. 1973-75, chairperson, 1975-77, adv. bd. com., pres. 1977-79, long range planning com. 1978-79, entry level task force 1981, nursing svc. adminstrn. exec. and legis. coms. 1981-82, nominating com. 1981-83), Sigma Theta Tau (Kappa Mu chpt.). Home: 2100 Valkyrie Dr NW Apt 108 Rochester MN 55901-2451 Office: Rochester Meth Hosp 200 1st St SW Rochester MN 55905-0001

FRY, ANNE EVANS, zoology educator; b. Phila., Sept. 11, 1939; d. Kenneth Evans and Nora Irene (Smith) F. AB, Mount Holyoke Coll., 1961; MS, U. Iowa, 1963; PhD, U. Mass., 1969. Instr. Carleton Coll., Northfield, Minn., 1963-65; asst. prof. Ohio Wesleyan U., Delaware, 1969-74, assoc. prof., 1974-80, prof., 1980—, Helen Whitelaw Jackson univ. prof., 1999—. Contbr. articles to profl. jours. Recipient Welch Teaching award Ohio Wesleyan U., 1976. Mem. AAAS, Am. Inst. Biol. Scis., Soc. for Integrative and Comparative Biology, Ohio Acad. Sci., Soc. Devel. Biology, Sigma Xi. Office: Ohio Wesleyan U Delaware OH 43015 E-mail: AEFry@owu.edu.

FRY, CHARLES GEORGE, theologian, educator; b. Piqua, Ohio, Aug. 15, 1936; s. Sylvan Jack and Lena Freda (Ehle) F. BA, Capital U., 1958; MA, Ohio State U., 1961, PhD, 1965; BD, Evang. Lutheran Theol. Sem., 1962, MDiv, 1977; DMin, Winebrenner Theol. Sem., 1978; DD, Cranmer Sem., 2001. Ordained to ministry Lutheran Ch. U.S.A, 1963; diplomate Am. Psychotherapy Assn. Pastor St. Mark's Luth. Ch. and Martin Luther Luth. Ch., Columbus, Ohio, 1961-62, 63-66; instr. Wittenberg U., 1962-63, 71-72, Capital U., 1963-75, asst. prof. history and religion, 1966-69, assoc. prof., 1969-75; theologian-in-residence North Community Luth. Ch., Columbus, 1971-73; assoc. prof. hist. theology, dir. missions edn. Concordia Theol. Sem., Ft. Wayne, Ind., 1975-84; sr. minister First Congl. Ch., Detroit, 1984-85; Protestant chaplain St. Francis Coll., Fort Wayne, 1982-92; prof. philosophy and theology Luth. Coll. of Health Professions, Ft. Wayne, 1992-98, U. St. Francis, Ft. Wayne, 1998-99, Winebrenner Theol. Sem., U. Findlay, Ohio, 1999—. Interim min. Arbor Grove Congl. Ch., Jackson, Mich., 1980, hon. minister emeritus 1996, First Presbyn. Ch., Huntington, Ind., 1988-89, St. Luke's Luth. Ch., Ft. Wayne, 1989-90, Mt. Pleasant Luth. Ch., 1990-91, St. Mark's Luth. Ch., 1990-91, Mt. Zion Luth. Ch., Ft. Wayne, 1991-93; interim min. Cmty. Christian Ch., New Carlisle, Ind., 1993-94, First Luth. Ch., Stryker, Ohio, 1994-95, Zion Luth. Ch., West Jefferson, Ohio, 1994-97, 98-2000, Agape Congl. Ch., Bowling Green, Ohio, 1997-98; interim min. Fairfield Parish, Lancaster, Ohio, 2000—; vis. prof. Damavand Coll., Tehran, 1973-74, bd. dirs., 1976-94; vis. prof. Ref. Bible Coll., 1975-80, Concordia Luth. Sem. at Brock U., summers 1977, 79, Grad. Sch. Christian Min., Huntington (Ind.) Coll., 1986-89, Wheaton Coll., 1987-88; vis. scholar Al Ain U., United Arab Emirates, 1987; theologian-in-residence, tchg. theologian Queentown Luth. Ch., Singapore, 1991, 99, 2000, 02; adj. faculty history Ind. U./Purdue U., Ft. Wayne, 1982-98, Winebrenner Theol. Sem., Findlay, Ohio, 1992, 99, 2000, Holy Trinity Coll. and Sem., 1999—, Tung Ling Bible Coll., Singapore, 2000, 02, North Tenn. Bible Inst., 1998—; pastor-in-residence Wittenberg U., Springfield, Ohio, 1992, Deaconess Cmty. Evang. Luth. Ch. Am., Phila., 1993. Author books including Age of Lutheran Orthodoxy, 1979, Lutheranism in America, 1979, Islam, 1980, 2d edit. 1982, The Way, The Truth, The Life, 1982, Great Asian Religions, 1984, Francis: A Call to Conversion, 1988, Brit. edit., 1990, The Middle East: A History, 1988, Congregationalists and Evolution: Asa Gray and Louis Agassiz, 1989, Pioneering a Theology of Evolution: Washington Gladden and Pierre Teilhard de Chardin, 1989, Avicenna's Philosophy of Education: An Introduction, 1990, Explorations in Protestant Theology, 1992, Life's Little Lessons, 1997, Kant's Three Questions, 1997, Four Little Words, 1997, Goethe: Life and Truth, 2001, others; co-producer Global Perspectives, IPFW-TV, Ft. Wayne, 1987-97. Bd. dirs. Luth. Liturgical Renewal, 1983-90, 94-2000, pres., 1999-2000; v.p. Internat. Luth. Fellowship, 1995-98, pres., 1998-2001; consecrated bishop, so. region Internat. Luth. Fellowship, 1996; assoc. St. Augustine's Fellowship, 1996—; bd. dirs. Zwemer Inst., Ft. Wayne, Ind., 1997—. Recipient Praestantia award Capital U., 1970, Concordia Hist. Inst. citation, 1977, Archbishop Robert Leighton award Nat. Anglican Ch., 1997; Regional Coun. for Internat. Edn. rsch. grantee, 1969; Joseph J. Malone postdoctoral fellow Egypt, 1986, Malone postdoctoral fellow, United Arab Emirates, 1987; named Ky. Col., 1999. Fellow Brit. Interplanetary Soc., Coll. Pastoral Counseling (diplomate), Am. Assn. Integrated Medicine (diplomate, bd. coll. pastoral counseling 2001-), Oxford Soc. Scholars; mem. Am. Hist. Assn., Am. Acad. Religion, Mid. East Inst. Gen. Soc. War of 1812 (compatriot 1994—, chaplain Ohio chpt. 1996—, chaplain gen. 2001-), German Soc. Md., Mil. and Hospitaller Order of St. Lazarus of Jerusalem (chaplain 2000—), Phi Alpha Theta. Democrat. Home: 158 W Union St Circleville OH 43113-1965 Office: PO Box 478 701 E Melrose Ave Findlay OH 45840-4416

FRY, CRAIG R. state legislator; b. Mishawaka, Ind., Oct. 6, 1952; s. Harold L. and Sonna Kay (wilson) F.; m. Carol Sue Granning, 1973; children: Courtney Lynn, Lucas Craig. Student, Ball State U., 1970, 72, Ind. U., South Bend, Ivy Tech. Coll. Bus. agt. N.E. Indt. Coun. of Carpenters, 1988—, svc. rep.; rep. Dist. 5 Ind. Ho. of Reps., 1988—, mem. age and aging com., environ. affairs com., mem. fin. inst. com.; chmn. ins. and corps., small bus. and labor coms.; ranking minority mem. Exec. dir. apprenticeship tng. Ivy Tech. State Coll. Pres. Carpenters #413, 1988; mem. Healthy Mothers/Healthy Babies; mem. Mishawaka/Penn Dem. Club.; mem. Penn Twp. Adv. Bd., 1987-88; mem. rules com. Ind. and Nat. Dem. Conv. Home: 637 Bay View Dr Mishawaka IN 46544-4157

FRY, DONALD LEWIS, physiologist, educator; b. Des Moines, Dec. 29, 1924; s. Clair V. and Maudie (Long) F.; children— Donald Stewart, Ronald Sinclair, Heather Elise, Laurel Virginia. M.D., Harvard U., 1949. Rsch. fellow Univ Minn Hosp., Mpls., 1952-53; sr. asst. surgeon gen. NIH, Bethesda, Md., 1953-56, surgeon, 1956-57, sr. surgeon, 1957-61, med. dir., 1961-80; prof. Ohio State U., Columbus, 1980—. Contbr. numerous articles and papers on physiology and biophysics of pulmonary mechanics, blood vascular interface, transvascular mass transport and the genesis of atherosclerosis to profl. jours., books. Mem. AAAS, Am. Physiol. Soc., Am. Soc. Clin. Investigation, Biophys. Soc., N.Y. Acad. Scis. Office: Ohio State U Coll Medicine 2025 Wiseman Hall 400 W 12th Ave Columbus OH 43210-1214

FRY, RICHARD E. architectural firm executive; BArch, U. Mich. Registered arch. Mich., Minn., Colo.; cert. Nat. Coun. Archtl. Registered Bds. Pres., prin.-in-charge Fry & Ptnrs. Archs., Inc., Aspen, Col. and Ann Arbor, Mich., 1970—. Adj. prof. U. Mich. Coll. Archtl. and Urban Planning; archtl. instr. Washtenaw C.C.; rep. Mich. archs. Nat. AIA Bd., Washington. Prin. works include U. Mich. Vis. Ctr., No. Brewery Office Bldg., Ann Arbor, Mich. League-U. Mich., Ann Arbor Art Assn., U. Mich. Dental Sch. Sindecuse Mus., We. Mich. U. Bookstore, Burns Park Elem. Sch., Ann Arbor Ctrl. Fire Sta., Heydon Wash. St. Properties, Ann Arbor, pvt. residences, others. Past mem. Ann Arbor Planning Commn.; bd. dirs. Bldg. Bd. Appeals; mem. art acquisition com. Washtenaw C.C. Fellow AIA (pres. Mich. chpt., chmn. design awards & recognition com. Mich. chpt., chmn. design retreat com. Mich. chpt., chmn. mid-summer conf. Mich. chpt., regional dir. Mich. chpt., pres. Huron Valley chpt.). Office: Fry & Ptnrs Archs Inc 450 S Wagner Rd Ann Arbor MI 48103-1944

FRY, ROY H(ENRY), librarian, educator; b. Seattle, June 16, 1931; s. Ray Edward and Fern Mildred (Harmon) F.; m. Joanne Mae Van de Guchte, Sept. 12, 1970; 1 child, Andrea Joy. BA in Asian Studies, BA in Anthropology, U. Wash., 1959; MA in Libr. Sci., Western Mich. U., 1965; MA in Polit. Sci., Northeastern Ill. U., 1977; archives cert., U. Dever, 1970; advanced studies program cert., Moody Bible Inst., 1990. Cert. tchr., Wash.; cert. pub. libr., N.Y.; cert. Med. Libr. Assn. Libr. and audio-visual coord. Zillah (Wash.) Pub. Schs., 1960-61; libr. Mark Morris H.S., Longview, Wash., 1961-64; evening reference libr. Loyola U. of Chgo., 1965-67, head reference libr., 1967-73, bibliog. svcs. libr., 1973-74, head circulation libr., 1974-76, coord. pub. svcs., 1976-85, gov. documents libr., 1985-91; ind. libr. cons., 1991-94; ref. libr. Trinity Evang. Divinity Sch., Deerfield, Ill., 1994—2001, reference, archives libr., 2001—. Tchg. asst. in anthropology Loyola U. of Chgo., 1966-67, instr. libr. sci. program for disadvantaged students, 1967, 68, univ. archivist, 1976-78, bibliographer for polit. sci., 1973-91, instr. corr. study div., 1975-85. Mem. Niles Twp. Regular Rep. Orgn., Skokie, Ill., 1982-98, sec. 1986-98; mem. Skokie Caucus Party, 1981-98; vol. Dep. Registration Officer, 1986—; mem. Skokie Traffic Safety Commn., 1984—, Skokie 4th July Parade com., 1986—; election judge Niles Twp., 1983-98, Avon Twp., 1999—. With USNR, 1951-52. Mem. Nat. Librs. Assn. (founding mem., bd. dirs. 1975-76), Asian/Pacific Am. Librs. Assn. (founding mem.), Chgo. Area Theol. Librs. Assn., Pacific N.W. Libr. Assn., Chgo. Area Archivists (founding mem.), Midwest Archives Conf. (founding mem.), ALA, Assn. Coll. and Rsch. Librs., Ill. Prairie Path Assn., Royal Can. Geog. Soc., Skokie Hist. Soc. (recording sec. 1986—), Ballard Hist. Soc. (Seattle), Macon County Hist. Soc. (Decatur, Ill.), Nat. Right to Life Com., Ill. Fedn. for Right to Life, Am. Legion, VFW, Korean War Vets. Assn., Pi Sigma Alpha. Republican. Evangelical Free. Office: Trinity Evang Divinity Sch Rolfing Meml Libr 2065 Half Day Rd Deerfield IL 60015-1241 Address: 335 S Arrowhead Ct Round Lake IL 60073-4209 E-mail: rfry@tiu.edu.

FRYDRYK, KARL ALLEN, financial executive; b. Sept. 8, 1954; m. Nancy J. Frydryk, May 5, 1984; 3 children. BS, Miami U., Oxford, Ohio, 1976. CPA, Ohio. Mgr. Touche Ross & Co., Dayton, Ohio, 1976-84; v.p. fin., sec., dir. Nord Resources Corp., 1984—. Mem. AICPA, Ohio Soc. CPAs, Optimist Internat. (pres. Centerville 1994). Office: Genesis Worldwide Inc 2600 Kettering Tower Dayton OH 45423

FRYKENBERG, ROBERT ERIC, historian, educator; b. India, June 8, 1930; s. Carl Eric and Doris Marie (Skoglund) F.; m. Carol Enid Addington, July 1, 1952; children: Ann Denise Leinis, Brian Robert, Craig Michael. B.A., Bethel Coll., Minn., 1951; M.A., U. Minn., 1953; M.Div., Bethel Theol. Sem., 1955; Ph.D. (Rockefeller fellow 1958-61), London U., 1961. Research asst. U. Calif., Berkeley, 1955-57; instr. Oakland (Calif.) Jr. Coll., 1957-58; Ford and Carnegie research and teaching fellow U. Chgo., 1961-62; mem. faculty U. Wis., Madison, 1962—, prof. history and S. Asian studies, 1971-97, emeritus prof. history and South Asian studies, 1997—, chmn. dept., dir. Center S. Asian Studies, 1970-73. Vis. prof. U. Hawaii, summer 1968; Radhakrishwan Meml. lectr. Oxford U., 1998; dir. Pew India Rsch. Advancement Projects, 1994-01. Author: Guntur District, 1978-1848: A History of Local Influence and Central Authority in South India, 1965, History and Belief: The Foundations of Historical Understanding, 1996; editor: Land Control and Social Structure in Indian History, 1969, 77, Land Tenure and Peasant in South Asia: An Anthology of Recent Research, 1977, Studies of South India, 1985, Delhi Through the Ages, 1986, 93; co-editor: Studies in the History of Christian Missions series, 1997—; contbr. articles to revs. and profl. publs. Trustee Am. Inst. Indian Studies, 1971-81; dir. summer seminar NEH, 1976. Rsch. fellow Am. Coun. Learned Socs.-Social Sci. Rsch. Coun. 1962-63, 67, 73-74, 83-84, 88-89, Guggenheim fellow, 1968-69, HEW Fulbright Hays sr. fellow, 1965-66, NEH fellow, 1975, fellow Wis. Inst. Rsch. Humanities, 1975, Wilson Ctr., 1986, 91-92, Pew Rsch. fellow, 1997. Fellow Royal Hist. Soc., Royal Asiatic Soc.; mem. Internat. Conf. and Seminars, Soc. S. Indian Studies (pres. 1968-70, 82-84), Am. Hist. Assn. (pres. conf. faith and history 1970-72), Assn. Asian Studies, Inst. Hist. Studies India, Inst. Asian Studies India, Assn. South Asian Studies Australia, Inst. Advanced Christian Studies (dir. 1979-83, 87-91, pres. 1981-83) Office: Univ Wis 4134 Humanities Bldg Madison WI 53706 E-mail: frykenberg@mhub.history.wisc.edu.

FRYLING, VICTOR J. energy company executive; Pres., COO CMS Energy Corp., Dearborn, Mich., 1991—. Office: CMS Energy Corp Fairlane Plz S Ste 1100 330 Town Center Dr Dearborn MI 48126

FRYMAN, DAVID TRAVIS, professional baseball player; b. Lexington, Ky., Mar. 25, 1969; With Detroit Tigers, 1987—. Recipient Silver Slugger award, 1992; mem. Sporting News All-Star Team, 1993, Am. League All-Star Team, 1992-93, 94, 96. Office: Cleveland Indians Jacobs Field 2401 Ontario St Cleveland OH 44115-4003*

FRYXELL, DAVID ALLEN, publishing executive; b. Sioux Falls, S.D., Mar. 8, 1956; s. Donald Raymond and Lucy (Dickinson) F.; m. Lisa Duaine Forman, June 16, 1978; 1 child, Courtney Elizabeth. B.A., Augustana Coll., 1978. Assoc.-sr. editor TWA Ambassador, St. Paul, 1978-80, mng. editor, 1980-81; sr. editor Horizon, Tuscaloosa, Ala., 1981-82; circuit writer Telegraph Herald, Dubuque, Iowa, 1982-85; contbg. editor Horizon mag., 1982-85; dir. publs., exec. editor Pitt mag. U. Pitts., 1985-90; editl. dir. Quad/Creative Group Milwaukee Mag., 1991-92; exec. features editor, dir. new ventures St. Paul Pioneer Press, 1992-95, sr. editor technology and new ventures, 1995-96; sr. editor bus. and tech., 1996; exec. producer Twin Cities Sidewalk Microsoft Corp., 1996-98; mag. editl. dir. F & W Publs., Cin., 1998—2001, editor-in-chief, 2001—. Chief judge mags. Golden Quill awards, Pitts., 1980; nonfiction columnist Writer's Digest, 1994—; faculty Maui Writers Conf., 2000—02. Author: Double-Parked on Main Street, 1988, How to Write Fast While Writing Well, 1992, Elements of Article Writing: Structure and Flow, 1996; editor: Family Tree Mag., 2000—, Comair Navigator Mag., 2001—; contbr. articles to mags. including Travel & Leisure, Playboy, Passages, AAA World, Savvy, Online Access, Diversion, Easy Living, Readers Digest, Link Up, others. Chief writer Anderson for Pres. Com., Minn., 1978. Mem. Iowa Newspaper Assn. (2d award master columnist 1983, 2d award best feature writing 1983, 2d award best series 1983), Chgo. Art Dirs. Club (Merit award for editing 1981), Coll. and Univ. Pub. Relations Assn. of Pa., Council for Advancement and Support of Edn. (Periodicals Improvement award 1987, 90, 91, Top Ten Mag. award 1990, 91, Articles of Yr. award 1990, Periodical Spl. Issues award 1991, Instl. Rels. Publs. award 1991, Periodical Resource Mgmt. award, 1990, 91), Augustana Coll. Fellows, Augustana Alumni Assn. (Decades of Leadership award 1978), Blue Key, Internat. Assn. Bus. Communicators (Golden Triangle award 1987, 89, best spl. publ. award 1988), Women in Communications (Matrix award 1990, hon. mention 1990, 91), City and Regional Mag. Assn. (Gen. Excellence award 1992, Spl. Sect. award 1992, Commentary award 1992, Investigative Writing award 1992), Mo. Lifestyle Awards (2d Gen. Excellence award 1994, 95). Democrat. Unitarian. Office: F & W Publs 4700 E Galbraith Rd Cincinnati OH 45236-6708 E-mail: davidfryxell@fwpubs.com.

FU, PAUL SHAN, law librarian, consultant; b. Shien-Yang, Liao-Ning, China, Sept. 7, 1932; came to U.S., 1961; s. Mu-Shia and Shih-Wei (Chang) F.; m. Doris S. Ku, Jan. 15, 1963; children: Eugene Y., Vincent Y. LLB, Soochow U., 1960; MCL, U. Ill., 1962; MSLS, Villanova U., 1968. Asst. libr., law lectr. Detroit Coll. of Law, 1968-69; law libr., asst. prof. law Ohio No. U., Ada, 1969-71, law libr., assoc. prof. law, 1971-72; law libr. Supreme Ct. of Ohio, Columbus, 1972—; pres. Asian-Am. Law Librs. Caucus, 1994. Dir. Nat. Conf. on State Ct. Librs., Columbus, 1993; cons. Supreme Ct. of Ill. Law Libr., Springfield, 1988, N.H. State Law Libr., Concord, 1987; judge West Pub. Excellence in Law Librarianship Awards Com., 1996. Author: Law Library Handbook of Ohio Supreme Court, 1974; columnist Ohio Lawyer, 1988—; contbr. articles to profl. jours. Recipient Award of Merit Columbus Bar Assn., 1996; U. Ill. fellow, 1961-62. Mem. ALA, Am. Assn. Law Librs. (sec. 1989-93, chair state, ct., and county law librs. sect. 1977-78), Am. Soc. Internat. Law, Univ. Club, Kiwanis (Columbus). Avocations: piano, oil painting, fiction, tennis. Home: 940 Evening St Worthington OH 43085-3051 Office: Ohio State Supreme Ct Law Libr 30 E Broad St Fl 4 Columbus OH 43215-3414

FUCHS, ELAINE V. molecular biologist, educator; b. Hinsdale, Ill., May 5, 1950; d. Louis H. and Viola L. (Lueck) F.; m. David T. Hansen, Sept. 10, 1988. BS in Chemistry with honors, U. Ill., Urbana, 1972; PhD in Biochemistry, Princeton U., 1977. Postdoctoral fellow dept. biology MIT, 1977-80; asst. prof. U. Chgo., 1980-85, assoc. prof., 1985-88, prof. dept. molecular genetics and cell biology, 1989—, Amgen prof. basic scis., 1993—, investigator, Howard Hughes Med. Inst., 1988—. Assoc. editor Jour. Cell Biology, 1993—; contr. numerous articles to profl. jours. Recipient R.R. Benesely award Am. Assn. Anatomists, 1988, Searle Scholar award Chgo. Cmty. Trust, 1981-84, Presdl. Young Investigator award NSF, 1984-89, NIH Merit award, 1993, 98, Wm. Montagna award Soc. Investigative Dermatology, 1995, Keith Porter Lecture award Am. Soc. Cell Biology, 1996, Sr. Woman Achievement award, 1997; named Harvey Lectr., 1999. Fellow Am. Acad. Arts and Scis., Am. Assn. Microbiology; mem. NAS (elected mem.), Inst. Medicine of NAS, Phi Beta Kappa. Office: U Chgo Howard Hughes Med Inst Dept Molecular Genetics 5841 S Maryland Ave Rm 314N Chicago IL 60637-1463

FUERSTNER, FIONA MARGARET ANNE, ballet company executive, ballet educator; b. Rio de Janeiro, Apr. 24, 1936; d. Paul G. and Agnes Ethel (Stothard) F.; m. Dane LaFontsee, June 7, 1969 (div. 1992); 1 child, Liana Marie. Studied with San Francisco Ballet, Royal Ballet (London), Ballet Rambert (London) Ballet Theatre Sch. (N.Y.C.), Sch. Am. Ballet (N.Y.C.). With corps de ballet San Francisco Ballet, 1952-55, soloist, 1955-58, prin. dancer, 1958-62; toured with Walter Terry's Am. Dances, 1962-63; prin. dancer Les Grands Ballets Can., Montreal, 1963-64, Am. Choreographer's Co. of N.Y., 1964, Pa. Ballet, 1965-68, 1968-74, ballet mistress, instr. co. class, apprentice class, 1974-77, ballet mistress, instr. co. class, 1977—86; ballet mistress Nashville Ballet, 1986-87, ballet mistress, asst. to artistic dir., 1987-91; ballet mistress Milw. Ballet, 1990-95, asst. to artistic dir. ballet mistress, 1995—. Guest dancer Ballet Concerto, Miami, 1967, 68, Erie Civic Ballet, 1969; guest instr. Marsha Woody Dance Acad., Beaumont, Tex., 1974, U. Louisville, 1977-78, co. class San Francisco Ballet, 1985, Tenn. Assn. Dance Nashville Conf., 1988, So. Regional Workshop Chgo., Nat. Assn. Dance Masters in Nashville, 1989, BalletMet, 1991, Memphis Classical Ballet, 1992, 97, 99, Nashville Ballet, 1992; guest ballet mistress BalletMet, 1993; faculty tchr. Sch. of Pa. Ballet, 1977-78, 78-86; organized concert group, ballet mistress, dancer Pa. Ballet, 1971; mem. dance panel Nat. Found. Advancement in the Arts, 1995-98; master tchr. South Eastern Regional Ballet Assn. Festival, 1998, Nat. Found. for Advancement in the Arts, 1999, 2001; guest tchr. Ind. U. Ballet Dept., 2000, Western Mich. U., 2002; dance panelist Midwest Regional, Nat. Found. for Advancement in the Arts, May and July 2001. Staged Allegro Brillante, Sch. Pa. Ballet Student Showcase, 1986, Nashville Ballet, 1988, Madrigalesco, Pacific NW Ballet, 1981, (parts) Nutcracker, Nashville Ballet, 1989, Scotch Symphony, Pa. Ballet, 1993, Carmina Burana, Alberta Ballet, 1993, Concerto Barocco, Ballet Omaha, 1994, Ballet Met, 1995, Serenade, Milw. Ballet Sch., 1994, 95, 96, Serenade Milw. Ballet, 1998-99, Serenade Western Mich. U., 1999-2000; staged Concerto Barocco, The Four Temperaments for Milw. Ballet, 1999-2000, Allegro Brillante, 2000-01.

FULGONI, GIAN MARC, market research company executive; b. Crickhowell, Brecon, England, Jan. 24, 1948; came to U.S., 1970; s. Romeo and Maria F. B.Sc. in Physics (with honors), Manchester U., 1969; M.A. in Mktg., Lancaster U., 1970. Exec. v.p. Mgmt. Sci. Assocs., Inc., Pitts., 1970-81; pres. Info. Resources, Inc., Chgo., 1981-89, CEO, 1986-98, vice chmn., 1989-90, chmn., 1991-95, bd. dirs. Bd. dirs. Platinum Tech., Inc. Mem. Young Pres. Orgn. Mem. Am. Mktg. Assn. Avocations: scuba diving; jogging; skiing. Home: 65 E Bellevue Pl Chicago IL 60611-1114 Office: 65 E Bellevue Pl Chicago IL 60611-1114

FULLER, HARRY LAURANCE, retired oil company executive; b. Moline, Ill., Nov. 8, 1938; s. Marlin and Mary Helen (Ilsley) F.; m. Nancy Lawrence, Dec. 27, 1961; children: Kathleen, Laura, Randall. BSChemE,

Cornell U., 1961; JD, DePaul U., 1965. Bar: Ill. 1965. With Standard Oil Co. (and affiliates), 1961-2000, sales mgr., 1972-74, gen. mgr. supply, 1974-77; exec. v.p. Standard Oil Co. (Amoco Oil Co. div.), Chgo., 1977-78; pres. Amoco Oil Co., 1978-81; exec. v.p. Standard Oil Co. of Ind., 1981-83; pres. Amoco Corp., 1983-91, chmn., CEO, 1991-2000, also dir., 1999-2000; co-chair BP Amoco p.l.c., 1999-2000; ret., 2000. Bd. dirs. Chase Manhattan Corp., Chase Manhattan Bank N.A., Abbott Labs., Motorola, Inc. Bd. dirs. Chgo. Rehab. Inst.; trustee Orchestral Assn. Mem. Am. Petroleum Inst. (bd. dirs.). Republican. Presbyterian. Clubs: Mid-Am, Chgo. Golf, Chicago.

FULLER, HOWARD, education educator, academic administrator; Supt. Milw. Sch. Dist.; dist. prof. edn., dir. Inst. Transformation Learning Marquette U., Milw., 1996—. Office: Marquette U Schroedor Complex PO Box 1881 Milwaukee WI 53201-1881

FULLER, JACK WILLIAM, writer, publishing executive; b. Chgo., Oct. 12, 1946; s. Ernest Brady and Dorothy Voss (Tegge) F.; m. Alyce Sue Tuttle, June 2, 1973; children: Timothy, Katherine. BS, Northwestern U., 1968; JD, Yale U., 1973. Bar: Ill. 1974. Reporter Chgo. Tribune, 1973-75, Washington corr., 1977-78, editorial writer, 1978-79, dep. editorial page editor, 1979-82, editorial page editor, 1982-87, exec. editor, 1987-89, v.p. and editor, 1989-93, pres., CEO, 1993-97, pub., 1994-97; pres. Tribune Pub. Co., 1997—. Spl. asst. to atty. gen. U.S. Dept. Justice, Washington, 1975-77. Author: Convergence, 1982 (Cliff Dwellers award 1983), Fragments, 1984 (Friends of Am. Writers award 1985), Mass, 1985, Our Fathers' Shadows, 1987, Legends' End, 1990, News Values, 1996, The Best of Jackson Payne, 2000. Mem. Pulitzer Prize Bd., 1991—2000; trustee U. Chgo., Field Mus.; Bd. dirs. McCormick Tribune Found. With U.S. Army, 1969—70. Recipient Gavel award ABA, 1979, Pulitzer prize for editl. writing, 1986. Fellow Am. Acad. Arts and Scis.; mem. Am. Soc. Newspaper Editors, Newspaper Assn. Am., Inter-Am. Dialogue, Inter-Am. Press Assn. (v.p.), Comml. Club of Chgo. Office: Chgo Tribune Co 435 N Michigan Ave Chicago IL 60611-4066

FULLER, MARTHA, professional sports team executive; b. Dec. 17, 1962; Office: 317 Washington St Saint Paul MN 55102

FULLER, PERRY LUCIAN, lawyer; b. Central City, Nebr., Oct. 26, 1922; s. Perry L. and Ruth (Howorth) F.; m. Alice Moorman, Mar. 6, 1948; 1 child, Leslie Ann Fuller. Student, U. Chgo. Law Sch., 1946-47; AB, U. Nebr., 1947, JD, 1949. Bar: Ill. 1950, U.S. Supreme Ct. Mem. staff Chgo. Crime Commn., 1949; sr. ptnr. Hinshaw & Culbertson and predeccessors, Chgo., 1956—. Lectr. in law U. Chgo., 1970-76, mem. vis. com., 1991-93. Vice chmn. exec. com. Law in Am. Soc. Found., 1966, chmn., 1967—69, pres., 1969—95; chmn. Cook County CSC, 1967—69; mem. Ill. Law Enforcement Commn., 1971—72; v.p. Fed. Defender, Inc., 1964; trustee Village of Winnetka, 1992—96; bd. dir. Winnetka Cmty. Chest, Ill., 1966—69, Ill. Humane Soc., 1978—, pres., 1986. 1st lt. USMC, 1942—46, Capt. USMC, 1952—53. Decorated Air medal. Fellow Am. Coll. Trial Lawyers (state chmn. 1972-74), Am. Bar Found., Ill. Bar Found.; mem. ABA (chmn. pub. relations com. 1968-69, gavel awards com. 1974-77, chmn. 1976-78), Ill, Fed., 7th Cir. Chgo. (bd. mgrs. 1967-69) bar assns., Am. Law Inst., Am. Judicature Soc., Internat. Assn. Def. Counsel (chmn. Continuing Legal Edn. bd. 1982-86, exec. com. 1983-86), Soc. Trial Lawyers Ill. (bd. dirs. 1967-68, 73-74, sec. 1975-76, pres. 1977-78), Def. Rsch. Inst. (chmn. insts. com. 1986-90), Scribes , Legal Club, Law Club (pres. 1987-88). Republican. Home: 1093 Fisher Ln Winnetka IL 60093-1503 Office: Hinshaw & Culbertson 222 N La Salle St Ste 300 Chicago IL 60601-1081

FULLER, SAMUEL ASHBY, lawyer, mining company executive; b. Indpls., Sept. 2, 1924; s. John L.H. and Mary (Ashby) F.; m. Betty Winn Hamilton, June 10, 1948; children— Mary Cheryl Fuller Hargrove, Karen E. Fuller Wolfe, Deborah R. BS in Gen. Engring, U. Cin., 1946, JD, 1947; cert. fin. planner, Coll. for Fin. Planning, 1989. Bar: Ohio 1948, Ind. 1951, Fla. 1984. Cleve. claims rep. Mfrs. and Mchts. Indemnity Co., 1947-48; claims supr. Indemnity Ins. Co. N.Am., 1948-50; with firm Stewart, Irwin, Gilliom, Fuller & Meyer (formerly Murray, Mannon, Fairchild & Stewart), Indpls., 1950-85, Lewis Kappes Fuller & Eads (name changed to Lewis & Kappes), Indpls., 1985-89, of counsel, 1990—; pres., dir. Irsugo Consol. Mines, Ltd., 1953-80. Dir. Ind. Pub. Health Found., Inc., 1972-84; staff instr. Purdue U. Life Ins. and Mktg. Inst., 1954-61; instr. Am. Coll. Life Underwriters, Indpls., 1964-74; mem. Ind. State Bd. Law Examiners, 1984-96, treas. 1987-88. Bd. dirs. Southwest Social Centre, Inc., 1965-70; pres., dir. Westminster Village North, Inc., 1981-89. Fellow: Indpls. Bar Found.; mem.: Fla. Bar, 7th Cir. Bar Assn., Ind. State Bar Assn. (bd. mgrs. 1986—88), Lincoln Hills Golf Club, Sun City Ctr. Golf and Racquet Club, Masons, Beta Theta Pi. Republican. Roman Catholic. Home: 306 Thornhill Pl Sun City Center FL 33573-5842 E-mail: samuel105@peoplepc.com.

FULLER, WAYNE ARTHUR, statistics educator; b. Corning, Iowa, June 15, 1931; s. Loren Boyd and Eva Gladys (Darrah) F.; m. Evelyn Rose Steinford, Dec. 22, 1956; children: Douglas W., Bret E. BS, Iowa State U., 1955, MS, 1957, PhD, 1959. Asst. prof. Iowa State U., Ames, 1959-62, assoc. prof., 1962-66, prof., 1966-83, disting. prof. stats., 1983—2001, disting. prof. emeritus, 2001—. Cons. Doane Mktg. Rsch., Inc., St. Louis. Author: Introduction to Statistical Time Series, 1976, 2d ed. 1996, Measurement Error Models, 1987; also articles. Served as cpl. U.S. Army, 1952-54 Fellow Am. Statis. Assn. (v.p. 1991-93), Inst. Math Stats., Econometric Soc.; mem. Internat. Statis. Inst. Biometric Soc., Royal Statis. Soc., Am. Agr. Econ. Assn. Home: 3013 Briggs Cir Ames IA 50010-4705 Office: Iowa State U Statis Lab 221 Snedecor Hall Ames IA 50010 E-mail: waf@iastate.edu.

FULLERTON, CHARLES WILLIAM, retired insurance company executive; b. Columbus, Ohio, May 18, 1917; s. Paul O. and Marvina (Groom) F.; m. Anne Hoddy, Jan. 21, 1940; children— Gary, Lynn Fullerton Johnson. B.S., Ohio State U., 1938. C.P.A., Ohio. Dist. financial dir. FSA, Columbus, 1938-40; office mgr. Goodyear Tire & Rubber Co., Huntington, W.Va., 1940-41; chief accountant to v.p. finance Landmark Farm Bur., Columbus, 1941-66; v.p., sec., treas. Nationwide Devel. Co., 1966-71; with Nationwide Ins. Affiliates, 1971-82, exec. v.p., 1972-73, pres., 1973-82; v.p. Nationwide Ins. Co., 1973-82. Dir. Nationwide Devel. Co., Nationwide Comm., Inc., Nationwide Consumer Svcs., Inc., Heritage Securities, Inc.; bd. govs. Investment Co. Inst., Washington. Mem. steering com. Devel. Com. for Greater Columbus, 1977-79; bd. dirs. Greater Columbus Arts Coun., Ohio Dominican Coll., Players Theatre of Columbus; active Downtown Action Com., Capitol Sq. Com. Mem. AICPA, Ohio Soc. CPA, Treas. Club of Columbus (past pres.), Nat. Soc. Accts. for Coops. (past pres.), Ohio Coun. Farmer Coops. (v.p.), Columbus Contrs. Club. Methodist. Club: Masons. Home: Apt 331 4590 Knightsbridge Blvd Columbus OH 43214-4334

FULLMER, PAUL, public relations counselor; b. Evanston, Ill., June 4, 1934; s. Joseph Charles and Marie (Guirsch) F.; m. Sandra Lewars Clifford, Apr. 22, 1961; children: Monica, David. AB, U. Notre Dame, 1955. Newspaper reporter Aurora (Ill.) Beacon News, 1955-57; account exec. Selz/Seabolt Comms., Chgo., 1957-64; v.p. Selz/Seabolt Comms., Inc., 1964-72, exec. v.p., 1972-79, pres., 1979-99, chmn., 1999-2000, Publicis Dialog Chicago, Chgo., 2000. Bd. dirs. Pinnacle Worldwide, pres. 1990-92, chmn., 1992-93. Pres. Notre Dame Club Chgo., 1964-65, hon. pres., 1992-93; co-chmn. jr. bd. NCCJ, Chgo., 1962; chmn. Amate House, Chgo., 1985-87; chmn. bd. trustees St. Mary's Acad., 1985-88; co-chmn. Bus. Execs. for Econ. Justice, 1992-94; chmn. exec. com. Holy Family Ch., 1989-93. Sgt. USAR, 1957. Fellow Pub. Rels. Soc. Am. (pres. Chgo. chpt. 1988-89); mem. Internat. Pub. Rels. Assn. Roman Catholic. Home: 87 Heatherdowns Ln Galena IL 61036 Office: Publicis Dialog Chicago 221 N La Salle St Chicago IL 60601-1206 E-mail: paul.fullmer@publicis-USA.com.

FULTON, WILLIAM, mathematics educator; b. Aug. 29, 1939; BA, Brown U., 1961; PhD, Princeton U., 1966. Instr. Princeton (N.J.) U., 1965-66; from instr. to asst. prof. Brandeis U., 1966-69; assoc. prof. Brown U., 1970-75, prof., 1975-87, U. Chgo., 1987-98, Charles L. Hutchinson Disting. Svc. prof., 1995-98; Keeler prof. math. U. Mich., Ann Arbor, 1998—. Vis. asst. prof. Princeton U., 1969-70; vis. prof. U. Genoa, 1969, Aarhus U., 1976-77, Orsay, 1987; vis. mem. Inst. des Hautes Etudes Scis., 1981, Inst. Advanced Study, 1981-82, 94, Math. Scis. Rsch. Inst., 1992-93, Ctr. Advanced Study, Oslo, 1994; Erlander prof. Mittag-Leffler Inst., 1996-97; lectr. in field. Author: Intersection Theory, 1984, Introduction to Intersection Theory in Algebraic Geometry, 1984, Introduction to Toric Varieties, 1993, Algebraic Topology, 1995, Young Tableaux, 1997; (with R. MacPherson) A Categorical Framework for the Study of Singular Spaces, 1981; (wih S. Lang) Riemann-Roch Algebra, 1985, (with J. Harris) Representation Theory; a first course, 1991; (with S. Bloch and I. Dolgachev, editors) Proceedings of the US-USSR Symposium in Algebraic Geometry, Univ. of Chicago, June-July, 1989, 1991; assoc. editor Duke Math. Jour., 1984-93, Jour. Algebraic Geometry, 1992-93; editor Jour. Am. Math. Soc., 1993-99, mng. editor, 1995-98; mem. editl. bd. Cambridge Studies in Advanced Math., 1994—, Chgo. Lectures in Math., 1994-98. Grantee NSF, 1976—, Sloan Found., 1981-82; Guggenheim fellow, 1980-81; named Erlander prof. Swedish Sci. Found., 1996-97. Mme. AAAS, NAS. Office: U Mich 525 E University Ave Ann Arbor MI 48109-1109

FULTZ, DAVE, meteorology educator; b. Chgo., Aug. 12, 1921; s. Harry T. and Ora L. (Voyles) F.; m. Jean Laura McEldowney, Apr. 6, 1946; children: Martha M., David L., Katherine R. BS, U. Chgo., 1941, cert. in meteorology, 1942, PhD, 1947. Emergency asst. U.S. Weather Bur., Chgo., 1942; research asst. U. Chgo. and U.S. Weather Bur., 1943-44; mem. faculty U. Chgo., 1945-46, dir. hydrodynamics lab., 1946—, prof. meteorology, 1960-91, prof. emeritus, 1991—. Cons. sci. adv. bd. USAF, 1959-64; mem. nat. com. fluid mechanics films Ednl. Services, Inc., Newton, Mass., 1962-71; research grants adv. com. Nat. Air Pollution Control Adminstrn., 1969-72. Contbr. articles to profl. jours. Served with USAAF, 1945. Fellow Guggenheim Found., 1950-51, NSF, 1957-58; recipient Golden Plate award Am. Acad. Achievement, 1968. Fellow Am. Meteorol. Soc. (Meisinger award 1951, C.G. Rossby Research medal 1967), Am. Geophys. Union, AAAS; mem. Royal Meteorol. Soc., Nat Acad. Scis., Phi Beta Kappa, Sigma Xi (sec., treas. Chgo. chpt. 1946, pres. 1975-76). Home: 5550 S South Shore Dr Chicago IL 60637-5051

FUNK, CARLA JEAN, library association executive; b. Wheeling, W.Va., Sept. 21, 1946; d. David H. and Jean (Duffy) Belt. BA in Psychology, Northwestern U., 1968; MLS, Ind. U., 1973; MBA, U. Chgo., 1985. Libr. adult svcs. Northbrook (Ill.) Pub. Libr., 1973-77; dir. Warren-Newport Pub. Libr. Dist., Gurnee, Ill., 1977-80; cons. Suburban Libr. Sys., Burr Ridge, 1980-83; dir. automation and tech. svcs., med. student svcs. AMA, Chgo., 1983-92; exec. dir. Med. Libr. Assn., 1992—. Adj. faculty Dominican U., 1986—; adv. com. Bicentennial Campaign U. S.C. Coll. Libr. and Info. Sci., Dominican U. Health Sci. com. Contbr. articles to profl. jours. Mem. Internat. Fedn. Libr. Assns. and Insts. (treas., U.S. nat. organizing com.), Am. Soc. Assn. Execs. (cert. assn. exec.), Ill. Libr. Assn., Assn. Forum of Chicagoland, Beta Phi Mu, Delta Zeta. Home: 6110 Golfview Dr Gurnee IL 60031-4701 Office: 65 E Wacker Pl Ste 1900 Chicago IL 60601-7246 E-mail: funk@mlahq.org.

FURLANE, MARK ELLIOTT, lawyer; b. Joliet, Ill., Aug. 2, 1949; s. Francis Emilio and Tosca (Cipriani) F.; m. Susan M. Keegan, July 4, 1987; children: Gahan Patricia, Michael Keegan. BA magna cum laude, Ctrl. Coll., 1971; JD with honors, George Washington U., 1974; MBA in Finance Specialization, U. Chgo., 1982. Bar: Ill. 1974, U.S. Dist. Ct. (no. dist.) Ill. 1979, U.S. Ct. Appeals (5th, 6th, 7th, 9th and 11th cirs.), U.S. Ct. Mil. Appeals, U.S. Supreme Ct. Ptnr. Gardner Carton & Douglas, Chgo., 1979—. Bd. mem. Ctr. for Disability and Elder Law, 2000—, Pub. Interest Law Initiative, 2001—; bd. dirs. Friends of Lincoln; local sch. counsel Lincoln Elem. Sch. Capt. USMCR. Mem. FBA (labor and employment com. 1996—, trustee 1999—), Chgo. Bar Assn. (chmn. labor and employment com. 1994-95), GSB Chgo. Club. Democrat. Roman Catholic. Office: Gardner Carton & Douglas 321 N Clark St Ste 3200 Chicago IL 60610-4719 E-mail: mfurlane@GCD.com.

FURLONG, MARK F. bank executive; BS in Acctg., Fin. and Bus., So. Ill. U. CPA, Mich. Sr. v.p. fin. First Exec. Corp.; first v.p. H.F. Ahmanson/Home Savings Am.; audit ptnr. Deloitte & Touche, L.A.; sr. v.p., CFO Old Kent Bank, 1998-99, exec. v.p., 1998-99; CFO Old Kent Fin. Corp., 1999—. Office: Old Kent Fin Corp 111 Lyon St NW Grand Rapids MI 49503

FURMAN, ANDY, radio personality; b. Bklyn. Radio host 700 WLW, Cin. Avocation: running. Office: 70 WLW 1111 St Gregory St Cincinnati OH 45202*

FURNEY, LINDA JEANNE, state legislator; b. Toledo, Sept. 11, 1947; d. Robert Ross and Jeanne Scott (Hogan) F. BS in Edn., Bowling Green State U., 1969; postgrad., U. Toledo. Tchr. Washington Local Schs., Toledo, 1969-72, Escola Americano do Rio de Janiero, 1972-74, Springfield Schs., Holland, Ohio, 1977-83; council mem. City of Toledo, 1983-86; mem. Ohio Senate from 11th dist., Columbus, 1987—. Mem. edn. com., rules com., reference and oversight com., fin. com., econ. devel. com. hwys. and transp. com., state and local govt. and vet. affairs com., asst. minority leader Ohio State Senate, Columbus, 1997-99. Dem. precinct committeewoman Toledo, 1980-90; mem. Toledo Bd. Edn., 1982-83. Recipient Citizen award Ohio Assn. Edn. Young Children, Stanley K. Levinson award Planned Parenthood Northwest Ohio, Educator of Yr. award Phi Delta Kappa, Milestone award Toledo YMCA, Pres. award Ohio Rehab. Assn.; named Person of Yr., Ohio Vocational Assn. Mem. NOW, AAUW, NAACP, ACLU (Found. award), Toledo Mus. Art, Toledo Zoo, Manhattan Dance Co. Home: 2626 Latonia Blvd Toledo OH 43606-3620 Office: Ohio Senate Senate Bldg Rm 051 Columbus OH 43215

FURST-BOWE, JULIE, academic administrator; BA in Journalism magna cum laude, U. Wis., Eau Claire, 1985; MS in Media Tech., U. Wis.-Stout, 1986; cert. in tng. and human resource devel., U. MInn., 1995. Media dir. libr. and media svcs. U. Wis., Waukesha, 1986—87, media specialist Media Devel. Ctr. Eau Claire, 1987—90; mem. faculty U. Wis.-Stout, Menomonie, 1990—94, assoc. prof., 1999, prof., 1999—, dir. grad. program, 1995—97, chmn. dept. comms., 1996—98, assoc. vice chancellor divsn. acad. and student affairs, 1998—, acting dir. Office Continuing Edn., 1998—99. Presenter in field. Contbr. articles to mags. and profl. publs., chpts. to books. Vol. Bolton Refuge House, 1988—98, Challenges and Chouces Career Workship for Young Women, 1988—98, Eau Claire Devel. and Tng. Ctr., 1997; mem. steering com. Eau Claire Women's Network, 1992, 1996; mem. Leadership Chipewa Valley, 1995, Inst. for Learning in Retirement, 1998—99; co-chmn. Menomonie Plan Com., 1997—99. Grantee, U. Wis.-Stout, 1994—97, U. Wis. Sys., 1997—2000. Mem.: AAUW, Wis. Vocat. Assn., Wis. Women in Higher Edn. Leadership., Wis. Edn. Media Assn. (bd. dirs. 1993—96, chmn. pub. rels. com. 1993—96, editor Wis. Ideas in Media jour. 1992—96), Profl. and Orgnl. Devel. Network, Profl. and Orgnl. Devel. Network (reviewer To Improve the Academy 1998—), North Ctrl. Assn. Summer Schs., Midwest Assn. Grad. Schs., Assn. Ednl. Comms. and Tech. (del. nat. leadership conf. 1994, Ednl. Found. Mentor scholar 1993), Acad. Human Resource Devel. (proposal reviewer, session facilitator 1997—2000, reviewer Internat. Jour. Tng. and Devel. 1998—), Am. Assn. Adult and Continuing Edn., ASTD (HRD prof.'s forum editor 1997, bd. dirs. N.W. Wis. chpt. 1994—97). Office: U Wis-Stout 303 Adminstrn Bldg 712 S Broadway Menomonie WI 54751-0790

FURSTE, WESLEY LEONARD, II, surgeon, educator; b. Cin., Apr. 19, 1915; s. Wesley Leonard and Alma (Deckebach) F.; m. Leone James, Mar. 28, 1942; children: Nancy Dianne, Susan Deanne, Wesley Leonard III. AB cum laude (Julius Dexter scholar 1933-34); Harvard Club scholar 1934-35), Harvard U., 1937, MD in Anatomy, 1941. Diplomate: Am. Bd. Surgery. Intern Ohio State U. Hosp., Columbus, 1941-42; fellow surgery U. Cin., 1945-46; asst. surg. resident Cin. Gen. Hosp., 1946-49; sr. asst. surg. resident Ohio State U. Hosps., 1949-50, chief surg. resident, 1950-51; limited practice medicine specializing in surgery Columbus, 1951—; instr. Ohio State U., 1951-54, clin. asst. prof. surgery, 1954-66, clin. assoc. prof., 1966-74, clin. prof. surgery, 1974-85, clin. prof. emeritus, 1985—. Mem. surg. staff Mt. Carmel Med. Center, chmn. dept. surgery, 1981-85, dir. surgery program, 1981-82; mem. surg. staff Children's, Grant Med. Ctr., Univ., Riverside, Meth. Hosps., St. Anthony Med. Ctr., Park Med. Ctr. (all Columbus); surg. cons. Dayton (Ohio) VA Hosp., Columbus State Sch., Ohio State Penitentiary, Mercy Hosp., Benjamin Franklin Hosp., Columbus, Columbus Cmty. Hosp.; regional adv. com. nat. blood program ARC, 1951-68, chmn., 1958-68; invited participant 2d Internat. Conf. on Tetanus, WHO, Bern, Switzerland, 1966, 3d, São, Paulo, Brazil, 1970, 4th, Dakar, Sénégal, 1975, 5th, Ronneby Brunn, Sweden, 1978, 6th, Lyon, France, 1981, 7th, Copanello, Italy, 1984, 8th, Leningrad, USSR, 1987, 9th, Granada, Spain, 1991; invited rapporteur 4th Internat. Conf. on Tetanus, Dakar, Sénégal, 1975; mem. med. adv. com. Medic Alert Found. Internat., 1971-73, 76-80, bd. dirs., 1973-76; Douglas lectr. Med. Coll. of Ohio, Toledo; founder Digestive Disease Found; lectr. U.S. Army M.C. on WWII Chinese activities during 1943-46; invited orator for new citizens at naturalization ceremonies U.S. Dist. Ct. (so. dist.) Ohio. Prime author: Tétanos; Tetanus: A Team Disease; contbg. author: Advances in Military Medicine, 1948, Management of the Injured Patient, Immediate Care of the Acutely Ill and Injured, 1978, Anaerobic Infections, 1989, Procs. of Internat. Tetans Confs. in Switzerland, Brazil, Sweden, Sénégal, France, Italy, USSR, Current Therapy in Emergency Medicine, Surgical Infectious Diseases (3 edits.), Currenty Emergency Therapy, Surgical Infections, Current Diagnosis (multiple edits.), Current Therapy (multiple edits.), Surgical Infections, 5 Minute Clinical Consult, 8 edits. (4 and 5 CD-Rom, Internet), Medical Microbiology and Infectious Diseases, editor Surgical Monthly Review; contbr. articles to profl. jours. Mem. Ohio Motor Vehicle Med. Rev. Bd., 1965-67, Pres. Club, Ohio State Univ.; bd. dirs. Am. Cancer Soc. Franklin County, pres., 1964-66; adv. coun. Upper Arlington Sr. Ctr., 2000. Served to maj., M.C. AUS, 1942-46, CBI, 1951-53. Recipient China Liberation medal, 2 commendations for surg. service in China U.S. Army; cert. of merit Am. Cancer Soc.; award for outstanding achievement in field clostridial infection dept. surgery Ohio State U. Coll. Medicine, 1984, Outstanding Service award, 1985; award for outstanding and dedicated service Mt. Carmel Med. Ctr., 1985; award for over 25 yrs. service St. Anthony Med. Ctr., U.S.A. Nat. Softball Squash Champion for age group, (1975—), Houston, 1992, (1980—), Denver, 96. Mem. AMA, AAAS, APHA, Cen. Surg. Assn., Surgical Infection Soc., Internat. Biliary Assn., Shock Soc., Soc. Am. Gastrointestinal Endoscopic Surgeons (com. on stds. of practice, resident and fellow edn., com. legis. review), Soc. Surgery of Alimentary Tract, A.C.S. (gov.-at-large, chmn. Ohio com. trauma; nat. subcom. prophylaxis against tetanus in wound mgmt., Ohio chapter Disting. Service award 1987; regional credentials com.), Am. Assn. Surgery of Trauma, Ohio Surg. Assn., Columbus Surg. Assn. (hon. mem.; pres. 1983), Am. Trauma Soc. (founding mem., dir.), Ohio Med. Assn., Acad. Medicine Columbus and Franklin County (Award of Merit for 17 yrs. service, chmn. blood transfusion com., 50 Year Svc. award), Acad. Medicine Cin., Am. Med. Writers Assn., Grad. Surg. Soc. U. Cin., Robert M. Zollinger Surg. Ohio State U. Surg. Soc., Mont Reid Grad. Surg. Soc., Am. Geriatrics Soc., N.Y. Acad. Scis., Assn. Program Dirs. in Surgery, Assn. Physicians State of Ohio, Collegium Internationale Chirurgiae Digestivae, Assn. Am. Med. Colls., Internat. Soc. Colon and Rectal Surgeons, Soc. Internat. de Chirurgie, Am. Assn. Sr. Physicians, Société Internationale sur le Tétanos, Am. Physicians Art Assn., Am. Assn. Retired Persons (bd. dirs. Franklin County Unit), China-Burma-India Vets., Assn. Columbus Basha (vice comdr. 1992-93, comdr. 1993-94, V-J Day coord., surgeon gen. 1994—), Am. Legion NW Post # 443, Am. Med. Golfing Assn., Internat. Brotherhood Magicians, Soc. Am. Magicians, N.Y. Cen. System Hist. Soc., U.S. Squash Racquets Assn. (mem. ranking com., med. adv. com.),(Nat. Softball Champion, 1992, 1996), Am. Platform Tennis Assn., Columbus Squash Racquets Assn. (bd. dirs.), VFW of U.S. (lectr.), Pres.'s Club (Ohio State U.). Presbyterian. Home and Office: Ohio State Univ 3125 Bembridge Rd Columbus OH 43221-2203 Fax: 614-457-5119. E-mail: wfursteii@aol.com.

FURTH, YVONNE, advertising executive; Pres. Draft Worldwide, Chgo. Office: Draft Worldwide 142 E Ontario St Chicago IL 60611-2818

FUSARO, RAMON MICHAEL, dermatologist, researcher; b. Bklyn., Mar. 6, 1927; s. Angelo and Ida (Pucci) F.; m. Lavonne Johnsen, Nov. 6, 1971; children: Lisa Ann, Toni Ann; stepsons: Jeff, Scott. BA, U. Minn., 1949, BS, 1951, MD, 1953, MS, 1958, PhD, 1965. Diplomate Am. Bd. Dermatology. Intern Mpls. Gen. Hosp., 1953-54, resident in internal medicine, 1954-57; from instr. to assoc. prof. U. Minn., 1957-70, dir. outpatient dermatology clinic, 1962-70; prof., chmn. dept. dermatology U. Nebr. Med. Center, Omaha, 1970-82; prof. dermatology sect. dept. internal medicine U. Nebr. Med. Ctr., 1982-91, acting chief sect. dermatology, 1991-94; prof., chmn. dept. dermatology Creighton U., 1975-87; prof. dermatology dept. internal medicine Creighton U. Sch. Medicine, 1983-89; prof. Creighton U., 1989—; dir. dermatology residency program Creighton/Nebr. Univs. Health Found., 1975-83; prof. dept. pub. health and preventive medicine Hereditary Cancer Inst., Creighton U., 1984—. Contbr. over 300 articles to profl. jours., 25 chpts. to books. With USN, 1944-46. Mem. Am. Acad. Dermatology, Sigma Xi. Home: 908 Beaver Lake Blvd Plattsmouth NE 68048-4500 Office: 984360 Nebr Med Ctr Omaha NE 68178-0403 also: Creighton U Med Sch Criss III Dept Prev Med 2500 California Plz Omaha NE 68178-0001 E-mail: rmfusaro@Creighton.edu.

FUSFELD, DANIEL ROLAND, economist; b. Washington, May 23, 1922; s. Irving Sidney and Cecile (Leban) F.; m. Harriet Miller, Aug. 30, 1947; children: Robert, Sarah, Yaakov Sadeh. BA, George Washington U., 1941; MA, Columbia U., 1947, PhD, 1953. Instr. Hofstra Coll., Hempstead, N.Y., 1947-53, asst. prof., 1953-56, Mich. State U., East Lansing, 1956-60; assoc. prof. U. Mich., Ann Arbor, 1960-64, prof., 1964-87, prof. emeritus, 1987—. Lectr. USAF Inst. Tech., Dayton, Ohio, 1958-59; vis. assoc. prof. Columbia U., N.Y.C., 1960; bd. dirs. Spectrum Human Svcs., 1992-98, Avalon Housing, Inc. Author: Economic Thought of Franklin D. Roosevelt, 1956, The Age of the Economist, 1966, 9th edit. 2001, Economics, 1972, The Basic Economics of the Urban-Racial Crisis, 1973, Rise and Repression of Radical Labor, 1877-1918, 1985; co-author: The Political Economy of the Urban Ghetto, 1984; co-editor: The Soviet Economy, 1962; also articles. With U.S. Army, 1943—46. Mem. Am. Econ. Assn., Assn. for Evolutionary Econs. (v.p. 1970, pres. 1971), Internat. Network for Econ. Method (chmn. 1989-92), Hist. Econ. Soc. Home: 3975 Ridgmaar Sq Ann Arbor MI 48105-3046 Office: U Mich Dept Econs Ann Arbor MI 48109 E-mail: hadafusf@umich.edu.

FUSSICHEN, KENNETH, computer scientist; b. Bklyn., Aug. 3, 1950; s. Lorenzo Anthony and Sue (Treppiedi) F.; m. Bobbie J. Ezra, May 18, 1974; children: Matthew, David, Vanessa, Natalie, Adam, Michael. AS in Data Processing, San Antonio Coll., 1975; BS in Bus., Ind. U., Indpls., 1980; MS in Mgmt., Ind. Wesleyan U., 1991. Programmer, analyst Computer Mgmt. Sys., Indpls., 1976-81; sr. programmer, analyst Jefferson Nat. Life, 1981-84; project leader Healthcare Adminstrv. Sys., Inc., 1984-87; sr. computer scientist Computer Scis. Corp., 1987-96; computer scientist Data Networks Corp., Dayton, Ohio, 1996; with Adecco Tech. Svcs., Cin., 1997—. Assoc. prof. computer scis. Ind. U.-Purdue U., Indpls., 1981-88; tech. advisor U.S. del. Internat. Stds. Orgn. on Ada 95 and Info. Systems, 1992-94. Info. Systems mgr. Cerebral Palsy Support Group, Indpls., 1987-89; computer cons. United Cerebral Palsy Ctrl. Ind., 1984-85; participant Ada 95 Lang. Rev., 1990-95 Mem. IEEE, Assn. Computing Machinery, Indpls. Computer Soc. (pres. 1989-90). Home: 130 Massie Dr Xenia OH 45385-3740

FYE, W. BRUCE, III, cardiologist; b. Meadville, Pa., Sept. 25, 1946; s. W. Bruce Jr. and Anne Elizabeth (Schreck) F.; m. Lois Eileen Baker, May 10, 1969; children: Katherine Anne, Elizabeth Jane. AB, Johns Hopkins U., 1968, MD, 1972, MA in Med. History, 1978. Diplomate Am. Bd. Internal Medicine, Am. Bd. Cardiovascular Diseases. Intern N.Y. Hosp.—Cornell Med. Ctr., N.Y.C., 1972-73, asst. resident, 1973-74, sr. asst. resident, 1974-75, fellow cardiology, 1975; fellow in cardiology Johns Hopkins U. Sch. Medicine, Balt., 1975-77, postdoctoral fellow in med. history, 1976-78, instr. in medicine, 1977-78; dir. cardiographics lab. Marshfield (Wis.) Clinic, 1978-99, chmn. dept. cardiology, 1981-99, dir. noninvasive cardiology, 1999; assoc. prof. medicine Med. Coll. Wis., Milw., 1988-99; prof. medicine and history medicine Mayo Med. Sch., Rochester, Minn., 2000—. Vice chief of staff St. Joseph's Hosp., Marshfield, 1989-99, exec. com., bd. dirs., 1994-97; clin. prof. medicine, adj. prof. history medicine U. Wis., Madison, 1990—; sr. assoc. cons. Mayo Clinic, Rochester, 2000, cons., 2001—. Author: The Development of American Physiology, 1987; editor: William Osler's Collected Papers on the Cardiovascular System, 1985, Classic Papers on Coronary Thrombosis and Myocardial Infarction, 1991; editor-in-chief: Classics of Cardiology Library, 1985—; author: American Cardiology; The History of a Specialty and Its College, 1996; mem. editl. bd. Marshfield Med. Bull., 1985-95, Am. Jour. Cardiology, 1990—, Clin. Cardiology, 1994—. Fellow Am. Coll. Cardiology (chmn. libr. com. 1991, historian 1991—, gov. Wis. chpt. 1993-96, steering com. bd. govs., 1994—, nominating com., 1994-96, chair govt. rels. com. 1996-99, trustee 1997—, v.p. 1999—, pres. 2002—); mem. Am. Assn. for History of Medicine (program chair 1987), State Med. Soc. Wis. (alt. del. 1990-94), Am. Hist. Assn., Am. Osler Soc. (pres. 1988-89), Am. Heart Assn. (exec. com. coun. on clin. cardiology 1991-97, chmn. membership com. coun. on clin. cardiology 1994-97, chair credentials com. coun. on clin. cardiology 1994-97), Inst. for Study of Cardiovascular Medicine (bd. dirs. 1994—), Phi Beta Kappa, Alpha Omega Alpha, Grolier Club. Presbyterian. Avocation: collecting and selling antiquarian medical books. Home: 1533 Seasons Ln SW Rochester MN 55902 Office: Mayo Clinic 200 1st St SW Rochester MN 55905-0002 Fax: 507-266-0103. E-mail: fye.bruce@mayo.edu.

GAAR, NORMAN EDWARD, lawyer, former state senator; b. Kansas City, Mo., Sept. 29, 1929; s. William Edward and Lola Eugene (McKain) G.; children: Anne, James, William John; m. Marilyn A. Wiegraffe, Apr. 12, 1986. Student, Baker U., 1947-49; AB, U. Mich., 1955, JD, 1956. Bar: Mo. 1957, Kans. 1962, U.S. Supreme Ct. 1969. Assoc. Stinson, Mag, Thomson, McEvers & Fizzell, Kansas City, 1956-59; ptnr. Stinson, Mag & Fizzell, 1959-79; mng. ptnr. Gaar & Bell, Kansas City, St. Louis, Overland Park, Wichita, Kans., 1979-87; ptnr. Burke, Williams, Sorensen & Gaar, Overland Park, L.A., Camarillo, Fresno, Costa Mesa, Calif., 1987-96; shareholder McDowell, Rice, Smith & Gaar, Overland Park, 1996—. Mem. Kans. Senate, 1965-84, majority leader, 1976-80; faculty N.Y. Practising Law Inst., 1969-74; adv. dir. Panel Pubs., Inc., N.Y.C. Mcpl. judge City of Westwood, Kans., 1959-63, mayor, 1963-65. With USN, 1949-53. Decorated Air medal (2); named State of Kans. Disting. Citizen, 1962. Fellow Am. coll. Bd. Coun.; mem. ABA, Am. Radio Relay League, Nat. Assn. Bond Lawyers, Calif. Assn. Bond Lawyers (charter), Russian-Am. Internat. Studies Assn. (dir. 2000--), Flying Midshipmen Assn., Assn. Naval Aviators, Tailhook Assn., Antique Airplane Assn., Exptl. Aircraft Assn., People to People. Republican. Episcopalian. Office: 7101 College Blvd Ste 200 40 Executive Hills Shawnee Mission KS 66210-1891 E-mail: ngaar@earthlink.net., ng@mrsg.com.

GABARRA, CARIN LESLIE, professional soccer player; b. East Orange, N.J., Jan. 9, 1965; m. Jim Gabarra. Degree in bus. mgmt., U. Calif., Santa Barbara, 1987. Mem. U.S. Nat. Women's Soccer Team, 1987-96; head coach, women's soccer Westmont Coll., 1987-88; assist. coach, women's soccer Harvard U., Boston, 1988-93; head coach, women's soccer Navy, 1993—. Mem. U.S. Olympic World Festival team, 1986-89; women's soccer U.S. Naval Acad., 1993. Ranked as 3d-leading goal scorer in U.S. women's history; mem. CONCACAF Championship team, 1993, 94; named U.S. Soccer's Female Athlete of Yr., 1987, 92, Golden Ball, FIFA Women's World Championship, China, 1991; named to U. Calif.-Santa Babara Athletic Hall of Fame; won Gold Medal in 1996, Atlanta Summer Olympic Games. Office: c/o US Soccer Fedn 1801 S Prairie Ave # 1811 Chicago IL 60616-1319

GABBARD, GLEN OWENS, psychiatrist, psychoanalyst; b. Charleston, Ill., Aug. 8, 1949; s. Earnest Glendon and Lucina Mildred (Paquet) G.; children: Matthew, Abigail, Amanda, Allison; m. Joyce Eileen Davidson, June 14, 1985. BS, Eastern Ill. U., 1972; MD, Rush Med. Coll., 1975; degree in psychoanalytic tng., Topeka Inst. for Psychoanalysis, 1984. Diplomate Am. Bd. Psychiatry and Neurology. Resident in psychiatry Menninger Sch. Psychiatry, Topeka, 1975-78, mem. faculty, 1978—; staff psychiatrist C.F. Menninger Hosp., 1978-83, sect. chief, 1984-89. Med. dir., 1989-94; tng. analyst Topeka Inst. for Psychoanalysis, 1989-2001, dir., 1996-2001; v.p. for adult svcs. Menninger Clinic, 1991-94; clin. prof. psychiatry U. Kans. Med. Sch., 1991-2001; Callaway Disting. prof. Menninger Clinic and Karl Menninger Sch. Psychiatry, 1994-2001; prof. psychiatry Baylor Coll. Medicine, 2001—. Author: With the Eyes of the Mind, 1984, Psychiatry and the Cinema, 1987, 2d edit., 1999, Medical Marriages, 1988, Sexual Exploitation in Professional Relationships, 1989, Psychodynamic Psychiatry in Clinical Practice, 1990, Portuguese transl., 1992, Italian transl., 1992, 2d edit., 1994, Korean transl., 1996, Japanese transl., 1997, 3rd edit., 2000, Treatments of Psychiatric Disorders: the DSM-IV Edition, 1995; meml. editl. bd. Am. Jour. Psychiatry, Am. Psychiat. Press; joint editor-in-chief Internat. Jour. Psychoanalysis; contbr. articles to profl. jours. V.p. Topeka Civic Theatre, 1981-82, pres. 1982-83, bd. dirs. 1981-83. Named one of Outstanding Young Men in Am. U.S. Jaycees, 1984. Mem. AAAS, Am. Psychoanalytic Assn. (assoc. editor jour., mem. editl. bd.), Am. Psychiat. Assn. (Falk fellow 1976, Edward A. Strecker award 1994, Disting. Psychiatrist lectr. 1995, C. Charles Burlingame award 1997, Mary S. Sigourney award 2000), Sch. Psychotherapy Rsch., Menninger Sch. Psychiatry Alumni Assn. (pres. 1982-83), Alpha Omega Alpha. Avocations: theater, music. Home: 1290 Jimmy Phillips Blvd Angleton TX 77515 Office: Dept Psychiatry Baylor Coll Medicine One Baylor Plz MS 350 Houston TX 77030

GABLE, KAREN ELAINE, health occupations educator; b. Des Moines, Nov. 12, 1939; d. John E. and Mabel I. (Davis) Clay; m. Robert W. Gable, Jr., Feb. 4, 1961; children: Susan Kay, Barbara Lynne, R.J. Kent. AS, Ind. U., Indpls., 1969, BS in Edn., 1976, MS in Edn., 1979, EdD, 1985. Registered dental hygienist, Ind.; cert. dental asst., Ind. Clin. instr. dental hygiene program Sch. Dentistry, Ind. U., 1976; asst. prof., coord. program dir. health scis. edn. Sch. Medicine, Ind. U., 1977-81; asst. prof. Sch. Edn. Ind. U., 1981-94, assoc. prof. health scis. edn. Sch. Allied Health & Medicine, 1994—, program dir., 1994—. Contbr. articles to profl. jours. Recipient Disting. Dental Hygiene Alumna award Ind. U. Sch. Dentistry. Mem. Assn. Health Occupations Tchr. Educators (treas., pres.), Ind. Allied Health Assn. (pres.-elect, pres.), Ind. Health Careers Assn. (pres.-elect, pres.), Ind. Dental Hygienists Assn. (sec.), Ind. Career and Tech. Edn. Assn. (Outstanding Svc. awards), Assn. Career and Tech. Edn. (profl. devel. com.), ACTE/Health Occupations Edn., Sigma Phi Alpha.

GABOURY, DAVID, engineering company executive; BSCE, U. Mass.; MSCE, MIT; grad. in bus., Harvard U. Pres. Woodward Clyde Cons.; with Terracon, Lenexa, Kans., 1997—, pres., COO, 2000—. Mem.: ASCE, Water Environ. Fedn. Office: Ferracon 16000 College Blvd Shawnee Mission KS 66219

GABRIEL, LARRY EDWARD, state legislator; b. Philip, S.D., Oct. 10, 1946; s. Floyd O. and Tressa (Coleman) G.; m. Charlotte Ann Burns, 1967; children: Malynda Sue, Jeffrey Allen. BS, S.D. State U., 1970. Mem. Haakon County Commn., S.D., 1974-82, S.D. Ho. of Reps., 1985-92, 93—, asst. majority whip, 1992-98, chmn. taxation com., mem. local govt. com., mem. legis. procedure and state affairs com.; rancher Cottonwood, S.D., 1970—; agrl. sec. State of S.D., 2000—. Mem. S.D. Stockgrower's Assn. (dir. 1982). Home: HC 84 Box 22 Cottonwood SD 57775-9421

GABRIEL, MICHAEL, psychology educator; b. Phila., May 5, 1940; s. Michael and Josephine (Alesio) G.; m. Linda Prinz, June, 1967 (div.); 1 child, Joseph Michael; m. Sonda S. Walsh, 1984. AB in Psychology, St. Joseph's Coll., 1962; MA, U. Wis., 1965, Ph.D., 1967. Asst. prof. Pomona Coll., Claremont, Calif., 1967-70; staff psychologist Pacific State Hosp., Pomona, 1968-70; NIMH sr. postdoctoral fellow U. Calif.-Irvine, 1970-72; asst. prof. U. Tex.-Austin, 1973-77, assoc. prof., 1977-82; prof. psychology U. Ill., Urbana, 1982—, appointee Ctr. for Advanced Study, 1990-91. Area chmn. Biol. Psychology Program, U. Tex., Austin, 1979-82; mem. rev. panel in behavioral and neural scis. NSF, 1988-91, prin. investigator database system for neuronal pattern analysis project, 1992—, ad hoc mem. biopsychology rev. panel, 1997-98; faculty Beckman Inst., U. Ill., Urbana, 1989—; chmn. Neuronal Pattern Analysis Group, Beckman Inst. Co-editor: (with J. Moore) Learning and Computational Neuroscience: Foundations of Adaptive Networks, 1989, (with B. Vogt) Neurobiology of Cingulate Cortex and Limbic Thalamus, 1993; mem. editl. bd. Neural Plasticity, Neurobiology of Learning and Memory. Grantee NIMH, 1978-88, 98—, NIH, 1988—, Air Force Office Sci. Rsch., 1988-91, NSF, 1992—, NIDA, 1996—. Fellow Am. Psychol. Soc., Internat. Behavioral Neurosci. Soc.; mem. Sigma Chi. Office: U Ill Beckman Inst 405 N Mathews Ave Urbana IL 61801-2325 E-mail: mgabriel@uiuc.edu.

GADDY, OSCAR LEE, electrical engineering educator; b. Republic, Mo., July 18, 1932; s. Oscar Franklin and Ruth Winnie (Cowart) G.; m. Mary Margaret Vaeth, Aug. 8, 1953; children: Oscar Franklin, John Anton, William Lee. BS, U. Kans., 1957, MS, 1959; PhD, U. Ill., 1962. Rsch. asst., instr. dept. elec. engring. U. Kans., Lawrence, 1957-59; rsch. asst. dept. elec. and computer engring. U. Ill., Urbana, 1959-62, asst. prof., 1962-65, assoc. prof., 1965-69, assoc. head, 1971-84, prof. dept. elec. and computer engring., 1969-93, prof. emeritus, 1993—. Contbr. articles to profl. jours. Fellow IEEE. Avocations: skeet and trap shooting, antique firearm restoration. Home: 609 E Evergreen Ct Urbana IL 61801-5930 Office: U Ill Dept Elec & Computer Engring 1406 W Green St Urbana IL 61801-2918 E-mail: o-gaddy@uiuc.edu.

GAD-EL-HAK, MOHAMED, aerospace and mechanical engineering educator, scientist; b. Tanta, El-Gharbia, Egypt, Feb. 11, 1945; came to U.S., 1968; s. Mohamed Gadelhak and Samira (Hosni) Ibrahim; m. Dilek Karaca, July 19, 1976; children: Kamal, Yasemin. BSc in Mech. Engring. summa cum laude, Ain Shams U., Cairo, 1966; PhD in Fluid Mechanics, Johns Hopkins U., 1973. Instr. Ain Shams U., Cairo, 1966-68; postdoctoral fellow Johns Hopkins U., Balt., 1973, U. So. Calif., L.A., 1973-74; asst. prof. engring. sci. & systems U. Va., Charlottesville, 1974-76; program mgr. Flow Rsch. Co., Seattle, 1976-86; prof. aerospace & mech. engring. U. Notre Dame, Ind., 1986—2002; Inez Caudill prof. bioengring., chmn. mech. engring. Va. Commonwealth U., Richmond, 2002—. Cons. USN, Washington, 1990-91, UN, N.Y.C., 1991, many others; lectr. in field. Author: Flow Control, 2000, Flow Control: Passive, Active, and Reactive Flow Management; assoc. tech. editor AIAA Jour., 1988-91; assoc. editor Applied Mechanics Revs., 1988—; contbg. editor: Springer Verlag's Lecture Notes in Engineering, 1988—; reviewer Jour. Fluid Mechanics, Physics of Fluids, AIAA Jour., Jour. of Aircraft, many others; editor: Advances in Fluid Mechanics Measurements, 1989, Frontiers in Experimental Fluid Mechanics, 1989, Flow Control: Fundamentals and Practices, 1998, The CRC MEMS Handbook, 2002; contbr. numerous articles to profl. jours. Recipient Alexander von Humboldt prize, 1999; Whitehead fellow Johns Hopkins U., Balt, 1968-73; Freeman scholar, 1998; professeur invité Univ. de Grenoble, France, 1991-92; sr. guest NATO, Paris, 1991, USN Disting. Faculty fellow, 1993; professeur exceptionnel univ. de Poitiers, France, 1994; rsch. grantee USN, 1976-80, USCG, 1976-78, NASA-Ames, 1981, NASA-Langley, 1985-87, 86, ONR, 1981-85, AFOSR, 1982-85, 85, Boeing Co., 1984, NSF, 1986, 95, Flow Industries, Inc., 1986-88, Cortana Corp., 1989-90, ONR, 1991, DARPA, 1991, Bourse de Haut Niveau Ministere de la Recherche et de la Technologie, Paris, 1991-92, NATO, 1991-92, others. Fellow AIAA, Am. Acad. Mechanics, ASME, Am. Phys. Soc. Achievements include patents on method and apparatus for controlling bound vortices in the vicinity of lifting surfaces, for reducing turbulent skin friction, for controlling turbulent boundary layers, for micropumping. Office: Va Commonwealth U 303 Engring Bldg Richmond VA 23284-3015 E-mail: gadelhak@vcu.edu.

GAEDE, JAMES ERNEST, physician, medical educator; b. Calgary, Alta., Can., July 2, 1953; s. John Ernest and Florence Eleanor (Hilmer) G.; married, Dec. 23, 1994; children: Graham, Jason, Nikki, Mary Frances, Sydney, Camille. BA, Augustana Coll., 1975, MA, 1976; MD, U. S.D., 1980. Diplomate Am. Bd. Family Practice. Staff physician Queen of Peace, Mitchell, S.D., 1983—, chief of staff, 1988, med. dir., 1988-89, St. Joe's Med. Assn., Howard, S.D., 1988—, Women's Health Clinic, Mitchell, 1983—; assoc. prof. U. of S.D. Sch. Medicine. Presenter U.S. Senate, Washington, 1991. Contbr. articles to profl. jours. Bd. dirs. Dakota Weslayan U., Mitchell, 1986-89, Dakota Mental Health, Mitchell, 1988-90; mem. Commn. 2000 S.D., Sioux Falls, 1988—; pub. health officer City of Mitchell, 1983—. Fellow Am. Acad. Family Practice (Active Tchrs. award 1984—); mem. AMA, S.D. Assn. Family Practice, S.D. State Med. Assn. (del. 1983—, sec. 1998-2000, v.p. 2000—), Mitchell C. of C., Mayo Alumni Assn., Doctors Mayo Soc. Avocations: sailing, music, auto restoration. Home: 2525 N Farrell Dr Palm Springs CA 92262-2601 Office: 2525 N Farrell Dr Palm Springs CA 92262-2601

GAERTNER, DONELL JOHN, retired library director; b. St. Louis, Sept. 30, 1932; s. Elmer Henry and Norine Helen (Colomb) G.; m. Darlene Oberbeck, Mar. 17, 1956; children: Karen Elaine, Keith Alan. A.B. in Econs., Washington U., 1954; M.L.S., U. Ill., 1955. Adminstrv. asst. St. Louis County Library, 1957-64, asst. dir., 1964-68, dir., 1968-97; ret., 1997. Past pres. bd. dirs. Emmaus Homes Inc. (for adult mentally retarded). Served to 1st lt. U.S. Army, 1955—57. Mem.: ALA (past pres.), Spl. Libr. Assn., Mo. Libr. Assn., Order Eastern Star, Masons, Omicron Delta Gamma, Phi Beta Mu. United Ch. Of Christ. E-mail: dgaertner@prodigy.net.

GAGE, EDWIN C., III (SKIP GAGE), travel and marketing services executive; b. Evanston, Ill., Nov. 1, 1940; s. Edwin Cutting and Margaret (Stackhouse) G.; m. Barbara Ann Carlson, June 26, 1965; children—Geoff, Scott, Christine, Richard B.S. in Bus. Adminstrn., Northwestern U., 1963, M.S. in Journalism, 1965. Account exec. Foote, Cone and Belding, 1965-68, dir. mktg. devel. & rsch., 1968-70; v.p. direct mktg. Carlson Mktg. Group of Carlson Cos., Mpls., 1970-75, exec. v.p., 1975-77, pres., 1977-83, also bd. dirs.; exec. v.p., COO Carlson Cos. Inc., 1983, pres., CEO, 1984-89, pres., chief exec. officer, 1989-91; now chmn., CEO Gage Marketing Group. Bd. dirs. Gage Mktg. Group, Carlson Holdings Inc., Carlson Real Estate, Carlson Real Estate Co., Inc., Supervalu Stores Inc., Fingerhut Cos., Kellogg adv. bd. Northwestern U., Minn. Coun. Quality, Mpls. Inst. Arts. Lt. USN. Mem. Young Pres. Orgn., Minn. Execs. Orgn. Avocations: music folk and popular, tennis, golf, hunting, fishing. Office: Gage Marketing Group 10000 Highway 55 Ste 100 Minneapolis MN 55441-6365

GAGE, FRED KELTON, lawyer; b. Mpls., June 20, 1925; s. Fred K. and Vivian L. G.; m. Dorothy Ann, Sept. 7, 1974; children: Deborah, Penelope, Amy, Lawrence. BS, U. Minn., 1948, LLB, 1950. Bar: Minn. 1950. Assoc. Wilson, Blethen & Ogle, Mankato, 1950-55; ptnr. Blethen, Gage, Krause, Blethen, Corcoran, Berkland & Peterson and predecessor firms, 1955-90, of counsel, 1991—. Mem. State Bd. Profl. Responsibility, Minn. Supreme Ct., 1974-82, mem. legal svcs. adv. com., 1996—. Mem. Mankato Sch. Bd., 1957-66, Minn. State Coll. Bd., 1960-64; mem. Minn. Senate from 11th Legis. Dist., 1966-72; Mem. Minn. Sports Facilities Commn., 1976-84. Served with USN, 1943-46. Named Mankato Outstanding Young Man of Yr., 1956, Outstanding Man of Minn., Mankato Jr. C. of C., 1958 Fellow Am. Bar Found.; mem. ABA (assembly del. 1980-86), Minn. Bar Assn. (chmn. tax sect. 1956-58, pres. 1977-78), Order of Coif. Methodist. Office: Blethen Gage & Krause PO Box 3049 127 S 2nd St Mankato MN 56001-3658 E-mail: kgage@bglow.com.

GAGEL, BARBARA JEAN, health insurance administrator; b. Celina, Ohio, Nov. 19, 1943; d. Vincent James and Theresa Barbara (Goettermoeller) G. BA, Miami U., 1965; MBA, U. Chgo., 1977. Asst. dir. for internat. trade State of Ill., Chgo., Brussels, Hongkong and Sao Paulo, Brazil, 1973-76; dir. office of mgmt. and planning Office Human Devel. Svcs., Chgo., 1976-79; dep. regional adminstr. Health Care Financing Adminstrn., 1979-82, regional adminstr., 1982-87, dir. bur. of prog. ops. Balt., 1987-92; dir. health stds. and quality bur. Health Care Fin. Adminstrn., 1992-96; pres., CEO AdminaStar, Inc., Indpls., 1996-2001. Recipient Presdl. Disting. Rank award 1988, 94, Presdl. Meritorious Rank award 1987, 92; named Fed. Exec. of Yr., 1987. Home: 114 Cherry Valley Rd Reisterstown MD 21136 E-mail: bgagel@home.com.

GAGGIOLI, RICHARD ARNOLD, mechanical engineering educator; b. Highwood, Ill., Dec. 3, 1934; s. Gustavo and Constantina Lucille (Mordini) G.; m. Anita Catherine Sage, Nov. 9, 1957; children: Catherine Anne, Michael James, Daniel Richard, Edward Thomas, Mary Esther. BME, Northwestern U., 1957, MS (NSF fellow), 1958; PhD (Gen. Electric, NSF fellow), U. Wis., 1961. Registered Profl. Engr., Wis. Coop. student engr. Abbott Labs. (pharms.), North Chicago, Ill., 1954-58; asst. prof. mech. engring. U. Wis., Madison, 1962-66, assoc. prof., 1966-69; prof., chmn. dept. mech. engring. Marquette U., Milw., 1969-72, prof., 1969-81, 90—; dean engring. and architecture Cath. U. Am., Washington, 1981-84; prof. mech. engring. U. Mass., Lowell, 1985-89. Mem. U.S. Army Math. Research Ctr., Madison, 1964-66; NSF-Soc. Indsl. and Applied Math. vis. lectr., 1969-72, engring. cons., 1970—. Author: (with E.F. Obert) Thermodynamics, 1963; editor: Thermodynamics-Second Law Analysis, Vol. 1, 1980, Vol. 2, 1983, Analysis of Energy Systems, 1985, Computer-Aided Engineering of Energy Systems, 1986; (with M.J. Moran) Analysis and Design of Advanced Energy Systems: Fundamentals, 1987; (with G. Tsatsaronis) Fundamentals of Thermodynamics and Energy Analysis, 1990; (with G.M. Reistad) Thermodynamics and Energy Systems: Fundamentals, 1991, (with R.F. Boehm et al.) Thermodynamics and the Design of Energy Systems, 1992; hon. editor Internat. Jour. Applied Thermodynamics, 1998—; contbr. articles to profl. jours. Chmn. bd. trustees Montrose Sch., Westwood, Mass., 1987-89. Recipient Emil H. Steiger Meml. Teaching award U. Wis., 1965, Pere Marquette award for faculty excellence Marquette U., 1976, Best Paper award Am. Chem. Soc. Chem. Tech. jour. 1977; NSF postdoctoral fellow chem. engring. U. Wis., 1961-62; vis. fellow Battelle Meml. Inst., 1968-69; invited lectr., Rome, 1987, 95, Beijing 1986, 89, 97, Zaragoza 1993, Florence, 1989, Athens, 1991, Istanbul, 1995, Krakow, 1994, 98, Tokyo, 1999, others. Fellow ASME (James Harry Potter gold medal 1988, advanced energy sys. divsn. best paper award 1991, E.F. Obert best paper award 2000); mem. AIChE, Summit Edn. Assn. (sec., trustee 1993—), Sigma Xi, Pi Tau Sigma, Tau Beta Pi. Roman Catholic. Office: Marquette U Dept Mech Engring Milwaukee WI 53201-1881 Home: W2202 Wilmers Grove Rd East Troy WI 53120

GAGNON, CRAIG WILLIAM, lawyer; b. St. Cloud, Minn., Dec. 19, 1940; s. Marvin Sylvester and Signa Gunhild (Johnson) G.; children: Nicole, Jeffrey, Camille; m. Pam Peglow, Nov. 8, 1980; children: Claire, Jillian, Jane. BA, U. Minn., 1964; JD magna cum laude, William Mitchell Coll. Law, 1968. Bar: Minn. 1968, U.S. Dist. Ct. Minn. 1968, U.S. Tax Ct. 1972, U.S. Supreme Ct. 1970. Ptnr. Oppenheimer, Wolff & Donnelly, Mpls., 1968—. Chmn. bd. Equity Bank. Trustee William Mitchell Coll. Law, St. Paul. 1989—, chmn. bd., 1999-2000. Named Alumnus of Notable Achievement, U. Minn. Fellow Am. Coll. Trial Lawyers; mem. Metro Breakfast Club (pres. 1993), Am. Bd. Trial Advocates (assoc.), Am. Law Inst. Avocations: hunting, fishing, golf. Home: 4807 Sunnyside Rd Edina MN 55424-1109 Office: Oppenheimer Wolff & Donnelly 45 S 7th St Ste 3400 Minneapolis MN 55402-1609 E-mail: cgagnon@oppenheimer.com.

GAINES, ROBERT DARRYL, lawyer, food services executive; b. Kansas City, Mo., May 27, 1951; s. Ralph Robert and Betty June (Crawford) G.; m. Shanette Carrol Kirch, Aug. 14, 1977; 1 child, Ariel Kirch. BA, U. Ariz., 1972; MBA, Mich. State U., 1973; JD, U. Mo., Kansas City, 1983. Bar: Mo. 1983, Ariz. 1983. Pvt. practice law, Kansas City, 1983—; pres. Colony Lobster Pot Co., 1984—, Colony Pla Co., Kansas City, 1985—. Mem. ABA, Mo. Bar Assn., Ariz. Bar Assn., Kansas City Bar Assn., Nat. Restaurant Assn., Mo. Restaurant Assn., Phi Delta Phi (treas. 1982-83). Avocations: flying, racquetball. Home: 11201 Madison Ave Kansas City MO 64114-5238 also: 8821 State Line Rd Kansas City MO 64114-2704 E-mail: robertgaines@cs.com.

GAINES, RUTH ANN, educator; BA in Drama and Speech, Clarke Coll.; MA in Dramatic Art, U. Calif., Santa Barbara. Tchr. drama East High Sch., Des Moines, 1971—. Host Classroom Connection Cable TV; former TV/radio prodr., talk show host TCI of Ctrl. Iowa, WHO; diversity facilitator Heartland Area Edn. Agy., Des Moines, 1979—; instr. speech and drama Des Moines Area C.C., 1971—. Bd. dirs. Very Spl. Arts, Hospice of Ctrl. Iowa, Westminster Ho.; former bd. dirs. YWCA of Greater Des Moines, Polk County Mental Health Assn., Drama Workshop, Des Moines Tutoring Ctr.; vice chair City Wide Strategic Plan, 1994-95; state senate candidate, 1994; racial justice coord. YWCA, 1992-93; chair Cross Cultural Rels., Des Moines Area Religious Coun., 1988-89; dir. religious edn. St. Ambrose Cathedral, 1981-83; grad. Leadership Iowa Class of 1997. Recipient Wal-Mart Tchr. of Yr., 1998, Iowa Tchr. of Yr., 1998. Mem. Iowa Edn. Assn., Des Moines Edn. Assn., Delta Kappa Gamma, Phi Delta Kappa, Delta Sigma Theta, Delta Kappa Pi. Home: 3501 Oxford St Des Moines IA 50313-4562 Office: East High Sch 815 E 13th St Des Moines IA 50316-3499

GAINES, WILLIAM CHESTER, journalist; b. Indpls., Nov. 1, 1933; s. Philip Damon and Georgia Agnes (Smith) G.; m. Nellie Gilyan; children: Michael, Michelle, Matthew. BS in Broadcasting, Butler U., 1956. TV announcer Sta. WKZO-TV, Kalamazoo, 1958-59; reporter Sta. WWCA Radio, Gary, Ind., 1959-60, Sta. WJOB Radio, Hammond, 1960-63; pres. Sta. WAMJ Radio, South Bend, 1983-88; from reporter to investigative reporter Chgo. Tribune, 1963—. Instr. Columbia Coll., Chgo., 1974-98; bd. advisors Fund for Investigative Journalism, Inc.; prof. journalism, Knight chair investigative/enterprise journalism, U. Ill., 2001—. Author: Investigative Reporting in Print and Broadcast, 1992. Recipient Pulitzer prize in Journalism, Columbia U., N.Y.C., 1976, 1988, Peter Lisagor award Chgo. Headline Club, 1986, 87. Office: Chgo Tribune 435 N Michigan Ave Chicago IL 60611-4066

GAINEY, HARVEY NUETON, transportation executive; b. Nicholls, Ga., Nov. 20, 1942; s. Lloyd Fryar and Rita Mae (Tanner) G.; m. Annie Ereveene, Nov. 9, 1962; children: Angela Marie, Harvey Neuton Jr. Student, Jacksonville (Fla.) U., 1964. Traffic mgr. Ryder Truck Lines, Jacksonville, 1964-70; v.p. sales Helms Express, Irwin, Pa., 1970-80; pres. Interstate Motor Freight, Grand Rapids, Mich., 1980-84; pres., prin., chmn. bd. dirs. Gainey Transportation Services Inc., 1984—. Bd. dirs. Cen. States Motor Bur., Chgo., Am. Trucking Assn., Washington, Eastern Cen. Motor Carriers, Akron, Ohio. Republican. Home: 7295 Leyton Dr SE Grand Rapids MI 49546-7340 Office: Gainey Transportation Services Inc 5976 Clay Ave SW Grand Rapids MI 49548-5790

GAITAN, FERNANDO J., JR. federal judge; b. 1948; Student, Kansas City (Kans.) C.C., 1966-67, Donnelly Coll., 1967-68, Pittsburg State U., 1968-70; JD, U. Mo., Kansas City, 1974. Atty. Southwestern Bell Telephone Co., 1974-80; judge 16th jud. cir. Jackson County Cir. Ct., 1980-86; judge Mo. Ct. Appeals (we. dist.), 1986-91; fed. judge U.S. Dist. Ct. (we. dist.) Mo., Kansas City, 1991—. Past pres. bd. dirs. De La Salle Edn. Ctr., Inc., 1985-87, active, 1983—; active Kansas City Mus., 1988—, St. Luke's Hosp., Kansas City, 1984—, NAACP, 1982—, NCCJ, 1984—. Mem. ABA, Mo. Bar Assn., Kansas City Met. Bar Assn., Lawyers' Assn., Jackson County Bar Assn., Univ. Club, Hillcrest Country Club, U. Mo. Kansas City Law Found., KCMC Child Devel. Corp., Kappa Alpha Psi. Office: US Dist Ct 7952 US Cthouse 400 E 9th St Kansas City MO 64106-2607

GAITHER, JOHN FRANCIS, JR. lawyer; b. Evansville, Ind., Mar. 31, 1949; s. John F. and Marjilee G.; m. Christine Luby, Nov. 26, 1971; children: John F. III, Maria Theresa. BA in Acctg., U. Notre Dame, 1971, JD, 1974. Bar: Ind. 1974, Ill. 1975, U.S. Ct. Appeals (7th cir.) 1975, U.S. Ct. Mil. Appeals 1977. CPA, Ind. Law clk. to Hon. Wilbur F. Pell, Jr. Ct. of Appeals 7th Cir., Chgo., 1974-76; assoc. atty. Bell, Boyd & Lloyd, 1979-82; sr. atty. Baxter Healthcare Corp., Deerfield, Ill., 1982-83, asst. sec., sr. atty., 1983-84, asst. sec., asst. gen. counsel, 1984-85; sec., assoc. gen. counsel Baxter Internat. Inc., 1985-87, sec., dep. gen. counsel, 1987-91; v.p. law/devel. Baxter Diagnostics Inc., 1991-92; v.p. law, strategic planning Baxter Global Businesses, 1992-93; dep. gen. counsel, v.p. strategic planning Baxter Internat. Inc., 1993-94, corp. v.p., corp. devel., 1994-2001; v.p., sec., gen. counsel Global Healthcare Exch., LLC, Westminster, Colo., 2001—. Editor-in-chief Notre Dame Lawyer, 1973-74; contbr. articles to profl. jours. Lt. comdr. USNR, 1976-79. Mem. ABA, Ill. Bar Assn., Ind. Bar Assn., Chgo. Bar Assn., Ind. Assn. CPAs. Avocations: sailing, skiing. Office: Global Healthcare Exch LLC 1627 Lake Cook Rd Deerfield IL 60015 also: 10385 Westmoor Dr Westminster CO 80021 E-mail: jgaither@ghx.com.

GAJL-PECZALSKA, KAZIMIERA J. retired surgical pathologist, pathology educator; b. Warsaw, Poland, Nov. 15, 1925; came to U.S., 1970; d. Kazimierz Emil and Anna Janina (Gervais) Gajl; widowed; children: Kazimierz Peczalski, Andrew Peczalski. Student, Jagiellonian Univ., Cracov, Poland, 1945-47; MD, Warsaw U., Poland, 1951, PhD in Immunopathology, 1964. Diplomate Polish Bd. Pediatrics, Polish Bd. Anatomic Pathology, Am. Bd. Pathology. Attending pediatrician Children's Hosp. for Infectious Diseases, Warsaw, Poland, 1953-58, head, pathology lab. Poland, 1958-65; adj. prof. Postgrad. Med. Sch., Poland, 1965-70; fellow U. Minn., Mpls., 1970-72, asst. prof. dept. pathology, 1972-75, assoc. prof. dept. pathology, 1975-79, prof. dept. pathology, 1979-00, dir. immunophenotyping and flow lab., 1974-00, dir. cytology dept. pathology, 1976-95; ret., 2000. Author chpts. to book; contbr. of numerous papers to profl. jours. Fellow WHO, Paris, 1959, London, 1962, Paris, 1967, U.S. Pub. Health Svcs. fellow, 1968-69; recipient Scientific Com. award Polish Ministry of Health and Social Welfare, 1964. Mem. Am. Soc. Experimental Pathology, Am. Soc. Cytology, Internat. Acad. Pathology, British Soc. Pediatric Pathology, Polish Soc. Pathology, Polish Soc Pediatricians. Roman Catholic. Avocations: music, skiing. Office: U Minn Dept Pathology U Health Ctr PO Box 609 Minneapolis MN 55455

GALAMBOS, THEODORE VICTOR, civil engineer, educator; b. Budapest, Hungary, Apr. 17, 1929; s. Paul and Magdalena (Potzner) G.; m. Barbara Ann Asp, June 25, 1957; children: Paul, Ruth, Ronald, John. BSCE, U. N.D, 1953, MSCE, 1954; PhD in CE, Lehigh U., 1959; Dr. honoris causa, Tech. U., Budapest, 1982; PhD (hon.), U. N.D., 1998; DSc (hon.), U. Minn., 2001. Registered profl. engr., Pa., Minn., Mo. From asst. to assoc. prof. civil engring. Lehigh U., Bethlehem, Pa., 1959-65; prof. Washington U., St. Louis, 1965-81, head dept., 1970-78; prof. U. Minn., Mpls., 1981-96, emeritus prof., 1997—. Cons. engr. Steel Joist Inst., Myrtle Beach, S.C., 1965—; vis. prof. U.S. Mil. Acad., West Point, 1990. Author, co-author 4 books in field; editor 1 book; contbr. over 100 articles to profl. jours. Served with U.S. Army, 1954-56. Recipient T.R. Higgins award Am. Inst. Steel Constrn., 1981. Mem. ASCE (hon., Norman medal 1983, Shortridge Hardesty award 1988, E.E. Howard award 1992), NAE, Internat. Assn. Bridge and Structural Engrs. Democrat. Baptist. Avocation: photography. Home: 4375 Wooddale Ave Minneapolis MN 55424-1060 Office: U Minn Civil Engring Dept Minneapolis MN 55455 E-mail: galam001@tc.umn.edu.

GALASK, RUDOLPH PETER, obstetrician and gynecologist; b. Fort Dodge, Iowa, Dec. 23, 1935; s. Peter Otto and Adeline Amelia (Maranesi) G.; m. Gloria Jean Vasti, June 19, 1965 BS, Drake U., 1959; MD, U. Iowa, 1964, MS, 1967. Diplomate Am. Bd. Obstetrics and Gynecology. Research fellow in microbiology U. Iowa, Iowa City, 1965-67, resident in ob-gyn., 1967-70, asst. prof., 1970-74, asst. prof. microbiology, 1973-74, assoc. prof. obstetrics and gynecology microbiology, 1974-78, prof., 1978—, chmn. exec. com. Coll. Medicine, 1992-93, prof. dermatology, 1999—. Cons. various pharm. and diagnostic cos. Editor: Infectious Diseases in the Female Patient, 1986-89; contbr. numerous articles to profl. jours. Served to staff sgt. USNG, 1954-64 Recipient I.D.S.O.G./Ortho McNeil award for outstanding contbns. to field of infectious diseases in ob-gyn., A.P.G.O. Excellence in Tchg. award, 1997; numerous grants to study the efficacy of various antibiotics and chemotherapeutics. Fellow Am. Gynecol. and Obstet. Soc., Am. Coll. Obstetricians and Gynecologists, Infectious Disease Am.; mem. AAAS, Cen. Assn. for Obstetricians and Gynecologists, Infectious Disease Soc. for Ob-Gyn. (pres. 1982-84, founding mem.), Soc. Gynecol. Investigation (coun. 1987-90), Queens Gynecol. Soc. (hon.), Tex. Assn. Obstetricians and Gynecologists (hon.), Am. Soc. Microbiology, Izaac Walton League, Ducks Unltd. Club (sponsor), Sigma Xi. Roman Catholic. Office: Univ Iowa Hosps Dept Ob-Gyn Iowa City IA 52242

GALE, JOHN A. secretary of state; b. Omaha, 1940; m. Carol Gale; 1 child Dave. BA in govt. internat. relations, Carleton Coll., Northfield, Minn. , 1962; JD in govt. internat. relations, Univ. Chgo. Law Sch., Northfield, Minn. , 1965. Sec. state State of Nebr., 2000—; pvt. practice of law 30 yrs.; elected state chmn. Nebr. State Rep. Party, 1986; asst. U.S. atty. Lincoln, 1971; legis. asst. Wash. , DC, 1968; asst. U.S. atty. Omaha, 1965. Republican. Office: NE Sec State State Capitol Ste 2300 Lincoln NE 68509*

GALE, NEIL JAN, Internet professional; b. Chgo., Jan. 12, 1960; s. Jack and Adele (Field) G. AA in Computer Sci., Wright Coll., 1980; D of Bus. Mgmt. (hon.), London Inst. Applied Rsch., 1993; diploma, Academia Argentina de Diplomacia, 1994; diploma (hon.), Institut Des Affaires Internationales, Paris, 1994; D of Bus. Mgmt. (hon.), World Acad., Monchengladbach, Germany, 1994. Mgr. Gen. Fin. Co., Chgo., 1980-84; mktg. mgr. Midland Fin. Co., 1984-85; mktg. dir. Diamond Mortgage Corp., 1985-86; sr. fin. analyst McKay Mazda-Nissan, Evanston, Ill., 1987-88; pres., CEO, Nat. Consumer Credit Cons., Chgo., 1988—; webmaster Everything Internet (merger with Millenium Techs. Inc. 1998), Naperville, Ill., 1996-98; pres. DrGale.com, Carol Stream, 1998—. Hon. prof. bus. mgmt. Inst. des Hautes Etudes Econs. et Sociales, Brussels, 1993; hon. prof. fin. Australian Inst. Coordinated Rsch., 1994; mem. adv. coun. Internat. Biog. Ctr., Cambridge, Eng.; mem. bd. govs., Continental gov. Am. Biog. Inst., 1990—, mem. rsch. bd. advisors, 1989—; notary pub. Ill., 1986-90. Contbr. articles to profl. jours. First aid chmn. Walk with Israel, 1977; notary pub., Ill., 1986-90; mem. computer com. Village of Hanover Park, Ill., 1997-2000. Decorated Knight of Order of San Ciriaco; recipient Bus. in Urban Environment award Chgo. Bd. Edn. and Ill. Bell Tel. Co., 1978, Outstanding Achievement award Chgo. Pub. Libr., 1979. Mem. Auto Credit (hon.), Friendship Cir. Club (treas. 1976-78). Avocation: antique Chgo. postcard and book collection. Home and Office: DrGale.com 780 W Army Trail Rd PMB 208 Carol Stream IL 60188-9297 E-mail: drgale@drgale.com.

GALL, ERIC PAPINEAU, physician, educator; b. Boston, May 24, 1940; s. Edward Alfred and Phyllis Hortense (Rivard) G.; m. Katherine Theiss, Apr. 20, 1968; children: Gretchen Theiss Gall, Michael Edward. AB, U. Pa., 1962, MD, 1966. Asst. instr. U. Pa., Phila., 1970-71, post doctoral trainee, fellow, 1971-73; asst. prof. U. Ariz., Tucscon, 1973-78, assoc. prof., 1978-83, prof. internal medicine, 1983-94, prof. surgery, 1983-94, prof. family/community medicine, 1983-94, chief rheumatology allergy and immunology, 1983-93, dir. arthritis ctr., 1986-94; Herman Finch Univ. of Health Scis. prof. of medicine The Chgo. Med. Sch., North Chicago, Ill., 1994—, prof. microbiology and immunology, 1994—, chmn. dept. medicine, 1994—, chief rheumatology sect., 1994-98, assoc. dean clin. affairs, 1996-97, dir. metabolic bone unit, 1998—. Author, editor: Rheumatoid Arthritis: Illustrated Guide to Path DX and Management of Rheumatoid Arthritis, 1988, Rheumatic Disease: Rehabilitation and Management, 1984, Primary Care, 1984; editor Clin. Care in The Rhematic Diseases, 1996; contbr. numerous articles to profl. jours. Chmn. med. and scientific com. Arthritis Found., Tucson, 1979-81. Maj. M.C., U.S. Army; Vietnam. Decorated Bronze Star; recipient Addie Thomas Nat. Svc. award Arthritis Found., 1988. Fellow ACP (coun. Ill. chpt. 1995—), Am. Coll. Rheumatology (founding chair ednl. materials com. 1986-89, bd. dirs. 1992-95, chmn. rehab. sect. 1992-95), Chgo. Inst. Medicine; mem. AMA (rep. sect. on med. schs. 1995—), Arthritis Health Professions Assn. (nat. pres. 1982-83), Am. Assn. Med. Colls., Am. Fedn. Clin. Rsch., Inst. Medicine of Chgo., Ctrl. Soc. Clin. Investigation, Arthritis Found. (nat. vice chmn. 1982-83, chmn. profl. edn. com. 1996—, chmn. ednl. materials com. 1991-96, blue ribbon com. on quality of life, bd. trustees Greater Chgo. chpt. 1997—, exec. com. 1998—), Assn. Profs. Medicine (bd. dirs.), Ill. Med. Soc., Lake County Med. Soc. (treas. 1998-99, sec. 2000—), Sigma Xi, Alpha Omega Alpha (regional counselor 1998—), Alpha Epsilon Delta. Avocations: photography, fishing. E-mail: (home) (office). Office: The Chgo Med Sch Dept Medicine 3333 Green Bay Rd North Chicago IL 60064-3037 E-mail: egall@aol.com., ericgall@finchcms.edu.

GALLAGHER, BOB, newscaster; b. Clarendon Hill, ill. BA in Journalism and Mktg., Marquette U., 1990. News editor/prodr., weekend morning news anchor WTMJ-TV, 1992—94; weekend sports anchor/reporter News-Center 13, WEAU, 1994—98, weekend sports dir., anchor, 1998—. Avocations: reading, golf. Office: WEAU PO Box 47 Eau Claire WI 54702

GALLAGHER, GERALD RAPHAEL, venture capitalist; b. Easton, Pa., Mar. 17, 1941; s. Gerald R. and Marjorie A. G.; m. Ellen Anne Mullane, Aug. 8, 1964; children: Ann Patrice, Gerald Patrick, Megan Ann. BS in Aero. Engring., Princeton U., 1963; MBA (Exec. Club Chgo. fellow 1969), U. Chgo., 1969. Dir. strategic planning Metro-Goldwyn-Mayer, N.Y.C., 1969; v.p. Donaldson, Lufkin & Jenrette, 1969-77; from v.p. to sr. v.p. planning and control Dayton Hudson Corp., Mpls., 1977-79; exec. v.p., chief adminstrv. officer subs. Mervyn's, Hayward, Calif.; then vice chmn., chief adminstrv. officer, 1979-85; vice chmn., chief adminstrv. office parent co., 1985-87; also dir.; gen. ptnr. Oak Investment Ptnrs., Mpls., 1987—. Bd. dirs. Baja Fresh, eStyle, Gaiam.com, Lucy Activewear, Ulta, Vicinity Corp. Mem. Fairview Hosp. and Healthcare Svcs. With USN, 1963-67. Mem. N.Y. Soc. Security Analysts, Mpls. Club, Interlachen Country Club, Beta Gamma Sigma. Roman Catholic. Office: Oak Investment Ptnrs 4550 Wells Fargo Ctr. 90 S 7th St Minneapolis MN 55402-3903 E-mail: jerry@oakvc.com.

GALLAGHER, JOHN SILL, III, astronomer; b. Boston, Mar. 26, 1947; s. John Sill Jr. and Caroline Eaton (Campbell) G.; m. Mary Lewis Ames, Aug. 29, 1970; children: Daphne E., Julia F. BA, Princeton U., 1969; MS, U. Wis., 1971, PhD, 1972. Vis. asst. prof. dept. physics and astronomy U. Nebr., Lincoln, 1972-74; asst. prof. Sch. Physics and Astronomy U. Minn., Mpls., 1974-77; assoc. prof. to prof. astronomy U. Ill., Urbana, 1977-84; astronomer Kitt Peak Nat. Obs., Tucson, 1984-86; dir. Lowell Obs., Flagstaff, Ariz., 1986-89; v.p. Associated Univs. for Rsch. in Astronomy, Inc., Washington, 1989-90; prof. astronomy U. Wis., Madison, 1990—. Fellow Am. Assn. Adv. Sci.; mem. Am. Astron. Soc. (councilor 1987-90), Internat. Astron. Union, Astron. Soc. of Pacific, AAAS. Office: U Wis Dept Astronomy 5534 Sterling Hall 475 N Charter St Madison WI 53706-1507

GALLAGHER, PATRICK FRANCIS XAVIER, public relations executive; b. Cleve., Feb. 9, 1952; s. Patrick Francis and Eileen (Brennan) G.; m. Anne Platek, May 3, 1980; children: Molly Anne, Kate Louise. Student, Holy Cross Coll., Worcester, Mass., 1970-72; BA, U. Pa., 1974; MBA, Cleve. State U., 1991. Accredited in pub. rels. Staff editor Penton Pub. Co., Cleve., 1975-80, editor, 1980-83; mgr. corp. communications Leaseway Transp. Corp., 1983-84, dir. pub. rels., 1984-85; sr. account exec. Edward Howard & Co., 1985-89, v.p., 1990-94, sr. v.p., 1994—. Trustee Project LEARN, Cleve. Mem. Pub. Rels. Soc. Am., Nat. Investor Rels. Inst. (v.p. Cleve.-No. Ohio chpt.), Cleve. Soc. Security Analysts-Assn. for Investment Mgmt. and Rsch. Office: Edward Howard & Co 7th Fl 1360 E 9th St Fl 7 Cleveland OH 44114-1716

GALLAGHER, RICHARD SIDNEY, lawyer; b. Minot, N.D., May 10, 1942; s. J.W.S. and Esther T. (Tappon) G.; m. Ann Rylands Larson, June 24, 1972; children: Elizabeth, Catherine. BSBA, Northwestern U., 1964; JD, Harvard U., 1967. Ptnr., chmn. dept. tax and individual planning Foley & Lardner, Milw., 1967—. Bd. dirs. Badger Meter Found., Milw. Bd. chmn. Milw. Youth Symphony Orchs., Milw., 1980-82; bd. chmn. Milw. County Performing. Arts Ctr., Milw., 1986-91; dir. Curative Rehab. Ctr., Milw., 1988-93, United Performing Arts Fund, 1991-99; pres. Donors Forum of Wis., 1997-2000. Lt. comdr., USN, 1967-69, Vietnam. Fellow Am. Coll. Tax Counsel, Am. Coll. of Trust and Estate Coun., Am. Law Inst.; mem. ABA (chmn. exempt orgns. com., sect. of taxation 1989-91, chmn. com. on adminstrn. of trusts and estates, sect. probate and trust law 1996-98). Office: Foley & Lardner Firstar Ctr 777 E Wisconsin Ave Milwaukee WI 53202

GALLAGHER, ROBERT E. risk management marketing company executive; b. 1923; CEO Arthur J. Gallagher & Co., Itasca, Ill., 1963-94, chmn. bd. Office: The Gallgher Ctr Two Pierce Pl Itasca IL 60143-3141 Fax: 630-285-4000.

GALLEGOS, MARCELO, chef; With Spiaggia, Chgo.; exec. chef Vivere; with Tuttaposto; chef Dal Pescatore, Italy. Office: Vivere 71 W Monroe St Chicago IL 60603

GALLGHER, J. PATRICK, JR. risk management marketing company executive; b. 1952; m. Anne Murphy; four children. Bachelor's Degree, Cornell U., 1974. Joined Arthur J. Gallagher & Co., Itasca, 1974, v.p. ops., 1985, dir., 1986, COO, pres., 1990, CEO, 1995. Bd. dirs. Gallagher Plumer Ltd.; underwriting mem. Lloyd's Syndicates. Mem. Sunset Ridge Country Club, Meadow Club, Dairymen's Country Club. Office: The Gallagher Ctr Two Pierce Pl Itasca IL 60143-3141 Fax: 630-285-4000.

GALLMAN, JOHN GERRY, publisher; b. Danzig, Mar. 31, 1938; s. Waldemar John and Marjorie (Gerry) G.; m. Elizabeth Ann Stratton, Apr. 29, 1961; children— John Waldemar, Sylvia Elizabeth, David Edward B.A., Yale U., 1960. Reporter Worcester Telegram, Mass., 1960-62; assoc. editor Johns Hopkins Press, Balt., 1962-65, Washington editor, 1965-70; editorial dir. Ind. U. Press, Bloomington, 1970-76, dir., 1976-2001; ret., 2001. Cons. U. Iowa, Iowa City, 1983-84, NEH, U. Mich., 1985 Mem. exec. com. ACLU, 1974-76; bd. dirs. Sycamore Valley Land Trust, 2001—. Mem. Assn. Am. Univ. Presses (pres., bd. dirs. 1986-87, past pres. bd. dirs. 1987-88), Ducks Unltd. (exec. com. local chpt. 1976-83) Democrat Avocations: reading; wilderness camping; jogging; hunting; fishing. Home: 2111 E Queensway Dr Bloomington IN 47401-6845

GALLO, DONALD ROBERT, retired English educator; b. Paterson, N.J., June 1, 1938; s. Sergio and Thelma Mae (Lowe) G.; m. C.J. Bott, Feb. 14, 1997; 1 child, Brian Keith; 1 stepchild, Christian Perrett. BA in English, Hope Coll., 1960; MAT in English Edn., Oberlin Coll., 1961; PhD in English Edn., Syracuse U., 1968. English tchr. Bedford Jr. High Sch., Westport, Conn., 1961-65; rsch. assoc. Syracuse (N.Y.) U., 1965-67; from asst. prof. to assoc. prof. edn. U. Colo., Denver, 1968-72; reading specialist Golden Jr. High Sch., Jefferson County Pub. Schs., Colo., 1972-73; prof. English Cen. Conn. State U., New Britain, 1973-97. Instr. composition Onondaga C. C., Syracuse, 1967; vis. faculty grad. liberal studies program Wesleyan U., 1983; staff writer reading assessment Nat. Assessment Ednl. Progress, Denver, 1972-73; speaker in field; cons. to schs. and librs. Mem. edit. bd. Nat. Coun. Tchrs. English, 1985-88; compiler, editor: Speaking for Ourselves, 1990, Speaking for Ourselves, Too, 1993; editor: Connections: Short Stories by Outstanding Writers for Young Adults, 1989, Visions: Nineteen Short Stories by Outstanding Writers for Young Adults, 1987, Center Stage: One-Act Plays for Teenage Readers and Actors, 1990, Sixteen: Short Stories by Outstanding Writers for Young Adults, 1984, Books for You, 1985, Authors' Insights: Turning Teenagers into Readers and Writers, 1992, Short Circuits: Thirteen Shocking Stories by Outstanding Writers for Young Adults, 1992, Within Reach: Ten Stories, 1993, Join In: Multiethnic Short Stories by Outstanding Writers for Young Adults, 1993, Ultimate Sports: Short Stories by Outstanding Writers for Young Adults, 1995, No Easy Answers: Short Stories About Teenagers Making Tough Choices, 1997, Time Capsule: Short Stories About Teenagers Throughout the Twentieth Century, 1999, On The Fringe, 2001; author: Presenting Richard Peck, 1989, Bookmark Reading Program, Seventh and Eighth Grade Texts and Workbooks, 1979, Heath Middle Level Literature, 1995; co-author: (with Sarah K. Herz) From Hinton to Hamlet: Building Bridges Between Young Adult Literature and the Classics, 1996. Recipient Disting. Svc. award Conn. Coun. Tchrs. English, 1989, ALAN award Assembly on Lit. for Adolescents of the Nat. Coun. Tchrs. English, 1992, Cert. of Merit award Cath. Libr. Assn., 1995, Ted Hipple Svc. award NCTE, 2001. Mem. Nat. Coun. Tchrs. English, Assembly on Lit. for Adolescents, Ohio Coun. Tchrs. English Lang. Arts, Soc. Children's Book Writers and Illustrators, Authors Guild. Avocations: gardening, cooking, traveling, photography. Address: 34540 Sherbrook Park Dr Solon OH 44139-2046 E-mail: gallodon@aol.com.

GALLOP, JANE (ANNE), women's studies educator, writer; b. Duluth, Minn., May 4, 1952; d. Melvin Gordon and Eudice Zelda (Titch) G.; children: Max Blau Gallop, Ruby Gallop Blau. BA, Cornell U., 1972, PhD, 1976. Lectr. French Gettysburg (Pa.) Coll., 1976; asst. prof. Miami U., Oxford, Ohio, 1977-81, assoc. prof., 1981-85; prof. women's studies Rice U., Houston, 1985-87, Autrey prof., 1987-90; prof. English U. Wis., Milw., 1990-92, Disting. prof., 1992—. NEH vis. prof. Emory U., Atlanta, 1984-85; Hill vis. prof. U. Minn., Mpls., 1987; dir. seminar for coll. tchrs. NEH, Milw., 1985, 88; instr. Sch. of Criticism and Theory, Dartmouth Coll., 1991. Author: Intersections, 1981, The Daughter's Seduction, 1982, Reading Lacan, 1985, Thinking Through the Body, 1988, Around 1981, 1992, Feminist Accused of Sexual Harassment, 1997,Anecdotal Theory, 2002; editor: Pedagogy, 1995. Guggenheim fellow, 1983-84. Mem. MLA. Office: U Wis PO Box 413 Milwaukee WI 53201-0413 E-mail: jg@uwm.edu.

GALOWICH, RONALD HOWARD, real estate investment executive, venture capitalist; b. Peoria, Ill., Feb. 18, 1936; s. Louis J. and Leah (Kahn) G.; m. Eleanor Bernstein, June 16, 1957 (div. Aug., 1977); children: Jeffrey, Robert, Pamela; m. Susan E. Loggans, Sept. 11, 1977 (div. Apr. 1988); m. Linda L. Kroupa, Oct. 18, 2000. BS in Commerce and Law, U. Ill., 1957, JD, 1959. Bar: Ill. 1959, U.S. Supreme Ct. 1963. Pres. Twin Oaks-Burr Oaks Realty, Joliet, Ill., 1961-81; ptnr. Galowich & Galowich, 1960-81; dir. real estate ops. Pritzker & Pritzker, Chgo., 1981-90; chmn. Madison Realty Group, Inc., 1985—, Madison Group Holdings, Inc., Chgo., 1990—; founder, chmn. CEO Madison Info. Technologies, Inc., 1994—. Co-founder, dir. First Health Group Corp. (formerly Health Care Compare Corp.), Downers Grove, Ill., 1982—; commr. Ill. Supreme Ct., 1968-70. Bd. visitors U. Ill. Coll. Law, 1996—, pres., 1998-2000; mem. leadership com. Cancer Inst., Rush-Presbyn. St. Lukes Med. Ctr., Chgo., 1993—; bd. dirs. Athletes Against Drugs, 1992—; bd. mgrs. Riverside Hosp. Cancer Ctr., Kankakee, Ill., 1999—. Fellow Am. Judicature Soc., Ill. Bar Found.; mem. ABA, Ill. Bar Assn., Urban Land Inst., Chgo. Bar Assn. Jewish. Avocation: lic. airline transport pilot. Home: 1248 N Astor St Chicago IL 60610-2308 Office: Madison Group Holdings Inc 200 W Madison St Ste 2800 Chicago IL 60606-3463 E-mail: rhgalo@ix.netcom.com., rgalowich@madison-info.com.

GALVIN, CHRISTOPHER B. electronics company executive; b. 1951; BA, Northwestern U., MBA, 1977. With Motorola, Inc., 1973—, sr. exec. v.p., asst. COO Ill., 1989-95, pres., COO, 1995—, now CEO. Office: Motorola Inc 1303 E Algonquin Rd Schaumburg IL 60196-1079*

GALVIN, KATHLEEN MALONE, communication educator; b. N.Y.C., Feb. 9, 1943; d. James Robert and Helen M. (Sullivan) G.; m. Charles A. Wilkinson, June 19,1973; children: Matthew, Katherine, Kara. BS, Fordham U., 1964; MA, Northwestern U., 1965, 80, PhD, 1968. Tchr. Evanston (Ill.) Township High Sch., 1967-72; asst. prof. Northwestern U., Evanston, 1968-73, assoc. prof., 1973-78, prof., 1978—, assoc. dean, 1988-2001. Presenter workshops in field. Author: Listening by Doing, 1986; sr. author: Family Communication, 5th edit., 2000; co-author: Person to Person, 5th edit., 1996, Basics of Speech, 3d edit., 1998; co-editor: Making Connections, 1996, 2d edit., 1999, Communication Works!, 2000; contbr. articles to profl. jours.; developer, instr. 26-video series on Family Communication (PBS Adult Satellite Sys.). Office: Northwestern U Sch Speech 2299 N Campus Dr Evanston IL 60208-3545

GALVIN, MICHAEL JOHN, JR. lawyer; b. Winona, Minn., July 8, 1930; s. Michael John Sr. and Margaret Elizabeth (O'Donohue) G.; m. Frances Dennis Culligan, Sept. 7, 1957; children: Sean, Kevin, Kathleen, Nora, Mary, Margaret, Patricia. BA, U. St. Thomas, 1952; LLB, U. Minn., 1957. Bar: Minn. 1957, U.S. Dist. Ct. Minn. 1957, U.S. Supreme Ct. 1961. With sales and svc. Badger Machine Co., Winona, 1950-56; mgr. Oaks Hotel Inc., 1950-56; ptnr. Briggs & Morgan, P.A., St. Paul, 1957—. Pres. St. Paul Winter Carnival Assn., 1970; sec. St. Paul Area C. of C., 1968-71; trustee U. St. Thomas, 1978-85, Coll. St. Catherines, St. Paul, 1999—; nat. chmn. U. Minn. Law Sch. Ptnrs. in Excellence Program, 2000-01; chmn. elect Indianhead Coun. Boy Scouts Am., 2001—. Lt. USAF, 1952-54, USAFR, 1954-60. Named Oustanding Young Man, City St. Paul, 1964, Boss of Yr., St. Paul Jaycees, 1990; recipient Disting. Alumnus award, U. St. Thomas, 1983, Great Living St. Paulite award, St. Paul Area C. of C., 2000, Eugene and Mary Fry Cmty. award, Cretin-Derham Hall Schs., 2000, Disting. Alumnus award, U. Minn. Law Sch., 2001. Mem. ABA (labor and employment law sect.), Minn. Bar Assn. (treas. 1991-93, pres.-elect 1993, pres. 1994-95, labor and employment law sect.), Ramsey County Bar Assn. (exec. coun. 1965-68, 83-86, pres. 1984-85), Minn. Vol. Attys. Corp. (pres. 1993-94), Univ. Club (pres. 1962), Minn. Club (pres. 1971), St. Paul Athletic Club (pres. 1986), St. Paul Area C. of C. (bd. dirs. 1995—, chmn. 1997-98). Republican. Roman Catholic. Office: Briggs & Morgan 2200 1st St N Saint Paul MN 55109-3210 E-mail: mgalvin@briggs.com.

GALVIN, PAT G. state legislator; m. Carol Galvin; 2 children. Student, Barber Coll. Barber; rep. Dist. 33 N.D. Ho. of reps., mem. human svcs., natural resources coms. Mem. Hazen City Commn., Hazen City Sch. Bd. With N.D. N.G. Mem. Am. Legion, Eagles. Home: PO Box 31 Hazen ND 58545-0031

GALVIN, WALTER J. electrical equipment manufacturing executive; CFO Emerson Electric Co., St. Louis, exec. v.p., CFO, 2000—. Office: Emerson Electric Co PO Box 4100 Saint Louis MO 63136-8506

GAMBLE, E. JAMES, lawyer, accountant; b. Duluth, Minn., June 1, 1929; s. Edward James and Modesta Caroline (Reichert) G.; m. Lois Kennedy, Apr. 3, 1954; children: John M., Martha M., Paul F. AB, U. Mich., 1950, JD, 1953. Bar: Mich. 1953, D.C. 1980; CPA, Mich. Tax acct. Ernst & Ernst, Detroit, 1957-59; assoc. Dykema, Gossett, Spencer, Goodnow & Trigg, 1959-67; ptnr. Dykema Gossett, 1967-94, Gamble, Rosenberger & Joswick LLP, Bloomfield Hills, 1994—. Adj. prof. law Wayne State U., Detroit, 1964-79; adj. lectr. law U. Mich., Ann Arbor, 1979-81, 93; co-reporter Uniform Principal and Income Act (1997); mem. adv. com. Restatement of the Law, 3rd, Property, Wills and Other Donative Transfers, Restatement of the Law, 3rd, Trusts; counsel Mich. State Bd. Accountancy, Lansing, 1973-77. Author: (handbook) The Revised Uniform Principal and Income Act, 1966; contbr. articles to profl. jours. Trustee Rehab. Inst., Inc., Detroit, 1961-84, chmn. bd. trustees, 1974-77; bd. dirs., sec. Jr. Achievement Southeastern Mich., 1973-86; trustee Walsh Coll. Accountancy and Bus. Adminstrn., Troy, Mich., 1975-87, Alma (Mich.) Coll., 1981-91; mem. Fin. and Estate Planning Coun. Detroit, bd. dirs., 1969-76, pres., 1975. Lt. USN, 1953-57. Recipient Bronze Leadership award Jr. Achievement, Inc., 1985 Fellow Am. Coll. Tax Counsel, Am. Coll. Trust and Estate Counsel (bd. regents 1988—, chmn. estate and gift tax com. 1989-92, pres. 1998-99), Academician, Internat. Acad. Estate and Trust Law (exec. coun. 2001—), Am. Bar Found. (life), Mich. State Bar Found.; mem. ABA (mem. spl. com. on profl. rels. with AICPA 1968-70), Mich. Bar Assn. (mem. various coms.), Detroit Bar Assn. (chmn. taxation com. 1968-74), Detroit Bar Assn. Found. (trustee, treas. 1973-79), Birmingham Athletic Club, Leland Country Club. Presbyterian.

GANASSI, CHIP, professional race car executive, owner; b. Pitts., May 24, 1958; m. Cara Ganassi; 1 child, Tessa. BA in Fin., Duquesne U., 1982. Exec. v.p. FRG Group, Pitts.; ptnr. Pitts. Pirates; promoter, co-mgr. Chgo. Motor Speedway; co-owner Target/Chip Ganassi Racing, 1990—. Former profl. race car driver, fastest of 9 rookies at Indpls. 500, 1982; 8 top-10 finishes in 28 Indy car appearances, 1986; ret. 1986; co-owner Patrick Racing, 1988-89; established Reynard N.Am., Indpls., 1993. Office: c/o Target/Chip Ganassi Racing 7777 Woodland Dr Indianapolis IN 46278-1794

GAND, GAYLE, chef; m. Rick Tramonto. Ry chef, owner Tru, Chgo., 1999—; chef Jam's, N.Y.C., 1985, Gotham Bar & Grill, N.Y.C., Strathallen Hotel, Rochester, Carlos', Highland Park, Ill.; pastry chef The Pump Room, Chgo.; chef Cafe 21, Chgo., Bice, Chgo., Bella Luna, Chgo., Stapleford Park, London, Charlie Trotter's, Chgo.; chef, owner Trio, 1993, Brasserie T, Chgo., 1995, Vanilla Bean Bakery, Chgo., 1996—98. (appeared on TV programs): Baker's Dozen, Chef du Jour, Ready, Set, Cook!, Cooking With Julia. Named one of Top Ten Best New Chefs, Food & Wine, 1994; recipient award, James Beard Found., 2001. Office: 676 N St Clair Chicago IL 60611

GANDHI, HAREN S. chemical engineer; b. Calcutta, India, May 2, 1941; B in Engring., Mumbai U., India. Rsch. engr. Ford Motor Co., Dearborn, Mich., 1967, various rsch. engring. and staff scientist positions, mgr. dept. chem. engring. Ford Rsch. Lab., head emission and fuel economy core team, 1997, Ford tech. fellow. Mem. adv. com. Ministries of Industry and Environment. Contbr. numerous articles to profl. jours. Mem. NAE. Achievements include more than 40 U.S. patents. Office: 20000 Rotunda Dr Rm 3437 Dearborn MI 48124-3958

GANDRUD, ROBERT P. retired fraternal insurance executive; b. 1943; Mem. actuarial staff Lutheran Brotherhood, Mpls., 1965-75, asst. v.p., 1975-76, v.p., 1976-80, sr. v.p., 1980-86, sr. exec. v.p., COO, 1986-87, pres., CEO, 1987-99, chmn. & CEO, 1999-2000, ret., 2000. Office: Lutheran Brotherhood 625 4th Ave S Ste 100 Minneapolis MN 55415-1665

GANNON, SISTER ANN IDA, retired philosophy educator, former college administrator; b. Chgo., 1915; d. George and Hanna (Murphy) G. A.B., Clarke Coll., 1941; A.M., Loyola U., Chgo., 1948, LL.D., 1970; Ph.D., St. Louis U., 1952; Litt.D., DePaul U., 1972; L.H.D., Lincoln Coll., 1965, Columbia Coll., 1969, Luther Coll., 1969; LHD, Augustana Coll., 1969; L.H.D., Marycrest Coll., 1972, Ursuline Coll., 1972, Spertus Coll. Judaica, 1974, Holy Cross Coll., 1974, Rosary Coll., 1975, St. Ambrose Coll., 1975, St. Leo Coll., 1976, Mt. St. Joseph Coll., 1976, Stritch Coll., 1976; LHD, Stonehill Coll., 1976, Elmhurst Coll., 1977, Manchester Coll., 1977, Marymount Coll., 1977; L.H.D., Governor's State U., 1979; LHD, Seattle U., 1981, St. Michael's Coll., 1984, Nazareth Coll., 1985, Holy Family Coll., 1986, Keller Grad. Sch. Mgmt., Our Lady of Holy Cross Coll., New Orleans, 1988. Mem. Sisters of Charity, B.V.M.; tchr. English St. Mary's High Sch., Chgo., 1941-47; residence, study abroad, 1951; chmn. philosophy dept. Mundelein Coll., 1951-57, pres., 1957-75, prof. philosophy, 1975-85, emeritus faculty, 1987—, archivist, 1986—. Contbr. articles philos. jours. Mem. adv. bd. Sec. Navy, 1975—80, Chgo. Police Bd., 1979—89; bd. dirs. Am. Coun. on Edn., 1971—75, chmn., 1974—75; nat. bd. dirs. Girl Scouts USA, 1966—74, nat. adv., 1976—85; trustee St. Louis U., 1974—87, Ursuline Coll., 1978—92, Cath. Theol. Union, 1983—89, DeVry, Inc., 1987—98, Duquesne U., 1989—91, Montay Coll., 1993—95; bd. dirs. Newberry Libr., 1976—, WTTW Pub. TV, 1976—, Parkside Human Svcs. Corp., 1983—89. Recipient Laetare medal, 1975, LaSallian award, 1975, Aquinas award, 1976, Chgo. Assn. Commerce and Industry award, 1976, Hesburgh award, 1982, Woman of Distinction award Nat. Conf. Women Student Leaders, 1985, Outstanding Svc. award Coun. Ind. Colls., 1989, Woman of History award for edn. AAUW, 1989; named One of 100 Oustanding Chgo. Women, Culture in Action, 1994, Alpha Sigma Nu, 1996. Mem. Am. Cath. Philos. Assn. (exec. coun. 1953-56), Assn. Am. Colls. (bd. dirs. 1965-70, chmn. 1969-70), Religious Edn. Assn. Am. (pres. 1973, chmn. bd. 1975-78), North Cen. Assn. (commn. on colls. and univs. 1971-78, chmn. exec. bd. 1975-77, bd. dirs.), Assn. Governing Bds. Colls. and Univs. (bd. dirs. 1979-88, hon. bd. dirs. 1989-92). Home: Wright Hall 6364 N Sheridan Rd Chicago IL 60660-1726 Office: Loyola U Office Archives Sullivan Ctr 6525 N Sheridan Rd Chicago IL 60626-5344 E-mail: aganno2@luc.edu.

GANNON, JEFFREY P. trucking/relocation services executive; BE, Villanova U. V.p. internat. bus. devel. Gen. Electric Co.; pres., CEO Zenith Electronics Co.; CEO Allied Worldwide. Former pres., CEO GE Lighting Asia Pacific, GE China, GE Mex., GE Latin Am., GE USSR. Office: Allied Worldwide 215 W Diehl Rd Naperville IL 60563

GANNON, MICHAEL J. printing company executive; CFO, sr. v.p. Flint Ink Corp., Detroit. Office: Flint Ink Corp 4600 Arrowhead Dr Ann Arbor MI 48105-2773

GANNON, THOMAS A. trucking executive; BS in Bus. Econs., Marquette U., 1976; JD, U. Wis., 1978. CFO Schneider Nat. Inc., Green Bay, Wis. Office: Schneider Nat Inc PO Box 2545 Green Bay WI 54306-2545

GANSKE, J. GREG, congressman, plastic surgeon; b. New Hampton, Iowa, Mar. 31, 1949; s. Victor Wilber and Mary Jo (O'Donnell) G.; m. Corrine Mikkelson, 1976; children: Ingrid, Briget, Karl. BA, U. Iowa, 1972, MD, 1976. Diplomate Am. Bd. Plastic Surgery, Am. Bd. Surgery. Intern U. Colo. Med. Ctr., Denver, 1976-78; resident in gen. surgery U. Oreg. Health Sci. Ctr., Portland, 1978-81, chief resident in gen. surgery, 1981-82; resident in plastic surgery Harvard Med. Sch., Boston, 1982-84; chief resident plastic surgery Brigham and Women's Hosp. and Children's Hosp., 1983-84; pvt. practice Des Moines, 1984-94; mem. U.S. Congress from 4th Iowadist., Washington, 1994—; mem. energy and commerce com. Staff Iowa Luth. Hosp., Iowa Meth. Med. Ctr., Mercy Hosp. Med. Ctr., Vets. Hosp., Charter Cmty. Hosp., Des Moines Gen. Hosp. Lt. col. M.C., USAR, 1984—. Fellow ACS, Am. Soc. Plastic and Reconstructive Surgeons; mem. AMA, Am. Assn. Plastic Surgeons, Iowa Med. Soc., Polk County Med. Soc., Iowa Soc. Plastic and Reconstructive Surgeons, Am. Assn. Hand Surgery, Midwestern Assn. Plastic Surgeons, Am. Soc. for Surgery of the Hand, Iowa Acad. Surgery, Am. Cleft Palate-Craniofacial Assn. Republican. Roman Catholic. Home: 5206 Waterbury Rd Des Moines IA 50312-1922 Office: US Ho Reps 1108 Longworth Hob Washington DC 20515-0001*

GANSLER, ROBERT, professional soccer coach; b. Mucsi, Hungary, July 1, 1941; came to U.S., 1952; m. Nancy Gansler; children: Robert, MIchael, Peter, Daniel. Grad., Marquette U., 1964. Head coach Kansas City Wizards/MLS, 1999—. Office: care Kansas City Wizards 706 Broadway St Ste 100 Kansas City MO 64105-2306

GANTZ, RICHARD ALAN, museum administrator; b. Ft. Wayne, Ind., July 28, 1946; m. Ruth Ann Kennell; 1 child, Sally Elizabeth. BS in Edn. with honors, Ball State U., 1968; MA, George Washington U., 1971; PhD, Ind. U., 1986. Social studies tchr. Ft. Wayne (Ind.) Community Schs., 1969-73; Nat. Park Svc. seasonal hist. Homestead Nat. Monument, Beatrice, Nebr., 1972; assoc. instr. Ind. U., Bloomington, 1975-76; asst. state hist. preserv. officer dept. natural resources State of Ind., 1976-90, asst. dir. divsn. mus. and memls., 1978-81, acting dir., 1982-83, dir. divsn. hist. preservation and archeology, 1981-90, acting dir. divsn. state mus. and hist. sites, 1989, dir. divsn. state mus. and hist. sites and Ind. State Mus., 1990—2001; dir. spl. projects Ind. Dept. Natural Resources, Indpls., 2001—. Mem. adj. faculty history dept. Butler U., Indpls., 1988—; mem. steering com. Dept. Commerce Heritage, Tourism and Edn., 1991-94; mem. project com. Ind. Heritage Trust, 1992—; chmn. Ind. Hist. Exchange Coun., 1984-91, Ind. Hist. Bridge Com., 1984-90. Contbr. articles to profl. jours. Active Ind. Main State Coun., 1985-98; sec. New Harmony State Commn., 1989-2001; mem. White River State Park Commn., 1993-2001, Ind. Gov.'s Millennium Task Force, 1998-2000, Ind. Gov.'s Residence Adv. Com., 1998—; mem. Ind. Gov.'s 2016 Task Force, 2001-; bd. dirs. Ind. Med. History Mus., 2001-. Mem. Orgn. Am. Hists., Nat. Trust Hist. Preservation, Ind. Assn. Hists., Ind. State Mus. Soc., Assn. Ind. Mus., Midwest Mus. Conf. Office: Dept Natural Resources Exec Office 402 W Washington St Indianapolis IN 46204

GAPPA, JUDITH M. university administrator; Student, Wellesley Coll., 1957-60; BA in Music, George Washington U., 1968, MA in Musicology, 1970; EdD in Ednl. Adminstrn., Utah State U., 1973; cert. Inst. for Ednl. Mgmt., Harvard U., 1980. Lectr. George Washington U., Washington, 1968-69; dir. fine arts program The York Sch., Monterey, Calif., 1970; program cons. Western Interstate Commn. for Higher Edn., Boulder, Colo., 1973; coord. affirmative action program Utah State U., Logan, 1973-75, dir. affirmative action/equal opportunity programs, asst. prof., 1975-77, 78-80, project dir., 1979-81; sr. staff assoc. Nat. Ctr. for Higher Edn. Mgmt. Systems, Inc., Boulder, 1977-78; assoc. v.p. for faculty affairs, dean of faculty, prof. San Francisco State U., 1980-91; sr. assoc. Am. Assn. Higher Edn., 1995-97; prof. Purdue U., West Lafayette, Ind., 1991—, v.p. human rels., 1991-98. Served on numerous coms., couns. Utah State U., San Francisco State U.; cons. Assn. Governing Bds., 1994, U. Mich., Duluth, 1992, Calif. State U. Human Resources Mgmt. Office, 1992, Am. U., Washington, 1987, No. Rockies Consortium for Higher Edn. Conf., 1985, So. Utah State Coll., 1982, Nat. Ctr. for Rsch. in Vocat. Edn., 1980-81, Hood Coll., 1982-84, Am. Insts. for Rsch. in Behavioral Scis., 1980-81; condr. workshops on edn. Co-author: The Invisible Faculty, 1993; mem. editl. bd. Rev. of Higher Edn., 1994-97; contbr. numerous articles to profl. jours. Grantee Lilly Endowment, 1995, United Techs. Corp., 1992, TIAA-CREF/Lilly Endowment, 1990, Calif. State U., 1985, San Francisco State U., 1981, HEW, 1979-81, Nat. Inst. Edn., 1977, Utah State U., 1977, Fed. workshop grant, 1976, State of Utah, 1975, 76. Mem. Western Assn. Schs. and Colls. (accreditation team mem. Calif. State U.-L.A. 1990), Am. Assn. for Higher Edn. (sr. assoc. Washington chpt. 1995-97), Assn. for Study of Higher Edn. (nat. adv. bd. ASHE-ERIC Higher Edn. Report Series 1990-91, editl. bd. Rev. of Higher Edn. 1994-97, nominating com. 1986-87, program com. for 1986 nat. conf., membership com. 1982-84, conf. com. 1983, editl. bd. Rev. of Higher Edn. 1994-97), Am. Coun. on Edn. Nat. Identification Program (No. Calif. state coord. 1988-91). Office: Purdue Univ Sch Edn 1446 Liberal Arts Rd West Lafayette IN 47907-1075

GAPSTUR, SUSAN MARY, cancer epidemiologist, educator, researcher; b. Mpls., Nov. 14, 1960; d. Michael and Mary Monica Gapstur. BS, U. Wis., La Crosse, 1983; MPH, U. Minn., 1989, PhD, 1993. Rsch. technician Mayo Clinic and Found., Rochester, Minn., 1984-87; rsch. assoc. U. Ariz., Tucson, 1993-94; asst. prof. dept. preventive medicine Northwestern U., Chgo., 1994—. Grant reviewer NIH, 1996—, Dept. Def., 1998—. Contbr. over 30 articles to med. jours., including Jour. AMA, Am. Jour. Physiology, Am. Jour. Epidemiology, Cancer Epidemiology. Predoctoral fellow U. Minn., 1990-92; rsch. grantee Lynn Sage Breast Cancer Found., 1996, Washington Square Health Found., 1998-00, Nat. Cancer Inst., 1998-02. Mem. Soc. for Epidemiologic Rsch., Am. Assn. Cancer Rsch., Am. Soc. Preventive Oncology (session chmn. 1993, 97). Avocations: hiking, canoeing. Office: Northwestern U Dept Preventive Medicine 680 N Lake Shore Dr 1102 Chicago IL 60611-4402

GARBER, DANIEL ELLIOT, philosophy educator; b. Schenectady, N.Y., Sept. 26, 1949; s. William and Laura Sarah (Coplon) G.; m. Susan McClary, 1972 (div. 1982); m. Susan Joyce Paul, 1982; children: Hannah Laura, Elisabeth Sarah. AB, Harvard U., 1971, AM in Philosophy, 1974, PhD in Philosophy, 1975. Asst. prof. U. Chgo., 1975-82, assoc. prof., 1982-86, prof. dept. philosophy, 1986—, chair dept., 1987-94, chair conceptual and hist. studies of sci., 1994-95, 99—, Lawrence Kimpton Disting. Svc. prof., 1995—, assoc. provost rsch. and edn., 1995-98. Vis. asst. prof. U. Minn., Mpls., 1979, Johns Hopkins U., Balt., 1980-81, Princeton (N.J.) U., 1982-83; mem. Inst. Advanced Study, Princeton, 1985-86, Ecole Normal Superieure, Lyon, France, 2000. Author: Descartes' Metaphysical Physics, 1992, Descartes Embodied, 2000; co-editor: The Cambridge History of 17th Century Philosophy, 1998, The Yale Leibniz; co-translator, co-editor: Leibniz: Philosophical Essays, 1989; contbr. articles to profl. jours. Fellow Am. Coun. Learned Socs., 1985-86; grantee NEH, 1986-94, NSF, 1991-94. Mem. Am. Philos. Assn., History of Sci. Soc., Philosophy of Sci. Assn. (bd. govs. 1990-93), Brit. Soc. for History of Philosophy, Internat. Berkeley Soc. (bd. officers), Leibniz Soc. Am. (pres.). Office: U Chgo Dept Philosophy 1010 E 59th St Chicago IL 60637-1512 E-mail: garb@midway.uchicago.edu.

GARBER, SAMUEL B. lawyer, business/turnaround management consultant; b. Chgo., Aug. 16, 1934; s. Morris and Yetta G.; m. Marietta C. Bratta; children: Debra Lee, Diane Lori. JD, U. Ill., 1958; MBA, U. Chgo., 1968. Bar: Ill. 1958. Ptnr. Brown, Dashow and Langluttig, Chgo., 1960-62; corp. counsel Walgreen Co., 1962-69; v.p., gen. counsel, exec. asst. to the pres. Carlyle & Co., 1969-73; dir. legal affairs Stop & Shop Co., Inc., 1973-74; gen. counsel Goldblatt Bros., Inc., 1974-76; v.p., sec., gen. counsel, dir. Evans, Inc., 1976-99, pres., CEO, 1999-2000; prof. mgmt. DePaul U., 1975—; prin. The Garber Group, Bus. Cons. and Turnaround Management Firm, Chgo., 2000—. Adj. prof. bus. law grad. sch. bus. U. Chgo., 1993; arbitrator N.Y. Stock Exch., 1996, Chgo. Merc. Exch., 1996, Am. Stock Exch., 1997, Nat. Futures Assn., 1997; columnist Garber's Gurus Tribune Media Svcs., 1999—. With U.S. Army, 1958-60. Mem. ABA, NYSE (arbitrator 1996—), Am. Arbitration Assn. (arbitrator 1993—), Nat. Retail Fedn., Ill. Retail Mchts. Assn. Home: 2626 N Lakeview Ave Chicago IL 60614-1809 Office: DePaul U 1 E Jackson Blvd Ste 7010 Chicago IL 60604-2287 E-mail: thegarbergroup@yahoo.com.

GARBERDING, LARRY GILBERT, retired utilities companies executive; b. Albert City, Iowa, Oct. 29, 1938; s. Gilbert D. and Lavern Marie Garberding; m. Elizabeth Ann Hankens, Aug. 20, 1961; children: Scott Richard, Kathryn Ann, Michael John. BS, Iowa State U., 1960. CPA, Nebr. Ptnr. Arthur Andersen & Co., Chgo., 1960-71; chief fin. officer Kans.-Nebr. Natural Gas Co., Inc., Hastings, Nebr., 1971-81, Tenn. Gas Transmission, Houston, 1981-83, exec. v.p., 1983-87; pres. Tenn. Gas Mktg., 1987-88, NICOR Inc., Naperville, Ill., 1988-90; exec. v.p., chief fin. officer Detroit Edison Co., 1990—2001; ret., 2001. With U.S. Army, 1961. Mem. AICPA. Republican. Lutheran. Lutheran.

GARCIA, ASTRID J. newspaper executive; b. Caguas, Puerto Rico, Sept. 6, 1950; m. Robert Gillespie; children: Robert, Richard. BA with distinction, Barnard Coll., 1972; JD, Bklyn. Law Sch., 1980. Bar: N.Y. 1980. Dir., lighting designer various theatres, N.Y.C., 1972-74; equal employment opportunity specialist Gen. Svcs. Adminstrn. Fed. Govt., Region II, 1974-76; paralegal So. Dist. N.Y. U.S. Atty.'s Office, 1976-80; atty. Puerto Rican Legal Def. and Edn. Fund, 1980-81, NLRB, N.Y.C. and Hartford, Conn., 1981-85; mgr. employee rels. dept. human resources The Hartford Courant, 1985-87; asst. dir. human resources The Miami (Fla.) Herald, 1987-90; v.p., dir. employee rels. St. Paul Pioneer Press, 1990-94; sr. v.p. human resources and labor, dir. labor rels. Jour. Comm., Milw., 1994-97; sr. v.p. ops. Milw. Jour. Sentinel, 1997—. Mem. N.Y. Bar Assn. Office: Milw Jour Sentinel PO Box 661 Milwaukee WI 53201-0661

GARCIA, GERSON, radio personality; b. Malaga, Spain, Aug. 10, 1963; m. Juanita Garcia; children: Thomas, Jonathan, Victoria Esperanza. Radio host, program dir. for Radio Esperanza Sta. WMBI Radio, Chgo. Avocation: cooking. Office: WMBI 820 N LaSalle Blvd Chicago IL 60610*

GARCIA, JESUS G. state legislator; b. Apr. 12, 1956; BA, U. Ill., Chgo., 1980. Paralegal Legal Assistance Found., 1977-80; asst. dir. Little Village Neighborhood Housing Svc., 1980-84; dep. commr. Dept. of Water, 1984-86; alderman City of Chgo., 1986-92; mem. Ill. State Senate, 1993—. Chmn. aviation com., mem. budget and govt. ops. com., mem. edn. com., mem. fin. com. Home: 2500 S Saint Louis Ave Chicago IL 60623-3925

GARCIA, MARCELO HORACIO, engineering educator, consultant; b. Cordoba, Argentina, Apr. 22, 1959; came to U.S., 1983; s. Juan Carlos Jose and Beatriz Alba Garcia; m. Estela Beti Rodriguez-Canga, May 17, 1984; children: Blas Ignacio, Emma Paina. Diploma in Engring., U. Litoral, Santa Fe, Argentina, 1982; MS in Civil Engring., U. Minn., Mpls., 1985; PhD in Civil Engring., 1989. Registered profl. engr., Argentina. Tech. asst. Agua y Energia Electrica, Santa Fe, Argentina, 1979-85; rsch. asst. St. Anthony Falls Lab., Mpls., 1983-87; rsch. fellow, 1988-89; asst. prof. U. Ill., Urbana, 1990-96, assoc. prof., 1996—; vis. prof. Calif. Inst. Tech., Pasadena, 1997—. Cons. Govt. Taiwan, Taipei, 1993, U.S. Army of Engrs., Vicksburg, Miss., 1993—, Electricite de France, Toulousse, 1996; tech. adv. U.S./Taiwan Sedimentation, Washington, 1992-94; vis. prof. U. Litoral, Santa Fe, Argentina, 1993—; disting. lectr. Hokkaido River Disaster Prevention Inst., Japan, 1990; guest lectr. U. Essen, Germany, 1995. Author: Environmental Hydrodynamics, 1996; contbr. articles to profl. jours. Recipient Karl Emil Hilgard hydraulics prize ASCE, N.Y.C., 1996, Alvin Anderson award U. Minn., Mpls., 1989; named Disting. Vis. Prof. U. Genoa, Italy, 1993. Mem. ASCE (Walter L. Huber Rsch. prize 1998), Am. Geophys. Union, Internat. Assn. for Hydraulic Rsch., Internat. Water Resources Assn., Sigma Xi. Achievements include development of the first model for sediment mixtures transport by turbidity currents in the ocean. Office: U Ill 205 N Mathews Ave Urbana IL 61801

GARCIA, OSCAR NICOLAS, computer science educator; b. Havana, Cuba, Sept. 10, 1936; s. Oscar Vicente and Leonor (Hernandez) G.; m. Diane Ford Journigan, Sept. 9, 1962; children: Flora, Virginia. BSEE, N.C. State U., 1961, MSEE, 1964; PhDEE, U. Md., 1969. Engr. IBM Corp., Endicott, N.Y., 1962-63; asst. prof. Old Dominion U., 1963-66, assoc. prof., 1969-70; research asst., instr. U. Md., 1966-69; assoc. prof. U. South Fla., Tampa, 1970-75, prof. computer sci., chmn. dept., 1975-85; prof. dept. elec. engring. and computer sci. George Washington U., Washington, 1985-95; disting. NCR prof. Wright State U., Dayton, Ohio, 1995—. Chmn. dept. computer sci. and engring. Wright State U., 1995—; dir. interactive sys. program in info., robotics and intelligent sys. divsn. Computer and Info. Sci. and Engring. Directorate, Intergovtl. Pers. Act, NSF, Washington, 1992-94; cons. and lectr. in field. Author: (with Y.T. Chien) Knowledge-Based Systems: Fundamentals and Tools, 1991. Fellow IEEE (bd. dirs. 1984-85, mem. U.S. activities bd. 1984, Profl. Leadership award 1991, Richard M. Emberson award 1994), Computer Soc. of IEEE (pres. 1981-83, Richard E. Merwin Disting. Svc. award 1988, Meritorious Svc. award 1991), AAAS; mem. Assn. Computing Machinery, Am. Soc. Engring. Edn., Am. Assn. Artificial Intelligence, Sigma Xi, Eta Kappa Nu, Phi Kappa Phi, Tau Beta Pi. Home: 1917 S Highgate Ct Beavercreek OH 45432-1880 Office: Russ Center Rm 303 Dept Comp Sci & Engring Wright State Univ Dayton OH 45435

GARCIA C. ELISA DOLORES, lawyer; b. Bklyn., Nov. 8, 1957; d. Vincent Garcia, Jr. and Dolores Elizabeth (Canedo) Marmo; m. John Jay Hasluck, Feb. 28, 1987; children: Brooke Elisabeth, John Neville. BA, MS, SUNY, Stony Brook, 1980; JD, St. John's U., 1985. Bar: N.Y. 1986. Cons. Energy Devel. Internat., Pt. Jefferson, N.Y., 1980-83; assoc. Willkie Farr & Gallagher, N.Y.C., 1985-89; sr. counsel GAF Corp./Internat. Specialty

Products, Wayne, N.J., 1989-94; regional counsel for L.Am., Philip Morris Internat., Rye Brook, N.Y., 1994-2000; exec. v.p., gen. counsel Domino's Pizza, LLC, Ann Arbor, Mich., 2000—. Mem. Glen Rock (N.J.) Planning Bd., 1992-95, chmn., 1994-95. Mem. ABA, N.Y. State Bar Assn., Mich. Bar Assn., Am. Corp. Counsel Assn. (dir. Mich. chpt.). Roman Catholic. Avocations: gardening, scuba diving. Office: Domino's Pizza LLC PO Box 997 30 Frank Lloyd Wright Dr Ann Arbor MI 48106-0997 Home: 52 Old Lyme Rd Chappaqua NY 10514-3806 E-mail: garciae@dominos.com.

GARD, BEVERLY J. state legislator; b. N.C., Mar. 8, 1940; m. Donald Gard; children: David, Doug. BS, U. Tenn., Chattanooga; grad. studies, U. Tenn. Biochemist Eli Lilly & Co.; councilwoman City of Greenfield, Ind., 1976-88; mem. Ind. State Senate from 28th dist., 1988—. Mem. Hancock Assn Retarded Citizens, Ind. Assn. Cities and Towns. Republican. Methodist. Office: Ind Senate Dist 28 200 W Washington St Indianapolis IN 46204-2728

GARD, JOHN, state legislator; b. Milw., Aug. 3, 1963; m. Cathy Zeuske; 2 children. BA, U. Wis., La Crosse, 1986. Mem. from dist. 89 Wis. State Assembly, Madison, 1987—, mem. joint com. rev. adminstrv. rules, 1987-98, mem. tourism and recreation conf., 1987-98, mem. select com. welfare reform, 1987-98, chmn. assembly welfare reform com., 1987-98, co-chair joint com. on fin., mem. legis. coun., audit coms., mem. joint. com. on employment rels. Mem. KC, Ducks Unltd., Sportsmen's Club, Lions. Office: PO Box 119 481 Aubin St Peshtigo WI 54157-1142

GARDEBRING, SANDRA S. academic administrator; Grad., Luther Coll., Decorah, Iowa; JD, U. Minn. Dir. Region 5 U.S. EPA; commr. Minn. Pollution Control Agy., Minn. Dept. Human Svcs.; judge Minn. Ct. Appeals; assoc. justice Minn. Supreme Ct., 1991-98; v.p. U. Minn., 1998—. Chmn. bd. regional planning agy. Met. Coun. Mem. Ctr. Victims of Torture; mem. Minn. Advocates, LWV; past bd. dirs. St. Paul United Way, Camp DuNord, Project Environment Found., Clean Sites. Office: U Minn 11 Morrill Hall 100 Church St SE Minneapolis MN 55455-0110

GARDIN, JULIUS MARKUS, cardiologist, educator; b. Detroit, Jan. 14, 1949; s. Abram and Fania (Toba) G.; m. Susan Deanne Kelemen, Dec. 19, 1982; children: Adam Lev, Tova Michal, Margot Anne. BS with high distinction, U. Mich., 1968, MD cum laude, 1972. Diplomate Am. Bd. Internal Medicine; cert. cardiovascular diseases. Intern then resident in medicine U. Mich., Ann Arbor, 1972-75; fellow in cardiology Georgetown U., Washington, 1975-77; dir. cardiology noninvasive lab., staff cardiologist Lakeside VA Med. Ctr., Chgo., 1977-79; staff cardiologist, asst. prof. Med. Sch. Northwestern U., 1978-79; dir. cardiology noninvasive lab. Irvine Med. Ctr. U. Calif., Orange, 1979-2000, from asst. prof. to assoc. prof. Irvine Med. Ctr., 1979-89, prof., 1989-2000, chief cardiology Irvine, 1994-99; prof. Wayne State U., Detroit, 2000—; St. John Guild disting. chair, chief div. cardiology St. John Hosp. and Med. Ctr., 2000—. Acting chief cardiology Long Beach (Calif.) VA Med. Ctr., 1982-84. Co-editor: Textbook of Two-Dimensional Echocardiography, 1983; editor: Update on Cardiovascular Diagnostics, 1982; assoc. editor Am. Jour. Cardiac Imaging, 1985-97; assoc. editor (text): Preventive Cardiology, 2000; mem. editl. bd. Archives of Internal Medicine and Chest, 1978-88, Am. Jour. Noninvasive Cardiology, 1985—, Am. Jour. Cardiology, 1987-94, 96—, Cardiovascular Imaging, 1988—, Echocardiography, 1985—, Jour. Am. Coll. Cardiology, 1990-94, 2001—; cardiovasc. area editor Jour. Clin. Ultrasound, 1989-94, Jour. Am. Soc. Echocardiography, 1992-2001; contbr. articles to profl. jours. Maj. Med. Svc. Corps, USAR. Grantee Am. Heart Assn., 1980-82, 83-84, 99—, Nat. Heart Lung and Blood Inst., 1988—. Fellow ACP, Am. Coll. Cardiology (physician workforce adv., health care reform and echocardiography coms., 1993-99), Am. Heart Assn. (fellow coun. clin. cardiology, coun. epidemiology and prevention, coun. cardiovascular radiology), Soc. Geriatric Cardiology (v.p. 1990-92, pres. 1992-93); mem. Internat. Cardiac Doppler Soc. (sec., bd. dirs., chmn. Pan-Am. sect. 1984—, v.p. 1988-90, pres. 1990-92), Am. Soc. Echocardiography (bd. dirs., treas. 1989-91, v.p. 1991-93, pres. 1993-95, chmn. nomenclature and stds. 1991-95, chmn. task force on standardized echo report 1999—), U. Mich. Med. Ctr. Alumni Assn. (bd. govs. 1979-81), Phi Beta Kappa, Alpha Omega Alpha, Phi Delta Epsilon. Jewish. Office: St John Hosp and Med Ctr PBII Ste 470 22201 Moross Rd Detroit MI 48236 E-mail: julius.gardin@stjohn.org.

GARDINER, JOHN ANDREW, political science educator; b. Niagara Falls, N.Y., July 10, 1937; s. William Cecil and Anne Charlotte (Hicks) G.; m. Jane Enstrom, Nov. 6, 1993; children: Margaret, Allison, Barrett. BA, Princeton U., 1959; MA, Yale U., 1962; LLB, Harvard U., 1963, PhD, 1966. Bar: Mass. 1963. Asst. prof. U. Wis., Madison, 1965-68; assoc. prof. SUNY, Stony Brook, 1968-69; chief rsch. planning Nat. Inst. Justice, Washington, 1969-71, dir. rsch. ops., 1971-73, asst. dir., 1973-74; prof. polit. sci. U. Ill., Chgo., 1974—, head dept. polit. sci., 1974-76, dir. office social sci. rsch., 1987—2002, acting assoc. dean Liberal Arts and Scis., 1991—92, 2000—02. Author: Fraud Control Game, 1984, Decisions for Sale, 1978, Politics of Corruption, 1970, Traffic and the Police 1969; contbr. articles to profl. jours. V.p. Ill. Citizens for Better Care, Chgo., 1988—90; rsch. dir. Chgo. Ethics Project, 1986—88. Rsch. fellow Am. Judicature Soc., 1985-86. Mem. Phi Beta Kappa. Office: U Ill Office Pol Sci M/C 276 1007 W Harrison St Chicago IL 60607-7137 E-mail: gracelan@uic.edu.

GARDNER, BRIAN E. lawyer; b. Des Moines, July 13, 1952; s. Lawrence E. and Sarah I. (Hill) G.; m. Rondi L. Veland, Aug. 7, 1976; children: Meredith Anne, Stephanie Lynn, John Clinton. BS, Iowa State U., 1974; JD, U. Iowa, 1978. Bar: Iowa 1978, Mo. 1978, Kans. 1979, U.S. Ct. Appeals (10th cir.) 1980, U.S. Dist. Ct. Kans. 1979, U.S. Dist. Ct. (we. dist.) Mo. 1978. Assoc. Morrison, Hecker, Curtis, Kuder & Parrish, Kansas City, Mo., 1978-80, Parker & Handsaker, Nevada, Iowa, 1980-81, Morrison, Hecker, Curtis, Kuder & Parrish, Overland Park, Kans., 1981-83; ptnr. Morrison & Hecker, Kansas City, Mo., 1983—, mng. ptnr., 1990-93, 96—; city atty. Mission Hills, Kans., 1992—. Bd. dirs. Overland Park Conv. and Visitors Bur., 1985-97, chmn., 1988-90; dir., mem. exec. com. Johnson County C.C. Found., Overland Park, 1990—, pres., 1997-98; bd. dirs. KCPT, 1993-99, 2000—, chmn., 1997-98; active Kansas City Area Devel. Coun., 1992—, Civic Coun. Greater Kansas City, 1998—. Mem. Kans. Bar Assn., Kans. Assn. Def. Counsel, Kansas City Met. Bar Assn., Mo. Bar Assn., Johnson County Bar Assn., Blue Hills Country Club, Cardinal Key, Phi Beta Kappa. Lutheran. Avocation: golf. Office: Morrison & Hecker LLP 2600 Grand Blvd Kansas City MO 64108-4606

GARDNER, CHARLES OLDA, plant geneticist and breeder, design consultant, analyst; b. Tecumseh, Neb., Mar. 15, 1919; s. Olda Cecil and Frances E. (Stover) G.; m. Wanda Marie Steinkamp, June 9, 1947; children— Charles Olda, Jr., Lynda Frances, Thomas Edward, Richard Alan B.S., U. Nebr., 1941, M.S., 1948; M.B.A., Harvard U., 1943; Ph.D., N.C. State U., 1951. Asst. extension agronomist U. Nebr., Lincoln, 1946-48, assoc. prof., 1952-57, chmn. statis. lab., 1957-68, prof., 1957-70, regents prof., 1970-89, prof. emeritus, 1989—, interim head Biometrics Ctr., 1988-89; asst. statistician N.C. State U., Raleigh, 1951-52. Vis. prof. U. Wis., 1962-63; cons. CIMMYT and Rockefeller Found., Mex., Latin Am., 1964—, cons., CIBA-GEIGY, Eastern half of U.S., 1983; cons., lectr. Dept. Agr., Queensland, Australia, 1977; cons., lectr. maize program Kasetsart U. and Ministry of Agr., Bangkok, 1990; spl. lectr. advanced maize breeding course for leaders of nat. maize programs in developing countries Internat. Ctr. for Maize and Wheat Improvement, El Batan, Mex., 1989, 91, 93. Contbr. articles to profl. jours. Elder, Eastridge Presbyterian Ch.; pres. Eastridge PTA. Served to capt., U.S. Army, 1943-46 Recipient Outstanding Research and Creativity award U. Nebr., 1981, USDA Disting. Service award, 1988, Award of Merit U. Nebr. Alumni Assn., 1996. Fellow Am. Soc. of Agronomy (pres. 1982, agronomic service award, 1988), Crop Sci. Soc. of Am. (pres. 1975, recipient Crop Sci. award, 1978, DeKalb-Pfizer Crop Sci. Disting. Career award 1984), AAAS (chmn. sect. O com. 1987); mem. Am. Genetic Assn., Genetic Soc. of Am., Biometric Soc. (mem. regional com.), Sigma Xi, Gamma Sigma Delta (Internat. Disting. Svc. Agr. 1977). Republican. Presbyterian Avocations: photography; golf; fishing; gardening. Home: 5835 Meadowbrook Ln Lincoln NE 68510-4026 Office: U Neb Dept Biometry Lincoln NE 68583-0712

GARDNER, CHESTER STONE, electrical and computer engineering educator, consultant; b. Jamaica, N.Y., Mar. 29, 1947; s. Frederick Rothrick and June Marie (Miller) G.; m. Nancy Christine Cunningham, Sept. 14, 1968; children: Nathan Fredrick, Jeremy Collin. BS, Mich. State U., 1969; MS, Northwestern U., 1971, PhD, 1973. Mem. tech. staff Bell Telephone Labs., Naperville, Ill., 1969-71; asst. prof. U. Ill., Urbana, 1973-77, assoc. prof., 1977-81, prof., 1981—, assoc. dean engring., 1987—, acting dean engring., v.p. acad. affairs, 1988-89. Sr. v.p. Quantum Labs., Inc., Laurel, Md., 1983-88; Beckman assoc. U. Ill. Ctr. Advanced Study.; cons. Caterpillar, Inc., 1978-85, Deere & Co., Ill., 1981-85, C.E. U.S. Army, 1978-88, USN, Washington, 1981-84, No. Ill. Gas Co., 1980-82, Sandia Nat. Lab., N.Mex., 1985, Booz-Allen & Hamilton, 1984, TRW value div., Ohio, 1982-84, GE Astro Space div., Pa., 1988—. Contbr. over 240 pub. articles, tech. reports and conf. papers; patentee in field. Summer fellow Air Force Geophysic Lab., 1985. Fellow IEEE (chair region 4 tech. activities 1979-80), Optical Soc. Am. (chair atmospheric optics tech. group 1982-84); mem. Am. Geophys. Union, Am. Meteorol. Soc. (com. on laser atmospheric studies), Sigma Xi, Tau Beta Pi, Eta Kappa Nu. Avocations: canoeing, hiking, skiing. Home: 1904 Trout Valley Dr Champaign IL 61822-9784 Office: U Ill 506 S Wright St Urbana IL 61801-3620

GARDNER, HOWARD ALAN, travel marketing executive, travel writer and editor; b. Rockford, Ill., June 24, 1920; s. Ellis Ralph and Leanor (Roseman) G.; m. Marjorie Ruth Klein, Sept. 29, 1945; children: Jill, Jeffrey. B.A., U. Mich., 1941. With advt. dept. Chgo. Tribune, 1941-43; mgr. promotion dept. Esquire mag., 1943-46; advt. mgr. Mrs. Klein's Food Products Co., 1946-48; pres. Sales-Aide Service Co., 1948-56, Gardner & Stein, 1956-59, Gardner, Stein & Frank, Inc., Chgo., 1959-83, Fun-derful World, Chgo., 1983—. Mem. Travel Industry Assn. Am., Confrerie de la Chaine des Rotisseurs (bailli hon., officier commandeur), Am. Geog. Soc., Nat. Geog. Soc., Connoisseurs Internat. (bd. dirs.), Phi Beta Kappa. Clubs: Travelers' Century, Carlton, International. Home: 100 E Bellevue Pl Chicago IL 60611-1157 Office: Fun-derful World 100 E Bellevue Pl Chicago IL 60611-1157

GARDNER, LEE M. automotive parts executive; Pres., co-COO Masco Tech, Taylor, Mich., pres., COO, 1998—. Office: Masco Tech Inc 21001 Van Born Rd Taylor MI 48180

GARDNER, RANDALL, state legislator, realtor; b. Bowling Green, Ohio, Aug. 20, 1958; s. Dallas E. and Velma (Brownson) G.; m. Sandra Kay Ford; children: Brooks, Christine, Austin. BS, Bowling Green State U., 1981, MA, 1987. Journalist Daily Sentinel-Tribune, Bowling Green, 1981-86; tchr. Otsego (Ohio) Local Schs., 1981-86; realtor, Bowling Green; mem. Ohio Ho. of Reps., Columbus, 1985-2000, asst. minority whip; mem. Ohio Senate from 2nd dist., Columbus, 2001—. Pres. Wood County Young Reps. Club, 1976-80; co-chmn. 5th Dist. Reagan for Pres. Com., 1980; dist. del. Rep. Nat. Conv., 1980, 84; vice chmn. Wood County Bd. Elections, 1982-85; exec. com. Wood County Rep. Com., 1982-86. Recipient Watchdog of Treasury award; Jennings scholar. Mem. Ohio Assn. Election Ofcls., Ohio Edn. Assn., Wood County Hist. Soc., Wood County Farm Bur., Legis. Exch. Coun., Sons Am. Legion, Omicron Delta Kappa. Home: 14900 Mitchell Rd Bowling Green OH 43402-8900

GARDNER, ROBERT A. state legislator; b. Algeria, Sept. 22, 1945; BA, postgrad, Bowling Green State U., Clev. State U., Kent State U. Mem. 18th dist. Ohio Senate, Columbus, 1997—. Trustee Madison Twp., 1982-96; commr. Lake County, 1987-96. Mem. Mason, Am. Legion. Office: Senate Bldg Rm 034, Ground Fl Columbus OH 43215

GARDNER, WILLIAM EARL, university dean; b. Hopkins, Minn., Oct. 11, 1928; s. William Henry and Ida (Swenson) G.; m. Crystal K. Meriwether, July 5, 1990; children by previous marriage: Mary Gardner Fenwick, Bret, Anne Gardner Smith, Eric. B.S., U. Minn., 1950, M.A., 1959, Ph.D., 1961. Tchr. pub. schs., Balaton, Rockford, New Ulm, Minn., 1950-54; instr. Univ. High Sch., U. Minn., Mpls., 1954-61; prof. edn. U. Minn., 1961—; assoc. dean U. Minn. (Coll. Edn.), 1970-76, dean, 1976-91, dean emeritus, 1991—; dir. Minn. Curriculum Lab., 1965-67. Vis. prof. U. York, Eng., 1967-68; Mem. Bd. Edn., St. Louis Park, Minn., 1971-77; mem. Tchr. Standards and Certification Commn., 1973-80; mem. Nat. Council Accreditation of Tchr. Edn., 1979-85; chmn. Minn. Council Econ. Edn., 1985-87; trustee Joint Council Econ. Edn., 1985— . Author: (with others) Education and Social Crisis, 1967, Social Studies in Secondary Schools, 1970, Selected Case Studies in Am. History, 1971, The Education of Tchrs., 1982. Mem. Nat. Coun. Social Studies, Am. Ednl. Rsch. Assn., Am. Assn. Colls. for Tchr. Edn. (bd. dirs. 1984-87, pres. 1987-88), Assn. Supervision and Curriculum Devel., Luth. Human Rels. Assn., Phi Delta Kappa. Lutheran. Office: U Minn Coll Edn 136 B Burton Hall 178 Pillsbury Dr SE Minneapolis MN 55455-0296

GARDOCKI, CHRISTOPHER, professional football player; b. Stone Mountain, Ga., Feb. 7, 1970; m. Sally Gardocki. Student, Clemson U. Punter Chgo. Bears, 1991-94, Indpls. Colts, 1995-98, Cleve. Browns, 1998—. Co-creator game NFL Trivia Blitz. Named to Pro Bowl, 1996. Office: Cleve Browns 1085 W 3rd St Cleveland OH 44114-1001 also: Cleveland Browns 76 Lou Groza Blvd. Berea OH 44017

GARDUNIO, JOSEPH, landscaping company executive; b. Chgo., Feb. 12, 1955; m. Marta Salas; children: Joey, Ricky, Alex, Selena. Pres. Unico Landscaping Inc., 1991—. Office: Unico Landscaping Inc 5119 S Hoyne Ave Chicago IL 60609-5513

GARFINKEL, JANE E. lawyer; b. N.Y.C., Dec. 2, 1952; d. Albert E. and Rita H. (Halpern) G.; m. Louis F. Solimine, May 20, 1979. BA, Wheaton Coll., 1974; MA, U. Mich., 1975, JD, 1979. Bar: Ohio 1980. Assoc. Smith & Schnacke, Cin., 1980-88, ptnr., 1988-89, Thompson Hine LLP, Cin., 1989—. Office: Thompson Hine LLP 312 Walnut St Ste 1400 Cincinnati OH 45202-4089 E-mail: jane.garfinkel@thompsonhine.com.

GARLAND, JAMES C. college president; b. Columbia, Mo., Aug. 11, 1942; BA in Physics, Princeton U., 1964; D in Solid State Physics, Cornell U., 1969; postgrad., Cambridge U., 1969-70. Asst. prof. physics Ohio State U., 1970-75, assoc. prof. physics, 1975-80, prof., 1980-96, chairperson dept. of physics; pres. Miami U., Oxford, Ohio, 1996—. Acting vice pres. for rsch. and grad. studies Ohio State U., dir. materials rsch. lab., 1986-90; pres., bd. dirs. Ohio State U. Rsch. Found., 1982-83. Contbr. articles to profl. jours. Recipient numerous rsch. grants; postdoctoral fellowship NSF. Fellow Am. Phys. Soc. Office: Miami U McGuffey Hall Oxford OH 45056

GARMAN, RITA B. judge; b. Aurora, Ill., Nov. 19, 1943; m. Gill Garman; children: Sara Ellen, Andrew Gill. BS in econs. suma cum laude, U. Ill. , 1965; JD with distinction, U. Iowa, 1968. Asst. state atty. Vermilion County, 1969—73; pvt. practice Sebat, Swanson, Banks, Lessen & Garman, 1973; assoc. cir. judge, 1974—86; cir. judge Fifth Jud. Cir., 1986—95, presiding cir. judge, 1987—95; judge Fourth Dist. Appellate Ct., 1996—2001; Supreme Ct. justice Ill. State Supreme Ct., 2001—. Mem.: Ill. Judge's Assn., Vermilion County Bar Assn., Iowa Bar Assn., Ill. State Bar Assn. Office: 3607 N Vermilion Ste 1 Danville IL 61832*

GARMAN, TERESA AGNES, state legislator; b. Ft. Dodge, Iowa, Aug. 29, 1937; d. John Clement and Barbara Marie (Korsa) Lennon; m. Merle A. Garman, Aug. 5, 1961; children: Laura Ann Garman Hansen, Rachel Irene Garman Coder, Robert Sylvester, Sarah Teresa Garman Powers. Grad. high sch., Ft. Dodge. With employee relations dept. 3M Co., Ames, Iowa, 1974-86; mem. Iowa Ho. of Reps., Des Moines, 1986—. Asst. majority leader, mem. platform com., del. Rep. Nat. Conv., 1988, del., mem. platform com., 1992, del., 1996; mem. Iowa Rep. Ctrl. Com. Mem. Rep. Farm Policy Coun., Story County Rep. Women, Story County Pork Prodrs., Farm Bur., Story City C. of C., Nev. C. of C. Roman Catholic. Avocations: horseback riding, gardening. Home: 1799 Old Bloomington Rd Ames IA 50010-9469 Office: State Capitol Des Moines IA 50319-0001

GARMEL, MARION BESS SIMON, retired journalist; b. El Paso, Tex., Oct. 15, 1936; d. Marcus and Frieda (Alfman) Simon; m. Raymond Lewis Garmel, Nov. 28, 1965 (dec. Feb. 1986); 1 child, Cynthia Rogers; 1 stepchild, Christine Blum. Student, U. Tex., El Paso, 1954-55; BJ, U. Tex., Austin, 1958. Exec. sec. Nat. Student Assn., Phila., 1958-59, pub. rels. dir., 1960-61; sec. World Assembly Youth, Paris, Brussels, 1959-60; dictationist Wall Street Jour., Washington, 1961; libr., staff writer Nat. Observer, Silver Spring, Md., 1961-70; art critic Indpls. News, 1971-91, editor Free Time sect., 1975-91, critic radio and TV, 1991-95; theater critic Indpls. Star and News, 1995-99; television critic Indpls. News, 1995-99; theater critic Indpls. Star, 1999—2002, ret., 2002. Mem. Nat. Fedn. Press Women (1st Place Critics award 1974), Hadassah Women's Zionist Orgn. Am. (life), Women's Press Club Ind. (1st Place Critics award 1995, 2002). Jewish. Avocation: tennis. Home: 226 E 45th St Indianapolis IN 46205-1712 E-mail: marion.garmel@indystar.com.

GARN, STANLEY MARION, physical anthropologist, educator; b. New London, Conn., Oct. 27, 1922; s. Harry and Sadie Edith (Cohen) G.; m. Priscilla Crozier, Apr. 8, 1950; children: Barbara, William David. AB, Harvard U., 1942, AM, 1947, PhD, 1948. Rsch. assoc. chem. engring. Chem. Warfare Svc. Devel. Lab. MIT, 1942-44; tech. editor Polaroid Co., 1944-46; cons. applied anthropology, 1946-47; rsch. fellow cardiology Mass. Gen. Hosp., Boston, 1946-52; instr. anthropology Harvard U., 1948-52; anthropologist Forsyth Dental Infirmary, Boston, 1947-52; dir. Forsyth face size project Army Chem. Corps, 1950-52; chmn. dept. growth and genetics Fels Rsch. Inst., Yellow Springs, Ohio, 1952-68; fellow Ctr. Human Growth and Devel. U. Mich., Ann Arbor, also prof. nutrition and anthropology, 1968-92, prof. emeritus, 1993—. Raymond Pearl lectr. Human Biol. Coun., 1992—; E.B.D. Neuhauser lectr. Soc. Pediatric Radiology, 1981. Author: Human Races, 1970, Gain and Loss of Cortical Bone, 1970; also contbr. over 1000 articles to profl. jours.; editorial bds. numerous jours. Recipient Disitng. Svc. award, U. Mich., Charles Darwin Lifetime Achievement award, Am. Assn. Phys. Anthropologists, 1994, Franz Boas award, Human Biol. Coun., 2002. Fellow AAAS, Am. Acad. Pediatrics (hon. assoc.), Am. Anthropol. Assn., Am. Acad. Arts and Scis., Human Biology Coun., Am. Soc. Clin. Nutrition, Am. Soc. Nutrition Scis.; mem. NAS, Am. Assn. Phys. Anthropologists, Internat. Assn. Dental Rsch., Internat. Orgn. Study Human Devel., Am. Soc. Naturalists, Internat. Assn. Human Biologists (coun.). Office: U Mich Ctr Human Growth & Devel 300 N Ingalls St Ann Arbor MI 48109-2007 Home: 827 Asa Gray Dr #258 Ann Arbor MI 48105-2566

GARNER, JIM D. state legislator, lawyer; b. Coffeyville, Kans., June 14, 1963; s. Wayne W. and Carol L. Garner. AA with honors, Coffeyville C.C., 1983; BA in History with distinction, U. Kans., 1985, JD, 1988. Bar: Kans. 1988. Jud. clk. for Dale E. Saffels U.S. Dist. Judge, Kans., 1988-90; atty. Hall, Levy, Lively, DeVore, Belot and Bell, Coffeyville, 1990-92; pvt. practice, 1992—; mem. Kans. Ho. of Reps., 1991—. Minority leader Kans. House of Reps., 1999—; mem. assembly on fed. issues Nat. Conf. of State Legislatures; mem. Program for Emerging Polit. Leaders, Darden Sch. of Bus., U. Va., 1994, Bowhay Inst. for Legis. Leadership Devel., Coun. of State Govts., U. Wis., 1995. Active cmty. co-chair, City of Coffeyville's Youth Focus Task Force, 1998; adv. com. Youth and Bus. Tng. Program; bd. dirs. Hospice Care Inc., Coffeyville, 1993-97, Pioneer chpt. ARC, 1998—; mem. task force Coffeyville C.C. Honors Program, 1998—; leadership Coffeyville Class of 1995; mem. legis. adv. bd. Dem. Leadership Coun., 1999—; mem. bd. govs. U. Kans. Law Sch., 2000—. Mem. Kans. Bar Assn., Order of Coif, Phi Alpha Theta, Phi Kappa Phi, Lions, Rotary. Home: 902A Lewark St Coffeyville KS 67337-3108 Office: PO Box 538 114 W 9th St Coffeyville KS 67337-5810

GARNER, PHIL, professional baseball manager; b. Jefferson City, Tenn., Apr. 30, 1949; m. Carol; children: Eric, Bethany, Ty. BS, U. Tenn., Knoxville, 1973. Profl. baseball player Oakland Athletics, 1973-76, Pitts. Pirates, 1977-81, Houston Astros, 1981-87, L.A. Dodgers, 1987, San Francisco Giants, 1988; coach Houston Astros, 1989-91; mgr. Milw. Brewers, 1991-99, Detroit Tigers, 1999—. Named to All-Star team, 1976, 80, 81. Office: Detroit Tigers 2100 Woodward Ave Detroit MI 48201-3474*

GARNETT, JESS, former state legislator; Pres. Garnett Wood Products, 1965—. Home: PO Box 801 West Plains MO 65775-0801

GARNETT, KEVIN, professional basketball player; Profl. basketball player Minnesota Timberwolves, 1995—. Named to All-NBA Third Team, 1998-99, NBA Player of Week, USA Basketball Sr. Nat. Team, 1999, All-Rookie Second Team, 1995-96. Office: Minnestoa Timberwolves 600 1st Ave N Minneapolis MN 55403-1400*

GAROFALO, DONALD R. window manufacturing executive; CEO, pres. Andersen Corp., Bayport, Minn. Office: Andersen Corp 100 4th Ave N Bayport MN 55003-1096

GARON, PHILIP STEPHEN, lawyer; b. Duluth, Minn., Nov. 11, 1947; s. Lawrence and Helen (Cohen) G.; m. Phyllis Sue Ansel, Mar. 22, 1970; children: Edward B., Sara B. BA summa cum laude, U. Minn., 1969, JD summa cum laude, 1972. Bar: Minn. 1972, D.C. 1973, U.S. Dist. Ct. Minn. 1974. Assoc. Covington & Burling, Washington, 1972-74, Faegre & Benson, Mpls., 1974-79, ptnr., 1980—. Mem. mgmt. com. Faegre & Benson, 1992—, chmn., 2001—. Co-author: Minnesota Corporation Law & Practice, 1996 (Burton award for legal writing 2001). Bd. dirs. Herzl Camp, Webster, Wis., 1985-91, Beth El Synagogue, Mpls., 1989-99, v.p., 1993-96. Mem. Minn. Bar Assn. (pres. exec. coun. bus. law sect. 1996-97). Avocations: tennis, reading, bridge. Office: Faegre & Benson 2200 Wells Fargo Ctr 90 S 7th St Ste 2200 Minneapolis MN 55402-3901

GARPOW, JAMES EDWARD, retired financial executive; b. Detroit, July 30, 1944; s. Roy Joseph and Jeanne Beechner (Brader) G.; m. Elizabeth Marie Conte, Aug. 30, 1969; children: Barbara Jean, Susan Marie. BBA, U. Mich., 1968. CPA, Mich. Audit mgr. Ernst & Young, Detroit, 1966-73; mgr. corp. acctg. Fed. Mogul Corp., 1973-79; corp. contr. LOF Plastics, Inc., 1979-80; treas., CFO, KMS Industries, Inc., Ann Arbor, Mich., 1980-83; asst. sec., corp. contr. Simpson Industries, Inc., 1983—, treas., 1995-99; ret., 1999. Mem. AICPA, Mich. Assn. CPAs, Fin. Execs. Inst., Beta Alpha Psi, Alpha Kappa Psi. E-mail: jgarpow@attbi.com.

GARR, DANIEL FRANK, restaurateur; b. Chgo., Sept. 4, 1950; s. Daniel Jacob and Sophie Evelen (Kurranty) G.; m. Dawn Marie Ciciora, May 7, 1983. AA, No. Ill. U., 1970; cert. recording engr., Inst. Audio Research,

1974. V.p. Garbaczewski Corp., Chgo., 1979-89, pres., 1989—; treas., chief exec. officer Gemtech Packaging Inc., 1990—. Pres. Fantasy Food Corp., Chgo., 1985-93; v.p. Dynamic Design Products, 1990; pres. Proline Tools, Md., 1998—. Bd. dirs. Am. Cancer Soc., 1993. Republican. Roman Catholic. Avocations: music, racquetball, photography. Home: 13713 Cavecreek Ct Lockport IL 60441-8653 Office: Chesdan Restaurant 4465 S Archer Ave Chicago IL 60632-2845

GARRATT, REGINALD GEORGE, electronics executive; b. Birmingham, Eng., Sept. 25, 1929; came to the U.S., 1974; s. Wallace Thomas and Beatrice Maud (Round) G.; m. Gwendoline Jean Parry (dec. 1986); children: Mark, Jonathan, Sean; m. Gail Elizabeth Mansfield, July 1, 1989. Degree in mech. engring., Aston U., 1951. Dir. mktg. Honeywell (UK) Ltd., London, 1965-70; mng. dir. Honeywell (South Africa) Ltd., Johannesburg, 1970-74; gen. mktg. mgr. components divsn. Honeywell, Freeport, Ill., 1974-77; v.p. mktg. Knowles Electronics, Inc., Itasca, 1977-89, pres., COO, 1989-91, pres., CEO, 1991-97, chmn., CEO, 1997—. Bd. dirs. Hear Now, Denver, 1993—, Hearing Industries Assn., Washington, 1983—, Better Hearing Inst., Washington, 1981-90. Avocations: squash, tennis, bridge, golf, antiques. Home: 138 Circle Ridge Dr Burr Ridge IL 60527-8379 Office: Knowles Electronics Inc 1151 Maplewood Dr Itasca IL 60143-2071

GARRETT, BOB, radio personality; Radio personality WEBN, Cin. Office: WEBN 1111 St Gregory St Cincinnati OH 45202

GARRETT, DEAN, professional basketball player; b. L.A., Nov. 27, 1966; s. Robert and Bobbie G.; m. Natasha Taylor; 1 child, Devyreau. Student, San Francisco City Coll., 1984-86; B of Criminal Justice, Ind. U., 1988. Center PAOK, Greece, 1995-96, Minn. Timberwolves, Minneapolis, 1996-97, 98—, Denver Nuggets, 1997-98. Avocations: baseball, football. Office: c/o Minn Timberwolves 600 1st Ave North Minneapolis MN 55403-9801

GARRETT, DWAYNE EVERETT, veterinary clinic executive; Office: Wentzville Veterinary 602 E Pearce Blvd Wentzville MO 63385-1538

GARRIGAN, RICHARD THOMAS, finance educator, consultant, editor; b. Cleve., Mar. 4, 1938; s. Walter John and Priscilla Marie (Hill) G.; m. Kristine Ottesen, Dec. 26, 1962; 1 child, Matthew Osborne. BS summa cum laude, Ohio State U., 1961, MA, 1963; MS, U. Wis., 1966, PhD, 1973. Asst. prof. fin. U. Wis., Whitewater, 1974-76, assoc. prof., 1976-77; v.p. rsch. Real Estate Rsch. Corp., Chgo., 1975-76; presdl. exch. exec. Fed. Home Loan Bank Bd., Washington, 1977-78; assoc. prof. DePaul U., Chgo., 1978-83, prof., 1983—. Mem. Midwestern regional adv. bd. Fed. Nat. Mortgage Assn., 1993-96; mem. adv. bd. Fed. Home Loan Bank, Chgo., 1996-98; bd. dirs. Fed. Home Loan Bank Chgo., 1983-86. Co-editor: The Handbook of Mortgage Banking, 1985, Real Estate Investment Trusts, Structure, Analysis and Strategy, 1998; editor Dow Jones-Irwin Series in Real Estate, 1987-90; contbr. articles to profl. jours. Served with U.S. Army, 1955-58. Alfred P. Sloan scholar, 1959-61; recipient Excellence award Haskins and Sells, 1960, Achievement award Pres.'s of U.S. Commn. on Exec. Exchange, 1978; fellow Mershon Nat. Security, Ohio State U., 1961-62, urban studies Ford Found., 1964-65, bus. Ford Found., 1965-66. Mem. Am. Real Estate Soc., Am. Real Estate and Urban Econs. Assn., Bldg. Owners and Mgrs. Assn. of Chgo. (adv. bd. 1994-98), Sphinx, Univ. Club Chgo., Lambda Alpha Internat. (Ely chpt. sec. 1984, v.p. 1985, pres. 1986), Beta Gamma Sigma, Phi Kappa Phi, Phi Eta Sigma. Home: 10002 Meadowdale Cir Spring Grove IL 60081-8687 Office: DePaul U Fin Dept 1 E Jackson Blvd Chicago IL 60604-2201

GARRIGAN, WILLIAM HENRY, III, firefighter, paramedic; b. Evergreen Park, Ill., Apr. 5, 1954; s. William Henry Jr. and Mary Jane (O'Connell) G.; m. Melissa Ann Vaughan, Aug. 2, 1980; children: William, Vaughan, Amanda. AA, Coll. of DuPage, Glen Ellyn, Ill., 1975; grad. paramedic tng., Loyola Med. Ctr., Maywood, Ill., 1976; student, No. Ill. U., 1976-77; BS, So. Ill. U., 1987. Cert. instr. CPR, Am. Heart Assn.; adv. cert. fire fighter III; cert. fire apparatus engr.; cert. fire svc. instr. I. Firefighter/paramedic North Palos (Ill.) Fire Dept., 1977-78, Oak Brook (Ill.) Fire Dept., 1979—, asst. coord. emergency med. svcs., 1983-87, coord. emergency med. svcs., 1987-97. Mem. edn. com. for paramedic edn. Village of Downers Grove, Ill., 1990—; mem. safety com. Village of Oak Brook, 1987—; mem. ambulance report com. Good Samaritan Hosp., Downers Grove, 1988—. ACLs provider Heart Assn. South Cook County, Ill., 1986—; com. mem., advancement chmn. Troop 699, Boy Scouts of Am., Palos Park, Ill., AYSO coach, 1994, active Quigley South High Sch. Alumni Assn., 1972—; trainer, coach Palos Panthers Soccer Club, 1999. Recipient acknowledgement of contbn. Dept. Pub. Health, State of Ill., 1987, recognition and appreciation of dedication and svc. Village of Oak Brook, 1989. Mem. Nat. Assn. EMTs, Ill. Profl. Firefighters Assn., North Palos Firemen's Assn. (pres. 1982-84, Outstanding Svc. award 1988), Profl. Assn. Specialty Divers, Dive Rescue Inc. Internat., Phi Kappa Sigma Alumni Assn. Republican. Roman Catholic. Avocations: golf, water skiing, scuba diving, swimming. Office: Oak Brook Fire Dept 1212 Oak Brook Rd Oak Brook IL 60523-4603

GARRIGUS, UPSON STANLEY, animal science and international agriculture educator; b. Willimantic, Conn., July 2, 1917; s. Harry Lucien and Bertha May (Patterson) B.; m. Olive Tyler, July 2, 1942; children— Beth Ellen, Mark Tyler B.S. with high honors, U. Conn., 1940; M.S., U. Ill., 1942, Ph.D., 1948; cert., Washington and Lee U., 1943, Sorbonne, 1944. Asst. U. Conn., Storrs, 1936-40; grad. asst. U. Ill., Urbana-Champaign, 1940-42, 46-48, asst. prof., then assoc. prof., 1948-55, prof., 1955—, head Sheep divsn., 1949-64, head Runinant divsn., 1964-70, prof. animal sci., internat. agr., assoc. head dept. animal sci., 1972-87, prof. emeritus, 1987—. Mem. Am. Dehydrator's Rsch. Coun., 1958-70; mem. Nutrient Requirements of Sheep Com., NRC, 1953-75, Nonprotein Nitrogen Utilization Com., NRC, 1970-76; cons. Midwest Univs., Consortium Internat. Activities Higher Edn., Indonesia, 1980, AID, Thailand, 1981, U. New Eng., Australia, Higher Edn. Indonesia, 1989. Contbr. numerous articles to profl. jours. Active Cmty. United Ch. of Christ; bd. dirs. Univ. YMCA, Champaign, Ill., 1956-62, 64-70; chmn. Baily Scholarships, 1972-76. Lt. maj. U.S. Army, 1942-46. Decorated Bronze Star. Recipient Nat. Block and Bridle Merit trophy, 1940; Service award Eastern States Exposition, 1959; Disting. Service award YMCA, 1970, 77; Animal Sci. Teaching and Counseling award U. Ill., 1980; Nat. Feed Ingredients Assn. travel fellow, 1971; outstanding alumni award Coll. Agriculture & Natural Resources U. Conn., 1996. Fellow AAAS, Am. Soc. Animal Sci. (Jean Claude Bouffault Meml. award in internat. animal agriculture 1994); mem. Soc. Exptl. Biology and Medicine, Am. Inst. Nutrition, Am. Inst. Biol. Sci., Coun. Agr. Sci. and Tech., Am. Registry Profl. Animal Scientists, Sigma Xi, Phi Kappa Phi, Phi Sigma, Gamma Sigma Delta. Home: 811 W William St Champaign IL 61820-5832 Office: 186 Animal Scis Lab 1207 W Gregory Dr Urbana IL 61801-4733 E-mail: garrigus@uiuc.edu.

GARRISON, CHARLES EUGENE, retired automotive executive; b. New London, Conn., Apr. 9, 1943; s. Charles Westel and Thelma Rae (Coleman) G.; m. Trudy Elizabeth Thorburn, Aug. 26, 1967 (div.); children: Matthew Charles, Mark Andrew; m. Beverley Halcyone Watkins, Apr. 19, 1991. BA, Mich. State U., 1965, MBA, 1966. Supr. service garage and motor pool Mich. State U., East Lansing, 1972, mgr. automotive services dept., 1972-2001, ret., 2001. Co-owner The Latest Scoop, 1980—; fleet mgmt. instr. various agys., 1985—; cons. in field, 1985—. Elder Holt Presbyn. Ch., 1975-77, mem. various coms., 1977-85; divsn. coord. United Way, 1972-73; mem. East Lansing Mass Transit com., 1972-75; judge Ingham County Fair, 1977-80. Capt. USAF, 1967-72. Recipient Vol. Achievement award United Way, 1984, 85, Cost Reduction Incentive award Nat. Assn. Coll. and Univ. Bus. Officers, Gov. Mich. Energy Mgmt. award, 1988, Spl. Energy Innovation award U.S. Dept. of Energy, 1990. Mem. Nat. Assn. Fleet Adminstrs., Big Ten Transp. Assn., U. Club. Mich. State U. (bd. dirs., pres. 1986-94), Kiwanis (sec. 1995-97, Internat. Diamond Single Svc. award 1982, Mich. dist. Disting. Pres. award 1982, Outstanding Bull. Editor 1983, Disting. Sec. award 1997). Lodge: Kiwanis (Internat. Diamond Single Service award 1982, Mich. dist. Disting. Pres. award 1982, Outstanding Bulletin Editor 1983). Avocations: golf, bowling, bridge, spectator sports. Home: 3730 Lott Ave Holt MI 48842-9414 E-mail: garris09@msu.edu., cegarris@pplant.msu.edu.

GARRISON, LARRY RICHARD, accounting educator; b. Kansas City, Mo., Jan. 10, 1951; s. Robert Milton and Virginia Claire (Huntington) G.; m. Sheila Caroline Murry, Aug. 10, 1973. BBA, Cen. Mo. State U., 1973; MS in Acctg., U. Mo., 1982; PhD, U. Nebr., 1986. CPA, Mo. Mgr. Garrison & Co., CPAs, Kansas City, 1973-79; controller G.F. & F. Enterprises, 1979-82; instr. U. Nebr., Lincoln, 1983-86; prof. U. Mo., Kansas City, 1986—. Exec. dir. Tax Policy Rsch. Project. Contbr. articles to profl. jours. Recipient Disting. Teaching award U. Nebr., 1984-85. Mem. Am. Inst. CPA's, Am. Taxation Assn., Mo. Soc. CPA's (Outstanding Educator of Yr. award 1999), Am. Acctg. Assn., Beta Alpha Psi, Beta Gamma Sigma. Office: U Mo 5100 Rockhill Rd Kansas City MO 64110-2481

GARSCADDEN, ALAN, physicist; b. Glasgow, Scotland, June 10, 1937; came to U.S., 1962; s. Andrew and Sarah Florence (Black) G.; m. Avril Margaret Thompson Garscadden, Jan. 24, 1962; children: A. Graeme, A.K. Neil, A.K. Gael, A.E. Hilary. BS (hon.), Queens U., Belfast, Ireland, 1958; PhD in Physics, 1962. Rsch. physicist Aerospace Rsch. Labs, Wright-Patterson AFB, 1962-73; lab. dir., 1973-75; rsch. physicist Aero Propulsion and Power Divsn., 1975-91; chief scientist Aero Propulsion Directorate, 1991-94, Wright Lab., 1995-97, Propulsion Directorate/Air Force Rsch. Lab., Wright-Patterson AFB, 1997—, Edwards AFB, Calif., 1997—. Adj. prof. physics Air Force Inst. Tech., Wright Patterson AFB, 1969—; bd. dirs. Von Karman Inst., Brussels; trustee Ohio Aerospace Inst., 1996-98. Contbr. articles to profl. jours. Commr. Planning Commn., Village of Yellow Springs, 1985-96. Recipient Disting. Svc. medal USAF, 1998. Fellow IEEE, Am. Phys. Soc., Inst. Physics, (U.K.);assoc. fellow AIAA. Avocation: history of colonial science. Office: AFRL/PR Air Force Rsch lab 1950 5th St Wright Patterson AFB OH 45433-7251

GARSON, ARNOLD HUGH, publishing executive; b. Lincoln, Nebr., May 29, 1941; s. Sam B. and Celia (Stine) Garson; m. Marilyn Grace Baird, Aug. 15, 1964; children: Scott Arnold, Christopher Baird, Gillian Grace, Megan Jane. BA, U. Nebr., 1964; MS, UCLA, 1965. Reporter Omaha World-Herald, 1965-69, Des Moines Tribune, 1969-72, city editor, 1972-75; reporter Des Moines Register, 1975-83, mng. editor, 1983-88; editor San Bernardino (Calif.) County Sun, 1988-96; pub., pres. Sioux Falls (S.D.) Argus Leader, 1996—; v.p. Gannett Pacific Newspaper Group, 2000—. V.p. S.D. Symphony Orch. Recipient Pub. Svc. Reporting award, Am. Polit. Sci. Assn., 1969, Mng. Editors Sweepstakes award, Iowa AP, 1976, John Hancock award for excellence in bus. and fin. journalism, 1979, Calif.-Nev. AP award for column writing, 1995. Mem.: S.D. Newspaper Assn. (past pres., bd. dirs.), Soc. Profl. Journalists, Am. Soc. Newspaper Editors. Jewish. Home: 5 S Riverview Hts Sioux Falls SD 57105-0252 Office: Sioux Falls Argus Leader PO Box 5034 Sioux Falls SD 57117-5034

GARTENHAUS, SOLOMON, physicist, educator; b. Kassel , Germany, Jan. 3, 1929; came to U.S., 1937, naturalized, 1943; s. Leopolt and Hanna (Brandler) G.; m. Johanna Lore Weisz, Aug. 30, 1953; children: Michael M., Kevin M. B.S., U. Pa., 1951; M.S., U. Ill., 1953, Ph.D., 1955. Instr. Stanford U., 1955-58; faculty physics Purdue U., Lafayette, Ind., 1958—, prof., 1963—; asst. dean Grad. Sch., 1972-77, sec. of faculties, 1980—. Disting. vis. prof. USAF Acad., Colo., 1977-78; dir. Purdue-Ind. Studienprogram, U. Hamburg, W. Ger., 1979-80; cons. Lockheed, summers 1958-60; officer, dir. Advanced Research Corp., 1961-65 Author: Elements of Plasma Physics, 1964, Physics-Basic Principles, 1975; contbr. articles to profl. jours. Fellow Am. Phys. Soc.; mem. N.Y. Acad. Scis., Am. Assn. Physics Tchrs., Phi Beta Kappa, Sigma Xi. Home: 2102 S 9th St Lafayette IN 47905-2132 Office: Purdue U Dept Physics Lafayette IN 47907 E-mail: garten@physics.purdue.edu.

GARTH, BRYANT GEOFFREY, law educator, foundation executive; b. San Diego, Dec. 9, 1949; s. William and Patricia (Feild) G.; m. Gwendolyn Sessions; children: Heather, Andrew, Daniela. BA magna cum laude, Yale U., 1972; JD, Stanford U., 1975; PhD, European U. Inst., Florence, Italy, 1979. Bar: Calif. 1975, Ind. 1988. Law clk. to judge U.S. Dist. Ct. (no. dist.) Calif., San Francisco, 1978-79; asst. prof. Ind. U., Bloomington, 1979-82, assoc. prof., 1982-85, prof., 1985-92, dean Law Sch., 1986-90; dir. Am. Bar Found., Chgo., 1990—. Cons. Ont. Law Reform Commn., 1984-85, 94, World Bank Argentina Project, 1993-94, World Bank Peru Project, 1996; vis. assoc. prof. U. Mich., Ann Arbor, 1983-84; bd. dirs. Internat. Human Rights Law Inst.; mem. bd. visitors Stanford U. Law Sch., 1993-2000. Author: Neighborhood Law Firms for the Poor, 1980; co-editor: Access to Justice: A World Survey, 1978, Access to Justice: Emerging Issues and Perspectives, 1979, Dealing in Virtue, 1996, Internationalization of Palace Wars, 2002; contbr. articles to profl. jours. V.p. H.G. & K.F. Montgomery Found. Rsch. grantee NSF, 1982, 91, 92, 95, 99, 2001, Nat. Inst. Dispute Resolution, 1985, Ind. Supreme Ct., 1989, Italian Coun. Rsch., 1989, Keck, 1995, MacArthur, 1997. Mem. Am. Law Inst., Law and Soc. Assn., Internat. Assn. Procedural Law. Democrat. Office: Am Bar Found 750 N Lake Shore Dr Chicago IL 60611-4403 E-mail: bggarth@abfn.org.

GARTNER, MICHAEL GAY, editor, television executive, baseball executive; b. Des Moines, Oct. 25, 1938; s. Carl David and Mary Marguerite (Gay) G.; m. Barbara Jeanne McCoy, May 25, 1968; children: Melissa, Christopher (dec.), Michael. BA, Carleton Coll., 1960; JD, NYU, 1969; LittD (hon.), Simpson Coll., 1984; LLD (hon.), James Madison U., 1989; LittD (hon.), Grand View Coll., 1990, Iowa Wesleyan Coll., 1997; LLD (hon.), Drake U., 2001. Bar: NY, Iowa. With Wall St. Jour., N.Y.C., 1960-74, page one editor, 1970-74; exec. editor Des Moines Register and Tribune, 1974-76, editor, 1976-82, editl. chmn., 1982-85, v.p., 1975-76, exec. v.p., 1977, pres., COO, 1978-85; editor Courier-Jour. and Louisville Times, 1986-87; gen. news exec. Gannett Co., 1987-88; pres. NBC News, 1988-93; editor, co-owner Ames (Iowa) Daily Tribune, 1986-99; chmn., majority-owner Iowa Cubs, 1999—; chmn., co-owner New West Newspapers, 2000—. Chmn. New West Newspapers, 2000—. Syndicated columnist on lang., 1978-95; columnist USA Today, 1993-98. Trustee Freedom Forum First Amendment Ctr. at Vanderbilt U.; dir. People for the Am. Way, Wells Fargo Banks Inc.; commentator Iowa Pub. Radio; hon. trustee Simpson Coll.; mem. Pulitzer Prize Bd., 1982-92, chmn., 1991-92. Recipient Pulitzer prize for editl. writing, 1997. Mem. ABA, Iowa Bar Assn., Assn. Bar City N.Y., Am. Soc. Newspaper Editors (pres. 1986-87), columnist Wall St. Jour., 1986-89; Wakonda Club, Garden of Gods Club. Home: 5315 Waterbury Rd Des Moines IA 50312-1923 also: 366 W 11th St New York NY 10014-6225 Office: 350 SW 1st St Des Moines IA 50309-4631 E-mail: mggartner@aol.com.

GARTON, ROBERT DEAN, state legislator; b. Chariton, Iowa, Aug. 18, 1933; s. Jesse Glenn and Ruth Irene (Wright) G.; m. Barbara Hicks, June 17, 1955; children: Bradford, Brenda. BS, Iowa State U., 1955; MS, Cornell U., 1959. Pers. rep. Cummins Engine Co., Columbus, Ind., 1959-61; owner Garton Assocs. Mgmt. Cons., 1961-96; dean profl. devel. Ivy Tech. State Coll., 1996—; mem. Ind. Senate, Indpls., 1970—, minority caucus chmn., 1976-78, majority caucus chmn., 1978-80, pres. pro tempore, 1980—. Bd. dir. Rural Water Sys., Ind. Coll. of Ind. Mem. exec. com. Nat. Conf. State Legislatures, 1989-92; chmn. Mid-West Conf. State Legislatures, Coun. State Govts., 1984-85, mem. gov. bd., 1985—; chmn. Ind. Civil Rights Commn., 1969-70; mem. exec. com. Nat. Fedn. Young Reps., 1966; trustee Franklin Coll.; bd. dirs. Independent Colls. of Ind. With USMCR, 1955-57. Co-recipient William M. Bulger Excellence in State Legis. Leadership award, 1999; named Hon. Citizen, Iowa, 1962, Tenn., 1977, winner internat. speech contest, Toastmasters, 1962, Small Bus. Champion, Ind. Small Bus. Coun., 1997, Pub. Servant of the Yr., Ind. Assn. Rehab. Facilities, 2000; named one of 5 Outstanding Young Men in Ind., 1968; recipient Man of Yr., Ind. Rep. Mayor's Assn., 1991, Disting. Svc. award, Jr. C. of C. Columbus, 1968, Guardian Small Bus. award, Nat. Fedn. for Ind. Bus., 1990, 1993, 1994, Lee Atwater Leadership award, Nat. Rep. Legislator Assn., 1991, Outstanding Pub. Svc. award, Podiatric Assn., 1993, United Sr. Action Legis. Leadership award, 1994, Outstanding Govt. Leader award, Apt. Assn. Ind., 1998, Legislator of the Yr. award, Ind. Civil Liberties Union, 2000, Freedom of Road award, ABATE of Ind., 2000, Senator of Yr. award, Ind. Primary Health Care Assn., 2001, Friend of Edn. award, N. Ctrl. Bus. Edn. Assn., 2001, Disting. Pub. Svc. award, Am. Legion, 2001, Pub. Sector award, Benjamin Harrison Medallion, 2001, Benjamin Harrison medallion, 2001. Mem. Rotary, Beta Theta Pi. Office: Ivy Tech State Coll PO Box 1111 Columbus IN 47202-1111 E-mail: gprice@iga.state.in.us.

GARTON, THOMAS WILLIAM, lawyer; b. Ft. Dodge, Iowa, Jan. 19, 1947; s. H. Boyd and Ruth A. (Porter) G.; m. Marcia K. Hoover, June 21, 1969; children: Geoffrey, Matthew. BA, Carleton Coll., 1969; JD magna cum laude, U. Minn., 1974. Assoc. Fredrikson & Byron, PA, Mpls., 1974-80, shareholder, 1980—, chmn. corp. practice group. Adj. prof. William Mitchell Coll. Law, St. Paul, Minn., 1977-80, U. Minn. Law Sch., Mpls., 1980; bd. dirs. RS/Eden Programs; presenter continuing legal edn. seminars on tax, mergers and acquisitions, and bus. planning, 1977—. With U.S. Army, 1969-71. Mem. ABA (tax sect.), Minn. Bar Assn. (dir. tax coun. 1987-89). Office: Fredrikson & Byron PA 1100 International Ctr 900 2nd Ave S Minneapolis MN 55402-3314 E-mail: tgarton@fredlaw.com.

GARVER, THOMAS HASKELL, curator, art consultant, writer; b. Duluth, Minn., Jan. 23, 1934; s. Harvie Adair and Margaret Hope (Foght) G.; m. Natasha Nicholson, Apr. 13, 1974. BA, Haverford Coll., 1956; MA, U. Minn., 1965. Asst. to dir. Krannert Art Mus., U. Ill., Urbana, 1960-62; asst. dir. fine arts dept. Seattle World's Fair, 1962, Rose Art Mus., Brandeis U., Waltham, Mass., 1962-68; dir. Newport Harbor Art Mus. (now Orange County Mus. Art), Calif., 1968-72, 77-80; curator exhbns. Fine Arts Mus. of San Francisco, 1972-77; dir. Madison (Wis.) Art Ctr., 1980-87; asst. prof. Calif. State U., 1970-71, 79-80. Curator art collection Rayovac Corp., Madison, 1985—. Author: Twelve Photographers of the American Social Landscape, 1967, Just Before the War: Urban American from 1935-41, 1968, The Paintings of George Tooker, 1985, rev. edit., 1992, The Last Steam Railroad in America: Photographs by O. Winston Link, 1995; exhbn. catalogues including Robert Rauschenberg, 1969, Tom Wesselmann, 1971, Reginald Marsh, 1972, Joseph Raffael, Paintings From the California Years, 1977, George Herms, 1978, 83, Nathan Oliveira, 1984, George Tooker, Paintings, 1983-87, 88, Mind and Beast: Contemporary Artists and the Animal Kingdom, 1992, Flora: Contemporary Artists and the World of Flowers, 1995, Trains that Passed in the Night: The Railroad Photographs of O. Winston Link, 1998, WATER: Contemporary Artists Who Use Water as a Theme in Their Art, Gibbes Mus. of Art, Charleston, S.C., 1999. Trustee U.S.S. Mass. Meml. Commn., Fall River, 1965-68; trustee South Coast Repertory Co., Costa Mesa, Calif., 1970-72; trustee Wis. Citizens for Arts, 1985-87; mem. Newport Beach Art Commn., 1978-79; mem. steering com. Archives Am. Art, San Francisco, 1977-80; mem. Madison Com. for Arts, 1984-87. Mem. Western Assn. Art Mus. (pres. 1970-71, trustee 1970-73), Art Mus. Assn. Am. (pres. 1979-82, trustee 1979-85). Home and Office: 1962 Atwood Ave Madison WI 53704-5221 E-mail: thgart@aol.com.

GARVEY, JOHN CHARLES, violist, conductor, retired music educator; b. Canonsburg, Pa., Mar. 17, 1921; s. Frank Sherwood and Esther (Gegenheimer) G.; m. Evelyn Ficarra, Mar. 13, 1947; children: Deborah, Frank, Deirdre. Student, Temple U., 1940-43. Prof. music Sch. Music, U. Ill., Urbana, 1948-91. Violinist, violist Jan. Savitt and Jerry Wald Jazz orchs., 1943-45; prin. violist Columbus Philharm. Orch., 1945-48, Aspen Festival Orch., 1964; condr. NIRTV Chamber Orch., Iran, 1973; founder, dir. Jazz Band, 1959, Chamber Orch., 1964, Russian Folk Orch., 1974; violist Walden Quartet, 1948-69, State Dept. Jazz Tours, 1968-69; condr. Harry Partch Ensemble, 1959-63 (Wihner Nat. Coll. Jazz Band champaionships 1967-69, Russian Ctr. grantee for study balalaika in Moscow 1970, 72, Ctr. for Advanced Studies grantee for study ethnic music 1972-73, recipient Ill. Gov.'s award in arts 1980); dir. U. Ill. Jazz Band tour of USSR, 1990; guest condr. Belarus State Jazz Band, Minsk, 1992; condr. New Ill. Jazz Band, 1995-96. Balinese Gamelan study grantee K.O.K.A.R., Bali, 1979, 87; grantee for study of Catalan Sardana music, Barcelona, 1986. Mem. Am. Fedn. Musicians (Local 196), Soc. for Ethno-musicology, Internat. Assn. Jazz Educators, Balalaika and Domra Assn. Am. Home: 10707 Lombardy Rd Silver Spring MD 20901-1632 Office: Nomad Imports 402 N Draper Ave Champaign IL 61821-2425

GARVIN, PAUL JOSEPH, JR. toxicologist; b. Toledo, Nov. 16, 1928; s. Paul Joseph and Laura Mary (Blanchet) G.; m. Priscilla Ann Haines, Aug. 23, 1952; children: Peter, Thomas, Paul III, Peggy, Priscilla, Polly. BA, St. John's U., 1950; MS, U. Minn., 1958. Rsch. assoc. Sterling-Winthrop Rsch. Inst., Renssaeler, N.Y., 1954-58; sr. rsch. pharmacologist Baxter-Travenol Inc., Morton Grove, Ill., 1958-72, mgr. safety evaluation, 1972-77; dir. toxicology Amoco Corp., Chgo., 1977-88, sr. health sci. advisor, 1988-92; toxicology cons. pvt. practice, Mt. Prospect, Ill., 1992—. Mem. adv. com. ctr. risk analysis Harvard U. Sch. Pub. Health, Boston, 1991-92; sci. adv. panel hazardous substance mgmt. rsch. ctr. U. Medicine and Dentistry, Newark, 1988-91, adv. panel ctr. alternatives to animal testing Johns Hopkins U. Sch. Hygiene and Pub. Health, Balt., 1990-92, scientific adv. com. CIIT, Research Triangle Park, N.C., 1986-88. Contbr. over 50 articles to profl. jours. Chmn. Mt. Prospect Bd. Health, 1960-70. Mem. AAAS, Am. Indsl. Hygiene Assn., Am. Soc. Pharmacology & Exptl. Therapeutics, N.Y. Acad. Sci., European Soc. Toxicology, Soc. Toxicology. Home and Office: 309 N Wille St Mount Prospect IL 60056-2454

GARWOOD, JULIE, writer; b. 1946; Author: (novels for young adults) A Girl Named Summer, 1985, (as Emily Chase) What's A Girl to Do, 1985, (historical romance novels) Gentle Warrior, 1985, Rebellious Desire, 1986, Honor's Splendor, 1987, The Lion's Lady, 1988, The Bride, 1989, Guardian Angel, 1990, The Gift, 1990, The Prize, 1991, The Secret, 1992, Castles, 1993, Saving Grace, 1993, Prince Charming, 1994, For the Roses, 1995, The Wedding, 1996, One Pink Rose, One White Rose, One Red Rose, Come the Spring, 1997, The Wedding, 1998, Ransom, 1999, Heartbreaker, 2000. Office: PO Box 7574 Leawood KS 66207-0574

GARZIA, SAMUEL ANGELO, lawyer; b. Highland Park, Mich., July 7, 1920; s. Angelo and Josephine G.; m. Josephine Lupo, June 6, 1946; children: Sanuel Angelo, Sandra Jo, Frank. J.D., Wayne State U., Detroit, 1943. Bar: Mich. 1943. Asst. friend of ct., Wayne County, Mich., 1946-48; practice law Detroit, 1948-97; sr. ptnr. Vandeveer Garzia, 1960-97. Served with AUS, 1943-45, ETO. Decorated Bronze Star; Croix de Guerre Luxembourg). Mem. ABA, Mich. Bar Assn., Detroit Bar Assn. (dir. 1976-83), Oakland Bar Assn., Assn. Def. Counsel Mich. (1st pres.

1966-67), Internat. Assn. Ins. Counsel, Am. Coll. Trial Lawyers, Am. Legion (judge advocate Mich. 1958) Roman Catholic. Home: 5229 Greenbriar Ct West Bloomfield MI 48323-2322 Office: 333 W Fort St Detroit MI 48226-3115

GASCOIGNE, WILLIAM M. research executive; BS in Computer Sci., Durham U. Regional dir. Philips Electronic & Assoc. Industries; maj. accts. dir. Olivetti; v,o, worldwide mktg., mng. dir. Europe Schlumberger Techs.; mgr. No. Europe Structural Dynamics Rsch. Corp., Milford, Ohio, 1990—, now sr. v.p., mng. dir. Europe. Office: Structural Dynamics Rsch Corp 2000 Eastman Dr Milford OH 45150-2712

GASH, LAUREN BETH, lawyer, state legislator; b. Summit, N.J., June 11, 1960; d. Ira Arnold and Sondra Regina (Stetin) G.; m. Gregg Allen Garmisa, June 12, 1983; children: Sarah, Benjamin. BA in Psychology, Clark U., 1982; JD, Georgetown U., 1987. Bar: Ill. 1989. Projects dir. U.S. Senator Alan Dixon, Washington, 1981-83; statewide constituency coord., dir. Women for Simon, U.S. Senator Paul Simon, Chgo., 1990; aide State Rep. Grace Mary Stern, Highland Park, Ill.; atty. Prairie State Legal Svcs., Waukegan; mem. Ill. State Ho. of Reps., chair judiciary-criminal com. Mem. women's health adv. bd. Highland Park Hosp., southeast adv. bd Coll. Lake County, JUF govt. agencies divsn. campaign cabinet, 1999, chair, Highland Park 2000 com., human needs subcom. Women in Law as 2d Career grantee; recipient Disting. Svc. award Ill. Com. for Honest Govt., 1996, Best Legis. Record Voting award Ind. Voters Ill., 1996; named Legis. of Yr. Alliance for the Mentally Ill, 1997. Mem. Ill. State Bar Assn. (mem. com. cmty. involvement), Formerly Employed Mothers at the Leading Edge (co-founder North Shore chpt.), Chgo. Women in Govt. Rels., Women Employed, Ravinia PTA (bd. dirs., polit. action chair), Com. for Interdist. Cooperation, North Shore Synagogue Beth El (social action com.) LWV (bd. dirs. Highland Park chpt., bd. dirs. Lake County chpt.). Avocations: flute, French, Spanish. also: 2052-l Stratton Bldg Springfield IL 62706-0001 Office: 1345 Forest Ave Highland Park IL 60035-3456

GASKILL, E. THURMAN, state legislator; b. Algona, Iowa, Apr. 4, 1935; m. Geraldine; children: Elizabeth, Mark, David. Student, Iowa State U. Owner farm; dir. First Fed. Savings Bank of Midwest; appointed by USDA sec. agr. Fed. Agrl. Energy Adv. Com., 1973, USDA Users Adv. Bd., 1988; mem. Ag Promotion Bd., 1974-85, Iowa Dept. Natural Resources, 1989-92, Iowa Senate from 8th dist., Des Moines, 1997—. Mem. White House Transition Team, 1988, County Bd. of Edn., U.S. Agr. Fed. Energy Commn.; chair Farmers for Nixon and Ford Campaigns; co-chair Iowa Farmers for Reagan/Bush and Bush/Quayle; nat. dep. dir. George Bush Ag Campaign, 1992; past commr. Iowa Devel. Commn.; mem. honors award selection com. USDA; spkr. in field; charter mem. bd. dirs. Iowa Peace Inst. Mem. adv. com. Iowa State U. Coll. Agr.; bd. dirs. United Meth. Ch.; past supt. Sunday Sch. With U.S. Army, 1954-56. Named to Iowa State U. Agr. Hall of Fame, 1975. Mem. Iowa Farm Bus. Assn. (past pres.), Nat. and Iowa Corn Growers (past pres.), U.S. Feed Grain Coun. (chair), Iowa Corn Promotion Bd. (past pres.), Agr. Coun. Am. (vice-chair), U.S. Feed Grains Coun. (mem. trade team to China 1981), Iowa Farm Bur., Shriners, Am. Legion, Rotary (mem. group study exchange team to Australia 1969). Republican. Methodist. Home: 1320 Birch Ave Corwith IA 50430-8045 Office: State Capitol 8th Dist 3 9th And Grand Des Moines IA 50319-0001 E-mail: thurman_gaskill@legis.state.ia.us.

GASKILL, SAM, state legislator; Mem. Mo. Ho. of Reps. Dist. 131, Jefferson City, 1995—. Republican.

GASPER, GEORGE, JR. mathematics educator; b. Hamtramck, Mich., Oct. 10, 1939; s. George Gregory and Anastasia Gasper; m. Brigitta Gasper, July 1, 1967; children: Karen, Kenneth. BS, Mich. Technol. U., 1962; MA, Wayne State U., 1964, PhD, 1967. Predoctoral traineeship NASA, 1966-67; vis. lectr. U. Wis., Madison, 1967-68; postdoctoral fellow U. Toronto, Ont., Can., 1968-69, vis. asst. prof. Can., 1969-70; asst. prof. math. Northwestern U., Evanston, Ill., 1970-73, assoc. prof., 1973-77, prof., 1977—. Co-author: Basic Hypergeometric Series, 1990; assoc. editor Jour. Math. Analysis and Applications, 1985-95, The Ramanujan Jour., 1995—. Fellow Alfred P. Sloan Found., 1973-75. Mem. Am. Math. Soc., Soc. Indsl. and Applied Math. (assoc. editor Jour. Math. Analysis 1984-85, vice chair activity group on orthogonal polynomials and spl. functions 1993-95). Office: Northwestern U Dept Math Lunt Bldg Evanston IL 60208-0001

GASPER, JOSEPH J. insurance company executive; b. Steubenville, Ohio; m. Jill; two children. Degree in econs., Ohio State U. Group underwriter Nationwide Ins., Columbus, 1966-72; mgmt. mktg. Columbus Ins., 1972-95; pres., COO Nationwide Fin. Svcs., Columbus, Ohio, 1996—. Bd. dirs. BalletMet, Columbus Children's Hosp., Otterbein Coll. Mem. Nat. Assn. Variable Annuities (chmn. bd. dirs.), Am. Coun. Life Ins. (bd. dirs.), Assn. Ohio Life Ins. Cos., Ins. Marketplace Standards Assn. Office: One Nationwide Plz Nationwide Fin Svcs Columbus OH 43215-2220

GASPER, RUTH EILEEN, real estate executive; b. Valparaiso, Ind., July 16, 1934; d. Reuben John and Effie (Wesner) Tenpas; m. Ralph L. Gasper, May 25, 1957. Student, Purdue U., 1952-56; BA, Govs. State U., 1982. Analyst computer sys. Leo Burnett Advt., Chgo., 1958-69; nat. adminstr. registrars Sports Car Club Am., Denver, 1977-79; pres. Ainslie Inc., Fla., 1982—. Mem. North River Commn. Housing Com., Chgo., 1982-83, fin. com. Mayor's Task Force on Homelessness City of Chgo. Area coord. Concerned Action party, Lansing, Ill., 1977; chief race registrar Ind. N.W. Region Sports Car Club Am., 1969-80; co-founder, Single Rm. Operators Assn., 1987-98. Mem. Dolphin Beach Club Condo Assn., Fantasy Island II Condo Assn. (sec.). Avocations: sports car racing, classical music.

GASS, RAYMOND WILLIAM, lawyer, consumer products company executive; b. Chgo., Apr. 6, 1937; s. William Frederick and Clara Gertrude (Grotman) G.; m. Patricia Ann Thomas, Apr. 20, 1968; children: Elizabeth Ann, Katharine Patricia, Christina Susanne. BS, Purdue U., 1959; LLB, U. Ill., 1962. Bar: Ill. Patent examiner U.S. Patent Office, Washington, 1962-63; atty. Armour and Co., Chgo., 1963-70; sr. atty. Greyhound Corp., 1970-71; sr. v.p., gen. counsel, sec. John Morrell & Co., 1971-89; v.p., gen. counsel Alberto-Culver Co., Melrose Park, Ill., 1989-98. Bd. dirs. Am. Chemet Corp., Columbia Paint and Coating Co. Mem. ABA, Chgo. Bar Assn. (chmn. com. corp. law depts. 1975-77)

GASS, WILLIAM H. writer, educator; b. Fargo, N.D., July 30, 1924; s. William Bernard and Claire (Sorensen) G.; m. Mary Patricia O'Kelly, 1952 (div.); children: Richard, Robert, Susan; m. Mary Alice Henderson, 1969; children: Elizabeth, Catherine. AB, Kenyon Coll., 1947, LHD (hon.), 1973, 85; PhD, Cornell U., 1953. Instr. philosophy Coll. of Wooster, Ohio, 1950-54; asst. prof. Purdue U., Lafayette, 1954-60, assoc. prof., 1960-66, prof. philosophy, 1966-69, Washington U., St. Louis, 1969-79, David May Disting. Univ. prof. in humanities, 1979-99; dir. Internat. Writers Center, 1990—2001. Vis. lectr. U. Ill., 1958-59; mem. Rockefeller Commn. on Humanities, 1978-80; mem. literature panel Nat. Endowment for the Arts, 1979-82. Author: Omensetter's Luck, 1966, In the Heart of the Heart of the Country, 1968, Willie Masters' Lonesome Wife, 1968, Fiction and the Figures of Life, 1970, On Being Blue, 1974, The World Within the Word, 1978, The Habitations of the Word: Essays, 1984, The Tunnel, 1995, Finding a Form, 1996, Cartesian Sonata, 1998, Reading Rilke, 1999, Tests of Time, 2002; contbr. to periodicals including N.Y. Rev. of Books, N.Y. Times Book Rev., New Republic, TriQuar., Salmagundi, others. Office: 6304 Westminster Pl Saint Louis MO 63130

GASSERE, EUGENE ARTHUR, lawyer, business executive; b. Beaumont, Tex., Oct. 20, 1930; s. Victor Eugene and Althea June (Haight) G.; m. Mary Alice Engelhard, Aug. 4, 1956; children— Paul, John, Anne. B.S., U. Wis., 1952, J.D., 1956; postgrad., Oxford U., 1956-57. Bar: Wis. bar 1956. Asst. counsel Wurlitzer Co., Chgo., 1958-61, Campbell Soup Co., Camden, N.J., 1961-65; asst. to pres. Thilmany Pulp & Paper Co., Kaukauna, Wis., 1966-68; with Skyline Corp., Elkhart, Ind., 1968-92, v.p., gen. counsel, asst. sec., 1973-92, ret., 1992—. Pres., bd. dirs. Elkhart Urban League, 1972-73, Elkhart Symphony, 1975-76, Elkhart Concert Club, 1976-77. Served with U.S. Army, 1952-54. Mem. Wis. Bar Assn., Phi Mu Alpha. Home: PO Box 165 Mindoro WI 54644-0165 Office: Skyline Corp 2520 Bypass Rd Elkhart IN 46514-1584 E-mail: pelt2ridge@aol.com.

GAST, HARRY T., JR. state legislator; b. St. Joseph, Mich., Sept. 20, 1920; s. Harry T. Sr. and Fern (Shearer) G.; m. Vera Jean Warren, 1944; children: Barbara Gast Moray, Linda, Dennis. Student, Mich. State U., 1939-41. Treas, then supervisor Lincoln Twp., 1946-70; mem. Mich. Ho. of Reps. from 43rd dist., Lansing, 1970-78, Mich. Senate from 20th dist., 1978—. County supervisor Berrien County, Mich., 1965-69; mem. Berrien County Bd. Pub. Works, Berrien County Bd. Health, 1965-70. Mem. Lions, Farm Bur., Jaycees (hon.), Mich. United Conservation Clubs. Office: S-324 Capitol Bldg Lansing MI 48913-0001

GATER, CHRIS, advertising executive; With Christian Brann Ltd., 1977-94; CEO, vice chmn. Brann Worldwide (formerly Christian Brann Ltd.), Deerfield, Ill., 1994-97, chmn., CEO, 1997—. Office: Brann Worldwide 540 Lake Cook Rd Ste 150 Deerfield IL 60015-5604

GATES, STEPHEN FRYE, lawyer, business executive; b. Clearwater, Fla., May 20, 1946; s. Orris Allison and Olga Betty (Frye) G.; m. Laura Daignault, June 10, 1972. BA in Econs., Yale U., 1968; JD, MBA, Harvard U., 1972. Bar: Fla. 1972, Mass. 1973, Ill. 1977, Colo. 1986. Assoc. Choate Hall & Stewart, Boston, 1973-77; atty. Amoco Corp., Chgo., 1977-82, gen. atty., 1982-86; regional atty. Amoco Prodn. Co., Denver, 1987-88; asst. treas. Amoco Corp., Chgo., 1988-91, assoc. gen. counsel, corp. sec., 1991-92; v.p. Amoco Chem. Co., 1993-95; v.p., gen. counsel Amoco Corp., Chgo., 1995-98; exec. v.p., group chief of staff BP Amoco p.l.c., London, 1999-2000; sr. v.p., gen. counsel, sec. FMC Corp., Chgo., 2000—01; ptnr. Mayer Brown Rome & Maw, 2002—. Bd. dirs. Nat. Legal Ctr. Pub. Interest, Wash., 1999—. Trustee Newberry Libr., Chgo., 1998—; bd. dirs. Chgo. Sister Cities Internat. Program, Inc., Friends of Prentice Hosp., 1994-98; mem. adv. coun. Chgo. Schweitzer Urban Fellows Program, 1996—; mem. adv. bd. Chgo. Vol. Legal Svcs. Found., 1996-98; mem. Chgo. Crime Commn., 2000—, bd.dirs. 2000—. Knox fellow, 1972-73. Fellow: Royal Soc. Arts (London); mem.: ABA, Yale Club, Chgo. Club, Univ. Club. Office: Mayer Brown Ropme & Maw 190 S LaSalle St Chicago IL 60603

GATES, WALTER EDWARD, small business owner; b. Glens Falls, N.Y., Aug. 15, 1946; s. William B. and Dawn K. (Preston) G.; m. Toni A. Naren, June 26, 1945; children: Lindsey Erin, Ryan Walter. BS, SUNY, Albany, 1968; EdM, Boston U., 1972; MBA, Harvard U., 1974. Asst. mgr. Wilson Sporting Goods Inc., River Grove, Ill., 1974-76, mgr., 1976-79; dir. Pizza Hut Inc., Wichita, Kans., 1979, sr. dir., 1979-80, v.p., 1980-82, sr. v.p., 1982-85; exec. v.p. Rent-A-Ctr. Inc., 1985-86, pres., chief operating officer, 1986-87, pres., chief exec. officer, chief operating officer, 1987-92; pres., CEO THORN Americas, 1991, chmn., CEO, 1992-96; CEO Gates Enterprises, Wichita, 1996—. Pres., CEO Gates Enterprises, 1985—. Bd. dirs. Wichita Symphony, 1984-87, Wichita Children's Theater, 1984-87; active Wichita Music Theatre, 1987—, Boy Scouts of Am., 1989—. Mem. Wichita C. of C. Avocations: skiing, water skiing, golf. Office: Gates Enterprises 8100 E 22nd St N Ste 2100-3 Wichita KS 67226-2330

GATTO, LOUIS CONSTANTINE, retired educational association administrator; b. Chgo., July 4, 1927; s. Louis S. and Marie (Bacigalupo) Gatto; m. Kathleen M. Paquette, July 7, 1951 (dec.); children: Christine Gatto Glasgow, Beth Gatto Roberts, Mark Gregory, Janine, Sandra Gatto Minniear; m. Marilyn R. Bennett, Feb. 9, 1991. Student, Amherst Coll., 1945-46; BA, St. Mary's Coll., Minn., 1950; postgrad., U. Minn., 1950-51; MA, DePaul U., 1956; PhD, Loyola U., Chgo., 1965; LittD (hon.), Marian Coll., Indpls., 1989; LHD (hon.), Martin U., Indpls., 1996. Speech asst. St. Mary's Coll., 1949-50; staff artist TV Times, Mpls., 1950-51; chmn. dept. English Zion-Benton H.S., Ill., 1951-56; tchr. New Trier H.S., Winnetka, 1956-57; instr. English St. Josephs Coll., Rensselaer, Ind., 1957-58, asst. prof., 1958-63, assoc. prof. Medieval and Renaissance lit., 1963-66, prof., 1966-71, asst. acad. dean, dir. summer session, 1967, acad. dean, 1968, v.p. acad. affairs, 1969-71; pres., prof. English Marian Coll., Indpls., 1971-89; dir. spl. projects, cons. svc. Independent Colls. of Ind., 1989—; amb. Independent Colls. Ind. Found., 1989—91; dir. Ind. Compact, 1989-99, West Point liaison officer, 1990—, dir. Operation Expanded Horizons, 1992—. Mem. Ind. N.W. Consortium Pvt. and Pub. Instns., 1968—71; selection com. Ind. Fulbright Found., 1968—70; mem. cmty. adv. coun. Indpls. Pub. Schs., 1976—77; mem. policy adv. coun. parent/child devel. project Bank St. Coll. Edn., 1976—79; mem. Hist. Landmarks Found. Ind., 1973—89; mem. long range devel. plan adv. com. Ind. Vocat. Tech. Coll., 1985—86; mem. adv. com. Alcohol Safety Action Project, 1972—75; mem. exec. com. adv. bd. Ctr. Econ. Edn., Ind. U.-Purdue U., Indpls., 1978—89; mem. exec. com. Ind. Conf. Higher Edn., 1973—75, 1978—81, 1987—89, pres., 1979—80; chmn. coun. pres. Consortium Urban Edn., 1974—75, pres., 1975—89; dir. spl. projects Ind. Conf. Higher Edn., 1992—94, exec. sec., 1994—. Contbr. articles to profl. jours. Vice chair Hamilton County ARC, 1999; bd. dirs., treas. Associated Colls. Ind., 1976—78, v.p., 1984—86; mem. Benjamin Harrison Meml. Commn., 1987—91; mem. adv. bd. Sta. WYFI; mem. gov.'s commn. Hoosier Celebration, 1988; Ind. lobbyist Ind. Higher Edn., 1989—90; chmn. Ind. Ameritech. Partnership Awards Program, 1990—95; asst. dir. Edml. Facilities Auth., 1991—93, exec. dir., 1994—; with Army War Coll., 1974; mem. Senator Lugar's merit selection com. West Point, 1995—; mem. adv. com. 21st century scholars program State Student Assistance Commn., 1998—; mem. adv. com. Ind. Coun. Quality Tchg. Student Learning, 2000—; bd. dirs. Greater Indpls. Progress Com., ARC, Hosp. Audiences Inpls., 1974—76, Ind. Higher Edn. Telecom. Sys., 1987—95, Hamilton County ARC, Ind. Colls. and Univs. Ind., chmn., 1979—80, 1986—88. Recipient Sagamor of the Wabash award, State of Ind., 1980, 1989, Outstanding Svc. award, Ind. Health Careers, 1983, Cir. award, Ind. Coalition Blacks in Higher Edn., 1986, Oustanding Contbns. award, Army Career And Alumni Assn., 1994; fellow ACE, 1966—67. Mem.: Ind. Conf. Higher Edn. (Dedicated Svc. award 1994), Am. Coun. Edn. (Ind. coord. fellow program 1999—), Friends of West Point Membership, West Point Soc. Ind., Heslar Naval Armory Club (life), Alpha Phi Omega. Home: 24 Apple Tree Cir Fishers IN 46038-1110 E-mail: iefa@msn.com.

GAUEN, PATRICK EMIL, newspaper correspondent; b. St. Louis, July 15, 1950; s. Louis Otto and Wilma Ellen (Rogers) G.; m. Patti Lynn Seib, Dec. 8, 1972 (div. 1992); children: Bethany, Heather; m. Karen Earhart, July 11, 1992; 1 stepchild, Christopher Stephenson. Student, So. Ill. U., 1968-70. Reporter, photographer Collinsville (Ill.) Herald, 1969-72, news editor, 1972-78; reporter St. Louis Globe-Democrat, 1978-84, mng. editor, 1984-85; reporter Ill. affairs St. Louis Post-Dispatch, 1985-89, polit. corr., 1989—, pub. safety team leader, 2000—; faculty univ. coll. Washington U., St. Louis, 1991—. Pub. safety reporting team leader St. Louis Post Dispatch, 2000. Recipient Outstanding Med. News Series award Ill. State Med. Soc., 1970, Best Feature Story award Suburban Newspapers Am., 1971, Best News Story award Suburban Newspapers Am., 1973, Best Spot News Story award UPI Editors Ill., 1972, Best Pub. Svc. Reporting award Ill. Press Assn., 1974, Best Feature Story award, 1975, Bar-News Media award Bar Assn. Met. St. Louis, 1987, Bob Hardy award Southern Ill. Chiefs of Police and Southwestern Law Enforcement, 1996, Terry Hughes award St. Louis chpt. Newspaper Guild, 1996, Liberty Bell award Madison County Bar Assn., 1999. Mem. Mid-Am. Press Inst. (bd. dirs. 1985—), Press Club Met. St. Louis (bd. dirs. 1985—), Sigma Delta Chi (bd. dirs. St. Louis chpt. 1985—, chpt. pres. 1985-86, 86-87). Avocations: reading; photography. Home: 30 Meadowlark Ln Highland IL 62249-3000 Office: St Louis Post Dispatch 900 N Tucker St Saint Louis MO 63101 E-mail: pgauer@post-dispatch.com.

GAUGHAN, PATRICIA ANNE, judge; b. Cleve., Oct. 21, 1953; d. John James and Alma Marie (Friedmann) G.; m. Roger Andrew Andrachik, Apr. 24, 1987; children: Brett Gaughan, Kathryn Gaughan. BA, St. Mary's Coll., 1975; JD, U. Notre Dame, 1978. Bar: Ohio 1978, Ind. 1978. Asst. county pros. Cuyahoga County Pros. Office, Cleve., 1978-83, 84-87; asst. U.S. atty. U.S. Atty.'s Office, 1983-84; assoc. Reid, Johnson, Downes, Andrachik & Webster, 1984-87; judge Common Pleas Ct. Cuyahoga County, 1987-96, exec. com., 1993-96; judge U.S. Dist. Ct. (no. dist.) Ohio, Eastern divsn., 1996—. Adj. prof. trial advocacy Cleve. Marshall Coll. of Law, 1983-87; mem. rules adv. com. Supreme Ct. of Ohio, Columbus, 1991-97; mem. paralegal studies adv. bd. Notre Dame Coll., Cleve., 1991—. Bd. dirs. Nat. Conf. Met. Cts., 1993—, Newburgh House of Hope, Cleve., 1994-96, Conflict Resolution Ctr., Cleve., 1995-98; mem. children's trust fund bd. Cuyahoga County Commrs., Cleve., 1984-92; v.p. Leukemia Soc., Lymphoma Soc. Mem. Ohio State Bar Assn., Ohio Jud. Conf. Assn., Cleve. Bar Assn. (trustee 1994-97), Cuyahoga County Bar Assn., Fed. Judges Assn., Fed. Cir. Bar Assn., Am. Judicature Soc., Common Pleas Ct. Judges Assn., Harold H. Burton Inn of Ct. (master of the bench 1991-96), Kappa Gamma Pi. Office: US Dist Ct 201 Superior Ave E Ste 202 Cleveland OH 44114-1201

GAULKE, EARL H. religious publisher and editor, clergyman; b. Milw., July 18, 1927; s. Albert and Olga (Reinhardt) G.; m. Margaret Elaine Preuss, Aug. 5, 1951; children: Cheryl, Stephen. BS in Edn., Concordia U., River Forest, Ill., 1950; BA, MDiv, Concordia Sem., St. Louis, 1956; MA, Washington U., St. Louis, 1965, PhD, 1970; DD, Concordia U., Irvine, Calif., 1995. Ordained minister Lutheran Ch., 1956. Prin., tchr. Pilgrim Luth. Sch., Santa Monica, Calif., 1950-52; tchr., dept. head Detroit Luth. High Sch., 1956-57; assoc. pastor Faith Luth. Ch., L.A., 1957-58; editor bd. of parish svcs., 1958-75; dir. editorial svcs. Luth. Ch.-Mo. Synod, St. Louis, 1975-92; v.p. edit. Concordia Pub. House, 1992—. Vis. instr. Washington U., U. Mo., St. Louis, Concordia Sem., Concordia Coll., Mpls.; rsch. assoc. Ctrl. Lab. (CEMREL), St. Louis, 1967-68. Author: You Can Have A Family, 1975, First Chance for the Church, 1978; contbr. articles to profl. jours. Recipient Epphatha award Detroit Inst. for Deaf, 1992. Mem. Am. Edn. Assn., Luth. Edn. Assn. (exec. editor 1978-79, Christus Magister 1989). Avocations: gardening, making wine. Home: 2447 Camberwell Ct Des Peres MO 63131-2118 Office: Concordia Pub House 3558 S Jefferson Ave Saint Louis MO 63118-3910 E-mail: earl.gaulke@cph.org.

GAUNCE, MICHAEL PAUL, insurance company executive; b. Paris, Oct. 17, 1949; s. Paul D. and Mary E. (Gardner) G.; m. Annette Beauchamp. BA, U. Ky., 1971. Cert. Life Underwriters Tng. Coun. Agt., mgr. Equitable Life of N.Y., Lexington, Ky., 1972-74; agt., regional mgr. Assn. Ins. Marketers, Inc., Indpls., Cin., South Bend, Ind., 1974-77; pres., chmn. Ins. Corp. Am., Indpls., 1977—. Chmn. bd. Argent Ins. Corp., Indpls., Alternative Healthcare Marketers, Inc., Indpls.; dir., past chmn. Brokers Ins. Corp., Indpls.; dir. Brokers Ins. Corp. Tenn., Nashville, Brokers Ins. Agy., Atlanta; dir., Brokers Ins. Corp., Ky., Agy. Mgmt. Corp., Indpls.; cons. adv. bd. Blue Cross/Blue Shield, Indpls., 1982-89; mem. adv. bd. Acordia, Inc., Indpls., 1996-98; mem. adv. group Trustmakr Ins. Co., 2000. Active Rep. Nat. Com. Mem. Ind. Assn. Employee Benefit cons. (pres. 1984-88), Elks, Greenwood C. of C., Franklin C. of C., Seymour C. of C. Republican. Avocations: fishing, swimming, reading, investments, travel. Office: Ins Corp Am 5140 Commerce Cir Indianapolis IN 46237-9744

GAVIN, MARY JANE, medical and surgical nurse; b. Prairie Du Chien, Wis., Sept. 1, 1941; d. Frank Grant and Mary Elizabeth Wolf; m. Alfred William Gavin, Nov. 9, 1963; children: Catherine Heidi Elizabeth, Carl Alfred Eric. Student, North Cen. Coll., Naperville, Ill., 1959-61; BS, RN, U. Wis., 1964; postgrad., Deepmuscle Tng. Ltd., 1980; postgrad. in deep muscle therapy. RN, Wis. Staff nurse U. Wis. Hosps., Madison; RN home response VA, Milw. Unit chair Badger Girls State, 1991—; mem. Wis. Am. Legion Aux.; mem. task force for handicapped Eastside Wis. Evang. Luth. Ch., Madison, 1993. U. Wis. scholar. Mem. Monona Grove Am. Legion Aux. (pres. Unit 429 1990—). Home: 702 Fairmont Ave Madison WI 53714-1424

GAVIN, ROBERT MICHAEL, JR. education consultant; b. Coatesville, Pa., Aug. 16, 1940; s. Robert Michael and Helen Regina (Finnegan) G.; m. Charlotte Marie Dugan, June 2, 1962; children— Anne, Patricia, Robert, Charles, Sean. B.A., St. John's U., Collegeville, Minn., 1962; Ph.D., Iowa State U., 1966; DSc (hon.), Haverford Coll., 1986, St. John's U., 1996. Mem. faculty Haverford (Pa.) Coll., 1966-84, prof. chemistry, 1975-84, dir. computing, 1979-80, provost, dean faculty, 1980-84, interim pres., 1996-97; pres. Macalester Coll., St. Paul, 1984-96, Cran Brook Edml. Cmty., Bloomfield Hills, Mich., 1997—2001; ret., 2001. Bd. dirs. Hartford Funds, SCT Corp., St. John's U., Minn. Author papers in field. Pres. Haverford Twp. Sch. Bd., 1975. Recipient Dreyfus Tchr.-Scholar award, 1973; NSF fellow, 1969-70 Democrat. Roman Catholic. Home: 751 Judd St Marine On Saint Croix MN 55047

GAVIN, SARA, public relations executive; b. Minn. Degree in History and Polit. Sci., Coll. St. Catherine, St Paul, Minn. Investor rels. programs Doremus & Co.; v.p. Hill and Knowlton/Twin Cities, Dorn Swenson Meyer, 1985-86; exec. v.p. Mona Meyer McGrath, 1986-93; pres. Mona Meyer McGrath & Gavin (Shandwick), Minn., 1993-95; mgr. dir. Shandwick Internat., 1995—. Bd. dirs. Minn. Women's Economic Round Table; trustee Coll. of St. Catherine, Minn. Pub. Radio. Recipient various awards PRSA, IABC. Mem. PRSA, Recognized Phi Beta Kappa. Office: Shandwick Ste 500 8400 Normandale Lake Blvd Minneapolis MN 55437-3889

GAW, ROBERT STEVEN, lawyer, state representative; b. Moberly, Mo., July 7, 1957; s. William Robert and Julia Marie (Bentley) G.; m. Fannie Beth Bowdish, Aug. 18, 1990. BS in Physics summa cum laude, N.E. Mo. State U., 1978; JD, U. Mo., 1981. Bar: Mo. 1981. Atty. State of Mo., Jefferson City, 1982-84, James Wheeler, Keytesville, Mo., 1984, City of Moberly, 1985-92, Schirmer & Gaw, Moberly, 1984-94, Schirmer, Suter & Gaw, 1994—. Elected spkr. Mo. House of Reps., 1996. State rep. Dist. 22, Mo., 1993—; chmn. Dem. Ctrl. Com., Randolph County, Mo., 1984-89; bd. dirs. Am. Diabetes Assn., Randolph County, 1990—; mem. com. Huntsville (Mo.) Horse Show, 1980's—, Mo. Children's Svcs. Commn., KIDS COUNT adv. com., Mo. Bar Commn. Children & the Law. Recipient award Am. Cancer Soc., 1993, award United Way; nominee Truman scholarship N.E. Mo. State U., 1977, Charles Dick Medal of Merit Nat. Guard Assn. of the U.S., 1995, Geyer award for pub. svc. to higher edn. U. Mo. Alumni Assn. and U. Mo.-Columbia; named Alumni of Yr., Truman State U., 1996. Mem. Mo. Bar Assn., Randolph County Bar Assn. (pres. 1984—), Moberly Area C. of C. (bd. dirs. 1991—), Moberly Rotary Club. Methodist. Avocations: singing, hunting, saddlebred horses. Office: Mo Ho of Reps State Capitol Building Jefferson City MO 65101-1556

GAY, DUANE, reporter; m. Teri Gay. Degree, U. Wis., Green Bay. News dir. TV and radio news, La Crosse, Oskkosh, Wausau, Green Bay and Milw., Wis.; reporter The Inside Story WISN 12, Milw. Recipient Emmy award, awards, Milw. Press Club, Milw. Assn., N.W. Broadcast News Assn., Radio and TV News Dirs. Assn. Office: WISN PO Box 402 Milwaukee WI 53201

GAY, WILLIAM ARTHUR, JR. thoracic surgeon; b. Richmond, Va., Jan. 16, 1936; s. William Arthur and Marion Harriette (Taylor) G.; m. Frances Louise Adkins, Dec. 17, 1960; children— William Taylor, Mason Arthur. BA, Va. Mil. Inst., 1957; MD, Duke U., 1961. Intern Duke U. Med. Ctr., Durham, NC, 1961—63, resident in surgery, 1965—71; asst. prof. surgery Cornell U. Med. Coll., N.Y.C., 1971—74, assoc., prof., 1974—78; cardiothoracic surgeon-in-chief N.Y. Hosp., 1976—84; prof., chmn. dept. surgery U. Utah Sch. Medicine, 1984—92; v.p. for health scis. U. Utah, 1990—91; chmn. Am. Bd. Thoracic Surgery, 1995—97; thoracic surgeon Barnes Hosp., St. Louis. Prof. surgery Sch. Medicine Washington U., St. Louis. Contbr. Recipient Career Scientist award, Irma T. Hirschl Charitable Trust, 1972. Mem. ACS, Soc. Vascular Surgery, Soc. Thoracic Surgery, Am. Assn. Thoracic Surgery (treas. 1989-94), Am. Surg. Assn., Soc. Univ. Surgeons (treas. 1977-80) Office: 1 Barnes Hospital Plz Saint Louis MO 63110-1036 E-mail: gayw@msnotes.wustl.edu.

GAYLE, MONICA, broadcast journalist; b. Wenatchee, WA, Mar. 3, 1960; BA Journalism, Wash. State U., 1982. Anchor, gen. assingment reporter KNSD-TV, San Diego, 1990-92; co-anchor CBS News Up to the Minute, 1992-93, CBS Morning News, 1993—. Recipient 2 Emmys and 3 Sigma Delta Chi awards. Office: CBS Morning News 524 W 57th St New York NY 10019-2924*

GAYLORD, EDSON I. manufacturing company executive; Chmn., pres. Ingersoll Milling Machine Co., Rockford, Ill. Recipient M. Eugene Merchant Mfg. medal ASME/SME, 1991. Office: Ingersoll Intl 707 Fulton Ave Rockford IL 61103-4069

GAYLORD, EDWARD LEWIS, publishing company executive; b. Denver, May 28, 1919; s. Edward King and Inez (Kinney) G.; m. Thelma Feragen, Aug. 30, 1950; children: Christine Elizabeth, Mary Inez, Edward King II, Thelma Louise. A.B., Stanford U., 1941; LL.D., Oklahoma City U., Okla. Christian Coll., Pepperdine U., 1984. Chmn. Okla. Pub. Co., Oklahoma City; editor, pub. Daily Oklahoman, Sunday Oklahoman; pres. OPUBCO Resources, Inc., OPUBCO Devel. Co.; past chmn. Gaylord Entertainment, Nashville. Chmn. bd. Gayno, Inc., Colorado Springs; ptnr. Cimarron Coal Co., Denver; past chmn., bd. dirs. Broadmoor Hotel, Colorado Springs. Chmn., trustee Okla. Industries Authority; hon. chmn. bd. govs. Okla. Christian Coll.; bd. dirs. Okla. State Fair, pres., 1961-71; past chmn. bd. dirs. Nat. Cowboy and Western Heritage Mus.; past chmn. Okla. Med. Rsch. Found.; past trustee Casady Sch., Oklahoma City U. Served with AUS, 1942-46. Recipient Brotherhood award NCCJ, 1961, Humanitarian award NCCJ, 1971, Disting. Svc. award U. Okla., 1981, Golden Plate award Am. Acad. Achievement, 1985, Pathmaker of Oklahoma County award Oklahoma City/County Hist. Soc., 1996, Pres.'s award for 50 Yrs. of Svc., 4-H and Future Farmers Am., 1996, Disting. Citizen award Last Frontier Coun. Boy Scouts Am., 1996, Silver Buffalo award, 1999; Adam Smith award Hillsdale Coll. and Shavano Inst., 1996; named to Okla. Hall of Fame, 1974, Okla. Journalism Hall of Fame, 1994; first recipient Spirit of Am. award U.S. Olympic Com., 1984. Mem. Oklahoma City C. of C. (dir., past pres.), So. Newspaper Pubs. Assn. (past pres.) Congregationalist. Home: 1506 Dorchester Dr Oklahoma City OK 73120-1203 Office: The Daily Oklahoman 9000 Broadway Ext Oklahoma City OK 73114-3799 also: Oklahoma Publishing Co. Box 25125 Oklahoma City OK 73125

GEAKE, RAYMOND ROBERT, psychologist; b. Detroit, Oct. 26, 1936; s. Harry Nevill and Phyllis Rae (Fox) G.; m. Carol Lynne Rens, June 9, 1962; children: Roger Rens, Tamara Lynne, William Rens. BS in Spl. Edn., U. Mich., 1958, MA in Guidance and Counseling, 1959, PhD in Edn. and Psychology, 1963. Coord. child devel. rsch. Edison Inst., Dearborn, Mich., 1962-66; dir. psychology dept. Plymouth (Mich.) State Home and Tng. Sch., Mich. Dept. Mental Health, 1966-69; pvt. practice ednl. psychology Northville, Mich., 1969-72; mem. Mich. Ho. of Reps., 1973-76, Mich. Senate, 1977-98. Adj. asst. prof. edn./psychology dept. Madonna Coll., Livonia, Mich., 1984-86. Co-author: Visual Tracking, A Self-instruction Workbook for Perceptual Skills in Reading, 1962. Trustee-at-large Schoolcraft C.C., 1969-72, chmn. bd. trustees, 1971-72; vice chmn. nat. adv. com. on mental health and illness of elderly HEW, 1976-77; vice chmn. human svcs. com., assembly fed. issues Nat. Conf. State Legislatures, 1994-95. Recipient Recognition award Found. for Improvement of Justice, 1993. Fellow Mich. Psychol. Assn.; mem. NEA (life), APA, Rotary. Republican. Office: Mich Office Children's Ombudsman PO Box 30026 Lansing MI 48909-7526

GEALT, ADELHEID MARIA, museum director; b. Munich, May 29, 1946; came to U.S., 1950; d. Gustav Konrad and Ella Sophie (Daeschlein) Medicus; m. Barry Allen Gealt, Mar. 15, 1969. BA, Ohio State U., 1968; MA, Ind. U., 1973, PhD, 1979. Registrar Ind. U. Art Mus., Bloomington, 1972-76, curator Western art, 1976—, acting/interim dir., 1987-89, dir., 1989—. Adj. assoc. prof. H.R. Hope Sch. Fine Arts, Ind. U., Bloomington, 1985—89, assoc. scholar, 1986, assoc. prof., 1989—; mem. nat. adv. coun. Valparaiso U. Art Mus.; commr. Indiana Arts Commn., 1997—2001. Author: Looking at Art, 1983, Domenico Tiepolo The Punchinello Drawings, 1986; co-author: Art of the Western World, 1989, Painting of the Golden Age: A Biographical Dictionary of Seventeenth-Century European Painters, 1993, Domeinco Tiepolo: Master Draftsman, 1996, Giandomenico Teipolo, Disegni dal mondo, 1996; contbg. author Critic's Choice, 1999. Grantee Nat. Endowment for Arts, 1982, 83, Am. Philos. Soc., 1985, NEH, 1985, Samuel H. Kress Found., 1999-2000. Mem. Assn. Art Mus. Dirs. Office: Ind U Art Mus 7th St Bloomington IN 47405-3024

GEALT, MICHAEL A. environmental microbiologist, educator; b. Phila., Nov. 27, 1948; s. Edward Leonard Gealt and Lillian Rose Brenner; m. Maryjanet McNamara, Jan. 2, 1981; 1 child ; m. Antonia Malandrucco, May 12, 1967 (div. 1977); 2 children. BA, Temple U., 1970; PhD, Rutgers U., 1974. Rsch. assoc. Med. Sch. Rutgers U., Piscataway, N.J., 1974-76; postdoct. assoc. Inst. Cancer Rsch., Phila., 1976-78; asst. prof. biol. scis. Drexel U., 1978-84; assoc. prof., 1984-90; prof., 1990-2000; dir. Sch. environ. Sci., Engring. and Policy, 1994-2000; dean Sch. Engring., Math. and Sci. Purdue U. Calument, Hammond, Ind., 2000—, prof. biology, 2000—. Contbr. articles to profl. jours. Grantee EPA, 1983, 85, 89, NSF, 1981, 94, 97. Mem. AAAS, Am. Soc. Microbiology (chair environ. and applied micro divsn. 1995), Am. Soc. Cell Biology, Assn. Environ. Engrs. & Science Profs., Am. Assn. Higher Educ., Am. Soc. Engring. Educ., Sigma Chi. Avocations: motorcycles, photography. Office: Purdue U Calumet Sch Engring Math and Sci 2200 169th St Hammond IN 46323-2068

GEAREN, JOHN JOSEPH, lawyer; b. Wareham, Mass., Sept. 1, 1943; BA, U. Notre Dame, 1965; MA (Rhodes Scholar), Oxford U., 1967; JD, Yale U., 1970. Bar: Ill. 1972. Ptnr. Mayer, Brown & Platt, Chgo., 1970—. Democrat. Roman Catholic. Home: 179 Linden Ave Unit 2 Oak Park IL 60302-1661 Office: Mayer Brown & Platt 190 S La Salle St Ste 3100 Chicago IL 60603-3441 E-mail: jgearen@mayerbrown.com.

GEARHART, MARILYN KAYE, mathematics and biology educator; b. Tucson, Apr. 11, 1950; d. Raymond Fred and Joan Gazell (White) Hagerty; m. Lon David Gearhart, Mar. 22, 1975; children: Amanda Kaye, Shannon Leigh. BA in Elem. Edn. with distinction, Manchester Coll., 1972; MS in Elem Edn. summa cum, Ind. U., 1976; BS in Math. with high honors, Tri-State U., 1985; postgrad., Ind. U., 1983-89, postgrad., 2001—, Purdue U., 1998-99, Loyola U., Chgo., 1999. Sub. tchr. South Bend (Ind.) Community Sch. Corp., 1971-72; tchr. DeKalb County Ea. Community Sch. Dist., Butler, Ind., 1972-77; founder, tchr. Pleasant View Christian Early Learning Ctr., Angola, 1981-85, also bd. dirs.; micro computer tchr. Purdue U., Ft. Wayne, Ind., 1984; substitute tchr. Met. Sch. Dist. Steuben County, Angola, 1985; tchr. math. and biology DeKalb County Cen. United Sch. Dist., Auburn, Ind., 1985—2001, maths. dept. chair, 1999—2001. Assoc. prof. math. Purdue U., 1998-2001. Author: (textbook) The Impossibility of Achieving and Maintaining an Utopia, 1971. Sponsor freshman class DeKalb H.S., 1987-89, sophomore class, 1989-96, Students Against Drunk Driving, Auburn, 1985-90, Butler Elem. Little Hoosiers, 1973-77; mem. attendance and gifted and talented coms. DeKalb H.S., 1989-90; coach Acad. Decathlon and Hoosier Acad. Super Bowl, 1989-97, Hoosier Spell Bowl, 1993-97; leader Girl Scouts U.S., 1986-91, mem., coord. product sales svc. Unit, 1989-90; del. Rep. State Conv., 1996; mem. DeKalb Band and Show Choir Parents. Recipient Dir's. award Ind. Jr. Hist. Soc., 1981-85; math. and sci. scholar Tri-State, 1985; grantee Tchrs. Retng. Fund. Ind.-State, 1983-85. Mem. NEA, AAUW (treas. 1987-89), Ind. Tchrs. Assn. (dist. del. to rep. assembly 1997, 99, 2000), DeKalb Edn. Assn. (bldg. rep. 1997-98, dist. membership chair 1998-2001), Beta Beta Beta. Mem. Christian Ch. Avocations: reading, swimming, canoeing, computers, working with young people. Home: 6121 #B Augusta Dr N Indianapolis IN 46224

GEARY, RICHARD, retired construction company executive; b. Portland, Oreg., Mar. 21, 1935; s. Arthur McCornack Geary and Martha Alice (Dorman) Smith; m. Patricia Leone Lehto, 1952 (div. Jan. 1972); children: Arthur Raymond, Elizabeth Diane Gearyr; m. Janet Lee Hendrickson, March 10, 1972; 1 child, Suzanne Janet Paymar; stepchilden: Sarah Anne Geary Ottem, David Walter Garner. BSCE with great distinction, Stanford U., 1956, MSCE, 1957. Engr. Peter Kiewit Sons' Co., Vancouver, Wash., 1957-59, supt., 1959-64, area mgr., 1964-69, Northwest dist. mgr., 1969-84, mgr. Pacific divsn., 1984-98—, also dir. Omaha, exec. v.p., divsn. mgr. Vancouver. Mem. Oreg.-Columbia Associated Gen. Contractors (bd. dirs. 1971—, pres., 1977), Phi Beta Kappa. Republican. Presbyterian. Avocations: duck and goose hunting, skiing, tennis, golf.

GECHT, MARTIN LOUIS, physician, bank executive; b. Chgo., July 12, 1920; s. Max and Sarah (Rolnick) G.; m. Francey Ann Heytow; children: Lauren Paula Gecht Kramer, Susan Ellen Gecht Rieser, Robert David. B.A., U. So. Calif., 1941; M.D., U. Health Sci./Chgo. Med. Sch., 1945; DHL (hon.), U. Health Scis., 2000. Intern Brookdale Med. Center, N.Y.C., 1944-45; resident in dermatology Cook County Hosp., 1955-58; gen. practice medicine, 1946-59; practice medicine specializing in dermatology, 1959-99; organized Allport Med. Group, 1948, now pres. Chmn. bd. Albany Bank & Trust Co. N.A., 1976— Trustee, mem. exec., fin. coms., chmn. audit com. Finch U. Health Sci./Chgo. Med. Sch.; participant numerous activities Jewish Fedn. Chgo.; Chgo. Com. Weizmann Inst. Sci., internat. bd. dirs.; mem. adv. com. on prints and drawings Art Inst. Chgo.; bd. dirs. Lyric Opera of Chgo. Recipient Disting. Service award Anti-Defamation League, B'nai B'rith, 1975, 83 Mem. Am. Bankers Assn., Ill. Bankers Assn., AMA, Ill. Med. Soc., Chgo. Med. Soc. Councilors, Am. Acad. Dermatology (life), Soc. Indsl. Medicine and Surgery. Jewish. Clubs: Metropolitan, Standard, High Ridge (Palm Beach, Fla.). Home: 1110 N Lake Shore Dr Apt 37 Chicago IL 60611-1054 Office: Albany Bank & Trust Co NA 3400 W Lawrence Ave Chicago IL 60625-5188

GEDDES, LANELLE EVELYN, nurse, physiologist; b. Houston, Sept. 15, 1935; d. Carl Otto and Evelyn Bertha (Frank) Nerger; m. Leslie Alexander Geddes, Aug. 3, 1962. BSN, U. Houston, 1957, PhD, 1970. Staff nurse Houston Ind. Sch. Dist., 1957-62; instr. to asst. prof. physiology Baylor U. Coll. Medicine, 1972-75; asst. prof. nursing Tex. Women's U., 1972-75; prof., head Purdue U. Sch. Nursing, Lafayette, Ind., 1975-91. Contbr. chpts. to books, articles to med. jours. Recipient tchg. awards. Mem. Am. Nurses Assn., Am. Assn. Critical-Care Nurses, AAAS, N.Y. Acad. Scis., Phi Kappa Phi, Sigma Theta Tau, Iota Sigma Pi. Lutheran. Office: Purdue Univ West Sch Nursing Lafayette IN 47907 E-mail: leg@nursing.purdue.edu.

GEDDES, LESLIE ALEXANDER, bioengineer, physiologist, educator; b. Scotland, May 24, 1921; s. Alexander and Helen (Humphrey) G.; m. Irene P. Bloomer; 1 child, James Alexander; m. La Nelle E. Nerger, Aug. 3, 1962. BEE, MEngring., ScD (hon.), McGill U.; PhD in Physiology, Baylor U. Med. Coll. Demonstrator in elec. engring. McGill U., 1945, research asst. dept. neurology, 1945-52; cons. elec. engring. to various indsl. firms Que., Can.; biophysicist dept. physiology Baylor Med. Coll., Houston, asst. prof. physiology, 1956-61, assoc. prof., 1961-65, prof., 1965-74; dir. Lab. of Biophysics, Tex. Inst. Rehab. and Research, Houston, 1961-65; prof. physiology Coll. Vet. Medicine, Tex. A. and M. U., College Station, 1965-74, prof. biomed. engring., 1969-74; Showalter Disting. prof. bioengring. and elec. engring. Purdue U., West Lafayette, Ind., 1974-91, Showalter Disting. prof. emeritus, 1991—. Cons. NASA Manned Spacecraft Center, Houston, 1962-64, USAF, Sch. Aerospace Medicine, Brooks AFB, 1958-65; expert witness, 1981—. Author: 22 books; cons. editor: Med. and Biol. Engring., 1969—, Med. Research Engring., 1964-74, Med. Electronics and Data, 1969—; mem. editorial bd.; Jour. Electrocardiology, 1968—, med. instr., 1974—; contbr. over 750 articles to bioengring. Mem. Soc. Free Space Floaters, 1961. Fellow: IEEE (Leadership award, Edison medal, IEEE 3d Millennium award, World of Difference award, Lee De Forest award 2001), AAAS, Royal Soc. Medicine, Am. Inst. for Med. and Biol. Engring., Am. Coll. Cardiology, Nat. Acad. Forensic Engrs., Australasian Coll. Physicists in Biology and Medicine; mem.: NAE, NSPE, Am. Physiol. Soc., Assn. for Advancement Med. Instrumentation (Leadership award), Biomed. Engring. Soc., Tex. Soc. Profl. Engrs., Radio Club Am., Phi Zeta, Tau Beta Pi, Sigma Xi. Achievements include patents for Holder 23 U.S. patents. Home: 400 N River Rd Apt 701 West Lafayette IN 47906-3131 Office: Purdue U POTR Bldg West Lafayette IN 47907-1296 E-mail: geddes@ecn.purdue.edu.

GEE, ROBERT LEROY, agriculturist, dairy farmer; b. Oakport Twp., Moorhead, Minn., May 25, 1926; s. Milton William and Hertha Elizabeth (Paschke) G.; m. Mae Valentine Erickson, June 18, 1953 B.S. in Agronomy, N.D. State U., 1951, postgrad., 1955, Colo. A&M U., 1954. Farm labor controller Minn. Extension Service, Clay County, 1944-45, county 4-H agt., 1951-57; rural mail carrier U.S. Postal Service, Moorhead, Minn., 1946-47; breeder registered shorthorn cattle and registered southdown sheep, 1950-63; owner, operator Gee Dairy Farm (Oak Grove Farm), 1957—. Asst. prof. status U. Minn., 1951-57; bd. dirs. Red River Valley Fair, West Fargo, N.D., 1960-86, Minn. Dairy Promotion Bd., St. Paul, 1968-69; bd. dirs. Red River Valley Devel. Assn., Crookston, Minn., 1973—, v.p., 1992—; bd. dirs. Red River Milk Producers Pool, Minn., N.D., 1963-78, treas., 1968-78; bd. dirs. Cass Clay Creamery Inc., Fargo, N.D., 1969-96, chmn. bd., 1982-85, 92-95, v.p., 1990-91; bd. dirs. U.S. Meat Animal Rsch. Ctr., Clay Ctr., Nebr., 1970; mem. Nat. Dairy Promotion Bd., Washington, 1984-88. Treas. Oakport Twp., 1974-82, supr., 1986—, v.p., 1987—; mem. Clay County Planning and Zoning Commn., 1991, vice chmn., 1992-96, chmn., 1996-2000; mem. Clay County Bd. Adjustment, 1995-2000, chmn., 1996-2000. With USN, 1945-46. Recipient Grand Champion Farm Flock award Man. Expn., 1960, Clay County's Outstanding Agriculturist award, 1996; named Clay County King Agassiz, Red River Valley Winter Shows, 1966, Grand Champion forage exhibit Red River Valley Winter Shows, 1979, 82; co-recipient Clay County Dairy Farm Family of Yr. award Red River Valley Dairymen's Assn., 1979. Mem. Minn. Milk Producers Assn. (bd. dirs. 1977-88, 93-97, sec. 1972-78, treas. 1977-87), Minn. Assn. Coops. (bd. dirs. 1984-96), State Coop. Assn. (dairy council 1975-96), Am. Farm Bur. Fedn., Nat. Farmers Union, Kragnes Farmers Elevator Assn., Red River Valley Livestock Assn., Am. Shorthorn Breeders Assn., Am. Southdown Breeders Assn., Holstein-Friesian Assn. Am. Republican. Mem. United Ch. of Christ. Club: Agassiz (v.p. 1979-81, pres. 1981-82) (Moorhead) Avocations: hunting; fishing; skiing. Home and Office: 8595 2nd St N Moorhead MN 56560-7103

GEFKE, HENRY JEROME, lawyer; b. Milw., Aug. 4, 1930; s. Jerome Henry and Frances (Daley) G.; m. Caroline Ann Lawrence, June 25, 1955 (div. Jan. 1968); children: Brian Lawrence, David Jerome; m. Mary Clare Nuss, Aug. 28, 1976; children: Lynn Marie, James Scott. B.S., Marquette U., 1952, LL.B., 1954; postgrad., Ohio State U., 1955-56. Bar: Wis. 1954, Tax Ct. U.S 1969; C.P.A., Wis. Accountant-auditor John G. Conley & Co. (C.P.A.s), Milw., 1956-59; with J.I. Case Co., Racine, Wis., 1959-68, corp. sec., asst. gen. counsel, 1965-68; assoc. Maier & Mulcahy, S.C., Milw., 1968-69; prin. Mulcahy, Gefke & Wherry, S.C., 1969-73; individual practice law, 1973—. Corp. officer, dir. various bus. corps. Pres., bd. dirs. Big Bros., Greater Racine, 1965-67; trustee Racine County Instns., 1960-63; bd. dirs., sec., legal counsel Racine Transitional Care, Inc., 1973-76; bd. dirs., legal counsel Our Home Found., Milw., 1979-82; bd. dirs. Racine County Mental Health Assn., 1963-67, Alliance for Mentally Ill Milw. County, 1986-88; bd. dirs., sec., legal counsel Glendale Econ. Devel. Corp., 1996—; bd. dirs. Glendale Bus. Coun., 1996-97; bd. dirs. Glendale Assn. of Commerce, Inc., 1997—, treas., 1998-2000, pres. 2000-02. Mem. Wis. Bar Assn., Milw. Bar Assn., Wis. Inst. CPA's, Delta Sigma Pi, Delta Theta Phi. Home: 5521 N Lydell Ave Glendale WI 53217-5042 Office: 400 W Silver Spring Dr Milwaukee WI 53217-5053 E-mail: hjgjdcpa@aol.com.

GEHA, ALEXANDER SALIM, cardiothoracic surgeon, educator; b. Beirut, June 18, 1936; came to U.S., 1963; s. Salim M. and Alice I. (Hayek) G.; m. Diane L. Redalen, Nov. 25, 1967; children— Samia, Rula, Nada BS in Biology, Am. U. Beirut, 1955, MD, 1959; MS in Surgery and Physiology, U. Minn.-Rochester, 1967; MS (privatum), Yale U., 1978. Asst. prof. U. Vt., Burlington, 1967-69; asst. prof. Washington U., St. Louis, 1969-73, assoc. prof., 1973-75, Yale U., New Haven, 1975-78, prof., chief cardiothoracic surgery, 1978-86, Case Western Res. U. and U. Hosp. of Cleve., 1986-98; Jay L. Ankeney prof. cardiothoracic surgery Case We. Reserve U., 1994-98; pres. Univ. Cardiothoracic Surgeons, Inc., Cleve., 1986—; prof., chief cardiothoracic surgery U. Ill., Chgo., 1998—; chief cardiothoracic surgery Mt. Sinai Hosp. Med. Ctr., 2000—. Cons. VA Hosp., West Haven, Conn., 1975-86, VA Hosp., Cleve., 1986-98, Westside VA Hosp., Chgo., 1998—, Cleve. Met. Health Med. Ctr., 1986-98, Mt. Sinai Med. Ctr., Cleve., 1990-98, Waterbury Hosp., 1976-86, Sharon Hosp., 1981-86, Michael Reese Hosp., 2002—; mem. study sect. Nat. Heart Lung and Blood Inst., 1981-85. Editor: Glenn's Thoracic and Cardio-vascular Surgery, 4th edit. 1983, 5th edit. 1991, 6th edit. 1996; editor Basic Surgery, 1984. Bd. dirs. New Haven Heart Assn., 1981-85 Mem. AMA, Assn. Clin. Cardiac Surgery (chmn. membership com. 1978-80, sec.-treas. 1980-83, pres. 1988), Am. Heart Assn. (bd. dirs. 1981-85. councils on basic sci., cardiovascular surgery), Am. Coll. Chest Physicians (steering com. 1980-84), Am. Assn. Thoracic Surgery, Am. Coll. Cardiology, ACS (chmn. coordinating com. on edn. in thoracic surgery, chmn. 1992-95), Am. Lung Assn., Am. Physiol. Soc., Am. Surg. Assn., Assn. Acad. Surgery, Central Surg. Assn., European Assn. Cardiothoracic Surgery, Internat. Soc. Heart and Lung Transplantation, Internat. Soc. Cardiovascular Surgery, Lebanese Order Physicians, New Eng. Surg. Soc., Pan Am. Med. Assn., Halsted Soc., Soc. Thoracic Surgeons (govt. rels. com., manpower com., program com., edn. and resources com.), Soc. for Vascular Surgery, Soc. Univ. Surgeons, Chgo. Surg. Soc., also others. Home: 854 W Fullerton Ave Chicago IL 60614-2413 Office: ILL Chgo 840 S Wood St Chicago IL 60612-7317 E-mail: ageha@uic.edu.

GEHAN, MARK WILLIAM, lawyer; b. St. Paul, Dec. 19, 1946; s. Mark William and Jean Elizabeth (McGee) G.; m. Lucy Lyman Harrison, Aug. 25, 1971; children: Hark Harrison, Alice McGee. BA, U. Notre Dame, 1968; JD, U. Minn., 1971. Bar: Minn. Asst. county atty. Ramsey County Atty.'s Office, St. Paul, 1972-76; prosecutor, Met. Area Dist. Urban County Attys. Bd., 1976-77; ptnr. Collins Buckley Sauntry & Haugh, 1978—. Bd. dirs. Minn. State Bd. Pub. Def., St. Paul, 1982-90. Pres. St. Paul Charter Commn., 1986-94. Mem. Minn. Bar Assn. (pres. 1998-99), Ramsey County Bar Assn. (pres. 1990-91). Avocations: scuba diving, tennis, guitar. Office: Collins Buckley Sauntry & Haugh First Nat Bank Bldg 332 Minnesota St Ste W1100 Saint Paul MN 55101-1379 E-mail: mgehan@cbsh.net.

GEHL, WILLIAM D. manufacturing company executive; b. 1947; Bar: Wis., Fla. With The Ziegler Co., Inc., West Bend, Wis., 1978-92, sr. v.p., gen. counsel, 1985-92, exec. v.p., COO, gen. counsel, sec., 1990-92, also bd. dirs.; dir. Gehl Co., 1987—, chmn. nominating com., mem. compensation and benefits com., pres., CEO, 1992—, also chmn. bd. dirs. Office: Gehl Co PO Box 179 143 Water St West Bend WI 53095-3400

GEHM, DAVID EUGENE, construction and environmental management executive; b. St. Louis, Nov. 15, 1952; s. John Francis and Rosemary Helen (Krupp) G. Cert. civil engring. tech., St. Louis Community Coll. Florissant Valley, 1973. Quality control inspector Fla. Testing and Engr., Ft. Lauderdale, 1973-76; surveyor Wunderlich Co., Union, Mo., 1976-77; quality control inspector The Binkley Co., Warrenton, 1977-78, Daniel Internat., Fulton, 1978-79; project mgr. Booker Assocs., Inc., St. Louis, 1979-86; pres. GEHM Corp., Boonville, Mo., 1986—. Mem. Nat. Inst. Cert. Engring. Techs., Inst. Cert. Engr. Techs., Tau Alpha Pi, Sons of Am. Legion. Avocations: hunting, fishing. Home: PO Box 265 Boonville MO 65233-0265 Office: 1480 W Ashley Rd Boonville MO 65233-2141 E-mail: dgehm@gehm.com.

GEHO, WALTER BLAIR, biomedical research executive; b. Wheeling, W.Va., May 18, 1939; s. Blair Roy and Susan (Yonko) G.; m. Marjorie Cooper, Aug. 25, 1962; children: Hans, Alison, Robert, David, Daniel. BS, Bethany Coll., 1960; PhD in Pharmacology, Western Res. U., 1964, MD, 1966. Instr. pharmacology Sch. of Medicine Western Res. U., Cleve., 1966-67; pres., CEO SDG Inc., 1993-2001, chief sci. officer, dir., 2001—; staff researcher Procter & Gamble Co., Cin., 1968-74, head pharmaceutical rsch. sect., 1974-81; v.p., dir. rsch. Tech. Unltd., Inc., Wooster, Ohio, 1981-89, pres., 1989-93; chmn., chief sci. officer, dir. AMDG, Inc., Cleve., 1997-2001, chief sci. officer, dir., 2001—. Contbr. articles to Phamacology of Bisphosphates, Clin. Pharmacology of Didronel, Genetics of Myositis Ossificans. Recipient 2 Ohio Innovator awards Edison Fund Ohio, 1987, Innovation award Enterprise Devel. Inst., 1995. Mem. AMA, Am. Chem. Soc. Achievements include patents in pharmaceuticals; contributions to development of osteoscan and didronel, and targeted drug delivery systems, commercialization of liposome inventions into consumer and pharmaceutical products. Office: SDG Inc PO Box 91023 Cleveland OH 44101-3023

GEHRING, FREDERICK WILLIAM, mathematician, educator; b. Ann Arbor, Mich., Aug. 7, 1925; s. Carl E. and Hester McNeal (Reed) G.; m. Lois Caroline Bigger, Aug. 29, 1953; children: Kalle Burgess, Peter Motz. BSE in Elec. Engring., U. Mich., 1946, MA in Math, 1949; PhD (Fulbright fellow) in Math, Cambridge U., Eng., 1952, ScD, 1976; PhD (hon.), U. Helsinki, Finland, 1977, U. Jyväskylä, 1990, Norwegian U. Sci. &

Technology, 1997. Benjamin Peirce instr. Harvard U., Cambridge, Mass., 1952-55; instr. math. U. Mich., Ann Arbor, 1955-56, asst. prof., 1956-59, assoc. prof., 1959-62, prof., 1962-96, T.H. Hildebrandt prof. math., 1984-96, prof. emeritus, 1996, chmn. dept. math., 1973-75, 77-84, disting. univ. prof., 1987—; hon. prof. Hunan U., Changsha, People's Republic of China, 1987. Vis. prof. Harvard U., 1964-65, Stanford U., 1964, U. Minn., 1971, Inst. Mittag-Leffler, Sweden, 1972, Mittag-Leffler, Sweden, 1990; Lars Onsager prof. Norwegian Tech. Hochschule, Norway, 1995; chair program in Geo Function Theory, Math. Scis. Rsch. Inst., Berkeley, 1986. Editor Duke Math. Jour., 1963-80, D. Van Nostrand Pub. Co., 1963-70, North Holland Pub. Co., 1970-94, Springer-Verlag, 1974—; editl. bd. Procs. Am. Math. Soc., 1962-65, Ind. U. Math. Jour., 1967-75, Math. Revs., 1969-75, Bull. Am. Math. Soc., 1979-85, Complex Variables, 1981—, Mich. Math. Jour., 1989, Annales Academiae Scientiarum Fennicae, 1996, Conformal Geometry and Dynamics, 1997—; contbr. numerous articles on rsch. in pure math. to sci. jours. With USNR, 1943-46. Decorated comdr. Finnish White Rose; NSF fellow, 1959-60; Fulbright fellow, 1958-59; Guggenheim fellow, 1958-59; Sci. Rsch. Coun. sr. fellow, 1981; Humboldt fellow, 1981-84; U. Auckland Found fellow, 1985; Finnish Acad. fellow U. Helsinki, 1989. Mem. NAS, Am. Acad. Arts and Scis., Assn. Women in Math., Math. Assn. Am., Am. Math. Soc. (coun. 1969-75, 80-83, trustee 1983-93, mem. editl. bd. 1997-98), Inst. for Math. and Its Applications (gov. 1981-84), Swiss Math. Soc., Finnish Math. Soc., London Math. Soc., European Math. Soc., Finnish Acad. Sci., German Math. soc., Royal Norwegian Soc. Scis. and Letters. Home: 2139 Melrose Ave Ann Arbor MI 48104-4067

GEHRKE, CHARLES WILLIAM, biochemistry educator; b. N.Y.C., July 18, 1917; s. Henry Edward and Louise (Mader) G.; m. Virginia Dorothy Horcher, Dec. 25, 1941; children: Charles William, Jon Craig, Susan Gay. BA in Biochemistry, Ohio State U., 1939, BS in Edn, MS in Biochemistry and Bacteriology, Ohio State U., 1941, PhD in Agrl. Biochemistry, 1947. Prof., head dept. chemistry Missouri Valley Coll., Marshall, Mo., 1942-49; instr. agrl. chemistry Ohio State U., Columbus, 1945-46; assoc. prof. agrl. chemistry U. Mo., Columbia, 1949-54, prof. biochemistry, 1954-87, prof. emeritus, 1987—, mgr. Expt. Sta. Chem. Labs., 1954-87, dir. interdisciplinary chromatography Mass Spectrometry Facility, 1982-87; founder, chmn. bd. dirs. Bioscis. and Tech. Internat., Inc., 1992. Founder, chmn. bd. dirs. Analytical Biochemistry Labs., Columbia, 1968-92, dir., 1992—; USA co-chmn. colloquium on A Lunar-Based Chem. Analysis Lab., 1989, 93; co-investigator lunar samples NASA, 1969-75; lectr., Japan, China, Taiwan, The Philippines, Hong Kong, 1982, 87, France, Fed. Republic of Germany, Switzerland, Italy, Egypt, 1986, 89. Author: 75 Years of Chromatography--A Historical Dialogue; author-editor: Amino Acid Analysis by Gas Chromatography, 3 vols., 1987, Chromatography and Modification of Nucleosides, 3 vols., 1990, A Lunar-Based Chemical Analysis Laboratory, 1992, A Lunar-Based Analytical Laboratory, 1997, Chromatography a Century of Discovery, 2001; mem. editorial bd. Jour. Chromatographic Sci., Jour. Chromatography; contbr. 260 articles to sci. jours. Recipient Faculty Alumni Gold medal award U. Mo., 1975, Chromatography Meml. medal Sci. Council on Chromatography of USSR Acad. Scis., 1980, Ohio State Alumni Profl. Achievement award, 2001; Ohio State Outstanding scholar, 1996. Fellow Am. Inst. Chemists, Assn. Ofcl. Analytical Chemists (Harvey W. Wiley award 1971, chmn. Magruder standard sample subcom. 1958-79, bd. dirs., mem. editl. bd. 1979-82, pres.-elect 1983, pres. centennial yr. 1984); mem. AAAS, Am. Soc. Biol. Chemists, Am. Chem. Soc. (pres. Mo. sect. 1958-59, 78-79, Spencer award 1980, Midwest Chemist award 1986, Dal Nogare award in chromatography 1995, U. Mo. Faculty Retiree of Yr. award 1993, nat. award in separations sci. and tech. 1999, Nat. award in Chromatography 2000), Am. Dairy Sci. Assn. (chmn. com. on protein nomenclature 1961-62), Fedn. Am. Socs. Exptl. Biology, Internat. Soc. Study of Origin of Life, N.Y. Acad. Sci., Cosmopolitan Luncheon Club (chmn. adv. coun. 1976—), Sigma Xi. Home: 708 Edgewood Ave Columbia MO 65203-7410 Office: Cancer Rsch Ctr 3501 Berrywood Dr Columbia MO 65201-6570

GEIER, PETER E. bank executive; With Merchants Nat. Bank and Trust, Indpls., 1979-84; v.p. nat. divsn. Huntington Nat. Bank subs. Huntington Bancshares, Columbus, Ohio, 1984-96, pres., COO, 1996—, Huntington Bancshares Inc., Columbus, 1999—. Office: Huntington Nat Bank & Huntington Bancshares Inc 41 S High St Columbus OH 43215-6101

GEIGER, TERRY, state legislator; BA in Pub. Svc., Alma Coll. Rep. Mich. State Dist. 87, 1995—. Address: 351 Capitol Bldg Lansing MI 48909-7514

GEIMAN, J. ROBERT, lawyer; b. Evanston, Ill., Mar. 5, 1931; s. Louis H. and Nancy O'Connell-Crowe G.; m. Ann L. Fitzgerald, July 29, 1972; children: J. Robert, William Patrick, Timothy Michael. BS, Northwestern U., 1953; JD, Notre Dame U., 1956. Bar: Ill. 1956, U.S. Ct. Appeals (7th cir.) 1956, U.S. Supreme Ct. 1969. Assoc. Eckert, Peterson & Lowry, Chgo., 1956-64; ptnr. Peterson, Lowry, Rall, Barber & Ross, 1964-70, Peterson & Ross, Chgo., 1970-96, of counsel, 1996—. Mem. com. on civil jury instructions Ill. Supreme Ct., 1979-81. Case editor Notre Dame Law Rev., 1956. Bd. advisors Cath. Charities of Archdiocese of Chgo., 1973-96. Fellow Internat. Acad. Trial Lawyers, Am. Coll. Trial Lawyers, Ill. Bar Found.; mem. ABA (aviation com., tort and ins. practice sect. 1980-90), Ill. Bar Assn. (sec. 1969-70, sec. bd. govs. 1969-71), Chgo. Bar Assn. (aviation law com. 1970-73), Bar Assn. of 7th Fed. Ct. (meetings com. 1968-70, vice chmn. membership com. 1973-75), Soc. Trial Lawyers, Cath. Lawyers Guild of Chgo. (bd. advisors 1973-96), Law Club Chgo., Chgo. Athletic Assn. (pres. 1973). Republican. Home: 900 SW Bay Point Cir Palm City FL 34990-1758 Office: Peterson & Ross 200 E Randolph St Ste 7300 Chicago IL 60601-7012

GEIS, JEROME ARTHUR, lawyer, legal educator; b. Shakopee, Minn., May 28, 1946; s. Arthur Adam and Emma Mary (Boegemann) G.; m. Beth Marie Bruger, Aug. 11, 1979; children: Jennifer, Jason, Joan, Janice. BA in History, Govt. magna cum laude, St. John's U., Collegeville, Minn., 1968; JD cum laude, U. Notre Dame, 1973; LLM in Taxation, NYU, 1975. Bar: Minn. 1973, U.S. Dist. Ct. Minn. 1973, U.S. Tax Ct. 1973, U.S. Ct. Appeals (8th cir.) 1973. Law clk. to presiding justice Minn. Supreme Ct., St. Paul, 1973-74; assoc. Dudley & Smith, 1975-76, Briggs & Morgan P.A., St. Paul, 1976-79, chief tax dept., 1983-95. Prof. tax law William Mitchell Coll. of Law, St. Paul, 1976—. Columnist Minn. Law Jour., 1986-89, Bench & Bar, 1990—; editl. cons.: Sales and Use Tax Alert; former reviewer Summary Reporter: Finance and Commerce, Minnesota State Bar Assn.; corr. State Tax Notes. Bd. dirs. Western Townhouse Assn., West St. Paul, 1979, St. Matthews Cath. Ch., West St. Paul, 1981; adv. bd. Minn. Inst. of Legal Edn., 1984—. Served to specialist 4th class U.S. Army, 1969-71. Fellow Am. Coll. Tax Counsel; mem. ABA, Am. Law Inst., Tax Inst. Am. (chmn. sales and use tax commn. 1988-90), Nat. Tax Assn., Am. Judicature Soc., Minn. Bar Assn. (bd. dirs. tax coun. sect. 1984-93, 94-97, 99—, chmn. 1990-91), Ramsey County Bar Assn., Minn. Taxpayers Assn. (bd. dirs. 1988—), Inst. Property Taxation, Supreme Ct. Hist. Soc., Nat. Assn. State Bar Tax Sects. (exec. com. 1993—), Citizens League, Minn. Club (bd. dirs. 1997-2000), KC, Kiwanis (bd. dirs. 2000--). Home: 1116 Dodd Rd Saint Paul MN 55118-1821 Office: Briggs & Morgan PA 2200 1st St N Saint Paul MN 55109-3210 E-mail: Geiger@Briggs.com.

GEISSINGER, FREDERICK WALLACE, investment banking executive; b. Huntingdon, Pa., Oct. 3, 1945; s. Harry Lloyd and Elizabeth Gertrude (Munkelt) G.; m. Anne Beth Lawrenz, Feb. 14, 1970; children: Amy Elizabeth, Jacqueline Marie. AB, Dartmouth Coll., 1967; MBA, U. Chgo., 1969. Lic. in securities and real estate, N.Y.C. Corp. banking officer Chase Manhattan Bank, N.Y.C., 1969-74, dir. corp. planning, 1974-76, asst. gen. mgr. Tokyo, 1976-80, chief staff Western Hemisphere N.Y.C., 1980-83, budget dir., 1983-86, sr. v.p. real estate, 1986-90; exec. v.p. Daiwa Securities Am. Inc., 1990-92; prin. Geissinger and Assocs., 1993; CEO Am. Gen. Land Devel. Inc., Houston, 1994-95, Am. Gen. Mortgage and Land Devel. Inc., 1995; chmn., CEO Am. Gen. Finance, Evansville, Ind., 1995—; vice chmn., group exec. Am. Gen. Corp., Houston, 1998—. Trustee Pelham (N.Y.) Bd. Edn., 1983-86. Mem. Urban Land Inst. (coun. 1986—), Real Estate Bd. N.Y., Pelham Country club (bd. govs. 1987-92, pres. 1990-92). Republican. Presbyterian. Avocations: skiing, golf, tennis, coaching girls soccer, classical music.

GELATT, CHARLES DANIEL, manufacturing company executive; b. La Crosse, Wis., Jan. 4, 1918; s. Philo Madison and Clara (Johnson) G.; m. Jane Leicht, Mar. 6, 1942 (div. 1972); children: Sarah Jane Gelatt Gephart, Charles D., Philip Madison; m. Paula Jo Evans, Aug. 22, 1973 (div. 1978); m. Sue Anne Jimieson, Dec. 11, 1983. BA, MA, U. Wis., 1939. V.p. Gelatt Corp., La Crosse, 1940-52, pres., 1952-95, chmn., 1995—99; pres. No. Engraving Corp., Sparta, Wis., 1958-67, chmn., 1967-96, chmn. emeritus, 1996—; pres. N.E. Co. Ltd., 2000—. Trustee Northwestern Mut. Life Ins. Co., Milw., 1960-88, mem. exec. com., 1961-77; chmn. North Ctrl. Trust Co., La. Crosse, 1989-93; mem. bd. regents U. Wis., 1947-74, pres. bd. regents, 1955-57, v.p., 1964-68, pres., 1968-69; mem. Wis. Coordinating Com. for Higher Edn., 1955-59, 64-69, chmn., 1956; chmn. Assn. Governing Bds. Univs. and Colls., Washington, 1971-72; trustee Carroll Coll., Waukesha, Wis., 1971-79, Viterbo Coll., La. Crosse, 1972-2002; trustee Gundersen Found., La Crosse, 1973-95. Mem. Phi Beta Kappa. Home: 9133 Collins Ave Surfside FL 33154 Office: PO Box 1087 La Crosse WI 54602-1087

GELBER, BRIAN, commodities trader; b. 1954; With Thomson Mc Kinnon Securities, Chgo., 1975-82, Gelber Group Inc., Chgo., 1982—, pres. Office: Gelber Group Inc 141 W Jackson Blvd Lbby 1 Chicago IL 60604-2904

GELBKE, CLAUS-KONRAD, nuclear physics educator; b. Celle, Germany, May 31, 1947; came to the U.S., 1976; s. Heinz and Gertraud Gelbke; m. Brigitte Zabeschek, Apr. 6, 1973; children: Susanne, Martin. Diploma für physik, U. Heidelberg, Germany, 1970, doctor rerum naturalium, 1973. Wissenschaftlicher asst. Max-Planck-Inst für Kernphysik, Heidelberg, 1973-76; physicist Lawrence Berkeley (Calif.) Lab., 1976-77; assoc. prof. physics Mich. State U., East Lansing, 1977-81, prof. physics, 1981-87, assoc. dir. nuclear sci. Nat. Superconducting Cyclotron Lab., 1987-90, disting. prof., 1990—, dir. Nat. Superconducting Cyclotron Lab., 1992—. Summer visitor Brookhaven Nat. Lab., Upton, N.Y., 1974, U. Washington, Seattle, 1975. Alfred P. Sloan fellow, 1979-83; Scholarship Studienstiftung des Deutschen Volkes, 1971-72; Humboldt Rsch. award U.S. Scis. Fellow Am. Physical Soc. Office: Mich State U Cyclotron Lab S Shaw Ln East Lansing MI 48824 E-mail: gelbke@nscl.msu.edu.

GELDER, JOHN WILLIAM, lawyer; b. Buffalo, Aug. 7, 1933; s. Ray Horace and Grace Catherine (Kelly) G.; m. Martha J. Kindleberger, June 12, 1953; William R., Mark S., Cathryn J. Gelder Brooks, Carolyn G. Gelder Bird B.B.A., U. Mich., 1956, J.D. with distinction, 1959. Bar: Mich. 1960, D.C. 1981, U.S. Supreme Ct. 1982. Assoc. Miller, Canfield, Paddock and Stone, P.L.C., Detroit, 1959-68, mng. ptnr., 1975-81, 90-93, ptnr., 1968-93, prin., 1994—. Bd. dirs. Tecumseh Products Co., 1989—. Asst. editor Mich. Law Rev., 1958, 59 Trustee, officer Herrick Found., Detroit, 1989—. Mem. State Bar Mich. (coun. mem. bus. law sect. 1984-90), Order of Coif, Bloomfield Hills Country Club. Home: 30845 River Crossing St Bingham Farms MI 48025-4656 Office: Miller Canfield Paddock & Stone PLC 840 W Long Lake Rd Ste 200 Troy MI 48098-6358 E-mail: gelder@millercanfield.com.

GELEHRTER, THOMAS DAVID, medical and genetics educator, physician; b. Liberec, Czechoslovakia, Mar. 11, 1936; married 1959; 2 children. BA, Oberlin Coll., 1957; MA, U. Oxford, Eng., 1959; MD, Harvard U., 1963. Intern, then asst. resident in internal medicine Mass. Gen. Hosp., Boston, 1963-65; rsch. assoc. in molecular biology NIAMD NIH, Bethesda, Md., 1965-69; fellow in med. genetics U. Wash., 1969-70; asst. prof. human genetics, internal medicine and pediatrics Sch. Medicine Yale U., 1970-73, assoc. prof., 1973-74, U. Mich., Ann Arbor, 1974-76, prof. internal medicine and human genetics, 1976-87, dir. divsn. med. genetics, 1977-87, chmn. dept. human genetics, prof. human genetics and internal medicine, 1987—. Josiah Macy, Jr. Found. faculty scholar and vis. scientist Imperial Cancer Rsch. Fund Labs., London, 1979-80; vis. fellow Inst. Molecular Medicine; Keeley vis. fellow Wadham Coll., U. Oxford, Wellcome Rsch. Travel grantee, 1995. Mem. editl. bd. Jour. Biol. Chemistry, 1995-2000. Trustee Oberlin Coll., 1970-75 Rhodes scholar, 1957-59. Fellow AAAS, Am. Coll. Med. Genetics; mem. Am. Soc. Human Genetics (bd. dirs. 1994-96), Am. Soc. Clin. Investigation, Am. Soc. Biochemistry and Molecular Biology, Assn. Am. Physicians. Office: 1241 Catherine St PO Box 618 Ann Arbor MI 48106-0618 E-mail: tdgum@umich.edu.

GELLMAN, SAMUEL HELMER, chemist, educator; b. Evanston, Ill., Sept. 12, 1959; s. Aaron Jacob and Susanne Gellman; m. Julie Ann Plotkin, Dec. 30, 1990. AB, Harvard U., 1981; PhD, Columbia U., 1986. Postdoctoral fellow Calif. Inst. Tech., Pasadena, 1986-87; asst. prof. chemistry U. Wis., Madison, 1987-93, assoc. prof., 1993-95, prof., 1995—. Contbr. articles to Jour. Am. Chem. Soc., Nature. Office Naval Rsch. young investigator, 1990; NSF presdl. young investigator, 1991; Alfred P. Sloan fellow Alfred P. Sloan Found., 1993. Mem. AAAS, Am. Chem. Soc. (Arthur C. Cope scholar 1997). Office: U Wis Dept Chemistry 1101 University Ave Madison WI 53706-1322 E-mail: gellman@chem.wisc.edu.

GELMAN, ANDREW RICHARD, lawyer; b. Chgo. s. Sidney S. and Beverly Gelman; m. Amy H., 1985; children: Stephen S., Adam P., Elizabeth F. BA, U. Pa., 1967; JD, U. Va., 1970. Bar: Va. 1970, Ill. 1971. Assoc. Roan & Grossman Law Firm, Chgo., 1971-74, McBride, Baker & Coles Law Firm, Chgo., 1974-77, ptnr., 1978—. Mem. com. on character and fitness of Ill. Supreme Ct., Chgo., 1979-95. Bd. dirs. Scholarship and Guidance Assn., Chgo., 1979—, Inst. for Edn. and Rsch. of Children's Meml. Hosp., Chgo., 1991—, vice-chair, 1998—; chmn. Med. Rsch. Inst. Coun., 1983-86, 91-92; trustee Michael Reese Hosp. and Med. Ctr., Chgo., 1987-91. Recipient Weigle award Chgo. Bar Found., 1980. Mem. ABA (standing com. jud. selection, tenure and compensation 1982-87, pub. understanding about the law com. 1987-91, chair probate and estate planning com. gen. practice sect. 1994-97, commn. on mental and phys. disability law 1995-97), Chgo. Bar Assn. (past chmn. divsn. probate practice com., bd. mgrs. 1978-80, chmn. young lawyers sect. 1976-77), Chgo. Estate Planning Coun. Office: McBride Baker & Coles 500 W Madison St Fl 40 Chicago IL 60661-2511 E-mail: gelman@mbc.com.

GEMIGNANI, JOSEPH ADOLPH, lawyer; b. Hancock, Mich., Apr. 17, 1932; s. Baldo A. and Yolanda M.; m. Barbara A. Thomson, Sept. 5, 1953; children: Joseph, Jon. BSME, Mich. Technological U., 1953; JD, U. Mich., 1958. Bar: Wis. 1959, Mich. 1960, U.S. Dist. Ct. (ea. and we. dists.) Wis., U.S. Ct. Appeals (7th cir.), U.S. Ct. Appeals (fed. cir.). In-house counsel McGraw Edison Co., Milw., 1958-60; ptnr. Michael, Best & Friedrich, 1960—. 1st lt. USAF, 1953-55. Home: 616 E Day Ave Milwaukee WI 53217-4841 Office: Michael Best & Friedrich 100 E Wisconsin Ave Ste 3300 Milwaukee WI 53202-4108

GENETSKI, ROBERT JAMES, economist; b. N.Y.C., Dec. 26, 1942; s. Alex and Helen Genetski. BS, Ea. Ill. U., 1964; MA, NYU, 1968, PhD, 1972. Tchr. English St. Procopius Acad., Lisle, Ill., 1965-66; research analyst Nat. Econ. Research Assn., N.Y.C., 1967-68; lectr. econs. NYU, 1969-70; econ. analyst Morgan Guaranty Trust Co., 1969-71; sr. v.p., economist Harris Trust & Savs. Bank, Chgo., 1971-88; pres. Stotler Econs., 1988-90; sr. v.p., chief economist The Chgo. Corp., 1990-91; pres. Robert Genetski & Assocs., 1991—; sr. mng. dir. Chgo. Capital, 1995-2000. Lectr. econs. NYU, 1969-70, U. Chgo., 1973; vis. prof. Wheaton (Ill.) Coll., 1986; mem. census adv. com. U.S. Dept. Commerce, 1983-86; bd. dirs. Fin. Security Corp., Suburban Fed. Savs. Bank. Author: (with Beryl Sprinkel) Winning with Money, 1977, Taking the Voodoo out of Economics, 1986, 88, A Nation of Millionaires, 1997. Chmn. ednl. com. Sch. Bd. Dist. 25, West Chicago, Ill., 1973-79; bd. dirs. Ctrl. DuPage Health Svcs., 1988-94. Mem. Am. Statis. Assn., Am. Econ. Assn. (fin. com. 1983—), Nat. Assn. Bus. Economists (editor Newsletter 1978), Western Econ. Assn., Am. Bankers Assn. (econ. adv. com. 1980-83), U.S. C. of C. (econ. adv. com. 1985—) Office: 195 N Harbor Dr Ste 4903 Chicago IL 60601 E-mail: rgenetski@earthlink.net.

GENOWAYS, HUGH HOWARD, systematic biologist, educator; b. Scottsbluff, Nebr., Dec. 24, 1940; s. Theodore Thompson and Sarah Louise (Beales) G.; m. Joyce Elaine Cox, July 28, 1963; children: Margaret Louise, Theodore Howard. AB, Hastings Coll., 1963; postgrad., U. Western Australia, 1964; PhD, U. Kans., 1971. Curator Mus. of Tex. Tech U., Lubbock, 1972-76, lectr. Mus. Sci. Program, 1974-76; curator Carnegie Mus. Natural History, Pitts., 1976-86; dir. U. Nebr. State Mus., Lincoln, 1986-94; chair mus. studies program U. Nebr., 1989-95, 97—, prof. state mus., 1986—, prof. natural resource scis., 1997—. Author, editor: Mammalian Biology in South America, 1982, Natural History of the Dog, 1984; contbns. in Vertebrate Paleontology, 1984, Species of Special Concern in Pennsylvania, 1985, Current Mammalogy, 1987, 90, Biology of the Heteromyidae, 1993, Storage of Natural History Collections: A Preventive Conservation Approach, 1996, Mammalogy: A Memorial Volume Honoring Dr. J. Knox Jones, Jr., 1996, (with Ted Genoways) A Perfect Picture of Hell: Eyewitness Accounts by Civil War Prisoners from the 12th Iowa, 2001. Packmaster Allegheny Trails coun. Boy Scouts Am., 1981-83, asst. scoutmaster, 1983-86. Grantee Fulbright Found., 1964, NSF, 1977-86, R.K. Mellon Found., 1981-86, Smithsonian Fgn. Currency Program, 1983-84, Inst. Mus. Svcs., 1989-96. Mem. Am. Soc. Mammalogists (pres. 1984-86, C. Hart Merriam award 1987, editor Spl. Pubs. 1995-96, historian 1997—), Internat. Theriological Congress (steering com. 1985—), Southwestern Assn. Naturalists (pres. 1984-85), Am. Assn. Mus., Nebr. Mus. Assn. (pres. 1990-92, 1st Hugh H. Genoways Achievement award 1994, sec. 1997-2000), Assn. Systematics Collections (bd. dirs. 1993-94), Nat. Inst. for Conservation Cultural Property (bd. dirs. 1993-94), Sociedad Argentina para Estudio Mamiferos, Lincoln Attractions and Mus. Assn. (chair 1987-94), Soc. Systematic Biologists, Rotary (bd. dirs. Lincoln N.E. club 1990-92). Office: U Nebr-Lincoln State Mus W436 Nebraska Hall Lincoln NE 68588-0514

GENT, ALAN NEVILLE, physicist, educator; b. Leicester, Eng., Nov. 11, 1927; came to U.S., 1961, naturalized, 1972; s. Harry Neville and Gladys (Hoyle) G.; m. Jean Margaret Wolstenholme, Sept. 1, 1949; children: Martin Paul Neville, Patrick Michael, Andrew John; m. Ginger Lee, Sept. 4, 1997. BS, U. London, 1946, BS in Physics, 1949, PhD in Sci., 1955; DHC, U. Haute-Alsace, France, 1997; DSc (hon.), De Montfort U., Eng., 1998. Lab. asst. John Bull Rubber Co., Leicester, Eng., 1944-45; research physicist Brit. (now Malaysian) Rubber Producers' Research Assn., 1949-61; prof. polymer physics U. Akron, Ohio, 1961-88, Dr. Harold A. Morton prof. polymer physics and polymer engring., 1988-94; prof. emeritus, 1994—; dean grad. studies and research U. Akron, 1978-86. Vis. prof. dept. materials Queen Mary Coll., U. London, 1969-70; vis. prof. dept. chem. engring. McGill U., 1983; Hill vis. prof. U. Minn., 1985; cons. Goodyear Tire & Rubber Co., 1963—, Gen. Motors, 1973-87. Contbr. articles to profl. pubis. Served with Brit. Army, 1947-49. Recipient Mobay award, Cellular Plastics divsn. Soc. of Plastics Industry, 1963, Colwyn medal Plastics and Rubber Inst. Gt. Brit., 1978, Adhesives award Com. F-11, ASTM, 1979, Internat. Rsch. award Soc. Plastics Engrs., 1980, Whitby award Rubber Chem. divsn. Am. Chem. Soc., 1987, Pub. Svc. medal NASA, 1988, Charles Goodyear medal Rubber Chem. divsn. Am. Chem. Soc., 1990; installed Ohio Sci. Tech. and Industry Hall of Fame, 1993. Mem. NAE, Soc. of Rheology (pres. 1981-83, Bingham medal 1975), Adhesion Soc. (pres. 1978-80, 3M award 1987, Pres.'s award 1997), Am. Phys. Soc. (chmn. divsn. high polymer physics 1977-78, High Polymer Physics prize 1996). Democrat. Office: U Akron Inst Polymer Science Akron OH 44325-3909 E-mail: angent@goodyear.com., angent@netzero.com.

GENTINE, LEE MICHAEL, marketing professional; b. Plymouth, Wis., Feb. 18, 1952; s. Leonard ALvin and Dolores Ann (Becker) G.; m. Debra Ann Suemnicht, Dec. 29, 1973; children: Amanda, Joshua, Jonathan. BBA, U. Notre Dame, 1974; MBA, DePaul U., 1977. Acct. Hurdman & Cranston, Chgo., 1974-75; sales rep. Sargento Cheese Inc., Plymouth, 1975-78, mktg. mgr., 1978-81, sr. v.p. mktg., 1981-84, exec. v.p. mktg., 1984-89, pres. consumer products divsn., 1989-97. Mem. adv. bd. Kaytee Products Inc., Chilton, Wis., 1994-98; mng. ptnr. Dairyland Investors Group, L.L.P., 1997—; bd. dirs. Sargento Foods Inc. Bd. dirs. Plymouth Softball Assn., 1980—; pres. Plymouth Indsl. Devel. Corp., 1981-85, Parish Coun., 1989-90; chmn. Plymouth Advancement Com., 1992-96, pres., 1992-2002; mem. adv. bd. St. Nicholas Hosp., 1998—; pres. Quit Qui Oc Athletic Alliance, Inc., 1999—. Named One of 100 Best and Brightest Advt. Execs., Advt. Age, 1986. Mem. Am. Mktg. Assn., Sheboygan County C. of C. (bd. dirs. 1987-89), Beta Gamma Sigma. Roman Catholic. Avocations: softball, golf, home rehabilitation. Office: Dairyland Investors Group LLP 601 Eastern Ave Plymouth WI 53073-1913

GENTRY, DON KENNETH, academic dean; b. Crawfordsville, Ind., Mar. 1, 1939; m. Carol A. Kern; children: Alynn, Alan, Andrew. BS in Animal Sci. & Agr. Edn., Purdue U., 1962, MS in Secondary Edn. & Ednl. Adminstrn., 1967; EdD in Ednl. Adminstrn., Ind. U., 1979; D (hon.), Vincennes U., 1983. Instr. in vocat. agr. North Montgomery Community Schs., Linden, Ind., 1962-67; state supr. agrl. edn. Ind. State Dept. Pub. Instruction, 1967-69, chief program planning, rsch. & evaluation divsn. vocat. edn., 1969, asst. dir. divsn. vocat. edn., 1969-70, dir. divsn. vocat. edn., 1970-71, exec. officer, state dir. vocat. edn., 1971-83; dir. Purdue Statewide Tech. Program Purdue U., West Lafayette, Ind., 1983-87, prof. indsl. tech., 1984—, asst. dean sch. tech., 1985-86, assoc. dean sch. tech., 1986-87, dean sch. tech., 1987—. Univ. rep. to Nat. Engring. Tech. Coun., 1989—. Contbr. articles to profl. jours.; over 20 papers & presentations in field. Bd. dirs. Ind. Corp. for Sci. & Tech., 1982-83. Recipient Outstanding Svc. award Ind. Distbv. Edn. Clubs Am., 1972, Disting. Hoosier award Gov. Edgar D. Whitcomb, 1972, Hon. Future Homemaker award Future Homemakers Am., 1973, Outstanding Hoosier award Gov. Otis R. Bowen, 1975, Sagamore of Wabash award, 1980, Outstanding Svc. awards Ind. Vocat. Assn., 1973, Nat. Office Edn. Assn., 1975, Nat. Vocat. Edn. Spl. Needs Assn., 1980, Ind. Employment & Tng. Assn., 1982, Outstanding Leadership award Ind. Vocat. Adminstrs. Assn., 1983, Appreciation award U.S. Dept. Def., 1991. Mem. Am. Soc. for Engring. Edn. (engring. tech. divsn.), Am. Vocat. Assn. (life mem.), Engring. Tech. Leadership Inst., Engring. Tech. Coun., Nat. Consortium for Four Year Degree Engring. Tech. Schs., Indiana Health Careers, Inc. (membership chmn. 1980-83), Nat. Assn. State Dirs. Vocat. Edn. (bd. dirs., sec. 1979, pres. 1980, past pres. 1981), Nat. Consortium for Vocat. Ednl. Leadership (devel.-charter pres. 1980, bd. dirs. 1979-82), Office Edn. Assn. (hon. life mem.), John Purdue Club, Ceres, Alpha Zeta, Alpha Tau Alpha, Tau Alpha Phi. Office: Purdue U Sch Tech West Lafayette IN 47907

GEO-KARIS, ADELINE JAY, state legislator; b. Tegeas, Greece, Mar. 29, 1918; Student, Northwestern U.; LLB, DePaul U. Bar: Ill. Founder Adeline J. Geo-Karis and Assocs., Zion, Ill.; former mcpl., legis. atty. Mundelein, Vernon Hills, Libertyville Twp., Twp. Long Grove (Ill.) Sch. Dist. Justice of peace; former asst. state's atty.; mem. Ill. Ho. of Reps., 1973-79; mem. Ill. Senate, 1979—, asst. majority leader, 1992—; former mayor City of Zion, Ill. Served to lt. comdr. USNR, Res. ret. Recipient Americanism medal DAR; named Woman of Yr. Daughters of Penelope, Outstanding Legislator Ill. Fedn. Ind. Colls. and Univs., 1975-78, Legis. award Ill. Assn. Park Dists., 1976; Sponsor Guilty but Mentally Ill law. Greek Orthodox. Office: Ill State Senate State Capitol Springfield IL 62706-0001

GEORGE, FRANCIS CARDINAL, archbishop; b. Chgo., Jan. 16, 1937; Ordained priest Roman Cath. Ch., 1963. Provincial ctrl. region Oblates of Mary Immaculate, 1973-74, vicar gen., 1974-86; bishop Diocese of Yakima, Wash., 1990-96; archbishop Archdiocese of Portland, Oreg., 1996-97, Archdiocese of Chgo., 1997—. Chancellor Cath. Ch. Extension Soc., U. St. Mary of the Lake, 1997; mem. Congregation Divine Worship and the Discipline of the Sacraments, Congregation Insts. Consecrated Life and Socs. of Apostolic Life, and Pontifical Coun. "Cor Unum", 1998, Congregation Evangelization of Peoples; mem. Congregation for Oriental Chs., 2001--; mem. Pontifical Commn. for the Cultural Heirtage of the Ch., 1999--. Mem. Coll. Cardinals. Office: Archdiocese of Chicago Pastoral Ctr PO Box 1979 Chicago IL 60690-1979

GEORGE, GARY RAYMOND, state legislator; b. Milw., Mar. 8, 1954; s. Horace Raymond and Audrey C. (Chevalier) G.; children: Alexander, Daniel Raymond. BBA, U. Wis., 1976; JD, Mich. Law. Sch., 1979. With tax dept. Arthur Young & Co., Milw., 1979-81; mem. Wis. Senate from 6th dist., Madison, 1981—; pres. pro tempore Wis. Senate, 1999—, chair judiciary and consumer affairs com., 1999—, co-chair joint com. on audit, 1999—. Democrat. Roman Catholic. Home: 1100 W Wells St Apt 1711 Milwaukee WI 53233-2341 Office: State Capitol 118 S PO Box 7882 Madison WI 53707-7882

GEORGE, JAMES W. travel company executive; MBA in Acctg., Ohio U. CPA. Managerial level acctg. positions with British Petroleum, Deloitte Haskins and Sells; sr. v.p., CFO, sec. TravelCtrs. of Am. Inc., Westlake, Ohio, 1993. Office: TravelCtrs Am Inc Ste 200 24601 Center Rigde Rd Westlake OH 44145

GEORGE, JOYCE JACKSON, lawyer, judge emeritus; b. Akron, Ohio, May 4, 1936; d. Ray and Verna (Popadich) Jackson; children: Michael Eliot, Michelle René. BA, U. Akron, 1962, JD, 1966; postgrad., Nat. Jud. Coll., Reno, 1976, NYU, 1983. Bar: Ohio 1966, U.S. Dist. Ct. (no. dist.) Ohio 1966, U.S. Ct. Appeals (6th cir.) 1968, U.S. Supreme Ct. 1968. Tchr. Akron Bd. Edn., 1962-66; asst. dir. law City of Akron, 1966-69, pub. utilities advisor, 1969-70, asst. dir. law, 1970-73; pvt. practice Akron, 1973-76; referee Akron Mcpl. Ct., 1975, judge, 1976-83, 9th dist. Ct. Appeals, Akron, 1983-89, Peninsula, Ohio, 1989; U.S. atty. No. Dist., 1989-93; v.p. adminstrn. Telxon Corp., Akron, 1993-96; pres. Ind. Bus. Info. Svcs., Inc., 1996—. Tchr., lectr. Ohio Jud. Coll., Nat. Jud. Coll.; cons. in field. Author: Judicial Opinion Writing Handbook, 1981, 3d edit., 1993, Referee's Report Writing Handbook, 1992; contbr. articles to profl. publs. Recipient Outstanding Woman of Yr. award Akron Bus. and Profl. Women's Club, 1982; Alumni Honor award U. Akron, 1983, Alumni award U. Akron Sch. Law, 1991; Dept. Treasury award, 1992; named Woman of Yr. in politics and govt. Summit County, Ohio, 1983. Mem.: ABA, Akron Bar Assn., Ohio Bar Assn. Fax: 330-668-2910.

GEORGE, THOMAS FREDERICK, chemistry educator; b. Phila., Mar. 18, 1947; s. Emmanuel John and Veronica Mather (Hansel) G.; m. Barbara Carol Harbach, Apr. 25, 1970. BA in Chemistry and Math., Gettysburg (Pa.) Coll., 1967; MS in Chemistry, Yale U., 1968, PhD, 1970. Rsch. assoc. MIT, 1970; postdoctoral fellow U. Calif., Berkeley, 1971; mem. faculty U. Rochester, N.Y., 1972-85, prof. chemistry, 1977-85; dean Faculty Natural Sci. and Math., prof. chemistry and physics SUNY-Buffalo, 1985-91; provost, acad. v.p., prof. chemistry and physics Wash. State U., Pullman, 1991-96; chancellor, prof. chemistry and physics U. Wis., Stevens Point, 1996—; Disting. vis. lectr. dept. chemistry U. Tex., Austin, 1978; lectr. NATO Advanced Study Inst., Cambridge, Eng., 1979; Disting. speaker dept. chemistry U. Utah, 1980; Disting. lectr. Air Force Weapons Lab., Kirtland AFB, N.Mex., 1980; mem. com. recommendations U.S. Army Basic Sci. Research, 1978-81; lectr. NATO Summer Sch. on Interfaces under Photon Irradiation, Maratea, Italy, 1986; organizer NSF workshop on theoretical aspects of laser radiation and its interaction with atomic and molecular systems Rochester, N.Y., 1977; vice chmn. 6th Internat. Conf. Molecular Energy Transfer, Rodez, France, 1979; chmn. Gordon Rsch. Conf. Molecular Energy Transfer, Wolfeboro, N.H., 1981. Adj. rsch. prof. physics Korea U., Seoul, 1994-99; Dow lectr. polymer sci. U. Detroit Mercy, 1996; mem. program com. Internat. Conf. on Lasers, San Francisco, 1981-83, ACS Symposium on Recent Advances in Surface Sci., Rochester sect., 1982, Internat. Laser Sci. Conf., Dallas, 1985, external rev. com. for chemistry Gettysburg Coll., 1984, awards com. ACS Procter and Gamble student prizes in chemistry, 1982-83, Free-electron Laser peer rev. panel Am. Inst. Biol. Sci. Med., alt., bd. trustees alt. Calspan-UB Rsch. Ctr., 1989-91; organiser APS Symposium on Laser-Induced Molecular Excitation/Photofragmentation, N.Y., 1987; co-organizer ACS Symposium on Phys. Chemistry High-Temp. Supercondrs., L.A., 1988; co-organizer MRS Symposium on High-Temperature Superconductors, Alfred, N.Y., 1988; chmn. SPIE Symposium on Photochemistry in Thin Films, L.A., 1989; mem. internat. program adv. com. Internat. Sch. Lasers and Applications, Sayanogorsk, East Siberia, USSR, 1989; lectr. on chemistry at cutting edge Smithsonian Instn./Am. Chem. Soc., Washington, 1990; Musselman lectr. Gettysburg Coll., 1999; mem. internat. adv. com. Xth Vavilov Conf. Nonlinear Optics, Novosibirsk, USSR, 1990; Am. coord. NSF Info. Exchange Seminar for U.S.-Japan Program of Cooperation in Photoconversion and Photosynthesis, Honolulu, 1990; mem. program com. Optical Soc. Am. Topical Meeting on Radiative Processes and Dephasing in Semiconductors, Coeur d'Alene, Idaho, 1998; mem. sci. com. Sixth Brijuni Internat. Conf. on Interdisciplinary Topics in Physics and Chemistry, Brijuni Isles, Croatia, 1998; mem. exec. bd. N.Y. State Inst. on Superconductivity, 1990-91; mem. ONT/ASEE rev. panel for Engring. Edn. postdoctoral fellowship program, 1990; mem. rev panel rsch. experiences for undergrads of sci. and tech. rsch. ctrs., NSF, 1989, mem. rev. panel grad. res. traineeships NSF, 1992; cons., lectr. in field. Co-author: (with Blackwell) Notes in Classical and Quantum Physics, 1990, (with Kluwer) Fundamentals in Chemical Physics, 1998; also over 580 papers in field; mem. editl. bd. Molecular Physics, 1984-90, Jour. Cluster Sci., 1989-97; mem. adv. bd. Jour. Phys. Chemistry, 1980-84; mem. adv. editl. bd. Chem. Physics Letters, 1979-81, Chem. Materials, 1989; mem. editl. bd. Jour. Quantum Nonlinear Phenomena (Soviet jour), 1991-96, Nova Jour. Theoretical Physics, 1996-97; editor-at-large Marcel Dekker, 1989; editor: Photochemistry in Thin Films, 1989; co-editor Internat. Jour. Theoretical Physics, Group Theory, and Nonlinear Optics, 1999—; co-editor: Chemistry of High-Temperature Superconductors, Vol. I, 1987, vol. II, 1988, ACS Symposium Series, Computational Studies of New Materials, 1999, Optics of Nanostructural Materials, 2001, Modern Topics in Chemical Physics, 2001; feature editor Jour. of Optical Soc. of Am., Spectrochimica Acta, Optical Engring. Tchr., scholar Camille and Henry Dreyfus Found., 1975-85; bd. mgrs. Buffalo Mus. Sci., 1986-92; mem. exec. bd. N.Y. State Inst. on Superconductivity, 1990-91; mem. canvassing com. ACS; mem. external rev. com. for chemistry Gettysburg Coll., 1984; mem. NEASC site visit team Boston U., ten-yr. accreditation, 1989; bd. dirs. Wash. State Inst. for Pub. Policy, 1991-96; trustee Wash. State U. Found., 1991-96; bd. dirs. Wash. Tech. Ctr., 1992-96; mem. exec. com. Northwest Acad. Forum, 1992-96, chmn. 1994-95; mem. rev. panel Grad. Rsch. Traineeships, NSF, 1992, mem. rev. panel for sci. and tech. ctr. proposals, 1998, rev. panel for preproposals for sci. and tech. ctrs., 1998; mem. Project 435 Dist. Leadership Coun., Wis. Assn. Biomed. Rsch. and Edn./Research America!, 1997; mem. Commn. on the Future of Gettysburg Coll., 1997-98; bd. dirs. Portage County Bus. Coun., 1998—, Stevens Point Area YMCA, 1998—, United Way Portage County, Wis., 1997—, chmn. 1999 campaign, Tech. Alliance State Wash., 1996, U. Wis.-Stevens Point Found., 1996—, Paper Sci. Found., 1996—; bd. trustees/dirs. (alt.) Assoc. Western Univs., 1993-96; bd. dirs. alt. Joint Ctr. Higher Edn., Spokane, 1996; mem steering com. Ctr. for Advanced Tech. in Healthcare Instruments and Devices, 1988-90; with Midwestern Higher Edn. Commn., 1999—; exploring chair Mushkodany Dist. Wis. Samoset Coun. Boy Scouts Am., 1998, finance chair, 1999, pres.-elect, 2001; bd. dirs. St. Michael's Hosp., Stevens Point, Wis., 1999-2000, Midwestern Higher Edn. Commn., 1999—, Distributed Learning Workshop, Midwestern Higher Edn. Commn., 1999-, Wis. Ctr. Acad. Talented Youth, 2001-; bd. trustees WiSys Tech. Found., 2000-; bd. commnrs. Acad. Advanced Distributed Learning Lab. (UW-US Dept. Def.), 2001; adv. coun. Ednl. Directories Unlimited, 2001-. Sloan fellow, 1976-80, postdoctoral fellow, 1990, Guggenheim fellow, 1983-84; recipient Disting. Alumni award Gettysburg Coll., 1987. Fellow AAAS, Soc. Photo-Optical Instrumentation Engrs., Am. Phys. Soc., N.Y. Acad. Scis., Inst. Superconductivity (steering com. 1987-91); mem. Am. Chem. Soc. (exec. com. phys. div. 1979-82, 85-89, 94-97, vice chmn. 1985-86, chmn.-elect 1986-87, chmn. 1987-88), Am. Assn. State Colls. and Univs. (acad. affairs subcom. on sci. edn. rsch. and tng., coun. state reps.), Wis. Assn. for Biomed. Rsch. and Edn., European Phys. Soc., Royal Soc. Chemistry (Marlow medal and prize 1979), Phi Beta Kappa, Sigma Xi (exec. com. U. Rochester 1984-85, faculty scholar award 1999). Democrat. Lutheran. Office: U Wis Office of Chancellor 213 Old Main Stevens Point WI 54481-3897 E-mail: tgeorge@uwsp.edu.

GEORGE, WILLIAM WALLACE, manufacturing company executive; b. Muskegon, Mich., Sept. 14, 1942; s. Wallace Edwin and Kathryn Jean (Dinkeloo) G.; m. Ann Tonnlier Pilgram, Sept. 6, 1969; children: Jeffrey, Jonathan. BS in Indsl. Engring. with honors, Ga. Inst. Tech., 1964; MBA with high distinction, Harvard U., 1966. Asst. to asst. sec. Dept. Def., Washington, 1966-68; spl. civilian asst. to sec. Navy, 1968-69; with Litton Industries, 1969-78, dir. long-range planning, 1969-70, v.p., 1976—; with Litton Microwave Cooking Products, 1970-78, v.p., 1970-71, exec. v.p., 1971-73, pres., 1973-78; v.p. corp. devel. Honeywell, Mpls., 1978-80, exec. v.p., 1983-87; pres. Honeywell Europe (S.A.), 1980-82, Indsl. Automation, 1987, Space and Aviation Systems, Mpls., 1988-89; pres., chief oper. officer Medtronic Inc., 1989-91, pres., CEO, 1989-96, chmn., CEO, 1996—. Bd. dirs. Dayton-Hudson, Imation. Bd. dirs. Minn. Symphony Orch., 1976-80, United Way, 1976-79, 96—, nat. chmn., Belgium, 1982-83, campaign chair, 1997; bd. dirs., pres., treas. Guthrie Theater, 1977-84; vice-chmn. United Theol. Sem., 1977-80, Abbott-Northwestern Hosp., 1984—, vice-chair, 1989-91, chair, 1991-93, Health Span, 1989-94; trustee Macalaster Coll., 1987-93, Allin Health Sys., 1994—, vice-chair, 1997—, Mlps. Inst. Arts, 1993—, chmn. Minn. Thunder Pro Soccer, 1994—. Recipient Meritorious Civilian Service Award Sec. Navy, 1969 Mem. Sigma Chi (Internat. Balfour award 1964, trustee 1971-77, Disting. Alumni award Harvard U., 1997). Episcopalian. Clubs: Minneapolis, Minikahda. Home: 2284 W Lake Of The Isles Pky Minneapolis MN 55405-2434 Office: Medtronic Inc 7000 Central Ave NE # Ms-400 Minneapolis MN 55432-3576

GEPHARDT, RICHARD ANDREW, congressman; b. St. Louis, Jan. 31, 1941; s. Louis Andrew and Loreen Estelle (Cassell) G.; m. Jane Ann Byrnes, Aug. 13, 1966; children: Matthew, Christine, Katherine. BS, Northwestern U., 1962; JD, U. Mich., 1965. Bar: Mo. 1965. Ptnr. Thompson & Mitchell, St. Louis, 1965-76; alderman 14th ward City of St. Louis, 1971-76; mem. U.S. Congress from 3d Mo. dist., 1979—; Dem. leader, mem. house dem. policy com.; minority leader. Dem. committeeman 14th ward, St. Louis, 1968-71; pres. Children's Hematology Rsch. Assn., St. Louis Children's Hosp., 1973-76; candidate for Dem. nomination for Pres. of U.S., 1987-88. Mem. Mo. Bar Assn., St. Louis Bar Assn., Am. Legion, Young Lawyer's Soc. (chmn. 1972-73), Kiwanis. Club: Mid-Town (St. Louis). Office: US Ho of Reps 1236 Longworth House Office Bldg Washington DC 20515-0001 also: Office of Dem Leader H-204 The Capitol Washington DC 20515-0001*

GERARD, JULES BERNARD, law educator; b. St. Louis, May 20, 1929; s. John Baptist and Faith Vera (Clinton) G.; m. Camilla Roma Smith, Aug. 8, 1953; children— Lisa, Karen Julia Student, Iowa State Coll., 1947-49; AB, Washington U., St. Louis, 1957, JD, 1958. Bar: N.Y. 1959, U.S. Supreme Ct. 1979. Assoc. Donovan, Leisure, Newton & Irvine, N.Y.C., 1958-60; asst. prof. law U. Mo., Columbia, 1960-62; asst. prof., assoc. prof. law Washington U., 1962-67, prof., 1967-99, prof. emeritus, 1999—. Author: Local Regulation of Adult Businesses, 1992, Proposed Washington D.C. Amendment, 1979, (with others) Sum and Substance Constitutional Law, 1976, (with others) Federal Land Use Law, 1986; editor: 100 Years of 14th Amendment, 1973; editor-in-chief Washington U. Law Quar., 1958; contbr. articles to profl. jours., chpts. to books. Mem. Mo. Adv. com. U.S. Commn. on Civil Rights, 1987-92. Served to 1st lt. USAF, 1950-54 Mem. ABA Republican Avocations: collecting scrimshaw and antique photographica, photography. Home: 1564 Yarmouth Point Dr Chesterfield MO 63017-5639 Office: PO Box 1120 Saint Louis MO 63188-1120 E-mail: gerard@law.wustl.edu.

GERBER, EUGENE J. bishop; b. Kingman, Kans., Apr. 30, 1931; s. Cornelius John and Lena Marie (Tiesmeyer) G. B.A., St. Thomas Sem., Denver; B.S., Wichita State U.; B.S.Th., Catholic U. Am.; S.T.L., Angelicum, Rome. Ordained priest Roman Catholic Ch., 1959; asst. chancellor Wichita Diocese, 1963, sec. to bishop, 1964, vice chancellor, 1967, mem. diocesan bd. adminstrn., 1973, diocesan cons., 1973, chancellor, 1975; chaplain, mem. governing bd. Holy Family Center for Mentally Retarded; bd. dirs. Cursillo; bishop of Dodge City, Kans., 1976-82, Diocese of Wichita, 1982—. also: Diocese of Wichita Chancery Office 424 N Broadway St Wichita KS 67202-2310

GERBER, JOHN J. real estate executive; Investment broker midwest region Mark Goodman Assocs., CB Comml.; founder Nat. Equity Advisors, 1992; pres. PM Realty Group Investment Svcs. LLC, Chgo. Office: PM Realty Group Investment # 1410 500 N Michigan Ave Chicago IL 60611-3777

GERBER, LAWRENCE, lawyer; b. Chgo., Oct. 2, 1940; BBA, Loyola U. Chgo., 1962; JD, Northwestern U., 1965. CPA Ill.; bar: Ill. 1965. Ptnr. McDermott, Will & Emery, Chgo., mng. ptnr., 1991—. Author: Hospital Restructuring: Why, When and How, 1983. Mem.: Ill. Assn. Hosp. Attys., Am. Acad. Hosp. Attys. Office: McDermott Will & Emery 227 W Monroe St Ste 3100 Chicago IL 60606-5096

GERBER, PHILLIP, advertising executive; b. 1963; Formerly with Edward H. Weiss & Co., Chgo.; mng. ptnr., media ops. dir. Duro RSCG Tatham, 1983—. Office: Euro RSCG Tatham 980 N Michigan Ave Chicago IL 60611-4501

GERBERDING, MILES CARSTON, lawyer; b. Decatur, Ind., Oct. 25, 1930; s. Arnold H. and Luella E. (Lapp) G.; m. Ruth H. Hostrup, Aug. 20, 1955 (dec. Mar. 1992); children: Karla M. Smith, Greta E. Cowart, Kent E., Brian K.; m. Joan W. Fackler, Jan. 2, 1993; stepchildren: Stephen W. Fackler, Deborah E. Holbrook. BS, Ind. U., 1954, JD, 1956. Bar: Ind. 1956, U.S. Dist. Ct. (so. and no. dists.) Ind. 1956, Mich. 1984. Ptnr. Nieter & Smith, Ft. Wayne, Ind., 1956-58, Barrett, Barrett & McNagny, Ft. Wayne, 1958-85, Barnes & Thornburg, Ft. Wayne, 1985-97; pvt. practice Frankfort, Mich., 1998—. Lectr., writer Ind. Continuing Legal Ednl. Forum. Contbr. articles to profl. jours. Pres. Luth. Assn. Elem. Edn., 1968-69; vice chmn., mem. Ind. Supreme Ct. Commn. on Continuing Legal Edn., sec.; bd. dirs. Big Bros., Ft. Wayne, Jr. Achievement, Ft. Wayne, United Way Allen County; pres. Concordia Ednl. Found., Greater Ft. Wayne C. of C. Found.; chmn. bd. visitors Ind. U. Sch. Law, Bloomington, 1984-85, mem. 1979-94; vice chmn. United Way of Allen County Campaign, 1990-92, chmn., 1992-93, dir., 1992-98; trustee Boys and Girls Club Ft. Wayne; sec. Willoughby Rotary Found., 1999. With USMC, 1950-52. Decorated UN medal, Korean Svc. medal with star; recipient Christus Magister award Luth. Edn. Assn., 1971, Disting Svc. award Ind. U. Sch. Law, 1999; named Grad. of Yr., Concordia Alumni Assn., 1993. Fellow: Mich. Bar Found., Ind. Bar Found. (dir.), Am. Coll. Trust and Estate Counsel, Am. Coll. Tax Counsel, Am. Bar Found.; mem.: VFW, ABA (rep. Nat. Conf. Lawyers and CPAs 1980—86, nominating com., ho. dels. credentials com., chmn. Ind. del. 1985—94, ho. dels. mem. com., standing com. on bar svc., coordinating com. on outreach, med. profl. liability com., com. on pub. understanding about law, vice-chmn. com. on state and local bars-sr. lawyers divsn., marital deduction com. taxation sect.), Korean War Vets. Assn., Mich. State Bar Found., Nat. Conf. Bar Pres. (exec. coun. 1983—86), Ind. CLE Forum (pres. 1978—79), Am. Judicature Soc., Allen County Bar Found. (former bd. dirs., sec.), Lawyer-Pilot Bar Assn., Allen County Bar Assn. (dir.), Benzie County Bar Assn. (pres. 1999—2000), State Bar Mich. (treas. Sr. Lawyers 1999—2000, chmn.-elect 2000—01, chmn. 2001—, com. on mandatory CLE, com. on quality profl. life), Ind. Bar Assn. (pres. 1979—80, del. ABA 1979—94), Am. Legion, TerraLex (former co-vice chmn. N.Am., dir. 1993—96), Benzie Area Hist. Soc. (dir.), Frankfort Rotary Club, Arcadia Lions Club (bd. dirs.). Republican. Lutheran. Home: 17726 N Ridgewood PO Box 6 Arcadia MI 49613-0006 Office: PO Box 272 Frankfort MI 49635-0272 also: PO Box 118 Arcadia MI 45613-0118 E-mail: mcgerb@northlink.net., jupnorth@northlink.net.

GERBERICH, WILLIAM WARREN, engineering educator; b. Wooster, Ohio, Dec. 30, 1935; s. Harold Robert and Clarissa Thelma (Ross) G.; m. Susan Elizabeth Goodwin, Aug. 15, 1959; children— Bradley Kent, Brian Keith, Beth Clarice. BS in Engring. Adminstrn, Case Inst. Tech., 1957; MS in Indsl. Engring, Syracuse U., 1959; PhD in Materials Sci. and Engring, U. Calif., Berkeley, 1971. Registered profl. engr. Calif. Research engr. Jet Propulsion Lab., Calif. Inst. Tech., Pasadena, Calif., 1959-61; research scientist Aeronutronic, Newport Beach, 1961-64; engring. research specialist Aerojet Gen., Sacramento, 1964-67; lectr. U. Calif., Berkeley, 1967-71; dir. materials sci. U. Minn., Mpls., 1972—, assoc. prof., dept. chem. engring. and materials sci., 1971-75, prof., 1975—, assoc. head dept., 1980-2000. Cons. material rev. bd. Argonne Nat. Labs., steel, med. products and aerospace cos.; chmn. bd. Inst. Mechanics and Materials U. Calif., San Diego, 1994—. Chmn. bd. Acta Metallurgica publs., 1986-89; co-editor 7 books; contbr. articles to tech. jours. Recipient Teleen English prize Case Inst. Tech., 1959, William Spraragen award Welding Jour., 1968, Outstanding Paper award Acta Met. Jour., 1994. Fellow Am. Soc. Metals; mem. AIME, Materials Rsch. Soc., Sigma Xi, Tau Beta Pi, Pi Delta Epsilon, Phi Delta Theta. Home: 21035 Radisson Inn Rd Christmas Lk Excelsior MN 55331 Office: U Minn Chem Engring Materials Minneapolis MN 55455

GERBERRY, RONALD VINCENT, state legislator; b. Youngstown, Ohio, Jan. 10, 1953; s. Edward S. and Erma (Timko) G.; m. Kathryn M. Schrum, 1976; children: Deanna Lynn, Ronald Vincent Jr., Daniel Schrum. AB, Youngstown State U., 1975. Tchr. social studies Beaver Local Sch. Dist., Columbiana County, Ohio, 1978-79, Trumbull County (Ohio) Joint Vocat. Sch., 1978-81, Hubbard Exempted Village Schs., Trumbull County, 1981-82; mem. Ohio Ho. of Reps., Columbus, 1982. Mem. Austintown (Ohio) Bd. Edn., 1974-82, v.p., 1977, pres., 1978, 81. Named hon. county supt. Ohio County Sypts. Assn., Legislator of Yr. Ohio Assn. Elem. Sch. Adminstrs., Educator of Yr., Mahoning County Elem. Sch. Adminstrs., Legislator of Yr. Ohio Acad. Trial Lawyers, 1996. Democrat. Home: 2940 Whispering Pines Dr Canfield OH 44406-9628

GERBIE, ALBERT BERNARD, obstetrician, gynecologist, educator; b. Toledo, Nov. 20, 1927; s. Louis and Fay (Green) G.; m. Barbara Hirsch, June 29, 1952; children: Gail Diane, Stephen Ralph. MD, George Washington U., 1951. Intern Michael Reese Hosp., Chgo., 1951-52; preceptorship in Ob-Gyn under Drs. R.A. Reis, J.L. Baer, E.J. DeCosta, 1952-55; practice medicine specializing in Ob-Gyn, 1955—; mem. faculty Northwestern U. Med. Sch., 1952—, prof. Ob-Gyn, 1972—, dir. continuing grad. edn., 1975—. Mem. staff Northwestern Meml. Hosp., 1955—; chief divsn. ob-gyn. Children's Meml. Hosp.; v.p., dir. Am. Bd. Ob-Gyn, 1976—, chmn. 1988—, pres. 1990, historian, 1998; chmn. liaison com. for ob-gyn., 1989; rep. Am. Bd. Med. Specialties; bd. dirs. Chgo. Maternity Ctr. Author textbooks; assoc. editor Surgery, Gynecology, and Obstetrics, Am. Jour. Ob-Gyn.; editor ACOG Current Jour. Rev.; contbr. chpts. to books, articles to profl. jours. Served with U.S. Army, 1946-47. Mem. ACS (bd. govs.), ACOG (chmn. learning resources commn.), AMA, Am. Gynecol. Soc., Am. Assn. Obstetricians and Gynecologists, Am. Gynecol. and Obstet. Soc., Am. Bd. Med. Specialties, Am. Coll. Sports Medicine, Ctrl. Assn. Ob-Gyn, Soc. Human Genetics, Southwestern Ob-Gyn. Soc., Chgo. Gynecol. Assn. (pres. 1977-78). Office: Ste 900 251 E Huron St Chicago IL 60611-4814

GERDES, DAVID ALAN, lawyer; b. Aberdeen, S.D., Aug. 10, 1942; s. Cyril Fredrick and Lorraine Mary (Boyle) G.; m. Karen Ann Hassinger, Aug. 3, 1968; children: Amy Renee, James David. BS, No. State Coll., Aberdeen, 1965; JD cum laude, U. S.D., 1968. Bar: S.D. 1968, U.S. Dist. Ct. S.D., 1968, U.S. Ct. Appeals (8th cir.) 1973, U.S. Supreme Ct. 1973. Assoc. Martens, Goldsmith, May, Porter & Adam, Pierre, S.D., 1968-73; ptnr. successor firm May, Adam, Gerdes & Thompson, 1973—. Chmn. disciplinary bd. S.D. Bar, 1980-81, mem. fed. practice com. U.S. Dist. Ct., S.D., 1986-91, 94—; mem. fed. adv. com. U.S. Ct. Appeals (8th cir.), 1989-93; bd. dirs. U.S.D. Law Sch. Found., 1973-84, pres., 1979-84. Mng. editor U. S.D. Law Rev., 1967-68. Chmn. Hughes County Rep. Ctrl. Com., 1979-81; del. Rep. State Conv., co-chair platform com., 1988, 90; state ctrl. committeeman, 1985-91. Served to lt. Signal Corps, AUS, 1965-68. Mem. ABA, Nat. Coun. Bar Pres., Internat. Assn. Def. Counsel, Assn. Def. Trial Attys., Am. Judicature Soc., Am. Bd. Trial Advocates, State Bar S.D. (chmn. professionalism com. 1989-90, pres. 1992-93), Pierre Area C. of C. (pres. 1980-81), S.D. C. of C. (bd. dirs. 1998—), Lawyer-Pilots Bar Assn., Def. Rsch. Inst., Am. Soc. Med. Assn. Counsel, Kiwanis, Elks. Republican. Methodist. Author: Physician's Guide to South Dakota Law, 1982. Office: May Adam Gerdes & Thompson PO Box 160 503 S Pierre St Pierre SD 57501-4522

GERDES, NEIL WAYNE, library director, educator; b. Moline, Ill., Oct. 19, 1943; s. John Edward and Della Marie (Ferguson) G. AB, U. Ill., 1965; BD, Harvard U., 1968; MA, Columbia U., 1971; MA in Libr. Sci., U. Chgo., 1975; DMin, U. St. Mary of the Lake, 1994. Ordained to ministry Unitarian Universalist Assn., 1975. Copy chief Little, Brown, 1968-69; instr. Tuskegee Inst., 1969-71; libr. asst. Augustana Coll., 1972-73; editl. asst. Library Quar., 1973-74; libr., prof. Meadville Theol. Sch., Chgo., 1973—; libr. program dir. Chgo. Cluster Theol. Schs., 1977-80; dir.

Hammond Libr., 1980—; prof. Chgo. Theol Sem., 1980—. Mem. exec. bd. Sem. Coop. Bookstore, Chgo., 1982—, Ctr. for Religion and Psychotherapy, Chgo., 1984-97, Ind. Voters of Ill., 1986-89, Hyde Park-Kenwood Cmty. Orgn., Chgo., 1988-89; pres. Hyde Park-Kenwood Interfaith Coun., 1986-90; chair libr. coun. Assn. Chgo. Theol. Sch., 1984-88, 96-98; trustee Civitas Dei Found., 1994—; mem. alumni coun. Harvard Divinity Sch., 1999—, sec., 2001. Mem. ALA, Am. Theol. Library Assn., Chgo. Area Theol. Library Assn., Unitarian Universalist Mins. Assn. (sec., treas. nat. body 1990-94), Assn. Liberal Religious Scholars (sec., treas. 1975—), Phi Beta Kappa Office: Chgo Theol Sem Hammond Libr 5757 S University Ave Chicago IL 60637-1507

GERDES, RALPH DONALD, fire safety consultant; b. Cin., Aug. 11, 1951; s. Paul Donald and Jo Ann Dorothy (Meyer) G. BArch, Ill. Inst. Tech., 1975. Registered architect, Ill. Architect Schiller & Frank, Wheeling, Ill., 1976; sr. assoc. Rolf Jensen & Assocs., Inc., Chgo., 1976-84; pres. Ralph Gerdes & Assocs., Inc., Indpls., 1984-88, chmn., 1988—; gen. mgr. Ralph Gerdes Cons., LLC. Lectr. Purdue U., Ind. U., Ill. Inst. Tech., Butler U., Ball State U.; bd. dirs. Ind. Fire Svcs. Inst. Co-author: Planning and Designing the Office Environment, 1981. Recipient Joel Polsky prize Am. Soc. Interior Designers, 1983. Mem. ASHRAE, AIA (bldg. performance and regulations com. liaison to Nat. Fire Protection Agy., liaison to Internat. Code Coun.), Soc. Fire Protection Engring. (assoc., exec. com. Ind. chpt. 1992—, pres. 1995-96), Nat. Fire Protection Assn. (tech. coms.), Bldg. Ofcls. and Code Adminstrs., Internat. Conf. Bldg. Ofcls., Ind. Fire Safety Assn. (bd. dirs. 1986-92, 94-95, pres. 1989-91), Archs. and Engrs. Bldg. Ofcls. (bd. dirs. 1994—, Ind. code devel. com.), Maple Creek Country Club, Indpls. Soc. Roman Catholic. Home: 556 Lockerbie Cir N Indianapolis IN 46202-3600 Office: 127 E Michigan St Ste 400 Indianapolis IN 46204-1518

GERDIN, RUSSELL A. transportation executive; Chmn., pres., founder Heartland Express, Coralville, Iowa, 1978—. Office: Heartland Express 2777 Heartland Dr Coralville IA 52241-2731

GEREN, GERALD S. lawyer; b. Chgo., Nov. 10, 1939; s. Ben and Sara (Block) G.; m. Phyllis Freeman, Feb. 11, 1962; children: Suzanne, Gregory, Bradley. BSMetE, Ill. Inst. Tech., 1961; JD, DePaul U., 1966. Bar: Ill. Supreme Ct. 1966, U.S. Ct. Customs and Patent Appeals 1967, U.S. Patent and Trademark Office 1967, U.S. Dist Ct. (no. dist.) Ill. 1969, U.S. Supreme Ct. 1972, U.S. Ct. Appeals (7th cir.) 1972, U.S. Ct. Appeals (fed. cir.) 1982. Engr. Internat. Harvester, Chgo., 1961-64; atty. Corning Glass Works, Corning, N.Y., 1966-69; assoc. Silverman & Cass, Chgo., 1969-70, Siegal & Geren, Chgo., 1970-71; ptnr. Epton, Mullin & Druth, 1971-84, Hill, Steadman & Simpson, Chgo., 1984-94, Gerald S. Geren Ltd., Chgo., 1994-96, Lee, Mann, Smith, McWilliams, Sweeney & Ohlson, 1997—. Contbr. articles to Indsl. Rsch. and Devel., Design News mags. Pres. Chgo. High Tech. Assn., 1981-86, v.p., 1986-87; mem. strategic planning com. Econ. Devel. Commn., Chgo., 1986-91; mem. Ill. Ctr. for Indsl. Tech., 1984-90, Ill. Mfg. Tech. Network, Chgo., 1986-91; mem. pres.' coun., rsch. coun., alumni bd. Ill. Inst. Tech., 1991—, The Leukemia Soc. Am. (Ill. chpt. bd. mem. 1988-90). Mem. ABA, Ill. Bar Assn., Chgo. Bar Assn., Patent Law Assn. Chgo., Am. Intellectual Property Law Assn., Execs. Club, Chgo. Econ. Club, Comml. Club Chgo. (small bus. com. 1985—), Met. Club Chgo. Office: Lee Mann Smith McWilliams Sweeney & Ohlson 209 S La Salle St Ste 410 Chicago IL 60604-1203

GERGIS, SAMIR DANIAL, anesthesiologist, educator; b. Beni-Suef, Egypt, Sept. 24, 1933; came to U.S., 1968; s. Danial and Hekmat (Assaad) G.; m. Dorothy K. Auen, June 16, 1973 (div. 1983); 1 child, Michael M.B., Ch. B., Cairo U., 1954, D.A., 1957, D.M., 1958, M.D. in Anesthesia (Ph.D.), 1962; D.A., U. Copenhagen, 1963. Intern Cairo U. Hosp., 1955-56, resident, 1957-59; instr. dept. anesthesia U. Iowa Coll. Medicine, Iowa City, 1968-69, asst. prof., 1969-72, assoc. prof., 1972-76, prof., 1976—. Fellow Am. Coll. Anesthesiology; mem. AAAS, Am. Soc. Anesthesiologists, Internat. Anesthesia Rsch. Soc., N.Y. Acad. Scis., Am. Soc. Pharmacology and Exptl. Therapeutics, Soc. Exptl. Biology and Medicine, Nat. Soc. Med. Rsch., Soc. for Neurosurgery, Anesthesia and Neurologic Supportive Care Assn., Assn. Anesthesia Clin. Dirs., Am. Soc. Clin. Pharmacology, Assn. Univ. Anesthesiologists. Coptic Orthodox Christian Home: 1019 Sunset St Iowa City IA 52246-4938 Office: U Iowa Dept Anesthesia Coll Medicine Iowa City IA 52242 E-mail: sgergis@hotmail.com., samir-gergis@uiowa.edu.

GERHARD, LEE CLARENCE, geologist, educator; b. Albion, N.Y., May 30, 1937; s. Carl Clarence and Helen Mary (Lahmer) G.; m. Darcy LaFollette, July 22, 1964; 1 dau., Tracy Leigh. BS, Syracuse U., 1958; MS, U. Kans., 1961, PhD, 1964. Exploration geologist, region stratigrapher Sinclair Oil & Gas Co., Midland, Tex. and Roswell, N.Mex., 1964-66; asst. prof. geology U. So. Colo., Pueblo, 1966-69, assoc. prof., 1969-72; assoc. prof., asst. dir. West Indies Lab. Fairleigh Dickinson U., Rutherford, N.J., 1972-75; asst. geologist State of N.D., Grand Forks, 1975-77, geologist, 1977-81; prof., chmn. dept. geology U. N.D., 1977-81; mgr. Rocky Mountain div. Supron Energy Corp., Denver, 1981-82; owner, pres. Gerhard & Assocs., Englewood, Colo., 1982-87; prof. petroleum geology Colo. Sch. Mines, Denver, 1982—, Getty prof., 1984-87; state geologist, dir. geol. survey State of Kans., Lawrence, 1987-99, prin. geologist, 1999—; founder, co-dir. Energy Rsch. Ctr., U. Kans., 1990-94. Presdl. appointee Nat. Adv. Com. on Oceans and Atmosphere, 1984-87. Contbr. articles to profl. jours. Served to 1st lt. U.S. Army, 1958-60. Danforth fellow, 1970-72; named to Kans. Oil and Gas Hall of Fame, 2002. Fellow Geol. Soc. Am.; mem. Am. Assn. Petroleum Geologists (hon. mem., Disting. Svc. award 1989, Journalism award 1996, pres. divsn. environ. geosci. 1994-95, hon. mem. divsn. environ. geoscis. 1998, Pub. Outreach award 1999), Am. Inst. Profl. Geologists, Rocky Mountain Assn. Geologists, Colo. Sci. Soc., Kans. Geol. Soc. (hon.), Sigma Xi, Sigma Gamma Epsilon. Home: 1628 Alvamar Dr Lawrence KS 66047-1714 Office: Kans Geol Survey 1930 Constant Ave Lawrence KS 66047-3724 E-mail: lee@kgs.ukans.edu.

GERHARDT, KENNETH W. agricultural company executive; Diploma, Acad. of Music, Vienna, Austria; BS, Emporia State U.; MS, Ind. U. Former chief info. officer, v.p. PepsiCo Food Svcs.; former chief info. officer, sr. v.p. AmeriServe Distbrn., Inc., Dallas; sr. v.p., chief info. officer ConAgra, Inc., Omaha, 1998—. Office: ConAgra Inc 1 ConAgra Dr Omaha NE 68102

GERHART, PETER MILTON, law educator; b. Milw., July 4, 1945; s. Howard Leon and Ann (Baker) G.; m. Virginia Ann Herold, Feb. 9, 1969 (div. Oct. 1980); 1 child, Matthew; m. Ann Tarbutton, Apr. 9, 1983; children: Mary Elizabeth, Margaret Ann, Grace Kendall. BA, Northwestern U., 1967; JD, Columbia U., 1971. Bar: N.Y. 1971, U.S. Dist. Ct. (so. dist.) N.Y. 1973. Assoc. Weil, Gotshal & Manges, N.Y.C., 1971-75; prof. law Ohio State U., Columbus, 1975—, assoc. dean, 1983-86; dean Case Western Res. U., Cleve., 1986-96, prof., 1996—. Cons. Pres.'s Commn. Antitrust, Washington, 1978-79, Adminstrv. Conf., Washington, 1976-77. Contbr. articles to profl. jours. Mem. ABA (cons. com. to study FTC 1969). Democrat. Presbyterian. Avocations: piano, jogging. Home: 14400 Shaker Blvd Cleveland OH 44120-1611 Office: Case Western Res U Sch Law 11075 East Blvd Cleveland OH 44106-5409

GERHART, PHILIP MARK, engineering educator; b. Kokomo, Ind., Aug. 5, 1946; BS in Mech. Engring., Rose-Hulman Inst. Tech., 1968; MS, U. Ill., 1969, PhD, 1971. Registered profl. engr. Ohio, Ind. Asst. prof. mech. engring. U. Akron (Ohio), 1971-76, assoc. prof., 1976-82, prof., 1982-84; dept. chair U. Evansville, Ind., 1984-95, dean coll. engring. and computer sci., 1995—. Summer faculty fellow NASA Lewis Rsch. Ctr., Cleve., 1972, 73, aerospace engr., summer 1974; engr. NED performance tech. Babcock & Wilcox Co., Barberton, Ohio, summers 1978, 79; co-devel., instr. tng. program for performance engrs. Ohio Edison Co., Akron, summer 1981-84; cons. Goodyear Aerospace Co., Buffalo Forge Co., Elec. Power Rsch. Inst., Bristol-Meyers USPNG, George Koch Sons Inc., Mohler Techs. Inc.; presenter papers in field. Author: (with R.J. Gross) Fundamentals of Fluid Mechanics, 1985, (with R.J. Gross and J.I. Hochstein) 2d edit., 1992; contbr. articles to profl. jours. Asst. scoutmaster, scoutmaster, troop com. chmn., scouting coord., unit commr., Boy Scouts Am., 1968—; deacon, Bible sch. supt., chmn. bldg. com., elder Northwest Ave. Ch. of Christ, Tallmadge, Ohio, 1973-84; chmn. corp., elder Cullen Ave. Christian Ch., Evansville, 1985-92. Recipient Outstanding Tchr. award Bd. Higher Edn. United Meth. Ch., 1994, 25 Yr. Vet. Cert. from Boy Scouts Am. Mem. ASME (Dedicated Svc. award 1986, Performance Test Codes Gold medal 1993, Student Sect. Outstanding Tchr. 1983, 84, performance test code 11 on fans 1975—, vice chair 1989—, performance test code 4.1 steam generators 1981—, bd. performance test codes 1990—, instr. profl. devel. course 1991—), Am. Soc. Engring. Edn., Lambda Chi Alpha, Tau Beta Pi, Pi Tau Sigma (founding advisor U Evansville chpt.), Sigma Xi, Phi Kappa Pi, Phi Beta Chi. Office: Coll Engring & Computer Sci Univ of Evansville 1800 Lincoln Ave Evansville IN 47722-0001

GERINGER, GERALD GENE, state legislator; m. Dorothy M. Geringer. State rep. Dist. 65 Kans. Ho. of Reps., 1996—. Mem. econ. devel. com., tourism com., SRS transition oversight com., vice chairperson health and human svcs. Kans. Ho. of Reps.; health care cons., 1996—. Office: 720 Rockledge Dr Junction City KS 66441-3974 E-mail: geringer@house.state.ks.us.

GERLACH, JOHN B. business executive; b. Columbus, Ohio, Jan. 28, 1927; s. John Joseph and Pauline (Pollitt) G.; m. Dareth Axene, Sept. 30, 1949; children: John B., David P., Susan. Student, Ohio State U., 1945-47, Ohio U., 1947-49. Ptnr. John Gerlach & Co., Columbus, from 1949; pres. Lancaster Glass Corp. (Ohio), from 1958, dir.; pres. Ind. Glass Co., Dunkirk, from 1952, dir.; pres. Lancaster Colony Corp., Columbus, Ohio, 1963—, dir., CEO, 1996—. Sec.-treas., dir. Pretty Products Inc., Coshocton, Ohio, Nat. Glove Inc., Coshocton, Ohio; dir. Columbus Dental Mfg. Co., Mills Inc., Columbus, Jackson Corp. (Ohio), Beverage Mgmt. Inc., Columbus Trustee Columbus Gallery Fine Arts. Clubs: Univ, Columbus, Scioto Country, Coshocton Country. Home: 2320 Onandaga Dr Columbus OH 43221-3690 Office: Lancaster Colony Corp 37 W Broad St Ste 500 Columbus OH 43215-4177

GERLITS, FRANCIS JOSEPH, lawyer; b. Chgo., Mar. 29, 1931; s. John T. and May (Cameron) G.; m. Suzanne Long, June 20, 1953; children: Kathleen, Karen, Mary Cameron, Francis Jr. Ph.B., U. Notre Dame, 1953; J.D., U. Chgo., 1958. Bar: Ill. 1958. Ptnr. Kirkland & Ellis, Chgo., 1964-95, of counsel, 1995; gen. counsel Internat. Harvester Co. (now Navistar Internat. Corp.), 1985-90. Mem. ABA, Order of Coif, Tavern Club, Chicago Club Office: Kirkland & Ellis 200 E Randolph St Fl 54 Chicago IL 60601-6636

GERLITZ, CURTIS NEAL, business executive; b. Jan. 26, 1944; s. Gustav Albert and Elna G.; m. Audrey Jean D'Almaine, Oct. 6, 1973. BSBA, U. Minn., 1966; MBA, No. Ill. U., 1990. Purchasing agt. I. S. Berlin Press, Chgo., 1973-75; asst. purchasing agt. Daubert Chem. Co., Oak Brook, Ill., 1975-78; purchasing mgr. IBG Internat., Wheeling, 1978-86; dir. purchasing Advance Process Supply Co., Chgo., 1986-91; pres. Selectech, Mount Prospect, Ill., 1991—. Decorated Purple Heart. Mem. Nat. Assn. Purchasing Mgmt., Purchasing Assn. Chgo., Mfrs. Agts. Nat. Assn., United Assn. Mgrs. Reps. (mem. nat. bd. advisors 1994-96), Beta Gamma Sigma, Sigma Iota Epsilon. Home: 404 S Helena Ave Mount Prospect IL 60056-2854 Office: Selectech Internat Inc 119 S Emerson St Ste 142 Mount Prospect IL 60056

GERMANN, STEVEN JAMES, museum director; b. Dayton, Ohio, Sept. 4, 1947; s. James Howard and Doris Olive (Smith) G.; m. Elizabeth Haifley, Oct. 13, 1979; children: Alison Haifley, Andrew Ryan. BA in History, Wright State U., 1969, MA in History, 1973, cert. Mus. Adminstrn., 1977. Dir. edn. svcs. Montgomery County Hist. Soc., Dayton, Ohio, 1976-82; mus. adminstr. Mont. Hist. Soc., Helena, 1982-89; dir. Alfred P. Sloan Mus., Flint, Mich., 1989-2000. Exec. v.p. Midwest Mus. Conf., St. Louis, 1992-96. Bd. dirs. Flint Area Conv. and Visitors Bureau. Mem. Am. Assn. Mus. (mus. accreditation vis. com. 1989—), Mich. Mus. Assn., Flint Rotary, Phi Alpha Theta (hon. Rho Sigma chpt.). Office: Sloan Museum 1221 E Kearsley St Flint MI 48503-1988 Home: 13 Rue Royale Dayton OH 45429-1463

GERRARD, JOHN M. state supreme court justice; b. Schuyler, Nebr., Nov. 2, 1953; BS, Nebr. Wesleyan U., 1976; MPA, U. Ariz., 1977; JD, U. of Pacific, 1981. Pvt. practice, Norfolk, 1981-95; city atty. City of Battle Creek, Nebr., 1982-95; justice Nebr. Supreme Ct., Lincoln, 1995—. Office: Nebr Supreme Ct 2219 State Capitol Lincoln NE 68509-8000 also: PO Box 98910 Lincoln NE 68509*

GERRY, MARTIN HUGHES, IV, federal agency administrator, lawyer; b. San Francisco, Jan. 3, 1943; s. Martin Hughes III and Emily (Kuhl) G.; m. Robin Lucile MacAskill, Sept. 9, 1963 (div. June 1971); 1 child, Carol Elizabeth; m. Beatrice Ann Borowski, Apr. 28, 1984; children: Emily Irena, David Edward. BA, Stanford U., 1964, JD, 1967. Bar: N.Y. 1967, D.C. 1977, U.S. Dist. Ct. D.C. 1979, U.S. Supreme Ct. 1985. Assoc. Nixon, Mudge, Rose, Guthrie, Alexander & Mitchell, N.Y.C., 1967-69; exec. asst. to dir. Office for Civil Rights, HEW, Washington, 1969-70; asst. to sec. HEW, 1970-74; dir. Office for Civil Rights, HEW, 1975-77; pres. Policy Ctr. for Children and Youth, Bethesda, Md., 1978-89; asst. sec. for planning and evaluation HHS, Washington, 1990-93; exec. dir. The Austin (Tex.) Project, 1993-95; rsch. prof., dir. Ctr. for Study of Family and Cmty. Policy U. Kans., 1995—; mem. adv. bd. on welfare indicators U.S. Dept. HHS, 1996-98. Spl. counsel Wednesday Group, U.S. Ho. of Reps., Washington, 1977-89, vice chair Commn. on Spl. Needs of Children, 1982-83; vice chair Nat. Legal Ctr. for Medically Dependent, Indpls., 1986-90; sr. cons. Orgn. for Econ. Cooperation and Devel., Paris, 1986-90; vis. rsch. scholar U. Md., 1988-89; vis. scholar Stanford U., 1989-90; dir. Nat. Tech. Assistance Ctr. on Welfare Reform, 1997—. Contbr. numerous articles on social policy, edn., pub. financing, and civil rights related subjects to profl. jours. Mem. disability adv. coun. Social Security Adminstrn., HHS, Washington, 1986-88; edn. expert Superior Ct. D.C., Washington, 1986-90; sr. policy advisor Bush-Quayle '88. Oscar Cushing Law fellow Stanford U., 1965. Mem. Fed. Bar Assn. Republican. Episcopalian. Avocations: sailing, hiking. Office: U Kans 1315 Wakarusa Dr Lawrence KS 66049

GERSHENSON, DENNIS, property company executive; Pres., CEO, trustee Ramco-Gershenson Properties, Southfield, Mich., 1989—. Office: 27600 Northwestern Hwy Ste 200 Southfield MI 48034-8466

GERSHENSON, JOEL, property company executive; Chmn., trustee Ramco-Gershenson Properties, Southfield, Mich., 1989—. Office: 27600 Northwestern Hwy Ste 200 Southfield MI 48034-8466

GERSHON, RICHARD A. commmunications educator; b. Apr. 20, 1952; s. Phillip and Sylvia Gershon; m. Casey, Aug. 25, 1978; 1 child, Matthew. BA in English, Goddard Coll., Plainfield, Vt., 1974; MEd in Edn., U. Vt., 1980; PhD in Mass Communication, Ohio U., 1986. Instr. English and Mass Communication Rice Meml. High Sch., Burlington, Vt., 1976-81; sr. bus. editor Telecom. Mag., Dedham, Mass., 1984-86; asst. prof. telecommunications SUNY, New Paltz, 1986-89; prof. telecommunications Western Mich. U., Kalamazoo, 1989—. Chair Policy and Planning Task Force for Greater Kalamazoo Telecity Project. Author: Transnational Media Corporation: Global Markets and Free Market Competition, 1997, Telecommunications Management: Industry Structures and Planning Strategies, 2001 (Nat. Cable TVs Mus.'s Book of Yr. award); contbr. articles to profl. jours. Mem. Broadcast Edn. Assn. (chair elect for internat. div.). Office: Western Mich U Dept Comm Kalamazoo MI 49008 E-mail: Richard.Gershon@wmich.edu.

GERSIE, MICHAEL H. insurance company executive; Actuarial trainee The Prin. Fin. Group, Des Moines, 1970, officer, 1975, sr. v.p., 1994, CFO, exec. v.p., 1996—. Office: The Prin Fin Group 711 High St Des Moines IA 50392-0001

GERSTNER, ROBERT WILLIAM, structural engineering educator, consultant; b. Chgo., Nov. 10, 1934; s. Robert Berty and Martha (Tuchelt) G.; m. Elizabeth Willard, Feb. 8, 1958; children: Charles Willard, William Mark. B.S., Northwestern U., 1956, M.S., 1957, Ph.D., 1960. Registered structural and profl. engr., Ill. Instr. Northwestern U., Evanston, Ill., 1957-59, research fellow, 1959-60; asst. prof. U. Ill., Chgo., 1960-63, assoc. prof., 1963-69, prof. structural engring., architecture, 1969-92, prof. emeritus, 1992—. Structural engr. cons., 1959—; mem. State of Ill. Structural Engring. Bd., 1992-94. Contbr. articles to profl. jours. Pres. Riverside Improvement Assn., 1973-77, 79-82. Mem. AAUP, ACLU, ASCE, Am. Soc. Engring. Edn., Structural Engrs. Assn. Ill. (bd. dirs. 1986-89, 92-94, sec. 1989-91, pres. 1991-92). Home: 2628 W Agatite Ave Chicago IL 60625-3011

GERVASON, ROBERT J, advertising executive; Exec. v.p. Campbell Ewald Advertising, Warren, Mich. Office: Campbell Ewald Advt 30400 Van Dyke Ave Warren MI 48093-2368

GESKE, JANINE PATRICIA, law educator, former state supreme court justice; b. Port Washington, Wis., May 12, 1949; d. Richard Braem and Georgette (Paulissen) Geske; m. Michael Julian Hogan, Jan. 2, 1982; children: Mia Geske Berman, Sarah Geske Hogan, Kevin Geske Hogan. Student, U. Grenoble, U. Rennes; BA, MA in Tchg., Beloit Coll., 1971; JD, Marquette U., 1975, LLD, 1998, LLD (hon.), 1994; DHL (hon.), Mt. Mary Coll., 1999. Bar: Wis. 1975, U.S. Dist. Ct. (ea. & we. dists.) Wis. 1975, U.S. Supreme Ct. 1978. Tchr. elem. sch., Lake Zurich, Ill., 1970-72; staff atty., chief staff atty. Legal Aid Soc., Milw., 1975-78; asst. prof. law, clin. dir. Law Sch. Marquette U., 1978-81; hearing examiner Milw. County CETA, 1980-81; judge Milw. County Circuit Ct., 1981-93; justice Supreme Ct. Wis., 1993-98; disting. prof. law Marquette U. Law Sch., Milw., 1998—. Dean Wis. Jud. Coll.; mem. faculty Nat. Jud. Coll.; instr. various jud. tng. programs, continuing legal edn. Fellow ABA, mem. Am. Law Inst., Am. Arbitration Assn., Soc. Profls. in Dispute Resolution, Wis. Bar Assn., Wis. Assn. Mediators, Milw. Bar Assn., Nat. Women Judges Assn., 7th Cir. Bar Assn., Alpha Sigma Nu. Roman Catholic. Office: Marquette U Law Sch PO Box 1881 Milwaukee WI 53201-1881

GEST, HOWARD, microbiologist, educator; b. London, Oct. 15, 1921; m. Janet Olin, Sept. 8, 1941 (dec. 1994); children: Theodore Olin, Michael Henry, Donald Evan; m. Virginia Davies Ollis, Jan. 6, 1998. B.A. in Bacteriology, UCLA, 1942; postgrad. in biology (Univ. fellow), Vanderbilt U., 1942; Ph.D. in Microbiology (Am. Cancer Soc. fellow), Washington U., St. Louis, 1949. Rsch. asst. Metall. Lab. (Manhattan Project) U. Chgo., 1943; from jr. to assoc. chemist Clinton Labs. (Manhattan Project), Oak Ridge, 1943-46; Instr. microbiology Western Res. U. Sch. Medicine, 1949-51, asst. prof. microbiology, 1951-53, asso. prof., 1953-59; USPHS spl. research fellow in biology Calif. Inst. Tech., 1956-57; prof. Henry Shaw Sch. Botany, Washington U., 1959-64, dept. zoology, 1964-66; prof. Ind. U., Bloomington, 1966-78, disting. prof. microbiology, 1978—, disting. prof. emeritus microbiology, 1987—, adj. prof. history and philosophy of sci., 1983—, chmn. dept. microbiology, 1966-70, disting. faculty rsch. lectr., 1987. NSF sr. postdoctoral fellow Nat. Inst. Med. Rsch., London, 1965-66; Guggenheim fellow Imperial Coll., London, U. Stockholm, U. Tokyo; vis. prof. dept. biophysics and biochemistry U. Tokyo and Japan Soc. Promotion Sci., 1970; mem. study sect. bacteriology and mycology NIH, 1966-68, chmn. study sect. microbial chemistry, 1968-69, mem. study sect. microbial physiology and genetics, 1988-90; mem. com. microbiol. problems of man in extended space flight Nat. Acad. Scis.-NRC, 1967-69 Guggenheim fellow Imperial Coll., London, UCLA, 1979-80. Cummings Lecturer, Bucknell U., 1997; Fellow AAAS, Am. Acad. Microbiology; mem. Am. Soc. Microbiology (hon.); Am. Acad. Arts and Sci. Office: Ind U Dept Biology Bloomington IN 47405

GESWEIN, GREGORY T. electronic company executive; married; 2 children. BBA, MBA in Fin., U. Cin. V.p., corp. contr., corp. treas. Mead Corp., Dayton, Ohio; sr. v.p., CFO Pioneer-Standard Electronics, Inc., Cleve., Diebold, Inc., North Canton, Ohio, 2000—. Office: Diebold Inc 5995 Mayfair Rd North Canton OH 44720-8077

GETTELFINGER, GERALD ANDREW, bishop; b. Oct. 20, 1935; Ordained priest Roman Cath. Ch., 1962, ordained bishop, 1989. Bishop Diocese of Evansville, Ind., 1989—. Home: 3980 Woodcastle Dr Evansville IN 47711-2776 Office: Cath Ctr PO Box 4169 Evansville IN 47724-0169

GETTLEMAN, ROBERT WILLIAM, judge; b. Atlantic City, May 5, 1943; s. Charles Edward and Beulah (Oppenheim) G.; m. Joyce Reinitz, Dec. 23, 1964; children: Lynn Katheryn, Jeffrey Alan. BSBA cum laude, Boston U., 1965; JD cum laude, Northwestern U., 1968. Bar: Ill. 1968, U.S. Dist. Ct. (no. dist.) Ill. 1968, U.S. Ct. Appeals (7th cir.) 1968, U.S. Dist. Ct. (ea. dist.) Wis. 1972, U.S. Supreme Ct. 1973. Law clk. to presiding justice U.S. Ct. Appeals, Chgo., 1968-70; assoc. D'Ancona & Pflaum, 1970-74, ptnr., 1974-94; judge U.S. Dist. Ct., Ill., 1994—. Bd. dirs. John Howard Assn., Chgo., 1973-94, pres., 1978-81, chmn. legal and policy coms.; commr., chmn. devel. disabilities and individual rights coms. Gov.'s Commn. to Revise Mental Health Code of Ill., 1973-77; chmn. steering com. Chgo. Project on Residential Alternatives, 1984-85; mem. Cook County State's Atty.'s Profl. Adv. Com., 1984—; treas. Ill. Guardianship and Advocacy Commn., 1984, vice chmn., 1985, chmn., 1986; bd. dirs., chmn. legal com. Pact, Inc., 1985—; mem. mcpl. officers election bd. Village of Lyons, Ill., 1985. Contbr. articles to law revs. Bd. dirs. Ill. divsn. ACLU, 1973-78. Recipient August W. Christmann award Mayor of Chgo., 1994. Fellow Am. Bar Found.; mem. ABA, Ill. Bar Assn., Chgo. Bar Assn., 7th Fed. Cir. Bar Assn., Chgo. Council Lawyers. Office: US Dist Ct 1788 Dirksen Bldg 219 S Dearborn St Fl 17 Chicago IL 60604-1702

GETTLER, BENJAMIN, lawyer, manufacturing company executive; b. Louisville, Sept. 16, 1925; s. Herbert and Gertrude (Cohen) G.; m. Deliaan Angel, Mar. 1972; children: Jorian, Thomas, Gail, John, Benjamin. BA in Econs. with high honors, U. Cin., 1945; JD (Frankfurter scholar), Harvard U., 1948. Bar: Ohio 1949, U.S. Supreme Ct. 1955. Ptnr. Brown & Gettler, Cin., 1951-73, Gettler, Katz & Buckley, Cin., 1973-87; chmn. bd. Am. Controlled Industries Inc., 1973-86; chmn. bd. dirs., pres. Colorpac Inc., Franklin, Ohio, 1973-86; chmn. bd., pres. Vulcan Internat. Corp., Wilmington, Del., 1988—, Vulcan Corp., Clarksville, Tenn., 1988—; chmn. exec. com. Valley Industries, Inc., Cin., 1973-86; vice chmn. bd. Cin. Southern R.R., 1987-91; chmn. bd. Trusthouse, Inc., Cin., 1987—. Chmn. bd. dirs. ACI Internat., Inc., Cin., 1990—; spl. counsel U. Cin., 1975-77, trustee, 1994—, vice chmn. bd., 1999-2000, chmn., 2000—; bd. dirs. PNC Bank, Ohio, 1988-96. Chmn. bd. Jewish Inst. Nat. Security Affairs, 1994-98, chmn. policy com., 1998—; chmn. Cin. Bonds for Israel, 1969; chmn. Nat. Israel Commn., Nat. Jewish Cmty. Rels. Adv. Coun., 1981-82; mem. Ohio, Ky. and Ind. Mass Transit Policy Com., 1970-75; pres. Cin. Jewish Cmty. Rels. Coun., 1978-80; trustee Jewish Hosp. Cin., 1978-92, chmn., 1991-92; chmn. Midwest Hosp. Sys., Inc., 1987-90, 92-93; pres. Jewish Found. Cin., 1995-99, chmn., 1999—; trustee Health Alliance Greater Cin., 1995-96, 2000-2001; chmn. Cin. Coalition for Reagan, 1980; co-chmn. Hamilton County Reagan Bush Campaign Ohio, 1984; chmn. Rep. Fin. Com., Hamilton County, 1991-92; mem. Hamilton County Rep. Policy Com., 1990—; trustee Rockwern Found., 1998—. Capt. U.S. Army, 1955-56. Mem. ABA, Cin. Bar Assn., Shoe Last Mfrs. Assn. (pres. 1984-85), Footwear Industries Am. (bd. dirs. 1989-2000), Phi Beta Kappa, Omicron Delta Kappa. Clubs: Coldstream Country, Harvard. Office: Vulcan Corp 30 Garfield Pl Ste 1040 Cincinnati OH 45202-4322

GETZ, GODFREY SHALOM, dean, pathology educator; b. Johannesburg, S. Africa, June 18, 1930; came to U.S., 1963; naturalized, 1971; s. Judah Nathan and Fay (Lakofski) G.; m. Millicent Lorraine Cohen; children: Edwin A., Andrew R., Keith S., Jonathan D. BSc, Witwatersrand U., Johannesburg, 1952; BSc (hon.), Witwatersrand U., 1955, MB, BCh, 1954; PhD, Oxford U., 1963. Lectr. Witwatersrand U., 1956, 59-63; Nuffield demonstrator Oxford U., Eng., 1956-59; rsch. assoc. Harvard Med. Sch., Boston, 1963-64; asst. then assoc. prof. U. Chgo., 1964-72, prof., 1972—; now dean. U. Chgo., Pritzker Sch. Med.; acting dean U. Chgo. divsn. biol. studies, 1999—. Office: U Chicago Pritzker Sch. Med. Office of the Dean Chicago IL 60637-1470 Home: Apt 1805 445 E North Water St Chicago IL 60611-5550

GETZ, JAMES EDWARD, legal association administrator; b. Shelbyville, Ill., June 8, 1950; s. William Forrest and Betty Jean (Mitchell) G.; m. Rita Genevieve Boyd, June 16, 1973; children: Christopher Brandon, Sarah Lynne. BS in Edn., Eastern Ill. U., 1972, MA, 1974. Grad. asst. Political Sci. Dept. Eastern Ill. U., Charleston, 1972-73; tchr. Plano (Ill.) Community Schs., 1973-74; conservation police officer Ill. Dept. Natural Resources, Office Law Enforcement, Springfield, Ill., 1974-77, region IV Ops. supr.; region IV comdr. Ill. Dept. Conservation Div. Law Enforcement, 1980-82; deputy chief Ill. Dept. Natural Resource, Office Law Enforcement, 1982-86, region II comdr., 1986-90; Lake Mich. enforcement ops. comdr. Ill. Dept. Natural Resources divsn. Law Enforcement, 1990—. Boating law adminstr. State Ill., 1984-86; chmn. several coms. Nat. Assn. State Boating Law Adminstrs.; mem Nat. Boating Safety Adv. Coun. U.S. Coast Guard; pres. Conservation Police Lodge #146, Fraternal Order Police, 1993-96. Author: Illinois Public Act 84-515, 1985; Illinois Public Act 85-147, 1987. Mem. Nat. Marine Mfr. Assn. Boat Cert. Com., Gt. Lakes Fisheries Commn. Law Enforcement Com. (vice chmn. 1986-90, chmn. 1990-92), Am. Boat & Yacht Coun. (bd. dirs. 1992-99). Avocations: boating, history, genealogy, Civil War reenacting. Home: 1709 N Orleans St Mchenry IL 60050-3885 Office: Ill Dept Natural Resources 701 N Point Dr Winthrop Harbor IL 60096-1371 E-mail: jgetz@dnrmail.state.il.us.

GETZ, ROBERT LEE, newspaper columnist; b. Francesville, Ind., Oct. 1, 1943; s. Benjamin Jacob and Helen Juanita (Thomas) G.; m. Lisa Gale Schneller, Sept. 11, 1972 (div. June 1988); children: Chase H., Page L., Tracy M.; m. Jeannie McCoy, Mar. 17, 1994 (div. June 2000). Student, Andrews U., 1962. Reporter Logansport (Ind.) Pharos-Tribune, 1964; sports editor Rochester (Ind.) Sentinel, 1965; sports writer, columnist Bloomington (Ind.) Herald-Telephone, 1967-70; sports editor Boca Raton (Fla.) News, 1972-74, columnist, feature writer, 1973-74; columnist Wichita (Kans.) Eagle, 1975—. Author: A Bookful of Bob Getz, 1992. With U.S. Army, 1965-67. Avocations: tennis, basketball. Office: Wichita Eagle 825 E Douglas Ave Wichita KS 67202-3594

GETZENDANNER, SUSAN, lawyer, former federal judge; b. Chgo., July 24, 1939; d. William B. and Carole S. (Muehling) O'Meara; children— Alexandra, Paul. B.B.A., J.D., Loyola U., 1966. Bar: Ill. bar 1966. Law clk. U.S. Dist. Ct., Chgo., 1966-68; assoc. Mayer, Brown & Platt, 1968-74, ptnr., 1974-80; judge U.S. Dist. Ct., 1980-87; ptnr. Skadden, Arps, Slate, Meagher & Flom, 1987—. Recipient medal of excellence Loyola U. Law Alumni Assn., 1981 Mem. ABA, Chgo. Council Lawyers. Office: Skadden Arps Slate Meagher Flom 333 W Wacker Dr # 2100 Chicago IL 60606-1220

GEWEKE, JOHN FREDERICK, economics educator; b. Washington, May 11, 1948; s. Robert William and Winnifred Lois (Quies) G.; m. Lynne Marie Osborn, Aug. 22, 1970; children: Andrew Robert, Alan Reid. BS, Mich. State U., 1970; PhD, U. Minn., 1975. Asst. prof. U. Wis., Madison, 1975-79, assoc. prof., 1979-82, prof., 1982-83, Duke U., Durham, N.C., 1983-86, William R. Kenan Jr. prof., 1986-90, dir. Inst. Stats. and Decision Scis., 1987-90; prof. U. Minn., Mpls., 1990—. Editor Jour. Bus. and Econs. Stats., 1989-92; co-editor Jour. Applied Econometrics, 1993—; assoc. editor Econometrica, 1984-88, 95—. Rsch. fellow Sloan Found., N.Y.C., 1982. Fellow Econometric Soc., Am. Statis. Assn.; mem. Am. Econ. Assn., Internat. Soc. for Bayesian Analysis (pres. 1999). Office: U Minn Dept Econs Minneapolis MN 55455

GEWERTZ, BRUCE LABE, surgeon, educator; b. Phila., Aug. 27, 1949; s. Milton and Shirley (Charen) G.; children: Samantha, Barton, Alexis; m. Diane Weiss, Aug. 31, 1997. BS, Pa. State U., State Coll., 1968; MD, Jefferson Med. Coll., Phila., 1972. Diplomate Am. Bd. Surgery. Surg. resident U. Mich., Ann Arbor, 1972-77; asst. prof. U. Tex., Dallas, 1977-81; assoc. prof. U. Chgo., 1981-87, prof. surgery, 1988—, faculty dean med. edn., 1989-92, Dallas Phemister prof., chmn. dept. surgery, 1992—. Teaching scholar Am. Heart Assn., Dallas, 1980-83; pres. Assn. Surg. Edn., 1983-84. Author: Atlas of Vascular Surgery, 1989, Surgery of the Aorta and its Branches, 2000; editor Jour. Surg. Rsch., 1987—; patentee removable vascular filter. Recipient Jobst award Coller Surg. Soc., 1975, Coller award Mich. chpt. Am. Coll. Surgeons, 1975. Mem. Soc. Vascular Surgery, Midwestern Vascular Soc. (pres. 1993, 94-95), Soc. Clin. Surgery, Soc. Univ. Surgeons, Chgo. Surg. Soc. (treas. 1989-92), Am. Surg. Assn., Point O'Woods Club (Benton Harbor, Mich.). Office: U Chgo MC 5029 5841 S Maryland Ave Chicago IL 60637-1463

GHERLEIN, GERALD LEE, lawyer, former diversified manufacturing company executive; b. Warren, Ohio, Feb. 16, 1938; s. Jacob A. and Ruth (Matthews) G.; m. Joycelyn Hardin, June 18, 1960; children: David, Christy. Student, Ohio Wesleyan U., 1956-58; B.S. in Bus. Adminstrn, Ohio State U., 1960; J.D., U. Mich., 1963. Bar: Ohio 1963. Assoc. Taft Stettinius & Hollister, Cin., 1963-66; corp. atty. Eaton Corp., Cleve., 1966-68, European legal counsel Zug, Switzerland, 1968-71, asst. sec., assoc. counsel Cleve., 1971-76, v.p., gen. counsel, 1976-91, exec. v.p., gen. counsel, 1991-2000, ret., 2000. Pres. Citizens League Greater Cleve., 1979-81; trustee Cleve. Ballet, 1983-88, vice chmn. 1985-87; trustee WVIZ Pub. Television, 1990-99, Armada Funds, 1997—. Mem. ABA, Greater Cleve. Bar Assn. (pres. 1989, trustee), Ohio Bar Assn., Am. Soc. Corp. Secs. (pres. Ohio regional group 1977), Pepper Pike Country Club, Union Club, Mayfield Country Club. Clubs: Union, Tavern, Mayfield Country. Home: 3679 Greenwood Dr Cleveland OH 44124-5502

GHERTY, JOHN E. food products and agricultural products company executive; b. 1944; married. BBA, U. Wis., 1965, JD, 1968, MA, 1970. Lawyer corp. law dept. Land O' Lakes Inc., Arden Hills, Minn., 1970-79, asst. to pres., 1979-81, group v.p., 1981-89, pres., CEO, 1989—. Bd. dirs. CF Industries, Long Grove, Ill., Minn. Life Inst., St. Paul. Bd. dirs. Grad. Inst. Coop. Leadership, Greater Twin Cities United Way. Mem.: 4-H Found. (bd. dirs.), Minn. Bus. Partnership, Nat. Coun. Farmer Coops. (chmn.). Office: Land O'Lakes PO Box 64101 Saint Paul MN 55164-0101 also: 4001 Lexington Ave N Saint Paul MN 55126-2934

GHETTI, BERNARDINO FRANCESCO, neuropathologist, neurobiology researcher; b. Pisa, Italy, Mar. 28, 1941; s. Getulio and Iris (Mugnetti) G.; m. Caterina Genovese, Oct. 8, 1966; children— Chiara, Simone. M.D. cum laude, U. Pisa, 1966, specialist in mental and nervous diseases, 1969. Lic. physician, Italy; cert. Edn. Council for Fgn. Med. Grads.; diplomate Am. Bd. Pathology. Postdoctoral fellow U. Pisa, 1966-70; research fellow in neuropathology Albert Einstein Coll. Medicine, Bronx, N.Y., 1970-73, resident, clin. fellow in pathology, 1973-75, resident in neuropathology, 1975-76; asst. prof. pathology Ind. U., Indpls., 1976-77, asst. prof. pathology and psychiatry, 1977-78, assoc. prof. pathology and psychiatry, 1978-83, prof. pathology, psychiatry, assoc. dir. program in med. neurobiology, 1983—, assoc. dir. divsn. neuropathology, 1989-93, prof. pathology, psychiatry, med. and molecular genetics, 1991-97, dir. Alzheimer Disease Ctr., 1991—, dir. divsn. neuropathology, 1993—, Disting. prof. pathology and lab. medicine, psychiatry, med. and molecular genetics, neurology, 1997—. Mem. Nat. Inst. Neurol. Disorders and Stroke rev. com. NIH, 1985-89; mem. NIH Reviewers Res., 1989-93. Contbr. articles and abstracts to profl. jours. Mem. Alzheimer's disease rsch. scientific rev. com. Am. Health Assistance Found., 1998—. Recipient Potamkin Prize, 1999. Mem. Internat. Soc. Neuropathology (v.p. 2000—), Am. Acad. Neurology, Am. Neurol. Assn., Am. Assn. Neuropathologists (pres. 1996-97), Soc. Neurosci., Assn. Research in Nervous and Mental Diseases, Internat. Brain Research Orgn., Am. Soc. Cell Biology, Italian Soc. Psychiatry, Italian Soc. Neurology, Sigma Xi Roman Catholic Home: 1124 Frederick Dr S Indianapolis IN 46260-3421 Office: Ind U 635 Barnhill Dr Rm 138 Indianapolis IN 46202-5126 E-mail: bghetti@inpui.edu.

GHIA, KIRTI N. fluid mechanics engineer, educator; b. Bombay, India; BS, Gujarat U., India, 1960; MS, Ill. Inst. Tech., 1965, PhD in Mechanical & Aerospace Engring., 1969. Rsch. engr. Premier Automobiles Ltd., India, 1960-61; rsch. asst. fluid dynamics Ill. Inst. Tech., 1961-65, instr., 1962, asst., 1962-69; from asst. prof. to assoc. prof. U. Cin., 1969-78, prof. fluid dynamics, 1978—. Cons. Huyck Corp., 1965-67, Kenner Prod Co., Cin., 1972-76, GE Co., Cin., 1973—, Air Force Flight Dynamics Lab., Wright Patterson AFB, 1976—, Naval Ship R&D Ctr., Bethesda, Md., 1977—, Reynolds Metal Co., Ala., 1978—; co-prin. investigator NSF grants, 1972-79, Aerospace Rsch. Lab., 1972-75, GE Co. grants, 1974-75, 76-77, Off Sci. Rsch. grants, 1978-79. Fellow ASME (Freeman scholar award 1995); mem. AIAA, Am. Soc. Engring. Edn., Sigma Xi. Achievements include research in analysis and numerical solutions of three-dimensional viscous internal flow problems; use of numerical coordinate transformations and higher-order spline techniques and direct solvers in the solution of navier-stokes equations. Office: Univ of Cincinnati Aerospace/Engring Mech Baldwin 759 Cincinnati OH 45221-0001

GHIARDI, JAMES DOMENIC, lawyer, educator; b. Gwinn, Mich., Nov. 10, 1918; s. John B. and Margaret M. (Trosello) G.; m. Phyllis A. Lindmeier, Sept. 5, 1945; children— Catherine, Jeanne, Mary. PhB, Marquette U., 1940, LLB, 1942, JD, 1968. Bar: Wis. bar 1942. Prof. law Marquette U. Law Sch., Milw., 1946-89, prof. law emeritus, 1990—; research dir. Def. Research Inst., Milw., 1962-72; of counsel firm Kluwin, Dunphy, Hankin & McNulty, 1972-87. Author: Personal Injury Damages, Wisconsin, 1964, Punitive Damages, Vol. I, 1981, Vol. II, 1985; contbr. articles to profl. jours. Served to capt. Med. Adminstrv. Br. U.S. Army, 1942-45. Recipient award for teaching excellence Marquette U. Faculty, 1971, Edward A. Uhrig Found., 1971, Alumni of Yr. award Marquette U. Law Sch., 1971, Charles L. Goldberg award for outstanding pub. svc. Wis. Law Found., 1986, Charles C. Pinckney award for legal scholarship and svc. to the legal profession N.Y. Def. Bar Assn., 1986. Fellow Am. Bar Found.; mem. ABA (mem. ho. of dels. 1967-80, Disting. Prof. Torts and Ins. Law award Torts and Ins. Practice sect. 1989), Milw. Bar Assn. (Lifetime Achievement award 1993), State Bar Wis. (gov., mem. exec. com. 1962-72, pres. 1970-71), Am. Law Ins., Wis. Bar Found., Am. Legion. Office: Sensenbrenner Hall Marquette U Law Sch PO Box 1881 Milwaukee WI 53201-1881

GHOSHAL, NANI GOPAL, veterinary anatomist, educator; b. Dacca, India, Dec. 1, 1934; came to U.S., 1963; s. Priya Kanta and Kiron Bala (Thakurata) G.; m. Chhanda Banerjee, Jan. 24, 1971; 1 child, Nupur G.V.Sc., B.V.C., India, 1955; DTVM, U. Edinburgh, 1961; Dr. med. vet., Tieraertzliche Hochschule Hannover, Fed. Republic Germany, 1962; PhD, Iowa State U., 1966. Vet. asst. surgeon West Bengal State Govt., India, 1955-56; instr. Bengal Vet. Coll., U. Calcutta, 1955-56; research asst. M.P. Govt. Coll. Vet. Sci. and Animal Husbandry, Mhow, India, 1956-59; research officer ICAR, India, 1963; instr. Iowa State U., Ames, 1963-66, asst. prof., 1967-70, assoc. prof., 1970-74, prof. vet. gross anatomy, 1974—. Chmn. Internat. Vet. Medicine Com., 1967-79; cons. Morocco-Minn. project U. Minn. Internat. Agrl. Programs, AID, 1983-88; adj. prof. Inst. Agronomique et Veterinaire, Hassan II, Rabat, Morocco, 1984-88. Co-author, editor: Getty's Anatomy of Domestic Animals, 5th edit., 1975; author: (with Tankred Koch, Peter Popesko) Venous Drainage of Domestic Animals, 1981; contbr. chpts. to books, articles to profl. jours. Recipient German Acad. Exchange Service award Govt. Fed. Republic of Germany, Bonn, 1961-62, Norden Disting. Tchr. award, 1978, Dr. William O. Reece award for outstanding advising Coll. of Vet. Medicine, 1997; various scholarships and grants. Fellow Royal Zool. Soc. Scotland (life); mem. World Assn. Vet. Anatomists, Am. Assn. Vet. Anatomists, AAAS, Am. Assn. Anatomists, Pan Am. Assn. Anatomy, N.Y. Acad. Scis., Iowa Vet. Med. Assn., Sigma Xi, Phi Zeta, Gamma Sigma Delta, Phi Kappa Phi Home: 1310 Glendale Ave Ames IA 50010-5526 Office: Iowa State U Coll Vet Medicine 2086 Dept Biomed Scis Ames IA 50011-1250 E-mail: nghoshal@iastate.edu.

GIACOLETTO, LAWRENCE JOSEPH, electronics engineering educator, researcher, consultant; b. Clinton, Ind., Nov. 14, 1916; s. Pete and Antonia (Savio) G.; m. Maxine Lorraine Dicks, May 31, 1941; 1 child, Carol Giacoletto. BSEE, Rose-Hulman Inst. Tech., 1938; MS in Physics, State U. Iowa, 1939; PhDEE, U. Mich., 1952. Rsch. engr. RCA Labs., Princeton, N.J., 1946-56; rsch. mgr. sci. lab. Ford Motor Co., Dearborn, Mich., 1956-61; prof. elec. engring. Mich. State U., East Lansing, 1961-87, prof. emeritus, 1987—; owner CoRes Inst., Okemos, Mich., 1965—. Author: Differential Amplifiers, 1970; editor: Electronics Designers' Handbook, 1977; patentee in field. Lt. col. USAR, 1941-87. Fellow IEEE (bd. dirs. 1964-65), AAAS (del. 1977-79), University Club (Lansing, Mich.), Sigma Xi. Republican. Roman Catholic. Home: 4465 Wausau Rd Okemos MI 48864-2741 Office: CoRes Inst 4465 Wausau Rd Okemos MI 48864-2741 E-mail: giacolet@pilot.msu.edu.

GIAMPIETRO, WAYNE BRUCE, lawyer; b. Chgo., Jan. 20, 1942; s. Joseph Anthony and Jeannette Marie (Zeller) G.; m. Mary E. Fordeck, June 15, 1963; children: Joseph, Anthony, Marcus. BA, Purdue U., 1963; JD, Northwestern U., 1966. Bar: Ill. 1966, U.S. Dist. Ct. (no. dist.) Ill. 1966, U.S. Ct. Appeals (7th cir.) 1967, U.S. Tax Ct. 1977, U.S. Supreme Ct. 1971. Assoc. Elmer Gertz, Chgo., 1966-73; mem. firm Gertz & Giampietro, 1974-75; sole practice, 1975-76; ptnr. Poltrock & Giampietro, 1976-87, Witwer, Burlage, Poltrock & Giampietro, 1987-94, Witwer, Poltrock & Giampietro, 1995—. Former cons. atty. Looking Glass divsn. Traveler's Aid Soc. Contbr. articles to profl. jours. Pres. Chgo. 47th Ward Young Republicans, 1968; bd. dirs. Ravenswood Conservation Commn. Lutheran. Avocation: stamp collecting. Home: 23 Windsor Dr Lincolnshire IL 60069-3410 Office: Witwer Poltrock & Giampietro 200 S Wacker Dr Ste 3100 Chicago IL 60606-4401 E-mail: wgiampietro@wpglawyers.com.

GIANCOLA, JAMES J. banking executive; Grad., Harvard U.; postgrad., Suffolk U., Boston; student, U. Colo. Pres. Gainer Bank, Ind.; exec. v.p. CNB Bancshares, Inc., 1992, pres., COO, 1994. Cmty. work U. So. Ind., U. Evansville, Evansville Dance Theatre, United Way, Leadership Evansville. Mem. Methodist Temple. Office: CNB Bancshares Inc PO Box 778 Evansville IN 47705-0778

GIANITSOS, ANESTIS NICHOLAS, surgeon; b. Chios, Greece, Aug. 31, 1961; came to U.S., 1966; s. Dimitrios and Soultani (Zannikos) G.; m. Laurie S. Hallmark, children: Alexia Soultani, Dimitri Jacob. BA summa cum laude, Boston U., 1983, MD, 1987. Physician U. Wis. Hosp., Madison, 1987-92; pres. Tricorp Informational Svcs., Williams Bay, Wis., 1989-93; staff urologist Riverview Clinic, Janesville, 1992-98; pres. Geneva Mktg. Sys., Lake Geneva, 1996—; med. dir. Men's Health Ctr. Mercy Health Sys., So. Wis., No. Ill., 1998—; staff urologist Mercy Regional Urology Ctr., Janesville, 1998—. Cons. Rural Wis. Hosp. Coop., Sauk City, 1989-93; staff urology Mercy Health Sys., Janesville, 1998—; med. dir. So. Wis. chpt. US TOO, 1993—. Contbr. articles to profl. jours. Commonwealth scholar, Augustus Howe Buck scholar. Fellow Internat. Coll. Surgeons; mem. Am. Assn. Clin. Urologists, Am. Urologic Assn., Wis. Med. Soc. Republican. Greek Orthodox. Avocations: photography, travel, baseball, investing, rare wine. Home: 1237 Geneva National Ave W Lake Geneva WI 53147-5009 Office: Mercy Men's Health Ctr 1000 Mineral Point Ave Janesville WI 53545-2940 E-mail: lshang@elknet.net., ngianitsos@mhsjvl.org.

GIANNETTI, LOUIS DANIEL, film educator, film critic; b. Natick, Mass., Apr. 1, 1937; s. John and Vincenza (Zappitelli) G.; m. Justine Ann Gallagher, Sept. 7, 1963 (div. 1980); children: Christina, Francesca. B.A., Boston U., 1959; M.A., U. Iowa, 1961, Ph.D., 1967. Asst. prof. English Emory U., Atlanta, 1966-70; prof. English and film Case Western Res. U., Cleve., 1970—2001, prof. emeritus English and film, 2002—. Author: Understanding Movies, 1972, rev. 9th edit., 2002, Godard and Others, 1975, Masters of the American Cinema, 1981, (with S. Eyman) Flashback, 1986, 4th rev. edit., 2000. Democrat. Office: Case Western Res U Dept English Euclid Ave Cleveland OH 44106-2706

GIBALA, RONALD, metallurgical engineering educator; b. New Castle, Pa., Oct. 3, 1938; s. Steve Anthony and June Rose (Frank) G.; m. Janice Claire Grichor; children: Maryellen, Janice, David, Kristine. B.S., Carnegie Inst. Tech., 1960; M.S., U. Ill., 1962, Ph.D., 1964. Engring. technician Crane Co., New Castle, Pa., 1956-59; engr. U.S. Steel Rsch. Labs., Monroeville, 1960; rsch. asst. U. Ill., Urbana, 1960-64; asst. prof. metallurgy Case Western Res. U., Cleve., 1964-69, assoc. prof., 1969-76, prof. metallurgy and materials sci. and macromolecular sci., 1976-84, co-dir. materials rsch. lab., 1981-84; dir. metallurgy program NSF, 1982-83; prof., chmn. dept. materials sci. and engring. U. Mich., Ann Arbor, 1984-94, L.H. and F.E. Van Vlack prof. materials sci. and engring., 1998—. Dir. electron microbeam analysis lab. U. Mich., Ann Arbor, 2002—. Contbr. articles to profl. jours.; editor: Hydrogen Embrittlement and Stress Corrosion Cracking, 1984. Pres. Woodhaven Hills Homeowners Assn., 1989-91. Recipient Alfred Noble prize ASCE, 1969, NASA Materials Sci. Divsn. Paper award, 1992; named Outstanding Young Mem. Cleve. chpt. Am. Soc. Metals, 1971; Tech. Achievement award Cleve. Tech. Socs. Council, 1972; vis. research fellow C.E.N.G. Labs., Grenoble, 1973-74; Matthias fellow Los Alamos Nat. Lab., 1991-92, Disting. Merit award U. Ill., 1998; vis. scientist Sandia Nat. Labs., 1998-99. Mem. TMS/AIME (dir. 1981-87), Am. Soc. Metals (chpt. chmn. 1975-76, Life Mem. award 1998), AAAS, Materials Research Soc. (councillor 1995-97, v.p. 1998, pres. 1999), Am. Ceramic Soc., Sigma Xi, Tau Beta Pi, Alpha Sigma Mu. Democrat. Club: Suburban Ski (pres. 1981-82). Home: 1543 Stonehaven St Ann Arbor MI 48104-4149 Office: U Mich Dept Materials Sci Engring Ann Arbor MI 48109-2136

GIBANS, JAMES DAVID, architect; b. Akron, Ohio, Feb. 10, 1930; s. Myer Jacob and Sylva (Hirsch) G.; m. Nina Freedlander, July 16, 1955; children: David Myer, Jonathan Samuel, Amy, Elisabeth. BA, Yale U., 1951, BArch, MArch, Yale U., 1954. Architect George K. Raad & Assocs. et al, San Francisco, 1958-63; project architect Ward and Schneider, Cleve., 1964-68; sr. assoc. William A. Gould and Assocs., 1968-74, Don M. Hisaka and Assoc., Cleve., 1974-76; pvt. practice architecture, 1976-81; v.p. Teare Herman & Gibans, Inc., 1981-89; v.p., treas. Herman Galvin Gibans, Inc., 1989-91, HGG, Inc., Cleve., 1991-94, Herman Gibans Fodor, Inc., 1994—2000, v.p., 2000—. Faculty Edn. for Aesthetic Awareness Cleve. State U., 1977—79. Trustee, mem. exec. com., 1st v.p. Cleve. Chamber Music Soc., 1970-78; mem. adv. bd. Environ. Resource Ctr., Cleve. Pub. Libr., 1973-76; mem. design rev. com. Shaker Square Hist. Dist., 1991-93; mem. Cleve. Landmarks Commn., 1993—; bd. dirs. Cleve. Soc. Contemporary Art, 1985-86, Friends of Shaker Square, 1994-96, Shaker Square Area Devel. Corp., 1996—, v.p., 1996-97, treas., 1997-2001, pres. 2001—; trustee Cleve. Found. for Arch., 1999—, chair focus com., 1999-2001, pres., 2001—. With U.S. Army, 1955-57. Fulbright grantee, 1954-55. Fellow AIA (sec. Cleve. chpt. 1972-74, bd. dirs. 1984-86, treas. 1989, v.p. 1990, pres. 1991); mem. Architects Soc. Ohio (trustee 1975-76, bd. dirs. 1985-88), Cleve. City Club, Rowfant Club, Fulbright Assn. (bd. dirs. N.E. Ohio chpt. 1995-99, treas. 1998-99), N.E. Ohio Jazz Soc. (bd. dirs. 1991-96, v.p. 1993-95, pres. 1995-96). Democrat. Jewish. Avocations: music, art, jogging, cross-country skiing. Home: 13800 Shaker Blvd Cleveland OH 44120-1585 Office: Herman Gibans Fodor Inc 1304 W 6th St Cleveland OH 44113-1304 E-mail: jgibans@hgfarchitects.com.

GIBARA, SAMIR G. tire manufacturing executive; CEO, chmn. Goodyear Tire & Rubber Co., Akron, Ohio. Office: Goodyear Tire & Rubber Co 1144 E Market St Akron OH 44316-0002

GIBBONS, JOHN, mortgage company executive; BA in Social Studies, PhDin Govt., Harvard U.; MBA, U. Pa. Asst. prof. social scis. U. Chgo.; rating specialist Std. & Poor's Corp.; dir. mortgage fin. group, v.p. mortgage fin. Merrill Lynch, v.p. mortgage rsch. group, dir. fin. instns. group; v.p. fin. rsch. Freddie Mac, 1991, acting CFO, sr. v.p. corp. rels., CFO, 1996—. Office: Fed Home Loan Bank Chgo 111 E Wacker Dr Ste 800 Chicago IL 60601

GIBBONS, MICHAEL RANDOLPH, state legislator, lawyer; b. Kirkwood, Mo., Mar. 24, 1959; s. Michael and Folsta Sara (Bailey) G.; m. Elizabeth Weddell, Jan. 30, 1988; children: Danny, Meredith. BA, Westminster Coll., 1981; JD, St. Louis U., 1984. Bar: Mo. 1984. Assoc. Michael Gibbons, Kirkwood, 1984-86; ptnr. Gibbons and Gibbons, 1986—; mem. Mo. Ho. of Reps. from 88th dist., Jefferson City, 1992-2000; mem. various coms.; mem. Mo. Senate from 15th dist., Jefferson City, 2001—. Mem. coun. City of Kirkwood, 1986-92; dep. mayor, 1990-92; mem. Bonhomme Twp. Rep. Club, v.p., 1985-87, bd. dirs.; vestry mem. Grace Episcopal Ch., Kirkwood, 1986-88; bd. dirs. Edgewood Children's Ctr., 1996—, Citizens for Modern Transit, 1996—. Mem. Bar Assn. of Met. St. Louis, Kirkwood C. of C. (bd. dirs. 1986-88), Kiwanis (pres. Kirkwood chpt. 1986-87). Republican. Avocations: sports. Home: 651 Pearl Ave Kirkwood MO 63122-2721 Office: Gibbons & Gibbons PC 214 N Clay Ave Kirkwood MO 63122-4004

GIBBONS, WILLIAM JOHN, lawyer; b. Chgo., Jan. 22, 1947; s. Edward and Lottie (Gasiorek) G.; children: Maximilian Clay, Bartholomew David, Ariel Katherine. BA, Northwestern U., 1968, JD, 1972. Bar: Ill. 1972, U.S. Dist. Ct. (no. dist.) Ill. 1972, U.S. Ct. Appeals (9th cir.) 1980, U.S. Supreme Ct. 1982, U.S. Ct. Appeals (7th cir.) 1984. Assoc. Kirkland and Ellis, Chgo., 1972-76; ptnr. Hedlund, Hunter and Lynch, 1976-82, Latham and Watkins, Chgo., 1982—, mng. ptnr. Chgo. office, 1995-2000. Bd. dirs. Pegasus Players, Chgo. Served with USAR, 1968-74. Mem.: ABA, Chgo. Coun. Lawyers, Seventh Cir. Bar Assn., Chgo. Bar Assn. (chair class action com. 1994—95), Riverpark Club (Chgo.). Home: 4900 S Kimbark Ave Chicago IL 60615-2922 Office: Latham & Watkins Sears Tower Ste 5800 Chicago IL 60606-6306

GIBBONS, WILLIAM REGINALD, JR. poet, novelist, translator, editor; b. Houston, Jan. 7, 1947; s. William Reginald and Elizabeth (Lubowski) G.; m. Virginia Margaret Harris, June 8, 1968 (div. July 1982); m. Cornelia Maude Spelman, Aug. 18, 1983. AB, Princeton U., 1969; MA, Stanford U., 1971, PhD, 1974. Instr. Spanish Rutgers U., Brunswick, N.J., 1975-76; lectr. creative writing Princeton U., 1976-80, Columbia U., N.Y.C., 1980-81; prof. English Northwestern U., Evanston, Ill., 1981—, editor TriQuarterly, 1981-97; prof. MFA Program for Writers Warren Wilson Coll., 1989—. Author: Roofs Voices Roads, 1979 (Quar. Rev. prize), The Ruined Motel, 1981, Saints, 1986, Maybe It Was So, 1991, Five Pears or Peaches, 1991, William Goyen: A Study of the Short Fiction, 1991, Sweetbitter, 1994, Sparrow: New and Selected Poems, 1997, Homage to Longshot O'Leary, 1999; translator: Selected Poems of Luis Cernuda, 1978, Guillén on Guillén, 1979, Euripides' Bakkhai, 2001; editor: The Poet's Work, 1979; (with G. Graff) Criticism in the University, 1985, The Writer in Our World, 1986, Fiction of the Eighties, 1990, Thomas McGrath: Life and the Poem, 1991, New Writing from Mexico, 1992. Woodrow Wilson fellow Stanford U., 1969-70; Fulbright fellow Spain, 1971-72; Guggenheim fellow, 1983-84; NEA fellow, 1984; Ill. Arts Coun. fellow, 1988; recipient Translation prize Denver Quar., 1977, Short Story award Tex. Inst. Letters, 1986, Carl Sandburg award, 1992, Anisfield-Wolf Book award, 1995, Jesse Jones award Tex. Inst. Letters, 1995, Ill. Arts Coun. Lit. awards, 1996, 97, Balcones Poetry prize, 1998, others. Mem. PEN Am. Ctr., Poetry Soc. Am. (John Masefield Meml. award 1991), Associated Writing Programs (bd. dirs. 1984-87), The Guild Complex (bd. dirs. 1989—). Office: Northwestern U Dept English Univ Hall 215 Evanston IL 60208-0001 E-mail: rgibbons@northwestern.edu.

GIBSON, BENJAMIN F. federal judge; b. Safford, Ala., July 13, 1931; s. Eddie and Pearl Ethel (Richardson) G.; m. Lucille Nelson, June 23, 1951; children: Charlotte, Linda, Gerald, Gail, Carol, Laura. B.S., Wayne State U., 1955; J.D. with distinction, Detroit Coll. Law, 1960. Bar: Mich. 1960. Acct., City of Detroit, 1955-56, Detroit Edison Co., 1956-61; asst. atty. gen. Mich., 1961-63; asst. pros. atty. Ingham County, 1963-64; pvt. practice law Lansing, from 1964; prof. Thomas Cooley Law Sch., 1979; judge U.S. Dist. Ct. West Dist. Mich., Grand Rapids, 1979—, chief judge U.S. Dist. Ct., 1991-95, now sr. judge, 1996-99. Bd. dirs. Cooley Law Sch.; adj. prof. Cooley Law Sch. Mem. United Way Project Blueprint; mem. bd. dirs. YMCA. Mem. Fed. Bar Assn., Mich. State Bar Assn., Grand Rapids State Bar Assn., Black Judges of Mich., Floyd H. Skinner Bar Assn., Fed. Judges Assn., Sigma Pi Phi. Club: Peninsular Club.

GIBSON, DAVID THOMAS, microbiology educator; b. Wakefield, Yorkshire, Eng., Feb. 16, 1938; U.S. citizen; married; two children. BSc in Biochemistry 1st class honors, U. Leeds, Eng., 1961, PhD in Biochemistry, 1964. Lectr. in biology Leeds Tech. Coll., 1962-63; rsch. assoc. U. Wis. Coll. Pharmacy, Madison, 1964-65; rsch. assoc. dept. microbiology U. Ill., Champaign-Urbana, 1965-67; asst. prof. microbiology dept. U. Tex., Austin, 1967-68, 69-71, assoc. prof. microbiology dept., 1971-75, prof. microbiology dept., 1975-88, dir. Ctr. for Applied Microbiology, 1981-88; prof., Edwin B. Green prof. biocatalysis and microbiology Coll. Medicine, U. Iowa, Iowa City, 1988—. Rsch. biochemist pharms. divsn. I.C.I. Ltd., Aderley Park, Cheshire, Eng., 1968-69; L.Am. vis. prof. Nat. Poly. Inst., Mexico City, 1976; mem. microbial chemistry study sect. NIH, 1977-80; mem. sci. adv. bd. AMGEN, 1981-88; mem. various univ. coms. Assoc. editor Devels. in Indsl. Microbiology, 1975-79; mem. editl. bd. Jour. Bacteriology, 1979-83, 88-91, 95-97, Jour. Biol. Chemistry, 1980-88, Biodegradation, 1989-96; contbr. numerous articles to profl. jours. Recipient Career Devel. award USPHS, 1972-77; grantee NIH, 1995—, USAF, 1996-99. Fellow AAAS; mem. Am. Soc. for Microbiology (Found. lectr. 1981-82, Procter and Gamble award in appled and environ. microbiology 1997), Am. Chem. Soc., Soc. for Indsl. Microbiology, Fedn. Am. Socs. for Exptl. Biology, Am. Acad. Microbiology (mem. nominating com. 1988-90), Sigma Xi, Phi Kappa Phi. Office: U Iowa Dept Microbiology 3733 Bowen Science Building Iowa City IA 52242-1109 E-mail: david.gibson@ulowa.edu.

GIBSON, JOHN ROBERT, judge; b. Springfield, Mo., Dec. 20, 1925; s. Harry B. and Edna (Kerr) G.; m. Mary Elizabeth Vaughn, Sept. 20, 1952 (dec. Aug. 1985); children: Jeanne, John Robert; m. Diane Allen Larrison, Oct. 1, 1986; stepchildren: Holly, Catherine. AB, U. Mo., 1949, JD, 1952. Bar: Mo. 1952. Assoc. Morrison, Hecker, Curtis, Kuder & Parrish, Kansas City, Mo., 1952-58, ptnr., 1958-81; judge U.S. Dist. Ct. (we. dist.) Mo., 1981-82, U.S. Ct. Appeals (8th cir.), Kansas City, 1982-94, sr. judge, 1994—. Mem. Mo. Press-Bar Commn., 1979-81; mem. com. on adminstrn. of magistrate sys. Jud. Conf. U.S., 1987-91, mem. security and facilities com., 1995—. Vice chmn. Jackson County Charter Transition Com., 1971-72; mem. Jackson County Charter Commn., 1970; v.p. Police Commrs. Bd., Kansas City, 1973-77. Served with AUS, 1944-46. With U.S. Army, 1944—46. Recipient Citation of Merit award U. Mo. at Columbia Sch. of Law, 1994. Fellow Am. Bar Found.; mem. ABA, Mo. State Bar (gov. 1972-79, pres. 1977-78; Pres.' award 1974, Smithson award 1984), Kansas City Bar Assn. (pres. 1970-71), Lawyers Assn. Kansas City (Charles Evan Whittaker award 1980), Fed. Judges Assn. (bd. dirs. 1991-97), Phi Beta Kappa, Omicron Delta Kappa. Presbyterian. Presbyterian. Office: US Ct Appeals 8th Cir 400 E 9th St Ste 1040 Kansas City MO 64106-2695

GIBSON, MCGUIRE, archaeologist, educator; b. Bushwood, Md., Nov. 6, 1938; s. Thomas Laurie and Essie Mae (Owens) G. BA, Fordham U., 1959; MA, U. Chgo., 1964, PhD, 1968. Asst. prof. anthropology U. Ill.-Chgo., 1968-71; asst. prof. anthropology U. Ariz., Tucson, 1971-72; asst. prof. U. Chgo., 1972-73, assoc. prof., 1973-81, prof., 1981—. Ann. prof. Am. Schs. Oriental Rsch., Baghdad, Iraq, 1969-70; dir. Nippur Expdn., Iraq, 1972—; dir. Dhamar Expdn., Yemen, 1978-98, Hamoukar Expedition, Syria, 1999—; chmn. Coun. Am. Overseas Rsch. Ctrs., 1984-88, treas., 1988-92, mem. exec. com., 1995—; dir. Hamoukar Expdn., Syria, 1999—. Author: The City and Area of Kish, 1972; author, editor: Excavations at Nippur, 12th Season, 1978, Uch Tepe I, 1981; editor: Irrigation's Impact on Society, 1974, Seals and Sealing in the Ancient Near Est, 1977, The Organization of Power: Aspects of Bureaucracy in the Ancient Near East, 1987, Uch Tepe II, 1990, Nippur III, 1993. Mem. arts com. Union League Civic and Arts Found., Chgo., 1984-86. Recipient Yemeni Arch. Svc. award, 1998; grantee Am. Numismatic Soc., 1966, Am. Philos. Soc., 1969, Nat. Geog. Soc., 1978, 89, NSF, 1994, NEH, 1995-98. Fellow Brit. Sch. Archaeology in Iraq, Royal Anthrop. Inst., Deutsche Orient-Gesellschaft; mem. AAAS, Am. Inst. Archaeology, Am. Anthrop. Assn., Am. Inst. for Yemeni Studies (pres. 1978-80, 92-96), Middle East Studies Assn., Am. Assn. Rsch. in Baghdad (pres. 1989—), Civil War Landscapes Assn. (pres. 2000—), Quadrangle Club, Sigma Xi. Democrat. Club: Quadrangle Avocations: architectural restoration; study of Oriental rugs. Office: U Chgo Oriental Inst 1155 E 58th St Chicago IL 60637-1540 E-mail: m-gibson@uchicago.edu.

GIDWITZ, GERALD, retired hair care company executive; b. Memphis, 1906; married; 5 children. PhB, U. Chgo., 1927. Co-founder, former chmn. bd. and chmn. exec. com. Helene Curtis Industries, Inc., Chgo.; ret. Trustee Roosevelt U., Auditorium Theatre Coun.; bd. dirs. Chgo. Crime Commn., Jamestown Found.; founder learning for earning that educates adults on pub. aid and gets them jobs at no cost to the students, 2001-. Mem. Ill. Mfg. Assn. (past bd. dirs.). Office: 325 N Wells St Chicago IL 60610-4705

GIERTZ, J. FRED, economics educator; b. Wichita, Kans., Jan. 18, 1943; s. Joe L. and Frieda J. (Hamblin) G.; m. Donna Hyland, Sept. 13, 1969; children: Seth H., Gabrielle H. BA, Wichita U., 1964; MA, Northwestern U., 1966, PhD, 1970. Instr. econs. Miami U., Oxford, Ohio, 1968-70, asst. prof., 1970-73, asso. prof., 1973-78, prof., 1978-80; prof. econs. Inst. Govt. and Public Affairs, U. Ill., Urbana, 1980—; acting dir. Inst. Govt. and Pub. Affairs U. Ill., 1993-94; exec. dir. Nat. Tax Assn., 2000—. Rsch. dir. Ill. Tax Reform Commn., 1982-83; dir. Ameritech fellowship program U. Ill., 1987-93; adviser Transition Team of Ill. Gov. Jim Edgar, 1990-91; trustee State Univs. Retirement System, 1995—; cons. in field. Mem. editorial bd.: Quarterly Rev. Econs. and Bus, 1979-88; contbr. articles in field to profl. jours. Mem. athletic bd. U. Ill., 1998—. Mem. Midwest Econs. Assn. (v.p. 1978-79), Am. Econ. Assn., Ill. Econ. Assn. (pres. 1986-87), Pub. Choice Soc., Nat. Tax Assn., Univ. Club Chgo., Champaign Country Club. Home: 601 Park Lane Dr Champaign IL 61820-7630 Office: U Ill Inst Govt Pub Affairs 1007 W Nevada St Urbana IL 61801-3812 E-mail: j-goertz@uiuc.edu.

GIESEN, RICHARD ALLYN, business executive; b. Evanston, Ill., Oct. 7, 1929; s. Elmer J. and Ethyl (Lillig) G.; m. Jeannine St. Bernard, Jan. 31, 1953; children: Richard Allyn, Laurie J., Mark S. B.S., Northwestern U., 1951. Research analyst new bus. and research depts. Glore, Forgan & Co., Chgo., 1951-57; asst. to pres. Gen. Dynamics Corp., N.Y.C., 1957-60, asst. treas., 1960-61, asst. v.p. ops. and contracts, 1961-63; fin. cons. IBM Corp., 1963, exec. asst. to sr. v.p., 1964-65; treas. subs. Sci. Research Assocs., Inc., Chgo., 1965-66, v.p. fin. and adminstrn., 1966-67, exec. v.p., chief operating officer, 1967-68, pres., chief exec. officer, 1968-80; pres., chief exec. officer, chmn. exec. com., dir. Field Enterprises, Inc., 1980-83; pres. RLM Investments, 1983-93; chmn., pres., CEO Am. Appraisal Assocs., Inc., 1984-93; chmn., CEO Continental Glass & Plastic, Inc., Chgo., 1988—, Continere Corp., 1988—. Bd. dirs. Smurfit Stone Container Corp., GATX, Inc.; bd. trustees Asia House Funds, 1994-98. Bd. trustees Asia House Fund, 1994-98; mem. bus. adv. coun. Chgo. Urban League, 1968-83; prin. Chgo. United, 1980-83; mem. adv. coun. Technol. Inst., Northwestern U.; mem. pres.'s coun. Nat. Coll. Edn., Evanston, Ill., 1977-86; bd. dirs. Am. Cancer Soc.; mem. adv. coun. J.L. Kellogg Grad. Sch. Mgmt., Northwestern U.; dir. Jr. Achievement Chgo., 1993—; trustee Chgo. Edn. TV Assn., 1975-81, Inst. Internat. Edn., 1997—, chmn. midwest adv. bd. Mem. Chgo. Pres. Orgn., Chief Execs. Orgn., Chgo. Assn. Commerce and Industry (bd. dirs.), Chgo. Coun. Com. Fgn. Rels., Webhannet Golf Club, Chgo. Club, Shoreacres (Lake Bluff, Ill) Club, Milw. Club, Alpha Tau Omega, Beta Gamma Sigma. Clubs: Chicago, Shoreacres (Lake Bluff, Ill.), Milw. Office: Continental Glass & Plastic 841 W Cermak Rd Chicago IL 60608-4582 Fax: 312-666-7501. E-mail: richard.giesen@cgppkg.com.

GIFFIN, MARY ELIZABETH, psychiatrist, educator; b. Rochester, Minn., Mar. 30, 1919; d. Herbert Ziegler and Mary Elizabeth (Nace) G. BA, Smith Coll., Northampton, Mass., 1939; MD, Johns Hopkins, 1943; MS, U. Minn., 1948. Diplomate Am. Bd. Psychiatry and Neurology. Cons. in neurology and psychiatry Mayo Clinic, Rochester, 1949-58; med. dir. Josselyn Clinic, Northfield, Ill., 1958-89; pvt. practice psychiatry, 1989—. Mem. faculty Inst. for Psychoanalysis, Chgo., 1963-89. Contbr. numerous articles to profl. jour. Mem. Ill. Psychiat. Soc., Am. Acad. Child Psychiatry. Republican. Mem. Am. Bapt. Ch. Avocation: creative writing. Home: 1190 Hamptondale Ave Winnetka IL 60093-1812 Office: 1 Northfield Plz Ste 300 Northfield IL 60093-1214

GIFFORD, DALE L. human resources executive; b. May 30, 1950; BS, U. Wis., 1971. With Hewitt Assocs. LLC, Lincolnshire, Ill., 1972—, now CEO. Office: Hewitt Associates 100 Half Day Rd Lincolnshire IL 60069-3242

GIFFORD, JOHN IRVING, retired agricultural equipment company executive; b. Lockport, N.Y., July 23, 1930; s. John Jacob and Carrie (McAdam) G.; m. Sara Jane Bauer, Jan. 28, 1955; children: John Hutchins, James Scott. BS, Purdue U., 1952, MS, 1956. Sales trainee Am. Nat. Foods, Inc., L.A., 1956; economist Deere & Co., Moline, Ill., 1956-65, pers. adminstr., 1965-70, mgr. data svcs., 1970-96; stats. cons. to cos. and trade assns., 1996—. Mem. USDA Agrl. Stats. adv. com., 1997—. Bd. dirs., Rock Island (Ill.) sect. Easter Seal Found., 1981-87; v.p. coun., St. John Luth. Ch., Rock Island, 1981-82; pres., Rock Island Little League, 1981-82; v.p. Babe Ruth Baseball, Rock Island, 1983; mem. agrl. census adv. com. U.S. Dept. Commerce, 1997-98; mem. adv. com. stats. USDA, 1999—. 1st lt. U.S. Army, 1952-54, Korea. Recipient Leadership recognition Equipment Mfrs. Inst. Mem. Nat. Assn. Bus. Econs., Equipment Mfrs. Assn., Farm and Indsl. Equipment Inst., Constrn. Industry Mfrs. Assn., Outdoor Power Equipment Inst., Engine Mfrs. Assn., Internat. Farm Tractor Com., Internat. Harvesting Equipment Com. (chmn. statistics com. 1994-95). Avocations: reading, golf. E-mail: gifford@revealed.net.

GILBERT, ALLAN ARTHUR, manufacturing executive; b. Chgo., Jan. 7, 1925; s. Allan T. and Elizabeth (Boyce) G.; m. Gwendolyn M. Moore, June 24, 1950; children: Debora D. and Elizabeth (twins), Allan M. Buyer Carson Pirie Scott & Co., Chgo., 1949-55; v.p. George Fry & Assocs., 1956-65; v.p. mktg. Chamberlain Mfg. Corp., Elmhurst, Ill., 1966-68; v.p. Lester B. Knight & Assocs., Chgo., 1968-75; v.p. manpower devel. Emerson Electric Co., St. Louis, 1975-92, cons., 1992-2000. Asst. prof. Roosevelt U., 1951-52. Mem. Gov.'s Adv. Council, Ill., 1969-70; fund raiser Ill. Republicans., 1966-67. Lt. (j.g.) USNR, 1944-46. Mem. Soc. Colonial Wars (dep. gov. Mo.), Glen View Club, Old Warson Club, Univ. Club, Princeton Club, Harvard Bus. Club. Office: Emerson Electric Co PO Box 4100 Saint Louis MO 63136-8506

GILBERT, DAVID R. public relations executive; Press sec. to Gov. James Thompson, Ill.; pres. David R. Gilbert & Assocs.; gen. mgr. Golin/Harris Comms., Chgo., 1993-96; pres. Golin/Harris Internat., 1996—. Office: Golin/Harris Internat 10th Fl 111 E Wacker Dr Fl 10 Chicago IL 60601-4305

GILBERT, ELMER GRANT, aerospace engineering educator, control theorist; b. Joliet, Ill., Mar. 29, 1930; s. Harry A. and Florence A. (Otterstrom) G.; m. Lois M. Verbrugge, Dec. 27, 1973. BSEE, U. Mich., 1952, MSEE, 1953, PhD in Instrumentation Engring., 1956. Instr. U. Mich., Ann Arbor, 1954-56, asst. prof., 1957-59, assoc. prof., 1959-63, prof. aerospace engring., 1963—. Founder, Applied Dynamics Inc., Ann Arbor. Patentee computer devices, 1968-74. Fellow IEEE (Control Engring. Field award 1994), AAAS; mem. Nat. Acad. Engring., Soc. Indsl. and Applied Math. Office: U Mich Dept Aerospace Engring Ann Arbor MI 48109-2140 E-mail: elmerg@umich.edu.

GILBERT, GLENN GORDON, linguistics educator; b. Montgomery, Ala., Sept. 17, 1936; s. William H. and Margaret (Christensen) G.; m. Erika Wrede, Aug. 8, 1964 (div. Nov. 1993); children: Alexander Martin, Christa Selene; m. Sharon Wright Page, July 23, 1994. AB in German Lang. and Lit., U. Chgo., 1957; postgrad., U. Frankfurt, Fed. Republic Germany, 1957-59; Diplôme de la Langue Française with honors, Sorbonne, U. Paris, 1960; PhD in Linguistics, Harvard U., 1963. Instr. Germanic langs. and lits. U. Tex., Austin, 1963-66, asst. prof. Germanic langs., 1967-70; vis. asst. prof. linguistics Can. Summer Sch. Linguistics, U. Alta., Edmonton, summer 1966; Fulbright lectr. linguistics U. Marburg, Fed. Republic Germany, 1966-67; assoc. prof. So. Ill. U., Carbondale, 1970-74, prof., 1975—, chmn. dept. linguistics, 1987—89, 1999—2002; Fulbright lectr. linguistics U. Mainz, Fed. Republic Germany, 1973-74; Z.W.O. research fellow in creole langs. U. Nijmegen, The Netherlands, 1984-85. Active numerous univ. linguistics coms. and councils; bd. dirs., mem. editorial bd., Ill. bus. rep. Papers in Linguistics, 1979-87; pres. Linguistic Research Inc., 1983-87. Founder, editor Journal of Pidgin and Creole Languages, 1985-2001; author: Linguistic Atlas of Texas German, 1972; editor: (books) Texas Studies in Bilingualism, 1970, The German Language in America, 1971, Pidgin and Creole Languages: Essays in Memory of John E. Reinecke, 1987, Pidgin and Creole Linguistics in the Twenty-First Century, 2002; co-editor (with Jacob Ornstein) Problems in Applied Educational Sociolinguistics, 1978; editor and translator: Pidgin and Creole Languages: Selected Essays by Hugo Schuchardt, 1980; editor: (book series) Studies in Ethnolinguistics, 1993—; contbr. numerous articles to profl. jours. and chpts. to books in field; also reviews. Translator, interpreter various cmty. orgns. NDEA fellow in Swedish, Harvard U., 1961-63; research grantee U. Tex.-Austin, 1963-70, Nat. Carl Schurz Meml. Fund, 1968, So. Ill. U.-Carbondale, 1970-84, NEH, 1981, Am. Philos. Soc., 1982; numerous invited lectures. Mem. Soc. Caribbean Linguistics, Soc. for Pidgin and Creole Linguistics. Home: 166 Union Grove Rd Carbondale IL 62901-7687 Office: So Ill U Dept Linguistics Carbondale IL 62901 E-mail: ggilbert@siu.edu., glennggilbert@msn.com.

GILBERT, HOWARD N(ORMAN), lawyer, director; b. Chgo., Aug. 19, 1928; s. Norman Aaron and Fannie (Cohn) G.; m. Jacqueline Glasser, Feb. 16, 1957; children: Norman Abraham, Harlan Wayne, Joel Kenneth, Sharon. PhB, U. Chgo., 1947; JD, Yale U., 1951. Bar: Ill 1951, U.S. Dist. Ct. (no. dist.) Ill. 1955, U.S. Ct. Appeals (7th cir.) 1956. Ptnr. Rusnak, Deutsch & Gilbert, Chgo., 1962-79, Aaron, Schimberg, Hess & Gilbert, Chgo., 1980-84; sr. ptnr. Holleb & Coff, 1984-2000, Wildman, Harrold, Chgo., 2000—. Bd. dirs. Jewish Fedn. Met. Chgo., 1977-83; chmn. bd. dirs., pres. Mt. Sinai Hosp. Med. Ctr., Chgo., 1968-69; trustee Chgo. Hosp. Coun., 1979-84; mem. bd. Jewish Edn., 1972-77; mem. vis. com. Coll. of U. Chgo., 1997—. Mem. ABA, Chgo. Bar Assn., Chgo. Coun. Lawyers, Ill. Soc. Health Lawyers, Standard Club, Bryn Mawr Country Club. Democrat. Jewish. Office: Wildman Harrold Allen & Dixon 225 W Wacker Dr Ste 3000 Chicago IL 60606-1224 E-mail: gilbert@wildmanharrold.com.

GILBERT, J. PHIL, federal judge; b. 1949; BS, U. Ill., 1971; JD, Loyola U., Chgo., 1974. Ptnr. Gilbert & Gilbert, Carbondale, Ill., 1974-83, Gilbert, Kimmel, Huffman & Prosser, Carbondale, 1983-88; circuit judge First Jud. Circuit, Ill., 1988-92; fed. judge U.S. Dist. Ct. (so. dist.) Ill., Benton, 1992—, chief judge, 1993—. Spl. asst. atty. gen. Pub. Aid Enforcement Divsn., 1974-75; asst. city atty. City of Carbondale, 1975-78; active Nat. Coun. Govt. Ethics Laws, 1988—; mem. Ill. State Bd. Elections, 1982, vice chmn., chmn., 1983-85. Bd. dirs. Friends of Morris Libr., 1988—; active Edn. Coun. 100, 1989—, Boy Scouts Am. Mem. Ill. State Bar, Jackson County Bar Assn., Ill. Judges Assn. (mem. com. jud. retention), Phi Alpha Delta. Office: US Dist Ct 301 W Main St Benton IL 62812-1362

GILBERT, JAMES H. judge; b. Mpls., Mar. 11, 1947; s. Kenneth H. and Virginia E. (Ekstrand) G.; m. Mary M. Makepeace, Sept. 17, 1971; children: Alisson K., Erica M., Kristina L. BA, U. Minn., 1969, JD, 1972. Bar: Minn. 1972, Wis. 1984, U.S. Dist. Ct. Minn. 1974, U.S. Tax Ct. 1978, U.S. Ct. Appeals (8th cir.) 1989, U.S. Supreme Ct. 1988. Lawyer, v.p., mng. ptnr. Meshbesher, Singer & Spence Ltd., Mpls., 1971—; assoc. justice Minn. State Supreme Ct., 1998—. Park Commr. City of Orono, Minn., 1988—; bd. dirs. Minn. Drug Abuse Resistance Edn. Inc. Mem. Minn. Bar Assn., Minn. Trial Lawyers Assn., Lafayette Club. Avocations: skiing, hunting, golf, tennis, snowmobiling. Office: Minn Judicial Ctr 25 Constitution Ave Rm 422 Saint Paul MN 55155

GILBERT, JAY, radio personality; Radio host WEBN, Cin. Named Personality of the Yr., Marconi Awards, 1999. Office: WEBN 111 St Gregory St Cincinnati OH 45202

GILBERT, JOHN OREN, insurance company executive; b. Morris, Minn., Aug. 30, 1942; s. Oren Lincoln and Thelma (Hall) G.; m. Marilyn Jean Erickson, Nov. 26, 1966; children: Brad, Erica. BA, U. Minn., Morris, 1964; MBA, U. Wis., Oshkosh, 1978. Asst. v.p. managerial reporting Aid Assn. for Luths., Appleton, Wis., 1981-85, asst. vp. info. mgmt., 1985-86, v.p. field svcs., 1986-90, v.p., gen. mgr., 1990-91, sr. v.p., mem. ins. svcs., 1992-94, exec. v.p., 1995—, chmn., pres., CEO, 1997—. Mem. U. Wis. Alumni Assn. (Disting. Alumni award 1992), Beta Gamma Sigma. Lutheran. Avocations: travel, wood-working. Office: Aid Assn for Luths 4321 N Ballard Rd Appleton WI 54919-7729 Home: Apt 1404 110 Bank St SE Minneapolis MN 55414-3904

GILBERT, PAUL W. retail executive; b. 1945; With Jacobson Stores, Inc., Jackson, Mich., 1975—, sr. v.p., CFO, exec. v.p., CFO, treas., vice chmn. bd., 1993—. Office: Jacobson Stores Inc 3333 Sargent Rd Jackson MI 49201-8847 Fax: (517) 764-1479.

GILBERT, RONALD RHEA, lawyer; b. Sandusky, Ohio, Dec. 29, 1942; s. Corvin and Mildred (Millikin) G.; children: Elizabeth, Lynne, Lisa. BA, Wittenberg U., 1964; JD, U. Mich., 1967, postgrad., 1967-68, Wayne State U., 1973-74. Bar: Mich. 1968, U.S. Dist. Ct. (ea. and we. dists.) Mich. 1968, U.S. Ct. Appeals (6th cir.) 1968, U.S. Ct. Appeals (9th cir.) 1977, U.S. Ct. Appeals (7th cir.) 1984, U.S. Ct. Appeals (3d cir.) 1988, U.S. Ct. Appeals (4th cir.) 1989, U.S. Ct. Appeals (8th cir.) 1990, U.S. Ct. Appeals (10th cir.) 1991, U.S. Ct. Appeals (11th cir.) 1992, U.S. Ct. Appeals (2nd cir.), 1992. Assoc. prosecutor Wayne County, Mich., 1969; assoc. Rouse, Selby, Dickinson, Shaw & Pike, Detroit, 1969-72; ptnr. Charfoos, Christensen, Gilbert & Archer, P.C., 1972-84; sole practice, 1984—. Instr. Madonna Coll., Detroit, 1977-81; mem. faculty Inst. Continuing Legal Edn., 1977—; speaker symposium on social security law Detroit Coll. Law, 1984; state bar grievance investigator; vol. chmn. Aquatic Injury Safety Found; mgr. web sites Found. for Spinal Cord Injury Prevention, Care and Cure (fscip.org), Found. for Aquatic Injury Prevention (aquaticisf.org). Co-author: Social Security Disability Claims, 1983; contbr. articles to legal jours. Founder, chmn. Aquatic Injury Safety Group, 1982, chmn., 1982-89; founder, chmn. Found. for Aquatic Injury Prevention, 1988, Found. for Spinal Cord Injury Prevention, 1988, founder websites; chmn. aquatic safety com. Nat. Safety Coun., 1987; mem. data collection subcom. of Nat. Swimming Safety Com. for Consumer Products Safety Commn.; bd. dirs. Nat. Coordinating Coun. on Spinal Cord Injuries; patron Detroit Art Inst., Detroit Zool. Soc.; mem. Pres.' Club U. Mich.; mem. Detroit Council on World Affairs, 1968-73, Council for Nat. Coop. in Aquatics; mem. combined fed. campaign Nat. Health Agy. Mich.; founder Spinal Cord Injury Traumatic Brain Injury Adv. Com. Mich. Pub. Health Chronic Adv. Com.; co-founder Safe Kids Coalition Southeastern Mich.; mem. Nat. Safe Kids Coalition. Mem. Assn. Trial Lawyers Am., Mich. Trial Lawyers Assn., System Safety Soc., ABA, Mich Bar Assn., Detroit Bar Assn., Am. Arbitration Assn., Am. Judicature Soc., Nat. Spinal Cord Injury Assn. (sec. 1988, bd. dirs., exec. com., chmn. prevention com.), Nat. Head Injury Assn., Mich. Head Injury Assn., Am. Standards and Testing Materials (com. F-24 on water parks and playgrounds, mem. com. F-8), World Water Parks Assn., Nat. Environ. Health Assn., Nat. Pub. Health Assn., Nat. Eagle Scout Assn. (alumni), Blue Key, Pi Kappa Alpha, Pi Sigma Alpha, Pi Delta Epsilon, U. Mich. Club, Spring Meadows Country Club. Office: 19223

Roscommon Harper Woods MI 48225 Office Fax: 313-245-0812. E-mail: ron@fscip.org., ron@aquaticisf.org., rrgpc@aol.com.

GILBERT, RUBY, state legislator; m. Booker Gilbert. Kans. state rep. Dist. 89, 1993—. Home: 2629 N Erie St Wichita KS 67219-4739 Office: Kans Ho of Reps State Capitol Topeka KS 66612

GILBERT, SAMUEL LAWRENCE, business owner; b. Chgo., Mar. 3, 1950; s. Robert Augustus and Ruby Elizabeth (Gammon) G.; m. Sharon Faye Warner, Nov. 3, 1972 (div. Oct. 1984); children: Shaundra, Shari, Sharita. AA in Health Care, Malcolm X Coll., Chgo., 1969; cert. in acctg., Bryant Stratton Coll., Chgo., 1989. Mail/shipping coord. Natural Gas Pipeline Co. Am., Chgo., 1970-82; mailroom asst. IBM Corp., 1982-83; CEO Genesis Comics Group, Inc., 1986-94; chmn., pub., CEO Genesis Pub., Ltd., 1994—; pub. Gilben Comics, 2000—; sr. v.p. creative design Gilben Prodn. Ltd., 2000—. Sr. v.p. creative design Gil Ben Comics. Editor: Gil Ben Prodns. Deacon Christ the King Temple Ch., Chgo., 1985-87; asst. pastor Greater Holy Rock MBC, Chgo., 1988-92, St. Titus MBC, Chgo., 1994—; assoc. min. Greater New Mt. Carmen, Chgo., 1992-94. Mem. Am. Mgmt. Assn., Rsch. Inst. Am. Democrat. Baptist. Avocation: building model aircraft.

GILBERT, SUZANNE HARRIS, advertising executive; b. Chgo, Mar. 8, 1948; d. Lawrence W. and Dorothea (Wilde) Harris: children: Kerry, Elizabeth, Gregory. BS, Marquette U.; MBA, U. Chgo., 1985. Fin. analyst Leo Burnett Co., Chgo.; sr. v.p., fin. administrn., sec.-treas. Clinton E. Frank Inc., 1975-85; with Campbell-Ewald Co., Detroit, 1985—, grp. sr. v.p Warren, Mich., exec. v.p., chief fin. and administrv. officer, 1990—. Bd. dirs.; bd. dirs., mem. fiscal control and investment audit coms. AAAA Ins. Co. Ltd. Bd. dirs. Detroit Workforce Devel.; mem. bd. advs. U. Detroit Mercy Coll. of Bus. Recipient Profl. Achievement award Marquette U., 2000. Mem. Am. Assn. Advt. Agys. (fiscal control com.), Econ. Club Detroit, Fin. Execs. Inst. (bd. dirs. Detroit chpt., pres.). Office: Campbell-Ewald 30400 Van Dyke Ave Warren MI 48093-2368

GILBERTSON, DAVID, state supreme court justice; Former judge S.D. Cir. Ct. (5th jud. cir.), Pierre; assoc. justice S.D. Supreme Ct., 1995—2001, chief justice, 2001—. Office: 500 E Capitol Ave Pierre SD 57501-5070*

GILBERTSON, ERIC RAYMOND, academic administrator, lawyer; b. Cleve., Mar. 5, 1945; s. Ewald R. and Esther V. (Johnson) G.; m. Cynthia F. Forrest, Jan. 25, 1974; children: Sara, Seth. BS, Bluffton Coll., 1966; MA in Econs., Ohio U., 1967; JD cum laude, Cleve. State U., 1970; DLitt (hon.), U. Mysore, Karnataka, India, 1993. Bar: Ohio 1970, Vt. 1984, U.S. Dist. Ct. (no. and so. dists.) Ohio 1971, U.S. Supreme Ct. 1981. Instr. econs. Kent State U., Ohio, 1969-70; law clk. Supreme Ct. of Ohio, Columbus, 1970-71; asst. atty. gen. State of Ohio, 1971-73; exec. asst. to pres. Ohio State U., 1973-79; assoc. Vorys, Sater, Seymore & Pease, 1979-81; pres. Johnson State Coll., Vt., 1981-89, Saginaw Valley State U., University Center, Mich., 1989—. Bd. dirs. Citizens Bank. Contbr. articles to profl. jours. Bd. dirs. Bay County Alliance for Schs., Midland County Econ. Growth and Devel. Corp.; mem. exec. com. Mich. Campus Compact. Mem. Am. Assn. State Colls. and Univs. (com. on policies and purposes), Saginaw County C. of C., Torch Club, Saginaw Club, Bay City Country Club. Home: 7371 Glen Eagle Dr Bay City MI 48706-9316 Office: Saginaw Valley State U Office Of Pres University Center MI 48710-0001 E-mail: erg@svsu.edu.

GILBERTSON, JOEL WARREN, lawyer; b. Valley City, N.D., Nov. 9, 1949; s. Roy W. and Gwen D. (Haugen) G.; m. Jan Erikson, June 11, 1972; children: David, Lisa. BA, Concordia Coll., Moorhead, Minn., 1972; JD, U. N.D., 1975. Bar: N.D. 1976, U.S. Dist. Ct. N.D. 1976. Ptnr. Binek & Gilbertson, Bowman, N.D., 1976; atty. N.D. Supreme Ct., Bismarck, 1976-78; exec. dir. N.D. Bar Assn., 1978-81; ptnr. Pearce & Durick, 1981-97; exec. v.p., gen. counsel Ind. Cmty. Banks of N.D., 1997—. Served with U.S. Army N.G., 1972-78. Mem. N.D. Bar Assn. (bd. govs. 1989-95, pres. 1992-93), N.D. Bar Found. (vice chmn. 1982-84, chmn. bd. dirs. 1986-89), South Cen. Dist. Bar Assn. (pres. 1987-89). Republican. Lutheran. Avocations: piano, softball. Home: 1025 Crescent Ln Bismarck ND 58501-2463 Office: Ind Comty Banks ND PO Box 6128 Bismarck ND 58506-6128

GILBY, STEVE, metallurgical engineering researcher; b. Dayton, Ohio, Sept. 22, 1939; BS, U. Cin., 1962; PhD in Metall. Engring., Ohio State U., 1966. Rsch. engr. steelmaking Youngstown Steel Co., 1966-76; rsch. engr. Armco Steel Co., 1967-69, sr. rsch. engr., 1969-72, rsch. assoc., 1972-75, mgr. steelmaking rsch., 1975-82, dir. process rsch., 1982-93; mng. dir. Armco Rsch. and Tech., Pitts., 1993-95, v.p. rsch. & tech., 1995—, asst. pres. Middletown, Ohio, 1996—. Chmn. external adv. commn. materials sci. and engring. dept. Ohio State U., 1988—. Mem. Am. Iron and Steel Soc., Am. Soc. Metals Internat. Achievements include research in steel-making and continuous casting process development. Office: Armco Inc Rsch & Tech 705 Curtis St Middletown OH 45044-5812

GILCHREST, THORNTON CHARLES, retired association executive; b. Chgo., Sept. 1, 1931; s. Charles Jewett Gilchrest and Patricia (Thornton) Thornton; m. Barbara Dibbern, June 8, 1952; children: Margaret Mary, James Thornton. B.S. in Journalism, U. Ill., 1953. Cert. tchr., Ill. Tchr. pub. high sch., West Chicago, Ill., 1957; exec. dir. Plumbing-Heating-Cooling Info. Bur., Chgo., 1958-64; asst. to pres. A.Y. McDonald Mfg. Co., Dubuque, Iowa, 1964-68; exec. dir. Am. Supply Assn., Chgo., 1968-77, exec. v.p., 1977-82, Nat. Safety Coun., Chgo., 1982-83, pres., 1983-95; chmn. Internat. Safety Coun., 1992-95. Pres. Nat. Safety Coun. Found. for Safety and Health, 1986-95. Bd. dirs. Prevent Blindness Am., 1993. With USN, 1953-55. Mem. Am. Soc. Assn. Execs., Chgo. Soc. Assn. Execs. Methodist.

GILCHRIST, GERALD SEYMOUR, pediatric hematologist, oncologist, educator; b. Springs, Transvaal, South Africa, May 25, 1935; arrived in U.S.A., 1962; s. David and Anne (Lipschitz) G.; m. Antoinette E. Besset, May 7, 1967; children: Daniel J., Michael A., Lauren D. MB BCh, U. Witwatersrand Med. Sch., Johannesburg, South Africa, 1957; Diploma in Child Health, Royal Coll. Physicians and Surgeons, London, 1961. Diplomate Am. Bd. Pediatrics (chmn. Sub-Bd. Pediatric Hematology-Oncology 1990-92). Intern Johannesburg Gen. Hosp., 1958-59; resident Transvaal Meml. Hosp. for Children and Baragwanath Hosp., Johannesburg, 1959-60; resident in pediatrics Hosp. for Sick Children, London, 1961, Children's Hosp., Cin., 1962-63; fellow pediatrics, hematology/oncology Children's Hosp. of L.A., 1963-65, cons. hematology and blood banking, 1965-71; attending physician Childrens Hosp. L.A., 1968-71; asst. prof. pediatrics U. So. Calif., Los Angeles, 1966-71; assoc. prof. pediatrics Mayo Med. Sch., Rochester, Minn., 1972-78, chmn. dept. pediatrics, 1984-96; cons. pediatric hematology/oncology Mayo Clinic and Found., 1971-2000; prof. pediatrics Mayo Med. Sch., Mayo Clinic and Found., Minn., 1978-2000; Helen C. Levitt prof. Mayo Clinic and Found., 1987-2000; prof. emeritus Mayo Found. and Med. Sch., 2000—. Mem. Commn. on Cancer, ACS, 1982-85; bd. dirs. Hemophilia Ctr., Dept. Maternal and Child Health, Rockville, Md., 1978-2000; prin. investigator Childrens Cancer Study Group, Nat. Cancer Inst., Bethesda, 1981-99. Co-author: You and Leukemia, 1976; contbr. chpts. to books, numerous articles to profl. jours. Med. advisor Northland Childrens Oncology Svcs., Rochester, Minn., 1978-80; bd. dirs. Minn. chpt. Nat. Hemophilia Found. Found., Mpls., 1981-84; chpt sec. Physicians for Social Respinsibility, Rochester, 1982-85; bd. dirs. Nat. Childhood Cancer Found., 1990-97; chair med. and scientific adv. bd. Nat. Children's Cancer Found., 1995-97. Fellow Am. Acad. Pediatrics (chmn. sect. on pediatric hematology-oncology 1988-90, chair coun. on sects. 1999-2002); mem. Am. Soc. Clin. Oncology, Am. Soc. Hematology, Am. Pediatric Soc., Am. Bd. Pediatrics (bd. dirs. 1990-91, chmn. sub bd. pediatric hematology-oncology 1989-91), Soc. for Pediatric Rsch. (mem. accreditation coun. grad. med. edn. residency rev. com. pediatrics 1997-2002), Am. Soc. Pediatric Hematology/Oncology (trustee 1996-98). Democrat. Jewish. Avocations: sailing, bicycling, kayaking, scuba diving.

GILCHRIST, GRACE, television station executive; V.p., gen. mgr. WXYZ-TV, Detroit. Office: Sta WXYZ-TV PO Box 789 20777 W Ten Mile Rd Southfield MI 48037-0789

GILCHRIST, JAMES A. communication educator; Chmn. dept. comms. Western Mich. U., Kalamazoo, assoc. dean coll. arts scis., 1999—. Office: We Mich U Coll Arts Sci Kalamazoo MI 49008

GILES, CALVIN LAMONT, state legislator; b. Chgo., July 10, 1962; BA in Mgmt, Northeastern Ill. U. Mem. from dist. 8 Ill. Ho. Reps., 1993—, chmn. local govt. com. Office: 5255 W North Ave Chicago IL 60639-4429

GILES, EUGENE, anthropology educator; b. Salt Lake City, June 30, 1933; s. George Eugene and Eleanor (Clark) G.; m. Inga Valborg Wikman, Sept. 9, 1964; children: Eric George, Edward Eugene. AB, Harvard U., 1955, AM, 1960, PhD, 1966; MA, U. Calif., Berkeley, 1956. Diplomate Am. Bd. Forensic Anthropology (bd. dirs. 1996—). Instr. in anthropology U. Ill., Urbana, 1964-66, assoc. prof., 1970-73, prof., 1973-99, head dept. anthropology, 1975-80; asst. prof. Harvard U., Cambridge, Mass., 1966-70; assoc. dean Grad. Coll. U. Ill., 1986-89, assoc. dean Liberal Arts and Scis. Coll., 1995-99, prof. emeritus, 1999—. Editor: (with J.S. Friedlaender, jr. editor) The Measures of Man: Methodologies in Biological Anthropology, 1976. Served with U.S. Army, 1956-58. NSF postdoctoral fellow, 1967-68; NSF grantee, 1970-72, NIH grantee, 1965-68 Fellow Am. Anthropol. Assn., AAAS, Am. Acad. Forensic Scis.; mem. Am. Assn. Phys. Anthropologists (exec. com. 1973-76, v.p. 1979-80, pres. 1981-83), Human Biology Assn. (exec. com. 1974-77), Phi Beta Kappa, Sigma Xi. Avocations: history of biological anthropology; rsch. in Papua New Guinea and Australia; forensic anthropology. Home: 1106 S Lynn St Champaign IL 61820-6331 Office: U Ill Dept Anthropology 607 S Mathews Ave Urbana IL 61801-3635 E-mail: e-giles1@uiuc.edu.

GILFORD, STEVEN ROSS, lawyer; b. Chgo., Dec. 2, 1952; s. Ronald M. and Adele (Miller) G.; m. Anne Christine Johnson, Jan. 2, 1974; children: Sarah Julia, Zachary Michael, Eliza Rebecca. BA, Dartmouth Coll., 1974; JD, M of Pub. Policy Scis., Duke U., 1978. Bar: Ill. 1978, U.S. Dist. Ct. (no. dist.) Ill. 1978, U.S. Ct. Appeals (7th cir.) 1981, U.S. Ct. Appeals (D.C. cir.) 1984, U.S. Ct. Appeals (5th cir.) 1988, U.S. Dist. Ct. (ea. dist.) Mich. 1995. Assoc. Isham, Lincoln & Beale, Chgo., 1978—85, ptnr., 1985—87, Mayer, Brown, Rowe & Maw, Chgo., 1987—. Adminstrv. law editor Duke Law Jour., 1976-77. Participating atty. ACLU, 1983—2000; sec. Evanston (Ill.) YMCA, 1985, vice chmn., 1986—92; v.p. ACLU, 1995—96; elected mem. bd. edn. dist. 202 Evanston Twp. H.S., 1993—, v.p., 1995—96, pres., 1996—98, mem. joint task force on safety, 1995—96; mem. Met. Family Svcs., Evanston Skokie Valley Cmty. Adv. Bd., 1997; mem., bd. dirs. Met. Family Svcs., 1998—; mem. Legal Aid Soc., 2001—; chmn. fin. com. Evanston Twp. H.S., 2001—; mem. exec. com. ED-RED, 2002—; Bd. dirs. Evanston (Ill.) YMCA, 1982—92; bd. dirs. Ill. ACLU, 1991—96; bd. dirs. Roger Bawldwin Found., 1993—96. Mem. ABA, Ill. Bar Assn., Chgo. Bar Assn. Home: 2728 Harrison St Evanston IL 60201-1216 Office: Mayer Brown Rowe & Maw 190 S La Salle St Ste 3100 Chicago IL 60603-3441

GILL, RICHARD LAWRENCE, lawyer; b. Chgo., Jan. 8, 1946; s. Joseph Richard and Dolores Ann (Powers) G.; m. Mary Helen Walker, July 14, 1990; children: Kyla Marie, Matthew Joseph. BA, Coll. of St. Thomas, St. Paul, 1968; JD, U. Minn., 1971. Bar: Minn. 1971, U.S. Dist. Ct. Minn. 1971, U.S. Supreme Ct. 1979, U.S. Ct. Appeals (8th cir.) 1983, U.S. Ct. Appeals (4th cir.) 1990, Ill. 1992. Spl. asst. atty. gen. State of Minn., St. Paul, 1971-73; assoc. Maun, Hazel, Green, Hayes, Simon & Aretz, 1974-77; ptnr. Gill & Brinkman, 1978-84, Robins, Kaplan, Miller & Ciresi, Mpls., 1984—. Vol. Courage Ctr., Golden Valley, Minn., 1981—; youth football coach Maplewood (Minn.) Athletic Assn., 1978-80; youth basketball coach Orono (Minn.) Athletic Assn., 1999—. Mem. ABA, Minn. Bar Assn., Hennepin County Bar Assn., Ramsey County Bar Assn., Assn. Trial Lawyers Am., Minn. Trial Lawyers Assn., Town and Country Club. Avocations: skiing, tennis, golf. Office: Robins Kaplan Miller & Ciresi 800 Lasalle Ave Ste 2800 Minneapolis MN 55402-2015 E-mail: rlgill@rkmc.com.

GILLESPIE, GARY DON, physician; b. Jackson, Mich., Apr. 23, 1943; s. Harold Don and Marion Estella (Diemer) G.; m. Nancy Bliven Hinkle, June 29, 1969 (div. July 1980; children: Brian James, Julie Elizabeth; m. Elaine Marie Beard, July 25, 1984. BS, U. Mich., 1966, D of Medicine, 1971. Diplomate Am. Bd. Family Practice. Intern Edward W. Sparrow Hosp., Lansing, Mich., 1971-72, resident in family practice, 1971-74; physician Dept. Family Practice, USN Med. Corps., Orlando, Fla., 1974-76; pvt. practice Okemos, Mich., 1976—. Chmn. continuing edn., dept. family practice Edward W. Sparrow Hosp., 1976-91; asst. clin. prof. dept. family practice Mich. State U. Coll. Medicine, East Lansing, 1981—. Lt. comdr. USN, 1974-76. Mem. AMA, Am. Acad. Family Physicians, Am. Bd. Family Practice, Mich. Acad. Family Physicians (treas. Capitol chpt. 1982-92). Republican. Avocations: reading, music, photography, travel, golf.

GILLESPIE, ROBERT WAYNE, banker; b. Cleve., Mar. 26, 1944; s. Robert Walton and Eleanore (Parsons) G.; m. Ann L. Wible, June 17, 1967; children: Laura, Gwen. B.A., Ohio Wesleyan U., 1966; M.B.A., Case Western Res. U., 1968; postgrad., Harvard U., 1979. Credit analyst Soc. Nat. Bank, Cleve., 1968-70, v.p., 1970-76, sr. v.p., 1976-79; exec. v.p. Soc. Nat Bank, 1979-81; vice-chmn., chief operating officer Soc. Nat. Bank, 1981-83, pres., chief operating officer, 1983-85, CEO, 1985—, pres., 1987-94; pres., CEO, Key Corp., 1995—, chmn., 1996—, CEO, 1996—. Trustee Case Western Res. U., Ohio Wesleyan U., Cleve. Mus. Art, Cleve. Initiative for Edn. and Musical Arts, Greater Cleve. Roundtable, Cleve. Tomorrow and North Coast Harbor; bd. dirs. Greater Cleve. Growth Assn. Office: Key Corp 127 Public Sq Cleveland OH 44114-1306

GILLET, PAMELA KIPPING, special education educator; EdB in Elem. Edn., Chgo. Tchrs. Coll., 1963; MA in Mental Retardation, Northeastern Ill. U., 1966; PhD in Gen. Spl. Edn./Adminstrn., Walden U., 1976. Cert. elem. edn., early childhood edn., learning disabled, mental retardation, behavior disorders, supt., supr. and dir. spl. edn. 4th grade tchr. Dist. # 83 Mannheim, Frankling Park, Ill., 1963-64; high sch. spl. edn. tchr. Dist. # 207 Maine Township, Park Ridge, 1964-67, prevocational coord., 1967-69, dept. chmn. spl. edn. dept., 1969-70; dir. EPDA Tchr. Tng. Program Chgo. Consortium Colls. and Univs., Northwest Ednl. Coop., Palatine, 1970-71; prin. West Suburban Spl. Edn. Ctr., Cicero, 1971-73; supr. West Suburban Assn. Spl. Edn., 1973-75; asst. dir. Northwest Suburban Spl. Edn. Orgn., Palatine, 1975-78, supt. Mt. Prospect, Ill., 1978-96; spl. edn. cons., 1996—. Adj. coll. instr. Northeastern Ill. U., Chgo. State U., Corcordia Coll., Barat Coll., Nat. Coll. of Edn., Roosevelt U.; mem. task forces ISBE, 1975-97, cons. career edn. project, 1977-78, mem. spl. edn. demandate study group, 1983-85; cons. Ednl. Testing Svc.; mem. tchr. edn. coun. Northeastern Ill. U., 1981-97, dean's grant program, 1982-97; leader of workshops, 1974—; lectr., cons. in field. Author: Auditory Processes, 1974, Career Education for Children, 1978, Of Work and Worth: Career Education Programming for Exceptional Children and Youth, 1981, Auditory Processes, Revised, 1992; contbr. articles to profl. jours., chpts. to books. Bd. dirs. Found. Exceptional Children, 1996—, pres., 1999—. Recipient Cmty. Svc. award Am. Legion, 1976, 80, Alumnus of Yr. award Northeastern Ill. U., 1984, Learning Disabilities of Am. Contributors award Coun. Understanding Learning Disabilities, 1992, Those Who Excel award of excellence Ill. State Bd. of Edn., 1994, Outstanding Svc. award Divsn. Mental Retardation and Devel. Disabilities, 1994; Sleznick award, Coun. of Admin. of Spl. Edn., 1996, Outstanding Contbr. award Coun. Exceptional Children, 1996, Burton Blatt award Divsn. on Metal Retardation and Devel. Disabilities, 1997, Outstanding Spl. Edn. Adminstr. of Yr. award Ill. Adminstrs. of Spl. Edn., 1997, Spl. Edn. Leadership award, 1995. Mem.: ASCD, Found. for Exceptional Children (pres. 2000—), Ill. Adminstrs. Spl. Edn. 1994—95, Coun. Exceptional Children (pres. Ill. chpt. 1975—77, bd. govs. 1977—80, 1996—2000, pres. mental retardation divsn. 1983—85, bd. govs. 1986, exec. com. 1989—92, v.p. internat. 1992—93, pres.-elect 1993—94, pres. 1994—95, bd. dirs. 2000—, Meritorious Svc. award Ill. 1983), Assn. Children with Learning Disabilities, Am. Assn. Sch. Adminstrs. Home and Office: 413 Courtley Oaks Blvd Winter Garden FL 34787

GILLIES, DONALD RICHARD, marketing and advertising consultant, educator; b. Sioux Falls, S.D., Jan. 14, 1939; s. Donald Franklin and Gladys O. (Gullickson) G.; m. Twyla Elaine Bloomquist, Apr. 7, 1962; children: Dawn, Trent, Tara. BA in Journalism/Advt., U. Minn., 1961. Writer, producer Sta. WCCO-TV, Mpls., 1954-60; mgmt. supr., sr. v.p., bd. dirs. Campbell-Mithun Advt., 1960-86; pres., chief oper. officer Colle & McVoy Inc., 1987-89; prin. Gillies group inc. (Gg), Minnetonka, Minn., 1989—. Adj. prof. U. St. Thomas, 1990-97, asst. prof., 2001—. Bd. dirs. Guthrie Theater, Mpls., 1979-84; mem. ch. coun. Mt. Olivet Ch., Mpls., 1988-94; mem. Minn. adv. rev. bd. BBB, 1996—. With USAR, 1961-69. Mem. Am. Assn. Advt. Agencies (regional gov.), Minn. Advt. Fedn. (bd. dirs. 1973-76). Lutheran. Home and Office: Gillies group inc (Gg) 5942 Fairwood Ln Minnetonka MN 55345-6533 E-mail: gilliesgroup@usa.net.

GILLIGAN, SANDRA KAYE, private school director; b. Ft. Lewis, Wash., Mar. 22, 1946; d. Jack G. and O. Ruth (Mitchell) Wagoner; m. James J. Gilligan, June 3, 1972 (div. June 1998); 1 child, J. Shawn Gilligan. BS in Edn., Emporia State U., 1968, MS in Psychology, 1971; postgrad., Drake U., 1976, U. Mo., St. Louis, 1977-79. Tchr. Parklane Elem. Sch., Aurora, Colo., 1968-69, Bonner Springs (Kans.) Elem., 1970; stewardess Frontier Airlines, Denver, 1969; grad. teaching asst. Emporia (Kans.) State U., 1970-71; lead tchr. Western Valley Youth Ranch, Buckeye, Ariz., 1971-74; staff mem. program devel., lead tchr. The New Found., Phoenix, 1974; ednl. therapist Orchard Pl., Des Moines, 1974-76; ednl. cons. Spl. Sch. Dist. of St. Louis County, 1976-79; founding dir. The Churchill Sch., St. Louis, 1978—. Instr. Webster Coll., Webster Groves, Mo., 1978-80; adj. prof. Maryville Coll., St. Louis, summer 1985; mem. profl. adv. bd. Learning Disabilities Assn., St. Louis Learning Disabilities Assn.; keynote spkr. Miss. Learning Disabilities Assn. Conv., 1991; site visitor blue ribbon schs. program U.S. Dept. Edn., 1992; mem. Evaluation Review Com. Indep. Sch. of Ctrl. States; cert. trainer Human Potential Seminars; presenter in field. Mem. profl. adv. com. Solomon Schechter Sch., St. Louis. Mem. Learning Disabilities Assn., Internat. Dyslexia Assn., St. Louis Jr. League. Avocations: gardening, painting. Office: The Churchill Sch 1035 Price School Ln Saint Louis MO 63124-1596

GILLIS, RUTH ANN M. electric company executive; BS in Econs., Smith Coll.; MBA, U. Chgo. Formerly with U. Chgo. Hosps. and Health Sys., 1st Chgo. Corp.; sr. v.p., CFO Unicom Corp. (now Exelon Corp.). Office: Exelon Corp 37th Fl 10 S Dearborn St Chicago IL 60603

GILLISPIE, HAROLD LEON, minister; b. Levant, Kans., May 11, 1933; s. Harold Leon and Agnes Anne (Dryden) G. BA in Bus. Adminstrn., Kans. Wesleyan U., 1955. Youth dir. Cen. YMCA, Des Moines, 1957-61; exec. dir. West Des Moines br. YMCA, 1961-65; exec. dir. Aurora Br. YMCA, Denver, 1965-69, YMCA, McCook, Nebr., 1969-75, Junction City, Kans., 1975-79; owner H & R Block Franchise, Manhattan, 1979-91; lay pastor Presbyn. Ch., Oak Hill, 1996—; vice moderator Presbytery of No. Kans., 1999-00, moderator, 2000-01. Proofreader text H & R Block, Kansas City, Mo., 1986-92. Bd. dirs. Flint Hills Breadbasket, Manhattan, Kans., 1982-89, treas., 1987; bd. dirs. Big Bros. Big Sisters, Manhattan, 1981-85, pres., 1983-85; pres. Downtown Manhattan, Inc., 1986; bd. dirs. Manhattan Main Street, 1986-89; bd. dirs. Ecumenical Campus Ministry, Kans. State U., 1995-99, 2002—, chmn., 1996-98. Republican. Presbyterian. Avocations: theology, tennis, baking, working with youth. Home: 710 Bertrand St Manhattan KS 66502-5156 E-mail: pastogil@flinthills.com.

GILLMING, KENNETH, church administrator; Pres. Bapt. Bible Fellowship Internat., Springfield, Mo. Office: Bapt Bible Fellowship Internat PO Box 191 Springfield MO 65801-0191

GILLMOR, KAREN LAKO, state agency administrator, strategic planner; b. Cleve., Jan. 29, 1948; d. William M. and Charlotte (Sheldon) Lako; m. Paul E. Gillmor, Dec. 10, 1983; children: Linda D., Julie E., Paul Michael, Connor W., Adam S. BA cum laude, Mich. State U., 1969; MA, Ohio State U., 1970, PhD, 1981. Asst. to v.p. Ohio State U., Columbus, 1972-77, spl. asst. dean law, 1979-81; asst. to pres. Ind. Cen. U., Indpls., 1977-78; rsch. asst. Burke Mktg. Rsch., 1978-79; v.p. pub. affairs Huntington Nat. Bank, Columbus, 1981-82; fin. cons. Ohio Rep. Fin. Com., 1982-83; chief mgmt. planning and rsch. Indsl. Commn. Ohio, 1983-86; mgr. physician rels. Ohio State U. Med. Ctr., 1987-91; cons. U.S. Sec. Labor, Washington, 1990-91; mem. Regional Bd. Rev./Indls. Commn., Ohio, 1991-92; assoc. dir. Ctr. Healthcare Policy and Rsch./Ohio State U., 1991-92; state senator Ohio Gen. Assembly, 1993-97; vice-chair State Employment Rels. Bd., 1997—. Legis. liaison Huntington Bancshares, Ohio, Ohio State U., Columbus; trustee Heidelberg Coll., 1999—. Grantee Andrew W. Mellon Found. 1978, Carnegie Corp. 1978; named Outstanding Freshman Ohio Legislator, 1994, Watchdog of the Treasury, 1994, 96; recipient Pres. award Ohio State Chiropractic Assn., 1994, Pub. Svc. award Am. Heart Assn., 1995, Outstanding Nat. Freshman Legislator of Yr., 1995; Ctr. Advancement and Study of Ethics award Capital U. and Trinity Luth. Seminary, 1996, U.S. Dept. of Army Cert. of Ach., 1997, Friend of Medicine award Ohio State Med. Assn., 1997, Legis. Ach. award Am. Acad. Pediatrics (Ohio chpt. 1997); inducted Hall of Fame, Rocky River H.S., 1998, Spirit of Women award, 1999. Mem. Women in Mainstream, Women's Roundtable, Ohio Fedn. Rep. Women, Am. Assn. Higher Edn., Coun. Advancement and Support Edn., DAR, Phi Delta Kappa. Methodist. Office: 65 E State St Ste 1200 Columbus OH 43215-4209

GILLMOR, PAUL E. congressman, lawyer; b. Tiffin, Ohio, Feb. 1, 1939; s. Paul Marshall and Lucy Jeannette (Fry) G.; m. Karen Lee Lako, Dec. 10, 1983; children: Linda Dianne, Julie Ellen, Paul Michael, Connor Sheldon, Adam William B.A., Ohio Wesleyan U., Delaware, 1961; J.D., U. Mich, 1964; LL.D. (hon.), Tiffin U., Ohio, 1985. Bar: Ohio, 1965. Mem. Ohio Senate, 1967-89, minority leader, 1978-81, 83-85, pres., 1981-83, 85-88; mem. U.S. Congress from 5th Ohio dist., Washington, 1989—; mem. energy and commerce com., fin. svcs. com., dep. majority whip. Assoc. firm Tomb and Hering, Tiffin, 1967-88; bd. dirs. Old Fort Banking Co., Ohio. Pres. Ohio Electoral Coll., Columbus, 1984. Served to capt. USAF, 1965-67. Recipient Gov.'s award, Ohio, 1980; Phillips medal of pub. service Ohio U. Coll. Osteopathy, 1981; Exec. Order, Ohio Commodores Assn., 1981; Disting. Citizen award Med. Coll. Ohio, 1982; named

Legislator of Yr., Ohio VFW, 1994. Mem. ABA, Ohio State Bar Assn., Nat. Republican Legislators Assn. (named Outstanding Legislator of Yr. 1983). Methodist. Office: US Ho of Reps Office House Mems 1203 Longworth Bldg Washington DC 20515-3505*

GILMAN, ALAN B. restaurant company executive; b. South Bend, Ind., Sept. 24, 1930; s. Sol M. and Lee R. (Rintzler) G.; m. Phyllis Schrager, Feb. 16, 1951; children: Bruce, Jeffrey, Lynn. A.B. with highest honors (Raymond Charles Stoltz scholar), Ind. U., 1952, M.B.A. (John H. Edwards fellow), 1954. With Lazarus Co. div. Federated Dept. Stores, Inc., Columbus, Ohio, 1954-60, div. mdse. mgr., 1961-64; with Sanger Harris div., 1965-74, chmn. bd., chief exec. officer, 1970-74, corp. v.p., 1974-80; with Abraham & Straus div., 1975-80, chmn. bd., chief exec. officer, 1978-80; pres. Murjani Internat. Ltd., N.Y.C., 1980-85; pvt. investor, 1985-87; chmn. At Ease of Newport Beach (Calif.) Inc., 1988-91; pres., chief exec. officer Consol. Products Inc., 1992—, Steak 'n Shake Inc. Vice chmn. bd. dirs. Ind. U. Found., nat. chmn. ann. giving, 1983, mem. presdl. search com., 1987-88; chmn. dean's adv. coun. Ind. U. Grad. Sch. Bus., 1976-86; mem. dean's adv. coun. Coll. Arts and Scis., Ind. U., 1989—, pres.'s cabinet, 1995; bd. dirs., pres., mem. exec. com. Greater N.Y. Fund-United Way, 1984-87; bd. dirs., mem. exec. com., chmn. strategic planning com. United Way of N.Y.C., 1982-88; dir. Corp. Comty. Coun., Indpls., Greater Indpls. Progress Com., Kelley Restaurants, Inc. Recipient Humanitarian of Yr. award Juvenile Diabetes Found., 1979, Disting. Alumni Svc. award Ind. U., 1996. Mem. Young Pres. Orgn. 49'er, Ind. U. Acad. Alumni Fellows, World Bus. Council, Phi Beta Kappa Assocs., Phi Alpha Theta, Beta Gamma Sigma (charter mem. dirs. table) Home: 2730 Brigs Bnd Bloomington IN 47401-4402 Office: Consolidated Products Inc 500 Century Bldg 36 S Penn Ave Indianapolis IN 46204

GILMAN, KENNETH B. retail executive; Formerly v.p., corp. contr. The Limited Inc., Columbus, Ohio, exec. v.p., chief fin. officer, 1998; vice chmn. Intimate Brands, Inc., OH, 1998; CEO Lane Bryant, Reynoldsburg, Ohio, 2001—. Office: Lane Bryant 5 Limited Pkwy Reynoldsburg OH 42068

GILMAN, SANDER LAWRENCE, German language educator; b. Buffalo, Feb. 21, 1944; s. William and Rebecca (Helf) G.; m. Marina von Eckardt, Dec. 28, 1969; children: Daniel, Samuel. BA, Tulane U., 1963, PhD, 1968; postgrad., U. Berlin and U. Munich, Ger.; LLD (hon.), U. Toronto, Ont., 1997. Lectr. German St. Mary's Dominican Coll., New Orleans, 1963-64; instr. Dillard U., 1967-68; asst. prof. Case Western Res. U., 1968-69; mem. faculty Cornell U., 1969-94, prof. German, 1976-94, prof. Near Eastern studies, 1984-91, prof. humane studies, 1984-87, Goldwin Smith prof., 1987-94, chmn. dept. German lit., 1974-81, 83-84; fellow dept. psychiatry Cornell U. Med. Coll., 1977-78; prof. history of psychiatry Cornell U., 1978-94; prof. German, history of sci. and psychiatry U. Chgo., 1994-2000, Henry R. Luce prof. Liberal Arts in Human Biology, 1995-2000, disting. svc. prof., 1999-2000; disting. prof. liberal arts & scis. and medicine U. Ill., Chgo., 2000—. O'Connor prof. Colgate U., 1982-83; Mellon prof. Tulane U., 1988, Old Dominion prof. English, Princeton U., 1988; Northrup Frye prof. of comparative lit. U. Toronto, Ont., Can., 1989; vis. prof. German lit. Free U. Berlin, 1989; vis. hist. scholar Nat. Libr. Medicine, 1991-92; vis. Rudolph prof. Jewish studies Syracuse (N.Y.) U., 1992; vis. prof. U. Witwatersrand, South Africa, 1994, U. Potsdam, 1996, U. Cape Town, 1996, Ctr. for Advanced Studies in the Behavioral Scis., 1996-97, Getty Inst. for Art and the Humanities, 1998. Author, editl. 50 books including Bertolt Brecht's Berlin, 1975, Nietzschean Parody, 1976, The Face of Madness, 1976, Klingers Werke, 1978, On Blackness Without Blacks, 1982, Begegnungen mit Nietzsche, 1981, Wahnsinn, Text Difference and Pathology, 1985, Jewish Self-Hatred, 1986, Oscar Wilde's London, 1987, Conversations with Nietzsche, 1987, Diseases and Representation, 1989, Sexuality: An Illustrated History, 1989, Nietzsche on Rhetoric and Language, 1989, The Jew's Body, 1991, Inscribing the Other, 1991, Rasse, Seuche, Sexualitat, 1992, Freud, Race, Gender, 1993, The Case of Sigmund Freud, 1993, Reading Freud Reading, 1993, Reemerging Jewish Culture in Germany, 1994, Jews in Today's German Culture, 1995, Health and Illness, 1995, Franz Kafka: The Jewish Patient, 1996, L'Autre et Le Moi, 1996, Smart Jews, 1996, Yale Companion to Jewish Writing and Thought in German Culture, 1997, Love and Marriage with Death, 1998, Creating Beauty to Cure the Soul, 1998, Making the Body Beautiful, 1999; also essays; mem. editl. bd. Diacritics, 1971-72, Lessing Yearbook, 1974—, German Quar., 1977-86; assoc. editor Confinia Psychiatrica, 1978-80. Guggenheim fellow, 1972-73, IREX exch. fellow German Democratic Republic, 1976, Soc. for Humanities faculty fellow Cornell U., 1981-82, Nat. Libr. Medicine sr. historian, fellow, 1990-91, Ctr. for the Adv. Study of the Behaviorial Scis. fellow, Stanford, 1996-97, Am. Acad., Berlin, 2000—. Mem. MLA (pres. 1995), Lessing Soc., Am. Assn. Tchrs. German, Soc. Internat. d'Études Littéraires et Psychiatres, Internat. Assn. Germanists. Democrat. Jewish. Home: 5701 S Dorchester Ave Chicago IL 60637-1726 E-mail: sander34@aol.com.

GILMAN, SID, neurologist, department chairman; b. L.A., Oct. 19, 1932; s. Morris and Sarah Rose (Cooper) G.; m. Carol G. Barbour. B.A., UCLA, 1954; M.D., 1957, FRCP, 2001. Intern UCLA Hosp., 1957-58; resident in neurology Boston City Hosp., 1960-63; from instr. to assoc. in neurology Harvard Med. Sch., 1965-68; from asst. prof. to prof. neurology Columbia U., N.Y.C., 1968-76; H. Houston Merritt prof. neurology, 1976-77; William J. Herdman prof., chair dept. neurology U. Mich., Ann Arbor, 1977—. Cons. VA Hosp., Ann Arbor, 1977—; mem. peripheral and ctrl. nervous sys. drugs adv. com. FDA, 1983-85, 86-87, 90-94, chmn., 1996-2000; adj. attending neurologist Henry Ford Hosp., Detroit; mem. chronic disease adv. com. Mich. Dept. Pub. Health, 1988-94; mem. neurol. sci. rsch. and tng. com. NIH, mem. neurol. disorders program project B com., mem. sci. programs adv. com. Nat. Inst. Neurol. Diseases, Communicative Disorders and Stroke, 1982-84, mem. nat. adv. neurol. disorders and stroke coun., 1994-97; dir. Mich. Alzheimer's Disease Rsch. Ctr., 1991—; mem. rsch. adv. coun. United Cerebral Palsy Found.; mem. sci. adv. coun. Nat. Ataxia Found., Nat. Amyotrophic Lateral Sclerosis Found., Inc.; mem. profl. adv. bd. Epilepsy Found. Am.; mem. rsch. adv. com. Nat. Multiple Sclerosis Soc., 1986-90; mem. exec. bd. Nat. Coalition for Rsch., 1989-95, Nat. Found. for Brain Rsch., 1989-95; mem. rsch. adv. com. Dana Alliance; mem. sci. adv. bd. Merck, Inc., 2000—; mem. sci. adv. bd. PPD Devel., 1999—; Henry Russel lectr. U. Mich., 2001. Author: (with J.R. Bloedel and R. Lechtenberg) Disorders of the Cerebellum, 1981, (with S.W. Newman) Manter and Gatz's Essentials of Clinical Neuroanatomy and Neurophysiology, 9th edit., 1996, (with J.C. Mazziotta) Clinical Brain Imaging: Principles and Applications, 1992, Clinical Examination of the Nervous System, 2000; sect. editor editl. bd. Exptl. Neurology, Current Opinion in Neurology and Neurosurgery, Neurology, Annals Neurology, Jour. Neuropathology and Exptl. Neurology, Neurobase Arbor Pub. Co.; editor-in-chief MedLink Neurology, 1992, Contemporary Neurology Series, 1995—, Neurology Network Commentary, 1996-2000, Lancet Neurology Network, 2000—; contbr. articles to profl. jours. Dir. Mich. Dem. Program, 1994-2000. With USPHS, 1958-60. Recipient Lucy G. Moses prize Columbia U., 1973, Weinstein Goldenson award United Cerebral Palsy Assn., 1981, UCLA Alumni Profl. Achievement award, 1992, UCLA Med. Alumni Profl. Achievement award, 1992. Fellow AAAS, Royal Soc. of Medicine, Royal Coll. Physicians, Am. Acad. Arts and Scis.; mem. Am. Neurol. Assn. (hon.; 1st v.p. 1985-86, pres.-elect 1987-88, pres. 1988-89), Mich. Neurol. Assn. (pres. 1987-88), Soc. Clin. Investigation, Am. Physiol. Soc., Am. Assn. Neuropathologists, Soc. Neurosci., Am. Acad. Neurology (vice chmn. geriatric neurology subcom. 1992-94, chmn. 1994-96, chmn. Decade of Brain com. 1990-95), Am. Epilepsy Soc., Assn. Rsch. in Nervous and Mental Disease, Inst. Medicine, Nat. Acad. Scis., Phi Beta Kappa, Alpha Omega Alpha. Home: 3411 Geddes Rd Ann Arbor MI 48105-2518 Office: U Mich Dept Neurology Ann Arbor MI 48109 E-mail: sgilman@umich.edu.

GILMER, GARY D. credit services company executive; Group exec. Household Internat. Inc., Prospect Heights, Ill., 1996—. Office: 2700 Sanders Rd Prospect Heights IL 60070-2701

GILMORE, HORACE WELDON, former federal judge; b. Columbus, Ohio, Apr. 4, 1918; s. Charles Thomas and Lucille (Weldon) G.; m. Mary Hays, June 20, 1942; children— Lindsay Gilmore Feinberg. A.B., U. Mich., 1939, J.D., 1942. Bar: Mich. bar 1946. Law clk. U.S. Ct. Appeals, 1946-47; practiced in Detroit, 1947-51; spl. asst. U.S. atty., 1951-52; mem. Mich. Bd. Tax Appeals, 1954; dep. atty. gen. State of Mich., 1955-56; circuit judge 3d Jud. Circuit, Detroit, 1956-80; judge U.S. Dist. Ct. (ea. dist.) Mich., 1980—, now sr. judge. Adj. prof. law Wayne State U. Law Sch., 1966-82; lectr. law U. Mich. Law Sch., 1969-90; faculty Nat. Coll. State Judiciary, 1966-83; mem. Mich. Jud. Tenure Commn., 1969-76; chmn. Mich. Com. to Revise Criminal Code, 1965-82, Mich. Com. to Revise Criminal Procedure, 1971-79; trustee Inst. for Ct. Mgmt. Author: Michigan Civil Procedure Before Trial, 2d edit, 1975; contbr. numerous articles to legal jours. Served with USNR, 1942-46. Mem. ABA, State Bar Mich., Am. Judicature Soc., Am. Law Inst., Nat. Conf. State Trial Judges.

GILMORE, KATHI, state treasurer; b. Dec. 23, 1944; m. Richard Gilmore; children: Suzi, Barb, Jeff, Amy. Mem. N.D. Ho. of Reps. from Dist. 6, 1989-92; treas. State of N.D., 1993—. Mem. Bd. Tax Equalization, State Hist. Bd., State Investment Bd., Tchrs. Fund for Retirement Bd., State Canvassing Bd., Bd. of Univ. and Sch. Lands Mem.: Assn. Securities Profls. (hon. co-chair pension fund conf. 1994, Task Forces Orgnl. Planning and Coordinating Com. 1993), Retirement and Investment Office Internal Audit Com., Nat. Assn. State Treas. (pension com.). Democrat. Presbyterian. Methodist. Office: State Treasurer 600 E Boulevard Ave Bismarck ND 58505-0660

GILMORE, PHYLLIS, state legislator; m. Kenneth Gilmore. Social worker; mem. Kans. State Ho. of Reps. Dist. 27, 1994-99; exec. dir. regulatory bd. State of Kans., Topeka, 1999—. Office: State Kans Regulatory Bd Topeka KS 66601

GILMORE, RONALD M. bishop; b. Apr. 23, 1942; Ordained priest Roman Cath. Ch. Consecrated bishop; bishop Diocese of Dodge City, Kans. Office: 910 Central Ave # 137 Dodge City KS 67801-4905

GILROY, SUE ANNE, state official; b. Ind. m. Dick Gilroy; children: Emily (dec.), Grant. Grad. cum laude, DePauw U.; MA, Ind. U. Ordained elder Presbyn. Ch. Former profl. assoc. Office of Mayor Lugar; former dir. Parks and Recreation; asst. to pres. Ind. Ctrl. U. (now U. Indpls.); chair Mayor Steve Goldsmith's Transition Team, 1991-92; state dir. for Senator Richard Lugar, Ind., 1990-93; sec. of state State of Ind., 1994—. Cons. in fundraising and bus. adminstrn. Tabernacle Presbyn. Ch.; bd. dirs. St. Vincent Hosp Found., Cathedral H.S., U. Indpls.; mem. adv. bd. Salvation Army. Mem. Indpls. Rotary Club. Office: Office of the Sec of State 201 State House Indianapolis IN 46204*

GILSTRAP, MARK, state legislator; b. Kansas City, Sept. 6, 1952; m. Joanne Gilstrap; 3 children. BSBA, Rockhurst Coll. Mem. Kans. Senate from 5th dist., Topeka, 1996—; mem. jud. com., ranking mem. transp. and tourism com.; mem. ways and means com.; mem. joint com. on spl. claims against the state; mem. joint com. on state gaming compacts. Democrat. Roman Catholic. Office: 300 SW 10th Ave Rm 138-n Topeka KS 66612-1504

GIN, SUE LING, retail executive; Chmn. Flying Food Co., Chicago. Mem. Womens Leadership Forum (bd. dirs.). Office: Flying Food Fare Inc 212 N Sangamon St Chicago IL 60607-1700

GINDER, GORDON DEAN, physician, educator; b. Jacksonville, Ill., Feb. 20, 1949; s. Clyde Delbert and Helen L. Ginder; m. Georgianne Schuller, May 31, 1975. BS, U. Ill., 1971; MD, Johns Hopkins U., 1975. Resident Case Western Res. U., Cleve., 1975-77; rsch. assoc. NIH, Bethesda, Md., 1977-79; fellow U. Iowa, Iowa City, 1979-80, asst. prof. div. hematology oncology, 1980-85, assoc. prof., 1985-89, prof., assoc. dir., 1989-90; prof., dir. div. med. oncology U. Minn., Mpls., 1990-97; prof., dir. Massey Cancer Ctr. Med. Coll. Va. Commonwealth U., Richmond, 1997—. Lt. comdr. USPHS, 1977-79. Mem. Am. Soc. Hematology, Am. Fedn. Clin. Rsch., Cen. Soc. Clin. Rsch. (councillor 1989-92), Am. Soc. Clin. Investigation, Am. Assn. Cancer Rsch., Assn. Am. Physicians. Office: Massey Cancer Ctr PO Box 980037 401 College St Richmond VA 23298-5017 E-mail: gdginder@hsc.vcu.edu.

GINGERICH, PHILIP DERSTINE, paleontologist, evolutionary biologist, educator; b. Goshen, Ind., Mar. 23, 1946; s. Orie Jacob and Miriam (Derstine) G.; m. B. Holly Smith, 1982 AB, Princeton U., 1968; PhD, Yale U., 1974. Prof. U. Mich., Ann Arbor, 1974—, dir. Mus. Paleontology, 1981-87, 1989—, prof. paleontology, 2001—. Contbr. articles to sci. jours. Recipient Henry Russel award U. Mich., 1980; Shadle fellow Am. Soc. Mammalogists, 1973-74, NATO fellow, 1975, Guggenheim fellow, 1983-84 Fellow Am. Assn. Adv. Scis., Geol. Soc. Am.; mem. Paleontol. Soc. (Schuchert award 1981), Soc. Study Evolution, Am. Soc. Mammalogists, Soc. Vert. Paleontology. Office: U Mich Mus Paleontology 1109 Geddes Ave Ann Arbor MI 48109-1079

GINN, ROBERT MARTIN, retired utility company executive; b. Detroit, Jan. 13, 1924; s. Lloyd T. and Edna S. (Martin) G.; m. Barbara R. Force, 1948; children: Anne, Martha, Thomas. BS in Elec. Engring., MS in Elec. Engring., U. Mich., 1948. With Cleve. Electric Illuminating Co., 1948-89, contr., 1959-62, v.p. gen. svcs., 1963-70, exec. v.p., 1970-77, pres., 1977-83, chief exec. officer, 1979-88, chmn., 1983-89; chmn., CEO Centerior Energy Corp., Toledo Edison Co., 1986-88. Mem. Shaker Heights Bd. Edn., (Ohio), 1968-75, pres., 1973-74; pres. Welfare Fedn. Cleve., 1968-69; chmn. Cleve. Commn. on Higher Edn., 1983-86; trustee John Carroll U., 1983-89, exec.-in-residence, 1989—; trustee Martha Holden Jennings Found., 1975—; chmn. Cleve. Opera, 1986-91. With USAAF, 1943-46. Office: 1120 Chester Ave # 470 Cleveland OH 44114-3514

GINSBERG, DONALD MAURICE, physicist, educator; b. Chgo., Nov. 19, 1933; s. Maurice J. and Zelda Ginsberg; m. Joli D. Lasker, June 10, 1957; children: Mark D., Dana L. BA, U. Chgo., 1952, BS, 1955, MS (NSF fellow), 1956; PhD (NSF fellow), U. Calif. at Berkeley, 1960. Mem. faculty U. Ill., Urbana, 1959-97, prof. physics, 1966-97, prof. emeritus, 1997—. Vis. scientist in physics Am. Assn. Physics Tchrs.-Am. Inst. Physics, 1965-71; vis. scientist IBM, 1976; mem. evaluation com. for Nat. High-Field Magnet Lab., NSF, 1977-79, 85, 91; mem. rev. com. for solid state sci. div. Argonne Nat. Lab., 1977-83, chmn., 1980; mem. rev. panel for basic energy scis. div. Dept. Energy, 1981 Editor: Physical Properties of High Temperature Superconductors, Vols. 1, 2, 3, 4, and 5, 1989, 90, 92, 94, 96; contbr. to Ency. Britannica, 1971, 82, 88, 94, 96, Concise Ency. of Magnetic and Superconducting Materials, 1992. Alfred P. Sloan rsch. fellow, 1960-64, NSF fellow, 1966-67; U. Ill. scholar, 1994; recipient Daniel C. Drucker award U. Ill. Engring. Coll., 1992. Fellow Am. Phys. Soc. (winner Oliver E. Buckley Consensed Matter Physics prize 1998); mem. AAAS, Phi Beta Kappa, Sigma Xi. Achievements include research and publications on low temperature physics, superconductivity, cryogenic instrumentation. Home: 2208 Grange Cir Urbana IL 61801-6607 Office: Loomis Lab 1110 W Green St Urbana IL 61801-9013

GINSBURG, DAVID, human genetics educator, researcher; b. Newburgh, N.Y., Aug. 11, 1952; s. Leonard and Ruth Helena Henrietta (Falkson) G.; m. Maureen Rose Kushinsky, June 7, 1981; children: Daniel William, Leah Beth. BA magna cum laude, Yale U., 1974; MD, Duke U., 1977. Diplomate Am. Bd. Internal Medicine, subspecialties in med. oncology and hematology; diplomate Am. Bd. Med. Genetics. Resident in pathology Presbyn. Hosp., San Francisco, 1977-78; intern, resident in internal medicine Peter Bent Brigham Hosp., Boston, 1978-81; fellow tng. program in hematology and med. oncology Brigham and Women's Hosp., Harvard Med. Sch., 1981-84, instr. medicine, 1984-85; asst. prof. dept. medicine U. Mich., Ann Arbor, 1985-89, assoc. prof. with tenure, 1989-93, assoc. prof. human genetics, 1989-93; asst. investigator Howard Hughes Med. Inst. Howard Hughes Med. Inst., 1985-89, assoc. investigator, 1989-93; prof. internal medicine and human genetics, 1993—; dir. divsn. med. genetics, dept. medicine, 1993—; investigator Howard Hughes Med. Inst., 1993—. Contbr. numerous articles to profl. jours. Named to Inst. Medicine Nat. Acad. Scis., 1999, E. Donnall Thomas lectr. and prize Am. Soc. Hematology, 2000. Mem. ACP, Am. Soc. Human Genetics, Am. Soc. Hematology, Am. Heart Assn. (thrombosis coun.), Assn. Am. Physicians, Am. Soc. for Clin. Investigation, Alpha Omega Alpha. Jewish. Office: Howard Hughes Med Inst 1150 W Medical Center Dr Ann Arbor MI 48109-0650 E-mail: ginsburg@umich.edu.

GIOVACCHINI, PETER LOUIS, psychoanalyst; b. N.Y.C., Apr. 12, 1922; s. Alex and Therese (Chicca) G.; m. Louise Post, Sept. 29, 1945; children: Philip, Sandra, Daniel. BS, U. Chgo., 1941, MD, 1944; postgrad., Columbia U., 1939; cert., Chgo. Inst. Psychoanalysis, 1954. Diplomate Am. Bd. Psychiatry and Neurology. Intern Fordham Hosp., N.Y.C., 1944-45; resident U. Chgo. Clinics, 1945-46, resident and research fellow, 1948-50; candidate Chgo. Inst. Psychoanalysis, 1949-54, clin. assoc., 1957—; clin. prof. U. Ill. Coll. Medicine, 1961-92, prof. emeritus, 1992—. Chief cons. psychodynamic unit Barclay Hosp., Chgo., 1979-81; cons. Wilmette (Ill.) Family Svc. Ctr. and United Charities, Boyer-Marin Lodge, Marin County, Calif., 1986—, Mario Martin Inst. for Psychotherapy, 1989—, Psychoanalytic Ctr. Calif., L.A., 1990—; vis. prof. Smith Coll., Mass.; tng. and supervising analyst Chgo. Ctr. for Psychoanalytic Studies, 1994—. Author: (with L.B. Boyer) Psychoanalytic Treatment of Schizophrenia and Characterological Disorders, 1967, Psychoanalytic Treatment, 1971, also several books on character structure, primitive mental states, psychopathology and psychoanalytic technique, psychoanalysis; also articles.; Co-editor: Annals of Adolescent Psychiatry, 1972-80. Capt. M.C. AUS, 1946-48. Fellow Am. Psychiat. Assn., Am. Orthopsychiat. Assn. (bd. dirs. 1979-83), Am. Coll. Psychoanalysts; mem. Am. Soc. Adolescent Psychiatry, Chgo. Soc. Adolescent Psychiatry (pres. 1972-73), Internat. Psychoanalytic Soc. (chmn. standing com. on rsch. in psychosis 1994—), Am. Psychoanalytic Assn., Chgo. Psychoanalytic Soc. Home: 270 Locust Rd Winnetka IL 60093-3609 Office: 505 N Lake Shore Dr Chicago IL 60611-3427

GIRARD, JIM, former state legislator; b. Marshall, Minn., June 12, 1953; s. Louis Felix and Beatrice (Barnady) G.; m. Becky; children: Chrsitine Marie, Ryan James. BS, Dakota State U., 1975, MS, 1971. Chmn. Lyon County Rep. Com., 1987-88; mem. Minn. State Rep. Ctrl. Com., 1987-89; state rep. Minn. Ho. Reps., Dist. 21A, 1989-97; sr. ptnr. Cookhill Gerard Assocs., St. Paul, 1999—. Mem. agrl. capital investments, fin. inst. & ins. & Tex. coms., Minn. Ho. Reps.; agrl. rep. Western Bank & Trust, 1977—; nutritionist Feeders Choice Foods, 1977-79; owner Girard Farms, 1979-99. Recipient Key Press award Minn. Jaycees, 1983, Disting. Svc. award Marshall Area Jaycees, 1984. Mem. Marshall Area C. of C. (chmn. agrl. com. 1987-88), Minn. Park Producers Assn. (legis. chmn. exec. com. 1986-89), Minn. Farm Bur., Alpha Gamma Rho. Home: 7677 Nottingham Pkwy Maple Grove MN 55311-1506

GIRARDI, JOSEPH ELLIOTT, baseball player; b. Peoria, Ill., Oct. 14, 1964; BS in Indsl. Engring., Northwestern U., 1986. Baseball player N.Y. Yankees, 1995-2000; catcher Chgo. Cubs, 2000—. Achievements include member of N.Y. Yankees World Series Champions, 1996. Office: Chgo Cubs Wrigley Field 1060 W Addison St Chicago IL 60613-4383*

GISLASON, ERIC ARNI, chemistry educator; b. Oak Park, Ill., Sept. 9, 1940; s. Raymond Spencer and Jane Ann (Clifford) G.; m. Nancy Brown, Sept. 11, 1962 (dec. June 1994); children: Kristina Elizabeth, John Harrison; m. Sharon McKevitt Fetzer, Apr. 25, 1998. BA summa cum laude, Oberlin Coll., 1962; PhD, Harvard U., 1967. Postdoctoral fellow U. Calif-Berkeley, 1967-69; asst. prof. chemistry U. Ill., Chgo., 1969-73; assoc. prof. U. Ill.-Chgo., 1973-77, prof., 1977—; acting head chemistry dept. U. Ill., Chgo., 1993-94, head chemistry dept., 1994-99, interim dean Coll. Liberal Arts and Scis., 1997-98, interim vice chancellor rsch., 1999-2001, vice chancellor rsch., 2001—. Vis. scientist FOM Inst. Atomic and Molecular Physics, Amsterdam, 1977-78; prof. associé U. Paris South, 1985. Contbr. articles to profl. jours. Recipient Silver Circle Teaching award U. Ill., 1982, Excellence in Teaching award U. Ill., 1990. Mem. Am. Chem. Soc. (vis. assocs. program), Am. Phys. Soc., Phi Beta Kappa, Sigma Xi, Phi Kappa Phi. Congregationalist Achievements include rsch. in theoretical studies of ion-molecule reactions, collision-induced dissociation, nonadiabatic transitions, molecular energy transfer and isotope effects. Home: 7227 Oak Ave River Forest IL 60305-1935 Office: U Ill-Chgo OCVR M/C 672 Rm 310 1737 W Polk St Chicago IL 60612-7727 E-mail: Gislason@uic.edu.

GITNER, GERALD L. air transportation executive, investment banker; b. Boston, Apr. 10, 1945; s. Samuel and Sylvia (Berkovitz) Gitner; m. Deanne Gebell, June 24, 1968; children: Daniel Mark, Seth Michael. BA cum laude, Boston U., 1966. Staff v.p. TransWorld Airlines, N.Y.C., 1972-74; sr. v.p. mktg. and planning Tex. Internat. Airlines, Houston, 1974-80; pres., founder People Express Airlines, Newark, 1980-82; chmn. Pan Am. World Svcs. Inc., N.Y.C., 1982-85, exec. v.p., chief fin. officer, 1983-85; vice chmn. Pan Am. World Airways, 1982-85, Pan Am Corp., 1984-85; pres. Tex. Air Corp., Houston, 1985-86; CEO, pres. ATASCO USA, Inc., aircraft trading firm, N.Y.C., 1986-89; chmn. D. G. Assocs. Inc., 1986—, Avalon Group, Ltd., N.Y.C., 1990-98; co-chmn. Global Aircraft Leasing Ltd., 1991-98, 1990—; dir. TWA, Inc., 1993—, CEO, 1996-99, chmn., 1997—. Bd. advisers econs. dept. Boston U.; dir. ICTS Internat. N.V., Factory Card Outlet, Inc.; mem. chancellors coun. U. Mo., St. Louis, 1997—2000. Trustee, mem. exec. com. Boston U., 1984—96; trustee Rochester (N.Y.) Inst. Tech., 1999—. Recipient Disting. Alumni award, Boston U., 1982, 1984. Mem.: Cornell Club N.Y., Sky Club, Phi Alpha Theta.

GITTELMAN, MARC JEFFREY, manufacturing and financial executive; b. N.Y.C., Nov. 26, 1947; s. Sidney and Trudy (Eidus) G.; m. Nanci V. Geiger, Apr. 9, 1988; 1 child, Brandon Michael. BBA, Hofstra U., 1969; MBA in Fin., Adelphi U., 1972; postgrad., U. Colo., Denver. Credit analyst Security Nat. Bank Long Island, Melville, N.Y., 1969-72; dir. adminstrn. Tiger Leasing Group Inc., Chgo., 1973-78; asst. treas. Storage Tech. Corp., Louisville, 1979-83; v.p., treas. Holnam Inc. (formerly Ideal Basic Industries), Dundee, Mich., 1984-91, Andrew Corp., Orland Park, Ill., 1992—. Bd. dirs. Food Bank of Rockies. Mem. Nat. Assn. Corp. Treas. Republican. Jewish. Office: Andrew Corp 10500 153rd St Orland Park IL 60462-3071 E-mail: jeffrey.gittelman@andrew.com.

GITTLEMAN, NEAL, orchestra conductor; b. Ancon, Panama Canal Zone, June 29, 1955; s. Edwin and Rosalyn (Leinwand) G.; m. Lisa Fry, Dec. 21, 1984. BA in Music, Yale U., 1975; postgrad., Manhattan Sch. Music, 1977-81; artist's diploma in orch. conducting, Hartt Sch. Music, Hartford, Conn., 1983. Asst. condr. Oreg. Symphony, Portland, 1983-86; music dir. Marion (Ind.) Philharm., 1987-86; assoc. condr. Syracuse (N.Y.) Symphony, 1986-89, Milw. Symphony Orch., 1989-95, resident condr., 1995-98; music dir. Dayton (Ohio) Philharm. Orch., 1995—. Guest condr. San Francisco Symphony, 1989, Rochester Symphony, 1989, Oreg. Symphony, 1990, San Jose Symphony, 1992, Minn. Orch., 1992, 93, Telemann Chamber Orch., Osaka, Japan, 1994, Shinsei Nihon Symphony, Tokyo, 1994, San Antonio Symphony, 1994, Indls. Symphony, 1994, UNAM Philharm., Mexico City, 1995, Grant Park Orch., Chgo., 1995, Buffalo Symphony, 1995, Chgo. Symphony, 1995, 97, Edmonton (Alta., Can.) Symphony, 1996, Augsburg Symphony, 1997. Recipient 2d prize Ernest Ansermet Internat. Conducting Competition, Geneva, 1984, 3d prize Leopold Stokowski Internat. Conducting Competition, N.Y.C., 1985; Karl Böhm fellow Hartt Sch. Music, 1982. Avocations: golf, squash, t'ai chi ch'uan. Office: Dayton Philharm Orch 125 E 1st St Dayton OH 45402-1214

GIUNTA, JOSEPH, conductor, music director; b. Atlantic City, May 8, 1951; m. Cynthia Reid, June 5, 1982. MusB in Theory, Northwestern U., 1973, MusM in Conducting, 1974; DFA (hon.), Simpson Coll., 1986. Condr., music dir. Waterloo/Cedar Falls Symphony and Chamber Orch. of Iowa, 1974-89; music dir. Des Moines Symphony Orch., 1989—. Guest condr. numerous symphonies, orchs. including Chgo. Symphony, London Philharm., Philharmonia Orch. of London, Minn. Orch., Indpls. Orch., Phoenix Symphony, Fla. Symphony, Akron (Ohio) Symphony, Syracuse (N.Y.) Symphony, R.I. Philharm. Recipient Helen M. Thompson award; named Outstanding Young Condr. in U.S., 1984. Mem. Phi Mu Alpha, Pi Kappa Lambda. Office: Des Moines Symphony 221 Walnut St Des Moines IA 50309-2101

GIVAN, RICHARD MARTIN, retired state supreme court justice; b. Indpls., June 7, 1921; s. Clinton Hodel and Glee (Bowen) G.; m. Pauline Marie Haggart, Feb. 28, 1945; children: Madalyn Givan Hesson, Sandra Givan Chenoweth, Patricia Givan Smith, Elizabeth Givan Whipple. LL.B., Ind. U., 1951. Bar: Ind. 1952. Ptnr. with Clinton H. Givan, 1952-59, Bowen, Myers, Northam & Givan, 1960-69; justice Ind. Supreme Ct., 1969-74, chief justice, 1974-87, assoc. justice, 1987-95; ret.; dep. pub. defender Ind., 1952-53; dep. atty. gen., 1953—64; dep. pros. atty. Marion County, 1965-66; ret., 1995. Mem. Ind. Ho. Reps., 1967-68 Served to 2d lt. USAAF, 1942-45. Mem. Ind. Bar Assn., Indpls. Bar Assn., Ind. Soc. Chgo., Newcomen Soc. N.Am., Internat. Arabian Horse Assn. (past dir., chmn. ethical practices rev. bd.), Ind. Arabian Horse Club (pres. 1971-72), Indpls. 500 Oldtimers Club, Lions, Sigma Delta Kappa. Mem. Soc. of Friends. Home: 6690 S County Road 1025 E Indianapolis IN 46231-2495

GIVENS, HENRY, JR. academic administrator; m. Belma Evans; children: Stacey G., Keith Alan. Bachelor, Lincoln U., Mo.; Master, U. Ill.; PhD, St. Louis U. Tchr. Webster Groves (Mo.) Sch. Dist., prin. magnet sch., asst. to supt. to schs.; pres. Harris-Stowe State Coll., St. Louis, 1979—. Interim pres. Lincoln U., 1987; cons. U.S. State Dept. Bd. dirs. Mo. Arts Coun., St. Louis Symphony Orch., St. Louis Zoo. Mem. Am. Assn. State Colls. and Univs., Nat. Alliance Black Sch. Educators, Nat. Assn. Equal Opportunity, North Ctrl. Assn. Colls. and Secondary Schs., Phi Delta Kappa, Sigma Pi Phi, Phi Delta Sigma. Office: Harris-Stowe State Coll 3026 Laclede Ave Saint Louis MO 63103-2136

GJOVIG, BRUCE QUENTIN, entrepreneur coach, consultant, entrepreneur; b. Crosby, N.D., Mar. 24, 1951; s. Ronald Daniel and Agnes (Smedberg) G.; children: Mike Mohn, Todd Chaffee. BA, BS, U. N.D., 1974. Rsch. chemist Man-in-the-Sea Project, Grand Forks, N.D., 1975-76; campaign advisor Elkin for Gov. Com., Bismarck, 1976; exec. officer Grand Forks Bd. Realtors, 1977-81; devel. officer U. N.D. Found., 1981-84; founder, dir. Ctr. for Innovation, Grand Forks, 1984—. Bd. dirs. 1st Seed Capital Co., Grand Forks, SBIR Project West, Phoenix; founder, chmn. N.D. Entrepreneur Hall of Fame, 1985—; founder Rural Tech. Incubator, 1994—, N.D. Angel Capital Network, 1998—. Editor: The Business Plan: Step-by-Step, 1988, The Marketing Plan: Step-by-Step, 1990; author, editor: Boxcar of Peaches: Nash Finch Co., 1990, Pardon Me, Your Manners are Showing!, 1992; contbr. articles to profl. jours. Founder, sponsor 67th Patent & Trademark Depository Libr., 1991—; chair N.D. Mus. Art, U. N.D. Nordic Initiative. Named Friend of Sml. Bus., Fargo C. of C., 1988; named U. N.D. Outstanding Greek Alumnus, 1990, Outstanding Svc. award, U. N.D. Alumni Assn., 1984, Western U.S. SBIR Support Person, 1997, Tibbetts award SBA, 1998, Kauffamn Leadership award 1998, SBA Nat. Vision 2000 award, 1999, others; named to N.D. Entrepreneur Hall of Fame, 2001. Mem. Assn. Univ. Tech. Mgrs., Assn. Univ. Related Rsch. Pks., Univ. Small Bus. Tech. Consortium (state dir. 1986-90), Alumni Inter-Fraternity Coun. (chmn. 1982-86, 90-95, Outstanding Alumnus 1990), Rotary, Delta Tau Delta. Republican. Episcopalian. Avocations: reading, politics, art collector, fund raising, entrepreneur history collector. Home: Condo # 31 2501 26th Ave S Grand Forks ND 58201-6454 Office: Ctr for Innovation PO Box 8372 Rural Tech Ctr Grand Forks ND 58202-8372 E-mail: bruce@innovators.net.

GLADDEN, DEAN ROBERT, arts administrator, educator, consultant; b. Columbus, Ohio, Dec. 27, 1953; s. Cyril Robert and Eileen (Faulkner) G.; m. Jane Frances Tellers, Aug. 27, 1953; children: John Dean, Catherine Eileen. B in Music Edn., Miami U., Oxford, Ohio, 1976; MS in Urban Arts Mgmt., Drexel U., 1978; postgrad., Harvard U., 1998. Exec. dir. Council for Arts of Greater Lima, Ohio, 1977-80, Arts Comm. Greater Toledo, 1980-82; dir. devel. and adminstrn. Great Lakes Theater Festival, Cleve., 1982-86; assoc. mng. dir. The Cleve. Play House, 1986, mng. dir., 1987—. Cons. Ohio Arts Coun., Cleve., 1977—, chmn. sponsor/touring panel, 1981-83; adj. assoc. prof. U. Akron, Ohio, 1984-87; mem. adv. com. Mandel Sch. of Non-Profit Mgmt., Case Western Res. U., Cleve. Author booklets on the econs. of arts in Ohio, 1981, 83, 85, 87, 89, 91, 93. Mem. League Resident Theatres (exec. com.), Ohio Citizens for Arts (v.p.), Rotary (pres.). Episcopalian. Avocations: piano, drums. Home: 2687 Rocklyn Rd Cleveland OH 44122-2112 Office: The Cleve Play House 8500 Euclid Ave Cleveland OH 44106-2032

GLADDEN, JAMES WALTER, JR. lawyer; b. Pitts., Feb. 23, 1940; s. James Walter and Cynthia Unice (Hales) G.; m. Patricia T. Kuehn, Aug. 21, 1993; children: James, Thomas, Robert. AB, DePauw U., 1961; JD, Harvard U., 1964. Bar: Ill. 1964, U.S. Sup. Ct. 1978. Ptnr. Mayer, Brown & Platt, Chgo., 1964—. Mem. ABA. Home: 1426 Chicago Ave Apt 5N Evanston IL 60201 Office: Mayer Brown & Platt 190 S La Salle St Ste 3900 Chicago IL 60603-3441 E-mail: jgladden@mayerbrownrowe.com.

GLADSTONE, WILLIAM SHELDON, JR. radiologist; b. Des Moines, Dec. 19, 1923; s. William Sheldon and Wanda (Rees) G.; m. Ruth Alice Jensen, June 19, 1944; children— Denise Ann, William Sheldon, Stephen Rees B.A., State U. Iowa, 1954, M.D., 1947. Diplomate Am. Bd. Radiology. Intern Hurley Hosp., Flint, Mich., 1947-48; gen. practice medicine Iowa Falls, Iowa, 1948-49; asst. dept. pathology State U. Iowa Coll. Medicine, Iowa City, 1949-50; resident in radiology Univ. Hosp., 1950-51, 53-54; practice medicine specializing in radiology Kalamazoo, 1954—. Exec. v.p. Kalamazoo Radiology; clin. asst. prof. radiology Mich. State U. Coll. Human Medicine; chief radiology Bronson Meth. Hosp., Kalamazoo, 1973-75, 77-79 Bd. dirs. Kalamazoo County Tb Soc., 1955-59, Mich. Children's Aid, 1960-62, Am. Cancer Soc., Kalamazoo, 1964-66. Served with AUS, 1943-46; served to capt. USAF, 1951-53 Fellow Am. Coll. Radiology; mem. Kalamazoo Acad. Medicine, AMA, Mich. Radiologic Soc. (pres. W. Mich. sect. 1976), Mich. State Med. Soc., SW Mich. Surg. Soc., Am. Roentgen Ray Soc., Phi Beta Kappa (pres. SW Mich. chpt. 1963) Republican. Episcopalian. Club: Kalamazoo Country. Lodges: Masons, Shriners Home: 1029 Essex Cir Kalamazoo MI 49008-2349 Office: 524 S Park St Kalamazoo MI 49007-5118

GLANCY, ALFRED ROBINSON, III, retired public utility company executive; b. Detroit, Mar. 14, 1938; s. Alfred Robinson and Elizabeth A. (Tant) G.; m. Ruth Mary Roby, Sept. 15, 1962; children: Joan C., Alfred R. IV, Douglas Roby, Andrew Roby. BA, Princeton U., 1960; MA, Harvard U., 1962. V.p. corp. planning Am. Nat. Gas Svc., Detroit, 1976-79; econ. and fin. planning staff Mich. Consol. Gas Co., 1962-64, supr. econ. studies and rates, 1965-67, mgr. econ. and fin. planning dept., 1967-68, treas., 1969-72, v.p., treas., 1972-73, v.p. customer and mktg. svcs., 1976-79, v.p. mktg./dist. ops., 1979-81, sr. v.p. mktg./customer svcs., 1981-83, sr. v.p. utility ops., 1983-84, chmn., CEO, 1984-92, MCN Energy Group Inc., Detroit, 1989-2001; ret., 2001. Bd. dirs., exec. com. UNICO Properties, Inc., Seattle. Past chmn. Detroit Symphony Orch., Detroit Renaissance Inc., exec. com.; past chmn. Detroit Med. Ctr., New Detroit, Inc. Mem. Princeton Club Mich., Country Club Detroit, Detroit Athletic Club. Republican. Office: Ste 405 400 Maple Park Blvd Saint Clair Shores MI 48081

GLANZMANN, THOMAS H. healthcare company executive; B in Polit. Sci., Dartmouth Coll.; MBA, Inst. Mgmt. Devel., Lausanne, Switzerland. With Baxter Healthcare, 1988—, asst. gen. mgr. Switzerland, v.p. bus. devel. and planning, blood therapy/immunotherapy, v.p. bus. devel. and planning Biotech Group, pres. Biotech Group in Europe, CEO Immuno Internat., 1996, pres. Hyland Immuno, 1998—, corp. v.p. Office: Baxter Healthcare One Baxter Pkwy Deerfield IL 60015-4633

GLASER, GARY A. bank executive; Grad., Baldwin-Wallace, Case Western Res. U. With Nat. City Corp., 1967-84; pres., CEO Nat. City Bank, Columbus, Ohio, 1984—, chmn., 2000—. Office: Nat City Bank 155 E Broad St Columbus OH 43215-3609

GLASER, ROBERT EDWARD, lawyer; b. Cin., Jan. 12, 1935; s. Delbert Henry and Rita Elizabeth (Arlinghaus) G.; m. Kathleen Eileen Grannen, June 17, 1961; children— Petra M., Timothy X., Mark G., Bridget M., Christopher D., Jenny M., Michael F. BS in Bus. Adminstrn. cum laude, Xavier U., Cin., 1955; LLB, U. Cin., 1960; LLM, U. Chgo., 1962; postgrad., U. Tuebingen, Fed. Republic of Germany, 1961. Bar: Ohio 1960, U.S. Dist. Ct. (no. dist.) Ohio 1963, U.S. Ct. Appeals (6th cir.) 1964, U.S. Tax Ct. 1970, U.S. Ct. Internat. Trade 1971, U.S. Ct. Fed. Claims 1992, U.S. Ct. Appeals (fed. cir.) 2000. Assoc. Arter & Hadden, Cleve., 1963-69, ptnr., 1970-2001, chmn., 1983-92; ret., 2001. Arbitrator Cuyahoga County Ct. Common Please, Ohio, 1972—, Med. Malpractice Panel, 1985—, Mediator Settlement Week, 1990; lectr. Cleve. Tax Inst., 1966—, mem. exec. com., 1980—84, chmn., 1982; lectr. Can.-U.S. Law Inst., 1980, Res. Officers Assn., 1970—, Ret. Officers Assn., 1995—. Contbr. articles to legal jours. Sec. Bay View Hosp., 1972-81; trustee Mental Health Rehab. and Rsch., Inc., 1975-86, mem. exec. com., 1977-81, pres., 1979-81; mem. men's com. Cleve. Play Ho., 1965—; mem. joint mental health and corrections com. Fedn. Cmty. Planning, 1978-81; mem. Cleve. Coun. on Fgn. Affairs, 1987-2002; mem. vis. com. Coll. Law Cleve. State U., 1987-97; mem. Soc. of Benchers, Case Western Res. Univ. Coll. Law, 1988—; trustee Univ. Circle, Inc., 1989-99, mem. exec. com., 1989-99. Col. U.S. Army, ret. Ford Found. grantee, 1960. Fellow Am. Bar Found. (life); mem. Ohio Bar Assn. (gen. tax com. 1998—, lawyer assistance com. 1999—), Nat. Bar Assn., Cleve. Bar Assn. (trustee 1983-87, chmn. bd. of com. grievance and discipline trial com. 1993—, gen. tax com. 1983—, lawyer assistance com. 1999—), Legal Aid Soc. Cleve., Am. Judicature Soc., 8th Jud. Conf. (life), Am. Arbitration Assn. (nat. and internat. panel arbitrators 1969—), Citizens League Greater Cleve., Order of Coif, Union Club, Pentagon Officers Athletic Club, Serra Internat., Cleve. Club (exec. com. 1987-88, 90-91, 93-98, 2000—, pres. 1994-96), KC. Democrat. Roman Catholic. Home: 22895 Mastick Rd Cleveland OH 44126-3145 Office: Arter & Hadden 1100 Huntington Bldg 925 Euclid Ave Cleveland OH 44115-1475

GLASER, RONALD, microbiology educator, scientist; b. N.Y.C., Feb. 27, 1939; s. Irving and Pauline G.; m. Janice Kiecolt, Jan. 17, 1980; children: Andrew, Erik. BA, U. Bridgeport, 1962; MS, U. R.I., 1964; PhD, U. Conn., 1968; postgrad., Baylor Coll. Medicine, 1968-69. Asst. prof. microbiology Pa. State U., Hershey, 1970-73, assoc. prof., 1973-77, prof., 1977-78; prof. chmn. dept. med. microbiology and immunology Coll. Medicine Ohio State U., Columbus, 1978-92; reviewer NIH and NASA study sects.; assoc. dean for rsch. and grad. edn. Ohio State U. Med. Ctr., Columbus, 1992-94, assoc. v.p. health sci. rsch., 1994-2001, Gilbert and Kathryn Mitchell chair in medicine, 1995—, assoc. v.p. rsch., 2001—, 2001—. Editor: (with T. Gottleib-Stematsky) Human Herpes Virus Infections: Clinical Aspects, 1982; (with others) Epstein-Barr Virus and Human Disease, 1987; (with J. Jones) Human Herpes Virus Infections, 1994; (with J. Kiecolt-Glaser) Handbook of Human Stress, 1994. NIH fellow, 1968-69; Franco-Am. Exch. Program; Fogarty Internat. Ctr.; NIH and INSRM fellow, 1975, 77; Leukemia Soc. Am. scholar, 1974. Fellow: Acad. Behavioral Medicine Rsch. (pres.-elect psychoneuroimmunology rsch. soc. 2002); mem.: AAAS, Am. Soc. Microbiology. Office: Ohio State U 2175 Graves Hall 333 W 10th Ave Columbus OH 43210-1239 E-mail: glaser.1@osu.edu.

GLASS, HENRY PETER, industrial designer, interior architect, educator; b. Vienna, Austria, Sept. 24, 1911; came to U.S., 1939; s. Ernst and Berta (Zaitschek) G.; m. Eleanor C. Knopp, Mar. 4, 1937; children: Ann Karin, Peter. Diploma architect, Wiener Tech. Hochschule, Vienna, 1933; M.Arch., Meisterschule Prof. Theiss, Vienna, 1935; Indsl. Design, Sch. Design, Chgo., 1953. Prin. architect Studio H. Glass, Vienna, 1935-38; designer Office Gilbert Rohde, N.Y.C., 1939-40, Morris Sanders, N.Y.C., 1940; head design dept. W.L. Stensgaard Assocs., Chgo., 1941-45; prin. Henry P. Glass, Assocs., Northfield, Ill., 1946—; prof. indsl. design Chgo. Art Inst., 1946-69. Designs include, Swingline, Children's Furniture; patentee in field; author: Design & Consumer, 1981, The Shape of Manmade Things, 1996, 100 Travel Sketches, 2000; one-man shows Hochschule Für Angewandte Kunst, Vienna, Austria, 1997, Chgo. Art Inst., 1999-2000; represented in private and permanent collections. Trustee Bd. of Northfield, 1966-67; pres. Am. Friends of Austria, 1990—. Recipient Ann. award Fine Hardwoods Assn., 1955, 56, Best Booth award Ski Show Expo Ctr., Chgo., 1972, Excellence in Design award Indsl. Design Mag., 1978, Golden Merit award City of Vienna, 1986, Cross of Honor for Arts and Scis., Republic of Austria, 1987, Good Design award Chgo. Atheneum, 1992. Fellow Indsl. Design Soc. Am. (chmn. Chgo. chpt. 1959-60, nat. vice chmn. 1960-62) Roman Catholic. Clubs: Am. Friends of Austria (v.p. 1976, then pres.); Austro Am. Council for the Mid-West (Chgo.) (pres. 1983-84). Home: 245 Dickens St Northfield IL 60093-3224 Office: Henry P Glass Assocs PO Box 52 Northfield IL 60093-0052

GLASS, KENNETH EDWARD, management consultant; b. Ft. Thomas, Ky., Sept. 28, 1940; s. Clarence E. and Lucille (Garrison) G.; m. Nancy Romanek, May 9, 1964; children: Ryan, Lara. ME, U. Cin., 1963, MS, 1965, grad. student, 1967. Registered profl. engr., Ohio. With Allis Chalmers Mfg. Co., Cin. and Eng., 1963-73; v.p. mfg. Fiat Allis Contrn. Machinery, Inc., Chgo., 1973-75; pres. Perkins Diesel Corp., Canton, Ohio, 1975-77; pres., chief exec. officer Massey-Ferguson, Inc., Des Moines, 1978, v.p., gen. mgr. N.Am. ops. Massey Ferguson Ltd., Des Moines, 1978; chmn., pres., chief exec. officer Union Metal Mfg. Co., Canton, Ohio, 1979-85; pres. Glass & Assocs. Inc., 1985—, chmn., 1996—; pres. Stony Point Group, Inc., 1996—, also bd. dirs.; chmn. Utica Corp., 2001—, UCA Holdings, 2001—, TECT Corp.; bd. dirs. Thames Water Holdings, Turnaround Mgmt. Assn.; trustee U. Cin. Found. Mem. Young Presidents Orgn., ASME, Soc. Automotive Engrs., Turnaround Mgmt. Assn., Assn. Cert. Turnaround Profls. (bd. dirs., v.p. 1993-94, pres. 1995-96), Am. Bankrupcy Inst., Pi Tau Sigma. Patentee in field.

GLASS, RICHARD MCLEAN, psychiatry educator, medical editor; b. Phoenix, Sept. 25, 1943; s. Richard Kirkpatrick and Harriet Margaret (Bradshaw) G.; m. Rita Mae Catherine Denk, Mar. 4, 1967; children: Kathryn, Brendan Neil. BA, Northwestern U., 1965, MD, 1968. Diplomate Am. Bd. Psychiatry and Neurology. Asst. prof. psychiatry U. Chgo., 1975-82, assoc. prof., 1982-95, clin. prof., 1995—. Dir. adult psychiatry clinic U. Chgo., 1985-89. Mem. editorial bd. Archives of Gen. Psychiatry, 1984—; cons. editor JAMA, 1987-89, dep. editor, 1989—; contbr. numerous articles to profl. jours. Served to major U.S. Army, 1970-72. Fellow Am. Psychiat. Assn.; mem. AAAS, AMA. Presbyterian. Avocations: tennis, music, trombone. Office: JAMA 515 N State St Chicago IL 60610-4325 E-mail: richard_glass@ama-assn.org.

GLASSCOCK, JOYCE H. state official; BJ magna cum laude, U. Mo., 1985; postgrad., George Washington U., 1993. Adminstrv. asst. Bailey, Deardourff, Sipple Polit. cons., McLean, Va., 1986; legis. corr. U.S. Senator John C. Danforth of Mo., Washington, 1987; press sec. Danforth for U.S. Senate, St. Louis, 1988; field rep. Dole for Pres., 1988; comms. cons. Eisenhower Centennial Found., Washington, 1989; dir .pub. affairs Econ. Devel. Adminstrn., U.S. Dept. Commerce, 1989-93; press sec. Congress Dave Hobson of Ohio, 1993-94; campaign dir. Bill Graves for Gov., Topeka, 1994; chief of staff Kans. Gov. Bill Graves, 1994—2001; Sec. of Adminstrn. State of Kans., 2001—. Office: Sec of Aminstrn Curtis Bldg Topeka KS 66612

GLASSCOCK, KENTON, state legislator; m. Joyce Glasscock. BA, Kans. State U., 1976. State rep. Dist. 62 Kans. Ho. of Reps., 1991—, mem. taxation and energy and natural resources com., mem. joint com. on adminstrv. rules and regulations, chairperson calendar and printing com., vice-chairperson interstate cooperation com., majority leader. Pres. Kans. Lumber Homestore. Home: PO Box 37 Manhattan KS 66505-0037 E-mail: glasscock@house.state.ks.us., kentglas@flinthills.com.

GLASSCOCK, LARRY CLABORN, insurance company executive; b. Cullman, Ala., Apr. 4, 1948; s. Oscar Claborn and Betty Lou (Norman) G.; m. Lee Ann Roden, Sept. 13, 1969; children— Michael, Carrie B.A., Cleve. State U., 1970; postgrad., Am. Inst. Banking, Columbia U. Vice pres. personnel and orgn. AmeriTrust Co., Cleve., 1974-75, v.p. nat. div., 1976-78, v.p., mgr. credit card ctr., 1978-79, sr. v.p. consumer fin., 1980-81, sr. v.p. nat. div., 1981-83, exec. v.p. corp. banking adminstr., 1983-87; group exec. v.p. AmeriTrust Corp. and AmeriTrust Co., 1987-92; pres., CEO Anthem Ins., Indpls., 1992—. Bd. dirs. AT Fin. Corp., AT Capital Corp., AmeriTrust Internat. Banking, AmeriTrust Devel. Bank, CT Leasing Corp., Community Mut. Ins. Co., The Gt. Lakes Constrn. Co. Trustee Cleve. State U. Devel. Found.; campaign chmn. Geauga County United Way, 1989; mem. adv. bd. Northeast Ohio Employee Ownership Ctr. Kent State U., 1987—. Served with USMC, 1970-76. Mem. Am. Inst. Banking, Am. Bankers Assn. (vice chmn. exec. com. comml. lending div.), Assn. Res. City Bankers, Greater Cleve. Growth Assn., Cleve.State U. Alumni Assn. (pres. 1987). Clubs: Union (Cleve.); Hillbrook (Chagrin Falls, Ohio); The Country (Pepper Pike, Ohio). Office: Anthem Ins 120 Monument Cir Indianapolis IN 46204-4906

GLASSER, JAMES J. leasing company executive, retired; b. Chgo., June 5, 1934; s. Daniel D. and Sylvia G.; m. Louise D. Rosenthal, Apr. 19, 1964; children: Mary, Emily, Daniel. A.B., Yale U., 1955; J.D., Harvard U., 1958. Bar: Ill. 1958. Asst. states atty., Cook County, Ill., 1958-61; mem. exec. staff GATX Corp., Chgo., 1961-69, pres., 1974-96, chmn. bd., CEO, 1978-96, chmn. emeritus, 1996—, also dir. Gen. mgr. Infilco Products Co., 1969-70; v.p. GATX Leasing Corp., San Francisco, 1970-71, pres., 1971-74; bd. dirs. B.F. Goodrich Co., Harris Bankcorp, Inc., Harris Trust & Savs. Bank, Mut. Trust Life Ins. Co. Bd. dirs. Lake Forest Hosp., Northwestern Meml. Corp., Voices for Ill. Children; trustee Better Govt. Assn., Chgo. Zool. Soc., U. Chgo. Mem. Chgo. C. of C. (dir.), Chgo. Cen. Area Com. (dir.), Econ. Club of Chgo., Commercial Club, Casino Club, Chgo. Club, Racquet Club, Onwentsia Club (Lake Forest, Ill.), Shoreacres (Lake Bluff, Ill.), Tucson Country Club, Chi Psi. Home: 464 N Mayflower Rd Lake Forest IL 60045-2306 Office: 500 W Monroe St Chicago IL 60661-3630

GLASSHEIM, ELIOT ALAN, editor, state legislator; b. N.Y.C., Feb. 10, 1938; s. Raymond S. and Edith (Ruthizer) G.; m. Patricia Sanborn, July 20, 1969 (div. Feb. 1979); children: Eagle, Don; m. Dyan Rey, Feb. 14, 1996. BA, Wesleyan U., 1960; MA, U. N.Mex., 1966, PhD, 1972. Copy boy, book reviewer Wash. Post, 1960-61; editl. proofreader Wall St. Jour., N.Y.C., 1962-64; mgmt. trainee Accessory Fashions, 1964-66; asst. prof. English, Augusta (Ga.) Coll., 1968-70; fellow U. N.D., Grand Forks, 1971-73; mem.. N.D. Ho. of Reps., 1975-76, 93—; grant writer, dir. oral history project of 97 flood N.D. Mus. Art, 1993-99; owner used bookstore and Internet sales Dr. Eliot's Twice Sold Tales, 1992—; policy analyst No. Great Plains, Inc., 1999—. Dir. Population/Food Fund, Grand Forks, 1977-79; housing coord., grantswriter N.D. Migrant Coun., Grand Forks, 1979-81; mem. house appropriations com. N.D. Ho. of Reps., 2001—. Editor: Population and Food Issues, 1977, 1978, Voices from the Flood, 1999, Behind the Scenes, 2002, Toward New Horizons: Moving the Northern Great Plains Region to a Stronger Economic Future, 2002; author (poems): The Restless Giant, 1968. Exec. dir. Quad County Cmty. Action Agy., Grand Forks, 1981—87; field rep., office mgr. U.S. Senator Quentin Burdick, 1987—92; mem. Grand Forks City Coun., 1982—, Grand Forks Planning and Zoning Com., 1984—96, mem. flood response com., 1997—2000, chmn. population task force, 2001; chmn. interim legis. Commerce Commn., 1999—2000; founder, dir. Red River Valley Habitat for Humanity, Grand Forks, 1988—99; chmn. Dist. 17/18 Dems., 1980—81; bd. dirs. Prairie Pub. TV, 1997—2000. Home: 619 N 3rd St Grand Forks ND 58203-3203 E-mail: eglasshe@state.nd.us.

GLASSMAN, ERIC I. retail executive; Grad., U. Cin., 1981. CFO, v.p. DIY Home Warehouse, Inc., Valley View, Ohio. Office: DIY Home Warehouse Inc 5811 Canal Rd Valley View OH 44125

GLAZIER, ROBERT CARL, publishing executive; b. Brandsville, Mo., Mar. 26, 1927; s. Vernie A. and Mildred F. (Beu) G.; m. Harriette Hubbard, June 5, 1949; children: Gregory Kent, Jeffrey Robert. Student, Drury Coll., 1944-46; BA, U. Wichita, 1949. Reporter Springfield (Mo.) Daily News, 1944-46; asst. city editor Wichita Eagle, 1946-49; journalism instr. U. Wichita, 1949-53; dir. pub. relations Springfield (Mo.) Pub. Schs., 1953-59; asso. dir. dept. radio and TV The Methodist Ch., Nashville, 1959-61; gen. mgr. WDCN-TV (Channel 2), 1961-65, KETC (Channel 9), St. Louis, 1965-76; also exec. dir. St. Louis Ednl. TV Commn.; pres. So. Ednl. Communications Assn., 1976-80; chmn. bd. Springfield Communications, Inc., Mo., 1980—. Bd. dirs. Systematic Savs. & Loan Assn.; pres., bd. dirs. Cox Health Systems. Bd. dirs. Adult Edn. Council Greater St. Louis, 1965-76, United Meth. Communications, 1980-86, Springfield Area Council of Chs., 1980-86, Lester E. Cox Med. Ctrs., 1988—. Served with AUS, 1945-46. Mem. Nat. Sch. Public Relations Assn. (past regional dir.), Nat. Acad. TV Arts and Scis. (gov.), Mo. Instructional TV Council, Ill.

Instructional TV Commn., Nat. Assn. Ednl. Broadcasters. Methodist. Club: Rotary Internat. Home: 2305 E Meadow Dr Springfield MO 65804-4536 Office: 520 S Union Ave Springfield MO 65802-2660

GLEASON, JOHN PATRICK, JR. trade association executive; b. N.Y.C., Nov. 11, 1941; s. John Patrick Sr. and Ruth T. (Madigan) G.; m. Judith Peper (dec. 1980); children: John P. III, Megan K.; m. Susan Leigh Collier, Mar. 31, 1984; children: Kevin M., Colin P. BS in Fgn. Service, Georgetown U., 1963; PMD, Harvard Bus. Sch., 1972. Gen. mgr. Pappagallo, Inc., Washington, 1964-67; export project mgr. U.S. Dept. Commerce, 1967-68; investment banker Blyth, Eastman Dillon, Inc., 1968-70; with U.S. Dept. Commerce, 1970-77, chief staff domestic and internat. bus. adminstrn., 1970-77, dep. asst. sec. commerce, 1970-77; pres. Brick Inst. Am., Reston, Va., 1977-86, Portland Cement Assn., Skokie, Ill., 1986—. Bd. dirs., chmn. Coun. Masonry Rsch., Reston, 1985—, Masonry Industry Com., Washington, 1984—. Recipient Silver medal U.S. Dept. Commerce, Washington, 1978. Mem. Am. Soc. Assn. Execs., Chgo. Soc. Assn. Execs., River Bend Country Club (Great Falls, Va.), Carlton Club (Washington), Skokie Country Club (Glencoe, Ill.). Republican. Office: Portland Cement Assn 5420 Old Orchard Rd Skokie IL 60077-1053

GLEESON, PAUL FRANCIS, retired lawyer; b. Bronx, June 20, 1941; s. William Francis and Julia Anne (Dargis) G.; children: Kevin F., Sean W., Brendan J., Colleen J. AB in History, Fordham U., 1963; JD, U. Chgo., 1966. Bar: Ill. 1966, Fed. Trial Bar Ill. 1969, U.S. Ct. Appeals (6th cir.) 1972, U.S. Ct. Appeals (7th cir.) 1973, U.S. Ct. Appeals (8th cir.) 1997. Assoc. Vedder, Price, Kaufman & Kammholz, Chgo., 1966-73, ptnr., 1973-2000; ret., 2000. Adj. prof. DePaul U. Sch. of Law, 1991. Co-author (with Day, Green & Cleveland) The Equal Employment Opportunity Compliance Manual, 1978; columnist: (with B. Alper) Gleeson and Alper on Employment Law, Merrill's Illinois Legal Times, 1988-90. Capt. U.S. Army, 1966-68, Vietnam. Decorated Bronze Star; Floyd Russell Mechem scholar, 1963-66. Mem. Order of Coif, Phi Beta Kappa. Roman Catholic.

GLEICH, GERALD JOSEPH, immunologist, medical scientist; b. Escanaba, Mich., May 14, 1931; s. Gordon Joseph and Agnes (Ederer) G.; m. Elizabeth Louise Hearn, Aug. 16, 1955 (div. 1976); children: Elizabeth Genevieve, Martin Christopher, Julia Katherine; m. Kristin Marie Leiferman, Sept. 25, 1976; children: Stephen Joseph, David Francis, Caroline Louise, William Gerald B.A., U. Mich., 1953, M.D., 1956. Diplomate: Am. Bd. Internal Medicine. Intern Phila. Gen. Hosp., 1956-57; resident Jackson Meml. Hosp., Miami, Fla., 1959-61; instr. in medicine and microbiology U. Rochester, N.Y., 1961-65; cons. in medicine, prof. immunology and medicine Mayo Clinic-Med. Sch., Rochester, Minn., 1965—2001; chmn. dept. immunology Mayo Clinic, 1982-90, George M. Eisenberg prof., 1995—2001; disting. investigator Mayo Found., 1988—2001; prof. medicine & dermatology U. Utah, Salt Lake City, 2001—. Mem. bd. sci. counselors Nat. Inst. Allergy and Infectious Disease, 1981-83; chmn. subcom. on standardization allergens WHO, Geneva, 1974-75; lectr. Am. Acad. Allergy, 1976, 82; mem., chmn. immunological scis. study sect. NIH, 1984-87; John M. Sheldon Meml. lectr., 1976, 82, 88; Steve Lang Meml. Lectureship, 1980, Stoll-Stunkard lectr. Am. Soc. Parasitologists, 1986, David Talmage Meml. lectureship, 1987, Disting. lectr. Med. Scis. Mayo Clinic, 1988. Contbr. articles on eosinophilic leukocyte to profl. jours. Served to capt. USAF, 1957-59. Recipient Landmark in Allergy award, 1990; grantee Nat. Inst. Allergy and Infectious Disease, 1970—; AAAS fellow for studies of structure, biol. properties and role in pathogenesis of disease of basic proteins present in cytoplasmic granules of eosinophilic leukocytes, 1993. Fellow ACP, Am. Acad. Allergy and Immunology (hon. fellow award 1992), AAAS; mem. Am. Soc. Clin. Investigation, Am. Assn. Immunologists, Assn. Am. Physicians, Phi Beta Kappa, Phi Kappa Phi, Alpha Omega Alpha. Roman Catholic. Home: 4313 S Zarahemla Dr Salt Lake City UT 84124 Office: Univ Utah 4B454 Sch Medicine 30 North 1900 East Salt Lake City UT 84132-2409

GLEICHMAN, JOHN ALAN, safety and loss control executive; b. Anthony, Kans., Feb. 11, 1944; s. Charles William and Caroline Elizabeth (Emch) G.; m. Martha Jean Cannon, July 1, 1966; 1 son, John Alan Jr. BS in Bus. Mgmt., Kans. State Tchrs. Coll., 1966. Cert. hazard control mgr.; cert. safety profl. with a speciality in constrn. safety; cert. safety exec. Office mgr. to asst. supt. Barton-Malow Co., Detroit, 1967-72, safety coord., 1972-76, corp. mgr. safety and security, 1976-89, dir. corp. safety and loss control, 1989—. Instr. U. Mich., Wayne State U., 1977-81, Lawrence Tech. U., 1994-96; mem. constrn. safety stds. commn. adv. com. for concrete constrn. and steel erection Bur. of Safety and Regulations, Mich. Dept. Labor, 1977—; rep. constrn. stds. com. Am. Nat. Stds. Inst., 1984—. Author: (with others) You, The National Safety Council, and Voluntary Standards, 1981, Construction Accident Analysis: The Inductive Learning Approach, 1991; mem. editl. adv. bd. Safety and Health: The Internat. Safety, Health and Environ. Mag., 1989—. Instr. multimedia first aid ARC, 1976-89; past trustee Apostolic Christian Ch., Livonia, Mich. Recipient Safety Achievement awards Mich. Mut. Ins. Co., 1979-83; Cameron award Constrn. sect. Indsl. divsn. Nat. Safety Coun., 1982, 87. Mem. Mich. Safety Conf. (pres. 1984-85), Am. Soc. Safety Engrs. (pres. Detroit chpt. 1982, nat. adminstr. constrn. divsn. 1988-89, bd. dirs. 1988-90, Safety Profl. of Yr. 1984), Nat. Safety Coun. (chmn. tech. rev. constrn. sect. indsl. divsn. 1980-84, chmn. stds. com. indsl. divsn. 1983-85, chmn. assn. com. indsl. divsn. 1986-87, dir. sects. group indsl. divsn. 1987-89, chmn. elect indsl. divsn. 1989-90, chmn. 1990-91, bd. dirs. 1987-92, Disting. Svcs. to Safety award 1993), Am. Arbitration Assn. (panel arbitrators 1985). Office: Barton Malow Co 26500 American Dr Southfield MI 48034 Office Fax: 248-436-5403. E-mail: john.gleichman@bartonmalow.com.

GLEIJESES, MARIO, holding company executive; b. Italy, Feb. 27, 1955; came to U.S., 1985; s. Luigi Gleijeses and Rosalba Catanoso; m. Betsy L. Miller, Mar. 14, 1992; children: Rosalba, Caterina. Student, U. Naples, 1973-77. Chartering mgr. Itex subs. Italgrani, Zurich, 1977-82; asst. to pres. Italgrani Spa, Naples, Italy, 1982-85; exec. v.p., bd. dirs. Italgrani USA Inc. and Italgrani Elevator Co., St. Louis, 1985-89; v.p., bd. dirs. New Eng. Milling Co., Ayer, Mass., 1987-89; bd. dirs. Green Bay Elevator Co., Burlington, Iowa; v.p., bd. dirs. Mayco Export, Inc., Mpls., 1988-89; pres., bd. dirs. McLean Elevator Co., Benedict, N.D., 1989; founder, pres., bd. dirs. Agricorp Holding Inc., 1989-92; pres., bd. dirs. Granicorp Inc., 1989-92, Granicorp Export, Inc., U.S. Virgin Islands, 1989-92; chmn., CEO, bd. dirs. Granicorp France, S.A., Paris, 1991-92; founder, pres., bd. dirs. Gleijeses, Inc., 1993—; founder, chmn. bd. dirs. Lithoflex Corp., 1994—; pres. Hoky-Contico, LLC, 1995-96.

GLEISSER, MARCUS DAVID, writer, lawyer, journalist; b. Buenos Aires, Argentina, Feb. 14, 1923; s. Ben and Riva (Kogan) G.; m. Helga Marianne Rothschild, Oct. 23, 1955; children: Brian Saul, Julia Lynne Wainblat, Hannah Tanya Sharnsky, Ellyn Ruth Klein. B.A. in Journalism, Case Western Res. U., 1945, M.A. in Econs., 1949; J.D., Cleve. State U., 1958. Bar: Ohio 1958, U.S. Dist. Ct. (no. and ea. dists.) Ohio 1981, U.S. Supreme Ct. 1962. Police reporter Cleve. Press, 1942-44, copy editor, 1944-47; advt. copy writer McDonough-Lewy, Inc., 1947-50; copy editor Cleve. Plain Dealer, 1950-52, gen. assignment reporter, 1952-57, court-house reporter, 1957-63, real estate editor, 1963-81, fin. writer and investment columnist, 1981—. Author: The World of Cyrus Eaton, 1965, Juries and Justice, 1968; also articles.; editor in chief: Cleve.-Marshall Law Rev., 1956, 57. Trustee Cleve. Coll. Alumni Assn., 1968, Euclid Mayor's Exec. Council, 1973-76, Euclid Charter Commn., 1975-76. Recipient Nat. Bronze medal Am. Newspaper Pubs. Assn., 1944, Nat. Silver Gavel award ABA, 1958, Bronze medal Nat. Legal Aid and Defender Assn., 1963, Loeb award for disting. bus. and fin. writing U. Conn., 1966; cert. of recognition NCCJ, 1967, Silver Medal award consistently outstanding spl. feature columns Nat. Headliners club, 1969, award Ohio Bar Assn., 1957, 58, 59, 60, 61, 62, award pub. svc. Cleve. Newspaper Guild, 1959, award for best column, 1976, award Nat. Assn. Real Estate Editors, 1965, 71, 72, 73, 80, 91, award Nat. Assn. Real Estate Bds., 1966, 67, 68, 69, 70, 71, 73, award Nat. Assn. Home Builders, 1970, 1st prize Nat. Assn. Realtors, 1980, Bus.-Fin. Writing award Press Club Cleve., 1969, Disting. Merit award Cleve. Assn. Real Estate Brokers, 1976, Excellence in Bus. Journalism award Press Club Cleve., 1983, 85, Fin. Writing award Pannell, Kerr & Forster, 1985; runner-up Pulitzer Prize in Journalism for local reporting, 1973; named to N.E. Ohio Apt. Assn. Hall of Fame, 1996. Mem. Am. Newspaper Guild, Soc. Profl. Journalists (Disting. Svc. award Cleve. chpt. 1994), City Club. Club: City (Cleve.) Home: 647 Grand View Ln Aurora OH 44202 Office: 1801 Superior Ave E Cleveland OH 44114-2107 E-mail: gleisser@stratos.net.

GLENDENING, EVERETT AUSTIN, architect; b. White Plains, N.Y., May 20, 1929; s. Gilbert Leslie and Elsie Jane (Fanjoy) G.; m. Wilhelmina Louise Hanley, Nov. 26, 1949; children: Nancy, James, Thomas, Terry, Susan. B.Arch., U. Cin., 1953; M.Arch., M.I.T., 1954. With Duffy Constrn. Co., Cleve., 1951-55, SIS Architects, Cin., 1956-58, T.J. Moore (architect), Denver, 1959; prof. architecture U. Cin., 1960-67; pvt. practice architecture Cin., 1959—. Prin. works include Queen's Towers, Cin., 1964, Summit Chase, Columbus, Ohio, 1966, Norwood High Sch., Cin., 1972, W.Va. State Mus., 1978, Douglass Montessori Sch., Cin., 1979, Christie Lane Workshop, Norwalk, Ohio, 1980, Coll. Law U. Cin., 1981, Elks Lodge, Columbus, Ind., 1981, Geology/Physics Sci. Ctr. U. Cin., 1983, U. Rio Grande Dormitory, 1989, U. Rio Grande Student Ctr., 1994, U. Rio Grande Math-Sci.-Nursing Bldg., 1995, Planetarium, Shawnee State U., 1998, Sch. for Creative and Performing Arts Auditorium, Cin. Pub. Schs., 1997. Served as 1st lt. USAF, 1954-56. Fellow AIA (honor awards Ohio chpt. 1966-70, 74, 82, 90, 91, Cin. chpt. 1966-68, 70, 76, Bronze medal 1969, Apple award for arch. 1995, mem. U.S. delegation of architects to People's Republic China and Hong Kong 1990); mem. Architect's Soc. Ohio, Scarab. Methodist. Office: 8050 Montgomery Rd Cincinnati OH 45236-2950 Fax: (513) 791-2794.

GLENISTER, BRIAN FREDERICK, geologist, educator; b. Albany, Western Australia, Sept. 28, 1928; came to U.S., 1959, naturalized, 1967; s. Frederick and Mabel (Frusher) G.; m. Anne Marie Treloar, Feb. 16, 1956; children: Alan Edward, Linda Marie, Kathryn Grace. BSc, U. Western Australia, Perth, 1949; MSc, U. Melbourne, Australia, 1953; PhD, U. Iowa, 1956. Lectr., then sr. lectr. geology U. Western Australia, 1956-59; asst. prof. U. Iowa, Iowa City, 1959-62, assoc. prof., 1962-66, prof., 1966-74, chmn. geology dept., 1968-74, A.K. Miller prof. geology, 1974-97, A.K. Miller prof. geology emeritus, 1997—. Mem. AAAS, Paleontol. Soc. (pres. 1988-89), Geol. Soc. Am., Geol. Soc. Iowa (pres. 1991), Paleontol. Rsch. Inst. Home: 2015 Scales Bend Rd NE North Liberty IA 52317-9331 E-mail: brian-glenister@uiowa.edu.

GLENN, GERALD MARVIN, marketing, engineering and construction executive; b. Greenville, S.C., Aug. 20, 1942; s. Oscar Marvin and Lorene (Ashmore) G.; m. Candice Wilson, Oct. 24, 1986; children: Regina Lynn, Gerald Marvin II, Charles Wilson. BSCE, Clemson U., 1964. With Daniel Constrn. Co., Greenville, S.C., 1964-77, Fluor Corp., Santa Ana, Calif., 1977-94, sr. v.p. mktg., 1982-85, pres. U.S. ops., 1985-86, exec. v.p., 1986, group pres., dir. Irvine, 1986-94; owner, prin. The Glenn Group LLC, Cimarron, Colo., 1994—, Eagle Glen Ranch LLC, Cimarron, 1994—; chmn., pres., CEO, Chgo. Bridge & Iron Co. N.V., The Woodlands, Tex., 1996—. Chmn. bd. dirs. Chgo. chpt. Am. Heart Assn., 1999—2001. Mem.: TAPPI, AIChE, Inst. Gas Tech. (dir.), Ill. Bus. Roundtable, Am. Petroleum Inst., Chgo. Soc., Chgo. Coun. Fgn. Rels. (mem. Chgo. com.), Econ. Club Chgo., Mid-Am. Club, Club at Carlton Woods, Woodlands Country Club, Ruth Lake Country Club, Univ. Club Houston, Execs. Club Chgo., Olympia Fields Country Club, Fairway Pines Golf Club. Republican. Methodist. Home: 23 Cypress Lake Pl The Woodlands TX 77382 Office: CB&I Ste 300 10200 Grogans Mill Rd The Woodlands TX 77380 Fax: 832-513-1778.

GLENN, JOHN HERSCHEL, JR. former senator; b. Cambridge, Ohio, July 18, 1921; s. John Herschel and Clara (Sproat) G.; m. Anna Margaret Castor, Apr. 1943; children: Carolyn Ann, John David. Student, Muskingum Coll., 1939-42, B.Sc., 1962; naval aviation cadet, U. Iowa, 1942; grad. flight sch., Naval Air Tng. Center, Corpus Christi, Tex., 1943, Navy Test Pilot Tng. Sch., Patuxent River, Md., 1954. Commd. 2d lt. USMC, 1943, assigned 4th Marine Aircraft Wing, Marshall Islands campaign, 1944, assigned 9th Marine Aircraft Wing, 1945-46; with 1st Marine Aircraft Wing, North China Patrol, also Guam, 1947-48; flight instr. advanced flight tng. Corpus Christi, 1949-51; asst. G-2/G-3 Amphibious Warfare Sch., Quantico, Va., 1951; with Marine Fighter Squadron 311, exchange pilot 25th Fighter Interceptor Squadron USAF, Korea, 1953; project officer fighter design br. Navy Bur. Aero. Washington, 1956-58; astronaut Project Mercury, Manned Spacecraft Center NASA, 1959-65; pilot Mercury-Atlas 6, 1st orbital space flight launched from Cape Canaveral, Fla., Feb. 1962; ret. as col., 1965; v.p. corp. devel. and dir. Royal Crown Cola Co., 1966-74; pres. Royal Crown Internat.; U.S. senator from Ohio, 1975-99; mem.-at-large Ohio State Dem. Com., 1999—. Mem. Spl. Com. on Aging, Armed Svcs. Com., Senate Dem. Tech. and Comm. Com., Intelligence Com.; ranking minority mem. Govtl. Affairs Com.; vice-chmn. Senate Dem. Policy Com. Co-author: We Seven, 1962; author: P.S., I Listened to Your Heart Beat. Made first supersonic transcontinental flight, July 16, 1957; trustee Muskingum Coll. Decorated D.F.C. (six), Air medal (18); recipient Astronaut medal USMC, Navy unit commendation, Korean Presdl. unit citation, Disting. Merit award Muskingum Coll., Medal of Honor N.Y.C., Congl. Space Medal of Honor, 1978, Centennial awd., Nat. Geographic Soc., 1988, other decorations, awards and hon. degrees. Mem. Soc. Exptl. Test Pilots, Internat. Acad. of Astronautics (hon.) Democrat. Presbyterian. Office: Ohio State U John Glenn Inst 100 Bricker Hall 190 N Oval Mall Columbus OH 43210-1321

GLENNEN, ROBERT EUGENE, JR. retired university president; b. Omaha, Mar. 31, 1933; s. Robert E. and La Verda (Elledge) G.; m. Mary C. O'Brien, Apr. 17, 1958; children: Maureen, Bobby, Colleen, Billy, Barry, Katie, Molly, Kerry A.B., U. Portland, 1955, M.Ed., 1957; Ph.D., U. Notre Dame, 1962. Asst. prof. U. Portland, 1956-60; asst. prof., assoc. prof. Eastern Mont. Coll., Billings, 1962-65; assoc. dean U. Notre Dame, South Bend, Ind., 1965-72; dean, v.p. U. Nev.-Las Vegas, 1972-80; pres. Western N.Mex. U., Silver City, 1980-84, Emporia (Kans.) State U., 1984-97; acting vice-chancellor U. Ark., Montecello, 1999; interim provost U. So. Colo., 1999-2000, interim pres., 2001—. Bd. dirs. Emporia Enterprises; cons. HEW, Washington, 1964-84 Author: Guidance: An Orientation, 1966. Contbr. articles to profl. jours. Pres. PTA, South Bend, Ind., 1970-71; bd. trustees Am. Coll. Testing Corp., Iowa City, 1977-80; chmn. Kans. Regents Coun. of Pres., 1986-87, 92-93, 95-96. Recipient award of excellence Nat. Acad. Advising Assn., Disting. Alumnus award U. Portland, 1993, Kans. Master Tchr. award, 1994; named Coach of Yr., Coach and Athletic mag., 1958, Pub. Adminstr. of Yr., 1994, Athletic Hall of Fame, Portland, 1995; Rotary Paul Harris fellow, 1995, Ford Found. fellow, 1961-62. Mem. Kans. C. of C. (bd. dirs.), Emporia C. of C. Regional Devel. Assn. (bd. dirs., Bank IV), Am. Personnel and Guidance Assn., Am. Assn. State Colls. and Univs. (chair pres's. commn. on tchr. edn.), Am. Assn. Higher Edn., Nev. Personnel and Guidance Assn., Assn. Counselor Educators and Suprs., Am. Assn. Counseling and Devel., Nat. Assn. Student Personnel Adminstrs. Republican. Roman Catholic. Avocations: racketball, walking, reading; hiking.

GLICKMAN, CARL DAVID, banker; b. Cleve., July 29, 1926; s. Jack I. and Dora R. (Rubinowitz) G.; m. Barbara H. Schulman, Oct. 16, 1960; children: Lindsay Dale, David Craig, Robert Todd. Student, U. Minn., 1944, Inst. Fin. Mgmt., Harvard U., 1970. Pres. Glickman Orgn., Cleve., 1953—; chmn. bd., chief exec. officer Computer Research, Inc., Pitts., 1964-67, Am. Steel & Pump Corp., N.Y.C., 1968-71, Shelter Resources Corp., Cleve., 1971-75; pres. Leader Bldg., Inc., 1959—, Capital Bancorp., Cleve., 1971-75, Real Property Corp., Cleve., 1975—; spl. ltd. ptnr. Bear Stearns & Co., 1978-85, dir., 1985—. Chmn. exec. com. Franklin Corp., N.Y.C., 1986-98, Cook United Inc., Cleve., 1986-87, Capital Nat. Bank Cleve., 1970-75, bd. dirs., 1975-80; chmn. bd. dirs. Univ. Nat. Bank, Chgo., 1968-70; ltd. ptnr. S.B. Lewis & Co., N.Y.C., 1980-89; gen. ptnr. Millbrook Assocs., Chester Union Assocs.; founding gen. ptnr. Park Ctrl. Assocs.; pres., bd. dirs. LGT Industries, Durham, N.C., 1987-95; bd. dirs. Royal Petroleum Properties Corp., Jerusalem Econ. Corp., Israel, Custodial Trust Co., Alliance Tyre and Rubber Co., Tel Aviv,Tnuport Ltd., Tel Aviv, Indsl. Structures, Inc., Tel Aviv, Lexington Corp. Properties, N.Y.C., Office Max, Inc., InfoTech, Englewood Cliff, N.J. Mem. Mayor's Com. Urban Renewal, 1965-67; mem. Mayors Task Force on Higher Edn., 1967-69; trustee Cleve. Growth Assn., 1972-75; co-chmn. Herzog Loan Fund Cleve. State U., 1970-76; chmn. Med. Arts Hosp., Houston, 1976-86 ; bd. visitors Case Western Res. Sch. Law; trustee Montefiore Home Aged, Mt. Sinai Hosp.; mem. grievance com. Cleve. Bar Assn., 1982-85; foreman Cuyahoga County Grand Jury, Cleve., 1984-85; trustee Cleve. State U., ARC, 2000—. Served with USAAF, 1944-46. Mem. Am. Bankers Assn., Am. Arbitration Assn. (arbitrator), Phi Sigma Delta, Phi Eta Sigma. Clubs: Beechmont Country, City, Union (Cleve.); Standard (Chgo.); Harmonie, Town (N.Y.C.), Friars, Palm Beach (Fla.) Yacht. Lodge: Masons. Office: 1140 Leader Bldg Cleveland OH 44114 also: 383 Madison Ave New York NY 10167-0002 also: 1 N Breakers Row Palm Beach FL 33480-4021

GLICKMAN, ROBERT JEFFREY, banking executive; b. Mpls., Feb. 10, 1947; s. Joseph Charles and Beverly (Willis) G.; m. Hardye Simons Moel (div. 1983); children: Kate, Adam; m. Caryn Chernick, June 26, 1988. BA, Cornell U., 1969. Pres. River Forest Bancorp, Inc., Chgo., 1969—. Mem. Young Presidents Orgn. Jewish. Office: Corus Bancshares Inc 3959 N Lincoln Ave Chicago IL 60613-2431

GLIDDEN, JOHN REDMOND, lawyer; b. Sanford, Maine, July 24, 1936; s. Kenneth Eugene and Kathryn (Gilpatrick) G.; m. Jacqueline R. Scales, Aug. 6, 1964; children— Ian, Claire, Jason Student, U. Wis., 1954-55; B.S., Coe Coll., 1958; LL.B., U. Iowa, 1961. Bar: Iowa 1961, Ill. 1965. Assoc. firm Williams & Hartzell, Carthage, Ill., 1965-67; ptnr. Hartzell, Glidden, Tucker & Hartzell and predecessor firms, 1969—. City atty. City of Carthage, 1969— Capt., judge advocate USAF, 1961-65. Mem. ABA, Fed. Bar Assn., Ill. Bar Assn., Iowa Bar Assn., Hancock County Bar Assn., Am. Trial Lawyers Assn., Ill. Trial Lawyers Assn. (governing bd. 1973-80), Am. Legion, Carthage Golf Club (bd. dirs. 1967—), Phi Delta Phi, Sigma Nu. Home: PO Box 70 1625 N Highway 94 Carthage IL 62321-3435 Office: PO Box 70 Carthage IL 62321-0070

GLIDDEN, ROBERT BURR, university president, musician, educator; b. Rippey, Iowa, Nov. 29, 1936; s. Burr Harold and Lora Elsie (Groves) Glidden; m. Rene Colete Siefken, Apr. 26, 1964; children: Melissa, Michele, Briana. BA, U. Iowa, 1958, MA, 1960, PhD, 1966. Tchr. instrumental music Morrison Community High Sch., Ill., 1958-63, Univ. Schs., Iowa City, 1963-66; asst. prof. music Wright State U., Dayton, Ohio, 1966-67, Ind. U., Bloomington, 1967-69; also asst. dir. bands, 1969-72; assoc. prof. music U. Okla., Norman; dir. grad. studies in music, exec. dir. Nat. Assn. Schs. Music, Washington, 1972-75, treas., 1977-82, v.p., 1982-85, pres., 1985-88; dean Coll. Musical Arts, Bowling Green State U., Ohio, 1975-79; dean Sch. Music Fla. State U., Tallahassee, 1979-91, provost, v.p. for acad. affairs, 1991-94; pres. Ohio U., Athens, 1994—. Cons., higher edn., condr.; chmn. Coun. Specialized Accrediting Agys., 1976—77; chair Am. Coun. Edn. Commn. Leadership and Instnl. Effectiveness, 1998—2000; chair coun. pres. Mid-Am. Conf., 1997—99. Bd. dirs. Coun. on Postsecondary Accreditation, 1977—84, exec. com., 1979—84, chmn., 1981—83; bd. dirs. Arts, Edn. and Ams., Inc., 1978—81; chmn. advanced placement music com. Coll. Bd., 1977—79; mem. Coun. on Arts Task Force on Edn. Tng. and Devel. Profl. Artists and Art Educators, 1977—78; mem. adv. coun. on accreditation Nat. League for Nursing, 1977—81; mem. edn. adv. com. Nat. Endowment for Arts, 1987, adv. com. for arts in edn., 1989—90. Mem.: Ohio Inter-Univ. Coun. (chair 2001—02), Ohio Campus Compact (exec. com. 2000—), Ohio Aerospace Inst. 1995—, (chair 1998—2000), Ohio Supercomputer Ctr. (governing bd. 1996—), Ohio Higher Edn. Funding Commn., Ohio Sci. and Tech. Coun. (biotech. com.), So. Assn. Colls. and Schs. (commn. on coll. 1993—94), Coun. for Higher Edn. Accreditation (chair bd. dirs. 1996—98), Assn. Specialized and Profl. Accreditors (bd. dirs. 1994—96), Coll. Music Soc. (chmn. govt. rels. com. 1976—78, task force on edn. coll. music tchrs. 1987), Mortar Bd., Pi Kappa Lamda (nat. v.p. 1979—81, pres. 1981—85), Omicron Delta Kappa, Phi Kappa Phi, Phi Beta Kappa. Episcopalian. Home: 29 Park Pl Athens OH 45701-2910 Office: Ohio Univ Cutler Hall Athens OH 45701-2979 E-mail: gliddenr@ohio.edu.

GLIEBERMAN, HERBERT ALLEN, lawyer; b. Chgo., Dec. 6, 1930; s. Elmer and Jean (Gerber) G.; m. Evelyn Eraci; children— Ronald, Gale, Joel Student, U. Ill., 1947, Roosevelt U., 1948-50; J.D., Chgo. Kent Coll. Law, 1953. Bar: Ill. 1954, D.C. 1987. Pvt. practice, Chgo., 1954—; lectr. Chgo. Kent. Coll. Law, Ill. Inst. Continuing Legal Edn. Lectr. in field. Author: Some Syndromes of Love, 1965, Know Your Legal Rights, 1974, Confessions of A Divorce Lawyer, 1975, Closed Marriage, 1978, Four Weekends to an Ideal Marriage, 1981; former host 2 radio shows for NBC Sta. WMAQ: Ask the Lawyer, Law and Controversy; contbr. articles to profl. jours. Former trustee Chgo. Kent. Coll. Law; former bd. dirs. Chgo. Coun. on Alcoholism. Mem. Am. Acad. Matrimonial Lawyers (cert. of appreciation 1967), Decologue Soc. Lawyers (cert. of appreciation 1965, 66, 68), Assn. Trial Lawyers Am. (cert. of appreciation 1973), Ill. Trial Lawyers Assn. (cert. of appreciation 1974), ABA, Ill. State Bar Assn., Chgo. Bar Assn. Jewish (bd. dirs., pres. Temple) Home: 180 E Pearson St Chicago IL 60611-2130 Office: 19 S La Salle St Chicago IL 60603-1401 Fax: (312) 236-3417. E-mail: hglieber@gateway.net.

GLOVER, JAMES TODD, manufacturing company executive; b. Aberdeen, S.D., Apr. 30, 1939; s. Fay and Vi (Bruns) G.; m. Joann Elizabeth House; children: Jason, Jeffrey, Jamie. Student, S.D. State U.; BS in Math., No. State Coll., Aberdeen, 1961. Inside sales engr. Aberdeen Ops. Safeguard, 1961-64, asst. sales engr., 1965-67, mktg. mgr., 1968-72, gen. mgr., 1973-77; v.p. ops. Safeguard PowerTech Systems, Aberdeen, 1978-83, exec. v.p., 1984-85, pres., 1986-89; pres., chief exec. officer, chief ops. officer, dir. Hub City, Inc., 1989—. Officer Safeguard Sci. Co., Inc.; v.p. corp. devel. Regal-Beloit (Wis.) Corp., 1990-93; v.p. HQ Cos., Mpls., 1993-98, gen. mgr. Pixall Ltd. Partnership, Clear Lake, Wis., 1993-98; pres. JTG Solicitors, Inc., Peoria, Ariz., 1998--. Bd. mem. S.D. Swimming Assn.; S.D. Dist. Export Council. Export Devel. Authority; bd. dirs. No. State Found., James River Water Devel.; bd. mem., chmn. James River Water Devel. Dist. Recipient Ernie Gunderson award S.D. Swimming Assn. Mem. Power Transmission Distbrs. Assn. (past bd. dirs., past chmn. allied adv. bd.), Power Transmission Rep. Assn. (past bd. dirs., past chmn. allied adv. bd.), Aberdeen C. of C., S.D. Mfrs. Assn. (past dir.). Republican. Roman Catholic. Avocations: hunting, fishing, music.

GLOYD, LAWRENCE EUGENE, retired diversified manufacturing company executive; b. Milan, Nov. 5, 1932; s. Oran C. and Ruth (Baylor) G.; m. Delma Lear, Sept. 10, 1955; children: Sheryl, Julia, Susan. BA, Hanover Coll., 1954, Hon, D in Bus. Adminstrn., 1994; Hon. D, Rockford

Coll., 1999. Salesman Shapleigh Hardware, St. Louis, 1956-60, W. Bingham Co., Cleve., 1960-61, Amerock Corp., Rockford, Ill., 1961-68, regional sales mgr., 1968-69, dir. consumer products mktg., 1969-71, dir. merchandising, 1971-72, dir. mktg. and sales, 1972-73, v.p. mktg. and sales, 1973-81, exec. v.p., 1982—86, pres., gen. mgr., 1982-86; v.p. Hardware Products Group, Anchor Hocking Corp., Lancaster, Ohio, 1986—88; pres., COO, CEO CLARCOR, Rockford, Ill., 1988—2000, chmn. bd., CEO, 1988-2000, also bd. dirs., chmn. emeritus, 2000—. Bd. dirs. Amcore Fin. Inc., Rockford, Thomas Industries Inc., Louisville, Woodward Gov. Co., Rockford, Ill., Genyte Thomas Group, Louisville, Group Dekko, Kendalville, Ind.; past. chmn. bd. trustees Rockford Coll.; bd. dirs., past chmn. SwedishAm. Corp. Past chmn. bd. dirs. Coun. of 100; past mem. bd. dirs. Ill. Coun. on Econ. Edn.; nat. bd. dirs. Big Bros./Big Sisters; bd. trustees Hanover (Ind.) Coll. Recipient Master Entrpreneur of Yr. Ill./N.W. Ind. award Ernst & Young, 1999, Lambda Chi Alpha Nat. Order Achievement award, 1999, Alumni Achievement award Hanover Coll., 1994. Mem. Am. Hardware Mfrs. Assn., Ill. Mfrs. Assn., Nat. Assn. Mfrs., Hardware Group Assn., Pres. Assn., Masons. Republican. Office: Clarcor Inc 6367 Sebring Way Loves Park IL 61111

GNAT, RAYMOND EARL, librarian; b. Milw., Jan. 15, 1932; s. John and Emily (Syperek) Gnat; m. Jean Helen Monday, June 19, 1954; children: Barbara, Richard. BBA, U. Wis., 1954, postgrad., 1959; MS, U. Ill., 1958; MPA, Ind. U., Indpls., 1981. Page Milw. Pub. Libr., 1950-53, jr. libr., 1954, librarian, 1958-63; circulation asst. U. Ill., 1956-57, serials cataloger, 1957-58; asst. dir. Indpls.-Marion County Pub. Libr., 1963-71, dir., 1972-94. Exec. dir. Ind. Nat. Libr. Week, 1965. Mem.: ALA, Bibliog. Soc. Am., Ind. Libr. Assn. (pres. 1980), Portfolio Club, Lit. Club. Home: 8246 Shadow Cir Indianapolis IN 46260-2761

GO, ROBERT A. management consultant; b. July 29, 1955; s. Michael and Sabina (Tan) G. BS, U Detriot, 1977; MBA, U. Santa Clara, 1981. Ptnr. Deloitte & Touche (formerly Touche Ross & Co.), Detroit, 1977—. Contbr. articles to profl. jours. Mem. Health Care Fin. Mgt. Assn., Am. Hosp. Assn., Renaissance Club. Office: Deloitte & Touche 600 Renaissance Ctr Fl 10 Detroit MI 48243-1804

GODDU, ROGER, retail executive; b. Springfield, Mass., June 23, 1950; m. Kate Goddu; 5 children. Student, Adrian Coll., U. Toledo; grad., Harvard Bus. Exec. Program, 1995. Mdse. adminstr. LaSalle and Koch divsn. R.H. Macy & Co., 1970-75; v.p., gen. mdse. mgr. Rikes/Lazarus Dept. Stores, 1975-80; mdse. mgr. Dayton Hudson divsn. Target Stores, 1980-83, v.p. Dayton Hudson divsn., 1983-85, sr. v.p., gen. mdse. mgr. Dayton Hudson divsn., 1985-89; exec. v.p., gen. mdse. mgr. Toys R Us, Paramus, N.J., 1989-95, pres. U.S. merchandising, 1996-97; chmn., CEO Montgomery Ward, LLC, Chgo., 1997—. Dir. Kids in Distressed Situations, Project Pride in Living, Mpls.; founder The Nat. Conf., Bergen County, N.J. Office: Montgomery Ward LLC 535 W Chicago Ave Chicago IL 60671-0001

GODFREY, MAURICE, biomedical scientist; b. Addis Ababa, Ethiopia, June 11, 1956; s. Robert and Liliana (Gandolfi) G.; m. Matilde Elena Almeida, July 5, 1985; children: C. Maximilian, R. Alessandro, D. Guillermo. BS, Monmouth Coll., 1977; MS, Columbia U., 1980, M in Philosophy, 1983, PhD, 1986. Postdoctoral fellow Oreg. Health Sci. U., Shrine Hosp., Portland, 1986-89; assoc. prof. pediatrics, dir. connective tissue lab. U. Nebr. Med. Ctr., Omaha, 1990—. Author: (with others) McKusick's Heritable Disorders of Connective Tissue, 1993, The Metabolic Basis of Inherited Disease, 1995; contbr. articles to profl. jours. Recipient grant-in-aid Am. Heart Assn., 1989, 93; Basil O'Connor scholar March of Dimes, 1991; established investigator Am. Heart Assn., 1995. Mem. AAAS, Am. Soc. of Human Genetics, Am. Fedn. for Clin. Rsch., Basic Sci. Coun. of the Am. Heart Assn. Achievements include co-discovery of fibrillin gene the cause of the Marfan syndrome. Office: UNMC Dept Pediatrics 982168 Nebr Med Ctr Omaha NE 68198-0001 also: Nat Marfan Found 382 Main St Port Washington NY 11050-3136

GODFREY, ROBERT GORDON, physician; b. Wichita, Kans., June 11, 1927; s. Henry Robert and Pearl Madeline (Gaston) G.; m. Margaret Scott Ingling, June 24, 1951; children: Timothy, Katherine, Gwendolyn, Melissa. B.A., U. Wichita, 1952; M.D., U. Kans., 1958. Intern Boston City Hosp., 1958-59; resident in internal medicine Peter Bent Brigham Hosp., Boston, 1959-60, Colo. Gen. Hosp., Denver, 1961-63; asst. in medicine Peter Bent and Robert Brigham Hosp.-Harvard Med. Sch., 1959-61; fellow in rheumatology Robert B. Brigham Hosp., 1960-61, U. Colo., Denver, 1963-64; instr. medicine U. Kans. Med. Ctr., Kansas City, 1964-65, asst. prof. med., 1965-95, staff physician, chief arthritis sect., 1965-75; ret., 1995; assoc. chief of staff for ambulatory care VA Med Ctr., Kansas City, Mo., 1978-80; staff physician, sr. rheumatologist VA Med. Ctr., 1980-84; chief rheumatology sect., assoc. chief med. service ambulatory care Leavenworth VA Med. Ctr., Kans., 1984-88; cons. rheumatology Physicians Associated, Overland Park, 1988-93; pvt. cons. rheumtology, 1995—. Served with M.C., U.S. Army, 1945-47. Recipient Disting. Service award Kans. Arthritis Found., 1975 Fellow ACP, Am. Coll. Rheumatology (founding fellow original Am. Rheumatism Assn.); mem. Am. Soc. Clin. Rheumatology, Sigma Xi, Alpha Omega Alpha. Republican Office: U Kans Med Ctr Divsn Allergy Clin Immunol Rheumatol 3901 Rainbow Blvd Kansas City KS 66160-0001 E-mail: rgodfrey@sound.net.

GODFREY, WILLIAM ASHLEY, ophthalmologist; b. Arkansas City, Kans., May 19, 1938; BA, U. Kans., Lawrence, 1960; MD, U. Kans., Kansas City, 1965. Diplomate Am. Bd. Ophthalmology. Intern Tulane U., New Orleans, 1965-66; resident U. Kans. Sch. Medicine, 1968-71; rsch. fellow U. Calif., San Francisco, 1971-73; asst. prof., then assoc. prof. U. Kans. Sch. Medicine, 1973-84, prof. ophthalmology, 1984—. Mem. staff St. Luke's Hosp., Kansas City, Mo., 1973— , Kansas U. Med. Ctr., Kansas City, 1973— ; cons. Kansas City Vets Hosp., Mo., 1973-89. Contbr. articles to profl. publs. With USAF, 1966-68. NIH fellow, 1971-73. Fellow ACP, Am. Acad. Ophthalmology (honor ward 1983), Am. Uveitis Soc.; mem. Am. COll. Physicians, AMA, Am. Fedn. Clin. Rsch., Am. Rheumatism Assn., Assn. Rsch. in Vision and Ophthalmology, Am. Math. Soc., Ocular Immunology and Microbiology Soc., Kansas City Soc. Ophthalmology, Kans. Med. Soc., Mo. Ophthalmology Soc., Jackson County Med. Soc., Am. Ophthal. Soc., Wyandotte County Med. Soc., Johnson County Med. Soc., Soc. Heed Fellows, Assn. Proctor Fellows, Kans. Ophthal. Soc., Alpha Omega Alpha. Office: Hunkeler Vision Ctr 4321 Washington St Ste 6000 Kansas City MO 64111-5933

GODICH, JOHN PAUL, federal magistrate judge; b. Indpls., Nov. 30, 1944; m. Suzanne Steffen Geringer, Sept. 7, 1974. AB cum laude, Princeton U., 1966; JD, Yale U., 1969. Assoc. Barnes Hickam Pantzer & Boyd (now Barnes & Thornburg), Ind., 1971-73; law clk. U.S. Dist. Ct. (so. dist.) Ind., 1969-71; chief U.S. magistrate judge U.S. Dist. Ct. (so. dist.) Inc., 1973—, chief magistrate judge, 1986. Apptd. to Jud. Conf. U.S. com. Adminstrn. U.S. Magistrate Judges, 1987, 90, com. Local Rules so. dist. Ind., 1989—, com. to Implement Civil Justice Reform Act, 1991—; chmn. Fed. Jud. Ctr. advanced seminar for U.S. Magistrate Judges, Warren, Vt., 1991, Orientation seminar Newly Apptd. U.S. Magistrates, 1988. Mem. bd. editors Yale Law Jour., 1967-69. Mem. ABA, FBA, Am. Judicature Soc., Ind. State Bar Assn., Indpls. Bar Assn., Fed. Magistrate Judges Assn., 7th Cir. Bar Assn. (mem. edn. com. 1991—, ad hoc com. on high cost of litigation, 1978-79), Phi Beta Kappa. Office: US Dist Ct Rm 230 US Courthouse 46 E Ohio St Indianapolis IN 46204-1903

GODINER, DONALD LEONARD, lawyer; b. Bronx, N.Y., Feb. 21, 1933; s. Israel and Edith (Rubenstein) G.; m. Caryl Mignon Nussbaum, Sept. 7, 1958; children: Clifford, Kenneth. AB, NYU, 1953; JD, Columbia U., 1956. Bar: N.Y. 1956, Mo. 1972. Gen. counsel Stromberg-Carlson, Rochester, N.Y., 1965-71; assoc. gen. counsel Gen. Dynamics Corp., St. Louis, 1971-73; v.p., gen. counsel Permaneer Corp., 1973-75; ptnr. Gallop, Johnson, Godiner, Morganstern & Crebs, 1975-80; sr. v.p., gen. counsel, sec. Laclede Gas Co., 1980-98; of counsel Stone, Leyton and Gershman, P.C., 1999—. Editor Columbia U. Law Rev., 1955-56. Served with U.S. Army, 1956-58. Mem.: Assn. of Bar of City of N.Y., ABA. Home: 157 Trails West Dr Chesterfield MO 63017-2553 Office: Stone Leyton & Gershman PC 7133 Forsyth Blvd Ste 500 Saint Louis MO 63105-2122

GODWIN, HAROLD NORMAN, pharmacist, educator; b. Ransom, Kans., Oct. 9, 1941; s. Harold Joseph and Nora Elva (Welsh) G.; m. Judy Rae Ricketts, June 9, 1963; children: Paula Lynn, Jennifer Joy. BS in Pharmacy, U. Kans., 1964; MS in Hosp. Pharmacy, Ohio State U., 1966. Lic. pharmacist, Kans., Ohio. Instr. Ohio State U. Coll. Pharmacy, Columbus, 1966-69; asst. dir. pharmacy Ohio State U., 1966-69; dir. pharmacy U. Kans. Med. Ctr., Kansas City, 1969—; asst. prof. U. Kans. Sch. Pharmacy, 1969-74, assoc. prof., 1974-80, prof. pharmacy, 1980—, asst. dean pharmacy, 1975-89, assoc. dean pharmacy, 1989—, chmn. pharmacy practice, 1984—. John W. Webb lectr., vis. prof. Northeastern U., 1999; chmn. pharmacy exec. com. H. HealthSys. Consortium, 2001—. Author: Implementation Guide to IV Admixtures, 1977; (with others) Remington's Pharmaceutical Sciences, 1980, 85, 90, 95, 2000; contbr. over 100 articles to profl. jours. Bd. dirs. Rsch. and Edn. Found., 2002—. Recipient Clifton J. Latiolais award Ohio State U. Residents Alumni, 1986, Disting. Alumni award Ohio State U. Coll. Pharmacy, 1995; named Tchr. of the Yr., U. Kans. Sch. of Pharmacy, 2001. Fellow: Am. Soc. Hosp. Pharmacists (bd. dirs. 1978—81, pres. 1982—83, Harvey A.K. Whitney award 1991); mem.: Am. Coun. Pharm. Edn. (bd. dirs. 1988—2000, pres. 1992—96), Greater Kansas City Soc. Hosp. Pharmacists 1972, Kans. Soc. Hosp. Pharmacists (Kans. Hosp. Pharmacist of Yr. 1982, Harold N. Godwin award 1984), Kans. Pharmacists Assn. (pres 1977, Kans. Pharmacist of Yr. 1982), Am. Pharm. Assn. (Disting. Achievement award 2000). Republican. Methodist. Avocations: tennis, biking, cooking, wine tasting. Home: 10112 W 98th St Shawnee Mission KS 66212-5238 Office: U Kans Med Ctr Rainbow Blvd At 39th St Kansas City KS 66106-7231

GOEBEL, JOHN J. lawyer, director; b. St. Charles, Mo., Feb. 3, 1930; s. Francis Joseph and Elizabeth (Lawler) G.; m. Margaret Mary Rooney, May 10, 1958; children— Laura, Margaret, John, Matthew B.S., LL.B., St. Louis U., 1953. Bar: Mo. 1953, U.S. Dist. Ct. (ea. dist.) Mo. 1957. Jr. exec. Constrn. Escrow Service Inc., St. Louis, 1955-56; jr. ptnr. Bryan Cave LLP, 1956-66, ptnr., 1966-98, sr. counsel, 1998—. Bd. dirs. Stifel Fin. Corp., St. Louis. Served to 1st lt. USAF, 1953-55 Mem. ABA, St. Louis Bar Assn., Mo. Bar Assn., Bellerive Country Club, Noonday Club, Port Royal Club. Roman Catholic. Home: 245 Little Harbour Ln Naples FL 34102-7606 Office: Bryan Cave 1 Metropolitan Sq Ste 3600 Saint Louis MO 63102-2750 E-mail: jjgoebel@bryancavellp.com.

GOEDERT, RAYMOND E. bishop; b. Oct. 15, 1927; Ordained priest Roman Cath. Ch., 1952. Consecrated bishop, 1991; aux. bishop Archdiocese of Chgo., 1991—. Office: 155 E Superior St Chicago IL 60611-2911

GOEHNER, DONNA MARIE, retired university dean; b. Chgo., Mar. 9, 1941; d. Robert and Elizabeth (Cseke) Barra; m. George Louis Goehner, Dec. 16, 1961; 1 child, Michelle Renee. BS in English, So. Ill. U., 1963; MSLS, U. Ill., 1966, CAS in L.S., 1974; PhD in Edn., So. Ill. U., 1983. Rsch. assoc. U. Ill., Urbana, 1966-67; high sch. librarian St. Joseph-Ogden Sch. System, St. Joseph, Ill., 1967-68; curriculum lab librarian Western Ill. U., Macomb, 1968-73, periodicals librarian, 1974-76, coordinator for tech. svcs., 1977-78, acquisitions and collection devel. librarian, 1979-86, acting dir. library, 1986, dean library svcs., 1988-97; assoc. Univ. librarian for tech. and adminstrv. svcs. Ill. State U., Normal, 1986-88; ret., 1998. Contbr. articles to profl. jours. Mem. ALA, Assn. Coll. and Rsch. Libraries (chmn. univ. libraries sect. 1988-89), Ill. Assn. Coll. and Rsch. Libraries (pres. 1985-86), Ill. Library Assn. (Acad.Librarian of Yr. 1989). Home: 1001 Wigwam Hollow Rd Macomb IL 61455-1035 Office: Univ Library Western Ill U Macomb IL 61455

GOETSCH, ROBERT GEORGE, state legislator; b. Juneau, Wis., Aug. 5, 1933; 010s. Elmer Allen and Dorothy (Stein) G.; m. Carolyn Helen Koboski, 1974; children: Chad Evan, Shana Renee. BS, U. W. Madison, 1975. Farmer, Juneau; mem. from dist. 39 Wis. State Assembly, Madison, 1982—. Exch. del. to Rhodesia, Internat. Farm Youth Exch., 1962-63; county supr., Dodge County, Wis., 1972-83; chmn. Town of Oak Grove, Wis., 1971-82. Mem. Nat. Farmers Orgn., Am. Legion, Elks, Phi Kappa Phi. Home: N6485 High Point Rd Juneau WI 53039-9750 Office: State Capitol 314 North St Madison WI 53704-4921

GOETSCHEL, ARTHUR W. industrial manufacturing executive; Treas. Griffin Wheel; pres. Griffin Wheel & Griffin Can., Chgo., 1991-95; corp. v.p. Amstead, 1995-97; pres. Amstead Industries, 1997—; chmn., CEO Amstead Industries Inc., Chgo., 1999—. Office: Amstead Industries Inc 205 N Michigan Ave Chicago IL 60601

GOETTSCH, KIRK E. lawyer; b. Holstein, Iowa, July 21, 1960; BS, Iowa State U., 1982; JD, Drake U., 1985. Bar: Iowa, U.S. Tax Ct, U.S. Dist. Ct. (no. and so. dists.) Iowa. Ptnr. Clark Hasting, Ames, Iowa, 1985-90, Forristal & Goettsch, Holstein, 1990—. Part-time county atty., Holstein, 1990—. Chmn. Story County Rep. Party, 1988, del. state convention; active local Evangelical Ch. Mem. Holstein C. of C., Holstein Country Club, Holstein Cmty. Club. Avocations: golf, computers. Office: Forristal & Goettsch PO Box 160 Holstein IA 51025-0160

GOETZ, WILLIAM G. state legislator; b. Hazen, N.D., Jan. 6, 1944; s. Otto E. and Elfrieda (Knoop) G.; m. Marion R. Schock, 1970; children: Marcia, Paul, Mark. AA, Bismarck Jr. Coll., 1964; BA, Minot State Coll., 1966; MA, U. N.D., 1967. Asst. mgr. Medora divsn. Gold Seal Co., 1963-70; dean sch. bus. and adminstrn. Dickinson State U., 1967; state rep. dist. 37, 1975-90; state senator, 1990-97; chief of staff for gov. of N.D. Dickenson, N.D., 1997—. Chmn. Rep. Ho. Caucus; asst. majority leader, vice chmn. fin. and tax. com. N.D. Ho. Reps., 1975-90; asst. minority leader; mem. appropriations com., asst. majority leader N.D. State Senate, 1990—. Chmn. dist. 37 Rep. com., 1976—, mem. exec. com.; appointed by pres. to Nat. Coun. for Edn. Rsch. and Improvement. Recipient Pub. Svc. award N.D. Lignite Coun. Mem. Greater N.D. Assn. (formerly bd. dirs., Educator of Yr.), Nat. Conf. State Legislators. Republican. Home: 3642 Hackberry St Bismarck ND 58503-0299

GOETZMAN, BRUCE EDGAR, architecture educator; b. Rochester, June 6, 1931; s. Benjamin Byron and Illa Flowers G.; m. Jane Grady McRae,June 25, 1955; children: Adam Brit, Ben Evan. BArch, Carnegie Mellon U., 1954; MS in Architecture, Columbia U., 1956; M in Cmty. Planning, U. Cin., 1965; postgrad., U. London, 1968. Asst. prof. Univ. Cin., 1956-66; prin. Bruce Goetzman & Assocs., Cin., 1965-77; acting chmn. grad. div. Univ. Cin., 1966-67, assoc. prof., 1967-99; prof. emeritus, 1999; ptnr. Goetzman & Follmer Architects, Cin., 1977-85; prin. Bruce Goetzman, Restoration Architect, 1985--. Trustee Miami Purchase Assn. Hist. Preservation, Cin., 1972-91, Ohio Hist. Sites Preservation Adv. Bd., 1980-92; trustee Ohio Hist. Soc., 1986-96, pres., 1995-96; pres. Ohio Preservation Alliance, 1986-88; trustee Cin. Preservation Assn., 1993-2000. Mem.: AIA, Assn. Preservation Tech., Architects Soc. Ohio, Cincinnatus Assn. Democrat. Home: 187 Greendale Ave Cincinnati OH 45220-1223

GOFF, WILMER SCOTT, retired photographer; b. Steubenville, Ohio, July 11, 1923; s. Floyd Orville and Ellen Armenia (Funk) G.; m. Mary Elizabeth Fischer, Dec. 7, 1950; children: Carolyn, Christopher. BFA with honors, Ohio U., 1949. Photographer Columbus (Ohio) Dispatch, 1949-52, Warner P. Simpson, Columbus, 1952-53; owner Willy Goff Photo Studio, Grove City, Ohio, 1954-59; photographer N.Am. Rockwell, Columbus, 1953-70; supr. Transp. Rsch. Ctr. Ohio, East Liberty, 1970-89; adult edn. instr. photography Upper Arlington and Worthington Schs., 1989-99. Photography instr. Columbus Coll. Art and Design, 1949-71; photography judge Ohio State Fair, 1966-68; judge Greater Columbus Film Festival, 1970-72; photographer John Glenn campaign, 1974. One man shows include 100 print exhibit Southern Hotel, Columbus, 1953. Recipient Public's Choice award Columbus Art Gallery, 1958, Photo-Pictoral 1st Pl. award Dix Newspapers, 1960, Best of Show award Balloon Show Competition, 1985. Mem. Aircraft Camera Club (pres. 1954-55), Grove City Camera CLub (pres. 1959-60). Republican. Roman Catholic. Avocations: stamp collecting, recording, cycling. Home: 6110 Darby Ln Columbus OH 43229-2628

GOFFMAN, WILLIAM, mathematician, educator; b. Cleve., Jan. 28, 1924; s. Sam and Mollie (Stein) G.; m. Patricia McLoughlin, Feb. 7, 1964. B.S., U. Mich., 1950, Ph.D., 1954. Math. cons., 1954-59; research asso. prof. Case Western Res. U., Cleve., 1959-71; dean Case Western Res. U. (Sch. Library Sci.), 1971-77; dir. Case Western Res. U. (Complex Systems Inst.), 1972-75. Contbr. numerous publs. to sci. jours. Served with USAAF, 1943-46. Recipient research grants NSF, research grants NIH, research grants USAF, research grants others. Fellow AAAS Home: 2 Bratenahl Pl Bratenahl OH 44108-1183 Office: Case Western Res Univ Cleveland OH 44106

GOINS, FRANCES FLORIANO, lawyer; b. Buffalo, Jan. 30, 1950; d. William and Anita (Graziano) Floriano; m. Gary Mitchell Goins; children: Matthew W., Mark W. MusB, Cleve. Inst. Music, 1971; MusM, Case Western Res. U., 1973, JD, 1977. Bar: Ohio 1977, U.S. Dist. Ct. Ohio 1978, U.S. Ct. Appeals (6th cir.) 1979, N.Y. 1984, U.S. Ct. Appeals (2d cir.) 1984. Law clk to Hon. Frank J. Battisti U.S. Dist. Ct. (no. dist.) Ohio, Cleve., 1977-78; ptnr. Squire, Sanders & Dempsey, 1986—. Mem. vis. com. bd. overseers Case Western Res. U., Cleve., 1984-2000; faculty Nat. Inst. Trial Advocacy, Cleve.; faculty, lectr. trial advocacy seminar Cleve. State U. Sch. Law, 1989-90. Editor-in-chief law rev. Case Western Res. Sch. Law, 1976-77. Trustee, chairperson devel. com. Lyric Opera Cleve., 1985-92; founding trustee Shoreby Club Cleve.; v.p. bd. trustees Bay Village Montessori Sch., 1994-96. Mem. ABA (bus. law sect., bus. lit. com., subcom. on corporate governance 1995—, fed. regulation of securities com., subcom. on civil litigation and SEC enforcement matters 1992—), Ohio Women's Bar Assn. (founding mem.), Ohio State Bar Assn. (ad hoc com. on bus. cts. 1994-99), Cleve. Bar Assn. (com. on women and the law 1987-2000, ethics com. 1988-90, securities law inst., jud. selection com. 1996-2001). Democrat. Roman Catholic. Office: Squire Sanders & Dempsey 4900 Key Tower 127 Public Sq Ste 4900 Cleveland OH 44114-1304

GOLAN, STEPHEN LEONARD, lawyer; b. Chgo., Oct. 22, 1951; s. Leonard Walter and Carol (Pepper) G.; m. Sharon D. Robson, Aug. 16, 1980; children: Brianna, Jenna, Melissa. BA, Claremont (Calif.) Men's Coll., 1974; MBA, JD, Northwestern U., 1978. Bar: Ill. 1978, U.S. Dist. Ct. (no. dist.) Ill. 1978, U.S. Ct. Appeals (7th cir.) 1993. Ptnr. Seyfarth, Shaw, Fairweather & Geraldson, Chgo., 1978-93; founding ptnr. Field & Golan, 1993—. Mem. ABA, AICPA, Nat. Assn. JD-MBA Profls. (bd. dirs. 1984-86), Ill. Bar Assn., Chgo. Bar Assn., Tavern Club (mem. jr. com. 1984-86), Exmoor Country Club (Highland Park, Ill.), Lake Forest Caucus. Republican. Episcopalian. Office: Field & Golan 15th Fl 3 First National Plz Chicago IL 60602 E-mail: slgolan@fieldgolan.com.

GOLD, CAROL R. dean, nursing educator; PhD, Northwestern U. Assoc. prof., acting dean Marcella Nieff Sch. Nursing Loyola U., Chgo. Contbr. articles to profl. jours. Mem. ANA, Am. Acad. of Ambulatory Care Nursing, Ill. Nurses Assn., Sigma Theta Tau Internat. Office: Loyola U Chgo Niehoff Sch Nursing 6525 N Sheridan Rd Chicago IL 60626-5344

GOLD, EDWARD DAVID, lawyer; b. Detroit, Jan. 17, 1941; s. Morris and Hilda (Robinson) Gold; m. Francine Sheila Kamin, Jan. 8, 1967; children: Lorne Brian, Karen Beth. Student, Wayne State U., 1958-61; JD, Detroit Coll. Law, 1964. Bar: Mich. 1965, U.S. Dist. Ct. (ea. dist.) Mich. 1965, U.S. Ct. Appeals (6th cir.) 1965, D.C. 1966. Atty. gen. counsel FCC, Washington, 1965-66; ptnr. Conn, Conn & Gold, Detroit, 1966-67, May, Conn, Conn & Gold, Livonia, 1967-69, Hyman, Gurwin, Nachman, Gold & Alterman, Southfield, 1971-88, Butzel Long, Bloomfield Hills, 1988—. Mem. Oakland County Criminal Justice Coordinating Coun., 1976—77; chmn. Freind Ct. Adv. Com., Lansing, Mich., 1982—88; contbr. lectr. Inst. Continuing Legal Edn., Ann Arbor, Mich., 1981—, Mich. Trial Lawyers Assn.; adj. prof. U. Detroit Mercy Sch. Law, 2001—. Author: (book) Michigan Family Law, 1988; contbr. articles to legal jours. Mem. Southfield Transp. Commn., 1975—77; chairperson atty. disp. bd. Tri-County Hearin Panel 71, 1994—2002; chmn. attys.' divsn. Jewish Welfare Fedn., Detroit; mem. nat. young leadership cabinet United Jewish Appeal, N.Y.C., 1978—80; pres. Jewish Family Svc., Detroit, 1988—90; bd. dirs. Oakland County Legal Aid Soc., 1979—84. Scholar Tau Epsilon Rho, 1963. Fellow: Am. Acad. Matrimonial Lawyers (bd. dirs. 1988—93, pres. Mich. chpt. 1992—93, nat. bd. govs. 1988—2001, nat. v.p. 2001—), Am. Coll. Family Trial Lawyers; mem.: Am. Arbitration Assn., Bar Assn. D.C., Southfield Bar Assn. (pres. 1975—76), Oakland County Bar Assn. (bd. dirs. 1984—93, pres. 1992—93), Mich. Bar Assn. (coun. real property law sect. 1973—81, coun. family law sect. 1974—75, 1977—82, chmn. family law sect. 1981—82, rep. assembly 1978—82, Lifetime Achievement award), Alpha Epsilon Pi (nat. pres. 1976—77, Order of Lion award 1986). Avocation: golf. Office: Butzel Long Ste 200 100 Bloomfield Hills Pkwy Bloomfield Hills MI 48304 E-mail: Gold@Butzel.com.

GOLD, GERALD SEYMOUR, lawyer; b. Cleve., Feb. 2, 1931; s. David N. and Geraldine (Bloch) G.; 1 child, Anne; m. Rosemary Grdina, 1994. AB, Case-Western Res. U., 1951, LLB, 1954. Bar: Ohio 1954, U.S. Supreme Ct. 1961. Practiced in, Cleve., 1954-60; chief asst. legal aid defender Cuyahoga County, 1960-61, chief legal aid defender, 1961-65; assoc. Ulmer, Byrne, Laronge, Glickman & Curtis, Cleve., 1965-66; ptnr. Gold, Rotatori, Schwartz & Gibbons, 1966—. Instr. in law Case-Western Res. U., 1965-66, Cleve. State Law Sch., 1968-69, Case-Western Res. Law-Medicine Center, 1961-77; lectr. to bar assns. commr. Cuyahoga County Pub. Defender, 1977-81. Contbg. author: American Jurisprudence Trials, 1966; Contbr. articles to law revs. Fellow Am. Coll. Trial Lawyers, Am. Bd. Criminal Lawyers, Ohio State Bar Found., Internat. Soc. Barristers; mem. ABA (criminal justice coun.), Cuyahoga County Criminal Ct. Bar Assn. (chmn., Lifetime Achievement award 1995), Ohio Bar Assn. (chmn. criminal law sect. 1974-78, ho. of dels. 1986—), Greater Cleve. Bar Assn. (Merit award 1974, trustee 1978—, pres. 1982-83), Nat. Assn. Criminal Def. Lawyers (pres. 1977, Merit award 1975), Ohio Acad. Trial Lawyers (chmn. criminal law sect. 1970-75), Ohio Assn. Criminal Def. Lawyers (bd. dirs. 1990), Case-Western Res. U. Law Alumni Assn. (pres. 1974-75, Outstanding Alumnus award 1991), Soc. Benchers, Court of Nisi Prius Club, Cleve. Skating Club. Home: 33000 Pinetree Rd Pepper Pike OH 44124-5514 Office: 1500 Leader Bldg Cleveland OH 44124-3337

GOLD, PAUL ERNEST, psychology educator, behavioral neuroscience educator; b. Detroit, Jan. 7, 1945; s. Hyman and Sylvia Gold; children: Scott David Gold, Zachary Alexander Korol-Gold. BA, U. Mich., 1966; MS, U. N.C., 1968; PhD, 1971. NIH postdoctoral fellow, lectr. psychobiology U. Calif., Irvine, 1972-76; asst. prof. U. Va., Charlottesville, 1976-78, assoc. prof., 1978-81, prof., 1981-97, Commonwealth prof., 1997—, dir. neurosci. grad. program, 1991-95; prof. Binghamton (N.Y.) U., 1999-2000, U. Ill., Urbana-Champaign, 2000—. Dir. Med. Scholars Program U. Ill. Coll. Medicine, Urbana-Champaign, 2000—. Editor Psychobiology, 1990-97, Neurobiology of Learning and Memory, 1998—; contbr. numerous articles to sci. publs. Mem. Commonwealth of Va. Alzheimer's and Related Disorders Commn., 1998-99. Recipient James McKeen Cattell award, 1983, Sesquicentennial Assn. award, U. Va., 1983, 90-93, Disting. Alumni award U. N.C., Chapel Hill, 2000; named APA Master Lectr., 2000; NIH fellow, 1967. Fellow APA (com. animal rsch. & ethics), AAAS, Am. Psychol. Soc. (mem. com. 1990-91, program com. 1991); mem. Soc. for Neurosci. (com. on animals in rsch. 1993-98), NSF Adv. Panel for Behavioral and Computational Neurosci., 1993-96. Office: U Ill at Urbana-Champaign Dept Psychology Champaign IL 61820 E-mail: pgold@uiuc.edu.

GOLDBERG, ANNE CAROL, physician, educator; b. Balt., June 12, 1951; d. Stanley Barry and Selma Ray (Freiman) G.; m. Ronald M. Levin, July 29, 1989. AB, Harvard U., 1973; MD, U. Md., 1977. Diplomate Am. Bd. Internal Medicine, Am. Bd. Endocrinlolgy and Metabolism. Intern in medicine Michael Reese Hosp., Chgo., 1977-78, resident in medicine, 1978-80; fellow in endocrinology Washington U., St. Louis, 1980-83, instr. medicine, 1983-85, asst. prof. medicine, 1985-94, assoc. prof. medicine, 1994—, clin. dir. lipid reseach clinic, 1987-96. Mem. steering com. Cholesterol Coalition, St. Louis, 1988-93. Fellow ACP; mem. AMA, Am. Diabetes Assn., Am. Heart Assn., Am. Med. Women's Assn., Endocrine Soc., Alpha Omega Alpha. Democrat. Jewish. Avocation: needlepoint. Office: Washington U Med Sch Box 8046 660 S Euclid Ave Saint Louis MO 63110-1010 E-mail: agoldber@im.wustl.edu.

GOLDBERG, ARNOLD IRVING, psychoanalyst, educator; b. Chgo., May 21, 1929; s. Morris Henry and Rose (Auerbach) G.; m. Constance Obenhaus; children: Andrew, Sarah. BS, U. Ill., 1949; MD, U. Ill., Chgo., 1953. Diplomate Am. Bd. Psychiatry and Neurology; cert. psychoanalyst. Intern Cin. Gen. Hosp., 1954-55; psychiat. resident Michael Reese Hosp., Chgo., 1957-59; tng. and supervising analyst Chgo. Inst. for Psychoanalysis, 1970—, dir., 1990-92; assoc. psychiatrist Rush Presbyterian St. Lukes Hosp., Chgo., 1982—; prof. psychiatry Rush Med. Coll., 1982-97, Cynthia Oudejans Harris MD prof. psychiatry, 1997—. Author: Models of the Mind, 1973, A Fresh Look at Psychoanalysis, 1988, The Prisonhouse of Psychoanalysis, 1990, The Problem of Perversion, 1995, Being of Two Minds, 1999; editor: Future of Psychoanalysis: Progress in Self Psychology, Vols. 1-16, 1976-99, Errant Selves, 2000; contbr. numerous articls to profl. jours. Capt. U.S. Army, 1955-57. Fellow Am. Psychiat. Assn. (life); mem. Am. Psychoanalytic Assn. Home: 844 W Chalmers Pl Chicago IL 60614-3223 Office: Inst for Psychoanalysis Chgo 122 S Michigan Ave Ste 1305 Chicago IL 60603-6107 E-mail: Docaiq@aol.com.

GOLDBERG, VICKI COMM, employment services executive; b. Chicago, Ill., Oct. 21, 1945; d. Julius and Esther (Kennon) Comm; m. Sheldon Goldberg, Aug 16, 1970; children: Felicia, Sharisse. BA in Psychology, Northeastern Ill. U., 1967. Lic. employment counselor, Ill.; cert. teacher, Ill. Elem. sch. tchr. Sch. Dist. 21, Wheeling, Ill., 1967-70; community svc. rep. Welcome Wagon, Memphis, 1977-80; mktg. rep. McDonald's Corp., Oakbrook, Ill., 1980-83; staff supr. Debbie Temps, Niles, 1983-85; day care ctr. dir. Kinder Care, Palatine, 1985-86; office mgr. Casey Svcs. Inc., Des Plaines, 1986-89; regional mgr. Profl. Resources Internat., Oakbrook Terrace, 1989-92; mgr. acctg. ops. Kelly Fin. Resources, Downers Grove, 1992—. Guest facilitator Northeastern Ill. U., Elmhurst Coll., Ill. Dept. Employment Securities, Ill. CPA Soc., Inst. Mgmt. Accts., U. Ill. Chgo. Advisor Morton Grove (Ill.) Pk. Dist., 1981; columnist Vol. Svcs. of Skokie (Ill.) Valley, 1988-94. Mem. Nat. Assn. Pers. Cons., Nat. Assn. Job Search Trainers. Avocations: traveling, reading. Office: Kelly Tech Svcs 7250 N Cicero Ave Ste 202 Lincolnwood IL 60712-1627

GOLDBERGER, ARTHUR STANLEY, economics educator; b. N.Y.C., Nov. 20, 1930; s. David M. and Martha (Greenwald) G.; m. Iefke Engelsman, Aug. 19, 1957; children: Nina Judith, Nicholas Bernard. B.S., N.Y.U., 1951; M.A., U. Mich., 1952, Ph.D., 1958. Acting asst. prof. econs. Stanford U., 1956-59; assoc. prof. econs. U. Wis., 1960- 63, prof., 1963-70, H.M. Groves prof., 1970-79, Vilas research prof., 1979-98, prof. emeritus, 1998—. Vis. prof. Center Planning and Econ. Rsch., Athens, Greece, 1964-65, U. Hawaii, 1969, 71, Stanford U., 1990, 96, 2000; Keynes vis. prof. U. Essex, 1968-69. Author: (with L.R. Klein) An Econometric Model of the United States, 1929-52, 1955, Impact Multipliers and Dynamic Properties, 1959, Econometric Theory, 1964, Topics in Regression Analysis, 1968, Functional Form and Utility, 1987, A Course in Econometrics, 1991, Introductory Econometrics, 1998; editor: (with O.D. Duncan) Structural Equation Models in the Social Sciences, 1973, (with D.J. Aigner) Latent Variables in Socioeconomic Models, 1976; Assoc. editor: Jour. Econometrics, 1973-77; bd. editors: Am. Econ. Rev, 1964-66, Jour. Econ. Lit, 1975-77. Fulbright fellow Netherlands Sch. Econs., 1955-56, 59-60; fellow Ctr. for Advanced Study in Behavioral Scis., Stanford, 1976-77, 80-81; Guggenheim fellow Stanford U., 1972-73, 85. Fellow Am. Statis. Assn., Econometric Soc. (council 1975-80, 82-87), Am. Acad. Arts and Scis., AAAS; mem. Am. Econ. Assn. (Disting. fellow 1988), Nat. Acad. Scis., Royal Netherlands Acad. Scis. Home: 2828 Sylvan Ave Madison WI 53705-5228 Office: U Wis Dept Econs 1180 Observatory Dr Madison WI 53706-1320 E-mail: asgoldbe@facstaff.wisc.edu.

GOLDBERGER, ROBERT D. food products company executive; b. 1935; V.p. King Foods, Inc., Newport, Minn., 1956-73; with GFI America, Mpls., 1973—, pres., CEO. Office: GFI America 2815 Blaisdell Ave Minneapolis MN 55408-2385

GOLDBLATT, STANFORD JAY, lawyer; b. Chgo., Feb. 25, 1939; s. Maurice and Bernice (Mendelson) G.; m. Ann Dudley Cronkhite, June 17, 1968; children: Alexandra, Nathaniel, Jeremy. BA magna cum laude, Harvard U., 1960, LLB magna cum laude, 1963. Bar: Ill. 1963. Law clk. U.S. Ct. Appeals, 5th Jud. Circuit, New Orleans, 1963-64; mem. firm Winston & Strawn, Chgo., 1964-67; v.p. Goldblatt Bros., Inc., 1967-76, pres., chief exec. officer, 1976-77, chmn. exec. com., 1977-78; ptnr. Hopkins & Sutter, 1978-97, Winston & Strawn, Chgo., 1997—. Dir. MacLean-Fogg Co. Trustee U. Chgo., Louis A. Weiss Meml. Hosp., Cancer Rsch. Found., U. Chgo. Hosps. Mem. Econ. Club, Racquet Club, Comml. Club. Office: Winston & Strawn 35 W Wacker Dr Ste 4200 Chicago IL 60601-1695

GOLDEN, BRUCE PAUL, lawyer; b. Chgo., Dec. 4, 1943; s. Irving R. and Anne K. (Eisenberg) G. SB in Elec. Sci. and Engring., MIT, 1965, SM in Elec. Engring., 1966; JD, Harvard U., 1969. Bar: Ill. 1969, U.S. Dist. Ct. (no. dist.) Ill. 1970, U.S. Ct. Appeals (7th cir.) 1994, U.S. Supreme Ct. 1995, cert.: (arbitrator); lic. real estate broker. Assoc. McDermott, Will & Emery, Chgo., 1970-75, ptnr., 1976-91; of counsel Fishman & Merrick, P.C., 1991-92, Coffield, Ungaretti & Harris, Chgo., 1992-96; Bruce P. Golden and Assocs., 1996—; gen. counsel Piranha, Inc., 2000—. Officer, dir. various corps.; speaker bank law, securities law, venture capital seminars Contbr. articles to Banking Law Jour., contbg. editor, 1979— Chmn. MIT Enterprise Forum Chgo.; bd. dirs. Entrepreneurship Inst. Chgo., Chgo. chpt. U.S. Entrepreneurs Network, Ill. Small Bus. Devel. Ctr., Kellogg Sch. Bus. community services com. Mem. MIT Alumni of Chgo. (dir. 1993—), Union League. Home and Office: 4137 N Hermitage Ave Chicago IL 60613-1820

GOLDEN, CHARLES E. pharmaceutical company executive; CFO Eli Lilly and Co., Indpls. Office: Eli Lilly and Co Lily Corp Ctr Indianapolis IN 46285-0001

GOLDEN, WILLIAM C. lawyer; b. N.Y.C., Oct. 27, 1936; s. Edwin and Sue (Lipman) G.; m. Rachel Epstein; children: Rebecca, Naomi, Nathaniel, David. BS, Wharton Sch., U. Pa., 1957; LLB, Columbia U., 1960. Bar: N.Y. 1961, Ill. 1967. Atty. Dept. Justice, Tax Div., Washington, 1960-61, Dept. Treasury, Washington, 1962-65; assoc. prof. of law Ind. U., Bloomington, 1965-67; assoc., then ptnr. Sidley and Austin, Chgo., 1967—. Bd. dirs. ALAMCO, Clarksburg, W.Va., 1980-85. Author: Attorneys' Guide to Charitable Giving, 1967. Bd. dirs. Self Help Ctr., Evanston, Ill., 1985-86; chmn. Info. Tech. Resource Ctr., Chgo., 1987—. Mem. ABA, Chgo. Bar Assn. (chmn. fed. tax com. 1979-80). Office: Sidley & Austin 1 S First National Plz Chicago IL 60603-2000

GOLDENBERG, KIM, university president, internist; BS, SUNY, Stonybrook, 1968; MS, Polytech. Inst. N.Y., 1972; MD, Albany (N.Y.) Med. Coll., 1979. Test engr. lunar lander and naval jets, Grumman, N.Y., 1968-75; resident internl medicine Western Res. Care Sys., Youngstown, Ohio, 1979-82; dir. gen. internal medicine Wright State U. Sch. Medicine, Dayton, 1983-89, vice chair medicine, 1988-89, assoc. dean for students and curriculum, 1989-90, dean, 1990-98, pres., 1998—. Office: Wright State U Office of Pres Dayton OH 45435

GOLDFARB, BERNARD SANFORD, lawyer; b. Cleve., Apr. 15, 1917; s. Harry and Esther (Lenson) Goldfarb; m. Barbara Brofman Goldfarb, Jan. 4, 1966; children: Merdeith Stacy, Lauren Beth. A.B., Case Western Res. U., 1938, J.D., 1940. Bar: Ohio 1940. Since practiced in, Cleve.; sr. ptnr. firm Goldfarb & Reznick, 1967-95; pvt. practice Cleve., 1997—. Spl. counsel to atty. gen. Ohio, 1950, 1971—74; mem. Ohio Commn. Uniform Traffic Rules, 1973—80. Contbr. legal jours. Served with USAAF, 1942-45. Mem.: ABA, Cuyahoga County Bar Assn., Greater Cleve. Bar Assn., Ohio Bar Assn. Home: 39 Pepper Creek Dr Pepper Pike OH 44124-5279 Office: 55 Public Sq Ste 1500 Cleveland OH 44113-1998

GOLDFARB, ERIC DANIEL, information technology executive, computer industry analyst; b. Kalamazoo, Apr. 29, 1964; s. Russell Marshall and Clare Sara (Rosett) Goldfarb; m. Gwen Julia Oberman, Aug. 20, 1989; children: Adam, David. Bachelors, U. Mich., 1986. Project leader Domino's Pizza, Inc., Ann Arbor, Mich., 1986—90; mgr. info. systems Interpublic Group (Lintas), Warren, 1990-91; mgr. bus. sys. The Ltd. Inc. (Express), Columbus, Ohio, 1991-94; v.p., CIO Elder-Beerman Stores Corp., Dayton, 1994—96; v.p., CIO/CTO Pearson plc (Viacom-Macmillan), Indpls., 1996—2001; CIO (worldwide) Global Knowledge Inc., Cary, NC, 2001—. Chmn. Bus. & Industry Adv. Coun., Ann Arbor, 1988-89; speaker in field. Contbr. articles to profl. jours. Recipient nat. Arthur D. Little "Best of the Best" award. Republican. Avocations: sailing, golfing. Office: Global Knowledge Inc. 9000 Regency Parkway Cary NC 27512

GOLDFEIN, IRIS, financial company executive; Vice chmn., human resources Coopers & Lybrand, Chgo.; leader of Price Waterhouse Coopers Kwasha HR Solutions, 1998—; group pres. HR Innovations. Office: Price Waterhouse Coopers 203 N La Salle St Chicago IL 60601-1210

GOLDGAR, BERTRAND ALVIN, literary historian, educator; b. Macon, Ga., Nov. 17, 1927; s. Benjamin Meyer and Annie (Shapiro) G.; m. Corinne Cohn Hartman, Apr. 6, 1950; children: Arnold Benjamin, Anne Hartman. BA, Vanderbilt U., 1948, MA, 1949, Princeton U., 1957, PhD, 1958. Instr. in English Clemson (S.C.) U., 1948-50, asst. prof., 1951-52; instr. English Lawrence U., Appleton, Wis., 1957-61, asst. prof., 1961-65, assoc. prof., 1965-71, prof. English, 1971—, John N. Bergstrom prof. humanities, 1980—. Mem. fellowship panel NEH, 1979 Author: The Curse of Party: Swift's Relations with Addison and Steele, 1961, Walpole and the Wits: The Relation of Politics to Literature, 1722-1742, 1976; editor: The Literary Criticism of Alexander Pope, 1965, Henry Fielding's The Covent-Garden Jour., 1988, Henry Fielding's Miscellanies, Vol. 2, 1993, Jonathan Wild, 1997, The Grub Street Jour. 1730-1733, 2002; adv. editor: 18th Century Studies, 1977-82. With AUS, 1952-54. Fellow, Am. Coun. Learned Socs, 1973-74, NEH, 1980-81. Mem. Am. Soc. 18th Century Studies, Johnson Soc. Cen. Region. Home: 914 E Eldorado St Appleton WI 54911-5536 Office: Lawrence U Dept English Appleton WI 54912 E-mail: bertrand.a.goldgar@lawrence.edu.

GOLDIN, MARTIN BRUCE, financial executive, consultant; b. Teaneck, N.J., May 18, 1938; s. Arthur Daniel and Shirley Edith (Holland) G.; m. Joyce Anne Rossin, Aug. 22, 1960; children: Melissa Beth, Julie Amber, Kevin James, Sabrina Nicole. BBA, U. Miami, 1960; postgrad., Detroit Coll. Law, 1967. Fin. analyst Chrysler Corp. Detroit, London, 1967-70; chief fin. officer Chrysler de Mex., Mexico City, 1971-77, Chrysler Australia Ltd., Adelaide, 1978-80, Internat. Harvester De Mex., Mexico City, 1980-85; compt. Citicorp Diners Club, Denver, 1985-87, chief fin. officer, exec. v.p. Chgo., 1988-96; v.p. fin. Deluxe Corp., Shoreview, Minn., 1997-98. Fin. cons. Rossin-Goldin, Detroit, 1960—, La Torre de Acapulco (Mex.), 1980-88. Office: Rossin-Goldin Co 2634 Red Arrow Dr Las Vegas NV 89135 E-mail: mbgcfo@aol.com.

GOLDMAN, ALLEN MARSHALL, physics educator; b. N.Y.C., Oct. 18, 1937; s. Louis and Mildred (Kohn) G.; m. Katherine Virginia Darnell, July 31, 1960; children: Matthew, Rachel, Benjamin AB, Harvard U., 1958; PhD, Stanford U., 1965. Rsch. asst. Stanford U., Calif., 1960-65, rsch. assoc., 1965; asst. prof. physics U. Minn., Mpls., 1965-67, assoc. prof., 1967-73, prof., 1974—, inst. tech. prof., 1992—, dir. Ctr. for Sci. and Application of Superconductivity, 1989—, head Sch. of Physics and Astronomy, 1996—. Co-chmn. Gordon Conf. on Quantum Liquids and Solids, 1981; dir. NATO Advanced Study Inst., 1983; mem. materials rsch. adv. com. NSF, 1985-88; mem. vis. com. Francis Butter Nat. Magnet Lab., 1986-89, chmn., 1987-89; mem. vis. com. Nat. Nanofabrication Facility at Cornell, 1988-90, mem. user com., 1997-99; mem. vis. com. U. Chgo. Materials Program of Argonne Nat. Lab., 1992-98, chmn. 1995; mem. Buckley prize com., 1994-95, London prize com., 1994-98; mem. Helium Res. com. NAS/NRC, 1998-99. Mem. publs. oversight com. Am. Phys. Soc., 1996-99, chair 1997; mem. pub. policy com. Am. Inst. Physics, 1999—, assoc. editor Revs. of Modern Physics, 1999—; contbr. articles to profl. jours. Com. of vis. divsn. materials rsch. NSF, 1999. Alfred P. Sloan Found. fellow, 1966-70. Fellow AAAS, Am. Phys. Soc. (divisional councilor divsn. condensed matter physics 1994-96, 99—, mem. exec. com. 2001—, London Meml. prize 2002). Jewish. Home: 1015 James Ct Mendota Heights MN 55118-3640 Office: U Minn Sch Physics and Astronomy 116 Church St SE Minneapolis MN 55455-0149 E-mail: goldman@physics.umn.edu., amgoldman@mn.mediaone.net.

GOLDMAN, LOUIS BUDWIG, lawyer; b. Chgo., Apr. 11, 1948; s. Jack Sydney and Lorraine (Budwig) G.; m. Barbara Marcia Berg, Oct. 2, 1983; children: Jacqueline Ilyse, Annie Dara, Michael Louis. BA magna cum laude, U. Calif., Berkeley, 1970; JD cum laude, U. Chgo., 1974. Bar: Calif. 1975, U.S. Dist. Ct. (no. dist.) Calif. 1975, U.S. Ct. Appeals (9th cir.) 1975, N.Y. 1976, U.S. Dist. Ct. (so. and ea. dists.) N.Y. 1976, U.S. Ct. Appeals (2nd cir.) 1976, Ill. 1991, Czech Republic, 1997; registered fgn. lawyer, Eng. 1999, Wales 1999. Law clk. U.S. Dist. Ct., San Francisco, 1974-75; assoc. Cleary, Gottlieb, Steen & Hamilton, N.Y.C. and Paris, 1975-81, Edwards & Angell, N.Y.C., 1981-83, ptnr., 1986-88, Wald, Harkrader & Ross, N.Y.C., 1983-86, Altheimer & Gray, Chgo., 1989—, co-chmn., 1999—. Mng. dir. Abacus & Assocs. Inc., N.Y.C.; supervisory bd. Pudliszki S.A. Mem. U. Chgo. Law Rev.; contbr. articles to profl. jours. Mem. Chgo.-Prague Sister Cities Com., Chgo.-China Sister Cities Com.; bd. dirs. Lyric Opera Ctr. for Am. Artists, New Trier Swim Club; sec. class of 1970, U. Calif., Berkeley; bd. trustees The Ravinia Festival. Mem. ABA (com. on privatization), Calif. Bar Assn., N.Y. State Bar Assn. (com. on internat. banking, securities and fin. transactions), Assn. of the Bar of City of N.Y., N.Y. County Lawyers Assn., Chgo. Bar Assn., Ill. State Bar Assn., Internat. Bar Assn., Order of Coif, Northwestern Assocs., Chgo. China Sister Cities Comm., Old Willow Club, The Law Club, Phi Beta Kappa. Home: 465 Grove St Glencoe IL 60022-1844 Office: Altheimer & Gray 10 S Wacker Dr Ste 4000 Chicago IL 60606-7407 E-mail: goldmanl@altheimer.com.

GOLDMAN, MARC L. federal judge; b. 1948; BA, U. Mich., 1969; JD, Wayne State U., 1973. Atty. State Appellate Defender Office, 1973-74, Washtenaw County Pub. Defender, Ann Arbor, Mich., 1974-76; asst. U.S. atty. U.S. Dist. Ct. (ea. dist.) Mich., 1980-83, magistrate judge, 1983—. Asst. prof. Wayne State U. Law Sch., 1973-74; vis. asst. prof. U. Mich. Law Sch., 1979-80. Office: US Dist Ct Ea Dist Mich Fed Bldg 231 W Lafayette Chamber 704 Detroit MI 48226 Fax: 810-341-7859.

GOLDMANN, MORTON AARON, cardiologist, educator; b. Chgo., July 11, 1924; s. Harry Ascher and Frieda (Cohon) G.; m. Doris-Jane Tumpeer, July 18, 1951; children: Deborah, Jory, Erica, Leslie BS, U. Ill., 1943, MD, 1946. Diplomate Am. Bd. Internal Medicine. Intern Cook County Hosp., Chgo., 1946-47, resident physician, 1949-52; practice medicine specializing in internal medicine and cardiology Skokie, Ill., 1952—; chief of medicine Rush North Shore Med. Ctr. (formerly Skokie Valley Hosp.), 1964-65, also trustee, 1968—, pres. med. staff, 1968-69, attending physician, med. dir. heart sta. and cardiac rehab. unit, 1973-96, bd. dirs., 1970—; former attending physician Ill. Research Hosp.; former assoc. prof. Abraham Lincoln Sch. Medicine, U. Ill., Chgo.; prof. Cook County Grad. Sch. Medicine. Pres. Heart Assn. North Cook County, 1978-81, North Suburban Assn. Health Resources, 1974-77 Contbr. numerous articles to profl. jours. Capt. M.C., AUS, 1947-49, PTO Fellow ACP, Inst. Medicine Chgo., Am. Coll. Cardiology; mem. AMA, Am. Soc. Internal Medicine, Am. Heart Assn., Ill. Med. Soc., Chgo. Med. Soc., Chgo. Heart Assn. (bd. govs., bd. dirs. 1978-87, bd. trustees 1979-83). Office: 667 Carriage Hill Dr Glenview IL 60025-5402

GOLDRING, NORMAN MAX, advertising executive; b. Chgo., June 22, 1937; s. Jack and Carolyn (Wolf) G.; m. Cynthia Lois Garland, Dec. 20, 1959; children: Jay Marshall, Diane. BS in Bus., Miami (Ohio) U., 1959; MBA, U. Chgo., 1963. Advt. account mgr. Edward H. Weiss & Co., Chgo., 1959-61; sr. v.p., dir. mktg. svcs. Stern, Walters & Simmons, Inc., 1961-68; chmn. Goldring & Co., Inc., 1968-89; pres., CEO CPM, Inc., 1969-93, chmn., 1994-99; pres. CPO Inc., 1994—. Dir. Creative Works, Inc., 1994-97; instr. mktg. and advt. mgmt. Roosevelt U., 1965-68. Mem. editorial bd. Jour. Media Planning. Commr. Ridgeville Park Dist., Evanston, Ill., 1971-75, pres. 1974-75; bd. dirs., v.p. Mus. Broadcast Comm., 1983-92; bd. dirs. Chgo. Chamber Musicians 1988—, Chgo. Metro History Fair, 1990, The Lake Forest Grad. Sch. Mgmt., 2000—; trustee Chgo. Assn. Dirs. Mktg. Ednl. Found., 2001—. Mem. Am. Mktg. Assn. (speaker), Advt. Coun. Inc. (Midwest adv. bd. 1983-90), Am. Mgmt. Assn., Direct Mktg. Assn. (mem. chmn., broadcast coun.), Chgo. Assn. Dirs. Mktg., Elec. Ret. Assn. Home: 855 Beverly Pl Lake Forest IL 60045-3901 Office: CPO Inc # 16 233 N Michigan Ave Chicago IL 60601-5519 E-mail: ngoldring@cpodirect.com.

GOLDSBOROUGH, ROBERT GERALD, publishing executive, author; b. Chgo., Oct. 3, 1937; s. Robert Vincent and Wilma (Janak) G.; m. Janet Elizabeth Moore, Jan. 15, 1966; children: Suzanne Joy, Robert Michael, Colleen Marie, Bonnie Laura. BS, Northwestern U., 1959, MS with honors, 1960. Reporter A.P., 1959, City News Bur., Chgo., 1959; with Chgo. Tribune, 1960-82, reporter neighborhood news sect., asst. editor Sunday mag. and TV sect., 1963-66, editor TV Week mag., 1966-67, asst. to features editor, 1967-71, asst. to editor, 1971-72, Sunday editor, 1972-75, editor Sunday mag., 1975-82; exec. editor Advt. Age Mag., Chgo., 1982-88, spl. projects dir., 1988-91; corp. projects editor Crain Communications, 1991-96, spl. projects dir., 1997—. Author: Great Railroad Paintings, 1976, The Crain Adventure, 1992, Nero Wolfe Mysteries: Murder in E-Minor, 1986, Death on Deadline, 1987, The Bloodied Ivy, 1988, The Last Coincidence, 1989, Fade to Black, 1990, Silver Spire, 1992, The Missing Chapter, 1994. Served with AUS, 1961. Recipient Northwestern U. Alumni Svc. award, 2001. Mem. Arts Club. Presbyterian. Office: 360 N Michigan Ave Chicago IL 60601 E-mail: rgoldsborough@crain.com.

GOLDSCHMIDT, LYNN HARVEY, lawyer; b. Chgo., June 14, 1951; d. Arthur and Ida (Shirman) H.; m. Robert Allen Goldschmidt, Aug. 27, 1972; children: Elizabeth Anne, Carolyn Helene. BS with honors, U. Ill., 1973; JD magna cum laude, Northwestern U., 1976. Bar: Ill. 1976. Ptnr. Hopkins & Sutter, Chgo., 1976-2001, Foley & Lardner, Chgo., 2001—. Articles editor Northwestern U. Law Rev. Mem. Airport Coun. Internat., N. Am., Order of Coif. Office: Foley and Lardner 3 1st National Plz Ste 4100 Chicago IL 60602 E-mail: LGoldschmidt@foleylaw.com.

GOLDSCHMIDT, PASCAL JOSEPH, medical educator, cardiologist; b. Brussels, Belgium, Apr. 12, 1954; m. Emily Ann Boches. BS, Univ. Libre de Bruxelles, 1976, MD, 1980. Lic. physician Md., Ohio, Belgium. Intern and resident in medicine/cardiology Erasme Acad. Hosp./U. Libre de Brussels, 1980-83; rsch. fellow dept. immunology and microbiology Med. U. S.C., Charleston, 1983-86; resident in medicine Union Meml. Hosp., Balt., 1986-88; clin. and rsch. fellow cardiology/cell biology/anatomy Johns Hopkins U., 1988-91, assoc. prof. dept. medicine/cardiology divsn., 1991-96, dir. Bernard Lab. Vascular Biology, 1991-96; attending CCU Johns Hopkins Hosp., 1991-96, co-dir. Thrombosis Ctr., 1994-96; co-dir. Henry Ciccarone Ctr. for Prevention Heart Disease, 1991-96; prof. medicine, dir. Heart and Lung Inst. Ohio State U., Columbus, dir. divsn. cardiology, 1998—. Lectr. in field. Contbr. numerous articles and abstracts to profl. jours., chpts. to books; reviewer New Eng. Jour. Medicine, Annals of Internal Medicine, Biochemistry, Blood, Cell, Cell Adhesion and Comm., Circulation Rsch., Jour. Cell Biology, Molecular Biology of the Cell, Am. Heart Assn., NIH. Recipient NATO Sci. award, 1983, 84; grantee Clinician Scientist Award, 1991-93, Syntex Scholars Program, 1992-95, Am. Heart Assn., 1992-94, 95—, NIH, 1992-96, 94-96, 95—; Am. Heart Assn. fellow, 1990, Med. U. S.C., 1984, 85. Mem. AAAS, Am. Heart Assn., Am. Soc. Clin. Investigators. Home: 3725 Foxwood Pl Durham NC 27705-1992 Office: Ohio State U Heart/Lung 514 Med Rsch Facility 420 W 12th Ave Columbus OH 43210-1214

GOLDSMITH, ETHEL FRANK, medical social worker; b. Chgo., May 31, 1919; d. Theodore and Rose (Falk) Frank; m. Julian Royce Goldsmith, Sept. 4, 1940; children: Richard, Susan, John. BA, U. Chgo., 1940. Lic. social worker, Ill. Liaison worker psychiat. consultation service U. Chgo. Hosp., 1964-68; med. social worker Wyler Children's Hosp., Chgo., 1968-98. Treas. U. Chgo. Service League, 1958-62, chmn. camp Brueckner Farr Aux., 1966-72; pres. Bobs Roberts Hosp. Service Commn., 1962; bd. dirs. Richardson Wildlife Sanctuary, 1988-2000; mem. Field Mus. Women's Bd., 1966—; bd. dirs. Hyde Park Art Ctr., 1964-82, Chgo. Commons Assn., 1967-77, Alumni Assn. Sch. Social Service Adminstrn., 1976-80,

Self Help Home for Aged, 1985-2000, U. Chgo. Svc. League, 2002—,; vol. Chgo. Found. for Edn.; mem. womens bd. U. Chgo., 1999—. Recipient Alumni Citation Pub. Service, U. Chgo., 1972. Mem. Phi Beta Kappa. Home: 5631 S Blackstone Ave Chicago IL 60637-1827

GOLDSMITH, JOHN ANTON, linguist, educator; b. N.Y.C., Nov. 7, 1951; s. Simon Albert and Thelma Margaret (Ettesvold) G.; m. Jessie Elizabeth Pinkham, Nov. 20, 1982; children: Elizabeth, Paul, Julia. BA, Swarthmore Coll., 1972; PhD, MIT, 1976. Asst., assoc. then prof. Ind. U., Bloomington, 1976-84; prof. U. Chgo., 1984—, Edward Carson Waller Disting. Svc. prof., 1997—. Bd. dirs. U. Chgo. Press, 1990-94. Author: Autosegmental and Metrical Phonology, 1990, (with G. Huck) Ideology and Linguistic Theory, 1995, (with J. Komlos and P. Gold) The Chicago Guide to Your Academic Career; editor, translator Syntax and Human Experience, 1991; editor: The Last Phonological Rule, 1993, Handbook of Phonological Theory, 1995, Phonological Theory: The Essential Readings, 1999. Mem. Linguistics Soc. Am. (mem. exec. com. 1988-91). Office: U Chgo Dept Linguistics 1010 E 59th St Chicago IL 60637-1512

GOLDSMITH, STEPHEN, mayor; b. Indpls., Dec. 12, 1946; s. Joseph F. and Marjorie (Holmes) G.; m. Margaret McDaniel, June 15, 1988; children: Reid, Elizabeth, Devereaux, Olivia. AB, Wabash Coll., 1968, hon. LLD, 1993; JD with honors, U. Mich., 1971. Pvt. practice atty., 1972-78, 91; dep. corp. counsel City of Indpls., 1974-75, chief trial dep., 1976-78; pros. atty. Marion County, Ind., 1979-90; mayor Indpls., 1991—. Chmn. Ctr. Civic Innovation, Manhattan Inst.; adv. bd. Bur. Justice and Stats.; chmn. Indpls. & Ctrl. Ind. Tech. Partnership; co-chmn. domestic strategy group, Aspen Inst.; hon. co-chmn. Nat. Coun. Pub.-Pvt. Partnerships; mem. def. reform group, Dept. Def.; various adv. and peer rev. bds., Nat. Inst. Justice; adv. bd. Office Juvenile Justice and Delinquency; adv. bd. Pres.'s Commn. on Missing and Exploited Children; vice chmn. Pres.'s Commn. on Model State Drug Laws; rsch. fellow in criminal justice & mgmt., Harvard U. Kennedy Sch. Govt.; asst. and adj. prof. I.U.,; adj. fellow The Manhattan Inst.; adj. faculty, Columbia U. Author: The Twenty-first Century City; editor (Jour.) Prosecutor's Perspective; contbr. Jerusalem Post, Harvard Bus. Rev., Wall St. Jour., others. USAR, 1968-74. Office: Office of Mayor 2501 City-County Bldg 200 E Washington St Indianapolis IN 46204-3307

GOLDSTEIN, ALFRED GEORGE, retail and consumer products executive; b. N.Y.C., Sept. 22, 1932; s. Milton and Pauline M. G.; m. Hope D. Perry, July 5, 1959; children: Mark, Robert. AB, CCNY, 1953; MS, Columbia U., 1954. With Sears, Roebuck & Co., Chgo., 1956-79, v.p. mdse, group nat. mdse. mgr., 1976-79; sr. v.p. consumer bus. Am. Can Co., Greenwich, Conn., 1979-81, sr. v.p. waste recovery bus., 1981-82, exec. v.p. plastics packaging bus., 1982-83, pres. splty. retailing sector, 1983-87; pres. splty. merchandising and direct mktg. group, Sears Logistics Svc. Sears, Roebuck & Co., Chgo., 1987-93; pres., CEO AG Assocs., 1993 —; bd. dirs. Sears Mdse. Group, Sears Can., Ltd. Former vice chmn., CEO, bd. dirs. Fingerhut Corp.; chmn. bd. dirs. Pickwick Internat.; chmn., CEO, Musicland Group; bd. dirs. Gander Mountain Corp., 1994. Exec. editor: Internat. Jour. Addictions, 1975-80. Trustee Archeus Found., 1978-90, Com. Econ. Devel., 1998—; bd. dirs., mem. exec. com. United Negro Coll. Fund, 1991—, vice chmn., 2001—; mem. exec. com. Columbia U. Grad. Sch. Bus. Alumni Assn., 1980-85, Am. Can Co. Found.; mem. mktg. com. bd. trustees Art Inst., Chgo., 1988-2002; mem. adv. bd. J.L. Kellogg Sch. Mgmt. Ctr. Study Ethical Issues in Bus., Northwestern U., 1992-2001, Gozuieta Bus. Sch. Ctr. Leadership and Career Studies, Emory U., 1990-97; bd. dirs. Art Americana, 1996. With AUS, 1954-56. Mem. Am. Arbitration Assn. (arbitrator).

GOLDSTEIN, JONATHAN AMOS, retired ancient history and classics educator; b. N.Y.C., July 19, 1929; s. David Aaron and Rose Frances (Berman) G.; m. Helen Charlotte Tunik, Feb. 1, 1959; children— Rise Belle, Rachel Sarah AB cum laude, Harvard U., 1950, AM, 1951; M of Hebrew Lit., Jewish Theol. Sem., 1955, D of Hebrew Letters (hon.), 1987; PhD, Columbia U., 1959. Instr. Columbia U., N.Y.C., 1960-62; prof. U. Iowa, 1962-97; ret., 1997. Author: The Letters of Demosthenes, 1968, I Maccabees, 1976, II Maccabees, 1983, Semites, Iranians, Greeks, and Romans, 1990, Peoples of an Almighty God, 2001. Pres. Congregation Agudas Achim, Iowa City, 1969-70 Fulbright scholar U.S. State Dept., Israel, 1959-60; sr. faculty fellow U. Iowa, 1984 Fellow Am. Acad. for Jewish Rsch.; mem. AAUP, Am. Philol. Assn., Assn. Ancient Historians, Archaeol. Inst. Am., Phi Beta Kappa. Democrat. Jewish. Avocations: singing; Jewish community activities. Home: 312 Windsor Dr Iowa City IA 52245-6044 Office: U Iowa Dept History Schaeffer Hall Iowa City IA 52242

GOLDSTEIN, MARVIN EMANUEL, aerospace scientist, research center administrator; b. Cambridge, Mass., Oct. 11, 1938; s. David and Evelyn (Wilner) G.; m. Priscilla Ann Beresh, July 5, 1965; children: Deborah, Judy. BS in Mech. Engring., Northeastern U., 1961; MS in Mech. Engring., MIT, 1962; PhD in Mech. Engring., U. Mich., 1965. Engr. Arthur D. Little, Inc., Cambridge, 1958-61; rsch. asst. MIT, 1961-63, rsch. assoc., 1965-67; aerospace engr. Lewis Rsch. Ctr., NASA, Cleve., 1967-79, chief scientist, 1980—. Adj. prof. math dept. Case Western Res. U., 1998—. Author: Aeroacoustics, 1976; contbr. articles to profl. jours. Fellow AIAA (assoc. editor jour. 1977-79, chmn. aeroacoustics tech. com., 1979-81, mem. publs. com. 1980-83, Aeroacoustics award 1983, Pendray award 1983), Am. Phys. Soc. (exec. com. div. fluid dynamics 1991-93, Otto Laporte award in fluid mechanics 1997); mem. NAE. Avocation: automobile racing and rebuilding. Office: NASA Lewis Rsch Ctr MS 3-17 21000 Brookpark Rd Cleveland OH 44135-3191

GOLDSTEIN, NORMAN RAY, international trading company executive, consultant; b. Chgo., Nov. 20, 1944; s. Max and Rose (Weiner) G.; m. Bonnie A. Brod, Aug. 31, 1969; children: Russell, Matthew, Jamie. AA, Wright Jr. Coll., 1965; BS in Fin., No. Ill. U., DeKalb, 1967; MS in Acctg. cum laude, Roosevelt U., 1986. Gen. bus. mgr. Greenstreet Corp., Whiting, Ind., 1967; wholesale credit mgr. Atlantic Richfield Co., Chgo., 1968-74; v.p. fin., treas. Barton Inc. (Barton Brands, Ltd.), 1974-96; chmn., CEO Gold Internat., 1996—. Spl. master U.S. Dist. Ct., 1998; chmn. ABC Fin. Communications Forum, Chgo., 1987-88; v.p., bd. dirs. Consort Corp., Chgo., 1971-80; spl. master U.S. Dist. Ct., 1998; adj. prof. fin. No. Ill. U., 2000-01; speaker on treasury and fin. mgmt. Contbg. author: Handbook of Cash Flow and Treasury Management, 1987; contbr. articles to profl. publs. Bd. dirs. Maine Twp. Jewish Congregation Shaare Emet, Des Plaines, 1986—, pres. 1989-91. Named Outstanding Credit Exec. of Yr., Nat. Assn. Credit Mgmt., 1987, Disting. Alumnus Coll. of Bus. No. Ill. U., 1998. Fellow Nat. Inst. Credit; mem. Treasury Mgmt. Assn., Fin. Mgrs. Assn. Chgo. (treas. 1991-92), Treasury Mgmt. Assn. Chgo. (chmn. ednl. scholarship com. 1995-99, chmn. Windy City Summit Treasury Conf. 1999-2000), Distillers Imports and Vintners (chmn. 1980-82), N.Y. Credit and Fin. Mgmt. Assn., Chgo. Midwest Credit Mgmt. Assn. (bd. dirs. 1984-87).

GOLDSTEIN, RICHARD JAY, mechanical engineer, educator; b. N.Y.C., Mar. 27, 1928; s. Henry and Rose (Steierman) G.; m. Barbara Goldstein; children: Arthur Sander, Jonathan Jacob, Benjamin Samuel, Naomi Sarith. BME, Cornell U., 1948; MS in Mech. Engring., U. Minn., 1950, MS in Physics, 1951, PhD in Mech. Engring., 1959; DSc (hon.), Israel Inst. Tech., 1994; Dr. honoris causa, U. Lisbon, 1996; hon. doctorate, A.V. Luikov Heat and Mass Transfer Inst., Minsk, Belarus, 1997. Instr. U. Minn., Mpls., 1948-51, instr., rsch. fellow, 1956-58, mem. faculty, 1961—, prof. mech. engring., 1965—, head dept., 1977-97, James J. Ryan prof., 1989—, Regents' prof., 1990—; devel. rsch. engr. Oak Ridge Nat. Lab., 1951-54; sr. engr. Lockheed Aircraft, 1956; asst. prof. Brown U., 1959-61. Vis. prof. Technion, Israel, 1976, Imperial Coll., Eng., 1984; cons. in field, 1956—; chmn. Midwest U. Energy Consortium; chmn. Coun. Energy Engring. Rsch.; NSF sr. postdoctoral fellow, vis. prof. Cambridge (Eng.) U., 1971-72; Prince lectr., 1983, William Gurley lectr., 1988, Hawkins Meml. lectr., 1991; disting. lectr. Pa. State U., 1992; mem. acad. com. internat. bd. govs. Technion; hon. mem. sci. bd. A.V. Luikov Heat and Mass Transfer Inst., Minsk, 1997. Editorial adv. bd. Experiments in Fluids, Heat Transfer-Japanese Rsch., Heat Transfer-Soviet Rsch., Bull of the Internat. Centre for Heat andMass Transfer, Internat. Archives of Heat and Mass Transfer; hon. editorial adv. bd. Internat. J. Heat and Mass Transfer, Internat. Communications in Heat and Mass Transfer. 1st U.S. Army lt. AUS, 1954-55. Recipient NASA award for tech. innovation, 1977, MUEC Dist. Svc. award, 1986, NAE, 1985, George Taylor Alumni Soc. award, 1988, A.V. Lykov medal, 1990, Max Jakob Meml. award ASME/AICE, 1990, Nusselt-Reynolds prize, 1993, Dr. Scientiarum Honoris Causa award Technion-Israel Inst. Tech., 1994, Thermal Engring. Internat. award Japan Soc. Mech. Engring.; NATO fellow, Paris, 1960-61, Lady Davis fellow Technion, Israel, 1976. Fellow AAAS, ASME (Heat Transfer Meml. award 1978, Svc. award 1978, Centennial medallion 1980, BEG v.p. 1984-88, 50th anniv. award of heat transfer divsn. 1988, sr. v.p. 1989-93, hon. mem. 1992, BOG 1993-97, pres. 1996-97, sr. v.p. COE 1988-92, Dedicated Svc. award 2001), Royal Acad. Engring. (fgn.), Am. Soc. Engring. Edn., Assembly for Internat. Heat Transfer Confs. (pres. 1986-90), Internat. Ctr. for Heat and Mass Transfer (exec. com. 1985—, chmn. 1992, pres.), Am. Phys. Soc., Japan Soc. Promotion of Sci., Royal Acad. Engring. (fgn.); mem. Am. Phys. Soc., Minn. Acad. Sci., Nat. Acad. Engring., Nat. Acad. Engring.-Mex. (corr. 1991), Golden Key Nat. Honor Soc., Sigma Xi, Tau Beta Pi, Pi Tau Sigma ISROMAC award 2002). Achievements include research and publications in thermodynamics, fluid mechanics, heat transfer, optical measuring techniques. Home: 4241 Bassett Creek Dr Golden Valley MN 55422-4257 Office: U Minn Dept Mech Engring 111 Church St SE Minneapolis MN 55455-0150

GOLDSTEIN, SIDNEY, pharmaceutical scientist; b. Phila., Mar. 27, 1932; s. Israel and Gertrude (Stein) G.; m. Janice Levy, June 19, 1955; children: Rhonda, David, Nina. BSc in Pharmacy, Phila. Coll. Pharmacy & Sci., 1954, MSc in Pharmacy, 1955, DSc in Pharmacy, 1958. Cardiovascular unit head Eaton Labs, Norwich, N.Y., 1958-59; anti-inflammatory unit head Lederle Labs, Pearl River, 1959-61; with Merrell Dow Rsch. Inst., Cin., 1961-93; v.p. global pharm. and analytical scis. Marion Merrell Dow Inc., Kansas City, Mo., 1991-93; v.p. sci. and tech. Duramed Pharm., Inc., Cin., 1994-98, v.p. bus. devel., sci. & tech., 1998—. Adj. assoc. prof. U. Cin. Coll. Pharmacy, 1984-98, mem. dean's adv. coun., 1998—; lectr. pharmacology Phila. Coll. Pharmacy, 1967-70; chair PQRI-drug product tech. com. AAPS, 1997—; mem. So. Ohio Life Sci. Task Force, 1999-2001, GPhA sci. com., 2001. Contbr. articles to profl. jours. Bd. trustees Glen Manor Home for Aged, Cin., 1983-89. Recipient Award for Nicoderm, R&D Mag., 1992. Mem. Am. Assn. Pharm. Scientists, Am. Soc. Clin. Pharmacology and Therapeutics, Soc. Exptl. Biology and Medicine, Am. Soc. Pharmacology and Exptl. Therapeutics, B'nai B'rith (chpt. v.p. 1978). Home: 1125 Fort View Pl Cincinnati OH 45202-1713 Office: Duramed Pharmaceuticals 5040 Duramed Dr Cincinnati OH 45213-2520 E-mail: sgoldstein@duramed.com., goldsts@fuse.net.

GOLDSTEIN, STEVEN, lawyer; b. St. Louis, Sept. 8, 1950; s. Alexander Julius and Dorothy Lea (Matier) G.; m. Laura Lou Staley, July 20, 1980. BS in Speech, Northwestern U., Evanston, Ill., 1972; JD, U. Mich., 1975. Bar: Mo. 1975. Prin. Goldstein & Pressman, P.C., St. Louis, 2000—. Mem. ABA, Mo. Bar Assn. (chmn. bankruptcy com. 1983-85), Bar Assn. of Met. St. Louis. Home: 712 Swarthmore Ln Saint Louis MO 63130-3618 Office: Goldstein & Pressman PC 121 Hunter Ave Ste 101 Saint Louis MO 63124-2082 E-mail: stg@goldsteinpressman.com.

GOLDSTEIN, STEVEN ALAN, medical and engineering educator; b. Reading, Pa., Sept. 15, 1954; m. Nancy Ellen Gehr, Aug. 22, 1976; children: Aaron Michael, Jonathan David. BS in Mech. Engring., Tufts U., 1976; MS in Bioengring., U. Mich., 1977, PhD in Bioengring, 1981. Rsch. investigator dept. surgery U. Mich., Ann Arbor, 1981-83, asst. prof. surgery, 1983-88, assoc. prof. surgery, 1988-92, prof. surgery, 1992—. Co-dir. orthopaedic biomechanics lab. U. Mich., 1981-82, dir. orthopaedic rsch. labs. U. Mich., 1982—; prof. mech. engring. and applied mechanics, 1992—, mem. faculty bioengring. program, 1982-96, prof. biomed. engring., 1996—, interim chmn., 1985-89, rsch. scientist Inst. Gerontology, 1993—, asst. dean rsch. & grad. studies U. Mich. Med. Sch., 1993-98, assoc. dean, 1999—; rsch. asst. bioengring. ctr. Tufts New England Med. Ctr., 1974-76; mem. calcium homeostasis adv. group NASA, 1987-89; cons. Libbey-Owens Ill., Gen. Tire & Rubber, Upjohn, Ethyl Corp., Norwich Eaton, KMS Fusion, Whitby Pharmaceuticals, Norian Corp., Genetics Inst., Therics Inc., Osteo Biologics Inc., Matrigin Inc.; chair NIH study sect. on orthopaedics and musculoskeletal diseases, 1993-95. Author: Advances in Engineering, 1991; author (with others) Biomechanics of Diathrodial Joints, 1990, Molecular Biology of the Cardiovascular System, 1991, Surgery: Scientific Principles and Practice, 1993, Limb Development and Regeneration, 1993, Accidental Injury: Biomechanics and Prevention, 1993; reviewer Math. Bioscis., 1982—, Annals of Biomed. Engring., 1983—, Clin. Orthopaedics and Related Rsch., 1983—, Jour. Rehab. Rsch. and Devel., 1987—; reviewer Jour. Biomechanics, 1982—, editorial cons., 1992—; reviewer Jour. Biomech. Engring., 1982—, assoc. editor, 1991-97; reviewer Jour. Orthopaedic Rsch., 1984—, mem. bd. assoc. editors , 1992—; reviewer Jour. Bone and Joint Surgery, 1987—, mem. bd. assoc. editors for rsch., 1989—; reviewer, mem. study section NIH, NSF, NASA, Nat. Inst. Occupational Health & Safety, 1983—; contbr. more than 100 articles to profl. jours. Recipient Young Rsch. Investigator award 3M Corp., 1984, Nicolas Andre award Assn. Bone & Joint Surgeons, 1987-88. Mem. ASME (chair program com. 1989-92, sec.-elect 1993, exec. com. bioengring. divsn. 1989—, chair bioengring. divsn. 1995-96, Y.C. Fung Young Investigator award 1987), Am. Soc. Biomechanics (exec. bd. 1984-85), Am. Acad. Orthopaedic Surgeons (com. biomed. engring. 1991—, Kappa Delta award 1989-90), Orthopaedic Rsch. Soc. (adj. program com. 1990-91, program com. 1992, sec. 1997—), Biomed. Engring. Soc., Engring. Soc. Detroit (Young Engr. of Yr. award 1987), The Knee Soc. Achievements include patents (with other) for Intracone Reamer, Instacone Prosthetic Surface, Flexible Connecting Shaft for Intramedullary Reamer, Tissue Pressure Measurement Transducer System, Continuous Flow Tissue Pressure Measurement Transducer System, Prosthesis Interface Surface and Method of Implanting, Direct Gene Transfer in Wounds. Office: U Mich Orthopaedic Rsch Labs 400 N Ingalls St Rm G161 Ann Arbor MI 48109-2003

GOLDSTICK, THOMAS KARL, biomedical engineering educator; b. Toronto, Ont., Can., Aug. 21, 1934; came to U.S., 1955; s. David and Iva Sarah (Kaplan) G.; m. Marcia Adrienne Jenkins, July 4, 1982. BS, MIT, 1957, MS, 1959; PhD, U. Calif., Berkeley, 1966, U. Calif., San Francisco, 1966-67. Asst. prof. Northwestern U., Evanston, Ill., 1967-71, assoc. prof. chem. engring. and biol. sci., 1971-81, prof. chem. engring., neurobiology and physiology, 1981-85, prof. chem. engring., biomed. engring., neurobiology and physiology, 1985-99, prof. emeritus, 1999—. Adj. prof. ophthalmology U. Ill., Chgo., 1981-91. Editor: Oxygen Transport to Tissue V, 1983, VII, 1985, X, 1988, XI, 1989, XII, 1990, XIII, 1992. Rsch. grantee NIH, 1968—; Spl. Rsch. fellow U. Calif., San Diego, LaJolla, 1971-73. Mem. Internat. Soc. Oxygen Transport to Tissue (sec. 1980-86, exec. com. 1986-93), Biomed. Engring. Soc. (bd. dirs. 1983-86, chmn. publs. bd. 1985-86). Home: 2025 Sherman Ave Apt 504 Evanston IL 60201-3269 Office: Chem Engring Dept Northwestern U Evanston IL 60208-3120 E-mail: t-goldstick@northwestern.edu.

GOLDWASSER, EDWIN LEO, physicist; b. N.Y.C., Mar. 9, 1919; s. I. Edwin and Edith (Goldstein) G.; m. Elizabeth Weiss, Oct. 27, 1940; children: Michael, John, Katherine, David, Richard. BA, Harvard U., 1940; PhD, U. Calif., Berkeley, 1950. Rsch. asst. and rsch. assoc. U. Calif., Berkeley, 1946-51; rsch. assoc., prof. physics U. Ill., Urbana, 1951-88; dep. dir. Fermi Nat. Accelerator Lab., Batavia, Ill., 1967-78; vice chancellor for rsch. U. Ill., Urbana, 1978-80, vice chancellor acad. affairs, 1979-86, acting dir. internat. programs, 1988-89, acting dir. Computer-based Edn. Rsch. Lab., 1989-92; assoc. dir. Superconducting Super Collider Cen. Design Group, Berkeley, 1986-88; disting. fellow Calif. Inst. Tech., 1993-94. Mem., chmn. Nat. Rsch. Coun. div. Phys. Scis., Washington, 1961-69; chmn. sci. policy com. Stanford (Calif.) Linear Accelerator Ctr., 1980-84; chmn. sci. and ednl. adv. com. U. Calif., Berkeley, 1986-92. Author: Optics, Waves, Atoms and Nuclei, 1965; contbr. articles to profl. jours. Westinghouse fellow, 1949-50; Guggenheim fellow, 1957-58; Fulbright fellow, 1957-58. Fellow: AAAS; mem.: Phi Kappa Phi, Xigma Xi, Phi Beta Kappa. Avocations: tennis, swimming, opera. Home: 612 W Delaware Ave Urbana IL 61801-4805 Office: U Ill Dept Physics 1110 W Green St Urbana IL 61801-9013 E-mail: egoldwas@uiuc.edu.

GOLDWASSER, EUGENE, biochemist, educator; b. N.Y.C., Oct. 14, 1922; s. Herman and Anna (Ackerman) G.; m. Florence Cohen, Dec. 22, 1949 (dec.); children— Thomas Alan, Matthew Laurence, James Herman; m. Deone Jackman, Feb. 15, 1986 B.S., U. Chgo., 1943, Ph.D., 1950; ScD (hon.), N.Y. Med. Coll. Am. Cancer Soc. fellow U. Copenhagen, Denmark, 1950-52; rsch. assoc. U. Chgo., 1952-61, mem. faculty, 1962—, prof. biochemistry, 1963-91, prof. emeritus biochemistry and molecular biology, 1991—, chmn. com. on devel. biology., 1976-91, chmn. biochemistry and molecular biology, 1994-98. Served with AUS, 1944-46. Recipient Esther Langer medal for cancer rsch. Internat. Soc. Blood Purification, 1987, Simpson award Wayne State U., Lucerne award Fedn. European Physiol. Soc., Karl Landsteiner award Am. Assn. of Blood Banks; Guggenheim fellow Oxford (Eng.) U., 1966-67. Fellow AAAS, Am. Acad. Arts and Scis.; mem. Am. Soc. Biol. Chemists, Biochem. Soc., Internat. Soc. Exptl. Hematology, Am. Soc. Hematology, Sigma Xi. Achievements include purification of human erythropoietin; rsch. in biochemistry and red blood cell formation. Home: 5656 S Dorchester Ave Chicago IL 60637-1706 E-mail: egoldwas@midway.uchicago.edu.

GOLER, MICHAEL DAVID, lawyer; b. Cleve., June 29, 1952; s. George G. and Harriet (Zellen) G.; children: Jonathan A. Jennifer S. BA in Classics (Greek), Union Coll., 1974; JD, Case We. Reserve U., 1977. Bar: Ohio 1977, U.S. Dist. Ct. Ohio 1977, U.S. Ct. Appeals (6th cir.) 1982. Assoc. Persky, Marken, Konigsberg & Shapiro, Cleve., 1977-81; assoc. counsel Cardinal Fed. Savings Bank, 1981-84; assoc. Arter & Hadden, 1984-86, Kohrman, Jackson & Krantz, Cleve., 1988-86, ptnr., 1988-94; of counsel Goodman Weiss Miller LLP, 1994—. Mem. ABA (sect. real property probate and trust law, chmn. com. enforcement of creditor's rights and bankruptcy, 1991-95, vice chair com. on econs., tech. and practice methods 1995-97, chair 1997-2001, mng. editor EDirt online newsletter 1999—, mem. coun. 2001-), Cleve. Bar Assn. (founder, chmn. environ. law sect. 1991-95, chmn. real estate sect. 1989-90). Avocations: music, golf, squash, bicycling, skiing. Home: 6809 Mayfield Rd #1272 Mayfield Heights OH 44124 Office: Goodman Weiss Miller LLP 100 Erieview Plz Fl 27 Cleveland OH 44114-1824 E-mail: goler@goodmanweissmiller.com.

GOLIN, ALVIN, public relations company executive; b. Chgo., June 19, 1929; s. Charles and Jeanette G.; m. June Kerns, Aug. 25, 1961; children: Barry, Karen, Ellen. B.J., Roosevelt U., 1950. Publicity rep. MGM Pictures, N.Y.C., 1951-54; chmn. Golin/Harris Communications Inc., Chgo., 1975—. Lectr. to numerous univs. Advisor Chgo. council Boy Scouts Am.; advisor Nat. Multiple Sclerosis Soc., U. Tenn. Mem. Pub. Relations Soc. Am., Publicity Club of Chgo. Office: Golin/Harris Communications Inc 111 E Wacker Dr Fl 10 Chicago IL 60601-4305

GOLOMB, HARVEY MORRIS, oncologist, educator; b. Pitts., Feb. 13, 1943; s. Russell Austin and Dorothy (Simon) G.; m. Lynne Rooth, Dec. 28, 1965; children: Adam, Sara. BA, U. Chgo., 1964; MD, U. Pitts., 1968. Diplomate Am. Bd. Internal Medicine, Am. Bd. Med. Oncology. Intern Boston City Hosp., 1968-69; resident Johns Hopkins U., Balt., 1971-72, fellow, 1972-73, U. Chgo., 1973-75, asst. prof. dept. medicine, 1975-79, assoc. prof., 1979-83, prof., 1983—, chief sect. hematology/oncology, 1981-98, chmn. dept. medicine, 1998—. Chmn. subspecialty bd. med. oncology Am. Bd. Internal Medicine, 1991-95. Contbr. over 300 articles, papers to profl. publs.; co-editor: Lung Cancer, 1988. Capt. U.S. Army, 1971-73. Mem. Am. Soc. Hematology (bd. dirs. 1987-91), Am. Soc. Oncology (pres. elect 1989-90, pres. 1990-91). Office: U Chgo MC 6092 5841 S Maryland Ave Chicago IL 60637-1463 E-mail: hgolomb@medicine.bsd.uchicago.edu.

GOLOMSKI, WILLIAM ARTHUR JOSEPH, consulting company executive; b. Custer, Wis. s. John Frank and Margaret Sophie (Glisczinski) G.; m. Joan Ellen Hagen; children: Gretchen E., William A. Jr. MS, Marquette U.; MBA, U. Chgo; MS in Engring. Mgmt., Milw. Sch. Engring; MA, Roosevelt U. Registered profl. engr., Calif. Prin. W.A. Golomski & Assocs., Algoma, Wis., 1949—, pres., 1971—. Judge Malcolm Baldridge Nat. Quality award, 1988; sr. lectr. Grad. Sch. Bus., U. Chgo., 1990-95. Author chpts. in books; co-editor A Quality Revolution in Manufacturing, 1989; founding editor Quality Mgmt. Jour., 1993. Mem. Avoca Sch. Bd., Wilmette, Ill.; adv. bd. Milw. Sch. Engring., 1967-72, 83-87, indsl. engring. com. Hon. mem. Philippine Soc. Quality Control, 1992. Fellow AAAS, Am. Soc. Quality Control (Eugene L. Grant award 1991, Edwards medal, William A. Golomski rsch. award named in his honor 1986, Am. Deming medal met. sect., hon. mem. 1993), N.Y. Acad. Scis., Royal Soc. Health, Am. Statis. Assn., Inst. Indsl. Engrs. (Frank and Lillian Gilbreth Indsl. Engring. award 1999), World Assn Productivity Sciences; mem. NAE. Achievements include devel. of world class orgns.; first jour. for quality mgmt. and quality in higher edn. Office: N9690 County Road U Algoma WI 54201-9528

GOLUSIN, MILLARD R. obstetrician and gynecologist; b. Detroit, Feb. 14, 1947; s. Raddie and Joan (Lalich) G.; m. Yvonne Marie Cronovich, Sept. 29, 1974; children: Milan, Marko, Matthew. BS with honors, Wayne State U., 1968, MS, 1970, MD, 1975. Diplomate Am. Bd. Obstetrics and Gynecology. Intern, then resident William Beaumont Hosp., Royal Oak, Mich., 1975-78; practice medicine specializing in obstetrics and gynecology Village Gynecologic and Obstetric Assocs., P.C., Southfield and Troy, 1978-92; pvt. practice specializing in obstetrics and gynecology Troy, 1992-98; assoc. Wilshire Obstetrics-Gynecol. Assocs. PC, 1998—. Mem. quality assurance com. William Beaumont Hosp., Royal Oak, Mich., 1979—, mem. gynecol. quality assurance com., 1993—; charter mem., pres. Preferred Ob-Gyn. Mgmt. Group L.L.C. Trustee, mem. credentials com. Preferred Provider Network, 2000; trustee United Beaumont Physicians Group, 1993—. Served with U.S. Army, 1969-71. Fellow ACOG; mem. Am. Soc. Reproductive Medicine, Mich. State Med. Soc., Am. Inst. Ultrasound Medicine, Serbian Singing Soc., Ravanica (musical dir. 1967—, pres. 1981-82). Republican. Serbian Eastern Orthodox. Avocations: music, golf. Office: Wilshire Obstetrics-Gynecol Assocs PC 4600 Investment Dr Ste 170 Troy MI 48098-6369

GOMBERG, EDITH S. LISANSKY, psychologist, educator; b. N.Y.C., Jan. 14, 1920; d. Barnet and Dorothy (Resnick) Silverglied; m. Henry Jacob Gomberg, June 24, 1967; children: Stephen, Judith, Eugene, Richard, Robert. M.A., Columbia U., 1940; Ph.D., Yale U., 1949. Lectr., rsch. asst., rsch. assoc. Center Alcohol Studies, Yale U., New Haven, 1949-67; assoc. prof. dept. psychology U. P.R., 1968-71; prof. Sch. Social Work, U. Mich.,

Ann Arbor, 1974-90; prof. psychology, dept. psychiatry U. Mich., 1988-99, prof. emerita, 1999—. Author: Gender and Disordered Behavior, 1979, Alcohol, Science and Society Revisited, 1982, Current Issues in Alcohol/Drug Studies, 1989, Drugs and Human Behavior: A Sourcebook for the Helping Professions, 1991, Women and Substance Abuse, 1993, Alcohol and Aging, 1995; contbr. chpts. to books, articles to profl. jours. Mem. Rep. Town Meeting, Hamden, Conn., 1964-65; mem. Blue Ribbon Study Commn. on Alcoholism and Aging, Nat. Council on Alcoholism, 1979-82; chmn. panel on prevention, study to assess sci. opportunities of alcohol-related research Inst. Medicine, Nat. Acad. Sci.; mem. alcohol psychosocial research rev. com. Nat. Inst. Alcohol Abuse and Alcoholism, 1981-82. Mary E. Ives fellow, 1944; AAUW Elizabeth Avery Colten fellow, 1955 Mem. Psychonomic Soc., Sociedad Interamericana de Psicología, Rsch. Soc. on Alcoholism, Sigma Xi. Jewish. Home: 430 Hillspur Rd Ann Arbor MI 48105-1049 Office: U Mich Alcohol Rsch Ctr 400 E Eisenhower Pkwy Ann Arbor MI 48108-3318 E-mail: a2edith@aol.com.

GOMER, ROBERT, chemistry educator; b. Vienna, Mar. 24, 1924; m. Anne Olah, 1955; children: Richard, Maria. B.A., Pomona Coll., 1944; Ph.D. in Chemistry, U. Rochester, 1949; AEC fellow chemistry, Harvard, 1949-50. Instr. dept. chemistry James Franck Inst. U. Chgo., 1950-51, asst. prof., 1951-54, assoc. prof., 1954-58, prof., 1958-96, Carl William Eisendrath Disting. Service prof., 1984-96, prof. emeritus, 1996—. Dir. James Franck Inst. U. Chgo., 1977-83 Bd. dirs. Bull. Atomic Scientists, 1960-84. Served with AUS, 1944-46. Recipient Kendall award in surface chemistry Am. Chem. Soc., 1975, Davisson Germer prize Am. Phys. Soc., 1981, Medard W. Welch award Am. Vacuum Soc., 1989, Arthur W. Adamson award Am. Chem. Soc., 1996; Sloan fellow, 1958-62, Guggenheim fellow, 1969-70; Bourke lectr. Eng., 1959. Mem. Leopoldina Acad. Scis., Nat. Acad. Scis., Am. Acad. Arts and Sci. Home: 4824 S Kimbark Ave Chicago IL 60615-1916 Office: 5640 S Ellis Ave Chicago IL 60637-1433 E-mail: r-gomer@uchicago.edu.

GOMES, EDWARD CLAYTON, JR. construction company executive; b. Terre Haute, Ind., Nov. 15, 1933; s. Edward Clayton Sr. and Jewel Margaret (James) G.; m. Pamela Thompson, Jan. 11, 1958; children: Hilary T., Valerie C. BBA, Washington U., St. Louis, 1955, MBA, 1968. Pres. Mo. Petroleum Products Co., St. Louis, 1969-80; pres., CEO Lionmark, Inc., 1980—. Bd. dirs. Martin K. Eby Constrn., Inc., Wichita, Magna Bank, St. Louis, Rightchoice Managed Care, Inc.; internat. dir. Young Pres.'s Orgn., N.Y.C., 1975-80; trustee Blue Cross Blue Shield Mo., 1991-94. Bd. dirs. Acad. of Sci., St. Louis, 1977-80; trustee St. Louis Art Mus., 1988-92, The Hawthorne Found., Jefferson City, Mo., 1983-86; commr. St. Louis Sci. Ctr., 1980-83. Mem. World Bus. Coun., Chief Execs. Orgn. (bd. dirs.), Whittemore House, St. Louis Club, Beta Gamma Sigma. Episcopalian. Avocations: swimming, tennis, reading, travel. Office: Lionmark Inc 1620 Woodson Rd Saint Louis MO 63114-6129

GOMEZ, LUIS OSCAR, Asian and religious studies educator; b. Guayanilla, P.R., Apr. 7, 1943; s. Manuel Gomez and Lucila Rodriguez; m. Ruth Cedenia Maldonado, Dec. 24, 1963; children: Luis Oscar, Jr., Miran Ruth. BA, U. P.R., 1963; PhD Asian Langs. and Lit., Yale U., 1967; MA in Clin. Psychology, U. Mich., 1991, PhD, 1998. Lic. clin. psychologist. Vis. asst. prof. U. P.R., Rio Piedras, 1967, lectr., 1969-70, assoc. prof., 1970-73; assoc. prof. dept. Asian langs. and cultures U. Mich., Ann Arbor, 1973-80, prof. Buddhist studies, dept. Asian langs. and cultures, 1980—, chmn. dept., 1981-89; prof. psychology dept. psychology, 1999—. Vis. asst. prof. U. Wash., Seattle, 1967-68; Evans-Wentz Disting. lectr. Stanford (Calif.) U., 1983, vis. prof., 1985; vis. prof. Otani U. Kyoto, Japan, 1991-94. Author: The Land of Bliss, 1996; co-editor: Barabudur, Problemas de Filosofia, Studies in the Literature of the Great Vehicle, 1989. Mem. Am. Psychol. Assn., Soc. for Sci. Study Religion, Am. Acad. Religion, Internat. Assn. Buddhist Studies (gen. sec. 1986-89), Assn. Asian Studies. Home: 3204 Lockridge Dr Ann Arbor MI 48108-1722 Office: U Mich Dept Asian Langs & Cultures 105 S State St Ann Arbor MI 48109-1285

GOMEZ, MANUEL RODRIGUEZ, physician; b. Minaya, Spain, July 4, 1928; came to U.S., 1952, naturalized, 1961; s. Argimiro Rodriguez Herguedas and Isabel Gomez Torrente; m. Joan A. Stormer, Sept. 25, 1954; children: Christopher, Gregory, Douglas, Timothy. M.D., U. Havana, Cuba, 1952; M.S. in Anatomy, U. Mich., 1956. Intern Michael Reese Hosp., 1952-53, asst. resident in pediatrics, 1953-54; resident in neurology U. Mich., 1954-56; fellow in pediatric neurology U. Chgo. Med. Sch., 1956-57; instr. neurology U. Buffalo Med. Sch., 1957-58, 59-60; clin. clk. neurology Inst. Neurology, U. London, 1958-59; asst. prof., then assoc. prof. neurology Wayne State U. Med. Sch., 1960-64; mem. faculty Mayo Med. Sch., Rochester, Minn., 1964—, prof. pediatric neurology, 1975—, emeritus prof. pediatric neurology Minn., 1994—. Cons. pediatric neurology, head sect. Mayo Clinic, 1964-84, sr. cons. 1992—; vis. prof. King Faisal Hosp., Riyjadh, Saudia Arabia, 1994, Children's Hosp. Miami, 1995, Seville, Spain, 1995. Author: Tuberous Sclerosis, 1979, 2nd edit., 1988, 3d edit., 1999, Neurocutaneous Diseases, 1987; co-editor: Tuberous Sclerosis and Allied Disorders, 1991, Neurologia y Neuropsicologia Pediatrica, 1996; adv. bd. Brain and Devel., Pedriatrika. Recipient Ramón y Cajal award Academia Iberoamericana de Neuropediatría, 1995. Mem. Am. Acad. Neurology, Am. Neurol. Assn., Child Neurology Assn. (founder, former pres., Hower award 1989), N.Y. Acad. Scis., Philippine Pediatric Soc. (hon.), Sociedad Española de Neurologia (hon.), Sociedad Española de Neuropediatria (hon.), Assn. Research Nervous and Mental Disease, Orton-Dyslexia Soc. (adv. bd.), Am. Epilepsy Soc., Internat. Child Neurology Soc. (founder), Cen. Soc. Neurol. Research, Nat. Tuberous Sclerosis Assn. (hon. profl. advisor, Leadership award 1994), Sociedad Centroamericana de Neurologia y Neurociugia, Colombian Neurologic Soc. (hon.), Soc. Psiquiatría y Neurologia de Infancia y Adolescencia Chile (hon.), Costarican Neurol. Sci. Soc. (hon.), soc. Argentina de Neurologia Infantil (hon.). Home: 4225 Meadow Ridge Dr SW Rochester MN 55902-6640 Office: Mayo Clinic 200 1st St SW Rochester MN 55905-0001

GONZALEZ, JUAN (ALBERTO VAZQUEZ), professional baseball player; b. Vega Baja, Puerto Rico, Oct. 16, 1969; Outfielder Tex. Rangers, 1989-99; designated hitter Detroit Tigers, 2000—. Named Am. Assn. MVP, 1990; named to Am. League Silver Slugger Team, 1992-93, Sporting News Am. League All-Star team, 1993, 96. Named Am. League MVP, Baseball Writer's Assn. of Am., 1996. Achievements include leading Am. League in home runs, 1992-93. Office: Detroit Tigers 2100 Woodward Ave Detroit MI 48201-3474

GONZALEZ, TONY, football player; b. Huntington Beach, California, Feb. 27, 1976; Attended , Univ. Calif. Tight end Kans. City Chiefs, 1997—. Two-time participant Pro Bowl; spokesperson Midwest Donor Organ Bank, U.S. Dept. Transp. Safety Campaign, Sch. Safety Hotline, Kans. Cons. (movie) Any Given Sunday, appeared (HBO episode) Arliss , 2000, host (TV series) KCTV-5, appeared Buckle Up: Football is a Game, Your Life is Not. Founder Tony Gonzalez Found.; contbr. Shadow Buddies Program, Boys & Girls Clubs; donator Kans. City Boys & Girls Club, 1999. Recipient Mack Lee Hill award. Office: 1 Arrowhead Dr Kansas City MO 64129*

GONZALEZ, WILLIAM G. healthcare advisor; b. Hackensack, N.J., Mar. 28, 1940; s. William G. and Blanche Irene (Saffery) G.; m. Shirley Ann Mos, Aug. 15, 1964; children: Dana Lynn, Liane Renee. BA, Rutgers U., 1964; MBA, Cornell U., 1966; cert., Sloan Inst. Hosp. Adminstrn., 1966; MPA, NYU, 1980. Bus. adminstr. U. Calif.-San Francisco Med. Ctr., 1966-68, asst. dir., various positions, 1968-74; dep. dir. Capital Dist. Psychiat. Ctr., Albany, N.Y., 1974-79; instr. Albany Med. Coll., 1974-79; adj. asst. prof. SUNY-Albany, 1978-79; dir. U. Calif.-Irvine Med. Ctr., Orange, 1979-85; sr. lectr. Grad. Sch. Mgmt. and Calif. Coll. Medicine, U. Calif., Irvine, 1980-85; bd. dirs. Hosp. Coun. So. Calif., 1983-85; pres., chief exec. officer Butterworth Health Corp. and Butterworth Hosp., Grand Rapids, Mich., 1985-99; pres., CEO Spectrum Health, 1999-2000; healthcare advisor Wm. Gonzalez & Assocs., Chgo., 2000—. Adj. prof. health svcs. adminstrn. Mich. State U. Coll. Human Medicine, 1985—; mem. gov.'s Task Force on Access to Health Care, 1987-89; mem. nursing task force Joint Commn. on Accreditation Health Care Orgns., 1988-90; trustee Mich. Hosp. Assn., 1990-96; chmn. M in Mgmt. adv. coun. Aquinas Coll., Grand Rapids, 1992-95; bd. dirs. Grand Rapids Area Med. Edn. Ctr., chmn., 1995-97; mem. accreditation coun. grad. med. edn., Am. Hosp. Assn., coordinating Com. on Med. Edn.; regent ACHE Area B., Mich., 1994-98. Bd. dirs. Grand Rapids Pub. Edn. Fund, 1993-99; bd. dirs. Old Kent Fin. Corp., 1994-2000; active Health Professions Coun., San Francisco, 1971-74; active Planned Parenthood-World Population, Alameda Calif. and San Francisco, 1972-74; mem. coun. of dels. sect. on met. hosps. Gov.'s Coun., 1989-92; mem. regional policy bd. AHA, 1990-93. Served with M.C. U.S. Army, 1961-64. William Stout scholar, 1964; Alfred P. Sloan scholar, 1964-65; N.Y. State Regents scholar, 1964-65; Rotary Internat. exchange fellow in hosp. adminstrn. Australia, summer 1982

GOOCH, U. L. state legislator; m. Augusta Gooch. Kans. state senator Dist. 29, 1993—. Address: Capitol Office Bldg 300 SW 10th Ave Rm 404-n Topeka KS 66612-1504 also: 12 Crestview Lakes Est Wichita KS 67220-2914

GOOD, TIMOTHY JAY, medical equipment services company executive; b. Lima, Ohio, May 3, 1947; s. Marion Edward and Erma Mae (Sibold) G.; m. Ruth Ann Wray, July 22, 1967; children: Lucinda, Kelley, Ryan, Evan, Andrew. Student, Sinclair Community Coll., Dayton, Ohio, 1976-78, Ohio U., 1976-80, BioSystems Inst., Phoenix, 1982-86. Cert. cardiopulmonary technologist; cert. respiratory therapy technician; cert. pulmonary function technician; registered cardiopulmonary technologist, nat. managed care cert. level I and II. Asst. dir. respiratory therapy Bethesda Hosp., Zanesville, Ohio, 1968; dir. respiratory therapy Mount St. Mary Hosp., Nelsonville, 1968-75, Hocking Valley Hosp., Logan, 1972-81, Med. Ctr. Hosp., Chillicothe, 1975-78; pres. Cardiopulmonary Care, Inc., Logan, 1976—, Patient Evaluation Services, Logan, 1986-95. Cons. respiratory therapy S.E. Ohio Tb Hosp., Nelsonville, 1970-72, Ohio Lung Assn., 1978; mem. adv. com. and clin. faculty Shawnee State Coll., Portsmouth, Ohio, 1976-78; affiliate med. staff Hocking Valley Cmty. Hosp., Logan, Ohio, 1992—, Drs. Hosp., Nelsonville, 1994—. Pres. Hocking County (Ohio) Heart Assn., 1977; trustee Green Twp. (Ohio), 1980-82; chmn. Hocking, Vinton and Athens Counties (Ohio) Mental Health Bd., 1986, Hocking County Regional Planning Commn., 1986; mem. adv. coun. Faith Builders Ednl. Programs, Guys Mill, Pa., 1988-2000. Mem. Am. Assn. Respiratory Care (bd. dirs. 1982-84), Nat. Soc. Cardiopulmonary Technologists, Nat. Assn. Med. Equipment Suppliers, Ohio Soc. Respiratory Care (pres. 1978), Kiwanis (pres. Logan chpt. 1986—), Gideons Internat. (pres. Lancaster Ohio Camp 1999-2001, camp performance program asst. area 8-2, 2000). Republican. Mennonite. Avocations: reading, politics. Home: 3290 Stoney Hill Rd SW Lancaster OH 43130-8594 Office: 450 State Route 664 N Logan OH 43138-8541 E-mail: stoneyhill2@juno.com.

GOOD, WILLIAM ALLEN, professional society executive; b. Oak Park, Ill., May 29, 1949; s. Fred Clifton and Dorothy Helen (Stockdale) G.; m. Julianne Doggett, Jan. 8, 1972 (div. Apr. 1980); m. Paulette Edith Gordon, Apr. 23, 1983 (div. Apr. 1991); m. Laura Elizabeth Wellbank, Sept. 25, 1993. MBA, U. Chgo., 1992. Supr. Dun & Bradstreet, Inc., Chgo., 1972-73; gen. mgr. Nat. Roofing Contractors Assn., 1973-85, exec. v.p., Rosemont, Ill., 1987—; dir. mktg. Rand Devel. Corp., San Antonio, 1985-86; co-owner GT Communications, Inc., Dallas, 1985-87. Mem. Am. Soc. Assn. Execs. (cert.), Inst. for Orgn. Mgmt. (chmn. 1990-91), Chgo. Soc. Assn. Execs. (pres. 1996-97). Republican. Roman Catholic. Avocations: tennis, photography. Office: Nat Roofing Contractors Assn 10255 W Higgins Rd Rosemont IL 60018-5606 E-mail: bgood@nrca.net.

GOODE, WAYNE, state legislator; b. St. Louis, Aug. 20, 1937; s. Peter Wayne and Helen Celeste (McManus) G.; m. Jane Margaret Bell, July 27, 1963; children: Peter Wayne III, Jennifer Jacquelyn. BS in Banking and Fin., U. Mo., 1960. Mem. Mo. Ho. of Reps., Jefferson City, 1962-84, Mo. State Senate, Jefferson City, 1984—. Chair senate appropriations com.; mem. Commerce and Environ. Com., Civil and Criminal Juris Prudence Com., State Budget Control, Nat. Conf., Nat. Conf. State Legis. Found. for State Legis. Former mem. dean's coun. Sch. Bus. and Pub. Adminstrn. U. Mo., Focus St. Louis Conf. on Edn.; former bd. dirs. St. Louis Art Mus.; mem. St. Louis Econ. Conversion Project; mem. Citizen's for Mo.'s Children; bd. dirs. Mo. Hist. Soc.; mem. Sierra Club, Wilderness Soc., Audubon Soc. Lt. U.S. Army, 1960-61. Recipient numerous awards including Chancellor's Medallion, U. Mo., Mo. Assn. Counties Legis. award, Dr. Martin Luther King, Jr. St. Louis Co. Awareness Com. award, V.I.P. award Advt. Club, Recognition Meritorious Svc. award St. Louis Indsl. Rels. Assn., Disting. Svc. award Mo. Assn. for Children with Learning Disabilities, Outstanding Contribution in Improving Mental Health Care award Mental Health Assn., 1980 Globe Dem. award; named Conservation Legislator of Yr. Mo. Conservation Fedn., 1st Ann. Friend of Edn. Mo. NEA, Outstanding Legislator Mo. Assn. Pub. Employees, One of Ten Best Legislators St. Louisan Mag., Among Best and Brightest Columbia (Mo.) Daily Tribune, 1983 Ten Best Legislators Mo. Times. Home: 7231 Winchester Dr Saint Louis MO 63121-2623 Office: State Senate State Capitol Rm 333 201 W Capitol Ave Jefferson City MO 65101-1556

GOODENBERGER, DANIEL MARVIN, medical educator; b. McCook, Nebr., Apr. 24, 1948; s. Marvin Eugene and Mary Ellen (Marshall) G.; m. Janet Ann King, July 30, 1979; children: James Michael, Katherine Elizabeth. BS, U. Nebr., 1970; MD, Duke U., 1974. Diplomate Am. Bd. Internal Medicine, Am. Bd. Emergency Medicine (examiner 1983-95), Am. Bd. Pulmonary Disease, Am. Bd. Critical Care Medicine. Intern Peter Bent Brigham Hosp., Boston, 1974-75, resident in internal medicine, 1975-76; clin. assoc. Nat. Cancer Inst., Bethesda, Md., 1976-78; fellow pulmonary and critical care medicine Boston U. Med. Ctr., 1985-88; assoc. dir. emergency dept. Arlington (Va.) Hosp., 1979-82; edn. dir. emergency dept. Georgetown U. Hosp., Washington, 1982-85; dir. emergency svcs. U. Hosp., Boston, 1986-87; dir. pulmonary and critical care fellowship Washington U. Med. Schs., St. Louis, 1989-93; dir. pulmonary cons. svcs. Barnes Hosp., 1990-93, dir. internal medicine residency program, 1992—; assoc. prof. medicine Washington U., 1995-99; dir. divsn. med. edn. Washington U. Sch. Medicine, 1998—, prof. medicine, 1999—. Chief Wood-Moore Firm, Barnes-Jewish Hosp., 1996-2001. Editor Careers, 1996-98. Lt. comdr. USPHS, 1973-78. Winthrop Breon and Am. Coll. Chest Physicians scholar, 1987. Fellow ACP, Am. Coll. Chest Physicians; mem. AMA, Am. Thoracic Soc., Assn. Program Dirs. Internal Medicine (nominating and publs. com. 1991-98), St. Louis Met. Med. Soc. (councilor 1997-2000), Phi Beta Kappa, Alpha Omega Alpha. Methodist. Avocations: theatre, symphony music, travel, sailing. Home: 4355 Maryland Ave Saint Louis MO 63108-2737 Office: Washington U Sch Medicine Box 8121 660 S Euclid Ave Saint Louis MO 63110-1010

GOODIN, JULIA C. forensic pathologist, state official, educator; b. Columbia, Ky., Mar. 10, 1957; d. Vitus Jack and Geneva Goodin. BS, Western Ky. U., 1979; MD, U. Ky., 1983. Diplomate Am. Bd. Clin. and Anatomic Pathology, Am. Bd. Forensic Pathology. Intern Vanderbilt U. Med. Ctr., Nashville, 1983, resident in anatomic and clin. pathology, 1984-87; fellow in forensic pathology Med. Examiner's Office, Balt., 1987-88; asst. med. examiner Office of Chief Med. Examiner, 1988-90; dep. chief med. examiner State of Tenn., 1990-94; asst. med. examiner Nashville, 1990-93; chief med. examiner, 1993-94; asst. med. investigator State of N.Mex., Albuquerque, 1994-96; asst. prof. U. N.Mex., 1994-96; clin. assoc. prof. U. of South Ala. Sch. Medicine, 1996-99; state med. examiner Ala. Dept. Forensic Scis., Mobile, 1996-99; chief state med. examiner State of Iowa, Des Moines, 1999—. Clin. prof. U. Md. Med. Sch., Balt., 1988-90, Vanderbilt U. Med. Ctr., 1990-94. Capt. USNR, 1985—. Mem. Am. Acad. Forensic Sci., Assn. Mil. Surgeons of U.S., AMA. Avocations: long-distance running, weight lifting, photography, studying French. Home: 100 Market St Unit 414 Des Moines IA 50309-4765 Office: 321 E 12th St Des Moines IA 50319-0075

GOODKIND, CONRAD GEORGE, lawyer; b. Arlington, Va., Aug. 8, 1944; s. Bernard Arthur and Sylvia (Lieber) G.; m. Sandra Timme, Aug. 27, 1966; children: Carley M., Adam B., Erica L., Anne G. BS, U. Wis., 1966, JD, 1969. Bar: Wis. 1969, U.S. Dist. Ct. (ea. and we. dists.) Wis. 1969. Assoc. Kivett & Kasdorf, Milw., 1969-71; counsel Citizens' Study Com. on Jud. Orgn., Madison, 1971-73; dep. commr. securities State of Wis., 1973-79; assoc. Quarles & Brady, Milw., 1979-81, ptnr., 1981—, mem. exec. com., 1983—. Adj. prof. securities law U. Wis. Law Sch., Madison, 1975-79, Marquette U. Law Sch., Milw., 1981-83; mem. Gov.'s Bus. Cts. Task Force, 1994-98, state regulation com. Nat. Assn. Securities Dealers, Inc., Washington, 1986-92; bd. dirs. Able Distbg. Corp.; bd. dirs., sec. Cade Industries, Inc., 1989-99; sec. Brady Corp., 1999—. Bd. dirs. Milw. Repertory Theatre, 1995-2001, exec. com. mem., 1997-2001. Mem. ABA (vice chmn. state regulation securities com. 1986-89, chmn. 1989-92, vice chmn. bus. law sect. com. on insts. and seminars 2001—), Wis. Bar Assn. (chmn. securities com., 1981-95, bd. dirs. sect. bus. law 1991—, vice chair sect. bus. law 1996-98, chair 1998-2000). Office: Quarles & Brady LLP 411 E Wisconsin Ave Ste 2550 Milwaukee WI 53202-4497

GOODMAN, ALLEN CHARLES, economics educator; b. Cleve., Oct. 28, 1947; s. Nathan and Pearl (Dorfman) G.; m. Janet Hankin, July 22, 1984; 1 child, Sara. AB, U. Mich., 1969; PhD, Yale U., 1976. Asst. prof. Lawrence U., Appleton, Wis., 1975-78; rsch. scientist Johns Hopkins U., Balt., 1978-86; economist Dept. Housing and Urban Devel., Washington, 1985-86; assoc. prof. Wayne State U., Detroit, 1986-88, prof. econs., 1988—, chmn. dept., 1988-96. Author: Changing Downtown, 1987, Economics of Housing Markets, 1989, Economics of Health and Health Care, 2001, 3d edit. Mem. Mayor's Coord. Coun. on Criminal Justice, Balt., 1984-86. Mem. APHA, Am. Econs. Assn., Am. Real Estate and Urban Econs. Assn. Office: Wayne State U Dept Econs Detroit MI 48202

GOODMAN, BERNARD, physics educator; b. Phila., June 14, 1923; s. Louis and Fannie (Solomon) G.; m. Joyce Janet Willoughby, Mar. 3, 1950; children— David Nathan, Jonathan Bernard, Mark William AB, U. Pa., 1943, PhD, 1955. Stress analyst Internat. Harvester Co., Chgo., 1947-52; research assoc. U. Mo., 1952, asst. prof. physics, 1954-58, assoc. prof., 1958-64, prof., 1964—; prof. physics U. Cin., 1965-93, prof. emeritus, 1993—. Vis. sci. Argonne Nat. Lab., 1956-57, 61-62, 65-66, 70, Brookhaven Nat. Lab., 1960, Bell Telephone Lab., 1967, Ohio U., 1969; Nordita guest prof. Inst. Theoretical Physics, Uppsala, Sweden, 1962-63, Gothenberg, Sweden, 1971-72; vis. prof. Inst. Theoretical Physics, Gothenberg, 1985. Guggenheim fellow, 1962-63, Gordon Godfrey fellow U. NSW, Sydney, Australia, 1990; Fulbright scholar Inst. Theoretical Physics, Trieste, Italy, 1979-80 Fellow Am. Phys. Soc.; mem. AAAS, Phi Beta Kappa, Sigma Xi Achievements include rsch. on condensed matter theory. Home: 3411 Cornell Pl Cincinnati OH 45220-1501 Office: U Cin Dept Physics Cincinnati OH 45221-0011 E-mail: goodman@physics.uc.edu.

GOODMAN, DONALD JOSEPH, dentist; b. Cleve., Aug. 14, 1922; s. Joseph Henry and Henrietta Inez (Mandel) G.; BS, Adelbert Coll., 1943; DDS, Case-Western Reserve U., 1945; m. Dora May Hirsh, Sept. 18, 1947; children: Lynda (Mrs. Barry Allen Levin), Keith, Bruce; m. Ruth Jeanette Weber, May 1, 1974. Pvt. practice dentistry, Cleve., 1949-86; lectr. in field. With Dental Corps, USNR, 1946-48. Mem. Am. Acad. Gen. Dentistry, ADA Ohio State Dental Assn., Cleve. Dental Soc., Fedn. Dentaire Internationale, Cleve. Council on World Affairs, Greater Cleve. Growth Assn., Council of Smaller Enterprises, Phi Sigma Delta, Zeta Beta Tau, Alpha Omega. Clubs: Masons (32 deg.), Shriners, Travelers' Century (Gold award, special award), Circumnavigators. Home: 29099 Shaker Blvd Pepper Pike OH 44124-5022

GOODMAN, DWIGHT, manufacturing executive; Pres. Glas-Craft subs. Cohesant Techs. Inc., Indpls.; exec. v.p., CFO Cohesant Techs. Inc., pres., COO, 1996-98, CEO, 1998—. Office: Cohesant Techs Inc 5845 W 82d St Ste 102 Indianapolis IN 46278

GOODMAN, ELIZABETH ANN, lawyer; b. Marquette, Mich., Aug. 11, 1950; d. Paul William and Pearl Marie Goodman; m. Herbert Charles Gardner, Sept. 24, 1977. Student, U. Munich, 1970-71; BA cum laude, Alma (Mich.) Coll., 1972; JD cum laude, U. Mich., 1977. Bar: Minn. 1978, Mich. 1978, U.S. Dist. Ct. Minn. 1979. Cert. real property law specialist, real property sect. Minn. Bar Assn. High sch. tchr. Onaway (Mich.) High Sch., 1973-74; assoc. Dorsey & Whitney LLP, Mpls., 1978-82; ptnr. Dorsey & Whitney, 1983-99; v .p., chief gen. counsel Ryan Cos , 2000—. Mem. Am. Corp. Counsel Assn., Minn. Bar Assn., Hennepin County Bar Assn. Office: Ryan Cos 50 S 10th St Ste 300 Minneapolis MN 55403-2012

GOODMAN, ERIK DAVID, engineering educator; b. Palo Alto, Calif., Feb. 14, 1944; s. Harold Orbeck and Shirley Mae (Lillie) G.; m. Denise Rowand Dyktor, Aug. 10, 1968 (div. 1976); m. Cheryl Diane Barris, Aug. 27, 1978; 1 child, David Richard. BS in Math., Mich. State U., 1966, MS in Systems Sci., 1968; PhD in Computer Communication Sci., U. Mich., 1972; Hon. Doctorate, Dneprodzerzhinsk State Tech U., Ukraine, 1996. Asst. prof. elec. engring. Mich. State U., East Lansing, 1972-77, assoc. prof. elec. engring., 1977-84, dir. case ctr. for computer aided engring. and mfg., 1983—, prof. elec. engring., dir., 1984—, prof. mech. engring., 1992—. Dir. Mich. State U. Mfg. Rsch. Consortium, 1993—; v.p., Applied Computational Design Assocs., Inc., Okemos, Mich.; pres. Tech. Gateway, Inc., East Lansing; cons. Chinese Computer Comms., Inc., Lansing, 1988—; gen. chair First Internat. Conf. on Evolutionary Computation and its Applications, Moscow, 1996, Seventh Internat Conf. on Genetic Algorithms, 1997, Genetic and Evolutionary Computation Conf., 2001; gen. co-chmn. Internat. Computer Graphics Conf., Detroit, 1986. Author: (with others) SYSKIT: Linear Systems Toolkit, 1986; patentee in field. Academician, Internat. Informatization Acad. (Russia), 1993—. Mem. AIAA (chair rsch. and future dirs., subcom. CAD/CAM tech. com. 1987-89, Outstanding Svc. 1990), IEEE Computer Soc., Soc. Mfg. Engrs., Aircraft Owners and Pilots Assn., Acad. Engring. Scis. Ukraine (adv. prof. East China Normal U., 2002-), Internat. Soc. for Genetic and Evolutionary Computation (exec. com. 2001—, chair 2001--). Avocations: musician, tennis, studying Chinese. Office: Mich State U Dept Elec & Computer Engring 2308M Engineering Bldg East Lansing MI 48824 E-mail: goodman@tcimet.net., goodman@egr.msu.edu., e.goodman@acdassoc.com.

GOODMAN, GARY ALAN, lawyer; b. Memphis, Nov. 27, 1947; s. Louis H. and Margie (Evensky) G.; m. Teresa E. Berry, July 2, 1987. AB, Cornell U., 1969; JD, Columbia U., 1972. Bar: N.Y., 1973, U.S. Dist. Ct. (so. dist.) N.Y. 1973, Ill. 1979, U.S. Dist. Ct. (no. dist.) Ill. 1979, U.S. Cir. Ct. (2d cir.), U.S. Cir. Ct. (7th cir). Assoc. Sullivan & Cromwell, N.Y.C., 1972-79;

ptrn., gen. counsel Winston & Strawn, Chgo., 1979—. Bd. dirs. Lyric Opera Chgo., 1998—. Home: 219 E Lake Shore Dr Chicago IL 60611-1352 Office: Winston & Strawn 35 W Wacker Dr Ste 4200 Chicago IL 60601-1695

GOODMAN, HAROLD S. lawyer; b. St. Louis, Aug. 17, 1937; s. David and Eva Katherine (Wasserman) G.; m. Karen K. Mauldin, Aug. 5, 1979; 1 child, James Richardson. AB, U. Mo., 1960; LLB, JD, Washington U., St. Louis, 1963. Bar: Mo. 1963. Asso. firm Bishop & Goodman, St. Louis, 1963-70; v.p., gen. counsel, sec. World Color Press, Inc., 1970-75; pvt. practice, 1975-81; ptnr. Gallop, Johnson & Neuman, L.C., 1981—. Mem. St. Louis County CSC, 1976-80; trustee Cystic Fibrosis Found., 1971— , pres., 1975; mem. Mo.-St. Louis Met. Airport Authority, 1980-86; trustee-at-large Nat. Cystic Fibrosis Found., 1984-90; mem. Laumeier Sculpture Park, 1996—, chmn. bd. trustees, 2001—; mem. Cmty. in Partnership., 1986-88. Mem. ABA, Mo. Bar Assn., Bar Assn. St. Louis, Washington U. Law Alumni Assn. (pres. 1976-77), Zeta Beta Tau (pres. trustee corp. 1964-69), Phi Delta Phi. Home: 340 Falling Leaves Ct Saint Louis MO 63141-7405 Office: Gallop Johnson & Neuman LC 101 S Hanley Rd Ste 1600 Saint Louis MO 63105-3489 E-mail: hsgoodman@gjn.com.

GOODMAN, JULIE, nurse midwife; b. Dec. 14, 1937; m. Michael B. Goodman; children: Julia, Christopher, Jennifer. BAin Nursing, Coll. St. Catherine, 1960; MSN, U. Minn., 1975, PhDin Adult Edn., 1990. RN, Minn.; cert. nurse midwife. Staff nurse St. Joseph's Hosp., St. Paul, 1960-61; pub. health nurse Family Nursing Svc., 1961-63; instr. nursing U. S.D., Vermillion, 1963-66, Saint Mary's Sch. Nursing, Rochester, Minn., 1966-68, Rochester (Minn.) C. C., 1970-83; nurse practitioner Planned Parenthood, Rochester, Minn., 1978-81; dir. nursing cont. edn. Rochester (Minn.) C. C., 1983-88, dir. nursing, 1989-90, assoc. dean acad. affairs, 1994-95, dean of nursing and allied health, 1995—. Adv. bd. Family Consultation Svc., Rochester, Minn., 1983-86. Author, editor: Child and Family, 1982, 2nd edit. 1987; contbr. articles to profl. jours. Recipient Faculty Svc. award Mayo Med. Ctr., 1996, Main Achievement award, 1989. Mem. Am. Nurses Assn. (nat. del., Book of Yr. 1983), Nat. League Nursing, Minn. Orgn. Assoc. Degree Nursing (co-pres. 1994-96), Minn. Nurses Assn. (chair nursing edn. com. 1982-87, 87-89, bd. dirs. 6th dist.), Great Plains Perinatal Assn., Sigma Theta Tau Office: Rochester Cmty and Tech Coll 851 30th Ave SE Rochester MN 55904-4915

GOODMAN, STANLEY, lawyer; b. Cin., June 16, 1931; s. Sol and Ethel (Barsman) G.; m. Diane Elaine Kassel, Apr. 15, 1956; children: Julie Lerner, Jeffrey Stephen, Richard Paul. BA, U. Cin., 1953, JD, 1955. Bar: Ohio 1955, Ky. 1976. Ptnr. Goodman & Goodman, Cin., 1955—. Dir. Winbco Tank Co., Ottumwa, Iowa; lectr. Ohio Bar Continuing Legal Edn. Series. Mem. ABA, Am. Health Lawyers Assn., Ohio State Bar Assn. (chair eminent domain com. 1997-2000), Ky. Bar Assn., Cin. Bar Assn., Bankers Club, Losantiville Country Club. Jewish. Office: 123 E 4th St Cincinnati OH 45202-4003 E-mail: sgoodman@goodlaw.com.

GOODNO, KEVIN P. state legislator; b. Oct. 22, 1962; m. Linda Goodno; 1 child. BA in Bus. Adminstrn., Concordia Coll., 1985, BA in Polit. Sci. State rep. Dist. 9Ad Minn. Ho. of Reps., 1991—. Mem. regulated industry com., tax com., labor mgmt. rels. com., crime prevention com., health and human svcs. finance com., health and human svcs. policy com., gov.'s jobs & tng. coun., state coun. vocat. tech. edn., advantage Minn., Minn. Ho. of Reps. Mem. Moorhead C. of C., Ducks Unltd. Home: Box 478 Moorhead MN 56561 Office: 563 State Office Bldg Saint Paul MN 55155 E-mail: rep.Kevin.Goodno@house.leg.state.mn.us.

GOODRICH, JAMES WILLIAM, historian, association executive; b. Burlington, Iowa, Oct. 31, 1939; s. Martin Glenn and Marion Elizabeth (Prasse) G.; m. Linda Marlyse Andreoli, Aug. 31, 1963 (div. Aug. 1989); children: Anne Marlyse, Kimberly Ann. BS in Edn., Cen. Mo. State U., 1962; MA, U. Mo., 1964, PhD, 1974. Archivist Sec. of State, Mo., 1966; asst. then assoc. editor State Hist. Soc. Mo., Columbia, 1967-78, assoc. dir., 1978-85, dir., 1985—. Cons. USDA Soil Conservation Svc., Columbia, 1976, Mus. History and Sci., Kansas City, Mo., 1978, Mo. State Mus., 1989, Mo. Dept. Conservation, 1990, 91, 95, 97; mem. Mo. Hist. Records Adv. Bd., Jefferson City, 1985—, State Records Commn., Jefferson City, 1984—, Mo. Bd. Geographic Names, 1995; dir. Western Hist. Manuscript Collection, 1985—; adj. prof. history U. Mo., Columbia, 1988—. Co-author: Historic Missouri, 1988; editor: Report on a Journey to North America, 1980; assoc. editor Mo. Hist. Rev., 1967-85, editor 1985—; co-editor: German-American Experience in Missouri, 1986; co-editor, contbr. Marking Missouri History, 1998; contbr. articles to profl. jours. Mem. Planning and Zoning Commn., Columbia, 1975-77; councilman City of Columbia, 1977-79, 79-81; chmn. city audit com., Columbia, 1981-88; v.p. Friends of Mo. St. Archives, 1989-94; mem. 13th Jud. Cir. Bar Rev. Com., 1991-97; bd. dirs. Mo. Mansion Preservation Inc., 1991—; bd. dirs. Boone County Cmty. Trust, 1992—; mem. exec. com. Mo. State U. Alumni Assn., 1988-92, pres. 1991; mem. 6th Regional Disciplinary Com. Mo. Judiciary, 1997—; mem. Mo. Lewis and Clark Bicentennial Com., 1997—. Mem. Orgn. Am. Historians, Western History Assn., Am. Assn. for State & Local History, Conservation Fedn. Mo., Ducks Unlimited, Mo. Mus. Assn., Mo. Press Assn., Wild Canid Survival and Rsch. Ctr. Avocations: decoy collecting, waterfowl hunting, orinthoscopy. Office: State Hist Soc Mo 1020 Lowry St Columbia MO 65201-7207

GOODRICH, JOHN BERNARD, lawyer, consultant; b. Spokane, Wash., Jan. 4, 1928; s. John Casey and Dorothy (Koll) G.; m. Therese H. Vollmer, June 14, 1952; children— Joseph B., Bernadette M., Andrew J., Philip M., Thomas A., Mary Elizabeth, Jennifer H., Rosanne M. J.D., Gonzaga U., 1954. Bar: Wash, 1954, Ill. 1955. Indsl. traffic mgr. Pacific N.W. Alloys, Spokane, 1950-54; asst. to gen. counsel Cromium Mining & Smelting Corp., Chgo., 1954-56; with Monon R.R., 1956-69, atty., gen. solicitor, 1956-66, sec., 1957-69, treas., 1959-66, v.p. law, 1966-69; also dir.; sec.-treas. I.C.G.R.R., Chgo., 1970-79, sec., gen. atty., 1979-85; gen. counsel Ill. Devel. Fin. Authority, Chgo., 1985-92, spl. counsel, 1993; atty., cons. pvt. practice, Park Forest, Ill., 1994—. Mem. Park Forest Traffic and Safety Commn., 1963-66; mem. Park Forest Recreation Bd., 1966-77, chmn., 1969-70; trustee Village of Park Forest, 1977-80; mem. bd. Sch. Dist. 163, 1984-89; pres. South Cook Orgn. for Pub. Edn., 1988-89; conf. and meeting planner The Compassionate Friends, Inc., Oak Brook, Ill., 1991-94; bd. dirs. Park Forest Art Ctr., 1993-95, Ill. Philharm. Orch., 1994-98, treas., 1995-98; mem. adv. bd. Chgo. Self Help Ctr., 1993-94; bd. dirs. Ill Self Help Coalition, 1994-96; treas. Bereaved Parents of the U.S.A., 1995-2000, bd. dirs. 2000—, Tall Grass Arts Assn., 1999—; trustee Chgo. South Suburban Mass Transit Dist., 1996—, treas., 2000—. Inducted into Park Forest Hall of Fame, 1998. Mem. KC, The Parkforesters, Inc. (pres. 1998—, dir.), Kiwanis. Republican. Roman Catholic. Home and Office: 35 Cunningham Ln Park Forest IL 60466-2094

GOODRIDGE, ALAN GARDNER, research biochemist, educator; b. Peabody, Mass., Apr. 2, 1937; s. Lester Elmer and Gertrude Edith (Gardner) G.; m. R. Ann Funderburk, Aug. 19, 1960; children— Alan Gardner Jr., Bryant C. BS in Biology, Tufts U., 1958; MS in Zoology, U. Mich., 1963, PhD in Zoology, 1964. Rsch. fellow dept. biochemistry Harvard Med. Sch., Boston, 1964-66; asst. prof. physiology U. Kans. Med. Ctr., Kansas City, 1966-68; assoc. prof. Banting and Best dept. med. rsch. U. Toronto, Ont., Can., 1968-76, prof. Banting and Best dept. med. rsch., 1976-77; prof. pharmacology and biochemistry Case Western Res. U., Cleve., 1977-87; prof., head dept. biochemistry U. Iowa, 1987-96; prof. biochemistry Ohio State U., 1996—, dean Coll. Biol. Scis., 1996-2001, exec. dean Colls. of Arts and Sci., 1999-2001. Assoc. editor Jour. Biol. Chemistry, 1990—, Ann. Rev. of Nutrition, 1994-99, Jour. Lipid Rsch., 1995-99; contbr. numerous articles to profl. jours. Served with USN, 1958-61 Grantee Med. Rsch. Coun. Can., 1968-77, NIH, 1966-68, 77-97, USDA 1986-90, 93-97; Josiah Macy Jr. faculty scholar, 1975-76. Mem. AAAS, Am. Soc. Biochemistry and Molecular Biology, Thyroid Assn. Home: 844 W Orange Rd Delaware OH 43015-7978 Office: Ohio State U Coll Biol Scis 484 W 12th Ave Columbus OH 43210-1214 E-mail: goodridge.4@osu.edu.

GOODSTEIN, AARON E. federal magistrate judge; b. Sheboygan, Wis., Apr. 28, 1942; BA, U. Wis. Madison, 1964; JD, U. Wis., 1967. Bar: Wis. 1967, U.S. Dist. Ct. (ea. and we. dists.) Wis. 1967, U.S. Ct. Appeals (7th crct.) 1968. Law clk. to Hon. Myron L. Gordon U.S. Dist. Ct., Ea. Dist. Wis., 1967-68; shareholder Chernov, Croen & Goodstein, S.C., Milw., 1968-79; U.S. magistrate judge Ea. Dist. Wis., 1979-87, reapptd., 1987-95, 95—. Panelist Current Issues Relating to the Fourth, Fifth and Sixth Amendments, Jud. Conf. of 7th Cir., 1991; speaker fed. ct.'s class Marquette Law Sch., 1992; moderator probation and pretrial svcs. divsn. U.S. Cts., 1992; chair magistrate judges edn. com. Fed. Jud. Ctr., 1990-98, mem. magistrate judges com. of Jud. Conf. of U.S., 1993-99; adv. com. local rules and practice Ea. Dist. Wis., mem. adv. panel under Civil Justice Reform Act 1990; faculty mem. in field. Prodr: (video) Complaints, Warrants for Arrest and Search Warrants, 1992, Administrative Matters Pertaining to Magistrate Judges and Their Staff, 1993, Social Security: Process and Problems, Parts One and Two, 2000; mem. editl. adv. panel Handbook of Federal Civil Discovery and Disclosure, 1998; contbr. articles to profl. jours. Bd. dirs. Milw. Legal Aid Soc., 1974-79, Milw. Jewish Coun., 1977-79; pres. Milw. Forum, 1979-80, alumni mem.; pres. Congregation Shalom, 1990-92. Recipient Pro Bono award Gene and Ruth Posner Found., 1988. Mem. ABA (former chair magistrate judges com. Nat. Conf. Fed. Trial Judges), Fed. Magistrate Judges Assn. (1st v.p.), State Bar Wis. (pres. young lawyer's divsn. 1975-76, bd. govs. 1975-77), Milw. Bar Assn. (exec. bd. 1978-79, sec. 1979-82), U. of Wis. Law Sch. Alumni Assn. (bd. dirs. 1989-98), Order Coif, Phi Kappa Phi. Office: US Magistrate Judge 258 US Courthouse 517 E Wisconsin Ave Milwaukee WI 53202-4500

GOODSTEIN, SANDERS ABRAHAM, scrap iron company executive; b. N.Y.C., Oct. 3, 1918; s. Samuel G. and Katie (Lipson) G.; m. Rose Laro, June 28, 1942; children: Peter, Esther, Jack, Rachel. Student, Wayne State U., 1934-36; AB, U. Mich., 1938, MBA, 1939, JD, 1946; postgrad., Harvard, 1943. Bar: Mich., 1946. Sec. Laro Coal & Iron Co., Flint, Mich., 1946-60, pres., 1960—; owner, operator Paterson Mfg. Co., 1953-94. Gen. ptnr. Indianhead Co., Pontiac, Mich., 1955-70, pres., 1965-70; sec. Amatac Corp., Erie, Pa., unitl 1969; chmn. bd. Gen. Foundry & Mfg. Co., Flint, 1968—, pres., 1970-92; pres. Lacron Steel Co., Providence, 1975-80, ETL Corp., Flint, 1983-91, Can. Blending and Processing, Windsor, 1988-97; mem. corp. body Mich. Blue Shield, 1970-76. Served to lt. comdr. USNR, 1942-46. Mem. Fed. Bar Assn., Am. Bar Assn., Bar Mich., Am. Pub. Works Assn., Am. Foundrymen's Soc., Order of Coif, Beta Gamma Sigma, Phi Kappa Phi. Jewish. Home: 2602 Parkside Dr Flint MI 48503-4662 Office: 6301 N Dort Hwy Flint MI 48505-2348

GOODWIN, BECKY K. secondary education educator; Sci. tchr. Kansas Sch for the Deaf, Olathe, Kans. Christa McAuliffe fellowship grantee State of Kans., 1992, 94, 97; named Kans. Tchr. of Yr., 1995; recipient Presdl. award for Excellence in Sci. and Math. Secondary Sci. for Kans., 1992, Outstanding Biology Tchr. award Nat. Assn. Biology Tchrs., 1992, Sci. Teaching Achievement Recognition Star award NSTA, 1993, Milken Nat. Educator award, 1995, Tandy Tech. Tchr. award, 1998. Office: Kansas Sch For the Deaf 450 E Park St Olathe KS 66061-5410

GOODWIN, DANIEL L. real estate company executive; b. 1943; BS, No. Ill. U., De Kalb, 1964, MA, 1966. Chmn. bd., CEO The Inland Group Inc., Oak Brook, Ill. Office: The Inland Group Inc 2901 Butterfield Rd Oak Brook IL 60523-1190

GOODWIN, GRETA HALL, state legislator; m. James G. Goodwin. Legal asst., 1988—; mem. Kans. Ho. of Reps from 78th dist., Topeka, 1993-97, Kans. Senate from 32nd dist., Topeka, 1997—. Home: 420 E 12th Ave Winfield KS 67156-3721 Office: Kans Senate Chambers State Capitol Topeka KS 66612 E-mail: ggoodwin@ink.org.

GOODWIN, JAMES E. air transportation executive; BBA, Salem Coll. With United Airlines, 1967, sr. v.p. internat., 1992, sr. v.p. N.Am., pres., COO, 1998; former chmn., CEO UAL Corp., Elk Grove Twp., Ill. Trustee Lewis U.; bd. dirs. Chgo. Coun. Fgn. Rels. Mem. Exec. Club Chgo. (bd. dirs.), Comml. Club Chgo. (civic com.). Office: UAL Corp 1200 E Algonquin Rd Elk Grove Village IL 60007

GOODWIN, WILLIAM MAXWELL, financial executive; b. Muncie, Ind., Oct. 13, 1939; s. Donald Dunkin and Beth Virginia (Maxwell) G.; m. LaDonna Sherry Erickson, June 9, 1962; children: Lauri Michelle, Lisa Dianne. AB, Ind. U., 1961, MBA, 1966. CPA, Ind. Staff acct., supr. Ernst & Whinney (now Ernst Whinney & Young), Indpls., 1966-72; contr. Lilly Endowment, Inc., 1972-82, treas., sec., 1983-95, v.p. cmty. devel., 1996—. Advisor Sch. Bus., Ind. U., Bloomington, Ind., 1980-95; fin. advisor U.S. Gymnastic Fedn., Indpls., 1983-89; treas., dir. Nat. Gymnastics Found. Inc., Indpls., 1988-89. Contbr. articles to profl. jours. Treas., dir. Ind. Sports Corp., Indpls., 1979-88; dir. Youth Works, Inc., Indpls., 1977-85, Greater Indpls. Progress Com., 1996—; treas. Nat. Sports Festival, Indpls., 1982; treas., mem. exec. com. 1987 Pan Am. Games, Indpls.; chmn. AAU Sullivan Award Dinner, Indpls., 1983-94, mem. award selection com., 1993—. Capt. U.S. Army, 1962-64. Mem. AICPA, Ind. Assn. CPAs, Beta Gamma Sigma, Delta Phi Alpha. Republican. Methodist. Home: 3586 Inverness Blvd Carmel IN 46032-9380 Office: Lilly Endowment Inc PO Box 88068 Indianapolis IN 46208-0068 E-mail: goodwinb@lei.org.

GOOGASIAN, GEORGE ARA, lawyer; b. Pontiac, Mich., Feb. 22, 1936; s. Peter and Lucy (Chobanian) G.; m. Phyllis Elaine Law, June 27, 1959; children— Karen Ann, Steven George, Dean Michael B.A., U. Mich., 1958; J.D., Northwestern U., 1961. Bar: Mich. 1961. Assoc. Marentay, Rouse, Selby, Fischer & Webber, Detroit, 1961-62; asst. U.S. Atty. U.S. Dept. Justice, 1962-64; assoc. Howlett, Hartman & Beier, Pontiac and Bloomfield Hills, Mich., 1964-81; ptnr. Googasian Hopkins Hohauser & Forhan, Bloomfield Hills, 1981-96, The Googasian Firm, Bloomfield Hills, 1996—. Mem. bd. law examiners State of Mich., 1997—2002, pres., 2001—02. Author: Trial Advocacy Manual, 1984, West Groups Michigan Practice Torts, vols. 14 and 15, 2001. Pres. Oakland Parks Found., Pontiac, 1984-89; chmn. Oakland County Dem. party, Pontiac, 1964-70; state campaign chmn. U.S. Senator Philip A. Hart, Detroit, 1970; bd. dirs. Big Bros. Oakland County. 1968-73 Fellow Am. Bar Found., Am. Coll. Trial Lawyers, Internat. Acad. Trial Lawyers; mem. ABA (del. 1992-93, exec. coun. nat. conf. bar pres. 1993-96), ATLA, Am. Bd. Trial Advocates, State Bar Mich. (pres. elect 1991-92, pres. 1992—), Oakland County Bar Assn. (pres. 1985-86), Oakland Bar Found. (pres. 1990-92). Presbyterian. Club: U. Mich. Club Greater Detroit Home: 3750 Orion Rd Oakland MI 48363-3029 Office: 6895 Telegraph Rd Bloomfield Hills MI 48301-3138

GOOLDY, PATRICIA ALICE, retired elementary education educator; b. Indpls., Nov. 23, 1937; d. Harold Emanuel and Emma Irene (Wade) VanTreese; m. Walter Raymond Gooldy, May 4, 1968. BS, U. Indpls., 1959; MS, Butler U., 1963. Tchr. Franklin Twp. Cmty. Schs., Indpls., 1959-68, 72-99, USA Dep. Schs., Bad Kreuznach, Germany, 1969-72; ret., 1999. Co-owner Ye Olde Genealogie Shoppe, Indpls., 1972—; lectr. in field. Author: 21 Things I Wish I'd Found, 1984; editor: Indiana Wills to 1880: Index to Indiana Wills, 1987; co-editor: Indiana Manual For Gen, 1991, Illinois Manual For Gen, 1994. Mem. Franklin Twp. Geneal. Soc. (founder), Ind. Geneal. Soc. (chartered). Office: Ye Olde Genealogie Shoppe PO Box 39128 Indianapolis IN 46239-0128 E-mail: yogs@iquest.net.

GOOREY, NANCY JANE, dentist; b. Davenport, Iowa, May 8, 1922; d. Edgar Ray and Glenna Mae (Williams) Miller; m. Douglas B. Miller, Sept. 12, 1939 (div. 1951); children: Victoria Lee, Nickola Ellen, Douglas George, Melahna Marie; m. Louis Joseph Roseberry Goorey, Feb. 22, 1980. Student, Wooster (Ohio) Coll., 1939-40; DDS, Ohio State U., 1955. Cert. in gen. anesthesiology. Mem. faculty coll. dentistry Ohio State U., Columbus, 1955-86, dir., chmn. div. dental hygiene coll. dentistry, 1969-86, asst. dean coll. dentistry, 1975-86, mem. grad. faculty colls. dentistry and medicine, 1980-86, asst. dean, prof. emeritus colls. dentistry, 1986—. Moderator, prodn. chmn. Lifesavers 40 Prodns., 1981—; mem. task force on sch. based-linked oral health project Ohio Dept. Health, 1999—; mem. Franklin County Task Force on Access to Dental Care. Producer, video program Giving Your Mouth a Sporting Chance, 1990, video Operation TACTIC. Chmn. State Planning Com. for Health Edn. in Ohio, Columbus, 1976-77, 87-88, 95-97; founder Coun. on Health Info., Columbus, 1980, del., 1981-85, chmn., pres., 1985-86, chmn. prodn. com., 1986—, chmn. Capital Campaign; trustee Caring Dentists Found., Mayor's Drug Edn. and Prevention Program, Columbus, 1980—; mem. edn. com. Franklin County Rep. com., exec. com., 1993—; mem. human svcs. com. The Columbus Found.; pres. Worthington Arts Coun., 1998-2000. Recipient Vol. of Yr. award Columbus Health Dept., 1988-89, Dental Hygiene Nancy J. Goorey award Ohio State U., 1988, Drug Free Sch. Consortium award, 1996, Champion of Children's Oral Health award Ohio Dept. of Health Dental Divsn., 1997, Disting. Alumnus award Ohio State U. Coll. Dentistry, YWCA Women of Achievement award, 2000. Fellow: Internat. Coll. Dentists, Am. Soc. Dental Anesthesiology, Am. Coll. Dentists (chmn.-elect 1989—90, chmn. Columbus sect.); mem.: ADA (nat. consumer advisor 1975—78, coun.. edn. and licensure 1997—), Cols. Med. Assoc. Mem. Sports Med. Comm., Ohio Dept. Health (sch. linked oral health project 1999), Ohio State Med. Assn. Alliance (chmn. state com. legis. affairs 1993—94, chmn. state health promotions com. 1994—95, v.p. 1995—97, pres.-elect 1997, pres. 1998), The Found. of the Acad. of Medicine (v.p. 1993—94), Columbus Dental Soc. (chmn. coun. on constn. and bilaws on jud. affairs 1989—, pres. bd. dirs. 1986—87, 1989—91, chmn. sports dentistry com. 1995—), Ohio Dental Assn. (cons. 1979—, mem. subcoun. on dentists concerned for dentists 1994—96, chmn. subcoun. chem. dependency, prin. investigator, chair smokeless tobacco rsch., Ohio Disting. Dentist 1983), Am. Assn. Dental Schs. (pres. 1972—77, v.p.), Caring Dentists Found. (trustee), The Columbus Found. (human svcs. com.), Acad. of Medicine Aux. (pres. 1992—93, 1996—97, chair mouthguard project), Ohio State U. Faculty and Profl. Womens Club (pres. 1971—72), Ohio State U. Starling Womens Club 1982—83, Omicron Kappa Upsilon. Republican. Episcopalian. Avocations: camping, travel, bridge, cooking, wine. Office: Ohio State U Coll Dentistry 305 W 12th Ave Columbus OH 43210-1267

GORCYCA, DAVID G. lawyer; b. Feb. 20, 1962; BA in Polit. Sci., 1984, JD, 1988. House counsel Beresh & Prokopp, Liberty Mut. Ins. Co., 1985-88; asst. prosecuting atty. Oakland County Prosecutor's Office, 1988-90; assoc. Alan R. Miller, P.C., 1990-91; pvt. practice Valenti, Bolger & Gorcyca, 1991-96; prosecuting atty. Oakland County Prosecutor's Office, 1996—. Legis. aide to Sen. Richard D. Fessler, Mich. State Capital and Dist. Office, 1983-84; city liaison to crime prevention coun. sr. citizens adv. bd. Royal Oak City Commr., 1993—; del. Rep. State Conv.; precinct del. City of Royal Oak; del. Rep. County Conv.; mem. Lincoln Club Com., Bylaws Com.; active Boys and Girls Club, Mich. Cancer Found., Am. Heart Assn. Recipient Am. Jurisprudence Book award; Edward H. Rakow scholar FBA, Mfr.'s Nat. Bank of Detroit scholar, Mich. tuition scholar. Mem. Mich. Bar Assn., Mich. Rep. Lawyers Assn., Advocacy Bar Assn., Oakland County Bar Assn., Mich. State U. Pre-Law Assn., Mich. State U. Student Found., Sigma Alpha Epsilon (pres.), Intrafraternity Coun. Avocations: exercising, golf, basketball. Office: Office of Prosecuting Atty Courthouse Tower Pontiac MI 48341

GORDER, WILLIAM E. state legislator; m. Marlene Gorder; 4 children. BA, MEd, U. N.D. Tchr.; farmer; state rep. dist. 16, 1981—. Vice chmn. natural resources com.; mem. edn. and human svcs. com. N.D. Ho. Reps. Mem. Grafton C. of C., Grafton Gideon Camp, Walsh Hist. Soc., Farm Bur., Am. Legion. Republican. Home: 1345 Lawler Ave Grafton ND 58237-1764

GORDON, DAN, food service executive; Pres. Gordon Food Svc. Inc., Grand Rapids, Mich. Office: Gordon Food Svc Inc PO Box 1787 Grand Rapids MI 49501-1787

GORDON, EDWARD EARL, management consultant, educator; b. Evergreen Park, Ill., Feb. 28, 1949; s. Earl and Estelle (Biehn) G.; m. Elaine Huarisa, Aug. 6, 1983. BA in History, Edn., DePaul U., 1971, MA in History, 1972; postgrad., U. Chgo., 1972-73; PhD in History of Edn./Psychology, Loyola U., 1988. Founding pres. Imperial Consulting Corp., Oak Lawn, Ill., 1968—; exec. dir. North Am. Inst. for Tng. and Ednl. Rsch., 1972—. Arbitrator Coun. Better Bus. Burs., Chgo., 1977—, Ill. Bd. Edn., 1986—; lectr. Sch. Edn., DePaul U., Chgo., 1979-92, Northwestern U., Chgo., 1999, Conf. Bd. Basic Skills Devel. in the Workplace Conf., 2000; adj. prof., dir. grad. program in tng. and devel. Roosevelt U., Chgo., 1990-91; instr. adult corp. instrn. mgmt. program Loyola U., Chgo., 1992-98; mem. Conf. Bd. Bus. Edn. Conf., 1996; keynote spkr. Partnerships in Learning at Work program U. B.C., Vancouver, Can., 1990, ednl. conf. Assn. Legal Adminstrs., 1999, Corp. Univ. Forum, Chgo., 1996, Measuring Performance and Profit for Workforce Edn. Programs, Palm Springs, Calif. Author: Educators' Consumer Guide to Private Tutoring Services, 1989, Centuries of Tutoring: A History of Alternative Education in America and Western Europe, 1990, Closing the Literacy Gap in American Business: A Handbook for Trainers and Human Resources Development Specialists, 1991, The Need for Work Force Education, 1993, FutureWork: The Revolution Reshaping American Business, 1994, Ethics for Training and Development, 1995, Enhancing Learning in Training and Adult Edn., 1998, Opportunities in Training and Development Careers, 1996, Skill Wars: Winning the Battle for Productivity and Profit, 2000; contbr. articles to profl. jours.; mem. editl. adv. bd., columnist Corp. Univ. Forum Mag., 1995-98. Bd. dirs. Ill. Literacy Resource Devel. Ctr., BBB of Chgo. and No. Ill., 1996—; mem. bus.-edn. partnerships bd. Ill. Bd. Edn., 1995—; mem. Pvt. Industry Coun. of Cook County, 1994—. Mem. ASTD (pres.-elect. Chgo. chpt. 1989-90, dir. manuscript rev. bd. 1988—), Am. Ednl. Rsch. Assn., Am. Hist. Assn., Internat. Reading Assn., Am. Mgmt. Assn. (presenter New Strategic Corp. Model 1993), Internat. Soc. Performance Improvement, Midwest History of Edn. Soc. (pres.), Phi Delta Kappa (pres. DePaul U. chpt. 1986-88). Roman Catholic. Office: # 8E 220 E Walton St Chicago IL 60611-1649 E-mail: imperialcorp@juno.com.

GORDON, ELLEN RUBIN, candy company executive; d. William B. and Cele H. (Travis) Rubin; m. Melvin J. Gordon, June 25, 1950; children: Virginia, Karen, Wendy, Lisa. Student, Vassar Coll., 1948-50; B.A., Brandeis U., 1965; postgrad., Harvard U., 1968. With Tootsie Roll Industries, Inc., Chgo., 1968—, corp. sec., 1970-74, v.p. product devel., 1974-76, sr. v.p., 1976-78, pres., COO, 1978—; v.p., dir. HDI Investment Corp. Mem. coun. on divsn. biol. scis. and Pritzker Sch. Medicine U. Chgo.; mem. med. sch. adv. coun. for cell biology and pathology Harvard U.; mem. bd. fellows Faculty of Medicine, Harvard Med, Sch. Mem. dean's coun. J.L. Kellogg Grad. Sch. Mgmt. at Northwestern U.; mem. bd fellows Harvard U. Med. Sch.; mem. univ. resources and overseers com. Harvard U.;bd. advisors Women Inc. Recipient Kettle award, 1985. Mem. Nat. Confectioners Assn. (bd. dirs.). Office: Tootsie Roll Industries Inc 7401 S Cicero Ave Chicago IL 60629-5885

GORDON, GILBERT, chemist, educator; b. Chgo., Nov. 11, 1933; s. Walter and Catherine Gordon; m. Joyce Elaine Masura; children: Thomas, Lyndi. B.S., Bradley U., 1955; Ph.D., Mich. State U., 1959. Postdoctoral research assoc. U. Chgo., 1959-60; asst. prof. U. Md., College Park, 1960-64, assoc. prof., 1964-67, prof., 1967; prof. chemistry U. Iowa, Iowa City, 1967-73; prof., chmn. dept. Miami U., Oxford, Ohio, 1973-84, Volwiler Disting. Research prof., 1984—. Mem. editl. bd. synthesis inorganic metal, organic chemistry; contbr. articles to chem. jours. Editor: catalysis kinetics sect. Chem. Abstracts, 1970— ; editorial bd. synthesis inorganic metal, organic chemistry: catalysis kinetics sect. Ohio Jour. Sci, 1971— ; contbr. articles to chem. jours. Named Cin. Chemist of Yr., 1981 Mem.: Faraday Soc., Chem. Soc. London, Am. Chem. Soc., Internat. Ozone Assn. (treas., pres.), Phi Kappa Phi, Sigma Xi. Home: 190 Shadowy Hills Dr Oxford OH 45056-1441 Office: Miami U Dept Chemistry Oxford OH 45056 E-mail: gordong@muohio.edu.

GORDON, JULIE PEYTON, foundation administrator; b. Jacksonville, Fla., June 21, 1940; d. Robert Benoist Shields and Bessie (Cavanaugh) Peyton; m. Robert James Gordon, June 22, 1963. BA, Boston U., 1963; MA, Harvard U., 1965, PhD, 1969. Asst. prof. English Ill. Inst. Tech., Chgo., 1968-75, assoc. prof., 1975-77, asst. dean students, 1975-78; asst. dean acad. affairs Northwestern U., Evanston, Ill., 1978-80, lectr. English, Univ. Coll., 1978—, assoc. dean Univ. Coll., 1980-85, sec. Econometric Soc., 1975—, exec. dir. Econometric Soc., 1985—. Mem. nat. adv. com. ALA, Chgo., 1983-86. Author: Seasons in the Contemporary American Family, 1984. Grantee NEH, 1971-73; project scholar NEH, 1983-86. Mem. Phi Beta Kappa. Avocation: writing fiction and poetry. Home: 202 Greenwood Evanston IL 60201-4714 Office: Northwestern U Dept Econs Econometric Soc Evanston IL 60208-2600

GORDON, MYRON L. federal judge; b. Kenosha, Wis., Feb. 11, 1918; m. Peggy Gordon, Aug. 16, 1942 (dec. Mar. 1973); children: Wendy, John, Polly; m. Myra Gordon, Mar. 30, 1979. BA, MA, U. Wis., 1939; LLB, Harvard U., 1942. Judge U.S. Ct. Appeals, Milw., 1951-62, Wis. State Supreme Ct., Madison, 1966-67, U.S. Dist. Ct., Milw., 1967—; now sr. judge. Office: US Dist Ct 271 US Courthouse 517 E Wisconsin Ave Milwaukee WI 53202-4500

GORDON, PHILLIP, lawyer; b. Potgietersrust, South Africa, July 11, 1943; BA, U. Witwatersrand, 1964, BA honors, 1965; BA, Oxford U., Eng., 1967, MA, 1973; JD, U. Chgo., 1969. Bar: Ill. 1969, N.Y. 1973. Co-chmn. Altheimer & Gray, Chgo. Tchg. assoc. Northwestern U. Sch. Law, 1967-68. Mem. ABA, Ill State Bar, Chgo. Bar Assn. Office: Altheimer & Gray 10 S Wacker Dr Ste 4000 Chicago IL 60606-7407

GORDON, ROBERT JAMES, economics educator; b. Boston, Sept. 3, 1940; s. Robert Aaron and Margaret (Shaughnessy) G.; m. Julie S. Peyton, June 22, 1963. A.B., Harvard U., 1962; M.A., Oxford U., Eng., 1969; Ph.D., MIT, 1967. Asst. prof. econs. Harvard U., 1967-68; asst. prof. U. Chgo., 1968-73; prof. econs. Northwestern U., Evanston, Ill., 1973—, Stanley G. Harris prof. social scis., 1987—, chair econs. dept., 1992-96. Rsch. assoc. Nat. Bur. Econ Rsch., 1968—; mem. Brookings Panel Econ. Activity, 1970—; co-chmn. Internat. Seminar Macroecons., 1978-94; mem. exec. com. Conf. Rsch., Income and Wealth, 1978-83; mem. panel rev. productivity measures NAS, 1977-79; cons. bd. govs. Fed. Res. Sys., 1973-83, U.S. Dept. Treasury, 1967-80, U.S. Congl. Budget Office, 1996—, U.S. Bur. Econ. Analysis, 1999—; mem. Nat. Commn. on Consumer Price Index, 1995-97. Author: Macroeconomics, 1978, 8th edit., 2000, Milton Friedman's Monetary Framework, 1974, Challenges to Interdependent Economies, 1979, The American Business Cycle: Continuity and Change, 1986, The Measurement of Durable Goods Prices, 1990, International Volatility and Economic Growth, 1991, The Economics of New Goods, 1997; editor Jour. Polit. Economy, 1970-73. Recipient Lustrum prize Erasmus U., 1999; Marshall fellow, 1962-64; fellow Ford Found., 1966-67; grantee NSF, 1971—; fellow Guggenheim Meml. Found., 1980-81; rsch. fellow German Marshall Fund, 1985-86. Fellow AAAS, Econometric Soc. (treas. 1975—); mem. Am. Econ. Assn. (bd. editors 1975-77, mem. exec. com. 1981-83), Phi Beta Kappa Office: Northwestern U Dept Econs Evanston IL 60208-0001 E-mail: rjg@northwestern.edu.

GORDON, WILLIAM A. lawyer; b. Bklyn., Feb. 6, 1940; m. Joyce Kahler, Aug. 26, 1962; children: Kyle Robert, Michael Stuart, David Andrew. BS, Northwestern U., 1960; LLB, Harvard U., 1963. Bar: Ill. 1963, U.S. Dist. Ct. (no. dist. trial bar) Ill. 1965, U.S. Ct. Appeals (7th cir.) 1971, U.S. Supreme Ct. 1971, U.S. Tax Ct. 1971, U.S. Ct. Appeals (2nd cir.) 1983, U.S. Ct. Appeals (6th cir.) 1987. Law clk. U.S. Dist. Ct. (no. dist.) Ill., 1963-66; ptnr. Mayer, Brown & Platt, Chgo., 1970—. Office: Mayer Brown & Platt 190 S La Salle St Ste 3100 Chicago IL 60603-3441

GORENCE, PATRICIA JOSETTA, judge; b. Sheboygan, Wis., Mar. 6, 1943; d. Joseph and Antonia (Marinsheck) G.; m. John Michael Bach, July 11, 1969; children: Amy Jane, Mara Jo, J. Christopher Bach. BA, Marquette U., 1965, JD, 1977; MA, U. Wis., 1969. Bar: Wis. 1977, U.S. Dist. Ct. (ea. and we. dists.) Wis. 1977, U.S. Ct. Appeals (7th cir.) 1979, U.S. Supreme Ct. 1980. Asst. U.S. atty. U.S. Atty.'s Office, Milw., 1979-84, 1st asst. U.S. Attys., 1984-87, 89-91, U.S. Atty., 1987-88; dep. atty. gen. State of Wis. Dept. Justice, Madison, 1991-93; assoc. Ginbel, Reilly, Guerin & Brown, Milw., 1993-94; U.S. magistrate judge U.S. Dist. Ct. Wis., 1994—. Bd. dirs. U. Wis.-Milw. Slovenian Arts Coun., 1989—, treas., 1989—, Milw. Dance Theatre, 1993-98; bd. chair Bottomless Closet, 1999—. Recipient Spl. Commendation, U.S. Dept. Justice, 1986, IRS, 1988. Mem. ABA, Am. Law Inst., Am. Judicature Soc., Nat. Assn. Women Judges, Fed. Magistrate Judges Assn. (cir. dir. 1997-2000), Milw. Bar Assn. (chair cmty. rels. com. 2000—, Prosecutor of Yr. 1990), State Bar Wis. (chair lawyer dispute resolution com. 1986—, chair professionalism com. 1988-2000, vice chair legal edn. commn. 1994-96, Pres. award 1995), 7th Cir. Bar Assn. (chair rules and practices com. 1991-95), Assn. for Women Lawyers, Profl. Dimensions (sec. 1998-2000, v.p. adminstrn. 2000-2002).

GORHAM, EVILLE, ecologist, biogeochemist; b. Halifax, N.S., Can., Oct. 15, 1925; s. Ralph Arthur and Shirley Agatha (Eville) G.; m. Ada Verne MacLeod, Sept. 29, 1948; children: Kerstin, Vivien, Jocelyn, James. BSc in Biology with distinction, Dalhousie U., 1945, MSc in Zoology, 1947, LLD (hon.), 1991; PhD in Botany, U. London, Eng., 1951; DSc (hon.), McGill U., 1993, U. Minn., 1999. Lectr. botany U. Coll., London, Eng., 1951-54; sr. sci. officer Freshwater Biol. Assn., Ambleside, Eng., 1954-58; lectr., asst. prof. botany U. Toronto, 1958-62; assoc. prof. botany U. Minn., Mpls., 1962-65, prof., 1966-75, head dept., 1967-71, prof. ecology, 1975-84, Regents' prof. ecology and botany, 1984-98, Regents' prof. emeritus, 1999—; prof., head dept. biology U. Calgary, Alta., Can., 1965-66. Mem. for Can., Internat. Commn. on Atmospheric Chemistry and Radioactivity, 1959-62; mem. vis. panel to rev. toxicology program NAS-NRC, 1974-75, mem. com. on inland aquatic ecosys. Water Sci. and Tech. Bd., 1994-96, mem. com. to evaluate indicators for monitoring aquatic and terrestrial environments Water Sci. and Tech. Bd., 1997-99, mem. com. on hydrologic sci. bd. on Atmospheric Scis. and Climate, 1998-99; mem. coordinating com. for sci. and tech. assessment environ. pollutants Environ. Studies Bd., 1975-78; mem. com. on med. and biologic effects of environ. pollutants Assembly Life Scis., 1976-77; mem. com. to recommend nat. program for assessing problem of atmospheric deposition (acid rain) President's Coun. on Environ. Quality, 1978; mem. com. on atmosphere and biosphere Bd. Agr. and Renewable Resources, 1979-81; mem. panel on environ. impact diesel impact study com. NAE-NRC, 1980-81; mem. U.S.-Can.-Mex. joint sci. com. on acid precipitation Studies Bd., NAS-NRC, Royal Soc. Can., Mex. Acad. Scis., 1981-84; mem. health and environ. rsch. adv. com. U.S. Dept. Energy, 1992-94; mem. Water Sci. and Tech. Bd. NAS-NRC, 1996-99; mem. coun. sci. advisors Marine Biol. Lab., Woods Hole, Mass., 1996-99. Mem. editl. bd. Ecology, 1965-67, Limnology and Oceanography, 1970-72, Conservation Biology, 1987-88, Ecol. Applications, 1989-92, Environ. Revs., 1992—; contbr. articles on limnology, ecology, and biogeochemistry to profl. jours. Bd. dirs. Acid Rain Found., 1982-87, sec.-treas. 1982-84 Recipient Regents' medal U. Minn., 1984, Benjamin Franklin medal in earth sci. Franklin Inst., Phila., 2000; Royal Soc. Can. rsch. fellow State Forest Rsch. Inst., Stockholm, Sweden, 1950-51; grantee NSF, AEC, NIH, ERDA, NASA, Dept. of Energy, NRC Can., Ont. Rsch. Found., Environment Can., Office Water Resources Rsch., Dept. Interior, Andrew W. Mellon Found., N.Y.C. Fellow AAAS, Royal Soc. Can., Am. Acad. Arts and Scis.; mem. NAS, Am. Soc. Limnology and Oceanography (G. Evelyn Hutchinson medal 1986), Ecol. Soc. Am., Internat. Assn. Theoretical and Applied Limnology, Soc. Wetland Scientists, Swedish Phytogeog. Soc. (hon.), Gown in Town Club. Home: 1933 E River Ter Minneapolis MN 55414-3673

GORLIN, ROBERT JAMES, medical educator, educator; b. Hudson, N.Y., Jan. 11, 1923; s. James Alter and Gladys Gretchen (Hallenbeck) G.; m. Marilyn Alpern, Aug. 24, 1952; children: Cathy, Jed. AB, Columbia U., 1943, postgrad., 1947-50; DDS, Washington U., St. Louis, 1947; MS, State U. Iowa, 1956; DSc (hon.) , U. Athens, Greece, 1982, U. Thesallonike, 1993, U. Md., 1999, U. Minn., 2002. Oral pathologist VA Hosp., Bronx, N.Y., 1950-51; instr. dentistry Columbia U., N.Y.C., 1950-51; dental dir., pathologist Op. Blue Jay, Thule, Greenland, 1951-52; mem. exec. faculty, chmn. oral pathology and genetics Sch. Dentistry U. Minn., Mpls., 1956-90, assoc. prof. div. oral pathology Sch. Dentistry, 1956-58, prof. Sch. Dentistry, 1958-93, prof. pathology and dermatology Sch. Medicine, Sch. Dentistry, 1971-93, prof. pediatrics, ob-gyn, otolaryngology Sch. Medicine, 1973-93, Regents' prof. oral pathology, 1978-93; Fulbright exch. prof., Guggenheim fellow Royal Dental Coll., Copenhagen, 1961; 1st Lingamfelter lectr. dermatology U. Va., 1971; 1st Boyle lectr. Case Western Res. U. Med. Ctr., Cleve., 1972; vis. prof. UCLA-Harbor Gen. Hosp., 1972; asst. chief dental service Glenwood Hills Med. Ctr., 1959-61, chief, 1962-64, cons., 1969-73; Regents' prof. emeritis U of Minn. Sch. of Dentistry, Mpls, 1994-. Cons. oral pathology Mpls. VA Hosp., 1958—, Mt. Sinai Hosp., Mpls., 1958—91; cons. pediatrics Hennepin County Gen. Hosp., St. Paul's Children's Hosp., Ramsey County Gen. Hosp., Mpls. Children's Hosp., Gillette State Hosp. Crippled Children; mem. Minn. Adv. Bd. Human Genetics, 1959—73; Minn. mem. U.S. Congl. Liaison Com. for Dentistry, 1963—80; mem. Ctr. Histologic Nomenclature and Classification of Odontogenic Tumors and Allied Lesions WHO, 1966—80; mem. adv. com. periodontal disease and soft tissue study NIH, 1967—78, mem. dental sect., 1970—73; mem. adv. com. Nat. Found. Clin. Rsch., 1974—; vis. prof. Tel Aviv U., 1980, Sch. Dentistry, Jerusalem, 1981; 2nd Edward Sheridan lectr., Dublin, 89; Windemere lectr. Brit. Paediatric Assn., 1990; founder, bd. dirs. Found. for Devel. and Med. Genetics, 1994. Author: (with M. Cohen) Syndromes of the Head and Neck, 1964, 76, 90, 2001 (with R. Goodman) The Face in Genetic Disorders, 1970, 77, The Malformed Infant and Child, 1983, (with B. Konigsmark) Genetic and Metabolic Disorders, 1977, Hereditary Hearing Loss and Its Syndromes, 1995; co-contbr.: Computer Assisted Diagnosis in Pediatrics, 2d edit., 1971; editor: (with H. Goldman) Thoma's Oral Pathology, 1970, Chromosomes and Human Cancer (J. Cervenka and B. Koulischer), 1972; editorial cons. Jour. Dental Rsch., Geriatrics, Archives of Oral Biology, Jour. Pediats., Pediats., Am. Jour. Diseases of Children, Syndrome Identification, Radiology; editor oral pathology Oral Surgery, Oral Medicine, Oral Pathology, Clin. Pediats.; assoc. editor Am. Jour. Human Genetics, 1970-73, Jour. Oral Pathology, 1972-83, Jour. Maxillofacial Surgery, 1973—, Cleft Palate Jour., 1976—, Clin. Pediat., 1985—; mem. bd. Excerpta Medica, 1976-80, Jour. Craniofacial Genetic Devel. Biology, 1980—, Jour. Clin. Dysmorphology, 1982-86, Gerodontics, 1984-86, Birth Defects Ency., 1986—, Dysmorphology Clin. Genetics, 1987—; cons. editor Stedman's Med. Dictionary, 1959—; contbr. numerous articles to profl. jours. Bd. dirs. Minn. div. Am. Cancer Soc., 1959-60, mem. nat. clin. fellowship com., 1962-65. With U.S. Army, 1943-44; lt. USNR, 1953-55. Named Spinoza chair, U. Amsterdam, 1995, Disting. lectr., Am. Soc. Human Genetics, 2001, Royal Soc. Medicine, London, 2001; recipient Fredrick Birnberg Rsch. award, Columbia U., 1987, Lifetime Achievement award, March of Dimes, 1989, award, Am. Cleft Palate Assn., 1993, Norton Ross prize, ADA, 1995, Disting. Alumni award, Washington U., 1997, Goldhaber award, Harvard U., 1997, Premio Anni Verdi award, Spoleto, Italy, 1997; fellow, Columbia U., 1947—48, NIH, 1948—49, Nat. Insts. Dental Rsch., 1949—50. Fellow: Royal Soc. Surgeons of Eng., Royal Soc. Surgeons of Ireland, Am. Bd. Oral Pathology, Am. Acad. Oral Pathology (v.p. 1957—58, sec. 1958—64, v.p. 1964—65, pres. 1966—67, award 1993, diplomate), Am. Coll. Med. Genetics (hon.); mem.: ADA (cons. coun. dental edn. 1967—), Internat. Soc. Craniofacial Biology (bd. dirs. 1966—67, v.p. 1967—68, pres. 1969—70), Hollywood Acad. Medicine (hon.), Nat. Inst. Medicine NAS (sr.), Internat. Assn. Oral Pathology (hon.), Skeletal Dysplasia Soc. (hon.), Internat. Skeletal Soc., Royal Soc. Medicine London (Burrough Wellcome fellow 1991, R. Abercrombie award in med. genetics 1994, Disting. lectr. 2001), Am. Soc. Human Genetics (Disting. lectr. 2001), Minn. Soc. Pathologists, Internat. Assn. Dental Rsch. (sec. Minn. divsn. 1958—59, pres. 1959—60), Omicron Kappa Upsilon, Sigma Xi. Office: U Minn 16-206 Health Sci Unit A Minneapolis MN 55455 E-mail: gorli002@tc.umn.edu.

GORMAN, JAMES CARVILL, pump manufacturing company executive; b. Mansfield, Ohio, Apr. 16, 1924; s. James Carville and Ruth (Barnes) G.; m. Marjorie Newcomer, Apr. 10, 1950; children: Jeff, Gayle. BS, Ohio State U., 1949. Sales engr. Gorman Rupp Co., Mansfield, Ohio, 1949-58, sales mgr., 1958-64, pres., 1964-89, chmn., CEO, 1989-99, chmn., 1999—. Pres. Manairco, Inc., 1952-85, chmn. bd., 1985—; chmn. Mansfield Airport Commn., 1954-2000; treas. EAA Aviation Found., Oshkosh, Wis., 1980—. Capt. USAAF, 1942-46. Mem. Constrn. Industry Mfrs. Assn. Episcopalian. Home: PO Box 2599 Mansfield OH 44906-0599 Office: Gorman Rupp 305 Bowman St Mansfield OH 44903-1600

GORMAN, JOHN R. auxiliary bishop; Ordained priest Roman Cath. Ch., 1952. Aux. bishop Roman Cath. Ch., Chgo., appointed aux. bishop, titular bishop of Catula, 1988—, consecrated, 1988—. Home and Office: Archdiocese of Chgo-Vicariate V 2330 W 118th St Chicago IL 60643-4710

GORMAN, JOSEPH TOLLE, automotive parts manufacturing executive; b. Rising Sun, Ind., 1937; BA, Kent State U., 1959; LLB, Yale U., 1962. Assoc. Baker, Hostetler & Patterson, Cleve., 1962-67; with legal dept. TRW Inc., 1968-69, asst. sec., 1969-70, sec., 1970-72, v.p. sr. counsel automotive worldwide ops., 1972-73, v.p., asst. gen. counsel, 1973-76, v.p., gen. counsel, 1976-80, acting head communications function, 1978, exec. v.p. indsl. and energy sector, 1980-84, exec. v.p., asst. pres., 1984-85, pres., CEO, 1985-88, chmn., CEO, 1988—, also bd. dirs. Bd. dirs. Aluminum Co. Am., Procter & Gamble Co.; mem. adv. bd. BP Am. Inc.; bd. dirs. U.S.-China Bus. Coun., bd. dirs.; mem. Bd. of The Prince of Wales Bus. Leaders Form; mem. hon. com. Fedn. Internat. des Soc. d'Ingenieurs des Tech. de l'Automobile; mem. Def. Industry Initiative Steering Com.; chmn. Internat. Trade and Investment Task Force; mem. strengthening of Am. Initiative Ctr. for Strategic and Internat. Studies; adv. com. Nat. Security Telecom.; mem. Conf. Bd., Bus. Coun., Trilateral Commn., Bus. Roundtable's Policy Com., Coun. on Fgn. Rels., Pres.'s Export Coun., Coun. on Competitiveness. Trustee New Ohio Inst., Cleve. Tomorrow, Mus. Arts Assn., Cleve. Inst. Art, United Way Svcs., Cleve. Clinic Found., Com. for Econ. Devel., com. for econ. devel. and the Malcolm Baldrige Nat. Quality Award Found.; mem. Ohio Gov.'s Edn. Mgmt. Coun., Kent State U. Found.; bd. mem. The New Am. Schs. Devel. Corp., The Bus.-Higher Edn. Forum, Civic Vision 2000 and Beyond. Recipient Japan Prime Minister's Trade award, 1994. Fax: (212) 334-2463. E-mail: nhgall@mindspring.com.

GORMAN, STEPHEN E. airline executive; Former v.p. ops. Aviall Inc., Dallas; former gen. mgr. JT8D engines Pratt & Whitney; v.p. engine maintenance ops. Northwest Airlines, St. Paul, 1996, v.p. engine maintenance ops. and component maintenance, 1997-99, sr. v.p. tech. ops., 1999—. Office: Northwest Airlines Corp 5101 Northwest Dr Saint Paul MN 55111-3027

GORMAN, STEPHEN THOMAS, former state legislator; b. Fargo, N.D., Dec. 4, 1924; m. Mary K. Sullivan Johnson; 3 children. Student, St. John's U., Collegeville, Minn., N.D. State Sch. Sci., Wahpeton. Chmn. Knight Printing Co., ret.; state rep. dist. 46, 1987-97. Vice chmn. fin. and taxation com.; mem. natural resources com., appropriations com., edn. and environ. divsn. com. N.D. Ho. Reps. Recipient Silver Metal award Advtg. Fedn. Fargo/Moorhead, Disting. Svc. award Jaycees. Mem. Fargo C. of C., Elks, Rotary, K.C., Am. Legion. Republican. Home: 810 Southwood Dr Fargo ND 58103-6020

GORSKI, JACK, biochemistry educator; b. Green Bay, Wis., Mar. 14, 1931; s. John R. and Martha (Kenney) G.; m. Harriet M. Fischer, Sept. 9, 1955; children: Michael, Jo Anne. Student, Calif. Poly. Coll., 1949-50; B.S., U. Wis., 1953; postgrad., U. Utah, 1957; M.S., Wash. State U., 1956, Ph.D., 1958. NIH postdoctoral fellow U. Wis., 1958-61; asst. prof., asso. prof. physiology U. Ill., Urbana, 1961-66, prof. physiology, 1967—, prof. biochemistry, 1969—; prof. biochemistry and animal scis. U. Wis., Madison, 1973—, Wis. Alumni Research Found. prof., 1985. NSF research fellow Princeton, 1966-67; mem. endocrinology study sect. NIH, 1966-70, molecular biology study sect., 1977-81; mem. biochemistry adv. com. Am. Cancer Soc., 1973-76, mem. personnel for research com., 1983— Contbr. articles to profl. jours. Recipient NIH Merit award, 1986. Fellow Am. Acad. Arts and Sci.; mem. NAS, Am. Soc. Biol. Chemists, Endocrine Soc. (Oppenheimer award 1971, Disting. Leadership award 1987, pres. 1990-91, F.C. Koch award 1995). Democrat. Unitarian. Office: U Wis Dept Biochemistry 433 Babcock Dr Madison WI 53706-1544

GORSLINE, STEPHEN PAUL, security firm executive; b. Washington, Aug. 22, 1954; s. Robert William and Patricia Ann (Ketchum) G. AAS in Criminal Justice, Coll. of Lake County, 1987; BS in Criminal Justice, Madonna U., 1998. Dir. safety ops. Thielenhaus Corp., Novi, Mich., 1998-99. Vol. Nat. Rep. Com., Washington, 1992. Staff sgt. USAF, 1977-82. Mem. Safety/Security Mgmt. Assn. (exec. dir. 1996-99), Fraternal Order Police. Roman Catholic. Avocations: collecting stamps, old coins and postcards. E-mail: stevegorsline@yahoo.com.

GORTER, JAMES POLK, investment banker; b. Balt., Dec. 10, 1929; s. T. Poultney and Swan (Deford) G.; m. Audrey Fentress; children: James Jr., David F., Mary H. A.B., Princeton U., 1951; postgrad., London Sch. Econ., 1951-52. Ptnr. Goldman, Sachs & Co., 1956-88, ltd. ptnr., 1989-99; chmn. Baker, Fentress & Co., Chgo., 1987—. Bd. dirs. Caterpillar Inc. Trustee Lake Forest Coll. Served with USN, 1952-55. Clubs: Chicago Commonwealth, Chicago, Economic, Commercial. Office: Baker Fentress & Co 1 Rockefeller Plz Fl 25 New York NY 10020-2102

GOSCHKA, MICHAEL JOHN, state legislator; b. Saginaw, Mich., Oct. 21, 1953; s. Arthur Clarence and Ethel Marie (Alden) G.; m. Maryann Louise Sielaff, 1979. Student, Delta Coll., 1972, Cornerstone Coll., 1974-77. Forklift operator Dow Corning Corp., 1984-92; mem. Mich. Ho. of Reps. from 94th dist., Lansing, 1993-98, Mich. Senate from 33rd dist., Lansing, 1999—. Vice chmn. tourism & recreation com. Mich. Ho. Reps., 1993—, agriculture & forestry com., 1993—, edn. com., 1993—, mental health com., 1993—, house oversight com., 1993—, ethics com., 1993—, tax policy com., 1995—. Exec. com. Saginaw County Rep. Com., 1982—, del. to state, 1982—, rep. precinct, 1982—. Mem. Mich. Farm Bur., Sons Am. Legionnaires, Saginaw Right to Life. Home: 16393 W Schroeder Rd Brant MI 48614-8781 Office: 1010 Farnum Bldg 125 W Allegan St Lansing MI 48933-1702

GOSLEE, DWIGHT J. agricultural company executive; BS in Acctg., U. Minn. CPA. Formerly with Touche Ross & Co.; asst. corp. controller to v.p./controller internat. divsn. ConAgra, Inc., Omaha, 1985-97, sr. v.p. mergers and acquisitions, 1997—. Office: ConAgra Inc 1 ConAgra Dr Omaha NE 68102

GOSNELL, DAVINA J. dean, nursing educator; BSN, U. Pitts.; MS, PhD, Ohio State U. Dean Sch. Nursing, prof. Kent (Ohio) State U. Chair Ohio Pub. Health Coun. Recipient U. Pitts. Sch. Nursing Disting. Alumni award. Mem. ONA, NLN, STT, GSA, Delta Kappa Gamma. Office: Kent State U Sch Nursing PO Box 5190 Kent OH 44242-0001 E-mail: dgasnell@kent.edu.

GOSS, RICHARD HENRY, lawyer; b. Worcester, Mass., Oct. 24, 1935; s. George Lee and Marion Bernadine (Henry) G.; children: Margaret Elizabeth, Richard Henry Eric, Emily Charlotte; m. Eleanor Kirsten Berg, Nov. 27, 1971. Student, Mich. State U., 1952-54; BA in Econs., Clark U., 1956; JD, Northwestern U., 1959. Bar: Ill. 1959, U.S. Supreme Ct. 1970. Asst. cashier Nat. Blvd. Bank of Chgo., 1959-61; v.p. Paul D. Speer & Assocs. Inc., Mcpl. Fin. Cons., Chgo., 1962-68; mng. ptnr. Chapman and Cutler, Attys. at Law, 1968-95. Bd. dirs. Japan Am. Soc. Chgo., 1987-96, v.p., chmn. mem. com., 1988-90; chmn. bd. dirs. Brays Island Plantation Colony, Inc., 1995-97. Mem. Eastman (N.H.) Golf Club. Republican. Episcopalian. Avocations: hunting, skeet, sporting clays and trap shooting, travel, Oriental studies. Home: 7 Par Brae Eastman Box 1316 Grantham NH 03753

GOTTLIEB, GIDON ALAIN GUY, law educator; b. Paris, Dec. 9, 1932; m. Antoinette Rozoy Countess de Roussy de Sales, May 12, 1965. LLB with honors, London Sch. Econs., 1954, Cambridge (Eng.) U., 1956, diploma in comparative law, 1958; LLM, Harvard U., 1957, SJD, 1962. Bar: Called to bar Lincoln Inn, London 1958. Lectr. govt. Dartmouth Coll., 1960-61; assoc. firm Shearman & Sterling, N.Y.C., 1962-65; mem. faculty N.Y. U. Law Sch., 1965-76; Leo Spitz prof. internat. law and diplomacy U. Chgo. Law Sch., 1976—. UN rep. Amnesty Internat., 1966-72; mem. founding com. World Assembly Human Rights, 1968; adv. bd. Internat. League Rights of Man; disting. vis. fellow Hoover Instn., Stanford, Calif., 1991-94, 97—. Author: The Logic of Choice: An Investigation of the Concepts of Rule and Rationality, 1968, Nation Against State, 1993. Fellow N.Y. Coun. on Fgn. Rels. (sr. fellow, dir., Middle East Peace Project 1988-94); mem. Am. Soc. Internat. Law, Century Assn. (N.Y.C.). Office: U Chgo Law Sch 1111 E 60th St Chicago IL 60637-2776

GOTTLIEB, RICHARD DOUGLAS, media executive; b. Davenport, Iowa, June 12, 1942; s. David and Elaine Gottlieb; m. Harriet Barg; children: Michael, Jason, Allison, Meghan. BS, U. Ariz., 1964. Mgr.-in-tng. Madison (Wis.) Newspapers, Inc., 1965-68, prodn. coordinator, 1968-72, treas., dir., 1972-80, gen. mgr., 1973-80; pub. Racine (Wis.) Journal-Times, 1980-85; v.p. Lee Enterprises, Inc., Davenport, 1985-86, pres., chief oper.

officer, 1986—. Bd. dirs. Madison Newspapers, Inc., NAPP Systems, Inc., San Marcos, Calif., Newspaper Advt. Bur., Washington. Avocations: hunting, tennis. Office: Lee Enterprises Inc 215 N Main St Ste 400 Davenport IA 52801-1924

GOTTRON, FRANCIS ROBERT, III, small business owner; b. Youngstown, Ohio, Dec. 26, 1953; s. Francis R. Jr. and Norma J. (Giba) G.; m. Joyce L. Garling, Nov. 25, 1975. BSBA cum laude, Youngstown State U., 1978. With Commonwealth Land Title Youngstown, Inc., 1972-87, Lender's Svc., Inc., 1979—, Title Agy. Michaels, 1984—; examiner delinquent tax Mahoning County Prosecutor's Office, 1989—; owner, prin. Mahoning County Recorder's Office, Youngstown, 1978—; examiner Fed. Title Agy., 1982—; pres. M&G Title Search Inc. Appraiser Probate Ct., 1989—. Democrat. Lutheran. Avocations: fantasy baseball, camping, forestry, environment. Home: 9165 New Rd North Jackson OH 44451-9707 Office: PO Box 268 Youngstown OH 44501-0268 E-mail: f_gottron@yahoo.com.

GOTTSCHALK, ALEXANDER, radiologist, diagnostic radiology educator; b. Chgo., Mar. 23, 1932; s. Louis R. and Fruma (Kasden) G.; m. Jane Rosenbloom, Aug. 13, 1960; children: Rand, Karen, Amy. B.A. magna cum laude, Harvard U., 1954; M.D., Washington U., St. Louis, 1958. Diplomate: Am. Bd. Radiology, Am. Bd. Nuclear Medicine. Intern U. Ill. Research and Edn. Hosps., Chgo., 1958-59; resident U. Chgo., 1959-62, asst. prof., 1964-66, assoc. prof., 1966-68, prof. radiology, 1968-74, chmn. dept. radiology, 1971-72; research assoc. Donner Lab., Lawrence Radiol. Lab., Calif., 1962-64; dir. Franklin McLean Meml. Research Hosp., 1967-74; prof. and dir. nuclear medicine Sch. Medicine Yale U., New Haven, 1974-77, acting chmn. radiology, 1980-81, vice-chmn. radiology, 1977-89; prof. radiology Mich. State U., East Lansing, 1990—. Contbr. chpts. to books, articles to publs. in field. Fleischner lectr., 1983 Fellow Am. Coll. Radiology, Am. Coll. Chest Physicians; mem. Radiol. Soc. N.Am. (2d v.p. 1977), Assn. Univ. Radiologists (pres. 1971), Soc. Nuclear Medicine (pres. 1974-75), Am. Roentgen Ray Soc., Fleischner Soc. (treas. 1978-83, pres. 1989-90), Phi Beta Kappa, Alpha Omega Alpha. Home: 4246 Van Atta Rd Okemos MI 48864-3137 Office: Radiology Bldg Rm 120 Mich State U East Lansing MI 48824-1303 E-mail: alex.gottschalk@radiology.msu.edu.

GOTTSCHALK, GUY, agricultural products executive; Grad., U. Wis. Owner, pres. Gottschalk Cranberry, Inc., Wisconsin Rapids, Wis., Biron Cranberry Co., Wisconsin Rapids. Mem. bd. regents U. Wis., Wis., 1998—. Office: Conifer Ctr 412 Dalay Ave Wisconsin Rapids WI 54494

GOTTSCHALK, JOHN E. newspaper publishing executive; b. 1943; Pub. Sidney (Nebr.) Newspaper, 1966-74; with Omaha World Herald Co., 1975—, pres., CEO, 1989—. Office: Omaha-World Herald Co World-Herald Sq Omaha NE 68102-1138

GOTTSCHALK, STEPHEN ELMER, lawyer; b. Rochester, Minn., Oct. 9, 1947; s. Elmer H. and Ruth F. (Thurley) G.; m. Lorilyn J. Dopp, Feb. 14, 1970; children: Andrew Stephen, Stephanie Beth, Lorissa Christine, Michael Donald. BS, Valparaiso U., 1969, JD, 1972. Bar: Minn. 1972, U.S. Dist. Ct. (Minn.) 1972. Jud. clk. Minn. Supreme Ct., St. Paul, 1972-73; assoc. Dorsey & Whitney, Minn., 1973-78, ptnr., 1979—, dept. head employee benefits dept., 1986-91, 98—. Adj. prof. employee benefits Sch. Law U. Minn. Mem. pres. adv. coun., Valparaiso U., 1983—; bd. dirs. Twin Cities Habitat for Humanity, Inc. Recipient Svc. award Valparaiso Alumni Assn., 1986. Mem. Midwest Pension Conf. Avocation: squash. Home: 4339 Fremont Ave S Minneapolis MN 55409-1720 Office: Dorsey & Whitney 50 S 6th St Ste 1500 Minneapolis MN 55402-1498 E-mail: gottschalk.steve@dorseylaw.com.

GOTTSCHALK, THOMAS A. lawyer; b. Decatur, Ind., July 5, 1942; s. John Simson and Edith (Liechty) G.; m. Barbara J. Risen, Aug. 28, 1965; children: Deborah, Diane. AB, Earlham Coll., 1964; JD, U. Chgo., 1967. Bar: Ill. 1967, D.C. 1986, U.S. Supreme Ct. Assoc. Kirkland & Ellis, Chgo., 1967-73, ptnr., 1973-94; sr. v.p., gen. counsel Gen. Motors Corp., 1994—. Trustee Earlham Coll., Richmond, Ind., 1972—, chmn., 1985-91. Mem. ABA (mem. litigation, antitrust and criminal law sects.), D.C. Bar Assn., Chgo. Coun. of Lawyers, Conf. Bd. Coun. of Chief Legal Officers. Office: Gen Motors Corp 300 Renaissance Ctr Detroit MI 48265-0001

GOTTSCHALL, JOAN B. judge; b. Oak Ridge, Tenn., Apr. 23, 1947; d. Herbert A. and Elaine (Reichbaum) G. BA cum laude, Smith Coll., Mass., 1969; JD, Stanford Univ., Calif., 1973. Bar: Ill. 1973. Assoc. Jenner & Block, 1973-76, 78-81, ptnr., 1981-82; staff atty. Fed. Defender Program, 1976-78, Univ. of Chgo., Office of Legal Counsel, 1983-84; magistrate judge U.S. Dist. Ct. (no. dist.) Ill., Chgo., 1984—96, judge, 1996—2002. Mem. vis. com., past chair Divinity Sch., U. Chgo., 1984—97. Bd. dirs. Constl. Rights Found. Chgo., Martin Marty Ctr., U. Chgo. Div. Sch. Mem.: Divinity Sch. (vis. com.), Women's Bar Assn. Ill., Chgo. Bar Assn., Am. Bar Assn. Office: Everett McKinley Dirksen Bldg 219 S Dearborn St Ste 1978 Chicago IL 60604-1877

GOTTSCHLICH, GARY WILLIAM, lawyer; b. Dayton, Ohio, Aug. 27, 1946; s. William Frederick and Rosemary Teresa Gottschlich; m. Sharon Melanie Plunkett, Oct. 7, 1978; children: David W., Andrew J., Thomas M. Bs, U. Dayton, 1968; cert., Univ. Coll., London, 1970; JD, U. NNotre Dame, 1971. Bar: Ohio 1971. Asst. pros. atty. Montgomery County, Dayton, 1971-73; assoc. Young, Pryor, Lynn & Jerardi, 1973-80, ptnr., 1980-84, Louis & Froelich, Dayton, 1984-87, Porter, Wright, Morris & Arthur, Dayton, 1987-97, Gottschlich & Portune, Dayton, 1997—. Capt. USAR. Mem. ABA, ATLA, Ohio Bar Assn. (bd. govs. litigation sect.), Dayton Bar Assn. (treas. 1981-82), Miami Valley Trial Lawyers Assn. (founding). Roman Catholic. Avocations: golf, sailing, squash. Home: 5260 Little Woods Ln Dayton OH 45429-2124 Office: Gottschlich & Portune LLP The Historic Armory 201 E Sixth St Dayton OH 45402-2836

GOUGEON, JOEL, state legislator; b. Bay City, Mich., Jan. 13, 1943; m. Kaye; 1 child, Amy. Grad., Gen. Motors Inst., 1966. Commr. Bay City Bd. Commrs., 1984-90; mem. Mich. Senate from 34th dist., Lansing, 1993—. Families com. State Capitol, Lansing, Mich., 2002—, mental health & human svc. com., 2002—, v.chmn. farming com., 2002—, agribusiness & food sys. com., 2002—, chmn. cmty. health com., 2002—, retirement com., 2002—, chmn. capital outlay com., 2002—, mem. family ind. agy., 2002—. Mem. Bay City Lions, Bay County Crime Stoppers, Elks, Am. Legion, Vietnam Vets, John Glenn Boosters. Address: 1005 Farnum Bldg PO Box 30036 Lansing MI 48909-7536

GOUGH, PAULINE BJERKE, magazine editor; b. Wadena, Minn., Jan. 7, 1935; d. Luther C. and Zita Pauline (Halbmaier) Bjerke; children: Mary Pauline, Sarah Elizabeth, Philip Clayton. BA, U. Minn., Mpls., 1957; BS, Moorhead (Minn.) State Coll., 1970; MS, Ind. U., Bloomington, 1972; EdD, Ind. U., 1977. Reporter women's page San Jose (Calif.) Mercury-News, 1957-58; with rsch. dept. Campbell-Mithun Advt., Mpls., 1958-60; tchr. Univ. Elem. Sch., Bloomington, 1970-79; freelance writer Agy. Instrnl. TV, 1974-80; asst. editor Phi Delta Kappa, 1980-81, mem. profl. staff, 1981—, mng. editor, 1981-88, editor, 1988—. Mem. adj. faculty Ind. U.-Purdue U., Indpls., summers 1976, 77; leader insts. on writing for publ. Contbr. articles to profl. publs. Recipient Disting. Alumna award Moorhead State U., 1982. Mem. Phi Beta Kappa, Phi Delta Kappa. Home: 3570 S Oakridge Dr Bloomington IN 47401-8926 Office: Phi Delta Kappa PO Box 789 408 N Union St Bloomington IN 47405-3800 E-mail: pgough@kiva.net.

GOULD, JOHN PHILIP, economist, educator; b. Chgo., Jan. 19, 1939; s. John Philip and Lillian Gould; children: John Philip III, Jeffrey Hayes; m. Kathleen A. Carpenter. BS with highest distinction, Northwestern U., 1960; MBA, U. Chgo., 1963, PhD, 1966. Faculty U. Chgo., 1965—, prof. econs., 1974—, disting. service prof. econs., 1984—, dean Grad. Sch. Bus., 1983-93, v.p. planning, 1988—91; Steven G. Rothmeier prof., disting. svc. prof. econs., 1996—; exec. v.p. Lexecon Inc., Chgo., 1994—; pres. Cardean, 1999—2001. Vis. prof. Nat. Taiwan U., 1978; spl. asst. econ. affairs to sec. labor, 1969-70; spl. asst. to dir. Office Mgmt. and Budget, 1970; past chmn. econ. policy adv. com. Dept. Labor; bd. dirs. DFA Investment Dimensions Group, Harbor Capital Advisors, First Prairie Funds, 1985-96; chmn. Pegasus Funds, 1996-99, Milw. Mutual, 1997—, Unext.com, 1999—. Author: (with E. Lazear) Microeconomic Theory, 6th edit, 1989; contbg. author: Microeconomic Foundations of Employment and Inflation Theory, 1970; editor: Jour. of Bus. , 1976-83, Jour. Fin. Econs., 1976-83, Jour. Accounting and Econs., 1978-81; contbr. articles to profl. jours. Bd. dirs. United Way/Crusade of Mercy, 1986-91, Lookingglass Theatre Co., 1994-96. Recipient Wall St. Jour. award, 1960, Am. Marketing Assn. award, 1960; Earhart Found. fellow. Mem. Am. Econs. Assn., Econometric Soc. (chmn. local arrangements 1968), Econ. Club of Chgo., Comml. Club of Chgo., Beta Gamma Sigma. Home: 100 E Huron St Apt 2105 Chicago IL 60611-5903 Office: U Chgo Grad Sch Bus 1101 E 58th St Chicago IL 60637-1511

GOULD, PHILLIP LOUIS, civil engineering educator, consultant; b. Chgo., May 24, 1937; m. Deborah Paula Rothholtz, Feb. 5, 1961; children: Elizabeth, Nathan, Rebecca, Joshua. BS, U. Ill., 1959, MS, 1960; PhD, Northwestern U., 1966. Structural designer Skidmore, Owings & Merrill, Chgo., 1960-63; prin. structural engr. Westenhoff & Novick, 1963-64; NASA trainee Northwestern U., Evanston, Ill., 1964-66; asst. prof. civil engring. Washington U., St. Louis, 1966-68, assoc. prof., 1968-74, prof., 1974—, chmn. dept. civil engring., 1978-98, Harold D. Jolly prof. civil engring., 1981—. Vis. prof. Ruhr U., Fed. Republic Germany, 1974-75, U. Sydney, Australia, 1981, Shanghai Inst. Tech., Peoples Republic of China, 1986; dir. Earthquake Engring. Rsch. Inst., exec. coun. Internat. Assn. for Shell and Spatial Structures, pres. Great Lakes chpt. and New Madrid chpt. Earthquake Engring. Rsch. Inst. Author: Static Analysis of Shells: A Unified Development of Surface Structures, 1977, Introduction to Linear Elasticity, 1984, Finite Element Analysis of Shells of Revolution, 1985, Analysis of Shells and Plates, 1987, 2d edit., 1999; co-author: Dynamic Response of Structures to Wind and Earthquake Loading, 1980; co-editor: Environmental Forces on Engineering Structures, 1979, Natural Draught Cooling Towers, 1985; editor: Engineering Structures, 1979—. Dir. Earthquake Engring. Rsch. Inst., 1993—95; vice chmn. Mo. Seismic Safety Commn., 1998—99, chmn., 2000—01; St. Louis regional dir. Mid-Am. Earthquake Ctr. Recipient Sr. Scientist award Alexander von Humboldt Found., Fed. Republic Germany, 1974-75 Fellow ASCE (bd. dirs. St. Louis sect. 1985-87, Otto Nutli award); mem. Am. Soc. Engring. Edn., Internat. Assn. Shell Structures, Structural Engrs. Assn. Ill., Mo. Soc. Profl. Engrs. (Outstanding Engr. in Edn. award), Civil Engring. Alumni Assn. U. Ill., Urbana-Champaign (Disting. Alumnus award). Home: 102 Lake Frst Saint Louis MO 63117-1303 Office: Washington U Dept Civil Engring PO Box 1130 Saint Louis MO 63188-1130 E-mail: pgoul@seas.wustl.edu.

GOULD, SAMUEL HALPERT, pediatrics educator; b. Balt., June 14, 1922; s. Herman and Theresa Gould; m. June Linda Walter, June 17, 1952; children: Hallie, Phyllis, Cynthia, Nancy. MD, State U. Iowa, 1951. Diplomate Am. Bd. Pediat. Intern Balt. City Hosp., 1951-52, Johns Hopkins Hosp., Balt., 1952-53; resident U. Iowa Hosps., Iowa City, 1953-54; pvt. practice, Benton Harbor, Mich., 1957-86; assoc. prof. pediat. U. Chgo., 1986—, chief sect. gen. pediat., 1993-99. Mem. Alpha Omega Alpha. Home: 1555 N Astor St Chicago IL 60610-1673 Office: U of Chgo Pritzker Sch of Medicine 5841 S Maryland Ave MC 1057 Chicago IL 60637-1463

GOULDEY, GLENN CHARLES, manufacturing company executive; b. N.Y.C., July 28, 1952; s. George Howard and Jeannette Ruth Williamson; m. Leslie Jeanne Ruth, Oct. 2, 1982; children: Jeremy Charles, Nicholas Glenn, Alexander James George. BS in Bus., Coll. N.J., 1976; postgrad., Portland State U., 1980; MBA, Rider U., 1981; postgrad., Dartmouth Coll., 1994-95. Cert. in purchasing mgmt., cert. in prodn. and inventory control. Sr. planner Eaton Corp., Flemington, N.J., 1975-77, pricing mgr., distbn., 1977-79, inventory control mgr., 1979-80, materials mgr., purchasing Beaverton, Oreg., 1980-81, mfg. and materials mgr., 1981-83, mktg. and materials mgr., 1983-87, plant and gen. mgr., 1987-88, v.p. sales and mktg. Carol Stream, Ill., 1988-89, mgr. ops. divsn., 1989-93, gen. bus. mgr., 1993-95; pres., gen. mgr. Lectron Products divsn. Eaton, Rochester Hills, Mich., 1995-99; v.p. technology, planning strategy IT Eaton Automotive Group Worldwide, 2000—. Patentee in field. Mem. bd. advisors Oakland U. Bus. Sch., Mich. Colls. Found.; bd. dirs., vice chair Rochester Cmty. Schs. Found.; asst. coach lacrosse Rochester Hills United H.S. Mem. Am. Prodn. Inventory Control Soc., Nat. Youth Sports Coaches Assn. (cert.), Soc. Automotive Engrs. Internat. Republican. Lutheran. Office: Eaton Corp 1400 S Livernois Rd Rochester MI 48307-3362 E-mail: GlennGouldey@eaton.com.

GOULET, DENIS ANDRÉ, development ethicist, writer; b. Fall River, Mass., May 27, 1931; s. Fernand Joseph and Lumena (Bouchard) G.; m. Ana Maria Reynaldo, Nov. 21, 1964; children: Andrea, Sinane. BA in Philosophy, St. Paul's Coll., Washington, 1954, MA in Philosophy, 1956; MA in Social Planning, Institut de Recherche et de Formation en Vue du Développement, Paris, 1960; PhD in Polit. Sci., U. São Paulo, Brazil, 1963. Laborer, France, Spain, Algeria, 1956-59; planning advisor AID, Recife, Brazil, 1964-65; vis. prof. U. Sask., Regina, Can., 1965-66; assoc. prof. Ind. U., Bloomington, 1966-68; vis. fellow Ctr. for Study of Dem. Instns., Santa Barbara, Calif., 1969; fellow Ctr. for Study Devel. & Social Change, Cambridge, Mass., 1970-74; vis. prof. U. Calif., San Diego, 1969-70; sr. fellow Ctr. for Study Devel. and Social Change, Cambridge, Mass., 1970-74; vis. fellow Overseas Devel. Coun./OAS, Washington, 1974-76; sr. fellow Overseas Devel. Coun., 1976-79; O'Neill chair in edn. for justice, dept. econs. U. Notre Dame, Ind., 1979—2002; faculty fellow Kellogg Inst. for Internat. Study, Krock Inst. for Internat. Peace Studies; prof. econs. Coll. Arts & Letters U. Notre Dame. Vis. prof. U. Warsaw, Poland, 1989-90. Author: The Cruel Choice, 1971, The Uncertain Promise, 1977, Mexico: Development Strategies for the Future, 1983, Incentives for Development: The Key to Equity, 1989, Development Ethics: A Guide to Theory and Practice, 1995. Exec. bd. Internat. Dev. Ethics Assn.; editl. bd. Jour. of Health and Population in Developing Countries; internat. adv. coun. TODA Inst. for Global Peace and Policy Rsch.; internat. adv. bd. Internat. Centre for Islamic Political Economy. Decorated chevalier Odre Nat. du Cèdre (Lebanon), 1960; OAS grantee, 1961-62, Fulbright grantee, 1986; recipient Reinhold Niebuhr award U. Notre Dame, 1988. Democrat. Roman Catholic. Avocations: racquetball, piano. Home: 825 Ashland Ave South Bend IN 46616-1307 Office: U Notre Dame Dept Econs Notre Dame IN 46556-5677

GOULETAS, EVANGELINE, investment executive; m. Hugh L. Carey, 1981. M.A. in Math, Northeastern Ill. State Coll. Formerly mem. faculty dept. Chgo. Bd. Edn.; prin. Am. Invsco Corp., Chgo., 1969—; ptnr. Electronic Realty Assn., IMB (Internat. Mcht. Banking), N.Y.C., 1969—. Formerly trustee DePaul U.; trustee Chgo. City Library, Com. for Thalassemia Concern; chairperson Combined Cardiac Research Women's Found., U. Chgo., N.Y. State Watch Com.; mem. exec. bd. Chgo. City Ballet, N.Y.C. Meals-On-Wheels, LaGuardia Community Coll. Recipient Great Am. award B'nai B'rith, 1977, Businesswoman of Yr. award Soc. of the Little Flower, 1979, Exec. Businesswoman of the Yr. Internat. Orgn. of Women Execs., 1980, Tree of Life Honor, Jewish Nat. Fund, 1981, Myrtle Wreath award, Nassau County Hadassah, 1981, Paedia award DePaul U., 1982, Eleanor Roosevelt Humanities award, State of Israel Bonds, 1983, humanitarian award Assn. for Children with Retarded Mental Devel., 1985, Woman of Distinction Pan Euboean Soc. of Am., 1985; two residences named in her honor Fedn. of P.R. Orgns., Bronx, United Cerebral Palsy, Staten Island; Evangeline Gouletas-Carey Leadership award presented annually in her name by LaGuardia Community Coll. of CUNY. Mem. Nat. Assn. Realtors, Inst. Real Estate Mgmt., Pres.'s Assn. of Am. Mgmt. Assn. Greek Orthodox.

GOVE, SAMUEL KIMBALL, political science educator; b. Walpole, Mass., Dec. 27, 1923; Student, Mass. State Coll., 1941-43; B.S. in Econs, U. Mass., 1947; M.A. in Polit. Sci, Syracuse U., 1951. Research asst. govt. and pub. affairs U. Ill., 1950-51, research asso., 1951-54, mem. faculty, 1954—, prof. polit. sci., 1966-89, prof. emeritus, 1989—; dir. Inst. Govt. and Pub. Affairs, 1967-85, dir. emeritus, 1987—. Staff asst. Nat. Assn. Assessing Officers, 1949; mem. rsch. staff Ill. Commn. Study State Govt., 1950—51; staff fellow Nat. Mcpl. League, 1955—56; exec. asst. Ill. Auditor Pub. Accounts, 1957; program coord. Ill. Legis. Staff Intern Program, 1962—70; mem. com. financing higher edn. Ill. Master Plan Higher Edn., 1963; mem. Ill. Commn. Orgn. Gen. Assembly, 1965—69, 1970—73, Ill. Commn. State Govt., 1965—67; cons. elections ABC, 1964, 66, 68; chmn. Champaign (Ill.) County Econ. Opportunity Coun., 1966—67; state legis. rsch. fellow Am. Polit. Sci. Assn., 1966—68; cons. Am. Council Edn., 1966—67; sec. Local Govts. Commn., 1967—69; staff dir. Ill. Constn. Study Commn., 1968—69; exec. sec. Gov. Ill. Constn. Research Group, 1969—70; mem. Ill. Constn. Study Commn., 1969—70; chmn. Citizens Task Force on Constl. Implementation, 1970—71; mem. Gov. Elect's Task Force on Transition, 1972, 1991—92; adv. coun. Ill. Dept. Local Govt. Affairs, 1969—79, Gov.'s Human Resources , 1991—93, Ill. Commn. on Regulatory Rev., 1994—98, Ill. Bd. Higher Edn., 1998—, Ill. Issues Bd. , 1974, chmn. bd. dirs. , 1974—85. Author numerous books, monographs and articles. Chmn. Champaign-Urbana Study Commn. on Intergovtl. Coop., 1976-78. Served to lt. (j.g.) USNR, 1943-46. Fellow Nat. Acad. Pub. Adminstrn.; mem. AAUP (past chpt. pres., mem. nat. com. R 1969-75, 78-84, nat. coun. 1978-80), Am. Polit Sci. Assn., Am. Soc. Pub. Adminstrn. (past chpt. chmn.; chmn. univs. govtl. rsch. conf. 1969-71), Govtl. Rsch. Assn. (dir. 1969-71), Ill. Hist. Soc., Midwest Polit. Sci. Assn. (v.p. 1978-80), Nat. Mcpl. League (council 1972-80, 81-84, 85), Nat Civic League (coun. advisors 1987-89), Cosmos Club. Home: 2006 Bruce Dr Urbana IL 61801-6419 Office: 1007 W Nevada St Urbana IL 61801-3812 E-mail: s.gove@uiuc.edn.

GOVINDJEE, biophysics, biochemistry, and biology educator; b. Allahabad, India, Oct. 24, 1933; came to U.S., 1956, naturalized, 1972; s. Vishveshvar Prasad and Savitri Devi Asthana; m. Rajni Varma, Oct. 24, 1957; children: Anita Govindjee, Sanjay Govindjee. BSc, U. Allahabad, 1952, MSc, 1954; PhD, U. Ill., 1960. Lectr. botany U. Allahabad, 1954-56; grad. fellow U. Ill., Urbana, 1956-58, research asst., 1958-60, USPHS postdoctoral trainee biophysics, 1960-61, mem. faculty, 1961—, assoc. prof. botany and biophysics, 1965-69, prof. biophysics and plant biology, 1969-99, disting. lectr. Sch. Life Scis., 1978, emeritus prof. biophysics, plant biology and biochemistry, 1999—. Author: Photosynthesis, 1969; editor: Bioenergetics of Photosynthesis, 1975, Photosynthesis: Energy Conversion by Plants and Bacteria Carbon Assimilation and Plant Productivity, 2 vols., 1982 (Russian transl. 1987), The Oxygen evolving system of photosynthesis, 1983, Light Emission by Plants and Bacteria, 1986, Excitation Energy and Electron Transfer in Photosynthesis, 1989, Molecular Biology of Photosynthesis, 1989, Photosynthesis: From Photoreactions to Productivity, 1993, Concepts in Photobiology: Photosynthesis and Photomorphogenesis, 1999; editor Hist. Corner: Photosynthesis Rsch., 1989—; guest editor spl. issue Biophys. Jour., 1972, Photochemistry and Photobiology, 1978, Photosynthesis Research, 1993, 96, 2002-; editor-in-chief Photosynthesis Rsch., 1985-88; series editor: Advances in Photosynthesis, vol. 1, 1994, vol. 2, 1995, vols. 3, 4 and 5, 1996, vols. 6 and 7, 1998, vol. 8, 1999, vol. 9, 2000, vols. 10 and 11, 2001, vol. 12, 2002; contbr. articles to profl. jours., also Sci. Am. Fulbright scholar, 1956-61, 96-97. Fellow AAAS, NAS (India); mem. Am. Soc. Plant Physiologists, Biophys. Soc. Am., Am. Soc. Photobiology (coun. 1976, pres. 1981), Internat. Photosynthesis Soc. (exec. com., publ. com. 1995-01), Sigma Xi. Home: 2401 Boudreau Dr Urbana IL 61801-6655 E-mail: gov@uiuc.edu.

GOWARD, RUSSELL, former state legislator; b. St. Louis, Aug. 25, 1935; s. William and Zenobia (Askew) G.; m. Dolores Jean Thornton, 1957; children: Russell II, Monika. Cert., Hubbard's Bus. Coll., 1959; student, Harris Tchrs. Coll. Divsn. leader 21st Ward Dem. Orgn., Mo., 1963-65; rep. Mo. State Ho. Reps. Dist. 60, 1967-97; pres., treas. Goward's & Assocs., Inc., 1967-99; ret. Active Boy Scouts Am. Decorated Nat. Def. Svc. Ribbon, European Occupl. medal. Mem. Masons. Home: 5000 Tyus Ct Saint Louis MO 63115-1553

GOWEN, RICHARD JOSEPH, electrical engineering educator, academic administrator; b. New Brunswick, N.J., July 6, 1935; s. Charles David and Esther Ann (Hughes) G.; m. Nancy A. Applegate, Dec. 28, 1955; children: Jeff, Cindy, Betsy, Susan, Kerry. BS in Elec. Engring., Rutgers U., 1957; MS, Iowa State U., 1961, PhD, 1962. Registered profl. engr., Colo. Rsch. engr. RCA Labs., Princeton, N.J., 1957; commd. USAF; ground electronics officer Yaak AFB, Mont., 1957-59; instr. USAF Acad., 1962-63, rsch. assoc., 1963-64, asst. prof., 1964-65, assoc. prof., 1965-66, tenured assoc. prof. elec. engring., 1966-70, tenured prof., 1971-77, dir., prin. investigator NASA instrumentation group for cardiovascular studies, 1968-77; mem. launch and recovery med. team Johnson Space Ctr., NASA, 1971-77; v.p., dean engring., prof. S.D. Sch. Mines and Tech., Rapid City, 1977-84, pres., 1987—, Dakota State U., Madison, 1984-87. Prin. investigator program in support space cardiovascular studies NASA, 1977-81; co-chmn. Joint Industry, Nuclear Regulatory IEEE, Am. Nuclear Soc. Probabilistic Risk Assessment Guidelines for Nuclear Power Plants Project, 1980-83; mem. Dept. Def. Software Engring. Inst. Panel, 1983; mem. Congl. Web-based Edn. Commn., 1999—. Contbr. articles to profl. jours.; patentee in field. Bd. dirs. St. Martins Acad., Rapid City, S.D., Journey Mus., 1998—, Greater Rapid City Econ. Devel. Partnership, 1991—, Rapid City C. of C., 1998—; mem. U.S. Web Edn. Commn., 1999—. Fellow IEEE (Centennial Internat. pres. 1984, bd. dirs., 1976-75), USAB/IEEE Disting. Contbns. to Engring. Professionalism award 1986); mem. Am. Assn. Engring. Socs. (bd. dirs., 1983-87, chmn. 1988), Rapid City C. of C. (bd. dirs. 1998—), Rotary, Sigma Xi, Phi Kappa Phi, Tau Beta Phi, Eta Kappa Nu (bd. dirs., 1994, pres. 1998—) Pi Mu Epsilon. Roman Catholic. Home: 1609 Palo Verde Dr Rapid City SD 57701-4461 Office: SD Sch Mines & Tech Office of Pres Rapid City SD 57701

GOWLER, VICKI SUE, newspaper editor, journalist; b. Decatur, Ill., Apr. 16, 1951; d. Carroll Eugene and Audra Janet (Briggs) G. BS in Journalism, U. Ill., 1973. Reporter Iroquois County Daily Times, Watseka, Ill., 1973-75, Quincy (Ill.) Herald-Whig, 1975-78; from reporter to mng. editor Miami (Fla.) Herald, Stuart, Delray Beach, West Palm Beach, 1089-88; asst. news editor Knight-Ridder Washington Bur., 1988-93; exec. editor Duluth (Minn.) News-Tribune, Knight-Ridder newspaper, 1993—. Recipient numerous awards for journalistic works, including RFK award, staet AP awards in all categories. Mem. Am. Soc. Newspaper Editors. Methodist. Avocations: reading, tennis, playing clarinet, travel, visiting with his family. Home: 1688 Highland Pkwy Saint Paul MN 55116-2103

GRABEMANN, KARL W. lawyer; b. Chgo., Apr. 27, 1929; s. Karl H. and Trude (Stockram) G.; m. Mary Darr, Dec. 6, 1958; children: Robert S., Lisa D. B.S., Northwestern U., 1951, J.D., 1956. Bar: Ill. 1957, U.S. Supreme

Ct. 1960, U.S. Ct. Appeals for D.C. 1957, U.S. Ct. Appeals for 7th Circuit 1957, U.S. Ct. Appeals for 5th Circuit 1967, U.S. Dist. Ct. for D.C. 1957, U.S. Dist. Ct. for No. Dist. Ill. 1957. Atty. NLRB, Chgo., 1956-60; ptnr. firm Turner, Hunt & Woolley, 1960-69, Keck, Mahin & Cate, Chgo., 1969-79, McDermott, Will & Emery, Chgo., 1979-89; of counsel Murphy, Smith & Polk, 1990—. Mem. ABA, Ill. Bar Assn., Chgo. Bar Assn. Republican. Club: Metropolitan (Chgo.). E-mail: karl.grabemann@odnss.

GRABER, RICHARD WILLIAM, lawyer; b. Lakewood, Ohio, July 31, 1956; s. Richard Allen and Lynn Carol (Hurschman) G.; m. Alexandria Ahlquist Richardson, Apr. 28, 1984; children: Scott Bailey, Erik Richard. AB magna cum laude, Duke U., 1978; JD, Boston U., 1981. Bar: Wis. 1981. Mem. Reinhart Boerner Van Deuren Norris & Rieselbach, S.C., Milw., 1981—. Bd. dirs. Crane Mfg. & Svc. Corp., Cudahy, Wis. Mem. bd. of governors, Wis. Patient Compensation Fund, 1988-97; chmn. fin. com. Wis. Rep. Party, 1993-97, chmn., 1999—; mem. exec. com. North Shore Rep. Club, Milw., 1988—, Reps. of Wis., 1991; mem. Am. Coun. Young Polit. Leaders, 1990; candidate for Wis. Assembly, 1990; chmn. Kasten for Senate com. 1993; mem. bd. of appeals, Village of Shorewood, 1991—, mem. bd. of trustees of the Medical College of Wis., 1997—. Mem. Rotary (pres. Milw. 1988-89, Paul Harris fellow 1990). Avocations: politics, softball, basketball. Home: 2726 E Shorewood Blvd Milwaukee WI 53211-2458 Office: Reinhart Boerner Van Deuren Norris & Rieselbach PO Box 51400 Milwaukee WI 53203-3400*

GRABER, THOMAS M. orthodontist, researcher; b. St. Louis, May 27, 1917; Diplomate Am. Bd. Orthodontics. DMD, Washington U., St. Louis, 1940; MS in Dentistry, Northwestern U., 1946, PhD in Anatomy, 1950; Doctorate (hon.), U. Gothenberg, 1989; DSc (hon.), Washington U., 1991, U. Mich., 1994, U. Kunming, 1996. Diplomate Am. Bd. Orthodontics (Recognition award 1990, Dewel award, 1992). Mem. faculty Northwestern U. Dental Sch., 1946-58, assoc. prof. orthodontics, 1954-58; dir. research Northwestern U. Dental Sch. (cleft lip and palate Inst.), 1947-58; assoc. attending orthodontist Children's Meml. Hosp., Chgo., 1951-58; vis. lectr. U. Mich. Dental Sch., 1958-67; dir. Kenilworth Research Found., Ill., 1967—; prof. orthodontics Zoller Dental Clinic; pediatrics research assoc. prof. anthropology and anatomy U. Chgo., 1969-81, assoc. prof. plastic and reconstructive surgery, 1980-82; research scientist ADA Research Inst., Chgo., 1980-90; dir. G.V. Black Inst. for Continuing Edn., 1967—; vis. prof. U. Mich., 1984-94; clin. prof. orthodontics U. Ill. Coll. Dentistry, Chgo., 1994—. Northcroft lectr., Birmingham, Eng., 1989; cons. in field. Author textbooks, articles; editor-in-chief Am. Jour. Orthodontics, 1985-2000, World Jour Orthodontics, 2000—. Served as capt. Dental Corps AUS, 1941-45. Recipient Alumni Merit award Northwestern U., 1977; named Disting. Alumnus Washington U., 1980; NIH grantee, 1954, 56-60, 76, 77, 79, 80, 85, 86. Fellow Royal Coll. Surgeons (Eng.), Am. Coll. of Dentists, Internat. Coll. of Dentists; mem. Am. Dental Soc., Ill. Dental Soc., Am. Assn. Orthodontists (gen. chmn. 1960, 77, 80, founding mem., chmn. coun. on orthodontic edn. and audio visual com. 1962, 67, gen. chmn. jour. 1977, trustee, Grieve Meml. award 1964, 84, Disting. Service award 1970, Ketcham award 1975, Salzmann award 1979, 75th Anniversary citation 1990, Mershon award 1989, Horace Hayden award 1991, Jarabak Internat. Teaching and Rsch. award 1994, Heritage award 1998, 99), Internat. Assn. Research (chmn. Chgo. sect. 1973-74), Chgo. Orthodontists Assn. (pres. 1961-62), European Orthodontists Soc.(hon.life mem. 2002), Ill. Orthodontists Soc. (pres. 1969-70, Outstanding Tchg. award 1999), Angle Soc. (pres. 1968), Japan Orthodontists Soc., World Fedn. Orthodontists (hon., Millenium award 2000), Ill. Soc. Orthodontists, SAR. Republican. Presbyterian. Home: 2895 Sheridan Pl Evanston IL 60201-1725 Office: U Ill Coll Dentistry MC842 801 S Paulina St # Mc842 Chicago IL 60612-7210 E-mail: tgraber@uic.edu., tmgraber@attbi.com.

GRABOW, STEPHEN HARRIS, architecture educator; b. Bklyn., Jan. 15, 1943; s. Philip and Ida (England) G.; 1 child, Nicole Elizabeth. BArch., U. Mich., 1965; MArch., Pratt Inst., 1966; postgrad., U. Calif.-Berkeley, 1966-67; PhD, U. Wash., 1973. Architect-planner U.S. Peace Corps, Tunisia, 1967-69; regional planning cons. Teheran, Iran, 1969; asst. prof. architecture U. Ariz., 1969-70; teaching assoc. U. Wash., 1970-72; lectr. town and regional planning Duncan of Jordanstone Coll. Art, U. Dundee, Scotland, 1972-73; asst. prof. architecture and urban design U. Kans.-Lawrence, 1973-76, assoc. prof., 1976-82, prof., 1982—, dir. architecture, 1979-82, 83-86; vis. fellow U. Calif.-Berkeley, 1977; research and design cons. Design Build Architects, Lawrence; bd. dirs. Assn. Collegiate Schs. Architecture, 1982-87. Vis. lectr. Royal Danish Acad. Fine Arts, Copenhagen, 1987-88. Author: Christopher Alexander and the Search for a New Paradigm in Architecture, 1983; mem. editorial bd.: Jour. Archtl. Edn., 1982-84. Recipient award Nat. Endowment for Arts, 1974, citation for excellence in design rsch. NEA, 1980, Biennial Svc. award Denmark's Internat. Studies Program, 1997, Bradley Tchg. award in architecture U. Kans., 1998; Fulbright Scholar award, 1987-88; NEH fellow, 1976-77. Mem. Nat. Archtl. Research Council (appointee 1986-87). Home: 1518 Crossgate Dr Lawrence KS 66047-3504 Office: U Kans Sch Architecture & Urban Design 1465 Jayhawk Blvd Lawrence KS 66045-7614 E-mail: sgrabow@ku.edu.

GRACE, (WALTER) CHARLES, prosecutor; b. Elmira, N.Y., Mar. 4, 1947; s. Claude Henry and Grace Anne (Richardson) G.; m. Barbbara Lynn Eaglen, Oct. 3, 1981; children: Katherine Anne, Charles Brigham. BA History, Duke U., 1969; JD, U. Tenn., 1972. Bar: Ill., 1972; U.S. Dist. Ct. (ea. and so. dists.) Ill., 1972. Asst. state's atty. Jackson County, Murphysboro, Ill., 1972-73; assoc. Donald R. Mitchell Law Office, Carbondale, 1973-74; atty. Jackson County Pub. Defender, Murphysboro, 1974-77; ptnr. Lockwood & Grace, Carbondale, 1977-78, pvt. practice, 1978-79; ptnr. Hendricks, Watt & Grace, Murphysboro, 1979-82; assoc. Feirich, Schone, Mager, Green & Assocs., Carbondale, 1982-83, Feirch, Schoen, Mager, Green & Assocs., Carbondale, 1983-88; state's atty. Jackson County State's Atty., Murphysboro, 1988-93; U.S. Atty. U.S. Atty.'s Office, Fairview Heights, Ill., 1993—. Chmn. Jackson County Child Advocacy Adv. Bd., 1988-93; adv. bd. Ill. State Violent Crime Victim's Adv. Bd., 1988-90; com. mem. Jackson County Juv. Justice Task Force, 1988-93; exec. com. Ill. State's Atty.'s Assn., 1991-93; legis. com. Ill. Sate's Atty.'s Assn., 1992-93; co-chmn. Jackson County SAFE Policy/Gang Policy Interagy. Steering Com. Adv. Bd., 1991-93; master So. Ill. Am. Inn. of Ct., 1992—; others. Active NAACP,, Carbondale; mem. Jackson County Heart Fund Campaign, 1976-77; bd. dirs. Carbondale United Way, 1978-80, capt. campaign drive, profl. div., 1980; mem. planning com. John A. Logan Coll.-Jackson County Bar Assn. Continuing Edn. Programs; mem. adv. com. to Corrections and Law Enforcment Programs, So. Ill. U. Sch. of Tech. Careers, 1978-89; mem. Hill House Board, Inc., 1979-84; pres. 1980-82; lector St. Francis Xavier Ch., Carbondale. Mem. Jackson County Bar Assn. (sec. 1978-79, pres. 1980-81), Ill. State Bar Assn. (mem. criminal law sect., family law sect., tort law sect.), ABA (family law and criminal law sects.), Assn. Trial Lawyers of Am., Nat. Legal Aid and Defender Assn., Ill. Pub. Defenders Assn., So. Ill. Am. Inns of Ct. (barrister 1993-95). Democrat. Roman Catholic. Avocations: golf, swimming, cooking, enology. Home: 431 Phillips Rd Carbondale IL 62901-7459 Office: US Attys Office 9 Executive Dr Ste 300 Fairview Heights IL 62208-1344

GRACE, MARK EUGENE, baseball player; b. Winston-Salem, N.C., June 28, 1964; Student, Saddleback C.C., San Diego State U. First baseman Chgo. Cubs, 1988—. Mem. Nat. League All-Star Team, 1993, 95. Recipient Golden Glove award, 1992-93; named Sporting News Rookie Player of Yr., MVP Ea. League, 1987; assist leader for 1st basemen, 1990-92; ranked 1st in Nat. League for put-outs, 1991-92. Office: Chgo Cubs Wrigley Field 1060 W Addison St Chicago IL 60613-4383*

GRACE, RICHARD EDWARD, engineering educator; b. Chgo., June 26, 1930; s. Richard Edward and Louise (Koko) G.; m. Consuela Cummings Fotos, Jan. 29, 1955; children: Virginia Louise, Richard Cummings (dec.). BS in Metall. Engring., Purdue U., 1951; PhD, Carnegie Inst. Tech., 1954. Registered profl. engr., N.J. Asst. prof. Purdue U., West Lafayette, Ind., 1954-58, assoc. prof., 1958-62, prof., 1962-2000, head sch. materials sci. and metall. engring., 1965-72, head div. interdisciplinary engring. studies, 1970-82, head freshman engring. dept., asst. dean engring., 1981-87, v.p. for student services, 1987-95, dir. undergrad. studies program, 1995-2000, prof. emeritus, v.p. emeritus, 2000—. Cons. to Midwest industries. Contbr. articles to profl. jours. Pres. Lafayette Symphony Found. Bd., 1993-95. Named Sagamore of Wabash, Gov. of Ind., 1995. Fellow Am. Soc. Metals (tchr. award 1962), Am. Soc. Engring. Edn. (Centennial medallion 1993), Accreditation Bd. Engring. and Tech. (past dir. and officer engring. edn. and accreditation com., related engring. com., Grinter award 1989); mem. Minerals, Metals and Materials Soc. (bd. dirs. 1987-90), Lafayette Country Club, Rotary, Elks, Sigma Xi, Tau Beta Pi, Omicron Delta Kappa, Phi Gamma Delta. Home: 2175 Tecumseh Park Ln West Lafayette IN 47906-2118 Office: Purdue U 1289 MSEE Bldg West Lafayette IN 47907-1289

GRACEY, DOUGLAS ROBERT, physician, physiologist, educator; b. Fort Dodge, Iowa, Aug. 7, 1936; s. Warren Robert and Areta Mary (Thompson) G.; m. Edith Ann Haas, Dec. 23, 1961; children— Laura, Douglas Robert B.A., Coe Coll., 1958; M.D., Northwestern U., 1962; M.S., U. Minn., 1968. Diplomate Am. Bd. Internal Medicine. Intern Cook County Hosp., Chgo., 1962-63; resident Mayo Grad. Sch. Medicine, 1963-66, 68-69; asst. prof. medicine Northwestern U. Med. Sch., 1969-75; assoc. prof. medicine Mayo Med. Sch., Rochester, Minn., 1975-83, prof., 1983—, vice chmn. pulmonary div., 1982-87; vice chmn. for practice dept. medicine Mayo Clinic, Rochester, 1983-93, dir. critical care medicine div., 1985-89, chmn. revenue systems com., chmn. divsn. pulmonary and critical care medicine. Author: (with W.W. Addington) Tuberculosis, 1972, Flying Lessons, Ambulances and orther Air Force Vignettes, 2000; editor: Pulmonary Diseases in the Adult, 1981; contbr. articles to profl. jours. Trustee Coe Coll., 1976-92. Served to capt. M.C., USAF, 1966-68 Am. Thoracic Soc. tng. fellow, 1968-69 Fellow ACP, Am. Coll. Chest Physicians, AMA. Republican. Lodges: Masons, Shriners Office: Mayo Clinic Chmn Div Pulmonary & Critical Care Med Rochester MN 55901

GRACZ, GREGORY L. labor union administrator; AA, Milw. Area Tech. Coll.; grad., Marquette U. Firefighter City of Milw. Fire Dept., 1978—, capt., 1998—; pres., contract adminstr. Milw. Profl. Fire Fighters Assn. Local 215. Mem. bd. regents U. Wis., Wis., 1999—. Office: Milw Profl Fire Fighters Assn Local 215 5625 W Wisconsin Ave Milwaukee WI 53213

GRADE, JEFFERY T. manufacturing company executive; b. Chicago, 1943; BS, Ill. Inst. Tech., 1966; MBA, DePaul U., 1972. With Plasto Mfg. Corp., 1965-66, Motorola Inc., 1966-67, Bell and Howell, 1967-68, Ill. Cen. Gulf R.R., 1968-73; v.p. fin. IC Industries, 1973-83; with Harnischfeger Corp., Milw., 1983-99, pres., COO, bd. dirs., 1986—, CEO, 1991-99, also chmn., CEO. Served with USN, 1865-66. Office: Harnischfeger Industries Ste 2780 100 E Wisconsin Ave Milwaukee WI 53202-4127

GRADWOHL, DAVID MAYER, anthropology educator; b. Lincoln, Nebr., Jan. 22, 1934; s. Bernard Sam and Elaine (Mayer) G.; m. Hanna Rosenberg, Dec. 29, 1957; children: Steven Ernst, Jane Mayer Nash, Kathryn Mayer Flaminio. BA in Anthropology and Geology, Nebr. U., 1955; postgrad., Edinburgh (Scotland) U., 1955-56; PhD in Anthropology, Harvard U., 1967. Instr. anthropology Iowa State U., Ames, 1962-66, asst. prof., 1966-67, assoc. prof., 1967-72, coord. anthropology, 1968-75, chair Am. Indian studies program, 1981-85, prof. anthropology, 1972—; asst site supr. Winchester (Eng.) Excavations Com., 1965. Advisor Nat. Register Hist. Sites, Des Moines, 1969-88, Office of State Archaeologist, Iowa City, 1983—; commr. Ames Hist. Preservation Commn., 1988-91. Co-author: The Worlds Between Two Rivers, 1987, 2d edit., 2000, Exploring Buried Buxton, 1990; co-author (audio visual programs) Blacks and Whites in Buxton, 1986, Iowa's Indian Heritage, 1972. With U.S. Army, 1957-59. Fulbright fellow U.S. Ednl. Commn., Edinburgh, 1956; recipient Faculty Citation, Iowa State Alumni Assn., Ames, 1980, Charles Irby Disting. Svc. award Nat. Assn. Ethnic Studies, 1990, Career Achievement award for undergrad. teaching AMOCO, 1992, Alumni Achievement award U. Nebr., 2001. Fellow Am. Anthropol. Assn., Assn. Iowa Archaeologists (chair 1977-78), Nebr. Assn. Profl. Archaeologists; mem. Soc. Am. Archaeology, Soc. Hist. Archaeology, Nebr. Jewish Hist. Soc., Nebr. State Hist. Soc., Plains Anthropol. Soc. (bd. dirs. 1969-72, 87-90, Disting. Svc. award 1998), Nat. Assn. Ethnic Studies (mem. editorial bd. 1987—), Iowa Archaeol. Soc. (mem. editl. bd. 1992—, Keyes-Orr Disting. Svc. award 1997), Iowa Jewish Hist. Soc. (co-founder, bd. dirs. 1996—). Democrat. Jewish. Avocations: hiking, mountain climbing, music. Home: 2003 Ashmore Dr Ames IA 50014-7804 Office: Iowa State U Dept Anthropology Ames IA 50011-0001 E-mail: gradwohl@iastate.edu.

GRADY, JOHN F. federal judge; b. Chgo., May 23, 1929; s. John F. and Lucille F. (Shroder) G.; m. Patsy Grady, Aug. 10, 1968; 1 child, John F. BS, Northwestern U., 1952, JD, 1954. Bar: Ill. 1955. Assoc. Sonnenschein, Berkson, Lautmann, Levinson & Morse, Chgo., 1954-56; asst. U.S. atty. No. Dist. Ill., 1956-61, chief criminal divsn., 1960-61; assoc. Snyder, Clarke, Dalziel, Holmquist & Johnson, Waukegan, Ill., 1961-63; practice law, 1963-76; judge U.S. Dist. Ct. (no. dist.) Ill., Chgo., 1976-86, chief judge, 1986-90, sr. judge, 1994—. Mem. com. criminal law U.S. Jud. Conf., 1982-87, adv. com. civil rules, 1984-90, chair, 1987-90; mem. bench book com. Fed. Jud. Ctr., 1988-93; mem. Nat. State-Fed. Jud. Coun., 1990-92, Jud. Panel on Multidist. Litigation, 1992-2000. Assoc. editor: Northwestern U. Law Rev. Mem. Phi Beta Kappa Office: US Dist Ct Rm 2286 219 S Dearborn St Ste 2286 Chicago IL 60604-1802

GRAEBER, CLYDE D. former state legislator; b. Aug. 29, 1933; m. Pauline Graeber. BA, U. Tulsa, 1954, JD, 1959. City commr. Leavenworth, Kans., 1978-84, mayor, 1983-84; Kans. state rep. Dist. 41, 1985-97; chmn. Rep. House Caucus; lawyer, banker, 1996—; sec. of health & environment Kansas City, 1999—. Mem. Am. Legis. Exch. Coun., Okla. Bar Assn. Home: 2400 Kingman St Leavenworth KS 66048-4230 Office: Capital Towers 400 SW 8th Ave Ste 200 Topeka KS 66603-3925

GRAF, ROBERT ARLAN, retired financial services executive; b. Bethlehem, Pa., Dec. 8, 1933; s. Rudolph Bernard and Edith May (Crossman) G.; m. Bernice Irene Garman, Dec. 21, 1957; 1 child, R. Mark. AB, U. Pa., 1955; JD, Temple U., 1958. Bar: Mass. 1963. Mgr. annuities The Paul Revere Life Ins. Co., Worcester, Mass., 1960-68; v.p. mass coverage adminstrn. Bankers Security Life Ins. Soc., Washington, 1968; regional dir. group pension Participating Annuity Life Ins. Co., McLean, Va., 1968-69; pres. LNC Equity Sales Corp., Ft. Wayne, Ind., 1969-84; 2d v.p. Lincoln Nat. Corp., 1969-84; sr. v.p. personal fin. services mktg. and tng. The No. Trust, Chgo., 1984-86; sr. v.p. Kemper Fin. Services Inc., Kemper Investors Life Ins. Co., 1986-90; pres. Investors Brokerage Svcs., Inc., 1987-90; v.p. fin. instns. div. Rollins Splty. Group, 1990-91; nat. sales dir. fin. instns. Paul Revere Ins. Group, Worcester, Mass., 1991-99; ret., 1999. Vol. Boy Scouts Am., Ft. Wayne, Sci. Ctrl., Ft. Wayne, St. Francis U., Ft. Wayne; vol. fundraiser United Way, Ft. Wayne, 1982-83, Fine Arts Found., Ft. Wayne, 1984. Served with USMC, 1958-60. Mem. Life Ins. Mktg. and Rsch. Assn. (chmn. investment products com. 1981-83, mem. mktg. through supplemental distbn. systems com.), Nat. Assn. Securities Dealers (prin.), Chgo. Bar Assn. (employee benefits com., fin. svcs. com., ins. com.), Bank Mktg. Assn., Fin. Instns. Ins. Assn., Assn. of Banks in Ins., Met. Club Chgo., Chgo. Shell Club, Masons, Delta Tau Delta, Phi Delta Phi. Presbyterian. Avocations: collecting specimen seashells, tennis, reading, collecting fossils.

GRAF, TRUMAN FREDERICK, agricultural economist, educator; b. New Holstein, Wis., Sept. 18, 1922; s. Herbert and Rose (Sell) G.; m. Sylvia Ann Thompson, Sept. 6, 1947; children: Eric Kindley, Siri Lynne, Peter Truman. BS, U. Wis., 1947, MS, 1949, PhD, 1953. Mktg. specialist, coop. agt. USDA and U. Wis., 1948-50; instr. agrl. econs. U. Wis., Madison, 1951-53, asst. prof., 1953-56, assoc. prof., 1956-61, prof., 1961-85, prof. emeritus, 1985—. Expert witness, 1982—; mem. Gov.'s Com. on Wis. Dairy Mktg.; mem. 3-man team to make mktg. analysis in Nigeria, USDA, 1962, made U.S. milk mktg. study, 1971; made mktg. analyses in 13 Carribbean countries, 1964; made mktg. analysis U. Wis., Mex., 1965; made mktg. analyses U.S. Ednl. Found., Finland, 1970, Rumanian Ministry Edn., U.S. Dept. State, Rumania, USSR, 1976, France, 1981, Russia, 1992, Ukraine, 1992, 98, Bulgaria, 1992, 93, Hungary, 1993, Poland, 1993, Zimbabwe, Africa, 1994, Ukraine, 1998; rschr. for internat. agrl. mktg. agys., Kazakhstan, 1999, Uganda, 2000, U.S. Treasury Dept., Cuba, 2002, U. Tchg. on Internat. Trade., 1963-93. Contbr. articles to profl. jours. Active Cub Scouts; bd. dirs. Univ. Houses Assn., 1955-56, Univ. Hill Farm Assn., 1958-59, Univ. Hill Farm Swim Club, 1959-60, Oakwood Retirement Homes, 1992-2001. Recipient Uhlman award Chgo. Bd. Trade, 1952, recipient Man of Yr. award World Dairy Expn., 1976, Disting. Svc. award U. Wis. Extension, 1981, Coop. Builder award Fedn. Coops., 1982, Internat. Trade Spl. award Gov. Wis., 1983. Mem. AARP (econ. security adv. com.), Am. Agrl. Econs. Assn. (Published Rsch. award 1974), Am. Mktg. Assn., Madison Naval Res. Assn. (pres. 1968—), Am. Econ. Assn., Hist. Soc., United Dairy Industries Assn. (adv. com.), Wis. Fedn. Coops., Lakeshore Federated Dairy Coop., Wis. Ret. Educators Assn. (bd. dirs.), Wis. Coalition of Annuitants (vice chair), Civil War Club, Kiwanis. Lutheran. Achievements include applied rsch. study for dairy firms, orgns. state ed. regulatory agys. and agrl. bus. firms. Home: 5007 Prairie Rose Ct Middleton WI 53562-2385 Office: U Wis Dept of Agr Dept Agriculture Madison WI 53706

GRAHAM, CHARLES, research psychologist; b. Atlantic City, Nov. 21, 1937; s. Charles Leroy and Margery (Kaplan) G.; m. Sally Jones, Dec. 8, 1962 (div. Apr. 1974); children: Ronna, Christopher, Glen; m. Mary R. Cook, May 18, 1996; 1 child, Sheri J. BS, U. Md., 1966; MS, Pa. State U., 1968, PhD, 1970. Rsch. assoc. Inst. Pa. Hosp., Phila., 1970-74; instr., lectr. dept. psychiatry U. Pa., 1970-74; sr. exptl. psychologist Midwest Rsch. Inst., Kansas City, 1974-78, prin. exptl. psychologist, 1979-94, sr. advisor for life scis., 1994—, prin. advisor for life scis., 1998—. Mgr. Bioelectromagnetics Rsch. Program, 1998—; tech. review panel Dept. of Energy, EPA, NIH, WHO, Internat. Commn. on Non-Ionizing Radiation Protection. With U.S. Army, 1960-62. NIH grantee, 1975-2000. Mem. Am. Psychol. Assn., Soc. Psychophysiol. Rsch., Claude Bernard Soc., Bioelectromagnetics, Sigma Xi. Avocations: travel, photography, gardening. Office: Midwest Rsch Inst 425 Volker Blvd Kansas City MO 64110-2299 E-mail: mcg@planetkc.com., cgraham@mriresearch.org.

GRAHAM, DAVID BROWNING, lawyer; b. Wildwood, N.J., Dec. 20, 1942; s. William Browning and Mary Graham; m. Linda Lea Beasley, Feb. 20, 1971; children: Owen, Mary. BS, La. State U., 1966, JD, 1969. Bar: La. 1969, D.C. 1972, U.S. Ct. Appeals (D.C. cir.) 1974, Ill. 1980, Ohio 1999. Atty. U.S. EPA, Washington, 1972-73; corp. counsel Nat. Rural Elec. Coop. Assn., 1973-77; dir. office hearing and appeals U.S. Dept. Interior, Arlington, Va., 1977-79; dep. gen. counsel Velsicol Chem. Corp., Chgo., 1979-84; ptnr. Freedman, Levy, Kroll & Simonds, Washington, 1984-89, Kaye, Scholer, Fierman, Hays & Handler, Washington, 1989-92, Howrey & Simon, Washington, 1992-98, Baker & Hostetler, Cleve., 1998—. Mem. bd. advisors Toxics Law Reporter, Washington, 1987—, Chem. Waste Litigation Reporter, Washington, 1986—. Co-author: Environmental Justice and Underlying Societal Problems, 1997, New Approaches to Environmental Law and Agency Regulation: The Daubert Litigation Approach, 2000; contbr. articles to profl. jours. Mem. parents bd. Bucknell U. Mem. ABA (former officer sect. environ., energy & environ. law), D.C. Bar Assn., Ohio Bar Assn., Cleve. Bar Assn. Presbyterian. Avocations: running, skiing. Office: Baker & Hostetler 1900 E 9th St 3200 National City Ctr Cleveland OH 44114-3485

GRAHAM, DAVID F. lawyer; b. Chgo., Sept. 14, 1953; BA with high honors, Haverford Coll., 1975; JD, U. Chgo., 1978. Bar: Ill. 1978. Law clk. to Hon. Charles Levin Mich. Supreme Ct., 1978-79; Bigelow teaching fellow, lectr. on law U. Chgo., 1979-80; ptnr. Sidley & Austin, Chgo. Office: Sidley & Austin 1 S First National Plz Chicago IL 60603-2000

GRAHAM, DIANE E. newspaper editor; b. Gary, Ind., June 29, 1953; d. William M. and Mary Jane (Shreve) G.; m. Daniel Kevin Miller, Oct. 18, 1986. Bachelor's degree, Drake U., 1974. Reporter Des Moines Tribune, 1974-78, Des Moines Register, 1978-84, bus. editor, 1984-86, dep. mng. editor, 1986-95, mng. editor, 1995—. Pres. Iowa Freedom of Info. Coun., Des Moines, 1992-93; chair adv. bd. Drake U. Sch. Journalism, Des Moines, 1995—. Davenport fellow for bus./econ. reporting U. Mo., 1983. Avocations: pipe-organ playing, gardening. Office: Des Moines Register 715 Locust St Des Moines IA 50309-3767

GRAHAM, EDWARD HENRY, retired lawyer; b. Belleville, Kans., June 15, 1935; AB, U. Kans., 1957, LLB, 1960, JD, 1968. Bar: Kans. 1960, Iowa 1969. Assoc. Lilleston, Spradling, Gott, Stallwitz & Hope, Wichita, Kans., 1964-67, ptnr., 1967-69; gen. counsel Massey-Ferguson, Inc., Des Moines, 1969-82, AGRI Industries, Des Moines, 1982-85; asst. atty. gen. Iowa Dept. Justice, 1985-86; assoc. counsel Maytag Corp., Newton, Iowa, 1986-89, assoc. gen. counsel, 1989-90, v.p., gen. counsel, 1990-2000, retired, 2000. Maj. USAF, 1961-63. Home: 4150 Greenwood Dr Des Moines IA 50312

GRAHAM, JAMES, state legislator; b. Ironton, Mo., June 22, 1960; AS in Bus. Mgmt., Mineral Area Coll., 1980; degree, Mo. FFA State Farmer. Former tchr., Fredericktown, Mo.; state rep. Dist. 106 Mo. Ho. of Reps., 1991—. Mem. agr. com., appropriations com., correctional insts. com., mines and mining com., banks and fin. instns. com., budget com., A+ schs. com., capital improvements and leasing oversight com.; cattle farmer. Del. Am. Coun. Young Polit. Leaders, China and Taiwan, 1993; active Little Vine United Bapt. Ch. Mem. NRA, Marcus Lodge 110 AF&AM (master), Optimist Club, Rotary Club, C. of C. Office: Mo Ho of Reps Rm 105B 201 W Capitol Ave Jefferson City MO 65101 Fax: 573-751-5123. E-mail: jgraham@servics.state.mo.us.

GRAHAM, JAMES LOWELL, federal judge; b. 1939; BA, JD summa cum laude, Ohio State U., 1962. Pvt. practice Crabbe, Brown, Jones, Potts & Schmidt, Columbus, Ohio, 1962-69, Graham, Dutro, Nemeth, and predecessors, Columbus, 1969-86; judge U.S. Dist. Ct. (so. dist.) Ohio, 1986—. Faculty Ohio Jud. Coll., Ohio Legal Inst. Chmn. Ohio Bar Examiners, 1974, Devel. Commn. City of Columbus, 1976-77; mem. legal svcs. Salvation Army of Columbus, 1967-77, legal sect. United Way Campaign, 1976-80. Fellow Am. Coll. Trial Lawyers; mem. Capital U. Coll. of Law Assn. (dean's coun.), Ohio State U. Alumni Assn. Office: US Dist Ct 169 US Courthouse 85 Marconi Blvd Columbus OH 43215-2823

GRAHAM, JEWEL FREEMAN, social worker, lawyer, educator; b. Springfield, Ohio, May 3, 1925; d. Robert Lee and Lula Belle Freeman; m. Paul N. Graham, Aug. 8, 1953; children: Robert, Nathan. BA, Fisk U., 1946; student, Howard U., 1946-47; MS in Social Svc. Adminstrn., Case

Western Res. U., 1953; JD, U. Dayton, 1979; LHD (hon.), Meadville-Lombard Theol. Sch., 1991. Bar: Ohio; cert. social worker. Assoc. dir. teenage program dept. YWCA, Grand Rapids, Mich., 1947-50, coord. met. teenage program Detroit, 1953-56; dir. program for interracial edn. Antioch Coll., Yellow Springs, Ohio, 1964-69, from asst. prof. to prof., 1969-92, prof. emeritus, 1992—. Mem. Ohio Commn. on Dispute Resolution and Conflict Mgmt., 1990-92. Mem. exec. com. World YMCA, Geneva, 1975-83, 87—, pres., 1983; bd. dirs. YWCA of the U.S.A., 1970-89, pres., 1979-85; bd. dirs. Antioch U., 1994-96. Named to Greene County Women's Hall of Fame, 1982, Ohio Women's Hall of Fame, 1988; named 1 of 10 Outstanding Women of Miami Valley, 1987; recipient Ambassador award YWCA of the U.S.A., 1993. Mem. ABA, Nat. Assn. of Social Workers (charter), Nat. Coun. of Negro Women (life), Alpha Kappa Alpha. Democrat. Unitarian Universalist. Avocations: bicycling, swimming, walking, needlework. Office: Antioch Coll Livermore 51 Yellow Springs OH 45387 E-mail: jewelg@aol.com.

GRAHAM, JOHN DALBY, public relations executive; b. Maryville, Mo., Aug. 24, 1937; s. Kyle T. and Irma Irene (Dalby) G.; m. Linda Mills Graham, Dec. 21, 1996; children: Katherine Elizabeth, David Landon. B.J., U. Mo., 1959. Editor Hallmark Cards, Inc., Kansas City, Mo., 1959-62; dir. pub. relations St. Louis Met. YMCA, 1962-66; chmn., chief exec. officer Fleishman-Hillard, Inc., St. Louis, 1966—; chmn. Fleishman-Hillard Europe. Bd. dirs. Fleishman-Hillard/U.K. Ltd. Trustee St. Louis U.; mem. exec. bd. St. Louis Area coun. Boy Scouts Am. Capt. U.S. Army, 1959-66. Fellow Pub. Rels. Soc. Am.; mem. Internat. Pub. Rels. Assn., Nat. Investor Rels. Inst., Round Table, Arthur Page Soc., Log Cabin Club. Home: PO Box 8797 Saint Louis MO 63101-8797 Office: Fleishman Hillard Inc 200 N Broadway Saint Louis MO 63102-2796

GRAHAM, JOHN W. advertising executive; b. 1946; With Richfield (Ohio) Properties, 1969-83, Nationwide Advt. Svc., Cleve., 1983—, pres., CEO. Office: Nationwide Advt Svc Inc 1228 Euclid Ave Ste 600 Cleveland OH 44115-1845

GRAHAM, JORIE, writer; b. N.Y.C., May 9, 1950; d. Curtis Bell and Beverly (Stoll) Pepper; m. James Galvin. BFA, NYU, 1973; MFA, U. Iowa, 1978. Asst. prof. Murray (Ky.) State U., 1978-79, Humboldt State U., Arcata, Calif., 1979-81; instr. Columbia U., N.Y.C., 1981-83; mem. staff U. Iowa, Iowa City, 1983—, prof. English, dir. poetry workshop, 1999—. Poetry editor Crazy Horse, 1978-81; Bayelston chair Harvard U., 1998-99. Author: Hybrids of Plants and of Ghosts, 1980 (Great Lakes Colls. Assn. award 1981), Erosion, 1983, The End of Beauty, 1987, Region of Unlikeness, 1991, Materialism, 1993, The Dream of the Unified Field: Selected Poems 1974-94, 1995, The Errancy, 1997, Swarm, 1999; editor: Earth Took of Earth: 100 Great Poems of the English Language, 1996; editor: (with David Lehman) The Best American Poetry 1990, 1990. Recipient Am. Acad. Poets award, 1977, Young Poet prize Poetry Northwest, 1980, Pushcart prize, 1980, 82, American Poetry Review prize, 1982, Pulitzer prize in poetry, 1996, Lavan award Acad. Am. Poets, 1991, Martin Zaubel award Acad. and Inst. of Arts and Letters, 1992; Bunting fellow Radcliff Inst., 1982, Guggenheim fellow, 1983, John D. and Catherine T. MacArthur Found. fellow, 1990; grantee Ingram-Merrill Found., 1981. Office: U Iowa 102 Dey House 507 N Clinton St Iowa City IA 52245

GRAHAM, ROBERT, medical association executive; b. Pueblo, Colo., Feb. 15, 1943; married. AB, Earlham Coll., 1965; MD, U. Kans., 1970. Asst. adminstr. agy. goals Health Svc. & Mental Health Admn. Dept. Health Edn. & Welfare, Washington, 1970—73; resident in family practice Bapt. Meml. Hosp., 1974—75; asst. dir. divsn. edn. Am. Acad. Family Physicians, Kansas City, Mo., 1973—76; dep. dir. Bur. Health Manpower, Health Resources Adminstrn. Dept. Health Edn. & Welfare, 1976—78, dep. adminstr., 1978—79; profl. staff mem. subcom. health & sci. rsch. Comty. Labor & Human Resources, U.S. Senate, 1979—80; acting adminstr. health resources adminstrn. Dept. Health & Human Svc., 1981—82, adminstr., 1982—85; exec. v.p. Am. Acad. Family Physicians, Kansas City, Mo., 1985—. Mem. staff Program Health Mgmt. Baylor Coll. Medicine, 1976; exec. sec. Grad. Med. Edn. Nat. Adv. Com., 1978—79; bd. dirs. Alliance for Health Referendum, 1994—, Sun Valley Forum Nat. Health. Contbr. articles. Mem.: AMA, Am. Soc. Assn. Execs., Am. Assn. Med. Soc. Execs., Am. Acad. Med. Dirs., Am. Acad. Family Physicians, Assn. Am. Med. Colls., Inst. Medicine of NAS (exec. v.p., CEO 1985—2000). Office: Am Acad Family Physicians 11400 Tomahawk Creek Pky Leawood KS 66211-2672

GRAHAM, WILLIAM B. pharmaceutical company executive; b. Chgo., July 14, 1911; s. William and Elizabeth (Burden) G.; m. Edna Kanaley, June 15, 1940 (dec.); children: William J., Elizabeth Anne, Margaret, Robert B.; m. Catherine Van Duzer, July 23, 1984. SB cum laude, U. Chgo., 1932, JD cum laude, 1936; LLD, Carthage Coll., 1974, Lake Forest Coll., 1983; LLD (hon.), U. Ill., 1988; LHD, St. Xavier Coll. and Nat. Coll. Edn., 1983; LHD (hon.), Barat Coll., 1997, DePaul U., 1998. Bar: Ill. 1936. Patent lawyer Dyrenforth, Lee, Chritton & Wiles, 1936-40; mem. Dawson & Ooms, 1940-45; v.p., mgr. Baxter Internat., Inc., Deerfield, Ill., 1945-53, pres., 1953-71, CEO, 1960-80, chmn. bd. Ill., 1980-85, sr. chmn., 1989-95, chmn. emeritus, 1995—. Prof., chair Weizmann Inst. Sci., Rehoboth, Israel, 1978; lectr. U. Chgo., 1981-82. Chmn. bd. dirs. Lyric Opera Chgo.; bd. dirs. Big Shoulders, Wendy Will Care Fedn., Chgo. Hort. Soc.; trustee Orchestral Assn., U. Chgo., Evanston (Ill.) Hosp.; past pres. Cmty. Fund of Chgo. Recipient V.I.P. award Lewis Found., 1963, Disting. Citizen award Ill. St. Andrew Soc., 1974, Decision Maker of Yr. award Am. Statis. Assn., 1974, Marketer of Yr. award AMA, 1976, Found. award Kidney Found., 1981, Chicagoan of Yr. award Chgo. Boys Club, 1981, Bus. Statesman of Yr. award Harvard Bus. Sch. Club Chgo., 1983, Achievement award Med. Tech. Svcs., 1983, Disting. Fellows award Internat. Ctr. for Artificial Organs and Transplantations, 1982, Chgo. Civic award DePaul U., 1986, Internat. Visitors Golden Medallion award U. Ill., 1988, Chgo. medal U. Chgo., 1992, Laureate award Lincoln Acad. Ill., 1992, Lyric Opera Carol Fox award, 1992, Good Scout award N.E. Coun. Boy Scouts Am., 1993, Making History award Chgo. Hist. Soc., 1996; recognized for pioneering work Health Industry Mfrs. Assn., 1981; inducted Jr. Achievement Chgo. Bus. Hall of Fame, 1986, Modern Healthcare Hall of Fame, 1994, Art Alliance Legend award Dreihaus Found., 2000. Mem. Am. Pharm. Mfrs. Assn. (past pres.), Ill. Mfrs. Assn. (past pres.), Pharm. Mfrs. Assn. (past chmn., award for spl. distinction leadership 1981), Chgo. Club (past pres.), Commonwealth Club, Comml. Club, Indian Hill Club, Casino Club, Old Elm Club, Seminole Club, Everglades Club, Bath and Tennis Club, Links Club, Phi Beta Kappa, Sigma Xi, Phi Delta Phi. Home: 40 Devonshire Ln Kenilworth IL 60043-1205 Office: Baxter Internat Inc 1 Baxter Pkwy Deerfield IL 60015-4625

GRAHN, BARBARA ASCHER, retired publishing executive; b. Chgo., Mar. 26, 1929; d. Harry L. and Eleanor (Simon) Ascher; m. Robert D. Grahn, Dec. 23, 1952; children: Susan Grahn Gantz, Nancy Lee, Wendy Grahn O'Brien. BA, Miami U., Oxford, Ohio, 1950. Promotion dir. George Williams Coll., Chgo., 1950-52; sales mgr. Chatham Mfg., 1952-54; research asst. Standard Rate and Data Service, Skokie, 1968-70, adminstr. editorial services, 1970-75, asst. editor, 1975-77, editor Wilmette, 1977-87; assoc. pub. Std. Rate and Data Svc., 1987-95, quality assurance mgr., 1995—2002; ret., 2002. Precinct capt. Ill. Reps., 1956-58; pres. Cmty. Club of Jewish Women, Skokie, 1958-60; bd. dirs., treas. North Shore Towers Condo Assn., Skokie, 1986-90, 93-99, 2002-. Mem. NAFE, Chgo. Ad Club, Alpha Epsilon Phi. Avocations: choreography, swimming, spending time with grandchildren. E-mail: cjmmk@aol.com.

GRAINGER, DAVID WILLIAM, distribution company executive; b. Chgo., Oct. 23, 1927; s. William Wallace and Hally (Ward) G. BSEE, U. Wis., 1950. With W.W. Grainger, Inc., Chgo., 1952—, chmn. bd., 1968-97, sr. chmn., 1997—. Office: WW Grainger Inc 100 Grainger Pkwy Lake Forest IL 60045-5201

GRALEN, DONALD JOHN, lawyer; b. Oak Park, Ill., Mar. 18, 1933; s. Oliver Edwin and Rosalie Marie (Buskens) G.; m. Jane Walsh, Dec. 29, 1956; children: Alana, Mark, Paul, Ann, Sarah. BS, Loyola U., Chgo., 1956; JD with honors, Loyola U., 1957. Bar: Ill. 1958. Assoc. Sidley & Austin, Chgo., 1959-65, ptnr., 1966-94, counsel, 1994-99. Co-author chpts. in books. Trustee Village of LaGrange, Ill., 1973-77; chmn. LaGrange Zoning Bd., 1971-73, LaGrange Econ. Devel. Com., 1982, Cmty. Meml. Found., 1995—; bd. dirs. Carson Pirie Scott Found., Chgo., 1980-89, Jr. Achievement, 1978-88, Met. Housing and Planning Coun., 1982-89, Cmty. Family Svc. and Mental Health Assn., 1983-87, Chgo. Youth Conservation Corps, 1988-92, LaGrange Meml. Found., 1990-95, YMCA Met. Chgo., 1990—. 1st lt. U.S. Army, 1957-59. Mem. Ill. Bar Assn., Univ. Club, Big Foot Country Club. Home: 42 Durham Ct Burr Ridge IL 60527-7938 Office: Sidley & Austin 1 S First National Plz Chicago IL 60603-2000 E-mail: dgralen@aol.com.

GRAMS, RODNEY D. former senator, former congressman; b. 1948; Student, Anoka-Ramsey Jr. Coll., Brown Inst., Minneapolis, Minn., Carroll Coll., Helena, Mont. Engrng. cons. Orr-Schelen Mayeron & Assoc., Mpls.; anchor, producer Sta. KFBB-TV, Great Falls, Mont., Sta. WSAU-TV, Wausau, Wis., Sta. WIFR-TV, Rockford, Ill., Sta. KMSP-TV, Mpls.; mem. 103d Congress from 6th Minn. Dist., 1993-94; U.S. Senator from Minn., 1995—2001. Pres., CEO Sun Ridge Builders. Republican. Office: US Senate 257 Dirksen Senate Office Washington DC 20510-2304

GRANBERG, KURT, state legislator, lawyer; b. Breese, Ill., June 16, 1953; s. Marnen George and Agnes Mary (Vahlkamp) G. BS, U. Ill., Chgo., 1975; postgrad., Ill. Inst. Tech., 1980. Bar: Ill. 1980, U.S. Dist. Ct. (so. dist.) Ill. 1983. Legis. intern Ill. Ho. Reps., Springfield, 1975-76, mem. staff, 1975-77; assoc. James Donnewald Law Office, Breese, 1980-83; asst. pub. defender Clinton County, Ill., 1981-83; ptnr. Donnewald & Granberg, Breese, 1983—; spl. asst. atty. gen. State of Ill., 1983—; registered lobbyist, 1984—; mem. Ill. Ho. Reps., 1986—; asst. Dem. majority leader. Mem. fin. com. Ill. Inst. Tech.-Chgo. Kent. Sch. Law, 1979-80. Dem. precinct committeeman, Carlyle, Ill., 1982-84; mem. Clinton County Bd., Carlyle, 1984—, Carlyle Lake Adv. Com.; bd. dirs. Ctrl. Comprehensive Mental Health Ctr., Centralia, Ill., 1984—. Mem. ABA, Ill. Bar Assn., Clinton County Bar Assn., Jaycees, Carlyle Bus. and Profl. Assn., K.C., Optimists. Roman Catholic. Home: 17918 Oakwood Dr Carlyle IL 62231-2918 Office: Ill Ho of Reps 300 E Capitol Ave Springfield IL 62701-1710

GRANDGUIST, BETTY L. former director elder affairs; 5 children. Nursing, Mercy Hosp. Sch. Nursing, Des Moines; BA in Psychology, Drake U.; MA in Social Work, U. Iowa, 1976. Divsn. adminstr. Iowa Dept. Pub. Health, Des Moines; exec. dir. Iowa Dept. Elder Affairs, 1987—. Adj. instr. U. Iowa Sch. Social Work. Recipient Nat. Govs. Assn. award, 1992. Mem. Nat. Assn. State Units Aging (v.p.), Iowa Health Care Reform Council, Govs. Task Force Affirmative Action, Long Term Care Coordinating Unit (Issues Scanning Bd.), Drake U. Arts, Scis. Adv. Bd.

GRANHOLM, JENNIFER MULHERN, state attorney general; b. Vancouver, B.C., Can., Feb. 5, 1959; arrived in U.S., 1962; d. Civtor Ivar and Shirley Alfreda (Dowden) Granholm; m. Daniel Granholm Mulhern, May 23, 1986; children: Kathryn, Cecelia, Jack. BA, U. Calif., Berkeley, 1984; JD, Harvard U., 1987. Bar: Mich. 1987, U.S. Dist. Ct. (ea. dist.) Mich. 1987, U.S. Ct. Appeals (6th cir.) 1987. Jud. law clk. 6th Cir Ct. Appeals, Detroit, 1987—88; exec. asst. Wayne County Exec., 1988—89; asst. U.S. atty. Dept. Justice, 1990—94; corp. counsel Wayne County, 1994—98; elected atty. gen., 1999. Gen. counsel Detroit/Wayne County Stadium Authority, 1996—98. Contbr. articles to profl. jours. Commr. Great Lakes Commn.; mem. bd. Cyberstate.org YWCA. Mem.: Inc. Soc. Irish Lawyers, Women's Law Assn., Detroit Bar Assn. Roman Catholic. Avocations: running, family, laughing. Office: Atty Gen PO Box 30212 Lansing MI 48909-7712

GRANOFF, MARK HOWARD, insurance company executive; b. Bklyn., May 29, 1946; s. Leo A. and Harriett (Golden) G.; m. Dale Blash, Aug. 25, 1968; 1 child, Hal P. BA in Econs., CUNY, 1968, MA, 1972. With Union Mut. Ins. Co., Portland, Maine, 1973-84, dir. life policy owner svcs., 1981-82, dir. bus. analysis, 1982-84, dir. disability mktg., 1984; dir. mktg. Maccabees Mut. Life Ins. Co., Southfield, Mich., 1984-88; v.p. employee benefits mktg. Bus. Men's Assurance Co. Am., Kansas City, Mo., 1988-90; v.p. mktg. Blue Cross and Blue Shield United of Wis., Milw., 1990—; pres., COO United Wis. Group, 1991—. Bd. dirs. Alzheimer's Assn. Southeastern Wis., Miw., 1992—, Wis. chpt. Arthritis Found. Mem. Self Ins. Inst. Am. (chair promotion com. 1988), Life Ins. Mktg. Rsch. Assn. (tng. subcom. 1987), Ins. Acctg. and Statis. Assn. (chpt. v.p. promotions 1980). Home: 5692 Salisbury Dr Roanoke VA 24018-3876 Office: United Wis Group 401 W Michigan St Milwaukee WI 53203-2804

GRANSEE, MARSHA L. federal agency executive; b. Youngstown, OH, Sept. 26, 1952; m. Wallace A. Witkowski, Jan. 1, 1987; two children: BA in anthropology, Ohio State U., Columbus, 1974; JD, Cleveland-Marshall Coll. Law, 1978. Bar: Va. 1978, Ohio 1979, D.C. 1987. Assoc. legal editor Pub. Utilities Fortnightly, 1979-83; clerk office adminstrv. law judges Fed. Energy Regularoty Commn., 1983-85; assoc. Rose, Schmidt, Chapman, Duff and Hasley, 1985-87; atty. adviser Electric Rates and Corp. Regulation, 1987-88, sr. trial atty. gas and oil litig., 1988-92, legal adviser commr., 1992-94, legal adviser chair, 1994—, assoc. gen. counsel, 1994—. Contbg. author: Energy Law and Transactions. Mem. Fed. Energy Bar Assn. Office: Off Gen Counsel Fed Energy Reg Commn 888 First St Rm 10D-01 Youngstown OH 20426

GRANT, DAVID JAMES WILLIAM, pharmacy educator; b. Walsall, Eng., Mar. 26, 1937; came to U.S., 1988; s. James and Attie Hilda May (Stringer) G. BA in Chemistry with 1st class honors, Oxford U., Eng., 1961, MA, DPhil in Phys. Chemistry, 1963, DSc in Phys. Sci., 1990. Lectr. chemistry U. Coll. of Sierra Leone, Freetown, 1963-65; lectr. then sr. lectr. pharm. chemistry U. Nottingham, Eng., 1965-81; prof. phys. pharmacy Sch. Pharmacy, U. Toronto, Ont., Can., 1981-88, assoc. dean grad. studies and rsch. Can., 1984-87; endowed prof. pharmaceutics Coll. Pharmacy, U. Minn., Mpls., 1988—. Bd. dirs. Hosokawa Micron Internat., Inc., 1998-2001; mem. grants com. for pharm. sci. Med. Rsch. Coun. Can., Ottawa, 1983-87; mem. com. on health rsch. Ont. Univs., Toronto, 1985-87; vis. prof. Med. Rsch. Coun. Can.; mem. stds. expert com. for excipients: test methods for U.S. Pharmacopeia, 1991—; cons. to numerous chem. and pharm. cos. Co-author: Physical Chemistry for Students of Pharmacy and Biology, 1977, Solubility Behavior of Organic Compounds, 1990; mem. editl. bd. Jour. Pharm. Scis., 1990-93, assoc. editor, 1994—; mem. editl. adv. bd. Pharm. Devel. and Tech., 1995—, Kona, 1996—, AAPS Pharm. Sci., 1999—; contbr. more than 200 articles to sci. jours Lt. Brit. Army, 1955-57. Recipient Rsch. award Leverhulme Found., U.K., 1969, Pharmaceutics award of excellence PhRMA Found., 1999; grantee rsch. couns. and indsl. cos., U.K., Can., U.S. Fellow Royal Soc. Chemistry, Am. Assn. Pharm. Scientists (sustaining charter mem. 1986—), AAAS, Internat. Union Pure and Applied Chemistry; mem. Am. Inst. Chem. Engrs., Am. Pharm. Assn., Am. Chem. Soc., Am. Assn. Coll. Pharmacy. Achievements include showing how small amounts of additives or impurities modify the physical properties of crystalline drugs and excipients; development of crystal engineering of pharmaceutical substances. Office: U Minn Weaver-Densford Hall 308 Harvard St SE Minneapolis MN 55455-0353

GRANT, DENNIS, newspaper publishing executive; Dir. advt. Chgo. Tribune. Office: Chgo Tribune Co 435 N Michigan Ave Chicago IL 60611-4066

GRANT, EDWARD ROBERT, chemistry educator, company executive; b. Tacoma, Sept. 23, 1947; s. Melven Edwin and Estelle Muriel (Glueck) G.; m. Catherine Janine Carey, Aug. 10, 1980; children: Alexander Edward, Janine Catherine. BA in Chemistry, Occidental Coll., 1969; PhD in Chemistry, U. Calif., Davis, 1974. Asst. prof. Cornell U., Ithaca, N.Y., 1977-83, assoc. prof., 1983-86; prof. chemistry Purdue U., West Lafayette, Ind., 1986—, assoc. head dept. chemistry, 1989-93; CEO SpectraCode, Inc., 1996—. Vis. prof. Laboratoire Photophysique Moleculaire, Universite de Paris-Sud, 1991; vis. prof. Technische Universitat Munchen, 1992-93; directeur de recherche associe (5 éme) échelon CNRS Laboratoire Aimé-Cotton, Paris. Contbr. numerous articles to profl. jours. Recipient Nobel Laureate Signature award, 1986, Humbuldt Rsch. award for sr. U.S. scientists, 1992, R & D 100 award, 1998, Henry Ford Tech. award, 1999; Fulbright sr. scholar, 1988. Fellow Am. Phys. Soc. Office: Purdue U Dept Chemistry West Lafayette IN 47907 E-mail: edgrant@purdue.edu.

GRANT, JOHN THOMAS, retired state supreme court justice; b. Omaha, Oct. 25, 1920; s. Thomas J. and Mary Elizabeth (Smith) G.; m. Marian Louise Saner, Dec. 27, 1947 (dec. 1995); children: Martha Grant Bruckner, John P., Susan J., Joseph W., Timothy K.; m. Zella Forehead, June 7, 1997. LLB, JD, Creighton U., 1950. Bar: Nebr. 1950. Sole practice law, Omaha, 1950-74; judge State Dist. Ct., 1974-83; justice Nebr. Supreme Ct., Lincoln, 1983-92. Served with Signal Corps, U.S. Army, 1942-45, PTO Home: 912 S 118th Plz Omaha NE 68154-3404

GRANT, PAUL BERNARD, industrial relations educator, arbitrator; b. Chgo., Mar. 18, 1931; s. Paul B. and Catherine (Flyke) G.; m. Madeleine Grant, Aug. 15, 1959 (dec. Nov. 2000); children: Maura, Elizabeth, Paul, Francis, Timothy. BS, Loyola U., Chgo., 1952; MS, Inst. Indsl. Rels., Chgo., 1954. Asst. prof. Loyola U., Chgo., 1959-89, assoc. prof. indsl. rels., 1989-96, asst. v.p., 1977-85, dir. employee rels., 1967-76, sec. retirement com., 1967-95; expert witness Employment Matters, 1993—; prof. emeritus Loyola U., 1996—. Labor arbitrator Am. Arbitration Assn., Chgo., 1972—, Fed. Mediation Conciliation Svc., Washington, 1976—, Ill. Labor Rels. Bd., Chgo., 1984—, Ill. Edni. Labor Rels. Bd., Chgo., 1987—, Nat. Mediation Bd., Chgo., Washington, 1988—, Social Security Adminstrn.; mediator Ctr. for Employment Dispute Resolution, 1993—; U.S. arbitrator, del. N.Am. Agreement on Labor Cooperation, 1993—; expert witness employment and civil rights. Author: Cutting Health Care Costs, 1987. Sgt. U.S. Army, 1954-56. Mem. Am. Arbitration Assn., Assn. for Conflict Resolution, Indsl. Rels. Rsch. Assn., Am. Legion, Ill. Labor History Soc. Roman Catholic. Avocation: history. Home and Office: 3300 W Rance Ter Lincolnwood IL 60712-3831

GRANT, ROBERT NATHAN, lawyer; b. Newburgh, N.Y., Mar. 7, 1930; s. Henry and Helen (Berkowitz) Grusky; m. Barbara Weil, Feb. 10, 1952; children— Susan, Elizabeth Grant Ellerton, Nancy Grant Gray. BA, Yale U., 1951; LLB, Harvard U., 1956. Bar: Ill. 1956, N.Y. 1990; registered fgn. lawyer, U.K. Assoc. Sonnenschein Nath & Rosenthal, Chgo., 1956-65; ptnr. Sonnenschein, Nath & Rosenthal, 1965—. Sec. UNR Industries, Inc., Chgo., 1979-90; sec. San Diego Padres Prof. Baseball Team, 1974-78. Contbr. articles to profl. jours. Pres. Winnetka (Ill.) Bd. Edn., 1980—81; mem. Winnetka Planning Commn., 1975—77, New Trier Twp. Caucus, 1974; bd. dirs. United Charities, 1984—94; mem. legal aid com., 1982—; vice-chmn., 1986—87; chmn., 1987—94; pres. Legal Aid Soc. Ill., 1988—94; trustee The Nature Conservancy-Ill., 1978—88; pres. Winnetka Pub. Schs. Found., 1995—98, Winnetka Cmty. House, 2000—01; bd. dirs. New Trier High Sch. Edni. Found., 2001—, Winnetka (Ill.) Bd. Edn., 1974—81. 1st lt. USAF, 1951—53. Recipient William H. Avery award for 10 yrs. svc. as chmn. Legal Aid Soc., 1994. Mem. ABA (vice-chmn. commercial leasing com.), Scholarship and Guidance Assn. (bd. dirs. 1968-92, pres. 1979-83), Harvard Law Sch. Spl. Gifts, Yale Alumni Recruiting Com., Standard Club, Yale Club (N.Y.C.), Phi Beta Kappa. Avocations: tennis, jogging, travel, reading. Home: 1165 Hamptondale Ave Winnetka IL 60093-1811 Office: Sonnenschein Nath & Rosenthal 233 S Wacker Dr Ste 8000 Chicago IL 60606-6491 E-mail: rngrant@sonnenschein.com.

GRANT, W. THOMAS, II, insurance company executive; b. 1950; BA, U. Kans., 1972; MBA, U. Pa., 1976. With Bus. Men's Assurance Co. Am., Kansas City, Mo., 1976—, dir. planning, 1980-81, v.p., dir. corp. planning, 1981-83, sr. v.p. corp. research, 1983-84, pres., bd. dirs., 1984-86, pres., chief exec. officer, 1986-90; Chmn., Pres. and CEO Labone Inc., Lenexa, Kans. Office: LabOne Inc 10101 Renner Blvd Lenexa KS 66219

GRANTHAM, JARED JAMES, nephrologist, educator; b. Dodge City, Kans., May 19, 1936; married, 1958; 4 children. AB, Baker U., 1958; MD, U. Kans., 1962. Assoc. prof. med. U. Kans., Kansas City, 1969-76, head nephrology sect., 1970-96, prof., 1976-96, disting. prof., 1996—. Founder and chmn. Polycystic Kidney Rsch. Found.; dir. Kidney Inst., 2000. Fellow NIH, 1964-66; grantee Nat. Inst. Diabetes Digestive and Kidney Diseases, 1969-03; recipient Homer Smith award Am. Soc. Nephrology and Am. Heart Assn., 1992, David Hume award Nat. Kidney Found., 1998. Mem. Am. Soc. Nephrology, Am. Soc. Clin. Investigation, Am. Physiol. Soc., Am. Fedn. Clin. Rsch., Assn. Am. Phys. Achievements include research in fluid and electrolyte metabolism, electrolyte transport, mechanism of action of antidiuretic hormone and polycystic kidney disease. Office: U Kans Dept Medicine/ Nephrology 3901 Rainbow Blvd Kansas City KS 66160-0001 E-mail: jgrantha@kumc.edu.

GRASSLEY, CHARLES ERNEST, senator; b. New Hartford, Iowa, Sept. 17, 1933; s. Louis Arthur and Ruth (Corwin) G.; m. Barbara Ann Speicher; children: Lee, Wendy, Robin, Michele, Jay. BA, U. No. Iowa, 1955, MA, 1956; postgrad., U. Iowa, 1957-58. Farmer; instr. polit. sci. Drake U., 1962, Charles City Community Coll., 1967-68; mem. Iowa Ho. of Reps., 1959-75, U.S. Ho. Rep. 94th-96th Congresses from 3d Iowa Dist.; senator from Iowa U.S. Senate, Washington, 1981—; chmn. Senate Fin. Com., 2001—. Mem. Am. Farm Bur., Iowa Hist. Soc., Masons, Pi Gamma Mu, Kappa Delta Pi. Republican. Baptist. Office: US Senate 135 Hart Senate Bldg Washington DC 20510-0001

GRATZ, RONALD G. real estate development executive; Degree, Ohio State U. CPA, Ohio. With Coopers & Lybrand, Columbus, Ohio; CFO Borror; v.p., CFO Zaring Homes, Cin. Office: Zaring Nat Corp 11300 Cornell Park Dr Ste 500 Cincinnati OH 45242-1885

GRATZ, WILLIAM W. state legislator; State rep. Dist. 113 Mo. State Congress, 1993—; owner Gratz Real Estate & Auction Svc., Jefferson City, 1978—.

GRAUER, DOUGLAS DALE, civil engineer; b. Marysville, Kans., June 27, 1956; s. Norman Wayne and Ruth Ann (Schwindaman) G.; m. Bette Lynn Bohnenblust, Aug. 16, 1980; children: Diana Kathryn, Laura Jaclyn. Student, Baker U., 1976; BSCE, Kans. State U., 1979. Registered profl. engr., Iowa, Kans., Nebr., Okla. Pipeline engr. Cities Service Pipeline Co., Shreveport, La., 1979-80; products terminal engr. Cities Service Co., Braintree, Mass., 1980-81, project engr. Tulsa, 1981-83; staff engr. Cities

Service Oil and Gas Corp., 1983-85; asst. products pipeline and terminal supt. Nat. Coop. Refinery Assn., Blue Rapids, Kans., 1985-90, supt. products pipeline and terminal, 1990—. Mem. ASCE, NSPE, Kans. Soc. Profl. Engrs., Nat. Assn. Corrosion Engrs., Chi Epsilon. Republican. Avocations: golf, fishing, woodworking. Home: 1321 Ranch Rd Mcpherson KS 67460-2313 Office: Nat Coop Refinery Assn PO Box 1404 Mcpherson KS 67460-1404

GRAUPE, DANIEL, electrical and computer engineering educator, systems and biomedical engineer; b. Jerusalem; came to U.S., 1970, naturalized, 1976. s. Heinz M. and Hella N. (Neumann) G.; m. Dalia Smilansky, July 9, 1968; children: Menachem-Henny, Pelleg-Pinhas, Oren. BSME, Technion, Israel Inst. Tech., Haifa, 1958, BSEE, 1959, Dipl. Ing. Elec. Engring., 1960; PhDEE, U. Liverpool, Eng., 1963. Lectr. U. Liverpool, Eng., 1963-67; sr. lectr. Technion, Israel Inst. Tech., Haifa, 1967-70; assoc. prof. elec. engring. Colo. State U., Ft. Collins, 1970-74, prof. elec. engring., 1974-78; prof. elec. and computer engring. Ill. Inst. Tech., Chgo., 1978-84, Bodine chair disting. prof. elec. and computer engring., 1984-85; Sr. U. Ill. scholar U. Ill., 1988—; prof. elec. engring., computer sci., 1991—. Adj. prof. rehab. medicine U. Ill., Chgo., 1985—; vis. prof. elec. engring. Notre Dame U., Ind., 1976; Springer vis. chair prof., dept. mech. engring. U. Calif.-Berkeley, 1977; vis. prof. Sch. Medicine, Tel Aviv U., summers 1982, 83, 84, Swiss Fed. Inst. Tech., Zurich, 1988, 89, 91, 92, 96; vis. prof. Northwestern U., Evanston, Ill., 1995-96; founder, v.p. Intellitech Inc., Northbrook, Ill., 1982-88; founder, chief scientist, bd. dirs. Sigmedics Inc., Northfield, Ill., 1988-95; bd. dirs. GS Systems Inc., Skokie, Ill. Author: Identification of Systems (transl. into Russian and Serbo-Croat), 1972, 2d edit., 1976, Time Series Analysis Identification and Adaptive Filtering, 1984, 2d edit., 1989, Chinese translation, 1987; (with K.H. Kohn) Functional Electrical Stimulation for Ambulation by Paraplegics, 1994, (Spanish transl.), 1998, Principles of Artificial Neural Networks, 1997; assoc. editor Internat. Jour. Software Engring. and Knowledge Engring., 1996—, Neurol. Rsch., 1998—, Psychline, 1998—; contbr. articles to profl. jours.; patentee in field. Trustee Knowledge Systems Ins., Skokie, Ill., 1988—; chmn. Chgo. chpt. Leo Baeck Inst., 1992—. With Israel Air Force, 1952-55 Recipient Anna Frank prize Hebrew U. Jerusalem and Technion, Haifa, 1961 Fellow IEEE; mem. IEEE Cirs. and Systems Soc. (chmn. tech. com. on image and signal processing in medicine 1988-92, assoc. editor IEEE Transactions on Cirs. and Systems 1989-92), Internat. Orgn. Neurol. Socs. (mem. internat. adv. bd. 1999—), N.Y. Acad. Scis. Jewish Avocations: reading; history; philosophy. Home: 496 Hillside Dr Highland Park IL 60035-4826 Office: U Ill Dept Elec Engring and Sci 851 S Morgan St Chicago IL 60607-7042 E-mail: graupe@eecs.uic.edu.

GRAVELLE, JOHN DAVID, secondary education educator; Tchr. math, Eng. grades 10-12 Merrill (Wis.) High Sch., to 1997, technology coord., 1997—. Recipient State Tchr. of Yr. Math/Eng. award Wis., 1992. Office: Merrill High Sch 120 N Sales St Merrill WI 54452-2648

GRAVES, RAY REYNOLDS, retired judge; b. Tuscumbia, Ala., Jan. 10, 1946; s. Isaac and Olga Ernestine (Wilder) Graves; children: Claire Elise, Reynolds Douglass. BA, Trinity Coll., Hartford, Conn., 1967; JD, Wayne State U., 1970. Bar: Mich. 1971, U.S. Dist. Ct. (ea. dist.) Mich. 1971, U.S. Ct. Appeals (6th cir.) 1972, U.S. Supreme Ct. 1976, D.C. 1977. Defender Legal Aid and Defender Assn., Detroit, 1970-71; assoc. Liberson, Fink, Feiler, Crystal & Burdick, 1971-72, Patmon, Young & Kirk, 1972-73; ptnr. Lewis, White, Clay & Graves, 1974-81; mem. legal dept. Detroit Edison Co., 1981; judge U.S. Bankruptcy Ct., Ea. Dist. Mich., Detroit, 1982-2002; chief judge U.S. Bankruptcy Ct., 1991-95; prin. BBK, Ltd., Southfield, Mich., 1995—. Mem. U.S. ct. com. State Bar Mich. Trustee Mich. Opera Theatre, 1986—88; vestry Christ Ch. Episcopal, Grosse Pointe, Mich., 1994—97; del Diocesan Conv. Episcopal Ch., 1997; bd. dirs. Mich. Cancer Found. Fellow: Am. Coll. Bankruptcy; mem.: D.C. Bar Assn., Detroit Bar Assn., Wolverine Bar Assn., Assn. Black Judges Mich., World Peace Through Law Conf., World Assn. Judges, Nat. Conf. Bakruptcy Jduges (bd. govs. 1984—88), Iota Boulè (Sire Archon 1999—2001), Sigma Pi Phi, Delta Kappa Epsilon. Episcopalian. Office: 300 Galleria Officentre # 103 Southfield MI 48034 Office Fax: 248-603-8374. Business E-Mail: rgraves@e-bbk.com.

GRAVES, SAM, congressman, former state legislator; State rep. Dist. 4 Mo. Gen. State Assembly, 1993-94, state senator Dist. 12, 1995-2001; mem. U.S. Congress from 6th Mo. dist., 2001—. Office: US Ho Reps 1407 Longworth Ho Office Bldg Washington DC 20515*

GRAVES, SAM, communications media executive; Bur. chief Indpls. Metro Network News, 1998—. Office: Metro Network News 6081 E 82nd St Ste 419 Indianapolis IN 46250-1535

GRAVES, WALLACE BILLINGSLEY, retired university executive; b. Ft.Worth, Feb. 10, 1922; s. Ellery George and Edith (Billingsley) G.; m. Barbara Jeanne Abey, Nov. 20, 1943; children: David W., Emily Graves Hay, John R., Julie Graves Williams. BA, U. Okla., 1943; MA, Tex. Christian U., 1947; PhD, U. Tex., 1953; LLD (hon.), Ind. State U., 1970, Valparaiso U., 1972; LHD (hon.), Morningside Coll., 1971, U. Evansville, 1989. Teaching fellow Tex. Christian U., Ft. Worth, 1946-47, U. Tex., Austin, 1947-50; prof. polit. sci. DePauw U., Greencastle, Ind., 1950-58; Armstrong prof. govt., dean of men Tex. Wesleyan Coll., Ft. Worth, 1958-63, asst. to pres., 1963-65; acad. v.p. U. Pacific, Stockton, Calif., 1965-67; pres. U. Evansville, Ind., 1967-87, chancellor, 1986-89, pres. emeritus, 1989—. Vis. prof. Butler U., summer 1956; bd. dirs. Citizens Nat. Bank, Evansville, Herrburger Brooks P.L.C., Nottingham, Eng. Author: The United Nations, Great Britain and the British Non-Self Governing Territories, 1954, The One Semester Course in International Relations, 1956, Harlaxton College: The Camelot of Academe, 1990; contbr. articles to profl. jours. Mem. exec. bd. Tarrant County chpt. ARC, 1960-65, chmn. home svc. com.; chmn. ARC of Southwestern Ind., 1994—; midwest region com. ARC, 2000-02; bd. dirs. Ft. Worth Assn. Retarded Children, 1963-65; mem. Met. Ft. Worth Devel. Coordinating Com., World Affairs Coun., Chgo. and Stockton, adv. bd. Supplementary Edn. Ctr., Stockton; v.p. Buffalo Trace coun. Boy Scouts Am., Evansville, 1968, exec. bd., 1968-74, adv. coun, 1974—; bd. dirs. Jr. Achievement Inc., Evansville, 1968-73; mem. commn. ecumenical affairs United Meth. Ch., Evansville, 1968-72, univ. senate, 1972-76, Ind. area study commn., 1972-74; bd. dirs. Evansville Day Sch., 1967-76; mem. Ind. State Scholarship Commn., 1969-77, adv. bd. St. Mary's Med. Ctr., Evansville, 1970—, Evansville's Future Inc., 1967—, pres., 1974-77; bd. dirs. Ind. Health Careers Inc., 1974-75; mem. Govs. Adv. Com. Pub. Health, 1971-72; bd. dirs. Leadership Evansville, 1975-71, Evansville Mus., 1978—, Lincolnland Hist. Trust, 1978—; pres. Beethoven Found., Indpls., 1980-88; mem. organizing com. Pan Am. Games, 1987; bd. dirs. Sta. WNIN Pub. TV, Evansville, 1973—, chmn. bd., 1982-84. With U.S. Army, 1943. Recipient Best Tchr. award DePauw U., 1954, medal of honor U. Evansville, 1977, medal of merit Govt. Thailand, 1984, medal of honofr DAR, 1999; Wallace B. Graves Day named in his honor Office Mayor City Evansville, 1977; rsch. scholar U. Tex., 1947; Ford Found. fellow, summer 1951, 55; Paul Harris (Rotary) fellow, 1995. Mem. AAUP, Am. Assn. Acad. Deans, Am. Coll. Pub. Relations Assn., Am. Polit. Sci. Assn., Ind. Colls. and Univs. Ind. Inc. (pres. 1970-71, 76-77), North Cen. Assn. Colls. and Secondary Schs. (cons., investigator), Am. Assn. Pres. Ind. Colls. and Univs. (exec. com. 1969-70), Am. Assn. Colls. (various coms.), Associated Colls. Ind. (pres. 1972-74), Carl Duisberg Soc. (pres. Am. assn. 1973-74), Internat. Assn. Univ. Pres. (bd. dirs. N.Am. council 1975-87), Ind. Consortium Computer and High Tech. Edn., Ft. Worth C. of C. (chmn. econ. edn. com. 1963-64), Gold Key, Blue Key, Phi Kappa Phi, Phi Mu Alpha, Alpha Sigma Lambda, Pi Sigma Alpha, Sigma Nu. Clubs: Knife and Fork (pres. 1964-65) (Ft. Worth); Commonwealth (San Francisco); Columbia (Indpls.); Petroleum; Evansville Country, Kennel (Evansville). Lodge: Rotary (pres. Ft. club 1964-65).

GRAVES, WILLIAM PRESTON, governor; b. Salina, Kans., Jan. 9, 1953; s. William Henry and Helen (Mayo) G.; m. Linda Richey, Apr. 1990; 1 child, Katie. BBA, Kans. Wesleyan U., Salina, 1975; postgrad., U. Kans., 1978-79. Dep. asst. sec. of state State of Kans., Topeka, 1980-85, asst. sec. of state, 1985-87, sec. of state, 1987-95, gov., 1995—. Mem. Competitiveness Policy Coun. Mem. Kans. Cavalry; trustee Kans. Wesleyan U., 1987—; bd. trustes Sunflower State Games. Named Outstanding Young Alumnus, Kans. Wesleyan U., Salina, 1975, Outstanding Young Kansan, Salina Jaycees, 1986, Kans. Jaycees, 1986, Outstanding Kans. Citizen, Jayhawk area BSA, 2002; named to Athletic Hall of Fame, Kans. Wesleyan U., Salina, 1986. Mem. Kans. C. of C. and Industry. Republican. Methodist. Avocations: running, reading, traveling. Office: Office of Gov 2nd Fl State Capitol Topeka KS 66612

GRAY, DAWN PLAMBECK, work-family consultant; b. Chgo., Aug. 23, 1957; d. Raymond August and Eunice Eve (Fox) Plambeck; m. Richard Scott Gray, Apr. 13, 1985; children: Zachary, Rae. BS, Northwestern U., 1979. Desk asst. Sta. WCFL, Chgo., 1979-80; writer UPI Internat., 1980; asignment editor Cable News Network, 1980-81; account exec. Aaron Cushman and Assoc., 1981-83, Ruder Finn & Rotman, Chgo., 1983-84, account supr., 1984-86, dir. consumer group, 1986-87; dir. pub. rels. Tassani Communications, 1987-90; v.p. Marcy Monyek & Assoc., 1990; pres. Moments Inc., 1991—. Avocation: dance. Office: Moments Inc 1028 W Monroe St Chicago IL 60607-2604

GRAY, HANNA HOLBORN, history educator; b. Heidelberg, Germany, Oct. 25, 1930; d. Hajo and Annemarie (Bettmann) Holborn; m. Charles Montgomery Gray, June 19, 1954. AB, Bryn Mawr Coll., 1950; PhD, Harvard U., 1957; MA, Yale U., 1971, LLD, 1978; LittD (hon.), St. Lawrence U., 1974, Oxford (Eng.) U., 1979; LLD (hon.), Dickinson Coll., 1979, U. Notre Dame, 1980, Marquette U., 1984; LittD (hon.), Washington U., 1985; HHD (hon.), St. Mary's Coll., 1974; LHD (hon.), Grinnell (Iowa) Coll., 1974, Lawrence U., 1974, Denison U., 1974, Wheaton Coll., 1976, Marlboro Coll., 1979, Rikkyo (Japan) U., 1979, Roosevelt U., 1980, Knox Coll., 1980, Coe Coll., 1981, Thomas Jefferson U., 1981, Duke U., 1982, New Sch. for Social Research, 1982, Clark U., 1982, Brandeis U., 1983, Colgate U., 1983, Wayne State U., 1984, Miami U., Oxford, Ohio, 1984, So. Meth. U., 1984, CUNY, 1985, U. Denver, 1985, Am. Coll. Greece, 1986, Muskingum Coll., 1987, Rush Presbyn. St. Lukes Med. Ctr., 1987, NYU, 1988, Rosemont Coll., 1988, Claremont U. Ctr. Grad Sch., 1989, Moravian Coll., 1991, Rensselaer Poly. Inst., 1991, Coll. William and Mary, 1991, Centre Coll., 1991, Macalester Coll., 1993, McGill U., 1993, Ind. U., 1994, Med. U. of S.C., 1994; LLD (hon.), Union Coll., 1975, Regis Coll., 1976, Dartmouth Coll., 1978, Trinity Coll., 1978, U. Bridgeport, 1978, Dickinson Coll., 1979, Brown U., 1979, Wittenburg U., 1979, Dickinson Coll., 1979, U. Rochester, 1980, U. Notre Dame, 1980, U. So. Calif., 1980, U. Mich., 1981, Princeton U., 1982, Georgetown U., 1983, Marquette U., 1984, W.Va. Wesleyan U., 1985, Hamilton Coll., 1985, Smith Coll., 1986, U. Miami, 1986, Columbia U., 1987, NYU, 1988, Rosemont Coll., 1988, U. Toronto, Can., 1991; LDH, LHD, Haverford Coll., 1995; LDH, Tulane U., 1995; LLD, LLD, Harvard U., 1995; LHD, McGill U., 1993, Macalester Coll., 1993, Ind. U., 1994, Med. U. S.C., 1994, Haverford Coll., 1995, Tulane U., 1995; LLD, Harvard U., 1995, U. Chgo., 1996. Instr. Bryn Mawr Coll., 1953-54; tchg. fellow Harvard, 1955-57, instr., 1957-59, asst. prof., 1959-60, vis. lectr., 1963-64; asst. prof. U. Chgo., 1961-64, assoc. prof., 1964-72; dean, prof. Northwestern U., Evanston, Ill., 1972-74; provost, prof. history Yale U., 1974-78, acting pres., 1977-78; pres. U. Chgo., 1978-93, prof. dept. history, 1978—, Harry Pratt Judson disting. svc. prof. history, 1994—. Fellow Ctr. for Advanced Study in Behavioral Scis., 1966-67, vis. scholar, 1970-71; vis. prof. U. Calif., Berkeley, 1970-71. Editor: (with Charles Gray) Jour. Modern History, 1965-70; contbr. articles to profl. jours. Mem. Nat. Coun. on Humanities, 1972-78; trustee Yale Corp., 1971-74; fellow Harvard Corp.; chmn. bd. Howard Hughes Med. Inst., Marlboro Sch. Music; chmn. bd. dirs. Andrew W. Mellon Found.; mem. bd. regents The Smithsonian Instn. Decorated Grosse Verdienstkreuz (Germany); fellow Newberry Libr., 1960-61, hon. fellow St. Anne's Coll., Oxford (Eng.) U., 1978—; Fulbright scholar, 1950-51; recipient Grad. medal Radcliffe Coll., 1976, Yale medal, 1978, Medal of Liberty award, 1986, Medal of Freedom, 1991, Frontrunner award Sara Lee, 1991, Laureate Lincoln Acad. Ill., 1988, Charles Frankel prize, 1993, Centennial medal Harvard U., 1994, Disting. Svc. award in edn. Inst. Internat. Edn., 1994, Medal of Distinction Barnard Coll., 2000. Fellow Am. Acad. Arts and Scis.; mem. Renaissance Soc. Am., Am. Philos. Soc. (Jefferson medal 1993), Nat. Acad. Edn., Coun. Fgn. Rels. Chgo., Coun. on Fgn. Rels. N.Y., Phi Beta Kappa (vis. scholar 1971-72). Office: U Chgo Dept History 1126 E 59th St Chicago IL 60637-1580

GRAY, HELEN THERESA GOTT, religion editor; b. Jersey City, July 2, 1942; d. William E. and Cynthia B. (Williams) Gott; m. David L. Gray, Aug. 15, 1976; 1 child, David Lee Jr. BA, Syracuse U., 1963; M in Internat. Affairs, Columbia U., 1965. Editor religion sect. The Kansas City (Mo.) Star, 1971—; owner Pub. Co. and Christian Bookstore. Tchr. Bible sch. Pleasant Green Bapt. Ch., Kansas City, Kans., 1975—, counselor, 1978—. Co-author, editor several books; contbr. articles. Recipient writing award Valley Forge Freedom Found., 1967-97; John Hay Whitney Found. grantee, 1963-64; named 100 Most Influential African Ams. in Greater Kansas City. Mem. Religion Newswriters Assn., Kansas City Assn. Black Journalists (life achievement award 1998). Office: The Kansas City Star 1729 Grand Blvd Kansas City MO 64108-1458 E-mail: hgray@kcstar.com.

GRAY, JOHN WALKER, mathematician, educator; b. St. Paul, Oct. 3, 1931; s. Clarence Walker and Helen (Ewald) G.; m. Eva Maria Wirth, Dec. 30, 1957; children— Stephen, Theodore, Elisabeth. BA, Swarthmore Coll., 1953; PhD, Stanford U., 1957. Temp. mem. Inst. for Advanced Study, Princeton, N.J., 1957-59; Ritt instr. Columbia U., 1959-62; asst. prof. math. U. Ill., Urbana, 1962-64, assoc. prof., 1964-66, prof., 1966—, dir. grad. studies, 1995—2000, prof. emeritus, 2000—. Organizer Category Theory Session, Oberwolfach, Germany, 1971, 72, 73, 75, 77, 79 Contbr. to: Springer Lecture Notes in Mathematics, 1974. NSF sr. fellow, 1966-67; Fulbright-Hays sr. lectr., 1975-76 Mem. Am. Math. Soc., AAAS. Home: 303 W Michigan Ave Urbana IL 61801-4945 Office: U Ill Dept Math Urbana IL 61801

GRAY, RICHARD, art dealer, consultant, holding company executive; b. Chgo., Dec. 30, 1928; s. Edward and Pearl B. Gray; m. Mary Kay Lackritz, Mar. 28, 1953; children— Paul, Jennifer, Harry Student, U. Ill., 1951. Pres. The Grayline Co., 1952-63; sec.-treas. The Edward Gray Corp., 1952-63; prin., dir. GrayCor, 1963—; dir. The Richard Gray Gallery, Chgo. and N.Y.C., 1963—. Lectr., juror, panelist Guggenheim Mus., N.Y.C., Art. Inst. Chgo., Harvard U., U. Ill., Mich. State U., Milw. Art Mus., New Sch. for Social Research, N.Y., Met. Mus., N.Y.C., Colloquium-The Getty Mus., U. Chgo., Seattle Art Mus.; mem. art adv. panel U.S. Internal Revenue Svc. Contbr. articles to Chgo. Tribune, Chgo. Daily News, Crain's Chgo. Bus., Chgo. Mag., Collector Investor Mag. Bd. dirs. Sta. WFMT-FM, 1992-98, Ill. Humanities Coun.; trustee, vice chmn. WTTW Channel 11—Chgo. Pub. TV; bd. dirs. Goodman Theatre, Chgo.; trustee Chgo. Symphony Orch.; former chair bd. Chgo. Internat. Theater Festival; adv. com. Smithsonian Inst.; bd. dirs. Old Masters Soc., Art Inst. Chgo.; mem. steering com. Friends of the Libraries, Art Inst Chgo.; mem. capital devel. bd. State of Ill., pub. arts adv. com., former mem. selection com. Gov.'s Awards for Arts; former mem. nat. adv. bd. Ohio State U. Wexner Ctr. for Visual Arts; pres. Art Dealers Assn. Am.; former pres. Chgo. Art Dealers Assn.; former chmn. Navy Pier Task Force, City of Chgo., 1986-88; mem. vis. com. U. Chgo. Humanities Div., chmn., bd. govs. Alfred Smart Mus. U. Chgo.; vice-chmn., bd. dirs. Chgo. Humanities Festival. Mem. Chgo. Pub. Schs. Alumni Assn. (former chmn. bd. dirs.), Chgo. Coun. Fgn. Rels. (Chgo. com.), Chgo. Club, Quadrangle Club, Arts Club of Chgo. Achievements include specializing in contemporary, modern and impressionist masters. Office: Richard Gray Gallery 875 N Michigan Ave Ste 2503 Chicago IL 60611-1876 also: 1018 Madison Ave New York NY

GRAY, VIRGINIA HICKMAN, political science educator; b. Camden, Ark., June 10, 1945; d. George Leonard and Ethel Massengale (Bell) Hickman; 1 child, Brian Charles. BA with honors, Hendrix Coll., 1967; MA, Washington U., St. Louis, 1969, PhD, 1972. Asst. prof. polit. sci. U. Ky., Lexington, 1971-73; from asst. prof. to assoc. prof. U. Minn., Mpls., 1973-83, prof., 1983-2000, chairperson dept. polit. sci., 1985-88; Winston Disting. prof. polit. sci. U. N.C., Chapel Hill, 2000—. Guest scholar Brookings Inst., Washington, 1977-78; vis. prof. U. Oslo, 1985, Nankai U., 1988, U. B.C., 1992, U. N.C., 1993-94; NSF vis. prof. for women, 1993-94. Co-author: The Organizational Politics of Criminal Justice, 1980, Feminism and the New Right, 1983, Politics in the American States, 1983, 7th edit., 1999, American States and Cities, 1991, 2d edit., 1997, The Population Ecology of Interest Representation, 1996, Minnesota Politics and Government, 1999. Bd. dirs. Health Ptnrs. Inc., 1992-2001, chair, 1999-2001. Fellow Woodrow Wilson Found., 1970, NDEA, 1969-70; grantee Swedish Bicentennial Found., 1985; recipient rsch. assistantship NSF, 1968-69, rsch. grant NSF, 1997-2001; scholar in residence Rockefeller Ctr., Bellagio, Italy. Mem. Am. Polit. Sci. Assn. (coun. 1990-92), Midwest Polit. Sci. Assn. (coun. 1984-86, v.p. 1997-99), Policy Studies Orgn. (coun. 1977-79), So. Polit. Sci. Assn., Western Polit. Sci. Assn. Democrat. Unitarian. Home: 2 Heather Ct Chapel Hill NC 27517 Office: U NC Dept Polit Sci CB 3265 Hamilton Hall Chapel Hill NC 27599-3265

GRAY, WILLIAM GUERIN, civil engineering educator; b. San Francisco, Jan. 9, 1948; BS, U. Calif., 1969; MA, Princeton U., 1971, PhD, 1974. Asst. prof. dept. civil engring. Princeton U., N.J., 1975-80, dir. grad. studies dept. civil engring., 1977-84, assoc. prof. dept. civil engring., 1980-84; prof. dept. civil engring. U. Notre Dame, Ind., 1984-88, chmn. civil engring., geol. scis., 1984-95, Massman prof. civil engring. and geol. scis., 1988—. Office: U Notre Dame Dept Civil Engring Sc Notre Dame IN 46556

GRAYHACK, JOHN THOMAS, urologist, educator; b. Kankakee, Ill., Aug. 21, 1923; s. John and Marie (Keckich) G.; m. Elizabeth Houlehin, June 3, 1950; children: Elizabeth, Anne Marie, Linda Jean, John, William. B.S., U. Chgo., 1945, M.D., 1947. Diplomate Am. Bd. Urology. Intern medicine Billings Hosp., Chgo., 1947; intern gen. surgery Johns Hopkins Hosp., 1947-48, asst. resident, 1948-49, fellow urology, 1949-50, asst. resident, 1950-52; resident urology, 1952-53; dir. Kretschmer Lab., Northwestern U. Med. Sch., 1956-75, prof. urology, 1963—, chmn. dept., 1961-90. Cons. VA Rsch. Hosp. Editor Year Book of Urology, 1963-78; editor Jour. Urology, 1985-94. Served to capt. USAF, 1954-56. Recipient Outstanding Achievement award USAF, Ferdinand C. Valentine award N.Y. Acad. Medicine, Disting. Svc. award U. Chgo., 1978, Pioneer award Internat. Symposium Biology Prostate Growth, 1998; fellow Am. Cancer Soc., 1949-50, Damon Runyon Fund, 1953-54, Johns Hopkins Soc. Scholars. Mem. AMA, Ill., Chgo. med. socs., Am. Assn. Genitourinary Surgeons (Barringer medal, Keyes medal), Am. Urology Assn. (Hugh H. Young award, Fuller award, Mary Hugh and Russell Scott award, Ramon Guiteras award 1994), Chgo. Urology Soc. (John T. Grayhack lectr.), Endocrine Soc., Clin. Soc. Genitourinary Surgeons, Am. Surg. Assn., Soc. Univ. Urologists, Nephrology Soc., Phi Beta Kappa, Alpha Omega Alpha. Home: 95 N Park Rd La Grange IL 60525-5938 Office: Northwestern Meml Hosp Superior St Fairbanks Ct Chicago IL 60611

GRAYSON, EDWARD DAVIS, lawyer, manufacturing company executive; b. Davenport, Iowa, June 20, 1938; s. Charles E. and Isabelle (Davis) G.; m. Alice Ann McLaughlin; children: Alice Anne, Maureen Isabelle, Edward Davis Jr. B.A., U. Iowa, 1960, LLB, 1964. Bar: Iowa 1964, Mass. 1967. Atty. Goodwin, Procter & Hoar, Boston, 1967-74; sr. v.p., gen. counsel Wang Labs., Inc., Lowell, Mass., 1974-92; v.p., gen. counsel Honeywell, Inc., Mpls., 1992—. Trustee U. Lowell, Mas., 1981-87, chmn. bd. trustees, 1982-85, 87; dir. Bus. Econs. Edn. Found., 1992—. Capt. USAF, 1964-67. Mem. ABA (com. corp. law depts.), Mass. Bar Assn. (bd. dels. 1977-80), Greater Mpls. C. of C. (dir. 1992—). Office: Honeywell Inc Honeywell Plz PO Box 524 Minneapolis MN 55440-0524

GRAZIANO, FRANK MICHAEL, medical educator, researcher; b. Easton, Pa., June 5, 1942; s. Michael and Grace (Farace) G.; m. Mary Helen Ashton, Feb. 4, 1967; children: Teresa Ann, Frank Jr., Alicia Grace. BS, St. Joseph's Coll., 1964; MS, Villanova Univ., 1967; PhD, Univ. Va., 1970, MD, 1973. Diplomate Am. Bd. of Internal Medicine, Am. Bd. of Allergy and Clinical Immunology. Internship Univ. Wis. Hosp., Madison, 1973-74; residency in medicine Univ. Wis., 1974-76, asst. prof., 1978-84, assoc. prof., 1984-89, prof. medicine, 1989—, chief section of Rheumatology, 1989—. Author numerous books, articles, papers in field. Admissions com. Univ. Wis. Medical Sch., 1983-86, Minority subcom. chmn., 1985-86; medical and scientific com. Wis. Arthritis Found., 1979-80, Univ. Wis. Madison AIDS Task Force Com., 1986-89; Bd. dirs. Wis. Arthritis Found., 1990—, Wis. Com. Based Rsch. Consortium, 1990—. Recipient Am. Acad. Travel grant, 1978, NIH Young Investigator award, 1980, NIH Allergic Disease Acad. award, 1985. Fellow Am. Acad. Allergy/Immunology, Am. Coll. Physicians; mem. Am. Assn. Immunologists, Am. Assn. Advancement of Sci., Am. Thoracic Soc., Am. Coll. Pheumatology, Clinical Immunology Soc., Wis. Allergy Soc., Wis. Rheumatism Assn., Sigma Xi. Home: 853 Tipperary Rd Oregon WI 53575-2641 Office: Univ Wis Hosp & Clinics 600 Highland Ave # H6 363 Madison WI 53792-0001

GRAZIN, IGOR NIKOLAI, law educator, state official; b. Tartu, Estonia, June 27, 1952; came to U.S., 1990; s. Nikolai V. and Dagmar R. (Kibe) G.; 1 child, Anton. Jurist degree, U. Tartu, Estonia, 1975; candidate of sci. in law, Moscow Inst. Law, 1979; DSc in Law, Inst. State and Law, Moscow, 1986. Cert. jurist, USSR. Lectr., prof. U. Tartu, Estonia, 1977-86, prof. Estonia, 1986-89, assoc. dean Law Sch. Estonia, 1986-89; mem. of the coun. Popular Front of Estonia, Tallinn, 1988-90. Prof. U. Notre Dame, Ind., 1990-2000; faculty fellow Kellogg Inst. for Internat. Studies, Notre Dame, 1994—; adj. fellow Hudson Inst., 1994—; dir. Estonian Privatization Trust Fund; dean U. Nord. Author: Law as Text, 1983, Jeremy Bentham, 1990, Anglo-American Philosophy of Law, 1983, Right Course, 1994; editor: Studia Juridica, 1988-90; contbr. articles to profl. jours. Dep., Congress of Peoples Deps. of USSR, 1989-91; mem. Supreme Soviet, Moscow, 1989-91; counsellor to Pres., Republic of Estonia, 1993-97, V.P., pres. nat. assembly, 1999—; mem. Nat. Parliament of Estonia, 1995-99. Mem. AAUP, AALS (bd. dirs.), Estonian Bar Assn., Federalist Soc. U.S.A., Acad. Soc. of Estonian Lawyers (co-founder, vice chmn. 1989-90), Acad. Arts (Estonia, bd. dirs.), Rotary, Roman Club (founding). Republican. Lutheran. E-mail: igorveel@hotmail.com.

GRBAC, ELVIS, football player; b. Cleve., Aug. 13, 1970; m. Lori; children: Jack, Calvin, Ella. Football player San Francisco 49ers, 1993-1997, Kans. City Chiefs, 1997—. Office: Kans City Chiefs One Arrowhead Dr Kansas City MO 64129

GREASER, MARION LEWIS, science educator; b. Vinton, Iowa, Feb. 10, 1942; s. Lewis Levi and Elisabeth (Sage) G.; m. Marilyn Sue Pfister, June 12, 1965; children— Suzanne, Scott B.S., Iowa State U., 1964; M.S., U. Wis., 1967, Ph.D., 1969. Postdoctoral fellow Boston Biomed. Research Inst., 1968-71; asst. prof. sci. U. Wis., Madison, 1971-73, assoc. prof., 1973-77, prof., 1977—. Contbr. articles to profl. jours. Recipient Outstanding Researcher award Am. Heart Assn.-Wis., 1985 Mem. AAAS, Am. Soc. Biochem. Molecular Biology, Biophys. Soc., Inst. Food Technologists, Am. Meat Sci. Assn. (Disting. Research award 1981), Am. Soc. Animal Sci. (Meat Rsch. award 2000). Home: 2374 Branch St Middleton WI 53562-2809 Office: U Wis Muscle Biology Lab 1805 Linden Dr W Madison WI 53706-1110 E-mail: mgreaser@facstaff.wisc.edu.

GREBE, MICHAEL W. lawyer; b. Peoria, Ill., Oct. 25, 1940; BS, U.S. Mil. Acad., 1962; JD magna cum laude, U. Mich., 1970. Bar: Wis. 1970. Ptnr. Foley & Lardner, Milw. Note and comment editor: U. Mich. Law Rev., 1969—70. Mem.: Milw. Bar Assn., State Bar Wis., Order of Coif. Office: Foley & Lardner 777 E Wisconsin Ave Ste 3800 Milwaukee WI 53202-5367

GREDEN, JOHN FRANCIS, psychiatrist, educator; b. Winona, Minn., July 24, 1942; m. Renee Mary Kalmes; children: Daniel John, Sarah Renee, Leigh Raymond. BS, U. Minn., 1965, MD, 1967. Diplomate Am. Bd. Psychiatry and Neurology. Assoc. dir. psychiat. research Walter Reed Army Med. Ctr., Washington, 1972-74; asst. prof. Dept. Psychiatry U. Mich., Ann Arbor, 1974-77, assoc. prof., 1977-81, dir. clin. studies unit for affective disorders, 1980-85, prof., 1981—, chmn., sr. research scientist, 1985—; chmn. faculty group practice U. Mich. Contbr. 188 articles to profl. jours., 28 chpts. to books. Served to maj. U.S. Army, 1969-74. Recipient A.E. Bennett research award Cen. Neuropsychiat. Found., 1974, Nolan D.C. Lewis Vis. Scholar award Carrier Found., 1982. Fellow Am. Psychiat. Assn.; mem. AAAS, Soc. Biol. Psychiatry (past pres., co-editor-in-chief Jour. Psychiatry Rsch. 1984-2000), Am. Coll. Neuropsychopharmacology, Psychiat. Rsch. Soc. (past pres., sr. editor scientific pubs., 1999—). Office: U Mich Med Ctr Dept Psychiatry 1500 E Medical Center Dr Ann Arbor MI 48109-0005

GREEK, DAROLD I. lawyer; b. Kunkle, Ohio, Mar. 30, 1909; s. Albert F. and Iva (Shaffer) G.; m. Catherine Johnson, Oct. 12, 1935 (dec. 1962); 1 child, Darold I (dec.); m. Elizabeth Tracy Ridgley, Sept. 18, 1970 (dec. May 1972); stepchildren— Thomas B., David Ridgley; m. Nadine Berry Weisheimer Bivens, Dec. 23, 1976; stepchildren— Richard A. Weisheimer, Jon B. Weisheimer. Student, Bowling Green State U., 1926-28; LL.B., Ohio State U., 1932. Bar: Ohio 1932. Treas., Williams County, Ohio, 1932-33; atty. Ohio Dept. Taxation, 1934-36; practiced in Columbus, 1937-89; ptnr. George, Greek, King, McMahon & McConnaughey (and predecessors), 1937-79; of counsel Baker & Hostetler, 1979-89. Mem. Ohio Bar Assn., Columbus Bar Assn. (pres. 1966-67), Columbus Country Club, The Golf Club, Naples Yacht Club, Hole in the Wall Golf Club. Presbyterian. Home: 6635 Lake of Woods Pt Galena OH 43021 also: 2901 Gulf Shore Blvd N Naples FL 34103-3937 Office: 65 E State St Columbus OH 43215-4213

GREELEY, ANDREW MORAN, sociologist, author; b. Oak Park, Ill., Feb. 5, 1928; s. Andrew T. and Grace G. AB, St. Mary of Lake Sem., 1950, STL, 1954; MA, U. Chgo., 1961, PhD, 1962; LHD (hon.) , Bowling Green State U., 1986, No. Mich., 1993; HHD (hon.) , St. Louis U., 1991; LHD, LLD, Ariz. State U., 1998; LHD (hon.) , U. San Francisco, 2002, Bard Coll., 2002. Ordained priest Roman Cath. Ch., 1954. Asst. pastor Ch. of Christ the King, Chgo., 1954-64; sr. study dir. Nat. Opinion Rsch. Ctr., 1962-68; dir. Ctr. for Study Am. Pluralism, from 1973; lectr. sociology U. Chgo., 1963-72; prof. sociology U. Ariz., Tucson, from 1978, now adj. prof.; prof. social sci. U. Chgo., 1991—. Cons. Hazen Found. Commn. Syndicated columnist People and Values, N.Y. Times Religious News Svc.; columnist Daily Southtown; guest columnist Chgo. Sun Times, 1985—; Author: The Church and the Suburbs, 1959, Strangers in the House, 1961, Religion and Career, 1963, (with Peter H. Rossi) Education of Catholic Americans, 1966, Changing Catholic College, 1967, Come Blow Your Mind With Me, 1971, Life for a Wanderer: A New Look at Christian Spirituality, 1971, The Denominational Society: A Sociological Approach to Religion in America, 1972, Priests in the United States: Reflections on A Survey, 1972, That Most Distressful Nation, 1972, New Agenda, 1973, Jesus Myth, 1971, Unsecular Man, 1974, Ethnicity in the United States: A Preliminary Reconnaissance, 1974, Ecstasy: A Way of Knowing, 1974, Building Coalitions: American Politics in the 1970's, 1974, Sexual Intimacy, 1975, Denomination Society, 1975, The Great Mysteries: An Essential Catechism, 1976, The Communal Catholic: A Personal Manifesto, 1976, Death and Beyond, 1976, The American Catholic: A Social Portrait, 1977, The Making of the Popes, 1978, 79, The Magic Cup: An Irish Legend, 1979, Women I've Met, 1979, Why Can't They Be Like Us?, 1980, Death In April, 1980, The Cardinal Sins, 1981, Religion: A Secular Theory, 1982, Thy Brother's Wife, 1982, Ascent Into Hell, 1983, Lord of the Dance, 1984, Virgin & Martyr, 1985, Piece of My Mind on Just About Everything, 1985, Happy are the Meek, 1985, The Magic Cup, 1985, God Game, 1986, Happy Are the Clean of Heart, 1986, Confessions of a Parish Priest, 1986, Patience of a Saint, 1987, Rite of Spring, 1987, Angels of September, 1986, Happy Are Those Who Thirst For Justice, 1987, The Final Planet, 1987, Angel Fire, 1988, (photography) Andrew Greeley's Chicago, 1989, Love Song, 1989, St. Valentine's Night, 1989, The Bible and Us, 1990, The short stories All About Women, 1990, (photography) The Irish, 1990, The Catholic Myth: The Behavior and Beliefs of American Catholics, 1990, The Cardinal Virtues, 1990, Faithful Attraction: Discovering Intimacy, Love, and Fidelity in American Marriage, 1991, The Search for Maggie Ward, 1991, An Occasion of Sin, 1991, Happy Are the Merciful, 1992, Wages of Sin, 1992, Fall from Grace, 1993, Sacraments of Love: A Prayer Journal, 1994, Irish Gold, 1994, Happy are the Poor Spirit, 1994, Happy are Those Who Mourn, 1995, Angel Light: An Old-Fashioned Love Story, 1995, Windows: A Prayer Journal, 1995, Religion as Poetry, 1995, Sociology and Religion, 1995, White Smoke, 1996, Irish Lace, 1996, Happy Are The Oppressed, 1996, Summer at the Lake, 1997, Star Bright!, 1997, The Bishop at Sea, 1997, I Hope You're Listening, God: A Prayer Journal, 1997, Irish Whiskey, 1998, Contract with an Angel, 1998, The Bishop and the Three Kings, 1998, A Mid-Winter's Tale, 1998, Furthermore! Memories of a Parish Priest, 1999, 2000, The Bishop and the Missing L Train, 2000, Christmas Wedding, 2000, Irish Love, 2001, The Bishop and the Begger Girl of St. Germain, 2001, September Song, 2001, Irish Stew, 2002, The Bishop in the West Wing, 2002; (with J. Neusner) Common Ground: A Priest and a Rabbi Read Scripture Together, 1996, others; (with Chilton, Green, and Neusner) Forging a Common Future, 1996, The Catholic Imagination, 2000, (with Albert Bergesen) God in the Movies, 2000, My Love: A Prayer Journal, 2001, Letters to a Loving God, 2002; contbr. articles to profl. jours. Recipient Cath. Press Assn. award for best book for young people, 1965, Thomas Alva Edison award for radio broadcast, 1962, C. Albert Kobb award Nat. Cath. Edn. Assn., 1977, Mark Twain award Soc. Study Midwestern Lit., 1987, Popular Culture award Ctr. Study of Popular Culture, 1988, Freedom to Read award Friends Chgo. Pub. Libr., 1989, U.S. Cath. award, 1993, Ill. Outstanding Citizen award Coll. Lake County, 1993, Quigley Disting. Alumni award, 1997; named to Top 100 Irish Ams. Irish Am. Mag, 1992, named Irish Am. of Century Irish Am. Mag., 1999. Mem. Am. Sociol. Assn., Soc. for Sci. Study Religion, Religious Research Assn. Address: Rosner & Walsh 650 N Dearborn St Chicago IL 60610-3873

GREELEY, TIMOTHY P. federal judge; BS, Western Mich. U., 1976; JD magna cum laude, Wayne State U., 1980. Bar: Mich. 1982, U.S. Dist. Ct. (we. Mich.) 1982. Law clk. to Hon. Phillip Pratt U.S. Dist. Ct. (ea. dist.) Mich., Marquette, 1980-82; atty. Foster, Swift, Collins & Coey, P.C., Lansing, Mich., 1982-87; magistrate judge U.S. Dist. Ct. (we. dist.) Mich., Marquette, 1988—. Office: US Dist Ct We Dist Mich 330 Fed Bldg 202 W Washington St Marquette MI 49855-4357 Fax: 906-226-6231.

GREEN, AHMAN, football player; b. Omaha, Feb. 16, 1977; Running back Green Bay Packers, 2000—, Seattle Seahawks, 1998—2000. Office: Green Bay Packers PO Box 10628 Green Bay WI 54307-0628*

GREEN, DARLENE, controller, municipal official; b. St. Louis; BSBA, Washington U. Budget dir. City of St. Louis, comptroller, chief fiscal officer, 1995—. Vol. St. Louis Pub. Schs., St. Louis Crisis Nursery, Big Bros. & Big Sisters, YWCA Greater St. Louis; mem. Airport Commn.; trustee City of St. Louis Retirement Sys.; bd. dirs. Employment Connection, St. Louis Cmty. Edn. Task Force. Mem.: NAACP, Govt. Fin. Officers Assn., Nat. Assn. Black Accts., Zeta Phi Beta. Office: City of St Louis 1200 Market St Rm 212 Saint Louis MO 63103-2805 Fax: 314-622-4026.

GREEN, DAVID WILLIAM, chemist, educator; b. Hudson, Mich., Nov. 19, 1942; s. Francis Harger and Dorotha Louise (Onweller) G.; m. Mary Sarah McCullough, July 8, 1967; children: Laura, Brenda, Mark, Brian, William. BA, Albion Coll., 1964; PhD, U. Calif., Berkeley, 1968; MBA, U. Chgo., 1985. Instr. U. Calif., Berkeley, 1968; rsch. assoc. U. Chgo., 1968-71; asst. prof. Albion (Mich.) Coll., 1971-75; chemist Argonne (Ill.) Nat. Lab., 1975-82, mgr. analytical chemistry, 1982—2001; prof. chemistry Coll. DuPage, Glen Ellyn, Ill., 1991-93. Vis. prof. chemistry Albion Coll., 2001—. Editor Mng. the Modern Lab, 1995—, mem. editl. bd., 1994—. Pres. Dist. 58 Bd. Edn., Downers Grove, Ill., 1976-79. Mem. Analytical Lab. Mgrs. Assn. (pres. 1986-87, treas. 1989). Home: 602 Bidwell Albion MI 49224- Office: Putnam Hall Albion College Albion MI 49224- E-mail: dwgreen@albion.edu.

GREEN, DENNIS, professional football coach; b. Harrisburg, Pa., Feb. 17, 1949; BS, U. Iowa, 1971. Asst. coach U. Iowa, 1972, 74-76, U. Dayton, 1973, Stanford U., 1977-78, 80, San Francisco 49ers, 1979; head coach Northwestern U., 1981-85; asst. coach San Francisco 49ers, 1986-88; head coach Stanford U., 1989-91, Minn. Vikings, 1992—. Office: Minnesota Vikings 9520 Viking Dr Eden Prairie MN 55344-3898

GREEN, DENNIS JOSEPH, lawyer; b. Milw., Sept. 28, 1941; m. Janet McQueen; children: Karla Pope, Cheryl Ashley, Deborah. BS in Mgmt., U. Ill., 1963, JD, 1968. Bar: Ill. 1968, Mo. 1968. Atty. Monsanto Co., St. Louis, 1968-75, asst. co. counsel, 1975-76, counsel, 1976-79; gen. counsel, sec. Fisher Controls Internat. Inc., Clayton, Mo., 1979-85, v.p., gen. counsel, sec., 1985-93; v.p., assoc. gen. counsel Emerson Electric Co., St. Louis, 1992—. 1st lt. U.S. Army, 1963-65. Office: Emerson Electric Co PO Box 4100 8000 W Florissant Ave Saint Louis MO 63136-1494 E-mail: dennis.green@emrsn.com.

GREEN, DON WESLEY, chemical and petroleum engineering educator; b. Tulsa, July 8, 1932; s. Earl Leslie and Erma Pansy (Brackins) G.; m. Patricia Louise Polston, Nov. 26, 1954; children: Guy Leslie, Don Michael, Charles Patrick. BS in Petroleum Engring., U. Tulsa, 1955; MSChemE, U. Okla., 1959, PhD in Chem. Engring., 1963. Rsch. scientist Continental Oil Co., Ponca City, Okla., 1962-64; asst. to assoc. prof. U. Kans., Lawrence, 1964-71, prof. chem. and petroleum engring., 1971-82, chmn. dept. chem. and petroleum engring., 1970-74, 96-200, co-dir. Tertiary Oil Recovery project, 1974—, Conger-Gabel Disting. prof., 1982-95, Deane E. Ackers Disting. prof., 1995—. Faculty rep. to NCAA. Editor: Perry's Chemical Engineers' Handbook, 1984, 97; contbr. articles to profl. jours. 1st lt. USAF, 1955-57. Fellow Am. Inst. Chem. Engrs.; mem. Soc. Petroleum Engrs. (Disting. Achievement award 1983, chmn. edn. and accreditation com. 1980-81, Disting. mem. 1986, Disting. lectr. 1986). Democrat. Avocations: handball, baseball, mountain hiking. Home: 1020 Sunset Dr Lawrence KS 66044-4546 Office: U Kans Dept Chem & Petroleum Engring 4008 Learned Hall Lawrence KS 66045-7526

GREEN, HAROLD DANIEL, dentist; b. Scranton, Pa., Feb. 4, 1934; s. Harold Charles and Viola Mildred (Brown) G.; m. Cornelia Ann Ellis, Aug. 1, 1959; children: Scott Alan, Mary Ann. BA, Beloit Coll. (Wis.), 1956; DDS, Northwestern U., 1960. Gen. practice dentistry, Beloit, Wis., 1964—. Dir. Beloit Savs. Bank, chmn. trust com., 1989—; mem loan com. Blackhawk State Bank, mem. fin. com., 1993. Contbr. articles to profl. jours. Active Wis. div. Am. Cancer Soc., 1964-75; 1st pres., co-organizer Citizen's Council Against Crime, Beloit; past officer, chmn. membership Beloit YMCA; pres. Beloit Brewers, chmn. bd., 1988-91, class A midwest league affiliate of Milw. Brewers baseball team, 1986-87; chmn. Student Achievers Program, Wis., No. Ill.; mem. adv. bd. Salvation Army; chmn. Beloiters for Coun.-Mgr., 1989; stateline chmn. Student Achiever Program, 1988, 93; bd. dirs. Greater Beloit Found., 1989—; chmating com. Greater Beloit Community Trust, Inc., 1991,93; chmn. adminstrv. bd., chmn. Council of Ministries, First United Methodist Ch., Beloit, pastor parish rels., 1995—; chmn. ann. dinner, bd. dirs., nominating com., fundraising, pub. speakers Beloit Crime Stoppers, 1993—, chmn., 1995-96; chmn. facilities study com. Sch. Dist. Beloit, 1991—; chmn. Eagle Scout bd. rev. Sinnisippi coun. Boy Scouts Am., 1995-96; vice chair spkrs. bur. Beloit Sports Hall of Fame, 1998-99, chmn., 1999. Recipient award for creativity in dentistry Johnson & Johnson Co., 1970; 3 citations for Cmty. Svc. United Givers Fund, 1970-75; Disting. Svc. citation Greater Beloit Assn. Commerce; named to Rock County Hall of Honor, 2000 Fellow Acad. Gen. Dentistry, Internat. Coll. Dentists. (Wis. editor), Am. Acad. Dental Practice Adminstrn. (past chmn. profl. liaison; mem. ADA (chmn. council on dental practice 1982-84), Wis. Dental Assn. (pres. 1979-80, trustee 1968-74), Wis. Dental Assn. Found., Rock County Dental Soc. (pres. 1976), Wis. Council of Professions (bd. dirs. 1974-80, pres. 1973-75), Chgo. Dental Soc., Greater Milw. Dental Assn., Fedn. Dentaire Internationale, Pierre Fauchard Acad., Am. Acad. History of Dentistry, Lions (beloit programs, 1993—, past pres.), Delta Sigma Delta. Avocations: cycling, golf, basketball, running, fishing. Home: 2207 Collingswood Dr Beloit WI 53511-2332 Office: 419 Pleasant St Beloit WI 53511-6249

GREEN, JOHN LAFAYETTE, JR. education executive; b. Trenton, N.J., Apr. 3, 1929; m. Harriet Hardin Hill, Nov. 8, 1962; 1 child, John Lafayette III BA, Miss. State U., 1955; MEd, Wayne State U., 1971; PhD, Rensselaer Poly. Inst., 1974. Asst. to treas. Internat. Paper Co., 1955-57; mem. faculty U. Calif., Berkeley, 1957-65; v.p. U. Ga., Athens, 1965-71, Rensselaer Poly. Inst., Troy, N.Y., 1971-76; exec. v.p. U. Miami, 1976-80; sr. v.p. U. Houston, 1980-81; pres. Washburn U., Topeka, 1981-88; exec. dir. Assn. Collegiate Bus. Schs. and Programs, Overland Park, 1988-95. Pres., chmn. bd. dirs. Strategic Planning/Mgmt. Assocs., Inc., Overland Park, Kans., 1981—; CEO Internat. Assembly for Collegiate Bus. Edn., Overland Park, 1997—; past. pres. Kansas City and Topeka chpts. Planning Forum. Author: Budgeting, 1967, (with others) Cost Accounting, 1969, Administrative Data Processing, 1970, Strategic Planning, 1980, Strategic Planning: A System for Businesses, 1986, A Strategic Planning System for Higher Education, 1987, Strategy Development and Implementation for Banks, 1988, co-author: Outcomes Assessment in Higher Education Linked to Strategic Planning and Budgeting, 1997. Bd. dirs. Boy Scouts Am., Topeka, 1983-85. With U.S. Army 1951-53 Recipient Disting. Kansan of Yr. in Pub. Adminstrn. award Topeka Capital Jour., 1984, Kans. Pub. Adminstr. of Yr. award Am. Soc. Pub. Adminstrn., 1984, Disting. Exec. award Mktg. Exec. Kans., 1984, Edn. Leader's Hall of Fame award, 1995. Mem. AAUP, Conf. Bd., Am. Mgmt. Assn., Fin. Execs. Inst., Demographics Inst., Masons, Shriners, Royal Order of Jesters, Phi Delta Kappa, Beta Alpha Psi, Phi Kappa Phi, Pi Kappa Alpha, Delta Sigma Pi. Republican. Presbyterian. (elder, deacon). Avocations: golf, tennis. Home: 12568 Farley Overland Park KS 66213-2526 Office: PO Box 25217 Shawnee Mission KS 66225-5217

GREEN, JOYCE, book publishing company executive; b. Taylorville, Ill., Oct. 22, 1928; d. Lynn and Vivian Coke (Richardson) Reinerd; m. Warren H. Green, Oct. 8, 1960. AA, Christian Coll., 1946; BS, MacMurray Coll., 1948. Pres. Warren H. Green, Inc., St. Louis, 1992—; editor Affirmative Action Register, 1977—; pres. InterContinental Industries, Inc., 1980—; chief exec. officer Pubs. Svc. Ctr. Mem. St. Louis C. of C., Jr. League Club, Media Club, Mo. Athletic Club. Home: 10000 Ocean Blvd Apt 90 Jensen Beach FL 34957 Office: 8356 Olive Blvd Saint Louis MO 63132-2814 E-mail: JRG1036@aol.com.

GREEN, KEVIN PATRICK, career officer; b. Aug. 28, 1949; m. Kate Donohue; 3 children. Grad., U.S. Naval Acad., 1971; MS, Naval Postgrad. Sch., 1977; Grad., Nat. War Coll., 1992. Ensign USN, 1971, advanced through grades to rear adm., 1996; assigned to frigate USS Voge (DE 1047), 1971-74; weapons officer USS Richard L. Page (FFG 5), 1978-80; ops. officer USS Preble (DDG 46), 1980-82; exec. officer USS Dahlgren (DDG 43), 1984-85; comdr. USS Taylor (FFG 50), 1989-91; comdr. destroyer squadron twenty-three, 1994-95; duty in spl. ops. br. Atlantic fleet hqrs., 1982-84; instr. combat sys., tactics prospective comdg. officer course, 1985-88; mil. asst. office of Sec. of Def., 1992-94; dir. surface officer disbn. divsn. bur. naval personnel, 1995-97; comdr. Naval Tng. Ctr., Great Lakes, Ill., 1996-98, Cruiser-Destroyer Group Three, 1998-99, U.S. Naval Forces So. Command, 1999—. Decorated Legion of Merit. E-mial. Office: Rear Adm USN COMUSNAVSO PSC 813 Box 2 FPO AA 34099-6004 E-mail: greenk@navstarr.navy.mil.

GREEN, MARK ANDREW, congressman, lawyer; b. Boston, June 1, 1960; s. Jeremy Raleigh and Elizabeth Pamela (Roome) G.; m. Susan Keske, Aug. 5, 1985; children: Rachel Eve Libinu, Anna Faith Kitali, Alexander Mark Amutavi. BA, U. Wis., Eau Claire, 1983; JD, U. Wis., Madison, 1987. Bar: Wis. 1987. Tchr., intern World Teach Project, Kakamega, Kenya, 1987-88; of counsel Godfrey & Kahn, S.C., Green Bay, Wis., 1989-98; mem. Wis. Assembly, Madison, 1992-98, chmn. assembly majority caucus, chmn. assembly jud. com., 1994-98; state chmn. Am. Legis. Exch. Coun.; mem. U.S. Congress from 8th Wis. dist., 1999—; mem. fin. svcs. com., judiciary com. Legal counsel Rep. Assembly Campaign Com., Madison, 1993—. Chmn. mcpl. affairs Brown County Taxpayers Assn., Green Bay, 1990-92; chmn. Brown County Rep. Party, 1991-92; bd. dirs. Nat. R.R. Mus., Green Bay, 1992—; chmn. resolutions com. Wis. Rep. Conv., Milw., 1993. Recipient Wis. award Ind. Bus. Assn., 1996; named Wis. Outstanding Legislator of 1995, Wis. Builders Assn., Healthcare Leader of Wis., State Med. Soc., 1996; scholar U. Wis., Eau Claire, 1982. Mem. ABA, Wis. Bar Assn., Am. Legis. Exch. Coun., Nat. Conf. State Legislators, Brown County Home Builders Assn., Kiwanis. Office: Ho of Reps 1218 Longworth Ho Office Bldg Washington DC 20515-4908*

GREEN, MAURICE, molecular biologist, virologist, educator; b. N.Y.C., May 5, 1926; s. David and Bessie (Lipschitz) G.; m. Marilyn Glick, Aug. 20, 1950; children: Michael Richard, Wendy Allison Green Lee, Eric Douglas B.S. in Chemistry, U. Mich., 1949; M.S. in Biochemistry and Chemistry, U. Wis.-Madison, 1952, Ph.D. in Biochemistry and Chemistry, 1954. Instr. biochemistry U. Pa. Med. Sch., Phila., 1955-56; asst. prof. St. Louis U. Health Scis. Ctr., 1956-60, assoc. prof., 1960-63, prof. microbiology, 1963-77; prof., chmn. Inst. for Molecular Virology, 1964—. Office: St Louis U Health Sci Ctr Inst for Molecular Virology 3681 Park Ave Saint Louis MO 63110-2511

GREEN, MIKE, state legislator; b. Risco, Miss., Sept. 28, 1948; Student, Flint Jr. Coll., 1966-68. Tool and die worker; mem. from dist. 84 Mich. State Ho. of Reps., Lansing, 1995—, minority vice chmn. agr. com., mem. transp., ins. and mental health coms.; chair agr. and resource mgmt. com., 1999-2000; mem. conservation and outdoor recreation com.; mem. constl. law and ethis, health policy com. Address: PO Box 300014 Lansing MI 48909-7514 Also: House Office Bldg S-1188 Lansing MI 48909

GREEN, MORRIS, physician, educator; b. Indpls., May 27, 1922; s. Coleman and Rebecca (Oleinick) Green; m. Janice Barber Gorton, Mar. 11, 1955; children: David Schuster, Alan Coleman, Carolyn Ann, Susan Elaine, Marcia Ruth, Sylvia Rebecca. AB, Ind. U., 1942, MD, 1944. Intern Ind. U. Med. Ctr., 1945; resident pediat. U. Ill. Rsch. and Ednl. Hosps., 1947—49; instr. pediat. U. Ill. Coll. Medicine, 1949—52; asst. prof. Yale Sch. Medicine, 1952—57; faculty Ind. U. Sch. Medicine, Indpls., 1957—, Perry W. Lesh prof. pediat., 1963—; chmn. dept. pediat., physician-in-chief James Whitcomb Riley Hosp. for Children, 1967—88. Commr. health State of Ind., 1990—91. Author: Pediatric Diagnosis, 6th edit., 1998; co-editor: Ambulatory Pediatrics, 1968, 5th edit., 1999, Bright Futures, 2d edit., 2000; mem. editl. bd.: Pediat. Rev., mem. editl. bd.: Contemporary Pediat., mem. editl. bd.: Current Problems Pediat., mem. editl. bd.: Jour. Devel. Behavioral Pediat., mem. editl. bd.: Jour. Ambulatory Pediat. Assn., mem. editl. bd.: Social Work in Health Care, nat. adviser: Children Today. Served to capt. M.C. U.S. Army, 1945—47. Recipient George Armstrong award in ambulatory pediat., 1971, C. Anderson Aldrich award in child devel., 1982, Irving S. Cutter award, Phi Rho Sigma, 1984, Ross award for pediat. edn., 1985, Simon Wile award, Am. Acad. Child and Adolescent Psychiatry, 1990, Joseph W. St. Geme award, Fedn. Pediat. Orgns., 1992, Disting. Career award, Ambulatory Pediat. Assn., 1996. Mem.: AMA (Abraham Jacobi award 1990), Soc. Rsch. Child Devel., Inst. Medicine, Am. Orthopsychiat. Assn., Am. Acad. Pediat. (Abraham Jacobi award 1990), Am. Fedn. Clin. Rsch., Soc. Pediat. Rsch., Am. Pediatric Soc., Alpha Omega Alpha, Sigma Xi, Phi Beta Kappa. Home: 1840 Brewster Rd Indianapolis IN 46260-1561 Office: 702 Barnhill Dr Indianapolis IN 46202-5128

GREEN, NANCY LOUGHRIDGE, newspaper executive; b. Lexington, Ky., Jan. 19, 1942; d. William S. and Nancy O. (Green) Loughridge. BA in Journalism, U. Ky., 1964, postgrad., 1968; MA in Journalism, Ball State U., 1971; postgrad., U. Minn., 1968. Tchr. English, publs. adv. Clark County H.S., Winchester, Ky., 1965-66, Pleasure Ridge Park H.S., Louisville, 1966-67, Clarksville (Ind.) H.S., 1967-68, Charleston (W.Va.) H.S., 1968-69; asst. publs., pub. info. specialist W.Va. Dept. Edn., Charleston, 1969-70; tchr. journalism, publs. dir. Elmhurst H.S., Ft. Wayne, Ind., 1970-71; adviser student publs. U. Ky., Lexington, 1971-82; gen. mgr. student publs. U. Tex., Austin, 1982-85; pres., pub. Palladium-Item, Richmond, Ind., 1985-89, News-Leader, Springfield, Mo., 1989-92; asst. to pres. newspaper divsn. Gannett Co., Inc., Washington, 1992-94; exec. dir. advancement Clayton State Coll., Morrow, Ga., 1994-96; v.p. advancement Clayton Coll. & State U., 1996-99; v.p. comm. Ga. GLOBE U. Sys., 1999-2000; dir. circulation/distbn., sales & mktg. Lee Enterprises, Davenport, Iowa, 2000—. Dir. urban journalism program Harte-Hanks, 1984, various Louisville and Lexington newspaper pubs., 1976-82; pres. Media Cons., Inc., Lexington, 1980; sec. Kernel Press, Inc., 1971-82. Contbr. articles to profl. jours. Bd. dirs. Richmond Cmty. Devel. Corp., 1987-89, United Way of the Ozarks, 1990-92, ARC, 1990-92, Springfield Arts Coun., 1990-91, Bus. Devel. Corp., 1991-92, Bus. Edn. Alliance, 1991-92, Caring Found., 1991-92, Cox Hosp. Bd., 1990-92, Springfield Schs. Found., 1991-92, Jr. League, Lexington, 1980-82, Manchester Ctr., 1978-82, pres., 1979-82; chmn. Greater Richmond Progress Com., 1986-87, bd. dirs., 1986-89; pres. Leadership Wayne County, 1986-87, bd. dirs. 1985-89; adv. bd. Ind. U. East, 1985-89, Richmond C. of C., 1987-89, Ind. Humanities Coun., 1988-89, Youth Comm. Bd., 1988-92, Opera Theatre

No. Va., 1992-94, Atlanta chpt. AIWF, 1995—. Recipient Coll. Media Advisers First Amendment award, 1987, Disting. Svc. award Assn. Edn. Journalism and Mass Comm., 1989; named to Ball State Journalism Hall of Fame, 1988, Coll. Media Advisers Hall of Fame, 1994. Mem. Student Press Law Ctr. (bd. dirs. 1975—, pres. 1985-87, 94-96, v.p. 1992-94), Assoc. Collegiate Press, Journalism Edn. Assn. (Carl Towley award 1988), Nat. Coun. Coll. Publs. Advs. (pres. 1979-83, Disting. Newspaper Adv. 1976, Disting. Bus. Adviser 1984), Columbia Scholastic Press Assn. (Gold Key 1980), So. Interscholastic Press Assn. (Disting. Svc. award 1983), Nat. Scholastic Press Assn. (Pioneer award 1982), Soc. Profl. Journalists, Clayton County C. of C. (adv. bd. 1995-99, internat. com. chmn. 1996-98). E-mail: nancy.green@lee.net.

GREEN, PETER MORRIS, classics educator, writer, translator; b. London, Dec. 22, 1924; came to U.S., 1971; s. Arthur and Olive Emily (Slaughter) G.; m. Lalage Isobel Pulvertaft, July 28, 1951 (div.); children: Timothy Michael Bourke, Nicholas Paul, Sarah Francesca; m. Carin Margreta Christensen, July 18, 1975. BA, Cambridge U., 1950, MA, PhD, Cambridge U., 1954. Dir. studies in classics Selwyn Coll., Cambridge, Eng., 1952-53; freelance writer, journalist, translator, London, 1954-63; lectr. Greek history and lit. Coll. Yr. in Athens, 1966-71; prof. classics U. Tex., Austin, 1971-97, James R. Dougherty Centennial prof., 1982-97, prof. emeritus, 1997—. Vis. prof. classics UCLA, 1976; vis. prof. history U. Iowa, 1997-98, adj. prof. classics, 1998—; vis. prof. history, Athens, 1999; Mellon chair in humanities Tulane U., 1986; vis. fellow, writer-in-residence Hellenic studies program Princeton U., fall semester, 2001. Fiction critic: Daily Telegraph, London, 1954-63; sr. cons. editor: Hodder & Stoughton Ltd., London, 1959-63; cons.: (Odyssey project) Nat. Radio Theatre, Chgo., 1980-81; author: The Sword of Pleasure, 1957 (Heinemann award for Lit. 1957), The Laughter of Aphrodite, 1965, Armada from Athens, 1970, The Shadow of the Parthenon, 1972, Alexander of Macedon 356-323 BC: A Historical Biography, 1974, 2d edit., 1991, Classical Bearings, 1989, ed edit., 1998, Alexander to Actium: The Historical Evolution of the Hellenistic Age, 1990, rev. edit., 1993, The Greco-Persian Wars, 1996; translator, editor: Juvenal, The Sixteen Satires, 1967, 3d edit., 1998, Ovid: The Erotic Poems, 1982, Yannis Ritsos: The Fourth Dimension, 1993, Hellenistic History and Culture, 1993, Ovid: The Poems of Exile, 1994, Apollonios Rhodios, The Argonautika, 1997; editor-in-chief Syllecta Classica, 1999—. Served to sgt. RAF, 1943-47. NEH fellow, 1983-84; Craven scholar Cambridge U., 1950; Obermann Ctr. for Advanced Rsch. fellow U. Iowa, 1997; recipient 1st prize Nat. Poetry Libr., 1997. Fellow Royal Soc. Lit. (council 1959-63); mem. Soc. for Promotion of Hellenic Studies (U.K.), Classical Assn. (U.K.), Am. Philol. Assn., Archaeol. Inst. Am., Mem. Liberal Party. Club: Savile (London). Office: Dept Classics U Iowa Iowa City IA 52242 E-mail: peter-green-1@uiowa.edu.

GREEN, RICHARD CALVIN, JR. electric power and gas industry executive; b. Kansas City, Mo., May 6, 1954; s. Richard C. and Ann (Gableman) G.; m. Nancy Jean Risk, Aug. 6, 1977; children: Allison Thompt, Ashley Jean, Richard Calvin III. BSBA, So. Methodist U., 1976. With Mo. Pub. Service, Kansas City, 1976-85, exec. v.p., 1982-85; pres., chief exec. officer UtiliCorp United Inc., 1985-89, pres., chmn. bd., from 1989, now CEO, chmn. bd. Bd. dirs. Midwest Rsch. Inst., The BHA Group, Inc., Urban Inst. Washington.

GREEN, ROBERT K. energy executive; BS in Engring., Princeton U.; JD, Vanderbilt U. Atty. Blackwell, Sanders, Matheny, Weary & Lombardi, Kansas City, 1987-88; asst. divsn. counsel Mo. Pub. Svc. divsn. UtiliCorp United, divsn. counsel Mo. Pub. Svc. divsn., v.p. adminstrn. Mo. Pub. Svc. divsn., sr. v.p. ops. Mo. Pub. Svc. divsn., pres. Mo. Pub. Svc. divsn., 1991—; exec. v.p., bd.d irs. UtiliCorp, Kansas City, Mo., 1993-96, pres., COO, 1996—. Bd. dirs. United Mo. Bank, CompGeeks.com.; chmn. United Energy, Melbourne, Australia, 1995, UnitedNetworks, Auckland, New Zealand, 1998, Aquila Energy, 1999. Chmn. Initiative for Competitive Inner City, Kansas City. Mem. ABA, Mo. Bar Assn., Kansas City Met. Bar Assn. Office: UtiliCorp United 20 W 9th St Kansas City MO 64105-1704

GREEN, SAUL A. lawyer; B.A., U. Mich. , 1969; J.D., U. Mich. Law , 1972. Asst. U.S. Atty., eastern dist. Mich U.S. Dept Justice, Mich., 1973—76; chief counsel Us. Dept. of Housing and Urban Devel., Detroit, 1976—89; corp. counsel Wayne County, 1989—93; U.S. atty. Ea. Dist. Mich., Detroit, 1994—2001; sr. counsel Miller, Canfield, Paddock and Stone, PLC , 2001—, dir., Minority Bus Practice Group, 2001—. Office: Miller, Canfield, Paddock and Stone, PLC 150 West Jefferson, Suite 2500 Detroit MI 48226 Office Fax: 313-496-8453. E-mail: greens@millercanfield.com.

GREEN, TIMOTHY P. state legislator; b. North Saint Louis, Mo., June 29, 1963; m. Lisa Ann Green, 1990. BBA, U. Mo. St. Louis. State rep. Dist. 73 Mo. Ho. of Reps., 1988—. Mem. appropriations health and mental health com., ins. com., munic com.; vice chmn. labor com.; constrn. electrician. Office: Capitol Bldg 201 W Capitol Ave Jefferson City MO 65101-1556

GREEN, TRENT JASON, football player; b. Cedar Rapids , Iowa, July 9, 1970; m. Julie Green; children: T.J., Derek Green. Degree in Bus. , Ind. U. Football player San Diego Chargers, 1993, Washington Redskins, 1995—99, St. Louis Rams, 1999—2001, Kans. City Chiefs, 2001—. Established Trent Green Family Found., 1999; supporter Star Bright Rm. at Kans. Children's Mercy Hosp. Avocations: basketball, golf, hunting, fishing. Office: 1 Arrowhead Dr Kansas City MO 64129 Office Fax: 816-923-4719.*

GREEN, WILLIAM, archaeologist; b. Chgo., May 30, 1953; s. David and Lillian (Kerdeman) G. AB, Grinnell Coll., 1974; MA, U. Wis., 1977, PhD, 1987. Staff archaeologist State Hist. Soc. of Wis., Madison, 1978-86; asst. prof. archaeology Western Ill. U., Macomb, 1980, 81; state archaeologist U. Iowa, Iowa City, 1988-2001, adj. asst. prof. anthropology, 1988-94, adj. assoc. prof. anthropology, 1994-2001; dir. Logan Mus. Anthropology, Beloit (Wis.) Coll., 2001—, adj. prof. anthropology, 2001—. Editor jour. The Wis. Archaeologist, 1983-88; editor: Midcontinental Jour. Archaeology, 1998—; contbr. articles and revs. to profl. jours. Chair Johnson County Hist. Preservation Commn., Iowa, 1991-93. Grantee NSF, 1990-91, State Hist. Soc. Iowa, Leopold Ctr. for Sustainable Agr., Iowa Acad. Sci., 1988-91, 95. Fellow Am. Anthropol. Assn. Jewish. Office: Logan Mus Anthropology Beloit Coll Beloit WI 53511

GREENBAUM, STUART I. economist, educator; b. N.Y.C., Oct. 7, 1936; s. Sam and Bertha (Freimark) G.; m. Margaret E. Wache, July 29, 1964; children: Regina Gail, Nathan Carl. BS, NYU, 1959; Ph.D., Johns Hopkins U., 1964. Fin. economist Fed. Res. Bank of Kansas City, Mo., 1962-66; sr. economist Office of the Comptroller of the Currency, Washington, 1966-67; assoc. prof. econs. U. Ky., Lexington, 1968-74, prof., 1974-76, chmn. dept. econs., 1975-76; vis. prof. fin. Kellogg Grad. Sch. Mgmt., Northwestern U., Evanston, Ill., 1974-75, prof. fin., 1976-78, Harold L. Stuart prof. banking and fin., 1978-83, Norman Strunk disting. prof. fin. instns., 1983-95, dir. Banking Research Ctr., 1976-95, assoc. dean for acad. affairs, 1988-92; dean John M. Olin Sch. of Bus. Washington U., St. Louis, 1995—, Bank of Am. prof. mgrl. leadership, John M. Olin Sch. bus., 2000—. Cons. Fed. Res. Bank Chgo., 1994-95; mem. Fed. Savs. and Loan Adv. Coun., 1986-89; vis. prof. banking and fin. Leon Recanati Grad. Sch. Bus. Adminstrn., Tel Aviv (Israel) U., 1980-81. Assoc. editor Nat. Banking Rev., 1966-67, So. Econ. Jour., 1977-79, Jour. Fin., 1977-83, Jour. Banking and Fin., 1980-92, Jour. Fin. Rsch., 1981-87, Fin. Rev., 1985-89, Managerial and Decision Econs., 1989-94, Jour. Econs., Mgmt. and Strategy, 1991-95; founding and mng. editor Jour. Fin. Intermediation, 1989-96. With U.S. Army, 1958-64. Mem. Am. Econ. Assn., Am. Fin. Assn. Office: Washington U Campus Box 1133 One Brookings Dr Saint Louis MO 63130-4899 E-mail: greenbaum@olin.wwtl.edu.

GREENBERG, BERNARD, entomologist, educator; b. N.Y.C., Apr. 24, 1922; s. Isidore and Rose (Gordon) G.; m. Barbara Muriel Dickler, Sept. 1, 1949; children: Gary, Linda, Deborah, Daniel. B.A., Bklyn. Coll., 1944; M.A., U. Kans., 1951, Ph.D., 1954. Asst. prof. biology U. Ill. Med. Center, Chgo., 1954-61, assoc. prof., 1961-66, prof. Geophys. Scis., 1966-90, prof. emeritus, 1990—. Vis. sci. Istituto Superiore di Sanitá, Rome, 1960-61, Fulbright-Hays sr. research scholar, 1967-68; vis. sci. Instituto de Salubridad y Enfermedades Tropicales, Mexico City, 1962, 63; cons. in field; cons., expert witness in forensic entomology; pres. Bioconcern; nat. lectr. Sigma Xi Hon. Sci. Rsch. Soc., 1996—. Author: Flies and Disease, vol. 1, 1971, Flies and Disease, vol. 2, 1973, Flies as Forensic Indicators: , 2001; contbr. articles. Pvt. USAF, 1944—46. NSF grantee, 1959-60, 79-81; NIH grantee, 1960-67; U.S. Army Med. Research and Devel. Command grantee, 1966-72, 85; Electric Power Research Inst. grantee, 1976-85; Office Naval Research grantee, 1977-78. Fellow AAAS; mem. Entomol. Soc. Am., Chgo. Acad. Sci. (sci. gov. 1981—), Home: 1463 E 55th Pl Chicago IL 60637-1875 Office: Dept Biol Scis M/C 066 U Ill Chgo Chicago IL 60607 E-mail: bugaboo@uic.edu.

GREENBERG, BRADLEY SANDER, communications educator; b. Toledo, Aug. 3, 1934; s. Abraham and Florence (Cohen) G.; m. Delight Thompson, June 7, 1959; children: Beth, Shawn, Debra. B.A. in Journalism; Univ. scholar, Bowling Green State U., 1956; M.S. in Journalism; Univ. fellow, U. Wis., 1957, Ph.D. in Mass Communication, 1961. Postdoctoral fellow Mass. Comms. Rsch. Ctr., 1960-61; research asso. Inst. Communication Research, Stanford U., 1961-64; asst. prof. Mich. State U., East Lansing, 1964-66, assoc. prof., 1966-71, prof. dept. communication, 1971—, Univ. Disting. prof., 1990, chmn. dept., 1977-84, prof. telecommunication, 1975—, chmn. dept., 1984-90. Vis. prof. U. Ga., Athens, 1999, U. Calif., Berkeley, 1992; fellow Ctrs. Disease Control and Prevention, Atlanta, 1999; sr. fellow East-West Ctr., Comms. Inst., Honolulu, 1978-79, 81; rsch. fellow Ind. Broadcasting Authority, London, 1985-86; cons. Pres.'s Commn. on Causes and Prevention Violence, 1968-69, Surgeon Gen.'s Sci. Adv. Com. on TV and Social Behavior, 1970-72, 82. Author: The Kennedy Assassination and the American Public: Social Communication in Crisis, 1965, Use of Mass Media by the Urban Poor, 1970, Life on Television, 1980, Mexican Americans and the Mass Media, 1983, Cableviewing, 1988, Teletext in the U.K., 1988, Mass Media, Sex and the Adolescent,1993, Desert Storm and the Mass Media, 1993, The Alphabet Soup of TV Ratings, 2001. Served to maj. U.S. Army Res., 1973. Recipient Chancellors award for disting. svc. in journalism U. Wis., 1978, disting. faculty award Mich. State U., 1979; named to Journalism Hall of Fame Bowling Green State U., 1980; rsch. grantee NIH, NSF, USPHS, Carnegie Corp., Hoso Bunka Found., Nat. Assn. Broadcasters. Fellow Internat. Comm. Assn. (pres. 1994-95); mem. Assn. for Edn. in Journalism, Phi Kappa Phi (pres. 1993-94). Home: 350 Winterberry Ln Okemos MI 48864-4166 Office: Mich State U Dept Telecommunication 477 Communication Arts Sci East Lansing MI 48824-1212 E-mail: bradg@msu.edu.

GREENBERG, DAVID BERNARD, chemical engineering educator; b. Norfolk, Va., Nov. 2, 1928; s. Abraham David and Ida (Frenkil) G.; m. Helen Muriel Levine, Aug. 15, 1959 (div. Aug. 1980); children: Lisa, Jan, Jill BS in Chem. Engring., Carnegie Inst. Tech., 1952; MS in Chem. Engring., Johns Hopkins U., 1959; PhD, La. State U., 1964. Registered profl. engr., La. Process engr. U.S. Indsl. Chem. Co., Balt., 1952-55; project engr. FMC Corp., 1955-56; asst. prof. U.S. Naval Acad., Annapolis, Md., 1958-61; from instr. to prof. La. State U., Baton Rouge, 1961-74; prof. chem. engring. U. Cin., 1974—, head dept., 1974-81. Program dir. engring. divsn. NSF, Washington, 1972-73, chem. and thermal scis. divsn., 1989-90; sr. scientist Chem. Sys. Lab., Dept. Army, Edgewood, Md., 1981-83; cons. Burk & Assocs., New Orleans, 1970-78. Contbr. numerous articles on chem. engring. to profl. jours. Mem. Cin. Mayor's Energy Task Force, 1981— . Served to lt. USNR, 1947-52 Esso research fellow, 1964-65, NSF fellow, 1961 Fellow Am. Soc. for Laser Medicine and Surgery; mem. Am. Inst. Chem. Engrs., Am. Chem. Soc., Am. Soc. for Engring. Edn., Sigma Xi, Tau Beta Pi, Phi Lambda Upsilon. Jewish. Home: 8547 Wyoming Club Dr Cincinnati OH 45215-4243 Office: Univ Cin Dept Chem Engring PO Box 210171 Cincinnati OH 45221-0171 E-mail: David.Greenberg@uc.edu.

GREENBERG, GERALD STEPHEN, lawyer; b. Phila., July 27, 1951; s. Bernard and Elaine Alice (Shapiro) G.; m. Pamela Sue Meyers, Aug. 24, 1975; children: David Stuart, Allison Brooke. BA, Dickinson Coll., 1973; JD, Harvard U., 1976. Bar: N.Y. 1977, U.S. Dist. Ct. (so. dist.) N.Y. 1977, Ohio 1988. Assoc. Kaye, Scholer, Fierman, Hays & Handler, N.Y.C., 1976-86; atty. Exxon Corp., 1986-87; assoc. Taft, Stettinius & Hollister LLP, Cin., 1987-89; ptnr. Taft, Stettinius & Hollister, 1990—. Mem. ABA, Assn. of Bar of City of N.Y., Cin. Bar Assn. Office: 1800 Firstar Tower 425 Walnut St Cincinnati OH 45202-3923 E-mail: greenberg@taftlaw.com.

GREENBERG, JACK M. food products executive; b. 1942; s. Edith S. Scher; m. Donna; children: David, Ilyse, Allison. BSc in Acctg., DePaul U., Chgo., 1964, JD, 1968. Bar: Ill; CPA, Ill. With Arthur Young & Co., 1964-82; chief fin. officer, exec. v.p. McDonald's Corp., Oakbrook, Ill., 1982—, vice chmn., chief fin. officer Oak Brook, CFO, exec. v.p., 1982, vice chmn., CFO, 1992, bd. dirs., pres & ceo, 1997—, chmn & ceo, 1999—. Bd. dirs. Abbott Labs., Harcourt Gen., Boston. Bd. dirs. DePaul U., IIT, Kent Coll. Law. Mem. AICPA, Ill. Inst. Cert. Pub. Accts. Office: McDonald's Corp 1 Mcdonalds Plz Oak Brook IL 60523-1911

GREENBERG, STEVE, brokerage house executive; Pres. Alaron Trading Corp., Chgo. Office: Alaron Trading Corp 822 W Washington St Chicago IL 60607-2302

GREENBERGER, NORTON JERALD, physician; b. Cleve., Sept. 13, 1933; s. Sam and Lillian (Frank) G.; m. Joan Narcus, Aug. 10, 1964; children: Sharon, Rachel, Wendy. A.B., Yale U., 1955; M.D., Western Res. U., 1959. Diplomate: Am. Bd. Internal Medicine (sec.-treas. 1980-82). Intern Univ. Hosps., Cleve., 1959-60, resident internal medicine, 1960-62; USPHS fellow in gastroenterology Harvard U., 1962-65, Mass. Gen. Hosp., Boston, 1962-65; with Ohio State U., Columbus, 1965-72, dir. div. gastroenterology, 1967-72, prof., 1971-72; prof., chmn. dept. medicine U. Kans., Kansas City, 1972-2000, sr. assoc. dean acad. affairs, 2000—02; clin. prof. medicine Harvard Med. Sch., 2002—. Mem. Nat. Bd. Med. Examiners, 1971-75; mem. gen. medicine study sect. A, NIH, 1973-76 Author: Gastrointestinal Disorders: A Pathophysiologic Approach, 1976, rev. edit., 1989,Medical Book of Lists, 5th edit., 1998, History Taking and Physical Examination: Essentials and Clinical Correlates, 1992; co-editor gastroent. sect. Yearbook of Medicine, 1969-98; editor Yearbook of Digestive Diseases, 1984-98; contbr. articles to med. jours. Recipient Outstanding Teaching award House Staff Dept. Medicine Ohio State U., 1970-71, Outstanding Teaching award Kans. U. Med. Sch. Class of 1978, Outstanding Med. Educator, 1984, 85, 90, 91, 98, 99. Fellow ACP (editorial com. gastoenterology sect. 1975-77, regent 1984-92, chmn. bd. regents 1988-89, pres. 1990-91, Disting. Tchg. award 2001); mem. Am. Fedn. Clin. Rsch. (pres. Midwestern sect. 1973-74), Ctrl. Soc. Clin. Rsch. (councillor 1975, pres. 1979-80), Midwestern Gut Club, Am. Gastroent. Assn. (pres.-elect 1983-84, pres. 1984-85, Disting. Educator award 1995), Am. Soc. Clin. Investigation, Am. Soc. Pharmacology and Exptl. Therapeutics, Assn. Am. Physicians, Assn. Profs. Medicine (pres. 1986-87, Williams award 2000), Phi Beta Kappa, Sigma Xi, Alpha Omega Alpha. Office: Brigham & Womens Hosp Boston MA 02115

GREENBLATT, DEANA CHARLENE, elementary education educator; b. Chgo., Mar. 13, 1948; d. Walter and Betty (Lamasky) Beisel; BEd., Chgo. State U., 1969; MA in Guidance and Counseling, Roosevelt U., 1973; m. Mark Greenblatt, June 22, 1975. Tchr., counselor Chgo. Pub. Schs., 1969-75, City Colls. of Chgo. GED-TV, 1976; tchr. Columbus (Ohio) Pub. Schs., 1976-86; tchr. Chgo. Pub. Schs., 1993—; participant learning exchange, Chgo. Active B'nai B'rith; vol. Right-to-Read, Columbus; mem. Community Learning Exchange, Acad. Yr. in U.S.A. Com. Counselor, 1989—. Columbus. Cert. tchr. K-9, Ill., Ohio; cert. personnel guidance, Ill., Ohio; cert. Chgo. Bd. Edn. Mem. Am. Personnel and Guidance Assn., Internat. Platform Assn., B'nai B'rith Women Club (chpt. v.p.). Democrat. Home: 3820 W Touhy Ave Lincolnwood IL 60712-1026

GREENBLATT, WILLIAM, photographer; b. St. Louis, June 9, 1954; BS in Edn., U. Mo., 1977, MEd, 1981. Pres. William Greenblatt Photography, Inc., St. Louis, 1972—; photographer UPI, 1977—, Getty Images; bureau chief, St. Louis UPI, St. Louis. Mem. adv. bd. Salvation Army, St. Louis, 1996—, Harbor Light. Recipient 1st pl., 2d pl., Baseball Hall of Fame, 1991. Mem.: Press Club Met. St. Louis (bd. dirs.), Soc. Environ. Journalists, Soc. Profl. Jouranalists, Investigative Reporters and Editors, Nat. Press Photographers Assn., Am. Soc. Media Photographers. Home and Office: 20 Nantucket Ln Saint Louis MO 63132-4135 Office: United Press Internat St. Louis Bureau 20 Nantucket Ln Saint Louis MO 63132-4135 Fax: 314-991-9320.

GREENE, JOSEPH E. material science researcher; PhD in Materials Sci., U.S.C., 1971. Prof. U. Ill., 1971—; Erlander prof. Physics Linkping U., Sweden. Editor: CRC Critical Revs. in Solid State and Materials Sci., Thin Solid Films. Recipient Tage Erlander Physics prize 1992-95, Tech. Excellence award Semiconductor Rsch. Corp. 1994, Dept. Energy Sustained Outstanding Rsch. award 1996, David Adler Lectrship. award 1998. Mem. Am. Vacuum Soc. (bd. dirs., pres.), Am. Inst. Physics (gov. bd. mem.), Am. Physical Soc., AVS, TMS, MRS. Office: Dept Materials Sci and Engring U Ill 1101 W Springfield Ave Urbana IL 61801-3005

GREENE, LAURA HELEN, physicist; b. Cleve., June 12, 1952; d. Sam and Frances (Kain) G.; children: Max Greene Giannetta, Leo Greene Giannetta. BS cum laude in Physics, Ohio State U., 1974, MS in Physics, 1978; MS in Exptl. Physics, Cornell U., 1980, PhD in Physics, 1984. Mem. tech. staff Hughes Aircraft Co., Torrance, Calif., 1974-75; teaching asst. Ohio State U., Columbus, 1975-76, rsch. asst., 1976-77; teaching asst. Cornell U., Ithaca, N.Y., 1977-79, rsch. asst., 1979-83; postdoctoral mem. tech. staff Bellcore (formerly Bell Labs.), Red Bank, N.J., 1983-85, Murray Hill, 1983-85, mem. tech. staff Red Bank, 1985-92; prof. dept. physics U. Ill., Urbana, 1992—, Swanlund endowed chair, 2000, Ctr. for Advanced Study resident assoc., 2000—. Beckman assoc. Ctr. Advanced Study U Ill. at Urbana-Champaign, 1996-97, mem. provost's com. on sexual harassment edn., 1999-2000, mem. physics adv. com., 1999—; mem. McMillan award com. 1994-96, chair, 1995-97; co-chair Gordon Rsch. Conf., 1996, chair, 1998; mem.-at-large Coun. Gordon Rsch. Confs., 1999—, mem. schedule and selection com.; mem. Basic Energy Scis. Adv. Com., 2000; interim and founding bd. trustee Inst. for Complex and Adaptive Materials, Los Alamos and U. Calif.; mem. various rev. panels and workshops NSF and Dept. Energy; presenter in field; resident assoc. ctr. for advanced study U. Ill., Urbana, Ill., 2000-01; review panel Can. Inst. Advanced Rsch., Superconductivity Review, 2002; mem. provost com. sexual harrassment edn. U. Ill., 1999-2001, oversight com. for vice chancellor rsch., U. Ill., 2001-02, Sloan Found. Selection Com. for Physics, 2001-; adv. com. Sec. of Energy Bill Richardson, 2000-. Contbr. over 150 articles to profl. jours.; presenter over 150 domestic and internat. invited talks. Mem. selection com. in physics Sloan Found. Recipient Beckman award U. Ill. Campus Rsch. Bd., 1993, E.O. Lawrence award Dept. Energy, 1999, 2001; rsch. grantee NSF, 1991—, ONR, 1995—, Dept. Energy, 1995—. Fellow AAAS (electorate nominating com. of sect. B physics 2000—, chmn. nominating com. for physics, 2001-02), Am. Acad. Arts and Scis., Am. Phys. Soc. (gen. councilor 1992—, congl. fellow screening com. 1993, exec. bd. 1995—, com. on coms. 1995—, chair 1997, search com. The Phys. Rev. 1996, nominating com. divsn. condensed matter physics 1998—, Maria Goeppert-Mayer award 1994, Centennial Spkr. 1997); mem. Materials Rsch. Soc. (symposium chair 1992), Am. Assn. Physics Tchrs., Internat. Union Pure and Applied Physicists (commr., U.S. liaison com. 1996—, U.S. del. to Low-Temperature Physics Commn. 1996—), Phi Kappa Phi. Avocations: children, physics, working out, music. Office: U Ill Loomis Lab Physics 1110 W Green St Urbana IL 61801-9013 E-mail: lhg@uiuc.edu.

GREENE, ROBERT BERNARD, JR. (BOB GREENE), broadcast television correspondent, columnist, author; b. Columbus, Ohio, Mar. 10, 1947; s. Robert Bernard and Phyllis Ann (Harmon) G.; m. Susan Bonnet Koebel, Feb. 13, 1971; 1 dau., Amanda Sue. B.S., Northwestern U., 1969. Reporter Chgo. Sun-Times, 1969-71, columnist, 1971-78; syndicated columnist Field Newspaper Syndicate, Irvine, Calif., 1976-81, Tribune Co. Syndicate, N.Y.C., 1981—; contbg. corr. ABC News Nightline, from 1981; columnist Chgo. Tribune, 1978—. Lectr. fine arts U. Chgo. Contbg. editor: Esquire Mag., 1980— ; books include We Didn't Have None of Them Fat Funky Angels on the Wall of Heartbreak Hotel and Other Reports from America, 1971; Running: A Nixon-McGovern Campaign Journal, 1973, Billion Dollar Baby, 1974, Johnny Deadline, Reporter: The Best of Bob Greene, 1976, (with Paul Galloway) Bagtime, 1977, American Beat, 1983, Good Morning, Merry Sunshine, 1984, Cheeseburgers, The Best of Bob Greene, 1985, Be True to Your School, 1987, Homecoming: When the Soldiers Returned From Vietnam, 1989, Hang Time: Days and Dreams With Michael Jordan, 1992. Recipient Nat. Headliner award for best newspaper column in U.S., 1977, Peter Lisagor award, 1981 Office: Chgo Tribune 435 N Michigan Ave Chicago IL 60611-4066

GREENE, TERRY J. legislative staff member; m. Tricia; children: Patrick, Brady, Douglas, Teddy. Student, Ariz. State U.; BA in Speech Comm., Drury Coll. Press sec. Congressman Thomas Ewing, Washington, 1991-95, dist. adminstr., 1995-96, chief of staff, chief advisor pub. policy, legis. matters, 1996—. Baseball scholar Ariz. State U. Office: 509 W Dunbar St Mahomet IL 61853-9244

GREENER, RALPH BERTRAM, lawyer; b. Rahway, N.J., Sept. 23, 1940; s. Ralph Bertram and Mary Ellen (Esch) G.; m. Jean Elizabeth Wilson, Mar. 21, 1964; children: Eric Wilson, Erin Hope, Nicholas Christian. BA, Wheaton Coll., 1962; JD, Duke U., 1968. Bar: Minn. 1969, U.S. Dist. Ct. 1969, U.S. Tax Ct. 1988. With Fredrikson & Byron P.A., Mpls., 1969—. Chmn. Minn. Lawyers Mutual Ins. Co., Mpls. 1981—; pres. Nat. Assn. of Bar-Related Ins. Cos., 1989-90. 1st Lt. USMCR, 1962-65. Recipient award of profl. excellence Minn. State Bar Assn., 1993. Mem. Rotary Club. Home: 1018 W Minnehaha Pky Minneapolis MN 55419-1161 Office: Fredrikson & Byron PA 4000 Pilsbury cntr 200 south 6th St Minneapolis MN 55402-1425 E-mail: rgreener@fredlaw.com.

GREENFIELD, JOHN CHARLES, bio-organic chemist; b. Dayton, Ohio, 1945; s. Ivan Ralph and Mildred Louise (House) G.; m. Liga Miervaldis, aug. 2, 1980; children: John Hollen, Mark Richard. BS cum laude, Ohio U., 1967; PhD, U. Ill., 1974. Instr. sci. area h.s., Dayton, 1968-71; grad. rsch. asst. U. Ill., 1971-74; postdoctoral rsch. fellow Swiss

Fed. Inst. Tech., Zurich, 1975-76; rsch. chemist infectious diseases rsch. Upjohn Co., Kalamazoo, 1976-82, sr. rsch. scientist drug metabolism rsch., 1982-93; sr. project mgr. Upjohn Labs., 1993-95, Pharmacia & Upjohn Inc., Kalamazoo, 1995-96; acquisitions review specialist, bus. devel. Pharmacia and Upjohn, Inc., 1996-98, clin. monitor, U.S. market co. med. affairs, 1998-2000; dir. global med. svcs. Pharmacia Inc., 2000—. Contbr. articles to sci. jours.; patentee in field. Adult leader Boy Scouts Am. Am.-Swiss Found. for Sci. Exchange fellow, 1975; NSF-NATO postdoctoral fellow, 1975-76 Mem. AAAS, Am. Chem. Soc. (chmn. Kalamazoo sect. 1994, Disting. Svc. award 1996), N.Y. Acad. Scis., Am. Assn. Pharm. Scientists, Am. Assn. Microbiology, Drug Info. Assn., Am. Soc. Hematology, Sigma Xi, Phi Eta Sigma, Blue Key, Phi Lambda Upsilon, Delta Tau Delta. Achievements include identification, evaluation, and management of worldwide research and development projects for new pharmaceutical agents. Home: 6695 E E Ave Richland MI 49083-9471 Office: Pharmacia Inc 7000 Portage Rd Kalamazoo MI 49001-0199

GREENFIELD, LAZAR JOHN, surgeon, educator; b. Houston, Dec. 14, 1934; s. Robert G. and Betty B. (Greenfield) Heath; m. Sharon Dee Bishkin, Aug. 29, 1956; children: John, Julie, Jeff. Student, Rice U., 1951-54; M.D., Baylor U., 1958. Diplomate: Am. Bd. Surgery (dir. 1976-82), Am. Bd. Thoracic Surgery, cert. gen. vascular surgery, 1991. Intern Johns Hopkins Hosp., Balt., 1958-59, resident, 1961-66; chief surgery VA Hosp., Oklahoma City, 1966-74; prof. dept. surgery U. Okla. Med. Center, 1971-74; Stuart McGuire prof., chmn. dept. surgery Med. Coll. Va., Richmond, 1974-87; F.A. coller prof., chmn. dept of surgery U. Mich., 1987—. Mem. surgery A study sect. NIH. Author: Surgery in the Aged, 1975; editor-in-chief Surgery, Scientific Principles and Practice, 1993; editor Complications in Surgery and Trauma, 1983, 2d edit., 1990; contbr. to profl. publs. Served with USPHS, 1959-61. Thomas R. Franklin scholar, 1952; John and Mary Markle scholar in med. sci., 1968-73 Mem. Inst. of Medicine of NAS, Am. Surg. Assn., Am. Assn. Thoracic Surgery, Assn. Acad. Surgery, Soc. Univ. Surgeons, Phi Delta Epsilon. Home: 505 E Huron St Ann Arbor MI 48104-1573 Office: U Mich Med Sch 2101 Taubman Ctr Ann Arbor MI 48109-0346

GREENFIELD, LEE, state legislator; b. Bklyn., July 29, 1941; s. Solomen and Edith (Herschman) G.; m. Marcia Greenfield, Nov. 25, 1965. BS in Physics, Purdue U., West Lafayette, Ind., 1963; postgrad., U. Minn., 1963-73. Instr. applied math. U. Minn., Mpls., 1964-73; prin. asst. Hennepin County Bd. Commrs., 1975-77; mgmt. analyst Office of Planning & Devel., Hennepin County, 1977; rep. Minn. Ho. of Reps., St. Paul, 1979-2000; prin. adminstrv. asst. Hennepin County Ctr. for Health Policy/Cmty. Svcs. Integration, 2001—. Mem. steering com. Reforming State Group, N.Y.C., 1993, chmn., 1994-96. Bd. dirs. Twin City Cmty. Program for Affordable Health Care, Mpls., 1982-84, Arthritis Found., Mpls., 1988-90, Freeport West, Mpls., 1982—, Ams. for Dem. Action, Mpls., 1979—, v.p., 1976-78. Recipient Dwight V. Dixon award Mental Health Assn. Minn., 1994. Mem. Mental Health Assn. Minn. (Disting. Svc. award 1987), Planned Parenthood of Minn. (Pub. Svc. award 1993). Mem. Democratic-Farmer-Labor Party. Jewish. Office: Hennepin County Health Policy Ctr A-1702 Government Center Minneapolis MN 55487-0172 E-mail: lee.greenfield@co.hennepin.mn.us.

GREENFIELD, NORMAN SAMUEL, psychologist, educator; b. N.Y.C., June 2, 1923; s. Max and Dorothy (Hertz) G.; m. Marjorie Hanson Klein, May 17, 1969; children— Ellen Beth, Jennifer Ann, Susan Emery. BA, NYU, 1948; MA, U. Calif., Berkeley, 1951, PhD, 1953. Fellow med. psychology Langley Porter Clinic, U. Calif. Med. Center, 1949-50; VA Mental Health Clinic trainee San Francisco, 1950-53; instr. clin. psychology U. Oreg. Med. Sch., 1953-54; from asst. prof. to prof. psychiatry U. Wis. Med. Sch. at, Madison, 1954—; assoc. dir. Wis. Psychiat. Inst., U. Wis. Center for Health Scis., 1961-74. Emeritus prof. psychiatry, 1991—. Co-editor: The New Hospital Psychiatry, Handbook of Psychophysiology, Psychoanalysis and Current Biological Thought; contbr. articles to profl. jours. Served with USAAF, 1943-46. Mem. AAUP, Am. Psychol. Assn., Soc. Psychophysiol. Rsch., Am. Psychosomatic Soc. Office: U Wis Psychiat Inst 6001 Research Park Blvd Madison WI 53719-1176 E-mail: ngreen5921@aol.com.

GREENGUS, SAMUEL, academic administrator, religion educator; b. Chgo., Mar. 11, 1936; s. Eugene and Thelma (Romirowsky) G.; m. Lesha Bellows, Apr. 30, 1957; children: Deana, Rachel, Judith. Student, Hebrew Theol. Coll., Chgo., 1950-58; MA, U. Chgo., 1959, PhD, 1963. Prof. semitic langs. Hebrew Union Coll.-Jewish Inst. Religion, Cin., 1963-89, Julian Morgenstern prof. bible and near eastern lit., 1989—, dean rabbinic sch., 1979-84, dean Cin. campus, 1985-87, dean sch. grad. studies, 1985-90, dean faculty, 1987-98, v.p. for Acad. affairs, 1990-96. Vis. lectr. U. of Dayton, Ohio, 1964-69, Leo Baeck Coll., London, 1976-77; area supr. Tel Gezer Excavation, Israel, 1966-67; mem. bd. editors Hebrew Union Coll. Ann. Author: Old Babylonian Tablets from Ishchali and Vicinity, 1979, Studies in Ishchali Documents, 1986; mem. bd. editors Zeitschrift fur Altorientalische und Biblische Rechtsgeschichte; contbr. articles to profl. jours. Mem. Cin. Community Hebrew Schs. Bd., 1970-75; mem. vis. com. Sch. for Creative and Performing Arts, Cin., 1980-82; chmn. acad. officers, Greater Cin. Consortium Colls. and Univs., 1984-85, mem. exec. com., 1989-96. Am. Council Learned Socs. fellow, 1970-71, Am. Assn. Theol. Schs. fellow, 1976-77. Mem. Am. Oriental Soc., Assn. Jewish Studies, Soc. Bibl. Lit., Phi Beta Kappa. Jewish. Office: Hebrew Union Coll Jewish Inst Religion 3101 Clifton Ave Cincinnati OH 45220-2404

GREENHILL, H. GAYLON, retired academic administrator; Chancellor U. Wis., Whitewater, 1991-99, chancellor emeritus, 1999—. Address: PO Box 507 Whitewater WI 53190-0507 E-mail: greenhig@mail.uww.edu.

GREENKORN, ROBERT ALBERT, chemical engineering educator; b. Oshkosh, Wis., Oct. 12, 1928; s. Frederick John and Sophie (Phillips) G.; m. Rosemary Drexler, Aug. 16, 1952; children: David Michael, Eileen Anne, Susan Marie, Nancy Joanne. Student, Oshkosh State Coll., 1951-52; BS, U. Wis., 1954, MS, 1955, PhD, 1957. Postdoctoral fellow Norwegian Tech. Inst., 1957-58; rsch. engr. Jersey Prodn. Rsch. Co., Tulsa, 1958-63; lectr. U. Tulsa, 1958-63; assoc. prof. theoretical and applied mechanics Marquette U., Milw., 1963-65; assoc. prof. chem. engring. Purdue U., Lafayette, Ind., 1965-67, prof., head chem. engring. dept., 1967-72, asst. dean engring., 1972-76, assoc. dean engring., dir. engring. expt. sta., 1976-80, v.p., assoc. provost, 1980-86; v.p. programs Purdue Rsch. Found., 1980-94, v.p. rsch., 1986-92, v.p. rsch., dean grad. sch., 1993-94, spl. asst. to the pres., 1994-2000, v.p. spl. programs, 1994-2000, R. Games Slayter disting. prof. chem. engring., 1995-2000, R. Games Slayter disting. prof. emeritus chem. engring., 2000—. Rsch. coord. Ind. Clean Mfg. and Safe Materials Inst., 1994-2000; dir. Tech. Assistance Program, 1996-2000. Author: (with D.P. Kessler) Transfer Operations, 1972, (with K.C. Chao) Thermodynamics of Fluids: An Introduction to Equilibrium Theory, 1975, (with D.P. Kessler) Modeling and Data Analysis for Engineers and Scientists, 1980, Flow Phenomena in Porous Media, 1983, Momentum, Heat and Mass Transfer Fundamentals (with D.P. Kessler), 1999; contbr. articles to profl. jours. Served with USN, 1946-51. Decorated D.F.C., Air medal with two oak leaf clusters; recipient Fellow Members awd., Am. Soc. for Engineering Education, 1992. Fellow AIChE, Am. Soc. Engring. Edn.; mem. AAAS, Soc. Petroleum Engrs., Am. Chem. Soc., Am. Geophys. Union, Sigma Xi, Phi Eta Sigma, Tau Beta Pi, Phi Gamma Delta. Roman Catholic. Achievements include patents in field. Home: 151 Knox Dr West Lafayette IN 47906-2147

GREENLER, ROBERT GEORGE, physics educator, researcher; b. Kenton, Ohio, Oct. 24, 1929; s. Dallas George and Ruth Edna (Mallett) G.; m. Barbara Stacy, May 30, 1954; children: Leland S., Karen R., Robin A. BS in Physics, U. Rochester, 1951; PhD in Physics, Johns Hopkins U., 1957. Research scientist Allis-Chalmers Mfg. Co., Milw., 1957-62; assoc. prof. physics U. Wis., 1962-67, prof., 1967-91, adj. prof., 1991-98, prof. emeritus, 1998—. Sr. vis. fellow U. East Anglia, Norwich, Eng., 1971-72; traveling lectr. Optical Soc. Am., 1973-74; lectr. Coop. Edn. Program, Malaysia, 1990-91; organizer pub. outreach program Sci. Bag; prodr. 25 ednl. videos; did field rsch. on optical atmospheric effects at U.S. Antarctic Rsch. Station, South Pole, 1976-77, 97-98, 98-99. Author: Rainbows, Halos and Glories, 1980, Chasing the Rainbow: Recurrences in the Life of a Scientist, 2000; contbr. 80 articles to profl. jours. Sr. Fulbright scholar Fritz Haber Inst. of Max Planck Soc., West Berlin, 1983; grantee NSF, Petroleum Research Fund, Am. Chem. Soc. Fellow AAAS, Optical Soc. Am. (v.p. 1985, pres.-elect 1986, pres. 1987, 1st Esther Hoffman Beller award 1993); mem. Am. Assn. Physics Tchrs. (Milikan Lectr. award 1988). Achievements include research in surface science, infrared spectroscopy of adsorbed molecules, meteorological optics, iridescent colors in biological systems. Home: 1901 W Pioneer Rd Mequon WI 53097-1737 Office: U Wis Milw Dept Physics PO Box 413 Milwaukee WI 53201-0413 E-mail: greenler@uwm.edu.

GREENOUGH, WILLIAM TALLANT, psychobiologist, educator; b. Seattle, Oct. 11, 1944; s. Harrison and Maryon C. (Whitten) G.; 1 dau., Jennifer Anne. B.A., U. Oreg., 1964; M.A., UCLA, 1966, Ph.D., 1969. Instr. U. Ill., Urbana-Champaign, 1968-69, asst. prof., 1969-73, assoc. prof., 1973-77, chair neural and behavioral biology program, 1977-87, prof. psychology, psychiatry, cell and structural biology, 1978—; assoc. dir. Beckman Inst. for Advanced Sci. and Tech., 1987-91; prof. U. Ill. Ctr. Advanced Study, 1997—, Swanlund prof. psychology, psychiatry, cell biology, bioeng., 1998—, prof. neurosci. program, 1998—, dir., 2000—. Vis. prof. psychobiology U. Calif., Irvine, 1972; vis. prof. psychology U. Wash., 1975-76; program chmn. Winter Conf. on Brain Rsch., 1984-85, conf. chair, 1994-95; panel mem. integrative neural sys. NSF, 1987-91; dir. NSF Ctr. of Neurobiology of Learning and Memory, 1989-94; v.p., exec. com. Forum on Rsch. Mgmt., Fed. Behavioral, Psychol. and Cognitive Scis., 1991-93; mem. sci. adv. bd. Am. Psychol. Assn. Sci. Directorate; mem. NSF Biol. Sci. Directorate Adv. Com. Editor: (with R.N. Walsh) Environments as Therapy for Brain Dysfunction, 1976, (with J.M. Juraska) Developmental Neuropsychobiology, 1987; co-editor jour. Neurobiol. Learning and Memory, 1984—; contbr. numerous articles to profl. jours. Recipient William Rosen award for rsch. Nat. Fragile X Found., 1998; Cattell Found. fellow, 1975-76; USPHS and NSF grantee, 1969— ; U. Ill. sr. scholar, 1985-88. Fellow AAAS (chair sect. I, Psychology 2001-02), APA (Disting. Sci. Contbn. award 1999), Am. Psychol. Soc. (William James Fellow award), Soc. Exptl. Psychology; mem. NAS, Soc. Neurosci. (councilor 1990-94), Soc. Devel. Neurosci., Soc. Devel. Psychobiology (bd. dirs. 1977-80), Sigma Xi. Achievements include research interests in morphological plasticity of cerebellum, experience and learning-based synapse formation, molecular mechanisms of mental retardation, and plasticity of glial cells. Home: 1919 Melrose Dr Apt C Champaign IL 61820-2013 Office: U Ill Beckman Inst 405 N Mathews Ave Urbana IL 61801-2325 E-mail: wgreenou@psych.uiuc.edu.

GREENSTEIN, JULIUS SIDNEY, zoology educator; b. Boston, July 13, 1927; s. Samuel and Helen (Shriber) G.; m. Joette Mason, Aug. 23, 1954; children: Gail Susan, Jodi Beth, Jay Mason, Blake Jeffrey, Joette Elise. BA, Clark U., 1948; MS, U. Ill., 1951, PhD, 1955; postgrad., Harvard U., 1966. Mem. faculty U. Mass., Amherst, 1954-59; faculty Duquesne U., Pitts., 1959-70, chmn. dept. biol. scis., 1961-70, prof., 1964-70; prof., chmn. dept. biology State SUNY, Fredonia, 1970-74, acting dean arts and scis., 1973-74; dean math. and natural scis. Shippensburg (Pa.) U., 1974-80; also dir. Ctr. for Sci. and the Citizen; pres. Ctrl. Ohio Tech. Coll., 1980-94, pres. emeritus, 1994—; dean, dir. Ohio State U., Newark, 1980-94, prof. zoology, 1980—. Vis. lectr. Am. Inst. Biol. Scis., 1966-76; disting. vis. prof. USAF Acad., 1994-95. Author: Contemporary Readings in Biology, 1971, Readings in Living Systems, 1972; spl. editor Internat. Jour. Fertility, 1958-69, Contraception, 1970-77; columnist Newark Advocate, 1981-93, Licking Countian, 1993-94; contbr. articles to profl. jours. Mem. Carnegie Civic Symphony Orch.; mem. sci. adv. bd. Human Life Found.; trustee Licking Meml. Hosp., Licking County Symphony Orch.; mem. campaign cabinet United Way Licking County; exec. bd. Cen. Ohio Rural Consortium and Pvt. Industry Coun.; mem. higher edn. panel Am. Coun. on Edn., labor com. Higher Edn. Coun. Ohio. Served in armored div. AUS, World War II. Recipient Wisdom award honor, 197O Mem. AAAS, Am. Assn. Acad. Deans, Am. Assn. Univ. Admintrs., Am. Assn. Anatomists, Am. Inst. Biol. Scis., Internat. Fertility Assn., Am. Soc. Zoologists, Am. Fertility Soc., Soc. Study Fertility (Eng.), Coun. Biol. Editors, Pa. Acad. Sci. (editorial bd. 1963-70), N.Y. State Acad. Sci., Soc. Study Devel. Biology, Ohio Assn. Regional Campuses (vice chair 1988-89, chair 1989-90, pres.), North Cen. Assn. Colls. and Schs. (cons., evaluator), Newark C. of C., Rotary, Sigma Xi. Achievements include contributions to understanding of causes and prevention of reproductive failure in mammals by studying early developmental stages of embryo, nature of male and female reproductive organs and endocrine glands; developed new techniques for staining specimens and smears; first to demonstrate that estradiol injections cause corpus luteum regression, hence early termination of pregnancy; investigated relationship of specific diseases to normal reproductive performance. Home: 1284 Howell Dr Newark OH 43055-1742 Office: Ohio State U at Newark University Dr Newark OH 43055-1797

GREENSTREET, ROBERT CHARLES, architect, educator; b. London, June 8, 1952; s. Joseph Philip Henry and Joan (Dean) G.; m. Karen Eloise Holland, Sept. 6, 1975. Diploma in architecture, Oxford Brookes U., 1976, PhD in Architecture, 1983. Registered architect, Eng. Vis. asst. prof. Kans. State U., 1978-79; asst. prof. U. Kans., 1979-80; vis. prof. Ball State U., Muncie, 1980-81; prof. U. Wis., 1981—, asst. vice chancellor, 1985-86, chmn. dept. architecture, 1986-90, dean Sch. Architecture and Urban Planning, 1990-2000, dep. chancellor for campus and urban design, 2000—. Author, co-author 7 books; contbr. more than 150 articles to profl. jours. Fellow Royal Soc. Arts; mem. AIA (assoc.), Royal Inst. Brit. Architects, Wis. Soc. Architects, Chartered Inst. Arbitrators; mem. Am. Arbitration Assn., Assn. Collegiate Schs. of Architecture (pres. 1995-96). Anglican. Office: U Wis Dept Architecture PO Box 413 Milwaukee WI 53201-0413

GREENWALD, GERALD, air transportation executive; b. St. Louis, Sept. 11, 1935; s. Frank and Bertha G.; m. Glenda Lee Gerstein, June 29, 1958; children: Scott, Stacey, Bradley, Joshua. BA Cumlaude (Univ. scholar), Princeton U., 1957; MA, Wayne State U., 1962. With Ford Motor Co., 1957-79; pres. Ford Venezuela; dir. non-automotive ops. Europe; vice chmn. Chrysler Corp., Highland Park, Mich., 1979-85; chmn. Chrysler Motors, 1985-88; vice chmn. Chrysler Corp., 1988-90; chief exec. officer United Employee Acquisition Corp., 1990; pres., mng. dir. Dillon, Read & Co. Inc., N.Y.C., 1991-92; pres., co. CEO Olympia & York, Toronto, 1992-93; chmn. Tatra, 1993-94; chmn., CEO, UAL Corp., Elk Grove Township, Ill., 1994-98. Bd. dirs. Aetna and Princeton, AOL Time Warner. Civic Com. of Chgo., USAF, 1957-60. Mem. Econ. Club Chgo., Princeton (trustee).

GREENWALD, GILBERT SAUL, physiologist; b. N.Y.C., June 24, 1927; s. Morris M. and Celia G.; m. Pola Gorsky, Sept. 9, 1950; children: Susan Greenwald Waxman, Elizabeth Greenwald Jordan, Douglas. AB with honors, U. Calif., Berkeley, 1949, PhD in Zoology, 1954. Postdoctoral fellow dept. embryology USPHS Carnegie Inst. Washington, 1954-56; instr., then asst. prof. anatomy U. Wash. Med. Sch., Seattle, 1956-61; mem. faculty U. Kans. Med. Ctr., Kansas City, 1961-96, disting. prof. physiology, 1977-96, univ. disting. prof., 1995, disting. prof. emeritus, 1996—, chmn. dept. physiology, 1977-93, prof. ob-gyn., 1977-93, prof. anatomy, ob-gyn., 1965-77, rsch. prof. in human reprodn., 1961-77. Mem. reproductive biology study sect. NIH, 1966-70, mem. population rsch. adv. com., 1967-71; mem. regulatory biol. panel NSF, 1984-86 Editor Biology of Reprodn., 1974-77. With USNR, 1944-45. Recipient Higuchi Biomed. Sci. award U. Kans., 1984; USPHS fellow Carnegie Instn., 1954-56. Mem. AAAS, Soc. Study of Reprodn. (pres. 1971, Disting. Svc. award 1988, Carl Hartman award 1993), Endocrine Soc., Brit. Soc. Study Fertility, Am. Physiol. Soc., Soc. Exptl. Biology and Medicine (councillor 1991-95), Sigma Xi. Office: U Kans Med Ctr 39th and Rainbow Blvd Kansas City KS 66103 E-mail: ggreenwa@kumc.edu.

GREENWALT, TIBOR JACK, physician, educator; b. Budapest, Hungary, Jan. 23, 1914; arrived in U.S., 1920, naturalized, 1943; s. Bela and Irene (Foldes) Greenwalt; m. Shirley Johnson, Aug. 6, 1960 (dec. Sept. 1970); 1 child Peter H. ; m. Pia Glas, Feb. 27, 1971 (dec. July 1996). BA summa cum laude, MD, NYU, 1937. Diplomate Am. Bd. Internal Medicine. Intern pathology and bacteriology Mt. Sinai Hosp., N.Y.C., 1937—38; rotating intern Kings County Hosp., Bklyn., 1938—40; resident medicine Montefiore Hosp., N.Y.C., 1940—41; research asso. New Eng. Med. Center, Boston, 1941—42; med. dir. Milw. Blood Center, 1947—66; faculty medicine Marquette U. Sch. Medicine, 1948—66, prof. medicine, 1963—66; cons. hematology VA Hosp., Wood, Wis., 1946—66, Milw. County Gen. Hosp., 1948—66; dir. blood program ARC, 1967—78, sr. sci. adviser blood program, 1978—79; clin. prof. medicine George Washington U. Sch. Medicine, 1967—79; prof. medicine U. Cin. Med. Center, 1979—84, prof. emeritus medicine and pathology, 1984—; dir. Hoxworth Blood Center, 1979—87, dir. research, 1987—. Chmn. com. blood and transfusion problems NAS-NRC, 1963—66; mem. hematology study sect. NIH, 1960—63, chmn., 1970—72; vis. prof., spkr. throughout U.S., 1960—; mem. Med. Rsch. Srv. Merit Rev. Bd. for Hematology, VA, 1981—83; mem. blood diseases and resources adv. com. Nat. Heart, Lung and Blood Inst., 1983—87, adv. coun., 1986—90, coordinating com. Nat. Blood Resources Edn. Program, adv. com. Office of Prevention Edn. and Control, 1987—91. Author (with others): Hemolytic Syndromes, 1942; author: (with Shirley Greenwalt) Coagulation and Transfusion in Clinical Medicine, 1965; editor (with Graham A. Jamieson): The Red Cell Membrane, 1969; editor: Formation and Destruction of Blood Cells, 1970, Glycoproteins of Plasma and Membranes, 1971, The Human Red Cell in Vitro, 1974, Transmissible Disease and Blood Transfusion, 1974, Trace Proteins of Plasma, 1976, The Granuloctye, 1977, Blood Substitutes and Plasma Expanders, 1978, The Blood Platelet in Transfusion Therapy, 1978, Methods in Hematology: Blood Transfusion, 1988, History of International Society of Blood Transfusion, 2000; editor, contbr.: Immunogenetics, 1967, editor-in-chief: Transfusion, 1960—66, assoc. editor: , 1966—86, mem. editl. bd.: Gen. Prins. of Blood Transfusion, 1962—83, mem. editl. bd.: Vox Sanguinis, 1956—76, mem. editl. bd.: Haematologia, 1968—90, mem. editl. bd.: Blood, 1979—84; contbr. articles to profl. lit. Maj. M.C. U.S. Army, 1942—46. Recipient Gold medal, Caduceus Soc., NYU, 1933, Jr. Achievement award for outstanding contbn. sci., 1958, 1st Charles R. Drew award, ARC, Washington, 1981, Disting. Citizen's award, Allied Vets. Coun., 1963, award pioneer blood group rsch., Ctr. for Immunology, SUNY, Buffalo, 1976, Witebsky lectureship, 1994, Albion O. Bernstein award, Med. Soc. State N.Y., 1997. Fellow: AAAS, N.Y. Acad. Scis.; mem.: ACP, Am. Soc. Human Genetics, Soc. Exptl. Biology and Medicine, Am. Assn. Immunologists, Am. Soc. Hematology (treas. 1963—67), Ohio Sci. Roundtable, Internat. Soc. Haemostasis and Thrombosis (life), Inst. Medicine (sr.), Ctrl. Soc. Clin. Rsch., Am. Soc. Clin. Pathologists, Internat. Soc. Blood Transfusion (pres. 1966—72, historian 1975—96), Internat. Soc. Hematology, Am. Assn. Blood Banks (v.p. 1959—60, med. dir. ctrl. file rare donors 1960—66, 50th anniversary com., John Elliot award 1966, Grove-Rasmussen award 1988, Bernard Fantus medal 1993, Tibor J. Greenwalt lectr. 1997—), Cosmos Club, Alpha Omega Alpha, Sigma Xi. Home: 2444 Madison Rd #1501 Cincinnati OH 45208-1228 Office: Hoxworth Blood Ctr 3130 Highland Ave Cincinnati OH 45267-0001 E-mail: tjgreenwalt@aol.com.

GREENWOOD, DANN E. lawyer; b. Dickinson, N.D., Sept. 21, 1952; s. Lawrence E. and Joyce E. (Henley) G.; m. Debra K. Ableidinger, June 15, 1975; children: Jay, Lindsey, Paige. BSBA magna cum laude, U. N.D., 1974, JD, 1977. Bar: N.D. 1977, U.S. Dist. Ct. N.D. 1980. Ptnr. Greenwood, Greenwood & Greenwood and predecessor firms, Dickinson, 1977-98, Greenwood & Ramsey PLLP, 1998—. Mem. N.D. Supreme Ct. Disciplinary Bd., 1983-89, Northern Lights Boy Scouts Council, Dickinson, 1985—; bd. dirs. Legal Assistance N.D., Bismarck, 1980-86. Mem. N.D. Bar Assn. (pres. 1998-99), Stark-Dunn County Bar Assn., N.D. Trial Lawyers Assn. (sec. 1983-84, treas. 1984-85, v.p. 1985-86, pres. 1987-88). Lutheran. Lodges: Kiwanis, Masons, Shriners, Elks. Home: PO Box 688 Dickinson ND 58602-0688 E-mail: shadyln@pop.ctctel.com., grlawdg@ndsupernet.com.

GREENWOOD, TIM, former state legislator, lawyer; m. Linda J. Greenwood; children: Kelly, Katharine. BA, Denison U., 1971; JD, U. Toledo, 1978. Bar: Ohio 1978. Ptnr. Spengler & Nathanson, Toledo, Spengler, Nathanson, Heyman, McCarthy & Durfee, Toledo; mem. Ohio Senate, Columbus, 1994-97, Ohio Turnpike Commn, Mem. Ho. Ho. of Reps., Columbus, 1989-92, 93-94; active United Way, Toledo-Northwestern Ohio Foodbank. Named Freshman Legislator of Yr., 1990. Mem. Ohio Bar Assn., Toledo Bar Assn., Toledo Jr. Bar Assn. (pres.), Sylvania C. of C., Legis. Exch. Coun. Republican. Home: 4325 Mockingbird Ln Toledo OH 43623-3218

GREER, CARL CRAWFORD, petroleum company executive; b. Pitts., June 12, 1940; s. Joseph Moss and Gene (Crawford) G.; m. Jerrine Ehlers, June 16, 1962 (div.); children: Caryn, Michael, Janet; m. Patricia Taylor, Feb. 4, 1989. B.S., Lehigh U., 1962; Ph.D., Columbia U., 1966; PsyD, Ill. Sch. Profl. Psychology, Chgo., 1993. Lic. clin. psychologist and Jungian analyst. Assoc. in bus. Columbia U., 1964-66, asst. prof. banking and finance, 1966-67; retail mktg. mgr. Martin Oil Service Inc., Alsip, Ill., 1967-68, exec. v.p., 1968, pres., dir., 1968-76, chmn. bd., pres., 1976-85; pres., dir. Martin Mktg. Corp. GP Martin Oil Mktg. Ltd., 1982, MEMCO Mgmt. Corp. GP Martin Exploration Mgmt. Co., 1985. Bd. dirs. Fin. Assocs., Inc., Source Precision Medicine. Mem. Beta Theta Pi, Tau Beta Pi, Beta Gamma Sigma, Omicron Delta Kappa. Presbyterian.

GREER, NORRIS E. lawyer; b. San Francisco, June 21, 1945; BA, U. Mo., Kansas City, 1967, JD, 1974. Bar: Mo. 1974. Atty. Shughart Thomson & Kilroy, Kansas City, Mo. Mem. ABA, Nat. Assn. Coll. and Univ. Attys., The Mo. Bar, Kansas City Met. Bar Assn., Lawyers Assn. Kansas City. Office: Shughart Thomson & Kilroy 12 Wyandotte Plz 120 W 12th St Ste 1500 Kansas City MO 64105-1929

GREER, RICHARD, radio personality; b. Syracuse, N.Y., July 11, 1950; children: Bill, Sarah. Radio host WNWV, Elyria, Ohio, 1990—. Avocations: singing, guitar, photography. Office: WNWV 538 W 2d St PO Box 4006 Elyria OH 44036*

GREER, THOMAS H. newspaper executive; b. Nashville, July 24, 1942; s. Thomas H. and Eliza (Scruggs) G.; children: Kasey Lynn, Janna Whitney. BA in Polit. Sci., Dillard U., 1963. News/sports reporter Trenton (N.J.) Evening Times, 1965-73; news reporter The Plain Dealer, Cleve., 1973-75, sports editor, 1983-86, mng. editor, 1986-89, exec. editor, 1989-92, v.p., sr. editor, 1992-98; sr. v.p., 1998—; sports writer, columnist

Phila. Daily News, 1977-80; sports columnist N.Y. Daily News, 1980-83. Judge Scripps-Howard Founds. Walker Stone/Editl. Writing award, 1993; nominating jury mem. Pulitzer Prize, 1989-90. Bd. dirs. Greater Cleve. Roundtable, Cleve., Bus. Volunteerism Coun., ARC, Cleve., Cuyahoga Plan, Plain Dealer Credit Union, Am. Cancer Soc. Named Paul Miller Disting. Journalism Lectr., Oklahoma State U., 1993. Mem. Am. Press Inst., Nat. Assn. Minority Media Execs. (bd. dirs.), Freedom Forum's Adv. Coun. for Sports Journalism, Am. Soc. Newspaper Editors, Nat. Assn. Black Journalists, AP Mng. Editors Assn., AP Sports Editors' Assn., Cleve. Zool. Soc., Cleve. Press Club, Omega Psi Phi. Office: The Plain Dealer 1801 Superior Ave E Cleveland OH 44114-2198

GREER, WILLIS ROSWELL, JR. accounting educator; b. Memphis, Nov. 16, 1938; s. Willis Roswell and Myra Bell (Bridges) G.; m. Melinda S. Scott, June 28, 1963; children: Howard Willis, Catherine Irene Grubbs, Charles Walker. BS, Cornell U., 1961, MBA with distinction, 1966; PhD in Acctg., U. Mich., 1971. Cert. Mgmt. Acct., Cert. Bus. Appraiser. Lectr. acctg. and stats. U. West Indies, Trinidad, 1966-67; teaching asst., Paton fellow U. Mich., 1967-71; asst. prof. acctg. U. Oreg., 1971-75, assoc. prof., 1975-76; vis. prof. acctg. Dartmouth Coll., Amos Tuck Sch., 1976-77, assoc. prof., 1976-82; vis. scholar Manchester (Eng.) Bus. Sch., 1981; prof. acctg. Naval Postgrad. Sch., 1982-88, acad. assoc. fin. mgmt., 1983-84, chmn. dept. adminstrv. scis., 1984-87; prof. acctg. U. Iowa, Iowa City, 1988-96, assoc. dean grad. programs, 1989-92, head dept. acctg., 1992-95; lectr. acctg. and fin. analysis Tohoku U., Japan, 1993-94; dean Coll. Bus. Adminstrn. U. No. Iowa, Cedar Falls, 1996—. Cons. U.S. Small Bus. Adminstrn. Minority Bus. Devel. Program, several large firms in various mfg. and svc. industries; presenter numerous seminars and workshops. Co-author: (with Paul Wasserman) Consultants and Consulting Organizations, 1966, (with J. Peter Williamson) Interim Inventory Estimation Error, 1979, (with Shu Liao) Cost Analysis for Dual Source Weapon Procurement, 1983, Cost Analysis for Competitive Major Weapon Systems Procurement: Further Refinement and Extension, 1984; author: A Method for Estimating and Controlling the Cost of Extending Technology, 1988; editor: (with Dan Nussbaum) Cost Analysis and Estimating: Tools and Techniques, 1990; contbr. articles to profl. jours. Treas. Oaknoll Retirement Cmty., 1993—. Mem. Inst. Mgmt. Accts. (dir. Cedar Rapids chpt. 1990—), Am. Acctg. Assn., Decision Scis. Inst., Inst. Bus. Appraisers, Inc. Republican. Achievements include research on conditions under which dual source procurement of major weapon systems is beneficial to goverment; building an accurate model for forecasting research and development costs for specified technology advancement; avocations: travel, photography. Home: PO Box 224 Rollins MT 59931-0224

GREFE, ROLLAND EUGENE, lawyer; b. Ida County, Iowa, June 27, 1920; s. Alfred William and Zoma Corrine (Lasher) G.; m. Mary Arlene Cruikshank, June 12, 1943; 1 son, Roger Frederick. BA, Morningside Coll., 1941; JD, State U. Iowa, 1946. Bar: Iowa 1946. Assoc. Schaetzle, Williams & Stewart, Des Moines, 1946-48, Schaetzle, Swift, Austin & Stewart, Des Moines, 1948-52; ptnr. Schaetzle, Austin & Grefe (and related firms), 1952-60, Austin, Grefe & Sidney, Des Moines, 1960-71; sr. ptnr. Grefe & Sidney, 1971-95; mem. Grefe & Sidney P.L.C., 1995—. Dir. Freeman Decorating Co., 1969— , Cowles Syndicate, Inc., 1982-86; mem. bd. mgrs. Lawyers Com. Network, L.L.C., 1997-2000, chair, 1998-2000. Bd. dirs. Des Moines Area C.C., 1966-76, pres., 1967-76; bd. dirs. Westminster Presbyn. Ch. Found., 1975-89, Iowa State Bar Found., 1979-91; trustee Des Moines Water Works, 1984-99, pres., 1987, 91, 96. Lt. USNR, 1942-45. Fellow Am. Bar Found., Am. Coll. Trust and Estate Counsel; mem. ABA (ho. of dels. 1982-96, Iowa state del. 1992-93, bd. govs. 1993-96, standing com. on tech. and info. systems 1998-2001, sr. lawyers divsn. chair internet and tech. com. 2000-02), Assn. Endowment Found. Coll. (mem. pension plan adminstrn. com. 1994-2000), Polk County Bar Assn. (pres. 1971-72), Iowa State Bar Assn. (bd. govs. 1972-76, pres. 1978-79, chmn. com. on long-range planning 1979-81, Award of Merit 1982), Des Moines Estate Planners, Lincoln Inne. Republican. Presbyterian. Clubs: Sertoma (Des Moines), Des Moines (Des Moines), Wakonda (Des Moines). Home: 3524 Grand Ave Apt 803 Des Moines IA 50312-4344 Office: PO Box 10434 2222 Grand Ave Des Moines IA 50312-5306 E-mail: Rgrefe@grefesidney.com.

GREGERSON, LINDA KAREN, poet, language educator; b. Elgin, Ill., Aug. 5, 1950; d. Olaf Thorbjorn and Karen Mildred Gregerson; m. Steven Mullaney, 1980; children: Emma Mullaney, Megan Mullaney. BA, Oberlin Coll., 1971; MA, Northwestern U., 1972; MFA, U. Iowa, 1977; PhD, Stanford U., 1987. Actress Kraken, 1972-75; staff editor Atlantic Monthly, Boston, 1982-87; asst. prof. English U. Mich., Ann Arbor, 1987-94, assoc. prof., 1994—2001, prof., 2001—. Dir. MFA program in creative writing U. Mich., 1997—2000; mem. usage panel Am. Heritage Dictionary; vis. mem. Inst. for Advanced Study, Princeton, NJ, 1993—94. Author (poetry): Fire in the Conservatory, 1982, The Woman Who Died in Her Sleep, 1996, Waterborne, 2002; author: The Reformation of the Subject: Spenser, MIlton and the English Protestant Epic, 1995, Negative Capability: Contemporary American Poetry, 2001, (work represented in) The Pushcart Prize XIX: Best of the Small Presses, 1994, Nature's Ban: Women's Literature about Incest from the Twelfth Century to the Present, New Bread Loaf Anthology of Contemporary Americn Poetry, 1999; contbr. , poetry to lit. mags. Recipient Levison Prize award Poetry, 1991, Consuelo Ford award, Poetry Soc. Am., 1992, Acad. award in Lit., Am. Acad. Arts and Letters, 2002; fellow, Nat. Endowment Arts, 1985, 1992, Mellon, Nat. Humanities Ctr., 1991—92, Guggenheim, 2000; grantee Arts Found., Mich., 1994. Mem.: MLA, Inst. Advanced Study (vis. mem. 1993—94), Milton Soc., Internat. Spenser Soc. (Isabel MacCaffrey award 1992), Renaissance Soc.Am., Shakespeare Assn. Am. Office: U Mich Dept English Lang and Lit 3187 Angell Hall Ann Arbor MI 48109-1045 Address: 4881 Hidden Brook Ln Ann Arbor MI 48105-9663 E-mail: gregerso@umich.edu.

GREGG, JOHN RICHARD, lawyer, state legislator; b. Sandborn, Ind., Sept. 6, 1954; s. Donald Richard and Beverly June (Blackwood) G.; m. Sherry L. Biddinger, Nov. 18, 1989; children: John Blackwood, Hunter W. AS, Vincennes U., 1974; AB, Ind. U., 1976, JD, 1984; MPA, Ind. State U., 1978. Real estate agt. Peabody Coal, Jasonville, Ind., 1978-79; govt. affairs agt. Amax Coal, Evansville, Indpls., 1979-85; ptnr. Gregg & Brock, Vincennes, 1985—; mem. Ind. Gen. Assembly, 1986—, house majority leader, 1990-94, minority leader, 1994-96, spkr., 1996—. Adj. prof. Vincennes (Ind.) U., 1985—. Active United Meth. Ch.; del. Nat. Dem. Conv. Mem. Wabash Valley Human Svcs. (bd. dirs. 1982-85), Knox County Bar Assn. (pres. 1993), Columbia Club, Indpls. Press Club, Torpedo Club, Knights of Pythias, Sandborn Masonic Lodge (past master 1979), Sigma Pi. Democrat. Home: PO Box 301 Sandborn IN 47578-0301 Office: Indiana House Reps State Capitol Rm 3-2 Indianapolis IN 46204 : 20566 East Jerico Road, PO Box 301 Sandborn IN 47578*

GREGG, LAUREN, women's soccer coach; b. Rochester, Minn., July 20, 1960; BS in Psychology, U. N.C.; MS in Counseling and Consulting Psychology, Harvard U. Asst. soccer coach U. N.C., 1983; asst. coach Harvard U., Cambridge, Mass.; head coach U. Va., 1987-95; asst. coach U.S. Women's Nat. Soccer Team, 1996—. Named Coach of Yr. Nat. Soccer Coaches Assn. Am., 1990; recipient Gold medal Atlanta Olympics, 1996; Marie Jane postgrad. scholar. Office: US Soccer Fedn US Soccer House 1801 S Prairie Ave Chicago IL 60616-1319

GREGG, ROBERT LEE, pharmacist; b. White River, S.D., Mar. 2, 1932; s. C.W. and Margaret (Maguire) G.; m. Julie D. Tyler, June 7, 1956; children: Allen, Mark, Susan. BS, S.D. State U., 1958. Registered pharmacist, S.D. Owner, mgr., pharmacist Kennebec (S.D.) Drug, 1958-79, Gregg Drug, Chamberlain, S.D., 1978—. Adv. coun. Coll. Pharmacy, S.D. State U., Brookings, 1985-98; pres. S.D. Bd. Pharmacy, Pierre, 1992-93. Past sec. Indsl. Devel. Corp., Kennebec; pres. Lake Francis Case Devel. Corp., Chamberlain, 1984-85, Brule County unit Am. Cancer Soc., 1992—. With Med. Svc. Corps, U.S. Army, 1953-55, Korea. Named S.D. Horsepeson of Yr., S.D. Horse Coun., 1999. Mem. S.D. Pharm. Assn. (pres. 1985-86, Bowl of Hygeia award 1992, S.D. Pharmacist of Yr. 1996), Nat. Assn. Retail Druggists, Chamberlain C. of C., NRA (life), VFW (life, quartermaster Kennebec 1965-76, Outstanding Post Quartermaster award 1965), Am. Legion (life), Am. Quarter Horse Assn., S.D. Trail Riders (bd. dirs. 1986-97), KC (4th degree). Republican. Roman Catholic. Avocations: equestrian activities, trail riding, big game hunting. Home: PO Box 459 220 N Grace St Chamberlain SD 57325-1002 Office: PO Box 459 200 N Main St Chamberlain SD 57325-1326

GREGOR, CLUNIE BRYAN, geology educator; b. Edinburgh, Scotland, Mar. 5, 1929; came to U.S., 1968; s. David Clunie Gregor and Barbara Mary Moller-Beilby; m. Suzanne Assir, Apr. 24, 1955 (div. Apr. 1969); 1 child, Andrew James; m. Anna Bramanti, Apr. 15, 1969 (dec. Oct. 1993); children: Thomas James, Matthew James. BA, Cambridge (Eng.) U., 1951, MA, 1954; DSc, U. Utrecht, The Netherlands, 1967. Instr. Am. U. Beirut, 1958-64; rsch. asst. Delft (The Netherlands) Inst. Tech., 1964-65, dir. Crystallographic Lab., 1965-67; vis. prof. Case Western Res. U., Cleve., 1968-69; prof. West Ga. Coll., Carrollton, 1969-72, Wright State U., Dayton, Ohio, 1972—. Chmn. USA work group on geochem. cycles, 1972-88, vice chmn. panel on geochem. cycles NAS, 1988-90. Author: (monograph) Geochemical Behaviour of Sodium, 1967; editor: Chemical Cycles in the Evolution of the Earth, 1988. Grantee NSF, 1977-82, Sicily, 1978-80. Fellow Geol. Soc. (London); mem. Geol. Soc. Am., Am. Geophys. Union, Geochem. Soc. (sec. 1983-89). Home: 136 W North College St Yellow Springs OH 45387-1563 Office: Wright State U Dept Geol Scis Dayton OH 45435

GREGORY, VALISKA, writer; b. Chgo., Nov. 3, 1940; d. Andrej and Stephania (Lascik) Valiska; m. Marshall W. Gregory, Aug. 18, 1962; children: Melissa, Holly. BA cum laude, Ind. Ctrl. Coll., 1962; MA, Univ. Chgo., 1966; postgrad., Vassar Inst. Pub. Writing, 1984, Simmons Coll., 1986. Music and drama tchr. White Oak Elem. Sch., Whiting, Ind., 1962-64; tchr. Oak Lawn (Ill.) Meml. H.S., 1965-68; lectr. English U. Wis., Milw., 1968-74; adj. prof. English U. Indpls., 1974-83, Butler U., Indpls., 1983-85, writer-in-residence, 1993—; fellow Butler Writer's Studio, 1989-92. Founding dir. Butler U. Midwinter Children's Litf. Conf., 1989—; spkr., workshop leader schs., libr., confs., 1993—. Author: Sunny Side Up, 1986 (Chickadee Mag. Book of Month award 1986), Terribly Wonderful, 1986 (Grandparent's Mag. Best Book award 1986), The Oatmeal Cookie, 1987 (Best of Best Book list Chgo. Sun-Times), Riddle Soup, 1987 (Best of Best Book list Chgo. Sun-Times), Through the Mickle Woods (named Pick of List Am. Booksellers Assn. 1992, Parent's Choice award, 1992; State Ind. Read Aloud-List 1993), Happy Burpday, Maggie McDougal!, 1992 (State Ind. Read-aloud List 1993), Babysitting for Benjamin (Parent's Choice Honor award 1993), Kate's Giants, 1995, Loooking for Angels, 1996, (named Picked of the List Am. Book Sellers Assn., 1996), When Stories Fell Like Shooting Stars, 1996, (Family Circle Mag. Critics Choice, 1996), A Valentine for Norman Noggs, 1999, Shirley's Wonderful Baby, 2000. Recipient Ill. Wesleyan U. Poetry award, 1982, hon. mention Billee Murray Denny Nat. Poetry Award Bilee Murray Denny Poetry Found., 1982, Hudelson award Children's Fiction Work-In-Progress, 1982, Artistic Excellence and Achievement award State Art Treasure Arts Ind., 1989; Individual Artist Master fellow Ind. Arts Commn. and Nat. Endowment for Arts, 1986. Mem. AAUW (Creative Writer's pres. 1984-86), Author's Guild, Authors League Am., Soc. Children's Book Writers and Illustrators, Nat. Book Critic's Circle, Children's Reading Round Table, Soc. Midland Authors. Democrat. Office: Butler U 4600 Sunset Ave Indianapolis IN 46208-3487

GREILING, MINDY, state legislator; b. Feb. 1948; m. Roger Greiling; 2 children. BA, Gustavus Adolphis Coll.; MEd, U. Minn. State rep. Minn. Ho. Reps., Dist. 54B, 1993—. Office: 100 Constitution Ave Saint Paul MN 55155-1232

GRENDELL, DIANE V. state legislator, lawyer, nurse; m. Tim Grendell; children: James, Kate. Grad. in nursing, St. John's Coll.; JD, Cleve. Marshall Coll. Law; postgrad., Baldwin Wallace Coll. Bar: Ohio; RN, Ohio. Mem. Ohio Ho. of Reps., Columbus, 1993—. Recipient Seven Seals award, Wilson achievement award. Mem. Ohio Bar Assn., Ohio Nurses Assn., Chester C. of C., Chester and Geauga County Hist. Soc., Farm Bur. (chmn.), Sierra Club. Republican. Home: 7413 Tattersall St Chesterland OH 44026-2036 Office: OH House of Reps State House Columbus OH 43215

GREPPIN, JOHN AIRD COUTTS, philologist, editor, educator; b. Rochester, N.Y., Apr. 2, 1937; s. Ernest Haquette and Edna Barbara (Kill) G.; m. Mary Elizabeth Cleland Hannan, Sept. 30, 1961; children: Sarah Cleland Coutts, Carl Hannan Haquette. AB in Greek, U. Rochester, N.Y., 1961; MA in Classics, U. Wash., 1966; PhD in Indo-European Studies, UCLA, 1972; postdoctoral student, Yerevan State U., USSR, 1974-75. Tchr. Greek, Latin Stowe (Vt.) Prep. Sch., 1961-62; tchr. Woodstock (Vt.) Country Sch., 1962-65, admissions dir., 1968-69; interim asst. prof. U. Fla., Gainesville, 1971-72; tchr. Isidore Newman Sch., New Orleans, 1972-74; from asst. to assoc. to prof. linguistics Cleve. State U., 1975—, dir. program in linguistics, 1979-83, 99—. Vis. prof. linguistics Philipps U., Marburg, Germany, 1993. Author: Initial Vowel and Aspiration in Classical Armenian, 1973, Classical Armenian Nominal Suffixes, 1975, Classical and Middle Armenian Bird Names: A Taxonomic and Mythological Study, 1978, An Etymological Dictionary of the Indo-European Components of Classical Armenian, 1984, Bark Galianosi: The Greek Armenian Dictionary to Galen, 1985, A Handbook of Armenian Dialectology, 1986, An Arabic-Armenian Pharmaceutical Dictionary, 1997, The Diffusion of Greco-Roman Medicine into the Middle East and the Caucasus, 1999; editor: Proc. of 1st Internat. Conf. on Armenian Linguistics, Phila., 1979, (with others) Interrogativity: A Colloquium of the Grammar, Typology and Pragmatics of Questions in Seven Diverse Languages, 1984, When Worlds Collide: The Indo-Europeans and the Pre-Indo-Europeans: The Bellagio Papers, 1990, Studies in Classical Armenian Literature, 1994, Studies in Honor of Jaan Puhvel, Part One: Ancient Languages and Philology, 1997, Part Two: Mythology and Religion, 1997; founding editor Ann. Armenian Linguistics, 1980—, Armenian and Anatolian Studies, 1979—, Proc. 4th Internat. Conf. on Armenian Linguistics, 1992, Classical Armenian Literature: Studies in Early Armenian Authors; mng. editor Raft, A Jour. of Armenian Poetry and Criticism, 1987-2000; contbr. over 200 articles to Am., European and Soviet jours., over 260 revs. to London Times Lit. Supplement, N.Y. Times Book Rev., others. Recipient Silver medal Congregazione Mekhitarista, Venice, Italy, 1978; fellow Am. Coun. Learned Socs., 1965, NEH, 1978-79, NIH, 1984, Internat. Rsch. and Exchs. Bd., 1974-75, grantee, 1979-81, 84-87, 89, 92, 94, 98; grantee AGBU Manoogian Fund, 1977, 79-2001, Gulbenkian Found., 1982, 85, 96, Rockefeller Found., 1987, Am. Coun. Learned Socs., 1987. Mem. Assn. Internat. des Études Arméniennes, Soc. for Study of the Caucasus, Am. Philol. Soc., Linguistic Soc. Am., Soc. for Armenian Studies (mem. exec. bd. 1982-86, sec. 1983-85), Am. Oriental Soc., Soc. Caucasologia Europaea. Avocations: pianist, chamber music assns., bird watching. Home: 3349 Fairmount Blvd Cleveland OH 44118-4262 Office: Cleve State U Dept Linguistics Cleveland OH 44115 Office Fax: 216-687-9214. E-mail: j.greppin@csuohio.edu.

GREVE, JOHN HENRY, veterinary parasitologist, educator; b. Pitts., Aug. 11, 1934; s. John Welch and Edna Viola (Thuenen) G.; m. Sally Jeanette Doane, June 21, 1956; children— John Haven, Suzanne Carol, Pamela Jean B.S., Mich. State U., East Lansing, 1956, D.V.M., 1958, M.S., 1959; Ph.D., Purdue U., West Lafayette, Ind., 1963. Assoc. instr. Mich. State U., East Lansing, 1958-59; instr. Purdue U., West Lafayette, 1959-63; asst. prof. Iowa State U., Ames, 1963-64, assoc. prof., 1964-68, prof. dept. vet. pathology, 1968-99, interim chair dept. vet. pathology, 1992-95, counselor acad. and student affairs, 1991-92. Cons. to Dean on alumni affairs, Coll. Vet. Medicine; cons. parasitologist various zoos Mem. editl. bd. Lab. Animal Sci., 1971-83, Vet. Rsch. Comm., 1977-84, Vet. Parasitology, 1984-98; contbr. articles to sci. jours., chpts. to books. Dist. chmn. Broken Arrow Dist., Boy Scouts Am., Ames, Iowa, 1975-77 Named Disting. Tchr. Norden Labs., 1965, 99, Outstanding Tchr. Amoco Oil, Iowa State U., 1972, Faculty Mem. of Yr., Coll. Vet. Medicine, 1999; recipient Faculty Citation Iowa State U. Alumni Assn., 1978. Mem. AVMA (mem. editl. bd. jour. 1975-98, Excellence in Teaching award student chpt. 1990), Iowa Vet. Med. Assn., Am. Soc. Parasitologists, Midwestern Conf. Parasitologists (sec.-treas. 1967-75, presiding officer 1975-76), Am. Assn. Vet. Parasitologists (pres. 1968-70), Helminthological Soc. Washington, World Assn. for Advancement Vet. Parasitology, Am. Assn. Vet. Med. Colls., Izaak Walton League (bd. dirs. Iowa 1968-70), Honor Soc. Cardinal Key, Gamma Sigma Delta, Phi Eta Sigma, Phi Kappa Phi, Phi Zeta. Republican. Lodges: Kiwanis (Town and Country-Ames pres. 1967, Nebr.-Iowa lt. gov. 1972-73) Avocations: philately, camping, gardening. Office: Iowa State U Coll Vet Med Found Ames IA 50011-1250 E-mail: sdgreve@isunet.net.

GREW, PRISCILLA CROSWELL, university official, geology educator; b. Glens Falls, N.Y., Oct. 26, 1940; d. James Croswell and Evangeline Pearl (Beougher) Perkins; m. Edward Sturgis Grew, June 14, 1975. BA magna cum laude, Bryn Mawr Coll., 1962; PhD, U. Calif., Berkeley, 1967. Instr. dept. geology Boston Coll., 1967-68, asst. prof., 1968-72; asst. rsch. geologist UCLA, 1972-77, adj. asst. prof. environ. sci. and engring., 1975-76; dir. Calif. Dept. Conservation, 1977-81; commr. Calif. Pub. Utilities Commn., San Francisco, 1981-86; dir. Minn. Geol. Survey, St. Paul, 1986-93; prof. dept. geology U. Minn., Mpls., 1986-93; vice chancellor for rsch. U. Nebr., Lincoln, 1993-99, prof. dept. geoscis., 1993—, prof. conservation/survey divsn. Inst. Agr., 1993—; coord. Native Am. Graves Protection and Repatriation Act, 1998—. Vis. asst. prof. geology U. Calif., Davis, 1973-74; chmn. Calif. State Mining and Geology Bd., Sacramento, 1976-77; exec. sec., editor Lake Powell Rsch. Project, 1971-77; cons., mem. vis. staff Los Alamos (N.Mex.) Nat. Lab., 1972-77; mem. com. on minority participation in earth sci. and mineral engring. Dept. Interior, 1972-75; chmn. Calif. Geothermal Resource Task Force, 1977, Calif. Geothermal Resources Bd., 1977-81; mem. earthquake studies adv. panel U.S. Geol. Survey, 1979-83, mem. adv. com., 1982-86; mem. adv. coun. Gas Rsch. Inst., 1982-86, mem. rsch. coord. coun., 1987-98, vice chmn., 1994-96, chmn., 1996-98, mem. sci. and tech. coun., 1998-2001; mem. bd. on global change rsch. NAS, 1995-99, mem. subcom. on earthquake rsch., 1985-88, mem. bd. on earth scis. and resources, 1986-91, mem. bd. on mineral and energy resources, 1982-88, Minn. Minerals Coord. Com., 1986-93, mem. U.S. nat. com. on geodesy and geophysics 2001—; mem. adv. bd. Sch. Earth Scis., Stanford U., 1989—, Sec. of Energy Adv. Bd., 1995-97; mem. com. on equal opportunities in sci. and tech. NSF, 1985-86, mem. adv. com. on earth scis., 1987-91, mem. adv. com. on sci. and tech. ctrs. devel., 1987-91, mem., adv. com. on sci. and tech. ctrs., 1996, adv. com. on geoscis., 1994-97; mem. State-Fed. Tech. Partnership Task Force, 1995-99, Fed. Coun. for Continental Sci. Drilling, 1992-98, Gt. Plains Partnership Coun., 1995-99; trustee Am. Geol. Inst. Found., 1988— (Ian Campbell medlist 1999). Contbr. articles to profl. jours. Bd. dirs. Abendmusik:Lincoln, 1995-97; trustee 1st Plymouth Congl. Ch., Lincoln, 1997-2000. Fellow NSF, 1962-66. Fellow AAAS (chmn. electorate nominating com. sect. E 1980-84, mem.-at-large 1987-91, chmn.-elect 1994, chmn. 1995, coun. del. 1997-98), Geol. Soc. Am. (nominations com. 1974, chmn. com. on geology and pub. policy 1981-84, audit com. 1988-90, chair 1990, com. on coms. 1986-87, 91-92, chmn. com. on coms. 1995, chair Day medal com. 1990, councilor 1987-91), Mineral. Soc. Am. (mem. Roebling medal com. 1999—), Geol. Assn. Can.; mem. Am. Geophys. Union (chmn. com. pub. affairs 1984-89), Soc. Mayflower Descs., Nat. Parks and Conservation Assn. (trustee 1982-86), Nat. Assn. Regulatory Utility Commrs. (com. on gas 1982-86, exec. com. 1984-86, com. on energy conservation 1983-84), U.S. Nat. Com. on Geology (at-large 1985-93), Cosmos Club, Country Club of Lincoln. Congregational. Office: U Nebr NAGPRA Coordinator 301 Bessey Hall Lincoln NE 68588-0381

GREWCOCK, WILLIAM L. mining company executive; b. 1925; married BCE, U. Nebr., 1950. With Peter Kiewit Sons, Inc., Omaha, 1950—, mgr. Grand Island dist., 1960-65, v.p., 1965-82, sr. v.p., 1982-86, vice chmn., 1986—, also bd. dirs.; pres. Kiewit Mining Group, Inc. subs. Peter Kiewit Sons, Inc., now chmn.; sr. v.p. Kiewit U.S. Co. subs. Peter Kiewit Sons, Inc., Omaha, 1982—, also bd. dirs. Office: Kiewit Constrn Group Inc 1000 Kiewit Plz Omaha NE 68131

GRIEMAN, JOHN JOSEPH, communications executive; b. St. Paul, Sept. 7, 1944; s. Roy and Agnes (Thell) G.; m. Joan Schultz, Sept. 12, 1964; children: Nancy, Amy, Angie, Ginette. BS in Acctg., Coll. of St. Thomas, St. Paul, 1966. Supr. Coopers & Lybrand, Mpls., 1966-72; treas. 1st Midwest Corp., 1972-75; pvt. practice fin. cons. Mpls., 1975-76; dir. corp. planning and systems, asst. controller constrn. equipment, group mgr. corp. acctg. Am. Hoist & Derrick Co., St. Paul, 1976-82; controller Cowles Media Co., Mpls., 1982, v.p., 1983; controller Mpls. Star and Tribune Co., 1983-96; v.p., CFO Mpls. Star and Tribune, 1983-96; cons. bus. improvement New Brighton, Minn., 1996—. Bd. dirs. Jr. Achievement Upper Midwest, 1987—, Project for Pride in Living, Mpls., 1994—, Lifetrac Resources, 1999—, Mpls. Pub. Sch. Found., 2000—. Mem. Am. Inst. CPA's (chmn. mems. in industry com. 1979-81), Minn. Soc. CPA's (bd. dirs., treas. 1980-81, mem. of month 1977). Home and Office: 1410 18th St NW New Brighton MN 55112-5407

GRIESHEIMER, JOHN ELMER, state representative; b. St. Clair, Mo., July 19, 1952; s. Elmer Augustus and Mary (Middleton) G.; m. Rita Ann Maune, June 15, 1974; children: Sean, Aaron, Michelle. Cert. auto mechanics, East Cen. Coll., Union, Mo., 1971, AAS, 1973. Councilman ward II City of Washington, Mo., 1982-88; county commr. Franklin County, Union, 1989-92; state rep. State of Mo., Jefferson City, 1993—. Chmn. Solid Waste com., 1984-88; vice chmn. East Ctrl. Solid Waste Task Force Waste com., 1990-92. Bd. dirs. Washington Lions Club; adv. bd. dirs. 4 Rivers Vo-Tech. Sch., Washington, Mo. Mem. KC (4th degree). Republican. Roman Catholic. Home: 33 Oxford Dr Washington MO 63090-4609 Office: State of Mo State Capitol Building # PO Jefferson City MO 65101-1556

GRIEVE, PIERSON MACDONALD, retired specialty chemicals and services company executive; b. Flint, Mich., Dec. 5, 1927; s. P.M. and Margaret (Leamy) G.; m. Florence R. Brogan, July 29, 1950; children: Margaret, Scott, Bruce. BSBA, Northwestern U., 1950; postgrad., U. Minn., 1955-56. Staff engr. Caterpillar Tractor Co., Peoria, Ill., 1950-52; mgmt. cons. A.T. Kearney & Co., Chgo., 1952-55; pres. Rap-in-Wax, Mpls., 1955-62; exec. AP Parts Corp., Toledo, 1962-67; pres., CEO Questor Corp., 1967-82; CEO Ecolab Inc., St. Paul, 1983-96; ret. Bd. dirs. St. Paul Cos. Inc., Mesaba Aviation; ptnr. Paladium Equity Ptnrs. LLC. Mem. adv. coun. J.L. Kellogg Grad. Sch. Mgmt., Northwestern U.; bd. dirs. Guthrie Theatre; bd. trustees St. Thomas U. With USNR, 1945-46. Mem. Chevaliers du Tastevin, Mpls. Club, Beta Gamma Sigma (dirs. table). Episcopalian.

GRIFFEY, KEN, JR. (GEORGE KENNETH GRIFFEY JR.), professional baseball player; b. Donora, Pa., Nov. 21, 1969; Grad. high sch., Cin. Outfielder Seattle Mariners, 1987-99, Cin. Reds, 1999—. Recipient Gold Glove award, 1990-96; named to All-Star team, 1990-95, All-Star game MVP, 1992, , Sporting News Am. League Silver Slugger team, 1991, 93-94, 96 Sporting News All-Star team, 1991, 93-94. Office: Cincinnati Reds 100 Cinergy Fld Cincinnati OH 45202-3543*

GRIFFIN, J. TIMOTHY, air transportation executive; With Am. Airlines; sr. v.p., schedules, pricing Continental Airlines; sr. v.p., market planning, systems Northwest Airlines, 1993—, exec. v.p., mktg., distbn., 1999—. Office: Northwest Airlines Corp 5101 Northwest Dr Saint Paul MN 55111-3027

GRIFFIN, JAMES ANTHONY, bishop; b. Fairview Park, Ohio, June 13, 1934; s. Thomas Anthony and Margaret Mary (Hanousek) Griffin. BA, Borromeo Coll., 1956; JCL magna cum laude, Pontifical Lateran U., Rome, 1963; JD summa cum laude, Cleve. State U., 1972; DHL (hon.), Ohio Dominican Coll., 1994. Ordained priest Roman Catholic Ch., 1960, bishop, 1979; asso. pastor St. Jerome Ch., Cleve., 1960-61; sec.-notary Cleve. Diocesan Tribunal, 1963-65; asst. chancellor Diocese of Cleve., 1965-68, vice chancellor, 1968-73, chancellor, 1973-78, vicar gen., 1978-79; pastor St. William Ch., Euclid, Ohio, 1978-79; aux. bishop Diocese of Cleve., vicar of western region Ohio, 1979-83; bishop Diocese of Columbus (Ohio), 1983—. Mem clergy relations bd Diocese Cleveland, Ohio, 1972—75, mem clergy retirement bd, Ohio, 1973—78, mem clergy personnel bd, Ohio, 1979—83. Author (with A J Quinn): (book) Thoughts for Our Times, 1969, Thoughts for Sowing, 1970; author: (with others) Ashes from the Cathedral, 1974, Sackcloth and Ashes, 1976, The Priestly Heart, 1983, Reflections on the Law of Love, 1991, Summary of the New Catholic Catechism, 1994. Chmn bd govs N Am Coll, Rome, 1984—88; co-chair Columbus Community Relations Comn, 1992—95; mem Am's Promise, Columbus, Ohio, 1997—2001, Columbus Coalition Domestic Violence, 2001—; mem. adv. coun. Cmty. Shelter Bd., 2001—; mem. adv. team Cmtys. in Sch., 2002—; chmn Mayor's Coun Youth, 1986—90; trustee St Mary Sem, 1976—78; bd dirs, mem pension comt Cath Cemeteries Asn, 1978—83; vice-chancellor Pontifical Col Josephinum, 1983—; treas Cath Relief Serv Bd, 1988—91, pres, 1991—96; bd dirs Holy Family Cancer Home, 1973—78, Meals on Wheels, Euclid, 1978—79, Franklin County United Way, 1984—90. Decorated Knight of the Holy Sepulchre; recipient Human Rights Award, Anti-Defamation League B'nai B'rith, 1987, Gov's Award, State of Ohio, 1994, Jessing Award, Pontifical Col, 1993, Don Bosco Medal, 1997, NG Minuteman Award, 1999, Cmty. Svc. award, Columbus Urban League, 1999, Bronze Pelican award, Cath. Boy Scouts, 2002, Charity Newsies award, 2002. Mem.: Columbus Bar Asn (chmn jud advt comt 1987—91, Liberty Bell Award 1989), Am Canon Law Soc.

GRIFFIN, JEAN LATZ, commn. strategist; b. Joliet, Ill., Mar. 6, 1943; d. Carl Joseph and Helene Monica (Bradshaw) Latz; m. Dennis Joseph Griffin, Sept. 16, 1967; children: Joseph, Timothy, Peter. BS in Chemistry, Coll. St. Francis, Joliet, 1965; MS in Journalsim, U. Wis., 1967. Clin. investigation coord. Baxter Labs., 1967-68; reporter Joliet Herald News, 1968-70, Raleigh (N.C.) Times, 1974-75, Suburban Trib, Hinsdale, Ill., 1976-78, regional edn. reporter, 1978-82; gen. assignment reporter Chgo. Tribune, 1982-84, edn. writer, 1984-88, pub. health writer, 1988-94, govt., politics, and pub. policy reporter, 1994-97, econ. devel. reporter, 1997; strategist The Strategy Group, Chgo., 1998—; owner CyberINK, 1998—; adj. journalism instr. Roosevelt U., Chicago, 2001—. Bd. dirs. Residents for Emergency Shelter, Chgo., 1978-82, Genesis House, Chgo., 1995-98, vol. cook, 1994-98; devel. com. mem. Hope Now, Inc., 1998-2000; membership chair Arlington Hts. C. of C., 2001—; vol. Taoist Tai Chi instr., 2001—. Recipient Writing award Am. Dental Assn., 1969, Alumna Profl. Achievement award Coll. St. Francis, Joliet, 1985, First Prize in edn1. writing Edn. Writers Am., 1986, Grand prize, 1988, Benjamin Fine award Nat. Assn. Secondary Sch. Prins., 1988, Edward Scott Beck award for reporting Chgo. Tribune, 1988, Peter Lisagor award for pub. svc. Soc. Profl. Journalists, Chgo. chpt., 1988, Mark of Excellence Chgo. Assn. Black Journalists, 1992, Cushing award for Journalistic Excellence, Chgo. Dental Soc., 1992, Human First award Horizon Cmty. Svcs., Chgo., 1993, Robert F. Kennedy Grand Prize in Journalism, 1994, Editl. Excellence award Ill. Merchandising Coun., 1994; finalist Pulitzer Prize, 1994. Mem. Women's Leadership Coun., Taoist Tai Chi Soc. USA-Ill., Dynamic Link Arlington Heights C. of C. E=mail. Office: The Strategy Group 730 N Franklin St Chicago IL 60610-3563 E-mail: jlgrif@earthlink.net.

GRIFFIN, MICHAEL J. former state legislator; b. Jackson, Miss., May 12, 1933; m. Janet Stark; children: Margaret, John, Martin, Michael, Robert, Gerald, Maureen. BA, Jackson C.C., 1959. City commr., Jackson, 1967-73; rep. Mich. Dist. 50, 1972-92, Mich. Dist. 64, 1993-98. Alt. chmn. joint com. on adminstrv. rules Mich. Ho. Reps., legis. coun., corps. & fin. com., tourism, fisheries, and wildlife com.; product mgr. Rhemm Mfg. Home: 1616 Cascade Ct Jackson MI 49203-3808

GRIFFIN, ROBERT PAUL, former United States senator, state supreme court justice; b. Detroit, Nov. 6, 1923; s. J.A. and Beulah M. G.; m. Marjorie J. Anderson, 1947; children— Paul Robert, Richard Allen, James Anderson, Martha Jill. AB, BS, Central Mich. U., 1947, LLD, 1963; JD, U. Mich., 1950, LLD, 1973; LL.D., Eastern Mich. U., 1969, Albion Coll., 1970, Western Mich. U., 1971, Grand Valley State Coll., 1971, Detroit Coll. Bus., 1972, Detroit Coll. Law, 1973; L.H.D., Hillsdale (Mich.) Coll., 1970; J.C.D., Rollins Coll., 1970; Ed.D., No. Mich. U., 1970; D. Pub. Service, Detroit Inst. Tech., 1971. Bar: Mich. 1950. Pvt. practice, Traverse City, Mich., 1950-56; mem. 85th-89th congresses from 9th Dist. Mich., Washington, 1957-66; mem. U.S. Senate from Mich., 1966-79; counsel Miller, Canfield, Paddock & Stone, Traverse City, 1979-86; assoc. justice Mich. Supreme Ct., Lansing, 1987-95. Trustee Gerald R. Ford Found. Served with inf. AUS, World War II, ETO. Named 1 of 10 Outstanding Young Men of Nation U.S. Jaycees, 1959 Mem. ABA, Mich. Bar Assn., D.C. Bar Assn., Kiwanis.

GRIFFITH, DONALD KENDALL, lawyer; b. Aurora, Ill., Feb. 4, 1933; s. Walter George and Mary Elizabeth G.; m. Susan Smykal, Aug. 4, 1962; children: Kay, Kendall. Grad. in history with honors, Culver Mil. Acad., 1951; BA, U. Ill., 1955, JD, 1958. Bar: Ill. 1958, U.S. Supreme Ct. 1973. Assoc. Hinshaw & Culbertson, Chgo., 1959-65, ptnr., 1965-98, of counsel, 1999—. Spl. asst. atty. gen. Ill., 1970-72; lectr. Ill. Inst. Continuing Legal Edn., 1970-90. Mem. editl. bd. Ill. Civil Practice After Trial, 1970; co-editor The Brief, 1975-83; contbg. author Civil Practice After Trial, 1984, 89; contbr. articles to legal jour. Trustee Lawrence Hall Youth Svcs., 1967—, v.p. for program, 1969-74; bd. dirs. Child Care Assn. Ill., 1970-73; mem. Lake Forest H.S. Bd. Edn., 1983-84. 2d lt. USAF, 1956. Fellow Am. Acad. Appellate Lawyers; mem. ABA (chmn. appellate advocacy com., tort and ins. practice sect. 1983-84), Ill. Bar Assn., Chgo. Bar Assn., Appellate Lawyers Assn. Ill. (pres. 1973-74), Univ. Club Chgo., Knollwood Club, Alpha Chi Rho (chpt. pres.), Phi Delta Phi. Office: Hinshaw & Culbertson 222 N LaSalle St Ste 300 Chicago IL 60601-1081 E-mail: kgriffit@hinshawlaw.com.

GRIFFITH, G. LARRY, lawyer; b. Keokuk, Iowa, Mar. 6, 1937; s. Charles Floyd and Lillian Mae (McClinton) G.; children: Randall Dale, Kristin Lin, Barry Wynn. BA, DePauw U., 1959; JD, U. Iowa, 1962. Bar: Iowa 1962, Minn. 1963. Ptnr. Dorsey & Whitney, Mpls., 1962-2000, chair real estate dept., 1991-95, of counsel, 2001—. Instr. modern real estate transactions U. Minn., Mpls., 1970-71; bd. dirs. Brock-White Co. Comment editor U. Iowa Law Rev., 1961-62. Scout master Boy Scouts Am., Mpls., 1965-69; bd. dirs. Jr. Achievement, 1991—. Rector scholar De Pauw U., 1955-59 Mem. ABA, Minn. Bar Assn., Hennepin County Bar Assn., U.S. Ski Assn. (alpine competition com. cen. div. 1981-87, chmn. region I 1984-86), Mpls. Athletic Club, Burnsville Athletic Club (bd. dirs., legal advisor 1980-92), Phi Alpha Delta. Avocations: skiing, tennis, hunting, scuba diving, golf. Home: 8308 40th Ave N New Hope MN 55427 Office: Dorsey & Whitney LLP Ste 1500 50 S 6th St Minneapolis MN 55402-1553 E-mail: griffith.larry@dorseylaw.com.

GRIFFITH, JOHN FRANCIS, pediatrician, administrator, educator; b. Humboldt, Sask., Can., Feb. 14, 1934; came to U.S., 1963; s. J. Stuart and Grayce M. (Reid) G.; m. Shirley Shaw, Sept 2, 1961; children: Kathleen Ann, Karen Elizabeth, Kristine M., James Stuart. BA, U. Sask., 1956, MD, 1958. Diplomate Am. Bd. Pediatrics (chmn. bd. 1989—). Intern Montreal (Can.) Gen. Hosp., 1958-59, resident, 1959-60, gen. practice medicine, 1960-61; pediatric resident Montreal Children's Hosp., 1961-63, Case Western Res. U., Cleve., 1963-64, Mass. Gen. Hosp., Boston, 1964-67; research fellow neurology Harvard U. Med. Sch., 1964-66, research fellow neuropathology, 1966-67, teaching fellow neurology, 1967-69; research infectious diseases Children's Hosp. Med. Ctr., 1967-69; asst. prof. pediatrics Duke U. Med. Ctr., Durham, N.C., 1969-71, assoc. prof., 1971-76, assoc. prof. medicine, 1975-76; prof., chmn. dept. pediatrics U. Tenn., Memphis, 1976-86; prof. pediatrics and neurology Georgetown U., Washington, 1986-96. Emeritus prof. pediat. and neurology Georgetown U., Washington, 1996—; examiner, mem. written exam com. Am. Bd. Pediat., Chapel Hill, NC, 1979—83, mem. task force on recert., 1979—80, bd. dirs., 1985—89, exec. com. of bd. dirs., 1986, chair program dir. liaion com. and new directions com., 1985—86, chair rsch. and rev. com. and chair guidelines for combined tng. program, 1987—88, sec.-treas., 1986—87; mem. residency rev. com. Accreditation Coun., Chgo., 1982—86, chmn. evaluation com. on pediat. scientist tng. program, 1982—86; sr. v.p. univ. and acad. affairs Health Alliance Greater Cin.; assoc. dean U. Cin. Coll. Medicine. Contbr. articles to profl. jours. Howard Hughes Found., 1971-74; Multiple Sclerosis grantee, 1969-71; Benjamen Miler Meml. grantee, 1971-74; FDA grantee, 1978-80 Mem. Assn. Am. Med. Colls. (com. on AIDS 1987), Irish-Am. Pediatrics Soc., Soc. Pediatrics Rsch., Am. Pediatric Soc., AOA, Am. Acad. Pediatrics, Assn. Med. Sch. Pediatrics Dept. Chmn., Royal Coll. Physicians and Surgeons, Am. Bd. Pediatrics (chmn., bd. dirs. 1989-90), Sigma Chi. Office: Health Alliance 3200 Burnet Ave Cincinnati OH 45229-3099

GRIFFITH, JOHN RANDALL, health services administrator, educator; b. Balt., Mar. 22, 1934; s. Richard Robinson and Eleanor (Bond) G.; m. Helen Klenner, Sept. 17, 1955; children: Julia, Alison, Richard. BS Indsl. Engring., The Johns Hopkins U., 1955; MBA Hospital Adminstrn., U. Chgo., 1957. From asst. prof. to prof. U. Mich. Sch. Pub. Health Dept. Health Mgmt. Policy, Ann Arbor, 1960—, interim dept. chair, 1987-88, dept. chair, 1988-91, Andrew Pattullo Collegiate prof. Hosp. Adminstrn., 1982—; dir. program, chmn. dept. Bur. Hosp. Adminstrn., Mich., 1970-82. Examiner Baldridge Nat. Quality Award, 1997—98. Author: Quantitative Techniques for Hospital Planning and Control, 1972, Measuring Hospital Performance, 1978, The Well Managed Community Hospital, 1987 (award, 1988), Moral Challenges of Health Care Management, The Well-Managed Health Care Organization, 1995 (award, 1999, award, 2000), The Well-Managed Health Care Organization, 5th edit., 2002, Designing 21st Century Healthcare: Leadership in Hospitals and Health Systems, 1998; author: (with others) Re-Engineering Health Care: Building on Continuous Quality Improvement, 1995. Bd. dirs., pres., Assn. Univ. Programs Health Adminstrn., 1974-75, Pattullo lectr., 1999; bd. dirs. Accredation Commn., 1977-83. Recipient Filerman Prize for Ednl. Leadership, Assn. Univ. Programs in Health Adminstrn., 2002. Fellow Am. Coll. Health Care Execs. (gold medal 1992, James A. Hamilton award), Tau Beta Pi, Omicron Delta Kappa. Home: 333 Rock Creek Ct Ann Arbor MI 48104-1857 Office: U Mich SPH II 109 Observatory St Ann Arbor MI 48109-2029

GRIFFITH, MARY H. corporate communications executive; b. Ky. BA in English, Centre Coll., Danville, Ky. Sr. v.p., dir. pub. rels. 1st Nat. Bank Louisville, until 1990; with Nat. City Corp., Cleve., 1990—, sr. v.p. mktg. comm., 1992—. Bd. dirs. Centre Coll.; active numerous city and state civic orgns. Recipient Disting. Alumni award Centre Coll., 1991. Office: Nat City Corp Nat City Ctr 1900 E 9th St Cleveland OH 44114-3401

GRIFFITH, OWEN WENDELL, biochemistry educator; b. Oakland, Calif., June 19, 1946; s. Charles H. and Gladys C. (Farrar) G. BA, U. Calif., Berkeley, 1968; PhD, Rockefeller U., 1975. Asst. prof. Cornell U. Med. Coll., N.Y.C., 1978-81, assoc. prof., 1981-87, prof., 1987-92; prof., chmn. biochemistry Med. Coll. of Wis., Milw., 1992-2001, prof. biochemistry, 2001—; sci. founder, bd. dirs., chmn. ArgiNOx, Inc., 2000—. Mem., chmn. med. biochemistry study sect. NIH, Bethesda, Md., 1988-92. Contbr. more than 160 articles to profl. jours. Grantee NIH. Mem. Am. Chem. Soc., Am. Soc. Biochemistry and Molecular Biology, Am. Soc. Pharmacology and Exptl. Therapeutics. Achievements include more than 40 patents and patent applications in biomedical research. Office: Med Coll Wis Dept Biochemistry 8701 W Watertown Plank Rd Milwaukee WI 53226-3548 E-mail: griffith@mcw.edu.

GRIFFITH, ROGER, professional sports team executive; m. Jean Griffith; 1 child. Grad. Magna cum laude, Augsburg Coll., 1984; MBA in Gen. Mgmt., U. Minn., 1988. Dir. internal audit Northwest Airlines; divsn. mgr. ad specialty direct mail divsn. Taymark, a Taylor Corp. co.; exec. pres., CFO Minn. Timberwolves & Lynx, Mpls., 1994—, COO. Office: 600 1st Ave N Minneapolis MN 55403

GRIFFITH, SIMA LYNN, investment banking executive, consultant; b. N.Y.C., Sept. 7, 1960; d. Morris Benjamin and Mary (Buberoglü) Nahum; m. Clark Calvin Griffith, Sept. 13, 1987. BA in English, Amherst Coll., 1982. Account exec. D.F. King & Co., Inc., N.Y.C., 1982-84, asst. v.p., 1984-86, v.p., 1986-88, Wells & Miller, Mpls., 1988; with Griffith, Levi Capital, Inc., 1988-96; principal Aethlon, Capital LLC, 1996—. Co-chmn. PRSA, IR seminars, 1987; bd. advisors Pacer, Inc.; bd. govs. Children's Theater Co. Mem. Internat. Assn. Bus. Communicators (bd. govs. 1987-88), Pub. Relations Soc. Am. (bd. govs. investor relations sec. 1987-89), Nat. Investor Relations Inst. Office: Aethlon Capital LLC 4920 IDS Ctr 80 S 8th St Minneapolis MN 55402-2100

GRIFFITHS, CHARLES H., JR. career officer; BS in Engring., U.S. Naval Acad., 1971; Disting. Grad., Naval War Coll.; postgrad., Harvard's Kennedy Sch. Govt., 1991, Harvard Bus. Sch., 1994. Commd. ensign USN, advanced through ranks to rear adm.; various assignments to spl. asst. to dep. dir. Naval Nuclear Propulsion Program; exec. asst. to Chief of Naval Personnel; dir. combat plans, dep. dir., plans and policy U.S. Strategic Command, Offutt AFB, Nebr., 1999—. Decorated Def. Superior Svc. medal, Legion of Merit (2 times), Bronze Star, Meritorious Svc. medal (3 times), Joint Svc. Commendation medal, Navy Commendation medal (4 times), others. Office: 901 Sac Blvd Ste 2e10 Offutt A F B NE 68113-5455

GRIFFITHS, DAVID NEAL, utility executive; b. Oxford, Ind., Sept. 11, 1935; s. David Scifres and Lorene Francis Griffiths; m. Alice Anne Goodpasture, Aug. 9, 1959 (div. 1972); children— Beth Anne, David Douglas; m. Barbette Suzanne Goetsch, June 7, 1975; children— Michael, Megan BS in Indsl. Econs., Purdue U., 1957. Various positions Delco Remy div. Gen. Motors Corp., Anderson, Ind., 1957-69; dep. commr. revenue State of Ind., Indpls., 1969-71, adminstrv. asst. to gov., 1971-72; exec. dir. Environ. Quality Control, Inc., 1972-75; project mgr. EDP Corp., Sarasota, Fla., 1975-76, v.p. adminstrn., 1977-78; asst. to pres. Citizens Gas and Coke Utility, Indpls., 1978-80, v.p. pub. affairs, 1980-82, sr. v.p. adminstrn., 1982-92, exec. v.p., 1995-98, exec. v.p., COO, 1998—, pres., CEO, 1999—. Mem. ind. Energy Devel. Bd., Indpls., 1980-92, Midwest Govs.' Energy Task Force, 1972-75; chmn. Fed. Home Loan Bank of Indpls., 1990-93; bd. dirs. Ind. Farmers Mut. Ins. Co., Midwest Energy Assn., Meth. Med. Group, Rose-Hulman Inst. Tech. Author: Implementing Quality with a Customer Focus, Management in a Quality Environment. Pres. Indsl. Mgmt. Club, Anderson and Madison County, Inc., 1961; Cen. Coun. Indsl. Mgmt. Clubs 1966; bd. dirs., chmn. Environ. Quality Conrol, Inc., Indpls., 1983-98, Life/Ledership Devel., Inc.; bd.dirs. Greater Indpls. Progress Com., Goodwill Industries Found., Indpls. Econ. Devel. Corp. Recipient Exchange Industrialist with USSR award YMCA, 1963; named Sagamore of Wabash, Gov. of Ind., 1971, 75. Mem. Govtl. Affairs Soc. Ind. (past pres.), Ind. Gas Assn. (bd. dirs.), Indpls. C. of C. (bd. dirs.). Republican. Methodist. Clubs: Columbia (Indpls.), Downtown Kiwanis (Indpls.). Avocations: golf, swimming. Home: 8158 Brent Ave Indianapolis IN 46240-2725 Office: Citizens Gas & Coke Utility 2020 N Meridian St Indianapolis IN 46202-1393

GRIFFITHS, ROBERT PENNELL, banker; b. Chgo., May 6, 1949; s. George Findley and Marion E. (Winterrowd) G.; m. Susan Hillman, Jan. 31, 1976. BA, Amherst Coll., 1972; MS in Mgmt., Northwestern U., 1974. Comml. banking officer No. Trust Co., Chgo., 1978-80, 2d v.p., 1980-83, v.p., 1983-85; sr. v.p. comml. lending UnibancTrust Co., 1985-88; pres., CEO Old Kent Bank (formerly Ill Regional Bank Naperville, Ill.), 1988-90; sr. v.p. Old Kent Bank, Chgo., 1991-92, UnibankTrust/Hawthorne (merged with Old Kent Bank), 1987-89; pres., CEO Uptown Nat. Bank Chgo., 1993—. Mem. Univ. Club (Chgo.), Onwentsia Club. Office: Uptown Nat Bank 4753 N Broadway St Chicago IL 60640-4993 Home: Apt 311 625 Deerfield Rd Deerfield IL 60015-3238

GRIGGS, LEONARD LEROY, JR. airport executive; b. Norfolk, Va., Oct. 13, 1931; s. Leonard LeRoy and Mary (Blair) G.; m. Denise Ziegler, Mar. 18, 1977; children: Margaret Rosalyn, Virginia Lorraine Williams, Julia Blair Havey, Deborah Branham Taylor. BS, U.S. Mil. Acad., 1954; MS in Aero. Engring., Air Force Inst. Tech., 1960; MS in Internat. Affairs, George Washington U., 1967; disting. grad., Naval War Coll., 1967, Army War Coll., 1971. Registered profl. engr., Mo. Commd. 2d lt. U.S. Army, 1954; advanced through grades to col. USAF, 1970; served in Vietnam; ret., 1977; dir. Lambert St. Louis Internat. Airport, 1977-87; v.p. Ross & Baruzzini, Inc., 1987-89, Bangert Bros. Constrn. Co., St. Louis and Denver, 1989—; asst. adminstr. for airports FAA, Washington, 1990-93; airport dir. St. Louis Internat. Airport, 1993—. Adj. prof. St. Louis U.; apptd. to Nat. Civil Aviation Rev. Commn., 1997. Bd. dirs. USO, St. Louis/Lambert, Airports Coun. Internat., 1997-98. Decorated Silver Star, D.F.C. with 4 oak leaf clusters, Bronze Star, Meritorious Service medal, Air medal with 22 oak leaf clusters, Purple Heart, Air Force Commendation medal with 2 oak leaf clusters, Army Commendation medal; Medal of Honor; Medal of Gallantry (Vietnam); recipient Aviation Engring. Safety award FAA, 1979 Mem. Airport Operators Coun. Internat., Am. Assn. Airport Execs., Profl. Engring. Soc. St. Louis, Order of Dadelians, St. Louis Air Force Assn., Engr. Club, Mo. Athletic Club, Army Navy Club, Univ. Club., Order DeMolay. Home: 4400 Lindell Blvd Apt 17M Saint Louis MO 63108-2427 Office: Lambert-St Louis Intl Airport PO Box 10212 Lambert Airport MO 63145-0212

GRIMLEY, JEFFREY MICHAEL, dentist; b. Alton, Ill., Feb. 3, 1957; s. John Richard and Joyce Imogene (Mallin) G.; m. Julie Ellen Gardner, Aug. 2, 1980; children: Joel Michael, Christopher Mark, Benjamin Jeffrey. BS, U. Iowa, 1979, DDS, 1983; cert., Miami Valley Hosp, Dayton, Ohio, 1984. Gen. practice dentistry, Naperville, Ill., 1984—. Mem. ADA, Acad. Gen. Dentistry, Ill. Dental Soc., Chgo. Dental Soc. Methodist. Avocations: sports, photography. Office: 14 S Main St Naperville IL 60540-5365

GRIMM, LOUIS JOHN, mathematician, educator; b. St. Louis, Nov. 30, 1933; s. Louis and Florence Agnes (Hammond) G.; m. Barbara Ann Mitko, May 6, 1967; children: Thomas, Mary. BS, St. Louis U., 1954; MS, Ga. Inst. Tech., 1960; PhD, U. Minn., 1965. Chemist USPHS, Savannah, Ga., 1958-61; asst. prof. U. Utah, Salt Lake City, 1965-69; assoc. prof. U. Mo., Rolla, 1969-74, prof., 1974—, chmn. dept. math. and stats., 1981-87, dir. Inst. Applied Math., 1983-87. Vis. asst. prof. U. Minn., Mpls., 1966; vis. prof. U. Nebr., Lincoln, 1978-79, U. So. Calif., L.A., 1987-88; exch. scientist Polish Acad. Scis., Warsaw, Poland, 1981. Contbr. articles to profl. jours. With Med. Svc. Corps, AUS, 1956-58. Jefferson Smurfit fellow Univ. Coll. Dublin (Ireland), 1984; NSF rsch. grantee. Mem. AAUP, Soc. for Indsl. and Applied Math., Polish Math. Soc., Gesellschaft für angewandte Mathematik und Mechanik, Math. Assn. Am. (disting. tchg. award, 2001), Sigma Xi. Office: U Mo Dept Math & Stats Rolla MO 65409-0001

GRIMSHAW, LYNN ALAN, lawyer; b. Portsmouth, Ohio, Sept. 14, 1949; s. Vaughn Edwin and Margaret (Jordan) G.; m. Beverly Gay Moore, Oct. 21, 1978; children: Jordan, Stuart. BS in Indsl. Mgmt., Purdue U., 1971; JD, U. Cin., 1975. Bar: Ohio 1978. Atty. Gerlach & Grimshaw, Portsmouth, 1975-76; pros. atty. Scioto County, 1977—. Mem. Gov.'s Organized Crime Cons. Com., Ohio, 1984. Chmn. Scioto County Dem. Party, 1980-81. Mem. Ohio Pros. Atty. Assn. (pres. 1985), Nat. Dist. Atty.'s Assn. (bd. dirs. 1987), Scioto County Bar Assn. (pres. 1997), Kiwanis. Democrat. Methodist. Office: Scioto County Courthouse 6th and Courts Sts Portsmouth OH 45662

GRINDBERG, TONY, state legislator; m. Vanessa Grindberg; 1 child. Student, N.D. State Coll. Sci., Wahpeton, Moorehead State U. Dir. Interstate Bus. Coll.; mem. N.D. Senate from 41st dist., Bismark, 1993—. Vice chmn. edn. com.; mem. govt. and vet. affairs com. N.D. State Senate. Mem. Midwestern Bus. Coll. Assn. (pres.), Rotary. Republican. Home: 2832 39 1/2 Ave S Fargo ND 58104-7014

GRINTER, DONALD W. metal processing executive; b. 1936; married BA, Mich. State U., 1961, MBA, 1962. With Borg-Warner Corp., 1962-81; v.p. Abex Corp., Stamford, Conn., from 1981, exec. v.p., 1984—, also bd. dirs. Office: ABC-NACO Inc Ste 502 201 Butterfield Rd Downers Grove IL 60515

GRISKO, JEROME P., JR. diversified financial services company executive; Ptnr. Baker & Hostetler, LLP, 1987-98; sr. v.p. mergers and acquisitions and legal affairs Century Bus. Sys., Cleve., 1998—, interim pres., 2000—. Office: Century Bus Sys Ste 330 6480 Roxside Woods Blvd Cleveland OH 44131

GRISSOM, MARQUIS DEON, professional baseball player; b. Atlanta, Apr. 17, 1967; Student, Fla. A & M. Outfielder Montreal Expos, 1988-94; with Atlanta Braves, 1994-97, Milwaukee Brewers, 1997—2000, Los Angeles Dodgers, 2001—. Named to Nat. League All-Star team, 1993, 94; recipient Golden Glove award, 1993-96. Achievements include leading the Nat. League in stolen bases, 1991-92. Office: Los Angeles Dodgers Dodger Stadium 1000 Elysian Park Avenue Los Angeles CA 90012-1199*

GRISWELL, J. BARRY, insurance company executive; b. Ga. Bachelor's, Berry Coll., 1971; master's, Stetson U., 1972. Pres., CEO MetLife Mktg. Corp. (subs. MetLife Ins. Co.); agy. v.p. The Prin. Fin. Group, Des Moines, 1986-91, sr. v.p. individual ins. dept., 1991-96, exec. v.p., 1996-98, pres., 1998—, pres., CEO, 1999—. Past chair LIMRA Internat.; past chair bd. trustees Life Underwriting Tng. Coun.; trustee Ctrl. Coll., Pella, Iowa, dir. bus. com. for arts. Office: The Prin Fin Group 711 High St Des Moines IA 50392-0002

GRISWOLD, TOM, radio personality; b. Cleve., 1953; Radio host morning show Sta. WFBQ-FM, Indpls. Office: WFBQ 6161 Fall Creek Rd Indianapolis IN 46220*

GROBSCHMIDT, RICHARD A. state legislator; b. Milw., May 3, 1948; married; 1 child. BS, U. Wis., Oshkosh, 1972; MS, U. Wis., Milw., 1979. Polit. sci. tchr. South Milwaukee H.S., 1972-85; mem. from dist. 21 Wis. State Assembly, Madison, 1984-95; mem. Wis. Senate from 7th dist., 1995—; chmn. edn. com. Wis. Senate. Mem. Local Hist. Soc., Nature Conservancy. Home: 912 Lake Dr South Milwaukee WI 53172-1736

GROETHE, REED, lawyer; b. Indpls., Mar. 21, 1952; s. Alfred Philip and Kathryn (Skerik) G.; m. Nancy Jayne Radefeld, June 2, 1974; children: Jacob Peter, Eric Alfred. BA, St. Olaf Coll., 1974; JD, U. Chgo., 1977. Bar: Wis. 1977. Law clk. to judge U.S. Ct. Appeals (5th cir.), Montgomery, Ala., 1977-78; assoc. Foley & Lardner, Milw., 1978-86, ptnr., 1986—. Pres. Bay Shore Luth. Ch., Whitefish Bay, Wis., 1985-89. Mem. ABA (tax sect.), Nat. Asn. Bond Lawyers, Wis. Bar Assn. Lutheran. Office: Foley & Lardner 777 E Wisconsin Ave Ste 3800 Milwaukee WI 53202-5367

GROETZINGER, JON, JR. lawyer, consumer products executive; b. N.Y.C., Feb. 12, 1949; s. Jon M. and Elinor Groetzinger; m. Carol Marie O'Connor, Jan. 24, 1981; 3 children. AB magna cum laude, Middlebury Coll., 1971; JD in Internat. Legal Affairs, Cornell U., 1974. Bar: N.H. 1974, N.Y. 1980, Mass. 1980, Fla. 1982, Md. 1985, Ohio 1991, U.S. Supreme Ct. 1980. Assoc. McLane, Graf, Greene, Raulerson and Middleton, P.A., Manchester, N.H., 1974-76; atty. John A. Gray Law Offices, Boston, 1978-81; pvt. practice N.H., Boston, 1977-81; chief internat. counsel Martin Marietta Corp., Bethesda, Md., 1981-88; pres., exec. v.p. Martin Marietta Overseas Corp., 1984-88; sr. v.p., gen. counsel, corp. sec. Am. Greetings Corp., Cleve., 1988—. Chmn. internat. adv. bd. Case Western Res. U. Law Sch., 1995—, disting. adj. prof., 1998—. Trustee Middlebury (Vt.) Coll., 1974—76, mem. bd. overseers, 1977—; bd. dirs. Cleve. Coun. on World Affairs, 1991—98, 1999—, chmn. strategic planning com., 2000—02, mem. exec. com., 2000—02; bd. dirs. Can.-U.s. Law Inst.; mem. exec. com. The Conf. Bds. Coun. Chief Legal Officers, 1996—, membership chmn., 1997—98, program chair, 1999—2000, coun. chmn., 2000—02; chmn. Greater Cleve. Gen. Counsel Assn., 2001—, pres., 2001—; vice chmn. Cleve. Coun. on World Affairs, 2002—, vice chmn. bd., 2002—. Mem. ABA, N.H. Bar Assn., Fla. Bar Assn., Ohio Bar Assn., Cleve. Bar Assn., Md. Bar Assn., Am. Soc. Corp. Secs. (sec. Ohio chpt. 1995—, v.p. 1996-97, pres. 1997-98, adv. com. 1998--), Soc. of Benchers, Phi Beta Kappa. Office: Am Greetings Corp 1 American Rd Cleveland OH 44144-2301 E-mail: jgroetzi@yahoo.com.

GROISS, FRED GEORGE, lawyer; b. Glen Cove, N.Y., Mar. 12, 1936; s. Frederick F.W. and Dorothy C. (Roberts) G.; m. Jacqueline C. Grosse; children— Frederick C., Katherine E., Jennifer L. A.B., Cornell U., 1958, LL.B., 1961. Bar: N.Y. 1961, Wis. 1963, U.S. Dist. Ct. (ea. dist.) Wis., 1963, U.S. Ct. Appeals (7th cir.) 1965. Assoc. Sage, Gray, Todd & Sims, N.Y.C., 1961-63; assoc. Porter, Quale, Porter & Zirbel, Milw., 1963-65, Brady, Tyrrell, Cotter & Cutler, Milw., 1965-70; ptnr. Quarles & Brady, 1970-2000; ret. Lectr. various labor law confs. Mem. Gov.'s Commn. on Civil Service Reform, Madison, Wis., 1977-78 Mem.: Wis. Bar Assn. (bd. dirs. labor law sect. 1975—77), Greencroft ACAC Club. Republican. Avocation: sports. Home: 2460 Dunmore Rd Charlottesville VA 22901-9447

GRONEMUS, BARBARA, state legislator; b. Nov. 21, 1931; d. Erwin J. and Irene (Resch) Barry; m. Lambert N. Gronemus, 1949; children: Michelle (Mrs. Jerome J. Carroll), Jacqueline (Mrs. Eric Baken), Margaret Susan (Mrs. David Williams). Former dir. nursing home activity; mem. from dist. 91 Wis. State Assembly, Madison, 1982—, mem. state affairs, small bus. coms., 1993, mem. agr. com., 1983—, vice chmn., 1985, chmn. subcom. on swing psuedorabies, 1985, vice chmn. commerce and consumer affairs, 1983, mem. excise/fees, tourism, recreation & forest productivity, 1985, mem. Minn.-Wis. boundary commn. legis. adv. com., 1983—, chmn. agr., forestry and rural affairs coms. Chmn. Trempealeau County Dem. Com., 1981-82, 3d Congl. Dist. Dem. Com., 1982-83. Mem. Am. Legion, Farmers Union, Whitehall Women's Club, Whitehall Rod and Gun Club, Trempealeau County Homemakers Club. Home: PO Box 676 36301 West St Whitehall WI 54773-8512 Office: Wis House of Reps Office Of House Mems Madison WI 53702-0001

GRONSTAL, MICHAEL E. state legislator; b. Council Bluffs, Iowa, Jan. 29, 1950; m. Connie Meisenbach. BA, Antioch Coll.; student, Loyola U. With Dem. Party State Ctrl. Com. 5th Dist.; chair Pottawattamie County Dem. Party, 1986-88; mem. Iowa Senate from 42nd dist., Des Moines, 1984—; asst. majority leader 71st, 72d Gen. Assemblies; majority whip 73rd Gen. Assembly; pres. of the senate 74th Gen. Assembly; minority leader 77th and 78th Gen. Assembly. Former mem. Govs. Drug Treatment Lic. Bd.; bd. dirs. River Bluffs Cmty. Mental Health Ctr., Chem. Dependency Agy. Democrat. Home: 220 Bennett Ave Council Bluffs IA 51503-5205 Office: State Capitol Dist 42 Des Moines IA 50319-0001 E-mail: mgronst@legis.state.ia.us.

GROSE, CHARLES FREDERICK, pediatrician, infectious disease specialist; b. Faribault, Minn., Apr. 15, 1942; s. Frederick G. and Marie A. (Swelland) G. BA, Beloit Coll., 1963; MD, U. Chgo., 1967. Bd. cert. in pediatric infectious disease. Resident Albert Einstein Coll. Medicine, Bronx, N.Y., 1967-68, fellow, 1970—75, U. Calif., San Francisco, 1975-76; asst. prof. Health Sci. Ctr. U. Tex., San Antonio, 1976-84; prof. pediatrics U. Iowa Hosp., Iowa City, 1985—. Cons. NIH, Bethesda, Md., 1988—. Mem. editorial bd. Pediatric Infectious Disease Jour., 1991—, Virology Jour.; contbr. articles to profl. and sci. jours. Capt. U.S. Army Med. Corps., Vietnam, 1968-70. Grantee NIH, 1978—. Fellow Infectious Disease Soc. Am., Pediatric Infectious Disease Soc., Am. Acad. Pediatrics, Am. Soc. Virology. Achievements include research on diagnosis and treatment of chickenpox and shingles, and on the etiologic agent which is varicella virus. Office: U Iowa Hosp Pediatrics 200 Hawkins Dr Iowa City IA 52242-1009 E-mail: charles-grose@uiowa.edu.

GROSFELD, JAY LAZAR, surgeon, educator; b. N.Y.C., May 30, 1935; m. Margie Faulkner; children: Lisa, Denise, Janice, Jeffrey, Mark. AB cum laude, NYU, 1957, MD, 1961. Diplomate Am. Bd. Surgery (spl. qualification Pediatric Surgery). Intern in gen. surgery dept. surgery Bellevue and Univ Hosps. NYU, N.Y.C., 1961—62; resident in gen. surgery Bellevue and Univ. Hosps. NYU, 1962—66; resident in pediatric surgery Ohio State U. Coll. Medicine, Children's Hosp., 1968—70; instr. surgery Ohio State U. Coll. Medicine, 1968—70; clin. instr. surgery NYU Sch. Medicine, N.Y.C., 1965—66, asst. prof. surgery and pediatrics, 1970—72; prof., dir. pediatric surgery Ind. U. Sch. Medicine, Indpls., 1972—, Lafayette F. Page prof., 1981—, chmn. Dept. Surgery, 1985—; surgeon-in-chief James Whitcomb Riley Hosp. Children. Author: Common Problems in Pediatric Surgery, 1991, Central Surgical Association: The First 50 Years, 1991, Progress in Pediatric Trauma, 1992, Essentials of Pediatric Surgery, 1995, Pediatric Surgery, 5th edit., 1998, The Surgery of Childhood Tumors, 1999; contbr. ; editor-in-chief : Jour. Pediat. Surgery; editor: Seminars in Pediat. Surgery. Capt. M.C. U.S. Army, 1966—68. Recipient Commendation medal, recipient numerous fellowships, grants, teaching awards. Fellow: ACS (bd. govs. 1985—91), Royal Coll. Physicians and Surgeons Glasgow, Am. Acad. Pediats. (exec. com. surg. sect. 1989—95, chmn. surg. sect. 1994—95, sec. surg. sect., Ladd medal 2002—), Royal Coll. Surgeons of Eng. (hon.); mem.: AMA, Halsted Soc. (v.p. 1995—96, pres. 1996—97), Accreditation Coun. Grad. Med. Edn. (vice chair surg. residency rev. com. 2000—01), Am. Bd. Med. Specialities, World Fedn. Assns. Pediat. Surgeons (pres. 1998—2001, v.p.), Am. Bd. Surgery (bd. dirs. 1989—97, vice chair 1995, chmn. 1996—97, chmn.-elect), Am. Pediatric Surg. Assn. Found. (chmn. bd. dirs.), Internat. Soc. Surgery (sec., treas. Internat. Soc. Surgery Found. 2001—), Western Surg. Assn. (pres. 1997—98), Soc. Surg. Oncology, Brit. Assn. Pediat. Surgeons (exec. com. 1990—93, Denis Browne Gold medal 1998), Ctrl. Surg. Assn. (sec. 1987—, pres.-elect 1988, pres. 1990), Soc. Surgery Alimentary Tract, Am. Trauma Soc., Ind. State Med. Assn., Marion County Med. Soc., Soc. Univ. Surgeons, Am. Surg. Assn., Am. Pediat. Surg. Assn. 1994—95, (bd. govs., pres.-elect), N.Y. Cancer Soc., Assn. Acad. Surgery, Pediat. Surgery Biology Club, Alpha Omega Alpha, Phi Beta Kappa. Office: J W Riley Childrens Hosp 702 Barnhill Dr Rm 2500 Indianapolis IN 46202-5128 also: Ind U Med Ctr Dept Surgery 545 Barnhill Dr Dept Surgery Indianapolis IN 46202-5112 E-mail: jgrosfel@iupui.edu.

GROS LOUIS, KENNETH RICHARD RUSSELL, university chancellor; b. Nashua, N.H., Dec. 18, 1936; s. Albert W. and Jeannette Evelyn (Richards) Gros L.; m. Dolores K. Winandy, Aug. 28, 1965; children: Amy Katherine, Julie Jeannette. BA, Columbia U., 1959, MA, 1960; Ph.D. (Knapp fellow), U. Wis., 1964. Asst. prof. Ind. U., Bloomington, 1964—67, assoc. prof. English and comparative lit., 1967—73, prof., 1973—, assoc. chmn. comparative lit. dept., 1967—69, assoc. dean arts and scis., 1970—73, chmn. dept. English, 1973—78, dean arts and scis., 1978—80, v.p., 1980—88, chancellor, 1988—2001, v.p. acad. affairs, 1994—2001, trustee prof., 2001—. Bd. dirs. Anthem, Inc.; exec. coun. acad. affairs Nat. Assn. Univ. and Land Grant Colls., 1986-97—, bd. dirs. Bd. dirs. Editor Yearbook of Comparative and Gen. Lit., 1968—, Vol. I: Literary Interpretations of Biblical Narratives, 1974, Vol. II, 1982; contbr. articles to profl. jours. Bd. dirs. Assoc. Group, 1983-95, Anthem Blue Cross and Blue Shield, 1995—; mem. Ind. Com. Humanities, chmn., 1980-81; chmn. Com. on Instnl. Coop., 1986-2000; mem. Nat. Commn. on Libr. Preservation and Access, 1986-93; vice chmn., bd. dirs. Ctr. for Rsch. Librs., 1986—, chmn. bd. dirs., 1987-88. Recipient Disting. Teaching award Ind. U., 1970 Mem. MLA, Nat. Coun. Tchrs. English, AAUP, Phi Beta Kappa. Home: 4965 E Heritage Woods Rd Bloomington IN 47401-9313 Office: Ind U Wylie Hall Bloomington IN 47405 E-mail: grosloui@indiana.edu.

GROSS, CHARLES ROBERT, bank executive, state senator; b. St. Charles, Mo., Aug. 20, 1958; s. Jack Robert and Margaret Ellen (Stumberg) G.; m. Leslie Ann Goralczyk, May 27, 1984; children: Megan Marie, Madelynn Ann. BS in Pub. Adminstrn., U. Mo., 1981, MPA, 1982. Pers. mgr. Army and Air Force Exch. Svc., various cities, 1983-89; pers., safety dir. Ever-Green Lawns Corp., St. Charles, 1989-92; state rep. Mo. Legislature, Jefferson City, 1993—; real estate appraiser, 1994—2001; v.p. UMB Bank, 2001—. Pres. St. Charles County Young Reps., 1990-92; active Youth in Need, Bridgeway Counseling. Mem. St. Charles DARE, Kiwanis, Pacaderms, Alpha Kappa Psi (life). Lutheran. Avocations: golf, scuba diving, ice hockey. Home: 3019 Westborough Ct Saint Charles MO 63301-4550 E-mail: chuckgross58@hotmail.com.

GROSS, DAVID LEE, geologist; b. Springfield, Ill., Nov. 20, 1943; s. Carl David and Shirley Marie (Northcutt) G.; m. Claudia Cole, June 11, 1966; children: Oliver David, Alexander Lee AB, Knox Coll., 1965; MS, U. Ill., 1967, PhD, 1969. Registered profl. geologist, Ill., Calif. Asst. geologist Ill. State Geol. Survey, Champaign, 1969-73, assoc. geologist, 1973-80, geologist, 1980—, coord. environ. geology, 1979-84, head environ. studies, 1984-89, asst. chief, 1991-99, sr. geologist, 1999—. Exec. dir. Gov.'s Sci. Adv. com., Chgo., 1989-91; bd. dirs. First State Bank, Beardstown, Ill. Contbr. numerous articles to profl. jours. Bd. govs. Channing-Murray Found., 1973-76, pres., 1976; trustee Unitarian Universalist Ch., Urbana, 1977-80, 99—, chmn., 1977-79, 99—; bd. dirs. Vol. Action Ctr., 1981-85, chmn., 1984-85; bd. dirs. United Way Champaign County, 1984-89, exec. com., 1984-85, chmn. United Way Campaign, U. Ill., 1986; bd. dirs. Vol. Ctr., 1994-97; mem. Gov.'s Sci. Adv. Com., 1989-97; vol. summer camp counselor for teenage youth, 1984-96, 97, 98, 99; bd. dirs. Ill. Prairie chpt. ARC, 1997—. NDEA fellow, 1969 Fellow Geol. Soc. Am., AAAS; mem. Internat. Union Quaternary Rsch., Am. Quaternary Assn., Internat. Assn. Gt. Lakes Rsch., Am. Inst. Profl. Geologists (pres. Ill.-Ind. sect. 1980), Ill. State Acad. Sci., Rotary (pres. Urbana, Ill. chpt. 1986-87), Columbia (Chgo.) Yacht Club, Sigma Xi. Home: 3 Flora Ct Champaign IL 61821-3216 Office: Ill State Geol Survey 615 E Peabody Dr Champaign IL 61820-6918

GROSS, JAMES HOWARD, lawyer; b. Springfield, Ohio, Sept. 21, 1941; s. Cyril James and Virginia (Stieg) G.; m. Gail Sue Helmick, July 13, 1968; children: Karin G. Cramer, David James. BA, Ohio State U., 1963; LLB, Harvard U., 1966. Bar: Ohio 1966, D.C. 1975. Assoc. Vorys, Sater, Seymour and Pease, Columbus, Ohio, 1966-75, resident ptnr. Washington, 1975-77; ptnr. Vorys, Sater, Seymour and Pease LLP, Columbus, 1975—. White House fellow, spl. asst. to sec. HUD, Washington, 1972-73; city atty. City of Bexley, Ohio, 1985—. Mem. Franklin County Rep. Cen. Com., 1973-75, Bexley City Coun., 1981-85. Lt. comdr. USNR, 1968-74. Mem. ABA, Ohio Bar Assn. (corp. law com.), Columbus Bar Assn. (securities law com.), D.C. Bar Assn. Lutheran. Home: 5 Sessions Dr Bexley OH 43209-1440 Office: Vorys Sater Seymour and Pease LLP 52 E Gay St # 1008 Columbus OH 43215-3161

GROSS, MICHAEL LAWRENCE, chemistry educator; b. St. Cloud, Minn., Nov. 6, 1940; s. Ralph J. and Margaret T. (Iten) G.; m. Kathleen M. Trammer, June 13, 1966 (div. 1981); children: Matthew R. and Michele R. (twins); m. Judith L. Stewart, 1994. BA, St. John's U., St. Cloud, 1962; PhD, U. Minn., 1966. Postdoctoral fellow U. Pa., Phila., 1966-67, Purdue U., Lafayette, Ind., 1967-68; asst. prof. chemistry U. Nebr., Lincoln, 1968-72, assoc. prof., 1972-78, prof., 1978-83, 3M alumni prof., 1983-88, C. Petrus Peterson prof., 1988-94; dir. Midwest Ctr. for Mass Spectrometry, 1978-94; prof. chemistry, pathology, and medicine Washington U., St. Louis, 1994—. Mem. metallobiochemistry study sect. NIH, Washington, 1985-88; mem. bd. on chem. scis. and tech. NRC, 1986-91; vis. prof. Internat. Grad. Sch., U. Amsterdam, The Netherlands, 1990, U. Warwick, Eng., 1988. Editor: (book) High Performance Mass Spectrometry, 1978, Biological Mass Spectrometry: A Tutorial, 1991, Biological Mass Spectrometry: Present and Future, 1994, Practical Electrospray Ionization Mass Spectrometry, 2001; editor Mass Spectrometry Revs., 1982-90, Jour. Am. Soc. Mass Spectrometry, 1990—; contbr. 400 chpts. to books and numerous articles to profl. jours. Mem. instnl. rev. bd. St. Elizabeth, Lincoln Gen. and Bryan Meml. hosps., 1982-90. Recipient award for disting. teaching U. Nebr., 1978, Pioneer award Commonwealth of Mass., 1987; identified as one of Top 50 Cited Chemists in World, 1984-91. Mem. Am. Chem. Soc. (Field and Franklin award 1999), Am. Soc. for Mass Spectrometry, Union Concerned Scientists, Sigma Xi, Phi Lambda Upsilon. Democrat. Roman Catholic. Home: 6958 Waterman Ave Saint Louis MO 63130-4332 Office: Washington U Dept Chemistry Saint Louis MO 63130 E-mail: mgross@wuchem.wustl.edu.

GROSS, THEODORE LAWRENCE, university administrator, author; b. Bklyn., Dec. 4, 1930; s. David and Anna (Weisbrod) G.; m. Selma Bell, Aug. 27, 1955 (dec. 1991); children: Donna, Jonathan; m. Jody Gross. BA, U. Maine, 1952; MA, Columbia U., 1957, PhD, 1960. Prof. English CCNY, 1958-78, chmn. dept., 1970-72, assoc. dean and dean humanities, 1972-78, v.p. instl. advancement, 1976-77; provost Capitol Campus, Pa. State U., Middletown, 1979-83; dean Sch. Letters and Sci. SUNY Coll., Purchase, 1983-88; chmn. SUNY-Purchase Westchester Sch. Partnership, 1984-88; pres. Roosevelt U., Chgo., 1988—. Vis. prof., Fulbright scholar, Nancy, France, 1964-65, 68-69, Dept. State lectr., Nigeria, Israel, Japan, Austria. Author: Albion W. Tourgée, 1964, Thomas Nelson Page, 1967, Hawthorne, Melville, Crane: A Critical Bibliography, 1971, The Heroic Ideal in American Literature, 1971, Academic Turmoil: The Reality and Promise of Open Education, 1980, Partners in Education: How Colleges Can Work with Schools to Improve Teaching and Learning, 1988; also essays, revs.; editor: Fiction, 1967, Dark Symphony: Negro Literature in America, 1968, Representative Men, 1969, A Nation of Nations, 1971, The Literature of American Jews, 1973; gen. editor: Studies in Language and Literature, 1974, America in Literature, 1978. With AUS, 1952-54. Grantee, Rockefeller Found., 1976-77, Am. Coun. Learned Socs. Mem. MLA, PEN, Nat. Coun. Tchrs. of English (chmn. lit. com.), Century Assn., Univ. Club, Chgo. Club. Home: 1100 N Lake Shore Dr Chicago IL 60611-1070 E-mail: tgross@roosevelt.edu.

GROSSBERG, GEORGE THOMAS, psychiatrist, educator; b. Hungary, Aug. 20, 1948; came to the U.S., 1957; s. Henry and Barbara (Rothman) G.; m. Darla Jean Brown, June 13, 1976; children: Jonathan, Anna-Leah, Aviva, Aliza Rebecca, Jeremy. BA, Yeshiva U., 1971; MD, St. Louis U., 1975. Diplomate Am. Bd. Psychiatry and Neurology. Chief resident in psychiatry St. Louis U., 1978-79, instr., 1979-81, asst. prof., 1982-86, assoc. prof., 1986-90, prof., 1990-98, Samuel W. Fordyce prof. and chmn. dept. psychiatry, 1995-98, Samuel w. Fordyce prof., dir. divsn. geriat. psychiatry, 1998—. Cons. on aging U.S. VA Hosps. Assn., Washington, 1990—. Contbr. articles to profl. jours. Adv. bd. St. Louis Alzheimers Assn., 1983—. Recipient Pub. Svc. award, St. Louis Alzheimers Assn., 1989, Donovan-Sheer award, St. Louis Mental Health Assn., 1999, Fleischman-Hilliard award, Jewish Ctr. for Aged, 2000, Physician of Year award, Mo. Adult Daycare Assn., 2001. Mem. Am. Assn. Geriat. Psychiatry (pres. 1989-90), Am. Psychiat. Assn. (cons. on aging 1990—, Falk fellow 1977-79), Am. Geriat. Soc., Gerontol. Soc. Am., Internat. Psychogeriat. Assn. (treas. 1997—, pres.-elect 2001). Avocations: collectibles, art, skiing. Office: Saint Louis U Med Ctr 1221 S Grand Blvd Saint Louis MO 63104-1016 E-mail: grossbgt@slu.edu.

GROSSBERG, MICHAEL LEE, theater critic, writer; b. Houston, Sept. 7, 1952; s. Fred Samuel and Esther R. (Rosenstein) G. BA, U. Tex., 1979, BS in Journalism, 1983. Film, theater critic, reporter Victor Valley Daily News, Victorville, Calif., 1983-85; film, theater critic Columbus (Ohio) Dispatch, 1985-87, theater critic, 1987—. Co-founder Free Press Assn., Mencken awards for outstanding journalism, dir., 1981-94. Contbr. Otis Guernsey/Burns Mantle Theater Yearbook: Best Plays, 1993-01; regional report columnist Backstage, 1997—. Mem. Outer Critics Cir., Am. Theatre Critics Assn. (chmn. awards new plays com. 1993-99, exec. com. 1996-2002, vice chmn. 2001-02), Libertarian Futurist Soc. (chmn. Prometheus award judges com. 1997—, pres. bd. 2000—). Avocations: reading, traveling, meditation, public speaking. Home: 3164 Plymouth Pl Columbus OH 43213-4236 Office: Columbus Dispatch 34 S 3rd St Columbus OH 43215-4241 E-mail: mikegrossb@aol.com., mgrossberg@dispatch.com.

GROSSI, FRANCIS XAVIER, JR. lawyer, educator; b. Somerville, Mass., May 8, 1943; s. Francis Xavier and Angela Mary (LoGiudice) G.; m. Betty Morene Ballenger, May 12, 1962 (div. 1987); children: Francis Xavier III, Gina Maria, Andrea Mary, Cynthia Marie; m. Milada Dvorak, Dec. 31, 1987; children: Lukas Paolo, Anna Milada. BS, U. Mo., 1964; JD, U. Mich., 1967. Bar: D.C. 1968, U.S. Ct. Appeals (7th and 9th crcts.) 1969, U.S. Tax Ct. 1970, U.S. Ct. Appeals (4th crct.) 1972, U.S. Ct. Appeals (2d crct.) 1973, Ill. 1977. Appellate atty. U.S. Dept. Justice, Washington, 1967-69; assoc. Williams & Connolly, 1970-76; ptnr., chmn. litigation dept. Katten Muchin & Zavis, Chgo., 1977-95; ptnr. Bates, Meckler, Bulger & Tilson, 1995—. Adj. prof. Loyola U. Law Sch., Chgo., 1979-81, DePaul Law Sch., Chgo., 1981-94; faculty Nat. Inst. Trial Advocacy, Chgo., 1989—; chmn. com. Chgo. Coun. Lawyers, 1991-92. Contbg. author: Survey Bankruptcy Law, 1981; author, editor (legal publ.) Evidence Practice Guide. Mem. Joint Civic com. Italian Ams., 1988; bd. dirs. Italian Am. Polit. Coalition, 1995-96; pres. Univ. Village Assn., Chgo., 1992-95. With USMCR, 1960. Fellow Am. Coll. Trial Lawyers; mem. Chgo. Bar Assn., Justinian Soc. Democrat. Roman Catholic. Avocations: writing, camping, workshop. Address: 7322 Exner St Darien IL 60561

GROSSMAN, JEROME BARNETT, retired service firm executive; b. Kansas City, Kans., Sept. 9, 1919; m. Marian Navran, Sept. 19, 1945; children: Jean Zeldin, Janet Zwillenberg. AB, U. Mich., 1941. Exec. v.p., gen. mgr. Helzberg's Diamond Shop Inc., 1941-66; dir. mktg. H & R Block, Inc., Kansas City, Mo., 1966-69, asst. to pres., 1969-71, exec. v.p., chief oper. officer, 1971-88, sr. exec. v.p., chief oper., 1988-89, vice chmn. of the bd., 1989-92, vice chmn. emeritus, 1992—. Bd. dirs. Spherion Corp. Served to maj. USAF, 1941-45. Office: H & R Block Inc 4400 Main St Kansas City MO 64111-1812

GROSSMAN, JOEL B(ARRY), political science educator; b. N.Y.C., June 19, 1936; s. Joseph and Selma G.; m. Mary Hengstenberg, Aug. 23, 1964; children: Alison, Joanna, Daniel. BA, Queens Coll., 1957; MA, U. Iowa, 1960, PhD, 1963. Faculty dept. polit. sci. U. Wis., Madison, 1963-96, prof., 1971-96, chmn. dept., 1975-78; prof. Johns Hopkins U., 1996—. Fellow in law and polit. sci. Harvard Law Sch., Cambridge, Mass., 1965-66; Fulbright lectr. U. Strathclyde, Glasgow, 1968-69; vis. prof. law U. Stockholm, 1973, John Hopkins U., 1995-96. Editor: Law and Soc. Review, 1978-82; author: Lawyers and Judges, 1965, Frontiers of Judicial Research, 1969, Law and Change in Modern America, 1971, Constitutional Law and Judicial Policy Making, 1972, 80, 88; contbr. articles to profl. jours. Chmn. Wis. Jud. Commn. 1985-87. Served with USAR, 1960-66. Mem. Wis. Civil Liberties Union (vice chmn. 1970-72), Am. Polit. Sci. Assn., Midwest Polit. Sci. Assn. (v.p. 1988-90), So. Polit. Sci. Assn., Law and Soc. Assn. Democrat. Home: 6606 Walnutwood Cir Baltimore MD 21212-1213 E-mail: jbgrossm@jhunix.hcf.jhu.edu.

GROSSMAN, LISA ROBBIN, clinical psychologist, lawyer; b. Jan. 22, 1952; d. Samuel R. and Sarah (Kruger) G. BA with highest distinction & honors, Northwestern U., 1974, JD cum laude, 1979, PhD, 1982. Bar: Ill. 1981; registered psychologist, Ill. Jud. intern U.S. Supreme Ct., Washington, 1975; pre-doctoral psychology intern Michael Reese Hosp. and Med. Ctr., Chgo., 1979-80; therapist Homes for Children, 1980-83; psychologist Psychiat. Inst. Cir. Ct. Cook County, 1981-87; pvt. practice, 1984—. Invited participant workshop HHS, Rockville, Md., 1981. Contbr. articles to profl. jours. Mem.: APA (coun. reps. 2000—, com. on legal issues 1992—95, com. on profl. practice and stds. 1996—99, chair 1998, state leadership organizing com. 1996—98, bd. profl. affairs 2001—, mem. exec. com. caucus of state and provincial reps. 2000—02, chair 2001), ABA, Soc. Personality Assessment, Chgo. Bar Assn., Ill. State Bar Assn., Chgo. Assn. for Psychoanalytic Psychologists (parliamentarian 1982), Ill. Psychol. Assn. (pres. 1995—96), Alpha Lambda Delta, Shi-Ai, Phi Beta Kappa, Mortar Bd. Office: 500 N Michigan Ave Ste 1520 Chicago IL 60611-3758 E-mail: LRGrossman@aol.com.

GROSSMAN, MARY MARGARET, elementary education educator; b. East Cleveland, Ohio, Sept. 26, 1946; d. Frank Anthony and Margaret Mary (Buda) G. Student, Kent State Univ., 1965-67; BS in Elem. Edn. cum laude, Cleveland State Univ., 1971; postgrad, Lake Erie Coll., 1974-77, John Carroll Univ., 1978, 81, 82, 83, 85, Cleveland State Univ., 1985. Cert. elem. sch. tchr. grades 1 to 8, Ohio; cert. data processing, Ohio. Tchr. Cleve. Catholic Diocese, Cleve., 1971-72, Willoughby-Eastlake Sch. Dist., Willoughby, 1972—. Participant Nat. Econ. Edn. Conf., Richmond, Va., 1995. Eucharistic min. St. Christine's Ch., Euclid, 1988—, mem. parish pastoral coun., 1995-00. Recipient Samuel H. Elliott Econ. Leadership award, 1986-87, Consumer Educator award N.E. Ohio Region, 1986, 1st pl. award for excellence in tchg. Tchrs. in Am. Enterprise, 1984-85, 89-90;

Martha Holden Jennings scholar, 1984-85. Mem. NEA, Ohio Edn. Assn. (human rels. award 1986-87, cert. merit 1987-88), Northeast Ohio Edn. Assn. (Positive Tchr. Image award 1988). Roman Catholic. Avocations: racquetball, softball, walking, tennis, bicycling. Home: 944 E 225th St Cleveland OH 44123-3308 Office: McKinley Elem Sch 1200 Lost Nation Rd Willoughby OH 44094-7324

GROSSMAN, THEODORE MARTIN, lawyer; b. N.Y.C., Dec. 31, 1949; s. Albert and Sylvia Pia (Greenstein) G.; m. Linda Gail Steinbook, Dec. 5, 1976; children: Andrew Scott, Michael Steven. AB, Cornell U., 1971, JD, 1974. Bar: N.Y. 1975, U.S. Ct. Appeals (D.C. cir.) 1981, U.S. Ct. Appeals (2nd cir.) 1982, U.S. Ct. Appeals (5th cir.) 1984, U.S. Dist. Ct. (no. dist.) Ohio 1986, Ohio 1987, U.S. Dist. Ct. (so. dist.) N.Y. 1988, U.S. Dist. Ct. (ea. dist.) N.Y. 1988, U.S. Ct. Appeals (6th cir.) 1988. Assoc. Debevoise, Plimpton, Lyons & Gates, N.Y.C., 1974-77, Rosenman Colin Freund Lewis & Cohen, N.Y.C., 1977-80; trial and appellate counsel fed. programs br. of civil div. U.S. Dept. Justice, Washington, 1980-84; assoc. Jones, Day, Reavis & Pogue, Cleve., 1984-86, ptnr., 1987—. Editor Cornell U. Law Rev., 1974. Trustee Cleve. Ctr. for Contemporary Art, 1992-96, treas., 1992-94. Mem. ABA. Home: 2979 Broxton Rd Cleveland OH 44120-1819 Office: Jones Day Reavis & Pogue 901 Lakeside Ave E Cleveland OH 44114-1190 E-mail: tgrossman@jonesday.com.

GROTHMAN, GLENN, state legislator; b. July 3, 1955; BA, U. Wis. Tax & estate planning atty.; assemblyman Wis. State Dist. 59, 1993—. Active Washington County Vol. Ctr. Mem. Washington County Bar Assn., Kiwanis, Moose. Address: 111 S 6th Ave West Bend WI 53095-3308

GROTZINGER, LAUREL ANN, librarian, educator; b. Truman, Minn., Apr. 15, 1935; d. Edward F. and Marian Gertrude (Greeley) G. BA, Carleton Coll., 1957; MS, U. Ill., 1958, PhD, 1964. Instr., asst. libr. Ill. State U., 1958-62; asst. prof. Western Mich. U., Kalamazoo, 1964-66, assoc. prof., 1966-68, prof., 1968—, asst. dir. Sch. Librarianship, 1965-72, chief rsch. officer, 1979-86, interim dir. Sch. Libr. and Info. Sci., 1982-86, dean grad. coll., 1979-92, prof. univ. libr., 1993—. Author: The Power and the Dignity, 1966; mem. editl. bd. Jour. Edn. for Librarianship, 1973-77, Dictionary Am. Libr. Biography, 1975-77, Mich. Academician, 1990—; contbr. articles to profl. jours., books. Trustee Kalamazoo Pub. Libr., 1991-93, v.p., 1991-92, pres., 1992-93; pres. Kalamazoo Bach Festival, 1996-97, bd. dirs. 1992-98, exec. com. 1996-98. Mem. ALA (sec.-treas. Libr. History Round Table 1973-74, vice chmn., chmn-elect 1983-84, chmn. 1984-85, mem.-at-large 1991-93), Spl. Librs. Assn., Assn. Libr. Info. Sci. Edn., Mich. acad. Sci., Arts and Letters (mem.-at-large, exec. com. 1980-86, pres. 1983-85, exec. com. 1990-94, pres. 1991-93, vice chmn. libr./info. scis. 1996-97, chair 1997-98), Internat. Assn. Torch Clubs (v.p. Kalamazoo chpt. 1992-93, pres. 1993-94, exec. com. 1989-95), Soc. Collegiate Journalists, Phi Beta Kappa (pres. S.W. Mich. chpt. 1977-78, sec. 1994-97, pres. 1997-99), Beta Phi Mu, Alpha Beta Alpha, Delta Kappa Gamma (pres. Alpha Psi chpt. 1988-92), Phi Kappa Phi. Home: 2729 Mockingbird Dr Kalamazoo MI 49008-1626 E-mail: grotzinger@wmich.edu.

GROVE, RICHARD CHARLES, retired power tool company executive; b. Bethlehem, Pa., Aug. 13, 1940; s. Dale Addison and Mary Elizabeth (Ripple) G.; m. Cynthia Ann Dimmick, Dec. 7, 1963; 1 child, Jeffrey. BEE, Cornell U., 1962; MBA, U. Pitts., 1967. Mgmt. cons. Touche Ross & Co., Detroit, 1967-72; mgr. bus. planning Amstar Corp., N.Y.C., 1972-75, treas. Spreckels Sugar div. San Francisco, 1975-82, treas. N.Y.C., 1983-84, v.p., controller Stamford, Conn., 1985-88, v.p., chief fin. officer, 1988-89; sr. v.p. Esstar Inc., New Haven, 1989, exec. v.p., dir., 1995; exec. v.p. Milw. Electric Tool Corp., 1990-91, pres., chief exec. officer, 1991-2000. Bd. dirs. Rental Svc. Corp. Bd. dirs. Carolinas Concert Assn. Served to 1st lt. U.S. Army, 1964—66. Mem.: The Point Lake and Golf Club. Republican. Avocations: golf, reading, travel. E-mail: richardgrove@adelphia.net.

GROWE, JOAN ANDERSON, former state official; b. Mpls., Sept. 28, 1935; d. Lucille M. (Brown) Johnson; children: Michael, Colleen, David, Patrick. B.S., St. Cloud State U., 1956; cert. in spl. edn., U. Minn., 1964; exec. mgmt. program State and local govt., Harvard U., 1979. Tchr. elem. pub. schs., Bloomington, Minn., 1956-58; tchr. for exceptional children elem. pub. schs. St. Paul, 1964-65; spl. edn. tchr. St. Anthony Pub. Schs., Minn., 1965-66; mem. Minn. Ho. of Reps., 1973-74; sec. of state State of Minn., St. Paul, 1975-98. Mem. exec. coun. Minn. State Bd. Investment. Mem. Women Execs. in State Govt., Women's Polit. Caucus, Minn. Women's Econ. Roundtable; candidate U.S. Senate, 1984; bd. dirs. Minn. Internat. Ctr.; mem. Nat. Commn. for the Renewal of Am. Democracy (Project Democracy); bd. dirs. Nat. Dem. Inst. for Internat. Affairs; mem. adv. bd. Hubert H. Humphrey Inst. for Pub. Affairs; bd. dirs. Mpls. Found. Recipient Minn. Sch. Bell award, 1977, YMCA Outstanding Achievement award, 1978, Disting. Alumni award St. Cloud State U., 1979, Charlotte Striebel Long Distance Runner award Minn. NOW, 1985, The Woman Who Makes a Difference award Internat. Women's Forum, 1991, Esther V. Crosby Leadership award Greater Mpls. Girl Scout Coun., 1992, Pathfinder award for Innovative Solutions, Ctr. for Policy Alternatives, 1996, Breaking the Glass Ceiling award Women Execs. in State Govt., 1998. Mem. Nat. Assn. Secs. of State (pres. 1979-80), Internat. Womens Forum. Roman Catholic.

GROWNEY, ROBERT L. communications company professional; BSME, MBA, Ill. Inst. Technology. Various mgr. positions to gen. mgr. Fixed Products Divsn. Motorola, Inc., Schaumburg, Ill., 1966-89, sr. v.p., gen. mgr. Radio Technologies Group, 1989-91, sr. v.p., gen. mgr. Paging and Telepoint Systems Group, 1991-92, exec. v.p., gen. mgr. Paging and Wireless Data Group, 1992-94, pres., gen. mgr. Messaging, Info. and Media Sector, 1994-97, pres., CEO, 1997—, COO. Office: Motorola Inc 1303 E Algonquin Rd Schaumburg IL 60196-4041

GRUBB, FLOYD DALE, state legislator; b. June 26, 1949; BS, Purdue U., 1985. Agrl. economist; cash grain commodity broker; rep. Dist. 42 Ind. Ho. of Reps., mem. agr. com., chmn. Fin. Inst.; vice chmn. pub. health com. Farmer. Precinct committeeman, 1968—; chmn. Dem. Caucus, Ind. Named Outstanding Freshman House Dem., 1988. Mem. Am. Legion (adj. and comdr.), Nat. Fedn. Ind. Bus., Purdue U. Alumni Assn., Harry Truman Club, Ferguson Club. Home: PO Box 9 Covington IN 47932-0009

GRUBB, ROBERT L., JR. neurosurgeon; b. Charlotte, N.C., May 9, 1940; MD, U. N.C., 1965. Intern Barnes Hosp., St. Louis, 1965-66, resident in gen. surgery, 1966-67, resident in neurosurgery, 1969-73; fellow NIH, Bethesda, Md., 1968-69; mem. staff Barnes-Jewish Hosp., St. Louis, St. Louis Children's Hosp.; prof. neurosurgery Washington U., St. Louis. Fellow ACS; mem. Am. Acad. Neurol. Surgery, AANS, CNS, SNS. Office: Washington U Sch Medicine 660 S Euclid Ave Box 8057 Saint Louis MO 63110-1010 E-mail: grubbr@nsurg.wustl.edu.

GRUBBS, J. PERRY, church administrator; Pres. Ch. Extension of the Ch. of God, Anderson, Ind., 1987—. Office: Church of God PO Box 2069 Anderson IN 46018-2069

GRUBBS, ROBERT W. computer services company executive; Pres. Anixter U.S.A.; pres., CEO, Anixter Inc. subs. Anixter Internat. Inc., Anixter Internat. Inc. Office: Anixter Internat Inc 4711 Golf Rd Skokie IL 60076-1224

GRUBER, JOHN EDWARD, editor, railroad historian, photographer; b. Chgo., May 18, 1936; s. Edward David and Leah Elizabeth (Diehl) G.; m. Bonnie Jean Barstow, May 12, 1962; children: Richard J., Timothy J. BA in Journalism, U. Wis., 1959, postgrad., 1981-84. Editor, writer U. Wis., Madison, 1960-95; editor Vintage Rails, Waukesha, Wis., 1995-99. Author: Focus on Rails, 1989, (pamphlet) Madison's Pioneer Buildings, 1987; co-author: Caboose, 2001; acting editor Rail News, 1999; also articles; contbr. photographs to Trains mag., 1960—; contbg. editor: Classic Trains, 2000—. Dir. Historic Madison, Inc., 1981-89. Recipient Nat. Award in R.R. History for photography Rwy. and Locomotive Hist. Soc., 1994; James J. Hill rsch. grantee Hill Reference Libr., 1986. Mem. Mid-Continent Railway Hist. Soc. (bd. dirs. 1984-87, 88-97, pres. 1988-89, sec. 1990-95, v.p. 1995-97, editor Mid-Continent Railway Gazette 1982-99), Ctr. for R.R. Photography and Art (pres. 1997—). Home: 1430 Drake St Madison WI 53711-2211

GRUBERG, MARTIN, political science educator; b. N.Y.C., Jan. 28, 1935; s. Benjamin and Mollie (Stolnitz) G.; m. Rosaline Kurfirst, Mar. 25, 1967 (dec. 1980); m. Humaira Sayeed, Aug. 15, 1983. BA, CCNY, 1955; PhD, Columbia U., 1963. Agt.-adjudicator Passport Agy., Dept. State, N.Y.C, 1960-61; tchr. social studies Pelham (N.Y.) High Sch., 1961-62; instr. polit. sci. CUNY-Hunter Coll., 1961-62; tchr. social studies James Monroe and Seward Park High Schs., N.Y.C., 1962-63; asst. prof. polit. sci. U. Wis., Oshkosh, 1963-66, assoc. prof., 1966-69, prof., chmn. dept., 1969-72, dir. pre-law program, 1966-69, 83—, coord. criminal justice program, 1983-87. Author: Women in American Politics, 1968, A Case Study in U.S. Urban Leadership: The Incumbency of Milwaukee Mayor Henry Maier, 1996, A History of Winnebago County Government, 1998; newspaper column: Women: Our Largest Minority, The Paper for Ctrl. Wiso., 1970-71, Spotlight on Women for Oshkosh Northwestern, 1971-73; Broadcast 16 weeks Civil Rights Revolution, Wis. State FM Network, 1974; editor: Wis. Polit. Scientist, 1986-91; contbr. articles to encys., profl. jours. Pres. Oshkosh Human Rights Coun., 1966-68; v.p. Winnebago chpt. NOW, 1970-71, sec. Oshkosh chpt., 1980-81, pres., 1981-83; pres. Women's Caucus of Midwest Polit. Scientists, 1980-81; pres. Fox Valley ACLU, 1985—. Recipient Am. Legion Aux. Americanism award, 1949, Buckvar award, 1955, Steigman award, 1955; N.Y. State scholar, 1952; Columbia grantee, 1961, 62, Wis. Regents' rsch. grantee, 1964-70, 73-75. Mem. AAUP (state sec. 1975-81, pres.-elect 1981-82, 91-92, pres. 1982-83, 92-93), Am. Polit. Sci. Assn., Midwest Polit. Sci. Assn., Wis. Polit. Sci. Assn. (pres. 1974-75), Law and Soc. Assn., Acad. Criminal Justice Scis., Candlelight Club, Optimists. Home: 2121 Oregon St Oshkosh WI 54902-7058 Office: U Wis Clow Hall Oshkosh WI 54901 E-mail: gruberg@uwosh.edu.

GRUEBELE, MARTIN, chemistry, physics, and biophysics educator; b. Stuttgart, Federal Republic of Germany, Jan. 10, 1964; came to U.S., 1980; s. Helmut and Edith Victoria (Berner) G.; m. Nancy Makri, July 10, 1992; 2 children. BS in Chemistry, U. Calif., Berkeley, 1984, PhD in Chemistry, 1988. Rsch. fellow Calif. Inst. Tech., Pasadena, 1989-92; asst. prof. dept. chemistry U. Ill., Urbana, 1992-98, assoc. prof., 1998-99, prof. chemistry and biophysics, 1999—, prof. chemistry, physics, and biophysics, 2000—. Sr. editor Jour. Phys. Chemistry; mem. editl. bd. Jour. Chem. Physics., Chem. Phys. Lett., Ann. Rev. Phys. Chem. Recipient New Faculty award Dreyfus Found., 1992, Nat. Young Investigator award NSF, 1994, Coblentz award, 2000; fellow IBM, 1986-87, Dow Chem. Co., 1987-88, David and Lucile Packard Found., 1994, Sloan fellow, 1997; Cottrell scholar, 1995, Camille and Henry Dreyfus scholar, 1998, Alfred P. Sloan fellow, 1998; Univ. scholar U. Ill., 1998. Mem. Am. Phys. Soc., Am. Chem. Soc., Biophys. Soc., Sigma Xi. Achievements include research of theoretical and experimental studies of novel transient molecular species, studies in laser-control of chemical reactions and molecular vibrational relaxation, as well as fast time-resolved protein folding dynamics. Office: U Ill Dept Chemistry Box 5-6 600 S Mathews Ave Urbana IL 61801-3602

GRUEN, GERALD ELMER, psychologist, educator; b. Granite City, Ill., July 19, 1937; s. Elmer George and Velma Pearl G.; m. Karol Jane Selvidge, Mar. 20, 1960; children— Tami Jane, Christy Lynn. B.A., So. Ill. U., 1959; M.A., U. Ill., 1963, Ph.D., 1964. Postdoctoral fellow Heinz Werner Inst. of Developmental Psychology, Clark U. and Worcester (Mass.) State Hosp., 1964-66; asst. prof. dept. psychol. scis. Purdue U., West Lafayette, Ind., 1966-69, assoc. prof., 1969-74, prof., 1974—, head dept. psychol. scis., 1987-97. Author: (with T. Wachs) Early Experience and Human Development; contbr. chpt. to The Structuring of Experience, 1977; contbr. articles to profl. jours. Deacon Calvary Baptist Ch., West Lafayette. Recipient USPHS rsch. awards, 1968-71, Nat. Rsch. Svc. award NIMH, 1976-80, Research award Nat. Insts. Child Health and Human Devel., 1981—; recipient Ind. Psychol. Assn. Gordon Barrows award for disting. career contbns., 2000. Fellow APA, Am. Psychol. Soc. (charter mem.); mem. Midwestern Psychol. Assn., Soc. for Rsch. in Child Devel., Sigma Xi. Home: 3738 Westlake Ct West Lafayette IN 47906 Office: Purdue U Psychology Dept West Lafayette IN 47907 E-mail: gruen@psych.purdue.edu.

GRUHN, ROBERT STEPHEN, retired parole officer; b. N.Y.C., Dec. 9, 1938; s. Jerome and Beatrice (Fuchs) G.; m. Shirley Darlene Brayfield, Sept. 14, 1984. BS, NYU, 1961; MA in Criminology, Sam Houston State U., 1975; AB in Legal Studies, Drury Coll., 1987. Cert. criminal investigator, gang crime specialist, State of Ill. Collection mgr. Sears, Roebuck & Co., Albuquerque, 1961-64; adjuster Gen. Adjustment Bur., 1964-65; indsl. engr. LTV Aerospace Corp., Dallas, 1965-66; agy. sec. Am. Nat. Ins., 1966-72; parole officer Tex. Bd. Parole, Dallas and Houston, 1974-80, Mo. Bd. Parole, Springfield, 1980-99; investigator Greene County (Mo.) Prosecuting Atty. Office, 1999—. With Springfield Police Dept. Tng. Acad. Facility, 1984-90; presenter Gang Awareness Program, S.W. Mo., 1992-99, Mo. State Hwy. Patrol Tng. Acad., 1997-99. Author Collision Course, 1984. Bd. dirs. Wayback Halfway House, Dallas, 1977-80; chmn. Gang Task Force, Springfield, 1996-97, So. Mo. Fugitive Task Force, Springfield, 1992-93; bd. dirs. youth svcs. Mo. Dept. Corrections, 1993—; sr. v.p. One Missing Link, Children Non-Profit Orgn., 1994—, active P.E.A.C.E. Project, Springfield, 1994-95; mem. Missing Persons Task Force, 2000—, Utility Theft Divsn. Task Force, 2000—. Recipient commendation cert. N.Y. Police Dept., 1961, Cert. of Achievement in Extremism and Terrorism, Mo. Dept. Corrections, 1986, Cert. of Achievement in Satanism and the Occult, Mo. Dept. Corrections, 1989, Cert. of Achievement in Dangerous Gangs, 1989, Cert. Achievement, Mid States Organized Crime Info. Ctr., 1990, Cert. of Appreciation, U.S. Treasury Dept., 1992. Mem. Am. Mgmt. Assn. (internat. v.p. 1971-74), Soc. for Advt. Mgmt. (sec. 1968-71, pres. 1971-72), Soc. for Advancement of Mgmt. (Profl. Achievement award 1972), Mo. Corrections Assn., Midwest Gang Investigations Assn., Mu Gamma Tau. Avocation: writing. Home: 6226 N State Hwy 2 Willard MO 65781-9720 Office: 1010 N Boonville Ave Springfield MO 65802-3804

GRUMBO, HOWARD, state legislator; m. Joyce Helgeson; 3 children. BS, U. N.D., 1958; MA, Long Beach State U., 1972. Tchr. Lidgerwood (N.D.) Pub. Sch., 1958-90; ret., 1990; state rep. dist. 27, 1991—. Mem. industry, bus. and labor com., transp. com. N.D. Ho. Reps., 1993-95, polit. subcom. and judiciary, 1991, edn. com. and transp. com., 1995-97, 99-2001. Mem. Pk. Bd. Commn.; chmn. Cmty. Devel. Corp. Mem. Lions (pres.). Democrat. Home: PO Box 435 Lidgerwood ND 58053-0435

GRUNDBERG, BETTY, state legislator, property manager; b. Woden, Iowa, Feb. 16, 1938; d. Edwin and Eva Ruth Meyer; m. Arnie Grundberg, Dec. 31, 1960; children: Christine, Julie, Michael, Susan. BA, Wartburg Coll., 1959; MA, U. Iowa, 1969; postgrad., Drake U. Cert. tchr. Property mgr. and renovator, Des Moines, 1973—; with Des Moines Sch. Bd., 1975-90; legis. State of Iowa, Des Moines, 1993—. Chmn. edn. com.; mem. human resources com., labor com. Active LWV, Des Moines, 1972—. Republican. Home and Office: 224 Foster Dr Des Moines IA 50312-2540

GRUNDHOFER, JERRY A. bank executive; BA, Loyola Marymount U., 1967. With Union Bank, 1967-81; pres. Alliance Bank, 1981-83; sr. v.p. So. Calif. corp. banking, sr. v.p. So. Calif. retail banking ops. Wells Fargo Bank, 1983-85, exec. v.p. 440 br. statewidef retail banking sys., 1985-87; vice chmn. Security Pacific Nat. Bank, 1987-90, pres., CEO, 1990-93, Star Banc Corp., Cin., 1993—, also chmn. bd. dirs.; pres., CEO Star Bank, N.A., 1993—, also bd. dirs.; CEO Firstar Corp., Milw.; chmn. U.S. Bancorp (formerly Firstar Corp.), Minneapolis, 2001—. Bd. dirs. Arete Assocs., Cin. Equity Fund, L.L.C., Hennegan Co., Visa Internat., Visa U.S.A., Inc., mem. exec. com. Trustee Children's Hosp. Med. Ctr., Health Found. Greater Cin., Cin. Symphony Orch., United Appeal/Cmty. Chest, United Way, U. Cin. Found., Xavier U.; co-chair Fine Arts Fund Campaign, 1995, chmn., 1996; co-chmn. Urban Capital Campaign, 1995, 96; chmn. corp. exec. com. 13th ann. tribute dinner Jewish Inst. Rel. Hebrew Union Coll., 1995; chmn. ann. dinner Nat. Conf. Christians and Jews, 1997; bd. dirs. Nat. Underground Railroad Freedom Ctr. Honoree 15th ann. tribute dinner Jewish Inst. Rel. Hebrew Union Coll., 1997. Mem. Am. Bankers Assn. (bd. dirs.), Internat. Fin. Conf. (bd. dirs.), Bankers Roundtable (bd. dirs.), Greater Cin. C. of C. (bd. dirs.), Over-the-Rhine C. of C. (bd. dirs.), Birnan Woods, Cin. Country Club, Comml. Club (mem. exec. com.), Double Eagle Golf Club, Queen City Club. Office: US Bancorp US Bank Pl 601 2nd Ave S Minneapolis MN 55402

GRUNDHOFER, JOHN F. banking executive; b. L.A., 1939; Student, Loyola U., 1960, U. So. Calif., 1964. Formerly with Wells Fargo & Co., San Francisco, also vice chmn.; now chmn., pres., CEO U.S. Bancorp (formerly First Bank System, Inc.), Mpls., 1990—; also dir. First Bank System, Inc. Office: US Bancorp 601 2nd Ave S Minneapolis MN 55402-4303

GRUNDY, KENNETH WILLIAM, political science educator; b. Phila., Aug. 6, 1936; s. William and Alma (Hahn) G.; m. Martha Jonet Paxson, June 25, 1960; children: William MacIntyre, Thomas Paxson, Anne Edmunds. BA with honors, Ursinus Coll., 1958; MA, Pa. State U., 1961, PhD, 1963. Asst. prof. polit. sci. San Fernando Valley State Coll., Northridge, Calif., 1963-66; assoc. prof. Case Western Res. U., Cleve., 1966-74, prof., 1974-88, Marcus A. Hanna prof., 1988—, chmn. dept. polit. sci., 1974-76, dir. Ctr. for Policy Studies, 1998-2000. Vis. sr. lectr. Makerere U. Coll., Kampala, Uganda, 1967-68; vis. scholar Inst. Social Studies, The Hague, The Netherlands, 1972-73, U. Pretoria, 1998; vis. Fulbright prof. U. Zambia, Lusaka, 1977, Nat. U. Ireland, Galway, 1979-80; vis. adj. prof. Cleve. State U., 1992—; editl. adv. bd. Ctr. Internat. Race Rels., 1968—. Author: Conflicting Images of the Military in Africa, 1968, Guerrilla Struggle in Africa, 1971, Confrontation and Accommodation in Southern Africa, 1973, (with Weinstein) The Ideologies of Violence, 1974, We're Against Apartheid, But, 1974, Defense Legislation and Communal Politics, 1978, (with V. McHale and B. Hughes) Evaluating Transnational Programs in Government and Business, 1980, Soldiers Without Politics, 1983, The Militarization of South African Politics, 1986, rev. edit., 1988, South Africa: Domestic Crisis and Global Challenge, 1991, The Politics of the National Arts Festival, 1993; also articles; book rev. editor Internat. Jour. Comparative Sociology, 1973-83; assoc. editor Jour. African Policy Studies, 1991—; contbg. editor Current History, 1982—; mem. editl. adv. bd. African Affairs, 1983-93; mem. editl. bd. Jour. Third World Studies, 1988—, South African Jour. Internat. Affairs, 1993-98. Fellow NDEA, 1959-62, Rhodes U., Grahamstown, South Africa, 1989-90, Ctr. Internat. Race Rels., 1969-70; 1st Bradlow fellow South African Inst. Internat. Rels., 1982; grantee Rockefeller Found., 1967-68, Social Sci. Rsch. Coun., 1972, 79-80, Earhart Found, 1979. Mem. African Studies Assn. (mem. exec. coun.), Inter-Univ. Seminar on Armed Forces and Soc., Internat. Studies Assn. Home: 2602 Exeter Rd Cleveland OH 44118-4246 Office: Case Western Res U Dept Polit Sci Cleveland OH 44106

GRUNSFELD, ERNEST ALTON, III, architect; b. Chgo., June 5, 1929; s. Ernest Alton Jr. and Mary Jane (Loeb) G.; m. Sally Riblett, July 10, 1954 (dec. 1999); children: Marcia Grunsfeld Henner, John Mace. Student, Inst. Design, Chgo., 1945, Art Inst. Chgo., 1946; BArch, MIT, 1952. Registered architect, Ill., Conn., Ind., Mich., N.C., Ohio, Mo., Tex., Wis. Ptnr. Yerkes & Grunsfeld, Chgo., 1956-65; owner Grunsfeld & Assocs., Architects, 1965-75, sr. ptnr., 1975-84, owner, 1984—2001; prin. Grunsfeld Shafer Architects, LLC, 2001—. Corp. mem. Woodlawn Hosp., Chgo., 1968-70; mem. Highland Park (Ill.) Planning Commn., 1969-75; pres. Grunsfeld Meml. Fund, Chgo., 1970—. Contbr. articles to profl. jours. Bd. dirs. Urban Gateways, Chgo., 1968-89, mem. adv. bd., 1989—; life mem. Field Mus. Natural History, Chgo., 1970—, Chgo. Symphony Orch. Assn., 1975—, governing mem., 1995—; mem. exec. com. Coun. for Arts MIT, Cambridge, 1977-89, bd. dirs., 1977—; hon. life mem. Chgo. Hort. Soc., 1995—; benefactor, hon. governing mem. Art Inst. Chgo., 1980—. Recipient 1st Honor award Burlington Mills, 1968. Fellow AIA (corp. mem. Chgo. chpt., Honor award 1962, citation of merit 1969); mem. Tavern Club, Lake Shore Country Club, Arts Club of Chgo. Office: Grunsfeld Schafer Architects LLC 211 E Ontario St Chicago IL 60611-3219

GRUPPEN, LARRY DALE, psychologist, educational researcher; b. Zeeland, Mich., Jan. 27, 1955; s. Howard Melvin and Gertrude Jean (Huizenga) G.; m. Mary Louise Shell, May 27, 1978; children: Timothy Andrew, Matthew Scott. MA, U. Mich., 1984, PhD, 1987. Rsch. investigator U. Mich. Med. Sch., Ann Arbor, 1987-88, asst. rsch. scientist, 1988—. Contbr. articles to Jour. AMA, Acad. Medicine, other profl. publs. Grantee Agy. Health Care Policy and Rsch., 1991—, Mich. Alzheimer's Disease Rsch. Ctr., 1992—, NIH, 1993—. Mem. APA, Am. Ednl. Rsch. Assn., Soc. Med. Decision Making, Soc. Judgement and Decision Making. Achievements include investigation of foundation and development of medical expertise, clinical reasoning and expert judgment, development of computer-based educational methods in medical education, exploration of process of innovation dissemination. Office: U Mich Med Sch G1211 Towsley Ln Ann Arbor MI 48105-9573

GRZESIAK, KATHERINE ANN, primary educator; BS, Ctrl. Mich. U., 1968; MA in Tchg., Saginaw Valley State U., 1975; postgrad., various univs., 1975—. 6th grade tchr. Buena Vista Sch. Dist., Saginaw, Mich., 1968-69, 70-71; tchr. Carrollton Pub. Schs., 1972-80, St. Peter and Paul Elem. Sch., Saginaw, 1981-84, Sch. Dist. of City of Saginaw, 1984-90; instr. Ctr. for Innovation in Edn., Saratoga, Calif., 1989—; tchr. Midland (Mich.) Pub. Schs., 1991—; 5th grade tchr. Eastlawn Elem., Midland. Adj. faculty Saginaw Valley State U., University Center, Mich., 1976-80, 88-90; presenter in field. Contbr. articles to profl. jours. Recipient Presdl. award for Excellence and Math. Tchg., 1994, Top Tchr. in Mich. Met. Woman mag., 1997, Nat. Educator award Milken Family Found., 1998, Presdl. award for excellence in sci. and math. tchg.; named Mich. Tchr. of Yr., 1998. Home: 3115 Mcgill St Midland MI 48642-3928 Office: Eastlawn Elem Sch 115 Eastlawn Dr Midland MI 48640-5561 E-mail: grzesiak@mindnet.org.

GSCHNEIDNER, KARL ALBERT, JR. metallurgist, educator, editor, consultant; b. Detroit, Nov. 16, 1930; s. Karl and Eugenie (Zehetmair) Gschneidner; m. Melba E. Pickenpaugh, Nov. 4, 1957; children: Thomas, David, Edward, Kathryn. BS, U. Detroit, 1952; PhD, Iowa State U., 1957. Mem. staff Los Alamos Sci. Lab., 1957-62, sec. chief, 1961-62; vis. asst. prof. U. Ill., Urbana, 1962-63; assoc. prof. materials sci. and engring. Iowa

State U., Ames, 1963-67, prof., 1967-79, Disting. prof., 1979—, metallurgist, 1963-67, sr. metallurgist, 1967—, dir. Rare-earth Info. Ctr., 1966-96; vis. prof. U. Calif.-San Diego, La Jolla, 1979-80; cons. Los Alamos Nat. Lab., 1981-86, Teltech, 1987-2000. Author: Rare Earth Alloys, 1961, Scandium, 1975, others; editor: (32 vol. book) Handbook on the Physics and Chemistry of Rare Earths, 1978-2001, Industrial Applications of Rare Earth Elements, 1981; contbr. numerous chpts. in books and articles to profl. publs. Recipient William Hume-Rothery award AIME, Warrendale, Pa., 1978, Burlington No. award for Excellence in Rsch., Iowa State U., 1989, Significant Implication for Energy Related Techs. in Metallurgy and Ceramics award Dept. Energy, 1997; co-recipient Outstanding Sci. Accomplishment in Metallurgy and Ceramics award Dept. Energy, Washington, 1982, Frank H. Spedding award Rare Earth Rsch. Confs., 1991, Russell B. Scott Meml. award Cryogenic Engr. Conf., 1995, David R. Boyland Eminent Faculty award in Rsch. Coll. Engring., Iowa State U., 1997; named Sci. Alumnus of 2000, U. Detroit-Mercy. Fellow Minerals, Metals and Materials Soc., Am. Soc. for Materials Internat.; mem. AAAS, Am. Chem. Soc., Am. Crystallographic Assn., Materials Rsch. Soc., Am. Phys. Soc., Iowa Acad. Sci., Materials Rsch. Soc. India (hon.), Cryogenic Soc. Am., Japan Inst. Metals (hon. mem.). Roman Catholic. Office: Iowa State U Ames Lab Ames IA 50011-3020 E-mail: cagey@ameslab.gov.

GUAN, KUN-LIANG, biochemist, educator; b. Tongxian, China, Apr. 28, 1963; s. Xian Xiu and Mei Wen (Zhang) G.; m. Yuli Wang, Apr. 25, 1986; children: Jean, Eric. BS, Hangzheu U., 1982; PhD, Purdue U., 1989. Rsch. asst., postdoctoral fellow Purdue U., West Lafayette, Ind., 1983-91; lectr., asst. prof. U. Mich., Ann Arbor, 1991—, asst. rsch. scientist, 1992—, assoc. prof., 1996—. Patentee in field; contbr. articles to profl. jours. Grantee Am. Cancer Soc., 1993, NIH, 1994; McArthur fellow, 1998. Achievements include DNA encoding in 18 kd CDK6 inhibiting protein, discovering the essential disease gene in bulbonic plague is an tyrosine phosphatase, discovering the dual specific phosphatase class, determining the mechanism of MAP Kinase kinase activation. Office: Dept Biol Chemistry Univ Mich Ann Arbor MI 48109

GUBOW, DAVID M. state legislator; AB in Urban Studies, U. Mich., 1971; JD, U. Detroit, 1974. Assoc. Zeff & Zeff, Detroit, 1975-76; ptnr. Gubow & Sirlin, Southfield, Mich., 1977-80, May, Gowing & Simpson, P.C., Bloomfield Hills, 1980-89; of counsel May, Simpson & Strote, P.C., 1989-91, Reosti, James & Sirlin, P.C., Detroit, 1991—; mem. dist. 35 Mich. Ho. of Reps., Lansing, 1985-98, asst. clerk, 1999—. Majority whip Mich. Ho. of Reps., 1985-94, former chmn. ins. and mental health com., vice chair judiciary com., mem. health policy, pub. utilities, tax policy, corrections and sr. citizens and retirement coms., chair spl. ad-hoc physician licensure com., adoption sub-com.; lectr. Inst. Continuing Legal Edn., Mich., Mich. Orgn. Diabetes Educators, Am. Soc. Indsl. Security, Mich. Pub. adminstr. Oakland County Mich., 1977-81; vice-chair, sec.-treas. Oakland County Bldg. Authority, Pontiac, Mich., 1976-80. Mem. State Bar Mich., Oakland County Bar Assn. (past chmn.), Judicial Conf. of 6th Cir. (life), Jewish Cmty. Coun., Jewish Welfare Fedn. Home: 26728 York Rd Huntington Woods MI 48070-1358 Address: Capitol Bldg Lansing MI 48909

GUDEMAN, STEPHEN FREDERICK, anthropology educator; b. Chgo., June 29, 1939; s. Edward and Frances (Alschuler) G.; m. Roxane Harvey, Sept. 20, 1965; children: Rebecca, Elise, Keren AB, Harvard U., 1961, MBA, 1965; MA, Cambridge U., Eng., 1963, PhD, 1970. Asst. prof. anthropology U. Minn.-Mpls., 1969-74, assoc. prof. anthropology, 1974-78, prof. anthropology, 1978—, chmn. dept., 1984-89, 96-97, 98-2001; mem. Inst. Advanced Study, Princeton, N.J., 1978-79; fellow Ctr. for Advanced Study, Palo Alto, Calif., 1995-96. Sr. fellowship NEH, 1983-84; mem. selection com. Marshall Scholarships, 1983-86; Benedict Disting. vis. prof. Carleton Coll., 1981; Hardy Chair lecture Hartwick Coll., 1985 Author: Relationships, Residence and the Individual, 1976, Demise of a Rural Economy, 1978, Economics As Culture, 1986, Conversations in Colombia, 1990; editor Cambridge Studies in Anthropology, 1989-96; contbr. numerous articles to profl. jours. Marshall scholar, 1961-63. Fellow Am. Anthropol. Assn. (bd. dirs. 1987-91), Am. Ethnological Soc. (pres. 1989-91, bd. dirs. 1987-91, assoc. editor 1981-84), Royal Anthropol. Inst. (sec., chmn. N.Am. com. 1983-88, Curl Bequest Essay prize 1971), Soc. Econ. Anthropology Avocations: tennis, jogging, music. Home: 1650 Dupont Ave S Minneapolis MN 55403-1101

GUELICH, ROBERT VERNON, retired management consultant; b. Dayton, Ohio, Oct. 30, 1917; m. Jane E. Schory, Dec. 6, 1941; children: Susan MacKenzie, Robert V. Jr., Helen Jane. B.A., Ohio Wesleyan U., 1938; M.B.A., Harvard U., 1940. Reporter Dayton Jour., 1935-37; overseas corr., staff editor Air Force mag., 1942-46; asst. dir. public relations Firestone Co., Akron, Ohio, 1946-57; sr. v.p. pub. relations Montgomery Ward & Co., Chgo., 1957-81; sr. mgmt. cons. Hill & Knowlton, 1981-83; asst. to chmn. Nat. Fitness Found., 1981-90; pres. Robert V. Guelich & Assocs., Inc., 1981—; pub. rels. cons. Exec. Svc. Corp. of Chgo., 1983-89. Chmn. Nat. Pub. Rels. Seminar, 1981. Bd. dirs. Nat. 4-H Coun., 1972-81; pres. bd. edn. New Trier Twp. High Sch., 1965-70. Maj. USAF, 1941-46. Recipient George Washington Honor medal Freedoms Found., 1977 Mem. Pub. Rels. Soc. Am. (bd. dirs. 1976-79, 3 Silver Anvil awards, 4 Presdl. Citations 1976, Outstanding Film award 1977), Chgo. Yacht Club, Mich. Shores Club, Phi Beta Kappa, Phi Gamma Delta, Sigma Delta Chi. Presbyterian. Home and Office: 380 Sterling Rd Kenilworth IL 60043-1048

GUENO, BARBARA, radio personality; Radio host Sta. WGCI-FM, Chgo. Office: WGCI 332 S Michigan Ave Ste 600 Chicago IL 60604*

GUEQUIERRE, JOHN PHILLIP, manufacturing company executive; b. Milw., Sept. 10, 1946; s. Gerald Herbert and Louise Ann (Fenske) G.; m. Mary Rowlands Speer, Aug. 17, 1968; children: William Edward, Robert John, Elizabeth Louise. BA, U. Wis., 1968; MBA, U. Chgo., 1972. Systems analyst Inland Steel Co., East Chgo., Ind., 1968-72; analyst inventory INRYCO, Milw., 1972-73, supr. material planning, 1973-74, mgr. contract adminstrn., 1974-76; mgr. fin. Inland Steel Devel. Corp., Washington, 1976-78; mgr. fin. analysis Inland Steel Urban Devel. Corp., Chgo., 1978-80; v.p. adminstrn. Scholz Homes Inc., Tol., 1980-83; sr. v.p. adminstrn., dir. Schult Homes Corp., Middlebury, Ind., 1983-92, sr. v.p. ops., dir., 1992-95, pres. manufactured housing group, 1995-99; sr. v.p. mfg. Oakwood Homes, 1999-2000; pres., CEO Pleasant St. Homes, LLC, 2000—. Chmn. budget subcom. United Way, Elkhart, Ind., 1983-89, bd. dirs. 1989-2000, treas., 1990-92, chmn. 1992; adult leader 4H, Elkhart County, 1983—; bd. dirs. Elkhart Chamber Found., 1993-98; bd. dirs. Ind. Assn. United Ways, 1993-2000, vice chmn., 1995-97, chmn., 1997. Mem.: Beta Gamma Sigma, Phi Kappa Phi, Phi Beta Kappa. Republican. Presbyterian. Office: Pleasant St Homes LLC 51700 Lovejoy Dr Middlebury IN 46540

GUERRI, WILLIAM GRANT, lawyer; b. Higbee, Mo., Mar. 30, 1921; s. Grant and Pearl (Zambelli) G.; m. Millicent K. Branding; children: Paula Ann Guerri Baker, Glenda Kay, William Grant. AB, Central Meth. Coll., 1943; LLB, Columbia, 1946. Bar: NY 1946, Mo. 1947. Ptnr. Thompson Coburn LLP, St. Louis, 1956—. Mem. bd. editors: Columbia Law Rev, 1945-46. Hon. mem. bd. dirs. St. Louis Heart Assn., chmn., 1972-73; bd. dirs. United Way Greater St. Louis, 1976-94; curator Ctrl. Meth. Coll., 1981-97. Fellow The Fellows of Am. Bar; mem. ABA, Mo. Bar Assn. (trustee 1984-92), Bar Assn. Met. St. Louis, Assn. of Bar of City of N.Y., Am. Law Inst., Am. Judicature Soc., Noonday Club, Round Table Club, Phi Delta Phi. Home: Apt 308 14300 Conway Meadows Ct E Chesterfield MO 63017-9612 Office: Thompson Coburn LLP Ste 3000 1 US Bank Plz Saint Louis MO 63101-1643 E-mail: wguerri@thompsoncoburn.com.

GUFFEY, EDITH ANN, religious organization administrator; Asst. to dir. student records U. Kans., 1984-90, assoc. dir. admissions, 1990-91; sec. United Ch. of Christ, Cleve., 1991—. Office: United Ch of Christ 700 Prospect Ave E Cleveland OH 44115-1131

GUIMOND, RICHARD JOSEPH, communications executive; b. Massena, N.Y., Oct. 28, 1947; BSMechE, U. Notre Dame, 1969; M Engring., Rensselaer Poly. Inst., 1970; MS in Environ. Health, Harvard U., 1973. Registered profl. engr., D.C. Commd. officer USPHS, 1970, advanced through grades to rear adm. (upper half), 1995, ret., 1996; with EPA, Washington, 1971-93; spl. asst. Office Radiation Programs, 1971-74, environ. project leader, Criteria and Standards div., 1974-78; chief engr. Office of Chem. Control, 1978-79; chief spl. reports br. Office of Toxic Substances, 1981, chief chem. control br., 1981-82; dir. Criteria & Standards div. Office Radiation Programs, 1982-86, dir. Radon div., 1986-88, dir. Office Radiation Protection, 1988-91; dep. asst. adminstr. Office Solid Waste and Emergency Response, Washington, 1991-93, acting asst. adminstr., 1993; prin. dept. asst. sec. Office Environ. Mgmt. Dept. Energy, 1993-96; corp. dir. environ. health & safety Motorola, Inc., Schaumburg, Ill., 1996—; vice pres. Motorola Inc., 1999—. Mem.: Res. Officers Assn., Commd. Officers Assn. USPHS, Health Physics Soc. Roman Catholic. Home: 1009 Oakland Ct Barrington IL 60010-6310 Office: Motorola Inc 1303 E Algonquin Rd Schaumburg IL 60196-1079

GUISEWITE, CATHY LEE, cartoonist; b. Dayton, Ohio, Sept. 5, 1950; d. William Lee and Anne (Duly) G. BA in English, U. Mich., 1972; LHD (hon.), R.I. Coll., 1979, Eastern Mich. U., 1981. Writer Campbell-Ewald Advt., Detroit, 1972-73; writer Norman Prady, Ltd., 1973-74, W.B. Doner & Co., Advt., Southfield, Mich., 1974-75, group supr., 1975-76, v.p., 1976-77; creator, writer, artist Cathy comic strip Universal Press Syndicate, Mission, Kans., 1976—. Author, artist: The Cathy Chronicles, 1978, What Do You Mean, I Still Don't Have Equal Rights??!!, 1980, What's a Nice Single Girl Doing with a Double Bed??!, 1981, I Think I'm Having a Relationship with a Blueberry Pie!, 1981, It Must Be Love, My Face Is Breaking Out, 1982, Another Saturday Night of Wild and Reckless Abandon, 1982, Cathy's Valentine's Day Survival Book, How to Live through Another February 14, 1982, How to Get Rich, Fall in Love, Lose Weight, and Solve all Your Problems by Saying "NO", 1983, Eat Your Way to a Better Relationship, 1983, A Mouthful of Breath Mints and No One to Kiss, 1983, Climb Every Mountain, Bounce Every Check, 1983, Men Should Come with Instruction Booklets, 1984, Wake Me Up When I'm a Size 5, 1985, Thin Thighs in Thirty Years, 1986, A Hand to Hold, An Opinion to Reject, 1987, Why Do the Right Words Always Come Out of the Wrong Mouth?, 1988, My Granddaughter Has Fleas, 1989, $14 in the Bank and a $200 Face in My Purse, 1990, Reflections (A Fifteenth Anniversary Collection), 1991, Only Love can Break a Heart, but a Shoe Sale Can Come Close, 1992, Revelations From a 45-Pound Purse, 1993; TV work includes 3 animated Cathy spls. (Emmy award 1987). Recipient Reuben award Nat. Cartoonists Soc., 1992. Office: Universal Press Syndicate 4520 Main St Ste 700 Kansas City MO 64111-7701

GULDA, EDWARD JAMES, business acquisitions executive; b. Detroit, Oct. 28, 1945; s. Alfred and Lucy Irene (Ball) G.; m. Nancy Mary Greenlee, Nov. 28, 1964; children: Kimberly Sue Marsh, Nicholas Edward. BS in Aerospace Engring., U. Mich., 1968, MBA, 1979. Systems engr. LTV Aerospace Corp., Sterling Heights, Mich., 1966-72; mgr. systems engring. Ford Motor Co., Dearborn, 1972-78; mgr., prodn. plan. Rockwell Internat. Corp., 1978-79, dir. prod. plan. Troy, 1979-80, dir. mkt. electronics, 1980-81, gen. mgr. auto electronics, 1981-84, v.p. rsch. and engring., 1984-85; pres. ITT Teves Am., 1985-87; group v.p. engring. ITT Auto, Inc., 1987-88; pres., chief exec. officer Dayton Walther (Varity) Corp., Dayton, Ohio, 1988-89; pres. Varity Brake Group Kelsey-Hayes Brake Group N.Am., Romulus, Mich., 1989-94; pres. Kelsey-Hayes Co., 1994-95, chief exec. Livonia, 1995; chmn. and CEO Peregrine Inc., Southfield, 1996-98; pres. Kinnick Group LLC, 1998—. Mem. MENSA, Birmingham Country Club, Golf Club Fiddler's Creek, Tarpon Bay Club. Avocations: hunting, golf. Office: 2706 Horseshoe Dr S Naples FL 34104 E-mail: ed@ejgulda.com.

GULLESON, PAM, state legislator; Home: PO Box 215 Rutland ND 58067-0215 Office: ND Ho of Reps State Capitol Bismarck ND 58505

GULLICKSON, GLENN, JR. physician, educator; b. Mpls., July 9, 1919; s. Glenn and Grace (Stellwagen) G.; m. Glenna A. Swore, May 18, 1957; children: Mary, Glenn III. B.A., U. Minn., 1942, M.D., 1945, Ph.D., 1961. Diplomate: Am. Bd. Phys. Medicine and Rehab. Intern Gallinger Municipal Hosp., Washington, 1944-45; faculty U. Minn. Med. Sch., Mpls., 1946—, assoc. prof. phys. medicine and rehab., 1961-66, prof. phys. medicine and rehab., 1966-86, prof. emeritus, 1986—, acting head dept., 1974-75, interim head, 1982-85, asst. dir. Rehab. Center, 1954-61, dir. Rehab. Center, 1961-86. Exec. dir. Am. Congress Phys. Medicine and Rehab., 1960-66; mem. exam. com. phys. therapists Minn. Bd. Med. Examiners, 1961-71, pres., 1968-71; mem. med. adv. com. Minn. Soc. for Crippled Children and Adults, 1967-72; fellow stroke council Am. Heart Assn., mem. exec. com., 1971-74; mem. neurol. scis. research tng. com. Nat. Inst. Neurol. Diseases and Blindness, 1965-69; exec. com. Joint Com. Stroke Facilities, 1969-78. Served to lt. (s.g.), M.C. USNR, 1945-46, 53-54. Mem. AMA (prin. rep. interspity. com. 1968-72, mem. residency review com. phys. medicine, rehab. 1971-79), AAUP, Minn. Med. Soc., Hennepin County Med. Soc., Minn. Med. Found., Am. Acad. Phys. Medicine and Rehab. (gov., v.p. 1968-69, pres. 1970-71), Am. Bd. Phys. Medicine and Rehab. (chmn. 1976-81, asst. to exec. dir. 1987-90), Am. Congress Rehab. Medicine (v.p. 1978-84, pres. 1984-85), Assn. Acad. Physiatrists, Sigma Xi. Home: # 225 9550 Collegeview Rd Bloomington MN 55437-2175 Office: Health Scis Ctr Univ Minn Minneapolis MN 55455

GUMBLETON, THOMAS J. bishop; b. Detroit, Jan. 26, 1930; Student, St. John Provincial Sem., Mich., Pontifical Lateran U., Rome. Ordained priest Roman Cath. Ch. 1956. Apptd. titular bishop Ululi and aux. bishop Roman Catholic Arch Diocese, Detroit, 1968—; pastor St. Leo Ch.

GUND, GORDON, venture capitalist, sports team executive; b. Cleve., Oct. 15, 1939; s. George and Jessica (Roesler) G.; m. Llura Liggett; children: Grant Ambler, Gordon Zachary. BA, Harvard U., 1961; DPubSvc (hon.), U. Maryland, 1980; DHL, Whittier Coll., 1993; LLD (hon.), U. Vt., 1994; PhD (hon.), Goteburg U., Sweden, 1997. Pres., chmn., CEO Gund Investment Corp., Princeton, N.J.; prin. owner Cleve. Cavaliers, NBA, 1983—; co-owner San Jose Sharks, NHL, 1990—. Mem. bd. govs. NHL, NBA; bd. dirs. Kellogg Co., Corning Inc.; mem. U.S. Olympic com. Co-founder The Found. Fighting Blindness, 1971, also chmn.; pres., trustee Gund Collection of Western Art; mem. Nat. Adv. Eye Coun., 1980-84. Office: Gund Investment Corp PO Box 449 14 Nassau St Princeton NJ 08542-4523

GUNDERSON, RICHARD L. insurance company executive; b. 1933; BSME, S.D. State U., Brookings, 1958; MBA, Northwestern U., 1961. V.p. investments St. Paul (Minn.) Cos., 1961-74, v.p. and asst. to the pres., 1974-76; pres. Western Life Ins. Co., St. Paul, 1976-85; pres., CEO Aid Assn. Luths., Appleton, Wis., 1985-95, chmn. bd., 1996—. With U.S. Army, 1954-57

GUNDERSON, SCOTT LEE, state legislator; b. Oct. 24, 1956; m. Lisa Gunderson, Oct. 17, 1981; children: Joshua, Hannah, Rebecca. Grad. H.S., Waterford, Wis. Former supr. Town of Waterford, Wis.; assemblyman Wis. State Dist. 83. Owner Gundy's Sport. Mem. Racine County Fair Bd., Wis. State Fair Park Bd. Mem. Wind Lake C. of C. (past pres.), Waterford Lions, Wings Over Wis. Address: State Capitol Rm 7W PO Box 8952 Madison WI 53708 E-mail: rep.gunderson@legis.state.wi.us.

GUNDRY, STANLEY N. publishing company executive; b. July 12, 1937; m. Patricia Smith, Aug. 3, 1958; 4 children. BA summa cum laude, L.A. Bapt. Coll., 1959; BD summa cum laude, Talbot Theol. Sem., 1963; STM, Union Coll., U. B.C., 1968; STD, Luth. Sch. Theology, 1975. Ordained to ministry Bapt. Ch., 1963. Pastor Nooksack Valley Bapt. Ch., Everson, Wash., 1963-68; prof. theology Moody Bible Inst., 1968-79; v.p., editor-in-chief Zondervan Pub., Grand Rapids, Mich., 1980—. Adj. prof. theology Trinity Evang. Divinity Sch., 1975-80. Pub. Wycliffe Bible Encyclopaedia, 1975, Love Them In: The Life and Theology of D.L. Moody, 1982; pub., co-editor: Tensions in Contemporary Theology, 1983, Perspectives on Evangelical Theology, 1979; co-author: NAS Harmony of the Gospels, 1986, NIV Harmony of the Gospels: A Revision of A.T. Robertson's Harmony, 1988. Mem. Am. Theol. Soc., Am. Soc. Ch. History, Evang. Theol. Soc. (pres. 1978), Soc. Scholarly Pub. Home: 4142 Burton St SE Grand Rapids MI 49546-6119 Office: Zondervan Pub House 5300 Patterson Ave SE Grand Rapids MI 49512-9512

GUNN, ALAN, law educator; b. Syracuse, N.Y., Apr. 8, 1940; s. Albert Dale and Helen Sherwood (Whitnall) G.; m. Bertha Ann Buchwald, 1975; 1 child, William BS, Rensselaer Poly. Inst., 1961; JD, Cornell U., 1970. Bar: D.C. 1970. Assoc. Hogan & Hartson, Washington, 1970-72; asst. prof. law Washington U., St. Louis, 1972-75, assoc. prof., 1975-76; assoc. prof. law Cornell U., Ithaca, N.Y., 1977-79, prof., 1979-84, J. duPratt White prof., 1984-89; prof. law U. Notre Dame, Ind., 1989-96, John N. Matthews prof., 1996—. Author: Partnership Income Taxation, 1991, 3d edit., 1999; (with Larry D. Ward) Cases, Text and Problems on Federal Income Taxation, 4th edit., 1998; (with Vincent R. Johnson) Studies in American Tort Law, 1994, 2d edit., 1999. Methodist. Office: U Notre Dame Law Sch Notre Dame IN 46556

GUNN, JAMES E. English language educator; b. Kansas City, Mo., July 12, 1923; s. J. Wayne and Elsie M. (Hutchison) G.; m. Jane Frances Anderson, Feb. 6, 1947; children: Christopher Wayne, Kevin Robert. BS, U. Kans., 1947, MA, 1951. Editor Western Printing and Litho, Racine, Wis., 1951-52; asst. dir. Civil Def., Kansas City, Mo., 1953; instr. U. Kans., Lawrence, 1955, mng. editor Alumni Assn., 1956-58, adminstrv. asst. to the chancellor for univ. rels., 1958-70, lectr. English, 1970-74, prof., 1974-93, emeritus prof., 1993—. Cons. Easton Press, Norwalk, Conn., 1985-98; lectr. in field. Author over 25 books including Station in Space, 1958, The Immortals, 1962, The End of the Dreams, 1975, Alternate Worlds: The Illustrated History of Science Fiction (World Sci. Fiction Conv. Spl. award 1976, Pilgrim award Sci. Fiction Rsch. Assn. 1976), The Listeners, 1972, The Dreamers, 1980, Isaac Asimov: the Foundations of Science Fiction, 1982 (Hugo award World Sci. Fiction Conv. 1983), The Science of Science - Fiction Writing, 2000, The Millennium Blues, 2001, numerous plays, screenplays, radio scripts; editor The Road to Sci. Fiction, 6 vols., 1977-2002, 8 other books; contbr. 98 stories to mags.; contbr. articles to profl. jours. Dir. Ctr. for Study Sci. Fiction, Lawrence, 1984—. Lt. (j.g.) USN, 1943-46, PTO. Recipient Eaton award Eaton Conf., 1992, Hugo award, 1983; Mellon fellow U. Kans., 1981, 84. Mem. Author's Guild, Sci. Fiction and Fantasy Writers Am. (pres. 1971-72), Sci. Fiction Rsch. Assn. (pres. 1981-82, Pilgrim award 1976)., Avocations: golf, bridge (ACBL N.Am. Open Pairs champion). Home: 2215 Orchard Ln Lawrence KS 66049-2707 Office: U Kans English Dept Lawrence KS 66045-0001

GUNN, MARY ELIZABETH, retired English language educator; b. Great Bend, Kans., July 21, 1914; d. Ernest E. and Elisabeth (Wesley) Eppstein; m. Charles Leonard Gunn, Sept. 13, 1936 (dec. Apr. 1985); 1 child, Charles Douglas. AB, Ft. Hays State U., 1935, BS in Edn., 1936, MA, 1967. Tchr. English Unified Sch. Dist. 428, Great Bend, 1963-80, Barton County C.C., Great Bend, 1977-84, tchr. adult edn., 1985-87, tchr. ESL, 1988-94; ret., 1994. Conf. Am. Studies fellow De Pauw U., 1969; recipient Nat. Cmty. Svc. award DAR, 1996. Mem. AAUW (Outstanding Mem. 1991), NEA, Bus. and Profl. Women (Woman of Yr. 1974), Kans. Adult Edn. Assn. (Master Adult Educator 1986), Kans. Assn. Tchrs. English, PEO, Delta Kappa Gamma, Alpha Sigma Alpha. Democrat. Mem. United Ch. of Christ. Avocations: travel, driving, needlepoint, crossword puzzles, reading. Home: 3009 16th St Great Bend KS 67530-3705

GUNN, MICHAEL PETER, lawyer; b. St. Louis, Oct. 18, 1944; s. Donald and Loretto Agnes (Hennelly) G.; m. Carolyn Ormsby Ritter, Nov. 27, 1969; children: Mark Thomas, Christopher Michael, John Ritter, Elizabeth Jane. JD, St. Louis U., 1968. Bar: Mo. 1968, U.S. Dist. Ct. (ea and we. dists.) Mo. 1968, U.S. Tax Ct. 1972. Assoc. Gunn & Gunn, St. Louis, 1968-81; ptnr. Gunn & Lane, 1981-86; pvt. practice Ballwin, Mo., 1986—. Rep. ea. dist. Mo. Ct. Appeals. Sgt. U.S. Army, 1969-75. Mem. ABA (del. Ho. of Dels. 1988—), St. Louis Bar Assn., The Mo. Bar (bd. govs. 1990—, exec. com. 1993-94, pres.-elect 1998-99, pres. 1999-2000), Lawyers Assn. St. Louis (pres. 1981-82), St. Louis Bar Found. (pres. 1988-89), Bar Assn. Met. St. Louis (pres. 1987-88), Nat. Conf. Bar Founds. (trustee 1990—, pres. elect 1993-94). Roman Catholic. Home: 2232 Centeroyal Dr Saint Louis MO 63131-1910 Office: Gunn & Rossetes PC Ste 240 1714 Deer Tracks Trail Saint Louis MO 63131

GUNTER, G. JANE, state legislator; 3 children. Grad. high sch. Rep. Dist. 7 N.D. Ho. of Reps., mem. human svcs. and polit. subdivsn. coms. Mem. Gov.'s Coun. Human Resources, Com. Children and Youth. Home: PO Box 449 Towner ND 58788-0449

GUPTA, KRISHNA CHANDRA, mechanical engineering educator; b. 1948; m. Karuna Gupta; 1 child, Anupama B.Tech. with distinction, Indian Inst. Tech., 1969; M.S. in M.E., Case Inst. Tech., 1971; Ph.D. in M.E., Stanford U., 1974. Grad. asst. Case Inst. Tech., Cleve., 1969-71; research asst. Stanford U., Calif., 1971-74; from asst. prof. mech. engring. to assoc. dean U. Ill., Chgo., 1974—2002, assoc. dean, 2002—. Mem. editorial adv. bd. Jour. Applied Mechanisms and Robotics; assoc. editor Mechanism and Machine Theory; contbr. articles to profl. jours. Recipient award of merit Procter & Gamble Co., 1978, South Pointing Chariot award, 1989, AM&R G.N. Sandor award, 1997; grantee in field. Fellow ASME (assoc. editor Jour. Mech. Design 1981-82, mem. editorial adv. bd. Applied Mechanics Rev. 1985-93, chmn. mechanisms com. 1989-90, gen chmn. 1990 design tech. conf., chmn. 1990 mechanisms conf., mem. design divsn. exec. com. 2001—, best paper computers in engring. conf. 1991, Henry Hess award 1979, editor newsletter divsn. design engrng.). Avocations: investments, speed reading. Office: Univ Ill Coll of Engring m/c 159 851 S Morgan St Chicago IL 60607-7043 Fax: 312-413-3365. E-mail: kcgupta@uic.edu.

GUPTA, SURAJ NARAYAN, physicist, educator; b. Haryana, India, Dec. 1, 1924; came to U.S., 1953, naturalized, 1963; s. Lakshmi N. and Devi (Goyal) G.; m. Letty J.R. Paine, July 14, 1948; children: Paul, Ranee. MS, St. Stephen's Coll., India, 1946; PhD, U. Cambridge, Eng., 1951. Imperial Chem. Industries fellow U. Manchester, Eng., 1951-53; vis. prof. physics Purdue U., 1953-56; prof. physics Wayne State U., Detroit, 1956-61, disting. prof. physics, 1961-99, disting. prof. emeritus physics, 1999—. Researcher on high energy physics, nuclear physics, relativity and gravitation. Author: Quantum Electrodynamics, 1977. Fellow Am. Phys. Soc., Nat. Acad. Scis. of India. Achievements include quantum theory with negative probability and quantization of the electromagnetic field; flat-space interpretation of Einstein's theory of gravitation and quantization of the gravitational field; regularization and renormalization of elementary particle interactions; development of the theory of bound states in quantum electrodynamics and quantum chromodynamics; mass matrix formulation of quark mixing and CP violation in weak interactions; investigation of phenomena at supercollider energies. Home: 30001 Hickory Ln Franklin MI 48025-1566 Office: Wayne State U Dept Physics Detroit MI 48202

GUPTA, SURENDRA KUMAR, chemical firm executive; b. Delhi, India, Apr. 5, 1938; came to U.S., 1963, naturalized, 1971; s. Bishan Chand and Devki G.; m. Karen Patricia Clarke, Oct. 12, 1968; children— Jay, Amanda. B.Sc. with honors, Delhi U., 1959, M.Sc., 1961; M.Tech., Indian Inst. Tech., Bombay, 1963; Ph.D., Wayne State U., 1968. Research assoc. Western Mich. U., Kalamazoo, 1968-73; indsl. postdoctoral fellow Starks Assocs., Buffalo, 1973-74; group leader New Eng. Nuclear Co., Boston, 1974-80, Pathfinder Labs., St. Louis, 1981-83; chmn. bd., chemist Am. Radiolabeled Chem., Inc., St. Louis, 1983— . Contbr. numerous articles to internat. sci. jours. Mem. Am. Chem. Soc. (chmn. pub. relations com. 1970-73). Hindu. Avocations: table tennis; stamp collecting; traveling. Home: 22 Muirfield Ln Saint Louis MO 63141-7380 Office: Am Radiolabeled Chems Inc 11624 Bowling Green Dr Saint Louis MO 63146-3506

GUPTA, VINOD, business lists company executive; b. New Delhi, July 4, 1946; came to U.S., 1967; BTech., I.I.T., Kharagpur, India, 1967; MS, U. Nebr., 1969, MBA, 1971. Chief exec. officer Am. Bus. Lists Inc., Ralston, Nebr. Office: Info USA Inc 5711 S 86th Cir Omaha NE 68127-4146

GURALNICK, SIDNEY AARON, civil engineering educator; b. Phila., Apr. 25, 1929; s. Philip and Kenia (Dudnik) G.; m. Eleanor Alban, Mar. 10, 1951; children: Sara Dian, Jeremy. BSc, Drexel Inst. Tech., Phila., 1952; MS, Cornell U., 1955, PhD, 1958. Registered profl. engr., Pa.; lic. structural engr., Ill. Instr., then asst. prof. Cornell U., 1952-58, mgr. structural research lab., 1956-58; mem. faculty Ill. Inst. Tech., Chgo., 1958—, prof. civil engring., 1967—, disting. prof. engring., 1982—, dir. structural engring. labs., 1968-71, dean Grad. Sch., 1971-75, exec. v.p., provost, 1975-82, trustee, 1976-82, dir. Advanced Bldg. Materials and Sys. Ctr., 1987—. Devel. engr. Portland Cement Assn., Skokie, Ill., 1959-61; participant internat. confs.; cons. to govt. and industry. Author numerous papers in field. Trustee Inst. Gas Tech., 1976-81, Rsch. Inst. of Ill. Inst. Tech., 1976-82; commr.-at-large North Ctrl. Assn. Schs. and Colls., 1985-89, cons., evaluator, 1989-93. With C.E., U.S. Army, 1950-51. McGraw fellow, 1952-53; Faculty Rsch. fellow Ill. Inst. Tech., 1960; European travel grantee, 1961 Fellow ASCE (Lifetime Achievement award Ill. sect. 1997, Civil Engr. of Yr. award Ill. sect. 1998, Collingwood prize 1961); mem. Am. Concrete Inst., Am. Soc. for Engring. Edn., Soc. Exptl. Mechanics, Structural Engrs. Assn. Ill. (bd. dirs., pres.-elect 1989-90, pres. 1990-91, John F. Parmer award 1993), Transp. Rsch. Bd., Ill. Univs. Transp. Rsch. Consortium (adminstrv. com. 1983-93), Sigma Xi, Phi Kappa Phi, Tau Beta Pi, Chi Epsilon. Office: Ill Inst Tech 3300 S Federal St Chicago IL 60616-3793 E-mail: guralnick@iit.edu.

GURNETT, DONALD ALFRED, physics educator; b. Cedar Rapids, Iowa, Apr. 11, 1940; s. Alfred Foley and Velma (Trachta) G.; m. Marie Barbara Schmitz, Oct. 10, 1964; children: Suzanne, Christina. B.S. in Elec. Engring., U. Iowa, 1962, M.S. in Physics, 1963, Ph.D. in Physics, 1965. Prof. physics and astronomy U. Iowa, Iowa City, 1965-75, 76-79, 80—; rsch. scientist Max-Planck Inst., Garching, Fed. Republic Germany, 1975-76; vis. prof. UCLA, 1979-80; mem. space physics com. Nat. Acad. Sci., Washington, 1975-78, mem. com. on solar terrrestrial research, 1976-79, mem. com. on planetary and lunar exploration, 1982-85. Recipient Alexander von Humboldt Found. award, 1975, Disting. Sci. Achievement award NASA, 1981, Space Act award NASA, 1986, Sci. Achievement medal Gov. of Iowa, 1987, Disting. Iowa Scientist award Iowa Acad. Sci., 1989, Marion L. Huit award U. Iowa, 1990, Iowa Bd. Regents award for faculty excellence, 1994. Fellow Am. Geophys. Union (assoc. editor Jour. Geophys. Rsch. 1974-77, Fleming medal 1989), Am. Phys. Soc. (award for excellence in plasma physics 1989); mem. Internat. Union Radio Sci. (Dellinger gold medal 1978), Soaring Soc. Am. (Iowa State gov. 1983-86), Nat. Acad. of Sci. Home: 4664 Canterbury Ct Iowa City IA 52245 Office: U Iowa Dept Physics and Astronomy 715 Van Allen Hall Iowa City IA 52242-1403

GUSEWELLE, CHARLES WESLEY, journalist, writer, documentary maker; b. Kansas City, Kans., July 22, 1933; s. Hugh L. and Dorothy (Middleton) G.; m. Katie Jane Ingels, Apr. 17, 1966; children— Anne Elizabeth, Jennifer Sue. BA in English, Westminster Coll., 1955; LHD (hon.), Park Coll., 1990. Reporter Kansas City (Mo.) Star, 1955-66, editorial writer of fgn. affairs, 1966-76, fgn. editor, 1976-79, asso. editor, columnist, 1979—. Author: A Paris Notebook, 1985, An Africa Notebook, 1986, Quick as Shadows Passing, 1988, Far from Any Coast, 1989, A Great Current Running, 1994, Another Autumn, 1996, The Rufus Chronicle, 1998, A Buick in the Kitchen, 2000, On the Way to Other Country, 2001; contbr. short stories to Brit., Am. lit. quars.; writer, narrator, host: A Great Current Running, This Place Called Home (Regional Emmy 1998), Water and Fire: A Story of the Ozarks. 1st lt. AUS, 1956-58. Recipient Aga Khan prize for fiction, 1977, Thorpe Menn Lit. award, 1989; inducted Writers Hall of Fame, 2000. Home: 1245 Stratford Rd Kansas City MO 64113-1325 Office: 1729 Grand Ave Kansas City MO 64108-1413

GUSHEE, RICHARD BORDLEY, lawyer; b. Detroit, Aug. 25, 1926; s. Edward Tisdale and Norine Amelia (Bordley) G.; m. Marilyn Lucy Flynn, June 9, 1951; children: Jacqueline Lowe (dec. 1977), Peter Hale. BA, Williams Coll., 1947; JD, U. Mich., 1950. Bar: Mich. 1951, U.S. Supreme Ct. 1961. Assoc. Miller, Canfield, Paddock and Stone, Detroit, 1950-58, ptnr., 1959-93, of counsel, 1994—. Chmn. Tri-county Hearing Panel #18 of Atty. Discipline Bd. Former trustee United Community Svcs.; former chancellor Episc. Diocese Mich. With USAF, 1945. Mem. ABA, Detroit Met. Bar Assn. Office: Miller Canfield Paddock & Stone 150 W Jefferson Ave Ste 2500 Detroit MI 48226-4416 E-mail: gushee@millercanfield.com.

GUSTAFSON, COLE RICHARD, agricultural economics educator; b. St. Croix Falls, Wis., Nov. 21, 1955; s. Richard A. and Darelyne (Peroff) G.; m. Nancy J. Anderson, Mar. 17, 1979; children: Ana, Kelsey. BS, U. Minn., St. Paul, 1978, MS, 1980; PhD, U. Ill., 1986. Rsch. asst. U. Minn., St. Paul, 1978-80; agrl. economist Dept. Agriculture, Washington, 1980-86; assoc. prof. agrl. econs. N.D. State U., Fargo, 1986-98, asst. dean rsch., 1998—. Mem. Am. Agrl. Econs. Assn., So. Agrl. Econs. Assn., Western Agrl. Econs. Assn., Am. Econs. Assn., Phi Kappa Phi, Gamma Sigma Delta, Sigma Xi. Lutheran. Avocations: woodworking, constrn., farming. Office: ND State U Dept Agrl Experiment Sta Fargo ND 58105-5435

GUSTAFSON, DAN, state legislator; State rep. Dist. 67 Mich. Ho. of Reps., 1993-98; chief of staff Lt. Gov. Dick Posthumus, Lansing, Mich., 1998—. Home: 5537 Wild Iris Ln Haslett MI 48840-8685 Office: Lt Govs Office 505 Romney Bldg Lansing MI 48909

GUSTAFSON, DAVID HAROLD, industrial engineering and preventive medicine educator; b. Kane, Pa., Sept. 11, 1940; s. Harold Edward and Olive Albertina (McKalip) G.; m. Rea Corina Anagnos, June 23, 1962; children: Laura Lynn, Michelle Elaine, David Harold B.S. in Indsl. Engring., U. Mich., 1962, M.S. in Indsl. Engring, 1963, Ph.D., 1966. Dir. hosp. div. Community Systems Found., Ann Arbor, Mich., 1961-64; asst. prof. indsl. engring. U. Wis.-Madison, 1966-70, assoc. prof., 1970-74, prof., 1974—, Robert A. Ratner prof. indsl. engring. $D, 2000—, dir., founder Ctr. for Health Systems and Analysis, 1974—, chmn. dept. indsl. engring., 1984-88, adminstrv. com. Grad. Sch., 1995-98, mem. athletic bd., 2000—; sr. analyst Dec. and Designs Inc., McLean, Va., 1974. Dir. rsch. Govt. Health Policy Task Force, State of Wis., 1969-71; prin. cons. Medicaid Mgmt. Study Team, 1977-78; prin. investigator Nursing Home Quality Assurance System, 1979, Computer System for Adolscent Health Promotion, 1983, Computer System to Support Breast Cancer and People with AIDS, 1993; vis. prof. London Sch. Econs., 1983, Harvard U., 1999; developer computer-based support to measure and improve health care quality. Author: Group Techniques, 1975, Health Policy Analysis, 1992; contbr. articles to profl. jours. Adviser conflict resolution Luth. Ch., 1973-79; active numerous civic orgns. Recipient numerous grants, 1968—, Ragnar Onstad award for cmty. svc., 1990. Fellow Assn. for Health Svcs. Rsch., Inst. for Health Care Improvement (bd. mem. 1990—); mem. Inst. Indsl. Engring., Ops. Rsch. Soc., Med. Decision Making Avocations: jogging, guitar, water sports, cross country skiing, parenting. Office: U Wis Ctr Health Systems 610 Walnut St Madison WI 53705-2336

GUSTAFSON, WINTHROP ADOLPH, aeronautical and astronautical engineering educator; b. Moline, Ill., Oct. 14, 1928; s. Gustav A. and Katherine (Wenger) G.; m. Sarah Elizabeth Garner, Aug. 3, 1957; children: Charles Lee, Stanley Scott, John Winthrop, Richard Neil. B.S., U. Ill., 1950, M.S., 1954, Ph.D., 1956. Research scientist Lockheed Missiles & Space Co., Palo Alto, Calif., 1956-60; asso. prof. Sch. Aeros. and Astronautics, Purdue U., Lafayette, Ind., 1960-66, prof., 1966-98, assoc. head sch., 1980-98, acting head sch., 1984-85, 93, prof. emeritus, 1998—. Vis. prof. U. Calif. at San Diego, 1968; research engr. Allison div. Gen. Motors Co., Indpls., summer 1962; mem. tech. staff Bell Telephone Labs., Whippany, N.J., summer 1966, NASA-Dryden Flight Research Center, summer 1976; cons. Goodyear Aerospace Corp., Akron, Ohio, 1964, Los Alamos Sci. Lab., 1977, U.S. Army, 1986-87. Contbr. articles to profl. jours. Served to 1st lt. USAF, 1951-53. Mem. AIAA. Home: 209 Lindberg Ave West Lafayette IN 47906-2109 Office: Purdue U Sch Aeros & Astronautics Lafayette IN 47907

GUTH, SHERMAN LEON (S. LEE GUTH), psychologist, educator; b. N.Y.C., s. Arthur and Caroline (Laub) G.; children from previous marriage: Melissa, Victoria; m. Ling Zhao; 1 child, Lillian. B.S., Purdue U., 1959; M.A., U. Ill., 1961, Ph.D., 1963. Lectr. dept. psychology Ind. U., Bloomington, 1962-63, instr., 1963-64, asst. prof., 1964-67, assoc. prof., 1967-70, prof., 1970—; dir. research and grad. devel. Sch. Optometry, 1980-88, chmn. dept. visual scis., 1982-85. Vis. assoc. prof. psychology Mich. State U., 1968-69; NIH spl. research fellow in psychology U. Calif., Berkeley, 1971-72; NSF program dir. for sensory physiology and perception, 1977-78 NIH research grantee, 1964-70, NSF research grantee, 1963-86. Fellow Optical Soc. Am. Achievements include being the creator of the ATD model for visual adaption and color perception. Office: Ind U Sch Optometry or Dept Psychology Bloomington IN 47405

GUTHERY, JOHN M. lawyer; b. Broken Bow, Nebr., Nov. 22, 1946; s. John M. and Kay G.; m. Diane Messineo, May 26, 1972; 1 child, Lisa. BS, U. Nebr., 1969, JD, 1972. Bar: Nebr. 1972. Pres. Perry, Guthery, Haase & Gessford, P.C., L.L.O., Lincoln, Nebr., 1972—. Mem. ATLA, ABA (mem. litigation section), Nebr. Bank Attys. Assn. (past pres., 1985-86), Nebr. Assn. Trial Attys., Nebr. State Bar Assn. (pres. 1998-99, mem. Nebr.State Bar Found. mem. ho. dels. 1979-83, 87-95, exec. coun. 1988-94 pres. elect. 1997-98, chair Nebr. bankruptcy sect.), Lincoln Bar Assn. (bd. trustees, 1985-88, pres. 1990-91). Office: Perry Guthery Haase & Gessford PC LLO 233 S 13th St Ste 1400 Lincoln NE 68508-2003 E-mail: jguthery@perrylawfirm.com.

GUTHMAN, JACK, lawyer; b. Cologne, Germany, Apr. 19, 1938; came to U.S., 1939, naturalized, 1945; s. Albert and Selma (Cahn) G.; m. Sandra Polk, Nov. 26, 1967. B.A., Northwestern U., 1960; LL.B., Yale U., 1963. Bar: Ill. bar 1963. Law clk. to dist. judge U.S. Dist. Ct. No. Ill., 1963-65; since practiced in Chgo.; ptnr. Sidley & Austin, 1970-94, Shefsky & Froelich Ltd., Chgo., 1995—. Mem. City Chgo. Zoning Bd. Appeals, 1970-75, chmn., 1975-87. Democrat. Jewish. Office: Shefsky & Froelich Ltd 444 N Michigan Ave Ste 2600B Chicago IL 60611-3998

GUTHRIE, CARLTON L. automotive manufacturing company executive; b. Atlanta; m. Danielle Guthrie; children: Carille, Adam. BA with honors in Econs., Harvard U., 1974, MBA in Gen. Mgmt., 1978. With Phila. Nat. Bank, Procter & Gamble; mgmt. cons. Jewel Cos., Chgo.; sr. cons. consumer group McKinsey & Co.; exec. v.p., COO James H. Lowry & Assocs.; co-owner, pres., CEO, chmn. bd. Trumark, Inc., Lansing, Mich. Bd. dirs. Shorebank Corp., Chgo. and Detroit. Founder, chmn. bd. Single Parent Family Inst., Lansing, Mich.; corp. sponsor YMCA's Y Achievers Program, Lansing; bd. dirs. Joyce Found., Chgo., Ctrs. for New Horizons, Chgo.; adv. bd. Governor's State U. Sch. Bus., University Park, Ill.; nat. bd. dirs. Initiative for a Competitive Inner City, Boston; adv. com. mem. Joint Ctr. for Polit. and Econ. Studies, Washington. Recipient Chivas Regal Extrapreneur of the Yr. award, 1989. Mem. Nat. Assn. Black Automotive Suppliers (v.p., bd. dirs.), Runners' Club Chgo. (co-founder). Office: Trumark Inc 1101 N Shiawassee St Owosso MI 48867-1640 Fax: 517-482-0795.

GUTHRIE, DIANA FERN, nursing educator; b. N.Y.C., May 7, 1934; d. Floyd George and A. May (Moler) Worthington; m. Richard Alan Guthrie, Aug. 18, 1957; children: Laura, Joyce, Tammy. AA, Graceland Coll., 1953; RN, Independence (Mo.) Sanitarium, 1956; BS in Nursing, U. Mo., 1957, MS in Pub. Health, 1969; EdS, Wichita State U., 1982; PhD, Walden U., 1985. Cert. diabetes educator, bd. cert. advanced diabetes mgmt.; RN Mo., Kans., cert. holistic nursing, RN advanced practitioner; lic. profl. counselor Kans., cert. stress mgmt. edn., clin. hypnosis, healing touch, lic. marriage and family therapist. Instr. red cross U.S. Naval Sta., Sangley Point, Philippines, 1961-63; acting head nurse newborn nursery U. Mo., Columbia, 1963-64, birth defect nurse dept. pediat., 1964-65, nursing dir. clin. research ctr., 1965-67, research asst., 1967-73; diabetes nurse specialist Sch. Medicine U. Kans., Wichita, 1973—, asst. then assoc. prof. Sch. Medicine, 1974-85, prof. dept. pediat. and psychiatry Sch. Medicine, 1985-99, prof. emeritus, 2000; prof. dept. nursing Kans. U. Med. Ctr., 1985-99, ret., 1999. Nurse cons. diabetes Mo. Regional Med. Program, Columbia, 1970-73; nat. advisor Human Diabetes Ctr. for Excellence, Lexington, Ky., 1982-90, Phoenix, 1983-92, Charlottesville, Ky., 1990-95; adj. prof. Sch. Nursing Wichita State U., 1985—. Author: Nursing Management of Diabetes, 1977, Nursing Management of Diabetes, 5th edit., 2002, The DiabetesSource Book, 1990, 5th edit., 2002, Alternative and Complementary Diabetes Case, 2000; contbr. articles to profl. jours. Mem. health adv. bd. Mid-Am. All Indian Ctr., Wichita, 1978-80; bd. dirs. Wichita Urban Indian Health Clinic, 1980-82; bd. trustees Graceland Coll., Lamoni, Iowa, 1996—. Fellow: Am. Acad. Nursing; mem.: APHA, ANA, Am. Assn. Med. Psychotherapists (profl. adv. bd. 1985—), Am. Assn. Diabetes Educators (Kans. area Disting. Svc. award 1999), Am. Diabetes Assn. (Kans. area prof. edn. and youth com. 1988—, affiliate bd. dirs. 1979—83, pres. Kans. affiliate 1980—81, 1990—91, Outstanding Educator award 1979, Regional Outstanding Svc. award 1984), Sigma Theta Tau (Exemplary Recognition award Epsilon Gamma chpt. 1996). Democrat. Mem. Community of Christ Ch. Avocations: harp, piano, oil painting, crafts, reading. Office: 200 S Hillside Wichita KS 67211-2127 E-mail: dguthrie@kumc.edu.

GUTHRIE, FRANK ALBERT, chemistry educator; b. Madison, Ind., Feb. 16, 1927; s. Ned and Gladys (Glick) G.; m. Marcella Glee Farrar, June 12, 1955; children: Mark Alan, Bruce Bradford, Kent Andrew, Lee Farrar. AB, Hanover Coll., 1950; MS, Purdue U., 1952; PhD, Ind. U., 1962. Mem. faculty Rose-Hulman Inst. Tech., Terre Haute, Ind., 1952—, assoc. prof., 1962-67, prof. chemistry, 1967-94, prof. emeritus, 1994—, chmn. dept., 1969-72, chief health professions adviser, 1975-94. Kettering vis. lectr. U. Ill., Urbana, 1961-62; vis. prof. chemistry U.S. Mil. Acad., West Point, N.Y., 1987-88, 93-94, admissions coord., 1989—; vis. prof. chemistry Butler U., spring 2000. Mem. exec. bd. Wabash Valley council Boy Scouts Am., 1971-87, adv. bd., 1988—, v.p. for scouting, 1976; selection chmn. Leadership Terre Haute, 1978-80. Served with AUS, 1945-46. Recipient Vigil Honor Order of Arrow, Wabash Valley coun. Boy Scouts Am., 1975, Wood badge, 1976, Dist. award of merit, 1976, Silver Beaver award, 1980. Fellow Ind. Acad. Sci. (pres. 1970, chmn. acad. found. trustees 1986—); mem. Am. Chem. Soc. (sec. 1973-77, editor directory 1965-77, chmn. divsn. analytical chemistry 1979-80, chmn. 1958, councilor Wabash Valley sect. 1980—, local sect. activities com. 1982-86, nominations and elections com. 1988-94, sec. 1992-94, coun. policy com. 1995, constn. and bylaws com. 1996—, steering com. for Joint Ctrl.-Gt. Lakes Regional Meetings, Indpls., 1978, 91, vis. assoc. com. profl. tng. 1984—, chmn. analytical chemistry exam. inst. std. exam. 1994), Coblentz Soc., Midwest Univs. Analytical Chemistry Conf., Hanover Coll. Alumni Assn. (pres. 1974, Alumni Achievement award 1977), Sigma Xi (treas. Wabash Valley chpt. 1994-98), Phi Lambda Upsilon, Phi Gamma Delta, Alpha Chi Sigma (E.E. Dunlap scholarship selection com. 1986—, chmn. 1990—, dir. expansion 1995-99, profl. rep. 1997-2000). Presbyterian. Club: Masons (32 deg.). Home: 120 Berkley Dr Terre Haute IN 47803-1708 Office: Rose Hulman Inst Tech 5500 Wabash Ave Terre Haute IN 47803-3999 E-mail: frank.guthrie@rose-hulman.edu., fguthrie@onemain.com.

GUTHRIE, RICHARD ALAN, physician; b. Pleasant Hill, Ill., Nov. 13, 1935; s. Merle Pruitt and Cleona Marie (Weaver) G.; m. Diana Fern Worthington, Aug. 18, 1957; children: Laura, Joyce, Tamara. AA, Graceland Coll., 1955; MD, U. Mo., 1960. Diplomate Am. Bd. Pediatrics, Am. Bd. Pediatric Endocrinology; cert. Nat. Bd. for Diabetes Educators. Intern U.S. Naval Hosp., Camp Pendleton, Calif., 1960-61, dir. dependent svcs. Sangley Point, The Philippines, 1961-63; asst. instr., resident in pediatrics U. Mo., 1963-65, NIH fellow in endocrinology and metabolism, 1965-68, asst. prof., dir. newborn svcs., 1968-71, assoc. prof. pediat., 1971-73; prof., chmn. dept. pediatrics U. Kans. Med. Sch., Wichita, 1973-82; exec. dir. Kans. Regional Diabetes Ctr., 1982-84; pres. Mid-Am. Diabetes Assocs., 1984—. Dir. Robert L. Jackson Diabetes Treatment, Edn. and Rsch. Ctr., 1985—. Author: Nursing Management in Diabetes Mellitus, 1976, 3rd edit., 1991, 4th edit., 1997, The Child with Diabetes, 1970, Physiologic Management of Diabetes in Children, 1986, Diabetes Source Book, 1990, 2d edit., 1994, 3rd edit., 1997, 4th edit., 1999; mem. editl. bd. Practical Diabetology, 1982-92, Diabetes Self-Management, 1984-97, Diabetes Educator, 1985-89; assoc. editor Diabetes Spectrum, 2000—; contbr. articles to profl. jours. Mem. health ministries bd. Reorganized Ch. Jesus Christ Latter-day Saints; mem. adv. bd. Kans. Action for Children, 1978—, Kans. State Diabetes, 1988-93, 95—. With USN, 1960-63. Recipient grants NIH, 1968—, Outstanding Faculty award Wichita State U., 1976, 2000, Disting. alumnus award Graceland Coll., 1984, Humanitarian award Wesley Med. Found., 1997, award for outstanding cmty. svc. Am. Diabetes Assn., 2001; Dr. McIver Furman Disting. lectureship in health scis. Del Mar Coll., Corpus Christi, Tex., 1986. Fellow Am. Acad. Pediatrics, Am. Coll. Endocrinology; mem. AMA, Am. Diabetes Assn. (bd. dirs. 1972-77, Outstanding Contbn. to Camping award 1992), Kans. Diabetes Assn. (pres. 1974, chmn. bd. 1974-77, 85-87), Kans. State Med. Soc., Sedgewick County Med. Soc., Am. Pediat. Soc., Soc. Pediat. Rsch., Wichita Pediat. Soc. (bd. dirs. 1988, pres. 1990-92), Lawson Wilkins Pediat. Endocrinology Soc., Midwest Soc. Pediat. Rsch., Internat. Soc. for Pediat. and Adolescent Diabetes (edn. com. 1995—), Am. Assn. Diabetes Educators (bd. dirs. 1994-97), Am. Assn. Clin. Endocrinology 1992—), Sigma Xi, Alpha Omega Alpha. Home: 14210 SW 60th St Andover KS 67002-8237 Office: Mid-Am Diabetes Assocs 200 S Hillside St Wichita KS 67211-2127 E-mail: rag33@hotmail.com.

GUTIERREZ, CARLOS M. grocery manufacturing company executive; Student, Monterrey Inst. Tech., Queretaro, Mex. Sales rep.m various sales and mktg. positions Kellogg de Mex., Mexico City, 1975-82, gen. mgr., 1984-89; pres., CEO, Kellogg Can., 1989-90; supr. L.Am. mktg. svcs. Kellogg Co., Battle Creek, Mich., 1982-83, mgr. internat. mktg. svcs., 1983-84, corp. v.p. product devel., 1990, v.p., 1990-93, exec. v.p., 1994-96, exec. v.p. bus. devel., 1996-98, pres., COO, 1998-99, pres., CEO, 1999—, also bd. dirs. Exec. v.p. sales and mktg. Kellogg USA, Battle Creek, 1990-93, exec. v.p., 1993-94, gen. mgr. cereal divsn., 1993-94; pres. Kellog Asia-Pacific, 1994-96. Mem. Grocery Mfrs. Am. (bd. dirs.). Office: 1 Kellogg Sq Battle Creek MI 49017-3534

GUTIERREZ, LUIS V. congressman, elementary education educator; b. Chgo., Dec. 10, 1953; BA magna cum laude in English, Northeastern Ill. U., 1975. Social worker Ill. Dept. Children and Family Svcs.; adminstrv. asst. Mayor's Subcom. on Infrastructure, 1984-85; alderman for 26th ward Chgo. City Coun., 1986-93, pres. pro tempore, 1992; mem. U.S. Congress from 4th Ill. Dist., 1993—; mem. banking and fin. svcs. com., vet. affair com. Chmn. Housing, Land Acquisition and Disposition com., 1989-93. Democrat. Office: US Ho of Reps 2452 Rayburn House Off Bldg Washington DC 20515-0001*

GUTKNECHT, GILBERT WILLIAM, JR. congressman, former state legislator, auctioneer; b. Cedar Falls, Iowa, Mar. 20, 1951; s. Gilbert William Sr. and Joan (Kerns) G.; m. Mary Catherine Keefe, June 3, 1972; children: Margaret, Paul, Emily. BA, U. No. Iowa, 1973. Sales rep. J. S. Latta, Cedar Falls, 1973-78, Valley Sch. Supplies, Appleton, Wis., 1978-81; auctioneer Rochester, Minn., 1978-95; state legis. State of Minn., 1982-95; mem. U.S. Congress from 1st Minn. dist., 1995—, mem. sci. com., budget com., agriculture com., 1997—. Avocations: fishing, boating, baseball. Office: US House Reps 425 Cannon House Office Bldg Washington DC 20515-2301 also: Midway Office Plaza 1530 Greenview Dr SW Ste 108 Rochester MN 55902-1080*

GUTMANN, DAVID LEO, psychology educator; b. N.Y.C., Sept. 17, 1925; s. Isaac and Masha (Agronsky) G.; m. Joanna Redfield, Aug. 18, 1951; children: Stephanie, Ethan. MA, U. Chgo., 1956, PhD, 1958. Lectr. psychology Harvard U., Cambridge, Mass., 1960-62; prof. U. Mich., Ann Arbor, 1962-76, Northwestern U., Chgo., 1976-97, prof. emeritus, 1998—, chief of psychology, 1976-81, dir. older adult program, 1978-95. Vis. emeritus prof. Hebrew U., Jerusalem, 1997. Author: Reclaimed Powers: Toward a New Psychology of Men and Women in Later Life, 1987, Reclaimed Powers: Men and Women in Later Life, 1994, The Human Elder in Nature, Culture, and Society, 1997; co-author: (with Bardwick, Douvan and Horner) Feminine Personality and Conflict, 1979. With U.S. Mcht. Marine, 1943-46. Recipient Career Devel. award NIMH, 1964-74. Fellow Gerontol. Soc. Am.; mem. Am. Vets. of Israel, Nat. Assn. Scholars. Jewish. E-mail: d-gutmann@northwestern.edu., dgutmann@aol.com.

GUTOWICZ, MATTHEW FRANCIS, JR. radiologist; b. Camden, N.J., Feb. 23, 1945; s. Matthew F. and A. Patricia (Walczak) G.; m. Alice Mary Bell, June 27, 1977; 1 child, Melissa. BA, Temple U., 1968; DO, Phila. Coll. Osteo. Medicine, 1972. Diplomate Am. Bd. Radiology, Am. Bd. Nuclear Medicine. Intern Mercy Hosp., Denver, 1972-73; resident in diagnostic radiology Hosp. of U. Pa., Phila., 1973-76, fellow in nuclear medicine, 1976-77; chief dept. radiology and nuclear medicine Fisher Titus Med. Ctr., Norwalk, Ohio, 1977—; pres. Firelands Radiology, Inc., 1977—. Ptnr. Pacifica in the Desert Restaurant, Palm Desert, Calif. Republican. Roman Catholic. Avocations: photography, tennis, scuba diving. Home: 23 Patrician Dr Norwalk OH 44857-2463 Personal E-mail: mattg@nwonline.net.

GUTSTEIN, SOLOMON, lawyer; b. Newport, R.I., June 18, 1934; s. Morris Aaron and Goldie Leah (Nussbaum) G.; m. Carol Feinhandler, Sept.

3, 1961; children: Jon Eric, David Ethan, Daniel Ari, Joshua Aaron. AB with honors, U. Chgo., 1953, JD, 1956. Bar: Ill. 1956, U.S. Dist. Ct. (no. dist.) Ill. 1957, U.S. Ct. Appeals (7th cir.) 1958, U.S. Ct. Appeals (5th cir.) 1971, U.S. Supreme Ct. 1980; rabbi, 1955. Assoc. Schradzke, Gould & Ratner, Chgo., 1956-60; ptnr. firm Schwartz & Gutstein, 1961-65, Gutstein & Cope, Chgo., 1968-72, Gutstein & Schwartz, Chgo., 1980-83, Gutstein & Sherwin, Chgo., 1983-85; ptnr. Arvey, Hodes, Costello & Burman, 1991-92, Tenney & Bentley LLc, Chgo., 2000—. Spl. asst. atty. gen. State of Ill., 1968-69; adj. prof. law John Marshall Law Sch., 1993-96; lectr. bus. law U. Chgo. Grad. Sch. Bus., 1973-82; cons. Ill. Real Property Svc., Bancroft Whitney Co., 1988-89; lectr. in field; real estate broker. Author: Illinois Real Estate, 2 vols., 1983, rev. ann. updates, 1984—95; co-author: Construction Law in Illinois, annually, 1980—84, Judaism in Art (The Windows of Shaare Tivkah), 1995, Illinois Real Estate Practice Guide, 2 vols., 1996, rev. ann. edit., 1997—2001; contbr. chpt. to Commercial Real Estate Transactions, 1962-76; assoc. editor U. Chgo. Law Rev., 1954—56, editl. advisor Basic Real Estate I, also Advanced Real Estate II, 1960—70; author: Analysis of the Book of Psalms, 1962; contbr. articles to profl. publs. Mem. Cook County Citizens Fee Rev. Com., 1965; alderman from 40th ward Chgo. City Coun., 1975-79; mem. govt. affairs adv. com. Jewish Fedn., 1984-94. Fuerstenberg scholar U. Chgo., 1950-56; Kosmerl fellow U. Chgo., 1953-56. Mem. Ill. State Bar Assn. (real estate law sect. coun. 2001), Chgo. Bar Assn., Decalogue Soc. Lawyers, B'nai B'rith. Office: Tenney & Bentley LLC 111 W Washington St Ste 1900 Chicago IL 60602-2769 E-mail: tenben@interaccess.com., sol.gut@prodigy.com.

GUTTAU, MICHAEL K. state agency administrator, banker; b. Council Bluffs, Iowa, Nov. 8, 1946; s. Detlef Hugo and Ethel Evelyn (Schmidt) G.; m. Judith Ann Frazier, June 28, 1968; children: Heidi Ann, Joshua Michael. BS in Farm Operation, Iowa State U., 1969; postgrad., U. Nebr., Omaha, 1975. Administrv. asst. to dean students, asst. instr. sociology Iowa State U., Ames, 1969; trainee, asst. cashier, cashier Treynor (Iowa) State Bank, 1972-78, pres., chmn., CEO, 1978—. Appt. Iowa Supt. Banking, 1995; bd. dirs. Mercy Midlands Corp., Omaha; advisor N.Y. Fed. Res. Bank, Russian Am. Bankers Forum Acad. for Advanced Studies in Banking and Fin.; presenter Internat. Russian Banking Conf. 1992-93, mem. steering com., 1992-93; mem. U.S. Dept. State-U.S./Slovakian Counterpart Team Agr. Fin. and Credit. Chmn. steering com. Pottawattamie County Riverbend Indsl. Site, Western Iowa Devel. Assn., Mercy Hosp., Council Bluffs, Treynor Cmty. Devel. Com.; bd. dirs. Deaf Missions Worldwide Christian Ministry for Deaf; mem. youth com. Pottawattamie County 4-H; founder, pres., bd. dirs. Treynor Devel. Found. Corp.; deacon, moderator, adult and H.S. Sunday sch. tchr. Zion Congl. Ch., Treynor. With U.S. Army, 1969-72, Vietnam; with Nebr. Army NG, 1972-80. Decorated DFC with oak leaf cluster, Bronze Star, Air medal with V device, 28 Air medals; Recipient Outstanding Citizen award Treynor Town and Country Club, Swords to Plowshares award Bus.-Banks Exch. Newspaper, Moscow, 1992. Mem. Am. Bankers Assn. (chmn. future of cmty. banking study, cmty. bankers adv. bd. and coun., dir. edn. coun., mem. adminstrv. com. govt. rels. com.), Iowa Bankers Assn. (pres.-elect 1994-95, chmn. legis. com., bd. dirs.), S.W. Iowa Bank Adminstrn. Inst. (pres.), Treynor Bus. Assn. (founder, past pres., bd. dirs.), Scabbard and Blade, Gamma Gamma, Theta Delta Chi. Republican. Avocation: aviation. Home: RR 2 Box 82B Council Bluffs IA 51503-9802 Office: Treynor State Bank 15 E Main St Treynor IA 51575

GUTTENBERG, ALBERT ZISKIND, planning educator; b. Chelsea, Mass., Nov. 6, 1921; s. Harry and Edith (Bernstein) G.; m. Mariella Mascardi, June 29, 1964. AB in Social Rels., Harvard U., 1948; postgrad. in sociology, U. Chgo., 1949-51; postgrad. in city planning, U. Pa., 1958-59. Planning asst. Planning Bd., City of Portland, Maine, 1954-56; planning analyst Planning Commn., City of Phila., 1956-60; chief gen. plans and programming sect. Comprehensive Planning div., 1960-61; sr. planner Nat. Capital Downtown Com., Washington, 1962-63; assoc. prof. urban planning U. Ill., 1964-69, prof. urban and regional planning, 1969-89; chair in urban and regional renewal Dept. Geodesy, Delft U. Tech., The Netherlands, 1977-78. Cons. in field. Author: (with others) Explorations Into Urban Structure, 1964, New Directions in Land use Classification, 1965, (with others) Human Ecology, 1975, The Language of Planning, 1993; editor Planning and Public Policy, 1974-89; contbr. articles on land use planning to profl. pubs. Served with U.S. Army, 1942-46. Guggenheim fellow, 1970-71; Brookings Inst. guest scholar, 1970-71; Gelderman Fund grantee Delft U. Tech., 1977; German Marshall Fund Travel grantee, Holland, 1979; recipient Fulbright Travel award Italy, 1986. Mem. Am. Planning Assn., Am. Inst. Cert. Planners (coll. fellows), Soc. Am. City and Regional Planning History, Fulbright Alumni Assn. Home: 711 Hamilton Dr Champaign IL 61820-6811 Office: 111 Temple Hoyne Buell Hall 611 E Lorado Taft Dr Champaign IL 61820-6921 E-mail: a-guttenb@uiuc.edu.

GUY, RALPH B., JR. federal judge; b. Detroit, Aug. 30, 1929; s. Ralph B. and Shirley (Skladd) G.. AB, U. Mich., 1950, JD, 1953. Bar: Mich. 1953. Sole practice, Dearborn, Mich., 1954—55; asst. corp. counsel City of Dearborn, 1955—58, corp. counsel, 1958—69; chief asst. U.S. Atty.'s Office (ea. dist.), Detroit and Mich., 1969—70, U.S. Atty., 1970—76; judge U.S. Dist. Ct. (ea. dist.) Mich., Ann Arbor, 1976—85, U.S. Ct. Appeals (6th cir.), Ann Arbor, 1985—94, sr. judge, 1994—. Treas. Detroit-Wayne County Bldg. Authority, 1966—73; chmn. sch. study com. Dearborn Bd. Edn., 1973; mem. Fed. Exec. Bd., 1970—, bd. dirs., 1971—73. Recipient Civic Achievement award, Dearborn Rotary, 1971, Distinguished Alumni award, U. Mich., 1972. Mem.: FBA (pres. 1974—75), ABA (state chmn. sect. local govt. 1965—70), Out-County Suprs. Assn. (pres. 1965), Mich. Municipal League, Mich. Assn. Municipal Attys. 1962—64, Nat. Inst. Municipal Law Officers (chmn. Mich. chpt. 1964—69), Am. Judicature Soc., Dearborn Bar Assn. (pres. 1959—60), Detroit Bar Assn., State Bar Mich. (commr. 1975—), U. Mich. Alumni Club (local pres. Dearborn 1961—62), Rotary (local pres. 1973—74), Lambda Chi Alpha, Phi Alpha Delta. Office: US Ct Appeals PO Box 7910 200 E Liberty St Rm 226 Ann Arbor MI 48107

GUYON, JOHN CARL, retired university administrator; b. Washington, Oct. 16, 1931; s. Carl Alexander and Sara Myrle (Bumgarner) G.; m. Elizabeth Joyce Smith, Nov. 12, 1955; children— Cynthia Joan, John Carl, II. B.A., Washington and Jefferson Coll., 1953; M.S., Toledo U., 1958; Ph.D., Purdue U., 1961. Mem. faculty U. Mo., 1961—71, prof. chemistry, chmn. dept., 1970—71, Memphis State U., 1971—74; dean Coll. Sci., So. Ill. U., Carbondale, 1974—75, Coll. Sci., So. Ill. U. (Grad. Sch.), assoc. v.p. research, 1976—80, v.p. acad. affairs and research, 1980; pres. So. Ill. U., 1987—95, chancellor, 1996—97; ret., 1997—. Author: Aanlytical Chemistry, 1965, Qualitative Analysis, 1966, Solution Equilbria, 1969; also articles, abstracts.; Gen. editor: Instrumental Methods of Analysis. Served with AUS, 41954-56. Eli Lilly Co. fellow, 1959-61; Owens Ill. Co. fellow, 1958; Jesse W. Lazear scholar, 1953 Mem. Am. Chem. Soc., AAAS, Phi Beta Kappa, Sigma Xi, Phi, Lambda Upsilon.

GWINN, ROBERT P. publishing executive; b. Anderson, Ind., June 30, 1907; s. Marshall and Margaret (Cather) G.; m. Nancy Flanders, Jan. 20, 1942 (dec. 1989); 1 child, Richard Herbert. PhB, U. Chgo., 1929. With Sunbeam Corp., Chgo., 1936-51, gen. sales mgr. elec. appliance div., 1951-52, v.p., dir., 1952-55, pres., chief exec. officer, 1955-71, chmn. bd., chief exec. officer, 1971-82, also bd. dirs.; chmn. bd., chief exec. officer Ency. Britannica, Inc., 1973-93, chmn. emeritus, 1993—. Chmn. bd., CEO Titan Oil Co., Riverside; bd. dirs. Continental Assurance Co., Continental Casualty Co., CNA/Fin. Corp., Inst. for Philos. Rsch., Alberto-Culver Corp. Trustee Chgo. Zool. Soc., U. Chgo.; mem. Citizens Adv. Com., Chgo.; bd. fellows Harvard Med. Sch., James Madison Coun., Libr. of Congress. Mem. Soc. Chgo., Internat. Food and Wine Soc. Chgo., Mid. Am. Club, Elec. Mfrs. Club (hon.), Comml. Club Chgo., Casino Club, Execs. Club, Bird Key Yacht Club, Riverside Golf Club, U. Chgo. Club, Alpha Sigma Phi.

GYLLENHAAL, ANDERS, editor; Editor News & Observer, Raleigh, N.C. Office: PO Box 191 Raleigh NC 27602-9150 also: Star Tribune 425 Portland Ave. Minneapolis MN 55488

GYSBERS, NORMAN CHARLES, education educator; b. Waupun, Wis., Sept. 29, 1932; s. George S. and Mabel (Landaal) Gysbers; m. Mary Lou Ziegler, June 23, 1954 (dec. July 1997); children: David, Debra, Daniel; m. Barbara K. Townsend, May 12, 2001. A.B., Hope Coll., 1954; M.A., U. Mich., 1959, Ph.D., 1963. Tchr. Elem. and Jr. High Sch., Muskegon Heights, Mich., 1954-56; lectr. edn. U. Mich., 1962-63; prof. counseling psychology U. Mo., Columbia, 1963—. Cons. U.S. Office Edn.; mem. nat. adv. coms. ERIC Clearinghouses in Career Edn. and Counseling and Personnel Services; research and devel. com. for CEEB, Am. Insts. for Research Project on Career Decision Making, Comprehensive Career Edn. Model, TV Career Awareness Project KCET-TV, Los Angeles; dir. 10 nat. research projects and state projects in career devel.-guidance; Francqui prof. Universite Libre de Bruxelles. Editor: Vocat. Guidance Quar. 1962-70; (with L. Sunny Hansen) spl. issue Personnel and Guidance Jour., May 1975, Jour. Career Devel., 1979— , (with E. Moore and W. Miller) Developing Careers in the Elementary School, 1973, (with E. Moore and H. Drier) Career Guidance: Practices and Perspectives, 1973; author: (with E. Moore) Improving Guidance Programs, 1981, Designing Careers, 1984, (with E. Moore) Career Counseling, 1987, (with P. Henderson) Developing and Managing Your School Guidance Program, 1988, 3d edit., 2000, (with C. McDaniels) Counseling for Career Development, 1992, (with P. Henderson) Guidance Programs that Work, 1997, (with M. Heppner and J. Johnston) Career Counseling, 1998, (with P. Henderson) Leading and Managing Your School Guidance Program Staff, 1998, (with P. Henderson) Implementing Comprehensive School Guidance Programs, 02; contbr. articles to profl. jours. and chpts. to textbooks. Elder Presbyn. Ch. Served with arty. U.S. Army, 1956-58. Recipient Am. Spirit award USAF, 1987. Mem.: ACA (pres. 1977—78, disting. profl. svc. award 1983), Internat. Assn. Ednl. and Vocat. Guidance, Mo. Guidance Assn. (outstanding svc. award 1978), Am. Vocat. Assn. (v.p. 1979—82, merit award guidance divsn. 1978), Am. Sch. Counselor Assn. (post-secondary sch. counselor of yr. 2001), Assn. for Counselor Edn. and Supervision, Nat. Career Devel. Assn. (pres. 1972—73, nat. merit award 1981, Eminent Career award 1989). Home: 4 Bingham Rd Columbia MO 65203 Office: U Mo 201 G Student Success Ctr Columbia MO 65211-6060 E-mail: gysbersn@missouri.edu.

HAAG, EVERETT KEITH, architect; b. Cuyahoga Falls, Ohio, Jan. 27, 1928; s. Arnold and Lois (Martz) H.; m. Eleanor Jean Baker, Nov. 1, 1961; children— Kurt, Paula, Pamela. B.S. in Architecture, Kent State U., 1951; B.Arch., Western Res. U., 1953. Founder, prin. firm Keith Haag & Assos. (architects), Cuyahoga Falls, 1955-72; founder, pres. Keith Haag Assos. Inc. (architecture-engring.-planning), 1972-81; archtl. and planning cons., 1981—. Instr. Kent State U., 1952-54 Pres. Tri-County Planning Commn., 1960-61; chmn. Urban Renewal Review Commn., Cuyahoga Falls, 1971—, Regional Planning Group, Northampton Twp., 1970— ; mem. Akron Regional Devel. Bd.; bd. dirs. Goodwill Industries, chmn. strategic planning com., 1988—, Akron, Stan Hywet Hall Found., Inc. (pres. 1991-92); chmn. Historic Bldgs. Com., 1988—; mem. alumni bd. Kent State U., 1970-72, co-developer Polymer Housing system, 1989. Recipient 46 archtl. design awards. Fellow AIA (past pres. Akron chpt., nat. com. on office practice); mem. Architects Soc. Ohio (exec. com., sec. 1975-76, v.p. 1977-78, pres. 1979, Gold medal 1986), Northampton C. of C. (pres. 1972), Summit County Hist. Soc. (dir. 1974—) Clubs: President's (Kent State U.), Hilltoppers (Akron U.). Home: 1007 W Steels Corners Rd Cuyahoga Falls OH 44223-3111 Office: PO Box 1147 Cuyahoga Falls OH 44223-0147

HAAN, PHILIP C. airline executive; Various positions Am. Airlines, Ford Motor Co.; Northwest Airlines Co., 1991-95, sr. v.p., internat., 1995-99, exec. v.p., internat. sales, info. svcs., 1999—. Office: Northwest Airlines Corp 5101 Northwest Dr Saint Paul MN 55111-3027

HAAS, BILL, state legislator; b. June 25, 1949; m. Joenie Haas; 2 children. AA, U. Minn., 1969. Employee benefits broker, 1971—; rep. Dist. 48A Minn. Ho. of Reps., 1994—, vice chair ways and means com.; mem. commerce, health and human svcs. coms.; mem. environment and natural resources com.

HAAS, HOWARD GREEN, retired bedding manufacturing company executive; b. Chgo., Apr. 14, 1924; s. Adolph and Marie (Green) H.; m. Carolyn Werbner, June 4, 1949; children: Jody, Jonathan. Student, U. Chgo., 1942; BBA, U. Mich., 1948. Promotion dir. Esquire, Inc., Chgo., 1949-50; advt. mgr. Mitchell Mfg. Co., 1950-52, v.p. advt., 1952-56, v.p. sales, 1956-58; sales mgr. Sealy, Inc., Chgo., 1959-60, v.p. marketing, 1960-65, exec. v.p., 1965-67, pres., treas., 1967-86, 87. Bd. dirs. Ingersoll Holding Co., Aurora Custom Machinery, Inc.; chmn. Howard Haas Assocs.; vis. prof. strategic mgmt. U. Chgo. Grad. Sch. Bus., 1989—. Author: The Leader Within, 1993. Past mem. nominating com. Glencoe Sch. Bd.; mem. print and drawing com. Art Inst. Chgo.; past chmn. parent's com. Washington U., St. Louis; past bd. dirs. Jewish Children's Bur.; mem. vis. com. Oriental Inst., U. Chgo., Northbrook Symphony, Meet the Composer. 1st lt. USAAF, 1943-45, ETO. Decorated Air medal with 3 oak leaf clusters; recipient Brotherhood award NCCJ, 1970, Human Relations award Am. Jewish Com., 1977 Mem. Nat. Assn. Bedding Mfrs. (past vice chmn., trustee), Birchwood Tennis Club (Highland Pk., Ill.), Masons. Jewish. Office: Howard Haas Assocs 208 S La Salle St Ste 1275 Chicago IL 60604-1101 E-mail: hghhaas@aol.com.

HAASE, ASHLEY THOMSON, microbiology educator, researcher; b. Chgo., Dec. 8, 1939; s. Milton Conrad and Mary Elizabeth Minter (Thomson) H.; m. Ann DeLong, 1962; children: Elizabeth, Stephanie, Harris. BA, Lawrence Coll., 1961; MD, Columbia U., 1965. Intern Johns Hopkins Hosp., Balt., 1965-67; clin. assoc. Nat. Inst. Allergy and Infectious Disease, Bethesda, 1967-70; vis. scientist Nat. Inst. Med. Rsch., London, 1970-71; chief infectious disease sect. VA Med. Ctr., San Francisco, 1971-84, med. investigator, 1978-83; prof. microbiology U. Minn., Mpls., 1984-99, head dept., 1984—, Regents' prof., 1999—. Mem. fellowship screening com. Am. Cancer Soc., San Francisco, 1978-81; mem. UNESCO Internat. Cell Rsch. Orgn., India, 1978; mem. nat. adv. coun. Nat. Inst. Allergy and Infectious Diseases, 1986-91, mem. task force on microbiology and infectious diseases, 1991, merit investigator, 1989—, chair AIDS rsch. adv. com., 1993-96, chmn. vaccine subcom.; Javits neurosci. investigator Nat. Inst. Neurol. and Communicative Disorders and Stroke, 1988-95; chmn. panel on AIDS, U.S.-Japan Coop. Med. Sci. Program, 1988-95; mem. OAR AIDS Rsch. Evaluation Working Group, 1995-96; mem. adv. com. for career awards in biomed. scis. Burroughs-Wellcome Fund, 1995-2000; trustee Lawrence U., 1997-2000; adv. coun. NIH Office AIDS Rsch., 2002-. Editor: Microbial Pathogenesis, 1988-94; contbr. articles on AIDS pathogenesis and other topics in neurovirology to profl. jours. Recipient Lucia R. Briggs Disting. Achievement award Lawrence Coll., 1990. Mem. Am. Soc. Microbiology, Assn. Am. Physicians, Am. Soc. Clin. Investigation, Am. Soc. Virology, Assn. Med. Schs. Microbiology Chmn., Infectious Diseases Soc. Am., Nat. Multiple Sclerosis Soc. (adv. com. 1978-84), Am. Assn. Immunologists, Phi Beta Kappa, Alpha Omega Alpha. Democrat. Home: 14 Buffalo Rd Saint Paul MN 55127-2136 Office: U Minn Dept Microbiology 420 Delaware St SE Minneapolis MN 55455-0374

HABERMAN, F. WILLIAM, lawyer; b. Princeton, N.J., Apr. 20, 1940; s. Frederick William and Louise (Power) H.; m. Carmen Marie Duffy, June 15, 1963; children: Frederick, Sarah. BA, U. Wis., 1962; LLB, Harvard Law Sch., 1965. Bar: Wis. 1965, Fla. 1993, U.S. Dist. Ct. (ea. dist.) Wis. 1966, U.S. Dist. Ct. (we. dist.) Wis. 1967. Ptnr. Michael, Best & Friedrich, Milw., 1965—. Mem. adv. bd. Johnson Bank, 1994—. Co-author: Marital Property Law in Wisconsin, 1986. Trustee Pub. Policy Forum, Milw., 1992—; bd. dirs. Ctrl. YMCA, Milw., 1988-93, Richard and Ethel Herzfeld Found., Milw., 1985—, Wis. affiliate Am. Heart Assn., 1993-97, Greater Milw. Com., 1999—; mem. adv. bd. Milw. Fair Housing Coun., 1989-90; mem. deferred giving adv. bd. Milw. Sch. Engring., 1989-93; bd. dirs. Milw. Children's Hosp. Found., 1994-98, Milw. Repertory Theater, 1997-2002. Fellow Am. Coll. Trust & Estate Counsel; mem. ABA, Wis. Bar Assn. Home: 2727 E Shorewood Blvd Milwaukee WI 53211-2459 Office: Michael Best & Friedrich 100 E Wisconsin Ave Ste 3300 Milwaukee WI 53202-4108

HABERMAN, SHELBY JOEL, statistician, educator; b. Cin., May 4, 1947; s. Jack Leon and Miriam Leah (Langberg) H.; m. Elinor Penny Levine, Feb. 18, 1979 (dec. 1996); children: Shoshanah, Chasiah, Sarah, Milcah, Boaz, Devorah. AB, Princeton U., 1968; PhD, U. Chgo., 1970. Asst. prof. to prof. U. Chgo., 1970-82; prof. Hebrew U., Jerusalem, 1982-84; prof. stats. Northwestern U., Evanston, Ill., 1984—, chmn. dept., 1986-88. Author: Analysis of Frequency Data, 1974, Analysis of Qualitative Data, Vol. I, 1978, Vol. II, 1979, Advanced Statistics, Vol. I, 1996; contbr. articles to profl. jours. Guggenheim fellow, 1977-78. Fellow AAAS, Inst. Math. Stats., Am. Statis. Assn. Home: 2935 W North Shore Ave Chicago IL 60645-4225 Office: Northwestern U Dept Stats 2006 Sheridan Rd Evanston IL 60208-0852 E-mail: haberman@gibbs.stats.nwu.edu.

HABIG, DOUGLAS ARNOLD, manufacturing company executive; b. Louisville, 1946; s. Arnold F. and Mary Ann (Jahn) H. B.S., St. Louis U., 1968; M.B.A., Ind. U., 1972. Comml. loan officer Ind. Nat. Bank, Indpls., 1972-75; exec. v.p., treas., chief fin. officer Kimball Internat. Inc., Jasper, Ind., 1975-81, pres., dir., 1981—. Office: Kimball Internat Inc 1600 Royal St Jasper IN 47549-1022

HACHEY, THOMAS EUGENE, British and Irish history educator, consultant; b. Lewiston, Maine, June 8, 1938; s. Leo Joseph and Margaret Mary (Johnson) H.; m. Jane Beverly Whitman, June 9, 1962. B.A., St. Francis Coll., 1960; M.A., Niagara U., 1961; Ph.D., St. John's U., 1965. Asst. prof. history Marquette U., Milw., 1964-69, assoc. prof., 1969-77, prof., 1977—, chmn. dept. history, 1979-93, dean Coll. Arts and Scis., 1993-2000; exec. dir. Irish programs, endowed chair dept. history Boston Coll., 2000—. Vis. prof. history Sch. Irish Studies, Dublin, 1977-78; cons. investments in Ireland Frost & Sullivan, N.Y.C., 1978-82; pres. Am. Conf. Irish Studies, 1983-85; dir. Bradley Inst. for Democracy and Pub. Values, 1988—. Author: Problem of Partition: Peril to World Peace, 1972, Britain and Irish Separatism, 1977; co-author: The Irish Experience, 1988, expanded edit., 1996, Perspectives of Irish Nationalism, 1988; editor: Voices of Revolution, 1972, Confidential Despatches, 1975; contbr. over 100 articles and revs. to Brit., Irish and Am. jours. and newspapers. Danforth assoc., 1979-85. Fellow Anglo-Am. Assocs. Roman Catholic. Home: 20 Deerpath Rd Dedham MA 02026 Office: Connolly House 300 Hammond St Chestnut Hill MA 02467-3951

HACHTEN, RICHARD ARTHUR, II, health system executive; b. L.A., Mar. 24, 1945; s. Richard A. and Dorothy Margaret (Shipley) H.; m. Jeanine Hachten, Dec. 12, 1970; children: Kristianne, Karin. BS in Econs., U. Calif., Santa Barbara, 1967; MBA, UCLA, 1969. Mgmt. intern TRW Systems Group, Redondo Beach, Calif., 1969-72; adminstrv. asst. Meth. Hosp., Arcadia, 1972-73, asst. adminstr., 1973-74, assoc. adminstr., 1974-76, v.p. adminstrn., 1976-80; exec. v.p., adminstr., 1980-81; pres., adminstr., 1981-84; CEO Tri-City Hosp. Dist., Oceanside, 1984-91; pres. Bergan Mercy Health Sys., Omaha, 1991-95, Algent Health, Omaha, 1996—. Instr. health care mgmt. Pasadena (Calif.) City Coll. Bd. dirs., pres. Hospice of Pasadena, Inc.; bd. dirs. ARC, Arcadia, Mercy Housing Midwest, Omaha; bd. dirs. Metropolitan Community College Found. Mem. Am. Coll. Healthcare Execs., Hosp. Coun. San Diego and Imperial Counties (chmn., bd. dirs.), Nebr. Assn. Hosp. and Health Sys. (chmn. bd. dirs., chmn. dist. 1), Calif. Assn. Hosps. and Health Sys. (bd. dirs.), Rotary, Beta Gamma Sigma. Republican. Methodist. Home: 2676 S 96th Cir Omaha NE 68124-1949 Office: Alegent Health 1010 N 96th St Ste 200 Omaha NE 68114-2595

HACKBARTH, TOM, former state legislator; b. Dec. 28, 1951; m. Mary Hackbarth; 3 children. Student, North Hennepin C.C. Rep. Dist. 50A Minn. Ho. of reps., 1994-96, 98—. Vice chair environment and natural resources fin. com.; mem. environment and natural resources policy com., jobs econ. devel. policy com. Office: 100 Constitution Ave Saint Paul MN 55155-1232

HACKBIRTH, DAVID WILLIAM, aluminum company executive; b. Butler, Ind., Jan. 25, 1935; s. Ernest William and Bessie Mae (Snyder) H.; m. Anna Katherine Shaffer, July 19, 1959; children: Cynthia Kay, David William. Student, Defiance Coll., 1953; B.S., Ind. U., 1959; J.D., Wayne State U., 1963, postgrad., 1965; M.B.A., U. Detroit, 1965. Bar: Mich. bar 1963. Auditor Ernst & Ernst, Indpls., 1958-59; fin. and budget analyst Ford Motor Co., Dearborn, Mich., 1959-62; legal adminstr. Chrysler Corp., Detroit, 1962-63, tax atty., 1963-66, Glidden Co., Cleve., 1966-67; asst. to treas. Alcan Aluminum Corp., 1967-70, asst. to group v.p. ops., 1970-73; pres., dir. Aluminio de Colombia S.A., 1973-76; v.p. Alcan Bldg. Products div. Alcan Aluminum Corp., Warren, Ohio, 1976-78, pres., 1978-83, Alcan Sheet and Plate div., 1983-86, Alcan Bldg Products div., 1986-89, Alcan Extrusions USA div., 1989-90; pres., dir. Alcan Aluminum Corp., 1990-95, Bus. Concepts, Inc., 1995—. Bd. dirs. Luxfer USA Ltd., Alcan-Toyo-Am., Inc., Lanxide Corp., Liberty Mutual Ins. Co. Bd. dirs. ARC, NCCJ. Served with U.S. Army, 1954-56. Mem. ABA, Am. Arbitration Assn., Mich. Bar Assn., Cleve. Growth Assn. (dir.), Akron Regional Devel. Bd., Pine Lake Trout Club, Country Club of Hudson, Union Club, Cotillion Soc. Cleve., Scottish Rite, Beta Alpha Psi, Delta Theta Phi. Home: 290 Bicknell Dr Hudson OH 44236-2922 Office: 920 Key Bldg 159 S Main St Akron OH 44308-1317

HACKEL, EMANUEL, science educator; b. Bklyn., June 17, 1925; s. Henry N. and Esther (Herbstman) H.; m. Elisabeth Mackie, June 24, 1950 (dec. Apr. 1978); children: Lisa M., Meredith Anne, Janet M.; m. Rachel A. Fisher, Oct. 18, 1981; stepchildren: Daniel E., Tabitha A., and Jessica K. Harrison. Student, N.Y. U., 1941-42; B.S., U. Mich., 1948, M.S., 1949; Ph.D., Mich. State U., 1953. Fisheries biologist Mich. Dept. Conservation, 1949; mem. faculty Mich. State U., East Lansing, 1949—, prof. natural sci., 1962-74, chmn. dept. natural sci., 1963-74, prof. medicine, 1974-95, prof. emeritus, 1995—, prof. zoology, 1974-95, prof. emeritus, 1995—. Asst. dean coll. 1958-63; rsch. fellow Galton Lab., U. Coll., London, 1970-71, 77-78; vis. investigator blood group rsch. unit Lister Inst., London, 1956-57; cons. Mpls. War Meml. Blood Bank, 1983-95. Author: Guide to Laboratory Studies in Biological Science, 1951, Studies in Natural Science, 1953, Natural Science, 1955, Vols. 1, 2, 3, 1952-63. Editor: The Search for Explanation-Studies in Natural Science, Vols. 1, 2, 3, 1967-68, Laboratory Manual for Natural Science, Vol. 1, 2, 3, 1967-68,

Human Genetics, 1974, Theoretical Aspects of HLA, 1982, Bone Marrow Transplantation, 1983, HLA Techniques for Blood Bankers, 1984, Human Genetics 1984: A Look at the Last Ten Years and the Next Ten, Transfusion Management of Some Common Heritable Blood Disorders, 1992, Advances in Transplantation, 1993, HLA Typing Section, Clinical Laboratory Medicine, 1994, Human Genetics '94: A Revolution in Full Swing, 1994; contbr. articles on genetics, human blood group immunology and chem. nature of blood group antigens, human biochem. genetics, tissue typing, human histocompatability antigens to sci. jours. Served to lt. (j.g.) USNR, 1943-47; now lt. comdr. USNR Ret. Recipient Cooley Meml. award Am. Assn. Blood Banks, 1969, Elliott Meml. award Am. Assn. Blood Banks, 1987, alumni disting. faculty award Coll. Natural Sci. Mich. State U., 1995. Mem. Assn. Gen. and Liberal Studies (sec.-treas. 1962-65), AAUP, AAAS, Genetics Soc. Am., Am. Soc. Human Genetics, Am. Assn. Blood Banks (dir. 1983-84, chmn. sci. sect. 1983-84), Mich. Assn. Blood Banks (v.p. 1970, pres. 1975-77), Am. Inst. Biol. Sci., Biometric Soc., Transplantation Soc. Mich. (dir. 1975-84), Am. Assn. for Clin. Histocompatability Testing, N.Y. Acad. Scis., Sigma Xi, Phi Kappa Phi. Home: 244 Oakland Dr East Lansing MI 48823-4747

HACKER, DOUGLAS A. air transportation executive; CFO UAL Corp., Chgo., exec. v.p., CFO. Office: UAL Corp 1200 E Algonquin Rd Elk Grove Village IL 60007

HACKETT, BARBARA (KLOKA), retired judge; b. 1928; B of Philosophy, U. Detroit, 1948, JD, 1950. Bar: Mich. 1951, U.S. Dist. Ct. (ea. dist.) Mich. 1951, U.S. Ct. Appeals (6th cir.) 1951, U.S. Supreme Ct. 1957. Law clk. U.S. Dist. Ct. (ea. dist.) Mich., 1951-52; chief law clk. Mich. Ct. Appeals, 1965-66; asst. pros. atty. Wayne County, Mich., 1967-72; pvt. practice Detroit, 1952-53, 72-73; assoc. Frasco, Hackett & Mills, 1984-86; U.S. magistrate U.S. Dist. Ct. (ea. dist.) Mich., Detroit, 1973-84, judge, 1986-2001; ret., 2000. Mem. Interstate Commerce Commn., 1964. Trustee U. Detroit, 1983-89, Mercy High Sch., Farmington Hills, Mich. 1984-86, Detroit Symphony Orch., Orch. Hall Assocs., Detroit Sci. Ctr., United Community Svcs. Recipient Pres.'s Cabinet award U. Detroit Mercy, 1991. Mem. ABA (spl. ct. judge discovery abuse com. 1978-79, com. on cts. in cmty. 1979-84), Am. Judicature Soc., Fed. Bar Assn. (sec. 1981-82), Fed. Judges Assn., Nat. Assn. Women Judges, Nat. Dist. Attys. Assn., Nat. Assn. R.R. Trial Counsel, State Bar Mich., Women Lawyers Assn. Mich. Pros. Attys. Assn. Mich. (Disting. Svc. award 1971), Oakland County Bar Assn., U. Detroit Law Alumni Assn. (officer 1970-75, pres. 1975-77, Alumni Tower award 1976), Washtenaw County Bar Assn., Women's Econ. Club (bd. dirs. 1975-80, pres. 1980-81, named Detroit's Dynamic Women 1992), Econ. Club Detroit (bd. dirs. 1979-85, 88—), Phi Gamma Nu. Home: Pmb 182 4195 Tamiami Trl S Venice FL 34293-5112

HACKETT, EARL RANDOLPH, neurologist; b. Moulmein, Burma, Feb. 16, 1932; s. Paul Richmond and Martha Jane (Lewis) H.; m. Shirley Jane Kanehl, May 25, 1953; children: Nancy, Raymond, Susan, Lynn, Laurie, Richard, Alicia. B.S., Drury Coll., Springfield, Mo., 1953; M.D., Western Res. U., 1957. Diplomate Am. Bd. Psychiatry and Neurology, Am. Bd. Electrodiagnostic Medicine. Intern, then resident in neurology Charity Hosp., New Orleans, 1957-62; resident in internal medicine VA Hosp., 1958-59; mem. faculty La. State U. Med. Sch., 1962—, prof. neurology, 1973-88, head dept., 1977-88; clin. prof. neurology U. Mo., Columbia, 1988—. Mem. med. adv. bd. Myasthenia Gravis Found. Fellow Am. Acad. Neurology; mem. Am. Assn. Electrodiagnostic Medicine, Soc. Clin. Neurologists, Mo. Med. Assn., Greene County Med. Soc., AOA. Methodist. Home: 2517 S Brentwood Blvd Springfield MO 65804-3201 Office: 1965 S Fremont Ave Ste 2800 Springfield MO 65804-2258

HACKETT, JAMES P. manufacturing executive; b. 1955; BA, U. Mich., 1977. With Proctor and Gamble Co., 1977-81; joined Steelcase Inc., Grand Rapids, Mich., 1981—, sr. v.p. sales and mktg., 1990, pres. Turnstone, 1993; exec. v.p. Steelcase Ventures, 1994; exec. v.p., CEO Steelcase N.Am., 1994, pres., CEO, 1995—. Office: 901 44th St SE Grand Rapids MI 49508-7594

HACKETT, JOHN THOMAS, retired economist; b. Fort Wayne, Ind., Oct. 10, 1932; s. Harry H. and Ruth (Greer) H.; m. Ann E. Thompson, July 24, 1954; children: Jane, David, Sarah, Peter. BS, Ind. U., 1954, MBA, 1958; PhD, Ohio State U., 1961. Instr. Ohio State U., 1958-61; asst. v.p., economist Fed. Res. Bank, Cleve., 1961-64; dir. planning Cummins Engine Co., Columbus, Ind., 1964-66, v.p. finance, 1966-71, exec. v.p., 1971-88, also dir.; v.p. fin. and adminstrn. Ind. U., Bloomington, 1988-91; mng. gen. ptnr. CID Equity Ptnrs., L.P., Indpls., 1991—2002, ret., 2002. Bd. dirs. Irwin Fin. Corp., Ball Corp., Ind. Corp. for Bus. Modernizationand Tech.; chmn. bd. dirs. Wabash Nat. Corp. 1st lt. AUS, 1954-56. Mem. Ind. Acad., Beta Gamma Sigma. Home: PO Box 2337 Columbus IN 47202-2337

HACKETT, ROGER FLEMING, history educator; b. Kobe, Japan, Oct. 23, 1922; s. Harold Wallace and Anna Luena (Powell) H.; m. Caroline Betty Gray, Aug. 24, 1946; children: Anne Marilyn, David Gray, Brian Vance. B.A., Carleton Coll., 1947; M.A., Harvard U., 1949, Ph.D., 1955. Prof. history Northwestern U., Evanston, Ill., 1953-61; prof. history U. Mich., Ann Arbor, 1961-93, prof. emeritus, 1993—, chmn. dept., 1975-77; dir. Center for Japanese Studies, 1968-71, 78, 79. Cons. Office of Edn., HEW; mem. sub-com., joint com. Social Sci. Research Council. Author: Yamagata Aritomo in the Rise of Modern Japan 1838-1922, 1971; Editor: Jour. Asian Studies, 1959-62; contbr. articles and chpts to profl. jours. and books. Served with USMC, 1942-46. Social Sci. Research Council fellow; Japan Found. fellow; Fulbright-Hays fellow; fellow St. Antony's Coll. Oxford U. Mem. Japan Soc., Assn. for Asian Studies (exec. com., bd. dirs. 1966-69), Internat. House of Japan, Phi Beta Kappa. Club: Racquet (Ann Arbor). Home: 2122 Dorset Rd Ann Arbor MI 48104-2604 Office: U Mich Dept History Ann Arbor MI 48109 E-mail: fhackett@umich.edu.

HACKETT, WESLEY PHELPS, JR. lawyer; b. Detroit, Jan. 3, 1939; s. Wesley P. and Helen (Decker) H.; children: Kelly D. Hackett Pell, Robin C. BA, Mich. State U., 1960; JD, Wayne State U., 1968. Bar: Mich. 1968, U.S. Dist. Ct. (we. dist.) Mich. 1971, U.S. Ct. Appeals (6th cir.) 1972, U.S. Dist. Ct. (ea. dist.) Mich. 1972, U.S. Supreme Ct. 1972, U.S. Ct. Mil. Appeals 1991. Law clk. Mich. Supreme Ct., Lansing, 1968-70; ptnr. Brown & Hackett, 1971-73; pvt. practice, 1973-84; ptnr. Starr, Bissell & Hackett, 1984-87; pvt. practice East Lansing, Mich., 1987-98, Saranac, 1998—. Adj. prof. Thomas M. Cooley Law Sch., Lansing, 1973—; instr. Lansing C.C., 1981-99. Author: Evidence: A Trial Manual for Michigan Lawyers, 1981, Hackett's Evidence: Michigan and Federal, 2d edit., 1995, Michigan Lawyers Manual Part L, 1994, revised, 2002; co-author: Hiring Legal Staff, 1990. Mem. City of East Lansing Planning Commn., 1969-72; mem. Village of Saranac Planning Commn., 2000—; bd. dirs. St. Vincent Home for Children, Lansing, 1974-82. 1st lt. USAF, 1961-65. Fellow Coll. Law Practice Mgmt.; mem. ABA (sec. gen. practice sect. 1990-91, vice-chair 1991-92, chair 1993-94, standing com. on lawyer referral and info. svcs. 1997-2000, sole practitioner of yr. 1994, founders award 1997), State Bar Mich. (chair legal econs. sect. 1990-91).

HACKL, DONALD JOHN, architect; b. Chgo., May 11, 1934; s. John Frank and Frieda Marie Hackl; m. Bernadine Marie Becker, Sept. 29, 1962; children: Jeffrey Scott, Craig Michael, Cristina Lynn. BArch., U. Ill., 1957, MS in Architecture, 1958. With Loebl Schlossman & Hackl Architects, Chgo., 1963—, assoc., 1967-74, exec. v.p., dir., 1974, pres., dir., 1975—. Prof. architecture Internat. Acad. Architecture, Sofia, Bulgaria; mem. Nat. Coun. Archtl. Registration Bds., 1980—; bd. dirs. Chgo. Bldg. Congress, 1983-94, v.p., 1985-94; design juries include: Reynolds Metals, Western Mont. Regional Design, Am. Inst. Steel Constrn., Precast Concrete Inst., Okla. Soc. Architects, UIA/UNESCO (4); chmn. Ariz. Soc. Architects, Midwest Design Conf., 1983; design critic dept. arch. U. Ill., 1975-76, 81; vis. critic sch. architecture U. Notre Dame, 1977, 78, 80, 82; adj. prof. Kent Coll. Law, Ill. Inst. Tech., 1983—; adj. faculty Shenzhen (China) U., 1998-; cons. Pub. Svcs. Adminstrn., Washington, 1974-76; cons. urban planning, Changchun, China. Prin. works include Water Tower Place, Chgo., 1976, King Faisel Specialist Hosp. and Rsch. Ctr., Riyadh, Saudi Arabia, 1978, Household Internat. Hdqrs., Prospect Heights, Ill., 1978, Shriners Hosp. for Children, Chgo., 1979, Square D Co. Hdqrs., Palatine, Ill., 1979, West Suburban Hosp., Oak Park, Ill., 1981, Allstate Pla. West, Northbrook, Ill., 1990, Sears Roebuck & Co. stores of future concept, 1985-89, Ford City Shopping Ctr. Redevel., Chgo., 1989, Commerce Clearing House, Riverwoods, Ill., 1986, Physicians' Pavilion Greater Balt. Med. Ctr., 1987, Two Prudential Plaza, Chgo., 1990, City Place with Omni Hotel, Chgo., 1990, 350 N. LaSalle, Chgo., 1990, Infinitec, Assistive Tech. Application Ctr. for United Cerebral Palsy Assn., Chgo., 1992, Shenzhen AVIC Plaza Bldg., Shenzhen, China, 1993, Ill. State U. Biol. and Chemistry Scis. Lab. Bldg., Normal, 1995, Old Orchard Shopping Ctr. Redevel., Skokie, Ill., 1994, Sun Comml. City, Changchun, China, 1993, Shekou Harbor Bldg., Shenzhen, 1995, East Shanghai Film and TV Ctr., 1995, Luo-Hu Comml. Ctr., Shenzhen, 1994, Shenzhen Internat. Exch. Plz., 1996, Jin Hui Plz., Shanghai, 1996, Shenzhen Cultural Ctr., 1997, Changchun Sun Housing Estates, China, 1999, Hdqrs. for Almacenes Paris LTDA, Santiago, Chile, 1999, Cook County Hosp. Replacement Facility, 2002, Grand Pier Ctr., Chgo., 1998, Computer/Engring. Bldg. U. Ill., 1999—, Bank of Mauritius, Port Louis, 1999. Mem. Met. Am. Cancer Crusade, 1973; life trustee West Suburban Hosp., 1983—, mem. exec. com., 1986-87; vice chmn. North Ctrl. Coll., 1990—; mem. Pres.'s Coun. U. Ill. Found.; mem. curricula adv. com. Dept. Architecture, U. Ill.; bd. dirs. World Trade Ctr., Chgo., 1995—. Fellow AIA (treas. Chgo. chpt. 1977-78, exec. com. 1978-81, v.p. 1981, pres. 1981, bd. dirs. Chgo. AIA Found. 1981-83, nat. v.p. 1985, 1st v.p. 1986, nat. pres. 1987, chmn. design com. 1985, exec. com. 1985-87, bd. dirs. 1981-87, documents com. 1974-79, chmn. 1980, exec. com. AIA Svc. Corp. 1983-84, chmn. internat. com. 1987-91), Royal Archtl. Inst. Can. (hon.), Colegios Architectos Mexicanos (hon.), Internat. Acad. Architecture (hon.); mem. Union Internat. Archs. (bd. dirs., del. 1987—, 1st v.p. 1990-93, coun. 1993-96, v.p. region III 1996-99, treas. 2000—), Union Bulgarian Archs. (hon.), Soc. Cuban Archs., Japan Inst. Archs. (hon.), Colegio Arquitectos Cochabamba (Bolivia), Colegios Arquitectos Espana (hon.), Instituto do Arquiteclos do Brazil (hon.), Art Inst. Chgo., Tavern Clubs, Carlton Club, Econ. Club, Lake Zurich Club. Office: Loebl Schlossman and Hackl Inc 130 E Randolph Dr Ste 3400 Chicago IL 60601-6313

HACKMAN, LARRY J. program director, consulant; m. Sandra McFarland, 1966; children: Alex, Kate. LHD (hon.), U. Mo., 1998. Former archivist State of N.Y., John F. Kennedy Libr., others; asst. commr. of edn. for archives and records adminstrn. N.Y. State; dir. Harry S. Truman Presdl. Libr., Independence, Mo., 1995-2000; retired, 2000; cons, 2000—. Lectr. in field; Mellon fellow in Modern Archives, U. Mich., Littauer fellow Sch. of Govt. at Harvard; past mem. governing bd. Rockefeller Archives Ctr.; pres. Truman Libr. Inst., 1998-2000. Recipient Disting. Pub. Svc. award Rockefeller Coll. of Pub. Affairs, SUNY, Albany, Disting. Svc. award Nat. Hist. Publs. and Records Commn., 1999. Office: Harry S Truman Libr 500 W Us Highway 24 Independence MO 64050-2481

HADAD, SAM, food products distribution executive; CFO Reyes Holding, Lake Forest, Ill. Office: Reyes Holding 225 E Deerpath Rd Lake Forest IL 60045 Office Fax: (847) 604-9972.

HADDAD, ABRAHAM HERZL, electrical engineering educator, researcher; b. Baghdad, Iraq, Jan. 16, 1938; came to U.S., 1963; s. Moshe M. and Masuda (Cohen) H.; m. Carolyn Ann Kushner, Sept. 9, 1966; children: Benjamin, Judith, Jonathan. BSEE, Technion-Israel Inst. Tech., Haifa, 1960, MSEE, 1963; MA in Elec. Engring., Princeton U., 1964, PhD in Elec. Engring., 1966. Asst. prof. elec. engring. U. Ill., Urbana, 1966-70, assoc prof., 1970-75, prof., 1975-81; sr. staff cons. Dynamics Research Corp., Wilmington, Mass., 1979; program dir. NSF, Washington, 1979-83; prof. Ga. Inst. Tech., Atlanta, 1983-88; Dever prof., chmn. elec. engring and computer sci. dept. Northwestern U., 1988-98, Dever prof. dept. elec. and computer engring., 1996—, interim chair dept., 2001—02, dir. master info. and tech., 1998—. Dir. Computer Integrated Mfg. Sys. Program, 1987—88; adv. U.S. Army Missle Command, Huntsville, Ala., 1969—79; vis. assoc. prof. Tel Aviv U., Israel, 1972—73; cons. Lockheed-Ga. Co., 1984—88; sec. Am. Automatic Control Coun., 1990—; gen chmn. Am. Control Conf., 1993; chmn. policy com. Internat. Fedn. Automatic Control, 1996—2002. Editor: Non-linear Systems, 1975; assoc. editor Control Engring. Practice, 1999—. Fellow AAAS, IEEE (editor Trans. on Automatic Control 1983-89, Centennial medal 1984, mem. awards bd. 1997-99, third millenium medal 2000); mem. Control Systems Soc. of IEEE (gen. chair 1984 Conf. on Decision and Control, Disting. mem. award 1985, v.p. fin. affairs 1989-90, pres.-elect 1991, pres. 1992). Jewish. Office: Northwestern U Dept Ece Evanston IL 60208-0001

HADDAD, GEORGE ILYAS, engineering educator, research scientist; b. Aindara, Lebanon, Apr. 7, 1935; came to U.S., 1952, naturalized, 1961; s. Elias Ferris and Fahima (Haddad) H.; m. Mary Louella Nixon, June 28, 1958; children: Theodore N., Susan Anne. B.S. in Elec. Engring, U. Mich., 1956, M.S., 1958, Ph.D., 1963. Mem. faculty U. Mich., Ann Arbor, 1963—, assoc. prof., 1965-69, prof. elec. engring., 1968—, Robert J. Hiller prof., 1991—, dir. electron physics lab., 1968-75, chmn. dept. elec. engring. and computer sci., 1975-87, 91-97, dir. ctr. for high-frequency microelectronics, 1987—. Cons. to industry. Contbr. articles to profl. jours. Recipient Curtis W. McGraw research award Am. Soc. Engring, Edn., 1970, Excellence in Research award Coll. Engring., U. Mich., 1985, Disting. Faculty Achievement award U. Mich., 1985-86, S.S. Attwood award, 1991, MTT-S Disting. Educator award, 1996. Fellow IEEE (editor proc. and trans.); mem. NAE, Am. Soc. Engring. Edn., Am. Phys. Soc., Acad. Engring., Sigma Xi, Phi Kappa Phi, Eta Kappa Nu, Tau Beta Pi. Office: U Mich Dept Elec Engring & Computer Sci 2309 EECS 1301 Beal Ave Ann Arbor MI 48109-2122 E-mail: jih@umich.edu.

HADDOCK, FRED(ERICK) T(HEODORE), JR. astronomer, educator; b. Independence, Mo., May 31, 1919; s. Fred Theodore Sr. and Helen (Sea) H.; m. Margaret Pratt, June 24, 1941 (div. Sept. 1976); children: Thomas Frederick, Richard Marshall. SB, MIT, 1941; MS, U. Md., 1950; DSc (hon.), Rhodes Coll., 1965, Ripon Coll., 1966. Physicist U.S. Naval Rsch. Lab., Washington, 1941-56; assoc. prof. elec. engring. and astronomy U. Mich., Ann Arbor, 1956-59, prof. elec. engring., 1959-67, prof. astronomy, 1959-88, emeritus prof., 1988—. Lectr. radio astronomy Jodrell Bank U. Manchester, Eng., 1962; vis. assoc. radio astronomy Calif. Inst. Tech., 1966; vis. lectr. Raman Inst., Bangalore, India, 1978; sr. cons. Nat. Radio Astron. Obs., W.Va., 1960-61; founder, dir. U. Mich. Radio Astron. Obs., 1961-84. Author: (chpts. in books) Space Age Astronomy, 1962, Radio Astronomy of the Solar System, 1966; contbr. articles to prof. jours. and publs. Mem. Union Radio Sci. Internat., nat. chmn. commn. on radio astronomy, 1954-57; trustee Associated Univs., Inc., 1964-68; prin. investigator, five Orbiting Geophys. Observatories, 1960-74, and Interplanetary Probe 9, 1964-77; co-investigator on Voyager planetary probes, 1970-86, NASA, Washington; mem. astronomy adv. panel NSF, Washington, 1957-60, 63-66. With USN, 1944-45. Fellow IEEE (life), Am. Astron. Soc. (v.p. 1961-63); mem. Internat. Astron. Union (commn. on radio astronomy 1948—), NAS (adv. panel astronomy facilities 1962-64), AIA (hon. mem. Huron Valley chpt. 1980—), Sigma Xi (past pres. U. Mich. chpt. 1956—). Achievements include design and development of first submarine periscope radar antenna, 1943-44; early discoveries in microwave astronomy, gaseous nebulae in 1953 and early space detection of kilometer waves from galaxy and the sun, 1962. Home: 3935 Holden Dr Ann Arbor MI 48103-9415 Office: U Mich Astronomy Dept Ann Arbor MI 48109 E-mail: fhaddock@umich.edu.

HADERLEIN, THOMAS M. retired lawyer; b. Chgo., Sept. 2, 1935; BSC, DePaul U., 1957; JD, Georgetown U., 1960, LLM, 1962. Bar: Ill. 1960, D.C. 1960. With Baker & McKenzie, Washington, 1959-64, ptnr. Chgo., ret., 2000. Office: Baker & McKenzie One Prudential Plz 130 E Randolph St Ste 3700 Chicago IL 60601-6342

HADLEY, LEONARD ANSON, appliance manufacturing corporation executive; b. Earlham, Iowa, July 4, 1934; s. Willard J. and Berneice (Cook) H.; children: Philip, Christine. Student, Drake U., 1952-53; BSc in Acctg., U. Iowa, 1958. Cost acct. Maytag Co., Newton, Iowa, 1959-61, sr. cost acct., 1961-63, mktg. budget supr., 1964-67, mgr. budgets, 1967-75, asst. contr., 1975-79, v.p. corp. planning, 1979-86, pres., 1986-89; exec. v.p., pres. Appliance Group Maytag Corp., 1989-90, exec. v.p., COO, 1990-91, pres., COO, 1991, pres., CEO, 1992, chmn., CEO, 1993—. Bd. dirs. Maytag Corp., Deere & Co., Norwest Bank, Snap-on Inc. Bd. visitors U. Iowa Bus. Sch., U. Iowa Found.; active Newton First United Meth. Ch. Served with U.S. Army, 1954-56. Mem. Newton C. of C., Iowa Bus. Coun. (chmn. 1998—), Nat. Assn. Mfrs., Iowa Coll. Found., Des Moines Club. Republican. Office: Maytag Corp 403 W 4th St N Newton IA 50208-3034

HADLEY, ROBERT JAMES, lawyer; b. Wilmington, Ohio, Oct. 27, 1938; s. Robert Edwin and Ethel Edith (Slade) H.; m. Judith Ellen Gilbert, Aug. 11, 1962; children: Scott, Laura, Stephen. BA in History cum laude, Ohio State U., 1960; LLB, Harvard U., 1963. Bar: Ohio 1963. Assoc. Smith & Schnacke, Dayton, 1963-69, ptnr., 1970-89, Thompson Hine LLP, Dayton, 1989—. Pres. Man-to-Man Assocs., 1978-84, Dayton Habitat for Humanity, 1988; v.p. COPE Halfway House, Dayton, 1982-85; dir., sec. Friendship Village of Dayton, 1985—; bd. dirs. Cmty. Blood Ctr., Dayton, 1987—; loaned exec. United Way, 1980-82, cabinet 2001-02; mem. Kettering Civic Band, 1968—, v.p. Parish Resource Ctr., 1996-99, pres., 1999-2000; bd. dirs. South Cmty. YMCA, 1996-98, Greater Dayton Youth for Christ, 1980-86, Dayton Area Peace Accords Project; mem., treas. Ministry of Money bd., 1992—. Named Kettering Man of the Yr., 1986; Rotary Found. grantee, Israel, 1974. Mem. ABA, Ohio Bar Assn., Dayton Bar Assn., Dayton Racquet Club, Rotary (pres. Kettering 1986-87, dist. gov., group rep. Dist. 667 1989-90, dist. gov. 1993-94), Phi Beta Kappa. Republican. Methodist. Avocations: music, travel, sports. Home: 4848 Glenmina Dr Dayton OH 45440-2002 Office: Thompson Hine LLP PO Box 8801 2000 Courthouse Plz NE Dayton OH 45401-8801 E-mail: bob.hadley@thompsonhine.com.

HADLEY, STANTON THOMAS, international manufacturing and marketing company executive, lawyer; b. Beloit, Kans., July 3, 1936; s. Robert Campbell and Helen (Schroeder) H.; m. Charlotte June Holmes, June 9, 1962; children: Gayle Elizabeth, Robert Edward, Stanton Thomas, Steven Holmes. B.S. in Metall. Engring., Colo. Sch. Mines, 1958; LL.B., U. Colo., 1962. Bar: Colo. 1962, U.S. Dist. Ct. 1962, U.S. Patent Office 1963. Metallurgist ASARCO, Leadville, Colo., 1957; tng. engr. Allis-Chalmers Co., West Allis, Wis., 1958-61; adminstrv. engr. Ball Corp., Boulder, Colo., 1961-62, atty., 1962-65; patent counsel Scott Paper Co., Phila., 1965-71, USG Corp., Chgo., 1971-76, gen. mgr. metals div., 1976-79, group v.p. indsl. group, 1979-84, sr. v.p. adminstrn., sec., 1984, sec., 1984-87, sr. v.p. staff services, 1987-89; pres. Ansco Photo-Optical Products Corp., 1989-93, Visador Co., Marion, Va., 1994-98. Bd. dirs. Masonite Corp., WJE Assocs. Inc., USG Found. Bd. dirs. Ill. Safety Council, North Suburban YMCA, Northbrook Symphony Orch.; former mem. founders' council Field Mus.; mem. Chgo. United, Chgo. Assn. Commerce and Industry. Served with U.S. Army, 1959. Mem. Am. Soc. Metals, Licensing Execs. Soc., Assn. Corp. Patent Counsel. Republican. Clubs: Union League, Sunset Ridge Country, Executives. Home: 555 Valley Way Northfield IL 60093-1067 Office: STH Cons 555 Valley Way Northfield IL 60093-1067

HAECK, JAMES F. company executive; Exec. v.p. The LTV Corp., Cleve., 1993—. Office: The LTV Corp PO Box 6778 Cleveland OH 44101-1778

HAENICKE, DIETHER HANS, university president emeritus, educator; b. Hagen, Germany, May 19, 1935; came to U.S., 1963, naturalized, 1972; s. Erwin Otto and Helene (Wildfang) H.; m. Carol Ann Colditz, Sept. 29, 1962; children: Jennifer Ruth, Kurt Robert. Student, U. Gottingen, 1955-56, U. Marburg, 1957-59; Ph.D. magna cum laude in German Lit. and Philology, U. Munich, 1962; DHL (hon.), Cen. Mich. U., 1986; DHL, We. Mich. U., 1998. Asst. prof. Wayne State U., Detroit, 1963-68, assoc. prof., 1968-72, prof. German, 1972-78, resident dir. Jr. Year in Freiburg (Ger.), 1965-66, 69-70, dir. Jr. Year Abroad programs, 1970-75, chmn. dept. Romance and Germanic langs. and lits., 1971-72, assoc. dean Coll. Liberal Arts, 1972-75, provost, 1975-77, v.p., provost, 1977-78; dean Coll. Humanities Ohio State U., 1978-82, v.p. acad. affairs, provost, 1982-85; pres. Western Mich. U., Kalamazoo, 1985-98. Asst. prof. Colby Coll. Summer Sch. of Langs., 1964-65; lectr. Internationale Ferienkurse, U. Freiburg, summers 1961, 66, 67 Author: (with Horst S. Daemmrich) The Challenge of German Literature, 1971, Untersuchungen zum Versepos des 20. Jahrhunderts, 1962; editor: Liebesgeschichte der schonen Magelone, 1969, Der blonde Eckbert und andere Novellen, 1969, Franz Sternbalds Wanderungen, 1970; contbr. articles to acad. and lit. jours. Mem. Mich. State Atty. Discipline Bd. Fulbright scholar, 1963-65 Mem. MLA, AAUP, Am. Assn. Tchrs. of German, Mich. Acad. Arts and Scis., Mich. Coun. for Arts and Cultural Affairs, Phi Beta Kappa. Office: Western Mich U 3019 Waldo Library Kalamazoo MI 49008-3804 E-mail: diether.haenicke@wmich.edu.

HAERING, EDWIN RAYMOND, chemical engineering educator, consultant; b. Columbus, Ohio, Dec. 8, 1932; s. Edwin Jacob and Mary Mildred (Kunst) H.; m. Suzanne Rowe, June 9, 1956; children: Cynthia, David Arthur, Elizabeth. BChemE, MS, Ohio State U., 1956, PhD, 1966. Mem. faculty Ohio State U., Columbus, 1959-91, assoc. prof., 1973-82, prof. chem. engring., 1982-91, prof. emeritus, 1991—, vice chmn. dept., 1974-76, chmn. dept., 1977-78. Cons. in field, 1966—. Author: Laboratory Manual for Unit Operations Laboratory, 1980; also tech. articles to profl. jours. Disaster svcs. vol. ARC, 1997—. Lt. (j.g.) USNR, 1956—59. NROTC scholar, 1951-56, Dow Chem. Co. scholar, 1956; Keppers tchg. fellow, 1962. Mem. AIChE (treas. Cen. Ohio sect. 1974-79), Am. Chem. Soc., Port Clinton Power Squadron, Sigma Xi, Tau Beta Pi, Ohio State U. Faculty Club (pres. 1988-89), Bay Point Yacht Club, Columbus Maennerrhor Club, Lake Erie South Shore Hunter Sailing Assn. (treas. 1997-99). Avocations: golf, gardening, sailing. Home: 701 Stoutenberg Dr Marblehead OH 43440-2049 Office: Ohio State Univ Dept Chem Engring 701 Stoutenberg Dr Marblehead OH 43440-2049

HAFFNER, CHARLES CHRISTIAN, III, retired printing company executive; b. Chgo., May 27, 1928; s. Charles Christian and Clarissa (Donnelley) H.; m. Anne P. Clark, June 19, 1970. BA, Yale U., 1950. With R.R. Donnelley & Sons Co., Chgo., 1951—, treas., 1962-68, v.p. and treas., 1968-83, vice-chmn. and treas., 1983-84, vice-chmn., 1984-90, ret., 1990. Bd. dirs. DuKane Corp. Chmn. Morton Arboretum, 1975-2001, Newberry Libr., 1986-2000, Sprague Found., 1996-2000; trustee Art Inst. Chgo., Latin Sch., Chgo., 1974-84, Ill. Cancer Coun., 1984-92, Chgo. City Day Sch., Lincoln Pk. Zool. Soc., Brooks Sch., 1987-95, Newberry Libr.; life trustee Sprague Found.; bd. govs. Nature Conservancy, 1973-84, chmn.

Ill. chpt., 1984-87, life trustee, 1987—; mem. Chgo. Plan Commn., 1986-91. 1st lt. USAF, 1952-54. Mem. Chgo. Club, Comml. Club, Commonwealth Club, Racquet Club, Caxton Club, Casino Club. Home: 1530 N State Pkwy Chicago IL 60610-1610 Office: 35 E Wacker Dr Ste 2650 Chicago IL 60601-2398

HAFFNER, DAVID S. business executive; Exec. v.p. Leggett & Platt, Inc., Carthage, Mo., 1990—, COO, 1999—. Office: Leggett & Platt Inc PO Box 757 1 Leggett Rd Carthage MO 64836-9649

HAGAN, JOHN CHARLES, III, ophthalmologist; b. Mexico, Mo., Oct. 7, 1943; s. John Charles Hagan II and Cleta L. (Book) Neely; m. Rebecca Jane Chapman, July 15, 1967; children: Carol Ann, Catherine Elizabeth. BA, U. Mo., 1965; MD, Loyola U., Chgo., 1969. Diplomate Am. Bd. Ophthalmology. Intern Med. Coll. Wis., Milw., 1969-70; resident in ophthalmology Emory U., Atlanta, 1972-75; practice medicine, Kansas City, Mo., 1975—. Cons. Am. Running and Phys. Fitness Assn., Washington, 1973—. Editor: Mo. Medicine: The Jour. of the Mo. State Med. Assn.; contbr. over 100 articles to med. jours. Capt. M.C., USAF, 1970-72. Fellow ACS; mem. AMA, Am. Intraocular Implant Soc., Mo. Soc. Eye Physicians and Surgeons (pres. 1998), Mo. Soc. Ophthalmology. Office: Discover Vision Ctrs 9401 N Oak Trafficway Kansas City MO 64155

HAGAN, MICHAEL CHARLES, transporation executive; Bachelor's, Brescia Coll., 1970. Mgmt. trainee Am. Comml. Barge Line Am. Comml. Lines, Jeffersonville, Ind., 1970-87, exec. v.p., 1989-90, pres., 1990, pres., CEO, 1992—; v.p. rail unit CSX, 1989-90. Office: Am Comml Lines 1701 Utica Pike Jeffersonville IN 47130-4747

HAGAN, ROBERT F. state legislator; b. Youngstown, Ohio, Mar. 31, 1949; m. Michele Hagan; children: Jennifer, Kristen, Thomas, James, Natalia. Engr. locomotive CSX Transp.; state rep. Dist. 53 Ohio Ho. of Reps., 1987-97; mem. Ohio Senate from 33rd dist., Columbus, 1997—. Vice chmn. Transp. and Urban Affairs com.; mem. commerce com., labor com., health and retirement com., human resources com. Trustee Northside Citizens Coalition. Named Pub. Ofcl. of Yr. Nat. Assn. Steel Workers Ohio, 1990, Ohioan of Yr. OCSEA, 1990, Legislators of Yr. Ohio Counseling Assn., 1991; recipient Legis. Leadership award Ohio Coalition for Edn. Handicapped Children, 1990, Legis. award Assn. Ohio Health Commrs., 1992. Mem. Nat. Fedn. Blind (chmn.), Steelworkers Oldtimers Club, Citizens League, United Transp. Union Local 604, Sierra Club. Office: Ohio Senate State Capitol Bldg Columbus OH 43215

HAGAN, SHEILA B. corporate lawyer; b. 1961; BA, Coll. St. Thomas; JD, U. Minn. Bar: 1987. V.p., gen. counsel IBP, Inc., Dakota Dunes, S.D. Office: IBP Inc 800 Stevens Port Dr Ste 836 Dakota Dunes SD 57049-5005

HAGAN-HARRELL, MARY M. state legislator; b. Cape Girardeau, Mo. m. Stan Harrell. BS in Elem. Edn. and Fine Arts, Southeast Mo. State U.; MLS, George Peabody Coll. Tchr., libr. Riverview Gardens (Mo.) Sch. Dist., 1960-86; committeewoman Ferguson Twp., 1972-89; state rep. Dist. 75 Mo. Ho. of Reps., 1986—. Chmn. retirement com., state employees com.; mem. appropriations, edn. and pub. safety com., govt. ogrn. com., higher edn. com., elem. and secondary edn. com., labor com., joint coms. pub. employees retirement, workers compensation and employment security com., health care contbns. for state employees com.; sec. St. Louis County Dem. Ctrl. Com., 1976-89. Mem. NEA, Nat. Orgn. Women Legislators, Women Polit. Caucus, Mo. Orgn. Women Legislators, Mo. Sch. Librs. Assn., Downettes Charitable Club. Office: Mo Ho of Reps Rm 316 201 W Capitol Ave Jefferson City MO 65101-1556 E-mail: mhaganha@services.state.mo.us.

HAGE, CHRISTINE LIND, library administrator; b. Detroit, Nov. 26, 1949; d. Richards I. and Letizia L. (Majorana) Lind; m. Robert M. Hage, Aug. 21, 1971; children: Paul R., Andrew M. BA in English, Oakland U., Rochester Hills, Mich., 1970; MLS, U. Mich., 1971. Cert. libr., Mich. Head of adult and circulation svcs. Troy (Mich.) Pub. Libr., 1971-77; dir. Shelby Twp. (Mich.) Libr., 1977-81; head of adult svcs. Rochester Hills Pub. Libr., 1981-88, dir., 1988-99, Clinton-Macomb Pub. Libr., Mich., 1999—. Chair Detroit Suburban Librs. Roundtable, 1981, 92; chair Oakland County Union List of Serials, 1989. Editor: Public Library Policy Resource Manual, 1987, Michigan Associations Directory, 1987. Bd. dirs. Greater Rochester Area Cmty. Found., 1994-98. Recipient Rose award AAUW, Utica, Mich., 1980; named Mich. Libr. of the Yr., 1997. Mem. Am. Libr Assn. (councilor), Pub. Libr. Assn. (bd. dirs. 1990-94, pres. 1998-99), Mich. Libr. Assn. (chair numerous units 1971—), Mount Clemens Rotary. Lutheran. Home: 1893 Ludgate Ln Rochester Hills MI 48309-2965 Office: Clinton-Macomb Pub Libr 43245 Garfield Rd Clinton Township MI 48038-1115 E-mail: christine@cmpl.org.

HAGEDORN, DONALD JAMES, phytopathologist, educator, agricultural consultant; b. Moscow, May 18, 1919; s. Frederick William and Elizabeth Viola (Scheyer) H.; m. Eloise Tierney, July 18, 1943; 1 child, James William BS, U. Idaho, 1941, DSc (hon.), 1979; MS, U. Wis., 1943, PhD, 1948. Prof. agronomy and plant pathology U. Wis., Madison, 1948-64, prof. plant pathology, 1964—. Courtesy prof. plant pathology Oreg. State U., Covallis, 1972-73; vis. scientist DSIR Lincoln Rsch. Ctr., Christchurch, N.Z., 1980-81; cons. Asgrow Seed Co., 1987-93; affiliate prof. plant pathology U. Idaho, 1991—. Contbr. chpts. to books, articles to profl. jours. With USAAF, 1943-46. Recipient Campbell award AAAS, 1961, CIBA-Geigy award, 1974, Meritorious Svc. award Nat. Pea Improvement Assn., 1979, Bean Improvement Coop., 1979, Forty-Niners award, 1983, Citation for Outstanding Sci. Achievement, Wis. Acad. Letters, Arts and Scis., 1986; NSF sr. fellow, 1957; named Disting. Centennial Alumnus, U. Idaho, 1989; named to U. Idaho Alumni Hall of Fame, 1990. Fellow Am. Phytopath, Soc.; mem. Kiwanis, Sigma Xi, Gamma Sigma Delta, Alpha Zeta. Methodist. Home: 927 University Bay Dr Madison WI 53705-2248 Office: U Wis 583 Russell Labs 1630 Linden Dr Madison WI 53706-1520

HAGEDORN, JAMES, company executive; Grad. AMP program, Harvard Bus. Sch. Sr. mgmt. roles Miracle-Gro; with The Scotts Co., 1995, pres. N.Am. ops., pres., COO domestic and indsl. bus., 2000—. Exec. v.p. Scotts' U.S. Bus. Groups. Officer USAF. Office: 41 S High St Ste 3500 Columbus OH 43215-6110

HAGEL, CHARLES, senator; b. North Platte, Nebr., Oct. 4, 1946; m. Lilibet Ziller; 2 children. Student, Brown Inst. Radio & TV, Minn., 1966; BA, U. Nebr., 1971. Dep. adminstr. VA, 1981-82; pres./CEO World USO, 1987-90; pres. McCarthy & Co., 1991-96; U.S. senator from Nebr., 1996—. Mem. internat. fin., fgn. rels. coms. U.S. Senate, chmn. senate global climate change observer group, mem. NATO observer group; mem. coms. banking, housing and urban affairs, 1997—, spl. com. on aging, 1997—; founder/dir. Vanguard Cellular Syss. Inc. Active Bellevue U., Red Cross, No Greater Love, World USO; chair Paralyzed Veterans of Am., 10 Anniversary Vietnam Vets. Meml. With U.S. Army, 1967-68. Mem. Am. Legion VFW, Omaha C. of C. (trustee). Office: 248 Russell Senate Office Bldg Washington DC 20510-0001

HAGELIN, JOHN SAMUEL, theoretical physicist; b. Pitts., June 9, 1954; s. Carl William and Mary Lee (Stephenson) H. AB summa cum laude, Dartmouth Coll., 1975; MA, Harvard U., 1976, PhD, 1981. Sci. assoc. European Lab. for Particle Physics, CERN, Geneva, 1981-82; rsch. assoc. Stanford (Calif.) Linear Accelerator Ctr., 1982-83; assoc. prof. physics Maharishi U. Mgmt., Fairfield, Iowa, 1983-84, prof. physics, 1984—. Pres., dir. rsch. Enlightened Audio Designs Corp., 1991—; dir. Inst. Sci., Tech. and Pub. Policy, 1992—. Contbr. numerous articles to scientific jours. Presdl. candidate Natural Law Party, 1992, 96, 2000. Tyndall fellow Harvard U., 1979-80, Kilby Young Innovator award 1992. Mem. Iowa Acad. Scis. Avocation: research. Home and Office: Maharishi Univ Mgmt Inst Sci Tech-Pub Policy Fairfield IA 52557-0001 E-mail: istpp@mum.edu.

HAGEN, DONALD FLOYD, university administrator, former military officer; b. Ambrose, N.D., Jan. 2, 1938; s. Alvin Hagen and Edith I. (Abell) Olsen; m. Karen Pizzino, May 11, 1973; children: Dana, Lisa Amanda. BA, Concordia Coll., Moorhead, Minn., 1959; BS in Medicine, U. N.D., 1961; MD, Northwestern U., Evanston, Ill., 1963. Diplomate Am. Bd. Surgery. Commd. ensign USN, 1964, advanced through grades to rear adm., 1989; internship L.A. County Gen. Hosp., 1963-64; residency gen. surgery Portmouth (Va.) Naval Hosp., 1970-73; staff surgeon Naval Aerospace Med. Ctr., Pensacola, Fla., 1973-75; chief surgery U.S. Naval Hosp., Yokosuka, Japan, 1973-79, dir. clin. svcs. Jacksonville, Fla., 1979-81, commdg. officer Camp Pendleton, Calif., 1984-86; dir. contingency planning div. Bur. Medicine and Surgery, Washington, 1981-82; dir. med. edn. and tng. Office of Surgeon Gen., 1982-84, dir. health care ops., 1986-88; dep. comdr. health care ops. Naval Med. Command, 1988; comdr. Nat. Naval Med. Ctr., Bethesda, Md., 1988-91; surgeon gen., vice admiral USN, 1991-95, retired, 1995; exec. vice chancellor U. Kans. Med. Ctr., Kansas City, 1995—. Mem. bd. regents Uniformed Svcs. U. Health Scis., Bethesda, 1988-90; asst. chief Navy Med. Corps., 1989-90. Decorated bronze star; recipient Fed. Exec. award of excellence Am. Hosp. Assn., 1989. Mem. AMA, Am. Coll. Physician Execs., Assn. Mil. Surgeons of the U.S. (Founder award 1984), Army-Navy Club (Washington). Republican. Avocations: piano playing, church choir. Office: U Kans Med Ctr 3901 Rainbow Blvd Kansas City KS 66160-0001

HAGEN, LAWRENCE JACOB, agricultural engineer; b. Rugby, N.D., Mar. 6, 1940; s. Lars and Alice (Hannem) H. BS, N.D. State U., 1962, MS, 1967; PhD, Kans. State U., 1980. Agrl. engr. USDA, Manhattan, Kans., 1967—. Contbr. tech. articles to profl. pubs. Capt. USAF, 1963-69. Mem. Am. Soc. Agrl. Engrs., Soil & Water Conservation Soc. Am. Office: USDA Agronomy Dept ARS Wind Erosion Kans State U 2004 Throckmorton Hall Manhattan KS 66506-5500 E-mail: hagen@weru.ksu.edu.

HAGEN, RICHARD E. (DICK), state legislator; b. Pine Ridge, S.D., Aug. 16, 1937; m. Mona Hagen; children: Shagne, Winona. Mem. S.D. Ho. of Reps., 1982-92, 93-2000, mem. health and human svc. com. and local govt. com.; painter, carpenter; mem. S.D. Senate from 27th dist., Pierre, 2001—. Mem. local govt. com., transportation com. S.D. House of Reps. Mem. Shannon County Sch. Bd. Democrat. Home: PO Box 3 Pine Ridge SD 57770-0003

HAGENLOCKER, EDWARD E. retired automobile company executive; b. 1939; married. BS, MS, Ohio State U., 1962, PhD, 1964; MBA, Mich. State U., 1982. With Ford Motor Co., 1964-98, chief engr., 1973-77, 78-80, dir., v.p. ops. Brazil, 1984-85, dir., pres. Brazil, 1985-86, v.p., gen. mgr. truck ops. Mich., 1986-92, exec. v.p. N.Am. automotive ops., 1992-94, pres. Ford automotive ops., 1994-96, vice chmn., 1996-98. Office: 39400 Woodward Ave Ste 165 Bloomfield Hills MI 48304-5151

HAGER, KENNETH VINCENT, accountant; b. Kansas City, Mo., Jan. 8, 1951; s. George D. and Elaine H. (Boutross) H.; m. Marilyn Jean Ricono, June 28, 1975; children: Christina, Joseph. BS in Bus. Adminstrn. and Acctg., U. Kans., 1972. CPA, Mo., Kans. From mem. audit staff to mgr. Arthur Young, Kansas City, Mo., 1973-82; v.p. fin. Kreeuncy Control Products, Olathe, Kans., 1982; internal audit mgr. Puritan Bennett Corp., Overland Park, 1982-84; supr. EDP, audit Kansas City (Mo.) So. Ind., 1984-86, internal audit mgr., 1986-88; v.p., chief fin. officer DST Systems, Inc., Kansas City, 1988—. Bd. dirs. Am. Cancer Soc., Kansas City, Mo., 1981—, chmn. pub. edn., 1984—. Mem. AICPA (pres. 1988). Roman Catholic. Avocations: baseball, golf, basketball. Home: 2801 W 127th St Leawood KS 66209-2415 Office: DST Systems Inc 333 W 11th St Kansas City MO 64105

HAGER, LOWELL PAUL, biochemistry educator; b. Girard, Kans., Aug. 30, 1926; s. Paul William and Christine (Selle) H.; m. Frances Erea, Jan. 22, 1949; children: Paul, Steven, JoAnn. AB, Valparaiso U., 1947; MA, U. Kans., 1950; PhD, U. Ill., 1953. Postdoctoral fellow Mass. Gen. Hosp., Boston, 1953-55; asst. prof. biochemistry Harvard U., Cambridge, Mass., 1955-60; mem. faculty U. Ill., Urbana, 1960—, prof. biochemistry, 1965—, head biochem. div., 1967-89, dir. Biotech. Ctr., 1987—. Chmn. physiol. chemistry study sect. NIH, 1965—; vis. scientist Imperial Cancer Rsch. Fund, 1964; cons. NSF, 1976. Editor life scis. Archives Biochemistry and Biophysics, 1966—; assoc. editor Biochemistry, 1973—; mem. editorial bd. Jour. Biol. Chemistry, 1874—. With USAAF, 1945. Guggenheim fellow U. Oxford, Eng., 1959-60, Max Planck Inst. Zellchemie, 1959-60. Mem. NAS (elected), Am. Chem. Soc., Am. Soc. Biol. Chemists, Am. Soc. Microbiology (chmn. physiology divsn. 1967). Achievements include rsch. in enzyme mechanisms, intermediary metabolism, tumor virus. Home: 5 Fields East Champaign IL 61822 E-mail: l-hager@uiuc.edu.

HAGERTY, THOMAS M. insurance executive; Grad., Harvard Bus. Sch. Mng. dir. Thomas H. Lee Ptnrs.; dir. Metris Co., Inc., Cott Corp., Freedom Securities Corp., ARC Holdings., Metris Co.; interim CEO Conseco, Inc., 2000—. Office: 11825 N Penn St Carmel IN 46032

HAGEVIK, BRUCE, radio personality; b. Ortonvile, Minn. m. Marvette Hagevik. Grad. Psychology, Moorhead State Coll. Announcer, Ortonville, Minn.; news dir. Faribault; radio host, news anchor Sta. WCCO Radio, Mpls., 1973—. Recipient award, AP, Northwest Broadcast News Assn., Radio and TV News Dirs. Assn. Office: WCCO 625 2nd Ave S Minneapolis MN 55402*

HAGG, REXFORD A. lawyer, former state legislatorr; b. Sioux Falls, S.D., May 10, 1957; m. Cindy Hagg; 1 child. Student, Nebr. U., S.D. State U. City atty. City of Box Elder, S.D., 1984—; mem. S.D. Ho. of Reps., 1988—98, vice chmn. judiciary com., mem. legis. procedure and taxation coms., speaker, 1997-98; atty. Whiting, Hagg & Hagg, Rapid City, S.D. Home: 1721 West Blvd Rapid City SD 57701-4555 Office: Whiting Hagg & Hagg 601 West Boulevard PO Box 8008 Rapid City SD 57709

HAGGARD, JOAN CLAIRE, church musician, piano instructor, accompanist; b. Ann Arbor, Mich., July 7, 1932; d. Clifford Buell and Bertha (Woodhurst) Wightman; m. Harold Wallace Haggard, June 30, 1956; children: Alan C., Stephen T., John A., Marian E. BA, Carleton Coll., 1954; postgrad., Ecole des Beaux Arts, Fontainebleau, France, 1954, U. Mich., 1954-55; A., Am. Guild Organists, 1980. Cert. pvt. piano tchr. Organist, choir dir. St. Paul's Episc. Ch., Riverside, Ill., 1955-59; dir. of music St. Andrew's Episc. Ch., Livonia, Mich., 1960-72; organist Christ Episc. Ch., Dearborn, 1973-83; dir. of music St. Philip's Episc. Ch., Rochester, 1983-92; organist, music coord. 1st United Meth. Ch., Farmington, 1992-2000. Pvt. piano tchr., Livonia, 1960—; piano instr. Southfield (Mich.) Sr. Adult Ctr., 1992-99; accompanist Creative and Performing Arts High Sch., Livonia, 1987-90; accompanist many solo instrumental and vocal performances, 1959—. Editor Livonia Youth Symphony Soc. newsletter, 1972-77; contbr. articles to profl. jours. Pres. Livonia Youth Symphony Soc., 1973-76; program dir. Episcopal Diocese Mich. Jr. Choir Camp, 1981-84, 87-89; coord. daily worship Triennial Conv. Episcopal Ch., Detroit, 1988. Mem. Am. Guild Organists (dean Detroit chpt. 1976-79, gen. chmn. nat. conv. 1986, councillor Region V 1986-92), Nat. Guild Piano Tchrs. (judge piano auditions 1987—), Music Tchrs. Nat. Assn., Assn. Anglican Musicians, Hymn Soc. in the U.S. and Can., Assn. Diocesan Liturgy and Music Commns., Music Commn. Episcopal Diocese Mich. (chmn. 1980-81), Mich. Fedn. Music Clubs (pres. eastern dist. 1998-2000), Mich. Music Tchrs. Assn. (local assn. chmn. 1996—), Piano Tchrs. Forum (Livonia area, pres. 1995-97), SAI Friend of Arts, PEO. Avocations: bird watching, nature, reading (especially murder mysteries). Home: 33974 Hampshire St Livonia MI 48154-2722

HAGGLUND, CLARANCE EDWARD, lawyer, publishing company owner; b. Omaha, Feb. 17, 1927; s. Clarance Andrew and Esther May (Kelle) H.; m. Dorothy Souser, Mar. 27, 1953 (div. Aug. 1972); children: Laura, Bret, Katherine; m. Merle Patricia Hagglund, Oct. 28, 1972. BA, U. S.D., 1949; JD, William Mitchell Coll. Law, 1953. Bar: Minn. 1955, U.S. Ct. Appeals (8th cir.) 1974, U.S. Supreme Ct. 1963; diplomate Am. Bd. Profl. Liability Attys. Ptnr. Hagglund & Johnson and predecessor firms, Mpls., 1973—; mem. Hagglund, Weimer and Speidel, PA; publ., pres. Common Law Publishing Inc., Golden Valley, Minn., 1991—. Pres. Internat. Control Sys., Inc., Mpls., 1979—, Hill River Corp., Mpls., 1976—; gen. counsel Minn. Assn. Profl. Ins. Agts., Inc., Mpls., 1965-86; CFO, Pro-Trac, software for profl. liability ins. industry. Contbr. articles to profl. jours. Served to lt. comdr. USNR, 1945-46, 50-69. Fellow Internat. Soc. Barristers; mem. Lawyers Pilots Bar Assn., U.S. Maritime Law Assn. (proctor), Acad. Cert. Trial Lawyers Minn. (dean 1983-85), Nat. Bd. Trial Advocacy (cert. in civil trial law, bd. dirs.), Douglas Amdahl Inns of Ct. (pres.), Ill. Athletic Club (Chgo.), Edina Country Club (Minn.), Calhoun Beach Club (Mpls.). Roman Catholic. Avocation: flying. Home: 3168 Dean Ct Minneapolis MN 55416-4386 Office: Common Law Publishing Inc 5101 Olson Memorial Hwy Golden Valley MN 55422-5149 E-mail: hagglund@pro-ns.net.

HAHM, DAVID EDGAR, classics educator; b. Milw., Sept. 30, 1938; s. Edgar David and Loraine Emily (Stebnitz) H.; m. Donna Lorraine Seifert, Aug. 8, 1964; children: Melanie Davida, Christopher David, Geoffrey Kenneth, Martha Maria. BA, Northwestern Coll., 1960; student, Wis. Luth. Sem., 1960-61; MA, U. Wis., 1962, PhD, 1966. Asst. prof. U. Mo., Columbia, 1966-69; asst. prof. classics Ohio State U., Columbus, 1969-72, assoc. prof., 1972-78, prof., 1978—, chmn., 1999—. Vis. fellow Corpus Christi Coll., Cambridge, Eng., 1990-91. Author: The Origins of Stoic Cosmology, 1977; contbr. articles to jours., chpts. to books. Trustee Dublin Hist. Soc., 1974-79, pres., 1974-76; active Archtl. Rev. Bd., Dublin, Ohio, 1976-83, chmn., 1980-82; mem. exec. bd. Worthington Hist. Soc., 1981-89, 93—; trustee Old Dublin Assn., 1996—, treas., 1997—. Fellow Ctr. Hellenic Studies; mem. AAUP, Am. Philol. Assn., Am. Philos. Assn., Classical Assn., Mid. West and South, History of Sci. Soc., Soc. Ancient Greek Philosophy. Lutheran. Office: Ohio State U Dept Greek and Latin 230 N Oval Mall Columbus OH 43210-1335 E-mail: hahm.1@osu.edu.

HAHN, DAVID BENNETT, hospital administrator, marketing professional; b. Louisville, June 5, 1945; s. Bennett E. and Betty J. (McGaughey) H.; m. Elizabeth Burdine, Oct. 4, 1975; children: Stephen, Sarah, Scott. BS in Agrl. Econs., Ohio State U., 1967; MBA, U. Toledo, 1977. Social worker, supr. Franklin County Welfare, Columbus, Ohio, 1968-71, pers. asst., 1971-73; pers. dir. Mansfield (Ohio) Gen. Hosp., 1973-76; adminstr. Kettering Hosp., Loudonville, Ohio, 1978-81; v.p. Marietta (Ohio) Hosp., 1981-92; CEO City Hosp., Bellaire, 1992-94, mktg. dir. med. integrated svcs., 1995-98; pres. Advanced Practice Systems, 1996—; v.p. Tech Risk Mat. Group, 1998—. Coach St. Clairsville H.S. Soccer. Mem. East Muskingham Civic Assn. Bd., 1982-92; bd. dirs., recreation coord. Marietta Soccer League; v.p. Mid-Ohio Mktg. Assn., 1992; bd. dirs. Belmont County Salvation Army, 1992—. Fellow Am. Coll. Health Care Execs.; mem. Assn. MBA Execs., Am. Mktg. Assn. (local chpt. bd. dirs.), Ohio Hosp. Assn. Com., Ohio Hosp. Soc. for Planning and Mktg., Loudonville C. of C. (pres. bd. dirs. 1981), Bellaire C. of C. (bd. devel. com.), Wheeling Soccer Assn. (coach), St. Clairsville Area Soccer Assn. (bd. pres.), Pioneer Alumni Ohio State U. (bd. dirs., pres.), Rotary (bd. dirs. Loudonville club 1978-81), Lions (1st v.p.), Shriners, Masons. Mem. Calvary Presbyterian. Avocations: soccer, reading, gardening, running. Office: Tech Risk Mgmt Group Inc 401 N Michigan Ave Ste 2600 Chicago IL 60611-4246

HAHN, EUGENE HERMAN, state legislator; b. Milw., July 21, 1929; s. L. Herman and Julia (Senft) H.; m. Lorraine Closs, 1949; children: Jeffrey, Robert, Eugene Jr., Andrew. Student, U. Wis., 1947-48. Town assessor Town of Cambria, Wis., 1957-61; county supr., 1972-91; mem. from dist. 47 Wis. State Assembly, Madison, 1991—. Chair consumer affairs com. Wis. Assembly, co-chair joint survey com. on tax exemptions, mem. agr., edn., transp. and correction and cts. coms.; dir. Fed. Land Bank, Sauk, Columbia, Dane, Adams, Juneau, Marquette, Green Lake, Wis., 1973-88. Committeeman Farmers Home Adminstrn., Columbia and Marquette Counties, 1969-72; chmn. county bd., Cambria, 1986-88. Mem. Wis. Farm Bur., Masons (past master, pardee), Wis. Corn Growers. Home: W3198 Old B Rd Cambria WI 53923-9757 Office: PO Box 8952 Madison WI 53708-8952

HAHN, FREDERIC LOUIS, lawyer; b. Chgo., Apr. 28, 1941; s. Max and Margery Ruth (Goodman) H.; m. Susan Firestone, Mar. 26, 1967; 1 child, Frederic Firestone. AB with highest distinction, Cornell U., 1962, MBA with highest distinction, 1963; JD magna cum laude, Harvard U., 1966. Bar: Ill. 1966; CPA, Ill. Assoc. Hopkins & Sutter, Chgo., 1966-72, ptnr., 1973-94, Mayer, Brown & Platt (now Mayer, Brown, Rowe & Maw), Chgo., 1994—. Bd. dirs. Lyric Opera of Chgo., 1988—. Recipient Gold medal (CPA exam) State of Ill., 1963. Mem. Phi Beta Kappa. Home: 1377 Scott Ave Winnetka IL 60093-1444 Office: Mayer Brown Rowe & Maw 190 S La Salle St Ste 3100 Chicago IL 60603-3441 E-mail: fhahn@mayerbrownrowe.com.

HAHN, GEORGE LEROY, agricultural engineer, biometeorologist; b. Muncie, Kans., Nov. 12, 1934; s. Vernon Leslie and Marguerite Alberta (Breeden) H.; m. Clovice Elaine Christensen, Dec. 3, 1955; children—Valerie, Cecile, Steven, Melanie. BS, U. Mo., Columbia, 1957, PhD, 1971; MS, U. Calif., Davis, 1961. Agrl. engr., project leader and tech. advisor Agrl. Research Service, U.S. Dept. Agr., Columbia, Mo., 1957, Davis, Calif., 1958-61, Columbia, 1961-78, Clay Center, Nebr., 1978—. Contbr. articles to profl. jours. and books on impact of climatic and other environ. factors on livestock prodn., efficiency, and well-being, evaluation of methods of reducing impact and techniques for measuring dynamic responses and characterizing stress in meat animals. Recipient award Am. Soc. Agrl. Engrs.-Metal Bldgs. Mfrs. Assn., 1976 Fellow Am. Soc. Agrl. Engrs. (dir. prof. coun. 1991-93); mem. Am. Meteorol. Soc. (award for outstanding achievement in bioclimatology 1976), Internat. Soc. Biometeorology (treas. 1999—), Am. Soc. Animal Sci. Office: US Meat Animal Rsch Ctr PO Box 166 Clay Center NE 68933-0166 E-mail: hahn@email.marc.usda.gov.

HAHN, KENNETH P. manufacturing executive; b. 1958; Grad., U. Wis., Milw. CPA. Audit mgr. Price Waterhouse; corp. contr. Gehl Co., West Bend, Wis., 1988—, officer, 1994, v.p. fin., treas., 1997—. Office: Gehl Co PO Box 179 143 Water St West Bend WI 53095-3400 Fax: 262-334-6603.

HAIDOSTIAN, ALICE BERBERIAN, concert pianist, civic volunteer and fundraiser; b. Highland Park, Mich., Sept. 21, 1925; d. Harry M. and Siroun Vartabedian Berberian; m. Berj H. Haidostian, Oct. 1, 1949; children: Cynthia Esther Haidostian Wilbanks, Christine Rebecca Haidostian Garry, Dicran Berj. MusB, U. Mich., 1946, MusM, 1949. Pvt. piano tchr., 1946-48; tchr. music Detroit Pub. Sch., 1953; dir. The Haidostians vocal trio, 1959-71; dir. Youth Choral Group Cultural Soc. Armenians from Istanbul, 1965-72. Chmn. adv. coun. Armenian Studies Program, U. Mich., 1984-99. Initiated: Operas Anoush, 1981—82, initiated: Operas, 2001—; dir.: (vocal trio) The Haidostians, 1959—71, Youth Choral Group Cultural Soc. Armenians from Istanbul, 1965—72; initiator: Transparent Manikin exhibit, 1976. Active Centennial Celebration U. Mich. Sch. Music, Detroit, 1980; mem. Armenian Gen. Benevolent Union Alex Manoogian Sch., 1981—91, Detroit chpt. core group com., 1992—; chmn. Marie Manoogian group, 1993—; mem. Detroit Symphony Orch., 1986—88, Detroit Women's Symphony Orch, Mich. Oprea, Mich. Opera Theatre, bd. trustees, 1982—; mem. Oakway Symphony Orch., Save Orch. Hall, Women's Divsn. Project Hope, 1964—, pres., 1995—96, Detroit Armenian Women's Club, 1964—65, 1973—75; mem. Armenian Gen. Benevolent Union, Detroit Women's Chpt., 1944—93; bd. dirs. Childhelp USA Greater Detroit Aux., 1998—; mem. Detroit Sci. Ctr., 1976—, bd. trustees, 1999—; organist, chour dir. Armenian Congl. Ch., Detroit, 1946—48; mem. Westminster Ch. Detroit Chancel Choir, 1965—80. Recipient Spirit of Detroit award, 1980, Heart of Gold award United Found. City Detroit, 1981, Nat. Svc. citation U. Mich. Alumnae Coun., 1980, Disting. Alumni Svc. award U. Mich., 1981, Magic Flute award Internat. Found. Mozarteum, Salzburg, Austria, 1989, Lifetime Achievement award Outstanding Woman Mich. Project HOPE, 1998, Cmty. Svc. award Wayne County Med. Soc. Alliance, 2000; named Armenian Mother of Yr., Internat. Inst. Detroit, 1981. Mem. Detroit Assn. Univ. Mich. Women (pres. 1969-71), Mich. Fedn. Music Clubs, Mich. State Med. Soc. Aux., Pro Mozart Soc. Greater Detroit (pres. 1982—), Pro Musica Detroit (sec. 1969-90, 1st v.p. 1990—), Tuesday Musicale Detroit (pres. 1970-72), Univ. Mich. Alumni Assn. (chmn. alumnae coun. 1977-79), Univ. Mich. Sch. Music Alumni Soc., Women's Assn. Detroit Symphony Orch. (pres. 1986-88), U. Mich. Alumni Assn. (bd. dirs.), U. Mich. Emeritus Club (pres. 1997-98). Avocation: playing piano by ear, travel. Home: 6838 Valley Spring Dr Bloomfield Hills MI 48301-2845

HAIG, SUSAN, conductor; b. ; Formerly condr. Windsor (Ont., Can.) Symphony Orch.; now music dir. S.D. Symphony Orch., Sioux Falls. Office: SD Symphony Orch 300 N Dakota Ave Sioux Falls SD 57104

HAILE, GETATCHEW, retired archivist, educator; b. Shenkora, Shewa, Ethiopia, Apr. 19, 1931; came to U.S., 1976; s. Haile Woldeyes and Asseggedetch Wolde Yohannes; m. Misrak Emitu Amare, July 12, 1964; children: Rebecca, Sossina, Elizabeth, Dawit, Mariam-Sena, Yohannes. BD, Coptic Theol. Coll., Cairo, 1957; BA, Am. U. at Cairo, 1957; PhD, Tübingen (Fed. Republic Germany) U., 1962. Advisor Middle Eastern affairs Ethiopian Ministry Fgn. Affairs, Addis Ababa, 1962; prof. Ethiopian studies Addis Ababa U., 1962-73; mem. parliament State of Ethiopia, Addis Ababa, 1974-75; cataloguer Oriental manuscripts Hill Monastic Manuscript Libr. St. John's U., Collegeville, Minn., 1976-99, regents prof. medieval studies, 1988-99, retired, 1999. Co-editor Acta Ethiopica, 1974-89; mem. internat. adv. bd. Jour. Ethiopian Studies, 1991—, Ethiopian Jour. of Edn., 1992—; contbg. editor Northeast African Studies; mem. adv. bd. Analecta Bellandiana, 1993—, Aethiopica, Zeitschrift für Äthiopistische Studien, 1996—; mem. Ethiopian Register, 1994—; author monographs and contbr. articles to scholarly jours. Mem. Cen. Com. of World Coun. of Chs., Geneva, 1968-74; mem. adv. bd. Ethiopian Orthodox Ch., Addis Ababa, 1973-74. MacArthur fellow, 1988. Corr. fellow Brit. Acad. Home: 17903 County Road 9 Avon MN 56310-8624 Office: St John's U Hill Monastic Manuscpt Libr Collegeville MN 56321 E-mail: ghaile@csbsju.edu., ghaile@albanytel.com.

HAILE, H. G. German language and literature educator; b. Brownwood, Tex., July 31, 1931; s. Frank and Neil (Goodson) H.; m. Mary Elizabeth Huff, Sept. 1, 1952; children: Jonathan, Christian, Constance Haile Hunsaker. B.A., U. Ark., 1952, M.A., 1954; student, U. Cologne, Germany, 1955-56; Ph.D., U. Ill., 1957. Instr. U. Pa., 1956-57; asst. prof., then asso. prof. U. Houston, 1957-63; mem. faculty U. Ill., Urbana, 1963—, prof. German, 1965—, head dept., 1964-73; asso. mem. U. Ill. (Center for Advanced Study), 1969—. Vis. prof. U. Mich., U. Ga. Author: Das Faustbuch nach der Wolfenbuttler Handschrift, 1963, 95, The History of Doctor Johann Faustus, 1965, 1996, Artist in Chrysalis: A Biographical Study of Goethe in Italy, 1973, Invitation to Goethe's Faust, 1978, Luther: An Experiment in Biography, 1983, We Are All Sonsabitches Now, 2000; contbr. numerous articles to profl. and popular jours. Fulbright fellow, 1955; Fellow Am. Council Learned Socs., 1961-62 Office: U Ill 3072 Foreign Languages Urbana IL 61801 E-mail: harryhaile@aol.com., harryhaile@home.com.

HAILEY, V. ANN, retail executive; CFO The Limited Inc., Columbus, Ohio. Office: The Limited Inc 3 Limited Pkwy Columbus OH 43230-1467

HAIMAN, IRWIN SANFORD, lawyer; b. Cleve., Mar. 19, 1916; s. Alfred W. and Stella H. (Weiss) H.; m. Jeanne D. Jaffee, Mar. 8, 1942; children: Karen H. Schenkel, Susan L. B.A., Western Res. U., 1937; LL.B., Cleve. Marshall Law Sch., 1941; J.D., Cleve. State U., 1969. Bar: Ohio 1941, U.S. Ct. Appeals (6th cir.) 1961, U.S. Supreme Ct. 1961. Asst. to pres. Tremco Mfg. Co., Cleve., 1936-42; house counsel William Edwards Co., 1947-48; pvt. practice, 1948-68; ptnr. firm Garber, Simon, Haiman, Gutfeld, Friedman & Jacobs, 1968-80; ptnr. McCarthy, Lebit, Crystal & Haiman, 1981—. Lectr. in speech Western Res. U., 1948-70; dir. Washington Fed. Savs. and Loan Assn.; asst. law dir., prosecutor City of Lyndhurst, Ohio, 1965-79, law dir., 1979-84. Trustee Montefiore Home, Cleve., 1974-88 (life trustee 1988—)—, East End Neighborhood House, 1962-68; councilman City of South Euclid, 1948-54, pres., 1952-54; pres. Young People's Congregation, Fairmount Temple, 1951-52; sec., trustee Surburban Temple, 1962-65, trustee, 1983— , pres., 1984-87; chmn. speakers div., bd. dirs. Cleve. chpt. ARC, 1959-62; chmn. speaker and film div. Cleve. United Appeal, 1961-62; chmn. speakers div. Jewish Welfare Fund Cleve., 1973-79. Served as 1st lt. AUS, 1943-47. Mem. Ohio, Cleve. bar assns., Assn. Trial Lawyers Am., Zeta Beta Tau. Clubs: Oakwood Country, Lake Forest Country (pres. 1971-72, 75-79). Home: 20201 N Park Blvd Cleveland OH 44118-5000

HAINES, JOSEPH E. state legislator; b. Greene County, Ohio, Sept. 30, 1923; m. Joy Haines; children: Thomas, Thaddeus, Jonathan, Barbara. BS, Ohio State U., 1949. Chmn. then commr. Greene County, 1968-76; state rep. Dist. 75 Ohio State Congress, 1981-92; state rep. Dist. 74 Ohio Ho. of Reps., 1993-99; dep. dir. Ohio Dept. Agriculture, 2000—. Farmer; mem. agr. and natural resources com., fin. and appropriations com., energy and environ. com., fin. inst. com., rules com., hwy. and hwy. safety com., reference com. Mem. Nat. Assn. County Commrs. (chmn.), SW Dist. County Commr. Assn. (chmn.), Ohio Shorthorn Breeders (past pres.), Farm Bur., Kiwanis (past pres.), YMCA (bd. dirs.).

HAINES, LEE MARK, JR. religious denomination administrator; b. Marion, Ind., Dec. 9, 1927; s. Lee M. Sr. and Anna (Stevens); m. Maxine Louise Shockey, June 8, 1948; children: Mark Edward, Rhoda Lynn. B of Religion, Ind. Wesleyan U., 1950; MDiv, Christian Theol. Sem., Indpls., 1959; ThM, Christian Theol. Sem., 1973; D Ministry, Bethel Theol. Sem., St. Paul, 1981; DD (hon.), Ind. Wesleyan U., 1981; LittD (hon.), Houghton Coll., N.Y., 1981; DD (hon.), So. Wesleyan U., 1996. Ordained to ministry Wesleyan Ch., 1950. Pastor Peru (Ind.) Wesleyan Meth. Ch., 1948-51, Blue River Wesleyan Meth. Ch., Arlington, Ind., 1951-56, Jonesboro (Ind.) Wesleyan Meth. Ch., 1956-61; editor Adult Sunday Sch. Lessons Wesleyan Meth. Ch., Marion, Ind., 1961-63; pastor Eastlawn Wesleyan Ch., Indpls., 1963-70; assoc. prof. religion Ind. Wesleyan U., 1970-80; gen. sec. edn. and the ministry The Wesleyan Ch., Indpls., 1980-88, gen. supt., 1988-2000, gen. supt. emeritus, 2000—. Historian The Wesleyan Ch., 1976-88; vice-chair Wesleyan World Fellowship, 1996-00. Assoc. editor/writer: The Wesleyan Bible Commentary; co-author: An Outline History of the Wesleyan Church; co-editor: Conscience and Commitment: History of the Wesleyan Methodist Church; Days of Our Pilgrimage: History of the Pilgrim Holiness Church; contbg. author Reformers and Revivalists: The History of the Wesleyan Church. Mem. Evang. Theol. Soc., Wesleyan Theol. Soc. (editor 1978-81), Christian Holiness Partnership (treas. 1994-97). E-mail: lmhmlh@aol.com.

HAINJE, DICK G. state legislator, fire fighter; b. Sioux Falls, S.D., Aug. 11, 1956; m. Becky Jones; 3 children. AA, S.D. State U., 1995. Fire fighter, asst. fire chief Sioux Falls Fire Rescue Dept., 1977—; EMT, 1978—; mem. dist. 11 S.D. Senate, Pierre, 1996—. Chair United Way City of Sioux Falls Employees; chair Fire Fighter Pension Fund, 1989—. Mem. S.D. EMT Assn., S.D. Fire Fighters Assn. Republican. Lutheran. Office: State Capitol Bldg 500 E Capitol Ave Pierre SD 57501-5070

HAJEK, BRUCE E. electrical engineer, educator; PhD, U. Calif., Berkeley, 1979. Prof. dept. elec. and computer engring. U. Ill., Urbana. Mem. NAE. Office: U Ill CSL 1308 W Main St Urbana IL 61801 E-mail: b_hajek@uiuc.edu.

HAKE, RALPH F. construction company executive; b. Cin. BBA, U. Cin.; MBA, U. Chgo. V.p. adminstrn.l. Mead Corp., Escababa, Mich., 1980-84, dir. corp. devel. Dayton, Ohio, 1984-87; various fin. and ops. positions including corp. v.p., contr. Whirlpool Corp., Benton Harbor, Mich., from 1987, pres. Bauknecht appliance group, exec. v.p. N.Am. appliance group, sr. exec. v.p. ops., until 1997, sr. exec. v.p., CFO, 1997-1999; exec. v.p., CFO Fluor Corp., Aliso Viejo, Calif., 1999—. With U.S. Army, 1971-73. Mem. NAM (bd. dirs.). Office: 1 Enterprise Aliso Viejo CA 92656-2606

HAKEL, MILTON DANIEL, JR. psychology educator, consultant, publisher; b. Hutchinson, Minn., Aug. 1, 1941; s. Milton Daniel and Emily Ann (Kovar) H.; m. Lee Ellen Pervier, Sept. 1, 1962; children: Lane, Jennifer BA, U. Minn., 1963, PhD, 1966. Diplomate in Indsl. and Organizational Psychology Am. Bd. Profl. Psychology. Prof. psychology Ohio State U., Columbus, 1968-85, U. Houston, 1985-91, chmn. dept., 1987-91; Ohio Bd. Regents eminent scholar, prof. Bowling Green State U., 1991—; pres. Organizational Research and Devel., 1977—; ptnr. Applied Research Group, 1984-87. Trustee Am. Bd. Profl. Psychology, 1987-90; mem. com. on assessment and tchr. quality NRC, 1999-00; mem. bd. testing and assessment NRC, 1999-02, mem. U.S. nat. com. for Internat. Union for Psychol. Sci., 1997-01, chair, 2001—. Co-author (sr.): Making It Happen: Doing Research with Implementation in Mind, 1982; author: Beyond Multiple Choice: Evaluating Alternatives to Traditional Testing, 1998; editor Current Directions in Psychol. Sci., 1998-99, Personnel Psychology, 1973-84, pub., 1984—; contbr. 40 articles to profl. jours. Chair Human Capital Initiative Coordinating Com., 1991-99, co-chair Applying Sci. Learning to U. Edu. conf. steering com. Recipient James McKeen Cattell award, 1965; Fulbright-Hays Sr. scholar, 1978; NSF grantee, 1966-73 Fellow Am. Psychol. Soc. (founding bd. dirs.); mem. Soc. for Indsl. and Orgnl. Psychology (pres. 1984, Disting. Svc. Contbrs. award 1995), Acad. Mgmt., Internat. Assn. Applied Psychology, Summit Conf. Presbyterian Home: 1435 Cedar Ln Bowling Green OH 43402-1476 Office: Bowling Green State U Dept Psychology Bowling Green OH 43403-0001 E-mail: mhakel@bgnet.bgsu.edu.

HALBERSTAM, HEINI, mathematics educator; b. Most, Czechoslovakia, Sept. 11, 1926; came to Eng., 1939, naturalized, 1998. s. Michael and Judith (Honig) H.; m. Heather M. Peacock, Mar. 11, 1950 (dec. 1971); children: Naomi Deborah, Judith Marion, Lucy Rebecca, Michael Welsford; m. Doreen Bramley, Sept. 28, 1972. B.S. with honours, Univ. Coll., London U., 1946, M.S., 1948, Ph.D., 1952. Lectr. math. U. Exeter, 1949-57; reader Royal Holloway Coll., London U., 1957-62; Erasmus Smith prof. Trinity Coll., Dublin, Ireland, 1962-64; prof. Nottingham U., England, 1964-80; prof. math. U. Ill., Urbana-Champaign, 1980-96, prof. emeritus, 1996—. Vis. lectr. Brown U., 1955-56; vis. prof. U. Mich., 1966, U. Tel Aviv, 1973, U. Paris-South, 1972 Co-author: Sequences, 1966, 2d edit., 1983, Sieve Methods, 1975; co-editor math. papers of, W.R. Hamilton, H. Davenport; contbr. articles to profl. jours. Mem. London Math. Soc. (v.p. 1962-63, 74-77), Am. Math Soc.

HALE, DAVID CLOVIS, former state representative; b. Sacramento, Aug. 14, 1964; s. Clovis Ray and Judy Garland (Lee) H.; m. Shannon Lynn Ruyle, June 19, 1993. BA in Social Sci., Cedarville Coll., 1986; M in internat. bus., St. Louis U., 1995. Asst. mgr. Assocs. Fin. Corp., Fairborn, Ohio, 1986-87; br. fin. rep. Am. Family Fin. Svc., St. Louis, 1987-88; state rep. State of Mo., Jefferson City, 1989-94; mgr. external affairs AT&T Wireless Svcs., St. Louis, 1995-97, mgr. corp. comm. and pub. affairs, 1998—. Mem. Am. Legis. Exch. Coun. Health Care Task Force, 1989-93, Trade, Travel and Tourism Task Force, 1993-94, Missourians First Task Force, 1992-94; allocator United Way, 1990-93; active First Evang. Free Ch., St. Louis. Mem. World Affairs Coun. (bd. dirs.), St. Louis World Trade Club St. Louis. Home: 850 La Bonne Pkwy Ballwin MO 63021-7058 Office: AT&T Wireless Svcs 400 S Woods Mill Rd Chesterfield MO 63017-3429 E-mail: david-hale@attws.com.

HALE, JAMES THOMAS, retail company executive, lawyer; b. Mpls., May 14, 1940; s. Thomas Taylor and Alice Louise (Mc Connon) H.; m. Sharon Sue Johnson, Aug. 27, 1960; children: David Scott, Eric James, Kristin Lynn. BA, Dartmouth Coll., 1962; LLB, U. Minn., 1965. Bar: Minn. Law clk. Chief Justice Earl Warren, U.S. Supreme Ct., 1965-66; asso. firm Faegre & Benson, Mpls., 1966-73, ptnr., 1973-79; v.p., dir. corp. growth Gen. Mills, Inc., 1979-80, v.p. fin. and control consumer non-foods, 1981; sr. v.p., gen. counsel, corp. sec. Dayton-Hudson Corp., Mpls., 1981-2000; exec. v.p., gen. counsel, corp. sec. Target Corp., 2000—. Adj. prof. U. Minn., 1967-73. Mem. exec. com. Fund Legal Aid Soc., others. Mem. Order of Coif, Phi Beta Kappa. Office: Target Corp 1000 Nicollet Mall Minneapolis MN 55403-2467

HALE, ROGER LOUCKS, manufacturing company executive; b. Plainfield, N.J., Dec. 13, 1934; s. Lloyd and Elizabeth (Adams) H.; m. Sandra Johnston, June 10, 1961 (div.); children: Jocelyn, Leslie, Nina, Deirdre; m. Eleanor L. Hall, Nov. 24, 1989. BA, Brown U., 1956; MBA, Harvard U., 1961. With Tennant Co., Mpls., 1961-99, pres., CEO, 1975-98, chmn., CEO, 1998-99, chmn., 1999, also bd. dirs. Bd. dirs. Walker Art Ctr., 1970—, Ploughshares Fund, 1996—; vice chmn. Neighborhood Employment Network, 1980; bd. dirs., chmn. Pub. Radio Internat., 1990; chmn. Minn. Bus. Partnership, 1993-95, Gov.'s Workforce Devel. Coun.; commr. Met. Airports Commn. Named Exec. of Yr., Corp. Report mag., 1988, One of Minn.'s 5 Outstanding Corp. Dirs., Twin Cities Bus. Monthly, 1996; recipient Mpls. Spl. Recognition award for Svc. to City of Mpls., 1993. Office: Union Plz 333 Washington Ave N Ste 313 Minneapolis MN 55401-1364

HALES, DANIEL B. lawyer; b. Oak Park, Ill., Sept. 29, 1941; s. Burton W. and Marion (Jones) H.; m. Deborah J. Dorr, June 4, 1966; children, Daniel R.J., Marion P., George B. BA in Econs., U. Mich., 1963; Juris Doctorate, Northwestern U., 1966. Bar: Ill.1966, U.S. Dist. Ct. (no. dist.) Ill. 1967, U.S. Ct. Appeals (7th cir.) 1968, U.S. Supreme Ct. 1977. Ptnr. Peterson, Ross, Schloerb & Seidel, Chgo. Gen. counsel The Philadelphia Soc., Chgo.; dir. Chgo. Crime Commn. Pres., dir. Americans for Effective Law Enforcement Inc., Chgo.; bd. dirs. Duncan YMCA, Chgo.; chmn. Ill. Lawyers for Reagan and Bush, 1980; gen. counsel New Trier Twp., Winnetka, Ill. Republican Orgn.; mem. bd. govs. United Rep. Fund of Ill. Mem. Chgo. Bar Assn. (trust law com. 1975—), Ill. State Bar Assn., The Law Club, N.E. Commonwealth Club, N.E. Federalist Soc. (advisor). Office: Peterson & Ross 200 E Randolph St Ste 7300 Chicago IL 60601-7012

HALEY, DAVID, state legislator; b. Kansas City, 1958; m. Michelle Haley. Mem. Kans. Ho. of Reps. from 34th dist., Topeka, 1994-2000, Kans. Senate from 4th dist., Topeka, 2001—. Pub. affairs cons. Address: 936 Cleveland Ave Kansas City KS 66101-1226

HALEY, DAVID ALAN, healthcare executive; b. St. Louis, Aug. 29, 1943; s. John David and Helen Ermyl (Richardson) H.; m. Donna Lee Davis, Nov. 24, 1965; children: Trisha Lynn, Jason Alan, Eric Nathan. BA, So. Ill. U., Edwardsville, 1966; MPH magna cum laude, UCLA, 1971. Adminstrv. asst. Kaiser Found. Hosp., Panorama City, Calif., 1971; assoc. adminstr. Our Lady of Lourdes Hosp., Pasco, Wash., 1971-74, Garfield Hosp., Monterey Park, Calif., 1974-75; assoc. exec. dir. Gen. Hosp., Ft. Walton Beach, Fla., 1976-79; v.p. ops. Our Lady of the Lake Regional Med. Ctr., Baton Rouge, 1979-88; pres. Phoenix Connection, 1988-89; CEO Gibson Gen. Hosp., Princeton, Ind., 1989-93; pres., CEO Four States Physicians Assn., Joplin, Mo., 1993-94; exec. dir. MedQuest Health Resources, Inc., 1995-96; pres., CEO, The Haley Group, Frankfort, Ill., 1996—. Mem. Four Rivers Comprehensive Health Planning Agy., Richland, Wash., 1972-74; treas. S.E. Wash. State Hosp. Coun., Pasco, 1973, v.p. 1974; corp. mem. Mid La. Health Systems Agy., Baton Rouge, 1979-82; gubernatorial appointee La. Statewide Health Coord. Coun., Baton Rouge, 1984, Ind. Healthcare Facility Adminstrn. Bd., Indpls., 1991-93; sec.-treas. S.W. Ind. Hosp. Coun., Evansville, 1992-93. Served with USNR, 1967-69. USPHS fellow, 1969-71. Fellow Am. Coll. Healthcare Execs.; mem. Healthcare Fin. Mgmt. Assn., La. Hosp. Assn. (council on planning, 1984-87), Ind. Hosp. Assn. (mem. coun. pub. rels. 1992-93), Vis. Nurse Assn. Southwestern Ind. (bd. dirs. 1992-93), La. Assn. Bus. and Industry (health care council 1987). Republican. Lodge: Kiwanis. Home and Office: The Haley Group 19142 66th Ct #102 Tinley Park IL 60477

HALEY, GEORGE, Romance languages educator; b. Lorain, Ohio, Oct. 19, 1929; s. George and Mary (Haley). AB, Oberlin Coll., 1948; MA, Brown U., 1951, PhD (Pres.'s fellow), 1956. Prof. U. Chgo., 1968—, chmn. dept. Romance langs., 1970-74. Author: Vicente Espinel and Marcos de Obregón, 1959, The Narrator in Don Quixote, 1965, Diario de un Estudiante de Salamanca, 1977, El Quijote de Cervantes, 1984; mem. editl. bd. Modern Philology, 1967-95. Guggenheim fellow, 1962-63 Mem. Hispanic Soc. Am., Phi Beta Kappa. Home: 901 S Plymouth Ct Chicago IL 60605-2059 Office: 1050 E 59th St Chicago IL 60637-1559

HALEY, JOHNETTA RANDOLPH, musician, educator, university official; b. Alton, Ill., Mar. 19; d. John a. and Willye E. (Smith) Randolph; children form previous marriage: Karen, Michael. MusB in Edn., Lincoln U., 1945; MusM, So. Ill. U., 1972. Cert. cons. 1995. Vocal and gen. music tchr. Lincoln High Sch., E. St. Louis, Ill., 1945-48; vocal music tchr., choral dir. Turner Sch., Kirkwood, Mo., 1950-55; vocal and gen. music tchr. Nipher Jr. High Sch., 1955-71; prof. music Sch. Fine Arts So. Ill. U., Edwardsville, 1972—; dir. East St. Louis Campus, 1982—. Adjudicator music festivals; area music cons. Ill. Office Edn., 1977-78; prgram splst. St. Louis Human Devel. corp., 1968. Interim exec. dir. St. Louis Coun. Black People, summer, 1970; bd. dirs. YWCA, 1975-80, Artist Presentation Soc., St. Louis, 1975, United Negro Coll. Fund, 1976-78; bd. curators Lincoln U., Jefferson City, Mo., 1974-82, pres., 1978-82; chairperson Ill. Com. on Black Concerns in Higher Edn.; mem. Nat. Ministry on Urban Edn. Luth. Ch.-Mo. Synod, 1975-80; bd. dirs. Coun. Luth. Chs. Stillman Coll.; pres. congregation St. Phillips Luth. Ch.; bd. dirs. Girls, Inc.; mem. Ill. Aux. Bd., United Way; v.p. East St. Louis Cmty. Fund, Inc. Recipient Cotillion de Leon award for Outstanding Cmty. Svc., 1977, Disting. Alumnae award Lincoln U., 1977, Disting. Svc. award United Negro Coll. Fund, 1979; SCLC, 1981; recipient Cmty. Svc. award St. Louis Drifters, 1979, Disting. Svc. to Arts award Sigma Gamma Rho, Nat. Negro Musicians award, 1981, Sci. awareness award, 1984-85, Tri Del Federated award, 1985, Martin Luther King Drum Maj. award, 1985, Bus. and Profl. Women's Club award, 1985-86, Fred L. McDowell award, 1986, Vol. of Yr. award Inroads Inc., 1986, Woman of Achievement in Edn. award Elks, 1987, Woman of Achievement award Suburban Newspaper of Greater St. Louis and Sta. KMOX-Radio, 1988, Love award Greeley Cmty. Ctr., Sammy Davies Jr. award in Edn., 1990, Yes I Can award in Edn., 1990, Merit award Urban League, 1994, Legacy award Nat. Coun. Negro Women, 1995; named Disting. Citizen St. Louis Argus Newspaper, 1970, Dutchess of Paducah, 1973; the Johnetta Haley Scholars Acad. minority scholarship named in her honor So. Ill. U. Mem. AAUP, Music Educators Nat. Conf., Nat. Choral Dirs. Assn., Nat. Assn. Negro Musicians, Coll. Music Soc., Coun. Luth. Chs., Ill. Music. Educators, Jack and Jill, Inc., Women of Achievement in Edn., Friends of St. Louis Art Mus., The Links, Inc., Las Amigas Social Club, Alpha Kappa Alpha (internat. parliamentarian, Golden soror award 1995), Mu Phi Epsilon, Pi Kappa, Lambda. Lutheran. Home: 1926 Bennington Common Dr Saint Louis MO 63146-2555

HALEY, PAT, state legislator; m. Irene Haley; 3 children. Student, U. Minn., St. John's U. Mem. S.D. Ho. of Reps., 1993-2000, mem. commerce and state affairs com. Writer and pub. Home: 766 Utah Ave SE Huron SD 57350-2906

HALEY, THOMAS WILLIAM, corporate executive; b. Bird Island, Minn., Oct. 23, 1936; s. Mildred (Driscoll) H.; m. Carolyn Marie Peterson, June 16, 1962; children: Sheila, Marie. BS in Bus., U. Minn., 1964. Rsch. technician Honeywell, Inc., Mpls., 1960-64; rsch. analyst J.M. Dain & Co., 1964-67; v.p. fin. Pawnee Corp., Pipestone, Minn., 1967-70; chmn., chief exec. officer Innovex, Inc., Hopkins, 1972—. Chmn. bd. Mag-Head Engring., Mpls., 1987—; bd. dirs. Precision Coatings, Mpls. Sgt. USMC, 1954-57. Mem. Phi Beta Kappa, Beta Gamma Sigma. Republican. Avocations: running, cooking, reading, golf. Office: Innovex Inc 5540 Pioneer Creek Dr Maple Plain MN 55359-9007

HALL, CARL LOREN, electrical distribution executive; b. Jenkins, Ky., Oct. 4, 1937; s. Carl Edwin and Josephine (Smith) H.; m. Barbara Kay Anderson, Aug. 21, 1956; children: Carl David, Michael, Elizabeth. BS, U. Cin., 1971. From warehouseman to sr. sales rep. Graybar Electric Co., Inc., Cin., 1959-74, br. mgr. Dayton, Ohio, 1975-76, dist. sales mgr. Cin., 1976-81, dist. mgr. Memphis, 1981-84, Houston, 1984-88, dist. mgr., dir. Chgo., 1988-94, exec. v.p. St. Louis, 1994-95, pres., CEO, 1995-2001. Bd. dirs. Boatmen's Nat. Bank, St. Louis, St. Louis Repertory Theatre, Nat. Assn. Elec. Distbrs. With USAF, 1955-59. Mem. Medinah Country Club, Bellerive Country Club, St. Louis Club. Avocation: golf. Office: Graybar Electric Co Inc 34 N Meramec Ave Clayton MO 63105-3882

HALL, DAVID CHARLES, retired zoo director, veterinarian; b. St. Paul, Aug. 12, 1944; s. Wilhelm Frank and Estelle Elizabeth H.; m. Sandra Jean Prink, Oct. 2, 1945; children: Jason Wilhelm, Jeremy Marvin. BME, U. Minn., 1966, DVM, 1976. Sr. mktg. engr. Rosemount Engring. Co., Eden Prairie, Minn., 1966-75; ptnr. Oregon (Wis.) Vet. Med. Clinic, 1976-86; dir. Henry Vilas Zool. Pk., Madison, Wis., 1986-2000; ret., 2000. Advisor Food divsn. Wis. Dept. Agrl. Trade and Consumer Protection, Madison, 1985-86, Exam. sect. Wis. Dept. Regulation and Licensing, Madison, 1981-82. Recipient Caleb Dorr acad. award, U. Minn., 1972-76. Mem. AVMA, Am.

Assn. Zoo Vets., Am. Assn. Zool. Pks. and Aquariums, Phi Kappa Phi, Phi Zeta. Lutheran. Lodge: Optimists (pres. 1980). Avocations: skiing, swimming, hiking, hunting, other outdoor sports. Home: 3162 Waucheeta Trl Madison WI 53711-5952

HALL, DONALD JOYCE, greeting card company executive; b. Kansas City, Mo., July 9, 1928; s. Joyce Clyde and Elizabeth Ann (Dilday) H.; m. Adele Coryell, Nov. 28, 1953; children: Donald Joyce, Margaret Elizabeth, David Earl. A.B., Dartmouth, 1950; LL.D., William Jewell Coll., Denver U., 1977. With Hallmark Cards, Inc., Kansas City, Mo., 1953—, adminstrv. v.p., 1958-66, pres., chief exec. officer, 1966-83, chmn. bd., 1983—, chief exec. officer, 1983-86. Dir. United Telecommunications, Inc., Dayton-Hudson Corp., William E. Coutts Co., Ltd.; past dir. Fed. Res. Bank Kansas City, Mut. Benefit Life Ins. Co., Business Men's Assurance Co., Commerce Bank Kansas City, 1st Nat. Bank Lawrence. Pres. Civic Council Greater Kansas City; past chmn. bd. Kansas City Assn. Trusts and Founds.; Bd. dirs. Am. Royal Assn., Friends of Art, Eisenhower Found.; bd. dirs. Kansas City Minority Suppliers Devel. Council, Kans. City Minority Suppliers Devel. Council,Kansas City Symphony; past pres. Pembroke Country Day Sch., Civic Council of Greater Kansas City; trustee, past chmn. exec. com. Midwest Research Inst.; trustee Nelson-Atkins Museum of Art. Served to 1st lt. AUS, 1950-53. Recipient Eisenhower Medallion award, 1973; Parsons Sch. Design award, 1977; 3d Ann. Civic Service award Hebrew Acad. Kansas City, 1976; Chancellor's medal U. Mo., Kansas City, 1977; Disting. Service citation U. Kans., 1980 Mem. Kansas City C. of C. (named Mr. Kansas City 1972, dir.), AIA (hon.) Office: Hallmark Cards Inc Office Chmn Bd 2501 Mcgee St Kansas City MO 64108-2600

HALL, FLOYD, retail executive; b. Duncan, Okla., Sept. 4, 1938; m. Janet Hall; children: Larry, Karen. Student, Bakersfield Jr. Coll., So. Meth. U., Harvard U., 1977. Nat. sales mgr. Montgomery Ward, Chgo., 1966-70; v.p., regional v.p. The Singer Co., Dallas, 1970-73; pres., CEO B. Dalton Book Seller, Mpls., 1973-81; chmn., CEO Target Stores, 1981-84, Grand Union Co., Wayne, N.J., 1984-89, also bd. dirs.; chmn., CEO The Museum Co., East Rutherford, N.J., 1989-95, also bd. dirs.; chmn., pres., CEO Kmart Corp., Troy, Mich., 1995-2000, also bd. dirs. Bd. dirs. Lynx Techs., Kenwood Prodns. Trustee Bklyn. Mus.; bd. dirs. Give Kids The World, Jundt Growth Fund. Served with U.S. Army. Office: Kmart Corp 3100 W Big Beaver Rd Troy MI 48084-3163

HALL, FRANKLIN R. entomology researcher, educator; b. Boston, Oct. 30, 1934; BS, Univ. Mass., 1956; MS, Syracuse Univ., 1961; PhD, Purdue Univ., 1967. Field rep. entomology Niagara Chemical Co., 1960-63; fruit crop specialist Chevron Chemical Co., Standard Oil Co. Calif., 1967-70; prof. devel. rep. agril. Chemagro Corp., 1970; head lab. pest control Applications Tech. Ohio State U., 1981—. Asst. prof. Ohio Agrl. Rsch. & Devel. Ctr. Ohio State Univ., 1970-73, assoc. prof., 1973-78, prof. entomology, 1978-2000, prof. emeritus, 2001. Mem. Entomology Soc. Am. Office: Ohio State U Lab Pest Control Application Tech Agrl R&D Ctr Wooster OH 44691

HALL, GLENN ALLEN, lawyer, state representative; b. Pekin, Ill., Oct. 22, 1955; s. Gerald Eugene and Vinetta Bell Hall; m. Mary Melodie Hall, Dec. 30, 1978; children: Kimberly, Jaired, Ellie, Chava, Justice. BS in Edn., U. Mo., 1980; JD, Regent U., 1989. Bar: Mo. 1989. Atty. Glenn Allen Hall, Atty. at law, Kans. City, Mo., 1989—2001; state rep. State of Mo., 1993-99; owner The Almond Branch, Salem, Mo., 2001—; atty. Glenn Allen Hall, Atty. at Law, 2001—. Author: No Justice in the Land, 1993, The Seperation, 1999, Food Sacrificed to Idols, 2000. Fax: 573-729-2344. E-mail: salemjustice@earthlink.net.

HALL, HANSEL CRIMIEL, communications executive; b. Gary, Ind., Mar. 12, 1929; s. Alfred McKenzie and Grace Elizabeth (Crimiel) H. BS, Ind. U., 1953; LLB, Blackstone Sch. Law, 1982. Officer IRS, 1959-64; gasoline svc. sta. operator, then realtor Chgo., 1964-69; program specialist HUD, 1969-73; dir. equal opportunity St. Paul, 1973-75; dir. fair housing Indpls., from 1975; human resource officer U.S. Fish and Wildlife Svc., Twin Cities, Minn. Cons. in civil rights; pres. bd. dirs. Riverview Towers Cooperative Assn., Inc., 1984-87; pres., CEO Crimiel Comms., Inc., 1988—; CFO, treas. Korean War Vets. Edn. Grant Corp., 1996—; del. U.S. parliamentarian to Russia and Czechoslovakia, 1992, to Cuba, 1999; bd. dirs. Nat. Korean War Vets. Assn., 1992. With USAF, 1951-53, Korea. Recipient Amb. for Peace cert. Korean Vets. Assn., 1991, Korean Svc. medal Rep. of Korea, 1991. Mem. NAACP (Golden Heritage life mem.), Res. Officers Assn., Am. Inst. Parliamentarians, Nat. Assn. Parliamentarians, Minn. State Assn. Parliamentarians (pres. 1997-99), Toastmasters DTM, Ind. U. Alumni Assn., Omega Psi Phi.

HALL, HOWARD ERNEST, lawyer; b. Cleve., Oct. 4, 1945; s. Howard Leland and Edna Mae (Geiss) H.; m. Jamie L. Sundheimer, Sept. 21, 1968; children— Matthew Reed, Jennifer Kathleen, Michael John. B.S., Bowling Green State U., Ohio, 1967; J.D., U. Toledo, 1970. Bar: Ohio 1970; U.S. Dist. Ct. (no. dist.) Ohio 1972; U.S. Dist. Ct. (so. dist.) Ohio 1978. Sole practice, Parma, Ohio, 1970-72; assoc. Thomas E. Ray Law Office, Cardington, Ohio, 1972-74; ptnr. Ray & Hall, Cardington, 1974-80, Howard E. Hall Law Office, Cardington, 1980-84, Hall & Elkin, Cardington, 1985— ; asst. prosecutor Morrow County, Ohio, 1977-82, prosecutor, 1985— ; solicitor Village of Cardington, 1974-77, 83-85. Trustee Morrow County chpt. ARC, Mt. Gilead, Ohio, 1981— ; pres. trustees Morrow County Council on Alcohol and Drugs, Inc., Mt. Gilead, 1982— . Mem. Am. Trial Lawyers Assn., ABA, Ohio State Bar Assn., Ohio Acad. Trial Lawyers, Morrow County Bar Assn. (pres. 1983-85). Republican. Methodist. Lodge: Rotary, Masons (master 1984-85). Avocations: Jogging; sports. Home: 2815 Township Road 167 Cardington OH 43315-9715 Office: Hall & Elkin Law Office Hall Elkin Law Ofc 126 E Cardington OH 43338

HALL, JOAN M. lawyer; b. Inman, Nebr., Apr. 13, 1939; d. Warren J. and Delia E. (Allyn) McClurg; m. George J. Cotsirilos, Dec. 4, 1988; children: Colin Michael, Justin Allyn BA, Nebr. Wesleyan U., 1961; JD, Yale U., 1965. Bar: Ill. 1965, U.S. Dist. Ct. (no. dist.) Ill. 1965, U.S. Ct. Appeals (7th cir.) 1965. Assoc. Jenner & Block, Chgo., 1965-71, sr. ptnr., 1971—. Chmn. character and fitness Ill. Supreme Ct., 1988-89; mem. dist. admissions com. U.S. Dist. Ct. (no. dist.) Ill. Mem. exec. com. Yale Law Sch. Assn., 1976-86, treas., 1982-85; bd. dirs. Yale Law Sch. FUnd, 1978—, chmn., 1984-86; bd. dirs. Chgo. Lawyer's Com. Civil Rights Under the Law, 1978—, chmn., 1983-84; bd. dirs. Legal Assistance Found. Chgo., 1979-82; trustee Rush-Presbyn. St. Luke's Hosp., 1984—; mem. Gannon-Proctor Commn., 1982-84; trustee, bd. govs. Nebr. Wesleyan U., 1983—; bd. dirs. Goodman Theatre, Ill. Sports Facility Authority, 1986-96; mem. vis. com. Northwestern U. Sch. Law, 1987-92; mem. adv. coun. De Paul U. Sch. Law, 1987-94; bd. govs. Chgo. Lighthouse for the Blind. Fellow Am. Coll. Trial Lawyers; mem. ABA (chmn. litig. sect. 1982-83, fed. judiciary com. 1985-91, resource devel. coun. 1984-85, Ho. of Dels. 1991-93), Comml. Club (sec. 1995—), Econ. Club (Chgo., dir.). Office: Jenner & Block 1 E Ibm Plz Fl 4000 Chicago IL 60611-7603

HALL, KATHY, nursing official; b. Covington, Ky., Feb. 15, 1953; d. Joseph B. and Mary Louise (Weindel) Dusing; m. Harold G. Hall, Oct. 6, 1973; children: Becky, Amy, Sarah. AA, Eastern Ky. U., 1973, BS in Nursing, 1978. Cert. in infection control. Med.-surg. staff nurse Good Samaritan Hosp., Lexington, Ky., 1973; orientation instr. Pattie A. Clay Hosp., Richmond, 1978-82, infection control nurse, 1975-93, quality assurance dir., 1982-93; nurse epidemiologist U. Ky. Chandler Med. Ctr., Lexington, 1993—. Mem. Assn. for Practitioners in Infection Control. Office: U Ky Hosp HG 608 800 Rose St Lexington KY 40536-0001

HALL, KATHY L. orchestra executive; b. Donnellson, Iowa; Prin. bassoonist Cedar Rapids (Iowa) Symphony Orch., exec. dir., 1992. Office: Cedar Rapids Symphony Orch 205 2nd Ave SE Cedar Rapids IA 52401-1213

HALL, TOM T. songwriter, performer; b. Olive Hill, Ky., May 25, 1936; s. Virgil Hall; m. Dixie Dean. Student, Roanoke Coll. Founder pub. co. Hallnote Music. With group Tom Hall and the Kentucky Travelers, disc jockey, Sta. WMOR, Morehead, Ky., songwriter with, Newkeys Music, Inc., rec. artist with Mercury Records until 1977, with RCA, Mercury, Polygram records, 1977—; performed with band, The Storytellers, Carnegie Hall, N.Y.C., 1973; performed at Smithsonian Instn., 1979, White House, 1980; albums include Magnificent Music Machine, Natural Dreams, 1984, Homecoming, I Witness Life, The Storyteller, Songs of Fox Hollow, Country Classics, Ol' T's in Town, Places I've Done Time, Everything From Jesus to Jack Daniels, many others; songs include Harper Valley P.T.A.; author: Songwriter's Handbook, Laughing Man of Woodmont Coves, Acts of Life, Christmas and the Old House, The Storyteller's Nashville, What a Book! Served in U.S. Army, 1957-61.

HALL, TONY P. congressman; b. Dayton, Ohio, Jan. 16, 1942; m. Janet Dick, 1973; 1 child, Jyl. Student, Ohio State U.; AB, Denison U., 1964; LLD (hon.), Asbury Coll., Eastern Coll. Vol. Peace Corps, Thailand, 1966-67; mem. Ohio Ho. of Reps., 1969-72, Ohio Senate, 1973-78, U.S. Congress from 3d Ohio dist., Washington, 1979—; mem. rules com., ranking minority mem. subcom. tech. and the house. Founder, mem. steering com. Congl. Friends of Human Rights Monitors; mem. bd. mgrs. Air Force Mus. Found.; trustee Holiday Aid; mem. adv. com. Emergency Resource Bank; chmn. Dem. Caucus Task Force on Hunger. Recipient Disting. Svc. Against Hunger award Bread for the World, 1984, 87, Tree of Life award Jewish Nat. Fund, 1986, Golden Apple award Nat. Assn. Nutrition and Aging Svcs. Programs, 1986, Freedom award Asian Pacific Am. C. of C., 1986, Presdl. End Hunger award, 1988, Silver Anniversary award NCAA, 1989, Silver World Food Day medal Food and Agriculture Orgn. of UN, Ptnrs. award Oxfam Am., 1992; nominated for Nobel Peace prize, 1998, 99, 2001. Mem. Nat. Assn. Women, Infants & Children (Leadership award 1991). Democrat. Office: 1432 Longworth Bldg Ofc Washington DC 20515-3503*

HALL, WAYNE F. engineering company executive; BS in Acctg., Calif. State Poly. U.; postgrad., Columbia U. Contr. CRM Books; founder Internat. Peripherals & Computer Corp.; mem. audit staff Arthur Andersen & Co., L.A.; CFO, mng. ptnr. Black & Veatch, LLP, Kansas City, Mo., 1991, vice chmn., CFO, pres. process bus. Mem. adv. bd. Emporia State U., Johnson County C.C., Kans. Mem. FEI, AICPA, Calif. Soc. CPAs. Office: Black & Veatch Holding Co 8400 Ward Parkway Kansas City MO 64114 Fax: 913 658-2936.

HALL, WILLIAM JOEL, civil engineer, educator; b. Berkeley, Calif., Apr. 13, 1926; s. Eugene Raymond and Mary (Harkey) H.; m. Elaine Frances Thalman, Dec. 18, 1948; children: Martha Jane, James Frederick, Carolyn Marie. Student, U. Calif., Berkeley, 1943-44, Kings Point, 1944-45; BSCE, U. Kans., 1948; MS, U. Ill., Urbana, 1951, PhD, 1954. Teaching asst. U. Kans., 1947-48; engr. Sohio Pipe Line Co., 1948-49; mem. faculty U. Ill., Urbana, 1949-93, prof. civil engring., 1959-93, head dept. civil engring., 1984-91; prof. emeritus, 1993—. Cons. structural dynamics, seismic, materials to govt. orgns. and industry. Author books, articles, chpts. in books, revs. Recipient A. Epstein Meml. award U. Ill., 1958, Halliburton Engring, Edn. Leadership award, 1980, Disting. Engring. Svc. award U. Kans., 1985; Univ. scholar, U. Ill., 1986-89. Fellow AAAS; mem. NAE, ASME, ASTM, ASCE (hon., pres. Ctrl. Ill. sect. 1967-68, chmn. structural divsn. exec. com. 1973—, chmn. tech. coun. on lifeline earthquake engring. exec. com. 1982—, Kans. sect. award 1948, Walter L. Huber award 1963, Howard award 1984, Newmark medal 1984, C. Martin Duke award 1990, Norman medal 1992), Am. Concrete Inst., Am. Welding Soc. (Adams Meml. membership award 1967), Earthquake Engring. Rsch. Inst. (Housner medal 1998), Seismol. Soc. Am., Structural Engrs. Assn. Ill. (John Parmer award 1990), Sigma Xi, Tau Beta Pi (Daniel C. Drucker eminent faculty award 1993), Sigma Tau, Chi Epsilon (nat. honor mem. 1998), Phi Kappa Phi. Home: 3105 Valley Brook Dr Champaign IL 61822-6111 Office: U Ill Civil Engring 2106 Newmark Lab 205 N Mathews Ave Urbana IL 61801-2350 E-mail: w-hall3@staff.uiuc.edu., wj-efhall@worldnet.att.net.

HALLAUER, ARNEL ROY, geneticist; b. Netawaka, Kans., May 4, 1932; s. Roy Virgil and Mabel Fern (Bohnenkemper) H.; m. Janet Yvonne Goodmanson, Aug. 29, 1964; children: Elizabeth, Paul B.S., Kans. State U., 1954; M.S., Iowa State U., 1958, Ph.D., 1960. Rsch. agronomist USDA, Ames, Iowa, 1958-60, geneticist Raleigh, N.C., 1961-62, rsch. geneticist Ames, 1963-89; prof. Iowa State U., 1990—, C.F. Curtiss Disting. prof. agr. emeritus, 1991—. Author: (with J.B. Miranda) Quantitative Genetics in Maize Breeding, 1981, 2d edit., 1988; editor: Specialty Corns, 1994, 2d edit., 2000. 1st lt. U.S. Army, 1954-56. Recipient Applied Rsch. and Ext. award 1981, Henry A. Wallace award for disting.svc. to agr., 1992, Disting. Alumni Achievement citation, 1996, Iowa State U., Genetics and Plant Breeding award Nat. Coun. Plant Breeding, 1984, Gov.'s Sci. medal State of Iowa, 1990, Burlington No. Career Rsch. Achievement award Iowa State Found., 1991, Centennial medal Phi Kappa Phi, 1997, Verdent Plant Genetics award Verdent Ptnrs., Chgo., 2001; USDA grantee, 1982, 85, 87, 90; named to USDA/Agrl. Rsch. Sci. Hall of Fame, 1992. Fellow Am. Soc. Agronomy (Agronomic Achievement award for crops 1989, Agronomic Rsch. award 1992), Crop Sci. Soc. (Dekalb Pfizer Crop Sci. award 1981), Iowa Acad. Sci. (disting. fellow 1985); mem. NAS, Nat. Agri-Mktg. Assn. (nat. award for excellence in rsch. 1993), Am. Genetic Assn., Am. Statis. Assn., Kans. State U. Alumni Assn. (alumni fellow 1997), Iowa State Alumni Assn. (faculty citation 1987, Disting. Achievement Citation 1995), Gamma Sigma Delta (Disting. Svc. to Agr. award 1990, Rsch. Award of Merit 1999, Verdant Ptnr.'s Crop Genetics award 2001). Republican. Lutheran Home: 516 Luther Dr Ames IA 50010-4735 Office: Iowa State U 1505 Dept Agronomy Ames IA 50010

HALLEY, JAMES WOODS, physics educator; b. Chgo., Nov. 16, 1938; m. Merile Hobbs; 2 children. BS, MIT, 1961; PhD, U. Calif., Berkeley, 1965. NSF predoctoral fellow U. Calif., Berkeley, 1963-65; NSF postdoctoral fellow Faculte des Scis., Orsay, France, 1965-66; asst. prof. U. Calif., Berkeley, 1966-68; assoc. prof. U. Minn., Mpls., 1968-77, prof. physics, 1977—, fellow Supercomputer Inst., 1989—, grad. faculty materials sci., 1989—. Vis. prof. Oxford U., 1973, Harwell AERE, 1973, U. Oreg., 1975, Yale U., 1976, Brookhaven N.L., 1976, 79, Harvard U., 1979, Mich. State U., 1980, Argonne, 1981—, Inst. for Theoretical Physics, Santa Barbara, 1983, 97, 98, chemistry dept. U. Calif., Santa Barbara, 1984, U. Calif., Berkeley, 1993; IBM Almaden Rsch. Ctr., 1987, Australian Nat. U., 1988; cons. 3M, 1985-89, UNESCO, 1986, GM Corp., 1989-90, Ednl. Testing Svc., 1989; mem. GRE bd. examiners Ednl. Testing Svc., 1991-96; physics bd. dirs. U.S. Com. for Sci. Coop. with Vietnam, 1985—. Author: Physics of Human Motion, 1981; editor 7 books; contbr. over 150 articles to profl. jours. Recipient George Taylor Tchg. award, 1979, McMillan professorship, 1979; Bush fellow, 1983-84; grantee NSF, 1972-79, 95—, Rsch. Corp., 1970-72, Corrosion Ctr., 1980-92, Ednl. Devel. Program, 1973, 79, 3M, 1982, IBM Advanced Edn. Project, 1985, Dept. Edn., 1986, US-Australia travel grantee NSF, 1987, rsch. grantee IBM, 1988-90, grantee Electric Power Rsch. Inst., 1988-90, Dept. Energy, 1990—, Sumitomo Metal Industries, 1992-93, NASA, 1992-95. Fellow Am. Phys. Soc.; mem. AAAS, Materials Rsch. Soc. Achievements include research in theory of disorder in condensed matter, statistics and dynamics of polymers, physics of the fluid-solid interface, high temperature superconductivity, condensate fraction in bose superfluids. Office: Univ Minn Sch Physics and Astronomy Minneapolis MN 55455

HALLINAN, JOHN CORNELIUS, mechanical engineering consultant; b. Phila., Feb. 12, 1919; s. John Joseph and Ellen Bridget (Sullivan) H.; m. Eleanor Ruth Denny, July 7, 1945; children: Ann, Mary, Kathleen, Claire (dec.), Joan, John, Patricia, Mark, Michael, Joseph, William, Theresa. BSME, Villanova U., 1940. Design and lab. engr. Am. Bosch, Springfield, Mass., 1946-47; lab. mgr. Baldwin Lima Hamilton, Eddystone, Pa., 1947-54; rsch. engr. Caterpillar Inc., Peoria, Ill., 1954-62, lab. mgr., 1962-72, engring. mgr., 1972-85; engring. cons., Washington, 1985—. Contbr. articles to profl. jours. Trustee St. Patrick Parish, Washington, 1962-93, lector, 1978—. With USN, 1943-46. Named Engr. of Yr., Peoria Engring. Coun., 1975, Recipient Internal Combustion Engine award Am. Soc. of Mechanical Engineers, 1995. Mem. ASME (chmn. ctrl. Ill. sect. 1962-63, other sectional and regional offices, chmn. Soichiro Honda medal com., divsn. for disting. tech. svc. to diesel engine industry 1992, Internal Combustion Engine award 1995), Soc. Automotive Engrs., Submarine Vets. WWII. Achievements include direction and management of the design and development of large engines, turbocharging of engines, conversion of diesel to spark ignited engines. Home and Office: 700 Crestview Dr Washington IL 61571-1605 E-mail: moonbream@aol.com.

HALLINAN, JOSEPH THOMAS, journalist, author; b. Barberton, Ohio, Sept. 3, 1960; s. Neil Patrick and Judith Ann (Tonovitz) H.; m. Pamela L. Taylor, Sept. 10, 2000. BS magna cum laude, Boston U., 1984. Reporter The Indpls. Star, 1984-91; nat. corr. Newhouse News Svc., Washington, 1991-99; reporter Chgo. Tribune, 1999-2000; staff reporter The Wall St. Jour., 2000—. Author: Going Up The River: Travels in a Prison Nation, 2001. Recipient Pulitzer prize for investigative reporting, 1991; named Disting. Alumni, Boston U., 1992; Nieman fellow Harvard U., 1997-98. Roman Catholic. Avocations: scuba diving, fishing, travel. Home: 3750 Lake Shore Dr Chicago IL 60613

HALLMAN, GARY L. photographer, educator; b. St. Paul, Aug. 7, 1940; s. Jack J. and Helen A. Hallman; 1 child, Peter J. BA, U. Minn., 1966, MFA, 1971. Mem. faculty dept. studio arts U. Minn., Mpls., 1970—, assoc. prof. photography, 1976—. Vis. adj. prof. R.I. Sch. Design, 1977-78; vis. exchange prof. U. N.Mex., 1984-85; vis. assoc. prof. The Colo. Coll., Colorado Springs, Colo., 1990; mem. visual arts adv. bd. Minn. State Arts Council, 1973-76; bd. dirs. Minn. Artists Exhbn. Program, 1989-91. Exhbns. include, Internat. Mus. Photography, George Eastman House, 1974, Light Gallery, N.Y.C., 1975, Balt. Mus., 1975, Mus. Modern Art, N.Y.C., 1978, Mpls. Inst. of Arts, Minn., 1996, B. Gray Gallery East Carolina Univ., Greenville, N.C., 1997, Nat. Mus. of Am., Washington, 1984. Frederick R. Weisman Art Mus., Mpls., 1998, The State Russian Mus., St. Petersburg, 1998, Barg Gallery/Teheran Mus. Contemporary Art, 2001, Risk/Revisit: The Photography of Gary Hallman, PARTs Gallery, Mpls., Minn., 2002; represented in permanent collections, Mus. Modern Art, N.Y.C., Internat. Mus. Photography, Rochester, N.Y., Nat. Gallery Can., Fogg Art Mus., Harvard U., Princeton U. Art Mus., Nat. Mus. Am. Art, Smithsonian Instn., Washington. Served with USN, 1958-61. Nat. Endowment Arts fellow, 1975-76; Bush Found. fellow, 1976-77; McKnight Found. fellow, 1982, 90, Artist Assistance fellowship grant, 1996. Mem. Soc. Photog. Edn., Coll. Art Assn. Am. Office: U Minn Dept Studio Arts Minneapolis MN 55455

HALLMARK, DONALD PARKER, museum director, lecturer; b. McPherson, Kans., Feb. 16, 1945; s. Daniel Clell and Esther Ione (Hart) H.; m. Linda Lorraine Lego, June 10, 1967; m. Monica Lynn, Amy Kristen. BFA, U. Ill., 1967; MA, U. Iowa, 1970; PhD, St. Louis U., 1980. From asst. prof. to prof. Greenville (Ill.) Coll., 1970-81, chmn. art dept., 1976-81; dir. Richard W. Bock Sculpture Collection, Greenville, 1975-81, Frank Lloyd Wright's Dana-Thomas House Hist. Site, Springfield, Ill., 1981—. Founding bd. mem. Frank Lloyd Wright Bldg Conservancy, Chgo., 1988-96; adj. prof. Sangamon State U., Springfield, 1986-90; lectr. FLW Bldg. Conservancy, Hollyhock House, L.A., The Gamble House, Pasadena, Calif., The High Mus., Atlanta, Decorative Arts Soc. SAH, Chgo., Indpls. Pub. Libr., The Natural Pattern of Structure Herberger Lectrs., Ariz. State U., Tempe, Art Inst. Chgo., FLW Bldg. Conservancy, Unity Temple, Oak Park, Ill,. FLW Home and Studio Lectrs., Oak Park Pub. Libr., Mus. of Our Nat. Heritage, Lexington, Mass., The Chgo. Arch. Found., Santa Fe Bldg., Chgo., Nat. Bldg. Mus., Washington Author: (booklet) The Dana-Thomas House: Its History, Acquisition and Preservation, 1992, (catalogue) Paul Ashbrook, 1990 (illustrated book) The Natural Pattern of Structure, 1995; TV interview appearances Bob Vila's Guide to Historic Homes, The Dana-Thomas House, 1996, The Homes of Frank Lloyd Wright, Home and Garden TV, 2000; interview The Homes of Frank LLoyd Wright, Home and Garden TV, 1990, interview Frank Lloyd Wright and the Prairie School, Films for Humanities and Scis., 1999; editor newsletter Guidelines for the Conservation of Frank Lloyd Wright Decorative Arts, 1996. Cons., sponsor Ill. Govt. Intern Program, Springfield, 1985—; libr. cons., vol. Michael Victor II Libr. Springfield Art Assn., 1988-93. Faculty grantee Shell Found., 1975; Grad. fellow St. Louis U., 1976. Mem. Am. Assn. Mus. Presbyterian. Avocations: slide library collecting, antique collecting, travel, ground and garden maintenance. Home: 605 W Sheridan St Petersburg IL 62675-1359 Office: Ill Hist Preservation Agy 301 E Lawrence Ave Springfield IL 62703-2232

HALLORAN, KATHLEEN L. financial executive, accountant; b. Sandwich, Ill., July 19, 1952; d. Oscar L. and Gertrude L. Huber; divorced. BA in Acctg., Lewis U., 1974; MBA, No. Ill. U., 1979. CPA, Ill. With NICOR, Inc., Naperville, 1974-84; asst. sec. No. Ill. Gas subs. NICOR, Inc., 1983-84, asst. contr., 1984; sec., treas. NICOR Inc., 1984-87; sec., contr. NICOR, Inc., 1987-89, v.p., sec., contr., 1989-92, v.p. info. svcs. and gen. acctg., 1992-94; v.p. info. svcs. and rates No. Ill. Gas, Aurora, 1994-95, v.p. info. svcs., rates and human resources, 1995-96; sr. v.p. info. svcs., rates and hours, 1996-98; sr. v.p. adminstrn., 1998-99; exec. v.p. fin. and adminstrn. No. Ill. Gas, Aurora, 1999—. Bd. dirs. Ctrl. DuPage Health, Nat. Assn. Child Advocates; mem. com. on dirs. Voices for Ill. Children; trustee Lewis U. Mem. Am. Gas Assn., Chgo. Econs. Club, Execs. Club Chgo., The Chgo. Network. Office: Nicor Gas Co PO Box 190 Aurora IL 60507-0190 E-mail: khallor@nicor.com.

HALLORAN, MICHAEL JOHN, lawyer; b. St. Louis, June 4, 1951; s. Edward Anthony Halloran and Helen M. (Kickham) Phillips; m. Gwen V. Carroll, July 25, 1983 (div. Oct. 1984). BS in Commerce, St. Louis U., 1972, JD, 1975. Bar: Ill. 1975, U.S. Dist. Ct. (no. dist.) Ill. 1975, U.S. Ct. Appeals (7th cir.) 1975. Assoc. Seyfarth, Shaw, Fairweather & Geraldson, Chgo., Washington, 1975-78; atty. Beinhauer & Rouhana, N.Y.C., 1978-79; assoc. William B. Hanley & Assocs., Chgo., 1979-81, Bell, Boyd & Lloyd, Chgo., 1981-83, ptnr., 1983-86; pvt. practice, 1987—. Home: 800 S Wells St Apt 552 Chicago IL 60607-4531 Office: 53 W Jackson Blvd Ste 319 Chicago IL 60604-3695 E-mail: mhalloran7@hotmail.com.

HALLWAS, JOHN EDWARD, English language educator; b. Waukegan, Ill., May 24, 1945; s. Emil Ferdinand and Ruth Edna (Wells) H.; m. Garnette Verna Stockstad, Jan. 3, 1966; children: John Darrin, Evan Bradley. BS in Edn., Western Ill. U., Macomb, 1967, MA, 1968; PhD, U. Fla., 1972. Grad. asst. Western Ill. U., Macomb, 1967-68, prof. English dept., 1970—. Author: Western Illinois Heritage, 1983, Illinois Literature: The 19th Century, 1986, Macomb: A Pictorial History, 1990, Spoon River

Anthology: An Annotated Edition, 1992, The Bootlegger: A Story of Small-Town America, 1998, others; editor Western Ill. Regional Studies, 1978-92; co-editor: Tales From Two Rivers book series, 1981—, Prairie State Books, 1987—; newspaper columnist Macomb Jour., 1981-84, Jacksonville (Ill.) Jour. Courier, 1984-85, 87-88. NDEA fellow U. Fla., Gainesville, 1968-70; recipient Faculty Svc. award Nat. U. Continuing Edn. Assn., 1981, Alumni Achievement award Western Ill. U., Macomb, 1983, MidAm. award, Soc. for Study of Midwestern Lit., 1994; named faculty lectr. Western Ill. U., Macomb, 1983, Disting. prof., 1992. Mem. Soc. for Study Midwestern Lit., Ill. State Hist. Soc. (adv. bd. 1990-96), McDonough County Hist. Soc. (pres. 1981-83), Phi Beta Kappa, Phi Kappa Phi. Avocations: nature study, fitness walking, skiing. Home: 31 Shorewood Dr Macomb IL 61455-9746 Office: Western Ill U Libr Macomb IL 61455

HALPERN, JACK, chemist, educator; b. Poland, Jan. 19, 1925; came to U.S., 1962, naturalized; s. Philip and Anna (Sass) H.; m. Helen Peritz, June 30, 1949; children: Janice Henry, Nina Phyllis. BS, McGill U., 1946, PhD, 1949; DSc (hon.), U. B.C., 1986, McGill U., 1997. Postdoctorate overseas fellow NRC, U. Manchester, Eng., 1949-50; instr. chemistry U. B.C., 1950, prof., 1961-62; Nuffield Found. traveling fellow Cambridge (Eng.) U., 1959-60; prof. chemistry U. Chgo., 1962-71, Louis Block prof. chemistry, 1971-83, Louis Block Disting. Svc. prof., 1983—. Vis. prof. U. Minn., 1962, Harvard, 1966-67, Calif. Inst. Tech., 1968-69, Princeton U., 1970-71, Max. Planck Institut, Mulheim, Fed. Republic Germany, 1983—, U. Copenhagen, 1978; Sherman Fairchild Disting. scholar Calif. Inst. Tech., 1979; guest scholar Kyoto U., 1981; Firth vis. prof. U. Sheffield, 1982, Phi Beta Kappa vis. scholar, 1990; R.B. Woodward vis. prof. Harvard U., 1991; numerous guest lectureships; cons. editor Macmillan Co., 1963-65, Oxford U. Press; cons. Am. Oil Co., Monsanto Co., Argonne Nat. Lab., IBM, Air Products Co., Enimont, Rohm and Haas; mem. adv. panel on chemistry NSF, 1967-70; mem. adv. bd. Am. Chem. Soc. Petroleum Rsch. Fund, 1972-74, Trans Atlantic Sci. and Humanities Program, 2001--; mem. medicinal chemistry sect. NIH, 1975-78, chmn., 1976-78; mem. chemistry adv. coun. Princeton U., 1982—; mem. univ. adv. com. Ency. Brit., 1985—; mem. chemistry vis. com. Calif. Inst. Tech., 1991—; chmn. German-Am. Acad. Coun., 1993-96, chmn. bd. trustees, 1996—. Assoc. editor: Inorganica Chimica Acta, Jour. Am. Chem. Soc.; co-editor: Collected Accounts of Transition Metal Chemistry, vol. 1, 1973, vol. 2, 1977; assoc. editor Procs. NAS; mem. editl. adv. bd. Oxford Univ. Press, Internat. Series Monographs on Chemistry; mem. editl. bd. Jour. Organometallic Chemistry, Accounts Chem. Rsch., Catalysis Revs., Jour. Catalysis, Jour. Molecular Catalysis, Jour. Coord. Chemistry, Gazzetta Chimica Italiana, Organometallics, Catalysis Letters, Kinetics and Catalysis Letters; contbr. articles to Ency. Britannica, rsch. jours. Trustee Gordon Rsch. Confs., 1968-70; bd. govs. David and Arthur Smart Mus., U. Chgo., 1988—; bd. dirs. Ct. Theatre. Recipient Young Author's prize Electrochem. Soc., 1953, award in catalysis Noble Metals Chem. Soc., London, 1976, Humboldt award, 1977, Richard Kokes award Johns Hopkins U., 1978, Willard Gibbs medal, 1986, Bailar medal U. Ill., 1986, Wilhelm von Hoffman medal German Chem. Soc., 1988, Chem. Pioneer's award Am. Inst. Chemists, 1991, Paracelsus prize Swiss Chem. Soc., 1992, Basolo Medal, Northwestern U., 1993, Robert A. Welch award, 1994, Henry J. Albert award Internat. Precious Metals Inst., 1995, award in Organometallic Chem. Am. Chem. Soc., 1995, Order of Merit Federal Republic of Germany, 1996. Fellow AAAS, Royal Soc. London, Am. Acad. Arts and Scis., Chem. Inst. Can., Royal Soc. Chemistry London (hon.), N.Y. Acad. Scis., Japan Soc. for Promotion Sci.; mem. NAS (fgn. assoc. 1984-85, mem. coun. 1990—, chmn. chemistry sect. 1991-93, v.p. 1993—, assoc. editor Proceedings NAS), Am. Chem. Soc. (editl. bd. Advances in Chemistry series 1963-65, 78-81, chmn. inorganic chemistry 1985, award in inorganic chemistry 1968, award for disting. svc. in advancement of inorganic chemistry 1985, award in organometallic chemistry 1995), Max Planck Soc. (sci. mem. 1983—), Art Inst. Chgo., Renaissance Soc. (bd. dirs.), New Swiss Chem. Soc. (Paracelsus prize 1992), Am. Friends of the Royal Soc. (bd. dirs.), Sigma Xi. Home: 5630 S Dorchester Ave Chicago IL 60637-1722 Office: U Chgo Dept Chemistry Chicago IL 60637 E-mail: jhjh@midway.uchicago.edu.

HALPIN, DANIEL WILLIAM, civil engineering educator, consultant; b. Covington, Ky., Sept. 29, 1938; s. Jordan W. and Gladys E. (Moore) H.; m. Maria Kirchner, Feb. 8, 1963; 1 son, Rainer. B.S., U.S. Mil. Acad., 1961; M.S.C.E., U. Ill., 1969, Ph.D., 1973. Research analyst Constrn. Engring. Research Lab., Champaign, Ill., 1970-72; faculty U. Ill., Urbana, 1972-73; mem. faculty Ga. Inst. Tech., Atlanta, 1973-85, prof., 1981-85; A.J. Clark prof., dir. Constrn. Engring. and Mgmt. U. Md., 1985-87; dir. div. Constrn. Engring. and Mgmt. Purdue U., 1987—, interim head Sch. Civil Engring., 2000—01; cons. constrn. mgmt. Vis. assoc. prof. U. Sydney, Australia, 1981; vis. prof. Swiss Fed. Inst. Tech., 1985, U. Karlsruhe, Germany, 1998; vis. scholar Tech. U., Munich, 1979; vis. lectr. Ctr. Cybernetics in Constrn., Bucharest, Romania, 1973; cons. office tech. assessment U.S. Congress, 1986-87; mem. JTEC Team to evaluate constrn. tech., Japan, 1990; juror emeritus Constrn. Innovation Forum, 1994; mem. rsch. com. Constrn. Industry Inst., 1995-2002. Author: Design of Construction and Process Operations, 1976, Construction Management, 1980, Planung und Kontrolle von Bauproduktionsprozessen, 1979, Constructo - A Heuristic Game for Construction Management, 1973, Financial and Cost Control Concepts for Construction Management, 1985, Planning and Analysis of Construction Operations, 1992, Construction Management, 2d edit., 1997. Served with C.E., U.S. Army, 1961-67. Decorated Bronze Star; recipient Walter L. Huber prize ASCE, 1979, Peurifoy Constrn. Rsch. award, 1992; grantee NSF, Dept. Energy. Mem. ASCE (past sect. pres. 1981-82, chmn. constrn. rsch. coun. 1985-86, Peurifoy Constrn. Rsch. award 1992), Am. Soc. Engring. Edn., Sigma Xi. Methodist. E-mail: halpin@ecn.purdue.edu.

HALPIN, MARY ELIZABETH, psychologist; b. Oak Park, ILl., June 4, 1951; d. Thomas Joseph and Rita Helen (Foley) H. BA, Marquette U., 1973, MEd, 1975, PhD, 1983. Lic. psychologist Ill., Calif., cert. sch. psychologist Ill. Staff psychologist Milw. Children's Hosp., 1975-83; postdoctoral intern El Dorado County Mental Health Ctr., Placerville, Calif., 1983-84; psychologist Inst. for Motivational Devel., Lombard, Ill., 1985-88; psychologist, founder, gen. ptnr. Assocs. for Adolescent Achievement, Deerfield, 1989-94; pvt. practice psychology, 1995—; sch. psychologist Winnetka (Ill.) Dist. 36, 2000—. Presenter Internat. Sch. Beijing, 1998. TV appearance Oprah Winfrey Show, 1995. Chmn., mem. peer rev. com. Charter Barclay Hosp., Chgo., 1991-93. Mem.: AAUW, APA, Ill. Psychol. Assn. (standing hearing panel ethics com. 1993, pub. rels. com. 1994, chair pub. rels. com. 1999—, area code rep. 1999—). Office: 420 Lake Cook Rd Ste 109 Deerfield IL 60015-4914

HALSO, ROBERT, real estate company executive; Pres. Pulte Homes of Michigan. Office: Pulte Home Corp 33 Bloomfield Hills Pkwy Bloomfield Hills MI 48304-2944

HALSTEAD, DAVID E. aeronautical engineer; s. Helen and George H. BS, MS, MS, Iowa State U. Lead engr. GE Aircraft Engines, Cin. Mem. ASME (Melville award 1998). Achievements include discovery (with others) that fluid flow through a gas turbine is orderly and predictable instead of turbulent as was once believed. Office: GE Aircraft Engines One Neumann Way Cincinnati OH 45215-6301

HALTER, JEFFREY BRIAN, internal medicine educator, geriatrician; b. Mpls., Aug. 25, 1945; s. Cyril Joel and Marcella (Medoff) H.; m. Ellen Laura Kuper, June 25, 1972; children: Alexander, Loren, Ethan, Amy. BA magna cum laude, U. Minn., 1966, BS, MD, 1969. Diplomate Am. Bd. Internal Medicine (test com. on geriatrics 1986-88), Am. Bd. Endocrinology and Metabolism. Intern, then resident in internal medicine Harbor Gen. Hosp., Torrance, Calif., 1969-71; resident U. Wash. Sch. Medicine, Seattle, 1973-74, fellow div. metabolism, endocrinology and gerontology, 1975-77, acting instr., asst. prof., then assoc. prof. dept. medicine, 1974-84; staff physician VA Med. Ctr., 1974-75, assoc. dir. Geriatric Rsch., Edn. and Clin. Ctr., 1978-84; prof. internal medicine, chief div. geriatric medicine U. Mich. Med. Sch., Ann Arbor, 1984—, rsch. scientist, med. dir. Inst. Gerontology, 1984—, dir. Geriatrics Ctr., 1988—. Chief geriatric sect. Ann Arbor VA Med. Ctr., 1984-92, dir. Geriatric Rsch., Edn. and Clin. Ctr., 1988-99; participant, presenter numerous congresses, symposia, confs., workshops in field; vis. prof. numerous univs., including Karolinska Inst., Stockholm, 1983, U. Copenhagen, 1983, Johns Hopkins U., 1985, 91, U. So. Calif., 1985, Harvard Med. Sch., 1987, 89, UCLA, 1991, U. Chgo., 1991, U. Melbourne, 1991, U. Adelaide, 1991, McGill U., 1991, U. Md., 1994; cons. Nat. Inst. on Aging; numerous others. Mem. editl. bd. Jour. Clin. Endocrinology and Metabolism, 1984-88, Am. Jour. Physiology: Endocrinology and Mebabolism, 1985-91, Diabetes, 1986-88, Yr. Book Endocrinology, 1986-91, Jour. Gerontology: Med. Scis., 1988-92; mem. editl. bd. Jour. Am. Geriatrics Soc., 1990-93, assoc. editor, 1993-97; guest editor Supplement on Diabetes in Elderly, Diabetes Care, 1990; contbr. over 300 articles and abstracts to med. jours., chpts. to books. With USPHS, 1971-73. AMA Goldberger fellow U. Geneva Inst. Clin. Biochemistry, 1969; grantee VA, 1978—, Nat. Inst. on Aging, 1985—, Nat. Inst. Diabetes, Digestive and Kidney Diseases, John A. Hartford Found., 1988-94, Am. Fedn. for Aging Rsch., 1994-95, Univers Found., 1991—. Fellow AAAS; mem. Am. Diabetes Assn. (chmn. com. on rsch. rev. 1989-90), Endocrine Soc., Am. Fedn. Clin. Rsch., Western Soc. Clin. Investigation, Am. Soc. Clin. Investigation, Gerontol. Soc. Am. (rsch., edn.-practice com. 1984-87, chmn. rsch. com. clin. medicine sect. 1986-87, chmn. clin. medicine sect., v.p. 1992-93), Am. Geriatrics Soc. (bd. dirs. 1990—, pub. policy com. 1993-97, chmn. long range planning com. 1995-97, pres. elect 1997-98, pres. 1998-99), Ctrl. Soc. Clin. Rsch. (chmn. endocrinology coun. 1993-94, chmn. geriatrics coun. 1995-96), Am. Physiol. Soc., Phi Beta Kappa, Alpha Omega Alpha. Avocations: running, swimming, skiing. Office: U Mich Geriatrics Ctr CCGCB Room 1111 1500 E Medical Center Dr Ann Arbor MI 48109-0005

HALVORSON, DEBBIE DEFRANCESCO, state legislator; b. Steger, Ill., Mar. 1, 1958; d. Richard Lavern and Joyce Winifred DeFrancesco; children: Stephanie, Matthew. Degree, Robert Morris Coll., Prairie State Coll.; postgrad., U. Va., 1997, Harvard U., 1999. Twp. clk. Crete (Ill.) Twp., 1993-96; rep. 40th dist. Ill. State Senate, 1996—. Mem. appropriations commn., local govt. commn., minority spokesman commerce and industry com. Dem. Whip Ill. State Senate. Named Edn. Hero, Ill. Edn. Assn., 1997, Freshman Legislator of Yr., Ill. Health Care Assn., 1997, Statesman of Yr., Ill., 1998. Mem.: LWV (Homewood-Flossmoor chpt.), Nat. Orgn. Women Legislators (bd. dirs.), Profl. Womens Network, Chgo. Heights Bus. and Profl. Women, Chgo. Southland C. of C., Crete Womens Club, Altrusa. Office: 417 Capitol Bldg Springfield IL 62706-0001 Address: 241 W Joe Orr Rd Chicago Heights IL 60411-1744

HAM, ARLENE H. state legislator; b. Belle Fourche, S.D., Aug. 1, 1936; widowed; 2 children. Owner, broker Real Estate bus.; chmn. S.D. Rep. Party, 1985-87; with Rep. Nat. Com., 1988-96; mem. S.D. Senate from 32nd dist., Pierre, 1996—. Bd. dirs. Luth. Social Svcs., U.S. West. Mem. 4-H Found., Wellspring. Mem. Nat. Realtors Assn., State Realtors Assn., Rapid City Realtors Assn. (bd. dirs.), Zonta Mental Health Assn., Vet. Bd. Examiners, S.D. Lottery Commn., S.D. Racing Commn., Rapid City C. of C. (Aethena award), Toastmistress. Republican. Lutheran. Home: 1116 Crestridge Ct Rapid City SD 57701-5381 Office: State Capitol Bldg Dist 32 500 E Capitol Ave Pierre SD 57501-5070

HAMADA, ROBERT S(EIJI), educator, economist, entrepreneur; b. San Francisco, Aug. 17, 1937; s. Horace T. and Maki G. Hamada; m. Anne Marcus, June 16, 1962; children: Matthew, Janet. BE, Yale U., 1959; SM, MIT, 1961, PhD, 1969. Economist Sun Oil Co., Phila., 1961—63; instr. U. Chgo., 1966—68, asst. prof. fin., 1968—71, assoc. prof., 1971—77, prof., 1977—89, Edward Eagle Brown prof., 1989—93, Edward Eagle Brown Disting. Svc. prof., 1993—, dir. Ctr. for Rsch. in Security Prices, 1980—85, dir. Ctr. Internat. Bus. Edn. and Rsch., 1992—94, dep. dean for faculty Grad Sch. Bus., 1985—90, dean, 1993—2001; CEO, dir. Merchants' Exchange, 2001—. Vis. prof. univs. including London Bus. Sch., 1973, 79-90, UCLA, 1971, U. Wash., Seattle, 1971-72, U. B.C., Vancouver, Can., 1976; bd. dirs. A.M. Castle & Co., Fleming Cos., Inc., No. Trust Corp.; pub. dir. Chgo. Bd. Trade, 1980-2000; cons. numerous fin. instns., banks, mfg., mgmt. cons., acctg. and law firms. Past assoc. editor Jour. Fin., Jour. Fin. and Quantitative Analysis, Jour. Applied Corp. Fin.; cons. editor Scott, Foresman & Co. fin. series; contbr. numerous articles to profl. jours. Bd. dirs. numerous neighborhood non-profit orgns., including Hyde Park Neighborhood Club, Chgo., Harper Ct. Found., Chgo., Hyde Park Co-op, U. Chgo. Lab. Schs., Window to the World Comms., Inc. (WTTW-TV), Terra Found. for the Arts. Named to 8 Outstanding Bus. Sch. Profs., fortune Mag., 1982; recipient 1st Outstanding Tchr. award, Grad. Sch. Bus., U. Chgo., 1970, McKinsey Tchg. prize, 1981; fellow Sloan Found. fellow, 1959—61, Ford Found. fellow, 1963—65, Standard Oil Found. fellow, 1965—66; scholar MIT scholar, 1959—61, Yale scholar, 1955—59. Mem. Am. Fin. Assn. (bd. dirs. 1982-85), Econometric Soc., Nat. Bur. Econ. Rsch. (bd. dirs., mem. investment and exec. coms.), Am. Econ. Assn. (investment com.), Inst. Mgmt. Scis. (investment com.), Tau Beta Pi. Office: U Chgo Grad Sch Bus 1101 E 58th St Chicago IL 60637-1511

HAMALAINEN, PEKKA KALEVI, historian, educator; b. Finland, Dec. 28, 1938; s. Olavi Simeon and Aili Aliisa (Laiho) H.; children: Kim Ilkka, Leija-Lee Louise Aili, Timothy Pekka Olavi, Kai Kalevi Edward. A.B., Ind. U., 1961, Ph.D., 1966. Acting asst. prof. history U. Calif., Santa Barbara, 1965-66, asst. prof. history, 1966-70; assoc. prof. history U. Wis., Madison, 1970-76, prof., 1976—2001, prof. emeritus, 2001—, chmn. Western European area studies program, 1977—. Nat. screening com. Scandinavian area Inst. Internat. Edn., Fulbright Hays Program; cons. Dept. State., Washington, 1991—; chair grad. edn. coun. U. Wis., 1996—, Vilas assoc. Author: Kielitaistelu Suomessa 1917-1939, 1968, Nationalitetskampen och sprakstriden i Finland 1917-1939, 1969, In Time of Storm: Revolution, Civil War and the Ethnolinguistic Issue in Finland, 1978, Luokka ja Kieli Vallankumouksen Suomessa, 1978, Uniting Germany: Actions and Reactions, 1994; contbr. articles to profl. publs. and jours. Served to lt. Finnish Navy, 1957-58. Faculty research grantee U. Calif., 1966-69; faculty summer fellow, 1969; Ford Found. grantee, 1967; faculty research grantee U. Wis., Madison, 1970— ; Am. Philos. Soc. research grantee, 1973; Am. Council Learned Socs. fellow, 1976; research grantee, 1978 Mem. AAUP, Am. Hist. Assn., German Studies Assn., Soc. Advancement Scandinavian Study (adv. com. exec. coun.), Fin. Hist. Assn. (corr. emem.), Coun. European Studies, Paasikivi Seura, Ind. U. Alumni Assn. Office: U Wis 3211 Humanities 455 N Park St Madison WI 53706-1405

HAMANN, DERYL FREDERICK, lawyer, bank executive; b. Lehigh, Iowa, Dec. 8, 1932; s. Frederick Carl Hamann and Ada Ellen (Hollingsworth) Hamann Geis; m. Carrie Svea Rosen, Aug. 23, 1954 (dec. 1985); children: Karl E., Daniel A., Esther Hamann Brabec, Julie Hamann Bunderson; m. Eleanor Ramona Nelson Curtis, June 20, 1987. AA, Ft. Dodge Jr. Coll., Iowa, 1953; BS in Law, U. Nebr., 1956, JD cum laude, 1958. Bar: Nebr. 1958, U.S. Dist. Ct. Nebr. 1958, U.S. Ct. Appeals (8th cir.) 1958. Law clk. U.S. Dist. Ct. for Nebr., Lincoln, 1958-59; ptnr. Baird, Holm, McEachen, Pedersen, Hamann & Strasheim, Omaha, 1959—. Chmn. adv. com. Supreme Ct. Nebr., Omaha, 1986-95; chmn. bd. Midwestern Cmty. Banks. Past pres. Omaha Estate Planning Coun. Mem. Nebr. Bar Found. (pres. 1981-86), Nebr. Assn. Bank Attys. (pres. 1985-86). Republican. Lutheran. Avocations: boating, reading. Office: Baird Holm McEachen Pedersen Hamann & Strasheim 1500 Woodmen Tower Omaha NE 68102

HAMBRICK, ERNESTINE, retired colon and rectal surgeon; b. Griffin, Ga., Mar. 31, 1941; d. Jack Daniel and Nannie (Harper) Hambrick Rubens. BS, U. Md., 1963; MD, U. Ill., 1967. Diplomate Am. Bd. Colon and Rectal Surgery, Am. Bd. Surgery. Intern in surgery Cook County Hosp., Chgo., 1967-68, resident in gen. surgery, 1968-72, fellow colon and rectal surgery, 1972-73, attending surgeon, 1973-74, part-time attending surgeon, 1974-80; pvt. practice colon and rectal surgery, 1974-97; pres. med. staff Michael Reese Hosp., 1990-92, chief surgery, 1993-95; founder, chmn. STOP Colon/Rectal Cancer Found., 1997—. Mem. Nat. Colorectal Cancer Round Table, 1997—, steering com. 2000—. Contbr. articles to profl. jours. Trustee Rsch. and Edn. Found., Michael Reese Med. Staff, Chgo., 1994-98, treas., 1994-98. Mem. ACS, Am. Soc. Colon and Rectal Surgeons (v.p. 1992-93, trustee Rsch. Found. 1992-98), Am. Coll. Gastroenterology. Avocations: travel, photography, scuba diving, flying, writing. Office: 30 N Michigan Ave Ste 1118 Chicago IL 60602-3503 E-mail: ehcrsone@aol.com.

HAMBURG, MARC D. insurance company executive; CFO Berkshire Hathaway Inc., Omaha. Office: Berkshire Hathaway Inc 3555 Farnam St Ste 1440 Omaha NE 68131-3378

HAMEL, LOUIS REGINALD, systems analysis consultant; b. Lowell, Mass., July 23, 1945; s. Wilfred John and Angelina Lucienne (Paradis) H.; m. Roi Anne Roberts, Mar. 24, 1967 (dec.); 1 child, Felicia Antoinette; m. Anne Louise Staup, July 2, 1972 (div.); children: Shawna Michelle, Louis Reginald III; m. Melissa A. Truesdale, Sept. 24, 1999; stepchildren: Maxwell Craig, Meghan Briana, Mary Elizabeth. AA, Kellogg C.C., 1978. Cert. worker's compensation profl. Retail mgr. Marshall Dept. Stores, Beverly, Mass., 1972-73; tech. svc. rep. Monarch Marking Systems, Framingham, 1973—74; employment specialist Dept. Labor, Battle Creek, Mich., 1977-78; v.p. corp. Keith Polygraph Cons. and Investigative Svc., Inc., 1978-79; indsl. engr., engine components divsn. Eaton Corp., 1979-82; tooling and process engr. Kelley Tech. Svcs., 1983-84, Clark Equipment Inc., 1983-84; tooling and mfg. engr., mfg. mgr. Trans Guard Industries Inc., Angola, Ind., 1983-85; facilitator employee involvement, safety dir. Wohlert Corp., Lansing, Mich., 1985—, workers compensation adminstr., tng. dir., 1985—, system analysis cons., 1975—. Cons. in field. Mem. Calhoun County Com. on Employment of Handicapped, Battle Creek, Mich., 1977-78; mem. Capital Area Labor Mgmt. Com., 1986-91. With USN, 1963-71, Vietnam. Recipient Svcs. to Handicapped award Internat. Assn. Pers. in Employment Security, Mich. chpt. 1978. Mem. VFW, Nat. Geog. Soc., Mich. Assn. Concerned Vets. (dir.), Nat. Assn. Concerned Vets. Democrat. Roman Catholic. Home and Office: 12240 S M 66 Hwy Bellevue MI 49021-9639 E-mail: hamellm@prodigy.net.

HAMEL, WILLIAM JOHN, church administrator, minister; b. Marquette, Mich., July 30, 1947; s. John Peter and Jayne B. (Berklund) H.; m. Karen Margaret Holleen, Aug. 10, 1968; children: Krista Joy, Kari Elise. BS, Wheaton Coll., 1969; MDiv, Trinity Evang. Div. Sch., Deerfield, Ill., 1972; DD, Trinity Internat. U., 1998; DCM, Trinity Western U., 1998. Ordained minister Evang. Free Ch. Am., 1978. Pastor West Bloomington (Minn.) Evang. Free Ch., 1972-86; dist. supt. Midwest Dist. Evang. Free Ch. Am., Kearney, Nebr., 1986-90; exec. v.p. Evang. Free Ch. Am., Mpls., 1990-97, pres., 1997—. Office: Evang Free Ch Am 901 E 78th St Minneapolis MN 55420-1334

HAMERMESH, MORTON, physicist, educator; b. N.Y.C., Dec. 27, 1915; s. Isador J. and Rose (Kornhauser) H.; m. Madeline Goldberg, 1941; children: Daniel S., Deborah R., Lawrence A. B.S., Coll. City N.Y., 1936; Ph.D., N.Y.U., 1940. Instr. physics Coll. City N.Y., 1941, Stanford, 1941-43; research asso. Radio Research Lab., Harvard, 1943-46; asst. prof. physics N.Y.U., 1946-47, asso. prof., 1947-48; sr. physicist Argonne Nat. Lab., 1948-50, asso. dir. physics div., 1950-59, dir. physics div., 1959-63, assoc. lab. dir. basic research, 1963-65; prof. U. Minn., Mpls., 1965-69, 70-86, prof. emeritus, 1986—; head Sch. Physics and Astronomy, 1965-69, 70-73; prof. physics, chmn. dept. physics State U. N.Y., Stony Brook, 1969-70. Translator: Classical Theory of Fields (by Landau and Lifshitz), 1951; numerous papers in field. Fellow Am. Phys. Soc.; mem. Research Soc. Am. Office: Univ Minn Physics Dept Minneapolis MN 55455 E-mail: mort@physics.spa.umn.edu.

HAMEROW, THEODORE STEPHEN, history educator; b. Warsaw, Poland, Aug. 24, 1920; arrived in U.S.A., 1929, naturalized, 1930; s. Haim Schneyer and Bella (Rubinlicht) H.; m. Margarete Lotter, Aug. 16, 1954 (div. Dec. 27, 1996); children: Judith Margarete, Helena Francisca; m. Diane Franzen, Oct. 4, 1997. B.A., CUNY, 1942; M.A., Columbia U., 1947; Ph.D., Yale U., 1951. Instr. Wellesley Coll., 1950-51, U. Md., 1951-52; instr., asst. prof., then asso. prof. U. Ill, 1952-58; mem. faculty U. Wis., 1958-91, prof. history, 1961-91, G. P. Gooch prof. history, 1978-91, chmn. dept. history, 1973-76. Cons. editor Dorsey Press, 1961-71; mem. coun. Internat. Exch. Scholars, 1983-85, Nat. Coun. on Humanities, 1992-2000. Author: Restoration, Revolution, Reaction, 1958, Otto von Bismarck: A Historical Assessment, 1962, The Social Foundations of German Unification 1858-1871, 2 vols, 1969-72, The Birth of a New Europe: State and Society in the Nineteenth Century, 1983, Reflections on History and Historians, 1987, From the Finland Station: The Graying of Revolution in the Twentieth Century, 1990, On the Road to the Wolf's Lair: German Resistance to Hitler, 1997, Remembering a Vanished World: A Jewish Childhood in Interwar Poland, 2001; co-author: History of the World, 1960, A History of the Western World, 1969; editor: Otto von Bismarck, Reflections and Reminiscences, 1962, The Age of Bismarck, 1973; editorial bd.: Jour. Modern History, 1967-70, Central European History, 1968-72, Revs. in European History, 1974-78. Mem. Am. Hist. Assn., Conf. Group Central European History (sec.-treas. 1960-62, chmn. 1976), Wis. Assn. of Scholars (pres. 1989-91). Home: 885 Terry Pl Madison WI 53711-1956 Office: U Wisc Dept History Madison WI 53711 E-mail: dkhamerow@facstaff.wisc.edu.

HAMERS, ROBERT J. chemistry educator, researcher; Prof. chemistry U. Wis., Madison, Evan P. Helfaer chair, 1996—. Recipient Peter Mark Meml. award Am. Vacuum Soc., 1994; NSF fellow, 1992-97, John Simon Guggenheim Found. fellow, 2000, S.C. Johnson Co. Disting. fellow, 2000—. Fellow Am. Vacuum Soc. Office: U Wisconsin Dept Chemistry 1101 University Ave Madison WI 53706-1322 Fax: 608-262-0453. E-mail: rjhamers@facstaff.wisc.edu.

HAMERTON, JOHN LAURENCE, geneticist, educator; b. Brighton, Eng., Sept. 23, 1929; arrived in Can., 1969; s. Bernard John and Nora (Casey) H.; m. Irene Tuck; children: Katherine, Sarah. BS in Zoology, London U., 1951, DSc in Human Genetics, 1968. Sr. sci. officer Brit. Mus. (Natural History), London, 1956-60; lectr. Guys Hosp. Med. Sch., 1960-62, sr. lectr., 1962-69; assoc. prof. pediatrics dept. U. Man., Winnipeg, Can., 1969-72, prof. pediatrics dept. Can., 1972, assoc. dean. med. sch. Can., 1978-81, prof. dept. human genetics Can., 1985-96, head. dept. Can., 1985-93, Disting. prof. Can., 1987-96, Disting. prof. emeritus Can., 1996—, mem. univ. bd. govs. Can., 1976-82, 87-90, 91-93, 93-96. Vis. prof. Hebrew U., Jerusalem, 1975; rsch. prof. Med. Rsch. Coun. Can., 1981-82; v.p. Man. Health Rsch. Coun., Winnipeg, 1988-90, chmn., 1990-98; v.p. XIVth Internat. Congress of Genetics, Toronto, 1988; chair adv. com. Prov. Imaging, 1993-99. Author: Chromosomes in Medicine,

1962, Human Cytogenetics, Vols. I and II, 1971; contbr. over 180 articles to profl. jours. Chmn. Can. Sheep Coun., 1988, 89, 90, Man. Livestock Performance Testing Bd., 1988-90, 93-95. Recipient Robert Roessler de Villiers award Leukemia Soc. Am., 1956, Huxley Meml. medal Imperial Coll. Sci. and Tech., 1958, Teddy rsch. award Children's Hosp. Winnipeg Rsch. Found., Inc., 1987 Fellow Inst. Biology (U.K.), Can. Coll. Med. Geneticists (pres. 1990-94), Royal Soc. Can.; mem. Royal Coll. Sci. (assoc.), Man. Sheep Assn. (pres. 1986-89). Avocation: sheep farming. Home: RR 1 Box 27 Grp 7 Dugald MB Canada R0E 0K0 Office: U Man Dept Genetics 250-770 Bannatyne Ave Winnipeg MB Canada R3E 0W3

HAMIEL, JEFF, airport executive; Lic. comml. pilot. With Met. Airports Commn., Mpls., 1977—, exec. dir., 1985—. Lt. col. USAFR. Office: Met Airports Commn 6040 28th Ave S Minneapolis MN 55450-2701

HAMILTON, DAVID F. judge; b. 1957; BA magna cum laude, Haverford Coll., 1979; JD, Yale U., 1983. Law clk. to Hon. Richard D. Cudahy U.S. Ct. Appeals (7th cir.), 1983-84; atty. Barnes & Thornburg, Indpls., 1984-88, 91-94; judge U.S. Dist. Ct. (so. dist.) Ind., 1994—. Counsel to Gov. of Ind., 1989-91; chair Ind. State Ethics Commn., 1991-94. V.p. for litigation, bd. dirs. Ind. Civil Liberties Union, 1987-88. Fulbright scholar, 1979-80; recipient Sagamore of the Wabash, Gov. Evan Bayh, 1991. Mem.: Am. Inns. of Ct. (Sagamore chpt., pres. 2001—, criminal law com. jud. conf. 2000—). Office: US Dist Ct So Dist Ind 46 E Ohio St Rm 330 Indianapolis IN 46204-1921

HAMILTON, HAROLD PHILIP, fund raising executive; b. High Point, N.C., Apr. 26, 1924; s. Alfred McKinley and Dora Elizabeth (Surratt) H.; m. Agnes Marie Kametz, Sept. 4, 1944; children: Dawn Elizabeth, Deborah Anne, Harold Philip, Elaine Denise. Student, Lehigh U., 1943-44; B.A. cum laude, High Point Coll., 1947, L.H.D., 1965; B.D. (Myers Park scholar), Duke, 1950, Ph.D., 1954. Asst. prof. philosophy and religion N.C. State Coll., 1953-55; dean of faculty, asso. prof. Christian thought Ky. Wesleyan Coll., 1955-58, dean of coll., prof., 1958-59, dean of coll., acting pres., 1959-60, pres., prof. Christian thought, 1960-70; pres. Central Meth. Coll., 1970-76; asst. state treas. Commonwealth of Ky., 1976-80; adminstr. Timken Mercy Med. Center, 1980-83; pres. Deaconess Hosp. Found., 1983-85; v.p. planned giving Ohio Presbyn. Retirement Svcs. Found., 1985-95. Pres. Oxford Inst. Meth. Theol. Studies, 1958, Ctrl. Ohio Planned Giving Coun. Served with AUS, World War II. Mem. Am. Renaissance Soc., Central States Faculty Conf. (exec. com.), Am. Soc. Ch. History, Inst. Higher Edn., Fayette C. of C., NEA, Nat. Assn. for Hosp. Devel., Newcomen Soc. N.Am., Phi Delta Theta, Phi Alpha Theta, Phi Beta Patron, Omicron Delta Kappa. Methodist (lay leader, ofcl. bd., tchr., elder). Lodges: Rotary (v.p.), Round Table. Home: 1459 Firwood Dr Columbus OH 43229-3434 Office: Ohio Presbyn Retirement Svcs Found 1001 Kingsmill Pkwy Columbus OH 43229-1129

HAMILTON, JEAN CONSTANCE, judge; b. St. Louis, Nov. 12, 1945; AB, Wellesley Coll., 1968; JD, Washington U., St. Louis, 1971; LLM, Yale U., 1982. Atty. Dept. of Justice, Washington, 1971-73, asst. U.S. atty. St. Louis, 1973-78; judge 22d Jud. Circuit State of Mo., 1982-88; judge Mo. Ct. Appeals (ea. dist.), 1988-90, U.S. Dist. Ct. (ea. dist.) Mo., 1990—, chief judge, 1995—. Office: US Courthouse 111 S 10th St Saint Louis MO 63102

HAMILTON, PETER BANNERMAN, business executive, lawyer; b. Phila., Oct. 22, 1946; s. William George Jr. and Elizabeth Jane (McCullough) H.; m. Elizabeth Anne Arthur, May 8, 1982; children— Peter Bannerman, Jr., Brian Arthur. A.B., Princeton U., 1968; J.D., Yale U., 1971. Bar: D.C. 1972, Pa. 1972, Ind. 1985. Mem. staff Office Asst. Sec. Def. for Systems Analysis and Office Gen. Counsel, Dept. Def., Washington, 1971-74; mem. firm Williams & Connolly, 1974-77; gen. counsel Dept. Air Force, 1977-78; dep. gen. counsel HEW, 1979, exec. asst. to sec., 1979; spl. asst. to Sec. and Dep. Sec. Def., Washington, 1979-80; ptnr. Califano, Ross & Heineman, 1980-82; v.p., gen. counsel, sec. Cummins Engine Co., Inc., 1983-86, v.p. law and treasury, 1987-88, v.p., CFO, 1988-95; sr. v.p., CFO, Brunswick Corp., Lake Forest, Ill., 1996-98, exec. v.p., CFO, 1998-99; vice chmn., pres. Brunswick Bowling and Billiards, 2000—. Bd. dirs. Brunswick Corp., The Kemper Ins. Cos., The Talbots, Inc. Articles editor: Yale Law Jour, 1970-71. Served to lt. USN, 1971-74. Home: 970 E Deerpath Rd Lake Forest IL 60045-2212 Office: Brunswick Corp 1 N Field Ct Lake Forest IL 60045-4811

HAMILTON, ROBERT APPLEBY, JR. insurance company executive; b. Boston, Feb. 20, 1940; s. Robert A. and Alice Margaret (Dowdall) H.; m. Ellen Kuhlen, Aug. 13, 1966; children: Jennifer, Robert Appleby III, Elizabeth. Student, Miami U. (Ohio), 1958-62. CLU; chartered fin. cons. With Travelers Ins. Co., various locations, 1962-65, New Eng. Mut. Life Ins. Co., various locations, 1965-90, regional pension rep. Boston, 1968-71, regional mgr. Chgo., 1972-83, sr. pension cons., 1983-90; mktg. and fin. cons. Snowbeck Enterprises, Inc., Geneva, 1990-97, ret., 1997. Producer Sta. WCTV; mem. Rep. Town Com., Wenham, Mass., 1970-72, Milton Twp., Ill., 1973-75; mem. Wenham Water Commn., 1970-72. Mem. Midwest Pension Conf. (chmn. 1989-90), Am. Soc. Pension Actuaries (assoc.), Am. Soc. CLUs, Am. Assn. Fin. Planners, Profit Sharing Coun. Am., Chgo. Coun. Fgn. Rels., Alpha Epsilon Rho. Republican. Home: 110 Hamilton Ln Wheaton IL 60187-1807 also: HC 35 Box 764 Tenants Harbor ME 04860-9709 E-mail: erisabob@aol.com.

HAMILTON, ROBERT OTTE, lawyer; b. Marysville, Ohio, July 27, 1927; s. George Robinson and Annette (Otte) H.; m. Phyllis Eileen Clark, Dec. 16, 1962; children: Nathan Clark, Scott Robert. AB, Miami U., Oxford, Ohio, 1950; JD, U. Mich., 1953. Bar: Ohio 1953, U.S. Supreme Ct. 1960. Sole practice, Marysville, 1953—; pros. atty. Union County, Ohio, 1957-65; city atty. City of Marysville, 1956-81. Mem. Union, Morrow and Del. Mental Health Bd.,d 1957-72; pres. Marysville Jaycees, 1954; mem. Union County Rep. Exec. Com., 1955-65, sec., 1955-60. Served with USN, 1945-46, to lt. (j.g.) USNR, 1946-66. Mem. ABA, Ohio State BAr Assn. (chmn. jr. bar sect. 1961, ho. of dels. 1976-86, exec. com. 1983-86), Ohio State Bar Found. (pres. 1996), Union County Bar Assn. (pres. 1960), Ohio Acad. Trial Lawyers, Masons. Home: 432 W 6th St Marysville OH 43040-1464 Office: 116 S Court St Marysville OH 43040-1545

HAMILTON, WILLIAM MILTON, retired manufacturing executive; b. Phila., Feb. 5, 1925; s. Louis Valentine and Elsie Marie (Walter) H.; m. Edith Marie Busey, June 9, 1947; children: Barbara Marie, William Milton Jr., Patricia Ann. B.S. in Indsl. Mgmt., Ga. Inst. Tech., 1947. Asst. br. mgr. Swift & Co., Atlanta, 1947-48; treas. R.K. Price Co., Fayetteville, 1954-55; br. mgr. N.Y. Wire Cloth Co., Atlanta, 1955-56; from ops. mgr. to pres. Premier Indsl. Corp., Cleve., 1956-91, dir., cons., 1991-96, spl. asst. to chmn., 1998—, also bd. dirs.; CEO product mfg. group Premier Farnell, 1996-98, spl. asst. to CEO, 1998—, pres., COO, 1998-99, spl. asst. to chief exec., 1999—2001; ret., 2001. Served to lt. USN, 1943-46, 48-54. Mem.: Jonathan Landing Golf Club (Fla.), Elyria Country Club (Ohio). Methodist. Home: 2222 Pebblebrook Cleveland OH 44145-4378 Office: Premier Farnell 4500 Euclid Ave Cleveland OH 44103-3736 E-mail: hew1947@aol.com.

HAMISTER, DONALD BRUCE, retired electronics company executive; b. Cleve., Nov. 29, 1920; s. Victor Carl and Bess Irene (Sutherl) H.; m. Margaret Irene Singiser, Dec. 22, 1946; children: Don Bruce, Tracy. A.B. cum laude, Kenyon Coll., 1947, LLD (hon.), 1989; postgrad., Stanford U., 1948-49, U. Chgo., 1957; LLD (hon.), Kenyon Coll., 1989. Application engr. S.E. Joslyn Co., Cin., 1947-48; regional sales mgr. Joslyn Mfg. and Supply Co., St. Louis, 1950-52, mktg. mgr. Chgo., 1953-55, asst. to pres., 1956-57, mgr. aircraft arrester dept., 1958-62, gen. mgr. electronic systems div., 1962-71, v.p., gen. mgr., dir. Goleta, Calif., 1973-78, group v.p. indsl. products, 1974-78, pres., chief exec. officer, 1978-85, chmn., 1979-94, ret. chmn., 1994; chmn. Joslyn Mfg. and Supply Co. name changed to Joslyn Corp., 1986; also bd. dirs. Joslyn Corp., 1973—; pres. Joslyn Stainless; chmn. emeritus Joslyn Corp., Goleta, 1995—; pres., dir. Joslyn Stamping Co.; pres., chmn., dir. Joslyn Def. Systems, Inc., 1981—; dir. Brewer Tichener Corp.; chief exec. officer Joslyn Corp., Chgo., 1991-94, ret., 1994. Served to lt. USNR, 1942-46. Mem. IEEE, Airline Avionics Inst. (pres., chmn. 1972-74) Club: Univ. (Chgo.). E-mail: dbh1141@aol.com.

HAMM, CHARLES D. diversified financial services company executive; With KPMG Peat Marwick LLP, 1984-97, ptnr., 1996-97; CFO, treas. Century Bus. Svcs., Cleve., 1997—. Mem. AICPA, Ohio Soc. CPA. Office: Century Bus Svcs Ste 330 6480 Roxside Woods Blvd Cleveland OH 44131

HAMM, MARIEL MARGARET, soccer player; b. Selma, Ala., Mar. 17, 1972; m. Christian Corry. BS in Polit. Sci., U. N.C., 1994. Forward U.S. Women's Nat. Soccer Team, Chgo., 1987—. Named U.S. Soccer Female Athlete of Yr., 1994-95, MVP of U.S. Women's Cup, 1995; recipient Gold medal Atlanta Olympics, 1996; World Cup 1999. Office: US Soccer Fedn US Soccer House 1801 S Prairie Ave Chicago IL 60616-1319

HAMM, RICHARD L. church administrator; b. Crawfordsville, Ind., Dec. 21, 1947; m. Melinda Ann Fishbaugh; children: David Lee, Laura Ann. Student, St. Petersburg Jr. Coll., 1966-67; BA in Religion, Butler U., 1970; D of Ministry, Christian Theol. Sem., 1974. Pastor Abington (Ind.) Christian Ch., 1968, Little Eagle Creek Christian Ch., Westfield, Ind., 1970; assoc. pastor Ctrl. Christian ch., Kansas City, Kans., 1974; founding pastor North Oak Christian ch., Mo., 1975-82; sr. pastor 1st Christian Ch., Ft. Wayne, Ind., 1982-90; regional min. Christian Ch. (Disciples of Christ) Tenn., 1990-93; gen. min., pres. Christian Ch. (Disciples of Christ) U.S. and Can., 1993—. Bd. dirs. mid-Am. region Christian Ch. (Disciples of Christ), 1977-81, bd. dirs. Kans. region, 1980-81, bd. dirs. Ind. region, 1983-90, chair area new ch. com. Ind. region, 1984-87, 89, mem. commn. ministry Ind. region, 1985-87, 89, mem. gen. bd., 1986-90, bd. dirs. divsn. overseas ministries, 1991—, commn. on ministry, 1991—, mem. task force mission funding, 1992; moderator Christian Ch. Greater Kansas City, 1980-81; advisor/participant World Coun. Chs. Ctrl. Com., Geneva, 1992; convener Chs. Covenant Communion workshops, Tenn., 1992; v.p. Nat. Coun. Chs., 1996; mem. ctrl. com. World Coun. Chs., 1998—. Author: From Mainline to Front Line, 1997, 2020 Vision for the Christian Church (Disciples of Christ), 2001. Mem. Mayor's Task Force Domestic Violence, 1990. Recipient Recognition award North Kansas City Edn. Assn., 1979, Recognition award Ft. Wayne, Ind., Edn. Assn. and Ft. Wayne Community Schs., 1984, Ind. Region's Model Ministry award, 1990; named Ecumenist of Yr. of Tenn., 1993. Mem. Tenn. Assn. Chs. (pres.-elect 1992), Clergy United Action (pres. 1984-86), Associated Chs. Ft. Wayne and Allen County (bd. dirs., officer 1982-90), Rotary. Office: Christian Church (Disciples of Christ) PO Box 1986 Indianapolis IN 46206-1986

HAMMEL, HAROLD THEODORE, physiology and biophysics educator, researcher; b. Huntington, Ind., May 8, 1921; s. Audry Harold and Ferne Jane (Wiles) H.; m. Dorothy King, Dec. 29, 1948; children: Nannette, Heidi. BS in Physics, Purdue U., 1943; MS in Physics, Cornell U., 1950, PhD in Zoology, 1953; DSc (hon.), Huntington Coll., 1999. Jr. physicist Los Alamos (N.Mex.) Lab., 1944-46, staff physicist, 1948-49; from instr. to asst. prof. U. Pa., Phila., 1953-61; assoc. prof., fellow John B. Pierce Lab. Yale U., New Haven, 1961-68; prof. Scripps Instn. of Oceanography U. Calif., San Diego, 1968-88, emeritus prof., 1988—. Adj. prof. physiology and biophysics Ind. U., Bloomington, 1989—; fgn. sci. mem. Max Planck Inst. for Physiol. and Clin. Rsch., 1978—; U.S. sr. scientist Alexander von Humboldt Found., 1981. Author: (with Scholander) Osmosis and Tensile Solvent, 1976; contbr. over 200 articles to profl. jours. Fellow AAAS; mem. Am. Phys. Soc., Am. Chem. Soc., Am. Physiol. Soc. (Fifth August Krogh Disting. lectureship 1998, Honor award Environ. and Exercize sect. 1996), Am. Soc. Mammalogy, Norwegian Acad. Sci. and Letters. Democrat. Achievements include first measurement of phloem sap, and of xylem sap pressure in higher plants; research in osmosis and fluid transport in plants, thermal and metabolic responses to moderate cold exposure in Australian Aborigine, Kalahari Bushmen, Innuit, Alacalut Indians; explanation of freezing without cavitation in evergreen plants; extension and application of kinetic theory to Hulett's theory of solvent tension and to osmotic force in Starling's experiment; research in theory of adjustable set point and gain for regulation of body temperature in vertebrates, research in control of salt gland function in birds. Home: 1605 Ridgeway Dr Ellettsville IN 47429-9474 Office: Ind U Med Scis Program Bloomington IN 47405 E-mail: hhammel@indiana.edu.

HAMMER, DAVID LINDLEY, lawyer, writer; b. Newton, Iowa, June 6, 1929; s. Neal paul and Agnes Marilyn (Reece) H.; m. Audrey Lowe, June 20, 1953; children: Julie, Lisa, David. BA, Grinnell Coll., 1951; JD, U. Iowa, 1956. Bar: Iowa 1956, U.S. Dist. Ct. (no. dist.) Iowa 1959, U.S. Dist. Ct. (so. dist.) Iowa 1969, U.S. Ct. Appeals (8th cir.) 1996, U.S. Supreme Ct. 1977. Ptnr. Hammer Simon & Jensen, Galena, Ill., Dubuque, Iowa; mem. grievance commn. Iowa Supreme Ct., 1973-85, mem. adv. rules com., 1986-92. Author: Poems from the Ledge, 1980, The Game is Afoot, 1983, For the Sake of the Game, 1986, To Play the Game, 1986, The 22nd Man, 1989, The Quest, 1993, My Dear Watson, 1994, The Before Breakfast Pipe, 1995, A Dangerous Game, 1997, The Vital Essence, 1999, A Talent for Murder, 2000, Yonder in the Gaslight, 2000, Straight Up with a Twist, 2001, A Deep Game, 2001, The Game is Underfoot, 2002. Bd. dirs. Linwood Cemetery Assn., 1973—, pres., 1983-84; bd. dirs. Dubuque Mus. Art, 1998-2001, hon. dir.; bd. dirs., past pres. Finley Hosp., hon. dir.; bd. dirs. Finley Found., 1988-95; past campaign chmn., past pres. United Way; past bd. dirs. Carnegie Stout Pub. Libr. With U.S. Army, 1951-53. Fellow Am. Coll. Trial Lawyers; mem. ABA, Young Lawyers Iowa (past pres.), Iowa Def. Counsel Assn. (pres. 1991-92, del. to Def. Rsch. Inst. 1992-93), Assn. Def. Trial Attys. (exec. coun. 1983-86, past chmn. Iowa chpt.), Iowa State Bar Assn. (past chmn. continuing legal edn. com.), Iowa Acad. Trial Lawyers, Dubuque County Bar Assn. (past pres.), Baker St. Irregulars. Republican. Congregationalist. Office: 770 Main St Dubuque IA 52001

HAMMER, WILLIAM ROY, paleontologist, educator; b. Detroit, Nov. 15, 1949; BS, Wayne State U., 1971, MS, 1973, PhD, 1979. Asst. prof. geology Wayne State U., Detroit, 1980-81, Augustana Coll., Rock Island, Ill., 1981-87, assoc. prof., 1987-94, prof., chair dept. geology, dir. Fryxell Geology Mus., 1988—, Fritiof Fryxell endowed chair, 1998—. Rsch. assoc. Field Mus. Natural History, Chgo., 1993—; prin. investigator grants for Antarctic Rsch. NSF, Washington, 1981—; Am. Assn. Petroleum Geologists Disting. lectr., 1996-97. Contbr. articles to profl. jours.; contbg. author to 14 books and 3 field guidebooks. Mem. AAAS (mem.-at-large com. on geology and geography 1998—), Soc. Vertebrate Paleontology (chair Skinner prize com. 1998—), Paleontological Soc. (chair N/C sect. 1989-90), Soc. Econ. Paleontologists and Mineralogists (v.p. Great Lakes sect. 1985-86). Achievements include discovery of many new fossil reptiles and amphibians from Antarctica, including the first Jurassic dinosaurs from that continent. Office: Augustana Coll Dept Geology Rock Island IL 61201

HAMMERMAN, MARC RANDALL, nephrologist, educator; b. St. Louis, Sept. 29, 1947; s. Elmer and Lillian Hammerman; m. Nancy Tutt, Aug. 9, 1974; children: Seth, Megan. AB, Washington U., St. Louis, 1969, MD, 1972. Intern Barnes Hosp., St. Louis, 1972-73, resident, 1973-74, Mass. Gen. Hosp., Boston, 1976-77; instr. Washington U., St. Louis, 1977-78, asst. prof., 1979-84, assoc. prof., 1984-89, prof., 1989—, dir. renal div. Sch. Medicine, 1991—. Mem. study sect. NIH, 1990-95; investigator Am. Heart Assn., 1984. Contbr. over 100 sci. articles, revs. to profl. publs., chpts. to books. Lt. comdr. USPHS, 1974-76. NIH grantee, 1980—. Mem. Am. Fedn. for Clin. Rsch., Am. Soc. Clin. Investigation, Assn. Am. Physicians. Office: Washington U Sch Medicine Renal Div Box 8126 660 S Euclid Ave Saint Louis MO 63110-1010 E-mail: mhammerm@im.wustl.edu.

HAMMERSTROM, BEVERLY SWOISH, state legislator; b. Mineral Wells, Tex., Mar. 28, 1944; d. William Graham and Marjorie Wirth (Lillis) Swoish; m. Don Preston Hammerstrom, June 25, 1966 (div. Oct. 1976); children: Todd Preston, Rory Scott. BA, Adrian Coll., 1966; MPA, U. Toledo, 1994. Cert. mcpl. clk. Tchr. Geneva (N.Y.) Pub. Schs., 1966-69; substitute tchr. Darien (Wis.) Pub. Schs., 1970-71; tchr. Bedford Coop. Nursery Sch., Lambertville, Mich., 1975; retail mgr., buyer Gallerie, Toledo, 1975-78, Personal Touch, Toledo, 1978-80; clk. Bedford Township, Temperance, Mich., 1980-92; mem. Mich. Ho. of Reps., Lansing, 1993-98, Mich. Senate from 17th dist., Lansing, 1999—. Bd. dirs. Family Med. Ctr., Temperance; emergency mgmt. bd. Washtenaw County, Ypsilanti, Mich., 1993—, Monroe (Mich.) County, 1993—. Mem. Internat. Inst. Mcpl. Clks. (bd. dirs. Found. 1996), Mich. Assn. Clks. (life, pres. 1990-91), Am. Legis. Exch. Coun. (transp. task force), Coun. State Govt. (med. policies com., del. 1995—), Women in Govt. (state dir. 1999—). Republican. Roman Catholic. Home: 1183 Oakmont Dr Temperance MI 48182-9563 Office: Mich Senate PO Box 30036 Lansing MI 48909-7536

HAMMESFAHR, ROBERT WINTER, lawyer; b. Pittsfield, Mass., May 17, 1954; s. Frederick W. and Patricia Lue (Winter) H.; widowed; 1 child, Scott Gardner. BA, Colgate U., 1975; JD, Northwestern U., Chgo., 1978. Bar: Ill. 1978, U.S. Dist. Ct. (no. dist.) Ill. 1978, N.Y. 1991, U.S. Supreme Ct. 1989. Ptnr. Blatt, Hammesfahr & Eaton, Chgo., 1994-97, mng. ptnr., 1997-2000, chmn., 2000; mem. Cozen O'Connor, 2001—. Author: (with others) Punitive Damages: A Guide to the Insurability of Punitive Damages in the United States and Its Territories, 1988, Punitive Damages: A State-By-State Guide to Law and Practice, 1991, (pocket parts 1993, 96, Japanese edits., 1995, 99, 2000, 2001), 2d edit., 2002, The Law of Reinsurance Claims, 1994, Supplement 1997; editor, author: (with others) @Risk—Internet and E-commerce Insurance and Reinsurance, 2000, 2.0 version, 2002; contbr. articles to profl. jours. Mem. ABA, Chgo. Bar Assn. Avocations: tennis, skiing. Office: Cozen O'Connor 222 S Riverside Plz Ste 1500 Chicago IL 60606-6000 E-mail: rhammesfahr@cozen.com.

HAMMOND, EDWARD H. university president; b. McAllen, Tex., May 4, 1944; s. Will J. and Bergit A. (Lund) H.; m. Vivian hammeke, Aug. 26, 1967; children: Kelly Edvidge, Lance Edward, Julie Marie. BS in Speech, Kans. State Tchrs. Coll., 1966, MS, 1967; PhD, U. MO., 1971. Asst. dir. of field svcs. Kans. State Tchrs. Coll., Emporia, 1966-67; dir. student affairs Purdue U. North Cen. campus, Westville, Ind., 1967-68; counselor housing office U. Mo., Columbia, 1969-70; asst. dean of students So. Ill. U., Carbondale, 1970, asst. to pres. for student rels., 1970-73; v.p. student affairs Seton Hall U., S. Orange, N.J., 1973-76, U. Louisville, 1976-87; pres. Fort Hays State U., Hays, Kans., 1987—. Chair bd. trustees Boost Alcohol Consciousness Concerning the Health of U. Students of the U.S. Inc., 1987-93; trustee The Lincoln Found., 1979-87; mem. Inter-Assn. Task Force on Coll. Alcohol Abuse and Misuse, 1984—; vis. faculty mem. Ind. U., Bloomington, 1972-83; cons. in field. Contbr. articles to profl. jours. NDEA fellow U. Mo., 1968-70; named to Mid-Am. Edn. Hall of Fame, 1997. Mem. Am. Coun. on Edn., Am. Assn. State Colls. and Univs., Am. Assn. Univ. Adminstrs., Nat. Assn. Student Pers. Adminstrs. (nat. pres. 1983, John Jones award 1986), Kans. C. of C. and Industry (bd. dirs. 1990—), Pi Kappa Delta, Sigma Phi Epsilon. Avocations: golf, racquetball, water sports, tennis. Office: Fort Hays State U 600 Park St Bldg 1 Hays KS 67601-4099 E-mail: ehammond@fhsu.edu.

HAMMOND, HAROLD LOGAN, pathology educator, oral and maxillofacial pathologist; b. Hillsboro, Ill., Mar. 18, 1934; s. Harold Thomas and Lillian (Carlson) H.; m. Sharon Bunton, Aug. 1, 1954 (dec. 1974); 1 child, Connie; m. Pat J. Palmer, June 3, 1986. Student Millikin U., 1953-57, Roosevelt U., Chgo., 1957-58; DDS, Loyola U., Chgo., 1962; MS, U. Chgo., 1967. Diplomate Am. Bd. Oral and Maxillofacial Pathology. Intern, U. Chgo. Hosps., Chgo., 1962-63, resident, 1963-66, chief resident in oral pathology, 1966-67; asst. prof. oral pathology U. Iowa, Iowa City, 1967-72, assoc. prof., 1972-80, assoc. prof., dir. surg. oral pathology, 1980-83, prof., dir., 1983—; cons. pathologist Hosp. Gen. de Managua, Nicaragua, 1970-90, VA Hosp., Iowa City, 1977—. Cons. editor: Revista de la Asociation de Nicaragua, 1970-71, Revista de la Federacion Odontologica de Centroamerica y Panama, 1971-77. Contbr. articles to sci. jours. Recipient Mosby Pub. Co. Scholarship award, 1962. Fellow AAAS, Am. Acad. Oral and Maxillofacial Pathology; mem. Am. Men and Women of Sci., N.Y. Acad. Scis., AAUP, Internat. Assn. Oral Pathologists, Internat. Assn. Dental Rsch., N.Am. Soc. Head and Neck Pathologists, Am. Dental Assn., Am. Assn. for Dental Rsch. Avocations: collecting antique clocks, collecting gambling paraphernalia, collecting toys. Home: 1732 Brown Deer Rd Coralville IA 52241-1157 Office: U Iowa Dental Sci Bldg Iowa City IA 52242-1001

HAMMOND, JOHNIE, state legislator; b. Europa, Miss., Aug. 22, 1932; m. Earl Hammond. Student, U. Tex.; BA in Social Work, U. Minn., 1953; BBA in Bus. Mgmt., Iowa State U., 1981. With Story County Bd. of Suprs., 1975-79; mem. Iowa Ho. of Reps., 1982-94, Iowa Senate from 31st dist., 1994—. Mem. nat. adv. com. State Health Care Reform; bd. dirs. ICLU. Mem. First Bapt. Ch., Ames, Moingona Girl Scout Coun., Story County Battered Women's Shelter; bd. dirs. Caring Found. for Children. Mem. LWV, Nat. Coun. State Legislators, Iowa Women's Polit. Caucus, Ams. United for Separation of Ch. and State (mem. nat. adv. com.). Democrat. Home: 3431 Ross Rd Ames IA 50014-3961 Office: State Capitol Dist 31 3 9th And Grand Des Moines IA 50319-0001 E-mail: johnie_hammond@legis.state.ia.us.

HAMMONS, BRIAN KENT, lawyer, business executive; b. Wurzburg, Federal Republic Germany, Mar. 6, 1958; arrived in U.S., 1958; s. R. Dwain and Donna G. (Carender) H.; m. Kimberly M. Pflumm, July 26, 1980; children: April Michelle, David Dwain, Adam Carender. BS summa cum laude, S.W. Mo. State U., Springfield, 1980; JD cum laude, So. Meth. U., Dallas, 1985. Bar: Mo. 1985. Exec., treas., v.p. Hammons Products Co., Stockton, Mo., 1980-86, exec. v.p., sec., 1987-96, pres., COO, CEO, 1997—; assoc. Stinson, Mag & Fizzell, Kansas City, Mo., 1986-87. Mem. Stockton Airport Bd., 1987-89, Stockton City Coun., 1989-91; pres. Stockton Cmty. Found.; cub scout leader Boy Scouts Am.; Sunday sch. tchr.; soccer coach. Mem. Mo. Bar Assn., Masons (sec. 1980-81), Lions (pres. 1990-91), Leadership Mo., Young Presidents Orgn., Phi Delta Phi. Republican. Methodist. Avocations: running, flying, tennis, golf, hunting. Office: Hammons Products Co 105 Hammons Dr PO Box 140 Stockton MO 65785

HAMMONS, JOHN Q. hotel executive; Chmn., CEO John Q. Hammons Hotels, Inc. and Cos., Springfield, Mo. Office: John Q Hammons Hotels Inc & Cos #900 300 John Q Hammons Pkwy Springfield MO 65806

HAMNER, LANCE DALTON, prosecutor; b. Fukuoka, Japan, Sept. 18, 1955; parents Am. citizens; s. Louie D. and Mary Louise (Sloan) H.; m. Karla Jean Cleverly, Sept. 22, 1980; children: Lance Dalton Jr., Nicholas James, Louie Alexander, Samuel Sean, Victoria Jean. BS summa cum laude, Weber State Coll., 1984; JD magna cum laude, Ind. U., 1987. Bar: Ind., U.S. Dist. Ct. (no., so. dist.) Ind. 1988. Atty. Barnes & Thornburg,

Indpls., 1988-89; dep. prosecuting atty. Marion County Prosecutor's Office, 1989-90; pros. atty. Johnson County, Franklin, Ind., 1990—. Legal corr. WGGR Radio News, Indpls., 1995; adj. prof. law Sch. Law Ind. U., Indpls., 1995—96, Bloomington, 1996—98; frequent spkr. on legal topics including search and seizure and interrogation law; lectr. Ind. Continuing Legal Edn. Forum, Indpls., 1992; mem. faculty Newly-Elected Pros. Sch. Ind. Pros. Attys. Coun., 1999; mem. faculty Indpls. Police Acad., 1999, Ind. Police Corps, 2000—. Author: Indiana Search & Seizure Courtroom Manual, 2001—02; editor: Ind. Law Jour., 1987. Asst. scoutmaster Boy Scouts Am., Franklin, Ind., 1995-99, scoutmaster, 1999—. Mem. Nat. Dist. Attys. Assn., Assn. Govt. Attys. in Capital Litigation, Ind. Prosecuting Atty.'s Coun., Nat. Eagle Scout Assn., Order of the Coif. Republican. Mem. LDS Ch. Avocations: family, fitness, writing. Office: Prosecutor's Office Courthouse Annex N 18 W Jefferson St Franklin IN 46131-2353

HAMPEL, ROBERT EDWARD, advertising executive; b. Cin., Apr. 29, 1941; s. John Edward and Ruth Elizabeth (Pister) H.; m. Nanci Jean Nau, Aug. 24, 1963; 1 child, Jeffrey Braam. BBA, U. Cin., 1964; MBA, U. Evansville, 1980. Asst. account mgr. Procter and Gamble, Balt., 1965, corp. forecaster Cin., 1966-68; asst. contr. Keller-Crescent Co., Evansville, Ind., 1968-71; dir. mgmt. info. svcs. Keller-Crescent div. Am. Standards, 1971-76, exec. v.p. fin., 1976-85, sr. exec. v.p., 1985-86; sr. exec. v.p., sec., treas., CFO Keller-Crescent Co., Inc., 1987—, bd. dirs. Bd. dirs. Hahn, Inc. Pres. Jr. Achievement of S.W. Ind., Evansville, 1976-77, Evansville Philharm., 1981-82; pres. United Way of S.W. Ind., 1988-89; bd. dirs. Evansville Mus. Arts and Scis., 1988-95, treas., 1987-88; treas. Evansville Regional Econ. Devel. Corp., 1994—. Mem. Nat. Assn. Accts. (pres. Evansville chpt. 1980-81, nat. bd. dirs. 1984-85, nat. com. 1985-87). Home: 10727 Coach Light Dr Evansville IN 47725-8674 Office: Keller-Crescent Co Inc 1100 E Louisiana St PO Box 3 Evansville IN 47701-0003

HAMPER, ROBERT JOSEPH, marketing executive; b. Chgo., May 20, 1956; s. Robert William and Barbara Jean Hamper. BSBA with honors, Ill. State U., 1977, MBA with honors, 1979; ABD, Northern Ill. U., 1999. Fin. mgr. Ill. Bell, Chgo., 1979-82; staff mgr. AT&T, Basking Ridge, N.J., 1982-84; mem. tech. staff Bell labs., Homedale, 1983-84; sr. staff. mgr. market analysis Ameritech Svcs., Schaumburg, Ill., 1985-87; dir. strategic planning Ameritech Corp., Chgo., 1987-90; pres. R.J. Hamper Bus. Cons., River Forest, 1981—, mgr. investment fund, 1990—. Asst. prof. fin. and mktg. Dominican U., River Forest, 1983-98; adj. prof. fin. Loyola U., Chgo., 1988—; seminar presenter in field; career counselor, 1985—. Author: Developing a Profitable Marketing Plan: Text and Cases, 1987, Marketing and Planning Forms, 1987, Strategic Market Planning, 1990, 92, 94, 95, 97, 99, Handbook for Proposal Writing, 1995, 97, 98, 2000; contbg. author: College Business Math, 1995, 97, 99; contbr. articles to profl. jours. Leader Boy Scouts Am., Park Forest, Ill., 1979-83. Mem. Am. Mktg. Assn. (exec.), Am. Mgmt. Assn., Fin. Mgmt. Assn., Am. Fin. Assn., Am. Hosp. Assn. Home and Office: 730 Clinton Pl River Forest IL 60305-1914

HAMPTON, PHILIP MICHAEL, consulting engineering company executive; b. Asheville, N.C., Sept. 5, 1932; s. Boyd Walker and Helen Reba (Smith) H.; m. Wilma Christine Gross, July 7, 1951; children: Philip Michael, Deborah Lynn, Gregg Ashley. A.B. in Geology, Berea Coll., 1954. Draftsman-designer Johnson & Anderson, Inc., Pontiac, Mich., 1955-57, designer, also project mgr., 1957-59, dir. bus. devel., 1962-76, v.p., 1966-74, exec. v.p., 1974-76; v.p. Spalding G. DeDecker & Assos., Inc., Madison Heights, Mich., 1976-84; founder, pres. Hampton Engring. Assocs., Inc., 1985—; pres. HMA Consultants Inc., 1977—, Geo Internat., Inc., 1978—. V.p. JAVLEN Internat., 1971-73, Micuda-Hampton Assocs., Inc., 1985-86; co-founder, owner My World Shops and Hampton Galleries, Ltd., 1976-90; co-owner Hampton-Tyedten Galleries Ltd., 1979-81; mem. public adv. panel GSA, 1977-78; chmn. task force of com. fed. procurement of architect/engr. svcs. ABA, 1977-79. Editor: Total Scope, 1963-71. Pres. Waterford Bd. Edn., 1969-71; mem. state resolution com. Democratic Conv., 1972; exec. com. Oakland County Dem. Com., 1973-74; precinct del., 1972-76, 80—; trustee Environ. Research Assocs., sec.-treas., 1969-71, pres., 1971-73; chmn. Waterford Cable Communications Commn., 1981-88; mem. Cultural Council Pontiac, 1987-90; bd. dirs. Oakland C. of C., 1972-74, Readings for the Blind, Inc., 2002-; chmn. utilities com. Oakland Bus. Roundtable, 1993—; vice chmn. Pontiac Urban League, 1996—. Named to Honorable Order Ky. Colonels. Fellow Am. Cons. Engrs. Coun. (internat. engring. com. 1971-76, vice chmn. pub. rels. com. 1970-72, chmn. publs. com. 1972-74, chmn. ABA model procurement code com. 1977-79, nat. dir. 1986-89, mem. com. fellows 1988—, Pres. award 1990); ASCE, AAAS, mem. Nat. Water Well Assn. (chmn. tech. div. 1969-71), Cons. Engrs. Coun. Mich. (awards com. 1970-74), Am. Arbitration Assn. (comml. panel 1977—), Pontiac C. of C. (co-founder 1989), Oakland Bus. Roundtable (charter). Presbyterian. Clubs: Pontiac Exchange, Pontiac-Detroit Lions Quarterback Club (co-founder). Home and Office: 2440 Ostrum St Waterford MI 48328-1829 Office: 35 W Huron St Ste 801 Pontiac MI 48342-2128

HAMPTON, VERNE CHURCHILL, II, lawyer; b. Pontiac, Mich., Jan. 5, 1934; s. Verne Churchill and Mildred (Peck) H.; m. Stephanie Hall, Oct. 5, 1973; children: J. Howard, Timothy H., Julia C. Thibodeau. BA, Mich. State U., 1955; LLB, U. Va., 1958. Bar: Mich. 1958. Since practiced in, Detroit; ptnr. firm Dickinson Wright, 1967—. Bd. dirs., sec. Carhartt, Inc., R & R Radio Corp. Mem. Mich. Rep. Fin. Com.; bd. dirs. Detroit Bus./Edn. Alliance; corp. mem. Boys' Clubs Met. Detroit. Mem. ABA, State Bar Mich. (chmn. bus. law sect. 1980-84), Detroit Athletic Club, Country Club Detroit, Yondotega Club, Sigma Alpha Epsilon, Phi Alpha Delta. Republican. Episcopalian. Home: 360 Provencal Rd Grosse Pointe Farms MI 48236-2959 Office: Dickinson Wright PLLC 500 Woodward Ave Ste 4000 Detroit MI 48226-3416 E-mail: vhampton@dickinson-wright.com.

HAMRICK, LINDA L. educator; b. Fort Wayne, Ind., Feb. 14, 1954; BS in Edn., Ball State U., 1977; MS in Edn., Ind. U., 1980; EdD in Ednl. Leadership, Ball State U., 1991. Cert. tchr., sch. adminstr., supt., Ind. Tchr. Fort Wayne (Ind.) Cmty. Schs., 1978—; adminstrv. intern Ft. Wayne (Ind.) Cmty. Schs., 1997—; educator-YIC Whitley County Probation, Columbia City, Ind., 1997—. Assoc. faculty Ind. U., 1987, 88; sch. supt. internship N.W. Allen County Schs., Fort Wayne, 1990-91. Site dir. youth basketball Ft. Wayne YMCA, 1982-86; site supr. Ft. Wayne Park Dept., 1980-85. Mem. AAPHERD, Ind. Middle Level Educators Assn., Internat. Reading Assn., Am. Endurance Ride Conf., Internat. Arabian Horse Assn., Upper Midwest Endurance Ride Conf. Avocations: horse riding endurance, snowmobiling, downhill skiing, boating, water skiing. Office: South Side HS 3601 S Calhoun St Fort Wayne IN 46807-2006

HAN, KENNETH, dean; b. Seoul, Korea, July 3, 1938; came to U.S., 1965; s. Chyi-Kyung and Taeksoon (Shim) H.; m. Helen Hyi-won Rho, Sept. 1, 1967; children: Iris, Vincent, Allison. BS, Seoul Nat. U., 1961, MS, 1963, U. Ill., 1967; PhD, U. Calif., Berkeley, 1971. Lectr. Monash U., Melbourne, Australia, 1971-74, sr. lectr. Australia, 1974-81; assoc. prof. S.D. Sch. Mines, Rapid City, 1981-84, prof., 1984-87, dept. head metallurgy, 1987-94, dean, 1994-99, Bd. of Regents disting. prof., 1995—. Author: Mineral Processing and Extractive Metallurgy, 1981, Recovery and Sampling of Precious Metals, 1989; editor-in-chief Gordon & Breach, 1986—; patentee in field. Recipient Arthur F. Taggett award, 1995, Milton Wadsworth award, 1995, Ernest L. Buckley award, 1994, award for Excellence in Rsch., S.D. Bd. Regents, 1998. Mem. AIME (disting. mem., chmn. 1996-97, Mineral Industry Edn. award 2000), NAE, Soc. Mining, Metallurgy and Exploration. Republican. Home: SD Sch Mines 5499 Blue Stem Ct Rapid City SD 57702-8205 Office: SD Sch Mines 501 E Saint Joseph St Rapid City SD 57701-3901 E-mail: knah@silver.sdsmt.edu.

HANCOCK, JAMES BEATY, interior designer; b. Hartford, Ky. s. James Winfield Scott and Hettie Frances (Meadows) H. BA, Hardin-Simmons U., 1948, MA, 1952. Head interior design dept. Thornton's, Abilene, Tex., 1945-54; interior designer The Halle Bros. Co., Cleve., 1954-55; v.p. Olympic Products, 1955-56; mgr., interior designer Bell Drapery Shops of Ohio, Inc., Shaker Heights, 1957-78, v.p., 1979—. Lectr. interior design, Abilene and Cleve.; works include 6 original murals Broadway Theater, Abilene, 1940, mural Skyline Outdoor Theatre, Abilene, 1950, cover designs for Isotopics mag., 1958-60. Mem. Western Res. Hist. Soc., Cleve Mus. Art, Decorative Arts Trust. Served with AUS, 1942-46. Recipient 2d place award of oil painting West Tex. Expn., 1940, honorable mention, 1940. Mem. Abilene Mus. Fine Arts (charter) Cleve. Cir. of the Decorative Arts Trust (charter). Home and Office: 1 Bratenahl Pl Apt 103 Cleveland OH 44108-1152 E-mail: hancockjb@aol.com.

HANCOCK, MEL, former congressman; b. Cape Fair, Mo., Sept. 14, 1929; BS, S.W. Mo. State Coll., 1951. Chmn. bd. dirs. Fed. Protection Inc.; with Internat. Harvester Co.; mem. 101st-104th Congresses from 7th Mo. Dist., 1989-96; mem. ways and means com. Chmn. Taxpayer's Survival Assn. With USAF, USAFR. Mem. Nat. Rifle Assn. (life), Farm Bur., Am. Legion. Republican. Mem. Ch. of Christ. Office: 6220 W Farm Rd #140 Springfield MO 65802

HAND, ELBERT O. clothing manufacturing and retailing company executive; b. 1939; BS, Hamilton Coll., 1961. With Hart Schaffner and Marx, 1964-83; pres., chief exec. officer men's apparel group Hartmarx Corp., 1983-85, pres., 1985—, then pres., chief operating officer, chmn., chief exec. officer, 1992—. Office: Hartmarx Corp 101 N Wacker Dr Chicago IL 60606-1718

HAND, ROGER, physician, educator; b. Bklyn., Sept. 25, 1938; s. Morton and Angela (Belvedere) H.; children: Christopher, Jessica. BS, NYU, 1959, MD, 1962. Intern, then resident in internal medicine NYU Med. Ctr., 1962-68; postdoctoral fellow, asst. prof. Rockefeller U., N.Y.C., 1968-73; clin. asst. prof. medicine Cornell U. Med. Coll., 1970-73; asst. prof., then assoc. prof. medicine McGill U., Montreal, Que., Can., 1973-80; prof. medicine, dir. McGill Cancer Ctr., 1980-84; sr. physician Royal Victoria Hosp., Montreal, 1980-84; chmn. internal medicine Ill. Masonic Ctr., Chgo., 1984-88; prof. medicine U. Ill., 1984—, chief sect. gen. internal medicine, 1988-95, prof. health policy and adminstrn. Sch. Pub. Health, 1995—. Prin. clin. coord. Ill. Found. Quality Health Care, Chgo., 1996-2000; physician advisor OLR Med. Ctr., Chgo., 2000—. Contbr. articles to profl. jours. Brig. gen. USAR, 1963-71, 85—. Decorated Air medal, Meritorious Svc. medal, Army Commendation medal; med. rsch. grantee. Fellow ACP, Royal Coll. Physicians and Surgeons, Am. Coll. Med. Quality; mem. Am. Soc. Clin. Investigation, Am. Soc. Biol. Chemists, Am. Assn. Cancer Research, Am. Soc. Clin. Oncology, Infectious Disease Soc., Can. Soc. Clin. Investigation, Cen. Soc. Clin. Rsch., Am. Cancer Soc.(bd. dirs. Ill. div.), Am. Health Quality Assn. Office: OLR Med Ctr 5645 W Addison St Chicago IL 60634-4403 E-mail: rhand@reshealthcare.org.

HANDEL, DAVID JONATHAN, health care administrator; b. N.Y.C., Jan. 2, 1946; s. Milton M. and Ruth (Stamer) H.; m. Julia Elizabeth Noll, June 26, 1971; chldren: Daniel, Jennifer. BS, Cornell U., 1966; MBA, U. Chgo., 1968. Assoc. planning coordinator for health scis. Northwestern U., Chgo., 1970-73, adminstr. Northwestern U. Med. Clinics and Med. Assocs., 1973-76; dir. planning and implementation Mid-Ohio Health Planning Fedn., Columbus, Ohio, 1976-79; assoc. hosp. adminstr. Vanderbilt U. Hosps., Nashville, 1979-82, assoc. dir. ops., 1982-85; dir. Ind. U. Hosps., Indpls., 1985-96; exec. v.p., COO Clarian Health Ptnrs., Inc., 1997—. V.p. United Hosp. Svcs., Indpls., 1986-88, pres., 1989-90, Bedford Reg. Med. Ctr., 1997—, La Porte Regional Health Sys., Inc., 1998—, Rehab. Hosp. Ind., 1999—, v.p., 2002-; pres. Goshen Health Sys., 2000—. Contbr. articles to profl. jours. Sr. asst. health svcs. officer USPHS, 1968-70. Fellow Am. Coll. Health Care Execs.; mem. Ind. Hosp. Assn. (bd. dirs. 1994-97). Office: Clarian Health 550 University Blvd Indianapolis IN 46202-5149

HANDELMAN, HOWARD, political scientist, educator; b. N.Y.C., Apr. 29, 1943; s. Victor and Ruth (Goodman) H.; m. Nancy Rae Forster, Sept. 22, 1967; 1 child, Michael Jesse. Student, London Sch. Econs., 1963-64; BA, U. Pa., 1965; MA in polit. sci., U. Wis., 1967; PhD in polit. sci., U.Wis., 1971. Instr. Ctr. for Latin Am., U. Milw., 1970-71, asst. prof., 1971-76, assoc. prof., 1976-81, prof., 1981—. Faculty assoc. Am. Universities Field Staff, Hanover, N.H., 1978-80. Author: Struggle in the Andes, 1974, Military Rule and the Road to Democracy in South America, 1981, The Politics of Rural Change in Asia and Latin America, 1981; co-author, editor: Paying the Costs of Austerity in South America, 1989; co-author: Politics in a Changing World, 1993, 2d edit., 1998, The Challenge of Third World Development, 1996, Mexican Politics, 1997. Mem. Latin Am. Studies Assn. Jewish. Avocations: jogging, music, raquetball. Office: U Wis-Milw Polit Sci Dept PO Box 413 Milwaukee WI 53201-0413

HANDLEMAN, DAVID, audio products company executive; b. 1914; married. With Handleman Co., Inc., Troy, Mich., 1937—, sec.-treas., 1946-66, chmn., dir., 1966—, also CEO, 1966-91. Office: Handleman Co 500 Kirts Blvd PO Box 7045 Troy MI 48007-7045

HANDRICK, JOSEPH W. state legislator; b. Nov. 2, 1965; BA, U. Wis. Assemblyman Wis. State Dist. 34, 1994—, mem. census and redistricting com., 1999—, chair assembly com., 1999—. Mem. Oneida County, Wis. Mem. Wis. Equal Rights Coun. Mem. Minocqua Lakes Improvement Assn. (bd. dirs.). Address: PO Box 604 Minocqua WI 54548-0604

HANDY, RICHARD LINCOLN, civil engineer, educator; b. Chariton, Iowa, Feb. 12, 1929; s. Walter Newton and Florence Elizabeth (Shoemaker) H.; married, Apr. 18, 1964 (div. 1980); 1 child, Beth Susan.; m. Kathryn Etona Claussen, Feb. 13, 1982. BS in Geology, Iowa State U., 1951, MS, 1953, PhD in Soil Engring. and Geology, 1956. Asst. prof. civil engring. Iowa State U., Ames, 1956-59, assoc. prof., 1959-63, prof., 1963-87, disting. prof., 1987-91, disting. prof. emeritus, 1991—; prof.-in-charge Spangler Geotech. Lab., 1963-91; cons. in soil engring., soil and rock testing, landslide stabilization; v.p. research W.N. Handy Co., 1958-91, chmn. bd., 1986-90; pres. Handy Geotech. Instruments, Inc., 1980-93, chmn. bd. dirs., 1993—; mem., chmn. bd. dirs. Geopier Found. Co., L.C., 1993-95. Author: The Day the House Fell, 1995; co-author: (with M.G. Spangler) Soil Engineering 3rd edit., 1972, 4th edit. 1983; contbr. articles to profl. jours. Recipient faculty citation Iowa State U., 1976; named Anson Marston Disting. Prof. Engring., Iowa State U., 1987. Fellow AAAS, Geol. Soc. Am., Iowa Acad. Sci.; mem. ASCE (Thomas A. Middlebrooks award 1986), Soil Sci. Soc. Am., Internat. Soc. Soil Mech. and Found. Engrs. Achievements include patents in soils field. Home and Office: 1502 270th St Madrid IA 50156-7522 E-mail: rlhandy@pionet.net.

HANE, MIKISO, history educator; b. Hollister, Calif., Jan. 16, 1922; s. Ichitaro and Hifuyo (Taoka) H.; m. Rose Michiko Kanemoto, Sept. 19, 1948; children: Laurie Shizue, Jennifer Kazuko. BA, Yale U., 1952, MA, 1953, PhD, 1957. Asst. prof. history U. Toledo, Ohio, 1959-61, Knox Coll., Galesburg, Ill., 1961-66, assoc. prof. history, 1966-72, prof. history, 1972-92, prof. emeritus, 1993—. Author: Japan, A Historical Survey, 1972, Peasants, Rebels and Outcasts, 1982, Emperor Hirohito and His Chief Aide, 1982; editor, translator: Reflections on the Way to the Gallows, 1988, Eastern Phoenix: Japan Since 1945, 1996, Japan, A Short History, 2000. Fulbright grantee, 1957-58, Japan Found. grantee, 1973, NEH grantee, 1979-80. Mem. Assn. for Asian Studies (bd. dirs. 1985-88), Am. Hist. Assn. (teaching div. 1980-83), Midwest Conf. on Asian Affairs (pres. 1988), Nat. Coun. on Humanities. Buddhist. Home: 2285 N Broad St Galesburg IL 61401-1454 Office: Knox Coll History Dept South St Galesburg IL 61401 E-mail: mhane@knox.edu.

HANEY, TRACY, radio personality; b. Little Rock, Jan. 6, 1963; m. Lisa Haney; 1 child. Radio host of Midday Connection Sta. WMBI Radio, Chgo. Office: WMBI 820 N LaSalle Blvd Chicago IL 60610*

HANFORD, PAT, performing company executive; Exec. dir. Tulsa Ballet, Ballet Internationale, 2002—. Office: Ballet Internationale 502 N Capitol Ave Ste B Indianapolis IN 46204 Office Fax: 317-637-1637.*

HANKET, MARK JOHN, lawyer; b. Jan. 28, 1943; s. Laddie W. and Florence J. (Kubat) H.; m. Carole A. Dalpiaz, Sept. 14, 1968; children: Gregory, Jennifer, Sarah. AB magna cum laude, John Carroll U., 1965; JD cum laude, Ohio State U., 1968; MBA, Xavier U., 1977. Bar: Ohio 1968, Mich. 1993. Atty. Chemed Corp., Cin., 1973-77, asst. sec., 1977-82, sec., 1982-84, v.p., sec., 1984-86; v.p., gen counsel DuBois Chems. Divsn., 1986-87; v.p., sec. gen. counsel DuBois Chems., Inc., 1987-91; sec. gen. counsel Diversey Corp., 1991-94, v.p., sec. gen. counsel, 1994-96; v.p. law and people excellence, sec. Americlean Sys., Inc., 1996-99; asst. gen. counsel Diversey Lever, Inc., 1999—2002; sr. counsel JohnsonDiversey, Inc., Southfield, Mich., 2002—. Capt. U.S. Army, 1968—73. Decorated Meritorious Svc. medal, Army Commendation medal with oak leaf cluster. Mem. ABA, Mich. Bar Assn., Am. Corp. Counsel Assn., Ohio Bar Assn. Office: JohnsonDiversey Inc 29435 Northwestern Hwy Ste 400 Southfield MI 48034-8449 E-mail: mark.hanket@diverseylever.com.

HANKS, ALAN R. chemistry educator; b. Balt., Nov. 30, 1939; s. Raymond Hanks and Lillian (Simon) Miller; m. Beverly Jean Hinson, Jan. 17, 1961; children: Craig, Denise, Leta. BS in Physics, West Tex. State U., 1962; MS in Biophys. Chemistry, N. Mex. Highlands U., 1964; PhD in Biophysics, Pa. State U., 1967. Nuclear med. sci. officer Armed Forces Inst. Pathology, Washington, 1967-69; from asst. to prof. biochemistry, biophysics Tex. A&M U., Coll. Sta., Tex., 1969-82; state chemist, seed commnr., prof. Purdue U., West Lafayette, Ind., 1982—. Corr. mem., liaison Collaborative Internat. Pesticide Analytical Coun., 1988—; mem. FAO panel on pesticides UN, 1991—, mem. WHO panel on pesticides, 2001—. Contbr. articles to profl. jours. Fellow Assn. Ofcl. Analytical Chemists (chmn. methods bd. 1986-89, bd. dirs. 1990-96, sec.-treas. 1992-93, pres.-elect 1993-94, pres. 1994-95, immediate past pres. 1995-96, chmn. liaison com. 1997-2001); mem. Assn. Am. Feed Control Ofcls. (chmn. minerals com. 1985-96, pres.-elect 1998-99, pres. 1999-2000, immediate past pres. 2000-2001, lab. methods and svc. com. 1988-93, bd. dirs. 1996-2001), Assn. Am. Plant Food Control Ofcls. (chmn. Magruder check sample com. 1988-90, bd. dirs. 1989-94, chmn. environ. affairs com. 1990-99, pres.-elect 1991-92, pres. 1992-93, past pres. 1993-94). Avocations: fishing, gardening, sports, travel. Home: PO Box 2627 West Lafayette IN 47996-2627 Office: Purdue U 1154 Biochemistry West Lafayette IN 47907-1154 E-mail: hanksa@purdue.edu.

HANKS, CARL THOMAS, oral pathology educator, researcher; b. Cushing, Okla., Aug. 10, 1939; s. John Carl and Ruby Jewel (Bias) H.; m. Judith Melinda Sharp, Dec. 30, 1961; children: Stephanie Brett, John Conrad. BS, Phillips U., 1961; DDS, Washington U., St. Louis, 1964; PhD, SUNY, Buffalo, 1970. Diplomate Am. Bd. Pathology. Asst. prof. oral pathology SUNY, Buffalo, 1969-70; with Sch. of Dentistry U. Mich., Ann Arbor, 1970—, assoc. prof. Sch. of Medicine, 1978—, prof. oral pathology Sch. of Dentistry, 1979—. Contbr. articles to profl. jours. Fogarty Found. Internat. Fellow, 1976. Mem. Internat. Assn. for Dental Rsch. (pres. sect. 1989—), Am. Acad. Oral Pathology, Nat. Tissue Culture Assn., AAAS, Pulp Biology Group. Democrat. Home: 1276 Kuehnle Ct Ann Arbor MI 48103-2628 Office: U Mich 1011 E University Ave Ann Arbor MI 48104-3916

HANLEY, MICHAEL JOSEPH, state legislator; b. Saginaw, Mich., Dec. 9, 1955; s. Richard Albert and Doreen Ann (Goodrow) H.; m. Susi Arndt; 1 child, Nicholas. BA summa cum laude, Western Mich. U., 1987. Mayor pro tem, Saginaw, 1991-93; rep. Mich. State Dist. 95, 1995—. Saginaw City Coun., 1987-93; mem. Mich. Ho. Reps., 1995—, legis. coun., house minority leader 1999—, mem. ho. fiscal governing bd., house TV oversight. Mem. NAACP. Address: State Capitol Lansing MI 48913-0001

HANLEY, THOMAS PATRICK, obstetrician-gynecologist; b. St. Louis, Apr. 16, 1951; s. Thomas P. and Virginia Barbara (Lydon) H.; m. Patricia Ann McHargue, Dec. 27, 1975; children: Colleen, Thomas III, Timothy, Matthew. BA, St. Louis U., 1973, MD, 1977. Diplomate Am. Bd. Ob-gyn. Intern St. Louis U., 1977-78, resident, 1978-81; practice medicine specializing in ob-gyn St. Louis, 1981—; pres. med. staff St. Mary's Health Ctr., 1993; mem. staff Mo. Bapt. Hosp., Forest Park Hosp.; assoc. clin. prof. St. Louis U. Med. Sch., 1983—. Mem. exec. com. St. Louis Med. Group, 1995-2000. Mem. AMA (Physicians Recognition award 1981—), Am. Coll. Ob-Gyn. (Physicians Excellence award 1986—), Gynecol. Laser Soc., St. Louis Gynecol. Soc. (pres. 1989-90), St. Louis Met. Med. Soc., West Borough Country Club. Republican. Roman Catholic. Avocation: golf. Office: 1035 Bellevue Ave Ste 208 Saint Louis MO 63117-1846

HANNA, MARSHA L. artistic director; b. Tiffin, Ohio, Nov. 27, 1951; d. Willis Leondadis and Frances Lucille (Neeley) H. BS, Bowling Green State U., 1980. Drama specialist City of Dayton, Ohio, 1975-80; gen. mgr. Illumination Theatre, 1978-85; product analyst Mead Data Ctrl., 1980-86; instr. Sinclair C.C., 1986—; freelance stage dir., 1986—; resident dir. Human Race Theatre Co., 1986—, artistic dir., 1990—. Dir.: Equus, 1981, Beyond Therapy, 1983, The Diviners, 1984, Amadeus, 1985, The Fantasticks, 1986, Getting Out, 1987, Orphans, 1988, Fool for Love, 1989, A Shayna Maidel, 1990, A Christmas Carol, 1991, Steel Magnolias, 1992, The Elephant Man, 1993, Closer Than Ever, 1993, The Good Times Are Killing Me, 1994, Cloud Nine, 1995, Three Tall Women, 1996, The Cherry Orchard, 1996, Quilters, 1997, Taking Sides, Stonewall Jackson's House, 1998, On Golden Pond, 1999, Three Days of Rain, 1999, Art, 2000, Resident Alien, 2001, I Hate Hamlet, 2002. Office: The Human Race Theatre Co 126 N Main St Ste 300 Dayton OH 45402-1766

HANNA, MARTIN SHAD, lawyer; b. Bowling Green, Ohio, Aug. 4, 1940; s. Martin Lester and Julia Loyal (Moor) H.; m. Ann I. Amos; children: Jennifer Lynn, Jonathan Moor, Katharine Anne. Student, Bowling Green State U.; B.S., Purdue U., 1962; J.D., Am. U., 1965. Bar: Ohio 1965, D.C. 1967, U.S. Supreme Ct. 1969. Ptnr. Hanna, Middleton & Roebke, 1965-70; ptnr. Hanna & Hanna, Bowling Green, 1971—. Spl. counsel for atty. gen. Ohio, 1969-71, 82-85, Ohio Bd. Regents, 1974; instr. Bowling Green State U., 1970, Ohio Div. Vocat. Edn., 1970— , Ohio Peace Officer Tng. Council, 1968; legal adviser NW Ohio Vol. Firemen's Assn., 1970— Contbr. articles to profl. publs. Elder, lay minister Presbyn. Ch.; state chmn. Ohio League Young Republican Clubs, 1972-73; nat. vice chmn. Young Rep. Nat. Fedn., 1973-75, counselor to chmn., 1975-77; cive chmn. Wood County Rep. Exec. Com., Ohio, 1972-80, precinct committeeman, 1968-80; trustee Bowling Green State U., 1976-86; mem. Ohio State Fire Commn., 1979-87; mem. Ohio Rural Fire coun., 1993—. Recipient George Washington honor medal award Freedoms Found. at Valley Forge, 1969, award of merit Ohio Legal Ctr. Inst., 1973, Robert A. Taft Disting. Service award, 1974, James A. Rhodes Leadership award, 1975; named one of 10 Outstanding Young Men, Ohio Jaycees, 1968. Mem. ABA, D.C. Bar Assn., Ohio Bar Assn., Northwest Ohio Bar Assn., Wood County Bar Assn.,

Toledo Bar Assn., Am. Trauma Soc. (trauma and law com.), Phi Delta Phi, Pi Kappa Delta, Omicron Delta Kappa Home: PO Box 1137 Bowling Green OH 43402-1137 Office: Hanna & Hanna 700 N Main St Bowling Green OH 43402-1815

HANNA, MILFORD A. agricultural engineering educator; b. West Middlesex, Pa., Feb. 26, 1947; s. Clayton S. and Clara (Burrows) H.; m. Lenora J. Uhrmacher, May 13, 1978; children: Michelle L., Charles C., Susan R., Andrew A. BS, Pa. State U., 1969, MS, 1971, PhD, 1973. Asst. prof. Calif. Poly. State U., San Luis Obispo, Calif., 1973-75, U. Nebr., Lincoln, 1975-79, assoc. prof., 1979-85, prof., 1985—, prof. food engring., 1990—, dir. Indsl. Agrl. Products Ctr., 1991—. Contbr. more than 70 articles to profl. jours. Recipient Rsch. award of Merit, Gamma Sigma Delta, 1991. Fellow Am. Soc. Agrl. Engrs. (chmn. Food Processing Engring. Inst. 1991-92, Engr. of Yr. Nebr. sect. 1991), Am. Assn. Cereal Chemists, Coun. for Agrl. Sci. and Tech., Kiwanis (gov. Nebr.-Iowa dist. 1992-93) dist. chmn. Worldwide Srvs. Project, 1994. Achievements include patent pending on starch-based plastic foams. Office: U Nebr 211 L W Chase Hall W Lincoln NE 68583-0730

HANNA, NESSIM, marketing educator; b. Assiut, Egypt, Apr. 30, 1938; came to U.S., 1961, naturalized, 1973; s. Yanni and Lulu Shehata (Oweda) H.; m. Dana Lascu, Aug. 28, 1987 (div. 1988); m. Margaret Ann Curzan, 1996. BS in Commerce, Cairo U., 1958; MS in Mktg., U. Ill., 1964, PhD in Mktg, 1969. Asst. prof., chmn. dept. mktg. W.Va. Inst. Tech., Montgomery, 1968-69; asso. prof. bus. adminstrn. Middle Tenn. State U., Murfreesboro, 1969-70; prof. mktg. No. Ill. U., De Kalb, 1970—; mktg. cons. Arab Research and Admintrn. Center, 1975-77, Investments Cons. Internat., 1974-77. Vis. prof. mktg. U. Petroleum and Minirals, Dharan, Saudi Arabia, 1980-81, Norwegian Sch. Mgmt., Oslo, 1988; chmn. dept. mktg., dir. research inst. King Saud U., Kassim, Saudi Arabia, 1983-84; vis. scholar Hong Kong Bapt. U., fall 1991. Author: Marketing Opportunities in Egypt: A Business Guide, 1977, Principles of Marketing, 1985, Pricing Policies and Procedures, 1995, Winning Strategies, 1991, Consumer Behavior: An Applied Approach, 2001; contbr. articles to profl. jours. Named Outstanding Citizen Citizenship Council Met. Chgo., 1974 Mem. Southwestern Social Sci. Assn., Am. Mktg. Assn., Midwest Bus. Adminstrn. Assn., Assn. Egyptian-Am. Scholars (treas.), Acad. Mktg. Sci., Am. Inst. Decision Scis., Phi Beta Lambda, Beta Gamma Sigma, Phi Kappa Phi, Alpha Mu Alpha. Republican. Christian Orthodox. Avocation: overseas travel. Home: Ste 2402 5415 N Sheridan Rd Apt 2402 Chicago IL 60640-1939 Office: No Ill U Dept Mktg Dekalb IL 60115 E-mail: nhanna@niu.edu.

HANNAH, WAYNE ROBERTSON, JR. lawyer; b. Freeport, Ill., Aug. 18, 1931; s. Wayne Robertson and Edith (Biene) H.; m. Patricia Anne Matthews, June 1, 1957; children— Tamara Lee, Wendy, Wayne Robertson III B.A., Ill. Coll., 1953; J.D., NYU, 1957. Bar: Ill. 1957, U.S. Dist. Ct. (no. dist.) Ill., U.S. Supreme Ct. Ptnr. Sonnenschein, Nath & Rosenthal, Chgo., 1965—. Dir. Checker Motors Corp., N.Y.C. and Kalamazoo, 1982-86; lectr. Ill. Inst. Continuing Edn. Sec. 7th cir. Root-Tilden Scholarship Program NYU, 1967-94; chmn. Root-Tilden-Kern scholarship com., 1981-86, trustee law ctr., 1985—; pres. bd. Firman Cmty. Svcs, Chgo., 1972-75; trustee, pres., chmn. bd. Chgo. City Ballet, 1982-86. 2d lt. USMC, 1951-54. Root-Tilden scholar NYU, 1954-57; Fulbright scholar, 1953-54 Mem. ABA (real estate com.), Chgo. Bar Assn. (chmn. condominium subcom. real estate com. 1977-78, sec., dir. condominium assn. 1991—), Ill. Bar Assn. (real estate com.), Econ. Club (Chgo.), Skokie Country Club (Glencoe, Ill.). Presbyterian. Avocations: tennis; golf. Office: Sonnenschein Nath and Rosenthal 233 S Wacker Dr Ste 8000 Chicago IL 60606-6491 E-mail: wrh@sonnenschein.com.

HANNAY, WILLIAM MOUAT, III, lawyer; b. Kansas City, Mo., Dec. 3, 1944; s. William Mouat and Gladys (Capron) H.; m. Donna Jean Harkins, Sept. 30, 1978; children: Capron Grace, Blaike Ann, William Mouat IV. BA, Yale U., 1966; JD, Georgetown U., 1973. Bar: Mo. 1973, D.C. 1974, N.Y. 1975, Ill. 1980. Law clk. to Judge Myron Bright, U.S. Ct. Appeals, 8th Cir., St. Louis, 1973-74; law clk. to Justice Tom Clark U.S. Supreme Ct., Washington, 1974-75; assoc. Weil Gotshal & Manges, N.Y.C., 1975-77; asst. dist. atty. New York County Dist. Atty.'s Office, 1977-79; ptnr. Schiff Hardin & Waite, Chgo., 1979—. Adj. prof. IIT/Chgo.-Kent Law Sch., 1983—. Author: International Trade: Avoiding Criminal Risks, Designing an Effective Antitrust Compliance Program, Tying Arrangements; contbr. articles to profl. jours. Chmn. bd. dirs. Gilbert and Sullivan Soc. Chgo., 1984-87, Served with U.S. Army, 1967-68, Vietnam. Mem. ABA (chair sect. internat. law and practice 1998-99, chair Africa law initiative coun. 2000—), Chgo Bar Assn. (chmn. antitrust com. 1986-87), Yale Club (pres. 1987-89), Chgo. Yacht Club, Union League Club (Chgo.). Democrat. Episcopalian. Home: 591 Plum Tree Rd Barrington IL 60010-2329 Office: Schiff Hardin & Waite 7200 Sears Tower Chicago IL 60606 E-mail: whannay@schiffhardin.com.

HANNEMANN, TIMOTHY W. aerospace executive; BSEE, Ill. Inst. Tech., 1964, MSEE, 1966; completed exec. program, U. S.C., 1981. Various positions in mgmt. and devel. advanced sys. TRW Inc., Cleve., 1969, mgr. electronic devel. opers. comms. divsn., mgr. def. comms. divsn., 1986, v.p., gen. mgr. electronic sys. gorup, 1989-91, exec. v.p., gen. mgr. space and def. sector, 1991-95, exec. v.p., gen. mgr. space and electronics group, 1995—. Office: TRW Inc 1900 Richmond Rd Cleveland OH 44124-3760

HANNER, JOHN, retail executive; Exec. v.p., COO Clark Retail Group, Oakbrook, Ill., 2000—. Office: Clark Retail Group Inc 3003 Butterfield Rd Oak Brook IL 60523

HANNON, BRUCE MICHAEL, engineer, educator; b. Champaign, Ill., Aug. 14, 1934; s. Walter Leo and Kathleen Rose (Phalen) H.; m. Patricia Claire Coffey, Aug. 11, 1956; children: Claire, Laura, Brian. BSCE, U. Ill., 1956, MS in Engring. Mechanics, 1966, PhD in Engring. Mechanics, 1970. Engr. with chem. industry, 1957-66; instr. U. Ill., Urbana, 1966-71, assoc. prof. energy rsch., 1974-83, prof. regional sci., 1983—, Jubilee prof. liberal arts and scis., 1991—. Vis. prof. Nat. Ctr. for Supercomputing Applications; cons. NSF, NAS, NAE, chem. industry, various fed. energy agys; patentee in field. Contbr. articles to profl. jours. 1st lt. C.E. AUS, 1956-57. Named Engring. Tchr. of Yr., U. Ill., 1970, Man of Yr., Sierra Club, 1971; recipient 1st prize Mitchell Award Club of Rome, 1975. Home: 1208 W Union St Champaign IL 61821-3229 Office: U Ill 220 Daven Hall Urbana IL 61801

HANRATTY, THOMAS JOSEPH, chemical engineer, educator; b. Phila., Nov. 9, 1926; s. John Joseph and Elizabeth Marie (O'Connor) H.; m. Joan L. Hertel, Aug. 25, 1956; children: John, Vincent, Maria, Michael, Peter. BS Chem. Engring., Villanova U., 1947; hon. doctorate, 1979; M.S., Ohio State U., 1950; Ph.D., Princeton U., 1953; PhD (hon.), Polytechnic INst. Toulouse, 1999; doctorate (hon.) , Tolouse Poly. Inst., 1999. Engr. Fischer & Porter, 1947-48; research engr. Battelle Meml. Inst., 1948-50; engr. Rohm & Haas, Phila., summer 1951; research engr. Shell Devel. Co., Emeryville, Calif., 1954; faculty U. Ill., Urbana, 1953—, assoc. prof., 1958-63, prof. chem. engring., 1963—, James W. Westwater prof. chem. engring., 1989-97. Cons. in field; vis. assoc. prof. Brown U., 1962-63 Contbr. articles to profl. jours. NSF sr. postdoctoral fellow, 1962; recipient Curtis W. McGraw award Am. Soc. Engring. Edn., 1963, Sr. Research award, 1979; Disting. Engring. Alumnus award Ohio State U., 1984; Shell Disting. prof., 1981-86; 1st winner Internat. prize for rsch. in multiphase flow, 1998; Sr. Univ. Scholar, U. Ill., 1987, Lamme award Ohio State Univ., 1997. Fellow Am. Phys. Soc.; mem. NAE, Am. Acad. Arts and Scis., NAS. AIChE (Colburn award 1957, Walker award 1964, Profl. Progress award 1967, Ernest Thiele award Chgo. sect. 1986), Serra Internat. Club. Roman Catholic. Home: 1019 W Charles St Champaign IL 61821-4525 Office: U Ill 205 Roger Adams Lab 600 S Mathews Ave Urbana IL 61801-3602 E-mail: hanratty@scs.uiuc.edu.

HANREDDY, JOSEPH, stage director; b. L.A., Oct. 18, 1947; s. Harvey Joseph and Geraldine (Powers) H. BA, San Jose State U., 1969, MA, 1970. Artistic dir. Ensemble Theatre Project, Santa Barbara, Calif., 1979-85, Madison Repertory Theatre, 1987-1993, Milw. Repertory Theater, 1993—. Dir. San Diego Repertory Theatre, 1986, Cider Mill Playhouse, Binghamton, N.Y., 1985—, Santa Barbara Repertory Theatre, 1985. Office: Milwaukee Repertory Theatre 108 E Wells St Milwaukee WI 53202-3504

HANSELL, EDGAR FRANK, lawyer; b. Leon, Iowa, Oct. 12, 1937; s. Edgar Noble and Celestia Delphine (Skinner) H.; m. Phyllis Wray Silvey, June 24, 1961; children— John Joseph, Jordan Burke AA, Graceland Coll., 1957; BBA, U. Iowa, 1959, JD, 1961. Bar: Iowa 1961. Assoc. Nyemaster, Goode, McLaughlin, Voigts, West, Hansell & O'Brien, P.C., Des Moines, 1964-68, ptnr., shareholder, 1968—. Bd. dirs. The Vernon Co., Greater Des Moines Partnership, Downtown Cmty. Alliance, Inc., Des Moines Internat. Airport; mem. adv. com. to bd. dirs. The Lauridson Group, Inc.; adj. prof. law Drake U., Des Moines, 1990—98. Mem. editorial adv. bd. Jour. Corp. Law, 1985—. Bd. dirs. Des Moines Child Guidance Ctr., 1972-78, 81-87, pres., 1977-78; trustee Iowa Law Sch. Found., 1975-90, pres., 1983-87; bd. dirs. Iowa Natural Heritage Found., 1988-93, Iowa Sports Found., 1986-97; bd. dirs. Iowa State Bar Found., 1991-2000, pres., 1996-98. With USAF, 1961-64. Mem. ABA, Iowa Bar Assn. (pres. young lawyers sect. 1971-72, bd. govs. 1971-72, 85-87, mem. grievance commn. 1973-78, Merit award young lawyers sect. 1977, 98, chmn. corp. and bus. law com. 1979-85, pres. 1989-90), Polk County Bar Assn., Des Moines Club (pres. 1979-80). Home: 139-37th Des Moines IA 50312-4303 Office: Nyemaster Goode Voigts West Hansell & O'Brien PC 700 Walnut St Ste 1600 Des Moines IA 50309-3800 E-mail: efh@nyemaster.com.

HANSELL, RICHARD STANLEY, obstetrician, gynecologist, educator; b. Indpls., Nov. 18, 1950; s. Robert Mathey and Jewell (Martin) H.; m. Cathy C., Oct. 7, 1995; children: Elizabeth, Victoria. BA, DePauw U., 1972; MD, Ind. U., 1976. Cert. Am. Bd. Obstetrics and Gynecology. Practice medicine specializing in ob-gyn Cedarwood Med. Ctr., St. Joseph, Mich., 1980-86; asst. prof. ob-gyn. Ind. U., Indpls., 1986-93, assoc. prof., 1993—2002, prof., 2002—. Instr. Western Mich. U., Kalamazoo, 1980-86; med. bd. Planned Parenthood, Benton Harbor, Mich., 1980-86; med. dir. Planned Parenthood of Ctrl. Ind., 1991-95; examiner Am. Bd. Ob-gyn., 1994—. Mem. AMA, Am. Coll. Ob-Gyn, Assn. of Profs. of Gynecology and Obstetrics, Ind. State Med. Soc., Ctrl. Assn. Ob/gyn., Indpls. Med. Soc. Presbyterian. Lodge: Kiwanis. Avocations: golf, fishing. Office: Ind U Med Sch Dept Ob-Gyn 1001 W 10th St Indianapolis IN 46202-2859

HANSEN, CARL R. management consultant, b. Chgo., May 2, 1926; s. Carl M. and Anna C. (Roge) H.; m. Christia Marie Loeser, Dec. 31, 1952; 1 child, Lothar. MBA, U. Chgo., 1954. Dir. market rsch. Kitchens of Sara Lee, Deerfield, Ill., Earle Ludgin & Co., Chgo.; svc. v.p. Market Rsch. Corp. Am., 1956-67; pres. Chgo. Assoc. Inc., 1967—. Chmn. Ill. adv. coun. SBA, 1973-74; mem. exec. com. Ill. Gov.'s Adv. Coun., 1969-72; resident officer U.S. High Commn. Germany, 1949-52; vice chmn. Rep. Cen. Com. Cook County; chmn. Cook County Young Reps., 1957-58, 12th Congl. Dist. Rep. Orgn., 1971-74, 78-82, Suburban Rep. Orgn., 1974-78, 82-86; del. Rep. Nat. Conv., 1968, 84, 92; chmn. Legis. Dist. Ill., 1964—; del. Rep. State Conv., 1962-96; Elk Grove Twp. Rep. committeeman, 1962-2002; pres. John Ericsson Rep. League Ill., 1975-76; Rep. presdl. elector Ill., 1972; chmn. Viking Ship Restoration Com., mem. Cook County Bd. Commrs., 1970, 74—, chmn. legis. com., adminstrn. com.; mem. bd. dirs. Nat. Assn. Counties; mem. Am. Scandinavian Found. 1st lt. AUS, 1944-48, maj. Res. Mem. Am. Mktg. Assn., Am. Statis. Assn., Nat. Assn. Counties (dir.), Res. Officers Assn., Chgo. Hist. Soc., Planning Forum, Am. Legion, VFW, Dania Soc., Sons of Norway, Swedish Am. Hist. Soc., Lions, Masons, Shriners. Home: 110 S Edward St Mount Prospect IL 60056-3414 Office: 118 N Clark St Chicago IL 60602-1304

HANSEN, CHARLES, lawyer; b. Jersey City, May 23, 1926; s. Charles Henry and Katherine (Bensch) H.; m. Carolyn P. Smith, Sept. 26, 1953; children: Mark, Melissa. B.S., U. Mich., 1946; J.D., Mich. Law Sch., 1950. Bar: N.Y. 1951, Wis. 1961, Mo. 1980. Engr. Westinghouse Electric Co., 1946; assoc. Mudge, Stern, Williams & Tucker, 1950-53; chief labor counsel, div. counsel Sylvania Electric Products, 1953-61; sec., gen. counsel Trane Co., La Crosse, Wis., 1961-69, exec. v.p., 1968-73; pres. Cutler-Hammer World Trade, Inc., 1973-77; v.p. Cutler-Hammer, Inc., 1973-77, exec. v.p., 1977-79; sr. v.p. law Emerson Electric Co., 1979-84, sr. v.p., sec., gen. counsel, 1984-89; ptnr. Bryan Cave, 1989-95, of counsel, 1995—. Adj. prof. Sch. Law St. Louis U., 1987-99. Served to lt. (j.g.) USNR, 1943-46. Mem. ABA, Wis., Mo. bar assns., Am. Law Inst., Order of Coif, Tau Beta Pi. Home: 8 Wydown Ter Saint Louis MO 63105-2217 Office: 211 N Broadway 1 Metropolitan Sq Ste 3000 Saint Louis MO 63102-2741 E-mail: hansencih@aol.com.and., chansen@bryancavellp.com.

HANSEN, CLAIRE V. financial executive; b. Thornton, Iowa, June 3, 1925; s. Charles F. and Grace B. (Miller) H.; m. Renee C. Hansen, Aug. 17, 1946; children: Charles James, Christopher David, Peter Chrissis. BSc, U. Notre Dame, 1947; MBA, Harvard U., 1948. Chartered fin. analyst. With Salk, Ward & Salk, Inc.; v.p. Salk Inst. Agency, 1954-59; with Duff, Anderson & Clark, Chgo., 1959-67, v.p., dir., 1967-71; dir. Duff and Phelps, Inc., 1972-88; exec. v.p. Duff & Phelps, 1973-75, pres., chief exec. officer, 1975-84, chmn., chief exec. officer, 1984-87; chmn. bd. dirs. Duff & Phelps Utilities Income, Inc., Chgo., 1987—2001, CEO, 2000—01; chmn. bd. dirs. Duff & Phelps Select Income Fund, Inc., 2002—. Bd. dirs. Chgo. Lung Assn., 1962-80, pres. 1973-75; bd. dirs. Am. Lung Assn., 1971-83, Ctr. Religion and Psychotherapy in Chgo., 1979-83; trustee Glenwood Sch. for Boys, 1974-95, chmn., 1983-87; bd. dirs. Auditorium Theatre Coun., 1983-88, treas., 1987-88; bd. dirs. Schwab Rehab. Hosp., 1978-82, pres., 1980-82; bd. dirs. Pelican Bay Found. Inc., 1993-99, treas., 1993-96, pres., 1996-97. Mem. Inst. Chartered Fin. Analysts, Mid-Am. Club, Univ. Club, Chgo. Club, Olympia Fields Country Club, Club Pelican Bay, Hole-in-the-Wall Golf Club. Republican. Episcopalian. Home: 5601 Turtle Bay Dr Apt 2001 Naples FL 34108-2703 Office: 55 E Monroe St Ste 3600 Chicago IL 60603-5026

HANSEN, DAVID RASMUSSEN, federal judge; b. 1938; BA, N.W. Mo. State U., 1960; JD, George Washington U., 1963. Asst. clk. to minority House Appropriations Com. Ho. of Reps., 1960—61; adminstrv. aide 7th Dist. Iowa, 1962—63; pvt. practice Jones, Cambridge & Carl, Atlantic, Iowa, 1963—64; capt., judge advocate General's Corps U.S. Army, 1964—68; pvt. practice Barker, Hansen & McNeal, Iowa Falls, Iowa, 1968—76; ptnr. Win-Gin Farms, 1971—; judge Police Ct., 1969—73, 2d Jud. Dist. Ct., 1976—86, U.S. Dist. Ct. (no. dist.) , Cedar Rapids, 1986—91, U.S. Ct. Appeals (8th cir.), Cedar Rapids, 1991—. Office: US Courthouse 101 1st St SE Cedar Rapids IA 52401-1202

HANSEN, H. JACK, management consultant; b. Chgo., Mar. 28, 1922; s. Herbert Christian John and Laura Elizabeth (Osterman) Hansen; m. Joan Dorothy Norum, Nov. 28, 1980; children: Marilyn Joan, Gail Jean, Mark John. BSME, Ill. Inst. Tech., 1944. Cert. mgmt. cons. Mech. and indsl. engr. Harper Wyman Co., Chgo., 1944-51; chief indsl. engr. Shakeproof divsn. Ill. Tool Works, Des Plaines, 1951-53; cons., prin. A.T. Kearney & Co., Chgo. and N.Y.C., 1953-71; pres. H.J. Hansen Co., Elburn, Ill., 1971—2000. Acting mfg. engring. mgr. European Ops., Hobart Corp., 1974—78; owner, mgmt. cons. Hansen Mgmt. Search Co., Mt. Prospect, Ill., 1980—93; active turnaround cons., 1992—2000. Mem. Planning Commn. Village of Elburn, 1995—97, trustee, 1997—2001, chmn. Pers. Commn., mem. Fin. Commn., mem. Pub. Works Commn.; pres. Men's Club, 1987—90, Good Shepherd Luth. Ch., Des Plaines, Ill., 1988—90; active mem. mcpl. legis. com. DuKane Valley Coun. With U.S. Army, 1945—46. Inducted Tilden Tech. Alumni Assn. Hall of Fame, 2000. Mem. Inst. Mgmt. Cons. (founding), Methods-Time Measurement Assn. (bd. dirs. 1964-70, pres. 1967-68), Am. Arbitrtion Assn., Soc. Advancement Mgmt. (past bd. dirs.), coun. for Internat. Progress in Mgmt. (past bd. dirs.), Found. Internat. Progress in Mgmt. (past bd. dirs.), Econ. Devel. Com., Elburn C. of C. Office: H J Hansen Co 317 Prairie Valley St Elburn IL 60119-8977

HANSEN, HAL T. retired investment company executive; Pres. Cargill Investor Svcs., Chgo., ret. 1998. Founder Viking Investors Svcs., Lake Forest, Ill., 1998—; exec. cons. CP Risk Mgmt. (subs. Chgo. Ptnrs.), 1998—. Nat. Futures Assn. (former chmn.).

HANSEN, JAMES ALLEN, state agency administrator; b. West Point, Nebr., Jan. 10, 1939; s. Walter J. and Dorothy (Kay) H.; m. Janice A. Wenke, June 27, 1964 (div. 1975); m. Rebecca A. Bayer, Nov. 28, 1975. BA, Wayne State Coll., 1965. Pres. Farmers State Bank, Lexington, Nebr., 1972-80, No. Bank, Omaha, 1980-86, 1st Nat. Bank, Fremont, Nebr., 1986-87; regional v.p. Am. First Co., Omaha, 1987-90; mng. agt. FDIC/RTC, Burnsville, Minn., 1990; dir. Nebr. Dept. Banking & Fin., Lincoln, 1991-98; chmn., CEO Centennial Bank, Omaha, 1999—. Chmn., bd. dirs. Conf. of State Bank Suprs., Washington, 1992-97. Mem. group study exch. team to Australia, Rotary Internat., 1970. 1st lt. U.S. Army N.G., 1960-66. Home: 1233 S 116th Ave Omaha NE 68144-1717 Office: Centennial Bank 9003 S 145th St Omaha NE 68138-3636

HANSEN, JO-IDA CHARLOTTE, psychology educator, researcher; b. Washington, Oct. 2, 1947; d. Gordon Henry and Charlotte Lorraine (Helgeson) H.; m. John Paul Campbell. BA, U. Minn., 1969, MA, 1971, PhD, 1974. Asst. prof. psychology U. Minn., Mpls., 1974-78, assoc. prof., 1978-84, prof., 1984—, dir. Ctr. for Interest Measurement Rsch., 1974—, dir. counseling psychology program, 1987—, dir. Vocat. Assessment Clinic, 1997—, prof. human resources and indsl. rels., 1997—. Author: User's Guide for the SII, 1984, 2d edit., 1992, Manual for the SII, 1985 2d edit. 1994; editor: Measurement and Evaluation in Counseling and Development, 1993-2000; editor Jour. Counselling Psychology, 1999—; contbr. numerous articles to profl. jours., chpts. to books. Recipient early career award U. Minn., 1982, E.K. Strong, Jr. gold medal Strong Exec. Bd., 1984. Fellow APA (coun. reps. 1990-93, 97-99, pres. divsn. counseling psychology 1993-94, chmn. joint com. testing practices 1989-93, com. to revise APA/Am. Ednl. Rsch. Assn. nat. coun. measurement evalation testing stds. 1993-99, exam. com. Assn. State Provincial Psychology Bds. 1996-99, Leona Tyler award for rsch. and profl. svc. 1996); mem. ACA (extended rsch. award 1990, disting. rsch. award 1996), Assn. for Measurement and Evaluation (pres. 1988-89, Exemplary Practice award 1987, 90). Avocations: golf, theater, music, water and downhill skiing, spectator sports. Office: U Minn Dept Psychology Ctr Interest Measurement 75 E River Rd Minneapolis MN 55455-0280

HANSEN, KATHRYN GERTRUDE, editor, former state official; b. Gardner, Ill., May 24, 1912; d. Harry J. and Marguerite (Gaston) Hansen. BS with honors, U. Ill., 1934, MS, 1936. Sec. U. N.C., 1936-37, U. High Sch., U. Ill., 1937-44; personnel asst. U. Ill., Urbana, 1944-46, supr. tng. and activities, 1946-47, personnel officer, instr. psychology, 1947-52; exec. sec. U. Civil Service System, Ill.; also sec. for merit bd., 1952-61; adminstrv. officer, sec. merit bd., 1961-68; dir. system, 1968-72; lay asst. firm Webber, Balbach, Theis and Follmer, P.C., Urbana, Ill., 1972-74. Author: (with others) A Plan of Position Classification for Colleges and Universities: A Classification Plan for Staff Positions at Colleges and Universities, Grundy-Corners, 1982, Sarah, A Documentary of Her Life and Times, 1984, Ninety Years with Fortnightly, Vols. I and II, an historical compilation, 1986, Vol. III, 1995, Whispers of Yesterday, 1989, Through the Years with the Champaign-Urbana Business and Professional Women's Club, 1912-33, 1993, My Heritage, 1995, Presbyterian Women of First Presbyterian Church, Champaign, Illinois, An Historical Documentary, 1870-1995, 1996, (with Patricia Phillips) Fifty Golden Years, Altrusa International of Champaign-Urbana, Illinois, 1950-2000, 2001; editor: The Illini Worker, 1946-52, Campus Pathways, 1952-61, This is Your Civil Service Handbook, 1960-67; author, cons., editor publs. on personnel practices. Bd. dirs. U. YWCA, 1952-55, chmn., 1954-55; bd. dirs. Champaign-Urbana Symphony, 1978-81; mem., sec. Presbyn. Women 1st Presbyn Ch., Champaign, 1986-90, mem. coordinating team, 1986-91, hon. life mem., 1999. Mem. Coll. and Univ. Personnel Assn. for Human Resources (hon., life mem., editor jour. 1955-73, newsletter, internat. pres. 1967-68, nat. publs. award named in her honor 1987, Ill. State award 1996), Annuitants Assn. State Univs. Retirement System Ill. (state sec.-treas. 1974-75), U. Ill. Found., Pres.'s Coun. (life), Laureate Cir., U. Ill. Alumni Assn. (life), Friends of the Library (bd. dirs. 1987-91), Nat. League Am. Pen Women, AAUW (state 1st v.p. 1958-60, hon., life), Secretariat U. Ill. (life, named scholarship 1972—), Grundy County Hist. Soc. (life), Altrusa Internat., Fortnightly Club (Champaign-Urbana), Eastern Star, Delta Kappa Gamma (state pres. 1961-63), Phi Mu (life), Kappa Delta Pi, Kappa Tau Alpha. Presbyterian. Home: 1004 E Harding Dr Apt 307 Urbana IL 61801-6346

HANSEN, OLE VIGGO, chemical engineer; b. Detroit, May 6, 1934; s. Oluf Viggo and Carrie Alma (Wary) H.; m. Shirley Elizabeth Ford, Dec. 29, 1966; 1 child, Victoria Louisa. BSChemE, Wayne State U., 1956; equivalent of BS in Meteorology, Tex. A & M Univ., 1958. Registered profl. engr., Mich. Engr. tech. svcs. 3M Co., Detroit, 1956-57; chem. engr. Fisher Body div. Gen. Motors, 1960-64; mgr. mktg. Monsanto Co., St. Louis and Australia, 1964-76; dir. tech. mktg. Beltran Assocs., Inc., N.Y.C., 1976-78; leader mist eliminator profit ctr. Koch - Glitsch, Inc., Wichita, Kans., 1978-99; ret. Bd. dirs. Divmesh of Canada, Ltd., Calgary, Alta., 1984-85. Contbr. articles to profl. jours.; patentee in field. Served to capt. USAF, 1956-60. Mem. Am. Inst. Chem. Engrs. (session chmn. nat. meeting 1980), Am. Meteorol. Soc., Soc. Automotive Engrs. Australasia. Avocations: 19th century history, classical music, travel. Home: 7800 Killarney Pl Wichita KS 67206-1633

HANSEN, ROBYN L. lawyer; b. Terre Haute, Ind., Dec. 2, 1949; d. Robert Louis and Shirley (Nagel) Wieman; m. Gary Hansen, Aug. 21, 1971 (div. 1985); children: Nathan Ross Hansen, Brian Michael Hansen; m. John Marley Clarey, Jan. 1, 1986. BA, Gustavus Adolphus, 1971; JD cum laude, William Mitchell Coll. Law, 1977. Bar: Minn. 1977, U.S. Dist. Ct. Minn. 1977. Atty. Briggs and Morgan P.A., St. Paul, 1977-93, Leonard, Street and Deinard, Mpls., 1993—. Trustee Actors Theatre, St. Paul, 1980—88, Minn. Mus. Am. Art, 1994—97; mem. Minn. Inst. Pub. Fin., 1987—93, bd. dirs., 1993—95, pres., 1995; bd. dirs. St. Paul Downtown Coun., 1985—93, Met. State U. Found., 1993—, chair, 2000—02; bd. dirs. St. Paul Area Conv. and Vis. Bur., 1995—, chair, 1999—2001; bd. dirs. Capital City Partnership, 1997—. Mem. ABA, Minn. Bar Assn., Ramsey County Bar Assn., Nat. Assn. Bond Lawyers, St. Paul Area C. of C. (bd. dirs., exec. com. 1997-99). Office: Leonard Street and Deinard 380 St Peter St Ste 500 Saint Paul MN 55102 E-mail: robyn.hansen@leonard.com.

HANSEN, STEVEN D. state legislator; b. Sioux City, Iowa, Feb. 5, 1955; m. Glenda DenHerder. Student, Briar Cliff Coll.; BA, Morningside Coll., 1977; MA, U. S.D., 1988. Dir. Woodbury County Juvenile Detention Ctr., 1980-87; pvt. practice; mem. Iowa Senate from 1st dist., Des Moines, 1982—. Mem. Iowa Jaycees (past pres.), Sierra Club, Siouxland Ski Club. Democrat. Home: 3401 Military Rd Sioux City IA 51103-1263 Office: State Capitol 1st Dist 3 9th And Grand Des Moines IA 50319-0001 E-mail: steven_hansen@legis.state.ia.us.

HANSEN, THOMAS J. tool manufacturing company executive; BS in Mktg., No. Ill. U., 1971; MABA, Govs. State U., 1978. Zone sales mgr. GE; various positions including regional sales mgr. Singer Controls divsn. Eaton Corp.; joined Ill. Tool Works Inc., Glenview, 1980, nat. sales and mktg. mgr. Shakeproof Indsl. Products divsn., other mgmt. and exec. level positions including gen. mgr., then pres. metal fasteners and components bus., exec. v.p., 1998—. Mem. adv. bd. Century Moving and Storage. Active United Way, Jr. Achievment. Mem. Gen. Motors Supplier Coun., Indsl. Fastener Inst., Elgin Country Club. Office: Ill Tool Works Inc 3600 W Lake Ave Glenview IL 60025-5811

HANSEN, THOMAS NANASTAD, pediatrician, health facility administrator; b. Neenah, Wis., Oct. 11, 1947; m. Cheryl Bailey, June 9, 1979; children: Elaine Christ, William Thomas. BS in Physics summa cum laude, Tex. Christian U., 1970; MD, Baylor Coll. Medicine, 1973. Diplomate Am. Bd. Pediatrics. Intern in pediatrics Baylor Coll. Medicine, Houston, 1973-74, resident in pediatrics, 1974-76, postdoctoral fellow in neonatal perinatal medicine, 1976-78; postdoctoral fellow in pediatric pulmonary disease U. Calif., San Francisco, 1978-81; asst. prof. pediatrics Baylor Coll. Medicine, 1978-84, assoc. prof. pediatrics, 1984-89; prof. pediatrics and cell biology Tex. Children's Hosp. Found., Houston, 1989-95; head sect. on neonatology Baylor Coll. of Medicine, 1987-95, vice-chmn. rsch. dept. pediatrics, 1994-95, dir. child health rsch. ctr., 1994-95, co-dir. ctr. for tng. in molecular medicine, 1994-95; chmn. pediat., CEO Children's Hosp., Columbus, Ohio, 1995—. Mem. exam com. Am. Bd. Pediatrics, 1982—, sub-bd. neonatal-perinatal medicine, 1992—, chmn. credentials com., 1993—, chmn.-elect sub-bd. neonaatal perinatal medicine, 1994. Contbr. numerous articles to profl. jours. Trustee Tex. Women's Hosp., 1988-91. Mem. Western Soc. for Pediatric Rsch., So. Soc. for Pediaatric Rsch., Soc. for Pediatric Rsch. (sec.-treas. 1986-91, chmn. student rsch. com. 1990—, trustee internat. chpt. 1992—), Am. Physiol. Soc., Am. Pediatric Soc., Am. Fedn. for Clin. Rsch., Am. Thoracic Soc., Am. Acad. of Pediatrics, N.Y. Acad. of Scis., Am. Soc. for Cell Biology, Assn. of Med. Sch. Pediatric Dept. Chmn., Sigma Xi. Home: 4328 Vaux Link New Albany OH 43054-9681 Office: Med Dir's Office Childrens Hosp 700 Childrens Dr Columbus OH 43205-2664

HANSEN, W. LEE, economics educator, author; b. Racine, Wis., Nov. 8, 1928; s. William R. and Gertrude M. (Spillum) H.; m. Sally Ann Porch, Dec. 26, 1955; children— Ellen J., Martha L. BA, U. Wis., Madison, 1950, MA, 1955; PhD, Johns Hopkins U., 1958. Asst. prof. econs. UCLA, from 1958, assoc. prof., to 1965; assoc. prof. econs. U. Wis., Madison, from 1965, prof., prof. emeritus, 1996—. Sr. staff economist Pres.'s Coun. Econ. Advisers, Washington, 1964-65; trustee Nat. Coun. on Econ. Edn., N.Y.C., 1976-2000, sec., 1996-2000; mem. bd. founders NCEE, 2000—. Author: Benefits, Costs, and Finance of Public Higher Education, 1969, Education, Income, and Human Capital, 1970, The Labor Market for Scientists and Engineers, 1973, Perspectives on Economic Education, 1977, A Framework for Teaching Basic Economic Concepts, 1984, The End of Mandatory Retirement, 1989, Unemployment Insurance: The Second Half-Century, 1990, Academic Freedom on Trial: 100 Years of Sifting and Winnowing at the University of Wisconsin, 1998; contbr. articles to profl. jours. Sgt. U.S. Army, 1951-53. Recipient Amoco Disting. Tchg. award U. Wis., 1982, Hilldale award, 1988, Disting. Svc. award Nat. Coun. on Econs. Edn., 1991, Marvin Bower award, 1994, , Henry H. Villard Rsch. award, 2000, Tchr. Acad. U. Wis., 1994, Outstanding Postsecondary Educator award nat. Fedn. Ind. Bus. Found., 1992, Leavey award for excellence in pvt. enterprise edn. Freedoms Found., 1996; Guggenheim fellow, 1969-70; Fulbright sr. scholar, Australia, 1988. Mem. AAUP (chair com. on the econ. status of the profession 1979-86, mem. nat. coun. 1980-82, retirement com. 1985-95), Am. Econ. Assn. (chmn. com. on econ. edn. 1983-88, exec. sec. commn. grad. edn. econs. 1988-91), Indsl. Rels. Rsch. Assn., Midwest Econs. Assn. (pres. 1987), Phi Beta Kappa. Unitarian. Office: U Wis Dept Econs 1180 Observatory Dr Madison WI 53706-1320

HANSER, FREDERICK OTTO, professional sports team executive; b. St. Louis, Apr. 13, 1942; s. S. Albert Hanser and Olive D. Mullen; m. Katharine Thompson; children: Tim, Kara. BA in Econs., Yale U., 1963; JD, Washington U., St. Louis, 1966. Assoc. Fordyce & Mayne, 1966-78; ptnr. Armstrong & Teasdale, LLP, St. Louis, 1978-96; pres., dir. Gateway Group Inc., 1996—; chmn. St. Louis Cardinals, 1996—. Mem. exec. com., bd. dirs. Miss. Valley Bancshares Inc. Mem. exec. bd. Greater St. Louis area coun. Boy Scouts Am.; bd. dirs. St. Louis Children's Hosp., mem. devel. bd.; bd. dirs. St. Louis Country Day Sch., Easter Seal Soc. Office: St Louis Cardinals 250 Stadium Plz Saint Louis MO 63102-1722

HANSMAN, ROBERT G. art educator, artist; BFA, U. Kans., 1970. Asst. prof. Washington U., St. Louis. Instr. dept. parks and recreation Project Artspark, 1993, Arts Connection/City Faces, 1994—; instr. juvenile detention program Children's Art Cir., 1995; established Jermaine Lamond Roberts Meml. Art Studio, Clinton-Peabody Pub. Housing, 1997. One-man shows include St. Louis C.C. at Forest Park, 1988, MJF Arts Studio Gallery, 1990, University City Pub. Lib., 1992, 95, Bonsack Gallery, 1995. Mem. pub. housing revitalization focus group Darst-Webbe, 1995. Named Reader's Poll Best Local Artist, The Riverfront Times, 1995; recipient First Pl. award/Best of Show, St. Louis Artists Guild, 1988, 1992, Componere Gallery, 1990, Not Just An Art Dirs. Club, 1990, The Gallery Connection, 1991, Art St. Louis Gallery, 1991, World of Difference award City Faces, 1996, Mo. Arts award, Mo. Arts Coun., 1997, Excellence in Tchg. award, Emerson Electric, 2000, Disting. Faculty award, 2001, honoree, Colin Powell's Am. Promise, 1999, Mo. Ho. of Reps., 1997; grantee, Bi-State Arts in Transit Project, 1995, 1996, 1999. Office: Washington U Sch Arch Campus Box 1079 One Brookings Dr Saint Louis MO 63130 E-mail: hansman@architecture.wustl.edu.

HANSON, AL, financial newsletter editor and publisher; b. Mpls., May 15, 1930; s. Albert and Lillie (Hanse) H.; m. Janette Ladonna Vansickle, June 27, 1952; children: Sharon, Susan, Shirley, Sandra. BA, Augsburg Coll., 1952. Product mgr. Uniroyal, Indpls., 1960-70; mem., seat owner Mpls. Grain Exch., 1970-76, Intermountain Stock Exch., Salt Lake City, 1971-77; editor Al Hanson Newsletter, Ottertail, Minn., 1982—. Pres. Internat. Cons., Buenos Aires, 1989—. Author: Personal Witnessing in Jail, 1989; contbr. several hundred articles to profl. jours. Founder Lutheran Prison Ministry, 1980. Lt. U.S. Army, 1950-60. Home: 312 S College Dr Concordia MO 64020-8154 Office: Internat Cons PO Box 9 Ottertail MN 56571-0009 Address: PO Box 168 Concordia MO 64020-0168 E-mail: alhanson@ylm.org.

HANSON, ARTHUR STUART, health facility administrator, physician; b. Mpls., Mar. 10, 1937; s. Arthur Emanuel and Frances Elenor (Larson) H.; m. Gail Joan Taylor, June 16, 1963; children: Marta Eileen, Peter Arthur. BA, Dartmouth Coll., 1959; MD, U. Minn., 1963. Diplomate Am. Bd. Internal Medicine, Am. Bd. Pulmonary Disease. Intern Hennipen County Med. Ctr., 1963-64; resident in internal medicine U. Minn., 1964-65, 68-70, fellow pulmonary disease, 1970-71; cons. Park Nicollet Clinic, Mpls., 1971—, med. dir., 1975-82, v.p. legis. and cmty. affairs, 1982-86; dir. med. edn. Park Nicollet Med. Found., 1982-86; pres., CEO Park Nicollet Inst., 1986—2002. Bd. dirs. Minn. Health Data Inst., 1993—. Pres., bd. chair Minn. Smoke Free Coalition, 1985-88, 96-98; chmn. bd. Smoke Free Generation Minn., 1984-90. Recipient Cmty. Leadership award, Am. Lung Assn. Hennepin County, 1987, Harvey H. Rogers Meml. award, Minn. Pub. Health Assn., 1988, award for excellence in health promotion, Minn. Health Commr., 1989, Physician of Excellence award, Park Nicollet Health Svcs., 2000, Lynn Smith 25-Yr. award, Am. Cancer Soc., 2001. Fellow ACP, AMA (del., chmn.), Am. Coll. Chest Physicians; mem. Minn. Med. Assn. (pres. 1992-93, Stop the Violence award 1994, Disting. Svc. award 1998), Minn. Healthcare Coalition on Violence, Hennepin County Med. Soc. (pres. 1990-91, Charles Bolles Bolles-Rogers award 1998). Universalist. Avocations: birding, gardening, physical fitness, reading, traveling. Office: Park Nicollet Clinic Ste 300 6490 Excelsior Blvd Minneapolis MN 55426

HANSON, BRUCE EUGENE, lawyer; b. Lincoln, Nebr., Aug. 25, 1942; s. Lester E. and Gladys (Diessner) H.; m. Peggy Pardun, Dec. 25, 1972 (dec. Nov. 1989). BA, U. Minn., 1965, JD, 1966. Bar: Minn. 1966, U.S. Dist. Ct. Minn. 1966, U.S. Tax Ct. 1973, U.S. Ct. Appeals (8th cir.) 1973, U.S. Ct. Appeals (fed. cir.) 1983, U.S. Supreme Ct. 1970. Shareholder Doherty, Rumble & Butler, P.A., St. Paul, 1966-99; ptnr. Oppenheimer, Wolff & Donnelly, LLP, Mpls., 1999—. Dir., sec. Am. Saddlebred Horse Assn.; bd. trustees, chair United Hosp., 1996-98. Mem. ATLA, Hennepin County Bar Assn., Minn. State Bar Assn., Am. Health Lawyers Assn., Minn. Soc. Hosp. Attys., North Oaks Golf Club, Order of Coif, Phi Delta Phi. Home: 23 Evergreen Rd Saint Paul MN 55127-2077 Office: Oppenheimer Wolff & Donnelly LLP 45 S 7th St Ste 3300 Minneapolis MN 55402-1614 E-mail: BHanson@Oppenheimer.com.

HANSON, DALE S. retired banker; b. Milw., Nov. 11, 1938; s. Yngve Holger and Evelyn (Johnson) H.; m. Joan Benton, July 15, 1961; children— Thomas S., Tim B. B.A. in Econs., Carlton Coll., 1960; postgrad. Exec. Program, Credit and Fin. Mgmt. Stanford U., 1966-67. Asst. cashier First Bank, St. Paul, 1964-66, asst. v.p., 1966-68, v.p., 1968-82, sr. v.p., 1982-83, exec. v.p., 1983-84, pres., 1984-88; pres., mng. ptnr. FBS Mcht. Banking Group, 1987-90; mng. ptnr. Matrix Leasing Internat., 1989-90; exec. v.p. 1st Bank System, Mpls., 1984-91; v.p., treas., chief fin. officer C.H. Robinson Co., 1991-98, also bd. dirs.; ret., 1998. Bd. dirs. W.A. Lang Co., Edwards Mfg. Co. Mem. Corp. Health One, Inc.; bd. dirs. St. Paul Chamber Orch., Twin City Pub. TV, St. Paul Riverfront Devel. Corp., 1985-91. 1st lt. USNG, 1961-67. Mem. Robert Morris Assocs. (pres. 1982-83), Fin. Execs. Inst. (bd. dirs. Twin Cities chpt.), Somerset Golf Club, Mpls. Club, Minn. Club (St. Paul). Republican. Presbyterian. Avocations: Skiing; sailing; golfing; photography. Office: care C H Robinson Co 8100 Mitchell Rd Ste 200 Eden Prairie MN 55344-2178

HANSON, DAVID GORDON, otolaryngologist, surgeon; b. Seattle, Nov. 16, 1943; m. Terri Dangerfield, Jan. 22, 1976. BS, Wheaton Coll., 1966; MD, U. Wash., 1970; MS, U. Minn., 1976. Intern Hennepin County Gen. Hosp., Mpls., 1971-72; resident in surgery and otolaryngology U. Minn., 1972-76; sr. surgeon NIH, Nat. Inst. Neurol. and Communicative Disorders and Stroke, USPHS, Bethesda, Md., 1975-78; asst. prof. surgery UCLA Sch. Medicine, 1978-83, assoc. prof., vice chief divsn. head and neck surgery, 1983-89; prof., chmn. dept. otolaryngology Northwestern U. Med. Sch., Chgo., 1989—; chmn. otolaryngology Northwestern Meml. Hosp., 1989—. Chief sect. head and neck surgery VA Med. Ctr., West Los Angeles, 1983-89. Contbr. articles to profl. jours. Served to comdr. USPHS, 1975-78. NIH grantee, 1983—. Fellow ACS, Triological Soc., Am. Laryngological Assn, Am. Broncho-Esophagol. Assn., Am. Soc. Head and Neck Surgery, Am. Acad. Otolaryngology (Award of Honor, 1985); mem. AMA. Avocations: skiing, sailing.

HANSON, DAVID JAMES, lawyer; b. Neenah, Wis., July 20, 1943; s. Vernon James and Dorothy O. Hanson; m. Diana G. Severson, Aug. 25, 1965 (div. Sept. 1982); children: Matthew Vernon, Maja Kirsten, Brian Edward; m. Linda Hughes Bochert, May 28, 1983; children: Scott Charles, Sarah Katherine. BS, U. Wis., 1965, JD, 1968. Bar: Wis. 1968, U.S. Dist. Ct. (we. dist.) Wis. 1968, U.S. Dist. Ct. (ea. dist.) Wis. 1969, U.S. Ct. Appeals (7th cir.) 1970, U.S. Supreme Ct. 1971. Asst. atty. gen. State of Wis. Dept. of Justice, Madison, 1968-71, dep. atty. gen., 1976-81; asst. chancellor, chief legal counsel U. Wis., 1971-76; ptnr. Michael, Best & Friedrich LLP, 1981—. Lectr. Law Sch., U. Wis., Madison, 1972-75; chair govt. law sect. State Bar Wis., Madison, 1979-88. Contbr. articles to profl. jours. Bd. dirs. Sand County Found., Madison, 1988—, Wis. Ctr. for Academically Talented Youth, Madison, 1991-94, bd. trustees Edgewwod Coll., Madison, 1997—. Mem. ABA, Madison Club, Blackhawk Country Club. Democrat. Unitarian. Avocations: canoeing, skiing, golf, biking, hunting. Office: Michael Best & Friedrich PO Box 1806 Madison WI 53701-1806 E-mail: djhanson@mbflaw.com.

HANSON, DORIS J. state legislator; b. Oct. 24, 1925; Student, U. Wis. Former bus. mgr., now v.p. real estate co.; mem. from dist. 48 Wis. State Assembly, Madison, 1992-98; exec. dir. Teach Wis., 1998—. Former sec., now pres. Village of McFarland, Wis.; former chairwoman Dane County Regional Airport Commn. Home: 4101 Monona Dr Apt 304 Monona WI 53716-1677 Office: 101 E Wilson St Madison WI 53702-0004

HANSON, FLOYD BLISS, applied mathematician, computational scientist, mathematical biologist; b. Bklyn., Mar. 9, 1939; s. Charles Keld and Violet Ellen (Bliss) H.; m. Ethel Louise Hutchins, July 27, 1962; 1 child, Lisa Kirsten BS, Antioch Coll., 1962; MS, Brown U., 1964, PhD, 1968. Space technician Convair Astronautics, San Diego, 1961; applied mathematician Arthur D. Little, Inc., Cambridge, Mass., 1961; physicist Wright-Patterson AFB, Dayton, Ohio, 1962; assoc. research scientist Courant Inst., N.Y.C., 1967-68; asst. prof. U. Ill., Chgo., 1969-75, assoc. prof., 1975-83, prof., 1983—, assoc. dir. Lab. for Advanced Computing, 1990—, assoc. dir. Lab. for Control & Info., 1993—. Faculty rsch. participant Argonne (Ill.) Nat. Lab., 1985-87, faculty rsch. leave, 1987-88, rsch. assoc., 1988—; vis. prof., divsn. applied math. Brown U., 1994; mem. vis. faculty Sch. Civil and Environ. Engring., Cornell U., 1995. Assoc. editor-in-chief Applied and Computational Control Signals and Circuits, 1996—; author: (with others) Control and Dynamical Systems: Advances in Theory and Applications, 1996; contbr. articles in field to profl. jours. Recipient UIC CETL Tchr. Recognition award, 1999, UIC award for excellence in tchg., 2001; NSF rsch. grantee, 1970-83, 88—, NSF equipment grantee, 1973; Nat. Ctr. for Supercomputer Applications Computer grantee, 1986—; supercomputer grantee Los Alamos Nat. Lab., 1990-97, Cornell Theory Ctr., 1993-96, Pitts. Supercomputer Ctr., 1993-98, San Diego grantee Super Computer Ctr., 1998—. Mem. IEEE (sr., tech. com. on control edn. appointment, 2002), Soc. Indsl. and Applied Math., Computer Soc. of IEEE, Control Sys. Soc. of IEEE, Resource Modeling Assn. Home: 5435 S East View Park Chicago IL 60615-5915 Office: U Ill Dept Math Stats and Computer Sci M/C 249 851 S Morgan St Rm 322 Chicago IL 60607-7042 E-mail: hanson@uic.edu.

HANSON, GAIL G. physicist, educator; b. Dayton, Ohio, Feb. 22, 1947; married 1968 (div. 1998); 2 children. BS in Physics, MIT, 1968, PhD in Exptl. High Energy Physics, 1973. Rsch. assoc. Stanford Linear Accelerator Ctr., 1973-76, physicist, continuing staff mem., 1976-84, physicist, permanent staff mem., 1984-89; prof. physics Ind. U., Bloomington, 1989-97, disting. prof., 1997—. Mem. subpanel High Energy Physics Adv. Panel, 1989-90; mem. physics adv. com. Univs. Rsch. Assn. Fermilab, 1990-94, mem. bd. overseers, 1991-97, dir. rev. panel, 1993-94, mem. vis. com., 1995-97; mem. com. examiners GRE Physics Test, 1992-2000; mem. collaboration exec. com. U.S. ATLAS, 1994-95. Guggenheim fellow, 1995. Fellow AAAS (mem. electorate nominating com. physics sect. 1996—), Am. Phys. Soc. (W.K.H. Panofsky prize 1996). Office: Ind U Dept Physics Bloomington IN 47405 E-mail: gail@indiana.edu.

HANSON, HEIDI ELIZABETH, lawyer; b. Portsmouth, Ohio, Nov. 13, 1954; BS, U. Ill., 1975, JD, 1978. Bar: Ill. 1978, U.S. Dist. Ct. (no. dist.) Ill., U.S. Ct. Appeals (7th cir.). Atty. water, air and land pollution divs. Ill. EPA, Springfield, Ill., 1978-85, atty. water pollution div. Maywood, 1985-86; assoc. Ross & Hardies, Chgo., 1987-89, ptnr., 1990-94; founder H.E. Hanson Law Offices, Western Springs, Ill., 1994—. Named hon. Ky. Col., 2000. Mem.: Indsl. Water, Waste and Sewer Group, Air and Waste Mgmt. Assn., Chgo. Bar Assn., Chicagoland C. of C. Avocation: gardening. Office: 4721 Franklin Ave Ste 1500 Western Springs IL 60558-1720

HANSON, JOHN BERNARD, retired botanist, agronomy and plant biology educator; b. Denver, Mar. 24, 1918; BA, U. Colo., 1948; MS, State Coll. Wash., 1950, PhD in Botany, 1952. Asst. State Coll. Wash., 1948-51; NRC fellow Calif. Inst. Tech., 1952-53; from asst. prof. to prof. U. Ill., Urbana, 1953-85, head dept. botany, 1967-77, prof. emeritus agronomy and plant biology, 1985—. Fulbright Rsch. scholar Waite Agr. Experimental Sta., Australia, 1959-60; NATO sr. fellow U. East Anglia, Eng., 1968. Mem. Am. Soc. Plant Physiologists (Adolph E. Gude Jr. award 1989). Home: 101 W Windsor Rd Apt 2106 Urbana IL 61802-6663 Office: U Ill 284 Morrill Hall Urbana IL 61801 :

HANSON, JOHN NILS, industrial high technology manufacturing company executive; b. Berwyn, Ill., Jan. 22, 1942; s. Robert and Stephanie Ann (Kazluskas) H.; m. Stephanie Morgan, June 5, 1965; children: Laurel, Mark Nils. B.S. in Chem. Engring., MIT, 1964, M.S. in Nuclear Engring., 1965; Ph.D. in Nuclear Sci. and Engring., Carnegie-Mellon U., 1969. Sr. scientist Westinghouse Electric Corp., Bettis Atomic Power Labs., West Mifflin, Pa., 1965-70, asst. to gen. mgr. advanced test core, 1971-73; fellow White House, Washington, 1970-71; asst. to pres. Gould Inc., Rolling Meadows, Ill., 1973-74, pres., gen. mgr. electric motor div. St. Louis, 1974-78, group v.p. elec. products Rolling Meadows, 1978-80; v.p. Internat. Harvester, 1980-81; pres. Solar Turbines Internat., San Diego, 1980—; v.p. Caterpillar Tractor Co., Peoria, Ill., 1981—. Contbr. articles on indsl. tech. to profl. jours. Vice chmn. Friends of Scouting Fundraising-Boy Scouts Am., San Diego council, 1983— ; mem. Judge Wallace Longrange planning com., 1983— , vice chmn. fin. adv. com., 1983— ; mem. cabinet fund drive United Way, San Diego County Chpt., 1982— ; mem. exec. fin. com. Pete Wilson for Senate campaign, San Diego, 1982; vice chmn. Children's Hosp. Research Ctr., 1983— ; mem. vis. com. sponsored research MIT, Cambridge, 1978— ; mem. Pvt. Industry Council, 1983. Mem. White House Fellows Assn., Greater San Diego C. of C. (bd. dirs.) Office: Solar Turbines Inc PO Box 85376 San Diego CA 92186-5376 also: Caterpillar Inc 100 NE Adams St Peoria IL 61629-0001 also: Joy Techs Inc 301 Grant St Pittsburgh PA 15219-1407

HANSON, LYLE, state legislator; m. Betty; two children. BS, U. N.D.; MS, Moorehead State U. N.D. State rep. Dist. 48, 1979—; substitute tchr. Mem. edn. and natural resources coms.; Dem. caucus leader. Recipient Legis. Conservationist of Yr. award N.D. Wildlife Fedn., 1981, Jamestown United Sportsman of Yr., 1994; named to Ofcls. Hall of Fame. Mem. United Sportsman, Elks, Eagles, Safari Club Internat., N.D. Wildlife Fedn., Found. for N.Am. Wild Sheep. Home: 337 15th Ave NE Jamestown ND 58401-3830

HANSON, PAULA E. state legislator; b. Jan. 21, 1944; m. Jim Hanson; 3 children. Mem. Minn. State Senate, 1992—, mem. various coms. Democrat. Home: 2428 Bunker Lake Blvd NE Andover MN 55304-7129 Office: Minn State Senate 328 Capitol 75 Constitution Ave Saint Paul MN 55155-1601

HANSON, RICHARD A. former state commissioner; m. Sharon Kinney. B in Engring., Kans. State U.; MBA, Washington U.; postgrad., U. Mo. Engr. pvt. industry; dep. commr. Office of Adminstrn.; asst. state treas.; commr., chief adminstrv. officer Mo. Commr. Adminstrn., 1993-2000; interim Sec. of State, 1994. Bd. mem. State Employees Retirement Sys., Consol. Health Care Plan, Deferred Compensation Commn., Voluntary Life Ins. Commn., Pub. Entity Risk Mgmt. Bd., Commn. on Intergovernmental Rels., Minority Bus. Adv. Commn., Bd. Fund Commrs., Show Me State Games, others. Named State Exec. of Yr., Fed. Exec. Inst. Alumni Assn., Pub. Adminstr. of Yr., Mo. Inst. Pub. Adminstrs., Statesman of Month, Jefferson City Post-Tribune. Mem. Jefferson City Leadership Forum, Jefferson City Area C. of C. (bd. mem.). Office: Adminstrn Office PO Box 809 Jefferson City MO 65102-0809

HANSON, RICHARD WINFIELD, biochemist, educator; b. Oxford, N.Y., Nov. 10, 1935; s. John Vincent and Agatha Helen H.; m. Gloria M. Lucchesi, June 10, 1961; children: Paul, Benjamin, Daria. BS, Northeastern U., 1959; MS, Brown U., 1961, PhD, 1963. Asst. prof to prof. biochemistry Temple U. Sch. Medicine, Phila., 1965-78; prof., chmn. dept. biochemistry Case Western U. Sch. Medicine, Cleve., 1978-99, Leonard and Jean Sheggs prof. biochemistry, 1993—. Cons. USPHS, FDA. Assoc. editor Jour. Biol. Chemistry; contbr. articles to profl. jours. Served to capt. Med. Service Corps, U.S. Army, 1963-65. Recipient Mead-Johnson award, 1971, Kaiser Permenante award, 1982, Maurice Saltzman award, 1991, Osborne Mendel award, 1995, William C. Rose award, 1999. Mem. AAAS, Inst. Medicine NAS, Am. Soc. Biochemistry and Molecular Biology (pres. 1999-2000). Office: Case Western Res U Dept of Biochemistry, Rm W405 10900 Euclid Ave Cleveland OH 44106

HANSON, ROBERT ARTHUR, retired agricultural equipment executive; b. Moline, Ill., Dec. 13, 1924; s. Nels A. and Margaret I. (Chapman) H.; m. Patricia Ann Klinger, June 25, 1955. BA, Augustana Coll., Rock Island, Ill., 1948. Various positions Deere & Co., Moline, 1950-62, gen. mgr. Mexico, 1962-64, Spain, 1964-66, dir. mktg. overseas, 1966-70, v.p. overseas ops., 1972, sr. v.p. overseas div., 1973, dir., 1974—, exec. v.p., 1975-78, pres., 1978-85, chief oper. officer, 1979-82, chief exec. officer, 1982-89, chmn., 1982-90. With USMCR, 1943-46. Mem. Bus. Coun. Home: 2200 29th Avenue Court Dr Moline IL 61265-6926 Office: Deere & Co One John Deere Pl Moline IL 61265-8098

HANSON, ROBERT DUANE, civil engineering educator; b. Albert Lea., Minn., July 27, 1935; s. James Edwin and Gertie (Kvale) H.; m. Kaye Lynn Nielsen, June 7, 1959; children: Craig Robert, Eric Neil. Student, St. Olaf Coll., Northfield, Minn., 1953-54; BSE, U. Minn., 1957, MS in Civil Engring., 1958; PhD, Calif. Inst. Tech., Pasadena, 1965. Registered profl. engr., Mich., N.D. Design engr. Pitts.-Des Moines Stel, Des Moines, 1958-59; asst. prof. U. N.D., Grand Forks, 1959-61; rsch. engr. Calif. Inst. Tech., 1965; asst. prof. U. Calif.-Davis, 1965-66; from asst. prof. to prof. civil engring. U. Mich., Ann Arbor, 1966—2001, prof. emeritus, 2001—, chmn. dept. civil engring., 1976-84; sr. earthquake engr. Fed. Emergency Mgmt. Agy., 1994-2000. Vis. prof., dir. Earthquake Engring. Rsch. Ctr., U. Calif., Berkeley, 1991; dir. BCS divsn. NSF, Washington, 1989-90; cons. NSF, 1979-88, 92-94; cons. Bechtel Corp., Ann Arbor, 1976-87, Sensei Engrs., Ann Arbor, 1977-90, Bldg. Seismic Safety Coun., 1988-94, Fed. Emergency Mgmt. Agy., 1992-94, 2000—. Contbr. articles to profl. jours. Recipient Reese Rsch. award ASCE, 1980; recipient Disting. Svc. award U. Mich., 1969; tchg. award Chi Epsilon, 1985, Attwood Engr. Excellence award, 1986. Mem. NAE, ASCE (com. chmn. 1975-94), Earthquake

Engring. Rsch. Inst. (hon. v.p. 1977-79, bd. dirs. 1976-79, 88-92, pres.-elect 1988, pres. 1989-91, past pres. 1991-92). Lutheran. Home: 2926 Saklan Indian Dr Walnut Creek CA 94595-3911 E-mail: rdhanson2@aol.com.

HANSON, RONALD WILLIAM, lawyer; b. Aug. 3, 1950; s. Orlin Eugene and Irene Agnes Hanson; m. Sandra Kay Cook, Aug. 21, 1971; children: Alec Evan, Corinn Michele. BA summa cum laude, St. Olaf Coll., 1972; JD cum laude, U. Chgo., 1975. Bar: Ill. 1975, U.S. Dist. Ct. (no. dist.) Ill. 1975, U.S. Ct. Appeals (7th cir.) 1978, U.S. Ct. Appeals (10th cir.) 1989. Assoc. Sidley & Austin, Chgo., 1975-83, ptnr., 1983-88, Latham & Watkins, Chgo., 1988—. Ofcl. advisor to Nat. Conf. of Commrs. on Uniform State Laws; lectr. Ill. Inst. Continuing Legal Edn., Springfield, Am. Bankruptcy Inst., Washington, Banking Law Inst., Practicing Law Inst., Am. Law Inst. Contbr. articles to profl. jours. Mem. ABA, Ill. Bar Assn., Chgo. Bar Assn., Order of Coif, Met. Club, Phi Beta Kappa. Republican. Lutheran. Home: 664 W 58th St Hinsdale IL 60521-5104 Office: Latham & Watkins Sears Tower Ste 5800 Chicago IL 60606-6306 E-mail: ronaldhanson@lw.com.

HANTHORN, DENNIS WAYNE, performing arts association administrator; b. Lima, Ohio, Dec. 21, 1951; s. Floyd Wilber and June J. (Rummel) H.; m. Rebecca R. Hackler, Aug. 2, 1975; children: Rachel R., Micah A, Hanna. BS in Music Edn., Southwest Mo. State, Springfield, 1975; MusM in French Horn, U. Wis., 1977. Instr. U. Ala., 1978-79; gen. mgr. Cin. Chamber Orch., 1980-82; founder, dir. Queen City Brass, 1979-83; mng. dir. Dayton (Ohio) Opera, 1982-89; gen. dir. Florentine Opera Co., Milw., 1989—. Home: N75w5434 Georgetown Dr Cedarburg WI 53012-1557 Office: Florentine Opera Co 735 N Water St Ste 1315 Milwaukee WI 53202-4106

HANUS, JEROME GEORGE, archbishop; b. May 26, 1940; Attended, Conception Sem., Mo., St. Anselm U., Rome, Italy, Princeton Theol. Sem., Princeton U. Ordained priest Roman Cath. Ch., 1966. Abbot Conception Abbey, 1977-87; pres. Swiss Am. Benedictine Congregation, 1984-87; bishop Diocese of St. Cloud, Minn., 1987-94; coadjuctor archbishop Dubuque, Iowa, 1994-95; archbishop, 1995—. Office: PO Box 479 Dubuque IA 52004-0479

HAQUE, MALIKA HAKIM, pediatrician; b. Madras, India; came to U.S., 1967; d. Syed Abdul and Rahimunisa (Hussain) Hakim; m. C. Azeez Haque, Feb. 5, 1967; children: Kifizeba, Masarath Nashr, Asim Zayd. MBBS, Madras Med. Coll., 1967. Diplomate Am. Bd. Pediatrics. Rotating intern Miriam Hosp. Brown U., Providence, 1967-68; resident in pediatrics N.J. Coll. Medicine Childrens Hosp., 1968-70; fellow in devel. disabilities Ohio State U., 1970-71; acting chief pediat. Nisonger Ctr., 1973-74; staff pediatrician Children and Youth Project Children's Hosp., Columbus, Ohio; clin. asst. prof. pediatrics Ohio State U., 1974-80, clin. assoc. prof. pediatrics, 1981-99, clin. assoc. prof. dept. internat. health Coll. Medicine, 1993-99, clin. prof. pediatrics and internat. health Coll. Medicine, 1999—. Pediatrician in charge cmty. Children's Hosp. Cmty. Health Ctrs. Children's Hosp., Columbus, 1982—, dir. pediatric acad. assoc., Columbus Children's Hosp., Ohio State U., 1992—; cons. Ctrl. Ohio Head Start Program, 1974-79; med. cons. Bur. Rehab. and Devel. Disabilities for State of Ohio, 1990—. Contbr. articles to profl. jours. and newspapers. Charter founder Ronald Reagan Rep. Ctr.; trustee Asian Am. Health Alliance Network, Columbus, 1994—. Recipient Physician Recognition award, AMA, 1971—86, 1988—99, Gold medals in surgery, radiology, pediat. and ob-gyn., Presdl. medal of Merit, Pres. Ronald Reagan, 1982, Nat. Leadership award, Nat. Rep. Congl. Com., 2001. Fellow Am. Acad. Pediatrics; mem. Islamic Med. Assn., Am. Assn. of Physicians of Indian Origin, Ambulatory Pediatric Assn., Ctrl. Ohio Pediatric Soc., Islamic Med. Assn. Muslim. Achievements include research on enuresis and tumors caused by human papilloma viruses. Home: 5995 Forestview Dr Columbus OH 43213-2114 Office: 700 Childrens Dr Columbus OH 43205-2664

HARALDSON, TENA, newspaper editor; Bur. chief AP, Sioux Falls, S.D., 1989—. Office: 330 N Main Ave Ste 303 Sioux Falls SD 57104-6034

HARBERGER, ARNOLD CARL, economist, educator; b. Newark, July 27, 1924; s. Ferdinand C. and Martha (Bucher) H.; m. Ana Beatriz Valjalo, Mar. 15, 1958; children: Paul Vincent, Carl David. Student, Johns Hopkins U., 1941-43; MA, U. Chgo., 1947, PhD, 1950; Doctor honoris causa, U. Tucuman, 1979, Cath. U. Chile, 1988, Tech. U. Cen. Am., 1989. Asst. prof. polit. economy Johns Hopkins U., 1949-53; asso. prof. econs. U. Chgo., 1953-59, prof., 1959—, chmn. dept., 1964-71, 75-80, Gustavus F. and Ann M. Swift disting. svc. prof., 1977-91, prof. emeritus, 1991—, dir. Ctr. Latin Am. Econ. Studies, 1965-92. Vis. prof. MIT (Ctr. Internat. Studies), New Delhi, 1961-62, Econ. Devel. Inst., IBRD, 1965, Harvard U., 1971-72, Princeton U., 1973-74, UCLA, 1983, 84, U. Paris, 1986; prof. econs. UCLA, 1984—; cons. IMF, 1950, 89, U.S. Pres.'s Materials Policy Commn., 1951-52, U.S. Treasury Dept., 1961-75, Com. Econ. devel., 1961-78, Planning Commn., India, 1961-62, 73, Pan Am. Union, 1962-76, Dept. State, 1962-76, Cen. Bank, Chile, 1965-70, Dominican Republic, 1989, China, 1995, Ecuador, 1996, Planning Dept., Panama, 1963-77, Colombia, 1969-71, Nicaragua, 1990, Indonesia, 1997—; cons. Ford Found., 1967-77, Planning Commn., El Salvador, 1973-75, Budget and Planning Office, Uruguay, 1974-75, Can. Dept. Regional Econ. Expansion, 1975-77, Econ. Min. Argentina, 1994-2000, Fin. Ministry, Bolivia, 1976, Mex., 1976—; cons. Can. Dept. Employment and Migration, 1980-82, Indonesian Ministry Fin., 1981-82, 86, 97-2000, Can. Dept. Fin., 1982-88, Can. Dept. Industry, Sci. and Tech., 1991-99, Chinese Ministry Fin., 1983; ministry fin., Malawi, 1988, Venezuela, 1989, Colombia, 1991, 94, 2002, Dominican Republic, 1996, 97, Egypt, 2002, Nicaragua, 2002; mem. internat. adv. coun. Inst. Internat. Studies, Stanford U., 1991-99; v.p., chmn. adv. coun. Inst. for Policy Reform; cons. Office Econ. Adviser to the Pres. Russia, 2000—. Author: Project Evaluation, 1972, Taxation and Welfare, 1974; Editor: Demand for Durable Goods, 1960, The Taxation of Income from Capital, 1968, Key Problems of Economic Policy In Latin America, 1970, World Economic Growth, 1985; contbr. sci. papers to profl. jours. and govt. publs. With AUS, 1943-46. Guggenheim fellow; Fulbright scholar; faculty rsch. fellow Social Sci. Rsch. Coun.; Ford Found. faculty rsch. fellow, 1968-69. Fellow Econometric Soc., Am. Acad. Arts and Scis., Am. Econ. Assn. (mem. exec. com. 1970-72, v.p. 1992, pres.-elect 1996, pres. 1997, disting. fellow 1999), Western Econ. Assn. (v.p. 1987-88, pres. 1989-90), Royal Econ. Soc., Nat. Tax Assn., NAS, Phi Beta Kappa. Home: 136 Buckskin Rd Bell Canyon CA 91307-1125 Office: UCLA PO Box 951477 405 Hilgard Ave Los Angeles CA 90095-1477 E-mail: harberger@econ.ucla.edu.

HARBERT, NORMAN CARL, electric company executive; b. Cleveland, Ohio, Oct. 7, 1933; s. Carl J. and Jane O. Harbert; m. Donna Lea Bransuela, Sept. 8, 1936; children— Carl, Merritt, Scott, Ann. B.S. in Industrial Engring., U. Mich., 1956; M.S. in Engring. Admin., Case Inst., 1962. Engring. administr. Reliance Electric Co., Cleveland, 1959-67, chief industrial engr., 1967-70, plant mgr., Ashtabula, Ohio, 1970-72, div. mgr. motors, 1973-75, corp. dir. mfg., 1976-78, gen. mgr. rotating group, 1978-80; pres., chief exec. officer Ajax Magnethermic Corp., Warren, Ohio, 1980— ; dir. OsAir Inc., Mentor, Ohio, Second Nat. Bank, Warren, Roadway Services, Inc, Akron, Ohio, Wean United, Pitts., Lintern Corp., Mentor, Ohio, Maverick Tube Corp., St. Louis. Trustee Euclid Gen. Hosp., Cleveland, 1978-83, Crippled Children's Soc., Cleveland; loaned exec. United Appeal, Cleveland, 1964; chmn. United Appeal Campaign, Ashtabula, 1971, Euclid council Boy Scout Am. campaign, (Ohio), 1974. Served to lt. USAF 1959-61. Republican. Office: Hawk Corp 200 Public Sq Ste 30-5000 Cleveland OH 44114

HARDEN, OLETA ELIZABETH, English educator, university administrator; b. Jamestown, Ky., Nov. 22, 1935; d. Stanley Virgil and Myrtie Alice (Stearns) McWhorter; m. Dennis Clarence Harden, July 23, 1966. BA, Western Ky. U., 1956; MA in English, U. Ark., 1958, PhD, 1965. Teaching asst. U. Ark., Fayetteville, 1956-57, 58-59, 61-63; instr. S.W. Mo. State Coll., Springfield, 1957-58, Murray (Ky.) U., 1959-61; asst. prof. English Northeastern State Coll., Tahlequah, Okla., 1963-65; asst. prof. Wichita (Kans.) State U., 1965-66; asst. prof. English Wright State U., Dayton, Ohio, 1966-68, assoc. prof., 1968-72, prof., 1972-93, asst. chmn. English dept., 1967-70, asst. dean, 1971-73, assoc. dean, 1973-74, exec. dir. gen. univ. services, 1974-76, pres. of faculty, 1984-85, prof. emerita, 1993—. Pres. Wright State Retirees Assn., 1995-96. Author: Maria Edgeworth's Art of Prose Fiction, 1971, Maria Edgeworth, 1984; editor: The Extension, 1999—. Pres. Wright State Retirees Assn., 1995-96. R & D grantee Wright State U., 1969, 78, Ford Found. grantee, 1971, Wright State U. sabbatical grantee Oxford U., Eng., 1978-79, 86-87; recipient Presdl. award for outstanding svc. Wright State U., 1986, Alumni Teaching Excellence award, 1993. Mem. MLA, Coll. English Assn., AAUP, Women's Caucus for Modern Langs., Am. Conf. for Irish Studies (presenter 1989, 91, 94, 95). Office: Wright State U Dept English 7751 Colonel Glenn Hwy Dayton OH 45431-1674 Home: 2618 Big Woods Trl Dayton OH 45431-8704 E-mail: oharden@aol.com.

HARDEN, VAN, radio personality; Radio host morning show Sta. WHO-AM, Des Moines. Office: WHO Radio 1801 Grand Ave Des Moines IA 50309*

HARDENBURGER, JANICE, state legislator; m. William Hardenburger. Kans. state senator Dist. 21, 1993—; farm ptnr., 1996—. Home: 562 25th Rd Haddam KS 66944-9037

HARDER, ELAINE RENE, state legislator; b. Windom, Minn., Dec. 27, 1947; d. Russell Jacob and Eunice Rupp; m. Ronald Dale Harder, 1970; children: Graydon, Nicole. BS in Secondary Edn., Mankato State U., 1970. Tchr. secondary sch.; owner sml. bus.; sales rep.; rep. Dist. 22B Minn. Ho. of Reps., 1995—. Chair ethics com. Minn. Ho. of Reps., mem. agriculture policy com., agriculture and rural devel. finance com., taxes com., property tax divsn. com.; life and heatlh ins. profl. 4-H youth devel. agt. U. Minn. Ext. Svc. AAUW, Minn. Assn. Life Underwriters, Minn. Home Econ. Assn., Jackson C. of C., Kiwanis, Phi Upsilon Omicron, Delta Clovia. Office: 487 State Office Bldg Saint Paul MN 55155 E-mail: rep.Elaine.Harder@house.leg.state.mn.us.

HARDER, ROBERT CLARENCE, state official; b. Horton, Kans., June 4, 1929; s. Clarence L. and Olympia E. (Kubik) H.; m. Dorothy Lou Welty, July 31, 1953; children: Anne, James David. AB, Baker U., Baldwin, Kans., 1951; MTh, So. Meth. U., 1954; ThD in Social Ethics, Boston U., 1958; LHD (hon.), Baker U., 1983, Ottawa U., 1991. Ordained to ministry Meth. Ch., 1959; pastor East Topeka Meth. Ch., 1958-64; mem. Kans. Ho. of Reps., 1961-67; rsch. assoc. Menninger Found., Topeka, 1964-65; instr. Washburn U., 1964, 68, 69; dir. Topeka Office of Econ. Opportunity, 1965-67; tech. asst. coordinator Office of Gov. of Kans., 1967-68; dir. community resources devel. League of Kans. Municipalities, 1968-69; dir. Kans. Dept. Social Welfare, Topeka, 1969-73, sec., 1973-87; projects adminstr. Topeka State Hosp., 1987-89. Adj. prof. pub. adminstrn. Kans. U., 1987-95, instr. Sch. Social Welfare, 1971-87; cons. Menninger Topeka, 1991-92; sec. Kans. Dept. Health and Environment, 1992-95. Contbr. articles to profl. jours. Recipient Disting. Svc. award East Topeka Civic Assn., 1963, Romana Hood award, 1965, Cert. of Recognition, State of Kans., 1979, 87, Spl. Commendation award Kans. Senate, 1987, Spl. Commendation, Kans. Ho. of Reps., 1987, Outstanding Alumnus award Perkins Sch. Theology, So. Meth. U., 1994, Disting. Svc. award Kans. Children's Svc. League, 1998; named Outstanding Pub. Ofcl. of the Yr., 1987. Mem. Am. Soc. Public Adminstrs. (Public Adminstr. of Yr. Kans. chpt. 1980), Am. Public Welfare Assn., Kans. Health Care Commn., Kans. Conf. Social Welfare (Outstanding Person of Yr. 1987). Democrat.

HARDGROVE, JAMES ALAN, lawyer; b. Chgo., Feb. 20, 1945; s. Albert John and Ruth (Noonen) H.; m. Kathleen M. Peterson, June 15, 1968; children: Jennifer Anne, Amy Kristine, Michael Sheridan. BA, U. Notre Dame, 1967; cert. English law, U. Coll. Law, 1969; JD, U. Notre Dame, 1970. Bar: Ill. 1970, U.S. Ct. Appeals (7th cir.) 1970, U.S. Dist. Ct. (no. dist.) Ill. 1970, U.S. Dist. Ct. (cen. dist.) Ill. 1978, U.S. Supreme Ct. 1980. Law clk. to presiding justice U.S. Ct. Appeals (7th cir.), Chgo., 1970-71; assoc. Sidley & Austin, 1971-76, ptnr., 1977—. Mem. ABA, Ill. Bar Assn., Chgo. Bar Assn., Legal Club. Home: 948 Ridge Ave Evanston IL 60202-1720 Office: Sidley Austin Brown & Word Bank One Plz 10 S Dearborn St Chicago IL 60603-2000 E-mail: jhardgro@sidley.com.

HARDIN, CHRISTOPHER DEMAREST, medical educator; b. Syracuse, N.Y., July 31, 1961; BS, Cornell U., 1983; MS in Physiology, U. Rochester, 1986; PhD, U. Cin., 1989. Sr. fellow Dept. Radiology U. Wash., 1989-91, rsch. asst. prof., 1991—; asst. prof., then assoc. prof. physiology U. Mo., Columbia, 1993—. Tutor, mentor in field; spkr. in field. Contbr. articles to profl. jours. Albert J. Ryan fellow, 1986-89, tng. grant fellow U. Cin.,. 1985-86, univ. grad. fellow U. Rochester, 1983-85; recipient Jeffrey D. Doane Meml. award, 1987, Nat. Rsch. Svc. award, 1989-92, Dorsett L. Spurgeon Disting. Med. Rsch. award, 1999. Mem. AAAS, Internat. Soc. Heart Rsch. (N.Am. sect), Am. Heart Assn. Sci. Coun. (basic sci.), Am. Physiol. Soc., Harold Lamport award Outstanding Young Invesitgator 1995), Biophysical Soc. Home: 4480 Roemer Rd Columbia MO 65202-7060 Office: Univ of Missouri Dept of Physiology Ma415 Med Sci Bldg Columbia MO 65212-0001

HARDIN, CLIFFORD MORRIS, retired university chancellor, cabinet member; b. Knightstown, Ind., Oct. 9, 1915; s. James Alvin and Mabel (Macy) H.; m. Martha Love Wood, June 28, 1939; children: Susan Carol (Mrs. L.W. Wood), Clifford Wood, Cynthia (Mrs. Robert Milligan), Nancy Ann (Mrs. Douglas L. Rogers), James. BS, Purdue U., 1937, MS, 1939, PhD, 1941, DSc (hon.), 1952; Farm Found. scholar, U. Chgo., 1939-40; LLD, Creighton U., 1956, Ill. State U., 1973; Dr. honoris causa, Nat. U. Colombia, 1968; DSc, Mich. State U., 1969, N.D. State U., 1969, U. Nebr., 1978, Okla. Christian Coll., 1979. Instr. U. Wis., 1941-42, asst. prof. agrl. econs., 1942-44; assoc. prof. agrl. econs. Mich. State Coll., 1944-46, prof., chmn. agrl. econs. dept., 1946-48, dir. expt. sta., 1949-53, dean agr., 1953-54; chancellor U. Nebr., 1954-69; sec. U.S. Dept. Agr., Washington, 1969-71; vice chmn. bd., dir. Ralston Purina Co., St. Louis, 1971-80; dir. Center for Study of Am. Bus., Washington U., 1981-83, scholar-in-residence, 1983-85; cons., dir. Stifel, Nicolaus & Co., 1980-87. Bd. dirs. Gallup, Inc., Lincoln, Nebr., 1980-99; bd. dirs. Omaha br. Fed. Res. Bank of Kansas City, 1961-67, chmn., 1962-67. Editor: Overcoming World Hunger, 1969. Trustee Rockefeller Found., 1961-69, 72-81, Winrock, Internat., Morrilton, Ark., 1984-94, Am. Assembly, 1975—, U. Nebr. Found., 1975—; mem. Pres.'s Com. to Stregthen Security Free World, 1963. Mem. Assn. State Univs. and Land-Grant Colls. (pres. 1960, chmn. exec. com. 1961).

HARDIN, LOWELL STEWART, retired economics educator; b. nr. Knightstown, Ind., Nov. 16, 1917; s. J. Fred and Mildred (Stewart) H.; m. Mary J. Cooley, Sept. 21, 1940; children: Thomas Stewart, Joyce Ann, Peter Lowell. BS, Purdue U., 1939, DAgr (hon), 1990; PhD, Cornell U., 1943. Grad. asst., instr. Cornell U., 1939-43; instr., asst. and assoc. prof., prof. Purdue U., 1943-65, adj. prof. agrl. econs., 1965-66, prof., 1981-84, emeritus prof., asst. dir. internat. programs, 1984—, acting head dept. agrl. econs., 1954-57, head dept., 1957-65; also dir. Purdue Work Simplification Lab. Program adviser agr. Ford Found., 1965-66, program officer agr., 1966-81; former trustee Internat. Food Policy Rsch. Inst., Washington, Internat. Ctr. for Agrl. Rsch. in Dry Areas, Aleppo, Syria, Internat. Svc. for Nat. Agrl. Rsch., The Hague, The Netherlands, Winrock Internat. Inst. for Agrl. Devel., Morrilton, Ark. Author: (with L.M. Vaughan) Farm Work Simplification, 1949. Fellow AAAS, Am. Agrl. Econ. Assn. (pres. 1963-64); mem. Internat. Assn. Agrl. Economists, Sigma Xi, Alpha Gamma Rho, Phi Kappa Phi, Alpha Zeta, Sigma Delta Chi. Federated Church. Home: 2628 Calvin Ct W Lafayette IN 47906-1402

HARDIS, STEPHEN ROGER, retired manufacturing company executive; b. N.Y.C., July 13, 1935; s. Abraham I. and Ethel (Krinsky) H; m. Sondra Joyce Rolbin, Sept. 15, 1957; children: Julia Faye, Andrew Martin, Joanna Halley. B.A. with distinction, Cornell U., 1956; M.P.A. in Econs., Woodrow Wilson Sch. of Pub. and Internat. Affairs Princeton U., 1960. Asst. to controller Gen. Dynamics, 1960-61; fin. analyst Pfaudler Permutit Inc., 1961-64; staff asst. to controller, 1964; mgr. corp. long-range planning Ritter Pfaudler Corp., 1965-68, dir. corporate planning, 1968; treas. Sybron Corp., Rochester, N.Y., 1969—, v.p. fin., 1970-77, exec. v.p. fin. and planning, 1977-79; vice chmn., chief fin. and adminstrv. officer Eaton Corp., Cleve., 1979—, vice chmn., CEO, 1995, chmn., CEO, 1996-2000; ret., 2000; chmn. Axcelis Techs., 2000—. Bd. dirs. Progressive Corp., Nordson Corp., Lexmark Corp., Marsh & McLennan, Axcelis Techs., Inc., Steris Corp, Apogent Techs., Inc. Past mem. Gov.'s Task Force on High Tech. Industry; past mem. bd. dirs. Rochester Area Hosp. Corp., Rochester Area Ednl. TV Sta., Genesee Hosp.; trustee Cleve. Clinic, Inc., Playhouse Square Found., Musical Arts Assn. (Cleve. Orchestra). With USNR, 1956-58. Mem. Phi Beta Kappa. Office: Eaton Corp 1111 Superior Ave E Cleveland OH 44114-2507

HARDY, DEBORAH LEWIS, dean, educator, dental hygienist; b. Nov. 11, 1963; Student, Christopher Newport Coll., 1982-84; BS in Dental Hygiene, Old Dominion U., 1989, cert. in gerontol. studies, MS in Dental Hygiene, Old Dominion U., 1991; postgrad., U. Tex., Dallas, 1993. Cert. ADA Joint Commn. on Nat. Dental Exam.; lic. S.E. Regional Va., Tex., Va.; cert. in cardiopulmonary resuscitation. Assoc. prof. Caruth Sch. Dental Hygiene Baylor Coll., Dallas, 1991-95; assoc. dean health occupations-dental N.E. Wis. Tech. Coll., Green Bay, 1995-97, assoc. dean health and cmty. svc., 1997—. Dental asst. Dr. William Griffin, Newport News, Va., 1989; dental asst., dental hygienist Dental Power, Inc., Newport News, 1988-90; dental hygienist Dr. John Caudill, Virginia Beach, 1990-91, Drs. Cash and Weisburg, Norfolk, Va., 1990-91; dental hygienist, educator Riverside Regional Convalescent Ctr., Newport News, 1991; part-time dental hygienist East Dallas Clinic, 1992-95, Nelson-Tebedo Dental Clinic, Dallas, 1995, Oneida (Wis.) Dental Clinic, 1997; cons., educator Skilled Nursing Facility, Collins Hosp., Baylor U. Med. Ctr., Dallas, 1992; lectr. and spkr. in field. Author: (book) Preventive Oral Health Services Provided by Nurses' Aides to Nursing Home Residents, 1991, (book chpt.) Oral Health and the Older Adult, 1995; editor: (newsletter) Oral Examiner, 1993-95; mem. editl. bd. Profl. Devel. Quar. PDQ, 1994-95; contbr. numerous articles and abstracts to profl. jours. Dental hygienist, educator Operation Smile Internat., Ghana Med. Mission, Accra, 1989; vol. Ea. Va. Med. Sch.-Ea. Shore, 1988, Girls Inc., Dallas, 1992; coord. Spirit of Christmas Program, Caruth Sch. Dental Hygiene, 1991, Sr. Student Oral Health Edn., St. Philip's Episcopal Sch. and Comty. Ctr., Dallas, 1993, Health Fair, Dallas Marriott Quorum Hotel, 1993. Recipient Acad. Dentistry for the Handicapped award, 1989, award for phenomenal achievement and leadership Women Dentists' Awards Luncheon, 1993; fellow Old Dominion U., 1990; also numerous rsch. grants in field. Mem. Am. Vocat. Assn., Nat. Dental Hygienists' Assn., Am. Dental Hygienists' Assn., Am. Assn. Dental Schs., Student Nat. Dental Assn. (faculty facilitator 1992-95), N.E. Wis. African Am. Assn. (membership chair 1997), Dallas Dental Hygienists' Soc. (Mem. of Month 1993, 95), Sigma Phi Alpha. Office: NE Wis Tech Coll PO Box 19042 2740 W Mason St Green Bay WI 54303-4966

HARDY, MICHAEL LYNN, lawyer; b. St. Louis, Aug. 28, 1947; s. William Frost and Ruth (Shea) H.; m. Martha Bond, Sept. 2, 1972; children: Brian M., Kevin S. AB, John Carroll U., 1969; JD, U. Mich., 1972. Bar: Ohio 1972. Assoc. Guren, Merritt, et al, Cleve., 1972-77, ptnr., 1977-84, Thompson Hine LLP and predecessor, Cleve., 1984—. Editor-in-chief Ohio Environ. Monthly, 1989-94, Ohio Environ. Law, 1992; bd. advisors Harvard Environ. Law Rev., 1976-78, The Environ. Counselor, 1988—. Trustee Nature Ctr. at Shaker Lakes. Capt. U.S. Army, 1969-74. Mem. ABA (nat. resources sect.), Ohio State Bar Assn. (sec. environ. law com. 1983-84, vice-chmn. 1984-86, chmn. 1987-91), Def. Rsch. Inst. (chmn. industrywide litig. com. 1989-91), Canterbury Golf Club. Home: 30649 Summit Ln Cleveland OH 44124-5836 Office: Thompson Hine LLP 3900 Key Ctr 127 Public Sq Cleveland OH 44114-1216 E-mail: mike.hardy@thompsonhine.com.

HARDY, RICHARD ALLEN, mechanical engineer, diesel fuel engine specialist; b. Cleveland, Ohio, Sept. 16, 1928; s. Harry and Mae Hardy; m. Lois L. Fawcett, May 16, 1953 (dec. Dec. 1990); children: Pamela, Richard, James, Thomas. BSME, Case Inst. Tech., 1952. Founder, CEO Fluid Mechanics Inc., Cleve., 1957—. Designed and built largest dynamic fuel-injection pump test stand in Western hemisphere. Cpl. U.S. Army, 1946-48. Recipient Weatherhead 100 award Cleve., 1989. Mem. Assn. of Diesel Specialists (various coms. 1960—). Roman Catholic. Avocations: racquetball, scuba. Home: 26875 Hilliard Blvd Cleveland OH 44145-3213

HARDY, WILLIAM ROBINSON, lawyer; b. Cin., June 14, 1934; s. William B. and Chastine M. (Sprague) H.; m. Leslie Warrington Bailey, Apr. 16, 1999; children from previous marriage: Anita Christina, William Robinson Jr. AB magna cum laude, Princeton U., 1956; JD, Harvard U., 1963. Bar: Ohio 1963, U.S. Supreme Ct. 1975. Life underwriter New Eng. Mut. Life Ins. Co., 1956-63; assoc. Graydon, Head & Ritchey, Cin., 1963-68, ptnr., 1968-98. Mem. panel comml. arbitrators Am. Arbitration Assn., 1972—, mem. panel large complex case program, 1993—, panel of mediators, 1993—, comml. arbitrator tng. faculty, 1998—; reporter joint com. for revision of rules of U.S. Dist. Ct. for So. Dist. Ohio, 1975, 80, 83, mem., 1990—. Bd. dirs. Cin. Union Bethel, 1968-82, pres., 1977-82, emeritus, 1982—; bd. dirs. Ohio Valley Goodwill Industries Rehab. Ctr., Cin., 1970—, pres., 1981-92; mem. Cin. Bd. Bldg. Appeals, 1976-2001, vice chmn., 1983, chmn., 1983-2001; pres. Hamilton County (Ohio) Alcohol and Drug Addiction Svcs. Bd., 1990-92; trustee Substance Abuse Mgmt. and Devel. Inc., 1998-99. Capt. USAR, 1956-68; maj. gen. Ohio Mil. Res., insp. gen., 1988-89, TJAG, 1989-93, dep. comdr., 1993-96, comdr., 1996-2001. Recipient award of merit Ohio Legal Ctr. Inst., 1975, 76, Ohio Commendation medal, 1999. Mem. ABA, AAAS, Ohio Bar Assn., Cin. Bar Assn., Ohio Acad. Trial Lawyers, Am. Arbitration Assn., Assn. for Conflict Resolution, 6th Cir. Jud. Conf. (life), Ohio Soc. Colonial Wars (gov. 1979), Princeton (N.Y.C.) Club, Interlachen Country Club (Winter Park, Fla.), Phi Beta Kappa. Mem. Ch. Of Redeemer. Office: 432 Walnut St Ste 206 Cincinnati OH 45202-3909

HARDYMON, DAVID WAYNE, lawyer; b. Columbus, Ohio, Aug. 22, 1949; s. Philip Barbour and Margaret Evelyn (Bowers) H.; m. Monica Ella Sleep, Mar. 13, 1982; children: Philip Garnet, Teresa Jeanette. BA in History, Bowling Green State U., 1971; JD, Capital U., Columbus, Ohio, 1976. Bar: Ohio 1976, U.S. Dist. Ct. (so. dist.) Ohio 1976; U.S. Supreme Ct. 1980, U.S. Ct. Appeals (6th cir.) 1982, Ky. 1999, U.S. Dist. Ct. (no. dist.) Ohio 1999, W.Va. 2000, U.S. Dist. Ct. (so. dist.) W.Va. 2000. Asst. prosecuting atty. Franklin County Prosecuter's Office, Columbus, Ohio, 1976-81; assoc. Vorys, Sater, Seymour & Pease, 1981-86, ptnr., 1987—.

Mem. Chmn's. Club Franklin Country Rep. Orgn., 1983. Fellow Columbus Bar Found.; mem. Ohio State Bar Assn., Columbus Bar Assn. Avocations: sailing, archery. Office: Vorys Sater Seymour & Pease PO Box 1008 52 E Gay St Columbus OH 43215-3161

HARE, ROBERT YATES, music history educator; b. McGrann, Pa., June 14, 1921; s. Robert Deemar and Beulah (Yates) H.; m. Constance King Rutherford, Mar. 31, 1948; children: Stephen, Beverly, Madeleine. Mus.B., U. Detroit, 1948; M.A., Wayne State U., 1950; Ph.D., U. Iowa, 1959. Instr. Marietta (Ohio) Coll., 1949-51, Del Mar Coll., Corpus Christi, Tex., 1951-55; prof., chmn. grad. studies San Jose (Calif.) State U., 1956-65; prof., dean Eastern Ill. U. Music, 1965-74; prof. music history and lit. Ohio State U., Columbus, 1974-86, prof. emeritus, 1986—, dir. Sch. Music, 1974-78, dir. audio-rec. engring., 1979-82, arts adminstr. research and faculty devel., 1982-86. Cons. in field; Mem. council music edn. in higher edn. Ill. Music Educators Assn., 1969-74. Condr. coll. symphony band, 1956-63, San Jose Youth Symphony, 1957-59, univ. symphony, 1968-74, Ea. Ill. U. Symphony, 1968-74; French horn recitals, Carnegie Music Hall, Pitts., 1940, 42; French hornist, Pitts. Symphony Orch., 1941-43, 44-45, Buffalo Philharmonic, 1943-44, Cin. Summer Opera Co., 1945, Indpls. Symphony Orch., 1945-46, San Antonio Symphony Orch., 1947-49; orchestrator, San Antonio Symphony Orch., 1947-49; recs. include Pitts. Symphony Orch., Indpls. Symphony Orch. (as French hornist), San Jose State U. Symphonic Band (as condr.); contbr. articles to profl. jours. Mem. com. grad. and profl. edn. in arts and humanities Ill. Bd. Higher Edn., 1969-70; mem. performing arts commn. Ill. Sesquicentennial, 1967; mem. exec. bd. Greater Columbus Arts Council, 1974-76, Ohio Alliance for Arts in Edn., 1974-76; trustee Columbus Symphony Orch., 1975-79. Profl. Promise scholar Carnegie-Mellon U., 1939 Mem. Music Educators Nat. Conf. (publs. planning com. 1970-76), Am. Musicol. Soc., Coll. Music Soc., Phi Mu Alpha, Sinfonia (hon.), Pi Kappa Lambda (hon.), Delta Omicron (hon.). Lodges: Masons; Shriners. Home: 2624 SW Ashworth Pl Topeka KS 66614-2507 Office: Ohio State U Coll Arts 305 Mershon Auditorium Columbus OH 43210

HARKIN, THOMAS RICHARD, senator; b. Cumming, Iowa, Nov. 19, 1939; s. Patrick and Frances H.; m. Ruth Raduenz, 1968; children: Amy, Jenny. BS, Iowa State U., 1962; JD, Cath. U. Am., 1972. Mem. staff Ho. of Reps. Select Com. U.S. Involvement in S.E. Asia, 1970; mem. 94th-98th Congresses from 5th Iowa Dist., mem. sci. and tech. com., mem. agr., nutrition and forestry coms.; U.S. Senator from Iowa, 1984—. Mem. Dem. Steering Com., com. labor and human resources; chmn. Appropriations Subcom. on Labor, Health and Human Svcs and Edn.; ; chmn. Agr., Nutrition, and Forestry subcom. on Rsch., Nutrition, and Gen. Legis.; mem. Small Bus. Com.; prin. author Ams. with Disabilities Act. Co-author: (with C.E. Thomas) Five Minutes to Midnight: Why the Nuclear Threat is Growing Faster than Ever, 1990. Dem. candidate for Presidency of U.S., 1992. Served with USN, 1962-67. Named Outstanding Young Alumnus Iowa State U. Alumni Assn., 1974 Democrat. Office: US Senate 731 Hart Senate Bldg Washington DC 20510-0001

HARKNA, ERIC, advertising executive; b. Tallinn, Estonia, June 24, 1940; came to U.S., 1947; s. Erich K. Harkna and Adelaide Mender; children: Britt, Kristiana, Christian Erik; m. Tonise Paul. B.A., Colgate U., 1962; M.B.A., Columbia U., 1964. Account exec. Benton & Bowles, N.Y.C., 1965-68; v.p., account supr. Kenyon & Eckhart, 1969-71, BBDO, Inc., N.Y.C., 1973-74, v.p., mgmt. supr., 1974-76, sr. v.p., dir., 1977-82; exec. v.p., dir., 1979-82; pres., dir. BBDO, Inc., Chgo., 1982-84, pres., chief exec. officer, 1984-93; sr. v.p. BBDO Worldwide, 1993—. Chmn. ann. awards dinner Advt. Age, 1987; chmn. Media Subcom., Chgo.; guest lectr. Chgo. Coun. Fgn. Rels., World Econ. Forum. Bd. dirs. United Cerebral Palsy Found., Chgo., 1982-94, Friends of Prentice Hosp.; v.p. nat. fund raising exec. com. Juvenile Diabetes Found. Internat., 1987-95, bd. dirs., 1990-96, internat. long range planning com. 1995-98; bd. dirs. Chgo. Coun. Profl. Psychology, 1991-96, Mus. Broadcast Commn., 1992—, U.S. Baltic Found., 1996—, Del. Place Bank. Colgate U. Norwegian Study grantee, 1961; recipient Internat. Bus. award Columbia U., 1964 Mem. Am. Assn. Advt. Agys. (regional bd. govs. 1994), Am. Mktg. Assn., Chgo. Coun. Fgn. Rels., Chgo. Advt. Club, Chgo. Econs. Club, Lake Shore Soc. Clubs, Execs. Club Chgo., N.Y. Athletic Club (N.Y.C.), N.Y. A.C. Yacht Club (Pelham), Chgo. Estonia House, Chgo. Yacht Club, 410 Club (founder, chmn., bd. dirs., bd. govs.). Office: BBDO Worldwide Inc 410 N Michigan Ave Ste 8 Chicago IL 60611-4273

HARL, NEIL EUGENE, economist, lawyer, educator; b. Appanoose County, Iowa, Oct. 9, 1933; s. Herbert Peter and Bertha Catherine (Bonner) H.; m. Darlene Ramona Harris, Sept. 7, 1952; children: James Brent, Rodney Scott. BS, Iowa State U., 1955, PhD, 1965; JD, U. Iowa, 1961. Bar: Iowa 1961. Field editor Wallace's Farmer, 1957-58; research assoc. U.S. Dept. Agr., Iowa City and Ames, Iowa, 1958-64; assoc. prof. econs. Iowa State U., Ames, 1964-67, prof., 1967—, Charles F. Curtiss Disting. prof., 1976—, dir. Ctr. Internat. Agrl. Fin., 1990—. Mem. adv. group to commr. IRS, 1979-80; mem. adv. com. Heckerling Inst. on Estate Planning, Miami, Fla., 1983-96; mem. adv. com. Office Tech. Assessment, U.S. Congress, 1988-95, vice chair, 1992-93, chair, 1993-94; mem. exec. bd. U.S. West Comms., Iowa, 1989-90; mem. adv. com. on agrl. biotech. USDA, 2000-02; lectr. in field. Author: Farm Estate and Business Planning, 1973, Farm Estate and Business Planning, 15th edit., 2001, Legal and Tax Guide for Agricultural Lenders, 1984, Legal and Tax Guide for Agricultural Lenders, supplement, 1987, Agricultural Law, 15 vols., 1980—81, Agricultural Law, 15 vols., rev. edit., 2002, Agricultural Law Manual, 1985, Agricultural Law Manual, rev. edit., 2002, The Farm Debt Crisis of the 1980s, 1990; co-author: Farmland, 1982, Principles of Agricultural Law, 1997, 2002, Taxation of Cooperatives, 1999, Reporting Farm Income, 2000, Family Owned Business Deduction, 2001, Arrogance and Power: The Saga of WOI-TV, 2001, The Law of the Land, 2002; author, actor films and videotape programs; contbr. articles to profl. jours. Trustee Iowa State U. Agrl. Found., 1969-90. 1st lt. AUS, 1955-57. 1st lt. U.S. Army, 1955—57. Recipient Outstanding Tchr. award Iowa State U., 1973, Disting Svc. to Agr. award Am. Soc. Farm Mgrs. and Rural Appraisers, 1977, Iowa sect. 1996, Faculty Svc. award Nat. Univ. Ext. Assn., 1980, Disting. Svc. award Am. Agrl. Editors Assn., 1984, Disting. Achievement citation Iowa State U., 1985, Disting. Svc. to State Govt. award Nat. Gov.'s Assn., 1986, Disting. Svc. award Iowa State U., 1986, Farm Leader of Yr. award Des Moines Register, 1986, Henry A. Wallace award, 1987, Superior Svc. award USDA, 1987, Disting. Svc. to Iowa Agr. award Iowa Farm Bur., 1992, Faculty Excellence award, Iowa Bd. Regents, 1993, Charles A. Black award Coun. Agrl. Sci. Tech., 1997, Excellence in Internat. Agr. award Iowa State U., 1999, Disting. Svc. to Agr. award Chgo. Farmers Club, 1999, Exceptional Svc. to Agr. award Iowa Master Farmers, Wallaces Farmer, 2000, Pres.'s award for disting. svc. Iowa State U., 2002; named Seminar Leader of Yr. Nat. Assn. Accts., 2000. Fellow Am. Coll. Trusts and Estates Counsel, Am. Agrl. Econs. Assn. (exec. bd. 1979-85, pres. 1983-84, bd. dirs. Am. Agrl. Econs. Found. 1992-94, pres. 1993-94, Outstanding Ext. Program award 1970, Excellence in Communicating Rsch. Results award 1975, Disting. Undergrad. Tchr. award 1976), ABA Rsch. Found., Iowa State Bar Found.; mem. ABA, Iowa Bar Assn. (Pres. award 1991), Am. Agrl. Law Assn. (pres. 1980-81, Disting. Svc. award 1984). Home: 2821 Duff Ave Ames IA 50010-4709 also: 3001 Kanaloa 78-261 Manukai St Kailua Kona HI 96740 Office: Iowa State U Dept Econs Ames IA 50011-1070 E-mail: harl@iastate.edu.

HARLAN, ROBERT ERNEST, professional football team executive; b. Des Moines, Sept. 9, 1936; m. Madeline Harlan; children: Kevin, Bryan, Michael. BJ, Marquette U., 1958. Former gen. reporter UPI, Milw.; sports info. dir. Marquette U., 1959; dir. community rels. St. Louis Cardinals baseball team, 1966-68, dir. pub. rels., 1968-71; asst. gen. mgr. Green Bay (Wis.) Packers, 1971-75, corp. gen. mgr., 1975-81, corp. asst. to pres., 1981-88, exec. v.p. adminstrn., 1988-89, pres., chief exec. officer, 1989—. Bd. dirs. Firstar Bank, Green Bay. Mem. exec. bd. Packer 65 Roses Sports Club. Served with U.S. Army. Mem. bd. of trustees, St. Norbert Coll., Wis. Avocation: golf. Office: Green Bay Packers 1265 Lombardi Ave Green Bay WI 54304-3997 also: Green Bay Packers Lambeau Field PO Box 10628 Green Bay WI 54307-0628

HARLAN, TIMOTHY, state legislator; b. Boonville, Mo., Mar. 15, 1949; m. Linda Harlan; children: Reed, Brook. Degree in history, Westminster Coll.; degree in law, U. Mo., Columbia. Mem. Mo. Ho. of Reps., Jefferson City, 1994—. Mem. budget com., ethics com., joint rules com., fiscal rev. com., tobacco com., appropriations com., accounts, ops. and fin. com.; vice chmn. judiciary com.; chmn. critical issues com. Active Presbyn. Ch. Recognized as outstanding legislator by Mo. Assn. Osteopathic Physicians, LWV, Mo. State Med. Soc., Mo. Pharmacy Assn., Mo. Psychol. Assn., Mo. Coalition of Alliances for the Mentally Ill, Nat. Alliance for the Mentally Ill, St. Louis 2004, Jud. Conf. Mo., Mo. Bar, Mo. Optometric Assn., Mo. Nurses Assn., Mo. Perfusion Soc., Mo. Assisted Living Assn., Mo. Assn. Homes for the Aging. Democrat. Office: Mo House of Reps Rm 400CC 201 W Capitol Ave Jefferson City MO 65101 Fax: 573 526 1088. E-mail: tharlan@services.state.mo.us.

HARLESS, KATHERINE J. telecommunications company executive; m. Skip Harless; children: Skip Jr., Ely, Bill. B in Acctg., U. Tex., 1972. With GTE, 1973—, regional pres. telephone ops., 1994-96, pres. airfone, 1996—. Bd. dirs. U. Tex. Bus. Sch., Skytel Comms. Mem. Com. of 200 (tres. com. 200 found. bd.), Chgo. Network, Internat. Women's Forum, Execs. Club Chgo., Barbara Bush Found. (mem. celebration of reading com.), Leadership Am. Office: GTE Airfone 2809 Butterfield Rd Oak Brook IL 60523-1151 Fax: 630-572-0506.

HARMAN, JOHN ROYDEN, retired lawyer; b. Elkhart, Ind., June 30, 1921; s. James Lewis and Bessie Bell (Mountjoy) H.; m. Elizabeth Rae Crosier, Dec. 12, 1943 (dec. May 1995); 1 child, James Richard. B.S., U. Ill., 1943; J.D., Ind. U., 1949. Bar: Ind. 1949. Assoc. Proctor & Proctor, Elkhart, 1949-51; pvt. practice, 1952-60; ptnr. Cawley & Harman, 1960-65, Thornburg, McGill, Deahl, Harman, Carey & Murray, 1965-82, Barnes & Thornburg, Elkhart, 1982-89; ret., 1989. Atty. City of Elkhart, 1952-60. State del. Ind. Republican Com., 1962-70; pres., bd. dirs. Crippled Childrens Soc.; bd. dirs. United Community Services Elkhart County. 1st lt., F.A.,AUS, 1943-46, PTO. Fellow Ind. Bar Found; mem. ABA, Ind. Bar Assn. , Elkhart County Bar Assn. (pres. 1977), Elkhart City Bar Assn. (pres. 1970), Elkhart C. of C. (pres. 1977, bd. dirs. 1972-75), Elcona Country Club (bd. dirs.), Phi Kappa Psi, Alpha Kappa Psi, Phi Delta Phi. Republican. Presbyterian. Avocation: golf. Office: NBD Bank Bldg 121 W Franklin St Ste 200 Elkhart IN 46516-3200

HARMAN, MIKE, real estate broker, small business owner; b. Troy, Kans., Aug. 27, 1952; m. Sue Harman; 2 children. Libertarian candidate for U.S. House 7th Dist., Mo., 1996. Office: 675 E 380th Rd Dunnegan MO 65640-9622

HARMEL, PAUL, corporate executive; CEO Lifetouch, Eden Prairie, Minn. Office: Lifetouch 11000 Viking Dr Eden Prairie MN 55344-7257

HARMON, BUD GENE, animal sciences educator, consultant; b. Camden, Ind., July 2, 1931; s. Orvie M. and Margaret (Cooke) H.; m. Mary Lynne Jones, June 7, 1953; children: Brad Lee, Beth Ann, Jana Renee. BS, Purdue U., 1958; PhD, Mich. State U., 1962. Rsch. tchr. U. Ill., Urbana, 1962-75; rsch. dir. Ralston Purina, St. Louis, 1975-86; head dept. animal sci. Purdue U., West Lafayette, 1986-97, now prof. Mem. sci. adv. bd. Fats and Protein Found. Rsch. Bd., 1997—. With USN, 1951-55. Mem. Am. Soc. Animal Sci. (pres. 1994). Office: Purdue U Dept Animal Scis West Lafayette IN 47907

HARMON, PATRICK, historian, sports commentator; b. St. Louis, Sept. 2, 1916; s. Jack and Laura (Duchesne) H.; m. Anne M. Worland, Aug. 31, 1940; children— Michael, Timothy, Kathleen, Daniel, John, Sheila, Peggy, Brigid, Kevin, Teresa, Christopher. A.B., U. Ill., 1939. Sports editor News-Gazette, Champaign, Ill., 1942-47, Gazette, Cedar Rapids, Iowa, 1947-51, Post, Cin., 1951-85; ret., 1985; sports commentator Sta. WCPO-TV, 1953-56, Sta. WKRC, 1958, Sta. WLW-TV, 1958-68; curator, historian Coll. Football Hall of Fame, Kings Island, Ohio, 1986-95; historian, 1995—. Contbg. sports editor: World Book, 1959— . Recipient Fred Hutchinson Meml. award for community service, 1969; named Internat. Churchmen's Sports Writer of Year, 1973 Mem. Sigma Chi. Home and Office: 608 Maple Trace Cincinnati OH 45246

HARMON, ROBERT WAYNE, electrical engineering executive; b. Winchester, Ind., Oct. 22, 1929; s. Wayne and Theresa (Bishop) H.; m. Mary Louise Cobb; children: Wayne Charles, Keith Robert, Arthur Dean, Frederic Bruce. BSEE with highest distinction, Purdue U, 1951, MSEE, 1955. Engr. Aro, Inc., Tullahoma, Tenn., 1951-54; devel. engr. Ohio Brass Co., Barberton, Ohio, 1955-63, dir. new product devel., 1963-68; chief engr. A.B. Chance Co., Centralia, Mo., 1968-95. Cons. and legal tech. expert witness in field. Holder 30 patents in insulation, elect. apparatus. Fellow IEEE (life); mem. ASTM, Nat. Elec. Mfgrs. Assn. Avocations: geology, archaeology, whitewater canoeing. Home and Office: 19001 N Jay Jay Centralia MO 65240-3510 E-mail: robermon@aol.com.

HARMONY, MARLIN DALE, chemistry educator; b. Lincoln, Nebr., Mar. 2, 1936; s. Philip and Helen Irene (Michal) H. A.A., Kansas City (Mo.) Jr. Coll., 1956; B.S. in Chem. Engring., U. Kans., 1958; Ph.D. in Chemistry, U. Calif.-Berkeley, 1961. Asst. prof. U. Kans., Lawrence, 1962-67, assoc. prof., 1967-71, prof., 1971-98, chmn., 1980-88, prof. emeritus, 1998—. Panel mem. NRC-Nat. Bur. Standards., 1969-78; mem. review panel NSF, 1977, 92. Author: Introduction to Molecular Energies and Spectra, 1972; contbg. editor: Physics Vade Mecum, 1981; mem. editorial bd. Structural Chemistry, 1989-98; contbr. articles to profl. jours.; patentee in field. Postdoctoral fellow NSF Harvard U., 1961-62. Fellow AAAS; mem. Am. Chem. Soc., Am. Phys. Soc., Sigma Xi, Alpha Chi Sigma, Phi Lambda Upsilon, Tau Beta Pi Democrat. Home: 1033 Avalon Rd Lawrence KS 66044-2505 Office: U Kans Dept Chemistry Lawrence KS 66045-0001

HARMS, NANCY ANN, nursing educator; b. Holdrege, Nebr., Feb. 18, 1948; d. Orval M. and Ruth Marie (Nelson) H.; m. Gerhart J. Wehrbein. Diploma, Bryan Meml. Hosp., 1971; BS in Natural Sci., Nebr. Wesleyan U., 1971; BSN, U. Nebr., 1975, MSN, 1977, PhD, 1988. RN, Nebr. Staff nurse, asst. supr., ins. coord. Brewster Hosp., Holdrege, Nebr., 1971-72; instr. Immanuel Sch. Nursing, Omaha, 1972-75; coord. nursing care plan devel. Hosp. Info. System U. Nebr. Med. Ctr., 1975; asst. chair dept. Coll. St. Mary, 1975-80; curriculum coord. Midland Luth. Coll., Fremont, Nebr., 1980-88, chair nursing div., 1988—. Mem. ANA (mem. Ho. of Dels.), Nebr. Nurses' Assn. (Nurse Excellence award, Excellence in Writing award jour., adv. Nebr. Student Nurses Assn., mem. various coms.), Nat. League Nursing, Sigma Theta Tau (theta omega, gamma pi chpts.).

HARNESS, DAVID KEITH, pastor; b. Beech Grove, Ind., Nov. 25, 1946; s. George Lewis and Evelyn Pauline (Reeves) H.; m. Peggy Ann Kyle, Feb. 14, 1993; children: Jonathan D., Ronald K., Rebecca L. Harness Lewis, Timothy Mayfield, Kimberly Case. B in Theology, Apostolic Bible Inst., 1983. Pastor United Pentecostal Ch., Council Bluffs, Iowa, 1973-76, Internat. Ministerial Assn., Indpls., 1984-96; Global Network of Christian Ministries, 1997—; CEO Nat. Christian Outreach; pastor Compassion Ctr. Fellowship. Bd. dirs. Christian Super Hwy. Network, Indpls.; asst. chaplain Marion County Jail, Indpls., 1997; chaplain Homecroft Police Dept. Author: The Gospel According to a Grandpa, 1996. Pres. New Life Ch., Inc., Indpls., 1984-94; active Multiple Sclerosis Soc. Avocation: radio announcing. Home: 2864 Punto Alto Ct Indianapolis IN 46227-6146

HAROLD, TOM, advertising executive; CEO iPares (formerly Dillon New Media), Mpls. Office: iPares 5000 Union Plz 333 Washington Ave N Minneapolis MN 55401

HARPER, DONALD VICTOR, retired transportation and logistics educator; b. Chgo., Mar. 27, 1927; s. Victor Rudolph and Mildred Victoria (Safbom) H.; children: Christine Ann, Diane Elizabeth, David Victor. Student, Wright Jr. Coll., 1945, 46-47; B.S. in Journalism, U. Ill., Urbana, 1950, Ph.D. in Econs., 1957. Instr. Coll. Commerce and Bus. adminstrn. U. Ill., Urbana, 1953-56; lectr. Carlson Sch. Mgmt. U. Minn., Mpls., 1956, asst. prof. Carlson Sch. Mgmt., 1956-59, assoc. prof., 1959-65, prof. transp. and logistics, 1965-97, chmn. dept. mgmt. and transp., 1967-70, dir. MBA and PhD programs, 1970-79, dir. PhD program, 1979-80, chmn. dept. mktg. and logistics mgmt., 1991-96; prof. emeritus, 1997—; cons. to bus. and govt. agys. Author: Economic Regulation of the Motor Trucking Industry by the States, 1959, Price Policy and Procedure, 1966, Transportation in America: Users, Carriers, Government, 2d edit, 1982; contbr. articles to profl. jours. Served with USNR, 1945-46. Mem. Am. Econ. Assn. (Disting. Mem. award transp. and pub. utilities group 1988), Am. Mktg. Assn., Transp. Research Forum, Am. Soc. Transp. and Logistics, Transp. Club Mpls. and St. Paul, Assn. Transp. Law, Logistics and Policy. Home: 2451 Sheldon St Saint Paul MN 55113-3138 Office: U Minn Carlson Sch Mgmt 321 19th Ave S Minneapolis MN 55455-0438 E-mail: dharper@csom.umn.edu.

HARPER, PATRICIA M. retired state legislator; b. Cresco, Dec. 4, 1932; d. Patrick Mullaney and Martha Gossman; 1 child, Susan. BA, MA, U. No. Iowa. Tchr. secondary math. and sci., 1955-86; mem. Iowa Ho. of Reps., 1987-90, 92-96, Iowa Senate, 1997—2002. Bd. dir. Grin & Grow Day Care Ctrs. Mem. AAUW, LWV, Waterloo Edn. Assn., Alliance for Mentally Ill. Democrat. Home: 3336 Santa Maria Dr Waterloo IA 50702-5334 Office: Iowa Senate State Capitol Des Moines IA 50319-0001

HARPER, PATRICIA NELSEN, psychiatrist; b. Omaha, July 25, 1944; d. Eddie R. and Marjorie L. (Williams) Nelsen. BS, Antioch Coll., Yellow Springs, Ohio, 1966; MD, U. Nebr., 1975; grad., Topeka Inst. Psychoanalysis, 1997. Cert. psychiatrist. Psychiatric residency Karl Menninger Sch. of Psychiatry, Topeka, 1975-78; staff psychiatrist The Menninger Clinic, 1978-98. Faculty mem. Karl Menninger Sch. of Psychiatry, Topeka, 1982-98. Program dir. Addictions Recovery Program C.F. Menninger Meml. Hosp., Topeka, 1987-97. Mem. Am. Psychiatric Assn., Am. Med Women Assn., Am. Psychoanalytic Assn. Office: Pk Nicollet Clinic Health Sys Minn 3800 Park Nicollet Blvd Saint Louis Park MN 55416-2527

HARPER, W(ALTER) JOSEPH, financial consultant; b. Columbus, Ohio, Apr. 6, 1947; s. J. Joseph and Patricia A. (Whetzle) H.; m. J. Lynn Rutherford, Aug. 1, 1970; children: Tracy, Kelly, Brett. BS in Edn., Ohio State U., 1970. Cert. fin. planner; registered investment advisor, Ohio. Tchr., coach Lake Wales (Fla.) Schs., 1970-71, Westerville (Ohio) Pub. Schs., 1971-74; securities salesman, fin. planner Investors Diversified Svcs., Columbus, 1974-83; fin. planner, investment mgr. Harper Assocs., 1983—. Mem. golf team Ohio State U., 1966-69. Mem. Nat. Assn. Personal Fin. Advisors, Internat. Assn. Fin. Planning, Inst. Cert. Fin. Planners (bd. dirs., pres. Ctrl. Ohio Soc.), Rotary, Scioto Country Club, Worthington Hills Country Club. Republican. Avocations: sports, children's activities, duck hunting. E-mail: harps@jadeinc.com.

HARPER, WILLIAM WAYNE, broadcast executive; b. Peoria, Ill., 1943; BA, Sanamon State U., 1985; MSA, Ctrl. Mich. U., 1991. Dir. Sta. WAND-TV, Decatur, Ill., 1962-70; account exec. Sta. WTWD-TV, Terre Haute, 1970-74, Sta. WFIE-TV, Evansville, Ind., 1974-77, Sta. WAND-TV, Decatur, 1977-80; gen. sales mgr. Sta. WRSP-TV, Springfield, Ill., 1980-83; v.p., gen. mgr. Sta. WVFT-TV, Roanoke, Va., 1983-84, Sta. WSMH-TV, Flint, Mich., 1984-90, Sta. WBRE-TV, Wilkes-Barre, Pa., 1990-94; gen. mgr. Sta. WBBJ-TV, Jackson, Tenn., 1994-95, Sta. WRSP/WCCU-TV, Springfield, 1997—. Office: Sta WRSP/WCCO-TV 3003 Old Rochester Rd Springfield IL 62703-5664

HARP-JIRSCHELE, MARY, communications executive; Grad., St. Norbert Coll., 1976. Writer, reporter The Post-Crescent, Appleton, Wis.; media rels. specialist in corp. rels. Aid Assn. for Lutherans, 1984-87, dir. pub. info., 1987-93, asst. v.p. media and mem. rels., 1993-95, 2d v.p. comms. products and svcs., 1995-97, v.p. comms., 1997-99, v.p. comms. and facilities mgmt., 1999—2001; v.p. comm. Aid Assn. for Lutherans/ Luth. Brotherhood, Mpls., 2001—. Mem. Pub. Rels. Soc. Am., Internat. Assn. Bus. Communicators. Office: Aid Assn for Lutherans/Luth Brotherhood 625 Fourth Ave S Minneapolis MN 55415

HARR, LUCY LORAINE, public relations executive; b. Sparta, Wis., Dec. 2, 1951; d. Ernest Donald Harr and Dorothy Catherine (Heintz) Harr Vetter BS, U. Wis., Madison, 1976, MS, 1978. Lectr. U. Wis., Madison, 1977-82; from asst. editor to editor Everybody's Money Everybody's Money Credit Union Nat. Assn., 1979-84, mgr. ann. report, 1984-92, v.p. pub. rels., 1984-93, sr. v.p. credit union devel., 1993-96, sr. v.p. consumer rels. and corp. responsibility, 1996-97; owner Providing Solutions, Stoughton, Wis., 1997—; ptnr. Fourth Lake Comm., LLP. Dir. consumer appeals bd. Ford Motor Co., Milw., 1983-87. Author: Credit Union Basic Guide to Retirement Planning, 1998. Bd. dirs. Madison Area Crimestoppers, 1982-84. Recipient Clarion award, 1982. Mem. Women in Comm. (pres. Madison profl. chpt. 1982-83, nat. v.p. programs 1986-87, vice-chair/sec. nat. interim bd. 1996-97, chair nat. bd. dirs. 1997-2001), Internat. Assn. Bus. Communicators (program chair dist. meeting 1981), Am. Soc. Assn. Execs. (Gold Circle award 1984) Avocations: bicycling, reading. E-mail: lharr@providingsolutions.com.

HARR, MILTON EDWARD, civil engineering professor, engineering consultant; b. Chelsea, Mass., Oct. 19, 1925; s. Hyman and Ann (Kristal) H.; m. Florence Solomon, May 19, 1945; children: Faith, Karen, Robert. BS, Northeastern U., Boston, 1949; MS, Rutgers U., 1955; PhD, Purdue U., 1958; Docteur Honoris Causa, U. Brussels, 1987. Engr. Bureau of Reclamation, Provo, Utah, 1949, State Hwy. Dept., Beverly, Mass., 1949-53; asst. instr. Rutgers U., New Brunswick, N.J., 1953-55; instr. Purdue U., West Lafayette, Ind., 1955-58, asst. prof., 1958-60, assoc. prof., 1960-72, prof., 1972—. Jubilee prof. Chalmers Tech. Inst., Gothenburg, Sweden, 1996-97; cons. Bendix Corp., South Bend, Ind., Bougainville Copper Ltd., New Guinea, Brown and Root, Houston, Sandia Nat. Labs, Albuquerque, and many others; lectr. at many numerous colls. and univs. Author: Groundwater & Seepage, 1962, Foundations of Theoretical Soil Mechanics, 1966, Mechanics of Particulate Media, 1977, Reliability in Civil Engineering, 1987; editorial bd. Applied Ocean Research, 1978—, Internat. Jour. for Numerical and Analytical Methods in Geomechanics, 1978—; contbr. articles to profl. jours.; patentee in field. Bd. dirs. Ind. Joint Hwy. Research Project, 1969-72; adv. panel Am. Assn. State Hwy. Ofcls.; mem. Hwy. Research Bd. Com. on Stresses in Earth Masses, NASA Aeronautics Adv. Com., 1977-81, Task Force on Railway Maintenance Com., Transp. Research Bd., 1978-82, U.S. Com. on Large Dams; chmn. Track Structure Systems Design Com., 1976-79, Pavement Design Divsn.

of HRB, 1964-70. Served with USN, 1943, ETO, with USMC, 1944-45, PTO. Recipient U.S. Sr. Scientist award Alexander von Humbolt Orgn., Bonn, Germany, 1983, Bechtel award Bechtel Engring. Co., Houston, 1983, G. Ernest Brooks award ASCE-Cleve. sect., Cleve., 1987; named Shaw Lectr., N.C. State U., 1984. Fellow ASCE; mem. Nat. Acad. Engrs., Ind. Acad. Sci., Third Marine Div. Assn., Elks, Sigma Xi, Chi Epsilon. Avocations: music, art. Home: 4440 Exeter Dr Unit N204 Longboat Key FL 34228-2228 Office: Purdue U 1284 Civil Engineering West Lafayette IN 47907-1284

HARRE, ALAN FREDERICK, university president; b. Nashville, June 12, 1940; s. Adolph Henry and Hilda (Vogt) H.; m. Diane Carole Mack, Aug. 9, 1964; children: Andrea Lyn, Jennifer Leigh, Eric Stephen. BA, Concordia Sr. Coll., 1962; MDiv, Concordia Sem., St. Louis, 1966; MA, Presbyn. Sch. Christian Edn., Richmond, Va., 1967; PhD, Wayne State U., 1976. Ordained to ministry Luth. Ch. Asst. pastor St. James Luth. Ch. of Grosse Pointe, Grosse Pointe Farms, Mich., 1967-73; asst. prof. theology Concordia Tchrs. Coll., Seward, Nebr., 1973-78, asst. to pres., 1981, assoc. prof. theology, 1978-84, dean student affairs, 1982-84, acting pres., 1984; pres. Concordia Coll., St. Paul, 1984-88, Valparaiso (Ind.) U., 1988—. Author: Close the Back Door, 1984. Bd. dirs. Munster Med. Rsch. Found., Northwest Ind. Forum, Ind. Campus Compact, Independent Colls. Ind. Found., Luth. Ednl. Conf. Am., The Luther Inst., Christmas in April, Porter County Cmty. Found., Cmty. Devel. Corp., Quality Life Coun., Gary Accord; mem. adv. bd. YMCA. Recipient Disting. Cmty. Leader award, 1998, Sam Walton Bus. Leader award, 1999, Crystal Globe award, 1999. Mem. Am. Assn. Higher Edn., Ind. Conf. of Higher Edn., Ind. Soc. Chgo. Union League Club of Chgo. Home: 3900 Hemlock St Valparaiso IN 46383-1814 Office: Valparaiso U Office of the President Valparaiso IN 46383-9978 E-mail: alan.harre@valpo.edu.

HARRIMAN, GERALD EUGENE, retired business administrator, economics educator; b. Dell Rapids, S.D., May 30, 1924; s. Roy L. and Margaret (Schrantz) H.; m. Eileen Bernadine Bensman, June 10, 1950; children— G. Peter, Mary K., Margaret C., Elizabeth A. B.S., U. Notre Dame, 1947; A.M., U. S.D., 1949; Ph.D., U. Cin., 1957. Expediter Minn. Mining & Mfg. Co., 1947-48; from instr. to asst. dean, chmn. dept. bus. adminstrn. and finance Xavier U., 1949-66; prof. bus. adminstrn., chmn. div. bus. and econs. Ind. U. at South Bend, 1966-75, prof. bus. adminstrn. and econs., 1975-89, prof. emeritus, 1989—, dean faculties, 1975-87, acting chancellor, 1979, vice chancellor acad. affairs, 1987-89; ret., 1989. Vis. prof. fin. U. S.D., 1962; chmn. acad. deans Ind. Conf. Higher Edn., 1981-82; cons. in field. Mem. citizens adv. coun. long range fin. planning Coun. of City of Cin., 1963; mem. Community Edn. Roundtable, 1984—; mem. Scholarship Found. of St. Joseph County, Inc., 1992. Served with USNR, 1942-45. Mem. Am. Econs. Assn., Am. Finance Assn., Beta Gamma Sigma. Home: 16600 Gerald St Granger IN 46530-9579 Office: 1700 Mishawaka Ave South Bend IN 46615-1408

HARRINGTON, BERNARD J. bishop; b. Detroit, Sept. 6, 1933; s. John and Norah (Cronin) Harrington. MEd, Cath. U. Am. Ordained priest Roman Cath. Ch., 1959. Consecrated bishop, 1993; aux. bishop Archdiocese of Detroit, 1994-98, asst. supt. schs., pastor Holy Name Parish, pastor St. Rene Goupil Parish; bishop Diocese of Winona, Minn., 1998—. Office: PO Box 588 55 W Sanborn St Winona MN 55987-3655

HARRINGTON, BEVERLY, museum director; BS, Carnegie Mellon U., 1959; BAE, U. Wis., Oshkosh, 1967, MST, 1971; MSA, U. Wis., Milw., 1977. With art dept. U. Wis., Oshkosh, 1977-87; curator collections and exhibitions at arboretum Paine Art Ctr., 1983-90; dir. Hearthstone Mus., Appleton, Wis., 1991—. Office: Hearthstone Hist House Mus 625 W Prospect Ave Appleton WI 54911-6042

HARRINGTON, CAROL A. lawyer; b. Geneva, Feb. 13, 1953; d. Eugene P. and M. Ruth (Bowersox) Kloubec; m. Warren J. Harrington, Aug. 19, 1972; children: Jennifer Ruth, Carrie Anne. BS summa cum laude, U. Ill., 1974, JD magna cum laude, 1977. Bar: Ill. 1977, U.S. Dist. Ct. (no. dist.) Ill. 1977, U.S. Tax Ct. 1979. Assoc. Winston & Strawn, Chgo., 1977-84, ptnr., 1984-88, McDermott, Will & Emery, 1988—. Speaker in field. Co-author: Generation-Skipping Tax , 1996, Generation-Skipping Transfer Tax, Warren, Gorham & Lamont, 2000. Fellow Am. Coll. Trusts and Estate Coun. (bd. regents 1999—); mem. ABA (chmn. B-1 generation skipping transfer com. 1987-92, coun. real property, probate and trust law sect. 1992-98), Ill. State Bar Assn., Chgo. Bar Assn. (trust law com. divsn. 1), Chgo. Estate Planning Coun. Office: McDermott Will & Emery 227 W Monroe St Ste 3100 Chicago IL 60606-5096

HARRINGTON, JAMES TIMOTHY, lawyer; b. Chgo., Sept. 4, 1942; s. John Paul and Margaret Rita (Cunneen) H.; m. Roseanne Strupeck, Sept. 4, 1965; children: James Timothy, Roseanne, Maris Zajdela. BA, U. Notre Dame, 1964, JD, 1967. Bar: Ill. 1967, Ind. 1968, U.S. Dist. Ct. (no. dist.) Ill. 1967, U.S. Dist. Ct. (no. and so. dists.) Ind. 1968, U.S. Ct. Appeals (7th cir.) 1969, U.S. Ct. Appeals (4th cir.) 1977, U.S. Ct. Appeals (8th cir.) 1979, U.S. Ct. Appeals (3d cir.) 1981, U.S. Supreme Ct. 1979, U.S. Ct. Appeals (D.C. cir.) 1993. Law clk. U.S. Dist. Ct. (no. dist.) Ind., 1967-69; assoc. Rooks, Pitts & Poust, Chgo., 1969-75, ptnr., 1976-87, Ross & Hardies, Chgo., 1987—. Lectr. environ. law, fed. procedures, adminstrv. law, 1960—. Vice chmn. Mid Am. Legal Found.; chmn., bd. dirs. Ill. Safety Coun. Fellow Am. Bar Found.; mem. Ill. Bar Assn., Ind. Bar Assn., Chgo. Bar Assn. (environ. law com., real estate com.), Indsl. Water Waste and Sewer Group (past chmn.), Air and Waste Mgmt. Assn. (bd. dirs. Lake Mich. sect.), Assn. Environ. Law Inst., Lawyers Club Chgo., Exec. Club Chgo., Union League Club Chgo. Roman Catholic. Home: 746 Foxdale Ave Winnetka IL 60093-1908 Office: Ross & Hardies 150 N Michigan Ave Ste 2500 Chicago IL 60601-7567 E-mail: james.harrington@rosshardies.com.

HARRINGTON, JEREMY THOMAS, priest, publishing executive; b. Lafayette, Ind., Oct. 7, 1932; s. William and Ellen (Cain) H. BA, Duns Scotus Coll., 1955; postgrad., U. Detroit, 1955, Marquette U., 1961; MA, Xavier U., Cin., 1965; MS in Journalism, Northwestern U., 1967; LHD (hon.) , St. Bonaventure U., 1999. Ordained priest Roman Cath. Ch., 1959. Joined Order Friars Minor, 1950; tchr. Roger Bacon High Sch., Cin., 1960-64; assoc. editor St. Anthony Messenger, 1964-66, editor, 1966-81, pub., 1975-81, pub., CEO, 1991—; mem. bd. Franciscan Province Cin., 1969-72, 75-81, chief exec. bd., 1981-90. Author: Your Wedding: Planning Your Own Ceremony, 1974; Editor: Conscience in Today's World, 1970, Jesus: Superstar or Savior?, 1972. Mem. Catholic Press Assn. (pres. 1975-77, dir.), Kappa Tau Alpha. Home: 1615 Vine St Cincinnati OH 45202 Office: St Anthony Messenger 28 W Liberty St Cincinnati OH 45202 E-mail: JeremyH@AmericanCatholic.org.

HARRINGTON, JOHN TIMOTHY, retired lawyer; b. Madison, Wis., May 26, 1921; s. Cornelius Louis and Emily (Chisholm) H.; m. Deborah Reynolds, May 23, 1948; children— Elizabeth Chisholm, Samuel Parker, Hannah Quincy, Jane McRae B.S., Harvard U., 1942, LL.B., 1948. Bar: Wis. 1949. Assoc. Quarles & Brady and predecessor firms, Milw., 1948-58, ptnr., 1958-91; ret., 1991—. Served to lt. comdr. USNR, 1942-46, PTO Mem. ABA, Wis. Bar Assn., Milw. Bar Assn., Milw. Club. Republican. Home: 924 E Juneau Ave Milwaukee WI 53202-2748 Office: Quarles & Brady 411 E Wisconsin Ave Ste 2550 Milwaukee WI 53202-4497 E-mail: jtharrington@webtv.net.

HARRINGTON, MICHAEL FRANCIS, paper and packaging company executive; b. Butte, Mont., Aug. 6, 1940; s. Bernard Michael and Ruth Ann (Mullane) H.; m. Beverly Elaine Oswood, Dec. 30, 1967; children: Michael, Moria, Kevin. BS, Gonzaga U., Spokane, 1964, MBA, 1971; postgrad., Stanford U., 1985. Indsl. rels. rep. Kaiser Aluminum, Spokane, 1965-69; region indsl. rels. rep. Gen. Inst. Corp., Post Falls, Idaho, 1969-72; region employee rels.mgr. Boise Cascade Corp., Medford, Oreg., 1972-75, div. employee rels. mgr. Boise, Idaho, 1975-81, corp. dir. labor rels., 1981-91; v.p. human resources Smurfit Stone Container Corp. (formerly Jefferson Smurfit Corp.), St. Louis, 1991—. Mem. adv. bd. Gonzaga U. Sch. Bus., 1990—. Bd. dirs. Laumeier Sculpture Garden, St. Louis, 1995—, St. Joseph Sch. for Deaf, St. Louis, 1994—. Mem. Labor Policy Assn., Am. Forest and Paper Assn. (bd. dirs., chmn. employee rels. com. 1988—). Republican. Roman Catholic. Office: Jefferson Smurfit Corp 8182 Maryland Ave Saint Louis MO 63105-3769

HARRINGTON, NANCEY, state senator; m. Rex Harrington. Mem. Kans. State Senate Dist. 26, 1995—; vice chair fed. and state affairs com.; mem. judiciary com., transp. and tourism com.

HARRIS, BILL, state legislator; b. Fork Mountain, Tenn., Sept. 1, 1934; m. Mary C. Harris; children: Billy M. Jr., Lonny E., Scott, Sherry. Student, U. Ariz. Auto dealer, bus. owner, Ashland, Ohio; mem. Ohio State Ho. Reps., Columbus, 1995-2000, Ohio Senate from 19th dist., Columbus, 2000—. Vice chmn. Buick Nat. Dealers' Coun. Trustee Samaritan Hosp., Ashland. Mem. Ohio Automobile Dealers Assn. (trustee), Ashland Area C. of C.

HARRIS, BOB, radio personality; Radio host Sta. KFGO-AM, Fargo, ND. Office: KFGO 1020 25th St S Fargo ND 58103*

HARRIS, CHARLES ELMER, lawyer; b. Williamsburg, Iowa, Nov. 26, 1922; s. Charles Elmer and Loretto (Judge) H.; m. Marjorie Clark, Jul. 9, 1949 (div. June. 1969); m. Linda Rae Slaymaker, Nov. 25, 1992; children: Martha Ann, Julie Ann, Charles Elmer III. Student, St. Ambrose Coll., 1940-42; B.S.C., U. Iowa, 1946, J.D., 1949. Bar: Iowa 1949. Mem. firm Brody, Parker, Roberts, Thoma & Harris, Des Moines, 1949-66, Herrick, Langdon, Belin Harris, Langdon & Helmick, Des Moines, 1966-78, Belin Harris Helmick, P.C., Des Moines, 1978-91, Belin, Harris, Lamson , McCormick, P.C., Des Moines, 1991-96; pvt. practice, 1997-99; ret., 1999. Lectr. tax schs., meetings, 1951, 55, 67, 69, 77-84, 90, 91. Comments editor: Iowa Law Rev., 1948-49. Bd. dirs. NCCJ, 1964-67, Iowa Bar Found., 1977-92, Iowa Law Sch. Found., 1977-90, United Way Found., 1981-89. Lt. (j.g.) USNR, 1943-46. Fellow Am. Coll. Trust and Estate Counsel; mem. ABA, Iowa Bar Assn. (bd. govs. 1973-80, Merit award 1980), Polk County Bar Assn. (pres. 1972-73), Polk County Jr. Bar Assn. (pres. 1952-53), Order of Coif, Sigma Chi, Delta Theta Phi. Roman Catholic. Home: 5141 Robertson Dr Des Moines IA 50312-2170 E-mail: Harris5141@aol.com.

HARRIS, CHRISTINE, dance company executive; b. Milw. Mktg. dir. Milw. Symphony Orch., 1984-90, head Arts in Cmty. Edn. program, 1990-95; with Inst. Music, Health and Edn., Mpls., 1996-97; exec. dir. Milw. Ballet, 1997—. Office: Milw Ballet 504 W National Ave Milwaukee WI 53204-1746

HARRIS, DONALD RAY, lawyer; b. Lake Preston, S.D., Apr. 21, 1938; s. Raymond H. and Nona (Trousdale) H.; children: Beverly, Scott, Bradley, Lindi; m. Sharon K. Brown, Sept. 4, 1982. BA, State U. Iowa, 1959; JD, U. Iowa, 1961. Bar: Ill. 1963, U.S. Dist. Ct. (no. dist.) Ill. 1963, U.S. Ct. Appeals (3d, 4th, 6th, 7th, 9th and fed. cirs.) 1966-95, U.S. Dist. Ct. (we. dist.) Tex. 1989, U.S. Supreme Ct. 1977. Assoc. Jenner & Block, Chgo., 1963-70, ptnr., 1970—. Lt. inf. U.S. Army, 1961-63. Mem. ABA, Ill. Bar Assn., Chgo. Bar Assn., Bar Assn. 7th Cir., Chgo. Coun. Lawyers, Am. Coll. Trial Lawyers, Lawyers Club of Chgo. Office: Jenner & Block One IBM Plz Chicago IL 60611-3586 E-mail: dharris@jenner.com.

HARRIS, EARL L. state legislator; m. Donna J. Harris. Student, Purdue U., Ill. Inst. Tech. With Ky Package Store; rep. Dist. 12 Ind. Ho. of Reps., 1981-91, rep. Dist. 2, 1991—, mem. commerce com., govt. affairs com., aged and aging com., mem. ins. com., corp. and small bus. com.; chmn. ways and means com. Mem. NAACP; past pres. Chgo. Black Coalition, Chgo. Homeowners Assn., Sunnyside Homeowners Assn.; chmn. African-Am. Leadership Forum; mem. N.W. Urban League. Home: 4114 Butternut St East Chicago IN 46312-2943

HARRIS, GREGORY SCOTT, management services executive; b. Denver, June 5, 1955; s. Herbert E. and Marcia Jean (Raabe) H. B.S. in Journalism with honors, U. Colo., 1977; M.B.A., Loyola U., Chgo., 1981. Dir. public relations IMPACT Internat., Inc., Chgo., 1977-78; dir. edn. Nat. Home Furnishings Assn. (NHFA), 1978-79, v.p. industry affairs, 1981-87, exec. v.p., chief operating officer, 1987-88; exec. dir. Interior Design Soc., 1979-82; sec. NHFA Service Corp., 1986-87, v.p., 1986-87, pres., 1987-91, also bd. dirs.; pres. Open Hand: Chgo. Found., 1988-91; chief of staff Chgo. City Coun., 1992—. Mem. Devel. Adv. Coun. City of Chgo., 1990-92; bd. dirs. Nonprofit Fin. Ctr.; mem. advocacy and pub. policy com. AFC. Trustee Design Found., Chgo., 1980-88; chmn. bd. dirs. AIDS Walk Found., 1990-91; bd. dirs. AIDS Legal Coun., 1992-94, Heartland Alliance for Human Needs and Human Rights; fin. dir. Simpson for Congress Com., 1991-92; mem. adv. bd. The Neofuturists, 2000. Recipient Leadership in Mktg. award Newspaper Pubs. Assn., 1983, Outstanding Young Chicagoan award Chgo. Jaycees, 1992, Outstanding Svc. to Immigrant and Refugee Cmty. award, 1996, Uptown C. of C. Ann. award, 1996, Voice of People Cmty. award, 1994, Equality award Human Rights Campaign, 1997, W. Clement Stone award, 1998, Biggest Heart award Hearts Found., 1999, Food For Life award, Florence Bezazian Citizenship award, 1999, Greater Chgo. Com. Humanitarian Efforts award, 2000, Inst. Cultural Affairs USA cert. of appreciation, 2000; named to City of Chgo. Hall of Fame, 1996. Office: Chgo City Coun City Hall 121 N La Salle St Chicago IL 60602-1202

HARRIS, IRVING, lawyer; b. Cin., May 23, 1927; s. Albert and Sadye H.; m. Selma Schottenstein, June 18, 1950; children: Jeffrey Philip, Jonathan Lindley (dec.), Lisa Ann Hollister. Undergrad. degree, U. Cin., 1948, LLB, 1951. Ptnr. Cors, Hair & Hartsock, 1954-81, Hartsock, Harris & Schneider, Cin., 1981-82, Porter, Wright, Morris & Arthur, Cin., 1982-89; ptnr. firm Harris, Harris, Field Schacter & Bardach Ltd., 1989-2000. Mem. Ohio Trade Mission to Orient, 1973, to Eng. and Germany, 1974; spl. counsel to Atty. Gen. Ohio, 1963-71; life mem. 6th Cir. Jud. Conf.; lectr. Advising, Oper. and Rebuilding the Financially Distressed Co., 1991; bd. dirs. Bank One, Cin., 1993-2000, HRC Ltd. Partnership (Hyatt Regency (Cin.) Cin. Mem. Ohio Devel. Financing Commn., 1974—84, vice-chmn., 1978—79; spl. counsel Ohio Atty. Gen.'s Office for the Police and Firemen's Disability and Pension Fund, 1994—97; trustee Skidmore Coll., 1976—90, trustee emeritus, 1991—, Big Bros.; trustee Cin. Symphony Orch., 1989—96; bd. overseers U. Cin. Law Sch., 1998—; arbitrator Ct. of Common Pleas of Hamilton County, 2001—; mediator U.S. Dist. Ct. (so. dist.) Ohio Western divsn., 1999—. Mem. ABA (Sherman Act com., sect. on antitrust and bus. law 1969—, subcoms. on derivative actions, bankruptcy, litigation of bus. and corp. litigation 1992—), Ohio Bar Assn., Cin. Bar Assn., Am. Judicature Soc., Am. Arbitration Assn. (arbitrator), Potter Stewart Inn of Ct. (master of the bench), Queen City Club, Univ. Club, Camargo Hunt Club, Cin. Tennis Club, Snowmass Country Club. Home: 18 Grandin Ln Cincinnati OH 45208-3365 Office: Harris Interests 3801 Carew Tower 441 Vine St Cincinnati OH 45202-2806

HARRIS, IRVING BROOKS, investor, director; b. St. Paul, Aug. 4, 1910; s. William and Mildred (Brooks) H.; m. Joan White; children: Roxanne, Virginia, William. AB, Yale U., 1931, hon. degree, 1990, Loyola U., 1976, Kenyon Coll., 1986, Columbia Coll., 1987, Lesley Coll., 1988, Bank Street Coll. Edn., 1988, De Pauw U., 1989; hon. deg., U. Ill., 1992, Roosevelt U., 1996; hon. degree, Gov.'s State U., 1997. Exec. in finance business, 1931-42; aircraft part bus., 1944-46; exec. Toni Home Permanent Co., after 1946; (sold stockholdings in Toni Co. to Gillette Safety Razor Co.), 1948; dir. Gillette Safety Razor Co., 1948-60; exec. v.p. Toni Co., 1946-52; chmn. bd. Sci. Research Assos., 1953-58; pres. Michael Reese Hosp. and Med. Center, Chgo., 1958-61, Harris Group, Inc., 1959-76. Chmn. exec. com. Pittway Corp., 1962—2000; chmn. William Harris Investors, 1987—2000. Trustee U. Chgo., Nat. Ctr. Clin. Infant Programs, Chgo. Ednl. TV Assn.; chmn. emeritus Family Focus; chmn. Harris Found.; pres. emeritus Erikson Inst.; pres., co-founder The Ounce of Prevention Fund, 1982—, chmn. emeritus, 1997—; trustee Am. Jewish Com.; former chmn. adv. bd. Ill. Dept. Children and Family Svcs. Tng. Inst., Ill. Competitive Access and Reimbursement Equity Program; vice chmn. Gov.'s Task Force on Future of Mental Health in Ill.; spl. counselor to select com. on children Ill. Gen. Assembly; served with Bd. Econ. Warfare OPA, 1942-44. Recipient Chgo. UNICEF World of Children award, 1985, hon. membership award Chgo. Pediatric Soc., 1986, Am. Orthopsychiat. Assn. award, 1986, Salesman of Yr. award Harvard Club Chgo., 1989, Disting. Svc. to State Govt. award Nat. Gov.'s Assn., 1990, Amicus Certus award Luth. Soc. Svcs. of Ill., 1990, Cmty. Partnership award United Neighborhood Orgn., Chgo., 1990, As They Grow award Parents, 1991, Citizen fellow Inst. Medicine Chgo., 1990, Service to Young Children award Chgo. Met. Assn. for Edn. of Young Children, 1995; Clifford Beers lectr. Yale U., 1987. Fellow Am. Acad. Pediatrics (hon.), Am. Acad. Arts and Scis.; mem. NAS (pres.'s circle 1989), Am. Orthopsychiatric Assn. (award 1986, Marian F. Langer award 1995), Chgo. Pediatric Soc. (hon.), Standard Club, Midday Club. Home: 209 E Lake Shore Dr Chicago IL 60611-1307 Office: William Harris Investors Inc 2 N La Salle St Ste 400 Chicago IL 60602-3703

HARRIS, JAMES THOMAS, III, college administrator, educator; b. Findlay, Ohio, July 31, 1958; s. James Thomas II and Carolyn Sue (Cairns) H.; m. Mary Catherine Kurdila, June 27, 1981; children: Zachary James, Braden Gerald. BE in Secondary Edn., U. Toledo, 1980; MEd in Ednl. Adminstrn., Edinboro U., 1983; EdD in Higher Edn. Adminstrn., Pa. State U., 1988; postgrad. Inst. Ednl. Mgmt., Harvard U., 1993. Secondary tchr., dept. chair Highland H.S., Sparta, Ohio, 1980-81, Ctrl. Cath. H.S., Toledo, 1981-82; grad. asst., acad. advisor Edinboro (Pa.) State U., 1982-83; fin. aid adminstr. Pa. State U., University Park, 1983-86, assoc. dir. Corp. and Found. Rels. dept., 1986-88; v.p. Coll. Mt. St. Joseph, Cin., 1988-91, Wright State U., Dayton, 1991-94; pres. Defiance (Ohio) Coll., 1994—2002, Widener U., 2002—. Faculty mem. 10 Case Confs., 1986—; spkr., workshop presenter in field. Contbr. articles to profl. jours. Chair Vol. Connection of Defiance County, 1995-; vol. Leadership Defiance, Dayton, vice chair, 1992-94; bd. dirs. Defiance County United Way, 1998-2001; vol. ARC, Cin., 1988-91; bd. trustees Ohio Found. of Indep. Colls., 1994-; exec. com. Ohio Campus Compact, 1998-; vol. advisor St. Joseph Ch. and Elem. Sch., 1988-91; grad. Leadership Dayton, 1992; coach Nat. Collegiate Boxing Assn., Brunei, 1985, USSR, 1988. Recipient fellowship Am. Assn. Higher Edn. Edn. Resource and Index Ctr., 1987, Excellence in Edn. award Pa. State U., 2000, Alumni Leadershiip and Svc. award Pa. State U., 1996, Disting. Alumni award U. Toledo, 1999, Cmty. Leadership award NAACP Northwest Ohio chap., 1999; named to Top 50 Coll. and Univ. Presidents Templeton Found, 1999. Mem. NAACP, Am. Assn. Higher Edn., Assn. of Indep. Colls. and Univs. of Ohio, Rotary, Young President's Orgn., Alpha Kappa Delta, Pi Lambda Theta. Roman Catholic. Avocations: reading, blues music, walking. Office: Widener U 1 University Pl Chester PA 19013

HARRIS, JOHN EDWARD, lawyer; b. Mpls., Nov. 16, 1936; s. John Law and Harriet Comilla (Hunt) H.; m. Ruth Wilder Esty, Aug. 26, 1958; children— Jeffrey Langdon, Stowe John Wilder, Benjamin Wood B.A. summa cum laude, Lawrence Coll., 1959; J.D., Harvard U., 1962. Bar: Minn. 1962, U.S. Dist. Ct. Minn. 1962, U.S. Tax Ct. 1963. Assoc. Faegre & Benson, Mpls., 1962-69, ptnr., 1970-2000, head, trusts, estates and found. group, 1974-97. Trustee Ucross Found., Wyo., 1981-93, 97— Contbr. articles to Notre Dame Planning Inst., 1976, 78 Bd. dirs. Meth. Health Care Minn., 1986-93; chmn. Meth. Hosp., St. Louis Park, Minn., 1979-81, bd. dirs., 1993-94; pres. West Met. Hosp. trustee Coun., Mpls., 1980-81; chmn. Minn. Coun. on Founds., Mpls., 1985-88; bd. dirs. Twin Cities RISE!, 1995—. Mem. ABA (chmn. com. on charitable trusts, real property and trust law sect. 1973-77, exempt orgns. com., tax section 1991—), Minn. Bar Assn. (chmn. probate and trust law sect. 1979-80, mem. study com. Minn. Nonprofit Corps. 1986-91, mem. nonprofit corps. com. 1998—), Phi Beta Kappa Home: 713 Coventry Ln Minneapolis MN 55435-5653 Office: Faegre & Benson 2200 Wells Fargo Ctr 90 S 7th St Ste 2200 Minneapolis MN 55402-3901 E-mail: jharris@faegre.com., jharris331@excite.com.

HARRIS, JOHN WILLIAM, hematologist, educator; b. Boston, Mar. 30, 1920; s. Ulysses Sylvester and Lillian (Dennett) H.; m. Stephanie Jean Bunting, Apr. 7, 1951; children: Wendy Alexandra, Alison Dennett, Stephen Bunting. B.S., Trinity Coll., Hartford, Conn., 1941; M.D., Harvard, 1944. Intern Boston City Hosp., 1944-45, resident, 1947-48; research fellow medicine Thorndike Meml. Lab., Harvard Med. Sch., 1948-51, research assoc., 1951-52; sr. instr. medicine Western Res. U., Cleve., 1952-54, asst. prof., 1954-57, assoc. prof., 1957-62, prof., 1962-99, prof. emeritus, 1999—. Hematologist, vis. physician Cleve. Met. Gen. Hosp., 1952-99, assoc. dir. dept. medicine, 1967-81; attending physician VA Hosp., Cleve., 1953-58, sr. attending physician hematology, 1959-99; cons. staff Lutheran Hosp., 1965-99; mem. hematology study sect. NIH, 1962-66, chmn., 1983-85, mem. hematology tng. grants com., 1969-73; mem. com. blood and transfusion Nat. Acad. Scis.-NRC, 1963-65; chmn. Merit Rev. Bd. in Hematology, Med. Research Service, VA, 1977-80 Served to capt. U.S. Army, 1945-47. Recipient USPHS Research Career award, 1962, Martin Luther King, Jr. award for outstanding research in sickle cell anemia, 1972; Alfred Stengel Research fellow ACP, 1951-52; Markle scholar in medicine, 1955-60; named to Cleve. Med. Hall of Fame, 1998. Fellow ACP, Internat. Soc. Hematology (nat. counselor, Interam. div. 1986); mem. AAAS, Am. Fedn. Clin. Research, Am. Soc. Clin. Investigation (past v.p.), Central Soc. Clin. Research, Soc. Exptl. Biology and Medicine, Am. Soc. Hematology (pres. 1981-82), Acad. Medicine Cleve., Assn. Am. Physicians, Phi Beta Kappa, Alpha Omega Alpha. Home: Bruening Health Ctr Rm 603C 2181 Ambleside Dr Cleveland OH 44106 Office: 2500 Metrohealth Dr Cleveland OH 44109-1900

HARRIS, JOSEPH MCALLISTER, retired chemist; b. Pontiac, Ill., July 27, 1929; s. Fred Gilbert and Catherine Marguerite (McAllister) H.; m. Margot Jeanette L'Hommedieu, Feb. 17, 1952; children: Timothy, Kaye, Paula, Bruce, Anne, Martha, Rebecca. BA, Blackburn Coll., Carlinville, Ill., 1952; postgrad., So. Ill. U., 1953-54, U. Ill., 1956-61. Technician Olin Ind., Inc., Energy, Ill., 1953-54; quality control staff Union Starch and Refining Co., Granite City, 1954; rsch. asst. Ill. State Geol. Survey, Urbana, 1954-61; chemist II Water Pollution Control Bd., Annapolis, Md., 1961-63; phys. chemist Ball Bros. Rsch., Inc., Muncie, Ind., 1963-66; sr. engr. Radio Corp. Am., Marion, 1966-70; chemist OA Labs., Inc., Indpls., 1973-86, OA

Labs. & Rsch., Inc., Indpls., 1986-93, cons., 1993—. Bd. dirs. Tri-County Hearing Assn. for Children, Muncie, 1967-70. Mem. Am. Chem. Soc., AAAS, Soc. Applied Spectroscopy. Republican. Presbyterian. Avocations: gardening, camping. Home: 800 E Washington St Muncie IN 47305-2533

HARRIS, JULES ELI, medical educator, physician, clinical scientist, administrator; b. Toronto, Ont., Can., Oct. 12, 1934; came to U.S., 1978; s. George Joseph and Ida Harris; m. Josephine Leikin; children: Leah, Daniel, Adam, Sheira, Robin, Naomi. MD, U. Toronto, 1959. Intern, then resident Toronto (Can.) Gen. Hsp., 1959-65; asst. prof. medicine M.D. Anderson Hosp. Med. Ctr., Houston, 1966-69; prof. medicine U. Ottawa (Ont.), 1969-78; prof. medicine, prof. immunology Rush Med. Coll., Rush U., Chgo., 1978—; dir. Rush Cancer Ctr., 1986-92; dir. Rush sect. med. oncology, 1978-93. Mem. gov.'s adv. bd. for cancer control State of Ill., 1988—; chmn. bd. trustees Ill. Cancer Coun., Chgo., 1987-88; chmn. immunology devices panel FDA, 1995—. Author: Immunology of Malignant Disease, 1975; editor Prostaglandin Inhibitors in Tumor Immunology and Immunotherapy, 1994. Mem. internat. bd. govs. Ben Gurion U. of Negev, Beer-Sheva, Israel, 1986-95; pres. bd., chmn. sci. adv. com. Israel Cancer Rsch. Fund, Chgo. Fellow ACP, Royal Coll. Physicians Can. (cert. in internal medicine); mem. Am. Soc. Clin. Oncology (chmn. pub. rels. com. 1987-89), Univ. Club, Alpha Omega Alpha. Jewish. Office: Rush-Presbyn-St Luke's Med Ctr 1725 W Congress Pkwy Chicago IL 60612-3809

HARRIS, K. DAVID, senior state supreme court justice; b. Jefferson, Iowa, July 29, 1927; s. Orville William and Jessie Heloise (Smart) H.; m. Madonna Theresa Coyne, Sept. 4, 1948; children: Jane, Julia, Frederick. BA, U. Iowa, 1949, JD, 1951. Bar: Iowa 1951, U.S. Dist. Ct (so. dist.) Iowa, 1958. Sole practice Harris & Harris, Jefferson, 1951-62; dist. judge 16th Judicial Dist., Iowa, 1962-72; justice Iowa Supreme Ct., Des Moines, 1972-99, sr. justice, 1999—. Served with U.S. Army, 1944-46, PTO. Mem. VFW, Am. Legion, Rotary. Roman Catholic. Avocation: writing poetry. Office: Iowa Supreme Ct State Capitol Bldg Des Moines IA 50319-0001*

HARRIS, KING WILLIAM, manufacturing company executive; b. 1943; BA, Harvard U., 1964, MBA, 1965. With Pittway Corp., Northbrook, Ill., 1971—, v.p. alarm div., 1971-75, exec. v.p. electronics div., 1975-80, chmn. bd. dirs., chief exec. officer electronics div., 1980-84, now pres., chief exec. officer, bd. dirs. Office: Aptargroup Inc 475 W Terra Cotta Ave Crystal Lake IL 60014

HARRIS, NEIL, historian, educator; b. Bklyn., 1938; s. Harold and Irene Harris. AB, Columbia U., N.Y.C., 1958; BA, Cambridge U., Eng., 1960; PhD, Harvard U., 1965. From instr. to asst. prof. history Harvard U., Cambridge, Mass., 1965-69; assoc. prof. U. Chgo., 1969-72, prof., 1972-90, Preston and Sterling Morton prof. of history, 1990—, dir. Nat. Humanities Inst., 1975-77, chmn. dept. history, 1985-88. Mem. adv. bd. Temple Hoyne Buell Ctr., Columbia, 1984-89; mem. adv. com. dept. architecture Art Inst. Chgo., 1982—; mem. Smithsonian Council, 1978-84, chmn. 1984-92; visiting prof. Yale U., 1974; dir. d'etudes Ecole des Hautes Etudes en Sci. Sociales, Paris, 1985. Author: Artist in American Society, 1966, Humbug: The Art of P.T. Barnum, 1970, Cultural Excursions, 1990, Building Lives, 1999; editor: Land of Contrasts, 1970, the WPA Guide to Illinois, 1983; bd. editors New Eng. Quar., 1982—, Winterthur Portfolio, 1978-80, 85-88, Frederick Law Olmsted Papers, 1973, Am. Scholar, 1994-2000; mem. editorial adv. bd. History Today, 1978-86. Trustee H.F. DuPont Winterthur (Del.) Mus., 1978-87, Newberry Libr.; mem. Nat. Mus. Svcs. Bd., Washington, 1977-84; vis. com. J. Paul Getty Mus., 1995—; bd. dirs. Nat. Mus. Am. History, 1997-2000. Named Am. Coun. Learned Socs. fellow, 1972-73, NEH fellow, 1980-81, Guggenheim fellow, 1999-2000; Getty scholar, 1991, Nat. Mus. Am. Art scholar, 1995-96; Boucher lectr. Johns Hopkins U., 1971, Cardozo lectr. Yale U., 1974, Tandy lectr. Whitney Mus. Am. Art, 1982, Kemper lectr. Pitzer Coll., 1980, Buell lectr. Columbia U., 1993; recipient Joseph Henry medal Smithsonian Instn., 1991. Fellow Am. Acad. Arts and Scis.; mem. Am. Antiquarian Soc., Am. Coun. Learned Socs. (vice chmn. N.Y. 1978-89, chmn. 1989-93), Orgn. Am. Historians, Phi Beta Kappa (senator united chpts. 1985-97, vis. lectr. 1985-86). Home: 4950 S Chicago Beach Dr Chicago IL 60615-3207 Office: U Chgo Dept History 1126 E 59th St Chicago IL 60637-1580

HARRIS, NEISON, manufacturing company executive; b. St. Paul, Jan. 24, 1915; s. William and Mildred (Brooks) H.; m. Bette Deutsch, Jan. 25, 1939; children: Katherine, King, Toni. AB, Yale U., 1936. Founder Toni Home Permanent Co., 1936-46; pres. Toni divsn. Gillette Safety Razor Co., 1946-66; pres. Paper Mate divsn. Gillette Co.; pres., bd. dirs. Pittway Corp., Northbrook, Ill., 1959-84, chmn. bd., 1984-2000. Chmn. bd., dir. Standard Shares, Inc. Named One of Ten Outstanding Young Men U.S., Jr. C. of C., 1948. Mem.: Lake Shore Country Club (Chgo.), Standard Club (Chgo.). Died Sept. 7, 2001.

HARRIS, PATTI B. telecommunications executive; Pres., CEO Harris-McBurney Co., Jackson, Mich. Office: Harris McBurney Co PO Box 267 Jackson MI 49204-0267 Fax: 517-787-6809. E-mail: info@hmcb.com.

HARRIS, ROBERT BLYNN, civil engineer, educator; b. Dec. 31, 1918; m. Jean Margaret; children: William R., James F., David B., Peter S. BS, U. Colo., 1940; MS, Calif. Inst. Tech., 1947. Prof. engr., Mich. From instr. to prof., assoc. chmn. civil engring. U. Mich., Ann Arbor, 1947-87. Vis. prof. Nat. Inst. Constrn. Mgmt. and Rsch., Bombay, 1987-88, U. Utah, 1986, Calif. Inst. Tech., 1946-47, U. Conn., 1943-44, U. Colo., Boulder, 1972. Author: Precedence and Arrow Networking Techniques for Construction, 1978, Two Structural Theories — The Influence Line and Moment Distribution, 1971; contbr. articles to profl. jours. Mem. ASCE (Richard R. Torrens award 1996), Am. Soc. Engring. Edn., Tau Beta Pi, Chi Epsilon, Pi Mu Epsilon, Kappa Kappa Psi, Phi Kappa Phi. Home: 325Wilkinson St Apt 217 Chelsea MI 48118-1524 Office: 2350 GG Brown Lab U Mich Ann Arbor MI 48109-2125 E-mail: harris@engin.umich.edu.

HARRIS, THOMAS L. public relations executive; b. Dayton, Ohio, Apr. 18, 1931; s. James and Leona (Blum) H.; m. JoAnn K. Karch, Apr. 14, 1957; children: James Harris, Theodore Harris. BA, U. Mich., 1953; MA, U. Chgo., 1956. Exec. v.p. Daniel J. Edelman Inc., Chgo., 1957-67; v.p. pub. rels. Neddham Harper & Steers, 1967-72; pres. Foote Cone & Belding Pub. Rels., 1973-78, Golin-Harris Communications Inc., Chgo., 1978-89, also vice chmn.; adj. prof. Medill Sch. Journalism, Northwestern U., Evanston, Ill., 1987—; mng. ptnr. Thomas L. Harris & Co., Highland Pk., 1992—. Served with U.S. Army, 1953-55. Mem. Public Relations Soc. Am. (Gold Anvil award 2000). Home: 241 Melba Ln Highland Park IL 60035-1904 Office: Thomas L Harris & Co 600 Central Ave Highland Park IL 60035-3211 E-mail: ttlhco@aol.com.

HARRIS, ZELEMA M. academic administrator; b. Newton County, Tex., Jan. 12, 1940; d. James Robert and Gertrude Violet (Swearingen) Marshall; m. Manuel Holloway. BS, Prairie View A&M, 1961; MEd, U. Kans., 1972, EdD, 1976, U. Asst. dir. urban affairs U. Kans., Lawrence, 1970-72, asst. dir. Centennial Coll., 1970-72, dir. supportive edn. svcs., 1970-72; coord. curriculum evaluation Met. Community Coll., Kansas City, Mo., 1976-77, dir. curriculum evaluation, 1977-78, dir. edn. opportunity ctr., 1978-80, dir. dist. svcs., 1980; pres. Pioneer Community Coll., 1980-87, Pen Valley Community Coll., Kansas City, 1987-90, Parkland Coll., Champaign, Ill., 1990—. Co-author: Evaluation and Program Planning, 1978. Recipient Protestant award Kansas City Coun., 1987, Kansas City Spirit award Gillis Ctr. of Kansas City and Kansas City Star, 1987; named one of Women of Conscience, Panel of Am. Women, 1987. Mem. Nat. Inst. for Leadership Devel. Am. Assn. Women in Community Colls. (adv. bd.), Am. Assn. Community and Jr. Colls. (bd. dirs., Coun. on Black Am. Affairs), Black Women in Higher Edn., N. Cen. Assn. Colls. and Schs. (bd. dirs. N. Cen. region). Home: 7 Briar Hill Cir Champaign IL 61822-6137 Office: Parkland Coll Office of the President 2400 W Bradley Ave Champaign IL 61821-1806

HARRISON, DONALD CAREY, university official, cardiology educator; b. Blount County, Ala., Feb. 24, 1934; s. Walter Carey and Sovola (Thompson) H.; m. Laura Jane McAnnally, July 24, 1955; children—Douglas, Elizabeth, Donna Marie. B.S. in Chemistry, Birmingham So. Coll., 1954; M.D., U. Ala., 1958. Diplomate Am. Bd. Internal Medicine (cardiovascular disease). Intern, asst. resident Peter Bent Brigham Hosp., 1958-60; fellow in cardiology Harvard U., 1961, NIH, 1961-63; mem. faculty Stanford U. Med. Sch., 1963-86, chief div. cardiology, 1967-86, prof. medicine, 1971-86; chief cardiology Stanford U. Hosp., 1967-86, William G. Irwin prof. cardiology, 1972-86; sr. v.p., provost for health affairs U Cin. Med. Ctr., 1986—; prof. medicine, cardiology U. Cin. Coll. Medicine; CEO U. Cin. Med. Ctr., 1987—. Cons. to local hosps., industry and govt.; bd. dirs. Novoste, Inc., Heart Stent Inc., Enable, Inc., AtriCure Med., Venturi, LLP, , Uterine Muscle Dysfunction, Inc., Emerging Concepts Inc., Am. Heart Assn., U. Cin. Physicians, Health Alliance of Greater Cin., Univ. Health Systems Consortium, Inc. Mem. editorial bd. Brit. Jour. Clin. Practice, 1993—; mem. editorial bd. Drugs, 1980—, Am. Jour. Cardiology, 1984—, Health, 1988—, Inpharma, 19926; contbr. articles to med. jours., chpts. to books. Served with USPHS, 1961-63. Fellow Interam. Soc. Cardiology (v.p. 1980-86), Am. Coll. Cardiology (mem. chmn., v.p. 1972-73, sec. 1969-70, trustee 1972-78), Am. Heart Assn. (fellow coun. circulation, clin. cardiology and basic sci., chmn. program com. 1972-76, nat. chmn. publs. com. 1976-81, pres.-elect 1980-81, pres. 1982-83); mem. Am. Soc. Clin. Investigation, Am. Fedn. Clin. Rsch., Am. Assn. Physicians, ACP, Assn. U. Cardiologists, Am. Clin. and Climatol Assn., Brit. Cardiac Soc., Acad. Medicine Cin., Assn. Acad. Health Ctrs. (past chmn.). Home: 9250 Old Indian Hill Rd Cincinnati OH 45243-3438 Office: U Cin Med Ctr ML 663 250 Health Professions Bldg Cincinnati OH 45267-0663 Fax: (513) 558-2962. E-mail: don.harrison@uc.edu.

HARRISON, JEREMY THOMAS, dean, law educator; b. San Francisco, Dec. 23, 1935; s. James Gregory and Agnes Johanna (Patrick) H.; m. Roseanne E. Thomas, Dec. 29, 1962 (dec. Oct. 1983); children: James, Amelia, Roseanne, Jeremy, Alexandra, Nadya, Rachel; m. Laura Ellen Marrack, Apr. 28, 1990; children: Robert, Peter, Paul, Philip, John. BS, U. San Francisco, 1957, JD, 1960; LLM, Harvard U., 1962. Bar: Calif. 1961, Hawaii 1987. Assoc. Brobeck, Phleger & Harrison, San Francisco, 1960-61; law clk. to assoc. justice U.S. Ct. Claims, Washington, 1962-63; lectr. law U. Ghana, Accra, 1963-64, U. Ife, Ibadan, Nigeria, 1964-66; prof. law U. San. Francisco, 1966-85; dean Sch. Law U. Hawaii, Honolulu, 1985-94; dean Mich. State U. Detroit Coll. Law, East Lansing, 1996-98, prof. law, 1998—. Vis. prof. law Haile Sellassie I U., Addis Ababa, Ethiopia, 1971-74, U. Hawaii, 1977-79; Elips Disting. prof. law Gadjah Mada U., Yogyakarta, Indonesia, 1995-96. Author: Cases and Materials on Evidence, Africa, 1967, Cases and Materials on Ethiopian Civil Procedure, 1974. Counsel citizen's panel Hawaii's Jud. Adminstrn., Honolulu, 1985-86; bd. dirs. Straub Found., Honolulu; pres. Pacific Health Rsch. Inst., Honolulu, 1993-95. Mem. ABA, Am. Bar Found., Calif Bar Assn., Hawaii Bar Assn., Internat. 3d World Legal Studies Assn. Office: Mich State U Detroit Coll Law 465 Law College Bldg East Lansing MI 48824-1300

HARRISON, JOSEPH WILLIAM, state legislator; b. Chgo., Sept. 10, 1931; s. Roy J. and Gladys V. (Greenman) H.; m. Ann Hovey Gillespie, June 9, 1956; children: Holly Ann, Tracy Jeanne, Thomas Joseph, Amy Beth, Kitty Lynne, Christy Jayne. BS, U.S. Naval Acad., 1956; postgrad., Ind. U. Law Sch., 1968-70. Asst. to pres. Harrison Steel Castings Co., Attica, Ind., 1960-64, sales rsch. engr., 1964-66, asst. sec., 1966-69, sec., 1969-71, v.p., 1971-84, dir., 1968-74; mem. Ind. Senate, 1966—, majority leader, 1980—. Mem. Attica Consol. Sch. Bd., 1964-66, pres., 1966-67. Served with USN, 1956-60. Mem. Am. Legion, Sigma Chi. Republican. Methodist. Lodges: Elks, Eagles. Home: 504 E Pike St Attica IN 47918-1524 Office: PO Box 409 Attica IN 47918-0409 also: State Senate State Capitol 200 W Washington St Indianapolis IN 46204-2728

HARRISON, MARVIN, football player; b. Phila., Aug. 25, 1972; Degree in retailing, Syracuse Univ. Wide receiver Indpls. Colts, 1996—. Office: Indpls Colts 7001 W 56th St Indianapolis IN 46254*

HARRISON, MICHAEL GREGORY, judge; b. Lansing, Mich., Aug. 4, 1941; s. Gus and Jean D. (Fuller) H.; m. Deborah L. Dunn, June 17, 1972; children: Abigail Ann, Adam Christopher, Andrew Stephen. AB, Albion (Mich.) Coll., 1963; JD, U. Mich., 1966; postgrad., George Washington U. Bar: Mich. 1966, U.S. Dist. Ct. (ea. and we. dists.) Mich. 1967, U.S. Ct. Appeals (6th cir.). Asst. pros. atty. County of Ingham, Lansing, 1968-70, corp. counsel, 1970-76; judge 30th Jud. Cir. State of Mich., 1976-2000; chief judge 30th Jud. Cir. State of Mich., 1980-91; judge Ct. of Claims, 1979-2000; of counsel Foster, Swift, Collins and Smith, Lansing, 2000—. Counsel Capital Region Airport Authority, Lansing, 1970-76, Ingham Med. Ctr., Lansing, 1970-76; chmn. Ingham County Bldg. Authority, Mason, Mich., 1971-76; adj. prof. Thomas M. Cooley Law Sch., Lansing, 1976—. Editor Litigation Control, 1996; contbr. chpt. to Michigan Municipal Law, Actions of Governing Bodies, 1980; contbr. articles to profl. jours. Mem. shared vision steering com. United Way-C. of C.; mem. adv. bd. Hospice of Lansing, 1989—; pres. Greater Lansing Urban League, 1974-76, Lansing Symphony Assn., 1974-76; chmn. Mid. Mich. chpt. ARC, Lansing, 1984-86; bd. dirs., sec. St. Lawrence Hosp., Lansing, 1980-88; bd. dirs. ARC Gt. Lakes Regional Blood Svcs., 1991-95, Lansing 2000, 1987—; mem. exec. bd. Chief Okemos coun. Boy Scouts Am.; mem. criminal justice adv. com. Olivet Coll.; hon. bd. dirs. Lansing Area Safety Coun.; mem. State Bar Bd. Commrs., 1993-96; mem. felony sentencing guidelines steering com., chmn. caseflow mgmt. coordinating com., mem. juror use and mgmt. task force Mich. Supreme Ct. Recipient Disting. Citizens award Boy Scouts Am., Disting. Vol. award Ingham County Bar Assn., Disting. Alumni award Albion Coll. Fellow: Mich. Bar Found., Am. Bar Found.; mem.: ABA (coun. mem. judicial divsn., coun. mem. tort and ins. practice sect.), Mich. State Bar Found. (pres. 1991—2000), Nat. Conf. State Trial Judges (exec. com. 1991—94, vice chmn. 1995—96, chmn. 1997—98), Mich. Judges Assn. (treas. 1991, sec. 1992, 2d v.p. 1993, 1st v.p. 1994, pres. 1995), Mich. State U. Am. Inn of Ct. 2001—, (master), Am. Judicature Soc. (bd. dirs. 1996—), Rotary Club, Lansing (pres. 2001—, 2001—02), Country Club, Lansing. Republican. Congregationalist. Avocations: skiing, golf, tennis, travel, photography. Office: 313 S Washington Sq Lansing MI 48933-2193 E-mail: mharrison@fosterswift.com.

HARRISON, MICHAEL JAY, physicist, educator; b. Chgo., Aug. 20, 1932; s. Nathan J. and Mae (Nathan) H.; m. Ann Tukey, Sept. 1, 1970. A.B., Harvard, 1954; M.S., U. Chgo., 1956, Ph.D., 1960. Fulbright fellow and H. Van Loon fellow in theoretical physics U. Leiden, Netherlands, 1954-55; NSF fellow U. Chgo., 1957-59; research fellow math. physics U. Birmingham, Eng., 1959-61; asst. prof. Mich. State U., East Lansing, 1961-63, assoc. prof., 1963-68, prof., 1968—, faculty grievance officer, 1972-73, dean Lyman Briggs Coll., 1973-81, adj. prof. community health scis., 1988-93, adj. prof. epidemiology, 1993—. Vis. research physicist Inst. Theoretical Physics, U. Calif., Santa Barbara, 1980-81; with Air Force Cambridge Research Center, summer 1953, M.I.T. Lincoln Lab., summer 1954, RCA Sarnoff Lab., summers 1961-63; physicist Westinghouse Labs., summer 1956; cons. RCA Lab., 1961-64, United Aircraft Co., 1964-66, U.K. Atomic Energy Authority, Harwell Lab., summer 1960, Thailand project in Bangkok, Mich. State U.-AID, summer 1968; vis. research affiliate theoretical biology and biophysics, Los Alamos Nat. Lab., 1987-88. Contbr. articles to U.S., fgn. profl. jours. Am. Council on Edn. fellow U. Calif., Los Angeles, 1970-71. Fellow Am. Phys. Soc.; mem. AAUP (chpt. treas. 1966-67), N.Y. Acad. Scis., Harvard Club of Ctrl. Mich. (pres. 1988-93), Rotary, B'nai B'rith, Phi Beta Kappa, Sigma Xi. Jewish. Avocations: hiking, travel, photography. Home: 277 Maplewood Dr East Lansing MI 48823-4746 Office: Mich State U Physics Dept East Lansing MI 48824 E-mail: harrison@pa.msu.edu.

HARRISON, MOSES W., II, state supreme court chief justice; b. Collinsville, Ill., Mar. 30, 1932; m. Sharon Harrison; children: Luke, Clarence. BA, Colo. Coll.; LLB, Washington U., St. Louis. Bar: Ill. 1958, Mo. 1958. Pvt. practice, 1958-73; judge 3d Jud. Cir., Ill., 1973-79, 5th Dist. Appellate Ct., 1979-92; chief justice Ill. Supreme Ct., 1992—. Mem. ABA, Am. Judicature Soc., Ill. State Bar Assn. (former bd. govs.), Madison County Bar Assn. (former pres.), Tri-City Bar Assn., Met. St. Louis Bar Assn., Justinian Soc. Office: 333 Salem Pl Ste 170 Fairview Heights IL 62208-1363*

HARRISON, PATRICK WOODS, lawyer; b. St. Louis, July 14, 1946; s. Charles William and Carolyn (Woods) H.; m. Rebecca Tout, Dec. 23, 1967; children: Heather Ann, Heath Aaron. BS, Ind. U., 1968, JD, 1972. Bar: Ind. 1973, U.S. Dist. Ct. (so. dist.) Ind. 1973, U.S. Dist. Ct. Nebr. 1982, U.S. Supreme Ct. 1977. Assoc. Goltra, Cline, King & Beck, Columbus, Ind., 1972-73; ptnr. Goltra & Harrison, 1973-78; pvt. practice, 1979-80; ptnr. Cline, King, Beck and Harrison, 1980-85, Beck, Harrison & Dalmbert, Columbus, 1985—. Ind. Jud. Nominating Commn. nominee Ind. Supreme Ct., 1984. With U.S. Army, 1968-70. Fellow Ind. Trial Lawyers Assn. (bd. dirs. 1984, emeritus dir. 1999, Co-Trial Lawyer of Yr. 1999); mem. Am. Trial Lawyers Assn. Republican. Baptist. Avocation: golf. Home: 14250 W Mount Healthy Rd Columbus IN 47201-9309 Office: Beck Harrison & Dalmbert 320 Franklin St Columbus IN 47201-6732 E-mail: harrison@direcway.com., woodyh@bhdatty.com.

HARROLD, BERNARD, lawyer; b. Wells County, Ind., Feb. 5, 1925; s. James Delmer and Marie (Mounsey) H.; m. Kathleen Walker, Nov. 26, 1952; children— Bernard James, Camilla Ruth, Renata Jane. Student, Biarritz Am. U., 1945; AB, Ind. U., 1949, LLB, 1951. Bar: Ill. 1951. Since practiced in, Chgo.; assoc., then mem. firm Kirkland, Ellis, Hodson, Chaffetz & Masters, 1951-67; sr. ptnr. Wildman, Harrold, Allen & Dixon, 1967—. Note editor: Ind. Law Jour, 1950-51; contbr. articles to profl. jours. Served with AUS, 1944-46, ETO. Fellow Am. Coll. Trial Lawyers, Acad. Law Alumni Fellows Ind. U. Sch. Law; mem. ABA, Ill. Bar Assn. (chmn. evidence program 1970), Chgo. Bar Assn, Lawyers Club, Univ. Club, Order of Coif, Phi Beta Kappa, Phi Eta Sigma. Home: 809 Locust St Winnetka IL 60093-1821 Office: Wildman Harrold Allen & Dixon 225 W Wacker Dr Fl 28 Chicago IL 60606-1229

HARSDORF, SHEILA ELOISE, state legislator, farmer; b. St. Paul, July 25, 1956; d. Ervin Albert and Eloise Vivian (Sodergren) H.; m. Vernon Clark Bailey, Nov. 18, 1989. BS in Animal Sci., U. Minn., 1978; grad., Wis. Rural Leadership Program, 1986. Loan officer Prodn. Credit Assn. River Falls, Wis., 1978-80; dairy farmer, Beldenville, 1980-88; mem. Wis. Assembly from 30th dist., Madison, 1988-98, Wis. Senate from 10th dist., Madison, 2001—. Part-time dairy farmer; mem. adv. coun. for small bus., agrl. and labor Fed. Res. Bank Minn., Mpls., l988; mem. Wis. Agrl. Stblzn. and Conservation svc. Com., 1987-88. Mem., chairwoman Pierce County Dairy Promotion Com., 1986; mem. Congressman's Adv. Coun. on Agr., 1988—. First Covenant Ch., River Falls. Mem. Wis. Farm Bur. (co-treas. 1982-85, Discussion Meet winner 1986), Wis. Holstein Assn., Dairy Shrine. Republican. Home: N6627 County Rd E River Falls WI 54022-4036

HARSHMAN, RICHARD R. manufacturing executive; b. Apr. 22, 1947; BS, Fordham U, Bronx, N.Y. Lucy Ellen/F & F Labs.; v.p. sales, mktg. Tootsie Roll; CEO, pres. Storck USA, Storck North America, 1985-98; CEO Favorite Brands Internat., Lincolnshire, Ill., 1998—. Office: Favorite Brands Intl 100 Deforest Ave East Hanover NJ 07936-2813 Address: Favorite Brands 2121 Waukegan Rd Ste 300 Bannockburn IL 60015-1831

HART, CARL KISER, JR. county attorney; b. Madison, Wis., Oct. 30, 1955; s. Carl Kiser Sr. and Eleanor Katie (Pauls) H.; m. Barbara Ann Brooks, May 28, 1980; children: Elizabeth Ann, Daniel Keith. BA, U. Wis., 1977; JD, U. Tulsa, 1981. Bar: Okla. 1981, Nebr. 1989, Wis. 1991. Asst. dist. atty. Okla.'s 16th Dist., Poteau, 1981-82, Okla.'s 26th Dist., Woodward, 1983-87, 1st asst. dist. atty., 1987-90; dep. county atty. Seward County, Nebr., 1991-97, Butler County, 1995—, Colfax County, Nebr., 2000—02; atty. Butler County, 1996—2002. Trustee Woodward County Law Libr., 1987-90; bd. mem. Butler County Arts Coun., 1994-96, Butler County Cmty. Coalition, 1999-2002; trumpeter Columbus Jazz Orch., Seward Mcpl. Band, Concordia U. Cmty. Band. Mem. Okla. Bar Assn., Nebr. Bar Assn., Wis. Bar Assn., Rotary, Masons. Methodist. Avocation: trumpet playing. Home: 1209 N 4th St David City NE 68632-1105 Office: Butler County Attys Office Butler County Courthouse David City NE 68632

HART, CECIL WILLIAM JOSEPH, otolaryngologist, surgeon; b. Bath, Avon, Eng., May 27, 1931; came to U.S., 1957. s. William Theodore Hart and Paulina Olive (Adams) Gilmer; m. Brigid Frances Molloy, June 15, 1957 (dec. Nov. 1984); children: Geoffrey Arthur, Paula Mary, John Adams; m. Doris Crystel Katharina Alm, Mar. 14, 1987; children: Kristen-Linnea Alm, Erik Alm, Britt-Marie Alm. BA, Trinity Coll., Dublin, Ireland, 1952, MB, BCH, BAO, 1955, MA, 1958. Diplomate Am. Bd. Otolaryngology. Intern Dr. Steevens Hosp., Dublin, Ireland, 1956, Little Co. Mary Hosp., Evergreen Park, Ill., 1957, mem. staff, 1958-59; resident in otolaryngology U. Chgo. Hosp. and clinic, 1959-62; instr. U. Chgo. Med. Sch., 1962-64, asst. prof., 1964-65; practice medicine specializing in otolaryngology Chgo., 1958—; mem. staff Northwestern Meml. Hosp., 1972-97, Rehab. Inst. Chgo., 1965-97, Children's Meml. Hosp., 1972-97, Little Co. of Mary Hosp., 1977-94, LaGrange (Ill.) Comty. Meml. Hosp., 1977-94, Loyola U. Med. Ctr., 1997—. Tchg. assoc. Cleft Palate Inst., 1968, dir. otolaryngology, 1969-92; asst. prof. dept. otolaryngology-head and neck surgery Northwestern U. Med. Sch., 1965-75, assoc. prof., 1975-92, prof., 1992-97, prof. emeritus, 1997—; lectr. dept. otorhinolaryngology Loyola U., 1972, prof. otolaryngology, head and neck surgery, 1997—; med. adv. bd. So. Hearing and Speech Found., Nat. Inst. of Deafness and Other Communicative Disorders, 1989-95. Producer videos, movie; contbr. numerous articles to profl. jours. and mags.; also guest appearances various radio and TV talk shows. NIH fellow U. Chgo., 1962-63; NIH grantee, 1985-88. Fellow Am. Neurotology Soc. (pres. 1974-75, chmn. editorial review & publ. com. 1978-79, constn. and bylaws com. 1979-97), Am. Acad. Otolaryngology-Head and Neck Surgery (chmn. subcom. on Equilibrium 1980-86, computer com. 1987-90), ACS, Inst. Medicine Chgo., Soc. for Ear, Nose and Throat Advances in Children; mem. AMA, Brit. Med. Assn., Ill. State Med. Soc., Chgo. Med. Soc., Am. Cleft Palate Assn., Am. Council Otolaryngology, Am. Otological Soc., Chgo. Laryngological and Otological Soc. (v.p. 1975-76), Northwestern Clin. Faculty Med. Assn. (vice chmn. 1976-78, pres. 1979-81), Barany Soc., Royal Soc. Medicine, Irish Otolaryngological Soc., So. Hearing and Speech Found (med. adv. bd.), Chgo. Hearing and Balance Assn. (pres.), Sigma Xi. Roman Catholic. Avocations: travel, baroque music, symphony, opera, tennis. Office: Bldg 105 Rm 1870 2160 S 1st Ave Maywood IL 60153-3304

HART, DANIEL, orchestra executive; Bassist Peoria (Ill.) Symphony Orch., Colo. Springs (Colo.) Symphony, Baton Rouge Symphony Orch.; exec. dir. Va. Symphony Orch., Norfolk, 1994-98, Columbus (Ohio) Symphony Orch., 1998—. Office: Columbus Symphony Orch 55 E State St Columbus OH 43215-4203

HART, GEORGE ZAVEN, state legislator; b. Detroit, May 13, 1927; AA, Henry Ford C.C.; BA, Wayne State U., 1952. City councilman, Dearborn, Mich., 1957-71; county commr. Wayne County, 1972-78; mem. from dist. 10 Mich. Senate, Lansing, 1978-82, 87-94, mem. from dist. 6, 1995—. Chmn. Com. on Transp. & Tourism, Spl. Com. on Sports Violence Mich. State Senate; mem. Mcpl. & Election Com., Consumer Affairs Com., State Affairs, Transp. & Tourism Com., Local Govt. & Vet. Com., Energy Com., Farming Agribus. and Food Sys. Com., Families, Mental Health and Human Svcs. com. Mich. State Senate; mem. joint commn. Adminstrv. Rules. Recipient Steering Wheel award Automobile Clubh, 1981. Mem. Am. Legion, Mason, Moose, Kiwanis, Goodfellows, Pulaski Civic Orgn. Address: 4200 Roemer St Dearborn MI 48126-3421 Office: 1015 Farnum Bldg PO Box 30036 Lansing MI 48909-7536

HART, JAMES WARREN, university administrator, restaurant owner, former professional football player; b. Evanston, Ill., Apr. 29, 1944; s. George Ezrie and Marjorie Helen (Karsten) H.; m. Mary Elizabeth Mueller, June 17, 1967; children: Bradley James and Suzanne Elizabeth (twins), Kathryn Anne. B.S., So. Ill. U., 1967. Quarterback St. Louis Cardinals Profl. Football Team, 1966-83, Washington Redskins Profl. Football Team, 1984; radio sports personality Sta. KMOX, 1975-84, Sta. KXOK, 1985-86; sports analyst Sta. WGN Radio, Chgo., 1985-89; athletics dir. So. Ill. U., Carbondale, 1988-99, assoc. chancellor for external affairs, 1999-2000; head coach So. Ill. Spl. Olympics, 1973-90, Mo. Spl. Olympics, 1976-78; co-owner Dierdorf & Hart's Steak House (2 locations), St. Louis; spl. asst. to vice chancellor for instnl. devel. So. Ill. U., 1999—. Co-author: The Jim Hart Story, 1977. Gen. campaign chmn. St. Louis Heart Assn., 1974-88; hon. chmn. St. Louis Sr. Olympics, 1986-88. Named Most Valuable Player in Nat. Football Conf., 1974, Most Valuable Player with St. Louis Cardinals, 1973, 1975, 1978, Man of Yr., St. Louis Dodge Dealers, 1975, 1976, Miller High Life, 1980; named to So. Ill. U. Sports Hall of Fame, 1978, Mo. Sports Hall of Fame, 1998, Missouri Valley Conf. Hall of Fame, 2001; recipient Brian Piccolo-Nat. YMCA Humanitarian award, 1980. Mem.: AFTRA, NFL Players Assn. (Byron Whizzer White award 1976, Brian Piccolo Nat. YMCA Humanitarian award 1980), Fellowship Christian Athletes. Republican.

HART, JOHN, professional sports team executive; b. Tampa, Fla., July 21, 1948; m. Sandi DeVorak; 1 child, Shannon. Degree in History and Physical Edn., U. Cen. Fla., 1973. Minor league mgr. Montreal Expos, 1969-75, Balt. Orioles, 1975-88, third base coach, 1988; spl. assignment scout, interim mgr. Cleve. Indians, 1989-91, exec. v.p. and gen. mgr., 1991—. Named Major League Baseball Exec. of the Yr. The Sporting News, 1994, 1995. Office: Cleveland Indians Jacobs Field 2401 Ontario St Cleveland OH 44115-4003

HART, KATHERINE MILLER, college dean; b. Hinsdale, Ill., Jan. 31, 1943; d. Donald William and Katherine (Hiatt) H. BA, DePauw U., 1965; MPH, U. Ill., 1976. Mem. staff 1st Nat. Bank Chgo., 1965-68; dir. phys. placement svcs. AMA, Chgo., 1968-75; from staff assoc. to assoc. dean U. Ill., 1975-90, assoc. dean, 1990—. Mem. Chgo. Ill. Union bd., 1986-88. Mem. Assoc. Am. Med. Colls. (planning com. faculty affairs profl. dev. conference, 1998), U. ECOS Bus. Team. Office: Univ of Illinois Coll Medicine 1853 W Polk M/C 784 Chicago IL 60612

HART, MILDRED, retired counselor; b. Ever, Ky., Apr. 7, 1937; d. Dewey Otis and Malta Virginia (Adams) Cooper; m. Joseph Paul Surace, Oct. 26, 1956 (dec. Jan. 1966); children: Marisa Surace Craig, Vincent, Angela, Stephen (dec. 1994); m. James Robert Hart, June 26, 1994. BS in Edn., Ohio State U., 1974, MA in Guidance-Counseling, 1976. Cert. elem. and secondary tchr., secondary prin., supr., Ohio; lic. profl. counselor, Ohio. Sec. H.G. Snyder & Assocs., accts., Columbus, Ohio, 1958-63; tchr. Columbus Pub. Schs., 1974-79, counselor, 1977-99, chmn. student svcs. dept., 1985-99. Adjustor Bancohio Nat. Bank, Columbus, 1985-93. Author: (booklet) College Handbook for Independence High School Students, 1988. Leader Girl Scouts U.S., Columbus, 1969-73. Mem. NEA, Ohio State U. Alumni Assn., Nat. Honor Soc., Pi Lambda Theta (sec. Ctrl. Ohio chpt. 1985-93, 99—, treas. Ctrl. Ohio chpt. 1997-99), Phi Kappa Phi. Democrat. Roman Catholic. Avocations: travel, reading, cooking, antiques. Home: 2328 Sedgwick Dr Columbus OH 43220-5431

HART, WILLIAM THOMAS, federal judge; b. Joliet, Ill., Feb. 4, 1929; s. William Michael and Geraldine (Archambeault) H.; m. Catherine Motta, Nov. 27, 1954; children: Catherine Hart Fornero, Susan Hart DaMario, Julie Hart Boesen, Sally Hart Collins, Nancy Hart McLaughlin. JD, Loyola U., Chgo., 1951. Bar: Ill. 1951, U.S. Dist. Ct. 1951, U.S. Ct. Appeals (7th cir.) 1954, U.S. Ct. Appeals (D.C. cir.) 1977. Asst. U.S. atty. U.S. Dist. Ct. (no. dist.) Ill., Chgo., 1954-56; assoc. Defrees & Fiske, 1956-59; spl. asst. atty. gen. State of Ill., 1957-58; assoc. then ptnr. Schiff, Hardin & Waite, 1959-82; spl. asst. state's atty. Cook County, Ill., 1960; judge U.S. Dist. Ct. Ill., 1982—; now sr. judge. Mem. exec. com. U.S. Dist. Ct. (no. dist.) Ill., 1988-92; mem. com. on adminstrn. fed. magistrates sys., Jud. Conf. U.S., 1987-92, 7th cir. Jud. Coun., 1990-92; mem. edn. com. Fed. Jud. Ctr., 1994-99; chair No. Dist. Ill. Ct. Hist. Assoc., 1998—. Pres. adv. bd. Mercy Med. Ctr., Aurora, Ill., 1980-81; v.p. Aurora Blood Bank, 1972-77; trustee Rosary H.S., 1981-82, 93-98; bd. dirs. Chgo. Legal Asst. Found., 1974-76. Served with U.S. Army, 1951-53. Decorated Bronze Starl named to Joliet/Will County Hall of Pride, 1992. Mem. 7th Cir. Bar Assn., Law Club, Legal Club, Soc. Trial Lawyers, Union League Club of Aurora, Ill. (hon.), Inn of Ct., Serra Club of Aurora (v.p. 2000—). Office: US Dist Ct No Dist Ill US Courthouse Rm 2246 219 S Dearborn St Chicago IL 60604-1702

HARTKE, CHARLES A. state legislator; b. Effingham, Ill., May 7, 1944; m. Kathy Hartke; 2 children. Farmer; mem. from 108th dist. Ill. Ho. of Reps., 1985—. Vice chmn. agr. com.; chmn. counties and twps. com.; mem. appropriations com., elem. and secondary edn. com., transp. and motor vehicles com., children com., econ. devel. and legis. info. system com., pub. safety and infrastructure appropriations coms., vets. affairs com. Home: PO Box 1205 Effingham IL 62401-1205

HARTLEY, DAVID, state legislator, lawyer; b. Dec. 16, 1942; m. Vicki Mayes. BA, U. Louisville, 1967, postgrad.; JD, Capital U., 1983. State rep. Dist. 62 Ohio Ho. of Reps., 1973-92, state rep. Dist. 73, 1993—. Minority leader commerce and labor, mem. pub. utilities com., agriculture and natural resources com.; mem. Clark County Dem. exec. com. Mem. exec. com. Interfaith Hospitality Network. Named Legislator of Yr., Children for the Enforcement of Support, 1987, Top Legislator, Ohio Union of Patrolmen Assn., 1990, Ohio's Most Effective Legislator for the Environment, Ohio Environ. Coun., 1993; recipient Outstanding Achievement award Sierra Club, 1992, Spl. award of merit Ohio Acad. Trial Lawyers, 1992, Dir.'s award Ohio Victims of Crime Program, 1993, Disting. Svc. award Ohio State Bar Assn., 1993. Mem. UAW. Office: Riffe Ctr 77 S High St Fl 10 Columbus OH 43266-0603 Fax: 614 644 9494.

HARTLEY, DUNCAN, fundraising executive; b. Sept. 27, 1941; s. Harold Shephard and Catherine Carmichael (Hursley) H.; m. Adrienne Ashley, Aug. 19, 1971. BA, U. Mich., 1964; MA, Wayne State U., Detroit, 1966, PhD. Instr. English dept. Wayne State U., 1969-71; asst. prof. William Paterson Coll., 1971-74; adminstr. ednl. resources, chpt. liaison Young Pres.'s Orgn., N.Y.C., 1974-78; dir. planned giving Carroll Coll., Waukesha, Wis., 1978-80; dir. capital gifts Greater N.Y. Coun. Boy Scouts Am., N.Y.C., 1980-84; dir. individual giving, exec. dir. pres.'s coun. Meml. Sloan-Kettering Cancer Ctr., 1984-96; assoc. dean of devel. and alumni affairs Sch. Medicine Case Western Res. U., Cleve., 1996—. Co-editor, author: The Sociology of the Arts, 1974. Mem. Princeton Club of N.Y., Audiophile Soc. Presbyterian. Avocation: audio equipment reviewing. Home: 310 E Stonebrooke Ct Chagrin Falls OH 44022-2100 Office: Case Western Res U Sch Medicine 10900 Euclid Ave Cleveland OH 44106-1712

HARTNETT, D. PAUL, state legislator; b. Sioux City, Iowa, Sept. 29, 1927; m. Marjorie Sheehan, 1951; children: Debbie (Mrs. Burchard), Cindy (Mrs. Spagnola), Marcy (Mrs. Closner), Joan, Michael. BA, Wayne State Coll., 1951, MS, 1958; PhD, U. Nebr., 1966. H.S. tchr., coach, adminstr., Nebr.; coll. prof.; mem. Nebr. Legislature from 45th dist., Lincoln, 1984—; chmn. urban affairs com. Nebr. Legislature, mem. gen. affairs com., natural resources com., mem. edn. com. of the states, mem. exec. bd. Past mem. Bellevue Sch. Bd. Mem. C. of C., Eagles, KC, Phi Delta Kappa. Office: 407 Greenbriar Ct Bellevue NE 68005-4714 also: State Capitol 1445 K St Lincoln NE 68508-2731

HARTNETT, JAMES PATRICK, engineering educator; b. Lynn, Mass., Mar. 19, 1924; s. James Patrick and Anna Elizabeth (Ryan) H.; m. Shirley Germaine Carlson, July 14, 1945 (div. 1969); children: James, David, Paul, Carla, Dennis; m. Edith Zubrin, Sept. 10, 1971. BS in Mech. Engring, Ill. Inst. Tech., 1947; MS, MIT, 1948; PhD, U. Calif., Berkeley, 1954. Engr. gas turbine div. Gen. Electric Co., 1948-49; rsch. engr. U. Calif., Berkeley, 1949-54; asst. prof. to prof. mech. engring. U. Minn., 1954-61; Guggenheim fellow, vis. prof. U. Tokyo, Japan, 1960; cons. ICA, Seoul, Korea, 1960; Fulbright lectr., cons. mech. engring. U. Alexandria, Egypt, 1961; H. Fletcher Brown prof. mech. engring., chmn. dept. U. Del., 1961-65; engring. cons., 1954-74; prof., head dept. energy engring. U. Ill., Chgo., 1965-74; dir. Energy Resources Ctr., 1974-98. Sci. exch. visitor, Romania, 1969; vis. prof. Israel Inst. Tech., 1971; cons. Asian Inst. Tech., Bangkok 1977; 1st Dr. Arcot Ramachandran prof. heat transfer Indian Inst. Tech., Madras, 1995-96. Editor: Recent Advances in Heat and Mass Transfer, 1961; co-editor: Internat. Jour. Heat and Mass Transfer, 1960—, (with T.F. Irvine, Jr.) Advances in Heat Transfer, 1963—, Heat Transfer-Japanese Research, Soviet Research, 1971, Fluid Mechanics-Soviet Research, 1971; contbr. articles on heat transfer, fluid mechanics, energy to tech. jours. Mem. organizing com. and sci. coun. Internat. Centre Heat and Mass Transfer, Ankara, Turkey, 1969—; mem., sec. Ill. Energy Resources Commn., 1974-85; mem. sci. coun. Regional Center for Energy, Heat and Mass Transfer for Asia and Pacific, 1976—; sec. Midwest Univs. Energy Consortium, 1980—. Recipient Profl. Achievement award Ill. Inst. Tech. Alumni Assn., 1977; recipient Luikov medal Internat. Ctr. Heat and Mass Transfer, 1981; Japan Soc. for Promotion of Sci. fellow, 1987. Fellow ASME (Meml. award heat transfer divsn. 1969, 40th Anniversary award 1989, AIChE-ASME Max Jakob Meml. award 1989), Indian Nat. Acad. Engring., Japanese Soc. Mech. Engrs. (hon.); mem. Internat. Higher Edn. Acad. of Scis./Moscow (Disting. prof. 1997), Sigma Xi, Tau Beta Pi, Pi Tau Sigma. Address: Univ of Ill 1919 W Taylor St Chicago IL 60612-7246

HARTOG, JOHN, II, theology educator, librarian; b. Orange City, Iowa, Nov. 15, 1936; s. John and Gertrude Marie (Hofland) H.; m. Martha Griselda Nuñez, July 30, 1964; children: John III, Paul Anthony. AA, Northwestern Coll., 1956; student, Moody Bible Inst., 1956-57, Middle Coll. Langs., Middlebury, Vt., 1959; BA, Wheaton (Ill.) Coll., 1959; ThM, Dallas Theol. Sem., 1964; MSLS, East Tex. State U., 1970; ThD, Grace Theol. Sem., 1978; D in Ministry, Cen. Bapt. Theol. Sem., 1988. Ordained to ministry Gen. Assn. Regular Bapt. Chs., 1969. Min. religious lit. Immanuel Tract Soc., Dallas, 1964-66; pastor Lipscomb (Tex.) Community Ch., 1966-67; instr. libr. Mont. Inst. Bible, Billings, 1967-68, acad. dean Lewistown, 1973-77; prof., head libr. Calvary Bible Coll., Kansas City, Mo., 1984-89, acad. dean, 1987-89; prof., libr. Faith Bapt. Bible Coll., Ankeny, Iowa, 1968-70, 77-84, 89—; founding pastor Maranatha Bapt. Ch., Grimes, 1995—. Author: The Fall of a Kingdom, 1983, Enduring to the End, 1987, When the Church Was Young and Bold, 1988, Abounding Grace, 1991, The Biblical Qualifications of a Pastor, 1992, Alive in Christ, 1993. Mem. Pi Gamma Mu, Phi Theta Kappa. Republican. Avocation: gardening. Office: Faith Bapt Theol Sem 1900 NW 4th St Ankeny IA 50021-2152

HARTSFIELD, JAMES KENNEDY, JR. geneticist, orthodontist; b. Decatur, Ala., Feb. 12, 1955; s. James Kennedy and Shirley Joann (Bridwell) H.; m. Karen Lee Whitaker, May 8, 1977; 1 child, Kennedy Whitaker. BS, U. S.C., 1977; DMD, Med. U. S.C., 1981; MS, Ind. U., 1983; M in Med. Sci., Harvard U., 1987; PhD, U. South Fla., 1993. Diplomate Am. Bd. Med. Genetics. Intern Hillsborough Dental Rsch. Clinic, Tampa, Fla., 1981-82; clin. fellow Ind. U., Indpls., 1982-83; rsch. fellow Harvard U., Boston, 1983-86, Mass. Gen. Hosp., Boston, 1984-86; clin. fellow U. South Fla., Tampa, 1986-87, asst. prof., 1987-93; assoc. prof. Sch. Dentistry and Medicine Ind. U., Indpls., 1993—. Dir. Teratogen Info. Svc., U. South Fla., 1987-93; dir. oral facial genetics Sch. Dentistry Ind. U., 1993—. Contbr. articles to profl. jours. Recipient Physician-Scientist award NIH, 1989, 1st Ind. Rsch. Support and Transition award, 1996. Fellow Am. Coll. Med. Genetics (founding); mem. ADA, Am. Soc. Human Genetics, Am. Assn. for Dental Rsch., Soc. Craniofacial Genetics (pres. 1989-90), Am. Assn. Dental Schs., Am. Cleft Palate Assn., Am. Assn. Orthodontists. Presbyterian. Avocations: music, boating. Home: 8095 Sunfish Ct Indianapolis IN 46236-8887 Office: Ind U Schs Dentistry and Medicine 1121 W Michigan St Indianapolis IN 46202-5211 Also: 8801 N Meridian St Ste 313 Indianapolis IN 46260-5316

HARTUNG, JAMES H. airport authority executive; Pres. Toledo-Lucas County Port Authority. Office: Toledo Lucas County Port Authority 1 Maritime Plz Toledo OH 43604

HARTZLER, ED, state legislator; State rep. Dist. 123 Mo. Ho. of Reps., 1993—. Mem. appropriations com., banks and fin. instns. com., state rels. and vets. affairs com., govtl. orgn. and rev. com., ins. com., urban affairs com. Office: Mo House of Reps Rm 115D 201 W Capitol Ave Jefferson City MO 65101 Home Fax: 816 331 0171; Office Fax: 573 526 1313. E-mail: ehartzle@services.state.mo.us.

HARTZLER, GEOFFREY OLIVER, retired cardiologist; b. Goshen, Ind., Nov. 6, 1946; s. Robert Willis and Emma Irene (Blosser) H.; m. Lois Anne Kauffman, June 1967 (div. May 1983); children: Abigail, Christine, Amanda; m. Dorothy Eloise Arnn, July 1985. BA, Goshen Coll., 1968; MD with honors, Ind. U., 1972. Diplomate Am. Bd. Internal Medicine, Bd. in Cardiovascular Disease. Intern Mayo Grad. Sch. Medicine, Rochester, Minn., 1972-73, fellow in medicine, 1973-74, fellow in cardiology, 1974-76; assoc. cons. internal medicine and cardiovascular disease Mayo Clinic, 1976-77; instr. medicine Mayo Med. Sch. and Grad. Sch. Medicine, 1976-79; cons. cardiovascular disease and internal medicine Mayo Clinic and Mayo Found., 1977-80; dir. invasive diagnostic electrophysiology Mayo Clinic, Minn., 1979-80; cardiologist Cardiovascular Cons., Inc., Kansas City, Mo., 1980-93; clin. prof. medicine U. Mo., 1985-95. Cons. cardiologist Mid-Am. Heart Inst., Kansas City, 1980-95; dir. advanced angioplasty fellowship program St. Luke's Hosp., Kansas City, 1985-92, med. dir. cardiovascular clin. rsch. ctr. Mid-Am. Heart Inst., 1993-95; cons. Advanced Cardiovascular Systems, Inc., Santa Clara, Calif., 1983-95; past mem. editl. or rev. bd. Am. Jour. Cardiology, Jour. Am. Coll. Cardiology, Cath. and CV Diagnosis, others; co-founder Ventritex, Inc., Sunnyvale, Calif., 1985-88, Triax Internat., Inc., Lenexa, Kans., 1989-96; prin., bd. dirs. Kustom Signals, Inc., Lenexa, 1990-96, LMP Steel & Wire Co., Maryville, Mo., 1992—, Hartz Properties, Inc., Prarie Village, Kans., 1993—, Lett Electronics, Inc., Topeka, 1995-98, Intraluminal Therapeutics, Inc., Kansas City, Kans., 1997—. Contbr. articles to profl. jours., chpts. to books; made TV presentations to lay people on aspects of cardiology. Recipient KK Chen award, 1970, E.V. Allen scholarship, 1971, Osler award U. Miami, 1986, 1st Ann. Career Achievement award Cardiol. Rsch. Found., 1994. Fellow Am. Coll. Cardiology, Coun. on Clin. Cardiology of Am. Heart Assn., Soc. for Cardiac Angiography; mem. AMA, Mo. State Med. Assn., Jackson County Med. Assn., Am. Heart Assn., Alpha Omega Alpha. Avocations: music, motorcycling, reading, traveling, business. Office: 2600 Verona Rd Shawnee Mission KS 66208-1266

HARTZLER, VICKY J. state legislator; Mem. Mo. Ho. of Reps., Jefferson City, 1994-2000. Address: 22804 E 299th St Harrisonville MO 64701-6320

HARVEY, DAVID R. chemical company executive; With Sigma-Aldrich Corp., St. Louis, 1981—, pres., COO, 1995—, pres., CEO, 2000—, also bd. dirs. Office: Sigma-Aldrich Corp 3050 Spruce St Saint Louis MO 63103

HARVEY, JACK K. holding company executive; b. 1943; With Douglas County Bank & Trust Co., Omaha, 1960—; chmn. bd., exec. v.p. State Bank Holding Co. (now Great Western Bank). Office: Great Western Bank 14545 W Center Rd Omaha NE 68144-3276

HARVEY, JOHN GROVER, mathematics educator; b. Waco, Tex., Aug. 10, 1934; s. John Grover and Mary Inez (Davidson) H. AA, Navarro Jr. Coll., Corsicana, Tex., 1953; BS, Baylor U., 1955; MS, Fla. State U., 1957; PhD, Tulane U., 1961. Instr. math. U. Ill., Urbana, 1961-63, asst. prof., 1963-66; assoc. prof. math. U. Wis., Madison, 1966-75, prof., 1975-2001, prof. emeritus, 2001—. Prin. investigator Wis. R & D Ctr. for Cognitive Learning, Madison, 1968-78. Editor: Matching High School Preparation to College Needs: Prognostic and Diagnostic Testing, 1996.; editor, contbg. author: Models for Technology Teacher Education in Mathematics, 1997; contbr. chpts. to books. Mem. Math. Assn. Am. (assoc. editor 1969-74, chmn. com. on testing 1988-93), Am. Ednl. Rsch. Assn., Nat. Coun. Tchrs. of Math., Wis. Math. Coun. (Disting. Math. Educator award 1993). Democrat. Lutheran. Home: 330 Morgan St # 506 New Orleans LA 70114-1070

HARVEY, PAUL, news commentator, author, columnist; b. Tulsa, Sept. 4, 1918; s. Harry Harrison and Anna Dagmar (Christensen) Aurandt; m. Lynne Cooper, June 4, 1940; 1 child, Paul Harvey. Litt.D. (hon.), Culver-Stockton Coll., 1952, St. Bonaventure U., 1953; LL.D., John Brown U., Ark., 1959, Mont. Sch. Mines, 1961, Trinity Coll. Fla., 1963, Parsons Coll., 1968; H.H.D., Wayland Bapt. Coll., 1960, Union Coll., 1962, Samford U., 1970, Howard Payne U., Tex., 1978, Sterling Coll., 1982; Degree (hon.), Rosary Coll., 1996. Announcer radio sta. KVOO, Tulsa; sta. mgr. Salina, Kans.; spl. events dir. radio sta. KXOK, St. Louis; program dir. radio sta. WKZO, Kalamazoo, 1941-43; dir. news and information OWI, Mich., Ind., 1941-43; news commentator, analyst ABC, 1944—; syndicated columnist Los Angeles Times Syndicate (formerly Gen. Features Corp.), 1954—; TV commentator, 1968. Author: Remember These Things, 1952, Autumn of Liberty, 1954, The Rest of the Story, 1956, You Said It, Paul Harvey, 1969, Our Lives, Our Fortunes, Our Sacred Honor; Album rec. Yesterday's Voices, 1959, Testing Time, 1960, Uncommon Man, 1962. Bd. dirs. John D. and Catherine T. MacArthur Found.; mem. bd. govs. Orchestral Assn. Chgo. Symphony Orch. Recipient citation DAV, 1949, 11 Freedoms Found. awards, 1952-76, radio award Am. Legion, 1952, citation of merit, 1955, 57, Cert. of merit VFW, 1953, Bronze Christopher's award, 1953, award of honor Sumter Guards, 1955, nat. pub. welfare services trophy Colo. Am. Legion, 1957,Great Am. KSEL award, 1962, Spl. ABC award, 1973, Ill. Broadcaster award, 1974, John Peter Zenger Freedom award Eagles, 1975, Am. of Year award Lions Internat., 1975, Outstanding Broadcast Journalism award, 1980, Gen. Omar N. Bradley Spirit of Independence trophy, 1980, Man of Yr. award Chgo. Broadcast Advt. Club, 1981, Golden Radio award Nat. Radio Broadcasters Assn., 1982, Best Speaking Voice award Am. Speech, Lang. and Hearing Assn., 1982, Horatio Alger award, 1983, Outstanding Broadcast Personality award Advt. Club Balt., 1984, Meritorius Svc. award Am. Acad. Family Physicians, 1984, Cert. of Appreciation Humane Soc. of U.S., 1985, Genesis award The Fund for Animals, 1986, Okla. Assn. Broadcasters award, 1987, Henry G. Bennett Disting. Svc. award Okla. State U., 1987, James Herriot award Humane Soc. U.S., 1987, Lowell Thomas award, 1989, Gold medal Internat. Radio & TV Soc., 1989, Others award Salvation Army, 1989, Journalism award Internat. Radio Festival, 1989, Marconi award Network Personality of Yr., 1989, 91, 96, 98, Dante award, 1990, William Booth award Salvation Army, 1990, Journalism award Chgo. Hall of Fame, 1990, Bd. of Dirs. award Nat. Religious Broadcasters, 1991, Great Am. Race Legend's award Interstate, 1991, Good Guy award Am. Legion, 1992, Outstanding Pub. Spkr. award Toastmasters Internat., 1992, Paul White award Radio T.V. News Dirs., 1992, Peabody award 1993, 94, Spirit of Broadcasting award NAB, 1994, Silver award Am. Advertising Fedn., 1994, Hall of Fame award Broadcasting & Cable Mag., 1995, Am. Spirit award USAF, 1996, Lifetime Achievement award Radio Mercury, 1997, Lifetime Achievement award Gold Angel, 1998, Lifetime Achievement award Radio Mercury, 1997; elected to Okla. Hall of Fame, 1955, Nat. Assn. Broadcasters Hall of Fame, 1979; named Top Commentator of Yr. Radio-TV Daily, 1962, Laureate Lincoln Acad. of Ill., 1987 (Ill. highest honor); to Emerson Radio Hall of Fame, 1990, among 20th Century's Most Significant Americans George Mag., 1998. Mem. Washington Radio and Television Corrs. Assn., Aircraft Owners and Pilots Assn. Club: Chicago Press. Achievements include having broadcasts and columns reprinted in Congressional Record 102 times. Office: 333 N Michigan Ave Ste 1600 Chicago IL 60601-4005

HARVEY, RAYMOND CURTIS, conductor; b. N.Y.C., Dec. 9, 1950; s. Shirley Nathaniel and Doris Louise (Walwin) H. BMus, MMus, Oberlin Coll., 1973; M. in Musical Arts, Yale U., 1978, D in Musical Arts, 1984. Choral dir. Northfield (Mass.) Mt. Hermon Sch., 1973-76; asst. conductor Des Moines Metro Opera, Indianola, Iowa, 1977-80; music dir. Tex. Opera Theater, Houston, 1978-80; Exxon/arts endowment conductor Indpls. Symphony, 1980-83; assoc. conductor Buffalo Philharmonic, 1983-86; music dir. Marion (Ind.) Philharmonic, 1982-86, Springfield (Mass.) Symphony, 1986-94, Fresno Philharm. Orch., 1993-99, El Paso (Tex.) Opera, 1995—, Kalamazoo Symphony Orch., 1999—. Guest conductor Minn. Orch., 1991, 92, Detroit Symphony, 1990, 92, N.Y. Philharmonic, 1987, Atlanta Symphony, 1992, Louisville Orch., 1990, 93, Utah Symphony, 1993, Phila. Orch., 2001, Detroit Symphony, 1992, 2001. Democrat. Methodist. Avocations: running, fitness. Office: Kalamazoo Symphony Orch 359 S Burdick St Ste 100 Kalamazoo MI 49007

HARVEY, RONALD GILBERT, research chemist; b. Ottawa, Ont., Can., Sept. 9, 1927; came to U.S., 1948; s. Gilbert and Adeline (LeClair) H.; m. Helene H. Szpara, May 18, 1952; 1 child, Ronald Edward. BS in Biology, UCLA, 1952; MS in Chemistry, U. Chgo., 1956, PhD in Chemistry, 1960. Project leader Sinclair Rsch. Labs., Harvey, Ill., 1956-58; instr. U. Chgo., 1960-63, asst.prof., 1964-68, assoc. prof., 1968-75, prof., 1975-97, prof. emeritus, 1997—; postdoctoral fellow Imperial Coll., London, Eng., 1963-64. Cons. Nat. Cancer Inst., Washington, Farmacon Corp., Oakbrook, Ill., CIDAC, Palo Alto, Calif., 1978-80; OMNI Research Mayaguex, P.R., 1973-74, Nat. Inst. Environ. Health Sci., Washington, Am. Cancer Soc., Atlanta, U.S.-Israel Binational Sci. Found. Author: Polycyclic Aromatic Hydrocarbons Chemistry and Carcinogenesis, 1991, Polycyclic Aromatic Hydrocarbons, 1997; editor: Polycyclic Hydrocarbons and Carcinogenesis; mem. editl. bd. Polycyclic Aromatic Compounds; contbr. more than 430 articles to profl. jours. Recipient ISPAC award for rsch. in polycyclic hydrocarbon chemistry, 1995. Fellow Royal Chem. Soc., Am. Inst. Chemists; mem. AAAS, Am. Chem. Soc., Am. Assn. Cancer Rsch., Sigma Xi. Achievements include patents for synthesis of alpha-olefins, anti-androgen compounds. Home: 10550 Golf Rd Orland Park IL 60462-7420 Office: U Chgo Ben May Inst 5841 S Maryland Ave Chicago IL 60637-1463 E-mail: rharvey@huggins.bsd.uchicago.edu.

HARVIE, CRAWFORD THOMAS, lawyer; b. N.Y.C., Mar. 28, 1943; s. William Mead and Barbara Adele (Johnson) H.; m. Iris Ruth Alofsin, June 10, 1972; children: Katherine, Edward. AB, Stanford U., 1965; LLB, Yale U., 1968; cert. advanced mgmt. program, Harvard U., 1992. Bar: N.Y. 1969. Assoc. Debevoise & Plimpton, N.Y.C., 1971-75; counsel TRW, Inc., Cleve., 1976-77, sr. counsel, 1978-79, asst. gen. counsel, v.p., 1980-83; v.p. law TRW Automotive, 1983-90; v.p., assoc. gen. counsel TRW Inc., 1990-95; sr. v.p., gen. counsel, sec. Goodyear Tire and Rubber Co., Akron, Ohio, 1995—. Trustee Cleve. Inst. of Music, 1989—, Akron Art Mus.; bd. overseers Blossom Music Ctr. Mem. Am. Corp. Counsel Assn., Assn. of Gen. Counsel, Chief Legal Officer Roundtable-U.S. Home: 6537 Thornbrook Cir Hudson OH 44236-3552 Office: Goodyear Tire and Rubber Co 1144 E Market St Akron OH 44316-0001

HARWICK, DENNIS PATRICK, lawyer; b. May 27, 1949; s. T. Dale and Lois L. (Patrick) H.; m. Rebecca Cowgill, May 10, 1980. BA, U. Idaho, 1971, JD, 1974. Bar: Idaho 1974, U.S. Dist. Ct. Idaho 1974. Legal officer Idaho Bank & Trust, Pocatello, 1974-79, v.p. legal Boise, 1979-85; exec. dir. Idaho State Bar and Idaho Law Found., Inc., 1985-90, CEO Washington State Bar Assn., 1990-97, Kans. Bar Assn./Kans. Bar Found., Topeka, 1998—. Spokesman, 1983-85; mem. adv. coun. U. Idaho Coll. Letters and Sci., 1986-90; pres. Kans. Lawyers Svc. Corp., 1998—. Editor Corp. Newsletter, 1983-85. Bd. dirs. Boise Philharm., 1984-89, v.p. adminstrn., 1985-87; chmn. Idaho Commn. U.S. Constl. Bicentennial, 1986-88; chmn. Idaho Bus. Week Program, 1984; treas. Idaho State Dem. Conv., 1980. Mem. ABA, Nat. Assn. Bar Execs. (mem. exec. com., pres. 1996-97), Nat. Conf. Bar Founds. (trustee), Idaho State Bar (examiner/grader 1975-90), Idaho Bankers Assn. (spokesman), Am. Inst. Banking (state chmn. 1982-83), Idaho Assn. Commerce and Industry (chmn. coms.), Boise Bar Assn., Bar Assn. Adminstrn., Topeka Tennis Assn. (bd. dirs. 2000—), Phi Beta Kappa. Clubs: Boise Racquet and Swim (bd. dirs. 1988-90, pres. 1990). Democrat. Office: Kans Bar Assn PO Box 1037 Topeka KS 66601-1037

HARWOOD, JULIUS J. metallurgist, educator; b. N.Y.C., Dec. 3, 1918; m. Naomi Beitner, 1983; children: Dane L., Gail A., Caren L., Rochelle. BS, CCNY, 1939; MS, U. Md., 1953; D of Engring. (hon.), Mich. Tech. U., 1986. Materials engr. U.S. Naval Gun Factory, 1940-46; metall. Off Naval Rsch., 1946-60; mgr. metall. sci. lab. Ford Motor Co., Dearborn, Mich., 1960-69, mgr. rsch. planning engring. and rsch. staff, 1969-71, dir. Material Sci. Lab, engring. and rsch. staff, 1971-83; prof. engring. Wayne State U., Detroit, 1984; pres. Ovonic Synthetic Material Co., Troy, Mich., 1984-87, Harwood Cons., Orchard Lake, 1987—, West Bloomfield. Adj. prof. Wayne State U., Detroit, 1975. Contbr. articles to profl. jours. Fellow AAAS, Metall. Soc. (pres. 1973), Am. Soc. Metals (John H. Shoemaker award 1977), Engring. Soc. of Detroit (Gold Medal award 1983); mem. Am. Inst. Mining, Metall. and Petroleum Engrs. (pres. 1976, hon.), Am. Ceramic Soc. (Orton lectr. 1978), Nat. Acad. Engrs. Office: 5023 Pheasant Cv West Bloomfield MI 48323-2093

HASARA, KAREN A. mayor; b. Springfield, Ill., Oct. 17, 1940; m. Jerry Gott; 4 children. BA, Sangamon State U. Mem. Ill. Ho. of Reps., Springfield, 1986-91, 92-94, mem. appropriations I, elem. and sec. edn., counties and twps., agrl., children, aging, small bus., coal devel., mkt., fin. inst. and human svc. coms.; former spokesman on mental health; former vicespokesman on state govt. adminstrn.; mayor City of Springfield, 1995—. Office: City of Springfield 800 E Monroe St Ste 300 Springfield IL 62701-1699

HASE, DAVID JOHN, lawyer; b. Milw., Feb. 27, 1940; s. John Henry and Catherine Charlotte (Leekley) H.; m. Penelope Sue Pritchard, Sept. 2, 1964; children: Jeffrey David, Jennifer Anne, John Paul. AB, Dartmouth Coll., 1962; LLB, U. Wis., 1965. Bar: Wis. 1965, U.S. Dist. Ct. (ea. dist.) Wis. 1965, U.S. Ct. Appeals (7th cir.) 1971, U.S. Ct. Appeals (D.C. cir.) 1975, U.S. Ct. Appeals (9th cir.) 1989, U.S. Supreme Ct. 1975. Assoc. Grootemaat, Cook & Franke, Milw., 1965-67, ptnr., shareholder, 1968-70; shareholder Cook & Franke S.C., 1970-73; legal counsel to gov. Wis., Madison, 1973-74; dep. atty. gen. State of Wis., 1974-76; assoc. Foley & Lardner, Milw., 1976-77, ptnr., 1977-94; shareholder Cook & Franke S.C., 1994—. Mem. Sch. Bd., Mequon, Wis., 1971-94, treas., 1973-75, pres., 1975-94. Mem. ABA. Democrat. Home: 2108 W Raleigh Ct Mequon WI 53092-5416 Office: Cook & Franke SC 660 E Mason St Ste 401 Milwaukee WI 53202-3877 E-mail: hase@cf-law.com.

HASELKORN, ROBERT, virology educator; b. Bklyn., Nov. 7, 1934; s. Barney and Mildred (Seplowin) H.; m. Margot Block, June 23, 1957; children: Deborah, David. AB, Princeton U., 1956; PhD, Harvard U., 1959. Asst. prof. biophysics U. Chgo., 1961-64, assoc. prof., 1964-69, prof., chmn. dept., 1969-84, F.L. Pritzker Disting. Service prof. dept. molecular genetics and cell biology, 1984—; dir. Ctr. for Photochemistry and Photobiology, 1987—; pres. Integrated Genomics, Inc., 2000—01. Chmn. bd. dirs. Integrated Genomics, Inc., Chgo., 1997—; cons. virology and rickettsiology study sect. USPHS, 1969-73; mem. sci. adv. bd. Sloan-Kettering Inst., 1978-79; mem. nitrogen fixation panel U.S. Dept. Agr., 1978-79; mem. panel sci. advs. UNIDO Internat. Ctr. for Genetic Engring. and Biotech., 1984-94, 97—; mem. recombinant DNA adv. com. NIH, 1991-95; adj. scientist Woods Hole Oceanographic Instn., 1994—. Editor: Virology, 1973—; mem. editl. bd. Molecular Microbiology; contbr. articles to profl. jours. Recipient USPHS Rsch. Career Devel. award, 1963-69, Interstate Postgrad. Med. Assn. Rsch. award, 1967, Darbaker prize Bot. Soc. Am., 1982, Gregor Mendel medal in biol. scis. Acad. Scis. Czech Republic, 1996, Buzatti-Traverso lectr., CNR, Rome, 1997; Am. Cancer Soc. postdoctoral rsch. fellow ARC Virus Rsch. Unit, Cambridge, Eng., 1959-61, Guggenheim fellow Institut Pasteur, Paris, 1975, Sackler fellow Tel Aviv U., 1987. Fellow AAAS, Am. Acad. Arts and Scis. (chmn., midwest coun., v.p. 1993-99); mem. NAS, Internat. Soc. Plant Molecular Biology (pres. 1987-89). Home: 5834 S Stony Island Ave Chicago IL 60637-2060 Office: U Chgo 920 E 58th St Chicago IL 60637 E-mail: rh01@uchicago.edu.

HASELWOOD, ELDON LAVERNE, retired education educator; b. Barnard, Mo., July 19, 1933; m. Joan Haselwood; children: Ann, Karen, Polly, Amy. BS in Edn., U. Omaha, 1960; MA in Libr. Sci., U. Denver, 1963; PhD, U. Nebr., 1972. Libr. Omaha Pub. Schs., 1960-61, Lewis Cen. Community Schs., Council Bluffs, Iowa, 1961-63; documents libr. U. Omaha, 1963-66; prof. dept. tchr. edn. U. Nebr., Omaha, 1966—, coord. ednl. tech. Coll. Edn., 1993—2002, ret., 2002. Cons. Nat. Park Svc., Omaha, 1978—. Cpl. U.S. Army, 1953-55. Mem. ALA (councilor 1988-91, excellence in teaching award 1987), Am. Assn. Sch. Librs., Mountain Plains Libr. Assn. (rep. 1999—), Nebr. Libr. Assn. (pres. 1981, meritorious svc. award 1983, Mad Hatter award 1998), Nebr. Ednl. Media Assn. (disting. svc. award 1993), Iowa Assn. Ednl. Media, Nebr. Libr. Commn. (commr. 1981-86). Home: 615 S 122nd St Omaha NE 68154-3015

HASENOHRL, DONALD W. state legislator; b. Marshfield, Wis., Nov. 25, 1935; m. Kathleen Hasenohrl; children: Dena, Charles, Donald. Former farmer; mem. from dist. 70 Wis. State Assembly, Madison, 1974—, mem. hwy. com., 1979—, mem. excise and fees com., 1983—, chmn. transp. com., 1983—, mem. transp. project coms., mem. energy and commerce com., 1991—, mem. hwys., transp., excise and fees com., 1993, mem. consumer affairs, rural affairs & hwys. & transp. coms., 1995, mem. hwy. and transp., consumer affairs, rural affairs com., 1997. Chmn. Wood County Dem. Com., 1963-64; mem. Marshfield City Planning Com., 1966-67; bd. dirs. Ctrl. Wis. State Fair Assn. Named Outstanding Legislator of Yr., Wis. Mfr. Housing Assn., 1983. Mem. KC, Eagles, United Comml. Travelers, Marshfield Elks, Knights of Columbus, Lions Club, Bus. and Profl. Women's Club, Ctrl. Wis. Sportsmen's Club, Eau Pleine Boat Club. Roman Catholic. Office: PO Box 8952 Madison WI 53708-8952 Fax: 608-266-7038. E-mail: rep.hasenohrl@legis.state.wi.us.

HASHIMOTO, KEN, dermatology educator; b. Niigata City, Japan, June 19, 1931; came to U.S., 1956; m. Noriko Sakai, Oct. 3, 1961; children: Naomi, Martha, Eugene, Amy. MD, Niigata U., 1955. Cert. Am. Bd. Dermatology, 1968, Dermatopathology, 1972. Asst. prof. dermatology Tufts U. Sch. Medicine, Boston, 1965-68; assoc. prof. medicine, anatomy U. Tenn., Memphis, 1968-70, prof. medicine, assoc. prof. anatomy, 1970-77, dir., dermatopathology, prof., 1975-77; prof., dir. dermatology, prof. anatomy Wright State U., Dayton, Ohio, 1977-80; chief, dermatology sect., dir. elec. microscopy lab. VA Med. Ctr., 1977-80; dermatologist in chief Detroit Med. Ctr., 1987—; prof., chmn. dermatology Wayne State U., Detroit, 1980-99, prof. emeritus, 1999—. Mem. dermatol. drugs adv. com. FDA. Fulbright scholar, 1956-59; participant med. investigatorship career devel. program VA, 1969-77. Mem. Am. Soc. Dermatopathology (pres. 1986-87), Nat. Bd. Med. Examiners, Japanese Soc. Investigative Dermatology (hon.), Memphis Dermatological Soc. (pres. 1973-74), Soc. Investigative Dermatology (v.p. 1980-81, chmn. program com. 1985-86), Soc. Francaise de Dermatologie et de Syphilographie (corr. 1989), Japanese Assn. Dermatology (hon.). Office: Wayne State U Sch Medicine Dept Dermatology 540 E Canfield St Detroit MI 48201-1928

HASHMI, SAJJAD AHMAD, business educator, university dean; b. India, Dec. 20, 1933; m. Monica Ruggiero; children: Serena, Jason, Shawn, Michelle. BA, U. Karachi, 1953, MA, 1956; PhD in Ins., U. Pa., 1962. Lectr. Ohio State U., Columbus, 1962-64; asst. prof. Roosevelt U., Chgo., 1964-66; prof. Ball State U., Muncie, Ind., 1966-83, chmn. dept. fin., 1973-83; Jones disting. prof., dean Sch. Bus. Emporia (Kans.) State U., 1983—. Cons. and speaker to profl. ins. agts., Indpls., Louisville, Springfield, Ill.; tech. advisor Ind. Arts Commn.; vice chmn. bd. trustees Kans. Ins. Edn. Found.; bd. dirs. Blue Cross and Blue Shield of Kans.; appeared on TV and radio programs, testified before N.Y., Kans. and Ind. legis. coms. Author: Insurance is a Funny Business, 1972, Automobile Insurance, 1973, Contemporary Personal Finance, 1985, Make Every Second Count, 1989, Strategies for The Future, 1990; contbr. articles, revs., monographs to profl. publs. Named Prof. of Yr., Ball State U. Students, 1971, Outstanding Tchr. of Yr., Ball State U., 1970. Mem. Am. Risk and Ins. Assn., Midwest Fin. Assn., Fin. Mgmt. Assn., Emporia C. of C., Emporia Country Club, Rotary, Beta Gamma Sigma, Sigma Iota Epsilon, Alpha Kappa Psi, Gamma Iota Epsilon, Phi Kappa Phi. Home: 2909 Lakeridge Rd Emporia KS 66801-5982 Office: Emporia State U Sch of Bus 1200 Commercial St Emporia KS 66801-5087 E-mail: hashmisa@emporia.edu.

HASLANGER, PHILIP CHARLES, journalist; b. Menominee, Mich., May 11, 1949; s. Harry LeRoy and Agnes Gertrude (Seidl) H.; m. Rosemary Ann Raasch Carta, May 27, 1972 (div.); children: Brian David, Sarah Marie; m. Ellen Jean Reuter, Apr. 9, 1983; children: Michael Kenneth, Julia Jane. BA in Sociology, U. Wis., 1971, MA in Journalism, 1973. With The Capital Times, Madison, Wis., 1973—, mng. editor, 1998—. Author: Stories of Call, 1988. Mem. Nat. Conf. Editl. Writers (bd. dirs. 1993, 94, 97, officer 1999-2002), New Media Fedn. Avocations: reading, music, hiking. Home: 5409 Vicar Ln Madison WI 53714-3443 Office: The Capital Times 1901 Fish Hatchery Rd Madison WI 53713-1248 E-mail: phaslanger@madison.com.

HASSEBROOK, CHUCK, not-for-profit developer; m. Kate Borchman, Dec. 31, 1991; 2 children. BA, U. Nebr. Exec. dir. Ctr. for Rural Affairs, Walthill, Nebr. Mem. USDA Commn. on Small Farms, 1997—99, Nebr. Network 21 Food Sys. Com., 1993—97; former co-chmn. north ctrl. region tech. com. USDA Low Input Sustainable Agr. Rsch. Program; mem. agrl. sci. and tech. rev. bd. USDA, 1991—96. Mem. bd. regents U. Nebr., 1994—, vice chmn., 1999, chmn., 2000; mem. external adv. com. on bioethics Iowa State U., 1987—90; mem. Keystone Ctr. Structure of Agr. Group; bd. dirs. Bread for the World, 1988—94. Mem.: Agr. Builders Nebr. Mailing: 250 N 3d St Lyons NE 68038

HASSELBACHER, DARLENE M. human resources executive; b. Ill. Grad., Marycrest Coll., 1983; MBA, St. Ambrose U., 1985. Sr. v.p. Sears Mfg. Co., 1984-86; dir. human resources Lee Enterprises, Inc., 1986-97; v.p. human resources Aid Assn. for Luths., Appleton, Wis., 1997—. Vol. Emergency Shelter Bd.; mem. First English Luth. Ch.; bd. dirs. AAL Employee Credit Union. Mem. Media Human Resources Assn. (past pres.), Soc. for Human Resources Mgmt. Office: Aid Assn for Lutherans 4231 N Ballard Rd Appleton WI 54919-0001

HASSERT, BRENT, state legislator; Owner Hassert Landscaping; mem. from 83d dist. Ill. Ho. of Reps., 1993—. Formerly mem. Will County Bd. Commrs.; formerly chmn., exec. Pub. Works and Natural Resources Coms., Will County; formerly commr. Will County Forest Preserve; formerly mem. Ill. Task Force for Solid Waste Legislation. Home: 1413 Sherman Rd Ste 60 Romeoville IL 60446-4092

HASSKAMP, KRIS, state legislator; b. Apr. 5, 1951; AA, Brainerd C.C.; BS, Bemidji State U. State rep. Dist. 12A, Minn., 1988—. Mem. com. edn. judiciary & local govt. coms., vice chmn. energy com., com. & econ. devel.-tourism & small bus. divsn. com., mem. environ. & natural resources-fin. divsn. gen. legis., vet. affairs & elec. coms., tax com., property tax divsn. com., commerce, tourism, consumer affairs, ins. and banking coms. Minn. Ho. of Reps. Lead Dem. local govt. and met. affairs. Home: 405 Superior Ave Crosby MN 56441-1264 Office: 100 Constitution Ave Saint Paul MN 55155-1232

HAST, ADELE, editor, historian; b. N.Y.C., Dec. 6, 1931; d. Louis and Kate (Miller) Krongelb; m. Malcolm Howard Hast, Feb. 1, 1953; children: David Jay, Howard Arthur. BA magna cum laude, Bklyn. Coll., 1953; MA, U. Iowa, 1969, PhD, 1979. Rsch. assoc. Atlas Early Am. History Project, Newberry Library, Chgo., 1971-75; assoc. dir. Atlas Great Lakes Indian History Project, 1976-79, Hist. Boundary Data File Project, 1979-81; editor in chief Marquis Who's Who, Inc., Chgo., 1981-86; survey dir. Nat. Opinion Rsch. Ctr., U. Chgo., 1986-89; rsch. fellow Newberry Libr., Chgo., 1989-95, scholar in residence, 1995—; exec. editor St. James Press, 1990-92; mng. editor Hist. Ency. of Chgo. Women U. Ill., 1991-93, dir., editor Hist. Ency. of Chgo. Women project, 1993-2001, sr. rsch. assoc. Ctr. for Rsch. on Women and Gender, 1999—. Mem. faculty Newberry Libr. Summer Inst. Cartography, 1980. Author: Loyalism in Revolutionary Virginia, 1985, American Leaders Past and Present: The View from Who's Who in America, 1985; compiler: Iowa, Missouri, vol. 4 of Historical Atlas and Chronology of County Boundaries, 1788-1980, 1984; editor: International Directory of Company Histories, vols. 3-5, 1991-92, Women Building Chicago 1790-1990: A Biographical Dictionary, 2001; assoc. editor: Atlas of Great Lakes Indian History, 1987; contbr. articles to profl. jours. Mem. profl. adv. grad. program pub. history Loyola U., 1986—; treas., bd. dirs. Chgo. Map Soc., 1980-81, 93-95; mem. New Trier Twp. H.S. Bd. Caucus, 1972-74; mem. acad. coun. Am. Jewish Hist. Soc., 1985—; pres. Chgo. Jewish Hist. Soc., 1980-81, bd. dirs., 1977—. Recipient Alumna of Yr. award Bklyn. Coll., 1984, Colonial Williamsburg Found. grantee-in-aid, 1975, Brit. Acad. rsch. fellow, 1979; Am. Coun. Learned Socs. grantee-in-aid, 1980; NEH rsch. grantee, 1985, 87, 93-95, 97-98. Fellow Royal Hist. Soc., Phi Beta Kappa, Kappa Delta Pi; mem. Am. Hist. Assn., Orgn. Am. Historians, Chgo. Area Women's History Conf. (sec., treas. 1994—, bd. dirs. 1990—), Caxton Club (coun. 1990-93). Office: Newberry Library 60 W Walton St Chicago IL 60610-3380

HAST, MALCOLM HOWARD, medical educator, biomedical scientist; b. N.Y.C., May 28, 1931; s. Irving William and Rose Lillian (Berlin) H.; m. Adele Krongelb, Feb. 1, 1953; children: David Jay, Howard Arthur. B.A., Bklyn. Coll., 1953; postgrad., U. So. Calif., 1955-57; M.A., Ohio State U., 1958, Ph.D. (NIH fellow), 1961; CBiol, FIBiol, Gt. Britain, 1991. Instr. U. Iowa, 1961-63; NIH spl. fellow U. Iowa (Coll. Medicine), 1963-65, asst. prof., 1965-69; assoc. prof. otolaryngology-head and neck surgery Northwestern U. Feinberg Sch. Medicine, Chgo., 1969—74; prof. Northwestern U. Med. Sch., 1974—, dir. research otolaryngology, 1969-93, prof. cell and molecular biology (anatomy), 1977—; prof. basic and behavioral scis. Northwestern U. Dental Sch., 1989-2001; assoc. med. staff Northwestern Meml. Hosp., 1969-90, health profl., 1990-93; rsch. assoc. zoology Field Mus. Natural History, 1995—; guest scientist Max Planck Inst. für Psychiatrie, 1976; vis. prof. Royal Coll. Surgeons Eng., 1980-86, U. Edinburgh, 1987; assoc. editor Clinical Anatomy, 1995—. Mem. task force on new materials Am. Bd. Otolaryngology, 1969-72; dir. Ill. Soc. Med. Rsch., 1973-77; mem. Internat. Anat. Nomenclature Com., 1983-91; guest scientist Zoologisches Forschungsinstitut und Mus. A. Koenig, 1988; mem. Northwestern U. Med. Sch. Admissions com., 1991-, chmn., 1998-; Brodel meml. lectr. Assn. Med. Illustrators, 1995; mem. Chgo. Clin. Ethics Programs. Prin. investigator, editor Transation of Vesalius' Fabraic, 1995-; contbr. articles to profl. jours., chpts. to books. Mem. adv. bd. Ctr. Deafness, 1977-80; bd. dirs. Cliff Dwellers Arts Found., 1979-82; trustee Wilmette Libr. Bd., 1982-83, Wilmette Bd. Health, 1999-. Served with U.S. Army, 1953-55. NATO sr. fellow in sci. Oxford U., Eng., 1978; NIH rsch. grantee, 1964-84, 95—, NSF rsch. grantee, 1975-77, NEH grantee, 1995-2002; recipient Gould Internat. award, 1971, Disting. Alumnus award of Honor, Bklyn. Coll., 1977, Alumnus of Yr. award, 1984; Arnott demonstrator Royal Coll. Surgeons Eng., 1985. Fellow AAAS, Linnean Soc. London, Inst. Biology, Am. Speech-Hearing Assn., Royal Soc. Medicine; mem. AMA, AAUP (chpt. pres. 1977-82), Am. Physiol. Soc. (animal care and experimentation com. 1976-82), Am. Assn. Clin. Anatomists, Chgo. Laryngol. and Otol. Soc. (coun. 1988-89), Am. Soc. Mammalogists, Anat. Soc. Gt. Britain and Ireland, Am. Assn. History Medicine, Soc. Med. History Chgo., Amnesty Internat. (coord. Chgo. Health profls. group 1986-87), Am. Assn. Anatomists, Nat. Eagle Scout Assn., Sigma Xi (chpt. pres. 1971-72), Sigma Alpha Eta. Achievements include research on neuromuscular physiology, embryology and comparative anatomy of the larynx, history of medicine. Office: 303 E Chicago Ave Chicago IL 60611-3093

HASTAD, DOUGLAS NOEL, physical education educator; b. Fargo, N.D., Dec. 18, 1949; s. Harold Noel and Olive Adelaide (Nugent) H.; m. Nancy Jo Seljevold, June 11, 1972; children: Jacob Noel, Rebekah Josie. BA, Concordia Coll., 1971; MS, Wash. State U., 1972; EdD, Ariz. State U., 1980; postgrad., Harvard U., 1992. Elem. phys. edn. specialist Moorhead (Minn.) Pub. Schs., 1972-76; instr. Concordia Coll., Moorhead, 1976-78; grad. assoc. Ariz. State U., Tempe, 1976-79; asst. prof. No. Ill. U., DeKalb, 1979-84; dept. chmn., assoc. prof. Tex. Christian U., Ft. Worth, 1984-89, interim dean, 1987-89; prof., dean dept. health, phys. edn. and recreation U. Wis., La Crosse, 1989—. Coordinator statewide fitness evaluation project for youth, DeKalb, 1980-84; cons. U. Tex. Med. Br., Galveston, 1985-86. Author: Fitness in the Elementary School, 1986, 2d edit., 1989, Measurement and Evaluation in Physical Education and Exercise Science, 1989, 2d edit., 1994; editl. bd.: The Physical Educator, 1984—; contbr. articles to profl. jours. Vol. Spl. Olympics/Sr. Olympics, DeKalb, 1982-84; vice chmn. program com. Am. Heart Assn. Tex. br., Ft. Worth, 1985-86; dir. conf. on future directions for fitness Tarrant County Med. Soc., Ft. Worth, 1985, pub. sch. adv. bd., 1984-86; bd. dirs. Rotary Internat. Fellow Bush Foundation (hon.); mem. Am. Alliance for Health, Phys. Edn., Recreation and Dance, Golden Key Honor Soc. Home: N2166 Valley Rd La Crosse WI 54601-7118 Office: U Wis Coll Health Phys Edn and Recreation 124 Mitchell St La Crosse WI 54603-1205

HASTERT, DENNIS (J. DENNIS HASTERT), congressman; b. Aurora, Ill., Jan. 2, 1942; m. Jean Kahl, 1973; children: Joshua, Ethan. BA, Wheaton Coll., 1964; MS, No. Ill. U., 1967. Tchr., coach Yorkville (Ill.) High Sch.; mem. Ill. House Reps., Springfield, 1980-86, U.S. Congress from 14th dist. Ill., 1987—, chief dep. majority whip, 1994-99, speaker of the house, 1999—, mem. commerce com., mem. govt. reform and oversight com. Lodge: Lions (Yorkville). Office: US Ho of Reps 2369 Rayburn House Office Bldg Washington DC 20515-1314*

HASTINGS, BARRY G. trust company executive; Pres. No. Trust Corp., Chgo., 1993—. Office: No Trust Co 50 S Lasalle St Chicago IL 60675-0001

HASTINGS, JOYCE R. editor; Editor Wis. Lawyer, Madison. Office: State Bar Wis PO Box 7158 Madison WI 53707-7158

HASTINGS, WILLIAM CHARLES, retired state supreme court chief justice; b. Newman Grove, Nebr., Jan. 31, 1921; s. William C. and Margaret (Hansen) H.; m. Julie Ann Simonson, Dec. 29, 1946; children—Pamela, Charles, Steven. B.Sc., U. Nebr., 1942, J.D., 1948; LHD (hon.), Hastings Coll., 1991. Bar: Nebr. 1948. With FBI, 1942-43; mem. firm Chambers, Holland, Dudgeon & Hastings, Lincoln, 1948-65; judge 3d jud. dist. Nebr., 1965-79, Supreme Ct. Nebr., Lincoln, 1979-88, chief justice, 1988-95; ret., 1995. Bd. dirs. Nat. Conf. Chief Justices, 1989-91. Pres. Child Guidance Ctr., Lincoln, 1962, 63; v.p. Lincoln Community Coun., 1968, 69; vice chmn. Antelope Valley coun. Boy Scouts Am., 1968, 69; pres. 1st Presbyn. Ch. Found., 1968—; mem. Lincoln Parks and Recreation Adv. Bd., Govs. task force correctional dept. medical svcs., 2000; mem. Nebr. Pub. Employees Retirement Bd. Served with AUS, 1943-46. Named to Nebr. Jaycee Hall of Fame, 1998. Mem. ABA, Nebr. Bar Assn. (George H. Turner award 1991, Pioneer award 1992), Am. Jud. Soc., Lincoln Bar Assn., Nebr. Dist. Judges Assn. (past pres.), Nat. Conf. Chief Justices (past bd. dirs.), Am. Judicature Soc. (Herbert Harley award 1997), Phi Delta Phi. Republican. Presbyterian (deacon, elder, trustee). Club: East Hills Country (pres. 1959-60). Home: 1544 S 58th St Lincoln NE 68506-1407

HATCH, MICHAEL WARD, lawyer; b. Pittsfield, Mass., Nov. 19, 1949; s. Ward Sterling and Elizabeth (Hubbard) H.; m. Lisa Schilling, June 8, 1974; children: Stuart, Andrew, Gillian. AB in Econs., St. Lawrence U., 1971; JD, Yale U., 1974. Bar: Wis. 1974, N.Y. 1980. Ptnr., chmn. real estate group Foley & Lardner, Milw., 1974—. Mem. ABA, N.Y. State Bar Assn., Wis. Bar Assn., Milw. Bar Assn., Am. Coll. Real Estate Lawyers, Urban Land Inst., Nat. Multi Housing Coun., Mortgage Bankers Assn. Wis., Bldg. Owners and Mgrs. Assn., Local Initiatives Support Corp., Milw. Athletic Club, Town Club. Avocations: architecture, historic preservation. Office: Foley & Lardner 777 E Wisconsin Ave Ste 3800 Milwaukee WI 53202-5367

HATCH, MIKE, state attorney general; m. Patti Hatch; 3 children. BS in Polit. Sci. with honors, U. Minn., Duluth, 1970; JD, U. Minn., 1973. Commr. of commerce State of. Minn., 1983—89; pvt. practice law; atty. gen. State of Minn., 1999—. Office: Minn Atty Gen's Office 1400 NCL Tower 445 Minnesota St Saint Paul MN 55101

HATCH, NATHAN ORR, university administrator; b. May 17, 1946; m. Julia Gregg; 3 children. AB summa cum laude, Wheaton Coll., 1968; AM, Washington U., 1972, PhD, 1974. Postdoctoral fellow Johns Hopkins U., 1974-75; from asst. prof. to prof. history U. Notre Dame, Ind., 1975-88, dir. grad. studies dept. history, 1980-83, assoc. dean Coll. Arts and Letters, dir. Inst. for Scholarship in the Liberal Arts, 1983-89, acting dean Coll. Arts and Letters, 1988-89, v.p. for grad. studies and rsch., 1989-96, prof., 1989, provost, 1996—, Andrew V. Tackes prof. history, 1999—. Author: The Sacred Cause of Liberty: Republican Thought and the Millennium in Revolutionary New England, 1977, The Democratization of American Christianity, 1989 (Albert C. Outler prize Am. Soc. Ch. History 1989, 1989 Book prize Soc. for Historians of Early Am. Republic, co-winner John Hope Franklin Publ. prize Yale U. Press 1990); also articles; editor: The Professions in American History, 1988; co-editor: The Bible in America: Essays in Cultural History, 1982, Jonathan Edwards and the American Experience, 1988. Bd. dirs. United Way St. Joseph County, Ind., 1987-92; trustee St. Joseph's Med. Ctr., 1994, chair bd. trustees, 1997-99; mem. nat. adv. bd. Salvation Army, 1997-99; trustee Fuller Theol. Sem., 1998—; mem. Nat. Coun. Humanities, 2000—. Recipient Paul Fenlon Teaching award U. Notre Dame, 1981; Am. Coun. Learned Socs. fellow, 1976, Fred Harris Daniels fellow Am. Antiquarian Soc., 1977, Charles Warren fellow Harvard U., 1977-78; grantee Lilly Endowment, 1979, Ind. Com. for the Humanities, 1981-82, NEH, 1981-85. Mem. Johns Hopkins Soc. Scholars, Am. Soc. Ch. Hist. (pres. 1993), Phi Beta Kappa. Office: U Notre Dame Office of the Provost Notre Dame IN 46556

HATFIELD, JERRY LEE, plant physiologist, biometeorologist; b. Wamego, Kans., May 1, 1949; s. Virgil H. and Elsie L. (Fischer) H.; m. Patricia JoAnne Reigle, Sept. 1, 1968; children: Mark E., Andrew J. BS, Kans. State U., 1971; MS, U. Ky., 1972; PhD, Iowa State U., 1975. Biometeorologist U. Calif., Davis, 1975-83; plant physiologist USDA-Agrl. Rsch. Svc., Lubbock, Tex., 1983-89; lab. dir. Nat. Soil Tilth Lab., USDA-Agr. Rsch. Svc., Ames, Iowa, 1989—. Editor: Biometerology and Integrated Pest Management, 1982, Limitations to Plant Root Growth, vol. 19, Advances in Soil Science, 1992, Soil Biology: Impacts on Soil Quality, Advances in Soil Science, 1993, Crops Residue Management, Advances in Soil Science, 1994, Utilization of Manure as a Soil Resource, Advances in Soil Science, 1998, Innovative Weed and Soil Management, Advances in Soil Science, Nitrogen in the Environment, 2001; contbr. over 295 articles to profl. jours. Recipient Arthur S. Fleming award for outstanding svc. to fed. govt., 1997. Fellow Soil Sci. Soc. Am., Am. Soc. Agronomy (editor jour. 1989-95, editor-in-chief 1996—, Agronomic Svc. award 1999), Crop Sci. Soc. Am.; mem. Am. Geophys. Union, Am. Meteorol. Soc. (chair agrl./forest com. 1980-81, agrl. and forest meteorology com. 1999—), Indian Agrometeorol. Soc. (hon.), Soil & Water Conservation Soc. (program chair 1997-98, Pres. Leadership award 1998), Phi Kappa Phi. Republican. Avocations: golfing, reading, photography, landscaping. Office: USDA Agrl Rsch Svc Nat Soil Tilth Lab 2150 Pammel Dr Ames IA 50011-0001 E-mail: hatfield@nstl.gov.

HATLEN, ROE HAROLD, restaurant executive; b. Libby, Mont., Nov. 6, 1943; s. Knute Harold and Hilda Elizabeth H.; B.B.A., Pacific Lutheran U., 1965; M.B.A, U. Oreg., 1967; m. Beverly Joan Thompson, June 18, 1966; children— Kari, Erick, Lars. Auditor, Kohnen & Larson, Eugene, Oreg., 1966-67; auditor Herzinger, Porter, Addison & Blind, Eugene, 1967-73; controller Internat. King's Table, Inc., Eugene, 1973-76, v.p. fin., treas., 1976— . Pres. bd. dirs. Central Lutheran Found. Bd., 1979-82; mem. alumni bd. Pacific Luth. U., Tacoma, Wash., 1982— . Served with USAR, 1967-73. Mem. Am. Inst. C.P.A.s, (bd. accountancy), Portland Cash Mgrs. Assn., Oreg. Soc. C.P.A.s, Nat. Restaurant Assn. Home: 782 Kristen Ct Eugene OR 97401-2346 Office: Buffets Inc 1460 Buffet Way Eagan MN 55121-1133

HATLER, PATRICIA RUTH, lawyer; b. Las Vegas, Nev., Aug. 4, 1954; d. Houston Eugene and Laurie (Danforth) Hatler; m. Howard A. Coffin II; children: Sloan H. D. Coffin, Laurie H. M. Coffin. BS, Duke U., 1976; JD, U. Va., 1980. Bar: Pa. 1980, Ohio 2002. Assoc. Dechert, Price & Rhoads, Phila., 1980-83; assoc. counsel Independence Blue Cross, 1983-86, sr. v.p., gen. counsel, corp. sec., 1987-99, Nationwide, Columbus, OH, 1999—. Home: 170 N Drexel Ave Bexley OH 43209-1427 Office: Nationwide One Nationwide Plaza Columbus OH 43215 E-mail: hatlerp@nationwide.com.

HATTEBERG, LARRY MERLE, photojournalist; b. Winfield, Kans., June 30, 1944; s. Merle Lawrence and Mary Dorothy (Early) H.; m. Judy Beth Keller, June 6, 1965; children: Sherry Renee, Susan Michelle. Student, Kans. State Tchrs. Coll., 1962-63, Emporia-Wichita State U., 1963-66. Photographer Sta. KAKE-TV, Wichita, Kans., 1963, photojournalist, 1966-67, chief photographer, 1967-81, assoc. news dir., 1981-87, exec. news dir., 1987-88, co-anchor 5 p.m. newscast, 1988-92; co-anchor Evening News broadcasts KAKE-TV, 1992—. Co-chmn. faculty Nat. Press Photographers TV Workshop, U. Okla., 1975—. Author: Larry Hatteberg's Kansas People,1991; developed Hatteberg's People series for TV, 1974. Served with USAR, 1966-72. Regional semi-finalist NASA Journalist-in-Spece Program; recipient Brotherhood award Kans. region NCCJ, 1995, regional lifetime Emmy award TV segment Hatteberg's People, Regional Emmy, 2000. Life mem. Nat. Press Photographers Assn. (Nat. TV News Photographer of Yr. award 1975, 77, Joseph Sprague award 1983, Joseph Costa award 1991). Office: 1500 N West St Wichita KS 67203-1323

HATTERY, ROBERT RALPH, radiologist, educator; b. Phoenix, Dec. 15, 1939; s. Robert Ralph and Goldie M. (Secor) H.; m. D. Diane Sittler, June 18, 1961; children: Angela, Michael. BA, Ind. U., 1961, MD, 1964; cert. in diagnostic radiology, Mayo Grad. Sch. Medicine, 1970. Diplomate Am. Bd. Radiology. Intern Parkland Meml. Hosp.-Southwestern Med. Sch., Dallas, 1964-65; fellow Mayo Clinic, Rochester, Minn., 1967-70, cons., 1970-81, chmn. dept. diagnostic radiology, 1981-86; instr. radiology Mayo Med. Sch., 1973-75, asst. prof. radiology, 1975-78, assoc. prof. radiology, 1978-82, prof. radiology, 1982—. Chair Mayo Group Practice Bd., 1991-93; chmn. bd. govs Mayo Clinic, Rochester, 1994-98; trustee Mayo Found., 1992—; trustee Am. Bd. Radiology. Author numerous jour. articles and abstracts, book chpts. Capt. USAF, 1965-67, Willford Hall Hosp., San Antonio. Fellow Am. Coll. Radiology; mem. Radiol. Soc. N.Am. (bd. dirs. 1999—), Am. Roentgen Ray Soc., Soc. Computed Body Tomography (pres. 1982-83), Soc. Genitourinary Radiography (pres. 1986-88). Office: Mayo Clinic 200 1st St SW Rochester MN 55905-0002 E-mail: rhattery@mayo.edu.

HATTIN, DONALD EDWARD, geologist, educator; b. Cohasset, Mass., Nov. 16, 1928; s. Edward Arthur and Una Vestella (Whipple) H.; m. Marjorie Elizabeth Macy, July 15, 1950; children: Sandra Jane, Ronald Scott, Donna Jean. B.S., U. Mass., 1950; M.S., U. Kans., 1952, Ph.D. (Shell fellow), 1954. Asst. instr. geology U. Kans., 1950-52, instr., 1953-54; asst. prof. geology Ind. U., Bloomington, 1954-60, assoc. prof., 1960-67, prof., 1967-95, prof. emeritus, 1995—; asst. geologist Kans. Geol. Survey, 1952, research assoc., 1959-68, 70-74, 77-82, 86-87. Vis. prof. Ernst-Moritz-Arndt U., Greifswald, German Dem. Republic, 1985; geologist Ind. Geol. Survey, 1957-58; cons. in field, mem. N.Am. Commn. on Stratigraphic Nomenclature, 1987-90, 91-94; vis. disting. prof. U. Kans., 1991. Author: Stratigraphy of the Wreford Limestone, 1957, Stratigraphy of the Carlile Shale, 1962, Stratigraphy of the Graneros Shale in Central Kansas, 1965, Stratigraphy and Depositional Environment of Greenhorn Limestone of Kansas, 1975, Upper Cretaceous Stratigraphy and Depositional Environments of Western Kansas, 1978, Stratigraphy and Depositional Environment of Smoky Hill Chalk, Niobrara Chalk, Western Kansas, 1982. Capt. reserves USAF, 1950—59, capt. active USAF, 1955—57. Recipient Erasmus Haworth Disting. Alumni honors in geology U. Kans., 1976, Alumni Disting. Tchg. award Coll. Arts and Scis. Ind. U., 1988, Disting. Tchg. and Mentoring award Grad. Sch. Ind. U., 1995; NSF grantee, 1975-77, 88-90, Am. Chem. Soc. grantee, 1978-80, 84-86; NSF fellow, 1969. Fellow: Geol. Soc. Am. (grantee 1975); mem.: Paleontol. Soc., Soc. Econ. Paleontologists Mineralogists, Am. Assn. Petroleum Geologists (Outstanding Educator award Ea. sect. 1993). Office: Ind U Dept Geol Scis Bloomington IN 47405

HATTON, JANIE R. HILL, principal; Formerly prin. Milw. Trade and Tech. H.S.; cmty. supt. Milw. Pub. Schs., 1989-91; dir. Dept. Leadership Svcs., 1996-97; dep. supt. Leadership Svcs., Milw., 1997-99; prin. Pulaski H.S., 1999—. Recipient Milw. Prin. Yr. award Alexander Hamilton H.S., 1986, Nat. Principal of the Year award Nat. Assn. Secondary Sch. Principals and Met. Life Ins. Co., 1993, It Takes a Whole Village Leadership award, 1999. Mem. Milw. Links Inc., Delta Sigma Theta. Office: Pulaski HS 2500 W Oklahoma Ave Milwaukee WI 53215-4437

HAUG, EDWARD JOSEPH, JR. mechanical engineering educator, simulation research engineer; b. Bonne Terre, Mo., Sept. 15, 1940; s. Edward Joseph and Thelma (Harrison) H.; m. Carol Jean Todd, July 1, 1979; 1 child, Kirk Anthony. BSME, U. Mo., Rolla, 1962; MS in Applied Mechanics, Kans. State U., 1964, PhD in Applied Mechanics, 1966. Rsch. engr. Army Armaments Command, Rock Island, Ill., 1969; chief sys. analysis Army Weapons Command, 1970, chief sys. rsch., 1971-72, chief concepts and tech., 1973-76; prof. U. Iowa, Iowa City, 1976—, Carver Disting. prof., 1990—, dir. Ctr. for Computer Aided Design, 1983-95; dir. Nat. Advanced Driving Simulator and Simulation Ctr., 1992-98. Author 9 books on computer aided design and dynamics; editor 5 books; contbr. numerous papers to profl. jours. Capt. U.S. Army, 1966-68. Recipient Innovative Info. Tech. award Computerworld/Smithsonian Instn., 1989, Colwell Merit award Soc. Automotive Engrs., 1989. Fellow ASME (Design Automation award 1991, Machine Design award 1992), Am. Acad. Mechanics. Achievements include patents for Constant Recoil Automatic Cannon, and for Real-Time Simulation System. Home: 2440 County Road 500 Bayfield CO 81122-8729 Office: U Iowa Dept Mech Engring Iowa City IA 52242 E-mail: haug@nads-sc.uiowa.edu.

HAUGLAND, ERLING, political organization executive; b. Crosby, N.D. BA, U. N.D. Pres. Recreation Supply Co. Inc., Inpls., 1980—. Chmn. N.D. State Reps., Bismark, 1999—. Office: PO Box 1473 Bismarck ND 58502-1473

HAUPT, ROGER A. advertising executive; CEO Leo Burnett Co., Inc., Chgo., 1999-2000, BCom3, 2000—. Office: BCom3 Group 35 W Wacker Dr Chicago IL 60601

HAUPTMANN, RANDAL MARK, biotechnologist; b. Hot Springs, S.D., July 6, 1956; s. Ivan Joy and Phyllis Maxine (Pierce) H.; m. Beverly Kay Suko, May 22, 1975; 1 child, Erich William. BS, S.D. State U., 1979; MS, U. Ill., 1982, PhD, 1984. Postdoctoral rschr. Monsanto Corp. Rsch., St. Louis, 1984-86; vis. rsch. scientist U. Fla., Gainesville, 1986-88; asst. prof. No. Ill. U., DeKalb, 1988-90, dir. plant molecular biology ctr., 1989-90; sr. rsch. scientist Amoco Life Sci. Techs., Naperville, Ill., 1990-94; dir. advanced tech. Seminis Vegetable Seeds, Woodland, Calif., 1994-98; gen. mgr. Ball Helix, West Chicago, Ill., 1998—. Author: (with others) Methods in Molecular Biology, 1990; contbr. articles to profl. jours. Mem. Internat. Assn. Plant Tissue Culture, Internat. Soc. Plant Molecular Biology, Am. Soc. Plant Physiologists, Tissue Culture Assn. (Virginia Evans award 1982), Sigma Xi, Gamma Sigma Delta. Republican. Office: Ball Helix 622 Town Rd West Chicago IL 60185-2614

HAURY, DAVID LEROY, science education specialist; b. Salem, Oreg., Sept. 17, 1947; s. Hubert Oscar and Anna Lorane (Davis) H.; m. Arlene H. Friesen, Dec. 26, 1968. BA in Biology, U. Oreg., 1974, MA in Biology, 1978; PhD in Sci. Edn., U. Wash., 1983. Cert. tchr., Oreg., S. Australia. Sci. tchr. Grant High Sch., Mt. Gambier, S. Australia, 1974-77; teaching assoc. U. Wash., Seattle, 1979-82; asst. prof. biology Judson Bapt. Coll., The Dalles, Oreg., 1982-84; asst. prof. sci. edn. Tufts U., Medford, Mass., 1984-90; assoc. prof. sci. edn. U. Lowell (Mass.), 1990-91, Ohio State U., Columbus, 1991—, dir.Eric Clearinghouse for Sci., Math. and Environ. Edn., 1991—. Cons. in field; dir. Sci. Edn. Programs and Leadership, Lowell, 1988-91. Editor Jour. of Sci. Tchr. Edn., 1988-94. Mem. adv. bd. Project Learning Tree, Mass., 1986-91, Tsongas Indsl. History Ctr., Lowell, 1989-91. Sgt. U.S. Army, 1968-72. Mem. Assn. for Edn. Tchrs. of Sci., ASCD, Nat. Assn. Rsch. in Sci. Teaching, Nat. Sci. Assn., Nat. Sci. Tchrs. Assn., Phi Beta Kappa, Phi Delta Kappa. Avocations: photography, nature study, cycling, hiking. Office: Ohio State U 249 Arps Hall 1945 N High St Columbus OH 43210-1120 also: Ohio State U Eric Clearinghouse for Sci 1929 Kenny Rd Columbus OH 43210-1015

HAUSER, ELLOYD, finance company executive; CEO Solutran. Office: Solutran 3600 Holly Ln N Ste 60 Plymouth MN 55447-1286

HAUSER, STEPHEN CRANE, gastroenterologist; b. Oak Park, Ill., Oct. 6, 1951; s. Crane C. and Mary C. Hauser; m. Eleanor C. Blasi; 2 children. BA, Franklin & Marshall Coll., 1973; MD, U. Chgo., 1977. Fellow in gastroenterology Brigham and Women's Hosp., Boston, 1980-83, physician, 1983-98; clin. gastroenterologist and hepatologist Mayo Clinic, Rochester, Minn., 1998—. Mem. Am. Assn. for Study of Liver Disease, Am. Gastroenterol. Assn., Phi Beta Kappa, Alpha Omega Alpha. Office: Mayo Clinic Dept Gastroenterology and Hepatology 200 1st St SW Rochester MN 55905-0002

HAUSERMAN, JACQUITA KNIGHT, management consultant; b. Donalsonville, Ga., Apr. 23, 1942; d. Lendon Bernard and Ressie Mae (Robinson) Knight; m. Mark Kenny Hauserman, July 8, 1978 (div. Mar. 1998). BS in Math., U. Montevallo, Ala., 1964; MA in Tchg. Math., Emory U., 1973; MBA in Fin., Ga. State U., 1978. Fin. analyst Cleve. Electric Illuminating Co., 1982-83, gen. supr. employment svc., 1983-85, sr. corp. planning advisor, 1985-86, dir. customer svc., 1986-88, v.p. adminstrn., 1988-90; v.p. customer svc. & cmty. affairs Centerior Energy Corp., Independence, Ohio, 1990-93, v.p. customer support, 1993-95, v.p. bus. svcs., 1995-97; v.p., chief devel. officer Summa Health Sys., Akron, 1999-2000; prin. Arcadia Consulting, Pepper Pike, 2000—. Bd. dirs. Cascade Devel. Corp., Am. Stone Industries; ind. cons. Trustee John Carroll U., U. Heights, Ohio. Home and Office: 8440 Danbury Blvd #204 Naples FL 34120 E-mail: jkh2clev@aol.com.

HAUSLER, WILLIAM JOHN, JR. microbiologist, educator, public health laboratory administrator; b. Kansas City, Kans., Aug. 31, 1926; s. William John and Clifton (McCambridge) H.; m. Mary Lois Rice, Apr. 19, 1949 (dec. 1999); children: Cheryl Kaye Johnson, Kenneth Randall, Eric Rice, Mark Clifton; m. Jeanne Seeberger, May 26, 2001. AB in Microbiology, U. Kans., 1951, MA in Microbiology, 1953, PhD in Microbiology, Math., 1958. Diplomate Am. Bd. Med. Microbiology (chmn. 1979-82, Profl. Recognition award 1995). Asst. instr. U. Kans., Lawrence, 1951-56, rsch. asst., 1956-58; assoc. bacteriologist Iowa State Hygienic Lab., Iowa City, 1958-59, asst. dir., prin. bacteriologist, 1959-65, dir., 1965-95; dir. emeritus, 1995—; asst. prof. U. Iowa Coll. Medicine, Iowa City, 1959-66, assoc. prof., 1966-90, prof., 1990—; assoc. prof. U. Iowa Coll. Dentistry, 1966-90, prof., 1990—. Cons. to Iran WHO, 1969, U.S. EPA, 1970-72, CDC, 1965—, People's Republic China WHO, 1990, WHO Western Pacific Region, 1991, UNDP India, 1992; cons. to industry. Editor: Standard Methods for the Examination of Dairy Products, 1972, Manual Clinical Microbiology, 3d edit., 1980, 4th edit., 1985, 5th edit., 1991, Compendium of Methods for the Microbiological Examination of Foods, 1980, 2d edit., 1984, Diagnostic Procedures for Bacterial Mycotic and Parasitic Infections, 1981, Laboratory Diagnosis of Infections Diseases: Principles and Practice, 1988; co-editor: Topley & Wilson's Microbiology and Microbial Infections, 9th edit., 1997; mem. editl. bd. various profl. jours.; contbr. articles to profl. jours. Councilman City Govt., University Heights, Iowa, 1966-69; commr. Iowa Air Pollution Control Commn., 1967-74; mem. exec. com. Iowa Dept. Environ. Quality, 1974-80, Nat. Com. for Clin. Lab. Standards, bd. dirs., 1987-93. Lt. comdr. USNR, 1944-67. Recipient Henry Albert Meml. award Iowa Pub. Health Assn., 1974. Fellow APHA, Am. Acad. Microbiology (chmn. 1983-89, Profl. Recognition award 1995); mem. Am. Soc. Microbiology, Assn. State and Territorial Pub. Health Lab. Dirs. (pres. 1984-85, Lifetime Achievement award 1998), Sigma Phi Epsilon, Rotary (Paul Harris fellow). Avocations: photography; woodworking; wilderness backpacking. Home: 11 The Woods NE Iowa City IA 52240-7986 Office: U Iowa Hygienic Lab Oakdale Hall Iowa City IA 52242 E-mail: iahausler@yahoo.com.

HAUSMAN, ALICE, state legislator; b. July 31, 1942; M. Robert Hausman; 2 children. BS in Edn., Concordia Coll., 1963, MA in Edn., 1965. State rep. Dist. 66B Minn. Ho. of Reps., Minn., 1989—. Mem. econ. devel. com., transportation fin. com., transportation policy com., vice chmn. environ. & natural resources com., edn. fin. divsn. & regulated indsl. & energy coms., Minn. Ho. of Reps. Home: 1447 Chelmsford St Saint Paul MN 55108-1404 Office: 245 State Office Bldg Saint Paul MN 55155 E-mail: rep.Alice.Hausman@house.leg.state.mn.us.

HAVERKAMP, JUDSON, editor; AB in History, Earlham Coll., 1967; MEd, U. Mass., 1976, postgrad. With U.S. Peace Corps/Ministry of Pub. Helath, Bangkok, Thailand, 1967-70; asst. fgn. student advisor U. Mass., Amherst, 1971-75, publs. coord. Ctr. for Internat. Edn., 1975-79; dir. residence, acad. advisor Bradford (Mass.) Coll., 1979-81; freelance writer and editor Mpls., 1981-84; assoc. editor Minn. State Bar Assn., 1984-85, dir. publs., editor, 1985—. Office: Minn State Bar Assn 600 Nicollet Ave Ste 380 Minneapolis MN 55402-1641

HAW, BILL, association executive; Pres. Nat. Farms Inc., Kansas City, Mo. Office: National Farms Inc 1600 Genessee St Ste 846 Kansas City MO 64102-1079

HAWKINS, BRETT WILLIAM, political science educator; b. Buffalo, Sept. 15, 1937; s. Ralph C. and Irma A. (Rowley) H.; m. Linda L. Knuth, Oct. 31, 1974; 1 child, Brett William. A.B., U. Rochester, 1959; M.A., Vanderbilt U., 1962, Ph.D., 1964. Instr. polit. sci. Vanderbilt U., 1963; instr. in polit. sci. Washington and Lee U., 1963-64, asst. prof., 1964-65, U. Ga., Athens, 1965-68, assoc. prof., 1968-70, U. Wis., Milw., 1970-71, prof., 1971-99, ret, 2000. Author: Nashville Metro, 1964, The Ethnic Factor in American Politics, 1970, Politics in the Metropolis, 2d edit, 1971, Politics and Urban Policies, 1971, The Politics of Raising State and Local Revenue, 1978, Professional Associations and Municipal Innovation, 1981; contbr. articles to profl. jours., chpts. in edited vols. Mem. Phi Beta Kappa, Iota of N.Y. Home: 5318 N Kent Ave Whitefish Bay WI 53217-5109 E-mail: bretthwk@yahoo.com.

HAWKINS, JOSEPH ELMER, JR. retired acoustic physiologist, educator; b. Waco, Tex., Mar. 4, 1914; s. Joseph Elmer and Maude Burke (Schlenker) H.; m. Jane Elizabeth Daddow, Aug. 24, 1939; children: Richard Spencer Daddow, Peter Douglas Huntington, James Marion Davis, William Alexander Parmley, Priscilla Ann (Mrs. Philip A. Leach). Student, Altes Realgymnasium, Munich, 1929-30; AB, Baylor U., 1933; postgrad., Brown U., 1933-34; BA in Physiology, U. Oxford, 1937, MA, 1966, DSc in Clin. Medicine, 1979; PhD in Med. Sci., Harvard U., 1941. Tchg. fellow in physiology Harvard Med. Sch., 1937-41, instr., 1941-45; asst. investigator Nat. Def. Rsch. Com.-Office Sci. Rsch. & Devel., Harvard U., 1941-43; spl. rsch. assoc. Harvard Psycho-Acoustic Lab., Cambridge, Mass., 1943-45; asst. prof. physiology Bowman Gray Sch. Medicine, Wake Forest Coll., Winston-Salem, N.C., 1945-46; rsch. assoc. neurophysiology Merck Inst. for Therapeutic Rsch., Rahway, N.J., 1946-56; assoc. prof. otolaryngology NYU Sch. Medicine, 1956-63; prof. physiol. acoustics U. Mich., Ann Arbor, 1963-84, prof. otolaryngology emeritus, 1984—, chmn. grad. program in physiol. acoustics, 1969-81. Assoc. dir. Kresge Hearing Rsch. Inst., 1979-82; disting. vis. prof. biology Baylor U., Waco, Tex., 1985-93; mem. NIH sensory diseases study sect., 1958-61, communicative disorders rsch. tng. com., 1965-69, communicative scis. study sect., 1975-79; mem. Nat. Libr. Medicine Communicative Disorders Task Force, 1977-79; lectr. Armed Forces Inst. Pathology, 1969-74; cons. various pharm. cos. Contbr. to: Ency. Brit., 1974, 86, 99; editor: (with M. Lawrence and W.P. Work) Otophysiology, 1973, (with S.A. Lerner and G.T. Matz) Aminoglycoside Ototoxicity, 1981; contbr. sci. articles to profl. jours. Pres. Fleming Creek Neighborhood Assn., Washtenaw County, Mich., 1973-74; mem. Bd. Edn., Cranford, N.J., 1958-61. Rhodes scholar Tex. and Worcester Coll., U. Oxford, 1934-37; USPHS spl. fellow Öronkliniken, Sahlgrenska Sjukhuset U. Göteborg, Sweden, 1961-63; NAS exch. lectr. to Yugoslavia and Bulgaria, 1977; Chercheur étranger de l'INSERM, Lab. d'Audiologie Expérimentale, U. Bordeaux II, 1978; recipient Disting. Achievement award Baylor U., 1982, City of Pleven, Bulgaria medal, 1982, U. Bordeaux medal, 1983, Humboldt Rsch. award for sr. U.S. scientists U. Würzburg, 1991, Hon. Citizen award, Bordeaux, 1991, Disting. Alumnus award Baylor U., 1996. Fellow AAAS, Acoustical Soc. Am.; mem. Am. Physiol. Soc., Assn. for Rsch. in Otolaryngology (award of merit 1985), Collegium Oto-rhino-laryngologicum Amicitiae Sacrum, Bárány Soc., European Workshop for Inner Ear Biology, Am. Assn. for History of Medicine, Am. Otol. Soc. (assoc.), Prosper Menière Soc. (hon., Gold medal for basic sci. 1998), Pacific Coast Oto-ophthalmol. Soc. (hon.), Connétablie de Guyenne (Bordeaux, assoc.), Phi Beta Kappa, Sigma Xi. Anglican. Democrat. Avocations: Germanic and Romance languages and literature, gardening. Home: Glacier Hills Apt 258 1200 Earhart Rd Ann Arbor MI 48105 Office: U Mich Med Sch Kresge Hearing Rsch Inst Ann Arbor MI 48109-0506 E-mail: josehawk@umich.edu.

HAWKINS, LORETTA ANN, secondary school educator, playwright; b. Winston-Salem, N.C., Jan. 1, 1942; d. John Henry and Laurine (Hines) Sanders; m. Joseph Hawkins, Dec. 10, 1962; children: Robin, Dionne, Sherri. BS in Edn., Chgo. State U., 1965; MA in Lit., Governor's State U., 1977, MA in African Cultures, 1978; MLA in Humanities, U. Chgo., 1998. Cert. tchr., Ill. Tchr. Chgo. Bd. Edn., 1968—; lectr. Chgo. City Colls., 1987-89; tchr. English, Gage Park H.S., Chgo., 1988—. Mem. steering com. Mellon Seminar U. Chgo., 1990; tchr. adv. com. Goodman Theatre, Chgo., 1992, mem. cmty. adv. coun., 1996—; spkr. in field. Author: (reading workbook) Contemporary Black Heroes, 1992, (plays) Of Quiet Birds, 1993 (James H. Wilson award 1993), Above the Line, 1994, Good Morning, Miss Alex; contbr. poetry, articles to profl. publs.; featured WTTW-Educate, 1996. Mem. Chgo. Tchg. Connections Network, DePaul U. Ctr. Urban Edn., 2001, CPS Mentoring and Induction of New Tchrs. Program. Santa Fe Pacific Found. fellow, 1988, Lloyd Fry Found. fellow, 1989, Andrew W. Mellon Found. fellow, 1991, Ill. Arts Coun. fellow, 1993; Cmty. Arts Assistance Program Award grantee Chgo. Dept. Cultural Affairs; recipient Feminist Writers 3d pl. award NOW, 1993, Zora Neale Hurston-Bessie Head Fiction award Black Writer's Conf., 1993, numerous others; featured on WTTW-TV Educate, 1996. Mem. AAUW, Nat. Coun.

Tchrs. English (spkr. conv.), Am. Fedn. Tchrs., Women's Theatre Alliance, Dramatists Guild of Am., Internat. Women's Writing Guild. Avocations: films, coins, reading, walking. Home: 8928 S Oglesby Ave Chicago IL 60617-3047 Office: Gage Park HS 5630 S RockwellAve Chicago IL 60629

HAWKINS, RICHARD ALBERT, medical educator, administrator; b. Greenwich, Conn., Mar. 27, 1940; s. Albert Rice and Florence Marie Elizabeth (Hansen) H.; m. Enriqueta Elias, May 9, 1964; children: Richard Alfred, Paul Andrés. BSc magna cum laude, San Diego State U., 1963; PhD, Harvard U., 1969; LHD (hon.), U. Phoenix, 1994. Rsch. fellow Metabolic Rsch. Lab. Radcliffe Infirmary, Oxford (Eng.) U., 1969-71; staff fellow in neurochemistry St. Elizabeth Hosp., Washington, 1971-72, NIMH/NIAAA sr. staff fellow in neurochemistry, 1972-74; chief phys. sci. br. FDA, Rockville, Md., 1974-76; assoc. prof. neurosurgery and physiology NYU Med. Ctr., N.Y.C., 1976-77; prof. anesthesia and physiology Pa. State U., Hershey (Pa.) Med. Ctr., 1977-88; prof., chmn. physiology and biophysics Herman M. Finch U. Health Scis./Chgo. Med. Sch., North Chicago, Ill., 1988-93, exec. v.p. acad. affairs, chief academic officer, 1993-98, provost, 1998, pres., CEO, 1999—, Scholl Coll. Podiatric Medicine, 2001—. Hon. prof. U. Valencia, Spain, 1989—. Mem. editorial bd. Am. Jour. Physiology, Endocrinology and Metabolism; contbr. numerous articles to profl. jours. Recipient Meritorious Rsch. award Morris Parker Found., 1992. Fellow Am. Heart Assn.; mem. Am. Physiol. Soc., Am. Soc. Neurochemistry, Biochem. Soc., Soc. for Neurosci., Alpha Omega Alpha. Home: 150 Brierfield Ct Lake Bluff IL 60044-1917 Office: Finch U Health Scis Chgo Med Sch 3333 Green Bay Rd North Chicago IL 60064-3037 Fax: 847-578-3404.

HAWKINSON, CARL E. state legislator; b. Galesburg, Ill., Oct. 7, 1947; m. Karen Zeches; 3 chilren. BA, Park Coll.; JD, Harvard U. Law practice; mem. from 94th dist. Ill. Ho. of Reps., 1983-86; now mem. Ill. State Senate. Office: 4 Weinberg Arcade Galesburg IL 61401-4603 also: 1577 N Prairie St Galesburg IL 61401-1857

HAWKINSON, GARY MICHAEL, financial services company executive; b. Chgo., Oct. 30, 1948; s. Roy G. and June M. (Miller) H.; m. Patricia Kaye Schlievert, Jan. 9, 1971; children: Kenneth, Christopher. BBA in Fin., U. Toledo, 1971; postgrad., U. Harvard, 1989. Various mgmt. and analytical positions Toledo Edison Co., 1972-79, asst. treas., asst. sec., 1979-86; treas. Centerior Energy Corp., Independence, Ohio, 1986-96, dir. govtl. affairs, 1996-98; dir. fin. and adminstrn. Parkwood Corp., Cleve., 1998-99; dir. treasury Univ. Hosps. Health Sys., 1999—. Trustee Luth. Med. Ctr. Found. Served to 2d lt. U.S. Army, 1971-72. Mem. Cleve. Treas.'s Club (v.p. 1988-89, pres. 1989-90), Rotary. Avocations: skiing, sailing. Home: 26875 Kenley Ct Westlake OH 44145-1456 Office: Univ Hosps Health Sys 11100 Euclid Ave Cleveland OH 44106-1736

HAWLEY, ELLIS WAYNE, historian, educator; b. Cambridge, Kans., June 2, 1929; s. Pearl Washington and Gladys Laura (Logsdon) H.; m. Sofia Koltun, Sept. 2, 1953; children— Arnold Jay, Agnes Fay. B.A., U. Wichita, 1950; M.A., U. Kans., 1951; Ph.D. (research fellow), U. Wis., 1959. Instr. to prof. history North Tex. State U., 1957-68; prof. history Ohio State U., 1968-69, U. Iowa, 1969-94, prof. emeritus, 1994—, chmn. dept. history, 1986-89. Hist. cons. Pub. Papers of the Presidents: Hoover, 1974-78. Author: The New Deal and the Problem of Monopoly, 1966, The Great War and the Search for a Modern Order, 1979, (with others) Herbert Hoover and the Crisis of American Capitalism, 1973, Herbert Hoover as Secretary of Commerce, 1981, Federal Social Policy, 1988, Herbert Hoover and the Historians, 1989; contbr. articles to profl. jours., essays to books Investigator Project to Study Hist. in Iowa Pub. Schs., Iowa City, 1978-79; cons. Quad Cities hist. project Putnam Mus., Davenport, 1978-79. Served to 1st lt. inf. AUS, 1951-53 North Tex. State U. Faculty Devel. grantee, 1967-68, U. Iowa, 1975-76. Mem. Am. Hist. Assn., Orgn. Am. Historians, So. Hist. Assn., AAUP (mem. exec. coun. Iowa chapt. 1982-84), Iowa Hist. Soc. Democrat. Home: 2524 E Washington St Iowa City IA 52245-3724 E-mail: e-hawley@worldnet.att.net.

HAWLEY, RAYMOND GLEN, pathologist; b. Cambridge, Kans., Jan. 13, 1939; s. Pearl Washington and Gladys Laura (Logsdon) H.; m. Phyllis Ann Williams, Aug. 25, 1963; children: Bradford, Anthony, Douglas. BS, Kans. State U., 1961; MD, U. Kans., 1965. Intern Wesley Med. Ctr., Wichita, 1965-66; pathology resident Riverside Meth. Hosp., Columbus, Ohio, 1966-70; pathologist St. Joseph Hosp., Concordia, Kans., 1973-75, St. Joseph Med. Ctr., Wichita, 1975-82, Via Christi Regional Med. Ctr., Wichita, 1983-2000; Coffeyville (Kans.) Regional Med. Ctr., 2000—. Maj. U.S. Army, 1970-73. Fellow Am. Coll. Pathologists; mem. AMA, Am. Soc. Clin. Pathologists, Kans. Soc. Pathology (sec.-treas. 1989-99). Home: 512 Spruce St Coffeyville KS 67337-4834 E-mail: rhawley@KScable.com.

HAWORTH, DANIEL THOMAS, chemistry educator; b. Fond du Lac, Wis., June 27, 1928; s. Arthur Valentine and Mary Lena (Wattawa) H.; m. Mary Hormuth, Dec. 27, 1952; children: Daniel G., M. Judith, Steven T. BS, U. Wis., Oshkosh, 1950; MS, Marquette U., 1952; PhD, St. Louis U., 1959. Nuclear chemist Bur. of Ships, Washington, 1952-53; rsch. chemist All-Chalmer Mfg. Co., Milw., 1958-60; instr. chemistry Marquette U., 1955, from asst. prof. to assoc. prof., 1960-68, prof., 1968—. Contbr. numerous articles to profl. jours.; patentee in field. Served as cpl. U.S. Army, 1953-55. Recipient Pere Marquette award for tchg. excellence Marquette U., 1971, Nicolos Salgo Outstanding Tchr. award, 1971. Mem. Am. Chem. Soc. (emeritus), N.Y. Acad. Scis., Wis. Acad. Arts/Scis./Letters, Sigma Xi (emeritus). Roman Catholic. Avocation: philately. Home: 3483 N Frederick Ave Milwaukee WI 53211-2902 Office: Marquette Univ Dept Chemistry PO Box 1881 Milwaukee WI 53201-1881 E-mail: daniel.haworth@marquette.edu.

HAWORTH, GERRARD WENDELL, office systems manufacturing company executive; b. Alliance, Nebr., Oct. 9, 1911; s. Elmer R. and Lulu (Jones) H.; m. Dorcas A. Snyder, June 22, 1938 (dec.); children: Lois, Richard, Joan, Mary, Julie; m. 2d Edna Mae Van Tatenhove, Feb. 5, 1979. A.B., Western Mich. U., 1937; M.A., U. Mich., 1940. Tchr. Holland High Sch., Mich., 1937-48; founding chmn. Haworth Inc., Holland, 1948—. Office: Haworth Inc 1 Haworth Ctr Holland MI 49423-8820

HAWORTH, JAMES CHILTON, pediatrics educator; b. Gosforth, Eng., May 29, 1923; emigrated to Can., 1957, naturalized, 1972; s. Walter Norman and Violet Chilton (Dobbie) H.; m. Eleanor Marian Bowser, Oct. 18, 1951; children— Elizabeth Marian, Peter Norman James, Margaret Jean, Anne Ruth. M.B., Ch.B, U. Birmingham, Eng., 1945, M.D., 1960. House physician Birmingham Gen. and Children's Hosps., 1946-47; fellow Cin. Children's Hosp., 1949-50; house physician Hosp. for Sick Children, London, 1951; pediatric registrar Alder Hey Children's Hosp., Liverpool, Eng., 1951-52; sr. registrar Sheffield Children's Hosp., 1953-57; pediatrician Winnipeg (Man., Can.) Clinic, 1957-65; asst. prof. dept. pediatrics U. Man., Winnipeg, 1965-67, assoc. prof., 1967-70, prof., 1970-94, head dept. pediatrics, 1979-85, senate mem., 1985-90, prof. human genetics, 1987-94, prof. emeritus, 1994—, sr. scholar dept. biochemistry and med. genetics, 1999—. Mem. active staff Health Scis. Centre-Children's, 1957-93; cons. staff St. Boniface Hosp., 1974-93; hon. staff Health Sci. Ctr., 1993—. Contbr. numerous articles to profl. jours. Bd. dirs. Man. Med. Svc. found., 1988—, exec. dir., 1995—. Served with Royal Naval Vol. Res., 1947-49. Fellow Royal Coll. Physicians (Can., London), Can. Coll. Medical Geneticists (hon.); mem. Canadian Soc. Clin. Investigation, Am. Acad. Pediatrics, Am. Pediatric Soc., Soc. Pediatric Research, Canadian Pediatric Soc., Midwest Soc. Pediatric Research. Home: 301 Victoria Crescent Winnipeg MB Canada R2M 1X8 Office: Childrens Hosp Dept Pediatrics 678 William Ave Winnipeg MB Canada R3E 0W1

HAWORTH, RICHARD G. office furniture manufacturer; b. 1942; With Haworth Inc., Holland, Mich., chm. bd., 1975—. Office: Haworth Inc 1 Haworth Ctr Holland MI 49423-8820

HAWTHORNE, FRANK CHRISTOPHER, geologist, educator; b. Bristol, Eng., Jan. 8, 1946; arrived in Can., 1968; s. Frank and Audrey Patricia (Miles) H.; m. Robin Elizabeth Hoult, June 27, 1970 (div.); children: Beverly Ann, Christopher Richard James. BSc hon., U. London, 1968; A.R.S.M., Royal Sch. of Mines, London, 1968; PhD in Geology, McMaster U., Hamilton, Ont., Can., 1973. Post-doctoral fellow U. Man., Winnipeg, Can., 1973-75, rsch. assoc. in geology Can., 1975-80, univ. rsch. fellow Can., 1980-90, assoc. prof. Can., 1984-85, prof. Can., 1985—, disting. prof. Can., 1997—. Editor: Spectroscopy in Mineralogy, 1988; contbr. over 300 articles to profl. jours. Killam fellow, Can. Coun., 1991; Willet G. Miller Medal, 1993, Royal Soc. Can. Fellow Mineral. Soc. Am. (councillor 1988-91), Royal Soc. of Can. (Willet G. Miller medal 1993), Geol. Assn. of Can. (Past Pres. medal 1991, Logan medal 1996); mem. Mineral. Assn. of Can. (pres. 1990—, Hawley medal 1984, 94, 98), Mineral Soc. Great Britain (Schlumberger medal 1995), Sigma Xi (Sr. Rsch. award 1988, Rh Inst. Found. medal 1997). Avocations: poetry, history of science, running, weightlifting, dining. Office: U Man Dept Geological Scis 125 Dysart Rd Winnipeg MB Canada R3T 2N2

HAWTHORNE, TIMOTHY ROBERT, direct response advertising and communications company executive; b. Evanston, Ill., June 29, 1950; s. John and Marjie Phyllis (Horner) H.; 1 child, Jessica Hope. BA cum laude, Harvard U., 1973. Editor, prodr. Sta. WCCO-TV, Mpls., 1973-78; field prodr. Sta. KYW-TV, Phila., 1978-80; pres., founder Producer/Writer Network, Newtown, Pa., 1980-82; v.p. prodn. Teleimage, Inc., Phila., 1982-83; pres. Hawthorne Prodns., Phila., Los Angeles and Fairfield, Iowa, 1983—; co-founder, pres. Fairfield TV, 1984-86; pres. Hawthorne Comm., Inc., Fairfield, 1986—. Prodr., writer, dir.: (TV series) Real People, That's Incredible, Ripley's Believe It Or Not, Entertainment Tonight, 1979-85. Dir. Fairfield Cultural Soc., 1985-87; mem. Pres. Soc. Maharishi Internat. U., Fairfield, 1984—. Named Iowa/Nebr. Entrepreneur of Yr., 1996. Mem. Dirs. Guild Am., Nat. Info. Mktg. Assn. (founding mem., bd. dirs.), Direct Mktg. Assn., Fairfield C. of C. Avocations: travel, skiing. Home: 1825 Okra Blvd Fairfield IA 52556-8709 Office: Hawthorne Dir Inc 300 N 16th St Fairfield IA 52556-2604

HAWTHORNE, VICTOR MORRISON, epidemiologist, educator; b. Glasgow, Scotland, June 19, 1921; came to U.S., 1978; s. John Morrison and Isabel Stuart (Crowe) H.; m. Jean Christie Mackenzie, Aug. 19, 1948; children: Hilary June, Wendy Victoria, Joan Rosalind. MB ChB, U. Glasgow, 1951, MD, 1962, DSc (hon.), 1996; diploma, Scottish Coun. for Health Edn., 1976. Sr. lectr. dept. epidemiology U. Glasgow, 1967-78, sr. research fellow dept. community medicine, 1978-91; cons. physician Nat. Health Service, Glasgow Health Bd., 1966-78; coordinator Scottish MMR services Nat. Health Service Scotland, 1970-78; prof. epidemiology U. Mich., Ann Arbor, 1978-91, chmn. dept., 1978-86, prof. dept. family practice, 1982-91, prof. epidemiology emeritus, 1991—95. Chmn. epidemiology study sect. NIH, Bethesda, Md., 1979-83, active, 1979-93; chmn. kidney disease adv. com. Mich. Dept. Pub. Health, Lansing, 1979-95, mem. chronic disease adv. com., 1979; chmn. Continuing Med. Edn./Pub. Health Consortium Mich., 1987—2002; hon. dir. Bayer Rsch. unit Royal Coll. Physicians of Edinburgh, 1987-93, hon. cons. Royal Coll. Physicians of Edinburgh Diabetes Register, 1989-01, U. Mich. Complementary & Cardiovascular Rsch. Ctr., 1999-. Author: First Aid For Medical Students, 1978, Tuberculosis, Respiratory and Cardiovascular Risks of Dying in the West of Scotland, 1985; contbr. articles to profl. jours. Recipient Bronze medal U. Helsinki, 1985; Victor Hawthorne: Young Investigator Rsch. Award Program established in his honor Mich. Dept. Pub. Health, 1986. Fellow Royal Coll. Physicians and Surgeons of Glasgow, Royal Coll. Physicians of Edinburgh, Faculty of Pub. Health Medicine, Soc. Antiquaries of Scotland, Am. Coll. Epidemiology. Mem. Ch. of Scotland Avocations: sketching; gardening. Office: Univ Mich Sch Pub Health Dept Epidemiology 109 Observatory St Ann Arbor MI 48109-2029 E-mail: vmhaw@umich.edu.

HAYDEN, JOHN, radio director; b. Kansas City, Mo., May 1, 1962; m. Donna Hayden; children: Lindsey, Jeff, Tanner. Program dir. Sta. WMBI Radio, Chgo. Office: WMBI 820 N LaSalle Blvd Chicago IL 60610*

HAYDEN, JOHN W. real estate company executive; BA, Northwe. U.; MBA, Miami U. With Midland Co., 1981, v.p., 1987-96, sr. exec. v.p. Am. Home Groups, 1987=96, pres. Am. Modern Ins. Group, 1994-98, sr. exec. v.p., 1996-98, pres., CEO, 1998—, also bd. dirs. Office: Midland Co 7000 Midland Blvd Amelia OH 45102-2608

HAYDEN, JOSEPH PAGE, JR. company executive; b. Cin., Oct. 8, 1929; s. Joseph Page and Amy Dorothy (Weber) H.; m. Lois Taylor, Dec. 29, 1951; children: Joseph Page III, William Taylor, John Weber, Thomas Richard. B.S. in Bus, Miami U., Oxford, Ohio, 1951; student, U. Cin. Law Sch., 1952; DL (hon.), Miami U., 1986. With mobile home div. Midland-Guardian Co., Cin., 1952-61, v.p., 1954-60; pres., chief exec. officer, dir. Midland Co., Cin., 1961-80, chmn. bd., CEO, dir., 1980-98, chmn. exec. com., bd. dirs., 1998—. Bd. dirs. Firstar Corp., Cin. Mem. bus. adv. com. Miami U., Oxford, Ohio; mem. pres.'s council Xavier U., Cin.; bd. trustees Miami U. Found. Mem. Bankers Club, Met. Club (Cin., Ohio), Comml. Club (Ohio), Boca Bay Pass Club (Fla.), Lemon Bay Golf (Fla.), Useppa Island Club (Fla.), Sigma Chi. Clubs: Queen City, Hyde Park Golf and Country, University (Cin.); Boca Grande (Fla.). Office: 7000 Midland Blvd Amelia OH 45102-2608

HAYDEN, ROBERT W. business executive; V.p. Midland Co., Amelia, Ohio, 1988—. Office: Midland Co 7000 Midland Blvd Amelia OH 45102-2608

HAYDOCK, WALTER JAMES, banker; b. Chgo., Dec. 14, 1947; s. Joseph Albert and Lillian V. (Adeszko) H.; m. Bonnie Jean Thompson, Aug. 22, 1970; children: Nicole Lynn, Matthew Michael. Student, Harvard Bus. Coll., 1969-71, Daily Coll., 1971-73; BS in Acctg., DePaul U., 1976. Computer operator, jr. programmer Pepper Constrn. Co., Chgo., 1972-73; input analyst Continental Bank, 1973-76, data control supr., 1976-79, corp. fixed asset adminstr., 1979-83, properties sys. analyst, 1983-87, props. sr. sys. supr., 1987-91; unit chief conversions Fed. Deposit Ins. Corp., 1992-93, info. security specialist, 1993-96; info. security officer U. Ill., 1996—2001, info. sys. admin., 2001—. Pres. Wal-Bon., Inc.; distbr. Lic. Disney Character Mdse. Mem. Southwest Suburban Bd. Realtors. Home: 13525 Marissa Ct Lockport IL 60441 Office: 914 S Wood St M/C 807 Chicago IL 60612-7338

HAYES, BRENDA SUE NELSON, artist; b. Rockford, Ill., May 26, 1941; d. Reuben Hartvick and Mary Jane (Pinkston) Nelson; m. John Michael Hayes, Jan. 26, 1964; 1 child, Amy Anne. BFA in Graphic Design, U. Ill., 1964. Exec. officer JMH Corp., Indpls., 1971—. Exhibited at Art Source, Bethesda, Md., The Corp. Collection, Kansas City, Mo., The Hang Up Gallery, Sarasota, Fla., Art By Design, Inc., Indpls., Swan Coach House Gallery, Atlanta, Arnot Art Mus., Elmira, N.Y., Indpls. Mus. Art, Pindar Gallery, Soho, N.Y.; represented in permanent collections at Holy Family Hosp., Des Plaines, Ill., Lilly Endowment, Dow Venture Ctr. Internat. Hdqs., Wishard Hosp., Indpls., Deloitte Touche, Inc., USA Group, Indpls., Indpls. Art Ctr., IBM, AT&T, U.S. Sprint, NWS Corp., Chgo., Meth. Hosp., Indpls., Eli Lilly Corp., Indpls. and Chgo., Hewlett-Packard, Trammell Crow, Dow Consumer Products, Melvin Simon & Assocs., Dow Elanco Corp. Hdqs., Ikon Inc., Support Net, Bank One, NBDB Bank Processing Ctr. Lobby, Indpls., Mckinney Processing Bank Ctr., Indpls., Cellular One Regional Offices, Nat. City Plaza, 250 pvt. collections. Bd. dirs. Contemporary Art Soc. for Indpls. Mus. Art, 1993—, sec., 1992-94; charter mem. Nat. Mus. Women in Arts, Habitat for Humanity. Lydia Bates scholar U. Ill., 1961-63, Ill. Found. of Study scholar, 1963-64, resident schoar, 1960-64; recipient Panhellenic award for Study U. Ill., 1963-64, Gallery Exhbn. awards. Mem. Nat. Mus. Women in the Arts (charter), Gamma Alpha Chi (Outstanding Woman in Journalism 1964). Home: 157 E 71st St Indianapolis IN 46220-1011 Studio: 921 E 66th St Indianapolis IN 46220-1137

HAYES, CHARLES DEWAYNE, professional baseball player; b. Hattiesburg, Miss., May 29, 1965; Grad. high sch., Miss. With San Francisco Giants, 1988-89, 98-99; 3d baseman Phila. Phillies, 1989-91, 95; with N.Y. Yankees, 1992, 96-97, Colo. Rockies, 1993-94, Pitts. Pirates, 1996, Milwaukee Brewers, 2000—. Office: Milwaukee Brewers County Stadium PO Box 3099 Milwaukee WI 53201-3099

HAYES, DAVID JOHN ARTHUR, JR. legal association executive; b. Chgo., July 30, 1929; s. David J.A. and Lucille (Johnson) H.; m. Anne Huston, Feb. 20, 1963; children— David J.A. III, Cary AB, Harvard U., 1952, JD, 1961. Bar: Ill. Trust officer, asst. sec. First Nat. Bank of Evanston, Ill., 1961-63; gen. counsel Ill. State Bar Assn., Chgo., 1963-66; asst. dir. ABA, 1966-68, div. dir., 1968-69, asst. exec. dir., 1969-87, v.p., 1987-88, assoc. exec. v.p., 1989-90, sr. assoc. exec. v.p., 1990, exec. dir., 1990-94, exec. dir. emeritus, 1994—; exec. dir. Naval Res. Lawyers Assn., 1971-75; asst. sec. gen. Internat. Bar Assn., 1978-80, 90—, Inter-ABA, 1984—. Contbr. articles to profl. jours. Capt. JAGC, USNR Fellow Am. Bar Found. (life); mem. Ill. State Bar Assn. (ho. of dels. 1972-76), Nat. Orgn. Bar Counsel (pres. 1967), Chgo. Bar Assn., Michigan Shores Club. Home: 908 Pontiac Rd Wilmette IL 60091-1349 Office: ABA 750 N Lake Shore Dr Chicago IL 60611-4403 E-mail: djahayes@aol.com.

HAYES, JOHN FRANCIS, lawyer; b. Salina, Kans., Dec. 11, 1919; s. John Francis and Helen (Dye) H.; m. Elizabeth Ann Ireton, Aug. 10, 1950; children: Carl Ireton, Ann Chandler. A.B., Washburn Coll., 1941; LL.B., 1946. Bar: Kans. 1946, Mo. 1987. Pvt. practice, Hutchinson, Kans., 1946—; dir. Gilliland & Hayes, P.A. (and predecessors), 1946—. Mem. Commn. Uniform State Laws, 1975—; bd. dirs. Cen. Bank and Trust Co., Hutchinson, Cen. Fin. Corp., Waddell & Reed Funds. Mem. Kans. Ho. of Reps., 1953-55, 67-79, majority leader, 1975-77. Served as capt. AUS, 1942-46. Fellow Am. Bar Found., Am. Coll. Trial Lawyers; mem. Hutchinson C. of C. (pres. 1961), Kans. Assn. Def. Counsel (pres. 1972-73), Internat. Assn. Def. Counsel. Republican. Home: 31 Pawnee Dr Hutchinson KS 67502-2981 Office: 20 W 2nd Ave Fl 2 Hutchinson KS 67501-5246 also: 1211 Penntower Bldg 3100 Broadway St Kansas City MO 64111-2406 also: PO Box 49406 200 N Broadway St Ste 300 Wichita KS 67202-2324

HAYES, JOHN PATRICK, electrical engineering and computer science educator, consultant; b. Newbridge, Ireland, Mar. 3, 1944; s. Patrick Joseph and Christine (Duggan) H.; m. Joan Benson, June 7, 1969; children: Thomas, Michael. BE in Elec. Engring., Nat. U. Ireland, Dublin, 1965; MS in Elec. Engring., U. Ill., 1967, PhD in Elec. Engring., 1970. Systems engr. Royal Dutch Shell Co., The Hague, The Netherlands, 1970-72; asst. prof. elec. engring. and computer sci. U. So. Calif., L.A., 1972-77, assoc. prof., 1977-82; prof. U. Mich., Ann Arbor, 1982—. Cons. to various orgns., 1972— . Author: Computer Architecture and Organization, 1978, 3d edit., 1998, Digital System Design and Microprocessors, 1984, Hierarchical Modeling for VLSI Circuit Testing, 1990, Layout Minimization for CMOS Cells, 1992, Introduction to Digital Logic Design, 1993; contbr. articles to profl. jours. Fellow: IEEE (assoc. editor jour. 1989—94); mem.: Assn. Computing Machinery 1978—81, Sigma Xi. Office: U Mich Dept Elec Engring & Computer Sci Ann Arbor MI 48109 E-mail: jhayes@eecs.umich.edu.

HAYES, ROBERT E. former state legislator; b. Battle Creek, Mich., Oct. 18, 1933; m. to Marilyn Hayes; children: Eric, Jennifer. BS, N.E. Mo. U.; JD, Ind. U. Pvt. practice law; state rep. Dist. 59 Ind. Ho. of Reps., 1974-80, 82-97, asst. majority floor leader, mem. human affairs and edn. com., mem. judiciary com., cts. and criminal code com., mem. rules and legis. procedures com. Mem. Am. Legion, Kiwanis, Eagles, Phi Delta Phi. Home: 3221 Sherwood Pl Columbus IN 47203-2612

HAYES, SCOTT BIRCHARD, raw materials company executive; b. Washington, Apr. 2, 1926; s. Webb C. II Hayes and Martha Baker; m. Dorothy Walter, Oct. 27, 1951; children: Scott B. Jr., James W., Timothy W., Michael S. BS, Yale U., 1950. Sr. v.p. Pickands Mather & Co., Cleve., 1953-87, ret., 1987. Bd. dirs., v.p. Hayes Presdl. Ctr., Fremont, Ohio, 1965, pres., 1987—; trustee Ohio Hist. Soc., 1993-96. With USN, 1944-46. Mem. Kirtland Country Club. Avocations: golf, tennis, squash, fishing. Home: PO Box 1070 Boca Grande FL 33921-1070

HAYES, STEPHEN MATTHEW, librarian; b. Detroit, Sept. 30, 1950; s. Matthew Cleary and Evelyn Mary (Warren) H. BS in Psychology, Mich. State U., 1972; MLS, Western Mich. U., 1974; MS in Adminstrn., U. Notre Dame, 1979. Cons. Western Mich. U., Kalamazoo, 1974; libr. U. Notre Dame, Ind., 1974-76, ref. and pub. documents libr., 1976-94; libr. Bus. Svcs. Libr., 1994—. Author/contbr.: What is Written Remains: Historical Essays on the Libraries of Notre Dame, 1994; editor: Environmental Concerns, 1975; contbr.: Depository Library Use of Technology: A Practitioner's Perspective, 1993. Recipient Rev. Paul J. Foik award, 1998. Mem. AAUP, ALA (govt. documents roundtable 1978—, chair 1987-88, chair pubs. com. 1989-91, coord. com. on access to info. 1989-90, 93-95, exec. bd. dirs. 1988-91, awards com. 1991-93, chair Godort orgn. com. 1991-93, Godort legis. com., 1999-2002, bus. ref. and svc. sect. 1994—, bus. & adult ref. roundtable 1995—, edn. com. 1996-98, resolution com. 1997-99, ad hoc com. on govt. info. 2002-), Assn. Pub. Data Users (census com., steering com. 1987-96), Indigo (fed. rec. commn. chair 1992-93, apptd. depository libr. coun. to pub. printer 1994-97). Roman Catholic. Avocations: birdwatching, bicycling, racquetball, musician. Home: PO Box 6032 South Bend IN 46660-6032 Office: U Notre Dame L012 Mendoza Coll Of Business Notre Dame IN 46556-5646 E-mail: stephen.m.hayes.2@nd.edu.

HAYS, MICHAEL D. research company executive; Pres., CEO, founder Nat. Rsch. Corp., Lincoln, Nebr., 1981—. Office: Nat Rsch Corp 1033 O St Lincoln NE 68508-3636 Fax: 402-475-9061.

HAYS, PATRICK GREGORY, health care executive; b. Kansas City, Kans., Sept. 9, 1942; s. Vance Samuel and Mary Ellen (Crabbe) H.; m. Penelope Ann Hall, July 3, 1976; children: Julia L., Jennifer M., Emily J., Drew D. B.S. in Bus. Adminstrn, U. Tulsa, 1964; M.H.A., U. Minn., 1971; postgrad., U. Mich. Grad. Sch. Bus. Adminstrn., 1977. Mfg. analyst N.Am. Rockwell Corp., Tulsa, 1964-66; asst. adminstr., adminstr. for ops. Henry Ford Hosp., Detroit, 1971-75; exec. v.p. Meth. Med. Ctr. of Ill., Peoria, 1975-77; adminstr. Kaiser Found. Hosp., Los Angeles, 1977-80; pres. Sutter Community Hosps. and Sutter Health, Sacramento, 1980-95; pres., CEO Blue Cross Blue Shield Assn., Chgo., 1995—. Bd. dirs. VHA, Inc.; trustee Cen. Area Teaching Hosps., Inc., L.A., 1977-79; clin. preceptor U.

Minn.; clin. prof. grad. program in health svcs. adminstrn. U. So. Calif.; mem. exec. com. St. Jude Children's Rsch. Hosp. Midwest Affilate, Peoria, 1975-77; past chmn. adv. bd. grad. program in health svcs. adminstrn. U. So. Calif., Sacramento; bd.dirs. Hosp.Coun. No.Calif., 1986, The Healthcare Forum, 1987-89; bd. dirs., exec. com. Found. Health Inc., HMO, 1987-90; chmn. bd. Option Care Inc., 1986-90, Calif. Assn. Hosp. and Health Systems, 1991; regent Am. Coll. Healthcare Execs., 1989-95, founding pres. Sacramento Regional Purchasing Coun.; mem. adv. bd. the Governance Inst.; bd. dir. U.S. Bank of Calif., 1993-95, mem. civil justice reform act com., U.S. Dist. Ct., Ea. Calif. Contbr. articles on health services to publs. Mem. Pvt. Industry Coun., Sacramento Employment and Tng. Agy., 1984-85; bd. dirs. Consumer Credit Counselors Sacramento, 1984-87, Sacramento Area United Way, campaign chair, 1992-93; bd. dirs. Comstock Club, 1986-89; pres. Sacramento Camellia Festival Assn., 1987-88; chmn. Whitney M. Young Jr. Award, 1987; pres. Sacramento Regional Purchasing Coun., 1989-90. With U.S. Army, 1966-69. Decorated Army Commendation medal, cert. of appreciation Dept. Army; recipient Commendation resolution Calif. Senate, 1979, Whitney M. Young award Sacramento Urban League, 1983; named Chief Exec. Officer of Yr., Soc. for Healthcare Planning and Mktg. of Am. Hosp. Assn., 1991; USPHS fellow, 1969-71, Calif. Assn. Hosps. and Health Systems Walker fellow, 1989. Fellow Am. Coll. Healthcare Execs. (Calif. regent); mem. Calif. Assn. Hosps. and Health Systems (chmn. bd. dirs. 1991), Sacramento-Sierra Hosp. Assn. (exec. com., bd. dirs., pres. 1984), Royal Soc. Health (U.K.), Am. Mgmt. Assn. (Pres. Club), Hollywood C. of C. (revitalization com. 1979), Sacramento C. of C. (bd. dirs. 1982-85, 87-88), Vol. Hosps. Pacific (bd. dirs.), Rotary (bd. dirs. Sacramento 1987-89), Kappa Sigma (treas.). Presbyterian. Office: Blue Cross & Blue Shield 225 N Michigan Ave Lowr 9 Chicago IL 60601-7682

HAYS, RUTH, lawyer; b. Fukuoka, Japan, Sept. 20, 1950; d. George Howard and Helen Jincy (Mathis) H. AB, Grinnell Coll., 1972; JD, Washington U., 1978. Bar: Mo. 1978. Law clk. U.S. Ct. Appeals (8th cir.), St. Louis, 1978-80; assoc. Husch & Eppenberger, LLC, 1980-87, ptnr., 1987—. Articles editor Urban Law Annual, 1977-78. Bd. dirs. Childhaven, St. Louis, 1982-93, pres. 1987-88. Olin fellow Monticello Coll. Found., St. Louis, 1975-78; recipient Spl. Svc. award Legal Svs. Ea. Mo., 1993. Mem. ABA, Mo. Bar Assn., Bar Assn. Met. St. Louis, Employee Benefits Assn. (pres. 1995), Order of Coif, Phi Beta Kappa. E-mail:; ruth.hays.husch.com. Office: Husch & Eppenberger 100 N Broadway Ste 1300 Saint Louis MO 63102-2789

HAYS, THOMAS S. medical educator, medical researcher; b. Winter Haven, Fla., Dec. 20, 1954; married. BS in Zoology, U. N.C., 1976, PhD in Cell Biology, 1985. Rsch. asst. dept. zoology U. N.C., Chapel Hill, 1975—76; rsch. asst. dept. biol. scis. Duke U., Durham, NC, 1976—79; asst. instr. quantitative and analytical microscopy Marine Biol. Lab., Woods Hole, Mass., 1981—83; asst. instr. optical microscopy U. Calif., Santa Cruz, 1982; postdoctoral fellow dept. molecular, cellular and devel. biology U. Colo., Boulder, 1985—89; asst. prof. dept. genetics and cell biology U. Minn., St. Paul, 1989—95, assoc. prof. dept. genetics and cell biology, 1995—. External reviewer NSF, 1989—. Reviewer: Jour. Cell Biology, reviewer: Jour. Biol. Chemistry, reviewer: Molecular Biology of the Cell, reviewer: Molecular Cell Biology, reviewer: Proceedings Nat. Acad. Sci. USA, reviewer: Cell Motility and the Cytoskeleton, reviewer: Jour. Cell Sci., reviewer: Genetics; contbr. articles to profl. jours. Recipient Basil O'Connor Scholar award, March of Dimes, 1993, Establishe Investigator award, Am. Heart Found., 1996; fellow H.V. Wilson, U. N.C., 1983, R.J. Reynolds, 1983, Postdoctoral, NIH, 1985—88; grantee Tng., 1991—95, 1995—, Rsch. Tng., NSF, 1991—95, March of Dimes, 1995—; scholar Founders, Marine Biol. Lab., 1980. Mem.: Genetics Soc. Am., Am. Soc. Cell Biology. Office: U Minn Dept Genetics Cell Biology & Devel 6-160 Jackson Hall 321 Church St SE Minneapolis MN 55455

HAYWARD, EDWARD JOSEPH, lawyer; b. Springfield, Mo., Dec. 4, 1943; s. Joseph Hunter and Rosemary (Barber) H.; m. Ellinor Duffy, Aug. 30, 1968; children: Jeffrey, Stephen, Susan. Student, U. d'Aix Marseille, Aix-en-Provence, France, 1963-64; AB, Stanford U., 1965; JD magna cum laude, Harvard U., 1971. Bar: N.Y. 1972, Minn. 1980. Assoc. Cleary, Gottlieb, Steen & Hamilton, N.Y.C. and Brussels, 1971-74, Oppenheimer Wolff & Donnelly, Brussels, 1975-79, ptnr. Mpls., 1978—. Pres. Twin Cities Fgn. Trade Zone Inc., Mpls., 1983-84. Chmn. legis. com. Minn. World Trade Assn., Mpls., 1984-87. Served to capt. U.S. Army, 1965-68. Mem.: ABA, Minn. Bar Assn. (councillor internat. law sect. 1983—, sec. 1986—88, vice chmn. 1988—89, chmn. 1989—90), Dist. Export Coun. 1996—, German-Am. C. of C. (bd. dirs. 1994—99, 2000—), French-Am. C. of C. 1983—, (pres. 1985—87, 1996—2001, nat. sec. 1988—). Republican. Presbyterian. Avocations: languages, sports. Home: 6625 W Shore Dr Minneapolis MN 55435-1528 Office: Oppenheimer Wolff & Donnelly 45 S 7th St Ste 3300 Minneapolis MN 55402-1614 E-mail: ehayward@oppenheimer.com.

HAYWARD, THOMAS ZANDER, JR. lawyer; b. Oct. 21, 1940; s. Thomas Z. and Wilhelmina (White) H.; m. Sally Madden, June 20, 1964; children: Thomas Z., Wallace M., Robert M. BA, Northwestern U., 1962, JD, 1965; MBA, U. Chgo., 1970. Bar: Ill. 1966, Ohio 1966, U.S. Dist. Ct. (no. dist.) Ill. 1966, U.S. Supreme Ct. 1970. Assoc. Defrees & Fiske, Chgo., 1965-69, ptnr., 1969-81, Boodell, Sears, Giambalvo & Crowley, Chgo., 1981-87, Bell, Boyd, Lloyd, Chgo., 1987—. Mem. mgmt. and exec. coms. Bell, Boyd, Lloyd. Trustee Northwestern U., 1980-84, 97—, vice-chmn., 2000—; bd. dirs. Ill. Continuing Legal Edn., 1987-92, Chgo. area Found. for Legal Svcs., 1983—. Recipient Northwestern U. Alumni Svc. award, 1973. Mem. ABA (ho. of dels. 1984—, fed. jud. com. 1993-97, bd. govs., exec. com. 1998-2001, chmn. fin. com.), Ill. State Bar Assn., Chgo. Bar Assn. (pres. 1983-84), Chgo. Club, Casino Club, Barrington Hills Country Club (pres. 1985-87). Republican. Presbyterian. Home: 8 W County Line Rd Barrington IL 60010-2613 Office: Bell Boyd & Lloyd 3 1st Nat Plz 70 W Madison St Ste 3300 Chicago IL 60602-4284

HAYZLETT, GARY K. state legislator; b. Lakin, Kans., Sept. 4, 1941; s. Lester Madison and Juanita (Coder) H.; m. Helen Yakel, 1961; children: Teresa Jane, Jennifer Jill, Wendy Marie. Student, Garden City C.C., 1960-61. County commr. Kearny County, Kans., 1974—; chmn. Kans. Legis. Policy Group; Kans. state rep. Dist. 122; owner, operator Gary's AG Grocery, Lakin, 1965-79, Dairy Queen/Brazier, 1979—. Mem. Kans. County Commrs. Assn., Masons (Emerald Lodge No. 289), Scottish Rite, Shriners. Home: PO Box 66 Lakin KS 67860-0066

HAZELTINE, JOYCE, state official; b. Pierre, S.D. m. Dave Hazeltine; children: Derek, Tara, Kirk. Student, Huron (S.D.) Coll., No. State Coll., Aberdeen, S.D., Black Hills State Coll., Spearfish, S.D. Former asst. chief clk. S.D. Ho. of Reps.; former sec. S.D. State Senate; sec. of state State of S.D., Pierre, 1987—. Adminstrv. asst. Pres. Ford Campaign, S.D.; Rep. county chmn. Hughes County S.D.; state co-chair Phil Gramm for Pres., 1996. Mem. Nat. Assn. Secs. of State (exec. bd., pres.), Women Execs. in State Govts. (bd. dirs.). Office: Sec of State's Office 500 E Capitol Ave Ste 204 Pierre SD 57501-5070 E-mail: joyceh@sos.state.sd.us.

HAZELWOOD, JOHN A. lawyer; b. July 9, 1938; s. Clark John Adam and Katherine (Kletzsch) H.; m. Anne Messinger, Aug. 17, 1964; children: Katherine, Sara, Robin. BA, Yale U., 1960; JD, U. Mich., 1963; LLM in Taxation, NYU, 1964. Bar: Wis. 1963, U.S. Dist. Ct. (ea. dist.) Wis. 1964, U.S. Ct. Appeals (7th cir.) 1965, U.S. Tax Ct. 1965. Assoc. Quarles & Brady, Milw., 1964-70, ptnr., 1971-2000, ptnr.-in-charge bus. tax group, 1979-89, of counsel, 2000—. Vis. prof. corp. taxation U. Wis., 1971; dir., sec. 7 pvt. corps. Bd. dirs., chmn. bd. Zool. Soc. Milw., 1987-89; civilian participant joint civilian orientation conf. Dept. Def., 1990. Contbr. articles to legal jours. Chmn. PBS affiliate TV auction, 1976; assoc. fellow Pierson Coll., Yale U., 1986—. Mem. ABA, Wis. Bar Assn. (chair bd. tax sect. 1989-90), Yale Alumni Assn. (Wis. rep., bd. govs. 1986-89), Milw. Athletic Club (Iron Man champion 1992), Yale Club (N.Y.C.). Office: 701 Green Bay Rd Cedarburg WI 53012-9105

HAZLETON, RICHARD A. chemicals executive; b. 1941; Pres., ceo Dow Corning Corp, Midland, Mich., 1965—, chmn., CEO. Office: Dow Corning Corp PO Box 994 Midland MI 48686-0001

H'DOUBLER, FRANCIS TODD, JR. surgeon; b. Springfield, Mo., June 18, 1925; s. Francis Todd and Alice Louise (Bemis) H'D; m. Joan Louise Huber, Dec. 20, 1951 (dec. Dec. 1983); children: Julie H'Doubler Thomas and Sarah H'Doubler Muegge (twins), Kurt, Scott; m. Marie Ruth Duckworth, Jan. 18, 1986 Student, Washington U., St. Louis, 1943, Miami U., Oxford, Ohio, 1943-44; B.S., U. Wis., 1946, M.D., 1948. Intern Milw. Hosp., 1948-49; resident in surgery U.S. Naval Hosp., Oakland, Calif., 1950-51; practice medicine specializing in alternative medicine Springfield, Mo., 1952—; mem. courtesy staff St. John's Hosp., L.E. Cox Hosp., Springfield. Bd. dirs. Union Planters Bank. Active Singing Doctors; chmn. fundraising drive YMCA, 1960-61, Sch. Bond and Tax Levy Com., 1958, Greene County Rep. Com., 1974-75; past bd. trustees Shriners Hosps., past chmn. spinal cord injury com., past chmn. rsch. com., past chmn. long range planning com., emeritus mem. rsch. com.; mem. Commn. to Reapportion Mo. Senate, 1971, Rep. State Fin. Com., 1972-75, steering com. Wilson's Creekl Battlefield Nat. Park, 1951-61, pres.'s adv. coun. Sch. Ozarks, Point Lookout, Mo., 1975-89; trustee Cottey Coll., Nevada, Mo., past bd. chmn.; bd. trustees Forest Inst. With USNR, 1943-46, 49-51. Decorated Bronze Star with V, Purple Heart with oak leaf cluster; recipient Disting. Service award Mo. Jaycees, 1959; Humanitarian award S.W. Mo. Drug Travelers Assn., 1971; named Young Man of Yr., City of Springfield, 1959 Fellow Am. Coll. Nuclear Medicine (founder's group); mem. AMA, Greene County Med. Assn., Mo. Med. Soc., Southwestern Surg. Congress, Mo. Surg. Assn., Soc. Nuclear Medicine, Am. Thyroid Assn., Springfield Jr. C. of C. (past pres.), Springfield C. of C., DAV, VFW, SAR, Am. Legion, Green Gang (co-founder), Sigma Nu (Outstanding Alumnus nat. award 1980), Nu Sigma Nu. Presbyterian. Club: Hickory Hills Country. Lodges: Mason (33 deg.), Shriners (imperial potentate 1980-81), Red Cross of Constantine, Order DeMolay Legion Honor (hon.), Royal Order Scotland.

HEAD, PATRICK JAMES, lawyer; b. Randolph, Nebr., July 13, 1932; s. Clarence Martin and Ellen Cecelia (Magirl) H.; m. Eleanor Hickey, Nov. 24, 1960; children: Adrienne, Ellen, Damian, Maria, Brendan, Martin, Sarah, Daniel, Brian. A.B. summa cum laude, Georgetown U., 1953, LL.B., 1956, LL.M. in Internat. Law, 1957. Bar: D.C. 1956, Ill. 1966. Assoc. John L. Ingolsby (and predecessor firm), Washington, 1956-64; gen. counsel internat. ops. Sears, Roebuck & Co., Oakbrook, Ill., 1964-70, counsel midwest ter. Skokie, 1970-72; v.p. Montgomery Ward & Co., Inc., Washington, 1972-76, v.p., gen. counsel, sec. Chgo., 1976-81; v.p., gen. counsel FMC Corp., 1981-96; ptnr. Altheimer E. Gray, 1997—. Bd. visitors Northwestern Law, 1988-91. Mem. Chgo. Crime Commn.; bd. regents Georgetown U., Washington, 1981-87; bd. visitors Georgetown Law Sch., 1992—. Mem. ABA, D.C. Bar Assn., Chgo. Bar Assn., Am. Law Inst. Democrat. Roman Catholic. Clubs: Met. (Washington); Chgo, Internat. Office: Williams Montgomery & John Ltd 20 N Wacker Dr 21st Fl Chicago IL 60606-7407

HEADLEE, RAYMOND, psychoanalyst, educator; b. Shelby County, Ind., July 27, 1917; s. Ortis Verl and Mary Mae (Wright) H.; m. Eleanor Case Benton, Aug. 24, 1941; children: Sue, Mark, Ann. A.B. in Psychology, Ind. U., 1939, A.M. in Exptl. Psychology, 1941, M.D., 1944; grad., Chgo. Inst. Psychoanalysis, 1959. Diplomate: Am. Bd. Psychiatry and Neurology (examiner 1964—). Intern St. Elizabeth's Hosp., Washington, 1944-45, resident in psychiatry, 1945-46, Milw. Psychiat. Hosp., 1947-48, pres. staff, 1965-70; practice medicine specializing in psychiatry and psychoanalysis Elm Grove, Wis., 1949—; clin. asst. prof. psychiatry Med. Coll. Wis., 1958-59, clin. asso. prof., 1959-62, clin. prof., 1962-2000, chmn. dept. psychiatry, 1963-70; prof. psychology Marquette U., 1966-76; Bd. dirs. Elm Brook (Wis.) Meml. Hosp., 1969-71; ret., 2000. Author: (with Bonnie Corey) Psychiatry in Nursing, 1949, I Think, Therefore I Know, 1996; contbr. numerous articles to profl. jours. 1st lt. Ft. Knox Armored Med. Rsch. Lab., AUS, 1945, to col. USPHS. Fellow Am. Psychiat. Assn. (life), Am. Coll. Psychiatry (emeritus); mem. State Med. Soc. Wis. (editorial dir. 1971-77), Wis. Psychiat. Assn. (pres. 1971-72), Milw. Club. E-mail: 1amplg@mymailstation.com.

HEADRICK, DANIEL RICHARD, history and social sciences educator; b. Bay Shore, N.Y., Aug. 2, 1941; s. William Cecil and Edith (Finkelstein) H.; m. Rita Koplowitz, June 20, 1965 (dec. 1988); children: Isabelle, Juliet, Matthew; m. Kate Ezra, Aug. 23, 1992. B, Lycée de Garçons, Metz, France, 1959; BA, Swarthmore Coll., 1962; MA, Johns Hopkins U., 1964; PhD, Princeton U., 1971. Instr. history Tuskegee (Ala.) Inst., 1968-71, asst. prof., 1971-73, assoc. prof., 1973-75; assoc. prof. social scis. Roosevelt U., Chgo., 1975-82, prof., 1982—. Vis. NEH scholar Hawaii Pacific U., 2000. Author: Ejercito y Politica, 1981, The Tools of Empire, 1981, Tentacles of Progress, 1988, The Invisible Weapon, 1991, The Earth and Its Peoples, 1997, When Information Came of Age, 2000. Coll. Tchrs. fellow NEH, 1983-84, 88-89, Guggenheim fellow, 1994, Sloan fellow, 1998; recipient Faculty Achievement award Burlington No. Found., 1988, 92. Mem. Am. Hist. Assn., World History Assn. (exec. com. 1991—), Soc. for History Tech. (exec. com. 1992—). Home: 5483 S Hyde Park Blvd Chicago IL 60615-5827 Office: Roosevelt U Univ Coll 430 S Michigan Ave Chicago IL 60605-1394 E-mail: dan.headrick@att.net.

HEAGY, THOMAS CHARLES, banker; b. Fresno, Calif., Jan. 4, 1945; s. Clarence H. and Ruth (Geer) H.; m. Regina Victoria Polk, Apr. 12, 1980 (dec. Oct. 1983); m. Linda Anne Hutton, Jan. 10, 1987. BA in Physics, U. Chgo., 1967, MBA with honors, 1970; MSc in Fin., London Sch. Econs., 1970. Dep. mgr. mgmt. scis. First Nat. Bank Chgo., 1970-75; chmn. bd., chief exec. officer South Shore Nat. Bank, Chgo., 1975-80; exec. v.p. Exchange Nat. Bank Chgo., 1980-90; vice chmn. LaSalle Nat. Bank, 1990—, LaSalle Nat. Corp., 1990—. CFO ABN AMRO N.Am., 1996—. Bd. dirs. Chgo. Symphony, 1995—, The Regina V. Polk Scholarship Fund, Chgo., 1983—, Mus. Contemporary Art, Chgo., 1994—, Chgo. Music and Dance Theater, 1994—, Lyric Opera Chgo., 1999—; mem. vis. com. Oriental Inst., U. Chgo., 1988—; mem. Renaissance Soc., 1989—; bd. govs. Am. Rsch. Ctr. Egypt, 1996—. Home: 4939 S Greenwood Ave Chicago IL 60615-2815 Office: LaSalle Nat Bank 135 S Lasalle St Fl 5 Chicago IL 60603-4402

HEALEY, EDWARD HOPKINS, architect; b. Dubuque, Iowa, Jan. 3, 1925; s. George Beach and Marian (Hopkins) H.; m. Alice Letitia Dawson, Sept. 11, 1954; children: Susan Healey Toussaint, Carolyn Healey Olson, Ellen Hopkins Healey. BS in Architecture, U. Ill., 1950; cert., Ecoles D'Art Americaines, Fountainbleau, France, 1950. Registered architect, Iowa, Ill., Wis., Minn. Ptnr. Brown & Healey, Architects, Cedar Rapids, Iowa, 1953-60, Brown, Healey & Bock, Architects and Engrs., Cedar Rapids, 1960-81; pres. Brown, Healey & Bock, Architects, Planners, Interior Designers, 1981-90, Brown, Healey, Stone & Sauer, Architects, Planners, Interior Designers, Cedar Rapids, 1990-95. Del. The White House Conf. on Libraries and Info. Svcs., Washington, 1979, 91; pres. profl. adv. bd. dept. architecture Iowa State U., Ames, 1981-82; pres. East Cen. Regional Library Bd., Cedar Rapids, 1981-84; mem. Iowa Library Commn., Des Moines, 1987-90, chmn., 1987-89; bd. dirs. Iowa Cultural Affairs Adv. Coun., Des Moines, 1987-89; trustee Linn County Hist. Mus., 1990—, pres., 1995-96; trustee Brucemore, 1983-89. Fellow AIA (Iowa medal of Honor 1996, pres. Iowa chpt. 1965-66); mem. ALA, Nat. Coun. Archtl. Registration Bds. (bd. dirs. 1975-77), Literary Club (sec. 1980-86, pres. 1987-88). Avocations: sailing, swimming. Home: 2500 White Eagle Trl SE Cedar Rapids IA 52403-1548 Office: Brown Healey Stone & Sauer Architects PC 800 1st Ave NE Cedar Rapids IA 52402-5002

HEALY, BRYCE, state agency administrator; b. Chamberlain, SD, Jan. 28, 1971; m. Mary Healy. BS in Agrl. Bus., SD State U. Owner farm/ranch operation; dep. commr. SD Office Sch. and Pub. Lands, Pierre, SD; dir. equalization Marshall County, Britton; dir. field svcs. SD Farmers Union; dep. commr. SD Office Sch. and Pub. Lands, Pierre. Office: 500 E Capitol Ave Pierre SD 57501-5070

HEALY, SONDRA ANITA, consumer products company executive; b. 1939; married; 3 children. BFA, Goodman Sch. Drama, 1963; MA, Nat. Coll., 1964. Owner, chair Turtle Wax, Chgo., 1973—. Office: Turtle Wax 5655 S 73rd Ave Chicago IL 60638

HEANEY, GERALD WILLIAM, federal judge; b. Goodhue, Minn., Jan. 29, 1918; s. William J. and Johanna (Ryan) H.; m. Eleanor R. Schmitt, Dec. 1, 1945; children: William M., Carol J. Student, St. Thomas Coll., 1935—37; BSL, U. Minn., 1938, LLB, 1941. Bar: Minn. 1941. Lawyer securities div. Dept. of Commerce Minn., 1941—42; mem. firm Lewis. Hammer, Heaney, Weyl & Halverson, Duluth, 1946—66; judge U.S. Ct. Appeals (8th cir.), 1966—68, sr. judge, 1989—. Bd. regents U. Minn., 1964—65; Mem. Dem. Nat. Com. from Minn., 1955. Mem.: ABA, Am. Judicature Soc., Minn. Bar Assn. Roman Catholic. Office: US Ct Appeals 8th Cir US Courthouse & Federal Bldg 315 W 1st St Duluth MN 55802-1605

HEAP, JAMES CLARENCE, retired mechanical engineer; b. Trinidad, Colo. s. James and Elsie Mae (Brobst) H.; m. Alma Mae Swartzendruber. Registered profl. engr., Wis. Sr. mech. engr. Cook Electric Research Lab, Morton Grove, Ill., 1955-56; assoc. mech. engr. Argonne (Ill.) Nat. Lab., 1956-66; sr. project engr. Union Tank Car Co., East Chicago, Ind., 1966-71; sr. engr. Thrall Car Mfg. Co., Chicago Heights, 1971-77; research design engr. Graver Energy Systems, Inc., East Chicago, Ind., 1977-79; mech. cons. design engr. Pollak & Skan, Inc., Chgo., 1979-83, ret., 1983. Cons. mech. design and stress analysis, 1965-83. Author: Formulas for Circular Plates Subjected to Symmetrical Loads and Temperatures, 1966; contbr. tech. papers to profl. jour.; patentee in field. Served with USAF, 1946-47. Mem. ASME, Christian Businessmen's Com. U.S., The Gideon's Internat. Home: 1406 Ashton Ct Goshen IN 46526-4679

HEAPHY, JOHN MERRILL, lawyer; b. Escanaba, Mich., Apr. 27, 1927; s. John Merrill and Catherine R. (Feeney) H.; m. Martha Jean Knowles, Nov. 16, 1951; children— John Merrill III, Catherine Jean Heaphy DeThorne, Barbara H. Murphy. B.A., U. Mich., 1950; J.D., Wayne State U., 1953. Bar: Mich. 1954. Atty. office of gen. counsel HEW, Washington, 1954-57; ptnr. Vandeveer & Garzia, P.C. and predecessor firms, Detroit, 1958-86, pres. firm, 1986-92; ret. Served with USNR, 1945-46. Fellow Am. Coll. Trial Lawyers; mem. ABA, Internat. Assn. Def. Counsel, Mich. Bar Assn., Delta Theta Phi, Alpha Sigma Phi. Republican. Home: 14650 N Desert Rock Dr Tucson AZ 85737-7135 E-mail: JMHeaphy@aol.com.

HEARNE, GEORGE ARCHER, academic administrator; b. Tampa, Fla., Oct. 31, 1934; s. William Duncan and Marguerite Estelle (Archer) H.; m. Jean May Helmstadter, June 9, 1956; children: Diana Leslie, George Harrison. BA, Bethany Coll., 1955; MDiv, Yale U., 1958; MA, Ill. State U., 1968; HHD (hon.), Culver-Stockton Coll., 1986; LLD, Bethany Coll., 1997. Min. Arlington Christian Ch., Jacksonville, Fla., 1958-59; dir. admissions Eureka (Ill.) Coll., 1960-70, v.p. student devel., 1970-73, dean admissions and student devel., 1973-77, dean admissions and coll. rels., 1977-82, v.p. coll. rels., 1982-84, exec. v.p., 1984-85, pres., 1985—. Bd. dirs. Christian Ch., Ill., Wis. and Ind., 1985—, Higher Edn. divsn. Christian Ch., St. Louis, 1985—; pres. Eureka Bd. Edn., 1967-76; active various cmty. drives. Mem. Assoc. Colls. Ill. (bd. dirs. 1985—), Fedn. Ill. Ind. Colls. and Univs. (bd. dirs. 1985—, exec. com. 2000—), Coun. for Advancement and Support of Edn., Coun. Ind. Colls., Coun. of Pres. (higher edn. div.). Lodge: Rotary. Avocations: reading, music, antiques, golf. Office: Eureka Coll 300 E College Ave Eureka IL 61530-1562 E-mail: ghearne@eureka.edu.

HEATON, GERALD LEE, lawyer; b. Detroit, Feb. 28, 1952; s. Gerald and Bernice Johanna (Cromp) H.; m. Ilene Renee Mann, Oct. 25, 1975. AA, North Cen. Mich. Coll., 1972; BA, Albion Coll., 1974; JD, Ohio No. U., 1976. Bar: Ohio 1977, U.S. Dist. Ct. (so. dist.) Ohio 1977. Ptnr. Lile & Heaton, Bellefontaine, Ohio, 1977-79, MacGillivray & Heaton, Bellefontaine, 1979—. Asst. pros. atty. Logan County, Bellefontaine, 1977-84; soliciter Village of Belle Center, Ohio, 1982—, Village of De Graff, Ohio, 1982—. Pres. United Way, Bellefontaine, 1984, bd. dirs., 1982—. Mem. ABA, Ohio Bar Assn., Logan County Bar Assn., Assn. Trial Lawyers Am., Logan County C. of C. Republican. Roman Catholic. Lodges: Lions, Masons. Avocations: golf, tennis, crossword puzzles. Home: 2431 Carriage Hill Dr Bellefontaine OH 43311-9430

HEATWOLE, MARK M. lawyer; b. Pitts., Jan. 28, 1948; s. Marion Grove and Phyllis Adelle (Leiter) H.; m. Sarah Ann Collier, Dec. 30, 1970; children: Mary Phyllis, Elizabeth Collier, Anna Bell. BA, Washington and Lee U., 1969, JD, 1972. Bar: Ill. 1972, U.S. Dist. Ct. (no. dist.) Ill. 1972, U.S. Ct. Appeals (7th cir.) 1977, U.S. Supreme Ct. 1980, U.S. Tax Ct. 1987. Assoc. Chadwell & Kayser, Ltd., Chgo., 1972-79, ptnr., v.p., 1979-89; ptnr. Winston & Strawn, 1990—. Treas. Lyric Opera Chgo. Guild, 1980—81, v.p., 1980—81, chmn. fundraising, 1986; vice-chmn. Gorton Cmty. Ctr., 1986; chmn. bd. Gorton Cmty. Ctr. Found., 1986—89; trustee Barat Coll., 1982—85, The Admiral, Chgo., 1988—2001, Allendale Assn., 1991—2000; Mem. 1st ward Rep. com. on candidates Lake Forest (Ill.) Caucus, 1985—88, chmn., 1987—88, vice-chmn., 1989—90, chmn., 1990—91; mem. session Lake Forest Presbyn. Ch., 1978—84, chmn. ch. and society com., 1980; bd. dirs. Lyric Opera Chgo. Guild, 1976—, Lake Forest Symphony, 1987—91, Rehab. Inst. Chgo. Enterprises, 1991—2001, Gorton Community Ctr., 1982—88. Mem.: ABA (continuing legal edn. com. 1978—79, mem. antitrust com. young lawyers sect. 1978—81, com. on civil practice and procedure antitrust sect. 1980, bus. law sect. 1986—, patent trademark and copyright sect. 1990—), Chgo. Bar Assn. (chmn. profl. responsibility com. young lawyers sect. 1977—78, mem. exec. com. 1978—79, bd. dirs.), Lawyers Club, Winter Club, Econ. Club Chgo., Shoreacres Club (bd. govs. 1996—, pres. 2002—). Republican. Office: Winston & Strawn 35 W Wacker Dr Ste 4200 Chicago IL 60601-1695 E-mail: mheatwol@winston.com.

HEBDA, LAWRENCE JOHN, data processing executive, consultant; b. East Chicago, Ind., Apr. 9, 1954; s. Walter Martin and Barbara (Matczynski) H.; m. Cynthia Ruta Aizkalns, June 17, 1978. BS, Purdue U., 1976; MBA, U. Iowa, 1983. Cert. data processor. Programmer Inland Steel Co., East Chicago, 1976-77; data analyst Deere & Co., Moline, Ill., 1977-82, systems analyst, 1982-83, project mgr., 1983-84, dealer systems cons., 1984-85, corp. planning analyst, 1985-87, systems edn. adminstr., 1987-88, telecommunications analyst, 1988; info. systems sr. cons. Hewitt Assocs., Lincolnshire, 1988-93, MIS bus. mgr., 1994-97, mgr. software distbn./oper. sys., 1997-2000, mgr. client/server application support, 2000—02, application project mgr., 2002—. Instr. computer sci. dept. Coll. Lake County Ill., 1996—, mem. computer info. systems adv. bd., 1999—. Mem. Nat. Rep. Congl. Com., 1982-85; charter mem. Rep. Presdl. Task Force, 1980;

chmn. pastoral coun. Roman Cath. Ch., 1994-95. Recipient Cert. Recognition, Nat. Rep. Congl. Com., 1982-85, Presdl. Achievement award Rep. Nat. Com., 1984. Mem. Data Processing Mgmt. Assn., Am. Legion, Internat. Platform Assn., DAV Comdr.'s Club, King's Men Religious Orgn. (v.p. 1985, pres. 1986-87), Toastmasters (assoc. area gov. 1983-84), K.C. (3d degree coun. 8022, 2001). Roman Catholic. Club: Toastmasters Internat. (assoc. area gov. 1983-84). Home: 675 Sussex Cir Vernon Hills IL 60061-2123 Office: Hewitt Assocs 100 Half Day Rd Lincolnshire IL 60069-3242

HEBENSTREIT, JAMES BRYANT, agricultural products executive, bank and venture capital executive; b. Long Beach, Calif., Mar. 8, 1946; s. William Joseph and Jean (Stark) H.; m. Marilyn Bartlett, Aug. 23, 1986. AB, Harvard U., 1968, MBA, 1973. Pres. Terra-Light div. Butler Mfg. Co., Boston, 1980-82, Capital for Bus., Inc. (SB/C, venture capital affiliate Commerce Bancshares), St. Louis and Kansas City, Mo., 1982-87; sr. v.p. fin., CFO Commerce Bancshares, Inc., Kansas City, 1985-87, bd. dirs., 1987—; pres. Bartlett and Co., 1992—. Lt. USNR, 1968-71. Home: 1016 W 58th St Kansas City MO 64113-1133 Office: Bartlett & Co 4800 Main St Kansas City MO 64112-2510

HEBERMEHL, RODGER, executive director lutheran ministries; BA in Indsl. Engring., Purdue U. Supr. Internat. Harvestor Co., Wagoner, Okla., Rockwell Internat., McAlester; mgr. operations LORI, Inc., Tulsa; exec. dir. Internat. Lutheran Laymen's League, St. Louis, 1996—. Mem. Internat. Lutheran Laymen's League bd. govs. (exec. com.). Office: Lutheran Laymens League 2185 Hampton Ave Saint Louis MO 63139-2983

HECHLER, ROBERT LEE, financial services company executive; b. Galesburg, Ill., Nov. 12, 1936; s. Wesley Paul and Mildred (Paden) H.; m. Beverly Lockwood, Mar. 31, 1990; 1 child, Marcie Lee. BS, U. Ill., 1958; MBA, U. Chgo., 1967. Mgr. sales acctg. R.H. Donnelley, Chgo., 1960-64; mgr. profit plan Interstate United Corp., 1964-68; pres., CEO Waddell & Reed Inc., Kansas City, Mo., 1968—; chmn. Fiduciary Trust Co. N.H. Chmn. bd. dirs. ICI Mut. Ins. Co. Mem. Fin. Execs. Inst., Investment Co. Inst. (bd. govs.), Mission Hills Country Club, Kansas City Club. Office: Waddell & Reed Inc 6300 Lamar Ave Shawnee Mission KS 66202-4200

HECHT, HAROLD ARTHUR, orchidologist, chiropractor; b. St. Louis, Apr. 30, 1921; s. William Frederick and Myrtle Regina (Hugo) H.; m. Barbara Evelyne Ross, Nov. 19, 1942. D Chiropractic Medicine, Logan Coll. Sole practice, St. Louis, 1942-95; orchidologist, 1950—. Judge Orchid Digest Corp., 1959; internat. lectr., photographer in field radiotelephone engr., 1942. Contbr. articles to profl. jours. Mem. World Orchid Cong. (founding com. 1954), Mid-Am. Orchid Cong. (founder, pres. 1959, judge 1968), Am. Orchid Soc. (grand jurist, judge 1968), Mark Twain Orchid Soc. (pres. 1966, 90), Mo. Orchid Soc. (pres. 1959), European Orchid Congress (USA com. 1967). Republican. Avocations: philatilist, numismatist, amateur radio operator, antiquary, linguist.

HECK, RICHARD T. tree farmer; b. Madison, Ind., Sept. 16, 1924; s. Richard Charles and Virginia (Tevis) H.; m. Ruth Irwin Heck, June 27, 1948; children: Richard Gregory, Rebecca Jeanne. Student, Admiral Farragut Naval Acad., Pine Beach, N.J., 1942-43, Hanover Coll, 1947-48. Tree farmer, Hanover, Ind., 1943—. Vol. firefighter, 1946—; mem. arson investigation team Jefferson County, Ind., 1983-90, Hanover Twp. Vol. Fire Co., 1956—; trustee Hanover Coll., 1991-2000. With USN, 1944-54, WWII, Korea. Named to Hon. Order of Ky. Cols., 1971, Sagamore of Wabash, 1973; named Ind. Outstanding Tree Farmer, Ind. Tree Farm Commn., 1983, Nat. Outstanding Tree Farmer Am. Forest Found., 1984, Good Steward award Nat. Arbor Day Found., 1984, North Ctrl. Region Outstanding Tree Farmer, 1984, Ind. Conservationist of Yr., Ind. Dept. Natural Resources, 1985, Forest Conservationist of the Yr. Ind. Wildlife Fedn., 1987. Mem. Soc. Am. Foresters (hon.), Nat. Forestry Assn. (life), Ind. Foresty and Woodland Owners Assn. (bd. dirs. 1984-95, Ind. state tree farm com. 1984—), NRA (life), Ind. Vol. Firemans Assn. (life), Nat. Muzzle Loading Rifle Assn. (life), Internat. Assn. Arson Investigators, Inc., Nat. Eagle Scout Assn., Soc. Ind. Pioneers, Am. Legion, Wahpanipe Muzzle Loading Rifle Club, Connor Prairie Rifles Club, Masons, Elks. Republican. Presbyterian. Avocations: hunting, fishing, hiking, collecting Indian artifacts, competitive muzzle loading shooting. Address: 110 Clemmons St Hanover IN 47243-9659

HECKEL, JOHN LOUIS (JACK HECKEL), aerospace company executive; b. Columbus, Ohio, July 12, 1931; s. Russel Criblez and Ruth Selma (Heid) H.; m. Jacqueline Ann Alexander, Nov. 21, 1959 (div. 1993); children: Heidi, Holly, John; m. Linda Holleran, Aug. 1, 1994. BS, U. Ill., 1954; PhD with honors, Nat. U. San Diego, 1984. Divsn. mgr. Aerojet Divsn., Azusa, Calif., 1956-70, Seattle and Washington, 1956-70; pres. Aerojet-Space Gen. Co., El Monte, Calif., 1970-72, Aerojet Liquid Rocket Co., Sacramento, 1972-77; group v.p. Aerojet Sacramento Cos., 1977-81; pres. Aerojet Gen., La Jolla, Calif., 1981-85, chmn., CEO, 1985-87; pres., COO GenCorp., Akron, 1987-94, also bd. dirs. Bd. dirs. WD-40 Corp., Advanced Tissue Sci., Inc., San Diego, Applied Power Inc., Milw. Bd. dirs. San Diego Econ. Devel. Corp., 1983-86, Akron Regional Devel. Bd., Akron Gen. Hosp., Summit County United Way; pres. Summit Edn. Partnership Found., Akron. Recipient Disting. Alumni award U. Ill. Ann. Alumni Conv., 1979 Fellow AIAA (assoc.); mem. Aerospace Industries Assn. Am. (gov. 1981), Navy League U.S., Am. Def. Preparedness Assn., San Diego C. of C. (bd. dirs.)

HECKEL, RICHARD WAYNE, metallurgical engineering educator; b. Pitts., Jan. 25, 1934; s. Ralph Clyde and Esther Vera (Zoerb) H.; m. Peggy Ann Simmons, Jan. 3, 1959 (dec. Apr. 1998); children: Scott Alan, Laura Ann Rowe. BS in Metall. Engring., Carnegie Mellon, 1955, MS, 1958, PhD, 1959. Sr. research metallurgist E.I. duPont de Nemours & Co., Wilmington, Del., 1959-63; prof. metall. engring. Drexel U., Phila., 1963-71; head dept. materials sci. and engring. Carnegie Mellon, Pitts., 1971-76; pres., prof. emeritus dept. materials sci. and engring. Mich. Tech. U., Houghton, 1976—; tech. dir., owner Engring. Trends, 2000—. Commr. at large Engring. Workforce Commn., 1997—, with Engring. Trends (e-commerce). Contbr. articles to profl. jours. Served as 1st lt. Ordnance Corps, U.S. Army, 1959-60. Recipient Lindback Teaching award Drexel U., 1968; Research award Mich. Tech. U., 1985 Fellow ASM Internat. (life; Bradley Stoughton Young Tchr. of Metallurgy award 1969, Phila. Ednl. Achievement award 1967); mem. The Metals, Minerals and Materials Soc., Am. Welding Soc. (Adams Meml. mem. 1966), Am. Soc. Engring. Edn., Sigma Xi, Omicron Delta Kappa, Tau Beta Pi, Phi Kappa Phi, Alpha Sigma Mu. Address: Engring Trends 1281 Hickory Ln Houghton MI 49931-1609 E-mail: engtrend@up.net.

HECKEMEYER, ANTHONY JOSEPH, circuit court judge; b. Cape Girardeau, Mo., Jan. 20, 1939; s. Paul Q. and Frances E. (Goetz) H.; m. Elizabeth Faye Littleton, Feb. 13, 1964; children: Anthony Joseph, Matthew Paul, Mary Elizabeth, Andrew William, Sarah Kathryn. BS, U. Mo., 1962, JD, 1972; grad., Nat. Judicial Coll., 1980, Juvenile Coll., 1984. Bar: Mo. Mem. Mo. Ho. Reps., Jefferson City, 1964-72; sole practice Sikeston, Mo., 1972-81; presiding cir. judge State of Mo., Scott and Mississippi Counties, 1981—. Chmn. alcohol and substance abuse com. Nat. Council of Juvenile and Family Ct. Judges, Reno, 1987-88, presenter at U. Reno; majority party whip, chmn., vice chmn. agr. com., higher edn. com. as a miscellaneous resolution com. Named Outstanding Conservation Legislator Sears, 1968, Found. Mo. Wildlife Fedn., 1968, Man of Yr., Sikeston C. of C., 1989. Mem. Mo. Trial Judges Assn. (pres. 1995). Office: Presiding Cir Judge PO Box 256 Benton MO 63736-0256

HECKMAN, CAROL A. biology educator; b. East Stroudsburg, Pa., Oct. 18, 1944; d. Wilbur Thomas and Doris (Betts) H. BA, Beloit (Wis.) Coll., 1966; PhD, U. Mass., Amherst, 1972. Rsch. assoc. Yale U. Sch. Medicine, New Haven, 1973-75; staff mem. Oak Ridge (Tenn.) Nat. Lab., 1975-82; adj. assoc. prof. U. Tenn.-Oak Ridge Biomed. Grad. Sch., 1980-82; assoc. prof. Bowling Green (Ohio) State U., 1982-86, prof. biology, 1986—. Cons. NSF, Washington, 1977-80, NIH, Rockville, Md., 1996-98; dir. EM facility Bowling Green State U., 1982—; NSF trainee, Amherst, 1967-70; vis. prof. Univ. Coll. London. Contbr. articles to profl. jours., chpts. to books. Internat. Cancer Rsch. Tech. fellow Internat. Union Against Cancer, 1980, Heritage Found. fellow, 1982, guest rsch. fellow, Uppsala, Sweden, 1989-90; grantee NSF, 1981-84, 90-92, NIH, 1987-88, 98-2001, Dept. of Def., 2000—. Mem. AAAS, Am. Soc. Cell Biology, Microscopy Soc. Am., N.W. Ohio Microscopy (sec.-treas. 1986-90, pres. 1990-94), Soc. In Vitro Biology, Mid-Am. Drug Devel. (pres. 1999), Ohio Acad. Sci., Sigma Xi. Episcopalian. Achievements include research evaluation and development of in vitro anticarcinogens. Home: 861 Ferndale Ct Bowling Green OH 43402-1609 Office: Bowling Green State U Dept Biol Scis Bowling Green OH 43403-0001

HECKMAN, HENRY TREVENNEN SHICK, steel company executive; b. Reading, Pa., Mar. 27, 1918; s. H. Raymond and Charlotte E. Shick H.; AB, Lehigh U., 1939; m. Helen Clausen Wright, Nov. 28, 1946; children: Sharon Anita (dec.), Charlotte Marie. Advt. prodn. mgr. Republic Steel Corp., Cleve., 1940-42, editor Enduro Era, 1946-51, account exec., 1953-54, asst. dir. advt., 1957-65, dir. advt., 1965-82; partner Applegate & Heckman, Washington, 1955-56; advt. mgr. Harris Corp., 1956-57. Permanent chmn. Joint Com. for Audit Comparability, 1968-93; chmn. Media Comparability Coun., 1969-83; chmn. indsl. advertisers com. Greater Cleve. Growth Assn., 1973-76; chmn. publs. com. Lehigh U., 1971-76; pres.'s adv. coun. Ashland Coll., 1966-76; advt. adv. council Kent State U., 1976-81; exec. com. Cleve. chpt. ARC, 1968-74; mem. Republican Fin. Exec. Com., 1966-87; coord. adv. coun. pub. svcs. campaign Employer Support for Guard and Res., 1973-83, 90—. Comdr. USNR, 1942-46, 51-53; Korea. Named to Advt. Effectiveness Hall of Fame, 1967; named Advt. Man of Yr., 1969; recipient G.D. Crain, Jr. award, 1973; Disting. Alumnus award Lehigh U., 1979; elected to Cleve. Graphic Arts Council Hall of Distinction, 1981. Mem. Indsl. Marketers Cleve. (past pres., Golden Mousetrap award 1968), Bus. Mktg. Assn. (pres. 1968-69, Best Seller award 1966, Hall of Fame, 1973), Assn. Nat. Advertisers (chmn. shows and exhibits com. 1966-74, dir. 1969-72), Am. Iron and Steel Inst. (com. chmn. 1961-69), Steel Svc. Ctr. Inst. (advt. adv. com. 1965-77), New Eng. Soc., Western Res. Soc., SAR (pres. 1979, Archibald Willard award 1996), Ohio Soc. SAR (Hub Scott award 1995), Mil. Order World Wars (comdr. 1980), Early Settlers, Cleve. Advt. Club (pres. 1961-62, Hall of Fame 1980), Ctr. for Mktg. Comm. (chmn. bd. 1965), Internat. Platform Assn., Pi Delta Epsilon. Clubs: Cheshire Cheese (pres. 1982), Cleve. Grays (trustee 1980-82), Cleve. Skating. Home: 6000 Nob Hill Dr Apt 401 Chagrin Falls OH 44022-3358

HECKMAN, JAMES JOSEPH, economist, econometrician, educator; b. Chgo., Apr. 19, 1944; s. John Jacob and Bernice Irene (Medley) H.; m. Lynne Pettler, 1979; children: Jonathan Jacob, Alma Rachel. AB in Math. summa cum laude (Woodrow Wilson fellow), Colo. Coll., 1965, LLD (hon.), 2001; MA in Econs., Princeton U., 1968, PhD in Econs. (Harold Willis Dodds fellow), 1971; MA (hon.), Yale U., 1989; LLD (hon.), Colo. Coll., 2001; D (hon.) , U. Chile, 2002. From lectr. to assoc. prof. Columbia U., 1970-74; assoc. prof. econs. U. Chgo., 1973-76, prof., 1976—, Henry Schultz prof. of econ., 1985-95, Henry Schultz Disting. Svc. prof., 1995—, prof. econs. Harris Sch. Pub. Policy, 1990—, dir. Ctr. for Program Evaluation Harris Sch. Pub. Policy, 1991—, dir. Econs. Rsch. Ctr. Dept. Econs., 1997—; A. Whitney Griswold prof. econs. Yale U., New Haven, 1988-90, Sterling prof., 1990, prof., dept. stats., 1990; dir. Ctr. for Program Evaluation Harris Sch. Pub. Policy U. Chgo., 1991—, dir. Econs. Rsch. Ctr. Dept. Econs., 1997—. Rsch. assoc. Nat. Bur. Econs. Rsch., 1970-77, sr. rsch. assoc., 1977-85, 87—; Irving Fisher prof. econs. Yale U., 1984; treas. Chgo. Econ. Rsch. Assocs.; rsch. assoc. Econs. Rsch. Ctr.-NORC, 1985—; cons. in field; cons. Chgo. Urban League, 1978-86; mem. status Black Ams. com. NRC; lectr. in field.; hon. prof. U. Tucuman, Argentina, 1998, Hangzhou U. Sci. and Tech., Wuhan, China, 2001. Editor Jour. Polit. Economy, 1981-87; assoc. editor Jour. Econometrics, 1977-83, Jour. Labor Econs., 1983—, Econs. Revs., 1987—, Rev. of Econs. and Statistics, 1994—, Jour. Econ. Perspectives, 1989-96, Labor Econs., 1992—; author: (with B. Singer and G. Tsiang) Lecture Notes on Longitudinal Analysis, 1994; editor: (with B. Singer), Longitudinal Analysis of Labor Market Data, 1985; (with E. Leamer) Handbook of Econometrics, Vol. 5, Incentives in Govt. Bureaucracies: A Study of Performance Standards And Their Effects, The Economic Approach to Program Evaluation; Am. editor Rev. Econ. Studies, 1982-85; contbr. articles to profl. jours. Founding faculty and curriculum com. U. Chgo. Harris Sch. Pub. Policy. Recipient Louis Benezet Alumni prize Colo. Coll., 1985, Nobel Prize Economics, 2000; J.S. Guggenheim Found. fellow, 1978-79, Social Sci. Rsch. Coun. fellow, 1977-78, Ctr. for Advanced Study in Behavioral Scis. fellow, 1978-79. Fellow Am. Bar Found. (sr., rsch. affiliate 1989-91, sr. rsch. fellow 1991—), Econometric Soc. (mem. coun. 2001—), Am. Acad. Arts and Scis., Am. Statis. Assn.; mem. Nat. Acad. Scis. Am. Econ. Assn. (exec. com. 2000—, John Bates Clerk prize 1983), Midwest Econs. Assn. (pres.-elect 1996-97, pres. 1997-98), Am. Statis. Assn., Indsl. Rels. Rsch. Assn., Econ. Sci. Assn. (founder), Phi Beta Kappa. Home: 4807 S Greenwood Ave Chicago IL 60615-1913 Office: U Chgo Dept Econs 1126 E 59th St Chicago IL 60637-1580 E-mail: jjh@uchicago.edu.

HEDBERG, PAUL CLIFFORD, broadcasting executive; b. Cokato, Minn., May 28, 1939; s. Clifford L. and Florence (Erenberg) H.; m. Juliet Ann Schubert, Dec. 30, 1962; children: Mark, Ann. Student, Hamline U., 1959-60, U. Minn., 1960-62. Program dir. Sta. KRIB, Mason City, Iowa, 1957-58, Sta. WMIN, Mpls., 1959; staff announcer Time-Life broadcast Sta. WTCN-AM-TV, 1959-61, Crowell Collier Sta. KDWB, St. Paul, 1961-62; founder, pres. Sta. KBEW, Minn., 1963-81; founder, owner Sta. KQAD and KLQL-FM, Luverne, 1971-88; co-founder Sta. KMRS, KKOK-FM, Morris, 1956-94; pres. Sta. KMRS-AM, KKOK-FM, 1974-94; founder, pres. Courtney Clifford Inc., Mpls., 1977-79; founder, owner Market Quoters Inc., Blue Earth, 1974-96; pres. Complete Commodity Options Inc., 1977-91; pres., owner Sta. KEEZ-FM, Mankato, Minn., 1977-92; founder, pres. Sta. KUOO-FM, Spirit Lake, Iowa, 1984-99; owner Sta. KRIB and KLSS-FM, Mason City, 1984-97; owner, pres. Sta. KAYL-AM-FM, Storm Lake, 1990-99; pres. KLGA AM-FM, Algona, 1993-99; CEO Hedberg Broadcasting Group, Blue Earth, 1976-99; pres. KSOU AM-FM, Sioux Center, 1996-99. Bd. dirs. Minn. Good Roads, v.p., 1976-79, pres., 1979-81; bd. dirs. Blue Earth Indsl. Svcs. Corp., pres., 1970-76; dir. Spirit Lake Industries; mem. affiliates bd. NBC Radio Network, 1990-95, chmn., 1991-95; pres. CEO Arnolds Park (Iowa) Amusement Park, 1990-95; founder KUQQ-FM, Spirit Lake-Milford, Iowa, 1996-99, KIHK-FM Rock Valley, Iowa, 1997-99; founder, developer Bridgewater Devel., Spirit Lake, Iowa, 1999. Mem. Iowa Gt. Lakes Airport Commn., 1986-92; bd. dirs. Pavek Mus. Wonderful Wireless, St. Louis Park, Minn., 1987—. Recipient Disting. Service award Blue Earth Jaycees, 1971 Mem. Nat. Assn. Broadcasters (bd. dirs. 1985-89, 93-95), Minn. Assn. Broadcasters (radio bd. dirs. 1975-86, v.p. 1980-81, pres. 1983-84), Minn. AP Broadcasters (pres. 1966, bd. dirs. 1976-78), Iowa Broadcasters Assn. (Broadcaster of Yr. 1998), Iowa Lakes C. of C. (bd. dirs. 1985-86), Blue Earth C. of C. (pres. 1967, Leadership Recognition award 1967), Gredeh L.C. (founder 1995—), Masons, Shriners. Lutheran. Home: 4400 Gulf Shore Blvd N Naples FL 34103-2216 Office: Bridgewater Devel Office PO Box 157 Spirit Lake IA 51360-0157

HEDEEN, RODNEY A. manufacturing executive; BS in Indsl. Tech., U. Wis.; MBA, U. Louisville. With GE, Louisville, Hillenbrand Industries, Batesville, Ind., Cummins Engine Co., Columbus; from sr. v.p. mfg./distgn. to pres. bus. sys. divsn. Reynolds & Reynolds, Dayton, Ohio, 1987—97, pres. bus. sys. divsn., 1997—2000; pres., CEO The Relizon Co., 2000—. Bd. dirs. Dayton Area chpt. ARC. Mem. Internat. Bus. Forms Inst. (bd. dirs. N.Am. and internat. bd., mem. found. bd.). Office: Relizon 220 E Monument Dayton OH 45402-1223

HEDGE, H. KAY, state senator; b. Rose Hill, Iowa, Apr. 2, 1928; m. Alleen Hedge. Student, U. Iowa. Farmer; U.S. senator from Iowa, 1988—. Mem. Fremont United Meth. Ch., Iowa. Mem. Iowa Soybean Assn., Iowa Corn Growers, Iowa Cattlemen's Assn., Mahaska County Pork Prodrs., Mahaska County Farm Bur., Oskaloosa C. of C., Am. Legion. Republican. Home: 3208 335th St Fremont IA 52561-9796 Office: State Capitol Dist 48 3 9th And Grand Des Moines IA 50319-0001 E-mail: kay_hedge@legis.state.ia.us.

HEDIEN, WAYNE EVANS, retired insurance company executive; b. Evanston, Ill., Feb. 15, 1934; s. George L. and Edith P. (Chalstrom) H.; m. Colette Johnston, Aug. 24, 1963; 3 children. BSME, Northwestern U., 1956, MBA, 1957. Engr. Cook Electric Co., Skokie, Ill., 1957-64; bus. mgr. Preston Sci., Inc., Anaheim, Calif., 1964-66; security analyst Allstate Ins. Co., Northbrook, Ill., 1966-70, portfolio mgr., 1970-73, asst. treas., 1973-78, v.p., treas., 1978-80, sr. v.p., treas., 1980-83, exec. v.p., chief fin. officer, 1983-85, vice chmn., chief fin. officer, 1986, pres., 1986-89, chmn., 1989-94, The Allstate Corp., 1993-94, also bd. dirs.; retired, 1994. Mem. adv. coun. Kellogg Grad. Sch. Mgmt., Northwestern U.; bd. dirs. The PMI Group, Inc., Field Mus. Natural History, Morgan Stanley Dean Witter Funds. Mem. Comml. Club Chgo. Office: WEH Assocs 5750 Old Orchard Rd Ste 530 Skokie IL 60077-1081

HEDLUND, RONALD, baritone; b. Mpls., May 12, 1934; s. Cyril and Mildred H.; m. Barbara Smith, Nov. 12, 1974; children: Eric, Alexander. BA, Hamline U.; MusM, Ind. U. Mem. faculty dept. music U. Ill., 1970-74, 83—; bass soloist, instr. classical music seminar Eisenstadt and Vienna, Austria. Singing voice cons. Carle Clinic Speech Ctr., Urbana, 1994—. Appeared throughout U.S. including opera cos. of San Francisco, Chgo., Houston, Miami, Seattle, Dallas, Ft. Worth, Phila., Washington, Omaha, Santa Fe, Lake George, Boston, N.Y.C. Opera, Met. Opera Nat. Co., New Orleans, Spoleto Festival, Edinburgh Festival, Vancouver Opera, Conn. Opera, Aspen Festival, R.I. Opera, Chgo. Opera Theater, Opera Theatre St. Louis, Utah Opera, Peoria Civic Opera, Ill. Opera Theatre; soloist with numerous orchs., recitals throughout U.S. Served with USNR, 1958-63. Office: String Soc Artists 505 Eliot Dr Urbana IL 61801-6727

HEDREN, PAUL LESLIE, national park administrator, historian; b. New Ulm, Minn., Nov. 12, 1949; s. Thomas Harry and Muriel Mary (Kunz) H.; m. Janeen Margaret Wolcott, June 19, 1974 (div. 1997); children: Ethne Olivia, Whitney Elizabeth. BA, St. Cloud State Coll., 1972. Park ranger, historian Ft. Laramie (Wyo.) Nat. Hist. Site, 1971-76; historian Big Hole Nat. Battlefield, Wisdom, Mont., 1976-78; chief ranger, historian Golden Spike Nat. Hist. Site, Brigham City, Utah, 1978-84; supt. Fort Union Trading Post Nat. Hist. Site, Williston, N.D., 1984-97, Niobrara/Mo. Nat. Scenic Riverways, O'Neill, Nebr., 1997—. Author: First Scalp for Custer, 1980, With Crook in the Black Hills, 1985, Fort Laramie in 1876, 1988 (Best Book of 1988 Wyo. State Hist. Soc.); editor: Campaigning with King, 1991 (Merit award State Hist. Soc. Wis. 1991), The Great Sioux War 1876-77, 1991, Traveler's Guide to the Great Sioux War, 1996; contbr. articles to profl. jours. Bd. dirs. Conv. and Vis. Bur., Williston, 1984-96, pres., 1994-96. Mem. Co. Mil. Historians, Western History Assn. (mem. coun. 1990-93). Avocations: writing, lecturing on Am. western history. Office: Niobrara/Mo NSR PO Box 591 Oneill NE 68763-0591

HEDRICK, LARRY WILLIS, airport executive; b. Newton, Kans., Dec. 23, 1939; s. A.C. and Goldie (Kerns) H.; m. Nancy Cashin, July 21, 1962; children: Christina, Kathleen, Thomas. BL, U. LaSalle, Chgo., 1973. Lic. airport mgr., Mass, pilot and instrument technician. Airport mgr., dir. civil def. Newton City-County Airport, 1966-73; airport mgr. Barnes Mcpl. Airport, Mass., 1973-77, Niagara Falls Internat. Airport, 1977-81, Greater Buffalo (N.Y.) Internat. Airport, 1981-87; appointed airport adminstr. Pt. Columbus Internat. Airport, Columbus, Ohio, 1987-91; appointed exec. dir. Columbus Airport Authority, 1991-2000. Founding bd. mem. Airline Passengers of Am., 1987; guest speaker various univs. and airport confs. Bd. dirs. Greater Columbus Conv. and Visitors Bur., 1992; past squadron commdr. CAP Kans. Wing. With USN, 1958-62. Mem. Am. Assn. Airport Execs. (accredited 1973, nat. sec. 1982, treas. bd. dirs. 1983, 1st v.p. 1985, 2d v.p. 1984, nat. pres. 1986-87, Disting. Svc. award 1994), Nat. Fire Protection Assn. (airport industry's only rep.), Mass. Airport Mgmt. Assn. (pres. 1975-76). Office: Columbus Airport Authority 295 Crabapple Drive Howard OH 43028

HEFFELFINGER, THOMAS BACKER, lawyer; b. Mpls., Feb. 13, 1948; BA in History, Stanford U., 1970; JD, U. Minn., 1975. Bar: Minn. 1976, U.S. Dist. Ct. Minn. 1977, U.S. Ct. Appeals (8th cir.) 1983. Law clk. Office of the Hennepin County Atty. , 1974-76; asst. atty. juvenile divsn. Office of the Hennepin County Atty., 1976, asst. atty. criminal divsn. trial sect., 1977-82, asst. atty. major offender unit, 1978-81, supr. burglary unit, 1981-82; asst. U.S. atty. criminal divsn. Dist. Minn., U.S. Dept. Justice, 1982-88, atty. white collar crime sect., 1982-85, supr. narcotics and firemans sect., 1985-86; ptnr. Opperman Heins & Paquin, 1988-91; U.S. atty. Dist. Minn., U.S. Dept. Justice, 1991-93, 2001—; ptnr. Bowman and Brooke, 1993—2000, Best & Flanagan, 2000—01. Contbr. articles to profl. jours. Candidate Hennepin County Atty., 1986; bd. dirs. Mpls. Chpt. ARC, 1987—; mem. Hennepin County Task Force on Youth and Drugs, 1987-88, Minn. Ho. of Reps. Rep. Caucus Drug Task Force, 1989-90, Minn. Commn. on Violent Crime, 1991; chmn. Minn. Commn. on Jud. Selection, 1990-91; lectr. in field. Mem. Fed. Bar Assn., Minn. Bar Assn., Hennepin County Bar Assn. Office: 600 US Courthouse 300 S 4th St Minneapolis MN 55415

HEFFERNAN, NATHAN STEWART, retired state supreme court chief justice; b. Frederic, Wis., Aug. 6, 1920; s. Jesse Eugene and Pearl Eva (Kaump) H.; m. Dorothy Hillemann, Apr. 27, 1946; children: Katie (Mrs. Howard Thomas), Michael, Thomas. BA, U. Wis., 1942, LLB, 1948; postgrad. in bus., Harvard U. Sch. Bus. Adminstrn., 1943-44; LLD (hon.), Lakeland Coll., 1995; LLD, U. Wis., 1999. Bar: Wis. 1948, U.S. Dist. Ct. (we. dist.) Wis. 1948, U.S. Dist. Ct. (ea. dist.) Wis. 1950, U.S. Ct. Appeals (7th cir.) 1960, U.S. Supreme Ct. 1960. Assoc. firm Schubring, Ryan, Peterson & Sutherland, Madison, Wis., 1948-49; practice in Sheboygan, 1949-59; partner firm Buchen & Heffernan, 1951-59; counsel Wis. League Municipalities, 1949; research asst. to gov. Wis., 1949; asst. dist. atty. Sheboygan County, 1951-53; city atty. City of Sheboygan, 1953-59; dep. atty. gen. State of Wis., 1959-62; U.S. atty. Western Dist. Wis., 1962-64; justice Wis. Supreme Ct., 1964—, chief justice, 1983-95. Lectr. mcpl. corps., 1961-64, appellate procedure and practice U. Wis. Law Sch., 1971-83; faculty Appellate Judges Seminar, Inst. Jud. Adminstrn., NYU, 1972-87; former mem. Nat. Council State Ct. Reps., chmn., 1976-77; ex-officio dir. Nat. Ctr. State Cts., 1976-77, mem. adv. bd. appellate justice project; former mem. Wis. Jud. Planning Com.; chmn. Wis. Appellate Practice and Procedure Com., 1975-76; mem. exec. com. Wis. Jud. Conf.,

1978—, chmn., 1983; pres. City Attys. Assn., 1958-59; chair Citizens Panel on Election Reform; co-chair Equal Justice Coalition. Wis. chmn. NCCJ, 1966-67; past exec. bd. Four Lakes Coun., Boy Scouts Am.; gen. chmn. Wis. Dem. Conv., 1960, 61; mem. Wis. Found.; bd. dirs. Inst. Jud. Adminstrn.; visitors U. Wis. Law Sch., 1970-83, chmn., 1973-76; past mem. corp. bd. Meth. Hosp.; former curator Wis. Hist. Soc., curator emeritus, 1990; trustee Wis. Meml. Union, Wis. State Libr., William Freeman Vilas Trust Estate; v.p. U. Wis. Meml. Union Bldg. Assn.; former deacon Conglist. Ch. Lt. (s.g.) USNR, 1942-46, ETO, PTO. Recipient Disting. Svc. award NCCJ, 1968, Ann. Disting. Svc. award Wis. Mediation Assn., 1995, Lifetime Achievement award Milw. Bar Assn., 1995, Disting. Svc. award Dem. Party Sheboygan County, 1995; Disting. Jud. fellow Marquette U. Law Sch., 1996. Fellow Am. Bar Found. (life), Inst. for Jud. Adminstrn. (hon., bd. dirs., mem. faculty seminar), Wis. Bar Assn. (chmn. Wis. bar com. study on legal edn. 1995-96, hon. chmn. Equal Justice Coalition 1997—, Goldberg award for disting. svc.), Wis. Bar Found.; mem. ABA (past mem. spl. com. on adminstrn. criminal justice, mem. com. fed.-state delineation of jurisdiction, jud. adminstrn. com. on appellate ct., com. appellate time standards), Am. Law Inst. (life, adv. com. on complex litigation), Dane County Bar Assn., Sheboygan County Bar Assn., Am. Judicature Soc. (dir. 1977-80, chmn. program com. 1979-81), Wis. Law Alumni Assn. (bd. dirs., Disting. Alumni Svc. award 1989), Nat. Conf. Chief Justices (bd. dirs.), Nat. Assn. Ct. Mgmt., Wis. Rivers Alliance (bd. dirs.), Order of Coif, Iron Cross, U. Club (Madison, Wis.), Phi Kappa Phi, Phi Delta Phi. Clubs: Madison Lit. (pres. 1979-80); Harvard (Milw.); Harvard Bus. Sch. (Wis.). Home: 17 Thorstein Veblen Pl Madison WI 53705

HEFNER, CHRISTIE ANN, multi-media entertainment executive; b. Chgo., Nov. 8, 1952; d. Hugh Marston and Mildred Marie (Williams) H. BA summa cum laude in English and Am. Lit., Brandeis U., 1974. Freelance journalist, Boston, 1974-75; spl. asst. to chmn. Playboy Enterprises, Inc., Chgo., 1975-78, v.p., 1978-82, bd. dirs., 1979—, vice chmn., 1986-88, pres., 1982-88, COO, 1984-88, chmn., CEO, 1988—. Bd. dirs. Playboy Found.-Playboy Enterprises, Inc., Ill. chpt. ACLU, Mag. Pubs. Assn. Bd. dirs. Nat. Coalition on Crime and Delinquency, Creative Coalition, Rush-Presbyn.-St. Lukes Med. Ctr., MarketWatch.com, Inc., Canyon Ranch Bus. Com. for the Arts, NCTA Diversity Com. Recipient Agness Underwood award, L.A. chpt. Women in Comm., 1984, Founders award, Midwest Women's Ctr., 1986, Human Rights award, Am. Jewish Com., 1987, Harry Kalven Freedom of Expression award, ACLU, Ill., 1987, Spirit of Life award, City of Hope, 1988, Eleanor Roosevelt award, Internat. Platform Assn., 1990, Will Rogers Meml. award, Beverly Hills C. of C. and Civic Assn., 1993, Champion of Freedom award, ADL, 2000, Bettie B. Port Humanitarian award, Mt. Sinai, 2001, John Wayne Cancer Ctr. award, 2001, Christopher Reeve 1st Amendment award, Creative Coalition, 2001, Vanguard award, NCTA, 2002. Mem. Brandeis Nat. Women's Com. (life), Com. of 200, Young Pres. Orgn., Chgo. Network, Voters for Choice, Phi Beta Kappa. Democrat. Office: Playboy Enterprises Inc 680 N Lake Shore Dr Chicago IL 60611-4455

HEFNER, THOMAS L. real estate company executive; BA, Purdue U. With Continental Bank, Ind. Nat. Bank, Ind. Mortgage Corp.; mng. gen. ptnr. Duke Assocs., 1981-93; pres., CEO Duke Realty Investments (merged with Weeks Corp.), 1993-99; chmn., CEO Duke-Weeks Realty Corp., Indpls., 1999—. Bd. dirs. Project e. Mem. dean's adv. coun. Krannert Sch. Bus., Purdue U. Mem. Nat. Assn. Real Estate Investments Trusts (bg. govs.), Ctrl. Ind. Corp. Partnership (bd. dirs.), Nature Conservancy Ind. (bd. dirs.). Office: Ste 1200 8888 Keystone Crossing Indianapolis IN 46240

HEFT, JAMES LEWIS, academic administrator, theology educator; b. Cleve., Feb. 20, 1943; s. Berl Ramsey and Hazel Mary (Miller) H. BA in Philosophy, U. Dayton, 1965, BS in Edn., 1966; MA in Theology, U. Toronto, 1971, PhD in Hist. Theology, 1977. Prof. theology U. Dayton, Ohio, chmn. religious studies dept., 1983-89, provost, 1989-96, prof. faith and culture, chancellor, 1996—, lectr.; bd. dirs. Inst. Ednl. Mgmt., Harvard U., 1989. Author: John XXII (1316-1334) and Papal Teaching Authority, 1986; editor: Faith and the Intellectual Life, 1996; contbr. numerous articles to profl. jours. Trustee U. Dayton, 1970-77; bd. dirs. Nat. Conf., 1990—; trustee St. Mary's Univ., San Antonio, 1995—, Greater Dayton Pub. TV, 1995-97. U. Toronto scholar, 1969-77; recipient Excellence in Tchg. award U. Dayton, 1983, 1st Pl. prize Cath. Press Assn., 1990. Mem. Nat. Cath. Edn. Assn. (bd. dirs. 1994-95), Coll. Theology Soc., Cath. Theol. Soc. Am., Assn. Cath. Colls. and Univs. (bd. dirs. 1993-95, vice chmn. 1996—), Mariological Soc. Am. Roman Cath., Collegium (bd. dirs. 1990-94). Avocation: theatre. Office: U Dayton 300 College Park Ave Dayton OH 45469-0001

HEFTY, THOMAS R. insurance company executive; b. 1947; BA, U. Wis., 1968; MA, Johns Hopkins U., 1969; JD, U. Wis., 1973. Atty. Fed. Trade Commn., 1973-74, CMI Investment, 1974-76; asst. gen. counsel Sentry Ins., 1976-79; dep. commr. Wis. Ins. Commn., 1979-82; v.p., sec., gen. counsel Blue Cross Shield United of Wis., 1982-84, sr. v.p., 1984-87, pres., CEO, 1987—; pres. United Wis. Services. Office: Blue Cross Shield United of WI 401 W Michigan St Milwaukee WI 53203-2804

HEGARTY, MARY FRANCES, lawyer; b. Chgo., Dec. 19, 1950; d. James E. and Frances M. (King) H. BA, DePaul U., 1972, JD, 1975. Bar: Ill. 1975, U.S. Dist. Ct. (no. dist.) Ill. 1976, U.S. Supreme Ct. 1980. Ptnr. Lannon & Hegarty, Park Ridge, Ill., 1975-80; pvt. practice, 1980—. Dir. Legal Assistance Found. Chgo., 1983—. Mem. revenue study com. Chgo. City Coun. Fin. Com., 1983; mem. Sole Source Rev. Panel, City of Chgo., 1984; pres. Hist. Pullman Found., Inc., 1984-85; apptd. Park Ridge Zoning Bd., 1993-94. Mem. Ill. State Bar Assn. (real estate coun. 1980-84), Chgo. Bar Assn., Women's Bar Assn. Ill. (pres. 1983-84), NW Suburban Bar Assn., Park Ridge Women Entrepreneurs, Chgo. Athletic Assn. (pres. 1992-93), Park Ridge C. of C. (pres. 2002-). Democrat. Roman Catholic. Office: 301 W Touhy Ave Park Ridge IL 60068-4204

HEGEL, CAROLYN MARIE, farmer, farm bureau executive; b. Lagro, Ind., Apr. 19, 1940; d. Ralph H. and Mary Lucile (Rudig) Lynn; m. Tom Lee Hegel, June 3, 1962. Student pub. schs., Columbia City, Ind. Bookkeeper Huntington County Farm Bur. Co-op, Inc., Ind., 1959-67, office mgr., 1967-70; twp. woman leader Wabash County (Ind.) Farm Bur., Inc., 1970-73, county woman leader, 1973-76; dist. woman leader Ind. Farm Bur., Inc., Indpls., 1976-80, 2d v.p., bd. dirs., 1980—, chmn. women's com., 1980—, exec. com., 1988—. Farmer Andrews, Ind., 1962—; dir. Farm Bur. Ins. Co., Indpls., 1980—, exec. com., 1988; spkr. in field. Women in the Field columnist Hoosier Farmer mag., 1980—. Mem. rural task force Great Lakes States Econ. Devel. Commn., 1987-88, Ind. Farm Bur. Svc. Co., 1980—; bd. dirs. Ind. farm Bur. Found., Indpls., 1980—, Ind. Inst. Agr., Food and Nutrition, Indpls., 1982—, Ind. 4-H Found., Lafayette, 1983-86; mem. Ind. Rural Health Adv. Coun., 1993-96; com. mem. Hoosier Homestead Award Cert. Com., Indpls., 1980—; organizer farm divsn. Wabash County Am. Cancer Soc. Fund Dr., 1974; Sunday sch. tchr., bd. dir. children's activities Bethel United Meth. Ch., 1965—, pres. Bethel United Meth. Women, Lagro, 1975-81; bd. dirs. N.E. Ind. Kidney Found., 1984—, Nat. Kidney Found. of Ind., 1985-89, v.p., 1986—; active Leadership Am. Program, 1988. Named one of Outstanding Farm Woman of Yr. Country Woman Mag., 1987; recipient State 4-H Home Econs. award Ind. 4-H, 1960. Mem.: Am. Farm Bur. Fedn. (midwest rep. to women's com. 1986—93), Producers Mktg. Assn. (bd. dirs. 1980—94), Ind. Agrl. Mktg. Assn. 1980—94, Women in Comm., Inc. Republican. Home: 3330 N 650 E Andrews IN 46702-9616 Office: Ind Farm Bur Inc PO Box 1290 225 S East St Indianapolis IN 46202-4058 E-mail: chegel@infarmbureau.com.

HEGEMAN, DANIEL JAY, state legislator; b. Cosby, Mo., Mar. 4, 1963; s. Donald Jay and Margaret Joan (Kowitz) H.; m. Francine Marie Walker, 1990; children: Hannah Marie, Joseph Daniel, Heidi Joan. BSA, U. Mo. Columbia. State rep. Dist. 6 Mo. State Rep., 1991-92, state rep. Dist. 5, 1992—. Treas. Hegeman Farm, Inc., 1988—. Mem. NW Mo. Holstein Assn. (v.p. 1991-92, pres. 1993-94, bd. dirs. 1994-95), Mid-Am. Dairymen, Inc. Dist. 14 (v.p. 1991-92), Andrew County Ext. Coun. (pres. 1990), Andrew County Farm Bur., Buchanan & Andrew County Dairy Herd Improvement Assn. (treas.), Cosby Masonic Lodge 600 (Worshipful Master 1989-90); Alpha Zeta, Omicron Delta Kappa, Alpha Gamma Rho.

HEGENDERFER, JONITA SUSAN, public relations executive; b. Chgo., Mar. 18, 1944; d. Clifford Lincoln and Cornelia Anna (Larson) Hazzard; m. Gary William Hegenderfer, Mar. 12, 1971 (dec. 1978). BA, Purdue U., 1965; postgrad., Calif. State U., Long Beach, 1966-67, Northwestern U., 1969-70. Tchr. English, Long Beach (Calif.) Schs., 1965-68; editl. asst. Playboy Mag., Chgo., 1968-70; comms. specialist AMA, 1970-72; v.p. Home Data, Hinsdale, Ill., 1972-75; mktg. mgr. Olympic Savs. & Loan, Berwyn, 1975-79; sr. v.p. Golin/Harris Comms., Chgo., 1979-89; pres. JSH & A, 1989—. Bd. dirs. Chgo. Internat. Film Festival, 1989, 90. Author: Slim Guide to Spas, 1984, (video) PR Guide for Chicago LSCs, 1991; editor: Financial Information National Directory, 1972; contbr. articles to profl. jours. Co-chmn. pub. rels. com. Am. Cancer Soc., Chgo., 1984; mem. com. March of Dimes, Chgo., 1986; mem. pub. rels. com. Girl Scouts Chgo., 1989-90, bd. dirs., 1994-95; bd. dirs. Greater DuPage Women's Bus. Coun., 1992-93, Girl Scouts U.S. DuPage County, 1994—; vol. ctr. adv. com. United Way, Chgo., 1990-93; mem. cmty. svc. com. Publicity Club Chgo., 1990—. Recipient 5 Golden Trumpet awards Publicity Club Chgo., 1983, 96, 94, Silver Trumpet awards, 1984, 86, 88, Spectra awards Internat. Assn. Bus. Communicators, 1984, 85, 87, Gold Quill aard, 1985, Bronze Anvil award Pub. Rels. Soc. Am., 1985, award Nat. Creativity in Pub. Rels. award, 1995; named Influential Woman in Bus., 1998. Mem. Am. Mktg. Assn., Publicity Club Chgo., Pub. Rels. Soc. Am., Chgo. Women in Pub., Nat. Assn. Women Bus. Owners, DuPage Area Assn. Bus. Tech. (bd. dirs. 1997), Coun. on Fgn. Rels., Met. Women's Forum, Cinema Chgo. (bd. dirs. 1988-89). Avocations: travel, photography. Office: JSH & A Comms IS 450 Summit #320 Oakbrook Terrace IL 60181 E-mail: jonni@jsha.com.

HEGER, MARTIN L. bank executive; With Nat. Bank Detroit, Detroit, 1969-78, Fed. Home Loan Bank of Indpls., 1979-92, pres., 1992—. Office: Fed Home Loan Bank Indpls PO Box 60 8250 Woodfield Crossing Bld Indianapolis IN 46206

HEIBERG, ROBERT ALAN, lawyer; b. St. Cloud, Minn., June 29, 1943; s. Rasmus Adolph and Irene (Shaffer) H.; m. Sharon Ann Olson, Aug. 2, 1969; children— Eric Robert, Mark Alan, Maren Ann B.A. summa cum laude, U. Minn., 1965, J.D. summa cum laude, 1968. Bar: Minn. 1968. Law clk. to assoc. justice Minn. Supreme Ct., 1968-69; assoc. Dorsey & Whitney, Mpls., 1969-73, ptnr., 1974—; instr. Law Sch., U. Minn., 1968-72, instr. legal assts. program, 1972-77. Articles editor Minn. Law Rev., 1967-68 Mem. adv. com. U. Minn. Legal Assts. Program, 1977-84, bd. visitors Law Sch., 1991-96. Mem. ABA (sect. real property, probate and trust law), Minn. Bar Assn. (chmn. com. on legal assts. 1979), Hennepin County Bar Assn., Am. Rose Soc. (accredited judge 1996), Order of Coif, Phi Beta Kappa Republican. Lutheran Home: 4510 Wooddale Ave Minneapolis MN 55424-1137 Office: Dorsey & Whitney 50 S 6th St Ste 1500 Minneapolis MN 55402-1498 E-mail: heiberg.robert@dorseylaw.com.

HEICHEL, GARY HAROLD, crop sciences educator; b. Park Falls, Wis., Nov. 9, 1940; s. Harold H. and Bernice I. (Comp) H.; m. Iris Fehl Martin, Apr. 24, 1988. BS, Iowa State U., 1962; MS, Cornell U., 1964, PhD, 1968; D of Natural Scis. (hon.), Swiss Fed. Inst. Tech., Zurich, 1998. Asst. plant physiologist Conn. Agrl. Expt. Stat., New Haven, 1968-73, assoc. plant physiologist, 1973-76, plant physiologist, 1976, USDA Agrl. Rsch. Svc., St. Paul, 1976-90, acting rsch. leader, 1988-90; head agronomy dept. U. Ill., Urbana, 1990-95, interim head plant pathology dept., 1994-95, head crop scis. dept., 1995—. Adj. prof. agronomy U. Minn., 1976-90; program mgr. USDA Competitive Rsch. Grants Office, 1981. Contbr. chpts. to books, articles to profl. jours. Pres., mem. adminstrv. bd. Cheshire, Conn. United Meth. Ch., 1973-76, v.p. Cheshire Land Trust, 1975-76. Named Civil Servant of Yr., Twin Cities Fed. Exec. Bd., St. Paul, 1984. Fellow AAAS (chair sect. 0 1997-98), Crop Sci. Soc. Am. (pres. 1991-92, award 1987), Am. Soc. Agronomy (exec. com. 1990-92, pres. north ctrl. sect. 1991-93, pres. 1997-98, Svc. award 2001), Am. Soc. Plant Physiologists (trustee 1988-90), Urbana Rotary (bd. dirs. 1997-99). Avocations: classical music, reading, hiking, gardening. Office: U Ill Dept Crop Scis 1102 S Goodwin Ave AW-101 Urbana IL 61801-4730 E-mail: gheichel@uiuc.edu.

HEIDELBERGER, KATHLEEN PATRICIA, physician; b. Bklyn., Apr. 13, 1939; d. William Cyprian and Margaret Bernadette (Hughes) H.; m. Charles William Davenport, Oct. 8, 1977. B.S. cum laude, Coll. Misericordia, 1961; M.D. cum laude, Woman's Med. Coll. Pa., 1965. Intern Mary Hitchcock Hosp., Hanover, N.H., 1965-66, resident in pathology, 1966-70; mem. faculty U. Mich., Ann Arbor, 1970—, assoc. prof. pathology, 1976-79, prof., 1979—. Mem. Am. Soc. Clin. Pathologists, U.S.-Can. Acad. Pathology, Soc. for Pediatric Pathology, Coll. Am. Pathologists. Office: U Mich Box 0054 Dept Pathology UH 2G/332 Ann Arbor MI 48109

HEIGAARD, WILLIAM STEVEN, state senator; b. Gardar, N.D., May 18, 1938; s. Oliver and Gaufey (Erickson) H.; m. Paula Geston, 1960; children: Jody, Rebecca, Sara. BA, U. N.D., 1961, JD, 1967. Bar: N.D. 1967. Asst. atty. gen., Bismarck, N.D., 1970-75; mem. N.D. Ho. of Reps., 1980-81, N.D. State Senate, 1981-92, majority leader, 1987-92; chmn. N.D. State Dem. Party, 2000—. 1st lt. U.S. Army, 1962-64. Mem. Am. Legion, Eagles, Elks, Phi Delta Phi. Lutheran. Office: 1116 N 14th St Bismarck ND 58501-4201 also: ND Democratic Party 1902 E Divide Ave Bismarck ND 58501-2301

HEIKES, KEITH, science administrator; b. 1957; With Ralston Purina, Chilicothe, Mo., 1978—81, Kabsu, Inc., Manhattan, Kans., 1981—90, Noba Inc., Tiffin, Ohio, 1990—, now COO; v.p. internat. programs 21st Century Genetics; with Coop. Resources Internat., Shawano, Wis. Office: Coop Resources Internat 100 Mbc Dr Shawano WI 54166-6095

HEILICSER, BERNARD JAY, emergency physician; b. Bklyn., Jan. 19, 1947; s. Murray and Esther (Dubrow) H.; m. Marcia Cherry, June 2, 1976; children: Micah, Seth, Jacob. BA, SUNY, Binghamton, 1968; MS, Hahnemann Med. Coll., Phila., 1971; DO, Coll. Osteo. Medicine/Surgery, Des Moines, 1976. Diplomate Am. Bd. Emergency Medicine. Instr. anatomy and physiology U. Pa. and Hahnemann Med. Coll., Phila., 1971-73; staff physician Va. Inst. Tech., Blacksburg, 1977-78; asst. prof. emergency medicine Chgo. Coll. Osteo. Medicine, 1979; emergency physician St. Margaret Hosp., Hammond, Ind., 1979-83, Michael Reese Med. Ctr., Chgo., 1989-91, Ingalls Hosp., Harvey, Ill., 1983—; project med. dir. South Cook County Emergency Med. Svc., 1984—. Mem. faculty Chgo. Osteo. Med. Ctr., 1987—; faculty trauma nurse specialist St. James Hosp., Chicago Heights, Ill., 1980—; preceptor nurse practitioners Purdue U., Hammond, 1981—; fellow MacLean Ctr. Clin. Med. Ethics, U. Chgo., 1993-94; chmn. ethics com., hosp. med. ethicist Ingalls Hosp., Harvey, Ill., 1994—; cons. The Nat. Bd. Osteo. Med. Examiners, Harvey, 1994—, ethics com. Am. Coll. Osteo. Emergency Physicians, 1997—; chmn. disaster com. Ill. Region 7 Emergency Med. Svcs./Trauma, 1997—; chair Ill. Region VII EMS Adv. Coun., 2001—; mem. adj. faculty Coll. Health Professions, Govs. State U., 1999—; mem. exec. coun. Ill. Mobile Emergency Response Team, 1999—; med. advisor Combined Agy. Response Team, 1999—. Vol. fireman Flossmoor (Ill.) Fire Dept., 1985—, Matteson (Ill.) Fire Dept., 1980—; chmn. Ill. Regional 7 EMS Adv. Coun. Fellow Am. Coll. Emergency Physicians; mem. Am. Osteo. Assn., Nat. Assn. Emergency Med. Svcs. Physicians, Am. Coll. Osteo. Emergency Physicians (ethics com. 1996—), Nat. Assn. Emergency Med. Technicians, Prehosp. Care Providers Ill., Sigma Sigma Phi. Jewish. Avocations: running, basketball. Office: Ingalls Hosp One Ingalls Dr Harvey IL 60426

HEIMLICH, HENRY JAY, physician, surgeon, educator; b. Wilmington, Del., Feb. 3, 1920; s. Philip and Mary (Epstein) Heimlich; m. Jane Murray, June 3, 1951; children: Philip, Janet, Elisabeth. BA, Cornell U., 1941, MD, 1943; DSc (hon.) , Wilmington Coll., 1981, Adelphi U., 1982, Rider Coll., 1983, Alfred U., 1993. Diplomate Am. Bd. Surgery, Am. Bd. Thoracic Surgery. Intern Boston City Hosp., 1944; resident VA Hosp., Bronx, 1946—47, Mt. Sinai Hosp., N.Y.C., 1947—48, Bellevue Hosp., N.Y.C., 1948—49, Triboro Hosp., Jamaica, NY, 1949—50; attending surgeon divsn. surgery Montefiore Hosp., N.Y.C., 1950—69; dir. surgery Jewish Hosp., Cin., 1969—77; prof. advanced clin. scis. Xavier U., 1977—89; assoc. clin. prof. surgery U. Cin. Coll. Medicine, 1969—78. Pres. Heimlich Inst.; mem. Pres.'s Commn. on Heart Disease, Cancer and Stroke, 1965; pres. Nat. Cancer Found., 1963—68, bd. dirs., 1960—70; founder Heimlich Inst. Found. Author: Postoperative Care in Thoracic Surgery, 1962; author: (with M.O. Cantor, C.H. Lupton) Surgery of the Stomach, Duodenum and Diaphragm, Questions and Answers, 1965; contbr. chapters to books, articles to profl. jours.; prodr.(film): Esophageal Replacement with a Reversed Gastric Tube (Medaglione Di Bronzo Minerva, 1961), Reversed Gastric Tube Esophagoplasty Using Stapling Technique, How to Save a Choking Victim: The Heimlich Maneuver, 1976, 1982, How to Save a Drowning Victim: The Heimlich Maneuver, 1981, Stress Relief: The Heimlich Method, 1983, (video): Dr. Heimlich's Home First Aid Video, 1989 (Vira award, 1989); editl. bd. films Reporte's Medicos, 1962. Cmty. Devel. Found., 1967—70; Save the Chidlren FEdn., 1967—68; United Cancer Coun., 1967—70. Served to lt. (s.g.) USNR, 1944—46. Recipient Lasker award for Pub. Svc., Lasker Found., 1984, China-Burma-India Vets. Assn. Americanism award, 1988, 1st Heimlich Humanitarian award, Spirit of Am. Festival, 1994, Heimlich Inst. established in perpetuity by Deaconess Assns., Inc. Fellow: ACS (chpt. pres. 1964), Am. Coll. Gastroenterology, Am. Coll. Chest Physicians; mem.: AMA (cons. to jour.), Ctrl. Surg. Assn., Collegium INternat. Chirurgiae Digestive, Pan Am. Med. Assn., Am. Gastroent. Assn., Soc. Surgery Alimentary Tract, N.Y. Soc. Thoracic Surgery, Cin. Soc. Thoracic Surgery, Soc. Thoracic Surgeons (founding mem.). Achievements include development of Heimlich Operation (reversed gastric tube esophagoplasty) for replacement of esophagus;invention of Heimlich chest drain valve, Heimlich Micro-Trach (HMT) for COPD, emphysema and cystic fibrosis;development of Heimlich Maneuver to save lives of victims of food choking and drowning and prevents and overcomes asthma attacks (listed in Random House, Oxford Am. and Webster dictionaries);development of Computers for Peace, a program to maintain peace throughout world and A Caring World. Office: Heimlich Inst Found Deaconess Hosp 311 Straight St Cincinnati OH 45219-1018 E-mail: heimlich@iglou.com.

HEINEMAN, BEN WALTER, corporation executive; b. Wausau, Wis., Feb. 10, 1914; s. Walter Ben and Elsie Brunswick (Deutsch) H.; m. Natalie Goldstein, Apr. 17, 1935; children: Martha Heineman Pieper, Ben Walter. Student, U. Mich., 1930-33; LLB, Northwestern U., 1936; LLD (hon.), Lawrence Coll., 1959; LL.D. (hon.), Lake Forest Coll., 1966, Northwestern U., 1967; LHD, DePaul U., 1986. Bar: Ill. 1936. Pvt. practice law and govt. svc., Chgo., Washington, Algiers, 1936-56; chmn. bd. dirs. Four Wheel Drive Auto Co., 1954-57; chmn. C. & N.W. Ry. Co., 1956-72; founder, former chmn., CEO Northwest Industries, Inc., 1968-85. Dir., chmn. exec. com., bd. dirs. 1st Nat. Bank, Chgo.; chmn. orgn. com. First Chgo. Corp., 1965-86; Chmn. White House Conf. to Fulfill These Rights, 1966, Pres.'s Task Force on Govt. Orgn., 1966-67, Pres.'s Commn. Income Maintenance Programs, 1967-69 Life trustee U. Chgo.; chmn. Ill. Bd. Higher Edn., 1962-69; trustee, mem. investment com. Savs. and Profit Sharing Fund Sears Roebuck Employees, 1966-71; trustee, mem. exec. com., chmn. audit com. Rockefeller Found., 1972-78; life dir. Lyric Opera, Chgo.; life trustee Orchestral Assn.; sustaining fellow Art Inst. Chgo., 20th century acquisition com.; trustee emeritus The Corning (N.Y.) Glass Mus. Fellow ABA, AAAS, Am. Bar Found. (life); mem. Am. Law Inst. (life), Ill. Bar Assn., Chgo. Bar Assn., Ephraim Club (Wis.), Yacht Club, Mid-Am. Club, Chgo. Club, Wayfarers Club, Std. Club (life), Quadrangle Club, Comml. Club (life), Carlton Club, Order of Coif, Phi Delta Phi (hon.). Office: 180 E Pearson St Apt 4304 Chicago IL 60611-2171 E-mail: BWH@hmansr.net.

HEINEMAN, DAVID, state official; b. Falls City, Nebr., May 12, 1948; s. Jean Trevers and Irene Larkin H.; m. Sally Ganem, 1977. BS, U.S. Mil. Acad., 1970. Sales rep. Procter & Gamble, 1976-77; campaign mgr. Daub for Congress, 1977-78; dep. dir. Policy Rsch. Office, Nebr., 1979; dir. Nebr. State Rep. Exec. Com., 1979-81; chief of staff to Congressman Daub, 1983-88; office mgr. for Congressman Berenter, 1990-94; city councilman City of Fremont, Nebr., 1990-94; state treas. State of Nebr., 1995—. Decorated Army Commendation medal; recipient Outstanding Rep. Vol. award Douglas County Rep. Party, 1976, Outstanding Young Am. award Jaycees, 1980. Mem. Nat. Assn. State Treas. (pres. 1999-2000), Nat. Electronic Commerce Coordinating Coun. (exec. com. 1998—). Office: Treasurer's Office PO Box 94788 Lincoln NE 68509-4788 E-mail: dheineman@treasurer.org.*

HEINEMAN, PAUL LOWE, consulting civil engineer; b. Omaha, Oct. 24, 1924; s. Paul George and Annie L. (Lowe) H.; m. Gloria Nixon; children by previous marriage: Karen E., John F., Ellen F. Student, U. Omaha, 1942-43; B.S.C.E., Iowa State U., 1945, M.S., 1948. Registered profl. engr. Mo., Calif., N.Y., Kans., 25 other states and Republic of Colombia. Instr. Iowa State U., 1946-48; designer, project mgr. Howard, Needles, Tammen & Bergendoff (Cons. Engrs.), Kansas City, Mo., 1948-64, ptnr., 1965-86; exec. v.p. Howard, Needles, Tammen & Bergendoff Internat., Inc., Kansas City, 1967-84, pres., v.p. subs., 1983-86. Bd. dirs., sec.-treas. emeritus The Road Info. Program. Served with C.E. Corp USNR, 1945-46. Fellow ASCE, Am. Cons. Engrs. Coun., Inst. Traffic Engrs.; mem. NSPE, Am. Ry. Engring. Assn., Am. Concrete Inst., Am. Arbitration Assn., Engrs. Club (Kansas City). Presbyterian (elder 1958—). Home and Office: 2 J St Lake Lotawana MO 64086-9749

HEINEMAN, STEVEN, air transportation executive; b. 1940; BA, Tulane U.; JD, Northwestern U. Bar: Ill. 1971. Gen. atty. United Airlines, Elk Grove Village, Ill.

HEINEMAN, WILLIAM RICHARD, chemistry educator; b. Lubbock, Tex., Oct. 15, 1942; s. Ellis Richard and Edna (Anderson) H.; m. Linda Margaret Harkins, Oct. 25, 1969; children: David William, John Richard. BS, Tex. Tech. U., 1964; PhD, U. N.C., 1968. Rsch. chemist Hercules, Inc., Wilmington, Del., 1968-70; rsch. assoc. Case Western Res. U., Cleve., 1970-71, The Ohio State U., Columbus, 1971-72; asst. prof. U. Cin., 1972-76, assoc. prof., 1976-80, prof., 1980-88, dist. rsch. prof., 1988—. Mem. adv. bd. Analytical Chemistry, Washington, 1984-86, The Analyst, Eng., 1987-95, Selective Electrode Revs., 1987-92, Fresenius Jour. Analytical Chemistry, 199 1-94, Analytical Chimica Acta, 1991-93, Applied Biochemistry and Biotechnology, 1991—, Quimica Analitica, 1993—; U.S. editor Biosensors and Bioelectronics, Eng., 1987—; coun. Gordon Rsch. Confs. Author: Experiments in Instrumental Methods, 1984, Chemical Instrumentrumentation, 1989; editor: Laboratory Techniques in Electroanalytical Chemistry, 1984, Chemical Sensors and Microinstrumentation, 1989. Recipient Charles N. Reilley award in Electroanalytical Chemistry, 1995, Humboldt prize Humboldt Soc., 1989, Rieveschl award U. Cin., 1988, Japan Rsch. award, Japan, 1987, Award in Chem. Sensors 6th Internat. Meeting on Chem/ Sensors, 1996, Excellence in Teaching award ACS Divsn. of Analytical Chemistry, 1997, Torbern Bergman Medal in Analytical Chemistry, Swedish Chem. Soc., Analysdagarna, 1999; named Disting. Scientist Tech. Socs. Coun., 1984; fellow Japan Soc. for Promotion of Sci., 1981. Mem. Am. Chem. Soc. (treas. analytical chem. divsn. 1983-86, 96-97, councilor 1984-98, chair-elect 1996-97, chair 1997-98, named Chemist of Yr. 1983, divsn. analytical chemistry award for excellence in tchg. 1997), Soc. for Electroanalytical Chemistry (pres. 1984-85, bd. dirs. 1984-90). Office: U Cin Dept Chemistry PO Box 210172 Cincinnati OH 45221-0172

HEINEMANN, DAVID J. state legislator; b. West Point, Nebr., July 18, 1945; s. Lester Otto and Rita Charlotte (LaNoue) H.; m. Kristine Stroberg, 1972; children: Julie, Suzanne. BA cum laude, Augustana Coll., 1967; postgrad., U. Kans., 1967-68; JD, Washburn U., 1973. Rsch. asst. Govt. Rsch. Ctr. U. Kans., 1967-68; ptnr. Heinemann & Quint, 1973—; mem. Kans. Ho. of Reps., Topeka, 1968—, chmn. pension and investments, rules and jour., mem. juvenile matters com., vice-chmn. jud. com., mem. legis. post audit, assessment, mem. local govt., legis. and jud. reapportionment com., mem. social and rehab. svc. inst. spl. study com., mem. com. rev. plans for prison constrn., mem. joint com. handicapped accessibility, former chmn. energy and natural resources com., spkr. pro tem, 1985; gen. counsel Kans. Corp. Commn., until 1995. Bd. dirs. S.W. Devel. Svc. Inc.; author legis., 1977-82, Kans. Bar Assn. Jour., 1977-82. Contbr. articles to profl. publs. Pres. Garden City Cmty. Day Care Ctr., 1975—, bd. dirs., 1969-72; alt. del. Rep. Nat. Conv., 1972; dep. county atty. Finney County, 1975—; judge pro-tem Garden City Mcpl.; del. Kans. State Rep. Conv., 1972-78, 82; coord., primary and gen. campaigns for Sec. State Jakc Brier, 1978, 82; mem. Nat. Conf. State Legislators Pension Com., 1981-82, mem. Energy Com., 1983—; mem. Gov. Com. State Investment Practices. Named one of Outstanding Young Men of Am., 1982, Outstanding State Legis., Eagleton Inst. Polit., Rutgers U. Mem. Kans. Bar Assn., Garden City C. of C., Lions. Home: 3826 SW Cambridge Ct Topeka KS 66610-1166*

HEINEN, JAMES ALBIN, electrical engineering educator; b. Milw., June 23, 1943; s. Albin Jacob and Viola (DeBuhr) H. BEE, Marquette U., 1964, MS, 1967, PhD, 1969. Registered profl. engr., Wis. Data analyst Med. Sch. Marquette U., Milw., 1963, teaching asst. elec. engring. dept., 1964-65, 65-66, research asst., 1966, NASA trainee, 1966-69, research assoc. Provost's Office, 1970, asst. prof. and grad. adminstr., 1971-73, assoc. prof., chmn. elec. engring. dept., 1973-76, assoc. prof., 1976-80, prof. elec. engring. and computer sci., 1980-87, prof., dir. grad. studies elec. and computer engring., 1987-95, prof. elec. and computer engring., 1995-2000, prof. emeritus, 2000—, dir. signal processing rsch. ctr., 1990-99, co-dir. ctr. intelligent syss., controls, and signal processing, 1999—. Cons. in field Contbr. numerous articles and revs. on elec. engring. and computer sci. to profl. jours. Recipient Outstanding Engring. Tchr. award Marquette U., 1979, Teaching Excellence award Marquette U., 1985. Mem. IEEE (various coms., tech. reviewer Trans. Automatic Control 1969—, Trans. Circuits and Systems Soc. 1980—, Signal Processing Soc. 1980—, sr. mem., Meml. award Milw. sect. 1981, assoc. editor Trans. Circuits and Systems 1983-85, assoc. editor Trans. Indsl. Electronics 1996-2000), Am. Soc. Engring. Edn., Sigma Xi, Tau Beta Pi, Eta Kappa Nu (Most Outstanding Elec. Engring. Tchr. in U.S. award 1974), Pi Mu Epsilon, Alpha Sigma Nu. Home: 8200 W Menomonee River Pky Wauwatosa WI 53213-2537 Office: Marquette U Haggerty Hall Rm 298 PO Box 1881 Milwaukee WI 53201-1881 E-mail: james.heinen@marquette.edu.

HEININGER, S(AMUEL) ALLEN, retired chemical company executive; b. New Britain, Conn., June 13, 1925; s. Alfred D. and Erma Geraldine (Kline) H.; m. Barbara Ashenfelter Griffith, June 16, 1948 (dec. Oct. 6 1994); children: Janet, Kathryn, Kenneth, Keith; m. Margot Moran Danis, Nov. 27, 1998. A.B., Oberlin Coll., 1948; M.S., Carnegie Inst. Tech., 1951; D.Sc., 1952. Research chemist Monsanto Chem. Co., Dayton, Ohio, 1952-56, group leader, 1956-58, project mgr. devel. dept. Organic Chems. div. St. Louis, 1958-59, mgr. fine chems. intermediates and market exploration sect., 1959-65, dir. comml. devel., 1965-67, dir. food and fine chems., 1967-71, dir. corp. plans and devel., 1971-74; gen. mgr. plasticizers div. Monsanto Indsl. Chems. Co., 1974-76; dir. corp. research lab. Monsanto Chem. Co., 1977, v.p. research and devel., 1977-79, v.p. corp. plans and bus. devel., 1980-86, v.p. resource planning, 1986-90; retired, 1990. Contbr. articles to profl. jours.; U.S., fgn. patentee in field. Alderman, City of Warson Woods (Mo.), 1961-65, police commr., 1967-71, trustee St. Louis Sci. Ctr., 1997—, Repertory Theatre, 1998—; bd. dirs. Gen. Protestant Children's Home, 1999—, Episcopal City Mission, 1998—. Served to lt. USNR, 1943-46. Mem. Am. Chem. Soc. (pres.-elect 1990, pres. 1991), Indsl. Rsch. Inst. (pres. 1987-88), Soc. Chem. Industry, N.Y. Acad. Scis., U.S./Mex. Found. (bd. dirs.), Old Warson Country Club, Frontenac Racquet Club, Univ. Club (St. Louis), St. Andrews Club (Delray Beach). Republican. Episcopalian.

HEINLEN, RONALD EUGENE, lawyer; b. Delaware, Ohio, May 28, 1937; s. Carl Elwood and Evelyn Lucille (Scott) H.; m. Mary Pauline Turney, Dec. 28, 1955; children: James Michael, Deborah Lynn, Robert Christopher. AB, Harvard U., 1959, JD, 1962. Bar: Ohio 1962. Assoc. Frost & Jacobs, Cin., 1962-69, ptnr., 1969—. Lectr. Tax Inst. NYU. Contbr. articles to profl. jour. Trustee Cin. Nature Ctr., 1986-95. Fellow Am. Soc. Hosp. Attys.; mem. ABA, Ohio State Bar Assn., Cin. Bar Assn. (chmn. tax sect.), Cin. Country Club, University Club. Office: Frost & Jacobs 2500 PNC Ct 201 E 5th St Ste 2500 Cincinnati OH 45202-4182

HEINRICHS, APRIL, coach; b. Charlottesville, Va., Feb. 27, 1964; Student, U. N.C. Lic. U.S. Soccer Federation "A" coaching license. Full time asst. U.S. Women's Nat. Team, 1995-97; coaching staff 1995 Women's World Cup, 1996 Olympic Women's Soccer Team; head coach U.S. U-16 Nat. Team, 1997-2000; head coach, tech. dir. U.S. Women's Nat. Team, 2000—. Women's head coach U. Va., 1996, U. Md., 1991-96, Princeton U. Recipient U.S. Soccer Female Athlete of Yr. award, 1986, 89; voted female player of the 1980s Soccer America Magazine; first female inducted into Nat. Soccer Hall of Fame, 1998; named First Team All-American U. N.C. (3 times); inaugural recipient NSCAA Women's Com. award of Excellence, 2000. Office: US Soccer House 1801-1811 S Prairie Ave Chicago IL 60616

HEINRICHS, MARY ANN, former dean; b. Toledo, Mar. 28, 1930; m. Paul Heinrichs, Jan. 26, 1952; children: Paul, John, Nancy, James. PhD, U. Toledo, 1973. Prof. English U. Toledo, Ohio, 1965-77, dean, 1977-93; prof. emeritus Coll. Edn. Contbr. articles to profl. jours. Mem. Cmty. Planning Coun. Rsch. Project Employed Women, Ohio, 1982-84; mem. Coun. Family Violence, Toledo, 1981—; com. chmn. St. Joseph Sch. Bd., Toledo. 1976-79. Recipient Outstanding Scholarship award U. Toledo, 1965; AAUW scholar, 1984, Hunanities scholar, 1987—; named One of Foremost Women 20th Century, 1987, Outstanding Woman U. Toledo, 1991; inducted into Notre Dame Acad. Hall of Fame, 1991. Mem. AAUW (corp. rep. 1978-84), Internat. Tech. Comm. Soc. (chmn. 1979-80), Zonta,, Pi Lambda Theta (chpt. pres., del. 1974-76), Phi Kappa Phi (chpt. pres, del. 1969). Roman Catholic. Avocations: hiking, traveling, music. Office: U Toledo 2801 W Bancroft St Toledo OH 43606-3328

HEINZ, WILLIAM DENBY, lawyer; b. Carlinville, Ill., Nov. 26, 1947; s. William Henry and Margaret (Denby) H.; children: Kimberly, Rebecca, Elizabeth; m. Catherine Lamb Heinz. BS, Millikin U., 1969; JD, U. Ill., 1973. Bar: Ill. 1973, U.S. Dist. Ct. (no. dist.) Ill. 1974, U.S. Ct. Appeals (3d cir.) 1982, U.S. Ct. Appeals (5th cir.) 1973, U.S. Ct. Appeals (7th cir.) 1976, U.S. Supreme Ct. 1979. Law clk. to judge U.S. Ct. Appeals (5th cir.), Tuscaloosa, Ala., 1973-74; assoc. Jenner & Block, Chgo., 1974-80, ptnr., 1980—; mem. faculty NITA, 1981—. Adj. prof. Northwestern U. Sch. Law, 1995—; bd. visitors U. Ill. Coll. Law, 1990-93, pres.'s coun. U. Ill.; bd. dirs., chair Legal Aid Bur., Chgo.; bd. dirs. exec. com. Met. Family Svcs. Chgo. Recipient Disting. Grad. award U. Ill. Coll. Law, 1995. Fellow Am. Coll. Trial Lawyers; mem. ABA, Ill. Bar Assn. (civil practice and procedure sect. coun., com. on liaison with Ill. ARDC, task force on multi-disciplinary practice), Chgo. Bar Assn. (jud. evaluation com. 1990-93), ARDC Ill. Profl. Responsibility Inst., Cribbett Soc., U. Ill. Coll. Law, Legal Club (bd. dirs. 1998-2000), Westmoreland Country Club. Home: 437 Sheridan Rd Kenilworth IL 60043-1220 Office: Jenner & Block 1 E Ibm Plz Fl 46 Chicago IL 60611-3586 E-mail: wheinz@jenner.com.

HEIPLE, JAMES DEE, state supreme court justice; b. Peoria, Ill., Sept. 13, 1933; s. Rae Crane and Harriet (Birkett) H.; B.S., Bradley U., 1955; J.D., U. Louisville, 1957; Certificate in Internat. Law, City of London Coll., 1967; grad. Nat. Jud. Coll., 1971; LLM U. Va., 1988; m. Virginia Kerswill, July 28, 1956 (dec. Apr. 16, 1995); children: Jeremy Hans, Jonathan James, Rachel Duffield. Bar: Ill. 1957, Ky. 1958, U.S. Supreme Ct. 1962; partner Heiple and Heiple, Pekin, Ill., 1957-70; circuit judge Ill., 10th Circuit 1970-80; justice Ill. Appellate Ct., 1980-90; justice Ill. Supreme Ct., 1990—, ret., 2000. V.p., dir. Washington State Bank (Ill.), 1959-66; dir. Gridley State Bank (Ill.), 1958-59; village atty., Tremont, Ill., 1961-66, Mackinaw, Ill., 1961-66; asst. pub. defender Tazewell County, 1967-70., jud. clerk Ill. Appellate Ct., 1968-70. Chmn. Tazewell County Heart Fund, 1960. Pub. Adminstr. Tazewell County, Ill., 1959-61; sec. Tazewell County Republican Central Com. 1966-70; mem. Pekin Sch. Bd., 1970; mem. Ill. Supreme Ct. Com. on Profl. Responsibility, 1978-86. Recipient certificate Freedoms Found., 1975, George Washington honor medal, 1976, Bradley Centurion award Bradley U., 1995; named Disting. Alumnus, U. Louisville, 1992. Fellow ABA (life), Ill. Bar Found. (life), Ky. Bar Found. (life); mem. Ky., Ill. (chmn. legal edn. com. 1972-74, chmn. jud. sect. 1976-77, chmn. Bench and Bar Council 1984-85), Tazewell County Bar Assn. (pres. 1967-68), Ill. Judges Assn. (pres. 1978-79), Ky., Ill., Pa. hist. socs., S.A.R., War of 1812, Sons of Union Vets., Delta Theta Phi, Sigma Nu, Pi Kappa Delta. Methodist. Clubs: Filson; Union League (Chgo.), Country (Peoria). Lodge: Masons (33 degree). Office: 207 Main St Ste 500 Peoria IL 61602-1362*

HEIRD, ROBERT C. insurance executive human resources professional; Sr. v.p. human resources Anthem Ins. Cos., Inc., Indpls., 1998—. Office: Anthem Ins Cos Inc 120 Monument Cir Indianapolis IN 46204-4906

HEISE, MARILYN BEARDSLEY, public relations company executive; b. Cedar Rapids, Iowa, Feb. 26, 1935; d. Lee Roy and Angeline Myrtle Beardsley; m. John W. Heise, July 9, 1960; children: William Earnshaw, Steven James, Kathryn Kay Benninghoff. BA, Drake U., 1957. Account exec. The Beveridge Orgn., Chgo., 1958-60; editor, pub. The Working Craftsman mag., Northbrook, Ill., 1971-78; columnist Chgo. Sun-Times, 1973-78; pres. Craft Books, Inc., Northbrook, 1978-84; v.p. Sheila King Pub. Rels., Chgo., 1984-87, Aaron D. Cushman, Inc., Chgo., 1987-88; pres. Creative Cons. Assocs., Inc., Glencoe, Ill., 1989—, Heartfelt Charity Cards, 1991—. Mem. adv. panel Nat. Crafts Project, Ft. Collins, Colo., 1977; mem. adv. panel and com. Nat. Endowment for Arts, Washington, 1977; mem. editl. adv. bd. The Crafts Report, Seattle, 1978-86. Recipient achievement award Women in Mgmt., 1978. Mem. Pub. Rels. Soc. Am. (accredited). Office: Heartfelt 540 W Frontage Rd Ste 1060 Northfield IL 60093-1299

HEISLER, QUENTIN GEORGE, JR. lawyer; b. Jefferson City, Mo., June 30, 1943; s. Quentin George and Helen (Reynolds) H.; m. Susan Davis, Jan. 24, 1970; children: Sarah, Thomas, Margaret. AB magna cum laude, Harvard U., 1965, JD, 1968. Bar: Ill. 1968, U.S. Dist. Ct. (no. dist.) Ill. 1969, Fla. 1977. Assoc. McDermott, Will & Emery, Chgo., 1968-69, 70-75, ptnr., 1975—; legal counsel Office Minority Bus. Enterprise, Dept. Commerce, Washington, 1969-70. Mem. adv. bd. Entrepreneurship Inst., Chgo. Co-author: Working With Family Businesses, 1995; gen. editor: Trust Administration in Illinois, 1979. Chmn. Winnetka Caucus, Ill., 1983; mem. Winnetka Bd. Edn., 1985-89; trustee Hadley Sch. for the Blind, Winnetka, Shedd Aquarium; bd govs. Winnetka Cmty. House, 1998-99. Fellow Am. Coll. Trust and Estates Counsel; mem. ABA, Chgo. Coun. Estate Planning, Univ. Club, Harvard Club (bd. dirs. Chgo. chpt. 1984-95, pres. bd. 1989-91), Skokie Country Club (Glencoe, Ill.), Racquet Club. Office: McDermott Will & Emery 227 W Monroe St Ste 3100 Chicago IL 60606-5096

HEISLEY, MICHAEL E. manufacturing executive; Formerly with Robertson-Ceco Corp., Toms Foods, Inc., WorldPort Comm. Inc., Pettibone Corp.; chmn., CEO Heico Cos. LLC, St. Charles, Ill., 1979—. Chmn. Davis Wire Corp., Toms Foods, Inc. Mem. St. Patrick's Cath. Ch. Mem. Turnaround Mgmt. Assn., Union League Club, Chgo. Club. Office: Heico Cos 2075 Foxfield Saint Charles IL 60174

HEISS, RICHARD WALTER, former bank executive, consultant, lawyer; b. Monroe, Mich., July 8, 1930; s. Walter and Lillian (Harpst) H.; m. Nancy J. Blum, June 21, 1952; children: Kurt Frederick, Karl Richard. BA, Mich. State U., 1952; LLB, Detroit Coll., 1963, LLD (hon.), 1982; LLM, Wayne State U., 1969; cert., Stanford U. Exec. Program, 1979. Bar: Mich. 1963, U.S. Dist. Ct. (federal dist.) Mich. 1963. Asst. trust officer Mfrs. Nat. Bank of Detroit, 1960-62, trust officer, 1962-66; v.p., trust officer Mfrs. Nat. Bank Detroit, 1966-68, v.p., sr. trust officer, 1968-75, 1st v.p., sr. trust officer, 1975-77, sr. v.p., 1977-89, exec. v.p., 1989-92; vice chair Detroit Coll. Law Found., 1995—2000, chair, 2001—. Pres., CEO, Mfrs. Nat. Trust Co. Fla., 1984-88, chmn. bd., 1988-92; lectr. Inst. Continuing Legal Edn., Procknow Grad. Sch. Banking, U. Wis., Southwestern Grad. Sch. Bank, Am. Bankers Assn., Banking Sch. South; chmn. mem. exec. com. Trust Mgmt. Seminar, 1980; expert witness fiduciary law, 1993—. Mem. Legal-Fin. Network, Cmty. Found. S.E. Mich.; bd. dirs. Hist. Trinity, Inc., 1992—; trustee Detroit Coll. Law at Mich. State U., pres., 1983-94; pres. Mich. State U. Bus. Sch. Alumni Bd., 1983; mem. allocation and evaluation com. United Way S.E. Mich., 1989-92. 1st lt. AUS, 1952-57. Fellow State Bar Mich. Found.; mem. Mich. Bar Assn., Am. Bankers Assn. (pres. 1981, exec. com. trust divsn., pvt. banking com. 1984-89, investment adv. com. 1984-89), Mich. Bankers Assn. (chmn. trust divsn. exec. com. 1975), Detroit Golf Club (bd. dirs., pres. 1983), Mich. Srs. Golf Assn. (bd. govs. 1994-), Club at Seabrook Island, Delta Chi, Sigma Nu Phi. Republican. Lutheran. Home and Office: 30684 Sudbury Ct Farmington Hills MI 48331-1368

HEISTAD, DONALD DEAN, cardiologist; b. Chgo., Apr. 2, 1940; m. Sandra J.; children: Wendy, Dean. BS, U. Ill., 1959; MD, U. Chgo., 1963. Asst. prof. medicine U. Iowa Coll. Medicine, Iowa City, 1970-73, assoc. prof. medicine, 1973-76, prof. medicine, 1976—, prof. pharmacology, 1987—, prof. cardiology, dir. cardiovascular divsn., 1995—, Zahn prof. cardiology, 1999—. Bd. dirs. Iowa Ctr. on Aging. Editor: Cerebral Blood Flow: Effects of Nerves, 1982; assoc. editor: Hypertension, 1989-93, Circulation Rsch., 1980-85, consulting editor; editor-in-chief: Arteriosclerosis, Thrombosis, and Vascular Biology, 1999—; contbr. more than 400 papers to profl. jours. and chpts to books. Pres. U. Iowa Faculty Senate, Iowa City, 1980-81; vice-chair coun. on circulation Am. Heart Assn., 1994-96, chair, 1996-98. Capt. U.S. Army, 1967-70. Recipient Irving S. Wright award Stroke Coun., 1976, Harry Goldblatt award Coun. for High Blood Pressure Rsch., 1980, Merit award, 1987, Disting. Lecture award Coun. on Thrombosis, George E. Brown Meml. Lectr., Am. Heart Assn., 1999, Rsch. Achievement award, 2001; Disting. Alumni award U. Chgo., 1991, Novartis award Coun. High Blood Pressure Rsch., 1997; Landis award, Microcirculation Soc., 2001. Fellow Coun. for High Blood Pressure Rsch., Am. Soc. for Clin. Investigation, Assn. Am. Physicians, Assn. Univ. Cardiologists (sec.-treas. 1998-2001, pres. 2002-03), Am. Physiol. Soc. (chair cardiovascular sect. 1995-96, Wiggers award 1999); mem. Internat. Soc. and Fedn. Cardiologists. Democrat. Office: U Iowa Coll Medicine Dept Medicine Iowa City IA 52242 E-mail: donald-heistad@uiowa.edu.

HEITKAMP, HEIDI, state attorney general; b. Breckenridge, Minn. m. Darwin Lange; children: Althea Lange, Nathan Lange. BA, U. N.D., 1977; JD, Lewis and Clark Coll., 1980. Intern asst. Environ. Study Conf., Washington, 1976; legis. intern N.D. Legis. Coun., Bismarck, 1977; exec. dir. Northwestern Environ. Def. Ctr., Portland, 1978—79; rsch. asst. Nat. Resources Law Inst., 1979; atty. enforcement divsn. EPA, Washington, 1980—81; asst. atty. gen. Office of N.D. State Tax Commr., Bismarck, 1981—85, adminstrv. counsel, 1985—86, tax commr., 1986—92; atty. gen. State of N.D., 1993—. Del. Am. Coun. Young Polit. Leaders UK Internat. Def. Conf., 1988; trustee Fedn. Tax Adminstrs., 1991; presdl. appointee trade and environment policy adv. com. Office of Trade Reps., 1996. N.D. State Crusade chmn. Am. Cancer Soc., 1988—. Named One of 20 Young Lawyers Making a Difference, ABA Barrister mag., 1990; recipient Young Achiever award, Nat. Coun. Women, 1987; fellow Toll fellow, Coun. State Govts., 1986. Mem.: Nat. Assn. Atty. Gens. Office: Attorney General State Capitol 600 E Boulevard Ave Dept 125 Bismarck ND 58505-0040*

HEITKAMP, JOEL C. state legislator; b. Breckinridge, N.D., Nov. 2, 1961; m. Susan Heitkamp; 2 children. Student, U. N.D. Mem. N.D. Senate from 27th dist., Bismark, 1994—; mem. fin., taxation and natural resources coms. N.D. Senate. Recipient Operator's award N.D. State Health Dept. Mem. Richland County Pheasants, Hankinson Dollars for Scholars, Mantador Fire Dept. and Cmty. Club. Home: 16543 94 1/2 St SE Hankinson ND 58041-9538

HEJTMANEK, DANTON CHARLES, lawyer; b. Topeka, July 22, 1951; s. Robert Keith and Bernice Louise (Krause) H.; m. Julie Hejtmanek; 1 child, Brian J. BBA in Acctg., Washburn U., 1973, JD, 1975. Bar: Kans. 1976, U.S. Dist. Ct. Kans. 1976, U.S. Tax Ct. 1976. Ptnr. Schroer, Rice, Bryan & Lykins, P.A., Topeka, 1975-86, Bryan, Lykins & Hejtmanek, P.A., Topeka, 1986—. Mem. ABA (rep. young lawyers Kans. and Nebr.), ATLA, Kans. Bar Assn. (pres. young lawyers 1985), Kans. Trial Lawyers Assn., Sertoma (pres. 1983, internat. pres. 1998-99). Republican. Presbyterian. Avocations: snow skiing, travel. Home: 2800 SW Burlingame Rd Topeka KS 66611-1316 Office: Bryan Lykins & Hejtmanek PA 222 SW 7th St Topeka KS 66603-3734

HELDER, BRUCE ALAN, metal products executive; b. Grand Rapids, Mich., July 1, 1953; s. Harry Martin and Margaret (Ditmar) H.; m. Arlene Faye Docter, May 29, 1975; children: Amanda Joy, David Ryan, Joel Brent, Jonathan Bruce, Brandon Michael. Student, Calvin Coll., 1972-73, Grand Valley State Coll., Allendale, Mich., 1974. Lic. realtor assoc.; cert. media specialist. Indsl. sales rep. Newman Communications, Inc., Grand Rapids, 1971-81; v.p. sales and mktg. Best Metal Products Co., 1981—; pres. Venture Property Mgmt. Co. Mem. Real Estate Bd. Grand Rapids. Republican. Mem. Christian Reformed Ch. Home: PO Box 88153 Grand Rapids MI 49518-0153 Office: Best Metal Products Co PO Box 888-440 Grand Rapids MI 49588-8440

HELDMAN, JAMES GARDNER, lawyer; b. Cin., Mar. 7, 1949; s. James Norvin and Jane Marie (Gardner) H.; m. Wendy Maureen Saunders, Sept. 3, 1978; children: Dustin A., Courtney B. AB cum laude, Harvard U., 1971; JD with honors, George Washington U., 1974. Bar: D.C. 1975, U.S. Dist. Ct. (D.C. dist.) 1975, U.S. Ct. Appeals (D.C. cir.) 1975, U.S. Supreme Ct. 1980, Ohio 1981. Assoc. Perazich & Kolker, Washington, 1974-79, Wyman, Bautzer, Kuchel & Silbert, Washington, 1979-81, Strauss & Troy, Cin., 1981-83, ptnr., 1984—. Mem. ABA, Ohio State Bar Assn., Cin. Bar Assn. Avocations: tennis, platform tennis, biking. Office: Strauss & Troy The Fed Res Bldg 150 E Fourth St Cincinnati OH 45202-4018

HELDMAN, PAUL W. lawyer, grocery store company executive; BS, Boston U., 1973; JD, U. Cin., 1977. Bar: Ohio 1977. Assoc. Beckman, Lavercombe & Weil, 1977-82; atty. The Kroger Co., Cin., 1982-86; sr. atty. Kroger Co., 1986-87, sr. counsel, 1987-89, v.p., gen. counsel, 1989-92; v.p., sec., gen. counsel The Kroger Co., 1992-97, sr. v.p., sec., gen. counsel, 1997—. Office: The Kroger Co 1014 Vine St Ste 1000 Cincinnati OH 45202-1100

HELFER, MICHAEL STEVENS, lawyer, business executive; b. N.Y.C., Aug. 2, 1945; s. Robert Stevens and Teresa (Kahan) H.; m. Ricki Rhodarmer Helfer; children: Lisa, David, Matthew. BA summa cum laude, Claremont Men's Coll., 1967; JD magna cum laude, Harvard U., 1970. Bar: D.C. 1971. Law clk. to chief judge U.S. Ct. Appeals D.C., 1970-71; asst. counsel subcom. on constl. amendments Senate Judiciary Com., 1971-73; assoc. Wilmer, Cutler & Pickering, Washington, 1973-78, ptnr., 1978-2000, mgmt. com., 1990-98, chmn., 1995-98; exec. v.p. for corp. strategy Nationwide Ins./Fin. Svcs., Columbus, Ohio, 2000—; pres. Nationwide Strategic Investments, 2002—. Bd. dirs. Lawyers for Children Am., 1997–, Wexner Ctr. for Arts, 2002—. Mem. Am. Law Inst. Democrat. Home: 173 S Parkview Ave Columbus OH 43209 Office: Nationwide Ins/Fin Svcs Mail Code 1-37-09 Columbus OH 43215 E-mail: helferm@nationwide.com.

HELGERSON, HENRY, state legislator; b. Jan. 12, 1952; m. Nickoli A. Flynn. Grad., Rockhurst U. Kans. state rep. Dist. 86, 1983—. Dir. Children's Mus. Home: 4009 Hammond Dr Wichita KS 67218-1221

HELGESON, JOHN PAUL, plant physiologist, researcher; b. Barberton, Ohio, July 25, 1935; s. Earl Adrian and Marguerite (Dutcher) H.; m. Sarah Frances Slater, June 10, 1957; children: Daniel, Susan, James. AB, Oberlin Coll., 1957; PhD, U. Wis., 1964. NSF postdoctoral fellow Dept. of Chemistry, U. Ill., Urbana, 1964-66; from asst. to prof. botany and plant pathology U. Wis., Madison, 1966—. Plant physiologist USDA Argl. Rsch. Svc. plant disease resistance unit, Madison, 1966-90, rsch. leader, 1990—; program dir. USDA, Washington, 1982-83; vis. scientist Lab. of Cell Biology, Versailles, France, 1985-86. Lt. USAF, 1957-60. Mem. Bot. Soc. Am., Am. Phytopathol. Soc., Internat. Soc. Plant Molecular Biologists, Am. Soc. Plant Physiologists. Achievements include development of tissue culture procedures for studying interactions of plants and fungi, of somatic hybridizations to obtain new disease resistances in plants. E-mail: jph@plantpath.wisc.edu.

HELLAND, MARK DUANE, small business owner; b. Eldora, Iowa, May 19, 1949; s. Duane J. and Mary Carolyn (Bloomberg) H.; m. Lois Ann Lebakken, Aug. 15, 1970; children: Alissa, Jonathan. BA, Luther Coll., 1971; JD, U. Minn., 1974; postgrad., Harvard U., 1985, 88. Bar: Minn. 1974, Wis. 1980. Assoc. Berg Law Offices, Stewartville, Minn., 1974-77; v.p. Legal Systems, Inc., Eau Claire, Wis., 1977-78; sr. editor Lawyers Coop. Pub. Co., Rochester, N.Y., 1978-80; exec. dir. Profl. Edn. Systems, Inc., Eau Claire, 1980-81, chief exec. officer, 1981-88, pub., 1988-91, Wiley Law Publs., Colorado Springs, Colo., 1991-93; pres. PESI, Eau Claire, 1993—2001, PESI Law Publ., LLC, Eau Claire, 2001—. Author: Minnesota Probate System, 1980, Wisconsin Rules of the Road, 1985. Mem. Greater Eau Claire C. of C. Office: PESI 200 Spring St Eau Claire WI 54703-3225 E-mail: mhelland@pesi.com.

HELLER, ABRAHAM, psychiatrist, educator; b. Claremont, N.H., Mar. 17, 1917; s. David and Rose Heller; m. Lora S. Levy, June 16, 1957; 1 child, Judith Rose. BA, Brandeis U., 1953; MD, Boston U., 1957. Diplomate Am. Bd. Med. Examiners, Am. Bd. Psychiatry and Neurology. Resident in psychiatry U. Colo., Denver, 1958-61; chief in-patient psychiatry Denver Gen. Hosp., 1961-65, asst. dir. psychiat. services, 1965-70, assoc. dir. psychiat. services, 1970-73, dir., community mental health services, 1970-72; chief psychiatry, dir. community mental health ctr. Newport (R.I.) Hosp., 1973-77; clin. assoc. prof. psychiatry Brown U., Providence, 1973-77; prof. psychiatry, community health Wright State U., Dayton, Ohio, 1977-91, vice chmn. dept., 1980-91, prof. emeritus, 1991—. Fellow Am. Psychiat. Assn., Am. Orthopsychiat. Assn., Am. Assn. for Social Psychiatry. Jewish. Home: 1400 Runnymede Rd Dayton OH 45419-2924 Office: Wright State U Sch Medicine Dept Psychiatry PO Box 927 Dayton OH 45401-0927 E-mail: abraham.heller@wright.edu.

HELLER, FRANCIS H(OWARD), law and political science educator emeritus; b. Vienna, Austria, Aug. 24, 1917; came to U.S., 1938, naturalized, 1943; s. Charles A. and Lily (Grunwald) H.; m. Donna Munn, Sept. 3, 1949 (dec. Dec. 1990); 1 child, Denis Wayne. Student, U. Vienna, 1935-37; JD, MA, U. Va., 1941, PhD, 1948; DHL (hon.), Benedictine Coll., 1988. Asst. prof. govt. Coll. William and Mary, 1947; asst. prof. polit. sci. U. Kans., Lawrence, 1948-51, assoc. prof., 1951-56, prof., 1956-72, Roy A. Roberts prof. law and polit. sci., 1972-88, prof. emeritus, 1988—, assoc. dean Coll. Liberal Arts and Scis., 1957-66, assoc. dean of faculties, 1966-67, dean, 1967-70, vice chancellor for acad. affairs, 1970-72. Vis. prof. Inst. Advanced Studies, Vienna, 1965, U. Vienna Law Sch., 1985, 97, Trinity U., Tex., 1992. Author: Introduction to American Constitutional Law, 1952, The Presidency: A Modern Perspective, 1960, The Korean War: A 25-Year Perspective, 1977, The Truman White House, 1980, Economics and the Truman Administration, 1982, USA: Verfassung und Politik, 1987, NATO: The Founding of the Alliance and the Integration of Europe, 1992, The Kansas State Constitution: A Reference Guide, 1992, The United States and the Integration of Europe, 1996. Mem. Kans. Commn. on Constl. Revision, 1957-61, Lawrence City Planning Commn., 1957-63, ednl. adv. commn. U.S. Army Command and Gen. Staff Coll., 1969-72; bd. dirs. Harry S. Truman Libr. Inst., 1988-96, v.p., 1962-96; bd. dirs. Benedictine Coll., chmn., 1971-79; mem. nat. adv. coun. Ctr. for Study of Presidency, 1991-97. Pvt. to 1st lt. arty. AUS, 1942-47, capt. 1951-52, maj. USAR, ret. Decorated Silver Star, Bronze Star with cluster; recipient Career Teaching award Chancellor's Club, 1986, Silver Angel award Kans. Cath. Conf., 1987, Disting. Svc. citation U. Kans., 1998. Mem. Am. Polit. Sci. Assn. (exec. council 1958-60), Order of Coif, Phi Beta Kappa, Pi Sigma Alpha (mem. nat. council 1958-60) Home: 3419 Seminole Dr Lawrence KS 66047-1622 Office: U Kans Sch Law Green Hall Lawrence KS 66045-7577 E-mail: fheller@ku.edu.

HELLER, LOIS JANE, physiologist, educator, researcher; b. Detroit, Jan. 4, 1942; d. John and Lona Elizabeth (Stockmeyer) Skagerberg; m. Robert Eugene Heller, May 21, 1966; children: John Robert, Suzanne Elizabeth. BA, Albion Coll., 1964; MS, U. Mich., 1966; PhD, U. Ill., Chgo., 1970. Instr. med ctr. U. Ill., Chgo., 1969-70, asst. prof., 1970-71, U. Minn., Duluth, 1972-77, assoc. prof., 1977-89, prof., 1989—. Author: Cardiovascular Physiology, 4th edit., 1997; contbr. numerous articles to profl. jours. Mem. Am. Physiol. Soc., Am. Heart Assn., Soc. Exptl. Biology and Medicine, Internat. Soc. Heart Rsch., Sigma Xi. Avocation: birding. Home: 9129 Congdon Blvd Duluth MN 55804-0005 Office: Univ Minn Sch of Medicine Duluth MN 55812

HELLER, REINHOLD AUGUST, art educator, consultant; b. Fulda, Hesse, Germany, July 22, 1940; came to U.S., 1949; s. Friedrich Leonhard and Brigitte Hermine (Schuler) H.; m. Vivian Faye Hall, June 11, 1966; children: Frederik Andreas, Erik Reinhold. Student, George Washington U., 1958-59; B.S., St. Joseph's Coll., 1963; M.A., Ind. U., 1966, Ph.D., 1968. Asst. prof., prof. U. Pitts., 1968-78; prof. U. Chgo., 1978—. Acting dir. Smart Gallery, U. Chgo., 1983-86; cons., guest curator Nat. Gallery of Art, Washington, 1972,78 Author: Edvard Munch: The Scream, 1973, Munch: His Life and Work, 1984, Hildegard Auer: Ein Verlangen Nach Kunst, 1987, Am. edit., 1989, Toulouse-Lautrec: Painter of Montmarte, 1997; (catalogue) The Art of Wilhelm Lehmbruck, 1973, The Earthly Chimera and the Femme Fatale, 1981, Brücke: German Expressionist Prints from the Granvil and Marcia Specks Collection, 1988, Art in Germany from 1909 to 1936: From Expressionism to Resistance: The Marvin and Janet Fishman collection, 1990, Lyonel Feininger: Awareness, Recollection and Nostalgia, 1992, Stark Impressions: Graphic Prodns. in Germany, 1919-1933, 1994, Gabrielle Münter: The Years of Expressionism, 1905-1920, 1997. Am. Coun. Learned Socs. and Social Sci. Rsch. Coun. fellow, 1966-68, Fulbright fellow, 1966, Guggenheim fellow, 1975-76; Eisenmann Found. rsch. grantee, 1988-89. Mem. MLA, Coll. Art Assn., German Studies Assn., Historians of German and Ctrl. European Art. Office: U Chgo Dept Art Hist 5540 S Greenwood Ave Chicago IL 60637-1506 E-mail: rheller@midway.uchicago.edu.

HELLER, STANLEY J. lawyer, physician, educator; b. Phila., May 10, 1941; s. Albert Curtis and Blanche (Solton) H.; m. Martha Wright (div. 1975); children: Stephanie Gail, Michael Lawrence, Deborah Arlene; m. Brenda Anita West, Dec. 29, 1990. BA, Johns Hopkins U., 1962, MD, 1965; JD, Northwestern U., 1988. Diplomate Am. Bd. Internal Medicine, sub-bd. Cardiovascular Diseases; bar: Ill. 1988, Ga. 1996. Resident physician, medicine Rush-Presbyn. St. Lukes Hosp., Chgo., 1965-68; instr. U. Ill. Coll. Medicine, 1968-70; asst. prof. Rush Med. Coll., 1970-71; assoc. prof. Loyola Stritch Coll. Medicine, 1971-79; clin. assoc. prof. Northwestern U. Med. Sch., 1980—. Dir. cardiac diagnostic lab. St. Joseph Hosp., Chgo., 1971-84; pres. Northside Cardiology Group, Ltd., Chgo., 1973-84; ptnr. Thomas R. Cirignani & Assocs., Chgo., 1988—; attending physician St. Joseph Hosp., Chgo., 1971-85, Grant Hosp., Chgo., 1972-85, Augustana Hosp., Chgo., 1973-86; cons. physician Columbus Hosp., Chgo., 1980-84. Cardiology fellow USPHS, Chgo., 1968-70. Fellow ACP (meritus), Am. Coll. Cardiology (emeritus), Am. Heart Assn. (coun. clin. cardiology, emeritus); mem. ABA, ATLA, Ill. Bar Assn., Ill. Trial Lawyer Assn., Ga. Trial Lawyers Assn., Chgo. Bar Assn. Avocations: skiing, hiking, reading. Office: Thomas R Cirignani & Assocs 200 W Madison St Ste 3660 Chicago IL 60606-3417 E-mail: stan@cirignanl.com.

HELLIE, RICHARD, Russian history educator, researcher; b. Waterloo, Iowa, May 8, 1937; s. Ole Ingeman and Mary Elizabeth (Larsen) H.; children: Benjamin, Michael; m. Shujie Yu, Feb. 26, 1998. BA, U. Chgo., 1958, MA, 1960, PhD, 1965; postgrad., U. Moscow, 1963-64. Asst. prof. Rutgers U., 1965-66; asst. prof. Russian history U. Chgo., 1966-71, assoc. prof., 1971-80, prof., 1980-2001, dir. Ctr. for East European, Russian and Eurasian Studies, 1997—, Thomas E. Donnelley prof., 2001—. Author: Muscovite Society, 1967, Enserfment and Military Change in Muscovy, 1971 (Am. Hist. Assn. Adams prize 1972), Slavery in Russia 1450-1725, 1982 (Laing prize U. Chgo. Press 1985, Russian translation with new post-Soviet foreward Kholopstvo v Rossii, 1450-1725, 1998), 1982, The Russian Law Code (Ulozhenie) of 1649, 1988, The Economy and Material Culture of Russia 1600-1725, 1999; editor: The Plow, the Hammer and the Knout: An Economic History of Eighteenth Century Russia, 1985, Ivan the Terrible: A Quarcentenary Celebration of His Death, 1987, The Frontier in Russian History, 1993; editor quar. jour. Russian History. Fgn. area tng. fellow Ford Found., 1962-65, Guggenheim fellow, 1973-74, fellow NEH, 1978-79; grantee NEH, 1982-83, summer, 1988, NSF, 1988-90, Bradley Found., 1988-91. Mem. PEN, Nat. Hist. Soc., Am. Soc. Legal History, Am. Assn. Advancement Slavic Studies (editorial bd. Slavic Rev. 1979-81), Econ. History Assn., Assn. for Comparative Econ. Studies, Nat. Assn. Scholars. Home: 5807 S Dorchester Ave Apt 13E Chicago IL 60637-1729 Office: U Chgo Dept History 1126 E 59th St # 78 Chicago IL 60637-1580 E-mail: hell@midway.uchicago.edu.

HELLMAN, PETER STUART, technical manufacturing executive; b. Cleve., Oct. 16, 1949; s. Arthur Cerf and Joan (Alburn) H.; m. Alyson Dulin Ware, Sept. 18, 1976; children: Whitney Ware, Garrettson Stuart. BA, Hobart Coll., 1972; MBA, Case Western Res. U., 1984. V.p. Irving Trust Co., N.Y.C., 1972-79; fin. planning assoc. Std. Oil Co., Cleve., 1979-82, mgr. fin. planning, 1982-84, dir. ops. analysis, 1984-85, asst. treas., 1985-86, treas., 1986-87, gen. mgr. crude oil supply and trading, 1987-89; v.p., treas. TRW Inc., 1989-91, exec. v.p., CFO, 1991-94, asst. pres., 1994-95, pres., COO, bd. dirs., 1995-99; exec. v.p., CFO, chief adminstrv. officer Nordson Corp., Westlake, Ohio, 2000—. Bd. dirs. Nordson Corp., QWest Comm. Internat. Inc. Trustee Cleve. Zool. Soc., Ctr. for Families and Children; chmn. vis. com. Case Western Res. U. Weatherhead Sch. Mgmt.; trustee Case Western Res. U.; chmn. Cleve. Today. Office: Nordson Corp 28601 Clemens Rd Westlake OH 44145-1119

HELLMAN, SAMUEL, radiologist, physician, educator; b. N.Y.C., July 23, 1934; s. Henry Sidney and Anna (Egar) Hellman; m. Marcia Sherman, June 30, 1957; children: Jeffrey, Richard, Deborah Susan. BS magna cum laude, Allegheny Coll., 1955, DSc (hon.) , 1984; MD cum laude, SUNY, Syracuse, 1959, DSc (hon.) , 1993; MS (hon.) , Harvard U., 1968. Med. intern Beth Israel Hosp., Boston, 1959—60; asst. resident radiology Yale Sch. Medicine and Grace-New Haven Hosp., 1960—62, postdoctoral fellow radiotherapy and cancer research, 1962—64; postdoctoral fellow Inst. Cancer Research and Royal Marsden Hosp., London, 1965—66; asst. prof. radiology Yale Sch. Medicine, 1966—68; assoc. prof. radiology Harvard Med. Sch., 1968—70; dir. Joint Center for Radiation Therapy, 1968—83, assoc. prof., chmn. dept. radiation therapy, 1971, prof., chmn. dept., 1971—83, also Alvan T. and Viola D. Fuller-Am. Cancer Soc. prof.; physician-in-chief Meml. Sloan Kettering Cancer Ctr., 1983—88, Benno Schmidt chair in clin. oncology, 1983—88; dean div. biol. sci. and Pritzker Sch. Medicine, v.p. for Med. Ctr. U. Chgo., 1988—93, Pritzker Prof., 1988—93, Pritzker Disting. Svc. Prof., 1993—. Chmn. bd. sci. counselors divsn. cancer treatment Nat. Cancer Inst., 1980—84; bd. govs. Argonne Nat. Lab., 1990—93; trustee Brookings Inst., 1992—; bd. dirs. Varian Med. Systems Inc., Insightec; mem. sci. adv. bd. Ludwig Inst. for Cancer Rsch. Contbr. numerous articles to med. jours. Trustee Allegheny Coll., 1979—98, chmn. bd. trustees, 1987—93. Recipient Rosenthal award for cancer rsch., 1980, medal, City of Paris, 1986, award for Outstanding Contbns. to Cancer Care, Assn. Cmty. Cancer Ctrs., 1993. Fellow: AAAS; mem.: N.Y. Acad. Scis., Soc. Chmn. Acad. Radiology Depts., Inst. Medicine NAS, Assn. Am. Physicians, Am. Cancer Soc., Am. Soc. Hematology, Am. Assn. Cancer Rsch., Am. Soc. Clin. Oncology (David A. Karnovsky lectr. 1994, pres. 1986), Assn. Univ. Radiologists, Am. Coll. Radiology, Am. Soc. Therapeutic Radiologists 1983, (Gold medal 1991), Am. Radium Soc., Alpha Omega Alpha, Sigma Xi, Phi Beta Kappa. Home: 4950 S Chicago Beach Dr Chicago IL 60615-3207 Office: U Chgo Divsn Biol Scis 5841 S Maryland Ave Chicago IL 60637-1463 E-mail: s-hellman@uchicago.edu.

HELLMERS, NORMAN DONALD, historic site director; b. New Orleans, Feb. 3, 1944; s. Leonard H. and Meta J.C. (Wegener) H.; m. Patricia I. O'Brien, May 29, 1966; children: Jennifer I., Jeffrey N. BA, Concordia U., River Forest, Ill., 1966; postgrad., U. Iowa, 1966-67, La. State U., 1968. Writer, photographer Nebr. Game and Pks. Commn., Lincoln, 1969-71; ranger nat. pks. various locations, 1972-73; dist. naturalist Shenandoah Nat. Pk., Luray, Va., 1973-76; chief interpretation Grand Portage (Minn.) Nat. Monument, 1976-81; supt. Lincoln Boyhood Nat. Meml., Lincoln City, Ind., 1981-90, Lincoln Home Nat. Hist. Site, Springfield, Ill., 1990—. Lutheran. Avocations: photography, genealogy.

HELLMUTH, THEODORE HENNING, lawyer; b. Detroit, Mar. 28, 1949; s. George F. and Mildred Hellmuth; m. Laurie Hellmuth, May 29, 1970; children: Elizabeth Ann, Theodore Henning, Sara Marie. BA, U. Pa., 1970; JD cum laude, U. Mo.-Columbia, 1974. Bar: Mo. 1974, U.S. Dist. Ct. (ea. dist.) Mo. 1974, U.S. Ct. Appeals (8th cir.) 1978. Assoc., then ptnr. Armstrong Teasdale LLP, St. Louis, 1974—. Author: Missouri Real Estate, 1985, 2d edit., 1998, Lease Audits: The Essential Guide, 1994; editor Distressed Real Estate Law Alert, 1987-88, Litigated Commercial Real Estate Document Reports, 1987-95. Mem.: ABA, Am. Coll. Real Estate Lawyers, Order of Coif. Office: Armstrong Teasdale LLP 1 Metropolitan Sq Ste 2600 Saint Louis MO 63102-2740 E-mail: thellmuth@armstrongteasdale.com.

HELMAN, ROBERT ALAN, lawyer; b. Chgo., Jan. 27, 1934; s. Nathan W. and Esther (Weiss) H.; m. Janet R. Williams, Sept. 13, 1958; children: Marcus E., Adam J., Sarah E. Student, U. Ill., 1951-53; BSL, Northwestern U., 1954, LLB, 1956. Bar: Ill. 1956. Asso. firm Isham, Lincoln & Beale, Chgo., 1956-64, ptnr., 1965-66; ptnr. firm Mayer, Brown & Platt, 1967—. Bd. dirs. No. Trust Corp., The No. Trust Co., Dreyer's Grand Ice Cream Co., TCPL GP Inc., Brambles USA, Inc.; vis. com. U. Chgo. Law Sch. Co-author: Commentaries on 1970 Illinois Constitution, 1971; assoc. editor Northwestern U. Law Rev., 1955-56; contbr. articles to legal jours. Mem. Chgo. Fin. Rsch. and Adv. Com.; chmn. Citizens' Com. on Juvenile Ct., Cook County, 1969-81; pres. Legal Assistance Found., Chgo., 1973-76; chmn. vis. com. Northwestern U. Law Sch., 1989-92; bd. dirs. United Charities Chgo., 1967-73; hon. trustee Brookings Instn., Aspen Inst., 1986-92, Mus. of Contemporary Art. Mem. ABA, Chgo. Bar Assn., Am. Law Inst., Chgo. Coun. Lawyers, Legal Club Chgo., Law Club Chgo., Comml. Club (mem. civic com.), Chgo. Club, Cliffdwellers Club, Mid-Day Club, Econs. Club, Order of Coif. Home: 4950 S Chicago Beach Dr Chicago IL 60615-3207 Office: Mayer Brown Rowe & Maur 190 S La Salle St Ste 3100 Chicago IL 60603-3441

HELMHOLZ, R(ICHARD) H(ENRY), law educator; b. Pasadena, Calif., July 1, 1940; s. Lindsay and Alice (Bean) H.; m. Marilyn P. Helmholz. AB, Princeton U., 1962; JD, Harvard U., 1965; PhD, U. Calif., Berkeley, 1970; LLD, Trinity Coll., Dublin, 1992. Bar: Mo. 1965. Prof. law and hist. Washington U., St. Louis, 1970-81; prof. law U. Chgo., 1981—. Maitland lectr. Cambridge U., 1987; Goodhart prof. Cambridge U., 2000-01. Author: Marriage Litigation, 1975, Select Cases on Defamation, 1985, Canon Law and the Law of England, 1987, Roman Canon Law in Reformation England, 1990, Spirit of Classical Canon Law, 1996, The Ius Commune in England: Four Studies, 2001. Guggenheim fellow, 1986; recipient Von Humboldt rsch. prize, 1992. Fellow Brit. Acad. (corr.), Am. Acad. Arts and Scis., Am. Law Inst., Medieval Acad. Am.; mem. ABA, Am. Soc. Legal History (pres. 1992-94), Selden Soc. (v.p. 1984-87), Univ. Club, Reform Club. Home: 5757 S Kimbark Ave Chicago IL 60637-1614 Office: U Chgo Law Sch 1111 E 60th St Chicago IL 60637-2776 E-mail: dick_helmholz@law.uchicago.edu.

HELMKE, PAUL (WALTER PAUL HELMKE JR.), mayor, lawyer; b. Bloomington, Ind., Nov. 24, 1948; s. Walter P. and Rowene Mary (Crabill) H.; m. Deborah Jane Andrews, Aug. 23, 1969; children: Laura Andrews, Kathryn Elizabeth. BA with highest honors, Ind. U., 1970; JD, Yale U., 1973. Bar: Ind. 1973, Fla. 1982. Lawyer Helmke Beams Boyer Wagner, Ft. Wayne, Ind., 1973-87; mayor City Ft. Wayne, 1988-2000; atty. Barnes & Thornburg, Ft. Wayne, 2000—. Asst. county atty. Allen County, Ft. Wayne, 1974-87; pres. Nat. Rep. Mayors and Local Ofcls. Orgn., 1993; pres. U.S. Conf. of Mayors, 1997-98. Chmn. Allen-Wells chpt. ARC, Ft. Wayne, 1985-87; candidate for Rep. nomination 4th U.S. Congl. Dist.-Ind., 1980; Rep. nominee for U.S. Senate, Ind., 1998; bd. dirs. Nat. League of Cities, 1995-97, chair pub. safety and crime prevention com., 1995; candidate for Rep. nomination 3d U.S. Congl. Dist. Ind., 2002. Recipient J.C. Gallagher prize Law Sch. Yale U., New Haven, Conn., 1972 Mem. Ind. Assn. Cities and Towns (pres. 1996-97). Republican. Lutheran. Home: 1215 Korte Ln Fort Wayne IN 46807-2920 Office: Barnes & Thornburg 600 One Summit Sq Fort Wayne IN 46802-3119 E-mail: phelmke@btlaw.com., paulhelmke@aol.com.

HELQUIST, PAUL M. chemistry educator, researcher; b. Duluth, Minn., Mar. 5, 1947; s. Paul O. and Marie E. (Parent) H.; m. Christie M. Wick, June 11, 1970; children: Sandra Ann, Kristina Ann. BSc, U. Minn., Duluth, 1969; MSc, PhD, Cornell U., 1971; PhD honoris causa, U. Uppsala, Sweden, 1988. Postdoctoral fellow Harvard U., Cambridge, Mass., 1973-74; asst. prof. SUNY, Stony Brook, 1974-80, assoc. prof., 1980-84, prof., 1984-86, U. Notre Dame, Ind., 1986—, chmn. dept. chemistry and biochemistry, 1988-93. Mem. exam. bd. Ednl. Testing Svc., Princeton, N.J., 1989-98; cons. Proctor and Gamble Pharms., 1990—, Circagen, 1999—; head Walther Cancer Rsch. Ctr. Drug Devel., 1998—; dir. NSF workshops for coll. organic chemistry tchrs., 1999—. Author: Synthetic Organic Chemistry: Modern Methods and Strategy, 1989. Recipient Catacosinos Cancer Rsch. award, 1979, Walther Cancer Inst. award, 2001; grantee NIH, 1977—, NSF, 1979—; Am.-Scandinavian Found. fellow, 1982. Mem. Am. Chem. Soc. (instr. 1981—, Exceptional Achievement award 1991). Avocations: foreign languages, classical music, model building, amateur astronomy. Office: U Notre Dame Dept Chemistry & Biochemistry Notre Dame IN 46556 E-mail: helquist.1@nd.edu.

HELTNE, PAUL GREGORY, museum executive; b. Lake Mills, Iowa, July 4, 1941; s. Palmer Tilford and Grace Katherine (Hanson) H.; children— Lisa, Christian B.A., Luther Coll., Decorah, Iowa, 1962; Ph.D., U. Chgo., 1970. Asst. prof. Johns Hopkins U., Balt., 1970-82; dir. Chgo. Acad. Scis., 1982-91, pres., 1991—, co-dir. Nature Polis and Ethics Project, 1994—, pres. emeritus, 1999—. Cons. WHO, Am. Petroleum Inst. Author, editor: Neotropical Primates: Status and Conservation, 1976, Lion-Tailed Macaque, 1985, Science Learning in the Informal Setting, 1988, Understanding Chimpanzees, 1989, Chimpanzee Cultures, 1994. Trustee Balt. Zool. Soc., 1972-82. Mem. Am. Assn. Mus. (edn. task force, accreditation site visitor), Assn. Sci. Mus. Dirs. (sec.-treas. 1986-96), Am. Primatol. Soc., Internat. Primatology Soc., Soc. Integrative and Comparative Biology, Soc. for Study Evolution, Systematic Zoology Soc., Assn. Sci. and Tech. Ctrs. Office: Chgo Acad Scis 2060 N Clark St Chicago IL 60614-4713

HELVESTON, EUGENE MCGILLIS, pediatric ophthalmologist, educator; b. Detroit, Dec. 28, 1934; d. Eugene McGillis and Ann (Fay) H.; m. Barbara Hiss, June 15, 1959; children: Martha Hiss, Lisa Hiss. B.A., U. Mich., 1956, M.D., 1960. Intern St. Joseph Hosp., Ann Arbor, Mich., 1960-61; resident Ind. U. Hosps., Indpls., 1961-66; dir. pediatric opthalmology Ind. U. Sch. Medicine, 1967—, asst. prof., 1967-72, assoc. prof., 1972-76, prof., 1976—, chmn., 1981-83, dir. sect. pediatric ophthalmology, 1967—. Fellow in opthalmology Wilmer Inst., Balt., 1966-67 Author: Pediatric Ophthalmology Practice, 1973, Atlas of Strabismus Surgery, 4th edit., 1993, Strabismus: A Decision Making Approach, 1994; chief editor; Am. Orthoptic Jour., 1976-82; contbr. articles to profl. jours. Mem. med. adv. bd. Project Orbis, 1989—. Kellogg scholar, 1959; grantee Heed scholar Heed Found., Chgo., 1966; recipient Outstanding Heed Fellow award, 1975 Fellow ACS, Am. Acad. Ophthalmology, Am. Orthoptic Coun. (pres. 1976-80), Am. Assn. Pediat. Ophthalmology and Strabismus (pres. 1990), Internat. Strabismus Assn. (sec.-treas.). Office: Ind U Sch Medicine 702 Rotary Cir Indianapolis IN 46202-5133

HELVEY, WILLIAM CHARLES, JR. communications specialist; b. Springfield, Mo., Sept. 4, 1942; s. William C. Sr. and Alice (Essary) H.; m. Julia Faye Howard, June 16, 1962; children: Howard, Harold. BS in Art Edn., S.W. Mo. State U., 1965; MA in Art, U. Mo., 1970. Tchr. art Marshfield (Mo.) H.S., 1965-67; med. illustrator, program emphasis mgr. Mo. Regional Med. Program, Columbia, 1968-80; dir. instrl. media Ctrl. Meth. Coll., Fayette, Mo.; comm. cons., Columbia, 1981-83; state comm. sys. specialist Univ. Ext., Lincoln U., Jefferson City, Mo., 1983—. Freelance artist, photographer, presenter in field. One-man shows (50) in art and photography; group shows (over 100) in arts, including Arts Ctr. of the Ozarks, Boone County Hist. Mus., Columbia, Mo., Arrow Rock State Hist. Site, Rozier Gallery, Jefferson City, Mo., Columbia Art League, U.S. Social Security Adminstrn., Nat. 4-H Ctr., Silver Springs, Md.; contbr. numerous articles to profl. jours. Project leader Boone County 4-H Clubs, Columbia, 1977—. Recipient Unsung Hero award U.S. Dept. Agr., 1988, Mo. Specialist award Mo. State Extension, 1990, 93, numerous awards in art, photography, film and video prodn. Mem. Aircraft Owners and Pilots Assn., Columbia Art League (chmn. art show, 1975—, Lifetime Achievement award in art), St. Louis Artists' Guild, St. Charles Artists' Guild. Avocations: nature, aviation. Home: 908 Shepard Ct Columbia MO 65201-6135 E-mail: bhelvey@aol.com.

HEMANN, PATRICIA A. federal judge; b. 1942; BA summa cum laude, U. Ill., 1964; JD summa cum laude, Cleveland Marshall Coll. Law, 1980. Law clk. to hon. William K. Thomas U.S. Dist. Ct. (no. dist.) Ohio, 1980-82; assoc. Hahn Lowser & Parks, 1982-93; magistrate judge U.S. Dist. Ct. (no. dist.) Ohio, Cleve., 1993—. Summer intern strike force organized crime divsn. U.S. Dept. Justice, Cleve., 1979; mem. vis. com., hon. trustee Cleveland Marshall Coll. Law. Mem. ABA, Fed. Bar Assn., Nat. Assn. Women Judges (membership chair dist. 7), Ohio Women's Bar Assn., Greater Cleve. Bar Assn. (trustee). Office: US Dist Ct No Dist Ohio 414 US Courthouse 201 Superior Ave E Cleveland OH 44114-1201 Fax: (216) 522-2000.

HEMENWAY, ROBERT E. academic administrator, language educator; b. Sioux City, Iowa, Aug. 10, 1941; s. Myrle Emery and Katharine Leone (Cook) H.; m. Marilyn Wickstrom, June 16, 1962 (div. 1970); children: Gina, Jeremy; m. Mattie Fenter, May 12, 1972 (div. 1980); children: Robin, Karintha, Matthew, Langston; m. Leah Renee Hattemer, Dec. 19, 1981; children: Zachary, Arna. BA, U. Nebr., Omaha, 1963; PhD, Kent (Ohio) State U., 1966. Asst. prof. English U. Ky., Lexington, 1966-68; assoc. prof. Am. studies U. Wyo., Laramie, 1968-73; prof. U. Ky., Lexington, 1973-86; dean arts and scis. U. Okla., Norman, 1986-89; chancellor U. Ky., Lexington, 1989-95, U. Kans., Lawrence, 1995—. Dean Gov.'s Scholar's Program, Ky., 1984-86. Author: Zora Neale Hurston, 1977 (Best Biography of 1977 award Soc. Midland Authors 1978, Rembert Patrick prize Fla. Hist. Soc. 1978). Mem. Gov.'s Task Force on Literacy, Okla., 1987-89; bd. dirs. Okla. H.S. Sci. and Math., Oklahoma City, 1985-86, Coun. Colls. Arts and Scis., 1987-89. NEH fellow, 1974-75. Mem. MLA, Am. Studies Assn. (nat. coun.), South Atlantic Assn. Depts. English (pres. 1984-85). Lutheran. Avocation: duplicate bridge. Office: Univ Kansas Office of the Chancellor 230 Strong Hall Lawrence KS 66045-7501

HEMKE, FREDERICK L. music educator, university administrator; b. July 11, 1935; s. Fred L. and May H. (Rowell) H.; m. Junita Borg, Dec. 26, 1959; children: Elizabeth Hemke Shapiro, Frederic John Borg. Premiere prix, Cons. Nat. de Musique, Paris, 1956; BS in Music Edn., U. Wis., Milw., 1958; MusM in Music Edn., Eastman Sch. of Music, Rochester, N.Y., 1962; DMA in Musical Arts, U. Wis., 1975. Chmn. dept. preparatory wind and percussion Sch. of Music Northwestern U., Evanston, Ill., 1962-75, chmn. dept. music performance and studies, 1962-94, prof. of music (saxophone), 1963—, sr. assoc. dean, 1994—. Faculty athletics rep. Northwestern U., Big 10 Conf., NCAA; cons. La Voz Corp., Sun Valley, Calif., Frederick Hemke Saxophone Reeds, So. Music Co., San Antonio, Hemke Saxophone Series, The Selmer Co., Elkhart, Ind. Instrumental soloist (recordings) The American Saxophone, Music for Tenor Saxophone, Allan Pettersson, Symphony No. 15 (with Stockholm Philharmonic); Quintet for String Quartet & Saxo-Warren Benson, Concerto-Ross Lee Finney; author: The Early History of the Saxophone, Hemke Saxophone Series. Recipient Excellence in Teaching award Northwestern U. Alumni Assn., Music Alumni Achievement award, U. Wis., Milw.; grantee: Nat. Endowment for the Arts. Mem. Ill. Music Educators Assn., Pi Kappa Lambda, Kappa Kappa Psi, Phi Mu Alpha Sinfonia (past province gov.) Office: Northwestern U Sch of Music 1965 S Campus Dr Evanston IL 60208-0874

HEMMER, JAMES PAUL, lawyer; b. Oshkosh, Wis., Mar. 28, 1942; s. Joseph John and Margaret Louise (Nuernberg) H.; m. Francine M. Chamallas, June 4, 1967; children— James, Christopher, Sarah. A.B. summa cum laude, Marquette U., 1964; LL.B., Harvard U., 1967. Bar: Ill. 1967. Assoc. Bell, Boyd & Lloyd, Chgo., 1967-74, ptnr., 1975—, mng. ptnr., 1990-93; adj. prof. law Marquette U., 1985-86, Chgo. Kent Coll. Law, 1991-93; lectr. Ill. Inst. Continuing Legal Edn.; bd. dirs. Sanford Corp., Constrn. Projects Mgmt. Inc., Holco Corp. Mem. Kenilworth (Ill.) Sch. Dist. 38 Bd. Edn., v.p. 1985-87, pres. 1987-89, Kenilworth Citizens Adv. Caucus; bd. dirs. Joseph Sears Sch. Devel. Fund. Wickersham fellow; Fulbright scholar. Mem. ABA, Ill. Bar Assn. (editor banking and comml. law newsletter), Alpha Sigma Nu, Phi Theta Psi, Phi Sigma Tau, Sigma Tau Delta. Clubs: University, Law, Legal (Chgo.); Kenilworth. Contbr. articles to legal jours.

HEMMER, PAUL EDWARD, musician, composer, broadcasting executive; b. Dubuque, Iowa, Oct. 12, 1944; s. Andrew Charles and Elizabeth Marie (Goerdt) H.; m. Janet T. Demmer, Feb. 7, 1970; children: Michelle, Steven. BS in Music Edn., U. Wis., Platteville, 1966. Program dir. Sta. WDBQ-AM, Dubuque, Iowa, 1967-93; leader Paul Hemmer Orch., 1967-96; v.p. Radio DBQ, Inc., 2000—. Co-owner Dukes Place Jazz Club, 1999-2002. Composer: (musical comedies) Get the Lead Out, 1976, Joe Sent Me!, 1978, Key City Komedy Company, 1981, Steamboat Comin', 1991, Here's to Dubuque, 1998, Sketches from a Drawing Room, 1996; appeared in film Field of Dreams, 1989. Named Citizen of Yr., Dubuque Telegraph-Herald, 1976, disting. alumni U. Wis., Platteville, 1999. Mem. Internat. Radio Broadcasters Idea Bank, Rotary. Roman Catholic. Home: 2375 Simpson St Dubuque IA 52003-7720 Office: Radio DBQ 8th Bluff Dubuque IA 52001 E-mail: dbqpaul@mchsi.com.

HEMSLEY, STEPHEN J. healthcare company executive; Mng. ptnr. strategy and planning Arthur Andersen and Co.; sr. exec. v.p. UnitedHealth Group, 1997-99; pres., CEO United Am. Health Group, Detroit, 1999—. Office: United Healthgroup Ct 9900 Bren Rd E Minnetonka Mills MN 55343

HENDEE, WILLIAM RICHARD, medical physics educator, university official; b. Owosso, Mich., Jan. 1, 1938; s. C.L. and Alvina M. H.; m. Jeannie Wesley, June 16, 1960; children: Mikal, Shonn, Eric, Gareth and Gregory (twins), Lara and Karel (twins). B.S., Millsaps Coll., Jackson, Miss., 1959; Ph.D., U. Tex., 1962; DSc (hon.), Millsaps Coll., Jackson, Miss., 1988. Diplomate Am. Bd. Radiology, Am. Bd. Health Physics. AEC fellow Nat. Reactor Testing Sta., Idaho Falls, Idaho, 1960; asst. prof., then assoc. prof. physics Millsaps Coll., 1962-65, chmn. dept., 1964-65; instr. Miss. State U. (extension), 1963; asst. prof., then assoc. prof. radiology (med. physics) U. Colo. Med. Center, 1965-73, prof., 1974-85, chmn. dept., 1978-85; mem. staff VA Hosp., Denver, 1970-85, Mercy Hosp., 1971-85, Denver Gen. Hosp., 1971-85, Beth Israel Hosp., 1974-85; v.p. sci. and tech. AMA, Chgo., 1985-1991; prof. radiology, biophysics, radiation oncology, bioethics Med. Coll. Wis., Milw., 1991—, clin. prof. radiology and biophysics, 1985-91, sr. assoc. dean, v.p., 1991—, dean grad. sch., 1995—. Prof. bioengring. Marquette U., 1993—; vis. lectr. Oak Ridge Assoc. Univs., 1964; adj. prof. radiology Northwestern U. Sch. Medicine, 1986-91. Contbr. articles to profl. jours. Served with USMC, 1957-62. Recipient Disting. Alumnus award Millsaps Coll., 1967, Disting. Svc. award Nat. Wildlife Fedn., 1990, Wright Langham Meml. award U. Ky., 1991; Gilbert X-ray fellow, 1960-62, summer fellow NSF, AEC; campus assoc. Danforth Found. Fellow Am. Coll. Radiology, Am. Inst. Med. and Biol. Engring. (pres. 1998-99); mem. AAAS, Health Physics Soc. (chmn. coms., Elda E. Anderson award 1972), Am. Assn. Physicists in Medicine (pres. 1976-77, Robert S. Landauer Meml. award 1977, William D. Coolidge award 1989), Nat. Wildlife Fedn. (Disting. Svc. award 1990), Soc. Biomed. Engring., (sr. mem.), Soc. Nuclear Medicine (pres. 1980-81, Benedict Cassen Meml. award 1984), Am. Acad. Home Care Physicians (Disting. Svc. award 1991), Omicron Delta Kappa, Theta Nu Sigma. Office: Med Coll Wis 8701 W Watertown Plank Rd Milwaukee WI 53226-3548

HENDERSON, ANGELO B. journalist; m. Felecia Henderson; 1 child, Grant. BA in Journalism, U. Ky., 1985. Journalist Wall Street Jour., Detroit; sr. spl. writer Page One The Wall Street Jour. Deacon Hartford Meml. Bapt. Ch., Detroit. Recipient Journalism award Detroit Press Club Found., 1993, Unity award for excellence in minority reporting for pub. affairs/social issues, 1993, Best of Gannett award for bus. and consumer affairs reporting, 1996, Pulitzer prize for Feature Writing, 1999. Mem. Nat. Assn. Black Journalists (former pres. Detroit chpt., award for outstanding coverage of the black condition 1992). Office: c/o Wall Street Jour Det Bur 500 Woodward Ave Ste 1950 Detroit MI 48226-5497

HENDERSON, BRODERICK, state legislator; Parking control officer; mem. fron dist. 35 Kans. State Ho. of Reps., Topeka. Address: 2710 N 8th St Kansas City KS 66101-1108

HENDERSON, DONALD L. executive; Gen. mgr. Deere & Co., Moline, Ill. Fellow Am. Soc. Agrl. Engrs. Office: Deer & Co 1 John Deere Pl Moline IL 61265-8098

HENDERSON, JAMES ALAN, former engine company executive; b. South Bend, Ind., July 26, 1934; s. John William and Norma (Wilson) H.; m. Mary Evelyn Kriner, June 20, 1959; children: James Alan, John Stuart, Jeffrey Todd, Amy Brenton. AB, Princeton U., 1956; Baker scholar, Harvard U., 1961-63. With Scott Foresman & Co., Chgo., 1962; chmn., CEO Cummins Engine Co., Inc., Columbus, 1995; staff mem. Am. Rsch. & Devel. Corp., Boston, 1963; faculty Harvard Bus. Sch., 1963; asst. to chmn. Cummins Engine Co., Inc., Columbus, Ind., 1964-65, v.p. mgmt. devel., 1965-69, v.p. personnel, 1969-70, v.p. ops., 1970-71, exec. v.p., 1971-75, exec. v.p., COO, 1975-77, pres., 1977-94, pres., CEO, 1994-95; chmn., CEO, 1995-99; also bd. dirs. Cummins Engine Co., Inc., Columbus. Bd. dirs. Cummins Engine Found., Inland Steel Ind., Chgo., Ameritech, Chgo., Rohm and Haas Co., Phila., Landmark Comm., Norfolk; mem. policy com. The Bus. Roundtable, Washington; mem. The Bus. Coun., Washington. Author: Creative Collective Bargaining, 1965. Chmn. exec. com., trustee Princeton U., 1986-92; pres. bd. trustees Culver Ednl. Found. Presbyterian. Home: 301 Washington St Columbus IN 47201 Office: Cummins Engine Co Inc 500 Jackson St Columbus IN 47201

HENDERSON, JANET E. lawyer; BA, U. Okla., 1978; JD, Columbia U., 1982. Bar: Okla. 1982, U.S. Dist. Ct. (no. dist.) Okla. 1982, Ill. 1986, U.S. Dist. Ct. (no. dist.) Ill. 1986. Ptnr. Sidley & Austin, Chgo. Lectr. on lender liability issues and bankruptcy to legal orgns., including Midwest Assn. Secured Lenders. Harlan Fiske Stone scholar Columbia U., 1982. Mem. ABA, Chgo. Bar Assn., Am. Bankruptcy Inst., Phi Beta Kappa. Office: Sidley & Austin 1 S First National Plz Chicago IL 60603-2000 Fax: 312-853-7036.

HENDERSON, JOHN L. academic administrator; Sr. asst. to pres. instl. devel. Cin. Tech. Coll., until 1987, v.p. instl. devel., 1987-88; pres. Wilberforce U., Ohio, 1988—. Office: Wilberforce U President's Ofc 1055 N Bickett Rd Wilberforce OH 45384-3001

HENDERSON, RONALD, police chief; b. St. Louis, Dec. 24, 1947; A in Criminal Justice, Florissant (Mo.) Valley C.C.; grad. exec. strategic mgmt. program, Sr. Mgmt. Inst. for Police, Boston, 1992; student, Dignitary Protection Sch., Washington, 1994. appointee Mo. Emergency Response Commn.; program dir. St. Louis Met. Police Dept. Intern Program; initiated New Year's Eve safety campaign. Several divsns. including vice-narcotics, internal affairs St. Louis Police Dept., patrolman, sgt., lt. col., comdr. bur. of patrol support, 1970-92, chief, 1995—. Bd. dirs. St. Louis Cath. Charities. Recipient Robert Lamb Jr. Humanitarian award Nat. Orgn. of Black Law Enfocement Officers, 1997. Office: Met Police Dept 1200 Clark Ave Saint Louis MO 63103-2801

HENDON, RICKY, state legislator; b. Cleveland, Dec. 8, 1953; Formerly alderman City of Chgo.; mem. Ill. Senate from 5th dist., 1992—. Home: 538 N Western Ave Chicago IL 60612-1422

HENDRICKS, KENNETH, wholesale distribution executive; b. Sept. 8, 1941; CEO, chmn. ABC Supply, Beloit, Wis. Office: ABC Supply One ABC Pkwy Beloit WI 53511-4466

HENDRICKSON, BRUCE CARL, life insurance company executive; b. Holdrege, Nebr., Apr. 4, 1930; s. Carl R. and Ruth E. (Bosserman) H.; m. Carol Schepman, June 12, 1952; children: Julie, Mark Bruce. B.A., U. Nebr., 1952. C.L.U., chartered fin. cons. Sr. agt. Prin. Life Ins. Co., Holdrege, 1950—. Bd. govs. Central Nebr. Tech. Community Coll.; mem. Nebr. Edn. Commn. of States, Nat. Hwy. Safety Advisors Com.; elder First Presbyterian Ch., Holdrege, mem. gen. assembly coun., 1999—; pres. Holdrege City Council, 1979-86; pres. Phelps County Community Found.; trustee U. Nebr. Found.; moderator Cen. Nebr. Presbytery, Presbyn. Ch. USA, 1986-88, Gen. Assembly Coun., 1998-2002; dir. Nebr. Art Collection Found., 1996; mem. pres. club U. Nebr., mem. chancellors club. Served with USNR, 1953-56. Bruce Hendrickson Week declared by Gov. of Nebr., 1975; recipient Distinguished Alumni Achievement award U. Nebr., 1977, Disting. Svc. award Nebr. State Assn. Life Underwriters, 1998. Mem. Nat. Assn. Life Underwriters (pres. 1975-76), Assn. Advanced Life Underwriting, Am. Soc. C.L.U.s, Life Underwriters Polit. Action Com. (chmn. 1989), Life Underwriters Tng. Coun. (trustee 1979-82), Million Dollar Round Table, Phi Kappa Psi. Republican. Clubs: Rotary (pres. 1960-61), Holdrege Country (Holdrege); Am. Legion, Elks. Office: Prin Fin Group PO Box 765 Holdrege NE 68949-0765

HENDRICKSON, CARL H. state legislator; Mem. Mo. Ho. of Reps., Jefferson City. Republican.

HENDRICKSON, DAVID R. real estate executive; BBA in Fin., Iowa State U. Sr. real estate fin. officer CB Comml.; co-founder Nat. Equity Advisors, 1992-97; COO, PM Realty Group Investment Svcs., LLC, Chgo., 1997—. Office: PM Realty Group Investment # 1410 500 N Michigan Ave Chicago IL 60611-3777

HENDRICKSON, KENT HERMAN, university administrator; b. Radcliffe, Iowa, Mar. 4, 1939; s. Herman Oliver and Minnie Ida (Dubberke) H.; m. Rosemary Lee Bergeson, Sept. 12, 1960 (div. 1981); children: Justin K., Susan K.; m. Ellen J. Waite, Mar. 26, 1994 (div. Dec. 1995). BS in History, Iowa State U., 1961; MALS, U. Mich., 1964. Assoc. dir. for tech. svcs. U. Nebr. Librs., Lincoln, 1964-70, dean of librs., 1985-95, assoc. vice chancellor info. svcs., 1995—; mgr. west coast operations Richard Abel Co., Beaverton, Oreg., 1970-74; v.p. corp. opers. Blackwell N.Am. Inc., 1975-79, v.p., 1980-81; assoc. univ. libr. U. Ariz. Libr., Tucson, 1981-85, acting asst. univ libr. for pub. svcs., 1982-84, dir. ctrl. svcs., 1984-85. Mem. Nebr. Conf. on Libr. and Info. Svcs., 1991; mem. adv. com. on integrated postsecondary edn. data system Nat. Ctr. for Edn. Statistics, 1990-93; mem. rsch. librs. adv. com. Online Computer Libr. Ctr. Inc., 1990-96, chair, 1992-93. Contbr. articles to profl. jours.; mem. editorial bd. U. Nebr. Press, 1990-95. Trustee AMIGOS, 1984-85; mem. info. systems and comm. com. U. Nebr.-Lincoln, 1988—, mem. acad. planning com., 1988-93, mem. adv. com. to Sheldon Art Gallery, 1985—, mem. adv. com. to computing resource ctr., 1987—, mem. campus wide campaign for health and human svcs., 1986-87, vice chair, 1986, chair, 1987; bd. dirs. Great Plains Network, 1998—, MidNet, 1995—, mem. Edu. Counc. NE Info. Tech. Commn., 1998—. Mem. Assn. Rsch. Librs. (stats. com. 1989-92, chair 1991-92, mem. mgmt. com. 1992-96, chair 1993-96, chair office mgmt. svcs. adv. com. 1993-96, mem. collection devel. com. 1986-88, bd. dirs. 1993-96), Assn. Coll. and Rsch. Librs. (mem. exec. com. univ. librs. sect. 1992-95, chair pre-conf. planning com. 1992, chair univ. librs. stds. rev. com. 1986-89, chair acad. librs. stats. com. 1986-89), OCLC Users Coun. (mem. fin. com. 1991-92, pres. Users Coun. 1993-94), U. Nebr. Coun. on Librs., Nebr. State Libr. Commn. (mem. strategic planning task force 1987-88). Office: U Nebr-Lincoln University Libraries Lincoln NE 68588-0496 E-mail: khendrickson1@unl.edu.

HENDRIX, JON RICHARD, biology educator; b. Passaic, N.J., May 4, 1938; s. William Louis and Velma Lucile (Coleman) H.; m. Janis Ruth Rouhselange, Nov. 24, 1962; children— Margaret Susan, Joann Ruth, Amy Therese B.S., Ind. State U., 1960, M.S., 1963; Ed.D., Ball State U., 1974. Sci. supr. Sch. Town of Highland, Ind., 1960-71; instr. Ind. U., Gary, 1968-69; assoc. prof. biology Ball State U., Muncie, 1972-80, prof., 1980-98, prof. emeritus, 1998—. Cons. Ind. Dept. Pub. Instrn., 1967-71, Ctr. for Values and Meaning, 1971— ; mem. Ind. Sci. Edn. Adv. Bd., Dept. Pub. Instrn., 1967-71 Author: The Wonder of Somehow, 1974, The Wonder of Someplace, 1974, The Wonder of Sometime, 1974, Becomings: A Parent Guidebook for In-Home Experiences with Nine to Eleven Year Olds, 1974, Becomings: A Clergy Guidebook for Experiences with Nine to Eleven Year Olds and Their Parents, 1974; contbr. articles to profl. jours. Recipient Outstanding Young Educator award Highland Jr. C. of C., 1968, Outstanding Faculty award in edn. Ind. U. N.W. Campus, 1970, Outstanding Teaching Faculty award Ball State U., 1982, Ball State U. fellowship, 1971-73, Hon. Mem. award Nat. Assn. Biology Tchrs., 1992, Outstanding Undergrad. Sci. Tchr. in Nation, Soc. of Coll. Sci. Tchrs./Kendall Mgmt., 1997; named Ind. Prof. of Yr., Coun. for Advancement and Support of Edn./Carneige, 1997. Fellow Ind. Acad. Sci.; mem. Nat. Sci. Suprs. Assn. (dir. 1969-71), Ind. Sci. Suprs. Assn. (pres. 1968-69), AAUP, Assn. Suprs. and Curriculum Devel., Nat. Biology Tchrs. Assn. (bd. dirs. 1986, 91—), Nat. Sci. Tchrs. Assn. (life), Nat. Soc. Coll. Sci. Tchrs. (undergrad. tchg. award 1997), Central Assn. Coll. Biology Tchrs., Hoosier Assn. Sci. Tchrs. Inc. (bd. dirs. 1968-71, Disting. Svc. award 1997), Ind. Assn. Tchr. Educators, Ind. Assn. Suprs. and Curriculum Devel., Ind. Biology Tchrs. Assn., Kappa Delta Pi, Phi Delta Kappa, Sigma Xi. Home: 8800 W Eucalyptus Ave Muncie IN 47304-9365 E-mail: jonh49@iquest.net.

HENDRY, JOHN, state supreme court justice; b. Omaha, Aug. 23, 1948; BS, U. Nebr., 1970, JD, 1974. Pvt. practice, Lincoln, 1974-1995; county ct. judge 3d Jud. Dist., 1995-98; chief justice Nebr. Supreme Ct., 1998—. Office: Rm 2214 State Capitol Lincoln NE 68509*

HENG, STANLEY MARK, national guard officer; b. Nebraska City, Nebr., Nov. 4, 1937; s. Robert Joseph Sr. and Margaret Ann (Volkmer) H.; m. Sharon E. Barrett, Oct. 10, 1959; children: Mark, Nick, Lisa. Grad., Command and Gen. Staff Coll., 1969; student, Nat. Def. U., 1979; BA, Doane Coll., 1987. Commd. adj. Nebr. N.G., 1966, advanced through grade to maj. gen., 1966-87; adj. Nebr. Mil. Dept., Lincoln, 1966-77, adminstrv. asst., 1978-86; adj. gen., dir. emergency mgmt. State of Nebr., 1987—2000. Mem. N.G. Assn. U.S., N.G. Assn. Nebr. (exec. sec. 1967-71, Svc. award 1970), Adj. Gens. Assn., Am. Legion. Democrat. Avocations: softball, basketball, running.

HENIKOFF, LEO M., JR. academic administrator, medical educator; b. Chgo., May 9, 1939; m. Carole E. Andersen; children from previous marriage: Leo M. III, Jamie Sue. MD with highest honors, U. Ill., Chgo., 1963. Diplomate Am. Bd. Pediat., Am. Bd. Pediat. Cardiology. Intern Presbyn.-St. Luke's Hosp., Chgo., 1963-64, resident, 1964-66, fellow in pediatric cardiology, 1968-69; clin. instr. U. Ill. Coll. Medicine, 1964-66; clin. instr. pediatrics Georgetown U. Med. Sch., Washington, 1966-68, clin. asst. prof., 1968; asst. prof. U. Ill. Coll. Medicine, Chgo., 1968-71; asst. prof. pediat. Rush Med. Coll., 1971-74, assoc. prof., 1974-79, asst. dean admissions, 1971-74, assoc. dean student affairs, 1974-76, assoc. dean med. scis. and svcs., 1976-79, acting dean v.p. med. affairs, 1976-78, prof. pediatrics, prof. medicine, 1984—; v.p. inter-instl. affairs Rush-Presbyn.-St. Luke's Med. Ctr., 1978-79, pres., 1984—; pres., CEO; trustee Rush-Presbyn.-St. Luke's Med. Ctr., Chgo., 1984—; dean and v.p. med. affairs Temple U. Sch. Medicine, Phila., 1979-84, prof. pediat. and medicine, 1979-84; pres. Rush U., Chgo., 1984—. Adj. attending Presbyn.-St. Luke's Hosp., 1969, asst., 1970-72, assoc., 1973-76, sr. attending, 1977-79, 84—; staff Temple U. Hosp., 1979-84; assoc. staff St. Christopher's Hosp. for Children, 1979-84; mem. Ill. Coun. of Deans, 1977-79; vice chmn. Chgo. Tech. Pk., 1984-85, 86-87, chmn., 1985-86, 87-88; chmn. bd. dirs. Mid-Am. Health Programs, Inc., 1985—; bd. dirs. Harris Trust and Savs. Bank, Harris Bankcorp. Inc.; chmn. bd. dirs. Rush North Shore Health Svcs., 1988—, Rush/Copley Health Care Sys. Inc., 1988—. Contbr. chpts. to books, articles to profl. jours. Bd. dirs. Fishbein Found., 1975-79, Chgo. Regional Blood Program, 1977-79, Sch. Dist. 69, 1974-75, Johnston R. Bowman Health Ctr. for Elderly, 1984—; mem. bd. mgrs. St. Christopher's Hosp. for Children, 1979-84; mem. bd. govs. Temple U. Hosp., 1979-84, Heart Assn. S.E. Pa., 1979-84; trustee Episc. Hosp., 1983-84, Otho S.A. Sprague Meml. Inst., 1984—; mem. adv. bd. Univ. Village Assn., 1984—; mem. exec. com. Gov.'s Build Ill. Com., 1985—. Lt. comdr. USPHS, 1964-68, Res. 1968—. Recipient Roche Med. award, 1962, Mosby award, 1963, Raymond B. Allen Instructorship award U. Ill. Coll. Medicine, 1966, also Med. Alumni award, 1988, Phoenix award Rush Med. Coll., 1977. Fellow Am. Acad. Pediat., Inst. Medicine Chgo., Coll. Physicians Phila., Am. Coll. Physicians Execs.; mem. Assn. Am. Med. Colls. (chmn. nominating com. 1980, mem. coun. deans 1977-84, mem. audit com. 1984), Coun. Tchg. Hosps. (adminstrv. bd. 1987-90), Pa. Med. Sch. Deans Com., AMA (mem. coun. on ethical and jud. affairs 1984-88), Pa. Med. Soc., Philadelphia County Med. Soc., Assn. Acad. Health Ctrs. (bd. dirs. 1988-94, chmn.-elect 1991-92, chmn. 1992-93), Alpha Omega Alpha (chmn. nat. nominating com. 1981-90, nat. dir. 1979-90, pres. 1989-90), Omega Beta Pi, Phi Eta Sigma, Phi Kappa Phi. Office: Rush-Presbyn-St Luke's Med Ctr 1653 W Congress Pkwy Chicago IL 60612-3833

HENKE, JANICE CARINE, educational software developer and marketer; b. Hunter, N.D., Jan. 28, 1938; d. John Leonard and Adeline (Hagen) Hanson; children: Toni L., Tom L., Tracy L. BS, U. Minn., 1965; postgrad., misc. schs., 1969—. Cert. elem. tchr., Minn., Iowa. Tchr. dance, 1953-56; tchr. kindergarten Des Moines Pub. Schs., 1964-65; tchr. elem. Ind. Sch. Dist. 284, Wayzata, Minn., 1969-93; pvt. bus. history, 1978—; marketer, promoter health enhancement Jeri Jacobus Cosmetics Aloe Pro, Am. Choice Nutrition, Multiway, KM Matol, 1978—; developer ednl. software, marketer of software Computer Aided Teaching Concepts, Excelsior, Minn., 1983—; Edn. Minn. authorized rep. with Midwest Benefit Advisers, 1993—. Developer, author drug edn. curriculum, Wayzata, 1970-71; mem. programs com. Health and Wellness, Wayzata, 1988-93; chmn. Wayzata Edn. Assn. Ins. Com., 1991-93; mem. Staff Devel. Adv. Bd., Wayzata, 1988-93; coach Odyssey of the Mind, 1989-93. Author, developer computer software; contbr. articles to newspapers. Fundraiser Ind. Reps. Wayzata, 1976-79; mem. pub. rels. com. Lake Minnetonka (Minn.) Dist. Ind. Reps., 1979-81, fundraising chmn., 1981-82; chmn. Wayzata Ind. Reps., 1981-82; sec. PTO, Wayzata, 1981-82. Mem. NEA, Minn. Edn. Assn., Wayzata Edn. Assn. (bd. mem., ins. chairperson). Lutheran. Avocations: swimming, skiing, traveling, reading, learning. Office: Henke Services Inc 20380 Excelsior Blvd Excelsior MN 55331-8733 E-mail: jhenke8464@hotmail.com.

HENKIN, ROBERT ELLIOTT, nuclear medicine physician; b. Pitts., June 7, 1942; s. Hyman and Nettie (Jaffee) H.; m. Denise Dulberg, June 26, 1966 (dec. 1985); children: Gregory, Joshua, Steven; m. Renae Marley, Nov. 27, 1988. Student, Cornell U., 1960-62; BA, NYU, 1965, MD, 1969. Diplomate Am. Bd. Nuclear Medicine, Nat. Bd. Med. Examiners. Internship gen. surgery Bellevue Med. Ctr., NYU, NYC, 1969—70; resident in diagnostic radiology Northwestern U., Chgo., 1970—72, resident in nuc. medicine, 1972—74, asst. prof. radiology, 1974—76; from asst. prof. to assoc. prof. radiology Loyola U., Maywood, 1976—80, prof. radiology, 1980—, dir. nuc. medicine, 1976—98, 2002—, acting chair dept. radiology, 2000—02, vice chair dept. radiology, 2002—. Fellow Am. Coll. Radiology, Am. Coll. Nuc. Physicians (pres. 1990); mem. AMA, Am. Coll. Physician Execs., Soc. Nuc. Medicine (bd. dirs., trustee 1983-89, v.p. 1995-96, ho. dels. 1998—). Home: 875 E 22d St #202 Lombard IL 60148-5025 E-mail: unm@mindspring.com.

HENNESSY, WILLIAM JOSEPH, prosecutor; b. St. Paul, May 18, 1942; s. William E. and Julia R. (Luger) H.; m. Sandra Hennessy, July 3, 1965 (div. Jan. 7, 1977); m. Sally Ann Kroiss, Dec. 31, 1996; 1 child, Patricia Lee. BA, St. Thomas U., 1964; LLB, JD, William Mitchell U., 1968. Bar: Minn. 1968, U.S. Supreme Ct. 1975. Sr. ptnr. Hennessy & Richardson, St. Paul, 1970—93; chief prosecutor Cook County, Grand Marais, 1995—. Mem. adv. com. on the Criminal Rules, Minn. Supreme Ct., 1998—. Mem. Minn. County Attys. Assn. (bd. dirs. 1996-2001). Avocation: commercial and instrument airplane pilot. Office: Cook County Courthouse PO Box 1150 Grand Marais MN 55604-1150

HENNING, GEORGE THOMAS, JR. steel company executive; b. West Reading, Pa., Sept. 26, 1941; s. George Thomas and Helen Virginia (Spangler) H.; m. Susan Young, July 21, 1962; children: George Thomas III, Michael Kevin. B.A., Pa. State U., 1963; M.B.A., Harvard, 1965. Mgr. econ. analysis Eastern Gas & Fuel, Boston, 1967; mgr. gen. acctg. Ohio River Co., Cin., 1968; asst. to contr. Eastern Gas & Fuel Assos., Boston, 1969; dir. corp. planning Boston Gas Co., 1970; contr. Eastern Assoc. Coal Corp., Pitts., 1971-74; v.p., contr. Lykes Resources, Inc., 1974-78; asst. contr. Jones & Laughlin Steel Corp., 1979-85; gen. mgr. coal mine ops. and raw materials sales LTV Steel Co., Cleve., 1986, gen. mgr. asset mgmt., 1986-89; v.p., chief fin. officer Pioneer Chlor Alkali Co., Inc., Houston, 1988-95; v.p., CFO Pioneer Cos., Inc., 1995; v.p., contr. The LTV Corp., Cleve., 1995-99, v.p., CFO, 1999—2001, ret., 2001. Mem. Pa. State Alumni Council. Mem. Omicron Delta Kappa, Pi Gamma Mu. Presbyterian. E-mail: shenning@penn.com.

HENNINGSEN, PETER, JR. diversified industry executive; b. Mpls., Oct. 6, 1926; s. Peter and Anna O. (Kjelstrup) H.; m. Donna J. Buresh, June 19, 1948; children— Deborah, Pamela, James. BBA, U. Minn., 1950. Packaging engr. govt. and aero. products div. Honeywell, Inc., Mpls., 1950-72; mgr. packaging Internat. Tel. & Tel., N.Y.C., 1972-80; v.p. Raymond Eisenhardt & Son, Inc., 1980-90; ind. packaging and material handling cons., 1990—. Mem. Inst. Packaging Profls. (formerly Soc. Packaging and Handling Engrs.), 1951—, fellow, 1970, pres., 1970-71, chmn. bd., 1972-73, named Man of Yr., 1968. Editl. cons. mags. in field. With USNR, 1944-46. Elected to Packaging Hall of Fame, Packaging Edn.

Forum, 1995. Mem. ASTM, Aerospace Industries Assn. (chmn. packaging com. 1967), Masons, Shriners. Methodist. Home and Office: 15717 Woodgate Rd N Minnetonka MN 55345-4533

HENRICK, MICHAEL FRANCIS, lawyer; b. Chgo., Feb. 29, 1948; s. John L. and A. Madeline (Hafner) H.; m. Cissi F. Henrick, Aug. 9, 1980; children: Michael Francis Jr., Derry Patricia. BA, Loyola U., 1971; JD with honors, John Marshall Law Sch., 1974. Bar: Ill. 1974, U.S. Dist. Ct. (no. dist.) Ill. 1974, U.S. Supreme Ct. 1979, Wis. 1985, U.S. Dist. Ct. (ea. dist.) Wis. 1985. Ptnr. Hinshaw & Culbertson, Chgo., Waukegan, Ill., 1974—. Recipient Corpus Juris Secundum award West Publ. Co., 1974. Mem. ABA, Def. Rsch. Inst., Ill. Bar Assn., Lake County Bar Assn., Ill. Hosp. Attys. Assn., Internat. Assn. of Def. Counsel, Ill. Def. Attys. Assn., Soc. Trial Lawyers Def. Rsch. Inst., Am. Inns of Ct. Office: Hinshaw & Culbertson 110 N West St Waukegan IL 60085-4330 E-mail: m.henrick@hinshawlaw.com.

HENRY, BARBARA A. publishing executive; b. Oshkosh, Wis., July 23, 1952; d. Robert Edward and Barbara Frances (Aylesworth) H. BJ, U. Nev. Reporter Reno Newspapers, 1974-78, city editor, 1978-80, mng. editor, 1980-82; asst. nat. editor USA Today, Washington, 1982-83; exec. editor Reno Gazette-Jour., 1981-86; former editor, dir. Gannett Rochester Newspapers, Rochester, N.Y.; pub. Great Falls (Mont.) Tribune(part of the Gannett group), 1992-96; pres., pub. Des Moines Register, 1996—. Mem. Soc. Profl. Journalists, Associated Press Mng. Editors, Am. Soc. Newspaper Editors, Calif.-Nev. Soc. Newspaper Editors (bd. dirs.). Avocation: skiing. Mailing: The Indianapolis Star P.O. Box 145 Indianapolis IN 46206-0145

HENRY, BRIAN C. telephone company executive; V.p., CFO Mentor Graphics Corp., Oreg.; exec. v.p., CFO, Cin. Bell Inc., 1998; COO info. mgmt. group Convergys Corp., Cin., 1998-99; exec. v.p., CFO, Lante Corp, Chgo., 1999—. Office: Lante Corp # 400 600 W Fulton St Chicago IL 60661-1259

HENRY, COLLEEN, reporter; Student, Georgetown U., Northwestern U. Reporter WISN 12, Milw. Office: WISN PO Box 402 Milwaukee WI 53201-0402

HENRY, EDWARD FRANK, computer accounting service executive; b. East Cleveland, Ohio, Mar. 18, 1923; s. Edward Emerson and Mildred Adelia (Kulow) H.; m. Nicole Annette Peth, June 18, 1977. BBA, Dyke Coll., 1948; postgrad., Case Western Reserve U., 1949, Cleve. Inst. Music, 1972. Cert. Notary Public Ohio. Internal auditor E.F. Hauserman Co., 1948-51; sales and radio announcer Sta. WSRS, 1951; office mgr. Frank C. Grismer Co., 1951-52, Broadway Buick Co., 1952-55; sec., treas. Commerce Ford Sales Co., 1955-65; nat. mgr. Auto Acctg. divsn. United Data Processing Co., Cin., 1966-68; v.p. Auto Data Sys. Co., Cleve., 1968-70; pres. Profl. Mgmt. Computer Sys., Inc., 1970—, Profl. Mgmt. Computer Sys. Becane Internat., 1999—, ComputerEASE, Small Bus. Computer Ctrs. divsn. Profl. Mgmt. Computer Sys., Inc., 1985—, VideoEASE CompuAIDE Computerized Video Rental Sys. divsn. Profl. Mgmt. Computer Systems, Inc., 1987-89; pres. CompuPRINT divsn. Profl. Mgmt. Computer Sys., Inc., 1995—, pres. TravelEASE divsn., 1996—. Drum maj., musician Wurlitzer Marching Band, Cleve., 1939—42, The Ed Henry Dance Band, 1939—42; with USAF Marching Band, Kearns, Utah, 1943; dramatic dir., actor Euclid Little Theatres, Jewish Cmty. Ctr. ; actor Cleve. Playhouse, 1961—63; dramatic dir., actor various other theatres; exec. artistic dir. NorthCoast Cultural Ctr., 1989—. Contbr. photography, Travel Agents Internat. mag., 1990 (hon. mention, 1990); prodr., dir. (Jesters) (plays) National Book of the Play Acapulco, Mexico, 1985, nat. prodr., dir. (Jesters) Nat. Book of the Play Reno, 1988—, Bally's Celebrity Rm., Las Vegas, 1989—96, Hyatt Regency O'Hare, 1998, Millennium, 2000, Nat. Book of the Play Bally's Las Vegas. Charter pres. No. Ohio Coun. Little Theatre, 1954—56; founder, artistic and mng. dir. Exptl. Theatre, Cleve., 1959—63; bd. dirs. Cleve. Philharm. Orch., 1972—74, Cleve. Jazz Orch., 1991—, Cleve. Opera League. 1st lt. USAF, 1943—46, PTO, capt. USAF, 1946—57. Decorated Bronze Star with 3 oak leaf clusters; named in Showtime in Cleveland: The Rise of A Regional Theater Center (John Vacha). Mem.: APA, Res. Officers Assn., Internat. Soc. Photographers, Associated Photographers Internat., Internat. Platform Assn., Am. Soc. Profl. Cons., Nat. Assn. Profl. Cons., Data Processing Mgmt. Assn., Mil. Order World Wars (commdr. Cleve. chpt. 1994—95, adjutant 2001, dept. commdr. State of Ohio 2001), Inst. Mgmt. Accts., Am. Mgmt. Assn., Air Force Assn. (life), Art Inst. Chgo., Cleve. Mus. Art, Nat. Assn. Met. Mus. Art of N.Y., Mayfield Area C. of C., Ky. Cols., SOBIB, Deep Springs Trout Club, Univ. Club, Acacia Country Club, Hermit Univ. Club, Cleve. Grays Club, Rotary, Kachina, Jesters (dir. 1981, impresario 1984—99, impresario emertus 2000, dramatic dir. 1971—), Grotto, Cuyahoga County Meml. Lodge (worshipful master 1993—94), Heroes of '76 (comdr. Cleve. 1977), KT, VFW, Am. Legion, Masons (50 yr. hon. 1994, hon. 33d degree St. Bernard lodge, Doge City), Sojourners (Nat. President's cert. 1977—78, pres. Cleve. chpt. #23 1978), DeMolay (master Cleve. Chpt. 1942, Legion of Honor 1970), Scottish Rite (dramatic dir. 1967—, thrice potent master 1982—84, class maned in his hon. 1994), Shriners (dramatic dir. 1968—88), Cleave. Ct. #14, Phi Kappa Gamma (charter pres., past nat. pres.). Republican. Presbyterian. Home: 666 Echo Dr Gates Mills OH 44040-9606 Office: Profl Mgmt Computer Systems Inc 19701 S Miles Rd Cleveland OH 44128-4257 Fax: 216-663-9822. E-mail: pmcscomputerease@aol.com.

HENRY, FREDERICK EDWARD, lawyer; b. St. Louis, Aug. 28, 1947; s. Frederick E. and Dorothy Jean (McCulley) H.; m. Vallie Catherine Jones, June 7, 1969; children: Christine Roberta, Charles Frederick. AB, Duke U., 1969, JD with honors, 1972. Bar: Ill. 1972, U.S. Dist. Ct. (no. dist.) Ill. 1972, Calif. 1982. Assoc. Baker & McKenzie, Chgo., 1972-79, ptnr., 1979—. Elder, session mem. Fourth Presbyn. Ch., Chgo., 2000—02; bd. dirs. Lincoln Park Conservation Assn., 1983—85, Old Town Triangle Assn., Chgo., 1980—83, pres., 1984. Recipient Willis Smith award, Duke U. Law Sch., 1972. Mem.: ABA, Calif. State Bar, Chgo. Bar Assn., Order of Coif. Home: 164 W Eugenie St Chicago IL 60614-5809 Office: Baker & McKenzie 1 Prudential Plz 130 E Randolph St Ste 3700 Chicago IL 60601-6342 E-mail: frederick.e.henry@bakernet.com.

HENRY, GERALD T. state legislator; m. Linda M. Becker. Mem. from dist. 48 Kans. State Ho. of Reps., Topeka. Exec. dir. Achievement Svc. Address: 215 N 5th PO Box 186 Atchison KS 66002-0186 Also: 3515 Neosho Rd Cummings KS 66016-9032

HENRY, JOHN THOMAS, retired newspaper executive; b. St. Paul, May 30, 1933; s. Harlan A. and Roxane (Thomas) H.; m. Carla Joyce Lechthaler, Jan. 2, 1982; children: Alexandra, Elizabeth, J. Thomas, Catherine. B.B.A., U. Minn., 1955. With St. Paul Pioneer Press Dispatch, 1955—, asst. to publisher, then bus. mgr., 1971-76, gen. mgr., chmn., pub., 1985-92; ret., 1992. V.p. St. Paul Jr. C. of C., 1965-66; bd. dirs., chmn. St. Paul Jr. Achievement; bd. dirs. Better Bus. Bur. of Minn., Boy Scouts Am., Minn. Coop. Office, Minn. Mus. Art; chmn. St. Paul Chamber Orch.; bd. dirs. St. Paul Downtown Coun., United Hosps., Minn. Sci. Mus., St. Paul United Way. With USAF, 1956-59. Recipient Disting. Service award Classified Advt. Mgrs. Assn., 1971 Mem. St. Paul C. of C. (chmn. bd. dirs. 1987). Lodge: Rotary. Home: 4436 Oakmede Ln Saint Paul MN 55110-7603 Office: NW Publs Inc 345 Cedar St Saint Paul MN 55101-1004

HENRY, MICHAEL E. computer company executive; m. Cynthia Henry; children: Reese, Reagan, Winsley. Grad. H.S. Programmer, installer Jack Henry & Assocs., Monett, Mo., 1973, mgr. R&D, 1983, chmn., CEO, 1994—, also bd. dirs. Office: Jack Henry & Assocs Inc 663 Hwy 60 PO Box 807 Monett MO 65708-8215

HENRY, PHYLLISS JEANETTE, marshal; AA in Law Enforcement, Des Moines Area C.C., 1972; B Gen. Studies, U. Iowa, 1984, MA in Comm. Studies, 1986, PhD in Comm. Rsch., 1988. Police officer Des Moines (Iowa) Police Dept., 1972-82; state adminstrv. dir. Roxanne Conlin for Gov. campaign, Iowa, 1982; intern Police Found., Washington, 1984; comm. rsch. analyst Starr and Assocs., 1985; mgr. support svcs. Dept. Pub. Safety Iowa State U., 1990-94; U.S. marshal so. dist. Iowa, apptd. by Pres. Clinton U.S. Dept. Justice, 1994—. Adv. com. Dirs. Marshals, 1995-97. Named Woman of Yr., Metro. Woman's Network, 1991, Officer of Yr. Internat. Assn. of Women, 1991. Mem. Iowa Assn. Women Police (co-founder, Officer of Yr. 1991), Fed. Exec. Coun. Policy Com., Nat. Ctr. for Women and Policing (adv. bd.). Office: Office US Marshal US Courthouse 123 E Walnut St Rm 343A Des Moines IA 50309-2035 E-mail: Phylliss.Henry@usdoj.gov.

HENRY, RICK, broadcast executive; Degree in engring., Ripon (Wis.) Coll. Pres., gen. mgr. Sta. WISN-TV, Milw., 1997—. Office: Sta WISN-TV 759 N 19th St Milwaukee WI 53233-2126

HENRY, ROBERT JOHN, lawyer; b. Chgo., Aug. 1, 1950; s. John P. and Margaret P. (Froelich) Henry; m. Sara Mikuto; children: Cherylyn, Deanna, Laurin. BA cum laude, Loyola U., Chgo., 1973, JD cum laude, 1975. Bar: Ill 1975, U.S. Dist. Ct. (no. dist.) Ill. 1975. Atty. Continental Ill. Nat. Bank, Chgo., 1975-77, Allied Van Lines, Inc., Chgo., 1977-81, assoc. gen. counsel, 1981-88, gen. counsel, 1988-90, v.p. adminstrn., gen. counsel, 1990-93, v.p. gen. counsel, 1993-99; v.p., assoc. gen. counsel Allied Worldwide, Inc., 1999—. Gen. counsel NFC N.Am., 1996-99. Alt. scholar Weymouth Kirkland Found., 1971. Mem. ABA, Chgo. Bar Assn., Am. Corp. Counsel Assn. Office: Allied Van Lines Inc PO Box 4403 Chicago IL 60680-4403 E-mail: robert.henry@alliedvan.com.

HENRY, WILLIAM LOCKWOOD, former food products executive, brewery executive; b. Pasadena, Calif., July 2, 1948; s. Edward Lockwood and Jane (Post) H.; m. Pamela Ann Henry; children: Thomas Edward, Michael Lockwood. BS, UCLA, 1971, MS, 1973. Fin. exec. Ford Motor Co., Dearborn, Mich., 1973-81; dir. fin. Stroh Brewery Co., Detroit, 1981-82, v.p., fin. planner, 1982-84, v.p., sales, mktg. adminstr., 1985-1986, v.p. mktg. and plannig, 1987-89; exec. v.p. Stroh Brewery Co, 1989-91; pres., CEO Stroh Brewery Co., 1991-99. Bd. dirs. Met. Affairs Corp., Century Coun. Mem. Detroit Athletic Club. Office: The Stroh Brewery Co 100 River Place Dr Ste 100 Detroit MI 48207-4291

HENSELMEIER, SANDRA NADINE, retired training and development consulting firm executive; b. Indpls., Nov. 20, 1937; d. Frederick Rost Henselmeier and Beatrice Nadine (Barnes) Henselmeier Enright; m. David Albert Funk, Oct. 2, 1976; children: William H. Stolz, Jr., Harry Phillip Stolz II, Sandra Ann Stolz. AB, Purdue U., 1971; MAT, Ind. U., 1975. Exec. sec. to dean Ind. U. Sch. Law, Indpls., 1977-78; adminstrv. asst. Ind. U.-Purdue U., Indpls., 1978-80, assoc. archivist, 1980-81; program and comm. coord. Midwest Alliance in Nursing, Indpls., 1981-82; tng. coord. Coll./Univ. Cos., Indpls., 1982-83; pres. Better Bus. Comms., Indpls., 1983—; adj. lectr. lectr. U. Indpls. Center Continuing. Mgmt. Devel. and Edn., Indpls., 1984—. Author: Successful Customer Service Writing, Winning with Effective Business Grammar, Successful Telephone Communication and Etiquette, Management Writing; contbr. articles to profl. jours. Mem. Am. Soc. Indexers Soc., Soc. Tech. Comms., Econ. Club Indpls. Republican. Presbyterian. Avocations: traveling, walking, reading, learning new ideas.

HENSLEY, ANTHONY M. state legislator; b. Topeka, Sept. 2, 1953; s. Harland Leroy and Georgina (Haydon) H.; m. Deborah Hensley; 1 child, Kathleen. BS, Washburn U., 1975; MS, Kans. State U., 1985. Mem. from dist. 58 Kans. State Senate, 1977-92, mem. from dist. 19, 1992—, minority leader, 1997; spl. edn. tchr., 1975—. Chmn. Washburn U. Young Dems., 1972-73, Shawnee County Dem. Ctrl. Com., 1981-86, 2d Dist. Dem. Com., 1991-93; committeeman 8th precinct 4th Ward Dem. Com., Topeka, 1976—; mem. Breakthrough House. Named one of Outstanding Young Men in Am., 1978, 82. Mem. Optimists. Home: 2226 SE Virginia Ave Topeka KS 66605-1357

HENSON, C. WARD, mathematician, educator; b. Worcester, Mass., Sept. 25, 1940; s. Charles W. and Daryl May (Hoyt) H.; m. Faith deMena Travis, August 31, 1963; children: Julia Rebecca, Suzanne Amy, Claire Victoria. AB, Harvard U., 1962; PhD, MIT, 1967. Asst. prof. Duke U., Durham, N.C., 1967-74, N.Mex. State U., Las Cruces, 1974-75, U. Ill., Urbana, 1975-77, assoc. prof., 1977-81, prof., 1981—, chmn. dept. math., 1988-92. Vis. assoc. prof. U. Wis., Madison, 1979-80; vis. prof. RWTH Aachen, Fed. Republic Germany, 1985-86, Univ. Tübingen, Fed. Republic Germany, 1992-93. Mem. Assn. for Symbolic Logic (sec.-treas. 1982-2000, pub. 1999—), Am. Math. Soc., London Math. Soc., European Assn. Theoretical Computer Sci. Office: U Ill Dept Math 1409 W Green St Urbana IL 61801-2943 E-mail: henson@math.uiuc.edu.

HENSON, DAVID B. university administrator; b. Orlando, Fla. m. Earlene V. Ovletrea; children: Mary, Charles. BS in Biology, Fla. A&M U., 1961; MSEd in Chemistry, Tuskegee U., 1968; PhD in Biochemistry, U. Iowa, 1972. Acting chmn. dept. biochemistry, asst. dean student affairs Howard U. Coll. Medicine, assoc. prof. biochemistry; dean student affairs, assoc. dean Yale Coll.; lectr. molecular biophysics and biochemistry, fellow Timothy Dwight Coll., Yale U.; provost, prof. chemistry Fla. Atlantic U., Broward; vice chancellor acad. svcs./student support svcs. U. Colo., Boulder; pres., prof. chemistry Ala. A&M U., Huntsville; v.p. student svcs. Purdue U., West Lafayette, Ind.; pres., prof. biochemistry Lincoln U., Jefferson City, Mo., 1997—. Contbr. articles to profl. publs. Treas. Coun. on Pub. Higher Edn. Mo.; bd. dirs. Jefferson City C. of C.; bd. govs. Capital Region Med. Ctr.; mem. steering com. River Rendezvous. Diabetes rsch. fellow U. Tex. Med. Sch., Houston, fellow Am. Coun. Edn. Mem. Sigma Xi, Beta Kappa Chi, Alpha Phi Alpha. Office: Lincoln U 340 Tomahawak Rd Jefferson City MO 65101-4463

HENSON, ROBERT FRANK, lawyer; b. Jenny Lind, Ark., Apr. 10, 1925; s. Newton and Nell Edith (Kessinger) H.; m. Jean Peterson Henson, Sept. 14, 1946; children: Robert F., Sandra Henson Curfman, Laura, Thomas, David, Steven. BS, U. Minn., 1948, JD, 1950. Bar: Minn. 1950, U.S. Supreme Ct. 1972. Atty. Soo Line R.R., 1950-52; ptnr. Cant, Haverstock, Beardsley, Gray & Plant, Mpls., 1952-66; sr. ptnr. Henson & Efron, 1966-94, of counsel, 1995—; !. Chmn. Minn. Lawyers Profl. Responsibility Bd., 1981-86; co-chmn. Supreme Ct. Study Com. on Lawyer Discipline, 1992-94. Trustee Mpls. Found., 1974-85, Emma Howe Found, 1986-90; chmn. Hennepin County Mental Health and Mental Retardation Bd., 1968-70. Served with USN, 1943-46. Fellow Am. Bar Found.; mem. ABA, Hennepin County Bar Assn. (pres. 1968-69), Minn. Bar Assn., Order of Coif Unitarian. Office: 220 S Sixth St Ste 1800 Minneapolis MN 55402-4502 Personal E-mail: rhenson@mn.rr.com. Business E-mail: rhenson@henson.efron.com .

HENTGEN, PATRICK GEORGE, baseball player; b. Detroit, Nov. 13, 1968; Pitcher Toronto Blue Jays, 1991-99, St. Louis Cardinals, 2000—. Mem. Am. League All-Star Team, 1993-94; player World Series Games, 1993. Named Am. League Pitcher of Yr., The Sporting News, 1996; recipient Cy Young award Baseball Writers' Assn. Am., 1996. Office: St Louis Cardinals 250 Stadium Plz Saint Louis MO 63102-1722

HENZLIK, RAYMOND EUGENE, zoophysiologist, educator; b. Casper, Wyo., Dec. 26, 1926; s. William H. Henzlik and Adeline Adele (Brown) Wolff; m. Wilma Louise Bartels, Oct. 1, 1950; children: Randall Eugene, Nancy Jo. BS, U. Nebr., 1948, MS, 1952, PhD, 1960; postgrad., Cornell U., 1961-62. Tchr. biology and chemistry York (Nebr.) High Sch., 1948-50; sci. edn. supr. Tchrs. Coll., U. Nebr., Lincoln, 1951-53; tchr. biology Omaha North High Sch., 1953-56; instr. biology Nebr. Wesleyan U., Lincoln, 1957-59; asst. prof. zoology and biology U. Nebr., 1959-61; asst. prof. biology Ball State U., Muncie, Ind., 1962-67, assoc. prof. physiology, 1967-69, prof. physiology, 1970—. Adj. vis. prof. vet. physiology Tex. A&M U., College Station, 1984-85; anatomy cons. Nat. Prescription Footwear Applicators Assn., Muncie, 1962—; lectr. Pedorthics Tech. Program, Muncie, 1977—; cons. ednl. affairs Argonne (Ill.) Nat. Lab., 1970-76; dir. ednl. program Am. Diabetes Assn., Muncie, 1979-83; vis. prof. health sci. USAF European Ctr., Ramstein and Rhein Main, Germany, 1977-78; lectr. Ind. Health Care Assn., 1985-91. Author: Human Physiology Lab Manual, 1976-92; contbr. articles to profl. jours. Pres. Muncie Tech. Soc., 1975-80; mem. bd. Am. Diabetes Assn. Delaware County, Muncie, 1979-85. Radiation biology fellow NSF/AEC, U. Mich., 1960, Radiobiology fellow AEC/NSF, Cornell U., 1961-62, Radiation Biology Rsch. fellow U.S. Radiobiology Lab N.C. State U., 1965, P.R. Nuclear Ctr., 1967. Mem. AAAS, Nutrition Today Soc., Ind. Acad. Sci., Muncie Tech. Soc., Mensa, Sigma Xi, Phi Delta Kappa. Avocations: renting houses, reading, book collecting. Home: 5009 N Somerset Dr Muncie IN 47304-6501 Office: Ball State U Physiology and Health Sci Dept 2000 W University Ave Muncie IN 47306-0002

HEPNER, JAMES O. medical school director; BA, PhD, U. Iowa; MHA, Wash. U., St. Louis. Dir., 1967—; hosp. adminstr. Jewish Hosp., St. Louis; grant reviewer Dept. of Health and Human Svc.; dir. Interagy. Inst. for Fed. Healthcare Execs. Cons. Air Force Surgeon Gen. Co-editor-in-chief Best Practices and Benchmarking in Healthcare: A Practical Jour. for Client and Mgmt. Applications. Recipient Gold Medal for Excellence and Leadership Med. Svc. Corp., Outstanding Healthcare award Hosp. Assn. of Met. St. Louis. Mem. Assn. of Univ. Programs in Health Adminstrn. (past bd. chmn.), Am. Coll. of Healthcare Execs. (bd. chmn., Silver Medal award of excellence Office: Wash U Sch of Medicine 660 S Euclid Ave Saint Louis MO 63110-1010

HEPPNER, GLORIA HILL, medical science administrator, educator; b. Gt. Falls, Mont., May 30, 1940; d. Eugene Merrill and Georgia M. (Swanson) Hill; m. Frank Henry Heppner, June 6, 1964 (div. 1975); 1 child, Michael Berkeley. BA, U. Calif., Berkeley, 1962, MA, 1964, PhD, 1967. Damon Runyon postdoctoral fellow U. Wash., Seattle, 1967-69; asst. and assoc. prof. Brown U., Providence, 1969-79, Herbert Fanger meml. lectr., 1988; chmn. dept. immunology, dir. labs., sr. v.p. Mich. Cancer Found., Detroit, 1979-91; dir. breast cancer program Karmanos Cancer Inst., 1991—, dep. dir., 1994—; assoc. chairperson for rsch. dept. internal medicine Wayne State U. Sch. Medicine, Detroit, 1991-2001, asst. dean cancer program, 2002—, asst. dean for cancer rsch., 2002—. Mem. external adv. com. basic sci. program M.D. Anderson Hosp. and Tumor Clinic, Houston, 1984-94; mem. external adv. com. Case Western Res. U. Cancer Ctr., Cleve., 1988—, Roswell Park Meml. Inst., Buffalo, 1991-98; Sarah Stewart meml. lectr. Georgetown U., Washington, 1988; bd. sci. counselors Nat. Inst. Dental Rsch., 1993-97. Editor: Macrophages and Cancer, 1988; mem. editl. bd. Cancer Rsch., 1989-93, Jour. Nat. Cancer Inst., 1988, Sci., 1988-92; contbr. over 200 articles to sci. jours. Bd. dirs. Lyric Chamber Ensemble, 1996-99. Recipient Mich. Sci. Trail-Blazer award State of Mich., 1987; fellow Damon Runyon-Walter Winchell Found., 1967-69. Mem. AAAS, Am. Assn. for Cancer Rsch. (bd. dirs. 1983-86, chmn. long-range planning com. 1989-91), Am. Assn. Immunologists, Metastasis Rsch. Soc. (bd. dirs. 1985-89), Women in Cancer Rsch. (nat. pres.), Internat. Differentiation Soc. (v.p. 1990-92, pres. 1992-94), LWV (bd. dirs. Grosse Pointe, Mich. 1989-95). Democrat. Avocations: music, theater. Office: Karmanos Cancer Inst 2nd Fl 4100 John R Exec Office Detroit MI 48201

HERB, MARVIN J. food products executive; b. 1937; BS, U. Buffalo, 1959; MBA, U. Toledo, 1964. Mgmt. trainee Kroger Co., Toledo, 1960-65; with Pepsi-Cola Co., Inc., 1965-72; various positions including pres. Pepsi-Cola Bottling Co. Indpls, Inc.; with Borden, Inc., N.Y.C., 1972-76, v.p. dairy and svc. divsn., 1976-77, pres. dairy and svc. divsn., 1977-78, corp. v.p., pres. dairy and svc. divsn., 1978-81; chmn. bd. Hondo, Inc., Niles, Ill., 1981—. Office: Hondo Inc 7400 N Oak Park Ave Niles IL 60714-3818

HERBERT, EDWARD FRANKLIN, public relations executive; b. N.Y.C., Jan. 30, 1946; s. H. Robert and Florence (Bender) H.; m. Rhonda J. Scharf, Aug. 20, 1967; children: Jason Dean and Heather Ann (twins). B.S. in Comm., Syracuse U., 1967, M.S., 1969. Assoc. dir. pub. relations Am. Optometric Assn., Washington, 1971; community relations specialist Gen. Electric Co., Columbia, Md., 1971-73, pub. relations account supr., 1973-75; dir. pub. affairs Nat. Consumer Fin. Assn., Washington, 1975-78; regional dir. pub. relations Montgomery Ward Co., Balt., 1978-80, fin. info. services dir., Chgo., 1980-81, internal comm. dir., 1981-82, corp. comm. dir., 1982-83; regional dir. pub. relations MCI Comm. Corp., Chgo., 1983-84; dir. comm. MCI Midwest, MCI Telecom. Corp., 1985-93; prin. Edward F. Herbert & Assoc., 1993—; Bd. dirs. United Cerebral Palsy of Chgo., Better Bus. Bur. Served with U.S. Army, 1969-71. Mem. Pub. Relations Soc. Am., Execs. Club of Chgo., Info. Industry Council. E-mail: efherbert@aol.com. Home and Office: 830 Timberhill Ln Highland Park IL 60035-5121

HERBERT, VICTOR JAMES, foundation administrator; b. Follansbee, W.Va., Aug. 6, 1917; s. Oliver James and Gertrude Mae (Lazear) H.; m. Dorothy Clara Johnson, Sept. 2, 1942 (dec. 1997); children: Victor J., Dorothy Constance; m. Venita Foster, Oct. 10, 1998. A.B., Bethany (W.Va.) Coll., 1940. Adminstr., negotiator, airline employee orgns.; a founder Air Line Stewards and Stewardesses Assn., Internat., 1946, acting pres., 1946-51, asst. to pres., 1951-59; in charge edn. and orgn. dept. Air Line Pilots Assn. A.F.L., 1946-62. Pres. Airline Employees Assn. Editor: Air Line Employee. Pres. bd. dirs. Bus. Indsl. Ministry. Mem. Beta Theta Pi. Presbyn. Club: Mason. Home: 14730 Greenview Rd Orland Park IL 60462-1992 Office: Air Line Employees Assn Internat 6500 W 65th St Ste 201 Chicago IL 60638-4912 E-mail: aleaintl@aol.com.

HERBERT, WILLIAM CARLISLE, lawyer; b. Gainesville, Fla., Aug. 25, 1947; s. Thomas Walter and Jean Elizabeth (Linton) H.; m. Mary Lee Dedinsky. AB, Princeton U., 1969; MSJ, Northwestern U., 1970, JD cum laude, 1976. Bar: Ill. 1976, U.S. Ct. Appeals (7th cir.) 1977, Fla. 1978, U.S. Dist. Ct. (no. dist.) Ill. 1978, U.S. Supreme Ct. 1980, U.S. Tax Ct. 1982. Law clk. to Hon. Latham Castle U.S. Ct. Appeals (7th cir.), 1976-77; ptnr. Foley & Lardner, Chgo. Exec. editor Northwestern U. Law Rev., 1976. Mem. ABA, Ill. State Bar Assn., Fla. Bar, Chgo. Bar Assn., Legal Club Chgo., U. Club Chgo. Presbyterian. Office: Foley & Lardner 3 1st National Plz Chicago IL 60602

HERBRUCKS, STEPHEN, food products executive; b. 1950; s. Harry Herbrucks. Pres. Herbruck Poultry Ranch Inc., Saranac, Mich., Poultry Mgmt. Systems, Saranac, 1980—. Office: Herbruck Poultry Ranch Inc 6425 W Grand River Ave Saranac MI 48881-9669

HERBST, ARTHUR LEE, obstetrician, gynecologist; b. N.Y.C., Sept. 14, 1931; s. Jerome Richard and Blanche (Vatz) H.; m. Lee Ginsburg, Aug. 10, 1958. A.B. magna cum laude, Harvard Coll., 1953, M.D. cum laude, 1959; DSc (hon.), N.E. Ohio U., 2001. Diplomate Am. Bd. Ob-gyn. (bd. dirs. 1985-93, dir. div. gynecol. oncology 1989-91). Intern Mass. Gen. Hosp., Boston, 1959-60, resident, 1960-62; resident in obstetrics and gynecology Boston Hosp. for Women, 1962-65; instr., assoc. prof. obstetrics-gynecology Mass. Gen. Hosp. and Harvard U. Med. Sch., Boston, 1965-76; Joseph B. DeLee prof. obstetrics and gynecology U. Chgo., 1976-84; chmn. dept. obstetrics-gynecology Chgo. Lying In Hosp., 1976—; Joseph B. DeLee Disting. Service prof. U. Chgo., 1984—2001; chmn. exec. com. U. Chgo. Hosps. and Clinics, 1980-84. Contbr. articles to profl. jours. Fellow Royal Coll. Obstetricians and Gynecologists (hon.), Inst. Med., Nat. Acad. Scis.; mem. AMA, ACS, ACOG, Am. Gynecol. and Obstet. Soc. (pres. 1997-98), Am. Assn. Profs. Ob-Gyn., Ctrl. Assn. Obstetricians and Gynecologists, Chgo. Gynecologic Soc., Soc. Pelvic Surgeons, Endocrine Soc., Infertility Soc., Soc. Gynecologic Oncologists. Home: 1234 N State Pkwy Chicago IL 60610-2219 Office: U Chgo Med Ctr 5841 S Maryland Ave Chicago IL 60637-1463

HERBST, ERIC, physicist, astronomer; b. N.Y.C., Jan. 15, 1946; s. Stuart Karl and Dorothy (Polakoff) H.; m. Judith Strassman, Oct. 15, 1972; children: Elisabeth, Andrea, Seth. AB, U. Rochester, 1966; MA, Harvard U., 1969, PhD, 1972. Asst. prof. chemistry Coll. of William and Mary, Williamsburg, Va., 1974-79, assoc. prof.chemistry, 1979-80; assoc. prof. physics Duke U., Durham, N.C., 1980-86, prof. physics, 1986-91, Univ. zu Köln, Cologne, Germany, 1988-89, Ohio State U., Columbus, 1991—, prof. astronomy, 1992—. Cons. NASA, Washington, 1985-90, NSF, Washington, 1989-92. Contbr. over 200 articles and 25 revs. to profl. jours. Recipient Humboldt award Humboldt Found., 1988, Max Planck prize Max Planck Soc., 1993. Fellow Am. Phys. Soc.; mem. Am. Astron. Soc., Am. Chem. Soc., Sigma Xi. Achievements include theory of how organic molecules are formed in space; theory of floppy molecules. Office: Ohio State U Dept Physics 174 W 18th Ave Columbus OH 43210-1106 E-mail: herbst@mps.ohio-state.edu.

HERBST, JAN FRANCIS, physicist, researcher; b. Tucson, May 1, 1947; s. Alva and Frances Theresa (Feler) H.; m. Margaret Mae Priest, July 24, 1982; children: Helen, John, Mary. BA in Physics, MS, U. Pa., 1968; PhD, Cornell U., 1974. Postdoctoral rsch. assoc. Nat. Bur. Standards, Gaithersburg, Md., 1974-76; asst. physicist Brookhaven Nat. Lab., Upton, N.Y., 1976-77; assoc. sr. rsch. physicist GM Rsch. Labs., Warren, Mich., 1977-81, staff rsch. scientist, 1981-85, mgr. magnetic materials sect., 1984—, sr. staff rsch. scientist, 1985-93, prin. rsch. scientist, 1993—. Mem. basic energy scis. adv. com. Dept. Energy, 1996-2000; mem. panel for physics Nat. Rsch. Coun. bd. assessment NIST Programs, 2000—. Contbr. articles over 95 to profl. jours. Recipient Campbell award GM Rsch. Labs., 1983, McCuen award GM Rsch. Labs., 1987, Kettering award GM Corp., 1987. Fellow Am. Phys. Soc. (sec.-treas. div. condensed matter physics 1985-90, nominating com. 1996-98, Internat. prize for new materials 1986). Achievements include patents for in field. Office: Mc 480-106-224 30500 Mound Rd Warren MI 48092-2031

HERD, HAROLD SHIELDS, state supreme court justice; b. Coldwater, Kans., June 3, 1918; B.A., Washburn U., 1941, J.D., 1942. Bar: Kans. 1943. Partner firm Rich and Herd, Coldwater, 1946-53; individual practice law, 1953-79; justice Kans. Supreme Ct., 1979-93; ret., 1993; disting. jurist in residence Washburn Law Sch., Topeka, 1993—. Mayor, Coldwater, 1949-53, county atty., Comanche County, Kans., 1954-58; mem. Kans. Senate, 1965-73, minority floor leader, 1969-73. Bd. govs. Washburn Law Sch., 1974-78, disting. jurist in residence, 1993-94; mem. Kans. Com. for Humanities, 1975-80, chmn. 1980, Hall Ctr. for Humanities, adv. coun. Kans. U. Mem. S.W. Bar Assn. (pres. 1977), Kans. Bar Assn. (exec. council 1973-80). Office: Washburn Law Sch 1700 SW College Ave Topeka KS 66621-0001

HERINGTON, LEIGH ELLSWORTH, state legislator, lawyer; b. Rochester, N.Y., Aug. 8, 1945; s. Donald G. and Ethel (Buck) H.; m. Anita Dixon, Dec. 12, 1970; children: Laurie, Tanya. AAS, Alfred State Coll., 1965; BBA, Kent State U., 1967, MBA, 1971; JD, U. Akron, 1976. Bar: Ohio 1976. Asst. sports info. dir. Kent State U., Ohio, 1969-70, asst. coord. internal comm., 1970-71, asst. dir. alumni rels., 1971-72; dir. pub. rels. Walsh Coll., Canton, Ohio, 1972-73; dir. comm. Hiram Coll., 1973-77; sole practice Aurora, 1977-78; ptnr. Christley, Herington & Pierce, 1978—; mem. Ohio Senate from 28th dist., Columbus, 1994—. Instr. law Hiram Coll., 1978— . Pres. Crestwood Bd. Edn., Portage County, Ohio, 1981, Portage County United Way, 1984; chmn. crusade Am. Cancer Soc., Portage County. Served with U.S. Army, 1968-69. Recipient Pres.'s award Portage County United Way, 1983; named Alumnus of Yr., Kent State U. Bus. Coll., 1984, Vol. of Yr., Portage County, 1986. Mem. ABA, Ohio State Bar Assn., Portage County Bar Assn., Ohio Coun. Sch. Bd. Attys., Pub. Rels. Soc. Am., Aurora-Streetsboro Club (charter), Rotary. Democrat. Office: Christley Herington & Pierce 14 New Hudson Rd Aurora OH 44202-9350 Address: 4039 Hardin Rd Ravenna OH 44266-9313 Office: Ohio Senate Senate Bldg Columbus OH 43215

HERMAN, SIDNEY N. lawyer; b. Chgo., May 14, 1953; s. Leonard M. and Suzanne (Nierman) H.; m. Meg Dobies. BA, Haverford Coll., 1975; JD, Northwestern U., 1978. Bar: Ill. 1978, U.S. Dist. Ct. (no. dist.) Ill. 1978, U.S. Ct. Appeals (7th cir.) 1982, U.S. Supreme Ct. 1983. Assoc. Kirkland & Ellis, Chgo., 1978-84, equity ptnr., 1984-93; founding ptnr. Bartlit Beck Herman Palenchar & Scott, 1993—. Bd. dirs. Todd Shipyards Corp., Sigmatron, Inc., Chgo., Global Material Techs., Chgo. Lawyers' Com. for Civil Rights Under Law, Inc.; mem. law bd. Northwestern U. Sch. Law. Articles editor Northwestern U. Law Rev. Trustee Francis W. Parker Sch.; bd. mem. Chgo. Lawyers' com. for Civil Rights Under Law. Mem. ABA, Ill. Bar Assn. Jewish. Office: Bartlit Beck Et Al Courthouse Pl 54 W Hubbard St Ste 300 Chicago IL 60610-4668

HERMES, MARJORY RUTH, machine embroidery and arts educator; b. Caldwell, Kans., June 28, 1931; d. Truman Homer and Olive Ruth (Ridings) Brown; m. Ogden S. Jones, Jr., Dec. 17, 1949 (div. Aug. 1956); m. Richard Lawrence Hermes, July 18, 1963; children: Penelope, Peter, Deborah, Patricia, Pamela, Kristin. Student, U. Kans., 1949-50, Arkansas City Jr. Coll., 1953-54. Sec. Maurer-Neuer Corp., Arkansas City, Kans., 1954-56, Lesh, Bradley & Barrand, Lawrence, 1959-60; exec. sec. Houston Corp., Wichita, 1956-57; mgr. Ind. Ins. Co., Landstuhl, Fed. Republic Germany, 1960-62; sec. U. Kans., Lawrence, 1962-63; photograph restorer Herb's Studio, 1977-78; ptnr., agt. Hayes-Richardson-Santee Inc., 1978-83; instr. sewing and machine embroidery Self & Bob's Bernina, 1985-95. Mem. Lawrence Ins. Bd., 1980-83. Bd. dirs. United Way, Lawrence, 1981-83; host Am. Indian Athletic Hall of Fame, 1980-82; treas. local polit. campaigns, 1984, 88; leader Therapeutic Horse Riding Instrn., Lawrence, 1992-95; vol. Lawrence Sr. Ctr., 1999—. Mem. Nat. Machine Embroidery Instrs. Assn. (bd. dirs. for N.D., S.D., Nebr., Iowa, Mo., Minn. and Kans. 1987-90), Am. Sewing Guild, Am. Bus. Women's Assn. (v.p. Lawrence 1980-81, pres. 1981-82, Inner Circle award 1982, Woman of Yr. award 1984), Lawrence C. of C. (envoy 1978-83). Republican. Avocations: horsemanship, travel, sailing. Home: 2513 W 24th Ter Lawrence KS 66047-2818

HERNANDEZ, RAMON ROBERT, retired clergyman and librarian; b. Chgo., Feb. 23, 1936; s. Eleazar Dario and Marie Helen (Stange) H.; m. Fern Ellen Muschinske, Aug. 11, 1962; children: Robert Frank, Maria Marta. BA, Elmhurst (Ill.) Coll., 1957; BD, Eden Theol. Sem., St. Louis, 1962; MA, U. Wis., 1970. Co-pastor St. Stephen United Ch. Christ, Merrill, Wis., 1960-64; dir. youth work Wis. Conf. United Ch. Christ, Madison, 1964-70; dir. T.B. Scott Free Library, Merrill, 1970-75, McMillan Meml. Library, Wisconsin Rapids, Wis., 1975-83, Ann Arbor (Mich.) Pub. Library, 1983-94; pastor Comty. Congl. Ch., Pinckney, Mich., 1994-98. Seminar leader on pub. libr. long-range planning, budgeting and handling problem patrons. Editl. com. mem. Songs of Many Nations Songbook, 1970; contbr. articles to profl. jours. Treas. Ann Arbor Homeless Coalition, 1985-88; bd. dirs., sec., v.p. Riverview Hosp. Assn., Wisconsin Rapids, 1977-83; bd. dirs. Hist. Soc. Mich., 1988-90, Ind. Living, Inc., Dame County, Wis., 2001—; bd. trustees Madison Pub. Libr, Wis., 2000—. Mem. ALA, Wis. Libr. Assn. (Leadership award 1980, pres. 1980), Rotary (pres. Merrill chpt. 1974-75, Community Svc. award 1975, pres. Ann Arbor chpt. 1990-91, Paul Harris fellow 1994).

HERNANDEZ, ROBERTO, professional baseball player; b. Santurce, P.R., Nov. 11, 1964; Student, U. S.C. Pitcher CHW, 1991-97, SF, 1997, Tampa Bay Devil Rays, 1998—. Office: Tampa Bay Devil Rays Tropicana Field One Tropicana Dr Saint Petersburg FL 33705 Fax: 727-825-3111.*

HERPE, DAVID A. lawyer; b. Chgo., May 2, 1953; s. Richard S. and Beverly H.; m. Tina Demsetz, Aug. 21, 1977; children: Lauren E., Stacy P. BA in Econs., U. Ill., 1975; JD, U. Chgo., 1978. Bar: Ill. 1978, U.S. Dist. Ct. (no. dist.) Ill. 1979, U.S. Tax Ct. 1991. Assoc. then ptnr. Schiff, Hardin & Waite, Chgo., 1978-1996; ptnr. McDermott, Will & Emery, 1996—. Co-author: Illinois Estate Planning, Will Drafting and Estate Administration Forms-Practice, 2nd edit., 1994; contbr. articles to legal jours. Mem. and dir. Chgo. Estate Planning Coun. (pres. 2000-01). Fellow Am. Coll. of Trust and Estate Counsel; mem. ABA. Office: McDermott Will & Emery 227 W Monroe St Ste 3100 Chicago IL 60606-5096

HERRICK, KENNETH GILBERT, manufacturing company executive; b. Jackson, Mich., Apr. 2, 1921; s. Ray Wesley and Hazel Marie (Forney) H.; m. Shirley J. Todd, Mar. 2, 1942; children: Todd Wesley, Toni Lynn. Student public and pvt. schs., Howe, Ind.; LHD (hon.), Siena Heights Coll., 1974; HHD (hon.), Adrian Coll., 1975, Detroit Inst. Tech., 1980; LLD, Judson Coll., 1975; D Engring. (hon.), Albion Coll., 1981. With Tecumseh Products Co., Mich., 1940-42, 45—, v.p., 1961-66, vice chmn. bd., 1964-70, pres., 1966-70, chmn. bd., chief exec. officer, 1970-86, chmn. bd., 1986—. Bd. dirs. Howe Mil. Sch., 1970-81, from Herrick Found., 1970; mem. exec. adv. bd. St. Jude Children's Hosp., from 1978. Served with USAAC, 1942-45. Recipient Hon. Alumni award Mich. State U., 1975; Disting. Svc. award Albion Coll., 1975 Mem. Lenawee Country Club, Elks, Tecumseh Country Club, Masons. Presbyterian. Office: Tecumseh Products Co 100 E Patterson St Tecumseh MI 49286-2087

HERRICK, TODD W. manufacturing company executive; b. Tecumseh, Mich., 1942; Grad., U. Notre Dame, 1967. Pres., chief exec. officer Tecumseh (Mich.) Products Co. Office: Tecumseh Products Co 100 E Patterson St Tecumseh MI 49286-2087

HERRIFORD, ROBERT LEVI, SR. army officer; b. Lewistown, Ill., May 4, 1931; s. John and Lola (Braden) H.; m. Muriel Jean Davis, July 10, 1949; children: Robert Levi, Thomas Merle, David William, Deborah S., Traci Ann. B.S., U. Ariz., 1966, M.B.A., 1968. Enlisted in U.S. Army, 1948, commd. 2d lt., 1952, advanced through grades to maj. gen., 1979; service in Vietnam, 1966-67; comdr. 269th Ordnance Group Ft. Bragg, N.C., 1969-71; chief spl. items mgmt. Tank Automotive Command Detroit, 1971-72; comdr. Korean Procurement Agy. Seoul, 1973-74; dir. procurement Armaments Command Rock Island, Ill., 1974-76; comdr. Def. Contracts Region N.Y., 1976-78; asst. dep. chief of staff logistics Pentagon, 1978-80; dir. procurement and prodn. Devel. and Readiness Command Alexandria, Va., 1980-83; assoc. chief ops. officer, dir. support services Argonne Nat. Lab., 1983-95. Chmn. Minority Bus. Opportunity Council, N.Y.C., 1976-78. Decorated Legion of Merit, D.S.M., Def. Superior Service medal, Bronze Star, Airmedal, numerous others. Mem. Am. Def. Preparedness Assn., Assn. U.S. Army, Am. Legion, Nat. Contracts Mgmt. Assn. (chpt. pres. 1975-76) Office: 104 N Pittsburg Lndg Springfield IL 62707-7959 E-mail: Robe@famvid.com.

HERRIN, MORELAND, retired civil engineering educator, consultant; b. Morris, Okla., Nov. 14, 1922; s. Birney D. and Lucille (Moreland) H.; m. Nancy M. Jameson, Dec. 24, 1946; children— Jeannie N., Stanley M., Gwen M. BSCE, Okla. State U., 1947, MS, 1949; PhD, Purdue U., 1954. Instr. Okla. State U., 1947-49, assoc. prof., 1954-58; prof. civil engring. U. Ill., Urbana, 1958—; ret. Dir. Ill. Coop. Transp. Program; design engr. Hudgins, Thompson & Ball (engrs.), Oklahoma City, 1949-50; materials engr. Garnett, Fleming, Cordray and Carpenter, Belvidere, Ill., 1957; asst. materials engr., road test Am. Assn. State Hwy. Ofcls., Ottawa, Ill., 1958; cons. hwy. materials, pavement design, 1955— Contbr. articles to profl. jours. Served to capt. USAAF, 1943-46. Recipient Epstein award U. Ill., 1962 Mem. Transp. Research Bd., Assn. Asphalt Paving Technology (pres. 1978), ASCE, Am. Soc. Engring. Edn., ASTM, Chi Epsilon, Tau Beta Pi. Mem. Disciples of Christ Ch. Home: 1414 W William St Champaign IL 61821-4407 Office: 1208 NCEL 205 N Mathews Ave Urbana IL 61801-2350

HERRING, RAYMOND MARK, marketing professional, researcher; b. Nashville, Sept. 23, 1952; s. Raymond Benjamin and Alma Ruth (Murrell) H. BA, Baylor U., 1974, MA, 1976, EdD, 1983. Rsch. and evaluation specialist McLennan County Med. Edn. and Rsch. Found., Waco, Tex., 1979-82; dir. edn., pub. rels. Providence Hosp., 1982-85, dir. ctr. for health promotion, 1983-85; v.p. John Leifer, Ltd., Shawnee Mission, Kans., 1985-86; pres. Mark Herring Assocs., Inc., Overland Park, 1986—; rsch. dir. Qualitative Svcs. Market Directions, Inc., Kansas City, Mo., 2000—. Adv. bd. Upjohn Healthcare Svcs., Waco, 1984-85; mem. editorial bd. Healthcare Mgmt. Rev., Rockville, Md., 1986-90. Contbr. articles to profl. jours. Active HealthPlus, Overland Park; bd. dirs. Am. Diabetes Assn., Waco, 1984-85, Tex. Soc. Hosp. Educators, 1983-85. Mem. Qualitative Rsch. Cons. Assn. Office: Mark Herring Assocs Inc 2150 Diamond Rock Hill Rd Malvern PA 19355

HERRMANN, DAN, food products executive; CFO Schwan's Sales Ent., Marshall, Minn. Office: Schwan's Sales Enterprises 115 W College Dr Marshall MN 56258 Office Fax: (507) 537-8450.

HERRON, ORLEY R. college president; b. Olive Hill, Ky., Nov. 16, 1933; s. Orley R. and Hyllie W. (Weaver) H.; m. Donna Jean Morgan, Aug. 24, 1956; children: Jill Donette, Morgan Niles, Mark Weaver. BA, Wheaton Coll., 1955; MA, Mich. State U., 1959, PhD, 1965; LittD (hon.), Houghton Coll., 1972; LHD (hon.), Lesley Coll., 1983. Dean of students Westmont Coll., Santa Barbara, Calif., 1961-67; dir. doctoral program/student pers. U. Miss., 1967-68; asst. to pres. Ind. State U., 1968-70; pres. Greenville (Ill.) Coll., 1970-77, Nat Louis U. (formerly Nat. Coll. Edn.), Evanston, Ill., 1977-97; chmn. and pres. ORH group eBooks Interactive, 1998—; founder AutoeDirect.com, Inc., 2000—. Mem. Ill. Commn. for Improvement Elem. and Secondary Edn., 1983-1985; chmn. bd. Harris Bank, Wilmette, Ill., 1991—, also bd. dirs.; bd. dirs. Corp. Cmty. Schs. Am., 1989—. Author: Role of the Trustee, 1969, Input-Output, 1970, New Dimensions in Stude Personnel Administration, 1970, A Christian Executive in a Secular World, 1979, Who Controls Your Child?, 1980, Words to Live By, 1997, (cassette tape) Governing Higher Education in the 70's, 1970. Rep. of Pres. U.S. 25th Anniversary UNESCO, 1971; mem. adv. bd. Expt. on Internat. Living, Santa Barbara, 1961-67; mem. Gov.'s Task Force on Encouraging Citizen Involvement in Edn., 1986-87; nat. dir. educators for reelection of Pres., 1972; bd. dirs. Ch. Centered Evangelism; mem. Chgo. Sun. Evening Club, 1987-97. Lt. comdr. U.S. Naval Res., 1973-77. Recipient Crusader Christian Contbn. award Wheaton Coll., 1955, 74, Outstanding Citizen award Greenville Jaycees, 1971, Outstanding Educator award Religious Heritage of Am., 1987, Disting. Alumnus award Wheaton Coll., Outstanding Alumnus award New Philadelphia H.S., Amicus Polonae award, 1996. Mem. Am. Assn. Higher Edn., AAUP, Coun. on Inter-Instnl. Cooperation (pres.), Council Advancement Small Colls. (sec.), Christian Coll. Consortium (exec. com.), Fedn. Ind. Ill. Colls. (exec. bd. 1971-97), Assn. Free Meth. Ednl. Instns. (pres. 1973-75), Rotary, Kiwanis. Office: One Westminster Pl Ste 101 Lake Forest IL 60045 E-mail: orley@orhgroup.com.

HERRUP, KARL, neurobiologist; b. Pitts., July 16, 1948; s. J. Lester and Florence Bernice Herrup; m. Claire Morse, Aug. 20, 1972 (div. Jan. 1989); children: Rachael, Adam, Alex; m. Leslie Reinherz, Mar. 1, 1992; 1 adopted child, Leah. BA in Biology magna cum laude, Brandeis U., 1970; PhD in Neuro-and Behavioral Sci., Stanford U., 1974. Postdoctoral fellow in neurogenetics Harvard Med. Sch./Children's Hosp., Boston, 1974-77; postdoctoral fellow in pharmacology Biozentrum, Basel, Switzerland, 1978; asst. prof., then assoc. prof. human genetics Sch. Medicine Yale U., New Haven, 1978-84, assoc. prof. biology, 1986-88; assoc. prof. neurology Mass. Gen. Hosp., Boston, 1988-92; assoc. prof. neurosci. Harvard Med. Sch., 1988-92; dir. div. devel. neurobiology Eunice Kennedy Shriver Ctr. for Mental Retardation, Waltham, Mass., 1988-92; prof. Alzheimer Rsch. Ctr. Case Western Sch. Medicine, Cleve., 1992—, dir. Univ. Alzheimer Ctr., 1997—. Mem. staff Yale Comprehensive Cancer Ctr., New Haven, 1987-88. Contbr. articles to profl. publs.; mem. editorial bd. Jour. of Comprehensive Neurology, Neurobiology of Aging, Jour. of Neurosci. Fellow NSF, 1978, Med. Found., 1976, Jane Coffin Childs Meml. Rsch. Fund, 1974; recipient faculty award Andrew W. Mellon Found., 1982. Mem. Soc. for Neurosci. (mem. social issues com. 1987-90, program com. 1989-92, edn. com. 1992—, sec. Conn. chpt. 1982-84, v.p. 1987-88), Soc. for Devel. Biology, Sigma Xi. Office: Case Western Res Med Sch Alzheimer Rsch Lab 10900 Euclid Ave Cleveland OH 44106-1712

HERSETH, ADOLPH SYLVESTER (BUD HERSETH), classical musician; b. Lake Park, Minn., July 25, 1921; Student, New England Conservatory, Boston. Prin. trumpet player Chgo. Symphony Orch., 1948—. With U.S. Army, World War II. Named Instrumentalist of Yr., Musical Am., 1996. Office: care Chgo Symphony Orch Orchestra Hall 220 S Michigan Ave Chicago IL 60604-2596

HERSHER, RICHARD DONALD, management consultant; b. Atlantic City, May 24, 1942; s. Mayo Lawrence and Adele (Dahlman) H.; m. Betsy R. Schnitz, Mar. 15, 1970 (div. June 1983); children: Erin, Laura; m. Roza Khazina, Sept. 4, 1993. BS, U. Cin., 1966; MBA, U. Chgo., 1973. Indsl. engr. U.S. Steel Corp., Chgo., 1966-68; mfg. engr. Westinghouse Electric Corp., 1968-73; sr. indsl. engr. Abbott Labs., North Chicago, Ill., 1973-76; plant mgr. DeMert & Dougherty, Chgo., 1976-79; pres. Hersher Assocs., Deerfield, Ill., 1979-83; exec. cons. Inst. Mgmt. Resources, Westlake Village, Calif., 1983-87; v.p. ops. Rex Precision Products, Gardena, 1987; sr. cons. Morris Anderson & Assocs., Rosemont, Ill., 1987-92; pres. Hersher Cons., Glenview, 1992—. Mem. Inst. Mgmt. Cons., Inst. Indsl. Engrs., Am. Prodn. Inventory Control Soc.

HERSHMAN, BRANDT, state legislator; m. Lisa Hershman. Dist. ops. dir. U.S. Rep. Steve Buyer; mgr. Hershman Farms; ptnr. Wilkes Innovative Techs.; mem. Ind. State Senate, 2000—, mem. edn. com., pensions and labor com., others. Mem. governing bd. Ind. Rural Devel. Coun.; bd. dirs., v.p. Pi Kappa Phi. Mem. Ind. Econ. Devel. Assn. Republican. Office: 200 W Washington St Indianapolis IN 46204

HERTEL, CURTIS, state legislator; b. Detroit, Mar. 7, 1953; s. John and Marie (Kaufmann) H.; m. Vickie; children: Curtis Jr., Matthew. BS, Wayne State U., 1977. Precinct del. Mich. Dem. Party, 1976-78; legis. svc. dir. Detroit Health Dept., 1977-80; state rep. Dist. 12 Mich. Ho. of Reps., 1981-94, state rep. Dist. 2, 1995-97. Author: An Ethnic Profile, 1976.

HERZBERG, THOMAS, artist, illustrator; b. Chgo., Feb. 3, 1954; s. Carroll Alexander and Victoria Herzberg; m. Rosemary Ann Morrissey, Aug. 11, 1979; 1 child, Kyli Rose. BA, Northeastern U., 1975; MFA, Northern Ill. U., 1979. Instr. Am. Acad. Art, Chgo., 2000—. Illustrations appeared in Chgo. mag., Advertising Age, Playboy mag., World Book, Chgo. Tribune, Washington Post, Art Inst. Chgo., Goodman Theatre, Chg. Exhibited Art Inst. Chgo., 1978, 84, De Cordova Mus., Lincoln., Mass., 1978, 79, 83, Silvermine Guild Artists, New Canaan, Conn., 1980, Met. Mus. and Art Ctr., Coral Gables, Fla., 1980, 82, Hunterdon Art Ctr., Clinton, N.J., 1982, U. Dallas, 1983, 10th, 12th and 13th Ann. Soc. Newpaper Design, Am. Soc. Illustrators 28th, 39th and 41st Ann. Exhbns.; represented in permanent collections De Cordova Mus., Terrance Gallery, Palenville, N.Y., Met. Mus. and Art Ctr., Silvermine Guild Artists, Carnegie Inst., Art Inst. Chgo., Lincoln Park Zoo, Chgo. Symphony Orch.; over 1700 illustrations in newspapers, mags., books, mus. graphics, 1981—. Mem. Air Force Art Program, 1998—. Named Best of Show 3 Ann. Ill. Regional Print Show, 1980; recipient Award of Excellence New Horizons in Art North Shore Art League, 1980-82, Weston Press and Gallery award 8th Internat. Miniature Print Exhbn. Pratt Graphic Ctr., 1981, Cert. of Design Excellence Print's Regional Design Ann., 1994-96, 97, also numerous awards Art Direction mag. creativity show, 1992-93, Soc. Newspaper Design, Cert. of Merit Soc. Illustrators.

HERZENBERG, CAROLINE STUART LITTLEJOHN, physicist; b. East Orange, N.J., Mar. 25, 1932; d. Charles Frederick and Caroline Dorothea (Schulze) L.; m. Leonardo Herzenberg, July 29, 1961; children: Karen Ann, Catherine Stuart. SB, MIT, 1953; SM, U. Chgo., 1955, PhD, 1958; DSc (hon.), SUNY, Plattsburgh, 1991. Asst. prof. Ill. Inst. Tech., Chgo., 1961-66, research physicist ITT Research Inst., 1967-70, sr. physicist, 1970-71; lectr. Calif. State U., Fresno, 1975-76; physicist Argonne (Ill.) Nat. Lab., Ill., 1977-2001. Prin. investigator NASA Apollo Returned Lunar Sample Analysis Program, 1967-71; producer and host TV sci. series Camera on Sci.; disting. vis. prof. SUNY, Plattsburgh, 1991; mem. final selection com. 1993 Bower award and Prize for Achievement in Sci., 1993-94; bd. adv. the Bower award and Prize for Achievements in Sci.; mem. nat. panel of advisors PBS TV sci. series Bill Nye the Sci. Guy, 1991-95; steering com. mem. Midwest Consortium for Internat. Security Studies, 1994-95. Author: Women Scientists from Antiquity to the Present: An Index, 1986; co-author: (with R.H. Howes) Their Day in the Sun: Women of the Manhattan Project, 1999; contbr. articles to profl. jours. Candidate for alderman, Freeport, Ill., 1975; past chmn. NOW chpt., Freeport Am. Phys. Soc. Congl. Scientist fellow finalist, 1976-77; recipient award in sci. Chgo. Women's Hall of Fame, 1989. Fellow AAAS, Am. Phys. Soc. (past chmn. com., past sec.-treas. forum on Physics and Soc., past exec. bd. Forum on the History of Physics, panel pub. affairs), Assn. Women in Sci. (nat. sec. 1982-84, pres. 1988-90); mem. Sigma Xi. Home and Office: 1700 E 56th St Apt 2707 Chicago IL 60637-5092 E-mail: carol@herzenberg.net.

HERZIG, DAVID JACOB, pharmaceutical company executive, consultant; b. Cleve., Dec. 13, 1936; s. Marvin Laurence and Lillian Gertrude (Blaine) H.; m. Phyllis Glicksberg, Sept. 2, 1962; children: Michael, Pamela, Roberta, Karen. BA, Oberlin Coll., 1958; PhD in Chemistry, U. Cin., 1963. Vis. scientist NIH, Bethesda, Md., 1963-65, staff fellow, 1965-67; sr. rsch. assoc. NYU Sch. Medicine, N.Y.C., 1967-68, Warner Lambert, Parke-Davis Co., Ann Arbor, Mich., 1968-77, dir. immunopharmacology, 1977-81, dir. sci. devel., 1981-99; v.p. drug devel. and sci. devel.

Mich. Biotechnology Inst., also bd. dirs. Bd. dirs. Metabasis, Inc. Contbr. articles to profl. jours. Bd. dirs. Mich. Ctr. High Tech., 1992-95. Fellow Damon Runyon Meml. Fund. Mem. AAAS, Am. Soc. Pharmacology and Exptl. Therapeutics, Am. Acad. Allergy Immunology, Mich. Biotech. Assn. (bd. dirs. 1993-96, pres. 1994-96), N.Y. Acad. Scis., N.Y. Fencers Club (bd. dirs. 1970-77), Sigma Xi. Avocations: squash, fencing, furniture building. Home and Office: 3540 Windemere Dr Ann Arbor MI 48105-2842 E-mail: davidjhherzig@world.oberlin.edu.

HERZOG, FRED F. law educator; b. Prague, Czech Republic, Sept. 21, 1907; s. David and Anna (Reich) H.; m. Betty Ruth Cohen, Mar. 27, 1947 (dec. Sept. 1984); children: Stephen E., David R. Dr. Juris, U. Graz (Austria), 1931; JD with high distinction U. Iowa, 1942; LL.D. (hon.), John Marshall Law Sch., 1983. Bar: Iowa 1942, Ill. 1946, U.S. Supreme Ct. 1965. Judge, Vienna, Austria, 1937-38; prof. and dean Chgo.-Kent Coll. Law, 1947-73; spl. atty. Met. San. Dist. Greater Chgo., 1962-70; 1st asst. atty. gen. Ill., 1973-76; dean John Marshall Law Sch., Chgo., 1976-83, prof., 1976—. Recipient Americanism award DAR, 1978; Golden Doctor diploma U. Graz, 1981; award of Excellence, John Marshall Law Sch. Alumni Assn., 1981; cert. of Appreciation, Ill. Dept. Registration and Edn., 1978; Ill. Atty. Gen.'s award for Outstanding Pub. Service, 1976; Torch of Learning award Am. Friends of the Hebrew U., 1986; named to Sr. Citizens Hall of Fame, City of Chgo., 1983. Mem. ABA, Ill. Bar Assn., Chgo. Bar Assn., Ill. Appellate Lawyers Assn., Decalogue Soc. Lawyers, Mid-Am. Club, Internat. Club (Chgo.), Union League Club (Chgo.). Contbr. articles to legal jours. Office: John Marshall Law Sch 315 S Plymouth Ct Chicago IL 60604-3969

HESBURGH, THEODORE MARTIN, clergyman, former university president; b. Syracuse, N.Y., May 25, 1917; s. Theodore Bernard and Anne Marie (Murphy) H. Student, U. Notre Dame, 1934-37; PhB, Gregorian U., 1939; postgrad., Holy Cross Coll., Washington, 1940-43; STD, Cath. U. Am., 1945; 124 hon. degrees awarded between 1954-92. Joined Order of Congregation of Holy Cross, 1934, ordained priest Roman Cath. Ch., 1943. Chaplain Nat. Tng. Sch. for Boys, Washington, 1943-44; vets. chaplain U. Notre Dame, 1945-47, 138 hon. degrees awarded between 1954-98, 1948-49, exec. v.p., 1949-52, pres., 1952-87, pres. emeritus, 1987—, instr., asst. prof. religion, 1945-48, chmn. dept. religion, 1948-49. Fellow Am. Acad. Arts and Scis.; mem. Internat. Fedn. Cath. Univs., Commn. on Humanities, Inst. Internat. Edn. (pres., dir.), Cath. Theol. Soc., Chief Execs. Forum, Am. Philos. Soc., Nat. Acad. Edn., Coun. on Fgn. Rels. (trustee), Nat. Acad. Scis. (hon.), U.S. Inst. Peace (bd. dirs.). Author: Theology of Catholic Action, 1945, God and the World of Man, 1950, Patterns for Educational Growth, 1958, Thoughts for Our Times, 1962, More Thoughts for Our Times, 1965, Still More Thoughts for Our Times, 1966, Thoughts IV, 1968, Thoughts V, 1969, The Humane Imperative: A Challenge for the Year 2000, 1974, The Hesburgh Papers: Higher Values in Higher Education, 1979, God, Country, Notre Dame, 1990, Travels with Ted and Ned, 1992. Former dir. Woodrow Wilson Nat. Fellowship Corp.; mem. Civil Rights Commn., 1957-72; mem. of Carnegie Commn. on Future of Higher Edn.; chmn. U.S. Commn. on Civil Rights, 1969-72; mem. Commn. on an All-Volunteer Armed Force, 1970; chmn. with rank of ambassador U.S. delegation UN Conf. Sci. and Tech. for Devel., 1977-79 ; Bd. dirs. Am. Council Edn., Freedoms Found. Valley Forge, Adlai Stevenson Inst. Internat. Affairs; past trustee, chmn. Rockefeller Found.; trustee Carnegie Found. for Advancement Teaching, Woodrow Wilson Nat. Fellowship Found., Inst. Internat. Edn., Nutrition Found., United Negro Coll. Fund, others; chmn. Overseas Devel. Council; chmn. acad. council Ecumenical Inst. for Advanced Theol. Studies, Jerusalem. Decorated comdr. L'ordre des Arts et des Lettres. Recipient U.S. Navy's Disting. Pub. Service award, 1959; Presdl. Medal of Freedom, 1964, Gold medal Nat. Inst. Social Scis., 1969, Cardinal Gibbons medal Cath. U. Am., 1969, Bellarmine medal Bellarmine-Ursuline Coll., 1970; Meiklejohn award AAUP, 1970, Charles Evans Hughes award Nat. Conf. Christians and Jews, 1970; Merit award Nat. Cath. Ednl. Assn., 1971, Pres.' Cabinet award U. Detroit, 1971; Am. Liberties medallion Am. Jewish Com., 1971; Liberty Bell award Ind. State Bar Assn., 1971; Laetare medal Univ. Notre Dame, 1987, Pub. Welfare medal NAS, 1984; Pub. Svc. award Common Cause, 1984, Disting. Svc. award Assn. Cath. Colls. and Univs., 1982, Jefferson award Coun. Advancement and Support of Edn., 1982, Congl. Gold medal, 2000. Fellow Am. Acad. Arts and Scis.; mem. NAS (hon.), Internat. Fedn. Cath. Univs., Commn. on Humanities, Inst. Internat. Edn. (pres., bd. dirs.), Cath. Theol. Soc., Chief Execs. Forum, Am. Philos. Soc., Nat. Acad. Edn., Coun. on Fgn. Rels. (trustee). Office: U Notre Dame 1315 Hesburgh Libr Notre Dame IN 46556

HESCHEL, MICHAEL S. retail food products executive; b. June 18, 1941; m. Judi Heschel; 2 children. BS in Indsl. Engring., Ohio State U., 1964, MBA in Indsl. Engring., 1965, MS in Indsl. Engring., 1967; PhD in Indsl. Engring., Ariz. State U., 1970. Former sr. mgmt. systems analyst Boeing Aircraft Co.; former corp. mgr. ops. rsch. FMC Corp.; former corp. v.p. info. svcs. Am. Hosp. Supply Corp.; former corp. v.p. info. resources Baxter Internat. Inc.; former chmn., CEO Security Pacific Automation Co.; group v.p. info. systems The Kroger Co., Cin., 1991-94, sr. v.p., 1994-95, exec. v.p., chief info. officer, 1995—. Office: The Kroger Co 1014 Vine St Cincinnati OH 45202-1100

HESS, EVELYN VICTORINE (MRS. MICHAEL HOWETT), medical educator; b. Dublin, Ireland, Nov. 8, 1926; arrived in U.S., 1960, naturalized, 1965; d. Ernest Joseph and Mary (Hawkins) H.; m. Michael Howett, Apr. 27, 1954. MB, B.Ch, BAO, U. Coll., Dublin, 1949; MD, Univ. Coll., Dublin, 1980. Intern West Middlesex Hosp., London, Eng., 1950; resident Clare Hall Hosp., 1951-53, Royal Free Hosp. and Med. Sch., London, 1954-57; rsch. fellow in epidemiology of Tb Royal Free Med. Sch., 1955; asst. prof. internal medicine U. Tex. Southwestern Med. Sch., 1960-64; assoc. prof. dept. medicine U. Cin. Coll. Medicine, 1964-69, McDonald prof. medicine, 1969—, dir. div. immunology, 1964-95. Sr. investigator Arthritis and Rheumatism Found., 1963-68; attending physician Univ. Hosp., VA Hosp.; cons. Children's Hosp., Cin., 1967—, Jewish Hosp., Cin., 1968—; mem. various coms., mem. nat. adv. coun. NIH; mem. various coms. FDA, Cin. Bd. Health. Contbr. articles on immunology, rheumatic diseases to jours., chpts. to books. Active Nat. Pks. Assn., Smithsonian Instn., others. Recipient Arthritis Found., 1973, 78, 83, Am. Lupus Soc., 1979, Am. Acad. Family Practice, 1980, award for AIDS work State of Ohio, 1989, Spirit of Am. Women award, 1989, Daniel Drake medal U. Cin., 2001; travel fellow Royal Free Med. Sch., Scandinavia, 1956, Empire Rheumatism Coun., 1958-59. Master ACP (gov. Ohio chpt. 1999—, Master Tchr. award 1995), ACR (Disting. Rheumatologist award 1996); fellow AAAS, Am. Acad. Allergy, Royal Soc. Medicine; mem. Heberden Soc., Am. Coll. Rheumatology, Pan-Am. League Assns. for Rheumatology, Ctrl. Soc. Clin. Rsch., Am. Fedn. Clin. Rsch., Am. Assn. Immunologists, Am. Soc. Nephrology, Am. Soc. Clin. Pharmacology and Therapeutics, Transplantation Soc., N.Y. Acad. Scis., Soc. Exptl. Biology and Medicine, Rheumatological Soc. Colombia (hon.), Rheumatological Soc. Peru (hon.), Rheumatological Soc. Italy (hon.), Clin. Immunol. Soc. Japan (hon.), Alpha Omega Alpha. Home: 2916 Grandin Rd Cincinnati OH 45208-3418 Office: U Cin Med Ctr ML 563 MSB Cincinnati OH 45267-0001 E-mail: hessev@email.uc.edu.

HESS, FREDERICK J. lawyer; b. Highland, Ill., Sept. 22, 1941; s. Fred and Matilda (Maiden) H.; m. Mary V. Menkhus, Nov. 13, 1976; children—Frederick, M. Elizabeth. B.S. in Polit. Sci. and History, St. Louis U., 1963; J.D., Washburn Sch. Law, Topeka, 1971. Bar: Kans. 1971, Ill. 1975, U.S. Supreme Ct. 1975, D.C. 1977, U.S. Tax Ct. 1977. Asst. U.S. atty. Dept. Justice, East St. Louis, Ill., 1971-73, 1st asst. U.S. atty., 1973-76; ct. appt. U.S. Atty. E. Dist. of Ill., 1977; ptnr. Stiehl & Hess, Belleville, Ill., 1977-82; U.S. atty. U.S. Dist. Ct. (so. dist.) Ill., East St. Louis, 1982-93; pvt. practice Lewis Rice & Fingersh, Belleville, 1993—. Past pres. Nat. Assn. Former U.S. Attys., 1996; part-time judge Ill. Ct. of Claims, 1997—. Served to capt. USAF, 1964-68. Fellow ABA Found., ISBA Found., Ill. Bar Assn., Ill. Bar Found.; mem. Kans. Bar Assn., D.C. Bar Assn. Republican. Clubs: Tamarac Golf (Shilo, Ill.). Office: Lewis Rice & Fingersh 325 S High St Belleville IL 62220-2116

HESS, KARL, electrical and computer engineering educator; b. Trumau, Austria, June 20, 1945; came to U.S. 1977; naturalized 1988; s. Karl Joseph and Gertrude (Resch) H.; m. Sylvia Horvath, Sept. 1967; children: Ursula, Karl Ph.D., U. Vienna, Austria, 1970. Rsch. asst. U. Vienna, 1969-71, asst. prof., 1971-77, univ. lectr., 1977; vis. assoc. prof. U. Ill., Urbana, 1977-80, prof. elec. and computer engring., 1988—, adj. prof. supercomputing applications, 1990—, Swanlund Endowed chair, 1996—, prof. physics. Contbr. articles to profl. jours.; patentee in field Univ. scholar U. Ill., 1982-83; Fulbright scholar, 1973-74. Fellow AAAS, IEEE (J.J. Ebers award 1994, David Sarnoff field award 1995, H. Welker Meml. medal 2001), Am. Phys. Soc., Am. Acad. Arts and Scis., Nat. Acad. Engring. Avocations: classical music; chess. Home: 1805 Bentbrook Dr Champaign IL 61822-9220 Office: U Ill Beckman Inst 405 N Mathews Ave Urbana IL 61801-2325 E-mail: k-hess@uiuc.edu.

HESS, MARGARET JOHNSTON, religious writer, educator; b. Ames, Iowa, Feb. 22, 1915; d. Howard Wright and Jane Edith (Stevenson) Johnston; m. Bartlett Leonard Hess, July 31, 1937; children: Daniel, Deborah, John, Janet. BA, Coe Coll., 1937. Bible tchr. Cmty. Bible Classes, Ward Presbyn. Ch., Livonia, Mich., 1959-96, Christ Ch. Cranbrook (Episcopalian), Bloomfield Hills, 1980-93, Luth. Ch. of the Redeemer, Birmingham, 1993-99. Co-author: (with B.L. Hess) How to Have a Giving Church, 1974, The Power of a Loving Church, 1977, How Does Your Marriage Grow?, 1983, Never Say Old, 1984; author: Love Knows No Barriers, 1979, Esther: Courage in Crisis, 1980, Unconventional Women, 1981, The Triumph of Love, 1987; contbr. articles to religiouos jours. Home: 15191 Ford Rd Apt 302 Dearborn MI 48126-4696

HESS, SIDNEY J., JR. lawyer; b. Chgo., June 26, 1910; s. Sidney J. and Alma (Katz) H.; m. Jacqueline Engelhardt, Aug. 28, 1948; children—Karen E. Hess Freeman, Lori Ann. PhB, U. Chgo., 1930, JD, 1932. Bar: Ill. 1932. Practiced in, Chgo., 1932—; mem. firm Aaron, Schimberg & Hess, 1933-84, D'Ancona & Pflaum, 1985—. Bd. dirs., legal counsel Jewish Fedn. of Met. Chgo., 1968-77, v.p., 1972-74, pres., 1974-76; dir., legal counsel Jewish United Fund Met. Chgo., 1971-77, pres., 1974-76; legal counsel Jewish Welfare Fund Met. Chgo., 1969-73; bd. dirs. S. Silberman & Sons, Chgo. Metallic Products, Inc., Vienna Sausage Mfg. Co. Mem. exec. com. Anti-Defamation League, 1954-57, HIAS, 1974-90; mem. nat. devel. coun., aims com., citizens bd. U. Chgo.; bd. dirs. Schwab Rehab. Hosp., 1954-65, pres., 1959-64; trustee Michael Reese Founds., 1991—. Recipient Judge Learned Hand Human Rels. award Am. Jewish Com., Julius Rosenwald Meml. award Jewish Fedn. Met. Chgo., 1994, Army Commendation Medal (USAF); elected to Jewish Cmty. Ctrs. Hall of Fame, City of Chgo. Sr. Citizens Hall of Fame. Mem. ABA, Ill. State Bar Assn., Chgo. Bar Assn., Am. Judicature Soc., U. Chgo. Law Sch. Assn. (dir.), Std. Club (past pres., dir.), Mid-Day Club (Chgo.), Northmoor Country Club (Highland Park, Ill.), Tamarisk Country Club (Rancho Mirage, Calif.), Phi Beta Kappa, Pi Lambda Phi. Home: 1040 N Lake Shore Dr Chicago IL 60611-1165 Office: 111 E Wacker Dr Chicago IL 60601-3713 Fax: 312-602-3162. E-mail: shess@dancona.com.

HESSE, CAROLYN SUE, lawyer; b. Belleville, Ill., Jan. 12, 1949; d. Ralph H. Hesse and Marilyn J. (Midgley) Hesse Dierkes; m. William H. Hallenbeck. BS, U. Ill., 1971; MS, U. Ill., Chgo., 1977; JD, DePaul U., 1983. Bar: Ill. 1983, U.S. Dist. Ct. (no. dist.) Ill. 1983. Rsch. assoc. U. Ill., Chgo., 1974-77; tech. adviser Ill. Pollution Control Bd., 1977-80; environ. scientist U.S. EPA, 1980-84; assoc. Pretzel & Stouffer, Chartered, 1984-87, Coffield Ungaretti Harris & Slavin, Chgo., 1987-88; ptnr. McDermott, Will & Emery, 1988-99; pvt. practice Chgo., 1999-2001; with Barnes & Thornburg, 2001—. Frequent spkr. seminars on environ. issues. Contbr. articles on environ. sci. to profl. jours. Mem. ABA. Office: Barnes & Thornburg 2600 Chase Plaza 10 S LaSalle St Chicago IL 60603

HESSLER, DAVID WILLIAM, information and multimedia systems educator; b. Oak Park, Ill., May 9, 1932; s. William Wigney and Gwendolyn Eileen (Butler) H.; m. Helen Montgomery, Aug. 27, 1955; children: Leslie Susan, Laura Lynne. BA, U. Mich., 1955, MA, 1961; PhD, Mich. State U., 1972. Comml. photographer Oscar & Assocs., Chgo., 1950; equipment engr. Western Electric Co., 1958-59; dir. librs. and media Ann Arbor (Mich.) Pub. Schs., 1966-67; asst. prof. edn. Western Mich. U., 1967-72, assoc. prof., 1974-77; dir. instrnl. svcs., prof. edn. U. S.C., 1973-74; cons., asst. dir. Audio-Visual Edn. Ctr. U. Mich., Ann Arbor, 1960-66, prof. Sch. Info., 1977-98, prof. emeritus, 1998—, dir. instrnl. strategy svcs. for schs. of edn., libr. sci., 1979-81, pres. Ann Arbor sys. and tech., 1987—, exec. dir. for info. svcs. Info-Span, 1991-92; exec. v.p. Infotronix, 1993-97. Cons. Presdl. Commn. on World Hunger; cons. media and tech.; instrnl. designer and evaluator; bd. dirs. Kirsch Techs.; vis. prof., cons. dept. biblioteconomia U. Brazil, 1981. Author: (with J. Smith) Student Production Guide, 1975, Technology for Communication and Instruction, 1983; producer/dir. numerous films, filmstrips, TV programs and sound/slide programs for various ednl. levels. Lt. USAF, 1955-58; capt. Res. ret. Decorated Air Force Commendation medal; named Mich. Most Valuable Tchr. Chrysler Corp., 1965; Ednl. Profl. Devel. Act fellow, 1968-69. Mem. ALA, ASTD, Assn. Image and Info. Mgmt., M Club, Phi Kappa Phi. Home: 3677 Frederick Dr Ann Arbor MI 48105-2887 Office: Univ Mich Sch Info W Hall 550 E University Ave Ann Arbor MI 48109-1092 E-mail: dwh@umich.edu.

HESTER, DONALD DENISON, economics educator; b. Cleve., Nov. 6, 1935; s. Donald Miller and Catherine (Denison) H.; m. Karen Ann Helm, Oct. 24, 1959; children: Douglas Christopher, Karl Jonathan. BA, Yale U., 1957, MA, 1958, PhD, 1961. Asst. prof., assoc. prof. Yale U., New Haven, 1961-68; jr. vis. prof. Bombay Univ., India, 1962-63; econs. prof. U. Wis., Madison, 1968-2000, dept. chmn., 1990-93. Cons. Fed. Res., 1969-84; vis. prof. People's U. China, Beijing, 1987. Author: Indian Banks: Their Portfolios, Profits and Policy, 1964; co-author: Bank Management and Portfolio Behavior, 1975, Banking Changes in the European Monetary Union: An Italian Perspective, 2002; co-editor: Risk Aversion and Portfolio Choice, 1967; contbr. numerous articles to profl. jours. Mem. Wis. Coun. Econ. Affairs, 1983-87. Guggenheim fellow 1972, Econometric Soc. fellow, 1977; recipient faculty fellowship Ford Found., 1967, other rsch. awards. Avocations: classical music, art, hiking, traveling. Home: 2111 Kendall Ave Madison WI 53705-3915 Office: U Wis Dept Econs 1180 Observatory Dr Madison WI 53706-1320 E-mail: ddhester@facstaff.wisc.edu.

HESTER, THOMAS PATRICK, lawyer, business executive; b. Tulsa, Okla., Nov. 20, 1937; s. E.P. and Mary J. (Layton) H; m. Nancy B. Scofield, Aug. 20, 1960; children: Thomas P. Jr., Ann S., John L. BA, Okla. U., 1961, LLB, 1963. Bar: Okla. 1963, Mo. 1967, N.Y. 1970, D.C. 1973, Ill. 1975. Atty. McAfee & Taft, Okla. City, 1963-66, Southwestern Bell Telephone Co., Okla. City, St. Louis, 1966-72, AT&T, N.Y.C., Washington, 1972-75; gen. atty. Ill. Bell Telephone Co., Springfield, 1975-77, gen. solicitor Chgo., 1977-83, v.p., gen. counsel, 1983-87; sr. v.p., gen. counsel Ameritech, 1987-91, exec. v.p., gen. counsel, 1991-97; ptnr. Mayer, Brown & Platt, 1997—; sr. v.p., gen. counsel, sec. Sears, Roebuck and Co., 1998-99, FMC Corp., 2000. Corp. counsel ctr. adv. bd. Northwestern U., 1987-97. Mem. Taxpayers Fedn. Ill., Springfield, 1987-97, chmn. bd. trustees 1987-88; mem. adv. bd. Ill. Dept. Natural Resources, 1991-2000—, chmn., 1993-98; trustee Art Inst. Chgo., 1995-2000. Fellow Am. Bar Found.; mem. Am. Law Inst. Office: Mayer Brown Rowe and Maw 190 S LaSalle St Chicago IL 60603-3441 E-mail: thester@mayerbrownrowe.com.

HETLAGE, ROBERT OWEN, lawyer; b. St. Louis, Jan. 9, 1931; s. George C. and Doris M. (Talbot) H.; m. Anne R. Willis, Sept. 24, 1960; children: Mary T., James C., Thomas K. AB, Washington U., St. Louis, 1952, LLB, 1954; LLM, George Washington U., 1957. Bar: Mo. 1954, U.S. Dist. Ct. (ea. dist.) Mo. 1954, U.S. Supreme Ct. 1957. Ptnr. Hetlage & Hetlage, 1958-65, Peper, Martin, Jensen, Maichel & Hetlage, St. Louis, 1966-97, chmn., 1994-97; of counsel Blackwell Sanders Peper Martin LLP, 1998—. 1st lt. U.S. Army, 1954-58. Fellow Am. Bar Found. (life, bd. trustees 1996—); mem. ABA (chmn. real property, probate and trust law sect. 1981-82), Bar Assn. Met. St. Louis (pres. 1967-68), Mo. Bar (pres. 1976-77), Am. Coll. Real Estate Lawyers (pres. 1985-86), Am. Judicature Soc., Anglo-Am. Real Property Inst. (chmn. 1991). Office: Blackwell Sanders Peper Martin LLP 720 Olive St Saint Louis MO 63101-2338 E-mail: rohetlage@blackwellsanders.com.

HETLAND, JAMES LYMAN, JR. banker, lawyer, educator; b. Mpls., June 9, 1925; s. James L. and Evelyn E. (Lundgren) H.; m. Barbara Anne Taylor, Sept. 10, 1949; children: Janice E., James E., Nancy L., Steven T. B.S.L., U. Minn., 1948, J.D., 1950. Bar: Minn. 1950. Law clk. Minn. Supreme Ct., 1949-50; asso. firm Mackall, Crounse, Moore, Helmey & Palmer, Mpls., 1950-56; prof. U. Minn. Coll. Law, 1956-71; v.p. urban devel. First Nat. Bank Mpls., 1971-75, sr. v.p. law and urban devel., 1975-82, sr. v.p., gen. counsel, sec., 1982-88; sr. v.p. First Bank System, 1987-88; counsel to bd. and sec. First Bank, N.A., 1988-90; of counsel Rasmussen & Assocs., Ltd., 1990-99; adj. prof. Hubert Humphrey Inst., U. Minn., 1976-90, Bus. Coll. extension, 1975-81, Coll. Law, 1980-90. Labor arbitrator, 1967—; chmn. Minn. Citizens Coun. Crime and Delinquency, 1978-83; chmn. adv. coms. Minn. Supreme Ct., 1958-90; regents adv. com. Hubert Humphrey Inst., U. Minn., 1982-90; chmn. Telecommuters, Inc., 1992-96. Co-author: Minnesota Jury Instruction Guides, 1963, 2d edit., 1974, Minnesota Practice, 3 vols., 1970. Chmn. Met. Coun. Twin Cities, St. Paul, 1967-71, Mpls. Charter Commn., 1963-70; chmn. Mpls. Citizens League, 1963-64, bd. dirs., 1953-67; bd. dirs. Mpls. Downtown Coun., 1971—, vice chmn., 1978-82, chmn., 1982-83; chmn. bd. Minn. Zool. Garden, 1978-83; nat. v.p., mem. exec. com. Nat. Mcpl. League, 1979-82, pres., 1982-85, chmn. bd., 1985-87; vice chmn. Minn. Press Coun., 1973-81; vice chmn. bd. Minn. Health Care Cost Coalition, 1980; bd. dirs. Interstudy, 1972-79, chmn., 1974; mem. Bus. Urban Issues Coun., Conf. Bd., 1980-89; bd. dirs. Freshwater Biol. Rsch. Found., 1971-85, adv. bd., 1985—; bd. dirs. Mpls. Community Coll. Found., 1978-83, Minn. Exptl. City, 1972-75, Minn. Campfire Girls, 1974-79, Mpls. YMCA, 1957-76; bd. dirs. Health Central, Inc., 1973-87, exec. com., 1977-87; bd. dirs. Citizen Coun. on Crime and Justice, 1977—, chmn., 1979-82; bd. dirs. Ctr. for Policy Studies, 1983—, Twin Cities Habitat for Humanity, 1988-95; mem. exec. com. Partnership Dataline U.S.A., 1983; bd. dirs., exec. com. Health One, 1987-93; trustee Metro State U., 1989-98, Mpls. United Way, 1988-99; chmn. Mpls. Urban Tennis, 1987-94. With AUS, 1943-46. Mem. ABA, Am. Bankers Assn., Minn. Bar Assn., Hennepin County Bar Assn. Republican. Lutheran. Clubs: Mpls. Athletic, N.W. Tennis Assn. Lodge: Rotary. E-mail: jbh1and@aol.com.

HETZEL, WILLIAM GELAL, executive search consultant; b. New Rochelle, N.Y., May 19, 1933; s. William Gelal and Nan (Sanes) H.; m. Karen Marie Ross; children: William Gelal III, Tara L., John F., Janda B. Student, Washington Coll., 1949-51; B.B.A., U. Miami, 1953; postgrad., Xavier U., 1957-58; M.B.A., Northwestern U., 1962. Cons. McKinsey & Co., Inc., Chgo., 1961-64; various sales mgmt. positions Xerox Corp., Rochester, N.Y., Louisville, 1964-69; dir. mktg. Maremont Corp., Chgo., 1969-70; pres. Medelco, Inc., Schiller Park, Ill., 1970-72; div. gen. mgr., v.p. ITT Service Industries Corp., Cleve., 1972-74; v.p. Lamalie Assos., Inc., Chgo., 1974-78; sr. v.p. Eastman & Beaudine, 1978-81; pres. The Hetzel Group, Inverness, Ill., 1981—. Speaker in field. Contbr. numerous articles on exec. recruitment to profl. jours. Mem. found. bd. Northeastern Ill. U., 1993—. Served to lt. (j.g.) USN, 1953-56. Mem. Internat. Assn. Corp. and Profl. Recruitment, Am. Assn. Exec. Search Cons. Republican. Lutheran. Office: 157 K Helm Rd Barrington IL 60010-7632

HEUER, ARTHUR HAROLD, ceramics engineer, educator; b. N.Y.C., Apr. 29, 1936; s. William Jacob and Hannah (Kaye) H.; m. Roberta Feinstein, Dec. 22, 1956 (div. 1974); children: Howard, Michael, James; m. Joan McKnee Hulburt, May 8, 1976. BS, CCNY, 1956; PhD, U. Leeds, Eng., 1965, DSc, 1977. Rsch. chemist Ind. Gen. Corp., Keasbey, N.J., 1956-60; rsch. engr. Electron Tube Div. Bendix Co., Eatontown, 1960-61; staff scientist AVCO Space Systems Div., Lowell, Mass., 1965-67; asst. prof. ceramics div. metall. and materials Case Western Res. U., Cleve., 1967-70, assoc. prof., 1970-74, prof., 1974—, dir. materials rsch. lab. Case Inst. Tech., 1974-80, Kyocera Prof. Ceramics, 1985—. External sci. mem. Max-Planck Inst. fur Metalforschung, Germany, 1990—. Editor: Zirconia I, Zirconia II; contbr. over 420 articles to profl. jours. Recipient Alexander von Humboldt award Max-Planck Inst., 1983, Gold Medal award ASM. Fellow Am. Ceramic Soc. (chmn. basic sci. com., Sosman Meml. lectr. 1986, editor jour. 1988-90, John Jeppson award 1990, Orton lectr. 1991, Disting. Life mem. 1996), U.K. Inst. Physics; mem. AAAS, NAE, ASM (Gold medal). Achievements include research in transformation toughening in Zirconia, electron microscopy in ceramics, dislocations in ceramics, phase transformations in ceramics, biomimetic processing of materials, materials science aspects of MEMS, rapid prototyping technology/solid freeform fabrication of engineering materials, mechanical properties of hard and soft tissue; co-founder CAM-LEM Inc. Home: 2043 Random Rd Apt 303 Cleveland OH 44106-5916 Office: Case Western Res U Materials Sci and Engring 10900 Euclid Ave Cleveland OH 44106-7204 E-mail: heuer@cwru.edu.

HEUER, GERALD ARTHUR, mathematician, educator; b. Bertha, Minn., Aug. 31, 1930; s. William C. F. and Selma C. (Rosenberg) Heuer; m. Jeanette Mary Knedel, Sept. 5, 1954; children: Paul, Karl, Ruth, Otto. BA, Concordia Coll., 1951; MA, U. Nebr., 1953; PhD, U. Minn., 1958. Math. instr. Hamline U., 1955-56, Concordia Coll., Moorehead, Minn., 1956-57, asst. prof., 1957-58, assoc. prof., 1958-62, prof., 1962-95, Sigurd and Pauline Prestegaard Mundhjeld prof., 1988-95, chmn. dept., 1963-70, research prof., 1970-71, prof. emeritus, mathematician-in-residence, 1995—; mathematician Remington Rand Univac, summer 1958. Vis. prof. U. Nebr., 1960—61, Wash. State U., Pullman, 1980—81; mathematician Control Data Corp., 1960—62, cons., 1960—63; vis. lectr. Math. Assn. Am., 1964—66; cons. NSF-AID, India, 1968—69; guest spkr. Minn. sect. Math. Assn. Am., 1956, Nebr. sect. Math. Assn. Am., 1961, No. Ctrl. sect. Math. Assn. Am., 1974; vis. prof., scholar Math. Inst. Cologne (German) U., 1973—74; vis. prof., scholar Inst. Stats., Econs. and Ops. Rsch. Graz U., Austria, 1987—88, rsch. prof., Austria, 1990, vis. prof., Austria, 94, Austria, 97; dir. U.S. Math. Olympiad Tng. Session; leader U.S. team Internat. Math. Olympiad, 1988—90; invited plenary spkr. Internat. Symposium Ops. Rsch., Passau, Germany, 1995. Author (with Ulrike Leopold-Wildburger): (book) Balanced Silverman Games on General Discrete Sets, 1991, Silverman's Game, 1995; contbr. articles to profl. jours.; reviewer: Zentralblatt für Mathematik, 1967—, reviewer: Math. Revs., 1978—. Fellow Faculty, NSF, 1966—67; grantee Rsch., 1963, 1964, 1966; scholar Bush Rsch., Concordia Coll., 1983—84, Centennial Rsch., 1992, 1993, 1994, 1995. Mem.: Österreichische Math. Gesellschaft (Vienna), Deutsche Math.-Vereinigung E.V. (Berlin), Nat. Geographic Soc., Am. Math. Soc., Math. Assn. Am. (com. Am. math. competitions 1988—, nat. bd. govs. 1971—73, com. Putnam prize 1987—90, pres. Minn. sect. 1959—60, cert.

meritorious svc. 1994), Sigma Xi. Lutheran. Home: 1216 Elm St S Moorhead MN 56560-4049 Office: Concordia Coll Dept Math Moorhead MN 56562-0001 E-mail: heuer@cord.edu.

HEWES, PHILIP A. computer company executive; BA, Colo. State U., 1974; JD, John Marshall Law Sch., 1977. Bar: Ill. Asst. corp. counsel Comdisco, Inc., Rosemont, Ill., 1977-92, sr. v.p. legal, sec., 1992—. Office: Comdisco Inc 6111 N River Rd Rosemont IL 60018-5158

HEWITT, JAMES WATT, lawyer; b. Hastings, Nebr., Dec. 25, 1932; s. Roscoe Stanley and Willa Manners (Watt) H.; m. Marjorie Ruth Barrett, Aug. 8, 1954; children: Mary Janet, William Edward, John Charles, Martha Ann. Student, Hastings Coll., 1950-52; BS, U. Nebr., 1954, JD, 1956, MA, 1994. Bar: Nebr. 1956. Practice, Hastings, 1956-57, Lincoln, Nebr., 1960—; v.p., gen. counsel Nebco, Inc., 1961—. Vis. lectr. U. Nebr. Coll. Law, 1970—71; adj. instr. Am. history Nebr. Wesleyan U., 2001—. Mem. state exec. com. Rep. Party, 1967-70, mem. state ctrl. com., 1967-70, legis chmn., 1968-70; bd. dirs. Lincoln Child Guidance Ctr., 1969-72, pres., 1972; bd. dirs. Lincoln Cmty. Playhouse, 1967-73, pres., 1972-73; trustee Bryan Meml. Hosp., Lincoln, 1968-74, 76-82, chmn., 1972-74; bd. dirs. Lincoln Libr., 1990-97; trustee U. Nebr. Found., 1979—; dir. Bryan Meml. Hosp. Found., Lincoln, 1994—; pres, dir. Nebr. State Hist. Soc. Found., Lincoln, 1994—; dir. Nebr. state chpt. The Nature Conservancy, 1993-97. Capt. USAF, 1957-60. Fellow Am. Bar Found. (Nebr. state chmn. 1988-92, 99—, chmn. 1994-95); mem. ABA (Nebr. state del. 1972-80, bd. govs. 1981-83), Nebr. State Bar (chmn. ins. com. 1972-76, chmn. pub. rels. com. 1982-84, pres. 1985-86), Fed. Bar Assn., Lincoln Bar Assn., Newcomen Soc. (Nebr. chair 1995—), Am. Rose Soc., Nebr. Rose Soc., Lincoln Rose Soc., Nebr. Club, Country of Lincoln Club, Round Table, Beta Theta Pi, Phi Delta Phi. Congregationalist. Home: 2990 Sheridan Blvd Lincoln NE 68502-4241 Office: PO Box 80268 1815 Y St Lincoln NE 68508-1233

HEWITT, PAMELA S. human resources specialist; b. 1953; Sr. v.p. human resources The Quaker Oats Co., Chgo., 1998—.

HEYMAN, RALPH EDMOND, lawyer; b. Cin., Mar. 14, 1931; s. Ralph and Florence (Kahn) H.; m. Sylvia Lee Schottenstein, Jan. 2, 1984; children: Michael Cary, Cynthia Ann Heyman Eeg, Ginger Florence. A.B. magna cum laude (Rufus Choat scholar), Dartmouth Coll., 1953; LLB cum laude, Harvard U., 1956; LLM, U. Cin., 1957. Bar: Ohio 1956, Ill. 1957. Pvt. practice, Cin., 1956-58, Dayton, 1958—; assoc. Freiden & Wolf, 1956-58; from assoc. to ptnr. Smith & Schnacke, 1958-88; ptnr. Chernesky, Heyman & Kress, Dayton, Ohio, 1988—. Lectr. estate planning U. Cin., 1958-61; lectr. participant Southwestern Ohio Tax Inst., 1957-65; lectr., moderator Dayton Bar Assn. Tax Insts., 1975-79, 94; lectr. continuing edn. program U. Dayton, 1989; lectr. estate planning Dayton Area Tax Profls., 1993; lectr. on venture capital Miami Valley Venture Assn., 1998; dir., gen. counsel Towne Properties, Ltd., Sachs Mgmt. Corp., Inc., Aristocrat Products, Inc., K.k. Motorcycle Supply, Inc., The Sportsman's Guide. Recipient Robert A. Shapiro Vol. award 1998. Commr. Bd. Rural Zoning Commn. Montgomery County, 1969-71; bd. dirs., pres. Jewish Fedn. Dayton, 1993-97; nat. trustee NCCJ; past pres. Temple Israel; pres. Temple Israel Found., 1999-2001; dir. United Way Greater Dayton Area, 1999. Recipient Humanitarian award NCCJ, 1997, Robert A. Shapiro Vol. award, 1998. Mem. ABA, Ohio Bar Assn., Dayton Bar Assn. (chmn. tax com.), Cin. Bar Assn., Lawyers Club, Bicycle Club, Meadowbrook Club, Dayton City Club (past pres.), B'nai Brith, Phi Beta Kappa. Jewish. Office: Chernesky Heyman & Kress PLL PO Box 3808 1100 Courthouse Plz SW Dayton OH 45401-3808

HEYMANN, S. RICHARD, lawyer; b. Chgo., Sept. 18, 1944; s. Samuel R. and Ann (Menning) H.; m. Jane Ann Gebhart, June 14, 1980; children: Elizabeth Jane, Catherine Claire. BS, U. Wis., 1966; JD, U. Mich., 1969. Bar: Mo. 1969, Wis. 1988. Law clk. Minn. Supreme Ct., St. Paul, 1970-72; assoc. Bryan, Cave, McPheeters & McRoberts, St. Louis, 1972-79, ptnr., 1980-87, Foley & Lardner, Madison, Wis., 1987-99; dir. Inst. for Environ. Studies U. Wis., 1996—. Adj. prof. U. Wis. Law Sch. Mem. U. Wis. Found., Wis. Alumni Assn. (bd. dirs. 1985-87). Clubs: Madison, Maple Bluff Country. Office: Univ Wis Inst Environ Studies 550 N Park St Rm 70 Madison WI 53706-1404 E-mail: srheymann@facstaff.wisc.edu.

HIBBS, JOHN STANLEY, lawyer; b. Des Moines, Sept. 19, 1934; s. Ray E. Hibbs and Jean Waller (Lackey) Gravender; m. John S. II, Kari S. Hibbs Carroll, Jennifer R. Hibbs-Kraus. BBA, U. Minn., 1956, JD cum laude, 1960. Bar; Minn. 1960, U.S. Dist. Ct. Minn. 1960, U.S. Ct. Appeals (8th cir.) 1963, U.S. Tax Ct. 1965, U.S. Supreme Ct. 1970. Ptnr. Dorsey and Whitney, Mpls., 1960—, Health Practice Group. Chmn. Adv. Task Force on Minn. Corp. Law, Mpls., 1979-82, tax policy study group of Minn. Bus. Climate Task Force, Mpls., 1978-80; coun. Med. Group Practice Attys. Author: Minnesota Nonprofit Corporations-A Corporate and Tax Guide, 1979; contbr. over 150 profl. papers to publs. Served to capt. USAR, 1956-66. Fellow Am. Coll. Tax Counsel; mem. ABA (cons. com. on corp. laws 1981-82), Nat. Health Lawyers Assn., Am. Acad. Healthcare Attys., Coun. Med. Group Practice Attys., Minn. Bar Assn., Hennepin County Bar Assn. Republican. Lutheran. Avocations: sports, reading, travel, gardening. Home: 25 Cooper Cir Minneapolis MN 55436-1316 Office: Dorsey & Whitney 220 S 6th St Ste 2200 Minneapolis MN 55402-1498

HICKEY, DAMON DOUGLAS, library director; b. Houston, Oct. 30, 1942; s. Thomas Earl and Ethel Elizabeth (Place) Hickey; m. Mary Lyons Temple, May 27, 1967; 1 child Doralyn Temple Hickey Rossmann. BA, Rice U., 1965; MDiv, Princeton (N.J.) Theol. Sem., 1968; cert. in clin. pastoral care, Inst. of Religion, Houston, 1969; MSLS, U. N.C., 1975; MA, U. N.C., Greensboro, 1982; PhD, U. S.C., 1989. Assoc. pastor First Presbyn. Ch., Irving, Tex., 1969-71, Southminster Presbyn. Ch., Oklahoma City, 1971-72; pastor First Presbyn. Ch., Moore, 1971—72; catalog librarian U. N.C., Chapel Hill, 1972-73; acting curator rare books Duke U., Durham, N.C., 1973-74; assoc. libr. dir. Guilford Coll., Greensboro, 1975-91, curator Friends Hist. Collection, 1980-91; dir. libr. Coll. Wooster, Ohio, 1991—. Adj. asst. prof. history Guilford Coll., 1990—91. Author: Sojourners No More: The Quakers in the New South, 1865-1920, 1997, When Chage is Set in Store: An Analysis of Seven Academic Libraries, 2001; editor: (jour.) The Southern Friend, 1983—91; contbr. chapters to books, articles, book revs. to profl. jours. Chair fund distbn. com. United Way Wooster, 1998-99. Recipient Twiford Religious History Book award N.C. Soc. of Historians, Inc., 1998. Mem.: ALA, Assn. Coll. and Rsch. Librs. (chair leadership com., coll. librs. sect.), Hist. Soc. N.C. (elect), Friends Hist. Assn., So. Hist. Assn., Orgn. Am. Historians, N.C. Friends Hist. Soc. (bd. dirs. 1977—91), Beta Phi Mu, Phi Alpha Theta. Democrat. Espicopalian, Quaker. Avocations: church work, baseball. Office: Coll of Wooster Libraries Wooster OH 44691-2364 E-mail: dhickey@wooster.edu.

HICKEY, JOHN JOSEPH, state legislator; b. St. Louis, Feb. 23, 1965; State rep. Dist. 80 Mo. State Legislature, 1993—2002. Journeyman pipefitter. Mem. Northwest Twp. Airport Twp. and North County Young Dems., Pipefitters Local 562, North County Labor Club, Woodson Terr. Lions Club Internat.

HICKEY, JOHN THOMAS, JR. lawyer; b. Evanston, Ill., July 9, 1952; s. John Thomas and Joanne (Keating) H.; m. Candis Bailey, July 7, 1979; children: Alison, Jack, Patrick, Claire, Matthew. AB, Georgetown U., 1974; JD, U. Chgo., 1977. Bar: Ill. 1977, U.S. Dist. Ct. (no. dist.) Ill. 1977, U.S. Ct. Appeals (7th cir.) 1977, U.S. Ct. Appeals (10th cir.) 1987. Assoc. Kirkland & Ellis, Chgo., 1977-83, ptnr., 1983—. Fellow Am. Coll. Trial Lawyers. Achievements include being listed in Leading Ill. Attys. Office: Kirkland & Ellis 200 E Randolph St Fl 59 Chicago IL 60601-6609

HICKMAN, FREDERIC W. lawyer; b. Sioux City, Iowa, June 30, 1927; s. Simeon M. and Esther (Nixon) H.; m. Katherine Heald, July 15, 1964; children: Mary Sanders, Sara Ridder. AB, Harvard U., 1948, LLB magna cum laude, 1951. Bar: Ill. 1951. Asso. firm Sidley & Austin, Chgo., 1951-55; partner firm Hopkins & Sutter, 1956-71, 75-92, sr. counsel, 1993-2001. Asst. sec. for tax policy Dept. Treasury, Washington, 1972-75; draftsman Ill. Income Tax, 1969; author and lectr. on taxation. Mem. Ill. Humanities Council, 1977-82; mem. Citizens Commn. on Public Sch. Fin., 1977-78; chmn. bd. trustees Am. Conservatory Music, 1980-90; pres. Nat. Tax Assn., 1989-90. Served with USN, 1945-46. Mem. ABA (chmn. com. on depreciation 1966-68, com. on capital formation 1976-78, coun. 1980-83, chmn. com. on tax structure and simplification 1991-92, Internat. Fiscal Assn. (dr. 1973-77), Am. Coll. Tax Counsel (regent 1989-92), Comm. Club (Chgo.), Union League (Chgo.), Mid-Day (Chgo.), Cliff Dwellers (Chgo.), Legal (Chgo., pres. 1980-81), Chikaming Country (Lakeside, Mich.) Club. Republican. Methodist. Home: 360 Green Bay Rd # 4E Winnetka IL 60093-4032 Office: Foley & Lardner 3 First National Plz Chicago IL 60602

HICKMAN, JAMES CHARLES, business and statistics educator, business school dean; b. Indianola, Iowa, Aug. 27, 1927; s. James C. and Mabel L. (Fisher) H.; m. Margaret W. McKee, June 12, 1950; children— Charles Wallace, Donald Robert, Barbara Jean. B.A., Simpson Coll., 1950; M.S., U. Iowa, 1952, Ph.D., 1961. Actuarial asst. Bankers Life Co., Des Moines, 1952-57; asst. prof. dept. statistics U. Iowa, 1961-64, asso. prof., 1964-67, prof., 1967-72; prof. bus. and statistics U. Wis., Madison, 1972-93, dean Sch. Bus., 1985-90, emeritus prof. and dean, 1993—; Warren prof. U. Manitoba, 1990; Bowles prof. George State U., 1996. Mem. panel of cons. on social security fin. Senate Fin. and House Ways and Means Com., 1975-76; mem. adv. com. to Joint Bd. for Enrollment of Actuaries, 1976-78; mem. Actuarial Standards Bd., 1985-92; dir. Mems. Capital Advisors., Am. Med. Security. Mem. editl. bd. N.Am. Actuarial Jour., 1997—. Mem. bd. pensions Presbyn. Ch. in U.S.A., 1989-95. With USAAF, 1945-47. Recipient Alumni Achievement award Simpson Coll., 1979, David Halmstad award for actuarial rsch. Actuarial Ednl. Rsch. Fund, 1979, 81, Disting. Alumni award U. Iowa, 1993; Coll. Liberal Arts Alumni fellow, U. Iowa, 1999. Fellow Soc. Actuaries (v.p. 1975-77, bd. govs. 1971-74, 91-94, J.E. O'Connor Disting. Svc. award 2000); mem. Actuarial Found. (trustee 1994-2000), Casualty Actuarial Soc., Am. Acad. Actuaries (Jarvis Farley award for svc.), Am. Statis. Assn., Swiss Assn. Actuaries (corr. mem.), Beta Gamma Sigma (bd. govs. 1988-92). Presbyterian. Home: 2822 Marshall Ct #3 Madison WI 53705-2271 Office: U Wis Sch Bus 975 University Ave Madison WI 53706-1324

HICKS, CADMUS METCALF, JR. financial analyst; b. Hagerstown, Md., Dec. 21, 1952; s. Cadmus Metcalf Sr. and Marie Elizabeth (Keefauver) H.; m. Elizabeth Ann Dressel, May 31, 1980; children: Liza, Alethea, Cadmus III. BA, Wheaton (Ill.) Coll., 1974; MA, U. Chgo., 1976; PhD, Northwestern U., Evanston, Ill., 1980. Chartered fin. analyst. Rsch. analyst John Nuveen & Co. Inc., Chgo., 1980-85, asst. v.p., 1985-90, v.p., 1990—, asst. mgr. rsch. dept., 1993-96, mgr. rsch. dept., 1996-99, market strategist, 1999—. Author: (with others) The Municipal Bond Handbook, 1983, Bond Credit Analysis: Framework and Case Studies, 2001; contbr. articles to profl. jours. Mem. Nat. Fedn. of Mcpl. Analysts (bd. govs. 1991-93), Chgo. Mcpl. Analysts Soc. (pres. 1991-92), Investment Analysts Soc. of Chgo., Assn. for Investment Mgmt. and Rsch. Republican. Office: 333 W Wacker Dr Chicago IL 60606-1220

HICKS, IRLE RAYMOND, retail food chain executive; b. Welch, W.Va., Dec. 21, 1928; s. Irle Raymond and Mary Louise (Day) H. B.A., U. Va., 1950. Bus. mgr. Hicks Ford, Covington, Ky., 1952-58; acct. Firestone Plantations Co., Harbel, Liberia, 1958-60; auditor Kroger Co., Cin., 1960-66, gen. auditor, 1966-68, asst. treas., 1968-72, treas., 1972—. Bd. dirs. Old Masons' Home Ky. Served with AUS, 1950-52. Mem. Fin. Execs. Inst., Bankers Club, Alpha Kappa Psi, Phi Kappa Psi. Episcopalian. Clubs: Mason, Cincinnati. Home: 454 Oliver Rd Cincinnati OH 45215-2507 Office: 1014 Vine St Cincinnati OH 45202-1141

HICKS, JIM, secondary education educator; Tchr. Physics Barrington (Ill.) H.S. Recipient Innovative Teaching and Secondary Sch. Physics award, 1992. Office: Barrington HS 616 W Main St Barrington IL 60010-3015

HICKS, JUDITH EILEEN, nursing administrator; b. Chgo., Jan. 1, 1947; d. John Patrick and Mary Ann (Clifford) Rohan; m. Laurence Joseph Hicks, Nov. 22, 1969; children: Colleen Driscoll, Patrick Kevin. BSN, St. Xavier Coll., Chgo., 1969, U. Ill., 1975. Staff nurse Mercy Hosp., Chgo., 1969-70, nursing supr., 1970-73; cons. continuing edn. Ill. Nurses Assn., 1974-75; dir. ob-gyn. nursing Northwestern Meml. Hosp., 1975-81; v.p. nursing Children's Meml. Hosp., 1981-86; pres. Children's Meml. Home Health, Inc., 1986—2001, Children's Meml. Nursing Svcs., 1986—2001. Pres. Allied & Children's Home Health and Nursing Svcs., 1988, CM Healthcare Resources, Inc., 1988—2001, The Pediat. Pl., Inc., 1994—2001, Focused Health Solutions, Inc., 2001—; dir. Near North Health Corp., Chgo., 1982—85; pres. Pediat. Excellence Program Svc.; bd. dirs. Infant Welfare Soc. Chgo., Nat. Breast Cancer Assn. Recipient Jonas Salk Leadership award March of Dimes, 1998, Ernst and Young Outstanding Ill. Nurse Leader award, 1999. Mem. Am. Soc. Nursing Adminstrs., Women's Health Exec. Network (1984-85), Ill. Hosp. Assn. (chmn. coun. on nursing 1982-83), Inst. Medicine. Home: 2206 Beechwood Ave Wilmette IL 60091-1508 Office: CM Health Care Resources Ste 200 1000 Sunset Ridge Rd Northbrook IL 60062-4010

HICKS, KEN CARLYLE, retail executive; b. Tulsa, Jan. 6, 1953; s. Harold I. and Patricia Ann (Carlyle) H.; m. Lucile Catherine Boland, June 22, 1974. BS, U.S. Mil. Acad., 1974; MBA, Harvard U., 1982. Commd. 2d lt. U.S. Army, 1974, advanced through grades to capt., resigned, 1980; assoc. McKinsey & Co., Dallas, 1982-83; v.p., chief operating officer All-Flow, Inc., Buffalo, 1984; sr. engagement mgr. McKinsey Co., Dallas, 1984-87; sr. v.p. May Dept. Stores Co., St. Louis, 1987-90, GMM Home Furnishings, May Merchandising Co., N.Y.C.; sr.v.p. GMM Foley's Department Stores, Houston; exec. v.p. Home Shopping Network, FL; pres. and dir. Payless ShoeSource, Topeka, 1999—. Class agt. Harvard Bus. Sch., 1982—; co. exec. United Way, St. Louis, 1988. Mem. Harvard Club (N.Y.C.). Avocations: horseback riding, jogging. Home: 224 Fall Creek Rd Lawrence KS 66049-9066 Office: Payless ShoeSource Inc 3231 SE 6th Ave Topeka KS 66607-2260

HIEMSTRA, MICHAEL J. manufacturing executive; CFO, v.p. fin. and adminstrn. Parker Hannifin Corp., Cleve., 1988—. Office: Parker Hannifin Corp 6035 Parkland Blvd Cleveland OH 44124-4141

HIER, DANIEL BARNET, neurologist; b. Chgo., Mar. 23, 1947; s. Stanley W. and Jean (Schrager) H.; m. Myra Goldberg, Aug. 30, 1981 (dec. Jul. 1995); m. Linda Lesky (sep. 1998); children: Benjamin Philip, David Samuel. BA, Harvard U., 1969, MD, 1973. Medical intern Bronx Mcpl. Hosp., N.Y.C., 1973-74; neurology resident Mass. Gen. Hosp., Boston, 1974-77, neurology fellow, 1977-79; neurologist Michael Reese Hosp., Chgo., 1979-89, chmn. neurology, 1987-89; head neurology U. Ill., 1989—, assoc. prof. neurology, 1989-91; prof. Ul. Ill., 1991—. Fellow Am. Acad. Neurology, Am. Heart Assn. (stroke council). Home: 2210 Schiller Ave Wilmette IL 60091-2328 E-mail: dbhier@ameritech.net.

HIER, MARSHALL DAVID, lawyer; b. Bay City, Mich., Aug. 24, 1945; s. Marshall George and Helen May (Copeland) H.; m. Nancy Speed Brown, June 26, 1970; children: John, Susan, Ann. BA, Mich. State U., 1966; JD, U. Mich., 1969. Bar: Mo. 1969. Assoc. Peper, Martin, Jensen, Maichel and Hetlage, St. Louis, 1969-76, ptnr., 1976-95; prin. Bertram, Peper and Hier, P.C., 1996—. Bd. dirs. Gateway Ctr. Met. St. Louis, Mercantile Libr. Assn., St. Louis Soc. Blind and Visually Impaired. Contbr. articles to profl. jours. Mem. St. Louis Bar Assn. (editor jour. 1988—), St. Louis Civil Round Table (former pres.). Baptist. Home: 17141 Chaise Ridge Rd Chesterfield MO 63005-4457

HIETALA, ALLAN, retired advertising executive; b. 1932; With Northrup King Co., Mpls., 1964-69, Colle & McAvoy, Inc., Mpls., 1969-97, chmn., CEO, chmn. emeritus, 1997-98.

HIETT, EDWARD EMERSON, retired lawyer, glass company executive; b. Toledo, Nov. 24, 1922; s. Stanley J. and Clara I. (Jones) H.; m. Margaret J. Winter, July 1, 1944; 1 dau., Katherine L. B.B.A., U. Mich., 1946, M.B.A., LL.B., 1949. Bar: Ohio bar 1949. Practice in, Toledo, 1949-52; mem. legal dept. Libbey-Owens-Ford Co., 1952-63, sec., 1963-78, asst. gen. counsel, 1963-73, v.p. gen. counsel, 1973-78; sr. counsel Owens-Corning Fiberglas, 1978-86; sole practice, 1986-91; ret., 1991. Lectr. econs., bus. law U. Toledo, 1949-69 Served as officer USNR, 1942-46. Mem. Toledo Club. Home: 5446 N Citation Rd Toledo OH 43615-2160 E-mail: edhiett@msn.com.

HIGBY, GREGORY JAMES, historical association administrator, historian; b. Dearborn, Mich., Dec. 24, 1953; s. Warren James and Gertrude H.; m. Marian Fredal, June 2, 1979. BS in Pharmacy, U. Mich., 1977; MS in Pharmacy, U. Wis., 1980, PhD in Pharmacy, 1984. Staff pharmacist Higby's Pharmacy, Bad Axe, Mich., 1977-78; asst. to dir. Am. Inst. of the History of Pharmacy, Madison, Wis., 1981-84, asst. dir., 1984-86, assoc. dir., 1986, acting dir., 1986-88, dir., 1988—; rsch. assoc. U. Wis., 1984-86. Adj. asst. prof. U. Wis., Madison, 1984-94, adj. assoc. prof., 1994-2000, adj. prof., 2000—; cons. Smithsonian Instn., Washington, 1987, Am. Soc. Hosp. Pharmacists, Bethesda, Md., 1990, U.S. Pharmacopeial Conv., 1992-95, Am. Assn. Colls. Pharmacy, 1993-99; adv. com. Fed. Drug Law Inst., Washington, 1989-90. Author: In Service to American Pharmacy: The Professional Life of William Procter, Jr., U. Ala. Press, 1992; co-author: The Spirit of Voluntarism...The United States Pharmacopeia 1820-1995, 1995; editor: One Hundred Years of the National Formulary, 1989, Pill Peddlers: Essays on the History of the Pharmaceutical Industry, 1990, Historical Hobbies for the Pharmacist, 1994, The History of Pharmacy, A Selected Annotated Bibliography, 1995, The Inside Story of Medicines, 1997, Apothecaries and the Drug Trade, 2001, 150 Years of Caring: A Pictorial History of the APHA, 2002; author poetry; editor: Pharmacy in History Jour., 1986—; contbr. articles to profl. jours. Recipient Edward Kremers award 1995. Mem. Am. Pharm. Assn., Am. Chem. Soc. (assoc.), Am. Assn. for History of Medicine, Hist. Sci. Soc., Orgn. Am. Historians, Soc. for History of Tech., Internat. Acad. History of Pharmacy. Avocations: bird watching, cycling, racquetball, musician. Office: Am Inst of the History of Pharmacy 777 Highland Ave Madison WI 53705-2222 E-mail: greghigby@aihp.org.

HIGGINS, FRANCIS EDWARD, history educator; b. Chgo., Nov. 29, 1935; s. Frank Edward and Mary Alyce (Fahey) H. BS, Loyola U., Chgo., 1959, MA, 1964; postgrad., Exeter Coll., Oxford (Eng.) U., 1962, Am. U. Beirut, 1966, McGill U., Montreal, 1967; Adminstrn. Cert., St. Xavier Coll., 1971; EdD, U. Sarasota, 1977. Tchr. Washington Jr. H.S., Chicago Heights, Ill., 1959, Chgo. Vocat. H.S., 1960-68, dept. chmn., 1964; asst. prof. social sci. Moraine Valley C.C., 1968-69; tchr. history Hillcrest H.S., Country Club Hills, Ill., 1969-93. Instr. nursing continuing edn. St. Francis Coll., 1978—. Contbr. revs. to Am. Cath. Hist. Jour., History Tchr. Jour. Mem. pres.'s coun. St. Xavier Coll., 1978—; mem. St. Germaine Sch. Bd., 1972-73, St. Alexander Sch. Bd., 1978-84; active Chgo. coun. Boy Scouts Am., 1969-77, asst. dist. commr., 1971-75, mem. dist. scout com., 1976-77; co-historian Palos Hts. Silver Jubilee Com., 1984. Recipient Disting. Svc. award Chgo. coun. Boy Scouts Am., 1974; Brit. Univ. scholar, 1962; Fulbright fellow, summer 1966; English Speaking Union fellow, 1967. Mem. Ill. Hist. Soc., Del. Hist. Soc., Am. Cath. Hist. Soc., Nat. Coun. Social Studies, Ill. Coun. Social Studies, Nat. Curriculum and Supervisory Assn., Ill. Supervisory Assn., Ill. Assn. Supervision and Curriculum Devel. (editl. rev. bd. Jour. 1984-86), Chgo. Hist. Soc., Nat. Hist. Soc., Brit. Hist. Assn., Nat. Soc. Study Edn., Phi Delta Kappa, Phi Kappa Mu. Republican. Roman Catholic. Home: 7931 W Lakeview Ct Palos Heights IL 60463-2526

HIGGINS, JACK, editorial cartoonist; b. Chgo., Aug. 19, 1954; s. Maurice James and Helen Marie (Egan) H.; m. Mary Elizabeth Irving, Apr. 26, 1997; children: Thomas Patick, Brigid Kathleen. BA in Econs., Coll. Holy Cross, 1976. Editorial cartoonist The Daily Northwestern, Evanston, Ill., 1978-81; freelance editorial cartoonist Chgo. Sun-Times, 1980-84, editorial cartoonist, 1984—. Vol. worker Jesuit Vol. Corps, Washington, 1977. Recipient Peter Lisagor award Chgo. Soc. Profl. Journalists, 1984, 87, 91, 94, 96, 97, 98, 99, 2000, 1st prize Internat. Salon Cartoons, Montreal, Que., Can., 1988, Pulitzer prize for editl. cartooning, 1989, Disting. Svc. award Sigma Delta Chi, 1988, 98, John Fischetti editl. cartooning award, 1998, media svc. award Chgo. Lung Assn., 1993, Herman Kogan media awards Chgo. Bar Assn., 1993, 95; named Alumnus of Yr., St. Ignatius Coll. Prep. Sch., Chgo., 1992, Ill. Journalist of Yr., 1996; finalist for Pulitzer prize, 1986, for Robert F. Kennedy journalism award, 1993, 94, others. Roman Catholic. Avocations: oil painting, bicycling. Office: Chgo Sun-Times 401 N Wabash Ave Chicago IL 60611-5642

HIGGINS, JAMES JACOB, statistics educator; b. Canton, Ill., Oct. 31, 1943; married, 1967; 2 children. BS, U. Ill., 1965; MS, Ill. State U., 1967; PhD in Stats., U. Mo., 1970. Asst. prof. math. U. Mo., Rolla, 1970-74; from asst. prof. to assoc. prof. math. U. South Fla., 1974-80; prof. stats. Kans. State U., Manhattan, 1980—; dept. head, 1990-95. Fellow Am. Statis. Assn.; mem. Inst. Math. Stats. Achievements include research in reliability theory; classical and Bayesian estimation theory; statistical modelling; experimental design; textbook author. Office: Kans State U Stats Lab Dickens Hall Manhattan KS 66506 E-mail: jhiggins@ksu.edu.

HIGGINS, LINDA I. state legislator; b. Mpls., Nov. 11, 1950; AA, Iowa Lakes C.C.; BS, Mankato State Coll. Mem. Minn. Senate from 58th dist., St. Paul, 1996—. Home: 1715 Emerson Ave N Minneapolis MN 55411-3226 Office: 226 Capitol 75 Constitution Ave Saint Paul MN 55155-1601

HIGGINS, RUTH ELLEN, theatre producer; b. Streator, Ill., Jan. 23, 1945; d. Thomas Francis and Mary Madeline (Ahearn) H.; m. Byron L. Schaffer, Oct. 17, 1975 (dec. May 1990); 1 child, Kareth Madeline Schaffer. BS in Edn. and Theater, No. Ill. U., 1967; MA in Theater Arts, U. Nebr., 1968; postgrad., No. Ill. U., 1970-74. Instr. Glenbrook North H.S., Northbrook, Ill., 1968-69; dir. theatre Highland C.C., Freeport, 1969-73; co-prodr. Dinglefest Theatre Co., Chgo., 1972-77; arts cons. Chgo. Cmty. Trust, 1973-74; exec. dir., founder Chgo. Alliance for the Performing Arts, 1974-79; prodr. New Tuners Theatre, Chgo., 186402999; exec. dir., co-founder Chgo. Coalition for Arts in Edn., 1979-83; gen. mgr. Theatre Bldg., Chgo., 1981-97, North Shore Ctr. Performing Arts, Skokie, Ill.,

1997-99; dir. MBA arts mgmt. Roosevelt U., Chgo., 1999—. Cons. Office Cook County Assessor, Chgo., 1980, Donors Forum, Chgo., 1981, Paramount Fine Arts Ctr., Aurora, Ill., 1979-81, North Park Village, Chgo., 1982; mem. theatre adv. panel Ill. Arts Coun., 1992; bd. dirs. Nat. Alliance Mus. Theatre.; mem. theatre creation and presentation panel Nat. Endowment for Arts, 1992, 97; bd. mem. Nat. Alliance for Mus. Theatre, 1996-2000; co-chair New Works Panel 2000, Comm.'s Com., 1998-2000. Co-prodr. over 90 world premieres, plays and musicals, 1972—; host (TV program) Arts & The Community, NBC's Knowledge, 1978. Mem. Chgo. Coun. on Fine Arts, 1976-79; panel mem. Dance Adv. Panel/Ill. Arts Coun., Chgo., 1979; mem. Ill. Arts Coun. theatre adv. panel 1992; mem. Nat. Endowment for the Arts, Opera Musical Theatre New Am. Works Panel, 1993; bd. dirs. Community TV Network, Chgo., 1980-84, Performance Community, Chgo., 1974-2000; mem. adv. bd. Gospel Arts Workshop, Chgo., 1979-85. Recipient Svc. to Arts & Edn. award Ill. Alliance for Arts in Edn., Chgo., 1984, 1st place award for direction Readers Theatre Nat. Competition Jr. Colls. Avocation: sailing. Office: New Tuners Theatre Theatre Bldg 1225 W Belmont Ave Chicago IL 60657-3205

HIGGINSON, BOBBY, professional baseball player; b. Phila., Aug. 18, 1970; Baseball player Detroit Tigers, 1995—. Office: Detroit Tigers 2100 Woodward Detroit MI 48201*

HIGHLEN, LARRY WADE, music educator, piano rebuilder, tuner; b. Warren, Ind., Oct. 31, 1936; s. Lawrence Wade and Anna Belle (Dungan) H.; m. Camille Pence (div. 1975); children: Laurel, Wade, Jennifer, Tanna. Student, Niles Bryant Coll., 1967, Ivy Tech. Coll., Kokomo, Ind., 1975-76, Ivy Tech. Coll., Ft. Wayne, Ind., 1983-84. Pvt. piano tchr., Kokomo, 1967-85; piano tchr. Barbara Martin Piano Svc., Indpls., 1985-88, 1990—, Van Wezel Performing Arts Hall, Sarasota, Fla., 1988-90. Author: Piano Abstract, 1981. Fellow Ancient and Mystical Order Rosae Crucis. Avocation: building experimental musical instruments. E-mail: larry. Home and Office: 1912 W Defenbaugh St Kokomo IN 46902-6032 E-mail: glowinghealth@rainforestbio.com.

HIGI, WILLIAM L. bishop; b. Anderson, Ind., Aug. 29, 1933; Student, Mt. St. Mary of the West Sem., Xavier U. Ordained priest Roman Cath. Ch., 1959. Bishop Roman Cath. Diocese of Lafayette, Lafayette, Ind., 1984—. Home: 610 Lingle Ave Lafayette IN 47901-1740 Office: Bishops Office PO Box 260 Lafayette IN 47902-0260

HILBERT, STEPHEN C. former insurance company executive; b. 1946; Student, Ind. State U. Agent Aetna Life Ins. Co., Indpls., 1967-70, United Home Life Ins. Agy., Indpls., 1970-75, Aetna Life Ins., Indpls., 1975-79; chmn., CEO Conseco Inc. (now Conseco Cos.), Carmel, Ind., 1979-2000. Bd. dirs. Ind. State U. Found., Indpls. Conv. and Visitors Assn., Indpls. Zoo, St. Vincent Hosp. Found.; trustee Ctrl. Ind. Coun. on Aging Found., U.S. Ski Team; vol. Jr. Achievement, Multiple Sclerosis Soc., Park Tudor Sch., Indpls. Symphony Orch., Am. Heart Assn., Mental Health Assn. Marion County, Ind., Indpls. 500 Festival Com. Office: Conseco Cos 11815 N Pennsylvania St Carmel IN 46032-4555

HILBOLDT, JAMES SONNEMANN, lawyer, investment advisor; b. Dallas, July 21, 1929; s. Grover C. and Grace E. (Sonnemann) H.; m. Martha M. Christian, Sept. 5, 1953; children: James, Katherine Hilboldt Farrell, Susanna Jean, Thomas. AB in Econs., Harvard U., 1952; postgrad., U. Chgo., 1952-53; JD, U. Mich., 1956. Registered investment advisor. With comml. and trust dept. No. Trust Co., Chgo., 1952-53; pvt. practice Kalamazoo, 1956—; pvt. practice as investment advisor, 1971—. Bd. dirs. Lafourche Realty Co., Inc., Kalamazoo, pres., 1971—. Bd. dirs. Kalamazoo Tennis Patrons, Inc., 1974-95, Downtown Devel. Authority, Kalamazoo, 1982-88, Downtown Tomorrow, Inc., Kalamazoo, 1985—, sec., treas., 1995, Downtown Kalamazoo Inc., 1988-91; treas., trustee The Power Found., 1967—, sec., 1967-94. Sgt. USMC, 1946-48. Mem. ABA, Mich. Bar Assn., Kalamazoo County Bar Assn., Harvard Club Western Mich. (pres. 1972-74), Kalamazoo Country Club, Park Club, Harvard Club N.Y.C. Avocations: tennis, swimming. Home: 4126 Lakeside Dr Kalamazoo MI 49008-2814 Office: 136 E Michigan Ave Ste 1201 Kalamazoo MI 49007-3936

HILDEBRAND, ROGER HENRY, astrophysicist, physicist; b. Berkeley, Calif., May 1, 1922; s. Joel Henry and Emily (Alexander) H.; m. Jane Roby Beedle, May 28, 1944; children: Peter Henry, Alice Louise, Kathryn Jane, Daniel Milton. AB in Chemistry, U. Calif., Berkeley, 1947, PhD in Physics, 1951. Physicist, U. Calif., 1942-51; physicist Tenn. Eastman Corp., Oak Ridge Nat. Lab., 1945; asst. prof. dept. physics Enrico Fermi Inst., U. Chgo., 1952-55, asso. prof., 1955-60, prof., 1960—, prof. dept. astronomy and astrophysics, 1978—, Samuel K. Allison Disting. Service prof., 1985—, chmn. dept. astronomy and astrophysics, 1984-88; dir. Enrico Fermi Inst., 1965-68, dean coll., 1969-73. Assoc. lab. dir. for high energy physics Argonne (Ill.) Nat. Lab., 1958-64; chmn. sci. policy com. Stanford (Calif.) Linear Accelerator Ctr., 1962-66; mem. physics adv. com. Nat. Accelerator Lab., 1967-69; mem. sci. and ednl. adv. com. Lawrence Berkeley Lab., 1972-80; chmn. com. to rev. U.S. medium energy sci. AEC and NSF, 1974; chmn. airborne obs. users group NASA, 1983-84; chmn. sci. cons. group Stratospheric Obs. for Infrared Astronomy (SOFIA), NASA, 1985-89, mem. sci. working group, 1995-97, sci. coun., 1997—; mem. space astronomy and astrophysics Space Sci. Bd., 1987-90; mem. coun. Columbus Project, 1987-88; mem. sci. and tech. adv. panel for the submillimeter array Harvard/Smithsonian Ctr. for Astrophysics, 1989-95; mem. astronomy and astrophysics survey com. NAS Panel for Infrared Astronomy, 1989-90; chmn. Dannie Helneman prize com. Am. Inst. Physics, 1990; mem. sci. and tech. adv. group Large Millimeter Telescope, 1995—; mem. obs. vis. com. Assn. Univs. for Rsch. in Astronomy, 1993-96, chmn. Stratospheric Obs. Infrared Astronomy sci. coun., 1997—; mem. NASA review panel for Small Explorer (SMEX) Proposals, 2000; mem. NASA/JPL bd. for Planck High Frequency Instrument Detectors, 2000—; mem. faculty Canary Islands Winter Sch. Astrophysics, 2000. Guggenheim fellow, 1968-69, Alfred P. Sloan Found. fellow, 1975. Fellow Am. Phys. Soc., Am. Acad. Arts and Scis.; mem. Am. Astron. Soc., Internat. Astron. Union, Midwestern Univs. Rsch. Assn. (dir. 19956-58, 62-68), Phi beta Kappa, Sigma Xi. Office: U Chgo Enrico Fermi Inst 5640 S Ellis Ave Chicago IL 60637-1433

HILDING, JEREL LEE, music and dance educator, former dancer; b. New Orleans, Sept. 24, 1949; s. Oscar William and Loeta Dana (Boldra) H.; m. Krystyna Zofia Jurkowski, July 1, 1978; children: Dennis Jozef, Kristopher Jay. BA, La. State U., New Orleans, 1971. Prin. dancer Joffrey Ballet, N.Y.C., 1975-89; dir. arts in edn. N.J. Ballet, 1989-90; assoc. prof., dir. dance U. Kans., 1990—. Avocations: piano, sports. Office: U of Kansas Dept Music and Dance 460 Murphy Hall 1530 Naismith Dr Lawrence KS 66045-0001

HILER, JOHN PATRICK, former government official, former congressman, business executive; b. Chgo., Apr. 24, 1953; s. Robert J. and Margaret F. Hiler; m. Catherine Sands B.A., Williams Coll., 1975; M.B.A., U. Chgo., 1977. Mktg. dir. Charles O. Hiler and Son, Inc., Walkerton, Ind., 1977-80, Accurate Castings Co., La Porte, 1977-80; mem. 97th-101st congresses from 3d Ind. Dist., 1981-90; dep. adminstr. GSA, Washington, 1991-93; exec. Accurate Castings, Inc., La Porte, Ind., 1993—. Del. Ind. Rep. Conv., 1978, 90, 94, Rep. Nat. Conv., 1984, 88, White House Conf. on Small Bus., 1980; trustee Meml. Hosp. Mem. Ind. Mfrs. Assn., North Ctrl. Ind. Med. Edn. Found. Roman Catholic. Office: Accurate Castings Inc PO Box 639 La Porte IN 46352-0639

HILES, BRADLEY STEPHEN, lawyer; b. Granite City, Ill., Nov. 11, 1955; s. Joseph J. and Betty Lou (Goodman) H.; m. Toni Jonine Failoni, Aug. 12, 1977; children: Eric Stephen, Nina Catherine, Emily Christine. BA cum laude, Furman U., 1977; JD cum laude, St. Louis U., 1980. Bar: Mo. 1980, U.S. Dist. Ct. (ea. dist.) Mo., 1980, Ill. 1981. From assoc. to ptnr. Blackwell Sanders Peper Martin, St. Louis, 1980—. V.p., sec., gen. counsel Miss. Lime Co., 1992. Editor-in-chief St. Louis Univ. Law Jour., 1979-80; contbr. articles to profl. jours. Pres. Second Baptist Ch. of St. Louis, 1988. Mem. Bar Assn. of Met. St. Louis (chmn. environ. and conservation law com. 1993-94). Republican. Baptist. Avocations: gospel singing, cycling. Home: 34 Meditation Way Ct Florissant MO 63031-6535 Office: Blackwell Sanders Peper Martin 720 Olive St Fl 24 Saint Louis MO 63101-2338

HILGERT, JOHN A. state legislator; b. Omaha, Jan. 8, 1964; m. Cara Linden, Aug. 12, 1995; 1 child, John Linden Hilgert. BSBA, U. Nebr., 1986; grad., Creighton U., 1989; grad. officer basic course, U.S. Army Judge Adv. Gen. Sch., 1989, grad. trial advocacy course, 1990. V.p. instnl. advancement Cath. Charities, Omaha; mem. Nebr. Legislature from 7th dist., Lincoln, 1995—. Mem. Mandan Pk. Renovation Com., Dahlman Area Rehab. Effort, St. Frances Cabrini Cath. Ch.; former rep. Archdiocesan Pastoral Coun. With U.S. Army, 1989-92, Ops. Desert Storm. Decorated Bronze Star. Mem. ABA, Nebr. State Bar Assn., Omaha Bar Assn., Hanscom Pk. Neighborhood Assn., Columbus Pk. Neighborhood Assn., Nebr. Human Svcs. Assn., Spring Lake Pk. Neighborhood Assn., Deer Pk. Neighborhood Assn., S. Omaha Bus. Assn., Q St. Merchants Assn., VFW, Am. Legion, Sons of Italy, La Soc. Des 40 Hommes Et 8 Chevaux, KC, S. Omaha Optimists Internat., Christoforo Colombo Lodge, Fraternal Order Eagles. Home: 4116 S 19th St Omaha NE 68107-2001 Office: State Capitol Dist 7 PO Box 94604 Rm 1404 Lincoln NE 68509-4604

HILGERT, RAYMOND LEWIS, management and industrial relations educator, consultant, arbitrator; b. St. Louis, July 28, 1930; s. Lewis Francis and Frieda Christine (Keune) H.; m. Bernice Alice Nerl, Apr. 28, 1951; children— Brenda, Diane, Jeffrey BA, Westminster Coll., Fulton, Mo., 1952; MBA, Washington U., St. Louis, 1961; DBA, Washington U., 1963. Mgmt. positions with Southwestern Bell Telephone Co., 1956-60; mem. faculty Olin Sch. Bus. Washington U., St. Louis, 1963—, dir. summer workshop Olin Sch. Bus., 1964-68; dir. mgmt. devel. programs Olin Sch. Bus. Washington U., 1967-84; asst. dean, dir. undergrad. program Olin Sch. Bus. Washington U., 1968-69. Cons.; lectr.; labor arbitrator Author: (with C. Ling and Ed Leonard Jr.) Cases, Incidents and Experiential Exercises in Human Resource Management, 1990, 3d edit., 2000, (with David Dalto) Cases in Collective Bargaining and Industrial Relations: A Decisional Approach, 1969, 10th edit., 2002, Labor Agreement Negotiations, 1983, 6th edit., 2001; (with Ed Leonard Jr.) Supervision: Concepts and Practices of Management, 1972, 8th edit., 2001, (with Philip Lechbass and James Trueodell) Christian Ethics in the Workplace, 2001; contbr. articles to profl. jours. Mem. adv. coun. St. Louis region SBA, 1983-91. Served to 1st lt. USAF, 1952-56 Named Tchr. of Yr., Washington U. Sch. Bus., 1968, 81, 85, 89. Mem. Acad. Mgmt., Indsl. Rels. Rsch. Assn., Soc. for Human Resource Mgmt. (sr. profl. in human resource mgmt.), Am. Mgmt. Assn. Lutheran Avocations: sports, movies. Home: 1744 Lynkirk Ln Kirkwood MO 63122-2251 Office: Washington U Olin Sch Bus PO Box 1133 Saint Louis MO 63188-1133

HILKER, LYLE J. financial services organization executive; b. New London, Wis. BBA, U. Wis., Oshkosh, 1992. With Aid Assn. for Luths., Appleton, Wis., 1973—, dir. managerial acctg., 1985-88, asst. v.p. Expense Info. Svcs., 1988-92, 2d v.p. Expense Info. Svcs., 1992-93, 2d v.p. fin. and managerial reporting, 1993-95, 2d v.p. bus. process assurance and enhancement, 1995-97, v.p. bus. process assurance and enhancement, 1997; now also v.p. product svcs. Thrivent Finl. for Luths. (formerly known as Aid Assn. for Luths.). Past pres. Bethlehem Luth. Ch., Hortonville, Wis.; also past pres. local chpt. Aid Assn. for Luths., Hortonville; past mem. Fox Valley Tech. Coll. Acctg. Adv. Com.; bd. dirs. Fox Valley Symphony. Office: Thrivent Finl for Luths 4321 N Ballard Rd Appleton WI 54919-0001

HILL, ALLEN M. public utility executive; b. Dayton, Ohio, June 15, 1945; m. Chris Hill; children: Patricia, Brent. B.S. in Elec. Engring., U. Dayton, 1967, M.B.A., 1972. With Dayton Power & Light Co., 1965—, coordinator rate design, 1975-76, supr. gas services, 1976-78, mgr. planning, 1978-80, asst. v.p., 1980-81, treas., 1981-83, v.p., treas., 1983-86, group v.p., 1986-88, pres., former chief ops. officer, 1988—; pres. & CEO Dayton Power & Light Co. (now DLP Inc.). Treas. Miami Valley Coalition for Health Care Cost Effectiveness Mem. Edison Electric Inst. Office: DPL Inc PO Box 1247 Dayton OH 45401

HILL, BARON P. congressman; b. Seymour, Ind., 1954; m. Betty Schepman; children: Jennifer, Cara, Elizabeth. BS in History, Furman U., 1975. Fin. analyst Merrill Lynch; mem. U.S. Congress from 9th Ind. dist., 1999—. Mem. Agr., Armed Forces coms., Blue Dog Dems., New Dem. Coalition. Elected to Ind. Ho. Reps., 1982-90; appointed by Speaker of the House to serve as chmn. House Rules Com.; asst. whip for Dem. Caucus, as chmn. Ind. House Campaign Com. from 1985-89; exec. dir. State Student Assistance Commn., 1992. Office: 1208 Longworth Hob Washington DC 20515-0001*

HILL, BRUCE MARVIN, statistician, scientist, educator; b. Chgo., Mar. 13, 1935; s. Samuel and Leah (Berman) H.; m. Linda Ladd, June 18, 1958; children— Alec Michael, Russell Andrew, Gregory Bruce; m. Anne Edith Gardiner Bruce, Aug. 5, 1972. B.S. in Math., U. Chgo., 1956; M.S. in Stats., Stanford U., 1958, Ph.D. in Stats., 1961. Mem. faculty U. Mich., Ann Arbor, 1960—, assoc. prof. stats. and probability theory, 1964-70, prof., 1970—. Vis. prof. bus. Harvard U., 1964-65; vis. prof. systems engring. U. Lancaster, U.K., 1968-69; vis. prof. stats. U. London, 1976; vis. prof. econs. U. Utah, 1979; vis. prof. math. U. Milan, U. Rome, 1989. Author: Hill Tail index estimator; editor Jour. Am. Statis. Assn., 1977-83, Jour. Bus. and Econ. Stats., 1982—; contbr. articles to profl. jours., chpts. to books on stats, encys. Grantee NSF, 1962-69, 81-86, 89—, USAF, 1971-73, 87-89. Fellow Am. Statis. Assn. (pres. Ann Arbor chpt. 1986-91), Inst. Math. Stats.; mem. AAUP, Am. Math Assn., Rsch. Club U. Mich., Psi Upsilon, Sigma Chi. Office: U Mich Dept Stats Ann Arbor MI 48109-1027 Home: 1645 Polipoli Rd Kula HI 96790-7524 E-mail: bbbmhill@juno.com.

HILL, CARLOTTA H. physician; b. Chgo., Apr. 8, 1958; d. Clarence Kenneth and Vlasta (Cizek) Hayes; m. Chester James Hill III, June 10, 1967 (div. 1974); m. Carlos A. Rotman, July 31, 1980; children: Robin Mercedes. BA magna cum laude, Knox Coll., 1969; MD with honors, U. Ill., 1973. Diplomate Nat. Bd. Med. Examiners, 1974, Am. Bd. Dermatology, 1978. Intern Mayo Sch. Medicine, Rochester, Minn., 1973-74; resident U. Ill., Chgo., 1975-78, asst. prof. clin. dermatology Coll. Medicine, 1978-93, assoc. prof. clin. dermatology Coll. Medicine, 1993—. Sen. U. Ill. Senate, Chgo., 1986-91, 99— ; councilor Chgo. Med. Soc., 1990-96, 99—. Contbr. articles to profl. jours. Bd. dirs. Summerfest St. James Cathedral, Chgo., 1986-91, YWCA, Lake Forest, Ill., 1995—, pres., 1998-00; master gardner Chgo. Botanic Garden, Glencoe, Ill., 1994-98; bd. dirs. Lake Bluff Open Lands Assn., 1997—. Recipient Janet Glascow award Am. Women's Med. Assn., 1973. Mem. AMA, Am. Acad. Dermatology, Herb Soc. Am. (ways and means No. Ill. unit 1992-94, treas. N. Ill. unit 1996-00, v.c. 2000—), Ill. State Dermatologic Soc., Chgo. Med. Soc., Chgo. Dermatologic Soc., Phi Beta Kappa, Alpha Omega Alpha. Avocations: travel, cooking, gardening, reading. Office: Dept Dermatology 808 S Wood St Chicago IL 60612-7300

HILL, CHARLES, newspaper editor; Bur. chief AP, Detroit, 1991—. Office: 300 River Place Dr Ste 2400 Detroit MI 48207-5064

HILL, CHARLES GRAHAM, JR. chemical engineering educator; b. Elmira, N.Y., July 28, 1937; s. Charles Graham and Ethel Mayburn (Pfleegor) H.; m. Katharine Mertice Koon, July 11, 1964; children: Elizabeth, Deborah, Cynthia. BS, MIT, 1959, MS, 1960, ScD, 1964. Asst. prof. MIT, Cambridge, 1964-65, U. Wis., Madison, 1967-71, assoc. prof., 1971-76, prof. chem. engring., 1976—, John T. and Magdalen L. Sobota prof. chem. engring., 1995—, prof. food sci., 1989—, chmn. dept. chem. engring., 1989-92. Cons. A.D. Little, Cambridge, 1964-65, Joseph Schlitz Brewing Co., Milw., 1973-76, Nat. Bur. Stds., 1979-95. Author: Introduction to Chemical Engineering Kinetics and Reactor Design, 1977; contbr. articles to profl. jours. Capt. U.S. Army, 1965-67. Gen. Motors Nat. scholar, 1955-59; NSF fellow, 1959-62, Ford Found. fellow, 1964-65, Fulbright Sr. fellow, 2000. Fellow AIChE; mem. Am. Chem. Soc., Inst. Food Technologists, Am. Oil Chemists Soc., Sigma Xi, Tau Beta Pi, Phi Lambda Upsilon. Republican. Presbyterian. Office: U Wis Dept Chem Engring 1415 Engineering Dr Madison WI 53706-1607 E-mail: hill@engr.wisc.edu.

HILL, DAVID K., JR. construction executive; Chmn., CEO Kimball Hill Homes, Rolling Meadows, Ill., 1990—. Office: 5999 New Wilke Rd Bldg 5 Rolling Meadows IL 60008-4506

HILL, EMITA BRADY, academic administrator; b. Balt., Jan. 31, 1936; d. Leo and Lucy McCormick (Jewett) Brady; children: Julie Beck, Christopher, Madeleine, Vedel. BA, Cornell U., 1957; MA, Middlebury Coll., 1958; PhD, Harvard U., 1967. Instr. Harvard U., 1961-63; asst. prof. Western Reserve U., 1967-69; from asst. prof. to v.p. Lehman Coll. CUNY, Bronx, N.Y., 1970-91; chancellor, grad. faculty Ind. U., Kokomo, Ind., 1991-99, chancellor emerita, 1999—. Trustee Am. U. in Kyrgyzstan; mem. Women's Forum of NY. Mem. Internat. Assn. Univ. Pres., Phi Beta Kappa. Avocations: music, scuba diving, tennis. E-mail: chill@indiana.edu.

HILL, GARY, video artist; b. Santa Monica, Calif., Apr. 4, 1951; Student, Art Students League, Woodstock, 1969. Founder, dir. Open Studio Video, Tarrytown, N.Y., 1977-78; artist-in-residence Exptl. TV Ctr., Binghamton, N.Y., 1975-77, Portable Channel, Rochester, N.Y., 1978, Sony Corp., Hon. Atsugi, Japan, 1985, Chgo. Art Inst., 1986, Calif. Inst. Arts, Valencia, 1987, Hopital Ephémère, Paris, 1991; vis. assoc. prof. Ctr. Media, SUNY, Buffalo, 1979-80; vis. prof. art Bard Coll., Annandale-on-Hudson, N.Y., 1983; art faculty Cornish Coll. Arts, Seattle, 1985-92. One person shows include Mus. Modern Art, N.Y.C., 1980, 90, Whitney Mus. Am. Art, N.Y.C., 1983, Galerie des Archives, Paris, 1990, 91, Galerie Huset-Glyptotek Mus. Mus., Copenhagen & YYZ Artist's Outlet, Toronto, 1990, OCO Espace d'art contemporain, Paris, 1991, Watari Mus. Contemporary Art, Tokyo, 1992, Mus. Modern Art, Oxford, Eng., 1993, Mus. Contemporary Art, L.A., 1994, Mus. Contemporary Art, Chgo., 1994, Fundaicó La Caixa, Barcelona, Spain, Busch-Reisinger Mus., Harvard U. Art Mus, Cambridge, Mass., 1995, Moderna Museet, Stockholm, 1995, Inst. Contemporary Art, Phila., 1996, Kunst-und Ausstellungshalle der Bundesrepublik Deutschland (Forum), Bonn, Germany, 1996, Centro Cultural Banco do Brazil, Rio de Janeiro, 1997, Musée d'Art Contemporain de Montréal, Can., 1998, Donald Young Gallery, Seattle, 1998, Museu d'Art Contemporani, Barcelona, Spain, 1998, others; exhibited in group shows Am. Ctr., Paris, 1983, Whitney Mus. Am. Art, N.Y., 1986, St. Gervais, Geneva, 2d Seminar on Internat. Video, 1987, ELAC Art Contemporain, Lyon, France, 1988, Biennial Exhbn., Whitney Mus. Am. Art, 1991, 93, Performing Objects, Inst. Contemporary Art, Boston, 1992, Cocido y Crudo, Centro Reina Sofia, Madrid, 1994, Light Into Art, Contemporary Arts Ctr., Cin., 1994, Facts and Figures, Lannan Found., L.A., 1994, Multiplas Dimensoes, Centro Cultural de Belem, Lisbon, Portugal, 1994, Beeld, Mus van Hedendaagse Kunst, Ghent, Belgium, 1994, Crossings, Kunsthalle Wien, Austria, 1998, Voices, Witte de with Rotterdam, The Netherlands, 1998; author: Primarily Speaking, 1981-83, Whitney Mus. Am. Art, 1983, Primarily Speaking Communications, 1988, And if the Right Hand did not Know What the Left Hand is Doing, Illuminating Video, 1990, Unspeakable Images, Camera Obscura, 1991, Finnish Nat. Gallery, Helsinki, Finland, 1995, Mus. Modern Art, N.Y.C., 1995, Albert Knox Gallery, Buffalo, 1996, World Wide Video Festival, Amsterdam, The Netherlands, 1997. Recipient prize ARTEC 91 Internat. Biennale, Nagoya, Japan, 1991; Rockefeller Intercult Media Arts fellow, 1989-90, Guggenheim fellow, 1990; recipient JOhn D. and Catherine T. MacArthur grant. Office: Donald Young Gallery 933 W Washington Blvd Chicago IL 60607-2218

HILL, J. EDWARD, physician, educator; b. Omaha, Feb. 2, 1938; m. Jean Hill; 2 children. MD, U. Miss., 1964. Diplomate Am. Bd. Family Practice. Intern Naval Hosp., 1964-65; assoc. prof. U. Miss. Med. Sch.; rsch. dir. North Miss. Med. Ctr., Tupelo; pvt. practice. Dir. family practice residency program North Miss. Med. Ctr., med. dir. Pres. Miss. afiliate Am. Heart Assn.; adv. bd. Head Start Program; pres. Sch. Bd.; bd. dirs. local ch. Recipient Miss. Family Dr. of Yr. 1991, ruuner up Family Dr. of Yr. Good Housekeeping mag. 1977. Mem. AMA (bd. trustees 1996, chair bd. com. on membership, fin. com., pres. AMA Found., AMA del. 1984), Miss. State Med. Assn. (chmn. bd. trustees, pres.), Miss. Acad. of Family Physicians (pres.), Am. Acad. of Family Physicians (alternate delegate, delegate), So. Med. Assn. (pres.), C. of C. (chair indsl. devel. com.). Office: AMA 515 N State St Chicago IL 60610-4325

HILL, JAMES STANLEY, computer consulting company executive; b. Merrickville, Ont., Can., July 24, 1914; m. Doris C. Huelster, 1938; children: George, Janice, Mary, Beverly, Richard. With Minn. Life Ins. Co., 1930-69; sr. v.p., 1966-69; pres. Digiplan, Inc., White Bear Lake, Minn., 1969—, Red Oak Press, 1994—. Bd. dirs., chmn. audit com. Hadco Inc., 1981-98; pub. spkr., 1994—. Author: Confessions of an 80 Year Old Boy, 1994, Almost Immortal, 1996. Treas. Minn. State H.S. Math. League, St. Paul Area Coun. of Chs. Found.; bd. dirs. United Hosp., 1972-99. Fellow Soc. Actuaries (bd. govs., v.p.). Home and Office: Digiplan Inc 5011 Lake Ave Apt 205 Saint Paul MN 55110-2655

HILL, LANCE, meteorologist; BS, Marquette U.; postgrad., Lyndon State Coll. Meteorologist KMEG-TV, Sioux City, Iowa, WANE-TV, Ft. Wayne, Ind., WISN, Milw. Recipient seal, Nat. Weather Assn. Mem.: Am. Meteorol. Soc. Avocations: mountain biking, hiking, camping, storm chasing. Office: WISN PO Box 402 Milwaukee WI 53201-0402

HILL, LLOYD L. food service executive; Exec. v.p. Kimberly Quality Care, 1980-91, pres., 1991-94; exec. v.p., COO Applebee's Internat. Inc., Overland Pk., Kans., 1994—, also bd. dirs. Office: Applebees Internat Inc 4551 W 107th St Ste 100 Shawnee Mission KS 66207-4037 Fax: 913-341-1694.

HILL, LOWELL DEAN, agricultural marketing educator; b. Delta, Iowa, Apr. 27, 1930; s. Frederick Carl and Harriet Jane (Atwood) H.; m. Betty Elaine Carpenter, Dec. 9, 1951; children: Rebecca Elaine, Brent Howard. BS in Agrl. Edn., Iowa State U., 1951; MS in Agrl. Econs., Mich. State U., 1961, PhD in Agrl. Econs., 1963. Asst. prof., then assoc. prof. dept. agrl. econs. U. Ill., Urbana, 1963-72, prof., 1972-77, L.J. Norton prof. agrl.

mktg., 1977-98, L.J. Norton prof. emeritus, 1998—. Cons. Office Tech. Assessment, Washington, 1986-88, South Am. and Europe, 1995, FAO, Rome, 1978-80, U.S. AID, 1983, World Bank, Washington, 1989-90, 92-93, Argentina, Colombia, Chile, 1989-94, U.S. Feed Grains Coun., Venezuela, Japan, Korea, 1990-93, USDA, Russia, 1993-96; mem. adv. com. Fed. Grain Inspection Svc., USDA, 2000-2003. Author: Grain Grades and Standards: Historical Issues, 1990; editor: Role of Government in a Market Economy, 1982, Corn Quality in World Markets, 1985. Cpl. U.S. Army, 1952-54. Fellow East West Ctr.; recipient Quality of Comm. award, 1980, 88, Disting. Policy Contbr. award 1988, Extension Programs award, 1989, Disting. Svc. award USDA, 1989, Internat. Mktg. Support award Am. Soybean Assn., 1989, Faculty award for rsch. excellence, 1991; Univ. scholar, 1992. Fellow: Am. Agrl. Econ. Assn.; mem.: Coun. Agrl. Sci. and Tech. (chmn. 1989—90), Rotary. Office: Univ Ill Mumford Hall 1301 W Gregory Dr Urbana IL 61801-9015 E-mail: l-hill3@uiuc.edu.

HILL, LUTHER LYONS, JR. lawyer; b. Des Moines, Aug. 21, 1922; s. Luther Lyons and Mary (Hippee) H.; m. Sara S. Carpenter, Aug. 12, 1950; children— Luther Lyons III, Mark Lyons. BA, Williams Coll., 1947; LLB, Harvard U., 1950; LLD (hon.), Simpson Coll., 1979. Bar: Iowa 1951. Law clk. to Justice Hugo L. Black U.S. Supreme Ct., 1950-51; assoc., ptnr. Henry & Henry, Des Moines, 1951-69; mem. legal staff Equitable Life Ins. Co. of Iowa, 1952-87, exec. v.p., 1969-87, gen. counsel, 1970-87; of counsel Nyemaster, Goode, McLaughlin, Voigts, Wiest, Hansell O'Brien, Des Moines, 1992—. Counsel, adminstr. Iowa Life and Health Ins. Guaranty Assn. Bd. dirs., past pres. United Comty. Svcs. Greater Des Moines; past trustee, past chmn. Simpson Coll., Indianola, Iowa; bd. chmn. Iowa State Hist. Found., 1997-2001; trustee The Hoyt Sherman Pl. Found. Capt. M.I., AUS, WWII, ETO. Mem. ABA, Iowa Bar Assn., Polk County Bar Assn., Assn. Life Ins. Counsel, Des Moines Club, Wakonda Club. Republican. Avocation: walking in the Swiss mountains. Home: 2801 Park Ave Des Moines IA 50321-1515 Office: Ste 1600 700 Walnut St Des Moines IA 50309-3929

HILL, PAUL MARK, clergyman; b. Cin., Aug. 29, 1953; s. Paul Frederick and Helen Faith (Skeen) H.; m. Rebecca Sue Helm, Dec. 29, 1977; children: Aaron Israel Paul, Revkah Lauren Amara, Hadassah Sue Elizabeth. BA in Biology, Asbury Coll., 1975; DivM, Anderson Sch. Theology, 1981; postgrad., Covenant Theol. Sem. Ordained to ministry Meth. Ch., 1984. Sr. pastor United Meth. Ch., Marion, Ind., 1978—, camp dir., 1990—. Speaker and lectr. in field. Dir. TV show Offer Them Christ, 1986; partial designer grandfather clock, 1989. Actor Civic Theater, Logansport, Ind., 1981-82, Peru Civic Theater, 1981-82; coach baseball, basketball, soccer, Marion, Ind., 1986-89; baseball coach, Lafayette, Ind., 1995; organizer, dir. Stockwell Youth Orch., 1990; coach basketball, Lafayette, Ind., 1993-95. Named to Outstanding Young Men of Am., 1988. Avocations: basketball, skiing, wood working, running, baseball.

HILL, RAYMOND JOSEPH, packaging company executive; b. Chanute, Kans., May 4, 1935; s. Raymond Joseph and Emma Leona (Arthurs) H.; Asso. in Engring., Coffeyville (Kans.) Coll., 1955; m. Bettie Anne Handshumaker, Mar. 2, 1957; children: David, Dianne, Todd, Scott, Jennifer. MBA, U. Denver, 1977. Field engr. Phillips Petroleum Co., Bartlesville, Okla., 1957-59; design engr. Thiokol Chem. Corp., Brigham City, Utah, 1959-60; tech. supr. Hercules Chem. Corp., Salt Lake City, 1960-68; project mgr. aerospace div. Ball Corp., Boulder, Colo., 1968-70, plant mgr. and v.p. mfg. metal container div., Findlay, Ohio and Denver, Colo., 1970-78, pres. agrl. systems div., Westminster, Colo., 1978-85; v.p. plastic ops., sr. v.p. mfg. tech., ex. v.p. food metal, exec. v.p. food plastics Am. Nat. Can Corp., Chgo., 1985-90, sr. v.p. mfg. tech., 1990-93, exec. v.p. food plastics N.Am.; pres. Chesnee Assocs., Inc., Internat. Cons., 1993-97; exec. v.p. The PopStraw Co., also bd. dirs.; bd. dirs. Navaho Agrl. Products Industries, United Energy Devel., Packaging Adv. Coun., Flex Packing Assn., The Hallmark Group, Packaging Ptnrs., Classic Signatures, Inc., PopStraw Co.; mem. policy adv. com. to Office of U.S. Trade Rep., 1980—. Mem. Am. Ordnance Assn., Nat. Food Processors Assn., Soc. Tool Engrs., Irrigation Assn., Rotary. Republican. Episcopalian. Home: 889 Turnbridge Cir Naperville IL 60540-8342 Office: Chesnee Assocs Inc 2010 E Algonquin Rd Ste 210 Schaumburg IL 60173-4168

HILL, RICHARD A. advertising executive; b. Detroit; Student, Mich. State U.; MS in Mktg., Wayne State U. With J. Walter Thompson, Young & Rubicam; media supr. Buick/GMC Truck divsn., assoc. media dir. McCann-Erickson, Troy, Mich., 1970-75, sr. account exec. Buick account, 1975-77, v.p. media, mktg. dir. Detroit, 1977-79, account supr. multi-products group, 1979-81, account supr. Buick, 1981-86, sr. v.p., mgmt. rep., 1986-91, dep. mgr., chmn. mgmt. bd., 1991-93, exec. v.p., gen. mgr., 1993-97, dir. profl. devel., 1997—, also exec. v.p., 1993—. Avocation: golf. Office: McCann-Erickson 755 W Big Beaver Rd Ste 2500 Troy MI 48084-0230

HILL, ROBYN LESLEY, artist, designer; b. Sydney, Australia, Apr. 28, 1942; d. Frank Bragg and Florence Margorie (Turnham) H. Grad., Nat. Art Sch., Sydney, 1962; studied with Edward Betts, Claude Croney, Fred Leach, Maxine Masterfield, 1969-85. Art mistress S.C.E.G.G.S., Sydney, 1963-66; apprentice artist Am. Greetings, Cleve., 1967, conventional and specialities planning stylist, profl. designer and artist, 1967-73, mkgt. dept. gift wrap coord., 1973-75, prof. stylist books and stationery dept., 1976-78, art dir. creative devel., 1978-81; program dir. Those Characters from Cleve., 1982-94. Creative, designer (TV program) The Special Magic of Herself the Elf (Can. Emmy award 1982); exhibited at Catherine Lorillard Wolfe Nat. Exhbn., N.Y., Massillon Mus. Invitational, Ohio, Adirondacks Nat. Show, N.Y., Artists Soc. Internat., San Francisco, Am. Watercolor Soc. show and traveling show, Rocky Mountain Watercolor Nat. Exhbn., Internat. Art Expo, Dallas, Blue Grass 5th Biennial, Ky.; works included in The Best of Flower Painting, 1997. Mem. Nat. Watercolor Soc. (signature), Nat. Watercolor USA Hon. Soc. (award Springfield Art Mus. 1984, signature), Am. Watercolor Soc. (assoc.), Midwest Watercolor Soc. (assoc.), Ohio Watercolor Soc. (So. Ohio Bank award 1983, signature), Pa. Soc. Watercolor Painters, Ga. Watercolor Soc. (assoc.), North Coast Collage Soc. (signature), Ky. Watercolor Soc. (exhibiting mem.). Episcopalian. Home: 27004 Lake Shore Blvd Euclid OH 44132-1242

HILL, STEPHEN L., JR. lawyer, former prosecutor; m. Marianne Matteson; 2 children. BS in Polit. Sci., Southwest Mo. State U., 1981; JD, U. Mo., 1986; postgrad., London U. Staff U.S. Congressman Ike Skelton, 4th dist Mo., 1982; trial atty. Smith, Gill, Fisher & Butts, Kansas City, 1986-94; U.S. atty. Western Dist. Mo., 1993—2001; partner Blackwell Sanders Peper Martin, LLP, Mo., 2001—. Office: Blackwell Sanders Peper Martin, LLP Two Pershing Square 2300 Main St, Ste. 1000 Kansas City MO 64108 Office Fax: 816-983-8080. E-mail: shill@bspmlaw.com.

HILL, TESSA, president non profit environmental group; BA in Edn., Park Recreation Adminstrn., U. Minn., 1968. Tchr. elem. schs., 1970; founder Kids For Saving Earth, Mpls., 1989—. Adv. com. U.S. Environ. Protection Agy., Dept. Health Human Svcs. Agy. Toxic Substances Disease Registry. Editor CHEC Report, Kids for Saving Earth News/Programs. Bd. dirs. Children's Health Environ. Coalition, Nat. Coalition Against Misuse Pesticides. Home and Office: Kids for Saving Earth Worldwide 5425 Pineview Ln N Minneapolis MN 55442-1704 E-mail: KSEWW@aol.com.

HILL, THOMAS J. career officer; BBA, U. Notre Dame. Commd. ensign USN, advanced through ranks to rear adm.; various assignments to mobilization asst. to dep. comdr. U.S. Transp. Command; former sr. mktg. rep. IBM, to 1991; account exect. Dean Witter, Indpls., 1991—. Founding mem./past chmn. Cen. Ind. Naval Ball. Active United Way of Cen. Ind., Indpls. Children's Mus., Indpls. Black Expo Summer Exposition, December's Children and the Indpls. Ballet Theater; bd. dirs., past v.p. Devel. for the Indpls. Chamber Orchestra. Decorated Meritorious Svc. medal, DoD Joint Svc. Commendation medal, others. Mem. Navy Supply Corps Assn. (past nat. dir.), Navy Supply Corps Found. (mem. fin. com.), Kiwanis. Office: 508 Scott Dr Scott Air Force Base IL 62225-5313

HILL, TYRONE, professional basketball player; b. Cin., Mar. 19, 1968; BA in Comm. Arts, Xavier U., 1986-90. Forward Golden State Warriors, San Francisco, 1990-93, Cleve. Cavaliers, 1993-97, Milw. Bucks, 1997-99, Philadelphia 76ers, 1999—. Active NBA Stay In Sch. Program. All-time leading rebounder, scorer Xavier U.; leader Cleve. Cavaliers field-goal percentage, 1993-94; named to NBA All-Star Game Eastern Conf., 1995. Avocation: music. Office: Cleveland Cavaliers Gund Arena One Center Court Cleveland OH 44115*

HILL, WILLIAM A(LEXANDER), judge; b. Carmel, Calif., Aug. 21, 1946; s. R. William and Ruth M. (McDonald) H.; m. Diane K. Hartman, Apr. 25, 1981; children: Erin, Georgia. BS, U. N.D., 1968, JD, 1971; cert., Hastings Coll. Law Coll. Advocacy, 1977; grad. in fed. evidence, U. Mich. Law Sch., 1981. Bar: N.D. 1971, Minn. 1974, U.S. Dist. Ct. N.D. 1971, U.S. Tax Ct. 1973, U.S. Ct. Appeals (8th cir.) 1973. Dep. sec. of state State of N.D., 1971-72; law clk. to judge U.S. Dist. Ct. N.D., 1972-74; ptnr. Pancratz Law Firm, Fargo, N.D., 1974-83; magistrate U.S. Dist. Ct., 1975-83; judge U.S. Bankruptcy Ct., 1983—. Mem. 8th cir. bankruptcy appellate panel, 1996—; part-time magistrate U.S. Dist. Ct. N.D., 1975-83; active N.D. Supreme Ct. Joint Procedures Com. Commr., 1978-83. Mem. exec. bd. dirs. No. Lights coun. Boy Scouts Am., 1993-98; bd. dirs. Fargo Moorhead Symphony, 1995-2001, Heritage Hjemkomst Ctr., Moorhead, Minn.; chmn. Gethemane Episcopal Found., Fargo, 1981-83; pres. Plains Art Mus., Moorhead, 1982. E-mail: william. Office: US Bankruptcy Ct Quentin N Burdick US Courthouse 655 1st Ave N Ste 350 Fargo ND 58102-4952 E-mail: hill@ndb.uscourts.gov.

HILLARD, CAROLE, lieutenant governor; b. Deadwood, S.D., Aug. 14, 1936; m. John M. Hillard (dec.); children: David, Sue Ellen, Todd, Eddie, Lornell. BA in Edn., Univ. of Ariz., 1957; MA in Edn., S.D. State Univ., 1982; MA in Polit. Sci., Univ. of S.D., 1984. State rep. State of S.D., 34th dist., 1991-95; lt. gov. State of S.D., 1995—. Dir. Mich. Nat. Bank., Black Hills Regional Eye Inst., YMCA; mem. exec. bd. Nat. Crime Prevention Coun. Active Rapid City Common Coun., Rapid City C. of C., S.D. Bd. of Charities and Corrections, McGruff Crime Prevention Coun. (exec. bd.), S.D. Corrections Commn., Cmty. Care Ctr., S.D. Children's Home Soc., S.D. Assurance Alliance, Nat. Child Protection Partnership, First United Methodist Ch. (exec. bd.), Rapid City Econ. Devel. Partnership, F.L.A.G.S. Found.; mem. exec. bd. Bog Bros./Big Sisters. Recipient Pub. Svc. award, 1987, Gov.'s Outstanding Citizen award, 1988, George award Rapid City C. of C., 1994; named Outstanding Chirperson, United Way, 1986, S.D. Guardian Small Bus., 1994. Mem. LWV, Women's Network, Mt. Rushmore Soc., Indian-White Coun., Toastmasters, Ninety-niners, Rapid City Fine Arts Coun. Republican. Methodist. Avocations: flying (lic. pvt. pilot), snow skiing, scuba diving, reading. Office: Office of Lt Governor State Capitol 500 E Capitol Ave Ste 215 Pierre SD 57501-5070*

HILLARD, TERRY G. protective services official; b. South Fulton, Tenn. BS in Corrections, MS in Corrections, Chgo. State U. Police officer Chgo. Police Dept., Ill., 1968—, comdr. Gresham dist. patrol divsn., 1991—93, dep. chief of patrol area 2, 1993—95, supt. of police, 1998—. With USMC, 63. Office: Chgo Police Dept Office of Supt 3510 S Michigan Ave Chicago IL 60653

HILLEGONDS, PAUL, former state legislator; b. Holland, Mich., Mar. 4, 1949; s. William C. and Elizabeth (Romaine) H.; m. Nancy; 1 child, Sarah. BA, U. Mich., 1971; JD, Coolegy Law Sch., 1986. Legis. asst. U.S. Rep. Philip Ruppe, Mich., 1971-74, adminstrv. asst., 1974-78; mgr. Ruppe's Congl. Campaign, 1974, 76; state rep. Dist. 54 Mich. Ho. of Reps., 1978-94, state rep. Dist. 88, 1995-96; pres., CEO Detroit Renaissance. Asst. minority leader, 1983-85, minority leader, 1986—; mem. Workers Compensation & Unemployment Ins. Subcoms., Mich. Ho. of Reps.; chmn. Rep. Campaign Com., leader Rep. Policy Com., Mich. Ho. of Reps. Recipient Disting. Svc. award Holland Jaycees, 198, Disting. Svc. award Assn. Ind. Colls., 1985—; named One of Ten Outstanding Legislators of Yr., Nat. Rep. Legislators Assn., 1988—. Mem. Ripon Soc., Assn. Pub. Justice, Holland Jaycees, Common Cause, Kiwanis.

HILLER, DAVID DEAN, lawyer; b. Chgo., June 12, 1953; AB, Harvard U., 1975, JD, 1978. Bar: Ill. 1981. Law clk. to Hon. Judge Malcolm Wilkey U.S. Ct. Appeals (D.C. cir.), 1978-79; law clk. to Hon. Justice Potter Stewart U.S. Supreme Ct., 1979-80; ptnr. Sidley and Austin, Chgo., 1983—; v.p., gen. counsel, sr. v.p. dev., pres. Tribune Co., 1988—. Spl. asst. to U.S. Atty. Gen., 1981-82; assoc. dep. atty. gen., 1982-83. Editor Harvard Law Rev., 1977-78. Mem. ABA (internat. law and corp. sects.) Office: Tribune Interactive 435 N Michigan Ave Chicago IL 60611-4066 also: Sidley and Austin One First Nat Pl Chicago IL 60603 E-mail: dhiller@tribune.com.

HILLER, STEVE, radio personality; b. Des Moines, Dec. 22, 1973; m. Natasha Hiller; 1 child Darien. Radio music host Sta. WMBI Radio, Chgo. Avocations: golf, football, water sports, Superman, road trips. Office: WMBI 820 N LaSalle Blvd Chicago IL 60610*

HILLERT, GLORIA BONNIN, anatomist, educator; b. Brownton, Minn., Jan. 25, 1930; d. Edward Henry and Lydia Magdalene (Luebker) Bonnin; m. Richard Hillert, Aug. 20, 1960; children: Kathryn, Virginia, Jonathan. BS, Valparaiso (Ind.) U., 1953; MA, U. Mich., 1958. Instr. Springfield (Ill.) Jr. Coll., 1953-57; teaching asst. U. Mich., Ann Arbor, 1957-58; instr., dept. head St. John's Coll., Winfield, Kans., 1958-59; asst. prof. Concordia Coll., River Forest, Ill., 1959-63; vis. instr. Wright Jr. Coll., Chgo., 1974-76, Ill. Benedictine Coll., Lisle, 1977-78, Rosary Coll., River Forest, 1976-81; prof. anatomy and physiology Triton Coll., River Grove, 1982-92, prof. emeritus, 1992—; vis. asst. prof. Concordia U., 1993—. Vis. instr. Wheaton (Ill.) Coll., 1988; advisor Springfield Jr. Coll. Sci. Club, 1953-57, Concordia Coll. Cultural Group, 1959-62; program dir. Triton Coll. Sci. Lectr. Series, 1983-87; participant Internat. Educators Workshop in Amazonia, 1993. Dem. campaign asst., Maywood, Ill., 1972, 88; vol. Mental Health Orgn., Chgo., 1969-73, Earthwatch, St. Croix, 1987, Costa Rica, 1989, Internat. Med. Care Team, Guatemala, 1995, Earthwatch End of Dinosaurs, 1997. Mem. AAUW, Ill. Assn. Community Coll. Biol. Tchrs., Nat. Assn. Biol. Tchrs. Lutheran. Avocation: traveling. Home: 1620 Clay Ct Melrose Park IL 60160-2419 Office: Triton Coll 2000 N 5th Ave River Grove IL 60171-1907 E-mail: rwhillert@aol.com.

HILLMAN, DOUGLAS WOODRUFF, federal district judge; b. Grand Rapids, Mich., Feb. 15, 1922; s. Lemuel Serrell and Dorothy (Woodruff) H.; m. Sally Jones, Sept. 13, 1944; children: Drusilla W., Clayton D. (dec.). Student, Phillips Exeter Acad., 1941; A.B., U. Mich., 1946, LL.B., 1948. Bar: Mich. 1948, U.S. Supreme Ct. 1967. Assoc. Lilly, Luyendyk & Snyder, Grand Rapids, 1948-53; partner Luyendyk, Hainer, Hillman, Karr & Dutcher, 1953-65, Hillman, Baxter & Hammond, 1965-79; U.S. dist. judge Western Dist. Mich., Grand Rapids, 1979—, chief judge, 1986-91, sr. judge, 1991—. Instr. Nat. Inst. Trial Adv., Boulder, Colo; dir. Fed. Judges Assn.; mem. jud. conf. com. on Admisntrn. of Magistrate Judges Sys., 1993-99; chair 6th Circuit Standing Com. on Jud. Conf. Planning; mem. exec. com. ABA jud. adminstrn. divsn. Nat. Conf. Fed. Trial Judges, 1995-98. Co-author articles in legal publs. Chmn. Grand Rapids Human Relations Commn., 1963-66; chmn. bd. trustees Fountain St. Ch., 1970-72; pres. Family Service Assn., 1967. Served as pilot USAAF, 1943-45. Decorated Air medal DFC; named One of 25 Most Respected Judges, Mich. Laywers Weekly, Grand Rapids Med. Hall Fame, 2001; recipient Ann. Civil Liberties award, ACLU, 1970, Disting. ALumni award, Ctrl. High Sch., 1986, Raymond Fox Advocacy award, 1989, Champion of Justice award, State Bar Mich., 1990, Profl. & Cmty. Svc. award, Young Lawyers Sect., 1996, Svc. to Profession award, Fed. Bar Assn., 1991; grantee Paul Harris fellow, Rotary Internat. Fellow Am. Bar Found.; mem. ABA, Mich. Bar Assn. (chmn. client security fund), Grand Rapids Bar Assn. (pres. 1963), Am. Coll. Trial Lawyers (Mich. chmn. 1979, com. on teaching trial and appellate adv.), 6th Circuit Jud. Conf. (life), Internat. Acad. Trial Lawyers, Fedn. Ins. Counsel, Internat. Assn. Ins. Counsel, Internat. Soc. Barristers (pres 1977-78, chair annual Hillman Trial Adv. Seminar 1982—), M Club of U. Mich. (com. visitors U. Mich. Law Sch.), Univ. Club (Grand Rapids), Torch Club. Office: US Dist Ct 682 Fed Bldg 110 Michigan St NW Grand Rapids MI 49503-2363

HILLMAN, JORDAN JAY, law educator; b. 1924. M.A. in Polit Sci., U. Chgo., 1947, JD, 1950; SJD, Northwestern U., 1965. Bar: Ill. 1950. Mem. legal staff Ill. Commerce Commn., 1950-53; with Chgo. and Northwestern Ry., 1954-67, gen. counsel, 1963-67, v.p. law, 1966-67; prof. emeritus law Northwestern U., 1967-89, prof., rsch. counsel, prof. transp. ctr., 1989-91; sr. legal cons., gen. counsel U.S. Ry. Assn., 1974-76, spl. counsel, 1976-79; legal cons. Amtrak, 1978. Mem. Constn. Study Commn., State of Ill., 1963-67; mem. Zoning Amendment Com., Evanston, Ill., 1963-68; mem. Bd. Edn., Dist. 202, Evanston Twp. H.S., 1968-71; mem. Chgo. Transit Authority Bd., 1981-87. Mem. Phi Beta Kappa. Author: Competition and Railroad Price Discrimination, 1968; The Parliamentary Structuring of British Road-Rail Freight Coordination, 1973; The Export-Import Bank at Work; Promotional Financing in the Public Sector, 1982; Price Level Regulation for Diversified Public Utilities, 1989. Office: Northwestern U Sch Law 317 E Chicago Ave Chicago IL 60611-3008

HILLS, ALAN, performing company executive; Grad., Wright State U. Arranger, handling co. tours rock Ballet Blue Suede Shoes; bus. mgr. Lord of the Dance prodn. at Beau Rivage Resort and Casino, Biloxi, Miss.; former gen. mgr. Cleve./San Jose Ballet; exec. dir. Cin. Ballet, 2001—. Office: Cin Ballet 1555 Central Pkwy Cincinnati OH 45214 Office Fax: 513-621-4844.*

HILLS, ARTHUR W. architectural firm executive; BS in Horticulture, Mich. State U., 1953; student, U. Toledo, 1957-58; B of Landscape Architecture, U. Mich., 1961. Registered architect, Mich., Ohio, Fla. Prin. Arthur Hills, Landscape Architect, 1960-66, Arthur Hills and Assocs., Toledo, 1966—. Prin. works include (golf courses) Golf Club Ga. (Best New Pvt. Course Golf Digest 1992), Harbour Pointe (Best New Pub. Course Golf Digest 1991), The Champions, Lexington, Ky., Bighorn Golf Club, Palm Desert, Calif., Dunes West, Charleston, S.C., Arthur Hills Course at Palmetto Dunes and Palmetto Hall Plantation, Hilton Head Island, Bonita Bay's Marsh Course, Bonita Springs, Fla. (one of Top 100 Courses in U.S. Golf Digest 1988—), TPC at Eagle Trace, Coral Springs, Fla. (one of Top 100 Courses in U.S. Golf Digest), Egypt Valley Country Club, Grand Rapids, Mich., Wingpointe, Salt Lake City, River Islands Golf Club, Knoxville, Tenn., Walking Stick, Pueblo, Colo., Windsor Parke, Jacksonville, Fla., The Legacy at Green Valley, Las Vegas, Nev., others. With U.S. Armed Svcs., 1952-54. Mem. Am. Soc. Golf Course Architects (officer, trustee), Am. Soc. Landscape Architects, Golf Course Supt.'s Assn. Am., Nat. Golf Found., Nat. Reacreation and Pks. Assn., Ohio Pks. and Recreation Assn., Ohio Turfgrass Found., Urban Land Inst. Office: Arthur Hills & Assoc 7351 W Bancroft St Toledo OH 43615-3014

HILLS, RUSTY, state official; BA in Telecom., Mich. State U.; M in Govt. and Internat. Studies, U. Notre Dame. Dir. comm. Rep. Mich. chmn. Spencer Abraham, Mich. Gov. John Engler, Lansing, dir. pub. affairs, 1995—. Bd. dirs. Mich. chpt. Cath. Campaign Am.; chmn. Mich. Reps. Mem. Mayo Smith Soc. Office: Mich Rep State Com 2121 E Grand River Ave Lansing MI 48912-3231

HIMES, JOHN HARTER, medical researcher, educator; b. Salt Lake City, July 25, 1947; s. Ellvert Hiram and Mildred Anna (Harter) H.; children: Rachel Anne, Matthew Hiram, Sarah Elizabeth; m. LaVell Gold. BS, Ariz. State U., 1971; PhD, U. Tex., 1975; MPH, Harvard U., 1982. Rsch., sr. scientist Fels Rsch. Inst., Yellow Springs, Ohio, 1976-79; Fels asst. prof. Wright State U. Sch. Medicine, Dayton, 1977-79; sr. analyst, project dir. Abt Assocs., Cambridge, Mass., 1979-82; assoc. prof. CUNY, Bklyn., 1982-87; from assoc. prof. to prof. U. Minn. Sch. Pub. Health, Mpls., 1987—, dir. nutrition coord. ctr., 1995—. Expert com physical status WHO, Geneva, Switzerland, 1991-94, expert adv. panel nutrition, 1994—; mem. tech. working groups Ctrs. for Disease Control, Washington and Atlanta, 1988-97. Author: Parent-specific Adjustment for Assessment of Recumbent Length & Stature, 1981, Anthropometric Assessment of Nutritional Status, 1991; contbr. articles to profl. jours. Recipient Nathalie Masse Meml. prize Internat. Children's Ctr., Paris, 1979. Fellow Human Biology Coun.; mem. APHA, N.Am. Assn. Study Obesity, Internat. Assn. Human Auxology, Pan Am. Health Orgn. (tech. adv. nutrition 1994—), Nat. Ctr. Health Stats. (tech. working group 1994-97), Am. Soc. Nutritional Scis., Soc. for Study Human Biology, Sigma Xi, Phi Kappa Phi, Delta Omega. E-mail: himes@epi.umn.edu.

HIMMELBERG, CHARLES JOHN, III, mathematics educator, researcher; b. North Kansas City, Mo., Nov. 12, 1931; s. Charles John and Magdalene Caroline (Batliner) H.; m. Mary Patricia Hennessy, Jan. 27, 1962; children: Charles, Ann, Mary, Joseph, Patrick. BS, Rockhurst Coll., 1952; MS, U. Notre Dame, 1954, PhD, 1957. Assoc. analyst Midwest Rsch. Inst., Kansas City, Mo., 1957-59; asst. prof. math. U. Kans., Lawrence, 1959-65, assoc. prof., 1965-68, prof., 1968—, chmn. dept. math., 1978-99. Mem. editorial bd. Rocky Mountain Jour. Math, 1972-88; contbr. articles to profl. jours. Mem. Am. Math. Soc., Math. Assn. Am. Roman Catholic. Office: U Kans Dept Math Lawrence KS 66045-7523 E-mail: himmelberg@math.ukans.edu.

HINDERAKER, JOHN HADLEY, lawyer; b. Watertown, S.D., Sept. 19, 1950; s. Irving Alden and Eula Mae (Jertson) H.; m. Shannon Faye Smith, Jan. 3, 1981 (div. 1993); children: Eric, Laura, Alison, Kathryn; m. Loree Kay Miner, June 4, 1994. AB magna cum laude, Dartmouth Coll., 1971; JD cum laude, Harvard U., 1974. Bar: Minn. 1974. Assoc. Faegre & Benson, Mpls., 1974-81, ptnr., 1981—. Chmn. practice standards com., Faegre & Benson, 1986—; lectr. in field. Contbr. articles to profl. jours. Bd. dirs. Ctr. of the Am. Experiment, 1996—. Mem. ABA, Minn. State Bar Assn. (mem. ethics com. 1979-85), Hennepin County Bar Assn. Republican. Lutheran. Avocations: authoring commentaries on polit. and econ. issues, weightlifting. Office: Faegre & Benson 2200 Norwest Ctr 90 S 7th St Ste 2200 Minneapolis MN 55402-3901

HINER, GLEN HAROLD, JR. materials company executive; b. Morgantown, W.Va., July 22, 1934; s. Glen Harold and Dorothy M. (Brown) H.; m. Ann Hiner; children: Stephanie, Greg. BS, W.Va. U., 1957, DSc (hon.), 1989. Registered elec. engr. Sales mgr. GE, 1965-67, mgr. mktg., 1967-70, plant mgr., 1970-72, gen. mgr., 1972-77; mng. dir. GE Plastics, The Netherlands, 1977-78, v.p., gen. mgr. Pittsfield, Mass., 1978-81, sr. v.p., gen. mgr., 1981-83, sr. v.p., group exec., 1983-92; chmn., CEO Owens-Corning, Toledo, 1992—. Bd. dirs. Dana Corp., Huntsman Corp.

Bd. dirs. Toledo Symphony. Capt. USAF, 1957-60. Mem. Bus. Coun., Bus. Roundtable, The Toledo Club, Toledo Country Club, Links Club, Inverness Club. Republican. Methodist. Office: Owens Corning One Owens Corning Pkwy Toledo OH 43659-0002

HINES, ANTHONY LORING, automotive executive; b. Altus, Okla., Sept. 19, 1941; s. William A. and Edna Lee (Allen) H.; m. Nancy Campbell, Sept. 19, 1959 (div. 1962); children: William, Todd; m. Jo Ann Willoughby, June 22, 1963; children: Donna, Larry, Teresa, Toni, Michael. BSChemE, U. Okla., 1967; MSChemE, Okla. State U., 1969; PhDME, U. Tex., 1973. Registered profl. engr., Tex. Asst. prof. chem. engring. Ga. Inst. Tech., Atlanta, 1973-75; asst. to assoc. prof. chem. engring. Colo. Sch. Mines, Golden, 1975-80; prof. chem. engring., head dept. U. Wyo., Laramie, 1980-83; assoc. dean engring. rsch. Okla. State U., Stillwater, 1983-87; prof. chem. engring., dean engring. U. Mo.-Columbia, 1987-93; v.p. Honda of Am., Mfg., Inc., Marysville, Ohio, 1993-97; sr. v.p. Honda of Am., Mfg. Inc., 1997; v.p. mfg. Navistar Internat. Corp., Springfield, 1998, group v.p. engring. and mfg. ops., 1999; dean coll. engring. U. Iowa, Iowa City, 1999—. Site visitor NSF, 1988-90; mem. Mo. Corp. for Sci. & Tech., 1991—; mem. rev. panel on air quality Internat. Energy Agy., 1991; mem. rev. panel Laser, 1990; mem., lead reviewer Lumcon, 1990. Co-author: Mass Transfer Fundamentals and Applications, 1984, Mass Transfer Solutions Manual, 1985, Indoor Air, Quality and Control, 1993; contbr. articles to profl. jours. Mem. Okla. Coun. Sci. and Tech. Rsch. Task Force, 1984, Regional Commerce and Growth Assn., St. Louis, 1988—; assoc. mem. Columbia Regional Econ. Devel., Inc., 1989—; mem. Columbia Area Regional Econ. Devel., Inc., 1989—. Mem. NSPE, ASHRAE (com. on sorption 1988—), Nat. Inst. for Engring. Mgmt. and Systems (bd. govs. 1990—), Am. Inst. Chem. Engrs. (sec. separations div. 1991), Mo. Soc. Profl. Engrs., Am. Soc. Engring. Edn., Avocations: hunting, fishing, handball, basketball.

HINES, MARSHALL, construction engineering company executive; b. Chgo., Dec. 29, 1923; s. Herbert Waldo and Helen (Gartside) H.; m. Janet Young, July 28, 1945; children: Karen Lynn, Keith Douglas, Dori Hines Alton. BCE, Mich. State U., 1947, MCE, 1948. Registered profl. engr., Mich. Project engr. The Christman Co., Lansing, Mich., 1948-55, supt., 1955-70, gen. supt., 1971-83, exec. v.p., 1983—96, ret. cons., 1996—. With U.S. Army, 1943-45. Mem. NSPE, Mich. Soc. Profl. Engrs. (bd. dirs. 1986, Constrn. Engr. Yr. 1990, Engr. of Yr. award 1994), Builders Exch. of Lansing (pres. 1988), Rotary (bd. dirs. Lansing club 1986-87). Republican. Methodist. Home: 1137 Rebecca Rd East Lansing MI 48823-5210 Office: The Christman Co 408 Kalamazoo Plz Lansing MI 48933-1990

HINES, N. WILLIAM, dean, law educator, administrator; b. 1936; AB, Baker U., 1958; LLB, U. Kans., 1961; LLD, Baker U., 1999. Bar: Kans. 1961, Iowa 1965. Law clk. U.S. Ct. Appeals 10th cir., 1961-62; tchg. fellow Harvard U., 1961-62; asst. prof. law U. Iowa, 1962-65, assoc. prof., 1965-67, prof., 1967-73, disting. prof., 1973—, dean, 1976—. Vis. prof. Stanford U., 1974—75. Editor (notes and comments): Kans. Law Rev. Fellow, Harvard U., 1961—62. Fellow: Iowa State Bar Found., ABA Found.; mem.: Order of Coif, Environ. Law Inst. (assoc.), Jo. Co. Her. Trust (founder, pres.). Office: U Iowa Coll Law Iowa City IA 52242-0001

HINKELMAN, RUTH AMIDON, insurance company executive; b. Streator, Ill., June 4, 1949; d. Olin Arthur and Marjorie Annabeth (Wright) Amidon; m. Allen Joseph Hinkelman, Jr., Oct. 28, 1972; children: Anne Elizabeth, Allen Joseph III. AB in Econs., U. Ill., 1971. Underwriter Kemper Ins. Group, Chgo., 1971-75; acct. exec. Near North Ins. Agy., 1975-76; underwriter Gen. Cologne Reinsurance Corp., 1976-78, asst. sec., 1978-79, asst. v.p., 1979-83, 2nd v.p., 1983-87, v.p., 1987—. Home: 133 Linden Ave Wilmette IL 60091-2838 Office: Gen Cologne Reinsurance Corp 233 S Wacker Dr Ste 4100 Chicago IL 60606-6323 E-mail: rhinkelm@gcre.com.

HINKENS, KAY L. social services association executive; Student, U. Wis., Oshkosh. With Aid Assn. for Luths., Appleton, Wis., 1971—, with employee credit union, 1971-85, co-founder, mgr. lending and mktg., Member Credit Union, 1986-91, v.p. Member Credit Union, 1991-94, pres. Member Credit Union, 1994—. Past tchr. Sunday sch. Mem. Mktg. Coun., Luth. Missionary Soc. (past pres.), Fox Cities Chpt. Credit Unions (past pres., treas.), Credit Union Exec. Soc. Office: Aid Assn for Lutherans 4321 N Ballard Rd Appleton WI 54919-0001

HINKLEY, GERRY, newspaper editor; Dep. mng. editor Milw. Jour. Sentinel, 1995—. Office: Milw Sentinel 333 W State St PO Box 661 Milwaukee WI 53201-0661

HINOJOSA, RAUL, physician, ear pathology researcher, educator; b. Tampico, Tamulipas, Mexico, June 18, 1928; came to U.S., 1962, naturalized, 1968; s. Raul Hinojosa-Flores and Melida (Prieto) Hinojosa; m. Berta Ojeda, Sept. 25, 1953; children—Berta Elena, Raul Andres, Jorge Alberto, María de Lourdes B.S. in Biology, Inst. Sci. and Tech., Tampico, 1946; M.D., Nat. Autonomous U. Mexico, Mexico City, 1954. Asst. prof. U. Chgo, 1962-68, assoc. prof., 1968-97, assoc. prof. emeritus, 1998—, dir. temporal bone program for ear rsch., 1962—, rsch. assoc., 1968-88. Rsch. fellow biophysics Harvard U., Boston, 1963; rsch. assoc. in neuropathology, Harvard U., 1964, rsch. fellow in anatomy, 1965. Editor temporal bone histopathology update Am. Jour. of Otolaryngology, 1989-94. Recipient Rsch. Career Devel. award NIH, 1962-65, rsch. grantee, 1962—, hearing rsch. study sect. grantee, 1988-92. Mem. AAAS, Internat. Otopathology Soc., Microscopy Soc. Am., Midwest Soc. Electron Microscopists, Assn. Rsch. in Otolaryngology, Am. Otological Soc., N.Y. Acad. Scis. Home: 5316 S Hyde Park Blvd Chicago IL 60615-5706 Office: U Chgo 5841 S Maryland Ave Chicago IL 60637-1463

HINSHAW, ADA SUE, dean, nursing educator; b. Arkansas City, Kans., May 20, 1939; d. Oscar A. and Georgia Ruth (Tucker) Cox; children: Cynthia Lynn, Scott Allen Lewis. BS, U. Kans., 1961; MSN, Yale U., 1963; MA, U. Ariz., 1973, PhD, 1975; DSc (hon.), U. Md., 1988, Med. Coll. of Ohio, 1988, Marquette U., 1990, U. Nebr., 1992; D Sci. (hon.), Mount Sinai Med. Ctr. Instr. Sch. Nursing U. Kans., 1963-66; asst. prof. U. Calif., San Francisco, 1966-71; prof. U. Ariz., Tucson, 1975-87; dir. nursing rsch. U. Med. Ctr., 1975-87; dir. Nat. Inst. Nursing Rsch. Pub. Health Svc., Dept. Health and Human Svcs., NIH, Washington, 1987—; now dean Sch. Nursing U. Mich., Ann Arbor. Contbd. articles to profl. jours. Recipient Kay Schilter award U. Kans., 1961, Lucille Petry Leone award Nat. League for Nursing, 1971, Wolanin Geriatric Nursing Rsch. award U. Ariz., 1978, Alumni of the Yr award Sch. Nursing U. Kans., 1981, Disting. Alumni award Sch. Nursing Yale U., 1981, Alumni Achievement award U. Ariz., 1990, Disting. citation Kans. Alumni Assn., 1992, Health Leader of the Yr. award PHS, 1993, Centennial award Columbia Sch. Nursing, 1993. Mem. ANA (Nurse Scientist of the Yr. award 1985), Coun. on Nursing Rschrs. (Nurse Scientist of the Yr. award 1985), Md. Nurses Assn., Western Soc. for Rsch. in Nursing, Am. Acad. Nursing, Nat. Acad. Practice, Inst. Medicine, Sigma Xi, Sigma Theta Tau (Beta Mu Chpt. award of Excellence in Nursing Edn., 1980, Elizabeth McWilliams Miller award, 1987), Alpha Chi Omega. Avocations: hiking, camping, bicycling. Office: U Mich Sch Nursing 400 N Ingalls St Ann Arbor MI 48109-2003

HINSHAW, EDWARD BANKS, broadcasting company executive; b. Aurora, Ill., Feb. 27, 1940; s. Lorenzo M. and Emily (Roach) H.; m. Victoria Leone Biggers, Jan. 16, 1965; children: Eric, Brian. Student, Harvard Coll., 1958-59, U. Minn., 1959-62. Announcer Sta. KSTP-Radio-TV, Mpls., 1959-64; announcer Voice of America, Washington, 1964-65; reporter, anchorman Jour. Broadcast Group, Inc. (formerly Sta. WTMJ, Inc.), Milw., 1965-70, editorialist, 1970-74, editorial dir., 1974—, mgr. public affairs, 1979-90, mgr. pers. and editorial affairs, 1990-94, v.p. human resources, 1994—. Instr. broadcast journalism U. Wis., Whitewater, 1976, 79, 86. Trustee Nat. First Amendment congress, 1980-83; chair Wis First Amendment Congress, 1985; bd. chair Milw. Urban League, 1987; bd. dirs. Children's Outing Assn., 1987-90, Ko-Thi Dance Co., 1992-99, pres., 1994-96; bd. dirs. Richard and Ethel Herzfeld Found., 1997—. Recipient DuPont-Columbia Citation in Broadcast Journalism, 1978; Abe Lincoln Merit award So. Baptist Radio-TV Commn., 1978; NCCJ Gold Media Medallion, 1977 Mem. Nat. Broadcast Editorial Assn. (pres. 1980-81), Wis. Broadcasters Assn. Found. (treas. 2000—), Milw. Press Club (bd. dirs. 1990-95, pres.-elect 1992, pres. 1993, past pres. 1994), Knight of the Golden Quill, Sigma Delta Chi (Disting. Svc. award 1977, Excellence in Journalism award 1988, Freedom of Info. award 1994). Office: Jour Broadcast Group Inc 720 E Capitol Dr Milwaukee WI 53212-1308 E-mail: hinshaw@journalbroadcastgroup.com.

HINSHAW, JUANITA, electric distributor executive; CFO Graybar Elec., St. Louis, 2000—. Office: Graybar Electric PO Box 7231 Saint Louis MO 63177

HIPPEE, WILLIAM H., JR. lawyer; b. Des Moines, 1946; BS, U. Pa., 1968; JD, Stanford U., 1972. Bar: Minn. 1972. Ptnr. Dorsey & Whitney LLP, Mpls. Office: Dorsey & Whitney LLP 50 South 6th St Ste 1500 Minneapolis MN 55402-1498

HIRSCH, DAVID L. lawyer, corporate executive; BA, Pomona Coll., 1959; JD, U. Calif., Berkeley, 1962. Bar: Calif. 1963. V.p. Metaldyne/NI Industries, Inc., Taylor, Mich., 1966—. V.p. mem. commn. on Govt. Procurement for U.S. Congress, 1971. Mem. editorial bd. Bur. Nat. Affairs' Fed. Contracts Report. Fellow Am. Bar Found.; mem. ABA (life fellow of fellows, chair emerging issues com. sect. pub. contract law, sec. pub. contract law sect. 1977-78, mem. council 1978-80, chmn. 1981-82), Calif. Bar (bd. advisors pub. law sect.), Los Angeles County Bar Assn., Fed. Bar Assn., Nat. Contract Mgmt. Assn. (nat. bd. advisors), Fin. Exec. Inst. (legal advisor com. on govt. bus.). Office: Masco Tech Corp/NI Industries Inc 21001 Van Born Rd Taylor MI 48180-1340

HIRSCH, JOACHIM V. (JAKE), aeronautics company executive; Diploma, U. Reutlingen, Germany. Various mgmt. positions TRW Inc., v.p., mgr. dir. Occupant Restraint Sys. Group Europe; exec. v.p., COO Magna Europe AG; pres., COO Kautex Textron, Germany; chmn., pres., CEO Textron Fastening Sys., Troy, Mich. Office: 840 W Long Lake Rd Ste 450 Troy MI 48098-6372

HIRSCH, JUNE SCHAUT, chaplain; b. Green Bay, Wis., Sept. 30, 1925; d. Clifford Charles and Eleanor Josephine (Arts) Schaut; m. Marshall E. Gilette, Jan. 23, 1946 (div. 1974); children: Ronald Leigh, Patrick Allen, Vicki Jeanne Baumann; m. Hubert L. Hirsch, Nov. 7, 1975. Student, St. Mary's Sch. Nursing, Rochester, Minn., 1943-45, U. Wis., Sheboygan, 1974-75. Cert. med. asst., 1966. Med. asst. James W. Faulkner, M.D., Phoenix, 1953-56; med. office mgr. Edward E. Houfek, M.D., Sheboygan, Wis., 1956-75; med. office cons. Profl. Mgmt. Inc., Milw., 1975-77; office mgr., adminstrv. asst. Schroeder & Holt Architects Ltd., 1977-90; vol. chaplain St. Camillus Health Ctr., 1991—, Children's Hosp. and Froedent Meml. Hosp., Milw., 1991-95; staff chaplain Froedert Meml. Hosp., 1995—. Instr. med. asst. program Lake Shore Tech., 1975-76. Mem. Am. Assn. Med. Assts. (nat. trustee 1963-66), Wis. Soc. Med. Assts. (life, exec. bd. 1975-89), Lake ShoreMed. Assts. (exec. bd. 1959-75), Nat. Assn. Cath. Chaplains (cert.). Republican. Roman Catholic. Home: 10200 W Bluemound Rd Apt 918 Milwaukee WI 53226-4372 Office: Froedtert Meml Luth Hosp 9200 W Wisconsin Ave Milwaukee WI 53226-3522

HIRSCH, LAWRENCE LEONARD, physician, retired educator; b. Chgo., Aug. 20, 1922; m. Donna Lee Sturm; children: Robert, Edward, Sharon. BS, U. Ill., 1943; MD, U. Ill., Chgo., 1950. Diplomate: Am. Bd. Family Practice. Intern. Ill. Masonic Med. Ctr., Chgo., 1950-51; practice medicine specializing in family medicine, 1951-70; dir. ambulatory care Ill. Masonic Med. Ctr., 1970-71, dir. family practice residency program, 1971-75; prof., chmn. dept. family medicine Chgo. Med. Sch., 1975-89, prof. emeritus, 1989—. Mem. med. licensing bd. State of Ill., 1982-94, chmn., 1988-94, hosp. licensing bd., 1994—; bd. dirs. Ill. Coun. for continuing Med. Edn., 1981-85, pres., 1986-87; cons. recombinant DNA Abbott Labs., 1980-87; lectr. in field; staff pres. Ill. Masonic Med. Ctr., 1970. Book rev. editor: Soc. of Tchrs. Family Medicine, 1979-89; book reviewer: Jour. AMA, 1969— ; contbr. articles to profl. jours. Bd. dirs. Mid-Am. chpt. ARC, Chgo., 1978-88; nat. pres. Alpha Phi Omega, Kansas City, Mo., 1974-78; exec. com. Chgo. Found. Med. Care and PSRO, 1977-84, Ill. State Inter-Ins. Exchange, 1975— ; bd. dirs. Crescent Counties Found. for Med. Care, 1985-91; commr. Northbrook (Ill.) Park Dist., 1987-91, pres., 1990—; mem. Village of Northbrook Planning Commn., 1987-89. Served with U.S. Army, 1943-46. Recipient Silver Beaver award Boy Scouts Am., 1963; recipient Silver Antelope award Boy Scouts Am., 1967, Disting. Eagle award Boy Scouts Am., 1969, Brotherhood award Lakeview Interfaith Council, 1968, Physician Speaker award AMA, 1981; inducted into City of Chgo. Sr. Citizens Hall of Fame, 1991. Fellow AAAS, Am. Acad. Family Physicians (mem. congress of dels.); mem. Chgo. Med. Soc. (pres. 1979, Pub. Svc. award 1990), Ill. Acad. Family Physicians (pres. 1977), Assn. Depts. Family Medicine (exec. com.), Masons, Shriners, Kiwanis (dir. local club). Democrat. Unitarian. Office: 1324 Coventry Ln Northbrook IL 60062-4339

HIRSCH, RAYMOND ROBERT, chemical company executive, lawyer; b. St. Louis, Mar. 20, 1936; s. Raymond Winton and Olive Frances (Gordon) H.; m. Joanne Therese Dennis, Jan. 30, 1960; children: Amy Elizabeth, Thomas Christopher, Timothy Joseph, Mary Patricia. LL.B., St. Louis U., 1959. Bar: Mo. 1959. With Treasury Dept., 1960-62, Petrolite Corp., St. Louis, 1962—, sec., 1971—, v.p., gen. counsel, 1973-82, sr. v.p., gen. counsel, 1982-92; of counsel Guilfoil, Petzall & Shoemake, St. Louis, 1992-2000. Mem. Pub. Defender Commn., Mo. Mcpl. judge City of Bridgeton, Mo., 1970-73; mem. City of Des Peres Planning and Zoning Commn., 1974-78; mem. bd. edn. Spl. Sch. Dist. St. Louis County, 1981-83; mem. Mo. Air N.G., 1959-60; trustee Childhaven. Mem. ABA, Am. Soc. Corp. Secs., Mo. Bar Assn., Bar Assn. St. Louis, Mo. Athletic Club. Roman Catholic. Home: 3 W Walinca Walk Saint Louis MO 63105-2007 Office: Guilfoil Petzall & Shoemake 100 S 4th St Saint Louis MO 63102-1800 E-mail: r.r.hirsch@worldnet.att.net.

HIRSCH, STEVEN W. lawyer; b. Concordia, Kans., Jan. 14, 1962; s. Frederick J. and Dora Lee (Cooper) H.; m. Anita J. Richardson, Dec. 13, 1987. BA cum laude, Kans. State U., 1983; JD with honors, Washburn U., 1986. Bar: Kans. 1986, U.S. Dist. Ct. Kans. 1986. Adminstrv. asst. Kans. Dept. of Treasury, Topeka, 1985-87; ptnr. Morgan & Hirsch, Kans., 1987—. Author: Simpson-T6 1st Century, 1982. Vol. fireman Oberlin City Fire Dept., 1987—; chmn. Decatur County Dem. Com., 1987—; Oberlin Conv. and Vis. Bur., 1988—; treas. United Ch. Oberlin, 1987—. Mem. Kans. Bar Assn., Kans. Trial Lawyers Assn., NE Kans. Bar Assn. Democrat. Baptist. Club: Bohemian. Lodge: Masons. Avocation: bike riding. Office: 124 S Penn Ave Oberlin KS 67749-2243

HIRSCHHORN, AUSTIN, lawyer; b. Detroit, Feb. 20, 1936; s. Herman and Dena Grace (Ufberg) H.; m. Susan Carol Goldstein, June 30, 1963; children: Laura Elsie, Carol Helen, Paula Gail. B.A. with honors, Mich. State U., 1957; JD, Wayne State U., 1960. Bar: Mich. 1961. Assoc. Arnold M. Gold Law Offices, Detroit, 1960-63; ptnr. Gold & Hirschhorn, 1963-65; pvt. practice, 1965-68; ptnr. Boigon, Hirschhorn & Winston, 1968-69, Boigon & Hirschhorn, Detroit and Southfield, 1969-78; pvt. practice Southfield, 1979-80; ptnr. Zemke & Hirschhorn (P.C.), Mich., 1980-83, Austin Hirschhorn, P.C., Southfield, 1983-91; of counsel Rubenstein, Isaacs, Haroutunian & Sobel, P.C., 1991-92; pvt. practice Austin Hirschhorn, P.C., Birmingham, Mich., 1992-96, Troy, 1996—. Lectr. Inst. Continuing Legal Edn., Mich. Trustee The Internat. Sch., Farmington Hills, Mich. With AUS, 1960-62. Mem. ABA, Fed. Bar Assn., Mich. Bar Assn., Oakland County Bar Assn., Am. Bankruptcy Inst., Comml. Law League Am. Jewish. Home: 26903 York Rd Huntington Woods MI 48070-1361 Office: 201 W Big Beaver Rd Ste 710 Troy MI 48084-4152 E-mail: shirschhorn@msn.com., austinh@ix.netcom.com.

HIRSCHMAN, SHERMAN JOSEPH, lawyer, accountant, educator; b. Detroit, May 11, 1935; s. Samuel and Anna (Maxmen) H.; m. Audrey Hecker, 1959; children: Samuel, Shari. BS, Wayne State U., 1956, JD, 1959, LLM, 1968; D in Bus. Adminstrn., Nova Southeastern U., 1996. Bar: Mich. 1959, Fla. 1983; CPA, Mich., Fla.; cert. tax lawyer, Fla. Pvt. practice, Mich., 1959—; instr. comml. law Detroit Coll. Bus., 1971—. Adj. instr. Nova Southeastern U., 1997—, Ctrl. Mich. U., 1997—, Fla. Metro U., 2001—. With USAR, 1959-62. Mem. Mich. Bar Assn., Fla. Bar Assn., Am. Arbitration Assn., Am. Assn. CPA Attys. Office: 340 Woodlake Wynde Oldsmar FL 34677-2190 E-mail: rgwh2oa@aol.com.

HIRST, RICHARD B. lawyer; Sr. v.p., gen. counsel Northwest Airlines, 1990-94, sr. v.p. corp. affairs, 1994—. Office: Northwest Airlines Inc 5101 Northwest Dr Saint Paul MN 55111-3027

HISS, ROLAND GRAHAM, physician, medical educator; b. Newark, Oct. 9, 1932; s. George Crosby and Adrianne (Graham) H.; m. Margaret Barringer McGrath, Aug. 23, 1957; children: John Barringer, Meredith Graham Brown. BS, U. Mich., 1955, MD, 1957. Diplomate Am. Bd. Internal Medicine. Intern in medicine Phila. Gen. Hosp., 1957-58; resident in medicine U. Mich. Hosp., Ann Arbor, 1961-64; fellow hematology Simpson Meml. Inst., 1964-66; faculty medicine U. Mich. Med. Sch., 1966—, chmn. dept. med. edn., 1982—; coordinator edn. Mich. Diabetes Research and Tng. Ctr., 1977—. Contbr. 50 articles to profl. jours. Served to capt. USAF, 1958-61. Recipient Teaching award Kaiser Permanente Found. and U. Mich., 1976. Fellow ACP; mem. Am. Diabetes Assn., AMA, Mich. State Med. Soc. Home: 3551 Chatham Way Ann Arbor MI 48105-2827 Office: U Mich Med Sch Towsley Ctr Box 0201 G-1103 Ann Arbor MI 48109-0201 E-mail: redhiss@umich.edu.

HITCH, ELIZABETH, academic administrator; Dir. higher edn. Ctrl. Mich. U., assoc. dean Sch. Edn., Health and Human Svcs., prof. dept. human environ. studies; mgr. instrn. design Sch. Medicine U. Mich., Ann Arbor; dean Coll. Edn. and Profl. Studies Ea. Ill. U., Charleston, Ill.; provost, vice chancellor U. Wis., LaCrosse, 2002—. Office: U Wis LaCrosse 145 Main Hall 1725 State St La Crosse WI 54601

HITES, RONALD ATLEE, environmental science educator, chemist; b. Jackson, Mich., Sept. 19, 1942; s. Wilbert T. and Evelyn J.H.; m. Bonnie Rae Carlson, Dec. 26, 1964; children: Veronica, Karin, David BA in Chemistry, Oakland U., 1964; PhD in Analytical Chemistry, MIT, 1968. NAS fellow Agrl. Rsch., Peoria, Ill., 1968-69; mem. rsch. staff, dept. chemistry MIT, Cambridge, 1969-72, asst. prof. chem. engring., 1972-76, assoc. prof., 1976-79; prof. Ind. U., Bloomington, 1979-89, Disting. prof. pub. and environ. affairs and chemistry, 1989—, dir. Environ. Sci. Rsch. Ctr., 2001—. Cons. EPA, 1974—. Assoc. editor Environ. Sci. Tech., 1990—; mem. editorial bd. Chemosphere, 1979-99; contbr. articles to prof. jours. Grantee NSF, 1974—, EPA, 1974—, Dept. Energy, 1977-95. Fellow AAAS; mem. Am. Chem. Soc. (award in environ. sci. 1991), Am. Soc. for Mass Spectrometry (pres. 1988-90, mem. editl. bd. 1990-96), Soc. Environ. Toxicol. Chemistry (bd. dirs. 1997-2000, Founders award 1993), Sigma Xi. Office: Ind U Sch Pub and Environ Affairs 410H Bloomington IN 47405 E-mail: Hitesr@indiana.edu.

HLAVACEK, ROY GEORGE, publishing executive, magazine editor; b. Chgo., Sept. 17, 1937; s. George Louis and Lillian Barbara (Vasovic) H.; m. Nancy Elaine Wroblaski, Aug. 3, 1963; children: Carrie Lee Felix, Alexander Michael. BS, U. Ill., 1960; MBA, U. Chgo., 1969. Project engr. Research and Devel. Center, Swift & Co., Chgo., 1960-65; v.p., editor, pub. Food Processing mag., Foods of Tomorrow mag. Food Publs. div. Putman Pub. Co., 1965-92; v.p., group pub. Food Group, Delta Comms. Inc., 1992-2001; dir. publs. Inst. Food Technologists, 2001—. Adv. com. dept. food sci. U. Ill., Urbana-Champaign, 1988-93. Patentee in field. Commr. Oak Park (Ill.) Landmarks Commn., 1972-79, chmn., 1976-79; treas. Oak Park Bicentennial Commn., 1973-76, Ernest Hemingway Found. of Oak Park, 1983-2000. Mem. ASME, Food Processing Machinery and Supplies Assn. (dir. 1987-91), Inst. Food Technologists (councilor 1975-81, chmn. Chgo. sect.), Pi Tau Sigma, Sigma Tau. Home: 904 Forest Ave Oak Park IL 60302-1310 Office: Inst Food Technologists 525 W Van Buren Chicago IL 60607 E-mail: rghlavacek@ift.org.

HO, DAVID KIM HONG, educator; b. Honolulu, Mar. 5, 1948; s. Raymond T.Y. and Ellen T.Y. (Fong) H.; m. Joan Yee, July 6, 1968 (div. Apr. 1982); 1 child, Michael J.; m. Patricia Ann McAndrews, June 25, 1983. BS in Indsl. Engring., U. So. Calif., 1970; MBA, Butler U., 1976; MS in Acctg., U. Wis., Whitewater, 1981. Cert. fellow in prodn. and inventory mgmt. Indsl. engr. FMC Corp., L.A., 1970-73, mgr. prodn. planning and inventory control Indpls., 1973-77; materials mgr. Butler Mfg. Co., Ft. Atkinson, Wis., 1977-81, systems mgr. Kansas City, Mo., 1981-82; dir. materials and systems Behlen Mfg. Co., Columbus, Nebr., 1982-84, v.p. operations, bd. dirs., 1984-86; mgr. corp. materials Lozier Corp., Omaha, 1986-90, plant mgr., 1990-91; v.p. mfg. Heatilator Inc., Mt. Pleasant, Iowa, 1991-93; prof. profl. studies Bellevue (Nebr.) U., 1993—. Instr., Met. C.C., Omaha, 1989—, Iowa Wesleyan Coll, Mt. Pleasant, 1991-92. Mem. Nat. Assn. Purchasing Mgmt. (acad.), Am. Prodn. and Inventory Control Soc. Home: 11729 Fisher House Rd Bellevue NE 68123-1112 Office: Met CC PO 3777-Soc 121 Omaha NE 68103-0777 E-mail: dho@metropo.mccneb.edu.

HOAK, JONATHAN S. lawyer; BA, U. Colo., 1971; postgrad., Exeter (Eng.); JD, Drake U., 1977. With Heritage Comms., Des Moines, 1971-74; assoc. Sidley & Austin, 1979-85, ptnr., 1985-90; gen. atty. fed. sys. divsn. AT&T, 1990-93; sr. v.p., gen. counsel NCR Corp., Dayton, Ohio, 1993—. Bd. counselors Drake U. Law Sch., U. Dayton Sch. Law Adv. Coun. Mem. ABA, Fed. Cir. Bar Assn., Ohio Bar Assn. Office: NCR Corp 1700 S Patterson Blvd Dayton OH 45479-0002

HOARD, HEIDI MARIE, lawyer; b. Mt. Clemons, Mich., Feb. 8, 1951; d. Duane Jay and Elizabeth Hoard; m. John B. Lunseth II, Jan. 11, 1980; children: John B. III, Steven J. BA, Macalester Coll., 1972; JD cum laude, U. Minn., 1976. Bar: Minn. 1976, U.S. Dist. Ct. Minn. 1976. Assoc. Faegre & Benson, Mpls., 1976-83, ptnr., 1984-93; sr. legal counsel Medtronic, Inc., 1993-95; v.p., gen. counsel, corp. sec. The Musicland Group, Minnetonka, 1995—. Mem. State Bd. Women in the Legal Profession Task Force, State Bd. Legal Cert., 1986-88, pres. Tel-Law, Bar Assn. Com., Mpls., 1978-80; bd. dirs. Fund for Legal Aid Soc. Mem. Minn. Region G, Law Enforcement Assistance Assn. Com., 1971-72; vol. aide U.S. Senate Nursing Home Investigation and Hearing, Mpls., 1971-72; student dir.

Legal Aid Clinic, U. Minn., Mpls., 1975-76. Mem. Am. Soc. Corp. Secs. (bd. dirs. Minn. sect.), Am. Corp. Counsel Assn., Minn. Bar Assn., Phi Beta Kappa. Democrat. Office: Musicland Group 10400 Yellow Circle Dr Hopkins MN 55343

HOARD, LEROY, professional football player; b. New Orleans, May 15, 1968; Student, U. Mich. Running back Cleve. Browns, Minnesota Vikings, 1996—. Named to NFL Pro Bowl Team, 1994. Office: Minnesota Vikings 9520 Viking Dr Eden Prairie MN 55344-3898

HOBBINS, ROBERT LEO, lawyer; b. Des Moines, June 5, 1948; s. Leo Michael and Margaret Ellen Hobbins; m. Carmela Theresa Tursi, Dec. 27, 1974; children: Brian, Patrick, Edward. BA magna cum laude, Creighton U., 1970; JD, NYU, 1973. Bar: Minn. 1973. Assoc. Dorsey & Whitney, Mpls., 1973-78, ptnr., 1979—. Clin. faculty Law Sch. Hamline U., 1981—. Root-Tilden scholar. Mem. ABA (labor sect., EEO law com.), Minn. State Bar Assn., Hennepin County Bar Assn., Creighton U. Alumni Assn. (v.p. 1994). Office: Dorsey & Whitney 220 S 6th St Ste 1400 Minneapolis MN 55402-4502 E-mail: hobbins.robert@dorseylaw.com.

HOBBS, LEWIS MANKIN, astronomer; b. Upper Darby, Pa., May 16, 1937; s. Lewis Samuel and Evangeline Elizabeth (Goss) H.; m. Jo Ann Faith Hagele, June 16, 1962; children: John, Michael, Dara. B of Engring. Physics, Cornell U., 1960; MS, U. Wis., 1962, PhD in Physics, 1966. Jr. astronomer Lick Obs., U. Calif., Santa Cruz, 1965-66; faculty U. Chgo., 1966—, prof. astronomy and astrophysics, 1976—; dir. Yerkes Obs. Williams Bay, Wis., 1974-82. Bd. dirs. Assn. Univs. for Rsch. in Astronomy, Washington, 1974-85; mem. Space Telescope Inst. Coun., 1982-87; astronomy com. of bd. trustees Univs. Rsch. Assn., Inc., Washington, 1979-83, chmn., 1979-81; bd. govs. Astrophys. Rsch. Consortium, Inc., Seattle, 1984-91; mem. Users Com. for Hubble Space Telescope, NASA, 1990-94; mem. telescope allocation com. Nat. Optical Astronomy Obs., 1998-2000. Contbr. articles to profl. jours. Bd. dirs. Mil. Symphony Assn. of Walworth County, 1972-88. Alfred P. Sloan scholar, 1955-60. Mem.: Internat. Astron. Union, Am. Phys. Soc., Am. Astron. Soc. Office: U Chgo Yerkes Observatory Williams Bay WI 53191

HOBSON, DAVID LEE, congressman, lawyer; b. Oct. 17, 1936; m. Carolyn Alexander; children: Susan Marie, Lynn Martha, Douglas Lee. BA, Ohio Wesleyan U., 1958; JD, Ohio State Coll. Law, 1963; hon. degree, Ctrl. State U., Wittenberg U. Former resident counsel Kissell Co., Springfield, Ohio; former atty. Union Ctrl. Life Ins. Co., Cin.; mem. Ohio Senate, 1982-90, majority whip, 1986-88, pres. pro tem, 1988-90; mem. U.S. Congress from 7th Ohio dist., Washington, 1991—; mem. house appropriations com., def. subcom., VA, HUD and Ind. Agys. subcom., chmn. mil constrn. subcom. House coms. appropriations, budget, standards of ofcl. conduct. Former trustee Wilberforce U., Ohio, Urbana U.; trustee Ohio Wesleyan; bd. dirs. Ohio. Mem. ABA, AMVETS, Ky. Bar Assn., Ohio Bar Assn., Springfield Bd. Realtors, Springfield Area C. of C. (past bd. dirs.), Non-Commissioned Officers Assn., Masons (32 degrees), Am. Legion, VFW, Moose, Elks, Rotary, Shrine Club. Home: # 200 5 W North St # 200 Springfield OH 45504-2544 Office: US Ho of Reps 1514 Longworth Hob Washington DC 20515-3507*

HOCHMAN, KENNETH GEORGE, lawyer; b. Mt. Vernon, N.Y., Nov. 12, 1947; s. Benjamin S. and Lillian (Gilbert) H.; m. Carol K. Hochman, Apr. 8, 1979; children: Brian Paul, Lisa Erin. BA, SUNY, Buffalo, 1969; JD, Columbia U., 1972. Bar: Ohio 1973, Fla. 1977, N.Y. 1979. Assoc. Jones, Day, Reavis & Pogue, Cleve., 1972-79, ptnr., 1980—. Trustee Katharine Kenyon Lippitt Found., Cleve., 1988, Kenridge Fund, Cleve., 1989, Bolton Found., Cleve., 1990, Elisha-Bolton Found., Cleve., 1993. Trustee United Way of Cleve., 2002—. Harlan Fiske Stone scholar Columbia U., 1971, 72. Fellow Am. Coll. Trusts and Estate Counsel; mem. Phi Beta Kappa, Oakwood Club (Cleve.) (trustee 1997, officer 2000). Office: Jones Day Reavis & Pogue 901 Lakeside Ave E Cleveland OH 44114-1190

HOCHSTER, MELVIN, mathematician, educator; b. Bklyn., Aug. 2, 1943; s. Lothar and Rose (Gruber) H.; m. Anita Klitzner, Aug. 29, 1965 (div. Feb. 1983); 1 child, Michael Adam; m. Margie Ruth Morris, Dec. 20, 1987; children: Hallie Margaret Hochster Morris, Sophie Elinor Hochster Morris, Louis Jacob, Daniel Craig Morris. B.A., Harvard U., 1964; M.A., Princeton U., 1966, Ph.D., 1967. Asst. prof. math. U. Minn., Mpls., 1967-70, assoc. prof., 1970-73; prof. math. Purdue U., West Lafayette, Ind., 1973-77, U. Mich., Ann Arbor, 1977-84, Raymond L. Wilder prof. math., 1984-94, Robert W. and Lynn H. Browne prof. math., 1994—. Guest prof. Math. Inst. Aarhus, Denmark, 1973-74; trustee Math. Sci. Rsch. Inst., Berkeley, Calif., 1985-87, mem. sci. adv. coun., 1989-93; bd. govs. Inst. for Math. and its Application, Mpls., 1985-87. Chmn. editorial com. Math. Revs., 1984-89. Guggenheim fellow, 1982 Fellow Am. Acad. Arts and Scis.; mem. Am. Math. Soc. (Frank Nelson Cole prize 1980), Math. Assn. Am., Nat. Acad. Sci. Office: U Mich Math Dept East Hall Ann Arbor MI 48109-1109

HOCKADAY, IRVINE O., JR. greeting card company executive; b. Ludington, Mich., Aug. 12, 1936; s. Irvine Oty and Helen (McCune) H.; m. Mary Ellen Jurden, July 8, 1961; children: Wendy Helen, Laura DuVal. A.B., Princeton U., 1958; LL.B., J.D., U. Mich., 1961. Bar: Mo. 1961. Atty. firm Lathrop, Koontz, Righter, Clagett and Norquist, Kansas City, 1961-67; atty., asst. gen. counsel, asst. to pres., v.p. Kansas City So. Industries, Inc., 1968-71, pres., chief ops. officer, 1971-80, pres., chief exec. officer, 1981-83; exec. v.p. Hallmark Cards, Inc., 1983-85, pres., chief exec. officer, 1986—, also bd. dirs., 1978—. Bd. dirs. Ford Motor Co., UtiliCorp United, Dow Jones and Co., Sprint; trustee Hall Family Found., Aspen Inst.; past chmn. bd. dirs. 10th dist. Fed. Res. Bank; past chmn. Civic Coun. Kansas City, 1987-89, Midwest Rsch. Inst. Club: Kansas City Country. Office: 2501 Mcgee St Kansas City MO 64108-2615

HOCKENBERG, HARLAN DAVID, lawyer; b. Des Moines, July 1, 1927; s. Leonard C. and Estyre M. (Zalk) H.; m. Dorothy A. Arkin, June 3, 1953; children: Marni Lynn, Thomas Leonard, Edward Arkin. BA, U. Iowa, 1949, JD, 1952. Bar: Iowa 1952. Assoc. Abramson & Myers, Des Moines, 1952-58, Abramson, Myers & Hockenberg, Des Moines, 1958-64; sr. ptnr. Davis, Hockenberg, Wine, Brown, Koehn & Shors, 1964-95; shareholder, dir. Sullivan & Ward, P.C., 1995—. Bd. dirs. West Des Moines State Bank, Partnership for a Drug-Free Iowa, Rep. Jewish Coalition, Smoother Sailing Found. Mem. bd. editors U. Iowa Law Review. Mem. Citizens for Ind. Cts., Internat. Rels. and Nat. Security Adv. Coun., Rep. Nat. Com., 1978; chmn. Coun. Jewish Fedns., Small Cities Com., 1970-71; mem. exec. com. Am. Israel Pub. Affairs Com.; pres. Wilkie House, Inc., Des Moines, 1965-66, Des Moines Jewish Welfare Fedn., 1973-74; mem. Presdl. Commn. on White House Fellowships, 1988-92; mem. Mayor's Select Com. on Drug Abuse, co-chair prevention subcom.; mem. ins. devel. bd. Iowa Dept. Econ. Devel. With USNR, 1945-46. Mem. Iowa State Bar Assn. (past chair professionalism com.), Des Moines C. of C. (pres. 1986, chmn. bur. econ. devel. 1979, 80, bd. dirs. 1986, chmn. Metro Forum), Des Moines Club, Pioneer Club, Delta Sigma Rho, Omicron Delta Kappa, Phi Epsilon Pi. Home: 2880 Grand Ave Des Moines IA 50312-4274 Office: Sullivan & Ward PC 801 Grand Ave Ste 3500 Des Moines IA 50309-8005 E-mail: bhockenberg@sullivan-ward.com.

HODAPP, DON JOSEPH, food company executive; b. Madelia, Minn., Dec. 24, 1937; s. Philip Henry and Katherine Lillian (Quinn) H.; m. Dorothy Ann Berg, Sept. 7, 1959; children: Don Jr., Jennifer, Paul, Patrick, Laurie. BA in Math., St. John's U., Collegeville, Minn., 1959. Adv. mktg. rep. IBM Corp., Mpls., 1959-66; dir. data processing Geo. A. Hormel & Co., Austin, Minn., 1966-69, asst. controller, 1969-81, gen. mgr. Fremont, Nebr., 1981-85, v.p. strategic planning Austin, 1985-86, group v.p., 1986-92, exec. v.p., CFO, 1992—, also bd. dirs., 1986—. Bd. dirs., treasl. Hormel Found. Bd. regents St. John's U., Collegeville, Minn., 1990-99; bd. dirs. Ctr. for Rural Policy and Devel. Republican. Roman Catholic. Lodge: Rotary. Office: Hormel Foods Corp 1 Hormel Pl Austin MN 55912-3680

HODES, SCOTT, lawyer; b. Chgo., Aug. 14, 1937; s. Barnet and Eleanor (Cramer) H.; m. Maria Bechily, 1982; children— Brian Kenneth, Valery Jane, Anthony Scott. AB, U. Chgo., 1956; JD, U. Mich., 1959; LLM, Northwestern U., 1962. Bar: Ill. 1959, D.C. 1962, N.Y. 1981. Assoc. Arvey, Hodes, Costello & Burman, Chgo., 1959-61, ptnr., 1965-91, Ross & Hardies, Chgo., 1992—. Bd. dirs. First Investors Life Ins. Co. N.Y., Richardson Electronics, Ltd., State Ill. Savs. and Loan Bd. Author: The Law of Art and Antiques, 1966, What Every Artist and Collector Should Know About the Law, 1974; Assoc. news editor: Fed. Bar News, 1963-70; co-editor: Conf. Mut. Funds, 1966, Legal Rights in the Art and Collectors' World, 1986; Contbr. articles to profl. jours. Chmn. Philippine Exch. Nurses award com., 1966; nat. chmn. Lawbooks U.S.A., 1962-73; chmn. Mut. Funds and Investment Mgmt. Conf., 1966-75; co-chmn. Chgo. World Friendship Day, 1967; mem. Ill. Arts Coun., 1973-75; Committeeman Ill. 9th Dist. Dem. Com., 1970-82; bd. dirs. Michael Reese Hosp. Rsch. Inst., 1965-73, Found. of Fed. Bar Assn., 1970—, United Cerebral Palsy Chgo., 1976-84; governing bd. Chgo. Symphony Soc., 1978-1999; governing mem. Art Inst. Chgo., 1980—; mem. com. on internat. investment and tech. Dept. State, 1980-83; bd. dirs. Chgo. Neighborhood Theatre Found., 1980-92, The Harold Washington Found., 1988-2000; exec. com. Anti Defamation League, 1990-98; chmn. Mayor's Task Force on Neighborhood Land Use, 1986-88; chmn. Navy Pier Devel. Authority, 1988-89; mem. Ill. Atty. Gen. adv. com., 1991-95; spl. counsel Art in Embassies Program, Dept. State, 1992-94; co-chmn. Private Enterprise Rev. and Adv. Bd., Ill., 1992-94; pres. Lawyers Creative Arts, 2000—. Capt. JAGC, AUS, 1962-64. Decorated Army Commendation medal; named one of Chicago's ten outstanding young men Jr. Assn. Commerce and Industry, 1968, Chgo. Artist's award for Support of Visual Arts, 1996, Disting. Svc. award Lawyer's for the Creative Arts, 1997. 02169408, Fed. Bar Assn. (chmn. council financing 1966-71, chmn. younger lawyers div. 1963-64, nat. council 1965— , Distinguished Service award 1971, 75, 86, Earl Kintner award for Outstanding Service, 1998), Ill. Bar Assn., Chgo. Bar Assn., Chgo. Art Inst. (life), Chgo. Hist. Soc. (life), Judge Adv. Gens. Assn. (life), Zeta Beta Tau, Tau Epsilon Rho. Jewish. Clubs: Standard, Econ. (Chgo.), Mid-Day. Lodge: Masons (32 degree). Home: 1540 N Lake Shore Dr Chicago IL 60610-6684 Office: Ross & Hardies 150 N Michigan Ave Ste 2500 Chicago IL 60601-7567 E-mail: scott.hodes@rosshardies.com.

HODGE, ROBERT JOSEPH, retail executive; b. St. Louis, July 5, 1937; s. Joseph Edward and Alberta Marie (Oehler) H.; m. Carmen Maria Villalobos, Sept. 1, 1960; children: Ralph, Robert, Carmen. BS in Indsl. Relations, St. Louis U., 1959. Meat dept. merchandiser Kroger Co., Cleve., 1972-74, corp. v.p. deli/bakery Cin., 1981-83, v.p. Atlanta div., 1983-85, meat merchandiser, 1977-80, v.p. gateway region, 1985-87; v.p. meat ops. Ralph's Grocery Co., Los Angeles, 1974-77; gen. mgr. Super X Drug, Melbourne, Fla., 1980-81; sr. v.p. Dillon Co., Hutchinson, Kans., 1987-89; sr. v.p. merchandising, manufacturing Kroger Co., Cin., 1989-92, pres. Cin./Dayton mktg. area, 1992—. Sgt. U.S. Army, res., 1959-66. Avocations: golf, skiing. Home: 614 Watchcove Ct Cincinnati OH 45230-3777 Office: Kroger Co 150 Tri County Pkwy Cincinnati OH 45246-3246

HODGES, RICHARD, former state legislator; b. Oct. 12, 1963; BA with honors, Oberlin Coll., 1986; MPA, U. Toledo, 1991. Ind. fin. cons., 1986-89; treas. Fulton County, Ohio, 1987-92; state rep. 82d Dist., 1993-98. Co-regional coord. Voinovich for Gov., 1990; mem. Ohio adv. com. Bush for Pres., 1988; mem. Fulton County Republican Ctrl. and Exec. coms., 1986-90; mgr. Tom Van Meter for State Senator, 1986. Mem. Fulton County Farm Bur., Fulton and Defiance County Township Trustees Assn., Defiance County Pheasants Forever, Rotary. Republican. Address: 210 Larch Ln Swanton OH 43558-8699

HODGSON, JANE ELIZABETH, obstetrician and gynecologist, consultant; b. Crookston, Minn., Jan. 23, 1915; d. Herbert and Adelaide (Marin) H.; m. Frank Walter Quattlebaum, Feb. 22, 1940; children: Gretchen, Nancy. BS, Carleton Coll., 1934, DSc (hon.), 1994; MD, U. Minn., 1939, MS in Ob-Gyn., 1947. Diplomate Am. Bd. Ob.-Gyn. Fellow Mayo Clinic, Rochester, Minn., 1941-44; pvt. practice in ob-gyn. St. Paul, 1947-72; med. dir. Preterm Clinic, Washington, 1972-74; med. dir. fertility control clinic St. Paul Ramsey Med. Ctr., 1974-79; med. dir. Planned Parenthood Minn., St. Paul, 1980-82, Midwest Health Ctr. Women, Mpls., 1981-83, Women's Health Ctr., Duluth, Minn., 1981-84, mem. staff, 1986—, also bd. dirs.; ostetrician/gynecologist Project Hope, Grenada, West Indies, 1984; vis. prof. ob-gyn. project hope Zheijiang Med. Sch., Hangzhou, People's Republic of China, 1985-86; clin. assoc. prof. ob-gyn. U. Minn., Mpls., 1986—. Vis. med. educator Project Hope, Cairo, 1979-80; vis. prof. dept. ob-gyn. U. Calif., San Francisco, 1983. Editor: Abortion & Sterilization, 1981; contbr. numerous articles to profl. jours. Bd. dirs. Genesis II Women, Mpls., 1988—, Pro Choice Resources, Mpls., 1991—, Wellstone Alliance, Mpls., 1992—, Ctr. for Reproductive Law and Policy, N.Y.C., 1995—. Recipient Ann. Humanitarian award Nat. Abortion Fedn., 1981, Woman Physician of Yr. award Med. Women Minn. Med. Assn., 1983, Ann. Jane Hodgson Reproductive Freedom award Nat. Abortion Rights Action League, 1989, Hanah G. Solomon award Nat. Coun. Jewish Women, 1990, Margaret Sanger award Planned Parenthood Fedn. of Am., 1995, Harold Swanberg award Am. Med. Writer's Assn., 1996. Fellow Am. Coll. Ob-Gyn. (founding); mem. Am. Med. Women's Assn. (E. Blackwell award 1992, Reproductive Health award 1994), Minn. Ob-Gyn. Soc. (pres. 1967), Minn. Med. Assn. (So. Minn. Med. award 1952), Minn. Women's Polit. Caucus (16th Ann. Founding Feminist award 1988), Mayo Clinic Alumni Assn. Home and Office: 211 2nd St NW Apt 1405 Rochester MN 55901-2895 E-mail: janeEhodgson@aol.com.

HODGSON, PAUL EDMUND, surgeon, department chairman; b. Milw., Dec. 14, 1921; s. Howard Edmund and Ethel Marie (Niemi) H.; m. Barbara Jean Osborne, Apr. 22, 1945; children: Ann, Paul. BS summa cum laude, Beloit Coll., 1943; M.D. cum laude, U. Mich., 1945. Diplomate: Am. Bd. Surgery. Intern U. Mich. Hosp., 1945-46, resident in surgery, 1948-52; mem. faculty dept. surgery U. Mich., 1952-62, assoc. prof., 1956-62; prof. surgery U. Nebr. Coll. Medicine, Omaha, 1962-88, prof. emeritus, 1988—, asst. dean for curriculum, 1966-72, chmn. dept. surgery, 1972-84. Trustee Beloit Coll., 1977-80 Served to capt. M.C. U.S. Army, 1946-48. Mem. A.C.S., Frederick A. Coller Surg. Soc., Soc. Univ. Surgeons, Central Surg. Assn., Soc. Surgery Alimentary Tract, Am. Assn. Surgery Trauma, Western Surg. Assn., Am. Surg. Assn. Presbyterian. Office: U Nebr Med Ctr 600 S 42nd St Omaha NE 68198-3280

HODGSON, THOMAS RICHARD, retired healthcare company executive; b. Lakewood, Ohio, Dec. 17, 1941; s. Thomas Julian and Dallas Louise (Livesay) H.; m. Susan Jane Cawrse, Aug. 10, 1963; children: Michael, Laura, Anne. BSChemE, Purdue U., 1963, DEng. (hon.), 1993; MSE, U. Mich., 1964; MBA, Harvard U., 1969. Devel. engr. E.I. Dupont, 1964; assoc. Booz-Allen & Hamilton, 1969-72; with Abbott Labs., North Chicago, Ill., 1972—, gen. mgr. Faultless div., 1976-78, v.p. gen. mgr. hosp. div., 1978-80, pres. hosp. div., 1980-83, group v.p., pres. Abbott Internat. Ltd., 1983-84; also bd. dirs. Abbott Internat. Ltd.; exec. v.p. parent co., pres. Abbott Internat. Inc. Abbott Labs., North Chicago, Ill., 1985-90, pres., chief oper. officer Abbott Park, 1990-99. Mem. engring. vis. com. Purdue U., 1996—; bd. dirs. St. Paul Cos. Mem. Lake Forest (Ill.) Bd. Edn., 1986-90; trustee and mem. exec. com. Rush-Presbyn. St. Luke's Med. Ctr. Chgo., 1992—; overseer Harvard Bus. Sch. Club Chgo., 1993—. Baker scholar; NSF fellow; recipient Disting. Engring. Alumni award Purdue U., 1985 Mem. Chgo. Coun. Fgn. Rels., Econ. Club, Knollwood Club, Shoreacres Club, Chgo. Club, Phi Eta Sigma, Tau Beta Pi. Home: 1015 Ashley Rd Lake Forest IL 60045-3379 Office: Abbott Labs 100 Abbott Park Rd Abbott Park IL 60064-3502

HODNIK, DAVID F. retail company executive; b. 1947; Grad., Western Ill. U., 1970. Sr. auditor Paul Pettengill & Co., 1969-72; with Ace Hardware Corp., Hinsdale, Ill., 1972—, acct., 1972-74, mgr. acctg., 1974-76, controller, 1976-80, v.p., treas., 1980-82; v.p. fin., treas. ACE Hardware Corp., Oak Brook, 1982-88, sr. v.p., 1988-90, exec. v.p., 1990-93, exec. v.p., COO, 1993-95, pres., COO, 1995-96, pres., CEO, 1996—. Office: ACE Hardware Corp 2200 Kensington Ct Oak Brook IL 60523-2100

HODOWAL, JOHN RAYMOND, lawyer, holding company executive, utility company executive; b. Dayton, Ohio, Feb. 16, 1945; m. Caroline H. Norris. B.S. in Indsl. Engring., Purdue U., 1966; J.D., Ind. U., 1970. Bar: Ind. 1971, U.S. Dist. Ct. (so. dist.) Ind. 1971, U.S. Ct. Appeals (7th cir.) 1973. Jr. engr. Indpls. Power and Light Co., 1968-69, assoc. engr., 1969-71, atty., 1971-73, asst. sec., assoc. gen. counsel, 1973-76, asst. sec., asst. treas., 1976-77, treas., 1977-79, v.p., treas., 1979; sr. v.p. fin. Indpls. Power and Light subs. IPALCO Enterprises, 1979-87, exec. v.p., 1987-89, chief exec. officer, 1989—, chmn. bd., chief exec. officer, 1990—; v.p., treas. IPALCO Enterprises Inc., Indpls., 1984-89, chmn. bd., pres., 1989—; pres. Mid-Am. Capital Resources Inc. subs. IPALCO Enterprises, 1984—, pres., chmn. bd., 1989—. CEO, chmn. bd. Mid.-Am. Energy Resource, Inc. subs. Mid.-Am. Capital Resources, Inc., chmn. bd., pres. 1989-91; chmn. bd. Cleve. Thermal Energy Corps. subs. Mid-Am. Energy Resources, Inc., 1991—; bd. dirs. Bank One, Indpls., N.A., Associated Ins. Cos., Inc., Ind. Electric Assn. Chmn. Corp. Cmty. Coun.; gen. chmn. 4th Quadrennial Internat. Violin Competition Indpls.; Ind. state chmn. U.S. Savs. Bond Program. Recipient Disting. Engring. Alumnus award Purdue U., 1990. Mem. Am. Mgmt. Assn., Ind. State C. of C. (bd. dirs.), Purdue U. Alumni Assn., Ind. U. Alumni Assn., Edison Electric Inst. Office: IPALCO Enterprises Inc 1 Monument Cir PO Box 1595 Indianapolis IN 46206-1595

HOECKER, DAVID, engineering executive; b. Cin., July 7, 1948; s. Vernon and Ruth (Schnake) H.; m. Susan Ameling, Aug. 15, 1970; children: Sarah, Paul. B.S., Rose Poly. Inst., Terre Haute, Ind., 1969; M.S.I.A., Purdue U., 1970; grad. program for execs., Carnegie-Mellon U., 1991. Cert. quality engr.; cert. quality mgr. Project mgr. Timken Co., Canton, Ohio, 1970-73, gen. supr., 1973-78, chief quality control engring. Lincolnton, N.C., 1978-82, chief engr. engring. services. Canton, Ohio, 1982-84, mgr. European Rsch. Northampton, Eng., 1984-89, gen. mgr. product engring. Canton, Ohio, 1989-93; gen. mgr. Timken Tooling Bus., 1993-95, gen. mgr. quality & tech., 1996—; v.p. The Wilderness Ctr. Inc., 1995-97, pres., 1997—2002. V.p. Canton Jaycees, 1973-74, Trinity United Ch. of Christ, 1983-84, 91-92, pres., 1993, chmn. endowment com., 1996, Brit. Timken Sports Club, 1986-89; dir. Young Life, Canton, 1975-78. Named Spoke of Yr. Canton Jaycees, 1972; named Key Man Canton Jaycees, 1974 Mem. ASME, Am. Soc. Quality Control (sr. mem., sec. Charlotte sect. 1980-81, treas. 1981), Canton Club. Republican. Office: Timken Co Mail Drop BON-07 PO Box 6929 Canton OH 44706-0929

HOEFT, DOUGLAS L. state legislator; BA, Denison U., 1964; MAT, Northwestern U., 1965; EdD, No. Ill. U., 1975. Tchr. Am. history Flower H.S., Chgo., 1964-65; tchr. social sci. Elgin (Ill.) H.S., 1965-75; instr. Grad. Sch. Nat. Lewis U., Lombard, Ill., 1985-87; asst. regional supt. schs. Kane County, 1975-87, supt., 1987-93; Mem. Ill. Ho. of Reps., 1993—. Contbr. articles to profl. jours. Mem. Gov.'s Task Force on Drugs and Alcohol, 1984; mem. adv. bd. Ill. Dept. Children and Family Svc., 1987-90. Also: 1112 South St Elgin IL 60123-7239 Address: 216 King Arthur Ct Elgin IL 60120-9544

HOEFT, ROBERT GENE, agriculture educator; b. David City, Nebr., May 21, 1944; s. Otto O. Hoeft and Lula (Barlean) Pleskac; m. Nancy A. Bussen, Sept. 1, 1990; children: Jeffrey, Angela. BS, U. Nebr., 1965, MS, 1967; PhD, U. Wis., 1972. Asst. prof. S.D. State U., Rapid City, 1972-73, U. Ill., Urbana, 1973-77, assoc. prof., 1977-81, prof., 1981—. Author: Modern Corn Production, 1986, Modern Corn & Soybean Production, 2000; editor Jour. Prodn. Agr., 1986-92. Recipient Funk award U. Ill., 1990, Robert E. Wagner award Potash and Phosphate Inst., 1998. Fellow Soil Sci. Soc. Am., Am. Soc. Agronomy (CIBA-Geigy award 1978, Agronomic Extension award, grantee 1988, Agronomic Achievement award-soils 1995, Werner Nelson award for diagnosis of yield limiting factors 1996); mem. Coun. for Sci. and Tech. Office: U Ill 1102 S Goodwin Ave Urbana IL 61801-4730

HOEG, DONALD FRANCIS, chemist, consultant, former research and development executive; b. Bklyn., Aug. 2, 1931; s. Harry Herman and Charlotte (Bourke) H.; m. Patricia Catherine Fogarty, Aug. 30, 1952; children— Thomas Edward, Robert Francis, Donald John, Mary Beth, Susan Catherine. B.S. in Chemistry summa cum laude, St. John's U., N.Y., 1953; Ph.D. in Chemistry, Ill. Inst. Tech., 1957. Fellow in chemistry and chem. engring. Armour Research Found., 1953-54; grad. research asst. Ill. Inst. Tech., 1954-56; research chemist W.R. Grace & Co., 1956-58, sr. research chemist, 1958-61; group leader addition polymer chemistry Roy C. Ingersoll Research Center, Borg-Warner Corp., Des Plaines, Ill., 1961-64, mgr. polymer chemistry, 1964-66, assoc. dir., head chem. research dept., 1966-75, dir., 1975-88; pres. DFH Assocs., 1988—. Former mem. solid state scis. adv. bd. NAS; bd. overseers Lewis Coll. Scis. and Letters of Ill. Inst. Tech., 1980-91; bd. dirs. Ill. Inst. Tech. Alumni, 1979-82, Mt. Prospect Combined Appeal, 1963-65 Bd. editors: Research Mgmt. Mag, 1979-82; contbr. numerous articles tech. publs., chpts. in books; patentee in field. TaPing Lin scholar, 1955-56; AEC asst., 1954; Armour Research Found. fellow, 1953-54; Ill. Inst. Tech. Achievement award, 1983 Mem. Am. Chem. Soc., AAAS, N.Y. Acad. Scis., Dirs. Indsl. Research, Am. Mgmt. Assn. (v.p. council 1984-88), Research Dirs. Assn. Chgo. (pres. 1977-78), Indsl. Research Inst. (bd. dirs. 1986-88), Sigma Xi. E-mail: dfh1931@aol.com.

HOEKSTRA, PETER, congressman, manufacturing executive; b. Groningen, The Netherlands, Oct. 30, 1953; m. Diane M. Johnson; children: Erin, Allison, Bryan. BA, Hope Coll., 1975; MBA, U. Mich., 1977. Furniture exec. Herman Miller, Inc., 1977-92, project mgr., product mgr., dir. product mgmt., dir. dealer mktg., v.p. dealer mktg., 1988-92, v.p. product mgmt., 1992-93; mem. U.S. Congress from 2d Mich. dist., 1993—, mem. budget com., mem. edn. and the workforce com.; mem. budget com. 103rd-106th Congresses from 2d Mich. dist., chmn. select edn. subcom. edn. and the workforce com., 2001, mem. select com. on intelligence, 2001. Mem. Budget Com; chmn. edn. and the workforce ctr. subcom. on oversight and investigations. Contbr. to project devel. Equa Chair, recognized as outstanding product of 1980s by Time Mag. Republican. Office: US Ho of Reps Office Of Ho Mems 1124 Longworth Bldg Washington DC 20515-0004 E-mail: tellhoek@mail.house.gov.*

HOEKWATER, JAMES WARREN, treasurer; b. Grand Rapids, Mich., Nov. 4, 1946; s. William Harold and Sena (Hoeksema) H.; m. Roberta Joyce Paczala, July 12, 1975; children: William Paczala, Elizabeth Veronica. BA, Mich. State U., 1970. CPA, Mich. With Touche Ross & Co., Detroit, 1970-77; v.p., controller Great Lakes div. Nat. Steel Corp., 1977-83; treas. Nat. Steel Corp., Pitts., 1983-89, v.p., 1987-89; corp. contr.

ITT Rayonier Inc., Stamford, Conn., 1989-94; treas. Acme Metals Inc., Riverdale, Ill., 1994—. Mem. AICPA. Republican. Episcopalian. Home: 6420 Lane Ct Hinsdale IL 60521-5354 Office: Acme Metals Inc 13500 S Perry Ave Riverdale IL 60827-1148

HOENIG, JONATHAN, radio talk show host; b. Chgo., Sept. 20, 1975; s. David and Ann Hoenig. B of Comm. Arts, Northwestern U., 1997. Commentator "Marketplace" NPR, Chgo., 1992; film critic, Sneak Previews PBS, 1991-93; freelance prodr. WTTW-TV, 1991-95; talk show host WNUR-FM, Evanston, Ill., 1995—. Creator (radio show) Capitalist Pig, 1996. Mem. NATAS, Nat. Assn. Radio Talk Show Hosts. Home and Office: 150 Lapier St Glencoe IL 60022-1915*

HOENIG, THOMAS M. bank executive; b. Fort Madison, Iowa, Sept. 6, 1946; BA in Econs., St. Benedict's Coll., 1968; MA, PhD, Iowa State U. of Sci. & Tech., Ames, 1974. Economist banking supervision area Fed. Reserve Bank of Kansa City, Mo., 1973, v.p., 1981, sr. v.p., 1986, CEO, 1991, pres., CEO, 1991—. Mem. Free Open Market Com.; bd. dirs., mem. banking adv. bd. U. Mo., Kansas City; mem. banking adv. bd. U. Mo., Columbia. Trustee Benedictine Coll., Atchison, Kans., Midwest Rsch. Inst. Office: Fed Res Bank of Kans City 925 Grand Blvd Kansas City MO 64106-2006 Home: 615 W Meyer Blvd Kansas City MO 64113-1543

HOERNEMAN, CALVIN A., JR. economics educator; b. Youngstown, Ohio, Sept. 30, 1940; s. Calvin A. and Lucille A. (Leiss) H.; m. Cheryl L. Morand, Aug. 10, 1973; children: David, Jennifer, Christina. BA, Bethany Coll., 1962; MA, Mich. State U., 1964, postgrad., Cambridge U. Mem. faculty, Delta Coll., University Center, Mich., 1966—, prof. econs., 1976—; cons. Prentice-Hall, Acad. Press, Goodyear Pub., Random House Pub.; econ. expert witness; Author: Poverty, Wealth and Income Distribution, 1969; co-author: "Caper" Principles of Economics Software Study Guide; contbr. articles to various publs. Recipient Recognition award AAUP, 1972, Bergstein award Delta Coll. Grad. Class, 1972, Competition for Excellence award IBM and the League for Innovation, 1988. Mem. AAUP, Am. Econ. Assn., Midwest Econ. Assn., Nat. Assn. Forensic Economist. Home: 5712 Lamplighter Ln Midland MI 48642-3137 Office: Delta Coll Dept Econs University Center MI 48710-0001

HOERNER, ROBERT JACK, lawyer; b. Fairfield, Iowa, Oct. 12, 1931; s. John Andrew and Margaret Louise (Simmons) Hoerner; m. Judith Chandler, Apr. 21, 1954 (div. Feb. 1975); children: John Andrew II, Timothy Chandler, Blayne Marie Hoerner Murray, Michelle Margaret Hoerner Smith; m. Mary Paolano, June 3, 1989. BA, Cornell Coll., 1953; JD, U. Mich., 1958. Bar: Ohio 1960, US Supreme Ct 1964, US Ct Appeals (6th cir) 1972, US Ct Appeals (fed cir) 1990. Law clk. to hon. Chief Justice Earl Warren U.S. Supreme Ct., Washington, 1958-59; assoc. Jones, Day, Reavis & Pogue, Cleve., 1959-63, 65-66; chief evaluation sect. antitrust divsn. Dept. Justice, Washington, 1963-65; ptnr. Jones, Day, Reavis & Pogue, Cleve., 1967-93. Contbr. articles to profl jours; editor (editor-in-chief): (journal) Mich Law Rev. Trustee New Orgn Visual Arts, Cleveland, Ohio, 1976—80, 1987—90. With Counter Intelligence Corps U.S. Army, 1953—55. Mem.: ABA (antitrust sect, patent sect), Cleveland Intellectual Property Law Asn, Greater Cleveland Bar Asn, Ohio Bar Asn, Leland Country Club, Order of Coif. Democrat. Home: 360 Darbys Run Bay Village OH 44140-2968 Office: Jones Day Reavis & Pogue 901 Lakeside Ave E Ste N-334 Cleveland OH 44114-1190 Business E-Mail: rjhoerner@jonesday.com.

HOESSLE, CHARLES HERMAN, zoo director; b. St. Louis, Mar. 20, 1931; m. Marilyn Mueller, Jan. 5, 1952; children: Maureen, Kirk, Tracy, Bradley. AA, Harris Tchrs. Coll., 1951; student, Am. Assn. Zool. Parks and Aquariums Zoo Mgmt. Sch., 1976-77; LLD (hon.), Maryville Coll., 1986, St. Louis U., 1990, U. Mo., St. Louis, 1994. Reptile keeper St. Louis Zoo, 1963, asst. curator, 1964, curator reptiles and curator edn., 1968-69, gen. curator and dep. dir., 1969-82, dir., 1982—2002, dir. emeritus, 2002—. Adj. prof. dept. biology St. Louis U., 1973-74, 81-82, 83; owner, operator Exotic Pet Shop, St. Louis; host St. Louis Zoo Show, 1968-78 Chmn. Reptile Study Merit Badge counselors, St. Louis; mem. adv. bd. Mo. Coalition for Environment, 1977; state chmn. UN Day, 1982; mem. St. Louis County Counts; bd. dirs. Harris-Stowe State Coll. Found., City Mus.; mem. Bd. Regents Harris-Stowe State Coll. Recipient Disting. Alumnus award Harris-Stowe State Coll., 1987. Mem. Internat. Union Dirs. Zool. Gardens, Am. Zoo and Aquarium Assn. (bd. dirs. 1977-79, 85-87, v.p. 1988, pres. 1990-91, past pres. 1991-92, rep. to species survival commn. Internat. Union for Conservation Nature and Natural Resources), St. Louis Naturalists Club, St. Louis Ctr. for Internat. Rels. (bd. dirs. 1993—), St. Louis Mus. Collaborative (pres. 1993), Animal Protective Assn. (bd. dirs.), Internat. Friendship Alliance St. Louis County (chmn. cultural com.), Explorers, St. Louis Herpetological Society, Hawthorne Soc., St. Louis Rotary Club, St Louis Ambassadors Club (bd. dir.). Home: 10814 Forest Circle Dr Saint Louis MO 63128-2007 Office: St Louis Zoo Forest Park Saint Louis MO 63110-1380

HOEVEN, JOHN, governor; b. Bismarck, N.D., Mar. 13, 1957; m. Mical (Mikey); children: Marcela, Jack. B in history and econ., Dartmouth Coll., 1979; MBA, J.L. Kelloge Grad. Sch. Mngmt., Northwestern U., 1981. Exec. v.p. First Western Bank, Minot, N.D., 1986-93; pres. and CEO Bank of N.D. (BND), 1993-2000; gov. N.D., 2000—. Econ. adv. N.D. Univ.; trustee Bismarck State Coll.; regent Minot State U. Cmty. chair Mo. Slope Areawide Campaign, 1998; chair Minot Chamber Commerce AFB Retention com., Minot Area Devel. Corp.; dir. Minot Kiwanis Club, Souris Valley Humane Soc, State Fair Adv. com.; mem. bd. dirs. First Western Bank and Trust, N.D. Bankers Assn., State Bank Bd., N.D. Small Bus. Investment Co., Prairie Pub. Broadcasting, N.D. Econ. Devel. Assn., Bismarck YMCA, Harold Schafer Leadership Ctr. Rep.; Catholic. Office: Gov Office 600 E Blvd Ave Bismarck ND 58505-0001*

HOEY, RITA, public relations executive; b. Chgo., Nov. 4, 1950; d. Louis D. and Edith M. (Finnemann) Hoey; m. Joseph John Dragonette, Sept. 4, 1982 (dec.). BA in English and History, No. Ill. U., 1972. Asst. dir. Nat. Assn. Housing and Human Devel., Chgo., 1975; pub. rels. account exec. Weber Cohn & Riley, 1975-76; publicity coord. U.S. Gypsum Co., 1976-77; with Daniel J. Edelman, Inc., 1977-84, sr. v.p., 1981-84; exec. v.p. Dragonette, Inc., 1984-91, pres., 1991-99, GCI Dragonette, Chgo., 1999—. Mem. Pub. Rels. Soc. Am. Home: Ste 2200 680 North Lake Shore Dr Chicago IL 60611 Office: GCI Dragonette 205 W Wacker Dr Ste 2200 Chicago IL 60606-1215

HOFER, ROY ELLIS, lawyer; b. Cin., Oct. 10, 1935; s. Eric Walter and Elsie Katherine (Ellis) H.; m. Suzanne Elizabeth Sturtz, June 6, 1956 (div. 1974); m. Cynthia Ann Corson, June 5, 1981; children: Kimberly, Tracy, Eric. BChemE, Purdue U., 1957; JD, Georgetown U., 1961. Patent examiner U.S. Patent & Trademark Office, Washington, 1957-59; patent agt. Exxon Corp., 1959-61; ptnr. Brinks Hofer Gilson & Lione, Chgo., 1961—, pres., 1995-99. Adv. com. No. Dist. Ill., 1991-95. Contbr. articles to profl. jours. Bd. dirs. Chgo. Lung Assn., 1982-83, Ctr. for Conflict Resolution, 1983-88, 90-91, pres., 1991-97; bd. dirs. Union League Club Chgo., 1984-88, Boys and Girls Club, Chgo., 1985-89, Ill. Inst. CLE, Chgo., 1986-88. Mem. ABA (dir. litigation sect. 1982-87), Fed. Cir. Bar Assn. (pres. 1993-94), Chgo. Bar Assn. (pres. 1988-89), Intellectual Property Law Assn. Chgo., Am. Intellectual Property Law Assn., Legal Club Chgo., Phi Eta Sigma, Tau Beta Pi, Omega Chi Epsilon. Republican. Office: Brinks Hofer Gilson & Lione Ste 3600 455 N Cityfront Plaza Dr Chicago IL 60611-5599

HOFER, THOMAS W. landscape company executive; Pres. Spring Green Lawn Care Corp., Plainfield, Ill. Office: Spring Green Lawn Care Corp 11909 S Spaulding School Dr Plainfield IL 60544-9501

HOFF, JAMES EDWIN, university president; b. Milw., June 23, 1932; s. James E. and Lydia Elisabeth (Kuhn) H. BS in Biology, Spring Hill Coll., 1958, MA in Philosophy, 1959; MA in Theology, St. Louis U., 1966; PhD in Theology, Gregorian U., Rome, 1969. Joined S.J., Roman Cath. Ch., 1953, ordained priest, 1965. Lectr. Creighton Prep. Sch., Omaha, 1959-62; lectr. in theology St. Thomas Coll., St. Paul, 1970-75, dir. novices Jesuit Novitiate, 1970-75; assoc. prof. Creighton U., Omaha, 1976-91, acting dean Sch. Medicine, 1980-82, v.p. univ. rels., pres. Creighton Found., 1983-91; faculty Coll. Medicine, U. Nebr., 1980-86; pres. Xavier U., Cin., 1991—. Bd. dirs. 1st Franklin Savs., Cin.; lectr., presenter in field. Contbr. articles to profl. jours. Bd. dirs. Creighton U., St. Joseph's U., Phila., St. Xavier H.S., Cin.; retreat dir. Jesuit Retreat House, Lake Elmo, Minn.; mem. Leadership Omaha. Mem. Nat. Assn. Cath. Chaplains, Cath. Theol. Soc. Am., Coun. for Advancement and Support Edn., Nat. Assn. Ind. Colls. and Univs., Am. Coun. on Edn. Office: Xavier U 3800 Victory Pkwy Unit 1 Cincinnati OH 45207-1092

HOFF, JOHN SCOTT, lawyer; b. Des Moines, Jan. 2, 1946; s. John Richard and Valetta R. (Scott) H.; m. Susan Murial Felver, June 21, 1972 (div. 1975); m. Shirley Jo Ward, June 21, 1975; children: Jennifer Jo, John Baron. BSBA, Drake U., 1967; MBA, Calif. State U., Fullerton, 1971; postgrad., Oxford (Eng.) U., 1973; JD, Southwestern U., L.A., 1975; MA in Mil. History, Am. Mil. U., 1995. Bar: Iowa 1976, U.S. Ct. Claims 1976, U.S. Ct. Customs and Patent Appeals 1976, U.S. Ct. Mil. Appeals 1976, Ill. 1977, U.S. Dist. Ct. (no. dist.) Ill. 1977, U.S. Ct. Appeals (7th cir.) 1979, Calif. 1980, U.S. Supreme Ct. 1982, Nebr. 1983, D.C. 1983, Wis. 1984, U.S. Dist. Ct. (so. dist.) Iowa 1987, U.S. Ct. Appeals (9th and 10th cirs.) 1988, U.S. Dist. Ct. Ariz. 1990, U.S. Ct. Appeals (6th cir.) 1990, Mich. 1991, U.S. Ct. Appeals (8th cir.) 1991, N.Y. 1995, Minn. 1996, U.S. Dist. Ct. (cen. dist.) Ill. 1996; CPCU; chartered cost analyst. Staff atty. FAA Hdqrs., Washington, 1975-76; assoc. Lord, Bissell & Brook, Chgo., 1976-81; ptnr. Lapin, Hoff, Slaw & Laffey, 1981-92, John Scott Hoff & Assocs., P.C., Chgo., 1992—. Real estate broker Ill. Dept. Profl. Regulation, Springfield, 1980— Contbr. articles to profl. jours. Capt. USAF, 1967—75. Mem. Aviation Ins. Assn. (v.p. 1990-92, pres. 1992-94), Air Force Assn. (v.p., pres. 1980-93), Internat. Soc. Air Safety Investigation (v.p.), Aircraft Owners and Pilots Assn., Exptl. Aircraft Assn., Nat. Assn. Flight Instrs., Aero. Club Chgo. Republican. Presbyterian. Avocations: flying, military history. Office: 20 S Clark St Ste 2210 Chicago IL 60603-1805 E-mail: jsh@aviationattorney.com.

HOFF, JULIAN THEODORE, physician, educator; b. Boise, Idaho, Sept. 22, 1936; s. Harvey Orval and Helen Marie (Boraas) H.; m. Diane Shanks, June 3, 1962; children— Paul, Allison, Julia. BA, Stanford U., Calif., 1958; MD, Cornell U., N.Y.C., 1962. Diplomate Am. Bd. Neurol. Surgery (sec. 1987-91, chmn. 1991-92). Intern N.Y. Hosp., N.Y.C., 1962-63, resident in surgery, 1963-64, resident in neurosurgery, 1966-70; asst. prof. neurosurgery U. Calif., San Francisco, assoc. prof. neurosurgery, 1974-78, prof. neurosurgery, 1978-81, U. Mich., Ann Arbor, 1981—, head sect. neurosurgery, 1981—. Mem. Am. Bd. Neurol-Surgery, 1986-92, chmn., 1991-92; mem. bd. sci. councillors Nat. Inst. Neurol. Diseases and Stroke-NIH, 1993-97, nat. adv. coun., 1999—. Editor: Practice of Neurosurgery, 1979-85; Current Surgical Management of Neurological Diseases, 1980; Neurosurgery: Diagnostic and Management Principles, 1992, Mild to Moderate Head Injury, 1989; co-editor: Neurosurgery: Scientific Basis of Clinical Practice, 1985, 3rd edit., 1999; contbr. articles to profl. jours. Served to capt. US Army, 1964-66. Recipient Tchr.-Investigator award, NIH, 1972—77, Javits Neurosci. Investigator award, 1985—99, Macy Faculty scholar, London, 1979. Fellow: ACS (2d v.p.-elect 1998—99); mem.: Soc. Neurol. Surgeons (pres. 1999—2000, Grass prize 2001), Cen. Neurosurg. Soc. 1985—86, Am. Acad. Neurosurgeons (treas. 1989—92, sec. 1992—, pres. 1996—), Congress Neurol. Surgeons (v.p. 1982—83), Am. Surg. Assn., Am. Assn. Neurol. Surgeons (v.p. 1991—93, pres. 1993—94, Cushing medal 2001), Inst. Medicine NAS. Republican. Presbyterian. Home: 2120 Wallingford Rd Ann Arbor MI 48104-4563 Office: U Mich Hosp TC 2128 Ann Arbor MI 48109

HOFFER, ALMA JEANNE, nursing educator; b. Dalhart, Tex., Sept. 15, 1932; d. James A. and Mildred (Zimlich) Koehler; m. John L. Hoffer, Oct. 7, 1954; children: John Jr., James Leo, Joseph V., Jerome P. BS, Bradley U., 1970; MA, W. Va. Coll. Grad. Study Inst., 1975; EdD, Ball State U., 1981, MA, 1986. Reg. Nurse. Staff nurse St Joseph Hosp., South Bend, Ind., 1958-59, Holy Cross Cen. Sch., St Joseph Hosp., South Bend, 1959-63; sch. nurse South Bend Sch. Corp., 1970-72; faculty staff Morris Harvey Coll., Charleston, W.Va., W.Va. Inst. Tech., Montgomery, 1975-76; asst. prof. Ball State U., Ind., 1976-77, Ind. U.-Purdue U., Ft. Wayne, 1977-81; assoc. prof. U. Akron, Ohio, 1981-83, 91-95, asst. dean, grad. edn., 1983-90, assoc. prof., 1991-93; prof., chair Dept. of Nursing St. Francis Coll., Fort Wayne, Ind., 1993-95; prin. investigator rsch. project Well Begun is Well Done Children's Med. Ctr. Women's Bd. Akron, 1995-96. Trustee Akron Child Guidance, 1983-88, 89-95, chair planning com., 1988; nursing Blick Clin., Akron, 1988; rsch. cons. St. Joseph Hosp., Ohio, 1989; cons. Health Sense, 1996-98; rschr., presenter in field. Contbg. author: Family Health Promotion Theories and Assessment, 1989, Nursing Connections, 1992. Task force mem. Gov. Celeste's Employee Assistance Program for State U. Campuses, Ohio, 1983-84, del. People to People Citizen Amb. Program to Europe, 1988. Mem. ANA, Nat. League for Nursing, Midwest Nursing Rsch. Soc., Transcultural Nursing Soc. (chair certification and recertification com. 2000—), Portage Country Club, Cleve. Country Club, Sigma Theta Tau. Republican. Roman Catholic. Avocations: tennis, golf, skiing. bus. Office: PO Box 794 Bath OH 44210-0794 E-mail: ajhoffer@earthlink.net., ajh1@uakron.edu.

HOFFHEIMER, DANIEL JOSEPH, lawyer; b. Cin., Dec. 28, 1950; s. Harry Max and Charlotte (O'Brien) Hoffheimer; m. Elizabeth Lee Hoffheimer; children: Rebecca, Rachel, Leah. Grad., Phillips Exeter Acad., 1969; AB cum laude, Harvard Coll., 1973; JD, U. Va., 1976. Bar: Ohio 1976, U.S. Dist. Ct. (so. dist.) Ohio 1976, U.S. Ct. Appeals (6th crct.) 1977, U.S. Ct. Appeals (D.C. and fed. crcts.) 1986, U.S. Ct. Internat. Trade 1986, U.S. Tax Ct. 1992, U.S. Supreme Ct. 1980, U.S. Tax Ct. 1992. Assoc. Taft, Stettinius & Hollister, Cin., 1976-84, ptnr., 1984—. Lectr. law Coll. Law, U. Cin., 1981-83; trustee Judges Hogan & Porter Meml. Trust; mem. adv. bd. Ohio Dist. Ct. Rev. Editor-in-chief U. Va. Jour. Internat. Law, 1975-76; co-author: Practitioners' Handbook Ohio First District Court Appeals, 1984, 2d edit., 1991, Federal Practice Manual, U.S. 6th Circuit Court of Appeals, 1999, Manual on Labor Law, 1988; mem. editl. bd. Probate Law Jour. Ohio, 2000—; contbr. articles to profl. jours. Mem. Cin. Symphony Bus. Rels. Com., 1977-86, Cin. Composers Guild, 1988-93, Ohio Supreme Ct. Com. Racial Fairness, 1993-2000; trustee Underground R.R. Freedom Mus., 1995—; mem. adv. bd. for Consumer Protection, Cin., 1978-80, Hoxworth Blood Ctr. Univ. Cin. Hosp., 1994-99; mem. bd. Hebrew Union Coll. Jewish Inst. Religion, 1994—, WGUC-FM Pub. Radio, 1988—, vice chmn., 1993-96, chmn., 1996-98; trustee Cin. Chamber Orch., 1977-80, Seven Hills Sch., Cin., 1980-86, Internat. Visitors Ctr., Cin., 1980-84, Friends Coll. Conservatory of Music, Cin., 1985-86, Cin. Symphony Orch., 1988-94, 96—, sec., 1996-99, vice chair 1999-2000, chair, 2001—, Children's Psychiat. Ctr., Cin., 1986-89, treas., 1987-89; vice chmn. Jewish Hosp., Cin., 1989-92; Leadership Cin., 1989-90; sec., trustee Cin. Symphony Musicians Pension Fund, 1989-99, Jewish Cmty. Rels. Coun., 1990-98, v.p., 1996-98; sec. Nat. Conf. Commn. Justice, 1992-99, treas. 1999-2000, trustee emeritus, 2000—; counsel Cin. AIDS Commn., 1991—, Cin. Inst. Fine Arts Govt. Affairs Com., 1993-94, B'nai B'rith Nat. Coun. Legacy Devel., 1996-97; trustee Nat. Underground R.R. Freedom Ctr., 1995—. Named Outstanding Young Man, U.S. Jaycees, 1984, 98. Life fellow Am. Bar Found., Ohio Bar Found.; fellow Am. Coll. Trust and Estate Counsel; mem. ABA, Internat. Bar Assn., Internat. Trade Bar Assn., Internat. Arbitration Assn. (comml. arbitrator 1991-95), Fed. Bar Assn. (treas. 1984, sec. 1985, v.p. 1986-87, pres. 1987-88), Ohio State Bar Assn. (bd. govs. Est. Pl. Trust and Probate Law sect. 1996—), Cin. Bar Assn. (trustee 1988-93, v.p. 1990-91, pres. 1992-93, chair Cin. Acad. Leadership for Lawyers 1998-2000), Harvard Club of Cin. (bd. dirs. 1980-88, v.p. 1983-86, pres. 1986-87). Democrat. Avocations: music, tennis, Chinese and Japanese art. Home: 1 Forest Hill Dr Cincinnati OH 45208-1953 Office: 1800 Firstar Tower 425 Walnut St Cincinnati OH 45202-3923 E-mail: hoffheimer@taftlaw.com.

HOFFMAN, ALFRED JOHN, retired mutual fund executive; b. Amarillo, Tex., Apr. 16, 1917; s. Kurt John and Mabel (Beven) H.; m. Falice Mae Pittinger, Jan. 5, 1946 (dec. Feb. 1990); children: Susan Terry, John; m. Frances Ward, Sept. 15, 1990.. J.D., U. Mo., 1942. Atty. Prudential Ins. Co. Am., 1946-50, Kansas City Fire & Marine Ins. Co., 1950-59; CEO, founder Jones & Babson, Inc., Kansas City, 1959-85, vice chmn., 1985-93; pres., dir. Babson and UMB Mut. Funds, 1959-85, dir., 1985-93. Naval aviator USN, 1942-46. Mem. ABA, Mo. Bar Assn., Kansas City Golf Assn. (past pres., bd. dirs.), Kansas City Golf Found. (founder, chmn., bd. dirs.), Kansas City Srs. Golf Assn. (past pres., bd. dirs.), U.S. Golf Assn. (com.), Western Golf Assn. (past dir.). Home and Office: 6701 High Dr Shawnee Mission KS 66208-2260

HOFFMAN, BARRY PAUL, lawyer; b. Phila., May 29, 1941; s. Samuel and Hilda (Cohn) H.; m. Mary Ann Schrock, May 18, 1978; children: Elizabeth Barron, Hayley Rebecca. BA, Pa. State U., 1963; JD, George Washington U., 1968. Bar: Pa. 1972, Mich. 1983. Asst. U.S. Senator Wayne Morse, Oreg., Washington; spl. agt. FBI; asst. dist. atty. Phila. Dist. Atty.'s Office; exec. v.p., gen. counsel Valassis Communications, Inc., Livonia, Mich., also bd. dirs. 1st lt. U.S. Army, 1963-65, Korea. Home: 49933 Standish Ct Plymouth MI 48170-2882 Office: Valassis Communications Inc 19975 Victor Pkwy Livonia MI 48152-7001 E-mail: hoffmanb@valassis.com.

HOFFMAN, CHARLES STEVEN, fertilizer company executive; b. Pittsburg, Tex., Mar. 12, 1949; s. Harold Winfred and Catherine Sims (Galvin) H.; m. Denise Bedard, Sept. 23, 1978; 1 child, Sara Andrea. BBA, Stephen F. Austin State U., 1971. Sales trainee indsl. chems. div. Internat. Minerals & Chem. Corp., Mundelein, Ill., 1974-75, field sales rep. indsl. chems. div., 1975-78, dist. sales mgr. indsl. chems. div. Akron, Ohio, 1978-82; mgr. Latin Am., internat. div. IMC Fertilizer Inc., Mundelein, 1982-87, dir. Asia Pacific, internat. div., 1987, v.p. internat. div. Northbrook, Ill., 1987-89, v.p. domestic wholesale mktg., 1989-90, sr. v.p. wholesale mktg., 1990—. Mem. Phosphate Chem. Export Assn. (bd. dirs.), Phosphate Rock Export Assn. (bd. dirs.), Can. Potash Export Assn. (Saskatoon, Sask., bd. dirs.), Potash and Phosphate Inst. (Atlanta, bd. dirs.), Conway Farms Golf Club (Lake Forest, Ill.). Avocation: golf. Home: 12 Exmoor Ln Lincolnshire IL 60069-4018 Office: IMC Fertilizer Group Inc 2100 Sanders Rd Ste 200 Northbrook IL 60062-6141

HOFFMAN, GENE D. food company executive, consultant; b. East St. Louis, Ill., July 29, 1927; s. Edmund H. and Bee (Hood) H.; m. Nancy P. Claney, Oct. 27, 1951; children: Kim Elizabeth, Keith Murdock. B.J. in Advt, U. Mo., 1948. Asst. advt. mgr. Montgomery Ward Co., 1948; copywriter, asst. mgr. advt. promotion Chgo. Tribune, 1949-50; mgr. promotion Phila. Bull., 1951-56; with The Kroger Co., 1956-77, gen. mgr. St. Louis div., 1956-61; dir. mktg. processed foods div., Cin., 1961-63, v.p., gen. mgr., 1964-66; corp. v.p. St. Louis, 1966; v.p. food mfg. divs., 1966-69; pres. Kroger Food Processing Co., 1969-72, Kroger Brands Co., 1972-74; sr. corp. v.p. parent co., 1974-75; corp. pres., bd. dirs. parent co., 1975-77; with Super Valu Stores, Inc., Mpls., 1977-88; pres. Super Valu Wholesale Food Cos., 1977-87, chmn., 1985-88; sr. corp. v.p. Super Valu Stores Inc.; chmn., chief exec. officer Food Giant, Inc.; pres., chief exec. officer Corp. Strategies Internat., Mpls., 1987—; pres. Mktg. Assocs., Inc., 1987—; pres., chief exec. officer LeaderShape, Inc., Champaign, Ill., 1987—. Chmn., bd. dirs. Quality Containers Internat., Inc., 1989—; bd. dirs. Novate Enterprise, Inc., Americana Mag., Rural Ventures, Inc., Lewis Grocer Co., Vital Resources, Inc., WestCoast Grocery Co., Paragon Trade Brands, Inc. Chmn. Leader Shape Inst.; chmn., bd. govs. ATO Found. Served with AC USNR, 1945-46. Mem. Am. Mgmt. Assn., Food Mktg. Inst., Greater Cin. C. of C. (v.p., dir.), AIM, Alpha Delta Sigma, Alpha Tau Omega. Episcopalian. Clubs: Interlachen Country (Mpls.), Comml., Cin., Hyde Park Golf and Country, Queen City, Bankers (Cin.); Tonka Racquets, Camargo Racquet. Office: Corp Strategies Internat 2859 Gale Rd Wayzata MN 55391-2623

HOFFMAN, JAMES PAUL, lawyer, hypnotist; b. Waterloo, Iowa, Sept. 7, 1943; s. James A. and Luella M. (Prokosch) H.; 1 child, Tiffany K. B.A., U. No. Iowa, 1965, J.D. U. Iowa, 1967. Bar: Iowa 1967, U.S. Dist. Ct. (no. dist.) Iowa 1981, U.S. Dist. Ct. (so. dist.) Iowa 1968, U.S. Dist. Ct. (so. dist.) Ill, U.S. Tax Ct. 1971, U.S. Ct. Appeals (8th cir.) 1970, U.S. Supreme Ct. 1974. Sr. mem. James P. Hoffman, Law Offices, Keokuk, Iowa, 1967—; chmn. bd. Iowa Inst. Hypnosis. Fellow Am. Inst. Hypnosis; mem. ABA, Iowa Bar Assn., Lee County Bar Assn., Assn. Trial Lawyers Am., Ill. Trial Lawyers Assn., Iowa Trial Lawyers Assn. Democrat. Roman Catholic. Author: The Iowa Trial Lawyers and the Use of Hypnosis, 1980. Home and Office: PO Box 1087 Middle Rd Keokuk IA 52632-1087

HOFFMAN, JAY C. state legislator; b. Nov. 6, 1961; m. Laurie Hoffman; children: Emily, Katelyn. Grad., Ill. State U., 1983; JD, St. Louis U., 1986. Bar: Ill. 1986. Mem. from Dist. 112, Ill. Ho. of Reps., Dem. floor leader. Mem. exec. fin. inst., jud. criminal com., welfare reform task force Ill. H. of Reps. Dem Cand. for U.S. House, 20th district, I.L., 1996 Named Outstanding Legislator of Yr., Ill. State Atty. Assn., 1994. Address: 7 Driftwood Ln Collinsville IL 62234-5279 Also: 2099 M Stratton Bldg Springfield IL 62706-0001

HOFFMAN, JERRY IRWIN, dental educator, department chairman; b. Chgo., Nov. 20, 1935; s. Irwin and Luba Hoffman; m. Sharon Lynn Seaman, Aug. 25, 1963; children: Steven Abram, Rachel Irene. Student, DePaul U., 1953-56; BS in Biology and Chemistry, Roosevelt U., 1956; DDS, Loyola U., Chgo., 1960; M of Health Care Adminstrn., Baylor U., 1972. Certificate, General Practice Residency, U.S. Army, 1978. Commd. officer U.S. Army, 1960 (served to 1962, returned 1964), advanced through grades to col., 1978, hdqrs. rep. local dental tng. confs. Europe Fed. Republic Germany, 1965-67; cons. to Comdg. Gen. U.S. Army Med. Research and Devel. Command, Washington, 1972-76; cons. Office of Surgeon Gen. U.S. Army, 1972-76, liaison rep. to Nat. Adv. Council and Oral Biology and Medicine Study Sessions of the Nat. Inst. Dental Research and NIH, 1973-76, resident in Gen. Practice Residency, 1976-78; comdg. officer U.S. Army Dental Activity, Fort Monmouth, N.J., 1979-82; ret., 1982; pvt. practice dentistry Chgo., 1962-64; assoc. prof. operative dentistry Loyola U. Sch. Dentistry, Maywood, Ill., 1982-93, dir. gen. practice residency, 1982-85, coordinator extramural dental resources, 1983-85, assoc. dean for clin. affairs, 1985-93; dir. sci. programs Chgo. Dental Soc., 1993—. Staff dentist Silas B. Hayes Army Hosp., Fort Ord, Calif., 1976-79, Patterson Army Hosp., Ft. Monmouth, 1979-82; lectr., presenter seminars in field. Contbr. articles to profl. jours. Decorated Legion of Merit, Meritorious Svc. Medal with oak leaf cluster. Fellow: Am. Coll. Dentists, Internat. Coll. Dentists, Odontographic Soc.; master: Acad.

Gen. Dentistry; mem. ADA, Ill. Dental Soc., Chgo. Dental Soc., Am. Assn. Dental Schs., Am. Soc. Assn. Execs., Assn. Healthcare Execs., Profl. Conv. Mgmt. Assn., Omicron Kappa Upsilon.

HOFFMAN, JOEL HARVEY, composer, educator; b. Vancouver, B.C., Can., Sept. 27, 1953; came to U.S., 1964; s Irwin and Esther Beatrice (Glazer) H.; m. Dorotea Vittoria Vismara, Dec. 30, 1988. MusB summa cum laude, U. Wales, Cardiff, 1974; MusM, Juilliard Sch. Music, 1976, D of Mus. Arts, 1978. Prof. composition Coll./Conservatory Music U. Cin., 1978—. Mem. faculty U. Cin.; artistic dir. Music Ninety-Nine Festival; resident composer MacDowell Colony Yaddo, Rockefeller Found., Camargo Found., Hindemith Found.; new music advisor Buffalo Philharm., 1991-92; composer-in-residence Nat. Chamber Orch., 1993-94. Composer: Sonata for Cello and Piano, 1982, Chamber Symphony, 1983, Double Concerto, 1984, Duo for viola and piano, 1984, Between Ten, 1985, Violin Concerto, 1986, The Hancock Trio, 1987, Fantasia Fiorentina for violin and piano, 1988, Crossing Points for string orch., 1990, Partenze for violin solo, 1990, Cubist Blues for piano trio, 1991, Music in Blue in Green for orch., 1991, Each for Himself/90? for piano solo, 1991, Metasmo for percussion trio, 1992, String Quartet No. 2, 1993, Self-Portrait with Mozart, 1994, Music for chamber orch., 1994, ChiaSsO for orch., 1995, L'Immensita dell'Attimo for voice and piano, 1995, The Music Within the Words, Part I for flute, oboe, cello and piano, 1996, Part II for viola, cello, harp and piano, 1996, Portogruaro Sextet for clarinet, horn, string trio, piano, 1996, l'Chaim Chantata, 1996, Stone Soup for violin and narrator, 1996, Millennium Dances for Orchestra, 1997, Self-Portrait with Gebirtig, 1998, Krakow Variations for viola sola, 1999, Reyzele, A Portrait for chamber ensemble, 1999; (recs.) Duo for Viola and Piano, CRI, 1991, Partenze for violin solo, Koch Internat., 1992, Music for Two Oboes, Centaur, 1995, Fantasy Pieces, Gasparo, 1996, Tum-Balalayke EMA Records, 1996; pianist in various recitals and solo concerts, Italy, France, Great Britain, U.S; pianist and arranger Trio Gebirtig. Artistic dir. Music 2000 Festival. Recipient award Am. Acad.-Inst. Arts and Letters, 1987, commn. Nat. Endowment for the Arts, 1986, 91, Fromm Found., 1980, 82, Am. Harp Soc., 1982, Am. Music Ctr., 1991, Cin. Symphony Orch., 1993, Shanghai String Quartet, 1993, Nat. Chamber Orch., 1993; Ohio Arts Coun. fellow, 1983, 87, 91, 94, 96. Mem. ASCAP, Am. Music Ctr., Gruppo Aperto Musica Oggi, Coll. Music Soc., Composers Forum, Cin. Chamber Music Soc., U. Cin. Faculty Jewish Coun. (past pres.). Avocation: Chinese, Italian cooking. Office: U Cin Coll Conservatory Music Cincinnati OH 45221-0001 Fax: 513 556-0202. E-mail: joel.hoffman@uc.edu.

HOFFMAN, NATHANIEL A. lawyer; b. Cin., Mar. 4, 1949; s. Ralph H. and Betty (Goldfarb) H.; m. Sara Naomi Fishman, Aug. 3, 1980; children: Joshua, Rebecca, Esther, David. BA, Yale U., 1971; JD, U. Mich., 1975. Bar: Calif. 1975, Wis. 1983. Assoc. McDonough, Holland & Allen, Sacramento, 1975-78, Herz, Levin, Teper, Sumner & Croysdale, Milw., 1982-85; ptnr. Michael, Best & Friedrich, 1985—. Atty. N.Y.C. Pub. Devel. Corp., 1980-82. Mem. ABA, State Bar Wis., Milw. Bar Assn., State Bar Calif. Home: 3258 N 51st Blvd Milwaukee WI 53216-3236 Office: Michael Best & Friedrich 100 E Wisconsin Ave Ste 3300 Milwaukee WI 53202-4108 E-mail: nahoffman@mbf-law.com.

HOFFMAN, PHILIP EDWARD, state legislator; b. Jackson, Mich., Nov. 10, 1951; s. Ralph Jacob Jr. and Nancy Joan (Vanantwerp) H.; m. Dennise Fitzgerald, Jan. 29, 1977; children: R. Jacob, Benjamin, Philip. BS, Ferris State U., 1974; postgrad. in edn., Mich. State U., 1975. Undercover narcotics investigator Region II Metro Squad, 1974-77; deputy sheriff Jackson County Sheriff's Dept., Lansing, 1974-82; mem. Mich. Ho. of Reps., 1982-93, Mich. Senate from 19th dist., Lansing, 1993—; v.p. pro tempore Mich. Senate. Chmn. Transportation Com., State Police Com., Military Affairs Com. Hunting, Fishing, Fishing. Forestry Com.; mem. Reapportionment Com.; asst. pro tempore of Senate. Mem. Rep. Exec. Com.; pres. Great Sauk Trail coun. Boy Scouts Am., 1995-96, v.p. 1992-95; past pres. Land O'Lakes Coun., 1992-94; lifelong mem. NAACP; co-chmn. Mich. Fire Svcs. Caucus, 1993—. Named Outstanding Legislator of Yr., Mich. Assn. Chiefs Police, 1993, Legis. Conservationist of Yr., Mich. United Conservation Clubs, 1994, Guardian of Small Bus., Nat. Fedn. Ind. Bus., 1996, Legis. of Yr., Mich. Sheriff's Assn., 1997; Federalism Summit, 1995; Toll fellow, 1995; Fleming fellow, 1994, 95, fellow Coun. State Govts., Ctr. for Policy Alternatives; recipient Silver Beaver award Boy Scouts Am., 1997, Advocate of Yr. award Mich. Mfrs. Assn., 1998, Flame Leadership award Ferris State U., 1998, Star award Dep. Sheriff's Assn. Mich., 1999, Legis. Leadership award Mich. Soft Drink Assn., 1999, Disting. Svc. award Ind. Colls. and Univs. of Mich. Assn., 2000; Am. Legion Legislative award, 2000, Disting. Svc. medal Mich Dept. Mil. and Vets Affairs, 2001, Legis. Leadership award Internat. Brotherhood Elec. Workers and Mich. Chpt. Nat. Elec. Contractors Assn., 2001, Disting. Citizen of Yr. award, Boy Scouts Am., 2001, Legislator of Yr. award, Police Officers Assn. Mich., 2001, Adjutant Gen. Patriot award Mich. Dept. Mil. and Vets. Affairs, 2001, Presdl. Citation award Mich. Sheriff's Assn., 2002, others. Mem. NAACP (life), Am. Legis. Exch. Coun. (Outstanding Legis. Mem. of Yr. 1992, chmn. telecom. task force, 1992-95, bd. dirs. 1996), Jackson C.C. Alumni Assn. (Disting. Svc. award 1987), Ferris State U. Alumni Assn. (Disting. Alumnus 1990), Mich. Jaycees (1 of 10 Outstanding Young People in Mich. 1985), Eagles, Moose, Ducks Unltd., Pheasants Forever, Alpha Sigma Chi. Republican. Roman Catholic. Office: State Capitol Lansing MI 48913-0001

HOFFMAN, RICHARD BRUCE, lawyer; b. Columbus, Ohio, June 8, 1947; s. Marion Keith and Ruth Eileen (McLear) Hoffman; m. Sandra Kay Schenkel, July 26, 1975; children: Kipp Hunter, Tyler Blake. BS in Gen. Engring., U. Ill., 1970; JD, DePaul U., 1973; LLM, John Marshall Sch. of Law, 1981. Bar: Ill. 1973, U.S. Dist. Ct. (no. dist.) Ill. 1973, U.S. Patent and Trademark Office 1973, U.S. Ct. Appeals (7th cir.) 1979, U.S. Ct. Appeals (fed. and 9th cirs.) 1982. Assoc. McCaleb, Lucas & Brugman, Chgo., 1973-76, ptnr., 1976-84, Tilton, Fallon, Lungmus & Chestnut, Chgo., 1984-2001, Marshall, Gerstein & Borun, Chgo., 2001—. Mem.: ABA, Internat. Trademark Assn., Intellectual Property Law Assn., Chgo. Bar Assn., Ill. Bar Assn., Union League-Chgo., Lawyers Club Chgo. Office: Marshall Gerstein & Borun 6300 Sears Tower 233 S Wacker Dr Chicago IL 60606-6402 E-mail: rhoffman@marshallip.com.

HOFFMAN, RICHARD GEORGE, psychologist; b. Benton Harbor, Mich., Oct. 6, 1949; s. Robert Fredrick and Kathleen Elyce (Watts) H.; m. Julia Ann May, Dec. 18, 1970; children: Leslie Margaret, Michael Charles, Angela Lynn, Jennifer Elizabeth. BS with honors, Mich. State U., 1971; MA in Psychology, Long Island U., 1974, PhD in Clin. Psychology, 1980. Lic. con. psychologst. Instr. pediatrics U. Va., Charlottesville, 1977-80; asst. prof. pediatrics and family med. U. Kans., Wichita, 1980-84; asst. prof. behavioral sci. U. Minn., Duluth, 1984-90, assoc. prof. behavioral sci., 1990—, asst. dean for med. edn. and curriculum, 1997—, dir. neuropsychology lab., 1986—, co-dir. hypothermia and water safety lab., 1987—, co-dir. neurobehavioral toxicology lab., 1990—; vis. sr. fellow in human clin. neuropsychology U. Okla. Health Scis. Ctr., 1995-96. Assoc. dir. Child Evaluation Ctr., Wichita, 1981-82; dir. adminstrn. Comprehensive Epilepsy Clinic, Wichita, 1983-84; cons. psychologist U. Assocs., P.A., Duluth, 1984—. Contbr. articles to profl. jour. Pres. Home and Sch. Assn., St. Michael's Sch., Duluth, 1986. Grantee Rsch. grantee, NIH, 1985, USCG, 1986, Sch. Medicine U. Kans., 1984, U. Minn., 1984, U.S. Army Med. Rsch. Command, 1988—, Naval Med. Rsch. Command, 1988, Gt. Lakes Protection Fund, 1991—93, Agy. for Toxic Substances and Disease Registry, 1992—95, 1995—. Fellow Am. Psychol. Soc., Am. Assn. Applied and Preventive Psychology; mem. APA, Nat. Acad. Neuropsychologists. Democrat. Roman Catholic. Avocations: bicycling, hiking. Home: 219 Occidental Blvd Duluth MN 55804-1365 Office: U Minn Dept Behavioral Scis Duluth MN 55812 E-mail: rhoffman@d.umn.edu.

HOFFMAN, ROBERT BUTLER, ministry industry executive; b. Ithaca, N.Y., Dec. 11, 1936; m. Janet A. O'Brien, Nov. 14, 1987; 3 stepchildren. AB in Geology, Cornell U., 1958; MBA, Harvard U., 1964. Mgr. data processing conversion U.S. Nat. Bank, Denver, 1961-62; fin. analyst mergers and acquisitions dept. W.R. Grace & Co., N.Y.C., 1964-66, regional fin. officer Pacific-Far East Overseas Chem. divsn. Sydney, Australia, 1966-69; CFO W.R. Grace Australia Ltd., Melbourne, 1967-69; v.p. fin. European divsn. W.R. Grace & Co., Lausanne, Switzerland, 1970-75, Switzerland, 1970-75; v.p. fin., CFO, FMC Corp., 1975-84; exec. v.p., CFO, Castle & Cooks, Inc., 1984; exec. v.p., CFO, bd. dirs. Staley Continental, Inc., Chgo., 1985-88; cons. on bus. strategy and fin. structure and controls, 1988-90; v.p., head internat. bus. sector FMC, 1990-94; sr. v.p., CFO, Monsanto Co., St. Louis, 1994-97, vice chmn., 1997-99; chmn. Harnischfeger Industries, Inc., Milw., 1999—. Bd. dirs. Kemper Group Funds, Chgo., Harnischfeger Industries, Inc., Milw., St. Louis; mem. coun. fin. execs. Conf. Bd.; mem. pvt. client bd. NationsBank. Mem. coun. Cornell U.; bd. dirs. Mo. Hist. Soc.; mem. adv. com. Webster U. Sch. Bus., St. Louis; bd. dirs. Opera Theatre St. Louis, Better Govt. Assn., Chgo., United Way Greater St. Louis, 1995-97, St. Louis Area coun. Boy Scouts Am., 1994-97; past bd. dirs. Nat. Outdoor Leadership Sch.; mem. vis. com. U. Chgo. Grad. Sch. Bus., 1976-96. Capt. USAF, 1958-61. Mem. Sigma Gamma Epsilon. Presbyterian. Office: Harnischfeger Industries Ste 2780 100 E Wisconsin Ave Milwaukee WI 53202-4127

HOFFMAN, SHARON LYNN, adult education educator; b. Chgo. d. David P. and Florence Seaman; m. Jerry Irwin Hoffman, Aug. 25, 1963; children: Steven Abram, Rachel Irene. BA, Ind. U., 1961; M Adult Edn., Nat.-Louis Univ., 1992. High sch. English tchr. Chgo. Pub. Schs., 1961-64; tchr. Dept. of Def. Schs., Braconne, France, 1964-66; tchr. ESL Russian Inst., Garmisch, Fed. Republic Germany, 1966, 67; tchr. adult edn. Monterey Peninsula Unified Schs., Ft. Ord, Calif., 1977-79; tchr. ESL MAECOM, Monmouth County, N.J., 1979-80; lectr., tchr. adult edn. Truman Coll./Temple Shalom, Chgo.; tchr. homebound Fairfax County Pub. Schs., Fairfax, Va., 1976; entry operator Standard Rate & Data, Wilmette, Ill., 1986-87; rsch. editor, spl. projects editor Marquis Who's Who, 1987-92; mem. adj. faculty Nat.-Louis U., Evanston and Wheeling, Ill., 1993-99, tutor coord., then coord. learning specialist, 1993-99; pres. Cultural Transitions, Highland Park, Ill., 1992—. Mem.: TESOL, ASTD, Chgo. Drama League, Nat. Coun. Tchrs. English. Home and Office: 2270 Highmoor Rd Highland Park IL 60035-1702 E-mail: culturaltrans1@aol.com.

HOFFMAN, SUE ELLEN, elementary education educator; b. Dayton, Ohio, Aug. 23, 1945; d. Cyril Vernon and Sarah Ellen (Sherer) Stephan; m. Lawrence Wayne Hoffman, Oct. 28, 1967. BS in Edn., U. Dayton, 1967; postgrad., Loyolla Coll., 1977, Ea. Mich. U., 1980; MEd, Wright State U., 1988. Cert. reading specialist and elem. tchr., Ohio. 5th grade tchr. St. Anthony Sch., Dayton, Ohio, 1967-68, West Huntsville (Ala.) Elem. Sch., 1968-71; 6th grade tchr. Ranchland Hills Pub. Sch., El Paso, Tex., 1973-74; 3rd grade tchr. Emerson Pub. Sch., Westerville, Ohio, 1976, St. Joan of Arc Sch., Aberdeen, Md., 1976-78, Our Lady of Good Counsel, Plymouth, Mich., 1979-80; 5th grade tchr. St. Helen Sch., Dayton, 1980—. Selected for membership Kappa Delta Pi, 1988. Mem. Internat. Reading Assn., Ohio Internat. Reading Assn., Dayton Area Internat. Reading Assn., Nat. Cath. Edn. Assn. Roman Catholic. Home: 2174 Green Springs Dr Kettering OH 45440-1120 Office: St Helen Sch 5086 Burkhardt Rd Dayton OH 45431-2000

HOFFMAN, VALERIE JANE, lawyer; b. Lowville, N.Y., Oct. 27, 1953; d. Russell Francis and Jane Marie (Fowler) H.; m. Michael J. Grillo, Apr. 4, 1996. Student, U. Edinburgh, Scotland, 1973-74; BA summa cum laude, Union Coll., 1975; JD, Boston Coll., 1978. Bar: Ill. 1978, U.S. Dist. Ct. (no. dist.) Ill. 1978, U.S. Ct. Appeals (3rd cir.) 1981, U.S. Ct. Appeals (7th cir.) 1983. Assoc. Seyfarth Shaw, Chgo., 1978-87; ptnr. Seyfarth and Shaw, 1987—. Adj. prof. Columbia Coll., 1985. Contbr. articles to legal publs. Dir. Remains Theatre, Chgo., 1981-95, pres., 1991-93, v.p., 1991-95; dir. The Nat. Conf. for Cmty. and Justice, Chgo. Region, 1993—, nat. trustee, 1995—; trustee bd. advisors Union Coll., 1996-99, trustee, 1999—; dir. AIDS Found. of Chgo., 1997—, sec., 1999—; trustee Union Coll., 1999—. Mem. ABA, Chgo. Bar Assn., Law Club Chgo., Univ. Club Chgo. (bd. dirs. 1984-87), Phi Beta Kappa. Office: Seyfarth Shaw 55 E Monroe St Ste 4400 Chicago IL 60603-5713

HOFFMANN, CHARLES WESLEY, retired foreign language educator; b. Sioux City, Iowa, Nov. 25, 1929; s. John Wesley and Gertrude J. (Giessen) H.; m. Barbara Brandel Frank, Aug. 11, 1954; children: Eric Gregory, Karla Jennifer. B.A., Oberlin Coll., 1951; M.A., U. Ill., 1952, Ph.D., 1956. Fulbright fellow U. Munich, Germany, 1953-55; Instr. German UCLA, 1956-58, asst. prof., 1958-64; assoc. prof. Ohio State U., 1964-66, prof., 1966—92, chmn. dept. German, 1969-77, 86-87. Author: Opposition Poetry in Nazi Germany, 1962, Survey of Research Tool Needs in German Language and Literature, 1978; also: articles on 20th Century German lit; adv. editor: Dimension, 1968-74. Recipient Disting. Teaching award UCLA, 1962, Lou Nemzer award for def. acad. freedom, 1982, Exemplary Faculty award Ohio State U., 1991; Fulbright grantee Germany, 1953-55, 1981. Mem. MLA, Am. Assn. Tchrs. German, ACLU, AAUP (pres. Ohio State U. 1984-86). Home: 291 Mccoy Ave Worthington OH 43085-3748 Office: Dieter Cunz Hall Columbus OH 43210

HOFFMANN, THOMAS RUSSELL, business management educator; b. Milw., Sept. 10, 1933; s. Alfred C. and Florence M. (Morlock) H.; m. Lorna G. Gruenzel, Aug. 31, 1957; 1 child, Timothy Jay. BS, U. Wis., 1955, MS, 1956, PhD, 1959. Engring. trainee Allis-Chalmers Mfg. Co., 1956-59; asst. prof. U. Wis. Sch. Commerce, 1959-63; mem. faculty U. Minn. Sch. Mgmt., Mpls., 1963-99, prof., 1965-99, chmn. dept. mgmt. scis., 1969-78; dir. West Bank Computer Center, 1971-87. Cons. to industry. Author: Production Management and Manufacturing Systems, 2 edit., 1967-71, (with others) Fortran 77: A Structured, Disciplined Style, 1978, 83, 88, Production and Inventory Management, 1983, 2d edit., 1991, Production and Operations Management, 1989; editor-in-chief Jour. Ops. Mgmt., 1993-95; contbr. articles to profl. jours. Chmn. long range planning com. Luth. Ch., 1971, pres., 1974, 89, treas., 1977-82, 93-98. Mem. Am. Prodn. and Inventory Control Soc. (pres. Twin Cities chpt., 1970-71, internat. pres. 1998). Home: 4501 Sedum Ln Edina MN 55435-4051 Office: U Minn Carlson Sch Mgmt Minneapolis MN 55455 E-mail: thoffmann@csom.umn.edu.

HOFFMEISTER, DONALD FREDERICK, zoology educator; b. San Bernardino, Calif., Mar. 21, 1916; s. Percival George and Julia Bell (Hillgartner) H.; m. Helen E. Kaatz, Aug. 11, 1938; m. 2d Florence Williamson, Aug. 15, 1995; children: James Ronald, Robert George. A.B., U. Calif.-Berkeley, 1938, M.A., 1940, Ph.D., 1944; ScD (hon.), MacMurray Coll., Jacksonville, Ill., 2000. Research, curatorial asst. Museum Vertebrate Zoology, U. Calif.-Berkeley, 1941-44, teaching asst. zoology, 1943-44; assoc. curator modern vertebrates Mus. Natural History, U. Kans., 1944-46, asst. prof. zoology, 1944-46; dir. Mus. Natural History, U. Ill., 1946-84, dir. emeritus, 1984—, mem. faculty univ., 1946—, prof. zoology, 1959-84, prof. emeritus, 1984—; research assoc. Mus. No. Ariz., 1969—. Author: Mammals, 1955, 1963, Fieldbook of Illinois Mammals, 1957, Zoo Animals, 1967, Mammals of Grand Canyon, 1971, Mammals of Ariz., 1986, Mammals of Illinois, 1989; also articles, reports. Fellow Ariz.-Nev. Acad. Sci.; mem. Am. Soc. Mammalogists (hon., sec. 1946-52, v.p. 1961-64, pres. 1964-66, Hartley H.T. Jackson award 1987), Midwest Mus. Conf. (hon., exec. v.p. 1962-63, pres. 1963-64), Am. Assn. Mus. (coun. 1973-76), Assn. Sci. Mus. Dirs. Home: 20 Fields E Champaign IL 61822-6129 Office: U Ill Mus Natural History Urbana IL 61801

HOFMAN, LEONARD JOHN, minister; b. Kent County, Mich., Jan. 31, 1928; s. Bert and Dora (Miedema) H.; m. H. Elaine (Ryskamp) H., Aug. 19, 1949; children: Laurie, Janice, Kathleen, Joel. BA, Calvin Coll., 1948; BTh, Calvin Sem., 1951, MDiv, 1981. Pastor Wright Christian Reformed Ch., Kanawha, Iowa, 1951-54, Kenosha Christian Reformed Ch., Kenosha, Wis., 1954-59, North St. Christian Reformed Ch., Zeeland, Mich., 1959-65, Ridgewood Christian Reformed Ch., Jenison, 1965-77, Bethany Christian Reformed Ch., Holland; pres. bd. trustees Christian Reformed Ch., Grand Rapids, 1977-82; gen. sec. Christian Reformed Ch. in N.Am., 1982-94, adminstrv. sec. for interchurch rels., 1995—. Sec. bd. trustees Calvin Coll., Grand Rapids, 1970-76. Recipient Oustanding Service award Calvin Alumni Assn., 1978. Mem. Nat. Assn. Evangelicals (bd. dirs. 1986-98, exec. com. bd. dirs. 1990-98, 2d vice chmn., bd. dirs. 1993-94, 1st vice chmn., bd. dirs. 1995-96, chmn. bd. dirs. 1997-98). Home and Office: 2237 Radcliff Cir SE Grand Rapids MI 49546-7725

HOFSOMMER, DONOVAN LOWELL, history educator; b. Ft. Dodge, Iowa, Apr. 10, 1938; s. Vernie George and Helma J. (Schager) H.; m. Sandra Louise Rusch, June 13, 1965; children: Kathryn Anne, Kristine Beret, Knute Lars. BA, U. Northern Iowa, 1960, MA, 1966; PhD, Okla. State U., 1973. Tchr. Fairfield (Iowa) High Sch., 1961-65; instr. U. Northern Iowa, Cedar Falls, 1965-66, Lea Coll., Albert Lea, Minn., 1966-70; teaching asst. Okla. State U., Stillwater, 1970-73; assoc. prof. and dept. head Wayland Coll., Plainview, Tex., 1973-81; corp. historian So. Pacific Co., San Francisco, 1981-85; hist. cons. Burlington No. Inc., Seattle, 1985-87; vis. prof. U. Mont., Missula, 1986-87; exec. dir. ctr. Western studies Augustana Coll., Sioux Falls, S.D., 1987-89; prof. history St. Cloud (Minn.) State U., 1989—. Cons. Dyanelectron and Dynarail, Pueblo, Colo., 1979-81, Grand Trunk Corp., Detroit, 1988-95; mem. editl. bd. annals of Iowa, Iowa City, 1975-94, R.R. history, Akron, Ohio, 1975—. Author: Prairie Oasis, 1975, Katy Northwest, 1976, Southern Pacific 1901-1985, 1986; co-author: History of Great Northern Railway, 1988, Quanah Route, 1991, Grand Trunk Corp., 1995; editor: Lexington Group Transport History, 1975—; mem. editl. bd. Annals of Iowa, Iowa City, 1975-92, R.R. History, Akron, Ohio, 1975—. With U.S. Army, 1960-66. Mem. Okla. Hist. Soc. (Wright Heritage award 1979), Ry. and Locomotive Hist. Soc. (Book award 1988, Sr. Achievement award 1995), Western History Assn., Orgn. Am. Historians, State Hist. Soc. Iowa, Am. Assn. for State and Local History. Presbyterian. Home: 1803 13th Ave SE Saint Cloud MN 56304-2231 Office: St Cloud State U Dept History Saint Cloud MN 56301

HOFSTADTER, DOUGLAS RICHARD, cognitive scientist, educator, writer; b. N.Y.C., Feb. 15, 1945; s. Robert and Nancy (Givan) H.; m. Carol Ann Brush, 1985; children: Daniel Frederic, Monica Marie. B.S. in Math. with distinction, Stanford U., 1965; M.S., U. Oreg., 1972, Ph.D. in Physics, 1975. Asst. prof. computer sci. Ind. U., Bloomington, 1977-80, assoc. prof., 1980-84; Walgreen prof. Cognitive Sci. U. Mich., Ann Arbor, 1984-88; prof. cognitive sci., computer sci. Ind. U., Bloomington, 1988—. Adj. prof. psychology, philosophy, history and philosophy of sci., comparative lit., dir. Ctr. for Rsch. on Concepts and Cognition, Ind. U. Author: Gödel, Escher, Bach: an Eternal Golden Braid, 1979, Metamagical Themas, 1985, Ambigrammi, 1987, Fluid Concepts and Creative Analogies, 1995, Rhapsody on a Theme by Clément Marot, 1996, Le Ton beau de Marot, 1997; editor: (with Daniel C. Dennett) The Mind's I, 1981; columnist: Metamagical Themas in Sci. Am., 1981-83. Recipient Pulitzer prize for gen. nonfiction, 1980; Am. Book award, 1980; Guggenheim fellow, 1980-81 Mem. Cognitive Sci. Soc., Am. Assn. Artificial Intelligence, Am. Lit. Translators Assn. Office: Ctr Rsch Concepts & Cognition 510 N Fess St Bloomington IN 47408-3822

HOGAN, BRIAN JOSEPH, editor; b. Aberdeen, S.D., Apr. 11, 1943; s. Arthur James and Magdalena (Frison) H.; m. Jamie Isabelle Schwingel, June 21, 1987. BS in Aerospace and Mech. Engring., U. Ariz., 1965, BS in Geophysics-Geochemistry, 1968; MS in Journalism, U. Utah, 1972. Rsch. asst. U. Va. Rsch. Labs for Engring. Scis., Charlottesville, 1965-66; exploration geophysicist Anaconda Co., Tucson, 1968-71; assoc. editor Benwill Pub. Co., Brookline, Mass., 1973-74; asst. editor Design News, Boston, 1974-75, midwest editor Chgo., 1975-87, sr. editor Newton, Mass., 1987-89, mng. editor, 1989-97; chief editor Mfg. Engring.-Soc. Mfg. Engrs., Dearborn, Mich. Author stage plays The Young O'Neil, 1983, Awakening, 1984. Precinct worker Cook County Rep. Com., Oak Park, Ill., 1986-87; interpreter Frank Lloyd Wright Home and Studio Found., Oak Park, 1981-87. Recipient numerous awards Am. Soc. Bus. Press Editors, Soc. Tech. Communication, Aviation Space Writers Assn. Mem. Am. Soc. Bus. Press Editors, Am. Hist. Print Collectors Soc. Republican. Roman Catholic. Avocations: photography, print collecting, cycling, hiking. Office: Mfg Engring 1 SME Dr PO Box 930 Dearborn MI 48121-0930 E-mail: hogabri@sme.org.

HOGAN, MICHAEL RAY, life science executive; b. Newark, Apr. 21, 1953; s. Raymond Carl and Mary Adele (Whalen) H.; m. Martha Ann Gorman, July 24, 1976; children: Colleen Michael, Patrick Gorman, Mary Kate, Andrei Sean. BA, Loyola U., Chgo., 1978; M in Mgmt. with distinction, Northwestern U., 1980. Cert. FLMI, HIA. Assoc. McKinsey & Co., Inc., Chgo., 1980-81, engagement mgr., 1982-83; sr. v.p., treas. FBS Ins. Co., Mpls., 1984-85; group v.p., gen. mgr. Gen. Am. Life Ins. Co., St. Louis, 1986, v.p., 1987-89, exec. v.p., 1990-95; pres., CEO Cova Corp., 1995-96; corp. v.p., controller Monsanto Co., 1996-99; v.p., CFO, CAO Sigma-Aldrich Corp., 1999—. Cons. Swedish Trade Commn., Chgo., 1978, Lee Wards Creative Crafts Co., Elgin, Ill., 1979; chmn. Consultec, Inc., Atlanta, 1990-95, Cova Fin. Life Ins. Co., Oakbrook Terrace, 1995; chmn., CEO Genelco, Inc., St. Louis, 1990-95; mem. adv. bd. Integrated Hlth Svcs. Managed Care, Owings Mills, Md., 1994—; pres. GenCare Hlth Sys., Inc., 1990-95; bd. dirs. Allegiant Bancorporation, 2001—. Contb. articles to profl. jours. Active Experience St. Louis, 1986; mem. Leadership Ctr. of Greater St. Louis, 1987-95, bd. dirs., 1988-95, v.p. comms., 1989-90, pres., 1991-92; bd. dirs. Focus St. Louis, Inc., 1996—; treas., 1996-98; bd. dirs. Combined Health Appeal of Greater St. Louis, 1992-97, v.p. programs, 1992-94, pres., 1995-96; bd. dirs. St. Louis Coll. Pharmacy, 1995-2000, Wyman Ctr., 1997-2000, Combined Health Appeal of Am., 1997-98, United Way of Greater St. Louis, 1997—, vice-chmn., 1997-99, Small World Adoption Found., 1998—, pres., 2000—. Scholar F.C. Austin Found., 1978-80, Phi Gamma Nu, 1980; recipient Nat. Vol. of Yr. award Combined Health Appeal of Am., 1996, Person of Yr. award Juvenile Diabetes Assn. St. Louis chpt., 1998, Gala Honoree, 1998, Health Citizen of Yr. award Combined Health Appeal Greater St. Louis, 1998, Corp. Leadership Divsn. award United Way Gtr. St. Louis, 1993, 95, Employee Divsn. award, 1997, 98. Mem. Beta Gamma Sigma, Greenbriar Hills Country Club. Roman Catholic. Avocations: reading, family, golf, travel. Home: 9368 Robyn Hills Dr Saint Louis MO 63127-1316

HOGENKAMP, HENRICUS PETRUS CORNELIS, biochemistry researcher, biochemistry educator; b. Doesburg, Gelderland, The Netherlands, Dec. 20, 1925; came to U.S., 1958; s. Johannes Hermanus and Maria Margaretha J. (Abeln) H.; m. Lieke Ter Haar, Apr. 25, 1953; children: Harry Peter, Derk John, Margaret Angelina. BSA, U. B.C., Vancouver, 1957, MSc, 1958; PhD, U. Calif., Berkeley, 1961. Rsch. biochemist U. Calif., Berkeley, 1961-62; assoc. scientist Fisheries Rsch. Bd. Can., Vancouver, B.C., 1962-63; asst. prof. U. Iowa, Iowa City, 1963-67, assoc. prof., 1967-71, prof., 1971-76; prof., head dept. biochemistry U. Minn.,

Mpls., 1976-92, prof. dept. biochemistry, 1992—. Vis. prof. Australian Nat. U., Canberra, Australia, 1966-67, Philipps U., Marburg, Fed. Republic of Germany, 1986-87, 1988, 1990; guest scientist U. Calif. Los Alamos (N.Mex) Sci. Lab., 1974-75. Sgt. Royal Netherlands Army, 1946-50, Indonesia. Recipient Alexander von Humboldt-Stiftung award Philipps U.-Fachbereich Microbiology, Marburg, Fed. Republic of Germany, 1986-87; named to Minn. Acad. Medicine,Mpls., 1980--; Guggenheim fellow U. Iowa, Iowa City, 1974-75. Mem. AAAS, Am. Chem. Soc., Am. Soc. Biochemistry and Molecular Biology (mem. pub. affairs com. 1986-91), Assn. Med. Sch. Depts. Biochemistry, Internat. Union Biochemists (chmn. U.S. nominating com. 1988). Home: 2211 Marion Rd Saint Paul MN 55113-3805 Office: U Minn Med Sch Dept Biochem 4 225 Millard Hall 435 Delaware St SE Minneapolis MN 55455-0347

HOGG, ROBERT VINCENT, JR. mathematical statistician, educator; b. Hannibal, Mo., Nov. 8, 1924; s. Robert Vincent and Isabelle Frances (Storrs) H.; m. Carolyn Joan Ladd, June 23, 1956 (dec. June 1990); children: Mary Carolyn, Barbara Jean, Allen Ladd, Robert Mason; m. Ann Burke, Oct. 15, 1994. BA, U. Ill., 1947; MS, U. Iowa, 1948, PhD, 1950. Asst. prof. math. U. Iowa, Iowa City, 1950-56, assoc. prof., 1956-62, prof., 1962-65, chmn. dept. stats., prof. stats., 1965-83, 92-93, Hanson prof. mfg. productivity, 1993-95, prof. emeritus, 2001—. Co-author: Introduction to Mathematical Statistics, 1959, 5th edit., 1995, Finite Mathematics and Calculus, 1974, Probability and Statistical Inference, 1977, 6th edit., 2000, Applied Statistics for Engineers and Physical Scientists, 1987, 2d edit., 1992; assoc. editor Am. Stats., 1971-74; contbr. articles to profl. jours. Vestryman local Episc. ch., 1958-60, 66-68, 91-92, 2001—. With USNR, 1943-46. Grantee NIH, 1966-68, 75-78, NSF, 1969-74. Fellow Inst. Math. Stats. (program sec., bd. bd. 1968-74), Am. Statis. Assn. (pres. Iowa sect. 1962-63, coun. 1965-66, 73-74, vis. lectr. 1965-68, 77-85, chmn. tng. sect. 1973, assoc. editor jour. 1978-80, pres.-elect 1987, pres. 1988, past pres. 1989, Founders award 1991, Noether award 2001); mem. Math. Assn. Am. (pres. Iowa sect. 1964-65, 95-96, bd. govs. 1971-74, visa. lectr. 1976-81, Outstanding Tchg. award 1993), Internat. Statis. Inst., Rotary (pres. Iowa City 1984-85), Sigma Xi (pres. Iowa dist. chpt. 1970-71), Pi Kappa Alpha. Home: 30130 Trails End Buena Vista CO 81211 Office: U Iowa Dept Statis Acturial Sci Iowa City IA 52242 E-mail: bhogg@starband.net.

HOGLE, WALTER S. career officer; BA in Psychology, Hartwick Coll., 1966; Diploma, Squadron Officer Sch., 1970; MS in Counseling, Troy State U., 1975; Diploma, Armed Forces Staff Coll., 1980, Nat. War Coll., 1986. Commd. 2d lt. USAF, 1967, advanced through ranks to lt. gen., 1998; various assignments tocomdr. 437th Airlift Wing, Charleston AFB, S.C., 1994-95; dir. of plans Hdqtrs. Air Mobility Command, Scott AFB, Ill., 1995-98; vice-comdr. Air Mobility Command, 1998—. Decorated Disting. Svc. medal, Legion of Merit with oak leaf cluster, Disting. Flying Cross, Bronze Star, Meritorious Svc. medal with two oak leaf clusters, Air medal with five oak leaf clusters, Air Force Commendation medal with oak leaf cluster, Republic of Vietnam Gallantry Cross with Palm, others. Office: AMC/CV 402 Scott Dr Unit 3ec Scott Air Force Base IL 62225-5300

HOGUET, DAVID DILWORTH, rental furniture executive; b. Sharon, Conn., Aug. 16, 1951; s. Joseph Lynch Hoguet and Diana Wood (Dilworth) Wantz; m. Karen Meisel, Oct. 9, 1983; children: Jennifer Leigh, Laura Beth. BA in History, U. Pa., 1973; MBA in Fin., NYU, 1975. With W.R. Grace, N.Y.C., 1975-1980; treas. Chemed Corp., Cin., 1981-1983, v.p. fin., treas., 1984-86; pres. Globe Funriture Rentals, 1986-89, chmn., 1989—. Fundraiser Brooks Sch., North Andover, Mass., 1978—. Mem. Funriture Rental Assn. Am. (pres. 1991—), Young Pres. Orgn., Losantiville Club, Racquet Club. Avocation: squash. Home: 740 Crevelings Ln Cincinnati OH 45226-1713 Office: Globe Business Resources 1925 Greenwood Ave Cincinnati OH 45246-6247

HOGUET, KAREN M. retail department store executive; m. David Hoguet; 2 children. Grad., Brown U.; MBA, Harvard U., 1980. With Boston Cons. Group, Chgo.; sr. cons. mktg. and long-range planning Federated Dept. Stores, Inc., Cin., 1982-85, dir. capital and bus. planning, 1985-87, operating v.p. planning and fin. analysis, 1987-88, corp. v.p., 1988-91, sr. v.p. planning, 1991—, treas., 1992—, CFO, 1997—, sr. v.p., CFO. Mem. Phi Beta Kappa. Office: Federated Dept Stores Inc 7 W 7th St Cincinnati OH 45202-2424 Fax: 513-579-7555.

HOHULIN, MARTIN, state legislator; b. Ft. Scott, Kans., May 1, 1964; m. Marilyn Hohulin; 1 child, William. State rep. Dist. 126 Mo. State Congress, 1991—. Mem. agr.-bus. consumer protection com., ranking rep. appropriations and labor com.; farm owner and operator. Mem. Cattlemens Assn., Barton County Farm Bur., Lamar Metro Club.

HOITINK, HENRICUS A. plant pathology educator; PhD in Phytobacteriology, U. Wis. Prof. plant pathology and environ. grad. studies program Ohio State U., Wooster. Recipient Ruth Allen award Am. Phytopathol. Soc., 1998. Achievements include development of principles for conversion of solid wastes into products beneficial to society, to determine how beneficial microorganisms in composts provide biological control of plant diseases. Office: OARDC Plant Pathology 211 Selby Hall 1680 Madison Ave Wooster OH 44691-4096 E-mail: hoitink.1@osu.edu.

HOKENSTAD, MERL CLIFFORD, JR. social work educator; b. Norfolk, Nebr., July 21, 1936; s. Merl Clifford and Flora Diane (Christian) H.; m. Dorothy Jean Tarrell, June 24, 1962; children: Alene Ann, Laura Rae, Marta Lynn. B.A. summa cum laude, Augustana Coll., 1958; Rotary Found. fellow, Durham (Eng.) U., 1958-59; M.S.W., Columbia U., 1962; Ph.D., Brandeis U., 1969, Inst. Ednl. Mgmt., Harvard U., 1977. With Lower East Side Neighborhood Assn., N.Y.C., 1962-64; community planning assoc. United Community Services, Sioux Falls, S.D., 1964-66; instr. Augustana Coll., 1964-66; research assoc. Ford Found. Project on Community Planning for Elderly, Brandeis U., Waltham, Mass., 1966-67; prof., dir. Sch. Social Work, Western Mich. U., Kalamazoo, 1968-74; prof., dean Sch. Applied Social Scis., Case Western Res. U., Cleve., 1974-83, Ralph and Dorothy Schmitt prof., 1983—, chmn. PhD program, 1990-94; prof. internat. health Sch. of Medicine, 1994—. Vis. prof. Inst. Sociology, Stockholm U., 1978, Fulbright lectr., 1980; vis. prof. Nat. Inst. Social Work, London, 1981, Sch. Social Work, Stockholm U., 1982-86, Eotvos Lorand U., Budapest, Hungary, 1992, 95, 96, London Sch. Econs., 1994; Fulbright rsch. scholar Inst. Applied Social Rsch., Oslo, 1989; fellow U. Canterbury, Christchurch, New Zealand, 1994; mem. UN tech. com. World Assembly on Aging, 2000-02; mem. U.S. delegation UN World Assembly on Aging, 2002. Author: Participation in Teaching and Learning: An Idea Book for Social Work Educators; editor: Meeting Human Needs: An International Annual, Vol. V, Linking Health Care and Social Services: International Perspectives; editor-in-chief Internat. Social Work Jour., 1985-87; co-editor: Profiles in Internat. Social Work, 1992, Issues in International Social Work, 1997, (internat. issue) Jour. Gerontol. Social Work, 1988, (internat. mental health issue) Jour. Sociology and Social Welfare, 1990, Jour. Social Policy and Administration, 1993, Jour. Aging Internat., 1994, Jour. Applied Social Scis., 1996; contbr. articles to profl. jours., chpts. to books. Mem. alcohol tng. rev. com. Nat. Inst. Alcoholism and Alcohol Abuse, 1974-78; workshop leader Am. Assn. State Colls. and Univs., 1974; chmn. U.S. com. XVIII Internat. Congress Schs. Social Work, 1976; chmn. Kalamazoo County Cmty. Mental Health Svcs. Bd., 1971, vice chmn., 1972; mem. edn. and tng. task force Mich. Office Drug Abuse and Alcoholism, 1972-73; mem. Mich. Assn. Mental Health Bds., 1972; bd. dirs. Cleve. United Way Svcs., 1982-84, del. assembly, 1974-82, mem. periodic rev. oversight com., 1982, mem. leadership devel. com., 1978, cmty. resources com., 1988—; bd. dirs. Kalamazoo United Way, 1968-72; trustee Cleve. Internat. Program for Youth Workers and Social Workers, chmn. program com., 1985-87; mem. program devel. com. Cleve. Center on Alcoholism, 1976; trustee Alcoholism Services Cleve., Inc., 1977-86, v.p., 1982-85; trustee Cmty. Info./Vol. Action Ctr., 1982-88, chmn. leadership devel. com., 1984-86, chmn. unmet needs com., 1986-88, exec. com., 1985-88, v.p., 1986-88; exec. com. Western Reserve Geriatric Edn. Ctr., 1995—; mem. adv. com. Coun. for Internat. Exch. Scholars, 1991-93, Fedn. for Cmty. Planning Coun. on Older Persons, 1991—, chmn. caregiver support program initiative, 1995-96; mem. adv. coun. Cuyahoga County Dept. Sr. and Adult Svcs., 1998—, chair, 2001—; mem. task force of social transition in Soviet Union, U.S. State Dept. Bur. Human Rights and Humanitarian Affairs; mem. UN NGO Com. on Aging, 1996—; co-chmn. U.S. Com. for Internat. Yr. of Older Persons, 1999. Named Outstanding Alumnus, Augustana Coll., 1980, Ohio Soc. Worker of the Yr., 1992; Fulbright Research fellow; NIMH trainee, 1960-62; Vocat. Rehab. trainee, 1966; Gerontology trainee, 1967; Rotary Found. fellow, 1958-59 Mem. NASW (internat. com. 1989-93, chmn. 1992-93), Acad. Cert. Social Workers, Internat. Assn. Schs. Social Work (exec. bd. 1978-92, 98—, treas. 1978-86, v.p. N.Am. 1988-92, membership sec. 1996-2000), Internat. Coun. on Social Welfare (dir. U.S. com. 1982-92), Coun. on Social Work Edn. (del. 1972-75, 77-83, chmn. ann. program meeting 1973, chmn. com. on nat. legis. and adminstrv. policy 1975-79, mem. nominating com. 1978-81, internat. com. 1980-86, 96—, chmn. com. 1982-84, dir. 1979-82, exec. com. 1986-89, pres. 1986-89), Nat. Conf. on Social Welfare (bd. dirs. 1978-80, chmn. sect. V program com. 1977-78), World Future Soc. (area coord. 1972-74), Fulbright Assn. (v.p. N.E. Ohio chpt. 1990-91), Nat. Coun. on Aging (bd. dirs. 1991-97, internat. com. 1991-97, pub. policy com. 1992-97). Democrat. Episcopalian. Home: 2917 Weymouth Rd Cleveland OH 44120-2234 Office: Case Western Res U 10900 Euclid Ave Cleveland OH 44106-1712 E-mail: mch2@po.cwru.edu.

HOKIN, LOWELL EDWARD, biochemist, educator; b. Chgo., Sept. 20, 1924; s. Oscar E. and Helen (Manfield) H.; m. Mabel Neaverson, Dec. 1, 1952 (div. Dec. 1973); children: Linda Ann, Catherine Esther (dec.), Samuel Arthur; m. Barbara M. Gallagher, Mar. 23, 1978 (div. July 1998); 1 child, Ian Oscar. Student, U. Chgo., 1942-43, Dartmouth Coll., 1943-44, U. Louisville Sch. Medicine, 1944-46, U. Ill. Sch. Medicine, 1946-47; MD, U. Louisville, 1948; PhD, U. Sheffield, Eng., 1952. Postdoctoral fellow dept. biochemistry McGill U., 1952-54, faculty, 1954-57, asst. prof., 1955-57; mem. faculty U. Wis., Madison, 1957—, prof. physiol. chemistry, 1961-68, prof. pharmacology, 1968-99, prof., chmn. pharmacology, 1968-93, prof. emeritus, 1999—. Contbr. numerous articles to tech. jours., chpts. to numerous books on phosphoinositides, biol. transport, the pancreas, the brain and lithium in manic-depression. With USNR, 1943-45. Mem. AAAS, Am. Soc. Biochemistry and Molecular Biology, Biochem. Soc. (U.K.), Am. Soc. Pharmacology and Exptl. Therapeutics, N.Y. Acad. Scis. Home: 4021C Monona Dr Monona WI 53716 Office: U Wis Med Sch Dept Pharm 1300 University Ave Madison WI 53706-1510 E-mail: lehokin@facstaff.wisc.edu.

HOLABIRD, JOHN AUGUR, JR. retired architect; b. Chgo., May 9, 1920; s. John Augur and Dorothy (Hackett) H.; m. Donna Katharine Smith, Nov. 25, 1942 (div. 1969); children: Jean, Katharine, Polly, Lisa (dec.); m. Marcia Stefanie Fergestad, June 28, 1969 (dec. Mar. 1994); children: Ann, Lynn; m. Janet Nothhelfer Connor, May 7, 1996. BA, Harvard U., 1942, MArch, 1948. Archtl. designer Holabird & Root, Chgo., 1948-49, 55-64, assoc. firm, 1964-70, ptnr., 1970-87. Tchr. drama Francis Parker Sch., Chgo., 1949-55; stage designer NBC-TV, 1955 Major: archtl. works include Francis Parker Sch, Chgo., Ravinia Stage and Restaurant, Highland Park, Ill., 1970, Bell Telephone Labs, Naperville, Ill., 1975, Canal Bldg, Chgo., 1974. Pres. Park West Community Assn., 1962; dir. Lincoln Park Conservation Assn., 1960-64, Corlands, 1979-85; mem. Chgo. Commn. on Historic and Archtl. Landmarks, 1981-85; bd. dirs. Lincoln Park Community Conservation, 1964; trustee Francis Parker Sch., Ravinia Festival Assn., Ill. Inst. Tech., 1980-86. Served with U.S. Army, 1942-45. Decorated Silver Star, Bronze Star; Fourragère (Belgium); Order of William (The Netherlands). Fellow AIA (pres. Chgo. chpt. 1977-78); mem. Tavern Club, Harvard Club (dir. 1974-78), Phi Beta Kappa. Democrat. Home: 200 E Pearson St Apt 3W Chicago IL 60611-2352 Office: Holabird & Root 300 W Adams St Chicago IL 60606-5101

HOLBROOK, JOHN SCOTT, JR. lawyer; b. Milw., Oct. 27, 1939; s. John Scott Holbrook and Francesca Marie (Eschweiler) Davidson; m. Mary Lynn Lorenz, June 13, 1980. BA, StanfordU., Palo Alto, Calif., 1961; JD, U. Mich., 1964. Bar: Wis. 1964. Ptnr. Quarles & Brady, Madison, Wis., 1964—. Mem. ABA, State Bar of Wis., Nat. Assn. of Bond Lawyers, Am. Coll. Bond Counsel. Office: Quarles & Brady 1 S Pinckney St Madison WI 53703-2892

HOLBROOK, THOMAS ALDREDGE, state legislator; b. St. Louis, Nov. 23, 1949; Ill. state rep. Dist. 113, 1995—. Office: 9200 W Main St Ste 4 Belleville IL 62223-1710

HOLDEN, BOB, governor; b. Kansas City, Mo. m. Lori Hauser; children: Robert, John. BS in Polit. Sci., Southwest Mo. State; Degree Kennedy Sch. Govt. for Public Execs. and Flemming Fellow Leadership Inst., Harvard U. Former adminstrv. asst./liaison U.S. Congressman Richard Gephardt, St. Louis; mem. Mo. Ho. of Reps., 1983-89; now state treas. State of Mo., Jefferson City, 1993—. Chmn. gen. approations com.; co-sponsor Excellence in Edn. Act; mem. Bd. Fund Commrs., Mo. State Employees Retirement System, Mo. Bus. Coun., Mo. Rural Opportunities Coun.; past chmn. Mo. Housing Devel. Commn. Dean Am. Legion Mo. Boy's State Legislative Sch.; mem. Holden Scholarship Fund, Leadership St. Louis; former mem. Confluence's Edn. Implementation, Tower Grove Hgts. Neighborhood Assn., Save the Children's Program; mem. Mo. Coun. Econ. Edn., Coun. State Govts.; vice-chair Mo. Cultural Trust. Mem. Nat. Assn. State Treas. (legis. chair). Office: St Treasurer PO Box 210 Jefferson City MO 65102-0210

HOLDEN, ROBERT WATSON, radiologist, educator, university dean; b. Brazil, Ind., Mar. 31, 1936; s. John William and Naomi Ellen (Watson) H.; m. Miriam Ann Bognanno, June 20, 1964; children: Anne, Robert II, Jennifer. BS in Pharmacy, Purdue U., 1958; MD, Ind. U., 1963. Diplomate Am. Bd. Radiology. Intern L.A. County Gen. Hosp., 1963-64; resident radiology Vanderbilt U., Nashville, 1970-73; asst. prof. Ind. U. Sch. Medicine, Indpls., 1973-77, assoc. prof., 1977-82, prof., 1982—, prof., chmn. dept. radiology, 1991-95, dean, 1996—2000; ret., 2000. Chief vascular and interventional radiology Wishard Meml. Hosp., Indpls., 1973-79, chief radiology, 1977-91; counselor NIH, 1990-94. Contbr. over 100 articles to profl. jours. Chmn. bldg. com. 1st United Meth. Ch., Mooresville, 1988-95. Capt. U.S. Army, 1964-66. Recipient Gold medal Assn. Univ. Radiologists, 1999, Gold medal Am. Roentgen Ray Soc., 2000; named Disting. Alumnus, Purdue U. Sch. Phharmacy, 1992. Fellow Soc. Cardiovascular and Interventional Radiology, Am. Coll. Radiology (counselor), Radiologic Soc. N.Am. (counselor), Ind. Roentgen Soc. (past pres.). Republican. Avocations: forestry, agriculture, tennis. Office: Ind U Sch Medicine fH 302 1120 South Dr Rm 302 Indianapolis IN 46202-5135

HOLDERMAN, JAMES F., JR. federal judge; b. 1946; BS, U. Ill., 1968, JD, 1971. Judge U.S. Dist. Ct. (no. dist.) Ill., Chgo., 1985—; asst. U.S. atty. City of Chgo., 1972-78; ptnr. Sonnenschein, Carlin et al, Chgo., 1978-85. Lectr. law U. Chgo., 1983—. Office: US Dist Ct US Courthouse 219 S Dearborn St Ste 2146 Chicago IL 60604-1801

HOLIHEN, JENNIFER A. real estate development company executive; CFO, treas., sec. Crossman Cmtys., Inc., Indpls., 1996—. Office: Crossman Cmtys Inc 9202 N Meridian St Ste 300 Indianapolis IN 46260-1833

HOLLAND, EUGENE, JR. lumber company executive; b. Lincoln, Nebr., Dec. 13, 1922; s. Eugene and Louise (Bedwell) H.; m. Martha Randall, May 15, 1948; children: Diane Holland Drewry, Randall, Mary susan Boyd, Jean, Robert Lawrence. A.B., Princeton U., 1944. V.p., dir. Holland Lumber Co. Chmn. Chgo. bus. div. Am. Cancer Soc., 1961; dir. Kenilworth United Fund, 1961-63, Commerce and Industry div. Crusade of Mercy, 1972; Bd. dirs. Evanston Hosp. Served with USNR, 1943-46. Clubs: Princeton (Chgo.), Chicago (Chgo.); Princeton (N.Y.C.); Glen View. Home: 416 Sheridan Rd Kenilworth IL 60043-1221 Office: 231 S La Salle St Chicago IL 60604-1407

HOLLAND, JOHN MADISON, retired family practice physician; b. Holden, W.Va., Oct. 7, 1927; s. Ophia I. and Lou V. (Elliott) H.; m. Mary Louise Bourne, Sept. 2, 1950; children— David, Stephen, Nancy B.S., Eastern Ky. State U., Richmond, 1949; M.D., U. Louisville, 1952. Diplomate Am. Bd. Family Practice, Am. Bd. Hospice and Palliative Medicine. Intern St. Joseph Infirmary, Louisville, 1952-53; gen. practice family medicine Physicians Group, Springfield, Ill., 1955-80; med. dir. St. John's Hosp., 1971-94, St. John's Hospice, 1995—; clin. prof. family practice So. Ill. U., Springfield, 1978—; ret., 1995. Served to capt. USAF, 1953-55 Mem. Am. Acad. Family Physicians, Am. Acad. Hospice/Palliative Medicine. Baptist Home: 2131 Lindsay Rd Springfield IL 62704-3242 E-mail: docholl70@aol.com.

HOLLAND, JOY, health care facility executive; b. N.Y.C., Oct. 24, 1946; d. Harry Walson and Edna May (Simmons) H.; m. Chesley Roderick Richardson, Sept.21, 1985; children: Carl Allen Fields, Craig Anthony Fields. AA in Nursing, Olive-Harvey Coll., 1972; BS, St. Joseph Coll., Bklyn., 1976; M in Health Adminstrn., C.W. Post Coll., 1978. Staff nurse U. Chgo. Hosp. and Clinics, Chgo., 1972; head nurse N.Y. Hosp., N.Y.C., 1972; clinic adminstr. Morrisania-Montefiore Hosp., Bronx, N.Y., 1973; head nurse, supr. Pilgrim Psychiat. Hosp., Brentwood, 1974, assoc. dir. staff devel., 1974-76, dir. nursing, 1976-78; surveyor, cons Joint Commn. on Accrediation of Hosps., Chgo., 1978-82; dir. Ypsilanti (Mich.) Regional Psychiat. Hosp., 1986-90, Clinton Valley Ctr., Pontiac, Mich., 1990-93, Huron Valley Ctr., Ypsilanti, 1993-99, Southgate Ctr., 1999-2001; CEO St. Elizabeth's Hosp., 2001—. Dep. commr. dept. mental health State of Ohio, 1980-82; cons. Joint Commn. Accreditation of Hosps.; adj. lectr. Sch. Nursing, U. Mich.; cons. specialist, bd. dirs. Holland-Richardson Assocs., Detroit. Contbr. author (book) Guide to J.C.A.H. Nursing Standards, 1985, 86 edits. Bd. dirs. Women in Crisis, Inc., N.Y.C., 1979-85, Washtenaw County (Mich.) ARC; bd. dirs. psychiatry dept. Chelsea (Mich.) Hosp., 1989-91. Mem. N.Y. Acad. Sci. (life), Bus. and Profl. Women, Inc., Masons, Order Ea. Star, Alpha Kappa Alpha, Sigma Theta Tau. Republican. Avocations: chess, crochet, walking. Home: 425 8th St NW Apt 634 Washington DC 20004-2113 Office: St Elizabeths Hospital 2700 Martin Luther King Drive Washington DC 20004

HOLLAND, KEN, sports team executive; b. Vernon, B.C., Can. m. Cindy Holland; children: Brad, Julie, Rachel, Greg. Hockey player Medicine Hat, 1974-75, Toronto Maple Leafs, 1975-80, Hartford, 1980-83, Detroit Red Wings, 1983-84, Binghamton, Springfield, amateur scouting dir., asst. gen. mgr., gen. mgr., 1997—. Inductee Binghamton Hall of Fame, 1998. Office: c/o Detroit Red Wings 600 Civic Center Dr Detroit MI 48226-4408

HOLLAND, ROBERT, JR. food products executive; b. 1940; Married; 3 children. BSME, Union Coll.; MBA in Internat. Mktg., Baruch Coll. Assoc. McKinsey & Co., 1968-81; chmn., CEO Rokher-J, White Plains, N.Y. and, Mich., 1984-87, 91-95; chmn. Gilreath Mfg., 1987-91; pres., CEO Ben & Jerry's Homemade, Inc., Waterbury, Vt., 1995—. Bd. dirs. Olin Corp., Mut. N.Y., TruMark Mfg. Co., Middlesex Mut. Ins. Co., UNC Ventures. Chmn. bd. trustees Spelman Coll.; trustee Atlanta Univ. Ctr.; dir. Lincoln Ctr. Theater, Harlem Jr. Tennis Program. Office: Ben & Jerry's Homemade PO Box 240 Waterbury VT 05676-0240

HOLLANDER, ADRIAN WILLOUGHBY, accounting services company executive; b. Sumter, S.C., Oct. 12, 1941; s. Willard Fisher and Mildred Hanna (Willoughby) H.; m. Eleanor Busby Smith, May 26, 1963; children: Richard, David, Robert. BS, Iowa State U., 1963. CPA; cert. info. system auditor; cert. internal auditor; cert. bank auditor; cert. fin. svcs. auditor. Mem. audit and cons. staff Arthur Andersen and Co., Chgo., 1965-71; auditor Beverly Bancorporation, 1971-73; v.p. Cullinane Corp., 1973-78; auditor Cen. Nat. Bank in Chgo., 1978-79; pres. EDP Audit Assocs., Inc., Summit, Ill., 1980, Complus, Inc., Hickory Hills, 1982-87, Chgo., 1987—. Cons., owner EDP Audit Service, Chgo., 1979—. Contbr. articles to profl. jours. Trustee St. Paul's Union Ch., Chgo., 1973-75; bd. dirs. Beverly Improvement Assn., Chgo., 1972-88; council of dels. Beverly Area Planning Assn., Chgo., 1980-85; del. Chgo. Agenda for Pub. Edn., 1983-87. Served to 1st lt. U.S. Army, 1963-65. Mem. AICPA, Ill. CPA Soc. (sec. Chgo. South chpt. 1991-92, treas. 1992-93, v.p. 1993-94, sr. v.p. 1994-95, pres. 1995-96, del. 1996-97), Info. Systems Audit and Control Assn., Nat. Assn. Fin. Svcs. Auditors, Inst. Internal Auditors, Chgo. Beverly Ridge Lions Club (pres. 1992-93). Republican. Avocations: fishing, camping, scouting. Home: 9360 S Pleasant Ave Chicago IL 60620-5644 Office: Complus Inc 9500 S Vanderpoel Ave Chicago IL 60643-1228

HOLLE, REGINALD HENRY, retired bishop; b. Burton, Tex., Nov. 21, 1925; s. Alfred W. and Lena (Nolte) H.; m. Marla C. Christianson, June 16, 1949; children: Todd, Joan. BA, Capital U., 1946, DD (hon.), 1979; MDiv, Trinity Luth. Sem., 1949; D of Ministry, Ohio Consortium Religious Stdy, 1977; DD (hon.), Wittenberg U., 1989. Ordained minister Evang. Luth. Ch. Am., then bishop. Assoc. pastor Zion Luth. Ch., Sandusky, Ohio, 1949-51; sr. pastor Salem Meml. Luth. Ch., Detroit, 1951-72, Parma Luth. Ch., Cleve., 1973-78; bishop Mich. dist. Am. Luth. Ch., Detroit, 1978-87; bishop NW Lower Mich. Synod Evang. Luth. Ch., Lansing, 1988-95. Bd. dirs. Aubsburg Fortress Pub. House, Wittenberg U. Author: Planning for Funerals, 1978; contbr. to Augsburg Sermon Series. Bd. dirs. Ronald McDonald House Ctrl. Mich., 1995—, Planned Giving Luth. Social Svcs. Mich., 1995—. Recipient Pub. Svc. citation Harper Woods City Coun., 1976, Recognition for Community Svc., Detroit Pub. Schs., 1974. E-mail: rholle@juno.com.

HOLLENBAUGH, H(ENRY) RITCHEY, lawyer; b. Shelby, Ohio, Nov. 12, 1947; m. Diane Robinson Nov. 21, 1973 (div. 1989); children: Chad Ritchey, Katie Paige; m. Rebecca U., Aug. 8, 1995. BA, Kent State U., 1969; JD, Capital U., 1973. Bar: Ohio 1973, U.S. Dist. Ct. (so. dist.) Ohio 1974, U.S. Ct. Appeals (6th cir.) 1976, U.S. Supreme Ct. 1978. Investigator Ohio Civil Rights Com., Columbus, Ohio, 1969-72; legal intern City Atty.'s Office, 1972-73, asst. city prosecutor, 1973-75, sr. asst. city atty., 1975-76; ptnr. Hunter, Hollenbaugh & Theodotou, 1976-85, Delligatti, Hollenbaugh, Briscoe & Milless, Columbus, 1985-91, Climaco Seminatore Delligatti & Hollenbaugh, Columbus, 1991-93, Delligatti, Hollenbaugh & Briscoe, Columbus, 1993-95, Draper, Hollenbaugh, Briscoe, Yashko & Carmany, 1996-99, Carlile Patchen & Murphy, Columbus, 1999—. Mem. Ohio Pub. Defender Commn., 1988-94; chmn. Franklin County Pub. Defender Commn., 1986-92. Treas. The Gov's. Com., 1987-96, Friends With Celeste, Friends of Gov's. Residence, 1987-92, Participation 2000, 1987-91. Fellow ABA Found. (chair commn. on advt. 1993-97, ho. of dels. 1993—); mem. Ohio State Bar Assn. (bd. govs. 1989-94, pres. 1992-93), Columbus Bar Assn. (pres. 1987-88), Nat. Conf. Bar Pres., Nat. Assn.

Criminal Def. Lawyers, Capital Club. Democrat. Methodist. Avocations: golf, politics. Home: 8549 Glenalmond Ct Dublin OH 43017-9737 Office: Carlile Patchen & Murphy 336 E Broad St Columbus OH 43215-3202 E-mail: HRN@CPMCAW.com.

HOLLENBERG, PAUL FREDERICK, pharmacology educator; b. Phila., Sept. 18, 1942; s. Frederick Henry and Catherine (Dentzer) H.; m. Emily Elizabeth Vanootighem, May 6, 1967; children: Kathryn Mary, David Paul. BS in Chemistry, Wittenberg U., 1964; MS in Biochemistry, U. Mich., 1966, PhD in Biochemistry, 1969. Postdoctoral fellow U. Mich., Ann Arbor, 1969, U. Ill., Urbana, 1969-72; asst. prof. Northwestern U., Chgo., 1972-81, assoc. prof., 1981-84, prof. pathology and molecular biology, 1984-87; prof. pharmacology, chmn. dept. Wayne State U. Sch. Medicine, Detroit, 1987-94, U. Mich. Med. Sch., Ann Arbor, 1994—. Mem. pharmacology test com. Nat. Bd. Med. Examiners; mem. Chem. Pathology Study Sect. NIH, 1987-91. Co-founder, assoc. editor Chem. Rsch. in Toxicology, 1988—; assoc. editor Jour. Pharmacology and Exptl. Therapeutics; mem. editl. bd. Drug Metabolism and Disposition, British Jour. Pharmacology. Schweppe Found. research fellow, 1974-77; NIH research grantee, 1974—. Mem. Am. Chem. Soc., Am. Soc. Biochemists and Molecular Biologists, Am. Soc. Pharmacology and Exptl. Therapeutics (sec./treas. 1998-99, pres.-elect 2001-02, pres. 2002-)), Am. Assn. for Cancer Rsch., Soc. Toxicology, Internat. Soc. for Study of Xenobiotics. Avocations: reading, running, golf. Home: 1968 Woodlily Ct Ann Arbor MI 48103-9728 Office: Univ Mich 2301 MSRB III Sch Medicine 1150 W Medical Center Dr Ann Arbor MI 48109-0632 E-mail: phollen@umich.edu.

HOLLIMAN, W. G. (MICKEY), JR. furniture manufacturing executive; Founder, pres., CEO Action Industries subs. Furniture Brands Internat., 1970-96; pres., chmn., CEO, Furniture Brands Internat., St. Louis, 1996—. Office: Furniture Brands Internat Ste 1900 101 S Hanley Rd Saint Louis MO 63105-3493

HOLLINGSWORTH, PIERCE, publishing executive; Pub. Real Estate Bus., Wheaton, Ill., Real Estate Profiles, Wheaton, 1998—. Office: PO Box 300 Wheaton IL 60189-0300

HOLLINGTON, RICHARD RINGS, JR. lawyer; b. Findlay, Ohio, Nov. 12, 1932; s. Richard Rings and Annett (Kirk) H.; m. Sally Stecher, Apr. 4, 1959; children: Florence A., Julie A., Richard R. III. Peter S. BA, Williams Coll., 1954; JD, Harvard U., 1957. Bar: Ohio 1957. Ptnr. Marshman, Hornbeck & Hollington, Cleve., 1958-67, McDonald, Hopkins, Hardy & Hollington, Cleve., 1967-69; law dir. City of Cleve., 1971-72; sr. ptnr. Baker & Hostetler, Cleve., 1969-71, 73—. Chmn. bd. dirs. The Ohio Bank; lead bd. dirs. Sky Fin. Group; mem. Ohio Banking Commn., 2001—. Mem. Ohio Gen. Assembly, 1967-70, Cuyahoga County Rep. Ctrl. Com., 1962-66; exec. com. Ohio Rep. Fin. Com., 1971-98, Cuyahoga County Rep. Orgn., 1968-98, Geauga County Rep. Orgn., 1998—; trustee Cleve. State U., 1970-73, Greater Cleve. Hosp. Assn., 1976-82, Cleve. Mus. Natural History, 1969-81, Cleve. Zool. Soc., 1970-99, N. E. Ohio Regional Sewer Dist., 1972-73, Cuyahoga County Hosp. Found., 1968-73, Cleve. 500 Found., 1990-95, U. Findlay, 1991—, others; bd. commrs. grievance and discipline Ohio Supreme Ct., 1993-95. Mem. ABA, Ohio Bar Assn., Greater Cleve. Bar Assn., Sixth Cir. Jud. Conf. (life), Eighth Dist. Ohio Jud. Conf. (life), Ct. Nisi Prius, Union Club (Cleve.), The Country Club (Pepper Pike), Pepper Pike Club, Roaring Gap (N.C.) Club, Rolling Rock (Pa.) Club. Home: 13792 County Line Rd Chagrin Falls OH 44022-4008 Office: Baker & Hostetler 3200 National City Ctr 1900 E 9th St Ste 3200 Cleveland OH 44114-3475

HOLLINGWORTH, ROBERT MICHAEL, toxicology researcher; b. Yorkshire, England, Oct. 4, 1939; married; 1961; 2 children. BSc, Univ. Reading, 1962; PhD, Univ. Calif., 1966. Asst. prof. to prof. insect toxicology Purdue Univ., West Lafayette, Ind., 1966-87; dir. Pesticide Rsch. Ctr., prof. entomology Mich. State Univ., 1987—; dir. Nat. Food Safety Toxicol. Ctr., 1991-99. Vis. prof. Stauffer Chem. Co., 1974-75. Mem. Toxicology Study Sect, NIH, 1976-80; Environ. Protection Agy., sci. adv. panel, Fifra, 1982-84; chmn. Divsn. Pesticide Chem. Am. Chem. Soc., 1984. Fellow AAAS, Am. Chem. Soc., Soc. Toxicology, Am. Coun. Sci . Health; mem. Soc. Risk Analysis. Achievements include research on metabolism and mode of action of insecticides and related chemicals. Office: Mich State U 106 Ctr for Integrated Planet Systems East Lansing MI 48824-1302

HOLLINS, MITCHELL LESLIE, lawyer; b. N.Y.C., Mar. 11, 1947; s. Milton and Alma (Bell) H.; m. Nancy Kirchheimer, Mar. 27, 1977 (div. 1999); children: Herbert K. II, Dorothy Ann, Betsy Ann Mizell; m. Jan C. Philipsborn, Oct. 24, 1999; 1 child. BA, Case Western Res. U., 1967; JD, NYU, 1971. Bar: Ill. 1971, U.S. Dist. Ct. (no. dist.) Ill. 1971. Assoc. Sonnenschein Nath & Rosenthal, Chgo., 1971-78, ptnr., 1978—. Asst. sec., dir. Jr. Achievement Chgo., 1980—; bd. dirs. Young Men's Jewish Coun., 1973-75; bd. dirs. young people's div. Jewish United Fund Met. Chgo., 1972-76; bd. dirs. Med. Rsch. Inst. Coun. Mem. exec. com., 1979-92, sec., 1981-82, gen. counsel, 1983-86, vice chmn., 1987-92, chmn. jr. bd., 1978-79. Editor NYU Jour. Internat. Law and Politics, 1970-71. Asst. sec., dir. Jr. Achievement Chgo., 1980—; bd. dirs. Young Men's Jewish Coun., 1973-75; bd. dirs. young people's divsn. Jewish United Fund Met. Chgo., 1972-76; bd. dirs. Med. Rsch. Inst. Coun., mem. exec. com., 1979-92, sec., 1981-82, gen. counsel, 1983-86, vice chmn., 1987-92, chmn. jr. bd., 1978-79. Mem. ABA, Am. Coll. Investment Counsel, Chgo. Bar Assn., Standard Club, Lake Shore Country Club (mem. bd. govs. 1984-92, sec. 1985-92), Lawyers Club. Republican. Home: 265 Wentworth Ave Glencoe IL 60022-1931 Office: Sonnenschein Nath & Rosenthal 8000 Sears Tower Chicago IL 60606

HOLLIS, DONALD ROGER, strategy consultant; b. Warren, Ohio, Mar. 4, 1936; s. Louis and Lena (Succo) H.; m. Marilyn G. Morganti, Aug. 23, 1958; children— Roger, Russell Kirk, Gregory, Heather. B.S., Kent State U., 1959. Regional mgr. Glidden Corp., San Francisco, 1959-65, dir. mgmt. info. services Cleve., 1965-68, SCM Corp., N.Y.C., 1968-71; v.p. Chase Manhattan Bank, 1971-81; sr. v.p. First Chgo. Corp., 1981-85, exec. v.p., 1986-95, head systems, data processing, cash mgmt. and security products and quality programs, 1986-95; pres., CEO DRH Strategic Cons., Chgo., 1995—. Bd. dirs. Deluxe Corp., S2 Corp., Quickstream, E.K.I. Bd. dirs. Advocate Health Sys.; mem. Ill. Inst. Tech. Bd. Trustees; mem. Ill. Inst. Tech. Rsch. Inst. Office: 20 S Clark St Ste 620 Chicago IL 60603-1803 E-mail: hollis@bankone.com.

HOLLIS-ALLBRITTON, CHERYL DAWN, retail paper supply store executive; b. Elgin, Ill., Feb. 15, 1959; d. L.T. and Florence (Elder) Saylors; stepparent Bobby D. Hollis; m. Thomas Allbritton, Aug. 10, 1985. BS in Phys. Edn., Brigham Young U., 1981; cosmetologist, 1981. Retail sales clk. Bee Discount, North Riverside, Ill., 1981-82, retail store mgr., Downers Grove, Ill., 1982, Oaklawn, Ill., 1982-83, St. Louis, 1983; retail tng. mgr. Arvey Paper & Office Products (divsn. Internat. Paper), Chgo., 1984, retail store mgr., Columbus, Ohio, 1984—. Republican. Mem. LDS Ch. Avocations: writing, reading, travel. Office: Arvey Paper & Office Products 431 E Livingston Ave Columbus OH 43215-5586

HOLLISTER, NANCY, state legislator; Lt. gov. State of Ohio, 1995-98, rep. Ho. of Reps., 1999—. Office: State House 77 S High St Columbus OH 43266-0001

HOLLISTER, WINSTON NED, pathologist; b. Milw., Mar. 23, 1942; s. Harold Arthur and Jeannette Clara (Gastrav) H.; m. Carol Jean Potter, Dec. 7, 1963 (div. May 1978); children: Timothy Carl, David Andrew; m. Margaret Ravenel Papen, Oct. 29, 1988; children: Margaret Ravenel, Charles Davis. BS in Physics, U. Wis., 1964; MD, Med. Coll. Wis., 1971. Diplomate Am. Bd. Internal Medicine, Am. Bd. Pathology. Staff pathologist St. Joseph's Hosp., Milw., 1976—; pres., CEO Franciscan Shared Lab, Wauwatosa, Wis., 1988-90; med. dir., chmn. bd. dirs. Med. Sci. Labs., 1989—. Cons. in field. Contbr. articles to profl. jours. Vestry mem. St. Paul's Episcopal Ch., Milw., 1978-83. Lt. USN, 1964-67. Recipient Houghton & Houghton award Med. Soc. Wis., 1971. Fellow Coll. Am. Pathologists (clin. practice com. 1984-87); mem. ACP, Am. Pathology Found. (pres. 1994—), River Tennis Club (bd. dirs., pres. 1978-98), The Milw. Club, Univ. Club Milw. Republican. Episcopalian. Avocations: sailing, skiing, tennis, travel, music. Home: 9949 N Valley Hill Dr Mequon WI 53092-5350 Office: Med Sci Labs 11020 W Plank Ct Wauwatosa WI 53226-3279

HOLLORAN, THOMAS EDWARD, business educator; b. Mpls., Sept. 27, 1929; s. Edward Francis and Florence G. (Loftus) H.; m. Patricia M. Holloran, June 26, 1954; children: Mary Patricia Harley, Anne Florence. BS, U. Minn., 1951, JD, 1955. Bar: Minn. 1955, Fed. 1955. Ptnr. Wheeler and Fredrikson, Mpls., 1955-67; exec. v.p. Medtronic, Inc., 1967-73, pres., 1973-75; chmn., chief exec. officer Inter-Regional Fin. Group, Inc. (renamed Dain Rauscher Corp), Mpls., 1976-85; prof. Grad. Sch. Bus. U. of St. Thomas, St. Paul, 1985—. Bd. dirs. Flexsteel Industries, Inc., Dubuque, Iowa, Medtronic, Inc. Spl. judge Mcpl. Ct. of Shorewood, Excelsior, Tonka Bay, Greenwood and Deephaven, Minn., 1961-65; Mayor, City of Shorewood, 1971-74; chmn. Urban Coalition, Mpls., 1977-78, City of Mpls. Task Force on Tech., 1983-84; mem. Mpls.-St. Paul Met. Airports Commn., 1974-82, vice chmn., 1976-82, chmn., 1989-91; bd. trustees Coll. St. Scholastica, 1971-81, chmn., 1979-81; trustee Coll. St. Thomas, 1979-88, U. Minn. Found., 1983-85, Bush Found., 1982—, chmn. 1991-96; trustee Mpls. Art Inst., 1986-93, Mpls. Children's Health Ctr., 1983-84; pres. Upper M.W. Coun., Mpls., 1978-80; bd. dirs. InterStudy, Excelsior, 1975-85, Minn. Press Coun., 1982-87, mem. corp. bd. Cath. Archdiocese Mpls. and St. Paul, 1990—. With USN, 1952-54, Korea. Mem. ABA, Minn. State Bar Assn. Roman Catholic.

HOLLOWAY, DONALD PHILLIP, lawyer; b. Akron, Ohio, Feb. 18, 1928; s. Harold Shane and Dorothy Gayle (Ryder) H. BS in Commerce, Ohio U., Athens, 1950; JD, U. Akron, 1955; MA, Kent State U., 1962. Bar: Ohio 1955. Title examiner Bankers Guarantee Title & Trust Co., Akron, 1950-54; acct. Robinson Clay Product Co., 1955-60; libr. Akron-Summit Pub. Libr., 1962-69, head fine arts and music divsn., 1969-71, sr. libr., 1972-82; pvt. practice Akron, 1982—. Payroll treas. Akron Symphony Orch., 1957-61; treas. Friends Libr. Akron and Summit County, 1970-72. Mem. ABA, ALA, Ohio Bar Assn., Akron Bar Assn., Ohio Libr. Assn., Nat. Trust Hist. Preservation, Music Libr. Assn., Soc. Archtl. Historians, Coll. Art Assn., Art Librs. N.Am., Akron City Club, North Coast Soc. Republican. Episcopalian. Avocations: art and architecture, music, travel. Home: 293 Delaware Pl Akron OH 44303-1275

HOLMAN, C. RAY, medical products executive; BSBA, U. Mo., 1964; postgrad., Harvard U., 1978, 91. CPA. Sr. acct. Price Waterhouse & Co., 1966-68, audit mgr., 1969-76; asst. contr., fin. planning and control Mallinckrodt Med. Inc., 1976-77, v.p., contr., 1977-82, v.p. fin. administrn., treas., contr., 1978-79, v.p. fin., treas., CEO, 1979-82, group v.p. fin. and corp. devel., CFO, 1982-83, group v.p. hosp. and lab. products group, 1983-85, group v.p. med. products group, 1985-88, pres., 1988-90, pres., CEO, 1990-92, Mallinckrodt Inc., 1992-94, chmn., pres., CEO, 1994-95, chmn., CEO, 1995—. Bd. dirs. Laclede Gas Co., NationsBank, Barnes Hosp. 1st lt. U.S. Army, 1966-68. Office: Mallinckrodt Inc PO Box 5840 675 McDonnell Blvd Saint Louis MO 63134

HOLMAN, JAMES LEWIS, financial and management consultant; b. Chgo., Oct. 27, 1926; s. James Louis and Lillian Marie (Walton) H.; m. Elizabeth Ann Owens, June 18, 1948 (div. 1982); children: Craig Stewart, Tracy Lynn, Mark Andrew, Bonnie Gwen (dec.); m. Geraldine Ann Wilson, Dec. 26, 1982. BS in Econs. and Mgmt., U. Ill., Urbana, 1950, postgrad., 1950; postgrad. Northwestern U., 1954-55. Traveling auditor, then statistician, asst. controller parent buying dept. Sears, Roebuck & Co., Chgo., 1951-54; asst. to sec.-treas. Hanover Securities Co., Chgo., 1954-65; asst. to controller chem. ops. div. Montgomery Ward & Co. Inc., Chgo., 1966-68; controller Henrotin Hosp., Chgo., 1968; bus. mgr. Julian, Dye, Javid, Hunter & Najafi, Associated, Chgo., 1969-81, cons. 1981-84; vol. cons., adminstrv. asst. Fiji Sch. Medicine, Suva, 1984-86, cons., 1987-89; vol. bus. cons. U.S. Peace Corps, Honduras, 1989, cons., 1989—; cons., dir., sec.-treas. Comprehensive Resources Ltd., Glenview (Ill.), Wheaton (Ill.) and Walnut Creek, Calif., 1982; bd. dirs., sec.-treas. Medtran, Inc., 1980-83; sec. James C. Valenta, P.C., 1979-82; sponsored project adminstr. Northwestern U., Evanston, Ill., 1984. Sec., B.R. Ryall YMCA, Glen Ellyn, Ill., 1974-76, bd. dirs., 1968-78; trustee Gary Meml. United Meth. Ch., Wheaton, 1961-69, 74-77; bd. dirs. Goodwill Industries Chgo., 1978-79, DuPage (Ill.) Symphony, 1954-58, treas., 1955-58. Served with USN, 1944-46. Baha'i. Mem. Kiwanis (bd. dirs. Chgo. 1956-60, bd. dirs. youth found. 1957-60, pres. 1958-60). Home and Office: 1571 Burr Oak Ct # B Wheaton IL 60187-2709

HOLMAN, RALPH THEODORE, biochemistry and nutrition educator; b. Mpls., Mar. 4, 1918; s. Alfred Theodore and May Carlia Anna (Nilson) Holman; m. Karla Calais, Mar. 26, 1943; 1 child Nils Teodore. AA, Bethel Jr. Coll., 1937; BS, U. Minn., 1939; MS, Rutgers U., 1941; PhD, U. Minn., 1944. Instr., div. of biochemistry U. Minn., Mpls., 1944-46; NRC-Nat. Acad. Scis. fellow Med. Nobel Inst., Stockholm, Sweden, 1946-47; Am. Scandinavian Found. fellow U. Uppsala, Sweden, 1947; assoc. prof. biochemistry and nutrition Tex. A&M U., College Station, 1948-51; assoc. prof. biochemistry Hormel Inst., U. Minn., Austin, 1951-56, prof., 1956-88, exec. dir., 1975-85, emeritus prof., 1988—; also adj. prof. of biochemistry Mayo Med. Sch., Rochester, Minn., 1977—. Mem. nutrition study sect. NIH, 1959-63; pres., organizer Golden Jubilee Internat. Congress on Essential Fatty Acids and Prostaglandins, 1980; mem. adv. bd. Deul. Conf. on Lipids, 1960-86; Sinclair Meml. lectr. Third Internat. Congress on Essential Fatty Acids and Eicasanoids, Adelaide, 1992. Founding editor Progress in Lipid Research, 1951—; editor Lipids, 1974-85; mem. editl. bd. Jour. Nutrition, 1962-66; contbr. 400 publs. on nutritional biochemistry of lipids; initiated omega 3 and omega 6 nomenclature for essential fatty acids, 1963; current rsch. on essentiality of omega 3 fatty acids. Pres. Mower County Coun. Churches., Austin, 1953-57; mem. Hormel Found., Austin, 1979-86. Recipient Fachini award Italian Oil Chemists, Milan; named Disting. Alumnus Bethel Coll., 1998. Fellow Am. Inst. Nutrition (Borden award 1966); mem. NAS, Am. Chem. Soc., Am. Oil Chemists Soc. (pres. 1974-75, Lipid Chemistry award 1979, Baldwin Disting. Svc. award 2001), Am. Soc. Biol. Chemists, Am. Orchid Soc. (rsch. com. 1980-85), Am. Heart Assn. (bd. dirs. Minn. affiliate 1991-93). Democrat. Congregationalist. Achievements include original research on essential nature of omega 3 polyunsaturated fatty acids. Avocations: writing history, gardening, orchid culture, research on orchid fragrances, construction. Home: 1403 2nd Ave SW Austin MN 55912-1609 Office: U Minn Hormel Inst 801 16th Ave NE Austin MN 55912-3679 E-mail: rtholman@maroon.tc.umn.edu.

HOLMAN, WILLIAM BAKER, surgeon, coroner; b. Norwalk, Ohio, Mar. 22, 1925; s. Merlin Earl and Rowena (Baker) H.; m. Jane Elizabeth Henderson, June 24, 1951; children: Craig W., Mark E., John S. BS, Capital U., 1946; MD, Jefferson Med. Coll., 1950. Intern, St. Luke's Hosp., Cleve., 1950-51, resident in gen. surgery, 1951-52, 55-57; practice medicine specializing in surgery, Norwalk, 1957-92; coroner Huron County, Norwalk, 1962-95, health commr., 1985-95; asst. clin. prof. surgery Med. Coll. Ohio at Toledo, 1984-92; Bd. dirs. REMSNO, Toledo, 1974-92, Norwalk Profl. Colony, 1983-92 ; mem. exec. com. Huron County Republican Com., Norwalk, 1980; bd. dirs. Fisher-Titus Med. Ctr., 1977-82, chmn., 1982; bd. dirs. Norwalk Area Health Svcs., Inc., 1987-92, 94—; mem. Norwalk City Sch. Bd. Edn., 1962-78, pres., 1964, 67-71, 78. Served to 1st lt. U.S. Army, 1952-54; Korea. Fellow ACS; mem. AMA, Ohio State Med. Assn., Huron County Med. Soc. (pres. 1978), Ohio State Coroners Assn., Nat. Assn. Med. Examiners. Lutheran. Avocations: boating; photography; stamp collecting; gun collecting. Home: 39 Warren Dr Norwalk OH 44857-2447

HOLMBERG, RAYMON E. state legislator; b. Grand Fords, N.D., Dec. 10, 1943; s. Leslie Orwell and Nina Marchildon H.; children: Mariah Jay, Brady Jon. BS, U. N.D., 1965, MS, 1976. Mem. N. D. Senate from 17th dist., Bismark, 1977—; counselor, tchr. Grand Forks Pub. Sch. Mem. judiciary, polit. subdivns. and joint constrn. rev. coms.; formerly Rep. Caucus leader and mem. appropriations com. Mem. N.D. Centennial Commn., 1985-91; past bd. dirs., pres. Greater Grand Forks Comm. Theater. Named Champion of People's Right to Know, Legislator of Yr., NRA. Mem. Elks, Nat. and N.D. edn. assns. Office: 621 High Plains Ct Grand Forks ND 58201-7717

HOLMES, ARTHUR S. manufacturing executive; m. Christy Holmes. BS, MS, Pa. State U.; MBA, Northwestern U. Founder, chmn., CEO Chart Industries, Inc., Cleve., 1989—; chmn. ALTEC Internat. Ltd. Partnership. Bd. dirs. 1st Bank Milw. Mem. bd. advisors Biterbo Coll.; mem. La Crosse Area Devel. Com.; mem. sch. adv. bd. U. Wis. Named Pa. State Disting. Engring. Alumnus, 1993; recipient Pope John XXIII award Viterbo Coll., 1999. Office: Chart Industries 5885 Landerbrook Dr Ste 150 Cleveland OH 44124-4031 Fax: 440-753-1491.

HOLMES, CARL DEAN, state representative, landowner; b. Dodge City, Kans., Oct. 19, 1940; s. Haskell Amos and Gertrude May (Swander) H.; m. Willynda Coley, Nov. 29, 1986; 1 child from previous marriage, Randall; 1 stepson, Bret Carpenter. Student, Kans. U., 1958-60; BBA, Colo. State U., Ft. Collins, 1962. Mgr. Holmes Motor Co., Plains, Kans., 1962-65; v.p. Holmes Chevrolet, Inc., Meade, 1962-78; owner Holmes Sales Co., Plains, 1965-80; land mgr. Holmes Farms, 1962—; mem. Kans. Ho. of Reps., Topeka. Chmn. Greater S.W. Regional Planning Commn., Garden City, Kans., 1980-82; del. Rep. Dist. Conv., Great Bend, Kans., 1984, Rep. State Conf., Great Bend, Kans., 1984, Rep. State Conv., Topeka, 1984, Rep. Dist. Conv., Russell, Kans., 1988, Rep. State Conv., Topeka, 1988; City of Plains Councilman, 1977-82, Coun. pres., 1979-82, mayor, 1982-89; mem. 125 dist. Kans. Ho. Reps., Topeka, 1985—; precinct committeeman Meade County Reps., 1986-89; pres. Kans. Mayors Assn., 1984-85; pres. League Kans. Municipalities, 1987-88; chmn. Kans. Ho. of Reps. Energy & Natural Resources com., 1993-96, Kans. flood task force, 1993, Kans. Electric Utility Restructuring Task Force, 1996-97, Kans. Ho. of Reps. Fiscal Oversight Com., 1997—, Kans. Ho. of Reps. Utilities Com., 1999—; mem. tax partnership task force Nat. Conf. State Legislatures, 2001, chmn., 1998; mem. energy and transp. fed. assembly, 2001—; mem. energy standing com. Nat. Conf. State Legislatures State and Fed. Assembly, 1989-94, Kans. Ho. of Reps. Appropriations Com., 1997-98; mem. environ standing com. NCSL-SFA, 1995-2001; mem. Am. Legis. Exch. Coun., Nat. Task Force on Energy, Environ. and Natural Resources, Kans. Environ. Leadership Program, 1999. Recipient Fox award Kans. Water Office, 1998, Intergovtl. Leadership award League of Kans. Municipalities, 1994. Mem. Liberal C. of C., Lions, Masons (past master), Scottish Rite, R.A.M., K.T., S.A.R. Methodist. Avocations: flying, photography, genealogy. Home: PO Box 2288 Liberal KS 67905-2288 Office: Kansas House Reps State House Topeka KS 66612

HOLMES, DAVID RICHARD, computer and business forms company executive; b. Salt Lake City, Aug. 10, 1940; s. John Rulon and Evelyn Nadine (Schettler) H.; m. Nancy Alice Lewis, Sept. 11, 1965; children: David Matthew, Stephen Michael, Jeffrey Alan. BA, Stanford U., 1963; MBA, Northwestern U., 1965. Category mgr., strategic planning mgr. Gen. Foods Corp., White Plains, N.Y., 1965-77; dir. mktg. Standard Brands Inc., N.Y.C., 1977-78; mktg. mgr. Gen. Electric, Fairfield, Conn., 1978-81; v.p., gen. mgr. Nabisco Brands Inc., N.Y.C., 1981-84; pres. computer systems div. Reynolds & Reynolds Co., Dayton, Ohio, 1984-87, pres., chief operating officer, 1987—, pres., chief exec. officer, 1989, chmn., pres., chief exec. officer, 1990, also bd. dirs., chmn., CEO. Bd. dirs. Bank One, Dayton, Ohio. Co-chair Downtown Dayton Partnership; mem. Dayton Bus. Com., Area Progress Coun.; trustee J.L. Kellogg Grad. Sch. Mgmt. Alumni Adv. Bd. Northwestern U.; gen. chmn. United Way campaign, Dayton, 1992, YMCA, Dayton Performing Arts Fund, Sta. WDPR-FM, St. Elizabeth Med. Found. Served with USNR, 1966-74. Mem. Am. Mgmt. Assn., Dayton Phil. Orch. Assn. (trustee 1988-91), Dayton C. of c. (bd. dirs. 1988). Republican. Presbyterian. Clubs: Am. Yacht (Rye, N.Y.); Dayton Country. Avocations: building furniture, skiing, tennis, sailing.

HOLMES, GRACE ELINOR, retired medical educator, pediatrician; b. Crookston, Minn., Mar. 27, 1932; d. William August and Anne Erika (Ermisch) Foege; m. Frederick Franklin Holmes, June 26, 1955; children: Heidi, Cindy (dec.), Lisa, Theodore, Julia, Andrew. BA, Pacific Luth. U., 1953; MD, U. Wash., 1957. Diplomate Am. Bd. Family Practice. Missionary physician Luth. Ch. Clinics, Malaysia, 1959-63; pediat. cons. Kilimanjaro Christian Med. Ctr., Tanzania, 1970-72; instr. pediat. Med. Ctr. U. Kans., Kansas City, 1967-69, asst. prof., 1969-70, 72-80, asst. prof. preventive medicine, 1978-80, assoc. prof. depts. pediat. & preventive medicine, 1980-87, prof. depts. pediat. & preventive medicine, 1987-2000, prof. emeritus, 2000—. Author: Whither Thou Goest, I Will Go, 1992, On Safari: A Collection of Stories. Recipient Humanitarian Svc. award Med. Alumni Assn. U. Wash. Sch. Medicine, 1995; named Alumna of Yr. Pacific Luth. U., 1988. Avocations: writing, music, photography. Home: 4701 Black Swan Dr Shawnee KS 66216-1234 Office: U Kans Med Ctr Child Devel Unit 3901 Rainbow Blvd Kansas City KS 66160-7340 E-mail: holmesgef@aol.com.

HOLMES, NANCY ELIZABETH, pediatrician; b. St. Louis, Aug. 3, 1950; d. David Reed and Phyllis Anne (Hunger) Holmes; m. Arthur Erwin Kramer, May 15, 1976; children: Melanie Elizabeth Kramer, Carl Edward Kramer. BA in Psychology, U. Kans., 1972; MD, U. Mo., 1976. Diplomate Am. Acad. Pediatrics. Intern., resident in pediatrics St. Louis Children's Hosp., Washington U., St. Louis, 1976-81; pediatrician Ctrl. Pediatrics, 1981—. Sch. physician Sch. Dist. Clayton, Mo., 1985—92; asst. prof. clin. pediats. Washington U., St. Louis, 1993—2000, assoc. prof., 2000—; cons. 1st Congregational Preschool, Clayton, 1984—86, Jewish Hosp. Daycare Ctr., St. Louis, 1993—, Flynn Park EArly Edn. Ctr., University City, Mo., 1994—; cmty. outpatient experience Preceptor Hosp., St. Louis Children's Hosp., 1991—93, 1994—; mem. med. exec. com. St. Louis Children's Hosp., 1992—94. Vol. reading tutor Flynn Park Sch., University City, 1992—98, cub scout leader, 1993—98; mem. com. Troop 493 Boy Scouts Am., 2000—; elder Trinity Presbyn. Ch., University City, 1989—92, 1996—2001; bd. dirs. Children's Hosp. Care Group. Fellow Am. Acad. Pediatrics; mem. AMA, Mo. State Med. Assn., St. Louis Metro. Med. Soc, St. Louis Pediatric Soc. Presbyterian. Avocations: reading, gardening, photography, travel. Office: Ctrl Pediatrics Inc 8888 Ladue Rd Ste 130 Saint Louis MO 63124-2056

HOLMES, PRIEST, football player; b. Fort Smith, Ark., Oct. 7, 1973; children: De'Andre, Jekovan. Postgrad in sport mgmt. , Univ. Texas.

Running back Kans. City Chiefs, 2001—, Balt. Ravens, 1997—2001; winner Super Bowl 35, 2001. Spokesperson Md. Dept. Edn. Gear Up Program; contbr. Dr. Ben Carson Scholarship Fund; spkr. Ray Kroc youth achievement awards McDonald's Corp.; spokesperson McDonald House Charities; mem. Fellowship Christian Athletes; spkr. Youth Explosion, 2000; contbr. Children's Miracle Net.; spkr. Urban Youth Min. Office: 1 Arrowhead Dr Kansas City MO 64129*

HOLMGREN, MYRON ROGER, social sciences educator; b. Willmar, Minn., Mar. 19, 1933; s. Alfred and Cleora Victora (Scott) H.; m. Ellen Mary Shaheen, June 9, 1957; children: Brian, Mary Jo Haas. BA, Mankato State U., 1958; MA, No. Colo. State U., 1959. Instr. Grinnell (Iowa) H.S., 1959-62, Joliet (Ill.) Jr. Coll., 1962-66; instr., fin. advisor Am. Express Fin. Advisors, Joliet, 1966-72; instr. Benedictine Coll., Atchison, Kans., 1973, Moraine Valley C.C., Palos Hills, Ill., 1974-75, Minooka (Ill.) H.S., 1974-93, dept. chmn., 1984-87, dir., coach Scholastic Bowl Team, 1976-93. Local dir. Exrox Award in Humanities, 1988=93; chmn. philosophy and goals North Ctrl. Accreditation, 1987-88. Author: Profitable Pricing Techniques, 1973; contbr. articles to profl. jours. Block chmn. March of Dimes, Am. Cancer Soc., 1989, 92-93; treas. bd. dirs. The Family Counseling Agy. of Will and Grundy Counties, 1996-99. Asian Found. grant, 1962. Mem. Internat. Platform Assn. Republican. Episcopalian. Avocations: reading, writing, travel, gourmet cooking, market analysis. Home: 1314 Douglas St Joliet IL 60435-5814

HOLNESS, GORDON VICTOR RIX, engineering executive, mechanical engineer; b. London, Sept. 6, 1939; came to U.S., 1969; s. Ernest Arthur and Ivy A. (Rix) H.; m. Susan F. Sage (dec.); m. Audrey A. Bezz, Apr. 18, 1984. Cert., Croydon Tech. Coll., Surrey, Eng., 1962; diploma in environ. engring., Nat. Coll., London, 1964. Registered profl. engr. Mich., Minn., Tex., Conn., Calif., Kans., Colo., Fla., Ariz., N.Y., D.C., Ala., N.C., Ky., Ohio, Mo., Tenn., Ill., Ont., Can. Design engr. West Sussex County Coun., Chichester, Sussex, Eng., 1956-59, C. McKechnie Jarvis & Ptnrs., London, 1959-64, Barlow Leslie & Ptnrs., Croydon, 1964; sr. engr. R. J. Tamblyn & Ptnrs., Toronto, Ont., Can., 1964-66; asst. chief engr. Giffels Assocs., Windsor, Can., 1966-69; from asst. chief engr. to chmn. and CEO, bd. dirs. Albert Kahn Assocs. Inc., Detroit, 1969—2001, also bd. dirs.; ret. chmn. emeritus, 2001. Contbr. articles to profl. jours. Bd. dirs. YMCA, Mt. Clemens, Mich., 1980-82. Fellow ASHRAE (chmn. energy mgmt. com. 1987, chmn. govt. affairs com. 1989, bd. dirs.); mem. NSPE, Am. Cons. Engrs. Coun., Chartered Inst. Bldg. Svcs. of Eng., Engring. Soc. Detroit, Mich. Soc. Profl. Engrs. (v.p. 1986, fellow 1998), Detroit Econ. Club (bd. dirs.). Republican. Presbyterian. Avocations: golf, tennis, racquetball, chess, sailing. Home: 55 S Edgewood Dr Grosse Pointe Shores MI 48236-1226 Office: Albert Kahn Assocs Inc 7430 2nd Ave Ste 800 Detroit MI 48202-2798 E-mail: gordon.holness@akahn.com.

HOLONYAK, NICK, JR. electrical engineering educator; b. Zeigler, Ill., Nov. 3, 1928; s. Nick and Anna (Rosoha) Holonyak. BS, U. Ill., 1950, MS, 1951, PhD (Tex. Instruments fellow), 1954; DSc (hon.) , Northwestern U., 1992; DEng. (hon.) , Notre Dame U., 1994. Tech. staff Bell Telephone Labs., Murray Hill, NJ, 1954—55; physicist, unit mgr., mgr. advanced semiconductor lab. Gen. Electric Co., Syracuse, NY, 1957—63; prof. elec. engring. and materials research lab. U. Ill., Urbana, 1963—, John Bardeen chair prof. elec. & computer engring. & physics, 1993—; mem. Center Advanced Study, 1977—. Author (with others): Semiconductor Controlled Rectifiers, 1964, Physical Properties of Semiconductors, 1989. With U.S. Army, 1955—57. Recipient Cordiner award GE, 1962, John Scott medal, City of Phila., 1975, GaAs Conf. award with Welker medal, 1976, Monie A. Ferst award, Sigma Xi, 1988, Nat. Medal Sci., NSF, 1990, Indsl. Application Sci., NAS, 1993, Centennial medal, ASEE, 1993, 50th Ann. award, Am. Elec. Assn, 1993, Japan prize, 1995. Fellow: IEEE (life Morris Liebmann award 1973, Jack A. Morton award 1981, Edison medal 1989, Third Millennium medal), Internat. Engring. Consortium, Am. Phys. Soc., Am. Acad. Arts and Scis., Am. Phys. Soc., Optical Soc. Am. (Charles H. Townes award 1992, Frederic Ives medal 2001); mem.: NAS (Indsl. Application of Sci. award 1993), NAE, AAAS, Math. Assn. Am., Electrochem. Soc., Ioffe Inst. (hon.), Russian Acad. Scis. (fgn. mem.), Minerals, Metals and Materials Soc. (John Bardeen award 1995), Ioffe Inst. (hon. 1992), Math. Assn. Am., Electrochem. Soc. (Solid State Sci. and Tech. award 1983), Tau Beta Pi (Outstanding Alumnus award 1999), Eta Kappa Nu (eminent mem. 1998, Karapetoff Eminent Mems. award 1994, eminent mem. 1998). Home: 2212 Fletcher St Urbana IL 61801-6915 Office: U Ill Dept Elec/Computer Engring 1406 W Green St Urbana IL 61801-2918

HOLSCHER, ROBERT F. county official; With Kenton County Airport Bd, Hebron, Ky., 1961—; dir. avaiation Cincinnati-N. Kentucky Internat. Airport, 1975—. Office: Kenton County Airport Bd PO Box 752000 Cincinnati OH 45275-2000

HOLSCHUH, JOHN DAVID, federal judge; b. Ironton, Ohio, Oct. 12, 1926; s. Edward A. and Helen (Ebert) H.; m. Carol Eloise Stouder, May 25, 1952; 1 child, John David Jr. BA, Miami U., 1948; JD, U. Cin., 1951. Bar: Ohio 1951, U.S. Dist. Ct. (so. dist.) Ohio 1952, U.S. Ct. Appeals (6th cir.) 1953, U.S. Supreme Ct. 1956. Atty. McNamara & McNamara, Columbus, Ohio, 1951-52, 54; law clk. to Hon. Mell. G. Underwood U.S. Dist. Ct., 1952-54; ptnr. Alexander, Ebinger, Holschuh, Fisher & McAlister, Ohio, 1954-80; judge U.S. Dist. Ct. (so. dist.) Ohio, 1980—, chief judge, 1990-96. Adj. prof. law Ohio State U. Coll. Law, 1970; mem. com. on codes of conduct Jud. Conf. U.S., 1985-90. Pres. bd. dirs. Neighborhood House, Columbus, 1969-70; active United Way of Franklin County, Columbus. Fellow Am. Coll. Trial Lawyers; mem. Order of Coif, Phi Beta Kappa, Omicron Delta Kappa. Office: US Courthouse 85 Marconi Blvd Columbus OH 43215 also: US Dist Ct 109 US Courthouse 85 Marconi Blvd Rm 109 Columbus OH 43215-2823

HOLSTEIN, JOHN CHARLES, state supreme court judge; b. Springfield, Mo., Jan. 10, 1945; s. Clyde E. Jr. and Wanda R. (Polson) H.; m. Mary Frances Brummell, Mar. 26, 1967; children: Robin Diane Camacho, Mary Katherine Link, Erin Elizabeth Lary. BA, S.W. Mo. State Coll., 1967; JD, U. Mo., 1970; LLM, U. Va., 1995. Bar: Mo. 1970. Atty. Moore & Brill, West Plains, Mo., 1970-75; probate judge Howell County, 1975-78, assoc. cir. judge, 1978-82; cir. judge 37th Jud. Cir., 1982-87; judge so. dist. Mo. Ct. Appeals, Springfield, 1987-88, chief judge so. dist., 1988-89; judge Supreme Ct. Mo., Jefferson City, 1989—2002, chief justice, 1995-97; shareholder Thomson & Kilroy, P.C., Springfield, 2002—. Instr. bus. law S.W. Mo. State Coll., 1976-77, pub. sch. law S.W. Bapt. U., 1999-2000. Lt. col. USAR, 1969-87. Office: Shugart Thomson & Kilroy PC 901 St Louis St Ste 1200 Springfield MO 65806

HOLSTEN, MARK, state legislator; b. Sept. 5, 1965; m. Lisa; 1 child. BA, U. Minn. State rep. Minn. Ho. Reps., Dist. 56A, Minn., 1993—. Tchr. U. St. Thomas. Home: 7790 Minar Ln N Stillwater MN 55082-9363

HOLT, DONALD A. retired university administrator, agronomist, consultant, researcher; b. Minooka, Ill., Jan. 29, 1932; s. Cecil Bell and Helen (Eickoff) H.; m. Marilyn Louise Jones, Sept. 6, 1953; children: Kathryn A. Holt Stichnoth, Steven Paul, Jeffrey David, William Edwin. BS In Agrl. Sci., MS in Agronomy, U. Ill.; PhD in Agronomy, Purdue U. Farmer, Minooka, Ill., 1956-63; instr., asst. prof., assoc. prof. then prof. agronomy Purdue U., West Lafayette, Ind., 1964-82; prof., head dept. agronomy U. Ill., Urbana-Champaign, Ill., 1982-83, dir. Ill. Agr. Expt. Sta., assoc. dean Coll. Agr., 1983-96, sr. assoc. dean Coll. Agr., cons. environ. sci., 1996-2002; ret., 2002. Cons. Deere and Co., Ottumwa, Iowa, 1978, NASA, Houston, 1979, Control Data Corp., Mpls., 1978-79, EPA, Corvallis, Oreg., 1981-90. Town Bd. commr., Otterbein, Ind., 1972-76. Fellow AAAS, Am. Soc. Agronomy (pres. 1988), Crop Sci. Soc. Am.; mem. Agrl. Rsch. Inst. (pres. 1991), Am. Forage and Grassland Coun., Ill. Forage and Grassland Coun., Gamma Sigma Delta (internat. pres. 1974-76). Republican. United Methodist. Home: 1801 Moraine Dr Champaign IL 61822-5261 Office: U Ill 170 N5RC 1101 W Peabody Dr Urbana IL 61801-4723 E-mail: d-holt@uiuc.edu.

HOLT, GLEN EDWARD, library administrator; b. Abilene, Kans., Sept. 14, 1939; s. John Wesley and Helen Laverne (Schrader) H.; m. Leslie Edmonds, Jan. 29, 1994; children from previous marriage: Kris, Karen, Gordon. BA, Baker U., 1960; MA, U. Chgo., 1965, PhD, 1975. From instr. to asst. prof. Wash. U., St. Louis, 1968-82; dir. honors div. Coll. Liberal Arts, U. Minn., 1982-87; exec. dir. St. Louis Pub. Libr., 1987—. Cons. Chgo. Hist. Soc., 1976-79, Mo. Hist. Soc., St. Louis, 1979-87, Buffalo-Erie County Pub. Libr., 1997-98; mem. Online Computer Libr. Ctr. Pub. Libr. Adv. Com., 1991-95. Co-editor: St. Louis, 1975; co-author: Chicago, A Guide to the Neighborhoods, 1979. Bd. dirs. U. Mo. Sch. Libr. and Info. Sci., 1987—. Recipient Cmty. Svc. award Commerce Bank, 2001; named Woodrow Wilson Found. fellow, 1963-64, Danforth fellow, 1963-68. Mem. Am. Libr. Assn., Pub. Libr. Assn. (Charlie Robinson award 2001), Spl. Librs. Assn. (St. Louis com. on fgn. rels.), Mo. Athletic Club. Avocations: photography, collecting paperweights, books and midwestern art. Home: 4954 Lindell Blvd Apt 4W Saint Louis MO 63108-1520 Office: St Louis Pub Libr 1301 Olive St Saint Louis MO 63103-2389 E-mail: gholt@spl.lib.mo.us.

HOLT, LESLIE EDMONDS, librarian; b. Mpls. d. Peter Robert and Elizabeth Knox (Donovan) Edmonds; m. Glen Edward Holt, Jan. 29, 1994. BA, Cornell Coll., 1971; MA, U. Chgo., 1975; PhD, Loyola U., Chgo., 1984. Asst. children's libr. Indian Trails Libr. Dist., Wheeling, Ill., 1972-73; libr. Erikson Inst. for Early Edn., Chgo., 1973-75; youth svcs. libr. Rolling Meadows (Ill.) Libr., 1975-82; libr. multicultural head start resource ctr. Chgo. Pub. Libr., 1982-84; asst. prof. grad. sch. libr. and info. sci. U. Ill., Urbana, 1984-90, assoc. dean, 1988-89; dir. youth svcs. and family literacy St. Louis Pub. Libr., 1990—. Pre-sch. advisor Rolling Meadows (Ill.) Park Dist., 1978-85; cons. to reading program The Latin Sch., Chgo., 1980-82; vis. lectr. Loyola U. of Chgo., 1980-84, U. Ill. Extension, Belleville, 1992; product mgr. Mister Anderson's Co., McHenry, Ill., 1981-84; instr. Nat. Coll. Edn., Evanston, Ill., 1982-84, Webster U., Webster Groves, Mo., 1991; cons. for libr. devel. Ill. Math. and Sci. Acad., Aurora, Ill., 1986-90; peer reviewer, advisor U.S. Dept. Edn. Office Edn. Rsch. and Improvement, 1987-89; libr. cons. Reading Rainbow Resources Guide, Sta. WNET-TV, N.Y.C., 1987, 88; adj. instr. U. Mo., Columbia, 1991, 92, 93; literary advisor Grace Hill Neighborhood Svcs., 1991-95; cons. Paschen-Tishman-Jahn, 1988; presenter in field. Author: An Investigation of the Effectiveness of an On-Line Catalog in Providing Bibliographic Acccess to Children in a Public Library Setting, 1989, Family Lieracy Programs in Public Libraries, 1990; contbr. articles to profl. jours. Mem. Success by Six Com., United Way of Met. St. Louis, 1993—. Grantee in field. Mem. ALA (mem. Carroll Preston Baber award jury 1992-94, World Book award 1986), Nat. Assn. Edn. Young Children, Internat. Reading Assn., Mo. Libr. Assn. (mem. summer reading program com. 1991, mem. Mark Twain award com. 1992), USA Toy Libr. Assn. (charter mem.), Assn. Libr. Svc. to Children (mem. toys, games and realia evaluation com. 1983-85, chair local arrangements 1984-85, chair rsch. com. 1985-88, mem. Randolph Caldecott com. 1987, mem. software evaluation 1988-89, mem. svc. to children with spl. needs 1989-91, chair Charlemae Rollins pres. program 1990-91, active, 1991, chair edn. com. 1991-93, 93—, bd. dirs. 1993-96, v.p., pres.-elect 1997-98, pres. 1998-99, past pres. 1999-2000), Children's Reading Round Table (mem. spl. award com. 1987-88). Office: St Louis Pub Lib 1301 Olive St Saint Louis MO 63103-2325

HOLT, ROBERT THEODORE, political scientist, dean, educator; b. Caledonia, Minn., July 26, 1928; s. Oscar Martin and Olga Linnea (Mattson) H.; m. Shirley J. Russell, Dec. 14, 1957; children: Susan Jane, Ann Carol, Sharon Linnea. AB magna cum laude, Hamline U., 1950; MPA, Princeton U., 1952, PhD, 1957. Instr. dept. polit. sci. U. Minn., Mpls., 1956-57, asst. prof., 1957-60, assoc. prof., 1960-64, prof., 1964-2001, prof. emeritus, 2001—, chmn. dept., 1978-81, dir. Ctr. for Comparative Studies in Tech. Devel. and Social Change, 1967-80, dir. rsch. devel. Coll. Liberal Arts, 1975-78, dean Grad. Sch., 1982-91, chair rsch. exec. coun., 1988-91, interim dean Coll. Liberal Arts, 1996, prof. emeritus, 2001. Bd. dirs. Coun. Grad. Schs., 1984-90, chair, 1989-90; mem. Assembly Social and Behavioral Scis., NAS, 1972-75. Author: Radio Free Europe, 1958, (with F.W. Van de Velde) Strategic Psychological Operations, 1960, The Soviet Union: Paradox and Change, 1962, (with J.E. Turner) The Political Basis of Economic Development, 1966, The Methodology of Comparative Research, 1970, Political Parties in Action, 1971, (with Turner and Chase) American Government in Comparative Perspective, 1979 With U.S. Army, 1953-55. Fellow Ctr. for Advanced Studies in Behavioral Scis., 1961-62. Mem. Am. Polit. Sci. Assn., Internat. Studies Assn., Mid West Polit Sci. Assn., Assn of Grad. Schs. (exec. com. 1985-88, chair grad. student fin. assistance com. 1986-91), 39er's Club. Episcopalian. Office: U Minn Polict Sci Dept 1414 Social Sci Tower 267 19th Ave S Minneapolis MN 55455-0499

HOLT, RONALD LEE, lawyer; b. Reading, Pa., Dec. 23, 1952; s. Carl John and Mary Catherine (Rossi) H.; m. Sharon Louella Nelsen, June 2, 1973; children: Angela, Valerie, Jeremy. BS in Speech summa cum laude, Evang. Coll., Springfield, Mo., 1975; JD with highest honors, Rutgers U., 1979. Bar: Mo. 1980, U.S. Dist. Ct. (we. dist.) Mo. 1980, U.S. Ct. Appeals (5th and 10th cirs.) 1988, U.S. Ct. Appeals (8th cir.) 1992. Law clk. to presiding judge U.S. Dist. Ct. (we. dist.) Mo., Kansas City, 1979-81; assoc. Stinson, Mag & Fizzell, 1981-86, ptnr., 1986-88, Bryan Cave and predecessor firm Bryan, Cave, McPheeters & McRoberts, Kansas City, 1988—. Mng. editor Rutgers U. Law Rev., 1978-79. Bd. dirs. Christian Conciliation Svc. of Kansas City, 1986-95, pres., 1989-91); bd. dirs. Christian Legal Soc. (bd. dirs. 1991-95, pres. Kansas City chpt. 1990, Mo. state membership dir., 1991-93). Mem. Kansas City Met. Bar Assn., Christian Legal Soc. Office: Bryan Cave 1200 Main St 3500 One Kansas City Pl Kansas City MO 64105-2100

HOLTER, GARY S. finance executive; CPA. Exec. v.p. fin. Simmons Airlines, Inc., 1986-88; exec. v.p., COO Knapp Shoes, Inc., 1989-95; exec. v.p., CFO Bekins, 1995-96; CFO Internat. Logistics Ltd., Hillside, Ill., 1997—. Office: Apac Teleservices Inc 6 Pkwy N Ctr Deerfield IL 60015

HOLTZ, MICHAEL P. hotel executive; Pres., CEO Amerihost Properties, Inc, Arlington Heights, Ill. Office: Amerihost Properties Inc Ste 400 2355 S Arlington Heights Rd Arlington Heights IL 60005-4500

HOLTZMAN, ROBERTA LEE, French and Spanish language educator; b. Detroit, Nov. 24, 1938; d. Paul John and Sophia (Marcus) H. AB cum laude, Wayne State U., 1959, MA, 1973, U. Mich., 1961. Fgn. lang. tchr. Birmingham (Mich.) Sch. Dist., 1959-60, Cass Tech. H.S., Detroit, 1961-64; from instr. to prof. French and Spanish, Schoolcraft Coll., Livonia, Mich., 1964-84, chmn. French and Spanish depts., 1984—. Trustee Cranbrook Music Guild, Ednl. Community, Bloomfield Hills, Mich., 1976-78. Fulbright-Hays fellow, Brazil, 1964. Mem. AAUW, NEA, MLA, Nat. Mus. Women in Arts (co-founder 1992), Am. Assn. Tchrs. of Spanish and Portuguese, Am. Assn. Tchrs. of French, Mich. Edn. Assn. Avocations: swimming, book collecting, photography, travel. Office: Schoolcraft Coll 18600 Haggerty Rd Livonia MI 45152-2696 E-mail: rholtzma@schoolcraft.cc.mi.us.

HOLWAY, GEORGE J. holding company executive; b. St. Louis, Sept. 13, 1949; m. Diana; children: Paul, Susan, Lindsey. BS in Commerce, St. Louis U., 1971, MBA, 1986. Auditor Arthur Andersen & Co., St. Louis, 1971-79; controller South Ranch Oil Co., 1979-80; from asst. controller to treas., corp. controller Peabody Coal Co., 1980-83, treas., corp. controller, 1983-86; controller Peabody Holding Co., Inc., 1986-90, v.p., controller, 1990-92; controller Zeigler Coal Holding Co., 1992, v.p., CFO, 1992-96; v.p. Peabody Group, 1996-98, v.p., CFO, 1998—, v.p. bus. devel. Mem. Financial Execs. Inst. Office: Peabody Group 701 Market St Ste 9000 Saint Louis MO 63101-1850 Fax: 314-342-7597. E-mail: gholway@peabodygroup.com.

HOLZBACH, RAYMOND THOMAS, gastroenterologist, author, educator; b. Salem, Ohio, Aug. 19, 1929; s. Raymond T. and Nelle A. (Conroy) H.; m. Lorraine E. Cozza, May 26, 1956; children: Ellen, Mark, James. BS, Georgetown U., 1951; MD, Case Western Res. U., 1955. Diplomate Nat. Bd. Med. Examiners, Am. Bd. Internal Medicine. Intern, asst. resident U. Ill. Research and Edn. Hosps., Chgo., 1955-56; sr. asst. resident medicine Cleve. Met. Gen. Hosp., 1959-60; asst. chief gastroenterology Case Western Res U., 1961-63; physician Gastroenterology Unit U. Hosps. of Cleve., 1961-63; instr. medicine Case Western Res. U. Sch. Medicine, Cleve., 1961-64, clin. instr. medicine, 1964-71; head gastrointestinal research unit, assoc. physician div. medicine St. Luke's Hosp., Cleve., 1967-73, dir. div. gastroenterology, 1970-73; head gastrointestinal research unit dept. medicine Cleve. Clinic Found., 1973—. Vis. prof. numerous instns. including Mayo Med. Sch., 1974, U. Calif., San Diego, 1977, U. Heidelberg, 1978, U. Pa., 1979, U. Zurich, 1980, U. Munich, 1982, U. Minn. Med. Ctr., 1985, med. ctrs., numerous Japanese univs., 1985, 92, Karolinska Inst., 1986, Royal Soc. London, 1987, Pa. State U. Sch. Med., U. Helsinki, RWTH-Aachen, Düsseldorf, Fed. Republic of Germany, U. Groningen, Utrecht, U. Amsterdam, The Netherlands, 1989, U. Perugia, Italy, Va. Commonwealth U.-Med. Coll. Va., Richmond, Christ Ch. Sch. Medicine, U. Otago, New Zealand, SUNY, Buffalo Sch. Medicine, 1990, Pontifical/Cath. U. Chile Sch. Medicine, 1991, Hiroshima U. Sch. Medicine, 1992, Kyoto U. Sch. Medicine, 1992, Sch. Medicine U. Jikei, Tokyo, 1992, Tel Aviv U., Israel Sch. Medicine, 1995, U. Leipzig, Germany, 1996, U. Heidelberg, Germany, 1996; lectr. in field. Mem. editl. bd. Gastroenterology jour., 1984-89; contbr. revs. and articles to med. jours. Served to capt. USAF, 1957-59. Recipient Alexander von Humboldt Found. Spl. Program award, 1978, 82. Fellow ACP; mem. ABA, Am. Gastroent. Assn. (rsch. com. 1976-79), Ctrl. Soc. Clin. Rsch., Am. Assn. for Study of Liver Diseases, AAAS, Am. Soc. Biol. Chemists, Am. Physiol. Assn., Biophys. Soc., Internat. Assn. Study of Liver, Am. Fedn. Clin. Rsch., Midwest Gut Club, Am. Soc. Clin. Nutrition, Ohio State Med. Assn., Sigma Xi. Unitarian. Home: 39251 Lander Rd Chagrin Falls OH 44022-2146 Office: Cleve Clin Found 9500 Euclid Ave Cleveland OH 44195-0001

HOLZER, EDWIN, advertising executive; b. June 22, 1933; MusB, Yale U., 1954, MusM, 1955; postgrad., Ind. U., 1956. Acct. exec. Benton & Bowles Inc., N.Y.C., 1959-62; account supr. William Esty Co., 1962-66, Grey Advt. Inc., N.Y.C., 1966-68, mgmt. supr., 1968-70; exec. v.p. Grey Inc., 1970-73; pres., CEO, COO Grey-North Inc., Chgo., 1973-85; chmn., CEO, Grey Chgo. (name changed to LOIS/GGK 1988), 1988; chmn., CEO LOIS/EJL (formerly Lois/USA), Chgo., from 1988; chief marketing officer CornerDrugstore.com, 2000—.

HONG, HOWARD VINCENT, library administrator, philosophy educator, editor, translator; b. Wolford, N.D., Oct. 19, 1912; BA, St. Olaf Coll., 1934; postgrad., Wash. State Coll., 1934-35; PhD, U. Minn., 1938; postgrad., U. Copenhagen, 1938-39; D.Litt. (hon.), McGill U., Montreal, 1977; D.D. (hon.), Trinity Sem., Columbus, Ohio, 1983; D.H.L. (hon.), Carleton Coll., 1987; ThD (hon.), U. Copenhagen, 1992. With English dept. Wash. State Coll., 1934-35; with Brit. Mus., 1937; mem. faculty dept. philosophy St. Olaf Coll., Northfield, Minn., 1938-78, asst. prof. philosophy, 1940-42, assoc. prof., 1942-47, prof., 1947-78, chmn. Ford Found. self-study com., 1955-56, dir. Kierkegaard Library, 1972-84. Vis. lectr. U. Minn., 1955; mem. Nat. Lutheran Council Scholarship and Grant Rev. Bd., 1958-66; lectr. Holden Village, Washington, 1963-70; mem. Minn. Colls. Grant Rev. Bd., 1970 Author, editor, contbr.: Integration in the Christian Liberal Arts College, 1956, books most recent This World and the Church, 1955; editor, contbg. author: Christian Faith and the Liberal Arts, 1960; co-editor, translator: (with Edna H. Hong) works by Gregor Malantschuk, numerous works by Soren Kierkegaard, Soren Kierkegaard's Journals and Papers, Vol. I, 1968 (Nat. Book award for transl. 1968), Søren Kierkegaard's Journals and Papers, Vol. II, 1970, Søren Kierkegaard's Journals and Papers, Vol. III-IV, 1975, Søren Kierkegaard's Journals and Papers, V-VII, 1978, The Controversial Kierkegaard (Gregor Malantschuk), 1980, Two Ages (Søren Kierkegaard), 1978, The Sickness unto Death (Søren Kierkegaard), 1980, The Corsaair Affair (Søren Kierkegaard), 1981, Fear and Trembling-Repetition, 1983, Philosophical Fragments-Johannes Climacus, 1985, Either/Or, 1987, Stages on Life's Way, 1988, The Concept of Irony, 1989, For Self-Examination and Judge for Yourself!, 1990, Eighteen Upbuilding Discourses, 1990, Practice in Christianity, 1991, Concluding Unscientific Postscript, 1992, Three Discourses on Imagined Occasions, 1993, Upbuilding Discourses in Various Spirits, 1993, Works of Love, 1995, Without Authority, 1997, Point of View, 1998, The Moment and Late Writings, 1998, The Book on Adler, 1998, The Essential Kierkegaard, 2000; gen. editor Kierkegaard's Writings, 1972—. Field sec. War Prisoners Aid, U.S., Scandinavia, and Germany, 1943-46; sr. rep. Service to Refugees, Luth. World Fedn., Germany and Austria, 1947-49; sr. field officer refugee div. World Council Chs., Germany, 1947-48; curator Kierkegaard House Found., 1999—. Decorated Order of Dannebrog (Denmark), Order of the Three Stars, Latvia; recipient award Minn. Humanities Commn., 1983; fellow Am.-Scandinavian Found.-Denmark, 1938-39, Am. Council Learned Socs., 1952-53, Rockefeller Found., 1959, sr. research fellow Fulbright Commn., 1959-60, 64, sr. fellow NEH, 1970-71; grantee NEH, 1972-73; publ. grantee Carlsberg Found., 1974, 86, 88, editing-translating grantee NEH, 1978-90, 95-98. Home: 5174 E 90 Old Dutch Rd Northfield MN 55057 Office: St Olaf Coll Kierkegaard Libr Northfield MN 55057

HONHART, FREDERICK LEWIS, III, academic director; b. San Diego, Oct. 29, 1943; s. Frederick Lewis Jr. and Rossiter (Hyde) H.; m. Barbara Ann Baker, Aug. 27, 1966; children: David Frederick, Stephen Charles. BA, Wayne State U., 1966; MA, Case-Western Res. U., 1968, PhD, 1972. Cert. archivist. Field rep. Ohio Hist. Soc., Columbus, 1972-73; asst. dir. univ. archives & hist. collections Mich. State U., East Lansing, 1974-79, dir., 1979—. Mem. adv. bd. Mich. Nat. Hist. Publs. & Records Commn., Lansing, 1979—; cons. in field. Creator: (microcomputer sys.), MicroMARC:amc, 1986 (Coker prize 1988), MicroMARC for Integrated Format, 1995; contbr. articles to profl. jours. Mem. Internat. Coun. Archives (steering com. sci. and univ. archives sect. 2000), Soc. Am. Archivists, Mich. Archival Assn. (pres. 1984-86), Midwest Archives Conf. (chair program com. 1982, 94, chair Author Awards com. 2001). Avocations: reading, sports, flying. Office: Mich State U 101 Conrad Hall East Lansing MI 48824-1327

HONIG, GEORGE RAYMOND, pediatrician; b. Chgo., May 5, 1936; s. Joseph C. and Raymonde S. (Moses) H.; m. Karen R. Jacobson, Dec. 18, 1960 (dec.); children: Sharon, Debra, Robert; m. Olga M. Weiss, May 24, 1998. BS in Liberal Arts and Sci., U. Ill., 1959, MD, MS in Pharmacology, U. Ill., 1961; PhD in Biochemistry, George Washington U., 1966. Diplomate Am. Bd. Pediatrics, Nat. Bd. Med. Examiners. Intern Johns Hopkins Hosp., Balt., 1961-62, fellow in pediatrics, 1961-63, asst. resident in pediatrics, 1962-63; rsch. assoc. Nat. Cancer Inst. NIH, 1963-66; fellow in pediatric hematology U. Ill., Chgo., 1966-68, asst. prof. pediatrics, 1968-

69, assoc. prof., 1969-74, prof., 1974-75, attending physician, 1968-75, dir. pediatric hematology svc., 1972-75, prof., head dept. pediatrics Coll. Medicine, 1984—; prof. pediatrics Northwestern U., 1975-83. Attending physician, dir. div. hematology Children's Meml. Hosp., Chgo., 1975-83. Contbr. numerous articles to profl. jours. Mem. AAUP, Am. Acad. Pediatrics, Am. Assn. Cancer Rsch., Am. Soc. Biochemistry and Molecular Biology, Am. Soc. Hematology, Am. Pediatric Soc., Soc. Pediatric Rsch., Alpha Omega Alpha. Office: U Ill Coll Medicine 840 S Wood St Chicago IL 60612-7317

HONOLD, LINDA KAYE, human resources development executive; b. Lansing, Mich., Aug. 16, 1956; d. Ervin Charles and Patricia Kathleen (Couzzins) Gaulke; m. Reynolds Keith Honold, dec. 5, 1987; 1 child, Samatha Kaye. BA in Polit. Sci., U. Wis., Eau Claire, 1980; MS in Indsl. Relations, U. Wis., Madison, 1987. Editorial asst. Lake Pub. Co., Libertyville, Ill., 1980-81; econ. devel. rep. Projects With Industry, Menomonie, Wis., 1981-83; exec. dir. Am. Cancer Soc., Eau Claire, 1983-85; career counselor Hmong Assn., Sheboygan, Wis., 1985-87; mem. resource team personal devel. Johnsonville Foods, Sheboygan Falls, 1987—. Contbr. article to profl. jours. Sec. Civil Svc. Commn., Sheboygan, 1986—; del. Dem. Party, San Francisco, 1984. Mem. Am. Soc. Personnel Adminstrs., Am. Soc. Tng. and Devel., Sheboygan County S. of C. (chmn. edn. coun.), Mortar Bd., Altrusa (sec. 1987—), Sheboygan Svc. Club. Lutheran. Avocations: jogging, reading, sailing. Home: 1633 N Prospect Ave Unit 20B Milwaukee WI 53202-2482 Office: Johnsonville Foods PO Box 906 Sheboygan Falls WI 53085-0906*

HONSE, ROBERT W. agricultural company executive; b. 1943; With Farmland Industries Inc., Kansas City, Mo., 1983—, exec. v.p., 1990—, CEO, pres., 2000—. Office: Farmland Industries PO Box 7305 Dept 209 3315 N Oak Trfy Kansas City MO 64116-2798

HOOD, DENISE PAGE, federal judge; b. 1952; BA, Yale Univ., 1974; JD, Columbia Sch. of Law, 1977. Asst. corp. counsel City of Detroit, Law Dept., 1977-82; judge 36th Dist. Ct., 1983-89, Recorder's Ct. for the City of Detroit, 1989-92, Wayne County Circuit Ct., 1993-94; district judge U.S. Dist. Ct. (Mich. ea. dist.), 6th circuit, 1994—. Recipient Judicial Service award Black Women Lawyers Assn., 1994. Mem. Am. Bar Assn., State Bar of Mich., Detroit Bar Assn. (Chmn. of Yr. award 1988), Assn. of Black Judges of Mich., Mich. Dist. Judges Assn., Am. Inns of Ct., Wolverine Bar Assn. (bd. of dirs.), Women Lawyers Assn. of Mich., Fed. Bar Assn., Nat. Assn. of Women Judges, Nat. Bar Assn. Judicial Coun., Mich. Judicial Inst. Office: US Courthouse 231 W Lafayette Blvd Rm 251 Detroit MI 48226-2789

HOOD, RON, state legislator; BS, BA, Ohio State U. Mktg. cons., Canfield, Ohio; rep. dist. 57 Ohio Ho. of Reps., Columbus.

HOOK, JOHN BURNEY, investment company executive; b. Franklin, Ind., Sept. 6, 1928; s. Burney S. and Elsie C. (Hubbard) H.; m. Georgia Delis, Feb. 8, 1958; children— David, Deborah. BS, Ind. U., 1956, MBA, 1957. CPA, Ohio.; cert. fin. analyst. Store mgr. Goodman-Jester, Inc., Franklin, Ind., 1949-50; auditor Ernst & Ernst, Indpls., 1953-56; financial analyst Eli Lilly & Co., 1957-59; gen. ptnr. Ball, Burge & Kraus, Cleve., 1966-72; pres., dir. Cuyahoga Mgmt. Corp., 1966-81; mng. ptnr. Hook Ptnrs., Cleve., 1984—96. Mem. AICPA, Am. Inst. CFAs, Union Club (Cleve.), Westwood Country Club, Ironwood Country Club (Palm Desert, Calif.). Republican. Methodist. Home: 435 Bates Dr Bay Village OH 44140 Office: 73233 Ribbonwood Palm Desert CA 92260

HOOKER, JAMES TODD, manufacturing executive; b. Ashland, Ohio, Dec. 21, 1946; s. Melvin Todd and Harriett (Lutz) H.; m. Sallie Foulkrod Utz, Feb. 22, 1975; 1 child, Stephanie Rae. BSBA magna cum laude, Ashland U., 1973. Advt. mgr. The Gorman-Rupp Co., Mansfield, Ohio, 1974-76, mfg. engr., 1976-79, asst. service mgr., 1979-80, gen. service mgr., 1980-86, asst. sales mgr., 1986-90, mgr. Ohio, 1990-95, dir. mfg., 1995-98, v.p. mfg. and facilities, 1998—. Solicitor United Way, Mansfield; moderator, bd. deacons Presbyn. Ch., 1988-89, elder, mem. Session; chmn. bd. Trustees Richland County Leadership Unltd.; mem. Heritage Found.; plank owner USN Meml. Found.; chmn. bd. Mansfield Richland County Chamber Edn. Found. Decorated Vietnamese Gallantry Cross. Mem. Omicron Delta Epsilon. Republican. Home: 1090 Trout Dr Mansfield OH 44903-9144 Office: The Gorman-Rupp Co 305 Bowman St Mansfield OH 44903-1600

HOOPS, H. RAY, college president; BA, Eastern Ill. U.; MA in Audiology, Speech Scis., PhD in Audiology, Speech Scis., Purdue U.; MBA, Moorhead State U. Vice chancellor academic affairs U. Miss., 1988-94; pres. U. Southern Ind., Evansville, 1994—. Contbr. articles to profl. jours. Founder Project '95 State of Miss. (Nat. Council State Govt. Assn. award). Recipient two Nat. Service awards U.S. Dept. Health, Edn. Welfare; Sr. Fulbright-Hayes Rsch. scholar U. Philippines. Fellow Am. Speech Hearing Assn. (Nat. Rsch. award). Office: Univ Southern Indiana Office of the President 8600 University Blvd Evansville IN 47712-3590

HOOTON, JAMES G. finance company executive; CFO Arthur Andersen, Chgo. Office: Arthur Andersen 33 W Monroe St Chicago IL 60603 Office Fax: (312) 507-6748.

HOOVER, PAUL, poet; b. Harrisonburg, Va., Apr. 30, 1946; s. Robert and Opal (Shinaberry) H.; m. Maxine Chernoff, 1974; children: Koren, Philip, Julian. BA cum laude, Manchester Coll., 1968; MA, U. Ill., 1973. Asst. editor U. Ill. Press, Champaign, 1973-74; prof. English, Columbia Coll., Chgo., 1974—. Co-founder Poetry Ctr., Sch. of Art Inst. of Chgo., 1974, bd. mem. 1974-87, pres. 1975-78; editor OINK!, 1971-85; co-founder, editor New Am. Writing, 1986. Author: Letter to Einstein Beginning Dear Albert, 1979, Somebody Talks a Lot, 1983, Nervous Songs, 1986, Idea, 1987 (Carl Sandburg award Friends of Chgo. Pub. Libr. 1987), Saigon, Illinois, 1988, The Novel: A Poem, 1990; editor: Postmodern American Poetry, 1994, Viridian, 1997 (Georgia prize 1997), Totem and Shadow: New and Selected Poems, 1999, Rehearsal in Black, 2001, Winter (Mirror), 2002; contbr. to various periodicals including New Yorker, Partisan Rev., New Directions, Sulfur, Chgo. Rev., Triquarterly, Am. Poetry Rev., New Republic; author: (screenplay) Viridian, 1994. Nat. Endowment for Arts fellow, 1980; Ill. Arts Coun. fellow, 1983, 84, 86; recipient General Electric Found. award for Younger Writers, 1984. Mem. MLA. Office: Columbia Coll Dept of English 600 S Michigan Ave Chicago IL 60605-1900 Home: 369 Molino Ave Mill Valley CA 94941-2767

HOOVER, WILLIAM LEICHLITER, forestry and natural resources educator, financial consultant; b. Brownsville, Pa., July 29, 1944; s. Aaron Jones and Edith (Leichliter) H.; m. Peggy Jo Spangler, Aug. 30, 1976; children: Jennifer Mary, Monica Susan, Samuel Spangler. BS, Pa. State U., 1966, MS, 1971; PhD, Iowa State U., 1977. Rsch. asst. Pa. State U., Iowa State U., 1970-74; asst. prof. Purdue U., West Lafayette, Ind., 1974-79, assoc. prof. dept. forestry & natural resources, 1980-85, prof., 1986—, asst. dept. head & extension coord. Dir. Nat. Timber Tax website. Author: A Guide to Federal Income Tax for Timber Owners, Timber Tax Management; contbg. editor taxes Tree Farmer Mag. Mem. Boy Scouts Am., Silver Beaver. 1st lt. C.E., u.S. Army, 1967-69. Decorated Bronze Star. Mem. Internat. Soc. Ecol. Econs., Forest Products Soc., Soc. Am. Foresters, Soc. Range Mgmt. Republican. Presbyterian. Home: 206 Connolly St West Lafayette IN 47906-2724 Office: Purdue U Dept Forestry West Lafayette IN 47907 E-mail: billh@fnr.purdue.edu.

HOPEN, HERBERT JOHN, horticulture educator; b. Madison, Wis., Jan. 7, 1934; s. Alfred and Amelia (Sveum) H.; m. Joanne C. Emmel, Sept. 12, 1959; children: Timothy, Rachel. BS, U. Wis., 1956, MS, 1959; PhD, Mich. State U., 1962. Asst. prof. U. Minn., Duluth, 1962-64; prof. U. Ill., Urbana, 1965-85, prof., acting head, 1983-85; prof. horticulture U. Wis., Madison, 1985-97, prof. emeritus, 1997, chmn. dept. horticulture, 1985-91. Mem. Am. Soc. for Hort. Sci., Weed Sci. Soc. Am., North Ctrl. Weed Sci. Soc., Ygdrasil, Sigma Xi. Avocations: reading, gardening. Office: U Wis Dept Hort 1575 Linden Dr Madison WI 53706-1514 E-mail: hjhopen@facstaff.wisc.edu.

HOPKINS, JEFFREY P. federal judge; b. 1960; JD, Ohio State U., 1985. Law clk. to Hon. Alan E. Norris U.S. Ct. Appeals (6th cir.), 1985-87; assoc. Squire, Sanders & Dempsey, 1987-90; asst. U.S. atty. U.S. Dist. Ct. (so. dist.) Ohio, 1990-96, bankruptcy judge, 1996—. Office: US Dist Ct So Dist Ohio 221 E 4th St # 2 Cincinnati OH 45202-4124 Fax: 513-684-2028.

HOPKINS, LEWIS DEAN, planner, educator; b. Lakewood, Ohio, Feb. 20, 1946; s. W. Dean and Harriet (Painter) H.; m. Susan Brewster Cocker, Aug. 24, 1968; children: Joshua, Nathaniel. BA, U. Pa., 1968, postgrad., 1968-69, M of Regional Planning, 1970, PhD, 1975. Asst. prof. landscape arch. Inst. Environ. Studies/U. Ill., Urbana-Champaign, 1972-79, assoc. prof. landscape arch., urban and regional planning, 1979-84, prof., head dept. urban and regional planning, 1984-97, prof. landscape arch., 1984—. Vis. lectr. dept. town and regional planning U. Sheffield, Eng., 1980; coord. grad. program in landscape arch. U. Ill., 1976-79, chair search com. for head dept. landscape arch., 1985, chair com. to evaluate dir. Inst. Environ. Studies, 1990, com. pub. adminstrn. program, 1990, campus budget strategies com., 1991-94, chancellors strategic planning com., 1993-95, campus senate, 1976-79, 82-84, chair ednl. policy com. 1978-79, senate coun. 1978-79, 82-83, budget com. 1984-86; project dir. Ill. Streams Info. sys., 1981-90; fellow Com. Instnl. Coop. Acad. Leadership Program, 1989-90; external site visit team dept. landscape arch. and environ. planning, Ariz. State U., 1990; rsch. adv. com. Ill.-Ind. Sea Grant Program, 1991—; exec. com. Office of Solid Waste Rsch., 1992-95; Fulbright sr. scholar to Nepal, 1997-98. Co-editor: (with Gill-Chin Lim) Jour. Planning Edn. and Rsch., 1987-91; mem. editl. bd. Jour. Planning Lit., Computers, Environment and Urban sys., Urban and Regional Info. Sys. Assn. Jour., Jour. Planning Edn. and Rsch., others; reviewer: European Jour. Ops. Rsch., Geographical Analysis, Internat. Regional Sci. Rev., Landscape Jour., Mgmt. Sci., Transp. Rsch., others; contbr. articles to profl. jours. Fellow Am. Inst. Cert. Planners; mem. AAUP (pres. campus chpt. 1983-84), Am. Planning Assn. (chair nominating com. Ill. chpt. 1988), Assn. Collegiate Schs. of Planning (regional rep. to exec. bd. 1989-91), Inst. Mgmt. Scis., Regional Sci. Assn., Urban and Regional Inf. Sys. Assn. for Planning Accreditation Bd. (chair site visit teams 1988, 92, 94, team mem. 1995, com. on dual degree programs 1992-93), Planning Accreditation Bd. (chair 1997—). Achievements include research in human and computer problem solving processes for incompletely defined spatial problems; land and water resources management, information, and decision support systems; comprehensive planning processes and institutions. Office: U Ill Urbana-Champaign Dept Urban/Regional Plan 611 E Taft Dr Champaign IL 61820-6921

HOPKINS, ROBERT ELLIOTT, music educator; b. Greensboro, N.C., Oct. 2, 1931; s. Julian Setzer and Elizabeth Stewart (Daniel) H. MusB, U. Rochester, 1953, MusM, 1954, D Mus. Arts, 1959; postgrad., Acad. for Music, Vienna, Austria, 1959-60. Instr. Mars Hill Coll., 1954-57, 60-63; prof. music Youngstown (Ohio) State U., 1963-93; prof. emeritus, 1993—. Editor: Alexander Reinagle: The Philadelphia Sonatas, 1978; contbr. New Grove Dictionary of Music and Musicians, 1980, 2d edit., 2001, New Grove Dictionary of American Music, 1987, New Grove Dictionary of Opera, 1992. Music dir. various chs., N.C. and Ohio, 1954-81; chmn. Nat. Piano Concerto Competition, Youngstown Symphony Soc., 1986-90. Recipient Disting. Prof. award Youngstown State U., 1990; Fulbright-Hays grantee, 1959-60, rsch. grantee Youngstown State U., 1969-70, 83. Fellow Am. Guild. Organists (dean Youngstown chpt. 1968-69, 73-74, S. Lewis Elmer award 1962, 66); mem. Am. Musicological Soc., Soc. Am. Music. E-mail: dok109@zoominternet.net.

HOPP, ANTHONY JAMES, advertising agency executive; b. Detroit, Jan. 31, 1945; s. William J. and Beverly (Gildea) H.; m. Nancy Jane Dunckel, Nov. 11, 1969; children: Beth, Michael. BA in Advt./Mktg., Mich. State U., 1967, MA in Advt./Psychology, 1968. Asst. account exec. Campbell-Ewald Adv., Warren, Mich., 1968-70; account exec. Lintas Campbell-Ewald, 1970-74, account supr., 1974-75, v.p., account supr., 1975-79, sr. v.p., mgmt. supr., 1979-85, group sr. v.p., group mgmt. supr., 1985-88, exec. v.p., account dir., 1988-93, pres., 1993-95, vice chmn., 1995—, also bd. dirs., chmn. & CEO. Bd. dirs. C-E Comm., Warren, Lintas Ams. Recipient Robert E. Healy award Interpublic Group of Cos., 1989. Mem. Adcraft, Hunters Creek, Bloomfield Hills Country Club, Pine Lake Country Club. Avocations: golf, hunting, boating. Office: Lintas-Campbell-Ewald 30400 Van Dyke Ave Warren MI 48093-2368

HOPP, DANIEL FREDERICK, manufacturing company executive, lawyer; b. Ann Arbor, Mich., Apr. 14, 1947; s. Clayton A. and Monica E. (Williams) H.; m. Maria G. Lopez, Dec. 20, 1968; children: Emily, Daniel, Melissa. BA in English, U. Mich., 1969; JD, Wayne State U., 1973. Bar: Ill. 1974, Mich. 1980. Atty. Mayer, Brown and Platt, Chgo., 1973-79, Whirlpool Corp., Benton Harbor, Mich., 1979-84, asst. sec., 1984-85, sec., asst. gen. counsel, 1985-89, v.p., gen. counsel, sec., 1989-98, sr. v.p., corp. affairs and gen. counsel, 1998—. Past co-chmn. Conf. Bd. Legal Quality Coun. Mem. City of St. Joseph (Mich.) Planning Comm.; bd. dirs. Lakeland Regional Health Sys., Joseph, Mich., St. Joseph Today; mem. Coun. for World Class Cmtys. With U.S. Army, 1969-71. Mem. Am. Soc. Corp. Secs. (past pres., bd. dirs. Chgo. chpt.), Mich. Bar Assn. (mem. Open Justice Commn.), Ill. Bar Assn., Berrien County Bar Assn. Republican. Mem. Ch. of Christ. Avocation: golf. Office: Whirlpool Corp Adminstrv Ctr 2000 N M 63 Benton Harbor MI 49022-2692

HOPP, NANCY SMITH, marketing executive; b. Aurora, Ill., Nov. 1, 1943; d. C. Dudley and Margaret (McWethy) Smith; m. Edward Thompson Reid, July 19, 1963 (div. Feb. 1966); 1 child, Edward Thompson Jr.; m. James C. Hopp, Feb. 4, 1978. Cert., Chgo. Sch. Interior Design, 1965; BA in Social Scis., Aurora U., 1968, MS in Bus. Mgmt., 1982. Dir. pub. rels. Sta. WLXT-TV, Aurora, 1969-70; bookstore mgr. Waubonsee Coll., Sugar Grove, Ill., 1970-79, dir. purchasing, 1979-85, dir. pub. rels., 1984-85; dir. devel. Assn. for Individual Devel., Aurora, 1985-87; dir. pub. rels. Provena Mercy Ctr., 1988-95; dir. mktg. Dreyer Med. Clinic, 1995—. Ninety for the 90s com. Ill. Dept. Aging, 1989. Editor: Volunteers Make the Difference, 1982; author Pigeon Woods Cookbook; producer (film) Caring Counts; contbr. articles to profl. jours. Bd. dirs. Family Support Ctr., Aurora, 1984-90, Aurora Area United Way, 1990-96, Corridor Group, 1993-94, Assn. Individual Devel., 1996—, Suicide Prevention Svcs., 1998-2000; adv. coun. Mercy Ctr. Health Care, Aurora, 1985-87; moderator New Eng. Congl. Ch., Aurora, 1983; charter mem. bd. dirs. Aurora Cmty. Coordinating Coun., 1985-86; mem. Block Grant Working Com., Aurora, 1987-2000, Kane County Health Com., 1994, Kane County Womens Health Coalition, 1999—; bd. dirs., sec. Cities in Schs./Aurora 2000, Inc., 1993-94, A.I.D., 1999—, Paramount Arts Ctr. Endowment Bd., 1999—, Fox Valley Arts Hall of Fame, 2000-. Recipient citation U.S. Dept. HEW, 1969, Christian Svc. award, 1996; named Woman of the Day, Sta. WAIT-AM, Chgo., 1974, Optimist of Yr. for Cmty. Svc., 1987, Woman of Distinction, YWCA, 1990. Mem. Women in Mgmt. (Nat. Charlotte Danstrom Woman of Achievement award 1984), Nat. Soc. Fund Raising Execs. (ethics com. Chgo. chpt. 1987), Ill. Assn. Coll. Stores (pres. 1976), Nat. Assn. Ednl. Buyers (com. 1984)), Alliance for Healthcare Strategy, Exch. Club. Republican. Avocations: water sports, auto racing, billiards, art, music. Home: 175 S Western Ave Aurora IL 60506-4617 Office: Dreyer Med Clinic 1877 W Downer Pl Aurora IL 60506-7334

HOPPE, THOMAS J. state legislator; b. Evanston, Ill., Mar. 21, 1957; BA, Benedictine Coll., 1979. State rep. Dist. 46 Mo. State Congress, 1991—. Mem. edn., fees and salaries com., local govt. and related matters com., urban affairs com.; mktg. cons. Mem. KC, Grandview, Belton & Kansas City C. of C.

HOPPER, DAVID HENRY, religion educator; b. Cranford, N.J., July 31, 1927; s. Orion Cornelius and Julia Margaret (Weitzel) H.; m. Nancy Ann Nelson, June 10, 1967 (div. June 1984); children: Sara Elizabeth, Kathryn Ann, Rachel Suzanne. BA, Yale U., 1950; BD, ThM, Princeton Theol. Sem., 1953, ThD, 1959. Ordained Presbyn. minister, 1961. Asst. prof. Macalester Coll., St. Paul, 1959-67, assoc. prof., 1967-73, James Wallace prof. of religion, 1973—2001, prof. emeritus, 2001—. Author: Tillich: A Theological Portrait, 1967 (N.J. Authors award 1968), A Dissent on Bonhoeffer, 1975, Technology, Theology, and the Idea of Progress, 1991. With USN, 1945-46. Recipient Newberry ACM Faculty fellow, 1992-93, Templeton Found. Sci./Religion Course award, 1996. Mem. Am. Acad. Religion, Internat. Bonhoeffer Soc., Hist. of Sci. Soc., Kierkegaard Soc. Home: 1757 Lincoln Ave Saint Paul MN 55105-1954

HOPPER, JOHN D., JR. career officer; B in Gen. Studies, USAF, 1969; grad. (disting.), Squadron Officer Sch., 1974; M in Logistics Mgmt. (disting.), Air Force Inst. Tech., 1977; grad. (disting.), Air Command Staff Coll., 1982; grad., Indsl. Coll. of Armed Forces, 1988; cert. nat. security leadership, Syrcuse U., 1997; cert., John Hopkins U., 1997. Commd. 2d lt. USAF, 1969, advanced through grades to maj. gen., 1997; c-130 pilot Ching Chuan Kang Air Base, Taiwan, Vietnam, 1971-72; instr. pilot, acad. instr. class comdr. 71st Flying Tng. Wing, Vance AFB, Okla., 1972-76; dep. dir., cadet logistics, aide USAF Acad., Colorado Sprgs., 1977-81; chief, pilot, asst. ops. officer 18th Mil. Airlift Squadron, McGuire AFB, N.J., 1982-84; chief 438th Airlift Wing, 1984-85; comdr. 438th Field Maintenance Squadron, 1984-85; chief Hdqs. U.S. Forces Command, Fort McPherson, Ga., 1988-90; dep. comdr. ops. 63rd Mil. Airlift Wing, Norton AFB, Calif., 1990-91; comdr. 89th Ops. Group, Andrews AFB, Md., 1991-92, 63rd Airlift Wing, Norton AFB, Calif., 1992-93, 375th Airlift Wing, Scott AFB, Ill., 1993-94; commandant of cadets and comdr. 34th Tng. Wing, USAF Acad., Colo. Springs, 1994-96; vice dir. logistics Joint Staff, Washington, 1996-98; dir. ops. Hdqs. Air Mobility Command, Scott AFB, Ill., 1998-99; comdr. 21st Air Force, McGuire AFB, N.J., 1999—. Office: HQ AM/DO 402 Scott Dr Unit 3a1 Scott Air Force Base IL 62225-5300

HOPPER, PATRICK M. securities trader; b. Detroit, Apr. 9, 1970; BS in Fin., Hillsdale (Mich.) Coll., 1992; MBA in Fin., Wayne State U., 1995. Registered rep. East West Brokerage Firm, Harper Woods, Mich., 1993, 1st of Mich. Corp., Grosse Pointe Woods, 1993—. Mem. Grosse Pointe Crisis Club, 1994—; precinct del. Grosse Pointe Rep. Com., 1993—. Mem. Lions. Avocations: politics, tennis, boating, golf. Also: Little Switzerland Inc PO Box 930 Saint Thomas VI 00804

HOPPER, STEPHEN RODGER, hospital administrator; b. Chgo., Aug. 28, 1949; s. Rodger Patterson and Dorothy Ann (Newberg) H.; m. Janet Sue Waddill, June 10, 1972; children: Nathan John, Amanda Sue. BA, Ill. Coll., 1971; MHA, U. Minn., 1974. Adminstrv. resident Rochester (Minn.) Meth. Hosp., 1973-74; dir. support svcs. Jennie Edmundson Hosp., Council Bluffs, Iowa, 1974-78; asst. adminstr. Trinity Meml. Hosp., Cudahy, Wis., 1978-83, sr. v.p. med. svcs., 1983-84; pres., chief exec. officer McDonough Dist. Hosp., Macomb, Ill., 1985—. Bd. dirs. Midamerica Nat. Bank, Canton, Ill. Bd. dirs. Macomb Area Indsl. Devel., 1985—, Wesley Village, 1988-2000; bd. dirs. YMCA, Macomb, 1987-94, also past pres.; chmn. staff parish com. Wesley United Meth. Ch., Mcomb, 1990-92; dist. chmn. Medicine Lodge dist. Illowa coun. Boy Scouts Am., 1997-99. Fellow Am. Coll. Healthcare Execs.; mem. Ill. Hosp. Assn. (past pres. region 1-B, bd. dirs. 1992-95, mem. venture corp. bd. 1999—), Macomb C. of C. (bd. dirs. 1990-94), Rotary (pres.-elect Macomb 1995-96, pres. 1996-97, asst. dist. gov. 2000—). Avocations: golf, reading, computers, travel. Home: 112 W Totem Trl Macomb IL 61455-1272 Office: McDonough Dist Hosp 525 E Grant St Macomb IL 61455-3318 E-mail: srhopper@mdh.org.

HOPSON, JAMES WARREN, publishing executive; b. St. Louis, May 24, 1946; s. David Warren and Ruth L. (Dierkes) H.; m. Julie Ann Eastlack, Dec. 21, 1968; children: John, Benjamin, Gillian. BJ, U. Mo., 1968; MBA, Harvard U., 1973. Project mgr. Des Moines Register & Tribune, 1973-76, dir. ops., 1976-78, circulation dir., 1978-79; gen. mgr. Corpus Christi (Tex.) Caller Times, 1979-82; pub. Middlesex News, Framingham, Mass., 1982-88; pres. N.E. Group-Harte-Hanks Comms., 1984-88; pub. The Press of Atlantic City, N.J., 1989-94; pres. Community Newspaper Co., Boston, 1994-95, Thomson Ctrl. Ohio, Newark, 1995-2000; pub. Wis. State Jour., Madison, Wis., 2000—; v.p. publishing Lee Enterprises, 2000—. Pres. Vol. Ctr. Atlantic County, 1992—; treas. DeCordova Mus., Lincoln, Mass., 1983-89, dir., 1983-89; sec. Family Health Svc. Ctrl. Ohio, 1997—, treas.; bd. dirs. Audit Bur. of Circulations, 1999—; bd, dirs. Madison Art Ctr., United Way of Dane County. 1st lt. U.S. Army, 1968-73, Vietnam. Mem. New Eng. Newspaper Assn. (chmn. circulation com. 1986-88), Mass. Newspaper Pub. Assn. (dir. 1984-88), Metrowest C. of C. (chmn. 1987-88, dir. audit bur. of circulations 1999—), Greater Madison C. of C. (bd. dirs.) Office: 1901 Fish Hatchery Rd Madison WI 53713-1248

HORISBERGER, DON HANS, conductor, musician; b. Millersburg, Ohio, Mar. 2, 1951; s. Hans and Jeannette (Grossniklaus) H. MusB, Capital U., 1973; MusM, Northwestern U., 1974, MusD, 1985. Dir. music 1st Presbyn. Ch., Waukegan, Ill., 1976-88; with Chgo. Symphony Chorus, 1977—, sect. leader, 1984-91, asst. condr., 1990-98, assoc. conductor, 1998—; dir. Waukegan Concert Chorus, 1979-97; organist/choirmaster Ch. of the Holy Spirit, Lake Forest, Ill., 1988—. Lectr. in music Capital U., Columbus, Ohio, 1974-75; asst. to lang. coach Chgo. Symphony Chorus, 1978—. Fulbright-Hayes grantee 1975. Mem. Am. Choral Dirs. Assn. (chair community choruses cen. div. spl. interest 1988-91), Assn. Profl. Vocal Ensembles (chorus Am.). E-mail: DHorisberger@CHSLF.ORG.

HORN, CHARLES F. state senator, lawyer, electrical engineer; b. Bellefontaine, Ohio, July 20, 1924; s. Huber H. and Mary C. Horn; m. Shirley E. Horn, Aug. 1, 1953; children: Holly E., Charles J., Heidi E. BSEE, Purdue U., 1949; LLB, Cleve. State U., 1954. Application engr. Westinghouse Electric, Cleve., 1949-51; engr. Hertner Electric Co., 1951-53; owner, engr. Lease Equipment Engring., 1953-61; owner, ptnr. IRBATCO, 1953-61; atty. Dayton, Ohio, 1961—; city coun. mem. City of Kettering, 1963-69, mayor, 1969-80; county commr. Montgomery County, 1980-84; mem. Ohio State Senate, Columbus, 1985—. Adv. panel Office of Sci. and Tech.; chair Econ. Devel., Tech. and Aerospace Com.; senate rep. Thomas Edison Tech. Bd., Devel. Financing Policy Bd., Ohio Indsl. Tng. Program Bd.; 3-term chair Fed. Labs Consortium Adv. Bd., 1980-83; cons. NSF; participant U.S. Conf. Mayors.; chair Ohio Econ. Study, 1997, 98, 99. Organizer Miami Valley Coun. Govts., Montgomery County; trustee Nat. Aviation Hall of Fame, Cox Arboretum, Cmty. Devel. Corp.; past trustee Grandview Hosp., Kettering C. of C., Dayton Area Sr. Citizens, Kidney Soc., Leukemia Soc., Pub. Opinion Ctr.; founder, chmn. Camp for Kids Who Can't; past adv. bd. Kettering Meml. Hosp.; past chmn. mcpl. sect. United Way Campaign; promoter formation of Wright Tech. Network; founder and past chair of Regional Econ. Strategies Forum. Served with

U.S. Army Air Corps, 1942-45, CBI Theatre. Recipient numerous awards including Michael A. DeNunzio award U.S. Conf. of Mayors, 1980, Citizen award Pub. Children Svc. Assn. Ohio, 1988, Legislator of Yr. award Nat. Assn. Social Workers, 1989, Tech. award Dayton Area Tech. Network, 1989, Disting. Legis. Svc. award Ohio Human Svcs. Dirs. Assn., 1989, Pub. Svc. award Quality Dayton, 1990, Tom Bradley Regional Leadership award Nat. Assn. Regional Coun., 1989, Vol. of Yr. award Camp Kern YWCA, Pub. Svc. award Ohio Computer Tech. Ctr., 1990, Topcat Tech. award State of Ohio, 1997, Guardian of Small Bus. award Nat. Fedn. of Ind. Bus., 1998. Mem. Eta Kappa Nu, Tau Beta Pi. Republican. Avocations: tennis, golf, bicycling, horticulture. Office: Horn Coen & Rife 2323 W Schantz Kettering OH 45409 also: State Senate Ohio Senate Bldg Ste 222 Statehouse Columbus OH 43215

HORN, JOAN KELLY, political research and consulting firm executive; b. St. Louis, Oct. 18, 1936; M. E. Terrence Jones; 6 children from previous marriage. BA, U. Mo., St. Louis, 1973, MA, 1975. Pre-sch., elem. sch. Montessori tchr.; founder pre-schs. St. Louis and St. Joseph, Mo.; adj. faculty dept. polit. sci. U. Mo., St. Louis, 1982-86; with St. Louis County Office Community Devel., 1977-80, St. Louis Housing Authority, 1980-82; pres. Community Cons. Inc., 1975-90; elected to 102nd Congress from 2nd dist. Mo., 1990, mem., 1991-92; dir. community devel. agy. City of St. Louis. Author articles on pub. policy issues. Mem. Dem. State Com.; Dem. candidate for U.S. House, 1992, 96. Mem. U. Mo. Alumni Alliance, U. Mo.-St. Louis Alumni Assn. (bd. dirs.). Roman Catholic. Office: 1015 Locust Ste 1200pt 2 Saint Louis MO 63101

HORN, WALLY E. state legislator; b. Bloomfield, Iowa, Nov. 28, 1933; m. Phyllis Peterson. BS, Northeastern Mo. State, 1958, MA, 1962; postgrad., Tex. A&M U., U. Iowa. Tchr., coach Jefferson Sr. High, Cedar Rapids, Iowa; facilitator info. office Cedar Rapids Cmty. Sch. Dist.; mem. Iowa Ho. of Reps., Des Moines, 1972-82, Iowa Senate from 27th dist., Des Moines, 1982—; majority leader Iowa Senate, 1992-97. Mem. Christian Ch.; former bd. dirs. Linn County Hist. and Mus. Assn.; bd. dirs. Cedar Rapids Kids League Baseball, Iowa. With U.S. Army, 1953-55. Mem. Cedar Rapids Edn. Assn., Am. Legion, Kiwanis (past pres.). Democrat. Home: 101 Stoney Point Rd SW Cedar Rapids IA 52404-1069 Office: State Capitol Dist 27 E 9th And Grand Des Moines IA 50319-0001 E-mail: wally_horn@legis.state.ia.us.

HORNBACK, JOSEPH HOPE, mathematics educator; b. Nevada, Mo., Apr. 20, 1910; s. Joseph Thomas and Geordia (Munn) H. A.B., Central Coll., 1932; M.A., Harvard, 1933; Ph.D., U. Ill., 1952; postgrad., U. Chgo., 1933-34, 41-42, 46-49. Tchr. math. Calumet City (Ill.) High Sch., 1934-37, U. Chgo. Lab Sch., 1937-42; asst. prof. math. U. Ala., 1952-57, asso. prof., 1957-63, prof., 1963-80, prof. emeritus, 1980—. Vis. scientist to high schs. for Ala. Acad. Sci. Chmn. gen. bd. 1st Christian Ch., Tuscaloosa, Ala., 1974-76; mem. world outreach com. Christian Chs. of Ala., 1973-75. Served as lt. USNR, 1942-46. Mem. Am. Math. Soc., Math. Assn. Am., Sigma Xi, Phi Kappa Phi. Club: Mason. Office: PO Box 151 Nevada MO 64772-0151

HORNBAKER, ALICE JOY, writer; b. Cin., Feb. 3, 1927; children: Christopher Albert, Holly Jo, Joseph Bernard III. BA cum laude and honors in Journalism, U. Calif., San Jose, 1949. Asst. woman's editor San Jose Mercury-News, 1949-55; columnist Life After 50, Cin. Post newspaper, 1993—2002; freelance writer Cin.; writer, broadcaster The Alice Hornbaker Show Sta. 89.3 WMKK-FM, 1996—; freelance feature writer www.grandparentworld.com. Owner, mgr. Frisch's Big Boy Restaurant, Cin., 1955-68; dir. pub. relations Children's Home Soc. Calif., Santa Clara, 1968-71; asst. dir. pub. relations United Fund Calif., Santa Clara, 1971—; editor Tristate Sunday Enquirer mag., 1986-89, columnist Generations Tristate mag.; editorial dir. Writers Digest Sch., Cin., 1971-75; columnist, critic, mag. writer, reporter, copy editor Tempo sec. Cin. Enquirer, 1975-93 , also book editor and critic, columnist for Aging, feature writer Tempo sect.; reporter news segments on aging Sta. WKRC-TV; tchr. adult edn. Forest Hills Sch. Dist., Thomas More Coll., 1973—; reporter, specialist on aging for Cin. Enquirer, 1989-93, commentator on aging Sta. WMLX-AM, 1991-93; broadcaster, writer Sta. WMKV-FM, 1995—. Author: (Book) Preventive Care: Easy Exercise Against Aging, 1974; columnist: internet 3 times weekly Life After 50; contbr. articles to various publs. including:, scientific papers fiction. Recipient Bronze award in Am. health journalism Am. Chiropractic Assn., 1977, 78, Golden Image award Assn. Ohio Philanthropic Homes, 1989; 1st pl. for feature writing Cin. Editors Assn., 1983, 1st and 3rd pl. feature writing awards Ohio Profl. Writers, Inc., 1992, Journalist of Yr. award Ohio chpt. Am. Coll. Health Care Adminstrs., 1993, Journalism award Greater Cin. Joint Coun. on Geriat. Care, 1993. Mem. Blue Pencil of Ohio State U. (pres. 1981-82), Women in Comm., Ohio Newspaper Women's Assn. (v.p. 1981-83, 1st pl. human interest story 1977-85, 2d pl. column award 1979, Tops in Ohio award 1982, M.M. McMullen 2d pl. award, 1982, Recognition award 1985, 4th pl. on aging Nat. Legacies contest 1994), Soc. Profl. Journalists (treas. 1981-82), Ohio Press Women, Inc. (1st and 3d pl. awards for feature writing 1992). E-mail: ajhornbaker@yahoo.com.

HORNE, JOHN R. farm equipment company executive; b. Gary, Ind., 1938; Grad., Purdue U., 1960, Bradley U., 1964. Group v.p., gen. mgr. Navistar Internat. Transp. Corp.; pres., COO, now CEO Navistar Internat. Corp., 1995—, also bd. dirs., 1995—; pres., CEO Navistar Internat. Corp. and Internat. Truck & Engine Corp., 1995—; also chmn. bd. dirs. Navistar Internat. Corp. Mem.Soc. Automotive Engrs. (chmn. fin. com.). Office: Internat Truck & Engine Corp 455 N Cityfront Plaza Dr Chicago IL 60611-5503

HORNER, WINIFRED BRYAN, humanities educator, researcher, consultant, writer; b. St. Louis, Aug. 31, 1922; d. Walter Edwin and Winifred (Kinealy) Bryan; m. David Alan Horner, June 15, 1943; children: Winifred, Richard, Elizabeth, David. AB, Washington U., St. Louis, 1943; MA, U. Mo., 1961; PhD, U. Mich., 1975. Instr. English U. Mo., Columbia, 1966-75, asst. prof. English, 1975-80, chair lower divorce studies, dir. composition program, 1974-80, assoc. prof., 1980-83, prof., 1984-85, prof. emerita, 1985—; prof. English, Radford chair rhetoric and composition Tex. Christian U., Ft. Worth, 1985-93, Cecil and Ida Green disting. prof. emerita, 1993-97. Disting. Vis. Prof., Tex. Woman's U. Editor: Historical Rhetoric: An Annotated Bibliography of Selected Sources in English, 1980, The Present State of Scholarship in Historical Rhetoric, 1983, Composition and Literature: Bridging the Gap, 1983, Rhetoric and Pedagogy: Its History, Philosophy and Practice, 1995; author: Rhetoric in a Classical Mode, 1987, Nineteenth-Century Scottish Rhetoric: The American Connection, 1993, Life Writing, 1996; co-author Harbrace Coll. Hancbook, 11th edit., 1990, 12th edit., 1994, 14th edit., 1998. Named Disting. prof. Tex. Woman's U., 1999, Disting. Alumna, Washington U.; Inst. for the Humanities fellow U. Edinburgh, 1987; NEH grantee, 1976, 87. Mem. Internat. Soc. for History Rhetoric (exec. coun. 1986), Rhetoric Soc. Am. (bd. dirs. 1981, pres. 1987), Nat. Coun. Writing Program Adminstrs. (v.p. 1977-85, pres. 1985-87), Coll. Conf. on Composition and Communication (exec. com.), Modern Lang. Assn. (mem. del. assembly 1981). Home and Office: 1904 Tremont Ct Columbia MO 65203-5467 Fax: 573-445-6896. E-mail: hornerw@missouri.edu.

HORNING, DANIEL D. underwriter; B Gen. Studies, U. Mich., 1982. Ptnr. Grand Haven (Mich.) group Northwestern Mut. Fin. Network. Bd. regents U. Mich., Ann Arbor, 1994—. Mem.: U. Mich. Alumni Club (past pres.), Pres.' Club, Victors Club, Mich. M Club. Republican. Office: 16964 Robbins Rd Ste 100 Grand Haven MI 49417

HOROWITZ, JACK, biochemistry educator; b. Vienna, Austria, Nov. 25, 1931; came to U.S., 1938; s. Joseph and Florence (Gutterman) H.; m. Carole Ann Sager, June 11, 1961; children— Michael Joseph, Jeffrey Frederick. B.S., CCNY, 1952; Ph.D., Ind. U., 1957. Rsch. assoc. Columbia U., N.Y.C., 1957-61; asst. prof. biochemistry Iowa State U., Ames, 1961-65, assoc. prof. biochemistry, 1965-71, prof. biochemistry, 1971-95, Univ. prof., 1995-2000, Univ. prof. emeritus, 2000—, chmn. dept. biochemistry, 1971-74, chmn. molecular, cellular and devel. biology program, 1977-80. Vis. scholar Rockefeller U., N.Y.C., 1968; vis. prof. Yale U., 1974-75; vis. scientist MIT, 1990-91; program dir. biophysics and biochemistry NSF, 1993-94. Contbr. articles to profl. jours. NSF fellow, 1952-54, 57-59; NIH and NSF grantee, 1961—; recipient faculty citation Iowa State U., 1989. Mem. RNA Soc., Am. Soc. Biochemistry and Molecular Biology, AAAS, Phi Beta Kappa, Sigma Xi, Phi Kappa Phi Jewish Home: 2014 Country Club Blvd Ames IA 50014-7013 Office: Iowa State U Dept Biochemistry Biophys Ames IA 50011-0001

HOROWITZ, SAMUEL BORIS, biomedical researcher, educational consultant; b. Perth Amboy, N.J., Aug. 26, 1927; s. Sol and Lillian (Levine) H.; m. Joan Hughes, June 15, 1956 (div. 1971); m. Marian Sylvia Herman, May 23, 1973 (div. 1986); 1 child, Ann Julia A.B., Hunter Coll., N.Y.C., 1951; Ph.D., U. Chgo., 1956. Research assoc. Eastern Pa. Psychiat. Inst., Phila., 1958-62; vis. investigator Inst. Physiol. and Med. Biophysics U. Uppsala, Sweden, 1962-63; head lab. A. Einstein Med. Ctr., Phila., 1963-72; chief cellular physiology lab. Mich. Cancer Found., Detroit, 1972-93, chmn. dept. biology, 1975-78, chmn. dept. physiology and biophysics, 1981-93. Contbr. articles to profl. jours. Served with U.S. Army, 1946-47 Fellow AAAS; mem. Am. Assn. Cancer Research, Am. Soc. Cell Biology, Sigma Xi. Home and Office: 4159 Woodland Dr Ann Arbor MI 48103-9775 E-mail: sbg3210@aol.com.

HORR, WILLIAM HENRY, retired lawyer; b. Portsmouth, Ohio, Sept. 23, 1914; s. Charles Chick and Effie (Amberg) H.; m. Marjorie Bell Marshall, Aug. 31, 1940; children— Robert W., Thomas M., Catherine, James C., Elizabeth; m. 2d Wilma Crawford, Mar. 12, 1988. A.B., Ohio Wesleyan U., 1936; J.D., U. Cin., 1939. Bar: Ohio 1939. Practice in, Portsmouth, 1939-42, 45-99; atty. Skelton, Kahl, Horr, Marshall & Burton, 1939-42, 45-78; spl. agt. FBI, Louisville, Indpls., Newark, 1942-45; substitute judge Mcpl. Ct., Portsmouth, 1955-80; gen. counsel Ohio Wesleyan U., 1966-70. Mem. Portsmouth Bd. Edn., 1947- 60; pres. Portsmouth YMCA.; trustee Ohio U. Portsmouth Br., Shawnee State C.C., 1975-80, Ohio Wesleyan U., 1953-68; chmn. bd. Hill View Retirement Ctr., 1973-85. Recipient Disting. Svc. award Portsmouth Jr. C. of C., 1947. Mem. Ohio Bar Assn. (past mem. exec. com.), Portsmouth Bar Assn. (past pres.), Phi Delta Phi, Phi Kappa Psi, Omicron Delta Kappa, Rotary (past pres.). Republican. Methodist. Home: 1732 Hillview Cir Portsmouth OH 45662-2673

HORRELL, KAREN HOLLEY, insurance company executive, lawyer; b. Augusta, Ga., July 10, 1952; d. Dudley Cornelius and Eleanor (Shouppe) Holley; m. Jack E. Horrell, Aug. 14, 1976. B.S., Berry Coll., 1974; J.D., Emory U., 1976. Bar: Ohio 1977. Corp. counsel Great Am. Ins. Co., Cin., 1977-80, v.p., gen. counsel, sec., 1981-85, sr. v.p., gen. counsel, sec., bd. dirs., 1985—; pres. corp. svcs. Great Am. Ins. Property & Casualty Group, 1999—; counsel Am. Fin. Corp., 1980-81; gen. counsel numerous subsidiaries Great Ins. Co.; sec., asst. sec. numerous other fin. and ins. cos. Bd. dirs. Tri-Health, Inc., Bethesda, Inc. Trustee Cmty. Chest, 1987—91, Seven Hills Sch., 1991—2000, v.p., 1995—99; mem. cabinet United Appeal, 1984; bd. dirs. YWCA, 1984—90, v.p. fin., 1986—89; mem. Hamilton County Blue Ribbon Task Force on Child Abuse and Neglect Svcs., 1989—91; trustee Ohio Ins. Inst., 1994—2000, chair, 1996—99, Bethesda Hosp. Inc.; chair Ohio Joint Underwriting Assn., 1992—97; trustee Berry Coll., 1999—; mem. Hamilton County Hosp. Commn., 1999—, vice chair, 2002—; bd. dirs. Children's Home, 2001—. Mem. ABA, Cin. Bar Assn. (admissions com. 1978-91, nominating com. 1987-90). Democrat. Home: 2355 Easthill Ave Cincinnati OH 45208-2608 Office: Great Am Ins Co 580 Walnut St Cincinnati OH 45202-3110

HORSCH, LAWRENCE LEONARD, venture capitalist, corporate revitalization executive; b. Mpls., Dec. 2, 1934; s. Leonard Charles and Cecilia May (Chamberlain) H.; m. Kathleen Joanne Simmer, Aug. 25, 1956; children: Daniel Lawrence, Timothy John, Christopher Girard, Catherine Jessica, Sarah Elisabeth. BA with honors, Coll. St. Thomas, 1957; MBA, Northwestern U., 1958. Investment banker Paine Webber Jackson & Curtis, Mpls., 1961-67; v.p. N.Am. Fin. Corp., 1967-71; pres. Eagle Investment Corp., 1971-87; chmn., chief exec. officer Munsingwear Inc., 1987-90; chmn. bd. Eagle Mgmt. & Fin. Corp., 1990—. Chmn. bd. dirs. Sci. Med. Life Sys., Maple Grove, Minn., 1971-94; bd. dirs. Boston Sci. Corp., Leuthold Funds, Inc., Gillette Specialty Heatlhcare. 1st lt. USAF, 1959-61. Mem. Fin. Analysts Fedn., Mpls. Rotary, Minikahda Country Club. Home: 1404 Hilltop Rdg Saint Joseph WI 54082-2013 Office: Eagle Mgmt & Fin Corp PO Box 235 Stillwater MN 55082-0235

HORSCH, ROBERT B. biotechnologist; b. Pitts. m. Linda Horsch; children: Elsa, Laura, Michael. BS in Biology, U. Calif., Riverside, 1974, PhD in Genetics, 1979. V.p. product and technology cooperation Monsanto, Middleton, Wis. Postdoctoral fellow plant physiology U. Sask, 1979—81. Recipient Nat. Medal Tech, 1998. Achievements include development of part of a team that developed the world's first practical system to introduce improved genes into crop plants and gene transfer capability to mostimportant crops including soybean, corn, wheat, cotton. Office: Monsanto Co 8520 University Green Middleton WI 53562 E-mail: robert.b.horsch@monsanto.com.

HORST, BRUCE EVERETT, manufacturing company executive; b. Three Rivers, Mich., Feb. 17, 1921; s. Walter and Genevieve (Turner) H.; m. Patricia Kranish, Oct. 4, 1969; children: Michael, Diane, Mark. BS in Bus. and Engring. Adminstrn, Mass. Inst. Tech., 1943. With Barber-Colman Co., Rockford, Ill., 1946-76, pres., 1965-75, vice chmn. bd., 1975-76; pres. Mid-States Screw Corp., 1976—. Bd. dirs. Rockford YMCA, 1964-75, pres., 1965-67. Served to 1st lt. USAAF, 1943-45. Decorated Air medal. Mem. Rotary, Univ. Club (Rockford), Forest Hills Country Club (Rockford) (past sec.), Moorings Country Club (Naples), Yacht Club at Lake Geneva (Wis.) E-mial. Home: 2625 Harlem Blvd Rockford IL 61103-4117 Office: Mid-States Screw Corp 1817 18th Ave Rockford IL 61104-7399 E-mail: msscrewco@aol.com.

HORST, DEENA LOUISE, state legislator; b. Sacramento, Feb. 14, 1944; s. Orlo John and Louise Helena (Schultze) Poovey; m. Gordon Lee Horst, 1966; children: Randall, Rebecca. BSE, Emporia State U., 1966, MA, 1972; postgrad., Kans. State U., 1993—. Elem. tchr. Peabody Sch., 1966-68; mid. sch. art tchr., dept. chmn. South Mid. Sch., Unified Sch. Dist. # 305, 1968—; mem. from dist. 69 Kans. State Ho. of Reps., 1995—. Vice chmn. Kans. 2000 com., Kans. House of Reps., chmn. State and nat. ofcl. U.S. Jaycee Women, 1968-84; sec. Saline County Rep. Ctrl. Com., Kans., 1992-95. Named Outstanding State Pres., U.S. Jaycee Women, 1979-80; co-recipient Master Tchr. award State of Kans., 1991. Mem. C. of C., Phi Alpha, Alpha Theta Rho, Phi Delta Kappa, Epsilon Sigma Alpha (Zone Outstanding Sister award 1990). Address: 920 S 9th St Salina KS 67401-4806 E-mail: deena@informatics.net.

HORSTMANN, JAMES DOUGLAS, college official; b. Davenport, Iowa, Oct. 2, 1933; s. Leonard A. and Agnes A. (Erhke) H.; m. Carol H. Griffiths, Sept. 8, 1956; children: Kent, Karen, Diane. BA, Augustana Coll., 1955. C.P.A., Ill., Wis. Staff acct., auditor Arthur Andersen & Co., Chgo., 1955-61; v.p., controller Harry S. Manchester, Inc., Madison, Wis., 1961-65; sr. v.p. fin., treas. H. C. Prange Co., Sheboygan, 1965-83, also dir.; dir. planned giving Augustana Coll., Rock Island, Ill., 1983-85, v.p. for devel., 1985-93, v.p. planned giving, 1993-98, v.p. emeritus, 1998—; pres. Schonstedt Instrument Co., 1993-95. Chmn. Wis. Mchts. Fedn.; dir. First Wis. Nat. Bank, Fond du Lac. Chmn. Sheboygan County (Wis.) Republican Party, 1969-70; vice chmn. Wis. 6th Congl. Dist., 1972-73, Rock Island County Reps., 2000—02; del. Nat. Rep. Conv., 1976; campaign chmn. Sheboygan United Way, 1977, treas., 1973-75, v.p., 1975-78, pres., 1978-79; bd. dirs. Public Expenditure Survey Wis., 1981-83, Rock Island YMCA, 1986-87, Christ Luth. H.S. Found., 2000—; v.p. Sheboygan Arts Found., 1973-75; v.p., bd. dirs. Sheboygan Retirement Home, 1977-83; bd. dirs. Franciscan Mental Health Ctr., 1984-94, pres., 1985-88; bd. dirs. Franciscan Health Care Systems, 1988-92; trustee Friendship Manor, 1993—, pres., 2000—; trustee Coun. on Children at Risk, 1989—, Franciscan Med. Ctr., 1990-92, Cmty. Found. at the Great River Bend, 2002-; trustee Villa Montessori Sch., 1999—, pres. 2000—; bd. dirs. Alternatives for the Older Adult, 2001—, German Am. Heritage Ctr. 2000—, Vis. Nurse/Homemakers Assn., 2001, Pathway Hospice, 2001; mem. Cmty. Found. of the Great River Bend, 2002-. With USN, 1955-57. Named Outstanding Fund Raising Exec. Nat. Soc. Fund Raising Execs., 1992; recipient Outstanding Svc. award Augustana Coll., 1979. Mem. Am. Heart Assn. (bd. dirs. Quad City chpt. 1999—, pres. 2002-), Am. Cancer Soc. (bd. dirs. Rock Island unit 1992—), Wis. Inst. CPAs, Ill. Soc. CPAs, Sheboygan County Assn. CPAs, Fin. Execs. Inst. (dir.), Quad-City Estate Planning Coun., Augustana Hist. Soc. (bd. dirs. 1999—), Augustana Coll. Alumni Assn. (pres. 1970-71), Rock Island Arsenal Golf Club, Econ. Club Sheboygan (pres. 1976-77), Kiwanis. Lutheran. Home: 1245 36th Ave Rock Island IL 61201-6022 Office: Augustana Coll 639 38th St Rock Island IL 61201-2210

HORTON, ALAN M. newspaper executive; Grad., Yale U., 1965. Reporter Cin. Post, 1965-67, Cleve. Press, 1967-70; Washington corr. Ohio daily newspapers, 1970-72; nat. corr. Scipps Howard News Svc., 1972-78; editor Shelbyville (Ind.) News, 1978-83; mng. editor Evansville (Ind.) Press, 1983-84; gen. mgr. Scripps/Knight-Ridder, 1985-86; pub. So. Calif. Pub. Co., 1986; editor Naples (Fla.) Daily News, 1987-91; v.p. newspaper ops. Scripps, Cin., 1991-94, sr. v.p. newspapers, 1994—. Trustee Found. Am. Comms. Mem. Newspaper Assn. Am. (bd. govs.), Am. Soc. Newspaper Editors (past chmn. ethics com.). Office: 312 Walnut St Cincinnati OH 45202-4024

HORTON, FRANK ELBA, university official, geography educator; b. Chgo., Aug. 19, 1939; s. Elba Earl and Mae Pauline (Prohaska) H.; m. Nancy Yocom, Aug. 26, 1960; children: Kimberly, Pamela, Amy, Kelly. BA, Western Ill. U., 1963; MS, Northwestern U., 1964, PhD, 1966. Faculty U. Iowa, Iowa City, 1966-75, prof. geography, 1966-75; dir. Inst. Urban and Regional Research, 1968-72, dean advanced studies, 1972-75; v.p. acad. affairs, research So. Ill. U., Carbondale, 1975-80; prof. geography and urban affairs, chancellor U. Wis., Milw., 1980-85; prof. geography, pres. U. Okla., Norman, 1985-88; prof. geography, higher edn. adminstrn., pres. U. Toledo, 1988-98, pres. emeritus, 1999—; prin. Horton & Assocs., Denver, 1999—; interim pres. So. Ill. U., 2000. Mem. commn. on leadership devel. and acad. adminstrn. Am. Coun. on Edn., 1983-85; mem. presdl. adv. com. Assn. on Governing Bds., 1986-98; dir. 1st Wis. Nat. Bank of Milw., 1980-85, Liberty Nat. Bank, Oklahoma City, 1986-89, Trustcorp. Bank, 1989-90; bd. dirs. Interstate Bakeries, GAC Corp. Author, editor: (with B.J.L. Berry) Geographic Perspectives on Urban Systems - With Integrated Readings, 1970, Urban Environmental Management - Planning for Pollution Control, 1974; editor: (with B.J.L. Berry) Geographical Perspectives on Contemporary Urban Problems, 1973; editorial adv. bd.: (with B.J.L. Berry) Transportation, 1971-78. Co-chmn. Goals for Milw. 2000, 1981-85, Greater Milw. Com., 1980; mem. bus. devel. sub-com. Okla. Coun. Sci. and Tech., 1985-88; mem. Harry S. Truman Library Inst., 1985-88, William Rockhill Nelson Trust, 1985-88; bd. govs. Am. Heart Assn., Wis., 1980-85, Ohio Supercomputer Ctr., 1993-97; mem. exec. com. Okla. Acad. State Goals, 1986-88; trustee Toledo Symphony Orch., 1989-96, Toledo Hosp., 1989-97, Pub. Broadcasting Found. Northwest Ohio, 1989-93, Key Bank, 1990-2000, Ohio Aerospace Inst., 1990-97; chair Inter-Univ. Coun. Pres. of Ohio Public Univs., 1992-93; mem. exec. com. Com. of 100, Toledo, 1989-92. Served with AUS, 1957-60. Mem. AAAs (nat. coun. 1976-78), Assn. Governing Bds. (mem. presdl. adv. commn. 1986-95), Assn. Am. Geographers, nat. Assn. State Univs. and Land Grant Colls. (chair urban affairs div. 1983-85, chmn. Coun. of Pres. 1987-88, exec. com. 1983-88), Nat. Hwy. Rsch. Soc., Okla. Coun. on Sci. and Tech., MidAm. State Univs. Assn. (pres. 1987-88), Ohio Supercomputer Ctr. (bd. govs. 1993), Ohio Aerospace Inst. (trustee 1990—), Okla. Acad. State Goals (pres. 1987-88), Okla. State C. of C. and Industry (v.p. 1987-88), Toledo Area C. of C. (vice chmn. bd. dirs. 1991-93). Home: 288 River Ranch Cir Bayfield CO 81122-8774 Office: Horton & Associates 825 E Speer Blvd Ste 300H Denver CO 80218-3719

HORVITZ, MICHAEL JOHN, lawyer; b. Cleve., Feb. 15, 1950; s. Harry Richard and Lois Joy (Unger) H.; m. Jane Rosenthal, Aug. 25, 1979; children: Katherine R., Elizabeth R. BS in Econs., U. Pa., 1972; JD, U. Va., 1975; LLM in Taxation, NYU, 1980. Bar: Ohio 1975, Fla. 1976. Assoc. Hahn, Loeser, Freedheim, Dean & Wellman, Cleve., 1975-78; counsel Hollywood, Inc., Fla., 1978-79; assoc. Jones, Day, Reavis & Pogue, Cleve., 1980-85, ptnr., 1985-2000, of counsel, 2001—. Mem. adv. bd. Kirtland Capital Ptnrs., L.P., 1992—; chmn. Parkland Mgmt. Co., 1992—; vice chmn. Horvitz Newspapers, Inc., 1994—; pres. H.R.H. Family Found., 1992—; chmn. H.R.H. Family Trust, 1992—; bd. dirs. Zephyr Mgmt., Inc.; corp. advisor Internat. Mgmt. Group, 1999—. Trustee Jewish Cmty. Fedn. Cleve., 1993—, Case Western Res. U., Musical Arts Assn., 1992—, Cleve. Ctr. Econ. Edn., 1992-95, Am. Cancer Soc., Cuyahoga County unit, 1989-95, Hathaway Brown Sch., Mt. Sinai Med. Ctr., Cleve. chpt. Am. Jewish Com., 1984-95, Montefiore Home for the Elderly, 1982-90, Health Hill Hosp. for Children, 1982-95, bd. pres., 1987-89; bd. dirs. Cleve. Mus. Art, 1991—, pres. bd., 1996-2001, chmn. bd., 2001—; bd. dirs. U. Va. Law Sch. Found., 1999-. Office: Jones Day Reavis & Pogue 901 Lakeside Ave E Cleveland OH 44114-1190 also: Parkland Mgmt Co 1001 Lakeside Ave E Ste 900 Cleveland OH 44114-1172

HORWICH, ALLAN, lawyer; b. Des Moines, Apr. 8, 1944; s. Joseph Maurice and Bernice (Davidson) H.; m. Carolyn Ruth Allen, Feb. 28, 1975; children: Benjamin, Diana, Eleanor, Flannery. AB, Princeton U., 1966; JD, U. Chgo., 1969. Bar: Ill. 1969, U.S. Dist. Ct. (no. dist.) Ill. 1969, U.S. Ct. Appeals (7th cir.) 1971, U.S. Ct. Appeals (10th cir.) 1983, U.S. Supreme Ct. 1976, U.S. Dist. Ct. (ctrl. dist.) Ill. 1990, U.S. Dist. Ct. (ea. dist.) Wis. 1995, U.S. Dist. Ct. (ea. dist.) Mich. 1995, U.S. Ct. Appeals (6th cir.) 1996. Assoc. Schiff Hardin & Waite, Chgo., 1969-74; ptnr. Schiff Hardin and Waite, 1975—, vice-chmn., 1989-95. Adj. prof. law Northwestern U. Sch. Law, 1999—2000, sr. lectr. law, 2000—. Home: 216 W Concord Ln Chicago IL 60614-5743 Office: Schiff Hardin & Waite 6600 Sears Tower Chicago IL 60606 E-mail: ahorwich@schiffhardin.com.

HORWICH, GEORGE, economist, educator; b. Detroit, July 23, 1924; s. Charles and Rose (Katzman) H.; m. Geraldine Lessans, Dec. 27, 1953; children: Ellen Beth, Karen Louise, Robert Lloyd, Susan Jean. Student, Wayne State U., 1942-43, 46, Ind. U., 1943-44; AM, U. Chgo., 1951, PhD, 1954. Lectr. econs. Extension Ctrs. Ind. U., Gar and Calumet, 1949-52, instr. econs. Bloomington, 1952-55; rsch. assoc. Nat. Bur. Econ. Rsch., N.Y.C., 1955-56; from asst. prof. to prof. econs. Purdue U., West Lafayette, Ind., 1956-99, chmn. econs. dept., 1974-78, Burton D. Morgan prof. for study pvt. enterprise, 1981-94, prof. emeritus, 1999—. Sr. rsch. assoc. Brookings Instn., Washington, 1958-62; sr. economist U.S. Dept. Energy,

Washington, 1978-80; spl. asst. for contingency planning U.S. Dept. Energy, 1984; adj. scholar Am. Enterprise Inst., 1984—; collaborating scientist energy divsn. Oak Ridge Nat. Lab., 1988-94; mem. U.S. Treasury Cons. Group, Washington, 1969; cons. Fed. Res. Bank, Chgo., 1971; vis. prof. econs. U. Calif., San Diego, 1971-72, People's Univ. of China, Beijing, 1992, Kobe (Japan) U. Commerce, 1996-97; vis. scholar Victoria U., New Zealand, 1997; staff Ind. Coun. Econ. Edn., West Lafayette, 1974—, Ctr. Pub. Policy and Pub. Adminstrn., Purdue U., West Lafayette, 1977—; advisor Econ. Inst. Rsch. and Edn., Boulder, Colo., 1977—; cons. U.S. Dept. Energy, 1980-88, Fortune 500 cos., 1965—, U.S. Dept. State, Washington, 1982, 92, Hudson Inst., 1991; vis. prof. Yokohama (Japan) City U., 2000. Author: Money, Capital and Prices, 1964; (with others) Costs and Benfits of a Protective Tariff on Refined Petroleum Products After Crude Oil Decontrol, 1980, Energy: An Economic Analysis, 1983; (with D.L. Weimer) Oil Price Shocks, Market Response and Contingency Planning, 1984; Responding to International Oil Crises, 1988; editor: Monetary Process and Policy, 1967, (with P.A. Samuelson) Trade, Stability, and Macroeconomics, 1974; (with J.P. Quirk) Essays in Contemporary Fields of Economics, 1981; (with E.J. Mitchell) Policies for Coping with Oil-Supply Disruptions, 1982, Energy Use in Transportation Contingency Planning, 1983; (with G.J. Lynch) Food, Policy and Politics, 1989; contbr. articles to profl. jours. With U.S. Army, 1943-46, ETO. NSF grantee; Fulbright rschr., 1996-97. Mem. Internat. Assn. Energy Econs., Am. Econ. Assn., Midwest Econs. Assn., Mont. Pelerin Soc., Nat. Assn. Scholars, Phila. Soc., Assn. Pub. Policy Analysis and Mgmt. Home: 120 Seminole Dr West Lafayette IN 47906-2116 Office: Purdue U Dept Econs West Lafayette IN 47907-1310

HORWITZ, IRWIN DANIEL, otolaryngologist, educator; b. Chgo., Mar. 31, 1920; s. Sol and Belle (Stern) H.; m. Isabel Morwitz, July 23, 1944; children— Steven, Judd, Clare. B.S., U. Ill., 1941, M.D., 1943. Intern Cook County Hosp., Chgo., 1944; resident Ill. Eye and Ear Infirmary, 1946-48; practice otolaryngology, 1948—; clin. prof., head divsn. otolaryngology Chgo. Med. Sch., 1969; prof. Rush Med. Sch., 1976—; formerly chief divsn. otolaryngology Mt. Sinai Hosp., former pres. med. staff. Contbr. articles profl. jours. Served to capt., M.C. AUS, 1944-46. Fellow A.C.S.; mem. AMA, Chgo. Otol. and Laryngol. Assn., Am. Acad. Ophthalmology and Otolaryngology, Ill., Chgo. med. socs. Home: 1633 2nd St #106 Highland Park IL 60035-5719 Office: 9669 Kenton Ave Skokie IL 60076-1266

HORWITZ, RONALD M. business administration educator; b. Detroit, June 25, 1938; s. Harry and Annette (Levine) H.; m. Carol Bransky, Mar. 30, 1961; children: Steven, Michael, David, Robert. BS, Wayne State U., 1959, MBA, 1961; PhD, Mich. State U., 1964. CPA, Mich. Prof. fin. U. Detroit, 1963-73, 75-79; healthcare cons., dir. personnel devel. Arthur Young & Co., Detroit, 1974-75; prof. fin., dean Sch. Bus. Adminstrn. Oakland U., Rochester, Mich., 1979-90, acting v.p. for acad. affairs, 1992-93, prof. fin., 1991-92, 93—. Contbr. articles to profl. jours. Bd. dirs. Providence Hosp. and Med. Ctr., 1995—, The Roeper Sch., 1996—; pub. mem. Greater Detroit Health Coun., 1980—; mem. fin. com. Ascension Health, St. Louis, 1998-2001, audit com., 2001—; audit com. Daus. of Charity Nat. Health System, 1988-93; mem. adv. bd. Providence Hosp., Southfield, 1980-95. Stonier fellow Am. Bankers Assn., 1963. Mem. Healthcare Fin. Mgmt. Assn. (bd. dirs. 1976-80), Mich. Assn. CPA's (grantee 1960), Fin. Mgmt. Assn., Am. Acctg. Assn., Acctg. Aid Soc. Detroit (founder), Mich. Bridge Assn. (pres. 1974-76). Avocation: bridge (life master). Office: Oakland U Sch Bus Adminstrn Rochester MI 48309-4493 E-mail: horwitz@oakland.edu.

HOSENPUD, JEFFREY, cardiovascular physician; b. Nov. 21, 1951; m. Janet Robbins, June 10, 1979; children: Jessica Sydney, Nathaniel Louis. BA with high honors, U. Calif., San Diego, 1973; MD, UCLA, 1977. Diplomate in internal medicine and cardiovascular medicine Am. Bd. Internal Medicine; diplomate Nat. Bd. Med. Examiners. Intern U. Wash., Seattle, 1977-78, resident in medicine, 1978-79, Med. Coll. Wis., Milw., 1979-80; fellow in cardiology Oreg. Health Scis. U., Portland, 1980-82, instr. medicine, 1982, instr.medicine, 1982, asst. prof. medicine, 1983-88, assoc. prof., 1988-93, prof., 1993-94; prof., chief divsn. cardiovascular medicine Med. Coll. Wis., Milw., 1994-98, Northwest Nut. Life prof. medicine, 1994—. Contbr. articles to profl. jours.; referee jours. USPHS fellow, 1981-83; Oreg. Heart Assn. rsch. fellow, 1981; NIH grantee; N.L. Tartar rsch. fellow, 1981, 82, other grants and awards. Fellow Am. Coll. Cardiology (coun. on clin. cardiology); mem. Am. Fedn. for Clin. Rsch., Internat. Soc. for Heart Transplantation, Western Soc. for Clin. Investigation, Pacific N.W. Transplant Soc., Am. Soc. Transplant Physicians, United Network for Organ Sharing, Trasnplantation Soc., Alpha Omega Alpha. Office: Med Coll Wis Cardiovascular Medicine Froedtert East FM Lit East 9200 W Wisconsin Ave Milwaukee WI 53226-3522

HOSKINS, RICHARD JEROLD, lawyer; b. Ft. Smith, Ark., June 19, 1945; s. Walter Jerold and Emma Gladys (Gaither) H.; children: Stephen Weston, Philip Richard. B.A., U. Kans., 1967; J.D., Northwestern U., 1970. Bar: N.Y. 1971, Ill. 1976, U.S. Supreme Ct. 1982. Assoc. Davis Polk & Wardwell, N.Y.C., 1970-73; asst. U.S. atty., So. Dist. N.Y., 1973-76; assoc. Schiff Hardin & Waite, Chgo., 1976-77, ptnr., 1978—. Adj. prof. U. Va. Law Sch., 1980-83, Northwestern U. Law Sch., 1992-98, sr. lectr., 1999—. Contbr. articles to profl. jours. Mem. vis. com. U. Chgo. Div. Sch.; bd. trustees Seabury-Western Theol. Sem.; Chancellor Episcopal Diocese of Chgo. Fellow Am. Coll. Trial Lawyers, Am. Bar Found.; mem. ABA, Ill. State Bar Assn., Chgo. Bar Assn., 7th Cir. Bar Assn., Assn. of Bar of City of N.Y., Chgo. Coun. Lawyers, Law Club Chgo., Met. Club (Chgo.), Univ. Club (Chgo.). Office: 6600 Sears Tower Chicago IL 60606

HOSMER, CRAIG WILLIAM, state legislator; b. Springfield, Mo., Mar. 16, 1959; BA, U. Mo. Columbia, 1982; JD, George Washington U., 1986. State rep. Dist. 138 Mo. State Congress, 1991—. Chmn. criminal law com., mem. higher edn. com., civil and adminstrv. law com., correctional insts. com., judiciary com. Office: State Capitol Rm 404 A Jefferson City MO 65101

HOSTETTLER, JOHN N. congressman; b. Evansville, Ind., July 19, 1961; s. Earl Eugene and Esther Aline (Hollingsworth) H.; m. Elizabeth Ann Hamman, Nov. 12, 1983; children: Matthew, Amanda, Jaclyn. BSME, Rose-Hulman Inst. Tech. Reg. profl. engr. Engr. So. Ind. Gas and Electric, Evansville, 1986-94; mem. U.S. Congress from 8th Ind. Dist., Washington, 1995—; mem. Agriculture and National Security coms. Deacon 12th Avenue Gen. Baptist, 1986—. Republican. Baptist. Office: US Ho of Reps 1507 Longworth HOB Washington DC 20515-0001*

HOTALING, ROBERT BACHMAN, community planner, educator; b. Syracuse, N.Y., July 19, 1918; s. Elliot Danforth and Florence (Bachman) Hotaling; m. M. Janet Kelley, Nov. 24, 1943 (dec.); children: Marilyn Kelley, Brock Elliot, William Austin, Richard Chapman; m. Jeanne Bryant, July 31, 1971 (dec.); m. Phyllis Hargrave, July 27, 2001. BS in Environ. Sci. and Forestry, Syracuse U., 1942; M of Urban and Regional Planning, Mich. State U., 1952. Staff dir. McFadzean, Everly Rose and Assocs., Chgo., 1946-49; dir. state and local planning R.I. Exec. Dept., Providence, 1952-55; tech. coord. for planning Interstate hwy. sytems through New England, R.I., Mass. and Conn., 1954-55; city planning dir., urban renewal planner Portland, Maine, 1955-57; acting dir., sec. Greater Portland Regional Planning Commn., 1956-57; prof. urban and regional planning Coll. Social Sci., Mich. State U., East Lansing, 1957-81; prof. lifelong edn. Inst. Community Devel., Mich. State U., 1957-81; prof. emeritus Mich. State U., 1981—; assoc. McKenna and Assocs., Farmington Hills, Mich., 1992—, Freeman, Smith & Assocs., Lansing, 1992—, Pub. Sector Cons., Lansing, 1992—. Pres. Urban Cons., Inc., 1962-66; pres., owner Robert B. Hotaling and Assoc., 1949—; expert witness to law firms, state and fed. agys., philanthropic orgns.; cons., lectr., seminarian Mich. Twp. Assn., 1963-81, Mich. Mcpl. League, 1978-94; mem. Mich. State Bd. of Registration for Profl. Community Planners, 1967-81, chmn., 1970-72, 76-79; cons. to state agys., polit. orgns. and corps. Author: Michigan Local Planning Commissioners Handbook (3 edits.), Michigan Township Planning and Zoning Handbook (2 edits.); chmn. editorial com. Mich. Laws Relating to Planning (3 edits.); contbr. articles to profl. jours. Mem. twp. planning commn. 1958-70, 87-94, 96-2001, chmn. 1969-70, 1998-2000, Meridian Twp., Ingham County, Mich.; mem. Meridian Twp. charter com., chmn., 1970-73; mem. Meridian Twp. Zoning Bd. of Appeals, 1969-70, 87, chmn. 1969-70; mem. strategic planning com. for planning future of Meridan Twp., Gov.'s State Legis. Zoning Revision Com., 1977-79; bd. dirs. Mich. Parks Assn., 1960-68; charter mem. Am. Inst. Cert. Profl. Community Planners, 1954-81; mem. Mich. State Bd. Registration for Profl. Community Planners State Examination Com., 1969-99, Am. Inst. Planners Nat. Examination Com. for Profl. Planners, 1977-78, 99. Capt. U.S. Army Corps. Engrs., 1942-46. Recipient Meritorious Svc. award Mich. Mcpl. League, 1994. Mem. Mich. Soc. Consulting Planners (bd. dirs. 1979—). Episcopalian. Home and Office: PO Box 304 Haslett MI 48840-0304 Fax: 517-702-9615. E-mail: rbhjbh@aol.com.

HOTCHKISS, EUGENE, III, retired academic administrator; b. Berwyn, Ill., Apr. 1, 1928; s. Eugene and Jeanette (Kennan) H.; m. Suzanne Ellen Troxell, Nov. 17, 1962; 1 dau., Ellen Sinclair. AB, Dartmouth Coll., 1950; PhD, Cornell U., 1960; LLD (hon.), Ill. Coll., 1976, Lake Forest Coll., 1993. Asst. to dean Dartmouth Coll., 1953-54, asst. dean, 1954-55, asso. dean, 1958-60; asst. dean Cornell U., Ithaca, N.Y., 1955-58; dean students, lectr. history Harvey Mudd Coll., Claremont, Calif., 1960-63, dean coll., 1962-68; exec. dean Chatham Coll., Pitts., 1968-70; pres. Lake Forest (Ill.) Coll., 1970-93, pres. emeritus, 1993—; interm pres. Eckerd Coll., 2000-01. Lt. (j.g.) USNR, 1950-53. Mem. Chgo. Coun. Fgn. Rels., Econ. Club, Chgo. Onnentsia Club, Caxton Club, Phi Beta Kappa, Phi Kappa Phi, Chi Phi. Office: Lake Forest Coll 555 N Sheridan Rd Lake Forest IL 60045-2338

HOTELLING, HAROLD, law and economics educator; b. N.Y.C., Dec. 26, 1945; s. Harold and Susanna Porter (Edmondson) H.; m. Barbara M. Anthony, May 4, 1974; children: Harold, George, James, Claire, Charles. AB, Columbia U., 1966; JD, U. N.C., 1972; MA, Duke U., 1975, PhD, 1982. Bar: N.C. 1973. Legal advisor U. N.C., Chapel Hill, 1972-73; instr. bus. law U. Ky., Lexington, 1977-79, asst. prof., 1980-84; asst. prof. dept. econs. Oakland U., Rochester, Mich., 1984-89; assoc. prof. econs. Lawrence Technol. U., Southfield, 1989—, chmn. dept. humanities social scis. and comm., 1994-99. Contbr. articles to profl. jours. Episcopalian. Home: 2112 Bretton Dr S Rochester Hills MI 48309-2952 Office: Lawrence Technol U Dept Humanities Southfield MI 48075 E-mail: hotelling@ltu.edu.

HOTH, STEVEN SERGEY, lawyer, educator; b. Jan. 30, 1941; s. Donald Leroy and Ina Dorothy (Barr) H.; m. JoEllen Maly, July 29, 1967; children: Andrew Steven, Peter Lindsey. AB, Grinnell Coll., 1962; JD, U. Iowa, 1966; postgrad., U. Pa., 1968, Oxford (Eng.) U., 1973. Bar: U.S. Ct. Appeals (8th cir.) 1966, U.S. Tax Ct. 1967, U.S. Ct. Claims 1967, U.S. Dist. Ct. Iowa 1968, U.S. Dist. Ct. N.D. 1968, U.S. Dist. Ct. S.D. 1968, U.S. Supreme Ct. 1973, U.S. Ct. Appeals (7th cir.) 1982. Law clk. to chief justice U.S. Ct. Appeals (8th cir.), Fargo, N.D., 1967-68; assoc. Hirsch, Adams, Hoth & Krekel, Burlington, Iowa, 1968-72, ptnr., 1972-91; pvt. practice, 1992—. Asst. atty. Des Moines County, Burlington, 1968-72, atty., 1972-83; alt. mcpl. judge, Burlington, 1968-69; lectr. criminal law Southeastern C.C., West Burlington, 1972-82; assoc. prof. polit. sci. Iowa Wesleyan Coll., Mt. Pleasant, 1981-82, Iowa Truck Rail; pres. Burlington Truck Rail, Burlington Short Line RR. Inc., Iowa Internat. Investments, Burlington Storage and Transfer; sec. Burlington Loading Co. Contbr. numerous articles to profl. jours. Chmn. Des Moines County Civil Svc. Commn.; trustee Charles H. Rand Lecture Trust; mem. Des Moines County Conf. Com., Des Moines County Conf. Bd.; dir. Burlington Med. Ctr. Staff Found.; moderator 1st Congl. Ch., Burlington; bd. dirs. UN Assn.; clk. Burlington North Bottoms Levy and Drainage Dist.; bd. mem., pres. Burlington Cmty. Sch. Dist. Bd. Edn., chmn. commn. on ministry, mem. exec. com. Nat. Assn. Congl. Christian Chs., moderator; treas. 1st dist. Dem. Com.; bd. dirs. Legal Aid Soc. Planned Parenthood Des Moines County. Recipient Chmn.'s award ARC, 1980; Reginald Heber Smith fellow in legal aid Cheyenne River Indian Reservation, Eagle Butte, S.D., 1967-68. Mem. Missionary Soc.-Nat. Assn. Congl. Christian Chs., ABA (internat. sect., tax sect.), Iowa State Bar Assn. (Med. Soc. liaison), Des Moines County Bar Assn., Am. Judicature Soc., Agrl. Law Com., Iowa Def. Coun., Iowa Archaeol. Soc., Soc. for German Am. Studies, Manorial Soc. Gt. Britain, Grinnell Coll. Alumni Assn. (bd. dirs.), Malawi Soc., Burlington-West Burlington C. of C. (bd. dirs.), Nat. Assn. Congrl. Christian Chs., Burlington Golf Club, New Crystal Lake Club (pres.), Elks, Eagles, Masons, Rotary. Office: PO Box 982 Hoth Bldg 200 Jefferson St Burlington IA 52601 E-mail: attorney@interl.net.

HOTTINGER, JAY, state legislator; b. Newark, Dec. 1, 1969; m. Cheri Moss, May 21, 1994. BA, BS summa cum laude, Capital U., Columbus, Ohio, 1992. Mgr. Jay Co.; councilman City of Newark, Ohio, 1992-94; pres. pro tem Newark City Coun., 1994; rep. dist. 77 Ohio Ho. of Reps., Columbus, 1995-98; mem. Ohio Senator from 31st dist., 1998—. Bd. dirs. East Mound Cmty. Devel. Corp., Am. Cancer Soc. (Newark). Named Outstanding Young Man of Licking County, 1992. Mem. Police Athletic League, Newark Area C. of C. Office: 042 State House Senate Bldg Columbus OH 43215-6108

HOTTINGER, JOHN CREIGHTON, state legislator, lawyer; b. Mankato, Minn., Sept. 18, 1945; s. Raymond Creighton and Hilda (Baker) H.; m. Miriam Jean Willging, Oct. 31, 1971; children: Julie, Creighton, Janna. BS, Coll. St. Thomas, St. Paul, 1967; JD, Georgetown U., 1971. Bar: Minn. 1972, U.S. Dist. Ct. Minn. 1977, U.S. Dist. Ct. (no. dist.) Ohio 1981, U.S. Ct. Appeals (5th cir.) 1991, U.S. Supreme Ct. 1992. Legis. asst. Hon. Donald M. Fraser, Washington, 1968-69, Dem. Study Group, Washington, 1969-73; ptnr. Farrish, Johnson, Maschka & Hottinger, Mankato, 1973-85; sr. ptnr. Hottinger Law Offices, 1985-91; ptnr. Gislason, Dosland, Hunter & Malecki, 1991-95; sr. ptnr. Hottinger Law Office, 1995—; of counsel MacKenzie and Gustafson, St. Peter, 1997—; mem. Minn. Senate, 1991—, asst. majority whip, 1993-95, majority whip, 1996-2000, chair health and family security com., 1997-2000, asst. majority leader, 2001—. Chair Bd. of Govt. Innovation and Cooperation, 1995. Dem. candidated Minn. Senate, 1982, U.S. Ho. of Reps., 1994; chair Midwestern Legis. Conf., 2000—; mem. exec. com. Coun. State Govts., 2000—, v.p., 2002. Mem. ABA, 5th Dist. Bar Assn., Minn. Bar Assn. Roman Catholic. Avocation: computer ops., writing. Office: Hottinger Law Office Box 3183 Mankato MN 56002-3183

HOUGHTON, DAVID DREW, meteorologist, educator; b. Phila., Apr. 26, 1938; s. Willard Fairchild and Sara Nancy (Holmes) H.; m. Barbara Flora Coan, June 22, 1963; children: Eric Brian, Karen Jeanette, Steven Andrew. BS, Pa. State U., 1959; MS, U. Wash., 1961, PhD, 1963. Rsch. scientist Nat. Ctr. Atmospheric Rsch., Boulder, Colo., 1963-68; exch. scientist USSR Acad. Scis., Moscow, 1966; vis. scientist Courant Inst. Math. Scis., N.Y.C., 1966; asst. prof. dept. meteorology U. Wis., Madison, 1968-69, assoc. prof., 1969-72, prof., 1972-2001, chmn. dept., 1976-79, 91-94, prof. emeritus, 2001—. Scientist Internat. Sci. and Mgmt. Group for Global Atmospheric Rsch. Program, Bracknell, Eng., 1972-73; lectr. Nanjing U., People's Republic of China, 1980 ; vis. sr. scientist Nat. Meteorol. Ctr., Washington, 1988; vis. scientist Inst. of Atmospheric Physics, Acad. of Scis., Beijing and Nanjing U., Nanjing, China, 1989; vis. cons. World Meteorol. Orgn., Geneva, 1997; vis. prof. Clark Atlanta U., 1998; trustee Univ. Corp. for Atmospheric Rsch., 1999-02. Contbr. articles to profl. jours.; editor-in-chief: Handbook of Applied Meteorology. Vice chmn. Planning Commn., Town of Dunn, Wis., 1977-81. NSF fellow, 1960-63. Fellow AAAS, Am. Meteorol. Soc. (chmn. edn. and human resources commn. 1987-93, pres. 1995-96); mem. Phi Beta Kappa, Sigma Xi, Phi Kappa Phi. Quaker. Office: U Wis Dept Atmos and Ocean Sci Madison WI 53706 E-mail: ddhought@facstaff.wisc.edu.

HOUK, JAMES CHARLES, physiologist, educator; b. Northville, Mich., June 3, 1939; s. James Charles and Elowene (Tower) H.; m. Antoinette Iacuzio, Dec. 28, 1963; children: Philip, Nadia, Peter. BSEE, Mich. Tech. U., 1961; MSEE, MIT, 1963; PhD, Harvard U., 1966. Instr. Harvard U. Med. Sch., 1967-69, asst. prof., 1969-73; lecturer Mass Inst. Tech., 1971-73; assoc. prof. Johns Hopkins U. Med. Sch., 1973-78; adjunct assoc prof. Univ. of North Carolina, 1975; prof., chmn. dept. physiology Northwestern Univ. Med. Sch., 1978—. Co-author: Medical Physiology 14th edit., 1980, Handbook of Physiology--The Nervous System II, 1981, Encyclopedia of Neuroscience, 1987, Models of Information Processing in the Basal Ganglia, 1995; contbr. chpts. to books. Recipient Javits award NIH, 1984-92. Mem. IEEE, AAAS, Soc. for Neurosci., Am. Physiol. Soc., European Neurosci. Assn., Assn. of Chmn. of Dept. of Physiology, Internat. Neural Network Soc. Office: Northwestern U 303 E Chicago Ave Chicago IL 60611-3093

HOUK, ROBERT SAMUEL, chemistry educator; b. New Castle, Pa., Nov. 23, 1952; s. Robert H. and Rose B. Houk; m. Linda Lembke, Oct. 3, 1981; children: Andrew, Mary. BS, Slippery Rock State Coll., 1974; PhD, Iowa State U., 1980. Asst. prof. chemistry Iowa State U., Ames, 1981-87, assoc. prof., 1987-91, prof., 1991—. Cons. Perkin Elmer Sciex, Norwalk, Conn., 1982—. Author: Handbook of ICP-MS, 1992; contbr. articles to profl. jours. Recipient M.F. Hasler award Spectroscopy Soc. Pitts., 1993, Wilkinson Teaching award Iowa State U., 1993. Mem. Am. Chem. Soc. (award in chem. instrumentation 1993), Soc. for Applied Spectroscopy (L.W. Strock award 1986, Maurice F. Hasler award 1993), Am. Soc. for Mass Spectrometry. Achievements include construction of first inductively coupled plasma-mass spectrometer for trace elemental analysis. Office: Iowa St Univ Ames Lab Ames IA 50011-0001

HOUPIS, CONSTANTINE HARRY, electrical engineering educator; b. Lowell, Mass., June 16, 1922; s. Harry John and Metaxia (Gourokous) H.; m. Mary Stephens, Aug. 28, 1960; children: Harry C., Angella S. Student, Wayne U., 1941-43; BS, U. Ill., 1947, MS, 1948; PhD, U. Wyo., 1971. Spl. rsch. asst. U. Ill., 1947-48; devel. elec. engr. Babcock & Wilcox Co., Alliance, Ohio, 1948-49; instr. elec. engring. Wayne State U., 1949-51; prin. elec. engr. Battelle Meml. Inst., Columbus, Ohio, 1951-52; prof. elec. engring. Air Force Inst. Tech., Wright-Patterson AFB, 1952-96, prof. emeritus, 1997—. Guest lectr. Nat. Tech. U. Athens, 1958, 99, U. Patras, 1984, Weizmann Inst. Sci., 1984, U. Strathclyde, 1995, Binghampton U., 1996; sr. rsch. assoc. Air Force Rsch. Lab., 1981-97, sr. rsch. assoc. emeritus, 1997—. Author: (with J.J. D'Azzo) Feedback Control System Analysis and Synthesis, 1960, 2d edit., 1966; Principles of Electrical Engineering: Electric Circuits, Electronics, Energy Conversion, Control Systems Computers, 1968; Linear Control Systems Analysis and Design: Conventional and Modern, 1975, 4th edit., 1995; (with J. Lubelfeld) Outline of Pulse Circuits; (with G.B. Lamont) Digital Control Systems: Theory Software, Hardware, 1985, 2d edit., 1992; (with S. Rasmussen) Quantitative Feedback Theory: Fundamentals and Applications, 1999, also articles on automatic controls in profl. jours. in U.S., U.K. and Europe. Served with AUS, 1942-46. Recipient Outstanding Engr. award Dayton Area Nat. Engrs. Week, 1962, Outstanding Civilian Career Svc. award, 1997. Fellow IEEE; mem. Am. Soc. Engring. Edn., Am. Hellenic Edn. Progressive Assn., Tau Beta Pi, Eta Kappa Nu. Greek Orthodox. Home: 1125 Brittany Hills Dr Dayton OH 45459-1415 Office: Air Force Inst Tech 2950 P St Bldg 642 Dayton OH 45433-7765

HOUSE, GEORGE, radio personality; m. Diane House. Radio host WIBM, Jackson, Mich., WEAQ, Eau Claire, Wis., WAXX, Eau Claire, WAYY, Eau Claire. Avocations: golf, fishing, acting, movies. Office: WAXX PO Box 1 Eau Claire WI 54702

HOUSE, JAMES STEPHEN, socialogical psychologist, educator; b. Phila., Jan. 27, 1944; s. James Jr. and Virginia Miller (Sturgis) H.; m. Wendy Fisher, May 13, 1967; children: Jeff, Erin. BA, Haverford Coll., 1965; PhD, U. Mich., 1972. From. instr. to assoc. prof. sociology Duke U., Durham, N.C., 1970-78; assoc. prof. sociology/assoc. rsch. scientist Survey Rsch. U. Mich., Ann Arbor, 1978-82, assoc. chair dept. sociology, 1981-84, prof. sociology, sr. rsch. scientist Survey Rsch. Ctr., 1982—, chair dept. sociology, 1986-90, dir. Survey Rsch. Ctr., Inst. Social Rsch., 1991-2001. Author: Work Stress and Social Support, 1981; co-editor: Sociological Perspectives on Social Psychology, 1995; assoc. editor Social Psychology Quar., 1988-91, Jour. Health & Social Behavior, 1997-2000; N.Am. editor Work and Stress, 1985-88; contbr. chpts. to books and articles to profl. jours. Guggenheim fellow, 1986-87. Fellow: AAAS, Soc. Behavioral Medicine, Am. Acad. Arts and Scis.; mem.: Soc. for Epidemiol. Rsch., Soc. for Psychol. Study of Social Issues, Acad. Behavioral Medicine Rsch., Am. Sociol. Assn., Inst. Medicine of Nat. Acad. Scis. Office: Univ Mich Inst Social Rsch PO Box 1248 Ann Arbor MI 48106-1248 E-mail: jimhouse@isr.umich.edu.

HOUSE, TED C. state legislator; b. Kansas City, Mo., Aug. 22, 1959; s. Keith and Ilene House; m. Mardi House. BA, Meth. Coll., 1981; JD, U. Mo. Kansas City, 1984. Intern legis. U.S. Congressman Ike Skelton, 1979; state rep. Mo. State Congress, 1980; atty. gen. State of Mo., 1982-84; mem. Mo. Ho. of Reps. from 15th dist., Jefferson City, 1988-94, Mo. Senate from 2nd dist., 1995—. Mem. appropriations com., edn. and pub. safety com., transp. com., labor and indsl. rels. com., conservation, parks and tourism com., econ. devel. com. Francis Howell Sch. Dist.; vice chmn. civil and criminal law com., ins. and housing com.; EMT Howard County Ambulance Svc.; legal investigator Trade Offense Divsn. Office Miss. Atty. Gen.; assoc. Heggs, Pryor & House. Mem. St. Charles C. of C. (govt. concerns com.), Salvation Army (bd. dirs.), Teen Parent Day Care Ctr., Phi Mu Alpha.

HOUSEHOLDER, LARRY, state official, small business owner; m. Taundra Householder; children: Derek, Adam, Matthew, Nathan, Luke. Grad. in polit. sci. , Ohio U., 1983. Commr. Perry County; Spkr. of Ho., Dist. 78 Ohio Ho. Rep., 2001—. Bd. chmn. Tri-County CAA; mem. L.F.C.P. Solid Waste Bd., Perry County Planning Commn. Coach Youth Baseball. Named Hon. chpt. farmer, 1995. Mem.: NFIB, C.of C., Rules and Ref. Com. (chmn.), 32nd Degree Scottish Rite, Shrine, Moose, Eagles, Lions, Grange, Farm Bur. Achievements include Speaker Householder running for state representative in 1996 where he has worked diligently to promote economic development, infrastructure, and improved education. Office: 77 South High St 14th Fl Columbus OH 43215-2500 Office Fax: 614-644-9494. Business E-Mail: rep78@ohr.state.oh.us.*

HOUSEMAN, GERALD L. political science educator, writer; b. Marshalltown, Iowa, Mar. 12, 1939; s. Lawrence D. and Mary N. (Smith) H.; m. Penelope Lyon, Feb. 11, 1961 (dec. 1994); children: Christopher, Elisabeth, Victoria; m. Juliana Sujata, 1999. BA, Calif. State U., Hayward, 1965, MA, 1967; PhD, U. Ill., 1971. Asst. prof. polit. sci. Ind. U., Ft. Wayne, 1971-76, assoc. prof., 1976-82, prof., 1982-2000. Vis. prof. New

Coll., Durham, Eng., 1975-76, Calif. State Polytech. U., San Luis Obispo, 1983-84, U. Calif., Irvine, 1984-85, St. Mary's Coll. Calif., 1985-86, Ind. U. Coop. Program in Malaysia, 1989-90, 94, 95, Fulbright Program, Indonesia, 1993-94, Malaysia, 2000-01. Author: (with H. Mark Roelofs) The American Political System 1983, G.D.H. Cole, 1979, The Right of Mobility, 1979, City of the Right, Urban Applications of American Political Thought, 1982, State and Local Government: The New Battleground, 1986; (with Michael W. MaCann) Judging the Constitution, 1989, Questioning the Law in Corporate Americia: Agenda for Reform, 1993, America and the Pacific Rim: Coming to Terms with New Realities, 1995. Mem. Transit Authority Bd., Ft. Wayne, 1973-75; city planning commr., 1982-83; Dem. candidate 4th dist. Ind. U.S. Ho. of Reps., 1996. With USMC, 1954-57. Grantee NSF, 1970, Ford Found., 1973, 74, NEH, 1977-78, 87, Ind. U. fellow 1973, 74, 77; recipient Wildavsky award Best Pub. Policy Article of Yr., 1994. Mem Am. Polit. Sci. Assn. (seminar grantee 1980, 81), Asian Studies Assn., Ind. Polit. Sci. Assn. (pres. 1979-80). E-mail: Houseman66@gateway.net.

HOUSER, DONALD RUSSELL, mechanical engineering educator, consultant; b. River Falls, Wis., Sept. 2, 1941; s. Elmont Ellsworth and Helen (Bunker) H.; m. Colleen Marie Collins, Dec. 30, 1967; children: Kelle, Kerri, Joshua. BS, U. Wis., 1964, MS, 1965, PhD, 1969. Registered profl. engr., Ohio. Instr. U. Wis., Madison, 1967-68; from asst. prof. to prof. Ohio State U., Columbus, 1968—, dir. Gear Dynamics and Gear Noise Rsch. Lab., 1979—, dir. Ctr. for Automotive Rsch., 1994-99. V.p. Gear Rsch. Inst., State Coll., Pa., 1990-99. Author: Gear Noise, 1991; contbg. editor Sound and Vibration mag., 1988-96; assoc. editor Jour. Mech. Design, 1993-94; mem. adv. bd. JSME Internat. Jour.; contbr. articles to profl. jours. Elder St. Andrews Presbyn. Ch., Columbus, 1972-75. Fellow ASME (legis. liaison Ohio coun. 1976-80, Century II medallion 1980); mem. Am. Gear Mfrs. Assn. (acad.), Soc. Automotive Engrs., Am. Helicopter Soc., Inst. Noise Control Engrs. Roman Catholic. Achievements include development of technology for measuring gear transmission error under load. Office: Ohio State U 206 W 18th Ave Columbus OH 43210-1189 E-mail: houser.4@osu.edu.

HOVDA, THEODORE JAMES, lawyer; b. Forest City, Iowa, Oct. 15, 1951; s. Ernest J. and Doris (Goodnight) H.; m. Susan J. Miller, Feb. 24, 1973; children: Theodore James III, Lee Joseph, Margaux Ann. BS, Iowa State U., 1973; JD, U. Iowa, 1977. Asst. county atty. Hancock County, Garner, Iowa, 1977-78, county atty., 1979-98; mem. Riehm & Hovda, 1977-98, Hovda Law Office, 1998—. County chmn. Hancock County Rep. Ctrl. Com., 1979-98. Mem. Iowa Bar Assn., Hancock County Bar Assn., Dist. 2A Bar Assn., Rotary, Masons. Republican. Methodist. Home: 785 11th Street Pl Garner IA 50438-1848 Office: Hovda Law Office PO Box 9 395 State St Garner IA 50438-1236 Fax: 641-923-3108. E-mail: tshovda@kalnet.com.

HOVEN, TIM, state legislator; b. Dec. 22, 1963; BA, U. Wis., Oshkosh. Assemblyman Wis. State Dist. 60, 1994—. Mem. Ozaukee County (Wis.) Bd., Port Washington (Wis.) Bd. Rev., Ozaukee County Econ. Devel. Corp. Mem. Ducks Unltd. Address: 204 S Webster St Port Washington WI 53074-2129

HOVER, GERALD R. state agency administrator; BA, Mich. U.; MS, PhD, Calif. State U., San Ann. Asst. state pk. Utah State Pk.; dir. Kans. Wildlife and Pk. Dept., Pratt, 1993—. Office: Kans Wildlife & Pk Dept 512 SE 25th Ave Pratt KS 67124-8174 Fax: 316-672-2972.

HOVERSON, ROBERT L. finance company executive; With Provident Fin. Group, Cin., 1985-92, sr. v.p., 1992-98, pres., CEO, 1998—. Office: Provident Fin Group Inc 1 E 4th St Cincinnati OH 45202-3717 Fax: 513-345-7185.

HOWARD, CLARK, radio personality; Owner travel agy. chain; radio host The Clark Howard Show WTMK radio, Milw., 1987—. Office: WTMJ 720 E Capital Dr Milwaukee WI 53212

HOWARD, DESMOND KEVIN, professional football player; b. Cleveland, OH, May 15, 1970; BA Comm. Studies, U. Mich. Wide receiver Washington Redskins, 1992-94; wide receiver, kick returner Jacksonville Jaguars, 1995, Green Bay Packers, 1996-97, Oakland Raiders, 1997-98; wide receiver Detroit Lions, 1998—. Named College Football Player of the Year, The Sporting News, 1991; recipient Heisman Trophy, 1991, Maxwell award, 1991, MVP Super Bowl XXXI, 1997. Office: Detroit Lions 1200 Featherstone Rd Pontiac MI 48342-1938 also: Detroit Lions, Inc. 222 Republican Drive Allen Park MI 48101

HOWARD, GLENN L. state legislator; b. Aug. 25, 1939; m. Florence Howard. Student, Ala. State U., U. Indpls. Mem. Ind. Senate from 33d dist. Mem. Judiciary, Planning & Pub. Svc., Transp., Health & Environ. Affairs, Pub. Policy and Internat. Cooperation Coms. Ind. State Senate. Mem. Indpls. City County Coun.; active Cmty. Affairs & News Media Rels., pub. affairs Indpls. Power & Light Co., Ind. State Black Expo and Urban League; bd. dirs. Noble Ctrs.; mem. Father Kelly's Youth Club; bd. dirs. Meals on Wheels, Indpls. Housing Strategy, Indpls. Campaign for Healthy Babies. Democrat. Home: 1005 W 36th St Indianapolis IN 46208-4129

HOWARD, JAMES JOSEPH, III, utility company executive; b. Pitts., July 1, 1935; s. James Joseph Jr. and Flossie (Wenzel) H.; m. Donna J. Fowler; children: James J. IV, Catherine A., Christine A., William F. BBA, U. Pitts., 1957; MS, MIT, 1970. With Bell Telephone of Pa., Pitts., 1957-78, v.p., gen. mgr., 1976-78; v.p. ops. Wis. Telephone Co., Milw., 1978-79, exec. v.p., chief operating officer, 1979-81, pres., chief exec. officer, 1981-83, chmn., chief exec. officer, 1983; pres., chief operating officer Ameritech, Chgo., 1983-87, dir.; pres., chief exec. officer No. States Power Co., Mpls., 1987—, chmn., 1988—, Xcel Energy, 2000-2001. Bd. dirs. Walgreen Co., Deerfield, Ill., No. States Power Co., Mpls., Honeywell, Mpls., Fed. Res. Bank of Mpls., Ecolab, St. Paul, ReliaStar Fin., Mpls., Edison Electric Inst., Electric Power Rsch. Inst., chmn. Nuclear Energy Inst. Trustee U. St. Thomas, St. Paul. Sloan fellow MIT, 1969. Mem. Conf. Bd. N.Y.

HOWARD, JANET C. former state legislator; m. Allen Howard; children: Shirle, Raymond, George. Student, Ea. Ky. U., U. Cin. Councilwoman City of Forest Park, Ohio; senator Ohio State Senate, Columbus. Mem. Nat. Fedn. Rep. Women; bd. dirs. Hamilton County Rep. Women's Club; mem. Beechwood PTA, Forest Park Commn. Forum, adv. coun. Winton Woods Sch., adv. bd. Hamilton County Human Svcs., task force Forest Park Quality of Life. Mem. Greenhills-Forest Park Kiwanis.

HOWARD, JERRY THOMAS, state legislator; b. Oak Ridge, Mo., Mar. 28, 1936; s. John Thomas and Sylvia Ann (Brecheisen) H.; m. Shirla Jean Rathjen McFaddin, 1973; children: Eliza Jane, John Trevor, Erin Penney, Michael Penney, Bill McFaddin. BS, Southeast Mo. U., 1960. Mem. from Dist. 156, Mo. State Ho. of Reps., 1973-77, 87-90; mem. Mo. State Senate, 1990—. Vice chmn. com. agr., conservation, parks and tourism; mem. com. fin. and govtl. orgn., com. judiciary, com. appropriations, com. adminstrv. rules; chmn. com. on aging, families and mental health, com. on wetlands, spl. com. on welfare reform, others. Mem. Elks, Am. Legion, Lions Internat., Masons, Scottish Rite, Shriners.

HOWARD, JOHN, former state legislator; m. Beverly; two children. Past mem. Carrington City Coun.; N.D. State rep. Dist. 29, 1989-96; svc. rep. Otter Tail Power Co. Mem. jud., polit. subdivsn. and ops. divsn. coms.; vice-chmn. appropriations-govt. Mem. Kiwanis, Am. Legion.

HOWARD, JOHN MALONE, surgeon, educator; b. Autaugaville, Ala., Aug. 25, 1919; s. Fontaine Maury and Mary Lorena (O'Brien) H.; m. Nina Lyman Abernathy, Dec. 22, 1943; children: John Malone Jr., Robert Fontaine, Nina Louise, George Glenn, Susan Elaine, Laura Leigh. BS, Birmingham So., 1941; MD, U. Pa., 1944. Resident in surgery U. Pa., 1944-50; mem. faculty Baylor U., Houston, 1950-55; prof., chmn. Emory U., Atlanta, 1955-57; chair surgery Hahnemann Med. Coll., Phila., 1958-62; dir. emergency med. svcs. Med. Coll. Ohio, Toledo, 1974-78, prof. surgery, 1974—, prof. emeritus; pvt. practice surgery, 1990—. Dir. U.S. army surg. rsch. team Korean War. Editor: Studies of Battle Casualties in Korea, vol. III, 1953, vol. I, 1955, vol. II, 1955, vol. IV, 1955 (with others) Surgical Diseases of the Pancreas, 1960, 3rd edit., 1997, The Chemistry of Trauma, 1963, Cardiovascular Surgery-Supplement to Circulation, 1963, Septic Shock. Clinical and Experimental Experiences, 1964, Studies of Ultraviolet Irradiation: Its Efficiency in Preventing Infections in Operative Wounds, 1964; contbr. chpts. to books, more than 400 articles to profl. jours. Capt. U.S. Army Med. Corps., 1951-53. Decorated Legion of Merit; recipient Distinction award Nat. Rsch. Coun., Disting. Achievement award Am. Trauma Soc. Mem. Royal Coll. Surgeons Edinburgh (hon.), Brazilian Coll. Surgeons (fgn.). Avocations: fishing, boating, history, gardening. Home: 11004 Winslow Rd Whitehouse OH 43571-9643 Office: Med Coll Ohio Dowling Hall 3065 Arlington Ave Toledo OH 43614-2570

HOWE, JONATHAN THOMAS, lawyer; b. Evanston, Ill., Dec. 16, 1940; s. Frederick King and Rosalie Charlotte (Volz) H.; m. Lois Helene Braun, July 12, 1963; children: Heather C., Jonathan Thomas Jr., Sara E. BA with honors, Northwestern U., 1963; JD with distinction, Duke U., 1966. Bar: Ill. 1966, U.S. Dist. Ct. (no. dist.) Ill. 1966, U.S. Ct. Appeals (7th cir.) 1967, U.S. Tax Ct. 1968, U.S. Supreme Ct. 1970, U.S. Ct. Appeals (D.C. cir.) 1976, U.S. Ct. Appeals (9th cir.) 1980, U.S. Ct. Appeals (4th, 5th, 11th dirs.) 1983, U.S. Claims Ct. 1990. Ptnr. Jenner & Block, Chgo., 1966-85, sr. ptnr. in charge assn. and adminstrv. law dept., 1978-85; founding and sr. ptnr., pres. Howe & Hutton, Chgo., Washington & St. Louis, 1985—. Exec. and adv. coms. to Ill. Sec. of State to revise the Ill. Not for Profit Act, 1983-86; dir. Pacific Mut. Realty Investors, Inc., 1985-86; dir. cable TV options for public Chgo. Access Corp., 1995-97, Bostrom Corp., 2001—. Contbg. editor Ill. Inst. for Continuing Legal Edn., 1973—, Sporting Goods Bus., 1977-91, Meeting News, 1978-88, Meetings Mgr., 1988—, Meetings and Convs., 1991—; contbr. articles to profl. jours.; legal editor Meetings and Convs., 1990—. Mem. Dist. 27 Bd. Edn., Northbrook, Ill., 1969-89, sec., 1969-72, pres., 1973-84; chmn. bd. trustees Sch. Employee Benefit Trust, 1979-85; founding bd. dirs., pres. Sch. Mgmt. Found. Ill., 1976-84; mem. exec. com. Northfield Twp. Rep. Orgn., 1967-71; bd. deacons Village Presbyn. Ch. Northbrook, 1975-78, trustee, 1981-83; mem. Arts and Music Forum, 4th Presbyn. Ch., Chgo., 1990-93; spl. advisor Pres.'s Coun. Phys. Fitness and Sports, 1983-87, Duke Univ. Sch. of Law Bd. of Visitors (life mem.). Named Industry Leader of Yr., Meeting Industry, 1987, Sch. Bd. Mem. Yr. (twice), Ill. State Bd. Edn.; recipient Internat. Found. PaceSetters award Hospitality Sales Mktg. Assn., 1996. Fellow Internat. Forum of Travel and Tourism Advs., Am. Soc. Assn. Execs. (vice-chmn. legal com. 1983-86); mem. Internat. Assn. Conv. and Hosp. Indsl. Attys. (founder), ABA (antitrust sect. Nat. Inst. com., trade assn. law com. corp. banking and bus. law sect., sect. on litigation, adminstrv. law sect.; mem. internat. law com., continuing edn. com., tort and ins. practice, vice-chmn. com. sports law 1986—, standing com. meetings and travel 1988-93, spl. advisor 1993—), Task Force on Membership Benefits for Disabled Lawyers, Ill. Bar Assn. (antitrust sect., civil practice sect., sch. law sect., adminstrv. law sect.; co-editor Antitrust Newsletter 1968-70), Chgo. Bar Assn. (def. of prisoners com. 1966-83, antitrust law com. 1971—, continuing edn. com. 1977—, chmn. assn. and non-profit soc. law com. 1984-86), Am. Soc. Assn. Execs. (vice-chmn. legal com., founding mem. legal sect.), N.Y. Soc. Assn. Execs., Acad. Hospitality Industry Attys. (founder, bd. dirs. 1994—, pres. 2001--), Nat. Sch. Bds. Assn. (nat. bd. dirs. 1979-89, exec. com. 1981-89, sec.-treas. 1983-85, 2d v.p. 1985-86, pres. 1987-88, chmn. devel. com. 1982-87, pres. 1987-88), D.C. Bar Assn., Am. Judicature Soc., Ill. Assn. Sch. Bds. (pres. 1977-79, bd. dirs. 1971-88), Chi Bar Found. (life), Assn. Forum Chicagoland (assoc., formerly Chgo. Soc. Assn. Execs.), Nat. Sch. Bds. Found. (pres./trustee 1995—), U.S. C. of C. (legal coun. 1998—), Greater Washington Soc. Assn. Execs., Legal Club, Law Club, Mid-Am. Club, Tower Club, Univ. Club Chgo., Psi Upsilon. Home: 126 W Delaware Pl Chicago IL 60610-3252 Office: 20 N Wacker Dr Ste 4200 Chicago IL 60606-3191 E-mail: jth@howehutton.com.

HOWE, STANLEY MERRILL, manufacturing company executive; b. Muscatine, Iowa, Feb. 5, 1924; s. Merrill Y. and Thelma F. (Corriel) H.; m. Helen Jensen, Mar. 29, 1953; children: Thomas, Janet, Steven, James. B.S., Iowa State U., 1946; M.B.A., Harvard U., 1948. Prodn. engr. HON Industries, Muscatine, Iowa, 1948-54, v.p. prodn., 1954-61, exec. v.p., 1961-64, pres., 1964-90, chmn., 1984-96, chief exec. officer, 1979-91. Trustee Iowa Wesleyan Coll. Gerard Swope fellow Harvard U., 1948. Mem. NAM, Bus. Instl. Furniture Mfrs. Assn. Methodist. Clubs: Rotary, Elks, 33. Office: Hon Industries Inc 414 E 3d St PO Box 1109 Muscatine IA 52761-0071

HOWE, WILLIAM HUGH, artist; b. Stockton, Calif., June 18, 1928; s. Edwin Walter and Eugenia (Mercante) H. AB, Ottawa (Kans.) U., 1951. Illustrator Western Auto Supply, Kansas City, Mo., 1952, Kansas City Mdse. Mart, 1953-56; comml. artist U.S. Army C.E., Kansas City, 1958-64, Howard Needles Tammen & Bergendoff Cons. Engrs., Kansas City, 1964-68, Urban & Regional Planning, 1968-70; freelance artist, 1970—. Exhibited paintings of butterflies Philbrook Art Ctr., Tulsa, Ft. Worth Children's Mus., Montserrat Gallery, N.Y.C., Witte Meml. Art Mus., San Antonio, Anthropology Mus., Chapultepec Park, Mexico City; represented in permanent collections: Smithsonian Instn., Washington, Franklin Mint (Pa.), Cranbook Inst., Bloomfield Hills, Mich., U. Mich. Exhibits Mus., Ann Arbor, Oak Knoll Mus., Clayton, Mo., Am. Mus. Natural History, N.Y.C., Denver Mus. Natural History, Am. Baptist Assembly, Green Lake, Wis., Mowbray Union, Ottawa U., Kans., Cen. Mo. State Coll., Warrensburg, Mich. State U., East Lansing, U. Wyo. Art Mus., Laramie, San Diego Mus. Nat. History, Balboa Park, U. Ariz., Tuscon, Ill. State Mus. Art, Springfield, Mont. Hist. Soc., Helena, Wyo. State Art Mus., Cheyenne, Ariz. State U., Tempe, Milw. Pub. Mus., State Capitol Bldg., Denver, Denver Pub. Libr., Kansas City (Mo.) Mus. History Sci., Presdl. Palace, Tamazunchale, San Luis Potosi, Mexico, Ottawa (Kans.) Jr. H.S., others; Am. Heritage Wildlife cards Am. Butterflies, 1983, U. Kans., 1994, U. Calif. Berkeley, Allyn Mus. Entomology, Sarasota, U. Colo., Colo. State U., Calif. Acad. Scis., San Francisco, Oakland (Calif.) Mus., James Ford Bell Mus., U. Minn. (Mpls), Coutts Art Mus., 1997; Author-artist: Our Butterflies and Moths, 1964, The Butterflies of North America, 1975, Butterfly Chart of North America, 1979, Butterfly sect. Readers Digest North American Wildlife, 1980; co-author (with Carlos R. Beutelspacher Baights), U.N.A.M., Mexico City, 1984; one man show Caroline Kingcade Gallery, North Kansas City, Mo., 1988, Coutts Mus. of Art, El Dorado, 1997, Dallas Mus. Natural History, Fair Park, 1999, George P. Spiva Art Ctr., Joplin, Mo., 1999; TV show Hoy Mismo, 1986. Mem. Ottawa Community Arts Coun., Leavenworth Arts. Coun.; mem. Larry Hatteberg's "Kans. People" KAKE-TV, Wichita. Named Am. Artist Am. References, 1990. Mem. Jour. Lepidopterists Soc., Burroughs Nature Club, Audubon Soc. Mo., Central States Entomo. Soc., Los Angeles County Mus., Spiva Art Ctr., Dallas Mus. Natural History, Mus. Culture and Natural History, Harvard Botanical Mus.. Democrat. Episcopalian. Avocation: collecting butterflies in Mexico and Guatemala. Home: 822 E 11th St Ottawa KS 66067-3138

HOWELL, ANDREW, state legislator; Law enforcement officer, Ft. Scott, Kans.; mem. from dist. 4 Kans. State Ho. of Reps., Topeka. Address: Apt 8 3404 SW 29th Ter Topeka KS 66614-2749

HOWELL, GEORGE BEDELL, equity investing and managing executive; b. Schenectady, Sept. 19, 1919; s. Jesse M. and Grace (Gerhaeusser) H.; m. Mary Barbara Crohurst, July 10, 1944; children: Raymond Gary, Terry Barbara, Janice Patricia, Nancy Jo, George Bedell Jr. BS in Adminstrv. Engring., Cornell U., 1942. With GE, 1946-59; v.p. mfg. Leece Neville Co., Cleve., 1959-61, Royal Electric Co., Pawtucket, R.I., 1961-62; dir. ops. packaging equipment and product devel. Acme Steel Co. (merged with Interlake Steel Corp. 1965), 1962-64; v.p. adminstrv. svc. Interlake Steel Corp., Chgo., 1964-66, v.p. internat. divsn., v.p. Acme Products divsn., 1966-70; CEO Golconda Corp., Chgo., 1970-72; v.p. devel. Internat. Minerals & Chems. Corp., 1972-73, sr. v.p., pres. industry group, 1974-77, exec. v.p., 1977-81; pres., CEO Wurlitzer Co., 1982-86, chmn., pres., CEO, 1986-87, vice chmn., 1987-88; prin. Mid West Ptnrs., Chgo., 1988-89; gen. ptnr. Pfingsten Ptnrs., 1989-94, ptnr., 1994—; chmn. Hallcrest Holding Corp., 1992-97, dir. exec. com., 1998—. Chmn. bd. trustees Village of Oak Brook, Ill., 1965-73, pres., 1973-79; trustee Christ Ch., Oak Brook, vice chmn., 1992-97, trustee emeritus, 1998. N.Y. State and Univ. scholar Cornell U., 1942. Mem. McGraw Wildlife Found., Chgo. Athletic Assn., Medinah Country Club, Econ. Club (Chgo.), Ocean Reef Club (Fla.). Home: 5 Brighton Ln Oak Brook IL 60523-2323 Office: 520 Lake Cook Rd Ste 375 Deerfield IL 60015-5632 E-mail: ghowell@pfingsten.com., howellgb@aol.com.

HOWELL, J. MARK, electronics company executive; Mgr. Ernst & Young LLP; corp. controller ADESA Corp., 1992-94; exec. v.p fin., CFO, treas., sec. Brightpoint, Inc., Indpls., 1994-96; COO, 1995—; pres., 1996—; also bd. dirs. Office: Brightpoint Inc # 575 600 E 96th St Indianapolis IN 46240-3788

HOWELL, JOEL DUBOSE, internist, educator; b. Tex., May 11, 1953; s. Wilson and Nora (Levitas) Howell; m. Linda C. Samuelson, June 26, 1976; children: Jonathan Samuelson, Benjamin Samuelson. BS, Mich. State U., 1975; MD, U. Chgo., 1979; PhD in History and Sociology of Sci., U. Pa., 1987. Intern, resident in internal medicine U. Chgo., 1979-82; Robert Wood Johnson clin. scholar U. Pa., Phila., 1982-84; instr. U. Mich., Ann Arbor, 1984-86, asst. prof., 1986-90, assoc. prof., 1990-97, prof., 1997—, Victor Vaughan prof. history medicine, 2001—. Editor: (book) Technology and American Medicine Practice: 1880-1930, 1988, Medical Lives and Scientific Medicine at Michigan; author: Technology in the Hospital, 1995. Scholar Henry J. Kaiser Family Fedn. Faculty, 1989—92, Charles E. Culpeper Found. Med. Humanities, 1992—96. Fellow: ACP, Am. Osler Soc., Am. Assn. History Medicine. E-mail: jhowell@umich.edu.

HOWELL, ROBERT EDWARD, hospital administrator; b. Marietta, Ohio, Jan. 19, 1949; married; 3 children. BS, Muskingham Coll., 1971; MS in Hosp. and Health Svcs. Adminstrn., Ohio State U., 1977. Assoc. dir. U. Minn. Hosps. and Clinics, Mpls., 1980-86; exec. dir. Med. Coll. Ga. Hosps. and Clinics, Augusta, 1986-94; dir., CEO, U. Iowa Hosps. and Clinics, Iowa City, 1994—. Mem. exec. com. Accreditation Coun. for Grad. Med. Edn. Mem. Coun. Tchg. Hosps. (past chmn.), Am. Assn. Med. Colls. (exec. com.), Am. Hosp. Assn. (coord. com. med. edn.), Univ. Health System Consortium (exec. com.). Office: U Iowa Hosps and Clinics 200 Hawkins Dr Iowa City IA 52242-1009

HOWELL, R(OBERT) THOMAS, JR. lawyer, former food company executive; b. Racine, Wis., July 18, 1942; s. Robert T. and Margaret Paris (Billings) H.; m. Karen Wallace Corbett, May 11, 1968; children: Clarinda, Margaret, Robert. AB, Williams Coll., 1964; JD, U. Wis., 1967; postgrad., Harvard U., 1981. Bar: Wis. 1968, Ill. 1968, U.S. Dist. Ct. (no. dist.) Ill. 1968, U.S. Tax Ct. Assoc. Hopkins & Sutter, Chgo., 1967-71; atty. The Quaker Oats Co., 1971-77, counsel, 1977-80, v.p., assoc. gen. corp. counsel, 1980-84, v.p., gen. corp. counsel, 1984-96, corp. sec., 1994-96; of counsel Seyfarth Shaw, 1997—. Bd. dirs. Ill. Inst. of Continuing Legal Edn., Lawyers for Creative Arts. Editor (mags.) Barrister, 1975-77, Compleat Lawyer, 1983-87. Bd. dirs. Metro. Family Svcs.; bd. dirs. Chgo. Bar Found., 1987—, pres., 1991-93; trustee 4th Presbyn. Ch., Chgo., 1989-92, pres., 1994-96; bd. dirs. Chgo. Equity Fund, 1992-96. Capt. USAR, 1966-72. Mem. ABA, Ill. Bar Assn., Wis. Bar Assn., Chgo. Bar Assn. (bd. mgrs. 1977-79, chmn. young lawyers sect. 1974-75), LawClub Chgo., Econ. Club Chgo., Univ. Club Chgo. (bd. dirs. 1982-85, 87-88, v.p.). Presbyterian. Home: 853 W Chalmers Pl Chicago IL 60614-3233 Office: Seyfarth Shaw 55 E Monroe St Ste 4200 Chicago IL 60603-5863 E-mail: thowell@seyfarth.com.

HOWERTON, JIM, state legislator; Mem. Mo. Ho. of Reps., Jefferson City. Republican.

HOWLAND, JOAN SIDNEY, law librarian, law educator; b. Eureka, Calif., Apr. 9, 1951; d. Robert Sidney and Ruth Mary Howland. BA, U. Calif., Davis, 1971; MA, U. Tex., 1973; MLS, Calif. State U., San Jose, 1975; JD, Santa Clara (Calif.) U., 1983; MBA, U. Minn., 1997. Assoc. librarian for pub. svcs. Stanford (Calif.) U. Law Library, 1975-83, Harvard U. Law Library, Cambridge, Mass., 1983-86; dep. dir. U. Calif. Law Library, Berkeley, 1986-92; dir. law libr., Roger F. Noreen prof. law U. Minn. Sch. of Law, 1992—, assoc. dean info. tech., 2001—. Questions and answers column editor Law Libr. Jour., 1986-91; memt. column editor Trends in Law Libr. Mgmt. & Tech., 1987-94. Mem. ALA, ABA (com. on accreditation 2001—), Am. Assn. Law Libra., Am. Assn. Law Schs., Am. Indian Libr. Assn. (treas. 1992—), Am. Law Inst. Office: U Minn Law Sch 229 19th Ave S Minneapolis MN 55455-0400

HOWLAND, WILLARD J. radiologist, educator; b. Neosho, Mo., Aug. 28, 1927; s. Willard Jay and Grace Darlene (Murphy) H.; m. Kathleen V. Jones, July 28, 1945; children: Wyck, Candice, Charles, Thomas, Heather AB, U. Kans., 1948, MD, 1950; MA, U. Minn., 1958; DSc (hon.), Coll. Med. N.E. Ohio, 1990. Intern U.S. Naval Hosp., Newport, R.I., 1950-51; pvt. practice medicine Kans., 1951-55; resident Mayo Clinic, Rochester, Minn., 1955-58; radiologist Ohio Valley Gen. Hosp., Wheeling, W.Va., 1959-67; prof., dir. diagnostic radiology Med. Units U. Tenn., Memphis, 1967-68; dir., chmn. dept. radiology Aultman Hosp., Canton, Ohio, 1968-87, pres. med. staff, 1978; prof., chmn. radiology coun. Coll. Medicine N.E. Ohio U., Rootstown, 1976-87, program dir. integrated radiology residency, 1976-87. Author, co-author three books and rsch. papers in field. With U.S. Army, 1945-46, USN, 1950-51. Fellow Am. Coll. Radiology; mem. AMA, Radiol. Soc. N.Am., Am. Roentgen Ray Soc., Ohio State Radiol. Soc. (pres. 1980-81), Masons. Republican. Presbyterian. Office: 1405 Harbor Dr NW Canton OH 44708-3098

HOWREY, EUGENE PHILIP, economics educator, consultant; b. Geneva, Dec. 1, 1937; s. Eugene Edgar and Ellen Pauline (Boord) H.; children: Patricia Marie, Richard Philip, Margaret Ellen, Mark McCall. A.B., Drake U., 1959; Ph.D., U. N.C., 1964; M.A. (hon.), U. Pa., 1972. Asst. prof. econs. Princeton U., N.J., 1963-69; assoc. prof. econs. U. Pa., Phila., 1969-73; prof. econs. U. Mich., Ann Arbor, 1973—, prof. stats., 1978—. Cons. Mathematica, Inc., Princeton, 1965-75; guest lectr. Inst. Advanced Studies, Vienna, 1974, 76. Contbr. articles to profl. jours.

Research grantee NSF, 1975, 79, 84 Mem. Ann Arbor Velo Club, Ann Arbor Bicycle Touring Club (pres. 1979-80), Phi Beta Kappa. Democrat. Roman Catholic. Avocation: bicycling. Home: 2152 Overlook Ct Ann Arbor MI 48103-2336 Office: U Mich Dept Econs Ann Arbor MI 48109 E-mail: eph@umich.edu

HOYE, DONALD J. hardware distribution company executive; b. 1949; Dealer acct. ServiStar, a predecessor of TruServ, from 1971, numerous positions, including v.p. sales, ops.-info. sys.; pres., CEO, Coast to Coast; pres., COO, TruServ Corp., Chgo., until 1999, pres., CEO, 1999—. Office: TruServ Corp 8600 W Bryn Mawr Ave Chicago IL 60631-3579

HOYT, JAMES LAWRENCE, journalism educator, athletic administrator; b. Wausau, Wis., July 18, 1943; s. Lawrence Beryl and Eleanor (Kischel) H.; m. Cheryl Johannes, July 23, 1966; children: Randall James, Rebecca Cheryl, Diane Caroline. BS, U. Wis., 1965, MS, 1967, PhD, 1970; postgrad., U. Pa., 1967-68. Reporter Sta. WTMJ-TV, Milw., 1965-67; prof. journalism Ind. U., Bloomington, 1970-73; writer, editor NBC News, Washington, 1972; prof. journalism U. Wis., Madison, 1973—; dir. U. Wis. Sch. Journalism, 1981-91. Chmn. athletic bd., faculty rep. NACC Big Ten Conf. Western Collegiate Hockey Assn., U. Wis., Madison, 1991—. Author: Mass Media in Perspective, 1984, Writing News for Broadcast, 1994; contbr. articles to profl. jours. Recipient Carol Brewer award Wis. Associated Press, 1996. Mem. Assn. for Edn. in Journalism and Mass Comm., Radio-TV News Dirs. Assn., Broadcast Edn. Assn., Internat. Radio-TV Soc. (Frank Stanton fellow 2001). Methodist Avocation: ice hockey. Home: 4709 Fond Du Lac Trl Madison WI 53705-4812 Office: U Wis Sch Journalism 821 University Ave Madison WI 53706-1412

HOYT, KENNETH BOYD, educational psychology educator; b. Cherokee, Iowa, July 13, 1924; s. Paul Fuller and Mary Helen (Tinker) H.; m. Phyllis June Howland, May 25, 1946; children: Andrew Paul, Roger Alan, Elinore Jane. B.S., U. Md., 1948; M.A., George Washington U., 1950; Ph.D., U. Minn., 1954; Ed.D. (hon.), Crete Coll., 1981. Tchr., counselor Northeast (Md.) High Sch., 1948-49; dir. guidance Westminster (Md.) High Sch., 1949-50; tchg. asst. U. Minn., 1950-51, instr. ednl. psychology, 1951-54; asst. prof. U. Iowa, Iowa City, 1954-57, assoc. prof., 1957-60, prof. edn., 1961-69; dir. Splty. Oriented Student Research Program, prof. edn. U. Md., Silver Spring, 1969-74; dir. office career edn. U.S. Office Edn., 1974-82; disting. vis. scholar Embry Riddle Aero. U., 1982-84; Univ. Disting. prof. edn. Kans. State U., 1984—; dir. counseling high skills vo-tech career options program Kansas State U., 1993-98. Cons. Ordnance Civilian Personnel Agy., 1954-60, Iowa Dept. Pub. Instrn., 1954-69, U.S. Dept. Labor, 1956-68, 65—, U.S. Office Edn., 1958—, Nat. Inst. Edn., 1973—. Author: (with L.A. Van Dyke) The Drop-Out Problem in Iowa High Schools, 1958, (with C.P. Froehlich) Guidance Testing, 1960, Selecting Employees for Developmental Opportunites and Guidance Services; Suggested Policies for Iowa Schools, 1963, Career Education: Contributions to an Evolving Concept, 1976, Career Education: Where It Is and Where It Is Going, 1981; co-author: Career Education: What It Is and How To Do It, 1972, Career Education and the Elementary School Teacher, 1973, Career Education in the Middle Junior High School, 1973, Career Education for Gifted and Talented Students, 1974, Career Education in the High School, 1977; Editor: Counselor Education and Supervision, 1961-65; Mem. editorial bd.: Personnel and Guidance Jour, 1960-63; Contbr. articles to profl. jours. Served with AUS, 1943-46. Fellow APA (divsn. 17); mem. Am. Counseling Assn. (pres. 1966-67, Arthur Hitchcock Outstanding Disting. Profl. Svc. award, 1994), Am. Vocat. Assn. (Outstanding Svc. award 1972), Assn. Counselor Edn. and Supervision (Disting. Svc. award 1965, Outstanding Career award 1990), Nat. Career Devel. Assn. (Eminent Career award 1981, pres. elect 1991-92, pres. 1992-93), Am. Sch. Counselors Assn., Am. Ednl. Rsch. Assn., Nat. Assn. for Industry Edn. Cooperation (vice-chmn. 1992—), Phi Delta Kappa. Home: 149 N Dartmouth Dr Manhattan KS 66503-3021 Office: Kans State U Coll of Edn 369 Bluemont Hall Manhattan KS 66506-5300 E-mail: khoyt@ksu.edu.

HRUBETZ, JOAN, dean, nursing educator; b. Collinsville, Ill., June 1, 1935; d. Frederick and Josephine (Nepute) H. RN, St. John's Hosp., St. Louis, 1956; BSN, St. Louis U., 1960, MA, 1970, PhD in Edn. and Counseling, 1975. Staff nurse St. John's Hosp., St. Louis, 1956-59; instr. med./surg. nursing St. Louis Mcpl. Sch. Nursing, 1960-63; asst. dir. nursing svc. Barnes Hosp., St. Louis, 1963-65, asst. dir. sch. nursing, 1965-68, ednl. cons., 1968-70, dir. sch. nursing, 1970-74; dir. undergrad. mprog. nursing St. Louis U., 1975-82, asst. to assoc. prof. nursing, 1975—, assoc. prof. pastoral health care, 1986—, dean Sch. Nursing, 1982—. Lectr. in field. Contbr. articles to profl. jours. Bd. dirs. Paraquad, Inc., Ctr. Independent Living, 1985-87, hon. mem., 1987—; bd. dirs. Kenrick-Glennon Seminar, 1988, sec. bd., 1989-90; mem. adv. com. project on Clin. Edn. in Care of Elderly, 1989. Group Health Found. grantee, 1987-88, 88-89, St. Louise U. Hosps. grantee, 1980-83, others. Mem. Mo. Assn. Adminstrs. of Baccalaureate and Higher Deg. Progs. in Nursing, St. Louis Assn. Deans and Dirs. of Schs. Nursing, Am. Assn. Colls. of Nursing (adv. com. to baccalaureate data project), Am. Nurses Assn., Mo. Nurses Assn., 3rd Dist. Mo. Nurses Assn., Nat. League Nursing, Mo. League for Nursing, St. Louis Reg. League for Nursing, Midwest Alliance in Nursing (governing bd. 1985-87, chair 1986-87, resolutions com. 1987-89), Conf. Jesuit Schs. Nursing, St. Louis Met. Hosp. Assn. Office: St Louis U Sch Nursing 3525 Caroline St Rm 222 Saint Louis MO 63104-1007

HUANG, THOMAS SHI-TAO, electrical engineering educator, researcher; b. Shanghai, China, June 26, 1936; came to U.S., 1958; s. Chien Liang and Allen (Chien) H.; m. Margaret Y. Nee, Apr. 4, 1959; children: Caroline B., Marjorie A., Thomas T., Gregory T. BS, Nat. Taiwan U., Taipei, 1956; MS, MIT, 1960, ScD, 1963. Asst. prof. MIT, Cambridge, Mass., 1963-67, assoc. prof., 1967-73; prof. Purdue U., West Lafayette, Ind., 1973-80, U. Ill., Urbana, 1980—, William L. Everitt Disting. Prof., 1996—. Vis. prof. Swiss Inst. Tech., Zurich, U. Hannover, Federal Republic of Germany, U. Que., Can., others; cons. IBM, AT&T Bell Labs., MIT Lincoln Lab., Kodak, others. Author 2 books; editor 12 books; contbr. more than 400 articles to tech. jours. Recipient A. V. Humboldt U.S. Sr. Scientist award Alexander V. Humboldt Found., 1976-77; Honda Lifetime Achievement award, 2000; Guggenheim fellow, 1971-72; fellow Japan Assn. for Promotion of Sci., 1986. Fellow IEEE (Signal Processing Soc. Tech. Achievement award 1987, Soc. award 1991, Third Millennium medal 2000, Jack S. Kilby medal 2001), Optical Soc. Am., Internat. Assn. for Pattern Recognition, Internat. Optical Engring. Soc.; mem. NAE, Chinese Acad. Engring. (fgn.). Office: Univ Ill Beckman Inst 405 N Mathews Ave Urbana IL 61801-2325

HUANG, VICTOR TSANGMIN, food scientist, researcher; b. Republic of China, Dec. 12, 1951; came to U.S., 1975; s. Shen Tan and Yeh Gee (Lai) H.; m. Jean Fong Chen, June 9, 1978; children: Hank Su, Andrea Su. BS, Hsing-Hua U., Hsin-Chu, Republic of China, 1973; MS, U. Chgo., 1977; PhD, Ohio State U., 1981. Teaching asst. U. Chgo., 1975-77; rsch. assoc. Ohio State U., Columbus, 1977-81; food scientist Pillsbury Co., Mpls., 1981—. Presenter dairy, baby and bakery product formulation field, 1977-94. Contbr. articles to profl. jours.; patentee frozen desserts and microwave food formulation fields in U.S. and Europe. Vice pres. Minn. Taiwanese Assn., Mpls., 1985. 2d lt. Taiwan Army, 1973-75. Mem. Am. Dairy Sci. Assn., Inst. Food Technologists, Am. Assn. Cereal Chemists, Am. Chem. Soc., Toastmasters (pres. Mpls. 1988). Office: Pillsbury Tech Ctr 330 University Ave SE Minneapolis MN 55414-1779

HUBBARD, DEAN LEON, university president; b. Nyssa, Oreg., June 17, 1939; s. Gaileon and Rhodene (Barton) H.; m. Aleta Ann Thornton, July 12, 1959; children: Melody Ann, Dean Paul John, Joy Marie BA, Andrews U., 1961, MA, 1962; diploma in Korean Lang., Yunsei U., Seoul, Korea, 1968; PhD, Stanford U., 1979. Dir. English Lang. Schs., Seoul, 1966-71; asst. to pres. Loma Linda U., Calif., 1974-76; acad. dean Union Coll., Lincoln, Nebr., 1976-80, pres., 1980-84, NW Mo. State U., Maryville, 1984—. Chair Acad. Quality Consortium, 1993-96; examiner Malcolm Baldridge Nat. Quality Award, 1993-96; judges panel Mo. Quality Award, 1994-96; adv. coun. edn. statistics U.S. Dept. Edn., 1997-99. Mem. ACE Leadership Devel. Coun., 1996—. Avocation: classical music. Office: NW Mo State U Office of President Maryville MO 64468-6001

HUBBARD, LINCOLN BEALS, medical physicist, consultant; b. Hawkesbury, Ont., Can., Sept. 8, 1940; s. Carroll Chauncey and Mary Lunn (Beals) H.; came to U.S., 1957; m. Nancy Ann Krieger, Apr. 3, 1961; children: Jill, Katrina. B.S. in Physics, U. N.H., 1961; Ph.D., MIT, 1967. Diplomate Am. Bd. Radiology; cert. health physicist Am. Bd. Health Physics. Postdoctoral appointee Argonne Nat. Lab., 1966-68; asst. prof. math. and physics Knoxville Coll. (Tenn.), 1968-70; asst. prof. physics Furman U., Greenville, S.C., 1970-74; chief physicist Mt. Sinai Hosp., Chgo., 1974-75, 79—, Cook County Hosp., Chgo., 1975-88; ptnr. Fields, Griffith, Hubbard & Broadbent, Inc., 1978-93; pres. Hubbard, Broadbent & Assoc., Ltd., 1993—; assoc. prof. med. physics, Rush U., 1986— . Mem. Am. Assn. Physicists in Medicine, Am. Coll. Radiology, Am. Phys. Soc. Author: (with S.S. Stefani) Mathematics for Technologists, 1979, (with G. B. Greenfield) Computers in Radiology, 1984. Home and Office: 4113 W End Rd Downers Grove IL 60515-2307

HUBBARD, STANLEY STUB, broadcast executive; b. St. Paul, May 28, 1933; s. Stanley Eugene and Didrikke A. (Stub) H.; m. Karen Elizabeth Holmen, June 13, 1959; children: Kathryn Elizabeth Hubbard Rominski, Stanley Eugene II, Virginia Anne Hubbard Morris, Robert Winston, Julia Didrikke Coyte. BA, U. Minn., 1955; hon. doctorate, Hamline U., 1995. With Hubbard Broadcasting, St. Paul, 1951—, pres., 1967—, chmn., CEO, 1983—; past chmn. U.S. Satellite Broadcasting Co., Inc., 1981-99. Mem. broadcast adv. com. on comm. subcom. Ho. of Reps., 1977—79; mem. adv. com. on advanced TV, FCC, 1988—95; mem. U.S. Nat. Inf. Infastructure Adv. Coun., 1994—96. Contbr. articles to profl. jours. Chmn. St. Croix Valley Youth Ctr., 1968—; trustee Hubbard Found.; bd. dirs. U. Minn. Found., Mpls., Am. Friends of Jamaica, Assn. Maximum Svc. TV, U. St. Thomas, Minn. Bus. Partnership; past advisor Gov.'s Crime Commn., Ramsey County Ice Arena Com.; past bd. dirs. The Guthrie Theater, The Psychoanalytic Found. of Minn., Sci. Mus. of Minn.; past mem. Hazelden Adv. Com.; mem. Met. Airports Pub. Found. Adv. Bd. Recipient Mitchell Charnley award Northwest Broadcast News Assn., 1991, Internat. Humanitarian award Am. Friends of Jamaica, 1989, Arthur C. Clarke award Satellite Broadcasting and Comm. Assn., 1994, DreamMaker award Children's Cancer Rsch. Fund, 1994, Disting. Svc. award Nat. Assn. Broadcasters, 1995, Spurgeon award Boy Scouts Am., 1985, Avatar award Broadcast Cable and Fin. Mgmt., 1995, Human Rights award Am. Jewish Com., 1995, Cmty. Leadership award Mpls./St. Paul chpt. Alzheimer's Assn., 1995, Most Innovative Product award Minn. High Tech. Coun., 1995, Journalism Innovator award U. Nebr., 1996, Minn. Family Bus. award U. St. Thomas, 1996, Disting. Alumnus award Breck Sch., 1996, Minn. and Dakotas Entrepreneur of Yr. award, 1996, Heritage award U.S. Hockey Hall of Fame, 1996, U. Minn. M Club Hall of Fame Lifetime Achievement award, 1996, Broadcasters' Found. Golden Mike award, 1997, Acad. of Achievement's Golden Plate award, 1997; named to Broadcasting and Cable Hall of Fame, 1991, Soc. Satellite Profls. Internat. Space Hall of Fame, 1992, Acad. Achievement's Golden Plate award, 1997, Broadcast Pioneer award Minn. Broadcasters Assn., 1998, John Hogan Disting. Svc. award Radio & TV News Dirs. Assn., 2000; inductee St. Croix Valley Athletics Hall of Fame, 2000. Mem. NATAS (chmn. bd. trustees), Broadcast Pioneers, Internat. Radio and TV Soc. Avocations: sailing and boating, reading, photography. Office: Hubbard Broadcasting Inc 3415 University Ave W Saint Paul MN 55114-2099

HUBER, SISTER ALBERTA, college president; b. Rock Island, Ill., Feb. 12, 1917; d. Albert and Lydia (Hofer) H. BA, Coll. St. Catherine, St. Paul, 1939; MA, U. Minn., 1945; PhD, U. Notre Dame, 1954. Mem. faculty Coll. St. Catherine, 1940—, prof. English, 1953-97; prof. emerita, 1997; chmn. dept. Coll. St. Catherine, 1960-63, acad. dean, 1962-64, pres., 1964-79. Trustee Avila Coll., Kansas City, Mo., 1986-97, St. Joseph's Hosp., St. Paul, 1971-80; pres. UN Assn. Minn., 1980-81; bd. dirs. St. Paul YMCA, 1986-92. Decorated Chevalier, Ordre des Palmes Acad.; recipient Outstanding Achievement award U. Minn. Alumni Assn., 1981. Mem. Phi Beta Kappa, Pi Gamma Mu. Office: 1724A Munster Ave Saint Paul MN 55116-3031

HUBER, DAVID LAWRENCE, physicist, educator; b. New Brunswick, N.J., July 31, 1937; s. Howard Frederick and Katherine Teresa (Smith) H.; m. Virginia Hullinger, Sept. 8, 1962; children: Laura Theresa, Johanna Jean, Amy Louise, William Hullinger. BA, Princeton U., 1959; MA, Harvard U., 1960, PhD, 1964. Instr. U. Wis., Madison, 1964-65, asst. prof., 1965-67, assoc. prof., 1967-69, prof., 1969—. Dir. Synchrotron Radiation Ctr., 1985-97, Phys. Scis. Lab, Stoughton, Wis., 1992—; disting. vis. prof. U. Mo., Kansas City, 1988. A.P. Sloan fellow, 1965-67, Guggenheim fellow, 1972-73, Nat. Assn. State Univs. and Land Grant Colls. fellow Office of Sci. and Tech. Policy, 1990-91. Fellow Am. Phys. Soc.; mem. AAAS, Sigma Xi. Office: Univ Wis Phys Scis Lab 3725 Schneider Dr Stoughton WI 53589-3034 also: U Wis Dept Physics 1150 University Ave Madison WI 53706-1302

HUBER, GREGORY B. state legislator; b. Jan. 25, 1956; MD, U. Wis., 1981. Asst. dist. atty. Marathon County Dist. Atty.'s Office; mem. from dist. 85 Wis. State Assembly, Madison, 1985, 88—. Pres. Rib Mountain State Park. Mem. Wausau Jaycees (past bd. dirs.), Wis. Alumni Club (bd. dirs.). Office: 406 S 9th Ave Wausau WI 54401-4541

HUBER, JOAN ALTHAUS, sociology educator; b. Bluffton, Ohio, Oct. 17, 1925; d. Lawrence Lester and Hallie (Althaus) H.; ; m. William Form, Feb. 5, 1971; children: Nancy Rytina, Steven Rytina. B.A., Pa. State U., 1945; M.A., Western Mich. U., 1963; Ph.D., Mich. State U., 1967. Asst. prof. sociology U. Notre Dame, Ind., 1967-71; asst. prof. sociology U. Ill., Urbana-Champaign, 1971-73, assoc. prof., 1973-78, prof., 1978-83, head dept., 1979-83; dean Coll. Social and Behavioral Sci., Ohio State U., Columbus, 1984-92; coordinating dean Coll. Arts and Sciences, Ohio State University, 1987-92, provost, 1992-93; sr. v.p., provost emeritus prof. Sociology emeritus, 1994. Author: (with William Form) Income and Ideology, 1973, (with Glenna Spitze) Sex Stratification, 1983. Editor: Changing Women in a Changing Society, 1973, (with Paul Chalfant) The Sociology of Poverty, 1974, Macro-Micro Linkages in Sociology, 1991. NSF research awardee, 1978-81 Mem. Am. Sociol. Assn. (v.p. 1981-83, pres. 1987-90), Midwest Sociol. Soc. (pres. 1979-80). Home: 2880 N Star Rd Columbus OH 43221-2959 Office: Ohio State U Dept Sociology 300 Bricker Hall 190 N Oval Mall Columbus OH 43210-1321 E-mail: huber.3@osu.edu.

HUBER, JOHN U. engineering executive; b. Saskatchewan, Can. B in Chem. Engring., U. Saskatchewan, 1960. With Internat. Nickel Co., 1960-63; various supr. positions Kalium Chems., Ltd., 1963-91; pres. Kalium Chems., Ltd. (subs. KCL Holdings, Inc.), 1991, KCL Holdings, Inc. (subs. Vigoro Corp.), 1991, Kalium Can. Ltd. (subs. KCL Holdings, Inc.), 1991; exec. v.p., officer Vigoro Corp. (now merged with IMC Global Inc.), 1996; corp. sr. v.p., pres. Crop Nutrients bus. unit IMC Global Inc., pres. IMC Potash bus. unit, 1999—, exec. v.p., officer Ill., 1999—. Mem. Can. Potash Export Assn. (dir. and chmn. bd. dirs.). Office: IMC Global Inc 2100 Sanders Rd Northbrook IL 60062-6139

HUBLER, MARY, state legislator; b. Milw., July 31, 1952; BS, U. Wis., Superior, 1973; JD, U. Wis., Madison, 1980. Former tchr., coach; atty.; mem. from dist. 75 Wis. State Assembly, Madison, 1984—, vice chairwoman tourism, recreation and forest product coms., 1985-98, mem. joint fin. com., until 1996; rural affairs & forestry State of Wis. Mem. Wis. Bar Assn. Office: PO Box 544 Rice Lake WI 54868-0544 also: Wis State Assembly State Capitol Madison WI 53702-0001

HUDEC, ROBERT EMIL, lawyer, educator; b. Cleve., Dec. 23, 1934; s. Emil and Mary (Tomcho) H.; m. Marianne Miller, Sept. 8, 1956; children: Michael Robert, Katharine Wright. B.A., Kenyon Coll., 1956, LL.D. (hon.), 1979; M.A., Cambridge U., 1958; LL.B., Yale U., 1961. Bar: D.C. 1963, Minn. 1974. Law clk. to Mr. Justice Potter Stewart, U.S. Supreme Ct., 1961-63; asst. gen. counsel Office Spl. Rep. for Trade Negotiations, Exec. Offices, 1963-65; Rockefeller Found. research fellow, 1965-66; asso. prof. law Yale U. Law Sch., 1966-72; prof. law U. Minn. Law Sch., Mpls., 1972—, Melvin C. Steen prof. law, 1986—. Author: The Gatt Legal System and World Trade Diplomacy, 1975, 2d edit., 1990, Developing Countries in the Gatt Legal System, 1987, Enforcing International Trade Law: The Evolution of the Modern GATT Legal System, 1993, Essays on the Nature of International Trade Law, 1999; contbr. articles to profl. jours. Mem. Am. Law Inst., Minn. Bar Assn. Office: U Minn Law Sch Minneapolis MN 55455

HUDKINS, CAROL L. state legislator; b. North Platte, Nebr., Feb. 21, 1945; m. Larry Hudkins; children: Janet, Kathy. Mem. Nebr. Legislature from 21st dist, Lincoln, 1992—; mem. agr. gen. affairs com.; mem. judiciary com. Mem. agr. gen. affairs com., judiciary com., rules com. (chair), natural resources com., transp. and comm. com, exec. bd., reference com. Mem. Saunders County Hist. Soc., Ned. Cattlemen, Saunders County Livestock Feeders; Neb. Cattlewomen. Republican. Methodist.

HUDNUT, ROBERT KILBORNE, clergyman, author; b. Cin., Jan. 7, 1934; s. William Herbert and Elizabeth (Kilborne) H.; m. Mary Lou Lundell; children by previous marriage: Heidi, Robert Kilborne, Heather, Matthew. B.A. with highest honors, Princeton, 1956; M.Div., Union Theol. Sem., N.Y.C., 1959. Ordained to ministry Presbyn. Ch., 1959; asst. minister Westminster Presbyn. Ch., Albany, N.Y., 1959-62; minister St. Luke Presbyn. Ch., Wayzata, Minn., 1962-73, Winnetka (Ill.) Presbyn. Ch., 1975-94. Exec. dir. Minn. Pub. Interest Research Group, 1973-75; Co-chmn. Minn. Joint Religious Legis. Coalition, 1970-75 Author: Surprised by God, 1967, A Sensitive Man and the Christ, 1971, A Thinking Man and the Christ, 1971, The Sleeping Giant: Arousing Church Power in America, 1971, An Active Man and the Christ, 1972, Arousing the Sleeping Giant: How to Organize Your Church for Action, 1973, Church Growth Is Not the Point, 1975, The Bootstrap Fallacy: What The Self-Help Books Don't Tell You, 1978, This People-This Parish, 1986, Meeting God in the Darkness, 1989, Emerson's Aesthetic, 1996, Call Waiting, 1999. Pres. Greater Met. Fedn. Twin Cities, 1970-72; chmn. Citizens Adv. Com. on Interstate 394, 1971-75; nat. chmn. Presbyns. for Ch. Renewal, 1971; Chmn. Democratic Party 33d Senatorial Dist. Minn., 1970-72, Minnetonka Dem. Party, 1970-72; fusion candidate for mayor, Albany, 1961; Bd. dirs. Minn. Council Chs., 1964-70; trustee Princeton U., 1972-76, Asheville (N.C.) Sch., 1979— . Rockefeller fellow, 1956; named Outstanding Young Man Minnetonka, 1967; recipient Distinguished Service award Minnetonka Tchrs. Assn., 1969 Mem. Phi Beta Kappa. Home and Office: 7145 65th St S Cottage Grove MN 55016-1130 E-mail: rkhudnut@aol.com.

HUDNUT, STEWART SKINNER, manufacturing company executive, lawyer; b. Cin., Apr. 29, 1939; s. William Herbert and Elizabeth Allen (Kilborne) H.; children: Alexander Putnam, Andrew Gerard, Nathaniel Parker. AB (summa cum laude), Princeton U., 1961; postgrad., Oxford U., Eng., 1962; JD, Harvard Law Sch., 1965; Environ. Law Cert., Pace U., 1991. Bar: N.Y. 1965, U.S. Dist. Ct. (so. and ea. dists.) N.Y., U.S. Ct. Appeals (2d cir.), U.S. Supreme Ct. Assoc. Davis Polk & Wardwell, N.Y.C., 1965-67, 71-73, Paris, 1968-70; v.p., counsel Bankers Trust Co., 1973-77; v.p., gen. counsel, sec. Scovill Mfg. Co., Waterbury, Conn., 1977-87; sr. v.p., gen. counsel, sec. Mcpl. Bond Investors Assurance Corp., White Plains, N.Y., 1987-89, Ill. Tool Works Inc., Glenview, Ill., 1992—. Bd. dirs., exec. com. Lyric Opera Guild of Chgo.; instr. Voyageur Outward Bound Sch., 1989-90. Woodrow Wilson fellow, Keasbey fellow Christ Ch. Oxford U., Eng., 1962. Mem. ABA, Ill. Bar Assn., Phi Beta Kappa. Republican. Presbyterian. Home: 56 Indian Hill Rd Winnetka IL 60093-3938 Office: Ill Tool Works Inc 3600 W Lake Ave Glenview IL 60025-5811

HUDSON, KATHERINE MARY, manufacturing company executive; b. Rochester, N.Y., Jan. 19, 1947; d. Edward Klock and Helen Mary (Rubacha) Nellis; m. Robert Orneal Hudson, Sept. 13, 1980; 1 child, Robert Klock. Student, Oberlin coll., 1964-66; BS in Mgmt., Ind. U., 1968; postgrad., Cornell U., 1968-69. Various postitions in fin., investor rels., communications, gen. mgr. instant photography Eastman Kodak Co., Rochester, 1970-87, chief info. officer, 1988-91, v.p., gen. mgr. printing and pub. imaging, 1991-93; pres., CEO W.H. Brady, Milw., 1994—, Brady Corp., Milw., 1999—. Bd. dirs. CNH Global N.V. Mem. adv. coun. Ind. U. Sch. Bus., 1994—; trustee Alverno Coll., 1994—; bd. dirs. Med. Coll. Wis., 1995—. Recipient Chief of the Yr. award Info. Week Mag., 1990, Athena award Rochester C. of C., 1992, WESG Breaking Glass Ceiling award, 1993, Sacajewea award, 1995; Lehman fellow N.Y. State, 1968; named Wis. Bus. Leader of Yr., 1995. Republican. Avocations: golf, fishing, creative writing. Office: Brady Corp 6555 W Good Hope Rd PO Box 571 Milwaukee WI 53201-0571 E-mail: kathy_hudson@bradycorp.com.

HUDSON, ROBERT PAUL, medical educator; b. Kansas City, Kans., Feb. 23, 1926; s. Chester Lloyd and Jean (Emerson) H.; m. Olive Jean Grimes, Aug. 1, 1948 (div. 1963); children: Robert E., Donald K., Timothy M.; m. Martha Isabelle Holter, July 10, 1965; children: Stephen, Laura. BA, U. Kans., 1949, MD, 1952; MA, Johns Hopkins U., 1966. Instr. U. Kans., Kansas City, 1958-59, assoc. in medicine, 1959-63, asst. prof., 1964-69, assoc. prof., 1969—, prof., chmn. history of medicine, 1969-95, ret. Author: Disease and Its Control, 1983; mem. editl. bd. Bull. History of Meidcine, Balt., 1981-94; contbr. articles to profl. jours. 1st lt. U.S. Army, 1953-55. Master ACP; mem. Am. Assn. for History of Medicine (pres. 1984-86), Am. Osler Soc. (bd. govs., pres. 1987-88). Home: 12925 S Frontier Rd Olathe KS 66061-8647 Office: Kans U Med Ctr 39th And Rainbow Blvd Kansas City KS 66160-0001 E-mail: rhudsonku@aol.com.

HUDSON, RONALD MORGAN, aviation planner; b. Anniston, Ala., May 7, 1954; s. James Alphus and Mildred Christine (Morgan) H.; m. Marsha Carol Smith, Dec. 27, 1974 (div. Aug. 1989); children: Jereme Brandon, Sara Elizabeth; m. Connie M. Luckey, Nov. 13, 1993. BS in Aviation Mgmt., Auburn U., 1976. Aviation planner Wainwright Engring. Co., Montgomery, Ala., 1978-81, Ralph Burke Assocs., Park Ridge, Ill., 1981-85; sr. assoc. mgr. aviation Knight Architects, Engrs., Planners, Inc., Chgo., 1985-96; sr. assoc. and aviation mgr. Hanson Profl. Svcs. Inc., Oak Brook, 1996—. Mem. Am. Planning Assn., Am. Inst. Cert. Planners, Am. Assn. Airport Execs., Ill. Pub. Airports Assn. Avocations: biking, travel. Home: 1710 E Oakton St Arlington Heights IL 60004-5000 E-mail: ronaldhudson@attbi.com.

HUDSON, STEVEN DANIEL, lawyer, judge; b. Trenton, Mo., Sept. 7, 1961; s. Jerry Daniel and Dorothy Louise (Wilhite) H.; m. Lora Sue Barnett, Dec. 21, 1986; children: Samantha Sue, Tanner Glen. BS in Bus. Adminstrn., William Jewell Coll., Liberty, Mo., 1983; JD, U. Mo., Kansas City, 1986. Bar: Mo. 1986, U.S. Dist. Ct. (we. dist.) Mo. 1986. Pvt. practice, Trenton, Mo., 1986—; pros. atty. Grundy County, 1995-99; assoc. cir. judge Grandy County Cir. Ct., 1999—. Mem. Trenton R-9 Vocat. Agr. Adv. Bd., 1990—; mem. North Ctrl. Mo. Coll. Office Occupations Adv. Bd., Trenton, 1991-93. Past pres., v.p. North Ctrl. Mo. Fair Bd., Trenton, 1987—; mem. Miss Trenton Scholarship Pageant Bd., 1988-95. Mem. Mo. Bar Assn., 9th Jud. Cir. Bar Assn. (pres. 1995), 3rd Jud. Cir. Bar Assn., Trenton Area C. of C. (mem. bd. 1988-90). Republican. Methodist. Avocation: sports. Office: 1013 Main St Trenton MO 64683-1839

HUDSON, THOMAS GEORGE, computer network executive; b. N.Y.C., Apr. 2, 1946; s. George Francis and Mary Hudson; m. Regina May Faulstich, Sept. 21, 1968; children: Gina, Tom, Anne, Matt. BSEE, U. Notre Dame, 1968; MBA in Fin., NYU, 1974; postgrad., Harvard U., 1990. Group dir. mktg. IBM Corp., Tokyo, 1984-87, v.p., gen. mgr., fin. industry exec. White Plains, N.Y., 1988-92, v.p. svcs. sector Stanford, Conn., 1992-93; sr. v.p., gen. mgr. McGraw Hill, N.Y.C., 1993-95, sr. v.p., 1995-96; pres., CEO Computer Network Tech., Mpls., 1996—, also bd. dirs. Mem. fin. com. World Econ. Coun., 1991, 92, 93. Mem. Info. Industry Assn. Roman Catholic. Avocations: skiing, boating, biking. Home: 45 Gideons Point Rd Excelsior MN 55331-9526 Office: Computer Network Technology Corporation 6000 Watham Ln N Plymouth MN 55442

HUEBSCH, MICHAEL D. state legislator; b. July 19, 1964; Grad., Oral Roberts U. Assemblyman Wis. State Dist. 94, 1994—. Mem. LaCrosse County Bd., Wis., LaCrosse Area Devel. Corp. Mem. Rotary. Address: 419 W Franklin St West Salem WI 54669-1531

HUELSKAMP, TIM, state legislator; b. Fowler, Kans., Nov. 11, 1968; m. Angela Huelskamp; 1 child, Natasha. BA, Coll. Santa Fe, 1991; PhD, Am. U., 1995. Mem. Kans. Senate, Topeka, 1996—, mem. elections and local govt. com., mem. energy and natural resources com., mem. transp. and tourism com., mem. joint com. on children and families. Republican. Office: 300 SW 10th Ave Rm 143N Topeka KS 66612-1504

HUELSMAN, JOANNE B. state legislator; b. Mar. 21, 1938; married. JD, Marquette U., 1980. Attorney, realtor, businesswoman; former mem. Wis. Assembly from 31st dist.; mem. Wis. Senate from 11th dist., Madison, 1990—. Republican. Home: 235 W Broadway Ste 210 Waukesha WI 53186-4826 Office: Wis State Senate PO Box 7882 Madison WI 53707-7882

HUENEKE, TERRY A. temporary services company executive; b. 1942; Degree in mktg., Milw. Area Tech. Coll., 1963, U. Wis., 1965. With Gt. Atlantic & Pacific Tea Co., Inc., 1960-69; asst. v.p. mktg. Career Acad., 1969-74; regional mktg. mgr., S.E. Manpower Inc., Milw., 1974-76, dir. U.S. field mktg., 1976-80, v.p. U.S., 1980-83, v.p. U.S. mktg., bus. devel., 1983-87, v.p., group exec. U.S. temporary svcs., 1987-88, exec. v.p., 1988—. Office: Manpower Inc 5301 N Ironwood Rd PO Box 2053 Milwaukee WI 53217-4982

HUETHER, ROBERT, state legislator; m. Karen; four children. Student, N.D. State U. N.D. State rep. Dist. 27, 1989—; dir. Cass County Elec./Minnkota Power; farmer. Mem. state and fed. govt. appropriations/human resources divsn., edn. and transp. coms. Democrat. Mailing: PO Box 679 Lisbon ND 58054-0679

HUFF, JOHN DAVID, church administrator; b. Muskegon, Mich., Nov. 20, 1952; s. Lucius Barthol and Marian (Brainard) H.; m. Diane Lynn Church, May 17, 1975; children: Joshua, Jason, Jessica. B in Religious Edn., Reformed Bible Coll., 1977; MA in Sch. Adminstrn., Calvin Coll., 1983; postgrad., Western Mich. U., 1984-93. Cert. ch. educator. Dir. edn. 1st Christian Reformed Ch., Visalia, Calif., 1977-79, Bethany Reformed Ch., Grand Rapids, Mich., 1979-83, Haven Reformed Ch., Kalamazoo, 1983-90, exec. dir. ops., 1990-93; exec. dir. Manitoqua Ministries, Frankfort, Ill., 1993—. Cons. David C. Cook Pubs., 1988-90, Office Evangelism Reformed Ch. in Am., 1987-91; tchr. trainer, mem. renewal forum Synod of Mich. Reformed Ch. in Am., 1987-90; regional evangelism trainer Synod of Mid-Am., 1995—; bd. dirs. Chgo. Christian Counseling Ctr., 1995-2000, bd. officer, 1996-2000; v.p. Illiana Classis Reformed Ch. in Am., 1999, pres., 2000; Denominational "Refocus Leaders" facilitator Classis Illiana, 1998-2000, Classis Chgo., 1999-2001; mem. adj. faculty Trinity Christian Coll., 1996; adj. prof. Reformed Bible Coll., 2000. Author: Effective Decision Making for Church Leaders, 1988, Leader's Guide for Out of the Saltshaker and into the World, 1988. Vice-chmn. Youth Com. Bill Glass Crusade, Visalia, 1978, chmn. Cen. Valley Ch. Workers Conf., Visalia, 1978; mem. Youth Com. City-Wide Easter Svcs., Visalia, 1979; trustee Reformed Bible Coll., Grand Rapids, 1984-91, exec. com., 1985-91, asst. sec. bd. dirs., 1986-87, sec. bd. dirs., 1987-90; chmn. S.W. Mich. Christian Discipleship Com., 1984-85. Recipient DeVos award Reformed Bible Coll., 1977; Mich. State scholar, 1970. Mem. Bibl. Archeol. Soc., Christian Educators-Reformed ch. Am., Inst. for Am. Ch. Growth (cons. 1986-93), Christian Mgmt. Assn. Cen. Valley Youth Ministers (sec. 1978-79), Alban Inst., Am. Camping Assn. (bd. dirs. Ill. chpt. 1995-98), Christian Camping Internat., Delta Epsilon Chi. Republican. Avocations: reading, racquetball, golf, civil war information. Home and Office: 8236 W Laraway Rd Frankfort IL 60423-7804 E-mail: huffjohn1@aol.com.

HUFF, MARSHA ELKINS, lawyer; b. Tulsa, Apr. 11, 1946; BA with honors, U. Tulsa, 1968, MA, 1970; JD cum laude, Loyola U. of Chgo., 1974. Bar: Wis. Ptnr. Foley & Lardner, Milw. Mem. editorial bd. Loyola U. Law Jour., 1973-74. Mem. ABA (mem. sect. taxation). Office: Foley & Lardner Firstar Ctr 777 E Wisconsin Ave Ste 3800 Milwaukee WI 53202-5367

HUGGINS, BOB, college basketball coach; b. Morgantown, W.Va., Sept. 21, 1953; m. June Ann Fillman; children: Jenna Leigh, Jacqueline. BS magna cum laude, U. W.Va., 1977, MA in Health Adminstrn., 1978. Grad. asst. basketball coach U. W.Va., Morgantown, 1977-78; asst. basketball coach Ohio State U., Columbus, 1978-90; head coach Walsh Coll., Canton, Ohio, 1980-83; asst. basketball coach U. Ctrl. Fla., Orlando, 1983-84; head basketball coach U. Akron, Ohio, 1984-89, U. Cin., 1989—. Mem. basketball coaching staff U.S. World Univ. Games team, 1993. Founder Bob Huggins Found., 1997-98. Named Coach of the Yr. dist. 22 NAIA, 1981-82, 1982-83, area 6, 1982-83, , Mid-Ohio Conf., 1981-82, 1982-83, Ohio Valley, 1984-85, Metro Conf., 1989-90, Dapper Dan Man of Yr., 1986-87, dist. 4 USBWA, 1991-92, Mideast Coach of Yr. Basketball Times, 1991-92, 95-96, Co-Nat. Coach of Yr., 1991-92 Hoop Scoop mag., finalist for AP Coach of Yr., 1991-92, Ohio Coll. Coach of Yr. Columbus Dispatch, 1991-92, 1995-96, Nat. Coll. Coach of Yr., Playboy Mag., 1992-93, Midseason Coach of Yr. USA Today, 1991-92 season; recipient Ray Meyer award Gt. Midwest conf., 1991-92, 92-93. Office: Univ Cincinnati Men's Basketball 340 Shoemaker Ctr Cincinnati OH 45221-0001

HUGHES, BARBARA BRADFORD, nurse, manufacturing executive; b. Bragg City, Mo., Jan. 21, 1941; d. Lawrence Hurl Bradford and Opal Jewel (Prater) Puttin; m. Robert Howard Hughes, Dec. 9, 1961; children: Kimberly Ann Hayden, Robert Howard II. ASN, St. Louis Community Coll., 1978; student, Webster U., 1980. RN, Mo. Med. surg. nurse Alexian Bros. Hosp., St. Louis, 1979-80; staff nurse Midwest Allergy Cons., 1980; nurse high altitude Aviation Nurse, Ltd., 1980-81; cardiac telemetry staff nurse Jefferson Meml. Hosp., Crystal City, Mo., 1992-94; vol. nurse Med. Ministry Internat., Plano, Tex., 1998-2001; CEO Supreme Tool & Die, Fenton, Mo., 2001—. Chmn. bd. dirs., CEO, ptnr. Supreme Tool & Die Co., Fenton, Mo., 1988—; pvt. practice real estate mgmt., 1962—; mem. nursing adv. com. Jefferson Coll., Hillsboro, Mo., 1999, mem. adv. bd., Mo., 2000—01. Vol. Luth. Hosp., St. Louis, 1967—70; mem. Mo. Bot. Garden, 1976—, Mo. Hist. Soc., 1976, St. Louis Zoo Friends Assn., 1986—87, Nat. Trust for Hist. Preservation, 1990—, Channel 9-Ednl. TV, St. Louis; vol. health tchr. Spartan Aluminum Products, Sparta, Ill., 1984; mem. Rosie the Riveter women's pilot group project, readying a DC3 for FAA recert. through Wings of Hope, TWA and Remote Area Med. Knoxville, for use in med. relief in remote areas of U.S. and the world; mem. med. missions to nat. and internat. remote areas sponsored by Wings of Hope, 2000—; mem. field and med. support team Wings of Hope, St. Louis, Remote ARea Medicad, Knoxville, Tenn. U. Mo. scholar, 1959. Mem.: AACN, Med. Ministries Internat., Nat. Tool and Machining Assn., U.S. Pilots Assn., Wings of Hope (St. Louis), Mo. Pilots Assn., Women in Aviation Internat. (charter), Tyospaye Club. Republican. Avocations: flying, gardening, reading. Office: Supreme Tool & Die 1536 Fenpark Dr Fenton MO 63026

HUGHES, CLYDE MATTHEW, religious denomination executive; b. Huntington, W.Va., Dec. 7, 1948; s. Donald Lee and Audrey Arlene (Stevers) H.; m. Linda May Daniels, June 10, 1972; children: Crystal, Dustin, Tina, Wesley, Timothy, Penny, Heidi, Robin. Diploma, Amb. Bible Inst., London, Ohio, 1972; BA, Cedarville (Ohio) Coll., 1974; MA, Meth. Theol. Sch. in Ohio, 1980; DD, Heritage Bible Coll., Dunn, N.C., 1994. Ordained to ministry Internat. Pentecostal Ch. of Christ, 1974. Pastor Internat. Pentecostal Ch. of Christ, Hillsboro, Ohio, 1981-82, nat. dir. Sunday sch. London, 1976-82, dir. ch. ministries, 1982-84, asst. gen. overseer, 1984-90, gen. overseer, chmn. gen. bd., 1990—. Mem. nat. com. Mission Am., 1997—; bd. dirs. Beulah Heights Bible Coll., Atlanta, 1982—, chmn. bd. 1990-96. Editor-in-chief The Pentecostal Leader; contbr. articles to religious publs. Chmn. bd. dirs. Locust Grove Rest Home, 1990-98. Mem. Nat. Assn. Evangs. (bd. dirs. 1990—2001), Madison County Evang. Assn. (bd. dirs. 1990-2001), London Ministerial Assn., Chs. United with Israel (bd. gov. 2002-), Mission Am. (nat. com. 1997-), Pentecostal/Charismatic Chs. N.Am. (bd. dirs. 1994—, exec. com. 2001), Internat. Pentecostal Press Assn. Home: 7040 Danville Rd London OH 43140-9766

HUGHES, DAN, professional basketball coach; Head coach Cleveland Rockers, 1999—. Office: Cleveland Rockers One Center Ct Cleveland OH 44115

HUGHES, EDWARD F. X. physician, educator; b. Boston, Jan. 10, 1942; s. Joseph Daniel and Elizabeth (Dempsey) H.; m. Susan Lane Mooney, Feb. 11, 1967; children: Edward, John, Dempsey BA in Philosophy, Amherst Coll., 1962; MD, Harvard U., 1966; MPH, Columbia U., 1969. Intern, resident surg. Columbia-Presbyn. Med. Ctr., N.Y.C., 1966-68; instr. to assoc. prof. Mt. Sinai Sch. Medicine, 1969-77; rsch. assoc. Nat. Bur. Economic Research, 1970-77; founder, dir. ctr. health svc. policy rsch. Northwestern U. Med. Sch., Chgo., 1977-94; prof. preventitive medicine J. L. Kellogg Grad. Sch. Mgmt., Northwestern U., Evanston, 1977—, dir. health svcs. mgmt. program Ill., 1977—. Cons. Nat. Ctr. Health Services Research, Rockville, Md., 1975-82, AMA, Chgo., 1981-83, Midwest Bus. Group on Health, Chgo., 1983-85. Editor: Hospital Cost Containment: A Policy Analysis, 1979, A Perspective on Quality in American health Care, 1988 (Bradley award 1962, Health Career Scientist award 1973-75); mem. editl. bd. Managed Care, Jour. Clin. Outcomes, Group Health News, Counseline; contbr. articles to profl. jours. Health Care Financing Adminstrn. grantee, Washington, 1978-84, Ford Found., 1983-86, Robert Wood Johnson Found, 1978-82, NIH, 1983-95, Pew Charitable Trusts, 1990-92, Baxter Found., 1991-96. Fellow N.Y. Acad. Medicine, Am. Coll. Physician Execs.; mem. APHA, Assn. Health Svcs. Rsch. (co-founder, v.p. 1981-83, bd. dirs. 1981-84), Assn. Tchrs. Preventive Medicine (bd. dirs. 1973-76), Med. Adminstrs. Conf., Nat. Assn. Managed Care Physicians (med. adv. bd.), Boston Latin Sch. Chgo. Club (bd. dirs. 1983-86), Chapoquoit Yacht Club (West Famouth, Mass., Latiolias Honor medal 1999), Beta Gamma Sigma. Home: 810 Lincoln St Evanston IL 60201-2405 Office: JL Kellogg Sch Mgmt 2001 Sheridan Rd Evanston IL 60208-0814

HUGHES, JEROME MICHAEL, education foundation executive; b. St. Paul, Oct. 1, 1929; s. Michael Joseph and Mary (Molloy) H.; m. Audrey M. Lackner, Aug. 11, 1951; children— Bernadine, Timothy, Kathleen, Rosemarie, Margaret, John BA, Coll. of St. Thomas, St. Paul, 1951; MA, U. Minn., 1958; EdD, Wayne State U., 1970; postdoctoral fellow, U. Minn., 1985. Tchr. Shakopee Sch. Dist., Minn., 1951-53, St. Paul Sch. Dist., 1953-61, counselor, 1963-66, rsch. asst., 1966-67, edn. cons., 1968-87; mem. Minn. Senate, St. Paul, 1966-93, chmn. edn. com., 1973-83, chmn. elections and ethics com., 1983-93, pres., 1983-93; mem. faculty U. Minn., 1986-95; pres. Minn. Edn. Found., Roseville, 1992—. Mem. Edn. Commn. of States, Denver, 1973-93; mem. Nat. Cmty. Edn. Adv. Coun., Washington, 1980-83; mem. Nat. Conf. State Legislature State/Fed. Assembly, 1983-93; adj. faculty U. Minn., 1986-95. Chair Goodwill/Easter Seals, 1993-95; bd. dirs. Nat. Parenting Assn. Minn., 1994-97, State Legis. Leaders Found., 1985-93. Mott fellow, 1967-68, Ford Found. fellow George Washington U., 1974-75, Bush Summer fellow, U. Calif., 1975; Disting. Policy fellow George Washington U., 1977-78; postdoctoral fellow U. Minn., 1980-81; recipient Pennell award Minn. Fedn. Tchrs., 1974; Disting. Svc. award Minn. Elem. Sch. Prins. Assn., 1982; named Community Educator of Yr. Minn. Community Edn. Assn., recipient other awards Mem. Phi Delta Kappa Democrat. Avocations: travel, reading, discussion, exercise. Office: Minn Edn Found PO Box 13643 Roseville MN 55113-0643

HUGHES, JOHN, chemical company executive; b. St. David's, Wales, Apr. 10, 1943; came to U.S., 1964; s. Essex James and Mary Ann (Harris) H.; m. Linda Kay Petersen; children: Stacey Ann, Bradford James. BS in Chemistry, U. Wales, 1964; MBA, U. Chgo., 1968. With AMCOL Internat., Arlington Heights, Ill., 1965—, now chmn. Office: AMCOL Internat 1500 W Shure Dr Arlington Heights IL 60004-1443

HUGHES, JOHN RUSSELL, physician, educator; b. DuBois, Pa., Dec. 19, 1928; s. John Henry and Alice (Cooper) H.; m. Mary Ann Dick, June 14, 1958; children: John Russell Jr. (dec.), Christopher Alan, Thomas Gregory, Cheryl Ann. AB summa cum laude, Franklin and Marshall Coll., 1950; BA with honors, Oxford (Eng.) U., 1952, MA with honors, 1955, DM (hon.), 1976; PhD, Harvard U., 1954; MD, Northwestern U., 1975. Neurophysiologist NIH, 1954-56; dir. electroencephalography dept. Meyer Hosp., SUNY, 1956-63; dir. div. lab. scis., including electroencephalography Northwestern U. Med. Center, 1963-77, prof. neurology, 1968—; dir. EEG and Epilepsy Clinic, U. Ill. Med. Center, 1977—; staff U. Ill. Hosp., Community Hosp., Geneva, Delnor Hosp., St. Charles; dir.neurophysiology Humana-Michael-Reese Med. Ctr., 1992—. Cons. Chgo. VA Westside Hosp., Mercyville and Copley Meml. Hosp., Aurora, Ill., others; participant debate on brain death BBC-TV; bd. dirs. Am. Bd. EEG and Neurophysiology; participant Am. Med. EEG Assn.; rep. Internat. Fedn. EEG and Clin. Neurophysiology lectr. tour of Africa, 1989; keynote speaker Internat. Course of Neurophusiology, Oxford U., 1993, invited speaker, 1996; invited spkr. Damascus Med. Sch., Syria, 1998. Author: Functional Organization of the Diencephalon, 1957, Atlas on Cerebral Death and Coma, 1976, Chinese Translation, 1997, Japanese Translation, 1998, EEG in Clinical Practice, 1982, 2d edit., 1994, EEG Evoked Potentials in Psychiatry and Behavioral Neurology, 1983; contbr. articles to profl. jours. Command Surgeon, USAR, 1986-90, with Army Med. R & D Command, 1990—, mobilization replacement for maj. gen., comdr. Recipient Alumni award Franklin and Marshall Coll., 1978, Lifetime Achievement award Am. EEG and Clin. Neurophysiol. Soc., 2000. Mem. Am. Electroencephalography Soc. (treas. 1965-68), Eastern Electroencephalography Soc. (sec.-treas. 1961-64), Ctrl. Electroencephalography Soc., Am. Med. EEG Assn. (bd. dirs.), Am. Bd. EEG and Neurophysiology (bd. dirs.), Internat. EEG and Clin. Neurophysiology (bd. dirs.), Am. Acad. EEG (bd. dirs.), Brit. Soc. of neurophysiology (hon.), Chgo. Acad. Medicine, Am. Epilepsy Soc., Am. Physiol. Soc., Soc. Neuroscis., Am. Acad. Neurology, Phi Beta Kappa, Sigma Xi (lectr. 1960—) Achievements include research on coding in central nervous system, new theory on neural mechanisms in olfaction, electro-clin. correlations in different types of epilepsy, organic aspects in juvenile delinquency. Home: 720 Roslyn Ter Evanston IL 60201-1722 Office: U Ill Consultation Clinic Epilepsy 912 S Wood St Chicago IL 60612-7325 E-mail: JHuhges@uic.edu.

HUGHES, LOUIS RALPH, automotive executive; b. Cleve., Feb. 10, 1949; s. Louis R. and Anna E. (Holland) H.; m. Candice A. Baranchik, May 20, 1972; children: Brian W., Brittany K. B of Mech. Engring., GM Inst., 1971; MBA, Harvard U., 1973. V.p. fin. GM Can., 1985-86, GM Europe, Switzerland, 1987-89; chmn., mng. dir. Adam. Opel, Germany, 1989-92; pres. GM Europe, 1992-94; exec.v.p. GM Corp., Detroit, 1992—; pres. GM Internat., Switzerland, 1994-98; exec. v.p. new bus. strategies Gen. Motors Corp., Detroit, 1998—. Avocations: skiing, mountain climbing, antiques. Office: Gen Motors Corp 300 Renaissance Ctr Detroit MI 48265-0001

HUGHES, T. LEE, newspaper editor; Bur. chief AP, Milw., 1993—. Office: 918 N 4th St Milwaukee WI 53203-1506

HUGOSON, GENE, state legislator, farmer; b. Sept. 1945; m. Patricia Hugoson; one child. BA, Augsburg Coll.; postgrad., Mankato State U. Farmer; Dist. 26A rep. Minn. Ho. of Reps., St. Paul, 1986-95; commr. Agr. Dept., 1995—. Former mem. econ. devel., internat. trade and redistricting coms., Minn. Ho. of Reps.; mem. Agr., rules and legis. adminstrn., transp. and transit, and taxes coms.; asst. minority leader. Office: State of Minn Dept of Agr 90 Plato Blvd W Saint Paul MN 55107-2004

HUHEEY, MARILYN JANE, ophthalmologist, educator; b. Cin., Aug. 31, 1935; d. George Mercer and Mary Jane (Weaver) H. BS in Math., Ohio U., Athens, 1958; MS in Physiology, U. Okla., 1966; MD, U. Ky., 1970. Diplomate Am. Bd. Ophthalmology. Tchr. math. James Ford Rhodes H.S., Cleve., 1956-58; biostatistician Nat. Jewish Hosp., Denver, 1958-60; life sci. engr. Stanley Aviation Corp., 1960-63, N.Am. Aviation Co., L.A., 1963-67; intern U. Ky. Hosp., 1970-71; emergency room physician Jewish Hosp., Mercy Hosp., Bethesda Hosp., Cin., 1971-72; ship's doctor, 1972; resident in ophthalmology Ohio State U. Hosp., Columbus, 1972-75; practice medicine specializing in ophthalmology, 1975—. Mem. staff Univ. Hosp., Grant Hosp., St. Anthony Hosp., 1975-79; clin. asst. prof. Ohio State U. Med. Sch., 1976-84, clin. assoc. prof., 1985—, dir. course ophthalmologic receptionist/aides, 1976; mem. Peer Rev. Sys. Bd., 1986-92, exec. com., 1988-92; mem. Ohio Optical Dispensers Bd., 1986-91; bd. dirs. Ctrl. Ohio Radio Reading Svc., 1997—; mem. Ohio Bd. Cosmetology, 1999—. Dem. candidate for Ohio Senate, 1982; mem. Wicked Investment Club, 1998—, pres. 1999—. Fellow Am. Acad. Ophthalmology; mem. AAUP, Am. Assn. Ophthalmologists, Ohio Ophthalmol. Soc. (bd. govs. 1984-89, del. to Ohio State Med. Assn. 1984-88), Franklin County Acad. Medicine (profl. rels. com. 1979-82, legis. com. 1981-89, edn. and program com. 1981-88, chmn. 1982-85, chmn. cmty. rels. com. 1987-90, chmn. resolution com. 1987-92, mem. fin. com. 1988-92), Ohio Soc. Prevent Blindness (chmn. med. adv. bd. 1978-80), Ohio State Med. Assn. (dr.-nurse liaison com. 1983-87), Columbus EENT Soc., Am. Coun. of the Blind (bd. dirs. 1995-96), Life Care Alliance (pres. sustaining bd. 1987-88), United Way (planning com. 1992-93), LWV, Columbus Coun. World Affairs, Columbus Bus. and Profl. Women's Club, Columbus C. of C., Grandview Area Bus. Assn., Federated Dem. Women Ohio, Columbus Area Women's Polit. Caucus, Columbus Met. Club (forum com. 1982-85, fundraising com. 1983-84, chmn. 10th anniversary com. 1986), Mercedes Benz Club (dir. 1981-83), Zonta (program com. 1984-86, chmn. internat. com. 1983), Herb Soc., Phi Mu. Home: 2396 Northwest Blvd Columbus OH 43221-3829 Office: 1335 Dublin Rd Ste 25A Columbus OH 43215-1000

HULBERT, SAMUEL FOSTER, college president; b. Adams Center, N.Y., Apr. 12, 1936; s. Foster David and Wilma May (Speakman) H.; m. Joy Elinor Husband, Sept. 3, 1960; children: Gregory, Samantha, Jeffrey. B.S. in Ceramic Engring., Alfred U., 1958, Ph.D., 1964. Registered profl. engr., La, S.C. Asst. varsity and freshman football coach Alfred U. (N.Y.), 1959-61; lab. instr. N.Y. State Coll. Ceramics, Alfred, 1958-59; instr. math and physics Alfred U., 1960-64; asst. prof. ceramic and metall. engring. Clemson U. (S.C.), 1964-68, head div. interdisciplinary studies, assoc. prof. materials and bioengring., 1968-71; assoc. dean engring research and interdisciplinary studies, prof. materials engring. and bioengring., dir. materials engring. and bioengring., 1970-73; prof. bioengring. and chmn. Sch. Engring. Tulane U., New Orleans, 1973-76; pres.-designate spl. asst. to pres. Rose-Hulman Inst. Tech., Terre Haute, Ind., 1976, pres., 1976—. Bd. dirs. Ind. Bus. Modernization & Tech. Corp., Integral Tech., Inc., Thomas & Skinner, Inc., Old Nat. Bank. Mem. editorial bd. Annals of Biomed. Engring., 1974, Jour. Biomed. Materials Rsch., 1970—; contbr. articles in field of biomaterials and artificial organ design to profl. jours. Mem. exec. com. Wabash Valley chpt. Boy Scouts Am.; mem. Ind. Humanities Coun., 1991—. Recipient medal Italian Soc. Orthopaedics, 1973, Delitala medal Instituto Ortopedico Rizzoli, 1973, Clemson award for outstanding contbns. to biomaterials, 1973, George Winters award European Soc. Biomaterials, 1982, Founder's award Soc. Biomaterials, 2001, Lifetime Achievement award Ind. Health Industry Forum, 1996, Ernst & Young Supporter of Indiana Entrepreneurship award, 1998, Chapman S. Root award Hospice of the Wabash Valley, 2000. Fellow Am. Inst. for Med. and Biol. Engring., Am. Biomaterials Scis. and Engring., Internat. Acad. Ceramics; mem. Am. Soc. Artificial Internal Organs, Biomed. Engring. Soc., Soc. Biomaterials (dir. 1974—, pres. 1975-76, founder's award 2001), Am. Ceramic Soc., Nat. Inst. Ceramics Engrs., Am. Soc. Engring. Edn., Ind. Colls. and Univ. Assn., Ind. Colls. of Ind., Ind. Conf. Higher Edn., Assn. Ind. Tech. Univs. (sec., treas. 1977-78, pres. 1987-90), Presidents of Ind. Colls. and Univs., Vigo County Hist. Soc. (dir. 1979—, pres. 1995—), Keramos, Blue Key, Ind. Acad., Internat. Acad. Ceramics, Rotary, Sigma Xi. Republican. Office: Rose Hulman Inst Tech Office of Pres 5500 Wabash Ave Terre Haute IN 47803-3999

HULIN, FRANCES C. prosecutor; AB, Northwestern U., 1957; JD, U. Ill., Urbana, 1971. Bar: Ill. 1973. Asst. states atty. Champaign County, IL, 1973-76, Macon County, Ill., 1977-78; prosecutor U.S. Attys. Office, Ctrl. Dist. Ill., 1978-93; U.S. atty. Dept. Justice, Springfield, Ill., 1993—. Office: US Attys Office 600 E Monroe St Ste 312 Springfield IL 62701-1675

HULL, BRETT A. professional hockey player; b. Belleville, Ont., Can., Aug. 9, 1964; s. Bobby Hull. Student, U. Minn., Duluth, 1984-86. Profl. hockey player Calgary Flames, 1986-88; with St. Louis Blues, 1988-96; forward Dallas Stars, Dallas, 1997-. Player NHL All-Star team, 1989-94, AHL All-Star first team, 1986-87, NHL All-Star first team, 1989-90, 91-92. Recipient Lady Byng Meml. Trophy 1989, 90, Hart Meml. trophy, 1990-91, WCHA Freshman of the Year award, 1984-85, Dudley Garrett Meml. trophy, 1986-87, Dodge Ram Tough award, 1989-90, 90-91, Lester B. Pearson award, 1990-91, Pro Set NHL Player of the Year award, 1990-91; named Sporting News NHL Player of Yr., 1990-91, Sporting News All-Star first team, 1989-90, 91-92, All-Star game Most Valuable

Player, 1992; Stanley Cup Champions, Dallas Stars, 1999. Led NHL in Goals Scored, 1989-92. Office: Detroit Red Wings Joe Louis Arena 600 Civic Center Detroit MI 48226*

HULL, CHARLES WILLIAM, retired special education educator; b. East St. Louis, Ill., Feb. 23, 1936; s. William Semple Hull and Jessie Marie (Brennan) Poole; m. Beverly Kay Julian, Aug. 19, 1967; 1 child, William Kenneth. BA in Econs., Cen. Meth. Coll., 1964; MEd, Olivet Nazarene Coll., 1974; AA (hon.), Joliet Jr. Coll., 1987. Tchr. elem. grades Taft Sch., Lockport, Ill., 1965-67; tchr. spl. edn. S.W. Cook County Coop. Assn. for Spl. Edn., Oak Forest, 1967-99; ret., 1999. Permanent exhibits include Tchr's Ret. Office Bldg., Springfield, Ill. Past bd. dirs., v.p., chmn. fund raising Easter Seals Will and Grundy Counties; dist. leader Am. Cancer Soc., 1984, residential campaign chmn., 1985; vol., mem. adv. bd. Big Bros.-Big Sisters Will County; Cub Scouts com. chmn. Boy Scouts Am., 1980-81, commr. Rainbow coun., bd. dirs. troop 61; mem. choir, past trustee Faith United Meth. Ch.; Will County walkathon chmn. March of Dimes, 1979; chmn. Canal Days events Will County Hist. Soc., 1987; active numerous other orgns.; mem. Nat. Trust for Hist. Preservation, Lockport Area Hist. Geneal. Soc. Cpl. USMC, 1955-58. Recipient Congl. Medal of Merit, 1985, Frederick Bartleson Meml. award Will County Hist. Soc., 1985, Citizen of Week award Sta. WBBM, Chgo., 1985, Leadership award Am. Cancer Soc., 1985, Outstanding Svc. award Big Bros.-Big Sisters Will County, letter of commendation Pres. of U.S., 1986, 89, Disting. Svc. award Joliet Jr. Coll., 1987, Citizen of Month award Southtown Economist, plaque KC. Mem. 1st Marine Div. Assn., Will County Old-Timers Baseball Assn., Am. Legion, Masons (32 degree), Shriners (pres. Joliet club 1983, Shriner of Yr. 1989), KC, Medina Temple, Lions (pres. Manhattan club 1984, chmn. youth and fgn. exch. dist. 1986-87, bd. dirs. Lockport chpt.), Will County Hist. Soc. (pres. 1989), Joliet Area Ret. Tchrs. Assn., Ill. Ret. Tchrs. Assn., Royal Order Scotland, Masons. Republican. Methodist. Home: 403 N Farrell Rd Lockport IL 60441-2404

HULL, ELIZABETH ANNE, retired English language educator; b. Upper Darby, Pa., Jan. 10, 1937; d. Frederick Bossart and Elizabeth (Schmik) H.; m. Dean Carlyle Beery, Feb. 5, 1955 (div. 1962); children: Catherine Doria Beery Pizarro, Barbara Phyllis Beery Wintczak; m. Frederik Pohl, July 1984. Student, Ill. State U., 1954-55; AA, Wilbur Wright Jr. Coll., Chgo., 1965; B in Philosophy, Northwestern U., 1968; MA, Loyola U., Chgo., 1970, PhD, 1975. Teaching asst. Loyola U., Chgo., 1968-71; prof. English, coord. honors program William Rainey Harper Coll., Palatine, Ill., 1971-2001; ret., 2001. Judge nat. writing competition Nat. Coun. Tchrs. of English, 1975—, John W. Campbell award, 1986—. Co-editor: (with F. Pohl) Tales from the Planet Earth; contbr. articles to profl. jours. Pres. Lexington Green Condominium Assn., Schaumburg, Ill., 1982-84; bd. dirs. Hunting Ridge Homeowner's Assn., Palatine, 1984-86; Dem. candidate for U.S. Ho. of Reps. for 8th Congl. Dist. Ill., 1996; bd. dirs. N.W. Cmty. Hosp. Aux., 2001—; steering com. Constituency on Vols. Ill. Hosp. Assn., 2001—. Recipient Northwestern U. Alumni award for Merit, 1995, Thomas Clareson award Sci. Fictin Rsch. Assn., 1998, Excellence award Nat. Inst. for Staff and Orgnl. Devel., 1998. Mem. MLA, Midwest MLA, Popular Culture Assn., Sci. Fiction Rsch. Assn. (editor 1981-84, sec. 1987-88, pres. 1989-90), Ill. Coll. English Assn. (pres. 1975-77), World Sci. Fiction Assn. (N.Am. sec. 1978—, pres. Honors coun. Ill. region 1992-93), Palatine Area LWV (bd. dirs. 1991—, v.p. 1995-96, pres. 1998-2000), Am. Assn. for Women in C.C. (v.p. comm., bd. dirs. Harper Coll. chpt. 1993-96), Northwest Comm. Hosp.Aux. Bd. of Dir., 2001, Vol. Steering Comm. for Ill. Hosp. Assn., 2002, Home: 855 Harvard Dr Palatine IL 60067-7026

HULL, KENNETH JAMES, retail bookstore/educ prod and services executive; b. Chgo., Oct. 21, 1936; s. Harold Raymond and Edna Carolyn (Weber) H.; m. Jacqueline Mary Oldham, June 27, 1970; children: Richard, Pamela. B.S., So. Ill. U., 1958. C.P.A., Ill. Audit staff Lawrence Scudder & Co., Chgo., 1962-63; audit mgr. Wolf & Co., 1963-68; acctg. mgr. Follett Corp., 1968-70, controller, 1970-77, v.p. fin., 1977—, dir., 1977—, chmn., CEO River Grove, Ill., 1997—. Dir. C.P.A.s Pub. Interest, Chgo., 1983-92, pres., 1987-90. Served with U.S. Army, 1958-62. Mem. AICPA (governing coun. 1984—, bd. dirs. 1991—), Ill. Soc. CPAs (sr. v.p. 1992-93, pres.-elect 1993-94). Lutheran. Office: Follett Corp 2233 West St River Grove IL 60171-1895 E-mail: kjhull@follett.com.

HULSHOF, KENNY, congressman; b. Sikeston, Mo., May 22, 1958; m. Renee Lynn Howell. BS, U. Mo., 1980; JD, U. Miss., 1983. Mem. U.S. Congress from Mo. 9th Dist., 1997—; mem. ways and means com. Rep. candidate for Boone County Prosecutor, 1992, U.S. House, 1994, 96. Roman Catholic. Office: Ho of Representatives 412 Cannon Washington DC 20515-0001*

HULSTON, JOHN KENTON, lawyer, director; b. Dade County, Mo., Mar. 29, 1915; s. John Fred and Myrtle Rosa (King) H.; m. Ruth Amis Luster, Dec. 18, 1944; 1 son, John Luster. AB, Drury Coll., Springfield, Mo., 1936; JD, Mo. U., Columbia, 1941, D (hon.), 1997. Bar: Mo. 1941, U.S. Supreme Ct. 1949. Tchr., coach Ash Grove (Mo.) High Sch., 1936-38; pvt. practice law Springfield, 1946—; co-founder, dir., v.p., sec. Reed Oil Co., Big Spring, Tex., 1951-68, Pioneer Oil Co., Ft. Worth, 1954-79; operator, chmn. Copperhead Hill farms (beef production), 1955-98; chmn. Bank of Ash Grove, 1959—, Citizens Home Bank, Greenfield, Mo., 1966—; pres. Bank of Springfield, 1968-69, Bank of Billings, 1987—; vice chmn., dir., mem. exec. com. Centerre Bank of Springfield, 1969-89; sec., dir., v.p., mem. exec. com. Ozark Air Lines Inc. (now Am. Air Lines), St. Louis, 1971-86, sec., dir., v.p., 1984-88; assoc. Hulston, Jones, Marsh & Shaffer, 1984—. Instr. real estate law Drury Coll., 1948-64; vis. lectr. corp. law E.R. Breech Sch. Bus., 1953. Author: West Point and Wilson's Creek 1861, 1955, An Ozarks Boy's Story, 1971, An Ozarks Lawyer's Story, 1976, History of Bank of Ash Grove, 1883-1983, 1983, A Look at Dade County, Missouri, 1905-85, 1985, Panhandle Profiles, 1889-1989, 1989, Lester E. Cox, 1895-1968, 1992, Moments in Time, 2001; (with Paul W. Barrett) Harry S. Truman v. J. William Chilton, 1991; contbr. articles to profl. jours. Chmn. Wilson's Creek Nat. Battlefield Commn., 1969-79; vice chmn. Springfield Home Rule Charter Commn., 1953; chmn. Springfield City Charter Commn., 1977; pres. Greene County Estate Planning Council, 1952; trustee Springfield Pub. Library, 1957-63, Drury Coll., 1966-95, State Hist. Soc. Mo., 1974—, life trustee, 1996—; trustee Cox Health Sys., 1959—, pres., 1966, vice chmn., 1967-2000, chmn., 2001—; chmn. Greene County Dems., 1947-48; introduced Pres. Harry S. Truman at 1st Whistle Stop Speech, Springfield, July 5, 1948; presdl. elector, 1948; mem. Mo. Civil War Centennial Commn., 1961-65; life trustee Drury Coll., 1966—; trustee Mo. U. Law Sch. Found., Columbia, pres., 1985-87; co-founder Civil War Round Table of the Ozarks, 1948, Wilson's Creek Battlefield Found., 1952, Greene County Hist. Soc., 1962, The Hist. Mus. Springfield-Greene County, 1974; mem. devel. fund bd. Mo. U., Columbia, 1986-90. Maj. U.S. Army, WWII, 1941-46. Recipient Springfield Young Man of Year award, 1950, Disting. Alumni award Drury Coll., 1974, Springfieldian of Year award, 1978, The Missourian award, 1998, Spl. commendation U.S. Dept. Interior, Nat. Park Service, 1981, Faculty-Alumni Gold medal award Mo. U., Columbia, 1988, Citation of Merit Mo. U. Law Sch., Disting. Svc. award Mo. U. Alumni Assn., 1993; inductee into Writers Hall of Fame, 1995. Fellow Am. Bar Found. (life); mem. ABA (real property, probate/trust reporter Mo. 1974-96), Am. Judicature Soc., Am. Acad. Hosp. Attys., Am. Soc. Law, Ethics and Medicine, Mo. Bar Assn. (1st chmn. legal aid 1952), Springfield Met. Bar Assn. (pres. 1973), Springfield C. of C. (pres. 1950, 51, 54), Supreme Ct. of Mo. Hist. Soc. (co-founder, trustee 1984-90), SAR, Order of Coif, Phi Delta Phi, Kappa Alpha Order. Democrat. Presbyterian. Clubs: Hickory Hills Country (Springfield); University of Mo. Jefferson (trustee 1976-82). Lodges: Masons (32 deg.), Shriners (potentate 1963), Jester. Home: 1300 E Catalpa St Springfield MO 65804-0134 Office: 2060 E Sunshine St Springfield MO 65804-1815

HULTGREN, DENNIS EUGENE, farmer, management consultant; b. Union County, S.D., Mar. 19, 1929; s. John Alfred and Esther Marie (Johnson) H.; m. Nelda Ethelyn Olson, Aug. 3, 1957; children: Nancy Hultgren Forsythe, Jean Hultgren Doty, Jahn Dennis, Ruth Dorothy Hultgren Henneman. Grad. high sch. Farmer, Union County, 1953—. Commr., chmn. Union County Planning and Zoning Bd., 1972-83; mem. bd. bylaw revision Union County Electric Co., 1983-85. Pres. bd. Union Creek Cemetry, 1958—; pres. bd. mgrs. Union-Sayles Watershed Dist., 1965-70; exec. bd. S.D. Farm Bur., Union County, 1996—, pres., 1998—; treas. Sioux Valley Twp., Union County, 1980—; treas., bd. dirs. W. Union Sch., 1957-67; chmn. Union County Sch. Bd., 1961-68; pres. Alcester (S.D.) Sch. Bd., 1970-77; chmn. Alcester PTA, 1967-68; mem. tech. bd. rev. Southeastern Coun. Govts., Sioux Falls, 1976-77; bd. dirs. Siouxland Interstate Met. Planning Coun., Sioux City, 1977-83, sec. coun. ofcls., 1978-83; bd. dirs. Old Opera House Cmty. Theater, Akron, Iowa, Akron Area Action Assn., 1983-85, Akron Devel. Corp., 1985-90; Rep. precinct committeeman, 1970, Union County Rep. Ctrl. Com., 1970—; chmn. S.D. State Bd. Equalization, 1987-95; mem. synod stewardship bd. Western Iowa Synod Luth. Ch., 1987-90, elected synod assembly bus. and coun. com., 1991-93, synod bus. and coun. com., 1997-99, synod coun. Western Iowa Synod, 1997-2000; S.D. del. Rep. nat. Conv., New Orleans, 1988. Served with AUS, 1951-53, Korea. Decorated Combat Infantry Badge, 3 Bronze Battle Stars; recipient Outstanding Dedication and Svc. award Old Opera House Cmty. Theatre, 1984, Sioux City Siouxland Disting. Citizen award Siouxland Interstate Met. Planning Coun., 1983, Jefferson award Sta. KELO-TV, 1985, Outstanding Cmty. Svc. award Lions Internat., 1985. Mem. S.D. State Resolutions Com., Farm Bur., Farmers Union (exec. bd. Union County 1987-90), S.D. Livestock Feeders Assn., Nat. Cattlemen's Assn., Associated Sch. Bds. S.D. (Merit award 1976), Am. Legion (exec. bd. Akron 1978-92, comdr. Akron 1980-81, 85-86, historian 1981-96, trustee 1983-90, 96—, vice comdr. 9th dist. 1989, chmn. athletics and contest com. Dept. of Iowa Am. Legion, 1991-92, 97-99, judge adv. 9th dist. Iowa 1993—), VFW (Alcester, S.D., vice-comdr. 1995-97, commdr. 2000—). Lutheran (mem. bd. 1967-70, 82-84, 90-93, 2001—, lay chmn. 1970, 82-93, chmn. centennial com. 1974, chmn. 125th anniversary com. 1999, chmn. ch. bd. 2001—). Address: Hulteboda Farm 47953 309th St Akron IA 51001-7575

HULTGREN, SCOTT J. microbiologist educator; PhD, Northwestern U., 1988. Postdoc. Umea U., Sweden; assoc. prof. Dept. Molecular Microbiology Wash. U. Sch. Medicine, St. Louis. Recipient Eli Lilly and Co. Rsch. award, 1998. Office: Dept Molecular Microbio Wash U Sch Medicine 660 S Euclid Ave # 8230 Saint Louis MO 63110-1010

HULTSTRAND, DONALD MAYNARD, bishop; b. Parkers Prairie, Minn., Apr. 16, 1927; s. Aaron Emmanuel H. and Selma Avendla (Liljegren) H.; m. Marjorie Richter, June 11, 1948; children— Katherine Ann, Charles John. B.A. summa cum laude, Macalester Coll., 1950; B.D. summa cum laude, Kenyon Coll., 1953; M.Div. summa cum laude, Colgate-Rochester Theol. Sem., 1974; D.D. honoris causa, Nashotah Divinity Sch., 1986. Ordained priest Episcopal Ch., 1953, consecrated bishop, 1982. Vicar St. John's Episcopal Ch., Worthington, Minn., 1953-57; rector Grace Meml. Ch., Wabasha, Minn., 1957-62, St. Mark's Episcopal Ch., Canton, Ohio, 1962-68, St. Paul's Episcopal Ch., Duluth, Minn., 1969-75; assoc. rector St. Andrew's Episcopal Ch., Kansas City, Mo., 1968-69; exec. dir. Anglican Fellowship of Prayer, 1975-79; rector Trinity Episcopal Ch., Greeley, Colo., 1979-82; bishop Episcopal Diocese of Springfield, Ill., 1982-91; exec. bd. Episcopal Radio (TV Found.), Atlanta, 1982-87, Anglican Fellowship of Prayer, 1968-93; adv. bd. Episcopal Boys' Homes, Salinas, Kans., 1983-91; com. of execs. Ill. Conf. Chs., 1982-91; mem. House of Bishops, 1982— , Minn. Standing Com., 1970-73; chmn. Minn. Examining Chaplains, 1954-61; chaplain Pewsaction Fellowships U.S.A., 1983-92; pres. Living Ch. Found., 1992—; advisor Diocesan Youth of Minn., 1956-60. Author: The Praying Church, 1978, And God Shall Wipe Away All Tears, 1968, Intercessory Prayer, 1972, Upper Room Dialogues, 1980, Revelations of Effective Prayer, 1995; co-author: The Parish as a Center of Prayer, 1996. Bd. dirs. Sr. Citizens Housing, Duluth, 1972-75, St. Luke's Hosp., Duluth, 1969-75; pres. Low-Rent Housing Project, Greeley, 1979-82. Served with USNR, 1945-46. Recipient Disting. Service award Young Life Minn., 1974; named hon. canon Diocese of Ohio, Cleve., 1967. Mem. Pi Phi Epsilon. Address: 1701 S Le Homme Dieu Dr NE Alexandria MN 56308-8504

HUME, LINDEL O. state legislator; b. Winslow, Ind., June 7, 1942; m. Judith Hume. BS, Oakland city Coll.; postgrad., U. Evansville. Mgr. internal auditing Potter & Brumfield; mem. Ind. Ho. of Reps., 1974-82, Ind. Senate from 48th dist., 1982—; minority whip; mem. agr. and small bus. com.; mem. ethics, interstate coop and transp. com.; ranking mem. elec. com.; mem. rules and legis. procedure com.; ranking minority mem. govt. and regulatory affairs com. Mem. adv. bd. Gibson County Salvation Army. Mem. Inst. Internal Auditors (past pres.), Kiwanis (past pres.). Home: 1797 Concord Dr Princeton IN 47670-9762 Office: State Senate State Capitol Indianapolis IN 46204

HUMERICKHOUSE, JOE D. state legislator; m. Thelma Humerickhouse. Ind. fee appraiser, Osage City, Kans.; mem. from dist. 59 Kans. State Ho. of Reps., Topeka. Address: 912 S 5th Osage City KS 66523 Also: 712 S 5th St Osage City KS 66523-1512

HUMKE, RAMON LYLE, utility executive; b. Quincy, Ill., Nov. 19, 1932; s. E.G. and Florence K. (Koch) H.; m. Carolyn Jacobs Humke, Nov. 20, 1955; 1 child, Steven K. Ed., Quincy Coll., 1952-53, Springfield (Ill.) Coll., Ill., 1956-58, Carleton Coll., 1968; LLD, U. Indpls., 1988. Various mgmt. positions Ill. Bell Telephone Co., 1951-73; dir. forecasting and productivity AT&T, N.Y.C., 1974-75; v.p. pers. Ill. Bell Tel. Co., Chgo., 1978-82; v.p. corp. affairs Ameritech, 1982-83; pres., CEO Ind. Bell Telephone Co. Inc., Indpls., 1983-89, Ameritech Svcs., Chgo., 1989-90; pres., COO Indpls. Power & Light Co., 1990—, also bd. dirs.; vice chmn. Ipalco Enterprises, Inc. Indpls., Indpls., 1991—; also bd. dirs. Ipalco Enterprises, Inc. Chmn. bd. Meridian Ins. Group, Meridian Mut. Ins. Co.; bd. dirs. LDI Mgmt. Chmn. Infrastructure Commn., 1990, Indpls.; bd. dirs. Indpls. Downtown, Inc., 1992—; adv. bd. Crossroads of Am. chpt. Boy Scouts Am. With U.S. Army, 1953-56, ETO. Named Ky. Col., 1983, Ark. Traveler, 1985, Sagamore of the Wabash, 1987, 89; recipient medal of merit U.S. Treasury Dept., 1984, 85, Charles Whistler award, 1989, Benjamin Harrison medallion award, 1990, Americanism award, 1991, Good Scout award Boy Scouts Am., 1993, Hoosier Heritage award, 1993, Ind. Acad., 1996. Mem. Indpls. C. of C. (chmn. 1997-98, dir.), Columbia Club, Crooked Stick Golf Club, Indpls. Athletic Club, Meridian Hills Country Club, Skyline Club (bd. govs.), Twin Lakes Golf Club. Avocations: golf, wilderness hiking, U.S. history.

HUML, DONALD SCOTT, manufacturing company executive; b. Lake Geneva, Wis., May 8, 1946; s. Robert Francis and Shirley (Roberts) H.; m. Joyce Cora Featherstone, Oct. 2, 1965; children: Tiffany Lynn, Alison Michelle, Andrew Scott. BBA, Marquette U., 1969; MBA, Temple U., 1980. Mgr. treasury ops. Allis-Chalmers Corp., West Allis, Wis., 1970-73; dir. fin. services CertainTeed Corp., Valley Forge, Pa., 1973-75, asst. treas., 1975-78, v.p., treas., 1978-81, v.p., comptroller, 1981-83, v.p., div. pres., 1983-86, v.p., group pres., 1986-89, v.p., chief fin. officer, 1989-90; v.p., CFO Saint-Gobain Corp., 1990-94; sr. v.p., CFO Snap-on Inc., Kenosha, Wis., 1994—2002; CFO Greif Corp., Delaware, Ohio, 2002—. Mem. adv. bd. Marquette U. Sch. Bus. Adminstrn. Mem. Am. Mgmt. Assn., Fin. Execs. Inst., Conf. Bd. CFO Coun., Leading CFOs, Beta Gamma Sigma. Republican. Roman Catholic. Avocations: tennis, running, reading. Home: 5695 Alvin Howe Rd Burlington WI 53105-9005 Office: Greif Corp 425 Winter Rd Delaware OH 43015 E-mail: dshuml@greif.com.

HUMMEL, GREGORY WILLIAM, lawyer; b. Sterling, Ill., Feb. 25, 1949; s. Osborne William and Vivian LaVera (Guess) H.; m. Teresa Lynn Beveroth, June 20, 1970; children: Andrea Lynn, Brandon Gregory. BA, MacMurray Coll., 1971; JD, Northwestern U., 1974. Bar: Ill. 1974, U.S. Dist. Ct. (no. dist.) Ill. 1974. Assoc. Rusnak, Deutsch & Gilbert, Chgo., 1974-78; ptnr. Rudnick & Wolfe, 1978-97; mem. Bell, Boyd & Lloyd LLC, 1997—. Editor Jour. Criminal Law & Criminology Northwestern U., 1973-74; co-author: Illinois Real Estate Forms, 1989; contbr. articles to law jours. Mem. gov. coun. Luth. Gen. Hosp. Advocate Health Care Sys.; trustee Mac Murray Coll., Jacksonville, Ill., 1986-2001; trustee, sec.-treas. Homes for Children Found; bd. advisors Chgo. area coun. Boy Scouts Am., ChildServ; trustee Nat. Inst. Constrn. Law and Practice. Mem. Internat. Bar Assn. (past co-chmn. com. internat. constrn. projects), Am. Coll. Constrn. Lawyers (past pres.), Urban Land Inst. (trustee), Urban Land Inst. Found. (gov.), Chgo. Dist. Coun. (past chmn.), Lambda Alpha Internat. (Ely chpt. past pres.). Office: Bell Boyd & Lloyd LLC 3 1st Nat Plaza 70 W Madison St Ste 3300 Chicago IL 60602-4207 E-mail: ghummel@bellboyd.com.

HUMPHREY, GEORGE MAGOFFIN, II, plastic molding company executive; b. Cleve., Mar. 19, 1942; s. Gilbert Watts and Louise (Ireland) H.; m. Marguerite Burton, June 19, 1964 (div. 1989); children: Mary O., Sandra; m. Patience Ryan, June 22, 1991. B.A., Yale U., 1964; J.D., U. Mich., 1967. Bar: Ohio 1967. Sales rep. Hanna Mining Co., Cleve., 1970-72, European rep., 1972-77, sales rep., 1977-78, mgr. sales, 1978, v.p. sales, 1978-80, sr. v.p. fin., 1980-81, sr. v.p. sales, dir., 1981-84; mng. dir. Russell Reynolds Assocs., 1984-87; gen. ptnr. Philips Industries, Ltd., 1987-94; pres. Extrudex, 1990—. Trustee Case Western Res. U., Cleve. Mus. Art, Cleve. Mus. Natural History, Cleve. Scholarship Programs, Inc., Univ. Hosps. Cleve. Served to capt. USMC, 1967-70. Mem. Union Club (Cleve.). Republican. Episcopalian. Home: 18 W Mather Ln Bratenahl OH 44108-1158 Office: Extrudex 310 Figgie Dr Painesville OH 44077-3028

HUMPHREY, KAREN ANN, college director; d. Martin and Eleanor (Schwartau) Annexstad; m. Charles W. Humphrey; children: Karna, Kirk. BA in Am. Studies, U. Minn. Cmty. affairs editor KRBI Radio, St. Peter, Minn., 1976-77; assoc. editor Dassel Cokato Enterprise and Dispatch, Dassel, 1979-89; legis. asst. to U.S. Sen. Dave Durenberger, 1989-95; comms. cons. Karen Humphrey and Co., Watertown, Minn., 1995-98; cmty. rels. mgr. Barnes & Noble, Minnetonka; pres. Minn. Hist. Soc., St. Paul, 1996-98; dir. planned giving Bethany Coll., Lindsborg, Kans., 1998—2002, coord. Disting. Professorship in Swedish Studies, 2000, v.p. instnl. advancement, 2002—. Mem. hon. com. for Vandringer Conf.: Norwegians in the Am. Mosaic, 2000. Active Bethany Luth. Ch., Bethany Coll. Symphonic Band, Lindsborg Cmty. Orch. Mem. Assn. Luth. Devel. Execs., U. Minn. Alumni Assn., Norwegian-Am. Hist. Assn. (bd. dirs.), Minn. Pub. Radio, Dassel Leikarring, Oral History Assn., Kans. State Hist. Soc. (bd. dirs.). Office: Bethany Coll 421 N 1st St Lindsborg KS 67456-1831 E-mail: khumphrey@ks-usa.net.

HUMPHREYS, KATIE, health agency administrator; b. South Bend, Ind. BS, Western Mich. U.; MS, Ind. U., South Bend; MBA, U. Notre Dame. Dir. health care policy Gov. Evan Bayh's adminstrn.; interim gen. mgr. Ind. Toll Rd.; commr. Ind. State Dept. Adminstrn.; dep. dir. Ind. State Budget Agy.; city contr., dir. adminstrn. and fin. City of South Bend; dep. commr. Ind. State Dept. Health, 1997—. With St. Joseph's Med. Ctr. South Bend, No. Ind. Health Sys. Agy., Logan Ctr. South Bend, No. Ind. State Hosp.; tchr. South Bend Comty. Schs. Office: Ind State Dept of Health 2 N Meridian St Indianapolis IN 46204-3003

HUMPHREYS, KIRK, mayor; b. 1950; BA, U. Okla., 1972. Pres. Gibraltar Ivestments, Inc., Oklahoma City, 1989—; mayor Oklahoma City, 1998—. Office: Office of the Mayor City Hall 200 N Walker Ave Ste 302 Oklahoma City OK 73102-2232*

HUNDLEY, ELAINE E. retired nursing education administrator; b. Mandan, N.D., Apr. 11, 1933; d. Valentine and Constantina Elisabeth (Braun) Helbling; m. James B. Hundley, Sept. 7, 1954; children: Mary Jo, Leslie, Jamie, John, Rachel. RN Diploma, Sisters of St. Joseph Sch. of Nursing of N.D., 1954; Coronary Care Cert., Parkland Coll., 1971; BA in Nursing, Sangamon State U., 1975; MA in Nursing Adminstrn./Edn., Columbia Pacific U., 1984. Cert. continuing edn. and staff devel., ANCC; cert. CNA instr. Clinic staff nurse Grand Forks (N.D.) Clinic, 1954-55; staff nurse med.-surg. units, house supr., nurse asst. instr. St. Michael's Hosp., Grand Forks, 1955-68; sch. nurse St. Michael's Sch., 1960-64; coronary care staff nurse Burnham Hosp., Champaign, Ill., 1972-73; mem. ICU staff St. John's Hosp., Springfield, 1975; dir. staff devel. Springfield Humana Hosp., 1977-80, ICU staff nurse, staff nurse recovery rm., med.-surg. units, emergency rm., 1975-77; dir. continuing edn. nursing/allied health Lincoln Land C.C., Springfield, 1981-97, ret., 1997. Mem. profl. edn. bd. Am. Cancer Soc., Am. Heart Assn. Active planning bd. Sangamon County Health Dept., Ill. Mem. ANA, Ill. Nurses Assn. (pres., program chair, bd. dirs. 9th dist. 1975—, chair commn. continuing edn. 1993-97, Staff Devel./Continuing Edn. award 1999), State Nurses Active in Politics in Ill., Health Svcs. Area Region Ill. Coun. Continuing Edn. (pres., v.p., sec., treas. 1978—). Roman Catholic. Avocations: music, reading, gardening, quilting, photography. Home: RR 1 Rochester IL 62563-9801 Office: Lincoln Land CC Shepherd Rd Springfield IL 62794

HUNHOFF, BERNIE P. state legislator; b. Yankton, S.D., Sept. 5, 1951; s. Bernard P. Sr. and Margaret (Modde) H.; m. Myrna Mulloy, 1974; children: Katie, Chris. BA, Mt. Marty Coll., 1974. Legis. aide U.S. Rep. Frank Denholm, 1974; chmn. Yankton County Dem. Party, 1984-86; mem. S.D. Senate, 1993—, mem. appropriations com.; pub. rels. dir. U. S.D. Sch.Medicine, 1977-79; editor, pub. The Observer, Yankton, S.D., 1979-85, S.D. Mag., Yankton, 1985—. Co-author: Uniquely S.D., 1989—. Home: PO Box 175 Yankton SD 57078-0175

HUNIA, EDWARD MARK, foundation executive; b. Sharon, Pa., Jan. 8, 1946; s. Edward and Estelle (Maleski) H.; m. Mary Sue Marburger, Sept. 25, 1976; children: Stephen, Adam. BSME, Carnegie Mellon U., 1967, MSME, 1968; MBA, U. Pitts., 1971. CFA. Sr. systems analyst Pitts. Plate Glass Industries, 1968-73; asst. to treas. Carnegie Mellon U., Pitts., 1973-76, dir. internal audit, 1976-78, asst. controller, dir. fin. systems, 1978-81, treas., 1981-90; v.p. for finance, treas. U. Pitts., 1990-92; sr. v.p., treas. The Kresge Found., Troy, Mich., 1992—. Mem. Assn. for Investment Mgmt. and Rsch., Fin. Analysts Soc. Detroit. Avocations: tennis, golf, running, books. Home: 4393 Barchester Dr Bloomfield Hills MI 48302-2116 Office: The Kresge Found PO Box 3151 Troy MI 48007-3151

HUNSBURGER, BILL, publishing executive; Pres., pub. The Clarion-Ledger, Jackson, Mich., 1993—. Office: 201 S Congress St Jackson MS 39201-4202

HUNT, EFFIE NEVA, former college dean, former English language educator; b. Waverly, Ill., June 19, 1922; d. Abraham Luther and Fannie Ethel (Ritter) H. A.B., MacMurray Coll. for Women, 1944; M.A., U. Ill., 1945, Ph.D., 1950; postgrad., Columbia U., 1953, Univ. Coll., U. London, 1949-50. Key-punch operator U.S. Treasury, 1945; spl. librarian Harvard U., 1947, U. Pa., 1948; Instr. English U. Ill., 1950-51; librarian Library of

Congress, Washington, 1951-52; asst. prof. English Mankato State Coll., 1952-59; prof. Radford Coll., 1959-63, chmn. dept. English, 1961-63; prof. Ind. State U., 1963-86; dean Ind. State U. (Coll. Arts and Scis.), 1974-86, dean and prof. emerita, 1987—. Author articles in field. Fulbright grantee, 1949-50 Mem. AAUP, MLA, Nat. Council Tchrs. English, Am. Assn. Higher Edn., Audubon Soc. Home: 3365 Wabash Ave Apt 4 Terre Haute IN 47803-1655 Office: Ind State U Root Hall Eng Dept Terre Haute IN 47809-0001

HUNT, HOLLY, small business owner; b. San Angelo, Tex., Nov. 19, 1942; d. Cagle O. and Zelma (Richardson) H.; m. Rowland Tackbary, Dec. 14, 1974 (div. 1987); children: Hunt Tackbary, Jett Tackberry, Trent Tackberry. BA in Eng. Lit., Tex. Tech., Lubbock, 1965. Buyer Foley's Dept. Store, Houston, 1965-68; designer Tempo, N.Y.C., 1969-73; owner, designer Holly Hunt Inc., 1973-83; owner, exec. v.p. Availco Equity Availco Syatems, Chgo.; owner, pres. Holly Hunt, Ltd., 1983--, 1986. Mem., art collector, Mus. Contrary art Chgo., 1978--. Mem. ASN, ISID. Republican. Presbyterian. Avocations: tennis, skiing, reading, art. Office: Holly Hunt Ltd 1728 Merchandise Mart Chicago IL 60654

HUNT, LAMAR, professional football team executive; b. 1932; s. H.L. and Lyda (Bunker) H.; m. Norma Hunt; children: Lamar, Sharron, Clark, Daniel. Grad., So. Meth. U. Founder, owner Kansas City Chiefs, NFL, 1959—, pres., 1959-76, chmn., 1977-78; founder, pres. AFL, 1959; (became Am. Football Conf.-NFL 1970); pres. Am. Football Conf., 1970—. Bd. dirs. Profl. Football Hall of Fame, Canton, Ohio. Named Salesman of Yr., Kansas City Advt. and Sales Execs. Club, 1963, Southwesterner of Yr., Tex. Sportswriters Assn., 1959. Office: Kans City Chiefs 1 Arrowhead Dr Kansas City MO 64129-1651

HUNT, LAWRENCE HALLEY, JR. lawyer; b. July 15, 1943; s. Lawrence Halley Sr. and Mary Hamilton (Johnson) H.; m. Katherine Collins; children: Caroline Smith, Laura Hamilton, Darwin Halley. AB, Dartmouth Coll., 1965; cert., l'Inst. d'Etudes Politiques, Paris, 1966; JD, U. Chgo., 1969. Bar: N.Y. 1970, Ill. 1971, U.S. Ct. Appeals (9th cir.) 1980, U.S. Ct. Appeals (2d cir.) 1981, U.S. Supreme Ct. 1981. Assoc. Davis Polk & Wardwell, N.Y.C., 1969-70, Sidley & Austin, Chgo., 1970-75; ptnr. Sidley Austin Brown & Wood, 1975—, mem. exec. com., 1985—. Adv. securities adv. com. Ill. Sec. of State, Springfield, Ill., 1977—87; prof. grad. program fin. svcs. law Ill. Inst. Tech.-Chgo.-Kent Coll. Law, 1987—99. Mng. editor U. Chgo. Law Review, 1968-69. James B. Reynolds scholar Dartmouth Coll., 1965-66. Mem.: ABA (com. on commodity regulation, past chmn. subcom. on futures commn. merchants, past mem. exec. coun.), Internat. Bar Assn. (past chmn. bus. law com. sub-com. futures and options), Indian Hill Club, Chgo. Club, Mid-Day Club. Office: Sidley Austin Brown & Wood Bank One Plz Chicago IL 60603 E-mail: lhunt@sidley.com.

HUNT, MICHAEL O'LEARY, wood science and engineering educator; b. Louisville, Dec. 9, 1935; s. George Henry and Tressie (Truax) H.; children: Elizabeth H. Schwartz, Lynne T. Lattimer, Michael O. Jr. BS, U. Ky., 1957; M.Forestry, Duke U., 1958; PhD, N.C. State U., 1970. Product engr. Wood Products div. Singer Co., Pickens, S.C., 1959-60; asst. prof. wood sci. Purdue U., West Lafayette, Ind., 1960-70, assoc. prof., 1970-79, prof. and dir. Wood Rsch. Lab., 1979—. Contbr. articles to over 70 sci. and tech. publs. Bd. mem. Wabash Valley Trust for Historic Preservation, Lafayette. Recipient Servaas Meml. award Hist. Landmarks Found. of Ind., 1994, H. Fannon award Lafayette Neighborhood Housing Svcs., 1998. Mem. Forest Products Soc. (pres. 1990-91, Fred Gottschalk Meml. award 1984), Soc. of Wood Sci. and Tech., Rotary. Achievements include patent for lightweight, high-performance structural particleboard. Office: Purdue Univ Wood Rsch Lab West Lafayette IN 47907-1200

HUNT, ROBERT CHESTER, construction company executive; b. Dayton, Ohio, 1923; Grad., Case Inst. Tech., 1942. With Huber Hunt & Nichols Inc., Indpls., 1947—, sec., 1950-51, gen. mgr., 1951-52, v.p., 1952-56, vice chmn., CEO, from 1956; chmn. bd. dirs. Hunt Constrn. Group, Inc., 2000—. Dir. Bank One Indpls., N.A., formerly Am. Fletcher Nat. Bank Office: Hunt Constrn Group Inc 2450 S Tibbs Ave Indianapolis IN 46241-4821

HUNT, ROBERT G. construction company executive; b. Feb. 15, 1948; BS in bus., Ball State U.; MS in Engring., Purdue U. Joined Huber, Hunt & Nichols Inc., Indpls., 1974, from field engr. to divsn. mgr., pres. Phoenix and Tampa, CEO Indpls., 1999—; pres. The Hunt Corp.

HUNT, ROGER, former state legislator; m. Sharon Hunt; 3 children. Student, Augustana Coll., U. S.D., George Washington U. Mem. S.D. Ho. of Reps., 1991—2001, mem. judiciary and edn. coms., spkr. of ho., 1999—2001; atty., tchr. S.D. State Legislature. Address: 48190 265th St Brandon SD 57005-7205

HUNT, ROGER SCHERMERHORN, healthcare administrator; b. White Plains, N.Y., Mar. 7, 1943; s. Charles Howland and Mildred Russell (Schermerhorn) H.; m. Mary Adams Libby, June 19, 1965; children: Christina Markle, David. BA, DePauw U., 1965; MBA, George Washington U., 1968. Adminstrv. resident Lankenau Hosp., Phila., 1966-68; asst. adminstr. Hahnemann Med. Coll. and Hosp., 1968-71, hosp. dir., 1971-74, assoc. v.p., hosp. adminstr., 1974-77; dir. Ind. U. Hosps., Indpls., 1977-84; pres. Luth. Gen. Hosp., Park Ridge, Ill., 1984-90; pres., CEO Fontbonne Health System, Toronto, 1990-92; sr. v.p. Northwestern Healthcare Network, Chgo., 1993-96; pres., CEO ViaHealth, Rochester, 1996-99; prin. Hunt Healthcare, Deerfield, Ill., 1999—2002; CEO, BroMenn Healthcare Sys., Bloomington, 2002—. Chmn. Alliance of Indpls. Hosps., 1981; pres. United Hosp. Services, 1979-81; assoc. prof. hosp. adminstrn. Ind. U. Sch. Medicine, 1977-84; vice chmn. Pa. Emergency Health Services Council, 1975-77; pres. Chester County Emergency Med. Service Council, 1971-77. Pres. Wayne Area Jr. C. of C., 1970-71, state dir., 1971-72; bd. dirs. Rochester Philharm. Orch., 1998-99. Fellow Am. Coll. Healthcare Execs. (regent for Ind. 1984, Ill. 1988-90, Postgrad. tng. award 1968); mem. Am. Hosp. Assn., Hosp. Assn. of N.Y. State (bd. dirs. 1998-99), Ind. Hosp. Assn. (bd. dirs. 1982-84), Met. Chgo. Healthcare Coun. (bd. dirs. 1986-95), DePauw U. Alumni Assn. (bd. dirs. 1988-94), Greater Rochester Metro C. of C. (bd. dirs. 1998-99). Office: BroMenn Healthcare PO Box 2850 Bloomington IL 61702-2850 E-mail: Rogerhunt@earthlink.net.

HUNT, V. WILLIAM (BILL), automotive supplier executive; b. Washington D.C., Sept. 26, 1944; BA, Ind. U., 1966, JD, 1969. Labor counsel TRW Automotive Worldwide; counsel Arvin, Inc., Columbus, Indiana, 1976-80, v.p. adminstrn. Troy, Mich., 1980-82, sec., 1982-90, exec. v.p., 1990-96, pres., 1996-98, CEO, 1998-2000, also bd. dirs.; vice chmn., pres. ArvinMeritor, Inc., 2000—. Chmn. Pres.'s Coun.; mem. dean's adv. coun. Ind. U. Sch. Bus., Ind. U. Well House Soc.; bd. dirs. Ind. U. Found.; co-chmn. Ctrl. Ind. Corp. Partnership. Mem. Mfrs. Alliance (trustee), Motor and Equipment Mfrs. Assn. (bd. dirs.).

HUNTER, BUDDY D. holding company executive; b. Wilsontown, Mo., Feb. 28, 1930; s. Harold H. and Marie (Miller) H.; (div.); children— Bruce, Beverly, Brenda, Brett B.S., Northeast Mo. State U., 1950. Pres. S.P. Wright & Co., Springfield, Ill., 1956-69; chmn. bd., pres., chief exec. officer AMEDCO Inc., St. Louis, 1969-86; chmn. Huntco Inc., Chesterfield, Mo., 1986—. Bd. dirs. Mark Twain BancShares, St. Louis, Svc. Corp. Internat., Houston, Cash Am. Investments, Ft. Worth, numerous other cos. Bd. dirs. Meml. Med. Ctr.; exec. adv. council Breech Sch. Bus., Drury Coll., Springfield, Mo. Capt. USAF, 1951-56 Mem. Masons, Shriners. Avocations: tennis; skiing; jogging. Office: Huntco Inc 14323 S Outer 40 Dr #600N Chesterfield MO 63017-5747

HUNTER, ELMO BOLTON, federal judge; b. St. Louis, Oct. 23, 1915; s. David Riley and Della (Bolton) H.; m. Shirley Arnold, Apr. 5, 1952; 1 child, Nancy Ann (Mrs. Ray Lee Hunt). AB, U. Mo., 1936, LLB, 1938; Cook Grad. fellow, U. Mich., 1941; PhD (hon.), Coll. of Ozarks, 1988. Bar: Mo. 1938. Pvt. practice, Kansas City, 1938-45; sr. asst. city counselor, 1939-40; ptnr. Sebree, Shook, Hardy and Hunter, 1945-51; state circuit judge Mo., 1951-57; Mo. appellate judge, 1957-65; judge U.S. Dist. Ct., Kansas City, Mo., 1965—, now sr. judge. Instr. law U. Mo., 1952-62; mem. jud. selection Elmo B. Hunter Citizens Ctr., Am. Judicature Soc. Contbr. articles to profl. jours. Mem. Bd. Police Commrs., 1949-51; Trustee Kansas City U., Coll. of Ozarks; fellow William Rockhill Nelson Gallery Art. 1st lt. M.I., AUS, 1943-46. Recipient 1st Ann. Law Day award U. Mo., 1964, Charles E. Whittaker award, 1994, SAR Law Enforcement Commendation medal, 1994, citation of Merit Mo. Law Sch., 1996. Fellow ABA; mem. Fed., Mo. bar assns., Jud. Conf. U.S. (mem. long range planning com., chmn. ct. adminstrn. com.), Am. Judicature Soc. (bd. govs., mem. exec. com., pres., chmn. bd., Devitt Disting. Svc. to Justice award 1987), Acad. Mo. Squires, Order of Coif, Phi Beta Kappa, Phi Delta Phi. Presbyterian (elder). Office: US Dist Ct 659 US Courthouse 811 Grand Blvd Ste 201 Kansas City MO 64106-1904

HUNTER, HARLEN CHARLES, orthopedic surgeon; b. Estherville, Iowa, Sept. 23, 1940; s. Roy Harold and Helen Iola (King) H.; m. JoAnn Wilson, June 30, 1962; children: Harlen Todd, Juliann Kristin. BA, Drake U., 1962; DO, Coll. Osteo. Med. and Surgery, Des Moines, 1967. Diplomate Am. Osteo. Bd. Orthop. Surgery, Am. Osteo. Acad. Sports Medicine. Intern Normandy Osteo. Hosp., St. Louis, 1967-68, resident in orthops., 1968-72, chmn. dept. orthops., 1976-77; founder Orthopedics and Sports Medicine, PC, Bedford, Ind. Founder, orthop. surgeon Mid-States Orthop. Sports Medicine Clinics of Am., Ltd. SPORTS Med. Ctrs., Chesterfield, Mo., Fairview Heights, Ill., Jerseyville, Ill., Herman, Mo., 1977-99, Hunter Trauma Team, 1988-92; founder, pres. Life Style Health Systems, 1992; assoc. prof. orthop. Kansas City Coll. Osteopathy, 1993; adj. prof. Lake Erie Coll. Osteo. Medicine, 1995—; mem. staff Normandy Osteopathic, 1972-90, Outpatient Surgery Ctr., St. Louis, 1990-99, Luth. Med. Ctr., 1989-99, St. Joe's of Kirkwood, 1990-99, Bedford Med. Ctr., Dunn Meml.; clin. instr. Kirksville Coll. Osteo. Medicine; orthop. cons., team physician to high schs.; pres. Health Specialists, Inc.; program dir. sports medicine Family Physicians, 1993, 94; sponsor, lectr. sports and occupl. emergency medicine, 1997—; host weekly TV program Raceology Weekly Spl. on Motorsports; mem. med. adv. bd. Mo. Athletic Activities Assn.; cons. sports medicine Sports St. Louis newspaper; founder Ann. Sports Medicine Clinic for Trainers and Coaches, 1 yr. fellowship in sports medicine; nat. lectr. various social, profl. orgns.; adj. clin. assoc. prof. Coll. Osteo. Surgery, Des Moines; orthop. surgeon Iowa State Boys Basketball Tournament, 1966-85; founder Mobile Sports Medicine Semi Truck, 1988, Hunter Sports Medicine Clinic, Belleville, Ill.; sponsor U.S. Biathalon Assn., 1989; staff photographer Ind. Motor Speedway, 1973—, Daytona Internat. Speedway, 1979-96; adv. bd. Motorsport Rsch. Group Human Performance Internat., Daytona Beach, Fla., 1990—; mem. Sports Medicine Commn. Ind. State Med. Assn. Co-author: Motorsports Medicine, 1992; host daily radio program Making a Difference; contbr. articles to profl. jours. Mem. adv. bd. Bedford Salvation Army. Recipient Clinic Spkr. award Iowa H.S. Baseball Coaches Assn., 1982, 83, Hall of Fame award Mo. Athletic Trainers Assn., 1987, Sibley Medallion award for outstanding svc. Lindenwood U., Ann. Outstanding Soccer Player of Yr. award Mo. Athletic Club, Hunter 100 Stock Car Race, Peveley, Mo.; Harlen C. Hunter Sports Complex named in his honor Lindenwood U., St. Charles, Mo., 1988. Fellow Am. Coll. Osteo. Surgeons, Am. Osteo Acad. Orthops. (past chmn. com. on athletic injuries), Am. Osteo. Acad. Sports Medicine; mem. Am. Osteo. Assn., Mo. Assn. Osteo. Physicians and Surgeons (medallion award 1990), Am. Coll. Sports Medicine, Am. Orthop. Soc. Sports Medicine (del. sports medicine exch. program to China 1985), AMA, Am. Coll. Occupational Medicine, Ind. Med. Assn. (sports medicine com. 1999—), Ind. Osteo. Assn., St. Louis Met. Med. Assn., Sports Car Club Am. (med. dir. pro racing 1989-91), World Congress Motorsport Scis., St. Louis Auto Racing Club (Amb. award 1989, 91), 500 Old Timers Club, The Butler Soc., Elks, Lions, Masons, Shriners. Republican. Methodist. Home: 604 Heltonville Rd E Bedford IN 47421-9250 Office: Ortho & Sports Medicine 2900 16th St Bedford IN 47421-3510

HUNTER, JAMES GALBRAITH, JR. lawyer; b. Phila., Jan. 6, 1942; s. James Galbraith and Emma Margaret (Jehl) H.; m. Pamela Ann Trott, July 18, 1969 (div.); children: James Nicholas, Catherine Selene; m. Nancy Grace Scheurwater, June 21, 1992. B.S. in Engring. Sci., Case Inst. Tech., 1965; J.D., U. Chgo., 1967. Bar: Ill. 1967, U.S. Dist. Ct. (no. dist.) Ill. 1967, U.S. Ct. Appeals (7th cir.) 1967, U.S. Ct. Claims, 1976, U.S. Ct. Appeals (4th and 9th cirs.) 1978, U.S. Supreme Ct. 1979, U.S. Dist. Ct. (cen. dist.) Ill. 1980, Calif. 1980, U.S. Dist. Ct. (cen. and so. dists.) Calif. 1980, U.S. Ct. Appeals (5th cir.) 1982, U.S. Ct. Appeals (fed. cir.) 1982. Assoc. Kirkland & Ellis, Chgo., 1967-68, 70-73, ptnr., 1973-76; ptnr. Hedlund, Hunter & Lynch, Chgo., 1976-82, Los Angeles, 1979-82; ptnr. Latham & Watkins, Hedlund, Hunter & Lynch, Chgo. and Los Angeles, 1982— . Served to lt. JAGC, USN, 1968-70. Mem. ABA, State Bar Calif., Los Angeles County Bar Assn., Chgo. Bar Assn. Clubs: Metropolitan (Chgo.), Chgo. Athletic Assn., Los Angeles Athletic. Exec. editor U. Chgo. Law Rev., 1966-67. Office: Latham & Watkins Sears Tower Ste 5800 Chicago IL 60606-6306 also: 633 W 5th St Los Angeles CA 90071-2005

HUNTER, J(AMES) PAUL, English language educator, literary critic, historian; b. Jamestown, N.Y., June 29, 1934; s. Paul W. and Florence I. (Walmer) H.; children: Debra, Lisa, Paul III, Anne, Ellen Harris. A.B., Ind. Central Coll., 1955; M.A., Miami U., Oxford, Ohio, 1957; Ph.D., Rice U., 1963. Instr., U. Fla., Gainesville, 1957-59, Williams Coll., Williamstown, Mass., 1962-64; asst. prof. U. Calif., Riverside, 1964-66; assoc. prof. English Emory U., Atlanta, 1966-68, prof., 1968-80, chmn. dept., 1973-79; prof. English, dean Coll. Arts and Sci., U. Rochester, N.Y., 1981-86; prof. English U. Chgo., 1987—, Chester D. Tripp prof. humanities, 1990-96, Barbara E. and Richard J. Franke prof. humanities, 1996—2001; dir. Franke Inst. for the Humanities, 1996—2001, Franke prof. emeritus, 2001—. Gen. editor Bedford Cultural Edits., 1994—. Author: The Reluctant Pilgrim, 1966, Occasional Form, 1975, Norton Introduction to Poetry, 8th edit., 1998, Norton Introduction to Literature, 7th edit., 2001, New Worlds of Literature, 2d edit., 1994, Before Novels, 1990; co-editor: Rhetorics of Order/Ordering Rhetorics, 1989; editor: Norton Critical Edition of Mary Shelley's Frankenstein, 1996. Sr. advisor Andrew W. Mellon Found., 1999—. Guggenheim fellow, 1976-77, NEH fellow, 1985-86, Nat. Humanities Ctr. fellow, 1986, 95-96. Mem. MLA, Am. Soc. 18th Century Studies (Louis Gottschalk prize 1991, 2d v.p. 1994-95, 1st v.p. 1995-96, pres. 1996-97), Southeastern Am. Soc. 18th Century Studies (pres. 1977-78), So. Atlantic MLA (pres. 1992-93), N.E. Am. Soc. 18th Century Studies (pres. 1982-83). Office: U Chgo Dept English 404 Wieboldt Hall Chicago IL 60637 E-mail: jph4@midway.uchicago.edu.

HUNTER, ROBERT TYLER, investment management company executive; b. Peoria, Ill., Jan. 14, 1943; s. Thomas Oakford and Joan (Sargent) H.; m. Mary Michelle Tyrrell, June 12, 1965. A.B., Harvard U., 1965. Pres. First Union Trust Co., Kansas City, Mo., 1973-81; sr. v.p., trust div. mgr. Centerre Bank, Kansas City, 1981-84; v.p., mgr. client services and mktg. DST Systems, Inc., Kansas City, 1984-85; sr. v.p. mktg. Waddell & Read Asset Mgmt. Co., Kansas City, 1985— Treas. M.S. Soc., Mission, Kans.; bd. dirs. Boys and Girls Club, Kansas City; trustee Menorah Hosp. Found., Kansas City; bd. govs. Kansas City Philharmonic Assn.; bd. dirs., com. chmn. Kansas City Youth Symphony. Fellow Fin. Analyst Fedn.; mem. Fin. Analyst Soc. Kansas City, Corp. Fiduciaries Soc. of Kansas City (past pres.), Estate Planning Assn. Republican. Roman Catholic. Clubs: Harvard/Radcliffe (pres. 1983-85); Kansas City Rcquet (Merriam, Kans.). Avocations: tennis; swimming; reading; coaching. Home: 8326 Mullen Rd Lenexa KS 66215-6019 Office: Midwest Trust Co. 10740 Nall Ave., Suite 100 Overland Park KS 66211

HUNTER, VICTOR LEE, marketing executive, consultant; b. Garrett, Ind., Mar. 1, 1947; s. John Joseph and Martha May (Brown) H.; m. Linda Ann Loudermilk, Dec. 19, 1969; children: Jed, Andrew, Matthew, Holly. BS, Purdue U., 1969; MBA, Harvard U., 1971. Dir. mktg. Kreuger, Inc., Green Bay, Wis., 1971-75; pres. B&I Furniture, Milw., 1975-81, Hunter Bus. Group, Milw., 1981—. Bd. dirs. Koss Corp., Milw., Wm. K. Walthers Co., Milw. Author: Business-to-Business Marketing: Creating a Community of Customers, 1997. Lay leader United Meth. Ch., Whitefish Bay, Wis., 1985; mem. exec. com. Greater Milw. Conv. and Visitors Bur. Mem. Direct Mktg. Assn., Wis. Pres.' Orgn., Bus. to Bus. Direct Mktg. Coun. Office: Hunter Business Group PO Box 12970 Milwaukee WI 53212-0970

HUNTINGTON, CURTIS EDWARD, actuary; b. Worcester, Mass., July 30, 1942; s. Everett Curtis and Margaret (Schwenzfeger) H. B.A., U. Mich., 1964, M.Actuarial Sci., 1965; J.D., Suffolk U., 1976. With New Eng. Mut. Life Ins. Co., Boston, 1965-93, v.p., auditor, 1980-84, corp. actuary, 1984-93; prof. math., dir. actuarial program U. Mich., Ann Arbor, 1993—. Treas. Actuarial Edn. and Rsch. Fund, 1986-89, chmn., 1989-92, dir. 1985—, exec. dir., 1994—. Trustee The Actuarial Found., 1998—. Served with USPHS, 1965-67. Mem. Soc. Actuaries (gen. chmn. edn. and exam. com. 1985-87, bd. govs. 1986-89, v.p. 1989-91), Am. Acad. Actuaries (bd. dirs. 1997-2000), Am. Soc. Pension Actuaries (dir. 1996—), Am. Coll. Life Underwriters, Internat. Actuarial Assn. (sec., nat. corr. U.S.), New Zealand Soc. Actuaries. Office: U Mich Dept of Math 2864 East Hall Ann Arbor MI 48109-1109

HUNTLEY, ROBERT STEPHEN, newspaper editor; b. Winston-Salem, N.C., Mar. 6, 1943; m. Linda Fabry; children: Kristine Elizabeth, Katherine Vallie. BA in Journalism, U. N.C., 1965. Reporter UPI, various locations, 1965-69, writer, editor broadcast and gen. news depts. Chgo., 1969-77, exec. editor nat. broadcast dept., 1977-78; bur. chief Commodity News Svc., 1978-79, U.S. News & World Report, Chgo., 1979-82, assoc. editor Washington, 1982-85, sr. editor, 1985-86; reporter, rewrite specialist Chgo. Sun Times, 1986-90, met. editor, 1990-91, asst. mng. editor/metro, 1991-97; editl. page editor, 1997—. Bd. dirs. City News Bur., Chgo, 1993-97, pres., 1996; media fellow Hoover Instit. Stanford U., 2001 Recipient Stick-O-Type award for feature writing Chgo. Newspaper Guild, 1987, Appreciation cert. for outstanding contbns. to freedom of info. Nat. Ctr. Freedom of Info. Studies at Loyola U.-Chgo., 1993; Media fellow Hoover Instn., Stanford U., 2001. Mem. Ill. Freedom of Info. Coun. (v.p. 1994). Office: Chgo Sun-Times 401 N Wabash Ave Chicago IL 60611-5642

HUNTLEY, THOMAS, state legislator, science educator; b. Feb. 1938; m. Gail Huntley; two children. BS, U. Minn.; PhD in Biochemistry, Iowa State U. Assoc. prof. biochemistry U. Minn., Duluth; Dist. 6B rep. Minn. Ho. of Reps., St. Paul, 1993—. Home: 1924 Wallace Ave Duluth MN 55803-2461

HUNTRESS, BETTY ANN, former music store proprietor, educator; b. Apr. 29, 1932; d. Emmett Slater and Catherine V. (Kihlmire) Brundage; m. Arnold Ray Huntress, June 26, 1954; children: Catherine, Michael, Carol, Alan. BA, Cornell U., 1954. Tchr. h.s., Bordentown, N.J., 1954-55; part-time asst. to prof. Delta Coll., Northwood Inst., Midland, Mich., 1968-2000; ret. tchr. Midland Pub. Schs. Owner, mgr. The Music Stand, Midland, 1979-82. Bd. dirs. Midland Ctr. for Arts, 1978-86; v.p. MCFTA (Arts Ctr.), 1980-84, Friends of the Ctr., 1985—; mem. charter bd. mgrs. Matrix Midland Ann. Arts and Sci. Festival, 1977-80; cons. Girl Scouts U.S., 1964-76; mem. Mich. Internat. Coun., 1975-76; bd. dirs. Literacy Coun. Midland County, 1986-94, sec., 1987-91; mem. Midland Hist. Soc., 1990—, mem. Dow Chem. Centennial Com., 1996-98; mem. Presbyn. ch. choir, 1963—. Named Midland Musician of Yr., 1977. Mem. AAUW (dir. 1962-73, pres. 1971-73, mem. Mich. state divsn. 1983-85, bd. dirs. 1993-95, Outstanding Woman as Agt. of Change award 1977, fellowship grant named in her honor 1976), LWV (bd. dirs. 1986-90, com. charter schs. 1995-99), Music Soc. Midland Ctr. for arts (dir. 1971-86, chmn. 1976-79), Midland Symphony League Soc. (2d v.p. 1995-99), Cmty. Concert Soc., Women's Study Club of Midland (pres. 1995-96), Friends of Libr., Kappa Delta Epsilon, Pi Lambda Theta, Alpha Xi Delta. Presbyterian. Home: 5316 Sunset Dr Midland MI 48640-2536 E-mail: arnhunt@concentric.net.

HURAS, WILLIAM DAVID, retired bishop; b. Kitchener, Ont., Can., Sept. 22, 1932; s. William Adam and Frieda Dorothea (Rose) H.; m. Barbara Elizabeth Lotz, Oct. 5, 1957; children— David, Matthew, Andrea BA, Waterloo Coll., Ont., 1954; BD, Waterloo Sem., Ont., 1963; MTh, Knox Coll., Toronto, Ont., 1968; MDiv, Waterloo Luth. U., 1973; DD (hon.), Wilfred Laurier U., Waterloo, 1980, Huron Coll., London, Ont., 1989. Ordained to ministry Luth. Ch. in Am., 1957. Pastor St. James Luth. Ch., Refrew, Ont., 1957-62, Advent Luth. Ch., North York, 1962-78; bishop Eastern Can. Synod Luth. Ch. in Am., Kitchener, 1978-85, Eastern Synod Evangel. Luth. Ch. in Can., 1986-98. Mem. exec. com. Can. sect. of Luth. Ch. in Am., 1969-79; mem. exec. com. Luth. Merger Commn., Can., 1978-85; pres. Luth. Council Can., 1985-88; chmn. Group Svcs. Inc., Evangelical Luth. Ch. in Can., 1993—2001; mem. Anglican-Luth. Jt. Working Group, 1995—2001. Bd. govs. Waterloo Luth. U., 1966-75, Waterloo Luth. Sem., 1973-75, 78—. Mem. Order of St. Lazarus of Jerusalem (Ecclesiastical Grand cross 1985). E-mail: huras@golden.net.

HURD, RICHARD NELSON, pharmaceutical company executive; b. Evanston, Ill., Feb. 25, 1926; s. Charles DeWitt and Mary Ormsby (Nelson) H.; m. Jocelyn Fillmore Martin, Dec. 22, 1950; children: Melanie Gray, Suzanne Dewitt. BS, U. Mich., 1946; PhD U. Minn., 1956. Chemist Gen. Electric Co., Schenectady, N.Y., 1948-49; R&D group leader Koppers Co., Pitts., 1956-57; rsch. chemist Mallinckrodt Chem. Works, St. Louis, 1957-63, group leader, 1963-66, Comml. Solvents Corp., Terre Haute, Ind., 1966-68, sect. head, 1968-71; mgr. sci. affairs G. D. Searle Internat. Co., Skokie, Ill., 1972-73, dir. mfg. and tech. affairs, 1973-77; rep. to internat. tech com. Pharm. Mfrs. Assn., 1973-77; v.p. tech. affairs Elder Pharms., Bryan, Ohio, 1977-81; v.p. rsch. & devel. U.S. Proprietary Drugs & Toiletries div. Schering-Plough Corp., Memphis, 1981-83; v.p sci affairs Moleculon, Inc., Cambridge, Mass., 1984-88; v.p. regulatory affairs Pharmaco-LSR, Inc., Austin, Tex., 1989-94; prin. Hurd & Assocs., Inc., Evanston, ILL., 1994—. Contbr. articles to profl. jours.; patentee in field. Mem. Ferguson-Florissant (Mo.) Sch. Bd., 1964-66; bd. dirs. United Fund of Wabash Valley (Ind.), 1969-71. With USN, 1943-46, 53-55. E.I. DuPont de Nemours & Co., Inc. fellow, 1956. Fellow AAAS; mem. Am. Acad. Dermatology (life), Am. Soc. Photobiology, Am. Chem. Soc., N.Y. Acad. Sci., Am. Pharm. Assn., Am. Assn. Pharm. Scientists, Food and Drug Law Inst., Drug Info. Assn., Sigma XI, Mich. Shores Club (Wilmette, Ill.). Presbyterian. Achievements include codevelopment of Ralgro and Oxsoralen; research in thioamides as a class of organic compounds; development of macrocyclic synthetic routes for natural products; development of psoralens for photochemotherapy of dermatologic disorders. E-mail: hurdreg@earthlink.net.

HURLEY, SAMUEL CLAY, III, investment management company executive; b. Peoria, Ill., Jan. 25, 1936; s. Samuel Clay Jr. and Wilmina Marie (Loveless) H.; m. Dorothy Jane Atkinson, Aug. 19, 1967; children: Samuel C. IV, Bruce Hilliard. AB in Econs., Brown U., 1958; MBA in Fin., Northwestern U., 1960; postgrad., Harvard U., 1984—. Portfolio mgr. Continental Ill. Nat. Bank, Chgo., 1960-62; mgr. bank rels. Internat. Harvester Co. (later Navistar), 1962-71; asst. treas. Internat. Harvester Credit Corp., 1962-71, Anchor Hocking Corp. (now owned by Newell Corp.), Lancaster, Ohio, 1971-74, treas., 1975—, v.p., 1983-87; gen. ptnr. Steele and Co. Ltd., Columbus, Ohio, 1988-90; pres. Hurley Investment Counsel Ltd., Lancaster, 1990—. Trustee Lancaster-Fairfield Cmty. Hosp., 1984-91, Fairfield County Hospice, Fairfield County Found.; mem. Fairfield County Bd. Mental Retardation and Devel. Disabilities, Lancaster, 1981-95. Mem. Lancaster Country Club, Rotary, Capitol Club (Columbus). Republican. Episcopalian. Home: 148 E Wheeling St Lancaster OH 43130-3705 Office: 109 N Broad St Ste 350 Lancaster OH 43130-3785 E-mail: hicl@hotmail.com.

HURN, RAYMOND WALTER, minister, religious order administrator; b. Ontario, Oreg., June 27, 1921; s. Walter H. and Bertha Sultana (Gray) H.; m. Madelyn Lenore Kirkpatrick, Dec. 30, 1941; children: Constance Isbell, Jacqueline Oliver. BA, So. Nazarene U., 1943; DD (hon.), So. Nazarene U, 1967; postgrad., U. Tulsa, 1946-47, Fuller Sem., Pasadena, Calif., 1978-81. Ordained to ministry Ch. of Nazarene, 1943. Pastor Ch. of Nazarene chs., Kans., Okla., Ga., Oreg., 1943-59; dist. supt. Ch. of Nazarene, West Tex. dist., Tex., 1959-68; dir. home missions and ch. extension Internat. Hdqrs. Ch. of Nazarene, Kansas City, Mo., 1968-85, gen. supt., 1985-93. Author: Mission Possible, 1973, Black Evangelism, Which Way from Here, 1973, Spiritual Gifts Workshop, 1977, Finding Your Ministry, 1980, Mission Action Sourcebook, 1980, Unleashing the Lay Potential in the Sunday School, 1986, The Rising Tide: New Churches for the New Millenium, 1997. Recipient Exec. award Am. Inst. Ch. Growth, 1980, B award Bethany So. Nazarene Univ., 1982, Heritage award So. Nazarene U., 1993, Lifetime Achievement award Assn. of Nazarene Bldg. Prof., 1993, Multicultural Fellowship award, 1993; named Gen. Supt. Emeritus, 23rd Gen. Assembly of the Ch. of the Nazarene, 1993.

HURST, DAN, radio personality; b. Ft. Worth; With KCMO-AM, Kansas City, Kans., KLSI-FM, Mix 93; radio host KUDL, Westwood, Kans., 1998—. Office: 4935 Belinder Westwood KS 66205*

HURT, JAMES RIGGINS, English language educator; b. Ashland, Ky., May 22, 1934; s. Joe and Martha Clay (Riggins) H.; m. Phyllis Tilton, June 5, 1958; children: Christopher, Ross, Matthew. AB, U. Ky., 1956, MA, 1957; PhD, Ind. U., 1965. Asst. prof. Ind. U., Kokomo, 1963-66; asst. prof. U. Ill., Urbana-Champaign, 1966-69, asso. prof., 1969-73, prof. English, 1973—. Author: Aelfric, 1972, Catiline's Dream, 1972, Film and Theatre, 1974, Writing Illinois, 1992, (play) Abraham Lincoln Walks at Midnight, 1980; co-editor: Literature of the Western World, 1984. Served with U.S. Army, 1957-59. Fellow Ill. Ctr. Advanced Study, 1979-80, 86-87. Mem. MLA, Ill. State Hist. Soc. Home: 1001 W William St Champaign IL 61821-4508 Office: 325 English Bldg 608 S Wright St Urbana IL 61801-3630 E-mail: j-hurt@uiuc.edu.

HURTER, ARTHUR PATRICK, economist, educator; b. Chgo., Jan. 29; s. Arthur P. and Lillian T. (Thums) H.; m. Florence Evalyn Kays; children— Patricia Lyn, Arthur Earl BSChemE, MSChemE, MA in Econs., PhD in Econs., Northwestern U. Chem. engr. Zonlite Rsch. Lab., Evanston, Ill., 1957-58; assoc. dir. Rsch. Transp. Ctr., Northwestern U., 1963-65; asst. prof. dept. Indsl. Engring. and Mgmt. Scis. Tech. Inst., Northwestern U., 1962-66, prof., 1970—; prof. of transp., 1992—; chmn. dept. Northwestern U., 1969-89, assoc. prof. fin. Grad. Sch. Mgmt., 1969-70, prof., 1970—. Faculty mem. Newspaper Mgmt. Ctr., Transp. Ctr., 1989—; cons. U. Chgo., ESCOR, Sears Roebuck & Co., Standard Oil of Ind., Ill.; bd. dirs. Ill. Environ. Health Rsch. Ctr., 1972-77; mem. com. Sci. Tech. Adv., Ill. Inst. Natural Resources, 1980-84. Author: The Economics of Private Truck Transportation, 1965, Facility Location and the Theory of Production, 1989; contbr. articles to profl. jours. Pres. Coun. St. Scholastical H.S., 1972-80; elder Granville Ave. Presbyn. Ch., 1976-89; deacon 1st Presbyn. Ch., Evanston. Grantee Resources for the Future, 1964, Office of Naval Research, 1965, NSF, Social Sci. Research Council dissertation fellow Mem. Am. Econ. Assn., Regional Sci. Assn., Ops. Research Soc. Am., Inst. Mgmt. Scis., Inst. Indsl. Engrs., Sigma Xi, Phi Lambda Upsilon, Tau Beta Pi, Alpha Pi Mu (Disting. Engr. award). Home: 1505 W Norwood St Chicago IL 60660-2414 Office: Dept Indsl Engring Mgmt Sci Technological Inst Northwestern U Evanston IL 60208-0001

HURWICZ, LEONID, economist, educator; b. Moscow, 1917; arrived in U.S., 1940; LLM, U. Warsaw, Poland, 1938; DSc (hon.) , Northwestern U., 1980; D honoris causa, U. Autónoma de Barcelona, Spain, 1989; D of Econs. honoris causa, Keio U., Tokyo, 1993; LLD (hon.) , U. Chgo., 1993; D honoris causa, Warsaw Sch. Econs., Poland, 1994. Rsch. assoc. Cowles Commn. U. Chgo., 1944—46; from assoc. prof. to prof. Iowa State U., Ames, 1946—49; prof. econ., math. and stats. U. Ill., 1949—51, U. Minn., Mpls., 1951—99, Regents' prof., 1969—88, Regent's prof. emeritus, 1988—, Carlson prof. econs., 1989—92, prof. econs., 1992—. Vis. prof. econs. Stanford U., Calif., 1955—56, 1958—59, Harvard U., Cambridge, Mass., 1969—71, U. Calif., Berkeley, 1976—77, Northwestern U., Evanston, Ill., 1988—89, U. Calif., Santa Barbara, 1998, Calif. Inst. Tech., 1999; Fisher lectr. U. Copenhaben, 1963; hon. prof. Ctrl. China U. Sci. and Tech., Wyhan, 1984; vis. lectr. People's U., Beijing, 1986, Tokyo U., 1982, Australian Econometric Mtgs., Melbourne, 1997; vis. Fulbright lectr. Bangalore U., India, 1965—66; vis. disting. prof. econs. U. Ill., 2001; invited lectr. Chuo U., Keio U., UN U., Inst. Adv. Studies (symposium participation), Tokyo, 1999, Symposium Devel. Western China, Chongqing, 2000, Pub. Econ. Theory Conf. Warwick U., England, 2000; cons. Econ. Design, Istanbul, 2000, Ctr. china U. Sci. and Tech., Wuhan, 2000, Peking U., 2000. Co-author (co-editor (with K.J. Arrow): Studies in Resource Allocation Processes, 1977; co-author: (co-editor (with K.J. Arrow and J. Uzawa) Studies in Linear and Non-Linear Programming, 1958; co-author: (co-editor (with J.S. Chipman) Prefences, Utility and Demand, 1971; co-author: (co-editor (D. Schmeidler and H. sonnenschein) Social Goals and Social Organization, 1985; editor: Econ. Design, 1993, Review of Econ. Design, 1997, Jour. of pub. Econ. Theory, 1999, Advances in Mathematical Economics, 1999, Econs. Bull., 2001; mem. adv. bd.: Jour. of Math. Econs.; contbr. articles to profl. jours. Recipient Nat. medal Sci., 1990; fellow, Ctr. Advances Studies in Behavioral Scis., 1955—56; scholar Sherman Fairchild Disting. scholar, Calif. Inst. Tech., 1984—85. Fellow: Am. Econ. Assn. (disting., lectr. 1972), Econometric Soc. (pres. 1969); mem.: NAS, Am. Acad. Arts and Scis. Office: Univ Minn Dept Econs 271 19th Ave S Minneapolis MN 55455-0430 E-mail: hurwicz@tc.umn.edu.

HUSAR, RUDOLF BERTALAN, mechanical engineering educator; b. Martonos, Yugoslavia, Oct. 29, 1941; came to U.S., 1966; s. Ga'bor and Ilona Huszar; m. Janja Djukic, Oct. 8, 1967; children: Maja, Attila. Degree in mech. engring., U. Zagreb, Croatia, 1962; diploma in mech. engring., Tech. U., Germany, 1966; PhDME, U. Minn., 1971. Design technician W. Hofer, Krefeld, Germany, 1962-63; rsch. asst. Tech. U., Berlin, 1963-66; from rsch. asst. to assoc. U. Minn., Mpls., 1966-71; rsch. fellow Calif. Inst. Tech., Pasadena, 1971-73; prof. Washington U., St. Louis, 1973—. Vis. prof. U. Stockholm, 1976; co-chmn. Interagy. Com. Health and Environ. Effects of Advanced Energy Tech., 1978; coop. program mem. Devel. and Appin. Space Tech. Air Pollution, EPA/NASA, 1978; dir. Ctr. for Air Pollution Impact and Trend Analysis (CAPITA), St. Louis, 1979—; mem. com. on atmospheric-biospheric interactions NAS, 1979-81. Editor: Atmospheric Environment, 1980, Indojaras, 1980; mem. adv. bd. Environ. Sci. Tech., 1980; contbr. chpt. to: Air Quality Criteria for Particulate Matter, EPA, 1995. Rsch. fellow U. Glasgow, Scotland, 1965, U. Minn., 1966-71; grantee, EPA, 1973—, NOAA, 1991—, U.S. Dept. Def., 1989-92. Mem. Air & Waste Mgmt. Assoc., Ges. Aerosolforschung. Office: Wash U CAPITA PO Box 1124 Saint Louis MO 63188-1124

HUSBY, DONALD EVANS, engineering company executive; b. Mpls., Nov. 30, 1927; s. Olaf and Elsie Louise (Hagen) H.; m. Beverly June Tilbury, Sept. 24, 1949. B.S., S.D. State U., 1952. Student engr., jr. asst., sr. engr., mgr. new products Westinghouse Electric Corp., Cleve., 1952-72; engring. mgr., v.p. engring. lighting div. Harvey Hubbell, Inc., Christiansburg, Va., 1972-76; pres. Elliptipar Inc., West Haven, Conn., 1976-78; fellow engr., mgr. engring. sect. Westinghouse Electric Corp., Vicksburg, Miss., 1978-82; engring. mgr. new products devel. Cooper Industries Crouse-Hinds LTG Products div., 1982-84; utility sales mgr. central region Cooper Lighting, Mpls., 1985-89; chief exec. officer Husby & Husby Inc., Madison, Minn., 1990—. Mem. indsl. adv. counsel Underwriters Labs.; provider ednl. seminars in lighting, tech. expert for NVLAP, NIST, U.S. Dept. Commerce. Contbr. articles to profl. jours.; patentee in field. With USN, 1945—47. Fellow Illuminating Engrs. Soc. (chmn., sec., dir., Disting. Service award 1989); mem. Internat. Municipal Signal Assn., Soc. Plastics Engrs., Nat. Elec. Mfrs. Assn., Am. Nat. Standards Inst., Am. Soc. Quality Control, Miss. Engring. Soc., D.C. Soc. Profl. Engrs., Designers Lighting Forum., Mensa Internat., Toastmasters Internat. Mem. Christian Ch. Home and Office: 705 5th Ave PO Box 66 Madison MN 56256-0066

HUSEBOE, ARTHUR ROBERT, American literature educator; b. Sioux Falls, S.D., Oct. 6, 1931; s. Carl and Lillian Ruth (Auby) H.; m. Doris Louise Eggers, May 27, 1953. BA, Augustana Coll., 1953; MA, U. S.D., 1956; PhD, Ind. U., 1963; LHD (hon.), Dana Coll., 1984. Teaching assoc. Ind. U., Bloomington, 1959-60; instr. U. S.D., Vermillion, 1960-61; prof. Augustana Coll., Sioux Falls, S.D., 1961—. Pres. S.D. Humanities Found., Sioux Falls, 1994-96, Fedn. of State Humanities Couns., Washington, 1988-91; exec. dir. Nordland Heritage Found., Sioux Falls, 1980—, Ctr. Western Studies, Augustana, 1989—; NEH regional chair, 1989—. Author: An Illustrated History of the Arts in South Dakota, 1989, Sir George Etherege, 1987, Herbert Krause, 1985, Sir John Vanbrugh, 1976. Bd. dirs. S.D. Symphony, Sioux Falls, 1966—; mem. Nordland Fest Assn., Sioux Falls, 1975—. With U.S. Army, 1953-55. Recipient Gov.'s award in the Arts State of S.D., 1989; NEH grantee, 1975-77, 79-83, 92-94; named to S.D. Hall of Fame, 2001. Mem. MLA, We. Lit. Assn. (pres. 1976-77), Norwegian-Am. Hist. Assn., S.D. Hist. Soc. Lutheran. Avocations: travel, theater, classical music. Home: 813 E 38th St Sioux Falls SD 57105-5939 Office: Ctr for Western Studies Augustana Coll Box Sioux Falls SD 57197-0001 E-mail: huseboe@inst.augie.edu.

HUSHEN, JOHN WALLACE, manufacturing company executive; b. Detroit, July 28, 1935; s. J. Wallace and Hilda Carol (Jean) H.; m. Margaret Corinne Aho, Apr. 25, 1959 (div. May 1978); children: Susan Lisa, Jane Louise, Peter Matthew; m. Lane Gay Johnston, Feb. 8, 1985; 1 child, John Case. BA, Wayne State U., 1958. Reporter The Detroit News, 1959-66; campaign press sec. Griffin for Senate, Mich., 1966; press sec. U.S. Senator Robert P. Griffin, Washington, 1967-70; dir. pub. info. U.S. Dept. Justice, 1970-74; dep. press sec. Pres. Gerald R. Ford, 1974-76; dir. govt. relations Eaton Corp., 1976-79, dir. pub. affairs Cleve., 1979-81, v.p. govt. rels. Washington, 1981-91, v.p. corp. affairs Cleve., 1991-99. Trustee Citizens League Rsch. Inst., Cleve., pres., 1998-2000; trustee YMCA, Cleve. Mem. Former Senate Aides, Senate Press Secs. Assn. (pres. 1969-70), Union Club, Capitol Hill Club. Avocations: skiing, golf.

HUSMAN, CATHERINE BIGOT, insurance company executive, actuary; b. Des Moines, Feb. 10, 1943; d. Edward George and Ruth Margaret (Cumming) Bigot; m. Charles Erwin Husman, Aug. 5, 1967; 1 child, Matthew Edward. BA with highest distinction, U. Iowa, 1965; MA, Ball State U., 1970. Actuarial asst. Am. United Life Ins. Co., Indpls., 1965-68, assoc. actuary, 1971-74, group actuary, 1974-84, v.p., corp. actuary, 1984-97, v.p., chief actuary, 1997—. Mem. group tech. com. Mut. Life Ins. Co., 1986-98; mem. profitability studies com. Life Office Mgmt. Assn. Inc., 1991-99. Mem. women's adv. com. United Way Cen. Ind., 1991-93; bd. dirs., mem. fin. com., St. Elizabeth's Home, 1991-99, sec., 1994, mem. exec. com., treas., 1995; bd. dirs., mem. adminstrv. svcs., mem. exec. com. Heritage Place, 1993-99, treas., 1995-99. Fellow Soc. Actuaries; mem. Am. Acad. Actuaries, Actuaries Club Ind., Ky. and Ohio, Actuarial Club Indpls. (pres. 1979-80), Kiwanis (bd. dirs.), Phi Beta Kappa. Republican. Roman Catholic. Avocations: reading, tennis. Home: 1411 N Claridge Way Carmel IN 46032-8333 Office: Am United Life Ins Co 1 American Sq Indianapolis IN 46282-0020 E-mail: c_husman@prodigy.net.

HUSSEY, DAVID HOLBERT, physician; b. Savanna, Ill., 1937; MD, Washington U., St. Louis, 1964. Intern MD Anderson Hosp., Houston, 1964-65, resident, 1965-68; physician U. Iowa Hosps. Office: U Iowa Hosps Rm W189-Z GH Iowa City IA 52242

HUSTED, RUSSELL FOREST, research scientist; b. Lafayette, Ind., Apr. 4, 1950; s. Robert Forest and Miriam Ruth (Jackson) H.; m. Nancy Lee Driscoll, Oct. 25, 1969 (div. Feb. 1986); children: Jacqueline Marie, Randall Forest; m. Ruth Elaine Hurlburt, Nov. 12, 1988. BS in Chemistry with highest distinction, Colo. State U., 1972; PhD in Pharmacology, U. Utah, 1976. Post-doctoral fellow dept. medicine U. Iowa, Iowa City, 1976-79, rsch. scientist dept. medicine, 1979-81, 1982—; asst. prof. U. Conn. Sch. Medicine, Farmington, 1981-82. Contbr. articles to profl. jours. Mallinckrodt scholar Colo. State U., 1968. Mem. AAAS, Am. Soc. Nephrology, Am. Physiol. Soc., Soc. Gen. Physiology, N.Y. Acad. Sci., Sigma Xi. Democrat. Methodist. Office: Univ Iowa 3180 Medical Labs Iowa City IA 52242 E-mail: russell-husted@uiowa.edu.

HUSTING, PETER MARDEN, advertising consultant; b. Bronxville, N.Y., Mar. 28, 1935; s. Charles Ottomar and Jane Alice (Marden) H.; m. Carolyn Riddle, Mar. 26, 1960; children: Jennifer, Gretchen, Charles Ottomar; m. Myrna Diaz, May 11, 1996. B.S., U. Wis., 1957; grad., Advanced Mgmt. Program, Harvard U., 1974. Sales rep. Crown Zellerbach Corp., San Francisco, 1958-59; media analyst Leo Burnett Co., Chgo., 1959-61, time buyer, 1961-62, asst. account exec., 1962-63, account exec., 1963-68, v.p., account supr., 1968-72, sr. v.p., account dir., 1972-79, group exec., 1979-86, exec. v.p., 1979-92, dir. human relations internat., 1986-92, also bd. dirs., ret., 1992; pres. Husting Enterprises, 1993—. Dir. Bernina of Am., Inc., Columbian Mutual Life Ins. Co., Efficient Mktg. Svcs., Inc., Harley-Davidson Customer Financing Corp. Trustee Shedd Aquarium Soc., Chgo., 1980-94, hon. life trustee, 1995—; bd. dirs. Chgo. Better Govt. Assn., 1976-92, Leadership Coun. Met. Open Cmtys., Chgo., 1980-86, Lyric Opera Guild, 1971-78, Chgo. Forum, 1969-76. Served with AUS, 1958. Clubs: Indian Hill (Winnetka) (bd. govs. 1975-79), The Valley Club (Montecito, Calif.), Coral Casino Club (Santa Barbara). Avocations: flying, swimming, hunting, trekking, golf. Office: Husting Enterprises 150 S Wacker Dr Ste 3100 Chicago IL 60606-4103

HUSTON, DEVERILLE ANNE, lawyer; b. Great Falls, Mont., Mar. 2, 1947; d. Orion Joseph and Beverly Rosemary (Mower) H. BA, U. Minn., 1969; JD, William Mitchell Coll. Law, 1975. Bar: Minn. 1975, Ill. 1976, U.S. Dist. Ct. (no. dist.) Ill. 1976). Assoc. Sidley & Austin, Chgo., 1977-83, ptnr., 1983—. Fellow Am. Bar Found.; mem. ABA, Chgo. Bar Assn., Chgo. Fin. Exch., Law Club. Office: Sidley & Austin Bank One Plz 425 W Surf St Apt 605 Chicago IL 60657-6139

HUSTON, JOHN LEWIS, chemistry educator; b. Lancaster, Ohio, Aug. 19, 1919; s. John Allen and Olive Blanche (Wilson) H.; m. Mary Margaret Lally, Sept. 12, 1964. A.B., Oberlin Coll., 1942; Ph.D., U. Calif. at Berkeley, 1946. Instr. chemistry Oreg. State U., Corvallis, 1946-49, asst. prof., 1949-52; mem. faculty Loyola U. at Chgo., 1952—, assoc. prof., 1954-68, prof., 1968-84, prof. emeritus, 1984—. Cons. Argonne (Ill.) Nat. Lab., 1964—. Contbr. articles to profl. jours. AEC grantee, 1947-52, NSF grantee, 1953-58 Mem.: Am. Chem. Soc., Sigma Xi, Phi Beta Kappa. Home: 4401 Keeney St Skokie IL 60076-3203 Office: Loyola U Dept Chemistry Chicago IL 60626

HUSTON, KATHLEEN MARIE, library administrator; b. Sparta, Wis., Jan. 7, 1944; BA, Edgewood Coll., 1966; MLS, U. Wis., Madison, 1969. Libr. Milw. Pub. Libr., 1969-90; city libr. Milw. Pub. Libr. System, 1991—. Office: Milwaukee Pub Libr 814 W Wisconsin Ave Milwaukee WI 53233-2309

HUSTON, MICHAEL JOE, lawyer; b. Logansport, Ind., Dec. 21, 1942; s. Harry Hobart and Dorothie Ann (Chew) H.; m. Joan Frances Jernigan, June 12, 1965; children: Scott Howard, Todd Michael, Julie Ann. BS, U.S. Military Acad., 1965; JD, Ind. U., 1972. Bar: Ind. 1972, U.S. Dist. Ct. (so. dist.) Ind. 1972, U.S. Dist. Ct. (no. dist.) Ind. 1975, U.S. Ct. Appeals (D.C. cir.) 1980. Commd. 2nd lt. U.S. Army, 1965, advanced through grades to capt., 1967, resigned, 1970; assoc. Baker & Daniels, Indpls., 1972-78, ptnr., 1979—. Contbr. articles to profl. jours. Bd. dirs., pres. Woodland Springs Homeowners Assn., Carmel, Ind., 1976-82; trustee Carmel United Meth. Ch., 1982-84. Fellow Ind. Bar Found. (master fellow 1991); mem. ABA, Ind. State Bar Assn., Indpls. Bar Assn., West Point Soc. Ind. (pres. 1996-98), Geist Sertoma Club (pres. 1996-97). Office: Baker & Daniels 300 N Meridian St Ste 2700 Indianapolis IN 46204-1782

HUSTON, SAMUEL RICHARD, health facility executive; b. Newton, Iowa, Apr. 21, 1940; s. Marshall Dwight and Miriam Evelyn (Peake) H.; m. Ann M. Huston; children: Carmen Colleen, Christopher Dwight. BA, U. No. Iowa, 1962; MA, State U. Iowa, 1964. Asst. adminstr. med. ctr. Hosp. of Vt., Burlington, 1964-66; assoc. dir. No. New Eng. Regional Med. Program, 1966-68; asst. adminstr. Univ. Hosp. Cleve., 1968-70, assoc. adminstr., 1974-78, sr. v.p., 1978-83, exec. v.p., chief oper. officer, 1983-86; assoc. dir. Duke Hosp., Durham, N.C., 1970-72; pres., chief exec. officer Lehigh Valley Hosp. Ctr., Allentown, Pa., 1986-87, Allentown Hosp.-Lehigh Valley Hosp. Ctr., 1987-90; chief exec. officer Lehigh Valley Health Network, Lehigh Valley Hosp., Allentown, 1990-93; pres., CEO St. Luke's Med. Ctr., Cleve., 1994-97, St. Luke's Found. of Cleve., 1997-99; prin. Jay Alix and Assocs., 1999-2000; COO ViaHealth System, Rochester, N.Y., 2000—. Avocations: reading, music, hunting, golf. Home: PO Box 22988 Beachwood OH 44122-0988 Office: ViaHealth System care Rochester Gen Hosp Portland Ave Rochester NY 14621 E-mail: sam.huston@viahealth.org.

HUSTON, STEVEN CRAIG, lawyer; b. Morris, Ill., June 3, 1954; s. Raymond P. and Evelyn M. (Bass) H. BA, Ill. Coll., 1977; JD, John Marshall Law Sch., 1980; MBA, Northwestern U., 1989. Bar: Ill. 1980, U.S. Dist. Ct. (no. dist.) Ill. 1980, U.S. Ct. Appeals (7th cir.) 1980. Assoc. Siegel, Denberg et al, Chgo., 1980-83; staff atty. Wm. Wrigley Jr. Co., 1983-84; asst. sec. legal William Wrigley Jr. Co., 1984-94, asst. v.p. legal, 1994-96, counsel North Am., 1996—2001; v.p., gen. counsel Symons Corp., 2002—. Mem.: ABA, Chgo. Bar Assn.

HUTCHINS, BECKY J. state legislator; m. Joel R. Hutchins. Mem. from dist. 50 Kans. State Ho. of Reps., Topeka. Address: 700 Wyoming Ave Holton KS 66436-1180

HUTCHINS, ROBERT AYER, architectural consultant; b. N.Y.C., Oct. 19, 1940; s. Robert Senger and Evelyn Reed (Brooks) Hutchins; m. Saran Niel Morgan, Jan. 4, 1964; children: Amey, Elisabeth, Margaret. BA, Harvard U., 1962, MArch, 1965; MDiv, McCormick Theol. Sem., 1992. Registered architect, Ill. Architect Skidmore, Owings & Merrill, Chgo., 1966—89, ptnr., 1980—89. Pres. Chgo. Architecture Found., 1983—86, v.p., 1986—89. Mem. Protestants for the Common Good, 2000—02; v.p., bd. dirs. Lincoln Park Zool. Soc., Chgo., 1976—91; bd. govs. Met. Planning Coun., 1977—; bd. trustees McCormick Theol. Sem., 1990—91. Mem.: AIA (corp.), Chgo. Presbytery Svc. Corps., Chgo. Cultural Affairs Adv. Bd. (vice chmn. 1984—90).

HUTCHINSON, DENNIS, radio director; m. Joy Hutchinson, 1994; children: Kelly, Ben. News dir. WUGN, Midland, Mich., 1998—. Coach ch. softball team; dir. Christian edn. local ch. Office: WUGN 510 E Isabella Rd Midland MI 48640

HUTCHISON, DAVE, state legislator; b. July 26, 1943; BA, St. Norbert Coll. Assemblyman Wis. State Dist. 1; chmn. info. policy com. Producer Touring All Canada Touring Show. Mem. Rotary, YMCA, Luxemburg C. of C. Address: N8915 State Highway 57 Luxemburg WI 54217-9600

HUTMACHER, JAMES K. state legislator, water drilling contractor; b. Chamberlain, S.D., Sept. 24, 1953; Water drilling contractor, Chamberlain, S.D.; mem. S.D. Senate from 25th dist., Pierre, 1994—; mem. agr., natural resources, edn. and taxation coms. S.D. Senate. Democrat.

HUTTNER, SIDNEY FREDERICK, librarian; b. Portal, N.D., Feb. 18, 1941; s. Frederick W. and Fern May (Nolting) H.; m. Elizabeth Ann Stege, Oct. 24, 1981; 1 child, Erica Marie. BA in Tutorial Studies, U. Chgo., 1963, MA in Philosophy, 1969. Asst. head spl. collections U. Chgo. Libr., 1970-80; head George Arents Rsch. Libr. Syracuse (N.Y.) Libr., 1980-84; curator spl. collections U. Tulsa Libr., 1984-98; head spl. collections U. Iowa Librs., 1999—. Author: A Register of Artists, Engravers, Booksellers, Bookbinders, Printers and Publishers in New York City, 1821-1842, 1993. Fellow Woodrow Wilson Found., 1963-64. Avocation: bookbinding. Home: 5 Glendale Cir Iowa City IA 52245-3208 Office: Spl Collections U Iowa Librs Iowa City IA 52240-1420 E-mail: sid-huttner@uiowa.edu.

HUTTON, CAROLE LEIGH, newspaper editor; b. Framingham, Mass., Aug. 23, 1956; d. James Hamilton and Norma Inez (Vitali) H. B Journalism, Mich. State U., 1978. Editor Natick (Mass.) Sun, 1978-79; reporter, city editor, mng. editor Hammond (Ind.) Times, 1979-87; dir. publs. CNA Ins. Cos., Chgo., 1987-88; day city editor, account editor Detroit News, 1988-90; city editor Detroit Free Press, 1992-95, dep. mng. editor for news, 1995-96, mng. editor, 1996—. Tutor Detroit Pub. High Schs., 1994. Recipient Local News Coverage award Hoosier State Press Assn., 1982, Commentary award Ill. Women's Press Assn., 1983, Newswriting award Ill. Women's Press Assn., 1983. Mem. IAP Mng. Editors, Am. Soc. Newspaper Editors, Mich. AP Editors Assn. (pres., bd. dirs. 2000—), Assoc. Press Mng. Editors. Office: Detroit Free Press 600 W Fort St Detroit MI 48226-2706

HUTTON, EDWARD LUKE, diversified public corporation executive; b. Bedford, Ind., May 5, 1919; s. Fred and Margaret (Drehobl) H.; m. Kathryn Jane Alexander; children— Edward Alexander, Thomas Charles, Jane Clarke B.S. with distinction, Ind. U., 1940, M.S. with distinction, 1941; LLD (hon.), Ind. U., Cumberland Coll., 1992. Dep. dir. Joint Export Import Agy. (USUK), Berlin, 1946-48; v.p. World Commerce Corp., 1948-51; asst. v.p. W.R. Grace & Co., 1951-53, cons., 1960-65, exec. v.p., gen. mgr. Dubois Chems. div., 1965-66, group exec. Specialty Products Group and v.p., 1966-68, exec. v.p., 1968-71; cons. internat. trade and fin., 1953-58; fin. v.p., exec. v.p. Ward Industries, 1958-59; pres., CEO Chemed Corp.,

Cin., 1971-2001, chmn., dir., 1993—; chmn. Omnicare, Inc., 1981—, dir.; chmn., dir. Roto-Rooter, Inc., 1984-96. Chmn. bd. dirs. Nat. San. Supply Co., 1983-97. Co-chmn. Pres.'s Pvt. Sector Survey on Cost Control, exec. com., subcom.; former trustee Millikin U., 1973-84. 1st lt., U.S. Army, 1945-47. Recipient Disting. Alumni Svc. award Ind. U., 1987. Mem. AAUP (governing bd. dirs. 1958—), Econ. Club, Princeton Club, Univ. Club, Queen City Club, Bankers Club. Home: 6680 Miralake Ln Cincinnati OH 45243-2722 Office: Chemed Corp 255 E 5th St Ste 2600 Cincinnati OH 45202-4700 E-mail: ehutton@chemed.com.

HUTTON, JOHN JAMES, medical researcher, medical educator; b. Ashland, Ky., July 24, 1936; s. John James and Alice (Virgin) H.; m. Mary Labach, June 13, 1964; children: Becky, John, Elizabeth. AB, Harvard U., 1958, MD, 1964. Diplomate Am. Bd. Internal Medicine. Sect. chief Roche Inst., Nutley, N.J., 1968-71; prof. medicine U. Ky., Lexington, 1971-79, U. Tex., San Antonio, 1980-84; prof. pediatrics U. Cin., 1984-87, dean Coll. Medicine, 1987—. Editor Internal Medicine, 1983—; contbr. articles to profl. jours. Mem. Am. Soc. Hematology, Assn. Am. Physicians, Am. Soc. Clin. Investigation. Office: U Cin Coll of Medicine PO Box 670555 Cincinnati OH 45267-0001

HVASS, SHERYL RAMSTAD, lawyer; BA, U. Minn., 1972; JD with honors, U. N.D., 1975. Bar: Minn. 1975, N.D. 1975, U.S. Dist. Ct. Minn. 1975, U.S. Dist. Ct. N.D. 1975, D.C. 1978, U.S. Ct. Appeals (8th cir.), U.S. Supreme Ct. 1978. Asst. Hennepin County Pub. Defender, 1975-78; asst. U.S. atty. U.S. Dist. Ct. Minn., 1978-81; assoc. Henson & Efron, PA, 1981-82; adj. prof. law sch. law Hamline U., 1983-86; judge Hennepin County Ct., Mpls., 1982-86; ptnr. Rider, Bennett, Egan & Arundel, 1986-99; commr. Dept. of Corrections, St. Paul, 1999—. Co-chair Fed. Practice Com. for Dist. Minn., 1980-82; mem. faculty Nat. Inst. for Trail Advocacy, 1983—; chmn. Minn. Sentencing Guidelines Commns. Active Greater Mpls. Girl Scouts Am. Coun., 1992—, nominations com. 1993; bd. dirs. Mpls. Children's Med. Ctr., 1992, ethics com., 1993; mem. adv. coun. Women's Intercollegiate Athletics, U. Minn., 1987—, vice chair, 1988-89, chair, 1989-91; bd. dirs. YMCA Met. Mpls., 1986—, co-chair program svcs. com. 1987-88, chair pub. rels./pub. affairs com. 1988-92, vice-chmn. 1992—; bd. mgmt. Downtown YMCA, 1984-87; bd. dirs. Search Inst., 1984-88; active Minn. Women's Econ. Roundtable, 1985—; bd. visitors U. N.D. Law Sch., 1982—, U. Minn. Law Sch., 1997—. Recipient Women to Watch award, 1983, Karen Gibbs Women of Achievement award Twin West C. of C., 1985, Civil Justice award Am. Bd. Trial Advocates, 1992. Fellow ABA (life, mem. exec. coun. nat. conf. bar pres. 1992-93, standing com. on assn. comm. 1992-95); mem. Fed. Bar Assn. (sec. Minn. chpt. 1981-83), Nat. Assn. Women Judges (chair site selection com. 1984-85, co-chair judicial selection com. 1985-86), Internat. Soc. Barristers, Minn. State Bar Assn. (chair young lawyers sect. 1981-81, chair legal edn. and admissions com. 1982-84, task force on minority hiring 1986-87, exec. com. 1990—, pres. 1997), Minn. Judges Assn. (chair jury instrn. com. 1984-86, exec. com. 1984-86), Minn. Women Lawyers (exec. com. 1978-83, chair speakers bur. 1978-79, pres. 1981-82), Hennepin County Bar Assn. (vice chair young lawyers com. 1977, sec. 1988-89, treas. 1989-90, pres. 1991-92), Assn. State Correctional Adminstrs. (chair rsch. adv. com.). Office: Commissioner/Department Corrections 1450 Energy Park Dr Ste 200 Saint Paul MN 55108-5227 E-mail: sramstadhvass@co.doc.state.mn.us.

HWANG, JENNIE S. business executive, author, inventor, consultant; married; children: Raymond, Rosalind. BA, Cheng-Kung U., Taiwan; MS, Kent State U.; MA, Columbia U.; PhD, Case Western Res. U. Rsch. scientist Martin Marietta Corp., Cleve., 1977-78, dir. rsch., 1978-80; dept. head Sherwin Williams Co., 1980-81; mgr. SCM Corp., 1981-88, dir., 1988-90; pres., chief exec. officer IEM-Fusion, Inc., 1990—; pres. and CEO H-Technologies Group, Cleveland, OH. Invited lectr. worldwide; U.S. rep. Internat. Electrotech. Commn.; bd. dirs. various profl. orgns. Author: Solder Paste in Electronic Packaging, 1989; contbg. author to three high tech. books.; patentee in field. Mem. Am. Chem. Soc., Am. Ceramic Soc., Am. Welding Soc., Am. Soc. Metals, Internat. Hybrid Microelectronics Soc., Inst. Packaging and Interconnecting Cirs., Sinfare Mount Tech. Assn, NAE, 1998—. Office: H- Technologies Group 5325 Naiman Pkwy Cleveland OH 44139-1011

HYDE, HENRY JOHN, congressman; b. Chgo., Apr. 18, 1924; s. Henry Clay and Monica (Kelly) H.; m. Jeanne Simpson, Nov. 8, 1947; children: Henry J., Robert, Laura, Anthony. Student, Duke U., 1943-44; BS, Georgetown U., 1946; JD, Loyola U., Chgo., 1949. Bar: Ill. 1950. Mem. Ill. Gen. Assembly, 1967-74, U.S. Congress from 6th Ill. dist., 1975—; mem. internat. rels. com., chmn. jud. com. With USN, 1944-46. Mem. Chgo. Bar Assn. Republican. Roman Catholic. Office: US Ho of Reps 2110 Rayburn Washington DC 20515-0001*

HYERS, THOMAS MORGAN, physician, biomedical researcher; b. Jacksonville, Fla., June 16, 1943; s. John and Joan (Clemens) H.; m. Elizabeth Mclean, June 12, 1965; children: Justin, Adam. BS, Duke U., 1964, MD, 1968. Diplomate Am. Bd. Internal Medicine, Am. Bd. Pulmonary Diseases. Intern in medicine Cleve. Met. Gen. Hosp., 1968-69; asst. chief Nat. Blood Resource Br., Nat. Heart, Lung and Blood Inst., NIH, 1971-72, pulmonary disease adv. com., 1983-86; resident in medicine U. Wash., Seattle, 1972-74; chief resident, instr. medicine, 1974-75; fellow in pulmonary diseases U. Colo. Health Scis. Ctr., Denver, 1975-76, research fellow Cardiovascular Pulmonary Research Lab., 1976-77, asst. prof. medicine, staff physician respiratory care, assoc. investigator, 1977-82; research assoc. Denver VA Med. Ctr., 1979-82; assoc. prof. medicine, dir. div. pulmonary diseases St. Louis U. Med. Ctr., 1982-85, prof. medicine, divsn. dir., 1985-98; dir. NIH Specialized Ctr. Research in Adult Respiratory Failure, 1983-93. Contbr. articles to profl. jours. Served to comdr. USPHS, 1969-71. Named hon. Ky. col. grantee NIH, Nat. Heart, Lung and Blood Inst. Fellow ACP, Am. Coll. Chest Physicians; mem. Am. Heart Assn. (mem. councils on thrombosis and cardiopulmonary disease), Internat. Soc. Thrombosis and Haemostasis, Am. Lung Assn. (Eastern Mo. chpt.), Am. Fedn. Clin. Research, Am. Physiol. Soc., Western Soc. Clin. Investigation, Am. Thoracic Soc., Phi Beta Kappa. Office: CARE Clin Rsch 533 Couch Ave Ste 140 Saint Louis MO 63122-5561

HYLLAND, RICHARD R. utility company executive; Sr. fin. cons. mgr. Arthur Andersen LLP; with NorthWestern Corp., Sioux Falls, S.D., 1989—, exec. v.p., pres., COO, 1998—, also bd. dirs. Vice chmn. NorthWestern Growth, CornerStone Propane Ptnrs., LLP, Blue Dot, Ex-planets; bd. dirs. LodgeNet Entertainment Corp., MDC Comms.; chmn. Franklin Industries. Office: NorthWestern Corp 125 S Dakota Ave Sioux Falls SD 57104

HYMAN, MICHAEL BRUCE, lawyer; b. Elgin, Ill., July 26, 1952; s. Robert I. and Ruth (Cohen) H.; m. Leslie Bland, Aug. 14, 1977; children: Rachel Joy, David Adam. BSJ with honors, Northwestern U., 1974, JD, 1977. Bar: Ill. 1977, U.S. Supreme Ct. 1989. Asst. atty. gen. Antitrust div. State of Ill., Chgo., 1977-79; trial atty. Much Shelist Freed Denenberg Ament & Rubenstein, 1979-85, ptnr., 1985—. Chmn. panelist various continuing legal edn. seminars. Columnist Editor's Briefcase, CBA Record, 1988-90, 93—, The Red Pencil, 1986-89; contbr. chpt. to book, articles to profl. jours.; host (cable TV program) You and the Law, 1995—. Trustee North Shore Congregation Israel, Glencoe, 1980-89, 95-2001, v.p., 1987-89. Mem. ABA (mem. sect. litigation, chmn. antitrust litigation com. 1987-90, editor-in-chief Litigation News 1990-92, mng. editor 1989-90, assoc. editor 1985-89, chmn. monographs and unpub. papers com. 1992-95, task force on civil justice reform 1991-93, editor-in-chief Litigation Docket, 1995-2001, Tips From the Trenches 2001-, mem. jud. divsn., lawyers conf., membership com. chair 1999-2002, exec. com. 2002--), Chgo. Bar Assn. (editor-in-chief CBA Record 1988-90, 93—, CBA News 1994-98, bd. mgrs. 1992-94, vice chair class action com. 1999-2000, chair 2000-01), Ill. Bar Assn. (rep. on assembly 1986-92, 94-99, 2001—, antitrust coun. 1981-87, chmn. coun. 1985-86, vice chair, sec., co-editor newsletter 1982-85, chmn. bench and bar sect. coun. 1990-91, bench and bar sect. coun. 1998—, professionalism com. 1992-95, chair 1993-94, vice chair ARDC com. 1995-96, chair ARDC com. 1996-97, mem. cable tv com. 1995—, chair 1997-99), Am. Soc. Writers on Legal Subjects (mem., chair book award com. 1997—), Decalogue Soc. Lawyers (trustee 2001—). Jewish. Avocations: writing, Abraham Lincoln. Office: Much Shelist Freed Denenberg Ament & Rubenstein 200 N La Salle St Ste 2100 Chicago IL 60601-1026 E-mail: mbhyman@muchlaw.com.

HYMOWITZ, THEODORE, plant geneticist, educator; b. N.Y.C., Feb. 16, 1934; s. Bernard and Ethel (Rose) H.; m. Ann Einhorn, Dec. 25, 1960 (div. 1985); children: Madeleine, Sara, Jessica; m. Barbara E. Bohen, June 11, 1989 (div. 1998). BS, Cornell U., 1955; MS, U. Ariz., 1957; PhD, Okla. State U., 1963. Agronomist IRI Rsch. Inst., Campinas, Brazil, 1964-66; from asst. to assoc. prof. U. Ill., Urbana, 1967-75, prof., 1975—. With U.S. Army, 1957-59. Recipient Rsch. award Land of Lincoln Soybean Assn., 1990, Funk award, 1991; scholar Loeb Found., Stillwater, Okla., 1961-62, Fulbright scholar, 1962-63. Fellow AAAS, Linnean Soc. London, Am. Soc. Agronomy, Crop Sci. Soc. Am. (Frank N. Meyer medal 1988). Achievements include research in the establishment of chromosomal map of the soybean, inheritance of the absence of seed lectin in soybeans, elucidation of genomic relationships among species in the genus Glycine, development of soybean cultivar lacking the Kunitz trypsin inhibitor, history of the introduction of the soybean to N.Am. Office: U Ill Dept Crop Sci 1102 S Goodwin Ave Urbana IL 61801-4730

HYSLOP, DAVID JOHNSON, arts administrator; b. Schenectady, June 27, 1942; s. Moses McDickens Hyslop; m. Sally Fefercorn, Aug. 12, 1995; 1 child, Alexander. BS in Music Edn., Ithaca Coll., 1965. Elem. sch. vocal music supr., Elmira Heights, N.Y., 1965-66; mgr. Elmira Symphony Choral Soc., 1966; asst. mng. dir. Minn. Orch., Mpls., 1969-72; gen. mgr. Oreg. Symphony Orch., Portland, 1972-78; exec. dir. St. Louis Symphony Soc., 1978-89, pres., 1989-91, Minn. Orch., 1991—. Bd. dirs. Am. Symphony Orch. League, 1988-96, chmn., 1994, mem. exec. and nominating coms., 1990-93; bd. dirs. Minn. Citizens for Arts, Mpls. Downtown Coun., 1992-97, Mpls. Visitors and Conf. Bur., 1996-98; mem., co-chmn. arts edn. task for Mo. Arts Coun., 1989-90; mem. rec. panel Nat Endowment for Arts, 1986-88, mem. challenge grant panel, 1987-88, mem. music overview panel, 1987-88, mem. music creation and presentation panel, 1999; chmn. music and performing arts com. Regional Commerce and Growth Assn., St. Louis, 1987-89; bd. dirs. Minn. State Fair Found., 2002--. Martha Baird Rockefeller grantee, 1966. Mem. Am. Symphony Orch. League (chmn. major mgrs. and policy com. 1985-87, orch. mgmt. fellowship program 1979-88, orch. assessment program 1988), Regional Orch. Mgrs. Assn. (founder), Minn. Orchestral Assn., Mpls. Club, Arena Club. Avocations: basketball, travel, reading, study of German. Home: 2019 Irving Ave S Minneapolis MN 55405-2521 Office: Minn Orch 1111 Nicollet Mall Minneapolis MN 55403-2406 E-mail: dhyslop@mnorch.org.

IACOBELLI, MARK ANTHONY, dentist; b. Cleve., Aug. 27, 1957; s. Anthony Peter and Irene Margaret (Pordash) I. BS, Case Western Res., 1979, DDS, 1982. Dentist, co-owner Iacobelli & Iffland, Canton, Ohio, 1982-85; gen. practice dentistry North Royalton, 1985—. Co-lectr. Jamison Cons. and Midwest Implant Inst. Named one of Outstanding Young Men Am., 1982. Fellow Acad. Gen. Dentistry; mem. ADA, Ohio Dental Assn., Cleve. Dental Assn., Am. Assn. Functional Orthodontics (Achievement award 1982), Padua Franciscan Alumni Assn. (chmn. devel. drive 1986, chmn. 1989, 90). Republican. Roman Catholic. Avocations: running, biking, skiing, golf. Office: 4480 Oakridge Dr Cleveland OH 44133-2069

IAMMARTINO, NICHOLAS R. corporate communications executive; B in Chem. Engring., Cooper Union; M in Chem. Engring., NYU; MBA in Fin., Adelphi U. Process engr. Esso Rsch. and Engring. Co., 1969-71; bus. and tech. news writer Chem. Engring. mag. McGraw-Hill, 1971-76; chem. industry securities analyst Merrill Lynch, 1976-78; from sr. writer to bus. pubs. mgr. dept. corp. comm. Celanese Corp., 1979-85; corp. mgr. fin. comm. and adminstrn. Philip Morris, Inc., 1985; dir. fin. comm. Borden, Inc., N.Y., 1986-89, dir. external comm., 1989, dir. pub. affairs, 1994-95, v.p. pub. affairs Ohio, 1995—. Bd. dirs. Borden Found., Inc.; mem. assn. bd. Columbus Zool. Pk. Assn. Office: Borden Inc 180 E Broad St Columbus OH 43215-3799

IATRIDIS, PANAYOTIS GEORGE, medical educator; b. Alexandria, Egypt, Dec. 10, 1926; naturalized citizen, 1975; m. Catherine Iatridis; children: Yanna, Mary. MD, U. Athens, Greece, 1951, DSc with honors in Physiology, 1968. Lic. physician Greece, Egypt, N.C., Ind., Ill. Resident Univ. Med. Clinic, Athens, 1951-53, Greek Hosp., Alexandria, Egypt, 1953-55, asst. dir. dept. medicine Egypt, 1959-62; rsch. assoc. dept. physiology U. N.C., Chapel Hill, 1963-66, asst. prof. physiology, 1969-72, faculty grad. sch., 1969-72; vis. rsch. scientist Protein Found./Harvard Sch. Pub. Health, Boston, 1966; rsch. scientist dept. physiology U. Athens, 1967-69; faculty Ind. U., prof. physiology, biophysics and medicine, asst. dean, dir. N.W. Ctr. for Med. Edn. Mem. search and screen com. Exec. Dir. of Lake County Med. Ctr. Devel. Agy., 1984; pres., CEO N.W. Ctr. Med. Svcs. Corp., 1985—; bd. dirs. Lake Shore Health Sys. of Ancilla Sys. Corp., 1986—, mem. quality assurance com., 1986—; lectr. in field; lectr. in field. Contbr. numerous articles and abstracts to profl. jours.; editl. bd. Ind. Medicine, 1992—. Mem. coun. St. Iakovos Greek Orthodox Ch., 1985; bd. dirs. World Affairs Coun. of N.W. Ind., 1985—; mem. ad hoc com. on AIDS Gary Cmty. Sch. Corp., 1985; bd. visitors Modern Greek Studies, Ind. U., Bloomington, 1985; mem. N.W. Ind. Forum Found., 1987—; chmn. Porter Starke Infection Control Com., 1988—; bd. dirs. N.W. Ind. Symphony, 1988-89; mem. N.W. Ind. Forum legis. Subcom., 1988, edn. com., 1992—; bd. dirs. N.W. Ind. chpt. Am. Lung Assn., 1977-84, exec. com., 1979-84; bd. dirs. Am. Cancer Soc., 1978-83, mem. med. edn. com., 1978-83; mem. coun. SS Constantine and Helen, Greek Orthodox Cathedral, Merrillville, Ind., 1979-81; vice chmn. Cmty. Health Assn., Lake County, 1979-81, chmn. med. adv. com., 1979-81, chmn. editl. bd., 1980-81; mem. rsch. com. Ind. affiliate Am. Heart Assn., 1982-84, vice chmn., 1983-84; mem. City of Gary Econ. Devel. Commn., 1984; group leader People to People Med. Edn. Delegation to People's Republic of China, 1984; founder, 1st pres. Greek Orthodox Ch. of Porter County, 1980-81. Recipient medal of St. Paul Greek Orthodox Archdiocese of North and South Am.; grantee Dept. HEW/NIH/USPHS, 1973-76, Lake County Med. Ctr. Devel. Agy., 1975-82, 82-85, 85, 85-86, 86-87, 86, 87, 88, 89, 90, 91, 92, Ind. State Bd. Health, Divsn. Maternal and Child Health, 1985, 858-86, 86-87, 87-89, Innkeepers Tax for Med. Edn., 1993, 94. Fellow ACP; mem. Acad. Athens (corr.), Ind. State Med. Soc. (commn. on med. edn. 1986—, vice chmn. commn. on conv. arrangements 1988), Porter County Med. Soc. (care of indigent com. 1986), Lake County Med. Soc. (care of indigent com. 1986), Rotary (chmn. membership devel. com. 1987-88). Office: Ind U NW Ctr for Med Edn 3400 Broadway Gary IN 46408-1101

IBEN, ICKO, JR. astrophysicist, educator; b. Champaign, Ill., June 27, 1931; s. Icko and Kathryn (Tomlin) I.; m. Miriam Genevieve Fett, Jan. 28, 1956; children: Christine, Timothy, Benjamin, Thomas. BA, Harvard U., 1953; MS, U. Ill., 1954, PhD, 1958. Asst. prof. physics Williams Coll., 1958-61; sr. rsch. fellow in physics Calif. Inst. Tech., Pasadena, 1961—64; assoc. prof. physics MIT, Cambridge, 1964-68, prof., 1968-72; prof. astronomy and physics, head dept. astronomy U. Ill., Champaign-Urbana, 1972-84, prof. astronomy and physics, 1972-89, disting. prof. astronomy and physics Urbana, 1989—99, disting. prof. emeritus, 2000; holder of Eberly family chair in astronomy Pa. State U., 1989-90. Vis. prof. astronomy Harvard U., 1966, 68, 70; vis. fellow Joint Inst. for Lab. Astrophysics U. Colo., 1971—72; vis. prof. astronomy and astrophysics U. Calif., Santa Cruz, 1972; vis. prof. physics and astronomy Inst. for Astronomy U. Hawaii, 1977; adv. panel astronomy sect. NSF, 1972—75; vis. com. Aura Observatories, 1979—82; vis. scientist astronomical coun. Union Soviet Socialist Rep. Acad. Sci., 1985; sr. vis. fellow Australian Nat. U., 1986; vis. prof. U. Bologna, Italy, 1986, Hokkaido U. Grad. Sch. Sci., 2001; sr. rsch. fellow U. Sussex, England, 1986; George Darwin lectr. Royal Astronomical Soc., London, 1984; McMillin lectr. Ohio State U., 1987; vis. eminent scholar U. Ctr. Ga., 1988; guest prof. Christian Albrechts U. Kiel, 1990. Contbr. articles to profl. jours. John Simon Guggenheim Meml. fellow, 1985-86; recipient Eddington medal Royal Astron. Soc., 1990. Fellow Japan Soc. for Promotion of Sci.; mem. Am. Astron. Soc. (councilor 1974-77, Henry Norris Russell lectr. 1989), U.S. Nat. Acad. of Scis., Internat. Astronom. Union. Home: 3910 Clubhouse Dr Champaign IL 61822-9280 Office: U Ill Dept of Astronomy 1002 W Green St Urbana IL 61801-3074

IBERS, JAMES ARTHUR, chemist, educator; b. Los Angeles, June 9, 1930; s. Max Charles and Esther (Imerman) I.; m. Joyce Audrey Henderson, June 10, 1951; children: Jill Tina, Arthur Alan. B.S., Calif. Inst. Tech., 1951, Ph.D., 1954. NSF post-doctoral fellow, Melbourne, Australia, 1954-55; chemist Shell Devel. Co., 1955-61, Brookhaven Nat. Lab., 1961-64; mem. faculty Northwestern U., 1964—, prof. chemistry, 1964-85, Charles E. and Emma H. Morrison prof. chemistry, 1986—. Recipient Disting. alumni award Calif. Inst. Tech., 1997. Mem. NAS, Am. Acad. Arts and Sci., Am. Chem. Soc. (inorganic chemistry award 1979, Disting. Svc. in the Advancement of Inorganic Chemistry award 1992, Linus Pauling award 1994), Am. Crystallographic Assn. Home: 2657 Orrington Ave Evanston IL 60201-1760 Office: Northwestern U Dept Chemistry Evanston IL 60208-3113 E-mail: ibers@chem.northwestern.edu.

ICHIISHI, TATSURO, economics and mathematics educator; b. Seoul, Dec. 16, 1943; came to U.S., 1970; s. Jitsuro and Tomiko (Tanaka) I.; m. Barbara Ann Franklin, Sept. 7, 1973 BA in Econs., Keio U., Tokyo, 1966, MA in Econs., 1968; MA in Math., U. Calif., Berkeley, 1973, PhD in Econs., 1974. Rsch. assoc. Keio U., Tokyo, 1968-73; vis. rsch. fellow Cath. U. Louvain, Heverlee, Belgium, 1974-75; lectr., rsch. assoc. Northwestern U., Evanston, Ill., 1975-76; asst. prof. Carnegie-Mellon U., Pitts., 1976-80; assoc. prof. U. Iowa, Iowa City, 1980-83, prof., 1983-86, Ohio State U., Columbus, 1987—, Hitotsubashi U., Tokyo, 2001—02. Vis. prof. Bilkent U., Ankara, Turkey, 1997; guest prof. Keio U., Tokyo, 1999. Author: Game Theory for Economic Analysis, 1983, The Cooperative Nature of the Firm, 1993, Microeconomic Theory, 1997; editor: (with Abraham Neyman and Yair Tauman) Game Theory and Applications, 1990, (with Thomas Marschak) Markets, Games, and Organizations: Essays on Honor of Roy Radner; series editor Math. Econs. and Game Theory, 2000—; assoc. editor Rev. of Econ. Design, 1997—; editl. bd. Internat. Jour. of Game Theory, 1997—, Advances in Mathematical Economics, 1998—, Games and Economic Behavior, 1998—; contbr. articles to profl. jours. Recipient Nikkei-Tosho Bunka Sho award Nihon Keizai Shinbun and Japan Ctr. for Econ. Rsch., 1994; CORE fellow, 1974-75; NSF grantee, 1978-82, 82-85, 92-96. Mem.: Game Theory Soc. Office: Ohio State U Dept Econs 1945 N High St Columbus OH 43210-1172

ICHINO, YOKO, ballet dancer; b. Los Angeles, Cali. Studied with Mia Slavenska, L.A. Mem. Joffrey II, N.Y.C., Joffrey Ballet, N.Y.C., Stuttgart Ballet, Fed. Republic Germany; tchr. ballet, 1976; soloist Am. Ballet Theatre, 1977-81; guest appearances, 1981-82; prin. Nat. Ballet Can., Toronto, Ont., 1982-90. Various guest appearances including World Ballet Festival, Tokyo, 1979, 85, Tokyo Ballet, 1980, with Alexander Godunov and Stars, summer, 1982, Sydney Ballet, Australia, N.Z. Ballet, summer 1984, Ballet de Marseille, 1985-87, Deutsche Opera Ballet Berlin, 1985-90, Munich Opera Ballet, 1987-90, Australian Ballet, 1987, 89, Staatsoper Berlin, 1989, 90, Komische Opera, Berlin, 1991-93, David Nixon's Dance Theater, Berlin, 1990, 91, Birmingham Royal Ballet, 1990-93, Deutsche Opera Ballet, Berlin, 1994-95; tchr. Australian Ballet, 1989, Birmingham Royal Ballet, 1991, 93, Nat. Ballet of Can., 1993, Cullberg Ballet, Sweden, 1994, Nat. Ballet Sch., 1994, 95, Ballet de Monte-Carlo, 1994, Geneva Ballet, 1995-98, Nederlands Dance Theater, 1995, Rambert Dance, 1995, Royal Winnipeg Ballet, 1999; tchr. numerous ballet workshops; dir. profl. program Ballet Met, 1995—. First Am. women recipient medal Third Internat. Ballet Competition, Moscow, 1977.

ICHIYAMA, DENNIS YOSHIHIDE, design educator, consultant, administrator; b. Aiea, Hawaii, May 28, 1944; s. Edwin Kiyotada and Florence Fusae (Inoshita) I. BFA, U. Hawaii, 1966; MFA, Yale U., 1968; postgrad., Allgemeine Gewerbeschule, Basel, Switzerland, 1975-77. Instr. U. Bridgeport, Conn., 1968-70; sr. graphic designer Graphic Communications Ltd., Hong Kong, 1970-71; instr. Carnegie-Mellon U., Pitts., 1971-74; asst. prof. Cornell U., Ithaca, N.Y., 1974-75; assoc. prof. Ind. U., Bloomington, 1977-78; asst. prof. U. Ill., Chgo., 1978-79; assoc. prof. Wichita (Kans.) State U., 1979-81; prof., chmn. divsn. art and design Purdue U., West Lafayette, Ind., 1985-92, head dept. visual and performing arts, 1993—. Design cons. U.S. Postal Svc., Washington, 1986, Purdue U. Press, West Lafayette, 1989—, Interior Design Educators Coun., Ithaca, 1985-87; vis. scholar U. Iowa Ctr. for the Book, 1990; fellow to Ctr. for Artistic endeavor Purdue U. Sch. Liberal Arts, 1992; artist-in-residence Hamilton Wood Type & Printing Mus., Wis., 1999-2000; bd. dir. Coll. Art Assn. Design work exhbns. in Can., U.S., Germany, Finland, France, Czechoslovakia; exhibited in shows at Centre Georges Pompidou, 1985, Poster Biennale, Warsaw, 1982, Biennale of Graphic Design, Brno, Czechoslovakia, 1982, 92; represented in collection of the Plakatsammlung of the Kunstgewerbemuseum, Zurich, Rochester Inst. of Tech. Libr., N.Y., Lahti Art Mus., Finland, Stevvi Book Arts and Spl. Collections Ctr., San Francisco Pub. Libr., Purdue U. Librs.; author essays in Contemporary Designers, 1985, T Y P O G R A M S Pure Type Forms, 2000, The Hamilton Type Specimen Sheets Portfolio, 2001, book revs.; book reviewer Choice (ALA, Assn. Coll./Rsch. Librs.). Grantee Nat. Endowment for Humanities, 1984; IAC master fellow Ind. Arts Commn., 1985, Nat. Endowment for Arts, 1989, Individual Artist program grantee, 2001—. Mem. Am. Ctr. for Design, Am. Inst. Graphic Arts, Graphic Design Educators Assn., Alliance Typographique Internat., Nat. Coun. Art Adminstrs. (nat. bd. dirs. 1998—), Internat. Coun. Fine Arts Deans, Coll. Art Assn. Am., Arts Ind. (state coun. 1993-99), Hui na opio o Hawaii (advisor 1986-93), Greater Lafayette Music Art Bd. Buddhist. Avocations: Swiss posters, artists books, Chinese and Japanese seals, printing history, hand bookbinding and letterpress printing. Office: Purdue U Dept Visual/Performing Arts CA # 1 West Lafayette IN 47907-1352 E-mail: diad@purdue.edu.

IDOL, ANNA CATHERINE, magazine editor; b. Chgo., July 8, 1941; d. Melvin Oliver and Louise Hildegard (Bullington) Lokensgard; m. William Ross Idol, Oct. 25, 1959 (div. Mar. 1962); 1 child, Laura Jeanne; m. Michael Wataru Sugano, Jan. 28, 1990. BS, Lake Forest (Ill.) Coll., 1980; MBA, Northwestern U., Evanston, Ill., 1982. treas. Chgo. Women in Pub., Chgo., 1970-71. Editor Rand McNally Co., Chgo., 1968-78, product mgr. adult reference, 1983-84; founder, pres. Bullington Laird, Inc., 1986—; mng. editor Elks Mag., 1997—. Pub.: Center Within, 1988 (award Heartsong Rev. 1989); writer, concept advt. alert, 1990 (Harvey Comm. award). Pres. Am. Buddhist Assn., 1985-93; mem. bd. Buddhist Temple

Chgo., 1985-93; v.p. Buddhist Coun. Midwest, 1985-89. Republican. Buddhist. Avocations: wilderness adventure, travel, reading. Office: Elks Mag 425 W Diversey Pkwy Chicago IL 60614-6196 E-mail: annai@elks.org.

IDOL, JAMES DANIEL, JR. chemist, educator, inventor, consultant; b. Harrisonville, Mo., Aug. 7, 1928; s. James Daniel and Gladys Rosita (Lile) I.; m. Marilyn Thorn Randall, 1977. A.B., William Jewell Coll., 1949; M.S., Purdue U., 1952, Ph.D., 1955, D.Sc. (hon.), 1980. With Standard Oil Co., Ohio, 1955-77, rsch. supr., 1965-68, rsch. mgr., 1968-77; mgr. venture rsch. Ashland Chem. Co., Columbus, Ohio, 1977-79, v.p., dir. corp. R & D, 1979-88; Disting. prof. materials sci. and ceramics Sch. Engring. Rutgers U., New Brunswick, N.J., 1988—, exec. dir. Ctr. for Packaging Sci. and Engring., 1988—, dep. dir. Ctr. for Plastics Recycle Rsch., 1988-95. Mem. adv. bd. NSF Presdl. Young Investigators Awards; cons. in field; lectr. chem. engring. dept. Northwestern U., 1978, Stanford U., 1982, 83, U. Calif., Berkeley, 1986, Yale U., 1988 U. Chgo., 1998; lectr. Lawrence Berkeley Lab., 1985, 86; mem. adv. bd. Petroleum Rsch. Fund, 1974-76; v.p., program coord. 1st N.Am. Chem. Congress, 1975; program coord. 1st Pacific Rim Chem. Cong., 1979; indsl. rep. Coun. for Chem. Rsch., 1983—, mem. governing bd., 1985—; mem. panel on frontiers in fossil fuel energy rsch. NRC, 1986, mem. com. on tracking toxic wastes, 1989-93, panel on polymers in the environ. Internat. Union of Pure and Applied Chemistry, 1996; mem. adv. bds. U. Tex., Tex. A&M, Ohio State U., Purdue U., Okla. State U., Ariz. State U., U. Mass., Case Western Reserve U., 1965-75; mem. com. on energy conservation in processing of indsl. materials; mem. adv. bd. Nat. Inst. Sci. and Tech., 1997—; mem. com. polymers recycling Internat. Union Pure and Applied Chem., 1993—; mem. U.S. Coun. Chem. Rsch., 1981-89, gov. bd. 1985-88. Chmn. editl. adv. bd.: Indsl. & Engring. Chemistry Jour., 1976—84, mem. editl. adv. bd.: Chem. and Engring. News, 1977—81, mem. editl. adv. bd.: Am. Chem. Soc. Symposium Series, 1978—84, mem. editl. adv. bd.: Advances in Chemistry Seris, 1979—84, mem. editl. adv. bd.: Chem. Week Mag., 1980—82, mem. editl. adv. bd.: Sci., 1986—91, mem. editl. adv. bd.: Jour. Applied Polymer Sci., 1988—; contbr. chapters to books, articles to profl. jours., handbooks and encys. Active Cleve. Welfare Fedn. Recipient Modern Pioneer award NAM, 1965, Disting. Alumnus citation William Jewell Coll., 1971 Fellow AAAS, Am. Inst. Chemists (life; bd. dirs. 1981—, vice chmn. 1986, chmn. 1987, Chem. Pioneer award 1968, Mems. and Fellows lectr. 1980); mem. Nat. Acad. Engring., Soc. Plastics Industry, Soc. Mfg. Engrs.-Composite Group, Am. Chem. Soc. (indsl. and engring. chemistry divsn., chmn. 1971, chem. innovator designation Chem. and Engring. News mag. 1971, Joseph P. Stewart Disting. Svc. award 1975, Creative Invention award 1975), Am. Mgmt. Assn. (R&D coun. 1985-88, Coun. award for Disting. Svc. pkg. coun. 1989-97, mfg. and tech. coun. 1997—), Dirs. of Indsl. Rsch., Am. Inst. Chem. Engrs., Licensing Execs. Soc., Soc. Plastics engrs., Indsl. Rsch. Inst. (rep., chmn. bd. editors 1983-86), Plastics Pioneers Assn., Soc. Chem. Industry (Perkin medal 1979), Ind. Acad. Sci., Catalysis Soc. (Ciapetti award/lectureship 1988), Cleve. Athletic Club, Cosmos Club (Washington), Worthington Hills Country Club, Masons, Shriners, Sigma Xi, Alpha Chi Sigma, Theta Chi Delta, Kappa Mu Epsilon, Alpha Phi Omega, Phi Gamma Delta. Mem. Christian Ch. (Disciples of Christ). Achievements include invention of ammoxidation process for manufacture acrylonitrile (over 80 plants in 30 countries-this ammoxidation process was designated as Nat. Hist. Chem. Landmark 1996 by Am. Chem. Soc;patents in field.

IGLAUER, BRUCE, record company executive; Educated, Lawrence U. Shipping clk. Delmark Records, 1970; founder, pres. Alligator Records, Chgo., 1971. Produced recording of Hound Dog Taylor and the House-rockers, 1971; producer for artists including Big Walter Horton, Son Seals and Fenton Robinson. Office: Alligator Records PO Box 60234 Chicago IL 60660-0234

IGNOFFO, CARLO MICHAEL, insect pathologist-virologist; b. Chicago Heights, Ill., Aug. 24, 1928; s. Joseph and Lucy (Sardo) I.; m. Florence F. Mielcarek, Sept. 3, 1949. B.S., No. Ill. U., 1950; M.S., U. Minn., 1954, Ph.D., 1957. Asst. prof. Iowa Wesleyan Coll., Mt. Pleasant, 1957-59; insect pathologist U.S. Dept. Agr., Brownsville, Tex., 1959-65; dir. entomology Internat. Minerals & Chems. Corp., Wasco, Calif. and Libertyville, Ill., 1965-71; lab. dir. U.S. Dept. Agr., Columbia, Mo., 1971-91; prof. dept. entomology U. Mo., 1974—. Served with Chem. Corps U.S. Army, 1954-56. Mem. AAAS, Internat. Orgn. Biol. Control (pres. 1974), Am. Inst. Biol. Scis., Soc. Invertebrate Pathology (editorial bd. 1965-68, assoc. editor 1992—, treas. 1968-70), Entomol. Soc. Am. Achievements include isolating, commercializing 1st viral pesticide; patentee in field. Office: Research Park 1503 S Providence Rd Columbia MO 65203-3535 E-mail: ignoffoc@missouri.edu.

IKENBERRY, STANLEY OLIVER, education educator, former university president; b. Lamar, Colo., Mar. 3, 1935; s. Oliver Samuel and Margaret (Moulton) Ikenberry; m. Judith Ellen Life, Aug. 24, 1958; children: David Lawrence, Steven Oliver, John Paul. BA, Shepherd Coll., 1956; MA, Mich. State U., 1957, PhD, 1960, LHD (hon.); LLD (hon.) , Millikin U.; LHD (hon.) , Millkin U.; LHD (hon.) , Ill. Coll., Rush U., W.Va. U.; LHD (hon.) (hon.) , Towson State U., U. Nebr., Bridgewater (Va.) Coll., Bradley U., Shepherd Coll., Roosevelt U.;. Instr. office evaluation svc. Mich. State U., 1958—60, instr. instl. rsch. office, 1960—62; asst. to provost for instl. rsch., asst. prof. edn. W.Va. U., 1962—65, dean coll. human resources and edn., assoc. prof. edn., 1965—69; prof., assoc. dir. ctr. study higher edn. Pa. State U., 1969—71, sr. v.p., 1971—79; pres. U. Ill., Urbana, 1979—95, pres. emeritus, Regent prof., 1995—; pres. Am. Coun. on Edn., Washington, 1996—2001. Bd. dirs. Pfizer, Inc., N.Y.C., Aquila Inc., Kansas City; pres. bd. overseers Tchrs. Ins. and Annutiy Assn./Coll. Retirement Equities Fund. Mem. Carnegie Found. Advancement Tchg. Named hon. alumnus, Pa. State U. Fellow: Am. Acad. Arts and Scis.; mem.: Assn. Am. Univs. (past chmn.), Tavern Club (Chgo.), Cosmos Club (Washington), Mid-Am. Club, Comml. Club Chgo. Office: U Ill 347 Education 1310 S 6th St Champaign IL 61820

ILGEN, DANIEL RICHARD, psychology educator; b. Freeport, Ill., Mar. 16, 1943; s. Paul Maurice and Marjorie V. (Glasser) I.; m. Barbara Geiser, Dec. 26, 1965; children: Elizabeth Ann, Mark Andrew. BS in Psychology, Iowa State U., 1965; MA, U. Ill., 1968, PhD in Indsl.-Orgnl. Psychology, 1969. Asst. prof. dept. psychology U. Ill., Urbana, 1969-70; instr. Dutchess County C.C., Poughkeepsie, NY, 1971-72; from asst. prof. to prof. dept. psychol. scis. Purdue U., West Lafayette, Ind., 1972-83, area head indsl.-orgnl. psychology, 1978-83; Hannah prof. organizational behavior depts. mgmt. and psychology Mich. State U., East Lansing, 1983—. Vis. assoc. prof. dept. mgmt. and orgn. U. Wash., Seattle, 1978-79; vis. prof. dept. mgmt. U. Western Australia, 1991, 2000. Co-author (with J.C. Naylor and R.D. Pritchard): A Theory of Behavior in Organizations, 1980; co-author: (with E.J. McCormick) Industrial Psychology, 1985; co-editor (with E. Pulakso): The Changing Nature of Performance, 1999; co-editor: (with C. Hulin) Computational Modeling of Behavior in Organizations, 2000; co-editor: (with W. Borman and R. Klimoski) Industrial and Organizational Psychology, The Comprehensive Handbook of Psychology, vol. 12, 2002; contbr. ; editor: Organizational Behavior and Human Decision Processes, 1998—2001. Capt. M.I., U.S. Army, 1970-72. Grantee Purdue U. Found., 81-82, U.S. Army Rsch. Inst., 1974-82, Office Naval Rsch., 1982-86, 90—. Fellow Am. Psychol. Assn. (edn. tng. com., coun. reps. 1985-87), Soc. Indsl. and Organizational Psychology of Am. Psychol. Assn. (pres. 1987-88, Disting. Sci. Contbn. award 2001), Am. Psychol. Soc.; mem. Acad. Mgmt., Soc. Organizational Behavior, Sigma Xi. Office: Mich State U Depts Mgmt And Psychol East Lansing MI 48824-1117 E-mail: Ilgen@msu.edu.

ILGEN, DOROTHY L. arts foundation executive; Asst. dir. Mo. Arts Coun.; exec. dir. Kans. Arts Commn., Ind. Arts Commn., Indpls., 1995—. Active numerous coms. and commns. various local, state, regional, and nat. orgns.; bd. dirs. Mid-Am. Arts Alliance, Arts Midwest, mem. program planning com.; bd. dirs., mem. planning and budget com., nominating com. Nat. Assembly of State Arts Agys.; panelist arts design panel NEA, Nat. Access Task Force. Office: Arts Commn 402 W Washington St Rm W072 Indianapolis IN 46204-2763

ILITCH, DENISE, food services executive; Pres. Bright Lites Inc., Detroit; vice chair Little Caesar Enterprises Inc., 1997—; pres. Olympia Devel. LLC, 1996—; exec. v.p. Ilitch Holdings, Detroit, 1999—. Bd. dirs. Detroit br. Fed. Res. Bank of Chgo. Office: Ilitch Holdings Inc 2211 Woodward Ave Detroit MI 48201-3467

ILITCH, MARIAN, professional hockey team executive, food service executive; m. Michael Ilitch; children: Denise Ilitch Lites, Ron, Mike Jr., Lisa Ilitch Murray, Atanas, Christopher, Carole. Owner, sec.-treas. Detroit Red Wings, Detroit Tigers Baseball Team, 1993—, also bd. dirs.; sec.-treas., vice chair Little Caesar Internat.; sec.-treas. Olympia Arenas, Inc., Fox Theatre. Recipient Pacesetter award, 1988, Michiganian of Yr. award, 1988, Nat. Preservation award Nat. Trust Hist. Preservation, 1990. Office: Little Ceasars Enterprises 2211 Woodward Ave Detroit MI 48201-3400 also: Detroit Tigers Tiger Stadium 2121 Trumbull St Detroit MI 48216-1343

ILITCH, MICHAEL, professional hockey team executive; m. Marian Ilitch; children: Denise Ilitch Lites, Ron, Mike Jr., Lisa, Atanas, Christopher, Carole. Founder, owner Little Caesars Restaurant, 1959—; owner, pres. Detroit Red Wings Hockey Team, 1982—; founder Blue Line Distributing, Am.'s Pizza Cafe; owner Olympia Arenas, Inc. (formerly Olympia Stadium Corp.), 1983—, Adirondack Red Wings Hockey Team, Detroit Drive of Arena Football League; owner, chmn., former pres. Detroit Tigers Baseball Team. With Detroit Tigers' farm system, 3 yrs. Founder Little Caesars Love Kitchen program, 1985—. With USMC, 4 yrs. Recipient a Lester Patrick trophy, 1991, Bus. Statesman award Harvard Bus. Sch. Club Detroit, 1990, Joe Louis award Sports Illustrated Mag. and Detroit Inst. Arts, Humanitarian of Yr. award March of Dimes, Nat. Preservation award Nat. Trust for Hist. Preservation, Pvt. Sector Initiative Presdl. citation Reagan Adminstrn., Volunteerism Presdl. citation Bush Adminstrn. Office: Detroit Red Wings 600 Civic Center Dr Detroit MI 48226-4419 also: Detroit Tigers Tiger Stadium 2100 Woodward Ave Detroit MI 48201-3470 also: Little Caesars Enterprizes 2211 Woodward Ave Detroit MI 48201-3467

ILTIS, HUGH HELLMUT, plant taxonomist-evolutionist, educator; b. Brno, Czechoslovakia, Apr. 7, 1925; came to U.S., 1939, naturalized, 1944; s. Hugo and Anne (Liebscher) I.; m. Grace Schaffel, Dec. 20, 1951 (div. Mar. 1958); children: Frank S., Michael George; m. Carolyn Merchant, Aug. 4, 1961 (div. June 1970); children: David Hugh, John Paul. B.A., U. Tenn., 1948; M.A., Washington U., St. Louis and Mo. Bot. Garden, 1950, Ph.D., 1952. Rsch. asst. Mo. Bot. Garden, 1948-52; asst. prof. botany U. Ark., 1952-55; asst. prof. U. Wis.-Madison, 1955-60, assoc. prof., 1960-67, prof., 1967-93, prof. emeritus, 1993—, curator herbarium, 1955-67, dir. univ. herbarium, 1967-93, dir. emeritus, 1993—. Vis. prof. U. Va., Biol. Sta., 1959; world-wide lectr. in field; expdns. to Costa Rica, 1949, 89, Peru, 1962-63, Mex., 1960, 71, 72, 77, 78, 79, 81, 82, 84, 87, 88, 90, 93, 94, 95, 96, Guatemala, 1976, Ecuador, 1977, St. Eustatius, P.R., 1989, USSR, 1975, 79, Nicaragua-Honduras, 1991, Venezuela, 1991, Hawaii, 1967; mem. adv. bd. Flora N.Am., 1970-73, Gov. Wis. Commn. State Forests, 1972-73; rsch. assoc. Mo. Bot. Gardens, Bot. Rsch. Inst. Tex.; co-instigator Reserva Biosfera Sierrra de Manantlán, Jalisco, Mex. Author: articles flora of Wis. and Mex., Capparaceae, biogeography, evolution of maize, human ecology, especially innate responses to, and needs for, natural beauty, diversity, wild nature and cultivated plant germ plasm preservation; co-author: Flora de Manantlan, 1995, Atlas of the Wisconsin Prairie and Savana Flora, 2000, Checklist of the Vascular Plants of Wisconsin; editor: Extinction or Preservation: What Biological Future for the South American Tropics?, 1978. With U.S. Army, 1944-46. Recipient Biologia award, U. Tenn., 1948, Feinstone Environ. award, SUNY, Syracuse, N.Y., 1990, Conservation award, Conservation Coun. Hawaii, 1990, Nat. Wildlife Fedn. Spl. Achievement award, 1992, Puga medal, U. de Guadalajara, Mex., 1994, Disting. Alumnus award, Missouri Bot. Gardens, 1999. Fellow AAAS, Linnean Soc. (London); mem. Am. Inst. Biol. Scis., Bot. Soc. Am. (Merit award 1996), Soc. Econ. Botany (Econ. Botanist of Yr. award 1998), Am. Soc. Plant Taxonomists (Asa Gray award 1994), Internat. Assn. Plant Taxonomy, Soc. Bot. Mex., Soc. Study Evolution, Ecol. Soc. Am., Wis. Acad. Arts, Sci. and Letters, Forum for Corr.-Internat. Ctr. Integrative Studies, Nature Conservancy (co-founder and trustee Wis. chpt., Nat. Oakleaf award 1963), Wilderness Soc., Sierra Club, Nat. Parks Assn., Citizens Natural Resources Assn. Wis., Natural Resource Def. Coun., Environ. Def. Fund, Friends of Earth, Cenozoic Soc., Zero Population Growth, Soc. Conservation Biology (Disting. Achievement award 1994), Natural Areas Assn., Sigma Xi, Phi Kappa Phi. Achievements include co-discoverer Zea diploperennis and Z. nicaragenensis. Home: 2784 Marshall Pky Madison WI 53713-1023 Office: U Wis Dept Botany 430 Lincoln Dr Madison WI 53706-1313 Fax: 608-262-7509. E-mail: hhiltis@facstaff.wisc.edu.

IMMELT, MARK W. bank executive; With Cen. Nat. Bank Cleve. (KeyCorp predecessor); exec. v.p. No. Ind. Key Bank; sr. v.p., sr. trust officer 1st Fin. Bancorp, 1996, sr. v.p.; pres., CEO 1st Nat. Bank Southwestern Ohio, Hamilton, 1999—. Office: 300 High St Hamilton OH 45011-6078

IMRAY, THOMAS JOHN, radiologist, educator; b. Milw., Nov. 11, 1939; s. George William and Genevieve (Bresnehan) I.; m. Carla Marie Rake, Aug. 17, 1963; children: John Scott, Jean Ann, Jeff William. BA, Marquette U., 1961, MD, 1965. Diplomate Nat. Bd. Med. Examiners, Am. Bd. Radiology (guest examiner 1975-76, 79, 85-2002). Intern St. Mary's Hosp., San Francisco, 1965-66; resident in radiology U. Minn., Mpls., 1966-70, instr., 1969-70; asst. prof. Med. Coll. of Wis., Milw., 1973-77, assoc. prof., 1977-80, U. Calif., Irvine, 1980-82; prof. and chmn. dept. radiology U. Nebr. Med. Ctr., Omaha, 1982-96, prof. dept. radiology, 1996—. Vis. prof. Vanderbilt U., Nashville, 1976, 82, U. Wis., Madison, 1978, SUNY Downstate Med. Ctr., Bklyn., 1978, Harvard Med. Sch., Boston, 1980, Loyola U. Sch. Medicine, Maywood, Ill., 1980, UCLA-Wadsworth VA Hosp., 1981, UCLA, 1982 Northwestern U. Sch. Medicine, Chgo., 1984, Meth. Hosp., Indpls., 1984, U. Mo., Kans. City, 1985, U. Iowa, Iowa City, 1986, U. Ark., Little Rock, 1987, Keio U. Sch. Medicine, Tokyo, 1989, Mich. State U., 1993. Contbr. articles to profl. jours. Mem. Tech. Task Force on Diagnostic Radiology Nebr. Dept. Health, 1983-84; Major U.S. Army M.C., 1970-73. Co-recipient Magna Cum Laude in Sci. Exhibits award Am. Soc. Neuroradiology, 1987; GE grantee, 1985-87. Fellow Am. Coll. Radiology; mem. AMA (rep. to radiology residency rev. com., 1987), Radiol. Soc. N. Am. (award 1981, 82), Am. Coll. Radiology (com. on satellite communications 1981-83), Am. Roentgen Ray Soc. (award 1986), Assn. Univ. Radiologists, Soc. Chmn. Acad. Radiology Depts., Am. Soc. Uroradiology, Nebr. State Radiol. Soc., Nebr. State Med. Assn., Omaha Metro Med. Soc., Omaha Mid-West Clin. Soc. (hosp. and svc. exhibits com. 1984, award 1986), Omaha C. of C. (task force on edn. 1983-85, edn. coun. steering com. 1984, edn. coun. 1985), Rotary Internat. (program com. 1986), Marquette U. Club (bd. dirs. Omaha chpt., 1987), Alpha Omega Alpha (alumni and faculty mems. com., 1986). Roman Catholic. Avocation: swimming. Office: Nebr Health Sys Dept Radiology 981045 Nebr Med Ctr Omaha NE 68198-1045

INCROPERA, FRANK PAUL, mechanical engineering educator; b. Lawrence, Mass., May 12, 1939; s. James Frank and Ann Laura (Leone) I.; m. Andrea Jeanne Eastman, Sept. 2, 1960; children: Terri Ann, Donna Renee, Shaunna Jeanne. BSME, MIT, 1961; MS, Stanford U., 1962, PhD, 1966. Jr. engr. Barry Controls Corp., Watertown, Mass., 1959; thermodynamics engr. Aerojet Gen. Corp., Azusa, Calif., 1961; heat transfer specialist Lockheed Missiles and Space Co., Sunnyvale, 1962-64; mem. faculty Purdue U., 1966-98, prof. mech. engring., 1973-98, head dept., 1989-98; dean of engring. U. Notre Dame, Ind., 1998—. Cons. in field. Author: Introduction to Molecular Structure and Thermodynamics, 1974, Fundamentals of Heat Transfer, 1985, 90, 96, 2001; Fundamentals of Heat and Mass Transfer, 1981, 85, 90, 96, 2001, Liquid Cooling of Electronic Devices by Single-Phase Convection, 1999; also articles. Recipient Solberg Teaching award Purdue U., 1973, 77, 86, Potter Teaching award, 1973, Von Humboldt sr. scientist award Fed. Republic Germany, 1988. Fellow ASME (Melville medal 1988, Heat Transfer Meml. award 1988, Worcester Reed Warner award 1995); mem. Am. Soc. Engring. Edn. (Ralph C. Roe award 1982, George Westinghouse award 1983), Nat. Acad. Engring. Achievements include invention of bloodless surg. scalpel. Office: U Notre Dame Coll Engring 257 Fitzpatrick Hall Notre Dame IN 46556 E-mail: fpi@nd.edu.

INGALLS, MARIE CECELIE, former state legislator, retail executive; b. Faith, S.D., Mar. 31, 1936; d. Jens P. and Ida B. (Hegre) Jensen; m. Dale D. Ingalls, June 20, 1955; children: Duane (dec.), Delane. BS, Black Hills State Coll., 1973, MS, 1978. Elem. tchr. Meade County Schs., Sturgis, S.D., 1957-72, Faith Sch. Dist. 46-2, 1973-76; elem. prin. Meade Sch. Dist. 46-1, Sturgis, 1976-81; owner, operator Ingalls, 1978-99; mem., asst. majority whip S.D. House Reps., Pierre, 1986-92; lobbyist S.D. Legislature. Former sec. S.D. Rep. Orgn; Rep. nominee S.D. Commr. Sch. and Pub. Lands, 1998. Recipient Woman of Achievement award City of Sturgis, 1986, Retail Bus. of Yr. 1998. Mem. S.D. Cattlewomen, S.D. Stockgrowers (edn. chair), S.D. Farm Bur. (bd. dirs. dist. V), Faith C. of C. (pres. 1989), Sturgis C. of C. (past bd. dirs.), Key City Investment Club. Republican. Lutheran. Avocations: knitting, crocheting, piano, reading. Home: 17054 Opal Rd Mud Butte SD 57758

INGERSOLL, ROBERT STEPHEN, former diplomat, federal agency administrator; b. Galesburg, Ill., Jan. 28, 1914; s. Roy Claire and Lulu May (Hinchliff) I.; m. Coralyn Eleanor Reid, Sept. 17, 1938; children: Coralyn Eleanor, Nancy, Joan (dec.), Gail, Elizabeth. Grad., Phillips Acad., 1933; BS, Yale U., 1937. With Armco Steel Corp., 1937-39, Ingersoll Steel & Disc div. (later Ingersoll Products div.), 1939-41, 42-54; pres. Ingersoll Products div., 1950-54; adminstrv. v.p. Borg-Warner Corp., 1953-56, pres., 1956-61, chmn., 1961-72, CEO, 1958-72, also dir.; with Cen. Rsch. Lab., 1941-42; U.S. amb. to Japan, 1972-73; asst. sec. state for East Asian Affairs U.S. Dept. State, Washington, 1974, dep. sec. state, 1974-76. Ptnr., past bd. dirs. First Chgo. Capital Mkts. Asia Ltd.; chmn. Panasonic Found.; former mem. Bus. Coun. Pres. Winnetka (Ill.) Sch. Bd., 1957-63; dep. chmn., life bd. trustees U. Chgo.; trustee Smith Coll., 1966-71, Aspen Inst. Humanistic Studies, Calif. Inst. Tech.; past bd. dirs. Johnson Found., Trilateral Commn. N.Am.; past mem. coun. Yale U.; past mem. adv. coun. Caterpillar Asia Pacific; past vice-chmn. Pacific adv. coun. United Techs. Nat. Park Found. Mem. Japan Soc. (chmn. N.Y.C. chpt. 1978-85), Chgo. Coun. Fgn. Rels., Coun. Fgn. Rels. N.Y.C., Indian Hill Club, Chgo. Club, Econ. Club (Chgo., Phoenix), Comml. Club, Bohemian Club, Desert Forest Golf Club, Desert Mountain Club, Old Elm Club. Home and Office: One Arbor Ln Apt 202 Evanston IL 60201

INGHAM, NORMAN WILLIAM, Russian literature educator, genealogist; b. Holyoke, Mass., Dec. 31, 1934; s. Earl Morris and Gladys May (Rust) I. AB, Middlebury Coll. in German and Russian cum laude, 1957; postgrad. Slavic philology, Free U. Berlin, 1957-58; MA in Russian lang. and lit., U. Mich., 1959; postgrad. in Russian lang. and lit., Leningrad (USSR) State U., 1961-62; PhD in Slavic langs. and lit., Harvard U., 1963. Cert. genealogist. Postdoctoral researcher Czechoslovak Acad. Scis., Prague, Czechoslovakia, 1963-64; asst. prof. dept Slavic langs. and lits. Ind. U., Bloomington, 1964-65; asst. prof. Harvard U., Cambridge, Mass., 1965-70, lectr., 1970-71; assoc. prof. U. Chgo., 1971-82, prof., 1982—, chmn. dept., 1977-83, dir. Eastern Europe and USSR lang. and area ctr., 1978-91. Mem. Am. Com. Slavists, 1977-83; mem. com. Slavic and Ea. European studies U. Chgo., 1979-91, chmn., 1982-91, also other coms.; dir. Ctr. for East European and Russian/Eurasian Studies, 1991-96; rep. internat. Rsch. and Exch. Bd.; cert. genealogist, 1994—. Author: E.T.A. Hoffman's Reception in Russia, 1974; editor: Church and Culture in Old Russia, 1991; co-editor: (with Joachim T. Baer) Mnemozina: Studia litteraria russica in honorem Vsevolod Setchkarev; mem. editorial bd. Slavic and East European Jour., 1978-87, adv. bd., 1987-89; assoc. editor Byzantine Studies, 1973-81; contbg. editor The Am. Genealogist, 1995—; contbr. and translator articles and book revs. Fulbright fellow, 1957-58, vis. fellow Dumbarton Oaks Ctr. for Byzantine Studies, 1972-73. Mem. Am. Assn. Advancement Slavic Studies (rep. coun. on mem. instns. 1985-96, area rep. nat. adv. com. for Ea. European lang. programs 1985-96), Am. Assn. Tchrs. Slavic and East European Langs., Early Slavic Studies Assn. (v.p. 1993-95, pres. 1995-97), Chgo. Consortium for Slavic and East European Studies (v.p. 1982-84, 98, pres. 1984-86, 98-2000, exec. coun. 1992-94), Phi Beta Kappa. Office: U Chgo Slavic Dept 1130 E 59th St Chicago IL 60637-1539 E-mail: n-ingham@uchicago.edu.

INGRAM, DONALD, insurance company executive, director; Acct. Nations Bank of Ga.; CEO Godwins Inc. (now called Aon Cons.), Chgo. Office: Aon Cons 123 N Wacker Dr Ste 1000 Chicago IL 60606-1700

INGRAM, WILLIAM THOMAS , III, mathematics educator; b. McKenzie, Tenn., Nov. 26, 1937; s. William Thomas and Virginia (Howell) I.; m. Barbara Lee Gordon, June 6, 1958; children: William Robert, Kathie Ann, Mark Thomas. BA, Bethel Coll., 1959; MS, La. State U., 1961; PhD, Auburn U., 1964. Instr. Auburn U., Ala., 1961-63; instr. math. U. Houston, 1964-65, asst. prof., 1965-68, assoc. prof., 1968-75, prof., 1975-89, U. Mo., Rolla, 1989—, chmn., 1989-98. Contbr. articles to profl. jours. Mem. Am. Math. Soc., Math. Assn. Am. Presbyterian. Avocation: photography. Home: 826 Oak Knoll Rd Rolla MO 65401-4714 Office: Univ Mo Rolla Dept Math and Statistics Rolla MO 65409-0020

INKLEY, JOHN JAMES, JR. lawyer; b. St. Louis, Nov. 7, 1945; s. John James Sr. and Morjorie Jane (Kenna) I.; m. Catherine Ann Mattingly, Apr. 13, 1971; children: Caroline Marie, John James III. BSIE, St. Louis U., 1967, JD, 1970; LLM in Taxation, Washington U., St. Louis, 1976. Bar: Mo. 1970, U.S. Dist. Ct. (we. dist.) Mo. 1970, U.S. Dist. Ct. (ea. dist.) Mo. 1975, U.S. Tax Ct. 1975, U.S. Supreme Ct. 1975. Assoc. Padberg, Raack, McSweeney & Slater, St. Louis, 1970-73; ptnr. Summer, Hanlon, Summer, MacDonald & Nouss, 1973-81; city atty. City of Town and Country, Mo., 1979-84, spl. counsel, 1984-88; ptnr. Hanlon, Nouss, Inkley & Coughlin, St. Louis, 1981-83; ptnr., chmn. banking and real estate dept. Suelthaus & Kaplan, 1983-91; ptnr. Armstrong Teasdale LLP (and predecessor firm), 1991—; co-chmn. bus. svcs. group, 1993-2000; exec. com. St. Louis, 1994—. Mem. ABA, Mo. Bar Assn., Bar Assn. Met. St. Louis. Roman Catholic. Home: 35 Muirfield Ln Saint Louis MO 63141-7382 Office: Armstrong Teasdale LLP 1 Metropolitan Sq Ste 2600 Saint Louis MO 63102-2740

INMAN, LORINDA K. nursing administrator; Exec. dir. Iowa Bd. Nursing, Des Moines. Office: Iowa Bd Nursing State Capitol Complex 1223 E Court Ave Des Moines IA 50309-5622

INMAN, MARIANNE ELIZABETH, college administrator; b. Berwyn, Ill., Jan. 9, 1943; d. Miles V. and Bessee M. (Hejtmanek), Plzak; m. David P. Inman; Aug 1, 1964. BA, Purdue U., 1964; AM, Ind. U., 1967; PhD, U. Tex., 1978. Dir. Comml. Div. World Instruction and Translation, Inc., Arlington, Va., 1969-71; program staff mem. Ctr. for Applied Linguistics, 1972-73; lectr. in French No. Va. Community Coll., Bailey's Crossroads, 1973; faculty mem., linguistic researcher Tehran (Iran) U., 1973-75; intern mgmt. edn. rsch. & devel. S.W Ednl. Devel. Lab., Austin, Tex., 1977-78; asst. prof., program dir. Southwestern U., Georgetown, 1978; dir. English lang. inst. Alaska Pacific U., Anchorage, 1980-87, chairperson all-U. requirements, 1984-88, assoc. dean acad. affairs, 1988-90; v.p. dean of coll. Northland Coll., Ashland, Wis., 1990-95; pres. Ctrl. Meth. Coll., Fayette, Mo., 1995—. Contbr. Pres. Commn. Foreign Lang. and Internat. Studies, Washington, 1978-79; manuscript evaluator The Modern Lang. Jour., Columbus, Ohio, 1979-84; cons. Anchorage Sch. Dist., 1984-90; cons., evaluator N. Cen. Assn. Colls. and Schs., Chgo., 1990—; mem. dean's task force Coun. on Ind. Colls., 1993-95; pres. Ind. Colls. and Univs. Mo., 1996-2000. Co-author: English for Medical Students, 1976; co-author and editor: English for Science and Engineering Students, 1977; contbr. articles to profl. jours. Treas. Alaska Humanities Forum, Anchorage, 1982-87; mem. Anchorage Matanuska-Susitna Borough Pvt. Industry Coun., 1983-86; mem. Sister Cities Commn., Anchorage, 1984-90; mem. Multicultural Edn. Adv. Bd., Anchorage, 1987-90; active speakers bur. Wis. Humanities Com., 1992-95, Mcpl. Libr. Bd., 1993-95; active Mo. Humanities Coun., 1997—; mem. bd. Great Rivers Coun. Boy Scouts Am., 1996—. Named Fellow of Grad. Sch., U. Tex. Austin, 1977-78, Nat. Teaching Fellow, Alaska Pacific U., Anchorage, 1980-81; recipient Pub. Svc. award Sister Cities Commn., Anchorage, 1987, Kellogg Found. Nat. fellowship, Battle Creek, Mich., 1988-91. Mem. League of Women Voters, Nat. Assn. Women in Edn., Am. Assn. for Higher Edn., Am. Coun on Teaching of Foreign Langs., Tchrs. of English to Speakers of Other Langs., Nat. Coun. Tchrs. of English, Alpha Chi, Alpha Lambda Delta, Delta Rho Kappa, Gold Peppers, Kappa Delta Pi, Mortar Bd., Omicron Delta Kappa, Phi Kappa Phi, Pi Delta Phi, Pi Lambda Theta, Sigma Delta Pi, Sigma Epsilon Pi, Sigma Kappa. Avocations: community theater, hiking, camping, fishing. Office: Ctrl Meth Coll 411 CMC Sq Fayette MO 65248-1198 E-mail: minman@cmc.edu.

INUI, THOMAS SPENCER, physician, educator; b. Balt., July 10, 1943; s. Frank Kazuo and Beulah Mae (Sheetz) Inui; m. Nancy Stowe, June 14, 1969; 1 child Tazo Stowe. BA, Haverford Coll., 1965; MD, Johns Hopkins U., 1969, ScM, 1973. Diplomate Am. Bd. Internal Medicine. Intern Johns Hopkins Hosp., Balt., 1969—70, resident in internal medicine, 1970—73; clin. scholar Johns Hopkins U., 1971—73, chief resident, instr., 1973—74; chief of medicine USPHS Indian Hosp., Albuquerque, 1974—76; chief gen. medicine, dir. health svc. rsch. Seattle VA Med. Ctr., 1976—86; dir. Robert Wood Johnson clin. scholars program U. Wash., Seattle, 1977—92, prof. dept. medicine and health svcs., 1985—92, head div. gen. internal medicine, 1986—92; prof., chmn. of dept. ambulatory care and prevention Harvard Med. Sch. and Harvard Pilgrim Health Care, Boston, 1992—2000; pres., CEO Fetzer Inst., 2000—01, Pegenstrief Inst., Kalamazoo, 2002—. Scholar-in-residence Assn. Am. Med. Coll., 2002. Contbr. articles to profl. publs. Surgeon USPHS, 1974—76. Fellow: ACP; mem.: APHA (mem. coun. 1988—90), Inst. Medicine, Soc. Tchrs. Family Medicine, Assn. Health Svcs. Rsch., Am. Fedn. Clin. Rsch., Soc. Gen. Internal Medicine (pres. 1988—89, mem. coun. 1983—89), Alpha Omega Alpha, Phi Beta Kappa. Office: Regenstrief 141 E Michigan Ave Ste 400 Kalamazoo MI 49007 E-mail: Thomasinui@aol.com.

IONESCU TULCEA, CASSIUS, research mathematician, educator; b. Bucharest, Rumania, Oct. 14, 1923; naturalized, 1967; s. Ioan and Ana (Caselli) Ionescu Tulcea. M.S., U. Bucarest, 1946; Ph.D., Yale, 1959. Mem. faculty U. Bucarest, 1946-57, assoc. prof., 1952-57; research assoc. Yale U., 1957-59, vis. lectr., 1959-61; assoc. prof. U. Pa., 1961-64; prof. U. Ill., Urbana, 1964-66, Northwestern U., Evanston, Ill., 1966-90, prof. emeritus, 1990—. Author: Hilbert Spaces (in Rumanian), 1956, A Book on Casino Craps, 1980, A Book on Casino Blackjack, 1982; co-author: Probability Calculus (in Rumanian), 1956, Calculus, 1968, An Introduction to Calculus, 1969, Honors Calculus, 1970, Topics in the Theory of Liftings, 1969, Sets, 1971, Topology, 1971, A Book on Casino Gambling, 1976; contbr. articles to profl. jours. Recipient Asachi prize Rumanian Acad., 1957. Office: Northwestern U 2033 Sheridan Rd Evanston IL 60208-0830

IQBAL, ZAFAR MOHD, cancer researcher, biochemist, pharmacologist, toxicologist, consultant, molecular biologist; b. Hyderabad, India, Dec. 12, 1938; came to U.S., 1965, naturalized, 1973; s. M.A. and Haleemunissa (Begum) Rahim. BSc, Osmania U., 1958, MSc, 1962; PhD, U. Md., 1970. Diplomate Am. Bd. Forensic Medicine, Am. Bd. Forensic Examiners. Fellow in molecular pharmacology Nat. Cancer Inst./NIH, Bethesda, Md., 1971-74; asst. prof. pharmacology Case Western Res. U., Cleve., 1974-76; assoc. dir. ERC programs in occupational toxicology U. Ill. Med. Ctr., Chgo., 1980-81, assoc. prof. microbiology, 1977-80, assoc. prof. occupational medicine and environ. health, 1976-93, assoc. prof. preventive medicine, 1982-93; faculty grad. coll. U. Ill., 1977-93, dir. Carcinogenesis Labs., 1983-93, chair recombinant DNA instnl. com., 1982-93; chair HIV hazards in rsch. com. U. Ill. Grad. Coll. Faculty, 1976-93; dir. Toxicology-Cancer, 1987—; affiliate Lurie Cancer Ctr. Northwestern U., 1996—. Cons. in field to OSHA, 1980-81, Clements Assocs., 1976-79, Expert Resources, 1982—, Ill. Cancer Coun., 1981-82, Toxicology Cancer, 1987—; lectr. continuing edn.; grant reviewer study sects. NIH; program project reviewer Nat. Cancer Inst., 2000; merit grant reviewer VA, 1981-82; mem. tech. bd. panel Gt. Lakes Protection Fund, 1989—; participant profl. confs.; NSF-Coun. Sci. and Indsl. Rsch. exch. scientist, 1981; sponsor, trainer India-U.S. exch. scientists NSF, 1985-86; peer reviewer: (jours.) Sci., Cancer Rsch., Jour. Biochem., Toxicology, Carcinogenesis, others, also books and films; spl. advisor RRL (India) Dirs., 1980-86; mem. U.S. AID's-Asia Environ. Partnership and Environ Tech. Network Asia, 1994—, Environ. and Tech. Network Asia-Latin Am. Program, 1996—; chair recombinant DNA com. U. Ill., Chgo., 1983-93; contbr. WHO Internat. Agy. for Rsch. Cancer, Tallinn, 1975, Budapest, 1979, Tokyo, 1981, Banff, 1983; mem. exec. bd. sci. and tech. advs. Am. Bd. Forensic Exams., 1997—. Author, editor: Molecular Mechanisms of Toxic Response; Pancreatic Carcinogenesis Mechanisms; editor Jour. Molecular Toxicology and Carcinogenesis; mem. editorial adv. bd. Forensic Examiner, 1995—; exec. bd. sci. and tech. advisors Am. Bd. Forensic Examiners, 1996—; contbr. more than 60 articles to profl. jours. NSF-CSIR exch. scientist, 1981; sponsor, trainer India-U.S. Exch. Scientists, NSF, 1985-86; spl. advisor RRL (India) Dirs., 1980—; pres. Rahim Meml. Found., 1995—. Fellow Coun. Sci. and Indsl. Rsch., India, 1963-65; Fogarty Internat. fellow Nat. Cancer Inst., NIH, 1970-71, staff fellow, 1971-74; grantee Nat. Cancer Inst./NIH, Nat. Inst. Occupational Safety and Health, EPA, State of Ill., 1974-93. Fellow Am. Coll. Forensic Examiners (life, diplomate, bd. cert. forensic medicine, editl. bd. advisors 1995—); mem. AAAS, Am. Assn. Cancer Rsch., Am. Pancreatic Assn., N.Y. Acad. Scis., Am. Chem. Soc., Soc. Toxicology, Am. Coll. Toxicology, Nat. Registry of Forensic Examiners, B.E.S.T. N.Am., Registry Global World Leaders, Soc. Toxicology (molecular biology, carcinogenesis and mechanism splty. sects.), NIHAA, Sigma Xi. Office: Toxicology-Cancer PO Box 60267 Chicago IL 60660-0267

IRONS, WILLIAM GEORGE, anthropology educator; b. Garrett, Ind., Dec. 25, 1933; s. George Randall and Eva Aileen (Veazey) I.; m. Marjorie Sue Rogasner, Nov. 4, 1972; children— Julia Rogasner, Marybeth Rogasner BA, U. Mich., 1960, MA, 1963, PhD, 1969; postgrad., London Sch. Econs., 1964-65. With Army C.E., 1956-58; asst. prof. social relations Johns Hopkins U., 1969-74; asst. prof. anthropology Pa. State U., 1974-78; assoc. prof. anthropology Northwestern U., Evanston, Ill., 1978-83, prof., 1983—. Cons. Nat. Geog. Soc., NSF, AAAS, Social Sci. Research Council, Time-Life Books, U. Wash. Press, Random House, Worth Pubs., Rutgers U. Press, U. Tex. Press, Pelenum Press, Oxford U. Press, Cornell U. Press. Author: Perspectives on Nomadism, 1972, The Yomut Turkmen, 1975, Evolutionary Biology and Human Social Behavior, 1979, Adaptation and Human Behavior, 2000; mem. bd. editors Evolution and Human Behavior. With AUS, 1954-56. Recipient Lifetime Achievement award Commn. on Nomadic Peoples, Internat. Union Anthropol. and Ethnological Scis.; grantee NSF, 1973, 76, 83, 85, 86, Ford Found., 1974, Harry Frank Guggenheim Found., 1976. Fellow AAAS, Am. Anthrop. Assn.; mem. Assocs. in Current Anthropology, Human Behavior and Evolution Soc. (pres. 2001—), Internat. Soc. Human Ethology, Internat. Soc. for Behavioral Ecology, Ctr. for Advanced Studies in Religion and Sci., Inst. for Religion in an Age of Sci., Phi Kappa Phi. Achievements include research on Turkmen of Iran, human behavioral ecology, evolutionary ethics. Home: 2604 Payne St Evanston IL 60201-2133 Office: Northwestern U Dept Anthropology 1810 Hinman Ave Evanston IL 60208-0809 E-mail: w-irons@northwestern.edu.

IRSAY, JAMES STEVEN, professional football team owner; b. Lincolnwood, Ill., June 13, 1959; s. Robert Irsay and Harriet Pogerzelski; m. Margaret Mary Coyle, Aug. 2, 1980; children: Carlie Margaret, Casey Coyle, Kalen. B in Broadcast Journalism, So. Meth. U., 1982. With Balt. Colts., from early 1970's; owner, CEO Indpls. Colts, 1972—. Bd. dirs. Noble Ind. Composer, performer single Hoosier Heartland, 1985, single and video Go Colts, 1985, Colors, 1990. Bd. dirs. United Way Ctrl. Ind.; dir. Greater Indpls. Progress Com. Avocations: weight lifting, guitar, songwriting. Office: Indpls Colts 7001 W 56th St Indianapolis IN 46254-9725 also: Indianapolis Colts P.O. Box 535000 Indianapolis IN 46253

IRVINE, GEORGE, professional basketball coach; b. Seattle, Feb. 1, 1948; children: Toby, Jaime; m. Jeanie Holmquist; stepchildren: Conor, Michael, Patrick. Grad., U. Wash., 1970. Guard, forward Va. Squires, Am. Basketball Assn., 1970-75; guard, forward Denver Nuggets, Am. Basketball Assn., 1975-76, asst. coach, 1976-80, Ind. Pacers, NBA, 1980-83, v.p., dir. basketball ops., 1983-84, coach, 1984-86, v.p., dir. basketball ops., 1986-94; asst. coach, 1994-95, Golden State Warriors, Oakland, Calif., 1995-97; head coach Detroit Pistons, 2000—. Team coach Goodwill Games, 1994. Office: Detroit Pistons 2 Championship Dr Auburn Hills MI 48326-1753

IRVINE, PHYLLIS ELEANOR, nursing educator, administrator; b. Germantown, Ohio, July 14, 1940; m. Richard James Irvine, Feb. 15, 1964; children: Mark, Rick. BSN, Ohio State U., 1962, MSN, 1979, PhD, 1981; MS, Miami U., Oxford, Ohio, 1966. Staff nurse VA Ctr., Dayton, Ohio, 1962-66; mem. nursing faculty Miami Valley Hosp. Sch. Nursing, 1968-78; teaching asst., lectr. Ohio State U., Columbus, 1979-82; assoc. prof. Ohio U., Athens, 1982-83; prof., dir. N.E. La. U., Monroe, 1984-88; prof., dir. sch. nursing Ball State U., Muncie, Ind., 1988—. Reviewer Health Edn. Jour., Reston, Va., 1987; contbr. articles to profl. jours. Mem. Mayor's Commn. on Needs of Women, La., 1984-88; 1st v.p., bd. dirs. United Way of Ouachita, La., 1986-88. Mem. ANA, Ind. Nurses Assn., Ind. Coun. Deans and Dirs. of Nursing Edn. (pres. 1992-98), Internat. Coun. Women's Health Issues (bd. dirs. 1986-92, 98-2000), Assn. for the Advancement Health Edn., Sigma Theta Tau. Office: Ball State U Cn418 Nursing Muncie IN 47306-0001

IRVING, LEE G. bank executive; Chief acctg. officer, exec. v.p. KeyCorp, Cleve. Office: KeyCorp 127 Public Square Cleveland OH 44114-1306

IRWIN, GERALD PORT, physician; b. Muncie, Ind., July 11, 1945; s. Francis Inlow and Helen Marcella (Morgan) I.; m. Martha Sue Vincent, Mar. 10, 1946; 1 child, Tamara Suzette. AB in Biol. Sci., Ind. U., 1968; MD, Ind. U., Indpls., 1972. Diplomate Am. Bd. Family Physicians. Intern and resident Ball Meml. Hosp., Muncie, Ind., 1972-73; pvt. practice Alexandria, 1973—. Med. dir. Richland Twp. Fire Dept., Anderson. Mem. AMA (Physician Recognition award 1992-95, 98-2001), Am. Acad. Family Physicians,Ind. State Med. Assn., Ind. Assn. Family Physicians, Lions, Elks. Methodist. Avocations: computers, backpacking. Office: PO Box 124 Alexandria IN 46001-0124

IRWIN, GLENN WARD, JR. medical educator, physician, university official; b. Roachdale, Ind., July 18, 1920; s. Glenn Ward and Elsie (Browning) I.; m. Marianna Ashby; children: Ann Graybill Irwin Warden, William Browning, Elizabeth Ashby Irwin Schiffli. BS, Ind. U., Bloomington, 1942; MD, Ind. U., Indpls., 1944; LLD (hon.), Ind. U., 1986, Marian Coll., 1987. Diplomate: Am. Bd. Internal Medicine. Intern Meth. Hosp., Indpls., 1944-45; resident in internal medicine Ind. U. Med. Ctr., 1945-46, 48-50; mem. faculty Ind. U., 1950—, instr. , asst. prof. then assoc. prof., 1950-61, prof. medicine, 1961-86, prof. emeritus, 1986, dean Sch. Medicine, 1965-73, dean emeritus, 1986, v.p., 1974-86; chancellor Ind. U.-Purdue U., 1973-74, chancellor emeritus, 1989. Sr. assoc. Ind. U. Found. Bd. dirs. Goodwill Industries of Ctrl. Ind., Indpls., Greater Indpls. Progress Com., Greater Indpls. YMCA, Walther Med. Rsch. Inst., Walther Oncology Ctr., Indpls. Health Inst., Eiteljorg Mus. Western Art and the Am. Indian; elder 2d Presbyn. Ch. Served to capt. M.C. U.S. Army, 1946-48. Recipient Disting. Alumnus award Ind. U. Sch. Medicine, 1972, Otis R. Bowen Physician County Service award, Benjamin Harrison award, Ind. Acad. award; named Sagamore of the Wabash, Gov. of Ind., 1961, 79, 86. Fellow ACP (gov. for Ind. 1964-70); mem. AMA, Ind. State Med. Assn., Marion County Med. Soc., Ind. Soc. of Chgo., 500 Festival Assn., James Whitcomb Riley Meml. Assn. (bd. govs. 1986—), Newcomen Soc., Sigma Xi, Alpha Omega Alpha, Beta Gamma Sigma, Sigma Theta Tau. Clubs: Columbia (Indpls.), Contemporary (Indpls.), Meridian Hills Country, Skyline (bd. dirs.). Lodge: Masons (33 degree), Rotary. Home: 8025 N Illinois St Indianapolis IN 46260-2938 Office: Ind U-Purdue U at Indpls 1120 South Dr Indianapolis IN 46202-5135 E-mail: drglenni@aol.com.

ISAACS, ROGER DAVID, public relations executive; b. Boston, Oct. 23, 1925; s. Raphael and Agnes (Wolfstein) I.; m. Joyce R. Wexler, Oct. 23, 1949; children: Gillian, Jan. Student, U. Wis., 1943; AB, Bard Coll., 1949. With Pub. Rels. Bd., Inc., Chgo., 1948—, account supr., 1948-51, ptnr., 1951-60, exec. v.p., 1960-66, pres., 1966-75, chmn., pres., 1975-86; chmn. PRB, a Needham Porter Novelli Co.; exec. v.p., gen. mgr. Doremus Porter Novelli, 1986-89; sr. counselor Porter/Novelli, 1989-91, The Fin. Rels. Bd., Inc., Chgo., 1991—. Bd. dirs. North Bank, Chgo. Past bd. dirs. Anti-Defamation League Chgo., Jewish Family and Cmty. Svc., Sr. ctrs. Met. Chgo., Highland Park Hosp., Met. Crusade of Mercy, Suburban Fine Arts Ctr., Asthma and Allergy Found., Spertus Coll.; cmty. adv. bd. Sta. WBEZ; bd. dirs. Chgo. Crime Commn.; libr. vis. com. Spertus Inst. With AUS, 1943-45. Decorated Purple Heart. Mem. Pub. Rels. Soc. Am. (accredited), Met. Club, Publicity Club Chgo. Home: 1045 Hillcrest Rd Glencoe IL 60022-1215 E-mail: joroisaacs@aol.com.

ISAACSON, DEAN LEROY, statistician; b. St. Cloud, Minn., Apr. 10, 1941; married. BS, Macalester Coll., 1963; MS, U. Minn., 1966, PhD, 1968. Asst. prof. math. and stats. Iowa State U., Ames, 1968, assoc. prof. math. and stats., 1972, prof. math. and stats., 1976—, acting dir. statis. lab, head of stats., 1984-86, dir. statis. lab., head stats., 1986—. Author book on Markov Chains; contbr. numerous articles to profl. jours. Fellow Am. Statis. Assn.; mem. Inst. of Math. Stats. Office: Iowa State U Sci and Tech Statis Lab 102 Snedecor Hl Ames IA 50011-0001 E-mail: dli@iastate.edu.

ISAACSON, MILTON STANLEY, research and development company executive, engineer; b. Dayton, Ohio, Apr. 23, 1932; s. Max and Sylvia Mariam (Kirsin) I.; m. Joan Sue Koor, Sept. 4, 1955; children: Julie Fay, Jill Ellen, Jan Lynn. BSEE, Ohio State U., 1955. Registered profl. engr., Ohio. Successively design engr., mgr. quality control, div. mgr., dir. R & D Globe Industries, Dayton, 1957-70; pres. Nu-Tech Industries, Inc., Trotwood, Ohio, 1970—. Officer, bd. dirs. Food Svcs., Dayton, 1970-95. Patentee brushless DC motors and medical devices. Bd. dirs. Grace House Sexual Abuse Resource Ctr., Dayton, 1985—, pres., 1985-89; bd. dirs. Temple Israel Found., 1987-90, pres., 1990; v.p. Jewish Fedn. Greater Dayton, 1984—; bd. dirs. Big Bros./Big Sisters of Greater Dayton, 1965-95, pres., 1978-79; bd. dirs. Old Time Newsies, 1969—, pres., 1991-92. 1st lt. USAF, 1955-57. Recipient Dr. Alan F. Wasserman Leadership award Jewish Fedn. Dayton, 1972, Boss of the Yr. award Nat. Trail chpt. Am. Bus. Womens Assn., 1975, Outstanding Pub. Svc. award Sta. WKEF, Dayton, 1979, Outstanding Svc. award Big Bros./Big Sisters of Greater Dayton, 1977, 88, Hon. Judge Carl D. Kessler Meml. award The Grace House, 1991. Mem. IEEE, Rotary (pres. Trotwood club 1989, sec. 1993—), Eta Kappa Nu. Avocations: fishing, traveling. Office: Nu-Tech Industries Inc 5905 Wolf Creek Pike Dayton OH 45426-2439

ISAAK, LARRY A. university system chancellor; m. Ruth Isaak; children: David, Corey. BSBA in Acctg., U. N.D., 1973, MBA, 1996. CPA. Asst. legis. budget analyst and auditor N.D. Legis. Coun., 1974-81; with Office of Mgmt. and Budget, 1981-84, state's exec. budget analyst; vice chancellor for adminstrv. and student affairs N.D. Univ. Sys., 1984-94, co-interim chancellor, 1994, chancellor, 1994—. Student affairs and liaison Student Affairs Coun., N.D. Student Assn.; dir. higher edn. computer network. Mem. AICPA, State Higher Edn. Exec. Officers Assn., N.W. Acad. Computing Consortium (past v.p., bd. dirs.), Nat. Assn. of State Higher Edn. Fin. Officers (chair 1994), State Soc. of Cert. Pub. Accts. (chair, mem. govtl. acctg. com.). Office: ND Univ Sys Dept 215 600 E Boulevard Ave Bismarck ND 58505-0230 E-mail: ndus_office@ndus.nodak.edu.

ISEMINGER, GARY HUDSON, philosophy educator; b. Middleboro, Mass., Mar. 3, 1937; s. Boyd Austin and Harriet Herring (Hudson); m. Andrea Louise Grove, Dec. 18, 1965; children: Andrew, Ellen. BA, Wesleyan U., 1958; MA, Yale U., 1960, PhD, 1961. Instr. Philosophy Yale U., 1961-62, Carleton Coll., Northfield, Minn., 1962-63, asst. prof., 1963-68, assoc. prof., 1968-73; prof., 1973-94; William H. Laird prof. philosophy and liberal arts Carleton Coll., Northfield, Minn., 1994—. Vis. fellow Kings Coll., London, 1966, U. Lancaster, 1991; chair student-faculty adminstrn. com. Carleton Coll., 1970-71, dept. philosophy, 1972-75, 86-89, 98—, ednl. policy com., 1973-74, English dept. rev. com., 1973-74, com. Lucas Lectrs. in Arts, 1977-81, presdl. inauguration, 1987, edn. dept. rev. task force, 1988, Am. studies program rev. com., 1992, mem. tenure and devel. rev. com., 1985-87, Coll. Coun., 1987, Coll. Marshall, 2001—; acad. vis. London Sch. Econs., 1971; vis. prof. philosophy U. Minn., 1979, Mayo Med. Sch., 1986, 87, U. Lancaster, 1994, Trinity Coll. Dublin, 2000; Belgum meml. lectr. St. Olaf Coll., 1997; panelist divsn. fellowships NEH, 1980, 91; commentator Minn. Pub. Radio, 1981; dir. London arts program Associated Colls. Midwest, 1982; cons. Harvard U. Press, Univ. Calif. Press, Prentice-Hall, Cornell U. Press, Holt, Rinehart and Winston, Vanderbilt U. Press, Jour. Aesthetics and Art Criticism, Dialogue, Notre Dame Jour. Formal Logic, Jour. of Philosophy and Phenomenological Rsch.; external reviewer, evaluator various philosophy depts.; presenter in field. Author: An Introduction to Deductive Logic, 1968, Logic and Philosophy: Selected Readings, 1968, 2d edit., 1980, Knowledge and Argument, 1984, Intention and Interpretation, 1992; mem. editl. bd. Am. Philos. Quar., 1989-92, Jour. of Aesthetics and Art Criticism, 1993—; contbr. articles, revs. to profl. jours. Active Minn. Humanities Commn., 1984-90, chair 1988-89 Grantee NSF Coun. Philos. Studies, 1968, Bush Found., 1983, Sloan Found. 1984, Faculty Devel. Endowment, 1989, 94, 2000, NEH, 1990, 91; recipient summer stipend NEH, 1971, 78, Disting. Alumnus award Wesleyan U., 1993; Woodrow Wilson fellow, 1958, fellow Univ. Coll., London, 1975, 78, Inst. Adv. Studies in the Humanities, U. Edinburgh, 1985; vis. scholar Cambridge U., 1996. Mem. AAUP (pres. Carleton chpt. 1967-68), Am. Philos. Assn. (program com. western divsn. 1982, task force on the philosophy major 1989-90, program com. ctrl. divsn. 1991, chmn. com. on tchg. philosophy 1993-96, com. to award Matchette prize in philosophy 1993-95, bd. officers 1993-96), Am. Soc. Aesthetics (trustee 1996-99), Minn. Philos. Soc. (pres. 1978-79), Phi Beta Kappa (pres. Carleton chpt. 1968-69). Avocations: classical percussion, jazz vibraphone, choral singing. Office: Carleton College One North College St Northfield MN 55057-4002

ISENBERG, HOWARD LEE, manufacturing company executive; b. Chgo., Dec. 21, 1936; children: Suzanne, Marc, Alan. BS, U. Pa., 1958. CPA, Ill. V.p. Conley Electronics, Chgo., 1960-63, Barr Co. div. Pittway Corp., Niles, Ill., 1963-68, pres. Barr Co. div., 1969-92; v.p. Pittway Corp., 1970-92, CCL Custom Mfg. (acquired Barr Co. in 1992), 1992—. Vice chmn., trustee Lake Forest (Ill.) Acad., 1986-98; trustee Providence-St. Mel H.S., Chgo., 1994—; chmn. The Barr Fund, 1993—. Home: 325 Oak Creek Dr Wheeling IL 60090-6741 Office: CCL Custom Mfg 6133 N River Rd Ste 800 Rosemont IL 60018-5175 E-mail: hisenberg@cclcustom.com.

ISENSTEIN, LAURA, library director; b. Toledo; BA in History, U. Mich., 1971, MA in Libr. Sci., 1972. Libr. Baltimore County Pub. Libr., 1972-81, area branch mgr., 1981-85, coord. info. svcs., 1985-94; founder, prin. LIA Assocs., Tng. Consultancy, 1988-95; dir. Pub. Libr. Des Moines, 1995-00. Mem. OCLC Adv. Coun. for Pub. Librs.; spkr. in field. Mem. editl. bd. Jewish Press; contbr. articles to profl. jours. Mem. cmty. edn. advt. coun. Des Moines Pub. Schs.; mem. Mayors' Select Com. Shared Svcs. Focus Group. Mem. ALA, Pub. Libr. Assn. (chmn., mem. various coms.), Urban Librs. Couns., Iowa Libr. Assn., Rotary Internat., Greater Des Moines Leadership Inst. Avocations: gourmet cooking, travel, reading mysteries. Office: Pub Libr Des Moines 100 Locust St Des Moines IA 50309-1767

ISON, CHRISTOPHER JOHN, investigative reporter; b. Crandon, Wis., Aug. 20, 1957; s. Luther Arnold Jr. and Penny (Koyn) I.; m. Nancy Cassutt, Aug. 1, 1988. BA, U. Minn., 1983. Editor in chief Minn. Daily, Mpls., 1982-83; reporter News-Tribune & Herald, Duluth, Minn., 1983-86, Star Tribune, Mpls., 1986—. Recipient Pulitzer prize for investigative reporting, 1990. Mem. Investigative Reporters and Editors. Office: Star Tribune 425 Portland Ave Minneapolis MN 55488-0002

ISRAEL, MARTIN HENRY, astrophysicist, educator, academic administrator; b. Chgo., Jan. 12, 1941; s. Herman and Anna Catherine I.; m. Margaret Ellen Mitouer, June 20, 1965; children: Elisa, Samuel. SB, U. Chgo., 1962; PhD, Calif. Inst. Tech., 1969. Asst. prof. physics Washington U., St. Louis, 1968-72, assoc. prof., 1972-75, prof., 1975—, assoc. dir. McDonnell Ctr. for Space Scis., 1982-87, acting dean faculty arts and scis., 1987-88, dean faculty, 1988-94, vice chancellor, 1994-95, vice chancellor acad. planning, 1995-97. Mem. com. on space astronomy and astrophysics NRC, 1976-79; mem. High Energy Astrophysics Mgmt. Ops. Working Group NASA, 1976-84, co-chair Cosmic Ray Program Working Group, 1980-87, mem. space and earth scis. adv. com., 1985-88, chair Particle Astrophysics Magnet Facility Definition Team, 1985-87, mem. astrophysics coun., 1986-87, prin. investigator Heavy Nuclei Expt. High Energy Astronomy Obs., 1971-89, mem. structure and evolution of the universe subcom., 1996-99, chair ACCESS steering com., 1998-2000, mem. Space Sta. Utilization adv. subcom., 1998—, mem. GSFC Space Sci. vis. com., 1997-2001, chair, 2000-01; mem. GSFC Ctr. Dir.'s Vis. Com., 2000-01; chair Space Sci. Working Group, Assn. Am. Univs., 1983-85; chair nat. organizing com. 19th Internat. Cosmic Ray Conf., 1985, 1982-85. Contbr.

articles on cosmic ray astrophysics and observation of elemental and isotopic composition of cosmic rays to profl. jours. Recipient Exceptional Sci. Achievement award NASA, 1980; Sloan Found. fellow, 1970. Fellow Am. Phys. Soc. (chair astrophysics divsn. 1980-81); mem. Am. Astron. Soc. (mem. exec. com. high energy astrophysics divsn. 1982-84), AAUP, AAAS. Home: 2 Valley View Pl Saint Louis MO 63124-1810 Office: Washington U Campus Box 1105 1 Brookings Dr Saint Louis MO 63130-4899 E-mail: mhi@wuphys.wustl.edu.

ISRAELOV, RHODA, financial planner, writer, entrepreneur; b. Pitts., May 20, 1940; d. Joseph and Fannie (Friedman) Kreinen; divorced; children: Jerome, Arthur, Russ. BS in Hebrew Edn., Herzlia Hebrew Tchrs. Coll., N.Y.C., 1961; BA in English Lang. and Lit., U. Mo., Kansas City, 1965; MS, Coll. Fin. Planning, 1991. CFP, CLU. Hebrew tchr. various schs., 1961-79; ins. agt. Conn. Mut. Life, Indpls., 1979-81; fin. planner, 1st v.p. investments Salomon Smith Barney, Inc., 1981—. Instr. for mut. fund licensing exams. Pathfinder Securities Sch., Indpls., 1983-87; cons. channel 6 News, 1984-85. Contbr. columns in newspapers, ; regular guest (Radio show) WTUX Radio, 1990—94. Recipient Gold Medal award Personal Selling Power, 1987; named Bus. Woman of Yr., Network of Women in Bus., 1986. Mem. Inst. Cert. Fin. Planners, Nat. Assn. Life Underwriters, Women's Life Underwriters' Conf. (treas. Ind. chpt. 1982, v.p. chpt. 1983), Internat. Assn. Fin. Planners (v.p. Ind. chpt. 1983-84, bd. dirs., sec.), Am. Soc. CLU, Women's Life Underwriters Conf., Nat. Coun. Jewish Women, Nat. Assn. Profl. Saleswomen, Nat. Spkrs. Assn. (pres. Ind. chpt. 1986-87, treas. 1984), Registry Fin. Planning Practitioners, Toastmasters (chpt. ednl. v.p. 1985-86), Soroptimists (bd. dirs.), Ctrl. Ind. Mensa. Avocations: piano, folk, square, folk and ballroom dancing, theatre. Office: Smith Barney Bank One Center Tower 111 Monument Cir Ste 3100 Indianapolis IN 46204-5193 E-mail: israelov@yahoo.com., rhoda.israelov@rssmb.com.

ISRAELS, LYONEL GARRY, hematologist, medical educator; b. Regina, Sask., Can., July 31, 1926; s. Simon and Sarah (Girtle) I.; m. Esther Hornstein, June 3, 1950; children: Sara, Jared. BA, U. Sask., 1946; MD, U. Man., 1949, MScawd, 1950, DSc (hon.), 1999. Intern Winnipeg Gen. Hosp., 1948-49; resident internal medicine and hematology Salt Lake County Hosp., 1950-52; fellow in hematology Kantonsspital, Zurich, 1952-53; dept. biochemistry U. Man., 1953-55, asst. prof. biochemistry, 1955-59, asst. prof. medicine, 1959-62, assoc. prof. medicine, 1962-66, prof. medicine, 1966—, Disting. prof., 1983—, acting head dept. medicine, 1977-79. Dir. Manitoba Inst. Cell Biology, 1970-73, sr. scientist, 1992—; exec. dir. Manitoba Cancer Treatment and Rsch. Found., 1973-92, 93—; attending physician Health Sci. Centre; cons. in hematology Children's Centre, Winnipeg; mem. Med. Rsch. Coun. Can., 1973-75; chmn. Manitoba Health Rsch. Coun., 1980-87; mem. sci. coun. Internat. Agy. Cancer Rsch., 1989-93, chmn., 1992-93. Contbr. articles on biochem. and immunol. aspects of blood, blood forming organs and cancer to sci. jours. Decorated Order of Can.; L.G. Israels chair in hematology at Ben Gurion U. in his honor, 1996. Fellow RCPC; mem. Am. Soc. Clin. Investigation, Can. Soc. Clin. Investigation (pres. 1968), Royal Coll. Physicians and Surgeons Can., Can. Hematol. Soc. (pres. 1972-74), Nat. Cancer Inst. Can. (pres. 1976-78), Manitoba Order of Buffalo Hunt. Decorated Order of Can.; L.G. Israels chair in hematology at Ben Gurion U. in his honor, 1996. Home: 502 South Dr Winnipeg MB Canada R3T 0B1 Office: 675 McDermot Ave Winnipeg MB Canada R3E 0V9 E-mail: lisraels@cc.umanitoba.ca.

ISSELHARD, DONALD EDWARD, dentist; b. Belleville, Ill., Apr. 11, 1941; s. Bertram Joseph and Margaret Eda (Dobbins) I.; m. Annette Scanaliato, Mar. 1, 1980; children: Kerstin, Nissa, Michele, Tara. Student, St. Louis U., 1959-62; BS in Dentistry, U. Ill., Chgo., 1970, DDS, 1966; MBA, Maryville U., 1994. Gen. practice dentistry, Clayton, Mo., 1967-70, Creve Coeur, 1970—. Assoc. instr. Forest Park C.C., St. Louis, 1973-77; asst. prof. Washington U., St. Louis, 1975-77; lectr. Continuing Edn. Ctrs. Am., 1977-79; pres. Tempo Condo. Investment Corp., 1994—, Strategic Empowerment Inc., 1994, Fortune Tempo Med. Condominium Assn., Inc., 1995—. Author: (with others) Anatomy of Orofacial Structures, 1977, 6th edit., 1998; contbg. author Comprehensive Rev. of Dental Hygiene, 1986. Fellow Acad. Gen. Dentistry Dentistry Internat., Masters Acad. Gen. Dentistry; mem. ADA, Mo. Acad. Gen. Dentistry (v.p. 1996, pres. 1997-99), Greater St. Louis Dental Assn., Gateway Practice Devel. Assn. (pres. 1986-90). Home: 17726 Drummer Ln Chesterfield MO 63005-4223 Office: 12401 Olive Blvd Saint Louis MO 63141-5448 E-mail: disselhard@aol.com.

ISTOCK, VERNE GEORGE, retired banker; b. Sept. 20, 1940; BA in Econs., U. Mich., 1962, MBA in Fin., 1963. Credit analyst trainee NBD Bancorp, Inc., Detroit, 1963-71, group head, 1971-77, head U.S. divsn., 1977-82, sr. v.p., 1979-82, exec. v.p., 1982-85, vice chmn., dir., 1985-93, chmn., CEO, 1994-95, also bd. dirs.; chmn. NBD Bank; pres., CEO First Chgo. NBD Corp., Chgo., 1995-98, chmn., 1996-98; chmn. bd. Bank One Corp., 1998-2000, pres., 2000; ret., 2000. Bd. dirs. Kelly Svcs. Inc., Masco Corp. Dir. Chgo. Coun. on Fgn. Rels. Mem. U. Mich. Alumni Assn. (past pres., lifetime dir.), Bankers Roundtable (past dir.), Econ. Club Chgo., Mich. Bus. Roundtable (former bd. dirs.), Comml. Club of Chgo., Econ. Club Detroit (past dir.), Ill. Bus. Roundtable (past dir.). Office: Bank One Corp 1 Bank One Plz Chicago IL 60670-0001 E-mail: verne_istock@bankone.com.

IVERS, MIKE, radio personality; Radio host WMJI, Cleve. Office: 6200 Oak Tree Blvd 4th Fl Cleveland OH 44131

IVERSON, STEWART E., JR. state legislator; b. Iowa Falls, Iowa, July 16, 1950; m. Vicki Bortell Iverson; 4 children. AA, Ellsworth C.C., Iowa Falls, Iowa, 1970; BA, Buena Vista Coll., 1987. Mem. Iowa Ho. of Reps., Des Moines, 1988-94, Iowa Senate from 5th dist., Des Moines, 1994—; senate majority leader, 1996—. Mem. First Luth. Ch.; former mem. Dows Cmty. Sch. Bd. With USMC, 1971-73. Mem. Soybean Assn., Pork Prodrs., Corn Growers, Farm Bur., Am. Legion, Elks. Republican. Home: 3020 Dows Williams Rd Dows IA 50071-7532 Office: State Capitol 5th Dist 3 9th And Grand Des Moines IA 50319-0001 E-mail: stewart_iverson@legis.state.ia.us.

IZANT, ROBERT JAMES, JR. pediatric surgeon; b. Cleve., Feb. 4, 1921; s. Robert James and Grace (Goulder) I.; m. Virginia Lincoln Root, Sept. 27, 1947; children: Jonathan G. II, Mary Root, Timothy Holman. AB cum laude, Amherst Coll., 1943; MD, Western Res. U., 1946. Diplomate: Am. Bd. Surgery, Am. Bd. Pediatric Surgery. Resident in surgery U. Hosp., Cleve., 1946-52; resident in pediatric surgery Boston Children's Med. Center, 1952-55; asst. prof. pediatric surgery Ohio State U., 1955-58; prof., dir. pediatric surgery and pediatrics Case Western Res.U., 1958-90, prof. emeritus pediatric surgery and pediatrics, 1990—. Dir. div. pediatric surgery Univ. Hosps. Cleve., Rainbow Babies and Children's Hosp.; also MetroHealth Ctr. Hosp., 1958-86; mem. adv. bd. Ohio State Services for Children with Med. Handicaps, 1957—. Co-author: The Surgical Neonate; contbr. articles to profl. jours. Bd. dirs. alumni Western Res. Acad. Served to lt. (j.g.) M.C. USNR, 1947-49. Fellow ACS, Am. Acad. Pediatrics; mem. Central Surg. Assn., Am. Assn. Surgery of Trauma, AMA, Am. Bd. Surgery, Cleve. Surg. Soc. (pres. 1971-72), Cleve. Acad. Medcine (dir. 1971-74), Am. Trauma Soc. (founding mem.), Teratology Soc., Lilliputian Surg. Soc., No. Ohio Pediatric Soc., Brit. Assn. Pediatric Surgery, Pediatric Surgery Biology Club, Am. Pediatric Surg. Assn. (founding mem., pres. 1987-88), Western Res. U. Sch. Medicine Alumni Assn. (pres. 1961-62), Am. Burn Assn., Sigma Xi, Alpha Omega Alpha, Nu Sigma Nu, Delta Kappa Epsilon. Home: 2275 Harcourt Dr Cleveland Heights OH 44106-4614 Office: Rainbow Babies and Childrens Hosp University Cir Cleveland OH 44106 Fax: (216) 795-4278. E-mail: rizant@aol.com.

IZZO, THOMAS, college basketball coach; b. Iron Mountain, Mich., Jan. 30, 1955; m. Lupe Izzo; 1 child, Raquel. Grad., No. Mich. U., 1977. Head coach Ishpeming (Mich.) H.S., 1977-79; asst. coach No. Mich. U., 1979-83; with Mich. State U., East Lansing, 1983—, head coach Spartans, 1995—. Named to No. Mich. U. Hall of Fame, 1990, Upper Peninsula Hall of Fame, 1998. Office: Mich State U Athletic Dept 222 Breslin Ctr Jensen Fieldhouse East Lansing MI 48824

JABERG, EUGENE CARL, theology educator, administrator; b. Linton, Ind., Mar. 27, 1927; s. Elmer Charles and Hilda Carolyn (Stuckmann) J.; m. Miriam Marie Priebe; children: Scott Christian, Beth Amy, David Edward. BA, Lakeland Coll., 1948; BD, Mission House Theol. Sem., 1954; MA, U. Wis., 1959, PhD, 1968. Ordained to ministry, United Ch. of Christ, 1959. Staff announcer WKOW-TV, Madison, Wis., 1955-58, 67-68; minister Pilgrim Congl. Ch., 1956-57; assoc. prof. speech Mission House Theol. Sem., Plymouth, Wis., 1958-62; asst. prof. communications United Theol. Sem., New Brighton, Minn., 1962-76, prof. communications, 1976-91, dir. admissions, 1984-87, dir. MDiv program, 1988-90, prof. emeritus, 1991—, acting dir. Masters programs, 1997-99. Bus. ptnr. Dimension 3 Media Svcs., Mpls., 1988-90; coord. spl. projects CTV North Suburbs Cable Access, 1992-2002; vis. scholar Cambridge U., Eng. Author, editor: A History of Lakeland-Mission House, 1962; author: The Video Pencil, 1980; contbr. articles, revs. to various publs.; producer films, videotapes. Artistic dir. Interfaith Players, Mpls., 1965-73; TV producer, moderator Town Meeting of Twin Cities, Mpls., 1967-70; producer, writer, host various radio and TV series, Mpls., 1970—; mem. Ctr. Urban Encounter, Mpls., 1972-74, New Brighton Human Rights Commn., 1975-77; bd. mem. office communications United Ch. Christ, N.Y.C., 1975-81; mem. North Suburban System Cable Access Commn., 1986-91. Corr. U.S. Army, 1949-50. Kaltenborn Radio scholar, 1957; grantee Assn. Theol. Sems., 1983; recipient Minn. Community TV award, 1993, Judges Choice award Alliance of Cmty. Media, 1999; named into Gallery of Distinction Lakeland Coll., 1996— Mem. Religious Speech Communication Assn. (co-chmn. 1972-74), World Assn. Christian Communication. Democrat. Avocations: travel, hiking, spectator sports, film. Home: 1601 Innsbruck Dr Minneapolis MN 55432-6046 Office: United Theol Sem 3000 5th St NW Saint Paul MN 55112-2507 E-mail: ecjaberg@aol.com., gjaberg@ctv15.org.

JABLONSKI, ROBERT LEO, architect; b. Chgo., Mar. 28, 1926; s. Leo Frank and Rose (Domian) J. BS, U. Ill., 1950. Lic. architect Nat. Coun. Archtl. Registration Bd., 1965. Chief planner Nat. Council YMCA, Chgo., 1957-64; assoc. univ. architect U. Ill., 1964-69; coordinator architect U. Chgo., 1969-70; dir. bldg. program City of Chgo., 1970-88; prin. Robert Jablonski Mgmt. Svcs., architect, Chgo., 1988—. Served with U.S. Army, 1940-46, ETO. Roman Catholic. Avocations: tennis, swimming.

JACHE, ALBERT WILLIAM, retired chemistry educator, scientist; b. Manchester, N.H., Nov. 5, 1924; s. William Frederick and Esther (Ruemely) J.; m. Lucy Ellen Hauslein, June 14, 1948; children: Ann Gail, Ellen Ruth, Philip William, Heidi Verena. BS, U. N.H., 1948, MS, 1950; PhD, U. Wash., 1952. Sr. chemist Air Reduction Co., Murray Hill, N.J., 1952-53; rsch. assoc. dept. physics Duke U., 1953-55; asst. prof. dept. chemistry Tex. A&M U., College Station, 1955-58, assoc. prof., 1958-61; cons. Ozark Mahoning Co., Tulsa, 1960-61, assoc. rsch. dir., 1961-64; sr. rsch. assoc. Olin Mathieson Chem. Corp. (now Olin Corp.), New Haven, 1964-67, sect. mgr., 1965-67, cons., 1967-75; prof. chemistry Marquette U., Milw., 1967-90, prof. emeritus, 1990—, chmn. chem. dept., 1967-72, dean Grad. Sch., 1972-77, assoc. acad. v.p. for health scis., 1974-77, assoc. v.p.-acad. affairs, 1977-85; scientist-in-residence Argonne (Ill.) Nat. Lab., 1985-86, scientist, 1991-96, temporary appointment, 1991-96; with Chem. Lab., 2000—. Program coordination com. Med. Center S.E. Wis.; lectr. U. Tulsa, 1963-64, New Haven Coll., 1967; cons. Allied Chem. Corp., 1977-78, 2000-; salt panel com. remediation buried and tank wastes NAS/NRC, 1996-97. Trustee Milw. Sci. Ednl. Found.; pres. Milw. Sci. Ednl. Trust, 1973—; trustee Argonne Univs. Assn., 1977-80; chmn. Assn. Grad. Schs. in Cath. Univs., 1973-75; mem. AUA nuclear engrng. edn. com. U. Chgo, 1977-89, chmn., 1984, sec., 1989; double bass player River Cities Symphony Orch., Evergreen Comty. Orch., 1997-2001, Evergreen String Ensemble, 1994-2000, Marietta Chamber Orch., 1994-97. With AUS, 1943-46. Fellow AAAS, Am. Inst. Chemists; mem. Am. Chem. Soc. (chmn.-elect, program chmn. div. fluorine chemistry 1981, chmn. div. fluorine chemistry 1982), Sigma Xi, Omicron Kappa Upsilon, Alpha Sigma Nu. Achievements include research and numerous patents in the area of inorganic fluorine chemistry with emphasis on anhydrous hydrogen fluoride as a solvent or reaction medium and Hypofluorite chemistry. Home: 301 Ohio St Marietta OH 45750-3139 Office: Marquette U Dept Chemistry Milwaukee WI 53233

JACHNA, JOSEPH DAVID, photographer, educator; b. Chgo., Sept. 12, 1935; m. Virginia Kemper, 1962; children: Timothy, Heidi, Jody. BS in Art Edn., Inst. Design, Ill. Inst. Tech., 1958, MS in Photography, 1961. Part-time photographic asst. Derwin Studio Darkroom, Chgo., 1953-54; photo-technician Eastman Kodak Labs., 1954; photographer's asst. DeSort Studio, 1956-58; free-lance photographer, 1961—; instr. photography Inst. Design, Ill. Inst. Tech., 1961—69; assoc. prof. U. Ill., 1969—75, prof., 1976—2001, prof. emeritus, 2001—. One-man shows include Art Inst. Chgo., 1961, St. Mary's Coll., Notre Dame, Ind., 1963, U. Ill., Chgo., 1965, 77, Lightfall Gallery Art Ctr., Evanston, Ill., 1970, U. Wis., Milw., 1970, Ctr. for Photog. Studies, Louisville, 1974, Nikon Photog. Salon, Tokyo, 1974, Afterimage Gallery, Dallas, 1975, Visual Studies Workshop Gallery, Rochester, N.Y., 1979, Chgo. Ctr. for Contemporary Photography, 1980, Focus Gallery, San Francisco, 1981, Photogenesis, Albuquerque, 1983, Andover (Mass.) Gallery, 1984, Chgo. State U., 1985, Tweed Mus. Art, Duluth, Minn., 1986, Gallery 954, Chgo., 1993, State of Ill. Galleries, Chgo., Lockport and Springfield, 1994, Fermilab, Batavia, Ill., 1995, Stephen Daiter Gallery, Chgo., 2000; exhibited in group shows at Art Inst. Chgo, 1963, 83, MIT, Cambridge, 1968, Walker Art Ctr., Mpls., 1973, 89, Renaissance Soc. Gallery U. Chgo., 1975, Mus. Contemporary Art, Chgo., 1977, 96—, Mus. Art RISD, Providence, 1978, Carpenter Ctr. Visual Arts, Harvard U., Cambridge, 1981, Nexus, Atlanta, 1983, Nat. Mus. Art., Washington, 1984, San Francisco Mus. Modern Art, 1985, Internat. Ctr. Photography, Tucson, 1992, Gallery 312, Chgo., 1996, Stockholm Subway, Sweden, 1999, Hyde Park Art Ctr., Chgo., 2001, Stephen Daiter Gallery, Chgo., 2002, Taken by Design: Photography at the Inst. fo Design, 1957-1971, 2002; represented in permanent collections, Mus. Modern Art, N.Y.C., Internat. Mus. Photography, George Eastman House, Rochester, N.Y., MIT, San Francisco Mus. Modern Art, Mpls. Inst. Arts, Art Inst. Chgo., Ctr. Photog. Studies, Louisville, Ctr. for Creative Photography, U. Ariz., Tucson. Ferguson Found. grantee, 1973; Nat. Endowment for Arts grantee, 1976; Ill. Arts Council, 1979; Guggenheim fellow, 1980 Home: 5707 W 89 Pl Oak Lawn IL 60453-1225 E-mail: iceman@uic.edu.

JACKMAN, ROBERT N. state legislator, veterinarian; b. Rushville, Ind., Feb. 7, 1943; m. Karen Jackman; 2 children. DVM, Purdue U., 1967. Vet., prin. Jackman Animal Clinic, Milroy, Ind.; mem. Ind. Senate from 42nd dist., Indpls., 1996—; mem. agrl. and small bus. com. Ind. Senate, mem. govtl. and regulatory affairs com., mem. transp. and interstate coop. com., mem. natural resources com. Mem. Milroy United Meth. Ch.; past pres. Milroy Econ. Devel. Com.; pres. Anderson Twp. Regional Sewer Dist.; mem. Rushville County Sch. Bldg. Coop. Mem. AVMA, Ind. Vet. Med. Assn., Am. Assn. Bovine Practitioners, Am. Assn. Swine Practitioners, Milroy Cmty. Club (Citizen of Yr. 1983, 91), Milroy Coyote Club (Man of Yr. 1981), Masons (past master # 139 club). Republican. Office: 200 W Washington St Indianapolis IN 46204-2728

JACKSON, BILLY MORROW, artist, retired art educator; b. Kansas City, Mo., Feb. 23, 1926; s. Alonzo David and Opal May (Morrow) J.; m. Blanche Mary Trice, June 12, 1949 (div. Jan. 1988); children: Lon Allan, Robin Jackson Todd, Aron Drew, Sylvia Marie; m. Siti Mariah, Feb. 1988. BFA, Washington U., St. Louis, 1949; MFA, U. Ill., 1954. Prof. art U. Ill., Champaign, 1954-87, ret., 1987. One man show Jane Haslem Gallery, Washington, 1990; represented in permanent collections at Smithsonian Inst., Washington, Nat. Gallery of Art, Washington, NASA Archives, Washington, Union League Club Chgo., Boston Pub. Libr., Met. Mus. Art, N.Y.C., Mus. of Legion of Honor, San Francisco, Libr. of Congress, Washington, Springfield (Mo.) Art Mus., Conn. Acad. of Fine Arts, Hartford, Artist's Guild, St. Louis, Phila., Free Libr., Evansville (Ind.) Mus. of Arts & Scis., Joslyn Art Mus., Omaha, Norfolk Mus., Omaha, Reading (Pa.) Pub. Libr. and Art Gallery, Lakeview Ctr. of Art, Peoria, Ill., Butler Inst. Am. Art, Youngstown, Ohio, Civic Ctr. Art Collection, Springfield, Ill., N.Y. Hilton, N.Y.C., Ill. State Mus., Springfield, World Book Ency., Chgo., Rockefeller Ctr., Dulin Gallery of Art, Knoxville, Tenn., Swope Mus., Terre Haute, Ind., Bur. of Peclamation, Washington, EPA, Washington, Krannert Art Mus., U. Ill., Champaign, Wichita (Kans.) Art Mus., Gov.'s State Coll., Park Forest South, Ill., Champaign Nat. Bank, Parkland Coll., Champaign, Sheldon Meml. Gallery of Art, U. Nebr., Lincoln, Busey First Nat. Bank, Champaign, 1st Nat. Bank, Champaign, Swanlund Bldg., Bechmann Inst., U. Ill., Champaign, Keday (Malaysia) State Mus.; commd. mural state Capitol Bldg., Springfield, Ill., Mara Inst. of Tech., Malaysia, Ill. Sch. for Deaf, Jacksonville, Quincy (Ill.) Vet. Hosp. and Home, Carle Hosp. Edn. Bldg., Urbana, Ill., Mural Agr. Libr., U. Ill., Champaign; subject of book Billy Morrow Jackson: Interpretations ot Time and Light (Howard E. Wooden), 1990, In Our Time, 1997, Krannert Art Mus., Champaign, Ill. Pvt. USMC, 1944—46, Okinawa. Democrat. Home: 706 W White St Champaign IL 61820-4706

JACKSON, CAROL E. federal judge; BA, Wellesley Coll., 1973; JD, U. Mich., 1976. With Thompson & Mitchell, St. Louis, 1976-83; counsel Mallinckrodt, Inc., 1983-85; magistrate U.S. Dist. Ct., Ea. Dist. Mo., 1986-92, dist. judge, 1992—. Adj. prof. law Washington U., St. Louis, 1989-92. Trustee St. Louis Art Mus., 1987-91; dir. bi-state chpt. ARC, 1989-91, Mo. Bot. Garden. Mem. Nat. Assn. Women Judges, Fed. Magistrate Judges Assn., Mo. Bar, St. Louis County Bar Assn., Bar Assn. Metro. St. Louis, Mound City Bar Assn., Lawyers Assn. St. Louis. Office: US Courthouse 1114 Market St Rm 812 Saint Louis MO 63101-2034

JACKSON, DARREN RICHARD, retail company executive; b. Detroit, Nov. 13, 1964; s. Richard Dennis and Connie May (Ellis) J.; m. Terry Ann Hall, May 28, 1988; children: Ryan David, Bridget Caffrey. BS in Acctg., Marquette U., 1986. CPA, Wis. Supr. KPMG Peat Marwick, Milw., 1985-89; dir. fin. reporting Carson, Pirie, Scott & Co., 1989-90, dir. treasury svcs., 1990-91, v.p., treas., CFO, 1992-1998; CFO, Full-line Store Div. Nordstrom, Inc.; sen. v.p. fin. & treas. Best Buy Co., Inc., Mpls., 2000-2001, CFO, 2001—. Office: Best Buy Co 7075 Flying Cloud Dr Eden Prairie MN 55344

JACKSON, DAVID D. state legislator; b. Topeka, Nov. 7, 1946; m. Annette Sorbeck; children: Chad, Traci. BS, Kans. State U., 1968. Housing mgmt. specialist HUD, 1971-83; v.p. Midwest Mgmt., Inc., 1983-85; pres. Jackson's Greenhouse & Garden Ctr., Inc., 1985—; mem. Kans. State Senate, 2000—. Bd. dirs. Seaman Unified Sch. Dist.-345 Sch. Bd., 1983-95; pres. Sunrise Optimist Club North Topeka, 1985-86, North Topeka on the Move, Inc., 1997—; comdr. Sons Am. Legion Post 400, 1985-86; clk. Soldier Twp. Bd., 1994—; v.p. North Topeka Bus. Alliance, 1998—; mem. Neighborhood Element Adv. Com. to the Topeka Shawnee County Consolidated Plan for 2025, 1999. Republican. Lutheran. Home: 2815 NE Rockaway Trail Topeka KS 66617 Office: State Capitol Rm 458-E Topeka KS 66612 Fax: 785-233-6348. E-mail: djack66617@networksplus.net.

JACKSON, DON, radio personality; Radio host WMJI, Independence, Ohio. Office: WMKI 6200 Oak Tree Blvd 4th Fl Cleveland OH 44131

JACKSON, EDGAR B., JR. medical educator; b. Rison, Ark., May 30, 1935; m. Thelma Jackson, 1957; children: Gary, David, Michael, Laura. BA, Case Western Res. U., 1962, MD, 1966. Intern Cleve. Met. Gen. Hosps., 1966-67, chief resident medicine, 1969-70; from sr. instr. medicine to asst. prof. to asst. clin. prof. Case Western Res. U., 1970-83, assoc. clin. prof., 1983-86, clin. prof. medicine, 1986—; chief of staff, sr. v.p. for clin. affairs Univ. Hosps. of Cleve. Asst. dean Case Western Res. U., 1971-74, asst. prof. comty. medicine, 1974-79, comty. health, 1977-88. Contbr. numerous articles to profl. jours. With U.S. Army, 1959-61. Carnegie Common Wealth Clin. scholar, 1970-72. Mem. APHA, Am. Sickle Cell Anemia Assn. Inc. Office: Univ Hosp 11100 Euclid Ave Cleveland OH 44106-1736

JACKSON, ERIC C. executive; Pres., CEO Internet, Inc., Milford, Ohio, 1999—. Office: Internet Inc 400 Techne Center Dr Ste 200 Milford OH 45150-2746

JACKSON, G. JAMES, protective services official; b. Columbus, Ohio; Student, Harvard U., Ohio State U., Northwestern U., FBI Acad. Patrolman Columbus Divsn. Police, 1958-67, sgt., 1967-71, lt., 1971-74, capt., 1974-77, dep. chief, 1977-90, chief, 1990—. With USMC. Office: Office Chief Police 120 Marconi Blvd Columbus OH 43215-2376

JACKSON, GREGORY WAYNE, orthodontist; b. Chgo., Sept. 4, 1950; s. Wayne Eldon and Marilyn Frances (Anderson) J.; m. Nora Ann Echtner, Mar. 17, 1973; children: Eric, David. Student, U. Ill., 1968-70; DDS with honors, U. Ill., Chgo., 1974; MSD, U. Wash., 1978. Practice dentistry specializing in orthodontics, Chgo., 1978—. Instr. orthodontic dept. U. Ill. Coll. Dentistry, Chgo., 1978-81. Coach Little League Baseball, Oak Brook, Ill., 1986-89. Served to lt. USN, 1974-76. Mem. ADA, Ill. State Dental Soc., Chgo. Dental Soc., Am. Assn. Orthodontists, Midwestern Soc. Orthodontists, Ill. Soc. Orthodontists, Omicron Kappa Upsilon. Evangelical. Avocations: golf, tennis, skiing. Office: 6435 S Pulaski Rd Chicago IL 60629-5148

JACKSON, ISAIAH, conductor; b. Richmond, Va., Jan. 22, 1945; s. Isaiah Allen and Alma Alverta (Norris) J.; m. Helen Tuntland, Aug. 6, 1977; children: Benjamin, Katharine, Caroline BA cum laude, Harvard U., 1966; MA, Stanford U., 1967; MS, Juilliard Sch. Music, 1969, DMA, 1973; DM (honoris causa), U. Dayton, 1999. Founder, condr. Juilliard String Ensemble, N.Y.C., 1970-71; asst. condr. Am. Symphony Orch., 1970-71, Balt. Symphony Orch., 1971-73; assoc. condr. Rochester (N.Y.) Philharmonic Orch., 1973-87; music dir. Dayton (Ohio) Philharm. Orch., 1987-95, 1987-95; prin. condr. Royal Ballet, Covent Garden, London, 1986, music dir., 1987-90; prin. guest condr. Queensland (Australia) Symphony Orch., 1993-96; music dir. Youngstown (Ohio) Symphony, 1996—, Pro Arte Chamber Orch. Boston, 2000—. Prin. guest condr. Canberra (Australia) Symphony Orch., 1996-98; guest condr. N.Y. Philharm. Orch., 1978, Boston Pops Orch., 1983, 90-94, Detroit Symphony Orch., 1983, 85, San Francisco Symphony, 1984, Toronto Symphony, 1984, 90, Orch. de la Suisse Romande, 1985, 88, BBC Concert Orch., 1987, Berlin Symp hony, 1989-95, Dallas Symphony, 1993, Royal Liverpool Philharm., 1995, Houston Symphony, 1995; numerous recordings for

Koch, Ivory Classics and Australian Broadcasting Corp. Recipient First Gov.'s award for arts in Va., Commonwealth Va., 1979, Signet Soc. medal for the arts Harvard U., 1991. Office: Thea Dispeker Inc 59 E 54th St New York NY 10022-4211

JACKSON, JAMES SIDNEY, psychology educator; b. Detroit, July 30, 1944; s. Pete James and Johnnie Mae (Wilson) J. BS, Mich. State U., 1966; MA, U. Toledo, 1970; PhD, Wayne State U., 1972. Probation counselor Lucas County Juvenile Ct., Toledo, 1967-68; tchg. and rsch. asst. Wayne State U., Detroit, 1968-71; from asst. prof. to prof. psychology U. Mich., Ann Arbor, 1971—, faculty assoc. Rsch. Ctr. Group Dynamics, 1971—, dir. Rsch. Ctr. Group Dynamics, 1996—, rsch. scientist, 1986—, faculty assoc. Inst. Gerontology, 1976—, faculty assoc. Ctr. Afro-Am. and African Studies, 1982—, dir. Ctr. Afro-Am. and African Studies, 1998—, assoc. dean Rackham Sch. Grad. Studies, 1987-92, prof. pub. health, 1990—, dir. program for rsch. on Black Ams., 1976—, Daniel Katz Disting. Univ. prof. psychology, 1995—, Daniel Katz Collegiate prof., 1994-95; Hill Disting. vis. prof. U. Minn., 1995. Chair sociol. psychology tng. program U. Mich., 1980-86, 93-96; cons. Emergency Sch. Aid Project, 1973-74, Commn. on Equal Opportunity in Psychology, 1970, Project to Provide Psychol. Svcs. to Head Start Programs, 1973-74, European Econ. Commn. Project on Racism, Xenophobia and Immigration, 1989—; mem. com. on aging and com. on status of Black Ams., NAS; mem. com. on African Am. Population Year 2000 and 2010 U.S. Census Bur.; mem. nat. adv. com. Boston Mus. Sci., 1998—; mem. Nat. Adv. Coun. on Aging, NIH, 1996-99; mem. bd. sci. counselors, Nat. Inst. Aging; invited rschr. Ecole des Hautes Etudes en Scis. Sociales, Paris, 1992—; disting. lectr. gerontology UCLA, 1992; mem. steering com. Nat. Acad. Aging Soc., 1995—. Author: The Black American Elderly: Research on Physical and Psychosocial Health, 1988, African American Elderly, 2d edit., 1997, (with Gurin P., Hatchett S.) Hope and Independence: Blacks Response to Electoral and Party Politics, 1989, Life in Black America, 1991, (with Chatters L., Taylor R.) Aging in Black America, 1993, (with H. Neighbors) Mental Health in Black America, 1996, (with R. Taylor and L. Clatters) Family Life in Black America, 1997, (with R. Gibson) Health in Black America, 1998; editor: New Directions: African Americans in a Diversifying Nation, 2000; editl. cons. Jour. Behavioral and Social Scientists; editl. bd. Jour. Gerontology, Applied Social Psychology Ann., Psychol. Bull., Jour. Social Issues; cons. editor Psychology and Aging; contbr. articles to profl. jours. Bd. dirs. Pub. Commn. on Mental Health, Ronald McDonald House, Ann Arbor, 1993—; bd. trustees Greenhills Sch., Ann Arbor, 1997—. Recipient Disting. Faculty Svc. award U. Mich., 1976, Harold R. Johnson Diversity Svc. award U. Mich., 2000; Urban Studies fellow Wayne State U., 1969-70; NSF fellow, 1969; Sr. Postdoctoral fellow Groupe d'Études et de Recherches sur la Science, École des Hautes Études en Sciences Sociales, 1986-87; Sr. Ford Found. Minority Postdoctoral fellow, 1986-87; Fogarty Sr. Internat. fellow, 1993-94; Robert W. Kleemeier award for rsch., Gerontol. Soc. Am. Fellow APA (divs. 9-20, policy and planning bd., fin. com. 1984-86, award for early contbns. 1983, Tenth Anniversary Peace and Social Justice award Soc. for the Study of Peace, Conflict and Violence, Peace Psychology divsn. 2000, com. on internat. relations, 1999-02, cahir 2001-02, Disting. Career Contbns. ro Rsch. award Divsn. 45, 2001), Am. Psychol. Soc., Gerontol. Soc. Am. (task force on minority issues in gerontology, chmn. 1988-92, ann. sci. conv. program com.); mem. AAAS (chair-elect sect. social, econ. and polit. scis.), Assn. Advancement of Psychology (trustee 1973-89, chmn. 1978-80), Black Students Psychol. Assn. (nat. chmn. 1970-71), Assn. Black Psychologists (nat. chmn. 1972-73), Soc. Psychol. Study of Social Issues, World Future Soc., Assn. Behavioral and Social Scientists, Gerontol. Soc. Am. (chair behavioral and social scis. sect. 1997-98), Internat. Platform Assn., NIMH (nat. mental health coun. 1989-93, panel on equal access com. on instl. cooperation 1989-92), Psi Chi, Alpha Phi Alpha. Home: 340 Orchard Hills Dr Ann Arbor MI 48104-1832 Office: U Mich 5110 Inst Social Rsch 426 Thompson St Ann Arbor MI 48104-2321

JACKSON, JANET ELIZABETH, city attorney, association executive; b. Randolph, Va. d. Robert and Joan (Morton) J.; 1 child, Harrison Michael Sewell. BA, Wittenberg U., 1975; JD, George Washington U., 1978. Bar: Ohio 1978, U.S. Dist. Ct. (so. dist.) Ohio 1979, U.S. Dist. Ct. (no. dist.) Ohio 1983. Asst. atty. gen. Office Ohio Atty. Gen., Columbus, 1978-80, chief crime victims compensation sect., 1980-82, chief workers compensation and civil rights sects., 1983-87; with Sindell, Sindell & Rubenstein, Cleve., 1982-83; judge Franklin County Mcpl. Ct., Columbus, 1987-97; city atty. City of Columbus, 1997—. Atty. gen.'s ethics and profl. responsibility adv. coun.; joint task force gender bias Ohio Supreme Ct. and Ohio State Bar Assn.; mem. com. to study impact of substance abuse on cts., Supreme Ct., 1989-90. Chair bd. trustees YWCA, 1988-95; vice-chair bd. trustees, mem. exec. com. United Way Franklin County; chair Right from the Start Community Forum; bd. dirs. Met. Women's Ctr., 1980-86, S.E. Community Mental Health Ctr., 1987, Columbus Urban League, 1987-90, Maryhaven, 1987-89, Riverside Meth. Hosp.; trustee Wittenberg U.; chair task force child care City of Columbus; vol. Columbus Pub. Schs.; past mem., chairperson Minority Task force on AIDS; mem. AIDS community adv. coalition, 1987-90, task force domestic violence, 1988; mem. svc. team Explorer Divsn. Boy Scouts Am.; trustee Franklin U. Recipient Sharon Wilkin award Met. Women's Ctr., Dr. Martin Luther King Jr. Humanitarian award Love Acad., 1987, Polit. Leadership award 29th Dist. Citizens' Caucus, 1987, Citizenship award Omega Psi Phi, 1987, Outstanding Accomplishments award Franklin County Dem. Women, 1988, Community Svc. award Met. Dem. Women's Club, 1989, Warren Jennings award Franklin County Mental Health Bd., 1989, Martin Luther King Jr. Humanitarian award Columbus Edn. Assn., 1991, Women of Achievement award YWCA, 1992, Citizen's award Columbus Assn. Edn. Young Children, 1993, Citations award Pi Lambda Theta, 1993, Blue Chip award Social Svcs., 1994, Peacemaker award Choices, David D. White award Black Alumni Assn. Capitol Law Sch., Cmty. Svc. award Columbus-Franklin County AFL-CIO. Mem. Internat. Mcpl. Lawyers Assn. (state chmn., mem. steering com. legislation and pub. policy and mgmt.), Nat. Conf. Black Lawyers (Disting. Barrister award 1988, John Mercer Langston award 1994), Ohio State Bar Assn. (coun. dels. 1993—, commn. racial and ethnic fairness, bd. govs. women in the profession sect.), Columbus Bar Assn., Women Lawyers Franklin County, The Links, Inc. (pres. Twin Rivers chpt. 1992-94), Columbus Mortar Bd. Alumni Club, Golden Key Nat. Honor Soc. (hon.). Office: Columbus City Atty City Hall 90 W Broad St Rm 200 Columbus OH 43215-9013

JACKSON, JESSE L., JR. congressman; b. Greenville, S.C., Mar. 11, 1965; m. Sandra Jackson. BS, N.C A&T U., 1987; MA, Chgo. Theol. Sem.; JD, U. Ill., 1993. Mem. U.S. Congress from 2d Ill. dist., Washington, 1995—, mem. house appropriations com., 1997—. Baptist. Office: US Ho of Reps 313 Cannon Office Bldg Washington DC 20515-0001*

JACKSON, JOHN CHARLES, retired secondary education educator, writer; b. Columbus, Ohio, Mar. 12, 1939; s. John Franklin and Mari Jane (Lusch) J.; m. Carol Nancy Tiggelbeck, June 24, 1990. Tchr. social studies Buckeye Local Sch., West Mansfield, Ohio, 1961-62, Grandview Heights (Ohio) City Schs., 1962-91; ret., 1991. Cooperating tchr. Project Bus. program Jr. Achievement, Grandview, 1984-91. Recipient Career Tchr. award Ohio State U. Coll. Edn. Alumni Soc., 1995; Martha Holden Jennings Found. scholar, 1968-69. Mem. Ohio Ret. Tchrs. Assn. (life.), Franklin County Ret. Tchrs. Assn. (life), Ohio State U. Alumni Assn. (life), Am. Mensa Ltd. Republican. Methodist. Avocations: reading, tennis, college football. Home: 5741 Aspendale Dr Columbus OH 43235-7506

JACKSON, MARCUS, electric power industry executive; Engr. Kansas City Power and Light Co., 1974-80, with, 1983—, asst. dir. power supply, sr. dir. power supply, v.p. power prodn., sr. v.p. power supply, exec. v.p., COO, 1996-99, exec. v.p., CFO, 1999—; project engr. Provo Arabia Ltd., Saudi Arabia, 1980-83. Pres., chmn. bd. KLT Power, Inc. Office: Kansas City Power & Light Co PO Box 418679 Kansas City MO 67201-8679

JACKSON, MARION LEROY, agronomist, soil scientist; b. Reynolds, Nebr., Nov. 30, 1914; s. Cleve L. and Belle Josephine (Hanson) J.; m. Chrystie Marie Bertramson, Sept. 2, 1937; children— Marjorie Lee, Virginia Lynn (Mrs. Bruce P. Conlon), Stanley Bertram, Douglas Mark. B.S. maxima cum laude with high distinction, U. Nebr., 1936, M.S., 1937, D.Sc. (hon.), 1974; Ph.D., U. Wis., 1939. Land classification aide U.S. Dept. Agr., Lincoln, Nebr., 1936-37; grad. research asst. U. Wis., Madison, 1937-39, postdoctoral fellow, 1939-41, instr., 1941-42, asst. prof., 1942-45, asso. prof., 1946-50, prof., 1950-74, Franklin Hiram King Disting. prof. emeritus, 1974—. Chemist Purdue U., 1945-46; vis. prof. Cornell U., 1959; disting. vis. prof. U. Wash., Seattle, 1973; mem. panel on disposition radioactive wastes Nat. Acad. Scis., 1976-77; lectr. U.S., Canadian govts., numerous univs. Author: Soil Chemical Analysis, 1958, Soil Chemical Analysis-Advanced Course, 1956, 2d edit., 1969; contbr. articles to profl. jours. Troop chmn. Four Lakes council Boy Scouts Am., 1965, scoutmaster, 1966. Recipient Soil Sci. Achievement award, 1958, Bouyoucos Soil Sci. Disting. Career award, 1986. Fellow AAAS, Am. Soc. Agronomy, Nat. Acad. Sci., Soil Sci. Soc. Am. (past pres.; Disting. Mem. award 1983, Career award 1986), Mineral Soc. Am.; mem. Clay Minerals Soc. (past pres., Disting. Mem. award 1977), Internat. Soc. Soil Sci., Nat. Acad. Sci., Mineral Soc. London, Phi Beta Kappa, Sigma Xi, Phi Lambda Upsilon, Alpha Zeta, Gamma Sigma Delta, Pi Mu Epsilon. Home: 309 Ozark Trl Madison WI 53705-2534 Office: U Wis 1525 Observatory Dr Madison WI 53706-1207

JACKSON, MICHAEL B. service company executive; Pres., CEO Specialized Svcs. Inc., Southfield, Mich., 1988—. Office: Specialized Svcs Inc 23077 Greenfield Rd Ste 470 Southfield MI 48075-3736 Fax: 248-557-0755.

JACKSON, MONICA DENEE, purchasing agent; b. Detroit, Aug. 18, 1966; d. Arthur James and Nossie Lucille Jackson. BS in Mktg., Bus. Logistics, Wayne State U., Detroit, 1999. Credit supr. 1st of Am. Bank, S.E. Mich., Detroit, 1990—93; fin. clk. County of Wayne, 1995—2000, purchasing agt., 2000—. Vol., Meals on Wheels, Detroit. Mem.: Nat. Assn. Purchasing Mgrs. Baptist. Avocation: bowling. Personal E-mail: jacksonmdj@hotmail.com. Business E-Mail: jacksonmdj@hotmail.com.*

JACKSON, PAUL HOWARD, multimedia producer, educator, minister, minister; b. Topeka, Nov. 10, 1952; s. Dwight Stover and Janice Ilona (Woeltje) J.; m. Elizabeth Ann McGhghy, July 23, 1977; children: Christopher, Jeremy, Catherine, Johanna, Caleb. BA, Washburn U., 1973; MLS, Emporia State U., 1974; MDiv, Concordia Sem., Clayton, Mo., 1979; postgrad., Ind. U., 1993-96; STM, Concordia Theol. Sem., Ft. Wayne, Ind., 1995. Ordained to ministry Luth. Ch.-Mo. Synod, 1979. Pastor St. Paul's Luth. Ch., Wakefield, Nebr., 1979-81, 1st Trinity Luth. Ch., Wayne, 1979-81; libr., tchr. Luth. High. Sch. Indpls., 1981-82; libr., prof. St. John's Coll., Winfield, Kans., 1982-85; libr. Winfield (Kans.) Pub. Library, 1985-88; pastor 1st Luth. Ch., Pond Creek, Okla., 1986-88; libr. Concordia Theol. Sem., Ft. Wayne, Ind., 1988-96; multimedia prodr. Concordia Publ. House, St. Louis, 1996-2000; pastor St. Paul Luth. Ch., Texhoma, Okla., 2000—. Adj. prof. Concordia U. Wis., Mequon, 1995-2000. Prodr. W3 Word Witness Worship, 1998-2000, Concordia Self-Study CD-ROM, Concordia Electronic Theological Libr., Luther's Works on CD-ROM; contbr. articles to religious jours. Bd. dirs. Trinity Ch. S.E. Asian Mission, Winfield, 1984-86, Wash. Luth. Sch. Assn., 1997-98, v.p. 1997-98; co-chair Winfield Com. for Commemorating the Bicentennial of the Constn., Winfield, 1987-88; chmn. Coalition for Purchase and Renovation, St. John's Coll., Winfield, 1988; sec., treas. exec. com. Area 3 Libr. Svc. Authority, Ft. Wayne, 1990-93; organizer Texhoma Christmas Effort, 2000-02. Mem. Rotary Internat., Phi Kappa Phi, Mu Alpha Pi. Republican. Home: RR 1 Box 114F Texhoma OK 73949-9730 Office: St Paul Luth Ch PO Box 465 Texhoma OK 73949 E-mail: stpaul@ptsi.net.

JACKSON, REBECCA R. lawyer; b. Ark., 1942; BA magna cum laude, St. Louis U., 1975, JD, 1978. Bar: Mo. 1978, Ill. 1979. Ptnr. Bryan Cave, St. Louis. Mem. ABA. Office: Bryan Cave One Met Sq 211 N Broadway Saint Louis MO 63102-2733

JACKSON, VALERIE PASCUZZI, radiologist, educator; b. Oakland, Calif., Aug. 25, 1952; d. Chris A. Pascuzzi and Janice (Mayne) Pacuzzi; 1 child Price Arthur III. AB, Ind. U., 1974, MD, 1978. Diplomate Am. Bd. Radiology. Intern, resident in diagnostic radiology Ind. U. Med. Ctr., 1978-82; from asst. prof. radiology to prof. radiology Ind. U. Sch. Medicine, Indpls., 1982-94, John A. Campbell prof. radiology, 1994—. Dir. residency program in radiology Ind. U. Sch. Medicine, 1994—; trustee Am. Bd. Radiology. Contbr. over 50 articles to profl. jours., chpts. to books. Fellow: Soc. Breast Imaging (pres. 1990—92), Am. Coll. Radiology (bd. chancellors, chair 3 coms.); mem.: AMA, Radiol. Soc. N.Am., Am. Roentgen Ray Soc., Am. Inst. Ultrasound in Medicine, Alpha Omega Alpha. Office: Indiana U Sch Med Dept Rad 1001 W 10th St Indianapolis IN 46202-2859

JACKWIG, LEE M. federal judge; b. 1950; BA, Loyola U. of Chgo., 1972; JD, DePaul U., 1975. Asst. atty. gen. State of Iowa, 1976-79, dep. indsl. commr., 1979-83; asst. U.S. atty. S.D. Iowa, Dept. Justice, 1983-86; bankruptcy judge U.S. Bankruptcy Ct. (so. dist.) Iowa, Des Moines, 1986—. Office: US Courthouse Annex 110 E Court Ave Ste 443 Des Moines IA 50309-2044

JACOB, BERNARD MICHEL, architect; b. Paris; naturalized; s. Paul and Therese (Abase) J.; m. Rosamond Gale Tryon; children: Clara, Paul. Diploma in architecture, Cooper Union; BArch, U. Minn. Registered architect, Minn. Sr. designer Ellerbe Assocs., St. Paul; head design Grover Dimond & Assocs.; co-founder Team 70 Architects, 1970—, pres., 1977—83, Bernard Jacob Architects Ltd., Mpls., 1983—. Mem. constrn. panel Am. Arbitration Assn., 1973— ; lectr. Sch. Architecture, U. Minn., Mpls., 1982— Editor: Architecture Minn. Mag., Minn. Soc. Architects, 1970-80; archtl. criticism columnist: Mpls. Star and Tribune, 1980-83, Corp. Report Mag., 1983; reviewer: (archtl. books) Choice Mag.; co-author: Skyway Typology/Mpls., Pocket Architecture/A Walking Guide to the Architecture Downtown Mpls. and St. Paul, 2d. rev. edit., 1988, Letters to Palladio, 1999. Founding chmn. Heritage Preservation Commn., St. Paul; past mem. St. Paul Planning Bd.; apptd. mem. Minn. State Designer Selection Bd., 1987-90; bd. dirs. Winslow House, 1995-97; chmn. archtl. subcom. Minn. Gov.'s Residence Coun., 1996-99. Fellow: AIA. Office: Bernard Jacob Architects Ltd 412 Foshay Tower 821 Marquette Ave Minneapolis MN 55402-2915 E-mail: palladio@skypoint.com.

JACOB, KEN, state legislator; b. St. Louis, Jan. 23, 1949; BS, U. Mo. Columbia. State rep. Dist. 25 Mo. Ho. of Reps., Jefferson City, 1983-96; mem. Mo. Senate from 19th dist., 1996—. Social worker.

JACOBI, FREDRICK THOMAS, newspaper publisher; b. Neenah, Wis., July 10, 1953; s. H. Paul and Patricia Mary (Steele) J.; m. Kim Lee Muenchow, Aug. 23, 1980; children: James Paul, Steven Thomas. AA in Bus., U. South Fla., 1973; BBA in Fin., Mktg., U. Wis., 1976; MBA in Mktg., U. Wis., Whitewater, 1980. Cert. newspaper circulation. City dist. mgr. Madison (Wis.) Newspapers Inc., 1977-79, city circulation mgr., 1979-80, circulation mgr., 1980-81, mktg. mgr., 1981-82, circulation dir., 1982-85, Gannett Co., Inc., Reno, 1985-88, regional circulation dir. Arlington, Va., 1988-90; pub., pres. Wausau (Wis.) Daily Herald, Gannett Co., Inc., 1990-92, Springfield (Mo.) News-Leader, 1993-96; v.p. Midwest region Gannett Co., Inc., 1993-96; pub., pres. Ft. Myers (Fla.) News-Press, 1996-2000, Rockford (Ill.) Register-Star, 2000—. Bd. dir. Coun. of 100, Rockford Coll., Inland Press Found.; com. chmn. Sales and Mktg. Exec., Madison, Ill., 1985. Editor Circulation-Central States, 1985. Program chmn. Jr. Achievement of Nev., Reno, 1987—88; pres. Springfield Bus. and Devel. Corp., 1996; bd. dir. Ozarks Press Assn., Make A Wish Mo., Horizon Econ. Devel. , 1997—2000, Lee County Pub. Schs. Found., 1997—2000. Mem.: Newspaper Assn. Am., Inland Press Assn., Ill. Press Assn., Young Pres.'s Orgn., The Exec. Com., Rotary. Republican. Roman Catholic. Avocations: micro-computers, running, gardening. Office: Rockford Register Star 99 E State St Rockford IL 61104

JACOBI, PETER PAUL, journalism educator, author; b. Berlin, Mar. 15, 1930; came to U.S., 1938, naturalized, 1944; s. Paul A. and Liesbeth (Kron) J.; m. Harriet Ackley, Dec. 8, 1956 (div. 1979); children: Keith Peter, John Wyn. BS in Journalism, Northwestern U., 1952, MS, 1953. Mem. journalism faculty Northwestern U., Evanston, Ill., 1955-81, profl. lectr., 1955-63, asst. prof., 1963-66, assoc. prof., 1966-69, prof. journalism, 1969-81, assoc. dean, 1966-74; communications cons. N.Y.C., 1980-84, Bloomington, Ind., 1985—; prof. journalism Ind. U., 1985-99, prof. emeritus, 1999. News assignment editor, newscaster, theatre and music reporter NBC, Chgo., 1955-61; news editor ABC, Chgo., 1951-53; radio commentator on music and opera, 1958-65; theatre and film critic Sta. WTTW, Chgo., 1964-74, arts critic, 1975-77; theatre and film critic Hollister Newspapers Suburban Chgo., 1963-70; music columnist Chicagoan mag., 1973-74; script cons. Goodman Theater, Chgo., 1973-75; syndicated commentator on arts and media N.Am. Radio Alliance, 1978-80; arts corr. Christian Sci. Monitor, 1956-81; music critic, columnist Bloomington (Ind.) Herald-Times, 1985—; columnist Arts Indiana, 1987—, Editors Only, 1994—, Editor's Workshop, 1995-98. Author: Writing with Style, The News Story and the Feature, 1982, The Messiah Book-The Life and Times of G.F. Handel's Greatest Hit, 1982, (with Jack Hilton) Straight Talk about Videoconferencing, 1986, The Magazine Article: How to Think It, Plan It, Write It, 1991, (with others) From Budapest to Bloomington, Janos Starker and the Hungarian Cello Tradition, 1999; contbg. essayist Lyric Opera Companion, 1991; editor Chgo. Lyric Opera News, 1958-61, Music Mag./Musical Courier, Chgo., 1961-62; contbr. articles on writing to Folio, Ragan Report, other mags., articles on arts to Sat. Rev., Chgo. Daily News, N.Y. Times, Highlights for Children, World Book, others. Mem. AAUP, NATAS, Assn. Edn. in Journalism, Soc. Profl. Journalists, Ind. Arts Commn. (chmn. 1990-93), Arts Midwest, Bloomington Arts Commn. Home: 3003 N Browncliff Ln Bloomington IN 47408-1317 Office: Ind U Sch Journalism Bloomington IN 47405

JACOBS, ALEXIS A. automobile company executive; With Columbus (Ohio) Fair Auto Auction, now owner, CEO, pres. Amb. Charity Newsies; mem. athletic dept. steering com. Ohio State U., Columbus; , also sponsor 3 athletic scholarships; bd. dirs. Salesian Boys and Girls Club, also former chmn. fundraising com.; formerly active Recreation Unltd., Dave Thomas Adoption Found. Three-Tour Challenge. Mem. Nat. Auto Auction Assn. (pres.). Office: Columbus Fair Auto Auction 4700 Groveport Rd Columbus OH 43207-5217 Fax: 614-497-1132.

JACOBS, ANDREW, JR. former congressman, educator; b. Indpls., Feb. 24, 1932; s. Andrew and Joyce Taylor (Wellborn) J.; m. Kim Hood; children: H.B. James Andrew, B.N. Steven Michael. B.S., Ind. U., 1955, LL.B., 1958. Bar: Ind. Practiced in Indpls., 1958-65, 73-74; mem. Ind. Ho. of Reps., 1958-60, 89th-92d congresses from 11th Dist., 1965-73, 94th-97th congresses from 11th Dist. Ind., 1975-83, 98th-103rd Congresses from 10th Dist. Ind., 1983-96. Ranking minority mem. ways & means subcom. on social security; adj. prof. Ind. U., 1996—. Author: The 1600 Killers: A Wake-Up Call for Congress, 1999. Served with USMC, 1950-52. Mem. Indpls. Bar Assn., Am. Legion. Democrat. Roman Catholic. Address: 1201 W 64th St Indianapolis IN 46260-4409

JACOBS, BRUCE E. business executive; Pres., CEO Grede Foundries, Milw., 1987—. Office: Grede Foundries PO Box 26499 9898 W Bluemound Rd Milwaukee WI 53226-4365 Fax: 414-256-9399.

JACOBS, DENNY, state legislator; b. Moline, Ill., Nov. 8, 1937; s. Oral G. and Caroline Harroun (Pinkerton) J.; m. Mary Ellen Duffy, June 10, 1955; children: Patricia, Denise, Elizabeth, Michael, J.P., Tory. BA, Augustana Coll., 1959. Co-owner J & J Music, 1966-82; mktg. dir. Group W Cable, 1985-86; mayor East Moline, Ill., 1973—; mem. Ill. State Senate, 1986—. Vice chmn. transp. com., mem. agr., conservation, energy and environment com., chmn. citizens coun. econ. devel., chmn. intergovt. com. Ill. State Senate. Mem. Moose, Elks (Disting. Citizen award 1986), Eagles, KC. Address: 3511 8th St East Moline IL 61244-3521 Also: 606 19th St Moline IL 61265-2142

JACOBS, DONALD P. dean emeritus, banking and finance educator; b. Chgo., June 22, 1927; s. David and Bertha (Nevod) J.; children: Elizabeth, Ann, David; m. Dinah Nemeroff, May 28, 1978. B.A., Roosevelt Coll., 1949; M.A., Columbia U., 1951, Ph.D., 1956. Mem. research staff Nat. Bur. Econ. Research, 1952-57; instr. Coll. City N.Y., 1955-57; mem. faculty to Morrison prof. fin. Northwestern U. Grad. Sch. Mgmt., 1970-78, chmn. dept., 1969-75, dean, 1975—, Gaylord Freeman Disting. prof. banking, 1978—. Bd. dirs. CDW Corp., Hartmarx Corp., Prologis Corp., Terex Corp., Conf. Savs. and Residential Financing; co-dir. fin. studies Presdl. Commn. Fin. Structure and Regulation, 1970-71; sr. economist banking and currency com. U.S. Ho. of Reps., 1963-64. Editor proc.: Conf. Savs. and Residential Financing, 1967, 68, 69; contbr. articles to profl. jours. Served with USNR, 1945-46. Ford Found. fellow, 1959-60, 63-64 Mem. Am. Econ. Assn., Am. Statis. Assn., Am. Fin. Assn., Econometrics Soc., Inst. Mgmt. Sci. Home: 617 Milburn St Evanston IL 60201-2407 Office: Northwestern Univ J L Kellogg Grad Sch Mgmt 2001 Sheridan Rd Evanston IL 60208-0814

JACOBS, DOUGLAS C. professional sports team executive; m. Georgia Jacobs; 3 children. BS, Miami U., Ohio; MBA, Case Western Res. U. CPA. Mng. ptnr. Arthur Andersen LLP, Cleve.; exec. v.p. Gucci Timepieces; exec. v.p. fin. The Cleve. Browns. Pres. Jr. Achievement Greater Cleve., Inc.; councilman Kirkland; chmn. Pacific Legan Found., Calif.; pres. Big Bros./Big Sisters Orange County; vice chmn. Orange County Performing Arts Ctr.; treas. Bowers Mus. Found. With USN. Office: The Cleveland Browns 76 Lou Groza Blvd Berea OH 44017*

JACOBS, FRANCIS ALBIN, biochemist, educator; b. Mpls., Feb. 23, 1918; s. Anthony and Agnes Ann (Stejskal) J.; m. Dorothy Caldwell, June 5, 1953; children: Christopher, Gregory, Paula, Margaret, John. BS, Regis Coll., Denver, 1939; postgrad, U. Denver, 1939-41; Fellow in Biochemistry, St. Louis U., 1941-49, PhD, 1949. Postdoctoral fellow Nat. Cancer Inst., Bethesda, Md., 1949-51; instr. physiol. chemistry U. Pitts. Sch. Medicine, 1951-52, asst. prof., 1952-54; asst. prof. biochemistry U. N.D. Sch. Medicine, Grand Forks, 1954-56, asso. prof., 1956-64, prof., 1964-87, prof. emeritus, 1987—. Dir., research supr. Nat. Sci. Research Participation Program in Biochemistry, 1959-63; advisor directorate for sci. edn. NSF. Contbr. articles to profl. jours. Mem. bishop's pastoral council Diocese of Fargo, N.D., 1979-86. Fellow AAAS, N.D. Acad. Sci. (editor 1967, 68); mem. Am. Soc. for Biochemistry and Molecular Biology, Am. Soc. for

Nutritional Scis., Soc. Exptl. Biology and Medicine, Am. Chem. Soc. (chmn. Red River valley sect. 1971), AAAS, AMA, Sigma Xi (pres. chpt. 1965-66, Faculty award for Outstanding Sci. Resch. U. N.D. chpt. 1982, cert. of recognition 1987), Alpha Sigma Nu, Phi Lambda Upsilon. Home: 1525 Robertson Ct Grand Forks ND 58201-7303 Office: U ND Sch Medicine Dept Biochemistry and Molecular Biology Grand Forks ND 58202 E-mail: fjacobs@medicine.nodak.edu.

JACOBS, IRWIN LAWRENCE, diversified corporate executive; b. Mpls., July 15, 1941; s. Samuel and Rose H. Jacobs; m. Alexandra Light, Aug. 26, 1962; children: Mark, Sheila, Melinda, Randi, Trisha. Student pub. schs. Chmn. Genmar Holdings, Inc., Mpls.; chmn. bd. Genmar Industries, Inc.; chmn. Jacobs Trading Co.; pres., CEO Jacobs Investors, Inc.; pres. Jacobs Realty II, Inc., 1993—, Jacobs Mgmt. Corp., 1983—, Gateway S/B, Inc., 1993—; chmn. Watkins Inc., Winona, Minn., Operation Bass, Inc., Gilbersville, Ky., 1996—, FLW Tour, Inc., Mpls., 1996—. Clubs: Mpls., Lafayette Country, Oakridge Country. Office: Genmar Holdings Inc 2900 IDS Ctr 80 S 8th St Minneapolis MN 55402-2100

JACOBS, JOEL, former state legislator, municipal official; m. Carol Jacobs; six children. BS, Moorhead State U.; postgrad., St. Cloud State U. Bus. instr.; Dist. 49B rep. Minn. Ho. of Reps., St. Paul, 1972-95; commr. of pub. utilities, 1995—. Chmn. regulated industries and energy com., vice chmn. ways and means com., mem. rules and legis. adminstrn. and taxes coms., Minn. Ho. of Reps. Office: 121 7th Pl E Ste 350 Saint Paul MN 55101-2163

JACOBS, JOHN PATRICK, lawyer; b. Chgo., Oct. 27, 1945; s. Anthony N. and Bessie (Montgomery) J.; m. Linda I. Grams, Oct. 6, 1973; 1 child, Christine Margaret. BA cum laude, U. Detroit, 1967, JD magna cum laude, 1970. Bar: Mich. 1970, U.S. Dist. Ct. Mich (ea. dist.) 1970, U.S. Ct. Appeals (6th cir.) 1974, U.S. Supreme Ct. 1978, U.S. Ct. Appeals (D.C. cir.) 1988, U.S. Ct. Appeals (4th cir.) 2001. Law clk. to chief judge Mich. Ct. Appeals, Detroit, 1970-71; assoc., then ptnr. Plunkett & Cooney P.C., 1972-92, also bd. dirs.; founding ptnr., prin. mem. O'Leary, O'Leary, Jacobs, Mattson, Perry & Mason P.C., Southfield, Mich., 1992-99; prin., owner John P. Jacobs, P.C., 1999—. Investigator Atty. Grievance Com., Detroit, 1975-84; mem. hearing panel Atty. Discipline Bd., Detroit, 1984-87, 94—; adj. prof. law Sch. Law, U. Detroit, 1983-84, faculty advisor, 1984-89, Pres.'s Cabinet, 1982—; elected rep. State Bar Rep. Assembly, Lansing, Mich., 1980-82, 91-92, 93-96; fellow Mich. State Bar Found., 1990-98; treas., mem. steering com. Mich. Bench-Bar Appellate Conf. Com., 1994—; apptd. mem. Mich. Supreme Ct. Com. on Appellate Fees, 1990; spl. mediator appellate negotiation program Mich. Ct. Appeals, 1995—; mem. exec. com. Mich. Appellate Bench-Bar Conf. Found., 1996—; appellate counsel to State Bar of Mich., mem. profl. ethics com., 1998, mem. multi-disciplinary practice com., 1999. Bd. editors Mich. Lawyers Weekly. Bd. dirs. Boysville of Mich., Clinton, 1988-95, 99—, chmn. pub. policy com., 1993-95, pub. policy liaison, 1999—; apptd. mem. State Bar Mich. Blue Ribbon Com. Improving Def. Counsel-Insurer Rels., 1998-99. Named Mgsr. Malloy Cath. Lawyer of Yr., Archdiocese of Detroit, 2001; recipient Robert E. Dice Med. Malpractice Def. Atty. award, Mich. Physicians, 1986; fellow Reginald Heber Smith fellow, 1971—72. Fellow Am. Acad. Appellate Lawyers, Mich. Std. Jury Instn. (subcom. employment law 1984-87); mem. ABA (litigation sect., appellate subcom., torts and ins. practice), Internat. Assn. Def. Counsel (v.p., amicus curiae com., med. and legal malpractice coms., product liability com.), Fedn. Ins. and Corp. Counsel, Mich. Def. Trial Counsel (chmn. amicus curiae com. 1986-88, chmn. future planning com., bd. dirs. 1989—, treas. 1993-94, sec. 1994-95, v.p. 1995-96, program chair 1990, 94, 95, pres., 1996-97), Def. Rsch. Inst. (state rep. 1997-98, Outstanding Performance Citation 1997, nat. appellate com. steering com. 1997—), Cath. Lawyers Soc. (bd. dirs. 1988-98, emeritus dir. 1998—, pres. 1994-95), Democrat. Roman Catholic. Avocations: collecting antique law books, film. Office: The Dime Bldg 719 Griswold Ste 600 Detroit MI 48226

JACOBS, LEONARD J. state legislator; m. Carol Jacobs; five children. Farmer and rancher; county commr., 1991—; rep. N.D. State Ho. Reps. Dist. 35, 1993—, mem. indsl., bus. and labor coms. Treas. S.W. Water Authority. Mem. Assn. Counties, N.D. Water Users, Adams County Social Svc., Lions, K.C.

JACOBS, LESLIE WILLIAM, lawyer; b. Akron, Ohio, Dec. 5, 1944; s. Leslie Wilson and Louise Francis (Walker) J.; m. Laurie Hutchinson, July 12, 1962; children— Leslie James, Andrew Wilson, Walker Fulton. Student, Denison U., 1962-63; B.S., Northwestern U., 1965; J.D., Harvard U., 1968. Bar: Ohio 1968, D.C. 1980, U.S. Supreme Ct. 1971, Brussels 1996. Law clk. to Chief Justice Kingsley A. Taft Ohio Supreme Ct., 1968-69; assoc. Thompson, Hine and Flory, Cleve., 1969-76, ptnr., 1976—, chmn. antitrust, internat. and regulatory area, 1988-99; chmn. bus. regulation and trade dept. Thompson Hine LLP and predecessor, 1999—. Lectr. conf. bd. Ohio Legal Ctr. Insts., Ohio State Bar Assn. Antitrust and Corp. Counsel Insts., Fed. Bar Assn., ABA, Canadian Inst., Internat. Assn. Young Lawyers, others; mem. Ohio Bd. Bar Examiners, 1990-94. Contbr. articles to profl. jours. Chmn. EconomicsAmerica, 1990-93; mem. vis. com. Case Western Res. U. Sch. Law, 1985-91; mem. Leadership Cleve., 1988. Lt. comdr. USNR, 1967-79. Fellow Am. Bar Found. (life), Ohio State Bar Found. (life, trustee 1985-87, Ritter award 1997); mem. ABA (ho. dels. 1986—, antitrust law sect. coun. 1985-88, officer 1991-97, state del. 1995-2001, nominating com. 1995-2001, bd. gov. 2001—), Ohio State Bar Assn. (pres. 1987, Ohio Bar medal 1990), Cleve. Bar Assn. (chmn. jud. selection com. 1982, trustee 1983-85), Am. Law Inst., Nat. Conf. Bar Pres., Internat. Club (Washington), Harvard Club (N.Y.C.), Chagrin Valley Hunt Club, Union Club (Cleve.), Castalia Trout Club. Republican. Presbyterian. Office: Thompson Hine LLP 3900 Key Ctr 127 Public Sq Cleveland OH 44114-1291

JACOBS, LLOYD A. cardiovascular surgeon; b. Holland, Mich., 1940; MD, Johns Hopkins U., 1968. Diplomate Am. Bd. Surgery. Intern Johns Hopkins Hosp., Balt., 1969-70, resident, 1970-71, U. Calif., San Diego, 1971-72, Wayne State U., Detroit, 1972-74; prof. surgery U. Mich. Sch. Medicine, Ann Arbor, 1974-, sr. assoc. dean, 1996—; COO U. Mich. Health Sys., 1997—. Hosp. appts.: VA Hosp., Ann Arbor, Mich., U. Mich. Hosp., Ann Arbor, chief of staff, VAH Med. Ctr., 1989-96. Fellow ACS; mem. AMA, Internat. Soc. Cardio Vascular Surgeons, Midwest Surgeons Assn. Office: 1500 E Medical Ctr Dr C246 Med Inn Ann Arbor MI 48109-0825

JACOBS, NORMAN JOSEPH, publishing company executive; b. Chgo., Oct. 28, 1932; s. Herman and Tillie (Chapman) J.; m. Jeri Kolber Rose, Jan. 2, 1977; 1 son, Barry Herman; children by previous marriage— Carey, Murray, Dale. B.S. in Mktg. U. Ill., 1954. Display salesman Chgo. Daily News, 1954-57; dist. mgr. Davidson Pub. Co., Chgo., 1957-62; v.p. Press-Tech, Inc., Evanston, Ill., 1962-69; pres. Century Pub. Co., 1969—. Bd. dirs. Chgo. Bulls Bd. dirs. United Cerebral Palsey Chgo. Served with USNR, 1951-59. Mem. B'nai B'rith, Birchwood Tennis Club, Alpha Delta Sigma, Tau Epsilon Phi. Jewish. Office: Century Pub Co 990 Grove St 4th Fl Evanston IL 60201-6510

JACOBS, RICHARD DEARBORN, consulting engineering company executive; b. Detroit, July 6, 1920; s. Richard Dearborn and Mattie Phoebe (Cobleigh) J.; divorced; children: Richard, Margaret, Paul, Linden. BS, U. Mich., 1944. Registered profl. engr., Ill., Mich., Wis., Miss. Engr. Detroit Diesel Engine divsn. Gen. Motors, 1946-51; mgr. indsl. and marine engine divsn. Reo Motors, Inc., Lansing, Mich., 1951-54; chief engr. Kennedy Marine Engine Co., Biloxi, Miss., 1955-59; marine sales mgr. Nordberg Mfg. Co., Milw., 1959-69, Fairbanks Morse Engine divsn. Colt Industries, Beloit, Wis., 1969-81; pres. R.D. Jacobs & Assocs., cons. engrs., naval arch. & marine engrs., Roscoe, Ill., 1981—. With AUS, 1944-46. Mem. ASTM, Soc. Naval Archs. and Marine Engrs. (chmn. sect. 1979-80), Soc. Automotive Engrs., Am. Soc. Naval Engrs., Soc. Am. Mil. Engrs., Navy League U.S., Propeller Club U.S., Masons. Unitarian. Office: 11405 Main St Roscoe IL 61073-9569

JACOBS, RICHARD E. real estate executive, sports team owner; 3 children from previous marriage. Ptnr. Jacobs, Visconsi & Jacobs; former chmn., chief exec. officer Cleve. Indians. Office: Richard E Jacobs Group 25425 Center Ridge Rd Cleveland OH 44145-4122

JACOBSEN, ARNOLD, archivist; b. N.Y.C., Nov. 6, 1913; s. Charles and Sylvia (Rosenfeld) J.; m. Hyla Sernick, 1943 (dec. 1983): children: Maurice, Howard (dec.), m. Elisabeth James. Investigator N.Y. Film Bd. of Trade, N.Y.C., 1933-39; film booker Universal Pictures, 1940-41; owner Memory Shop, Jackson Hgts., N.Y., 1947-50; publicity and promotions Grand Rapids (Mich.) Stadium, 1951-54; appliance sales Montgomery Ward, Grand Rapids, 1955-61; owner Arnold's Archives, 1960—; fin. coord. Consumers Power Co., 1962-78. Maker of cassettes of over 200,000 out-of-print hist. records for rsch. and ednl. purposes; organizer record catalogues Libr. Congress, 1980's; organizer record info., tapes Smithsonian Instn., 1980's; cataloguer supplier of most records of pvt. collection, archivist Chgo. Pub. Libr., 1980—. Libr. commr. E. Grand Rapids Pub. Libr., 1980's; vol. co-prodr. PBS-TV documentary, 1993. Sgt. U.S. Army, 1942-46. Mem. Am. Record Collectors Soc., Mich. Antique Phonograph Soc., Am. Record Collectors Assn. (membership com. 1960). Home and Office: Arnold's Archives 1106 Eastwood Ave SE Grand Rapids MI 49506-3580

JACOBSON, HOWARD, classics educator; b. Bronx, N.Y., Aug. 21, 1940; s. David and Jeannette (Signer) J.; m. Elaine Z. Finkelstein, June 10, 1965; children: Michael Noam, Daniel Benjamin, Joel Avram, David Moses. B.A., Columbia U., 1962, Ph.D., 1967; M.A., U. Chgo., 1963. Instr. Greek and Latin Columbia U., 1966-68; asst. prof. classics U. Ill., 1968-73, assoc. prof., 1973-80, prof., 1980—; Lady Davis vis. prof. Hebrew U., Jerusalem, winter 1983. Mem. Inst. for Advanced Study, Princeton, N.J., 1993-94. Author: Ovid's Heroides, 1974, The Exagoge of Ezekiel, 1983, A Commentary on Pseudo-Philo's Liber Antiquitatum Biblicarum (2 vols.), 1996; editor for Latin studies: Illinois Classical Studies Supplements. Nat. Endowment for Humanities fellow, 1971-72, 89; assoc. Ctr. for Advanced Study, U. Ill., 1983-84, spring 1994. Mem. Am. Philol. Assn. (Charles J. Goodwin Merit award 1985), Phi Beta Kappa. Jewish. Office: Dept Classics 4090 Foreign Languages Bldg 707 S Mathews Ave Urbana IL 61801-3625

JACOBSON, JEFF, state legislator; BA, Yale U., 1983; JD summa cum laude, Dayton Law Sch., 1988. Mem. Ohio Ho. of Reps. from 40th dist., Columbus, 1990-2000, Ohio Senate from 6th dist., Columbus, 2001—. Precinct capt. Montgomery County Reps., chmn.; exec. v.p. Ohioans for Fair Representation; lawyer. Mem. Antioch Temple Shrine, Mason (32d degree).

JACOBSON, LLOYD ELDRED, retired dentist; b. Madison, Minn., Mar. 9, 1923; s. Jacob Elton and Hilda Emily (Larson) J.; m. Ruth Solveig Skinsnes, Jan. 26, 1945; children: Rolf, Kathryn, Heidi. Student, St. Olaf Coll., 1943-44, 46-47, U. Chgo., 1945-46; DDS, U. Minn., 1951. Gen. practice dentistry, Kenyon, Minn., 1951-91; ret., 1991. Chmn. Am. Luth. Ch. Coun., Mpls., 1972-74; vol. World Brotherhood Exch., Bumbuli, Tanzania, 1965; treas. Kenyon Sch. Bd., 1958-60, Kenyon Devel. Corp., 1955-60. 1st lt. 14th Aif Force (Flying Tigers), USAAF, 1943-45, CBI. Recipient Outstanding Alumni award St. Olaf Coll., 1972, Disting. Alumni award U. Minn. Sch. Dentistry, 1987. Mem. Minn. Dental Assn. (treas. 1980-86), S.E. Dist. Dental Soc. (pres. 1979-80, sec.-treas. 1976-79), Rice County Dental Soc. (pres. 1969). Republican. Lodge: Lions (pres. Kenyon club 1952-54, dist. sec.-treas. 1974, Citizen of Yr. award 1986). Avocations: wood working, golf, stamp collecting. Home: 521 Spring St Kenyon MN 55946-1242 E-mail: rughnjake@aol.com.

JACOBSON, MARIAN SLUTZ, lawyer; b. Cin., Nov. 10, 1945; d. Leonard Doering and Emily Dana (Wells) Slutz; m. Fruman Jacobson, Sept. 21, 1975; 1 child, Lisa Wells. BA cum laude, Ohio Wesleyan U., 1967; JD, U. Chgo., 1972. Bar: Ill. 1972, U.S. Dist. Ct. (no. dist.) Ill. 1972, U.S. Ct. Appeals (7th cir.) 1973. Assoc. Sonnenschein Nath & Rosenthal, Chgo., 1972-79, ptnr., 1979—. Vis. com. U. Chgo. Law Sch., 1992-94. Mem. ABA, Chgo. Coun. Lawyers. Office: Sonnenschein Nath & Rosenthal 233 S Wacker Dr Ste 8000 Chicago IL 60606-6491 E-mail: msj@sonnenschein.com.

JACOBSON, NORMAN L. retired agricultural educator, researcher; b. Eau Claire, Wis., Sept. 11, 1918; s. Frank R. and Elma E. (Baker) J.; m. Gertrude A. Neff, Aug. 24, 1943; children: Gary, Judy. B.S., U. Wis., 1940; M.S., Iowa State U., 1941, Ph.D., 1947. Asst. prof. animal sci. Iowa State U., Ames, 1947-49, assoc. prof., 1949-53, prof., 1953, Disting. prof. agr., 1963-89, assoc. dean Grad. Coll., 1973-88, assoc. v.p. rsch., 1979-88, assoc. provost, 1988-89, dean Grad. Coll., 1988-89, emeritus disting. prof. agr., 1989—, interim chair Dept. Food Sci. and Human Nutrition, 1990-92. Contbr. articles to profl. jours., chpts. to books. Served to lt. USN, 1942-46, ETO, PTO. Fellow AAAS, Am. Inst. Nutrition, Am. Soc. Animal Sci. (Morrison award 1970), Am. Dairy Sci. Assn. (pres. 1972-73, Am. Feed Mfrs. Assn. award 1955, Borden award 1960, award of honor 1978, Disting. Svc. award 1989). Presbyterian. Home: 339 Hickory Dr Ames IA 50014-3430 Office: Iowa State U 313 Kildee Hl Ames IA 50011-3150 E-mail: nljacob@iastate.edu.

JACOBSON, RICHARD JOSEPH, lawyer; b. Ft. Benning, Ga., July 12, 1943; s. Harold Gordon and Ruth Fern (Enenstein) J.; m. Judy Josephine Dunbar, Sept. 17, 1966; 1 child, David Dunbar. AB, Harvard U., 1965, PhD, 1970; JD, U. Va., 1977. Bar: Ill. 1977, Va. 1977, D.C. 1979, U.S. Dist. Ct. (no. dist.) 1977, U.S. Ct. Appeals (7th cir.) 1991. Asst. prof. English U. Va., Charlottesville, 1970-74; assoc. Keck, Mahin & Cate, Chgo., 1977-83, ptnr., 1984-96; prin. Flaherty & Jacobson, P.C., 1996—. Author: Hawthorne's Conception of the Creative Process, 1965; contbr. articles to profl. jours. Pres. North Park Condominium assn., Chgo., 1978-80. Woodrow Wilson Nat. fellow, 1965. Mem. Va. State Bar Assn., D.C. Bar Assn., Chgo. Bar Assn. (chmn. com. preventing atty. malpractice 2000-2001), Assn. Profl. Responsibility Lawyers, Cliff Dwellers Club, Lawyers Club Chgo., Chgo. Literary Club. Home: 850 W Adams St Apt 3D Chicago IL 60607-3088 Office: Flaherty & Jacobson PC 134 N Lasalle St Ste 1600 Chicago IL 60602-1108 E-mail: rjacobson@fljlaw.com.

JACOBSON, ROBERT ANDREW, chemistry educator; b. Waterbury, Conn., Feb. 16, 1932; s. Carl Andrew and Mary Catherine (O'Donnell) J.; m. Margaret Ann McMahan, May 26, 1962; children: Robert Edward, Cheryl Ann BA, U. Conn., 1954; PhD, U. Minn., 1959. Instr. Princeton U., N.J., 1959-62, asst. prof., 1962-64; assoc. prof. Iowa State U., Ames, 1964-69, full prof., 1969-99, asst. dean Scis. and Humanities, 1982-85, prof. emeritus, 1999—. Chemist Ames Lab, Iowa, 1964-69, sr. chemist, 1969-99. Contbr. articles to profl. jours. Recipient Wilkinson Teaching award Iowa State U., Ames, 1974, 91. Mem. Am. Chem. Soc., Am. Crystallographic Assn. (chmn. apparatus and standards com. 1982-83) Avocations: gardening; painting. Home: 2732 Thompson Dr Ames IA 50010-4759 Office: Iowa State U 104 Gilman Ames IA 50011-3111 E-mail: raj@ameslab.gov.

JACOVER, JEROLD ALAN, lawyer; b. Chgo., Mar. 20, 1945; s. David Louis and Beverly (Funk) J.; m. Judith Lee Greenwald, June 28, 1970; children: Aric Seth, Evan Michael, Brian Ethan. BSEE, U. Wis., 1967; JD, Georgetown U., 1972. Bar: Ohio 1972, Ill. 1973, U.S. Ct. Appeals (7th cir.) 1974, U.S. Ct. Appeals (fed. cir.) 1983. Atty. Ralph Nader, Columbus, Ohio, 1972-73, Brinks Hofer, Gilson and Lione, Chgo., 1973—, pres., 2000—. Mem. ABA, Am. Intellectual Property Law Assn. (bd. dirs. 1994-98), Decalogue Soc. Lawyers, Intellectual Property Law Assn. Chgo. (bd. dirs. 1993-94, 98-99, pres. 2000), Intellectual Property Law Assn. Chgo. Ednl. Found. (pres. 1990-93), Am. Techion Soc. (pres. 1994-97). Office: Brinks Hofer Gilson & Lione Ste 3600 455 N Cityfront Plaza Dr Chicago IL 60611-5599 E-mail: jjacover@brinkshofer.com.

JACOVIDES, LINOS JACOVOU, electrical engineer, researcher; b. Paphos, Cyprus, May 10, 1940; s. Jacovos and Zoe (Evangelides) Jacovides; m. Katie McNamee; children: James, Michael, Christina, Julia. BS, U. Glasgow, Scotland, 1961, MS, 1962; PhD, U. London, 1965. Sr. rsch. engr. Def. Rsch. Labs. GM, Calif., 1965-67; sr. rsch. engr. elec. engring. GM Rsch. Labs., Warren, Mich., 1967-76, dept. rsch. engr. elec. engring. dept., 1975-85, asst. dept. head elec. engring. dept., 1985-87, prin. rsch. engr., 1987-88, head elec. and electronics dept., 1988-98; dir. Delphi Rsch. Labs., 1999—, Shelby Township, 1999—. Editor: Electric Vehicles, 1981; contbr. articles to profl. jours. Fellow: IEEE; mem.: Soc. Automotive Engrs., Industry Applications Soc. of IEEE (pres. 1990). Home: 154 Touraine Rd Grosse Pointe Farms MI 48236-3322 Office: M/C 483 478 103 51786 Shelby Pky Shelby Township MI 48315-1786 E-mail: linos@aol.com., linos.jacovides@delphiauto.com.

JACOX, ADA KATHRYN, nurse, educator; b. Centreville, Mich. d. Leo H. and Lilian (Gilbert) Jacox. BS in Nursing Edn., Columbia U., 1959; MS in Child Psychiat. Nursing, Wayne State U., 1965; PhD in Sociology, Case Western Res. U., 1969. RN. Dir. nursing Children's Hosp.-Northville State Hosp., Mich., 1961—63; assoc. prof., then prof. Coll. Nursing Univ. Iowa, Iowa City, 1969—76; prof., assoc. dean Sch. Nursing U. Colo., Denver, 1976—80; prof., dir. rsch. ctr. sch. nursing U. Md., Balt., 1980—90, dir. ctr. for health policy rsch., 1988—90; prof. sch. nursing, Independence Found. chair health policy Johns Hopkins U., 1990—95; prof., assoc. dean for rsch. Coll. Nursing Wayne State, Detroit, 1996. Co-chmn. panels to develop clin. guidelines for pain mgmt. U.S. Agy. for Health Care Policy and Rsch., 1990—94; chair AIDS study sect. NIH, 1990—92. Co-author: Organizing for Independent Nursing Practice, 1977 (named Book of Yr., Am. Jour. Nursing), A Process Measure for Primary Care: The Nurse Practitioner Rating Form, 1981 (named Book of Yr., Am. Jour. Nursing); editor: Pain: A Sourcebook for Nurses, 1977 (named Book of Yr., Am. Jour. Nursing). Recipient Disting. Achievement in Nursing Rsch. and Scholarship, Alumni Assn., Columbia U. Tchrs. Coll., 1975, Disting. award for spl. achievement, Nat. Coalition for Cancer Survivorship, 1994, Cameo award for rsch. excellence, Sigma Theta Tau, 1996, Rozella Schlotfeldt Leadership award, MAIN, 1997; fellow Carver fellow, U. Iowa, 1972. Fellow: Am. Acad. Nursing; mem.: Wayne State U. Alumni Assn. (Disting. Alumni award 1994), Inst. of Medicine, NAS (com. on nat. needs for biomed. and rsch. pers. 1984—87), Am. Acad. Nursing, Am. Health Quality Assn. (bd. dirs. 1998—2001), Am. Pain Soc. (chair clin. practice guidelines com. 1995—2000, bd. dirs. 1999—2001), Am. Nurses Found. (pres. 1982—85), AMA (mem. health policy agenda work group 1983—86), ANA (dir. 1978—82, 1st v.p. 1982—84). Office: Wayne State U Coll Nursing 5557 Cass Ave Detroit MI 48202-3615

JACOX, JOHN WILLIAM, retired mechanical engineer and consulting company executive; b. Pitts., Dec. 12, 1938; s. John Sherman and Grace Edna (Herbster) J.; 1 child, Brian Erik; m. Roma Jankauskaite, Sept. 3, 1993. BSME in Indsl. Mgmt., Carnegie Mellon U., 1962, BS in Indsl. Mgmt, 1962. Mfg. engr. Nuclear Fuel div. Westinghouse Elec. Co., Pitts., 1962-64; rsch. engr. Continental Can Co. Metal R&D Ctr., Pitts., 1964-65; data processing sales engr. IBM, Pitts., 1965-66; mktg. mgr. nuclear products MSA Internat., Pitts., 1966-72; v.p. Nuclear Cons. Svcs., Inc., Columbus, Ohio, 1973-84; v.p. NUCON Internat., 1981-84; bd. dirs. NUCON Europe Ltd., London, 1981—; pres. Jacox Assocs., Inc., 1984-2001; ret., 2001; cons., lectr. Nat. Ctr. for Rsch. in Vocat. Edn., 1978-84 ; author, presenter, session chmn. DOE/Harvard U. Nuclear Air Cleaning Confs., 1974—; lectr. Harvard U. Sch. Pub. Health Air Cleaning Lab., 1986—; co-chmn. program subcom. Tech. Alliance Cen. Ohio, 1984-85, vice-chmn., chmn.-elect dir. subcom., 1986-87, chmn. bd. trustees, 1986; tech. transfer com. Dayton Area Tech. Network; program com. World Trade Devel. Club; mem. legis. svcs. com. coop. edn. adv. com. Otterbein Coll., 1978-82; industry advisor Franklin U. Grad. Sch. Bus., 1994—. Mem. NRA (patron), ASHRAE (standards com. 3.2 and 9.4), ASTM (chmn. F-21), ASME (code com. nuclear air and gas treatment, main exec. com., chmn. subcom. field test procedures), Am. Nuclear Soc. (pub. info. com.), N.Y. Acad. Scis. (life), Ohio Acad. Sci. (life), Am. Nat. Stds. Inst., Internat. Soc. Nuc. Air Treatment Techs. (co-founder, officer), Columbus Area C. of C. (tech. roundtable 1983), Air Force Assn. (life), Mensa, Sun Bunch (pres. 1980-81), Dayton Area Tech. Network (subcom. on tech. transfer), Tech. Transfer Soc. Office: PO Box 29720 Columbus OH 43229-0720 Home: 4471 Summit Rd Pataskala OH 43062-8880

JAEGER, ALVIN A. (AL JAEGER), secretary of state; b. Beulah, N.D., 1943; m. Naomi Berg, 1969 (dec. 1979), m. Kathy Grangaard Anderson, 1986; children: Todd, Stacy, Heidi. Grad., Bismarck State Coll., 1963, Dickinson State U., 1966; postgrad., U. N.D., 1968, Mont. State U., 1970. Tchr. Killdeer High Sch., 1966-69, Kenmare High Sch., 1969-71; with Mobil Oil Corp., 1971-73; real estate broker, 1973-93; sec. of state State of N.D., 1993—. Active Charity Luth. Ch. With N.D. Army N.G. Named Realtor of Yr. Mem. Nat. Assn. Secs. State (exec. com., com. chmn.), Fargo-Moorhead Area Assn. Realtors (mem. coms. edn., profl. stds., bylaws, multiple listing svc.), N.D. Assn. Realtors (past chairperson state bylaws), Bismarck Kiwanis Club. Office: 600 E Boulevard Ave Bismarck ND 58505-0660

JAEGER, JEFF TODD, professional football player; b. Tacoma, Nov. 26, 1964; Student, Wash. Coll. With Cleve. Browns, 1987; kicker L.A. Raiders, 1989-96, Chgo. Bears, 1996—. Achievements inlude playing in Pro Bowl, 1991; shares single season record for most field goals made (35), 1993. Office: Chgo Bears 1000 Football Dr Lake Forest IL 60045-4829

JAFFE, HOWARD ALLEN, financial company executive; b. Chgo., June 17, 1953; s. Richard Lee Jaffe and Bette Carol (Steinberg) Whitehead; m. Beverly Ann Geisel, June 22, 1975; children: Victoria, Katharine. BS, No. Ill. U., 1974; MBA, Loyola U., Chgo., 1978. Various positions to sr. v.p. NBD Ill. Banks, Highland Park, Ill., 1975-90; exec. v.p., chief fin. officer No. States Fin. Corp., Waukegan, 1990-95; exec. v.p. and chief fin. officer Avondale Fed. Savings Bank, Chgo., 1995—; v.p. and chief fin. officer Avondale Fin. Corp., 1995—. Contbr. articles to profl. publs. Mem. Sch. Dist. 70 Bd. Edn., Libertyville, Ill., 1991-95; bd. dirs., treas. healthreach clinic for medically underserved, Waukegan, 1991—. Alumni scholar No. Ill. U., 1973-74. Mem. Rotary (pres.). Avocations: golf, personal computing. Home: 1129 Virginia Ave Libertyville IL 60048-4439 Office: Avondale Fed Savings Bank 20 N Clark St Chicago IL 60602-4109

JAGER, DURK I. retired marketing agency executive; b. Haskerland, The Netherlands, Apr. 30, 1943; BA, Erasmus U., Rotterdam, 1968, MBA, 1970. Asst. brand mgr., brand mgr. Procter & Gamble, The Netherlands, 1970-75, Cin., 1975-76, brand promotion mgr. The Netherlands, 1976-80, Austria, 1980-81, country mgr. Austria, 1981-82, advt./mktg. mgr. Japan, 1982-85, gen. mgr. Japan, 1985-86, divsn. mgr. Japan, 1986-87, v.p. Japan, 1987-88, group v.p. Far East and Asia Pacific divsns., 1988-89, exec. v.p. Soap, Chemicals, Health Care and Beauty Care divsns., 1990-91, exec. v.p. U.S. Business, 1991-95, pres., COO, 1995-99, chmn. bd., pres., chief exec., 1999-2000; ret., 2000. Mem. The Bus. Coun., The Bus. Roundtable, Internat. Coun., J.P. Morgan & Co., Inc. Bd. dirs. United Negro Coll. Fund, Inc., Eastman Kodak, Grocery Mfrs. of Am., U.S.-China Bus. Coun.; chmn. Greater Cin. Fine Arts Fund Campaign (1999), Japan-Am. Soc. of Greater Cin.; mem. bd. govs. Nature Conservatory; mem. Ohio Bus. Roundtable Steering Com. Mem. Commonwealth Club of Cin., Commercial Club of Cin., Hyde Park Country Club, Willow Pt. Golf and Country Club. Home: PO Box 599 Cincinnati OH 45201-0599

JAGER, MELVIN FRANCIS, lawyer; b. Joliet, Ill., Mar. 23, 1937; s. Melvin Van Zandt and Lucille Marie (Callahan) J.; m. Virginia Sue Maitland, Aug. 15, 1959; children: Lori, Jennifer, Scott, Christy. BSME, JD, U. Ill., 1962. Bar: Ill. 1962, D.C. 1962. Assoc. Iron, Birch, Swindler & McKie, Washington, 1962-65; ptnr. Hume, Clement, Brinks, Willian & Olds Ltd., Chgo., 1965-80, Lee, Smith & Jager, Chgo., 1981-83, Niro, Jager & Scavone, Chgo., 1984-85, Brinks, Hofer, Gilson & Lione Ltd., Chgo., 1985—. Adj. prof. law No. Ill. U. Sch. Law, 1979-80, John Marshall Law Sch., 1992, U. Ill. Coll. Law, Champaign, 1992—; chmn. Practicing Law Inst. Trade Secret Protection Symposium, 1986, 89. Author: Trade Secrets Law, 1984; editor U. Ill. Law Rev., 1961-62; contbg. author monograph: Sorting Out the Ownership Rights in Intellectual Property: A Practical Guide to Practical Counseling and Legal Representation, 1980. Mem. bd. edn. Glen Ellyn, Ill., 1974-80; chmn. Civic Betterment Party Nominating Com., Glen Ellyn, 1982-88; chmn. Glen Ellyn Environ. Protection Com., 1971-72; chmn. budget rev. com. Glen Ellyn United Fund, 1972, Glen Ellyn Ednl. Loan Fund trust, 1973. Mem. ABA (chmn. litigation sect. intellectual properties and patents com. 1984-88), Ill. State Bar Assn. (chmn. patent, trademark and copyright, coun. 1982-83, editor newsletter 1979-82), Chgo. Bar Assn., Am. Patent Law Assn., Intellectual Property Law Assn. of Chgo. (pres. 1997), Lic. Execs. Soc. (pres. U.S.A./Can. 1993-94), Am. Law Inst., Glen Ellyn Jaycees (life mem., pres. 1972, trustee), Chgo. Law Club, Union League Club, Phi Gamma Delta, Phi Delta Phi. Republican. Roman Catholic. Home: 440 N McClurg Ct Apt 313 Chicago IL 60611-4657 Office: Brinks Hofer Gilson & Lione Ltd Ste 3600 455 N Cityfront Plaza Dr Chicago IL 60611-5599

JAHN, HELMUT, architect; b. Nurnberg, Germany, Jan. 4, 1940; came to U.S., 1966; s. Wilhelm Anton and Karolina (Wirth) J.; m. Deborah Ann Lampe, Dec. 31, 1970; 1 child, Evan Dipl. Ing.-Architect, Technische Hochschule, Munich, 1965; postgrad., Ill. Inst. Tech., 1966-67; D.F.A. (hon.), St. Mary's Coll., Notre Dame, Ind., 1980. Registered architect, Ill., Calif., Colo., Fla., Ind., Minn., N.Y., Tex., Va., Nat. Coun. Archtl. Registration Bds. Germany. With P.C. von Seidlein, Munich, 1965-66; with C.F. Murphy Assocs., Chgo., 1967-81, asst. to Gene Summers, 1967-73, exec. v.p., dir. planning and design, 1973-81; prin. Murphy/Jahn, 1981-92, pres., 1982—, chief exec. officer, 1983—. Mem. design studio faculty U. Ill., Chgo., 1981; Elliot Noyes prof. archtl. design Harvard U., Cambridge, Mass., 1981; Davenport vis. prof. archtl. design Yale U., New Haven, 1983; thesis prof. IIT, Chgo., 1989-92. Prin. works include Kemper Arena, Kansas City, Mo., 1974 (Nat. AIA honor award, Am. Inst. Steel Constrn. award), Auraria Library, Denver, 1975, John Marshall Cts. Bldg., Richmond, Va. 1976, H. Roe Bartle Exhbn. Hall, Kansas City, Mo., 1976, Fourth Dist. Cts. Bldg., Maywood, Ill., 1976, Monroe Garage, Chgo., 1977, Michigan City (Ind.) Library, 1977 (AIA Ill. Council honor award, AIA-ALA First honor award, Am. Inst., Steel Constrn. award), St. Mary's Coll. Athletic Facility, South Bend, Ind., 1977 (AIA Ill. Council Honor award, AIA Nat. honor award, Am. Inst. Steel Constrn. award), Springfield Garage, Ill., 1977, Glenbrook Profl. Bldg., Northbrook, Ill., 1978, Rust-Oleum Corp. Hdqrs., Vernon Hills, Ill., 1978 (Am. Steel Constrn. award), La Lumiere Gymnasium, La Porte, Ind., 1978, Prairie Capital Convention Ctr.-Parking Garage, Springfield, Ill., 1979, W.W. Grainger Corp. Hdqrs., Skokie, Ill., 1979, Xerox Centre, Chgo., 1980, De La Garza Career Ctr., East Chicago, Ind., 1981 (ASHRAE Energy award), Area 2 Police Hdqrs., Chgo., 1981, Oak Brook (Ill.) Post Office, 1981, Commonwealth Edison Dist. Hdqrs., Downers Grove, Ill., 1981 (ASHRAE Energy award), First Source Ctr., South Bend, Ind., 1982, Argonne (Ill.) Program Support Facility, 1982 (Owens-Corning Fiberglass Energy Conservation award), One South Wacker Office Bldg., Chgo., 1982, Addition to Chgo. Bd. of Trade, 1982 (Reliance Devel. Group Inc. award for Disting. Arch., Am. Inst. Steel Constrn. award, Structural Engring. Assn. Ill. award), Mercy Hosp. Addition, Chgo., 1983, 11 Diagonal St., Johannesburg, Republic of South Africa, 1983, U. Ill. Agrl. Engring. Sci. Bldg., Champaign, 1984, Learning Resources Ctr., Coll. of DuPage, Glen Ellyn, Ill., 1984, Plaza East, Milw., 1984 (Disting. Architect award Milw. Art Commn.), Shand Morahan Corp. Hdqrs., Evanston, Ill., 1984, 701 Fourth Ave. S., Mpls., 1984, O'Hare Rapid Transit Sta., Chgo., 1984 (Nat. Honor award), State of Ill. Ctr., Chgo., 1985 (Structural Engring. Assn. Ill. award, AIA Chgo. chpt. award 1986), Parktown Stands, Johannesburg, 1986, Two Energy Ctr., Naperville, Ill., 1986, Hawthorne Ctr. Office Bldg., Vernon Hills, Ill., 1986, Park Ave. Tower, N.Y.C., 1986, 300 E. 85th St. Apts., N.Y.C., Northwestern Terminal, Chgo., 1987 (Structural Engring. Assn. of Ill. award 1987), United Airlines Terminal, 1987 (Structural Engring. Assn. of Ill. award, Nat. AIA Honor award, R.J. Reynolds Meml. award, 1988, AIA Chgo. chpt. award), One Liberty Place, Phila., 1987, Oakbrook (Ill.) Terr. Tower, 1987, O'Hare Internat. Airport, 1988 (AIA Chgo. chpt. award), Merchandise Mart Bridge, Chgo., 1988, Wilshire/Westwood Office Bldg., L.A., 1988, 425 Lexington Ave, N.Y.C., 1989, 750 Lexington Ave., 1989, Cityspire, N.Y.C., 1989, Messe Frankfurt Convention Ctr., Germany, 1989, Barnett Ctr., Jacksonville, Fla., 1990, Messe Frankfurt Tower, Germany, 1991 (AIA Chgo. chpt. award 1992), Livingston Plaza, Bklyn. Hgts., N.Y., 1991, Two Liberty Place, Phila., 1991 (AIA Chgo. chpt. award 1992), 120 N LaSalle, Chgo., 1992 (AIA Chgo. chpt. award 1992), One Am. Plz., Trolley Sta., San Diego, 1992 (AIA Chgo. chpt. award 1992), Mannheim (Germany) Ins. Bldg., 1992 (AIA Chgo. chpt. award 1992), Hyatt Roisy, Paris, 1992, Munich (Germany) Order Ctr., 1993 (AIA Chgo. Chpt. award, Nat. AIA Honor award), Hitachi Tower, Singapore, 1993, Caltex House, Singapore, 1993, Kempinski Hotel, Munich, 1994, (AIA Chgo. Chpt. award), Pallas, Stuttgart, Germany, 1994, 70 KU Damn, Berlin, 1994, (AIA Chgo. Chpt. award, Nat. AIA Honor award), Second Internat. Bangkok Airport, Charlemagne, Brussels, Century 21, Shanghai, China, FKB Airport, Köln, Germany; contbr. to numerous group and solo exhbns. of archtl. drawings and design. Recipient citation Progressive Architecture, 1977, award for Chgo. cen. area plan, 1985, Dean of Architecture award Chgo. design awards, 1991; Arnold W. Brunner meml. prize in architecture, 1982; Chgo. chpt. award AIA, 1975-79, 81-83, 86-88, nat. honor award, 1979, 87, N.Y. State award, 1986; 1st honor award ALA, 1978, energy award ASHRAE, 1981, Presdl. Desirn award Nat. Endowment Arts, 1988, R.S. Reynolds Meml. award, 1988; numerous others. Fellow AIA, Architecture Soc./Art Inst. Chgo., Chgo. Archtl. Club; mem. AIA (numerous Chgo. chpt. awards 1975—). Roman Catholic. Clubs: Comml. of Chgo., Economic of Chgo., Saddle & Cycle. Office: Murphy/Jahn 35 E Wacker Dr Ste 300 Chicago IL 60601-2157

JAHNS, JEFFREY, lawyer; b. Chgo., July 6, 1946; s. Maxim G. and Josephine Barbara (Czernek) J.; m. Jill Metcoff, Sept. 8, 1973; children: Anna Hope, Claire Martine, Elizabeth Grace. AB, Villanova U., 1968; JD, U. Chgo., 1971. Bar: Ill. 1971, U.S. Dist. Ct. (no. dist.) Ill. 1971, U.S. Ct. Appeals (7th cir.) 1973, U.S. Supreme Ct. 1974. Assoc. Roan & Grossman, Chgo., 1971-77, ptnr., 1977-81, Seyfarth Shaw, Chgo., 1981—. Mem. tax mgmt. adv. bd. Bur. Nat. Affairs, Washington, 1981--. Co-author: Corporate Acquisition Debt Interest Deduction, 1973; contbr. numerous articles to legal publs., chpts. to books. Trustee, chmn. Chgo. Architecture Found., 1982—; bd. dirs. Prairie Ave. House Mus., 1995-98; trustee Graham Found., 1998—. Ctr. for Urban Studies fellow U. Chgo., 1969-71. Mem. ABA, Chgo. Bar Assn. (chmn. various coms.), Internat. Coun. Shopping Ctrs., Mid-Day Club, Econ. Club Chgo., Lambda Alpha. Office: Seyfarth Shaw 55 E Monroe St Ste 4200 Chicago IL 60603-5863

JAHR, ARMIN N., II, clergy member, church administrator; Exec. dir. Luth. Brethren Home Missions, Fergus Falls, Minn. Office: Luth Brethren Home Missions PO Box 655 Fergus Falls MN 56538-0655

JAIN, NEMI CHAND, chemist, coating scientist, educator; b. Kota, Rajasthan, India, Oct. 15, 1951; came to U.S., 1983, naturalized, 1993; s. Chand Mal and Raj Devi (Nopra) J.; m. Shashi Bala Jain, Jan. 29, 1981; children: Nimisha, Seema. BSc, U. Rajasthan, 1971, MSc, 1973, PhD, 1978; postgrad., N.D. State U., 1990, McCorne Rsch. Inst., 1994, Baldwin-Wallace Coll., 1996. Lectr. chemistry Nat. Coun. of Edn. Rsch. Tng., Ajmer, India, 1976-77; asst. prof. U. Delhi, 1977-83; postdoctoral rsch. assoc. U. Va., Charlottesville, 1983-85; rsch. assoc./assoc. lab. dir. Colo. State U., Ft. Collins, 1985-89; rsch. scientist/team leader Sherwin-Williams Co., Chgo., 1989-96, sr. scientist, 1996—, sr. scientist, team leader Warrensville Heights, Ohio, 2000—. Advisor Harry Truman Coll., Chgo., 1999; cons. and lectr. in field. Developer waterborne coatings; developer coating test course Sherwin-Williams U., 1995; contbr. chpt. to book, numerous articles to profl. jours. Judge, Chgo. Sci. Fair, 1992, 95, 97, 98, 99, 2000, Competitive Leadership, Profl. Mgmt. Assn., 1997, 98, 1st Responder/Indsl. Med. Tech., 1995—, U. No. Colo, 1989, Am. Chem. Soc. H.S. Edn. Com., 1996—. CSIR fellow, 1973-76, Sardar Patel U. fellow, 1972, Lucknow U. tchr. fellow, 1979; recipient Disting. Nat. award for study abroad Govt. of India, 1983-85, State Govt. Rajasthan merit scholar, 1967-73, Bill Welch Excellence award Automotive Finishes, 2001. Fellow Am. Inst. Chemists; mem. ASTM, Am. Chem. Soc. (mem. h.s. edn. com. 1996-97), Internat. Union Pure and Applied Chemistry, Sigma Xi. Jain. Avocations: reading, walking, cooking, travel, computer, gardening. Home: 34423 Claythorne Rd Solon OH 44139-5627 Office: Sherwin Williams Co 4440 Warrensville Center Rd Warrensville Heights OH 44128 Fax: (216) 332-8670. E-mail: ncjain@sherwin.com.

JAKUBAUSKAS, EDWARD BENEDICT, college president; b. Waterbury, Conn., Apr. 14, 1930; s. Constantine and Barbara (Narstis) J.; m. Ruth Friz, Aug. 29, 1959; children— Carol, Marilyn, Mark, Eric. B.A., U. Conn., 1952, M.A., 1954; Ph.D., U. Wis., 1961. Economist FPC, 1956, Dept. Labor, 1956-58; instr. U. Wis., 1961-62, asst. prof. econs., 1962-63; asst. prof. Iowa State U., 1963-65, assoc. prof., 1965-66, prof., 1966-71; dean U. Wyo., 1971-76, prof. econs., 1971-79, v.p. acad. affairs, 1976-79; pres. SUNY, Geneseo, 1979-88, Cen. Mich. U., Mt. Pleasant, 1988-92; cons. in higher edn., 1992—. Author: Manpower Economics, 1971. Served with U.S. Army, 1954-56. Mem. Am. Assn. State Univs. and Colls. Mem. United Chs. of Christ.

JALLINGS, JESSICA, reporter, newscaster; b. Wis. BA in Journalism, U. Wis. With WISC-TV, Madison, Wis.; reporter WGBA-TV, Green Bay, WGLV-TV, Jacksonville, Fla.; reporter, anchor WISN, Milw., 2001—. Office: WISN PO Box 402 Milwaukee WI 53201-0402

JAMES, CHARLES FRANKLIN, JR. engineering educator, educator; b. Des Arc, Mo., July 16, 1931; s. Charles Franklin and Beulah Frances (Kyte) J.; m. Mollie Keeler, May 18, 1974; children: Thomas Elisha, Matthew Jeremiah. B.S., Purdue U., 1958, M.S., 1960, Ph.D., 1963. Registered profl. engr., Wis. Sr. indsl. engr. McDonnel Aircraft Co., 1963; asst. prof. U. R.I., 1963-66, prof., chmn. dept. indsl. engring., 1967-82, co-founder, mem Robotics Rsch. Ctr., 1980-83; C. Paul Stocker prof. engring. Ohio U., Athens, 1982-83; dean Coll. Engring. and Applied Sci., U. Wis.-Milw., 1984-95; v.p. academics Milw. Sch. of Engring., 1995-2000; ret., 2000. Cons. Asian Productivity Orgn.; arbitrator Fed. Mediation and Conciliation Service, Am. Arbitration Assn.; bd. dirs. Badger Meter Co., Milw. Contbr. articles to profl. jours. With USAF, 1951-55. Recipient Silver medal Tech. U. Budapest, Hungary, 1989. Mem. NSPE, ASME, Wis. Soc. Profl. Engrs. (pres. Milw. chpt. 1993-94, Outstanding Profl. Engr. in Edn. 1993, state-wide treas. 1994-96), Inst. Indsl. Engrs., Am. Soc. Engring. Edn., Soc. Mfg. Engrs., Am. Foundrymen's Soc., Engrs. and Scis. of Milw. (bd. dirs. 1988-95, v.p. 1991-93, pres.-elect 1993-94, pres. 1994-95).

JAMES, EDGERRIN, football player; Football player Inpls. Colts. Guest spkr. DARE prog. various schools; founder Edgerrin James Found. Named All-Pro 1st Team Assoc. Press, Coll. and Pro Football Newsweekly, Football Digest, Pro Football Weekly, Sporting News, USA Today, All AFC Team Football News, Pro Football Weekly, NFL All Rookie Team Coll. and Pro Football Newsweekly, Football Digest, Football News, Pro Football Weekly. Achievements include NFL rushing title, 1999, Pro Bowl player, 1999. Office: Inpls Colts PO Box 535000 Indianapolis IN 46253 also: Indianapolis Colts 7001 West 56th Street Indianapolis IN 46254

JAMES, ELIZABETH JOAN PLOGSTED, pediatrician, educator; b. Jefferson City, Mo., Jan. 15, 1939; d. Joseph Matthew Plogsted and Maxie Pearl (Manford) Plogsted Acuff; m. Ronald Carney James, Aug. 25, 1962; children: Susan Elizabeth, Jason Michael. BS in Chemistry, Lincoln U., 1960; MD, U. Mo., 1965. Diplomate Am. Bd. Pediat., Am. Bd. Neonatal-Perinatal Medicine. Resident in pediat. U. Mo. Hosps. & Clinics, Columbia, 1965-68, fellow in neonatology, 1968-69, dir. neonatal-perinatal medicine Children's Hosp., 1971—; fellow in neonatal-perinatal medicine U. Colo. Hosps., Denver, 1969-71; from asst. to assoc. prof. pediatrics and obstetrics sch. medicine U. Mo., 1971-83, prof. child health and obstetrics, 1983—. Dir. pediatric edn. program dept. child health sch. medicine U. Mo., Columbia, 1989—. Mem. editl. bd. Mo. Medicine, 1983—; contbr. chpts. to books and articles to profl. jours. Fellow Am. Acad. Pediat. (sect. neonatal-perinatal medicine); mem. Mo. State Med. Assn., Boone County Med. Soc., Alpha Omega Alpha. Roman Catholic. Avocations: classical music, bicycling, herb gardening. Office: U Mo Hosps & Clinics Childrens Hosp 1 Hospital Dr Columbia MO 65201-5276 E-mail: jamese@health.missouri.edu.

JAMES, FRANCIS EDWARD, JR. investment counselor; b. Woodville, Miss., Jan. 5, 1931; s. Francis Edwin and Ruth (Phillips) J.; m. Iris Senn, Nov. 3, 1952; children: Francis III, Barry, David. BS, La. State U., 1951; MS, Rensselaer Poly. Inst., 1966, PhD, 1967. Commd. 2d lt. USAF, 1950, advanced through grades to col., 1972; prof. mgmt. and statistics, chmn. dept quantitative studies Air Force Inst. Tech., Wright Patterson AFB, 1967-71, dir. grad. edn. div. mgmt. programs, 1972-74; ret. USAF, 1974; pres. James Investment Rsch., Inc., Alpha, Ohio, 1972—. Cons. math. modeling. Author: A Matrix Solution for the General Linear Regression Model; contbr. articles to profl. jours. Bd. dirs. James Capital Alliance, Inc. Decorated Legion of Merit, D.F.C., Air medal, Joint Services Commendation medal, Meritorious Service medal; recipient Outstanding Acad. Achievement award Rensselaer Poly. Inst., 1965, first Alumni Fellow appointment Rensselaer Poly. Inst. Mem. Am. Statis. Assn., Mil. Ops. Research Soc., Am. Fin. Assn., Investment Counsel Assn. Am., Mktg. Technicians Assn., Soc. Logistics Engring. (Eckles award 1973, tech. chmn.), Sigma Iota Epsilon, Epsilon Delta Sigma. Lodges: Masons; Rotary. Home: 2604 Lantz Rd Dayton OH 45434-6627 Office: James Investment Rsch Inc PO Box 8 Alpha OH 45301-0008

JAMES, GEORGE BARKER, II, investment executive; b. Haverhill, Mass., May 25, 1937; s. Paul Withington and Ruth (Burns) J.; m. Beverly A. Burch, Sept. 22, 1962; children: Alexander, Christopher, Geoffrey, Matthew. AB, Harvard U., 1959; MBA, Stanford U., 1962. Fiscal dir. E.G. & G. Inc., Bedford, Mass., 1963-67; fin. exec. Am. Brands Inc., N.Y.C., 1967-69; v.p. Pepsico, Inc., 1969-72; sr. v.p., chief fin. officer Arcata Corp., Menlo Park, Calif., 1972-82; exec. v.p. Crown Zellerbach Corp., San Francisco, 1982-85; sr. v.p., chief fin. officer Levi Strauss & Co., 1985-98. Bd. dirs. Pacific States Industries, Inc., Clayton Group Inc., Crown Vantage Corp (chmn.), Dresdner RCM Capital Corp, Sharper Image, Inc., Callious Software Inc., Canned Foods Inc.; dir. Il Fornaio Restaurants. Author: Industrial Development in the Ohio Valley, 1962. Mem. Andover (Mass.) Town Com., 1965-67; mem. Select Congl. Com. on World Hunger; mem. adv. coun. Calif. State Employees Pension Fund; chmn. bd. dirs. Towle Trust Fund; trustee Nat. Corp. Fund for the Dance, Cate Sch., Levi Strauss Found., Stern Grove Festival Assn., Zellerbach Family Fund, San Francisco Ballet Assn., Com. for Econ. Devel.; bd. dirs. Stanford U. Hosp., Calif. Pacific Med. Ctr. KQED; vice-chmn. World Affairs Coun.; mem. San Francisco Com. on Fgn. Rels. With AUS, 1960-61. Mem. Pacific Union Club, Bohemian Club, Menlo Circus Club, Harvard Club, N.Y. Athletic Club. Home: 207 Walnut St San Francisco CA 94118-2012 Office: Crown Vantage Inc 4445 Lakeforest Dr Ste 700 Cincinnati OH 45242

JAMES, J. BRADFORD, financial officer; BS in Acctg., Kent State U., 1969; MBA, Case Western Res. U., 1988. CPA. Acct. Arthur Andersen & Co., 1969-73; from corp. contr. to CFO Donn Corp., Westlake, Ohio, 1973-86; v.p. fin. USG Interiors, Inc., 1987-89, sr. v.p., CFO, 1991-94, group v.p. world wide ceilings, 1994-95, exec. v.p., 1995-98; sr. v.p., CFO IMC Global, Northbrook, Ill., 1998—. Office: IMC Global Inc PO Box 5037 Lake Forest IL 60045-5037

JAMES, JEFFERSON ANN, performing company executive, dancer, choreographer; b. July 12, 1943; d. Robert Mitchell and Dorothea Jefferson (Lewis) Miller; m. Martin Edward James, June 16, 1964; 1 child Rachel Eleanor. Student, Juilliard Sch. Music, N.Y.C., 1961—63; BFA, Coll. Connservatory Music, U. Cin., 1970. Vis. prof. Western Coll., Oxford, Ohio, 1970—72; artistic dir. Dance '70, Cin., 1970, Contemporary Dance Theater, Cin., 1972—. Bd. dirs. Cin. Commn. on Arts, 1981—87, OhioDance Assn., Cleve., 1984—92. Choreographer Corbett Awards Finalist, 1975, artist category, 1995; dir.: Corbett Awards (Arts Orgn. 1982, finalist 1990, 95). Mem. presenting/touring panel Ohoi Arts Coun., 1993—96; active Cin. Arts Allocation Com., 1994—2000, chmn., 1996—97; cmty. arts coord. for grand opening celebration Aronoff Ctr. for Arts, 1995; mem. steering com. Regional Cultural Planning Com. (Ohio, Ky., Ind.), 1996—98. Recipient Ohio Gov.'s award for the ARts, 1998, Ohio Dance award for contbns. to field, 1999. Office: Contemporary Dance Theater Inc 1805 Larch Ave Cincinnati OH 45224-2928

JAMES, MARILYN SHAW, secondary education educator, social service worker; b. Chgo., Apr. 6, 1926; d. Harry and Louise A. (Milkey) Shaw; m. Eugene Nelson James, June 17, 1950; children: Jim, Mark, Katherine, Caroline. BS, Carthage Coll., 1947; MA, U. Iowa, 1954. Tchr. home econs. Highland Park (Ill.) High Sch., 1947-50, Hampshire (Ill.) High Sch., 1950-51; instr. home econs. No. Ill. U., DeKalb, 1963-65; tchr. Winkie Bear, Sycamore, Ill., 1970-71; sub. tchr. DeKalb and Sycamore Sch. Dists., 1969—, Hinckley-Big Rock, Ill., 1973-80; homemaker coord. Family Svc. Agy., DeKalb, 1980-88, ret. V.p. Kishwaukee Symphony Assocs., 1988—90, pres., 1990; mem. Adv. Com. on Elder Concerns, 1991—, chmn., 1996—97; moderator First Congl. Ch., DeKalb, 1983—84; bd. dirs. Stage Coach Players, 1988—90, 2001—, stage mgr., 1954—; bd. dirs. Family Svc. Agy., 1971—79. Named Stage Coacher of Yr., Stage Coach Players, 1990. Mem. AAUW (v.p. scholar 1980, 90, 93, 94, 95, 96), LWV (legis. chair 1983), DeKalb County Home Economists, DeKalb Drama Club (pres. 1986-87), Univ. Women's Club (pres. 1991), Family Svc. Aux. (pres. 1998—), DeKalb Women's Club (bd. dirs.), Thursday Arts Lit. Club (pres. 1998—). Democrat. Home: 212 Tilton Park Dr Dekalb IL 60115-1942

JAMES, PHYLLIS A. lawyer; b. L.I., N.Y., Mar. 23, 1952; BA, Harvard U., 1974, JD, 1977. Bar: Calif. 1978. Mem. Pillsbury Madison & Sutro, San Francisco; corp. counsel City of Detroit Law Dept. Office: City of Detroit Law Dept 1650 First National Building 660 Woodward Ave Detroit MI 48226-3516

JAMES, SHERYL TERESA, journalist; b. Detroit, Oct. 7, 1951; d. Reese Louis and Dava Helen (Bryant) J.; m. Eric Torgeir Vigmostad, June 15, 1974; children: Teresa, Kelsey. BS in English, Ea. Mich. U., 1973. Staff writer, editor Lansing (Mich.) Mag., 1979-82; staff writer Greensboro (N.C.) News & Record, 1982-86, St. Petersburg (Fla.) Times, 1986-91, Detroit Free Press, 1991—. Cons. Poynter Inst., St. Petersburg, 1989—; cons. to high sch. newspapers, St. Petersburg, 1989—. Recipient Penney Missouri Awd. U. Missouri/J.C. Penney, 1985, 1st Pl. Feature Writing Awd. Fla. Soc. Newspaper Editors, 1991, Pulitzer Prize, Feature Writing, 1991, finalist, 1992, Alumna Achievement Awd. Eastern Michigan U., 1992. Democrat. Roman Catholic. Office: Detroit Free Press 600 W Fort St Detroit MI 48226-2706

JAMES, TROY LEE, state legislator; b. Texarkana, Tex. s. Samuel and Anniebell James; m. Betty Jean Winslow; 1 child, Laura. Student, Bethany Coll., Case We. Res. U., Fenton Coll. State rep. Dist. 12 Ohio Ho. of Reps., 1967-92, state rep. Dist. 10, 1993—. Chmn. environ. and natural resources com., econ. devel. and small bus. com.; mem. rules, aging and housing com., labor, hwys. and pub. safety com., select com. on Deinstitutionalization, select com. to investigate problems of maintaining basic utility rates; precinct committeeman Ward 11 Dem. Orgn., pres. Mem. Black Elected Dems. Ohio exec. com. Nat. Conf. State Legislatures, Common Fed. Taxation, Trade and Econ. Devel.; mem. Dem. Exec. Coun.; self-employed businessman; with Ohio Crankshaft; bd. dirs. Fedn. Cmty. Planning; mem. Citizen's League, Consumer Protection Agy. Cleve. Recipient Nat. award Nat. Soc. State Legislators, 1974, ENA award Nat. Assn. Career Women, 1978; named Legislator of Yr. Communicative Disorders Commn., 1988. Mem. NAACP, Nat. Soc. Social Workers, Ohio Soc. State Legislators, Phyllis Wheatly Assn. (bd. dirs.), Boy Scouts Am., 40th and 43d St. Neighborhood Block Club, 11th Ward Dem. Club. Fax: 614 644 9494.

JAMES, WILLIAM MORGAN, bishop; Bishop Ch. of God in Christ, Toledo. Office: St James Holiness Ch of God in Christ 3758 Chippendale Ct Toledo OH 43615-1111

JAMES, WILLIAM W. bank executive; b. Oct. 12, 1931; s. Will and Clyde (Cowdrey) James; m. Carol Ann Muenter, June 17, 1967; children: Saraw James Banks, David William. AB, Harvard U., 1953. Cert. trust and fin. advisor. Asst. to dir. overseas divsn. Becton Dickinson & Co., Rutherford, NJ, 1956-59; stockbroker Merrill Lynch, Pierce, Fenner & Smith, Inc., St. Louis, 1959-62; with trust divsn. Boatmen's Nat. Bank, 1962-90, v.p. in charge estate planning, sr. v.p., 1972-90; sr. v.p. Boatmen's Trust Co., 1989-96, fin., trust mktg. cons., 1996—. Mem. gift and bequest coun. Barnes Hosp., St. Louis, 1963—67, St. Louis U., 1972—78; dir. Mark Twain Summer Inst., 1987—92. With U.S. Army, 1953—55. Mem.: Am. Inst. Banking, Mo. Bankers Assn., Estate Planning Coun. St. Louis,

Harvard Alumni Assn. (bd. dirs. 1987—90), Noonday Club (St. Louis), Mo. Athletic Club, Harvard Club (Cambridge, Mass.), Harvard Club St. Louis (pres. 1972—73). Republican. Home: 1415 Michele Dr Saint Louis MO 63122-1404

JAMESON, J(AMES) LARRY, chemical company executive; b. Elizabethtown, Ky., 1937; s. William Kendrick and Ruth Helen (Krause) J.; m. Mary Louise Wojcik, June 26, 1965; children: Renee, Jennifer, Julie. BA in Math., Bellarmine Coll., 1959; BS in Chem. Engring., U. Detroit, 1963, MBA, 1970. Tech. mgr. automotive products Rinshed Mason et Cie, Paris, 1965-69; ops. mgr. vinyl coated fabrics Inmont Corp., Toledo, 1969-75, v.p., gen. mgr. European ops. London, 1975-79, v.p., gen. mgr. automotive finishes products Detroit, 1979-83, sr. v.p. worldwide automotive, 1983-86; pres. Coatings & Colorants div. BASF, Clifton, N.J., 1986-93; pres., CEO Pirelli Cable Corp., Florham Park, 1993-96; v.p. Ferro Chem. Corp., Cleve., 1996—. Mem. Soc. Automotive Engrs., Orchard Lake Country Club, The Country Club. Avocations: golf, tennis, skiing, hunting. Home: 17181 Hidden Point Dr Chagrin Falls OH 44023-2001 Office: Ferro Corp 1000 Lakeside Ave E Cleveland OH 44114-1147

JAMES-STRAND, NANCY LEABHARD, advertising executive; b. Oak Park, Ill., July 30, 1943; d. Arthur Ferdinand and Virginia Stella (Albertelli) Leabhard; m. Jack William Strand, July 1, 1971. Student, U. Madrid, 1963-64; BA in Teaching Spanish, U. Ill., 1965. With advt. sales Chgo. Tribune, 1968-69; asst. mgr. Nationwide Advt., Chgo., 1969-78, regional mgr., 1978—. Home: 140 S Grove Ave Oak Park IL 60302-2806 Office: Nationwide Advt 35 E Wacker Dr Chicago IL 60601-2103

JAMIESON, JAMES CHILLES, biochemist, educator; b. Aberdeen, Scotland, May 15, 1939; came to Can., 1967; s. John Munro Jamieson and Margaret Chilles; m. Muriel Margaret Shaw, Aug. 19, 1967. BS, Heriot Watt, Edinburgh, Scotland, 1963; PhD, Aberdeen U., 1967. Chartered chemist. Contbr. articles to profl. jours. Recipient grant NSERC, Manitoba, Can., 1995, IOR grant NSERC/Novopharm Bio., Manitoba, 1995. Fellow Chem. Inst. Can.; mem. Royal Inst. Chemistry. Achievements include research in field of glycobiology. Office: Univ of Manitoba Office Dean of Sci 250 Machray Hall Winnipeg MB Canada R3T 2N2

JAMISON, ROGER W. pianist, piano educator; b. Marion, Ohio, June 18, 1937; s. Harold Theodore and Martha Louise (Haas) J.; m. Caroline R. Hansley, Jan. 26, 1957; children: Lisa Renee, Eric Karl. BS, Ohio State U., 1959, MA (scholar), 1961; postgrad. Oberlin Conservatory, Oakland U.; student George Haddad, Columbus, Ohio, Mischa Kottler, Detroit. Piano faculty mem. Detroit Conservatory of Music, 1964-68, Cranbrook Schs., Bloomfield Hills, Mich., 1981-84; performer in one-man mus. presentation Spirits of Great Composers, 1979—; dir. music Birmingham Temple, Farmington Hills, Mich., 1984-95; soloist Brunch with Bach series Detroit Inst. Arts., Detroit Symphony Orch.'s Internat. Brahms Festival; regular soloist Christ Ch., Cranbrook, 1982-95; concert tour of Eng., 1991; condr. All Ohio Piano Ensemble, 1997; cons. Royal Oak Arts Council; adjudicator Am. Coll. Musicians. Mem. Nat. Guild of Piano Tchrs. (past pres. Oakland-Macomb chpt.) Address: 173 W Heffner St Delaware OH 43015-1258

JAN, GEORGE POKUNG, political science educator; b. Peking, Jan. 6, 1925; came to U.S., 1955; s. Yunan and Tehchieh (Lee) J.; m. Norma Yingchiang Wen, Sept. 28, 1946; children: Gregory, David, Daniel. BA, Nat. Chengchi U., Nanking, China, 1949; MA, So. Ill. U., 1956; PhD, NYU, 1960. Various positions including editor newspaper/mag., tchr., writer, dean, 1949-55; instr. Chinese NYU, N.Y.C., 1959-60; asst. prof. polit. sci. No. Ill. U., DeKalb, 1961; asst. to full prof. of govt. U. S.D., Vermillion, 1961-68, dir. Summer Inst. for Asian Studies, 1964-66; prof. polit. sci. U. Toledo, 1968-93, prof. emeritus, 1993—, chmn. Asian studies program, 1970-93, dir. Inst. for Asian Studies, 1990-93; pres. Am. Inst. Tech., Toledo, 1993-00. Vis. prof. polit. sci. Beijing U., China, 1988; hon. rsch. fellow Rsch. Ctr. for Contemporary China, Beijing U., 1988—; adviser to China U. Geol. Scis., Beijing, 1993—; hon. chmn. bd. Second H.S., Wenzhou Tchr's. Coll., China, 2000—. Author: The Chinese Commune Experiment, 1964, A Practical English Grammar for Junior Middle Schools, 1953, A Study of English Words, 1955, How to Do Business with China, 1994, Introduction to Political Science, 2000, others; editor: Government of Communist China, 1966, The International Politics of Asia, 1969, China Bus. Newsletter, 1993-98, International Relations of Asia, 1998, Political Development of China, 1998; bd. editors Asian Profile Jour., 1983-86, Jour. Econs. and Internat. Rels., 1986—, The New World of Politics, 1991—; contbr. articles to profl. jours., ency. and books. Pres. Chinese Assn. Greater Toledo, 1983-84; bd. dirs. Toledo Coun. on World Affairs, 1969-76; chmn. keynote session, Symposium on Chinese Ams. in the 1990s, Detroit, 1987; hon. chmn. bd. Second H.S. Wenzhou Tchrs. Coll., 2000—. Recipient Outstanding Svc. award The Internat. Inst. of Greater Toledo, 1983, teaching grants Asia Found., Japan Soc., 1964, 65, 66, rsch. grants U. Toledo, U. S.D., U. Mich., U. Chgo. numerous years, Significant Contribution award Pacific Cultural Found., Republic of China, 1988; named Hon. Rsch. Fellow, Rsch. Ctr. for Contemporary China, Beijing U., 1988, others. Mem. AAUP, Am. Polit. Sci. Assn., Midwest Polit. Sci. Assn., Assn. Asian Studies, Ohio Chinese Acad. and Profl. Assn. (bd. dirs. 1991—, pres. 1994-95), Mich. Chinese Acad. and Profl. Assn. (outstanding leadership award 1992), Am. Assn. Chinese Studies, Internat. Studies Assn., Ohio Internat. Edn. Assn. (chmn. planning and program com. 1976-77), Chinese Acad. and Profl. Assn. of Mid-Am. (bd. dirs. 1986-89), Am. Biog. Inst., Inc. (rsch. bd. advisors 1996—), Internat. Biog. Ctr. (hon. adv. coun.), Phi Beta Kappa, Pi Sigma Alpha, Phi Kappa Phi, Pi Gamma Mu, Phi Beta Delta. Avocations: gardening, photography, travel, swimming, chess. Home: 3041 Valley View Dr Toledo OH 43615-2237 E-mail: aitje@aol.com.

JANAK, PETER HAROLD, automotive company executive; b. Detroit; BS in Aerospace Engring., Miss. State U., 1963; grad. exec. program, Stanford U., 1994. Rsch. fluid amplifiers dept. aerospace engring. Miss. State U., State College, 1962—63; propulsion engr. space disvn. Chrysler Corp., New Orleans, 1963—65; from sr. engr. to chief performance analysis sect. Teledyne-Brown Engring., Hunstville, Ala., 1965—68; head propulsion tech. sect. TRW Def. and Space Sys. Group, Houston, 1968—71, mgr. surveillance sys. engring. McLean, Va., 1972—78, mgr. signal processing sys. dept., 1978—79, mgr. SURTASS engring., 1979—80, mgr. undersea surveillance projects and combat sys., 1980—83, mgr. def. sys. ops. Fairfax, 1987—90, mgr. tax modernization program, 1990—92, dep. gen. mgr. divsn. info svcs., 1992—94, v.p., gen. mgr. divsn. info. svcs., 1994—95; mgr. propulsion sys. dept. Technologieforschung, GmbH, Stuttgart, Germany, 1971—72; v.p., dep. gen. mgr. ea. divsn. PRC Sys. Svcs., McLean, 1983—84, pres., gen. mgr. divsn. sys. engring. and analysis, 1984—87; v.p., chief info. officer TRW Inc., Cleve., 1995—98; chief info. officer Delphi Automotive Sys., Troy, Mich., 1998—99; v.p., chief info. officer Delphi Corp., 1999—. Mem. external rsch. adv. bd. Miss. State U. Mem.: IEEE, Conf. Bd., Working Coun. Chief Info. Officers, Soc. Automotive Engrs., Soc. Mfg. Engrs. Office: Delphi Corp 5725 Delphi Dr Troy MI 48098-2815

JANEZICH, JERRY R. state legislator, small business owner; b. Mar. 16, 1950; m. Patricia Janezich; three children. BS, St. Cloud State U. Small bus. owner; former Dist. 5B rep. Minn. Ho. of Reps., St. Paul, 1992—; now senator Minn. State Senate. Vice chmn. judiciary, local govt. and met. affairs com., mem. commerce, regulated industries and taxes coms., Minn. Ho. of Reps. Home: 518 8th St NE Chisholm MN 55719-1338

JANICAK, PHILIP GREGORY, psychiatry educator, researcher; b. Chgo., Aug. 2, 1946; s. Edward and Josephine (Raskauskas) J.; m. Mary Judith Cray, Oct. 16, 1976; 1 child, Matthew Cray. BS in Psychology with honors, Loyola U., Chgo., 1969, MD, 1973. Diplomate Am. Bd. Psychiatry and Neurology. Asst. clin. prof. dept. psychiatry Loyola U., Maywood, Ill., 1976-78; research assoc. U. Chgo., 1979-81; asst. prof. U. Ill., Chgo., 1982-85, assoc. prof., 1986-92, prof., 1992—. Chief rsch. unit Ill. State Psychiat. Inst., Chgo., 1984-96; med. dir. psychiat. clin. rsch. ctr. U. Ill., 1996—. First author: Principles and Practice of Psychopharmacotherapy, 1993, 3d edit., 2001. NIMH grant co-investigator, 1986, 91, 93; NIMH grant prin. investigator, 1990; NIH grant assoc. program dir. 2000. Fellow Am. Psychiat. Assn. Roman Catholic. Avocation: voice. E-mail: pjanicak@psych.uic.edu.

JANICK, JULES, horticultural scientist, educator; b. N.Y.C., Mar. 16, 1931; s. Henry Spinner and Frieda (Tullman) Janick; m. Shirley Reisner, June 15, 1952; children: Peter Aaron, Robin Helen Janick Weinberger. BS, Cornell U., 1951; MS, Purdue U., 1952, PhD, 1954; DS in Agr. (hon.), U. Bologna, Italy, 1990; Doctor (hon.), Tech. U., Lisbon, Portugal, 1994. Instr. Purdue U., West Lafayette, 1954-56, asst. prof., 1956-59, assoc. prof., 1959-63, prof., 1963-88, James Troop Disting. prof. in horticulture, 1988—; dir. Purdue Ctr. for New Crops and Plant Products, 1990—. Cons. Food and Agrl. Orgn., Rome, Italy, 1988. Author: Horticultural Science, 4th edit., 1986, Classical Papers in Horticultural Science, 1989; co-author: Plant Science: An Introduction to World Crops, 3d edit., 1981; co-editor: Advances in Fruit Breeding, 1975, Methods in Fruit Breeding, 1983, Advances in New Crops, 1990, New Crops, 1993, Fruit Breeding (3 vols.), 1996; editor: Hort. Revs., Plant Breeding Revs., Progress in New Crops, 1996, Perspectives on New Crops and New Uses, 1999. Fellow AAAS, Portuguese Hort. Assn., Am. Soc. Hort. Sci. (pres. 1986-87), Interat. Soc. Hort. Sci., Sigma Xi, Phi Kapa Phi, Gamma Sigma Delta. Jewish. Avocation: drawing. Home: 420 Forest Hill Dr West Lafayette IN 47906-2316 Office: Dept Horticulture Purdue Univ West Lafayette IN 47907-1165 E-mail: jjanick@hort.purdue.edu.

JANIS, F. TIMOTHY, technology company executive; b. Chgo., Apr. 11, 1940; s. Fabian M. and Phyllis (Underwood) Janiszewski; m. Kathryn Dickey; children: Mark David, Paul Joseph, Melissa Ann. BS in Chemistry, Wichita State U., 1962, MS in Chemistry, 1963; PhD in Chemistry, Ill. Inst. Tech., 1968. Asst., then assoc. prof. chemistry Ill. Benedictine Coll., Lisle, Ill., 1969-74; asst. acad. dean Franklin (Ind.) Coll., 1974-77; divn. dir. Indpls. Ctr. for Advanced Rsch., 1977-92; founder and pres. ARAC, Inc., Franklin, Ind., 1992—. Cons. Argonne (Ill.) Nat. Lab., 1968-74, Office Pers. Mgmt., Denver, 1988-94; mem. adv. bd. R&D Enterprise Asia Pacific, 1999. Co-author: Moving R&D to Marketplace, 1993, rev. edit., 1995, 25 publs. on tech. transfer; internat. editor Tech. Bus. Mag., 1998-2000. Mem. Lisle Cmty. High Sch. Bd., 1970-72; bd. dirs. Near North Devel. Corp., Indpls., 1990-94. Named Sagamore of the Wabash, Gov. of State of Ind., 1990. Mem. Tech. Transfer Soc. (treas., pres. 1990-92, exec. dir. 1993-96). Roman Catholic. Avocations: golf, reading, sightseeing, grandchildren. Office: 604 Davis Dr Franklin IN 46131-7682 Fax: (317) 738-3980. E-mail: tjanis@aracinc.com.

JANKE, RONALD ROBERT, lawyer; b. Milw., Mar. 2, 1947; s. Robert Erwin and Elaine Patricia (Wilken) J.; m. Mary Ann Burg, July 3, 1971; children— Jennifer, William, Emily. B.A. cum laude, Wittenberg U., 1969; J.D. with distinction, Duke U., 1974. Bar: Ohio 1974. Assoc. Jones, Day, Reavis & Pogue, Cleve., 1974-83, ptnr., 1984—. Served with U.S. Army, 1970-71, Vietnam. Mem. ABA (chmn. environ. control com. 1980-83), Ohio Bar Assn., Greater Cleve. Bar Assn., Environ. Law Inst. Office: Jones Day Reavis & Pogue N Point 901 Lakeside Ave E Cleveland OH 44114-1190

JANKLOW, WILLIAM JOHN, governor; b. Chgo., Sept. 13, 1939; s. Arthur W. and LouElla Bernice (Gulbranson) J.; m. Mary Dean Thom, Sept. 3, 1960; children— Russell, Pam, Shonna. B.S.B.A., U. S.D., 1964, J.D., 1966. Bar: S.D. bar 1966, U.S. Supreme Ct. bar 1970. Staff atty. S.D. Legal Services, 1966-67, directing atty., chief officer, 1967-72; chief trial atty. S.D. Atty. Gen's. Office, Pierre, 1973-74, atty. gen., 1975-78; gov. S.D., 1979-87, 1995—. Lectr. in field Bd. dirs. Nat. Legal Services Corp. Served with USMC, 1956-59. Recipient Nat. award for legal excellence and skill Nat. Legal Aid and Defenders Assn., 1968 Mem. Nat. Assn. Attys. Gen., Am., S.D. trial lawyers assns., Am. Judicature Soc. Republican. Lutheran. Office: Office of the Governor 500 E Capitol Ave Pierre SD 57501-5070

JANOS, JAMES See **VENTURA, JESSE**

JANOVER, ROBERT H. lawyer; b. N.Y.C., Aug. 17, 1930; s. Cyrus J. and Lillian D. (Horwitz) J.; m. Mary Elizabeth McMahon, Oct. 23, 1966; 1 child, Laura Lockwood. BA, Princeton U., 1952; postgrad., U. Vienna, 1956; JD, Harvard U., 1957. Bar: N.Y. 1957, U.S. Supreme Ct. 1961, D.C. 1966, Mich. 1973. Practice law, N.Y.C., 1957-65; cons. Office of Edn., HEW, Washington, 1965; legis. atty. Office of Gen. Counsel, HEW, 1965-66; asst. gen. atty. Mgmt. Assistance Inc., N.Y.C., 1966-71; atty. Ford Motor Credit Co., Dearborn, Mich., 1971-74; mem. firm Freud, Markus, Slavin, Toohey & Galgan, Troy, 1974-79; pvt. practice Detroit, 1979-82, Bloomfield Hills, Mich., 1982—. Contbr. articles to profl. jours. Bd. dirs. Oakland Citizens League, 1976-96, v.p., 1976-79, pres., 1979-96; bd. dirs. Civic Searchlight, Inc., 1976-96. 1st lt., arty. U.S. Army, 1952-54, Korea. Mem.: ABA, Soc. 3d Inf. Divsn., Am. Inns Ct. (master of the bench 1996—99), Assn Bar of City of N.Y., Bar Assn. D.C., Detroit Met. Bar Assn., N.Y. State Bar, Mich. State Bar, Harvard Club (N.Y.C.), Nassau Club (Princeton, N.J.), Princeton Club of N.Y., Princeton Club of Mich. (pres. 1991—92). Home: 685 Ardmoor Dr Bloomfield Hills MI 48301-2415 Office: 100 W Long Lake Rd Ste 200 Bloomfield Hills MI 48304-2774 E-mail: rjanover@aol.com .

JANSEN, JAMES STEVEN, lawyer; b. Marshalltown, Iowa, Mar. 16, 1948; s. Virgil Charles and Virginia Rae (Hiatt) J.; m. Patricia Jean Beard, Nov. 24, 1984; children: Katherine, Emily, Ashley, Kristen. BS in Edn., U. Nebr., 1970; JD, Creighton U., 1973. Bar: Nebr. 1974, U.S. Dist. Ct. Nebr. 1974. Dep. county atty. County of Douglas, Omaha, 1974-78, county atty., 1991—; assoc. Naviaux, Kinney, Jansen and Dosek, 1979-83; assoc., then ptnr. Stave, Coffey, Swenson, Jansen and Schatz, 1984-90. Bd. dirs. Nebr. County Atty.'s Standards Adv. Coun., Lincoln, 1992--. Bd. dirs. Domestic Violence Coord. Coun. Greater Omaha, 1996--,co-chair, 1996-97, chmn., 1997-98; bd. dirs. Omaha Community Partnership, 1991—, chmn., 2000-01; mem. Nebr. Drug and Violent Crime Policy Bd., Lincoln, 1991-98, bd. dirs. Project Harmony Child Protection Ctr., 1996—, chmn., 1998. Mem. Nebr. State Bar Assn., Omaha Bar Assn., Nebr. County Atty.'s Assn. (bd. dirs. 1991—, pres. 1997-98), Nat. Dist. Atty.'s Assn. Democrat. Roman Catholic. Avocations: golf, reading. Office: Douglas County Attys Office Rm 100 Hall of Justice Omaha NE 68183

JANSSEN, RAMON E. state legislator; b. Hooper, Nebr., July 5, 1937; m. Nancy Janssen; children: Nick, Michael, Nola. Owner City Meat Market, Hooper, Nebr., Nickerson Meat Market; mem. Nebr. legislature from 15th dist., Lincoln, 1992—; mem. bldg. maintenance, edn., agrl. Nebr. Legislature, mem. govt., mil., and vet. affairs coms., chmn. gen. affairs com. Bd. dirs. Farmer's Home Ins. Co. Mem. Hooper Comml. Club, Elkhorn Valley Golf Club (past pres.), Lions Club. Address: Nebr State Senate State Capitol Rm 1015 Lincoln NE 68509 Also: PO Box 159 Nickerson NE 68044-0159

JANTZ, KENNETH M. construction executive; V.p., treas. Peter Kiewit Sons, Omaha. Office: Peter Kiewit and Sons 1000 Kiewit Plz Omaha NE 68131 Office Fax: (402) 271-2939.

JAQUA, RICHARD ALLEN, pathologist; b. Fort Dodge, Iowa, Apr. 15, 1938; s. John Franklin and Esther Constance (Rossing) J.; m. Mary Joanne Stewart, Dec. 29, 1969. B.A. magna cum laude, Yale U., 1960; M.D., Harvard U., 1965. Diplomate: Am. Bd. Pathology, Am. Bd. Nuclear Medicine. Teaching fellow pathology Harvard Med. Sch., 1965-67; resident clin. pathology NIH, 1967-69; intern pathology Mass. Gen. Hosp., Boston, 1965-66; fellow tumor pathology Meml.-Sloane Kettering Cancer Center, N.Y.C., 1969-70; asst. prof. pathology U. S.D. Sch. Medicine, Vermillion, 1970-73, asso. prof., 1973-74, asso. prof., acting chmn. dept. lab. medicine, 1974-77, prof., chmn. dept. lab. medicine, 1977—; dir. U. S.D. Sch. Medicine (Electron Microscopy Lab. and Clin. Virology Lab.), 1979—; pathologist VA Hosp., Sioux Falls, S.D., 1978—; practice medicine specializing in anatomic and clin. pathology and nuclear medicine Lab. Clin. Medicine, 1970—. Served with USPHS, 1967-69. Recipient Outstanding Prof. awards U. S.D. Med. Students, 1971, 75, 77, 90; VA grantee, 1980-82. U. S.D. Faculty Recogition award, 1986. Fellow Coll. Am. Pathologists, Am. Soc. Clin. Pathologists; mem. Electron Microscopy Soc. Am., Am. Assn. Cancer Edn., AAAS, Internat. Acad. Pathology, Soc. Nuclear Medicine, Sigma Xi, Alpha Omega Alpha. Home: 27546 483rd Ave Canton SD 57013-5511 Office: USD Health Sci Ctr 1400 W 22nd St Sioux Falls SD 57105-1505 E-mail: rjaqua@usd.edu.

JAQUES, DAMIEN PAUL, theater critic; b. Oak Park, Ill., Nov. 3, 1946; s. Norman Sands and Marion Esther (Werle) J.; m. Patricia A. Mehigan, July 7, 1976 (div. May 1989). BA, Marquette U., 1968. Field organizer, transp. aide Robert Kennedy Presdl. Campaign, Wis., Ind., Calif., 1968; campaign mgr. Carol Bauman Candidate for Congress, Milw., 1968; reporter Sheboygan (Wis.) Press, 1968-69, Evening Press, Binghamton, N.Y., 1969-72; reporter, music critic Milw. Jour., 1972-77, entertainment copy editor, 1977-80, theater critic, 1980—; corr. Back Stage, 1994—; host weekly radio prgm. Milwaukee Presents WHAD. Mem. Am. Theatre Critics Assn. (jurist Outstanding New Play award 1983-93, exec. bd., 1985-88, 1994-97, dir. Found., 1994-97). Avocations: travel, reading, cooking, fishing. Office: The Milwaukee Journal Sentinel PO Box 371 Milwaukee WI 53201-0371

JARAMILLO, CARLOS ALBERTO, civil engineer; b. Medellin, Colombia, Dec. 5, 1952; came to the U.S., 1986; s. Alberto and Maria Jaramillo; children: Daniel J., Nicolas. BCE, U. Nacional, Medellin, 1978; MS, U. Minn., 1980. Registered profl. engr., Wis., Colombia. Engr. Integral S.A., Medellin, 1977-79, sr. design engr., 1980-86; rsch. asst. St. Anthony Falls Lab., Mpls., 1979-80; civil engr. Mead & Hunt Inc., Madison, Wis., 1986-89; sr. geotech. engr. Harza Engring. Co., Chgo., 1989—2001, jr. ptnr., 1998—2001; sr. geotech. engr. , ptnr. MWH Global, 2001—. Prof. Escuela de Ingenieria de Antioquia, Medellin, 1981-86; designer numerous dams & underground structures. Cons. to public utilities, various countries 1994—; contbr. articles to profl. jours. Mem. ASCE (rock mechanics com.), U.S. Com. Large Dams, U.S. Nat. Soc. Soil Mechanics and Found. Engring., Phi Kappa Phi. Avocations: jogging, photography, philately, astronomy. Office: MWH Global Ste 1900 175 W Jackson Blvd Chicago IL 60604 Business E-Mail: carlos.a.jaramillo@mwhglobal.com.

JARBOE, MARK ALAN, lawyer; b. Flint, Mich., Aug. 19, 1951; s. Lloyd Aloysius and Helen Elizabeth (Frey) J.; m. Patricia Kovel, Aug. 20, 1971; 1 child, Alexander. Student, No. Mich. U., 1968-69; AB with high distinction, U. Mich., 1972; JD magna cum laude, Harvard U., 1975. Bar: Minn. 1975, U.S. Dist. Ct. Minn. 1975, U.S. Ct. Appeals (8th cir.) 1975, U.S. Ct. Appeals (7th cir.) 1993. Law clk. to presiding justice Minn. State Ct., St. Paul, 1975-76; from assoc. to ptnr. Dorsey & Whitney LLP, Mpls., 1976-81, ptnr., 1982—. Lectr. U. Minn. Law Sch., Hamline U. Sch. Law. Contbr. articles to profl. jours. Pres. parish coun. Ch. of Christ the King, Mpls., 1981-83. Mem. Fed. Bar Assn., Native Am. Bar Assn., Minn. Am. Indian Bar Assn., Mensa, Phi Beta Kappa. Republican. Roman Catholic. Home: 4816 W Lake Harriet Pky Minneapolis MN 55410-1903 Office: Dorsey & Whitney LLP 50 S 6th St Ste 1500 Minneapolis MN 55402-1498 E-mail: jarboe.mark@dorseylaw.com.

JAROS, MIKE, state legislator, administrative assistant; b. Apr. 12, 1944; m. Annette Nordine; three children. BA, U. Minn. Exec. asst. U. Minn., Duluth; Dist. 7B rep. Minn. Ho. of Reps., St. Paul, 1973-80, 85—. Former chmn. higher edn. divsn. edn. com., Minn. Ho. of Reps., former mem. labor-mgmt. rels. com.; chmn. commerce and econ. devel.-internat. trade, technology and econ. devel. divsn. coms., mem. taxes com. Recipient Nat. Scholastic Press award, Nat. Latin Testing award. Office: 559 State Office Bldg Saint Paul MN 55155-0001

JARTZ, JOHN G. food company executive; b. 1953; With Quaker Oats Co., Chgo., 1980—, sr. v.p. bus. devel., corp. sec., gen. counsel, 1997—. Office: Quaker Oats Co 321 N Clark St Ste Ll2 Chicago IL 60610-4790

JARVEY, JOHN A. federal judge; BS, U. Akron, 1978; JD, Drake U., 1981. Law clk. to Hon. Donald E. O'Brien U.S. Dist. Ct. (no. dist.) Iowa, Cedar Rapids, 1981-83; trial atty. U.S. Dept. Justice, Washington, 1983-87; chief magistrate judge U.S. Dist. Ct. (no. dist.) Iowa, Cedar Rapids. Office: 101 1st St SE Cedar Rapids IA 52401-1202

JARVI, NEEME, conductor; b. Tallinn , Estonia, June 7, 1937; came to U.S., 1980; s. August and Elss Jarvi; m. Liilia Jarvi, Sept. 2, 1961; children: Paavo, Kristjan, Maarika. Diploma in Music and Conducting, St. Petersburg (USSR) State Conservatorium, 1960; hon. doctorate, U. Aberdeen, Scotland, Music Conservatory of Talinn, Estonia, Gothenberg (Sweden) U., U. Mich. Condr. Estonian Radio Symphony Orch., 1960-63, chief condr., 1963-76, Estonian State Opera, 1963-76, Estonian State Symphony, 1976-80; prin. condr. Gothenburg (Sweden) Symphony Orch., 1982—; prin. condr., music dir., condr. laureate Royal Scottish Orch., Glasgow, 1984-88; music dir. Detroit Symphony Orch., 1990—. Prin. guest condr. Birmingham (Eng.) Symphony Orch., 1980-83; guest condr. N.Y. Philharm Orch., Boston Symphony Orch., Phila. Orch., Chgo. Symphony, Royal Concertgebow Amsterdam, The Philharmonia London, London Symphony, all Scandinavian Orchs., several operas at Met. Opera House, N.Y.C. Recs. include music of Ellington, Barber, Beach and Ives with DSO; complete symphonies of Sibelius, Stenhammar, Berwald, Dvorak, Gade, Svendsen, Brahms, R. Strauss, Glasounov, Eduard Tubin Schostakovitch, Prokoffiev, Rimski-Korsakov, Part, many others. Decorated knight comdr. North Star Order (Sweden); recipient 1st prize in conducting Accademia Nazionale di Santa Cecilia, 1971.

JARVIS, GILBERT ANDREW, humanities educator, writer; b. Chelsea, Mass., Feb. 13, 1941; s. Vernon Owen and Angeline M. (Burkard) J.; m. Carol Jean Ganter, Jan. 26, 1963; children: Vicki Lynn, Mark Christopher. BA, St. Norbert Coll., De Pere, Wis., 1963; MA, Purdue U., 1965, PhD, 1970. Prof. Ohio State U., Columbus, 1970-95, chmn. humanities edn., 1980-83, assoc. chmn. dept. ednl. theory and practice, 1983-87, chmn. dept. ednl. studies, 1987-95, dir. ESL programs, 1994-2000, chmn. prof. emeritus, 1995—. Cons. Internat. Edn. Program, U.S. Dept. Edn., Washington, 1977-84, many schs., agys. and pub. cos. Author: Et Vous?, 1983, 86, 89; Invitation, 1979, 2d edit., 1984, 3d edit., 1988, 4th edit., 1993, Y tu?, 1986, 2d edit., 1988, Connaitre et se connaitre, 3d edit., 1986, Invitation Essentials, 1991, 2d edit., 1995, Invitation au monde francophone, 2000; editor: The Challenge for Excellence, 1984; mem. editl. bd. Modern Lang. Jour., 1979-86; adv. bd. Can. Modern lang. Rev., 1982—.

Mem. Am. Coun. Tchg. Fgn. Langs. (editor Rev. Fgn. Lang. Edn. 1974, 75, 76, 77), Phi Delta Kappa. Avocations: travel, photography. Home: 8337 Evangeline Dr Columbus OH 43235-1136 E-mail: jarvis.3@osu.edu.

JASHEL, LARRY STEVEN (L. STEVEN ROSE), entrepreneur, media consultant; b. Dayton, Ohio, Jan. 21, 1950; s. Joseph John and Ruth Margarete (Race) J. Student, Harper Coll., Palatine, Ill., 1968-70. Pub.'s asst. Pub.'s Devel. Corp., Chgo., 1971-73; pub. rels. dir. Ill. Entertainer/Chgo. Star/Bankers' Guide, 1973-76; v.p. Internat. Media Prodns., Inc., 1976-78, Microdynamics Corp., Chgo., 1978-80; exec. v.p. Calif. Aqua Tech, Inc., The Solar Generation, L.A., 1980-82; pres., CEO Ra-Tel Comms. Corp., Ra-Tel Entertainment Corp./Cable Radio, Chgo., 1982-88; founder Steven Rose Prodns. and L.S. Jashel Assocs., 1988-98; founder, CEO Spuppets, Ltd., 1996, Children's Cultural Network, 2000—; exec. dir. Superior Benefit Solutions, 1998-2000. TV producer, dir., writer Ind. Broadcasting, Chgo., 1982—; radio producer, on-air personality Nat. Pub. Radio, Chgo. and Washington, 1982—, WJRC-AM, Chgo., 1987-88; music producer for ind. rec. artists, Chgo., 1982—; cons. Corp. for Pub. Broadcasting, 1982—; speaker in field. Musician, singer, composer over 175 copyrighted songs; author: Song of a New Age, 1990, A Bakers Dozen, 1995, Beyond Dreams, 2002; (book and TV script) Lovestar--The Exciting Adventures, 1994-95; author, producer, director Spuppets (puppets in space), 1997; co-author: Morning Song, 1997, The Best Poems of 1997, Planet Medieval, 1998, (musical acts) Mystic Blue and the Z-Generation, 2001, The Detours, Sudden, The Amboy Dukes, The Yellow Brick Road, J.J. Lee and the Radiants, 1964-72. Recipient Blue Ribbon Athlete award, Midwest Sports Assn., 1968, Film Festival award 1984, Am. Svc. award Am. Svc. Corp., 1988, Editor's Choice award Nat. Libr. Poetry, 1992, 97, Nat./Internat. award of Distinction for children's video and packaging, 1998, Videographer award, 1998, Telly award, 2000, Omni award, 2001; named delegation rep. to Presdl. Inaugaration Ball, Washington, 1980. Mem. ASCAP (award 1998-99, 2000), NARAS (Grammy awards 1982—), Nat. Assn. Pvt. Enterprise, Smithsonian Instn. (nat. assoc.), Nat. Cable TV Assn., Internat. Assn. Bus., Eckankar, Children's Entertainment Assn., Chgo. C. of C. Avocations: writing for children, bicycling, camping, hiking. Office: 15519B Keating Ave Oak Forest IL 60452-3616

JASIEK, JERRY, professional sports team executive; m. Tammy Jasiek. BS in Acctg., U. Ill., 1982. Sr. v.p., hockey adminstr. St. Loius Blues Hockey Club, 1997—. Office: Savvis Ctr 1401 Clark Ave Saint Louis MO 63103-2709

JAUDES, RICHARD EDWARD, lawyer; b. St. Louis, Feb. 22, 1943; s. Leo August Jr. and Dorothy Catherine (Schmidt) J.; m. Mary Kay Tansey, Sept. 22, 1967; children: Michele, Pamela. BS, St. Louis U., 1965, JD, 1968. Bar: Mo. Supreme Ct. 1968, U.S. Dist. Ct. (ea. dist.), Mo. 1973 U.S. Ct. Appeals (8th cir.) 1973, U.S. Supreme Ct. 1990. With Peper, Martin, Jensen, Maichel & Hetlage, St. Louis, 1973-97, mng. ptnr., 1990-93; lawyer, co-chair labor and employment practice group Thompson Coburn LLP, 1997—; mem. mgmt. com. Thompson Coburn. Bd. dirs. Baldor Electric Co. Vol. Civic Entrepreneurs Orgn., St. Louis, 1990; vol. counsel St. Louis chpt. MS Soc., 1990—, exec. com. Lt. USN, 1968-73; comdr. USNR, ret. Office: Thompson Coburn One Firstar Plz Saint Louis MO 63101-1693 E-mail: rjaudes@thompsoncoburn.com.

JAUDES, WILLIAM E. retired lawyer; b. St. Louis, 1937; s. August William and Gertrude Johanna (Simon) J.; m. Carol Joan Hurtgen, June 30, 1961; children: Phyllis Anne, Richard William, Suzanne Louise. AB, U. Mo., 1958; JD, St. Louis U., 1962, MBA, 1969. Bar: Mo. 1962, Ill. 1964, U.S. Dist. Ct. (ea. dist.) Mo. 1962, U.S. Supreme Ct. 1966, U.S. Ct. Appeals (8th cir.) 1980. Atty. Union Electric Co., St. Louis, 1963-73, gen. atty., 1973-80, gen. counsel, 1980-85, v.p. gen. counsel, 1985-88. Author: introduction to Mo. Bar Assn. book, Adminstrative Law, 1979. Home: Saint Louis, Mo. Died July 23, 2001.

JAURON, DICK, professional football coach; b. Peoria, Ill., Oct. 7, 1950; m. Gail Jauron; children: Kacy, Amy. Degree in History, Yale U. Profl. football player Detroit Lions, 1973-77, Cin. Bengal, 1978-80; co-owner health and fitness ctr. Cin.; with Nautilus; secondary coach Buffalo Bills, 1985; defensive backs coach Green Bay Packers; defensive coord. Jacksonville Jaguars; head coach Chgo. Bears, 1999—. Active numerous charities. Named 1974 Pro Bowl selection. Avocation: golf. Office: care Chicago Bears Halas Hall at Conway Park 1000 Football Dr Lake Forest IL 60045-4829

JAW, ANDREW CHUNG-SHIANG, software analyst; b. Tainan, Taiwan, Feb. 10, 1953; came to U.S., 1978; s. Ping-Tsen and Pey-Yuh Jaw; m. Amy Chi, July 30, 1979; children: Andrew, Anfin, Audrey. BS in Mech. Engring., Tatung Inst. Tech., Taipei, Taiwan, 1974; MS in Metallurgical Engring., Poly. Inst. N.Y., 1981; MSEE, Syracuse U., 1987. Engr. Tatung Co., Taipei, 1976-78; sr. assoc. engr. IBM Corp., Endicott, N.Y., 1980-89, Rochester, Minn., 1990-91; software cons. A BOC Health Care Co., Madison, Wis., 1991-92; sr. software engr. A Rockwell Internat. Co., Milw., 1992-94; staff software assurance analyst ARDIS Co., Lincolnshire, Ill., 1994-96, lead tech. programmer analyst, 1996-98, Am. Mobile Satellite Corp., Lincolnshire, 1998-2000; sr. network mgmt. sys. engr. Motient Corp., 2000—. Patentee in field. Recipient Cert. of Merit, Assembly of the State of N.Y., 1985; rsch. fellow Poly. Inst. N.Y., 1979. Mem. IEEE. E-mail: andrew.jaw@motient.com.

JAWORSKI, ERNEST G. retired biotechnologist; b. Mpls. m. Pauline Jaworski; children: Diane, David, Christopher. BS in Chemistry, U. Minn., 1948; MS in Biochemistry, Oreg. State U., 1950, PhD in Biochemistry, 1952. Ret. dir. biol. scis. Monsanto Co., St. Louis; scientist in residence St. Louis Sci. Ctr.; former interim dir. Donald Danforth Plant Sci. Ctr. Bd. dirs. Divergence. Recipient Nat. Medal Tech., 1998. Achievements include development of Assemblying and leading the team that developed the world's first practical system to introduce foreign genes into plants.

JAY, BURTON DEAN, insurance actuary; b. Sparta, Ill., Jan. 16, 1937; m. Eva May Eudy, Aug. 10, 1958; children— Cynthia Ann, Sylvia Ruth Putnam, Jon Russell. BA in Math, Ripon Coll., 1959. Actuarial student Northwestern Nat. Life Ins. Co., Mpls., summers 1957-59; various actuarial positions United of Omaha Life Ins. Co., Omaha, 1962-67, exec. v.p., chief actuary, 1967-91; sen., v.p. actuary Mut. of Omaha Ins. Co., 1991—. Bd. dirs. Omaha Ballet, 1986-95, exec. com., 1988-89, v.p. fin., 1988-89. 1st lt. AUS, 1959-62. Fellow Soc. Actuaries (part VI com. 1967-73, chmn. 1969-73, program com. 1975-80, chmn. 1980, planning com. 1986-88, task force on long term care valuation methods 1991-95, bd. govs. 1982-86, 88-90, v.p. 1985-86, 88-90, chmn. com. on health fin. issues 1993-98); mem. Am. Acad. Actuaries (com. on life ins. fin. reporting principles 1975-82, chmn. 1980-82, bd. dirs. 1981-88, treas. 1983-86, v.p. 1986-88, state health com. 1997—, chmn. 1997—, chmn. health orgn. risk based capital task force 1997-99, valuation task force 1997—), Life Ins. Mktg. Rsch. Assn. (fin. mgmt. rsch. com. 1974-78, chmn. 1977-78), Am. Coun. Life Ins. (actuarial com. 1983). Methodist (adminstrv. bd.). Home: 3056 Armbrust Dr Omaha NE 68124-2723 Office: Mutual of Omaha Ins Co Mutual Of Omaha Plz Omaha NE 68175-0001

JAYABALAN, VEMBLASERRY, nuclear medicine physician, radiologist; b. India, Apr. 3, 1937; came to U.S., 1970; s. Parameswaran and Janakay (Amma) Menon; m. Vijayam Jayabalan, May 2, 1963; children: Kishore, Suresh. B.Sc., Madras Christian Coll., India, 1955; M.B., B.S., U. Madras, 1961; Diploma in Med. Radioagnosis, U. Liverpool, Eng., 1967. Diplomate: Am. Bd. Radiology, Am. Bd. Nuclear Medicine. Intern Jipmer Hosp., Pondicherry, India, 1961-62; resident in cariology K.E.M. Hosp., Bombay, India, 1962-63; resident in radiology Mt. sinai Hosp., Chgo., 1970-72; fellow in nuclear medicine Michael Reese Hosp., 1972-73; dir. nuclear medicine Hurley Med. Ctr., Flint, Mich., 1973—. Assoc. clin. prof. radiology Mich. State U. Fellow Internat. Coll. Physicians; mem. Genesee County Med. Soc., Mich. Med. Soc., Radiol. Soc. N.Am., Am. Coll. Nuclear Physicians, Soc. Nuclear Medicine, Am. Coll. Internat. Physicians. Home: 6286 W Cimarron Trl Flint MI 48532-2018 Office: Hurley Med Ctr Flint MI 48503

JAYE, DAVE, state legislator; b. Feb. 2, 1958; BA with hons., U. Mich., 1981, MA with hons., 1982. Mem. Mich. Ho. of Reps from 26th dist., Lansing, 1988-94, Mich. Ho. of Reps. from 32nd dist., Lansing, 1994-97; real estate broker, 1996—; mem. Mich. Senate from 12th dist., Lansing, 1998—. Mem. Liquor Control, Corps. & Fins. Coms. Mich. Ho. of Reps. Named Man of Yr., State Young Reps., 1985. Mem. Macomb County Taxpayers, Kiwanis, KC. Home: 8303 Waschull Dr Washington MI 48094-2333 Address: PO Box 30036 Lansing MI 48909-7536

JAYE, DAVID ROBERT, JR. retired hospital administrator; b. Chgo., Aug. 15, 1930; s. David R. and Gertrude (Gibfried) J.; m. Mary Ann Scanlan, June 6, 1953; children— David, Jeffery, Kathleen. B.S., Loyola U. at Chgo., 1952; M.H.A., Northwestern U., 1954. Adminstrv. asst. Chgo. Wesley Meml. Hosp., 1953-54; asst. adminstr. Sharon (Pa.) Gen. Hosp., 1957-60, St. Joseph Hosp., Joliet, Ill., 1960-65; adminstr. Sacred Heart Hosp., Allentown, Pa., 1965-69; pres., chief exec. officer St. Joseph's Hosp., Marshfield, Wis., 1969-90; cons., 1990—. Regional v.p. Sisters of Sorrowful Mother Ministry Corp., Milw., 1989-91; bd. dirs. Marshfield Savs. and Loan; cons. Marshfield, Wis., 1991—. Past pres. North Central Wis. Hosp. Council; mem. Wis. State Health Policy Council; bd. dirs. Wis. Blue Cross, Marshfield Devel. Corp. Served as lt., Med. Service Corps USAF, 1954-57. Fellow Am. Coll. Hosp. Adminstrs. (coun. regents); mem. Am. Hosp. Assn. (coun. fed. rels., ho. of dels.), Cath. Hosp. Assn. (past trustee), Wis. Hosp. Assn. (past chmn. bd. trustees), Rotary, Elks, KC. Home and Office: 8925 W Minch Dr Minocqua WI 54548-9785

JAYNE, THOMAS R. lawyer; m. Patty Jayne; 4 children. BA, Westminster Coll., 1973; JD, U. Mo., 1976. Bar: Mo. 1976, Ill. 1979, Tex. 1995. Ptnr. Thompson Coburn LLP, St. Louis. Mem. exec. com. bd. mgrs. Ctrl. Inst. for the Deaf; bd. dirs. St. Louis Arts and Edn. Coun.; bd. govs. Truman State U., Kirksville, Mo., 2000—, v.p. bd. govs. Office: Thompson Coburn LLP One US Bank Plz Saint Louis MO 63101*

JEANNE, ROBERT LAWRENCE, entomologist, educator; b. N.Y.C., Jan. 14, 1942; s. Armand Lucien and Ruth (Stuber) Jeanne; m. Louise Grenville Bluhm, Sept. 18, 1976; children: Thomas Lucien, James McClure. BS in Biology, Denison U., 1964; postgrad., Justus-Liebig U., Giessen, Fed. Republic Germany, 1964-65; MA, Harvard U., 1968, PhD in Biology, 1971. Instr. biology U. Va., Charlottesville, 1970-71; asst. prof. biology Boston U., 1971-76; asst. prof. entomology U. Wis., Madison, 1976-79, assoc. prof., 1979-83, prof., 1983—. Rschr.: numerous publs. on social insects. Fellow Rotary Found., 1964—65, Guggenheim Meml., 1986—87; grantee NSF, 1972—. Mem.: Wis. Acad. Scis., Arts and Letters, Animal Behavior Soc., Internat. Union Study Social Insects (chmn. protempore, sec.-treas. 1979—80, pres. western hemisphere sect. 1981, assoc. editor insectes Sociaux 1986—2002), Assn. Tropical Biology, Phi Beta Kappa, Sigma Xi. Achievements include research in on insects. Office: U Wis Dept Entomology 1630 Linden Dr Madison WI 53706-1520 E-mail: jeanne@entomology.wisc.edu.

JEAVONS, NORMAN STONE, lawyer; b. Cleve., Apr. 18, 1930; s. William Norman and Mildred (Stone) J.; m. Kathleen Taze, Oct. 18, 1936; children: Kathleen Stone, Ann Lindsey. B.A., Dartmouth Coll., 1952; LL.B., Case Western Res. U., 1958. Bar: Ohio 1958. Atty. firm Baker & Hostetler, Cleve., 1958—, sr. ptnr., 1968—. Mem. policy com., trustee Laurel Sch., Shaker Hts., Ohio, 1980-99, Beech Brook, Cleve., 1972—, Storm King Sch., Cornwall-on-Hudson, N.Y. Served to lt. j.g. USCG, 1952-55. Mem. ABA, Ohio Bar Assn., Cleve. Bar Assn., Order of Coif, Ct. of Nisi Prius. Republican. Clubs: Univ. (Cleveland); Cleveland Racquet (Pepper Pike). Home: 32555 Creekside Dr Pepper Pike OH 44124-5223 Office: Baker & Hostetler 3200 National City Ctr 1900 E 9th St Ste 3200 Cleveland OH 44114-3475

JECKLIN, LOIS UNDERWOOD, art corporation executive, consultant; b. Manning, Iowa, Oct. 5, 1934; d. J.R. and Ruth O. (Austin) Underwood; m. Dirk C. Jecklin, June 24, 1955; children: Jennifer Anne, Ivan Peter. BA, State U. Iowa, 1992. Residency coord. Quad City Arts Coun., Rock Island, Ill., 1973-78; field rep. Affiliate Artists Inc., N.Y.C., 1975-77; mgr., artist in residence Deere & Co., Moline, Ill., 1977-80; dir. Vis. Artist Series, Davenport, Iowa, 1978-81; pres. Vis. Artists Inc., 1981-88; pres., owner Jecklin Assocs., 1988—. Asst. to exec. dir. Walter W. Naumburg Found., N.Y.C., 1990—; cons. writer's program St. Ambrose Coll., Davenport, 1981, 83, 85; mem. com. Iowa Arts Coun., Des Moines, 1983-84; panelist Chamber Music Am., N.Y.C., 1984, Pub. Art Conf., Cedar Rapids, Iowa, 1984; panelist, mem. com. Lt. Gov.'s Conf. on Iowa's Future, Des Moines, 1984. Trustee Davenport Mus. Art, 1975-98, hon. trustee, 1998—; trustee Nature Conservancy Iowa, 1987-88; mem. steering com. Iowa Citizens for Arts, Des Moines, 1970-71; bd. dirs. Tri-City Symphony Orch. Assn., Davenport, 1968-83; founding mem. Urban Design Coun., HOME, City of Davenport Beautification Com., 1970-72; bd. govs. Am. Craft Mus., N.Y.C., 1995—; mem. devel. coun. U. Iowa Mus. Art, 1996—. Recipient numerous awards Izaak Walton League, Davenport Art Gallery, Assn. for Retarded Citizens, Am. Heart Assn., Ill. Bur. corrections, many others; LaVernes Noyes scholar, 1953-55. Mem. Am. Symphony Orch. League, Crow Valley Golf Club, Outing Club, Rotary. Republican. Episcopalian. Home and Office: 2717 Nichols Ln Davenport IA 52803-3620 E-mail: jecklin@webtv.net.

JEDDA, JOHN, meteorologist; BS in Meteorology, St. Cloud State U. Morning and weekend meteorologist, Duluth, Minn.; morning weatherman KWWL-TV, Waterloo, Iowa; weekend weatherman KMSP-TV, Mpls.; weekend meteorologist, prodr., anchor NewsCenter 13 WEAU-TV. Recipient Seal of Approval for TV weathercasting, Am. Meteorology Assn. Avocations: golf, music, basketball. Office: WEAU-TV PO Box 47 Eau Claire WI 54702

JEFFERSON, JAMES WALTER, psychiatry educator; b. Mineola, N.Y., Aug. 14, 1937; s. Thomas Hutton and Alice (Withers) J.; m. Susan Mary Cole, June 25, 1965; children: Lara, Shawn, James C. BS, Bucknell U., 1958; MD, U. Wis., 1964. Cert. Am. Bd. Psychiatry and Neurology, Am. Bd. Internal Medicine. Asst. prof. psychiatry U. Wis. Med. Sch., Madison, 1974-78, assoc. prof., 1978-81, prof., 1981-92; disting. sr. scientist Dean Found. for Health, Rsch. and Edn., 1992-98; clin. prof. psychiatry U. Wis. Med. Sch., 1992—; disting. sr. scientist Madison Inst. Medicine, 1998—. Pres. Healthcare Tech. Sys., Madison, 1998—; co-dir. Lithium Info. Ctr., Madison, 1975—, Obsessive Compulsive Info. Ctr., Madison, 1990—; dir. Ctr. Affective Disorders, Madison, 1983-92. Co-author: Neuropsychiatric Features of Medical Disorders, 1981, Lithium Encyclopedia for Clinical Practice, 1983, 2nd edit., 1987, Depression and Its Treatment, 1984, 2nd edit., 1992, Anxiety and Its Treatment, 1986, Handbook of Medical Psychiatry, 1996. Served to maj. U.S. Army, 1968-71. Fellow ACP, Am. Psychiat. Assn.; mem. Collegium Internat. Neuropsychopharmacologium, Am. Soc. Clin. Psychopharmacology (nat. bd. trustees 1996—). Avocations: bicycling, travel. Office: Madison Inst Medicine 7617 Mineral Point Rd Madison WI 53717-1623 E-mail: jeffj@healthtechsys.com.

JEFFRIES, KIM, radio personality; b. Tex. m. Bruce Jeffries; 4 children. Grad. Theater and Speech, Northwestern U., Brown Inst. With Sta. WJON-Radio, St. Cloud; with Sta. KS95; reporter Sta. WCCO-TV, Mpls.; with Morning Show Sta. WCCO Radio, 1998, radio host midday live. Contbr. articles to profl. jours. Vol. Amicus, Teen Challenge; numerous other orgns. Avocations: church activities, sports, travel. Office: WCCO 625 2nd Ave S Minneapolis MN 55402*

JEFFRIES, MARY, public relations executive; Contr. Shandwick Internat., Mpls., 1988—, CFO, COO Shandwick U.S., 1993—, mng. dir. Shandwick U.S., 1996—. Office: Shadwick US Ste 500 8400 Normandale Lake Blvd Bloomington MN 55437-3889

JEFFRIES, MICHAEL S. apparel executive; b. 1945; m. Susan Jeffries; 1 child, Andrew. BA in Econs., Claremont Coll.; MBA, Columbia U. With Abraham and Straus, 1968; exec. v.p. merchandising Bullock's, 1980-83; pres., CEO Alcott & Andrews, 1983-89; exec. v.p. merchandising Paul Harris, 1990-92; pres., CEO Abercrombie & Fitch, Reynoldslang, Ohio, 1992—. Office: 4 Limited Pkwy E Reynoldsburg OH 43068-5302

JEFFS, THOMAS HAMILTON, II, retired banker; b. Grosse Pointe Farms, Mich., July 11, 1938; s. Thomas Raymond and Geraldine (Bogan) J.; m. Patricia Lucas, June 20, 1964; children: Leslie, Laura, Caroline BBA in Gen. Bus., U. Mich., 1960, MBA, 1961. With NBD Bank, 1962-99, pres., COO, until 1999; vice chmn., bd. dirs. First Chgo. NBD Corp., 1995-98. Bd. dirs. MCN Energy Group, Inc., Detroit, Intermet Corp., Local Initiatives Support Corp. Bd. dirs. Detroit Symphony, Econ. Club Detroit; chmn. New Detroit, Inc.; dir. Detroit Renaissance, Inc. With U.S. Army, 1960-62. Mem. Bankers Roundtable, Detroit Athletic Club, Detroit Club (pres. 1982), Detroit Country Club, Yondotega Club, Grosse Pointe Club. Republican. Episcopalian. Home: 27 Fair Acres Dr Grosse Pointe Farms MI 48236-3101 Office: NBD Bank 611 Woodward Ave Detroit MI 48226-3408

JEGEN, SISTER CAROL FRANCES, religion educator; b. Chgo., Oct. 11, 1925; d. Julian Aloysius and Evelyn W. (Bostelmann) J. BS in History, St. Louis U., 1951; MA in Theology, Marquette U., 1958, PhD in Religious Studies, 1968; hon. degree, St. Mary of the Woods, Terra Haute, Ind., 1977. Elem. tchr. St. Francis Xavier Sch., St. Louis, 1947-51; secondary tchr. Holy Angels Sch., Milw., 1951-57; coll. tchr. Mundelein Coll., Chgo., 1957-91; prof. pastoral studies Loyola U., 1991—. Adv. coun. U.S. Cath. Bishops, Washington, 1969-74; trustees Cath. Theol. Union, Chgo., 1974-84. Author: Jesus the Peace Maker, 1986, Restoring Our Friendship with God, 1989; co-author: (with Byron Sherwin) Thank God, 1989; editor: Mary According to Women, 1985. Participant Nat. Farm Worker Ministry, Fresno, Calif., 1977—; mem. Pax Christi, U.S.A., 1979—, Jane Addams Conf., Chgo., 1989. Recipient Loyola Civic award Loyola U., Chgo., 1981, Chgo. medallion for Excellence in Catechesis, 1996, Sor Juana award Hispanic Ministry, 2000; named one of 100 Women to Watch Today's Chgo. Woman, 1989. Mem. Cath. Theol. Soc. Am., Coll. Theology Soc., Cath.-Jewish Scholars Dialog, Liturgical Conf. Democrat. Roman Catholic. Avocations: music, gardening. Home: Wright Hall 6364 N Sheridan Rd Chicago IL 60660-1700 Office: Loyola U Inst Pastoral Studies 6525 N Sheridan Rd Chicago IL 60626-5385

JEGEN, LAWRENCE A., III, law educator; b. Chgo., Nov. 16, 1934; s. Lawrence A. and Katherine M. (Stibgen) J.; m. Janet M. Holmberg, Aug. 30, 1958; children: Christine M., David L. BA, Beloit Coll., 1956; JD, U. Mich., 1959, MBA, 1960; LLM, NYU, 1963. Bar: Ill. 1959, U.S. Dist. Ct. (no. dist.) Ill. 1959, U.S. Dist. Ct. (so. dist.) Ind. 1962, Ind. 1966, U.S. Tax Ct. 1966, U.S. Ct. Appeals (7th cir.) 1980, U.S. Supreme Ct. 1980. Tax cons. Coopers & Lybrand, N.Y.C., 1960-62; asst. prof. law Ind. U., Indpls., 1962-64, assoc. prof., 1964-66, prof., 1966—, Thomas F. Sheehan prof. tax law and policy, 1982—, prof. philanthropic studies Ctr. Philanthropy, 1992—, external tax counsel, 1997—. Ind. U. rep. to Nat. Assn. Coll. and Univ. Attys.; co-founder Annual Tax Inst. for Colls. and Univs.; bar rev. lectr., vis. prof. in field; spl. counsel Ind. Dept. Revenue, 1963-65, Gov.'s Commn. on Med. Edn., 1970-72; mem. commr.'s adv. com. IRS, 1981-82; advisor Notre Dame Estate Planning Inst.; mem. Ind. Corp. Law Survey Commn.; state tax notes corr. for tax analysts; contbg. editor Inst. Bus. Planning's Tax Planning Svc.; bd. dirs., officer Ind. Continuing Legal Edn. Forum; 1st chmn. bd. dirs. Baccalaureate Edn. Sys. Trust of Ind.; mem. Ind. Gen. Assembly Study Commn.-Ind. Gen. Corp. Act; mem. Ind. Corps. Survey Commn., 1965—; commr. Nat. Conf. Uniform State Laws, 1981-91; dir. N.Am. Wildlife Assn., 1981-90. Author: Indiana Will and Trust Manual, 1967-95; Lifetime and Estate, Personal and Business Planning, 1987; Estate Planning and Administration in Indiana, 1979, numerous other books, articles, chpts. Chmn. bd. dirs. Ind. Bar Ednl. Sys. Tchrs., 1988-89; mem. adv. bd. Ind. U. Ctr. on Philanthropy. Named hon. sec. of state, State of Ind., 1967, 1980, hon. dep. atty. gen., 1968, hon. state treas., 1969, Ford fellow, 1963; recipient Spl Alumni Tch. award, Ind. U. Alumni Assn., 1970, 1976, 1980, 1985, Excellence in Taxation award for improvement tax adminstrn., State of Ind. Quality for Ind. Taxpayers, Inc., 1990, The Thomas Hart Benton Mural medallion, 1993, 3 Sagamore of the Wabash awards, State Ind., Internat. award, Assn. Continuing Legal Administrators for Excellence in Continuing Legal Edn., Pres.'s Cir. Commemorative medallion Ind. U. Disting. Tchg. award . Fellow Am. Bar Found. (life), Am. Coll. Probate Counsel, Am. Coll. Tax Counsel; mem. ABA, FBA, Mid-West Inst. Estate and Tax Planning (adv. bd.), Ind. Bar Assn. (chmn. taxation sect. 1969-70, presdl. citation 1971), Indpls. Bar Assn. (Dr. Morton Finney Jr. Excellence in Legal Edn. award), Ind. Trial Lawyers Assn. (corp. taxation, estate taxation, state and local taxation). Office: Indiana Univ Sch Law 530 W New York St Indianapolis IN 46202-3225 E-mail: profjegen@aol.com.

JELINEK, JOHN JOSEPH, public relations executive; b. San Pedro, Calif., Sept. 3, 1955; s. Joseph Francis and Patricia Valerie (Powers) J.; m. Christl Michele Schneider, June 1986 (div. July 1997). BA, Loyola U., 1977; MA, Loyola-Marymount U., 1983; postgrad., Syracuse U. Assoc. editor E-Go Enterprises, Sherman Oaks, Calif., 1976-77; advt. dir. Select Promotions, Irvine, 1977-78; editor SCORE Internat., Westlake Village, 1978-79; exec. editor Petersen Pub. Co., L.A., 1979-82, editor, 1982-85; pub. rels. account exec. Hill and Knowlton Inc., 1985-87; acct. supr. Freeman/McCue Pub. Rels., Newport Beach, Calif., 1987-88; account supr. tech. div. Fleishman Hillard Inc., L.A., 1988-89; rep. pub. affairs corp. news dept. Ford Motor Co., Dearborn, Mich., 1989-90; product info. mgr. Ford of Can., Oakville, 1990-92; car product devel., pub. affairs mgr. Ford Motor Co., Dearborn, Mich., 1993-96, product devel., pub. affairs mgr., 1996-98, dir. car strategy comm., 1998-2001, Ford brand comm. mgr., 2001—02; v.p. pub. affairs Ford of Can., Oakville, 2002—. Author: (with others) Consumer's Guide to 1978 Trucks, 1978, Consumer's Guide to 1980 Trucks, 1979, Complete Guide to Used Cars, 1981, How to Buy the Best Compact Truck, 1984; columnist Guns & Ammo Mag., 1980-84, Petersen's Hunting Mag., 1986-87. Capt. Calif. State Mil. Res. 1982-89. Recipient 1st place award Calif. Newspaper Pub. Assn., 1977 Mem. NRA (life), L.A. County Mus. Natural History-Automobile Collection Coun., Aircraft Owners and Pilots Assn., Nat. Aeronautical Assn., Detroit Inst. Art. Republican. Roman Catholic Avocations: travel, flying, skiing, cooking. Office: Ford Motor Co Can The Canadian Rd Oakville ON Canada L6J 5E4 E-mail: jjelinek@ford.com.

JELLEMA, JON, state legislator, educator; b. Bloomington, Ind., Dec. 7, 1943; s. William Harry and Frances (Peters) J.; m. Betsy Zevalkink; children: Frances, Kate, Jon R., Elizabeth. BA, Calvin Coll., 1966; MA, Mich. State U., 1972. Prof. Grand Valley State U., Allendale, Mich., 1972-94; asst. dean William James Coll., Grand Valley State U., 1986-87;

dir. liberal studies program Grand Valley State U., 1988-89, chmn. English dept., 1989-91, prof. English dept., 1991-94; mem. Mich. Ho. of Reps., Lansing, 1994-2000; dean Arts and Humanities divsn. Grand Valley State U., Allendale, 2001—. Vice-chmn. appropriations com., vice chmn. subcom. on transp., chmn. joint capital outlay comm., chmn. policy comm., mem. edn. commn. states, mem. urban caucus. Pres. Grand Haven (Mich.) Pub. Sch. Bd., 1972-84; founder North Ottawa Cmty. Coalition. Mem. Assn. for Values in Higher Edn., Greater Grand Rapids Coun. for Arts, W. Shore Symphony Orch., Phi Kappa Phi. Avocations: sailing, skiing. Home: 510 Park Ave Grand Haven MI 49417-2107 Office: 290 LSH-GVSU Allendale MI 49401

JEN, ENOCH, electro-optical technology products executive; b. Phila., 1952; B in Math., Mich. State U., 1973, MBA in Acctg., 1974. CPA, Mich. With Ernst & Young, Grand Rapids, Mich.; contr., treas. Hi-Ram, Inc.; CFO Porter-Hadley Co., Am. Lumber Sales Corp.; sr. contr. The Hager Group Cos.; CFO Hope Rehab. Network, Inc.; contr. Gentex Corp., Zeeland, Mich., 1990; v.p. fin., treas. Gentex, 1991—. Mem. AICPA, Mich. Assn. CPA. Office: Gentex Corp 600 N Centennial St Zeeland MI 49464-1318 Office Fax: 616-772-7348. E-mail: publicrelations.ir@gentax.com.

JENEFSKY, JACK, wholesale company executive; b. Oct. 27, 1919; s. David and Anna (Saeks) Jenefsky; m. Beverly J. Mueller, Feb. 23, 1962; 1 child Anna Elizabeth 1 stepchild Cathryn Jean Mueller. BSBA, Ohio State U., 1941; postgrad., Harvard Bus. Sch., 1943; MA in Econs., U. Dayton, 1948. Surplus broker, Dayton, 1946—48; sales rep. Remington Rand-Univac, 1949—56, mgr. AF acct., 1957—59, br. mgr. Dayton, 1960—61, regional mktg. cons. Midwest region, 1962—63; pres. Bowman Supply Co., 1963—. Selection adv. bd. Air Force Acad., 3d congl. dist. chmn., 1974—82; chmn. 3d dist. screening bds. Mil. Acad., 1976—82; coord. Great Lakes region, res. assistance program CAP, 1970—73. CBI, maj. USAF, 1951—53. Mem.: Miami Valley Mil. Affairs Assn. (trustee 1985—, pres. bd. trustees 1987—88), Nat. Sojourners (pres. Dayton 1961—62), Ohio State U. Alumni Assn. (pres. Montgomery County, Ohio 1959—60), Dayton Area C. of C. (chmn. spl. events com. 1970—72, chmn. rsch. com. on mil. affairs 1983—87), Air Force Assn. (comdr. Ohio wing 1957—58, 1958—59), Res. Officers Assn. (pres. Ohio dept. 1956—57, nat. coun. 1957—58, chmn. R&D com. 1961—62), Harvard Bus. Sch. Club Dayton (pres. 1961—62, chmn. selection com., Fed. Govt. Employee of Yr. 1991, 1992), Lions. Jewish. Home: 136 Briar Heath Cir Dayton OH 45415-2601 Office: Bowman Supply Co PO Box 1404 Dayton OH 45401-1404 E-mail: bowmansupply@att.net.

JENKINS, DARRELL LEE, librarian; b. Roswell, N.Mex., Aug. 12, 1949; s. Lindon C. and Joyce (King) J.; m. Susan Jenkins. BA, Ea. N.Mex. U., 1971; MLS, U. Okla., 1972; MA, N.Mex. State U., 1976. Asst. edn., psychology, gift libr. N.Mex. State U., Las Cruces, 1972-73, edn. psychology libr., 1973-74, asst. reference libr., 1974-75, asst. catalog libr., 1975-76, asst. serials libr., 1976-77, acting head reference dept., 1977; adminstrv. svcs. libr. So. Ill. U., Carbondale, 1977-82, dir. libr. svcs., 1982-91, head social scis. div., 1992—. Cons. U.S. Naval Base, So. Ill. U., Groton, Conn., 1985-91; chmn. bd. dirs. CEC Comm., Inc., 1997-99. Author: Specialty Positions in ARL Libraries, 1982; co-author: Library Development and Fund Raising Capabilities, 1988; contbr. articles to profl. jours. Mem. ALA (chmn. libr. orgn. mgmt. sect. 1985-86), Am. Soc Info. Sci., Assn. Christian Librs., Ill. Libr. Computer System Orgn. (pres. 1985-86), Phi Kappa Phi, Beta Phi Mu, Phi Alpha Theta. Republican. Mem. Ch. Assembly God. Avocations: tennis, swimming.

JENKINS, GEORGE L. lawyer, entrepreneur; b. Wheeling, W.Va., Jan. 30, 1940; s. George Addison and Mildred Irene (Liggett) J. AB magna cum laude, Kent State U., 1963; JD with honors, U. Mich., 1966. Bar: Ohio 1966. Assoc. Vorys, Sater, Seymour & Pease, Columbus, Ohio, 1966-71, ptnr., 1975—; 1st asst. atty. gen. State of Ohio, 1971-75. Bd. dirs. Fleagane Enterprises, Inc., JMHS, Inc., Impex Logistics, Inc., Nat. Am. Logistics, Inc., ECNext, Inc., CP Techs., Inc., Spata Comm. Corp. Mem. ABA, Ohio Bar Assn., Columbus Bar Assn. (chmn. various coms. 1966—), Columbus Athletic Club, Muirfield Country Club, Desert Mountain Club, others. Democrat. Methodist. Avocations: tennis, jogging, travel, reading, golf. Office: Vorys Sater Seymour & Pease PO Box 1008 52 E Gay St Columbus OH 43215-3161 E-mail: gljenkins@vssp.com.

JENKINS, JAMES ROBERT, lawyer, corporate executive; b. Waukegan, Ill., June 10, 1945; s. William Ivy and Louise Elnora (Lampkins) J.; m. Anita Louise Horne, June 29, 1968; children: James R. II, Andrea Louise. AB in Philosophy, U. Mich., 1967, JD, 1973. Bar: Mich. 1973, Ill. 1974. Law clk., then assoc. Koster and Bullard, Ann Arbor, Mich., 1971-73; law clk. to Justice Seidenfeld 2d Dist. Ill. Ct. Appeals, Waukegan, 1973-74; asst. defender State of Mich. Appellate Defender Office, Detroit, 1974-75; dep. defender Fed. Defender Office, 1975-76; v.p., sec., gen. counsel, counsel sec. to corp. bd. dirs., counsel to exec. com., mem. fin. com. Dow Corning Corp., Midland, 1976—2000; sr. v.p., gen. counsel Deere & Co., Moline, Ill., 2000—. Trustee Alma Coll., 1985—. 1st lt. U.S. Army, 1967-70, Vietnam. Decorated Bronze Star. Fellow Mich. State Bar Found.; mem. Mich. State Bar Assn., Am. Law Inst., Am. Arbtration Assn. (bd. dirs.). Office: Deere Co 1 John Deere Pl Moline IL 61265-8098

JENKINS, JOHN ANTHONY, lawyer; b. Cin., Apr. 11, 1926; s. John A. and Norma S. (Snyder) J.; m. Margery N. Jenkins, May 24, 1997; children: Julie Anne, John Anthony III. BEE, Ohio State U., 1951, JD, 1953. Bar: Ohio, 1954, U.S. Supreme Ct. 1963. Assoc. Knepper White Richards & Miller, Columbus, Ohio, 1954-58, ptnr., 1958-78, Arter & Hadden, Columbus, 1978-94, of counsel, 1995—, mem. mgmt. com. Cleve., 1984-89. Dir. Gen. Exploration Co., Dallas, 1972-80; gen. ptnr. Columbus Lasher P/S, Columbus, Ohio, 1976— , Indian Bend Ltd. P/S, Phoenix, 1978— ; pres. Mummy Mountain Devel., Phoenix, 1978-89. Author: Ohio Public Contract law, 1989, 3d edit., 1994; contbr. articles to profl. jours. Trustee Citizens Rsch., Inc., Columbus, 1960-72; pres. Columbus Kiwanis Found., 1973-76; pres. Beta Theta Pi Bldg. Assn., Columbus, 1972-76. With U.S. Army, 1944-46. Fellow Am. Bar Found.; mem. ABA (chmn. com.), Ohio Bar Assn. (chmn. com.), Columbus Bar Assn. (chmn. com.), Capital Club, Muirfield Village Golf Club, Scioto Country Club, Golf Club (Gahanna, Ohio), Desert Mountain Club (Scottsdale, Ariz.) Masons, Shriners. Republican. Avocation: golf. Home: 10692 EHoney Mesquite Dr Scottsdale AZ 85262 Office: Arter & Hadden 10 W Broad St Ste 2100 Columbus OH 43215-3422

JENKINS, LYNN M. state legislator; b. Topeka, June 10, 1963; m. Scott M. Jenkins; children: Hayley, Hayden. AA, Kans. State U., 1984; BS, Weber State Coll., 1985. CPA. CPA, 1985—; rep. Kans. State Ho. Reps., 1998—; mem. Kans. State Senate, 2000—, mem. gen. govt. budget com., ins. com., post audit com., govt. orgn. and elections com., taxation com. Mem. adv. bd. Ct. Apptd. Spl. Advocate; bd. dirs. YMCA Metro, Family Svc. and Guidance Ctr.; treas., bd. dirs. Prince of Peace Presch.; active Jay Snideler PTO, Susanna Wesley United Meth. Ch. Mem. Kans. Soc. CPAs. Republican. Methodist. Home: 5940 SW Clarion Ln Topeka KS 66610 Office: State Capitol Rm 460-E Topeka KS 66612 Fax: 785-271-6585.

JENKINS, MELVIN LEMUEL, lawyer; b. Halifax, N.C., Oct. 15, 1947; s. Solomon Green and Minerva (Long) J.; m. Wanda Joyce Holly, May 20, 1972; children— Dawn, Shelley, Melvin, Holly Rae-Ann. B.S., N.C. Agrl. and State U., 1969; J.D., U. Kans., 1972. Bar: Nebr. 1973. US. Dist. Ct. Nebr. 1973. Atty., Legal Aid Soc., Kansas City, Mo., 1972, HUD, Kansas City, 1972-73; regional atty. U.S. Commn. on Civil Rights, Kansas City, Mo., 1973-79; regional dir. U.S. Commn. on Civil Rights, Kansas City, Mo., 1979— . Chmn. A.M. Roundtable, Kansas City, 1981-83; mem. Kansas City Human Relations Commn., 1980; Mem. Mo. Black Adoption Adv. Bd., Kansas City, 1981— ; bd. dirs. Joan Davis Spl. Sch. Mem. Nebr. Bar Assn., ACLU, Nat. Bar Assn., Fed. Bar Assn., ABA, Urban League. African Methodist Episcopalian. Lodge: Masons (master mason for civil rights 1979). E-mail: melvin.l.jenkins@worldnet.att.net. Home: 8015 Sunset Cir Grandview MO 64030-1461 Office: 911 Walnut St Kansas City MO 64106-2017 also: Commission on Civil Rights Central Regional Office 4th & State Ave #908 Kansas City KS 66101

JENKINS, THOMAS LLEWELLYN, physics educator; b. Cambridge, Mass., July 16, 1927; s. Francis A. and Henrietta (Smith) J.; m. Glen Pierce, July 8, 1951; children: Gale F., Phillip P., Matthew A., Sarah E. B.A., Pomona Coll., 1950; Ph.D., Cornell U., 1956. Physicist Lawrence Radiation Lab., Livermore, Calif., 1955-60; faculty Case Western Res. U., Cleve., 1960—, prof. physics, 1968-94, prof. emeritus physics, 1994—. Sci. and Engring. Research Council fellow Southampton U., (Eng.), 1983 Mem. Am. Phys. Soc., AAAS, Phi Beta Kappa, Sigma Xi. Home: 869 Belwood Dr Cleveland OH 44143-3239 Office: Case Western Res Univ Physics Dept Cleveland OH 44106

JENKINS, WILLIAM KENNETH, electrical engineering educator; b. Pitts., Apr. 12, 1947; s. William Kenneth and Edna Mae (Treusch) J.; m. Suzann Heinricher, Aug. 22, 1970 BSEE, Lehigh U., 1969; MSEE, Purdue U., 1971, PhD, 1974. Grad. instr., teaching asst. Purdue U., West Lafayette, Ind., 1969-74; research sci. assoc. Lockheed Corp., Palo Alto, Calif., 1974-77, cons., 1983—; asst. prof. elec. engring. U. Ill., Urbana, 1977-80, assoc. prof., 1980-83, prof., 1983-99, dir. coordinated sci. lab., 1986-99; prof., head elec. engring. Pa. State U., University Park, 1999—. Hon. vis. prof. U. York, U.K., 1995-96; vis. prof. Naval Postgrad. Sch., Monterey, Calif., 1996; cons. Ill. State Water Survey, Urbana, 1978, Siliconix, Inc., Santa Clara, Calif., 1979-81, Bell Labs., North Andover, Mass., 1984, AT&T Bell Labs, Lockheed Missiles and Space Co. Fellow IEEE (Millenium medal 2000); mem. IEEE Circuits and Systems Soc. (pres. 1985, editor reprint vol. 1986, Disting. Svc. award 1990), Signal Processing Soc. Avocations: tennis; swimming; sports cars; amateur musician. Home: 1517 Ridge Master Dr State College PA 16803-3164 Office: 129 EE East Bldg University Park PA 16802

JENKS, THOMAS EDWARD, lawyer; b. Dayton, Ohio, May 31, 1929; s. Wilbur L. and Anastasia A. (Ahern) J.; m. Marianna Fischer, Nov. 10, 1961; children— Pamela (dec.), William, David, Christine, Daniel, Douglas Student, Miami U., Oxford, Ohio, 1947-50; J.D. cum laude, Ohio State U., 1953; hon. grad., U.S. Naval Sch. Justice, 1953. Bar: Ohio 1953, U.S. Dist. Ct. (so. dist.) Ohio 1961, U.S. Supreme Ct. 1971, U.S. Ct. Appeals (6th cir.) 1984. Pvt. practice, Dayton, 1955—; of counsel Jenks, Surdyk & Oxley, Turner & Dowd. Lectr. med. malpractice law Served to 1st lt. USMC, 1953-55 Fellow Am. Coll. Trial Lawyers, Am. Bar Found., Ohio Bar Found.; mem. ABA (ho. of dels. 1985-88), Dayton Bar Assn. (pres. 1978-79), Ohio Bar Assn. (mem. bd. govs. litigation sect., 1990-98), Internat. Assn. Def. Counsel, Ohio Assn. Civil Trial Attys., Am. Bd. Trial Advs. (adv.), Nat. Conf. Bar Pres., Kettering C. of C. (past pres.), Kettering Holiday at Home Found. (past pres.), Order of Coif, Phi Delta Phi, Sigma Chi Republican. Roman Catholic. Clubs: Dayton Lawyers (pres. 1999—), Optimist (past pres. Oakwood chpt.). Office: Jenks Surdyk Oxley Turner & Dowd 900 1st Nat Plz Dayton OH 45402-1501

JENNINGS, LOREN G. state legislator, business owner; b. June 1951; m. Bonnie Jennings. Student, Vocat.-Tech. Sch. Bus. owner; Dist. 18B rep. Minn. Ho. of Reps., St. Paul, 1984—. Former vice chmn. appropriations com., Minn. Ho. of Reps., former mem. environ. and natural resources, housing and regulated industries coms.; vice chmn. health and human svcs.-human svcs. fin. divsn., mem. fin. instns. and ins. and regulated industries and energy coms. Address: PO Box 27 Rush City MN 55069-0027 Also: 3340 465th St Harris MN 55032-3701

JENNISON, ROBIN L. state legislator; s. Denise Jennison. Grad., Fort Hayes State U. Kans. state rep. Dist. 117, 1990—; farmer, stockman. Mem. Kans. Farm Bur., Kans. Livestock Assn., Kans. Wheat Growers Assn.

JENSEN, ADOLPH ROBERT, former chemistry educator; b. Elmhurst, Ill., Apr. 14, 1915; s. Adolph George William and Marie (Diener) J.; m. Nelle B. Willams, Sept. 5, 1950; children— Robert, Margaret. B.S., Wheaton Coll., Ill., 1937; M.S., U. Ill., 1940, Ph.D., 1942; postgrad., Ohio U., summer 1959, Rensselaer Poly. Inst., summer 1962, Purdue U., summer 1970, Duke, summer 1971. Head analytical chemistry sect. Lewis Flight Propulsion Lab., NASA, Cleve., 1942-46; prof. chemistry Baldwin-Wallace Coll., Berea, Ohio, 1946-83, prof. emeritus, 1983—, chmn. dept. chemistry, 1956-71. Vis. scientist Ohio Acad. Sci., 1960—64. Fellow AAAS; mem. Am. Chem. Soc., Ohio Acad. Sci. (v.p. chemistry sect. 1969-70), AAUP, Lutheran Acad. Scholarship, Sigma Xi, Phi Lambda Upsilon, Sigma Pi Sigma. Home: 25527 Butternut Ridge Rd North Olmsted OH 44070-4505

JENSEN, BAIBA, principal; Prin. Hawkins Elem. Sch., Brighton, Mich. Recipient Elem. Sch. Recognition awards U.S. Dept. Edn., 1989-90. Office: Hawkins Elem Sch 8900 Lee Rd Brighton MI 48116-2000

JENSEN, DICK LEROY, lawyer; b. Audubon, Iowa, Oct. 25, 1930; s. A.B. and Bernice (Fancher) J.; m. Nancy Wilson, June 30, 1956; children: Charles F., Sarah R. (dec.). LL.B., U. Iowa, 1954. Bar: Iowa 1954. Practice in, Audubon, Iowa, 1958-60; gen. counsel, sec. Walnut Grove Products, Co., Atlantic, 1960-64; legal staff W.R. Grace & Co., 1964-66; gen. counsel, v.p., sec. Spencer Foods, Inc., Iowa, 1966-72, dir., 1968-72; mem. Dreher, Simpson and Jensen, Des Moines, 1972—. Notes and legis. editor: Iowa Law Rev, 1953-54. Pres. S.W. Iowa Mental Health Inst., 1964-66. Served to lt. USNR, 1955-58. Mem. Masons, Sigma Nu, Phi Delta Phi. Republican. Presbyterian. Home: 3901 River Oaks Dr Des Moines IA 50312-4638 Office: Dreher Simpson & Jensen The Equitable Bldg Ste 222 Des Moines IA 50309-3723 E-mail: djensen@dreherlaw.com.

JENSEN, ERIK HUGO, pharmaceutical quality control consultant; b. Fredericia, Denmark, June 27, 1924; came to U.S. 1950; s. Alfred Marinus and Clara Krista (Sorensen) J.; m. Alice Emy Olesen, Oct. 8, 1949; children: Ian Peter, Lisa Joan, Linda Anne. BS, Royal Danish Sch. Pharmacy, Copenhagen, 1945, MS, 1948, PhD, 1954. Head product development AB Ferrosan, Malmo, Sweden, 1955-57; research scientist Upjohn Co., Kalamazoo, Mich., 1957-62, head quality control, 1962-63, mgr. quality control, 1963-66, asst. dir. quality control, 1966-81, dir. quality control, 1981-85, exec. dir. control devel. and adminstrn., 1985-86; pres., cons. Jensen Enterprises, 1986—. Author: A Study on Sodium Borohydride, 1954; contbr. articles to profl. jours.; patentee in field. Bd. dirs. Kalamazoo Inst. Arts, 1971-73, treas., 1973-74, pres., 1974-75. Mem. Pharm. Mfr.'s Assn. (quality control sect. recorder 1971-78, vice chmn. 1978-80, chmn. 1980-83), Acad. Pharm. Scis. (vice chmn. 1968-69, chmn. 1971-72) Lodge: Kiwanis (treas. 1962-65). Avocations: painting, sculpting, photography.

JENSEN, HAROLD LEROY, medical association administrator, physician; b. Mpls., Aug. 17, 1926; s. Harold Hans and Nell Irene (Cameron) J.; m. Nancy Elizabeth Scharff, Sept. 9, 1950 (div. 1976); children: Eric Richard, Kris Ann, Beth Susan; m. Sandra Lee Steinel, Oct. 18, 1976 B.S., U. Ill., 1950, M.D., 1955. Intern Ill. Central Hosp., Chgo., 1955-56, resident, 1956-57; practice medicine specializing in internal medicine Flossmoor, Ill., 1957-87; mem. staff Ingalls Meml. Hosp., Harvey, dir. continuing med. edn., 1979-87, v.p. med. affairs, 1987-2000, cons. med. affairs, 2000—. Asst. clin. prof. medicine U. Ill.; guest lectr. Gov.'s State U., University Park, Ill.; bd. dirs. HealthChicago HMO, 1989-92; bd. gov. ISMIE Mutal Ins. Co., 1986-, chmn., 1991-. Mem. editorial bd. Chgo. Healthcare, 1990-93; contbr. articles to profl. jours. Pres. bd. dirs. Homewood (Ill.) Pub. Libr., 1970-76; mem. policy bd. Cook County Healthcare Summit, 1990; chmn. Ill. Med. Polit. Action Com., 1990-92; chmn. Met. Chgo. Health Info. Network, 1995-2000. With U.S. Army, 1944-46. Mem. AMA (del. 1983-95), Chi. Med. Soc. (pres. 1985-86), Ill. Med. Soc. (trustee 1983-86, sec.-treas. 1986, trustee 1988-96, chmn. bd. trustees 1988-90), Chgo. Health Econ. Coun. (vice chmn. 1981-85), Am. Coll. Physicians Execs., Am. Coll. Utilization Rev. Physicians (cert., bd. dirs. 1985-89), Flossmoor Country Club (pres. 1972-73), Ill. Med. Physicians' Svc. Orgn. (bd. dirs. 1995-96). Republican. Office: ISMIG Mutual Ins Co 20 N Michigan Ave Chicago IL 60602-4811

JENSEN, JIM, state legislator; b. Omaha, Jan. 17, 1934; m. Joan Vecera, 1959; children: Jon, Jeff, Jill, Jay, Joel. Student, Omaha U. Contractor pvt. practice, Omaha, 1959—; mem. Nebr. Legislature, Lincoln, 1994—. Chmn. Omaha Zoning Bd. Appeals, 1987—; vice chmn. Papio/Mo. River Natural Resources Bd., 1990—. Mem. Pride Omaha (bd. dirs. 1989—), Met. Omaha Builders Assn. (bd. dirs. 1960—), Rotary Club.

JENSEN, JOHN W. state legislator; b. York, Nebr., Mar. 28, 1926; m. Myrtle L. Shipp; 5 children. Farmer, 1947—; mem. Iowa Senate from 11th dist., Des Moines, 1978—. Bd. dirs. Iowa Plastics Tech. Ctr. Mem. Bapt. Ch. With USMC, WWII. Mem. Corn Growers Assn., Cattlemen's Assn., Bremer County Farm Bur. Republican. Home: 1331 120th St Plainfield IA 50666-9646 Office: State Capitol 11th Dist 3 9th And Grand Des Moines IA 50319-0001 E-mail: john_jensen@legis.state.ia.us.

JENSEN, KATHRYN PATRICIA (KIT), public radio and television station executive; b. Fairbanks, Alaska, June 20, 1950; d. Edward Leroy and Doris Patricia (Fee) Bigelow; 1 child, Alexander Morgan. BA, U. Alaska, 1974. Sta. mgr., program dir. Sta. KUAC-FM, U. Alaska, Fairbanks, 1976-82; gen. mgr. Sta. KUAC-FM-TV, U. Alaska, 1982-87; pres., gen. mgr. Sta. WCPN-FM, Cleve. Pub. Radio, 1987-2001; COO, WVIZ/PBS and 90.3 WCPN, 2001—. Founding mem. Alaska Pub. Radio Network, 1978-85; bd. dirs. Nat. Pub. Radio, 1983-89, Pub. Radio Internat., 1997—. Bd. dirs. United Way, Cleve., 2001—. Recipient Elaine B. Mitchell award Alaska Pub. Radio Network, 1988, Oebie award, 1992, 95, William H. Kling Innovation and Entrepreneurship award Pub. Radio Internat., 1995, Leadership in Non-profit Mgmt. award Case We. Res. U., Mandel Ctr. Non-Profit Orgns., 1999; named Pub. Radio Gen. Mgr. of Yr., DEI/PRADO, 1999. Episcopalian. Avocations: reading, gardening. Office: WVIZ/PBS and 90.3 WCPN 3100 Chester Ave Ste 300 Cleveland OH 44114-4604

JENSEN, LYNN EDWARD, retired medical association executive, economist; b. Rock Springs, Wyo., May 27, 1945; s. Glen and Helen (Anderson) J.; m. Carol Jean Lombard, June 10, 1967 (dec. Dec. 2001); children: Chelsea, Kara. BA, Idaho State U., 1967; PhD, U. Utah, 1979. Rsch. assoc. Dept. Commerce, Washington, 1967, U. Utah, 1971-74, Utah State Planning Office, 1971-74; economist AMA Rsch. Ctr., Chgo., 1974-75, dir., 1975-85; v.p. health policy AMA, 1985-96, group v.p. strategic mgmt. and devel., 1996-97, COO, 1997-2000, interim exec. v.p., 1998, ret., 2000. Mem. Robert Wood Johnson Found. Adv. Com., Princeton, N.J., 1983-84, Johnson & Johnson Cmty. Health Program, 1985-88; health adv. com. GAO. Editor-in-chief Intermountain Econ. Rev., 1972-73; assoc. editor Jour. Bus. and Econ. Stats., 1981-85; contbr. articles to profl. jours. With U.S. Army, 1968-70. Mem. AMA, Assn. Am. Med. Soc. Execs., Am. Soc. Assn. Execs., Am. Econ. Assn., Nat. Assn. Bus. Economists. Presbyterian. Avocations: reading, computers, swimming, photography, biking.

JENSEN, RICHARD JORG, biology educator; b. Sandusky, Ohio, Jan. 17, 1947; s. Aksel Carl and Margaret (Wolfe) J.; m. Faye Robertson, May 30, 1970. BS, Austin Peay State U., 1970, MS, 1972; PhD, Miami U., 1975. Asst. prof. Wright State U., 1975-79; prof. St. Mary's Coll., 1979—. Guest prof. U. Notre Dame, Ind., 1981—, dir. Greene-Nieuwland Herbarium, 1988—; sr. rsch. fellow Ctr. for Field Biology, Austin Peay State U., 1986-88; vis. scholar dept. botany Miami U., 1987; panelist systematic biology program NSF, 1983-87. Assoc. editor Am. Midland Naturalist, 1988—; mem. exec. com. Am. Midland Naturalist, 1989—; mem. editl. bd. Plant Systematics and Evolution, 1990-96; assoc. editor Systematic Botany, 1996-2000. Recipient Award for outstanding tchg. Wright State U., 1978, Maria Pieta award for outstanding tchg. St. Mary's Coll., 1997; named to Austin Peay State U. Acad. Hall of Fame, 1998; NSF grantee, 1973, 79, 85, 87, 95, Rsch. Corp. grantee, 1984, Eli Lilly grantee, 1990. Fellow: Ind. Acad. Sci. (co-chair program com. 1988, fellow com., biol. survey com., publ. com., grantee 1983, 1991); mem.: Internat. Oak Soc. (bd. dirs. 1997—, webmaster 2000—), Soc. Systematic Biology, Internat. Assn. Plant Taxonomy, Bot. Soc. Am., Am. Soc. Plant Taxonomists (treas. 1991—96, rsch. com. 1987—90, chmn. 1989—90, coun. mem. at large 2000—, honors and awards com. 2000—, chair 2001, Disting. Svc. award 1996), Sigma Xi (grantee 1974). Democrat. Avocations: reading, computing, genealogy research. Home: 2044 Carrbridge Ct South Bend IN 46614-3514 Office: St Mary's Coll Dept Biology Notre Dame IN 46556 also: Greene-Nieuwland Herbarium Univ of Notre Dame Dept Biology Notre Dame IN 46556 E-mail: rjensen@saintmarys.edu., sparky0408@msn.com.

JENSEN, SAM, lawyer; b. Blair, Nebr., Oct. 30, 1935; s. Soren K. and Frances (Beck) J.; m. Marilyn Heck, June 28, 1959 (div. Jan. 1987); children: Soren R., Eric, Dana; m. Carmen Patton, Apr. 7, 1990. BA, U. Nebr., 1957, JD, 1961. Bar: Nebr. 1961. Mem. Smith Bros., Lexington, Nebr., 1961-63, Swarr, May, Smith and Andersen, Omaha, 1963-83, Erickson & Sederstrom, P.C., Omaha, 1983—. Chmn. bd. dirs., v.p. bd. dirs. Omaha Public Power Dist., 1979-81; chmn. Nebr. Coordinating Commn. for Postsecondary Edn., 1976-78. Del. Nat. Rep. Conv., 1960, mem. Nebr. Rep. Ctrl. Com., 1968-70; mem. Regents Commn. Urban U., U. Nebr., Omaha, chmn. Task Force on Higher Edn.; mem. Hwy Commn. State of Nebr., 1989-95; vice chmn. Opera Omaha, 1992-95, v.p., 1994-96. Recipient Disting. Service award U. Nebr., 1981 Mem. Omaha Bar Assn. (past exec. com.), Nebr. Bar Assn. (chmn. com. public relations 1973-76), Am. Bar Assn., U. Nebr. Alumni Assn. (pres. 1976-78), Rotary Club, Omaha Club, Beta Theta Pi, Phi Delta Phi. Clubs: Rotary, Omaha, Racquet. Office: 1 Regency Westpointe 10330 Regency Parkway Dr Omaha NE 68114-3774 E-mail: sj@eslaw.com., Jensen@tconl.com.

JENSEN, SCOTT R. state legislator; b. Waukesha, WI, Aug. 24, 1960; BA, Drake U., IA, 1982; MA, Harvard U., 1984. Pub. rels. exec.; aide Gov. Tommy Thompson, Madison, Wis.; mem. from dist. 23 Wis. State Assembly, 1992—, spkr. of the assembly, 1997—. Dir. assembly Rep. Caucus. Home: 850 S Springdale Rd Waukesha WI 53186-1412 Office: Madison Office Room 211 West State Capital PO Box 8952 Madison WI 53708-8952

JENSON, JON EBERDT, association executive; b. Madison, Wis., Aug. 1, 1934; s. Theodore Joel and Gertrude Beatrice (Edberdt) J.; m. Jeannette Marie Hasman, May 1, 1976; children: James, Peter. BS, U. Wis., 1956; postgrad., Goethe U., Frankfort, Germany, 1956; diploma, U. Cologne, West Germany, 1957. From staff rep. to dir. mktg. and tech. svcs. Forging Industry Assn., Cleve., 1959-75; exec. v.p., sec. Am. Metal Stamping

Assn., 1975-80; pres. Precision Metalforming Assn., Independence, Ohio, 1980-2000, pres. emeritus, 2000—; interim dir. Precision Machined Products Assn., Brecksville, Ohio. Interim dir. Precision Machined Products Assn., 2001—; exec. dir., sec. Forging Industry Ednl. and Rsch. Found., Cleve., 1967-75; lectr. NYU, 1973-75; Ohio bd. advisors Liberty Mut. Ins. Co. Author: Forging Industry Handbook, 1966; editor: Metal Forming mag, 1975-90, pub. 1990-2000. Bd. regents Insts. Orgn. Mgmt., U.S. C. of C., 1977-83, vice chmn., 1982, chmn., 1983; mem. bd. regents Marycrest Sch., Independence, Ohio, 1979-86; bd. dirs. Cleve. Conv. and Visitors Bur., 1988; chmn. Consuming Industries Trade Action Coalition, 1999—; mem. U.S. adv. trade com. With USNR, 1958-59. Rotary Internat. fellow, 1956 Mem. Am. Soc. Assn. Execs. (cert. assn. exec.), Cleve. Soc. Assn. Execs., Rockwell Springs Trout Club, Capitol Hill Club. Home: 5700 Brookside Rd Cleveland OH 44131-6013 E-mail: jjenson@pma.org.

JERGER, EDWARD WILLIAM, mechanical engineer, university dean; b. Milw., Mar. 13, 1922; s. Nickolaus and Ann (Huber) J.; m. Dorothy Marie Post, Aug. 2, 1944 (dec. 1981); children: Betty Ann Murphy, Barbara Lee Smyth; m. Elizabeth Cordiner Sweitzer, Mar. 27, 1982. B.S. in Mech. Engring, Marquette U., 1946; M.S., U. Wis., 1948; Ph.D., Iowa State U., 1951. Registered profl. engr., Iowa, Ind. Process engr. Wis. Malting Co., Manitowoc, 1946-47; asst. prof. mech. engring. Iowa State U., 1948-55; asso. prof. mech. engring. U. Notre Dame, 1955-61, prof., head mech. engring., 1961-68, asso. dean, 1968-82, prof. mech. engring., 1982-97, prof. emeritus, 1989—. Cons. U. Madre De Maestra Santiago, Dominican Republic, 1965-71 Bd. dirs. Beaufort County Schoolbook Found. Served with USAAF, 1943-46. Mem. ASME, Am. Soc. Engring. Edn., Nat. Soc. Profl. Engrs., Internat. Assn. Housing Sci. (dir.), Nat. Fire Protection Assn., Internat. Assn. Arson Investigators, Sigma Xi, Phi Kappa Phi, Pi Tau Sigma (nat. v.p. 1969-74, pres. 1974-78), Tau Beta Pi. Home: 4 Coburn Ct Okatie SC 29910-4560 Office: Univ Notre Dame Coll Engring Notre Dame IN 46556-5637 E-mail: profjerger@aol.com.

JERNSTEDT, RICHARD DON, public relations executive; b. McMinnville, Oreg., Feb. 26, 1947; s. Don and Catherine (Anderson) J.; m. Jean Diane Woods, Dec. 28, 1969; children: Ty Parker, Tiffin Kay BS, U. Oreg., 1969. Mgr. mktg. com. Container Corp. Am., Chgo., 1976-78; exec. v.p. Golin/Harris, 1983-85, pres., 1988-91; CEO Golin/Harris Comm., 1991—. Bd. dirs. Off the St. Club, Chgo., 1984; bd. govs. 410 Club, 1991—. Lt. (j.g.) USNR, 1968-72. Recipient Golden Trumpet award Publicity Club of Chgo.; named Outstanding Jr., U. Oreg., 1968 Mem. Internat. Assn. Bus. Communicators, Pub. Rels. Soc. Am. (Silver Anvil award 1986), Internat. Pub. Rels. Assn., Coun. Pub. Rels. Firms (bd. dirs., vice chmn.), Corp. Voice (bd. dirs.), Arthur Page Soc. Republican. Presbyterian. Avocations: sports, music, photography, traveling.

JEROME, JERROLD V. retired insurance company executive; BS, Linfield Coll., 1952; MBA, Stanford U., 1959. V.p. Teledyne, Inc., L.A., 1962-90; pres., CEO Unitrin, Inc., Chgo., 1990-92, vice chmn., 1992-94, chmn., 1994-99; ret., 1999. Office: Unitrin Inc 1 E Wacker Dr Chicago IL 60601-1802

JEROME, JOSEPH WALTER, mathematics educator; b. Phila., June 7, 1939; s. Joseph Walter and Hermena Josephine (Ostertag) J.; m. Sara Tobin, July 2, 1999. B.S. in Physics, St. Joseph's U., 1961; M.S., Purdue U., 1963, Ph.D., 1966. Vis. asst. prof. U. Wis., Madison, 1966-68; asst. prof. Case Western Res. U., Cleve., 1968-70; faculty Northwestern U., Evanston, Ill., 1970—, assoc. prof., 1972, prof. math., 1976—. Vis. fellow Oxford (Eng.) U., 1974—75; vis. prof. U. Tex. , Austin, 1978—79, Rush Med. Coll., Chgo., 1994—; cons. Bell Labs., NJ, 1981—; vis. scientist, 1982—83; vis. scholar U. Chgo.1, 0985; mem. adv. panel Internat. Workshops on Computational Electronics, 1990—. Author (with S. Fisher): Springer Lecture Series Math. 479, 1975, Approximation of Nonlinear Evolution Systems, 1983, Analysis of Charge Transport, 1995; mem. editl. bd.: Jour. Nonlinear Analysis, mem. editl. bd.: Jour. Computational Electronics. Br. Sci. Coun. sr. vis. fellow Oxford, 1974-75; NSF rsch. grantee, 1970—; recipient disting. alumnus award Purdue U. Sch. Sci., 1996. Mem. Am. Math. Soc., Soc. for Indsl. and Applied Math. Roman Catholic. Office: Northwestern U 2033 Sheridan Rd Evanston IL 60208-0830 E-mail: jwj@math.northwestern.edu.

JEROME, NORGE WINIFRED, nutritionist, anthropologist; b. Grenada, Nov. 3, 1930; arrived in U.S., 1956, naturalized, 1973; d. McManus Israel and Evelyn Mary (Grant) J. B.S. magna cum laude, Howard U., 1960; M.S., U. Wis., 1962, Ph.D., 1967. Cert. nutrition specialist; fellow Am. Coll. Nutrition. Asst. prof. U. Kans. Med. Sch., Kansas City, 1967-72, asso. prof., 1972-78, prof., 1978-95, dir. cmty. nutrition divsn., 1981-95, prof. emeritus, 1996—; dir. Office of Nutrition, AID, Washington, 1988-91; sr. rsch. fellow Univ. Ctr., AID, 1991-92; assoc. dean for minority affairs U. Kans. Sch. Medicine, 1996-98. Mem. tech. adv. group The Nat. Ctr. for Minority Health; dir. ednl. resource centers U. Kans. Med. Center, 1974-77, head community nutrition labs., 1978-95; cons. Children's TV Workshop, 1974-77; chairperson adv. bd. Teenage Parents Center, 1971-75; mem. planning and budget council, children and family sers. United Community Services, 1971-80; mem. panel on nutrition edn. White House Conf. on Food, Nutrition and Health, 1969; mem. bd. dirs., health care com. Prime Health, 1976-79; bd. dirs. Council on Children, Media and Merchandising; mem. consumer edn. task force Mid-Am. Health Systems Agy., 1977-79; commr. N.Am. working group Commn. Anthropology Food and Food Habits, Internat. Union Anthrop. and Ethnol. Scis., 1979-80; chmn. com. nutritional anthropology Internat. Union Nutritional Scis., 1979-80; mem. lipid metabolism adv. com. NIH, 1978-80; mem. nat. adv. panel multi-media campaign to improve children's diet U.S. Dept. Agr., 1979-81; bd. advisers Am. Council on Sci. and Health, 1985-88. Sr. author: Nutritional Anthropology, 1980; asso. editor: Jour. Nutrition Edn, 1971-77; adv. council, 1977-80; editor: Nutritional Anthropology Communicator, 1974-77; editorial adv. bd.: Med. Anthropology: Cross Cultural Studies in Health and Illness, 1976-88; adv. bd.: Internat. Jour. Nutrition Planning, 1977-88, Nutrition and Cancer: An Internat. Jour, 1978—2000, Jour. Nutrition and Behavior, 1981-86; contbr. articles to profl. jours. Mem. com. man-food sys. NRC, 1980-83; bd. dirs. Kansas City Urban League, 1969-77, Crittenton Ctr., Kansas City, Mo., 1979-80; mem. awards com. in nutrition edn. Met. Life Found., 1983-85; pres. Assn. for Women in Devel., 1991-93; trustee U. Bridgeport, Conn., 1992—; trustee Child Health Found., 1992-2000, chmn. bd. dirs., 1996-98; v.p., bd. trustees U. Bridgeport, Conn., 1997—; bd. dirs. Black Health Care Coalition of Kansas City, 1993—, Johnson County (Kans.) Found. on Aging, 2001--; bd. dirs. Solar Cookers Internat., 1992-2000, pres., 1998, 99; mem. Commn. on Aging, Johnson County, 1997--. Decorated Dau. Brit. Empire.; Recipient First Higuchi/Irvin Youngberg Research Achievement award U. Kans., 1982 Fellow Am. Soc. for Nutritional Scis., Am. Anthrop. Assn. (chairperson com. on nutritional anthropology 1974-77, founder com. nutritional anthropology 1974), Soc. Applied Anthropology, Am. Coll. Nutrition, Soc. Med. Anthropology, Am. Soc. Nutritional Scis., 1998; mem. Am. Public Health Assn. (food and nutrition council 1975-78, governing council 1982-85), Am. Inst. Nutrition (program com. 1983-86), Am. Soc. Clin. Nutrition, Am. Men and Women of Sci., Nat. Acad. Scis. (world food and nutrition study panel), N.Y. Acad. Scis., Inst. Food Technologists, Am. Dietetic Assn., Assn. for Women in Devel. (pres. 1991-93), Soc. Behavioral Medicine, Club of Rome (U.S. assoc.) Office: U of Kans Med Ctr 3901 Rainbow Blvd Kansas City KS 66160-7313

JERSILD, THOMAS NIELSEN, lawyer; b. Chgo., Dec. 12, 1936; s. Gerhardt S. and Martha M. (Beck) J.; m. Colleen Gay Campbell, June 15, 1963; children: Karen, Paul. BA, U. Chgo., 1957, JD, 1961. Bar: Ill. 1961, U.S. Dist. Ct. (no. dist.) Ill. 1961. Ptnr. Mayer, Brown & Platt, Chgo., 1969—. Author: Illinois Corporate and Business Forms, 2 Vols., 1989, with ann. supplements, Foreign Investment in U.S. Oil and Minerals, 1987; editor: U. Chgo. Law Rev., 1959-61. Past chmn. Ill. Sec. of State's Corp. Acts Adv. Com. Mem. ABA, Chgo. Bar Assn. (past chmn. corp. law com., past chmn. pub. utility law com.), Ill. State Bar Assn. (corp. and securities law sect.), Ea. Mineral Law Found., Legal Club Chgo. (past pres.), Law Club Chgo. (bd. dirs.). Office: Mayer Brown & Platt 190 S La Salle St Ste 3100 Chicago IL 60603-3441

JESCHKE, THOMAS, gifted education educator; Dir. spl. edn. Des Moines Pub. Schs., 1975-93, exec. dir. student and family svcs., 1993—. Recipient Coun. of Admin. of Spec. Edn. Outstanding Admin. award, 1994. Office: Des Moines ISD Adminstrv Office 1801 16th St Des Moines IA 50314-1902

JESSEN, LLOYD K. pharmacist, lawyer; BS in Pharmacy, S.D. State U., 1978; JD, Drake U., 1985. Lic. pharmacist, S.D., Minn., Iowa; bar: Iowa 1985. Staff phamacist K-Mart Corp., Mason City, Iowa, 1978-79; cmty. pharmacy mgr. People's Drug Stores, Inc., Spencer, 1979-82; hosp. pharmacist Mercy Hosp. Med. Ctr., Des Moines, 1982-86; legal rschr. Drake Legal Rsch. Svc., Drake U., 1983-84; staff atty. Iowa Supreme Ct., 1986-87; chief investigator Iowa Bd. of Pharmacy Examiners, 1987-90, exec. sec., dir. and drug control program adminstr., 1990—. Pharmacy/drug law lectr. Drake U., Des Moines, 1988-99, U. Osteo. Medicine and Health Sci., Des Moines, 1989-94, U. Iowa Coll. of Pharmacy, Iowa City, 1989-99, U. Iowa Coll. of Medicine, 1990-94, Am. Inst. of Bus., Des Moines, 1988-90; presenter in field. Editor (newsletter) Iowa Bd. of Pharmacy Examiners, 1990-99. Grantee Bur. of Justice Assistance/U.S. Dept. Justice, 1990-91, 91-92, 92-93, 93-94. Mem. Am. Soc. for Pharmacy Law, Iowa Pharmacists Assn., Nat. Assn. of Bds. of Pharmacy, Nat. assn. of State Controlled Substance Authorities. Office: Iowa Bd of Pharmacy Examiners 400 SW 8th St Ste E Des Moines IA 50309-4688

JESSUP, PAUL FREDERICK, financial economist, educator; b. Evanston, Ill., Apr. 16, 1939; s. Paul S. and Gertrude (Strohmaier) J.; m. Johanna A.M. Friesen, June 27, 1970; children: Christine Marieke, Paul Charles Friesen. BS, Northwestern U., 1960, PhD, 1966; AM, Harvard U., 1963; BA, U. Oxford, Eng., 1963; M.A., U. Oxford, 1983. Economist com. banking and currency U.S. Ho. of Reps., Washington, 1963-64; faculty U. Minn., Mpls., 1967-82, prof. fin., 1973-82; with Jessup & Co., Inc., St. Paul, 1982—; William Kahlert prof. mgmt. and econs. Hamline U., 1988—. Dir. Gerbill Inc.; Sabbatical prof. in residence Fed. Res. Bank, Mpls., 1973-74 Author: The Theory and Practice of Nonpar Banking, 1967, (with Roger B. Upson) Returns in Over-the-Counter Stock Markets, 1973, Competing for Stock Market Profits, 1974, Modern Bank Management: A Casebook, 1978, Modern Bank Management, 1980, Invest To Win: A Coach's Guide to Stocks, Bonds and Mutual Funds, 2001; editor: Innovations in Bank Management: Selected Readings, 1969; contbr. articles to profl. jours. Bd. dir. Assoc. of the James Ford Bell Libr. Mem. Midwest Fin. Assn. (past pres.) Clubs: Skylight (Mpls.); Univ. Club (Chgo.). Home: 1979 Shryer Ave W Saint Paul MN 55113-5414 Office: Hamline U 1536 Hewitt Ave Saint Paul MN 55104-1284

JETT, ERNEST CARROLL, b. Liberty, Tex., July 10, 1945; BA cum laude, Baylor U., 1967; MA, La. State U., 1969; JD, U. Tex., 1973. Bar: Tex. 1973, U.S. Dist. (so. dist.) Tex. 1979, U.S. Ct. Appeals (5th cir.) 1979, U.S. Supreme Ct. 1979, Mo. 1980. Mem. legal staff Cooper Industries, Inc., 1973-75, Tenneco, Inc., 1975-79; v.p., gen. counsel, sec. Leggett & Platt, Inc., Carthage, Mo., 1979—. Editor Tex. Internat. Law Jour. 1972-73. Mem. ABA, Am. Corp. Coun. Assn., Am. Soc. Corp. Secs., State Bar Tex., Mo. Bar Assn., Phi Alpha Theta, Alpha Chi, Phi Eta Sigma, Phi Delta Phi, Pi Gamma Mu. Office: Leggett & Platt Inc 1 Leggett Rd Carthage MO 64836-9649 E-mail: ernest.jett@leggett.com.

JETTER, ARTHUR CARL, JR. insurance company executive; b. Omaha, Oct. 9, 1947; s. Arthur Carl and Virginia Ann (Turner) J.; m. Jennifer Ann Jochim, Mar. 30, 1974; children: Arthur Carl III, Sarah Ann. BBA, Dana Coll., 1974. Registered health underwriter; CFP, CLU; registered employee benefits cons.; FLMI. Sales rep. life ins. Guarantee Mut., Omaha, 1974-81; pres. Art Jetter & Co., 1981—, Employers Mut. Acceptance Co., Omaha, 1981—. Capt., helicopter pilot inf. U.S. Army, 1968-72, Vietnam. Fellow Life Mgmt. Inst.; mem. CLU (cert., edn. chmn. Omaha chpt. 1984-91), Nat. Assn. Ind. Life Brokerage Agencies (chmn. 2000), Nat. Assn. Health Underwriters (pres. 1991-92, Gordon Merml. award 1995, Health Ins. Industry person of yr. 1995), Mass Mktg. Ins. Inst. (Person of Yr. award 1993). Republican. Lutheran. Home: 13624 Parker Cir Omaha NE 68154-3829 Office: Art Jetter and Co 11305 Chicago Cir Omaha NE 68154-2636 E-mail: art@jetter.com.

JETTKE, HARRY JEROME, retired government official; b. Detroit, Jan. 2, 1925; s. Harry H. and Eugenia M. (Dziatkiewicz) J.; m. Josefina Suarez-Garcia, Oct. 22, 1948; 1 child, Joan Lillian Clark. BA, Wayne State U., 1961; grad., Civilian Police Acad., Westlake, Ohio, 1999. Cert. drug specialist FDA. Owner, operator Farmacia Virreyes/Farmacias Regina, Toluca, Mexico, 1948-55; intern pharmacist Cunningham Drug Stores, Detroit, 1955-63; drug specialist, product safety specialist FDA, 1963-73; acting dir. for Cleve., U.S Consumer Pruduct Safety Commn., 1973-75, compliance officer, 1975-78, supr. investigations, 1978-82, regional compliance officer, 1982-83, sr. resident, 1983-90; ret., 1990. Served with Fin. Dept., U.S. Army, 1942-43. Mem. Am. Soc. for Quality Control (sr.; chmn. Cleve. sect. 1977-78, cert. quality technician, cert quality engr.), Asociacion Nacional Mexicana de Estadistica y Control de Calidad, Ohio Gun Collectors Assn., Cleve. Fed. Exec. Bd. (policy com.), Civilian Police Acad. Westlake Police Dept. Roman Catholic. Home: 25715 Yeoman Dr Cleveland OH 44145-4745

JETTON, GIRARD REUEL, JR. lawyer, retired oil company executive; b. Washington, Feb. 19, 1924; s. Girard Reuel and Hallie (Grimes) J.; m. Mera Riddell, Sept. 4, 1948 (dec. Dec. 1997); children: Mera Elizabeth, Robert Girard, James Thomas. BS in Engring., George Washington U., 1945, BA, 1947; JD, Harvard U., 1950. Bar: D.C. 1951, Md. 1959, Ohio 1960. Elec. engr. in rsch., 1944-45; patent atty. Washington, 1950-51; atty. IRS, 1951-54; trial atty. Dept. Justice, 1954-55; atty. then ptnr. McClure & McClure, 1955-60; with Marathon Oil Co., Findlay, Ohio, 1960-85, asst. to chmn. bd., 1969-73, corp. sec., 1973-85; pvt. practice, 1985—. With USNR, 1945-46. Mem. Bar Assn. D.C., Findlay/Hancock County Bar Assn., Met. Club (Washington). Home and Office: 170 Orchard Ln Findlay OH 45840-1130

JEWETT, JOHN RHODES, real estate executive; b. Indpls., Nov. 24, 1922; s. Chester Aten and Grace (Rhodes) J.; m. Marybelle Bramhall, June 12, 1946; children: John R., Jane B. B.A., DePauw U., 1944. Econ. research analyst Eli Lilly & Co., Indpls., 1946-48; with Pitman-Moore Co., 1948-65, v.p., asst. to pres., 1959-65; with F.C. Tucker Co., Inc., Indpls., 1965—, v.p., 1978-98, Colliers Turley Martin Tucker, Indpls., 1998—. Pres. Market Sq. Arena, 1974-79, Ind. Pacers (profl. basketball team), 1977-79 Served with AUS, 1943-46. Mem. Met. Indpls. Bd. Realtors, Ind. Assn. Realtors, Nat. Assn. Realtors. Clubs: Meridian Hills Country, Kiwanis. Home: 8504 Bent Tree Ct Indianapolis IN 46260-2348 Office: 2500 One American Sq Indianapolis IN 46282

JEZEK, KENNETH CHARLES, geophysicist, educator, researcher; b. Chgo., May 17, 1951; s. Rudolph and June J.; m. Rosanne M. Graziano, Jan. 27, 1984. BSc in Physics with honors, U. Ill., 1973; MSc in Geophysics, U. Wis., 1977, PhD in Geophysics, 1980. Observer Bartol Rsch. Found. Cosmic Ray Lab., McMurdo Sta., Antarctica, 1973-74; postdoctoral fellow Inst. Polar Studies Ohio State U., Columbus, 1980-81; project assoc. Geophysical and Polar Rsch. Ctr. U. Wis., 1981-83; geophysicist U.S. Army Cold Regions Rsch. and Engring. Lab., Hanover, N.H., 1983-85, 87-89; mgr. polar oceans and ice sheets program NASA, Washington, 1985-87; rsch. asst. prof. Thayer Sch. Engring. Dartmouth Coll., Hanover, 1987-89; assoc. prof. geology Ohio State U., Columbus, 1989-95, prof. dept. geol. sci., 1995—, dir. Byrd Polar Rsch. Ctr., 1989-95, 97-99. Prin. investigator Greenland, 1982, 85, Greenland Sea, 1988, Greenland Ice Sheet, 1991, 92; geophysicist Ross Ice Shelf, Antarctica, 1974-75, Devon Island Ice Cap, 1975, Camp Century Greenland, 1977, Southern Greenland Ice Sheet, 1981, East Antarctica, 1981-82; field leader Ross Ice Shelf, 1976-77, Dome C East Antarctica, 1978-79; cons. Polar Ice Coring Office, Greenland, 1983; mem. ad hoc com. remote sensing polar regions Nat. Rsch. Coun., 1985-89, geophys. data com., 1987-94, glaciology com. polar rsch. bd., 1988-95, glaciology rep. SCAR, 1990—, earth studies com. NAS, 1991-95, mem. NAS sci. panel rev. NASA earth obs. sys. data info. sys., 1992-95, mem. NAS sci. panel rev. nat. space sci. data ctr., 1992; mem. numerous NASA coms.; mem. Environ. Task Force, 1992; lab. coord. Sea Ice Electromagnetic Accelerated Rsch. Initiative Office Naval Rsch., 1992. Assoc editor: Jour. Geophys. Rsch., 1991-94; contbr. articles, abstracts to profl. jours. NSF grantee, 1982-83, 83-84, 95-97, Office Naval Rsch. grantee, 1984-89, CRREL grntee, 1985-86, NASA grantee, 1985-87, 87-89, 88-92, 90, 91-93, 95-98, ONR grantee, others. Mem. Am. Geophys. Union (chmn. snow, ice and permafrost com. 1992-94), Soc. Exploration Geophysicists, Internat. Glaciol. Soc. (coun. 1991—), Sigma Xi. Office: Ohio State U Byrd Polar Rsch Ctr 1090 Carmack Rd Columbus OH 43210-1002

JEZUIT, LESLIE JAMES, manufacturing company executive; b. Chgo., Nov. 4, 1945; s. Eugene and Tillie (Fleszewski) J.; m. Janet Diane Bushlus, Oct. 12, 1968; children— Douglas Blake, Kevin Lane B.S. in Mech. and Aerospace Engring., Ill. Inst. Tech., 1969, M.B.A., 1974. Mgr. engring. graphic systems group Rockwell Internat., Chgo., 1968-74, dir. comml. systems Cicero, 1974-75; v.p. mktg. and sales Mead Digital Systems, Dayton, Ohio, 1975-80; v.p. mktg. and sales Signal div. Fed. Signal Corp., University Park, Ill., 1980-81, pres. Signal div., 1981-85, v.p. corp. devel. Oak Brook, 1985-86; div. mgr. power distbn. div. Eaton Corp., Milw., 1986-87, gen. mgr. indsl. control and power distbn. div., 1987-88, v.p., 1988-91; pres., chief oper. officer Robertshaw Controls Co., Richmond, Va., 1991-95; pres., CEO, chmn. bd dirs. Quixote Inc., Chgo., 1995—; chmn. Transp. Mgmt. Techs., LLC, 1998-2001, Quixote Corp., 2001. Instr. Keller Sch. Mgmt., Chgo., 1982-83 Patentee in field Active United Way, Chgo., 1983-85; mem. Chgo. Crime Commn.; bd. dirs. Better Bus. Bur. of Milw., 1986, United Performing Arts Found of Milw., 1986, Greater Milw. Com., 1991-92. Mem. Gas Appliance Mfrs. Assn. (bd. dirs. 1994-96), Will County Local Devel. Co. (v.p. 1984-85, Bus. Man of Yr. award 1985), South Suburban C. of C., Monee C. of C., Am. Highway Users Assn. (bd.dirs. 2001—). Republican. Club: Metropolitan (Chgo.) Avocations: boating, fishing, cross country skiing, photography. Home: 26576 Countryside Lake Dr Mundelein IL 60060-3342 Office: Quixote Inc 1 E Wacker Dr Chicago IL 60601-1802 E-mail: quixpres@msn.com.

JHAWAR, SHIV RATAN, computer and tax consultant, computer software writer; b. Bikaner, India, Aug. 13, 1948; came to U.S., 1973; s. Dhanraj Harakchand and Ratan Devi (Bajaj) J. B in Commerce with honors, U. Calcutta, India, 1968; MS in Acctg., U. Ill., 1974. Enrolled agent, IRS. Accounts analyst CBS TV, Chgo., 1974-75; pvt. practice investment and tax cons., 1975—. Electronic tax transmitter IRS; lectr. income tax and acctg., India and U.S., 1971-80; cons., writer computer software. Creator FuturAccount. Mem. Nat. Soc. Pub. Accts., Am. Acctg. Assn., Inst. Chartered Accts. (cert. 1971), Chgo. Computer Soc. Avocations: writing, skating, chess, computer programming, meditation. Office: 6429 N Washtenaw Ave Chicago IL 60645

JIBBEN, LAURA ANN, state agency administrator; b. Peoria, Ill., Oct. 1, 1949; d. Charles Otto and Dorothy Lee (Skaggs) Becker; m. Michael Eugene Hagan, July 7, 1967 (div. Apr. 1972); m. Louis C. Jibben, July 14, 1972. BA in Criminal Justice, Sangamon State U., 1984; MBA, Northwestern U., 1990. Asst. to chief of adminstrn. Ill. Dept. Corrections, Springfield, 1974-77, exec. asst. to dir., 1977-80, dep. dir., 1980-81; mgr. toll services Ill. Tollway Dept., Oak Brook, 1981-86; chief adminstrv. officer Regional Transp. Authority, Chgo., 1986-90, fund mgr. loss financing plan, 1987-90, also, chmn. pension trust, exec. dir., 1990-96; v.p., gen. mgr. MTA, Inc., Chgo., 1996-99; ptnr. Hanson Engrs., Inc., Oak Brook, 1999-2000; sr. project mgr., cons. mgmt. Alfred Benesch & Co., 2000—02, v.p., 2002—. Cons. labor studies Sangamon State U., Springfield, 1981; bd. dirs. Chgo. Found. for Women. Apptd. mem. transp. adv. bd. City of Naperville, 1988-90; bd. dirs. Family Shelter Svcs., 1990-91; bd. dirs., chair devel. com. Govt. Assistance Program, 1997-2000, sec. bd. 1999; mem. surface transp. adv. panel U. Ill., 1997-2000; mem. nat. adv. bd. Women's Transp. Seminar, 1996—. Recipient Appreciation award VFW, Chgo., 1983, award Ill. State Toll Hwy. Authority, 1986; named Woman of Yr., Nat. Women's Transp. Seminar, 1991, AAUW, 1991. Mem. NAFE, Women's Transp. Seminar (Woman of Yr. award Chgo. chpt. 1991, Nat. Woman of Yr. 1991), Beta Sigma Phi (treas., v.p., corr. sec. Naperville and Easton, Ill. chpts.), Lambda Alpha. Avocations: reading, jogging, gardening. Office: Alfred Benesch & Co 401 Main St Ste 1110 Peoria IL 61602-1241 E-mail: ljibben@benesch.com.

JIMENEZ, BETTIE EILEEN, retired small business owner; b. LaCygne, Kans., June 8, 1932; d. William Albert and Ruby Faye (Cline) Montee; m. William R. Bradley, Aug. 21, 1947 (div. Sept. 1950); 1 child, Shirley; m. J.P. Jimenez, Feb. 20, 1951 (div. Nov. 1978); children: Pamela, Joe Jr., Robin Michelle. Student, Ft. Scott Jr. Coll., Paola, Kans., 1979-81. Reporter LaCygne Jour., 1943-45; union recorder I.L.G.W.U., Paola, 1956-57; mgr. Estes Metalcraft, Osawatomie, Kans., 1977-82; owner El Rey Tavern, 1980-95; ret., 1995. Home: 516 Walnut Ave Osawatomie KS 66064-1254 E-mail: bjozks@idir.net.

JINDRA, CHRISTINE, editor; b. Cleve., Sept. 18, 1947; d. Lad Joseph and Ann Frances (Makar) J.; m. Peter J. Junkin, Aug. 1, 1970 (div. Dec. 1987); children: William Patrick, Michael Lad. BS in Journalsim, Ohio State U., 1969. City reporter Buffalo News, 1969-70; metro reporter Plain Dealer, Cleve., 1970-82, assignment editor, nat. reporter, 1982-84, state editor, 1984-86, metro editor, 1986-88, feature editor, 1988-92, asst. mng. editor, 1992-2001, Sunday editor, 2001—. Mem. Women's Cmty. Found., Women's City Club. Avocations: skiing, gardening, traveling, cooking. Office: Plain Dealer 1801 Superior Ave E Cleveland OH 44114-2198

JISCHKE, MARTIN C. academic administrator; b. Chgo., Aug. 7, 1941; m. Patricia Fowler; children: Charles, Marian. BS in Physics with honors, Ill. Inst. Tech., 1963; MS in Aeronautics and Astronautics, MIT, 1964, PhD in Aeronautics and Astronautics, 1968. Engr. Rand Corp., Santa Monica, Calif., 1965; research engr. Battelle N.W. Lab., Richland, Washington, 1970; research fellow Donald W. Douglas Lab., 1971, Nat. Aeronautics and Space Adminstrn., Moffett Field, Calif., 1973; from asst. prof. to prof. aerospace, mech. and nuclear engring. U. Okla., 1968-75, prof., dir. Sch. Aerospace, Mech. and Nuclear Engring., 1977-81, interim pres., 1985, dean Coll. Engring., 1981-86, mem. various coms., 1985; White House fellow, spl. asst. to sec. of transp. U.S. Dept. Transp., Washington, 1975-76; chancellor U. Mo., Rolla, 1986-91; pres. Iowa State U., Ames, 1991-2000, Purdue U., 2000—. Bd. dirs. Kerr McGee Corp., Mo. Alliance for Sci., 1987-91, The Keystone Found., 1984-90, Mo. Corp. for Sci. and Tech., vice-chmn., 1990-91; participant Japanese Econ. Found. Vis. Leaders Program, 1983; mem. Gov.'s Coun. on Sci. and Tech. State of Okla.,

1983-84, Gordon Rsch. Conf. on Geophysics; mem. planning com. for 80's Okla. State Regents for Higher Edn.; mem. organizing com. 14th Midwestern Mechanics Conf.; mem. adv. com. for engring. sci. NSF Engring. Directorate, 1985-88; mem. com. on statewide postsecondary telecomm. policy Mo. Coordinating Bd. for Higher Edn., 1987-91; chmn. Congrl. Aero. Adv. Com., 1987-89; sci. adviser to Gov. of Mo., 1990-91; mem. Am. Coun. on Edn. Com. on Math. and Sci., 1990-91. Contbr. articles and reports to profl. publs. Civilian aide Sec. of Army, State of Mo. East, 1987-91; bd. dirs. Bankers Trust, 1995—, Iowa Spl. Olympics, Am. Coun. on Edn., 1996—, Nat. Merit Scholarship Corp., 1997—; mem. Kellogg Commn. on the Future of State and Land-Grant U., 1995—; founding pres. Global Consortium of Higher Edn. and Rsch. for Agr., 1999. Recipient Ralph Teetor award Soc. Automotive Engrs., 1971, Brandon H. Griffith award U. Okla., U. Okla. Regents award for superior teaching, 1975, IIT Prof. Achievement award, 1992, Delta Tau Delta Achievement award, 1992, Engrs. Club St. Louis Achievement award, 1991, Dept. Army Outstanding Civilian Svc. medal, 1991; NASA fellow, 1966; NSF fellow, 1965; AEC/NORCUS summer faculty fellow, 1970-71, NASA/ASEE fellow, 1973. Fellow AAAS, AIAA (assoc., sec.-treas. Okla. chpt., vice chmn., chmn.); mem. ASME, AAUP (v.p., pres. Okla. chpt.), NSPE, Am. Phys. Soc., Am. Soc. Engring. Edn. (Centennial Medallion 1993), Nat. Assn. State Univs. and Land Grant Colls. (bd. dirs., chair 1997-98), Assn. Big Twelve Univs. (pres. 1994-96), Mo. Soc. Profl. Engrs., Rotary, Phi Beta Kappa, Tau Beta Pi, Sigma Xi, Pi Tau Sigma, Sigma Gamma Tau, Sigma Pi Sigma, Phi Eta Sigma. Home: 500 McCormick Rd West Lafayette IN 47906 Office: Purdue U Office of the Pres West Lafayette IN 47906

JOBE, MURIEL IDA, medical technologist, educator; b. St. Louis, Apr. 17, 1931; d. Ernest William and Mable Mary (Hefflinger) Meissner; m. James Joseph Jobe, Sr., May 17, 1952 (dec. 1984); children: James J. Jr., Timothy D. (dec. 1976), Jonathan J., Daniel D. BS, Wash. U., St. Louis, 1971; med. technologist tng., Mo. Bapt. Hosp., St. Louis, 1973-74; postgrad., Webster U., St. Louis, 1981-83. Cytogenetic tech. St. Luke's Hosp., St. Louis, 1963-65; med. technologist Mo. Bapt. Hosp., 1974-76, 82-84, sr. instr., 1976-82, lead technologist, 1985; mgr., clin. instr. St. Louis U. Hosp., 1985-96; retired, 1996. Mem. student selection com. Mo. Bapt. Hosp. Med. Technologists, St. Louis, 1975-78; observer Nat. Com. Clin. Lab. Stds., Villanova, Pa., 1989-90, advisor, 1991-92, 93-95. Co-author: Clinical Hematology: Principles, Procedures, Correlations, 1991, 2d edit., 1997, 8th Revision PER Handbook, A Review Manual for Clinical Laboratory Exams., 1992. Counselor La Leche League; participant Ecology Day; community rels. chmn. The Life Seekers, St. Louis. Mem. Am. Soc. Clin. Pathologists (staff asst. 1984, 86, 88, 89, 94, 95, dir. workshops 1990, 91, bd. dirs. 1990-92, state advisor 1992-96, chmn. regional adv. com., adminstrv. bd. assoc. mem. sect., Regional Assoc. Mem. award 1994, Assoc. Mem. Sect. Disting. Svc. award 1997), Am. Assn. Clin. Chemists, Am. Soc. Med. Tech. (dir. workshop 1984), Mo. Soc. Med. Tech. (pres. 1985-86), Clin. Lab. Mgrs. Assn. (chmn. devel. St. Louis chpt.). Mem. United Ch. of Christ. Avocations: travel, cooking, gardening, dancing.

JOCK, PAUL F., II, lawyer; b. Indpls., Jan. 25, 1943; s. Paul F. and Alice (Sheehan) J.; m. Gail A. Webre, Sept. 16, 1967; children: Craig W., Nicole L. BBA, U. Notre Dame, 1965; JD, U. Chgo., 1970. Bar: Ill. 1970, N.Y. 1990. Ptnr. Kirkland & Ellis, Chgo. and N.Y.C., 1970-2001; v.p., gen. counsel GM Asset Mgmt., N.Y.C., 2000—. V.p. legal affairs Tribune Co., Chgo., 1981. Assoc. editor U. Chgo. Law Rev., 1969-70. Served to lt. USN, 1965-67. Mem. ABA, Chgo. Bar Assn., Assn. of the Bar of City of N.Y. Address: GM Asset Mgmt 767 Fifth Ave New York NY 10153 E-mail: paul.jock@gm.com.

JOCKETTY, WALT, professional sports team executive; m. Sue Jocketty; children: Ashley, Joey. BBA, U. Minn., 1974. Dir. minor league, scouting/asst. gen. mgr./player personnel Oakland A's, 1980-93; v.p., gen. mgr. St. Louis Cardinals, 1994—. Office: St Louis Cardinals 250 Stadium Plz Saint Louis MO 63102-1722

JOCKUSCH, CARL GROOS, JR. mathematics educator; b. San Antonio, July 13, 1941; s. Carl Groos and Mary English (Dickson) J.; m. Elizabeth Ann Northrop, June 17, 1964; children— William, Elizabeth, Rebecca. Student, Vanderbilt U., 1959-60; B.A. with highest honors, Swarthmore Coll., 1963; Ph.D., M.I.T., 1966. Instr. Northeastern U., 1966-67; asst. prof. math. U. Ill., Urbana-Champaign, 1967-71, assoc. prof., 1971-75, prof., 1975—. Contbr. articles to profl. jours.; editor Jour. Symbolic Logic, 1974-75, Proc. Am. Math. Soc., 1997—. Mem. Assn. Symbolic Logic, Am. Math. Soc., Math. Assn. Am. Home: 704 E Mchenry St Urbana IL 61801-6846 Office: Univ Ill Dept Math 1409 W Green St Urbana IL 61801-2943

JODARSKI, RICHARD R. social services association executive; m. Judith Jodarski; children: Jeremy, Jennifer. BS in Psychology, U. Wis., La Crosse, 1972. Account exec. Merrill, Lynch, Pierce, Fenner and Smith, 1975-78; bank trust officer, 1978-81; sr. trust officer First Nat. Bank of Manitowoc, Wis., 1981, v.p., sr. trust officer, 1998; pres., CEO Aid Assn. for Lutherans Trust Co., Appleton, 1998—. Pres. Stangel Found.; bd. dirs. Manitowoc Mut. Ins. Co. Active Manitowoc YMCA Endowment Fund, Capitol Civic Centre, Manitowoc Symphony Orch. Office: Aid Assn for Lutherans 4321 N Ballard Rd Appleton WI 54919-0001

JOEKEL, RONALD G. fraternal organization administrator; BA, Wesleyan U., Lincoln, Nebr., 1956; MEd, U. Nebr., 1959, EdD, 1966. Prin., tchr., DeWitt, Nebr., 1956-60; supt., 1960-63; supr., instr. Wesleyan U., Lincoln, 1963-65, asst. dir., asst. prin., 1966-67, assoc. prof., 1970-72, assoc. dir., assoc. prof., 1971-72, assoc. dean, assoc. prof., 1972-88, assoc. dean, acting chair, 1988-89, chair, 1989-95; exec. dir. Phi Delta Kappa Internat., Bloomington, Ind., 1995—. Cons. Workers Compensation, Ohio, 1976-79. Dir. Ohio Dept. Highway Safety, Columbus, 1985-90, Dept. Pub. Svc., Cleve., 1990—; exec. dir. Ohio State Employment Rels. Bd., Columbus, 1984; asst. dir. Ohio Dept. Adminstrv. Svcs., Columbus, 1984-85, Ohio Dept. Natural Resources, Columbus, 1984-85; chmn. Nuclear Power Emergency Evaluation Com., Columbus, 1985-90; bd. dirs. Ohio Retirement Study Commn., 1983-84, North East Ohio Regional Sewer Dist., Cleve., 1991—. Office: Phi Delta Kappa International PO Box 789 Bloomington IN 47402-0789

JOERRES, JEFFREY A. staffing company executive; BS, Marquette U. Various mgmt. positions IBM; v.p. sales and mtkg. ARI Network Svcs.; v.p. mktg. Manpower, Inc., Milw., from 1993, sr. v.p. European ops. and global account mgmt. and devel., until 1999, pres., CEO, 1999—. Office: Manpower Inc 5301 N Ironwood Rd Milwaukee WI 53217-4982

JOFFE, STEPHEN NEAL, surgical laser educator, medical executive; b. Springs, Transvaal, Republic of South Africa, Jan. 11, 1943; came to U.S., 1980; s. Hirshy N. and Pearl (Cohen) J.; m. Sandra Noche, Dec. 18, 1966; children: Heidi, Craig. BS, U. Stellenbosch, Cape Province, South Africa, 1963, MD, 1976; B in Medicine and Surgery, U. Witwatersrand, Johannesburg, South Africa, 1967. Fellow Coll. of Surgeons of South Africa, 1972, Royal Coll. Physicians and Surgeons of Glasgow, 1973, Royal Coll. of Surgeons of Edinburgh, 1973, Am. Coll. Surgeons, 1983; Diplomate Am. Bd. Laser Medicine and Surgery, 1986. Rotating registrar surgery Groote Schuur Hosp. Univ. of Capetown (South Africa), 1970-72, sr. registrar in surgery, 1972-73; sr. registrar 3 tutor in surgery dept. of surgery Hammersmith Hosp. and Royal Postgrad. Med. Sch., London, U.K., 1973-75, resident surg. officer U.K., 1974-75; hon. cons. surgeon, sr. lectr. in surgery Univ. of Glasgow (Scotland), 1975-80, Dept. of Surgery Glasgow Royal Infirmary, 1975-80; prof. of surgery U. Cin. Coll. of Medicine, 1980-90; esteemed quondam prof. surgery and medicine U. Cin. Med. Ctr., 1990—. House surgeon, house physician Johannesburg Gen. Hosp., 1968; resident surg. officer Hammersmith Hosp., 1974; courtesy staff and cons. surgeon various U.S. Hosps.; chmn. bd., dir. Surg. Laser Techs. (Japan) Co., Ltd., 1986, 88; pres. Laser Ctrs. Am., Inc., Cin., 1985—. Editor numerous med. books; contbr. articles to numerous publs., mags. and jours. Recipient Nash Meml. Prize, 1966, 1989 Enterprise award Cin. Bus. Courier; Barnes Agranat scholar, 1967. Mem. AAAS, AMA, Internat. Assn. Endocrine Surgeons, Internat. Duodenal Club, Internat. Fedn. Surg. Colls., Internat. Nd;Laser Soc. (chmn., founder 1983, co-chmn. 1985), Collegium Internat. Chirurgiae Digestivae, Internat. Soc. Surgery, Internat. Soc. Optical Engring. (co-chmn. Lasers in Medicine 1986, 87), Internat. Hosp. Fedn., European Soc. Surg. Rsch., Assn. Surgeons Great Britain and Ireland, British Soc. Gastroenterology, Pancreatic Soc. Great Britain, Surg. Rsch. Soc. (U.K.), Caledonian Soc. Gastroenterology, Scottish Soc. for Exptl. Medicine, Indian Soc. Gastroenterology, Assn. for Advancement Med. Instrumentation, Assn. for Gnotobiotics, Soc. U. Surgeons, Soc. for Surgery of Alimentary Tract, Royal Soc. Medicine, Endocrine Soc., Assn. Acad. Surgeons, Pancreas Club, Am. Assn. Clin. Anatomists, Am. Assn. Endocrine Surgeons, Am. Bd. Laser Surgery (examiner 1986), Am. Coll. Gastroenterology, Am. Coll. Healthcare Adminstrs., Am. Coll. Healthcare Mktg. Inst., Am. Coll. Med. Staff Affairs Inst., Am. Fedn. Clinic Rsch., Am. Gastroent. Assn., Am. Inst. Physics, Am. Physiol. Soc., Am. Soc. Gastrointestinal Endoscopy, Am. Soc. Laser Medicine and Surgery, N.Y. Acad. Scis., numerous others. Home: 8750 Red Fox Ln Cincinnati OH 45243-3731

JOHANNES, ROBERT J. lawyer; b. Milwaukee, Wis., July 31, 1952; BA summa cum laude, Marquette U., 1974; JD, U. Chgo., 1977. Bar: Wis. 1977. Mem. Michael, Best & Friedrich LLP, Milw., 1977—. Mem. ABA, Wis. Bar Assn., Phi Beta Kappa. Office: Michael Best Friedrich LLP 100 E Wisconsin Ave Ste 3300 Milwaukee WI 53202-4108

JOHANNESON, GERALD BENEDICT, office products company executive; b. May 11, 1940; BS, N.D. State U., 1962. With Internat. Harvester, Chgo., 1962-83, Uniroyal, Troy, Mich., 1983-85; exec. v.p. Haworth Inc., Holland, 1985-87, exec. v.p., chief oper. officer, 1987—, pres., COO, 1994-97, pres., CEO, 1997—. Office: Haworth Inc 1 Haworth Ctr Holland MI 49423-8820

JOHANNS, MICHAEL O. governor; b. Osage, Iowa, June 18, 1950; s. John Robert Sr. and Adeline Lucy (Royek) J.; m. Constance J. Weiss, June 10, 1972 (div. Dec. 1985); children: Justin Michael, Michaela Susan; m. Stephanie A. Suther, Dec. 24, 1986. BA, St. Mary's Coll., Winona, Minn., 1971; JD, Creighton U., 1974. Jud. law clk. Nebr. Supreme Ct., Lincoln, 1974-75; assoc. lawyer Cronin & Hannon, O'Neill, Nebr., 1975-76; ptnr. Office of Nelson Johanns, Lincoln, 1976-91; mayor City of Lincoln, 1991-98; gov. State of Nebr., 1999—. Mem. Lancaster County Bd., Lincoln, 1983-87; mem. City Coun. Lincoln, 1989-91. Mem. Nebr. Bar Assn. Roman Catholic. Avocations: skiing, biking, reading. Office: Office of Gov PO Box 94848 Lincoln NE 68509-4848 E-mail: mjohanns@notes.state.ne.us.

JOHANNSEN, CHRIS JAKOB, agronomist, educator, administrator; b. Randolph, Nebr., July 24, 1937; s. Jakob J. and Marie J. (Lorenzsen) J.; m. Joanne B. Rockwell, Aug. 16, 1959; children: Eric C., Peter J. BS, U. Nebr., Lincoln, 1959, MS, 1961; PhD, Purdue U., 1969. Program leader lab. for applications of remote sensing Purdue U., 1966-69, from asst. prof. to assoc. prof. agronomy, 1969-77, dir. ag data network, 1985-87, dir. lab. for applications of remote sensing, 1985—; prof. U. Mo., Columbia, 1977-84, dir. geogrpahic resources ctr., 1981-84; dir. Ag Data Network, Purdue U., 1985-87, Lab. for Applications of Remote Sensing, 1985—; prof. Purdue U., W. Lafayette, Ind., 1985—; dir. Nat. Resources Rsch. Inst., 1987-93, Environ. Scis. and Engring. Inst./Purdue U., West Lafayette, 1994-96. Vis. prof. U. Calif., Davis, 1980-81; cons. Lockheed Electronics, Houston, 1975-76, NOAA, Columbia, Mo., 1978-80, FAO UN, Nairobi, Kenya, 1983, 87, Rome, 1987, U.S. Agy. Internat. Devel., Eastern Africa, 1983, USDA-Soil Conservation Svc., Washington, 1984, 95-96, Space Sci. Corp., Washington, 1984-85, IBM, 1991, Ball Aerospace Corp., 1995, Space Imaging Inc., 1996—, Aventis CropSci. Inc., 1998—, RapidEye Corp., 2001-;pres., bd. dirs. Ecologistics Ltd., 2001; vis. chief scientist Space Imaging Inc., 1996-97; adj. prof. Katholique U. Lueven, Belgioum. Pres. coun. St. Andrew's Luth. Ch., Columbia, 1975-77; asst. scoutmaster Boy Scouts Am., Gt. Rivers coun., Columbia, 1979-84, West Lafayette, 1985-91; pres. Purdue Luth. Ministry, 1989-95; apptd. mem. West Lafayette Redevel. Authority, 2001-2004. Recipient Tech. Innovation Rsch. award NASA, 1979, Disting. Svc. award Mo. Assn. Soil and Water Conservation Dists., 1982, Agr. Alumni Merit award U. Nebr., 1995. Fellow Am. Soc. for Photogrammetry and Remote Sensing (Outstanding Svc. award 1992), Am. Soc. Agronomy, Soil Sci. Soc. Am., Soil Conservation Soc. Am. (pres. 1982-83); mem. World Assn. of Soil and Water, Internat. Union Soil Sci., Geosci. and Remote Sensing Soc. of IEEE, Ind. Acad. Scis., Rotary (Lafayette chpt. bd. dirs. 1995-98), Epsilon Sigma Phi (Internat. award 2000). Home: 209 Cedar Hollow Ct West Lafayette IN 47906-1671 Office: Lab Applications Remote Sensing 1202 POTR Hall Purdue U West Lafayette IN 47907-1202 E-mail: johan@purdue.edu.

JOHANSSON, NILS A. information services executive; b. 1948; Grad., U. Uppsala, Sweden, 1972; MBA, U. Ill., 1975. With Am. Hosp. Supply Corp., 1973-81; group contr. Bell & Howell Co., Skokie, Ill., 1981-87, treas., 1987-88, treas., v.p., 1988-89, bd. dirs., 1990—, v.p. fin., CFO, 1989—, bd. dirs., 1990, sr. v.p. fin., CFO, 1992-94. Office: Bell & Howell Co 5215 Old Orchard Rd Skokie IL 60077-1076

JOHN, GERALD WARREN, hospital pharmacist, educator; b. Salem, Ohio, Feb. 16, 1947; s. Harold Elba and Ruth Springer (Pike) J.; m. Jean Ann Marie Orris, Nov. 5, 1977; children: Patrick Warren, Jeanette Lynn. BS in Pharmacy, Ohio No. U., 1970; MS, U. Md., 1974. Registered pharmacist, Ohio, S.C. Staff pharmacist North Columbiana County Cmty. Hosp., Salem, 1970-72; asst. resident in hosp. pharmacy U. Md. Hosp., Balt., 1972-73, sr. resident, 1973-74, chmn. patient care pharmacies, 1974-76; dir. pharmacy Ohio Valley Hosp., Steubenville, 1976-97; exec. dir. Tri-State Health Svcs., Inc., 1997—. Mem. adv. bd. Contemporary Pharmacy Practice, 1977-83; preceptor profl. externship program Ohio No. U. Sch. Pharmacy, 1977—; adj. clin. instr. practical experience program Duquesne U. Sch. Pharmacy, 1976—; dir. pharmacy Trinity Med. Ctr., Steubenville, 1997—. Columnist Weirton Daily Times, 1990-94. Trustee, v.p. Valley Hospice Inc., 1985-98, 2000—. Named Hosp. Pharmacist of Yr., Md. Soc. Hosp. Pharmacists, 1976, Outstanding Young Man of Am., U.S. Jaycees, 1977. Fellow Am. Soc. Con. Pharmacists; mem. Am. Soc. Hosp. Pharmacists, Ohio Soc. Hosp. Pharmacists, Jefferson County Acad. Pharmacy, Southeastern Ohio Soc. Hosp. Pharmacists (pres. 1985-87), Rho Chi, Phi Eta Sigma. Methodist. E-mail: gjohn@trinityhealth.com.

JOHNS, DIANA, secondary education educator; BS, Mich. State U.; MS, U. Mich. Jr. high school tchr. Crestwood Dist. Schools, Dearborn Heights, Mich., sr. high sch. tchr., sci. dept. chair. Outstanding Earth-Sci. Tchr. award, 1992, Tchr. of the Year award Crestwood Sch. Dist., Scholarship award Crestwood High Sch. Chpt. NHS. Mem. Nat. Assn. Geology Tchrs., Mich. Earth Sci. Tchrs. Assn. Office: Crestwood Sr High Sch 1501 N Beech Daly Rd Dearborn Heights MI 48127-3403

JOHNS, JANET SUSAN, physician; b. Chgo., July 18, 1941; d. Nicholas C. and Doris Ann (Douglas) J.; m. Harlan R. Bullard; children: George, Sam. AB, Ind. U., 1963, MD, 1966. Diplomate Am. Acad. Family Practice. Intern Meml. Hosp., South Bend, Ind. Home: 3510 Woodcliff Dr Lafayette IN 47905-8834 Office: Purdue U Student Health 1826 Push West Lafayette IN 47905

JOHNS, WILLIAMS DAVIS, JR. geologist, educator; b. Waynesburg, Pa., Nov. 2, 1925; s. William Davis and Beatrice (VanKirk) J.; m. Mariana Paull, Aug. 28, 1948 (dec. Apr. 1993); children: Sydney Ann (dec.), Susan Helen, David William, Amy Matilda; m. Carla Waal, Nov. 6, 1999. BA, Coll. Wooster, 1947; MA, U. Ill., 1951, PhD, 1952. Spl. rsch. asst. petrology Engring. Expt. Sta., U. Ill., 1949-52; rsch. asst., then asst. prof. geology U. Ill., 1952-55; mem. faculty Washington U., St. Louis, 1955-69, prof. earth scis., 1964-69, chmn. dept., 1962-69; with dept. geology U. Mo., Columbia, 1970-97, prof. emeritus, 1997—. Vis. prof. U. Pitts., 1990-91, U. Vienna, 1994. Recipient U.S.-German Scientist award U. Goettingen, 1976-77; Fulbright fellow U. Goettingen, 1959-60, U. Heidelberg, 1968-69, U. Vienna, 1983-84. Fellow Geol. Soc. Am., Mineral. Soc. Am.; mem. Mineral. Soc. Great Britain and Ireland, Mineral. Soc. Can., Deutsches Mineralogisches Gesellschaft, Geochem. Soc., Phi Beta Kappa. Presbyterian (elder). Home: 2200 Yuma Dr Columbia MO 65203-1452

JOHNSEN, DAVID C. dean, dentistry educator; BS, U. Mich., 1965, DDS, 1970; MS in Pediat. Dentistry, U. Iowa, 1973. Diplomate Am. Bd. Pediat. Dentistry. Pediat. dentistry instr. U. Iowa, Iowa City, 1972-73, prof. pediat. dentistry, dean, 1995—; from asst. to assoc. prof. W.Va. U. Hosp., 1974-80, Case Western Res. U., Cleve., 1980-95, interim dean, 1993-95, dir. pediat. dentistry residency program, 1990-95. Contbr. articles to profl. jours. Mem. Head Start, World Vision, QualChoice Managed Health Care, Ctrs. for Disease Control, HHS Bur. Maternal and Child Health. Recipient numerous grants. Mem. Monongalia (Ohio) County Dental Soc., Iowa Pediat. Dentistry Alumni Assn., Am. Assn. for Dental Rsch., Am. Assn. Dental Schs., Am. Acad. Pediat. Dentistry. Office: U Iowa Coll Dentistry Rm 308 Iowa City IA 52242

JOHNSON, ALICE M. state legislator; b. Apr. 1, 1941; four children. AA, Mpls. Cmty. Coll., 1986; BA, Concordia Coll., St. Paul, 1993. Dist. 48B rep. Minn. Ho. of Reps., St. Paul, 1986—. Chair K-13 education fin. divsn.; mem. labor mgmt. rels., Internat. Trade Com. Minn. Ho. Reps. Home: 801 Ballantyne Ln NE Minneapolis MN 55432-2054 Office: Minn Ho of Reps State Capital Bldg Saint Paul MN 55155-0001

JOHNSON, ARTHUR GILBERT, microbiology educator; b. Eveleth, Minn., Feb. 1, 1926; s. Arthur Gilbert and Selma (Niemi) J.; m. Mildred Louise Anderson, June 15, 1951; children: Susan, Sally, Gary, Peter. B.A., U. Minn., 1950, M.Sc., 1951; Ph.D., U. Md., 1955. Biochemist Walter Reed Army Inst. Rsch., Washington, 1952-55; asst. prof. U. Mich., 1956-62, asso. prof., 1962-66, prof. microbiology, 1966-78; prof., head dept. med. microbiology/immunology U. Minn. Sch. Medicine, Duluth, 1978-99, prof. emeritus, 1999—. Mem. pre, postdoctoral and spl. fellowships study sect. NIH, 1968-70; mem. nat. adv. dental rsch. coun. NIH, 1972-75; mem. Nat. Bd. Med. Examiners, 1980-84; mem. bacteriology and mycology study sect. NIH, 1983-87, chmn., 1986-87; cons. microbiology. Editor Infection and Immunity, 1977-86. Served with US Merchant Marine, 1943-46. Mem. Am. Assn. Immunologists, Am. Soc. Microbiology, Infectious Diseases Soc. Am., Soc. Biol. Therapy, Immunocomprised Host Soc., Internat. Endotoxin Soc., Assn. Med. Sch. Microbiology and Immunology Chairs (pres. 1991-92). Achievements include research on immunology. Home: 209 Rockridge Cir Duluth MN 55804-1857 Office: U Minn Sch Medicine Dept Microbiology/Immunology Duluth MN 55812 E-mail: ajohnso1@d.umn.edu.

JOHNSON, BRUCE, state legislator; m. Kelley Johnson; children: Shane, Meagan, Connor, Morgan. BS, BA, Bowling Green State U.; JD, Capital U. Bar: Ohio. City prosecutor, Columbus; senator Ohio State Senate, chmn. decentralization com., co-chmn. deregulation com., chmn. ways and means com., co-chmn. spl. sch. funding task force, judicar joint legis. ethics com. Recipient Watchdog of the Treasury award United Conservatives of Ohio, 1996, Legislator of Yr. award Ohio Chem. Coun., 1997, award Ohio Victim Witness Assn., 1997. Mem. Ohio State Bar Assn., Columbus Bar Assn.

JOHNSON, BRUCE E. state legislator; b. Telpoli, Libya, May 25, 1960; m. Kelley; 4 children. BS, Bowling Green State U.; JD, Capital U. Mem. Ohio Senate from 3rd dist., Columbus, 1994—; attorney. Recipient Watchdog of the Treasury, Crime Victims Witness Assn award for Outstnading Legis. Mem. Columbus Bar Assn., Ohio Bar Assn. Office: State House 3d Dist Room 137 1st Fl Senate Bldg Columbus OH 43215

JOHNSON, C. NICHOLAS, dance company executive; MFA in Dance/Drama, U. Ariz.; studied with, Stefan Niedzialkowski, Frank Hatchett, Richard Levi, De Marco, N.Y.C. Assoc. artistic dir. Goldston & Johnson Sch. of Mimes; chief officer Mid-Am. Dance Theatre, Wichita, Kans.; asst. prof., dir. dance, modern dance, jazz, mime Coll. Fine Arts Wichita State U. Freelance tchr., dir., choreographer and performer various U.S. ballet schs. and univs. Performer Marcel Marceau World Ctr. Mime, Invisible People Mime Theatre, Internat. Children's Theatre Festival, Hong Kong. Kans. Arts Commn. fellow, 1999. Office: Wichita State U Sch Performing Arts-Dance PO Box 101 Wichita KS 67260-0001 E-mail: johnson2@twsuvm.uc.twsu.edu.

JOHNSON, C. TERRY, lawyer; b. Bridgeport, Conn., Sept. 24, 1937; s. Clifford Gustave and Evelyn Florence (Terry) J.; m. Suzanne Frances Chichy, Aug. 24, 1985; children: Laura Elizabeth, Melissa Lynne, Clifford Terry. AB, Trinity Coll., 1960; LLD, Columbia U., 1963. Bar: Ohio 1964, U.S. Ct. Appeals (6th cir.) 1966, U.S. Dist. Ct. (so. dist.) Ohio 1970. Legal dep. probate ct. Montgomery County, Dayton, Ohio, 1964-67; head probate dept. Coolidge Wall & Wood, 1967-79, Smith & Schnacke, Dayton, 1979-89, Thompson, Hine and Flory, Dayton, 1989-92; head estate planning and probate group Porter, Wright, Morris & Arthur, 1992—. Frequent lectr. on estate planning to various profl. orgns. Contbr. articles to profl. jours. Fellow Am. Coll. Trust and Estate Counsel; mem. Ohio Bar Assn. (bd. govs. estate planning, trust and probate law sect., chmn. 1993-95), Dayton Bar Assn. (chmn. probate com. 1992-94), Ohio State Bar Found. (trustee 1995-2000), Ohio CLE Inst. (trustee 1995-99, chair 1998-99), Dayton Legal Secs. Assn. (hon.), Dayton Bicycle Club. Home: 8307 Rhine Way Centerville OH 45458-3017 Office: Porter Wright Morris & Arthur 1 S Main St Ste 1600 Dayton OH 45402-2028 E-mail: CTJohnson@porterwright.com.

JOHNSON, CARL RANDOLPH, chemist, educator; b. Charlottesville, Va., Apr. 28, 1937; BS, Med. Coll. Va., 1958; PhD in Chemistry, U. Ill., 1962. NSF rsch. fellow chemistry Harvard U., 1962; from asst. to prof. chemistry Wayne State U., Detroit, 1962—90, Disting. prof., 1990—2001, chair dept. chemistry, 1997—2001, Disting. prof. emeritus, 2002—. Humboldt sr. scientist, 1991; bd. dirs. Organic Syntheses, Inc. Mem. adv. bd.: Jour. Organic Chemistry, 1976—81. Alfred P. Sloan fellow, 1965-68. Mem. Am. Chem. Soc. (assoc. editor jour. 1984-89, Harry and Carol Mosher award 1992), Royal Soc. Chemistry. Achievements include research in organic sulfur chemistry, especially sulfoxides and sulfoximines, exploratory synthetic chemistry, synthesis of compounds of potential medicinal activity, organometallic chemistry, synthesis of natural products, enzymes in synthesis. Office: Wayne State Univ Dept Chemistry Detroit MI 48202 E-mail: crj@chem.wayne.edu.

JOHNSON, CHERYL (C.J. JOHNSON), newspaper columnist; Gossip columnist Mpls. Star Tribune. Office: Mpls Star Tribune 425 Portland Ave Minneapolis MN 55488-1511

JOHNSON, CHRISTINE ANN, nurse; b. Omaha, Aug. 23, 1951; d. Ralph James and Marlene (Marlenee) Matney; m. Timothy Carl Johnson, Aug. 1, 1970; children: Erik Carl, Christine Nicole. Cert. practical nurse, Met. Tech. Community Coll., 1973; BA cum laude, Creighton U., 1989. LPN, Nebr.; cert. pregnancy exercise instr.; cert. lactation cons. EKG technician Bishop Clarkson Meml. Hosp., Omaha, 1971-74, lic. practical nurse, 1978—, instr. pregnancy exercise, 1984-86, instr. sibling preparation, 1985-86, instr. breastfeeding, 1985-95; LPN Cons. in Cardiology, P.C., 1974-78; tchr. asst. Creighton U. Dept. Psychology, 1987-88; lactation cons. Bergan Mercy Med. Ctr., 1994—. Teaching asst. dept. psychology, child psychology, adolescent psychology, devel. psychology Creighton U., 1987-88. Assoc. editor (cons.' corner) Jour. Human Lactation, 1994-96. Sec. United Meth. Women First United Meth. Ch., 1984-85, chmn. 1985-86; vol. Radio Talking Book, 1985; mem. Omaha Pub. Schs. Superintendent's Task Force on Human Growth and Devel., 1986, Project Linus, 1997—; vol. Paws for Friendship, 1997—, Dresses for Humanity Durham Western Heritage Mus., Omaha, 1999. Mem. Internat. Lactation Cons. Assn., Psi Chi. Methodist. Home: 4618 N 129th Ave Omaha NE 68164-1708 Office: Bergan Mercy Med Ctr 7500 Mercy Rd Omaha NE 68124-2319

JOHNSON, CURTIS J. state agency administrator; b. Platte, SD, Dec. 30, 1939; m. Mary Ellen Johnson; children: Kent, Craig. BS, U. SD; MS, SD State U. Sci. tchr., Huron, SD; prin. Dupree schs.; ins. agt. Huron; commr. SD Office Sch. and Pub. Lands, Pierre, 1990—. Mem.: NEA, Western States Land Commrs. Assn. (esec. bd.), Aircraft Owners and Pilots Assn., Beadle Club, Rotary Club, Shriners, Masons. Avocations: hunting, reading, flying. Office: 500 E Capitol Ave Pierre SD 57501-5070

JOHNSON, CURTIS LEE, publisher, editor, writer; b. Mpls., May 26, 1928; s. Hjalmar N. and Gladys (Goring) J.; m. Jo Ann Lekwa, June 30, 1950 (div. 1974); children: Mark Alan, Paula Catherine; m. Rochelle Miller Hickey, Jan. 11, 1975 (div. 1980); m. Betty Axelrod Fox, Aug. 28, 1982 (div. 1990). B.A., U. Iowa, 1951, M.A., 1952. Mag. and ency. editing and writing, Chgo., 1953-60; textbook and ednl. editing and writing, 1960-66; editor, pub. December Press, 1962—, pres., 1985—; free-lance editing and writing, 1966-72, 78—; mng. editor Aldine Pub. Co., 1972-73; v.p. St. Clair Press, 1973-77; sr. writer Bradford Exchange, 1978-81; mng. editor Regnery Gateway, 1981-82. Author: (with George Uskali) How to Restore Antique and Classic Cars, 1954; novels Hobbledehoy's Hero, 1959, Nobody's Perfect, 1973, Lace and a Bobbitt, 1976, The Morning Light, 1977, Song for Three Voices, 1984; The Mafia Manager, 1991, (with R. Craig Sautter) Wicked City Chicago, 1994, Thanksgiving in Vegas, 1995, 500 Years of Obscene...and Counting, 1997; editor: (with Jarvis Thurston) Stories from the Literary Magazines, 1970, Best Little Magazine Fiction, 1970, (with Alvin Greenberg), 1971, (with Jack Conroy) Writers in Revolt, 1973, (with Diane Kruchkow) Green Isle in the Sea, 1986, Who's Who in Writers, Editors & Poets, 1985-2000; essays The Forbidden Writings of Lee Wallek, 1978, (with R. Craig Sautter) A Book of Martyrs, 2002; also fiction, articles; cons. editor: Panache mag, 1967-76. Served with USN, 1946-48. Nat. Endowment Arts writing grantee, 1973, 81 Mem. Nat. Writers Union, Phi Beta Kappa, Club d'Ronde. Office: December Press PO Box 302 Highland Park IL 60035-0302

JOHNSON, CYNDA ANN, physician, educator; b. Girard, Kans., July 16, 1951; BA in Biology and German with honors, Stanford U., 1973; MD, UCLA, 1977; MBA, U. Mo., Kansas City, 1999. Diplomate Am. Bd. Family Medicine (bd. dirs., pres. 1999-2000). Tchg. fellow U. N.C., Chapel Hill, 1980-81; intern U. Kans. Med. Ctr., Kansas City, 1977-78, 1978-80, prof., acting chair dept. family medicine, 1998—99; prof., head dept. family medicine U. Iowa Coll. Medicine, Iowa City, 1999—. Mem. Am. Acad. Family Practice, Soc. Tchrs. Family Medicine, Iowa Acad. Family Physicians, Iowa Med. Soc. Office: U Iowa Coll Medicine 200 Hawkins Dr 01286-D PFP Iowa City IA 52242-1097 E-mail: cynda-johnson@uiowa.edu.

JOHNSON, DALE, contractor equipment company executive; With Graco Inc., Mpls., 1977—, v.p. contractor equipment divsn., 1996-2000, pres., COO, 2000—. Office: Graco Inc PO Box 1441 Minneapolis MN 55440-1441

JOHNSON, DAVE, state legislator; b. Aug. 21, 1963; m. Tracy Johnson; 1 child. BA, Augsburg Coll.; JD, U. Minn. Bar: Minn. Mem. Minn. Senate from 40th dist., St. Paul, 1996—. Home: 2400 W 112th St Bloomington MN 55431-3960 Office: 111 Capitol 75 Constitution Ave Saint Paul MN 55155-1601

JOHNSON, DAVID ALLEN, singer, songwriter, investor, minister; b. Indpls., Dec. 15, 1954; s. Eugene Robert and Vivian Claire (Moon) J. BA in English, Ind. U., 1977; cert., Columbia Sch. of Broadcasting, 1985. Ordained to ministry United Ch. of Christ, 1996. Founder, pres. Worldwide Assn. Disabled Entrepreneurs, Indpls., 1993—. Founder Global Access and Info. Network (GAIN), L.L.C. Singer, songwriter gospel and love songs; contbr. poems and articles to various publs.; concert promoter in field; founder DAJ Cons. Co.; CEO WebTeam. Bd. dirs. Christian Fellowship with the Disabled. Named 2000 Poet of the Yr., Famous Poets Soc. Mem. Am. Creativity Assn. (bd. dirs.), MENSA, Internat.-Nat. Ctr. for Creativity, Toastmasters (pres. 2000—). Republican. Avocations: reading, writing, biblical rsch., basketball. Home and Office: 5958 Devington Rd Apt 1 Indianapolis IN 46226 E-mail: DJohnson115@earthlink.net., coffeecupguy@aol.com.

JOHNSON, DAVID CHESTER, university chancellor, sociology educator; b. Jan. 21, 1933; s. Chester Laven and Olga Henriett (Resnick) J.; m. Jean Ann Lunnis, Sept. 10, 1955 (dec. 1996); children: Stephen, Andrew, Jennifer. BA, Gustavus Adolphus Coll., 1954; MA, U. Iowa, 1956, PhD, 1959; LLD, Luther Coll., 1993. Instr. to prof. sociology Luther Coll., Decorah, Iowa, 1957-69; dean arts and scis. East Stroudsburg (Pa.) U., 1969-76; v.p. acad. affairs St. Cloud (Minn.) State U., 1976-83; dean Gustavus Adolphus Coll., St. Peter, Minn., 1983-90; chancellor U. Minn., Morris, 1990-98; cons. to Scandinavian univs., 1999—. Leader of numerous hiking groups to Norwegian mountains. NSF sci. faculty fellow Inst. Social Rsch., Oslo, 1965-66, adminstrv. fellow Am. Coun. Edn., Luther Coll., 1968-69, Summer Leadership fellow Bush Found., Inst. Edn. Mgmt., Harvard U., 1981; Kennedy Swedish Fund grantee, 1976. Mem. Elder Learning Inst. U. Minn. (pres), U. Minn. Retirees Assn. (v.p.). Democrat. Lutheran. Home: 1235 Yale Pl Apt 1705 Minneapolis MN 55403-1948

JOHNSON, DAVID GALE, economist, educator; b. Vinton, Iowa, July 10, 1916; s. Albert D. and Myra Jane (Reed) J.; m. Helen Wallace, Aug. 10, 1938; children: David Wallace, Kay Ann. BS, Iowa State Coll., 1938, PhD, 1945; MS, U. Wis., 1939; student, U. Chgo., 1939-41; LHD (hon.), Iowa State U., 1995. Research assoc. Iowa State Coll., 1941-42, asst. prof. econs., 1942-44; with dept. econs. U. Chgo., 1944—, rsch. assoc. to assoc. prof., 1944-54, prof., 1954—, now emeritus prof., assoc. dean div. social scis., 1957-60, dean, 1960-70, chmn. dept. econs., 1971-75, 80-84, acting dir. library, 1971-72, dir. Office Econ. Analysis, 1975-80, v.p., dean of faculties, 1975, provost, 1976-80; acting dir. William Benton Fellowship in Broadcast Journalism, 1991-92; dir. Ctr. East Asian Studies, 1994-98. Economist OPA, 1942, Dept. State, 1946, Dept. Army, 1948; mem. food adv. com. Office of Tech. Assessment, U.S. Congress, 1974-76; cons. TVA and Rand Corp., AID, 1962-68; pres. Nat. Opinion Rsch. Ctr., 1962-75, 79-85; agrl. adviser Office of Pres.'s Spl. Rep. for Trade Negotiations, 1963-64; mem. Pres.'s Nat. Adv. Commn. on Food and Fiber, 1965-67; adv. bd. Policy Planning Coun. State Dept., 1967-69, Nat. Commn. on Population Growth and the Am. Future, 1970-72; mem. steering com. Pres.'s Food and Nutrition Study, NAS, 1975-77; chmn. bd. dirs. Univ. Savs. and Loan Assn., 1986-88, chmn. exec. com., 1988-92; mem. com. Econ. Edn. and Rsch. in China, 1984-94; co-chmn. working group on population growth and econ. devel. NAS, 1984-86, chmn. delegation to Bulgaria, 1991; team leader World Bank Food Sector Reform Mission to USSR and Republics, 1991-92; cons. European Bank for Reconstrn. and Devel., 1993; mem. internat. adv. com. China Ctr. for Econ. Rsch. Peking U., 1995—; hon. prof. Beijing U., 1999. Author: Forward Prices for Agriculture, 1947, Agriculture and Trade: A Study of Inconsistent Policies, 1950, (with Robert Gustafson) Grain Yields and the American Food Supply, 1962, The Struggle Against World Hunger, 1967, World Agriculture in Disarray, 1973, 2d edit., 1991, World Food Problems and Prospects, 1975, (with Karen Brooks) Prospects for Soviet Agriculture in the 1980's, 1983, The People's Republic of China: 1978-90, 1990, Long-Term Agricultural Policies for Central Europe, 1996; editor Economic Development and Cultural Change, 1986—. Bd. dirs. Wm. Benton Found., 1980-92; pres. S.E. Chgo. Commn., 1980—. Recipient Loyola-Mellon Social Sci. award Loyola U. Chgo., 1992. Fellow Am. Acad. Arts and Scis., Am. Agrl. Econs. Assn.; mem. NAS, Social Sci. Rsch. Coun. (dir. 1953-56), Am. Econ. Assn. (pres.-elect 1998, pres. 1999), Am. Farm Econ. Assn. (pres. 1964-65), Phi Kappa Phi, Alpha Zeta. Home: Apt 1406 5550 South Shore Dr Chicago IL 60637-5051 Office: U Chgo Dept Econs 1126 E 59th St Chicago IL 60637-1580 E-mail: dg-johnson@uchicago.edu.

JOHNSON, DAVID LYNN, materials scientist, educator; b. Provo, Utah, Apr. 2, 1934; s. David Elmer and Lucile (Maughan) J.; m. Rolla LaRae Page, June 26, 1959; children: Jeannette, David Page, Brice Aaron, Jeffrey Lynn, Karyn Rae. B.S., U. Utah, 1956, Ph.D., 1962. Mem. faculty dept. materials sci. and engring. Northwestern U., Evanston, Ill., 1962—, prof., 1971—, chmn. dept. materials scis. and engring., 1982-87, Walter D. Murphy Disting. prof., 1987—. Cons. in field. Contbr. articles to profl. jours. NSF grantee, 1971-77, 79— Fellow Am. Ceramic Soc. (chmn. basic sci. div. 1978-79, trustee 1980-81, 1990-93); mem. AAAS, Acad. Ceramics (charter), Metall. Soc., Materials Research Soc., Internat. Inst. for Sci. of Sintering, Am. Powder Metallurgy Inst., Sigma Xi, Alpha Sigma Mu, Phi Eta Sigma, Phi Kappa Phi, Tau Beta Pi. Mem. LDS Ch. Achievements include demonstration of ultra-rapid sintering of ceramics in high temperature gas plasmas; development of advanced sintering models. Office: Northwestern U Dept Materials Sci/Engring 2225 N Campus Dr Evanston IL 60208-3108 E-mail: dljohnson@northwestern.edu.

JOHNSON, DEAN ELTON, state legislator, Lutheran pastor; b. June 24, 1947; m. Avonelle Johnson. BA, Luther Coll.; MDiv, Luther Theol. Sem. Lutheran pastor; mem. Minn. Ho. of Reps., St. Paul, 1977-82, Minn. Senate from 15th dist., St. Paul, 1982—. Mem. elections and ethics, fin., gen. legis. and pub. gaming, transp., rules and adminstrn. and gaming regulation coms., Minn. State Senate; minority leader. Office: PO Box 996 605 E 4th St Willmar MN 56201

JOHNSON, DONALD CLAY, librarian, curator; b. Clintonville, Wis., Aug. 19, 1940; s. Everett Clay and Gertrude Edna Dorthea (Learmann) J. BA, U. Wis., 1962, PhD, 1980; MA, U. Chgo., 1967. Curator S.E. Asia Collection Yale U., New Haven, 1967-70; head reference libr. No. Ariz. U., Flagstaff, 1971-72; asst. libr. reader svcs. Nat. U. Malaysia, Kuala Lumpur, 1972-74; head reader svcs. Coll. William and Mary, Williamsburg, Va., 1980-87; curator Ames Libr. South Asia, U. Minn., Mpls., 1987—. Author: Southeast Asia: A Bibliography, 1970, Guide to Reference Materials on Southeast Asia, 1970, Index to Southeast Asian Journals, 1982, Agile Hands and Creative Minds, a Bibliography of Textile Traditions in Afghanistan, Bangladesh, Bhutan, India, Nepal, Pakistan, and Sri Lanka, 2000. Scholar Ford Found., 1963-64; rsch. grantee Am. Inst. Indian Studies, 1989, 90, 94. Mem. ALA (life), Assn. for Asian Studies (editor Resources for Scholarship series 1997-98). Avocation: textiles in South and Southeast Asia. Office: U Minn Ames Libr South Asia 309 19th Ave S Minneapolis MN 55455-0438 E-mail: d-john4@tc.umn.edu.

JOHNSON, DONALD LEE, retired agricultural materials processing company executive; b. Aurora, Ill., Mar. 9, 1935; s. Leonard F. and Fern J. (Johnson) J.; m. Virginia A. Wesoloski, Sept. 3, 1960; children: Joyce E., Janis M., Jolene G., Jay R. AS, Joliet Jr. Coll., 1959; BS, U. Ill., 1962; DSc, Washington U., 1966. Devel. engr. Petrolite Corp., Webster Groves, Mo., 1962-64; sr. devel. engr. A.E. Staley Co., Decatur, Ill., 1965-67, rsch. mgr. chem. div., 1967-75, dept. dir. rsch. div., 1975-87; v.p. product and process tech. Grain Processing Corp., Muscatine, Iowa, 1987-2000. Adv. coun. adult vocat. edn. State of Ill., Springfield, 1983—87; mem. organizing com. Am. Symposium on Biotech. for Fuels and Chems., 1985—97; departmental vis. com. botany dept. U. Tex., Austin, 1986—99; mem. applied sci. adv. coun. Miami U., Oxford, Ohio, 1987—97; chmn. rev. com. Solar Energy Rsch. Inst., Golden, Colo., 1988—89; mem. Sci. and Industry Adv. Bd., Nat. Renewable Energy Lab., Golden, Colo., 1993—99. Contbr. sci. papers to profl. jours.; patentee in field. Staff sgt. USAF, 1953-57. Mem. AAAS, AIChE, Am. Chem. Soc., Nat. Acad. Engring., Am. Legion, Rotary. Republican. Avocations: sailboat racing, running. Home: 29 Cape Fear Dr Hertford NC 27944-9218 E-mail: virdon@mchsi.com.

JOHNSON, DOROTHY PHYLLIS, retired counselor, art therapist; b. Kansas City, Mo., Sept. 13, 1925; d. Chris C. and Mabel T. (Gillum) Green; BA in Art, Ft. Hays. State U., 1975, MS in Guidance and Counseling, 1976, MA in Art, 1979; m. Herbert E. Johnson, May 11, 1945; children: Michael E., Gregory K. Art therapist High Plains Comprehensive Mental Health Assn., Hays, Kans., 1975-76; art therapist, mental health counselor Sunflower Mental Health Assn., Concordia, Kans., 1976-78, Pawnee Mental Health Svcs., 1978-91, co-dir. Project Togetherness, 1976-77, coord. partial hospitalization, 1978-82, out-patient therapist, 1982-91; pvt. practice, 1991-97, ret., 1997; dir. Swedish Am. State Bank, Courtland, Kans., 1960—, sec., 1973-77. Mem. Kans., Am. art therapy assns., Am. Mental Health Counselors Assn., Am. Counseling Assn., Kans. Counseling Assn., Assn. for Humanistic Psychologists, Assn. Transpersonal Psychologists, Assn. Specialists in Group Work, Phi Delta Kappa, Phi Kappa Phi. Contbr. articles to profl. jours. Home: PO Box 200 Courtland KS 66939-0200

JOHNSON, DOUGLAS J. state legislator, secondary education counselor; b. Aug. 17, 1942; AA, Va. Jr. Coll.; BS, U. Minn., Duluth; MEd, Wis. State U. H.s. counselor; mem. Minn. Ho. of Reps., St. Paul, 1970-74, Minn. Senate from 6th dist., St. Paul, 1976—. Chmn. tax laws and taxes com., Minn. State Senate, mem. elections and ethics, pub. utilities and energy, redistricting, rules and adminstrn., jobs, energy and cmty. devel. coms. Office: 1136 Lagoon Rd Tower MN 55790-8138 also: State Senate State Capitol Building Saint Paul MN 55155-0001

JOHNSON, E. PERRY, lawyer; b. Pa., 1943; BA, W. Va. U., 1965, JD, 1968. Bar: W. Va. 1968, D.C. 1981, Mo. 1983. Instr. Boston U. Sch. Law, 1973-74, asst. dir., 1977-79, bur. competition, exec. asst. to chmn., 1979, dep. dir., 1979-80, dir., 1980-81; ptnr. Bryan Cave, St. Louis. Vis. asst. prof. W. Va. U., 1972-73; adj. prof. St. Louis U. Sch. Law, 1985-86. With USN, 1968-72. Mem. ABA. Office: Bryan Cave 211 N Broadway Ste 3600 Saint Louis MO 63102-2733

JOHNSON, EARLE BERTRAND, insurance executive; b. Otter Lake, Mich., May 3, 1914; s. Bert M. and Blanche (Sherman) J.; m. Frances Pierce, 1940 (dec.); children: Earle Bertrand, Victoria, Julia, Sheryl; m. Peggy Minch Rust, Apr. 30, 1972. B.S., U. Fla., 1937, J.D., 1940. With State Farm Ins. Cos., Bloomington, Ill., 1940-95, regional agy. dir., 1958-60, regional v.p., 1960-65, v.p., sec. State Farm Mut. Automobile Ins. Co., 1965-80, dir., 1967-88; sr. v.p., treas. State Farm County Mut. Ins. Co. Tex., 1965-80, treas., 1963-80; chmn. State Farm Life Ins. Co., 1970-86, dir., mem. exec. com., 1965-88. V.p., mem. exec. com. State Farm Fire & Casualty Co., 1965-80, dir., 1965-95; dir. State Farm Investment Mgmt. Corp.; v.p., sec. State Farm Internat. Svcs., Inc., 1967-81; mem. exec. com. State Farm County Mut. Ins. Co. Tex., 1970-86. Mem. Agy. Officers Round Table (exec. coms.), Am., Fla. bar assns., Soc. Former FBI Agts., Life Ins. Mktg. and Research Assn. (dir. 1975-78), Life Underwriter Tng. Council (trustee 1974-77), Phi Alpha Delta, Phi Kappa Tau. Home: 59 N Country Club Pl Bloomington IL 61701-3450 Office: State Farm Life Ins Co One State Farm Plaza Bloomington IL 61701

JOHNSON, ERIC G. food products company executive; b. Chgo., Mar. 29, 1951; s. George Eillis and Joan Betty Johnson; m. Pamela Johnson, Apr. 8, 1979; children: Lecretia, Erin, Cara, John. BAS, Babson Coll., 1972; MBA, U. Chgo., 1977; LHD (hon.), Chgo. State U. With Proctor & Gamble, 1972-75; pres., CEO Johnson Products, 1988-92, Baldwin Ice Cream CO., 1992—, Baldwin Richardson Roods Co., Matteson, Ill., 1997—. Bd. dirs. Dr. Martin Luther King Ctr., Chgo. State U.; trustee Babson Coll., Glenwood Sch. for Boys. Recipient Leadership award Boy Scouts Am., Recognition award 100 Black Men of Am., Humanitarian award Willi Wilson Found., Jobs, Peace, Freedom award Lincoln Meml. Mem. NAACP (bd. dirs.), Olympia Fields Country Club. Office: Baldwin Richardson Foods Co 4440 Lincoln Hwy Matteson IL 60443-2349

JOHNSON, EUGENE LAURENCE, lawyer; b. Wisconsin Rapids, Wis., Nov. 30, 1936; s. Elmer Hilding and Claribel May Johnson; m. Barbara Dell Braley, June 18, 1960; children: Mark, Ben, Christopher. BSCE, U. Wis., 1960, JD, 1962. Bar: Minn. 1963, Calif. 1965, U.S. Patent Office 1963. Atty. Pillsbury Co., Mpls., 1962-64; assoc. Mellin, Hanscom & Hursh, San Francisco, 1964-66; ptnr. Dorsey & Whitney, Mpls., 1966-98, Eugene L. Johnson, PA, Wayzata, Minn., 1998—. Program founder, adj. prof. intellectual property law William Mitchell Coll. of Law, 1967-75. Capt. C.E. USAR, 1960. Mem. Minn. Bar Assn. (past bd. govs.), Am. Intellectual Property Law Assn., Minn. Intellectual Property Law Assn. (past pres.), Mpls. Athletic Club, Lafayette Country Club. Republican. Office: Eugene L Johnson PA 1500 Bohns Point Rd Wayzata MN 55391-9309

JOHNSON, EUGENE WALTER, mathematician, educator; b. El Paso, Tex., May 25, 1939; s. Walter Albert and Lillian Ann (Martinets) J.; m. Sandra Sue Gilbert, Oct. 16, 1959; 1 dau., Catherine Mary. Student, Riverside City Coll., 1958-60; BA, U. Calif., Riverside, 1963, MA, 1964, PhD, 1966. Asst. prof. Eastern N.Mex. State U., 1966; asst. prof. math. U. Iowa, Iowa City, 1966-70, asso. prof., 1970-75, prof., 1975—, chmn. dept., 1976-79. Author: Linear Algebra with Maple, 1993, Linear Algegra with Mathematics, 1995; co-author: Maple Flight Manual, 1992; contbr. articles to profl. jours. Mem. Am. Math. Soc., Math. Assn. Am. Democrat. Home: 4320 Oakridge Trl NE Iowa City IA 52240-7735 Office: Univ Iowa Dept Math Iowa City IA 52242 E-mail: eugene-johnson@uiowa.edu., eugene_johnson@home.com.

JOHNSON, G. ROBERT, lawyer; b. Mpls., July 2, 1940; BA, U. Minn., 1965, JD, 1968. Bar: Minn. 1968. Spl. asst. atty. gen. Minn. Pollution Control Agy., 1968-71; past ptnr. Popham, Haik, Schnobrich & Kaufman Ltd., Mpls.; ptnr. Oppenheimer, Wolff & Donnelly LLP, 1997—. Mem. ABA, Minn. Bar Assn. chmn. continuing legal edn. 1986-87), Nat. Coun. State Legislatures (liaison 1987—). Office: Oppenheimer Wolff & Donnelly LLP 3400 Plaza VII 45 S 7th St Ste 3400 Minneapolis MN 55402-1609

JOHNSON, GARY LEROY, publishing executive; b. Mpls., Aug. 19, 1938; s. Maurice Fred and Alta Elizabeth J.; m. Carol Ann Schlisler, Sept. 8, 1962. Diploma, Bethany Coll. of Missions, Mpls., 1959; student, Augsburg Coll., 1960-63. Mgr. Bethany Book Shop, Mpls., 1960-63, Bethany Printing Div., Mpls., 1963-76; pres. Bethany House Pubs., 1963—. Avocation: songwriting. Office: Bethany House Pubs 11400 Hampshire Ave S Minneapolis MN 55438-2852

JOHNSON, GARY M. lawyer; b. 1947; BS, Gustavus Adolphus Coll., 1969; JD, NYU, 1973. Law clk. to justice U.S. Ct. Appeals (3d cir.), Phila., 1973-74; assoc. Dorsey & Whitney, Mpls., 1974-79, ptnr., 1980—. Fellow Am. Coll. Trust and Estate Counsel; mem. Minn. Bar Assn., Hennepin County Bar Assn., Order of Coif. E-mail: johnson.gary#dorseylaw.com. Office: Dorsey & Whitney Ste 1500 50 South Sixth Street Minneapolis MN 55402-1498

JOHNSON, GARY R. corporate lawyer; MA, Ohio State U.; JD, U. Minn. Bar: Minn. 1974. V.p. law Northern St. Power Co., v.p., gen. counsel, 1991—. Office: Northern St Power Co PO Box 5th Fl 414 Nicollet Mall Minneapolis MN 55401-1927

JOHNSON, GARY THOMAS, lawyer; b. Chgo., July 26, 1950; s. Thomas G. Jr. and Marcia (Lunde) J.; m. Susan Elizabeth Moore, May 28, 1978; children: Christopher Thomas, Timothy Henry, Anna Louisa. AB, Yale U., 1972; Hons. BA, Oxford U., 1974, MA, 1983; JD, Harvard U., 1977. Ba: Ill. 1977, U.S. Dist. Ct. (no. dist.), Ill. 1977, U.S. Ct. Appeals (7th cir.) 1985, U.S. Supreme Ct. 1986, N.Y. 1993. Assoc. Mayer, Brown & Platt, Chgo., 1977-84, ptnr., 1985-94, Jones, Day, Reavis & Pogue, Chgo., 1994—. Mem. Spl. Commn. on Adminstrn. of Justice Cook County, Chgo., 1984-88; v.p. Criminal Justice Project of Cook County, 1987-91; bd. dirs. Lawyers' Com. for Civil Rights Under Law, 1992—, trustee, 1994—, regional co-chair, 1996-2001, co-chair, 2001—; mem. Ill. Supreme Ct. Spl. Commn. on the Adminstrn. of Justice, 1992-94. Bd. dirs. Chgo. Lawyers' Com. for Civil Rights Under Law, 1981-90, Legal Assistance Found., Chgo., 1987-96, pres., 1994-96. Rhodes scholar Oxford U., 1972-74. Fellow Am. Bar Found. (life), Ill. Bar Found. (life); mem. ABA (Ho. of Dels. 1991-97), Am. Judicature Soc. (bd. dirs. 1987-91), Ill. State Bar Assn., Chgo. Bar Assn., Chgo. Coun. Lawyers (pres. 1981-83), Internat. Bar Assn. Office: Jones Day Reavis & Pogue 77 W Wacker Dr Chicago IL 60601-1692

JOHNSON, GEORGE TAYLOR, training and manufacturing executive; b. Kansas City, Mo., Jan. 12, 1930; s. George Dewey and Geneva (Van Leu) J.; m. Pamela Kay Cole, Aug. 30, 1981; children: Van L., Victoria Johnson-Beineke, Wendell O., Marcella Johnson-Stewart, Julia I. BA, Columbia U., 1977. Enlisted U.S. Army, 1947; chief instr. rotary wing sect. U.S. Army Transp. Sch., Ft. Eustis, Va., 1965-67; ret. U.S. Army, 1967; group leader aerospace publs. Beech Aircraft Corp., Wichita, Kans., 1968-79, adminstr. aerospace logistics programs, 1979-87, staff asst. program mgmt., 1987-88, staff adminstr. program mgr., 1988-92, ret., 1992; pres., CEO Diversifieed Ednl. Tng. and Mfg. Co., 1992—. Founder U.S. Army Black Pilots Reunions, U.S. Army Black Aviators Assn.; mem. Cmty. Action Agy., Wichita, 1973-75, State of Kans. Aviation Adv. Com., 1991—, Pvt. Industry Coun., Wichita, 1994—; Kans. del. White House Conf. on Small Bus., Washington, 1995. Decorated DFC, Air medal with V and four oak leaf clusters; named Welfare to Work Small Bus. Owner of Yr., SBA, 1999; recipient Black Aviation Hall of Fame, 2001. Mem.: VFW, NAACP, Wichita Ind. Bus. Assn. (bd. dirs. 1996—2001), Wichita C. of C.

1996—99, 9th and 10th Cav. Assn., Army Aviation Assn. Am., Rotary Internat. Baptist. Home: 9430 Cross Creek St Wichita KS 67206 Office: 2102 E 21st St N Wichita KS 67214-1943 E-mail: gjohn97063@aol.com.

JOHNSON, HOLLIS RALPH, astronomy educator; b. Tremonton, Utah, Dec. 2, 1928; s. Ellwood Lewis and Ida Martha (Hansen) J.; m. Grete Margit Leed, June 3, 1954; children: Carol Ann Harrison, Wayne L., Lyle David, Charlotte Willian, Lise Marie Tyner, Richard L. BA in Physics, Brigham Young U., 1955, MA in Physics, 1957; PhD in Astrogeophysics, U. Colo., 1960. NSF postdoctoral fellow Paris Obs., 1960-61; rsch. assoc. Yale U., 1961-63; assoc. prof. astronomy Ind. U., Bloomington, 1963-69, prof., 1969-94, prof. emeritus, 1994—, chmn. dept. astronomy, 1978-82, 90-93. NAS/NRC sr. fellow NASA Ames Rsch. Ctr., 1982-83; vis. scientist High Altitude Obs., Boulder, Colo., 1971-72; F.C. Donders vis. prof. U. Utrecht, The Netherlands, 1989; vis. prof. Niels Bohr Inst., Copenhagen, 1990, 1994-97; bd. dirs. Assn. Univs. for Rsch. in Astronomy, 1991-94. Contbr. articles to profl. jours. Served with U.S. Army, 1951-53. Mem. Internat. Astron. Union, Am. Astron. Soc., AAAS, AAUP, Sigma Xi. Mem. LDS Ch. Office: Ind U Dept Astronomy Swain W 319 Bloomington IN 47405 E-mail: johnsonh@indiana.edu.

JOHNSON, HOWARD PAUL, agricultural engineering educator; b. Odebolt, Iowa, Jan. 27, 1923; s. Gustaf Johan and Ruth Helen (Hanson) J.; m. Patricia Jean Larsen, June 15, 1952; children: Cynthia, Lynette, Malcolm. BS, Iowa State U., 1949, MS in Agrl. Engring., 1950; MS in Hydraulic Engring., U. Iowa, 1954; PhD, Iowa State U., 1959. Engr., Soil Conservation Service, Sioux City, Iowa, 1949; instr. Iowa State U., Ames, 1950-53, 54-59, asst. prof., 1959-60, assoc. prof., 1960-62, prof. agrl. engring., 1962-80, head dept., 1980-88, prof. emeritus; cons., 1960-80. Contbr. numerous articles, papers to profl. lit. Co-editor Hydrologic Modeling, 1981. Patentee flow meter. Pres., Sawyer Sch. PTA, Ames, 1965; precinct rep. Republican party, Ames, 1980. Served with AUS, 1943-46, ETO. Recipient Iowa State U. Gamma Sigma Delta Merit award, 1983; EPA grantee, 1975-80; Anson Marston Disting. Prof. Engring., 1986. Fellow AAAS, Am. Soc. Agrl. Engrs. (div. chmn. 1969-70, tech. coun. 1974-76, Engr. of Yr. Iowa sect. 1981, Mid-Central sect. 1982, John Deere medal 1994). Baptist. Lodge: Rotary. Avocations: reading, photography, fishing, writing. Office: Iowa St U Dept Agrl Engring 100 Davidson Hall Ames IA 50014

JOHNSON, J. BRENT, insurance company executive; m. JoAnn Johnson; children: Steven, Jason, Justine. Degree in acctg., U. Wis., Milw. Auditor Wis. Pub. Svc. Commn.; budget dir. Am. Family Mutual Ins. Co., Madison, Wis., v.p., controller, 1987-98, exec. v.p. fin., treas., 1999—. Office: Am Family Ins Group 6000 American Pkwy Madison WI 53783-0001

JOHNSON, JAMES DAVID, concert pianist, organist, educator; b. Greenville, S.C., Aug. 7, 1948; s. Theron David and Lucile (Pearson) J.; m. Karen Elizabeth Jacobson, Feb. 1, 1975. MusB, U. Ariz., 1970, MusM, 1972, D of Mus. Arts, 1976; MusM, Westminster Choir Coll., 1986. Concert pianist, organist Pianists Found. Am., Boston Pops Orch., Royal Philharm., Nat. Symphony Orch., Leningrad Philharmonic, Victoria Symphony, others, 1961—; organist, choirmaster St. Paul's Episcopal Ch., Tucson, 1968-74, First United Meth. Ch., Fairbanks, Alaska, 1974-89, All Saints Episc. Ch., Omaha, 1995—; prof. music U. Alaska, Fairbanks, 1974-96, chair music dept., 1991-94; Isaacson prof. of music U. Nebr., Omaha, 1994—2001, chair dept. music, 1999—2001, Robert M. Spire chair in music, 2002—. Recordings include Moszkowski Etudes, 1973, Works of Chaminade Dohnanyi, 1977, Mendelssohn Concerti, 1978, Beethoven First Concerto, 1980, Beethoven, Reinecke, Ireland Trios with Alaska Chamber Ensemble, 1988, Kabalevsky Third Concerto, Muczynski Concerto, Muczynski Suite, 1990, Beethoven Third Concerto, 1993. Recipient Record of Month award Mus. Heritage Soc., 1979, 80; finalist mus. amb. program USIA, 1983. Mem. Music Tchrs. Nat. Assn., Phi Kappa Phi, Pi Kappa Lambda. Episcopalian. Avocations: painting, woodworking. Office: U Nebr Dept Music Omaha NE 68182-0001

JOHNSON, JAMES J. lawyer; BA, U. Mich.; JD, Ohio State U. Bar: Ohio 1972. V.p., gen. counsel Proctor & Gamble Co., Cin., 1991—, now sr. v.p., gen. counsel, 1991—, chief legal officer. Office: Procter & Gamble Co 1 Procter And Gamble Plz Cincinnati OH 45202-3393

JOHNSON, JAMES P. religious organization executive; Pres. Christian Ch. Found., Inc., Indpls. Office: Christian Ch Found Inc 130 E Washington St PO Box 1986 Indianapolis IN 46206-1986

JOHNSON, JANET HELEN, Egyptology educator; b. Everett, Wash., Dec. 24, 1944; d. Robert A. and Jane N. (Osborn) J.; m. Donald S. Whitcomb, Sept. 2, 1978; children: J.J., Felicia. BA, U. Chgo., 1967, PhD, 1972. Instr. Egyptology U. Chgo., 1971-72, asst. prof., 1972-79, assoc. prof., 1979-81, prof., 1981—; dir. Oriental Inst., 1983-89; research assoc. dept. anthropology Field Mus. of Natural History, 1980-84, 94-99. Author: Demotic Verbal System, 1977, Thus Wrote Onchsheshonqy, 1986, 3d revised edit., 2000, (with Donald Whitcomb) Quseir al-Qadim, 1978, 80; editor: (with E.F. Wente) Studies in Honor of G.R. Hughes, 1977, Life in a Multi-Cultural Society, 1992. Smithsonian Instn. grantee, 1977-83; NEH grantee, 1978-81, 81-85; Nat. Geog. Soc. grantee, 1978, 80, 82 Mem. Am. Rsch. Ctr. in Egypt (bd. govs. 1979—, exec. com. 1984-87, 90-96, v.p. 1990-93, pres. 1993-96). Office: U Chgo Oriental Inst 1155 E 58th St Chicago IL 60637-1540 E-mail: j-johnson@uchicago.edu.

JOHNSON, JAY WITHINGTON, former congressman; b. Bessemer, Mich., Sept. 30, 1943; s. Ruben W. and Catherine W. (Withington) J.; m. Jane Sholtz (div.); m. Jo Lee Works, June 26, 1982; stepchildren: Christopher, Joanna AA, Gogebic Community Coll., 1963; BA, No. Mich. U., 1965; MA, Mich. State U., 1970. Disk jockey Sta. WFMK, Lansing, Mich., 1968-69; news anchorman Sta. WILX-TV, 1969-70; radio news reporter Sta. WOWO, Ft. Wayne, Ind., 1970-73; news anchorman Sta. WPTV-TV, West Palm Beach, Fla., 1973-76; radio news reporter Sta. WVCG/WLVE-FM, Miami, 1976; TV producer Sta. WPLG-TV, 1976; news anchorman, mng. editor Sta. WPEC-TV, West Palm Beach, 1977-80; news anchorman Sta. WOTV-TV, Grand Rapids, Mich., 1980-81, Sta. WFRV-TV, Green Bay, Wis., 1981-87, Sta. WLUK-TV, Green Bay, 1987-96; mem. 105th Congress from 8th Wis dist., 1997-98, mem. agrl., transp. and infrastructure coms.; acting dep. asst. sec. congl. rels. USDA, 1999-2000; dir. U.S. Mint, Washington, 2000-2001. Vol. Big Bros./Big Sisters, Green Bay, 1982-87 (Vol. of Yr. 1985); pres., bd. dirs. Family Violence Ctr., Green Bay, 1982-87; v.p. communications United Way, Green Bay, 1987—; adv. bd. Libertas Alcohol Treatment Ctr., 1989—. With U.S. Army, 1966-68. Recipient Gov's award Gov. Tommy Thompson, 1988; named Citizen of Yr. Masons, 1987.

JOHNSON, JOANN MARDELLE, federal agency administrator; b. Massena, Iowa, Feb. 24, 1949; BA in Edn., U. No. Iowa, 1971. Former tchr.; grain and livestock prodr.; mem. Iowa Senate from 39th dist., Des Moines, 1994—2000; mem. appropriations com., mem. commerce com.; chair ways and means com.; mem. Nat. Credit Union Admin., Alexandria, Va., 2002—. Mem. 4-H, Local Devel. Bd.; vol. various cmty. orgns.; campaign mgr. Rep. Dwight Dinkle, 1992, Congressman Jim Lightfoot, 1990, orgn. dir., 1986-88. Mem. Am. Legis. Exch. Coun., Farm Bur., Cattleman's Assn. Republican. Office: Nat Credit Union Admin Off of the Bd 1775 Duke St Alexandria VA 22314-3428 Office Fax: 703-518-6319. E-mail: joann_johnson@legis.state.ia.us.

JOHNSON, JOEL W. food products executive; With General Foods Corp.; exec. v.p. sales and mktg. Hormel Foods Corp., 1991-92, pres., 1992-93, COO, CEO, 1993-95, chmn. bd., CEO, pres. Minn., 1995—. Bd. dirs. Overseers of The Carlson Sch. Mgmt. U. Minn.; trustee Hamilton Coll. Office: Hormel Foods Corp 1 Hormel Pl Austin MN 55912-3680

JOHNSON, JOHN WARREN, retired association executive; b. Mpls., Jan. 29, 1929; s. Walter E. and Eileen L. J.; m. Marion Louise Myrland; children— Daniel Warren, Karen Louise, Nancy Marie. B.A., U. Minn., 1951. CEO Am. Collectors Assn., Inc., Mpls., 1955-96; ret., 1996. Dir. Western Nat. Ins. Group, 1998—. Author: Political Christians, 1979, You Can Manage Your Money, 1981, 38 Days to Cape Town, 1981, Credit Guide for Collectors, 1984, The Pearls of Saigon, 1987, The Use of Humor in Public Speaking Is No Joke!, 1991, 53 Days to Beijing, 1991, The Strange Blood of East Africa, 1995. Mem. Mpls. City Coun., 1963-67; mem. Minn. State Ho. of Reps., 1967-74, asst. majority leader, 1972-74; Republican candidate for Gov. of Minn., 1974. With USNR, 1947-53. Mem. Am. Soc. Assn. Execs. (chmn. bd. 1986-87), U.S. C. of C. (chmn. bd. regents 1973, bd. dirs. 1990-92), Minn. Soc. Assn. Execs. (past pres.). Lutheran. Office: 4121 W 50th St Ste 1 Minneapolis MN 55424-1206

JOHNSON, JOHN D. grain company executive; b. Rhame, N.D. BBA, Black Hills State U. Feed cons. GTA divsn. Cenex Harvest States Cooperatives, Inver Grove Heights, Minn., 1976, regional sales mgr., dir. sales and mktg., gen. mgr. GTA Feeds, group v.p. Farm Mktg. and Supply, 1992, pres., CEO, 1995—, pres., gen. mgr., 1998—. Bd. dirs. Ventura Foods, Sparta Foods. Mem. NCRA (bd. dirs.). Office: Cenex Harvest States 5500 Cenex Dr Inver Grove Heights MN 55077

JOHNSON, JOHN FRANK, professional recruitment executive; b. Bklyn., Apr. 23, 1942; s. John Henry and Sirkka (Keto) J.; m. Martha Lear Fryer, Aug. 31, 1963 (div. Apr. 1988); children: Kristin Lin, Heather Alane; m. Virginia K. Yeaser, Nov. 16, 1989 BA in Econs., Tufts U., 1963; MBA in Indsl. Relations, Columbia U., 1964. Indsl. relations analyst Ford Motor Co., Dearborn and Livonia, Mich., 1964-67; various human resources positions Gen. Electric Co., Chgo. and Louisville, Ky., 1967-76; successively assoc., v.p., mng. dir., exec. v.p. and mng. dir. Lamalie Amrop Internat., Cleve., 1976-84; pres. LAI Ward Howell (formerly Lamalie Amrop Internat.), N.Y.C. and Cleve., 1984-95, pres., CEO Cleve., 1987-94, chmn., 1995-99; vice chmn. TMP Worldwide Exec. Search, 1999—. Mem. Human Resource Planning Soc., The Planning Forum, Assn. for Corp. Growth, Internat. Assn. Corp. and Profl. Recruiters, The Club (Cleve.), Union Club (Cleve.), Internat. Game Fishing Assn., Kirtland Country Club, Calusa Pines Club. Avocations: big game fishing, golf, travel, wine collecting, thoroughbred racing. Home: 12550 Lake Ave Ste 1607 Lakewood OH 44107-1571 Office: TMP Worldwide Exec Search 127 Public Sq Cleveland OH 44114-1216

JOHNSON, JOHN IRWIN, JR. neuroscientist; b. Salt Lake City, Aug. 18, 1931; s. John Irwin and Ann Josephine (Freeman) J. AB, U. Notre Dame, 1952; MS, Purdue U., 1955, PhD, 1957. Instr., then asst. prof. Marquette U., Milw., 1957-60; USPHS spl. research fellow U. Wis., Madison, 1960-63; Fulbright-Hays research scholar U. Sydney, Australia, 1964-65; asso. prof. biophysics, psychology and zoology Mich. State U., East Lansing, 1965-69, prof., 1969-81, chmn. dept. biophysics, 1973-78, prof. anatomy, 1981-99, prof. radiology and neurosci., 1999—. Vis. fellow psychology dept. Yale U., New Haven, 1975-76 Recipient Career Devel. award NIH, 1965-72, research grantee, 1966-79; research grantee NSF, 1969-71, 71-73, 73-76, 78-89, 91—; 3d hon. life mem. Anat. Assn. Australia and N.Z., 1973 Mem. Soc. Neurosci., Am. Assn. Anatomists, Soc. for Comparative and Integrative Biology, Am. Soc. Mammalogists, Animal Behavior Soc., AAUP, ACLU, Sigma Xi. Home: 2494 W Grand River Ave Okemos MI 48864-1447 Office: Mich State U Dept Radiology 519A E Fee Hall East Lansing MI 48824-1316 E-mail: johnij@aol.com., johnij4@yahoo.com.

JOHNSON, JOY ANN, diagnostic radiologist; b. New Richmond, Wis., Aug. 16, 1952; d. Howard James and Shirley Maxine (Eidem) J.que BA in Chemistry summa cum laude, U. No. Colo., 1974; D of Medicine, U. Colo., 1978. Diplomate Am. Bd. Radiology, Nat. Bd. Med. Examiners; cert. added qualification pediatric radiology. Resident in radiology U. Colo., 1978-81, fellow in radiology, 1981-82; asst. prof. diagnostic radiology and pediatrics, chief sect. pediatric radiology Clin. Radiology Found. U. Kans. Med. Ctr., Kansas City, 1982-87; radiologist Radiology Assocs. Ltd., Mo., 1987-92; mem. staff Bapt. Med. Ctr., 1987-92; radiologist Children's Mercy Hosp., 1992-95, Leavenworth-Kansas City Imaging, 1996—; assoc. prof. U. Mo., Kansas City, 1992—. Speaker Radiol. Soc. Republic of China, 1985. Contbr. articles to med. jours. Nat. Cancer Inst. fellow, 1982. Mem. AMA, Am. Coll. Radiology, Radiol. Soc. N.Am., Am. Inst. Ultrasound in Medicine (mem. program com. Kansas City 1984), Soc. Pediatric Radiology, Am. Assn. Women in Radiology, Lambda Sigma Tau. Avocations: horseback riding, jumping, physical fitness, sports, reading. Office: Leavenworth-Kansas City Imaging 9201 Parallel Pkwy Kansas City KS 66112-1528

JOHNSON, JULIA F. bank executive; Sr. v.p. Banc One Corp, Columbus, Ohio. Office: Banc One Corp Dept OH-0152 100 E Broad St Dept Oh-152 Columbus OH 43215-3607

JOHNSON, JULIE MARIE, lawyer, lobbyist; b. Aberdeen, S.D., Aug. 7, 1953; d. Howard B. and Jerauldine (Dilly) J.; m. Bryan L. Hisel. BA in Govt., Comm., U. S.D., 1974, MA in Polit. Sci., JD, U. S.D., 1976. Bar: S.D. 1977, U.S. Dist. Ct. S.D. 1977. Assoc. Siegel, Barnett Law Firm, Aberdeen, 1977; law clk. Fifth Judicial Circuit Ct., 1977-78; ptnr. Maloney, Kolker, Fritz, Hogan & Johnson, 1978-84; dep. sec. S.D. Dept. Labor, Aberdeen, Pierre, 1983-84, sec. Gov.'s Cabinet, 1985-87; pres. Industry and Commerce Assn. of S.D., Pierre, 1987-95; sec., Gov.'s Cabinet S.D. Dept. Revenue, 1995; exec. dir. S.D. Rural Devel. Coun., 1995—. Treas. S.D. Cmty. Found., Pierre, 1987-95; mem. Pvt. Industry Coun., 1985-87, S.D. Coun. on Vocat. Edn., 1985-87; bd. dirs. Mo. Shores Women's Resource Ctr., Pierre, 1988-89; chmn. S.D. Main St. Adv. Coun., 1987-91; bd. dirs. United Way, 1988-96, chmn., 1991; mem. Shortgrass Arts Coun., 1987—, South Dakotans for the Arts, 1981—, Solid Waste Mgmt. Plan Task Force, 1990, S.D. Citizens Adv. Coun. on Hazardous Waste, 1991-92, gov.'s adv. coun. on health care reform, 1992-93; bd. dirs. Hist. S.D. Found., 1996-99; founding mem., legal counsel Outdoor Women of S.D., Inc., 1995—; bd. trustees USD Found., 1992—; trustee, mem. bus. affairs com., 1996—, com. on trustees, Kelley Ctr. for Entrepreneurship adv. bd., presdl. search com. Dakota Wesleyan U., 1999-2000; founding mem., treas. S.D. Discovery Ctr. and Aquarium, Inc., bd. dirs., 1988-92; mem. S.D. Water Congress, 1990—97, bd. dirs., 1987-95; bd. dirs. Nyoda Girl Scout Coun., 1997-99; mem. adv. bd. W.O. Farber Ctr. for Excellence in Civic Leadership, 1998—; bd. dirs. Farber Fund, 1987—; founding mem. S.D. Chambers & Econ. Devel. Coun., 1989—; mem. Network Mgmt. Team Nat. Rural Devel. Partnership, 1998—2001; mem. Children's Care Hosp. and Sch. Found. Bd., 1997—, investment com., 1999—, bd. devel. com., 2000—; mem. Nat. Rural Devel. Partnership Presdl. Transition Team, 2000—, Agr. and Econ. Devel. Task Force, 2001—, S.D. Habitat for Humanity Bd., 2001—; bd. dir. Historic S.Dak. Found., 1995-98, Genesis of Innovation, 2000-, S.Dak. Habitat for Humanity, 2001-, ; acting exec. dir. S.Dak. Math., Sci. & Tech. Coun., 2000-; vol. chmn. S.Dak. WWII Meml. Dedication, 2001. RJR Nabisco fellow Women Execs. in State Govt., Harvard, 1986; named Outstanding Young Citizen Jaycees, Aberdeen, 1982, S.D. Jaycees, 1983. Mem. S.D. Bar Assn. (chmn. adminstrv. law com. 2001-, mem. CLE com., Worker's compensation com.), Industry and Commerce Assn. S.D. (bd. dirs. 1985-87), U. S.D. Alumni Assn. (exec. com. 1987-96, pres. 1990-92), AAUW, Bus. and Profl. Women U.S.A. (nat. legis. chmn. 1987-88, 92-94, nat. chmn. issues mgmt. 1991-93, pres. S.D. 1984-85, Woman of Yr. award Aberdeen chpt. 1982), Women Execs. in State Govt. (bd. didrs. 1985-87), Coun. State Mfrs. Assn., S.D. Mining Assn. (bd. dirs. 1991-95, Gold PAC, 1995-), Nat. Indsl. Coun., Coun. State C.'s of C., Ducks Unltd., Rotary, Zonta, ABC Investment Club, Rocky Mountain Elk Found. Republican. Lutheran. Address: 1100 E Church St Apt 352 Pierre SD 57501-2354 Office: Capitol Lake Plz 711 E Wells Ave Pierre SD 57501-3335 Home: 1414 Sharpstone Dr Mitchell SD 57301-6250 E-mail: juliem.johnson@state.sd.us.

JOHNSON, KENNETH HARVEY, veterinary pathologist; b. Hallock, Minn., Feb. 17, 1936; s. Clifford H. and Alma (Anderson) J.; Sept. 17, 1960; children: Jeffrey, Gregory, Sandra. BS, U. Minn., 1958, DVM, 1960, PhD, 1965. Jr. asst. health officer NIH, Bethesda, Md., 1958; practice vet. medicine Edina, Minn., 1960; USPHS-NIH non-service fellow U. Minn., St. Paul, 1960-65, asst. prof. dept. vet. pathology and parasitology, 1965-69, assoc. prof., 1969-73, prof., 1973-98, prof. emeritus dept. vet. pathobiology, 1998—, head, sect. pathology, dept. vet. biology, 1974-76, chmn. dept. vet. pathobiology Coll. Vet Medicine, 1976-83. Cons. Minn. Mining & Mfg. Co., Medtronic Inc., Natural-Y Surg. Specialties; principle and co-investigator several NIH grants, 1965-98. Mem. editl. bd. Amyloid, the Internat. Jour. of Exptl. and Clin. Investigation; contbr. chpts.: Veterinary Clinics of North America, 1971, Spontaneous Animal Models of Human Disease, 1979, Kirk's Current Veterinary Therapy; contbr. articles to sci. jours. Councilman Nativity Lutheran Ch., St. Anthony Village, Minn., 1972-75. Recipient Tchr. of Yr. award, 1968-69, Norden award for disting. tchr. in vet. medicine, 1970, Beecham award for rsch. excellence, 1989, Ralson Purina Small Animal Rsch. award, 1990, Phi Zeta faculty achievement award, 1992, Outstanding Achievement award Bd. of Regents of U. Minn., 2001. Mem.: AAUP, Am. Soc. Investigative Pathology, Am. Coll. Investigative Pathologists (hon.), Gamma Sigma Delta, Phi Zeta, Sigma Xi. Home: 3510 Skycroft Dr Minneapolis MN 55418-1780 Office: Univ Minn Coll Vet Medicine Dept Vet Diagnostic Med Saint Paul MN 55108 E-mail: johns049@tc.umn.edu.

JOHNSON, K(ENNETH) O(DELL), aerospace engineer; b. Harville, Mo., Aug. 31, 1922; s. Kenneth D. and Polly Louise (Wilson) J.; B.S. in Aero. Engring., Purdue U., 1950; m. Betty Lou Jones, Aug. 5, 1950; children— Cynthia Jo, Gregory Alan. Engr., design, quality and production mgmt. Gen. Lamp Co., Elwood, Ind., 1950-51; mem. staff aircraft gas turbine engine design Allison div. Gen. Motors Corp., Speedway, Ind., 1951-66; mem. turbofan aircraft engines plus marine, indsl. gas turbine engine design mgmt. staff Gen. Electric Co., 1966-86, cons. aerospace engring. Belcan Corp., Cin., 1986—. Served to capt. USAF, 1942-45. Assoc. fellow AIAA. Republican. Methodist. Holder over 20 patents in field. Recipient UDF Pioneer & Extraordinary Service award for unducted fan invention and patent, Gen. Electric Co., 1985, cert. recognition NASA, 1987; named Outstanding Aerospace Engr., Sch. Aeronautics and Astronautics, Purdue U., 2000; named to Gen. Electric Aircraft Engines Propulsion Hall of Fame, 1987. Home: 8360 Arapaho Ln Cincinnati OH 45243-2718 Office: Belcan Corp Dept Engring 10200 Anderson Way Cincinnati OH 45242-4718 Personal E-mail: kjohnson@one.net.

JOHNSON, LAEL FREDERIC, lawyer; b. Yakima, Wash., Jan. 22, 1938; s. Andrew Cabot and Gudney M. (Fredrickson) J.; m. Eugenie Rae Call, June 9, 1960; children: Eva Marie, Inga Margaret. AB, Wheaton (Ill.) Coll., 1960; JD, Northwestern U., 1963. Bar: Ill. 1963, U.S. Dist. Ct. (no. dist.) Ill. 1964, U.S. Ct. Appeals (7th cir.) 1966. V.p., gen. counsel Abbott Labs., Abbott Park, Ill., 1981-89, sr. v.p., sec., gen. counsel, 1989-94; of counsel Schiff Hardin & Waite, Chgo., 1995—. Mem. Law Sch. bd. Northwestern U. Mem. ABA, Chgo. Bar Assn., Assn. Gen. Counsel. Office: Schiff Hardin & Waite 6600 Sears Tower Chicago IL 60606

JOHNSON, LARRY WALTER, lawyer; b. Princeton, Minn., May 21, 1934; s. Alfred Herbert and Lillian Martha (Wetter) J.; m. Mary Ann Lindstrom, June 14, 1958; children: Lawrence W. II, Kristin Jane. BS in Law, U. Minn., 1957, LLB, 1959. Bar: Minn. 1959. Assoc. Dorsey & Whitney, Mpls., 1961-66, ptnr., 1967-95, of counsel, 1996—. Bd. dirs. Remmele Engring., Inc. Co-author, co-editor Minnesota Estate Administration, 1968. Bd. dirs. Minn. Bus. Found. Excellence in Edn., St. Paul. 1981-85, Walker Sponsor's Fund, Mpls., 1987; trustee Walker Meth. Residence and Health Services, Inc., Mpls., 1985-86. Served to 1st lt. U.S. Army, 1959-61. Mem. Minn. Bar Assn., Hennepin County Bar Assn., Mpls. Athletic Club. Republican. Congregationalist. Avocation: handball. Home: 5400 W Highwood Dr Minneapolis MN 55436-1225 Office: Dorsey & Whitney 220 S 6th St Ste 2200 Minneapolis MN 55402-1498

JOHNSON, LAWRENCE ALAN, cereal technologist, educator, administrator; b. Columbus, Ohio, Apr. 30, 1947; s. William and Wyoma (Swift) J.; m. Bernice Ann Miller, June 15, 1969; children: Bradley, David. BS, Ohio State U., 1969; MS, N.C. State U., 1971; PhD, Kans. State U., 1978. Rsch. chemist Durkee Foods div. SCM Corp., Strongsville, Ohio, 1973-75; assoc. rsch. chemist Food Protein R&D Ctr. Tex. A&M U., College Station, 1978-85; dir. Ctr. for Crops Utilization Rsch. Iowa State U., Ames, 1991—. Mem. rsch. com. Am. Soybean Assn., St. Louis, 1987-91, Nat. Corn Grower's Assn., St. Louis, 1990-91. Author: (with others) Handbook of Cereals, 1991; editor: (book/procs.) Technologies for Value-Added Products from Proteins and Co-Products, 1989; contbr. more than 130 articles to profl. jours. 1st lt. U.S. Army, 1971-73, Vietnam. Recipient Rsch. award Corn Refiners Assn., 1998. Mem. Am. Assn. Cereal Chemists (assoc. editor jour. 1982-85), Am. Soc. Agrl. Engrs., Am. Oil Chemists Soc. (assoc. editor jour. 1989—, Archer Daniels Midland Rsch. award 1986), Royal Swedish Acad. Agr. and Forestry (fgn. mem. 1999), Inst. Food Techs. Republican. Lutheran. Achievements include 11 patents. Home: 2226 Buchanan Dr Ames IA 50010-4368 Office: Ctr Crops Utilization Rsch Iowa State U Ames IA 50011-0001

JOHNSON, LAWRENCE EUGENE, lawyer; b. Morrison, Ill., Sept. 26, 1937; s. Frederick Eugene and Ruth Helen (Lorke) J.; m. Debby Karen McCaleb, June 17, 1961; children: Mark Lawrence, Eric Eugene, Lori Ann Johnson Purtzer. BS, No. Ill. U., 1960, MS, 1962; JD, U. Ill., 1965. Bar: Ill. 1965, U.S. Dist. Ct. (ctrl. dist.) Ill. 1965, U.S. Ct. Appeals (7th cir.) 1965; lic. pilot. Pvt. practice, 1965-68; states atty. County of Champaign, Ill., 1968-72; pvt. practice Champaign, 1972—. Spl. asst. atty. gen. litigation Ill. Dept. Revenue, 1982-86, Ill. Dept. Labor, 1982-86, Ill. Dept. Transp., 1986-90, Ill. Dept. Conservation, 1988-90, Ill. Dept. Nuclear Safety, 1989-90. Bd. mem. Ill. State Bd. Elections, 1990-95, vice chmn., 1993-95; chmn. Ill. Liquor Control Commn., 1972-73; hearing officer Ill. State Bd. Elections, 1988-90; mem. airport hazard zoning task force divsn. aeronautics Ill. Dept. Transp., 1987-88. With U.S. Army, 1955-57. Mem. U.S. Pilots Assn. (bd. dirs. 1989—), Ill. Pilots Assn. (pres. 1991-93, v.p., bd. dirs. 1989-91), Illini Area Pilots Assn. (pres. 1989-91), Ill. Trial Lawyers Assn., Champaign Urbana Kiwanis Early Risers, Champaign Urbana Ambucs, AMVETS (life). Office: Johnson & Assocs PO Box 1127 202 W Hill St Champaign IL 61824-1127 E-mail: lejai@shout.net.

JOHNSON, LINDA ARLENE, petroleum and flatbed semi-freight transporter; b. Sparta, Wis., Mar. 6, 1946; d. Clarence Julius and Arlene Mae (Yahnke) Jessie; children: Darrick, Larissa. With Union Nat. Bank & Trust Co., Sparta, 1964-69, Hill, Christensen & Co., CPA's, Tomah, Wis., 1969-75; owner Johnson of Wis. Oil Co., Inc., 1969-95; with Larry's Express, Inc., 1975-78; owner Johnson Rentals, 1979—, Johnson of Wis. Transport Co., Inc., Tomah, 1982—. Mem. Forward Tomah Devel., Inc., 1999—; active St. Paul's Luth Ch., Tomah. Mem. Petroleum Marketers Assn. Am., Nat. Assn. Convenience Stores, Am. Trucking Assn., Wis. Assn.

Convenience Stores, Petroleum Marketers Assn. Wis., Tomah Area C. of C., Tomah Area Credit Union (bd. dirs. 1993—, sec. 1993-94), Rotary Club Tomah (dir. 1997-99). Home and Office: 24011 Flatter Ave Tomah WI 54660-4424

JOHNSON, LLOYD PETER, retired banker; b. Mpls., May 1, 1930; s. Lloyd Percy and Edna (Schlampp) J.; m. Rosalind Gesner, July 3, 1954; children: Marcia, Russell, Paul. BA, Carleton Coll., Northfield, Minn., 1952; MBA, Stanford U., 1954. With Security Trust & Savs. Bank, San Diego, 1954-57; vice chmn. Security Nat. Bank, L.A., 1957-84; chmn., chief exec. officer Norwest Corp., Mpls., 1985-92, chmn. bd. dirs., 1993-95; ret., 1995. Mem. faculty Pacific Coast Banking Sch., 1969-72, chmn., 1979-80; bd. dirs. Valmont Industries Inc., Cargill Inc. Vice chmn. Carleton Coll. Mem. Calif. Bankers Assn. (pres. 1977-78).

JOHNSON, LOWELL C. state commissioner; b. Dodge County, Nebr., June 12, 1920; m. Ruth Marion Sloss, June 21, 1943; children: Mark C., Kent R., James S., Nancy L. BSME, U. Nebr., 1942. Farm and property mgmt. exec.; pres. Johnson-Sloss Land Co., North Bend, Nebr.; mem. Nebr. Legis., 1981-93, vice chmn. legis. appropriations com., mem. com. on coms.; commr. Nebr. Pub. Svc. Commn., 1995—; mem. coms. consumer affairs, fin. and tech. Nat. Assn. Regulatory Utility Commrs. Mem. Nebr. Telecomm. Relay Svc. adv. com., 1999—; mem. NECA Interstate Telcom Relay Svc. Fund adv. coun., 2001—. Former trustee Meml. Hosp. Dodge County; former mem. adv. coun. Nebr. Dept. Labor; former mem. behavioral scis. adv. com. Immanuel Hosp., Omaha; former mem. County Sch.. Reorgn. Com.; former field rep. Congressman Charles Thone; former pres. bd. dirs. North Bend Sr. Citizens Home, bd. edn. Mem. Am. Legion, Fremont and North Bend C. of C. Clubs: Masons (Scottish Rite), Shriners, Rotary. Home: PO Box 370 North Bend NE 68649-0370 Office: 1200 N St Lincoln NE 68508 E-mail: ljohnson@mail.state.ne.us.

JOHNSON, LYNN, liquor company wholesaler; CEO Johnson Bros. Wholesale Liquor, St. Paul. Office: Johnson Bros Wholesale Liqr 2285 University Ave W Saint Paul MN 55114-1604

JOHNSON, MARGARET ANN (PEGGY), library administrator; b. Atlanta, Aug. 11, 1948; d. Odell H. and Virginia (Mathiasen) J.; m. Lee J. English, Mar. 4, 1978; children: Carson J., Amelia J. BA, St. Olaf Coll., 1970; MA, U. Chgo., 1972; MBA, Met. State U., 1990. Music cataloger U. Iowa Librs., Iowa City, 1972-73; analyst Control Data Corp., Bloomington, Minn., 1973-75; br. libr. St. Paul Pub. Librs., 1975-77; head tech. svcs. St. Paul Campus Librs., U. Minn., 1977-86; collection devel. office U. Librs., U. Minn., Mpls., 1987-90; asst. dir. St. Paul Campus Librs., U. Minn., 1987-95; planning officer U. Librs. U. Minn., Mpls., 1993-97, asst. univ. libr., 1997—, interim univ. libr., 2002—. Libr. cons. Mekerere U., Kampala, Uganda, 1990, U. Nat. Rwanda, 1990, Inst. Agr. and Vet. Hassan II, Rabat, Morocco, 1992—, Ecole Nat. Agr., Meknes, Morocco, 2000, China Agrl. U., Beijing, 2001. Author: Automation and Organizational Change in Libraries, 1991, The Searchable Internet, 1996; editor: New Directions in Technical Services, 1997; editor Technicalities Jour., 2000—; editor Guide to Tech. Svcs. Resources, 1994, Recruiting, Educating and Tng. Librarians for Collection Devel., 1994, Collection Mgmt. and Devel., 1994, Virtually Yours, 1998; contbr. articles to profl. jours. Recipient Samuel Lazerow Rsch. fellowship Assn. Coll. and Rsch. Librs., Inst. for Sci. Info., 1987. Mem. ALA, Minn. Libr. Assn., Internat. Assn. Agrl. Librs. and Documentatists, U.S. Agrl. Info. Network, Assn. for Libr. Collections and Tech. Svcs. (pres. 1999-2000). Office: U of Minn Librs 499 Wilson Libr 309 19th Ave S Minneapolis MN 55455-0438 E-mail: m-john@tc.umn.edu.

JOHNSON, MARGARET KATHLEEN, business educator; b. Baylor County, Tex., Oct. 30, 1920; d. George W. and Julia Rivers (Turner) Higgins; m. Herman Clyde Johnson, Jr., July 27, 1949 (dec.); 1 child, Carolyn Kay. BS, Hardin-Simmons U., 1940; M in Bus. Edn., North Tex. State U., 1957, EdD, 1962. Clk. Farmers Nat. Bank, Seymour, Tex., 1940-41; adminstrv. sec. U.S. Navy, Corpus Christi, 1941-46; adminstrv. asst. Hdqrs. 8th Army, Yokohama, Japan, 1946-49; instr. Coll. Bus. Adminstrn., U. Ark., 1957-60; teaching fellow Sch. Bus. Adminstrn., North Tex. State U., 1960-62, instr., 1962-63; asst. prof. bus., tchr. edn. and secondary edn. Tchrs. Coll., U. Nebr., Lincoln, 1963-65, asso. prof., 1966-70, prof., 1970—. Guest lectr. U. N.Mex., 1967, Curriculum Devel. in Bus. Edn., N.S. Dept. Edn., 1969, North Tex. State U., 1970, East Tex. State U., 1972; in Policies Commn. for Bus. and Econ. Edn., 1979-83; mem. bd. devel. Hardin-Simmons U., 1994-97. Author: Standardized Production Typewriting Tests series, 1964-65, National Structure for Research in Vocational Education, 1966; co-author: Introduction to Word Processing, 1980, 2d edit., 1985, Introduction to Business Communication, 1981, 2d edit., 1988, Business Communication Principles and Applications, 1996; editor: Nat. Bus. Edn. Assn. Yearbook, 1980. Recipient United Bus. Edn. Assn. award as outstanding grad. student in bus. edn. North Tex. State U., 1957; award for outstanding service Nebr. Future Bus. Leaders Am., 1968; Mountain-Plains Bus. Edn. Leadership award, 1977; merit award Nebr. Bus. Assn., 1979 Mem. Nat. Bus. Edn. Assn. (exec. bd. 1975, 76-78), Mountain-Plains Bus. Edn. Assn. (exec. sec. 1970-73, pres. 1975), Nebr. Bus. Edn. Assn. (pres. 1966-67), Nebr. Council on Occupational Tchr. Edn., Delta Pi Epsilon. E-mail: margaretkh@aol.com.

JOHNSON, MARK ALAN, lawyer; b. Marysville, Ohio, June 5, 1960; s. Neil Raymond and Elizabeth Johnson; m. Deborah Anne Hillis, Sept. 21, 1984. BA, Otterbein Coll., 1982; JD, Ohio State U., 1985. Bar: Ohio 1985, U.S. Dist. Ct. (so. dist.) Ohio 1985, U.S. Ct. Appeals (6th cir.) 1987, U.S. Dist. Ct. (no. dist.) Ohio 1991, U.S. Ct. Appeals (5th cir.) 1998. Assoc. Baker and Hostetler LLP, Columbus, Ohio, 1985-92, ptnr., 1993—. Mem. ABA (litigation sect., mem. bus. torts litigation com., comml. and banking litigation com.), Ohio Bar Assn., Columbus Bar Assn. Office: Baker & Hostetler LLP 65 E State St Ste 2100 Columbus OH 43215-4215 E-mail: mjohnson@bakerlaw.com.

JOHNSON, MARK EUGENE, lawyer; b. Independence, Mo., Jan. 8, 1951; s. Russell Eugene and Reatha (Nixon) J.; m. Vicki Ja Lane, June 11, 1983. AB with honors, U. Mo., 1973, JD, 1976. Bar: Mo. 1976, U.s. Dist. Ct. (we. dist.) Mo. 1976, U.S. Ct. Appeals (8th cir.) 1984, U.S. Supreme Ct. 1993. Ptnr. Morrison & Hecker, LLP, Kansas City, Mo., 1976—. Editor Mo. Law Rev., 1974-76. Pres. Lido Villas Assn., Inc., Mission, Kans., 1979-81. Mem. ABA, Mo. Bar Assn., Kansas City Bar Assn., Lawyers Assn. Kansas City, Def. Rsch. Inst., Internat. Assn. Def. Counsel, Mo. Orgn. Def. Lawyers, Carriage Club, Order of Coif, Phi Beta Kappa, Phi Eta Sigma, Phi Kappa Phi, Omicron Delta Kappa. Republican. Presbyterian. Home: 4905 Somerset Dr Shawnee Mission KS 66207-2230 Office: Morrison & Hecker LLP 2600 Grand Blvd Ste 1200 Kansas City MO 64108-4606

JOHNSON, MARY ANN, computer training vocational school owner; b. Chgo., June 26, 1956; d. Truly and Pearlie Mae (Bell) J.; m. Russell Alan Jackson, May 18, 1976 (div. 1983); children: Pamela Ann, Russell Alan Jr. AA, Joliet (Ill.) Jr. Coll., 1990; student mgmt. info. systems, Governor State U. Student intern Argonne (Ill.) Nat. Lab., 1972-79, sec. II, 1979-82; word processor specialist SunGard Corp., Hinsdale, Ill., 1982-86; desktop designer, adminstrn. Amoco Chem. Corp., Naperville, 1988-89; desktop designer Travelers Corp., 1989-90; adminstrv. sec., computer operator Metromail Donnelly, Lombard, Ill., 1990-91; owner, pres. Tech. Soft Svcs., Chgo., 1991—. Lectr., condr. seminars on running small bus. Author: Running a Small Business, 1996. Avocations: self-defense, computer and software edn. Office: Tech Soft Svcs 160 E Illinois St Ste 603 Chicago IL 60611-3859

JOHNSON, MARYL RAE, cardiologist; b. Fort Dodge, Iowa, Apr. 15, 1951; d. Marvin George and Beryl Evelyn (White) Johnson. BS, Iowa State U., 1973; MD, U. Iowa, 1977. Diplomate Am. Bd. Internal Medicine, Am. Bd. Cardiovasc. Diseases. Intern U. Iowa Hosps., Iowa City, 1977-78, resident, 1978-81, fellow, 1979-82; assoc. in cardiology U. Iowa Hosps. and Clins., 1982-86, asst. prof. medicine cardiovasc. divsn., 1986-88; asst. prof. medicine Med. Ctr. Loyola U., 1988-92, assoc. prof., 1992-94, Rush. U., 1994-97, Northwestern U. Med. Sch., 1998—. Med. dir. cardiac transplantation U. Iowa Hosp., 1986—88; assoc. med. dir. cardiac transplantation Loyola U., 1988—94, assoc. med. dir. Rush Heart Failure and Cardiac Transplant Program, 1994—97; dir. Heart Failure Cardiac Transplant Program Northwestern U. Med. Sch., 1998—2001, dir. Heart Failure Program, 2001—. Editor (assoc. editor): Jour. Heart and Lung Transplantation, 1995—99; mem. editl. bd.: , 2000—. Mem. Nat. Heart Lung and Blood Adv. Coun., Bethesda, Md., 1979—83; mem. biomed. rsch. tech. rev. com. NIH, 1990—93, chairperson, 1992—93, chair biomed. rsch. tech. spl. emphasis panel, 1999—. Recipient Jane Leinfelder Meml. award, U. Iowa Coll. Medicine, 1977, Clin. Investigator award, NIH, 1981, New Investigator Rsch. award, 1981, 1986; scholar Barry Freeman, 1974. Mem.: ACP, AAAS, AMA, Am. Coll. Cardiology (bd. councillors Ill. chpt., heart failure and cardiac transplant com. 2002—), Am. Heart Assn., Chgo. Med. Soc., Ill Med. Soc., Ctrl. Soc. Clin. Rsch., Internat. Soc. Heart and Lung Transplantation, Order of Rose, Alpha Omega Alpha, Iota Sigma Pi, Phi Kappa Phi, Alpha Lambda Delta. Office: Northwestern U Med Sch 201 E Huron Galter 11-240 Chicago IL 60611-2958 E-mail: mrjohnso@nmh.org.

JOHNSON, MICHAEL O. window manufacturing executive; CFO, sr. v.p. corp. bus. svcs. Andersen Corp., Bayport, Minn. Office: Andersen Corp 100 4th Ave N Bayport MN 55003

JOHNSON, MILLARD WALLACE, JR. mathematics and engineering educator; b. Racine, Wis., Feb. 1, 1928; s. Millard Wallace and Marian Manilla (Rittman) J.; m. Ruth Pugh Gifford, Dec. 26, 1953; children: Millard Wallace III, Jeannette Marian Brooks, Charles Gifford, Peter Allen. BS in Applied Math. and Mechanics, U. Wis., 1952, MS, 1953; PhD in Math, MIT, 1957. Rsch. asst. MIT, 1953-57, lectr., 1957-58; mem. staff Math. Rsch. Ctr. U. Wis., Madison, 1958-94, prof. mechanics, 1958-63, prof. mechanics and math., 1964-94, mem. staff Rheology Rsch. Ctr., 1970—, mem. Engine Rsch. Ctr., 1985—, prof. emeritus, 1994—. Contbr. articles to profl. jours. Adv. bd. Internat. Math. and Statis. Librs. (IMSL), 1971-92. With USN, 1946-48. Fellow ASME; mem. Soc. Rheology, Soc. Indsl. and Applied Math., Am. Acad. Mechanics, Brit. Soc. Rheology, Wis. Acad. Scis., Arts and Letters, Phi Beta Kappa. Home: 802 Blue Ridge Pkwy Madison WI 53705-1148 Office: U Wis Dept Eng Phys 1500 Engineering Dr Madison WI 53706-1609

JOHNSON, NICHOLAS, writer, lawyer, lecturer; b. Iowa City, Sept. 23, 1934; s. Wendell A.L. and Edna (Bockwoldt) J.; m. Karen Mary Chapman, 1952 (div. 1972); children: Julie, Sherman, Gregory; m. Mary Eleanor Vasey, 1991. B.A., U. Tex., 1956, LL.B., 1958; L.H.D., Windham Coll., 1971. Bar: Tex. 1958, D.C. 1963, U.S. Supreme Ct. 1963, Iowa 1974; lic. radio amateur. Law clk. to judge John R. Brown, U.S. 5th Circuit Ct. Appeals, 1958-59; law clk. to U.S. Supreme Ct. Justice Hugo L. Black, 1959-60; acting assoc. prof. law U. Calif. at Berkeley, 1960-63; assoc. Covington & Burling, Washington, 1963-64; adminstr. Maritime Adminstrn., chmn. Maritime Subsidy Bd. U.S. Dept. Commerce, 1964-66; commr. FCC, 1966-73; adj. prof. law Georgetown U., 1971-73; Poynter fellow Yale U., 1971; vis. prof. U. Ill., Champaign-Urbana, 1976, U. Okla., Norman, 1978, Ill. State U., Normal, 1979, U. Wis., Madison, 1980, Newhouse Sch., Syracuse U., 1980, U. Iowa Coll. Law, 1981—; vis. prof. dept. communications studies U. Iowa, 1982-85; vis. prof. Western Behavioral Scis. Inst., U. Calif., San Diego, 1986-91. Vis. prof. Calif. State U., Los Angeles, 1986; regents prof. U. Calif., San Diego, 2000; co-dir. U. Iowa Inst. for Health, Behavior and Environ. Policy, 1990-93; chmn., dir. Nat. Citizens Comm. Lobby, 1975—, Nat. Citizens Com. for Broadcasting, 1974-78; pub. access, 1975-77; commentator Nat. Pub. Radio, 1975-77, 83-86, Sta. WRC-AM, Washington, 1977, Sta. WSUI, Iowa City, 1982-87; presdl. advisor White House Conf. on Libraries and Info. Services, 1979; exec. com. World Acad. Art and Sci., 1993-97. Author: Cases and Materials on Oil and Gas Law, 1962, How to Talk Back to Your Television Set, 1970, Japanese transl., 1971, Life Before Death in the Corporate State, 1971, Test Pattern for Living, 1972, Broadcasting in America, 1973, Cases and Materials on Communications Law and Policy, 1981, 82, 83, 84, 85, 86, Readings for Law of Electronic Media, 1993-94, (with David Loundy) Law of Electronic Media in a Cyberspace Age, 1996; syndicated columnist: Gannett News Service, 1982-84, Register and Tribune Syndicate, 1984, Cowles Syndicate, 1985-86, King Features Syndicate, 1986, Iowa City Press Citizen, 1998—; contbr. to legal, gen., internat. publs.; contbg. editor, host PBS The New Tech Times, 1983-84. Dem. candidate for U.S. Ho. of Reps. from 3d Iowa Dist., 1974; bd. dirs. Iowa City Cmty. Sch. Dist., Citizens for Ind. Public Broadcasting; mem. adv. bd. Ctr. for Media Edn., Cultural Environ. Movement, Fairness and Accuracy in Reporting, Inst. for Pub. Accuracy, Open Soc. Inst. Media Group, Project Censored, War and Peace Found.; mem. Broadband and Telecom. Commn., Iowa City, 1981-87. Named One of 10 Outstanding Young Men in U.S., U.S. Jaycees, 1967, recipient New Republic Pub. Defender award, 1970, Civil Liberties Award Ga. ACLU, 1972, DeWitt Carter Reddick award U. Tex., 1977, George Stoney award Nat. Fedn. Local Cable Programmers, 1987; fellow World Acad. Art and Sci., 1991—. Mem. D.C., Iowa bar assns., State Bar Tex., Golden Key, Order of Coif, Phi Beta Kappa, Phi Delta Phi, Phi Eta Sigma, Pi Sigma Alpha. Democrat. Unitarian. Home and Office: PO Box 1876 Iowa City IA 52244-1876 E-mail: njohnson@inav.net.

JOHNSON, NIEL MELVIN, archivist, historian; b. Galesburg, Ill., July 28, 1931; s. Clarence Herman and Frances Albertina (Nelson) J.; m. Verna Gail Applegate, May 1, 1952; children: Kristin, David. BA, Augustana Coll., 1953; MA, State U. Iowa, 1965, PhD, 1971. Tchr. Unit #115, Biggsville, Ill., 1954-57; asst. historian U.S. Army Weapons Command, Rock Island, 1957-60, chief historian, 1960-63; instr. Augustana Coll., 1967-69; asst. prof. Dana Coll., Blair, Nebr., 1969-74; vis. asst. prof. U. Nebr., Omaha, 1975-76; archivist, historian Harry S. Truman Libr., Independence, Mo., 1977-92. Pres. Portal to the Plains, Inc., Blair, Nebr., 1973-77, Am. Friends of Emigrant Inst. Sweden, East Moline, Ill., 1984-89. Author: George S. Viereck: German-American Propagandist, 1972, Portal to the Plains, 1974; co-author: Rockford Swedes: American Stories, 1993, Power, Money and Women: Words to the Wise from Harry S. Truman, 1999; contbr. articles in field to profl. jours., newspapers. Coord. New Sweden '88 com. of Greater Kansas City, Mo.; chmn. Historic Trails City Com., Independence, 1988-93. Recipient Commendation, Concordia Hist. Inst., St. Louis, 1977. Mem. Orgn. Am. Historians, Midwestern Archives Conf., Jackson County Hist. Soc., Scandinavian Assn. (pres. 1987-89). Democrat. Lutheran. Avocations: painting, writing, photography, golf, impersonator of Harry S. Truman. Home: 15804 Kiger Cir Independence MO 64055-3750

JOHNSON, OWEN VERNE, program director; b. Madison, Wis., Feb. 22, 1946; s. Verner Lalander Johnson and Marianne Virginia (Halvorson) Muse; m. Marta Kucerova, July 17, 1969 (div. Jan. 26, 2001); children: Eva, Hana; m. Ann Coonradt Tryon, May 12, 2001. BA in History with distinction, Wash. State U., 1968; MA in History, U. Mich., 1970, cert. in Russian Ea. European studies, PhD in History, U. Mich., 1978. Reporter Pullman (Wash.) Herald, 1961-67; reporter, announcer Sta. KWSU Radio-TV, Pullman, 1965-68; reporter, editor, producer Sta. WUOM, Ann Arbor, Mich., 1969-77; adminstrv. asst. Ctr. for Russian and Ea. European Studies U. Mich., 1978-79; asst. prof. sch. journalism So. Ill. U., Carbondale, 1979-80; asst. prof. Ind. U., Bloomington, 1980-87, assoc. prof., 1987—, acting dir. Polish studies, 1989-90, dir. grad. studies, 1990-91, dir. Russian and Ea. European Inst., 1991-95. Lectr. U. Mich., 1978-79; mem. Studia Academica Slovaca, Comenius U., Bratislava, Czechoslovakia, 1973; mem. Modern Sweden Seminar, Uppsala, 1967; field advisor journalism Am. Coun. Tchrs. of Russian, 1993-96; adj. prof. history Ind. U., Bloomington, 1996—. Author: Slovakia 1918-38: Education and the Making of a Nation, 1985; co-author: Eastern European Journalism Before, During and After Communism, 1999; contbr. articles to profl. jours.; corr. editor: Journalism History, 1985-2000; mem. editl. bd. Slovakia, 1978-89, Journalism Monographs, 1986-88, Kosmas, 1996—, Medigska istrazivanja, 2002-; cons. editor Slavic Rev., 1985-91. Capt. USAR, 1971-79. Grantee Nat. Coun. for Soviet and East European Rsch., 1988-90, Am. Coun. Learned Socs./Social Sci. Rsch. Coun. Joint Com. on Ea. Europe, 1983, Internat. Rsch. and Exchs. Bd., 1973-89; recipient Excellence in Journalism award Sigma Delta Chi, 1966. Mem. Am. Hist. Assn., Am. Assn. for Advancement of Slavic Studies (edn. com. 1988-90), Assn. for Edn. in Journalism and Mass. Comm. (head history divsn. 1985-86), Czechoslovak History Conf. (editor newsletter 1980-84, exec. com. 1988-92, Stanley Pech award 1987-88), Internat. Assn. for Media Comm. Rsch., Orgn. Am. Historians, Slovak Studies Assn. (pres. 1988-91). Democrat. Presbyterian. Office: Ind U Sch Journalism 222C Ernie Pyle Hall Bloomington IN 47405 Fax: 812-855-0901. E-mail: johnsono@indiana.edu.

JOHNSON, PATSY, nursing association administrator; Exec. administr. Kans. State Bd. Nursing, Topeka. Office: Kans State Bd of Nursing Landon State Office Bldg 900 SW Jackson St Rm 551 Topeka KS 66612-1225

JOHNSON, PAUL OREN, lawyer; b. Mpls., Feb. 2, 1937; s. Andrew Richard and LaVerne Delores (Slater) J.; children: Scott, Paula, Amy. BA, Carleton Coll., 1958; JD cum laude, U. Minn., 1961. Bar: Minn. 1961. Atty. Briggs & Morgan, St. Paul, 1961-62, Green Giant Co., Le Sueur, Minn., 1961-66, asst. sec., 1967-74, sec., 1975-79, v.p., gen. counsel, 1971-79, v.p. corporate rels., 1973-79, mem. mgmt. com., 1976-79; gen. counsel H.B. Fuller Co., St. Paul, 1979-84, sr. v.p., sec., 1980-90, mem. mgmt. com., 1981-90. Bd. dirs. The Fulcrum Group, chmn. bd. dirs. Coun. v.p., exec. com. Boy Scouts Am.; bd. dirs. Rep. County Com., 1965; bd. dirs. Minn. State U., 1979-82, v.p., 1980-82; chmn. bd. dirs. Minn. Com. Serving Deaf and Hard of Hearing; bd. dirs. vice chair Minn. Acads. Office: Lexington-Riverside 403-1077 Sibley Meml Hwy Saint Paul MN 55118-3680

JOHNSON, RICHARD FRED, lawyer; b. July 12, 1944; s. Sylvester Hiram and Naomi Ruth (Jackson) Johnson; m. Sheila Conley, June 26, 1970; children: Brendon, Bridget, Timothy, Laura. BS, Miami U., Oxford, Ohio, 1966; JD cum laude, Northwestern U., 1969. Bar: Ill. 1969, U.S. Dist. Ct. (no. dist.) Ill. 1969), U.S. Dist. Ct. (ctrl. dist.) Ill. 2000, U.S. Ct. Appeals (7th cir.) 1977, U.S. Ct. Appeals (2d cir.) 1980, U.S. Ct. Appeals (9th cir.) 1991, U.S. Ct. Appeals (5th cir.) 1993, U.S. Supreme Ct. 1978. Law clk. U.S. Dist. Ct. (no. dist.) Ill., Chgo., 1969-70; assoc. firm Lord, Bissell & Brook, 1970-77, ptnr., 1977—. Lectr. legal edn. Contbr. articles to profl. jours. Recipient Am. Jurisprudence award 1968. Mem. Chgo. Bar Assn., Union League. Home: 521 W Roscoe St Chicago IL 60657-3518 Office: Lord Bissell & Brook 115 S La Salle St Ste 3200 Chicago IL 60603-3902

JOHNSON, RICK, state official; m. Cindy Johnson. Former commr., bd. chmn. Osceola County; Spkr. of Ho. Mich. Ho. Reps., Dist. 102 , 2001—. Mem. Pine River Sch. Bd. Edn.; dist. dir. Mich. Farm Bur. Mem.: Osceola County Republican Party (chmn.). Office: 166 Capitol Bldg PO Box 30014 Lansing MI 48909-7514 Office Fax: 517-373-9371. Business E-Mail: rijohnson@house.state.mi.us.*

JOHNSON, ROGER, state agency administrator; b. Turtle Lake, N.D. Elected agrl. commr. N.D. Dept. Agrl., Bismarck, 1996—2000, re-elected, 2000—. Pres. Mid. Am. Internat. Agrl.-Trade Coun. Office: ND Dept Agrl 600 E Blvd 6th Fl Bismarck ND 58505-0200*

JOHNSON, SAMUEL CURTIS, chemical company executive; b. Racine, Wis., Mar. 2, 1928; s. Herbert Fisk and Gertrude (Brauner) J.; m. Imogene Powers, May 8, 1954; children: Samuel Curtis III, Helen Johnson-Leipold, Herbert Fisk III, Winifred Johnson Marquart. BA, Cornell U., 1950; MBA, Harvard U., 1952; LLD (hon.), Carthage Coll., 1974, Northland Coll., 1974, Ripon Coll., 1980, Carroll Coll., 1981, U. Surrey, 1985, Marquette U., 1986, Nijenrode U., 1992. With S.C. Johnson & Son, Inc., Racine, 1954—, internat. v.p., 1962-63, exec. v.p., 1963-66, pres., 1966-67, chmn., pres., chief exec. officer, 1967-72, chmn., chief exec. officer, 1972-88, chmn., 1988—; CEO S.C. Johnson Commercial Markets, 1996—. Bd. dirs. Deere & Co., Moline, Ill., H.J. Heinz Co., Phila., Mobil Corp., N.Y.C.; chmn. bd. dirs. Johnson Worldwide Assocs., Inc., Johnson Internat. Inc. Trustee Am. Mus. Natural History, N.Y.C.; trustee emeritus The Mayo Found., Cornell U., presdl. councillor; chm Johnson's Wax Fund, Inc., Johnson Found., Inc.; founding chmn. emeritus Prairie Sch., Racine; chmn. adv. coun. Cornell U. Grad. Sch. Mgmt.; regent emeritus Smithsonian Instn.; hon. mem. Bus. Coun.; mem. nat. bd. govs. The Nature Conservancy. Mem. Chi Psi. Clubs: Cornell (N.Y.C., Milw.); Univ. (Milw.); Racine Country. Home: 4815 Lighthouse Dr Racine WI 53402-2666 Office: S C Johnson Commercial Markets 8310 16TH St Sturtevant WI 53177

JOHNSON, SANKEY ANTON, manufacturing company executive; b. Bremerton, Wash., May 14, 1940; s. Sankey Broyd and Alice Mildred (Norum) J.; m. Carolyn Lee Rogers, Nov. 30, 1968; children: Marni Lee, Ronald Anton. B.S. in M.E, U. Wash.; M.B.A., Stanford U. V.p., gen. mgr. Cummins Asia Pacific, Manila, Philippines, 1974-78; v.p. automotive Cummins Engine Co., Columbus, Ind., 1978-79; v.p. North Am. Bus., 1979-81; pres., chief exec. officer Onan Corp., Mpls., 1981-85; exec. v.p. Pentair Inc., St. Paul, from 1985, chief operating officer, 1985—, pres., 1986-89; chmn. Hidden Creek Industries, Mpls., 1989—. Trustee Mfr.'s Alliance. Bd. advisors Stanford Grad. Sch. Bus. Mem. Minneapolis Club, Lafayette Club. Home: 2310 Huntington Point Rd W Wayzata MN 55391-9743 Office: Hidden Creek Industries 4508 Ids Ctr Minneapolis MN 55402

JOHNSON, SIDNEY B. state legislator; b. Sedalia, Mo., Aug. 19, 1942; m. Jean M. Turner; four children. BS, U. of Mo., Columbia. Farmer; county commr. Buchanan County, 1983-90; mem. Mo. Senate from 34th dist., Jefferson City, 1990—.

JOHNSON, STANLEY R. economist, educator; b. Burlington, Iowa, Aug. 26, 1938; married; 2 children. BA in Agrl. Econs., Western Ill. U., 1961; MS, Tex. Tech. U., 1962; PhD, Tex. A&M U., 1966. Asst. prof. dept. econs. U. Mo., Columbia, 1964-66, assoc. prof. depts. econs. and agrl. econs., 1967-70, prof., 1970-85, adj. prof., 1985—, chmn. dept. econs., 1972-74; assoc. prof. dept. agrl. econs. U. Conn., Storrs, 1966-67. Exec. dir. Food and Agrl. Policy Rsch. Inst., 1984-96; prof., dir. Ctr. Agrl. and Rural Devel. Iowa State U., Ames, 1985-97; vis. assoc. prof. agrl. econs. Purdue U., 1971-72; economist Agr. Can., Ottawa, 1975; vis. prof. econs. U. Ga., 1975-76, U. Calif., Berkeley, 1981; chmn. bd. Midwest Agribus. Trade Rsch. and Info. Ctr., 1987-96; vice provost Iowa State U., 1996—; hon.

prof. Ukrainian State Agrl. U., 1994, Chinese Acad. Scis., 1996. Author: Advanced Econometric Methods, 1984, Demand Systems Estimation, 1984, Advvanced Econemetric Methods, 1988, Industrial Policy for Agriculture in Global Economy, 1993, Agricultural Sector Models for U.S., 1993, Conservation of Great Plains Ecosystems: Current Scientific and Future Options, 1995; mem. internat. editl. bd. Advances in Agrl. Mgmt. and Econs., 1989; editor-in-chief: Agr. Econs., Jour. Internat. Assn. Agrl. Economists; mem editl. bd.: Internat. Review Econs. and Finance, 1997; contbr. chpts to books, articles to profl. jours. Chmn. bd. dirs. Inst. Policy Reform, 1990—; co-chair World Food Conf., 1988. Recipient Chancellor's award for outstanding rsch., 1980, Internat. Honor award Office of Internat. Cooperation and Devel./USDA, 1987, Charles F. Curtiss Disting. Professorship, 1990, Internat. Svc. award Wilton Park, 1993; named to Merlin Cole Meml. Professorship, 1994-97; numerous grants in econs. Fellow Am. Agrl. Econs. Assn.; mem. Am. Agrl. Econs. Assn. Found., V. I. All-Union Acad. Agrl. Scis. (fgn.), Ukrainian Acad. Agrl. Scis. (fgn. academician), Mo. Valley Econ. Assn. (bd. dirs. 1977-82, pres.-elect 1979-80, pres. 1980-81), Russian Acad. Agrl. Sci. (fgn. academician), Hungarian Acad. Sci. Office: Iowa State U 218 Beardshear Hl Ames IA 50011-0001

JOHNSON, STEVE, radio personality; Former news reporter AP Radio Network, UPI, USA News, CBS News, IMS Radio News; co-founder 30 station statewide radio network; announcer Sta. WUGN Radio, Midland, Mich. Office: WUGN 510 Isabella Rd Midland MI 48640*

JOHNSON, STEVEN R. state legislator; b. June 15, 1947; m. Shannon Johnson. BS, MBA, Ind. U. Supr. chem. lab. Ind. U., Kokomo; owner Tuess Inc., pres.; rep. Ind. Ho. of Reps., 1980-82, 84-86; mem. Ind. Senate from 21st dist., 1986—; mem. legis. appointment and elec. com. State Legis., ranking mem. ethics com., mem. corrections, crime and civil procedures com., chmn. planning and pub. svc. com. Chmn. Howard County Reps., 1988-91; mem. Cmty. Assistance Found. Mem. Kokomo c. of C., Christian Businessman's Com., Elks, Rotary. Office: State Senate State Capitol Indianapolis IN 46204

JOHNSON, TERRY CHARLES, biologist, educator; b. St. Paul, Aug. 8, 1936; s. Roy August and Catherine (McKigen) J.; m. Mary Ann Wilhelmy, Nov. 23, 1957; children: James, Gary, Jean. BS, Hamline U., 1958; MS, U. Minn., 1961, PhD, 1964. Postdoctoral fellow U. Calif., Irvine, 1964-66; asst. prof. Med. Sch., Northwestern U., Chgo., 1966-69, assoc. prof., 1969-73, prof., 1973-77; prof. div. biology Kans. State U., Manhattan, 1977—, dir. div. biology, 1977-92, Univ. Disting. prof., 1989. Dir. Konza Prairie Rsch. Area, Manhattan, 1977-92, Ctr. for Basic Cancer Rsch., Manhattan, 1980—, Ctr. for Space Life Scis., Manhattan, 1990-92; co-dir. Bioserve Space Techs., Manhattan, 1989—. Recipient Outstanding Tchr. of Yr. award Med. Sch., Northwestern U., 1975, Outstanding Tchr. award Ill. Coll. Pediatric Medicine, 1976, Disting. Grad. Faculty award Kans. State U., 1987, Outstanding Sci. award Sigma Xi Kans. State U. chpt., 1993, Outstanding Faculty Mem. award Panhellenic and Intrafraternity Couns., Kans., 1998. Mem. AAAS, Am. Soc. for Gravitational and Space Biology, Am. Soc. for Microbiology, Am. Soc. for Neurochemistry, Am. Soc. for Cell Biology, N.Y. Acad. Sci. Avocation: reading. Home: 205 Drake Dr Manhattan KS 66503-3029 Office: Kans State U Div Biology Ackert Hall Manhattan KS 66506

JOHNSON, THOMAS LEE, state legislator; b. Oakland, Calif., Apr. 30, 1945; s. WallaceJ.; m. Virginia Van Der Molen, 1968; children: Sorne, Derek, Kirk. BA, U. Mich., 1970; JD, DePaul U., 1974. Investigator State Atty.'s Office, DuPage County, Ill., 1970-74; assoc. Laraia, Solano, Berns & Kilander, Ltd., Wheaton, 1976-77; atty. Johnson, Westra, Broecker, Whittaker & Newitt, PC, Carol Stream, 1977—; mem. Ill. Ho. of Reps., 1993—, chmn. judiciary, criminal law, pub. utilities coms., also health care, human svcs., appropriations coms. Owner Buterfirld Hardware Store, Wheaton, 1977—. Past chmn. Winfield Twp. (Ill.) Rep. com.; past precinct committeeman Winfield Twp.; candidate U.S. Congress, 1984; del. Dole, 1988; campaign advisor Citizens to Elect Jim Ryan, 1990; mem. Sci. Tech. Mus., Wheaton Youth Outreach, Family Inst., Christian Legal Soc. Mem. ABA, Ill. Bar Assn., DuPage County Bar Assn., Am. Legion. Office: Ill State Rep 27w031 North Ave West Chicago IL 60185-5122

JOHNSON, TIMOTHY PATRICK, health and social researcher; b. Batavia, N.Y., July 14, 1954; s. Elmore Thomas and Sara (McKinsey) J.; m. LuEllen Doty, June 20, 1988; children: Sara Elizabeth, Elliott William. BA, Western Ky. U., 1977; MA, U. Wis., Milw., 1978; PhD, U. Ky., 1988. Sr. rsch. analyst dept. human resources State of Ky., Frankfort, 1979-80; rsch. analyst dept. medicine U. Ky., Lexington, 1980-82, rsch. coord. survey rsch. ctr., 1982-88; staff assoc. for psychometrics Am. Bd. Family Practice, 1988-89; asst. rsch. prof. epidemiology and biometry sch. pub. health U. Ill., Chgo., 1991—, project coord. survey rsch. lab., 1989-91, asst. dir. survey rsch. lab., 1991-93, assoc. dir., 1993-96, acting dir., 1996-98, dir., 1998—, assoc. prof. pub. adminstrn., 1996—. Contbr. articles to profl. jours. Mem. APHA, Am. Sociol. Assn., Am. Assn. Pub. Opinion Rsch., Am. Statis. Assn. Roman Catholic. Office: U Ill Survey Rsch Lab 412 S Peoria St Chicago IL 60607-7063 E-mail: tjohnson@srl.uic.edu.

JOHNSON, TIMOTHY PETER, senator; b. Canton, S.D., Dec. 28, 1946; s. Vandal Charles and Ruth Jorinda (Ljostveit) J.; m. Barbara Brooks, June 6, 1969; children: Brooks Dwight, Brendan Vandal, Kelsey Marie. BA, U. S.D., 1969, MA, 1970, JD, 1975; postgrad., Mich. State U., 1970-71. Bar: S.D. 1975, U.S. Dist. Ct. S.D. 1976. Fiscal analyst Legis. Fiscal Agy., Lansing, Mich., 1971-72; pvt. practice Vermillion, S.D., 1975-86; mem. S.D. Ho. of Reps., 1978-82, S.D. Senate, 1982-86, U.S. Ho. of Reps., 1987-97; U.S. senator from S.D., 1997—. Adj. inst. U. S.D., Vermillion, 1974-83; mem. S.D. Code Commn., Pierre, 1982-86. Mem. Vermillion City Planning Commn., 1977-78; treas. Clay County Dem. Com., Vermillion, 1978; del. Dem. Nat. Conv., 1988, 92, 96. NSF grantee, 1969-70. Mem. S.D. Bar Assn., Clay County Bar Assn., Phi Beta Kappa, Omicron Delta Kappa. Democrat. Lutheran. Office: 324 Hart Senate Ofc Bldg Washington DC 20510-0001 also: PO Box 1554 Aberdeen SD 57402-1554

JOHNSON, TIMOTHY VINCENT, congressman; b. Champaign, Ill., July 23, 1946; Mem. from 104th Dist. Ill. Ho. of Reps, 1976-2000; mem. U.S. Congress from 15th Ill. dist., Washington, 2001—; mem. agr. com., sci. com., transp. and infrastructure com. Home: 129 W Main St Urbana IL 61801-2714 Office: 1541 Longworth HOB Washington DC 20515*

JOHNSON, TOM MILROY, academic dean, medical educator, physician; b. Northville, Mich., Jan. 16, 1935; s. Waldo Theodore and Ruth Jeanette (Christensen) J.; m. Emily Chapin Rhoads, June 13, 1959 (div. Aug. 1983); children— Glenn C., Heidi R.; m. Jane Susan Robb, June 10, 1987; 1 stepchild, Elizabeth K. B.A. in Psychology with honors, Coll. of Wooster, 1956; M.D., Northwestern U., 1961; postgrad. in health systems mgmt., Harvard U., 1974. Rotating intern Detroit Receiving Hosp., 1961-62; resident in internal medicine U. Mich. Med. Ctr., Ann Arbor, 1962-65, fellow in pulmonary disease, 1967-68; asst. prof. internal medicine Mich. State U., East Lansing, 1968-71, assoc. prof., asst. dean Coll. of Medicine Grand Rapids, 1971-77; prof. medicine, dean Sch. of Medicine U. N.D., Grand Forks, 1977-88; prof., assoc. dean Coll. Human Medicine, Mich. State U., 1988-94; campus dean, CEO Kalamazoo Ctr. for Med. Studies Mich. State U., 1994-98, prof. emeritus medicine Mich., 1999—; cons. in med. edn. Fla. State U., 1999—2001. Bd. dirs. No. Mich. Regional Health Svcs., Petosky, 1991—2001. Contbr. articles to profl. jours. Capt. M.C., USAF, 1965-67. A. Blaine Brower Traveling scholar ACP, 1977; Tom M. Johnson lecture hall named in his honor Grand Rapids Med. Ctr., 1982; recipient Physician Leadership award Mich. Hosp. Assn., 1999. Fellow ACP (Laureate award Mich. chpt.); mem. AMA, Mich. State Med. Soc., Studebaker Drivers Club, Antique Automobile Club of Am., Alpha Omega Alpha. Club: Cosmos (Washington) Avocation: restoration of antique automobiles and older farm houses. Home and Office: 4815 Barton Rd Williamston MI 48895-9305 E-mail: tmjjsj@worldnet.att.net.

JOHNSON, WARREN DONALD, retired pharmaceutical executive, former air force officer; b. Blackwell, Okla., Sept. 2, 1922; s. Charles Leon and Vera Ruth (Tucker) J.; children: Richard Johnson, Patricia Suzanne Johnson Peak, Lindabeth Johnson Brown, Ross Anthony. Student, Oklahoma City U., 1940-41. Served to 1st lt. U.S. Army, 1942-45; commd. 1st lt. USAAF, 1945; advanced through grades to lt. gen. USAF; chief of staff SAC Offutt AFB, Nebr., 1971-73; dir. Def. Nuclear Agy., Washington, 1973-77; ret., 1977; corp. v.p. Baxter Internat. Inc., Deerfield, Ill., 1977-91. Cons., tchr. Lake Forest Grad. Sch. Mgmt., 1991-99; ptnr. Cort & Assoc. Aircraft Sales and Charter. Decorated D.S.M., Legion of Merit with 2 oak leaf clusters, Joint Commendation medal. E-mail: generaldon@aol.com.

JOHNSON, WILBUR CORNEAL (JOE JOHNSON), wildlife biologist; b. Kalamazoo, Nov. 16, 1941; BS, Mich. State U., 1964, MS, 1967. Cert. wildlife biologist. Wildlife technician W.K. Kellogg Bird Sanctuary, Mich. State U., Augusta, 1964-85, chief wildlife biologist, bird sanctuary mgr., 1985—. Recipient Miles B. Pirnie Meml. award Mich. Duckhunters Assn., 1993. Mem. Wildlife Soc., Pheasants Forever (nat. bd. 1988-2001), Miss. Flyway Coun. (tech. sect., chair swan com., mem. giant Can. goose com., rsch. com.). Office: WK Kellogg Bird Sanctuary Mich State Univ 12685 E C Ave Augusta MI 49012-9707

JOHNSON, WILLIAM HOWARD, agricultural engineer, educator; b. Sidney, Ohio, Sept. 3, 1922; s. Russell Earl and Dollie (Gamble) J.; m. Wyoma Jean Swift, Oct. 2, 1943; children: Lawrence Alan, Cheri Ellen, Dana Sue. B.S., Ohio State U., 1948, M.S., 1953; Ph.D., Mich. State U., 1960. Registered profl. engr. Mem. faculty Ohio Agrl. Expt. Sta., Wooster, 1948-64; mem. faculty Ohio Agrl. Research and Devel. Center, 1964-70, prof., asso. chmn. dept. agrl. engring., 1959-70; part-time prof. Ohio State U., 1964-70; prof., head dept. agrl. engring. Kans. State U., Manhattan, 1970-81, dir. Engring. Experiment Sta., 1981-87. Cons. farm equipment cos. Author: (with B.J. Lamp) Principles, Equipment and Systems for Corn Harvesting, 1966; also articles. Recipient Distinguished Alumnus award Coll. Engring., Ohio State U., 1974; named to Coll. Engring. Kans. State U. Hall of Fame, 1992; recipient Cyrus Hall McCormick-Jerome Increase Case medal Am. Society of Agricultural Engineers, 1994 Fellow Am. Soc. Agrl. Engrs. (pres. 1986-87, McCormick-Case Gold Medal award 1994), Kans. Engring. Soc. (pres. 1985-86), Sigma Xi, Tau Beta Pi. Achievements include research on soil-plant-machine relationships, harvesting, design for soiltillers, planters, harvesters. Home: 2121 Meadowlark Rd #131 Manhattan KS 66502 Office: Kans State Univ Dept Agrl Engring Seaton Hall Manhattan KS 66506

JOHNSON, WILLIAM J. state legislator; m. Elma Johnson; 4 children. Grad. high sch., Harding County, S.D. Mem. S.D. State Senate, 1993—, chmn. local govt. com., mem. appropriations, govt. oper. and audit coms.; tchr. Home: PO Box 185 Buffalo SD 57720-0185

JOHNSON, WILLIAM S. transportation executive; Mem. corp. fin. group Amoco; v.p. venture devel. Amoco Chem. Asia Pacific, Hong Kong; v.p. global bus. mgmt. Amoco Polyers, Inc.; pres. Amoco Fabrics and Fibers Co.; exec. v.p., CFO Budget Group, Inc., 2000—. Office: Budget Group Inc 4225 Naperville Rd Lisle IL 60532

JOHNSON-LEIPOLD, HELEN P. outdoor marine recreation company executive; b. 1957; V.p. consumer mktg. svcs. worldwide SCJ, 1992-95, exec. v.p. N.Am. businesses, 1995-97, v.p. personal and home care products, 1997-98, v.p. worldwide consumer products-mktg., 1998-99; chmn., CEO Johnson Outdoors (formerly Johnson Worldwide Assocs. Inc.), Miami Beach, Fla., 1999—. Office: 1326 Willow Rd Sturtevant WI 53177-0901 Office Fax: 262-884-1600.

JOHNSRUD, DUWAYNE, state legislator; b. Boscobel, Wis., Sept. 4, 1943; s. Gordon and Louise Johnsrud; m. Jacqueline Johnsrud, 1965; children: Jennifer, Jaret, Zachary. BS, U. Wis., La Crosse, 1970. Farmer, Eastman, Wis.; mem. from dist. 96 Wis. State Assembly, Madison, 1984—. Mem. Eastman Sch. Bd., 1982; mem. Crawford County Bd., 1982—; mem. Crawford County Farm Bur. Mem. Am. Legion, Prairie du Chien Lions Club, Eagles, Delta Sigma Pi. Office: RR 1 Box 91A Eastman WI 54626-9758

JOHNSTON, CYRUS CONRAD, JR. medical educator; b. Statesville, N.C., July 16, 1929; m. Marjorie Tarkington, Feb. 20, 1960; 2 children. BA, Duke U., 1951, MD, 1955. Diplomate Am. Bd. Internal Medicine. Intern Duke Hosp., Durham, N.C., 1955-56; resident in medicine Barnes Hosp., St. Louis, 1956-57; rsch. fellow in endocrinology and metabolism Ind. U., Indpls., 1959-61, instr. medicine, 1961-63, asst. prof., 1963-67, assoc. prof., 1967-69, prof. medicine, 1969-97, disting. prof. medicine, 1997—; assoc. dir. Gen. Clin. Rsch. Ctr. Ind. U. Med. Ctr., 1962-67, program dir., 1967-72, prin. investigator, 1968-88, dir. divsn. endocrinology and metabolism, 1968-94. Mem. aging rev. com. Nat. Inst. Aging, 1982-85, chmn. geriatrics rev. com., 1985-86; mem. nursing sci. rev. com. NIH, 1988-89; mem. com. for protection of human subjects Ind. U.-Purdue U., Indpls., 1966—, chmn., 1978—; chmn. Nat. Osteoporosis Found. Sci. Adv. Bd., 1986—; med. adv. panel Paget's Disease Found., 1989—; v.p. Nat. Osteoporosis Found., 1992—; mem. Nat. Adv. Coun. on Aging, 1992-95. Assoc. editor Bone and Mineral, 1985-94, Bone, 1995—; editl. bd. Jour. Bone and Mineral Rsch., Jour. Clin. Endocrinology and Metabolism, 1988-91. Capt. USAF, 1957-59. Recipient Career Rsch. Devel. award USPHS, 1963-68, Sandoz prize Internat. Assn. Gerontology, 1993. Mem. ACP, AAAS, AMA, Am. Assn. Clin. Endocrinologists (Yank D. Coble, Jr. M.D. Disting. Svc. award 1998), Am. Fedn. Clin. Rsch., Am. Soc. for Bone and Mineral Rsch. (Frederic C. Bartter award 1996), Am. Clin. and Climatological Soc., Ctrl. Soc. for Clin. Rsch., Endocrine Soc., Sigma Xi. Office: Indiana Univ Dept Medicine 541 N. Clinical Dr CL 459 Indianapolis IN 46202-5112 E-mail: cjohnsto@iupui.edu.

JOHNSTON, GLADYS STYLES, university official; b. St. Petersburg, Fla., Dec. 23, 1942; d. John Edward and Rosa (Moses) Styles; m. Hubert Seward Johnston, July 30, 1966. BS in Social Sci., Cheney U., 1963; MEd in Ednl. Adminstrn., Temple U., 1969; PhD in Ednl. Adminstrn.-Orgnl. Theory, Cornell U., 1974. Tchr. Chester (Pa.) Sch. Dist., 1963-66, West Chester (Pa.) Sch. Dist., 1966-67, asst. prin., elem. prin., dir. Summer Sch., 1968-71; dir. Head Start Chester County Bd. Edn., West Chester, 1967-69; teaching asst., rsch. asst. Cornell U., Ithaca, N.Y., 1971-74; asst. prof. ednl. adminstr. and supervision Rutgers U., New Brunswick, N.J., 1974-79, assoc. prof., chmn. dept. Grad. Sch. Edn., 1979-83, chmn. dept. mgmt. Sch. Bus., 1983-85; dean, prof. Coll. Edn., Ariz. State U., Tempe, 1985-91; provost, v.p. for acad. affairs DePaul U., Chgo., 1991-93, chancellor, 1993—. Disting. Commonwealth vis. prof. Coll. William and Mary Sch. Edn., Williamsburg, Va., 1982-83; manuscript reviewer Jour. Higher Edn., Jour. Ednl. Leadership, Prentice Hall Pub. Co., Englewood Cliffs, N.J.; speaker and conf. presenter in field; cons. AT&T, Ednl. Testing Svc., Prentice-Hall Pub. Co.; cons. to coordinating bd. Tex. Coll. and Univ. System. Author: Research and Thought in Administration Theory, 1986; mem. editorial bd. Ednl. Evaluation and Policy Analysis, Ednl. Adminstrn. Quar., Ednl. and Psychol. Rsch. Jour.; contbr. articles and book revs. to profl. jours., chpts. to books. Bd. dirs. Edn. Law Ctr., 1979-86, Sta. KAET-TV, Phoenix, 1987—, Found. for Sr. Living, 1990-91; mem. adv. coun. to bd. trustees Cornell U., 1981-86; trustee Middlesex Gen. Univ. Hosp., 1983-86. Recipient Outstanding Alumni award Temple U.; Andrew D. White fellow Cornell U. Mem. ASCD, Am. Assn. Colls. for Tchr. Edn., Nat. Conf. Profs. Ednl. Adminstrn., Am. Ednl. Rsch. Assn. (proposal reviewer 1979—, chmn. task force for participation and membership 1981—, chmn. E.F. Linquist award com. 1985, mem. govt. rels. com. 1986—, publ. com. 1986—), Phi Kappa Phi, Phi Delta Kappa, Alpha Phi Sigma. Office: U of Nebraska at Kearney Office of Chancellor 905 W 25th St Kearney NE 68845-4238

JOHNSTON, JAMES ROBERT, library director; b. Wheaton, Ill., June 3, 1947; s. Robert W. and Elizabeth S. (Townsend) J.; m. Carol Ann Trezza, June 14, 1969; children: Steven J., Julie M. BA, U. Notre Dame, 1969; MLS, Fla. State U., 1973. Head librarian Grande Prairie Library Dist., Hazel Crest, Ill., 1973-76; chief librarian Joliet (Ill.) Pub. Library, 1976—; pres. bd. dirs. Ill. Library Employees Benefit Plan. Mem. automation com. Heritage Trail Libr. Sys., Shorewood, Ill.; pres. Ill. Libr. Employees Benefit Plan, Joliet; bldg. cons. Co-author: Illinois Library Trustees Association Booklet "Selecting Consultants", 1986; contbr. speeches and articles in field. V.p. Joliet/Will County Project Pride; mem. events com. C. of C. Mem. Ill. Libr. Assn. (pub. libr. sect. 1977-78, legis. devel. com. 1977-82, jr. mems. roundtable 1976-77, regional planning com. 1996, Title III rev. com. 1996—, interlibr. coop. subcom.,), Kiwanis, Beta Phi Mu. Avocations: HO guage model railroading, softball, bowling, golf. Home: 2208 Graystone Dr Joliet IL 60431-8785 Office: Joliet Pub Library 150 N Ottawa St Joliet IL 60432-4192

JOHNSTON, JEFFERY W. publishing executive; b. Lockport, N.Y., Dec. 14, 1951; s. Sidney W. and Barbara (Jeffery) J.; m. Marcia Lynn Paca, Aug. 3, 1974; children: Paul W., Sarah E., David P. BA, Dartmouth Coll., 1974. Sales rep. John Hancock Ins., Boston, 1974-76; from sales rep. to editor edn., coll. textbooks Allyn Bacon Publ., Rochester, N.Y., 1976-85; from editor edn., coll. textbooks to exec. editor Merrill Publ., Columbus, Ohio, 1985-90; v.p., editor-in-chief Merrill Imprint-Macmillan Publ., 1990-94; v.p., publisher Merrill Imprint-Prentice Hall, 1994—. Republican. Avocations: running, reading. Office: Prentice Hall 445 Hutchinson Ave Columbus OH 43235-5677

JOHNSTON, LLOYD DOUGLAS, social scientist; b. Boston, Apr. 18, 1940; s. Leslie D. and Madeline B. (Irvin) J.; 1 child, Douglas Leslie. B.A. in Econs., Williams Coll., 1962; M.B.A., Harvard U., 1965, postgrad., 1965-66; M.A. in Social Psychology, U. Mich., 1971, Ph.D., 1973. Research asst. Grad. Sch. Bus. Adminstr., Harvard U., Boston, 1965-66; asst. study dir. Inst. Social Research, U. Mich., Ann Arbor, 1966-73, asst. research scientist, 1973-75, assoc. rsch. scientist, 1975-78, sr. rsch. scientist and program dir., 1978-98; disting. sr. rsch. scientist Inst. Social Rsch., U. Mich., 1998—; chmn. exec. com. U. Mich. Substance Abuse Rsch. Ctr. Excellence, 1990-95, acting dir., 1994-95. Prin. investigator Monitoring the Future: A Continuing Study of Lifestyles and Values of Am. Youth, 1975—, Youth, Education and Society, 1996—, also other nat. and internat. survey studies; cons. to WHO, UN, EEC, Coun. of Europe, Pan Am. Health Orgn., White House, U.S. Congress, various founds., numerous fgn. govts., fed. agys., univs., rsch. insts., TV networks, Nat. Partnership for Drug Free Am., 1975—; chmn. tech. planning group; mem. Resource Group for Goal Seven, Nat. Ednl. Goals Panel, 1991—; mem. extramural sci. adv. bd. Nat. Inst. on Drug Abuse, 1990-94; mem., also chmn. prevention subcom., Nat. Adv. Coun. on Drug Abuse, 1982-86, Presdl. appointee White House Conf. for a Drug-Free Am., 1987-88, Presdl. appointee Nat. Commn. for Drug Free Schs., 1989-90; chmn. drug epidemiology sect. Internat. Coun. on Alcohol and Addictions, 1982—; mem. Com. on Problems of Drug Dependence, 1982-86; mem. or chmn. various adv. coms. various univs., founds.; mem. various working groups NAS; mem. various coms. and adv. groups Nat. Inst. Drug Abuse, 1975—; mem. or chmn. 7 working groups WHO, 1975—; invited lectr. nat. and internat. confs. and convs.; testimony before Congress and fed. regulatory agys. Author: Drugs and American Youth, 1973, Student Drug Use in America, 1975-81, 82, Monitoring the Future Nat. Survey Results on Drug Use 1975-2000, vol. 1 and 2, 2001, 35 other books and monographs on drug use and lifestyles of Am. secondary sch. students and young adults, 1972—, 26 reference vols.; editor: Conducting Follow Up Research on Drug Treatment Programs, 1977; contbr. 100 chpts. to books, articles to profl. jours. Recipient Nat. Pacesetter award in rsch. Nat. Inst. on Drug Abuse, 1982, 1st Sr. Rsch. Scientist award and lectureship U. Mich., 1987, Regents award for disting. pub. svc., 1998. Fellow Coll. on Problems of Drug Dependence; mem. APA, Soc. for Psychol. Study Social Issues (sec.-treas. 1976-79), Am. Sociol. Assn., Am. Pub. Health Assn. Home: 5538 Lawrence Ct Pinckney MI 48169-9257 Office: U Mich Inst Social Rsch Ann Arbor MI 48109

JOHNSTON, MARILYN FRANCES-MEYERS, physician, medical educator; b. Buffalo, Mar. 30, 1937; BS, Dameon Coll., 1966; PhD, St. Louis U., 1970, MD, 1975. Diplomate Am. Bd. Pathology, Diplomate Nat. Bd. Med. Examiners. Fellow in immunology Washington U., St. Louis, 1970-72; resident in pathology Washington U. Hosp., 1975-77, St. John's Mercy Med. Ctr., St. Louis, 1977-79; research fellow hematology St. Louis U. Sch. Medicine, 1979-80; instr. biochemistry St. Louis U., 1972-75, asst. prof. pathology, 1980-87, assoc. prof., 1987-92, prof., 1992-99, prof. emeritus, 1999—, dir. transfusion svcs., 1980-99; staff pathologist Christian Hosp. Barnes Jewish Christian Hosps., St. Louis, 1999—. Med. dir. Mo./Ill. Regional Red Cross, 1983-88; area chmn. for inspection and accreditation Am. Assn. Blood Banks, Arlington, Va., 1984; med. dir. transfusion svc. Christian Hosps., Barnes-Jewish-Christian Hosp. Sys., St. Louis, 1999—. Author: Transfusion Therapy, 1985. Named Goldberger fellow, AMA, 1979; recipient Transfusion Medicine Acad. award, Nat. Heart, Blood and Lung Inst., 1984—. Mem. Am. Assn. Blood Banks, Am. Assn. Immunologists, Internat. Soc. Blood Transfusion, Am. Soc. Clin. Pathologists, Sigma Xi. Office: Christian Hosp NE 11133 Dunn Rd Saint Louis MO 63136

JOHNSTON, RICHARD FOURNESS, biologist, educator; b. Oakland, Calif., July 27, 1925; s. Arthur Nathaniel and Marie (Johnson) J.; m. Lora Lee Bliler, Feb. 7, 1948; children: Regan, Janet, Cassandra. BA, U. Calif., Berkeley, 1950, MA, 1953, PhD, 1955. Asst. prof. dept. biology N.Mex. State U., 1956-58; mem. faculty depts. zoology and ecology U. Kans., Lawrence, 1958—, prof., 1968-92, prof. emeritus, 1992—, chmn., 1979-82, editor mus. publs., 1974-76, 86-91; program dir. systematic biology NSF, Washington, 1968-69; editor Ann. Rev. Ecology and Systematics, 1968-92, Current Ornithology, 1981-87. Mem. adv. panel biol. scis. Smithsonian Fgn. Currency Program, 1969-71 Served with AUS, 1943-46. Am. Acad. Arts and Scis. grantee, 1957; nat. Acad. Sci. grantee, 1959; NSF grantee, 1959-83. Fellow Am. Ornithol. Union (Coues award 1975), AAAS, mem. Ecol. Soc. Am., Soc. Systematic Zoology (editor jour. 1967-70, pres. 1977), Soc. Study Evolution. Home: 615 Louisiana St Lawrence KS 66044-2337 Office: U Kans Mus Natural History Lawrence KS 66045-0001 E-mail: rjon@ku.edu.

JOHNSTONE, ROBERT PHILIP, lawyer; b. Bellefonte, Pa., Dec. 1, 1943; s. B. Kenneth and Helene (Hetzel) J.; m. Susan Alice Hardy, June 22, 1968; children: Natalie, Nancy. BS with honors, Denison U., 1966; JD magna cum laude, U. Mich., 1969. Bar: Ind. 1969. Assoc. Barnes, Hickam, Pantzer & Boyd, Indpls., 1969-75, ptnr., 1976-82, Barnes & Thornburg, Indpls., 1982—. Chmn. litigation dept. Barnes & Thornburg, 1988-89, mem. mgmt. com., 1988-89; lectr., panelist legal seminars and trial advocacy programs. Sec.-treas. Contemporary Art Soc. of Indpls. Mus. Art, 1983—84; v.p., bd. dirs. Friends of Herron Gallery, Herron Sch. Art, 1981—85; bd. dirs. Eagle Creek Park Found., 2001—. Fellow Am. Coll.

Trial Lawyers (state com. 1992-97, state chair 1995-96, award for courageous adv. com. 1996-2000)); mem. U.S. 7th Fed. Cir. Bar Assn., Ind. Bar Assn., Fed. Bar Assn., Indpls. Bar Assn., Order of the Coif, Woodstock Club (Indpls., bd. dirs. 1988-90, v.p. 1989, pres. 1990), Indpls. Art Ctr. (bd. dirs. 1991-97), Dramatic Club (Indpls.), Phi Beta Kappa, Omicron Delta Kappa. Home: 1065 W 52nd St Indianapolis IN 46228-2463 Office: Barnes & Thornburg 11 S Meridian St Indianapolis IN 46204-3535 E-mail: bob.johnstone@btlaw.com.

JOHO, JEAN, chef; Student, Hotel Restaurant Sch., Strasbourg, France. Apprentice L'Auberge de L'Ill, Alsace, France; sous chef Michelin three star restaurant; chef Maxim's, Chgo., Brasserie Jo, Chgo., 1995; owner, chef Everest; co-founder Corner Bakery. Named Best Am. Chef: Midwest, James Beard Found., Best Chef of Yr., Bon Appetit; recipient Best New Restaurant award, James Beard Found., 1995, Culinary award of excellence, Robert Mondavi. Mem.: Maitre Cuisiniers de France, Le Grande Table Du Monde Traditions and Qualite. Office: Everest 440 La Salle St 40th Fl Chicago IL 60605

JONAS, HARRY S. medical education consultant; b. Kirksville, Mo., Dec. 3, 1926; s. Harry S. and Sarah (Laird) J.; m. Connie Kirby, Aug. 6, 1949; children— Harry S., III, William Reed, Sarah Elizabeth. BA, Washington U., St. Louis, 1949, MD, 1952. Intern St. Luke's Hosp., St. Louis, 1952-53; resident Barnes Hosp., 1952-56; practiced medicine specializing in ob-gyn., Independence, Mo., 1956-74; prof. ob-gyn, chmn. dept. ob-gyn Truman Med. Center; asst. dean U. Mo-Kansas City Sch. Medicine, 1975-78, dean, 1978-87, med. edn. cons., 2000—, spl. cons. to the dean; asst. v.p. med. edn. AMA, Chgo., 1987-2000. Mem. Independence City Council, 1964-68; mem. Jackson County (Mo.) Legislature, 1973-74. Mem. ACOG (pres. 1986-87), Ctrl. Assn. Obstetricians and Gynecologists, Assn. Profs. Gynecology and Obstetrics, Assn. Am. Med. Colls., A.C.S., AMA, Mo. Med. Assn., Jackson County Med. Soc., Kansas City Gynecol. Soc., Chgo. Gynecol. Soc. Home: 207 NW Spruce St Lees Summit MO 64064-1430 Office: U Mo-Kansas City Sch Medicine 2411 Holmes St Kansas City MO 64108-2741

JONAS, JIRI, chemistry educator; b. Prague, Czechoslovakia, Apr. 1, 1932; s. Frantisek and Jirina (Vondrak) J.; m. Ana M. Masiulis, June 1, 1968. BSc, Tech. U. Prague, 1956; PhD, Czechoslovak Acad Sci., 1960. Research assoc. Inst. Organic Chemistry, Czechoslovak Acad. Sci., Prague, 1960-63; vis. scientist, dept. chemistry U. Ill., Urbana, 1963-65, from asst. to assoc. prof., 1966-72, prof. to prof. emeritus, 1972-2001, 01—, dir. sch. chem. scis., 1983-93; dir. to dir. emeritus Beckman Inst. Advanced Sci. and Tech., 1993-2001, 01—; sr. staff mem. Materials Research Lab. U. Ill., Urbana, 1970-93, prof. Ctr. for Advanced Study, 1996-2001. Mem. editl. bd. Jour. Magnetic Resonance, 1975-2000, Jour. Chem., 1980-83, Jour. Chem. Physics, 1986-89, , Ann. Rev. Phys. Chemistry, 1991-95, Accts. of Chem. Rsch., 1990-93; assoc. editor Jour. of Am. Chem. Soc.; contbr. more than 300 articles in field of chem. phys. to profl. publs. J.S. Guggenheim fellow, 1972-73, Alfred P. Sloan fellow, 1967-69; Univ. Sr. scholar U. Ill., 1985-88; recipient U.S. Sr. Scientist award Alexander von Humboldt Found., 1988 Fellow Am. Acad. Arts and Scis., AAAS, Am. Phys. Soc.; mem. Nat. Acad. Scis., Am. Chem. Soc. (Joel Henry Hildebrand award 1983), Materials Research Soc. Roman Catholic. Clubs: U. Ill. Tennis; NBTC (Naples, Fla.). Office: Univ of Ill 166 Roger Adams Lab 600 S Mathews Urbana IL 61801 E-mail: j-jonas@uiuc.edu.

JONASSON, OLGA, surgeon, educator; b. Peoria, Ill., Aug. 12, 1934; d. Olav and Swea C. (Johnson) J. MD, U Ill., Chgo., 1958; DSc, Newberry (S.C.) Coll., 1982. Diplomate Am. Bd. Surgery (bd. dirs. 1988-94). Intern and resident U. Ill. Rsch. & Ednl. Hosps., 1959-64; prof. surgery U. Ill., 1975-87; chief of surgery Cook County Hosp., Chgo., 1977-86; chmn., prof. dept. surgery Ohio State U., Columbus, 1987-93; mem. staff U. Ill. Hosps., Chgo., 1993—, dir. edn. and surg. dept., 1993—. Markle scholar John & Mary Markle Found., 1969. Fellow ACS; mem. Am. Surg. Assn. Office: Am Coll Surgeons Surg Svcs Dept 633 N Saint Clair St Chicago IL 60611-3234

JONCKHEERE, ALAN MATHEW, physicist; b. Howell, Mich., Feb. 12, 1947; s. August Peter and Elizabeth Gertrude (Nash) Jonckheere; m. Barbara Jean Minter, Aug. 16; children: Jessica, Susan, Laura Jean and Amanda Jean (twins). B.S., Mich. State U., 1969; M.S., U. Wash., 1970, Ph.D., 1976. Instr. physics dept. Fermi Nat. Accelerator Lab., Batavia, Ill., 1976-78, staff physicist, 1978—, assoc. dept. head meson dept., 1981-83, assoc. dept. head exptl. areas, 1983-84, Beams group coordinator, 1984-85, accelerator div. exptl. support dept., 1985-89, researcher div. D0 dept., 1989—. Researcher elem. particle physics Stanford Linear Accelerator Ctr., Lawrence Berkeley Lab., Calif. Contbr. papers to physics publs. Office: Fermi Natl Accelerator Lab PO Box 500 Batavia IL 60510-0500 E-mail: Jonckheere@fnal.gov.

JONDAHL, LYNN, foundation administrator; BA, Iowa State U., 1958; MDiv, Yale U., 1962. Ordained min. United Ch. of Christ, 62. Mem. ho. reps. State of Mich., Lansing, 1972—94, chmn. taxation com., mem. coll. and univ, consumers and judiciary coms., mem. juvenile justice subcom.; exec. dir. Mich. Prospect for Renewed Citizenship, Flint. Campus pastor Calif. State Coll., L.A.; co-dir. Christian Faith and Higher Edn. Inst. Mich. State U. Active Foster Grandparent Program, Student Advocat. Ctr., Ctr. Handicapped Affairs; corp. mem. United Ch. Bd. Nomeland Ministries. Named Legislator of Yr., Mich. Fedn. Pvt. Child and Family Agys., 1985, Mich. Twp. Assn., 1987, Citizens Alliance to Uphold Spl. Edn., 1990, Assn. Retarded Citizens Mich., 1990, Outstanding Legislator, AAUP, 1985, Outstanding Legislator of Yr., Mich. Assn. Deaf, Hearing and Speech Svcs., 1990; recipient Consumers Advocate award, Mich. Citizen's Lobby, 1974, Philip Hart award, Consumer Educators Mich., 1980. Mem.: ACLU, Mich. Women's Studies Assn., Mich. China Coun. Office: Northpart Center Ste 406 432 N Saginaw St Flint MI 48502

JONES, B. TODD, lawyer, former prosecutor; s. Paul and Sylvia Jones. Grad., Macalester Coll., 1979; JD, U. Minn., 1983. Mng. ptnr. Greene Espel, Mpls., 1996—97; asst. U.S. atty. for Minn., 1997—98; U.S. atty. Minn. dist. U.S. Dept. Justice, 1998—2001; ptnr. Robins, Kaplan, Miller & Ciresi, Mpls., 2001—. With USMC. Office: Robins Kaplan Miller & Ciresi 2800 LaSalle Plaza 800 LaSalle Ave Minneapolis MN 55402

JONES, BENJAMIN ANGUS, JR. retired agricultural engineering educator, administrator; b. Mahomet, Ill., Apr. 16, 1926; s. Benjamin Angus and Grace Lucile (Morr) J.; m. Georgeann Hall, Sept. 11, 1949; children: Nancy Kay Jones-Kepple, Ruth Ann Jones-Sommers. BS, U. Ill., 1949, MS, 1950, PhD, 1958. Registered profl. engr., Ill. Asst. prof., asst. ext. engr. U. Vt., Burlington, 1950-52; instr., agrl. engr. U. Ill., Urbana, 1952-54, asst. prof., agrl. engr., 1954-58, assoc. prof., agrl. engr., 1958-64, prof., agrl. engr., 1964-92, prof. emeritus, 1992—, assoc. dir., agrl. exptl. sta., 1973-92; assoc. dir. emeritus, 1992—, U. Ill., Urbana, 1992. Cons. various Ill. Drainage Dists., 1958—. Co-author: (textbook) Engineering Application in Agriculture, 1973; contbr. articles to Jour. Soil & Water Conservation, Encyclopedia Britannica, Agrl. Engring., Transactions of ASAE, Proceedings of ASCE, Soil Sci. Soc. Am. Proceedings, Crops and Soils, Jour. Hydrology, Water Resources Bulletin. Merit badge examiner Boy Scouts Am., Burlington, 1950-52; lay mem. Cen. Ill. Con. United Meth. Ch., 1978-81. With USN, 1944-46. NSF fellow. Fellow Am. Soc. Agrl. Engrs. (bd. dirs., trustee); mem. Soil and Water Conservation Soc., Am. Soc. for Engring. Edn., Sigma Xi, Gamma Sigma Delta, Alpha Epsilon. Home: 2012B Eagle Ridge Ct Urbana IL 61802-8617

JONES, C. PAUL, lawyer, educator; b. Grand Forks, N.D., Jan. 7, 1927; s. Walter M. and Sophie J. (Thorton) J.; m. Helen M. Fredel, Sept. 7, 1957; children— Katherine, Sara H. BBA, JD, U. Minn., 1950; LLM, William Mitchell Coll. of Law, 1955. Assoc. Lewis, Hammer, Heaney, Weyl & Halverson, Duluth, Minn., 1950-51; asst., chief dep. Hennepin County Atty., Mpls., 1952-58; asst. U.S. atty. U.S. Atty's. Office, St. Paul, 1959-60; assoc. Maun & Hazel, 1960-61; ptnr. Dorfman, Rudquist, Jones, & Ramstead, Mpls., 1961-65; state pub. defender Minn. State Pub. Defender's Office, 1966-90. Adj. prof. law William Mitchell Coll. of Law, St. Paul, 1953-70, prof. law, 1970—2001, prof. emeritus, 2001-. assoc. dean for acad. affairs, 1991-95; adj. prof. U. Minn., Mpls., 1970-90; mem. adv. com. on rules of criminal procedure Minn. Supreme Ct., 1970—. Author: Criminal Procedure from Police Detention to Final Disposition, 1981; Jones on Minnesota Criminal Procedure, 1955, 64, 70, 75; Minnesota Police Law Manual, 1955, 67, 70, 76 Mem. Minn. Gov.'s Crime Commn., St. Paul, 1970s, Minn. Fair Trial-Free Press Assn., Mpls., 1970s, Citizens League, Mpls., 1955—, Mpls. Aquatennial Assn., Mpls., 1955-60, Minn. Coun. on Crime and Justice, 1991—. Recipient Reginald Heber Smith award Nat. Legal Aid and Defender Assn., 1969 Fellow Am. Coll. Trial Lawyers; mem. Am. Bd. Trial Advs., ABA, Minn. State Bar Assn., Hennepin County Bar Assn., Ramsey County Bar Assn., Nat. Legal Aid & Defender Assn. Democrat. Lutheran. Clubs: Suburban Gyro of Mpls., Mpls. Athletic. Lodge: Rotary. Avocations: fishing; hunting; golfing; desert watching. Home: 5501 Dewey Hill Rd Edina MN 55439-1906 Office: William Mitchell Coll Law 875 Summit Ave Saint Paul MN 55105-3030

JONES, CHARLES W. labor union executive; b. Gary, Ind., Apr. 29, 1923; s. Charles Browning and Inez (Teegarden) J.; m. Ursula M. Wilden, Aug. 25, 1950; children: Charles Alan, Newton Browning, Donna Ruth, Doris Ursula. Grad. high sch., Gary. Boilermaker various constrn. contractors; organizer, then staff rep., rsch. & edn. dir., internat. v.p. Internat. Brotherhood of Boilermakers, Iron Ship Builders, Blacksmiths, Forgers and Helpers, Kansas City, Kans., now internat. pres. Chmn. bd. dirs. BB&T Co.; v.p. bldg. constrn. trades dept., v.p. metal trade dept. AFL-CIO. Office: Internat Brotherhood Boilermaker Iron Ship Bldrs Blacksmiths 753 State Ave Ste 570 Kansas City KS 66101-2511

JONES, CLAYTON M. computer and electronics company executive; b. Nashville; BS, U. Tenn.; MS, George Washington U. Former fighter pilot USAF; various exec.-level positions aerospace industry; with Rockwell Internat. Corp., Cedar Rapids, Iowa, 1995—, sr. v.p., pres. Rockwell Collins, 1999—. Mem. AIAA (bd. dirs.), Gen. Aviation Mfrs. Assn. Office: Rockwell Internat Corp 400 Collin Rd NE Cedar Rapids IA 52498-0001

JONES, COBI, professional soccer player; b. Detroit, June 16, 1970; Student, UCLA. Midfielder Coventry City, 1994-95, Vasco da Gama, 1995-96, L.A. Galaxy, 1996—, U.S. Nat. Team, 1996—. With gold medal U.S. team, Pan Am. Games, 1991, U.S. Olympic Team, 1992, U.S. Nat. Team, 1992-95, including victory over Ivory Coast, 1992; tied for all-time assist lead, with 11. Host (TV show) Megadose (MTV); guest appearance (TV show) Beverly Hills 90210, 1994. Office: c/o US Soccer Fedn 1801-1811 S Prairie Ave Chicago IL 60616 and: LA Galaxy 1640 S Sepulveda Blvd Los Angeles CA 90025-7510

JONES, DANIEL W. executive; Pres., cheif operating officer Zaring Nat. Corp., Cin., 1989—. Office: 11300 Cornell Park Dr Ste 500 Cincinnati OH 45242-1885

JONES, DAVID D., JR. marine engine equipment executive; BSME, MSME, PhD in Mech. Engring., N.C. State U. Various mgmt./exec. level positions, 1977—; v.p., gen. mgr. Force outboard Divsn. U.S. Marine; pres. Mercury Marine divsn. Brunswick Corp., 1989-97; CEO, pres. Outboard Marine, Waukegan, Ill., 1997—.

JONES, DOUG E. healthcare researcher, real estate broker, oil company owner; b. Parsons, Kans., Apr. 1, 1946; divorced; 2 children. BS, Southwest Mo. State U., 1969. Dem. candidate U.S. Senate, 1994, 96.

JONES, EDWARD, pathologist; b. Wellington, Kans., Mar. 21, 1935; s. Thomas S. and Grace W. (Sydebotham) Imel; m. Barbara A. Blount, Aug. 30, 1956; children: Kimberly Riegel, Sheila, Matt, Tom. AB in Chemistry, U. Kans., 1957, MD, 1961. Diplomate Am. Bd. Pathology in Anat. and Clin. Pathology. Intern St. Francis Hosp., Wichita, Kans., 1961-62; sr. asst. USPHS, Yuma, Ariz., 1962-64; gen. practice medicine Lawrence (Kans.) Meml. Hosp., 1964-65; resident in pathology St. Luke's Hosp., Kansas City, Mo., 1965-69; pathologist Ctrl. Kans. Med. Ctr., Gt. Bend, 1969-2001, dir., 1974-76, pres., 1976-78; ret., 2001. Physician cons. Hoisington Luth. Hosp., Kans., 1969— , St. Joseph's Meml. Hosp., Larned, Kans., 1969— , Edwards County Hosp., Kinsley, Kans., 1969—. Bd. dirs. Cedar Park Place, Gt. Bend, 1980-88. Fellow Coll. Am. Pathologists (del., foreman 1978-87), Am. Soc. Clin. Pathologists; mem. Kans. Soc. Pathologists (pres. 1980-81), Gt. Bend Cmty. Theater Club. Avocations: theater, musical theater. Home: 3208 Broadway Ave Great Bend KS 67530-3716

JONES, EDWIN CHANNING, JR. electrical and computer engineering educator; b. Parkersburg, W.Va., June 27, 1934; s. Edwin Channing and Helen M. J.; m. Ruth Carol Miller, Aug. 14, 1960; children: Charles, Cathleen, Helene. BSEE, W.Va. U., 1955; Diploma, U. London, 1956; PhD, U. Ill., 1962. Lic. profl. engr., W.Va. Engr. GE, Syracuse, N.Y. and Bloomington, Ill., 1955, 62, Westinghouse Electric Co., Balt., 1959; asst. prof. elec. engring. U. Ill., Urbana, 1962-66; asst. prof. Iowa State U., Ames, 1966-67, assoc. prof., 1967-72, prof., 1972—2001, univ. prof., 1995—2001, assoc. chair dept., 1997—2001, univ. prof. emeritus, 2001—. Mem. Accreditation Bd. Engring. Tech., N.Y.C., 1984-87. Author handbook chpts. on electronic engring. Lt. U.S. Army, 1956—58. Recipient Linton F. Grinter Disting. Svc. award, Accreditation Bd. Engring. Tech., 2001. Fellow AAAS, IEEE (pres. edn. soc. 1975-76, mem. ednl. activities bd. 1975-76, 78-81, 84-87, accreditation activity award), Am. Soc. Engring. Edn.; mem. Soc. History of Tech., Sigma Xi, Tau Beta Pi, Eta Kappa Nu, Phi Kappa Phi, Phi Beta Delta. Avocations: photography, slide rule collecting. Home: 111 Hunziker Cir Ames IA 50010-5022 Office: Iowa State U 2216 Coover Hl Ames IA 50011-0001

JONES, EMIL, JR. state legislator; b. Chgo., Oct. 18, 1935; s. Emil Sr. and Marilla (Mims) J.; m. Patricia Sterling, Dec. 14, 1974 (dec.); children: Debra, Renee, John, Emil III. A in Bus. Adminstrn., City Coll. Chgo., 1970. Mem. Ill. Ho. Reps., Springfield, 1972-82, Ill. Senate, Springfield, 1982—, Senate Dem. leader, mem. exec. com., mem. joint com. adminstrv. rules. Active Task Force on Long Term Care, Morgan Pk. Civic League, Chgo. Recipient Beautiful People award Chgo. Urban League, 1981, Friend of Edn. award Ill. State Bd. Edn., 1983, Legis. Leadership award Ill. Dept. Human Rights, 1984, Leadership award Nat. Bar Assn., 1985, Mem. Nat. Black Caucus State Legislators, Nat. Conf. State Legislators, Knights of St. Peter Claver, Shriners. Democrat. Roman Catholic. Home: 11357 S Lowe Ave Chicago IL 60628-4714 Office: 507 W 111th St Ste 16-600 Chicago IL 60628-4019 also: James R Thompson Ctr 100 W Randolph St Ste 16 600 Chicago IL 60601-3220

JONES, GEORGE HUMPHREY, retired healthcare executive, hospital facilities and communications consultant; b. Kansas City, Mo., July 10, 1923; s. George Humphrey and Mary R. (Marrs) J.; m. Peggy Jean Thompson, Nov. 23, 1943; children: Kenneth L., Daniel D., Kathleen Jones Smith, Carol R. Jones Johnson, Janet S. Jones Fitts. Student, U. Mo., Kansas City, 1940-43, Wis. State U., Oshkosh, 1943. Police officer Kansas City (Mo.) Police Dept., 1947-51; elec. contr. Paramount Elec. Svc., Kansas City, 1947-50; electrician Automatic Temp. Control Co., 1951-57; pres., chief ops. George H. Jones Co., 1957-65; sales mgr. Nycon Inc., Lee's Summit, Mo., 1965; design engr. Midland Wright Corp., Kansas City, 1966; dist. sales mgr. Comm. Electronics, 1967; plant ops. supr. Rsch. Med. Ctr., Coll. of Nursing and hdqrs. Health Midwest, 1968-77, dir. plant ops. and comm., 1977-90; hosp. facilities and comm. cons. Overland Park, Kans., 1990-99; ret. Guest lectr. Nat. U., San Diego, 1987. Vol. Salvation Army Emergency Svcs.; bd. dirs. Camellot Fine Arts Acad., 1974—76, v.p., bd. dirs., 1975—76; adv. dir. Rsch. Med. Ctr., 1990—; mem. Heart of Am. Wing Commemorative Air Force. With USAAF, 1946—46, with U.S. Army, 1950—51. Fellow Am. Soc. Hosp. Engring., Healthcare Info. and Mgmt. Systems Soc.; mem. Kansas City Area Hosp. Engrs. (pres. 1985, bd. dirs. 1985-89), Am. Legion, Alpha Phi Omega. Presbyterian. Avocations: fishing, photography. Home and Office: 6022 W 86th St Shawnee Mission KS 66207-1521

JONES, H. W. KASEY, financial planning executive, author, lecturer; b. Burlington, Iowa, Feb. 11, 1942; s. Herbert Warren and Mary Kathryn (Gardner) J.; m. Ellen E. Toon, Mar. 11, 1961 (div. Dec. 1969); children: Kari Lynne, Kevin C., Anthony W.; m. Janice C. Freyre, Jan. 9, 1994. Student, Bradley U., 1960-61, Coll. Fin. Planning, 1988. CFP. Gen. mgr. sales Wickstrom Chevrolet, Roselle, Ill., 1967-80; v.p. mktg. Re-Direct Svcs., Villa Park, 1980-81, pres., CEO, 1982-91, chmn. bd. dirs., 1983-91; registered rep. and prin. Long Grove Trading, Inc., Itasca, Ill., 1990—; midwest regional dir. Coll. Bound Student Athletes, Cedarburg, Wis., 1991-94; pres. Linchpin Fin. Group Ltd., McHenry, Ill., 1992—. Founding sponsor, mem. speakers' bur. Nat. Ctr. for Fin. Edn., San Francisco, 1984—; pres. Bus. Connection Mktg. Group; bd. dirs. The Cenegra Health System Found.; v.p. Landsport Corp. Mem. AARP, The Fin. Planning Assn., Kiwanis (bd. dirs., past pres.), Grand Geneva Resort and Spa (Lake Geneva, Wis.), Kiwanis, McHenry (Ill.) Country Club, McHenry C. of C. Avocations: golf, bowling. Home: 1202 S Green St Mchenry IL 60050-8186 E-mail: linchpin@mc.net.

JONES, JAMES E. state legislator; b. Ashby, Nebr., Nov. 19, 1931; m. Patricia Ann McConnell, 1953; children: Gordon, Steven, Vernon, Gregg. Farmer, rancher, Nebr.; mem. Nebr. Legislature from 43rd dist., Lincoln, 1992—; mem. banking, comml. and ins., natural resources coms. Nebr. Legislature. Address: Nebr State Senate State Capitol Rm 1117 Lincoln NE 68509 Also: HC 2 Box 79 Eddyville NE 68834-9410

JONES, JAMES EDWARD, JR. retired law educator; b. Little Rock, June 4, 1924; B.A., Lincoln U., Mo., 1950; M.A., U. Ill. Inst. Labor and Indsl. Relations, 1951; J.D., U. Wis., 1956. Bar: Wis., U.S. Supreme Ct. Indsl. relations analyst U.S. Wage Stabilization Bd., Region 7, 1951-53; legis. atty. Dept. Labor, Washington, 1956-63, counsel for labor relations, 1963-66, dir. office labor mgmt., policy devel., 1966-67, assoc. solicitor labor div. labor relations and civil rights, 1967-69; vis. prof. law and indsl. relations U. Wis.-Madison, 1969-70, prof., 1970-93, Bascom prof. law, 1983-91, Nathan P. Feinsinger prof. labor law, 1991-93, prof. emeritus, 1993—. Dir. Inst. Relations, Research Inst., 1971-73, assoc. Inst. for Research on Poverty, 1970, dir. Ctr. for Equal Employment and Affirmative Action, Indsl. Relations Research Inst., 1974-93; mem. research and edn. staff Pulp, Sulphite and Paper Mill Workers, AFL-CIO, 1958; mem. Fed. Service Impasses Panel, 1978-82; mem. pub. rev. bd. Internat. Union UAW, 1970—; mem. adv. com. NRC Nat. Acad. Scis., 1971-73; mem. Wis. Manpower Planning Council, 1971-76; mem. spl. com. on criminal justice, standards and goals Wis. Council Criminal Justice, 1975-76; bd. dirs. labor law sect. Wis. State Bar, 1976; mem. Fed. Mediation and Conciliation Arbitration Panel, 1975—; spl. arbitrator U.S. Steel and United Steel Workers, 1976-86; mem. expert com. on family budget revision Dept. Labor Series, 1978-79; cons. in field. Mem. Madison Police and Fire Commn., 1973-77, 94-95, pres., 1976-77. Recipient Sec. Labor Career Svc. award Dept. Labor, 1963, Hilldale award (Social Sci. Divsn.), 1990-91, Wis. Law Alumni Disting. Svc. award, 1995, tchr. of yr. award Soc. Am. Law Tchrs., 1998, disting. alumni award U. Ill., 1996; John Hay Whitney fellow, 1953, 54. Mem. Labor Law Group Trust (chmn. editorial policy com. 1978-82), Indsl. Relations Research Assn. (treas. Washington chpt. 1968-69, exec. bd. 1977-80), Fed. Bar Assn. (chmn. labor law com. 1967-69, dep. chmn. council on labor law and labor relations 1979-80), State Bar Wis., Nat. Bar Assn. (nat. adv. com. of equal employment clin. project 1970-79, Hall of Fame 1999), Nat. Acad. Arbitrators, Order of Coif, Phi Kappa Phi. Office: Univ Wisconsin Sch of Law Madison WI 53706

JONES, JAMES FLEMING, JR. college president, Roman language and literature educator; b. Atlanta, Apr. 9, 1947; s. James F. and Sarah Kate (Smith) J.; m. Jan Sheets, Nov. 15, 1969; children:Jennifer, Justin, Jason BA, U. Va., 1969; MA, Emory U., 1972; cert., U. Paris-Sorbonne, 1972; MPhil, Columbia U., 1974, Ph.D., 1975. Tchr., chmn. dept. fgn. langs. Woodward Acad., College Park, Ga., 1969-72; preceptor Columbia U., 1973-75; prof. Romance langs. and lit. Washington U., St. Louis, 1975-91, chmn. dept. Romance langs., 1982-91; vice provost, dean Dedman Coll., So. Meth. U., Dallas, 1991-96; pres. Kalamazoo Coll., 1996—. Sr. visitor for Hilary term, Oxford, 1987. Precentor, Ch. of St. Michael and St. George, Clayton, Mo., 1978-91. Decorated chevalier Ordre des Palmes Académiques; recipient Avis Blewett award Am. Guild Organists, 1989, Faculty award Washington U., 1990, Disting. Alumnus award Ga. Mil. Acad.-Woodward Acad. Alumni Assn., 1990; NEH fellow, 1976, Folger Inst. fellow, 1982. Mem. MLA, Am. Assn. Tchrs. of French, Am. Soc. 18th Century Studies, Soc. Rousseau Studies, Soc. Prévost d'Exiles Office: Kalamazoo Coll Office of Pres 1200 Academy St Kalamazoo MI 49006-3295

JONES, JEFFREY W. retail executive; Grad. summa cum laude, Mercyhurst Coll. CPA. Sr. acct. Arthur Anderson & Co., 1984-88; v.p., contr., treas. Dairy Mart Convenience Stores, Inc., 1988-94; v.p., contr., mktg. Clark Refining and Mktg. Inc., 1994-98; exec. v.p., CFO Clark Retail Group, Inc., Oak Brook, Ill., 1998—. Office: Clark Retail Group Inc. 3003 Butterfield Rd Ste 300 Oak Brook IL 60523

JONES, JOHN, professional sports team executive; b. New Orleans, Feb. 6, 1952; m. Cindy Jones. Grad., Loyola U. , New Orleans, 1973. Tchr., journalist; writer New Orleans Times-Picayune; editor Packer Report, 1974—75; instr. journalism Loyola U., New Orleans, 1976—78; dir. pub. rels. NFL Mgmt. Coun., 1987—94; exec. v.p., COO Green Bay (Wis.) Packers, 1999—. Bd. dirs. Green Bay Packer Hall of Fame, Bellin Hosp., Green Bay, Green Bay Boys & Girls Club. Office: 1265 Lombardi Ave Green Bay WI 54307

JONES, JOHN BAILEY, federal judge; b. Mitchell, S.D., Mar. 30, 1927; s. John B. and Grace M. (Bailey) J.; m. Rosemary Wermers; children: John, William, Mary Louise, David, Judith, Robert BSBA, U. S.D., 1951, LLB, 1953. Bar: S.D. 1953. Sole practice, Presho, S.D., 1953-67; judge Lyman County, Kennebec, 1953-56; mem. S.D. Ho. of Reps., Pierre, 1957-61; judge S.D. Cir. Ct., 1967-81, U.S. Dist. Ct. S.D., Sioux Falls, 1981—; now sr. judge. Mem. Am. Judicature Soc., S.D. Bar Assn., Fed. Judges Assn., VFW, Am. Legion Methodist. Lodges: Elks, Lions Avocation: golf. Office: US Dist Ct 400 S Phillips Ave Rm 302 Sioux Falls SD 57104-6851

JONES, JOHN O. state legislator; Ill. state rep. Dist. 107, 1995—. Office: PO Drawer 1787 1116 Main St Mount Vernon IL 62864-3819

JONES, LAWRENCE WILLIAM, retired educator, physicist; b. Evanston, Ill., Nov. 16, 1925; s. Charles Herbert and Fern (Storm) J.; m. Ruth Reavley Drummond, June 24, 1950; children: Douglas Warren, Carol

Anne, Ellen Louise. B.S., Northwestern U., 1948, M.S., 1949; Ph.D., U. Calif. at Berkeley, 1952. Research asst. U. Calif. Radiation Lab., Berkeley, 1950-52; mem. faculty U. Mich., Ann Arbor, 1952—, prof. physics, 1963-98, chmn. dept. physics, 1982-87, prof. emeritus, 1998—. Physicist Midwestern U. Rsch. Assn., 1956-57; vis. physicist Lawrence Radiation Lab., Berkeley, 1959—, cons., 1964-66; vis. scientist CERN, Geneva, Switzerland, 1961-62, 65, 85—, assoc., 1988—; vis. physicist Brookhaven Nat. Lab., Upton, N.Y., 1963—; vis. physicist Fermi Nat. Accelerator Lab., Batavia, Ill., 1971—; vis. prof. Tata Inst. Fundamental Rsch., Bombay, India, 1979, U. Sydney Australia, 1991; mem. elem. particle physics panel of physics survey com. NRC, 1984; cons. ctrl. design group Superconducting Super Collider Nat. Lab., 1985-87, vis. physicist, 1991-94; cons. NASA, 1974-81; trustee Univs. Rsch. Assn., 1982-87; disting. vis. scholar U. Adelaide, 1991; vis. scientist U. Auckland, 1991. Mem. adv. panel for Cosmic Rays Jour. of Physics G., 1991-95. Guggenheim fellow, 1965; Sci. Rsch. Coun. fellow, 1977. Fellow Am. Phys. Soc. Home: 2666 Parkridge Dr Ann Arbor MI 48103-1731 Office: U Mich Dept Physics Ann Arbor MI 48109-1120 E-mail: LWJones@umich.edu.

JONES, LEANDER CORBIN, educator, media specialist; b. Vincent, Ark., July 16, 1934; s. Lander Corbin and Una Bell (Lewis) J.; A.B., U. Ark., Pine Bluff, 1956; M.S., U. Ill., 1968; Ph.D., Union Grad. Inst., 1973; m. Lethonee Angela Hendricks, June 30, 1962; children: Angela Lynne, Leander Corbin. Tchr. English pub. high schs., Chgo. Bd. Edn., 1956-68; vol. English-as-fgn. lang. tchr. Peace Corps, Mogadiscio, Somalia, 1964-66; TV producer City Colls. of Chgo., 1968-73; communications media specialist Meharry Med. Coll., 1973-75; assoc. prof. Black Americana studies Western Mich., U., 1975-89, prof., 1989—, chmn. African studies program, 1980-81, co-chmn. Black caucus, 1983-84; pres. Corbin 22 Ltd., 1986—; dir. 7 art workshop Am. Negro Emancipation Centennial Authority, Chgo., 1960-63. Mem. Mich. Commn. on Crime and Delinquency, 1981-83; mem. exec. com. DuSable Mus. African Am. History, 1970—; mem. Prisoners Progress Assn., 1977-82, South African Solidarity Orgn., 1978—, Dennis Brutus Def. Com., 1980-83; chmn. Kalamazoo Community Relations Bd., 1977-79; bd. dirs. Kalamazoo Civic Players, 1981-83; pres. Black Theater of Kalamazoo, 1978-85; dir., dramaturg Mich. Black Repertory Theatre, 1987-90; exec. prodr. Ransom Street Playhouse, Kalamazoo, 1993—. Served with U.S. Army, 1956-58. Faculty Enrichment grantee Govt. Can., 1992. Mem. Assn. Study African-Am. History , NAACP (exec. com. Kalamazoo br. 1978-82), Theatre Arts and Broadcasting Skills Ctr. (pres. 1972—), AAUP, Mich. Orgn. African Studies, Nat. Council Black Studies, Popular Culture Assn., 100 Men's Club, Kappa Alpha Psi. Dir. South Side Ctr. of Performing Arts, Chgo., 1968-69, Progressive Theatre Unltd., Nashville, 1974-75, Mich. Black Repertory Theatre, 1987-90; chmn. Tenn. Region N.AM. Zone 2 of 2d World Festival Black and Artican Arts and Culture, 1975, Nat. Black Media Consortium, 1985; writer, producer, dir. TV drama: Roof Over my Head, Nashville 1975; designer program in theatre and TV for hard-to-educate; developer edn. programs in Ill. State Penitentiary, Pontiac, and Cook County Jail, Chgo., 1971-73. Writer, dir. 10 Score!, 1976, Super Summer, 1978; dir. Trouble in Mind, 1979, Day of Absence, 1981, 85, Happy Ending, 1981, Who's Got His Own, 1983, Take A Giant Step, 1985; producer For Colored Girls Who Have Considered Suicide When the Rainbow is Enuf, 1984; featured at Civic Theater, Kalamazoo, in Great White Hope, 1979, Dutchman, 1980, Moon On a Rainbow Shawl, 1980, Five on the Black Hand Side, 1982, Who's Got His Own, Guys and Dolls, Black Girl, Tambourines to Glory, 1983, Day of Absence, Take a Giant Step, 1985, Soldier's Play, 1986, Beef, No Chicken, 1989, Black Eagles, 1994; author: Roof Over My Head, 1975, Africa is for Reel, 1983, Journal of Black Studies, 1985; exec. producer and host TV series Fade to Black, 1986—. Home: PO Box 2404 Portage MI 49081-2404 Office: Western Mich U 3721 S Westnedge Ave Ste 222 Kalamazoo MI 49008-2979

JONES, LEE BENNETT, chemist, educator, university official; b. Memphis, Mar. 14, 1938; s. Harold S. and Martha B. J.; m. Vera Kramar, Feb. 8, 1964; children: David B., Michael B. BA magna cum laude, Wabash Coll, 1960; PhD, M.I.T., 1964; DSC (hon.), Wabash Coll., 1992. Faculty U. Ariz., Tucson, 1964-85, prof. chemistry, 1972-85, asst. head dept. chemistry, 1971-73, head dept., 1973-77, dean Grad. Coll., 1977-79, provost Grad. Studies and Health Scis., 1979-82, v.p. rsch., 1982-85; prof. chemistry, exec. v.p., provost U. Nebr., Lincoln, 1985—. Chmn. bd. dirs. Coun. Grad. Schs., 1986; mem. Grad. Records Exam. Bd., 1986-91; mem. Midwest Higher Edn. Commn., 1995—. Mem. editl. bd. Jour. Chem. Edn, 1975-79; contbr. numreous articles to sci. jours. Mem. Nebr. R&D Authority, 1985—, Midwest Higher Edn. Commn.; vice chmn. Nebr. Ednl. Telecomm. Commn., 1987-88, 91-92. NSF fellow, 1961-63, 64— Mem. AAAS, AAUP, Am. Chem. Soc., Chem. Soc. (London), N.Y. Acad. Scis., Phi Beta Kappa. Home: 1611 Kingston Rd Lincoln NE 68506-1526 Office: U Nebr 106 Varner Hall 3835 Holdrege St Lincoln NE 68503-1435

JONES, LOVANA S. state legislator; b. Mansfield, Ohio, Mar. 28, 1935; 2 chilren. BA, Ohio State U. Mem. from 5th dist. Ill. Ho. of Reps., formerly asst. majority leader. Mem. children and family law com., edn. fin. elections com., pub. safety and infrastructure appropriationcoms., chmn. reapportionment com., mem. state govt. com. Supr. anti-gang program Chgo. Intervention Network. Office: Ill State Senate State Capitol 109 State House Springfield IL 62706-0001

JONES, NATHAN JEROME, farm machinery manufacturing company executive; b. 1957; Grad., U. Wis.; MBA, U. Chgo. From acct. to various fin. assignments Deere & Co., Moline, Ill., 1978-91, asst. treas., 1991-94, treas., 1994-98, v.p., 1996-98, sr. v.p., CFO, 1998—. Office: Deere & Co 1 John Deere Pl Moline IL 61265-8098

JONES, NATHANIEL RAPHAEL, federal judge; b. Youngstown, Ohio, May 13, 1926; s. Nathaniel B. and Lillian (Rafe) J.; m. Lillian Graham, Mar. 22, 1974; children: Stephanie Joyce, Pamela Haley stepchildren: William Hawthorne, Rickey Hawthorne, Marc Hawthorne. A.B., Youngstown State U., 1951, LL.B., 1955, LL.D. (hon.) (hon.) , 1969, Syracuse U., 1972. Editor Buckeye Rev. newspaper, 1956; exec. dir. FEPC, Youngstown, 1956—59; practiced law, 1959—61; mem. firm Goldberg & Jones, 1968—69; asst. U.S. atty., 1961—67; asst. gen. counsel Nat. Adv. Commn. on Civil Disorders, 1967—68; gen. counsel NAACP, 1969—79; judge U.S. Ct. of Appeals, 6th Circuit, 1979—85, sr. judge, 1995—. Adj. prof. U. Cin. Coll. Law, 1983—; trial observer , South Africa, 1985; dir. Buckeye Rev. Pub. Co.; chmn. Con. on Adequate Def. and Incentives in Mil.; mem. Task Force-Vets. Benefits; lectr. South African Judges seminar, Johannesburg. Co-chmn. Cin. Roundtable, Black-Jewish Coalition Cin.; observer Soviet Union Behalf com. on Soviet Jewry; bd. dirs. Interights, USA. With USAAF, 1945—47. Mem.: FBA, ABA (co-chmn. com. constl. rights criminal sect. 1971—73), Nat. Conf. Black Lawyers, Urban League, Youngstown Area Devel. Corp., Am. Arbitration Assn., Nat. Bar Assn., Mahoning County Bar Assn., Ohio State Bar Assn., Houston Law Club (Youngstown), Elks, Kappa Alpha Psi. Baptist. Office: US Ct Appeals US Courthouse 100 E 5th St Ste 432 Cincinnati OH 45202-3911

JONES, NORMA LOUISE, librarian, educator; b. Poplar, Wis. d. George Elmer and Hilma June (Wiberg) J. BE, U. Wis.; MA, U. Minn., 1952; postgrad, U. Ill., 1957; PhD, U. Mich., 1965; postgrad., NARS, 1978, 79, 80, Nova U., 1983-96. Librarian Grand Rapids (Mich.) Public Schs., 1947-62; with Grand Rapids Public Library, 1948-49; instr. Central Mich. U., Mt. Pleasant, 1954, 55; lectr. U. Mich., Ann Arbor, 1954, 55, 61, 63-65, asst. prof., 1966-68; librarian Benton Harbor (Mich.) Public Schs., 1962-63; asst. prof. library sci. U. Wis., Oshkosh, 1968-70, assoc. prof., 1970-75, prof., 1975—, chmn. dept. library sci., 1980-84, exec. dir. librs. and learning resources, 1987-93; dir. Adult Ctr., 1993-95. Recipient Disting. Teaching award U. Wis.-Oshkosh, 1977 Mem. ALA (chmn. reference cons. 1975), Wis. Libr. Assn., Assn. Libr. and Info. Sci. Educators, Spl. Libr. Assn., Wis. Spl. Libr. Assn., Soc. Am. Archivists, Wis. Assn. Acad. Librs., Phi Beta Kappa, Phi Kappa Phi, Pi Lambda Theta, Beta Phi Mu, Sigma Pi Epsilon. Home: 1220 Maricopa Dr Oshkosh WI 54904-8121

JONES, PETER D'ALROY, historian, writer, retired educator; b. Hull, Eng., June 9, 1931; arrived in U.S., 1959, naturalized, 1968; s. Alfred and Madge (Rutter) d'Alroy; m. Johanna Maria Hartinger, Feb. 20, 1987; 1 child, Heather Marie; children from previous marriage: Kathryn Beauchamp Fly Ebert, Barbara Collier Rosenberg. BA, Manchester (Eng.) U., 1952, MA, 1953; PhD, London U. Sch. Econ., 1963; postgrad., U. Brussels, 1954. Freelance editor, London, 1953-56; lectr. U.S. history dept. Am. studies Manchester U., 1957-58; vis. asst. prof. econs. Tulane U., 1959-60; from asst. to full prof. Smith Coll., 1960-68; Kennan prof. Am. instns. and values Trinity Coll., Hartford, 1980-81; prof. history U. Ill., Chgo., 1968-98, prof. emeritus, 1998—. Vis. prof. Columbia U., U. Mass., U. Hawaii, U. Warsaw, Poland, U. Düsseldorf, Fed. Republic Germany, U. Salzburg, Austria; mem. com. examiners Grad. Record Exams. Ednl. Testing Svc., Princeton, N.J., 1966-70; mem. Am. studies com. Am. Coun. Learned Socs., 1973-75; lectr. U.S. Dept. State, 1973-87; adv. to publs. Author: Economic History of U.S.A. Since 1783, 1956, 2nd edit., 1965, The Story of the Saw, 1961, America's Wealth, 1963, The Consumer Society, 2d edit., 1967, The Christian Socialist Revival, 1968, The Robber Barons Revisited, 1968, Robert Hunter's Poverty: Social Conscience in the Progressive Era, 1965, La Sociedad Consumidora, 1968, Since Columbus: Poverty and Pluralism in the History of the Americas, 1975, The U.S.A.: A History of Its People and Society, 2 vols., 1976, Henry George and British Socialism, 1991; co-editor: Biographical Dictionary of American Mayors, 1820-1980, 1981, Ethnic Chicago, 1981, rev. and enlarged edit., 1984, 4th edit., 1995; contbr. several entries to Ency. World Biography, 1988, 94; contbr. numerous articles and book revs. to profl. jours., popular newspapers. R.W. Emerson prize com Phi Beta Kappa, 1991—94. Mem. London Sch. Econs. Soc. (life). E-mail: verdi1901@aol.com.

JONES, ROBERT BROOKE, microbiologist and immunologist educator; b. Knoxville, Tenn., Sept 14, 1942; s. Robert Melvin and Evaleen (Brooke) J.; m. Barbara Burgess McLawhorn, Sept. 7, 1963; children—Julia Ashley, Jonathan Davis, Quinnette Brooke. A.B. in Chemistry, U. N.C., 1964, M.D., 1970, Ph.D. in Biochemistry, 1970. Diplomate Am. Bd. Internal Medicine. Intern U. Wash., Seattle, 1970-71; resident U. Wash., Seattle, 1974-76; fellow in infectious diseases, 1976-78; asst. prof. Ind. U. Sch. Medicine, Indpls., 1978-83, assoc. prof. medicine, microbiology and immunology, 1983-86, prof., 1986—, assoc. dean, 1997—, CEO, med. dir. Wishard Health Svcs., Indpls.; dir. Midwest Sexually Transmitted Diseases Research Ctr., Indpls., 1983—; mem. NIH bacteriology rev. group, 1987. Contbr. sci. articles to profl. jours. Served to lt. comdr. U.S. Navy, 1971-74. NIH grantee, 1983. Fellow ACP; mem. Am. Venereal Disease Assn. (bd. dirs. 1983—), Am. Soc. Microbiology, Infectious Disease Soc. Am., Am. Fedn. Clin. Research, Order Golden Fleece, Sigma Xi, Alpha Omega Alpha. Republican. Mem. Society of Friends. Office: Ind U Fisler # 302 Dept Medicine Indianapolis IN 46202-5114 also: Wishard Health Svcs 1001 W 10th St Indianapolis IN 46202-2859

JONES, ROBERT E. company executive; m. Mary Jane Jones; 1 child, Tom. Student, Washington U. With The Jones Co., St. Louis, 1953—, pres., 1961—, chmn. bd. Bd. dir. St. John's Bank and Trust Co. Tech. advt. com. St. Louis County Planning Commn.; chmn. bd. Met. St. Louis Sewer Dist. Mem. Builders Assn. Greater St. Louis. (chmn. labor com.), Nat. Assn. Home Builders (life dir.). Office: Jones Company Ste 200 16640 Chesterfield Grove Ct Chesterfield MO 63005-1422

JONES, RONALD VANCE, health science association administrator; b. Springfield, Ill., Oct. 7, 1946; s. Dallas Vance and Bertha Henrietta (Bentley) J.; m. Patricia Ann O'Neill, Feb. 1, 1969; children: Devon Vance, Zachary Brice. BS, U. Ill., 1969, MEd, 1972. Tchr. English lang. Ottawa (Ill.) Twp. H.S., 1969-70; rsch. assoc. U. Ill., Urbana, 1970-73; dir. cmty. programs Ga. Dept. Youth Svcs., Atlanta, 1973-79; dir. planning Ga. Dept. Mental Health; capital project planner Ill. Dept. Mental Health, Springfield, 1979-85; bus. adminstr. Chester (Ill.) Mental Health Ctr., 1985-92; asst. supt. Malcolm Bliss Mental Health Ctr., St. Louis, 1992-96; chief operating officer Met. St. Louis Psychiatric Ctr., 1996—; pres., CEO RVJ Enterprises, Inc., 2000—. Editor: tchr. guidebooks for elem. schs., 1971-73. Vice-chmn., bd. dirs. Lullwater Sch. Atlanta; vol. St. Louis Easter Seal Soc., 1987-88. Mem. Ill. Health Facilities Planning Bd., Ill. Hosp. Licensing Bd., Ill. Long Term Care Facilities Bd., Gov's. State Bldgs. Energy Cons. Bd., Kappa Delta Pi, Phi Delta Kappa. Home: 7 Birnawoods Ln Olivette MO 63132-4405 Office: Metro St Louis Psychiatric Ctr Dept of Mental Health Saint Louis MO 63112

JONES, SHERMAN JARVIS, state senator; b. Winton, N.C., Feb. 10, 1935; s. Starkie Sherman and Gladys (Cherry) J.; m. Amelia Collins Buchanan, Dec. 16, 1956; children: Sheila C., Shelly C., Shelton C. Student, Kansas City C.C., 1976-77. Profl. baseball player, N.Y.C., Cin., S Francisco, 1953-65; police officer Kansas City (Kans.) Police Dept., 1965-88; state rep. Kans. Legislature, 1988-92, senator, 1993-00. Named one of Outstanding Young Men Am., 1970. Mem. Nat. Conf. State Legislators, Kans. Legis. Black Caucus (chmn. 1991—), Optimists (v.p. 1982-83), Masons. Democrat. Home: 3736 Weaver Dr Kansas City KS 66104-3763

JONES, SHIRLEY M. state legislator; b. Chgo., Nov. 9, 1939; 2 children. Ed., George Williams Coll. Mem. from Dist. 6, Ill. Ho. of Reps., 1987—, vice chmn. aging com. Also mem. higher edn., housing, human svc. appropriations, pub. utilities, revenue and state adminstrn. coms. Home: 541 W Roosevelt Rd Ste 2306 Chicago IL 60607-4915 Office: Ill State Senate State Capitol Springfield IL 62706-0001 Also: 47 W Polk St Ste M6 Chicago IL 60605-2088

JONES, STEPHANIE J. federal agency administrator; BA in English Lit. & Afro-Am. Studies, Smith Coll.; JD, U. Cin. Bar: Ohio 1986, U.S. Dist. Ct. Appeals (6th cir.) 1989, U.S. Dist. Ct. (so. dist.) Ohio 1987. Assoc. Graydon, Head & Ritchey, Cin., 1986-90; law prof. Salmon P. Chase Coll. Law Northern Ky. U.; chief edn. rep., spokesperson Dept. Edn. Region V, 1994—. Adj. prof. law Northwestern U. Sch. Law, Chgo.; lectr. in field; investigative, gen. news, feature reporter Cin. Post, 1982-83; exec. asst. Lionel Richie and the Commodores. Mem. Ohio Atty. Gen.'s Coun. on Ethics and Profl. Responsibility, 6th Cir. Jud. Conf. (life). Office: 111 N Canal St Ste 1094 Chicago IL 60606-7204

JONES, STEPHANIE TUBBS, congresswoman, lawyer; b. Cleve., Sept. 10, 1949; BA, Case Western Res. U., 1971, JD, 1974. Bar: Ohio 1974, U.S. Dist. Ct. (no. dist.) Ohio 1975, U.S. Ct. Appeals (6th cir.) 1981, U.S. Supreme Ct. 1981. Asst. gen. counsel, EEO adminstr. N.E. Ohio Regional Sewer Dist., 1974-76; asst. prosecutor Cuyahoga County Prosecutor's Office, 1976-79; trial atty. Cleve. dist. office EEO, 1979-81; judge Cleve. Mcpl. Ct., 1982-83, Cuyahoga County Ct. of Common Pleas, 1983-91; prosecutor Cuyahoga County, Cleve., 1991-98; mem. U.S. Congress from 11th Ohio dist., 1999—; mem. banking and fin. svcs. com., 1999—; mem. com. on small bus., 1999—. Mem. vis. com. bd. overseers Franklin Thomas Backus Sch. Law, Case Western Res. U. Bd. trustees Comty. Re-entry Program; bd. trustees class of 1984 Leadership Cleve. Alumnae; mem. Task Force on Violent Crime, Substance Abuse Initiative; trustee Cleve. Police Hist. Soc.; bd. trustees Bethany Bapt. Ch. Recipient Outstanding Vol. Svcs. in Law and Justice award Urban League Greater Cleve., 1986, Women of Yr. award Cleve. chpt. Nat. Assn. Negro Bus. and Profl. Women's Clubs, Inc., 1987, award in recognition of outstanding svc. to judiciary and black comty. Midwest region Nat. Black Am. Law Student Assn., 1988, Career Women of Achievement award YWCA, 1991, Disting. Svc. award Cleve. chpt. NAACP, 1997; named Black Profl. of Yr., Black Profl. Assn. Cleve., 1995, 1994 Ohio Dem. of Yr., Ohio Dem. Party, 1995; inductee Collinwood H.S. Hall of Fame, 1994, Soc. Benchers of Case Western Res. U. Sch. of Law, 1996. Mem. ABA, Nat. Black Prosecutor's Assn., Nat. Dist. Atty.'s Assn. (met. prosecutor's com.), Nat. Coun. Negro Women, Nat. Coll. Dist. Attys. (bd. regents), Ohio State Bar Assn. (Nettie Cronise Lutes award 1997), Ohio Prosecuting Attys. Assn. (exec. com.), Cleve. Bar Assn. (trustee), Norman S. Miner Bar Assn. (past treas.), Cuyahoga Women's Polit. Caucus, Delta Sigma Theta (Greater Cleve. Alumnae chpt., Althea Simmons award 1993). Office: Ho of Reps 1516 Longworth Hob Washington DC 20515-0001*

JONES, SUSIE, radio personality; Grad. Speech Comms., U. Minn. With Sta. KSTP, Sta. KARE, Sta. WCCO-TV, Mpls.; radio host afternoon drive Sta. KCCO-AM, 1996—, Saturday radio host. Office: WCCO 625 2nd Ave S Minneapolis MN 55402*

JONES, THOMAS FRANKLIN, protective services official; b. Atlantic City, Dec. 19, 1940; BA, Southeastern U., 1968. From agent to spl. agent in charge FBI, Cleve., 1968-95; ret., 1995; chief of police Cleve. Clinic Found., 1997—. Office: Police Dept Cleve Clinic Found 9500 Euclid Ave Cleveland OH 44195-0001

JONES, THOMAS WALTER, astrophysics educator, researcher; b. Odessa, Tex., June 22, 1945; s. Theodore Sydney and LaVerne Gertrude (Neis) J.; m. Karen Gay Cronquist, June 15, 1968 (div.); 1 child, Walter Brian. B.S. in Physics, U. Tex., 1967; M.S. in Physics, U. Minn., 1969, Ph.D. in Physics, 1972. Asst. physicist U. Calif., San Diego, 1972-75; asst. scientist Nat. Radio Astronomy Obs., Charlottesville, Va., 1975-77; asst. prof. dept. astronomy U. Minn., Mpls., 1977-80, assoc. prof., 1980-84, prof., 1984—, chmn. dept. astronomy, 1981-97. Contbr. articles to profl. jours. Mem. Am. Astron. Soc., Royal Astron. Soc., Internat. Astron. Union, Sigma Xi. Office: U Minn Dept Astronomy 116 Church St SE Minneapolis MN 55455-0149 Home: 1385 Eldridge Ave W Saint Paul MN 55113-5805

JONES, TREVOR OWEN, engineering executive; b. Maidstone, Kent, Eng., Nov. 3, 1930; came to U.S., 1957, naturalized, 1971; s. Richard Owen and Ruby Edith (Martin) J.; m. Jennie Lou Singleton, Sept. 12, 1959; children: Pembroke Robinson (dec.), Bronwyn Elizabeth. Higher Nat. Cert. in Elec. Engring., Aston Tech. Coll., Birmingham, Eng., 1952; Ordinary Nat. Cert. in Mech. Engring., Liverpool (Eng.) Tech. Coll., 1957. Registered profl. engr., Wis.; chartered engr., U.K. Student engr., elec. machine design engr. Brit. Gen. Electric Co., 1950-57; project engr., project mgr. Nuc. Ship Savannah, Allis-Chalmers Mfg. Co., 1957-59; with GM, 1959-78, staff engr. in charge Apollo computers, 1967, dir. electronic control sys., 1970-72, dir. advanced product engring., 1972-74; dir. GM Proving Grounds, 1974-78; v.p. engring., automotive worldwide TRW Inc., Cleve., 1978-80, v.p. transp. electronics group, 1980-87; chmn. bd. dirs. Libbey-Owens-Ford Inc., 1987-94; chmn., CEO Internat. Devel. Corp., 1987—; from vice chmn. to chmn. Echlin Inc., 1995-98, chmn. bd. dirs., interim pres. and CEO, 1997; chmn., founder, CEO Biomec Inc., 1998—. Vice chmn. Motor Vehicle Safety Adv. Coun., 1971; chmn. Nat. Hwy. Safety Adv. Com., 1976. Author, patentee automotive safety and electronics. Trustee Lawrence Inst. Tech., 1973-76; mem. exec. bd. Clinton Valley coun. Boy Scouts Am., 1975; mem. bd. govs. Cranbrook Inst. Sci., 1977; mem. Sec. of Def. Def. Sci. Bd. Task Force on Internat. Arms Devel. Cooperation, 1995-98; chmn. Nat. Rsch. Coun. Com. Partnership for a New Generation Vehicle, 1994-2001. Officer Brit. Army, 1955-57. Recipient Safety award for engring. excellence U.S. Dept. Transp., 1978. Fellow Brit. Instn. Elec. Engrs. (Hooper Mem. prize 1950), IEEE (life, exec. com. vehicle tech. soc. 1977-81), Royal Soc. of the Arts, Mfg. and Commerce, Soc. Automotive Engrs. (Arch T. Colwell paper award 1974, 75, Vincent Bendix Automotive Electronics award 1976, Edward N. Cole award 1988), Engring. Soc. Detroit, Engring. Soc. Cleve., Instn. Mech. Engrs. (hon.); mem. NAE, Union Club, Kirtland Country Club, Bloomfield Hills Country Club. Republican. Episcopalian. Home: Two Bratenahl Pl Bratenahl OH 44108 E-mail: tojones@biomec.com.

JONES, WELLINGTON DOWNING, III, banker; b. Topeka, Feb. 16, 1945; s. Wellington Downing Jr. and Nancy (Neiswanger) J.; m. Andrea Loftus, May 2, 1970; children: Wellington Downing IV, Heather, Lindsey. BSBA, Northwestern U., 1967; postgrad., Grad. Sch. Banking, Madison, Wis., 1980, Harvard U., 1987. Mktg. rep. IBM, Chgo., 1969-76; v.p. data processing 1st Bank & Trust (name 1st Source Bank 1981), South Bend, Ind., 1976-79, v.p. retail banking, 1979-81; sr. v.p. 1st Source Bank, 1981-88; pres. 1st Nat. Bank Mishawaka (acquired by 1st Source Bank 1983), Ind., 1983; exec. v.p. 1st Source Corp., South bend, 1988—; pres., 19989—; also bd. dirs. Bd. dirs. Trustcorp Mortgage, South Bend. Bd. dirs. Neighborhood Housing Svcs., South Bend, 1986—, Entertainment Dist. Bd., South Bend, 1991—, United Way St. Joseph County, South Bend, 1991—; chmn. South Bend Mayor's Housing Forum, 1991—; pres. No. Ind. Hist. Soc., South Bend, 1991—. Sgt. USMCR, 1967-73. Mem. Signal Point Club (Niles, Mich.), Morris Park Country Club. Presbyterian. Avocations: golf, platform tennis, reading, investments. Office: 1st Source Bank 100 N Michigan St South Bend IN 46601-1630

JONES, WENDELL E. state legislator; b. Nov. 4, 1937; m. Jane; 3 children. BS in Speech & Hearing Therapy, Ball State U. Speech therapist, dir. spl. edn. Dist. 15, Palatine, Ill.; mem. Ill. Senate, Springfield, 1998—. Rep. precinct capt.; pres. Village Palatine, 1973-77, trustee, 1967-73. Republican. Office: State Capitol 611 C Capitol Bldg Springfield IL 62706-0001 also: 110 W Northwest Hwy Palatine IL 60067-3558

JONES, WILL(IAM) (ARNOLD), writer, former newspaper columnist; b. Dover, Ohio, Jan. 29, 1924; s. Vinton W. and Eva M. (Ringheimer) J.; m. Ruth Hines Johnson, May 4, 1968; children by previous marriage—Judson D., Jeffrey B., Brinley W., Megan A., Snake C. Student, Ohio State U., 1942-45, U. Minn. Law Sch., 1945-46. Movie reviewer Tuscarawas County Republican News, Ohio, 1938-39; reporter Dover Daily Reporter, 1939-42, Columbus Citizen, Ohio, 1942-45, Mpls. Tribune, 1945-47, entertainment and food columnist, 1947-84. Creative cons., freelance writer advt. agencies 1962— . Author: cook book Wild in the Kitchen, 1961; also numerous articles. Founder S.H.A.M.E. Smokers, anti-smoking group, 1964. Served with USAAF, 1943. Home and Office: 2102 Cedar Lake Pkwy Minneapolis MN 55416-3616

JONES, WILLIAM AUGUSTUS, JR. retired bishop; b. Memphis, Jan. 24, 1927; s. William Augustus and Martha (Jones) J.; m. Margaret Loaring-Clark, Aug. 26, 1949; 4 children. B.A., Southwestern at Memphis, 1948; B.D., Yale U., 1951. Ordained priest Episcopal Ch., 1952; priest in charge Messiah Ch., Pulaski, Tenn., 1952-57; curate Christ Ch., Nashville, 1957-58; rector St. Mark Ch., LaGrange, Ga., 1958-65; asso. rector St. Luke Ch., Mountainbrook, Ala., 1965-66; dir. research So. region Assn. Christian Tng. and Service, Memphis, 1966-67; exec. dir. Assn. Christian Tng. and Service, 1968-72; rector St. John's, Johnson City, Tenn., 1972-75; bishop of Mo. St. Louis, 1975-93. Adj. staff Christ Ch., Wilmington, Del., 2001.

JONKER, BRUCE A. business executive; V.p., CFO Gradall Industries, Inc., New Philadelphia, Ohio. Office: Gradall Industries Inc 406 Mill Ave SW New Philadelphia OH 44663-3835

JORDAN, JAMES D. (JIM), state legislator; b. Feb. 17, 1964; m. Polly Jordan; children: Rachel, Benjamin, Jessie, Isaac. BS, U. Wis., 1986; MA, Ohio State U., 1991. Asst. wrestling coach Ohio State U., Columbus; rep. dist. 85 Ohio Ho. of Reps., 1994-2000; mem. Ohio Senate from 12th dist., 2001—. Mem. Champaign County Rep. Exec. Com., Mad River Valley Young Rep. Club, Citizens Against Govt. Waste, Right to Life Orgns. Big Ten and NCAA wrestling champion, 1985, 86. Address: 1709 S State Route 560 Urbana OH 43078-9637

JORDAN, JOHN W., II, holding company executive; b. 1948; With The Jordan Co., N.Y.C., 1982—; CEO Jordan Industries, Inc., Deerfield, Ill. Office: Jordan Industries 1751 Lake Cook Rd Ste 550 Deerfield IL 60015-5624 also: Jordan Industries Inc 875 N Michigan Ave Chicago IL 60611-1803

JORDAN, MICHELLE DENISE, lawyer; b. Chgo., Oct. 29, 1954; d. John A. and Margaret (O'Dood) J. BA in Polit. Sci., Loyola U, Chgo., 1974; JD, U. Mich., 1977. Bar. Ill. 1977, U.S. Dist. Ct. (no. dist.) Ill. 1978. Asst. state's atty. State's Attys. Office, Chgo., 1977-82; pvt. practice, 1983-84; with Ill. Atty. Gen.'s Office, 1984-90, chief environ. control div., 1988-90; ptnr. Hopkins & Sutter, 1991-93; apptd. dep. regional adminstr. region 5 U.S. EPA, 1994—. Active Operation Push, Chgo., 1971—. Recipient Kizzy Image Achievement and Svc. award, 1990, Suzanne E. Olive Nat. EEO award 1996; named in Am.'s Top 100 Bus. and Profl. Women, Dollars and SenseMag., Chgo., 1988. Mem. Ill. Bar Assn., Chgo. Bar Assn. (bd. mgrs., chmn. criminal law com. 1987-88, mem. hearing divsn., jud. evaluation com. 1987-88, exec. coun. 1987-88), Cook County Bar Assn., Nat. Bar Assn., Alpha Sigma Nu. Democrat. Baptist.

JORDAN, NICK M. state legislator, hotel, recreational facility executive; b. Kansas City, Mo., Dec. 2, 1949; s. Dwight M. and Joveta M. (Mills) J.; m. Linda Joyce Jarred, May 28, 1971; 1 child, Shelly Reneé. Grad. high sch., Overland Park, Kans. Restaurant mgr., asst. mgr., dir. mktg. Glenwood Manor Hotel, Overland Park, 1964-74; asst. dir. mktg. Radisson Muehlebach Hotel, Kansas City, Mo., 1974-79; dir. mktg. Grand Am. Hotel Corp., Overland Park, 1979-81, Regency Park Resort, Overland Park, 1981-83; pres. Overland Park Conv. and Visitors Bur., 1983-93; mem. Kans. Senate from 10th dist., 1995—. Vice chmn. Kans. Travel and Tourism Commn., Topeka, 1990—; appointee Johnson County (Kans.) Transp. Coun., 1988-92. Bd. dirs. Lakeview Village K.C. Coun. Prison Fellowship. Recipient Gov.'s Tourism award Kans. Assn. Broadcasters, 1987. Mem. Travel Industry Assn. Kans. (past pres., bd. dirs., Disting. Svc. award 1991), Internat. Assn. Conv. and Visitors Burs. (chmn. continuing edn. com. 1992-93), Rotary (bd. dirs. 1987-89). Avocations: reading, tennis, travel. Home: 7013 Albervan St Shawnee Mission KS 66216-2333 Office: The Hospitality Group 7013 Albervan Shawnee KS 66216 Address: Kansas Senate State Capitol Rm 143-N Topeka KS 66612

JORDAN, THOMAS FREDRICK, physics educator; b. Duluth, Minn., June 4, 1936; s. Thomas Vincent and Mildred (Nystrom) J. BA, U. Minn., 1958; PhD, U. Rochester, 1962. Rsch. assoc. U. Rochester, 1961-62, instr., 1962-63; NSF postdoctoral fellow U. Bern, Switzerland, 1963-64; asst. prof. U. Pitts., 1964-67, assoc. prof., 1967-70; prof. U. Minn., Duluth, 1970—. Vis. prof., workshop participant U. Wis., 1965, Aspen (Colo.) Inst. for Humanistic Studies, 1966, Summer Inst. for Theoretical Physics, U. Colo., 1967, Internat. Ctr. for Theoretical Physics, Trieste, Italy, 1968, U. Rochester, 1976-77, Syracuse U., Nat. Inst. for Nuclear Rsch., Firenze, Italy, U. Geneva., U. Paris 1982, Internat. Ctr. for Theoretical Physics, Trieste, workshop on early universe, Erice, Italy, Geneva, U. Bern, 1986, U. Calif. at Santa Barbara, 1968. Author: Linear Operators for Quantum Mechanics, 1969, Quantum Mechanics in Simple Matrix Form, 1985; contbr. numerous article to profl. jours. Rsch. fellow Alfred P. Sloan Found., 1965-67, Bush Found. fellow U. Tex., Temple U., 1984; Fulbright rsch. grantee U. Göttingen, Fed. Republic of Germany, 1991-92.

JORGENSEN, JAMES DOUGLAS, research physicist; b. Salina, Utah, Mar. 23, 1948; m. Ramona Gurr, June 6, 1970; children: Lynn Neilson, Michael Neilson, Kristeen Stenblik, Kathryn Brimball, Karen Russell, Scott Neilson. BS in Physics, Brigham Young U., 1970, PhD in Physics, 1975. Postdoctoral rsch. asst. Argonne (Ill.) Nat. Lab., 1974-77, asst. physicist solid state div., 1977-80, physicist material sci. div., 1980-89, sr. physicist, 1989—, group leader, 1988—. Mem. U.S. Nat. Com. for Crystallography, 1990-92, 94-97. Mem. editl. adv. bd. Jour. Solid State Chemistry, 1990—; contbr. over 300 articles to profl. jours. Bishop LDS Ch., Woodridge, Ill., 1984-89, stake pres., Naperville, Ill., 1998—. Recipient award for disting. performance at Argonne Nat. Lab., 1983, Barrett award, 1997; co-recipient Pacesetter award Argonne Nat. Lab., 1986, Dir.'s award, 1988; materials scis. rsch. competition award for outstanding sci. accomplishments in solid state physics U.S. Dept. Energy, 1987, 91; named honored alumnus Brigham Young U., 1992. Fellow Am. Phys. Soc.; mem. Materials Rsch. Soc., Am. Crystallographic Assn. (B.E. Warren Diffraction Physics award 1991). Office: Argonne Nat Lab Materials Sci Dv Bldg 223 Argonne IL 60439 E-mail: kkorgensen@anl.gov.

JORGENSON, MARY ANN, lawyer; b. Gallipolis, Ohio, 1941; BA, Agnes Scott Coll., 1963; MA, Harvard U., 1964; JD, Case Western Res. U., 1975. Bar: Ohio 1975, N.Y. 1982. Ptnr., chair firm's corp. practice Squire, Sanders & Dempsey, 1990—. Office: Squire Sanders & Dempsey LLP 127 Public Sq Ste 4900 Cleveland OH 44114-1284 E-mail: mjorgenson@ssd.com.

JORNDT, LOUIS DANIEL, retail drug store chain executive; b. Chgo., Aug. 24, 1941; s. Louis Carl and Margaret Estelle (Teel) J.; m. Patricia McDonnell, Aug. 1, 1964; children— Kristine, Michael, Kara B.S. in Pharmacy, Drake U., 1963; M.B.A., U. N.Mex., 1974. Various mgmt. positions Walgreen Co., Chgo., 1963-68, dist. mgr., 1968-75, regional dir. Deerfield, Ill., 1975-79, regional v.p., 1979-82, v.p., treas., 1982-85, sr. v.p., treas., 1985-89, pres., chief oper. officer, 1989-97, CEO, chmn., 1997—. Bd. dirs. Better Bus. Bur. Chgo., 1982—, Chgo. Assn. Commerce and Industry; nat. chmn. Drake U. Pharmacy Alumni Fund. Mem. Nat. Assn. Corp. Treas., Fin. Execs. Inst. Clubs: Economic (Chgo.); Glen View (Ill.) Golf. Avocations: golf; swimming; reading. Office: Walgreen Co 200 Wilmot Rd Deerfield IL 60015-4616

JORNS, DAVID LEE, retired university president; b. Tulsa, Jan. 10, 1944; s. Victor Lee and Nancy Jane (Pollard) J.; m. Audrey Parkes; children: Molly, Ben. BS in Radio and TV, Okla. State U., 1966, MA in Speech and Drama, 1968; PhD in Theatre History and Criticism, UCLA, 1973. Teaching asst. UCLA, 1970-73; asst. prof. U. Mo., Columbia, 1973-77, assoc. prof., 1977-80, dir. of theatre, 1977-80; chmn. theatre arts Mankato (Minn.) State U., 1980-84; dean fine arts and humanities West Tex. State U., Canyon, 1984-88; v.p. acad. affairs and provost No. Ky. U., Highland Heights, 1988-92; pres. Eastern Ill. U., Charleston, 1992-99. Contbr. articles, revs. to profl. publs.; producer 25 plays; editor The Jour. Opinion for the Performing Arts, 1975. Lt. USN, 1967-70. Mem. Ky. Coun. of Chief Acad. Officers, Soc. for Coll. & Univ. Planning, Assn. for Gen. & Liberal Studies, Am. Assn. for Higher Edn. Democrat. Avocations: computers, painting, reading.

JOSCELYN, KENT B(UCKLEY), lawyer; b. Binghamton, N.Y., Dec. 18, 1936; s. Raymond Miles and Gwen Buckley (Smith) J.; children: Kathryn Anne, Jennifer Sheldon. BS, Union Coll., 1957; JD, Albany (N.Y.) Law Sch., 1960. Bar: N.Y. 1961, U.S. Ct. Mil. Appeals 1962, D.C., 1967, Mich. 1979. Atty. adviser hdqts. USAF, Washington, 1965-67; assoc. prof. forensic studies U. Ind., Bloomington, 1967-76; dir. Inst. Rsch. in Pub. Safety, 1970-75; head policy analysis divsn. Highway Safety Rsch. Inst. U. Mich., Ann Arbor, 1976-81; dir. transp. planning and policy Urban Tech. Environ. Planning Program, 1981-84; prin. Joscelyn and Treat P.C., 1981—93, Joscelyn, McNair & Jeffrey P.C., Ann Arbor, 1993-2001. Cons. Law Enforcement Assistance Adminstrn., U.S. Dept. Justice, 1969-72; Gov.'s appointee as regional dir. Ind. Criminal Justice Planning Agy., 1969-72; vice chmn. Ind. Organized Crime Prevention Coun., 1969-72; commr. pub. safety City of Bloomington, Ind., 1974-76. Editor Internat. Jour. Criminal Justice. Capt. USAF, 1961-64. Mem. NAS, ABA, NRC, D.C. Bar Assn., N.Y. State Bar Assn., Internat. Bar Assn., Transp. Rsch. Bd. (chmn. motor vehicle and traffic law com. 1979-82), Am. Soc. Criminology (life), Assn. for Advancement Automotive Medicine (life), Soc. Automotive Engrs., Acad. Criminal Justice Scis. (life), Assn. Chiefs Police (assoc.), Nat. Safety Coun., Assn. Former Intelligence Officers (life), Product Liability Adv. Coun., Sigma Xi, Theta Delta Chi. Office: Kent B Joscelyn PC PO Box 130589 Ann Arbor MI 48113-0589 E-mail: kbjpc@earthlink.com.

JOSEPH, CHRIS, business services executive; BA, Miami U. Ohio; MBA, U. Chicago. Investment mgr. Wind Point Ptnrs., Chicago; co-founder, sr. v.p. ops. Integration Alliance Corp., 1994-98; CFO Parson Group, 1998—. Office: Parson Group Ste 1620 333 W Wacker Dr Chicago IL 60606-1246

JOSEPH, DANIEL DONALD, aeronautical engineer, educator; b. Chgo., Mar. 26, 1929; s. Samuel and Mary (Simon) J.; m. Ellen Broida, Dec. 18, 1949 (div. 1979); children: Karen, Michael, Charles; m. Kay Jaglo, Feb. 9, 1990. M.A. in Sociology, U. Chgo., 1950; B.S. in Mech. Engring, Ill. Inst. Tech., 1959, M.S., 1960, Ph.D., 1963. Asst. prof. mech. engring. Ill. Inst. Tech., 1962-63; mem. faculty U. Minn., 1963—, assoc. prof. fluid mechanics, 1965-69, prof. aerospace engring. and mechanics, 1969-90, Russell J. Penrose prof., 1990—. Author 4 books on stability and bifurcation theory and fluid dynamics; editor 3 books; editorial bd. SIAM Jour. Applied Math, Jour. Applied Mechanics, Jour. Non-Newtonian Fluid Mechanics, others; contbr. articles to sci. jours. Guggenheim fellow, 1969-70, Timoshenko medal Am. Soc. of Mechanical Engineers, 1995. Mem. NAS, ASME, NAE, Am. Phys. Soc., Am. Acad. Arts and Scis., Soc. Engring. Sci. (G.I. Taylor medal 1990, Bingham medal Soc. of Rheology). Achievements include contbns. to math. theory of hydrodynamic stability; rheology of viscoelastic fluids. Home: 1920 S 1st St Apt 2302 Minneapolis MN 55454-1279 Office: U Minn Dept Aerospace Engring 110 Union St SE Minneapolis MN 55455-0153

JOSEPH, DONALD W. health care products executive; B in Econs., MBA, Xavier U. With Baxter Healthcare, 1966—, terr. mgr., various positions Renal divsn., pres. Renal divsn., 1981, corp. v.p., 1990, group v.p. Renal, 1993—. With USAF, Ohio Air Nat. Guard. Recipient Health Advancement award N.Y./N.J. chpt. Nat. Kidney Found. Office: Baxter Healthcare One Baxter Pkwy Deerfield IL 60015-4633

JOSEPH, JULES K. retired public relations executive; b. Cin., Jan. 18, 1927; s. Leslie Bloch and Ellen (Kaufman) J.; m. Elizabeth Levy, Sept. 9, 1948; children— Ellen Beth, Barbara Ann, John Charles. B.A. in Journalism, U. Wis., 1948. Mem. press relations staff Gimbels, Milw., 1948-52; bur. chief Fairchild Publs., 1952-60; co-founder, chmn. emeritus Zigman-Joseph-Stephenson Assocs. in Pub. Rels., 1960-94; ret., 1994. Pres. Friends of Art of Milw. Art Ctr., 1961-62; v.p. Milwaukee County Mental Health, 1967; bd. dirs. Milw. Repertory Theatre, Camp Webb, Milw. Pks. Bd., St. John's Home for the Aged, Milw., DePaul Hosp., Charles Allis Art Libr., Wis. Olympics Com.; bd. dirs. Frank Lloyd Wright Heritage Tourism Program; adv. bd. Salvation Army. Recipient Chancellor's award for outstanding contbn. to mass communication U. Wis., 1988. Mem. Pub. Rels. Soc. Am. (accredited, treas. Wis. 1970-71, bd. dirs. counselors sect. 1991-92), Soc. for Profl. Journalists, Phi Kappa Phi. Episcopalian. Home: 10610 N Magnolia Dr Mequon WI 53092-5054 Office: 735 W Wisconsin Ave Milwaukee WI 53233-2413

JOSEPH, MARILYN SUSAN, gynecologist; b. Aug. 18, 1946; BA, Smith Coll., 1968; MD cum laude, SUNY Downstate Med. Ctr., Bklyn., 1972. Diplomate Am. Bd. Ob-Gyn, Nat. Bd. Med. Examiners. Intern U. Minn. Hosps., 1972-73, resident in ob-gyn, 1972-76; med. fellow specialist U. Minn., 1972-76, asst. prof. ob-gyn, 1976—, dir. women's clinic, 1984—. Med. dir. Boynton Health Svc., 1993—. Author: Differential Diagnosis Obstetrics, 1978. Fellow Am. Coll. Ob-Gyn (best paper dist. VI meeting 1981); mem. Hennepin County Med. Soc., Minn. State Med. Assn., Mpls. Council Ob-Gyn, Minn. State Ob-Gyn Soc. Avocations: cooking, bird watching, travel. Office: Boynton Health Svc 410 Church St SE Minneapolis MN 55455-0346

JOSEPH, ROBERT THOMAS, lawyer; b. June 12, 1946; s. Joseph Alexander and Clara Barbara (Francis) J.; m. Sarah Granger, May 22, 1971; children: Paul, Timothy. AB, Xavier U., 1968; JD, U. Mich., 1971. Bar: Mich. 1971, Ill. 1976, U.S. Dist. Ct. (no. dist.) Ill. 1976, U.S. Ct. Appeals (7th cir.) 1983. Staff atty. FTC Bur. Competition, Washington, 1971-76, asst. to dir., 1972-74; atty. Sonnenschein Nath & Rosenthal, Chgo., 1976—, ptnr., 1978—. Trustee Northbrook (Ill.) Libr. Bd., 1979-89, pres., 1983-85. Recipient Disting. Svc. award FTC, 1976. Mem. ABA (chair franchising com. of antitrust law sect. 1984-87, chair videotapes com. 1987-90, chair publs. com. 1991-94, coun. 1994-97, program officer 1997-99, com. officer 1999-2000, vice-chair 2000-2001, mem. governing bd. forum on franchising), Met. Club. Roman Catholic. Office: Sonnenschein Nath Rosenthal 233 S Wacker Dr Ste 8000 Chicago IL 60606-6491

JOSLIN, RODNEY DEAN, lawyer; b. Moline, Ill., May 18, 1944; s. Melvin Seth and Dorothy Ruth (Skaggs) J.; m. Ruth Anne Moody, Aug. 21, 1965 (div. July 1985); children: Amy Brooke, Eliot Dean; m. Jeanne Nowaczewski, Nov. 30, 1985; children: Benjamin Case, Cecelia Louise. AB, Augustana Coll., 1966; JD, U. Iowa, 1969. Bar: Iowa 1969, Ill. 1969, U.S. Dist. Ct. (no. dist.) Ill. 1970, U.S. Ct. Appeals (7th cir.) 1970, U.S. Supreme Ct. 1975. Assoc. Jenner & Block, Chgo., 1970-76, ptnr., 1976—. Bd. dirs. United Cerebral Palsy Assn., Chgo., 1988—, pres., 1992—; bd. dirs. Northwestern Libr. Coun., Chgo., 1988—, Augustana Coll., 1996—; chmn. Perspectives Charter Sch., 1998—. Address: 706 WHutchinson St Chicago IL 60613-1520

JOSLIN, ROGER SCOTT, insurance company executive; b. Bloomington, Ill., June 21, 1936; s. James Clifford Joslin and Doris Virginia (McLaflin) Joslin Browning; m. Stephany Moore, June 14, 1958; children: Scott, Jill, James BS in Bus., Miami U., 1958; JD, U. Ill., 1961. Bar: Ill. 1961. Assoc. Davis, Morgan & Witherell, Peoria, Ill., 1961-63; controller Union Ins. Group, Bloomington, 1963-64; asst. v.p. State Farm Mut., 1964-69, v.p., controller, 1969-77, v.p., treas., 1977-87, sr. v.p., treas., 1989-98, vice chmn., treas., 1998—. Chmn. bd. State Farm Fire and Casualty Co.; v.p., bd. dirs. State Farm Gen. Ins. Co.; bd. dirs. State Farm Mutual; treas. State Farm County Mut. Co. Tex.; v.p., treas., bd. dirs. State Farm Lloyds, Inc., State Farm Internat. Services, Inc., State Farm Investment Mgmt. Corp., State Farm Growth Fund, Inc., State Farm Balanced Fund, Inc., State Farm Interim Fund, Inc., State Farm Mcpl Bond Fund, Inc.; bd. dirs. State Farm Life Ins. Co., State Farm Life and Accident Assurance Co., State Farm Annuity and Life Ins. Co. Mem. Bloomington Bd. Edn., 1980-91, pres., 1983-84, 85-86; trustee 2d. Presbyn. Ch., 1971-74, pres. bd. trustees, 1973-74; bd. dirs. Brokaw Hosp., 1981-84; pres. BroMenn Healthcare, 1984-86, bd. dirs., 1984-89; bd. dirs. Western Ave. Cmty. Ctr., 1979-85, pres., 1981-83; bd. overseers RAND's Inst. for Civil Justice, 1989-98; chmn. Ins. Info. Inst., 1998—; chmn. bd. trustees Neighborhood Housing Svcs. Am., 1994—, The Social Compact, 1995-98, Natural Disaster Coalition, 1997-98—. Mem. ABA, Ill. State Bar Assn., McLean County Bar Assn., Ill. Soc. C.P.A.s, Miami U. Alumni Assn. (exec. council 1971-74) Presbyterian. Home: 2001 E Cloud St Bloomington IL 61701-5733 Office: State Farm Mut Automobile Ins Co 1 State Farm Plz Bloomington IL 61710-0001

JOST, LAWRENCE JOHN, lawyer; b. Alma, Wis., Oct. 9, 1944; s. Lester J. and Hazel L. (Johnson) J.; m. Anne E. Fisher, June 10, 1967; children— Peter, Katherine, Susan B.S.C.E., U. Wis., 1968, J.D., 1969. Bar: Wis. 1969, U.S. Dist. Ct. (ea. dist.) Wis. 1969, U.S. Ct. Appeals (7th cir.) 1969, U.S. Supreme Ct. 1980. Law clk. to judge U.S. Dist. Ct., Milw., 1969-70; assoc. firm Brady, Tyrrell, Cotter & Cutler, 1970-74; assoc. Quarles & Brady, 1974-76, ptnr., 1976—, coord. real estate group, 1985—. Vis. tchr. gen. practice Wis. Law Sch. Bd. dirs., Milwaukee Chamber Theatre, 1998-2001; Pres. Vis. Nurse Assn. Milw., 1982-85, VNA, Corp., 1982-86; bd. dirs. Wis. Heritage Inc., 1980-82, Vis. Nurse Found., 1986-95, pres., 1993-94; bd. dirs. Milw. Repertory Theater, 1987-95, 2001—, pres., 1990-92; bd. dirs. United Performing Arts Fund, 1989-93. Mem. ABA, Wis. Bar Assn. (lectr. seminars), Milw. Bar Assn., Am. Coll. Real Estate Lawyers. Mem. Plymouth United Ch. of Christ Office: Quarles & Brady 411 E Wisconsin Ave Ste 2550 Milwaukee WI 53202-4497

JOYAUX, ALAIN GEORGES, art museum director; b. East Lansing, Mich., Oct. 28, 1950; s. Georges Jules and Jane (Peckham) J.; 1 child, Daniel Edgar BFA in Studio Art, Mich. State U., 1973, MFA in Studio Art, 1976, MA in Art History, 1978. Acting dir. Kresge Art Mus., Mich. State U., East Lansing, 1978; asst. dir. Flint Inst. Arts, Mich., 1978-83; dir. Ball State U. Art Gallery (name changed to Mus. of Art), Muncie, Ind., 1983—. Author exhbn. catalogues, 1981—. Mem. Am. Assn. Mus., Intermus, Conservation Assn. (bd. dirs. 1985-93). Office: Ball State U Museum of Art 2000 W University Ave Muncie IN 47306-1022 E-mail: ajoyaux@bsu.edu.

JOYCE, JOSEPH M. lawyer; BSBA, U. Minn., 1973; JD, William Mitchell Coll. Law, 1977. Bar: Minn. 1977. Legal counsel Tonka Corp., Minnetonka, Minn., 1977-81, sec., gen. counsel, 1981-87, v.p., sec., gen. counsel, 1987—. Office: Best Buy Co Inc PO Box 9312 7075 Flying Cloud Dr Eden Prairie MN 55344-3538

JOYCE, MICHAEL PATRICK, lawyer; b. Omaha, Oct. 3, 1960; s. Thomas Hunt and Joan Clare (Berigan) J. Student, Miami U., Oxford, Ohio, 1978-79; BSBA, Creighton U., 1982; JD, U. Houston, 1988. Bar: Mo., Kans., U.S. Dist. Ct. (we. dist.) Mo. 1988, U.S. Dist. Ct. Kans. 1989, U.S. Ct. Appeals (8th and 10th cirs.) 1988, U.S. Supreme Ct. 1994. Assoc. mgr. Avco Fin. Svcs. Internat., Inc., Omaha, 1983-85; assoc. Wyrsch, Atwell, Mirakian, Lee & Hobbs, P.C. (formerly Koenigsdorf & Wyrsch, P.C.), Kansas City, Mo., 1988-94; shareholder Wyrsch, Hobbs, Mirakian, & Lee, PC, 1995-97; pvt. practice, 1997-98; pres. The Joyce Law Firm, LLC, Kansas City, Mo., 1998-2000; shareholder Van Osdol, Magruder Erickson & Redmond, PC, 2000—. Adj. prof. U. Mo. Kansas City Sch. Law, 1997—. Asst. editor (newsletter State Bar Tex.) Caveat Vendor, 1987-88. Grad. NITA, 1992; bd. dirs. Creighton U., 1997-99. Mem. ABA, Nat. Assn. Criminal Def. Lawyers, Am. Health Lawyers Assn., Mo. Bar Assn., Mo. Assn. Criminal Def. Lawyers, Kans. Bar Assn., Kansas City Metro Bar Assn., Johnson County Bar Assn., Creighton U. Alumni Assn. (dir. region IV nat. alumni bd. dirs. 1994-96, pres. 1997-99), Creighton U. Alumni Club (pres. Kansas City area 1992-94). Roman Catholic. Avocations: golf, basketball, community service. Office: 2400 Commerce Tower 911 Main St Kansas City MO 64105-2009 E-mail: mpjoyce@vomer.com.

JOYCE, MICHAEL STEWART, foundation executive, political science educator; b. Cleve., July 5, 1942; s. William Michael and Anna Mae (Stewart) J.; m. Mary Jo Olsen, June 2, 1989; children from previous marriage: Mary Therese, Martin Michael B.A., Cleve. State U., 1967; Ph.D., Walden U., 1974. Intake clk. Cuyahoga County Welfare Dept., Cleve., 1961-64, unit supr., 1964-65; tchr., athletic dir. St. Adelbert Sch., Berea, Ohio, 1965-67; tchr., coach St. Edward High Sch., Lakewood, 1965-67; social sci. research assoc. Ednl. Research Council Am., Cleve., 1970-73, asst. dir. social scis., 1973-74, asst. to pres., 1974-75; instr. polit. sci. Baldwin-Wallace Coll., 1972-73; exec. dir. Morris Goldseker Found., Balt., 1975-78, Inst. for Ednl. Affairs, N.Y.C., 1978-79, John M. Olin Found., N.Y.C., 1979-85; pres. Lynde and Harry Bradley Found., Milw., 1985—, also bd. dirs. Trustee John M. Olin Found., N.Y.C., 1982-85, Pinkerton Found., N.Y.C., 1984—, Found. for Cultural Rev., N.Y.C., 1983—, Md. Acad. Scis., Balt., 1976-78, Md. Hist. Soc., Balt., 1977-78; sec. Inst. for Ednl. Affairs, Washington, 1983—; panelist NEH grant rev., Washington, 1983, 84; chmn. Philanthropy Roundtable, 1987—; mem. selection com. Clare Booth Luce Fund, 1988—; bd. dirs. Blue Cross/Blue Shield United of Wis., 1996—. Author: (textbook) Youth and the Law, 1973; contbg. editor: (8 vols. textbook series) The Human Adventure, 1971, (2 vols. textbook series) The American Adventure, 1975; contbr. articles to profl. jours. and chpts. to books Mem. Nat. Commn. Civic Renewal, Cardinal's Com. on Laity Archdiocese N.Y., 1983— ; mem. commn. Catholic Social Teaching and U.S. Economy, 1984-85; nat. co-chmn. Scholars for Reagan-Bush, 1984; mem. exec. com. Pres.'s Pvt. Sector Study Cost Control the Grace Commn., 1983—; exec. com. Caths. for Bush, 1988; mem. adv. bd. USIA for Internat. Ednl. Exchange, 1982— ; mem. Eastern Regional Selection Panel on White House Fellowships, 1983— ; asst. to chmn. Nat. Productivity Adv. Com., 1982; mem. Presdl. task force on Pvt. Sector Initiatives, 1981; mem. Presdl. transition team, 1980-81; trustee N.Y. Foundling Hosp., 1982-86, Orch. Piccola, Balt., 1976-78; mem. Nat. Commn. on Civil Renewal, 1996—; bd. dirs. Blue Cross Blue Shield, 1996—, United of Wis., 1996—. Mem. Mt. Pelerin Soc., Sovereign Mil. Order Malta, Union League Club (N.Y.C.), Milw. Club., University Club. (Milw.). Republican. Roman Catholic. Address: The Lynde and Harry Bradley Found PO Box 510860 Milwaukee WI 53203-0153

JOYCE-HAYES, DEE LEIGH, lawyer; b. Lexington, Va., Aug. 29, 1946; d. Robert Newton and Dorothy Lucille (Markham) Joyce; m. Lester Stephen Vossmeyer, Dec. 28, 1971 (div. Apr. 1984); 1 child, Robert Stephen; m. Gary Lee Hayes, Aug. 29, 1986; 1 child, Elena. BA in Govt., Coll. William and Mary, 1968; JD, St. Louis U., 1980. Bar: Mo. 1980. Spl. asst. to dep. under sec. U.S. Dept. Transp., Washington, 1970-72; rsch. analyst Lee Creative Rsch., St. Louis, 1972-74; bank officer Mark Twain Banks, 1974-77; asst. cir. atty. Cir. Atty.'s Office St. Louis, 1981-92; cir. atty. Office of Cir. Atty., St. Louis, 1993—. Bd. dirs. Children's Advocacy Svcs. St. Louis, 1990—; bd. dirs. Backstoppers, St. Louis, 1994—; pres., 1996-97; gubernatorial appointee Mo. Sentencing Advs. Commn., 1995—; co-chmn. Operation Weed and Seed, St. Louis, 1994—; mem. disciplinary com. 22d Cir. Bar Com., St. Louis, 1992—; adj. prof. law Wash. U., 1997—. Bd. dirs. The Backstoppers, St. Louis, 1993—, pres. bd., 1996; mem. exec. com. Regional Violence Prevention Initiative, Mo. and Western Ill., 1994—; mem. nat. and St. Louis chpt. Women's Polit. Caucus; mem. com. on missions and social concerns Grace United Meth. Ch., St. Louis, 1988—. Mem. ACLU, Nat. Dist. Atty. Assn., Mo. Assn. Prosecuting Atty. (treas. 1996-97, v.p. 1997-98), Met. St. Louis Bar Assn., Mound City Bar Assn., Kappa Alpha Theta. Democrat. Avocations: gardening, travel, scuba diving, cooking, reading. Office: St Louis Cir Atty 1320 Market St Rm 330 Saint Louis MO 63103-2774

JUAREZ, MARTIN, priest; b. Kansas City, Kans., Mar. 23, 1946; s. Martin Huerta and Hermelinda (Rocha) J. AS, Colby Community Coll., 1971; BA in sociology, U. Mo., Kansas City, 1974; MDiv, St. Thomas Sem., Denver, 1985; cert. in Hispanic ministry, Oblate Sch. of Theology, San Antonio, 1991, Mexican-Am. Cultural Ctr., 1991. Priest Archdiocese of Kansas City, Kans., 1981—. Bd. dirs. Pioneer Village, Topeka, 1983-88; co-dir. El Centro, Topeka, 1989. Mem. Kans. Registered Animal Hosp. Techs. Assn., N.Am. Veterinary Tech. Assn., U. Mo. Alumni Assn., KC. Office: PO Box 410695 Kansas City MO 64141-0695

JUDD, WILLIAM ROBERT, engineering geologist, educator; b. Denver, Aug. 16, 1917; s. Samuel and Lillian (Israelske) J.; m. Rachel Elizabeth Douglas, Apr. 18, 1942; children: Stephanie (Mrs. Chris Wadley), Judith (Mrs. John Soden), Dayna (Mrs. Erick Grandmason), Pamela, Connie. A.B., U. Colo., 1941, postgrad., 1941-50. Registered profl. engr., Colo., engrng. geologist, Oreg. Engrng. geologist Colo. Water Conservation Bd., 1941-42; supervisory engrng. geologist Denver & Rio Grande Western R.R., Colo. and Utah, 1942-44; head geology sect. No. 1, acting dist. geologist-Alaska U.S. Bur. Reclamation, Office of Chief Engr., Denver, 1945-60; head basing tech. group RAND Corp., Santa Monica, Calif., 1960-65; prof. rock mechanics Purdue U., Lafayette, Ind., 1966-87, head geotech. engrng., 1976-86; tech. dir. Purdue U. Underground Excavation and Rock Properties Info. Center, 1972-79, prof. emeritus civil engrng., 1988—. Geotech. cons., U.S., Mexico, Cuba, Honduras, Greece, 1950— ; geoscience editor Am. Elsevier Pub. Co., 1967-71; chmn. panel on ocean scis. Com. on Instl. Cooperation, 1971-85; founder and chmn. Nat. Acad. Sci. U.S. Nat. Com. on Rock Mechanics, 1963-69, co-chmn. panel on research requirements, 1977-81, chmn. panel on awards, 1972-82; mem. U.S. Army Adv. Bd. on Mountain and Arctic Warfare, 1956-62, USAF Sci. Adv. Bd. Geophysics Panel Study Group, 1964-67; mem. com. on safety dams NRC, 1977-78, 82-83; Nat. dir. Nat. Ski Patrol System, Inc., 1956-62; Alex du Toit Meml. lectr., S.Africa and Rhodesia , 1967; owner Rayanbill Galleries, 1986—. Author: (with E.F. Taylor) Ski Patrol Manual, 1956, (with D. Krynine) Principles of Engineering Geology and Geotechnics, 1957, Sitzmarks or Safety, 1960; editor: Rock Mechanics research, 1966, State of Stress in the Earth's crust, 1964; co-editor: Physical Properties of Rocks and Minerals, 1981; editor-in-chief: Engrng. Geology, 1972-92, hon. editor, 1996—. Recipient Spl. Rsch. award NRC, 1982; named to Colo. Ski Hall of Fame, 1983; named hon. life mem. Nat. Ski Patrol System, Inc., 1988. Fellow ASCE, Geol. Soc. Am. (Disting. Practice award engrng. geology divsn. 1989), South African Inst. Mining and Metallurgy; mem. Assn. Engrng. Geologists (hon. 1990), Internat. Assn. Engrng. Geologists (Hans Cloos medal 1994), Ind. Soc. Engrng. Geology (life), U.S. Com. on Large Dams (exec. coun. 1977-83, com. on earthquakes 1976-90), U.S. Ski Assn. (hon. life), U.S. Recreational Ski Assn. (hon. life). Home and Office: 10 Elder Ct Lafayette IN 47905-3921

JUDGE, BERNARD MARTIN, editor, publisher; b. Chgo., Jan. 6, 1940; s. Bernard A. and Catherine Elizabeth (Halloran) J.; m. Kimbeth A. Wehrli, July 9, 1966; children: Kelly, Bernard R., Jessica. Reporter City News Bur., Chgo., 1965-66; reporter Chgo. Tribune, 1966-70, city editor, 1974-79, asst. mng. editor met. news, 1979-83; editor, gen. mgr. City News Bur. Chgo., 1983-84; assoc. editor Chgo. Sun-Times, 1984-88; from editor to pub. Chgo. Daily Law Bull., 1988—; pub. Chgo. Lawyer, 1989—; v.p. Law Bull. Pub. Co., Chgo., 1988—. Bd. dirs. Constnl. Rights Found., Chgo., 1992—, chmn. bd. dirs., 1995-97; trustee Fenwick Cath. Prep. H.S., Oak Park, Ill., 1989—. Named to Chgo. Journalism Hall of Fame, 2000. Mem. Sigma Delta Chi. Home: 360 E Randolph St Apt 1905 Chicago IL 60601-7335 Office: Law Bull Pub Co 415 N State St Chicago IL 60610-4631

JUDGE, JOHN, state legislator; m. Patty Judge, 1969; 3 children: Douglas, William Joseph. Farmer, cattleman; mem. Iowa Senate, Des Moines, 1999—, mem. agr. com., mem. local govt. com., mem. small bus., econ. devel. and tourism com., mem. transp. com. With USMC, Vietnam. Democrat. Office: State Capitol 9th And Grand Des Moines IA 50319-0001 E-mail: john_judge@legis.state.ia.us.

JUDGE, NANCY ELIZABETH, obstetrician, gynecologist; b. Holyoke, Mass., May 21, 1951; d. Martin P. and Barbara Judge; m. David B. Wood, Oct. 30, 1982; children: David, William, Elizabeth, Meredith. AB, Smith Coll., 1973; MD, U. Mass., 1977. Intern Case Western Res. U./MetroHealth Med. Ctr., Cleve., 1977-78, resident, 1978-81; staff physician MetroHealth Med. Ctr. Case Western Res. U. Hosps., 1981-90; dir. reproductive imaging ctr. Case Western Res. U. Hosps., 1990—, maternal-fetal medicine cons., 1990—. Asst. prof. reproductive biology Case Western Res. U., 1981—. Contbr. articles to profl. jours. Active Cleve. Art Mus., Playhouse Sq. Assn., Cleve. Garden Ctr. Fellow ACOG; mem. Cleve. Ob.-Gyn. Soc. (pres.).

JUENEMANN, SISTER JEAN, hospital executive; b. St. Cloud, Minn., Nov. 19, 1936; d. Leo A. and Teresa M. (Oster) J. Diploma, St. Cloud Sch. Nursing, 1957; student, Coll. St. Benedict, 1957-59; BSN cum laude, Seattle U., 1967; MHA, U. Minn., 1977. Dir. nursing svc. Queen of Peace Hosp., New Prague, Minn., 1963-65, 67-77, asst. adminstr., 1967-77, CEO, 1977—. Mem. bd. Bush Med. Fellows Program; spkr. at confs. Chmn. Cmty. Com. Prevention Chem. Abuse, New Prague, 1975-80; bd. dirs. St. Cloud (Minn.) Hosp., St. Benedict's Coll., St. Joseph, Minn. Recipient Disting. Svc. award Minn. Hosp. & Health Assn., 1996; Bush Found. Summer fellow Cornell U., U. Calif., Berkeley, 1982. Fellow Am. Coll. Healthcare Execs.; mem. AAUW (past pres. New Prague chpt.), Am. Hosp. Assn. (CEO of Yr. 1989), Soc. Health Care Planning & Mktg., Cath. Hosp. Assn., Women's Health Leadership Trust, New Prague Opportunities, Rotary (pres. New Prague chpt. 1994-95, asst. gov. dist. 1998-99), Sigma Theta Tau. Fax: (612) 758-5009. E-mail: Sjean@qofp.org.

JUERGENS, GEORGE IVAR, history educator; b. Bklyn., Mar. 20, 1932; s. George Odegaard and Magnhild (Julin) J.; m. Bonnie Jeanne Brownlee; children: Steven Erik, Paul Magnus. BA, Columbia Coll., 1953; BA, MA, Oxford U., 1956; PhD, Columbia U., 1965. Instr. Dartmouth Coll., Hanover, N.H., 1962-65; asst. prof. Amherst (Mass.) Coll., 1965-67; assoc. prof. Ind. U., Bloomington, 1967-80, prof. history, 1980—. Cons. Nat. Endowment Humanities, Washington, 1971— Author: Joseph Pulitzer and the New York World, 1966, News From The White House, 1981; assoc. editor: Jour. Am. History, 1968-69. With U.S. Army, 1956-58. Recipient Disting. Teaching award Amoco Found., 1982; Kellett fellow Columbia U., 1954-56; sr. faculty fellow Nat. Endowment Humanities, 1971-72; fellow Rockefeller Found., 1981-82 Mem. AAUP, Orgn. Am. Historians, Phi Beta Kappa Home: 2111 E Meadow Bluff Ct Bloomington IN 47401-6885 Office: Ind U Dept History Bloomington IN 47405 E-mail: juergens@indiana.edu.

JUGENHEIMER, DONALD WAYNE, advertising and communications educator, university administrator; b. Manhattan, Kans., Sept. 22, 1943; s. Robert William and Mabel Clara (Hobert) J.; m. Bonnie Jeanne Scamehorn, Aug. 30, 1970 (dec. 1983); 1 child, Beth Carrie; m. Kaleen B. Brown, July 25, 1987. BS in Advt., U. Ill.-Urbana, 1965, MS in Advt., 1968, PhD in Communications, 1972. Advt. copywriter Fillman & Assocs, Champaign, Ill., 1963-64, 66; media buyer Leo Burnett Co., Chgo., 1965-66; asst., assoc. prof. U. Kans., Lawrence, 1971-80, prof. jounralism, dir. grad. studies and rsch., 1980-85; Manship prof. journalism La. State U., Baton Rouge, 1985-87; prof., chmn. dept. communications and speech Fairleigh Dickinson U., Teaneck, N.J., 1987-89, 92-95, dean coll. liberal arts, 1989-92; chair dept. English, lang. and philosphy, 1995; prof., dir. Sch. Journalism So. Ill. U., Carbondale, 1995—. Adj. faculty Turku (Finland) Sch. Econs., 1999—; adv. cons. U.S. Army, Fort Sheridan, Ill., Pentagon, Washington, 1981-90, Am. Airlines, 1989-91, IBM Corp., 1989—, U.S. Dept. Def.; cons. editor Grid Publ., Columbus, Ohio, 1974-84; grad. and rsch. dir. U. Kans., 1978-84, adv. chmn., 1974-78; adj. prof. Turku (Finland) Sch. Econs. and Bus. Adminstrn., 1998—. Author: Advertising Media Sourcebook and Workbook, 1975, 3d edit., 1989, 4th edit. 1996, Strategic Advertising Decisions, 1976, Basic Advertising, 1979, 2d edit., 1991, Advertising Media, 1980, Problems and Practices in Advertising Research, 1982, Advertising Media: Strategy and Tactics, 1992; bd. editors Jour. Advt., 1985-89. Subscription mgr. Jour. of Advt., 1971-74, bus. mgr., 1974-79; chmn. U. Div. United Fund, Lawrence, 1971-72; pres. Sch.-Community Relations Council, Lawrence, 1974-75 Recipient Hope Teaching award U. Kans, 1977, 78 Kellogg Nat. fellow W.K. Kellogg Found., 1984-88; named Outstanding Young Men in Am. Nat. Jaycees, 1978 Mem. AAUP, Am. Acad. Advt. (pres. 1984-86), Assn. For Edn. in Journalism (head advertising div. 1977-78), Kappa Tau Alpha, Alpha Delta Sigma. Presbyterian Avocations: skiing; sailing; writing; travel; reading. Home: 110 Tecumseh Dr Carbondale IL 62901-7113 Office: So Ill U Sch Journalism Carbondale IL 62901-6601

JUHL, DANIEL LEO, manufacturing and marketing firm executive; b. Sioux City, Iowa, Aug. 18, 1935; s. Burnett Andrew and Margret Anne (Osinger) J.; m. Colleen Ann Eagan, Dec. 20, 1958; children: Gregory, Michael, Jennifer. Student, U. S.D., 1956; BSME, UCLA, 1959; postgrad., Harvard U., 1976. Design engr. Edler Industries, Newport Beach, Calif., 1959-61; v.p. mfg. Raybestos-Manhattan Corp. (now Rayteck Corp.), Trumbull, Conn., Can. and Europe, 1961-80; v.p. ops. Easco/KD Tools, Lancaster, Pa., 1980-83; mgr. ops. S.K. Wellman Corp., Bedford Heights, Ohio, 1983-86; gen. mgr. N.Am. Systems, 1986; indsl. mgmt. cons., 1987; pres., chief exec. officer Stanhope Products Co., Brookville, Ohio, 1987-2000, Nat. Extrusions Co., Bellefontaine, 1987—, Nathan Hale Furniture Co., 1987-2000; pres., CEO DJ Ventures Inc., Centerville, Ohio, 2000—. Contbr. numerous articles to trade jours.; patentee high temperature lightweight plastic insulation, molecular sieve used in auto air conditioning. Fund raiser United Way, 1980-2000. Recipient Disting. Alumni award UCLA, 1991. Mem. Soc. Automotive Engrs. (chmn. com. 1987), Soc. Plastics Industry, Elks. Avocations: travel, sports, woodworking.

JULIEN, THOMAS THEODORE, religious denomination administrator; b. Arcanum, Ohio, June 27, 1931; s. Russel Ray and Clara (Cassel) J.; m. Doris Mardella Briner, Aug. 21, 1953; children: Becky Jean, Terry Lee, Jacqueline Sue. BA, Bob Jones U., 1953; MDiv, Grace Theol. Sem., Winona Lake, Ind., 1957, DD (hon.), 1996; cert. French lang., U. Grenoble, France, 1960. Ordained to ministry Fellowship of Grace Brethren Chs., 1956. Pastor Grace Brethren Ch., Ft. Wayne, Ind., 1955-58; missionary Grace Brethren Fgn. Missions, Grenoble, 1959-64, field supt. Macon, France, 1964-78, dir. for Europe France, 1964-86; exec. dir. Grace Brethren Internat. Missions, Winona Lake, 1986-2000, spl. assignment Paris, 2000—. Author: Handbook for Young Christians, 1959, Inherited Wealth, 1976, Spiritual Greatness, 1979, Seize the Moment, 2000. Decorated chevalier de Republique (Ctrl. African Republic). Home: 545 S Circle Dr Warsaw IN 46580 Office: Grace Brethren Internat Missions PO Box 588 Winona Lake IN 46590-0588 E-mail: tomjulien@compuserve.com.

JULIUS, STEVO, physician, educator, physiologist; b. Kovin, Yugoslavia, Apr. 15, 1929; came to U.S., 1965, naturalized, 1971; s. Dezider and Jelena (Engel) J.; m. Susan P. Durrant, Sept. 17, 1971; children: Nicholas, Natasha. MD, U. Zagreb, 1953, ScD, 1964; MD (hon.), U. Goteborg, Sweden, 1979. Intern, then resident in internal medicine Univ. Hosp., Zagreb, 1953-60, sr. instr. internal medicine, 1962-64; rsch. asst. U. Mich. Med. Sch., 1961-62, mem. faculty, 1965—, prof. internal medicine, 1974—, assoc. prof. physiology, 1980-83, prof. physiology, 1983-98, chief divsn. hypertension, 1974-99, Frederick G.L. Huetwell prof. hypertension, 1996—. Co-editor: The Nervous System in Arterial Hypertension, 1976; contbr. articles to med. jours. Fellow Am. Coll. Cardiology; mem. Internat. Soc. Hypertension (v.p., Astra award 1984), Interam. Soc. Hypertension (treas. 1978-83), Am. Heart Assn. (couns. high blood pressure rsch. and epidemiology, life achievement award coun. for high blood pressure 1994), Am. Physiol. Soc. (adv. bd.), Am. Fedn. Clin. Rsch., Soc. Exptl. Biology and Medicine, Coun. for High Blood Pressure Rsch. (adv. bd.). Office: Univ Mich Med Sch Div Hypertension 3918 Taubman Ctr Ann Arbor MI 48109-0356

JUNEWICZ, JAMES J. lawyer; b. Oct. 1, 1950; s. John and Genevieve J.; m. Virginia Bornyas. BS, Georgetown U., 1972; JD, Duquesne U., 1976; LLM, NYU, 1978. Bar: Pa. 1977, D.C. 1978, Ill. 1984. Asst. gen. counsel SEC, Washington, 1982—84; ptnr. Mayer, Brown, Rowe & Maw, Chgo., 1987—. Office: Mayer Brown Rowe & Maw 190 S La Salle St Ste 3900 Chicago IL 60603-3410

JUNG, HOWARD J. retail executive; Chmn. Ace Hardware Corp., Oak Brook, Ill. Office: Ace Hardware Corp 2200 Kensington Ct Oak Brook IL 60523

JUNGE, MICHAEL KEITH, lawyer; b. Fargo, N.D., June 17, 1956; s. Herman Keith Jr. and Helen Beatrice (Perschke) J.; m. Ember Reighgott, Oct. 23, 1993. BA, St. Olaf Coll., 1978; JD, William Mitchell Coll., 1982. Bar: U.S. Dist. Ct. Minn. 1986. Asst. atty. McLeod County, Glencoe, Minn., 1982-87, county atty., 1987—. Instr. St. Olaf Coll., Northfield, Minn., 1993. Mem. Minn. County Atty. Assn. (treas. 1994-95), 8th Dist. Bar Assn. (pres. 1993-94). Office: McLeod County Atty 830 11th St E Ste 214 Glencoe MN 55336-2200

JURA, JAMES J. electric utility executive; b. Creston, Nebr., Dec. 9, 1942; s. Joseph James and Edna Helena (Mackenstadt) J.; children: Joseph, James, John, Fredericka. BA, U. Wash., Seattle, 1967; MBA, Seattle U., 1971; postgrad., Harvard U., 1985. With indsl. rels. staff Boeing Co., Seattle, 1968-71; with policy devel. staff OSHA, Washington, 1971-73; legis. and budget analyst Office Mgmt. and Budget, 1973-78; asst. adminstr. Bonneville Power Adminstrn., U.S. Dept. Energy, 1978-80, from exec. asst. adminstr. to adminstr. Portland, Oreg., 1980-91; CEO, gen. mgr. Assoc. Electric Coop. Inc., Springfield, Mo., 1991—. Bd. dirs. Assn. Mo. Elec. Coops., Mo. Employees Mut. Ins. Co. With U.S. Army, 1963-65. Republican. Office: Associated Electric Coop PO Box 754 Springfield MO 65801-0754

JURGENSEN, W.G. insurance company executive; BSBA, MBA, Creighton U. Corp. banking officer thru exec. v.p. corp. banking Northwest Investment Svcs.; mgmt. First Chicago NBD Corp.; exec. v.p. Bank One Corp.; CEO Nationwide Ins. Office: Nationwide Ins 1 Nationwide Plz Columbus OH 43215

JUST, DAVID GLEN, savings and loan association executive; b. Oskaloosa, Iowa, Feb. 10, 1944; s. Alvin E. and Ada L. (Hasty) J.; m. Barbara Ann Mahan; children: Michelle M. Just Grady, David G., Heather L. Just Jenkins. Dipl., Am. Inst. of Bus., Des Moines, 1963. CPA, Iowa. Acct. Daniel Gardiner, CPA, Des Moines, 1967-70, Alexander Grant & Co., Des Moines, 1970-71; account mgr. Fed. Home Loan Bank, 1971-77; pres. The Cameron Savs. & Loan Assn., Cameron, Mo., 1977—; Pres & CEO Cameron Fin. and Cameron Savs. Cameron Fin. Corporation, MO. V.p., dir. Del Lago Resort and Conf. Ctr., Montgomery, Tex., 1990—. Treas. Cameron Econ. Devel. Corp., 1990—, Com. to Promote Cameron, 1986-90. With USAF, 1963-67; bd. dirs. Cameron Community Hosp., 1983—; pres. Prince of Peace Luth. Ch., 1978-84, 1990—. Mem. Mo. League of Savs. Instns. (dir. 1988-90), Lions (pres., dir.). Democrat. Lutheran. Avocations: golf, hobby farming. Office: Cameron Fin. Corporation 1304 N Walnut St Cameron MO 64429-1327

JUSTEN, RALPH, museum director; b. Milw., Mar. 10, 1952; Exec. dir. Nat. R.R. Mus., Green Bay, Wis., 1997—. Office: Nat RR Mus 2285 S Broadway Green Bay WI 54304-4832 E-mail: rjjusten@nationalrrmuseum.org.

JUSTICE, BRADY RICHMOND, JR. medical services executive; b. Albertville, Ala., Dec. 26, 1930; s. Brady R. and Kate (McEachern) J.; m. Sandra Gearner, Dec. 29, 1956; children: David, Michael, Lori Blankenship, Kathryn Baker. BBA, Baylor U., 1953. CPA, Ind. Ptnr. Arthur Andersen & Co., Dallas, 1953-64, Indpls., 1964-72; exec. v.p. Basic Am. Industries, Inc., 1972-83; pres. Basic Am. Med., Inc., 1983-92; sr. v.p. Columbia Hosp. Corp., 1992-93; chmn. Heritage Capital Corp., Indpls., 1993—. Mem. Columbia Club, Lions (pres. Indpls. chpt.). Republican. Baptist. Home: 8037 Clymer Ln Indianapolis IN 46250-4236 Office: Heritage Capital Corp 6900 Gray Rd Indianapolis IN 46237-3209

KABARA, JON JOSEPH, biochemical pharmacology educator; b. Chgo., Nov. 26, 1926; s. John Stanley and Mary Elizabeth (Wielgus) K.; m. Virginia Christie (dec. 1974); children: Christie Anne, Mary K., Sheila Jon, Pat Lee; m. Annette Elser Sproull (dec. 1986), children: Timothy, Steven; m. Betty Z. Tabor, 1992. B.S., St. Mary's Coll., Minn., 1948; M.S., U. Miami, 1950; Ph.D. (Univ. scholar), U. Chgo., 1959. Prof. chemistry U. Detroit, 1957-68; prof., assoc. dean Mich. Coll. Osteo. Medicine, Pontiac, 1967-70; prof. assoc. dean pharmacology Mich. State U., E. Lansing, 1970-71, prof. biomechanics, 1971-89, prof. emeritus, 1989; dir. research and devel. Med.-Chem. Labs., Galena, Ill., 1950—, Kabe Realtor, 1986—; pres. div. research and devel. Galena's Kitchen Chemist, 1989—, Tech. Exch. Inc., 1989; co-owner, pres., dir. R&D Lil Gen. Miniature Golf Course, Galena, Ill., 1996—. Cons. in neurochemistry and microbiology. Contbr. over 200 articles to profl. jours.; editor: Cosmetic Preservation Preservative-Free Cosmetic & Drug Formulations and Korkies Cookbook, other books on lipid pharmacology; U.S. and fgn. patentee in field. Pres. Mich. NE PTA, 1959; active Little League, 1973-75. Damon Runyon Cancer fellow, 1949-50; Mt. Sinai fellow, 1949-51; Bishop Heffron awardee St. Mary's Coll., 1970; named Man of Year St. George High Sch. Alumni Club, 1970; recipient Disting. Alumni award 50th Anniversary, St. Mary's U., Minn., 1998. Fellow Am. Inst. Chemists; mem. Am. Oil Chem. Soc., N.Y. Acad. Sci., Detroit Physiology Soc., Assn. Analytical Chemists, AAAS, Am. Soc. Clin. Pathologists, Sigma Xi, other orgns. Home (Winter): 4350 Chatham Dr Longboat Key FL 34228-2342 E-mail: jonkab@aol.com.

KABAT, LINDA GEORGETTE, civic leader; b. Cleve., Nov. 26, 1951; d. Michael G. and Georgette (deVos) Paul; m. John Edward Kabat Jr., Apr. 23, 1977; 1 child, Susan Marie. Student, Cleve. Inst. Music, 1969-72. With sales dept. Higbee Co., Fairview Park, Ohio, 1972; customer svc. rep. Ashland Chem. Co., Cleve., 1972-74, Celanese Corp., Lakewood, Ohio, 1974-76; with sales dept. May Co., North Olmsted, 1979; customer svc. rep. Diamond Shamrock Corp., Cleve., 1979-82; in sales May Co., North Olmsted, 1989-97; with Concepts Direct, Longmont, Colo., 1999—. Chpt. pres. Cath. War Vets. Aux., Cleve., 1973-75, pres. Ohio, 1975-77, nat. sec., 1977-79, state sec., 1991-92. Mem. Mu Phi Epsilon (pres. 1971-72, historian 1970-71). Republican. Avocations: camping, traveling, needlework, music.

KACEK, DON J. management consultant; b. Berwyn, Ill., May 4, 1936; s. George J. and Rose (Krizik) K.m. Carolyn K. Hiner, July 22, 1961; children: Scott M., Stacey M. BSME, Ill. Inst. Tech., 1958. Engrng. sect. mgr. Sunstrand Corp., Rockford, Ill., 1958-72; group v.p. Kysor Indsl. Corp., Cadillac, Mich., 1972-76; dir. product devel. Ransburg Corp., Indpls., 1976-77, pres., 1977-88, CEO, chmn. bd. dirs., 1978-88; mgmt. cons., 1988—; owner, chmn. bd. dirs. Advanced Automation Techs., Inc., 1989-2000. Bd. dirs. Arvin Meritor Industries, Inc., Troy, Mich. Inventor Burn Rate Control Valve, 1966. With AUS, 1960. Recipient Sagamore of the Wabash award Gov. Ind., 1985.

KACKLEY, JAMES R. former financial services executive; b. Hammond, Ind. m. Barbe Kackley; children: Shannon, John. Grad., Northwestern U., 1964. Ptnr. Arthur Andersen & Co., Chgo., mng. ptnr.; mng. ptnr. fin. adminstrn. Andersen Worldwide, 1998-99. Bd. dirs. Chgo. Urban League, Cities in Schs., Adler Planetarium, Pres.'s Coun. for Mus. of Sci. and Industry; co-chmn. exec. coun. Inst. for Ill.; prin. Chgo. United; chmn. west div. campaign United Way, 1990; mem. adv. coun. Chgo. area coun. Boy Scouts Am.; chmn. fin. com. Winnetka Bible Ch. Mem. Mid-Am. Com., Nat. Strategy Forum, Attic Club, Chgo. Club, Econ. Club, , Indian Hill Club, Kenilworth Club, Univ. Club. Office: Andersen Worldwide 225 N Michigan Ave Fl 16 Chicago IL 60601-7600

KACZKA, JEFF, trucking/relocation services executive; CFO Allied Worldwide, Naperville, Ill., 1999—. Office: Allied Worldwide 215 W Diehl Rd Naperville IL 60563 Office Fax: (630) 717-4761.

KACZMARCZYK, JEFFREY ALLEN, journalist, classical music critic; b. Patuxent River Naval Air Base, Md., Jan. 7, 1963; s. Frank Joseph and Diane Catherine Kaczmarczyk; m. Cynthia L. Shimmel, Aug. 13, 1988; children: Jessica, Michael, David. BA, Western Mich. U., 1986; postgrad., Calif. State U. Editor-in-chief Western Herald, Kalamazoo, 1986-87; staff writer, acting editor Albion (Mich.) Recorder, 1987; staff writer, columnist Hastings (Mich.) Banner, 1987-92; arts writer, classical music critic The Grand Rapids (Mich.) Press., 1992—. Freelance arts writer, critic Kalamazoo (Mich.) Gazette, 1990-93; editor The Weekender, Hastings, 1991-93. Dir., sec. Thornapple Arts Coun., Hastings, 1992-97; dir. Grand Rapids Area Coun. for Humanities, 1995-2001; vestryman Emmanuel Episcopal Ch., Hastings, 1997-99, sr. warden, 1999. Episcopalian. Home: 314 S Park St Hastings MI 49058-1635 Office: The Grand Rapids Press 155 Michigan St NW Grand Rapids MI 49503-2353

KADANOFF, LEO PHILIP, physicist, educator; b. N.Y.C., Jan. 14, 1937; s. Abraham and Celia (Kibrick) Kadanoff; children: Marcia, Felice, Betsy. AB, Harvard U., 1957, MA, 1958, PhD, 1960. Fellow Neils Bohr Inst., Copenhagen, 1960—61; from asst. prof. to prof. physics U. Ill., Urbana, 1961—69; prof. physics and engrng., univ. prof. Brown U., Providence, 1969—78; prof. physics U. Chgo., 1978—82, John D. MacArthur Disting. Service prof., 1982—. Mem. tech. com. R.I. Planning Program, 1972—78, mem. human svcs. rev. com., 1977—78; pres. Urban Obs. R.I., 1972—78. Author: Electricity Magnetism and Heat, 1967; co-author: Quantum Statistical Mechanics, 1963; adv. bd. Sci. Year, 1975—79, editl. bd. Statis. Physics, 1972—79, Nuc. Physics, 1980—. Recipient Wolf Found. prize, 1980, Boltzmann medal, Internat. Union Pure and Applied Physics, 1990, Grande Medaille d'Or, Acad. Scis. Inst. France, 1998, Nat. med. Sci., 1999; fellow NSF, 1957—61, Sloan Found., 1963—67. Fellow: Am. Acad. Arts and Scis., Am. Phys. Soc. (Buckley prize 1977, Onsager prize 1998); mem.: NAS. Home: 5421 S Cornell Ave Apt 15 Chicago IL 60615-5678 Office: U Chgo James Franck Inst 5640 S Ellis Ave Chicago IL 60637-1433

KAESBERG, PAUL JOSEPH, virology researcher; b. Engers, Germany, Sept. 26, 1923; came to U.S., 1926, naturalized, 1933; s. Peter Ernst and Gertrude (Mueller) K.; m. Marian Lavon Hanneman, June 13, 1953; children— Paul Richard, James Kevin, Peter Roy. B.S. in Engrng, U. Wis., Madison, 1945, Ph.D. in Physics, 1949; D. Natural Scis. (hon.), U. Leiden, The Netherlands, 1975. Instr. biometry and physics U. Wis., 1949-51, asst. prof. biochemistry, 1956-58, assoc. prof., 1958-60, prof., 1960-63, prof. biophysics and biochemistry, 1963—, Beeman prof. biophysics and biochemistry, 1983-87, chmn. Biophysics Lab., 1970-88, Wis. Alumni Research Found. prof., 1981—, Beeman prof. molecular virology and biochemistry, 1987-90, prof. emeritus, 1990. Cons. in field. Contbr. chapts. to books and articles to profl. jours. Mem. NAS, Am. Soc. Virology (pres. 1987-88). Home: 5002 Bayfield Ter Madison WI 53705-4811 Office: U Wis Inst Molecular Virology 1525 Linden Dr Madison WI 53706-1534 E-mail: pjkaes@aol.com.

KAFARSKI, MITCHELL I. chemical processing company executive; b. Detroit, Dec. 15, 1917; s. Ignacy A. and Anastasia (Drzazgowski) K.; m. Zofia Drozdowska, July 11, 1967; children: Erik Michael, Konrad Christian. Student, U. Detroit, 1939-41, Shrivenham (Eng.) Am. U., 1946. Process engr. Packard Motor Car Co., Detroit, 1941-44; organizer, dir. Artist and Craftsman Sch., Esslingen, Germany, 1945-46; with Nat. Bank of Detroit, 1946-50; founder, pres. Chem. Processing Inc., Detroit, 1950-65, also bd. dirs.; chmn. bd., pres., treas. Aactron Inc., Madison Heights, Mich., 1965—; chmn. bd., pres. Imtech of Mich., Inc., 1988-92. Treas. Detroit Magnetic Insp. Co., 1960-65; also dir.; v.p. KMH Inc., Detroit, 1960-64; also dir.; treas. Packard Plating Inc., Detroit, 1962-67, also dir. Commr. Mich. State Fair, 1965-72; mem. com. devel. and planning to build Municipal Stadium State of Mich., 1965-88; benefactor, mem. Founders Soc., Detroit Inst. Arts, 1965— ; trustee Founders' Soc., Detroit Inst. Arts, 1982-90; sponsor, host world celebrity for World Preview Mich., 1965-66; mem. dist. adv. council SBA, 1971-73; del. White House Conf. on Aging, 1971; organizer, treas. Mich. Reagan for Pres. Com., 1980; treas. Straith Meml. Hosp., Southfield, Mich., 1972— , chmn. bd., 1976; trustee Mich. Opera Theater, 1982— ; bd. dirs. Gilbert and Sullivan Light Opera Soc., Palm Beach, Fla., 1985— ; White House rep. to opening of first U.S. Trade Center, Warsaw, Poland, 1972; chmn. fund-raising Bloomfield Arts Assn., Birmingham, Mich., 1973-74; mem. Space Theatre Consortium, Inc., Seattle, 1981-83; bd. regents Orchard Lake (Mich.) Schs., 1981-83; Vice chmn. Republican State Nationalities Council Mich., 1969-73; bd. dirs. Bloomfield Arts Assn., 1973-84, Friends of Kresge Library, Oakland U., 1973-86; presdl. appointee bd. dirs. U.S.A. Pennsylvania Ave. Devel. Corp., Washington, 1973-81; chmn. bd. Straith Meml. Hosp., Detroit, 1971— , Detroit Sci. Center, 1972— , corp. dir.; mem. Internat. Soc. Palm Beach; trustee Greater Palm Beach Symphony, 1986; mem. Citizen's Commn. to Improve Mich. Cts., 1986-88; contbr. Kravis Ctr. for Performing Arts, West Palm Beach, 1989; mem. Bus. Com. for the Arts, Palm Beacvh, 1991—. Served with AUS, 1944-46, ETO. Recipient Nat. award for war prodn. invention War Prodn. Bd., 1943; decorated knight's Cross Order of Poland's Rebirth Restituta, 1975, chevalier Chaine des Rotisseurs, 1982, Knight of Malta Order of St. John. Mem. Nat. Assn. Metal Finishers, Mich. Assn. Metal Finishers (dir., chmn. bd. 1976), N.A.M., Am. Electroplaters Soc., Cranbrook Acad. Arts, Am.-Polish Action Coun. (chmn. 1971-76), Am. Assn. Mus. (treas. Detroit), Poinciana Club, Village Club. Clubs: Capitol Hill (Washington); Detroit Athletic. Home: 21 Kingsley Manor Ct Bloomfield Hills MI 48304-3520 Office: Aactron Inc 29306 Stephenson Hwy Madison Heights MI 48071-2394

KAFOURE, MICHAEL D. food products executive; BS in Mgmt. and Adminstrn., Ind. U. Pres., COO U.S. baking ops. Interstate Bakeries Corp., Kansas City, Mo.; pres. Merico, Inc., St. Louis. Office: Interstate Bakeries Corp 12 E Armour Blvd Kansas City MO 64111

KAGAN, SIOMA, economics educator; b. Riga, Russia, Sept. 29, 1907; came to U.S., 1941, naturalized, 1950; s. Jacques and Berta (Kaplan) K.; m. Jean Batt, Apr. 5, 1947 (div. 1969). Diplom Ingenieur, Technische Hochschule, Berlin, 1931; M.A., Am. U., 1949; Ph.D. in Econs, Columbia U., 1954. Sci. asst. Heinrich Hertz Inst., Berlin, 1931-33; partner Laboratoire Electro-Acoustique, Neuilly-sur-Seine, France, 1933-48; chief French Mission Telecom. French Supply Council in N.Am., Washington, 1943-45; mem. telecom. bd. UN, 1946-47, econ. affairs officer, 1947-48; econs. cons. to govt. and industry; asso. prof. econs. Washington U., St. Louis, 1956-59; staff economist Joint Council Econ. Edn., N.Y.C., 1959-60; prof. internat. bus. U. Oreg., Eugene, 1960- 67, U. Mo., St. Louis, 1967-87, prof. emeritus, 1987—. Faculty leader exec. devel. programs Columbia, Northwestern U., NATO Def. Coll., Rome, others. Contbr. numerous articles profl. publs. Served with Free French Army, 1941-43. Decorated Legion of Honor (France). Recipient Thomas Jefferson award U. Mo., 1984 Fellow Latin Am. Studies Assn.; mem. Am. Econ. Assn., Acad. Polit. Sci., Assn. Asian Studies. Clubs: University (St. Louis); Conanicut Yacht (Jamestown, R.I.). Home: 8132 Roxburgh Dr Saint Louis MO 63105-2436 Office: U Mo Sch Business Saint Louis MO 63121

KAGAN, STUART MICHAEL, pediatrician; b. Milw., June 22, 1944; s. Harry and Bertha (Pittleman) K.; m. Gloria Jean Glass, Aug. 1, 1971; children: Jennifer Anne, Abigail Elizabeth. BS, U. Wis., 1966; MD, U. Utah, 1969; MPH, U. Kans., 1997. Diplomate Am. Bd. Pediat. Intern in pediats. Kans. U. Med. Ctr., Kansas City, 1969-70, resident in pediats., 1970-71, fellow in pediat. cardiology, 1971-73; pvt. practice Overland Park, Kans., 1975-88; occupational medicine physician Employer Health Svc., Kansas City, Mo., 1988—, med. rev. officer, 1994—, acting med. dir., 1994-99. Lt. comdr. USN, 1973-75. RecipientKans. Cardiology fellowship Kans. U. Med. ctr., 1972. Mem. Am. Coll. Occupational and Environ. Medicine, Am. Soc. Addiction Medicine, Great Plains Occupational and Environ. Medicine. Avocations: conservation, jogging, computers, astronomy. Office: Employer Health Svcs 8511 Hillcrest Rd Ste 100 Kansas City MO 64138-2776

KAHALAS, HARVEY, business educator; b. Boston, Dec. 3, 1941; s. James and Betty (Bonfeld) K.; m. Dianne Barbara Levine, Sept. 2, 1963; children: Wendy Elizabeth, Stacy Michele. BS, Boston U., 1965; MBA, U. Mich., 1966; PhD, U. Mass., 1971. Data processing coord. Ford Motor Co., Wayne, Mich., 1963-66; lectr. Salem (Mass.) State Coll., 1966-68; asst. prof. bus. Worcester (Mass.) Poly. Inst., 1970-72; asst. prof. Va. Poly. Inst. and State U., Blacksburg, 1972-75, assoc. prof., 1975-77, SUNY, Albany, 1977-79, assoc. dean, 1979-81, prof., 1979-89, dean, 1981-87; pres. HKE Inc., 1987-97; prof. U. Mass., Lowell, 1989-94, dean, 1989-94, exec. dir. Ctr. Indsl. Competitiveness, 1990-94, Commonwealth disting. prof., 1994-97; dir. Ctr. for Bus. Rsch. and Competitiveness, U. Mass., Dartmouth, 1994-97; prof., dean Wayne State U., 1997—. Program dir. Aspen Inst., 1994-97; cons. Aspen Inst./Fund for Corp. Initiatives, N.Y.C., 1980-94, GE, Schenectady, N.Y., 1981-85, GM, Tarrytown, N.Y., 1987-89; bd. dirs. Lumigen Inc., Southfield, Mich. Contbr. articles to profl. jours. Bd. dirs. Fund for Corp. Initiatives, N.Y.C., 1980—, Nat. Found. Ileitis and Colitis, Albany, 1982-89, Blue Cross Northeastern N.Y., Albany, 1983-89, Capital Dist. Bus. Rev., Albany, 1984—, Greater Detroit Area Health Coun., 1998—. Named Disting. Alumni, U. Mass., 1982, Disting. Lectr. USIA, 1985, Am. Participant USIA, 1989; Fulbright scholar, 1987, 88, Aspen Inst. scholar, 1997. Mem. Fulbright Assn. (life), Acad. Mgmt. (treas. 1971-73, mem. exec. com.), Human Resource Planning Soc. (hon.), Human Resource Systems Profls. (hon.), Pers. Accreditation Inst. (life), Beta Gamma Sigma, Sigma Iota Epsilon, Delta Tau Kappa. Office: Wayne State Univ Sch Bus Adm 226 Prentis Bld 5201 Cass Ave Detroit MI 48202-3930

KAHAN, MITCHELL DOUGLAS, art museum director; BA, U. Va., 1973; MA, Columbia U., 1975; M of Philosophy, CUNY, 1978, PhD, 1983. Mus. aide Nat. Mus. Am. Art, Washington, 1978; curator Montgomery (Ala.) Mus. Fine Art, 1978-82, N.C. Mus. Art, Raleigh, 1982-86; dir. Akron (Ohio) Art Mus., 1986—. Cons. La. World's Exposition, New Orleans, 1983-84. Author: Art Inc.: American Paintings in Corporate Collections, 1979, Roger Brown, 1981, Minnie Evans, 1986, Art Since 1850-Akron Art Museum, 2001. Columbia U. fellow, 1973, Smithsonian Inst. fellow, 1976-78, CUNY grad. research fellow, 1978, Nat. Endowment for Arts fellow, 1987. Mem. Coll. Art Assn., Intermus Conservation Assn. (trustee 1986-95, pres. 1990-92, 95), Assn. Art Mus. Dirs., Akron Roundtable (pres. 2001). Office: Akron Art Mus 70 E Market St Akron OH 44308-2084

KAHAN, PAUL, chef; BS in Applied Math. and Computer Sci., No. Ill. U. Chef Metropolis, erwin, Frontera Grill/Topolobampo, Chgo.; owner, chef Blackbird, 1997—. Named Best New Chef, Food & Wine, 1999. Office: Blackbird 619 W Randolph St Chicago IL 60606

KAHANA, EVA FROST, sociology educator; b. Budapest, Hungary, Mar. 21, 1941; came to U.S., 1957; d. Jacob and Sari Frost; m. Boaz Kahana, Apr. 15, 1962; children: Jeffrey, Michael. BA, Stern Coll., Yeshiva U., 1962; MA, CCNY, CUNY, 1965; PhD, U. Chgo., 1968; HLD (hon.), Yeshiva U., 1991. Nat. Inst. on Aging predoctoral fellow U. Chgo. Com. on Human Devel., 1963-66; postdoctoral fellow Midwest Council Social Research, 1968; with dept. sociology Washington U., St. Louis, 1967-71, successively research asst., research assoc., asst. prof.; with dept. sociology Wayne State U., Detroit, 1971-84, from assoc. prof. to prof., dir. Elderly Care Research Ctr., 1971-84; prof. Case Western Res. U., Cleve., 1984—, Armington Prof., 1989-90, chmn. dept. sociology, 1985—, dir. Elderly Care Research Ctr., 1984—, Pierce and Elizabeth Robson prof. humanities, 1990—. Cons. Nat. Inst. on Aging, Washington, 1976-80, NIMH, Washington, 1971-75. Author: (with E. Midlarsky) Altruism in Later Life, 1994; editor: (with others) Family Caregiving Across the Lifespan, 1994; mem. editl. bd. Gerontologist, 1975-79, Psychology of Aging, 1984-90, Jour. Gerontology, 1990-94, Applied Behavioral Sci. Rev., 1992—; contbr. articles to profl. jours., chpts. to books (recipient Pub.'s prize 1969). Bd. dirs. com. on aging Jewish Community Fedn., Cleve.; vol. cons. Alzheimer's Disease and Related Disorders Assn., Cleve. NIMH Career Devel. grantee, 1974-79, Nat. Inst. Aging Merit award grantee, 1989—; Mary E. Switzer Disting. fellow Nat. Inst. Rehab., 1992-93; recipient Arnold Heller award excellence in geriatrics and gerontology Menorah Park Ctr. for Aged, 1992; named Disting. Geontological Rschr. in Ohio, 1993. Fellow Gerontol. Soc. Am. (chair behavioral social sci. com. 1984-85, chair 2000—, Disting. Mentorship award 1987, Polisher award 1997); mem. Am. Sociol. Assn. (coun. sect. on aging 1985-87, Disting. Scholar award sect. on aging and life course 1997, chair sect. on aging and life course, 2000-2001), Am. Psychol. Assn., Soc. for Traumatic Stress, Wayne State U. Acad. Scholars (life), Sigma Xi. Avocations: reading, antiques, travel.

KAHLER, HERBERT FREDERICK, diversified business executive; b. St. Augustine, Fla., Sept. 20, 1936; s. Herbert E. and Marie (Strieter) K.; m. Erika Rozsypal, May 16, 1964; children: Erik, Stephen, Christopher, Michael, Craig. AB, Johns Hopkins, 1958; LLB, Harvard U., 1961. Bar: N.Y. bar 1962. With Simpson, Thacher & Bartlett, N.Y.C., 1961-65; sec., gen. counsel Insilco Corp., Meriden, Conn., 1965-70; pres., chief exec. officer W.H. Hutchinson & Son, Inc., Chgo., 1970-73, Miles Homes Co., Mpls., 1973-86; v.p., dir. Insilco Corp., 1979-88; pres. Kahler & Assocs., 1988—; pres., chief exec. officer Crown Fixtures, Inc., Plymouth, Minn., 1990—, Power Generation Svc., Inc., 1990—. Bd. corporators Meriden Hosp., 1965-70, Harvard, 1970; bd. govs. Meriden/Wallingford Hosp., 1987; bd. dirs. St. Paul Chamber Orch., 1974-87, St. Paul Opera Assn., 1975-77, Minn. Opera Co., 1977-87. Lt., arty. AUS, 1962-64. Mem. ABA, Newcomen Soc., Mpls. Club, Phi Beta Kappa. Office: Crown Fixtures Inc 10700 Highway 55 Ste 160 Plymouth MN 55441-6134

KAHN, DOUGLAS ALLEN, legal educator; b. Spartanburg, S.C., Nov. 7, 1934; s. Max Leonard and Julia (Rich) K.; m. Judith Bleich, Sept. 24, 1959; m. Mary Briscoe, June 12, 1970; children— Margery Ellen, Jeffrey Hodges B.A., U. N.C., 1955; J.D. with disting., George Washington U., 1958. Bar: D.C. 1958, Mich. 1965, U.S. Ct. Appeals (D.C. cir.) 1958, U.S. Ct. Appeals (5th and 9th cirs.) 1959, U.S. Ct. Appeals (3d, 4th and 6th cirs.) 1960, U.S. Supreme Ct. 1963. Atty. Civil and Tax div. U.S. Dept. Justice, 1958-62; assoc. Sachs and Jacobs, Washington, 1962-64; prof. law U. Mich., Ann Arbor, 1964—, Paul G. Kauper Disting. prof., 1984—. Vis. prof. Stanford Law Sch., 1973, Duke Law Sch., 1977, Fordham Law Sch., 1980-81, U. Cambridge, 1996. Author: (with Gann) Corporate Taxation, 1989, (with Lehman) Corporate Income Taxation, 2001, (with Waggoner and Pennell) Federal Taxation of Gifts, Trusts and Estates, 1997, Federal Income Tax, 1999; comment editor George Washington U. Law Rev., 1956-58; contbr. articles to profl. jours. Recipient Emil Brown Found. prize, 1969 Mem. ABA, Order of Coif. Republican. Jewish Office: U Mich Law Sch 625 S State St Ann Arbor MI 48109-1215 E-mail: dougkahn@umich.edu.

KAHN, EUGENE S. department store chain executive; BA, CCNY, 1971. Asst. buyer Gimbels East, 1971-73, buyer, 1973-76; various merchandising positions Bamberger's, from 1976, sr. v.p., gen. mdse. mgr., 1984-88; group sr. v.p. Macy's Northeast, 1988-89, Macy's South/Bullock's, 1989-90; pres., CEO G. Fox divsn. May Dept. Stores, 1990-92, pres., CEO Filene's divsn., 1992-98, vice chmn. parent co., 1996-97, exec. vice chmn., 1997-98, pres., CEO, 1998-2001, also bd. dirs., chmn., CEO, 2001—. Trustee Washington U., St. Louis; trustee, treas. Mary Inst./Country Day Sch., St. Louis. Office: May Dept Stores 611 Olive St Saint Louis MO 63101-1721

KAHN, JAMES STEVEN, retired museum director; b. N.Y.C., Oct. 14, 1931; 3 children. BS in Geology, CCNY, 1952; MS in Minerology, Pa. State U., 1954; PhD in Geol. Sci., U. Chgo., 1956. Instr. U. R.I., Kingston, 1957, asst. prof., 1958-60, research assoc. Narragansett Marine Lab., 1957-60; group leader U. Calif., Livermore, 1960-70; dept. head Physics Internat. Co., San Leandro, Calif., 1970-71; div. head geophysics U. Calif., Livermore, 1971-75, dep. assoc. dir. human resources, 1975-78, assoc. dir. nuclear testing, 1978-80, dep. dir. lab., 1980-87; pres., chief exec. officer, dir. Mus. Sci. and Industry, Chgo., 1987-97; retired, emeritus. Trustee Mus. Sci. and Industry; mem. math. scis. edn. bd. NAS, 1991-94; chmn. sci. adv. com. Gov. Ill., 1994-98; IMAX Corp. Co-author: Statistical Analysis in Geological Sciences, 1962; cntbr.: Microstructure, 1968; contbr. articles to scientific jours. Trustee Geol. Soc. Am., 1987-2002; bd. dirs. Franklin and Eleanor Roosevelt Inst., 1994-2001, Dubuque (Iowa) Art Inst., 1999—; rector sci. and medicine Lincoln Acad. Ill., 1994-2002; mem., vice-chmn. Bd. Natural Resources and Conservation, State of Ill. Centennial fellow Pa. State U. Coll. Earth and Mineral Scis., 1996. Mem. Quadrangle Club, Missions Hills (Calif.) Country Club, Sigma Xi. Unitarian. E-mail: j.bk@verizon.net.

KAHN, JAN EDWARD, manufacturing company executive; b. Dayton, Ohio, Aug. 29, 1948; s. Sigmond Lawrence and Betty Jane K.; m. Deborah Ann Deckinga, Nov. 28, 1975; children: Jason Edward, Justin Allen, Julie Ann. BS in Metall. Engring., U. Cin., 1971. Mgmt. trainee U.S. Steel Corp., Gary, Ind., 1971-72; plant metallurgist Regal Tube Co., Chgo., 1972-74, gen. foreman, 1974-76, supt., 1976-77, mgr. tech. svc., 1978-80, materials mgr., 1980-81; mgr. quality contrl Std. Tube Co., Detroit, 1977-78; dir. ops. Boye Needle Co., Chgo., 1981-82, v.p. ops., 1982-83, v.p., gen. mgr., 1984-85, pres., 1985-88; v.p. sales and mktg. Caron Internat., Washington, 1988—. Mem. Am. Soc. Metals, AIME, ASTM, Ravenswood Indsl. Coun. (bd. dirs. 1983-84, pres. 1985), hand Knitting Assn. (chmn. 1986-88), Triangle Club. Republican. Mem. Christian Reformed Ch. Home: 13909 Teakwood Dr Lockport IL 60441-8697 Office: Caron Internat PO Box 3000 Orland Park IL 60462-1099 E-mail: wa8lis@accesschicago.net.

KAHN, PHYLLIS, state legislator; b. Mar. 23, 1937; m. Don Kahn; two children. BA, Cornell U., 1957; PhD in Biophysics, Yale U., 1962; MPA, Harvard U., 1986. Dist. 59B rep. Minn. Ho. of Reps., St. Paul, 1972—. Former chmn. state dept. divsn. appropriations com., Minn. Ho. of Reps., former mem. econ. devel., agr., environ. and natural resources coms.; chmn. govt. op. com., state govt. fin. divsn. and edn.-higher edn. fin. divsn. coms. Home: 367 State Office Bldg Saint Paul MN 55155-0001 Office: Minn State Senate State Capitol Building Saint Paul MN 55155-0001

KAHN, SANDRA S. psychotherapist; b. Chgo., June 24, 1942; d. Chester and Ruth Sutker; m. Jack Murry Kahn, June 1, 1965; children: Erick, Jennifer. BA, U. Miami, 1964; MA, Roosevelt U., 1976. Tchr. Chgo. Pub. Schs., 1965-67; pvt. practice psychotherapy, Northbrook, Ill., 1976—. Host Shared Feelings, Sta. WEEF-AM, Highland Park, Ill., 1983—; author: The Kahn Report on Sexual Preferences, 1981, The Ex Wife Syndrome Cutting The Cord and Breaking Free After The Marriage Is Over, 1990; columnist Single Again mag. Mem. Ill. Psychol. Assn., Chgo. Psychol. Assn. (past pres. 1990). Jewish. Office: 801 Skokie Blvd Northbrook IL 60062-4039

KAHRILAS, PETER JAMES, medical educator, researcher; b. Culver City, Calif., June 9, 1953; s. Peter Jerome and Leticia (Llorett) K.; m. Elyse Anne Lambiase, Mar. 30, 1984; children: Genevieve Anne, Ian James, Miranda Elyse. Student, Yale U., 1971-75, U. Rochester, N.Y., 1975-79. Resident in medicine U. Hosp. of Cleve., 1979-82; fellow in gastroenterology Northwestern U., Chgo., 1982-84; rsch. fellow Med. Coll. of Wis., Milw., 1984-86, asst. prof. medicine, 1986-90, assoc. prof. medicine, 1990-95, prof. medicine, 1995-99; chief gastroenterology and hepatology Northwestrn U. Med. Sch., Chgo., 1999—. Contbr. articles to profl. jours. NIH grantee, 1990—. Fellow ACP, Ctrl. Soc. for Clin. Rsch., Am. Coll. Gastroenterology; mem. Am. Gastroenterol. Assn., Am. Fedn. for Clin. Rsch., Am. Soc. for Clin. Investigation, Am. Motility Soc. Democrat. Home: 203 Columbia Ave Park Ridge IL 60068-4923 Office: Northwestern U Searle Bldg 10-541 303 E Chicago Ave Chicago IL 60611-3093

KAHRL, ROBERT CONLEY, lawyer; b. Mt. Vernon, Ohio, June 2, 1946; s. K. Allin and Evelyn Sperry (Conley) K.; m. LaVonne Elaine Rutherford, July 12, 1969; children: Kurt Freeland, Eric Allin, Heidi Elizabeth. AB, Princeton U., 1968; MBA, JD, Ohio State U., 1975. Bar: Ohio 1975, U.S. Ct. Appeals (6th cir.) 1976, U.S. Dist. Ct. (no. dist.) Ohio 1977, U.S. Ct. Appeals (9th cir.) 1979, U.S. Ct. Appeals (fed. cir.) 1984, U.S. Ct. Appeals (D.C. cir.) 1986. Law clk. to presiding judge U.S. Ct. Appeals (6th cir.), Cleve., 1975-76; assoc. Jones, Day, Reavis & Pogue, 1976-84, ptnr., 1985—, chair intellectual property sect., 1991—. Mem. Hudson Park Bd. Served to lt. USN, 1968-72. Mem. Ohio State Bar Assn. (chmn. emeritus intellectual property sect.), Am. Intellectual Property Law Assn., Order of Coif, Am. Guild Organists. Republican. Presbyterian. Home: 7624 Red Fox Trl Hudson OH 44236-1926 Office: Jones Day Reavis & Pogue 901 Lakeside Ave E Cleveland OH 44114-1190 E-mail: rckahrl@jonesday.com.

KAISER, ANN CHRISTINE, magazine editor; b. Milw., Apr. 7, 1947; d. Herbert Walter and Annette G. (Werych) Gohlke; m. Louis Dan Kaiser; children: Richard L., Michael D. BS in Journalism, Northwestern U., 1969. Reporter Waco (Tex.) Tribune-Herald, 1969-71; editor Country Woman, Greendale, Wis., 1971—; mng. editor Taste of Home, 1993—. Named among People of the Yr., Milw. Mag., 1998. Lutheran. Avocations: sailing, tennis, golf, travel. Office: Reiman Publs 5400 S 60th St Greendale WI 53129-1404

KAISER, DANIEL HUGH, historian, educator; b. Phila., July 20, 1945; s. Walter Christian and Estelle Evelyn (Jaworsky) K.; m. Jonelle Marie Marwin, Aug. 10, 1968; children: Nina Marie, Andrew Eliot. AB, Wheaton Coll., 1967; AM, U. Chgo., 1970, PhD, 1977. Asst. prof. history U. Chgo., 1977-78, Grinnell (Iowa) Coll., 1979-84, assoc. prof., 1984-86, prof. history, 1986—, Joseph F. Rosenfield prof. social studies, 1984—, chair dept. history, 1988-90, 96-98. Mem. adv. bd. Soviet Studies in History, 1979-85; rsch. assoc. dept. Slavonic studies, vis. mem. Darwin Coll., Cambridge (Eng.) U., 1992-93; vis. prof. dept. Slavic langs. and lits. Ctr. for Medieval and Renaissance Studies, UCLA, 1996. Author: The Growth of the Law in Medieval Russia, 1980; editor: The Workers' Revolution in Russia, 1917, 1987; translator, editor: The Laws of Rus' Tenth to Fifteenth Centuries, 1992; co-editor: (with Gary Marker) Reinterpreting Russian History 860-1860s, 1994; editl. bd. Slavic Rev., 1996-2001. Elder 1st Presbyn. Ch., Grinnell, 1985, 87-89. Fellow Nat. Endowment Humanities, 1979, 92-93, 2000, John Simon Guggenheim Meml. Found., 1986, Fulbright-Hays Faculty Rsch. Abroad Found., 1986, Woodrow Wilson Internat. Ctr. Scholars, 1986, Internat. Rsch. Exchs. Bd. fellow to USSR/Russia, 1974-75, 78-79, 86, 93. Mem. Am. Assn. for Advancement Slavic Studies, Am. Hist. Assn., Early Slavic Studies Assn. (v.p. 1995-97, pres. 1997-99), Slavonic and East European Medieval Studies Group (U.K.), Study Group on 18th Century Russia (U.K.), 18th Century Russian Studies Assn. Office: Grinnell Coll Dept History Grinnell IA 50112-1670 E-mail: kaiser@grinnell.edu.

KAISER, MARTIN, newspaper editor; b. Milw., Oct. 11, 1950; Editor Milw. Jour.- Sentinel, 1997—. Office: Milwaukee Journal PO Box 661 333 W State St Milwaukee WI 53203-1309

KAISERLIAN, PENELOPE JANE, publishing company executive; b. Paisley, Scotland, Oct. 19, 1943; came to U.S., 1956; d. W. Norman and Magdalene Jeanette (Houlder) Hewson; m. Arthur Kaiserlian, June 29, 1968; 1 child, Christian BA, U. Exeter, Eng., 1965. Copywriter, sales rep. Pergamon Press, Elmsford, N.Y., 1965-68; exhibits mgr. Plenum Pub., N.Y.C., 1968-69; asst. mktg. mgr. U. Chgo. Press, 1969-76, mktg. mgr., 1976-83, assoc. dir., 1983-2001; dir. U. Va. Press, 2001—. Mem. Soc. for Scholarly Pub., Am. Geog. Assn., Colonnade Club. Office: Univ Va Press PO Box 400318 Charlottesville VA 22904-4318

KAKOS, GERARD STEPHEN, thoracic and cardiovascular surgeon; b. N.Y.C., Mar. 15, 1943; s. Stephen George Kakos and Margaret Misouic; m. Diana Toon, Dec. 19, 1964; children: Stephanie Lynn, Anna Katherine, Kristin Margaret. BA, Ohio State U., 1963, MD, 1967. Bd. cert. Am. Bd. Surgery, Am. Bd. Thoracic Surgery; lic., Ohio. NIH rsch. fellow in cardiovasc. surgery Duke U. Med. Ctr., Durham, N.C., 1970-71; intern in surgery Coll. Medicine Ohio State U., Columbus, 1967-68, asst. resident in surgery Coll. Medicine, 1969-73, sr. resident in surgery Coll. Medicine, 1971-72, adminstrv. chief resident in surgery Coll. Medicine, 1971-72, chief resident thoracic & cardiovasc. surgery Coll. Medicine, 1972-73, from asst. prof. to assoc. prof. surgery Coll. Medicine, 1970-85, assoc. clin. prof. surgery Coll. Medicine, 1985—. Chief divsn. thoracic surgery dept. surgery Ohio State U., Columbus, 1984-86, assoc. dir. working party for therapy of lung cancer (Nat. Cancer Inst.), 1973-76. Contbr. numerous articles to med. jours. Bd. dirs. Franklin County chpt. Cen. Ohio Heart Assn., 1978, Columbus Sch. for Girls, 1993-95. Capt. U.S. Army, 1968-76. Fellow ACS; mem. AMA, Internat. Soc. for Surgery, Am. Assn. Thoracic Surgery, Soc. for Vascular Surgery, Soc. Thoracic Surgery, Assn. for Acad. Surgery, Ohio State Med. Assn., Ohio State U. Hosps. Med. Soc., Columbus Surg. Soc., Acad. Medicine of Columbus and Franklin County, R. M. Zollinger Club, Alpha Epsilon Delta, Alpha Omega Alpha, Sigma Xi (Ohio state chpt.). Republican. Roman Catholic. Avocations: hunting, scuba diving. Office: Cardiothoracic Surgeons Inc 300 E Town St Fl 12 Columbus OH 43215-4620

KALAI, EHUD, decision sciences educator, researcher in economics and decision sciences; b. Tel Aviv, Dec. 7, 1942; came to U.S., 1963; s. Meir and Elisheva (Rabinovitch) K.; m. Marilyn Lott, Aug. 24, 1967; children: Kerren, Adam. AB with distinction, U. Calif. at Berkeley, 1967; MS, Cornell U., 1971, PhD in Applied Math., 1972. Asst. prof. dept. statistics Tel Aviv U., 1972-75; vis. asst. prof. decision scis. J.L. Kellogg Grad. Sch. Mgmt. Northwestern U., Evanston, Ill., 1975-76, assoc. prof. decision scis., 1976-78, prof. managerial econs. and decision scis., 1978-82, The Charles E. Morrison Chair prof. decision scis., 1982-2001, prof. math., 1990—, IBM rsch. chair managerial econs. Ill., 1980-81, J.L. Kellogg rsch. chair in decision theory, 1981-82, chmn. meds. dept., 1983-85; dir. Ctr. for

Strategic Decision-Making Kellogg Sch. Mgmt., Northwestern U., 1995—. Oskar Morgenstern rsch. prof. game theory NYU, 1991; expert testimony in ct. cases, 1982—; cons. Israeli Def. Forces, 1974-75, 1st Nat. Bank Chgo., 1987, Arthur Anderson, 1990, Kaiser Permanente, 1995, Nath Sonnenschein and Rosenthal, 1999, Baxter Healthcare Corp., 1999—; James J. O'Conner Distinguished Prof. of Decision and Game Scis., 2001—. Founder, editor Games and Econ. Behavior Jour., 1988—; editl. bd. Math. Social Scis., 1980-90, Jour. Econ. Theory, 1980-88, Internat. Jour. Game Theory, 1984—; contbr. numerous articles on game theory and econs. to profl. jours. Sgt. Israeli Def. Forces, 1960-63. NSF grantee, 1979—; Sherman Fairchild Disting. scholar, Calif. Inst. Tech., 1994-95. Fellow Econometrics Soc.; mem. Am. Math. Soc., Pub. Choice Soc., Game Theory Soc. (founder, exec. v.p. 1998—), Beta Gamma Sigma. Home: 1110 N Lake Shore Dr Apt 23S Chicago IL 60611-1023 Office: Kellogg Grad Sch of Mgmt Northwestern Univ Evanston IL 60208-0001 E-mail: kalai@kellogg.northwestern.edu.

KALAINOV, SAM CHARLES, insurance company executive; b. Steele, N.D., May 11, 1930; s. George and Celia Mae (Makedonsky) K.; m. Delores L. Holm., Aug. 10, 1957; children: John Charles, David Mark. B.S., N.D. State U., 1956. CLU. Life ins. agt. Am. Mut. Life Ins. Co., Fargo, N.D., 1956-60, supt. agys. Des Moines, 1960-70, sr. v.p. mktg., 1972-80, pres., chmn., CEO, 1980-95; v.p. agy. Western States Life Ins. Co., Fargo, 1970-72; chmn. bd. dirs. Am. Mut. Holding Corp., Amerus Life, 1995-2000. Bd. dirs. Am. Coun. Life Ins., Washington, Bankers Trust, Des Moines; past chmn. Des Moines Devel. Corp. Bd. dirs. Luth. Health Sys., Fargo, 1974-91, City Corp., Des Moines, 1981-95, Civic Ctr. Ct., 1981-95, Iowa Luth. Hosp., 1982-91; trustee Drake U.; past chmn. Des Moines Conv. and Visitors Bur.; civilian aide to Sec. Army at Large, 1991; past state dir. Selective Svc. Sys.; bd. mem. N.D. State U. Devel. Found. With inf. AUS, 1947-49, lt., 1952-55. Decorated Bronze Star; recipient Alumni Achievement award N.D. State U., 1983, Patrick Henry award Army Nat. Guard, 1998. Mem. Nat. Assn. Life Underwriters, Greater Des Moines C. of C. (past chmn., Nat. Leadership award 1978), Corp. for Internat. Trade (chmn.), Am. Legion, Rotary (past pres. Des Moines chpt.). Home: 681 50th St Des Moines IA 50312-1807 Office: AmerUs Group 699 Walnut St Des Moines IA 50309-3929

KALETA, PAUL J. corporate lawyer, oil industry executive; b. Queens, N.Y., Aug. 18, 1955; AB in Philosophy and English cum laude, Hamilton Coll., 1978; JD cum laude, Georgetown U., 1981. Bar: D.C. 1982, N.Y. 1993, U.S. Supreme Ct. 1987. Ptnr. Swidler & Berlin, 1985-91; v.p., gen. counsel Niagara Mohawk Power Corp., Syracuse, N.Y., 1991-98; v.p., gen. counsel, sec. Koch Industries, Inc., Wichita, Kans., 1998—. Vice chmn. Utility Law Commn. Mem. ABA, N.Y. State Bar Assn. Office: Koch Industries Inc 4111 E 37th St N PO Box 2256 Wichita KS 67201

KALIS, HENRY J. state legislator, farmer; b. Mar. 2, 1937; m. Violet Kalis; four children. Farmer; Dist. 26B rep. Minn. Ho. of Reps., St. Paul, 1974—. Former chmn. transp. com., Minn. Ho. of Reps.; former mem. agr., appropriations, health and human svcs. coms., former ex officio environ. and natural resources fin., health and housing, higher edn. human svcs., judiciary and state govt. divsn. coms.; chmn. capital investment com., mem. econ. devel., infrastructure and regulation fin., and ways and means coms. Address: RR 1 Box 55 Walters MN 56097-9601 Also: 10043 600th Ave Walters MN 56097-4703

KALISCH, BEATRICE JEAN, nursing educator, consultant; b. Tellahoma, Tenn., Oct. 15, 1943; d. Peter and Margaret Ruth Petersen; children— Philip P., Melanie J. BS, U. Nebr., 1965; MS, U. Md., 1967, PhD, 1970. Pediatric staff nurse Centre County Hosp., Bellefonte, Pa., 1965-66; instr. nursing Philipsburg (Pa.) Gen. Hosp. Sch. Nursing, 1966; pediatric staff nurse Greater Balt. Med. Center, Towson, Md., 1967; asst. prof. maternal-child nursing Am. U., 1967-68; clin. nurse specialist N.W. Tex. Hosp., Amarillo, 1970; assoc. prof. maternal-child nursing, curriculum coordinator nursing Amarillo Coll., 1970-71; chmn. baccalaureate nursing program, asso. prof. nursing U. So. Miss., 1971-74; prof. nursing, chmn. dept. parent-child nursing U. Mich. Sch. Nursing, Ann Arbor, 1974-86, Shirley C. Titus Disting. prof., 1977—, Titus Disting. prof. nursing mgmt., 1989—, dir. nursing bus. and health sys. program, 2000—; prin., dir. nursing consultation svcs. Ernst & Young, Detroit, 1986-89. Prin. investigator USPH grant to study image of nurses in mass media and the informational quality nursing news, U. Mich., 1977-86, prin. investigator to study intrahosp. transport of critically ill patients, 1991—; prin. investigator to study use of HIA nurse in N.Y.C. labor market, U. Mich.; prin. investigator to study the impact of managed care on critical care, U. Mich.; vis. Disting. prof. U. Ala., 1979, U. Tex., 1981, Tex. Christian U., 1983. Author: Child Abuse and Neglect: An Annotated Bibliography, 1978; co-author: Nursing Involvement in Health Planning, 1978, Politics of Nursing, 1982, Images of Nurses on Television, 1983, The Advance of American Nursing, 1986, revised, 1994, The Changing Image of the Nurse, 1987; co-editor: Studies in Nursing Mgmt.; contbr. articles to profl. jours. Recipient Joseph L. Andrews Bibliog. award Am. Assn. Law Libraries, 1979; Book of Yr. award Am. Jour. Nursing, 1978, 83, 86, 87, Outstanding Achievement award U. Md., 1987, Distinguished Alumni award U. Nebr., 1985, Shaw medal Boston Coll., 1986; USPHS fellow. Fellow Am. Acad. Nursing; mem. Am. Coll. Healthcare Execs., ANA, APHA, Am. Orgn. Nurse Execs., Sigma Theta Tau, Phi Kappa Phi. Presbyterian. Home: 27675 Chatsworth St Farmington MI 48334-1821 Office: U Mich Sch Nursing 400 N Ingalls St Ann Arbor MI 48109-0482 E-mail: bkalisch@umich.edu.

KALKWARE, KENT D. telecommunications professional; CPA, Mo. Sr. tax mgr. Arthur Andersen, St. Louis; v.p. fin. and acquisitions Charter Comms., 1995-96, sr. v.p. mergers and acquisitions, 1996-97, sr. v.p., CFO, 1997-2000; exec. v.p., CFO, 2000—. Office: Charter Comms Inc 12444 Powerscourt Dr Ste 400 Saint Louis MO 63131-3621 Fax: 314-965-5761.

KALKWARF, KENT D. communications company executive; BA in Acctg., Ill. Wesleyan U. CPA, Mo. Sr. tax mgr. Arthur Anderson; from v.p. finance & acquisitions to sr. v.p., CFO Charter Comms., St. Louis, 1995-97, exec. v.p., CFO, 1997—. Office: Charter Communications Inc 12444 Powerscourt Dr Ste 400 Saint Louis MO 63131-3621 Fax: (314) 965-5761.

KALLICK, DAVID A. lawyer; b. Chgo., Nov. 7, 1945; s. Joseph N. and Elizabeth A. (Just) K.; m. Arline E. Chizewer, Nov. 26, 1972; children: Michelle, Robert. AB in History, Princeton U., 1967; JD, Northwestern U., 1971. Bar: Ill. 1971, Calif. 1972. Law clk. to presiding justice Ill. Appellate Ct., Chgo., 1971-72; assoc. McCutchen, Doyle, Brown & Enersen, San Francisco, 1972-74; asst. dean U. So. Calif. Law Ctr., L.A., 1974-76, Ill. Inst. Tech.-Kent Coll. Law, Chgo., 1976-79; ptnr. Hurley Kallick & Schiller, Ltd., Deerfield, Ill., 1979-92, Tishler & Wald, Ltd., Chgo., 1992—. Bd. dirs. Capitol Bank and Trust, Chgo., Capitol Bank of Westmont, Ill. Bd. dirs. Congregation Solel, Highland Park, Ill., Birchwood Club, Highland Park; past bd. mem., pres. Sch. Dist. 107, Highland Park; former trustee Legacy 107 Edn. Found., Highland Park. With USAR, 1968-74. Mem. ABA, Calif. Bar Assn., Ill. Bar Assn., Chgo. Bar Assn., Princeton Univ. Club. Home: 1887 Spruce St Highland Park IL 60035-2150 Office: 200 S Wacker Dr Ste 2600 Chicago IL 60606-5807

KALLIK, CHIP, radio director; m. Sarah Kallik. BA Comm., Ohio State U. News anchor, reporter WEOL, Elyria, Ohio, WMJI, Cleve., 1991—94, dir. news ops., 1994—. Recipient Nat. Headline award Consistently Outstanding News Reporting, 1995. Avocations: golf, bowling, theater . Office: WMJI 6200 Oak Tree Blvd 4th Fl Cleveland OH 44131*

KALMAN, ANDREW, manufacturing company executive; b. Hungary, Aug. 14, 1919; came to U.S., 1922, naturalized, 1935; s. Louis and Julia (Bognar) K.; m. Violet Margaret Kish, June 11, 1949; children: Andrew Joseph, Richard Louis, Laurie Ann. With Detroit Engring. & Machine Co., 1947-66, exec. v.p., gen. mgr., 1952-66; exec. v.p. and dir. Indian Head, Inc., 1966-75, also dir. Dir. Acme Precision Products, 1959-80, Reef Energy Corp., 1980-84. Trustee emeritus Alma (Mich.) Coll.; bd. dirs. Am. Hungarian Found., New Brunswick, N.J.; mem. adv. coun., mem. exec. com., U. Mich. Ctr. for Communication Disorders. Home: 708 S Military St Dearborn MI 48124-2108 Office: 600 Woodbridge St Detroit MI 48226-4302

KALMAN, MARC, radio station executive; b. Appleton, Wis. m. Gail Thoen; children: Robert, Todd, Stacie. Student, Am. U. Disc jockey Sta. WJPD, Ishpeming, Mich., 1967, Sta. WMBD, Peoria, Ill., 1967; account exec. Sta. WMIN, 1968, Sta. KRSI, 1968-69, Sta. WDGY, 1969-74, gen. sales mgr., 1974-81; v.p./gen. mgr. Blair Radio, 1981-88; gen. sales mgr. Sta. WCCO, 1988-92; v.p./gen. mgr. Sta. WLOL, Mpls. Bd. dirs. Variety Children's Hosp. Mem. Minn. Broadcasters Assn. (bd. dirs.). Avocation: spectator sports. Office: WLOL 60 S 6th St Ste 930 Minneapolis MN 55402-4409

KALTER, ALAN, advertising agency executive; m. Chris Lezotte. With W.B. Doner & Co., Southfield, Mich., 1967—, exec. v.p., dir. retail divsn., 1990, vice chmn. account mgmt., 1990-92, pres., COO, 1992-95; CEO, chmn. W. B. Doner & Co., 1995—. Office: W B Doner & Co 25900 Northwestern Hwy Southfield MI 48075-1067

KALVER, GAIL ELLEN, dance company manager, musician; b. Chgo., Nov. 25, 1948; d. Nathan Eli and Alice Martha (Jaffe) K. BS in Music Edn., U. Ill., 1970; MA in Clarinet Chgo. Musical Coll., Roosevelt U., 1974. Profl. musician, Chgo., 1970-77; assoc. mgr. Ravinia Festival, Highland Park, Ill., 1977-83; exec. dir. Hubbard Street Dance Chgo., 1984—. Bd. dirs. Chicago Dance Coalition, Ill. Arts Alliance; mem. dance panel Ill. Arts Council, Chgo., 1983-85; mem. grants panels Chgo. Office Fine Arts, 1985. Editor: Music Explorer (for music edn.), 1983-86. Mem. grants panels NEA, 1992-94; cons. music Nat. Radio Theatre, Chgo., 1983—. Office: Hubbard St Dance Chgo 1147 W Jackson Blvd Chicago IL 60607-2905

KAMERICK, EILEEN ANN, corporate financial executive, lawyer; b. Ravenna, Ohio, July 22, 1958; d. John Joseph and Elaine Elizabeth (Lenney) K.; m. Victor J. Heckler, Sept. 1, 1990; 1 child, Connor Joseph Heckler. AB in English summa cum laude, Boston Coll., 1980; postgrad., Exeter Coll., Oxford, Eng., 1981; JD, U. Chgo., 1984, MBA in Finance and Internat. Bus. with honors, 1993. Bar: Ill. 1984, U.S. Dist. Ct. (no. dist.) Ill. 1985, Mass. 1986, U.S. Ct. Appeals (7th cir.) 1988, U.S. Supreme Ct. 1993. Assoc. Reuben & Proctor, Chgo., 1984-86, Skadden, Arps et al, Chgo., 1986-89; atty. internat. Amoco Corp., 1989-93, sr. fin. mgr. corp. fin., 1993—96, dir. banking and fin. svcs., 1996-97, v.p., treas., 1998-99, Whirlpool Corp., Benton Harbor, Mich., 1997; v.p., gen. counsel GE Capital Auto Fin. Svcs., Barrington, Ill., 1997-98; v.p., CFO BP Am., 1999-2000; exec. v.p. & CFO United Stationers Inc., Des Plaines, Ill., 2000—01; exec. v.p., CFO Bcom3, Chgo., 2001—. Advisor fin. com. Am. Petroleum Inst., 1992; bd. dirs. Heartland Alliance, Info. Resources, Inc. Vol. adv. 7th Cir. Bar Assn., Chgo., 1987—. Mem. Phi Beta Kappa. Roman Catholic. Home: 2658D N Southport Ave Chicago IL 60614-1228 Office: Bcom3 Ste 2200 35 W Wacker Dr Chicago IL 60601

KAMIN, BLAIR DOUGLASS, newspaper critic; b. Red Bank, N.J., Aug. 6, 1957; s. Arthur Z. and Virginia P. Kamin. BA, Amherst Coll., 1979; M in Environ. Design, Yale U., 1984. Reporter Des Moines Register, 1984-87, Chgo. Tribune, 1987-88, suburban affairs writer, 1988-92; culture news reporter, 1992; architecture critic, 1992—. Nominating juror Pulitzer Prize, 2000, 02. Author Why Architecture Matters: Lessons from Chicago, 2001, Why Architecture Matters, 2001; contbr. articles to profl. jours. Recipient Nat. Edn. Reporting award Edn. Writers Assn., 1985, Edward Scott Beck award Chgo. Tribune, 1990, George Polk award for criticism, 1996, Pulitzer Prize for Criticism, 1999, Inst. Honor for Collaborative Achievement, AIA, 1999, Peter Lisagor award for Exemplary Journalism, 1993, 94, 95, 96, 97, 98, 2001. Jewish.

KAMIN, CHESTER THOMAS, lawyer; b. Chgo., July 30, 1940; s. Alfred and Sara (Liebenson) K.; m. Nancy Schaefer, Sept. 8, 1962; children— Stacey Allison, Scott Thomas A.B. magna cum laude, Harvard Coll., 1962; J.D., U. Chgo., 1965. Bar: Ill. 1965, U.S. Dist. Ct. (no. dist.) Ill. 1965, U.S. Dist. Ct. D.C. 1994, U.S. Ct. Appeals (fed. cir.) 1967, U.S. Ct. Appeals (7th cir.) 1970, U.S. Ct. Appeals (5th cir.) 1975, U.S. Ct. Appeals (2d cir.) 1987, U.S. Ct. Appeals (6th cir.) 1996, U.S. Supreme Ct. 1971. Law clk. Ill. Appellate Ct., 1965-66; assoc. Jenner & Block, Chgo., 1966-72, ptnr., 1975—; spl. counsel to Gov. Ill., Springfield, 1973-74. Mem. steering com. Com. on Cts. and Justice, 1971— ; mem. Ill. Law Enforcement Commn., 1975-77; adj. prof. U. Chgo. Law Sch. Contbr. articles to profl. jours. Fellow Am. Bar Found., Am. Coll. Trial Lawyers; mem. ABA, Ill. State Bar Assn., Chgo. Bar Assn., Chgo. Coun. Lawyers, Lawyers Club, Quadrangle Club. Office: Jenner & Block 1 E Ibm Plz Fl 4700 Chicago IL 60611-3599 E-mail: ckamin@jenner.com.

KAMINS, JOHN MARK, lawyer; b. Chgo., Feb. 7, 1947; s. David and Beulah (Block) K.; m. Judith Joan Sperling, May 5, 1968; children— Robert, Heather. AB with high honors and distinction, U. Mich., 1968, JD, 1970. Bar: Mich. 1971, Fla. 1991. Assoc., Honigman Miller Schwartz and Cohn, Detroit, 1971-75, ptnr., 1976—; lectr. Inst. on Continuing Legal Edn. Pres. Mich. chpt. Leukemia Soc. Am., 1991-92, 93-96, nat. trustee, 1996—, nat. exec. com., 1997—; pres. Goodwill Industries of Greater Detroit Found., 2001, The Leukemia and Lymphoma Soc.; pres. Temple Beth El, Bloomfield Hills, Mich., 1994-96. Mem. Nat. Assn. Bond Lawyers (vice chmn. com. on opinions 1985-86), Mich. Bar Assn. (chairperson, pub. corp. law sect. 1992-93). Jewish. Home: 1315 Stuyvessant Rd Bloomfield Hills MI 48301-2144 Office: Honigman Miller Schwartz & Cohn 2290 First National Bldg Detroit MI 48226

KAMINSKI, DONALD LEON, medical educator, surgeon, gastrointestinal physiologist; b. Elba, Nebr., Nov. 9, 1940; s. Edwin and Irene (Syntek) K.; m. Maureen M. Cudmore, Nov. 28, 1964; children: Christian, Julie, Jane, Kathryn. B.S., Creighton U., 1962, M.D., 1966. Diplomate: Am. Bd. Surgery. Intern. St. Louis U., 1966-67, resident in surgery, 1967-71; attending surgeon St. Louis U. Hosp., 1972—, dir. gen. surgery, 1982—. Mem. Soc. Univ. Surgeons, Am. Physiol. Soc., Am. Gastroent. Assn., Am. Surg. Assn., Central Surg. Soc., Alpha Omega Alpha Republican. Roman Catholic. Home: 1025 Joanna Ave Saint Louis MO 63122-1821 Office: St Louis U 3635 Vista at Grand PO Box 15250 Saint Louis MO 63110-0250

KAMINSKY, MANFRED STEPHAN, physicist; b. Koenigsberg, Germany, June 4, 1929; came to U.S., 1958; s. Stephan and Kaethe (Gieger) K.; m. Elisabeth Moellering, May 1, 1957; children: Cornelia B., Mark-Peter. First diploma in physics, U. Rostock, Germany, 1951; Ph.D. in Physics magna cum laude, U. Marburg, Germany, 1957. German Research Soc. fellow and grad. asst. in physics U. Rostock, 1950-52; lectr. Rostock Med. Tech. Sch., 1952; German Research Soc. fellow and research asst. Phys. Inst., U. Marburg, 1953-57, sr. asst., 1957-58; research assn. Argonne (Ill.) Nat. Lab., 1958-59, asst. physicist, 1959-62, assoc., 1962-70, sr. physicist, 1970-86, dir. Surface Sci. Center-CTR Program, 1974-80, dir. Tribology Program, 1984-86; sole propr. Surface Treatment Sci. Internat., Hinsdale, Ill., 1986—. Cons. Office Tech. Assessment U.S. Congress, 1986, NRC com. on tribology, 1986-88; guest prof. Inst. Energy, U. Que., Montreal-Varennes, 1976-82; E.W. Mueller lectr. U. Wis., Milw., 1978; symposium chmn. Internat. Conf. Metall. Coatings, 1985-93. Author: Atomic and Ionic Impact Phenomena on Metal Surfaces, 1965; contbr. articles to profl. jours.; editor: Radiation Effects on Solid Surfaces, 1976; co-editor: Surface Effects on Controlled Fusion, 1974, Surface Effects in Controlled Fusion Devices, 1976, Dictionary of Terms for Vacuum Science and Technology, 1980; patentee in field. Bd. dirs. Com. 100, Hinsdale, 1970-75, 90-92, pres., 1973-74; pres. St. Vincent de Paul Soc., Hinsdale, 1972-73. Named Outstanding New Citizen of Year Citizenship Council Chgo., 1968; Japanese Soc. Promotion of Sci. fellow, 1982. Fellow Am. Phys. Soc.; mem. Am. Chem. Soc., Scientific Research Soc., Research Soc. Am., AAAS, Union German Phys. Socs., Am. Vacuum Soc. (sr., trustee 1982-84, chmn. Midwest sect. 1967-68, co-founder Gt. Lakes chpt., dir. 1968-70, chmn. fusion tech. div. 1980-81, editorial bd. jour. 1978-83, hon. 1986), Internat. Union Vacuum Sci., Techs. and Applications (chmn. fusion div. 1984-86), Sigma Xi. Home: 906 S Park Ave Hinsdale IL 60521-4519 also: 300 Galen Dr Apt 506 Key Biscayne FL 33149-2177 Office: Surface Treatment Sci Internat PO Box 175 Hinsdale IL 60522-0175

KAMISAR, YALE, lawyer, educator; b. N.Y.C., Aug. 29, 1929; s. Samuel and Mollie (Levine) K.; m. Esther Englander, Sept. 7, 1953 (div. Oct. 1973); children: David Graham, Gordon, Jonathan; m. Christine Keller, May 10, 1974 (dec. 1997); m. Joan Russell, Feb. 28, 1999. AB, NYU, 1950; LLB, Columbia U., 1954; LLD, CUNY, 1978. Bar: D.C. 1955. Rsch. assoc. Am. Law Inst., N.Y.C., 1953; assoc. Covington & Burling, Washington, 1955-57; assoc. prof., then prof. law U. Minn., Mpls., 1957-64; prof. law U. Mich., Ann Arbor, 1965-92, Clarence Darrow disting. univ. prof., 1992—. Vis. prof. law Harvard U., 1964-65; disting. vis. prof. law Coll. William and Mary, 1988; cons. Nat. Adv. Commn. Civil Disorders, 1967-68, Nat. Commn. Causes and Prevention Violence, 1968-69; mem. adv. com. model code pre-arraignment procedure Am. Law Inst., 1965-75. Reporter-draftsman: Uniform Rules of Criminal Procedure, 1971-73; author: (with J.H. Choper, S. Shiffrin and R.H. Fallon), Constitutional Law: Cases, Comments and Questions, 10th edit., 2002; (with W. LaFave, J. Israel and N. King) Modern Criminal Procedure: Cases and Commentaries, 10th edit., 2002, Criminal Procedure and the Constitution: Leading Cases and Introductory Text, 2002; (with F. Inbau and T. Arnold) Criminal Justice in Our Time, 1965; (with J. Grano and J. Haddad) Sum and Substance of Criminal Procedure, 1977, Police Interrogation and Confessions: Essays in Law and Policy, 1980; contbr. articles to profl. jours. Served to 1st lt. AUS, 1951-52. Recipient Am. Bar Found. Rsch. award, 1996. Home: 2910 Daleview Dr Ann Arbor MI 48105-9684 Office: U Mich Law Sch 625 S State St Ann Arbor MI 48109-1215

KAMPINE, JOHN P. anesthesiology and physiology educator; MD, PhD, U. Wis. Prof., chair dept. anesthesiology Med. U. Wis., Milw., prof. physiology. Mem.: Inst. Medicine-NAS. Office: Froedtert Meml Hosp PO Box 26099 9200 W Wisconsin Ave Milwaukee WI 53226-3596

KAMPOURIS, EMMANUEL ANDREW, retired corporate executive; b. Alexandria, Egypt, Dec. 14, 1934; came to U.S., 1979; s. Andrew George and Euridice Anne (Caralli) K.; m. Myrto Stellatos, July 4, 1959 (dec.); children: Andrew, Alexander Student, King's Sch., Bruton, Somerset, U.K., 1953; M.A. in Law, Oxford U., 1957; cert. in ceramic tech., North Staffordshire Coll. of Tech., U.K., 1962. Plant mgr., dir. "KEREM", Athens, Greece, 1962-64; dir. "HELLENIT", Greece, 1962-65; mng. dir. Ideal Standard, 1966-79; v.p., group exec. internat. and export Am. Standard Inc., New Brunswick, NJ, 1979-84, sr. v.p. bldg. products, 1984-89; pres., chief exec. officer Am. Standard Inc., Am. Standard Cos. Inc., N.Y.C., 1989-99, now chmn.; bd. dirs. Click Commerce Inc, Chgo. Bd. dirs. Ideal Refractories SAI, Athens, Ideal Standard Mexico, Am. Standard Sanitaryware (Thailand) Ltd., INCESA, San Jose, Costa Rica, Hoxan Corp., Sapporo, Japan. Bd. dirs. Greek Mgmt. Assn., Athens, 1975-77, Fedn. of Greek Industries, Athens. Mem. Young Pres. Orgn., Chief Execs. Orgn., Econ. Club of N.Y., Oxford Union, Oxford Law Soc., Am. Hellenic C. of C. (gen. sec. 1975-79), Chemists Club, Laurel Valley Golf Club. Greek Orthodox. Clubs: Spring Brook Country (Morristown, N.J.); Quogue Field, Quogue Beach (L.I., N.Y.). Avocations: golf; tennis; classical music. Office: Click Commerce Inc 200 E Randolph Dr Ste 4900 Chicago IL 60601

KAMPS, CHARLES Q. lawyer; b. Milw., Mar. 21, 1932; s. John G. and Mary (Quarles) K.; m. Mary B. Stehling, Sept. 28, 1963; children: Charles Jr., Louisa. LLB, Marquette U., 1959. Bar: Wis. 1959. Ptnr. Quarles & Brady, Milw., 1959—. Mem. U.S. Sailing Assn. (mem. sailing team, Olympic yachting com. of U.S.), Milwaukee Yacht Club (past commodore, 1971-72). Office: Quarles & Brady 411 E Wisconsin Ave Ste 2550 Milwaukee WI 53202-4497

KAMYSZEW, CHRISTOPHER D. museum curator, executive educator, art consultant; b. Warsaw, Poland, May 7, 1958; came to U.S., 1982; s. Mieczyslaw and Zofia (Kubik) K.; children: Oliver G., Samuel. BA, U. Warsaw, 1982, MA in Polish Lit. and Lang., 1984. Freelance writer and translator, Poland, 1977-81; freelance theatre dir. Dearborn Theatre Co., Chgo., 1982-83, Ossetynski Actors Lab., L.A., 1982-83; head lit. sect. Krag-Underground Publishers, Warsaw, 1980-83; head archives dept. Polish Mus. Am., Chgo., 1985-88, dir., curator, 1988-93; pres. Soc. for the Arts, 1993—. Bd. dirs. Gallery 58, Chgo.; pres. Inst. Symbological Rsch., Chgo., 1986-95, Internat. Ind. Theatre Found., Washington, 1985-86; exec. dir. Polish TV-USA, 1994-97. Co-author, editor: Collective Works of L.-F Celine, 1983, Literary Essays by L. Tyrmand, 1983; curated over 90 exhbts. in U.S. Dir., CEO Polish Film Festival, 1988—, Europe Film Festival, 1996—. Recipient Zycie Warszawy award, 1977, Audience award Edinburgh Theatre Festival, 1980, award for disting. translation Assn. Polish Translators, 1990, award Found. of Friends of Polish Mus., 1991, award of the Ministry of Fgn. Affairs of Poland, 1993, Laterna Magica award for disting. achievements in film, 1994; Wiehmann Found. scholar, 1982, Golden Cross of Merit, 2001, Copernican award, 2002. Avocations: reading, classical music, map collecting, cross-country skiing. Office: Society for Arts 1112 N Milwaukee Ave Chicago IL 60622-4017 E-mail: societyforarts@viprofix.com.

KANCELBAUM, JOSHUA JACOB, lawyer; b. Cleve., May 9, 1936; s. Charles P. and Bertha (Wigotsky) K.; m. Pamela Scotty, Nov. 21, 1973; 1 child, Barbara R. BA, Case Western Res. U., 1958, LLB, 1960. Bar: Ohio 1960, U.S. Ct. Mil. Appeals 1963, U.S. Supreme Ct. 1966, U.S. Tax Ct. 1976. Assoc. Ulmer, Berne, Laronge, Glickman & Curtis, Cleve., 1961-63, Berkman & Gordon, 1963-65; ptnr. Berkman, Gordon, Kancelbaum, Levy & Murray, 1966-79; pvt. practice Ohio, 1979—. Adj. prof. law Cleve. State U., 1979-80; spl. ch.-state counsel ACLU of Ohio, 1965-85. Pres. Am. Jewish Congress of No. Ohio, 1979-81, mem. nat. governing coun., chmn. commn. on law and social action, 1982-84. With U.S. Army, 1961. Mem. Ohio Bar Assn., Geauga County Bar Assn., Geauga County Law Libr. Assn. (trustee 1995-2000). Home: PO Box 657 Newbury OH 44065-0657 Office: 8228 Mayfield Rd Chesterland OH 44026-2542

KANE, JOHN C. retired health care products company executive; b. 1939; married BS, West Chester State Coll., 1961. With Merck Co., 1967-70; mgr. plant Schick Co., until 1974; gen. mgr. Lav Industries; ops. mgr. corp. procurement Abbott Labs., North Chicago, Ill., 1974-76, dir. corp. procurement, 1976-77, dir. ops., devel. corp. materials mgr., 1977-78, div., v.p. Puerto Rican site, 1978-79, dir. v.p. corp. materials mgmt., 1979-81, v.p. chem. and agrl. products, from 1981, exec. v.p. Ross Labs. div., COO, pres. Columbus, Ohio, 1989-2000; ret., 2000. Office: Cardinal Health Inc 7000 Cardinal Pl. Dublin OH 43017

KANE, LUCILE M. retired archivist, historian; b. Maiden Rock, Wis., Mar. 17, 1920; d. Emery John and Ruth (Coty) Kane BS, River Falls State Tchrs. Coll., 1942; MA, U. Minn., 1946. Tchr. Osceola (Wis.) High Sch., 1942-44; asst. publicity dept. U. Minn. Press, Mpls., 1945-46; rsch. fellow, editor Forest Products History Found., St. Paul, 1946-48; curator manuscripts Minn. Hist. Soc., 1948-75, sr. rsch. fellow, 1979-85, sr. rsch. assoc., 1985—, mem. hon. coun., 1988—. State archivist, 1975—79. Author, compiler: A Guide to the Care and Administration of Manuscripts, 2d edit., 1966, (with Kathryn A. Johnson) Manuscripts Collections of the Minnesota Historical Society, Guide No.2, 1955, The Waterfall That Built a City, 1966 (updated edit. pub. as The Falls of St. Anthony, 1987), (with Alan Ominsky) Twin Cities: A Pictorial History of Saint Paul and Minneapolis, 1983; transl., editor, Military Life in Dakota, The Jour. of Philippe Regis de Trobriand, 1951; editor: (with others) The Northern Expeditions of Major Stephen H. Long, 1978; contbr. articles to profl. jours. Recipient award of Merit Western History Assn., 1982, Disting. Svc. award Minn. Humanities Commn., 1983, award of Distinction Am. Assn. State and Local History, 1987; co-recipient Theodore C. Blegen award Minn. Hist. Soc., 1996. Fellow: Soc. Am. Archivists. Home: 1298 Fairmount Ave Saint Paul MN 55105-2703

KANE, ROBERT B. mathematics educator, academic dean; b. Oak Park, Ill., July 27, 1928; married; 5 children. BS in Math., U. Ill., 1950, MS in Math. Edn., 1958, PhD in Math. Edn., 1960. Secondary sch. math. tchr., 1950-51; math. analyst Armed Forces Security Agy., 1951-53; with mktg. dept. Standard Oil Co., 1953-57; exec. sec. Ill. Citizens' Edn. Com., 1957-58; rsch. assoc. U. Ill., Champaign, 1958-60; asst. prof. edn. & math. Purdue U., West Lafayette, Ind., 1960-63, assoc. prof., 1963-68, prof. edn. & math., 1968-93, chmn. math. & sci. edn., 1970-75, head dept. edn., dir. tchr. edn., 1975-88, dean sch. edn., 1988-91. Vis. rsch. prof. edn. U. Canterbury, Christchurch, New Zealand, 1969-70, dean edn. and prof. emeritus math. edn., 1993; pres., editor-in-chief Voyaging Press, 1982—; cons. Depts. Pub. Instrn., Ind., N.Y., N.C., Pa., Tex., N.J., also sch. dists. in 20 states and Washington, D.C.; cons. New Zealand Ministry Edn.; condr. 120 workshops for tchrs., suprs., sch. adminstrs.; math. cons. New Standard Encyclopedia; proposal evaluator NSF; mem. Edn. Senates Purdue U., Schs. Humanities, Social Sci. and Edn.; mem., chair area com. for social scis. & edn. Purdue U. Grad. Coun.; mem. select joint com. on minimal competency testing Ind. State Legislature; instl. rep., mem. steering com. Midwest region Holmes Group; mem., vice-chair curriculum standards com. Ind. Curriculum Adv. Coun.; editorial advisor jours. Arithmetic Tchr., Jour. Rsch. in Math. Edn., Math. Tchr. Co-author: The Modern Mathematics Series (108 total vols.), 1963-64, Operating with Mathematics, 1969, New Goals in Mathematics, 1969, Action Masters for Mathematics in Action (6 total vols.), 1969, Activity Books for Mathematics in Action (12 total vols.), 1970, Target: Meeting Mathematics (78 total vols.), 1973-74, Trigonometry, 1973, College Algebra and Trigonometry, 1974, Helping Children Read Mathematics, 1974, Algebra and Trigonometry, Structure and Method, 1977, 86, General Mathematics, 1977, Fundamentals of Mathematics, 1982, Pre-Algebra, 1985, 35 other math. texts, tchr's. edits.; contbr. over 50 articles to profl. jours. Recipient 18 grants USOE, NSF, Purdue Rsch. Found., Phi Delta Kappa, U.S. Dept. Edn., U.S. Info. Agy., 1959-90. Fellow AAAS; mem. Am. Ednl. Rsch. Assn., Ind. Coun. Tchrs. Math. (bd. dirs. 1967-70, editor Ind. Math. Newsletter 1963-65), Nat. Coun. Tchrs. Math. (speakers' core 1967-71), Math. Assn. Am., Ind. Assn. Colls. for Tchr. Edn. (exec. com. 1977, v.p. 1979-80, pres. 1980-82), Am. Assn. Colls. for Tchr. Edn. (chief instl. rep. 1975-91), Big Ten/Big Eight Dean's Network, Phi Delta Kappa. Address: 4122 Verdant Ln West Lafayette IN 47906-4673

KANE, ROBERT LEWIS, public health educator; b. N.Y.C., Jan. 18, 1940; m. Rosalie Smolkin, June 17, 1962; children: Miranda, Ingrid, Kate AB, Columbia Coll., N.Y.C., 1961; MD, Harvard U., 1965. Acting coordinator sr. clerkship program dept. community medicine U. Ky., Lexington, 1968-69; svc. unit dir. USPHS Indian Hosp., Shiprock, N.Mex., 1969-70; spl. asst. to regional health dir. USPHS HEW Region VIII, Denver, 1970-71; from asst. to assoc. prof. family and community medicine U. Utah Sch. Medicine, Salt Lake City, 1970-77; sr. researcher The Rand Corp., Santa Monica, Calif., 1977-85; from assoc. prof. to prof. medicine UCLA Sch. Medicine, 1978-85; prof. Sch. Pub. Health UCLA, 1980-85, U. Minn., 1985—, dean, 1985-90; intern U. Ky. Med. Ctr., Lexington, 1965-66, resident in community medicine, 1966-69. Adj. prof. Leonard Davis Sch. Gerontology, U. So. Calif., 1982-85; mem. expert com. on aging WHO, 1986—; Minn. endowed chair in long-term care and aging, 1989—; mem. adv. com. on Alzheimer's Disease, Washington, 1988-96; mem. com. on quality Inst. Medicine, 1988-90. Co-author: A Will and A Way, 1985, Long-term Care: Principles, Programs, and Policies, 1987, Essentials of Clinical Geriatrics, 4th edit., 1999, Understanding Health Care Outcomes Research, 1997, The Heart of Long Term Care, 1998, Assessing Older Persons, 2000. With USPHS, 1969-70. Home: 2715 E Lake Of The Isles Pky Minneapolis MN 55408-1053

KANER, HARVEY SHELDON, lawyer, executive; b. June 26, 1930; s. Rueben and Lillian Kaner; m. Caren Lee Gross, June 5, 1960; children: Amy B., Daniel E., Jason M. (dec.), Joshua A. B.B.A., U. Minn., 1952, LL.B., 1955. Bar: Minn. Sole practice, Mpls., 1956-58; asst. corp. counsel Farmers Union GTA (now Harvest States Cooperatives), St. Paul, 1958-59, corp. counsel, 1959-77, v.p. law, 1977-82, sr. v.p., corp. counsel, 1982-93; sr. v.p. and exec. counsel Harvest States Cooperatives, 1993-94; ret., 1994. Past sec. St. Louis Grain Corp.; lectr. extension program U. Wis., Madison; past dir. Farmers Export Co.; trustee Corp. Pension Funds Author publs. Products Liability, 1977 Served with USNG, 1947-49 Mem. ABA, Minn. State Bar Assn., Hennepin County Bar Assn., Nat. Council Farmer Coops. (mem. legal, tax and acctg. com.) Jewish Home: 4000 Royal Marco Way Apt 622 Marco Island FL 34145-7812

KANFER, FREDERICK H. psychologist, educator; married; 2 children. Student, Cooper Union Sch. Tech., Sch. Engring., 1942-44; BS cum laude, L.I. U., 1948; MA, Ind. U., 1952, PhD, 1953. Lic. psychologist, Oreg. Rsch. asst. Ind. U., 1949-52; asst. Psychol. Clinic, 1952-53, tchg. fellow in abnormal psychology, 1953; trainee VA Hosp., Indpls., 1951-52; asst. prof. psychology, dir. Psychoednl. Clinic, Washington U., St. Louis, 1953-57; cons. and asso. E.H. Parsons, M.D. and Assocs., 1955-57; assoc. prof. Purdue U., 1957-62; vis. prof. med. psychology U. Oreg. Med. Sch., summers 1958, 60, prof. psychiatry, 1962-69; vis. prof. psychology U. Oreg., Eugene, summers and winters 1967, 79; prof. psychology U. Cin., 1969-73; prof. U. Ill., Champaign, 1973-95, prof. emeritus, 1995—; sr. fellow, prof. U. Minn., Mpls., 1995-98. Fulbright lectr. Ruhr U., Bochum, Germany, 1968; guest prof. U. Salzburg, Austria, 1987; cons., spkr. in field; lectr., vis. prof. including univs. Oxford, Madrid, Heidelberg, Amsterdam, Berlin, Oslo, Cologne, Munich, Graz, Rome, Verona, Munster, Marburg, Wurzburg, London, Nijmegen, Copenhagen, Basel, Stockholm, Trondheim, Salzburg, Fribourg, Bern, Athens, Budapest; organizer, supr. postdoctoral tng. program for European psychologists univs. Cin. and Ill., 1969-87; vis. lectr. Inst. Environ. Health, U. Cin. Med. Sch., 1970-73, vis. prof. psychiatry, 1973-79; Morton vis. prof. Ohio U., 1976; sr. lectr. U. Bern, 1980-92; Disting. vis. prof. Dept. Air Force, 1983; adv. bd. Cambridge Ctr. for behavioral Studies, 1982-98; bd. advisors Internat. Alliance Health Edn., Stockholm, 1983—; mem. interna t. adv. bd. Max-Planck Inst. Psychiatry, 1985-90. Author: (with J.S. Phillips) Learning Foundations of Behavior Therapy, 1970, (with others) Premier Symposium Sobre Apprendizaje y Modificacion de Conducta en Ambientes educativos, 1975, (with Bruce K. Scheffi) Guiding the Therapeutic Change Process, 1988, (with H. Reinecker and D. Schmelzer) Selbstmanagement-Therapie, 1991, 3d rev. edit., 2000, (with D. Schmelzer) Wegweiser Verhaltenstherapie: Psychotherapie als chance, 2001; contbr. numerous articles to profl. publs.; editor: (with A.P. Goldstein) Helping People Change: A Textbook of Methods, 1975, 3d rev. edit., 1980, 4th rev. edit., 1991, Maximizing Treatment Gains: Transfer Enhancement in Psychotherapy, 1979, (with P. Karoly) The Psychology of Self-Management, 1982; (with S. Englund, C. Lenhoff and J. Rhodes) A Mentor Manual: For Adults Who Work With Pregnant and Parenting Teens, 1995; assoc. editor: Psychol. Reports, 1961-99, Jour. Addictive Behaviors, 1974-80; editl. bd. Behavior Therapy, 1969-74, Behavior Modification, 1975-84, Cognitive Therapy and Research, 1976-80, 83-92, Behavioral Assessment, 1979-81, Clin. Psychology Rev., 1980-85, 87-92, Revista de Psicologia Generaly Aplicada, 1980—, Jour. Social and Clin. Psychology, 1982-98, Jour. Clin. Psychology and Psychosomatics, 1982—; internat. editl. bd. Verhaltens Therapie (Behavior Therapy), study and editl. reviewer; adv. editor: Research Press, 1978-96. With U.S. Army, 1944-46. Recipient Alexander von Humboldt Sr. Scientist award, 1987-88; U. Ill. Rsch. Bd. grantee, 1973-78; U. Ill. Rsch. Bd. univ. scholar, 1990-93. Fellow Am. Psychol. Assn. (exec. council div. 12); mem. Midwestern Psychol. Assn., AAAS, Assn. Advancement Behavioral Therapies (dir. 1972-74), Am. Bd. Examiners Profl. Psychology (diplomate), Sigma Xi; hon. life mem. Italian Soc. Behavior Therapy, German Assn. Clin. Behavior Therapy, Orgn. Behavior Therapy Uruguay Office: U Ill Dept Psychology 603 E Daniel St Champaign IL 61820-6232 E-mail: fkanfer@s.psych.uiuc.edu.

KANG, EMIL J. orchestra executive; b. N.Y., 1969; BS in Econs., U. Rochester (N.Y.). Orch. mgr. Seattle Symphony Orch., 1996-99; v.p. ops. Detroit Symphony Orch., 1999-2000, pres., exec. dir., 2000—. Office: Detroit Symphony Orch 3663 Woodward Ave Ste 100 Detroit MI 48201-2444

KANG, SUNG-MO (STEVE KANG), electrical engineering educator; b. Seoul, Korea, Feb. 25, 1945; came to U.S., 1969; s. Chang-Shik and Kyung-Ja (Lee) K.; m. Myoung-A Cha, June 10, 1972; children: Jennifer, Jeffrey. BSEE, Fairleigh Dickinson U., 1970; MSEE, SUNY, Buffalo, 1972; PhD in Elec. Engring., U. Calif., Berkeley, 1975. Asst. prof. Rutgers U., Piscataway, N.J., 1975-77; mem. tech. staff AT&T Bell Labs., Murray Hill, 1977-82, supr., 1982-85; prof. U. Ill., Urbana, 1985-2000, head dept. electrical and computer engring., 1995-2000, assoc. Ctr. for Advanced Study, 1991-92, assoc. dir. microelectronics lab., 1988-95; univ. scholar U. Ill., 1995-96. Dir. Ctr. for ASIC R&D, dean sch. engring. U. Calif., Santa Cruz, 2001—. Author 8 books; contbr. over 300 papers to internat. jours. and confs.; 12 patents. Recipient Meritorious Svc. award Cirs. and Sys. Soc., 1994, Humboldt Rsch. award for Sr. U.S. Scientists, 1996, Grad. Teaching award IEEE, 1996, IEEE CAS Soc. Tech. Achievement award, 1997, KBS award in Sci. and Tech., 1998, SRC Tech. Excellence award, 1999, Alumnus award U. Calif., Berkeley, 2001. Fellow AAAS, ACM, IEEE (various offices in Circuits and Systems Soc. including pres. 1991, founding editor-in-chief Trans. on VSLI systems, Disting. lectr. 1994-97, Darlington award, SRC Inventor Recognition award 1993, 96, 99, 2001, Meritorious Svc. award Compuer Soc. 1990, CAS Soc. Golden Jubilee medal 1999, Millennium medal 2000), Nat. Acad. Engring. of Korea (fgn. mem.). Presbyterian. Avocations: tennis, travel. Office: U Calif Baskin Sch Engring Santa Cruz CA 95064 E-mail: kang@soe.ucsc.edu.

KANNE, MARVIN GEORGE, newspaper publishing executive; b. St. Louis, 1937; Student, St. Louis U. V.p., dir. ops. St. Louis Post-Dispatch. Mem. Am. Assn. Indsl. Mgmt., Am. Mgmt. Assn., IRRA Indsl. Rels. Rsch. Assn. Office: Saint Louis Post-Dispatch 900 N Tucker Blvd Saint Louis MO 63101-1099

KANNE, MICHAEL STEPHEN, judge; b. Rensselaer, Ind., Dec. 21, 1938; s. Allen Raymond and Jane (Robinson) Kanne; m. Judith Ann Stevens, June 22, 1963; children: Anne, Katherine. Student, St. Joseph's Coll., Rensselaer, 1957—58; BS, Ind. U., 1962, JD, 1968; postgrad., Boston U., 1963, U. Birmingham, Eng., 1975. Bar: Ind. 1968. Assoc. Nesbitt and Fisher, Rensselaer, 1968—71; sole practice, 1971—72; atty. City of Rensselaer, 1972; judge 30th Jud. Cir. of Ind., 1972—82, U.S. Dist. Ct. (no. dist.) Ind., Hammond, 1982—87, U.S. Ct. Appeals, Chgo., 1987—; chmn. U.S. Cts. Design Guide, 1988—95. Lectr. law St. Joseph's Coll., 1975—89, St. Frances Coll., 1990—91; faculty Nat. Inst. for Trial Advocacy, South Bend, Ind., 1978—88. Bd. visitors Ind. U. Sch. Law, 1987—, Ind. U. Sch. Pub. and Environ. Affairs, 1991—; trustee St. Joseph's Coll., 1984—. 1st lt. USAF, 1962—65. Named Outstanding Alumnus, Today's Cath. Tchr., 1991; recipient Disting. Svc. award, St. Joseph's Coll., 1973, Disting. Grad. award, Nat. Cath. Ednl. Assn. Mem.: FBA, Tippecanoe County Bar Assn., Jasper County Bar Assn. (pres. 1972—76), Ind. State Bar Assn. (bd. dirs. 1977—79, Presdl. citation 1979), Law Alumni Assn. Ind. U. (pres. 1980). Roman Catholic. Avocations: horseback riding, weightlifting. Office: Charles A Halleck Federal Building 234 N Fourth Street PO Box 1340 Lafayette IN 47902-1340 also: US Ct Appeals 219 S Dearborn St Ste 2722 Chicago IL 60604-1874

KANTROWITZ, ADRIAN, surgeon, educator; b. N.Y.C., Oct. 4, 1918; s. Bernard Abraham and Rose (Esserman) K.; m. Jean Rosensaft, Nov. 25, 1948; children: Niki, Lisa, Allen. AB, NYU, 1940; MD, L.I. Coll. Medicine, 1943; postgrad. physiology, Western Res. U., 1950. Diplomate: Am. Bd. Surgery, Am. Bd. Thoracic Surgery. Gen. rotating intern Jewish Hosp. Bklyn., 1944; asst. resident, then resident surgery Mt. Sinai Hosp., N.Y.C., 1947; asst. resident Montefiore Hosp., 1948, asst. resident pathology, 1949, fellow cardiovascular rsch. group, 1949, chief resident surgery, 1950, adj. surg. svc., 1951-55; USPHS fellow cardiovascular rsch., dept. physiology Western Res. U., 1951-52; asst. prof. surgery SUNY Coll. Medicine, 1955-56, assoc. prof. surgery, 1957-64, prof., 1964-70; dir. cardiovascular surgery Maimonides Med. Ctr., Bklyn., 1955-64, dir. surgery, 1964-70; chmn. dept. surgery Sinai Hosp. Detroit, 1970-75, chmn. dept. cardiovascular surgery, 1975-85; prof. surgery Wayne State U. Sch. Medicine, 1970—. Contbr. articles profl. jours. 1st lt. to capt., M.C. AUS, 1944-46. Recipient H.L. Moses prize to Montefiore Alumnus for outstanding rsch. accomplishment, 1949; 1st prize sci. exhibit Conv. N.Y. State Med. Soc., 1952; Gold Plate award Am. Acad. Achievement, 1966; Max Berg award for outstanding achievement in prolonging human life, 1966; Theodore and Susan B. Cummings humanitarian award Am. Coll. Cardiology, 1967 Fellow ACS, N.Y. Acad. Sci.; mem. Internat. Soc. Angiology, Am. Soc. Artificial Internal Organs (pres. 1968-69, Barney Clark award 1993), N.Y. County Med. Soc., Harvey Soc., N.Y. Soc. Thoracic Surgery, N.Y. Soc. Cardiovascular Surgery, Am. Heart Assn., Am. Physiol. Soc., Am. Coll. Cardiology, Am. Coll. Chest Physicians, Bklyn. Thoracic Surgery Soc. (pres. 1967-68), Pan Am. Med. Assn., Soaring Soc. Am., Am. Ski Assn. Achievements include being pub. pioneer motion pictures taken inside living heart, 1950; contbr. to devel. pump- oxygenators for human heart surgey; pioneer devel. mech., artificial hearts; performed 1st permanent partial mech. heart surgery in humans, 1966; 1st use phase-shift intra-aortic balloon pump in patient in cardiogenic shock; 1st human heart transplant in U.S., Dec. 1967. Home: 70 Gallogly Rd Auburn Hills MI 48326-1227 Office: 300 River Place Dr Detroit MI 48207-4233 E-mail: adriank3ak@aol.com.

KANZEG, DAVID GEORGE, radio station executive; b. Cleve., Apr. 9, 1948; s. George and Ida Marie Ada (Hienz) K. BA, Coll. Wooster (Ohio), 1970; MS, Syracuse (N.Y.) U., 1971; postgrad., SUNY, 1972. Cert. ESL lang. instr. Inst. English Meyer Lang. Ctr., Bogota, Colombia, 1969; grad. teaching asst. Syracuse U., 1971; instr. speech State U. Coll. at Buffalo, N.Y., 1971-73; exec. producer Sta. WCMU-FM Cen. Mich. U., Mt. Pleasant, 1973-76; radio program mgr. Sta. WLRH/Madison County Pub. Libr., Huntsville, Ala., 1976-77; radio program dir. Sta. WOUB-AM-FM Ohio U. Telecommunications, Athens, 1977-83; mgr. programming Sta. WNYC/N.Y. Pub. Radio, N.Y.C., 1983-86; sta. advisor Corp. for Pub. Broadcasting, Cleve., 1978-87; dir. programming Sta. WCPN/Cleve. Pub. Radio, 1987-99, v.p. programming divsn., 1999—2001; cons. Corp. for Pub. Broadcasting Mgmt. Consulting Svc., 1993—; sr. dir., sta. mgr. WCPN/Ideastream, 2001—. Participant seminars on future pub. radio, San Francisco and Washington, 1984-85; panel mem. Airlie IV Seminar on Art of Radio, N.Y.C., 1983; radio organizer Nat. Assn. Ednl. Broadcasters, Washington, 1976-78; exec. producer Future Forward Nat. Radio Series, 1985. Author: Transit Revisions, 1988, Ever Young: Douglas Moore and the Persistence of Legend, 1993; contbr. articles to publs; author, co-creator website. Mem. Isabella County sub-com. on transp., Mt. Pleasant, Mich., 1975; incorporator Mid-Mich. Opera Assn., Mt. Pleasant, 1975, Tenn. Valley Opera Assn., Huntsville, 1976; mem. media panel Ohio Arts Coun., Columbus, Ohio, 1979-80; active Airlie II Seminar on Art of Radio, 1979. Recipient Tech. Prodn. award Ohio Ednl. Broadcasting, 1980, Ohio State award, 1986. Mem. Ohio Pub. Radio Programming (group chmn. 1978-80), Assn. Inds. in Radio, No. Ohio Bibliophilic Soc., Sigma Delta Pi. Avocations: roller coasters, opera, traction, bicycling, travel. Home: 16253 Shurmer Rd Cleveland OH 44136-6115 Office: Sta WCPN/Cleve Pub Radio 3100 Chester Ave Ste 300 Cleveland OH 44114-4604

KANZLER, MICHAEL W. manufacturing company executive; CFO Ty, Oak Brook, Ill. Office: Ty PO Box 5377 Oak Brook IL 60522 Office Fax: (630) 920-8873.

KAO, WILLIAM CHISHON, dentist; b. Santiago, Chile, July 10, 1952; s. John S. and Mary Kao; m. Susie M. Moy, June 3, 1978; children: Jonathan, Kristen. BS with high honors, U. Ill., Chgo., 1974, BS in Dentistry with honors, 1976, DDS with honors, 1978. Comprehensive inst. U. Ill. Coll. Dentistry, Chgo., 1978-80; dentist, assoc. Dental Bldg., Oak Lawn, Ill., 1978-83; pvt. practice Carol Stream, 1978-82; dentist Preventive Dental Group, Glendale Heights, 1982-86; pvt. practice Roselle, 1986—. Mem. ADA (presiding chmn. ltd. attendance clinic at midwinter conv. 1980), Am. Acad. Implant Dentistry, U.S. Dental Inst., Ill. State Dental Soc., Chgo. Dental Soc., Ill. Dental Soc., Roselle C. of C., Bloomingdale Study Club, Bloomingdale Study Club (pres.). Avocation: tennis. Office: 1150 Lake St Roselle IL 60172-3385

KAPLAN, ARNOLD, health service organization executive; BS in Commerce, Engring., Drexel U., 1962; MS in Indsl. Adminstrn., Carnegie-Mellon U., 1964. Sr. v.p., CFO Air Products Chem., Inc.; CFO United Healthcare Corp., Mpls., 1998-2001. Past bd. dirs. Baum Sch. Art. Recipient Drexel 100 award, 1992. Mem. Fin. Execs. Rsch. Found. (bd. dirs.), Phi Kappa Phi. Office: United Healthcare Group Inc MN008-T910 PO Box 1459 Minneapolis MN 55440-1459

KAPLAN, HARVEY L. lawyer; b. Kansas City, Mo., Nov. 11, 1942; BS in Pharmacy, U. Mich., 1965; JD, U. Mo., 1968. Bar: Mo. 1968, U.S. Tax Ct. 1971, U.S. Supreme Ct. 1971. Ptnr. Shook, Hardy & Bacon LLP, Kansas City. Faculty mem. NITA Advanced Advocacy Program, 1988-89; mem. Kansas City-St. Louis Panel, CPR Inst. Dispute Resolution, 1989—. Mem. bd. editors Mo. Law Rev., 1967-68. Fellow Internat. Acad. Trial Lawyers (bd. dirs. 1991-97, 98—, sec.-treas. 2001—), Internat. Soc. Barristers, Am. Bar Found.; mem. Am. Soc. Pharmacy Law, Mo. Orgn. Def. Lawyers (bd. dirs. 1985-93), Internat. Assn. Def. Counsel (exec. com. 1991-94, def. counsel trial acad. 1989, dir.-elect 1992, dir. 1993, found. bd. dirs. 2000), Def. Rsch. Inst. (chmn. drug and med. device litigation com. 1991-94, bd. dirs. 1995-98, Law Inst. 1998-2001), Nat. Judicial Coll. (adv. coun. 1993—),Phi Delta Phi. Office: Shook Hardy & Bacon LLP 1 Kansas City Pl 1200 Main St Ste 2700 Kansas City MO 64105-2118 E-mail: hkaplan@shb.com.

KAPLAN, HENRY JERROLD, ophthalmologist, educator; b. N.Y.C., Dec. 29, 1942; s. Ralph and Henrietta (Davis) K.; m. Adele Lotner, June 26, 1966; children: Wendi Suzanne, Todd Daniel, Ariane Dev. AB, Columbia U., 1964; MD, Cornell U., 1968. Diplomate Am. Bd. Ophthalmology. Intern in medicine Lakeside Hosp., Univ. Hosps. Cleve., Case-Western Res. U., 1968-69; surg. resident Bellevue Hosp., NYU Med. Ctr., 1969-70; NIH rsch. fellow in immunology U. Tex. (Southwestern) Med. Sch., Dallas, 1972-74, asst. prof. dept. cell biology, 1974-75; resident in ophthalmology U. Iowa Hosps. and Clinics, Iowa City, 1975-78; retina-vitreous fellow dept. ophthalmology Med. Coll. Wis., Milw., 1978-79; assoc. prof. dept. ophthalmology Emory U. Sch. Medicine, Atlanta, 1979-84, prof., dir. rsch., 1984-88, assoc. prof. dept. microbiology, 1985-88; prof. dept. ophthalmology and visual scis. Washington U. Sch. Medicine, St. Louis, 1988-2000, chmn. dept. ophthalmology and visual scis., 1988-98; prof., chmn. dept. opthalmology and visual scis. U. Louisville (Ky.) Sch. Medicine, 2000—, William H. and Blondina F. Evans Prof. Ophthalmology, 2000—. Ophthalmologist in chief Barnes-Jewish Hosp., Washington U. Med. Ctr., 1988-98; affiliate scientist in pathology and immunology Yerkes Regional Primate Rsch. Ctr., Atlanta, 1981—; adj. prof. dept. small animal medicine U. Ga., Athens, 1985—; assoc. chief ophthalmology Emory U. Hosp., 1985-88; mem. visual scis. study sect. A-1 NIH, Bethesda, Md., 1985-89, chmn., 1987-89; pres. Barnes Eye Care Network, 1994-98; dir. Ky. Lions Eye Ctr., Louisville, 2000—. Author, co-author or editor, co-editor more than 200 med. textbooks, chpts. and articles on uveitis and macular degeneration and retinal degeneration pub. in refereed sci. and med. jours., 1974—; mem. sci. jour. rev. bds. Archives Ophthalmology, 1978—, Retina, 1982—, Am. Jour. Ophthalmology, 1983—, Ophthalmology, 1983—, Current Eye Rsch., 1986—, Exptl. Eye Rsch., 1986—; mem. sci. rev. bd. Investigative Ophthalmology and Visual Sci., 1983—, mem. editorial bd., 1990-92; co-editor Ocular Immunology and Inflammation, 1994-98; editor: Ocular Immunology and Inflammation, 1999—. Maj. M.C., USAF, 1970-72. Recipient sci. award Alcon Rsch. Inst., 1987; Olga Keith Weiss rsch. scholar to Prevent Blindness, Inc., N.Y.C., 1984. Fellow ACS, Am. Acad. Ophthalmology (Honor award 1984, Sr. Honor award 1994); mem. AMA, Assn. for Rsch. in Vision and Ophthalmology, Am. Assn. Immunologists, Macula Soc., Am. Uveitis Soc. (pres. 1997-99), Retina Soc., St. Louis Ophthal. Soc., St. Louis Met. Med. Soc., Mo. Ophthal. Soc. Jewish. E-mail: njkapl01@gwise.louisville.edu Office: U Louisville Sch Medicine Dept Opthalmol & Visual Sci 301 E Muhammad Ali Blvd Louisville KY 40202-1511 E-mail: hank.kaplan@louisville.edu.

KAPLAN, JARED, lawyer; b. Chgo., Dec. 28, 1938; s. Jerome and Phyllis Enid (Rieber) K.; m. Rosellen Engstrom, Dec. 28, 1964 (div. 1978); children: Brian F., Philip B.; m. Maridee Quanbeck, June 2, 1990. AB, UCLA, 1960; LLB, Harvard, 1963. Bar: Ill. 1963, U.S. Dist. Ct. (no. dist.) Ill. 1969, U.S. Tax Ct. 1978. Assoc. Ross & Hardies, Chgo., 1963-69, ptnr., 1970, Roan & Grossman, Chgo., 1970-83, Keck, Mahin & Cate, Chgo., 1983-94, McDermott, Will & Emery, Chgo., 1994—. Bd. dirs. ESOP (Employee Stock Ownership Plan) Assn., Washington, 1987-90, Family Firm Inst., Boston, 1996-99; adv. coun. Ill. Employee-Owned Enterprise, Chgo., 1984-98; chmn. Ill. Adv. Task Force on Ownership Succession and Employee Ownership, 1994-95. Editor in chief: Callaghan's Fed. Tax Guide, 1988; author: Employee Stock Ownership Plans, 1999. Nat. pres. Ripon Soc., Washington, 1975-76; adv. council mem. Rep. Nat. Com., Washington, 1978-80; alt. delegate Rep. Nat. Conv., Detroit, 1980; bd. dirs. Family Firm Inst., 1996-99. Fellow Ill. Bar Found.; mem. ABA (chmn. section of taxation, administrv. practice com. 1978-80), City Club, Chgo. (bd. govs. 1982-92), Univ. Club, Met. Club. Republican. Jewish. Home: 105 W Delaware Pl Chicago IL 60610-3200 Office: McDermott Will & Emery 227 W Monroe St Fl 44 Chicago IL 60606-5018 E-mail: jkaplan@mwe.com., jkaplan0@aol.com.

KAPLAN, JOSEPH, pediatrician; b. Boston, Mar. 7, 1941; Student, Dartmouth U., 1958-60; BA, NYU, 1962; MD, Johns Hopkins U., 1966.

Intern, resident in pediatrics Johns Hopkins Hosp., Balt., 1969-72; mem. staff Children's Hosp. Mich., Detroit, 1972—; prof. pediat., medicine and immunology-microbiology Wayne State U. Sch. Medicine, 1972—. Contbr. article to profl. publ. Maj. U.S. Army, 1969-72. Recipient Rsch. Career Devel. award NIH, 1975-80. Office: Children's Hosp 3901 Beaubien St Detroit MI 48201-2196 E-mail: jkaplan@med.wayne.edu.

KAPLAN, MANUEL E. physician, educator; b. N.Y.C., Nov. 6, 1928; s. Morris Jacob and Sylvia (Schiff) K.; m. Rita Goldman, May 22, 1955; children— Anne J., Eve D., Joshua M. BSc. Diplomate Am. Bd. Internal Medicine, Am. Bd. Hematology. Intern Boston City Hosp., 1954-55, resident, 1955-56, 58-59; fellow in hematology Thorndike Lab., 1959-62; attending hematologist Mt. Sinai Hosp., N.Y.C., 1962-65, asst. chief hematology, 1963-65; asst. prof. medicine Washington U. Sch. Medicine, St. Louis, 1965-69; asso. prof. medicine U. Minn. Sch. Medicine, Mpls., 1969-72, prof. medicine, 1972-97, prof. emeritus, 1997—. Chief hematology and oncology Mpls. VA Med Ctr., 1969-93; med. dir. physician asst. program Augsburg Coll., Mpls., 1995-2000. Contbr. numerous articles to profl. jours. Served with USPHS, 1956-58. Mem. Am. Fedn. Clin. Research, Am. Soc. Clin. Investigation, Am. Soc. Hematology, Am. Assn. Immunology, AAAS, others Jewish. Home: 2950 Dean Pky Apt 1201 Minneapolis MN 55416-4427 E-mail: mannykaplan@aol.com.

KAPLAN, MARJORIE ANN PASHKOW, school district administrator; b. Bronx, N.Y., Apr. 10, 1940; d. William B. and Laura (Libov) Pashkow; m. Marvin R. Kaplan, Aug. 16, 1962 (dec. 1980); children: Eliot, Mara; m. Timothy Sweeney, 1985 (div. 1986). BA, Smith Coll., 1962; MA, Ariz. State U., 1974, PhD, 1979. Presch. dir., tchr. Temple Beth Israel, Phoenix, 1967-72; tchr. Washington Sch. Dist., 1972-74, coord., 1974-75, prin., 1975-81; asst. supt. Paradise Valley Unified Sch. Dist., 1981-83, supt., 1984-92, Shawnee Mission Unified Sch. Dist., Overland Park, Kans., 1992—. Named Ariz. Supt. of Yr., 1992, Ariz. Sch. Bd. Assn. Supt. of Yr., 1987-88; named to Top 100 Educators, Exec. Educator mag., 1986. Mem. Am. Assn. Sch. Adminstrs. Office: Shawnee Mission Unified Sch Dist 512 7235 Antioch Rd Shawnee Mission KS 66204-1758

KAPLAN, RANDY KAYE, podiatrist; b. Detroit, Sept. 18, 1954; s. Earl Gene and Renee Joy (Sheftel) K. D of Podiatric Medicine, Ohio Coll., Cleve., 1979. Diplomate Am. Bd. Podiatric Surgery. Resident Kern Hosp., Warren, Mich., 1979-80; pvt. practice specializing in podiatric medicine, surgery Detroit, 1980—. Clin. instr., mem. staff Kern Hosp., Warren, 1980—; adj. prof. Ohio Coll. Podiatric Medicine, 1986—, Pa. Coll. Podiatric Medicine, 1986—; mem. staff Providence Hosp., 1995; lectr. in field. Contbr. articles to profl. jours. Co-founder The Great Lakes Conf., 1988. Recipient Earl G. Kaplan award for polit. action excellence, 1994; Inspector Gen's. Integrity award U.S. HHS, 1995. Fellow Am. Coll. Foot Surgeons; mem. Am. Diabetes Assn., Am. Podiatric Med. Assn. (mem. continuing edn. com. 1988-94, mem. labor rels. com. 1990-94), Mich. Podiatric Med. Assn. (bd. dirs. 1985—, 2nd v.p. 1988-90, pres. 1990-91, 92-93, Podiatrist of Yr. Southeastern divsn. 1987-88, Shining Star award for excellence 1992), Kern Hosp. Resident Alumni Assn., Mich. Pub. Health Assn., Phi Alpha Pi (Man of Yr. 1979). Jewish. Office: 25725 Coolidge Hwy Oak Park MI 48237-1307 E-mail: rklions@aol.com.

KAPLAN, SHELDON, lawyer, director; b. Mpls., Feb. 16, 1915; s. Max Julius and Harriet (Wolfson) K.; m. Helene Bamberger, Dec. 7, 1941; children— Jay Michael, Mary Jo, Jean Burton, Jeffrey Lee. BA summa cum laude, U. Minn., 1935; LLB, Columbia U., 1939. Bar: N.Y. 1940, Minn. 1946. Pvt. practice, N.Y.C., 1940-42, Mpls., 1946—; mem. firm Lauterstein, Spiller, Bergerman & Dannett, N.Y.C., 1939-42; ptnr. Maslon, Kaplan, Edelman, Borman, Brand & McNulty, Mpls., 1946-80. Chmn. Kaplan, Strangis and Kaplan, Mpls., 1980—; bd. dirs. Stewart Enterprises Inc., Creative Ventures Inc. Decisions editor Columbia Law Review, 1939. Served to capt. AUS, 1942-46. Mem. Minn. Bar Assn., Hazeltime Nat. Golf Club, Mpls. Club, Phi Beta Kappa. Home: 2950 Dean Pkwy Minneapolis MN 55416-4446 Office: Kaplan Strangis & Kaplan 5500 Wells Fargo Ctr Minneapolis MN 55402

KAPLAN, SIDNEY MOUNTBATTEN, lawyer; b. Bombay, Jan. 31, 1939; s. Charles von Pickens Kaplan and Jennie (Churchill) Goldberg; m. Donna Darrow, Feb. 14, 1989; children: Gary, Michael, Rory Patel. BA cum laude, Roosevelt U., 1960; JD, Ill. Inst. Tech., 1964. Bar: Ill., 1964, Minn., 1977, Colo., 1982, U.S. Dist. Ct. Ill. (no. dist.) 1964. Ptnr. Hess & Kaplan, Chgo., 1975-89, Baker & McKenzie, Chgo., 1989—. Bd. dirs. Jerome Gerson Meml. Found. Mem. Ill. Bar Assn., DuPage County Bar Assn., Cook County Bar Assn. Office: Baker & McKenzie 130 E Randolph Dr 1 Prudential Plz Chicago IL 60601

KAPLAN, STEVEN M. advertising executive; Pres., owner Sampling Corp. Am., 1989-97; pres., CEO Bounty Sampling Corp. Am. Worldwide, Glenview, Ill., 1997—. Spkr. Office: Bounty SCA Worldwide 4338 Di Paolo Ctr Glenview IL 60025-5201

KAPLAN, THOMAS ABRAHAM, physics educator; b. Phila., Feb. 24, 1926; s. Michael Jay and Nellie (Cohan) K.; m. Patricia Ruth Roe, Nov. 24, 1956; children: Melissa Ann, Andrea Jean, Laurie Michelle. BSME, U. Pa., 1948, PhD in Physics, 1954. Rsch. assoc. Engring. Rsch. Inst., U. Mich., Willow Run, 1954-56; rsch. assoc. Brookhaven Nat. Lab., Upton, N.Y., 1956-58; staff mem. Lincoln Lab., MIT, Lexington, Mass., 1959-70; prof. physics Mich. State U., East Lansing, 1970-95, prof. emeritus, 1995—. Cons. Naval Rsch. Lab., Washington, summer 1979-80; vis. scientist Max-Planck Inst. für Festkörperforschung, Stuttgart, Fed. Republic Germany, 1981-82, 88-89, summer 1983-84, Inst. für Festkörperforschung der Nuclear Physics Rsch. Inst. Jülich, Fed. Republic Germany, 1982; disting. vis. prof. U. Tsukuba, Ibaraki, Japan, 1989. Contbr. numerous articles on theoretical condensed matter physics to profl. jours. Petty officer 2nd class USN, 1944-46. Recipient Sr. Scientist award Alexander von Humboldt Stiftung, 1981. Fellow Am. Phys. Soc.; mem. Sigma Xi. Democrat. Jewish. Avocations: singing, playing piano and trumpet. Office: Mich State U Dept Physics Astronomy East Lansing MI 48824 E-mail: kaplan@pa.msu.edu.

KAPNICK, RICHARD BRADSHAW, lawyer; b. Chgo., Aug. 21, 1955; s. Harvey E. and Jean (Bradshaw) K.; m. Claudia Norris, Dec. 30, 1978; children: Sarah Bancroft, John Norris. BA with distinction, Stanford U., 1977; MPhil in Internat. Rels., U. Oxford, 1980; JD with honors, U. Chgo., 1982. Bar: Ill. 1982, N.Y. 1993. Law clk. to justice Ill. Supreme Ct., Chgo., 1982—84; law clk. to Justice John Paul Stevens U.S. Supreme Ct., Washington, 1984—85; assoc. Sidley, Austin, Brown & Wood, Chgo., 1985—89, ptnr., 1989—. Mng. editor U. Chgo. Law Rev., 1981-82. Trustee Chgo. Symphony Orch., 1995—, vice chmn., 2001—; vestryman Christ Ch., Winnetka, Ill., 2000—; bd. dirs., chmn. Civic Orch. Chgo., 1999—2001; bd. dirs. Cabrini Green Legal Aid Clinic, 1990—94, chmn. bd., 1991—93; mem., advisor, bd. dirs. Stanford Inst. for Econ. Policy Rsch., 1999—. Marshall scholar, 1978-80; fellow Leadership Greater Chgo., 1989-90. Mem. Order of Coif, Chgo. Club, Econ. Club Chgo., The Lawyers Club Chgo., Phi Beta Kappa. Republican. Episcopalian. Office: Sidney Austin Brown & Wood 10 S Dearborn St Chicago IL 60603

KAPP, C. TERRENCE, lawyer; b. Pine Bluff, Ark., Oct. 1, 1944; s. Robert Amos and Guenevere Patricia (DeVinne) K.; m. Betsy Langer, May 2, 1987. BA, Colgate U., 1966; JD, Cleve. State U., 1971; MA summa cum laude, Holy Apostles Coll., 1984. Bar: Ohio 1971, U.S. Dist. Ct. (no. dist.) Ohio 1973, U.S. Supreme Ct. 1980, U.S. Tax Ct. 1996. Ptnr. Kapp & Kapp, East Liverpool, Ohio, 1971-84; pvt. practice Cleve., 1984—; ptnr. Marshman, Snyder & Kapp, 1991-93, Kapp Law Offices, Cleve., 1994—. Contbr. articles to profl. jours. Pres., bd. dirs. Lake Erie Nature & Sci. Ctr., Bay Village, Ohio, 1991-92; chair St. John's Cathedral Endowment Trust, Cleve., 1992-94. Mem. ABA (commr. presdl. commn. on non-lawyer practice 1992-96; judge finals nat. appellate adv. competition 1987, nat. chmn. divorce laws and procedures com. Family law sect. 1989-93, vice-chmn. step families com. 1991-93, chmn. alternative funding com. 1992—, taxation com. exec. 1988—, task force on client edn. 1991—, chair nat. symposium on Image of Family law Atty.-Fact or Myth 1993, cert. Outstanding Svc. 1988, 89, 93, 95, domestic rels. taxation problems com. exec. Tax sect., Litigation sect.), Ohio State Bar Assn. (family law com. exec. 1987—, family law curriculum com. Ohio CLE Inst. 1992—), Cuyahoga County Bar Assn. (chair family law sect. 1991-92, bar admissions com. exec. 1986—, cert. grievance com. 1990—, jud. selection com. 1991—, unauthorized practice of law com. 1992—, cert. Outstanding Leadership 1992), Cleve. Athletic Club (pres., bd. dirs.), Bay Men's Club. Roman Catholic. Avocations: sailing, handball, racquet sports. Office: Kapp Law Offices PO Box 40447 Bay Village OH 44140-0447

KAPRAL, FRANK ALBERT, medical microbiology and immunology educator; b. Phila., Mar. 12, 1928; s. John and Erna Louise (Melching) K.; m. Marina Garay, Nov. 22, 1951; children: Frederick, Gloria, Robert. BS, U. of the Scis. in Phila., 1952; Ph.D, U. Pa., 1956. With U. Pa., Phila., 1952-66, assoc. in microbiology, 1958-66; assoc. microbiologist Phila Gen. Hosp., 1962-64, chief microbiology research, 1964-66, chief microbiology, 1965-66; asst. chief microbiol. research VA Hosp., Phila, 1962-66; assoc. prof. med. microbiology Ohio State U., Columbus, 1966-69, prof. med. virology, immunology and med. genetics, 1969—95, prof. emeritus dept. molecular virology, immunology and med. genetics, 1995—. Cons. Ctr. Disease Control, Atlanta, 1980, Proctor and Gamble Co., 1981-87. Contbr. articles to profl. jours.; patentee implant chamber. Active Ctrl. Ohio Diabetes Assn., 1992-93. With AUS, 1946-47. NIH rsch. grantee, 1959—; Ctrl. Ohio Diabetes Assn. grantee, 1992-93. Fellow Am. Acad. Microbiology, Infectious Diseases Soc. Am.; mem. AAAS, Am. Soc. for Microbiology, Am. Assn. for Immunologists, Sigma Xi. Democrat. Roman Catholic. Home: 873 Clubview Blvd S Columbus OH 43235-1771 Office: 2166B Gaver Ln Columbus OH 43223-3226

KAPSNER, CAROL RONNING, state supreme court justice; b. Bismarck, N.D. m. John Kapsner; children: Mical, Caithlin. BA in English lit., Coll. of St. Catherine; postgrad., Oxford U.; MA in English lit., Ind. U.; JD, U. Colo., 1977. Pvt. practice, Bismarck, 1977-98; justice N.D. Supreme Ct., 1998—. Mem. N.D. Bar Assn. (past bd. govs.), N.D. Trial Lawyers Assn. (past bd. govs.), Burleigh County Bar Assn. (past pres.). Office: Supreme Ct State Capitol 600 E Boulevard Ave Dept 180 Bismarck ND 58505-0530 Fax: 701-328-4480. E-mail: ckapsner@ndcourts.com.

KAPSON, JORDAN, automotive executive; b. 1923; Chmn. Jordan Motors, Inc. dba Jordan Ford, Mishawaka, Ind., 1947—, Jordan Toyota dba Jordan Volvo, Jordan Mitsubishi, 1981—, Jordan Motors, Inc. Office: Jordan Motors Inc 609 E Jefferson Blvd Mishawaka IN 46545-6524

KAPTUR, MARCIA CAROLYN, congresswoman; b. Toledo, June 17, 1946; B.A., U. Wis., 1968; M. Urban Planning, U. Mich., 1974; postgrad., U. Manchester, (Eng.), 1974, MIT; LLD (hon.), U. Toledo. Urban planner; asst. dir. urban affairs domestic policy staff White House, 1977-79; mem. U.S. Congress from 9th Ohio dist., Washington, 1983—; mem. appropriations com., Agr. subcom., D.C. subcom., VA, HUD, and indep. agys. subcom. Bd. dirs. Nat. Ctr. Urban Ethnic Affairs; adv. com. Gund Found.; exec. com. Lucas County Democratic Com.; mem. Dem. Women's Campaign Assn. Mem. Am. Planning Assn., Am. Inst. Cert. Planners, NAACP, Urban League, Polish Mus., U. Mich. Urban Planning Alumni Assn. (bd. dirs.), Polish Am. Hist. Assn. Roman Catholic. Clubs: Lucas County Dem. Bus. and Profl. Women's, Fulton County Dem. Women's. Office: US House of Reps 2366 Rayburn Washington DC 20515-0001*

KAPUSTA, GEORGE, botany educator, agronomy educator; b. Max, N.D., Nov. 20, 1932; m. 1958; 4 children. BS, N.D. State U., 1954; MS, U. Minn., 1957; PhD in Botany, So. Ill. U., 1975. Agronomist N.D. State U., 1958-64; assoc. prof. So. Ill. U., Carbondale, 1964-80, prof. agronomy, 1980—. Recipient Outstanding Rsch. & Exten award Land of Lincoln Soybean Assn., 1978. Fellow Weed Sci. Soc.; mem. Agronomy Soc. Am., Soil Sci. Soc. Am., Sigma Xi. Office: Southern Illinois Univ Plant & Soil Science Rsch Sta Mail Code 4415 Carbondale IL 62901-4415

KARANES, CHATCHADA, internist; b. Bangkok, 1948; came to U.S., 1972; MD, U. Bangkok, 1971. Bd. cert. in hematology, 1978. Intern St. Francis Hosp., Evanston, Ill., 1972-73, resident in internal medicine, 1973-75; fellow in hematology/oncology Washington U., St. Louis, 1975-79; staff Harper-Grace Hosp., Detroit, 1979; prof. medicine Wayne State U., 1979-2000; medical dir. Nat. Marrow Donor Prog., Minneapolis, 2000—. Mem. ACP, Am. Soc. Hematology, Am. Soc. Clin. Oncology, Am. Soc. Bone Marrow Transplant. Office: Nat Marrow Donor Program 3001 Broadway St NE Ste 500 Minneapolis MN 55413 E-mail: ckaranes@nmdp.org .

KARANIKAS, ALEXANDER, English language educator, author, actor; b. Manchester, N.H., Oct. 5, 1916; s. Stephen and Vaia (Olgas) K.; m. Helen J. Karagianes, Jan. 2, 1949; children: Marianthe Vaia, Diana Christine, Cynthia Maria. Student, U. N.H., 1934-36; A.B. cum laude, Harvard, 1939; M.A., Northwestern U., 1950, Ph.D. in English, 1953. With N.H. Writers Project, 1940-41; editor Allegheny-Kiski Valley Edit. The CIO News, 1941-42; radio news commentator Sta. WMUR, Manchester, 1946; grad. asst. Northwestern U., Evanston, Ill., 1950-52; instr. Kendall Coll., 1952-53, Northwestern U., Evanston, 1953-54, 57-58; mem. faculty U. Ill. at Chgo., 1954—, prof. English, 1974-82, prof. emeritus, 1982—; owner Deerhaven Orchard, 1974-96. Cons. in field. Author: When a Youth Gets Poetic, 1934, In Praise of Heroes, 1945, Tillers of a Myth: The Southern Agrarians as Social and Literary Critics, 1966 (Friends of Lit. award 1967), (with Helen Karanikas) Elias Venezis, 1969, Hellenes and Hellions: Modern Greek Characters in American Literature, 1981, Nashville Dreams (mus. comedy with songs by Larry Nestor), 1991, Stepping Stones (poems), 1994. Mem. nat. cabinet Am. Youth Congress, 1937-39; exec. sec. Mass. Youth Coun., 1939-40; co-chmn. Nat. Bicentennial Symposium on the Greek Experience in Am., 1976; Publicity dir. N.H. Ind. Voters, 1946; sec. Manchester Vets. Council, 1946; Candidate for Congress, 1948; mem. exec. com. United Hellenic Am. Congress, 1983—; exec. sec. Am. Coun. for Dem. Greece, 1947. Served with USAAF, 1942-45, Alaska corr. YANK, 1943-45. Mem. Hellenic Profl. Soc. Ill., Modern Greek Studies Assn., Screen Actors Guild, Friends of Lit., Harvard Club Chgo., Phi Eta Sigma, Order Ahepa (dist. sec. 1946). Mem. Greek Orthodox Ch. Home: 618 N Harvey Ave Oak Park IL 60302-1740 Office: Univ of Ill at Chicago English Dept Chicago IL 60680

KARCH, GEORGE FREDERICK, JR. lawyer; b. Cleve., Apr. 24, 1933; s. George Frederick, Sr. and Mary (Sargent) K.; m. Carolyn Biggar, Aug. 26, 1958; children— Geoffrey, George III, Margaret Ruth AB cum laude, Amherst Coll., 1955; LLB, U. Mich., 1959. Ptnr. Thompson, Hine and Flory, Cleve., 1959-98, ret., 1998. Adj. prof. litigation & trial tactics Case Western Reserve U. Sch. Law, 1993—. Trustee Geauga County Met. Housing Authority, Chardon, Ohio, 1960-84, chmn., 1981-83 Mem.: Tavern Club (Cleve.), Kirtland Country Club (Willoughby). Presbyterian. Avocations: reading history, golf, politics. Home: 1017 S Yachtsman Dr Sanibel FL 33957-5012 E-mail: CKarch1@aol.com.

KARDOS, PAUL JAMES, insurance company executive; b. North Vandergrift, Pa., Mar. 20, 1937; s. Joseph and Mary K.; m. Paulette Laura Sobota, Oct. 29, 1966; children— Diane, Brian. BS in Math, Grove City Coll., 1962. With Life Ins. Co. of N. Am., until 1977, v.p., until 1977; sr. v.p. Horace Mann Educators, Springfield, Ill., 1977-78, exec. v.p., 1978-79, pres., 1979—; dir., pres., CEO INA Corp. subs.

KARKHECK, JOHN PETER, physics educator, researcher; b. N.Y.C., Apr. 26, 1945; s. John Henry and Dorothy Cecilia (Riebling) K.; m. Kathleen Mary Shiels, Nov. 8, 1969; children: Lorraine, Michelle, Eric. BS, LeMoyne Coll., 1966; MA, SUNY, Buffalo, 1972; PhD, SUNY, Stony Brook, 1978. Various positions Grumman Corp., Bethpage, N.Y., 1964-68; grad. asst. SUNY, Buffalo, 1968-70; tchr. secondary schs. Mattituck (N.Y.) Sch. Dist., 1970-71, Shelter Island (N.Y.) Sch. Dist., 1971-73; grad. asst. SUNY, Stony Brook, 1973-78, postdoctoral fellow, 1978-79, rsch. assoc. N.Y., 1979-81; asst. prof. physics GMI Engring. and Mgmt. Inst., Flint, Mich., 1981-84, assoc. prof., 1984, prof., dir. physics, 1988-89, head. dept. sci. and math., 1989-93; prof., chmn. dept. physics Marquette U., Milw., 1993—. Physics assoc. Brookhaven Nat. Lab., Upton, N.Y., 1975-79, cons., 1979-85, STS, Hauppauge, N.Y., 1983, BID Ctr., Flint, 1985-90; acad. assoc. Mich. State U., 1988, 90, vis. scholar, 1989, vis. scientist, 1991; reviewer Addison-Wesley Pub., 1990, 93; regional dir. Mich. Sci. Olympiad, 1991-92, 92-93; co-dir. NATO Advanced Study Inst., 1998, editor, 1999-2000. Contbr. numerous articles to profl. jours. Den leader Cub Scouts Am., Flint, 1987-91; leader Boy Scouts Am., 1991-98; bd. dirs. Flint Area Sci. Fair, 1991-93; mem. sci. curriculum adv. com. Milw. Acad. Sci., 2000-; judge local sci. fairs. Dept. Energy rsch. grantee, 1977-79, NATO travel grantee, 1983-86, 89, NATO ASI grantee, 1998. Mem. Am. Phys. Soc., AAAS, AAPT, Sigma Xi (v.p. Marquette U. chpt. 1998-99, pres., 1999-2000). Roman Catholic. Avocations: swimming, reading, bicycling, travel, learning German. Home: 6592 N Bethmaur Ln Glendale WI 53209-3320 Office: Marquette Univ Dept Physics PO Box 1881 Milwaukee WI 53201-1881 E-mail: John.Karkheck@marquette.edu.

KARKUT, RICHARD THEODORE, clinical psychologist; b. Derby, Conn., Apr. 28, 1948; s. Harry Chester and Mary K. AB, William Jewell Coll., 1971; MA, U. Mo., Kansas City, 1976; D Psychology, Forest Inst. Profl. Psychology, 1988. Lic. psychologist, Ind.; cert. in biofeedback. Psychology intern Burrell Mental Health Ctr., Springfield, Mo., 1987-88; clin. psychologist Wabash Valley Hosp., Lafayette, Ind., 1989-91, Quinco Cons., North Vernon, 1991-93; CEO Adkar Assocs., Inc., Bloomington, 1993—. Cons. Div. Family Svcs., Lafayette, 1989-90. Guest editor jour. Ind. Psychologist; contbr. articles to profl. jours. Mem. Assn. Applied Psychophysiology and Biofeedback, Am. Counseling Assn. Anglican. Home: PO Box 1396 Bloomington IN 47402-1396

KARL, GEORGE, professional basketball coach; b. Penn Hills, Pa., May 12, 1951; m. Cathy Karl (div.); children: Kelci Ryanne, Coby Joseph. Grad., U. N.C., 1973. Guard San Antonio Spurs, NBA, 1973-78, asst. coach, head scout, 1978-80; coach Mont. Golden Nuggets, Continental Basketball Assn., 1980-83; dir. player acquisition Cleve. Cavaliers, 1983-84, coach, 1984-86; head coach Golden State Warriors, Oakland, Calif., from 1986, Albany (N.Y.) Patrons, 1988-89, 90-91, Real Madrid, Spain, 1991-92, Seattle Supersonics, 1992-98, Milwaukee Bucks, 1998—. Named Coach of Yr., Continental Basketball Assn., 1981, 83. Mem. Continental Basketball Assn. Office: care Milwaukee Bucks 1001 N 4th St Milwaukee WI 53203-1314

KARLEN, DOUGLAS LAWRENCE, soil scientist; b. Monroe, Wis., Aug. 28, 1951; s. Lawrence Herman and Marian Bertha (Trumpy) K.; m. Linda Sue Bender, June 9, 1973; children: Sarah Jean, Steven Douglas, Holly Lin. BS, U. Wis., 1973; MS, Mich. State U., 1975; PhD, Kans. State U., 1978. Rsch. soil scientist Coastal Plains Soil, Water Conservation Rsch. Ctr., USDA-ARS, Florence, S.C., 1978-88, Nat. Soil Tilth Lab. USDA-ARS, Ames, Iowa, 1988—. Team leader Leopold Ctr. for Sustainable Agr., Ames, 1989—94. Asst. scoutmaster, com. chmn. Boy Scouts Am., Ankeny, Iowa, 1991—. Fellow Am. Soc. Agronomy (bd. rep. Ag sys. 1997-99, Agronomic Rsch. award 2001, Werner L. Nelson award for diagnosis of Yeild limiting factors 2001), Crop Sci. Soc. Am. (assoc. editor 1988-93, tech. editor 1994-99), Soil Sci. Soc. Am. (Agronomic Achievement award-soils 1996); mem. Coun. Agrl. Sci. and Tech., Soil and Water Conservation Soc. Am., Internat. Soil Tillage Rsch. Orgn. Episcopalian. Office: USDA-ARS-MWA-NSTL 2150 Pammel Ct Ames IA 50014-4047 E-mail: karlen@nstl.gov.

KARLEN, GREG T. real estate executive; Pres. Madison Marquette Realty Svcs., Minnetonka, Minn., 1989—. Office: Madison Marquette Realty Svcs 11100 Wayzata Blvd Ste 601 Minnetonka MN 55305-5522

KARLIN, GARY LEE, insurance executive; b. Chgo., Jan. 18, 1934; s. Jack and Pearl (Malin-Weiss) K.; children: David, Paige; m. Cheryl Daneman; stepchildren: Chad, Brooke. Student, U. Ill., 1951-52, Roosevelt U., 1952. With Mut. of N.Y., 1956-62, sales mgr., 1958-62, regional trainer, 1962-63; pres. Exec. Motivation, Inc., 1964—; fin. planner, 1980—; chmn. field underwriters benefits/contracts com. MONY, 1974-85; v.p. Exec. Planning Svcs. divsn. Alexander & Alexander, Inc., 1990-96; dir., chmn. audit and compensation coms. Vasocor, Inc., Miami, Fla., 1990—; dir., chmn. audit com. Perception, Inc., 1993-98; v.p., treas. Exec. Fin. Group divsn. F.P.I.S., Inc., 1993-99. Pres. Karlin Bus. Group, 1998—; cons. in field; speaker numerous ins. seminars. Contbg. editor Profl. Mgmt. mag., 1965-67; subject of poem There Are No Heroes Anymore; contbr. articles to profl. jours.; subject of ins. film Impressions of Life. Named to MONY Hall of Fame, 1966; featured in Time mag., 1967. Mem. Internat. Assn. Fin. Planners, Chgo. Assn. Life Underwriters, (past bd. dirs.) Nat. Assn. Life Underwriters (life), Million Dollar Round Table (Top of Table), Ill. Leaders Round Table (past pres.), Emil Verban Soc., Carolina Club, Gov.'s Club (Chapel Hill). Home: 55230 Broughton Govs Club Chapel Hill NC 27514 E-mail: chergar@mindspring.com.

KARLIN, JEROME B. retail company executive; Grad., U. Ill. Coll. Pharmacy, 1965. Student, then pharmacist Walgreen Corp., Deerfield, Ill., 1963-67, store mgr., 1967-73, dist. mgr., 1973-79, dir. Health Svcs., 1979-82, western regional v.p., 1982-87, exec. v.p. store ops., 1998—, v.p. western store ops., 1987-98. Office: Walgreen Corp 200 Wilmot Rd Deerfield IL 60015-4620

KARLINS, M(ARTIN) WILLIAM, composer, educator; b. N.Y.C., Feb. 25, 1932; s. Theodore and Gertrude Bertha (Leifer) K.; m. Mickey Cutler, Apr. 6, 1952; children: Wayne, Laura. MusB, MusM, Manhattan Sch. Music, 1961; PhD in Composition, U. Iowa, Iowa City, 1965; studied with, Frederick Piket, Vittorio Giannini, Stefan Wolpe, Philip Bezanson, Richard Hervig. Asst. prof. music Western Ill. U., 1965-67; assoc. prof. theory and composition Northwestern U. Sch. Music, Evanston, Ill., 1967-73, prof., 1973—, dir., co-dir. Contemporary Music Ensemble, 1967—, apptd. Harry N./Ruth F. Wyatt prof. music theory/composition, 1998—. Vis. guest composer Ariz. State U., 1978, Ill. Wesleyan U., 1978; guest composer Nazareth Coll., Rochester, N.Y., 1978, Bowling Green State U., 1982, 89, Navy Band, Washington, 1988, Nat. Conf. for Condrs., Chgo., Ball State U., Bloomington, Composer's Symposium U. N.Mex., Albuquerque, 1991, Alta. (Can.) Coll. Conservatory Music, 1991, Sigma Alpha Iota Internat. Am. Music Awards Competition, 1993; featured guest composer We. Ill. U., Macomb, 1994; participant Coll. Band Dirs. Nat. Assn. Nat. Conf., Northwestern U., 1987; coord. composers workshops Internat. World Congress Saxophones, London; lectr., composer-in-residence World Saxophone Congress, Bordeaux, France, 1974, 6th summer festival Nat.

Saxophone Tng. Course, Duras, France, 6th Stage de Saxophone, Duras, France, 1991; panelist 43d Nat. Conf. Am. Symphony Orch. League; lectr., guest composer Franz Liszt Acad. Music, Franz Liszt Musical Coll., Györ, Hungary, 1995; panelist, guest composer Stefan Wolpe Festival, Temple U., Phila.; guest composer Budapest Spring Festival, 1999; honored composer, Sofia, Bulgaria, 1997; guest lectr., composer Vienna, Austria, 1999, Bowdoin Coll., Maine, 1999. Composer: Concert Music 1 through 5, Lamentations-In Memoriam, Elegy for Orchestra, Reflux (concerto for double bass and wind ensemble), Symphony No. 1, Concerto Grosso I and II, Academic Festival Fanfare for wind ensemble, Woodwind Quintet I and II, Saxophone Quartet I and II, Night Light Quartet No. 3 for Saxophones, 3 Plano Sonatas, Outgrowths-Variations for Piano, Suite of Preludes for piano, Humble Harvest for piano, Catena I (clarinet and chamber orch.), Catena II (soprano saxophone and brass quintet), Catena III (concerto for horn and orch.), Birthday Music I (flute, bass clarinet/clarinet and double bass) and II (flute and double bass), Under and Over (flute and double bass), Variations on Obiter Dictum (cello, piano and percussion), Music for Cello Alone I and II, Music for Oboe, Bass Clarinet and Piano, Music for Tenor Saxophone and Piano, Music for Alto Saxophone and Piano, Music for English Horn and Piano, Four Inventions and a Fugue for Bassoon, Piano and Female Voice, Infinity for Oboe d'amore, clarinet, viola and female voice, Song for Soprano with Alto Flute, Cello, Three Songs for Soprano, Flute and Piano, Chameleon for Harpsichord, Drei Kleine Cembalost+398cke (harpsichord), Celebration for Flute, Oboe and Harpsichord, Kindred Spirits for mandolin, guitar and harp, Quintet for Alto Saxophone and String Quartet, Impromptu for Saxophone and Organ, Nostalgie for 12 Saxophones Ensemble, Introduction and Passacaglia for 2 Saxophones and Piano, Just A Line From Chameleon, for 2 clarinets, Fantasia for tenor saxophone and percussion, Saxtuper for Saxophone, Tuba, and Percussion, Seasons for solo saxophonist, Concerto for Alto Saxophone and Orch., String Quartet with soprano in the last movement, Chidlren's Bedtime Songs for mixed chorus, Three Love Songs for male chorus, Three Poems for mixed chorus, Looking Out My Window for Treble Chorus and viola; recs. include Music for Tenor Saxophone and Piano, Music for Alto Saxophone and piano variations on Obiter Dictum for cello, piano and percussion, Introduction and Passsacaglia for 2 saxophones and piano, Solo Piece with Passacaglia for clarinet, Sonata No. 2, Sonata No. 3 for piano and Outgrowth Variations for Piano, Saxophone Quartets Nos. 1 and 2, Chameleon for harpischord, Drei Kleine Cembalostücke (harpsichord), Quintet for alto saxophone and string quartet, Nostalgie for 12 saxophone ensemble, Impromptu for alto saxophone and organ, Reflux (concerto for amplified double bass and winds), Quartet for Strings with soprano in the last movement, Song for Soprano, with alto flute and cello, Four Inventions and a Fugue for bassoon, piano, and soprano, Kindred Spirits for mandolin, guitar and harp, Concerto Grosso # 1 for 9 instruments, Catena II for soprano saxophone and brass quintet. Grantee MacDowell Colony, Nat. Endowment for Arts, 1979, 85, Meet the Composer, 1980, 84, 85, 90, 95, Ill. Arts Coun., 1985, 87, 90, 96, 98. Mem. Am. Music Ctr., Broadcast Music, Inc., Am. Woman Composers (trustee Chgo. chpt.), Pi Kappa Lambda, Sigma Alpha Iota (nat. arts. assoc.). Office: Northwestern U Sch Music Evanston IL 60208-0001 E-mail: m-karlins@northwestern.edu.

KARLL, JO ANN, state administrative law judge, lawyer; b. St. Louis, Nov. 16, 1948; d. Joseph H. and Dorothy Olga (Pyle) K.; m. William Austin Hernlund, Sept. 9, 1990. BS magna cum laude, Maryville U.; JD, St. Louis U. Bar: Mo. 1993. Ins. claims adjuster, 1967-88; mem. Mo. Gen. Assembly dist. 104, 1991-93; dir. Mo. State Divsn. Workers' Compensation, Jefferson City, 1993-2000, adminstrv. law judge, 2000—. Founder, 1st pres. scholarship fund Mo. Kids' Chance, Inc., 1995-96, bd. dirs., 1995—. Internat. Assn. of Indsl. Accident Bds. and Commns. (past pres.). Office: Mo St Divsn Worker's Compensation 3737 Harry S Truman Blvd Saint Charles MO 63301 Home: 727 Heatherstone Dr High Ridge MO 63049

KARMAN, JAMES ANTHONY, manufacturing executive; b. Grand Rapids, Mich., May 26, 1937; s. Anthony and Katherine D. Karman; m. Carolyn L. Hoehn, Aug. 29, 1959; children: Robb Thomas, Janet Ellen, Edward John, Christopher James. BS cum laude, Miami U., Oxford, Ohio, 1959; MBA, U. Wis., 1960. Instr. corp. fin. U. Wis., Madison, 1960-61; asst. mgr. investment dept. Union Bank & Trust Co., Grand Rapids, 1961-63; treas. RPM, Inc., Medina, Ohio, 1963-69, v.p., treas., 1969-72, v.p., sec.-treas., 1972-73, exec. v.p., sec.-treas., 1973-78, pres., 1978—, also bd. dirs., CFO, 1982-93, vice chmn., 1999—. Instr. Am. Inst. Banking, 1962; bd. dirs. Metro. Fin. Corp., Shiloh Industries, Inc., A. Schulman, Inc. Trustee Trinity Cathedral, Cleve., Western Res. Hist. Soc., Boys & Girls Club, Cleve., The Leelanau Sch., Glen Arbor, Mich.; past bd. trustees Cleve. Orch., Boys Hope, Cleve., Cleve. Playhouse; mem. adv. coun. Miami U. Sch. Bus. Adminstrn.; mem. bd. visitors U. Wis.; mem. corp. coun., fin. com. Cleve. Mus. Art.; mem. Bluecoats, Inc., Cleve. Mem. U.S. Power Squadron, Gt. Lakes Hist. Soc., Mayfield Country Club, Cleve. Playhouse Club, Pine Lake Trout Club, Union Club (Cleve.), St. Louis Club, Order of Artus, Phi Beta Kappa. Home: 2 Bratenahl Pl Apt 2A Cleveland OH 44108-1167 Office: RPM Inc PO Box 777 2628 Pearl Rd Medina OH 44256-7623

KARMEIER, DELBERT FRED, consulting engineer, realtor; b. Okawville, Ill., Apr. 2, 1935; s. Wilbert and Ida (Harre) K.; m. Naomi Firnhaber, Oct. 18, 1958; children: Kenton Howard, Dianne Jill. BSCE, U. Ill., 1957, MS in Transp. Engring., 1959. Rsch. assoc. U. Ill., 1958-59; traffic engr. St. Louis County, Mo., 1959-65, traffic commr., 1965-69; dir. transp. City of Kansas City, Mo., 1969-74, dir. aviation and transp., 1974-90; dir. pub. works City of Hartford, Conn., 1990-92; assoc. exec. dir. Am. Pub. Works Assn., Chgo., 1992-94; cons. Torres Cons. Engrs., Kansas City, Mo., 1994-95; assoc. J.D. Reece, Leawood, Kans., 1995—. Mem. Nat. Com. on Uniform Traffic Control Devices, 1971-85 Automotive Safety Found. fellow U. Ill., 1959. Mem. Inst. Transp. Engrs. (pres. Missouri Valley sect. 1965-66), Airport Operator's Coun. Internat., Am. Rd. and Transp. Builder's Assn. (dir. 1973-83, chmn. pub. transit adv. coun. 1980-83), Transp. Rsch. Bd., Am. Pub. Works Assn., U. Ill. Alumni Club Kansas City (pres. 1996—), Beta Sigma Psi (nat. editor 1963-69, pres. Kansas City alumni 1981-82, Disting. Alumnus award 1971, nat pres. 1986-88, nat. treas. 1996—). Lutheran. Home: 12206 Avila Dr Kansas City MO 64145-1750 Office: JD Reece 13002 State Line Rd Leawood KS 66209-1756 E-mail: delkarm@aol.com.

KAROL, NATHANIEL H. lawyer, consultant; b. N.Y.C., Feb. 16, 1929; s. Isidore and Lillian (Orlow) K.; m. Liliane Leser, July 20, 1967; children: David, Jordan. B.S. in Social Sci, CCNY, 1949; M.A. (fellow), Yale U., 1950; LL.B., N.Y. U., 1957, LL.M., 1959, J.D., 1966. Bar: N.Y. 1957. Mgmt. trainee Curtiss Wright Corp., Wood-Ridge, N.J., 1956-57; practiced in N.Y.C., 1957-58; contracting officer USAF, 1958-62; chief contract mgmt. survey and cost adminstrn. Office of Procurement, NASA, Washington, 1962-64; asst. dir. cost reduction, 1964-66; dep. asst. sec. Grants Adminstrn., HEW, Washington, 1966-69; univ. dean City U. N.Y.; exec. dir. Research Found., 1969-73; v.p. Hebrew Union Coll., Cin., 1973-75; partner, nat. chmn. cons. services for edn. Coopers & Lybrand (C.P.A.s), Chgo., 1975-81; pres. Nathaniel H. Karol & Assocs. Ltd., 1981—. Cons. to govt. agys. and ednl. instns., 1969— Author: Managing the Higher Education Enterprise. Served with U.S. Army, 1953-56. Recipient Outstanding Performance award HEW, 1968, Superior Performance award, 1969 Mem. N.Y. Bar, Nat. Assn. Coll. and Univ. Bus. Officers, Nat. Assn. Coll. and Univ. Attys. Home and Office: 1228 Cambridge Ct Highland Park IL 60035-1014

KARP, GARY, marketing and public relations executive; V.p. mktg. and pub. rels. Alliant Foodsvc., Deerfield, Ill., 1992-96, v.p. catagory mgmt., 1996—. Office: Alliant Foodsvc 1 Parkway N Deerfield IL 60015-2532

KARPIEL, DORIS CATHERINE, state legislator; b. Chgo., Sept. 21, 1935; d. Nicholas and Mary (McStravick) Feinen; m. Harvey Karpiel, 1955 (div.); children: Sharon, Lynn, Laura, Barry. AA, Morton Jr. Coll., 1955; BA, No. Ill. U., 1976. Real estate sales assoc. Bundy-Morgan BHG; coordinator Bloomingdale Twp. Republican Presdl. Hdqrs., Ill., 1960, 64, 68; former pres. Bloomingdale Twp. Rep. Orgn.; mem. Twp. Ofcls. of Ill.; trustee Bloomingdale Twp., 1974-75, supr., 1975-80; precinct committeewoman Bloomingdale Twp. Rep. Central Com., 1972, chmn., 1978-80; mem. Ill. Ho. of Reps., 1979-82, Ill. State Senate from 25th Dist., 1984—. Mem. Am. Legislators Exchange Council, Rep. Orgn. Schaumberg Twp.; former sec. DuPage County Suprs. Assn.; former sec. DuPage County Twp. Ofcls.; mem. DuPage County Women's Rep. Orgn., Meml. Hosp. Guild, Am. Cancer Soc. Mem. LWV, DuPage Bd. Realtors, Pi Sigma Alpha. Clubs: Bloomingdale Roselle and Streamwood Country, University Women's, St. Walters Women's. Office: Ill State Senate 123 Capitol Bldg Springfield IL 62706-0001 Address: 400 Lake St Ste 220 Roselle IL 60172-3572

KARR, GERALD LEE, agricultural economist, state senator; b. Emporia, Kans., Oct. 15, 1936; s. Orren L. and Kathleen M. (Keller) K.; B.S., Kans. State U., 1959; M.S. in Agrl. Econs., So. Ill. U., 1962, Ph.D. in Econs., 1966; m. Sharon Kay Studer, Oct. 18, 1959; children: Kevin Lee, Kelly Jolleen. Livestock mgr. Eckert Orchards Inc., Belleville, Ill., 1959-64; grad. asst. So. Ill. U., Carbondale, 1960-64; asst. prof. econs. Central Mo. State U., Warrensburg, 1964-67; asst. prof. agrl. econs., head dept. Njala U., Sierra Leone, West Africa, 1967-70; asst. prof. agrl. econs. U. Ill., Urbana, 1970-72; asso. prof. agrl. econs., chmn. dept., mgr. coll. farms Wilmington (Ohio) Coll., 1972-76; farmer, Emporia, Kans., 1976— ; mem. Kans. Senate, 1981-98, minority leader, 1991-96; rsch. advisor Bank of Sierra Leone, Freetown, summer 1967; agrl. sector cons. Econ. Mission to Sierra Leone, IBRD, 1973. Mem. Lyon County Farmer Union, Lyon County Livestock Assn., Omicron Delta Epsilon, Farm House. Contbr. articles to profl. jours. Democrat. Methodist. Club: Kiwanis.

KARRAKER, LOUIS RENDLEMAN, retired corporate executive; b. Jonesboro, Ill., Aug. 2, 1927; s. Ira Oliver and Helen Elsie (Rendleman) K.; m. Patricia Grace Stahlheber, June 20, 1952; children: Alan Louis, Sharon Elaine Cohen. BA, So. Ill. U., 1949, MA, 1952; postgrad., U. Wis., 1951-52, Washington U., St. Louis, 1954-56. V.p. personnel Am. Appraisal Assocs., Inc., Milw., 1969-73, v.p. adminstrn., 1973-74, group v.p., dir., 1974-77, exec. v.p., dir., 1977-79, pres., dir., 1979-82; bus. mgr. Concordia Coll., Ann Arbor, Mich., 1986-91. Cons. in field, 1982-86; asst. to chmn. Parker Pen Co., Janesville, Wis., 1967-69, personnel mgr., 1964-67; asst. to pres. Augustana Coll., Sioux Falls, S.D., 1962-64, acting chmn., dept. social scis., 1960-61, asst. prof. history, 1956-60. Columnist The Jour. Times, Racine, Wis., 1993-99; speaker Rep. and civic groups, Wis., 1993—. Trustee Better Bus. Bur., Milw., 1979-82, Citizens Govtl. Rsch. Bur., Milw., 1979-82; speaker, canvasser Rep. Party, S.D., 1956-60. With USNR, 1952-53, Korea. Mem. The Heritage Found., Hoover Presdl. Libr. Assn., Am. Legion. Lutheran. Avocation: church activities, travel, family activities, fishing. Home: 217 S 7th St Apt 11 Waterford WI 53185-4500 E-mail: karr217@webtv.net.

KARST, GARY GENE, retired architect; b. Barton County, Kans., Sept. 2, 1936; s. Emil and Clara (Nuss) K.; m. Loretta Marie Staub, Nov. 30, 1957; children: Kevin Gene, Sheri Lynn, Stacey Marie. BArch, Kans. State U., 1960. Registered profl. arch., Kans. Staff architect Horst & Terrill Architects, Topeka, 1960—64; ptnr. Horst, Terrill & Karst Architects, 1965—2001, dir. design, 1965—2001, sec., 1973—78, v.p., treas., 1978—92, v.p., 1992—99; pres., 1999—2001; ret., 2001; design architect Ruhnau, Evans, Brown & Steinman Architects, Riverside, Calif., 1964—65. Mem. Capital City Redevel. Agy., Topeka, 1978-86; mem. adv. bd. dept. architecture Kans. State U., Manhattan, 1986-87. Prin. works include Emporia (Kans.) H.S., 1972, (Kans. Soc. Architects award 1975), S.W. Bell Telephone Co. Equipment Bldg., 1974 (Bell Sys. award 1976), Durland Hall-Univ. Engring. Bldg., 1981 (Kans. Soc. Architects award 1983), Kans. State Prison Medium Security Facility, 1983 (Kans. Soc. Architects award 1985), Lansing H.S., 1988 (William W. Caudill citation Am. Sch. and Univ. Mag.), Leavenworth H.S., 1990 (citation Am. Sch. and Univ. Mag.), Plant Scis. Bldg., Kans. State U., 1994, Tomanek Hall, Ft. Hays State U., 1995; featured in publs. including Archtl. Record Mag. Recipient citation Am. Sch. and Univ. Mag.; Weigel scholar Kans. State U., 1958-60; Bales Organ Recital Hall U. Kans., 1995. Mem. AIA, Kans. Soc. Architects (pres. 1981-82), Coun. Edn. Facilities Planners Internat., Future Heritage Topeka, Optimists (pres. Topeka breakfast club 1970-71, lt. gov. Kans. dist. 1981-82). Avocations: woodworking, photography, sculpting. Home: 3535 SW Macvicar Ave Topeka KS 66611-1841 E-mail: gkarst@msn.com.

KARTER, ELIAS M. paper products company executive; b. 1940; married. BS, U. Maine, 1962, MS, 1963, PhD, 1967. Asst. mill mgr. Westvaco Corp., 1963-78; resident mgr. Boise So. Co., Deridder, La., 1978-80; with Ga. Kraft Co., Rome, from 1981, former pres., chmn., chief exec. officer, also bd. dirs.; now v.p. mfg. and tech. The Mead Corp., Dayton, Ohio, 1994-96, exec. v.p., 1996—. Served to capt. U.S. Army, 1968-70.

KARU, GILDA M(ALL), lawyer, government official; b. Oceanport, N.J., Dec. 1, 1951; d. Harold and Ilvy (Meriloo) K.; m. Frederick F. Foy, May 23, 1981. AB, Vassar Coll., 1974; JD, Ill. Inst. Tech., 1987. Bar: Ill. 1987, U.S. Dist. Ct. (no. dist.) Ill. 1987. Quality control reviewer Food and Nutrition Svc. USDA, Robbinsville, N.J., 1974-77, team leader, 1977-78, supr., 1978-81, sect. chief Food and Nutrition Svc. Chgo., 1991-2000, acting dir. field ops., 1998, acting dir. food stamp program, 1999; regional dir. civil rights/EEO for midwest region USDA Food and Nutrition Svc., 2000—. Employer adviser Ctr. for Rehab. and Tng. Disabled Persons, Chgo., 1986-93; chief mgmt. negotiator for collective bargaining agreement Nat. Treasury Employees Union, 1990; acting regional dir. Food Stamp program, 1999, 2000. Bd. dirs., legal counsel, regional dir. North Ctrl. Estonian Am. Nat. Coun., N.Y.C.; v.p. 1st Estonian Evang. Luth. Ch., Chgo., treas., 1994—; mem. Chgo. Vol. Legal Svcs., Friends of Arlington Heights Meml. Libr.; vol. dep. voter registration officer Cook County, Ill.; chair diversity adv. coun. Chgo. Fed. Exec. Bd., 2001—. Recipient cert. of recognition William A. Jump Meml. Found., 1987, Arthur S. Flemming award Washington Downtown Jaycees, 1987, Ill. Dem. Ethnic Heritage award, 1989, cert. of appreciation Assn. for Persons with Disabilities in Agr., 1992, Group Honor award for work on 1993 Miss. River Flood Disaster Relief, Sec. of USDA, 1994. Mem. ABA, AAUW, LWV (bd. dirs. 1992—, v.p. chpt. 2000—, newsletter editor), Ill. Bar Assn., Chgo. Bar Assn., Baltic Bar Assn., United Coun. on Welfare Fraud, Nat. Audubon Soc., Chgo. Area Seven Sisters Coll. Consortium (sec. 1995—), Mensa, Vassar Club (chpt. treas. 1988-90, v.p. 1990-91, coord. pub. rels. 1991—). Avocations: photography, reading, travel, crafts. Office: USDA Food and Nutrition Svc 77 W Jackson Blvd Fl 20 Chicago IL 60604-3591

KASER, BOB, radio personality; Pub. rels. asst., radio color commentator IHl Flint Generals, IHL Saginaw (Mich.) Gears, 1982, Easter League Erie Glades, 1983—84, Western League Seattle Thunderbirgs, 1984—89; radio announcer for IHL Grand Rapids Griffins Wood 1300, Grand Rapids, Mich., 1991—. Office: Woodradio 1300 77 Monroe Ctr Ste 1000 Grand Rapids MI 49503

KASHANI, HAMID REZA, lawyer, computer consultant; b. Tehran, Iran, May 1, 1955; came to U.S., 1976; s. Javad K. BSEE with highest distinction, Purdue U., 1978, MSEE, 1979; JD, Ind. U., 1986. Bar: Ind. 1986, U.S. Dist. Ct. (so. and no. dists.) 1986, U.S. Ct. Appeals (7th cir.) 1986, U.S. Supreme Ct. 1994, U.S. Ct. Appeals (9th cir.) 1996. Rsch. asst. Purdue U., West Lafayette, Ind., 1978-79, 80-81; engr. Cummins Engine Co., Columbus, 1981-82; assoc. faculty Ind. U.-Purdue U., Indpls., 1983-84; sr. software engr. Engineered System Devel., 1985-87; computer cons. Hamid R. Kashani, 1986—; pvt. practice law, 1986—; cons. Good Techs., 1987-90; pres. Virtual Media Techs., Inc., 1998—. Cons. Prism Imaging, Denver, 1990-93, Ind. Bar Assn., 1989-95. Editor: Computer Law Desktop Guide, 1995. Mem., bd. dirs. ACLU, 1997—, Ind. Civil Liberties Union, Indpls., 1987—, mem. legis. com., 1987—, mem. screening com., 1985—, del., 1989, 91, 93, 95, 97, 99, 2001, acting v.p. fundraising, 1995-96, v.p. edn., 1996—, chair long-range planning com., 1991-92, 96—, chmn. nominating com., 1997—, pres., 1999—; bd. dirs. ACLU, 1997—. Fellow Ind. U. Sch. Law, 1984; recipient Cert. of Appreciation Ind. Correctional Assn., 1988; named Cooperating Atty. of Yr. Ind. Civil Liberties Union, 1990, 95, 98. Mem. ABA (vice chmn. YLD computer law com. 1990-91, chmn. computer law exec. com. 1991-93, litigation exec. com. 1987-89, 90-93, YLD liaison standing com. on jud. selection, tenure and compensation 1992-94, 95-96, sci. & tech. co-chair first amendment rights in the digital age com., vice chair com. on opportunities for minorities and women, YLD liaison to ABA tech. coun. 1992-93, co-chmn. first amendment rights in the digital age com. 1997—, vice chmn. com. on opportunities for minorities women 1997—99, vice chmn. nat. info. infrastructure com. sect. sci. and tech. 1993-97, chair privacy info. and civil liberties ABA sect. of individual rights and responsibilities 1998—, mem. standing com. on jud. selection, tenure and compensation 1995-96, chair privacy info. and civil liberties sect. of individual rights and responsibilities 1998—), IEEE (Outstanding Contbns. award 1983), Indpls. Bar Assn. (chmn. articles and bylaws coms. 1994-95), Ind. State Bar Assn. (vice chair computer comms. com. 1995-98, chair computer comms. com. 1998—, chair computer comm. com. 1998—), Eta Kappa Nu, Tau Beta Pi, Phi Kappa Phi, Phi Eta Sigma. Office: 445 N Pennsylvania St Ste 600 Indianapolis IN 46204-1818 E-mail: hkashani@kashanilaw.com.

KASISCHKE, LOUIS WALTER, lawyer; b. Bay City, Mich., July 18, 1942; s. Emil Ernst and Gladys Ann (Stuady) K.; m. Sandra Ann Colosimo, Sept. 30, 1967; children: Douglas, Gregg. BA, Mich. State U., 1964, JD, 1967; LLM, Wayne State U., 1971. Bar: Mich. 1968, U.S. Dist. Ct. (southeastern dist.) Mich. 1968; CPA. Acct. Touche Ross & Co., Detroit, 1967-71; atty. Dykema Gossett, 1971—; pres. Pella Window and Door Co., West Bloomfield, Mich., 1990-98. Bd. dirs. Barton Malow Co., Southfield. Author: Michigan Closely Held Corporations, 1986; contbr. articles to profl. jours. Mem. ABA, AICPA, State Bar Mich. (editor column Mich. Bar Jour. 1971-83), Mich. Assn. CPAs, Am. Coll. Tax Counsel Republican. Lutheran. Avocations: mountaineering, skiing, running, squash, golf. Home: 3491 N Lakeshore Harbor Springs MI 49740 Office: Dykema Gossett 39577 Woodward Ave Ste 300 Bloomfield Hills MI 48304-5086

KASPAREK, JOHN ANTHONY, academic administrator; b. Detroit, June 14, 1943; s. John W. and Edna M. (Doll) K. BA in Philosophy, Kilroe Sem., Honesdale, Pa., 1966; MDiv., Sacred Heart Sch. Theology, 1991. Pastor Archdiocese of Detroit, 1969-77; provincial councilor Priests of the Sacred Heart, Hales Corners, Wis., 1977-92, dir. apostolates and fgn. missions, 1977-83, pers. dir., 1983-86; pres. Sacred Heart Sch. Theology, 1986—, also bd. dirs.; pastor Cathedral St. Ignatius Loyola, Palm Beach Gardens, Fla. Mem. KC (trinity coun. #4580 1986—), Equestrian Order of Holy Sepulchre Jerusalem, Cath. Knights Ins. Soc. (bd. dirs. 1992—). Roman Catholic. Office: Cathedral St Ignatius Loyola 9999 N Military Trl Palm Beach Gardens FL 33410-5460

KASPROW, BARBARA ANNE, biomedical scientist, writer; b. Hartford, Conn., Apr. 23, 1936; d. Stephen G. and Anna M. Kasprow. AB cum laude, Albertus Magnus Coll., 1958; postgrad., Laval U., 1958, Yale U., 1958-61; PhD, Loyola U., Chgo., 1969. Staff microbiology dept. Conn. State Dept. Health, 1957; lab. asst. dept. microbiology Yale U., New Haven, 1958-59; tng. scholar USPHS, 1959-60; asst. rsch. and editl. dept. anatomy Yale U., New Haven, 1961; rsch. assoc. N.Y. Med. Coll., 1961-62; rsch. assoc. Inst. for Study Human Reprodn. St. Ann Ob-Gyn. Hosp., Cleve., 1962-67; sr. rsch. assoc. dept. anatomy Stritch Sch. Medicine, Chgo., Hines, Ill., 1967-69; asst. prof. anatomy Loyola U., Chgo., 1969-75; asst. to v.p. University Rsch. Sys., 1975-79; v.p. med. topics Univ. Rsch. Sys., 1979—; asst. to pres. Internat. Basic and Biol.-Biomed. Curricula, Lombard, Ill., 1979—. Lectr. in field; invited U.S. del. on reprodn. to Vatican, 1964; round table leader Brazil-Israel Congress on Fertility and Sterility, Brazil Soc. Human Reprodn., São Paulo, 1972. Editl. asst. vol. VIII/3 Handbuch der Histochemie, Gustav Fischer Verlag, 1963; prodn. aide ednl. med. film The Soft Anvil, 1965-66; co-editor: Biology of Reproduction, Basic and Clinical Studies, 1973; contbr. articles to profl. jours. Recipient Certificate of Outstanding Achievement and Scholarship award Am. Assn. German Tchrs. and New Britain German Assn., 1954; named Honorary Citizen São Paulo, 1972. Mem. AAAS (life), Am. Assn. Anatomists, Am. Soc. Zoologists-The Soc. Integrative and Comparative Biology, Pan Am. Assn. Anatomy (co-organizer symposium on reproduction New Orleans 1972), Midwest Anatomists Assn. (program officer ann. meeting Chgo. 1974), Sigma Xi (life). Roman Catholic. Achievements include biological elucidation of growth horizons in uterine development, growth, and maturity; perfection of a hormonal model-system in highly controlled (surgerized) animals to ascertain quantitative relationships of purified estradiol-17beta and progesterone required for promotion of and duplication of these uterine growth horizons; development of experimental paradigms for the biomorphological elucidation of hormonally stimulated growth responses in endocrine target organs, and cyto- and histochemical elucidation of growth stimulants. Office: 607 E Wilson Ave Lombard IL 60148-4062

KASS, LAWRENCE, hematologist, oncologist, hematopathologist; b. Toledo, Sept. 30, 1938; AB magna cum laude, U. Mich., 1960; MD with hons., MS Anatomy, U. Chgo., 1964. Diplomate Nat. Bd. Med. Examiners, Am. Bd. Internal Medicine/Internal Medicine and Hematology, Med. Oncology, Am. Bd. Pathology/Hematology. Intern Peter Bent Brigham Hosp., Boston, 1964-65, asst. resident internal medicine, 1965-66; sr. asst. resident internal medicine U. Hosps. of Cleve., 1966-68; Elliott Hoyt fellow in hematology Univ. Hosps. of Cleve., 1967-68; various to rsch. assoc. U. Chgo., 1968-70; asst. prof. internal medicine U. Mich. Med. Sch., Ann Arbor, 1970-73, assoc. prof. internal medicine, 1973-78; prof. path., medicine Case Western Res. U. Sch. Medicine, Cleve., 1978—; head hematopathology MetroHealth Med. Ctr., 1978—. Cons. in medicine, VA Hosp., Ann Arbor; editorial cons. Williams and Wilkins Pubs., Balt., 1974—, Archives of Pathology and Lab. Medicine Blood, The Jour. of Hematology, The Jour. of Histochemistry and Cytochemistry, Western Jour. of Medicine, Am. Jour. of Hematology, Biotechnic & Histochemistry, 1975—. Rsch. Career Selection Rev. Com., VA, Washington, 1976—; active numerous coms. in field. Contbr. articles to profl. jours. Maj. med corps. U.S. Army, 1968-70. Recipient Internat. Giovanni DiGuglielmo prize, Giovanni DiGuglielmo Found., Accademia Nazionale Die Lincei, Rome, 1976, Diamond Cover award Nat. Soc. Histotechnologists and Jour. of Histotechnology, 1988, C.V. Mosby award, 1964, Merck award 1964. Fellow Am. Coll. Phys., Coll. Am. Pathologists; mem. AAAS, Am. Soc. Hematology, Am. Fedn. Clin. Rsch., Am. Soc. Clin. Oncology, Soc. Exptl. Biology and Medicine, Cen. Soc. Clin. Rsch., Histochem. Soc., Biol. Stain Commn., Am. Soc. Clin. Path., Phi Eta Sigma, Phi Beta Kappa, Alpha Omega Alpha. Office: MetroHealth Med Ctr 2500 Metrohealth Dr Cleveland OH 44109-1900 Fax: (216) 778-5701. E-mail: lkass@metrohealth.org.

KASS, LEON RICHARD, b. Chgo., Feb. 12, 1939; s. Samuel and Anna (Shoichet) K.; m. Amy Judith Apfel, June 22, 1961; children: Sarah, Miriam. B.S., U. Chgo., 1958, M.D., 1962; Ph.D. in Biochemistry, Harvard U., 1967. Intern Beth Israel Hosp., Boston, 1962-63; staff assoc. Lab. Molecular Biology, Nat. Inst. Arthritis and Metabolic Diseases, NIH, Bethesda, Md., 1967-69, staff fellow, 1969-70, sr. staff fellow, 1970; exec. sec. com. on life scis. and social policy NRC-NAS, Washington, 1970-72; tutor St. John's Coll., Annapolis, Md., 1972-76; Joseph P. Kennedy Sr. research prof. in bioethics Kennedy Inst., Georgetown U., 1974-76; Henry R. Luce prof. liberal arts of human biology in coll. U. Chgo., 1976-84, prof. com. on social thought, 1984-90, Addie Clark Harding prof. in coll. and com. on social thought, 1990—. Founding fellow, bd. dirs. Hastings Ctr., 1969-96; bd. govs. U.S.-Israel Binat. Sci. Found., 1982-88; mem. coun. Nat. Humanities Coun., 1984-91, vice chmn. 1987-89. Author: Toward a More Natural Science: Biology and Human Affairs, 1985, The Hungry Soul: Eating and the Perfecting of Our Nature, 1994, (James Q. Wilson) The Ethics of Human Cloning, 1998, (Amy A. Kass) Wing to Wing, Oar to Oar: Readings on Courting and Marrying; contbr. articles to profl. jours. Served with USPHS, 1967-69. NIH postdoctoral fellow, 1963-67, John Simon Guggenheim Meml. Found. fellow, 1972-73, Nat. Humanities Ctr. fellow, 1984-85, W.H. Brady, Jr. Disting. fellow Am. Enterprise Inst., 1991-92, 98-99; NEH grantee, 1973-74. Mem. Phi Beta Kappa, Alpha Omega Alpha. Jewish. Office: # Ae1 1150 17th St NW Washington DC 20036-4603

KASTEL, HOWARD L. lawyer, business executive; b. Chgo., June 11, 1932; s. William A. and Beatrice (Seltzer) K.; m. Joan Herron, Dec. 20, 1953; children: Mark Alan, Jeffrey Lawrence. BA, Harvard U., 1954; JD cum laude, Loyola U., Chgo., 1960. Bar: Ill. 1960, U.S. Dist. Ct. (no. dist.) Ill. 1960, U.S. Ct. Appeals (7th cir.) 1965, U.S. Ct. Appeals (2d, 3d, 4th, 5th, 8th and 9th cirs.), U.S. Supreme Ct. Assoc. Aaron, Aaron, Schimberg & Hess, Chgo., 1960-62; ptnr. Altheimer & Gray, 1962-80, Kastel & Rutkoff, Chgo., 1980-83, Holleb & Coff, Chgo., 1983-84, McDermott, Will & Emery, Chgo., 1984-97, of counsel, 1997—; pres., CEO Wanger Asset Mgmt. Ltd., 1998-99; ptnr. Wanger Asset Mgmt. LP, 1998-99. Mem. Fin. Acctg. Standards Bd. Task Force on Non-Bus. Orgns., 1981-83, mem. Labor Law Com., 1961-72, Civil Practice Com., 1971-88, Securities Law Com., 1981-88, Jud. Com., 1983—. Sgt. USMC, 1954-56. Mem. ABA (law and acctg. com. 1977—, chmn. subcom. internat. acctg., fed. regulations of securities subcom. on SEC practice and enforcement matters 1979—), Am. Arbitration Assn. (nat. panel arbitrators). Avocations: yacht racing, treking, cross country skiing, running. Home: 1501 N State Pkwy Chicago IL 60610-1676 Office: Apt 12A 1501 N State Pkwy Chicago IL 60610-5738

KASTEN, G. FREDERICK, JR. investment company executive; Pres., CEO, now chmn. Baird Fin. Corp., Milw. Office: Baird Fin Corp 777 E Wisconsin Ave Milwaukee WI 53202-5300

KASTEN, MARY ALICE C. state legislator; b. Matthews, Mo., June 6, 1928; d. Clarence Alvin and Ruth (Hill) Critchlow; m. Melvin C. Kasten, 1949; children: Mark, Michael, Margaret. BS, Southeast Mo. State U., 1949; postgrad., U. Pitts. State rep. Mo. State Congress. Del. Nat. Conf. Edn. and Citizenship; mem. Cape Girardeau Sch. Bd., Nat. Joint Com. Representing Sch. Bd. Assn., Mo. State Bd. Edn., State Adv. Com. on Vocat. Edn. Bd. Regents mem. Southeast Mo. State U. Mem. Nat. Sch. Bd. Assn., Mo. Sch. Bd. Assn. Office: Mo Ho of Reps State Capitol Building Jefferson City MO 65101-1556

KASTNER, CHRISTINE KRIHA, newspaper correspondent; b. Cleve., Aug. 27, 1951; d. Joseph Calvin and Grace (Weber) Kriha; m. Donald William Kastner, June 30, 1979; 1 child, Paul Donald. Assoc., Lakeland C.C., 1976; BA in Comms., Cleve. State U., 1983. Asst. editor, comms. specialist TRW, Inc., Cleve., 1978-85; editor Kaiser Permanente, 1985-87; dir. pub. rels. Northeastern Ohio chpt. Arthritis Found., 1991-92; newspaper corr. The Plain Dealer, 1992—. Contbg. author: Encyclopedia of Cleveland History, 1988. Recipient Gold Addy award Am. Advt. Fedn., 1986, Award of Excellence Women in Comms., Inc., 1987, Bronze Quill award Internat. Assn. Bus. Communicators, 1987. Mem. Soc. Profl. Journalists. Roman Catholic. Avocations: bicycling, reading. Home and Office: 5003 Clubside Rd Lyndhurst OH 44124-2540

KASTOR, FRANK SULLIVAN, English language educator; b. Evanston, Ill., Aug. 19, 1933; s. Herman Walker and Rebecca (Sullivan) K.; m. Tina Bennett, Oct. 28, 1979; children: Jeffrey, Mark, Harlan, Kristina, Patrick, Liam, Mary Elisabeth, Caroline. BA, U. Ill., 1955, MA, 1956; PhD, U. Calif., Berkeley, 1963. Teaching asst. U. Ill., 1955-56, U. Calif., Berkeley, 1960-63; asst. prof. English U. So. Calif., 1964-66, 67-68; assoc. prof. English No. Ill. U., 1968-69; prof. English, Wichita State U., 1969—, chmn. dept., 1969-75, prof. emeritus, 1998, ret., 1998. Contbr. to: The Milton Ency., The Dictionary of Literary Biography; author books, articles, revs., TV documentaries, C.S. Lewis study guides. Served with USAF, 1956-59. Rsch. grantee U. Calif., Berkeley, 1962, U. So. Calif., 1964, No. Ill. U., 1969, Wichita State U., 1970, 72, 73, 74, 84, 86, 92; Fulbright lectr., Spain, 1966-67; Kans. Com. for Humanities grantee, 1973, 74, 94; recipient NEH award, 1971, 84. Mem. MLA, Milton Soc. Am., Conf. on Christianity and Lit., AAUP, N.Y. C.S. Lewis Soc., C.S. Lewis Soc. of Kans. (founder, pres.), Phi Kappa Phi. Christian Ch. E-mail: kastor@wsuhub.uc.twsu.edu.

KASULIS, THOMAS PATRICK, humanities educator; b. Bridgeport, Conn., Mar. 5, 1948; s. Joseph John and Albina Anna (Checkanouskas) K.; m. Ellen Elizabeth Sponheimer, June 5, 1970; children: Telemachus, Matthias, Benedict. BA, Yale U., 1970, MPh, 1972, PhD, 1975; MA, U. Hawaii, 1973. Asst. prof. philosophy U. Hawaii, Honolulu, 1975-80; from asst. prof. to prof. philosophy and religion Northland Coll., Ashland, Wis., 1981-91; prof. comparative studies The Ohio State U., Columbus, 1991—, chair East Asian langs. and lit., 1993-95, chair comparative studies, 1995-98. Mellon faculty fellow in humanities Harvard U., Cambridge, Mass., 1979-80; vis. facility rschr. Osaka (Japan) U., 1982-83; Numata vis. prof. U. Chgo., Ill., 1988. Author: Zen Action/Zen Person, 1981; editor, co-translator: The Body: Toward an Eastern Mind-Body Theory, 1987; co-editor: Self as Body in Asian Theory and Practice, 1993, Self as Person in Asian Theory and Practice, 1994; contbr. chpts. to books and articles to profl. jours. Fellow Japan Found., 1982-83; NEH fellow for Coll. Tchrs., NEH, 1986-87; Sr. Rsch. fellow East West Ctr., Honolulu, 1988. Mem. Soc. for Asian and Comparative Philosophy (pres. 1988-91), Am. Soc. for the Study of Religion (pres. 1999—), Soc. for Values in Higher Edn. Home: 1465 Montcalm Rd Upper Arlington OH 43221-3450 Office: Comparative Studies Ohio State Univ 230 W 17th Ave Columbus OH 43210-1361 E-mail: kasulis.1@osu.edu.

KATCHER, RICHARD, lawyer; b. N.Y.C., Dec. 17, 1918; s. Samuel and Gussie (Applebaum) K.; m. Shirley Ruth Rifkin, Sept. 24, 1944; children: Douglas P., Robert A., Patti L. BA, U. Mich., 1941, JD, 1943. Bar: Mich. 1943, N.Y. 1944, Ohio 1946. Assoc. Noonan, Kaufman & Eagan, N.Y.C., 1943-46; from assoc. to ptnr. Ulmer, Berne & Laronge, Cleve., 1946-72; ptnr. Baker & Hostetler, 1972-95. Lectr. in fed. income taxation Case Western Res. U. Sch. Law, Cleve., 1953-69, 71-72; mem. bd. in control of intercollegiate athletics, U. Mich., 2001—. Contbr. articles on fed. tax to profl. jours. Recipient Disting. Alumni Service award U. Mich., 1987, Leadership medal Pres.' Soc. of U. Mich., 1991. Fellow ABA (coun. sect. taxation 1973-76), Am. Coll. Tax Counsel (regent); mem. Am. Bar Retirement Assn. (bd. dirs., v.p. 1986-87, pres. 1987-88), U. Mich. Pres. Soc. (chmn. exec. com. 1987-90), U. Mich. Cleve. Club (pres. 1959, Outstanding Alumnus award 1987), U. Mich. Alumni Assn. (dir. 1994-98, sec. 1997-98). Avocation: tennis. Home: 26150 Village Ln Apt 104 Beachwood OH 44122-7527 Office: Baker & Hostetler 3200 National City Ctr 1900 E 9th St Ste 3200 Cleveland OH 44114-3475 E-mail: RKatcher@baker-hostetler.com.

KATSIANIS, JOHN NICK, financial executive; b. Chgo., Oct. 27, 1960; s. John Nick and Rosalie A. (Kitzberger) K. BS in Acctg. and Fin., U. Ill., Chgo., 1982. CPA, Ill. Staff acct. gen. acctg. Svc. Master Industries, Inc., Downers Grove, Ill., 1983-84, staff acct. spl. projects, 1984-85; staff acct. Svc. Master Home Health Care Svcs., 1985, controller, 1985-89; dir. fin., asst. treas. Rush-Presbyn.-St. Luke's Med. Ctr., Chgo., 1989-93; sr. v.p., CFO NYLCare Health Plans of the Midwest, Oak Brook, Ill., 1993-98; regional pres. Avanti Health Sys. Ill., Inc., 1995-96; dir. fin. Elmhurst (Ill.) Meml. Health Sys., 1998—. Vice pres. Countryside (Ill.) Police Pension Bd., 1987-2001, pres. 2001--. Mem.: AICPA, Chgo. Healthcare Exec. Forum, Healthcare Fin. Mgmt. Assn. (bd. dirs. 2000—, treas. 2001—), Ill. CPA Soc. Baptist. Avocations: golf, snow skiing, swimming, softball. Home: 860 Tam Oshanter Bolingbrook IL 60440

KATZ, ADRIAN IZHACK, physician, educator; b. Bucharest, Romania, Aug. 3, 1932; came to U.S., 1965, naturalized, 1976; s. Ferdinand and Helen (Lustig) K.; m. Miriam Lesser, Mar. 31, 1965; children— Ron, Iris. M.D., Hebrew U., 1961. Research fellow Yale U., 1965-67, Harvard U., 1967-68; intern Belinson Med. Center, Israel, 1961, resident, 1962-65; practice medicine specializing in internal medicine and nephrology New Haven, 1966-67, Boston, 1967-68, Chgo., 1968—; attending physician U. Chgo. Hosps., 1968—, head nephrology sect., 1973-82; asst. prof. medicine U. Chgo., 1968-71, assoc. prof., 1971-74, prof., 1975—. Fogarty sr. internat. fellow, vis. scientist Lab Cell Physiology, Coll. de France, Paris, 1977-78; vis. prof. cellular and molecular physiology Yale U., 1988; vis. scientist dept. molecular medicine Karolinska Inst., Stockholm, 1994—. Co-author: Kidney Function and Disease in Pregnancy; contbr. chpts. to books, articles to profl. jours. Fellow A.C.P.; mem. Am. Physiol. Soc., Am. Soc. Clin. Investigation, Assn. Am. Physicians, Am. Soc. Nephrology, Internat. Soc. Nephrology, Central Soc. Clin. Research, N.Y. Acad. Scis. Home: 1125 E 53rd St Chicago IL 60615-4410 Office: U Chgo 5841 S Maryland Ave Chicago IL 60637-1463 E-mail: akatz@medicine.bsd.uchicago.edu.

KATZ, DAVID ALLAN, judge, former lawyer, business consultant; b. Nov. 1, 1933; s. Samuel and Ruth (Adelman) K.; m. Joan G. Siegel, Sept. 4, 1955; children: Linda, Michael S., Debra. BBA, Ohio State U., 1955, JD summa cum laude, 1957. Bar: Ohio 1957. Ptnr. Spengler Nathanson, Attys., Toledo, 1957-86, mng. ptnr., 1986-93; judge U.S. Dist. Ct. (no. dist.) Ohio, 1994—. Dir., corp. sec. Seaway Food Town, Inc., Maumee, Ohio, 1980-94; trustee St. Vincent Med. Ctr., 1987-96, sec., 1988-90, vice chmn.-treas., 1990-94, chmn., 1994-96, St. Vincent Med. Ctr. Found., chmn., 1990-92; trustee The Toledo Symphony; v.p. Jewish Edn. Service N.Am., 1985-91; trustee Mercy Health Sys. NW Ohio, 1996—. Pres. Temple B'nai Israel, Toledo, 1970-73, Jewish Welfare Fedn., Toledo, 1977-79, Toledo Bar Assn. Found., 1983-94. Fellow Ohio Bar Found., Toledo Bar Found.; mem. ABA, Toledo Bar Assn. (sec., trustee 1972-78), Ohio State Bar Assn. Office: US Court House 1716 Spielbusch Ave Ste 210 Toledo OH 43624-1347

KATZ, JOSEPH JACOB, chemist, educator; b. Apr. 19, 1912; s. Abraham and Stella (Asnin) K.; m. Celia S. Weiner, Oct. 1, 1944; children: Anna, Elizabeth, Mary, Abram. BSc, Wayne U., 1932; PhD, U. Chgo., 1942. Research asso. chemistry U. Chgo., 1942-43, asso. chemist metall. lab., 1943-45; sr. chemist Argonne Nat. Lab., Ill., 1945—; Tech. adviser U.S. delegation UN Conf. on Peaceful Uses Atomic Energy, Geneva, Switzerland, 1955; chmn. AAAS Gordon Research Conf. on Inorganic Chemistry, 1953-54. Am. editor Jour. Inorganic and Nuclear Chemistry, 1955-82. Recipient Distinguished Alumnus award Wayne U., 1955, Profl. Achievement award U. Chgo. Alumni Assn., 1983, Rumford Premium Am. Acad. Arts & Scis., 1992; Guggenheim fellow, 1956-57 Mem. Am. Chem. Soc. (award for nuclear applications in chemistry 1961, sec.-treas. div. phys. chemistry 1966-76), Nat. Acad. Scis., Phi Beta Kappa, Sigma Xi. Home: 1700 E 56th St Apt 1901 Chicago IL 60637-5085 Office: Argonne Nat Lab 9700 Cass Ave Argonne IL 60439-4803 E-mail: jjkatz@worldnet.att.net.

KATZ, LEWIS ROBERT, law educator; b. N.Y.C., Nov. 15, 1938; s. Samuel and Rose (Turoff) K.; m. Jan Karen Daugherty, Jan. 14, 1964; children: Brett Elizabeth, Adam Kenneth, Tyler Jessica. AB, Queens Coll., 1959; JD, Ind. U., 1963. Bar: Ind 1963, Ohio 1971. Assoc. Snyder, Bunger, Cotner & Harrell, Bloomington, Ind., 1963-65; instr. U. Mich. Law Sch., Ann Arbor, 1965-66; asst. prof. Case Western Res. U. Law Sch., Cleve., 1966-68, assoc. prof., 1968-71, prof., 1971—, John C. Hutchins prof. law, 1973—. Dir. Ctr. for Criminal Justice, Case Western Res. U., 1973-91, dir. fgn. grad. studies, 1992—; cons. criminal justice agys. Author: Justice is the Crime, 1972, The Justice Imperative: Introduction to Criminal Justice, 1979, Ohio Arrest Search and Seizure, ann. publ. 2001, (with J. Shapiro) New York Suppression Manual, 1991, Know Your Rights, 1994, (with P.C. Giannelli) Ohio Criminal Law, 1996, (with B.W. Griffin) Ohio Felony Sentencing Law, ann. publ., 2001, (with P.C. Giannelli) Ohio Criminal Justice, ann. publ., 2002. Mem. regional bd. Anti-Defamation League; trustee Women's Law Fund. Recipient Disting. Tchr. award Case West Res. U. Law Alumni Assn., Tchr. of Yr. award Case Western Res. U., 1999; Nat. Defender Project of Nat. Legal Aid and Defender Assn. fellow, 1968 Mem. ABA. Home: 29550 S Woodland Rd Pepper Pike OH 44124-5743 Office: Case Western Res U Law Sch Law Sch Cleveland OH 44106

KATZ, ROBERT STEPHEN, rheumatologist, educator; b. Balt., July 31, 1944; s. Irving Gilbert and Shirley Ann (Feldman) K.; m. Carlen Jo Levin, Dec. 12, 1972; children: Jeremy, Alexandra, Gena. BA, Columbia U., 1966; MD, U. Md., 1970. Diplomate Am. Bd. Internal Medicine. Fellow in rheumatology Johns Hopkins Hosp., Balt., 1974-76; assoc. prof. medicine Rush-Presbyn. St. Luke's Med. Ctr., Chgo., 1976—; intern Jewish Hosp. St. Louis/Washington U. Med. Ctr., 1970-71, resident in internal medicine, 1971-72. Mem., chmn. med. adv. bd. Lupus Found. Ill.; chmn. med. sci. com. No. Ill. chpt. Arthritis Found., 1985-87. Med. editor WBBM-TV, 1991-92, med. editor Fox TV WFLD, 1993—; chmn. Med. Adv. Bd. Chicago Sun-Times Medlife sect.; contbr. articles to profl. jours. Bd. dirs. Agers Found. Am. Lt. USN, 1970-72. Mem. AMA, Cen. Rheumatism Soc., Am. Coll. Rheumatology, Chgo. Med. Soc. Office: Dept Internal Medicine Rush Presbyn St Luke Med Ctr 1725 W Harrison St Ste 1039 Chicago IL 60612-3862

KATZ, SIDNEY FRANKLIN, obstetrician, gynecologist; b. Detroit, Sept. 5, 1928; m. Sally R. Katz. BS, Wayne State U., 1949; MD, U. Mich., 1953. Diplomate Am. Bd. Ob-Gyn. Intern Wayne County Gen. Hosp., Detroit; resident Grace Hosp., 1956—57; pvt. practice, Dearborn, 1959—. Capt. USAF, 1954—56. Fellow: ACS, ACOG; mem.: So. Mich. Surg. Soc., Mich. Soc. Gynecologists, Am. Soc. for Reproductive Medicine. Office: Ste 150 31500 Telegraph Rd Bingham Farms MI 48025-4313

KATZ, STUART CHARLES, lawyer, jazz musician; b. Chgo., June 9, 1937; s. Jerome H. and Sylvia L. (Singer) K.; m. Penny Schatz, Jan. 23, 1959; children: Steven, Lauren. BA, Roosevelt U., Chgo., 1959; JD with distinction, John Marshall Law Sch., 1964. Bar: Ill. 1964, U.S. Dist. Ct. (no. dist.) Ill. 1965, U.S. Supreme Ct. 1967. Exec. v.p. Heitman Fin. LLC, Chgo., 1972—. Mem. program com. Internat. Coun. Shopping Ctrs., U.S. Law Conf.; jazz pianist and vibraphonist, appeared in concerts with Benny Goodman, Gene Krupa, Bud Freeman. Mem. ABA, Ill. Bar Assn., Chgo. Bar Assn., Mortgage Bankers Am., Chgo. Assn. Realtors, Minn. Real Estate Bd. Jewish. Office: 180 N La Salle St Ste 3600 Chicago IL 60601-2805

KATZENELLENBOGEN, JOHN ALBERT, chemistry educator; b. Poughkeepsie, N.Y., May 10, 1944; s. Adolph Edmund Max and Elisabeth (Holzheu) K.; m. Benita Schulman, June 11, 1967; children: Deborah Joyce, Rachel Adria. MA, Harvard U., 1967, PhD, 1969. Asst. prof. chemistry U. Ill., Urbana, 1969-75, assoc. prof. chemistry, 1975-79, prof. chemistry, 1979—, prof. Beckman Inst., 1988—, Roger Adams prof. chemistry, 1992-96, Swanlund prof. of chemistry, 1996—. Chmn. BNP study section NIH, 1987-91; adv. com. AUI Brookhaven, 1986-90. Mem. editorial Biochemistry, Jour. Med. Chem., Steroids; contbr. articles to profl. jours. Recipient Berson Yalow award Soc. Nuclear Medicine, 1988, Paul Aebersold award Soc. Nuc. Medicine, 1995; Cope scholar ACS, 1999, Camille and Henry Dreyfus tchr. scholar, 1974-79, Univ. scholar, 1987-90; fellow Alfred P. Sloan Found., 1974-76, Guggenheim fellow, 1977-78. Fellow AAAS, Am. Acad. Arts and Scis.; mem. Am. Chem. Soc., Chem. Soc. (London). Office: U Ill 600 S Mathews Ave # Urbana IL 61801-3602

KATZMAN, RICHARD A. cardiologist, internist, consultant; b. Cleve., Mar. 22, 1931; s. Abraham N. and Anne Ruth (Kustin) K.; m. Roberta Brown, July 28, 1962; children: Audrey, Sharon, Naomi, Noah. BS, Case Western Reserve U., 1952; MD, U. Chgo., 1955. Diplomate Am. Bd. Internal Medicine. Prin. Richard A. Katzman M.D., Cleve., 1963—; dir. electrocardiography, dept. cardiology Metro Health Med. Ctr., 1992-97; staff cardiologist Mt. Sinai Hosp., Cleve., 1998-2000. Assoc. clin. prof. medicine Case Western Reserve U. V.p. Cleve. Coll. Jewish Studies, 1985-88. Capt. U.S. Army Med. Corps., 1956-58. Fellow Am. Coll. Physicians, Am. Coll. Chest Physicians. Home: 28950 Gates Mills Blvd Pepper Pike OH 44124-4744 Office: Parkway Med Bldg 3609 Park East Dr Beachwood OH 44122-4309

KAUFERT, DEAN R. state legislator; b. Neenah, Wis., May 23, 1957; Grad., Neenah H.S. Owner trophy and engraving shop, Neenah; mem. from dist. 55 Wis. State Assembly, Madison, 1990—. Bd. dirs. Neenah-Menasha Bowling Assn., Youth Go Bd. Mem. Optimists. Address: 1360 Alpine Ln Neenah WI 54956-4433

KAUFFMAN, ERLE GALEN, geologist, paleontologist; b. Washington, Feb. 9, 1933; s. Erle Benton and Paula Virginia (Graff) K.; children: Donald Erle, Robin Lyn, Erica Jean; m. Claudia C. Johnson, Sept. 1989. BS, U. Mich., 1955, MS, 1956, PhD, 1961; MSc (hon.), Oxford (Eng.) U., 1970; DHC, U. Göttingen, Germany, 1987. Teaching fellow, instr. U. Mich., Ann Arbor, 1956-60; from asst. to full curator dept. paleobiology Nat. Mus. Natural History Smithsonian Instn., Washington, 1960-80; prof. geology U. Colo., Boulder, 1980-96, chmn. dept. geol. scis., 1980-84, interim dir. Energy, Minerals Applied Rsch. Ctr., 1989-91; prof. geology Ind. U., 1996—. Adj. prof. geology George Washington U., Washington, 1962-80; cons. geologist, Boulder, 1980-96. Author, editor: Cretaceous Facies, Faunas and Paleoenvironments Across the Cretaceous Western Interior Basin, 1977; contbg. editor: Concepts and Methods of Biostratigraphy, 1977, Fine-grained Deposits and Biofacies of The Cretaceous Western Interior Seaway, 1985, High Resolution Event Stratigraphy, 1988, Paleontology and Evolution: Extinction Events, 1988, Extinction Events in Earth History, 1990, Evolution of the Western Interior Basin, 1993; also jour. articles. Recipient U.S. Govt. Spl. Svc. award, 1969, NSF Best Tchr. award U. Colo., 1985 named Disting. Lectr. Am. Geol. Inst., 1963-64, Am. Assn. Petroleum Geologists, 1984, 85, 91, 92; Fulbright fellow Australia, 1986. Fellow Geol. Soc. Am., AAAS; mem. Paleontol. Soc. (councilor under 40, pres. elect 1981, pres. 1982, past pres. 1983, chmn. 5 coms.); mem. NRC (rep.), Palaeontol. Assn., Internat. Paleontol. Assn. (v.p. 1982-88), Paleontol. Research Instn., Am. Assn. Petroleum Geol., Soc. Sedimentary Geology (com. mem., Spl. Svc. award 1985, Best Paper award 1985, Raymond C. Moore Paleontology medal 1991, William H. Twenhofel medal 1998), Rocky Mountain Assn. Geologists (project chief) (Scientist of Yr. 1977), Paleontol. Soc. Wash. (pres., sec., treas.), Geol. Soc. Wash. (councilor), Md. Acad. Scis. (hon. Paleontology sect.), Sigma Xi, Phi Kappa Phi, Sigma Gamma Epsilon. Democrat. Avocations: music, fishing, climbing, photography. Office: Dept Geol Sci Ind Univ 1001 E 10th St Bloomington IN 47405-1405 E-mail: kauffman@indiana.edu.

KAUFFMAN, SANDRA DALEY, state legislator; b. Osceola, Nebr., Jan. 26, 1933; d. James Richard and Erma Grace (Heald) Daley; m. Larry Allen Kauffman, Sept. 4, 1955; children: Claudia Kauffman Boosman, Matthew Allen. BA, U. Nebr., 1954; postgrad., U. Kansas City, summer 1957. Tchr. Falls City (Nebr.) High Sch., 1954-55, Westport High Sch., Kansas City, Mo., 1955-59; sales rep. Manson Industries, Topeka, 1974-75; dir. pub. affairs Bishop Hogan High Sch., Kansas City, 1985-86; mem. Mo. Ho. of Reps., Jefferson City, 1987-98. Mem. Kansas City Citizens Assn., 1981—, Kansas City Consensus, 1985—; mem. women's coun. U. Mo., Kansas City, 1986—; mem. rsch. mental health bd., bd. govs. Carondelet Aging Svcs., 1992—. Recipient Friend of Edn. award Ctr. Edn. Assn., 1986, Disting. Legislator award Mo. C.C. Assn.; named Mem. of Yr., Mo. Congress Parents and Tchrs., 1979. Mem. Am. Legis. Exch. Coun., Nat. Conf. State Legislatures, Network Bd., Nat. PTA (hon. life), Nat. Order Women Legislators, Mo. PTA (hon. life), South Kansas City C. of C., Grandview C. of C., Women C. of C., Mo. Women's Coun., Women Legislators Mo. (pres.). Republican. Methodist. Home: 620 E 90th Ter Kansas City MO 64131-2918 Office: Mo Ho of Reps State Capitol Building Jefferson City MO 65101-1556

KAUFMAN, ANDREW MICHAEL, lawyer; b. Boston, Feb. 19, 1949; s. Earle Bertram and Miriam (Halpern) K.; m. Michele Moselle, Aug. 24, 1975; children: Peter Moselle, Melissa Lanes, Caroline Raney. BA cum laude, Yale U., 1971; JD, Vanderbilt U., 1974. Bar: Tex. 1974, Ga. 1976, Ill. 1993, U.S. Ct. Appeals (5th and 11th cirs.) 1981. Assoc. Vinson & Elkins, Houston, 1974-76, ptnr., 1982-83, Austin, 1983-92, Dallas, 1992; assoc. Sutherland, Asbill & Brennan, Atlanta, 1976-80, ptnr., 1980-81, Kirkland & Ellis, Chgo., 1993—. Editor in chief Vanderbilt U. Law Rev., 1973-74. Mem. nat. alumni bd. Vanderbilt U.Law Sch., 1994—2000; Alumni fund raiser Yale U., 1971—; mem. Alumni Schs. Com. Yale U., 1986—92; mem. med. ethics coun. Seton Hosp., 1988—92; participant Leadership Austin, 1987—88; bd. dirs. KLRU-TV, 1989—93; mem. Austin (Tex.) Entrepreneurs Coun., 1991—92; mem. adv. bd. Dallas Bus. Com. Arts Leadership Inst., 1992—93; governing bd. mem. Chgo. Symphony Orch.; bd. dirs. United Way, Austin, Tex.; pub. TV Ballet Austin, 1986—92; mem. adv. bd. Austin Tech. Incubator, 1989—93. Mem. ABA (bus. law sect. 1978—, chmn. lease financing and secured transactions subcom. of com. devels. in bus. financing 1993-99, UCC com., legal opinions com., comml. fin. svcs. com.), Tex. Bar Assn., Yale U. Alumni Assn., Order of Coif, Headliners Club, Yale Club, N.Y.C. and Chgo., Knights of the Symphony Austin. Avocation: sailing. Office: Kirkland & Ellis 200 E Randolph St Fl 54 Chicago IL 60601-6636 E-mail: Andrew.Kaufman@chicago.kirkland.com.

KAUFMAN, BARTON LOWELL, financial services company executive; b. Shelbyville, Ind., Mar. 28, 1941; s. Nathan and Hortense (Schwartz) K.; m. Judy Dorman, June 17, 1962; children: Grant, Wendy Kaufman Siegel, Emily Kaufman Frank, Hannah. BS, Ind. U., 1962, JD, 1965. Bar: Ind. 1965. Agt. Kaufman Multi-Million Dollar Agy., Indpls., 1965-70; pres., CEO Kaufman Fin. Corp., 1970—. Pres. Twenty-Five Million Dollar Internat. Forum, Chgo., 1989. Republican. Jewish. Office: Kaufman Fin Corp 201 W 103rd St Ste 630 Indianapolis IN 46290-1126 E-mail: bartk@kaufin.com.

KAUFMAN, DONALD LEROY, building products executive; b. Erie, Pa., May 9, 1931; s. Isadore H. and Lena (Sandler) K.; m. Estelle Friedman, Aug. 15, 1954; children: Craig Ivan, Susan Beth, Carrie Ellen. B.S. in Bus. Adminstrn, Ohio State U., 1953, LL.B., 1955. Bar: Ohio 1955. Pres. Alside, Inc., Akron, Ohio, 1974—, chief exec. officer, 1982—. V.p., bd. dirs. Assoc. Materials Inc. Mem. adv. com. U. Akron; trustee Jewish Welfare Fund, Akron, 1958-65, young leaders div., 1961-65; trustee Akron City Hosp. Found., 1984-91, Menorah Park Home for Aged, Akron Children's Hosp. Found. Mem. Akron Bar Assn., Sigma Alpha Mu, Tau Epsilon Rho. Home: 2825 Roundhill Rd Akron OH 44333-2273 Office: PO Box 2010 Akron OH 44309-2010

KAUFMAN, DONALD WAYNE, research ecologist; b. Abilene, Tex., June 7, 1943; s. Leo Fred and Marcella Genevieve (Hobbie) K.; m. Glennis Ann Schroeder, Aug. 5, 1967; 1 child, Dawn. BS, Ft. Hays Kans. State Coll., 1965, MS, 1967; PhD, U. Ga., 1972. Postdoctoral fellow U. Tex., Austin, 1971-73; asst. prof. U. Ark., Fayetteville, 1974-75, SUNY, Binghamton, 1975-77; assoc. program dir. Population Biology, NSF, Washington, 1977-80; asst. prof. biology Kans. State U., Manhattan, 1980-84, assoc. prof. biology, 1984-91, prof. biology, 1991—; adj. curator mammals Sternberg Mus. Nat. History Ft. Hays State U., Hays, Kans., 2000—. Adj. prof. biology U. N.Mex., 1998; vis. scientist Savannah River Ecology Lab., Aiken, S.C., 1973-74; acting dir. Konza Prairie Rsch. Natural Area, 1986-87, coord., 1990-91; dir. Konza Prairie Long-Term Ecol. Rsch. Program, 1985-90; grant rev. panelist EPA, 1981-85, USDA, 1995-96; cons. NSF, 1984, Nat. Pk. Svc., 2000. Contbr. articles to profl. jours. Fellow NDEA, 1967—69. Mem. AAAS, Am. Soc. Mammalogists (award 1972, bd. dirs. 1989-92), Ecol. Soc. Am., Am. Inst. Biol. Scis., Soc. for the Study Evolution, The Wildlife Soc., Soc. Conservation Biology, Ctrl. Plains Soc. Mammalogists (bd. govs. 2000—), Sigma Xi. Office: Kans State U Div Biology Ackert Hall Manhattan KS 66506 E-mail: dwkaufma@ksu.edu.

KAUFMAN, JEFFREY ALLEN, publisher; b. Mpls., May 28, 1952; s. Theodore and Jean Louise (Tiegs) K. Student, Mankato State U., 1970-71, Ariz. State U., 1971-72; BA, U. Minn., 1975. Pres. Creative Resources, Inc., Mpls., 1976-80; sr. v.p. Literary Resources, Inc., Phoenix, 1980-81; pres. Multi-Media, 1981-83, Where To Go, Inc., Excelsior, Minn., 1983-86; v.p. The Old Utica Co., Mpls., 1986-88; chmn. Actif, Inc., Wayzata, Minn., 1988-89; ptnr. S&K Group, Mpls., 1989-90; editor in chief Spl. Events Pub., Inc., 1990-92; founder Electronic Claims Processing, Inc., Edina, Minn., 1992-96; co-owner BIO-Works, Inc., 1994—, Kaufman Capital Funding, 1997—. Cons. Control Data Corp. Mpls., 1978-81; dir. Nexus Inc. Mpls., 1978-81; founder ECP Inc., 1992. Author: (books) Where To Go in Minneapolis and Saint Paul, 1984, Where To Go in Los Angeles, 1985, (screenplay) Born To Be Chief, 1985. Avocations: golf, flying, equestrian. Home: PO Box 204 Excelsior MN 55331-0204 E-mail: seeme@pclink.com.

KAUFMAN, PAULA T. librarian; b. Perth Amboy, N.J., July 26, 1946; d. Harry and Clara (Katz) K.; m. L. Ratner, 1989. AB, Smith Coll., 1968; MS, Columbia U., 1969; MBA, U. New Haven, 1979. Reference libr. Columbia U., N.Y.C., 1969-70, bus. libr., 1979-82, dir. libr. svcs., 1982-86, dir. acad. info. svcs., 1986-87, acting v.p., univ. libr., 1987-88; dean of librs. U. Tenn., Knoxville, 1988-99; univ. libr. U. Ill., Urbana Champaign, 1999—. Reference coord. McKinsey & Co., N.Y.C., 1970—73; founder, ptnr. Info. for Bus., N.Y.C., 1973—76; prin. reference libr. Yale U., New Haven, 1976—79; bd. dir. Ctr. Rsch. Libr., 1994—2000, chmn., 1996—97; bd. dirs. CAUSE, 1996—98; bd. dir. Assn. Rsch. Libr., 1997—, v.p., pres.-elect, 2000—01, pres., 2001—02; bd. dir. ILCSO, 2000—02, chair, 2001—02; bd. dirs. Coun. on Libr. and Info. Resources, 2001—, vice chair, 2001—. Contbr. articles to mags., 1983—. Bd. dirs. Cmty. Shares, Knoxville, 1993—97, Lincoln Trails Libr. Sys., Champaign, Ill., 2001—. Mem. ALA, Soc. for Scholarly Pub., Solinet (bd. dirs., chmn. 1992-93).

KAUFMAN, PETER BISHOP, biological sciences educator; b. San Francisco, Feb. 25, 1928; s. Earle Francis and Gwendolyn Bishop (Morris) K.; m. Hazel Elizabeth Snyder, Apr. 5, 1958; children— Linda Myrl, Laura Irene B.S., Cornell U., 1949; Ph.D. in Botany, U. Calif.-Davis, 1954. Instr. botany U. Mich., Ann Arbor, 1956-58, asst. prof., 1958-62, assoc. prof., 1962-72, prof. botany, cellular and molecular biology and bioengring. program, 1972-97, emeritus prof. dept. biology, 1998—, instr. seminar Residential Coll., 1997—. Cons. NASA Space Biology Program; vis. prof. U. Lund, Sweden, 1964-65, U. Colo., Boulder, 1973-74; mem. faculty agr. Nagoya U., Japan, 1981 Author: Laboratory Experiments in Plant Physiology, 1975, Plants, People and Environment, 1979, Botany Illustrated, 1983, Practical Botany, 1983, Plants: Their Biology and Importance, 1989; co-author: Handbook of Molecular and Cellular Methods in Biology and Medicine, 1995, Methods in Gene Biotechnology, 1997, Natural Products from Plants, 1998, Creating a Sustainable Future Living in Harmony with the Earth, 2001. Mem. Mich. Natural Areas Coun.; mem. exec. com. U. Mich. Program in Scholarly Rsch. for Urban Minority Students. Grantee NSF, NASA Fellow AAAS; mem. Am. Inst. Biol. Scis., Am. Soc. Plant Physiologists, Am. Soc. for Gravitational and Space Biology (sec.-treas.), Internat. Soc. Plant Molecular Biologists, Bot. Soc. Am., Mich. Bot. Club (pres. 1985-89), Sigma Xi. Democrat. Presbyterian. Home: 8040 Huron River Dr Dexter MI 48130-9322 Office: U Mich 1270 Natural Sci Bldg 830 N University Ave Ann Arbor MI 48109-1048 E-mail: pbk@umich.edu.

KAUFMAN, RAYMOND L. energy company executive; b. Cleve., Mar. 9, 1940; s. Eugene and Elizabeth T. Kaufman; m. Janet Spangler, Sept. 1, 1962; 1 child, Jason. Student, Kent State U., 1958. Personnel dir. NESCO, Cleve., 1965-71; founder Advancement Corp., 1971—. Pres., owner Art Healan. Served with U.S. Army, 1961-63. Mem. AIC, Cleve. C. of C. Lodge: Rotary.

KAUTZMANN, DWIGHT C.H. federal magistrate judge; b. Bismarck, N.D., Dec. 30, 1945; m. Karen Ann Clausen, Aug. 19, 1972; children: Dreux, Don, DeAnn. BA, N.D. State U., 1968; JD, U. N.D., 1971. Bar: N.D. 1971, U.S. Ct. Appeals (8th cir.) 1977, U.S. Supreme Ct. 1994, U.S. Mil. Ct. Appeals. Pvt. practice, Mandan, N.D., 1971-96; judge Mandan Mcpl. Ct., 1973-76; chmn. Legal Svcs. Com. N.D., 1976-79; magistrate judge U.S. Dist. Ct. N.D., Bismark, 1978—. Mem. State Bar Assn. N.D. (pres. 1988), N.D. Trial Lawyers (pres. 1990-91), Bar Great Plains and Rocky Mountain States (chancellor 1992), Blue Key, Phi Alpha Delta. Office: US Courthouse PO Box 1578 220 E Rosser Ave Bismarck ND 58501-3867 Fax: 701-250-4259.

KAY, CRAIG, principal; Prin. Dassel (Minn.) Elem. Sch., 1981-2000; supt. Dassel-Cokato (Minn.) Sch. Dist., 2000—. Recipient Elem. Sch. Recognition award U.S. Dept. Edn., 1989-90. Office: Dassel-Cokato Sch Dist PO Box 370 Cokato MN 55321-0370

KAY, DICK, news correspondent; BS Speech Edn., Bradley U., 1962. With several radio and TV stas., Peoria, Ill.; news dir. Sta. KFRV-TV, Green Bay, Wis., 1965; news writer NBC 5, Chgo., 1968—70, reporter, 1970—, polit. editor, commentator. Named to Silver Cir. TV Acad., 2001; recipient Disting. Alumnus award, Bradley U., 1985, Regional Emmy award, 1996, George Foster Peabody medallion, 1984, award for Best Editl. or Commentary, AP, 1998—99, Peter Lisagor award, Soc. Profl. Journalists Chgo. chpt. The Chgo. Headline Club, 2000, Dante award, Joint Civic Com. Italian Ams., 1984, numerous others, 8 Chgo. Emmy awards. Office: NBC 454 N Columbus Dr Chicago IL 60611*

KAYE, GORDON ISRAEL, pathologist, anatomist, educator; b. N.Y.C., Aug. 13, 1935; s. Oscar Swarz and Rebecca (Schachman) K.; m. Nancy Elizabeth Weber, June 4, 1956; children: Jacqueline Elizabeth, Vivienne Rebecca. AB, Columbia U., 1955, AM, 1957, PhD, 1961. From rsch. asst. cytology to dir. Columbia U., N.Y.C., 1953—63, dir. F. Higginson Cabot Lab. Electron Microscopy, 1963—76; rsch. and tchg. asst. cytology Rockefeller Inst., 1957-58; from Alden March prof. to prof. emeritus Albany Med. Coll., 1976—99, prof. emeritus pathology, 1999—; prof. biomed. sci. SUNY Sch. Pub. Health, 1986-99; pres., CEO Waste Reduction by Waste Reduction, Inc., Troy, NY, 1993-98, chmn., 1998—, exec. v.p., 2002—. Mem. seminar on creative process Wenner-Gren Found., 1964-65; cons. electron microscopy dept. pathology N.Y. VA Hosp., 1965—; Raymond C. Truex Disting. lectr. Hahnemann U., 1987. Co-author: Key Facts in Histology, 1985, Histology: A Text and Atlas, 1995, 2d edit., 2002, Atlas der Histologie (in German), 1995, Histology, nat. med. series rev. series, 1997; editor: Current Topics in Cellular Anatomy, 1981; assoc. editor: The Anat. Record, 1972-98; editl. reviewer: Exptl. Eye Rsch., 1964, Cancer, 1972—, Investigative Ophthalmology, 1973—, Gastroenterology, 1969—; patentee (with Dr. Peter B. Weber) Method for Disposal of Radioactively Labeled Animal Carcasses, Methods for Treatment and Disposal of Regulated Med. Waste. Trustee Palisades free Libr., 1965-71; mem. Citizens Adv. Com., Sparkill Palisades Fire Dist., 1968-69; pres. Palisades Free Libr., 1969-71; trustee Orangetown Pub. Libr., 1971-73, Friends of Chamber Music, Troy, N.Y., 1988—; mem. citizens adv. com. Title III Program, S. Orangetown Ctrl. Sch. Dist., 1972-75; chmn. N.Y. State Low Level Waste Group, 1986-95; trustee Rockland Country Day Sch., 1974-78. Recipient Charles Huebschman prize in zoology Columbia U., 1954, Career Scientist award Health Rsch. Coun. N.Y.C., 1963-72, Rsch. Career Devel. award Nat. Inst. Arthritis and Metabolic Diseases, NIH, USPHS, 1972-76, Tousimis prize in biology, 1984; Ford Found. scholar, 1951-55; NSF predoctoral fellow, 1955-56, Nat. Inst. Neurol. Diseases and Blindness predoctoral fellow, 1959-61 Mem. Assn. Anatomy Chairmen (pres. 1980-81), Assn. Am. Med. Colls. (rep. council acad. socs. 1979—, mem. adminstrn. bd. CAS 1985-86), Am. Assn. Anatomists, Am. Soc. Cell Biology, Harvey Soc., Assn. Career Scientists Health Research Coun., Internat. Soc. Eye Research, N.Y. Soc. Electron Microscopists (dir. 1964-67), Arthur Purdy Stout Soc. Surg. Pathologists (hon.), Sigma Xi. Club: Waquoit Bay Yacht (Waquoit, Mass.). Achievements include patents for in field. Office: Waste Reduction by Waste Reduction 5711 W Minnesota St Indianapolis IN 46241-3825 E-mail: wr2kaye@aol.com.

KAYE, RICHARD WILLIAM, labor economist; b. Chgo., May 14, 1939; s. Albert Louis and Helen (Beckman) K.; m. Betty Ann Terry, Aug. 7, 1964; children: Ronald, William, Richard, Timothy. AB, Cornell U., 1960; MBA, Columbia U., 1962. Various fin. positions Inland Steel Co., Chgo., 1964-81; dir. info. svcs. No. Ind. Pub. Svc. Co., Hammond, 1981-86, dir. econ. analysis, 1986-88. Vis. dir. Purdue U., 1988; cons., ct. appointed receiver, 1989—; mgmt./fin. cons., 1990—. Advisor Calumet Coll., Whiting, Ind., 1985—; active Village Planning Commn., village trustee. Lt. (j.g.) USNR. Mem. Am. Mgmt. Assn., Cornell U. Alumni Assn., Columbia U. Alumni Assn., Rotary. Avocations: tennis, golf. Home: 2801 Cherrywood Ln Hazel Crest IL 60429-2126 Office: IDES 401 S State St Chicago IL 60605-1229

KAZA, GREG JOHN, economist, educator; b. Wyandotte, Mich., Nov. 11, 1960; s. John J. and Mary A. (Lazurek) K. BA in Econs., U. Detroit, 1989; MSF in Internat. Fin., Walsh Coll., Troy, Mich., 1998. V.p. policy rsch. The Mackinac Ctr., Midland, Mich., 1989-91; adj. prof. Northwood Inst. and Walsh Coll., Troy, 1998—; state rep. State of Mich., 1993-98; exec. dir. Citizen Legislators' Caucus Found., Washington, 1999-2000, Ark. Policy Found., Little Rock, 2000—. Author 9 state laws. Named Nat. Legislator of Yr., Rep. Liberty Caucus, 1994. Fellow Nat. Journalism Ctr.; mem. Highpointers Mountaineering Club. Republican. Roman Catholic. Office: 111 Center St Ste 1610E Little Rock AR 72201

KAZANOWSKI, LARRY, engineer; Degree in engring., MIT; MBA, Stanford U. With Ford Motor Co.; v.p. bus. strategy Visteon Automotive Sys.; CEO, pres. Cambridge Industries, Madison Heights, Mich., 1999—. Office: Cambridge Industries 2068 Lansing Pl Syosset NY 11791-9610

KAZIMIERCZUK, MARIAN KAZIMIERZ, electrical engineer, educator; b. Smolugi, Poland, Mar. 3, 1948; came to U.S., 1984; s. Stanislaw and Stanislawa (Tomaszewska) K.; m. Alicja Nowowiejska, July 5, 1973; children: Andrzej, Anna. MS, Tech. U. of Warsaw, Poland, 1971, PhD, 1978, DSc, 1984. Instr. elec. engring. Tech. U. of Warsaw, Poland, 1972-78, assoc. prof. Poland, 1978-84; project engr. Design Automation, Inc., Lexington, Mass., 1984; vis. prof. Va. Poly. Inst., Blacksburg, 1984-85, Wright State U., Dayton, Ohio, 1985—. Author: Resonant Power Converters, 1995; contbr. numerous articles to profl. jours. Recipient Univ. Edn. and Tech. award Polish Ministry of Sci. award, 1981, 84, 85, Polish Acad. Sci. award, 1983. Mem. IEEE (Harrel V. Noble award 1990), Assn. Polish Engrs., Polish Soc. Theoretical and Applied Elec. Scis. Roman Catholic. Home: 3620 Cypress Ct Dayton OH 45440-4515 Office: Wright State U Dept Elec Engring Dayton OH 45435

KEANE, WILLIAM FRANCIS, nephrology educator, research foundation executive; b. N.Y.C., Sept. 21, 1942; s. William F. and Theresa (Crotty) K.; m. Stephanie M. Gaherin, June 10, 1967; children: Alicia Anne, Elizabeth Gaherin. BS, Fordham U., 1964; MD, Yale U., 1968. Diplomate Am. Bd. Internal Medicine, Am. Bd. Nephrology. Intern Cornell N.Y. Hosp. Med. Ctr., 1968-69, resident, internal medicine, 1969-70, 72-73; fellow nephrology U. Minn. Hosps., Mpls., 1973-75; chmn. dept. Hennepin County Med. Ctr., 1991—; asst. prof. medicine U. Minn., 1976-82, assoc. prof., 1982-87, prof., 1987-89; pres. Minn. Med. Rsch. Found., 1989-95; nephrologist Hennepin County Med. Ctr., 1995. Chmn. dept. medicine Hennepin County Med. Ctr., 1992—. Mem. Am. Coll. Physicians, Am. Fedn. Clin. Rsch., Am. Soc. Clin. Pharmacology and Therapeutics, Am. Soc. Nephrology. Office: Hennepin County Med Ctr 701 Park Ave Minneapolis MN 55415-1623

KEANEY, WILLIAM REGIS, engineering and construction services executive, consultant; b. Pitts., Nov. 2, 1937; s. William Regis Sr. and Emily Elizabeth (Campi) K.; m. Sharon Lee Robinson, Feb. 23, 1956; children: William R., James A., Robert E., Susan Elizabeth. BBA in Mktg. and Internat. Mktg., Ohio State U., 1961. Sales engr. Burdett Oxygen Co., Cleve., 1961-64, A.O. Smith Co., Milw., 1964-66; pres. W.R. Keaney & Co., Columbus, Ohio, 1966-71, Power Equipment Service Corp., Columbus, 1971-80, Gen. Assocs. Corp., Worthington, Ohio, 1980—. Cons. Mannesmann, Houston, 1984-85, TVA, Knoxville, 1984-86, Power Authority of N.Y., White Plains, 1985-86, Utility Power Corp., Atlanta, 1985-86; mem. various task forces in the field. Vol. Cen. Ohio Lung Assn., Columbus, 1984-86. Mem. ASME (subgroups on nonferrous alloys, strenght/nonferrous alloys), ASTM (B2 com.), Am. Welding Soc., Welding Rsch. Coun., Worthington C. of C. (leadership program 1991-92), Mil. Vehicle Collectors Club, Masons. Democrat. Methodist. Avocations: antique cars, genealogy, camping, photography. Home: 1314 Oakview Dr Columbus OH 43235-1135 Office: Keaney & Co PO Box 762 Columbus OH 43085-0762 E-mail: bKEANEY@aol.com.

KEARNS, JAMES CANNON, lawyer; b. Urbana, Ill., Nov. 8, 1944; s. John T. and Ruth (Cannon) K.; m. Anne Shapland, Feb. 12, 1983; children: Rose, John. BA, U. Notre Dame, 1966; JD, U. Ill., 1975. Bar: Ill. 1975, U.S. Dist. Ct. (cen. dist.) Ill. 1975, U.S. Ct. Appeals (7th cir.) 1976, U.S. Supreme Ct. 1992. Ptnr. Heyl, Royster, Voelker & Allen, Peoria, Ill., 1975-81, Urbana, 1981—. Mem. ABA, Nat. Assn. RR Trial Coun., Ill. Bar Assn., Champaign County Bar Assn., Def. Rsch. Inst., Ill. Assn. Def. Trial Counsel, Am. Bar Found., Nat. Assn. Coll. and Univ. Attys., Internat. Assn. Defense Coun. Roman Catholic. Avocations: reading, jogging. Office: Heyl Royster Voelker & Allen PO Box 129 102 E Main St Ste 300 Urbana IL 61801-2733 E-mail: jkearns@hrva.com.

KEARNS, MERLE GRACE, state representative; b. Bellefonte, Pa., May 19, 1938; d. Robert John and Mary Katharine (Fitzgerald) Grace; m. Thomas Raymond Kearns, June 27, 1959; children: Thomas, Michael, Timothy, Matthew. BS, Ohio State U., 1960. Tchr. St. Raphael Elem. Sch., Springfield, Ohio, 1960-62; substitute tchr. Mad River Green Dist., 1972-78; instr. Clark Tech. Coll., 1978-80; commr. Clark County, Ohio, 1981-91; mem. Ohio Senate, Columbus, 1991-2000, Ohio Ho. of Reps., 2001—. Mem. edn. com., vice chair health and human svcs. com., mem. jt. com. agy. rule rev., mem. agr. com., chair legis. office of edn. oversight; co-chair domestic violence com. Ohio Supreme Ct.; pres. bd. county commrs., 1982, 83, 86, 87, 90, v.p., 1985, 88, 89. Sec. County Commrs. Assn. Ohio, 1988, 2d v.p., 1989—90, 1st v.p., 1990; mem. exec. com. Springfield Republicans, 1984; bd. pres. Ohio Children's Trust Fund, 1995—2000; chair Legis. Office of Edn. Oversight; mem. NCSL Welfare Reform Task Force, 2001—; vice-chair Policy Consensus Initiative Bd., 2002—; bd. dirs. Springfield Symphony, 1980—86, Arts Coun., 1980—85, County Commrs. Assn. Ohio, Nat. Conf. State Legislators. Recipient Pub. Policy Leadership award, 1997; named Woman of Yr., Springfield Pilot Club, 1981, Wittenberg Woman of Accomplishment, 1991, Watchdog of Treasury, 1991, 96, 2000, Legislator of Yr., Assn. Mental Health and Drug Addiction Svcs. Bds., 1996, Legislator of Yr., Pub. Childrens Svcs. Agencies Ohio, 1999, Legis. Co-Person of Yr., Assn. Joint Vocat. Sch. Supts., 1996, Ohio Cmty. Colls. Legis. of Yr., 1997, Disting. Svc. Pub. Officials award Assn. Ohio Philanthropic Homes, 1999, Mid Ohio Disting. Nurses Legis. of Yr., 2000, 1st Annual Jane Swart Disting. Svc. to Nursing, 2000, The Ohio State Univ. Coll. Human Ecology Citizenship award 2000; Ohio State U. scholar, 1957-59. Mem. LWV (bd. dirs. 1964-78, pres. 1975-78), Ohio Nurses Assn. (Legislator of Yr. 1995, 99), Rotary, Omicron Nu. Roman Catholic. Avocation: reading. Office: Ohio Ho of Reps 74th Dist 77 S High St Columbus OH 43215

KEARNS, WARREN KENNETH, business executive; b. Wilmington, Ohio, July 15, 1929; s. Roy William and Marie (Kay) K. B.S. in Civil Engring., Case Western Res. U., 1951. Registered profl. engr., Ohio, Pa. Supr. Pa. R.R. Co., 1951-56; exec. v.p. Pitts. & W.Va. Rwy. Co., 1956-64; mgr. mfg. services Wheeling Steel Corp., W.Va., 1964-67; v.p. L. B. Foster Co., Pitts., 1967-70, pres., 1979-85; v.p. Sharon Steel Co., Pa., 1970-73; pres. Ogden Steel Co., Cleve., 1973-79, Warren Kearns Assocs., 1985—. Bd. dirs. N.W. Pipe & Casing Co., Portland, Oreg., Erie (Pa.) Forge & Steel Co. Mem.: Sigma Xi, Tau Beta Pi. Avocation: music. Home: 2 High St Hudson OH 44236-2912 Office: Warren Kearns Assocs 1507 Guenevere St Streetsboro OH 44241-5025

KEATING, DANIEL LOUIS, law educator; b. Chgo., Oct. 14, 1961; s. Thomas Joseph and Joanne Clara (Shaughnessy) K.; m. Jane Marie Stevens, Aug. 2, 1986. BA, Monmouth Coll., 1983; JD, U. Chgo., 1986. Bar: Ill. 1986, U.S. Dist. Ct. (no. dist.) Ill. 1986. Lawyer 1st Nat. Bank Chgo., 1986-88; prof. law Washington U., St. Louis, 1988—, assoc. dean. Olin Found. John Olin Fellow, 1985. Mem. Order of Coif. Office: PO Box 1120 Saint Louis MO 63188-1120

KEEBLE, DONALD W. retail executive; Pres. store ops. U.S. Kmart Stores divsn. Kmart Corp., Troy, Mich., 1996—. Office: Kmart Corp 3100 W Big Beaver Rd Troy MI 48084-3163

KEEFER, J(AMES) MICHAEL, lawyer; b. Ft. Wayne, Ind., July 16, 1947; s. James Martin and Helen Patricia (Smith) K.; m. Jan Elaine McDonald, June 3, 1972; children: Christopher, Sean, Alison. AB in Hist., U. Notre Dame, 1969, JD, 1972. Bar: Ind. 1972, U.S. Dist. Ct. (no. and so. dists.) Ind. 1972. With legal dept. Lincoln Nat. Corp., Ft. Wayne, Ind., 1972—2002; 2d v.p., assoc. gen. counsel Lincoln Nat. Corp. and Lincoln Nat. Life Ins. Co., 1982-88, v.p., assoc. gen. counsel, 1988—2002; v.p., gen. counsel and dir. Lincoln Investment Mgmt., Inc., 1997-2000; v.p., dep. gen. counsel Lincoln Nat. Reassurance Co., 2001—02; of counsel Barres & Thornburg, 2002—. Bd. dirs. Allen County unit Am. Cancer Soc., Ft. Wayne, 1975-82, Embassy Theatre Found., 1998—, The Lincoln Mus., 1996—, Ft. Wayne-Allen County Hist. Soc., pres., 1993-95, Ft. Wayne Mus. Art, 1999—. Fellow Am. Coll. Investment Counsel, Ind. Bar Found.; mem. Ind. Bar Assn., Allen County Bar Assn. (bd. dirs., pres. 1996-97), Am. Coun. Life Ins. (various task forces), Am. Corp. Counsel Assn., Assn. Life Ins. Counsel (sec.-treas. 1994-2000, bd. govs. 2000—). Roman Catholic. Home: 1130 Woodland Xing Fort Wayne IN 46825-7239 Office: Barres & Thornburg 600 One Summit Sq Fort Wayne IN 46802-1110 E-mail: mkeefer@btlaw.com.

KEEGSTRA, KENNETH G. plant biochemistry administrator; Dir. dept. energy Plant Rsch. Lab. Mich. State U., East Lansing. Office: Mich State Univ Plant Rsch Lab Dept Energy 106 Plant Biology Lab East Lansing MI 48824-1312

KEEHN, SILAS, retired bank executive; b. New Rochelle, N.Y., June 30, 1930; s. Grant and Marjorie (Burchard) K.; m. Marcia June Lindquist, Mar. 26, 1955; children: Elisabeth Keehn Lewis, Britta Keehn Scott, Peter. AB in Econs, Hamilton Coll., Clinton, N.Y., 1952; MBA in Fin, Harvard U., 1957. With Mellon Bank N.A., Pitts., 1957-80, v.p., then sr. v.p., 1967-78, exec. v.p., 1978-79, vice-chmn., 1980; v.p. Mellon Nat. Corp., 1979-80, vice-chmn., 1980; chmn. bd. Pullman, Inc., Chgo., 1980; pres. Fed. Res. Bank Chgo., 1981-94; ret., 1994. Bd. dirs. ABN AMRO Bank, N.V., Amsterdam, ABN AMRO Holding, N.V., Amsterdam, Kewaunee Sci. Corp., Nat. Futures Assn., Chgo. Bd. Options Exch., Inc., TEPCO Resources, Inc. Trustee Rush-Presbyn.-St. Luke's Med. Ctr., Hamilton Coll., Clinton, N.Y. With USNR, 1953-56. Mem. Chgo. Club, Comml. Club Chgo., Econ. Club Chgo., Fox Chapel Golf Club (Pitts.), U. Club, Links Club (N.Y.C.), Rolling Rock Club (Ligonier, Pa.), Indian Hill Club. Office: 707 Skokie Blvd Ste 600 Northbrook IL 60062-2841

KEELING, JOE KEITH, religion educator, college official and dean; b. Muskogee, Okla., Apr. 21, 1936; s. William Lytle and Anna Madge (Watts) K.; m. Marjorie Ann Brotherton, 1957; children: Kara Kay, William Kent. BA in History, Northeastern State U., 1958; BD in Theology, So. Meth. U., 1962; MA in Theology, U. Chgo., 1967, PhD, 1974. Ordained to ministry United Meth. Ch., 1962. Dir. orientation, acad. advisor U. Chgo., 1964-68; asst. prof. religion Augustana Coll., Sioux Falls, S.D., 1968-72; from asst. to assoc. prof. philosophy and religion Rockford (Ill.) Coll., 1972-86, dean of spl. acad. programming, assoc. dean of coll., 1981-86; adj. assoc. prof. dept. medicine U. Ill. Coll of Medicine at Rockford, 1984-86; provost, dean, prof. religion and philosophy Baker U., Baldwin City, Kans., 1986-96; v.p., dean Ctrl. Meth. Coll., Fayette, Mo., 1996—. Mem. bd. ordained ministry Kans. Ea. Conf. United Meth. Ch., 1987-96; cons., evaluator, mem. accreditation rev. coun. North Ctrl. Assn. Colls. and Schs., Am. Conf. Acad. Deans, Midwest Bioethics Ctr. Author and lectr. in field. Mem. Kansas City Regional Coun. Higher Edn., 1986-94; mem. instnl. rev. com. Swedish-Am. Hosp., Rockford, 1981-86. Mem. Am. Acad. Religion (v.p., program chmn. Midwest region 1981-82, pres. 1982-83), Rockford C. of C. (bd. dirs. 1983-86), AAUP (Ill. state coun. mem. 1979-81), Archael. Inst. Am. (bd. dirs. Rockford chpt. 1984-86), Rotary. Democrat. Avocations: fishing, camping, canoeing. Home: PO Box 429 878 Highway 5 And 250 Fayette MO 65248-9509 Office: Ctrl Meth Coll Office of Vice Pres 411 Central Methodist Sq Fayette MO 65248-1129

KEENAN, JAMES GEORGE, classics educator; b. N.Y.C., Jan. 19, 1944; s. George F. and Cecilia Ann (Schmidt) K.; m. Laurie Haight; children: James, Kathleen, Kenneth, Mary, Lisa, Brian, Laura. A.B., Holy Cross Coll., 1965; M.A., Yale U., 1966, Ph.D., 1968. Asst. prof. Classics U. Calif., Berkeley, 1968-73; assoc. to full prof. Classics Loyola U. of Chgo., 1973—, chmn. classics, 1978-84, acting chmn., 1987-88. Cons. Petra Scrolls Conservation Project, 1995. Co-editor: edition of Greek papyri: The Tebtunis Papyri, vol. IV, 1976. Fellow Nat. Endowment for Humanities, 1973-74; travel grantee Am. Council Learned Socs., 1974, 83, 86; grant-in-aid Am. Philos. Soc., 1987. Mem. Am. Philol. Assn., Am. Soc. Papyrologists (pres. 1989-93), Chgo. Classical Club (pres. 1999-2001), Classical Assn. Midwest and South, Assn. Internat. des Papyrologues, Egypt Exploration Soc. Roman Catholic. Office: Loyola U Chgo Dept Classical Studies 6525 N Sheridan Rd Chicago IL 60626-5344 E-mail: jkeenan@luc.edu.

KEENEY, DENNIS RAYMOND, soil science educator; b. Osceola, Iowa, July 2, 1937; s. Paul N. and Evelyn L. (Beck) K.; m. Betty Ann Goodhue, June 20, 1959; children: Marcia, Susan. BS, Iowa State U., 1959; MS, U. Wis., 1961; PhD, Iowa State U., 1965. Postdoctoral research assoc. Iowa State U., Ames, 1965-66; prof. U. Wis., 1966-88, Romnes research prof., 1975—, chmn. dept. soil sci., 1978-83; chmn. land resources program Inst. Environ. Studies, 1985-88; prof. dept. agronomy Iowa State U., Ames, 1988—, dir. Leopold Ctr. for Sustainable Agr., 1988—; dir. Iowa State Water Resources Inst., 1991-98; sr. research scientist grasslands Dept. Sci. and Indsl. Research, Palmerston North, N.Z., 1975-76. Fellow Am. Soc. Agronomy (rsch. grantee 1986, pres. 1992-93), Soil Sci. Soc. Am. (pres. 1987-88, rsch. grantee 1981, Profl. Svc. award 1994). Office: Iowa State U 209 Curtiss Hl Ames IA 50011-0001

KEER, LEON MORRIS, engineering educator; b. Los Angeles, Sept. 13, 1934; s. William and Sophia (Bookman) Keer; m. Barbara Sara Davis, Aug. 18, 1956; children: Patricia Renee, Jacqueline Saundra, Harold Neal, Michael Derek. BS, Calif. Inst. Tech., 1956, MS, 1958; PhD, U. Minn., 1962. Registered profl. engr., Calif. Mem. tech. staff Hughes Aircraft Co., Culver City, Calif., 1956-59; research fellow, instr. U. Minn., Mpls., 1959-62; asst. prof. Northwestern U., Evanston, Ill., 1964-66, assoc. prof., 1966-70, prof. engring., 1970—, Walter P. Murphy prof. mech. and civil engring., 1994—, assoc. dean research and grad. studies, 1985-92, chmn. dept. civil engring., 1992-97. Preceptor Columbia U., N.Y.C., 1963—64; co-dir. Ctr. for Surface Entring. and Tribology, 1997—; dept. acad. advisor civil and structural engring. Hong Kong U., 1998—; Chau Wei-Yin meml. lectr. Hong Kong Poly. U., 2000. Co-editor: (monograph) Solid Contact and Lubrication, 1980; contbr. articles to profl. jours. Fellow, NATO, 1962, Guggenheim Found., 1972, JSPS, 1986. Fellow: NAE (elected 1997), ASME (life; tech. editor Jour. Applied Mechanics 1988—92, Innovative Rsch. award tribology divsn. 2001), ASCE (life; chmn. engring. mech. divsn. 1992—93), Am. Acad. Mechanics (sec. 1981—88, pres.-elect 1987—88, pres. 1988—89); mem.: Acoustical Soc. Am., Tau Beta Pi, Sigma Xi. Home: 2601 Marian Ln Wilmette IL 60091-2207 Office: Northwestern U Dept Civil Engring 2145 Sheridan Rd Dept Civil Evanston IL 60208-0834 E-mail: l-keer@northwestern.edu.

KEFAUVER, WELDON ADDISON, publisher; b. Canal Winchester, Ohio, Apr. 3, 1927; s. Ross Baker and Virginia Marie (Burtner) K. B.A., Ohio State U., Columbus, 1950. Mem. faculty Columbus Acad., 1956-58; mng. editor Ohio State U. Press, 1958-64, dir., 1964-84, dir. emeritus, 1984—. Dir. Am. Univ. Press Services, Inc., 1971-72, 76-79; mem. U.S. del. 2d Asian Pacific Conf. Publs., Taiwan, 1978 Author: Scholars and their Publishers, 1977; editorial adv. bd. Scholarly Publishing. Served with AUS, 1945-46. Recipient Centennial Service award Ohio State U., 1970; citation Ohioana Library Assn., 1974; Disting. Service award Ohio State U., 1986; recognized for service to Ohio State U. by Ohio Senate and Ohio Ho. of Reps., 1986. Mem. Assn. Am. Univ. Presses (v.p. 1971-72, dir. 1971-72, 76-79, pres. 1977-78), Soc. Scholarly Pub., Nathaniel Hawthorne Soc., AAUP, Phi Eta Sigma, Phi Kappa Phi Clubs: Torch (Columbus), Crichton (Columbus), Ohio State U. Faculty (Columbus). Home: 675 Eastmoor Blvd Columbus OH 43209-2252 Office: 1050 Carmack Rd Columbus OH 43210-1002

KEGERREIS, ROBERT JAMES, management consultant, marketing educator; b. Detroit, Apr. 2, 1921; s. I. G. and A. M. (Merry) K.; m. Katherine L. Falknor, Oct. 30, 1943; children: Merry, Duncan, Melissa. BA, BS, Ohio State U., 1943, MBA, 1946, PhD, 1968, U. Dayton, 1982, EdD (hon.), EdD (hon.), U. Dayton; LLD (hon.), U. Akron, Wilberforce U.; ScD (hon.), Cen. State U., Japan, 1992; EconD (hon.), Okayama U., Japan, 1992. Economist Fed. Res. Bank, Cleve., 1946-49; pres. KV Stores, Inc., Woodsfield, Ohio, 1949-69; v.p., sec. KBK Devel. Co., Inc., 1955-62; assoc. prof. Ohio U., Athens, 1967-69; dean Coll. Bus. and Adminstrn. Wright State U., Dayton, Ohio, 1969-71, v.p. adminstrn., 1971-73, pres., 1973-85; cons. RJK Co., 1985—. Bd. dirs. Robbins & Myers, Dayton, Bank One, Dayton, N.A., Miami Valley Rsch. Found., Tait Found. Exec. dir. Arts Ctr. Found., Dayton. Lt. (j.g.) USN, 1943-46. Mem. Moraine Country Club, Bicycle Club, Pelican Bay Country Club. Methodist. Avocations: flying, golf. Office: Kettering Tower Ste 1480 Dayton OH 45423-1000

KEIM, ROBERT BRUCE, lawyer; b. Nebraska City, Nebr., Jan. 10, 1946; s. Ernest Jacob and Ruby Rebecca (Mohr) K.; m. Barbara Ann Simmons, Aug. 10, 1968; 1 child, Robert Boyd. BS, U. Nebr., 1968; JD cum laude, Washburn U., 1974. Bar: Mo. 1974, Kans. 1985. Atty. Morris, Larson, King & Stamper, Kansas City, Mo., 1974-89, Shughart, Thomson & Kilroy, P.C., Overland Park, Kans., 1989-90, chmn. corp. fin. and transactional law dept., 1989-90; atty. Kutak Rock LLP, Kansas City, Mo., 1999—. Bd. dirs., mem. audit com. Osborn Labs., Olathe, Kans. Community advisor Jr. League of Johnson & Wyanadotte Counties, Overland Park, 1990—; active fin. com., deacon Rolling Hills Ch., Overland Park, 1990—, Econ. Devel. Coun. Overland Park, 1991—. Lt. U.S. Army, 1968-71. Avocations: running, golf, backpacking. Home: 10021 Juniper Ln Shawnee Mission KS 66207-3446 Office: Kutak/Rock LLP 1 Main Plz Ste 810 4435 Main St Kansas City KS 64111

KEISER, GEORGE J. state legislator; m. Kathy Keiser; four children. Owner Quality Printing Svc.; former commr. Bismarck City, N.D.; rep. N.D. State Ho. of Reps. Dist. 47, 1993—, vice chmn. indsl., bus. and labor com., mem. transp. com.

KEISER, JOHN HOWARD, university president; b. Mt. Olive, Ill., Mar. 12, 1936; s. Howard H. and Lorraine G. K.; m. Nancy Peterka, June 27, 1959; children: John, Sam, Joe. B.S. in Edn, Eastern Ill. U., 1958; M.A., Northwestern U., 1960, Ph.D. in History, 1964. Prof. history Westminster Coll., Fulton, Mo., 1963—65, Eastern Ill. U., Charleston, 1965—71; v.p. acad. affairs Sangamon State U., Springfield, Ill., 1971—78, acting pres., 1978; pres. Boise (Idaho) State U., 1978—93, S.W. Mo. State U., Springfield, 1993—. Author: Building for the Centuries, Illinois, 1865-1898, 1977, Illinois Vignettes, 1977. Bd. dirs. Abraham Lincoln coun. Boy Scouts Am., Springfield, Ore-Ida Council, Boise, Ozarks Trail coun. Springfield, NPR. Recipient Harry E. Pratt Meml. award Jour. Ill. History, 1970, 72; award of merit Ill. State Hist. Soc., 1980; award of merit Am. Assn. State and Local History, 1980, nat. medal of honor DAR, 1998, CEO Leadership award CASE, 1999. Mem.: Labor History Soc., Labor History Soc., Am. Hist. Soc., Orgn. Am. Historians, Boise C. of C. Roman Catholic. Club: Rotary. Roman Catholic. Office: SW Missouri St U Off Pres 901 S National Ave Springfield MO 65804-0027

KEITH, ALEXANDER MACDONALD, retired state supreme court chief justice, lawyer; b. Rochester, Minn., Nov. 22, 1928; s. Norman and Edna (Alexander) K.; m. Marion Sanford, April 29, 1955; children: Peter Sanford (dec.), Ian Alexander, Douglas Scott. BA, Amherst Coll., 1950; JD, Yale U., 1953. Assoc. counsel, mem. Mayo Clinic, Rochester, 1955-60; state sen. Olmstead County, St. Paul, 1959-63; lt. gov. State of Minn., 1963-67; pvt. practice, Rochester, 1960-73; ptnr. Dunlap Keith Finseth Berndt and Sandberg, 1973-89; assoc. justice Minn. Supreme Ct., St. Paul, 1989-90, chief justice, 1990-98; ret., 1998; of counsel Dunlap & Seeger P.A., Rochester, Minn., 1998—. Sen. del. White House Conf. on Aging, Washington, 1960; U.S. del. UN Delegation for Funding Developing Countries, Geneva, 1966; bd. dirs. Rochester Grad. Edn. Adv. Com., 1988-89, Ability Bldg. Ctr. Inc. 1st lt. USMC, 1953-55, Korea. Named Outstanding Freshman Senator, Minn. Senate, St. Paul. Home: 5225 Meadow Crossing Rd SW Rochester MN 55902-3506 Office: Dunlap & Seeger PA PO Box 549 Rochester MN 55903-0549 Fax: 507-288-9342.

KEITH, DAMON JEROME, federal judge; b. Detroit, July 4, 1922; s. Perry A. and Annie L. (Williams) K.; m. Rachel Boone Keith, Oct. 18, 1953; children: Cecile Keith, Debbie, Gilda. BA, W.Va. State Coll., 1943; JD, Howard U., 1949; LLM, Wayne State U., 1956; PhD (hon.) (hon.) , U. Mich., Howard U., Wayne State U., Mich. State U., N.Y. Law Sch., Detroit Coll. Law, W.Va. State Coll., U. Detroit, Atlanta U., Lincoln U., Marygrove Coll., Detroit Inst. Tech., Shaw Coll., Ctrl. State U., Yale U., Loyola Law Sch., L.A., Ea. Mich. U., Va. Union U., Ctrl. Mich. U., Morehouse Coll., Western Mich. U., Tuskegee U., Georgetown U., Hofstra U., DePaul U. Bar: Mich. 1949. Atty. Office Friend of Ct., Detroit, 1952—56; sr. ptnr. firm Keith, Conyers Anderson, Brown & Wahls, 1964—67; mem. Wayne County Bd. Suprs., 1958—63; dist. judge U.S. Dist. Ct. (ea. dist.) Mich., 1967—77, chief judge, 1975—77; judge U.S. Ct. Appeals (6th cir.), Detroit, 1977—95, sr. judge, 1995—. Mem. Wayne County (Mich.) Bd. Suprs., 1958—63; chmn. Mich. Civil Rights Commn., 1964—67; pres. Detroit Housing Commn., 1958—67; commr. State Bar Mich., 1960—67; mem. Mich. Com. Manpower Devel. and Vocat. Tng., 1964, Detroit Mayor's Health Adv. Com., 1969; rep. dist. judges 6th Cir. Jud. Conf., 1975—77; adv. com. on codes of conduct Jud. Conf. U.S., 1979—86; subcom. on supporting pers. Jud. Conf. Com. on Ct. Adminstrn., 1983—87; chmn. Com. on the Bicentennial of Constn. of Sixth Cir., 1985—; nat. chmn. Jud. Conf. Com. on the Bicentennial of Constn., 1987—; mem. Commn. on the Bicentennial of U.S. Constn., 1990; lectr. Howard U., 1972, Ohio State U. Law Sch., 1992, N.Y. Law Sch., 1992; guest lectr. Howard U. Law Sch., 1981; Bicentennial of Constn. lectr. W.Va. State Coll., 1987; keynote speaker Black Law Students Assn., Harvard Law Sch., 1987. Contbr. Trustee Med. Corp. Detroit, Interlochen Arts Acad., Cranbrook Sch., U. Detroit, Mich. chpt. Leukemia Soc. Am.; mem. Citizen's Adv. Com. Equal Ednl. Opportunity Detroit Bd. Edn.; gen. co-chmn. United Negro Coll. Fund Detroit; 1st v.p. emeritus Detroit chpt. NAACP; mem. com. mgmt. Detroit YMCA; mem. Detroit coun. Boy Scouts Am., Detroit Arts Commn.; vice chmn. Detroit Symphony Orch.; vis. com. Wayne State U. Law Sch.; adv. coun. U. Notre Dame Law Sch.; chmn. Citizen's Coun. for Mich. Pub. Univs.; deacon Tabernacle Missionary Bapt. Ch.; Deacon Bapt ch.; bd. dirs. Detroit Bd. Table, NCCJ. Named 1 of 100 Most Influential Black Ams., Ebony Mag., 1971—92, Damon J. Keith Elementary Sch. named in his honor, Detroit Bd. Edn., 1974, Damon J. Keith Ann. Civic and Humanitarian award established in his honor, Highland Park YMCA, 1984, 15th Mich. Legal Milestone The Uninvited Ear presented in honor of The Keith Decision, 1991; recipient Mich. Chronicle outstanding Citizen award, 1960, 1964, 1974, Alumni citation, Wayne State U., 1968, Ann. Jud. award, 1971, Citizen award, Mich. State U., Disting. Svc. award, Howard U., 1972, Jud. Independence award, 1973, Spingarn medal, NAACP, 1974, Fed. Judge of Yr. award, Black Law Students Assn., 1974, award for Outstanding Contbns. to Black Community, Nat. Assn. Black Social Workers, 1974, Judge of Yr. award, Nat. Conf. Black Lawyers, 1974, Bill of Rights award, Jewish Community Coun., 1977, A. Philip Randolph award, Detroit Coalition Black Trade Unionists, 1981, Human Rights Day award, B'nai B'rith Women's Coun. Met. Detroit, Robert L. Millender award, So. Christian Leadership Conf. Mich. chpt., 1982, Afro-Asian Inst. award, Histadrut in Israel, 1982, civil rights lectr. award, Creighton U. Ahmanson Law Ctr., 1983, Nat. Human Rels. award, Greater Detroit Roundtable of NCCJ, 1984, Knights of Charity award, Pontifical Inst. for Mission Extension, 1986, Disting. Pub. Svc. award, Mich. Anti-Defamation League of B'nai B'rith, 1987, Nat. Chpt. award, 1988, Black Achievement award, Equitable Fin. Cos., 1987, Menorah award, Afro-Asian Inst. Histadrut of Israel, 1988, Dr. George Derry award, Marygrove Coll. Detroit, One Nation award, The Patriots Found./GM, 1989, 1st Ann. Move Detroit Forward award, City of Detroit, 1990, Gov's. Minuteman award, Rotary Club Lansing, 1991. Mem.: ABA (coun. sect. legal edn. and admission to bar), Am. Judicature Soc., Nat. Lawyers Guild, Detroit Bar Assn. (pres'. award), Mich. Bar Assn. (champion of justice award), Nat. Bar Assn. (William H. Hastie award Jud. Coun., 8th Ann. equal Justice award), Detroit Cotillion Club, Alpha Phi Alpha. Office: US Ct Appeals US Courthouse 231 W Lafayette Blvd Rm 240 Detroit MI 48226-2779

KEITHLEY, JOSEPH FABER, electronic engineering manufacturing company executive; b. Peoria, Ill., Aug. 3, 1915; s. Giles E. and Elizabeth F. (Faber) K.; m. Nancy Jean Pearce, Jan. 17, 1948; children: Joseph Pearce, Elizabeth Margaret, Roy Faber. SB, MIT, 1937, SM, 1938. Registered profl. engr., Ohio. Mem. tech. staff Bell Telephone Labs., N.Y.C., 1938-40; engr., Naval Ordnance Lab., Washington, 1940-45, MASSA Labs., Cleve., 1945-46; pres., chmn. bd. Keithley Instruments, Inc., Cleve., 1946-73, chmn. bd., 1973—; mem. vis. com. Case Western Res. U. Sch. Mgmt., 1979—, elec. engring. and computer sci. dept. MIT, 1980—. Patentee station selecting system, method and apparatus for measuring and analyzing transient pressures in body of water, circuit interrupter. Recipient Disting. Civilian Service award U.S. Navy, 1945. Fellow IEEE (IECI Achievement medal 1976, Instrumentation and Measurement Soc. award 1983, Centennial medal 1984). Fellow AAAS; mem. NAE, Clubs: Union Club of Cleve., Mayfield Country, Cleve. Skating. Avocation: photography. Home: 1801 Chestnut Hills Dr # 211 Cleveland OH 44106-4643 Office: Keithley Instruments Inc 28775 Aurora Rd Cleveland OH 44139-1891

KEJR, JOSEPH, former state legislator; m. Geena Kejr. Kans. state rep. Dist. 67, until 1998; farmer. Home: 10143 W Stimmel Rd Brookville KS 67425-9719

KELCH, ROBERT PAUL, pediatric endocrinologist; b. Detroit, Dec. 3, 1942; s. Paul and Iona Bertha (Schmitt) Kelch; m. Jeri Anne Parker, Aug. 17, 1963; children: Randall Paul, Julie Marie. PhB, Wayne State U., Detroit, 1964; MD, U. Mich., Ann Arbor, 1967. Intern then Wyeth pediatric residency fellow U. Mich. Med. Center, 1967—70, research fellow, 1969—70, mem. faculty, 1972—94, prof. pediatrics, 1977—94, acting chmn. dept., 1979—80, chmn. dept., 1981—94; physician-in-chief C.S. Mott Children's Hosp. U. Mich., 1983—94; chief clin. affairs U. Mich. Hosps., 1989—92; NIH trainee pediatric endocrinology U. Calif. Med. Center, San Francisco, 1970—72; prof. pediat., dean U. Iowa Coll. Medicine, Iowa City, 1994—, v.p. statewide health svcs., 2001—. Co-author: A Practical Approach to Pediatric Endocrinology, 1975; contbr. articles to med. jours. With USNR. Fellow: Am. Acad. Pediat.; mem.: Midwest Soc. Pediat. Rsch. (pres. 1983—84), Lawson Wilkins Pediat. Endocrine Soc., Ctrl. Soc. Clin. Rsch., Assn. Med. Sch. Pediat. Dept. Chmn. 1989, Am. Soc. Clin. Investigation, Am. Fedn. Clin. Rsch., Endocrine Soc., Am. Bd. Pediat. (sec.-treas. 1992, chmn. 1995), Soc. Pediat. Rsch. (pres. 1988), Inst. Medicine NAS. Methodist. Home: 620 Larch Ln Iowa City IA 52245-3435 Office: U Iowa 312 CMAB Iowa City IA 52242-1101 E-mail: robert-kelch@uiowa.edu.

KELLEHER, TIMOTHY JOHN, publishing company executive; b. Massillon, Ohio, Jan. 4, 1940; s. John Joseph and Catherine Isabelle (Quinlan) K.; m. Mary Gray Thornton, Aug. 27, 1966; children— Catherine, Joseph, Sarah B.S. in Polit. Sci., Xavier U., Cin., 1962; postgrad., Xavier U., 1965, Morehead State U., Ky., 1975-76. Mgr. labor rels. GM, Norwood, Ohio, 1964-73; pers. mgr. Rockwell Internat., Winchester, Ky., 1973-77, dir. labor rels. Troy, Mich., 1977-82; v.p. human resources Detroit Free Press, 1982-89; sr. v.p. labor rels. Detroit Newspaper Agy., 1989—. Dir. Detroit Macomb Hosp. Corp. Bd. dirs. Greater Detroit Alliance of Bus., annually 1983-89, Winchester/Clark Hist. Soc., Ky., 1975, pres., 1976-77; bd. dirs. New Detroit Inc., annually 1983-89. Served to sgt. U.S. Army, 1962-64 Mem. Coop. Edn. Assn. Ky. (bd. dirs. 1975-77, Employer of Yr. award 1976), Indsl. Rels. Rsch. Assn., Xavier U. Alumni Assn. (pres. Detroit chpt. 1991-93), Forest Lake Country Club (bd. dirs. 1991-94, 2000-02, pres. 2001-02). Republican. Roman Catholic. Avocations: golf; fishing. Home: 4072 Cranbrook Ct Bloomfield Hills MI 48301-1714 Office: Detroit Newspaper Agy 615 W Lafayette Blvd Detroit MI 48226-3124 E-mail: TKelleher@dnps.com.

KELLER, DEBORAH KIM, former soccer player; b. Winfield, Ill., Mar. 24, 1975; Student in phys. edn., U. N.C. Mem. U.S. Nat. Women's Soccer Team, 1995—, inlcuding 3d-place 1995 FIFA Women's World Cup, Sweden; mem. U-20 Nat. Team, Nordic Cup, Germany, 1994; mem. gold-medal North team, 1995 U.S. Olympic Festival, Denver. Named Soccer Am. Player of Yr., 1996; voted Offensive Most Valuable Player, NCAA Tournament, 1996; named U. N.C. Athlete of Yr., 1997. Achievements: led U. N.C. to NCAA Championship, 1996. Office: US Soccer Fedn 1801-1811 S Prairie Ave Chicago IL 60616

KELLER, DENNIS JAMES, management educator; b. July 6, 1941; s. Ralph and Dorothy (Barckman) K.; m. Constance Bassett Templeton, May 28, 1966; children: Jeffrey Breckenridge, David McDaniel, John Templeton. AB, Princeton U., 1963; MBA, U. Chgo., 1968. Account exec. Motorola Comm., Chgo., 1964-67; v.p. fin. Bell & Howell Comm., Waltham, Mass., 1968-70; v.p. mktg. Bell & Howell Schs., Chgo., 1970-73; pres. Keller Grad. Sch. Mgmt., 1973-81, chmn., CEO, 1981—. Chmn. bd., chief exec. officer DeVry Inc., 1987—; cons., evaluator North Central Assn., Chgo., 1979-84; bd. dirs. Templeton Kenly & Co., Broadview, Ill., Nicor Inc. Trustee Glenwood (Ill.) Sch. for Boys, 1980—, Chgo. Zool. Soc., Brookfield, Ill., 1979—, Princeton (N.J.) U., 1994-98, 2000—, Lake Forest Acad.-Ferry Hall, Ill., 1980-87, George M. Pullman Found., Chgo., 1987—; bd. trustees U. Chgo., 1998—; bd. dirs. Great Books Found., Chgo., 1986-98; chmn. U. Chgo. Grad. Sch. Bus. coun., 1994—, Princeton U. Sch. Engring. and Applied Scis. Leadership Coun., 1992—; commr. North Cen. Assn.-Commn. on Instns. of Higher Edn., 1985-88. Nat. Merit scholar, 1959-63; U. Chgo. Grad. Sch. Bus. fellow, 1967-68. Mem. Hinsdale Golf Club, Econ. Club, Comml. Club Chgo., Chgo. Club, Nantucket Golf Club, Sankaty Head Golf Club. Republican. Mem. United Ch. of Christ. Office: DeVry Inc 1 Tower Ln Ste 1000 Oakbrook Terrace IL 60181 E-mail: dkeller@devry.com.

KELLER, ELIOT AARON, broadcasting executive; b. Davenport, Iowa, June 11, 1947; s. Norman Edward and Millie (Morris) K.; m. Sandra Kay McGrew, July 3, 1970; 1 child, Nicole. BA, U. Iowa, 1970; MS, San Diego State U., 1976. Corr. Sta. WHO-AM-FM-TV, Des Moines, 1969-70; newsman Sta. WSUI-AM, Iowa City, 1968-70; newsman, corr. Sta. WHBF-AM-FM-TV, Rock Island, Ill., 1969; newsman Sta. WOC-AM-FM-TV, Davenport, 1970; freelance newsman and photographer Iowa City, 1969-77; pres., dir. KZIA, Inc. (formerly KRNA, Inc. and Communicators., Inc.), 1971—; gen. mgr. Sta. KRNA FM, 1974-98, Sta. KQCR FM, Cedar Rapids, Iowa, 1994-95, Sta. KXMX FM, Cedar Rapids, 1995-98, Sta. KZIA-FM, Cedar Rapids, 1998—. Adj. instr. dept. comm. studies U. Iowa, Iowa City, 1983, 84. Named Broadcaster of Yr., Iowa Broadcasters Assn., 2001. Mem. Mid-Continent Ry. Hist. Soc. (bd. dirs.), R.R. Passenger Car Alliance, Iowa Assn. RR Passengers (excursion chair), Iowa City Area C. of C. (chair transp. com.). Jewish. Home: 1244 Devon Dr NE Iowa City IA 52240-9628 Office: Sta KZIA FM 1110 26th Ave SW Cedar Rapids IA 52404-3430 E-mail: eliot@kzia.com.

KELLER, JUAN DANE, lawyer; b. Cape Girardeau, Mo., Jan. 30, 1943; s. Irvin A. and Mercedes (Crippen) K.; m. Sandra Anne Solomon; children: Mary, John, Katharine, Robert, Michael, Cassandra. AB in History, U. Mo., l965, JD, l967; LLM, Georgetown U., l97l. Bar: Mo. Assoc. Bryan, Cave, St. Louis, 1971-78, ptnr., 1979—. Contbg. author: Missouri Bar Taxation Handbook, 1988-95. Capt. JAGC, U.S. Army, 1967-71. Mem. ABA, Mo. Bar (tax com. 1971—), Met. St. Louis Bar Assn., Order of Coif. Methodist. Office: Bryan Cave 1 Metropolitan Sq Ste 3600 Saint Louis MO 63102-2750 E-mail: jkeller@bryancave.com.

KELLER, KENNETH HARRISON, engineering educator, science policy analyst; b. N.Y.C., Oct. 19, 1934; s. Benjamin and Pearl (Pastor) K.; m. Dorothy Robinson, June 2, 1957 (div.); children: Andrew Robinson, Paul Victor; m. Bonita F. Sindelir, June 19, 1981; children: Jesse Daniel, Alexandra Amelie. AB, Columbia U., 1956, BS, 1957; MS in Engring., Johns Hopkins U., 1963, PhD, 1964. Asst. prof. dept. chem. engring. U. Minn., Mpls., 1964-68, assoc. prof., 1968-71, prof., 1971—, prof. Hubert H. Humphrey Inst. Pub. Affairs, 1996—, Charles M. Denny Jr. prof., assoc. dean Grad. Sch., 1973-74, 99—, acting dean Grad. Sch., 1974-75, head dept. chem. engring. and materials sci., 1978-80, v.p. acad. affairs, 1980-85, pres., 1985-88; Philip D. Reed sr. fellow for sci. and tech. Coun. on Fgn. Rels., 1990-96, sr. v.p., 1993-95. Cons. in field; mem. cardiology adv. com. NIH, 1982-86; mem. sci. and tech. adv. panel to dir. CIA, 1995-99; mem. commn. on phys. scis., math. and applications NRC, 1996-2000; bd. dirs. LASPAU: Acad. and Profl. Programs for the Ams., 1996—; trustee Sci. Mus. Minn., 1997—; chmn. Med. Technology Leadership Forum, 1998—. Mem. adv. com. program for Soviet emigré scholars, 1974-82; bd. govs. Argonne Nat. Lab., 1982-85; bd. dirs. Walker Art Ctr., 1982-88, Charles Babbage Found., 1991-99. Served from ensign to lt. USNR, 1957-61. NIH Spl. fellow, 1972-73; vis. fellow Woodrow Wilson Sch. of Pub. and Internat. Affairs, Princeton U., 1988-90. Founding fellow Am. Inst. for Med. and Biol. Engring.; fellow AAAS; mem. Am. Soc. Artificial Internal Organs (pres. 1980-81), AIChE (Food and Bioengring. award 1980), Am. Coun. for Emigrés in the Professions (dir. 1972-80), Nat. Acad. Engring., Mpls. C. of C. (bd. dirs. 1985-88), Coun. Fgn. Rels., Phi Beta Kappa, Sigma Xi (nat. lectr. 1978-80). Office: Hubert H Humphrey Inst U Minn 301 19th Ave S Ste 300 Minneapolis MN 55455-0411

KELLER, WILLIAM FRANCIS, publishing consultant; b. Meyersdale, Pa., May 22, 1922; s. Lloyd Francis and Dorothy Marie (Shultz) K.; m. Frances Jane Core, Mar. 31, 1944. A.A., Potomac State Coll. of W.Va. U., 1941; B.S., U. Md., 1943, M.S., 1945. Ednl. rep. Blakiston Co., 1945-51, assoc. editor, 1951-54; editor coll. div. McGraw Hill Book Co., N.Y.C., 1954-56; editor-in-chief Blakiston divsn. McGraw Hill Book Co., 1956-65, gen. mgr. div., 1965-68; pres. Year Book Med. Publs., Chgo., 1968-81, chmn. bd., 1968-82; pub. cons. Crystal Lake, Ill., 1982-95; adminstrv. sec. Am. Med. Pubs. Assn., 1985-91. Served with AUS, 1945-46. Office: 7916 W Hillside Rd Crystal Lake IL 60012-2939 E-mail: w.f.keller@world.net.att.com.

KELLERMEYER, ROBERT WILLIAM, physician, educator; b. Wheeling, W.Va., Sept. 4, 1929; s. William F. and Mabel I. (Keller) M.; m. Audrey L. Shanaberger, June 12, 1954; children: Suzanne, Scott, Mark. BA, Washington and Jefferson Coll., 1951; MD, Western Res. U., 1955. Diplomate Am. Bd. Internal Medicine, Am. Bd. Hematology, Am. Bd. Med. Oncology. Intern dept. medicine Univ. Hosps. Cleve., 1955-56, asst. resident, 1956-57, chief resident, 1962-63, co-dir. div. hematology and oncology, 1974-83; sr. instr. dept. medicine Univ. Hosps.-Case Western Res. U., 1963-66, asst. prof. medicine, 1965-68, assoc. prof., 1969-75, prof., 1975-96, emeritus prof., 1996—; David and Inez Myers prof. hematology Case Western Res. U., 1978-96; med. dir. Aultman Cancer Ctr. Aultman Hosp., Canton, Ohio, 1993—2000; prof. medicine N.E. Ohio Univs. Coll. Medicine, 1994—. Author: The Red Cell, 1970. With USPHS, 1957-59. Recipient Career Devel. award USPHS, 1966, Am. Cancer Soc. postdoctoral fellow, 1959-62; John and Mary R. Markle scholar, 1965. Mem. Am. Soc. Hematology, Cen. SOc. Clin. Rsch., Am. Fedn. Clin. Rsch., Am. Assn. Cancer Edn., Ea. Coop. Oncology Group, Am. Soc. Clin. Oncology. Office: Aultman Hosp 2600 6th St SW Canton OH 44710-1702

KELLEY, BRUCE GUNN, insurance company executive, lawyer; b. Phila., Mar. 17, 1954; s. Robb Beardsley and Winifred Elizabeth Gray (Murray) K.; m. Susan Aldrich Barnes, Oct. 1, 1983; children: Dashle Gunn, Barnes Gunn, Onnalee Kinkaid. AB, Dartmouth Coll., 1976; JD, U. Iowa, 1979. Bar: Iowa 1979; CPCU; CLU. Assoc. Bradshaw, Fowler, Proctor & Fairgrave, Des Moines, 1979-84, ptnr., 1984-85; gen. counsel Employers Mut. Casualty Co., 1985-89, exec. v.p., 1989-91, pres., 1991—, also bd. dirs. Trustee Am. Inst. for Chartered Property Casualty Underwiters/Ins. Inst. Am.; bd. dirs. Alliance Am. Insurers; chmn. adv. bd. Iowa Pub. Employees Retirement Sys. Trustee Nat. Com. on Drunk Drivers. Mem. Iowa Bar Assn., Des Moines Club, Rotary, Masons. Republican. Mem. United Church of Christ. Home: 14 Glenview Dr Des Moines IA 50312-2546 Office: EMC Ins Cos PO Box 712 Des Moines IA 50303-0712

KELLEY, FRANK NICHOLAS, dean; b. Akron, Ohio, Jan. 19, 1935; s. John William Kelley and Rose (Hadinger) Bates; m. Judith Carol Lowe, Jan. 1, 1960; children: Katherine Rose Bruno, Frank Michael, Christopher Patrick. BS, U. Akron, 1958, MS, 1959, PhD, 1961. Br. chief propellant devel. Air Force Rocket Propulsion Lab., Edwards AFB, Calif., 1965-69, chief of plans, 1969-70, chief scientist, 1970-73, Air Force Materials Lab., Wright-Patterson AFB, Ohio, 1973-77, dir., 1977-78; dir. Inst. Polymer Sci. U. Akron, 1978-88, dean Coll. Polymer Sci. and Engring., 1988—. Bd. dirs. Premix, Inc., North Kingsville, Ohio; cons. USAF, Thiokol Corp., others. Editor: Polymers in Space Research, 1965; contbr. articles to profl. jours. Lt. USAF, 1961-64; capt. USAF Res., 1964. Named Outstanding Alumnus, Tau Kappa Epsilon, 1991. Mem. Am. Chem. Soc. Mem. Disciples of Christ Ch. Avocation: woodworking. Office: U Akron Coll Polymer Sci and Polymer Engring Akron OH 44325-0001

KELLEY, JAMES, automotive sales executive; b. Decatur, Ind., June 13, 1918; m. Lavon Kelley; children: Suzanne Horton, Barbara Kraegel, Tom Kelley. Grad., G.E. Apprentice Sch. Early career positions with GE; founder Jim Kelley Buick, 1952; now chmn., co-CEO Kelley Automotive Group. Owner, developer Sycamore Hills Golf Club, 1989. Bd. dirs. Ft. Wayne Jr. Achievement, Big Bros. and Big Sisters, Boys and Girls club of Ft. Wayne, YMCA, Hoosier Celebrity Golf Tournament, Arthritis Found., Ft. Wayne Aviation Mus. Mem. Ft. Wayne C. of C. 9bd. dirs.), Sycamore Hills Golf Club (bd. dirs.), Ind. Golf Assn. (bd. dirs.), Western Golf Assn. (bd. dirs.). Avocations: aviation, Indy Car racing, health and fitness.

KELLEY, JOHN JOSEPH, JR. lawyer; b. Cleve., June 17, 1936; s. John Joseph and Helen (Meier) K.; m. Gloria Hill, June 20, 1959; children: John Joseph III, Scott MacDonald, Christopher Taft, Megan Meredith. B.S. cum laude in Commerce, Ohio U., 1958; LL.B., Case Western Res. U., 1960. Bar: Ohio bar 1960. Clk. firm Walter & Haverfield, Cleve., 1957-60; assoc. Walter, Haverfield, Buescher & Chockley, 1960-66, partner, 1967-72; chief exec. officer Fleischmann Enterprises, Cin., 1972-77; pvt. practice law, 1977-87; ptnr. Kohnen & Patton, 1988—. Chmn. bd. Basic Packaging Systems, Inc., 1982-87; dir. Orgamac Leasing Ltd; pres. Naples Devel. Inc., 1974-87, Yankee Leasing Co. Mem. Lakewood (Ohio) City Council, 1965-72, pres., 1972; mem. exec. com. Cuyahoga County (Ohio) Republican Central Com., 1965-72; mem. Hamilton County (Ohio) Rep. Policy Com.; Ohio chmn. Robert Taft, Jr. Senate Campaign Com., 1970, 76; bd. govs. Case Western Res. U., 1961, 84-87. Mem. Assn. Ohio Commodores, ABA, Ohio State Bar Assn., Cin. Bar Assn. Clubs: Cin. Country, Queen City (Cin.); Naples Bath and Tennis. Home: 5 Woodcreek Dr Cincinnati OH 45241-3255 Office: Kohnen & Patton Ohio Attorney General # 1400 Cincinnati OH 45202-2800 E-mail: jkelley@kohnenpatton.com.

KELLEY, JOSEPH E. career officer; BS, USAF Acad., 1974; MD, Rush U., 1977; student, Sch. Aerospace Medicine, Brooks AFB, Tex., 1984, Air Command and Staff Coll., 1986, Air War Coll., 1988, George Washington U., 1992; physician in mgmt. I, ACP Execs., Sheppard AFB, Tex., 1992, physician in mgmt. II, 1994, physician in mgmt. III, 1997. Diplomate Am. Bd. Surgery. Commd. capt. USAF, 1977, advanced through grades to brig. gen., 1997; intern then resident in gen. surgery David Grant Med. Ctr., Travis AFB, Calif., 1977-82; gen. surgeon then chief surgery Nellis USAF Hosp., Nellis AFB, Nev., 1982-84; chief hosp. svcs. Misawa USAF Hosp., Misawa Air Base, Japan, 1984-86; comdr. 90th Strategic Hosp., Francis E. Warren AFB, Wyo., 1986-89, 857th Strategic Hosp., Minot AFB, N.D., 1989-91, Fifth Med. Group, Minot AFB, 1991-92, Ehrling Bergquist Hosp., Offutt AFB, Nebr., 1992-93; chief med. resources, directorate med. programs/resources Office Air Force Surgeon Gen., Bolling AFB, D.C., 1993-95; command surgeon Pacific Air Forces, Hickam AFB, Hawaii, 1995-96; comdr. 74th Med. Group, Wright-Patterson AFB, Ohio, 1996—; lead agt. Dept. Def. Health Svc. Region 5, 1996—. Air Force state faculty mem. course ATLS. Decorated Legion of Merit. Mem. ACP Execs., Soc. Med. Cons. Armed Forces. Office: 74 MDG/CC 4881 Sugar Maple Dr Wright Patterson AFB OH 45433-5546

KELLEY, MARK ALBERT, physician, educator, health care executive; b. Boston, Oct. 31, 1947; s. Albert Joseph and Virginia Marie (Riley) Kelley; m. Gail Riggs Kelley, Aug. 4, 1974; children: Christopher Riggs, Amy Morgan. AB, Harvard U., Cambridge, Mass., 1969; MD, Harvard U., Boston, 1973. Diplomate Am. Bd. Internal Medicine, Am. Bd. Pulmonary Disease, Am. Bd. Critical Care. Intern Hosp. U. Pa., Phila., 1973—74, resident, 1974—76, chief med. resident, 1977—78, fellow in pulmonary diseases, 1976—77; dir. pulmonary fellowship U. Pa., 1979—82, from asst. to assoc. prof. medicine, 1979—92, prof., 1992-2000; dir. pulmonary fellowship tng. program, 1979—82; vice chmn. med. U. Pa. Sch. Medicine, Phila., 1986—90; dir. pulmonary fellowship tng. program, 1979—82; assoc. chmn. clin. svcs., dir. med. residency tng. program, 1982—86; dir. faculty group practice, 1985—90; vice dean clin. affairs U. Pa. Sch. Medicine, Phila., 1990—99; chief of medicine Phla. VA Med. Ctr., 1999—2000; exec. v.p., chief med. officer Henry Ford Health Sys., Detroit, 2000—; fellow in pulmonary disease Hosp. U. Pa., Phila., 1978—79. Spkr. in field. Mem. editl. bd. Critical Care Clinics, 1989—, Annals Internal Medicine, 1990—93, Critical Care Medicine, 1992—98. Fellow: ACP, Am. Coll. Chest Physicians; mem.: Am. Bd. Med. Specialties, Soc. Critical Care Medicine, Am. Bd. Internal Medicine (critical care medicine test com. 1988—93, chmn. 1990—93, bd. govs. 1990—98, exec. com. 1993—98, sec.-treas. 1994—96, chmn. 1997—98, sec.-treas. found. bd. 1999—), Am. Thoracic Soc. (chmn. nat. manpower study 1996—), Assn. Program Dirs. Internal Medicine, Alpha Omega Alpha. Office: 1 Ford Pl Detroit MI 48202-3450

KELLEY, PATRICK MICHAEL, minister, state legislator; b. Maryville, Mo., Oct. 27, 1948; s. Gilbert B. and Wilma M. K.; m. Nancy E. Schroeder, July 30, 1976; children: Ryan, Shane, Kristen. BS, William Jewell, 1970; MDiv, St. Paul, 1985. V.p. Kelley-Rickman Construction Col, 1970-72, pres., 1972-75; salesman Sequoia Supply Co., North Kansas City, Mo., 1975-77; owner, pres. Energy Expositions, 1977-83; pastor United Meth. Chs., Bates County, Mo., 1983-87, Aldersgate United Meth. Ch., Lee's Summit, 1987-90, Glenwood Park United Meth. Ch., Independence, 1990—; Rep. caucus chmn. Mo. State Ho. Reps., 1991, 92, minority floor leader, 1993, 94. Chmn. Lee's Summit D.A.R.E. task force; adv. bd. Community Mental Health Svcs., Lee's Summit; bd. dirs. Community Svcs. League, Lee's Summit. Mem. Lee's Summit Rep. Club (treas., pres.). Home: 3924 SW Windsong Dr Lees Summit MO 64082-4051 Office: Mo Ho Reps Capitol Bldg Jefferson City MO 65101 E-mail: pkelley@services.state.mo.us.

KELLEY, PATRICK WAYNE, prosecutor; b. Woodriver, Ill., Aug. 21, 1958; s. Merle Wayne and Alice Marilyn (Walker) K.; m. Tammie Ann Klein, Oct. 15, 1988; children: Andrew, Michael. B in Liberal Arts and Scis., Bradley U., 1980; JD, Cornell U., 1983. Bar: Ill. 1983, U.S. Dist. Ct. (ctrl. dist.) Ill. 1986. Assoc. Reinhard, Boener, Van Deren, Norris & Rieselbach, Milw., 1983-85; asst. state's atty. Sangamon County State's Atty., Springfield, Ill., 1985-87; assoc. Ensel, Jones, Blanchard & LaBarre, 1987-89; asst. U.S. atty. U.S. Atty. Ctrl. Dist. Ill., 1989-92; first asst. state's atty. Sangamon County State's Atty., 1992-94, state's atty., 1994—. Dir. Boys and Girls Club Springfield, 1992-97; treas., dir. Mental Health Ctr. Cen. Ill., Springfield, 1995—; mem. pattern jury instrns. com. Ill. Supreme Ct., Springfield, 1996—. Mem. Ill. State's Attys. Assn. (treas., legis. chmn. 1994—), Am. Bus. Club. Republican. Avocations: photography, running, bicycling, firearms. Office: Sangamon County States Atty 402 County Bldg Springfield IL 62701

KELLEY, STEVE, state legislator, lawyer; b. 1953; m. Sophie Kelley; two children. BA, Williams Coll.; JD, Columbia U. Lawyer; Dist. 44A rep. Minn. Ho. of Reps., St. Paul, 1992-96; mem. Minn. Senate from 44th dist., 1996—. Home: 121 Blake Rd S Hopkins MN 55343-2020 Office: 321 Capitol 75 Constitution Av Saint Paul MN 55155-0001

KELLEY, THOMAS WILLIAM, automotive sales executive; b. Ft. Wayne, Ind., Aug. 21, 1952; BS, Ind. U. Joined Jim Kelley Buick, 1974; various mgmt. and exec. level positions Kelley Automotive Group (formerly Jim Kelley Buick), Ft. Wayne, Ind., pres., co-CEO. Bd. dirs. Jr. Achievement, Big Bros. and Big Sisters, Boys and Girls Club of Ft. Wayne, YMCA. Mem. Ft. Wayne C. of C. (bd. dirs.). Avocations: golf, Indy car racing.

KELLEY, WILLIAM G. retail stores executive; CEO, chmn. bd. dirs. Consolidated Stores Corp., Columbus, Ohio, until 2000, strategic advisor, 2000—. Office: Consolidated Stores Corp PO Box 28512 300 Phillipi Rd Columbus OH 43228-0072

KELLOGG, WILLIAM S. retail executive; b. 1943; With Federated Dept. Stores, Inc., Cin., 1962-66, Kohl's Dept. Stores, Inc., Menomonee Falls, Wis., 1966-77, pres., 1977-82, chmn., 1982—. Office: Kohl's Dept Stores N56 W 17000 Ridgewood Dr Menomonee Falls WI 53051-7026

KELLY, A. DAVID, lawyer; b. St. Paul, June 8, 1948; s. David and Katherine (Tappins) K.; m. Elizabeth Woehrle, Oct. 25, 1978; children: Charles, George. BA, Carleton Coll., 1970; JD, Harvard U., 1973. Bar: Minn. 1973. Ptnr. Faegre & Benson, Mpls., 1973-90, Oppenheimer, Wolff & Donnelly, Mpls., 1990-95, Kelly, Hannaford & Battles, Mpls., 1995—. Trustee Carleton Coll., Northfield, Minn., 1972-76; chmn. Voyageurs Nat. Pk. Assn., Mpls., 1984-90; treas. Messiah Episc. Ch., St. Paul, 1988-96; pres. St. Paul Boys' and Girls' Club, 1992-95. Office: Kelly Hannaford & Battles 3900 Piper Jaffray Twr 222 South Ninth St Minneapolis MN 55402-3309

KELLY, ANASTASIA DONOVAN, lawyer; b. Boston, Oct. 9, 1949; d. Charles A. and Louise V. Donovan; m. Thomas C. Kelly, Aug. 23, 1980; children: Michael, Brian. BA cum laude, Trinity Coll, 1971; JD magna cum laude, George Washington U., 1981. Bar: D.C. 1982, Tex. 1982. Analyst Air Line Pilots Assn., 1971-74; dir. employee benefits Martin Marietta Corp., Bethesda, Md., 1974-81; assoc. Carrington, Coleman, Sloman & Blumenthal, Dallas, 1981-85, Wilmer, Cutler & Pickering, Washington, 1985-90, ptnr., 1990-95; sr. v.p., gen. counsel, sec. Fannie Mae, Washington, 1995-99; exec. v.p., gen. counsel, sec. Sears, Robuck & Co., 1999—. Named one of Outstanding Young Women of Am., 1980. Mem. Am. Bar Found., Order of Coif. Republican. Roman Catholic. Home: 9 Kensington Dr N Barrington IL 60010-6960 Office: Sears Roebuck & Co 3333 Beverly Rd Hoffman Estates IL 60179-0001

KELLY, ARTHUR LLOYD, management and investment company executive; b. Chgo., Nov. 15, 1937; s. Thomas Lloyd and Mildred (Wetten) Kelly; m. Diane Rex Cain, Nov. 25, 1978; children: Mary Lucinda, Thomas Lloyd, Alison Williams. BS with honors, Yale U., 1959; MBA, U. Chgo., 1964. With A.T. Kearney, Inc., 1959-75, mng. dir. Germany, 1964-70, v.p. for Europe Brussels, 1970-73, internat. v.p. London, 1974-75, ptnr., dir., 1969-75, mem. exec. com., 1972-75; pres., COO, dir. LaSalle Steel Co., Chgo., 1975-81; pres., CEO, dir. Dalta Corp., 1982—; mng. ptnr. KEL Enterprises L.P., 1983—. Dir. BASF Aktiengesellschaft, Ludwigshafen, Germany, BMW A.G., Munich, DataCard Corp., Minnetonka, Minn., Deere & Co., Moline, Ill., No. Trust Corp., Chgo., Snap-On, Inc., Kenosha, Wis., HSBC Trinkaus & Burkhardt KGaA, Dusseldorf; trustee U. Chgo.; mem. adv. coun. Ditchley Found., Oxford, England; bd. dirs. Chgo. Coun. Fgn. Rels. Fellow: Royal Geog. Soc. (life); mem.: Coun. Fgn. Rels. N.Y.C., World Pres.' Orgn., Yale Club, Racquet Club, Econ. Club, Comml. Club, Casino Club, Brook Club, Beta Gamma Sigma. Office: 20 S Clark St Ste 2222 Chicago IL 60603-1805

KELLY, CHARLES ARTHUR, lawyer; b. Evanston, Ill., Mar. 2, 1932; s. Charles Scott and Bess (Loftis) K.; m. Frances Kates, Sept. 9, 1961 (div. 1979); children: Timothy, Elizabeth, Mary; m. Patricia Lynn Francis, June 28, 1979. BA with honors, Amherst Coll., 1953; LLB, Harvard U., 1956. Bar: D.C. 1956, Ill. 1956. Assoc. Hubachek & Kelly, Chgo., 1956-64, ptnr., 1964-82, Chapman & Cutler, Chgo., 1982—. Sec.l Speedfam Internat., Inc., 1992-99, gen. counsel, 1998-99. Bd. dirs. Gads Hill Ctr., Chgo., pres., 1977—82; bd. dirs. Quetico Superior Found., Mpls., v.p., 1964—; bd. dirs. Lakeland Found., Chgo., 1960—96, pres., 1970—85, Ernest C. Oberholtzer Found., Mpls., 1962—, 1975—85, v.p., treas., 1998—; bd. dirs. Chgo. Hearing Found., 1990—94, Wilderness Rsch. Found., Chgo. Recipient Legion of Merit, USAF, 1982. Fellow Am. Coll. Trust and Estate Counsel; Mem. ABA, Chgo. Bar Assn., Ill. Bar Assn., Fed. Bar Assn., Univ. Club, Mid-Am. Club, Mich. Shores Club (Wilmette, Ill.), Harvard Club (Boston). Republican. Presbyterian. Office: Chapman and Cutler 111 W Monroe St Ste 1800 Chicago IL 60603-4096 E-mail: ckelly@chapman.com.

KELLY, CHARLES HAROLD, advertising agency executive; b. Omaha, Mar. 30, 1950; s. Kerwood Michael and Erma Lenore (Johnson) K.; m. Susan Marie Nielsen, Dec. 28, 1971; children: Matthew Michael, Laura Elizabeth. BA, Hastings Coll., 1972; MS, Iowa State U., 1973. Account exec. Kerker & Assocs., Mpls., 1977-80, v.p., dir. client services, 1983—; account exec. Foote, Cone & Belding, Chgo., 1980-82; account supr. Bozell, Jacobs, Kenyon & Eckhardt, Mpls., 1982-83; chmn. & CEO Kerker Mktg Communications Inc, Mlps. Bd. dirs. YMCA of Greater Mpls. Mem. Advt. Fedn. Mpls. (pres. 1987-88), Am. Assn. Advt. Agys. (past pres. Twin Cities). Republican. Lutheran. Avocations: jogging, golf, photography, music. Office: Kerker Mktg Communications Inc 7701 France Ave S Minneapolis MN 55435-5288

KELLY, DANIEL P. cardiologist, molecular biologist; b. Oct. 6, 1955; m. Therese J. Michelau; 3 children. BS in Biology, U. Ill., 1978, MD, 1982. Diplomate Am. Bd. Internal Medicine, Am. Bd. Cardiovasc. Disease. Intern in medicine Barnes Hosp., St. Louis, 1982—83, asst. resident in medicine, 1983—85; chief med. resident John Cochran VA Hosp., Washington U. Svc., 1984—85; rsch. postdoctoral fellow cardiovascular divsn. and dept. biol. chemistry Washington U. Sch. of Medicine, St. Louis, 1985—87, fellow in clin. cardiology, 1987—89, instr. of medicine cardiovascular divsn., 1989—90, asst. prof. medicine cardiovascular divsn., 1990—95, asst. prof. molecular biology and pharmacology, 1993—95, co-dir. Ctr. Adults with Congenital Heart Disease, 1993—, assoc. prof. medicine and molecular biology & pharmacology, 1995—, dir. Ctr. for Cardiovascular Rsch., 1996—. Lectr. rsch. and clin. fellowship program Washington U. Sch. Medicine, 1989, lectr. pharmacology and pathophysiology, 94; attending physician medicine and cardiology svcs. Barnes and Jewish Hosps., St. Louis, 1989. Contbr. chapters to books, articles to profl. jours. Recipient Lucille P. Markey Scholar award, Markey Found., 1989, Basal O'Connor Scholar award, March of Dimes, 1991, Rsch. Tng. grantee, NHLBI, 1994—, 1996—. Fellow: Am. Coll. Cardiology; mem.: AAAS, Am. Soc. for Clin. Investigation, Internat. Soc. Adult Congenital Heart Disease, Internat. Soc. Heart Rsch., Am. Heart Assn. (basic sci. coun., Established Investigator award 1995), Am. Fedn. Clin. Rsch., Alpha Omega Alpha, Phi Beta Kappa. Office: Washington U Sch of Medicine Ctr Cardiovasc Rsch 660 S Euclid Ave # 8086 Saint Louis MO 63110-1010

KELLY, DANIEL JOHN, physician; b. Binghamton, N.Y., June 23, 1940; s. William James and Mary Elizabeth (Schmitt) K.; m. Lois Ann Lanshe, Aug. 21, 1965; children: Britton James, Jeffrey Daniel, Reid William, Piper Ann. AB in History, Yale U., 1962; MD, Jefferson Med. Coll., 1966. Diplomate in Pathology, Nuclear Medicine, Dermatopathology. Intern Naval Hosp., Boston, 1966-67, resident Oakland, Calif., 1966-71, asst. chief lab. Great Lakes, Ill., 1971-73, chief lab. svcs., 1973-75; co-dir. lab. Highland Park (Ill.) Hosp., 1975-97, dir. lab., 1980-89, 96-97; co-dir. lab. Lake Forest (Ill.) Hosp., 1975-97, dir. lab., 1989-91; with Dean, Hoffman & Clark Pathologists S.C., Lake Forest, 1975-97, Associated Lab. Physician Svcs., Wauwatosa, Wis., 1997-99; chief of staff elect Highland Park (Ill.) Hosp., 1992-94, chief of staff, 1994-96, also bd. dirs.; with Consolidated Pathology Cons., S.C., Lake Bluff, Ill., 1999—. Med. exec. com. Highland Park Hosp., 1992-97, Lake Forest Hosp., 1989-91. Bd. dirs. Lake Forest Hist. Preservation Found., 1979-88; mem. bldg. rev. bd. City Govt., Lake Forest, 1989-93; mem. clin. lab. and blood bank adv. bd. Ill. Dept. Pub. Health, 1990-95; mem. Am. Pathology Found. Comdr. USNR, 1966-75. Fellow Coll. Am. Pathology, Am. Soc. Clin. Pathology, Internat. Acad. Pathologists, Am. Assn. Clin. Scientists; mem. AMA, Ill. Soc. Pathologists, Am. Soc. Microbiology, Am. Soc. Dermatopathology, Internat. Soc. Dermatopathology, Am. Acad. Dermatology, Assn. Military Surgeons. Roman Catholic. Avocations: reading, art, music, fishing. Home: 499 E Illinois Rd Lake Forest IL 60045-2364 Office: Dept Pathology Lake Forest Hosp 660 N Westmoreland Rd Lake Forest IL 60045-1659 Fax: 847-535-6237. E-mail: djdock@webtv.net.

KELLY, DENNIS MICHAEL, lawyer; b. Cleve., May 6, 1943; s. Thomas Francis and Margaret (Murphy) K.; m. Marilyn Ann Divoky, Dec. 28, 1967; children: Alison, Meredith. BA, John Carroll U., 1961-65; JD, U. Notre Dame, 1968. Bar: Ohio 1968. Law clk. U.S. Ct. Appeals (8th cir.), Cleve., 1968-69; assoc. Jones, Day, Reavis & Pogue, Cleve., 1969-75, ptnr., 1975—. Mem. Ohio Bar Assn., Bar Assn. Greater Cleve. Office: Jones Day Reavis & Pogue North Point 901 Lakeside Ave E Cleveland OH 44114-1190 E-mail: dmkelly@jonesday.com.

KELLY, DONALD PHILIP, entrepreneur; b. Chgo., Feb. 24, 1922; s. Thomas Nicholas and Ethel M. (Healy) K.; m. Byrd M. Sullivan, Oct. 25, 1952; children: Patrick, Laura, Thomas. Student, Loyola U., Chgo., 1953-54, De Paul U., 1954-55, Harvard U., 1965. Mgr. tabulating United Ins. Co. Am., 1946-51; mgr. data processing A.B. Wrisley Co., 1951-53, Swift & Co., 1953-65, asst. controller, 1965-67, controller, 1967-68, v.p. corporate devel., controller, 1968-70, fin. v.p., dir., 1970-73, Esmark, Inc., Chgo., 1973, pres., COO, 1973-77, pres., CEO, 1977-82, chmn., pres., CEO, 1982-84; pres. Kelly, Briggs & Assocs., Inc., 1984-86; chmn. Beatrice Co., 1986-88; chmn., CEO E-II Holdings Inc., 1987-88; pres., CEO D.P. Kelly & Assocs., L.P., Oak Brook, 1988—; chmn., pres., CEO Envirodyne Industries Inc., 1989-96. With USNR, 1942-46. Mem. Chgo. Club. Office: DP Kelly and Assocs LP 701 Harger Rd Ste 190 Oak Brook IL 60523-1490

KELLY, GLENDA MARIE, state legislator; b. San Diego, June 3, 1944; d. Glenn Adrian and Donna Louise (Embrey) Molsberry; m. Ronald Worth Campbell, June 3, 1962 (div. 1969); children: Gina Marie, Chad Loren; m. Dennis Patrick Kelly, Sept. 18, 1970. BS in Sociology cum laude, Mo. Western State Coll., 1989. Legal sec. Stanley S. Kalender, St. Joseph, Mo., 1960-88; dep. mayor City of St. Joseph, 1986-89, mayor, 1989-94; mem. Mo. Ho. Reps. 27th Dist., Mo., 1995—. Mem. Buchanan County Social Welfare Bd., 1979-85; mem. steering com. YWCA Women's Abuse Shelter, 1980; vice chair, chair budget com. Citizen's Adv. Commn., 1980-81; mem. task force Mo-Kan Regional Food Bank, 1981-83, City St. Joseph Fair Housing, 1984, Pony Express Region Tourist Info. Ctr., 1982, bd. dirs., 1983; bd. dirs. Pony Express Hist. Assn., 1983-84, Econ. Opportunity Corp., 1984-85, YWCA, 1985-86, Mo. Mcpl. League, 1990-94, St. Joseph Hist. Soc., 1979-80, sec., 1979-80; mem. St. Joseph City Coun., 1986, Governance Coun. Cmty. Based Health Care for Children, 1994—. Recipient Outstanding Community Vol. award United Way, Civic Recognition award City St. Joseph, Vol. award VFW Aux., 1980, Recognition award St. Joseph's br. NAACP, 1990, James C. Kirkpatrick Good Govt. award Northwest Mo. Press Assn., Historic Preservation award for Leadership in Historic Preservation Issues St. Joseph Landmark Commn., 1993; named Woman of Month by YWCA, 7/93, Outstanding Woman of Yr. YWCA, 1993. Mem. LWV (bd. dirs. St. Joseph area, co-chair local govt. com. 1978-79, chair budget com. 1979-80, 1st v.p. 1981, chair drug awareness com. 1981, pres. 1985-86), St. Joseph Area C. of C. (urban action com. 1985, econ. devel. coun. 1988—, bd. dirs. 1994—). Democrat. Roman Catholic. Avocations: reading, writing, fishing, drawing. Office: Mo Ho of Reps State Capitol Building Rm 312 Jefferson City MO 65101-1556

KELLY, J. PETER, steel company executive; b. 1941; AB, Harvard U., 1963; JD, Duquesne U., 1972. With LTV Steel Co., Inc., Cleveland, Ohio, 1963—, pres., COO, 1991-2000, chmn., pres. & CEO, 2000—.

KELLY, JAMES MICHAEL, plant and soil scientist; b. Knoxville, Feb. 2, 1944; s. Woodrow Wilson and Thelma Lucille (Miller) K.; m. Susan Kay Morris, Aug. 9, 1969; children: John Kip, Christopher Kenneth. BS, E. Tenn. State U., 1966; MS, U. Tenn., 1968, PhD, 1973. Cert. profl. soil scientist. Assoc. ecologist NUS Corp., Pitts., 1973-74; rsch. assoc. Forestry Dept. Purdue U., West Lafayette, Ind., 1975-76; program mgr. Tenn. Valley Authority, Oak Ridge, 1977-88, sr. rschr., 1990-94; sr. tech. specialist, team leader, 1994-95; prof., chair dept. forestry Iowa State U., Ames, 1995—. Vis. prof. agronomy Purdue U., 1988-89; adj. prof. U. Tenn., Knoxville, 1980-95, forestry dept. Purdue U., 1985-95. Author: Carbon Forms and Functions in Forest Soils, 1995; assoc. editor Soil Sci. Soc. Am. Jour., 1989-95, Forest Sci., 1998-2001; editl. bd. Forest Ecology and Management, 2001-; contbr. more than 100 articles to profl. jours. Head referee Ayso Youth Soccer, Oak Ridge, 1985-88; troop com. Boy Scouts Am., Oak

Ridge, 1989-95. Oak Ridge Assoc. Univ. fellow, 1970-72; Elec. Power Rsch. Inst. grantee, 1978, 82, 89, 91, 95, NSF grantee, 1995. Fellow Soil Sci. Soc. Am. (chmn. divsn. S7 1986-87, bd. dirs. 1988-89, awards com. 1992-93, fellows com. 1997-99, profl. svc. com. 2000-02); mem. AAAS, Ecol. Soc. Am., Soc. Am. Foresters, Exptl. Aircraft Assn. (chpt. pres. 1991-93), Trees Forever (bd. dirs. 1995—), Sigma Xi, Gamma Sigma Delta, Xi Sigma Pi. Achievements include research and application of environmental science. Office: Iowa State Univ Dept Forestry Ames IA 50011-0001

KELLY, JANET LANGFORD, lawyer; b. Kansas City, Mo., Nov. 27, 1957; BA, Grinnell Coll., 1979; JD, Yale U., 1983. Bar: N.Y. 1985, Ill. 1989. Law clerk to Hon. James J. Hunter III U.S. Ct. Appeals (3rd cir.), 1983-84; ptnr. Sidley & Austin, Chgo., 1984-89; sr. v.p., sec., gen. counsel Sara Lee Corp., 1995-99; exec. v.p. corp. devel., gen. counsel, sec. Kellogg Co., Battle Creek, Mich., 1999—. Sr. editor Yale Law Jour., 1983. Bd. dirs. Am. Arbitration Assn., Constl. Rights Found.; mem. adv. bd. Chgo. Vol. Legal Svcs. Found. Office: Kellogg Co PO Box 3599 1 Kellogg Sq Battle Creek MI 49016

KELLY, JOHN, advertising executive; Pres., CEO, founder Upshot, Chgo., 1994-98; CEO Ha-Lo Industries, Inc., Niles, Ill., 1999—. Office: Ha-Lo Industries Inc 5980 Touhy Ave Niles IL 60714

KELLY, JOHN TERENCE, architect; b. Elyria, Ohio, Jan. 27, 1922; s. Thomas Alo and Coletta Margaret (Conrad) K. BArch, Carnegie Mellon U., 1949; MArch, Harvard U., 1951, M of Landscape Architecture, 1952. Prin. architect John Terence Kelly, Cleve., 1954—. Vis. critic, lectr. U. Mich., U. Cin., Case Western Res. U., McGill U. Bd. dirs. Nova. With inf. AUS, 1943-46. Recipient Cleve. Arts prize in Architecture, 1968, hist. Bldg. award Architects Soc. Ohio, 1986; Charles Eliot Norton fellow, 1952, Fulbright fellow, Munich, Germany, 1953. Mem. AIA (nat. com. design). Home: 2646 N Moreland Blvd Cleveland OH 44120-1461 Office: 2646 N Moreland Blvd Cleveland OH 44120-1461

KELLY, KAY, social worker, administrator; B of Social Welfare, M of Social Welfare, U. Kans.; postgrad., Karl Menninger Sch. Psychiatry. Dir. social work Menninger, Topeka. Contbr. articles to profl. jours. Office: Menninger PO Box 829 Topeka KS 66601-0829

KELLY, MARILYN, state supreme court justice; b. Apr. 15, 1938; m. Donald Newman. BA, Ea. Mich. U., 1960, JD (hon.); postgrad., U. Paris.; MA, Middlebury Coll., 1961; JD with honors, Wayne State U., 1971. Assoc. Dykema, Gossett, Spencer, Goodnow & Trigg, Detroit, 1973-78; ptnr. Dudley, Patterson, Maxwell, Smith & Kelly, Bloomfield Hills, Mich., 1978-80; owner Marilyn Kelly & Assocs., Bloomfield Hills, Birmingham, 1980-88; judge Mich. Ct. of Appeals, 1989-96; justice Mich. Supreme Ct., 1997—. Tchr. lang., lit. Grosse Pointe Pub. Schs., Albion Coll., Ea. Mich. U.; past mem. rep. assembly, comms. com., family law coun. Mich. State Bar, now co-chair Open Justice Commn. Active Mich. Dem. Party, 1963—. Recipient Disting Alumni award Ea. Mich. U., Disting. Svc. award Mich. Edn. Assn. Mem. Soc. Irish-Am. Lawyers, Women Lawyers Assn. (past pres.), Oakland County Bar Assn. (past chair family law com.) Office: Mich Supreme Ct 3034 West Grand Blvd Ste 8-500 Detroit MI 48202

KELLY, RANDY C. state legislator; b. Aug. 2, 1950; m. Kathy Kelly; two children. BA, U. Minn. Mem. Minn. Ho. of Reps., St. Paul, 1974-90, Minn. Senate from 67th dist., St. Paul, 1990—. Vice chmn. fin. com., mem. crime prevention, fin. divsn. family svc., fin. state govt. divsn., and jobs, energy and cmty. devel. coms., Minn. State Senate. Address: 1630 David St Saint Paul MN 55119-3007 Also: 323 Capitol 75 Constitution Ave Saint Paul MN 55155-1601

KELLY, ROBERT J. supermarket executive; Exec. v.p. retailing Vons Co., Calif.; chmn. bd. dirs., pres., CEO Eagle Food Ctrs., Inc., Milan, 1995—. Office: Eagle Food Ctrs Inc PO Box 6700 Milan IL 61264-6700

KELLY, ROBERT VINCENT, JR. metal company executive; b. Phila., Sept. 29, 1938; s. Robert Vincent and Catherine Mary (Hanley) K.; m. Margaret Cecilia Taylor, Feb. 11, 1961; children: Robert V. III, Christopher T., Michael J., Tasha Marie. BS in Indsl. Mgmt., St. Joseph's U., Phila., 1960; postgrad., Roosevelt U., 1965-66. Gen. foreman prodn. Republic Steel Corp., Chgo., 1963-68; supt. prodn. Phoenix Steel Corp., Phoenixville, Pa., 1969-73; gen. supt. ops. Continental Steel Corp., Kokomo, Ind., 1973-77; gen. mgr. MACSTEEL div. Quanex Corp., Jackson, Mich., 1977-81; corp. v.p. Quanex Corp., Houston, 1979—, pres. MACSTEEL group Jackson, 1982—. Pres. La Salle Steel Co., Hammond, Ind., 1985-87, Arbuckle Corp., Jackson, 1984-88. Leader, com. mem. Boy Scouts Am., Jackson. Lt. USN, 1960-63. Mem. Am. Mgmt. Assn. (pres.), Inst. Indsl. Engrs., Assn. Iron and Steel Engrs., Am. Soc. for Metals, USN Inst., Jackson C. of C. Clubs: Jackson Country. Avocations: hiking, camping, sailing, scouting. Home: 1734 Metzmont Dr Jackson MI 49203-5379 Office: Macsteel, Quanex Corp 1 Jackson Sq Ste 500 Jackson MI 49201-1446

KELLY, THOMAS, state legislator; BS, Fordham U.; MS, L.I. U. Mem. from dist. 17 Mich. State Ho. of Reps., Lansing, 1995—, mem. edn., transp., house oversight and ethics coms., 1995—. City councilman City of Wayne, Mich. Address: PO Box 30014 Lansing MI 48909-7514

KELLY, THOMAS, advertising executive; V.p. media svcs. Hawthorne Direct, Fairfield, Iowa, pres., CEO. Office: Hawthorne Direct Inc PO Box 1366 300 N 16th St Fairfield IA 52556-2604

KELLY, TOM (JAY THOMAS KELLY), professional sports team manager; b. Graceville, Minn., Aug. 15, 1950; s. Joseph Thomas and Anna Grace (Heisenbottle) K.; children: Sharon Clare, Thomas John. Student, Mesa (Ariz.) Jr. Coll., 1968-69. Profl. baseball player Minn. Twins, Mpls., 1968-77, coach, 1982-86, mgr., 1987—, mgr. minor league team Toledo, 1978-82. Managed Minn. Twins team to World Series Championship, 1987, 91; named Am. League Mgr. of Yr. Sporting News, 1991. Mem. Assn. Profl. Baseball Players, U.S. Trotting Assn., Nat. Greyhound Assn. Avocation: harness racing. Office: Minn Twins Hubert H Humphrey Metrodome 34 Kirby Puckett Pl Minneapolis MN 55415-1596*

KELLY, WILLIAM GARRETT, judge; b. Grand Rapids, Mich., Nov. 30, 1947; s. Joseph Francis and Gertrude Frances (Downes) K.; m. Sharon Ann Diroff, Aug. 11, 1979; children: Colleen, Joseph, Caitlin, Meaghan and Patricia. BA, U. Detroit, 1970, JD, 1975. Bar: Mich. 1975, U.S. Dist. Ct. (we. dist.) Mich. 1975. Tchr. Peace Corps, Ghana, Republic of West Africa, 1970-72; asst. prosecutor Kalamazoo (Mich.) Prosecutor's Office, 1975-77; atty. Office of Defender, Grand Rapids, 1977-78; judge 62d B Dist. Ct., Kentwood, 1979—. Mem. faculty Mich. Jud. Inst., Lansing, 1985—, 2d Nat. Conf. on Ct. Tech., Denver, 1988; chmn.-elect Jud. Conf. State Bar Mich., 1990-91, chair, 1991-92; vice chmn. Nat. Conf. Spl. Ct. Judges, 1990-91, chair 1992-93. Bd. dirs. Nat. Ctr. for State Cts., 1994-2000; pres. Kentwood Jaycees, 1979-80. Named one of Five Outstanding Young Men of Mich., Mich. Jaycees, 1982. Mem. ABA (chair nat. conf. spl. ct. judges 1992-93), State Bar Mich., Grand Rapids Bar Assn., Cath. Lawyers Assn. Western Mich. (pres. 1987), Mich. Dist. Judges Assn. (pres. 1989). Roman Catholic. Office: 62d B Dist Ct PO Box 8848 4900 Breton Rd SE Kentwood MI 49518-8848

KELMAN, DONALD BRIAN, neurosurgeon; b. Brandon, Man., Can., Apr. 3, 1942; came to U.S., 1979; s. Alexander and May Marguerite (Ronayne) K.; m. Joan Ann Thompson, July 10, 1966 (div. Sept. 1985); children: Carl Michael, Melanie Catherine, Leslie Jane, Brian Andrew; m. Cynthia Marie Esser, Mar. 21, 1986; 1 child, Craig Richard. BA in Biology, U. Sask., 1964, MD, 1968. Diplomate Am. Bd. Neurol. Surgery. Intern St. Joseph's Hosp., Victoria, B.C., Can., 1968-69; pvt. practice, 1969-70; resident in neurosurgery Mayo Grad. Sch. of Medicine, Rochester, Minn., 1970-76; pvt. practice Prince George, B.C., Can., 1976-79; neurosurgeon Marshfield (Wis.) Clinic/St. Joseph's Hosp., 1979—. Chmn. neurosurgery dept. Marshfield Clinic, 1984-2000. Wis. rep. Coun. of State Neurol. Socs., 1990—; mem. adv. com. Seaman Mineral Mus., 1997-2000; bd. dirs. Seatec Found., 2000—. Mem. AMA, Am. Assn. Neurol. Surgeons, Wis. Med. Soc., Wis. Neurosurg. Soc. (sec., treas. 1987, pres. 1989). Avocations: rock and mineral collecting, lapidary art, painting, computers. Home: 1403 N Broadway Ave Marshfield WI 54449-1321 Office: Marshfield Clinic 1000 N Oak Ave Marshfield WI 54449-5702

KELPE, PAUL ROBERT, engineer, consultant; b. St. Louis, July 6, 1948; s. Robert Frederick and Doris Jean (Wood) K.; m. Janice Pauline Frey, Apr. 10, 1971; children: Brian Paul, Mark Robert. BA, Ottawa U., 1970; MS, U. Nebr., 1973; diploma in energy mgmt., Va. Poly. Inst., 1985. Cert. tchr., Nebr. Stationery engr. King Louie Corp., Overland Park, Kans., 1967-70; head tchr. sci. dept. Westside Community Schs., Omaha, 1970-81, energy dir., 1981-92. Apptd. mem. Nebr. Energy Coun., 1991-2002; sci. instr. Westside Middle Sch. Contbr. articles to profl. jours. Troop com. chmn. Boy Scouts Am., Omaha, 1987-92; bd. trustees Sanitary and Improvement Dist., 1980-84; candidate Sub-Dist. 7 PNRD, Omaha, 1988-89; mem. Gov.'s Energy Policy Coun., 1991-92. Recipient Energy award State of Nebr., 1987; grantee Nebr. Energy Office, 1982-92. Mem. ASHRAE (award 1988), Nebr. Acad. Scis., Nat. Sci. Tchrs. Assn., Nebr. State Tchr. Assn., NEA, Phi Delta Kappa. Republican. Lutheran. Avocations: camping, boating, swimming, water skiing, scuba diving. Office: Westside Community Schs 909 S 76th St Omaha NE 68114-4599 E-mail: pkelpe@westside66.org.

KELSCH, RAEANN, state legislator; m. Thomas D. Kelsch; 3 children. BBA, U. N.D. Mem. N.D. Ho. of Reps.; vice chmn. judiciary com.; mem. govt. and vets. affairs com. Bd. dirs. United Way; active AID, Inc. Republican. Home: 611 Craig Dr Mandan ND 58554-2353 Office: ND Ho of Reps State Capitol Bismarck ND 58505

KELSH, JEROME, state legislator; b. Fullerton, N.D., Oct. 25, 1940; s. George L. and Freda (Nelson) K.; m. Romona Keller; children: Scott, Jock, Steven. BS, U. N.D., 1962. Mem. N.D. Senate from 26th dist., Bismark, 1985—; chmn. agr. com. N.D. Senate, mem. edn. com., mem. transp. com. Agribusinessman. Mem. adv. bd. Ellenda Hosp.; past chmn. Fullerton Centennial Com.; past mem. Fullerton Sch. Bd.; mem. Fullerton Betterment Bd. Office: Rte 1 Box 27 Fullerton ND 58441 also: State Senate State Capitol Bismarck ND 58505

KELSO, BECKY, former state legislator; b. 1948; m. Michael Kelso; 2 children. BA in Comm., U. Minn. Mem. Minn. Ho. of Reps., 1986-98; mem. capital investment com.; mem. edn. com.; mem. regulated industries and energy com.; mem. transp. and transit com. Home: 60 S Shannon Dr Shakopee MN 55379-8025

KELSO, CAROL, state legislator; b. May 26, 1945; BA, Iowa State U. Assemblywoman Wis. State Dist. 88. Pres. Brown County Planning Commn.; mem. Brown County Harbor Commn., 2020 Hwy. Coalition. Address: 416 E Le Capitaine Cir Green Bay WI 54302-5153

KEMNITZ, JOSEPH WILLIAM, physiologist, researcher; b. Balt., Mar. 15, 1947; s. Harold Clarence Kemnitz and Alice Mae (Ziebarth) Delwiche; m. Amanda Marye Tuttle, Jan. 5, 1991; children: Julia Ellen, Joseph Andrew. BA, U. Wis., 1969, PhD, 1976. Rsch. assoc. Wis. Regional Primate Rsch. Ctr., Madison, 1976-79, asst. scientist, 1979-84, assoc. scientist, 1984-94, sr. scientist and assoc. dir., 1995-96; dir., 1996—; assoc. scientist dept. medicine U. Wis., Madison, 1991-94, sr. scientist dept. medicine, 1995-97, prof. dept. physiology. Cons. NIH, Bethesda, Md., 1981—; mem. Children's Diabetes Ctr., Madison, Wis., 1990—; steering com. Inst. on Aging, Madison, 1989—. Assoc. editor Hormones and Behavior, 1986-96; contbr. articles to profl. jours. Grantee (various) NIH, 1977—. Mem. Am. Physiol. Soc., Am. Inst. Nutrition, Am. Diabetes Assn., Am. Soc. Primatologists, Gerontol. Soc. Am., N.Am. Assn. Study of Obesity, Internat. Primatol. Soc. Office: Primate Rsch Ctr UW 1220 Capitol Ct Madison WI 53715-1237

KEMNITZ, RALPH A. lawyer; b. Aberdeen, S.D., Sept. 2, 1942; s. Ralph L. and Delphia F. (Benscoter) K.; m. Julianne K. Ufen, Jan. 19, 1965; children: Ralph, Candice, Kimberly. BS, No. State, 1966; JD, U. S.D., 1969. Bar: S.D. 1969. Atty. S.D. Legal Services, Ft. Thompson, 1969-71; assoc. Kemnitz Law Office, Philip, S.D., 1971-82; ptnr. Kemnitz & Barnett, 1982—. States atty. Haakon County, Philip, 1971-85. Chmn. S.D. Racing Commn., Pierre, 1984—; chmn., state del. Haakon County Reps., Philip, 1974-76. Named one of Outstanding Young Men in Am. Jaycees, 1973. Mem. ABA, S.D. Bar Assn., S.D. Trial Lawyers Assn., Philip City C. of C. (pres. 1972). Republican. Methodist. Home: PO Box 245 Philip SD 57567-0245 Office: Kemnitz & Barnett PO Box 489 Philip SD 57567-0489

KEMP, SHAWN T. professional basketball player; b. Elkhart, Ind., Nov. 26, 1969; Student, U. Ky., Trinity Valley C.C., 1988-89. Basketball player Seattle Supersonics, 1989-97; forward Cleveland Cavaliers, 1997. Named to NBA All-Star team, 1993, Dream Team II, 1994, All-NBA Second Team, 1994. Office: Portland Trailblazers Rose Quarter One Center Court Portland OR 97227

KEMPENICH, KEITH, state legislator; m. Melinda. Mem. N.D. Ho. of Reps., vice chmn. transp. com., mem. indsl., bus. and labor com. Rancher; crop adjuster. Mem. Lions, Farm Bur., Farmers Union, Aircraft Owners and Pilots Assn. Home: HC 4 Box 10 Bowman ND 58623-8810

KEMPER, ALEXANDER C. finance company executive; married Christine Kemper. BA in Am. History, Northwestern U. Credit analyst to pres. UMB Bank, n.a., Kansas City, Mo., 1987-94; pres. UMB Fin. Corp., 1995-96, pres., CEO, chmn. bd. dirs., 1996—. Bd. dirs. Greater Kans. C. of C., Pioneer Svc. Co., Kemper Realty Co., Stagecoach Inc., UMB Mortgage Co., UMB Bank South Banking Area, UMB Bank, n.a. - Metro Bank Area, UMB Fin. Corp., UMB Bank of Kansas City, UMB Bank of Colo. Mem. Am. Royal Assn. (bd. dirs.), Agr. Future of Am. (bd. dirs.). Office: UMB Fin Corp 1010 Grand Blvd Kansas City MO 64106-2225

KEMPER, DAVID WOODS, II, banker; b. Kansas City, Mo., Nov. 20, 1950; s. James Madison and Mildred (Lane) K.; m. Dorothy Ann Jannarone, Sept. 6, 1975; children: John W., Elizabeth C., Catherine B., William L. B.A. cum laude, Harvard U., 1972; M.A. in English Lit., Oxford, Worcester Coll., 1974; M.B.A., Stanford U., 1976. With Morgan Guaranty Trust Co., N.Y.C., 1975-78; v.p. Commerce Bank of Kansas City, Mo., 1978-79, sr. v.p., 1980-81; pres. Commerce Bancshares, Inc., 1982-86, pres., ceo, 1986-91, chmn., pres., ceo, 1991—; also dir. Commerce Bancshares, Inc; chmn. Commerce Bank N.A., St. Louis, 1985—. Bd. dirs. Kansas City, Tower Properties, Kansas City, Ralcorp Holdings, Inc. Contbr. articles on banking to profl. jours. Trustee Mo. Bot. Garden, St. Louis Symphony Orch., Washington U. Mem. Acad. Arts and Scis., Fin. Svcs. Roundtable, Kansas City Country Club, River Club (Kansas City), St. Louis Club, St. Louis Country Club, Racquet Club, Old Warson Country Club (St. Louis). Office: Commerce Bancshares Inc 8000 Forsyth Blvd Clayton MO 63105

KEMPER, JAMES DEE, lawyer; b. Olney, Ill., Feb. 23, 1947; s. Jack O. and Vivian L. Kemper; m. Diana J. Deig, June 1, 1968; children: Judd, Jason. BS, Ind. U., 1969, JD summa cum laude, 1971. Bar: Ind. 1971. Law clk. U.S. Ct. Appeals (7th cir.), Chgo., 1971-72; mng. ptnr. Ice Miller, Indpls., 1972—. Note editor Ind. U. Law Rev., 1970-71; contbr. articles to profl. jours. Past officer, bd. dirs. Marion County Assn. for Retarded Citizens, Inc., Indpls.; past bd. dirs. Cen. Ind. Easter Seal Soc., Indpls., Crossroads Rehab. Ctr., Inc, Indpls.; pres., bd. govs. Orchard Country Day Sch., Indpls.; mem. bd. Eiteljorg Mus. Native Americans, Butler U. Fellow Ind. Bar Found.; mem. ABA (employee benefit com.), Ind. Bar Assn., The Group, Inc., Midwest Pension Conf., U.S. C. of C. (employee benefit com.), Stanley K. Lacy Leadership Alumni. Office: Ice Miller 1 American Sq Indianapolis IN 46282-0020

KEMPER, JONATHAN MCBRIDE, banker; b. Kansas City, Mo., July 23, 1953; s. James Madison Jr. and Mildred (Lane) K.; m. Nancy Lee Smith, Nov. 26, 1983; children: Charlotte Lee, Nicolas Thornton, David Benjamin Royce. AB, Harvard U., 1975, MBA, 1979. Asst. bank examiner Fed. Res. Bank, N.Y.C., 1975-76; asst. treas. Second Dist. Securities, 1976-77; account officer Citicorp, Chgo., 1981-83; v.p. Commerce Bank of Kansas City, Mo., 1983-84, sr. v.p., 1984-85, pres., 1985—, chief exec. officer, 1988—, also bd. dirs. Bd. dirs. Tower Properties, Greater Kansas City Community Found.; vice-chmn. Commerce Bancshares, 1988—. Treas., bd. dirs. Truman Libr. Inst.; bd. dirs. Civic Coun. Kansas City. Office: Commerce Bank of Kansas City 1000 Walnut St PO Box 419248 Kansas City MO 64141-6248

KEMPER, RUFUS CROSBY, JR. banker; b. Kansas City, Mo., Feb. 22, 1927; s. Rufus Crosby and Enid (Jackson) K.; m. Mary Barton Stripp; children: Rufus Crosby III, Pamela Warrick Gabrovsky, Sheila Kemper Dietrich, John Mariner, Mary Barton, Alexander Charles, Heather Christian. Grad., Phillips Acad., Andover, Mass., 1942; student, U. Mo.; LL.D. (hon.), William Jewel Coll., 1976; DFA (hon.), Westminster Coll., 1983. Chmn., chief exec. officer, dir. United Mo. Bancshares, Inc., Kansas City, Mo., United Mo. Bank of Kansas City N.A.; dir. United Mo. City Bank; pres., dir. Kemper Realty Co., Pioneer Service Corp.; adv. dir. United Mo. Bank of Boonville, Overland Park Bancshares, Inc., Kans., Overland Park Bank and Trust Co.; dir. United Mo. Bank of St. Joseph; chmn. bd., dir. City Bancshares, Inc., Kansas City, Mo.; dir. Chgo. Title Ins. Co., United Mo. Mortgage Co., Kansas City So. Industries, Mo.; chmn., CEO United Mo. Bank of Kansas City, Kansas City. Past assoc. faculty mem. Baker U., Baldwin, Kans. Mem. adv. com. Research Med. Center; trustee Freedom's Found. Valley Forge, Kansas City Art Inst., U. Mo. Kansas City Conservatory; hon. trustee YWCA.; past trustee Kemper Mil. Sch. and Coll., Boonville, U. Kansas City, Frury Coll.; bd. dirs. Kansas City Indsl. Found., Heart of Am. council Boy Scouts Am., Heart of Am. United Way, Mid-Am. Arts Alliance, Starlight Theatre, Kansas City Symphony, Hist. Kansas City Found.; hon. bd. dirs. Albrecht Art Mus., St. Joseph, Mo.; treas., dir. Met. Performing Arts Funds; mem. dirs. council Lyric Opera; mem. community adv. council The Children's Mercy Hosp.; mem. nat. com. Whitney Mus. Am. Art, N.Y.C.; commr. Nat. Mus. Am. Art., Washington; past bd. dirs. and treas. C. of C. of Greater Kansas City; rep. candidate of U.S. Senate from Mo., 1962. Served with USNR, World War II. Recipient Key Man Kansas City Jr. C. of C., 1952, Distinguished Service, 1964, Man of Yr. award Kansas City Press Club, 1974, Outstanding Kansas Citian award Native Sons Kansas City, 1975, 82, 1st Advocacy award Mid-Continent Small Bus. Assn., 1980, Lester Milgram Humanitarian award, 1982, Man of Yr. award Downtown, Inc., 1982, Pirouette award Kansas City Ballet Guild and Kansas City Tomorrow Alumni Assn., 1983, Faculty Alumni award U. Mo. Columbia Alumni Assn., 1982, Mo. Arts Council award, 1984, Kansas City Chancellor's medal U. Mo., 1984, Disting. Service award St. Paul Sch. Theology, 1987, Advocacy award Mo. Citizens for the Arts, 1987; named Man of the Yr. Kansas City Press Club, 1974, Banker Advocate of Yr. Small Bus. Adminstrn., 1981, Man of the Yr. Downtown Inc., 1982. Mem. Am. Royal Assn. (v.p., bd. dirs.), Man of the Month Fraternity, Beta Theta Pi (Man of Yr. 1974) Republican. Episcopalian. Clubs: River, Carriage, Kansas City Country, Kansas City, 1021, Mo, Chathan, Mass., Garden of the Gods, Cheyenne Mountain Country (Colorado Springs, Colo.). Avocations: farming, tennis, sailing, horseback riding, raising cattle. Office: United Mo Bank Kans City PO Box 419226 Kansas City MO 64141-6226

KEMPF, DONALD G., JR. lawyer; b. Chgo., July 4, 1937; s. Donald G. and Verginia (Jahnke) K.; m. Nancy Kempf, June 12, 1965; children: Donald G. III, Charles P., Stephen R. AB, Villanova U., 1959; LLB, Harvard U., 1965; MBA, U. Chgo., 1989. Bar: Ill. 1965, U.S. Supreme Ct. 1972, N.Y. 1986, Colo. 1992. Assoc. Kirkland & Ellis, Chgo., 1965-70, ptnr., 1971-2000; exec. v.p., chief legal officer Morgan Stanley, N.Y.C., 2000—. Trustee Chgo. Symphony Orch., 1995—, Am. Inns of Ct. Found., 1997—; bd. govs. Chgo. Zool. Soc., 1975—, Art Inst. Chgo., 1984—; bd. dirs. United Charities Chgo., 1985—, chmn. bd., 1991-93. Capt. USMC, 1959-62. Fellow Am. Coll. Trial Lawyers; mem. Am. Econ. Assn., ABA, Chgo. Club, Econ. Club, Univ. Club, Mid-Am. Club, Saddle and Cycle Club (Chgo.), Snowmass (Colo.) Club, Quail Ridge (Fla.) Club, Westmoreland Club. Roman Catholic. Address: Morgan Stanley 1585 Broadway Fl 39 New York NY 10036-8200 E-mail: donald.kempf@morganstanley.com.

KEMPF, JANE ELMIRA, marketing executive; b. Phila., Sept. 28, 1927; d. Albert Thomas and Alice (Gaston) Mullen; m. Peter Kempf, Sept. 4, 1948 (dec. Mar. 1985); children: Peter Albert, Jan Michael, Richard Allen, Jeffery Val. Grad. high sch., Yeadon, Pa. News dir. Sta. WIFF, Auburn, Ind., 1968-69; city editor The Evening Star, 1969-76, columnist, 1969—2001; paralegal Warren Sunday Atty., 1977-85; mktg. mgr. City Nat. Bank, 1986-89; with communications mktg. Lincoln Fin. Corp., Ft. Wayne, Ind., 1989-90; prin. JK Communications Bus. Svcs., Auburn, 1990—, Auburn Pub. Co., 1997—. Prin. Auburn (Ind.) Pub. Author: Jane's Friends and Family Cookbook, vol. 1, 1997, vol. 2, 1999, vol. 3, 2002. Mem. Auburn Network Enterprising Women, Ladies Literary Club, PEO Sisterhood (past pres., treas.), Auburn C. of C. (past sec., bd. dirs.). Presbyterian. Home: 1117 Packard Pl Auburn IN 46706-1340 Office: Auburn Pub Inc 1117 Packard Pl Auburn IN 46706-1340 Fax: 260-927-1168. E-mail: jkempf@fwi.com.

KEMPSKI, RALPH ALOISIUS, bishop; b. Milw., July 16, 1934; s. Sigmund Joseph and Cecilia Josephine (Chojnacki) K.; m. Mary Jane Roth, July 30, 1955; children— Richard, Joan, John B.A., Augsburg Coll., 1960; M.Div., Northwestern Luth. Theol. Sem., 1963; D.Div., Wittenberg U., Springfield, Ohio, 1980. Pastor Epiphany Luth. Ch., Mpls., 1963-68, St. Stephen Luth. Ch., Louisville, 1968-71, Our Saviour Luth. Ch., West Lafayette, Ind., 1971-79; bishop Ind.-Ky. Synod Luth. Ch. Am., Indpls., 1979-87, Ind.-Ky. Synod Evang. Luth. Ch. Am., 1987-98. Bd. dirs. Ind. Coun. Chs., 1979-96, v.p., 1991-94, pres., 1994-96 ; bd. dirs. Ky. Coun. Chs., Luth. Sch. Theology, Chgo., Luth. Sch., Columbia, S.C., Wittenberg U., Springfield, Ohio, Suomi Coll.; governing bd. Nat. Coun. Chs. Christ U.S.A., N.Y.C., 1981-88, Luth. Theol. So. Sem., 1988-96, Trinity Sem., 1996-98. Mem. governing bd. Suomi Coll., Hancock, Mich., 1998-2001. Avocations: gardening, reading, camping, travelling, flying.

KENDALL, KAY LYNN, interior designer, consultant; b. Cadillac, Mich., Aug. 20, 1950; d. Robert Llewellyn and Betty Louise (Powers) K.; 1 child, Anna Renee Easter. BFA, U. Mich., 1973. Draftsman, interior designer store planning dept. Jacobson Stores, Inc., Jackson, Mich., 1974-79, sr. interior designer store planning dept., 1981-98; prin., pres. Kay Kendall Designs LLC (Kendall Interior Design and Devel.), 1979—; sr. interior designer Maddalena's Inc., 1998—; realtor Edward Surovell Realtors, Tecumseh, Mich., 2000—. Cons. in field. Big sister Big Bros./Big Sisters Jackon County. Mem. Am. Soc. Interior Designers (profl. mem., assoc. Ctrl. Mich. chpt.), Nat. Assn. Realtors, Jackson Area Assn. Realtors, Mich. Assn. Realtors. Avocations: tennis, golf, gardening, skiing. Home: 701 Church St Grass Lake MI 49240-9206 Office: Maddalena's Inc 2418 W Michigan Ave Jackson MI 49202-3920 also: Edward Surovell Realtors 145 E Chicago Blvd Tecumseh MI 49286-1546 E-mail: kkendall@quixnet.com.

KENDALL, LEON THOMAS, finance and real estate educator, retired insurance company executive; b. Elizabeth, N.J., May 20, 1928; m. Nancy O'Donnell; 6 children. BS in Acctg. magna cum laude, St. Vincent Coll., 1949; MBA in Mktg., Ind. U., 1950, DBA in Econs., 1956; LLD (hon.), Cardinal Stritch Coll., 1988. Teaching asso. Ind. U. Sch. Bus., 1950-53; economist Fed. Res. Bd., Atlanta, 1956-58, U.S. Savs. and Loan League, Chgo., 1958-64; v.p., economist N.Y. Stock Exchange, 1964-67; pres. Assn. Stock Exchange Firms, 1967-72, Securities Industry Assn., 1972-74; chmn., dir. Mortgage Guaranty Ins. Corp., Milw., 1974-89; vice chmn. MGIC Investment Corp., 1980-89; Norman Strunk prof. fin. instns. Kellogg Sch. of Mgmt., Northwestern U., Evanston, Ill., 1988—. Bd. dirs. Anthracite Capital, Inc., CoreCar, Inc., CBOE; commr. N.J. Mortgage Study, 1971-72; mem. Wis. Expenditures Study Commn., 1985-86. Author: (with Miles Colean) Who Buys the Houses, 1958, The Savings and Loan Business: Its Purposes, Functions and Economic Justification, 1962, Anatomy of the Residential Mortgage, 1964, Readings in Financial Institutions, 1965, The Exchange Community in 1975, 1965; editor: Thrift and Home Ownership: Writings of Fred T. Greene, 1962; contbr.: chpt. to American Enterprise: The Next Ten Years, 1961, The World Capital Shortage, 1977, Securitization Primer, 1996. Mem. deans adv. council Ind. U. Sch. Bus.; mem. adv. bd. Fed. Home Loan Mortgage Corp; vis. com. divsn. social scis. U. Chgo. Served with USAF, 1954-56. Grad. fellow Ind. U., 1950-53; Found. for Econ. Edn. fellow Pitts. Plate Glass Co., 1952 Mem. Acad. Alumni Fellows Ind. U. Sch. Bus., Lambda Alpha, Delta Epsilon Sigma, Beta Gamma Sigma. Office: MGIC Investment Corp MGIC Pla Milwaukee WI 53201

KENDALL, REBECCA O. lawyer, pharmaceutical company executive; BS, Ind. U., 1970, JD, 1975. Bar: Ind. 1975. Lectr. Ind. U. Sch. Bus., 1979-80; counsel Nat. Ins. Assn., 1980-81; atty. Eli Lilly and Co., Indpls., 1981-83, sec., gen. counsel Elanco Products co. divsn., 1983-88, sec., gen. counsel Pharm. divsn., 1988-93, dep. gen. counsel, asst. sec., 1993-95, v.p., gen. counsel, 1995-98, now sr. v.p., gen. counsel, 1998—. Office: Eli Lilly and Co Lilly Corp Ctr Indianapolis IN 46285-0001

KENDE, HANS JANOS, plant physiology educator; b. Szekesfehervar, Hungary, Jan. 18, 1937; came to U.S., 1965, naturalized, 1970; s. Istvan and Katalin (Grosz) K.; m. Gabriele F. Guggenheim, May 15, 1960; children: Benjamin R., Michael, Judith N. Nat. Ph.D., U. Zurich, Switzerland, 1960; DSc (hon.), U. Fribourg, Switzerland, 1995. Research Council fellow, Ottawa, Can., 1960-61; research fellow Calif. Inst. Tech., Pasadena, 1961-63; plant physiologist Negev Inst. of Arid Zone Research, Beersheva, Israel, 1963-65; assoc. prof. Mich. State U.-Dept. Energy Plant Research Lab., East Lansing, 1965-69, prof., 1969—; dir. Dept. Energy Plant Research Lab. Mich. State U., 1985-88; program mgr. for plant growth and devel. USDA, Washington, 1992. Vis. prof. Swiss Fed. Inst. Tech., Zurich, 1972-73, 79-80; vis. scientist Friedrich Miescher Institut, Basel, Switzerland, 1991. Mem. editorial bd. Plant Physiology, 1969-84, Biochemie und Physiologie der Pflanzen, 1975-93, Plant Molecular Biology, 1981-83, Planta, 1982-97; (editorial bd.) Jour. Plant Growth Regulation, 1982-84, Sci., 1997-2000, Plant Jour., 1998—; contbr. articles to profl. jours. Mem. adv. panel for devel. biology NSF, 1974-77. Guggenheim fellow, 1972-73 Fellow AAAS; mem. NAS, Am. Soc. Plant Biologists (Stephen Hales prize 1998), Leopoldina German Acad. Natural Scis. Home: 805 Virginia Ave East Lansing MI 48823-2835 Office: Mich State U Plant Rsch Lab East Lansing MI 48824

KENDZIOR, ROBERT JOSEPH, marketing executive; b. Mar. 24, 1952; s. Joseph W. and Josephine R. Kendzior. BArch, Ill. Inst. Tech., 1975. Account supr. Burger King Corp. Rogers Merchandising, Inc., Chgo., 1975-77; account exec. Walgreen Corp. Eisaman, Johns & Laws Advt., Inc., 1977-78; v.p. mktg. Dunkin Donuts Am., Inc., Randolph, Mass., 1978-95; v.p., chief mktg. officer Factory Card Outlet Am., Inc., Chgo., 1995-98; v.p. internat. mktg. Allied Domecq Retailing, 1999—; v.p. Internat. Mktg. and Retail Concepts, Randolph. Recipient Most Valuable Promotion award PepsiCo, 1984. Mem. Triangle Fraternity.

KENISON, RAYMOND ROBERT, fraternal organization administrator, director; b. Mo., Sept. 23, 1932; s. Raymond Roy and Emma Oleta (Holder) K.; m. Marjorie White, Feb. 1, 1955; children: Debra Kenison Brown, Peggy Kenison Crim, Raymond Roger, Robert B. AA, Hannibal LaGrange Coll., 1953; BA, U. Mo., 1961; postgrad., Cen. Bapt. Sem., Kansas City, 1957, Midwestern Bapt. Sem., 1965; cert. fin. planner, Coll. Fin. Planning, Denver; DivD, Hannibal LaGrange Coll., 1994. Cert. instr. Pastor First Bapt.Ch., Bates City, Mo., 1954-56, Friendship Bapt. Ch., Mexico, 1956-62, Immanuel Bapt. Ch., Hannibal, 1962-77; dir. devel. Mo. Bapt. Children's Home, Bridgeton, 1977-80, exec. dir., 1980—; pres., 1992—. Pres. bd. trustees Hannibal-Lagrange Coll.; co-founder, pres. Viability R & D Group. Mem. Child Welfare League of Am. Inc.; Nat. Soc. of Fund Raising Execs.; pres. Hannibal Coun. Alcohol and Drug Abuse; bd. dirs. Hannibal Cmty. Chest, 1974-79, pres. Hannibal Ministerial Alliance; bd. dirs. Alliance for Children and Families, Mo. Alliance for Children and Families. Kenison Complex named in his honor. Mem. Nat. Foster Parents Assn., So. Bapt. Child Care Execs. (pres.), Nat. Assn. of Homes for Children (sec.), Mo. Child Care Assn. (bd. dirs., pres. 1994—), S.W. Assn. of Child Care Execs., Inst. CFPs, Hannibal Investment Club (pres. 1976-78, 82-83), Viability R&D Group (co-founder, pres.). Home: 193 Lake Apollo Dr Hannibal MO 63401-6218 Office: Mo Bapt Children's Home 11300 Saint Charles Rock Rd Bridgeton MO 63044-2793

KENLEY, HOWARD, state legislator; b. Ft. Stockton, Tex., Mar. 28, 1945; s. Howard A. Jr. and Elvira (Hayten) K.; m. Sally Butler; children: John, Bill, Betsy. AB, Miami U., Oxford, Ohio, 1967; JD, Harvard U., 1972. Atty. Cadick, Burns, Duck & Neighbours, Indpls., 1972-73; pres., owner Kenley's Supermarkets, Noblesville, Ind., 1974-93; judge Noblesville City Ct., 1974-89; senator Dist. 20 Ind. State Senate, 1992—, mem. fin., judiciary, edn., planning and pub. policy coms., mem. fin. com., judiciary com., planning/pub. svc. com. Bd. dirs. Society Bank of Ind. Bd. dirs. Boys and Girls Club of Noblesville. With U.S. Army, 1969-71. Deocrated Army Commendation medal; named Bd. Mem. of Yr. Noblesville Boys and Girls Club, 1984-85. Mem. Ind. State Bar Assn., Hamilton County Bar Assn., 50 Club of Hamilton County, Elks, Beta theta Pi.

KENLEY, LUKE, state legislator; m. Sarah Butler; 3 children. Student, Miami U., 1967; JD, Harvard U., 1972. With law firm Cadick, Burns, Duck &@ Neighbours, 1972-74; pres. Kenley's Supermarkets Inc., 1974-98; mem. Ind. State Senate, 1992—, mem. pub. policy com., edn. com., budget subcom., chair pub. affairs subcom., mem. judiciary com., mem. probate code and trusts subcom., chmn. adminstrv. rules oversight com. Bd. dirs. Noblesville Boys and Girls Club; active First United Meth. Ch.; judge Noblesville City Ct., 1974-89. Office: 200 W Washington St Indianapolis IN 46204

KENLY, GRANGER FARWELL, marketing consultant, college official; b. Portland, Oreg., Feb. 15, 1919; s. F. Corning and Ruth (Farwell) K.; m. Suzanne Warner, Feb. 7, 1948 (div. Nov., 1977); children: Margaret F., Kenly Granger Farwell Jr.; m. Stella S. Angevin, Oct. 8, 1978. AB cum laude, Harvard U., 1941. Adminstrv. asst. to v.p. Poole Bros., Inc., Chgo., 1941-42; asst. advt. mgr. Sunset Mag., San Francisco, 1946-47; pub. relations, sales promotion mgr. Pabco Products, Inc., 1947-51; v.p. mgmt., supr. Needham, Louis & Brorby, Inc., Chgo., 1951-60; mgr. mktg. plans dept. Pure Oil Co., Palatine, Ill., 1961-62, v.p. pub. relations, personnel, 1962-66; v.p. pub. affairs Abbott Labs., North Chicago, Ill., 1966-71; v.p. corporate and investor relations IC Industries, Inc., Chgo., 1972-83; career devel. officer Lake Forest Coll., Ill., 1984—; chmn., exec. bd. Keystone-Garrett Properties, Houston, 1984—. Mem. 22d Ann. Global Strategy Conf. U.S. Naval War Coll., 1970; mem. pub. affairs council Am. Productivity Ctr., 1980-85. Bd. dirs. Evanston Hosp., 1963-82; trustee Ill. Soc. Prevention Blindness, 1958-64, Lawson YMCA, Chgo., 1972-83, Off the Street Boys Club, Chgo., 1978—; mem. Exec. Service Corps Chgo., 1984—. Served to maj. USAAF, 1942-46, ETO. Mem. Chgo. Club, Univ. Club (Chgo.), Onwentsia Club (Lake Forest, Ill.), Edgartown (Mass.) Yacht Club, The Reading Room (Edgartown), Hole-in-the-Wall Golf Club (Naples, Fla.), Naples Yacht Club. Republican. Episcopalian. Home: 945 Beverly Pl Lake Forest IL 60045-3903 Office: Lake Forest Coll Career Placement Officer Sheridan and College Rd Lake Forest IL 60045

KENNEDY, B(YRL) J(AMES), medicine and oncology educator; b. Plainview, Minn., June 24, 1921; s. Arthur Sylvester and Anna Margaret (Fassbender) K.; m. Margaret Bradford Hood, Oct. 21, 1950; children: Sharon Lynn, James Bradford, Scott Douglas, Grant Preston. BA, BS, U. Minn., 1943, MB, 1945, MD, 1946; MS in Exptl. Medicine, McGill U., Montreal, Que., Can., 1951. Diplomate Am. Bd. Internal Medicine, Am. Bd. Med. Oncology. Intern in medicine Mass. Gen. Hosp., Boston, 1945-46, resident in medicine, 1946, 51-52; fellow in medicine Harvard Med. Sch.-Mass. Gen. Hosp., 1947-49; rsch. fellow in medicine McGill U. Med. Sch., 1949-50; fellow in medicine Cornell U. Med. Sch., N.Y.C., 1950-51; asst. prof. medicine U. Minn. Med. Sch., Mpls., 1952-57, assoc. prof., 1957-67, prof., 1967-91, Masonic prof. oncology, 1970-91, prof. emeritus, 1991—, Regents prof. medicine, 1988-91, Regents prof. emeritus, 1991—. Contbr. articles to profl. jours. Past chmn. bd. Presbyn. Homes of Minn., St. Paul, bd. dirs., 1964-93. Recipient Nat. Divsn. award Am. Cancer Soc., 1975, Recognition award Assn. Comty. Cancer Ctrs., 1985, Spl. Recognition award Am. Soc. Internal Medicine, 1989, Charles Bolles Bolles-Roger award Hennepin Med. Soc., 1996; B.J. Kennedy Lectureship in Oncology named in his honor Minn. Med. Found., 1990, B.J. Kennedy Oncology Scholarship named in his honor Minn. Med. Found., 1998, B.J. Kennedy Chair in Med. Oncology named in his honor Minn. Med. Found., 1999. Fellow ACP (master 1996, Laureate award Minn. 1992); mem. AMA (Sci. Achievement award 1992), Am. Cancer Soc. (Disting. Svc. award 1991, Medal of Honor-Clin. Rsch. award 1996), Am. Soc. Clin. Oncology (pres. 1987-88), Am. Assn. Cancer Rsch., Am. Assn. Cancer Edn. (pres. 1982-83, Margaret Hay Edwards Achievement medal 1990), Minn. Med. Alumni (Harold S. Diehl award 1999), Town and Country Club (St. Paul). Avocation: photography. Home: 1949 E River Pky Minneapolis MN 55414-3675 Office: U Minn Med Sch and Hosp MMC 286 Mayo 420 Delaware St SE Minneapolis MN 55455-0374 E-mail: kenne018@tc.umn.edu.

KENNEDY, CHARLES ALLEN, lawyer; b. Maysville, KY, Dec. 11, 1940; s. Elmer Earl and Mary Frances Kennedy; m. Patricia Ann Louderback, Dec. 9, 1961; 1 child, Mimi Mignon. AB, Morehead State Coll., 1965, MA in Edn., 1968; JD, U. Akron, 1969; LLM, George Washington U., 1974. Bar: Ohio 1969. Asst. cashier Citizens Bank, Felicity, Ohio, 1961-63; tchr Triway Local Sch. Dist., Wooster, 1965-67; with office of gen. counsel Fgn. Agr. and Spl. Programs Divsn. USDA, Washington, 1969-71; ptnr. Kauffman, Eberhart, Cicconetti & Kennedy Co., Wooster, 1972-86, Kennedy, Cicconetti, Knowlton & BuyTendyk, LPA, Wooster, 1986—. Mem. ABA, FBA, ATLA, Am. Coll. Barristers, Ohio State Bar Assn., Ohio Acad. Trial Lawyers, Wayne County Bar Assn., Exch. Club, Lions, Elks, Phi Alpha Delta, Phi Delta Kappa. Republican. Home: 1770 Burbank Rd Wooster OH 44691-2240 Office: Kennedy Cicconetti & Know Ken 558 N Market St Wooster OH 44691-3406

KENNEDY, CORNELIA GROEFSEMA, federal judge; b. Detroit, Aug. 4, 1923; d. Elmer H. and Mary Blanche (Gibbons) Groefsema; m. Charles S. Kennedy, Jr. (dec.); 1 son, Charles S. III. B.A., U. Mich., 1945, J.D. with distinction, 1947; LL.D. (hon.), No. Mich. U., 1971, Eastern Mich. U., 1971, Western Mich. U., 1973, Detroit Coll. Law, 1980, U. Detroit, 1987. Bar: Mich. bar 1947. Law clk. to Chief Judge Harold M. Stephens, U.S. Ct. of Appeals, Washington, 1947-48; assoc. Elmer H. Groefsema, Detroit, 1948-52; partner Markle & Markle, 1952-66; judge 3d Judicial Circuit Mich., 1967-70; dist. judge U.S. Dist. Ct., Eastern Dist. Mich., Detroit, 1970-79, chief judge, 1977-79; circuit judge U.S. Ct. Appeals, (6th cir.), 1979-99, sr. judge, 1999—. Mem. Commn. on the Bicentennial of the U.S. Constitution (presdl. appointment). Recipient Sesquicentennial award U. Mich. Fellow Am. Bar Found.; mem. ABA, Mich. Bar Assn. (past chmn. negligence law sect.), Detroit Bar Assn. (past dir.), Fed. Bar Assn., Am. Judicature Soc., Nat. Assn. Women Lawyers, Am. Trial Lawyers Assn., Nat. Conf. Fed. Trial Judges (past chmn.), Fed. Jud. Fellows Commn. (bd. dirs.), Fed. Jud. Ctr. (bd. dirs.), Phi Beta Kappa. Office: US Ct of Appeals US Courthouse 231 W Lafayette St Rm 744 Detroit MI 48226-2700

KENNEDY, GEORGE DANNER, chemical company executive; b. Pitts., May 30, 1926; s. Thomas Reed and Lois (Smith) K.; m. Valerie Putis; children: Charles Reed, Jamey Kathleen, Susan Patton, Timothy Christian. BA, Williams Coll., 1948. With Scott Paper Co., 1947-52, Champion Paper Co., 1952-65; pres. Brown Co., 1965-71; exec. v.p. Internat. Minerals & Chem. Corp., Northbrook, Ill., 1971-78, pres., 1978-86; chmn. Mallinckrodt Group (formerly IMCERA), St. Louis, 1986—, CEO, 1983-91; also bd. dirs., chmn. exec. com. IMCERA (formerly Internat. Minerals & Chem. Corp.), Northbrook, Ill. Former bd. dirs. Kemper Found., Brunewick Corp., Smurfit Stone Corp., Ill. Tool Works; former chmn. nominting com. Kemper Nat.; former bd. dirs. Scotsman Industries, Inc.; former chmn. compensation com., bd. dirs. exec. com. Am. Nat. Can Co.; dir. Health Share, Acton, Mass; mng. ptnr. Berkshires Capital Investors, Willimstown, Mass. Bd. dirs. Children's Meml. Hosp. and Children's Meml. Med. Ctr., Inst. Internat. Edn., Sand County Found.; trustee Chgo. Symphony; gov. mem. Chgo. Orch. Assn.; dir. Lyric Opera Chgo., Ctr. for Workforce Preparation and Quality Edn.; regional trustee Boys and Girls Club of Am.; trustee Nat. Com. Against Drunk Driving. Mem. Indian Hill Club, Chgo. Club, Sleepy Hollow Country Club, Taconic Golf Club. Office: PO Box 559 Winnetka IL 60093-0559

KENNEDY, JACK, secondary education journalism educator; b. Iowa City, July 12, 1950; s. John William and Barbara Fern (Guffey) K.; m. Kathleen Ann Gowey, Sept. 25, 1971; children: Lesley Kathleen, Sara Ann, Philip John. BA in English, U. Iowa, 1976, MA in Edn., 1981. Tchr., journalism adviser Regina High Sch., Iowa City, 1976-80, City H.S., Iowa City, 1980-99, vice prin., 1999—2001; tchr. Heritage H.S., Littleton, Colo., 2002—. Journalism adv. Heritage H.S., 2002—. With USAF, 1971-74. Nat. HS Journalism Teacher of the Yr., Dow Jones Newspaper Fund, 1993. Mem.: NEA, Journalism Edn. Assn. Democrat. Avocations: reading, singing, coaching youth sports. Office: City High Sch 1900 Morningside Dr Iowa City IA 52245-4669 Home: 1473 N Camino Villa Bonita Tucson AZ 85715-5102

KENNEDY, JOHN PATRICK, lawyer, corporate executive; b. Oct. 2, 1943; s. Arch R. and Kathryn R. (Delahunty) K.; children: Kathleen, Elizabeth, Christina, Patrick, Lindsay. BA in Econs., U. Kans., 1965, JD, 1967; MBA, U. Mo., 1972, LLM, 1973. Bar: Kans. 1967, Mo. 1968, Ohio 1973, Wis. 1985, U.S. Supreme Ct. 1972, U.S. Dist. Ct. (we. dist.) Mo. 1972, U.S. dist. Ct. Kans. 1967. Trial atty. Kodas, Gingerich & Stites, Kansas City, Mo., 1967-69; sr. atty. Mobay Chem. Co., 1969-73; v.p., gen. counsel, corp. sec. Johnson Controls, Inc., Milw., 1984—. Small bus. advisor, venture capitalist. Contbr. articles to profl. jours. Served with USAR, 1967-73. Recipient Wall St. Jour. award, 1972, A. Jurisprudence awards, 1966-67. Mem. ABA, Ohio Bar Assn., Columbus Bar Assn., Wis. Bar Assn., Am. Corp. Counsel Assn. Democrat. Roman Catholic. Office: Johnson Controls Inc PO Box 591 5757 N Green Bay Ave Milwaukee WI 53201

KENNEDY, JOSEPH PAUL, polymer scientist, researcher; b. Budapest, Hungary, May 18, 1928; came to U.S., 1956; s. Laszlo and Rosa (Farkas) K.; m. Ingeborg G. Hausen, Feb. 10, 1956; children: Katherine, Cynthia, Julie PhD, U. Vienna, Austria, 1954; MBA, Rutgers U., 1961; hon. doctorate, Kossuth U., Hungary, 1989. Research fellow Sorbonne, U. Paris, 1955; research assoc. McGill U., Montreal, Que., Can., 1956; research chemist Celanese Corp., Summit, N.J., 1957-59; sr. research assoc. Esso Research Engring. Co., Linden, 1959-70; prof. polymer sci. U. Akron, Ohio, 1970-80, disting. prof. polymer sci. and chemistry, 1980—. Cons. Akron Cationic Polymer Devel. Co., 1983— Author: Cationic Polymerization, 1975, Carbocationic Polymerization, 1982, Designed Polymers by Carbocationic Macromolecular Engineering: Theory and Practice, 1992. Named Outstanding Researcher Alumni Assn. U. Akron, 1979; recipient Morley award and medal Cleve. Am. Chem. Soc., 1982, Am. Chem. Soc. award in Polymer Chemistry, 1995, award of disting. svc. in polymer sci. Soc. of Polymer Sci., Japan, 2000. Mem. Hungarian Acad. Scis., Am. Chem. Soc. (Polymer Chemistry award 1985, Applied Polymer Sci. award 1995, George Stafford Whitby award rubber divsn. 1996). Avocation: Japanese art of the Meiji. Home: 510 Saint Andrews Dr Akron OH 44303-1228 Office: U Akron Inst Polymer Sci Akron OH 44325-0001 E-mail: kennedy@polymer.uakron.edu.

KENNEDY, LAWRENCE ALLAN, mechanical engineering educator; b. Detroit, May 31, 1937; s. Clifford Earl and Emma Josephine (Muller) K.; m. Valaree J. Lockhart, Aug. 3, 1958; children: Joanne E., Julie A., Janet A., Raymond L., Jill M., Brian G. BS, U. Detroit, 1960; MS, Northwestern U., 1962, PhD, 1964. Registered profl. engr., N.Y. Chmn. dept., prof. mech. and aero. engring. SUNY-Buffalo, 1964-83; chmn. dept. mech. engring., prof. Ohio State U., Columbus, 1983-93, Ralph W. Kurtz disting. prof., 1992-95; dean coll. engring. U. Ill., Chgo., 1995—, prof. mech. engring. and chem. engring., 1995—. Vis. assoc. prof. mech. and aero. engring. U. Calif.-San Diego, 1968-69, VonKarman Inst., Rhode-St. Genese, Belgium, 1971-72; Goebel vis. prof. mech. and aero. engring. U. Mich., Ann Arbor, 1980-81; vis. prof. mech. & aerospace engring. Princeton U., 1993-94; cons. Cornell Aero. Lab., Buffalo, 1968-72, Tech. Adv. Service, Fort Washington, Pa., 1969— , Ashland Chem. Corp., Dublin, Ohio, 1983-90, Mech. Engring. Sci. and Application, Buffalo, 1972-83, Columbia Gas, 1987-92; vis. faculty fellow mech. and aerospace engring. Princeton U., 1994. Contbr. numerous articles on engring. to profl. jours.; editor: Progress in Astronautics and Aeros., Vol. 58, 1978, Exptl. Thermal and Fluid Scis., 1987-95; editor in chief Jour. Thermal & Fluid Scis., 1997—; assoc. editor Applied Mechanics Revs., 1985-88, Jour. Propulsion & Power, 1992-98. Recipient Ralph R. Teetor award 1984, AT&T Found. award, 1987, Ralph Coats Roe award, 1993; NATO fellow, 1971-72, NSF fellow, 1968-69, W.P. Murphy fellow, 1960-63; Agard lectr., 1971-72. Fellow AIAA, ASME, AAAS; mem. Am. Phys. Soc., Combustion Inst., Am. Soc. Engring. Edn., Soc. of Automotive Engrs. Roman Catholic. Avocations: skiing, squash, hiking, music. Home: 24306 Turnberry Ct Naperville IL 60564-8127 Office: Coll Engring M/C 159 851 S Morgan St Chicago IL 60607-7042

KENNEDY, MARK R. congressman; b. Benson, Minn., 1957; m. Debbie; 4 children. B.A, St. John's U., Minn.; MBA, U. Mich. CPA. Mem. U.S. Congress from 2nd Minn. dist., 2001—. Mem. Congressional com. Agriculture, Transportation and Infrastructure; subcom. Gen. Farm Commodities, Risk Mngmt., Conservation, Credit, Rural Devel. and Rsch., Aviation, Highways and Transit (vice ch.). Office: 1415 Longworth House Office bldg Washington DC 20515

KENNEDY, RAYMOND F. manufacturing executive; m. Mary Kennedy; 3 children. B in Bus. Mgmt., St. John's U.; postgrad., NYU. Pres. Delta and Peerless Faucet Cos., 1978-83; group pres. Masco Corp., 1983-88, pres. bldg. products, 1989-96, pres., COO, 1996—. Office: Masco Corp 21001 Van Born Rd Taylor MI 48180-1300

KENNELLY, SISTER KAREN MARGARET, retired academic administrator, church administrator, nun; b. Graceville, Minn., Aug. 4, 1933; d. Walter John Kennelly and Clara Stella Eastman. BA, Coll. St. Catherine, St. Paul, 1956; MA, Cath. U. Am., 1958; PhD, U. Calif., Berkeley, 1962. Joined Sisters of St. Joseph of Carondelet, Roman Cath. Ch., 1954. Prof. history Coll. St. Catherine, 1962-71, acad. dean, 1971-79; exec. dir. Nat. Fedn. Carondelet Colls., 1979-82; province dir. Sisters of St. Joseph of Carondelet, St. Paul, 1982-88; pres. Mt. St. Mary's Coll., L.A., 1989-2000, pres. emerita, 2000—; congl. dir. Sisters of St. Joseph of Carondelet, St. Louis, 2002—. Cons. N. Ctrl. Accreditation Assn., Chgo., 1974—84, Ohio Bd. Regents, Columbus, 1983—89; trustee colls., hosps., Minn., Wis., Calif., 1972—; chmn. Sisters St. Joseph Coll. Consortium, 1989—93. Editor, co-author: American Catholic Women, 1989; author (with others): Women of Minnesota, 1977; author: Women Religious and the Intellectual Life: The North American Achievement, 1996; co-editor: Gender Identities in American Catholocism, 2001; : Catholic Colleges for Women in America, 2002. Bd. dirs. Am. Coun. on Edn., 1997—99, Nat. Assn. Ind. Colls. and Univs., 1997—2000, Assn. Cath. Colls. and Univs., 1996—2000, Western Region Nat. Holocaust Mus., 1997—2000. Fellow Fulbright, 1964. Mem.: Western Assn. Schs. and Colls. (sr. commn. 1997—2000), Assn. Cath. Colls. and Univs. (exec. bd. 1996—2000), Am. Coun. Edn. (bd. dirs. 1997—99), Nat. Assn. Ind. Colls. and Univs. 1997—99, Am. Assn. Rsch. Historians Medieval Spain, Medieval Acad., Am. Cath. Hist. Soc., Am. Hist. Soc. Avocations: skiing, cuisine. Office: Congl Ctr 2311 Lindbergh Blvd Saint Louis MO 63131 E-mail: kkennelly33@hotmail.com.

KENNER, HOWARD A. state legislator; b. Chgo., Dec. 26, 1957; s. Tyrone and Emma (Payne) K. BS, U. Ill., 1980. CPA, Ill. Ill. state rep. Dist. 24. Mem. Appropriations, Gen. Svcs., Human Svcs., Health Care Availability and Access, Insurance Coms.; chmn. Com. on State Govt. Adminstr.; ptnr. Goodall, Kenner & Assoc. CPAs, Chgo. Office: 76 E 61st St Chicago IL 60637 also: 200 S Michigan Ave Chicago IL 60604-2402

KENNETT, ROBERT L. medical organization executive; V.p. pub. Jour. AMA, Chgo. Office: AMA 515 N State St Chicago IL 60610-4325

KENNEY, BRIAN A. financial services executive; BBA, U. Notre Dame, 1981; MBA in Fin., U. Mich., 1983. With Morton Internat., Inc., Peterson & Co., United Air Lines Corp.; mng. dir., corp. fin. & banking AMR Corp., 1990-95; treas. GATX Corp., Chgo., 1995-99, v.p., CFO, 1999—. Office: GATX Corp 500 W Monroe St Chicago IL 60661

KENNEY, CRANE H. lawyer; b. 1962; BA, U. Notre Dame; JD, U. Mich. Bar: Ill., 1988. Sr. v.p., gen. counsel and sec. Tribune Co., Chgo., 1996—. Office: Tribune Co 435 N Michigan Ave Ste 600 Chicago IL 60611-4001

KENNEY, FRANK DEMING, lawyer; b. Chgo., Feb. 20, 1921; s. Joseph Aloysius and Mary Edith (Deming) K.; m. Virginia Stuart Banning, Feb. 12, 1944; children: Claudia Kenney Carpenter, Pamela Kenney Voetberg, Sarah Kenney Swanson, Stuart Deming Kenney AB, U. Chgo., 1948, JD, 1949. Bar: Ill. 1948, U.S. Dist. Ct. (no. dist.) Ill. 1949. Assoc. J.O. Brown, Chgo., 1948-49; assoc., ptnr. Winston & Strawn, and predecessors, 1949-92, ret., 1992. 1st lt. AUS, 1942-46, CBI, PTO. Mem. ABA, Ill. Bar Assn., Chgo. Bar Assn. (chmn. real property law com. 1982-83), Lawyers Club Chgo., Fox River Valley Hunt Club, Quadrangle Club, Nat. Beagle Club Am. (bd. dirs. 1981-92), Spring Creek Basset Hunt Club (master 1977-93, chmn. bd., 1993-98, hon. chmn. bd. 1998—), Kappa Sigma (nat. housing fin. commr. for U.S. and Can., 1959-91). Republican. Roman Catholic. Home: PO Box 581 333 Old Sutton Rd Barrington IL 60010-9368 Office: Winston & Strawn 35 W Wacker Dr Ste 3800 Chicago IL 60601-1695

KENNEY, WILLIAM PATRICK, state legislator; b. San Francisco, Jan. 20, 1955; s. Charles Frances and Barbara Clare Kenney; m. Sandra Louise Ehrlich, Dec. 28, 1979; children: Kristin Allison, William Charles, Carlton Patrick, Elizabeth Alexandria. AA, Saddleback Jr. Coll., 1976; BA, U. No. Colo., 1978. Player Kansas City Chiefs, 1978-89, Washington Redskins, 1989; broker, officer Bill Kenney and Assocs., Lee's Summit, Mo., 1992—; mem. Mo. Senate from 8th dist., Jefferson City, 1995—. Named Most Valuable Player Kansas City Chiefs, 1983; named to Pro Bowl Am. Football Conf. NFL, 1983. Home and Office: 2808 SW Arthur Dr Lees Summit MO 64082-4062

KENNING, JOHN CHARLES, former marketing professional; b. Pitts., Mar. 10, 1961; s. Jack Charles and Barbara Ann (King) K. BS, Miami (Ohio) U., 1983. Mktg. rep. Lakewoy Mfg., Huron, Ohio, 1982-84, Cen. Ref., Chgo., 1984-85; regional v.p. mktg. Comdisco, St. Louis, 1985—. Mem. Glen Echo Club. Republican. Avocations: golf, investments, skiing. Office: Comdisco 11698 Lilburn Park Rd Saint Louis MO 63146-3535

KENNON, ROZMOND HERRON, retired physical therapist; b. Birmingham, Ala., Dec. 12, 1935; m. Gloria Oliver; children: Shawn, Rozmond Jr. BA, Talldega Coll., 1956; cert., U. Colo., 1957. Asst. chief phys. therapist St. John's Hosp., St. Paul, 1957-58, Creigthon Meml. St. Joseph's Hosp., Omaha, 1958-61; asst. chief, phys. therapist Sister Kenny Inst., Mpls., 1962, chief phys. therapy, 1962-64; cons. in phys. therapy Mt. Sinai Hosp., 1963-70; pvt. practice, 1964-98. Contbr. articles to profl. jours. Bd. dirs. Southdale YMCA, Edina Human Rights, Southside Med. Ctr., Mpls., Boy Scouts Am.; trustee Talladega (Ala.) Coll.; pres., CEO Daniel Kennon and Verna Herron Kennon Family Found.; chmn. fin. com. Talladega Bd. Trustees; exec. bd. dirs. Greater Ala. Coun. Boy Scouts Am. Mem. Am. Phys. Therapy Assn., Am. Registry Phys. Therapists, Ala. Phys. Therapy Assn. (mem. social-econ. com., past chmn. profl. practice com., bd. dirs., past sec.). Home: 5120 Lake Crest Cir Hoover AL 35226-5027

KENRICH, JOHN LEWIS, retired lawyer; b. Lima, Ohio, Oct. 17, 1929; s. Clarence E. and Rowena (Stroh) Katterheinrich; m. Betty Jane Roehll, May 26, 1951; children: John David, Mary Jane, Kathryn Ann, Thomas Roehll, Walter Clarence. BS, Miami U., Oxford, Ohio, 1951; LLB, U. Cin., 1953. Bar: Ohio 1953, Mass. 1969. Asst. counsel B.F. Goodrich Co., Akron, Ohio, 1956-65; asst. sec., counsel W.R. Grace & Co., Cin., 1965-68, v.p. Splty. Products Group divsn., 1970-71; corp. counsel, sec. Standex Internat. Corp., Andover, Mass., 1969-70; v.p., sec. Chemed Corp., Cin., 1971-82, sr. v.p., gen. counsel, 1982-86, exec. v.p., chief adminstrv. officer, 1986-91, ret., 1991. Trustee Better Bus. Bur., Cin., 1981-90; mem. bus. adv. coun. Miami U., 1986-88; mem. City Planning Commn., Akron, 1961-62; mem. bd. visitors Coll. Law U. Cin., 1988-92; mem. area coun. trustees Franciscan Sisters of Poor Found., Cin., 1989-93; bd. govs. Ohio River Valley chpt. Arthritis Found., 1992-95, 2000—; mem. Com. on Reinvestment City of Cin., 1991-93. 1st lt. JAGC U.S. Army, 1954-56. Mem. Cin. Bar Assn., Beta Theta Pi, Omicron Delta Kappa, Delta Sigma Pi, Phi Eta Sigma. Republican. Presbyterian. Home and Office: 504 Abilene Trl Cincinnati OH 45215-2515 E-mail: JKenrich@msn.com.

KENT, DEBORAH, automotive executive; div.; children: Jessica, Jordan. BA in Psychology, So. Ill. U.; MA in Indsl. Psychology, Washington U., St. Louis. Quality control supr., reliability engr. Ford Motor Co. Assembly Plant, Dearborn, Mich., area mgr. Wixom, 1987-92, mfg. mgr. Chgo., 1992-94, plant mgr. Avon Lake, Ohio, 1994—. Office: Ford Motor Co 650 Miller Rd Avon Lake OH 44012-2398

KENT, JERALD L. communications company executive; BA (hons.), MBA, Washington U. CPA, Mo. Tax mgr. Arthur Anderson & Co., 1979-83; from sr. v.p. to exec. v.p., CFO Cencom Cable Assocs., Inc., 1983-90, exec. v.p., CFO, 1990-93; prin., owner Charter Communications, St. Louis, 1993—. Bd. dirs. CCA Acquisition Corp., CCT Holdings Corp., CCA Holdings Corp., The Magic House Children's Mus. Chmn. finance com. Incarnate Word Ch. Recipient 1997 Regional Entrepreneurs of Yr. in Telecomms. and Entertainment award Ernst & Young, USA Today, DASDAQ, Kauffman Found., 1997. Mem. Young Pres. Orgn., Alumni Assn. Exec. com. Washington U. Office: Charter Communications Inc 12444 Powerscourt Dr Ste 100 Saint Louis MO 63131-3617 Fax: (314) 965-5761.

KEOUGH, MICHAEL J. paper manufacturing executive; b. 1952; With Internat. Paper, 1975-85, Crown Zellerbach, 1985; head multiwall and retail bag bus. Gaylord Container Corp., Deerfield, Ill., head corrugated container ops., 1993, v.p., gen. mgr. container ops., pres., COO, 2000—. Office: Gaylord Container Corp Ste 400 500 Lake Cook Rd Deerfield IL 60015-5269 Office Fax: 847-405-5628.

KERATA, JOSEPH J. secondary education educator; b. Cleve., Jan. 20, 1949; s. Joseph John and Lillian (Potocky) K.; m. Lynne E. Armington, July 20, 1990. BS in Edn., Ohio State U., 1971; MEd, Cleve. State U., 1978; postgrad., Ohio Wesleyan U., Princeton U. Tchr. sci. grades 7-8 Spellacy Jr. High Sch., Cleve., 1972-73; tchr. BSCS and gen. biology grades 10-12 Willoughby South High Sch., 1973-79; tchr. earth sci., physics, biology grades 10-12 Colegio Roosevelt, Lima, Peru, 1979-80; tchr. English adult edn. Academia Secretaria Y Typografia, 1980; tchr. gen. sci. grades 7-9 Eastlake Jr. High Sch., Willowick, Ohio, 1980-83; tchr. AP and honors biology Eastlake North High Sch., 1983—, chair dept. sci., 1984—. Mem. North Ctrl. Evaluation Team, 1978, cirriculum devel. and revision com., 1978, 85; judge sci. fairs several sch. dists., 1977—. Recipient Krecker Outstanding Sci. Dept. award, 1976, Outstanding Educator award Edinboro U., 1984, Sci. Tchr. of Yr. award Lubrizol Corp., 1991, Gov.'s Ednl. Leadership award, 1992, Ohio Tchr. of Yr. award, 1993; Martha Holden Jennings scholar, 1990; Woodrow Wilson Nat. fellow, 1992. Mem. NEA, Nat. Sci. Tchrs. Assn., Nat. Assn. Biology Tchrs., Ohio Edn. Assn., Ohio Acad. Sci., Willoughby-Eastlake Tchrs. Assn. (grievance chmn. 1981—), Cleve. Regional Assn. Biologists (original). Office: Eastlake North High Sch 34041 Stevens Blvd Eastlake OH 44095-2905

KERBER, LINDA KAUFMAN, historian, educator; b. N.Y.C., Jan. 23, 1940; d. Harry Hagman and Dorothy (Haber) Kaufman; m. Richard Kerber, June 5, 1960; children: Ross Jeremy, Justin Seth. AB cum laude, Barnard Coll., 1960; MA, NYU, 1961; PhD, Columbia U., 1968; DHL, Grinnell Coll., 1992. Instr., asst. prof. history Stern Coll., Yeshiva U., N.Y.C., 1963-68; asst. prof. history San Jose State Coll., (Calif.), 1969-70; vis. asst. prof. history Stanford U., 1970-71; asst. prof. history U. Iowa, Iowa City, 1971-75, prof., 1975-85, May Brodbeck prof., 1985—. Vis. prof. U. Chgo., 1991-92. Author: Federalists in Dissent: Imagery and Ideology in Jeffersonian America, 1970, paperback edit., 1980, 97, Women of the Republic: Intellect and Ideology in Revolutionary America, 1980, paperback edit., 1986, Toward an Intellectual History of Women, 1997, No Constitutional Right to Be Ladies: Women and the Obligations of Citizenship, 1998, paperback edit., 1999 (Littleton-Griswold prize in legal history Am. Hist. Assn., Joan Kelley prize in womens history Am. Hist. Assn.); co-editor: Women's America: Refocusing the Past, 1982, 5th edit., 2000, U.S. History As Women's History, 1995; mem. editl. bd. Signs: Jour. Women in Culture and Society; contbr. articles and book revs. to profl. jours. Fellow Danforth Found., NEH, 1976, 83-84, 94, Am. Coun. Learned Socs., 1975, Nat. Humanities Ctr., 1990-91, Guggenheim Found., 1990-91. Fellow Am. Acad. Arts and Scis.; mem. Orgn. Am. Historians (pres. 1996-97), Am. Hist. Assn., Am. Studies Assn. (pres. 1988), Am. Soc. for Legal History, Berkshire Conf. Women Historians, Soc. Am. Historians, Japan U.S. Friendship Commn., PEN/Am. Ctr. Jewish. Office: U Iowa Dept History Iowa City IA 52242

KERBER, RICHARD E. cardiologist; b. N.Y.C., May 10, 1939; s. Max and Pauline Kerber; m. Linda K. Kaufman; children: Ross, Justin. AB in Anthropology, Columbia U., 1960; MD, NYU, 1964. Diplomate Am. Bd. Internal Medicine, Am. Bd. Cardiology. Med. intern/resident Bellevue Hosp., N.Y.C., 1964—66; med. resident Stanford (Calif.) U. Hosp., 1968—69, cardiology fellow, 1969—71; asst. prof. internal medicine U. Iowa, Iowa City, 1971—74, assoc. prof. internal medicine, 1974—78, prof. medicine, 1978—. Editor: Echocardiography in Coronary Artery Disease, 1988. Capt. U.S. Army, 1966—68. Grantee RO1 grant, NHLBI, 1995—. Fellow: Am. Coll. Cardiology, Am. Heart Assn., Am. Coll. Cardiology (gov. for Iowa 1976—79, 1976—79), Am. Heart Assn. (chmn. coun. on cardiopulmonary and critical care 1997—99, 1997—99, award of Meritorious Achievement 1996, Scientific Coun. Dist. Achievement award 2001); mem.: Assn. Am. Physicians, Assn. Univ. Cardiologists, Assn. of Univ. Cardiologists, Am. Soc. for Clin. Investigation, Am. Soc. Echocardiology (sec. 1978—80, treas. 1993—95, v.p. 1995—97, pres. 1997—99, sec. 1978—80, treas. 1993—95, v.p. 1995—97, pres. 1997—99). Office: U Iowa Dept Medicine 200 Hawkins Dr Iowa City IA 52242-1009

KERBER, RONALD LEE, industrial corporation executive; b. Lafayette, Ind., July 2, 1943; s. John Andrew Kerber and Edith Helen (McMaster) Kerkhoff; children: John, Mark, Stephen, Jacqueline. BS, Purdue U., 1965; MS, Calif Inst. Tech., 1966, PhD, 1970. Registered profl. engr., Mich. Tech. staff Aerospace Corp., Los Angeles, 1971-72; prof. Mich. State U., E. Lansing, 1969-85, assoc. dean, 1984-85; program mgr. Defense Advanced Research Projects Agy., Arlington, Va., 1983-84; dep. undersec. U.S. Dept. Defense, Washington, 1985-88; v.p. advanced systems and tech. McDonnell Douglas Corp., St. Louis, 1988-89, v.p. tech. and bus. devel., 1989-91; exec. v.p., chief tech. officer Whirlpool Corp., Benton Harbor, 1991—. Contbr. articles to profl. jours. Mem. ASME, IEEE, Am. Phys. Soc.

KERBIS, GERTRUDE LEMPP, architect; m. Walter Peterhans (dec.); m. Donald Kerbis (div. 1972); children: Julian, Lisa, Kim. BS, U. Ill.; MA, Ill. Inst. Tech.; postgrad., Grad. Sch. Design, Harvard U., 1949-50. Archtl. designer Skidmore, Owings & Merrill, Chgo., 1954-59, C.F. Murphy Assocs., Chgo., 1959-62, 65-67; pvt. practice architecture Lempp Kerbis Assocs., 1967—; lectr. U. Ill., 1969; prof. William Rainey Harper Coll., 1970—95, Washington U., St. Louis, 1977, 82, Ill. Inst. Tech., 1989-91. Archtl. cons. Dept. Urban Renewal, City of Chgo.; mem. Northeastern Ill. Planning Commn., Open Land Project, Mid-North Community Orgn., Chgo. Met. Housing and Planning Council, Chgo. Mayor's Commn. for Preservation Chgo.'s Hist. Architecture; bd. dirs. Chgo. Sch. Architecture Found., 1972-76; trustee Chgo. Archtl. Assistance Ctr., Glessner House Found., Inland Architect Mag.; lectr. Art Inst. Chgo., U. N.Mex., Ill. Inst. Tech., Washington U., St. Louis, Ball State U., Muncie, Ind., U. Utah, Salt Lake City. Prin. archtl. works include U.S. Air Force Acad. dining hall, Colo., 1957, Skokie (Ill.) Pub. Library, 1959, Meadows Club, Lake Meadows, Chgo., 1959, O'Hare Internat. Airport 7 Continents Bldg, 1963; prin. developer and architect: Tennis Club, Highland Park, Ill., 1968, Watervliet, Mich. Tennis Ranch, 1970, Greenhouse Condominium, Chgo., 1976, Webster-Clark Townhouses, Chgo., 1986, Chappell Sch., 1993; exhibited at Chgo. Hist. Soc., 1984, Chgo. Mus. Sci. and Industry, 1985, Paris Exhbn. Chgo. Architects, 1985, Spertus Mus.; represented in permanent archtl. drawings collection Art Inst. Chgo. Active Art Inst. Chgo.. Recipient award for outstanding achievement in professions YWCA Met. Chgo., 1984 Fellow AIA (bd. dirs. Chgo. chpt. 1971-75, chpt. pres. 1980, nat. com. architecture, arts and recreation 1972-75, com. on design 1975-80, head subcom. inst. honors nomination); mem. Chgo. Women in Architecture (founder), Chgo. Network, Internat. Women's Forum, Arts Club Chgo., Cliff Dwellers (bd. dirs. 1987-88, pres. 1988, 89), Lambda Alpha. Office: Lempp Kerbis Assocs 172 W Burton Pl Chicago IL 60610-1310

KERIAN, JON ROBERT, retired judge; b. Grafton, N.D., Oct. 23, 1927; s. Cyril Robert and Elizabeth Antoinette (Kadlec) K.; m. Sylvia Ann Larson, Dec. 28, 1959; children: John, Ann. PhB, U. N.D., 1955, LLB, 1957, JD, 1971. Bar: N.D. 1957, U.S. Dist. Ct. N.D. 1958, U.S. Ct. Appeals (8th cir.) 1971, U.S. Supreme Ct. 1963. Pvt. practice law, Grand Forks, N.D., 1958-61; asst. atty. gen. State of N.D., Bismarck, 1961-67; ptnr. Bosard, McCutcheon, Kerian, Schmidt, Minot, N.D., 1967-80; dist. judge State of N.D., 1980-92, surrogate judge, 1993—. History instr. Bismarck State Coll., 1965-67; asst. city atty. City of Minot, 1968-76; atty. Zoning & Planning Commn., Minot, 1969-76; lectr. in field. Contbr. articles to profl. jours.; editor ABA newsletter, The Judges News, 1990—95. Mem. ABA (bd. editors Judges Jour. 1990-95), Western States Bar Conf. (pres. 1982-83), N.D. Bar Assn. (pres. 1979-80), Nat. Conf. State Trial Judges (exec. com. 1983-89). Home: 1800 8th St SW Minot ND 58701-6410 Office: PO Box 340 Minot ND 58702-0340

KERLEY, JAMES J. manufacturing executive; b. 1923; CFO Emmerson Electric Co., Inc., 1981-84, vice chmn., 1981-85, also bd. dirs.; acting chmn., CEO Rohr, Inc., Chula Vista, Calif., 1993, chmn., 1993—, also bd. dirs. Office: DT Industries Inc 907 W 5th St Dayton OH 45407-3306

KERLEY, JAMES JOSEPH, chemical company executive; b. Phila., Nov. 20, 1922; s. Philip William and Jane Veronica (Touey) K.; m. Dorothea Long Ickler, Oct. 24, 1944; children: Janet, James, Doris Ann, Suzanne. B.S. magna cum laude, Temple U., 1944; M.A., U. Pa., 1949, postgrad., 1949-51; LL.D., Temple U., 1969. Trainee Smith, Barney & Co., Phila., 1946-47; instr. finance Temple U., 1947-51; with Ford Motor Co., 1951-58; v.p., div. controller Crosley div. Avco Co., 1958-60; v.p., controller Ling-Temco-Vought Co., Dallas, 1960-62; v.p. finance Trans World Airlines, N.Y.C., 1962-65, sr. v.p., 1965-68, mem. exec. com., 1964-68; also dir.; fin. v.p. I.U. Internat. Corp., 1968-69; sr. v.p. fin. Lone Star Industries, Inc., 1969-70; former exec. v.p. Monsanto Co., chmn. fin. com., to 1980, also dir. Dir. Merc. Trust Co., Merc. Bancorp., both St. Louis, Mo. Pacific Corp., Rohr Industries, Inc., Assos. Corp. N.Am. Trustee St. Louis U. Served to 1st lt. USMCR, 1943-46, PTO. Mem. Beta Gamma Sigma. Office: DT Industries Inc 907 W 5th St Dayton OH 45407-3306

KERNAN, JOSEPH E. state official; BS, U. Notre Dame, 1968. Product mfg. mgr. Proctor & Gamble Co., 1976; sales exec. Schwarz Paper Co., 1976-80; city contr. South Bend, Ind., 1980-84; mayor, 1988; v.p., treas. MacWilliams Corp., 1984-88; lt. gov. State of Ind., Indpls., 1996—. Bd. trustees St. Joseph Med. Ctr. Bd. dirs. St. Joseph County Spl. Olympics, Notre Dame Club, Jr. Baseball Assn., Northside L.L.; campaign cabinet United Way, 1979-82; treas. Studebaker Music Inc. Comdr. USN, 1969-75. Recipient two Purple Heart medals, two Air medals, award for Individual Excellence.*

KERNS, BRIAN D. congressman; b. Ind., May 22, 1957; s. Noel and Rosalie K.; m. Lori Myers. BA in polit. sci., MPA, Ind. State U. Dir. publs. and pub. rels. St. Joseph's Coll., Rensselaer, Ind.; pub. info. specialist State Ind. Dept. Natural Resources; reporter, photographer WTWO TV, Terre Haute, Ind.; former Chief of Staff, Deputy Chief of Staff, Spokesman Capitol Hill; mem. U.S. Congress from 7th Ind. dist., 2001—. Mem. Congressional com. Transportation and Infrastructure, Internat. Rels., Policy; subcom. Highways and Transit, Water Resources and Environ., East Asia and Pacific, Nat. Security, Foreign Affairs, Retirement Security, Captial Markets, Tax Policy, Americas; Reg. Rep. for Ind., Ill. and Mich. Recipient Best Feature Story Yr., United Press Internat., Zorah Shrine Childrens Adv. award. Episc.; mem. Masonic, Elks, Eagles lodges. Office: 226 Cannon House bldg Washington DC 20515*

KERNS, STEVE, geneticist; Pres. Universal Pig Genes, Eldora, Iowa. Office: Universal Pig Genes 30355 260th St Eldora IA 50627-8201

KERR, ALEXANDER DUNCAN, JR. lawyer; b. Pitts., May 6, 1943; s. Alexander Duncan Sr. and Nancy Greenleaf (Martin) K.; m. Judith Kathleen Mottl, May 25, 1969; children: Matthew Jonathan, Joshua Brandon. BS in Bus., Northwestern U., 1965, JD, 1968. Bar: Ill. 1968, Pa. 1969, U.S. Dist. Ct. (ea. dist.) Pa. 1969, U.S. Dist. Ct. (no. dist.) Ill. 1969, U.S. Ct. Appeals (3rd and 7th cirs.) 1969, U.S. Supreme Ct. 1969. Assoc. Clark, Ladner, Fontenbaugh & Young, Phila., 1968-69, 73-74; asst. U.S. atty. U.S. Dept. Justice, Chgo., 1974-79; assoc., ptnr. Keck, Mahin & Cate, Chgo., Oak Brook, Ill., 1979-90; shareholder Tishler & Wald, Ltd., Chgo., 1990—. Staff atty. Park Dist. La Grange, Ill., 1985—; active Ill. St. Andrew Soc., North Riverside, 1982—, pres., 1995-97; vestryman, lay reader, chancellor, chalice bearer Emmanuel Episcopal Ch., 1980-99; mem. Pack 177, Troop 19, Order of the Arrow, Boy Scouts Am., La Grange, 1980—. With USN, 1969-75. Mem. Am. Legion, DuPage Club, Atlantis Divers. Home: 709 S Stone Ave La Grange IL 60525-2725 Fax: 708-354-1208. E-mail: akerr@tischlerandwald.com.

KERR, DAVE, state official, marketing professional; m. Patty Kerr; children: Ryan, Dan. Degree in Biol. Sci., Psychology, Kans. State U. , 1968; MBA, U. Kans., 1970. Leader com. on Econ. Devel., Edn.; candidate Kans. Senate, 1984; senator State of Kans., 1984—; served Kans. Senate, 1988, 1992, 1996, 2000; pres. Kans. State Senate Dist. 34, 2000—. Mem. bd. dirs. Hutchinson Hosp. Corp.; mem. bd. dirs. Reno County Mental Health Adv. Com.; with Hutchinson Hosp. Bd. Dirs., Bds. Leadership Hutchinson, Hutchinson C.of C., Healthy Families, Nickerson and Hutchinson HS booster clubs. Mem.: Kans. Tech. Enterprise Corp. (mem. bd. dirs. 1987—98), Republican Ctrl. Com. (sec. 1981—84), Kans. C. of C. and Industry, Kans. Farm Bur., Legis. Post Audit, Joint Pensions, Investments and Benefits (vice chmn.), Legis. Coordinating Coun. (chmn.), Interstate Coop., Ways and Means Com., Commerce Com., Calendar and Rules Com. Republican. Office: State Capitol Rm 359-E Topeka KS 66612 Business E-Mail: kerr@senate.state.ks.us.*

KERR, DAVID MILLS, state legislator; b. Pratt, Kans., May 4, 1945; s. Fred H. and Eleanor Mills (Barrett) K.; m. Mary Patricia O'Rourke, Aug. 24, 1979; children: Ryan, Daniel. BA, Kans. State U., 1968; MBA, U. Kans., 1970. Auditor Trans World Airlines, Kansas City, Mo., 1970-72, mgr. fin., 1972-76; pres. Agronomics Internat., Hutchinson, Kans., 1976-84; mem. Kans. State Senate, Topeka, 1984—, chmn. edn. com., 1992-95, chmn. ways and means com., chmn. joint budget com., 1996-2000, pres. state senate, 2001—. Bd. dirs. Kans. Tech. Enterprises Corp., Health Care, Inc.; chmn. Senate econ. devel. com., 1988, edn. com., 1993, Senate ways and means com., 1995; chmn. com. on econ. devel. Nat. Conf. State Legislatures; mem. Gov.'s Criminal Justice Coordinating Coun., 1988. Mem. Advanced Tech. Commn., Topeka, 1985; chmn. Task Force on Capitol Markets and Tax, Topeka, 1986; bd. dirs. Hutchinson Hosp. Corp., 1993, Kansas, Inc. Named Kans. Exporter of Yr., Internat. Trade Inst., 1981. Mem. Kans. C. of C. (bd. dirs. 1983-86). Republican. Presbyterian. Avocations: travel, reading, golf, hunting, fishing. Home: 72 Willowbrook St Hutchinson KS 67502-8948 Office: PO Box 2620 Hutchinson KS 67504-2620 also: State Senate State Capital Topeka KS 66612

KERR, GARY ENRICO, lawyer, educator; b. Kewanee, Ill., Feb. 8, 1948; s. Roy Harrison and Marietta (Dani) K.; m. Eileen Elizabeth Straeter, Aug. 18, 1978; 1 child, Victoria Elizabeth. BA, No. Ill. U., 1970; JD, Northwestern U., Chgo., 1973. Bar: Ill. 1974, U.S. Dist. Ct. (cen. dist.) Ill. 1982, U.S. Ct. Appeals (7th cir.) 1983, U.S. Supreme Ct. 1983. Adminstrv. asst. Office Supt. Pub. Instrn. State Ill., Chgo., Springfield, 1971-74; asst. legal advisor Ill. State Bd. Edn., Springfield, 1974-78; spl. counsel Ill. State Comptroller, 1978-79; pvt. practice, 1979—. Adj. faculty Sangamon State U. (now Ill. State U.), Springfield, Ill., 1994; pres., dir. counsel Kerr Products, Inc., Kewanee, Ill., 1980—; instr. paralegal program Robert Morris Coll., Springfield, 1992. Atty. South County Democrats, Sangamon County, Ill. Fellow Ednl. Policy program Inst. Ednl. Leadership, George Washington U., 1976-77. Mem. Ill. State Bar Assn. (chmn. sch. law sect. coun. 1983-84), Sangamon unty Bar Assn., Automotive Parts and Accessories Assn. (mem. govtl. affairs and internat. trade com. 1997). Avocations: snow skiing, tennis, fishing. Office: Gary Kerr Ltd 1020 S 7th St Springfield IL 62703-2417 E-mail: kerrltd@aol.com.

KERR, MICHAEL D. construction company executive; BSCE, Purdue U. With Huber, Hunt & Nichols Inc., Indpls., 1969—, from project engr., supt., project mgr., to exec. v.p., now pres., COO, 1999—. Mem. Associated Gen. Contractors, Indpls. Athletic Club.

KERR, SYLVIA JOANN, educator; b. Detroit, June 19, 1941; d. Frederic Dilmus and Maud (Dirst) Pfeffer; widowed; children: David, Kathleen. BA, Carleton Coll., 1963; MS, U. Minn., 1966, PhD, 1968. Asst. prof. Augsburg Coll., Mpls., 1968-71; instr. Anoka Ramsey Community Coll., Coon Rapids, Minn., 1973-74; from asst. prof. to full prof. Hamline U., St. Paul, 1974—. Contbr. numerous articles to profl. jours. NIH fellow U. Minn., 1972, 74-75. Office: Hamline U Dept Biology 1536 Hewitt Ave Saint Paul MN 55104-1205 E-mail: sKerr@piper.hamline.edu.

KERR, WILLIAM ANDREW, lawyer, educator; b. Harding, W.Va., Nov. 17, 1934; s. William James and Tocie Nyle (Morris) K.; m. Elizabeth Ann McMillin, Aug. 3, 1968 AB, W.Va. U., 1955, JD, 1957; LLM, Harvard U., 1958; BD, Duke U., 1968. Bar: W.Va. 1957, Pa. 1962, Ind. 1980. Assoc. McClintic, James, Wise and Robinson, Charleston, W.Va., 1958; assoc. Schnader, Harrison, Segal and Lewis, Phila., 1961-64; asst. prof. law Cleve. State U., 1966-67, assoc. prof. law, 1967-68, Ind. U., Indpls., 1968-69, 72-74, prof., 1974-98, prof. emeritus, 1998—; contract atty. Indpls. Pub. Defender Agy., 1998—. Asst. U.S. atty. So. Dist. Ind., Indpls., 1969-72; exec. dir. Ind. Jud. Ctr., 1974-86; dir. research Ind. Pros. Attys. Council, 1972-74; mem. Ind. Criminal Law Study Commn., 1973-89, sec., 1973-83; reporter speedy trial com. U.S. Dist. Ct. (so. dist.) Ind., 1975-84; trustee Ind. Criminal Justice Inst., 1983-86; bd. dirs. Indpls. Lawyers Commn., 1975-77, Ind. Lawyers Commn., 1980-83; mem. records mgmt. com. Ind. Supreme Ct., 1983-86. Author: Indiana Criminal Procedure: Pretrial, 1991, Indiana Criminal Procedure: Trial, 2 vols., 1998. Bd. dirs. Ch. Fedn. Greater Indpls., 1979-87. Served to capt. JAGC, USAF, 1958-61.

Decorated Air Force Commendation medal; Ford Found. fellow Harvard Law Sch., 1957-58; recipient Outstanding Prof. award Students Ind. U. Sch. Law, 1974, Disting. Service award Ind. Council Juvenile Ct. Judges, 1979, Outstanding Jud. Edn. Program award Nat. Council Juvenile and Family Ct. Judges, 1985. Mem. Ind. State Bar Assn., Indpls. Bar Assn., Phila. Bar Assn., W.Va. Bar Assn., Nat. Dist. Attys. Assn., Am. Judicature Soc., Fed. Bar Assn. (Outstanding Service award Indpls. chpt. 1975), Order of Coif, Phi Beta Kappa. Office: 55 Monument Cir Ste 1017 Indianapolis IN 46204-5901

KERR, WILLIAM T. publishing and broadcasting executive; b. Seattle, Apr. 17, 1941; m. Mary Lang, Oct. 15, 1966; 1 child, Susannah Gaskill Kerr Adler. B.A., U. Wash., 1963, Oxford U., Eng., 1965; MA, Harvard U., 1967, M.B.A., 1969. V.p. Dillon Read & Co., N.Y.C. and London, 1969-73; cons. McKinsey & Co., N.Y.C., 1973-79; v.p. New York Times Co., 1979-91; pres. New York Times Mag. Group, 1985-91; exec. v.p., pres. mag. group Meredith Corp., Des Moines, 1991-94, pres., chief oper. officer, bd. dirs., exec. com., 1994-96, pres., CEO, 1997-98, chmn., 1998—. Bd. dirs. Storage Tek Corp., Prin. Fin. Group, Maytag Corp. Mem. Mag. Pubs. Am. (bd. dirs. 1985—, chmn. 1994-95), Century Assn. (N.Y.C.), Union Club (N.Y.C.), The Brook Club (N.Y.C.), Quogue Field Club, Wakonda Club, Des Moines Club, Reform Club (London), Litchfield Country Club. Roman Catholic. Home: PO Box 1545 Litchfield CT 06759-1545 Office: Meredith Corp 1716 Locust St Des Moines IA 50309-3023

KERREY, BOB (J. ROBERT KERREY), academic administrator, former senator; b. Lincoln, Nebr., Aug. 27, 1943; s. James and Elinor Kerrey; m. Sarah Paley; children: Benjamin, Lindsey. BS in Pharmacy, U. Nebr., 1965. Owner, founder, developer Grandmother's Restaurants, Omaha, 1972—75; owner, founder Prairie Life Ctr., Lincoln and Omaha; gov. State of Nebr., Lincoln, 1983—87; ptnr. Printon, Kane & Co., Nebr., 1987—89; U.S. Sen. from Nebraska, 1989—2001; pres. New Sch. U., N.Y.C., 2001—. Mem. Agrl., Nutrition & Forestry Com.; ranking minority mem. appropriations subcom. Treasury, Postal Svc. & Gen. Govt.; select com. Intelligence, Fin., Prodn. & Price Comptetitiveness Com. Bd. dirs. Lincoln Ctr. Assn., Nebr. Easter Seal Soc. With USN, 1966—69, Vietnam. Decorated medal of Honor, Bronze Star, Purple Heart. Mem.: Lincoln C. of C., DAV, VFW, Am. Legion, Sertoma, Lions, Phi Gamma Delta. Congregationalist. Office: New Sch U Johnson and Kaplan Bldg Rm 800 66 W 12th St New York NY 10011*

KERRIGAN, JOHN E. academic administrator; Chancellor emeritus U. Wis., Oshkosh. Office: Gruenhagen Hall 208 Osceola St Oshkosh WI 54901 E-mail: kerrigan@uwosh-edu.

KERSHNER, RODGER A. corporate lawyer; BS, Wayne State U., 1971; JD, Detroit Coll. of Law, 1976. Bar: Mich. 1976. Assoc. gen. counsel ANR Pipeline Co., 1978-88; v.p., gen. counsel CMS Energy Corp., 1988-95, sr. v.p., gen. counsel, 1995—. Pres. Bay Harbor Co. Mem. bd. control Mich. Technol. U. Mem.: Bay Harbor Yacht Club (founding). Office: CMS Energy Corp 330 Town Center Dr Dearborn MI 48126-2738 E-mail: rkershner@cmsenergy.com.

KERTH, JACK D. otolaryngologist; b. Cin., July 28, 1933; MD, Ohio State U., 1958. Intern St. Luke's Hosp., Cleve., 1958-59; resident in otolaryngology Northwestern U., Chgo., 1959-63, fellow in otolaryngology, 1963, assoc. prof.; mem. staff Northwestern Meml. Hosp.; pvt. practice otolaryngoloty. Fellow ACP; mem. AMA, AAFRPS, AAOHNS, ABO. Office: 845 N Michigan Ave Chicago IL 60611-2252

KESLER, JAY LEWIS, academic administrator; b. Barnes, Wis., Sept. 15, 1935; s. Elsie M. Campbell Kesler; m. H. Jane Smith; children: Laura, Bruce, Terri. Student, Ball State U., 1953-54; BA, Taylor U., 1958, LHD (hon.), 1982; Dr. Divinity (hon.), Barrington Coll., 1977; DD (hon.), Asbury Theol. Sem., 1984, Anderson U., 1999; HHD (hon.), Huntington Coll., 1983; LHD, John Brown U., 1987; LLD (honoris causa), Gordon Coll., 1992; DD (hon.) , Union U., 2000, Trinity Internat. U., 2001; LHD (honoris causa), So. Wesleyan U., 2002. Dir. Marion (Ind.) Youth for Christ, 1955-58, crusade staff evangelist, 1959-60, dir. Ill.-Ind. region, 1960-62, dir. coll. recruitment, 1962-63, v.p. personnel, 1963-68, v.p. field coordination, 1968-73, pres., 1973-85, also bd. dirs.; pres. Taylor U., Upland, Ind., 1985-2000, chancellor, 2000—. Bd. dirs. Star Fin. Group, Christianity Today, Brotherhood Mut. Ins. Co., Nat. Ass. Evangs., Youth for Christ Internat., Youth for Christ U.S.A.; mem. bd. reference Christian Camps Inc.; mem. Council for Christian Colls. and Univs., bd. mem., 2001; chmn. United Christian Coll. Fund; mem. adv. bd. Christian Bible Soc.; co-pastor 1st Bapt. Ch., Geneva, 1972—85; mem. faculty Billy Graham Schs. Evangelism; lectr. Staley Disting. Christian Sch. Lecture Program; past gov.'s appointee Ind. Commn. on Youth. Speaker on Family Forum (daily radio show and radio program); mem. adv. com. Campus Life mag.; author: Let's Succeed With Our Teenagers, 1973, I Never Promised You a Disneyland, 1975, The Strong Weak People, 1976, Outside Disneyland, 1977, I Want a Home with No Problems, 1977, Growing Places, 1978, Too Big to Spank, 1978, Breakthrough, 1981, Parents & Teenagers, 1984 (Gold Medallion award), Family Forum, 1984, Making Life Make Sense, 1986, Parents and Children, 1986, Being Holy, Being Human, 1988, Ten Mistakes Parents Make With Teenagers (And How to Avoid Them), 1988, Is Your Marriage Really Worth Fighting For?, 1989, Energizing Your Teenagers' Faith, 1990, Raising Responsible Kids, 1991, Grandparenting: The Agony and the Ecstasy, 1993, Challenges for the College Bound, 1994, Emotionally Healthy Teenagers, 1998; contbr. articles to profl. jours. Bd. advisors Prison Fellowship Internat., Christian Camps Inc., Christian Educators Assn. Internat., Evangelicals for Social Action, Love and Action, Venture Middle East, Internat. Com. of Reference for New Life 2000. Named sr. fellow, Coun. Christian Coll., 2000, Sagamore of the Wabash, 2000; recipient Angel award, Religion in Media, 1985, Outstanding Youth Leadership award, Religious Heritage Am., 1989. Office: Taylor U Office Pres 236 W Reade Ave Upland IN 46989-1002

KESLER, STEPHEN EDWARD, economic geology educator; BS with honors, U. N.C., 1962; PhD, Stanford U., 1966. Asst. prof. econ. geology La. State U., Baton Rouge, 1966-70; assoc. prof. U. Toronto, Ont., Can., 1970-77; prof. U. Mich., Ann Arbor, 1977—, assoc. chair, 1998—. Vis. scientist Nat. Inst. Geography, Guatemala, 1966-69, Consejo Recursos Minerales, Mexico City, 1974-75; with Dirección General Minas, Santo Domingo, 1983-84; cons. exploration for metallic and non-metallic mineral deposits. Author: Our Finite Mineral Resources, 1975; (with others) Economic Geology of Central Dominican Republic, 1984, Mineral Resources: Economics and the Environment, 1994; assoc. editor Econ. Geology, 1981-91; mem. editorial bd. Jour. Geochem. Exploration, 1984-98. Pres. bd. trustees Lord of Light Luth. Ch., 1989-91. Fellow Geol. Soc. Am., Soc. Econ. Geologists (councillor 1983-86, internat. lectr. 1989-90, v.p. 1990-91, Thayer Lindsley lectr. 1994-95, pres. 1998-99); mem. Assn. Exploration Geochemists (councillor 1981-84), Soc. Mining Engrs. of AIME (program chmn. 1977). Lutheran. Office: U Mich Dept Geol Scis Ann Arbor MI 48109

KESSEL, RICHARD GLEN, zoology educator; b. Fairfield, Iowa, July 19, 1931; BS in Chemistry summa cum laude, Parsons Coll., 1953; MS in Zoology and Physiology, U. Iowa, 1956, PhD in Zoology and Cytology, 1959; postgrad., Marine Biol. Lab., 1957. Trainee dept. anatomy Bowman Gray Sch. Medicine, Wake Forest U., 1959-60; Nat. Inst. Gen. Med. Sci. postdoctoral rsch. fellow Bowman Gray Sch. Medicine, Wake Forest U., Winston-Salem, N.C., 1960-61, instr. anatomy, 1959-61, asst. prof., 1961; asst. prof. zoology U. Iowa, Iowa City, 1961-64, assoc. prof., 1964-68, prof., 1968—. Vis. investigator Hopkins Marine Sta., Pacific Grove, Calif., 1966; ind. investigator Marine Biol. Lab., Woods Hole, Mass., summers 1960, 62, 64 Author: (with C.Y. Shih) Scanning Electron Microscopy in Biology: A Students' Text-Atlas of Biological Organization, 1974, (with R.H. Kardon) Tissues and Organs: A Text-Atlas of Scanning Electron Microscopy, 1979, (with C.Y. Shih) Living Images, 1982, (with R. Roberts and H. Tung) Freeze Fracture Images of Cells and Tissues, 1991, Basic Medical Histology, 1998; assoc. editor Jour. Exptl. Zoology, 1978-82; mem. editorial bd. Jour. Submicroscopic Cytology, 1980—; mem. internat. bd. editors Scanning Electron Microscopy in Biology and Medicine; contbr. articles to profl. jours., chpts. to books Grantee USPHS, 1961-78, NSF, 1969-71, Whitehall Found., 1982-84; Bodine fellow; George Lincoln Seeley scholar; Nat Inst. Gen. Med. Sci.-USPHS, 1964-69. Mem. AAAS, Am. Soc. Cell Biology, Am. Assn. Anatomists, Electron Micros. Soc. Am., Am. Physiol. Soc., Soc. for Study of Reprodn., Am. Soc. Zoologists, Am. Inst. Biol. Sci., Soc. Devel. Biology, Sigma Xi, Phi Kappa Phi, Beta Beta Beta. Office: Univ Iowa Dept Biol Scis Iowa City IA 52242 E-mail: richard-kessel@uiowa.edu.

KESSINGER, MARGARET ANNE, medical educator; b. Beckley, W.Va., June 4, 1941; d. Clisby Theodore and Margaret Anne (Ellison) K.; m. Loyd Ernst Wegner, Nov. 27, 1971. MA, W.Va. U., 1963, MD, 1967. Diplomate Am. Bd. Internal Medicine and Med. Oncology. Internal medicine house officer U. Nebr. Med. Ctr., Omaha, 1967-70, fellow med. oncology, 1970-72, asst. prof. internal medicine, 1972-77, assoc. prof., 1977-90, prof., 1990—, assoc. chief oncology hematology sect., 1988-91, chief oncology hematology sect., 1991-99; assoc. dir. clin. rsch. U. Nebr. Med. Ctr./Eppley Cancer Ctr., 1999—. Contbr. articles to profl. publs. Fellow ACP, Am. Assn. Cancer Edn.; mem. Am. Soc. Clin. Oncology, Am. Assn. Cancer Rsch., Internat. Soc. Exptl. Hematology, Am. Soc. Hematology, Sigma Xi, Alpha Omega Alpha. Republican. Methodist. Avocations: aviation, gardening, canning, skiing. Office: U Nebr Med Ctr 987680 Nebraska Med Ctr Omaha NE 68198-0001 E-mail: makessin@unmc.edu.

KESSLER, JOAN F. lawyer; b. June 25, 1943; m. Frederick P. Kessler, Sept. 1967; 2 children. BA, U. Kans., 1961-65; postgrad., U. Wis., 1965-66; JD cum laude, Marquette U., 1968. Law clk. Hon. John W. Reynolds U.S. Dist. Ct. (ea. dist.) Wis., Milw., 1968-69; assoc. Warschafsky, Rotter & Tarnoff, 1969-71; pvt. practice, 1971-74; assoc. Cook & Franke, S.C., 1974-78; U.S. atty. Eastern Dist. Wis., 1978-81; ptnr. Foley & Lardner, 1981—. Lectr. profl. responsibility U. Wis. Law Sch., Marquette U. Law Sch., Milw., 1994-96; mem. bd. govs. State Bar of Wis., 1985-89, 90-92, 93-95, chair, 1993, bd. dirs. family law sect., 1991-94; mem. Jud. Coun. Wis., Madison, 1989-92; mem. Milw. Bd. Attys. Profl. Responsibility, 1979-85. Bd. dirs. Legal Aid Soc., 1974-78, v.p., 1978, Urban League, 1980-82, Women's Bus. Initiative Corp., 1989-91, Girl Scouts U.S., Milw., 1994-96; bd. dirs., pres. Voters for Choice in Wis., 1989-93. Fellow Am. Matrimonial Lawyers (bd. govs. 1990-96, v.p. 1996-99), Am. Law Inst., Am. Bar Found.; mem. ACLU (Best Lawyers in Am. 1993-98). Office: Foley & Lardner 777 E Wisconsin Ave Ste 3800 Milwaukee WI 53202-5367

KESSLER, JOHN WHITAKER, real estate developer; b. Cin., Mar. 7, 1936; s. Charles Wilmont and Elisabeth (Whitaker) K.; m. Charlotte Hamilton Power, Aug. 8, 1964; children: Catherine, Elizabeth, Jane. BS, Ohio State U., 1958. Mem. sales dept. Armstrong Cork Co., Lancaster, Pa., 1958-59; mgr. spl. products div. M & R Dietetics Labs., Columbus, Ohio, 1959-62; co-founder, mng. partner Multicon, 1962-70; pres. Multicon Communities div. Multicon Properties, Inc., 1970-72; prin. John W. Kessler Co., Columbus, 1972—; chmn. Marsh & McLennan Real Estate Advisors Inc., 1980—, New Albany Co., 1991—. Bd. dir. Bank One Corp., Abercrombie & Fitch. Office: New Albany Co PO Box 772 New Albany OH 43054-0772

KESSLER, PHILIP JOEL, lawyer; b. Detroit, Nov. 15, 1947; s. Herbert Jerome and Mary Rita (Bloomgarden) K.; m. Ruth Ann Kessler, Dec. 22, 1968 (div. 1981); children: Herbert Jeffrey, Jennifer Ann; m. Mary Ray Brophy, Jan. 29, 1988. AB in English with distinction, U. Mich., 1969; JD, U. Calif., Berkeley, 1972. Bar: Mich. 1972, U.S. Dist. Ct. (ea. dist.) Mich. 1972, U.S. Ct. Appeals (6th cir.) 1976, U.S. Dist. Ct. (no. dist.) Tex. 1990, U.S. Tax Ct. 1990. Assoc. Butzel Long Gust Klein & Van Zile, Detroit, 1972-79, ptnr., 1979-82; shareholder Butzel Long (and predecessor firms), 1982—, also bd. dirs. Legal rsch. tchg. fellow Detroit Coll. Law, 1975-77; asst. prof. law 1977-85; lectr. in field; local rules adv. com. U.S. Dist. Ct. for Ea. Dist. Mich., mem. 1991-95, chair 1994-95; life mem. Jud. Conf. U.S. Ct. Appeals for 6th Cir.; bd. dirs. The Beaumont Found., 1995-96, THAW Fund, 1995—. Mem. Founders Soc. Detroit Inst. Arts, 1988—. Fellow Am. Bar Found., Am. Coll. Trial Lawyers, Mich. Bar Found.; mem. Detroit Club, Franklin (Mich.) Hills Country Club. Avocation: golf. Home: 25612 Meadowdale St Franklin MI 48025-1101

KESSLER, ROBERT W. director license, inspections, environmental rules; BA in Urban Studies, U. Minn., St. Paul, 1974; MPA in Housing, Comty. Devel., U. So. Calif., Washington, Pub. Affairs Ctr., 1981; postgrad. studies in Project Mgmt., Program Evaluation U. Minn., 1978-94. City planner Office of the Mayor, St. Paul, 1973-74; devel. grant asst., comty. devel. divsn. City of St. Paul, 1975-80; program analyst HUD, Washington, 1980-81; asst. to chief of staff Mayor's Office City of St. Paul, 1982; comty. devel. specialist City of St. Paul, 1982-83, econ. devel. specialist neighborhood divsn., 1983-86; dir. St. Paul 503 Devel. Co., 1986-87; asst. to mayor City of St. Paul, 1987-88, dir. Mayor's info. and complaint office, 1988-90, license and permit mgr., 1990-92, dir. Office Lic., Inspections and Environ. Protection, 1992—. With U.S. Army Med. Bn., Vietnam, 1969-70. Decorated Bronze Star, U.S. Army, 1970. Mem. Internat. City/County Mgmt. Assn. (affiliate). Home: 2190 Dahl Ave Saint Paul MN 55119-5877 Office: Lics Inspections & Environ Protection 350 Saint Peter St Ste 300 Saint Paul MN 55102-1510

KETTELER, THOMAS R. retail executive; CFO Schottenstein Stores Corp., Columbus, Ohio. Office: Schottenstein Stores Corp 1800 Moler Rd Columbus OH 43207-1680

KETTERSON, ELLEN D. biologist, educator; b. Orange, N.J., Aug. 9, 1945; m. Val Nolan, Jr. BA in Botany, Ind. U., 1966, MA in Botany, 1968, PhD in Zoology, 1974. NIH fellow Wash. State U., 1975-77; asst. prof. biol. scis. Bowling Green State U., 1975-77; from vis. asst. prof. to asst. prof. biology Ind. U., Bloomington, 1977-84, from assoc. prof. to prof. biology, 1984—, co-dir. Ctr. for Integrative Study Animal Behavior, 1990—. Vis. scientist Purdue U., Lafayette, Ind., 1991, Rockefeller U., 1985, U. Va., 1984. Mem. editl. bd. Current Ornithology, 1989-94, editor, 1994-99; mem. editl. bd. Animal Behaviour, 1991-94, assoc. editor, 1997—; mem. editl. bd. Evolution, 1994, editor, 1994-99; editor: Jour. Avian Biology, 1999—. Grantee NSF, 1978—. Fellow Am. Ornithologists Union (v.p. 1995-96, coun. 1988-91, Elliot Coues award 1996), Animal Behavior Soc.; mem. AAAS, Internat. Ornithol. Com., Ecol. Soc. Am., Am. Soc. Naturalists, Animal Behavior Soc., Assn Field Ornithologists, Cooper Ornithol. Soc., Soc. Conservation Biology, Soc. Study of Evolution, Soc. Integrative and Comparative Biology, Soc. Behavioral Neuroendocrinology, Wilson Ornithol. Soc. (Margaret M. Nice award 1998), Sigma Xi. Office: Indiana U Dept Biology Bloomington IN 47405

KEVOIAN, BOB, radio personality; b. 1950; Grad., Long Beach State U., 1973. Radio host Sta. WFBQ-FM, Indpls. Office: WFBQ 6161 Fall Creek Rd Indianapolis IN 46220*

KEY, JACK DAYTON, librarian; b. Enid, Okla., Feb. 24, 1934; s. Ernest Dayton and Janie (Haldeman) K.; m. Virgie Ruth Richardson, Aug. 12, 1956; children— Toni, Scot, Todd. B.A., Phillips U., Enid, Okla., 1958; M.A., U. N.Mex., 1960; M.S., U. Ill., 1962. Staff supr. Grad. Library U. Ill., 1960-62; pharmacy librarian U. Iowa, 1962-64; med. librarian Lovelace Found. for Med. Edn. and Research, Albuquerque, 1965-70; dir. Mayo Med. Ctr. Librs., Rochester, Minn., 1970-94, dir. emeritus, 1994—; prof. emeritus biomed. comm. Mayo Med. Sch. Cons. in field; participant Naval War Coll. Conf., 1979; Alberta A. Brown lectr. Western Mich. U., 1979 Author: The Origin of the Vaccine Inoculation by Edward Jenner, 1977, William Alexander Hammond (1828-1900), 1979; editor: Library Automation: The Orient and South Pacific, 1975, Automated Activities in Health Sciences Libraries, 1975-78, Classics and Other Selected Readings in Medical Librarianship, 1980, Journal of a Quest for the Elusive Doctor Arthur Conan Doyle, 1982, Medical Vanities, 1982, William A. Hammond, M.D., 1828-1900: The Publications of an American Neurologist, 1983, Classics in Cardiology, Vol. 3, 1983, Vol. 4, 1989, Medical Casebook of Dr. Arthur Conan Doyle from Practitioner to Sherlock Holmes and Beyond, 1984, Medicine, Literature and Eponyms: An Encyclopedia of Medical Eponyms Derived from Literary Characters, 1989, Conan Doyle's Tales of Medical Humanism and Values, 1992; contbr. articles to profl. jours. Served with USN, 1952-55. U. N.Mex. fellow, 1958-59, N.Mex. Library Assn. Marion Dorroh Meml. scholar, 1960, Rotary Paul Harris fellow, 1979; recipient Outstanding Hist. Writing award Minn. Medicine, 1980, Spl. Svc. award Am. Acad. Dermatology, 1992, Farthing award Baker St. Jour., 1993; decorated knight Icelandic Order of Falcon, 1980; named to Phillips U. Hall Fame, 1988. Mem. Med. Library Assn., Am. Inst. History Pharmacy, Am. Assn. History Medicine, Am. Med. Writers Assn., Am. Osler Soc. (pres. 1990-91), Mystery Writers of Am., Alcuin Soc., Baker St. Irregulars, Ampersand Club, Sigma Xi (cert. of recognition 1982) Mem. Christian Ch. (Disciples of Christ). Home: PO Box 231 54 Skyline Dr Sandia Park NM 87047-0231 Office: Mayo Clinic Rochester MN 55905-0001

KEYES, JAMES HENRY, manufacturing company executive; b. LaCrosse, Wis., Sept. 2, 1940; s. Donald M. and Mary M. (Nodolf) K.; m. Judith Ann Carney, Nov. 21, 1964; children: James Patrick, Kevin, Timothy. BS, Marquette U., 1962; MBA, Northwestern U., 1963. Instr. Marquette U., Milw., 1963-65; CPA Peat. Marwick & Mitchell, 1965-66; with Johnson Controls, Inc., 1967—, mgr. sys. dept., 1967-71, divsn. contr., 1971-73, corp. contr., treas., 1973-77, v.p., CFO, 1977-85, exec. v.p., 1985-86, pres., 1986-99, chief operating officer, 1986-88, chief exec. officer, 1988—, also chmn. Bd. dirs. Baird Capital Devel. Fund. 1st Wis. Trust Co., LSI Logic, Inc., Universal Foods Corp. Active Milw. Symphony Orch., 1980—. Mem. Fin. Execs. Inst., Am. Inst. CPA's, Wis. Inst. CPA's., Machinery and Allied Products Inst. Office: Johnson Controls Inc 5757 N Green Bay Ave Milwaukee WI 53209-4408

KEYES, JEFFREY J. lawyer; BA magna cum laude, U. Notre Dame, 1968; JD cum laude, U. Mich., 1972. Bar: Minn. 1972. Shareholder Briggs and Morgan, P.A., Mpls.; fellow Am. Coll. Trial Lawyers. Mem. Gov.'s Task Force on Tort Reform, 1986; chmn. fed. practice com. U.S. Dist. Ct. Minn., 1990-93, chmn. adv. group on civil justice reform act U.S. Dist. Ct. Minn., 1991-93; trainer U.S. Magistrate Judges Tng. Conf. on Settlement, Mpls., 1992; lectr. numerous convs. and symposia in field. Contbr. articles to law jours. Mem. ABA (chmn. antitrust sect. franchise com. 1989-90, contbg. editor Antitrust Monograph 1987, co-editor Antitrust Sect. State Antitrust Law Handbook, Minn. chpt. 1990), Minn. State Bar Assn. (co-chair Women in the Legal Profn. task force 1996-97, chmn. civil litigation sect. 1985-86), Hennepin County Bar Assn. Office: Briggs and Morgan 2400 Ids Ctr Minneapolis MN 55402

KEYS, ARLANDER, federal judge; b. 1943; BA, DePaul U., 1972, JD, 1975. Trial atty. Nat. Labor Rels. Bd., 1975-80; regional atty. Fed. Labor Rels. Authority, Chgo., 1980-86; adminstrv. law judge SSA, Dept. of HHS, 1986-88, chief adminstrv. law judge, 1988-95; magistrate judge U.S. Dist. Ct. (no. dist.) Ill., 1995-98, presiding magistrate judge, 1998—. With USMC, 1963—67. Mem. ABA, Fed. Bar Assn., Ill. Jud. Coun., Chgo. Bar Assn., Cook County Bar Assn., 7th Cir. Bar Assn., Just the Beginning Found. Office: US Dist Ct 219 S Dearborn St Ste 2240 Chicago IL 60604-1802 Fax: 312-554-8546.

KEYSER, RICHARD LEE, distribution company executive; b. Harrisburg, Pa., Oct. 28, 1942; s. Harold L. and Mary J. (Raup) K.; m. Mary Ellen Carter, June 20, 1964; children: Jeffrey, Jennifer. BS, U.S. Naval Acad., 1964; MBA, Harvard U., 1971. Commd. ensign USN, 1964, advanced through grades to lt., 1966; resigned, 1969; mktg.-analysis mgr. Fleetguard, Inc., Dallas, 1971-72, dir. logistics Cookeville, Tenn., 1973-77; gen. mgr. parts ops. Cummins Engine Co., Inc., Columbus, Ind., 1977-83, exec. dir. mktg. ops., 1983-84; pres. NL-Hycalog, Houston, 1984-86; v.p. ops. W.W. Grainger, Inc., Chgo., 1986-87, exec. v.p., 1988-90, pres., 1991—, CEO, now chmn., 1995—. Bd. dirs. Morton Internat. County chmn. blood program ARC, Cookeville, 1976-77; bd. dirs. Preserve To Enjoy, Inc., Columbus, 1983-84, Irene Josselyn Clinic, Northfield, Ill., 1989-92, Lake Forest Grad. Sch. Mgmt., 1992—, Evanston Hosp. Corp., 1996—. Former lt. comdr. USNR. Fellow Am. Prodn. and Inventory Control Soc. (cert.); mem. Chgo. Club, Harvard Bus. Sch. Club Chgo. (v.p. 1988-89, pres. 1989-90), Comml. Club Chgo. Office: WW Grainger Inc 100 Grainger Pkwy Lake Forest IL 60045-5201

KHANDEKAR, JANARDAN DINKAR, oncologist, educator; b. Indore, India, Feb. 1, 1944; came to U.S., 1971; s. Dinker and Sulaochan (Dawlae) K.; m. Amita Oomen, Aug. 28, 1971; children: Manoj, Melin. MD, MBBS, U. Indore, 1969; sabbatical, Northwestern U., Baylor U., 1992. Diplomate Am. Bd. Internal Medicine, Am. Bd. Med. Oncology. Intern M.Y. Hosp., Indore, 1967-70; resident in medicine Allegheny Gen. Hosp., Pitts., 1972-73; head divsn. med. oncology Evanston (Ill.) Hosp., 1975-98, from asst. attending physician to assoc. attending physician, 1975-79, sr. attending physician, 1979—; fellow Med. Rsch. Coun., Montréal, Que., Can., 1970-71, Tufts U., Boston, 1973-75; asst. prof. medicine Northwestern U., Chgo., 1975-80, assoc. prof., 1980-86, prof. medicine, 1986—, Kellogg/Scanlon chair in oncology, 1991-98; dir. cancer control Northwestern U. Cancer Ctr., 1991—; assoc. dir. Kellogg Cancer Care Ctr. Evanston Hosp., 1979-87, dir., 1987—; Louise Coon chmn. dept. medicine Evanston Northwestern Healthcare, 1998—. Active NIH Ad Hoc Com. on Nat. Prostate Cancer Program, NIH Team for Audit Clin. Trials at Yale U., Roswell Park Meml. Inst., Mayo Clinic, etc.; chmn. rsch. com. and adv. com. Searle Clin. Pharmacology Unit; sr. investigator Eastern Coop. Oncology Group, 1976-83, Community Clin. Oncology Program, 1983—; lectr. in field. Author: (with others) Radiation-Associated Thyroid Carcinoma, 1977, Adjuvant Therapy of Cancer, 1977; contbr. over 135 articles to profl. jours. Recipient cert. of merit Nat. Cancer Inst.; grantee Ill. Cancer Coun., 1983-98, Duke U., 1983-90, Nat. Cancer Inst., 1983—, Women's Health Inst., 1993, Evanston Hosp., 1993—, NIH, 1988-91, 93—. Fellow ACP (laureate); mem. AAAS, Am. Soc. Clin. Oncology, Am. Fedn. Clin. Rsch., Am. Assn. Cancer Rsch., Inst. Medicine (Chgo.). Office: Evanston Hosp 2650 Ridge Ave Evanston IL 60201-1781

KHOURY, GEORGE GILBERT, printing company executive, baseball association executive; b. St. Louis, July 30, 1923; s. George Michael and Dorothy (Smith) K.; m. Colleen E. Khoury Czerny, Apr. 3, 1948; children: Colleen Ann, George Gilbert. Grad., St. Louis U., 1946. V.p. Khoury Bros. Printing, St. Louis, 1946—; exec. dir. George Khoury Assn. Baseball Leagues, Inc., 1967—. Served with U.S. Army, 1943-45, NATOUSA,

MTO. Decorated Purple Heart with oak leaf cluster. Roman Catholic. Office: George Khoury Assn Baseball Leagues 5400 Meramec Bottom Rd Saint Louis MO 63128-4624 E-mail: czernyce@msn.com.

KIBBIE, JOHN, state legislator; b. Palo Alto County, Iowa, July 14, 1929; m. Kathryn Kibbie; 6 children. Farmer; mem. Iowa Ho. of Reps., Des Moines, 1960-64, Iowa Senate, Des Moines, 1964-68, 88—; mem. nat. conv. platform com., 1968; mem. agr. com., mem. natural resources and environment com.; ranking mem. state govt. com.; mem. transp. com. Mem. Sacred Heart Ch.; trustee Kerber Milling Co.; bd. dirs. Benton Banks of Palo Alto County; bd. pres. Iowa Lake C.C.; former mediator Iowa Mediation Svc. With U.S. Army, Korea, 1951-53. Mem. VFW, Nat. Corn Growers, Farm Bur., Pork Prodrs., Iowa Soybean Assn., Pheasant Forever, Cattlemen's Assn., Farmer's Union, KC (dir. Ayrshire chpt.), Am. Legion, Moose. Democrat. Office: State Capitol 9th And Grand Ave Des Moines IA 50319-0001 E-mail: john_kibbie@legis.state.ia.us.

KIDD, DEBRA JEAN, communications executive; b. Chgo., May 13, 1956; d. Fred A. and Jean (Pezzopane) Winchar: m. Kim Joseph Kidd, July 22, 1978; children: Jennifer Marie, Michele Jean. AA in Bus. with high honors, Wright Jr. Coll., 1977. Legal sec. Sidley & Austin, Chgo., 1977-80; investment adminstr. Golder, Thoma & Co., 1980-81, exec. asst., 1981-84; sales rep. Dataspeed, Inc., 1984, midwestern regional mgr., 1985; comm. cons. Chgo. Comm., Inc., 1986-88; owner, founder Captain Kidd's Video, Niles, 1981-84. Editor: Lion's Roar, 1993-95. Vol. Am. Lung Assn., Chgo., 1979; vol. tchr. religious edn. Our Lady Mother of Ch., Norridge, Ill., 1981-83, St. Raymonds, Mt. Prospect, 1993-94, 2000—; vol. Parents Who Care, 1988-94, pres., 1991-93; vol. PTA Lion's Park Sch., 1993-95, bd. dirs., 1993-94; founder Young Journalist Club, 1994-95; leader Girl Scouts, 1992—, cons., 1994—, del., 1995—, registrar, 1996-97, organizer, 1996—, svc. unit mgr., 2000—; referee assignor Green White Soccer, 2001--; vol. Hearts Across Am., 2001--. Mem. NAFE, Nat. Assn. Bus. Women, Nat. Assn. Profl. Saleswomen, Phi Theta Kappa. Roman Catholic. Avocations: camping, skiing, snorkeling, sailing, reading. E-mail: dkidd739@aol.com.

KIDDER, C. ROBERT, food products executive; b. 1943; BSIE, U. Mich., 1966; MS, Iowa State U., 1968. With Ford Motor Co., Detroit, 1968-69, McKinsey & Co., N.Y.C., 1972-78, Dart Industries, 1978-80, Duracell Europe, 1980-81, Duracell Internat. Inc., 1981-95, pres., CEO, 1988-95, past chmn., CEO; chmn., CEO Borden, Inc., Columbus, Ohio, 1995—. With USN, 1969-72. Office: Borden Inc 180 E Broad St Columbus OH 43215-0003

KIDDER, FRED DOCKSTATER, lawyer; b. Cleve., May 22, 1922; s. Howard Lorin and Virgina (Milligan) K.; m. Eleanor (Hap) Kidder; children— Fred D. III, Barbara Anne Donelson, Jeanne Louise Haffeman. BS with distinction, U. Akron, 1948; JD, Case Western Res. U., 1950. Bar: Ohio 1950, Tex. 1985, U.S. Dist. Ct. (no. dist.) Ohio 1950, U.S. Dist. Ct. (no. dist.) Tex. 1985. Assoc. Arter & Hadden and predecessors, Cleve., 1950-79, ptnr., 1960-79, Jones, Day, Reavis and Pogue, Cleve., 1980-89, regional mng. ptnr. Tex., 1985-86; gen. counsel Lubrizol Corp., 1989-92, spl. counsel, 1993—. Contbr. articles to profl. jours. Mem. Cleve. Growth Assn., Shaker Heights Citizens Com., Citizens League Cleve.; former pres. Estate Planning Coun.; former co-chmn. bd. trustees Lake Erie Coll.; former bd. trustees, v.p., Alzheimer's Assn., Cleve.; mem., bd. trustees Cleve. Sight Ctr.; past mem. alumni coun. U. Akron; past. corp. coun. Dallas Mus. Art; past pres. Case Western Reserve U. Law Sch. Alumni Assn.; past chmn. Shaker Heights Recreation Bd. Mem. ABA, Nat. Assn. Corp. Secs., Tex. Bar Assn., Ohio State Bar Assn., Estate Planning Coun. (past pres.), Blue Coats, Soc. Benchers (past chmn.), Union Club, Pepper Pike Club (past sec.), The Country Club, Cleve. Skating Club, Order of Coif, Ct. of Nisi Prius (former judge), Phi Eta Sigma, Beta Delta Psi, Phi Sigma Alpha, Phi Delta Theta, Phi Delta Phi. Office: The Lubrizol Corp 29400 Lakeland Blvd Wickliffe OH 44092-2298

KIDDER, JOSEPH P. city service director; b. Akron, Ohio; m. Vicki Kidder; children: Raechel, Paul. Degree in acctg., U. Akron, 1980. Ward 6 councilman City of Akron, 1984-92, svc. dir., 1992—. Past chmn. budget and fin. com., Akron City Coun. Office: Office of Svc Dir Mcpl Bldg 166 S High St Rm 201 Akron OH 44308-1628

KIECOLT-GLASER, JANICE KAY, psychologist; b. Oklahoma City, June 30, 1951; d. Edward Harold and Vergie Mae (Lively) Kiecolt; m. Ronald Glaser, Jan. 18, 1980. BA in Psychology with honors, U. Okla., 1972; PhD in Clin. Psychology, U. Miami, 1976. Lic. psychologist, Ohio. Clin. psychology intern Baylor U. Coll. Medicine, Houston, 1974-75; postdoctoral fellow in adult clin. psychology U. Rochester, N.Y., 1976-78; asst. prof. psychiatry Ohio State U. Coll. Medicine, Columbus, 1978-84, assoc. prof. psychiatry and psychology, 1984-89, prof. psychiatry and psychology, 1989—, dir. divsn. health psychology, 1994—, active various coms. Mem. AIDS study sect. NIMH, 1988-91. Editl. bd. Brain, Behavior and Immunity jour., 1986—, Health Psychology jour., 1989—, Brit. Jour. Health Psychology, 1996—, Jour. Behavioral Medicine, 1994—, Psychosomatic Medicine, 1990—, Jour. Cons. and Clin. Psychology, 1992—, Jour. Gerontology, 1992—; reviewer Jour. Personality and Social Psychology, Psychiatry Rsch. jour.; contbr. articles to profl. jours., chpts. to books. NIMH grantee, 1985—; recipient Merit award NIMH, 1993; Ohio State Disting. scholar, 1994. Fellow Am. Psychol. Assn. (Outstanding Contbns. award 1988), Acad. Behavioral Medicine Rsch.; mem. Phi Beta Kappa. Avocations: jogging, fiction writing. Office: Ohio State U Coll Medicine Dept Psychiatry 473 W 12th Ave Columbus OH 43210-1252

KIEFER, GARY, newspaper editor; Now mng. editor features Columbus (Ohio) Dispatch. Office: Columbus Dispatch 34 S 3rd St Columbus OH 43215-4241

KIEL, FREDERICK ORIN, lawyer; b. Columbus, Feb. 22, 1942; s. Fred and Helen Kiel; m. Vivian Lee Naff, June 2, 1963; 1 child Aileen Vivian. AB magna cum laude, Wilmington Coll., 1963; JD, Harvard U., 1966. Bar: Ohio 1966, U.S. Supreme Ct. 1972. Assoc. Peck, Shaffer & Williams, Cin., 1966-71, ptnr., 1971-80, Taft, Stettinius & Hollister, Cin., 1980-89; pvt. practice law, 1990—. Lectr. and expert witness in field; co-founder Bond Attys.' Workshop, 1976. Editor: Bond Lawyers and Bond Law: An Oral History, 1993, Bondletter, 1991—, Anderson Insights, 1992—; contbr. articles on mcpl. bond fin. to profl. jours. Arbitrator Mcpl. Securities Rulemaking Bd., 1985-92; mem. Anderson Twp. Govtl. Task Force, 1986—; sec. Anderson Twp. Greenspace Adv. Com., 1990—; rep. precinct exec. Precinct H. Anderson Twp., 1991-92, 94-2001; twp. atty. Anderson Twp., 1997—; sec. Anderson Twp. Screening Com., 1999 Mem. Ohio State Bar Assn., Cin. Bar Assn., Nat. Assn. Bond Lawyers (dir. 1979-84, pres. 1982-83, hon. dir. 1984—, editor The Quar. Newsletter and The Bond Lawyer 1982—, Bond Atty.'s Workshop steering com. 1976, 83, 85, scrivener com. stds. of practice 1987-89), Queen City Club. Office: 1095 Nimitzview Dr Ste 103 Cincinnati OH 45230-4392

KIEL, SHELLEY, state senator; b. Galesburg, Ill., Aug. 16, 1950; m. Gary Kiel, Mar. 11, 1989; children: Darien, Brien, Joseph M.S., U. Nebr., Omaha, 1977. V.p. mktg. and ednl. design Flat Worl, Inc.; tchr.; state senator State of Nebr., Lincoln. Chmn. Metropolitan Cmty. Coll. (bd. govs.); mem. Save our LIbrs. STeering Com. Mem. Dundee Mem. Pk. Assn. (pres.), Omaha Neighborhood Courage, PTA bds. Lewis and Clark, Kennedy, Dundee schls., Omaha Libr. bd., Women's Fund.. Mem. Met. Cmty. Coll. Bd. Govs.,Pi Beta Phi House Corp. (pres.) Creighton U.; Leadership Omaha Alumni Assn. Congregationalist.

KIENBAUM, THOMAS GERD, lawyer; b. Berlin, Nov. 16, 1942; came to U.S., 1957; s. Gerd Wilhelm Kienbaum and Albertine Brigitte (Kramm) Kettler; m. Karen Smith, June 24, 1966 (div.); 1 child, Ursula; m. Elizabeth Hardy, Jan. 22, 1992. AB, U. Mich., 1965; JD magna cum laude, Wayne State U., 1968. Bar: Mich. 1968, Ill. 1991, U.S. Supreme Ct. 1983. Assoc. Dickinson, Wright, Moon, Van Dusen & Freeman, Detroit, 1968-76, ptnr., 1976-97; ptnr., founder Kienbaum Opperwall Hardy & Pelton, Detroit and Birmingham, 1997—. Contbr. legal articles to profl. publs. Bd. dirs. Wayne County Neighborhood Legal Svc., 1972-76, 87-88. Fellow ABA, State Bar of Mich. Found.; mem. Am. Judicature Soc., Coll. Labor and Employment Lawyers, State Bar Mich. (commr. 1987-96, sec. 1991-93, v.p. 1993-94, pres.-elect 1994-95, pres. 1995-96), Detroit Bar Assn. (pres. 1985-86), Barristers Assn. (pres. 1978-79), Oakland County Bar Assn., Order of the Coif. Avocations: reading, skiing, squash, sailing. Office: Kienbaum Opperwall Hardy & Pelton 325 S Old Woodward Ave Birmingham MI 48009-6202

KIENKER, JAMES W. marketing executive; CFO Boatmen's Bancshares Inc., Martiz Inc. Office: Maritz 1375 N Hgwy Dr Fenton MO 63099

KIERLIN, BOB, state legislator; b. June 1, 1939; 2 children. BSME, MBA, U. Minn. Mem. Minn. Senatefrom 32nd dist., St. Paul, 1999—. Republican. Office: 127 State Office Bldg 100 Constitution Ave Saint Paul MN 55155-1232 Home: PO Box 302 Winona MN 55987-0302

KIERSCHT, MARCIA SELLAND, academic administrator, psychologist; b. Rugby, N.D. d. Osmund Harold and Cynthia (Thoresen) Selland; m. Charles M. Kierscht, Aug. 19, 1961 (div. 1972); children: Cynthia Ann, Matthew Mason. BA, U. Iowa, 1960, MA, 1962; PhD, Vanderbilt U., 1975. Lic. psychologist, Ill., Minn. Sch. psychologist South Suburban Cook County, Homewood, Ill., 1962-64, Dist. 108, Highland Park, 1964-65, Spl. Edn. Dist. Lake County Ill., Gurnee, 1966-72; psychol. examiner John F. Kennedy Ctr., George Peabody Coll., 1972-73; instr. in pediatrics Med. Sch. Vanderbilt U., Nashville, 1975-76; assoc. prof. Moorhead (Minn.) State U., 1976-80, asst. to pres., 1980-86; provost, chief exec. officer Tri-Coll. U., Fargo, N.D., 1986-90; dean grad. and profl. sch. Hood Coll., Frederick, Md., 1990-93; v.p. Consortium of Univs. of the Washington Met. Area, 1993-94; pres. Stephens Coll., Columbia, Mo., 1994—. Contbr. articles to profl. jours. V.p. Plains Art Mus., Moorhead, 1986-88; chmn. bd. govs. Fargo-Moorhead Area Found., Fargo, 1983-90; bd. dirs. United Way, Columbia, 1994-2001. Recipient Pembina Trail award Minn. Hist. Soc., 1994. Mem. Am. Coun. on Edn., Coun. of Fellows, Fargo C. of C., Columbia C. of C. (bd. dirs.), Montgomery County High Tech. Coun., Rotary Club (Moorhead, Columbia, Fredericktowne), Cosmos Club, Washington. Office: Office of Pres 1200 E Broadway Columbia MO 65201-4978

KIESAU, JEAN, retail executive; Pres. Home of Economy, Grand Forks, N.D. Office: Home of Economy 1508 N Washington St Grand Forks ND 58203-1458

KIESSLING, LAURA LEE, chemist, researcher; b. Milw., Sept. 21, 1960; d. William E. and LaVonne V. (Korth) K. SB, MIT, 1983; PhD, Yale U., 1989. Teaching asst. MIT, Cambridge, Mass., 1982-83, Yale U., New Haven, 1983-84, rsch. asst., 1984-89; rsch. fellow Calif. Tech. U., Pasadena, 1989-91; asst. prof. chemistry U. Wis., Madison, 1991-97, assoc. prof., 1997-99, prof. chemistry, prof. biochemistry, 1999—. Cons. Ophidian, Inc., 1997-99, Alfred P. Sloan Found. Fellowships, 1997—; mem. bioorganic and natural products study sect. NIH, 1997—; sci. adv. bd. Promega Corp., 1999—; selection com. for editor Jour. Organic Chemistry, 1999. Mem. editl. bd. Chemistry and Biology, 1997—, Organic Reactions, 2000—; contbr. articles to profl. jours. Recipient Dow Chems. New Faculty award, 1992, Shaw Scientist award, 1992-97, Nat. Young Investigator award NSF, 1993-98, Beckman Young Investigator award, 1994-96, Zeneca Excellence in Chemistry award, 1996, Dreyfus Tchr.-Scholar award Dreyfus Found., 1996; Postdoctoral fellow Am. Cancer Soc., 1989-91, MacArthur fellow John D. and Catherine MacArthur Found., 1999, Alfred P. Sloan Found. fellow, 1997. Mem. AAAS, Am. Chem. Soc. (Cope scholar 1999, Isbell award 2000), Soc. Glycobiology, Am. Soc. for Biochemistry and Molecular Biology, Sigma Xi, Phi Lambda Upsilon. Avocations: canoeing, rowing, running. Office: U Wis Dept Chemistry 1101 University Ave Madison WI 53706-1322 Fax: 608-265-0764.

KIFFMEYER, MARY, state official; b. Balta, N.D., Dec. 29, 1946; m. Ralph Kiffmeyer; children: Christina, Patrick, James, John. RN, St. Gabriel's Sch. Nursing, Little Falls, Minn.; student, Anoka Ramsey C.C. RN, Minn.; cert. election judge. Co-owner RK Anesthesia, Big Lake, Minn.; sec. of state State of Minn., St. Paul, 1999—. Office: Office of Secretary of State 100 Constitution Ave Ste 180 Saint Paul MN 55155-1210

KIGGEN, JAMES D. telecommunications industry executive; Pres. Xtek, Inc., Cin., 1979-85, CEO, 1985-98; chmn. bd. dirs. Cin. Bell, Inc., 1999-2000; chmn. Broadwing Inc., Cincinnati, 2000—. Bd. dirs. 5th 3d Bancorp, U.S. Playing Card Co. Office: Broadwing Inc 201 E 4th St Cincinnati OH 45202-4122

KIKOLER, STEPHEN PHILIP, lawyer; b. N.Y.C., Apr. 24, 1945; s. Sigmund and Dorothy (Javna) K.; m. Ethel Lerner, June 18, 1967; children: Jeffrey Stuart, Shari Elaine. AB, U. Mich., 1966, JD cum laude, 1969. Bar: Ill. 1969, U.S. Dist. Ct. (no. dist.) Ill. 1969, U.S. Ct. Appeals (7th cir.) 1988, U.S. Ct. Appeals (11th cir.) 1994, U.S. Ct. Mil. Appeals 1970, U.S. Supreme Ct. 1994. Capt. Judge Advocate Gen.'s Corps U.S. Army, 1970-73; with Rosenthal & Schanfield, Chgo., 1973—2001, Much, Shelist, Freed, Denenberg, Ament & Rubenstein PC, Chgo., 2001—. Mem. ABA, Am. Land Title Assn., Ill. State Bar Assn., Chgo. Bar. Assn. (real property law com., mechanics' liens subcom.). Home: 2746 Norma Ct Glenview IL 60025-4661 Office: Much Shelist Freed Denenberg Ament & Rubenstein PC 200 N LaSalle St Ste 2100 Chicago IL 60601-1095 E-mail: skikoler@muchlaw.com.

KILBANE, CATHERINE M. lawyer; b. Cleve., Apr. 10, 1963; BA cum laude, Case Western Res. U., 1984, JD cum laude, 1987. Bar: Ohio 1987. Ptnr. Baker & Hostetler, Cleve., 1997—. Mem. Delta Theta Phi. Office: Baker & Hostetler 3200 Nat City Ctr 1900 E 9th St Ste 3200 Cleveland OH 44114-3475

KILBANE, THOMAS STANTON, lawyer; b. Cleve., Mar. 7, 1941; s. Thomas Joseph and Helen (Stanton) K.; m. Sally Conway Kilbane, June 4, 1966; children: Sarah, Thomas, Eamon, James, Carlin. BA magna cum laude, John Carroll U., 1963; JD, Northwestern U., 1966. Bar: Ohio 1966, U.S. Dist. Ct. (no. dist.) Ohio 1967, U.S. Supreme Ct. 1975, U.S. Ct. Claims 1981, U.S. Ct. Appeals (6th cir.) 1982, U.S. Ct. Appeals (3d cir.) 1990, U.S. Ct. Appeals (5th cir.) 1998, U.S. Ct. Appeals (7th cir.) 2002. Assoc. Squire, Sanders & Dempsey, Cleve., 1966-76, ptnr., 1976—, adminstrv. com., 1979-80, mgmt. com., 1981-83, 87-90, mng. ptnr. litigation practice area, 1991—. Fed. ct. panelist U.S. Dist. Ct. (no. dist.) Ohio. Mem. editl. bd. Northwestern U. Law Rev., 1965-66. Active Rep. Presdl. Task Force; bd. dirs. United Way Svcs. Capt. U.S. Army, 1967-69, Vietnam. Decorated Bronze Star; named Greater Cleve. Cath. Man of Yr., 1996. Fellow ABA, Am. Coll. Trial Lawyers, Internat. Acad. Trial Lawyers, Master Bencher of Anthony J. Celebrezze Inns of Ct.; mem. Fed. Bar Assn., Am. Coll. Barristers, Ohio Bar Assn. (AAA corp. counsel com., ctr. for pub. resources constrn. com.), Greater Cleve. Bar Assn., Def. Rsch. Inst., Jud. Conf. 8th Jud. Dist. Ohio (life), Union Club, The 50 Club, The Club, Alpha Sigma Nu. Republican. Roman Catholic. Office: Squire Sanders & Dempsey 4900 Key Tower 127 Public Sq Ste 4900 Cleveland OH 44114-1304 E-mail: tkilbane@ssd.com.

KILBRIDE, THOMAS L. judge; m. Mary Kilbride; 3 children. BA magna cum laude, St. Mary's Coll., 1978; JD, Antioch Sch. Law, 1981. Practicioner U.S. Dist. Ct., Ill., U.S. Seventh Cir. Ct. Appeals; Supreme Ct. justice Ill. State Supreme Ct., 2000—. Former mem. bd. dirs., former v.p., former pres. Ill. Twp. Attys. Assn. Vol. legal adv. Cmty. Caring Conf., Quad City Harvest Inc.; charter chmn. Quad Cities Interfaith Sponsoring Com.; former mem. Rock Island Human Rels. Com.; former vol. lawyer, charter mem. Ill. Pro Bono Ctr. Mem.: Rock Island County Bar Assn., Ill. State Bar Assn. Office: 1800 Third Ave Rm 202 Rock Island IL 61201*

KILBURG, PAUL J. federal judge; b. 1945; Chief bankruptcy judge U.S. Bankruptcy Ct. (no. dist.) Iowa, Cedar Rapids, 1993—; judge State of Iowa, 1978-93. Served in USAF, 1963-68. Office: Bankruptcy Ct 425 2d St SE Cedar Rapids IA 52407 Fax: (319) 286-2290.

KILDEE, DALE EDWARD, congressman; b. Flint, Mich., Sept. 16, 1929; s. Timothy Leo and Norma Alicia (Ullmer) K.; m. Gayle Heyn, Feb. 27, 1965; children: David, Laura, Paul. BA, Sacred Heart Sem., 1952; tchr.'s cert., U. Detroit, 1954; MA, U. Mich., 1961; postgrad. (Rotary Found. fellow), U. Peshawar, Pakistan, 1958-59. Tchr. U. Detroit H.S., 1954-56, Flint Central H.S., 1956-64; mem. Mich. Ho. of Reps., 1964-74, Mich. Senate, 1975-76, U.S. Congress from 7th Mich. dist., 1977-93, U.S. Congress from 9th Mich. dist., 1993—; mem. edn. and the workforce com., ranking minority mem. subcom. on early childhood, youth, & families; mem. resources com., mem. congl. auto caucus; mem. edn. and the workforce com. Mem. NAACP (life), Am. Fedn. Tchrs., Urban League, K.C., Optimists, Phi Delta Kappa. Lodges: K.C; Optimists. Office: US Ho of Reps 2107 Rayburn House Bldg Washington DC 20515-0001 also: 432 N Saginaw St Ste 410 Flint MI 48502-2018*

KILGARIN, KAREN, state official, public relations consultant; b. Omaha, Mar. 12, 1957; d. Bradford Michael and Verna Jane (Will) Kilgarin; 1 child Celeste Mattson Torrence. BA, U. Nebr., Kearney, 1979. With Real Estate Assocs., Inc., Omaha, 1979—84; capitol bur. chief Sta. KETV, 1984—92; dir. comm. and publs. Nebr. Edn. Assn., Lincoln, 1995—98, 1999—; dep. chief staff to gov., dir. pub. rels. State of Nebr., 1992—95, dir. dept. adminstrv. svcs., 1998—99. Mem. Nebr. Senate, Omaha, 1980—84; judicial nominating com. Gubernatorial appointment, 2000; mem. Capital Environment Commn. Mayor appointment, 2000. Mem. exec. com. Nebr. Dem. Com., Lincoln, 1995—98; trustee U. Nebr.-Kearney Found., 1992—95, mem. chancellor's adv. coun., 1995—. Recipient Oustanding Alumni award U. Nebr.-Kearney, 1993, Omaha South H.S., 1995, Wings award LWV, Omaha, 1995, President's award Nebr. Broadcasters Assn., 1995. Mem. NEA (pub. rels. coun. of states), Soc. Profl. Journalists, State Edn. Editors. Presbyterian. Avocations: photography, collecting, politics. Office: NSEA 605 S 14th St Lincoln NE 68508-2726

KILIAN, THOMAS J. insurance company executive; BS, U. Notre Dame. Pres. Pioneer Life Ins. Co.; sr. v.p. data processing Conseco, Inc., Carmel, Ind., 1989-96; pres. Conseco Svcs., L.L.C., 1996-98; pres., COO Conseco, Inc., 2000—. Office: Conseco Inc 11825 N Pennsylvania St Carmel IN 46032

KILLEEN, TIMOTHY L. aerospace scientist, research administrator; b. Cardiff, Wales, Jan. 21, 1952; came to U.S., 1978; married. BSc in Physics (1st class hons.), U. London, Eng., 1972, PhD in Atomic and Molecular Physics, 1975. Postdoctoral scholar U. Mich., Ann Arbor, 1978-79, asst. rsch. scientist, 1979-84, assoc. rsch. scientist, 1984-87, assoc. prof. atmospheric, oceanic and space scis., 1987-90, prof. atmospheric, oceanic and space scis., 1990-2000, dir. Space Physics Rsch. Lab., 1993-2000, assoc. v.p. rsch., 2000—; dir. Nat. Ctr. Atmospheric Rsch., Boulder, Colo., 2000—. Vis. scientist Nat. Ctr. for Atmospheric Rsch., 1983, 85, 86, 87 summers, affiliate scientist, 1988-92; cons. Rockwell Internat., Westinghouse GE Corp, 1989-92, PRC, Inc., NASA Headqtrs., NSF, Taiwanese Space Program; refereee for: Jour. Geophys. Rsch., Geophys. Rsch. Letters, NASA proposals, Applied Optics, Space Sci. Instrumentation, Phys. Scripta, Annales Geophysicae, Planetary and Space Scis, Radio Sci., AFOSR proposals, NSCF proposals, Cambridge U. Press, Am. Meteor. Soc., Nat. Rsch. Coun. Can., and others; co-dir. Rsch. Experiences for Undergrads. Site at U. Mich., 1986—; mem. U.S. Nat. Com. for Solar Terrestrial Energy Program, program rev. com. for NSF CFS and UAF programs, 1989, 90; chm. program review com. for the NSF Aeronomy program, 1986-88, 89; mem. COSPAR Commn. C task force on the CIRA-86 model atmosphere, vice chmn. COSPAR Commn. C.; chm. NSF CEDAR program sci. steering com., 1988-91; prin. investigator on projects for NASA, NSF, Phillip's Lab. Contbr. over 100 articles to profl. jours. including Jour. Geophys. Rsch., Applied Physics, Applied Optics, Space Sci. Instrumentation, Atomic Physics, Planetary and Space Scis., and others; assoc. editor Jour. Geophys. Rsch. (Space Physics), 1987-92, Jour. Atmopheric and Terrestrial Physics (N.Am.), 1995—; presenter papers at over 200 sci. meetings, confs., symposiums. Mem. U. Mich. Civil Liberties Bd., 1990-93, chmn. 1992-93; mem. U. Mich. faculty grievance bd. Mem. AAUP, Am. Geophys. Union (solar-planetary rels. exec. com., meetings com., fed. budget rev. com., pub. affairs com., chmn. solar-planetary rels. program com. fall 1987; convenor and presider for spl. sci. sessions at nat. meetings, convenor of Chapman conf. on the lower thermosphere and upper mesosphere 1992), Inst. Physics (Eng.), Am. Optical Soc. Office: U Mich Space Physics Rsch 2455 Hayward St Ann Arbor MI 48109-2143 also: Nat Ctr Atmospheric Rsch 1850 Table Mesa Dr Boulder CO 80305-5602

KILMAN, JAMES WILLIAM, surgeon, educator; b. Terre Haute, Ind., Jan. 22, 1931; s. Arthur and Irene (Piker) K.; m. Priscilla Margaret Jackson, June 20, 1968; children: James William, Julia Anne, Jennifer Irene. B.S., Ind. State U., 1956; M.D., Ind. U., 1960. Intern Ind.U. Med. Ctr., Indpls., 1960-61; resident surgery Ind.U. Med. Center, 1961-66, asst. prof., 1966-69, assoc. prof., 1969-73; prof. surgery Ohio State U. Coll. Medicine, 1973-91, prof. surgery emeritus, 1991—; chmn. dept. thoracic surgery Children's Hosp., 1975-91; aftending surgeon Univ. Hosp., Columbus, Ohio; attending staff Children's Hosp., pres. staff, 1978; attending staff Grant Hosp., Riverside Hosp. Cons. surgeon VA Hosp., Dayton; pres. Columbus Acad. Medicine, 1977 Trustee Central Ohio Heart Assn., Acad. Medicine Edn. Found., Children's Hosp., 1978— . Served with USNR, 1951-55. USPHS Cardiovascular fellow, 1963-64; recipient Alumni Achievement award, Ind. State U., 1989. Fellow ACS, Am. Coll. Cardiology, Am. Acad. Pediats., Coll. Chest Physicians; mem. Columbus Surg. Soc. (pres. 1974, hon. mem. 1993), Columbus Acad. Medicine (coun. 1971-73), Am. Surg. Assn., Soc. Univ. Surgeons, Am. Assn. Thoracic Surgery, Cen. Surg. Assn., Western Surg. Assn., Soc. Vascular Surgery, Internat. Cardiovasc. Soc., Internat. Soc. Surgeons, Chest Club, Cardiovasc. Surgery Club, City Club, Palm Aire Country Club, Faculty Club, Capital Club, Columbus Athletic Club, Pickaway County Country Club, Am. Boxer Club (bd. dirs. 2000—, pres. 2001—), Sigma Xi, Alpha Omega Alpha. Achievements include rsch., articles infant cardiopulmonary bypass and surgery for congenital heart lesions. Home and Office: 4231 Jackson Pike Grove City OH 43123-9198 Home: 7517 Fairlinks Ct Sarasota FL 34243-3846 E-mail: B16doc@aol.com.

KILPATRICK, CAROLYN CHEEKS, congresswoman; b. Detroit, June 25, 1945; d. Marvell and Willa Mae (Henry) Cheeks; divorced; children: Kwame, Ayanna. AS, Ferris State Coll., Big Rapids, Mich.., 1965; BS, Western Mich. U., 1972; MS in Edn., U. Mich., 1977. Tchr. Murray Wright High Sch., Detroit, 1972-78; mem. Mich. Ho. of Reps., Lansing, 1978-96, U.S. Congress from 15th Mich. dist., Washington, 1997—; mem. appropriations com. Del. Dem. Convs., 1980, 84, 88. Participant Mich. African Trade Mission, 1984, UN Internat. Women's Conf., 1986; del. participant Mich. Dept. Agr. to Nairobi (Kenya) Internat. Agr. Show, 1986. Recipient Anthony Wayne award Wayne State U., Disting. Legislator award U. Mich., Disting. Alumni award Ferris State U., Woman of Yr. award Gentlemen of Wall St., Inc., Burton-Abercrombie award 15th Dem. Congrl. dist. Mem. Nat. Orgn. 100 Black Women. Office: House of Reps 1610 Longworth House Office Bldg Washington DC 20515-2215*

KILPATRICK, KWAME, mayor; Doctorate , Detroit Coll. Law; BS in political sci., Fla. A&M Univ. Mayor City of Detroit , 2002—. Designer Clean Mich. Initiative , 1998. Democrat. Office: 1600 W Lafayette Blvd Detroit MI 48216*

KILROY, JOHN MUIR, lawyer; b. Kansas City, Mo., Apr. 12, 1918; s. James L. and Jane Alice (Scurry) K.; m. Lorraine K. Butler, Jan. 26, 1946; children: John Muir, William Terence. Student, Kansas City Jr. Coll., 1935-37; AB, U. Kansas City, 1940; JD, U. Mo., 1942. Bar: Mo. 1942. Practice in, Kansas City, 1946—; ptnr. Shughart, Thomson & Kilroy, 1948—, pres., 1977-86, chmn. bd. dirs., 1980-88, chmn. emeritus, 1988—. Instr. med. jurisprudence U. Health Scis., 1973-93; panelist numerous med.-legal groups ACS, Mo. Med. Assn., Kans. U. Med. Sch., S.W. Clin. Soc. Contbr. articles to profl. jours. Chmn. bd. dirs. Kansas City Heart Assn.; mem. adv. bd. Midwest Christian Counseling Svc.; bd. dirs., pres. Della Lamb Cmty. Svc., 1991, chmn. bd. dirs., 1993; bd. dirs. Laubach Literacy Coun., 1998-2001, Kingswood Manor, 1992-94, Mo. Meth. Found., 1993-2002. Named Man of Yr., Sigma Chi, 1989. Fellow Am. Coll. Trial Lawyers; mem. ABA, Mo. Bar Assn. (chmn. med. legal com.), Kansas City Bar Assn. (Litigator Emeritus award 1990), Internat. Assn. Barristers, Internat. Assn. Def. Counsel, Am. Coll. Legal Medicine, Am. Bd. Profl. Liability Attys., Fedn. Ins. Counsel, Law Soc. U. Mo., Order Barristers U. Mo., Lawyers Assn., Kansas City (pres. 1968), Kansas City C. of C., Univ. Club (v.p. 1984, pres. 1985), Indian Hills Country Club, Kansas City Club. Home: 6860 Tomahawk Rd Mission Hills KS 66208-2176 Office: Shughart Thomson & Kilroy 120 W 12th St Ste 1800 Kansas City MO 64105-1922

KILROY, WILLIAM TERRENCE, lawyer; b. Kansas City, Mo., May 24, 1950; s. John Muir and Katherine Lorraine (Butler) K.; m. Marianne Michelle Maurin, Sept. 8, 1984; children: Kyle E., Katherine A. BS, U. Kans., 1972, MA, 1974; JD, Washburn U., 1977. Bar: Mo. 1977. Assoc. Shughart, Thomson & Kilroy, Kansas City, Mo., 1977-81, mem., dir., 1981—. Contbr. articles to profl. publs. Mem. Kans. City Citizens Assn., 1980—; pres., bd. govs. Sch. Law Washburn, 1992-94; with Civic Coun. of Greater Kansas City, 1999—; legal coun. Heart of Am. Coun. Boy Scouts Am., 1988-92, mem. exec. com., 1988-95, Cmty. adv. Greater Kans. City Cmty. Found. and Affiliated Trusts, 1993-2000; bd. dirs. Kansas City Neighborhood Alliance, 1998—, Greater Kansas City Crime Commn. Mem. Lawyers Assn. Kansas City, Kansas City Bar Assn. (chmn. civil rights com. 1984), Mo. Bar Assn., ABA (subcom. on arbitration, labor law sect. 1977—), Greater Kansas City C. of C., Kansas City Club, Kansas City Country Club. Office: Shughart Thomson & Kilroy 12 Wyandotte Plz 120 W 12th St Ste 1500 Kansas City MO 64105-1929

KILZER, RALPH, state legislator; b. Bently, S.D., Aug. 30, 1935; m. Marcia; six children. BA, St. John U.; MD, Marquete U. Clin. prof. surgery UND Sch. Med.; mem. N.D. Ho. of Reps., Bismark, 1957, N.D. Senate from 47th dist., Bismark, 1996—. Founder Bone and Joint Ctr. Mem. Knight of the Holy Sepulchre; with U.S. ARmy. Recipient U. Mary McCarthy award. Mem. AMA, Am. Acad. Ortho. Surgeons, NFIB, Elks Club, Knights of Columbus; Legis. Chmn. N.D. Med. Assn. Republican; Roman Caholic. Office: 2040 N Grandview Ln Bismarck ND 58503-0845 E-mail: rkilzer@stae.nd.us.

KIM, BYUNG RO, environmental engineer; BSCE, Seoul Nat. U., 1971; MS in Environ. Engring., U. Ill., 1974, PhD in Environ. Engring., 1976. Registered profl. engr., Tenn. Environ. engr. Tenn. Valley Authority, Chattanooga, 1976-80; asst. prof. civil engring. Ga. Inst. Tech., Atlanta, 1980-85; staff rsch. engr. GM Rsch. Labs., Warren, Mich., 1985-90; staff tech., specialist Ford Rsch. Lab., Dearborn, 1990—. Adj. prof. environ. engring. Wayne State U., Detroit, 1994—. Contbr. articles to profl. jours. Office: PO Box 2053 Dearborn MI 48123-2087

KIM, CHONG LIM, political science educator; b. Seoul, Korea, July 17, 1937; came to U.S., 1962; s. Soo Myung and Chung Hwa (Moon) K.; m. Eun Hwa Park, Aug. 21, 1963; children: Bohm S., Lahn S., Lynn S. BA, Seoul Nat. U., 1960; MA, U. Oreg., 1964, PhD, 1968. Instr. U. Oreg., Eugene, 1965-67; asst. prof. U. Iowa, Iowa City, 1968-70, assoc. prof., 1970-75, prof., 1975—. Author: Legislative Connection, 1984, Legislative Process in Korea, 1981, Patterns of Recruitment, 1974; editor: Legislative Systems, 1975, Political Participation in Korea, 1980; contbr. numerous articles to profl. jours. Mem. Am. Polit. Sci. Assn., Midwest Polit. Sci. Assn. Avocations: reading, travel. Office: U Iowa Dept Polit Sci Iowa City IA 52242 E-mail: chong-kim@uiowa.edu.

KIM, E. HAN, finance and business administration educator; b. Seoul, Korea, May 27, 1946; came to U.S., 1966; s. Chang Yoon and Young Ja (Chung) K.; m. Tack Han, June 14, 1969; children— Juliane H., Elaine H., Deborah H. BS, U. Rochester, 1969; MBA, Cornell U., 1971; PhD, SUNY-Buffalo, 1975. Asst. prof. Ohio State U., Columbus, 1975-77, assoc. prof., 1979-80; assoc. prof., then prof. fin. and bus. adminstrn. U. Mich., Ann Arbor, 1980-84, Fred M. Taylor Disting. prof., 1984—, chmn. dept. fin., 1988-91; dir. Mitsui Life Fin. Rsch. Ctr., 1990—. Vis. assoc. prof. U. Chgo., 1978-79; vis. rsch. fellow Korea Devel. Inst., 1986-87; econ. cons. Govt. of Korea, 1985-87, 98; Cycle and Carriage vis. prof. Nat. U. Singapore, 1989; Yamaichi prof. econs. U. Tokyo, 1990-91; cons. Bank of Korea, 1985, U.S. Dept. Treasury, IRS, 1988-94, World Bank, 1989-91, 93, Posco, 1995-98, Korea Stock Exch., 1997-98; co-chair Citizens for Econ. Freedom, 1997-99; bd. dirs. Hana Bank, Found. Rsch. in Internat. Banking and Fin. Assoc. editor Jour. Fin., 1979-83, 88-92, Fin. Rev., 1982—, Internat. Jour. Fin., 1990—, Internat. Rev. Fin. Analysis, 1990-92, Rev. No. Am. Jour. of Econs. and Fin., 1990—, Rev. Quantitative Fin. and Acctg., 1990—, Pacific Basin Fin. Jour., 1991-96; edit. bd. Jour. Bus. Rsch., 1997—; adv. bd. Asia-Pacific Jour. Mgmt., 1990-96, Jour. Asian Bus., 1996—; contbr. articles to profl. jours. Mem. Korea-Am. Econ. Assn. (sec. gen. 1985, v.p. 1986, pres. 1996), Am. Econ. Assn., Am. Fin. Assn., Western Fin. Assn. Avocation: tennis, golf. Office: U Mich Sch Bus Adminstrn Ann Arbor MI 48109

KIM, MICHAEL CHARLES, lawyer; b. Honolulu, Mar. 9, 1950; s. Harold Dai You and Maria Adrienne K. Student, Gonzaga U., 1967-70; BA, U. Hawaii, 1971; JD, Northwestern U., 1976. Bar: Ill. 1977, U.S. Dist. Ct. (no. dist.) Ill. 1977, U.S. Ct. Appeals (7th cir.) 1981, U.S. Supreme Ct. 1986. Assoc. counsel Nat. Assn. Realtors, Chgo., 1977-78; assoc. Rudnick & Wolfe, 1978-83, Rudd & Assocs., Hoffman Estates, Ill., 1983-85; ptnr. Rudd & Kim, Hoffman Estates and Chgo., 1985-87; prin. Michael C. Kim & Assocs., Chgo. and Schaumburg, Ill., 1987-88; ptnr. Martin, Craig, Chester & Sonnenschein, Chgo. and Schaumburg, 1988-91, Arnstein & Lehr, Chgo., 1991—. Gen. counsel Assn. Sheridan Condo-Coop Owners, Chgo., 1988—; adj. prof. John Marshall Law Sch., Chgo. Author column Apt. and Condo News, 1984-87; co-author Historical and Practice Notes; contbr. articles to profl. jours. Bd. dirs. Astor Villa Condo Assn., Chgo., 1987-91, treas. 1987-89. Mem. ABA, Chgo. Bar Assn. (chmn condominium law subcom. 1990-92, chmn. real property legis. subcom. 1995-97, vice chmn. real property law com., 1998-99, chmn. real proprty law com. 1999-2000), Ill. State Bar Assn. (real estate law sect. coun. 1990-94, corp. and securities law sect. coun. 1990-92), Asian Am. Bar Assn. Greater Chgo. Area (bd. dirs. 1987-88, 90-91), Cmty. Assns. Inst. Ill. (bd. dirs. 1990-92, pres. 1992), Coll. Cmty. Assn. Lawyers (bd. govs. 1994-98), Univ. Club (Chgo.). Avocations: squash, photography, travel. Office: Arnstein & Lehr 120 S Riverside Plz Ste 1200 Chicago IL 60606-3910

KIM, YOON BERM, immunologist, educator; b. Pyongnam, Korea, Apr. 25, 1929; came to U.S., 1959, naturalized, 1975; s. Sang Sun and Yang Rang (Lee) K.; m. Soon Cha Kim, Feb. 23, 1959; children: John, Jean, Paul. MD, Seoul Nat. U., 1958; PhD, U. Minn., 1965. Intern Univ. Hosp. Seoul Nat. U., 1958-59; asst. prof. microbiology U. Minn., Mpls., 1965-70, assoc. prof., 1970-73; mem., head lab. ontogeny of immune system Sloan Kettering Inst. Cancer Research, Rye, N.Y., 1973-83; prof. immunology Cornell U. Grad. Sch. Med. Scis., N.Y.C., 1973-83, chmn. immunology unit, 1980-82; prof. microbiology, immunology and medicine, chmn. dept. micorbiology and immunology Finch U. Health Scis., Chgo. Med. Sch., 1983—, acting dean Sch. Grad. and Postdoctoral Studies, 1994-95. Mem. Lobund adv. bd. U. Notre Dame, 1977-88. Contbr. numerous articles on immunology to profl. jours. Recipient rsch. career devel. award USPHS, 1968-73, Morris Parker Meritorius Rsch. award U. Health Scis., Chgo. Med. Sch., 1984. Fellow Am. Acad. Microbiology; mem. AAAS, Korean Acad. Sci. and Tech., Assn. Gnotobiotics (pres.), Internat. Assn. for Gnotobiology (founding), Am. Assn. Immunologists, Am. Soc. Microbiology, Am. Assn. Pathologists, Korean-Am. Med. Assn., N.Y. Acad. Scis., Soc. for Leucocyte Biology, Internat. Soc. Devel. Comparative Immunology, Harvey Soc., Internat. Soc. Interferon and Cytokine Rsch., Korean Acad. Sci. and Tech., Chgo. Assn. Immunologists (pres.), Assn. Med. Sch. Microbiology and Immunology Chairs, Internat. Endotoxin Soc. (charter), Soc. Natural Immunity (charter), Sigma Xi, Alpha Omega Alpha. Achievements include discovery of the unique germfree dolostrum-deprived immunologically "virgin" piglet model used to investigate ontogenic development and regulation of the immune system including T/B lymphocytes, natural killer/killer cells, and macrophages; research on ontogeny and regulation of immune system, immunochemistry and biology of bacterial toxins, host-parasite relationships and gnotobiology. Home: 313 Weatherford Ct Lake Bluff IL 60044-1905 Office: Finch U Health Scis Chgo Med Sch 3333 Green Bay Rd North Chicago IL 60064-3037 E-mail: kimy@finchcms.edu.

KIMBALL, CLYDE WILLIAM, physicist, educator; b. Laurium, Mich., Apr. 20, 1928; s. Clyde D. and Gertrude M. (O'Neil) K. B.S. in Engring. Physics, Mich. Coll. Mining and Tech., 1950, M.S., 1952; Ph.D. in Physics, St. Louis U., 1959. Staff scientist aeronutronic div. Ford Co., 1960-62; assoc. physicist Argonne Nat. Lab., Ill., 1962-64; prof. physics No. Ill. U., De Kalb, 1964—, Presdl. rsch. chair, 1982-86, rsch. prof., 1986-88, disting. prof., 1989—, advisor to pres. sci. and tech., 1982-88. Program dir. low temperature physics Materials Research Div., NSF, Washington, 1978-79; chair, bd. govs. Consortium for Advanced Radiation Sources, 1994—; exec. com. Basic Energy Sci. Synchrotron Rsch. Ctr., 1994—. Contbr. articles to profl. jours. Served with U.S. Army, 1952-54 Fellow Am. Phys. Soc.; mem. AAAS, Am. Assn. Physics Tchrs., Sigma Xi. Home: PO Box 842 Dekalb IL 60115-0842 Office: No Ill U Dept Physics Faraday West 217 Dekalb IL 60115

KIMBALL, MARC KENNEDY, senatorial staff; b. Ely, Minn., Nov. 9, 1960; s. Robert W. and Susan K.; m. Michele Heigle, Oct. 5, 1991; children: Adam C., Amanda R. BA in Journalism, U. Minn., 1983. Reporter Minn. Daily, Mpls., 1983-85; tchr. English Helena Sch., Tsuchiura, Japan, 1984-85; dep. press. sec. U.S. Rep. Gerry Sikorski, Fridley, Minn., 1985-89; press. sec. U.S. Rep. Byron Dorgan, Washington, 1989-92, U.S. Senator Byron Dorgan, Washington, 1992-94, Ho. Budget Comm., Washington, 1994-95, minority press sec., 1995-97; press sec. U.S. Rep. Martin Sabo, 1997-98, U.S. Sen. Thomas Daschle, Washington, 1998-2001; dep. chief staff/comms. dir. U.S. Sen. Mark Dayton, 2001—. Democrat. Lutheran. Avocations: hockey, soccer. Home: 4415 Lily Ave Lake Elmo MN 55042 Office: US Sen Mark Dayton 298 Federal Bldg Fort Snelling MN 55111 E-mail: marc_kimball@dayton.senate.gov.

KIMBLE, BERNIE, radio director; b. Rochester, NY; Program dir. WNWV, Elyria, Ohio. Office: WMWV 538 W Broad St PO Box 406 Elyria OH 44036

KIMBLE, JUDITH E. molecular biologist, cell biologist; b. Providence, Apr. 24, 1949; BA, U. Calif., Berkeley, 1971; PhD, U. Colo., 1978; postgrad., MRC, Cambridge, Eng., 1978-82. Asst. prof. to assoc. prof. U. Wis., 1983-92; prof. molecular biology, biochemistry U. Wisc., Madison, 1992—, prof. med. genetics, 1994—. Investigator Howard Hughes Med. Inst., Md., 1994—. Mem. NAS, Am. Acad. Arts and Sci., Am. Soc. Cell Biology, Am. Soc. Biochemistry and Molecular Biology, Genetic Soc. Office: HHMI/Dept Biochemistry U Wisc-Madison 433 Babcock Dr Madison WI 53706-1544

KIMMEY, JAMES RICHARD, JR. foundation administrator; b. Boscobel, Wis., Jan. 26, 1935; s. James Richard and Frances Dale (Parnell) Kimmey; m. Sarah Webster Eastman, June 21, 1958; children: Elisabeth Webster, James Richard III. BS, U. Wis., 1957, MS, 1959, MD, 1961; MPH, U. Calif. at Berkeley, 1967. Diplomate Am. Bd. Preventive Medicine. Intern Univ. Hosps., Cleve., 1961-62; med. resident Univ. Hosp., Madison, 1962-63; served from surgeon to med. dir. USPHS, 1963-68, chief kidney disease br., 1964-66, regional health dir. N.Y., 1967-68; exec. dir. Cmty. Health Inc., N.Y.C., 1968-70, Am. Pub. Health Assn., 1970-73; sec. Health Policy Coun. Wis., 1973-75; pres. James R. Kimmey Assos., Inc., 1975-85; dir. Midwest Ctr. Health Planning, 1976-79; exec. dir. Inst. Health Planning, 1979-87; prof. pub. health, dir. Ctr. for Health Svcs. Edn. Rsch. St. Louis U. Med. Ctr., 1987-91; dean sch. pub. health St. Louis U., 1991-93, v.p. health scis., 1993-98, exec. v.p., 1998-2000; dir. Inst. Urban Health Policy, 2000-2001; pres. Mo. Found. for Health, 2001—. Adj. prof. NYU, N.Y.C., 1968—70; lectr. Johns Hopkins, 1971—73; clin. instr. U. Wis., 1974—87; pres. Inst. Health Planning, 1979—86; chair Task Force Accreditation Health Professions, 1997—99, St. Louis ConnectCare, 1998—2001; dir. Ctr. Engring. Tech., 1998—2001; vice chair St. Louis Access Health, 1999—2001. Editor: (book) The Nation's Health, 1972—73; mng. editor: Am. Jour. Pub. Health, 1970—73, mem. editl. adv. bd.: Health Cost Mgmt., 1983—87; contbr. articles to profl. jours. Pres. World Fedn. Pub. Health Assns., 1972—73; mem. sci. adv. bd. Gorgas Inst., 1970—73; bd. dirs. Internat. Union Health Edn., 1970—73. Decorated USPHS Commendation medal. Fellow: APHA (governing coun. 1978—81, chmn. cmty. health planning sect. 1979—80, governing coun. 1983—87, 1989—92), Am. Coll. Preventive Medicine; mem.: Prospective Payment Assessment Commn. (commr. 1991—97), Mo. Pub. Health Assn. (Mo. Communicator of the Yr. award 1994), Am. Coll. Health Adminstrs., Am. Health Planning Assn. (dir. 1974—75, 1977—78, corp. sec. 1977—78, pres. 1980—81, Richard H. Schlesinger award 1978, James R. Kimmey award 1994), Alpha Sigma Nu, Delta Omega, Alpha Omega Alpha, Phi Eta Sigma. Democrat. Episcopalian. Home: 1614 S 18th St Saint Louis MO 63104-2504 Office: 211 N Broadway Ste 2200 Saint Louis MO 63102 E-mail: jkimmey@mohealthfdn.org.

KINCAID, MARILYN COBURN, medical educator; b. Bennington, Vt., July 14, 1947; d. E. Robert and Jean A. (Flagg) Coburn; m. William Louis Kincaid, Dec. 21, 1970. AB, Mt. Holyoke Coll., 1969; MD, St. Louis U., 1975. Cert. Am. Bd. Ophthalmology, Am. Bd. Pathology. Asst. prof. ophthalmology & pathology U. Tex., San Antonio, 1982-86; assoc. prof. ophthalmology & pathology U. Mich. Med. Sch., Ann Arbor, 1986-87, St. Louis U. Sch. Medicine, 1989-94, prof., 1994—. Bd. dirs. Singular Vision Outreach, St. Louis. Author (book) Intraocular Lenses, 1989; contbr. articles to profl. jours. Fellow Am. Acad. Ophthalmology (Honor award 1990), Coll. Am. Pathologists; mem. Am. Assn. Ophthalmic Pathologists (sec.-treas. 1983-86). Avocations: sewing, embroidery. Office: St Louis U The Eye Inst 1755 S Grand Blvd Saint Louis MO 63104-1540

KIND, RON, congressman; b. La Crosse, Wis. s. Elroy and Greta Kind; m. Tawni Kind; 1 child, Johnny. Degree with honors, Harvard U., 1985; M, London Sch. Econs.; JD, U. Minn. Formerly with Quarles and Brady, Milw.; past prosecutor La Crosse County, numerous counties, Wis.; mem. U.S. Congress from 3d Wis. dist., 1997—; mem. house edn. and workforce com., resources com., agr. com. Active Freshman Bipartisan Campaign Fin. Reform Task Force; co-founder Upper Miss. River Congl. Caucus. Active Boys' and Girls' Club, La Crosse YMCA; bd. dirs. Coulee Coun. Alcohol or Other Drug Abuse. Mem. New Dem. Network, La Crosse Optimists Club. Lutheran. Office: 1713 Longworth Bldg Washington DC 20515-4903*

KINDER, PETER D. state legislator; b. Cape Girardeau, Mo., May 12, 1954; s. James A. and Mary Frances (Hunter) K. JD, St. Mary U., 1979; postgrad., U. Mo. Columbia, SE Mo. State U. Spl. asst. Rep. Bill Emerson, 1981-82; mem. Mo. Senate from 27th dist., Jefferson City, 1992—. Staff counsel, real estate rep., 1983-87; assoc. publ., 1987—; campaign mgr., 1980, 82. Mem. Mo. Bar Assn., Am. Cancer Soc., Mo. Farm Bur., Area Wide United Way, Lions Club.

KINDIG, FRED EUGENE, statistics educator, arbitrator; b. York, Pa., Sept. 5, 1920; s. Fred E. and Hattie (Keller) K.; m. Marie M. Doyle (dec. 1971); children: Pamela M., Bonita K., Gretchen A., Suzanne J.; m. Grace L. Mathison, Aug. 19, 1972 (dec. 1979); m. Susan S. Friend, Mar. 16, 1980. B.S., Pa. State U., 1942; M.S., U. Pitts., 1947, Ph.D., 1951. Indsl. engr., supr. Westinghouse Electric Corp., Pitts., 1942-51; asst. to exec. v. p. Phoenix Glass, Monaca, Pa., 1951-53; asst. and assoc. prof. U. Pitts., 1953-62; prof., coordinator quantitative methods Ohio State U., Columbus, 1962-81, prof. emeritus, 1981—; labor mgmt. arbitrator, 1953—. Author: Fundamentals of Statistical Controls and Fundamentals of Linear Programming, 1956; Contbr. articles to profl. jours. Pres. PTA, various times; mem. Franklin County 648 Bd., 1979-82; trustee, chmn. bd. trustees Columbus State Community Coll., 1982-92; trustee emeritus, 1992—. Mem. Am. Inst. Decision Scis. (v.p. 1969-71), Am. Arbitration Assn., Nat. Acad. Arbitrators, Am. Soc. Quality Control, Inst. Math. Stats., Am. Statis. Assn., Indsl. Relations Research Assn., Ops. Research Soc. Am., Soc. Profls. In Dispute Resolution, Alpha Sigma Phi, Tau Beta Pi, Beta Gamma Sigma. Clubs: Brookside Country, Univ. Home: 213 Saint Antoine St Columbus OH 43085-2242 Office: 207 St Jacques St Columbus OH 43085-2227

KINDLER, JEFFREY B. lawyer; b. May 13, 1955; JD, Harvard U., 1980. Bar: D.C. 1980. Pres. ptnr. brands McDonald's Corp., 1996-97, exec. v.p., gen. counsel Ill., 1997—; chmn., CEO Boston Mkt., 2000-2001; pres., ptnr. Brands McDonalds Corp., 2001—; chmn., CEO Boston Mkt., 2001—. Office: McDonalds Corp One Kroc Dr Oak Brook IL 60523 E-mail: jeff.kindler@mcd.com.

KINDRICK, ROBERT LEROY, academic administrator, dean, English educator; b. Kansas City, Mo., Aug. 17, 1942; s. Robert William and Waneta LeVeta (Lobdell) K.; m. Carolyn Jean Reed, Aug. 20 1965. BA, Park Coll., 1964; MA, U. Mo., Kansas City, 1967; PhD, U. Tex., 1971. Instr. Ctrl. Mo. State U., Warrenburg, 1967-69, asst. prof. to assoc. prof., 1969-78, prof., 1978-80, head dept. English, 1975-80; dean Coll. Arts and Scis.; prof. English Western Ill. U., Macomb, 1980-84; v.p. acad. affairs, prof. English Emporia State U., Kans., 1984-87; provost, v.p. acad. affairs, prof. English Eastern Ill. U., Charleston, 1987-91; provost, v.p. acad. affairs, dean grad. studies, dean grad. sch., prof. English, U. Mont., 1991-2000; v.p. for acad. affairs and rsch. Wichita State U. Author: Robert Henryson, 1979, A New Classical Rhetoric, 1980, Henryson and the Medieval Arts of Rhetoric, 1993, William Matthews on Caxton and Malory, 1997, The Poems of Robert Henryson, 1997; editor: Teaching the Middle Ages, 1981—, (jour.) Studies in Medieval and Renaissance Teaching, 1975-80; co-editor: The Malory Debate, 2000; contbr. articles to profl. jours. Chmn. bd. dirs. Mo. Com. for Humanities, 1979-80, Ill. Humanities Coun., 1991; pres. Park Coll. Young Dems., 1963; v.p. Mo. Young Dems., Jefferson City, 1964; campus coord. United Way, Macomb, Ill., 1983; mem. study com. Emporia Arts Coun., 1985-88; mem. NFL Edn. Adv. Ed., 1995—. U. Tex. fellow, 1965-66; Am. Coun. Learned Socs. travel grantee, 1975; Nat. Endowment for Humanities summer fellow, 1977; Medieval Acad. Am. grantee, 1976; Mo. Com. Humanities grantee, 1975-84; Assn. Scottish Lit. Studies grantee, 1979. Mem. Mo. Assn. Depts. English (pres. 1978-80), Mo. Philol. Assn. (founding pres. 1975-77), Medieval Assn. Midwest (councillor 1977—, ex officio bd. 1980—, v.p. 1987-88, exec. sec. 1988—), Ill. Medieval Assn. (founding exec. sec. 1983-93), Mid-Am. Medieval Assn., Rocky Mtn. MLA, Assn. Scottish Lt. Studies, Early English Text. Soc., Societe Rencesvals, Medieval Acad. N.Am. (exec. sec. com. on ctrs. and regional assns.), Internat. Arthurian Soc., Sigma Tau Delta, Phi Kappa Phi, Rotary (editor Warrensburg club). Home: PO Box 20110 Wichita KS 67208-1110 Office: Wichita State U 109 Morrison Hall Wichita KS 67208 E-mail: Robert.Kindrick@Wichita.edu.

KINDT, JOHN WARREN, lawyer, educator, consultant; b. Oak Park, Ill., May 24, 1950; s. Warren Frederick and Lois Jeannette (Woelffer) K.; m. Anne Marie Johnson, Apr. 17, 1982; children: John Warren Jr., James Roy Frederick. AB, Coll. William and Mary, 1972; JD, U. Ga., 1976, MBA, 1977; LLM, U. Va., 1978, SJD, 1981. Bar: D.C. 1976, Ga. 1976, Va. 1977. Advisor to gov. State of Va., Richmond, 1971-72; asst. to Congressman M. Caldwell Butler, U.S. Ho. of Reps., Washington, 1972-73; staff cons. White House, 1976-77; asst. prof. U. Ill., Champaign, 1978-81, assoc. prof., 1981-85, prof., 1985—. Cons. 3d UN Conf. on Law of Sea; lectr. exec. MBA program U. Ill. Author: Marine Pollution and the Law of the Sea, 4 vols., 1981, 2 vols., 1988, 92, Economic Impacts of Legalized Gambling, 1994; contbr. articles to profl. jours. Caucus chmn., del. White House Conf. on Youth, 1970; co-chmn. Va. Gov.'s Adv. Coun. on Youth, 1971; mem. Athens (Ga.) Legal Aid Soc., 1975-76. Rotary fellow, 1979-80; Smithsonian ABA/ELI scholar, 1981; sr. fellow London Sch. Econs., 1985-86. Mem. Am. Soc. Internat. Law, D.C. Bar Assn., Va. Bar Assn., Ga. Bar Assn. Home: 801 Brookside Ln Mahomet IL 61853-9545 Office: U Ill 350 Commerce W Champaign IL 61820

KING, ALBERT I. bioengineering educator; b. Tokyo, June 12, 1934; U.S. citizen; married; 2 children. BSc, U. Hong Kong, 1955; MS, Wayne State U., 1960; PhD in Engring. Mechanics, 1966. Demonstrator civil engring., Hong Kong, 1955-58; asst., instr. engring. mechanics Wayne State U., 1958-60, from instr. to assoc. prof., 1960-76, assoc. neurosurgery Sch. Medicine, 1971—, prof. bioengring., 1976—, Disting. Prof. mech. engring., 1990—. Recipient NIH Career Devel. award, Volvo award, 1984, H.R. Lissner award ASME, 1996. Mem. NAE, Am. Soc. Engring. Edn., Am. Soc. Mech. Engrs. (Charles Russ Richards Meml. award 1980), Am. Acad. Orthopaedic Surgeons, Sigma Xi. Achievements include rsch. in human response to acceleration and vibration, automotive and aircraft safety, biomechanics of the spine, mathematical modelling of impact events, low back pain rsch. Office: Bioengring Ctr 818 W Hancock St Detroit MI 48201-3719 E-mail: king@rrb.eng.wayne.edu.

KING, ANDRE RICHARDSON, architectural graphic designer; b. Chgo., July 30, 1931; s. Earl James and Margie Verdetta (Doyle) K.; children: Jandra Maria, Andre Etienne; m. Sally M. Ryan, Sept. 19, 1980. Student, Chgo. Tech. Coll., 1956-57, U. Chgo., 1956-59; B.A.E., Art Inst. Chgo., 1959; grad., Gemological Inst. Am., 1992. ARK, Archtl. & Environ. Graphic Design Firm est., 1982—; With Skidmore, Owings & Merrill, Chgo., 1956-82; ind. designer, cons., 1982—. Mem. alumni bd. Chgo. Art Inst. Served with USAF, 1951-55. Recipient Design award Art Inst. Chgo., 1959, DESI award, 1982; Hon. consul of Barbados, W.I., 1971— Mem. AIA (assoc.), Am. Inst. Graphic Designers, Soc. Environ. Graphic Designers, Soc. Topographic Arts, Chgo. Soc. Communicating Arts, Art Dirs. Club of Chgo. (pres. 1979-80, 80-82), Art Inst. Chgo. Alumni (bd. dirs.), Arts Club of Chgo., Consular Corps of Chgo., Sigma Pi Phi, Beta Boule. Home: 6700 S Oglesby Ave Chicago IL 60649-1301 Office: 6700 S Oglesby Ave Apt 2406 Chicago IL 60649-1387

KING, CHARLES ROSS, physician; b. Nevada, Iowa, Aug. 22, 1925; s. Carl Russell and Dorothy Sarah (Mills) K.; m. Frances Pamela Carter, Jan. 8, 1949; children— Deborah Diane, Carter Ross, Charles Conrad, Corbin Kent Student, Butler U., 1943; BS in Bus., Ind. U., 1948, MD, 1964. Diplomate Am. Bd. Family Practice. Dep. dir. Ind. Pub. Works and Supply, 1949-52; salesman Knox Coal Corp., 1952-59; rotating intern Marion County Gen. Hosp., Indpls., 1964-65; family practice medicine Anderson, Ind., 1965—. Sec.-treas. staff Cmty. Hosp., 1969-72, pres.-elect, dir., chief medicine, 1973—, bd. dirs., 1973-75; sec.-treas. St. John's Hosp., 1968-69, chief medicine, 1972-73, chief pediatrics, 1977—; bd. dirs. Rolling Hills Convalescnet Ctr., 1968-73; pres. Profl. Ctr. Lab., 1965—; vice chmn. Madison County Bd. Health, 1966-69, chmn., 1986—; chmn. bd. dirs. Star Fin. Bank, Anderson. Bd. dirs. Family Svc. Madison County, 1968-69, Madison County Assn. Mentally Retarded, 1972-76, Anderson Fine Arts Ctr., 1996—; trustee St. Johns Health System., 1898—; chmn. bd. dirs. Anderson Downtown Devel. Corp., 1980—; mem. Paramont Restoration Steering Com., 1994—; trustee, sec.-tread. St. John's Med. Ctr., 1989—; mem. exec. com. Madison United Way Fund, vice-chmn., 1995, chmn., 1996; mem. exec. com. Stop Teen Pregnancy Program, 1995—; exec. commr. Health Search Madison County, 1995—. With U.S. Army, 1944-46. Recipient Dr. James Macholtz award Spl. Olympics, 1986— Fellow Royal Soc. Health, Am. Acad. Family Practice (charter); mem. AMA (numerous Physicians Recognition awards), Ind. Med. Assn., Pan Am. Med. Assn., Am. Acad. Gen. Practice, Madison County Med. Soc. (pres. 1970), 9th Dist. Med. Soc. (sec.-treas. 1968), Anderson C. of C. (bd. dirs. 1979-82), Indpls. Mus. Art (corp. mem.), Anderson Country Club (bd. dirs. 1976-79), Phi Delta Theta (pres. Alumni Assn. 1952), Phi Chi. Methodist. Club: Anderson Country (bd. dirs. 1976-79) Home: 920 N Madison Ave Anderson IN 46011-1208 Office: 2015 Jackson St Anderson IN 46016-4337

KING, CLARK CHAPMAN, JR. lawyer; b. Quincy, Ill., May 18, 1929; s. Clark Chapman and Miriam Doris (Decker) K.; m. Joyce Jepson Jones, Jan. 5, 1955; children: Clark Chapman III, Jeffrey L., Stephen D., Carolyn Ann. BA cum laude, Amherst Coll., 1951; LLB, Harvard U., 1954. Bar: Ill. 1955, U.S. Dist. Ct. (no. dist.) 1955, (mid. dist.) Ill. 1960, U.S. Ct. Appeals (7th) 1957, (5th) 1982, (11th) 1985, (6th) 1984, U.S. Supreme Ct. 1977. Asst. atty. gen. State of Ill., Springfield, 1954, spl. asst. atty. gen., 1957-60; assoc. Robertson, Kepner, 1957-60, Hough, Young & Coale, Chgo., 1960-61; ptnr. Lord, Bissell & Brook, 1961-94, of counsel, 1994—. Active Northbrook Civic Assn.; vice-chmn. Cook County Young Reps., Chgo., 1960; area chmn. Northfield Twp. Rep. Orgn., 1960-70. Sgt. U.S. Army, 1954-57. Mem. Chgo. Bar Assn., Internat. Bar Assn., Agrl. Bar Assn. Avocations: fishing, hunting. Office: Lord Bissell & Brook 115 S La Salle St Ste 3200 Chicago IL 60603-3902

KING, DAVE, professional hockey coach; Formerly with Can. Nat. Hockey Program; head coach Calgary Flames, 1992-95; asst. coach, dir. European scouting Mont. Canadiens, 1996-99; head coach Columbus (Ohio) Blue Jackets, 2000—. Coached Calgary Flames to 2 straight division titles, 1993-94, 94-95. Office: c/o Columbus Blue Jackets Ste 235 150 E Wilson Bridge Rd Columbus OH 43085

KING, DONALD A., JR. company executive; Prin. ptnr. The RREEF Funds, Chgo., 1979—. Office: 41st Fl 875 N Michigan Ave Fl 41 Chicago IL 60611-1803

KING, G. ROGER, lawyer; b. Ashland, Ohio, Sept. 16, 1946; BS, Miami U., 1968; JD, Cornell U., 1971. Bar: Ohio 1971, D.C. 1972. Legis. asst. U.S. Senator Robert Taft Jr., Washington, 1971-73; profl. staff counsel Labor and Human Resources Com., U.S. Senate, 1973-74; ptnr. Jones, Day, Reavis & Pogue, Columbus, Ohio. Office: Jones Day Reavis & Pogue 1900 Huntington Ctr Columbus OH 43215-6103 E-mail: gking@jonesday.com.

KING, J. B. medical device company executive, lawyer; AB, Ind. U., 1951; LLB, Mich. U., 1954. Bar: Ind. 1954, Mich. 1954. Atty., ptnr. Baker & Daniels, 1954-87; v.p., gen. counsel Eli Lilly and Co., Indpls., 1987-95, Guidant Corp., Indpls., 1995—. Bd. dirs. Ind. Corp. Survey Commn., Bank One, Indpls, Indpls. Water Co.; conf. bd. Coun. Chief Legal Officers. Mem. bd. govs. Riley Meml. Assn. Fellow Ind. Bar Found.; mem. ABA, Ind. State Bar Assn., Indpls. Bar Assn., 7th Cir. Bar Assn., Nat. Tax Assn. (com. on multistate taxation), Assn. Gen. Counsel, Ind. Legal Found. (bd. dirs.), Ind. Fiscal Policy Inst. (bd. govs.), Ind. Corp.Survey Commn. Home: 5840 High Fall Rd Indianapolis IN 46226-1018 Office: Guidant Corp PO Box 44906 Indianapolis IN 46244-0906

KING, J. JOSEPH, electronics executive; Group v.p. internat. Molex, exec. v.p., pres., COO, 1999—, bd. dirs. Office: Molex Inc 2222 Wellington Ct Lisle IL 60532

KING, JAMES EDWARD, retired museum director, other: museums; b. Escanaba, Mich., July 23, 1940; s. G. Willard and Grace (Magee) K.; m. Frances Bartos, Jan. 15, 1973; 1 child, Scott E. BS, Alma Coll., 1962; MS, U. N.Mex., 1964; PhD, U. Ariz., 1972. Lab asst. in biology Alma Coll., Mich., 1960-62; rsch. asst. dept. biology U. N.Mex., Albuquerque, 1962-64; teaching asst. dept. botany and plant pathology Mich. State U., East Lansing, 1964-66; plant industry inspector Mich. Dept. Agriculture, Lansing, 1966-68; rsch. asst. dept. geochronology U. Ariz., Tucson, 1968-71, rsch. assoc. dept. geoscis., 1971-72; assoc. curator paleobotany Ill. State Mus., Springfield, 1972-78, head sci. sects. and full curator, 1978-85, asst. dir. for sci., 1985-87; adj. assoc. prof. dept. geology U. Ill., Urbana, 1979-88; dir. Carnegie Mus. Natural History, Pitts., 1987-96, Cleve. Mus. Natural History, 1996—2001; mus. cons., 2001—. Adj. prof. biology Sangamon State U., Springfield, Ill., 1983-87; adj. rsch. scientist Hunt Inst. Bot. Documentation, Carnegie Mellon U., Pitts., 1988—; adj. prof. dept. geology and planetary sci., U. Pitts., 1988-96; vis. scientist in residence Alma (Mich.) Coll., 1985. Author sci. papers on topics related to geology and paleobotany; mem. editorial bd. Jour. Archaeol. Sci., 1980-87. Bd. dirs. Western Pa. Conservancy, 1996-97, Allegheny Land Trust, 1995-96; trustee Chagrin River Watershed Ptnrs., 1997—; mem. exec. com. Univ. Cir., Inc., 1996—. Fellow Ill. State Acad. Sci. (pres. 1981-82); mem. Am. Assn. Mus. (bd. dirs. 1994-97), Am. Quaternary Assn., (treas., exec. com. 1976-84), Am. Assn. Stratigraphic Palynologists, Assn. Sci. Mus. Dirs. (v.p. 1992-93, pres. 1993-96), Assn. Systematics Collections (v.p. 1989-91, pres. 1991-93), Sigma Xi (pres. Springfield chpt. 1985-86). Home and Office: Ste 326 6336 N Oracle Rd Tucson AZ 85704

KING, JENNIFER ELIZABETH, editor; b. Summit, N.J., July 15, 1970; d. Layton E. and Margery A. (Long) K. BS in Journalism, Northwestern U., Evanston, Ill., 1992. Asst. editor Giant Steps Media, Chgo., 1992-93, assoc. editor Corp. Legal Times, 1993-94, dir. confs., 1994-95, mng. editor Corp. Legal Times, 1995-2001, v.p. editl. Corp. Legal Times, 2001—; acting mng. editor Ill. Legal Times, 1996-97; mng. editor U.S. Bus. Litig., 1997. Office: Corporate Legal Times LLC 656 W Randolph St # 500-e Chicago IL 60661-2114

KING, LARRY, editor; Exec. editor Omaha World-Herald. Office: Omaha World-Herald World-Herald Sq 1334 Dodge St Omaha NE 68102-1138

KING, LUCY JANE, retired psychiatrist, health facility administrator; b. Vandalia, Ill., Dec. 23, 1932; d. Ira and Lucy Jane (Harris) K. AB, Washington U., St. Louis, 1954, MD, 1958. Diplomate Am. Bd. Psychiatry and Neurology, subspecialty Addiction Psychiatry. From instr. to assoc. prof. psychiatry dept. Washington U., 1963-74; prof. dept. psychiatry Med. Coll. of Va., Richmond, 1974-79; clin. prof. dept. psychiatry George Washington U., Washington, 1981-84, Ind. U. Med. Sch., 1994-99. Mem. editorial bd. Annals of Clin. Psychiatry, 1989—. Author: (with others) Psychiatry in Primary Care, 1983; contbr. articles to profl. jours. Fellow Am. Psychiat. Assn.; mem. Am. Acad. Clin. Psychiatrists, Am. Med. Women's Assn., Am. Acad. Addiction Psychiatry, Am. Soc. Addiction Medicine (cert., dual diagnosis com. 1990—). Avocation: history. Office: Midtown CMHC 1001 W 10th St Indianapolis IN 46202-2859

KING, LYNDEL IRENE SAUNDERS, art museum director; b. Enid, Okla., June 10, 1943; d. Leslie Jay and Jennie Irene (Duggan) Saunders; m. Blaine Larman King, June 12, 1965. B.A., U. Kans., Lawrence, 1965; M.A., U. Minn.-Mpls., 1971, Ph.D., 1982. Dir. Univ. Art Mus., U. Minn.-Mpls., 1979—; dir. exhbns. and mus. programs Control Data Corp., 1979, 80-81; exhbn. coordinator Nat. Gallery of Art, Washington, 1980. Recipient Cultural Contbn. of Yr. award Mpls. C. of C., 1978; Honor award Minn. Soc. Architects, 1979. Mem. Assn. Art Mus. Dirs. (chair art issues com. 1998-2000, chair tech. comm. com. 2000, bd. trustees 1998—), Art Mus. Assn. Am. (v.p. bd. dirs. 1984-89), Assn. Coll. and Univ. Mus. and Galleries (v.p. 1989-92), Am. Assn. Mus., Internat. Coun. Mus., Upper Midwest Conservation Assn. (pres. bd. dirs. 1980—), Minn. Assn. Mus. (steering com. 1982), Am. Fedn. Arts Bd. Home: 326 W 50th St Minneapolis MN 55419-1247 Office: Weisman Art Mus 333 E River Rd Minneapolis MN 55455-0367

KING, MARCIA, management consultant; b. Lewiston, Maine, Aug. 4, 1940; d. Daniel Alden and Clarice Evelyn (Curtis) Barrell; m. Howard P. Lowell, Feb. 15, 1969 (div. 1980); m. Richard G. King Jr., Aug., 1980. BS, U. Maine, 1965; MSLS, Simmons Coll., 1967. Reference, field advisory and bookmobile libr. Maine State Libr., Augusta, 1965-69; dir. Lithgow Pub. Libr., 1969-72; exec. sec. Maine Libr. Adv. Com., Maine State Libr., 1972-73; dir. Wayland (Mass.) Free Pub. Libr., 1973-76; state libr. State of Oreg., Salem, 1976-82; dir. Tucson Pub. Libr., 1982-91; mgmt. cons. King Assocs., Tucson, 1991-2000; dir. Gary Pub. Libr., Ind., 2000—. Past chmn. bd. dirs. Tucson United Way; past chmn. adv. bd. com. Sta. KUAT (PBS-TV and Radio); mem. adv. bd. Resources for Women, Inc.; bd. dirs., past chmn. Salvation Army. Mem. ALA, Nat. Ctr. for Non-Profit Bds. Unitarian. Office: Gary Pub Libr 220 W 6th Ave Gary IN 46402 E-mail: marciak@gary.lib.in.us.

KING, MICHAEL HOWARD, lawyer; b. Chgo., Mar. 10, 1943; s. Warren and Betty (Fine) K.; m. Candice M. King, Aug. 18, 1968; children— Andrew, Julie. B.S. Washington U., St. Louis 1967, J.D. 1970. Bar: Ill. 1970, U.S. Dist. Ct. (no. dist.) Ill. 1970, U.S. Dist. Ct. (ea. dist.) Wis. 1972, U.S. Ct. Appeals (7th cir.) 1974, U.S. Ct. Appeals (5th cir.) 1979, U.S. Supreme Ct. 1975, U.S. Ct. Appeals (3d cir.) 1983, U.S. Tax Ct. 1987, U.S. Ct. Appeals (10th cir.) 1987, U.S. Dist. Ct. (no. dist.) Calif. 1987, U.S. Dist. Ct. Nebr. 1988, U.S. Dist. Ct. (ctrl. dist.) Ill. 1992, U.S. Dist. Ct. (no. dist.) N.Y. 1992, U.S. Ct. Appeals (2nd cir.) 1994. Spl. atty. organized crime, racketeering sect. U.S. Dept. Justice, Washington, 1970-73; asst. U.S. atty. No. Dist. Ill., Chgo., 1973-75; assoc. Antonow & Fink, Chgo., 1976, ptnr., 1977-79; ptnr. Ross & Hardies, Chgo., 1979-95; chmn. Bd. Commr. Office of State Appellate Defender. Co-author Model Jury Instructions in Criminal Antitrust Cases, 1982, Handbook on Antitrust Grand Jury Investigations, 1988. Bd. dirs. Chgo. Youth Ctrs., 1977-82; trustee Cove Sch., 1984-88, the Goodman Theatre, 1993—. Mem. ABA (litigation sect., antitrust sect., criminal practice procedure com.), Ill. Bar Assn., Chgo. Bar Assn. (judiciary com., antitrust com.), Am. Judicature Soc., Fed. Bar Assn., Assn. Trial Lawyers Am., Mid-Am. Club (bd. govs.), Econ. Club, Phi Delta Phi, Alpha Epsilon Pi. Home: 2025 Windy Hill Ln Highland Park IL 60035-4233 Office: Ross & Hardies 150 N Michigan Ave Ste 2500 Chicago IL 60601-7567

KING, NORAH MCCANN, federal judge; b. Steubenville, Ohio, Aug. 13, 1949; d. Charles Bernard and Frances Marcella (Krumm) McCann; married; 4 children. BA cum laude, Rosary Coll. (now Dominican U.), 1971; JD summa cum laude, Ohio State U., 1975. Bar: Ohio 1975, So. Dist. of Ohio 1980. Law clerk U.S. Dist. Ct., Columbus, Ohio, 1975-79; counsel Frost, King, Freytag & Carpenter, 1979-82; asst. prof. Ohio State U., 1980-82; U.S. magistrate judge U.S. Dist. Ct., 1982—, chief magistrate judge, 2000—. Recipient award of merit Columbus Bar Assn., 1990. Mem.: Columbus Bar Assn., Fed. Bar Assn., Coun. U.S. Magistrate Judges. Office: US Dist Ct 85 Marconi Blvd Rm 235 Columbus OH 43215-2837

KING, ORDIE HERBERT, JR. oral pathologist; b. Memphis, Aug. 11, 1933; s. Ordie Herbert and Hazel (Eaton) K.; m. Violette Papagianis, Mar. 21, 1974; children: Catherine Ann, Alexander Carlos; children by previous marriage: Anna LaVelle, Ordie Herbert III. BS, Memphis State U., 1957; DDS, U. Tenn., 1959, PhD, 1965. Diplomate Am. Bd. Oral Pathology. USPHS postdoctoral fellow U. Tenn., 1960-62, rsch. assoc. dept. pathology, 1963-65, asst. prof. pathology, 1965; resident oral pathology U. Tenn., City of Memphis Hosps., 1962-63; asst. prof. pathology Northwestern U., 1966; assoc. prof. oral pathology St. Louis U., 1967-69, prof., 1969-70, chmn. dept., 1967-70, chmn. dept. dentistry univ. hosps., 1967-70; acting chmn., vis. assoc. prof. oral pathology Washington U., St. Louis, 1969-70; prof. oral pathology, assoc. prof. pathology W.Va. U., Morgantown, 1970-74, prof. pathology, 1974, dir. Cytopathology Lab., Med. Ctr., 1971-74; prof. pathology So. Ill. U. Sch. Dental Medicine, Alton, 1974-97; chmn. dept. diagnostic specialties So. Ill. U., Edwardsville, 1979-92; clin. prof. pathology Washington U. Sch. Dental Medicine, St. Louis, 1979-80. Dir. So. Ill. Pathology Lab., Ltd., Godfrey, Ill., 1977—; dental cons. to chief med. examiner State of Tenn., 1963-65; mem. exec. com. St. Louis U. Hosps., 1967-70; mem. med. staff West Tenn. Cancer Clinic, 1962-65, W.Va. U. Hosp., 1970-74; mem. med./dental staff dept pathology Alton (Ill.) Meml. Hosp., 1986—; cons. VA Hosp., Clarksville, W.Va., 1973-74; dental cons. St. Louis County Med. Examiner, 1968-70; cons. cancer control program Nat. Ctr. for Chronic Disease Control, USPHS, 1967-70; mem. Mo. Bd. Dental Splty. Examiners, 1982-84. Fellow Am. Acad. Oral Pathology; mem. Am. Soc. Cytology, ADA, Am. Cancer Soc. (bd. dirs. W.Va. div. 1972-74), Tenn. Walking Horse Breeders and Exhibitors Assn., Spotted Saddle Horse Breeders and Exhibitors Assn., Delta Sigma Delta, Kappa Alpha, Phi Rho Sigma, Omicron Kappa Upsilon. Home: 6111 Vollmer Ln Godfrey IL 62035-1062 Office: So Ill Path Lab Ltd Godfrey IL 62035

KING, REATHA CLARK, community foundation executive; b. Ga. m. N. Judge King Jr.; children: N. Judge III, Scott. BS in Chemistry and Math., Clark Coll., 1958; PhD in Chemistry, U. Chgo., 1960; MBA, Columbia U., 1977; doctorate (hon.), Smith Coll., 1993, S.C. State U., 1995. Rsch. chemist Nat. Bur. Standards, Washington, 1963-68; mem. chemistry faculty York Coll. CUNY, Jamaica, 1968-77, assoc. dean divsn. natural scis. and math., 1970-74, assoc. dean acad. affairs, 1974-77; pres. Met. State U., St. Paul, Mpls., 1977-88; pres., exec. dir. Gen. Mills Found., Mpls., 1988—. Bd. dirs. Minn. Mut. Ins. Co., St. Paul, H.B. Fuller Co., St. Paul, N.W. Corp., Mpls.; cons., spkr. in field. Contbr. numerous articles to profl. jours. Bd. dirs. Coun. on Founds., Washington, Minn. Coun. on Found., H.B. Fuller Co. Found., St. Paul, Corp. Nat. and Cmty. Svc., vice-chair; chair corp. adv. coun. ARC; bd. overseers Clark Atlanta U.; mem. ministers and missionaries benefit bd. Am. Bapt. Ch., N.Y.C. Recipient Sisterhood award for disting. humanitarian svc. Nat. Conf. Christian and Jews, 1993, Woman of Distinction award St. Croix Valley Girl Scouts, 1995. Mem. NAACP (cmty. svc. award in edn. 1994), Delta Sigma Theta. Home: 110 Bank St SE Apt 2005 Minneapolis MN 55414-3905 Office: Gen Mills Found PO Box 1113 Minneapolis MN 55440-1113

KING, RICHARD ALLEN, lawyer; b. St. Joseph, Mo., July 4, 1944; s. Allen Welden and Lola (Donelson) K.; m. Deedee Gershenson, Apr. 19, 1986; children from previous marriage: Mary, Suzanne, Allen. BA, U. Mo., Columbia, 1966, JD cum laude, 1968. Bar: Mo. 1968. Law clk. Office of Chief Counsel, IRS, 1967; assoc. Reese, Constance, Slayton, Stewart & Stewart, Independence, Mo., 1968-73; ptnr. Constance, Slayton, Stewart & King, 1973-80, Cochran, Kramer, Kapke, Willerth & King, Independence, 1980-81; exec. asst. to gov. State of Mo., Jefferson City, 1981-82, dir. revenue, 1982-85; ptnr. Smith, Gill, Fisher and Butts, Inc., Kansas City, Mo., 1985-87, Wirken & King, Kansas City, 1988-93; chmn., CEO King Hershey, Mo., 1993—. Asst. city counselor City of Independence, 1968—69, mayor, 1974—78; vice chmn. Nat. Conf. Rep. Mayors, 1975—77; chmn. Mo. Gov.'s Task Force on Cmty. Crime Prevention, 1975—76, Kansas City Pub. Improvements Adv. Com., 1991—96, KC Team Effort, 1991—95; pres. Good Govt. League, Independence, 1972—73; mem. Mo. Commn. Human Rights, 1973—74; bd. dirs. Multistate Tax Commn., 1983—85, Chrisman Sawyer Bank, 1989—95. Contbr. articles to profl. jours. Bd. dirs. Am. Cancer Soc., Independence, 1973-79, chmn. crusade, 1973; bd. dirs. Independence Boys Club, 1972-79, Independence Cmty. Assn. Arts, 1973-76, Independence Sanitarium and Hosp., 1974-78, Jefferson City Meml. Hosp., 1981-85, NE Jackson County Mental Health Ctr., 1978-80, Greater Kansas City Nat. Coun. on Alcoholism, 1978-81, Am. Legion Boys State Mo., 1975—, Jefferson City United Way, 1982-85, Multi-State Tax Commn., 1982-85, Jackson County Hist. Soc., 1999—; pres. Friends U. Mo. Truman Campus, 1979-80, Kansas City Consensus, 1989-90; trustee Harry S. Truman Scholarship Found., 1975-78, Kansas City U., 1979-80, Andrew Drumm Inst., 1990—, pres. bd. trustees, 1992-94. Capt. U.S. Army, 1969-72. Recipient Outstanding Young Man of Mo. award Mo. Jaycees, 1975, award Mo. Inst. Pub. Adminstrn., 1983 Mem.: ABA, Independence C. of C. (pres. 1980—81), Mo. Econ. Devel. Fin. Assn. (pres. 1999—2001), Kansas City Bar Assn., Internat. Assn. Gaming Attys., Nat. Assn. Bond Lawyers, Kansas City Bar Assn. (chmn. real estate law com. 1988—89), Ea. Jackson County Bar Assn., Mo. Bar Assn., Order of Coif, Beta Theta Pi, Phi Delta Phi. Unitarian. Home: 206 E 30th St Kansas City MO 64108-3213 Office: King Hershey Ste 2100 2345 Grand Blvd Kansas City MO 64108-2619 E-mail: rking@kinghershey.com.

KING, ROBERT CHARLES, biologist, educator; b. N.Y.C., June 3, 1928; s. Charles James and Amanda (McCutchen) King. B.S., Yale U., 1948, Ph.D., 1952. Scientist biology dept. Brookhaven Nat. Lab., 1951-55; mem. faculty Northwestern U., 1956—, prof. biology, 1964-99, prof. emeritus, 2000—. Chmn. 8th Brookhaven Symposium in Biology, 1955; vis. investigator, fellow Rockefeller U., 1959; NSF sr. postdoctoral fellow U. Edinburgh, Scotland, 1958, Commonwealth Sci. and Indsl. Research Orgn. Div. Entomology, Canberra, Australia, 1963, Sericultural Expt. Sta., Tokyo, Japan, 1970 Author: Genetics, 2d edit., 1965, A Dictionary of Genetics, 6th edit., 2002, (with W.D. Stansfield) Ovarian Development in Drosophila melanogaster, 1970, also numerous papers; editor: Handbook of Genetics Series, 5 vols., (with H. Akai) Insect Ultrastructure, 2 vols., 1982. Fellow AAAS; mem. Am. Soc. Zoologists, Histochem. Soc., Am. Soc. Cell Biology (treas. 1972-75), Electron Microscopy Soc. Am., Genetics Soc. Am., Am. Soc. Naturalists, Soc. Devel. Biology, Entomol. Soc. Am., Genetics Soc. Can., Genetics Soc. Korea, Sigma Xi (pres. Northwestern U. chpt. 1966-67) Home: 2890 Fredric Ct Northbrook IL 60062-7504

KING, ROBERT HENRY, minister, church denomination executive, former educator; b. Sunny South, Ala., Apr. 1, 1922; s. Henry C. and Della S. (Bettis) K.; m. Edna Jean McCord, June 1, 1949; children: Jocelyn, Jann, Roger. BD, Immanuel Luth. Sem., Greensboro, N.C., 1949; MEd, U. Pitts., 1956; MA, Ind. U., 1968, PhD, 1969. Ordained to ministry Luth. Ch.—Mo. Synod, 1949. Pastor Victory Luth. Ch., Youngstown, Ohio, 1949-57, St. Philip Luth. Ch., Chgo., 1957-65; asst. prof. Concordia Tchrs. Coll., River Forest, Ill., 1968-70; prof. edn. Lincoln U., Jefferson City, Mo., 1970-87; v.p. Luth. Ch.—Mo. Synod, St. Louis, 1986—. Pastor Pilgrim Luth. Ch., Freedom, Mo., 1977-97; dir. lay ministry Concordia Coll., Selma, Ala., 1987-90; vis. instr. Concordia Sem., St. Louis, 1989—; dir. workshop Obot Idim Sem., Nigeria, 1990. Contbr. articles to religious jours. Mem. Jefferson City Sch. Bd., 1973-76. Lilly Found. fellow, 1965. Mem. Am. Assn. Adult Continuing Edn., Mo. Assn. Adult Continuing Edn., Phi Delta Kappa. Office: 901 Roland Ct Jefferson City MO 65101-3576

KING, SHARON LOUISE, lawyer; b. Ft. Wayne, Ind., Jan. 12, 1932; AB, Mt. Holyoke Coll., 1954; JD with distinction, Valparaiso U., 1957; LLM in Taxation, Georgetown U., 1961. Bar: Ind. 1957, D.C. 1958, Ill. 1962. Trial atty. tax divsn. U.S. Dept. Justice, 1958-62; sr. counsel Sidley & Austin, Chgo. Bd. dirs. Lawyer's Com. for Better Housing, Inc. Fellow Am. Coll. Tax Counsel; mem. ABA (chmn. com. closely-held corps. taxation sect. 1979-81, regulated pub. utilities com. taxation sect. 1982-83, coun. dir. taxation sect. 1983-86), Chgo. Bar Assn. (bd. mgrs. 1973-75, chmn. fed. tax com. 1983-84), Ill. State Bar Assn. (counsel dir. sect. fed. taxation 1989-91), Women's Bar Assn. Ill. Found. (bd. dirs., v.p., dir. scholarship). Office: Sidley & Austin Bank One Plz 425 W Surf St Apt 605 Chicago IL 60657-6139

KING, STEVE, state legislator; b. Storm Lake, Iowa, May 28, 1949; m. Marilyn King. Student, N.W. Mo. State U., 1967-70. Mem. Iowa Senate from 6th dist., Des Moines, 1996—; vice chair natural resources and environ. com.; mem. appropriations com., mem. bus. and labor rels. com.; mem. commerce com., mem. state govt. com. Mem. St. Martin's Cath. Ch.; bd. dirs. Odebolt Cmty. Housing. Mem. Iowa Cattleman's Assn., Land Improvement Contractors Am., U.S. C. of C., Odebolt C. of C., SAC County Farm Bur. Republican. Office: State Capitol 9th And Grand Ave Des Moines IA 50319-0001 E-mail: steve_king@legis.state.ia.us.

KING, WILLIAM CARL, automotive company executive; b. Lake City, Fla., May 23, 1944; s. William G. and Ruth O. (Barker) K.; m. Mary Lee Bray, June 24, 1966 (div. 1980); children: Julie Ann, Jeffrey Carl; m. Christine Nora Schieck, Aug. 14, 1981. BBA, Western Mich. U., 1966; MBA, Baldwin Wallace Coll., 1978. With purchasing div. Pontiac (Mich.) Motor Co., 1966-69; dir. planning dept. Kelsey Hayes, Romulus, Mich., 1969-74; dir. materials, mgmt. info. system Bendix, Elyria, Ohio, 1974-77; gen. mgr. Bendix HVS Ltd., London, Can., 1977-80; v.p., gen. mgr. Bendix FMD, Troy, N.Y., 1980-84; group v.p. Allied Automotive, Southfield,

Mich., 1985-89, v.p., group exec. Bendix automotive systems group, 1989—. Bd. dirs. Bendix Europe, Paris, Bendix France, Paris, Bendix Espana, Barcelona, Kalyani Brakd, Bendix India, Pune, Bendix Italia, Crema, Juride Werke, Glinde, Fed. Republic of Germany. Bd. dirs. Jr. Achievement, Albany, N.Y., 1980-82, officer, 1982-85; bd. dirs. Detroit area coun. Boy Scouts Am., 1990—. Mem. Soc. Automotive Engrs., Am. Prodn. Inventory Control Soc., Motor Equipment Mfrs. Assn. (pres. coun. 1989—, automotive/OEM coun. 1990—), Elks, Walnut Creek Country Club, Omicron Delta Kappa, Delta Chi. Republican. Methodist. Home: 41610 Fallbrook Ct Northville MI 48167-2902 Office: DETREX CORPORATION 24901 NORTHWESTERN HWY., STE 500 Southfield MI 48075

KINGDON, JOHN WELLS, political science educator; b. Wisconsin Rapids, Wis., Oct. 28, 1940; s. Robert Wells and Catherine (McCune) K.; m. Kirsten Berg, June 16, 1965; children: James, Tor BA, Oberlin Coll., 1962; MA, U. Wis., 1963, PhD, 1965. Asst. prof. polit. sci. U. Mich., Ann Arbor, 1965-70, assoc. prof., 1970-75, prof., 1975-98, prof. emeritus, 1998—, chmn. dept. polit. sci., 1982-87. Author: Candidates for Office, 1968, Congressmen's Voting Decisions, 1973, 3d rev. edit., 1989, Agendas, Alternatives and Public Policies, 1984, 2d edit., 1995, America the Unusual, 1998. NSF grantee, 1978-82, Soc. Sci. Research Council grantee, 1969-70; Guggenheim fellow, 1979-80, Ctr. for Advanced Study in Behaviorial Scis. fellow, 1987-88. Fellow Am. Acad. Arts and Scis.; mem. Midwest Polit. Sci. Assn. (pres. 1987-88). Office: U Mich Dept Polit Sci Ann Arbor MI 48109

KINGSLEY, JAMES GORDON, healthcare executive; b. Houston, Nov. 22, 1933; s. James Gordon and Blanche Sybil (Payne) K.; m. Martha Elizabeth Sasser, Aug. 24, 1956 (div. 1992); children: Gordon Alan, Craig Emerson; m. Suzanne H. Patterson, Oct. 30, 1993; 1 child, Aaron T. AB, Miss. Coll., 1955; MA, U. Mo., 1956; BD, ThD, New Orleans Bapt. Theol. Sem., 1960, 65; HHD (hon.), Mercer U., 1980; LittD (hon.), Seinan Gakuin U., Japan, 1989; postgrad., U. Louisville, 1968-69, Nat. U. Ireland, 1970, Harvard U., 1976. Asst. prof. Miss. Coll., 1956-58; instr. Tulane U., 1958-60; asst. prof. William Jewell Coll., Liberty, Mo., 1960-62; assoc. prof. Ky. So. Coll., Louisville, 1964-67, prof., 1967-69; prof. lit. and religion William Jewell Coll., 1969-93, dean, 1976-80, pres., 1980-93; v.p. Health Midwest, Kansas City, Mo., 1994-95, 96—; dep. dir. Nelson-Atkins Mus. of Art, 1995-96. Vis. fellow Cambridge (Eng.) U., 1988. Author: A Time for Openness, 1973, Frontiers, 1983, Conversations with Leaders for a New Millenium, 1991, A Place Called Grace, 1993, Kansas City Sesquicentennial: A Celebration of the Heart, 2001; contbr. articles to profl. jours. Bd. dirs. Mo. Repertory Theatre, Kansas City Symphony, Kansas City Art Inst., Episcopal Sem. S.W. LaRue fellow, 1976. Mem. English Speaking Union, Burren Conservancy, Friends of the Bog, Cambridge Soc. Episcopalian. Home: Lakewood 402 NE Point Dr Lees Summit MO 64064-1561 Office: Health Midwest 2310 E Meyer Blvd Kansas City MO 64132-1136

KINKEL, ANTHONY G. state legislator, educator; b. Nov. 1960; BA, U. Minn., Duluth. Educator; mem. Minn. Ho. of Reps. from dist. 4B, St. Paul, 1986-98, Minn. Senate from 4th dist., St. Paul, 1999—. Former mem. gen. legis., vet. affairs, and gaming coms., Minn. Ho. of Reps.; vice chmn. commerce and econ. devel. com., mem. edn.-higher edn. fin. divsn., and tourism and small bus. divsn. coms.

KINLIN, DONALD JAMES, lawyer; b. Boston, Nov. 29, 1938; s. Joseph Edward and Ruth Claire (Byrne) K.; m. Donna C. McGrath, Nov. 29, 1959; children: Karen J., Donald J., Joseph P., Kevin S. BS in Acctg., Syracuse U., 1968, MBA, 1970; JD, U. Nebr., 1975. Bar: Nebr. 1976, Ohio 1982, U.S. Supreme Ct. 1979, U.S. Claims Ct. 1982, U.S. Tax Ct. 1982, U.S. Ct. Appeals (5th and fed. cirs.) 1982. Atty. USAF, Mather AFB, Calif., 1976-78; sr. trial atty. Air Force Contract Law Ctr., Wright-Patterson AFB, Ohio, 1978-86, dep. dir., 1986-87; ptnr. Smith & Schnacke, Dayton, 1987-89, Thompson, Hine and Flory L.L.P., Dayton, 1989—. Mem. adv. bd. Fed. Publs. Inc. Govt. Contract Costs, Pricing & Acctg. Report. Contbr. articles to legal jours. Pres. Forest Ridge Assn., Dayton, 1984-96; sec., gen. counsel U.S. Air and Trade Show, 1994-98, chmn., 1998—; bd. dirs. Nat. Aviation Hall of Fame, 1998—. Mem. ABA (chmn. sect. pub. contract law 1993-94, sec., budget and fin. officer sect., coun. mem., chmn. fed. procurement divsn., vice chmn. acct., cost and pricing com., truth in negotiations com., chmn. cost Acctg. stas. subcom.), Fed. Bar Assn., Ohio Bar Assn., Nebr. Bar Assn., Contracts Appeals Bar Assn. (bd. govs. 1998-2001). Avocation: travel. Office: Thompson Hine & Flory LLP PO Box 8801 2000 Courthouse Pla NE Dayton OH 45401-8801

KINMAN, GARY, company executive; Owner, CEO Kinman Assocs., Inc. Office: Kinman Assocs Inc 7300 Industrial Pkwy Plain City OH 43064-8788 E-mail: kinman1@aol.com.

KINNEARY, JOSEPH PETER, federal judge; b. Cin., Sept. 19, 1905; s. Joseph and Anne (Mulvihill) K.; m. Byrnece Camille Rogers, June 26, 1950. BA, U. Notre Dame, 1928; JD, U. Cin., 1935, JD, 1967, LLD (hon.), 1991. Bar: Ohio 1935, U.S. Supreme Ct 1960. Pvt. practice in, Cin. and Columbus, 1935-61; asst. atty. gen. Ohio, 1937-39; 1st asst. atty. gen., 1949-51; spl. counsel to atty. gen., 1959-61; U.S. atty. So. Dist. Ohio, 1961-66; judge U.S. Dist. Ct. (so. dist.) Ohio, 1966—, chief judge, 1973-75, sr. judge. Lectr. law trusts Coll. Law, U. Cin., 1948 Del. Dem. Nat. Conv., 1952. Served to capt. AUS, World War II. Decorated Army Commendation ribbon. Mem. Phi Delta Phi. Roman Catholic. Home: 2440 Northwest Blvd Columbus OH 43221-3868 Office: US Dist Ct 319 US Courthouse 85 Marconi Blvd Columbus OH 43215-2823

KINNEY, EARL ROBERT, mutual funds company executive; b. Burnham, Maine, Apr. 12, 1917; s. Harry E. and Ethel (Vose) K.; m. Margaret Velie Thatcher, Apr. 23, 1977; children: Jeanie Elizabeth, Earl Robert, Isabella Alice. A.B., Bates Coll., 1939; postgrad., Harvard U. Grad. Sch., 1940. Founder, North Atlantic Pack Co., Bar Harbor, Maine, 1941, pres., 1941-42, treas., dir., 1941-64; with Gorton Corp. (became subs. Gen. Mills, Inc. 1968), 1954-68, pres., 1958-68; v.p. Gen. Mills, Inc., 1968-69, exec. v.p., 1969-73, chief fin. officer, 1970-73, pres., chief operating officer, 1973-77, chmn. bd., 1977-81; pres., chief exec. officer IDS Mut. Fund Group, Mpls., 1982-87. Bd. dirs. Idexx Labs., Inc. Trustee Bates Coll., also chmn. alumni drives, 1960-64. Office: 4900 IDS Ctr Minneapolis MN 55402

KINNEY, JOHN FRANCIS, bishop; b. Oelwein, Iowa, June 11, 1937; s. John F. and Marie B. (McCarty) K. Student, St. Paul Sem., 1957-63, N.Am. Coll., Rome, 1968-71; J.C.D., Pontifical Lateran U., 1971. Ordained priest Roman Catholic Ch., 1963. Assoc. pastor Ch. of St. Thomas, Mpls., 1963-66; vice chancellor of St. Paul and Mpls. Diocese, 1966-73; assoc. pastor Cathedral, St. Paul, 1971-74, chancellor, 1973; pastor Ch. of St. Leonard, from 1974; titular bishop of Caorle and aux. bishop Archdiocese of St. Paul and Mpls., 1977-82; bishop Diocese of Bismark, N.D., 1982-95, Diocese of St. Cloud, Minn., 1995—. Mem. Canon Law Soc. Am. Roman Catholic. Office: Chancery Office PO Box 1248 Saint Cloud MN 56302-1248

KINNEY, JON C. metal products executive; CFO, sr. v.p. Ill. Tool Works, Inc., Glenview, Ill., 1998—. Office: Illinois Tool Works Inc 3600 W Lake Ave Glenview IL 60025-5811

KINNEY, MARK BALDWIN, educator; b. Bangor, Maine, Dec. 27, 1944; s. Gerald Lewis and Virginia (Baldwin) K.; m. Nancy Pearson Kinney, June 6, 1964; children: Kathryn Louise Hahn, William Kinney. BA, U. Maine, Orono, 1962-66; MA, George Peabody Coll. for Tchrs, Nashville, 1970-71; PhD, George Peabody Coll. for Tchrs, 1971-76. Tchr. math. Hermon (Maine) Sch. Dist., 1967-70; rsch. assoc. Inst. of Gerontology U. Mich., 1974-76; asst. prof. U. Toledo, 1976-80, dir. off-campus edn., 1985-86, dir. student svcs., 1986-87, assoc. prof., 1980-99, dir. Ctr. for Internat. Studies and Programs, 1995-96, Lisle fellow (fellowship pres.), 1984-89; exec. dir. Lisle, Temperance, Mich., 1989—. Vis. lectr. Ea. Mich. U., Ypsilanti, 1973-75; cons. GM Corp., Toledo, Saginaw, 1990-94, U. Toledo Corp, 1993-94. Author: Staff Training in Geriatric Institutions, 1975, Skills in Interpersonal Comm., 1983, Exercises for the Older Adult, 1988, Empower Ourselves and Others, 1994. George Peabody Coll. Tchg. doctoral fellow U.S. Office of Edn., 1971-72. Mem. Phi Beta Delta, Phi Delta Kappa. Avocations: sailing, swimming, skiing, singing, boat building. Office: Lisle PO Box 87 Presque Isle MI 49777 E-mail: mkinney@utnet.utoledo.edu.

KINNEY, THOMAS J. adult education educator; BA in Psychology, Syracuse U., 1968; MSW in Mgmt., SUNY, Albany, 1974. Dir. profl. development program, Nelson A. Rockefeller coll. pub. affairs and policy U. Albany, SUNY, 1976-99, spl. asst. to provost, 1997-99; v.p. edn. Premier Health Alliance, Chgo., 1999—; CEO Kinney and Assoc., 2000—; bd. Synquest Technologies, Inc., 2001—. Mem. Task Force N.Y. State Work Force 21st Century; mem. SUNY 2000 Task Group Social Svcs.; dir. Ctr. Profl. Devel. and Continuing Edn. Rsch., chmn. quality forum Rockefeller Coll. Press; prof. Russian Acad. Edn.; co-founder Russian-Am. Ctr. Adult and Continuing Edn., Moscow; mem. task force employee assistance programs N.Y. State Assembly; mem. implementation adv. com. WorkKeys project Am. Coll. Testing; presenter in field. Editor Jour. Continuing Social Work Edn. Named Continuing Educator of Yr., Continuing Edn. Assn. N.Y., 1988; named to Internat. Adult and Continuing Hall of Fame, 1996 Fellow N.Y. State Acad. Pub. Adminstrn.; mem. Am. Assn. Adult and Continuing Edn. (treas., past chair commn. continuing profl. edn., Outstanding Svc. medallion 1994, pres. 1999—), Nat. Univ. Continuing Edn. Assn. (chair divsn. continuing edn. professions, mem. fin. com., mem. task force displaced profls.). Office: Premier Inc 201 N Birchwood Dr Naperville IL 60540 E-mail: thomaskinney@msn.com.

KINNISON, WILLIAM ANDREW, retired university president; b. Springfield, Ohio, Feb. 10, 1932; s. Errett Lowell and Audrey Muriel (Smith) K.; m. Lenore Belle Morris, June 11, 1960; children— William Errett, Linda Elise, Amy Elisabeth. A.B., Wittenberg U., 1954, B.S. in Edn., 1955; M.A., U. Wis., 1963; Ph.D. (1st Flesher fellow), Ohio State U., 1967; postgrad., Harvard U. Inst. Ednl. Mgmt., 1970; LL.D., Calif. Luth. Coll., 1983; Th.D., John Carroll U., 1983; LLD, Lenoir-Rhyne Coll., 1987; LHD, Capital U., 1995. Asst. dean admissions Wittenberg U., Springfield, 1958-65, asst. to pres., 1967-70, v.p. for univ. affairs, 1970-73, v.p. adminstrn., 1973, pres., 1974-95, pres. emeritus, 1995—; pres., CEO Heritage Ctr. of Clark County, 1997—. Author: Samuel Shellabarger: Lawyer, Jurist, Legislator, 1969, Building Sullivant's Pyramid: An Administrative History of the Ohio State University, 1970, Concise History of Wittenberg University, 1976, An American Seminary, 1980, Springfield and Clark County: an Illustrated History, 1985, also articles. Asst. to dir. Sch. Edn. Ohio State U., Columbus, 1965-67; past chmn. Assn. Ind. Colls. and Univs. Ohio; trustee Ohio Found. Ind. Colls., 1974-95, chair bd. trustees, 1995; chmn. standing com. Luth. World Ministries, 1976-82; mem. exec. coun. Luth. Ch. in Am., 1978-86; mem., chmn. Commn. for a New Luth. Ch., 1982-86; bd. dirs. Am. Assn. Colls., 1982-84. With U.S. Army, 1956-58. Mem. Clark County Hist. Soc. (trustee 1963—), Orgn. Am. Historians, Blue Key, Phi Beta Kappa, Phi Delta Kappa, Kappa Phi Kappa, Pi Sigma Alpha, Tau Kappa Alpha, Delta Sigma Phi, Omicron Delta Kappa. Clubs: Cosmos, Rotary. Home: 1820 Timberline Dr Springfield OH 45504-1236

KINNOIN, MEYER D. state legislator; m. Diane; 4 children. Mem. N.D. Senate, 1989—; vice chmn. state and fed. govt. com. Past mem. agr. com., fin. and tax. com. N.D. Senate; former mem. Mountrail County Park Commn., Housing Commn., U.S. Dept. Agr.; farmer Recipient Disting. Svc. Award Jaycees. Address: 6695 Clearlake Rd Palermo ND 58769-9314

KINS, JURIS, lawyer; b. Jelgava, Latvia, Apr. 24, 1942; came to U.S., 1949; s. Arnolds and Zenta (Dunis) K.; m. Olita Gita Kakis, Oct. 11, 1969; children: Aleksis A., Mikus N. BSChemE, U. Wis., 1964; MSChemE, U. Mich., 1965; JD, U. Wis., 1969. Bar: Wis. 1969, Ill. 1969. Assoc. ptnr. Chadwell & Kayser, Ltd., Chgo., 1969-90; ptnr. Vedder, Price, Kaufman & Kammholz, 1990-93; Abramson & Fox, 1993—. Pres. Latvian Peoples Support Group, Chgo., 1991—. Mem. ABA, Chgo. Bar Assn., Ill. Bar Assn., Wis. Bar Assn., Latvian Bar Assn. Avocations: tennis, skiing. Office: Abramson & Fox One E Wacker Dr Ste 3800 Chicago IL 60601 E-mail: juriskins@aol.com.

KINTNER, PHILIP L. history educator; b. Canton, Ohio, Jan. 23, 1926; s. William Wagner and Effie (Erwin) K.; m. Anne Genung, Dec. 27, 1951; children: Karen, Judith, Jennifer. BA, Wooster Coll., 1950; MA, Yale U., 1952, PhD, 1958. Instr. Trinity Coll., Hartford, Conn., 1954-56, Reed Coll., Portland, Oreg., 1957-58, Trinity Coll., 1958-59, asst. prof., 1959-64; vis. assoc. prof. U. Iowa, Iowa City, 1964-65; assoc. prof. Grinnell (Iowa) Coll., 1964-69; coll. entrance bd. exam commissioner European History, Princeton, N.J., 1968-70; chief reader advanced placement European history, 1969-72; ACM prof. Florence (Italy) Program, 1989-90; prof. Grinnell Coll., 1970-96, Rosenthal prof. humanities, 1976-96; prof. emeritus, 1996—. With U.S. Army, 1944-46. Recipient numerous travel/study grants for rsch. in Germany. Mem. Sixteenth Century Studies Conf. Avocations: woodworking, gardening, cooking, mineral hunting. Home: 716 Broad St Grinnell IA 50112-2226 Office: Grinnell Coll PO Box 805 Grinnell IA 50112-0805 E-mail: kintner@grinnell.edu.

KIPNIS, DAVID MORRIS, physician, educator; b. Balt., May 23, 1927; s. Rubin and Anna (Mizen) Kipnis; m. Paula Jane Levin, Aug. 16, 1953; children: Lynne, Laura, Robert. AB, Johns Hopkins U., 1945, MA, 1949; MD, U. Md., 1951. Intern Johns Hopkins Hosp., 1951—52; resident Duke Hosp., Durham, NC, 1952—54, U. Md. Hosp., 1954—55; asst. prof. medicine Washington U. Sch. Medicine, St. Louis, 1958—63, assoc. prof., 1963—65, prof., 1965—, Busch prof., chmn. dept. medicine, 1973—92; disting. prof. medicine Washington U. Sch. of Medicine, St. Louis, 1992—; asst. physician Barnes Hosp., assoc. physician, 1963—72, physician-in-chief, 1973—93, distinguished prof., 1993—. Chmn. endocrine study sect. NIH, 1963—64, diabetes tng. program com., 1970—; chmn. Nat. Diabetes Adv. Bd. Editor: Diabetes, 1973; mem. editl. bd.: Am. Jour. Medicine, 1973, mem. editl. bd.: Am. Jour. Med. Scis.; contbr. articles to profl. jours. Served with U.S. Army, 1945—46. Named Banting lectr., Brit. Diabetes Assn., 1972; scholar Markle scholar in med. scis., 1957—62. Mem.: NAS (coun. mem. 1997—), Nat. Acad. Scis., Inst. Medicine, Am. Acad. Arts and Scis., Am. Soc. Biol. Chemists, Endocrine Soc. (Oppenheimer award 1965), Am. Diabetes Assn. (Lilly award 1965, Banting medal 1977, Best medal 1981), Am. Fedn. Clin. Rsch., Assn. Am. Physicians (Kober medal 1994), Am. Soc. Clin. Investigation. Home: 7200 Wydown Blvd Saint Louis MO 63105-3023 Office: Barnes Hosp Dept Medicine PO Box 8212 660 S Euclid Ave Saint Louis MO 63110-1010

KIPPER, BARBARA LEVY, corporate executive; b. Chgo., July 16, 1942; d. Charles and Ruth (Doctoroff) Levy; m. David A. Kipper, Sept. 9, 1974; children: Talia Rose, Tamar Judith. BA, U. Mich., 1964. Reporter Chgo. Sun-Times, 1964-67; photo editor Cosmopolitan Mag., N.Y.C., 1969-71; vice chmn. Chas Levy Co., Chgo., 1984-86, chmn., 1986—. Trustee Spertus Inst. Jewish Studies, Chgo. Hist. Soc., Golden Apple Ind., Joffrey Ballet of Chgo.; bd. dirs. Lincoln Park Zoo, Shoah Visual History Found. Recipient Deborah award Com. Women's Equality, Am. Jewish Congress, 1992, Shap Shapiro Human Rels. award The Anti-Defamation League of B'nai B'rith, Personal PAC's Leadership award, 1996, Disting. Cmty. Leadership award, ADL, 1999; named Nat. Soc. Fund Raising Exec.'s Disting. Philanthropist, 1995. Mem.: Chgo. Network, Chgo. Coun. on Fgn. Rels., Com. of 200, Coun. on Founds., Internat. Women's Forum, Econ. Club of Chgo., Execs. Club of Chgo., The Standard Club. Jewish. Office: Chas Levy Co 1200 N North Branch St Chicago IL 60622-2449

KIRBY, DOROTHY MANVILLE, social worker; b. Burke, S.D., Oct. 23, 1917; d. Charles Vietz and Gail Lorena (Coonen) Manville; m. Sigmund Kirby, July 11, 1941 (div. 1969); children; Paul Howard, Robert Charles. BA, Wayne State U., 1970, MSW, 1972. Cert. social worker, Mich.; lic. marriage and family therapist, Mich. Pvt. practice social work, Allen Park, Mich., 1973—. Conduct seminars on stress, personal effectiveness and communication for various orgns., hosps. and bus. Pres. Allen Park Symphony Orch., 1990-92. Mem.: LWV (pres. Allen Park 1965—66), NASW (clin.), AAUW, Mich. Assn. Marriage and Family Therapy (sec. 1982), Nat. Assn. Marriage and Family Therapy, Soroptimists. Presbyterian. Avocation: playing violin. Home and Office: 15720 Wick Rd Allen Park MI 48101-1535 E-mail: dmkirby@ameritech.net.

KIRBY, RONALD EUGENE, fish and wildlife research administrator; b. Angola, Ind., Nov. 26, 1947; s. Robert Waye and Lorraine Alice (Hoag) K.; m. Dona J. Kirby; children: Cyrus Robert, William Emil, Peter Waye, Joshua M. Brosten, Emily A. Brosten, Andrew J. Brosten. BS, Duke U., 1969; MA, So. Ill. U., 1973; PhD, U. Minn., 1976. Staff biologist Coop. Wildlife Rsch. Lab., So. Ill. U., Carbondale, 1969-72; collaborating biologist U.S. Forest Svc., St. Paul and Cass Lake, Minn., 1970-72; rsch. biologist Antarctic Rsch. Program NSF, McMurdo Station, Antarctica, 1974; NIH rsch. trainee dept. ecology and behavioral biology U. Minn., Mpls., 1972-76; wildlife biologist, Patuxent Wildlife Rsch. Ctr. U.S. Fish and Wildlife Svc., Laurel, Md., 1976-80, population mgmt. specialist div. refuge mgmt. Washington, 1980-82, rsch. coord. Nat. Wildlife Refuge System, 1982-83, regional assistance biologist, office info. transfer Ft. Collins, Colo., 1983-88, leader info. transfer sect., 1988-90; asst. dir. No. Prairie Wildlife Rsch. Ctr., Jamestown, N.D., 1991-92, dir., 1993; dir. U.S. Nat. Biol. Svc. No. Prairie Sci. Ctr., 1993-96; dir. U.S. Geol. Survey No. Prairie Wildlife Rsch. Ctr., 1997-2001; dir. U.S. Geol. Survey Forest and Rangeland Ecosys. Sci. Ctr., Corvallis, Oreg., 2001—. Mem. waterfowl adv. com. Minn. Dept. Natural Resources, St. Paul, 1970-72; mem. black duck subcom. Atlantic Flyway Coun., 1976-80; mem. tech. sect. Central Flyway, 1991—. Contbr. to numerous profl. publs; editorial referee, sci. jours. and profl. reports. Active, Boy Scouts Am., 1984—. Grantee, AEC, 1972-76. Mem. The Wildlife Soc., Lambda Chi Alpha. Avocations: hiking, camping, bird watching, motorcycling, hunting. Office: Forest and Rangeland Ecosys Sci Ctr US Geol Survey 3200 SW Jefferson Way Corvallis OR 97331 E-mail: ronald_kirby@usgs.gov.

KIRBY, TERRY, professional football player; b. Hampton, Va., Jan. 20, 1970; B of Psychology, U. Va. Running back Miami (Fla.) Dolphins, 1993-95, San Francisco 49ers, 1996-98; NFC Championship Game, 1997; running back Cleve. Browns, 1999—. Office: c/o Cleve Browns 1085 W 3rd St Cleveland OH 44114

KIRCHER, JOHN JOSEPH, law educator; b. Milw., July 26, 1938; s. Joseph John and Martha Marie (Jach) K.; m. Marcia Susan Adamkiewicz, Aug. 26, 1961; children: Joseph John, Mary Kathryn. BA, Marquette U., 1960, JD, 1963. Bar: Wis. 1963, U.S. Dist. Ct. (ea. dist.) Wis. 1963, U.S. Ct. Appeals (7th cir.) 1992. Sole practice, Port Washington, Wis., 1963-66; with Def. Research Inst., Milw., 1966-80, research dir., 1972-80; with Marquette U., 1970—, prof. law, 1980—, assoc. dean acad. affairs, 1992-93. Chmn. Wis. Jud. Council, 1981-83. Author: (with J.D. Ghiardi) Punitive Damages: Law and Practice, 1981, 2d edit (with C.M. Wiseman), 2000; editor Federation of Defense and Corporate Counsel Quarterly; mem. editorial bd. Def. Law Jour.; contbr. articles to profl. jours. Recipient Teaching Excellence award Marquette U., 1986, Disting. Service award Def. Research Inst., 1980, Marquette Law Rev. Editors' award, 1988. Mem. ABA (Robert B. McKay Professor award 1993), Am. Law Inst., Wis. Bar Assn., Wis. Supreme Ct. Bd. of Bar Examiners (vice chair 1989-91, chair 1992), Am. Judicature Soc., Nat. Sports Law Inst. (adv. com. 1989—), Assn. Internationale de Droit des Assurances, Scribes. Roman Catholic. Office: PO Box 1881 Milwaukee WI 53201-1881

KIRCHICK, CALVIN B. lawyer; b. N.Y.C., Apr. 6, 1946; s. Jean Kirchick; m. Judith Madian, Apr. 28, 1968; children: Ross, Lisa, Joelle. BA magna cum laude, U. Mich., 1968, JD magna cum laude, 1972. Assoc. Baker & Hostetler, Cleve., 1972-81, ptnr., 1982—. Contbr. articles to profl. jours. Endowment counsel Coun. Jewish Fedns., N.Y.C., 1976-90, Cleve., 1996—; rec. sec. Green Rd. Synagogue, Beachwood, Ohio, 1982-85, trustee, 1981-86; founding trustee, v.p. Internat. Coun. Dati Tzioni Schs., 1994—; founding trustee Solomon Schecter Day Sch. leve., 1978-85; trustee Jewish Nat. Fund Cleve., 1984-94; co-founder, trustee Fuchs Bet Sefer Mizrachi, Cleve., 1984—. Angell scholar U. Mich., 1966. Fellow Am. Coll. Trust and Estate Coun.; mem. ABA (generation skipping transfer tax com. legis. and regulations planning and drafting 1988—, charitable deduction com. legis. 1987—, GSST com. 1987—, estate and gift tax com. 1987—), Ohio State Bar Assn., Greater Cleve. Bar Assn. (probate and trust law sect. com. 1987—), Phi Beta Kappa, Phi Kappa Phi, Order of Coif; mem. ACTEC (com. on Charitable Giving, 1995—). Republican. Jewish. Avocations: bicycling, skiing, swimming, modern history, Jewish religious studies. Office: Baker & Hostetler 3200 Nat City Ctr 1900 E 9th St Ste 3200 Cleveland OH 44114-3475

KIRK, BALLARD HARRY THURSTON, architect; b. Williamsport, Pa., Apr. 1, 1929; s. Ballard and Ada May (DeLaney) K.; m. Vera Elizabeth Kitchener, Mar. 13, 1951; children: Lisa Lee, Kira Alexandria, Dayna Allison, Courtlandt Blaine. BArch, Ohio State U., 1959. Pres. Kirk Assocs., Architects, Columbus, Ohio, 1963—. Mem. Ohio Bd. Bldg. Standards, Columbus, 1973-78, 92-99; pres. Nat. Coun. Archtl. Registration Bds., Washington, 1983-84, Ohio Bd. Examiners Architects, Columbus, 1973-93; bd. dirs. Nat. Archtl. Accrediting Bd., Washington, 1986-89. Mem. AIA (bd. dirs. Columbus chpt. 1988-92), Coll. of Fellows. Republican. Mem. Brethern Ch. Home: 2557 Charing Rd Columbus OH 43221-3673

KIRK, CAROL, lawyer; b. Henry, Ill., Dec. 23, 1937; d. Howard P. and Mildred Root McQuilkin; m. Robert James Kirk, Aug. 20, 1961; children: Kathleen, Nancy, Sally. BS in Music Edn., U. Ill., 1960; JD, Ind. U., Indpls., 1989. Bar: Ind. 1989. Pvt. piano tchr., 1957-85; pub. sch. music tchr., 1960-62; dir. Ind. State Ethics Commn., Indpls., 1989-97; atty. and investigator Disciplinary Commn., Supreme Ct. Ind., 1997—. Pres. Coun. on Govtl. Ethics Laws, (Internat.), 1993-94. Exec. editor Articles & Prodn. Ind. Law Rev., 1988-89. Mem. Met. Devel. Commn., Indpls., 1982-87; chairperson Pub. Radio Adv. Bd., Indpls., 1983-84, treas. Cmty. Svc. Coun., Indpls., 1988-91. Invitee to Nat. 4H Congress, Chgo., 1956; named 4H Family of Yr., Washington Twp., 4-H, Indpls., 1980, Vol. of Week, Voluntary Action Ctr., Indpls., 1980. Mem. LWV (pres. Indpls. 1979-83), Ind. Bar Assn., Indpls. Bar Assn., Phi Alpha Delta, Mu Phi Epsilon. Avocation: choir singing. Office: Discip Commn Supreme Ct Ind 1165 South Tower 115 W Washington St Indianapolis IN 46204-3420 E-mail: rkirk1937@aol.com.

KIRK, MARK STEVEN, congressman; b. Champaign, Ill., Sept. 15, 1959; s. Francis Gabriel and Judith Ann (Brady) K. BA, Cornell U., 1981; MS, London Sch. of Econs., 1982; JD, Georgetown U., 1992. Bar: Ill.

1992, D.C. 1993. Parliamentary aide Julian Critchley, London, 1982-83; chief of staff U.S. Rep. John Porter, Washington, 1984-90; officer World Bank, 1990; spl. asst. to asst. sec. of state State Dept., 1991-93; atty. Baker & McKenzie, 1993-95; counsel Ho. Internat. Rels. Com., 1995-99; mem. U.S. Congress from 10th Ill. dist., 2001—; mem. armed svcs. com., transp. and infrastructure com., budget com. Bd. dirs. Population Resource Ctr., Princeton, N.J. Contbr. articles to various newspapers. Organizer Bush/Quayle Campaign, No. Ill., 1988, Dole for Pres., 1988, various states; campaigner Porter for Congress, No. Ill., 1984-90. Lt. USNR, 1989—. Kellogg Fellow, Chgo., 1980, Radm James Fellow, Washington, 1984; recipient Coun. of Jewish Fedn. award Washington, 1988. Mem. Navy League, Naval Res. Assn., New Trier Rep. Orgn. Presbyterian. Avocations: backpacking, skydiving. Office: 1531 Longworth Ho Office Bldg Washington DC 20515 Home: 275 Whistler Rd Highland Park IL 60035-5947*

KIRK, NANCY A. state legislator, nursing home administrator; m. Henry Kirk. Nursing home adminstr.; mem. from dist. 56 Kans. State Ho. of Reps., Topeka. Address: 932 SW Frazier Ave Topeka KS 66606-1948

KIRK, THOMAS GARRETT, JR. librarian; b. Phila., Aug. 2, 1943; s. Thomas Garrett and Bertha (C.) K.; m. Elizabeth B. Walter, Aug. 29, 1964; children: Jennifer E., Cynthia M., Kristen A. BA, Earlham Coll., Richmond, Ind., 1965; MA, Ind. U., 1969; postgrad., Drexel U., 1987-88. Sci. libr. Earlham Coll., 1965-79; libr. cons. Richmond, Ind., 1972—; acting dir. librs. U. Wis., Parkside, Kenosha, 1979-80; dir. libr. Berea (Ky.) Coll., 1980-94, Earlham (Ind.) Coll., 1994-2000, dir. librs., coord. info. svcs., 2001—. Vis. instr. Ind. U. Libr. Sch., summers 1977, 78; bd. dirs SOLINET, 1981-84, 85-86, treas., 1982-84; bd. dirs. Ky. Libr. Network, 1985-87, 91-93, OCLC Users Coun., 1986-92, 99—, exec. com. 2001-02. Pvt. Acad. Libr. Network Ind., v.p. 1995-96, pres., 1996-97, OCLC Strategic Directions and Governance Adv. Com., 2000-2001; adv. bd. OCLC Coll. and Univ. Librs., 1995-98. Author: Library Research Guide to Biology, 1978; editor: Course-related Library and Literature Instruction, 1979, Increasing the Teaching Role of Academic Libraries, 1984; editl. bd. Coll. and Rsch. Librs., 1996-2002, Internet Reference Svcs. Quar., 1996—, Info. Literacy Adv. Coun., 2000—. Mem. ALA (coun. 1986-90), Assn. Coll. Rsch. Librs. (v.p., pres.-elect 1992-93, pres. 1993-94, past pres. 94-95, exec. com. 1984-85, 86-90, 92-95, rep. to Coalition for Networked Info. 1990-95, Miriam Dudley Bibliographic Instrn. Libr. of Yr. award 1984), Inst. for Info. Literacy (adv. com. 1998—), Ind. Libr. Fedn., Ind. Coop. Libr. Svcs. Authority (exec. com. 1999-2001), Ky. Libr. Assn. (Acad. Libr. of Yr. award 1984), Phi Kappa Phi. Mem. Soc. of Friends. Office: Earlham Coll Lilly Libr Richmond IN 47374

KIRKEGAARD, R. LAWRENCE, architectural acoustician; b. Denver, Dec. 11, 1937; s. Raymond Lawrence and Frances Jean (Stocking) K.; m. Joslyn Ann Hills, Mar 23, 1959; children: Dana Lawrence, Jonathan Eric, Bradford Andrew. AB cum laude, Harvard U., 1960, MArch, 1964. Cons. archtl. acoustics Bolt, Beranek & Newman, Cambridge, Mass., 1962-64; supervisory cons., regional mgr. Chgo., 1964-75; pres., prin. cons. R. Lawrence Kirkegaard & Assocs., Inc., 1976—. Frequent panelist for Nat. Endowment for Arts Design Arts Challenge Grant program. Prin. archtl. acoustics works: new projects include new Concert Hall for Tanglewood, Ordway Music Theatre, St. Paul, new performing arts cts. in Denver, Fort Lauderdale, Charlotte, N.C., Maui, Portand, Oreg., L.A., Greenville, S.C., Cin., New Concert Hall for Atlanta, Ga.; internat. projects include performing arts ctrs. in Taipei and Tainan, Taiwan, Bergamo, Italy, Edmonton, remodeling of the Tyl Theatre, Prague, Royal Philharmonic Hall, Liverpool, Eng., Barbican Concert Hall, London, Maison de Musique, Toulose, France; remodeling projects include Carnegie Hall (post-renovation), Orch. Hall, Chgo., Davies Symphony Hall, San Francisco, Heinz Hall, Pitts., Mahaffey Theatre, St. Petersburg, Fla., Guthrie Theatre, Oreg. Shakespeare Festival, Stratford Shakespeare Festival, Ont., Young Peoples' Theatre, Toronto; new schs. of music include Rice U., Northwestern U., U. Ala., Iowa State U., Pacific Luth. U., Red Deer Coll., Alta., Cin. Convervatory Mus., Luther Coll., N.D. State U.; remodeling projects include U. Chgo., Carleton Coll., Oberlin Conservatory. Co-founder Chestnut Hill Mental Health Ctr., Greenville, S.C. Mem. AIA (hon., nat. com. on arts and recreation), Acoustical Soc. Am., Harvard Grad. Sch. Design Alumni Coun., U.S. Inst. Theatre Tech., Am. Symphony Orch. League, Harvard Club (Chgo.). Home: 5200 Brookbank Rd Downers Grove IL 60515-4544 Office: R Lawrence Kirkegaard & Assocs Inc 801 W Adams St Fl 8 Chicago IL 60607-3013

KIRKHAM, JAMES ALVIN, manufacturing executive; b. Sumner County, Tenn., June 18, 1935; s. Shirley Barnes and Ouida Redempta (Bursby) K.; m. Shirley Ann Clouse, Sept. 3, 1954; children: Denise Anne, James Alvin II, Hughe Allan. Welder Ind. Wire Co., 1952-54; driver Arthur Lowe Cigar & Candy Co., 1954-56; time study Insley Mfg. Co., 1957; salesman Am. Chicle Co., 1958-59; mgr. Ace Battery, Inc., Indpls., 1967—; v.p. L P Industries, Inc., 1977—; pres. Rubber Recycling Corp., 1989—; ptnr. TKT Leasing, Indpls., 1978—, LDJ Leasing, Indpls., 1979—, Vets. Interstate Plan, Inc. Sec. Johnson County Pk. Bd.; bd. dirs. English Ave. Boys Club, State 4-H Horse and Pony Orgn.; pres. bd. dirs. Ind. Horse Coun. Found., Inc.; pres. PTO, Clark Twp. Sch. Dist.; v.p. Johnson County 4-H Fairboard; active Boy Scouts Am.; chmn. fundraising equestrian events 10th Pan Am. Games; treas. Ind. Horse Coun. Inc. Recipient Golden Boy award Indpls. Boys Club Alumni Assn., 1970; named Outstanding Show Mgr., Ind. State Fair, 1971; named to Ind. Horseman Hall of Fame, 1998. Mem. Am. Horse Show Assn., Ind. Saddle Horse Assn., Ind. Motor Truck Assn., Indpls. Motor Truck Assn., U.S. C. of C., Indpls. C. of C., Masons, Shriners, Moose Lodge, Ind. Pony Exhibitors Club, Am. Hackney Club, Ind. Pony of Am. Club, Ind. Shetland Pony Breeders Club. Home: 1213 N Matthews Rd Greenwood IN 46143-8343 Office: 2166 Bluff Rd Indianapolis IN 46225-1983

KIRKHAM, M. B. plant physiologist, educator; b. Cedar Rapids, Iowa; d. Don and Mary Elizabeth (Erwin) K. BA with honors, Wellesley Coll.; MS, PhD, U. Wis. Cert. profl. agronomist. Plant physiologist U.S. EPA, Cin., 1973-74; asst. prof. U. Mass., Amherst, 1974-76, Okla. State U., Stillwater, 1976-80; from assoc. prof. to prof. Kans. State U., Manhattan, 1980—. Guest lectr. Inst. Water Conservancy and Hydroelectric Power Rsch., Inst. Farm Irrigation Rsch., China, 1985, Inst. Exptl. Agronomy, Italy, 1989, Agrl. U. Wageningen, Inst. for Soil Fertility, Haren, The Netherlands, 1991, Massey U., New Zealand, 1991, Lincoln U., New Zealand, 1998, Environ. and Risk Mgmt. Group HortResearch, 1998, Palmerston North, New Zealand, 1998; William A. Albrecht seminar spkr. U. Mo., 1994; vis. scholar Biol. Labs., Harvard U., 1990; vis. scientist environ. physics sect. dept. sci and indsl. rsch., Palmerston North, New Zealand, 1991, The Horticulture and Food Rsch. Inst. New Zealand, Ltd., Crown Rsch. Inst., Palmerston North, 1998, Landcare Rsch., Lincoln, New Zealand, 1998; participant Internat. Grassland Congress, New Zealand, 13th Internat. Soil Tillage Rsch. Orgn. Conf., Aalborg, Denmark; spkr. Internat. Conf. Vadose Zone Hydrology, Davis, Calif., 1995, 4th Congress European Soc. for Agronomy, Veldhoven, The Netherlands, 1996, Internat. Workshop Characterization and Measurement of Hydraulic Properties of Unsaturated Soil, Riverside, Calif., 1997, Internat. Symposium on Plant Growth and Environ., Seoul, 1993, 15th Internat. Congress of Soil Sci., Acapulco, 1994, 16th Internat. Conf., Montpellier, France, 1998; invited paper Internat. Grasslands Congress, New Zealand; invited keynote spkr. 5th Internat. Conf. on Biogeochemistry Trace Elements, Vienna, Austria, 1999, 2d Internat. Conf. on Contaminants in Soil Environ. in Australasia-Pacific Region, New Delhi, 1999, Chem. Bioavailability in Terrestrial Environ. Workshop, Adelaide, Australia, 2001; peer rev. panel mem. USDA/Nat. Rsch. Initiative, Washington, 1994, rev. panel mem. USDA Office Sci. Quality Rev. Water Quality Nat. Program, 2001, appt. mem. U.S. Nat. Com. for Soil Sci. of the Nat. Acad. of Scis., 2001-. Editor: Water Use in Crop Production, 1999; co-editor: (with I.K. Iskandar) Trace Elements in Soil, 2001; cons. editor Plant and Soil Jour., 1979—; mem. editl. bd. BioCycle, 1978-82, Field Crops Rsch. Jour., 1983-91, Soil Sci., 1997—, Jour. Crop Prodn., 1998—, Jour. Environ. Quality, 2002--; mem. editl. adv. bd. Trends in Agrl. Scis.-Agronomy, 1992—; contbr. more than 180 articles and papers to sci. jours. Recipient Best Reviewer award, Water Resources Engring. divsn. Jour. Irrigation and Drainage Engring., ASCE, 1996; fellow NSF postdoctoral fellow, U. Wis., 1971—73, NDEA fellow, E.I. du Pont de Nemours and Co. summer faculty fellow, 1976; grantee, NSF, USDA, U.S. Dept. Energy, Dept. Sci. and Indsl. Rsch., New Zealand. Fellow AAAS, Am. Soc. Agronomy (editorial bd. 1985-90), Soil Sci. Soc. Am. (travel grantee to internat. congress Japan 1990), Royal Meteorol. Soc., Crop Sci. Soc. Am. (editorial bd. 1980-84); mem. Am. Soc. Plant Physiology (editorial bd. 1982-87), Am. Soc. Horticultural Sci., Internat. Soil Tillage Rsch. Organ., Internat. Soil Sci. Soc. (elected 1st vice chmn. commn. soil physics 1994-98), Bot. Soc. Am., Am. Meteorol. Soc., Société Française de Physiologie Végétale, Japanese Soc. Plant Physiology, Scandinavian Soc. Plant Physiology, N.Y. Acad. Sci., Soc. for Exptl. Biology (London), Growth Regulator Soc. Am., Water Environment Fedn., Phi Kappa Phi (scholar award 2000), Gamma Sigma Delta (Disting. Faculty award Kans. State U. chpt., 2001), Sigma Xi (sec. Kans. State U. chpt. 1997-99, Outstanding Sr. Scientist award 2002). Home: 1420 McCain Ln Apt 244 Manhattan KS 66502-4680 Office: Kans State U Dept Agronomy Throckmorton Hall Manhattan KS 66505-5501 E-mail: mbk@ksu.edu.

KIRKLAND, ALFRED YOUNGES, SR. federal judge; b. Elgin, Ill., 1917; s. Alfred and Elizabeth (Younges) K.; m. Gwendolyn E. Muntz, June 14, 1941; children: Pamela E. Kirkland Jensen, Alfred Younges Jr., James Muntz. BA, U. Ill., 1941, JD, 1943. Bar: Ill. 1943. Assoc. Mayer, Meyer, Austrian & Platt, Chgo., 1943; sr. ptnr. Kirkland, Brady, McQueen, Martin & Callahan and predecessor firms, Elgin, 1951-73; spl. asst. atty. gen. State of Ill., 1969-73; judge 16th Cir. Ct. Ill., 1973-74, U.S. Dist. Ct. (no. dist.) Ill., 1974-79, sr. judge, 1979—. Mem. Coun. Practicing Lawyers U. Ill. Law Forum, 1969—, mem. adv. bd., 1972-73, mem. adv. coun. continuing legal edn., 1959-62; chmn. Ill. Def. Rsch. Inst., 1965-66. Outdoor editor: Elgin Daily Courier-News, Kewanee Star-Courier; fishing editor: Midwest Outdoors Mag. Pres. Elgin YMCA, 1963, chmn. bd. trustees, 1995—. 2d lt. inf. AUS, 1943-46. Fellow Am. Coll. Trial Lawyers, Am. Bar Found.; mem. ABA (ho. of dels. 1967-70), Ill. State Bar Assn. (pres. 1968-69), Chgo. Bar Assn., Kane County Bar Assn. (pres. 1961-62), Elgin Bar Assn. (pres. 1951-52), Am. Judicature Soc. (bd. dirs. 1967—), Ill. Bar Found. (bd. dirs. 1961-69), Ill. Def. Counsel (bd. dirs. 1966-69), Soc. Trial Lawyers, Legal Club Chgo., Law Club Chgo., Internat. Assn. Ins. Counsel, Fed. Ins. Counsel, Assn. Ins. Counsel, Outdoor Writers Assn. Am. (gen. counsel), Assn. Gt. Lakes Outdoor Writers (v.p., bd. dirs.), Ill. C. of C. (bd. dirs. 1969-70), Phi Delta Phi, Sigma Nu. Republican. Congregationalist. Clubs: Elgin Country (pres. 1956), Cosmopolitan Internat. (past pres., judge advocate). Lodges: Elks, Moose. Home: 2421 Tall Oaks Dr Elgin IL 60123-4844 Office: 2421 Tall Oaks Dr Elgin IL 60123-4844

KIRKLAND, JOHN LEONARD, lawyer; b. Elgin, Ill., Aug. 8, 1926; s. Alfred Hines and Elizabeth Aurelia (Younges) Kirkland; m. Harriet Grose, Oct. 14, 1950; children: Karen Emily Kirkland Lazos, Kevin Grose, Robert John, Melissa Caroline Kirkland Glyman. BA, Lake Forest Coll., 1948; JD, Chgo.-Kent Coll. Law, 1952. Bar: Ill. 1951, U.S. Dist. Ct. (no. dist.) Ill. 1952. Assoc. Hinshaw, Culbertson, Moelmann, Hoban & Fuller, Chgo., 1952-60, ptnr., 1960-90, mng. ptnr., 1979-84; of counsel Hinshaw and Culbertson, 1991—. Lectr. Inst. Continuing Legal Edn. Ins. Law, 1968—75. Mem. Cook County Zoning Bd. Appeals, Ill., 1968—73, Arlington Heights Zoning Bd. Appeals, 1961—68, chmn., 1968—68. With USN, 1944—46. Fellow: Am. Coll. Trial Lawyers, Am. Bar Found.; mem.: Fedn. Ins. Counsel, Trial Lawyers Club Chgo. (pres. 1961), Soc. Trail Lawyers, Ill. State Bar Assn. (bd. govs. 1975—79, editor Policy ins. law publ. 1976—90), Big Foot Country Club (pres. 1978—79), Union League Club. Home: 7040 Pelican Bay Blvd # D303 Naples FL 34108-5520 Office: Hinshaw & Culbertson 222 N La Salle St Ste 300 Chicago IL 60601-1081

KIRKPATRICK, ANNE SAUNDERS, systems analyst; b. Birmingham, Mich., July 4, 1938; d. Stanley Rathbun and Esther (Casteel) Saunders; children: Elizabeth, Martha, Robert, Sarah. Student, Wellesley Coll., 1956-57, Laval U., Quebec City, Can., 1958, U. Ariz., 1958-59; BA in Philosophy, U. Mich., 1961. Systems engr. IBM, Chgo., 1962-64; sr. analyst Commonwealth Edison Co., 1981-97. Treas. Taproot Reps., DuPage County, Ill., 1977-80; pres. Hinsdale (Ill.) Women's Rep. Club, 1978-81. Club: Wellesley of Chgo. (bd. dirs. 1972-73). Home: 222 E Chestnut St Unit 8B Chicago IL 60611-2376 E-mail: acsaundersk@aol.com.

KIRKPATRICK, LARRY, radio personality; m. Terri Kirkpatrick, 1977; children: Mark, Bill, Amy, Scott, Timotny. Min., 1976—82; staff announcer WUGN, Midland, Mich., 1982—89, 2000—; min. Bay City, 1989—2000. Office: WUGN 510 Isabella Rd Midland MI 48640

KIRKPATRICK, R(OBERT) JAMES, geology educator; b. Schenectady, N.Y., Dec. 31, 1946; s. Robert James and Audrey (Rech) K.; m. Susan A. Wilson, Sept. 4, 1968 (div. 1984); children: Gregory Robert, Geoffrey Stephen; m. Carol A. Hanna, Sept. 3, 1985. AB, Cornell U., 1968; PhD, U. Ill., 1972. Asst. U.S. Geol. Survey, Denver, 1968; rsch. and teaching asst. U. Ill., Urbana, 1968-72, asst. prof. dept. geology, 1978-80, assoc. prof., 1980-83, prof., 1983-88, prof., head dept., 1988-97, exec. assoc. dean Coll. Liberal Arts & Scis., 1997—; sr. rsch. geologist prodn. rsch. div. Exxon, Houston, 1972-73; rsch. fellow in geophysics Harvard U., Cambridge, 1973-75; asst. rsch. geologist Scripps Instn. Oceanography, La Jolla, Calif., 1976-78. Mem. ocean crust panel Joint Oceanographic Instns. for Deep Earth Studies, 1977-78, active margin panel, 1978, downhole measurements panel, 1977-78; cons. various corps. Editor: Initial Reports of the Deep Sea Drilling Project, Vols. 46 and 55, 1979, 80; co-editor: Kinetics of Geochemical Processes, 1981; assoc. editor American Mineralogist, 1987-90; contbr. over 180 articles to profl. jours. Overseas fellow Churchill Coll., Eng., 1985-86; rsch. grantee NSF, 1977—, Dept. Edn., 2000—, various other orgns., 1978—. Fellow Geol. Soc. Am., Mineral. Soc. Am. (councillor 1990-93); mem. Am. Geophys. Union (VGP award com. 1985-88, chmn. 1986-88), Am. Cer. Soc., Internat. Mineral. Assn. (alt. U.S. del. 1982, coord. com. 1986 meeting, chmn. program com. 1986, U.S. rep. Commn. on Crystal Growth, v.p. 1986-90, sec. Commn. on Mineral Physics 1986-91). Office: U Ill Dept Geology Urbana IL 61801 E-mail: kirkpat@uiuc.edu.

KIRKPATRICK, SHARON MINTON, nursing educator, college administrator; b. Independence, Mo., Aug. 31, 1943; d. Charles Russell and Minnetta (Brotherton) Minton; m. John P. Kirkpatrick; children: John Brent, Kraig Russell. Grad. in nursing, Ind. Sanitarium and Hosp., Independence, 1965; AA, Graceland Coll., Lamoni, Iowa, 1965; BSN, Calif. State U., Sacramento, 1976; M in Nursing, U. Kans., 1981, PhD in Nursing, 1988. RN, Mo., Iowa. Office coordinator Family Practice Physicians, Cupertino, Calif., 1965-67; head nurse Truman Med. Ctr. East, Kansas City, Mo., 1977-79; teaching asst. U. Kans. Med. Ctr., 1980; asst. prof. nursing Graceland Coll., 1980-86, chmn. div. nursing, 1986-94, prof., dean Independence Campus, 1990-94, v.p., dean. of nursing, 1994—. Dir. cmty. health projects Haiti, Dominican Republic, Jamaica, Zambia, Zaire and Malawi. Contbr. articles to profl. jours. Trustee Independence Sanitarium and Hosp., 1977-86; mem. corp. body Truman Neurol. Ctr., Kansas City, 1979-86. Mem. ANA (coun. on cultural diversity), Mo. Nurses Assn. (bd. dirs., pres. 1991-93), Profl. Nurses Assn. (pres. 1982-84), Collegiate Nurse Educators Greater Kansas City (pres. 1991-92), Jr. Women's Club Cupertino (past pres.), Sigma Theta Tau. Mem. Reorganized LDS Ch. Avocations: traveling, cultural studies, backpacking, boating, reading. Home: 5665 NE Northgate Xing Lees Summit MO 64064-1240 Office: Graceland Coll Lamoni IA 50140

KIRKSEY, AVANELLE, nutrition educator; b. Mulberry, Ark., Mar. 23, 1926; BS, U. Ark., Fayetteville, 1947; MS, U. Tenn., Knoxville, 1950; PhD, Pa. State U., 1961; postdoctoral, U. Calif., Davis, 1976; DSc honoris causa, Purdue U., 1997. Assoc. prof. Ark. Polytechnic U., Russellville, 1950-55; research asst. Pa. State U., University Park, 1956-58, fellow Gen. Foods, 1958-60; assoc. prof. Purdue U., West Lafayette, Ind., 1961-69, prof. nutrition, 1970-85, disting. prof., 1985-96, disting. prof. emeritus, 1997. Prin. investigator nutrition project in rural Egypt; coord. nutrition program Indonesian Univs., 1987-91 Contbr. articles to profl. jours. Recipient Borden award Am. Home Econs. Assn., 1980. Fellow Am. Inst. Nutrition (Lederle award 1994); mem. N.Y. Acad. Scis., Phi Kappa Phi, Sigma Xi. Office: Purdue U Dept Food Nutrition West Lafayette IN 47907

KIRKWOOD, WILLIAM THOMAS, corporate professional; b. Marion, Ohio, Aug. 19, 1948; s. Hugh E. and Mildred M. (Schaeffer) K. Jr.; m. Deborah Hedges, Jan. 4, 1967 (div. Aug. 1980); children: Krista, Konni, Bobby; m. Beth C. Mitchell, May 30, 1981 (div. Aug. 1988). BS in Acctg., Franklin U., 1976. CPA. Acct. Worthington (Ohio) Foods, Inc., 1970-75, cost. supr., 1975-78, acctg. mgr., 1978-82, controller, 1982-86, asst. treas., 1986—; exec. v.p. and CFO Worthington Foods, Inc. Office: Worthington Foods Inc 900 Proprietors Rd Columbus OH 43085-3194

KIRSCHNER, BARBARA STARRELS, pediatric gastroenterologist; b. Phila., Mar. 23, 1941; m. Robert H. Kirschner. MD, Women's Med. Coll. Pa., 1967. Diplomate Am. Bd. Pediatrics; cert. in pediatric gastroenterology and nutrition. Intern U. Chgo., 1967-68, resident, 1968-70; mem. staff Wyler Children's Hosp., U. Chgo., 1977-83, asst. prof. pediatrics, 1984-88, prof. pediatrics and medicine, 1988—, mem. com. on nutrition and nutritional biology. Contbr. articles to profl. jours. Pediatric Gastroenterology fellow U. Chgo., 1975-77; recipient Davidson award in Pediatric gastroenterology Acad. Pediatrics, 1993, Joseph Brenneman award Chgo. Pediat. Soc., 2001. Mem. Am. Gastroenterologic Assn., N.Am. Soc. Pediatric Gastroenterology, Soc. Pediatric Rsch., Alpha Omega Alpha. Office: U Chgo Med Ctr 5839 S Maryland Ave # 4065 Chicago IL 60637-5417

KIRSCHNER, STANLEY, chemist; b. N.Y.C., Dec. 17, 1927; s. Abraham and Rebecca K.; m. Esther Green, June 11, 1950; children— Susan Joyce, Daniel Ross. BS magna cum laude, Bklyn. Coll., 1950; AM, Harvard U., 1952; PhD, U. Ill., 1954. Research chemist Monsanto Chem. Co., Everett, Mass., 1951; teaching asst. in chemistry Harvard U., 1950-52, U. Ill., Urbana, 1952-54; mem. faculty dept. chemistry Wayne State U., Detroit, 1954—, prof., 1960—, prof. emeritus, 1992—. Vis. prof. U. London, 1963-64, U. Florence, Italy, 1976, U. Sao Paulo, Brazil, 1969, Tohoku U., Sendai, Japan, 1978, Tech. U. Lisbon, Portugal, 1984, U. Porto, Portugal, 1984 Author: Advances in the Chemistry of Coordination Compounds, 1961, Coordination Chemistry, 1969, Inorganic Syntheses, Vol. 23, 1985; contbr. articles to profl. jours. Served with USN, 1945-46. Recipient Pres.'s award for excellence in teaching Wayne State U., 1979, Gold award Engring. Soc. of Detroit, 1995, Heyrovsky medal Czechoslovak Acad. Scis., 1978, Catalyst award in chem. edn. Chem. Mfrs. Assn., 1984, Faculty Svc. award Wayne State U. Alumni Assn., 1986; fellow Fulbright Found., 1963-64, NSF, 1963-64, Ford Found., 1969-70. Fellow AAAS, Am. Inst. Chemists, N.Y. Acad. Scis.; mem. AAUP, Am. Chem. Soc. (chmn. divsn. edn., bd. dirs. 1985-93, Henry Hill award 1995, Brazilian Acad. Scis., Internat. Conf. Coordination Chemistry (permanent sec. 1966-89, emeritus 1990), Internat. Union Pure and Applied Chemistry (com. nomenclature of inorganic chemistry 1991-93), Chem. Soc. Chile (hon.), Chem. Soc. (London). Home: 25615 Parkwood Dr Huntington Woods MI 48070-1424 Office: Dept Chemistry Wayne State Univ Detroit MI 48202

KIRSHENBAUM, JOSEPH, real estate developer; Pres. Noddle Devel. Co., Omaha, 1979—. Office: Noddle Devel Co PO Box 542010 Omaha NE 68154-8010

KIRSHNAN, RAAMA, electronics executive; V.p. fin. Cybertech Systems, Oak Brook, Ill. Office: Cybertech Systems 1135 W 22d St Oak Brook IL 60523

KIRSNER, JOSEPH BARNETT, physician, educator; b. Boston, Sept. 21, 1909; s. Harris and Ida (Waiser) K.; m. Minnie Schneider, Jan. 6, 1934; 1 son, Robert S. MD, Tufts U., 1933; PhD in Biol. Scis., U. Chgo., 1942; DSc (hon.), Tufts U., 1993. Intern Woodlawn Hosp., Chgo., 1933—34, resident in internal medicine, 1934—35; asst. in medicine U. Chgo., 1935—37, from asst. prof. to assoc. prof., 1937—51, prof., 1951—, Louis Black Distinguished Service prof. medicine, 1968—, chief of staff, also dep. dean for med. affairs, 1971—76. Cons. NIH, 1956-69; hon. pres. Gastrointestinal Research Found., 1961— ; Mem. drug efficacy adv. com. to NRC; chmn. adv. group Nat. Commn. on Digestive Diseases, 1978; chmn. emeritus sci. adv. com. Nat. Found. Ileitis and Colitis. Editor, author: Inflammatory Bowel Disease, 5th edit., 1999, The Growth of Gastroenterologic Knowledge During the 20th Century, 1994, Early Days of American Gastroenterology, 1996; contbr. more than 735 articles to profl. publs. Served with M.C. AUS, 1943-46, ETO; PTO. Recipient Julius Friedenwald medal disting. work gastroenterology, 1975, Horatio Alger award, 1979, hon. Gold Key for Disting. Service U. Chgo. Med. Alumni Assn., 1979, Alumni medal U. Chgo. Alumni Assn., 1989, Disting. Educator award Am. Gastroenterological Assn., 1999; Joseph B. Kirsner award for excellence in rsch. in clin. gastroenterology established in his honor, Am. Gastroent. Assn., 1990; G. Brohée lectr. World Cong. Gastroenterology, 1994, Laureate award Lincoln Acad. Ill. Mem. Am. Assn. Physicians, ACP (master, John Phillips award), Am. Gastroent. Assn. (past pres., governing bd.), Am. Gastroscopic Soc. (past pres.), Am. Soc. Gastrointestinal Endoscopy (Rudolf Schindler award), Am. Soc. Clin. Investigation, Ctrl. Soc. Clin. Rsch., Chgo. Soc. Internal Medicine (past pres.), Inst. Medicine Chgo. (George H. Coleman medal) Achievements include rsch. in gastrointestinal disorders, inflammatory disease of gastrointestinal tract. Home: 5805 S Dorchester Ave Chicago IL 60637-1730 Office: U Chgo Med Ctr 5841 S Maryland Ave Chicago IL 60637-1470

KIRWAN, WILLIAM ENGLISH, II, mathematics educator, university official, academic administrator; b. Louisville, Apr. 14, 1938; s. Albert Dennis Kirwan and Elizabeth (Heil) Kirwan; m. Patricia Ann Harper, Aug. 27, 1960; children: William English III, Ann Elizabeth. BA, U. Ky., 1960; MS (NDEA fellow 1960-63), Rutgers U., 1962, PhD, 1964. Instr. Rutgers U., 1963—64; mem. faculty U. Md., College Park, 1964, prof. math., 1972, chmn. dept., 1977—81, vice chancellor for acad. affairs, 1981—86, provost, 1986—88, acting pres., 1988—89, pres., 1989—98, Ohio State U., Columbus, 1998—. Vis. lectr. London U., 1966—67; program dir. NSF, 1975—76. Contbr. articles to profl. jours. MS 2000 Com. for NRC; mem. adv. bd. Montgomery County (Md.), 1975—79; bd. dirs. Nat. Assn. State Univs. and Land Grant Colls., 1995—, Greater Washington YMCA, 1994—; World Trade Ctr. Inst., 1990—. Decorated officer Order King Leopold II (Belgium); named Disting. Alumnus, U. Ky., 1989. Mem.: NCAA (pres. commn. 1995—), Coun. for the Internat. Exch. of Scholars, Math. Assn. Am., Am. Assn. Colls. and Univs. (bd. dirs. 1993—, 1994—), Am. Math. Soc. (coun. 1980—82, editor Proc. 1977—82). Office: University System of Maryland Chancellor's Office 3300 Metzerott Rd, Suite 2C Adelphi MD 20783

KIRWIN, KENNETH FRANCIS, law educator; b. Morris, Minn., May 10, 1941; s. Francis B. and Dorothy A. (McNally) K.; m. Phyllis J. Hills, June 2, 1962; children— David, Mark, Robert. B.A., St. John's U., 1963; J.D., U. Minn., 1966. Bar: Minn. 1966, U.S. Dist. Ct. Minn. 1968, U.S. Ct. Appeals (8th cir.) 1969. Law clk. to assoc. justice Supreme Ct., Minn., 1966-67; assoc. Lindquist & Vennum, Mpls., 1967-70; prof. law William Mitchell Coll. Law, St. Paul, 1970—. Staff dir. Uniform Rules Criminal Procedure, 1971-74, reporter, 1982-87; reporter Uniform Victims of Crime Act, 1991-92; adj. prof. U. Minn. Law Sch., 1977, 80; active Minn. Lawyers Profl. Responsibility Bd., 1975-81, Minn. Bd. Continuing Legal Edn., 1975-83. Author: (with Maynard E. Pirsig) Cases and Materials on Professional Responsibility, 1984. Mem. Ramsey County Bar Assn., Minn. State Bar Assn., ABA (mem. standing com. on discipline 1983-89), Am. Law Inst. Home: 1418 Brookshire Ct New Brighton MN 55112-6390 Office: William Mitchell Coll Law 875 Summit Ave Saint Paul MN 55105-3030 E-mail: kkirwin@wmitchell.edu.

KISCADEN, SHEILA M. state legislator; b. St. Paul, Apr. 21, 1946; d. Harvey Richard and Bea Mae (Conway) Martineau; m. Richard Craig Kiscaden, Sept. 12, 1970; children: Michael, Karen. BS in Edn., U. Minn., 1969; MS in Pub. Adminstrn., U. So. Calif., L.A., 1986. Tchr. So. St. Paul Secondary Schs., Minn., 1969-70, Jobs 70, Rochester, 1970-71; regional coord. Planned Parenthood, 1971-76; vol. svc. coord. Olmsted County, 1977-80, human svc. planner, 1980-82, legis. liaison, 1982-85; prin. Cons. Collaborator, 1987—; mem. Minn Senate from 30th dist., St. Paul, 1992—. Bd. dirs. Ability Bldg. Ctr. Found. Bd., Rochester, Minn., 1989-94, Dyslexia Inst. Minn., Rochester, Minn., 1989-94; team leader Global Vols., 1989—. Fulbright scholar, 1970. Mem. Phi Beta Kappa. Republican. Office: Minn State Senate 143 State Office Bldg Saint Paul MN 55155-0001

KISCHUK, RICHARD KARL, insurance company executive; b. Detroit, Mar. 14, 1949; s. Russell and Aubrey Ann (Artt) K.; m. Sandra Jean Dierkes, June 26, 1971; children: Robert Charles, Kirsten Grace, Erin Michelle, Danielle Laraine, Russell Olan, Erika Anne. BS, U. Mich., 1969, M in Actuarial Sci., 1971; MS in Bus. Adminstrn., Ind. U., 1979. Enrolled actuary. Actuarial trainee Lincoln Nat. Life, Ft. Wayne, Ind., 1971-72, actuarial asst., 1972-1973, asst. actuary, 1973-77, asst. v.p., 1977-80, 2d v.p., 1980-82; v.p. Lincoln Nat. Corp., 1982-86; v.p., dir. Lincoln Nat. Health and Casualty Ins. Co., 1985-87, Lincoln Nat. Life Reins. Co., 1985-87, Lincoln Nat. Adminstrv. Service; chief operating officer, dir. Lincoln Intermediaries, Inc., 1985-87, Spl. Pooled Risk Adminstrs., Inc., 1985-87, Underwriters and Mgmt. Services, Inc., 1985-87; pres. Crown Point Mgmt. Cons., Inc., 1987—, Beneficient Solutions, Inc., 1998—. Mem. editorial adv. bd. CLU Jour., 1983-91; contbr. articles to profl. jours. Fellow Soc Actuaries (chmn. fin. reporting sect. 1982-85, bd. govs. 1986-89), mem. Am. Acad. Actuaries. Avocations: camping, backpacking, canoing, photography. Office: Crown Point Mgmt Cons Inc PO Box 355 Pendleton IN 46064-0355

KISER, GERALD L. furniture company executive; Case goods divsn. mfg. mgr. Broyhill; v.p. ops. Kincaid Furniture Co. subs. La-Z-Boy Inc., Houston, La-Z-Boy Corp., Monroe, Mich., exec. v.p., COO, pres., COO. Mem. Am. Furniture Mfrs. Assn. Office: La-A-Boy Inc 1284 N Telegraph Rd Monroe MI 48162

KISHEL, GREGORY FRANCIS, federal judge; b. Virginia, Minn., Jan. 26, 1951; AB, Cornell U., 1973; JD, Boston Coll., 1977. Bar: Minn. 1978, U.S. Dist. Ct. Minn. 1978, U.S. Ct. Appeals (8th cir.) 1978, Wis. 1985, U.S. Dist. Ct. (we. dist.) Wis. 1985. Staff atty. Legal Aid Svc. of N.E. Minn., Duluth, 1978-81; pvt. practice, 1981-86; judge U.S. Bankruptcy Ct., St. Paul, 1986-2000, chief judge, 2000—. Judge U.S. Bankruptcy Ct., Duluth, 1984-86; pro tem mem. bankruptcy appellate panel 8th Cir. Ct., 1996—. Mem.: Minn. Bar Assn., Nat. Conf. Bankruptcy Judges, Polish Geneal. Soc. Minn. (pres. 1996—2000). Office: US Bankruptcy Ct 316 Robert St N Ste 210 Saint Paul MN 55101-1243

KISKA, TIMOTHY OLIN, newspaper columnist; b. Detroit, July 26, 1952; s. Edward Frederick and Mary Clare (Barnhart) K.; m. Patricia Irene Anstett, May 23, 1981; children: Caitlin, Amy, Eric. BA, Wayne State U., 1980, MA, 1995. Mem. staff Detroit Free Press, 1970-74, reporter, 1974-85, automotive writer, 1985-87; columnist Detroit News, 1987—. Adj. lectr. U. Mich., Dearborn, 2000—; mem. student newspaper publs. bd. Wayne State U., 1994-97, 99—. Author: Detroit's Powers and Personalities, 1989; contbr. articles to AutoWeek, 1985—. Mem. TV Critics Assn. Home: 20050 Marford Ct Grosse Pointe Woods MI 48236-2324 Office: Detroit News 615 W Lafayette Blvd Detroit MI 48226-3197

KISKER, CARL THOMAS, physician, medical educator; B.A., Johns Hopkins U., 1958; M.D., U. Cin. Coll. Medicine, 1962. Diplomate Am. Bd. Pediatrics, Am. Bd. Pediatric Hematology-Oncology. Lic. physician Ohio, Iowa. Intern U. Oreg. Coll. Medicine, 1962-63; sr. asst. surgeon NIH, 1963-65; jr. resident pediat. Children's Hosp., Cin., 1965-66, sr. resident pediat., 1966-67, fellow pediat. hematology, 1967-69, asst. attending pediatrician, 1968-69, attending pediatrician, 1969-73, dir. hemophilia project, 1971-73, dir. clin. hematology lab., 1972-73; asst. prof. pediat. U. Cin., 1969-72, assoc. prof. pediat., 1972-73, U. Iowa, Iowa City, 1973-79, dir. divsn. pediat. hematology-oncology, 1973-97, prof. pediat., 1979—. Med. lectr. various student and profl. groups; active mem. Pediat. Hematology-Oncology Group, Cin., Children's Cancer Study Group, L.A.; pres. Midwest Blood Club.; mem. adv. coun. Nat. Hemophilia Ctrs., 1979—.$D Mem. editl bd. Pediat. Today; contbr. numerous sci. papers to profl. jours. and chpts. in books. Mem. Iowa Found. Fund Raising Com. Lederle Med. Student Rsch. fellow, 1959; recipient state and fed. grants, Alumni of Yr. award U. Cin. Coll. Medicine, 2002. Mem. Am. Soc. Hematology, Mid-west Soc. for Pediat. RSch., Am. Fedn. for Clin. RSch., Am. Heart Assn., Internat. Soc. Thrombosis and Haemostasis (sub-com. on neonatal hemostasis), Ctrl. Soc. for Pediat. Rsch., Soc. Pediat. Rsch., Johnson County Med. Soc., Prairie Region Affiliated Blood Svcs., Am. Pediat. Soc. Office: Univ of Iowa Hosp 2520 Jcp Iowa City IA 52242 E-mail: c-kisker@uiowa.edu.

KISOR, HENRY DU BOIS, newspaper editor, critic, columnist; b. Ridgewood, N.J., Aug. 17, 1940; s. Manown and Judith (Du Bois) K.; m. Deborah L. Abbott, June 24, 1967; children: Colin, Conan. BA, Trinity Coll., 1962, LittD (hon.), 1991; MS in Journalism, Northwestern U., 1964. Copy editor Wilmington News-Jour. (Del.), 1964-65, Chgo. Daily News, 1965-73, book editor, 1973-78, Chgo. Sun-Times, 1978—. Adj. prof. Medill Sch. Journalism Northwestern U., Evanston, Ill., 1979-82 Author: What's That Pig Outdoors?: A Memoir of Deafness, 1990, Zephyr: Tracking a Dream Across America, 1994, Flight of the Gin Fizz; Midlife at 4,500 Feet, 1997. Bd. dirs. Chgo. Hearing Soc., 1975-76. Recipient Stick-O-Type award Chgo. Newspaper Guild, 1981, 85, Outstanding Achievement award Ill. UPI, 1983, 85, 1st pl. award Ill. UPI columns divsn., 1985, James Friend Meml. Critic award Friends of Lit., 1988, Best Non-fiction award, 1991; finalist Pulitzer Prize nomination in criticism Columbia U., 1981; named to Chgo. Journalism Hall of Fame, 2001; NEH seminar fellow, 1978. Office: Chgo Sun-Times 401 N Wabash Ave Chicago IL 60611-5642

KISSEL, EDWARD W. company executive; BS, Rensselaer Poly. Inst.; MS in Mgmt., MIT. Various positions including dir. ops. for Latin Am. region Goodyear Tire & Rubber Co., Akron, Ohio; v.p. mfg. and engring. Engelhard Corp., Iselin, N.J., 1987-90; exec. v.p., pres. passenger and light truck divsn. Continental-Gen. Tire, Inc.; CEO Kissel Group Ltd., 1993-99; pres., COO OM Group, Inc., 1999—. Office: 3500 Terminal Tower 50 Public Sq Cleveland OH 44113-2201

KISSEL, RICHARD JOHN, lawyer; b. Chgo., Nov. 27, 1936; s. John and Anne T. (Unichowski) K.; m. Donna Lou Heidersbach, Feb. 11, 1961; children: Roy Warren, David Todd, Audrey Anne. BA, Northwestern U., 1958; JD, Northwestern U., Chgo., 1961. Assoc. Peterson, Lowrey, Rall, Barber & Ross, Chgo., 1961-65; divsn. counsel Abbott Labs., North Chicago, 1965-70; mem. Pollution Control Bd., Chgo., 1970-72; adminstrv. asst. Gov.'s Staff, 1972; ptnr. Martin, Craig, Chester & Sonnenschein, 1973-88, Gardner, Carton & Douglas, Chgo., 1998—2000, chmn. mgmt. com., 1996-98, of counsel, 2000—. Adj. prof. U. Ill. Sch. Pub. Health, Chgo., 1973-76; instr. Kent. Sch. Law, Ill. Inst. Tech., Chgo., 1974-78; mem. vis. com. Northwestern U. Law Sch., 1996-99. Recipient Ill. award IAWA, 1996. Contbr. articles to legal jours. Active Sewer Task Force, Lake Forest, Ill. Fellow Internat. Soc. Barristers; mem. Ill. State Bar Assn., Chgo. Bar Assn., Ill. State C. of C. (chmn. environ. affairs 1973-76), Com. on Cts. for 21st Century, Knollwood Club (Lake Forest; gov. 1976-82), Lake Forest/Lake Bluff Sr. Citizens Found (bd. dirs., sr. adv. commn. Lake Forest, Ill.), Harbour Ridge Yacht & Country Club. Roman Catholic. Office: Gardner Carton & Douglas 321 N Clark St Ste 3000 Chicago IL 60610-4718 E-mail: rkissel@gcd.com.

KISSELL, DON R. state legislator; Mem. dist. 17 Mo. Ho. of Reps. Office: 121 Courtfield Dr O'Fallon MO 63366-4393

KITCH, FREDERICK DAVID, advertising executive; b. Chgo., Sept. 7, 1928; s. John Raymond and Mary Minerva (Wheeler) K.; m. Beverly Jane West, Nov. 24, 1976; children: William Mark, Stephen Neal, Michael Bruce Hile. BS in Journalism, Northwestern U., 1951. Mgmt. tng. Swift & Co., Chgo., 1954-55, dept. head Evansville, Ind., 1955-57; account exec. Keller-Crescent Co., 1957-60, sr. account exec., 1960-65, v.p. account supervision, 1965-72, v.p. direct client services, 1972-80, exec. v.p. client services, 1980-86, exec. v.p. mktg. and sales, 1986-93, also bd. dirs., ret., 1993; founder, chmn. Kitch & Schreiber, Inc., 1994—. Past pres. bd. dirs. Evansville Rescue Mission, 1981-97; pres. Welborn Hosp. Found., Evansville, 1984-91, Operation City Beautiful, Evansville, 1985-87; sec., treas. Vanderburgh County Redevel. Authority; v.p. Oak Meadow Homeowners Assn. Served to lt. U.S. Army, 1951-53. Recipient Silver Medal Tri State Advt. Club, 1980. Mem. Affiliated Advt. Internat. (sec.-treas.), 1980, Evansville Country Club (bd. dirs.). Republican. Episcopalian. Avocations: tennis, golf. Home: 4029 Fairfax Rd Evansville IN 47740 Office: Kitch & Schreiber Inc 320 NW King Jr Blvd Evansville IN 47735

KITE, STEVEN B. lawyer; b. Chgo., May 30, 1949; s. Ben and Dolores (Braver) K.; m. Catherine Lapinski, Jan. 13, 1980; children: David, Julia. BA, U. Ill., 1971; JD, Harvard U., 1974. Bar: Ga. 1974, U.S. Dist. Ct. Ga. 1974, U.S. Ct. Appeals (5th and 11th cirs.) 1981, Ill. 1985, Fla. 1986. Ptnr. Kutak Rock, Atlanta, 1974-84, Gardner, Carton & Douglas, Chgo., 1984—. Author, editor: Law For Elderly, 1978; author: Tax-Exempt Financing for Health Care Organizations, 1996; co-author: Bond Financing, 1994. Bd. dirs. Atlanta Legal Aid Soc., 1979-84; trustee Sr. Citizens Met. Atlanta, 1980-83. Mem. ABA, Ill. Bar Assn., State Bar Ga., Chgo. Bar Assn., Fla. Bar Assn., Nat. Assn. Bond Lawyers. Avocations: travel, sports, reading. Office: Gardner Carton & Douglas Quaker Tower 321 N Clark St Ste 3400 Chicago IL 60610-4795 E-mail: skite@gcd.com.

KITNA, JON, football player; b. Tacoma, Sept. 21, 1972; m. Jennifer Kitna; children: Jordan, Jada. Postgrad in math edn., Ctrl. Wash. Quarterback Cin. Bengals , 2001—, Seattle Seahawks , 1997—2000. Founder Christian Min. Remann Hall, Tacoma. Office: Cin Bengals One Paul Brown Stadium Cincinnati OH 45202*

KITT, WALTER, psychiatrist; b. N.Y.C., Dec. 18, 1925; s. Elias and Mary (Opiela) K.; m. Terry Escorcia, May 15, 1955 (dec. 1974); 1 child, Gregory; m. Sally Anderson Chappell, June 22, 1977. Student, CCNY, 1942-44; AB magna cum laude, Syracuse U., 1948; MD, Chgo. Med. Sch., 1952. Diplomate Am. Bd. Psychiatry and Neurology. Resident Neuropsychiat. Inst., Chgo., 1953-56; practice medicine specializing in psychiatry, 1956-64, Munster, Ind., 1963-80; psychiatrist Lakeside VA Med. Ctr., Chgo., 1981-92; practice medicine specializing in psychiatry Park Ridge, Ill., 1992-96, Schaumburg, 1996-97; acting chief psychiat. svcs. Lakeside VA Med. Ctr., Chgo., 1986-87; ret., 1998. Asst. prof. clin. psychiatry U. Ill. Med. Ctr., Chgo., 1958-64, Northwestern U., Chgo., 1974-96, asst. prof. emeritus 1996-2001; chmn. divsn. psychiatry Our Lady of Mercy Hosp., Dyer, Ind., 1970-72. Mem. Am. Psychiat. Assn. Home: 3750 N Lake Shore Dr Chicago IL 60613-4238

KITTLE, JIM, JR. state representative; m. Sherry Kittle; children: Sawyer, Kenzie. Postgrad. Ind. Univ., Ind. Univ. Sch. law. Chmn., CEO Kittle's Furniture Group, 1979—. Vice chair Bush for Pres. Team, 2000; delegate Three National Conventions; fin. chmn. McIntosh Campaign, 2000. Chmn. Retail Divsn. United Way Ctrl. Ind.; bd.dirs. Human Soc. Indpls.; adv. bd. St. Vincent Hosp.; bd. dirs. Ind. Chamber Commerce, Better Bus. Bur., Nat. Retail Fedn. Republican. Office: Ind State Rep Party 47 S Meridian St 2nd Fl Indianapolis IN 46204*

KITZKE, EUGENE DAVID, research management executive; b. Milw., Sept. 2, 1923; s. Leo R. and Regina R. (Tomczyk) K.; m. Lorraine Grace Shummon, Sept. 2, 1946; children: Mary Victoria, Paul Simon, Patrice Lynn, Jerome Peter. B.S., Marquette U., 1945, M.S., 1947. Instr. microbiology St. Mary's Sch. Nursing, Grand Rapids, Mich., 1946-47; assoc. prof. Aquinas Coll., 1947-51; lab researcher S.C. Johnson & Son, Inc., Racine, Wis., 1951-57, research mgr., 1957-76, v.p. corp. research and devel., 1976-81; pres. Oak Crete Block Corp., South Milwaukee, 1980—; developer Wind Crest Subdiv., Wind Lake, 1993. Asst. clin. prof. dept. environ. medicine Med. Coll. Wis., Milw., 1973-81; owner Danel Enterprise, South Milwaukee; bd. dirs. Songcards, Inc.; judge Marquette U. Sci. Fair. Author: For the Next Generation, 1986; patentee (in field); contbr. articles to tech. jours., fiction and poetry to mags. Mem. Pres.' Council Alverno Coll., 1979-87. Recipient H.F. Johnson Cmty. Svc. award, 1996; Disting. Scholar Marquette U., 1995. Mem. Palm Soc. (exec. bd., past pres.), AAAS, History of Sci. Soc., Sigma Xi, Phi Sigma, Sigma Tau Delta Roman Catholic. Home: 616 Aspen St South Milwaukee WI 53172-1702 Office: PO Box 413 South Milwaukee WI 53172-0413 also: 7101 S Pennsylvania Ave Oak Creek WI 53154-2439

KLAAS, PAUL BARRY, lawyer; b. St. Paul, Aug. 9, 1952; s. N. Paul and Ruth Elizabeth (Barry) K.; m. Barbara Ann Bockhaus, July 30, 1977; children: James, Ann, Brian. AB, Dartmouth Coll., 1974; JD, Harvard U., 1977. Bar: Minn. 1977, U.S. Dist. Ct. Minn. 1977, U.S. Ct. Appeals (8th cir.) 1979, U.S. Ct. Appeals (10th cir.) 1980, U.S. Supreme Ct. 1982, U.S. Ct. Appeals (9th cir.) 1989, U.S. Ct. Appeals (fed. cir.) 1994. Assoc. Dorsey & Whitney, Mpls., 1977-82, ptnr., 1983—. Chair trial dept., co-chair Internat. Arbitration and Litigation Practice Group; adj. prof. William Mitchell Coll Law, St. Paul, 1980-85. Fellow: Am. Coll. Trial Lawyers. Office: Dorsey & Whitney 50 S 6th St Ste 1500 Minneapolis MN 55402-1498 E-mail: klaas.paul@dorseylaw.com.

KLAASSEN, CURTIS D. toxicologist, educator; b. Ft. Dodge, Iowa, Nov. 23, 1942; s. Henry Herman and Luwene Sophie (Nieman) K.; m. Cherry Klaassen, Sept. 30, 1968; children: Kimberly, Lisa. BS, Wartburg Coll., Waverly, Iowa, 1964; PhD, U. Iowa, 1968. Diplomate Am. Bd. Toxicology. Prof. toxicology U. Kans. Med. Ctr., Kansas City. Editor: Casarett & Douls Toxicology, 1991. Recipient USPHS Rsch. Career Devel. award, 1971-76, Achievement award, Soc. Toxicology, 1976, Burroughs Wellcome scholar, 1982-87. Mem. Soc. of Toxicology (pres. 1990-91). Lutheran. Office: Univ of Kans Med Ctr 39 Rainbow Kansas City KS 66103-2071

KLAHR, SAULO, physician, educator; b. Santander, Colombia, June 8, 1935; came to U.S., 1961, naturalized, 1970; s. Herman and Raquel (Konigsberg) K.; m. Carol Declue, Dec. 29, 1965; children: James Herman, Robert David. B.A., Colegio Santa Librada, Cali, Colombia, 1954; M.D., U. Nat., Bogota, Colombia, 1959. Intern Hosp. San Juan de Dios, Bogota, 1958-59; resident U. Hosp., Cali, 1959-61; mem. faculty Washington U. Sch. Medicine, St. Louis, 1966—, prof. medicine, 1972-86, Joseph Friedman prof. renal disease, 1986-91, Simon prof. medicine, co-chmn. dept., 1991-97, dir. renal div., 1972-91; physician in chief Jewish Hosp., 1991-96; assoc. physician Barnes Hosp., 1972-75, physician, 1975-96, Barnes-Jewish Hosp., 1996—. Established investigator Am. Heart Assn., 1968-73; mem. adv. com. artificial kidney chronic uremia program USPHS, 1971—; bd. dirs. Eastern Mo. Kidney Found., 1973-75, chmn. med. adv. bd., 1973-74; rsch. com. Mo. Heart Assn., 1973-80, chmn., 1980-81; sci. adv. bd. Nat. Kidney Found., 1978, chmn., 1983-84, chmn. rsch. and fellowship com., 1979-81, v.p., 1986-88, pres., 1988-90; mem. gen. medicine B study sect. USPHS, 1979-83, chmn. gen. medicine B study sect., 1981-83; mem. cardiovascular and renal rev. group FDA, mem. VA Merit Rev. Bd. Nephrology, 1984-87, chmn., 1986-87; chmn. rsch. com. adv. bd. kidney, urology Nat. Inst. Diabetes and Digestive and Kidney Diseases, 1991-92, chmn. adv. bd., 1992-93; mem. adv. coun. Inst. Diabetes, Digestive Diseases and Kidney Diseases, 1995-98. Editor: Contemporary Nephrology, Chronic Renal Disease, Nutrition and the Kidney; editor in chief Am. Jour. Kidney Diseases, 1992-96; mem. editorial bd. Am. Jour. Nephrology, Am. Jour. Physiology and Renal and Electrolyte, Kidney and Body Fluids in Health and Disease, Internat. Jour. Pediatric Nephrology; assoc. editor Jour. Clin. Investigation; editor Kidney Internat., 1997—; contbr. articles to profl. jours., book chpts. USPHS postdoctoral fellow, 1961-63; recipient David M. Hume award Nat. Kidney Found., 1992, Thomas Addis medal Internat. Soc. Nutrition and Renal Metabolism, 1996. Fellow ACP, AAAS, Royal Coll. Physicians (London), Australian, Chilean, Colombian, Spanish, Polish and Italian Socs. Nephrology (hon.); mem. Am. Soc. Nephrology (councillor 1980-81, sec.-treas. 1981-84, pres. 1985-86, John P. Peters award 1998), Am. Soc. Clin. Investigation, Am. Physiol. Soc., Biophys. Soc., N.Y. Acad. Scis., Am. Soc. Renal Biochemistry and Metabolism (pres. 1982-84), Ctrl. Soc. Clin. Rsch., Soc. Exptl. Biology and Medicine, Assn. Am. Physicians, Soc. Gen. Physiologists, Internat. Soc. Nephrology (councillor 1987-95, mem. mgmt. com. 1987-95, chmn. program com. Sydney meeting 1997, mem. exec. com. 1997—), Sigma Xi, Alpha Omega Alpha. Home: 11544 Ladue Rd Saint Louis MO 63141-8341 Office: Barnes-Jewish Hosp Washington U Med Ctr 216 S Kingshighway Blvd Saint Louis MO 63110-1026

KLAPER, MARTIN JAY, lawyer; b. Chgo., Jan. 12, 1947; s. Carl and Kate F. (Friedman) K.; m. Julia Warner, Nov. 14, 1973. BS in Bus. summa cum laude, Ind. U., 1969, JD summa cum laude, 1971. Bar: Ind. 1971, U.S. Dist. Ct. (no. and so. dists.) Ind. 1971, U.S. Ct. Appeals (7th cir.) 1972, U.S. Supreme Ct. 1979. Law clk. to justice U.S. Ct. Appeals (7th cir.), 1971-72; ptnr. Ice Miller, Indpls., 1972—. Mem. ABA, Ind. Bar Assn. Office: Ice Miller PO Box 82001 Indianapolis IN 46282-2001 E-mail: Klaper@iquest.net., Klaper@Icemiller.com.

KLAPPERICH, FRANK LAWRENCE, JR. investment banker; b. Oak Park, Ill., Oct. 11, 1934; s. Frank Lawrence and Marjorie (Doan) K.; m. Margaret Monroe Touborg, Mar. 9, 1957; children: Margaret Friis, Susan Doane, Frank Lawrence III, Elizabeth Monroe. AB, Princeton U., 1956; MBA, Harvard U., 1961, postgrad., 1979. With Kidder, Peabody & Co., Inc., Chgo., 1961—, v.p., 1964—, dir., 1972-86, mng. dir., 1986-88, sr. v.p., 1988-90, ret., 1990; pres. Charter Capital Corp., 1991—. Bd. dirs. T.C. Mfg. Co., Inc. Governing mem. Orchestral Assn. Chgo. Symphony Orch., 1995—; vice chmn. governing mems., 1996-98. With USN, 1956—59, ret. LCDR USNR. Mem. Investment Analysts Soc. Chgo., Securities Industry Assn. (chmn. Ctrl. States dist. 1986-87), Inst. Chartered Fin. Analysts, Harvard Bus. Sch. Assn. Chgo., Princeton Club (Chgo., pres. 1970-71), Charter Club (governing bd. 1987-97), Chgo. Club, Mid-Day Club (trustee 1987-90), Bond Club (pres. 1983-84), Econ. Club, Forum Club S.W. Fla. (bd. dirs.), Harvard Club of Naples (Fla., bd. dirs. 1999-01, v.p. 2000-01, pres. 2001—), Princeton Club (N.Y.C.), Indian Hill Club (Winnetka, Ill.), Hole-in-the-Wall Golf Club (Naples) Home: 345 Woodley Rd Winnetka IL 60093-3740 Office: 125 S Wacker Dr Ste 300 Chicago IL 60606-4402

KLARE, GEORGE ROGER, psychology educator; b. Mpls., Apr. 17, 1922; s. George C. and Lee (Launer) K.; m. Julia Marie Price Matson, Dec. 24, 1946; children: Deborah, Roger, Barbara. Student, U. Nebr., 1940-41, U. Minn., 1941-43, U. Mo., 1943; B.A., U. Minn., 1946, M.A., 1947, Ph.D., 1950. Instr. U. Minn., 1948-50; staff psychologist Psychol. Corp., N.Y.C., 1950-51; research assoc. U. Ill., 1952-54; asst. prof. dept. psychology Ohio U., Athens, 1954-57, assoc. prof., 1957-62, prof., 1962-79, Disting. prof., 1979-89, Disting. prof. emeritus, 1989—, chmn. dept., 1959-63, acting dean Coll. Arts and Sci., 1965, 85-86, dean, 1966-71, media coordinator, 1972-75, acting assoc. provost for grad. and research programs, 1986-87; research assoc. Harvard U., 1968-69; vis. prof. State U. N.Y. at Stony Brook, 1971-72, U. Iowa, 1979-80. Staff mem. N.Y.C. Writers Conf., 1956-57; cons., lectr. Nat. Project Agr. Communication, 1957-59, Com. on World Literacy and Christian Lit., 1958-62; exec. asst., sr. rsch. engr. Autonetics, 1960-61; cons. Resources Devel. Corp., 1962-65, Boston Pub. Sch., 1968, D.C. Heath Co., 1971, Western Electric, 1973, Westinghouse, 1975, Human Resources Rsch. Orgn., 1978-79, U.S. Navy, 1975, Armed Svcs. Readability Rsch., 1975, Center for Ednl. Exptl., Devel. and Evaluation, 1978-79, 81, U.S. Army, 1979, Bell System Center for Tech. Edn., 1975-80, Time, Inc., 1977-79, AT&T, 1979-81, 83,84, Coll. Osteo Medicine, Ohio U., 1987-89; lectr. Open Univ., Eng., 1975, NATO Conf. Visual Presentation of Info., The Netherlands, 1978, Beijing Normal U., 1990. Author: (with Byron Buck) Know Your Reader, 1954, The Measurement of Readability, 1963, (with Paul A. Games) Elementary Statistics: Data Analysis for the Behavioral Sciences, 1967, A Manual for Readable Writing, 1975, 4th edit., 1980, How to Write Readable English, 1985, Assessing Readability-Citation Classic, 1988; mem. editorial bd. Info. Design Jour., 1979—, Instrl. Sci., 1975-93, Reading Tchr., 1981-82, Reading Rsch. and Instrn., 1985-87, The Literacy Dictionary, 1993 (invited essay 1995). Served to 1st lt. USAAF, 1943-45. Decorated Air medal, Purple Heart; Fulbright travel grantee U.S.-U.K. Ednl. Commn. to Open U., 1977-81 Fellow Am. Psychol. Assn.; mem. Nat. Reading Conf. (invited address 1975, Oscar Causey award for outstanding contbns. to reading research 1981), Internat. Reading Assn. (elected to Hall of Fame 1997), Am. Ednl. Research Assn., Phi Beta Kappa, Delta Phi Lambda, Psi Chi, Phi Delta Kappa. Home and Office: 8800 Johnson Rd Ste 108 The Plains OH 45780-1277 E-mail: klare@oak.cats.ohiou.edu.

KLARICH, DAVID JOHN, state legislator, lawyer; b. Hamilton, Ohio, July 17, 1963; s. Victor Martin and Janet Dawn (Carlson) K.; m. Cheryl Ruth O'Donnell, June 18, 1988. BA in Biology and Chemistry, U. Mo., 1985; MA in Pub. Policy, JD, Regent U., 1990. Bar: Mo. 1990. Mem. Mo. Ho. of Reps. from 92nd & 94th dists., Jefferson City, 1990-94, Mo. Senate from 26th dist., Jefferson City, 1994—; with Riezman and Berger, P.C. (and predecessor firm), Clayton, Mo., 1995—. Chmn. judiciary com. Mo. State Senate, 2001—. Active West County Rep. Orgn., Franklin and Washington County Reps., St. Louis Young Reps., Coll. Reps., Pachyderms; trustee Logan Coll. Chiropractic, 1998. Recipient Adminstrn. of Justice award Jud. Conf. Mo., 1991, 99, Mo. Bar award, 1993, 97, 2000, 01, Mo. Hosp. Assn. award, 1995, Jud. Conf. award, 2000, 01, Legal Svcs. award, 2000, award

Mo. Assn. Probate and Assoc. Cir. Judges, 2001; named Mo. Bar Outstanding Legis. of Yr., 1996, Voice of Bus. award Assoc. Industries, 1998. Mem. Bar Assn. Met. St. Louis, Young Lawyers Assn., Vol. Lawyers Assn., St. Louis Lawyers Assn., Mo. Assn. Trial Attys., ABA, St. Louis Eagle Scout Assn., Nat. Eagle Scout Assn., Jaycees, Lions, Mo. C. of C. (Spirit of Enterprise award 1997), Theta Xi. Mem. Assembly of God Ch. Office: Riezman and Berger PC 7700 Bonhomme Ave Fl 7 Clayton MO 63105-1924 Fax: (314) 727-6458. E-mail: klarich@reizmanberger.com.

KLASSEN, LYNELL W. rheumatologist, transplant immunologist; b. Gossel, Kans., Jan. 24, 1947; married; 4 children. AB, Tabor Coll., 1969; MD, U. Kans., 1973. Resident in internal medicine U. Iowa Hosps. and Clins., 1973-75, chief resident internal medicine, 1977-78, asst. prof., 1978-82, assoc. prof. rheumatology & immunology, 1982-90; prof., vice chmn. internal medicine U. Nebr. Med. Ctr., 1990—; rsch. assoc. immunology Arthritis & Rheumatism Br., NIH, 1975-77. Assoc. chief staff rsch., chief arthritis svc. rheumatology Omaha VA, 1982—; chmn. sci. rev. com. Nat. Inst. Alcohol Abuse, Alcoholism, 1989-95. Mem. Edn. Coun., Am. Coll. Rheumatology, Am. Coll. Physicians, Am. Assn. Immunology. Achievements include rsch. in mechanisms of hematopoietic allograft rejection, pathophysiology of graft-versus-host disease, use of cytotoxic therapy in non-malignant diseases. Office: Omaha Dept Vet Affairs Med Ctr 4101 Woolworth Ave Omaha NE 68105-1850

KLAUSER, JAMES ROLAND, lawyer; b. Milw., Feb. 16, 1939; s. Samuel and Ruth Shirley (Burmeister) K.; m. Shirley Krueger, Nov. 20, 1975; children: David James, James William. BS, U. Wis., 1961, JD, 1964, MA in Public Law, 1968. Bar: Wis. 1964. Atty. Chgo. Title & Trust Co., 1964-65; pvt. practice, Union Grove, Wis., 1965-68; counsel, staff atty. Wis. Legis. Coun., Madison, 1968-71, Senate Rep. Caucus, Madison, 1971-79; ptnr. DeWitt, Sundby, Huggett, Schumacher & Morgan SC, 1979-86; sec. Wis. Dept. Adminstrn., 1987-97; spl. counsel to gov. State of Wis., 1995-97; ptnr. DeWitt, Ross, Stevens, 1997—. Mem. Wis. State Investment Bd., Madison, 1987-97; chmn. Exec. Cabinet Quality Workforce, Madison, 1991-97. Een. chmn. Thompson for Wis., 1986—; mem. Gov.'s Commn. on Taliesin, Madison, 1988-92; bd. dirs. Wis. Housing and Econ. Devel. Authority, Madison, 1991-97. Recipient Disting. Svc. to State Govt. award Nat. Gov.'s Assn., 1991. Mem. Wis. Bar Assn. Republican. Lutheran. Avocations: reading, history, sailing, water sports. Office: DeWitt Ross & Stevens SC Two E Mifflin St Madison WI 53703

KLAVITER, HELEN LOTHROP, magazine editor; b. Lima, Ohio, Mar. 5, 1944; d. Eugene H. and Jean (Walters) Lothrop; m. Douglas B. Klaviter, June 7, 1969 (div. 1982); 1 child, Elizabeth B.A., Cornell Coll., Mt. Vernon, Iowa, 1966. Communication specialist Coop. Extension Service, Urbana, Ill., 1969-71; mng. editor Poetry Mag., Chgo., 1973—. Editorial cons. Harper & Row, N.Y.C., 1983-87. Bd. dirs. Ill. Theatre Ctr., 1989-95, St. Clement's Open Pantry, 1990—, Episc. Diocese of Chgo. Hunger Commn., 1992—, Comms. Commn., 1993—. Episcopalian Office: Poetry Mag Modern Poetry Assn 60 W Walton St Chicago IL 60610-7324 E-mail: hklaviter@poetrymagazine.org.

KLEBBA, RAYMOND ALLEN, property manager; b. Chgo., Apr. 16, 1934; s. Raymond Aloysius and Marie Cecelia (Tobin) K.; m. Barbara Ann Gurbal, Oct. 7, 1961; children: Anne, Daniel, Mary, Theresa. Student, Loyola U., Chgo., 1954-56; cert. property mgr., Inst. Real Estate Mgmt., 1970. Corr., rep. Western R.R. Assn., Chgo., 1956-61; pres. Midland Warehouses, 1961-68; v.p., gen. mgr. Strobeck, Reiss Sch. Mgmt. Co., 1968-70, real estate mgr. and broker, 1970-83; v.p., dir. Mid-Am. Nat. Bank, 1983-90; br. mgr. Bank of Highwood/Deerfield, Ill., 1990-94; v.p. sales First Colonial Mortgage Corp., Chgo., 1994-95; bus. mgr. St. Matthias Parish, 1995-98. Mem. Chgo. Bd. Realtors (vice chmn. comml. and indsl. leasing and property mgmt. coun.), Inst. Real Estate Mgmt. (life; chmn. chpt. of yr. com. 1975-76), Rotary, Moose, KC. Avocations: bowling, golf, gardening, fishing (Chicagoland individual casting champion 1999. Home: 4933 N Leavitt St Chicago IL 60625-1308

KLECKNER, ROBERT A. accounting firm executive; b. 1935; BS, U. Dayton; MBA, Ohio State U. With Grant Thornton Internat., Chgo., 1957—, mng. dir., internat.; CEO Grant Thornton. Office: Grant Thornton Internat 130 E Randolph St Ste 600 Chicago IL 60601-6144

KLECZKA, GERALD D. congressman; b. Milwaukee, Wis., Nov. 26, 1943; m. Bonnie L. Scott, 1978. Ed., U. Wis., Milw. Mem. Wis. Assembly, 1968-74; mem. Wis. Senate, 1974-84, U.S. Congress from 4th Wis. dist., Washington, 1984—. Mem. ways and means com., ways and means health subcom., house budget com. Mem. Wis. Dem. Com., Milwaukee County Dem. Com. With Air N.G., 1963-69. Mem. LaFarge Lifelong Learning Inst., Thomas More Found., Polish Nat. Alliance-Milw. Soc., Polish Am. Congress. Office: 2301 Rayburn Bldg Washington DC 20515-4904*

KLEEFISCH, REBECCA, reporter; b. Waterville, Ohio; m. Joel Kleefisch. B Journalism, U. Wis. Anchor WIFR-TV, Rockford, Ill.; reporter, anchor WISN 12, Milw., 1999—. Office: WISN PO Box 0402 Milwaukee WI 53201-0402

KLEIMAN, DAVID HAROLD, lawyer; b. Kendallville, Ind., Apr. 2, 1934; s. Isadore and Pearl (Wikoff) K.; m. Meta Dene Freeman, July 6, 1958; children: Gary, Andrew, Scott, Matthew. BS, Purdue U., 1956; JD, Northwestern U., 1959. Bar: Ind. 1959. Assoc. firm Bamberger & Feibleman, Indpls., 1959-61; ptnr. Bagal, Talesnick & Kleiman, 1961-73, Dann Pecar Newman & Kleiman, Indpls., 1973—; dep. pros. atty., 1961-62; counsel Met. Devel. Commn., 1965-75; Ind. Heartland Coordinating Commn., 1975-81. Editor: Jour. of Air Law and Commerce, 1958-59. Chmn. Young Leadership Coun., 1967; v.p. Indpls. Hebrew Congregation, 1973; pres. Jewish Cmty. Ctr. Assn., 1972-75; pres. Jewish Welfare Fedn., 1981-84; v.p. United Way Ctrl. Ind., 1982-86, pres., 1986, chmn. bd. dirs., 1987; bd. dirs. Jewish Fedn., 1972—, Ind. Symphony Soc., 1991-96; bd. dirs. Ind. Repertory Theatre, 1986—, pres. 1991-94; trustee Indpls. Found., 2000—; bd. dirs. Ctrl. Ind. Cmty Found., 2000—, English Found., 2000—. Recipient Young Leadership award, 1968, Isadore Fiebleman Man of Yr. award, 1987, Mossler Cmty. Svc. award, 1988, Chalfie Cmty. Svc. award, 1998. Mem. ABA, Ind. State Bar Assn., Indpls. Bar Assn., Comml. Law League Am., Columbia Club, Skyline Club (bd. dirs. 1993—), B'nai B'rith, Broadmoor Country Club. Office: Dann Pecar Newman & Kleiman One American Square PO Box 82008 Indianapolis IN 46282-2008

KLEIN, CHARLES HENLE, lithographing company executive; b. Cin., Oct. 5, 1908; s. Benjamin Franklin and Flora (Henle) K.; student Purdue U., 1926-27, U. Cin., 1927-28; m. Ruth Becker, Sept. 23, 1938 (dec. 1997); children— Betsy (Mrs. Marvin H. Schwartz), Charles H., Carla (Mrs. George Fee III). Pres., Progress Lithographing Co., Cin., 1934-59, Novelart Mfg. Co., Cin., 1960— ; dir. R.A. Taylor Corp. Founding mem. Chief Execs. Orgn., Losantiville Country Club, Queen City Club, Bankers Club. Home: Amberley Village 6754 Fair Oaks Dr Cincinnati OH 45237-3606 Office: Amberley Village 2121 Section Rd Cincinnati OH 45237-3509

KLEIN, GABRIELLA SONJA, retired communications executive; b. Chgo., Apr. 11, 1938; d. Frank E. Vosicky and Sonja (Kosner) Becvar; m. Donald J. Klein. BA in Comm. and Bus. Mgmt., Alverno Coll., 1983. Editor, owner Fox Lake (Wis.) Rep., 1962-65, McFarland (Wis.) Comty. Life and Monona Cmty. Herald, 1966-69; bur. reporter Waukesha (Wis.) Daily Freeman, 1969-71; cmty. rels. staff Waukesha County Tech. Coll., Pewaukee, Wis., 1971-73; pub. rels. specialist JI Case Co., Racine, 1973-75, corp. publs. editor, 1975-80; v.p., bd. dirs. publs. Image Mgmt. Valley View Ctr., Milw., 1980-82; pres. Comm. Concepts Unltd., Racine, 1983-98; ret., 1998. Past pres. Big Bros./Big Sisters Racine County; past v.p. devel. Girl Scouts Racine County, bd. dirs.; steering com. Racine Cmty. Coalition for Youth; bd. dirs. Leadership Racine; bd. dirs., v.p. mktg. Racine Cmty. Found. Recipient awards Wis. Press Assn., Nat. Fedn. Press Women; named Wis. Woman Entrepreneur of Yr., 1985, Vol. of Yr. Racine Area United Way, 1994, Woman of Distinction Bus., Racine YWCA, 1995, Edn. Cmty. Leader of Yr., Racine Area Mfrs. and Commerce, 2000, Thanks Badge Girl Scouts of Racine County, 2000, Outstanding Alumna award Alverno Coll., 1999. Mem. Internat. Assn. Bus. Communicators (accredited, bd. dirs. 1982-85, various awards), Soc. Profl. Journalists, Ad Club of Racine (Silver medal 1998). Home: 3045 Chatham St Racine WI 53402-4001

KLEIN, JERRY, state legislator; b. Nov. 21, 1951; m. Bev.; 4 children. , Bismarck Jr. Coll., Mary Coll. Pres. Fessenden Econ. Devel.; mem. N. D. Senate, Bismark, 1996—. Mem. Fessenden Vol. Fire Dept. Mem. N. D. Grocers Assn. (pres.); bd. dirs. CArrington Health Ctr. Office: Dist 14 PO Box 265 Fessenden ND 58438-0265 E-mail: jklein@state.nd.us.

KLEIN, KAREN K. federal judge; Magistrate judge U.S. Dist. Ct. N.D., Fargo. Office: 655 1st Ave N Ste 440 Fargo ND 58102-4952 Fax: 701-297-7075.

KLEIN, MATTHEW M. state legislator; m. Isabell; 6 children. Student, Ellendale Coll., Amarillo Jr. Coll., U. So. Calif., UCLA; BS, N.D. State U. Mem. N.D. Ho. of Reps., 1993—, mem. judiciary and industry, bus. and labor coms., mem. govt. and vet. affairs com.; chair govt. and vet. affairs com. Cons. in English. Recipient Worldwide Constrn. Mgr. of Yr. award. Mem. Am. Legion. Home: 1815 7th St NW Minot ND 58703-1314

KLEIN, MILES VINCENT, physics educator; b. Cleve., Mar. 9, 1933; s. Max Ralph and Isabelle (Benjamin) K.; m. Barbara Judith Pincus, Sept. 2, 1956; children: Cynthia Klein-Banai, Gail. BS, Northwestern U., 1954; PhD, Cornell U., 1961. NSF postdoctoral fellow Max Planck Inst., Stuttgart, Germany, 1961; prof. U. Ill., Urbana, 1962—. Co-author: Optics, 1986; contbr. articles to profl. jours. A.P. Sloan Found. fellow, 1963. Fellow AAAS, Am. Phys. Soc. (Frank Isakson prize 1990), Am. Acad. Arts and Scis.; mem. IEEE (Sr.), Nat. Acad. Scis. Office: Materials Rsch Lab 104 S Goodwin Ave Urbana IL 61801-2902 E-mail: m-klein5@uiuc.edu.

KLEINFELD, ERWIN, mathematician, educator; b. Vienna, Austria, Apr. 19, 1927; came to U.S., 1940; s. Lazar and Gina (Schönbach) K.; m. Margaret Morgan, July 2, 1968; children— Barbara, David. B.S., CCNY, 1948; M.A., U. Pa., 1949; Ph.D., U. Wis., 1951. Instr. U. Chgo., 1951-53; asst. prof. Ohio State U., 1953-56, asso. prof., 1957-60, prof., 1960-62; prof. math. Syracuse U., 1962-67, U. Hawaii, 1967-68, U. Iowa, 1968—. Vis. lectr. Yale, 1956-57; cons. Nat. Bur. Standards, summer 1953; research specialist U. Conn., summer 1955; research mathematician Bowdoin Coll., summer 1957; research asso. Cornell U., summer 1958, U. Calif. at Los Angeles, summer 1959, Stanford, summer 1960, Inst. Def. Analysis, summer 1961, 62, AID-India, summer 1964, 65; vis. prof. Emory U., 1976-77; Cons. Edn. IX Project, World Bank, U. Indonesia, 1985-86, Mucia/Ind. U.-(ITM) Shah Alam, Malaysia Project, 1988-89. Editorial bd. Jour. Algebra-Academic Press; cons. editor, Merrill Pub. Co.-Div. Bell & Howell. Contbr. articles research jours. Served with AUS, 1945-46. Wis. Alumni Rsch. Found. fellow, 1949-51, vis. rsch. fellow U. New Eng., Australia, 1992; grantee U.S. Army Rsch. Office, 1955-70, NSF, 1970-75. Mem. Am. Math. Soc., Sigma Xi. Home: 1555 N Sierra 120 Reno NV 89503 E-mail: kleinfld@math.uiowa.edu.

KLEINGARTNER, LARRY, agricultural association executive; b. Kulm, N.D., Mar. 14, 1945; s. William Fred and Elsie (Riebhagen) K.; m. Nancy Lee Brand, Sept. 2, 1978; children: Jessie Lee, Brita Paula, Anika Rae. AA, Bismarck Jr. Coll., 1965; BA, Jamestown Coll., 1967; MA, U. Hawaii, 1974. Vol. U.S. Peace Corps, Maharastra, India, 1968-71; dir. mktg. N.D. Dept. of Agr., Bismarck, N.D., 1975-79; exec. dir. Nat. Sunflower Assn., 1980—. Contbr. artilces on agr. to prof jours. V.p. New Horizons Fgn. Adoption Svcs., Bismarck, 1983—; bd. dirs. Bismarck Mandan Civic Chorus, 1980; Sunday sch. tchr. Lord of Life Luth. Ch., Bismarck, 1978—, coun. mem., 1984—. Nat. Def. Lang. fellow, 1972-74. Avocations: cross-country skiing, horseback riding, music. Home: 2823 Woodland Dr Bismarck ND 58504-8925 Office: Nat Sunflower Assn 4023 State St Bismarck ND 58503-0620

KLEINHENZ, CHRISTOPHER, foreign language educator, researcher; b. Indpls., Dec. 29, 1941; s. John Emory and Louise Eleanor (Ross); m. Margaret Ellen Zechiel, Aug. 1, 1964; children: Steven Russell, Michael Thomas. BA, Ind. U., 1964, MA, 1966, PhD, 1969. Asst. prof., dir. Bologna program Ind. U., 1970-71; instr. U. Wis., Madison, 1968-69, asst. prof., 1969-70, asst. prof., dept. French and Italian, 1971-75, assoc. prof., 1975-80, chmn. medieval studies program, 1975-80, 81-84, 89-95, 96—, prof., 1980—, chmn. dept., 1985-88, Carol Mason Kirk prof. Italian, 2000—. Dir. devel. grant NEH, Madison, 1976-79, co-dir. rsch. tools grant, 1980-84. Author: The Early Italian Sonnet, 1986; editor: Medieval Manuscripts and Textual Criticism, 1976, Medieval Studies in North America, 1982, Routledge Studies in Medieval Literature, 1986—, Dante Studies, 1988—; co-editor: Saint Augustine the Bishop: A Book of Essays, 1994, Routledge Medieval Casebooks, 1991—, Fearful Hope: Approaching the New Millennium, 1999; assoc. editor: Dante Encyvlopedia, 2000; chmn. editl. bd. Medieval Acad. Reprints for Teaching, 1981-93; bibliographer MLA, N.Y.C., 1981-88, BIGLLI, Rome, 1994—, Dante Studies, 1984—, ICLS, 2002–; book rev. editor Italica, 1984-93; co-translator: Dante Alighieri, Il Fiore and the Detto d'Amore, 2000. Chmn. com. on ctrs. and regional assns. Medieval Acad., 1993-99. Newberry Libr./NEH grantee, 1988-89. Mem. Medieval Assn. of Midwest (pres. 1984-85), Dante Soc. Am. (mem. coun. 1985-91), Am. Boccaccio Assn. (v.p. 1987-93, pres. 1993-97), Am. Assn. Tchrs. of Italian (v.p. 1993-98, pres. 1999—). Avocations: sports, stamp collecting, photography, travel. Home: 2247 Fox Ave Madison WI 53711-1922 Office: U Wis Dept French and Italian 1220 Linden Dr Madison WI 53706-1525 E-mail: ckleinhe@facstaff.wisc.edu.

KLEINMAN, BURTON HOWARD, real estate investor; b. Chgo., Nov. 19, 1923; s. Eli I. and Pearl (Cohan) K.; m. Shirley A. Freyer, Sept. 6, 1950 (div. Oct. 1969); children: Kim, Lauri. BS in Engring., U.S. Naval Acad., 1948. Commd. ensign USN, 1948, resigned, 1949; v.p. C.F. Corp., Chgo., 1958-80, pres., 1980-85; owner B.H. Kleinman Co., Northfield, Ill., 1955—. Bd. dirs. United Way Northfield, 1970-72, North Shore Mental Health Assn., 1978-82. Mem. Northfield C. of C. (bd. dirs. 1976-81), Kenosha Pilots Assn. Republican. Unitarian. Clubs: Deerfield Singles (pres. 1974-75), Winnetka Tennis Assn., Ridge & Valley Tennis. Avocations: tennis, scuba diving, sailing, flying. Home: 570 Happ Rd Northfield IL 60093-1112 Office: BH Kleinman Co 456 W Frontage Rd Northfield IL 60093-3034

KLEINMAN, MICHAEL A. trust company executive; BA English, Rockhurst Coll.; JD, St. Louis U. Cert. fin. planner. With legal sect. estate and gift tax divsn. IRS; dir. pub. rels. Nat. Assn. Intrecollegiate Athletics; with MidAm. Bank & Trust (now Firstar Bank), 1971, United Mo. Bank Kans. City; exec. v.p., mgr. employee benefit divsn. Midwest Trust, Overland Park, Kans. Chmn. planned giving com. Rockhurst U. Mem.: Internat. Assn. Fin. Planners, Estate Planning Soc. Kansas City, Mo. Bar Assn. Office: The Midwest Trust Co 10740 Nall Ave Ste 100 Overland Park KS 66211*

KLEINWORTH, EDWARD J. agricultural company executive; Pres. St. Ansgar Mills, Inc. Office: St Ansgar Mills Inc PO Box 370 Saint Ansgar IA 50472-0370

KLEIS, DAVID, state legislator; Mem. Minn. Senate from 16th dist., St. Paul, 1995—. Office: Minnesota State Senate 151 State Office Bldg Saint Paul MN 55155-0001 Also: 45 20th Ave N Saint Cloud MN 56303-4436

KLEMENS, THOMAS LLOYD, editor; b. Pitts., Mar. 28, 1952; s. Robert F. and Ann E. (Lacy) K.; m. Norreen McLellan, Aug. 4, 1973; children: Jonathan, Zachary. BFA, Carnegie-Mellon U., 1974; BSCE, U. Pitts., 1983; postgrad., Roosevelt U., Chgo., 1990-91. Registered profl. engr., Ill. Choir dir., tchr. Wellsville (Ohio) H.S., 1975-76; asst. band dir., tchr. North Hills H.S., Ross Twp., Pa., 1976-79; field engr. S.J. Groves & Sons, Pitts., 1983; structural engr. Sargent & Lundy, Chgo., 1983-87; field engr. Structural Preservation Systems, Inc., Margate, N.J., 1987; project mgr. Northwest Group, Inc., West Chicago, Ill., 1987; engr., purchasing agt. L.J. Keefe Co., Mt. Prospect, 1987-89; from assoc. editor to editor Hwy. & Heavy Constrn. Cahners Pub., Des Plaines, 1989-91, editor Hwy. & Heavy Constrn. Products, 1991-93, sr. editor Consulting/Specifying Engr., 1993-94; co-owner Wordwright, Palatine, 1993—. Instr. Motorola U., 1996-98; com. on constrn. equipment Transp. Rsch. Bd., Washington, 1991-93 adj. faculty William Rainey Harper Coll., Palatine, 1997—. Author Hwy. and Heavy Constrn., 1989-91, editor, 1991-92; author, editor Infrastructure, 1992-93; sr. editor Cons./Specifying Engr., 1993-94; editor PM Engr., Bus. News Pub., 1994-96, Plumbing Engr., TMB Pub., 1996—. Mem. ASCE, Am. Soc. Plumbing Engrs., Soc. Fire Protection Engrs. Office: 1838 Techny Ct Northbrook IL 60062-5474 E-mail: editor@plumbingengineer.com.

KLEMM, RICHARD O. state legislator; b. Chgo., May 05; s. Oren E. and Edythe (Neilsen) K.; m. Nancy Klemm; 7 children. BS, Purdue U., 1954. Pres., mem. Crystal Lake Dist. 46 Bd. Edn., 1964-71; trustee Nunda Twp., 1964-72; chmn., mem. McHenry County Bd., 1972-80; Ill. state rep. Dist. 63, 1981-92; Ill. state sen. Dist. 23, 1993—. Vice-spokesman Exec. Com.; mem. Labor and Commerce Com.; former minority spokesman, mem. Constnl. Officers Com., Vets. Affairs Com.; former mem. Environ. and Energy Com. Ill. Ho. of Reps.; pres., bd. chmn. Food Warming Equipment Co., Inc., Crystal Lake, 1972—. Recipient numerous comty. svc. awards. Mem. Sigma Nu.

KLEMM, RON, radio producer; b. Hammond, Ind. married; 1 child. BA Music and Comm., Dordt Coll. Ops. mgr. Classic 99, St. Louis. Avocation: golf. Office: Classic 99 85 Founders Ln Saint Louis MO 63105

KLENK, JAMES ANDREW, lawyer; b. Evergreen Park, Ill., July 18, 1949; s. Paul Theodore and Joan (Launspach) K.; m. Carol Evans, Aug. 26, 1972; children: Paul Andrew, Matthew Evans. BA, Beloit Coll., 1971; JD, U. Wis., 1974. Bar: Ill. 1974, Wis. 1974, U.S. Supreme Ct. 1978. Law clk. to Judge Thomas E. Fairchild U.S. Ct. Appeals (7th cir.), Chgo., 1974-75; assoc. Kirkland & Ellis, 1975-78; ptnr. Reuben & Proctor, 1978-86, Isham, Lincoln & Beale, Chgo., 1986-88, Sonnenschein, Nath & Rosenthal, Chgo., 1988—. Articles editor Wis. Law Rev. Mem. ABA (litigation sect., torts and ins. practice sect., bus. law sect.), Ill. Bar Assn. (anti-trust law sect., litigation sect., torts and ins. practice sect., intellectual prop.), Libel Def. Resource Ctr. (def. counsel sect.), Order of Coif, Phi Beta Kappa. Office: Sonnenschein Nath & Rosenthal 8000 Sears Tower Chicago IL 60606

KLEPPA, OLE J. chemistry educator; b. Oslo, Feb. 4, 1920; married; 2 children. MS, Norwegian Inst. Tech., 1946, DS, 1956. Union Carbon and Carbide postdoctoral fellow, instr. U. Chgo. Inst. Study of Metals, 1948-50; rsch. supr. divsn. chemistry and metallurgy Norwegian Def. Rsch. Establishment, 1950-51; asst. prof. U. Chgo., 1952-57, assoc. prof., 1958-62, prof. dept. chemistry, 1962-90, prof. dept. geophysical scis., 1968-90, prof. emeritus, 1990—, assoc. dir. James Franck Inst., 1968-71, dir., 1971-77, dir. materials rsch. lab., 1984-87. Cons. Argonne Nat. Lab., 1959-71; dir. The Calorimetry Conf., 1963-69, chmn., 1966-67; vis. prof. Japan Soc. Promotion of Sci., 1975, U. Paris, Orsay, 1977; presenter confs. in field. Bd. editors Jour. Chem. Physics, 1965-67, Jour. Chem. Thermodynamics, 1981-87, Jour. Phase Equilibria, 1995—; contbr. articles to profl. jours. Recipient Huffman Meml. award, 1982, U.S. Sr. Sci. Humboldt award, 1983-84. Fellow AAAS, Am. Soc. Metals; mem. Am. Chem. Soc., Am. Ceramic Soc., Soc. Norwegian Engrs., Royal Norwegian Soc. Sci. and Letters, Norwegian Acad. Tech. Scis., Minerals, Metals, and Materials Soc. (Hume-Rothery award 1994). Achievements include pioneering development of new technique of high-temperature oxide melt solution calorimetery; being the first person to extensively apply the Calvét-type twin microcalorimeter in high temperature thermochemistry; originator of a novel high-temperature reaction calorimeter suitable for continuous use at temperatures up to about 1500K; applying new calorimeter in extensive studies of binary alloys of early transition metals and rare earth metals with Group VIII transition metals and with noble metals. Office: U Chgo James Franck Inst 5640 S Ellis Ave Chicago IL 60637-1433 E-mail: Kleppa@control.uchicago.edu.

KLEVEN, MARGUERITE, state legislator; Mem. S.D. Senate from 29th dist., Pierre, 1995—; mem. appropriations com., chmn. govt. ops. and audit com. S.D. Senate. Republican.

KLIEBENSTEIN, DON, lawyer; b. Marshalltown, Iowa, May 3, 1936; s. Donald B. and Gertrude E. (Skeie) K.; m. Mary L. Delfs, June 11, 1960; 1 child, Julie Ann. Student, Grinnell Coll., 1953-55; BA, U. Iowa, 1957, JD, 1961. Bar: Iowa 1961, U.S. Dist. Ct. (no., so. dists.) Iowa 1961, U.S. Supreme Ct. 1971. Pvt. practice, Grundy Center, Iowa, 1961-67; ptnr. Kliebenstein & Heronimus, 1967-77, Kliebenstein, Heronimus & Schmidt, Grundy Center, 1977-98, Kliebenstein Heronimus Schmidt and Harris, Grundy Center, 1999—. Bd. dirs. Grundy Nat. Bank, Grundy Ctr.; county atty. Grundy County, 1965-98. Mem. ABA, Iows State Bar Assn., Grundy County Bar Assn. (pres. 1979-80), Nat. Dist. Attys. Assn., 1st Jud. Dist. Bar Assn. (pres. 1975-76). Republican. Methodist. Home: 701 9th St Grundy Center IA 50638-1238 Office: Kliebenstein Heronimus Schmidt & Harris 630 G Ave Grundy Center IA 50638-1500

KLIEBHAN, SISTER M(ARY) CAMILLE, academic administrator; b. Milw., Apr. 4, 1923; d. Alfred Sebastian and Mae Eileen (McNamara) K. Student, Cardinal Stritch Coll., Milw., 1945-48; B.A., Cath. Sisters Coll., Washington, 1949; M.A., Cath. U. Am., 1951, Ph.D., 1955. Joined Sisters of St. Francis of Assisi, Roman Catholic Ch., 1945; legal sec. Spence and Hanley (attys.), Milw., 1941-45; instr. edn. Cardinal Stritch Coll., 1955-62, assoc. prof., 1962-68, prof., 1968—, head dept. edn., 1962-67, dean students, 1962-64, chmn. grad. div., 1964-69, v.p. for acad. and student affairs, 1969-74, pres., also bd. dirs., 1974-91, chancellor, 1991—. Mem. TEMPO, 1982—2001; bd. dirs., 1986—89; bd. govs. Wis. Policy Rsch. Inst., 1987—97; bd. dirs. Goals for Milw. 2000, 1980—83; treas. Wis. Found. Ind. Colls., 1974—79, 1987—90, v.p., 1979—81, pres., 1981—83; bd. dirs. DePaul Hosp., 1982—91, Sacred Heart Sch. Theology, 1983—, Viterbo Coll., 1990—98, Milw. Cath. Home, 1991—2001, St. Ann Ctr. for Intergenerational Care, 1991—99, Wis. Psychoanalytic Found., 1989—96, St. Coletta's of Mass., 1995—98, Internat. Inst. Wis., 1984—94, Milw. Achiever Program, Inc., 1983—, Franciscan Pilgrimage Programs, Inc., 1997—, Friends of Internat. Inst. Wis., 1994—, Mental Hea.th Assn. Milwaukee County, 1983—87, Pub. Policy Forum, 1987—90, Better Bus. Bur. of Wis., Inc., 1989—2001, YWCA Greater Milw., 1996—2001, St. Camillus Campus, 1996—2001, mem. adv. bd., 1989—96. Mem. Am.

Psychol. Assn., Rotary Club of Milw. (v.p., pres. elect 1992-93, pres. 1993-94), St. Mary's Acad. Alumnae Assn., Phi Delta Kappa, Delta Epsilon Sigma, Psi Chi, Delta Kappa Gamma, Kappa Delta Pi.

KLIKA, CRISTINE M. state official; BS in Civil Engring., Purdue U. Registered profl. engr., Ind. With pvt. cons. firm designing rds. and bridges; county engr. Monroe County, Ind.; design engring. supr. Ind. Dept. Transp., cons. svcs. supr., design svcs. mgr. Design divsn., chief Tech. Svcs. divsn., mgr. Preliminary Engring. sect., to 1997, dep. commr. Office of Planning and Intermodal Transp., 1997—. Office: Ind Dept Transp 100 N Senate Ave Rm N755 Indianapolis IN 46204-2216

KLINCK, CYNTHIA ANNE, library director; b. Salamanaca, N.Y., Nov. 1, 1948; d. William James and Marjorie Irene (Woodruff) K.; m. Andrew Clavert Humphries, Nov. 26, 1983. BS, Ball State U., 1970; MLS, U. Ky., 1976. Reference/ young adult libr. Bartholomew County Libr., Columbus, Ind., 1970-74; dir. Paul Sawyier Pub. Libr., Frankfort, Ky., 1974-78, Washington-Centerville Pub. Libr., Dayton, Ohio, 1978—. Libr. bldg. cons.; libr. cons., trainer OPLIN Task Force. Contbr. articles to profl. mags. Bd. dirs. Bluegrass Comty. Action Agy., Frankfort, Ky., 1971-73; founder, bd. dirs. FACTS, Inc. (info. & referral), Frankfort, 1972-74; co-founder, bd. dirs. Seniors, Inc., Dayton, Ohio, 1980-81, 91—; trustee, officer South Comty., Inc. Mental Health Ctr., Dayton, 1980-89; pres. Miami Valley Librs.; mem. govt. affairs com., ann. conf. planning com., fin. resources task force conf. presenter Ohio Libr. Coun.; program presenter Ohio Libr. Coun. Confs. Recipient Vol. of Yr. So. Metro Regional C. of C. Mem. ALA, Am. Soc. for Info. Sci., Am. Soc. for Pers. Adminstrn., Ohio Libr. Assn. (chmn. legis. com.), South Metro Regional C. of C. (exec. com., bd. dirs., chmn. edn. com.), Rotary (bd. dirs.), Pub. Libr. Assn. Mng. for Results (trainer). Office: Washington-Centerville Pub Libr 111 W Spring Valley Rd Dayton OH 45458-3761

KLINE, FAITH ELIZABETH, college official; b. Lake Charles, La., Dec. 22, 1937; d. Walter Raymond and Erma Ruth (Gilbert) McClung; m. George Ellis Kline, Nov. 26, 1959; children: Alexandra M., George E. IV, Elizabeth A. BA, So. Nazarene U., 1960. Owner, ptnr. Country Peddler Gift Shop, Jackson, Mich., 1972-75; asst. dir. admissions Spring Arbor (Mich.) Coll., 1976-80; exec. sec. to pres. Camp Internat., Inc., Jackson, Mich., 1980-85; registered rep. IDS/Am. Express, 1985-86; investment broker A. G. Edwards & Sons, Inc., 1986-89; dir., trust and investment svcs., corp. asst. sec. The Free Meth. Found., Spring Arbor, 1989-92; adminstr. trusts and investments Hillsdale (Mich.) Coll., 1992—. Mem. Jackson County (Mich.) Hosp. Fin. Authority, 1987-92; pres. Hearthstone Enterprises, Inc., 1996—; co-owner Idyll Hour Coffeehouse, Spring Arbor, Mich., 1997—. Author: The Klines of Evanston: 1848 to 1968, 1970. Trustee Concord (Mich.) Bd. Edn., 1979-95, v.p., 1991-93, pres., 1993-94; sec. Jackson County (Mich.) County Reps., 1984-85, mem. exec. com., 1993-96; mem. Spring Arbor Twp. Hist. Com., Jackson Area Estate Planning Coun.; mem. Nat. Com. on Planned Giving, 1993—. Methodist. Avocation: 19th Century American antiques, piano music. Home: 223 Wickenham Dr Spring Arbor MI 49283 Office: Hillsdale Coll 33 E College St Hillsdale MI 49242-1205

KLINE, JAMES EDWARD, lawyer; b. Fremont, Ohio, Aug. 3, 1941; s. Walter J. and Sophia Kline; m. Mary Ann Bruening, Aug. 29, 1964; children: Laura Anne Kline, Matthew Thomas, Jennifer Sue. BS in Social Sci., John Carroll U., 1963; JD, Ohio State U., 1966; postgrad., Stanford U., 1991. Bar: Ohio, 1966, N.C., 1989, U.S. Tax. Ct., 1983. Assoc. Eastman, Stichter, Smith & Bergman, Toledo, 1966-70; ptnr. Eastman, Stichter, Smith & Bergman (name now Eastman & Smith), 1970-84, Shumaker, Loop & Kendrick, Toledo, 1984-88; v.p., gen. counsel Aeroquip-Vickers, Inc. (formerly Trinova Corp.), 1989-99; exec. v.p. Cavista Corp., 2000—01; dir. devel. The Toledo Mus. of Art , 2002—, Toledo Mus. Art, 2001—. Corp. sec. Sheller-Globe Corp., 1977—84; adj. prof. U. Toledo Coll. Law, 1988—94; bd. dirs. Plastic Techs., Inc.; trustee Promedica Health Edn. and Rsch. Corp., 2002—. Author: (with Robert Seaver) Ohio Corporation Law, 1988. Trustee Kidney Found. of Northwestern Ohio, Inc., 1972-81, pres., 1979-80; bd. dirs. Toledo Botanical Garden (formerly Crosby Gardens), 1974-80, pres., 1977-79; bd. dirs. Toledo Zool. Soc., 1983-96, 99—, pres., 1991-93; bd. dirs. Toledo Area Regional Transit Authority, 1984-90, pres., 1987-88; bd. dirs. Home Away From Home, Inc. (Ronald McDonald House NW Ohio), 1983-88; trustee Toledo Symphony Orch., 1981—, St. John's H.S., 1988-91, Ohio Found. Ind. Colls., 1991-2000; trustee Lourdes Coll., 1988-96, chmn., 1994-96; trustee ProMedia Health, Edn. and Rsch. Corp., 2002--. Fellow Ohio Bar Found.; mem. ABA, Nat. Assn. Corp. Dirs., Ohio Bar Assn. (corp. law com. 1977—, chmn. 1983-86), Toledo Bar Assn., Mfrs. Alliance (chair Law Coun. II 1997-99), Toledo Area C. of C. (trustee 1994—, chmn. 2000-01), Inverness Club, Toledo Club (trustee 1990-97), Stone Oak Country Club, Ottawa Skeet Club, Answer Club, Rotary. Roman Catholic. Home: 216 Treetop Pl Holland OH 43528-8451 Office: Toledo Mus Art 2445 Monroe St Toledo OH 43620 E-mail: jkline216@aol.com.

KLINE, KENNETH ALAN, mechanical engineering educator; b. Chgo., July 11, 1939; s. George Lester and Beverly Gretchen (Hanson) K.; m. Nancy Ann Bixler, June 25, 1960; children: Lisa Suzanne, John Kenneth, Jeffery Eastbury, Gretchen Mary. BS, U. Minn., 1961, PhD, 1965. Rsch. asst. U. Minn., Mpls., 1961-62, rsch. fellow, 1962-65; sr. rsch. engr. Esso Prodn. Rsch. Co., Houston, 1965-66; assoc. prof. Wayne State U., Detroit, 1966-73, prof. mech. engring., 1973—, interim chair dept. mech. engring., 1986-87, chair, 1987-95, interim dean of engring., 1996—, chair mech. engring., 1997—. Cons. Ford Motor Co., Detroit, 1976—, vis. scientist, 1984-85; vis. prof. U. Munich, 1972-73. Editor Proc. 6th Internat. Conf. Vehicle Structures, 1986; contbr. articles to profl. jours. Patentee ops. in submarine wells, layng pipes in water. Rep. precinct del., Grosse Pointe Park, Mich., 1982-84; vol. Grosee Pointe Neighborhood Club, 1973-82. A.P. Sloan Found. nat. scholar, 1959-61; NSF fellow 1961-64, NASA fellow 1964-65; recipient Sr. U.S. Sci. award Alexander von Humboldt-Stiftung, Fed. Republic Germany, 1972; prin. investigator NSF Rsch. Experiences for Undergrad. Sites, 1995—. Fellow ASME (chair 1974-75, 89-91, program chair winter ann. meeting 1993, gen. chair internat. mech. engring. congress & expo. 1994, nat. nominating com. 1997—, chair nat. dept. heads com., 1998—, Dedicated Svc. award 1996), AIAA, Soc. Automotive Engrs. (chair 1984-86, Forest R. McFarland award 1993), Soc. Rheology, Engring. Soc. (vice chair Detroit 1988—). Avocations: bird watching, tree farming, reading, swimming. Office: Wayne State U Engring Rm 2105 Detroit MI 48202

KLINE, PHILLIP D. state legislator, lawyer; b. Kansas City, Kans., Dec. 31, 1959; s. James R. and Janet S. (Shirley) K.; m. Deborah Suzanne Shattuck, July 22, 1989; 1 child, Jacqueline Hillary. BS in Pub. Rels. and Polit. Sci., Cen. Mo. State U., 1982; JD, U. Kans., 1987. Bar: Kans. 1987, U.S. Ct. Appeals (10th cir.), U.S. Dist. Ct. Kans. News reporter WHB Radio, Kansas City, Mo., 1981-82; pub. rels. rep. Mid-America, Inc., 1982-84; assoc. Blackwell, Sanders, Matheny, Weary & Lombardi, Overland Park, Kans., 1987—; legislator State of Kans. Nominee Kans. 2d Congl. Dist., 1986; mem. Kans. State Ho. of Reps. from 18th Dist., 1993—; chmn. taxation com., 1995—; fin. chmn. Johnson County Reps., 1990-91; chmn. Shawnee Reps., 1991-92; chmn., co-chmn. Corp. Woods Charity Jazz Festival, Overland Park, 1991-95; bd. dirs. Shawnee Mission Edn. Found., 1994-95, Rep. Ho. Campaign Com. Mem. Johnson County Bar Assn., Kans. Bar Assn., Rotary (bd. dirs., v.p. 1991-93, pres. 1994-95, Disting. Svc. award 1991). Methodist. Avocations: history, reading, athletics. Home: 10624 W 61st St Shawnee KS 66203-3016 Office: Blackwell Sanders Matheny Weary & Lombardi 9401 Indian Creek Pkwy Ste 1200 Overland Park KS 66210-2020

KLINEFELTER, SARAH STEPHENS, retired division dean, radio station manager; b. Des Moines, Jan. 30, 1938; d. Edward John and Mary Ethel (Adams) Stephens; m. Neil Klinefelter. BA, Drake U., 1958; MA, U. Iowa, Iowa City, 1968; postgrad., Harvard U., July, 1984, U. Wis., Sept., 1987, Vanderbilt U., 1991-92. Chmn. humanities dept. High Sch. Dist. 230, Orland Pk., Ill., 1958-68; chmn. communications and humanities div. Kirkwood Community Coll., Cedar Rapids, Iowa, 1968-78; prof. English Sch. of the Ozarks, Point Lookout, Mo., 1978-86; gen. mgr. Sta. KSOZ-FM, 1986-90; dean div. of performing and profl. arts Coll. of the Ozarks, 1989-2001. Commr. Skaggs Community Hosp., Branson, Mo., 1986—; chmn. Branson Planning and Zoning Commn., 1983; project dir. Mo. Humanities Bd.; commr., examiner North Cen. Assn. Higher Edn., 1978-85; commr. Iowa Humanities Bd., 1971-78; mem. Taney County Planning and Zoning Commn., 1989-98; pres. Branson Arts Coun., 1997—. Democrat. Presbyterian. Home: 182 Hensley Rd Forsyth MO 65653-5137 E-mail: sarahk@tri-lakes.net.

KLING, WILLIAM HUGH, broadcasting executive; b. St. Paul, Apr. 29, 1942; s. William Conrad and Helen A. (Leonard) K.; m. Sarah Margaret Baldwin, Sept. 25, 1976. B.A. in Economics, St. John's U., 1964; postgrad., Boston U., 1964-66. Pres. Minn. Pub. Radio, Inc., St. Paul, 1966—, Greenspring Co., 1986—, Am. Public Media Group, 1999—; founding dir. Nat. Pub. Radio, 1968-70, dir., 1977-80; founding pres. Public Radio Internat., 1982-86; vice chmn. Pub. Radio Internat., 1986-93. Bd. dirs. St. Paul Cos., Wenger Corp., Irwin Fin.; mem. various fund bds. Capital Group Am. Funds. Bd. dirs. Minn. Orch., 1987-93; trustee J.L. Found., 1988—; bd. dirs., chmn. Fitzgerald Theater Corp., 1983—; mem. The James Madison Coun. of Libr. of Congress, 1992-94. Recipient Edward R. Murrow award, 1981, award for Excellence Channels Mag., 1987; named Twin Citian of Yr., Twin Citian mag., 1987, Disting. Minnesotan, 1995, One of 100 Disting. Minnesotans of the Century, Mpls. Star Tribune, 2000. Mem. Mpls. Club. Office: Am Pub Media Group 45 7th St E Saint Paul MN 55101-2274

KLINGLER, GWENDOLYN WALBOLT, state representative; b. Toledo, May 28, 1944; d. L. Byron and Elizabeth (Brown) Walbolt; m. Walter Gerald Klingler, June 11, 1966; children: Kelly Michelle, Lance, Jeffrey. BA, Ohio Wesleyan U., 1966; MA, U. Mich., 1969; JD, George Washington U., 1981. Bar: Ill. Rsch. assoc. U. Mich., Ann Arbor, 1966-71; abstractor Year Book Med. Pub., Chgo., 1972-75; law clk. FDA, Rockville, Md., 1980; atty. Atty. Gen.'s Office State of Ill., Springfield, 1981-84, appellate prosecutor, 1984-92; ptnr. Boyle, Klingler & McClain, 1992-95. Mem. Springfield Bd. of Edn., 1987-91, pres., 1988; alderman Springfield City Coun., 1991-95; Rep. Ill. Ho. of Reps., 100th Dist., 1995—. Recipient Woman of Achievement award in Govt., Women-in-Mgmt., 1994, Disting. Alumni award Leadership Springfield, 1996. Mem. AAUW, Cen. Ill. Women's Bar Assn. (chair membership com.), Sangamon County Bar Assn., Greater Springfield C. of C., Women-in-Mgmt. Republican. Presbyterian (elder). Home: 1600 Ruth Pl Springfield IL 62704-3362 E-mail: klingler@housegopmail.state.il.us.

KLINKER, SHEILA ANN J. state legislator, middle school educator; m. Victor Klinker; children: Kerri, Kevin, Kelly. BS in Edn., MS in Elem. Edn., MS in Adminstrn. and Supervision, Purdue U. Outreach liaison Purdue U. Sch. Edn., 1982—; state rep. Ind. Ho. of Reps., Indpls., 1982—. Mem. St. Mary's Cathedral Parish; 1st woman appointee Tippecanoe Area Plan Commn.; bd. dirs. Lafayette Symphony, Opera de Lafayette, Tippecanoe County Chid Care, Purdue Musical Orgn.; past chairwoman pub. svc. divsn. United Way. Recipient Outstanding Svc. award Ind. Advocates for Children, Legis. award Assn. of BPW's Outstanding Woman in Politics, Woman of Distinction award Sycamore Girl Scout Coun., Salute to Women in Politics award, Outstanding Svc. for Pub. Interest award Ind. Optometric Assn., Pres.'s Spl. Svc. award Ind. Soc. Profl. Land Surveyors, Spl. Recognition award Ind. Chpt. NASW, Legis. Efforts Recognition award Ind. Residential Facilities Assn., Ind. Assn. for Counseling and Devel., Tippecanoe Arts Fedn. award, Purdue U. Musical Orgn. Alumni award, Marriage and Family Therapists Svc. award, 1998, Social Workers Svc. award, 1998, Ind. Assn. for Gifted Leadership award, 1998. Mem. Bus. and Profl. Women's Assn., Lafayette C. of C. (edn. com.), Delta Kappa Gamma, Phi Delta Kappa, Kappa Alpha Theta (mem. adv. bd.). Democrat. Home: 633 Kossuth St Lafayette IN 47905-1444 Office: Ind Ho of Reps State House Third Fl Indianapolis IN 46204

KLIPHARDT, RAYMOND A. engineering educator; b. Chgo., Mar. 18, 1917; s. Adolph Lewis and Hortense Marietta (Brandt) K.; m. Rhoda Joan Anderson, May 5, 1945; children: Janis Kliphardt Emery, Judith Kliphardt Ecklund, Jill Kliphardt White, Joan Kliphardt Quinn, Jennifer Kliphardt Miller. B.S., Ill. Inst. Tech., Chgo., 1938, M.S., 1948. Instr. North Park Coll., Chgo., 1938-43; asst. prof. Northwestern U., Evanston, Ill., 1945-51, assoc. prof., 1952-63, prof. engring. scis., 1964-87, prof. emeritus, 1987—, dir. U. Khartoum project, 1964-68, dir. focus program, 1975-78, chmn. engring. scis. and applied maths. dept., 1978-87. Cons. applied maths. div. Argonne Nat. Lab., Lemont, Ill., 1962-63; cons. on patent litigation Kirkland and Ellis, Chgo., 1976-77. Author: Analytical Graphics, 1957; Program Design in Fortran IV, 1970. Mem. bd. edn. Morton Grove, Ill., 1952-55, Niles Twp., Ill., 1957-58. Served as ensign USNR, 1943-45. Recipient Western Electric Fund award for excellence in instrn. of engring. students, Am. Soc. Engring. Edn., 1967. Office: Northwestern U Technol Inst Evanston IL 60208-0001

KLOBASA, JOHN ANTHONY, lawyer; b. St. Louis, Feb. 15, 1951; s. Alan R. and Virginia (Yager) K. BA in Econs., Emory U., 1972; JD, Wash. U., 1975. Bar: Mo. 1975, U.S. Dist. Ct. (ea. dist.) Mo. 1975, U.S. Ct. Appeals (8th cir.) 1976, U.S. Supreme Ct. 1979, U.S. Tax Ct. 1981, U.S. Ct. Appeals (9th cir.) 1990, U.S. Ct. Appeals (10th cir.) 1993. Assoc. Kohn, Shands, Elbert, Gianoulakis & Gilium LLP, St. Louis, 1975—80, ptnr., 1981—. Spl. counsel City of Town and Country, Mo., 1987; spl. counsel City of Des Peres, Mo., 1987, alderman, 1989-91. Mem. ABA, Mo. Bar Assn., Met. St. Louis Bar Assn., Order of Coif, Phi Beta Kappa. Republican. Office: Kohn Shands Elbert Gianoulakis & Gilium LLP 1 US Bank Plz Ste 2410 Saint Louis MO 63101-1643 E-mail: jklobasa@ksegg.com.

KLOEPPEL, DANIEL L. career officer; m. Debbie. BA in Econs., Northwestern U., 1970. Enlisted USN, 1970, advanced through grades to rear adm.; stationed at Naval Air Station, Cecil Field, Fla., 1973; stationed on USS Forestall; stationed at Naval Air Station, Kingsville, Tex., 1975-77, pilot New Orleans, 1977-79; various assignments VA-2082, 1979-89, VA-204, 1990-92; comdr. USS George Washington, Olathe, Kans., 1992; comdr. joint transportation reserve unit U.S. Transportation Command, Scott AFB, Ill., dir. plans and policy, 1998—; asst. dep. readiness Readiness Command Region 10, New Orleans; dep. commander Maritime Defense Zone Pacific, San Francisco, Naval Air Force Pacific Fleet, San Diego; comdr. Iceland Defense Force, 1998. Pilot Ozark Airlines, 1977-86, Trans World Airlines, 1986—. Decorated Legion of Merit, Meritorious Svc. medal with oak leaf cluster. Mem. Naval Reserve Assn., Reserve Officers Assn., Assn. Naval Aviation, Navy League, Phi Delta Theta Alumni Assn.

KLONGLAN, GERALD EDWARD, sociology educator; b. Nevada, Iowa, Apr. 1, 1936; s. Bernie R. and Willene Rebecca (Maland) K.; m. Donna Eileen Becvar, June 29, 1960; children: Jason, Suzanne. B.S., Iowa State U., 1958, M.S., 1962, Ph.D., 1963. Mem. faculty Iowa State U., Ames, 1963—2001, prof. sociology, 1972—2001, chmn. dept. sociology and anthropology, 1976-90, interim assoc. dean Coll. Sci. and Humanities, 1988-89; asst. dir. Iowa Agr. and Home Econ. Expt. Sta., 1990—2001; assoc. dean nat. programs Coll. Agr., 1995—2001; staff sociologist U.S. Dept. Agr., Coop. State Rsch. Svc., Washington, DC, 1991-93. Evaluation rschr. AID, Malawi, 1967, project cons., Ghana, 1976; ednl. cons. King Saud U., Saudi Arabia, 1981-83, Peking U., People's Republic of China, 1984-85; project implementor U. Zambia, Lusaka, 1982-83; family rsch., Norway, 1988, Czech Republic, 1995; project dir. mgmt. tng. Czech Republic and Slovak Republic, 1991-96; project dir. agr. rsch., Russia, Ukraine, other countries of former Soviet Union, 1992-99. Author: Social Indicators, 1972; (research monographs) Adoption Diffusion of Ideas, 1967; Creating Interorganizational Coordination, 1975, Communication Policy, 1983. Vol. scientist Am. Cancer Soc., 1969—; bd. dirs. Luth. Campus Ministry, Ames, 1972-78, chmn. bd., 1974-76; pres. Bethesda Luth. Ch., Ames, 1994-95. Recipient Wilton Park award Iowa State U., 1983 Mem. Rural Sociol. Soc. (coun. 1974-76, 91-92, v.p. 1977-78, pres. 1985-86), Am. Sociol. Assn. (com. on internat. sociology 1993-96), Midwest Sociol. Soc. (tng. com. 1975-78), Sigma Xi (pres. Iowa State U. chpt. 1983-84). Home: 1622 Maxwell Ave Ames IA 50010-5536 Office: Iowa State U Coll Agr 138 Curtiss Hl Ames IA 50011-0001 E-mail: klonglan@iastate.edu.

KLOPMAN, GILLES, chemistry educator; b. Brussels, Belgium, Feb. 24, 1933; came to U.S., 1965; s. Alge and Brana (Brendel) Klopman; m. Malvina Pantiel, Sept. 5, 1957. BA, Athenee d'Ixelles, Belgium, 1952; lic. chemistry, U. Brussels, 1956, D in Chemistry, 1960. Rsch. scientist Cyanamid European Rsch. Inst., Geneva, 1960-67; postdoctoral fellow U. Tex., 1964-65; assoc. prof. Case Western Res. U., Cleve., 1967-69, prof. chemistry, 1969—, chmn. dept., 1981-86, interim dean sci. and math., 1986-88, C.F. Mabery prof. of rsch., chmn. dept., 1988-95. V.p. Biofor, Ltd., PA, 1986-95; pres. Discovery Software Inc., 1991-93, Multicase, Inc., 1995—. Author: All Valence Electrons SCF Calculations, 1970, Chemical Reactivity and Reaction Paths, 1974; contbr. articles to profl. jours. Recipient Kahlbaum prize Swiss Chem. Soc., 1971; grantee NSF, NIH, EPA, PRF, ONR. Mem. AAUP, Am. Chem. Soc. (Morley medal 1993), Brit. Chem. Soc., Belgium Chem. Soc., Sigma Xi. Home: 22 Hyde Park Cleveland OH 44122-7536 Office: Case Western Res U 10900 Euclid Ave Cleveland OH 44106-1712 E-mail: gxk6@po.cwru.edu.

KLOS, JEROME JOHN, lawyer, director; b. La Crosse, Wis., Jan. 17, 1927; s. Charles and Edna S. (Wagner) K.; m. Mary M. Hamilton, July 26, 1958; children— Bryant H., Geoffrey W. B.S., U. Wis., 1948, J.D., 1950. Bar: Wis. 1950. Pres. Klos, Flynn and Papenfuss, La Crosse, 1950—. Bd. dirs. Union State Bank, West Salem, Wis. Mem. LaCrosse County Bd., 1957-74, vice chmn., 1972-74; pub. adminstr. La Crosse County, 1962-73; bd. dirs. West Salem Area Growth, Inc., La Crosse Area Growth, Inc.; trustee Sander and McKinly Scholarship Funds of West Salem Sch. Dist. Fellow Am. Coll. Real Estate Lawyers, Am. Coll. Probate Counsel, Wis. Law Found.; mem. Wis. Bar Assn., Elks, KC. Lodges: Elks, K.C. Home: 346 N Leonard St West Salem WI 54669-1238 Office: 800 Lynn Tower Bldg La Crosse WI 54601 E-mail: kfpatts@aol.com.

KLOSKA, RONALD FRANK, manufacturing company executive; b. Grand Rapids, Mich., Oct. 24, 1933; s. Frank B. and Catherine (Hilaski) K.; m. Mary F. Minick, Sept. 7, 1957; children: Kathleen Ann, Elizabeth Marie, Ronald Francis, Mary Josephine, Carolyn Louise. Student, St. Joseph Sem., Grand Rapids, Mich., 1947-53; PhB, U. Montreal, Que., Can., 1955; MBA, U. Mich., 1957. Staff acct. Coopers & Lybrand, Niles, Mich., 1957, staff to sr. acct., 1960—63; treas. Skyline Corp., Elkhart, Ind., 1963, v.p., treas., 1964—67, exec. v.p. fin., 1967—74, pres., 1974—85, pres., chief ops. officer, 1985—91, vice chmn., chief adminstrn. officer, 1991—94, vice chmn., chief adminstrn. officer, sec., 1994—95, vice chmn., dep. CEO, chief adminstrn. officer, 1995—98, vice chmn., CEO, chief adminstrn. officer, 1998—2001, dir., cons., 2001—. With U.S. Army, 1957—60. Mem. Mich. Soc. CPAs, Ind. Soc. CPAs, South Bend Country Club. Roman Catholic. Home: 1329 E Woodside St South Bend IN 46614-1455 Office: Skyline Corp 2520 Bypass Rd Elkhart IN 46514-1584

KLOSTER, CAROL GOOD, book and magazine distribution company; b. Richmond, Va., Aug. 18, 1948; d. David William and Lucy (McDowell) Good; m. John Kenneth Kloster III, Feb. 15, 1975; children: John Kenneth IV, Amanda Aileen. AB, Coll. William and Mary, 1970. Personnel supr. Charles Levy Circulating Co., Chgo., 1974-75, warehouse supr., 1976-77, warehouse mgr., 1978-80, dir. sales, 1980-83, asst. v.p., dir. mktg., 1984; v.p., gen. mgr. Video Trend of Chgo., 1985-86; v.p. gen. mgr. Levy Home Entertainment, 1986-92; pres., CEO Chas Levy Co., 1992—. Mem. bd., Family Focus Inc. Recipient Algernon Sidney Sullivan award Coll. William and Mary, 1970. Presbyterian. Home: 619 W North St Hinsdale IL 60521-3152 Office: Charles Levy Co 1200 N North Branch St Chicago IL 60622-2493

KLOSTERMAN, ALBERT LEONARD, technical development business executive, mechanical engineer; b. Cin., Oct. 22, 1942; s. Albert Clement and Mary J. Klosterman; m. Lynne Marie Gabelein, Jan. 4, 1964; children: Scott, Lance, Kimberly, Brad. BSMechE, U. Cin., 1965, MSMechE, 1968, PhD, 1971. Instr. U. Cin., 1966-70, adj. assoc. prof., 1974—; project mgr. Structural Dynamics Rsch. Corp., Milford, Ohio, 1970-72, mem. tech. staff, 1972-73, dir. tech. staff, 1973-78, v.p., gen. mgr., 1978-83, sr. v.p., chief tech. officer, gen. mgr., 1983-95; sr. v.p., chief scientist, 1995—. Mem. exec. steering com. Initial Graphics Exchange System/Product Data Exch. Speification of Nat. Standards Bd., Gaithersburg, Md., 1984—. Mem. editorial bd. Internat. Jour. Vehicle Design, 1979—. Recipient Disting. Alumnus award U. Cin., 1988. Mem. Assn. Computing Machinery, ASME (assoc.), Phi Kappa Theta. Republican. Roman Catholic. Home: 5444 Forest Ridge Cir Milford OH 45150-2821 Office: Structural Dynamics Rsch Corp 2000 Eastman Dr Milford OH 45150-2712

KLOTMAN, ROBERT HOWARD, music educator; b. Cleve., Nov. 22, 1918; s. Louis Klotman and Pearl (Warshawsky) Kaplan; m. Phyllis Helen Rauch, Apr. 4, 1943; children: Janet Lynn, Paul Evan. BS in Music Edn., Ohio No. U., 1940; MA in Music, Case-Western Res. U., 1950; EdD, Columbia U., 1956; MusD (hon.), Ohio No. U., 1984. Supr. music pub. schs., Dola, Ohio, 1940-42; tchr. instrumental, vocal music pub. schs. Euclid, 1942, 46; tchr. instrumental music pub. schs. Cleveland Heights, 1946-59; dir. music edn. pub. schs. Akron, 1959-63; divisional dir. music edn. pub. schs. Detroit, 1963-69; prof., chmn. dept. music edn. Ind. U., Bloomington, 1969-83, prof. emeritus, 1987—. Vis. prof. Shanghai Conservatory of Music, 1985, U. Alta., Edmonton, Can., summer 1991; guest lectr. U. Bar-Ilan, Israel, 1984; ednl. dir. firm Scherl & Roth (string importers), Cleve., 1956-70; mem. adv. bd. Contemporary Music Project, Ford Found., 1964-65; ednl. cons. Summy-Birchard Co. (music pubs.); mem. bicentennial com. J. C. Penney Co., 1974-76. Condr., Akron Youth Symphony Orch., 1959-63, Oak Park (Ill.) Symphony, 1967-69, Bloomington Youth Symphony Orch., 1969-75, Terre Haute Youth Symphony, 1992, Great Lake Music Camp Orch., 1982-96; author: Learning to Teach Through Playing: String Techniques and Pedagogy, 1971, The School Music Administrator and Supervisor: Catalysts for Change in Music Education, 1973, Teaching Strings, 1988, 2d. edit. 1996, (with others) Humanities Through the Black Experience, Foundations of Music Education, 1983, 2d edit., 1988; co-author: Administrating and Supervising Music, 1991; contbg. author: Ency. of Edn., 1971; editor: Orch. News, 1959-70; mem. editorial bd. Music Educators Jour., 1962-64, Instrumentalist, 1974-91; editor (with others) Scheduling Music Classes, 1968; editor, contbg. author: Music Performance Trust Funds Guide; composer: Action with Strings, 1962, Renaissance Suite, 1964, String Literature for Expanding Technique, 1973. Bd. dirs., sec. Ind. U. Credit Union, 1974-87; chmn. ednl. com. Chamber Music Am., 1993-95; chmn. Hall of Fame com. MENC, 1998—. With inf. AUS, 1942-46, ETO, PTO. Recipient citation

Nat. Assn. Negro Musicians Inc., 1966, citation Black Music Caucas, 1978, Outstanding Hoosier Musician award, 1986, Disting. Service award Am. String Tchrs. Assn., 1987, Sagamore of the Wabash Govs. award, 1991. Mem. Chamber Music Am. (chair edn. com. 1993-95), Am. String Tchrs. Assn. (pres. 1962-64, dir. pubs. 1985-94, chmn. past pres. coun. 1998-2000), Music Educators Nat. Conf. (chmn. commn. on tchr. edn. 1968-72, pres. 1976-78, Disting. Svc. award 1989, Hall of Fame com. 1996—), Rotary, Phi Mu Alpha Sinfonia, Phi Delta Kappa. Democrat. Jewish. Avocations: tennis, swimming, reading mystery novels. Home: 1234 Fenbrook Ln Bloomington IN 47401-4285 Office: Ind U Sch Music Bloomington IN 47405 E-mail: Klotman@indiana.edu.

KLOUCEK, FRANK JOHN, state legislator; b. Yankton, S.D., Sept. 27, 1956; s. Robert R. and Rose M. (Stekly) K.; m. Joan Marie Novak, 1980; children: Jennifer, Michelle, Kimberlee. BS, S.D. State U., 1978. Mem. S.D. Ho. of Reps., 1991-93, S.D. Senate, 1993—, vice chair senate agrl. com., 1993, 94, mem. health and human svcs., local govt. coms.; farmer; pres., chmn. resolution com. S.D. Farmers Union, 1992—. Committeeman Bon Homme County Dem. Com., 1986-88, pres. 1989—; mem. St. Georges Cath. Ch., Scotland. Recipient Disting. Svc. award S.D. Pharm. Assn., 1995. Mem. S.D. Farmers Union (county pres. 1986, Action Officer award 1989, 90), S.D.Soybean Growers Assn. (state sec. 1987, recognition plaque 1987), Lions (Bon Homme), K.C., Block and Bridle, Animal Agriculture Orgn., Alpha Zeta, Alpha Epsilon. Roman Catholic. Home: 29966 423rd Ave Scotland SD 57059-5714

KLUENDER, KEITH R. psychology educator; BS, Carroll Coll., 1979; MA, Northeastern U., 1981; PhD, U. Tex., 1988. Lectr. in psychology Northeastern U., 1981-82; rsch. asst. U. Tex., Austin, 1982-88, asst. instr., 1988-93; asst. prof. U. Wis., Madison, 1988-93, assoc. prof. psychology, 1993—, affiliate prof. neurophysiology, 1996—. Vis. scientist IBM Watso Rsch., 1983; presenter in field. Cons. editor Jour. Speech and Hearing Rsch., Perception and Psychophysics; reviewer various jours. in field; contbr. articles to profl. jours. Vilas assoc. prof., 1995; grantee U. Wis. Grad. Sch., 1989-90, 90-91, 96—, NIH-NIDCD, 1989-94, 94-99, Biomed. Rsch. Support, 1989-91, NSF, 1992-97, IBM, 1993, NIH, 1994—, NIDCD, 1990—; recipient Young Investigator award NSF, 1992-96, Troland Rsch. award NAS, 1997. Mem. APA, AAAS, Acoustical Soc. Am. (mem. speech tech. com.), Assn. for Rsch. in Otolaryngology, Behavioral and Brain Scis. Assoc., Internat. Soc. for Ecol. Psychology, psychonomic Soc., Sigma Xi. Office: U Wis Dept Psychology 1202 W Johnson St Madison WI 53706-1611

KLUES, JACK, communications executive; Exec. v.p. worldwide media svcs. Leo Burnett Co., Inc., Chgo.; CEO StarCom Worldwide, 1999—. Office: Leo Burnett Co Inc 35 W Wacker Dr Chicago IL 60601-1648

KLUG, SCOTT LEO, former congressman; b. Milwaukee, Wis., Jan. 16, 1953; s. Ralph William Klug and Josephine (Farrell) Weber; m. Tess Summers, Mar. 4, 1978; children: Keefe, Brett, Collin Phillip. BA, Lawrence U., 1975; MS in Journalism, Northwestern U., 1976; MBA, U. Wis., 1990. Reporter TV sta., Wausau, Wis., 1976-78; reporter Sta. KING-TV, Seattle, 1978-81; investigative reporter Sta. WJLA-TV, Washington, 1981-88; anchor, reporter Sta. WKOW-TV, Madison, Wis., 1988-90; v.p. pub. fin. dept. Blunt, Ellis & Loewi, 1990; mem. 102nd-105th U.S. Congress from 2d Wis. dist., Washington, 1991-98, mem. commerce com.; publ., CEO Trails Media Group Inc., Madison, 1999—; pub. affairs counsel Foley and Lardner, Washington, 1999—. Reporter, producer documentaries (Emmy awards 1989, 90). Named Nat. Humanitarian of Yr., Humane Soc., 1986; John McCloy fellow Columbia U. Sch. Journalism, 1987. Republican. Avocations: tennis, basketball, cooking. Office: Trails Media Group PO Box 317 Black Earth WI 53515 also: Foley and Lardner Verex Plaza 150 E Gilman St Madison WI 53703

KLUGMAN, STEPHAN CRAIG, newspaper editor; b. Fargo, N.D., May 11, 1945; s. Ted and Charlotte (Olson) K.; m. Julie Sue Terpening, Sept. 18, 1971; children: Josh, Carrie. BA in Journalism, Ind. U., 1967. Copy editor Chgo. Sun-Times, 1967-68, asst. telegraph editor, 1968-72, telegraph editor, 1972-74, city editor, 1974-76, asst. mng. editor features, 1976-78; asst. prof. Medill Sch. Journalism, Northwestern U., Evanston, Ill., 1978-79, dir. undergrad. studies, 1979-82; editor Jour.-Gazette, Ft. Wayne, Ind., 1982--. Mem. Am. Soc. Newspaper Editors. Office: Jour-Gazette 600 W Main St Fort Wayne IN 46802-1408

KLUSMAN, JUDITH, state legislator; b. Neenah, Wis., Dec. 14, 1956; m. Timothy A. Klusman; children: Charles, James. Student, Concordia Coll. Mem. from dist. 56 Wis. State Assembly, Madison, 1988—, asst. majority leader, co-chair joint survey com. retirement svc., mem. ways and means, assembly rules and orgn. coms. Mem. com. on agr. and internat. trade Nat. Conf. State Legislators; mem. task force on agr. and environ; mem. Legis. Coun. Spl. Com. on Child Custody, Support and Visitation Laws; mem. Legic. Coun. Spl. Com. on Remediation of Environ. Contamination. Mem. Outagamie County Local Emergency Planning Com.; mem. Wis. Rural Leadership Program; mem. World Dairy Ctr. Authority Bd. Recipient Key award 4-H, 1975, Outstanding Young Farm Couple award Winnebago County Farm Bur., 1983, Friend of Edn. award Neenah chpt. Wis. Edn. Assn., 1986-87, Friend of Agr. award Wis. Farm Bur. Fedn., 1990, 92, 94, Outstanding Alumni Winnebago County 4-H, 1992, Buardian of Small Bus. award Fedn. of Ind. Bus., 1992. Mem. Rotary Internat., Wis. Rural Leadership Alumni. Address: 7547 Green Meadow Rd Oshkosh WI 54904-9405

KMENTA, JAN, economics educator; b. Prague, Czechoslovakia, Jan. 3, 1928; came to U.S., 1963; m. Joan Helen Gaffney, Aug. 9, 1959; children: David, Steven. B in Econs. with 1st class honors, Sydney U., 1955; MA, Stanford U., 1959, PhD, 1964; hon. doctorate, U. Saarland, Germany, 1989. Lectr. U. N.S.W., Sydney, 1957-61; sr. lectr. Sydney U., 1961-63; asst. prof. U. Wis., Madison, 1963-65; prof. Mich. State U., East Lansing, 1965-73, U. Mich., Ann Arbor, 1973—. Vis. prof. U. Bonn, Germany, 1971-72, 1979-80, U. Saarland, Saarbrucken, Germany, 1984, 85, 86. Author: Elements of Econometrics, 2d edit., 1986; editor: (with others) Evaluation of Econometric Models, 1980, Large-Scale Macro-Econometric Models, 1981; contbr. articles to profl. jours. Recipient U.S. Sr. Scientist Prize, Humboldt Found., Bonn, 1979; Fulbright scholar, 1957-59. Fellow Am. Statis. Assn., Econometric Soc.; mem. Am. Econ. Assn., Czechozlovak Soc. Arts and Scis. in Am. Home: 2511 Londonderry Rd Ann Arbor MI 48104-4017 Office: U Mich Dept Econs Ann Arbor MI 48109

KNABE, GEORGE WILLIAM, JR. pathologist, educator; b. Grand Rapids, Mich., June 29, 1924; s. George William and Dorothy Emma (Fischofer) K., m. Lorine Jeanette Moffit, Jan. 16, 1954; children: Katharine J., Elizabeth J., Ann C., Dorothy M. Student, Mich. State U., 1942-43, The Citadel, Charleston, SC, 1943-44, Johns Hopkins U., 1944-45; MD, U. Md., 1949. Diplomate Am. Bd. Pathology. Intern Balt. City Hosp., 1949-50; resident pathology Cleve. Clin. Found., 1950-51, Henry Ford Hosp., Detroit, 1953-54; chief lab. svc. VA Ctr., Dayton, Ohio, 1955-57; vis. prof. pathology U. El Salvador Sch. Medicine, 1957-59; asst. prof. pathology U. P.R. Sch. Medicine, 1959-60; prof., chmn. dept. pathology Sch. Medicine, U. S.D., 1960-68, dean., 1967-72; dir. med. edn. St. Luke's Hosp., Duluth, 1972-78; prof. pathology U. Minn.-Duluth Sch. Medicine, 1972—, assoc. dean clin. affairs., 1972-76; chief. dept. pathology Virginia (Minn.) Regional Med. Ctr., 1978-98; pres. Range Pathology, 1998—. Bd. dirs Health Sys. Agy. of Western Lake Superior, Duluth 1975-82, No. Lakes Health Care Consortium, 1984—, U. Minn. Health and Med. Sch. Adv. Groups 1972—. 1st lt. to capt. M.C., USAF, 1951-53; surgeon to capt., USPHS Res., 1957—. Mem. AMA, U.S. and Can. Acad. Pathology, Am. Soc. Clin. Pathologists, Coll. Am. Pathologists. Avocations: art, horticulture, photography. Home: 1008 S 7th Ave Virginia MN 55792-3151 Office: Range Pathology 1008 7th Ave S Virginia MN 55792-3151

KNAPP, HOWARD RAYMOND, internist, clinical pharmacologist; b. Red Bank, N.J., Oct. 5, 1949; s. Howard Raymond and Jane Marie (Ray) K.; m. Brenda Louise Carr, 1984; 1 child, Matthew. AB in Biology, Washington U., St. Louis, 1971; MD, Vanderbilt U., 1977, PhD in Pharmacology, 1984. Diplomate Am. Bd. Internal Medicine. Asst. prof. medicine and pharmacology Vanderbilt U., Nashville, 1984-89, assoc. prof., 1990; assoc. prof. internal medicine and pharmacology U. Iowa, Iowa city, 1990-97, prof. internal medicine and pharmacology, 1997-2000, assoc. dir. NIH Clin. Rsch. Ctr., 1997-2000; exec. dir. Deaconess Billings (Mont.) Clin. Res. Divsn., 2000—. Mem. NIH Nutrition Study Sect., Bethesda, Md., 1994—96; cons. pharm. firms, grant orgns. and govtl. entities ; mem. applied pharmacol. task force Nat. Bd. Med. Examiners, 1997—2000; mem. expert panel on cardiovasc. and renal drugs U.S. Pharmacopeia, 2000—. Editor-in-chief Lipids, 1995—; contbr. numerous articles to profl. jours., chpts. to books. Grantee NIH, Am. Heart Assn., others. Fellow ACP, Am. Heart Assn. (vascular biol. rsch. rev. com. 1993-95, arteriosclerosis coun.); mem. Ctrl. Soc. for Clin. Rsch. (chair clin. pharmacol. sect. 1992-95), Am. Soc. for Clin. Pharmacology and Therapeutics. Achievements include first demonstration that calcium ionophores stimulate eicosanoid synthesis; first evidence that N-3 fatty acids reduce platelet activation and blood pressure in patients; first demonstration of the effects of 5-lipoxygenase inhibition in humans. E-mail: hknapp@billingsclinic.org.

KNAPP, JAMES IAN KEITH, judge; b. Bklyn., Apr. 6, 1943; s. Charles Townsend and Christine (Grange) K.; m. Joan Elizabeth Cunningham, June 10, 1967 (div. Mar. 1971); 1 child, Jennifer Elizabeth; m. Carol Jean Brown, July 14, 1981; children: Michelle Christine, David Michael Keith AB cum laude, Harvard U., 1964; JD, U. Colo., 1967; M in Law in Taxation, Georgetown U., 1989. Bar: Colo. 1967, Calif. 1968, U.S. Supreme Ct. 1983, D.C. 1986, Ohio 1995. Dep. dist. atty. County of L.A., 1968-79; head dep. dist. atty. Pomona br. office, 1979-82; dep. asst. atty. gen. criminal divsn. U.S. Dept. Justice, Washington, 1982-86, dep. assoc. atty. gen., 1986-87, dep. asst. atty. gen. tax divsn., 1988-89, acting asst. atty. gen. tax divsn., 1989, acting dep. chief organized crime sect. criminal divsn., 1989-91, dep. dir., asset forfeiture office criminal divsn., 1991-94; adminstrv. law judge Social Security Adminstrn., 1994—. Editor: California Uniform Crime Charging Standards and Manual, 1975 Vice chmn. Young Reps. Nat. Fedn., 1973-75; pres. Calif. Young Reps., 1975-77; mem. exec. com. Rep. State Ctrl. Com., Calif., 1975-77. Mem.: DC Bar Assn., Calif. Bar Assn. Episcopalian. Avocations: travel, reading. Office: Office of Hearings & Appeals 110 N Main St Ste 800 Dayton OH 45402-1786

KNAPP, PAUL RAYMOND, think tank executive; b. Long beach, Calif., Sept. 8, 1945; s. Franklin L. and Ella Jo (Andrews) K.; m. Shirley K. Wheeler, July 16, 1967 (div. 1987); children: Michele Ann, Erica Elizabeth, Matthew Gary; m. Nancy Jane Gift, May 1, 1988. BS, Calif. State U., Chico, 1970; MBA magna cum laude, U. Chgo., 1977. With Kemper Corp., various locations, 1969-77; sr. v.p., cFO Kemper Fin. Svcs., Inc., Chgo., 1977-87; pres., CEO Kessler Asher Group, 1988-90; dir., chmn., pres., CEO, Catalyst Inst., 1991—. Bd. dirs. Berger Mut. Funds, Denver, Futures Industry Inst., Washington, 1992—, Internat. Fedn. for Bus. Edn., Kansas City, Mo., 1993—. U.S. nat. com. for Pacific Econ. Cooperation, Washington, 1995—; bd. dirs. Allendale Assn., Lake Villa, Ill., 1988—. Home: 1410 N State Pkwy Chicago IL 60610-1512 Office: Catalyst Inst Ste 500 350 W Hubbard St Chicago IL 60610-6939

KNAPPENBERGER, PAUL HENRY, JR. science museum director; b. Reading, Pa., Sept. 5, 1942; s. Paul Henry and Kathryn (Medrick) K.; m. Naomi Knappenberger; children— Paul Charles, Timothy Alan, Shannon Rose Lalor, Heidi Kathrin. A.B. in Math, Franklin and Marshall Coll., 1964; M.A. in Astronomy (NASA fellow), U. Va., 1966, Ph.D. in Astronomy, 1968. Astronomer Fernbank Sci. Center, Atlanta, 1968-72; instr. Emory U. and Ga. State U., 1970-72; dir. Sci. Mus. of Va., Richmond, 1973-91; pres. The Adler Planetarium, Chgo., 1991—. Asst. prof. Va. Commonwealth U., U. Richmond, 1973-81; bd. dirs. Assn. Sci. and Tech. Centers, pres., 1985-87; instr. astronomy Yellowstone Inst.; former v.p. Midlothian Athletic Assn.; mem. council Nat. Mus. Act, 1984-86. Former mem. bd. dirs. Mus. Film Network, Exhibit Research Collaborative; co-founder Planetarium Show Network; dir. Informal Sci. Instructional Services, Ltd. NSF Sci. Edn. grantee, 1971-72; grantee NEH, Inst. Mus. Services. Mem. Am. Astron. Soc., AAAS, Internat. Planetarium Soc., Va. Acad. Sci., Va. Assn. Museums (council 1979-91), Am. Assn. Museums, Great Lakes Planetarium Assn. Home: 6n488 Splitrail Ct Saint Charles IL 60175-6928 Office: Adler Planetarium 1300 S Lake Shore Dr Chicago IL 60605-2489

KNAPSTEIN, MICHAEL, advertising executive; BS in Comm./Advt. and Pub. Rels., U. Wis., Stevens Point. Copywriter TAM Advt., Wausau, Wis., creative dir.; copy/contact Waldbillig & Besteman, Inc., Madison, 1979, co-owner, 1988, CEO, 1993—. Represented in permanent collections Nikon, Eastman Kodak. Active Start Smart, United Way Dane County. Mem. Madison Advt. Fedn. (bd. dirs.). Office: Waldbillig and Besteman Inc 7633 Ganser Way Madison WI 53719-2092 Fax: 608-829-0901.

KNEBEL, DONALD EARL, lawyer; b. Logansport, Ind., May 26, 1946; s. Everett Earl and Ethel Josephina (Hultgren) K.; m. Joan Elizabeth Vest, June 5, 1976 (div. 1980); 1 child, Mary Elizabeth; m. Jennifer Colt Johnson, Sept. 25, 1999. BEE with highest distinction, Purdue U., 1968; JD magna cum laude, Harvard U., 1974. Bar: Ind. 1974, U.S. Ct. Appeals (7th cir.) 1980, U.S. Ct. Appeals (3rd cir.) 1986, U.S. Ct. Appeals (6th cir.) 1987, U.S. Ct. Appeals (fed. cir.) 1988. Assoc. Barnes, Hickam, Pantzer & Boyd, Indpls., 1974-81; ptnr. Barnes & Thornburg, 1981—. Contbr. articles on intellectual property, antitrust and distbn. law to profl. publs. Trustee Indpls. Civic Theatre, 1986—95, chmn., 1988—91, hon. trustee, 1995—. Mem.: ABA, 7th Cir. Bar Assn., Indpls. Bar Assn., Ind. Bar Assn., Columbia Club, Kiwanis (pres. 1991—92). Presbyn. Office: Barnes & Thornburg 11 S Meridian St Ste 1313 Indianapolis IN 46204-3535

KNECHT, RICHARD ARDEN, family practitioner; b. Grand Rapids, Mar. 7, 1929; s. Fredrick William and Eva Rae (Blakley) K.; m. Joan Matson, Dec. 26, 1951 (div. 1975); children: Richard Arden, Karrie Jo, Jeffrey Paul; m. Patricia Irene Gilmore, Aug. 14, 1976; 1 child, Kimberly Kahler. BS, U. Mich., 1951, MD, 1955. Diplomate Am. Bd. Family Practice, Am. Bd. Geriatric Medicine; cert. med. dir. Intern St. Mary Hosp., Grand Rapids, Mich., 1955-56; pvt. practice, Fife Lake, 1956—. Fellow Am. Acad. Family Physicians, Am. Geriatric Soc., Royal Soc. Medicine; mem. Mich. Med. Soc. (com. on aging 1988—), Mich. Acad. Family Practice (chmn. com. on aging 1986-88, pub.'s award 1988), Mich. Med. Dirs. Assn. (pres. 1996-97). Avocations: archaeology, motorcycling, geology, hunting, fishing. Home and Office: PO Box 130 125 Morgan St Fife Lake MI 49633

KNEEN, JAMES RUSSELL, health care administrator; b. Kalamazoo, Dec. 16, 1955; s. Russell Packard and Joyce Elaine (Knapper) K.; m. Peggy Jo Howard, Aug. 4, 1979; children: Benjamin Russell, Katherine Elaine. BA, Alma Coll., 1978; MHA, U. Mo., 1982. Systems analyst Bronson Meth. Hosp., Kalamazoo, 1976-79; cons. U. Mo., Columbia, 1979-81; adminstrv. resident Meth. Hosp. Ind., Indpls., 1981-82; div. dir. psychiat. care svcs. Parkview Meml. Hosp., Ft. Wayne, Ind., 1982-88; exec. v.p. Meml. Hosp., Oconomowoc, Wis., 1988-90; exec. dir. Meml. Hosp. Found., Oconomowoc, 1988-90; pres., CEO Fostoria (Ohio) Community Hosp., 1990-94; pres. United Health Partnership, Toledo, 1995—. Bd. dirs. Washington House Alcoholism Treatment Ctr., 1983-88; bd. dirs., sec.-treas. Parkview Regional Outreach, 1985-88; bd. dirs., pres. Seneca County chpt. Am. Cancer Soc. Fellow Am. Coll. Healthcare Execs.; mem. Am. Hosp. Assn., Wis. Hosp. Assn. (coun. on health care delivery systems), Regent's Adv. Coun. Wis. (bd. dirs.), Ohio Hosp. Assn. (various coms.), Rotary (bd. dirs. Fostoria chpt). Office: United Health Ptrn 2200 Jefferson Ave Toledo OH 43624-1120

KNEIR, THOMAS J. federal agency administrator; b. Battle Creek, Mich., Feb. 10, 1949; m. Nadine S. Schaffer; 1 child Eric. BS in Acctg., U. Ill., Chgo., 1972. Asst. spl. agt.-in-charge, spl. agt.-in-charge FBI, Albuquerque, spl. agt. Dallas, Atlanta and Louisville, 1973, head govtl. fraud unit Washington, dep. asst. dir. criminal investigative divsn. Jacksonville, spl. agt.-in-charge Chgo., 2001—. Office: US Dept Justice FBI 219 S Dearborn St Ste 905 Chicago IL 60604

KNEPPER, GEORGE W. history educator; b. Akron, Ohio, Jan. 15, 1926; s. George W. and Grace (Darling) K.; m. Phyllis Watkins, Aug. 21, 1949; children— Susan Lynne, John Arthur. B.A., U. Akron, 1948; M.A., U. Mich., 1950, Ph.D., 1954. Mem. faculty U. Akron, 1948-49, 54-92, assoc. prof. history, head dept., 1959-62; dean U. Akron (Coll. Liberal Arts), 1962-67, prof. history, 1964-88, disting. prof. history, 1988-92. Author: New Lamps for Old, One Hundred Years of Urban Higher Education at the University of Akron, 1970, An Ohio Portrait, 1976, Akron: City at the Summit, 1981, Ohio and Its People, 1989, Summit's Glory: Sketches of Buchtel Coll. and the University of Akron, 1990; editor: Travels in the Southland; The Journal of Lucius Verus Biérce 1822-23, 1966. Served to ensign USNR, 1943-46. Fulbright fellow U. London, Eng., 1953-54 Mem. Am., So. hist. assns., Orgn. Am. Historians, Ohio Acad. History, Omicron Delta Kappa, Alpha Tau Omega, Phi Alpha Theta, Alpha Sigma Lambda. Home: 88 Ridge Side Ct Munroe Falls OH 44262-1076 Office: Univ Akron Coll Liberal Arts Dept History Akron OH 44325-0001

KNIFFEN, JAN ROGERS, finance executive; b. Herrin, Ill., Sept. 19, 1948; s. Paul Rogers and Evelyn Rose (Manering) K.; m. Janet Ann Rohn, Aug. 27, 1975; children: Julie Ann Meyer, Natalie Ann Meyer. Student, U. Ill., 1966-68; BS in Journalism, So. Ill. U., 1968-71; MBA in FIn., Lindenwood Coll., 1975-78; post-grad., St. Louis U., 1985—. Mgmt. trainee ACF Industries, St. Charles, Mo., 1972-73, order inquiry rep., 1973-75, sr. market analyst, 1975-77, sr. planner strategic planning, 1977-79, mgr. leasing, sales adminstrn. Earth City, 1979-81, dir. bus. planning, estimating, and scheduling, 1981-83, asst. treas., 1983-85, May Dept. Stores Co., St. Louis, 1985-86, v.p., treas., 1986-91, sr. v.p., treas., 1991—. Adj. prof. bus. adminstrn. Lindenwood Coll., 1978—; fin. advisor Job Network, St. Louis, 1987. Bd. mgrs. St. Charles (Mo.) County YMCA, 1981-86; bd. overseers Lindenwood Coll., 1986-93, bd. dirs., 1993—, alumni coun., 1983-86. Capt. USAF, 1970-75. Republican. Presbyterian. Club: Noon Day (St. Louis). Avocation: distance running. Office: May Dept Stores Co 611 Olive St Saint Louis MO 63101-1721

KNIGHT, BOB, college basketball coach; b. Massillon, Ohio, Oct. 25, 1940; s. Carroll and Hazel (Henthorne) K.; m. Nancy Lou Knight, Apr. 17, 1963 (div.); m. Karen Edgar, 1988. BS, Ohio State U., 1962. Asst. coach Cuyahoga Falls (Ohio) High Sch., 1962-63; freshman coach U.S. Mil. Acad., West Point, N.Y., 1963-65, head basketball coach, 1965-71, Ind. U., Bloomington, 1971-2000, Tex. Tech. U., Lubbock, 2001—. Speaker clinics in field; condr. tng. clinics for coaches and players. Trustee Naismith Meml. Basketball Hall of Fame. Served with U.S. Army. Recipient Big Ten Coach-of-Year award, 1973, 75, 76, 81, 89; named unanimously Nat. Coach of Year, 1975, 89, Nat. Coach of Yr. AP and Basketball Weekly, 1976; recipient appreciation plaque from team, 1979. Mem. Nat. Assn. Basketball Coaches (bd. dirs.) Methodist. Achievements include coaching U.S. team to gold medal 1984 Olympics; coached Ind. U. to NCAA Championship, 1976, 81, 87; college basketball's winningest active coach (one of only 12 NCAA coaches to have won 700 or more games). Office: Tex Tech U Mens Basketball United Spirit Ctr Indiana Ave Lubbock TX 79409

KNIGHT, CHARLES FIELD, electrical equipment manufacturing company executive; b. Lake Forest, Ill., Jan. 20, 1936; s. Lester Benjamin and Elizabeth Anne (Field) K.; m. Joanne Parrish, June 22, 1957; children: Lester Benjamin III, Anne Field Knight Davidson, Steven P., Jennifer Lee. B.S. in Mech. Engring., Cornell U., 1958, M.B.A., 1959. Mgmt. trainee Goetzewerke A.G., Burscheid, W. Ger., 1959-61; pres. Lester B. Knight Internat. Corp., 1961-63; exec. v.p. Lester B. Knight & Assocs., Inc., Chgo., 1963-67, pres., 1967-69, pres., CEO, 1969-73; vice chmn. bd. Emerson Electric Co., St. Louis, 1973, sr. vice chmn. bd., corp. exec. officer, 1973, CEO, 1973—, chmn., 1974—, also former pres., from 1973. Bd. dirs. Southwestern Bell Corp., Caterpillar Inc., Baxter Internat. Inc., Anheuser Busch Cos., Inc., The Brit. Petroleum Co. p.l.c. Mem. Civic Progress, 1973; bd. dirs. Arts and Edn. Coun.; bd. dirs., trustee Washington U., St. Louis, Olin Found. Mem. St. Louis Country Club, Log Cabin Club (St. Louis), Cristal Downs Club (Traverse City, Mich.), Glen View Golf Club (Ill.), Chicago Club, Sigma Phi Office: Emerson Electric Co 8100 W Florissant Ave Saint Louis MO 63136-1494

KNIGHT, CHARLIE, radio personality; Grad. high sch., Dallas. Radio host Oldies 95, Mission, Kans. Office: Oldies 95 FM 5800 Fatridge Dr 6th Fl Mission KS 66202*

KNIGHT, CHRISTOPHER NICHOLS, lawyer; b. New Haven, Sept. 7, 1946; s. Douglas Maitland and Grace Wallace (Nichols) K.; m. Emily Byrn Turner, Oct. 20, 1979; children: Ethan Douglas, Benjamin Walker Lester, Christopher N. Jr. BA, Yale U., 1968; JD, Duke U., 1971. Bar: Wis. 1971, U.S. Dist. Ct. (ea. dist.) Wis. 1973, U.S. Ct. Appeals (7th cir.) 1977, N.C. 1979, U.S. Dist. Ct. (mid. dist.) N.C. 1979, Minn., 1980, U.S. Supreme Ct. 1980, U.S. Ct. Appeals (4th, 8th cirs.) 1980, U.S. Dist. Ct. Minn. 1980, Ill. 1982, N.Y., 1996. Assoc. Quarles & Brady, Milw., 1971-78, ptnr., 1978-79, Smith Helms Mulliss & Moore, Greensboro, N.C., 1979-80, Kutak Rock, Mpls., 1980-82, Isham Lincoln & Beale, Chgo., 1982-88, Hopkins & Sutter, Chgo., 1988-2001, Foley & Lardner, Chgo., 2001—. Mem. ABA, Ill. State Bar Assn., Minn. State Bar Assn., N.Y. State Bar Assn., N.C. State Bar Assn., State Bar Wis., Nat. Assn. Bond Lawyers. Congregationalist. Office: Foley & Lardner Three First National Plz Chicago IL 60602 E-mail: cknight@foleylaw.com.

KNIGHT, FRANK BARDSLEY, mathematics educator; b. Chgo., Oct. 11, 1933; s. Frank Hyneman and Ethel Eunice (Verry) K.; m. Ingeborg G. Belz, Aug. 30, 1971; children: Marion A., Marc A., Ellen D. B.A., Cornell U., 1955; Ph.D., Princeton U., 1959. Instr. math. U. Minn., Mpls., 1960-61, asst. prof., 1962-63; asst. prof. math. U. Ill., Urbana, 1964-66, assoc. prof., 1967-71; prof. U. Ill, 1971-91, prof. emeritus, 1991—. Author: Essentials of Brownian Motion and Diffusion, 1981, Essays on the Prediction Process, 1981, Foundations of the Prediction Process, 1992. Sloan fellow, 1968-71; NSF grantee, 1981-89. Mem. Am. Math. Soc., Inst. Math. Stats., Am. Alpine Club. Office: U Ill 1409 W Green St Urbana IL 61801-2943 E-mail: f-knight@math.uiuc.edu.

KNIGHT, JEFFREY ALAN, finance executive; b. Bay City, Mich., Aug. 6, 1951; s. Dean Leroy and Mary Margaret (McLeod) K.; m. Ramona Margo Robins, Aug. 30, 1980; 1 child, Alexis. BBA in Acctg., Western Mich. U., 1973. CPA, Mich. Staff auditor Coopers & Lybrand, Detroit, 1973-75, supr., 1976-77; mgr. acctg. systems Guardian Industries Corp., Northville, Mich., 1978, asst. controller, 1979-80, corp. controller, 1981-83, v.p. fin., CFO, 1984—, now group v.p. fin., CFO. Mem. Fin. Execs. Inst., Am. Inst. CPA's, Mich. Assn. CPA's. Office: Guardian Industries Corp 2300 Harmon Rd Auburn Hills MI 48326

KNIGHT, JOHN ALLAN, clergyman, philosophy and religion educator; b. Mineral Wells, Tex., Nov. 8, 1931; s. John Lee and Beulah Mae (Bounds) K.; m. Justine Anne Rushing, Aug. 22, 1958; children— John Allan, James Alden, Judith Anne. B.A., Bethany Nazarene Coll., 1952; M.A., Okla. U., 1954; B.D., Vanderbilt U., 1957, Ph.D., 1966. Ordained to ministry Ch. of Nazarene, 1954; pastor Tenn. Dist. Ch. of Nazarene, 1953-61, 71-72; prof., chmn. dept. philosophy and religion Trevecca Nazarene Coll., Nashville, 1957-69; chmn. dept. philosophy and religion Mt. Vernon (Ohio) Nazarene Coll., 1969-71, pres., 1972-75; pastor Grace Nazarene Ch., Nashville, 1971-72; pres. Bethany (Okla.) Nazarene Coll., 1976-85; gen. supt. Internat. Ch. of the Nazarene, 1985—, vice chair Bd. Gen. Supts., 1990-92, chair Bd. Gen. Supts., 1992-94. Coordinator U.S. Govt. Project Studying Possible Coop. Ventures for Tenn. Colls. and Univs., 1969; mem. gen. bd. Internat. Ch. of Nazarene, 1980-85 Author: Commentary on Philippians, 1968, The Holiness Pilgrimage, 1971, In His Likeness, 1976, Beacon Bible Expositions, Vol. 9, 1985, What the Bible Says About Tongues - Speaking, 1988; co-author: Sanctify Them -- That the World May Know, 1987; co-author: Go -- Preach, The Preaching Event in the 90s; author: All Loves Excelling, 1995, Bridge to Our Tomorrows, 2000; editor-in-chief: Herald of Holiness, Kansas City, Mo., 1975-76. Pres. bd. govs. Okla. Ind. Coll. Found., 1979-81; trustee So. Nazarene U., Okla. Recipient Lily Found. Theology award Vanderbilt U., 1958-59; Carré fellow Vanderbilt U., 1960-62 Mem. Soc. Sci. Study Religion, Am. Acad. Religion, Wesley Theol. Soc. (pres. 1979), Evang. Theol. Assn. Club: Kiwanis Internat. Home: PO Box 368 Bethany OK 73008-0368 Office: Internat Ch of the Nazarene 6401 Paseo Blvd Kansas City MO 64131-1213 E-mail: jkharlo@aol.com.

KNIGHT, ROBERT G. mayor, investment banker; b. Wichita, Kans., July 31, 1941; s. Edwar G. and Melba (Barbour) K.; m. Jane Carol Benedick, Aug. 12, 1967; children— Jennifer, Amy, Kristin B.A., Wichita State U. Rep. First Securities Co., Wichita, Kans., 1970-76, v.p., 1984—, Mid-Continent Mcpls., Wichita, 1977-82, Ranson & Co., Wichita, 1982-84; mayor City of Wichita, 1980-81, 84—. Trustee Salvation Army, Wichita, 1980—, Urban Ministeries, Wichita, 1980—, Southwestern Coll., Winfield, Kans., 1980—; bd. dirs. Kans. Water Authority, Topeka, 1983—; commr. City of Wichita, 1979—. Served with USMCR, 1962-66 Recipient award of honor Concerned Citizens for Community Standards, 1982 Mem. Nat. League Cities, Kans. League Municipalities Republican. Methodist Avocation: sports. Office: Mayors Office City Hall 1st Fl 455 N Main St Wichita KS 67202-1600

KNIGHT, V. C. manufacturing executive; b. Landess, Ind., Aug. 12, 1904; s. Charles and Daisie (Farr) K.; m. Velma Cain, June 30, 1926; children: James, Marilyn. Student, Ind. State U., 1921-24; Ph.D. in Bus. Adminstrn., Adrian Coll., 1977, Hillsdale Coll., 1983. With McCray Refrigerator Co., 1926-47; v.p. ops.; exec. v.p. Betz Corp., Hammond, Ind., 1947-51; with Addison Products Co., 1951—, now chmn. bd. Past trustee Adrian Coll., present trustee emeritus. Office: Knight Refrigeration Co 215 Talbot St Addison MI 49220

KNIPSCHILD, ROBERT, artist, educator; b. Freeport, Ill., Aug. 17, 1927; s. Leon Francis and Alice (Walsh) K.; m. Patricia Ann O'Connor, Sept. 1, 1949; children— Abby Clare Knipschild Weber, Amy Louise Knipschild Wermeling, John Eliot, Jill Anne Knipschild Harsch, Sarah Kate. B.A., U. Wis., 1950; M.F.A., Cranbrook Acad. Art, 1951. Tchr. Balt. Mus. Art, 1951-52, Am. U., 1952, U. Conn., 1954-56, U. Wis., 1956-60, U. Iowa, 1960-66; prof. art, dir. grad. studies fine arts U. Cin., 1966-90, prof. emeritus fine arts, 1990—. Exhbns. include, Mus. Modern Art, Whitney Mus., Met. Mus., Corcoran Mus., Boston Mus., Carnegie Inst., also in Europe, Japan and, Australia. Served with AUS, 1945-47. Office: 1159 Hill Crest Rd Cincinnati OH 45224-3223

KNOEBEL, SUZANNE BUCKNER, cardiologist, medical educator; b. Ft. Wayne, Ind., Dec. 13, 1926; d. Doster and Marie (Lewis) Buckner. A.B., Goucher Coll., 1948; M.D., Ind. U.-Indpls., 1960. Diplomate: Am. Bd. Internal Medicine. Asst. prof. medicine Ind. U., Indpls., 1966-69, assoc. prof., 1969-72, prof., 1972-77, Krannert prof., 1977—. Asst. dean rsch. Ind. U., Indpls., 1975-85; assoc. dir. Krannert Inst. Cardiology, Indpls., 1974-90; asst. chief cardiology sect. Richard L. Roudebush VA Med. Ctr., Indpls., 1982-90; editor-in-chief ACC Current Jour. Rev., 1992-2000. Fellow Am. Coll. Cardiology (v.p. 1980-81, pres. 1982-83); mem. Am. Fedn. Clin. Research, Assn. Univ. Cardiologists Office: Ind U Sch Medicine 1111 W 10th St Indianapolis IN 46202-4800 E-mail: sknoebel@iupui.edu.

KNOKE, DAVID HARMON, sociology educator; b. Phila., Mar. 4, 1947; s. Donald Glenn and Frances Harriet (Dunn) Knoke; m. Joann Margaret Robar, Aug. 29, 1970; 1 child Margaret Frances. BA, U. Mich., 1969, MSW, 1971, PhD, 1972; MA, U. Chgo., 1970. Asst. prof. sociology Ind. U., Bloomington, 1972-75, assoc. prof., 1975-81, prof., 1981-85, dir. Inst. Social Rsch. and Ctr. for Survey Rsch., 1982-84; prof. sociology U. Minn., Mpls., 1985—, chmn., 1989-92, undergrad. dir., 1995-98, grad. dir., 1998—2002. Mem. sociology program rev. panel NSF, 1981-83; mem. sociology rev. panel Fulbright Scholars, 1993-95; mem. sociology com. Grad. Records Exams., 1998-2000. Author: Change and Continuity in American Politics, 1976, (with Peter J. Burke) Log-Linear Models, 1980, (with James R. Wood) Organized for Action, 1981, (with George W. Bohrnstedt and Alisa Potter Mee) Statistics for Social Data Analysis, 1982, 4th edit., 2002, (with James H. Kuklinski) Network Analysis, 1982, (with Edward O. Laumann) The Organizational State, 1987, Organizing for Collective Action, 1990, Political Networks, 1990, (with George W. Bohrnstedt) Basic Social Statistics, 1991, (with Franz Pappi, Jeffrey Broadbent and Yutaka Tsujinaka) Comparing Policy Networks, 1996, (with Arne Kalleberg, Peter Marsden and Joe Spaeth) Organizations in America, 1996, (with Peter Capelli, Laurie Bassi, Harry Katz, Paul Osterman and Michael Useem) Change at Work, 1997, Changing Organizations, 2001. Recipient NIMH Rsch. Scientist Devel. award, 1977-82; 11 rsch. grants NSF; Nat. Merit scholar, 1965-69, Fulbright Sr. Rsch. scholar, Germany, 1989, scholar of the Coll. U. Minn., 1996-99; Ctr. for Advanced Study in the Behavioral Scis. fellow, 1992-93. Mem. Am. Sociol. Assn. (chair orgns. and occupation sect. 1992-93), Sociol. Rsch. Assn., Acad. of Mgmt., Internat. Network for Social Network Analysis, European Group for Orgnl. Studies. Unitarian Home: 7305 Wooddale Ave S Minneapolis MN 55435-4157 Office: U Minn Dept Sociology Minneapolis MN 55455 E-mail: knoke@atlas.socsci.umn.edu.

KNOLL, GLENN FREDERICK, nuclear engineering educator; b. St. Joseph, Mich., Aug. 3, 1935; s. Oswald Herman and Clara Martha (Bernthal) K.; m. Gladys Hetzner, Sept. 7, 1957; children: Thomas, John, Peter. BS, Case Inst. Tech., 1957; MSChemE, Stanford U., 1959; PhD in Nuclear Engring., U. Mich., 1963. Asst. research physicist U. Mich., Ann Arbor, 1960-62, asst. prof. nuclear engring., 1962-67, assoc. prof., 1967-72, prof., 1972—, chmn. dept. nuclear engring., 1979-90, interim dean engring., 1995-96, also mem. bioengring. faculty. Vis. scientist Institut für Angewandte Kernphysik, Kernforschungszentrum Karlsruhe, Fed. Republic Germany, 1965-66; sr. vis. fellow dept. physics U. Surrey, Guildford, Eng., 1973; summer cons. Electric Power Research Inst., Palo Alto, Calif., 1974; cons. in field. Author: Radiation Detection and Measurement, 1979, 3d edit., 2000, Principles of Engineering, 1982; editor-in-chief IEEE/Nuclear and Plasma Scis. Soc., 1995-99; editor Nuclear Instns. and Methods in Physics Rsch., 1995—. Recipient excellence in rsch. award Coll. Engring., U. Mich., 1984, Atwood award, 2000, Ann. Merit award IEEE/NPSS, 1996, Millennium medal, 2000; Fulbright travel grantee, 1965-66; NSF fellow, 1958-60, Sci. Rsch. Coun. sr. fellow, 1973; vis. fellow Japan Soc. Promotion of Sci., 1987. Fellow IEEE, Am. Inst. Med. and Biol. Engring., Am. Nuclear Soc. (bd. dirs. 1989-91, Arthur Holly Compton award 1991); mem. Am. Soc. Engring. Edn. (Glenn Murphy award 1979), Nat. Acad. Engring., Sigma Xi, Tau Beta Pi. Achievements include patents in field. Office: U Mich Dept Nuclear Engring 121 Cooley Bldg Ann Arbor MI 48109 E-mail: gknoll@umich.edu.

KNOLLENBERG, JOSEPH (JOE KNOLLENBERG), congressman; b. Ill., 1934; m. Sandie Knollenberg; children: Martin, Stephen. Student, Eastern Ill. U. CLU. Agent, owner ins. co., 1960-93; mem. 103d-106th Congresses from 11th Mich. Dist., 1993—, mem. budget com. appropriations, mem. stds. of offcl. conduct coms. Past chmn., Birmingham Cable TV Community Adv. Bd., 18th Dist. Rep. Com., Rep. Com. Oakland County, 1978-86; past pres. St. Bede's Parish Coun., Evergreen Sch. PTA (Birmingham Sch. Dist.), Bloomfield Glens Homeowner's Assn., Cranbrook Homeowner's Assn.; past coord. Southfield Ad Hoc Park and Recreation Devel. Com.; past mem. Southfield Mayor's Wage and Salary Com.; chmn. Candidate Assistance Com./State Com., Oakland County Campaign, 1978; former regional/vice chair 17th Dist. Com., 1975-77; mem. Rep. State Com; exec. com. mem. and fin. com. Rep. Com. Oakland County; founder, mem. Rep. Leadership Com. Oakland County, 1984—; mem. Allstate Ins. Co's P.A.C.; del. Rep. Nat. Conv., 1980; del. to every state convention since 1974. Named chmn. of one of the top twenty-five counties in the country by Rep. Nat. Com. Mem. Am. Soc. Chartered Life Underwriters, Detroit Assn. Life Underwriters, Oakland County Lincoln Rep. Club, Troy C. of C. (current vice chmn.). Office: US Ho Reps 2349 Rayburn HOB Washington DC 20515-2211*

KNOPMAN, DAVID S. neurologist; b. Phila., Oct. 6, 1950; AB, Dartmouth Coll., 1972; MD, U. Minn., 1975. Diplomate Am. Bd. Psychiatry & Neurology. Intern Hennepin County Med. Ctr., 1975-76; resident U. Minn., 1976-79, asst. prof. neurology, 1980-86, assoc. prof. neurology, 1986-98, prof., 1998—2002; sr. assoc. cons. dept. neurology Mayo Clin., Rochester , 2002—. Prof. Mayo Med. Sch., Rochester, Minn., 2002—. Office: Mayo Clinic Dept Neurology Rochester MN 55905

KNORR, JOHN CHRISTIAN, entertainment executive, bandleader, producer; b. Crissey, Ohio, May 24, 1921; s. Reinhold Alfred and Mary (Rieth) K.; m. Jane Lucy Hammer, Nov. 8, 1941; children: Gerald William, Janice Grace Knorr Wilcox. Student, Ohio No. U., 1940-41. Violin soloist with Helen O'Connell, 1934-35; reed sideman Jimmy Dorsey, Les Brown and Sonny Dunham orchs., 1939-48; mem. theater pit orchs. and club shows, Ohio, 1949-57; leader Johnny Knorr Orch., Toledo, 1958—. Mgr. Centennial Ter.; owner Johnny Knorr Entertainment Agy.; bandleader, show producer; mem. Royal Ct. of Jesters #21, 1987. Recs. include Live at Franklin Park Mall, 1973, Let's Go Dancing, 1979, encore, 1984, (TV spl.) An Era of Swing, 1973, Live at Centennial Terrace, 1986, Let's Dance, 1989, Oh Johnny, 1997, One More Time, 2000. Trustee Presbyn. Ch. Served to cpl. AUS, 1944-45. Recipient outstanding dance band citations, Chgo., 1966, Des Moines, 1968, Las Vegas, 1969, Nat. Ballroom Operators Assn., Omaha, 1970, Entertainment Operators Assn., 1973; named Grand Duke of Toledo, King of the Hoboes, 1975; named to First Libbey H.S. Hall of Fame, 1994; winner in instrumental category Peoples Choice Awards for Performing Arts, 1997; inducted into Lake Erie West People's Choice Awards Hall of Fame, 1999. Mem. Am. Fedn. Musicians, Am. Legion, Exch. Club, Circus Fans Am., Masons, Shriners, Ind. Order Foresters. Home and Office: 1751 Fallbrook Rd Toledo OH 43614-3251

KNOTE, JOHN A. diagnostic radiologist; b. Marion, Ind., Aug. 4, 1938; m. Jan Knote; 3 children. MD, Ind. U., 1964. Diplomate Am. Bd. Nuclear Medicine, Am. Bd. Radiology. Intern Bapt. Meml. Hosp., Memphis, 1964-65; resident in radiology Ind. U., Indpls., 1965-68; diagnostic radiologist Arnett Clinic, Lafayeete, Ind.; dir. dept. radiology Purdue U. Student Hosp.; dir. radiology Lafayette Home Hosp., White County Meml. Hosp. Bd. dirs. YMCA, Boys Club; charter mem. Home Hosp. Found. Bd. Dirs. Fellow Am. Coll. Radiology (budget and fin. com., steering com., spkr. coun.), Am. Coll. of Nuclear Medicine; mem. AMA (vice spkr. ho. of dels. 1999, mem. coun. on med. svcs., chmn. subcom. on health care reform/fin., subcom. on managed care, del. from Ind.), Orgn. of State Med. Assn. Pres. (past pres.), Forum for Med. Affairs (past pres.), Ind. State Med. Assn. (trustee, chmn. bd., chmn. commn. on legislation, mem. future planning com.), Lafayette C. of C. (fed. govt. task force), Ind. Trotting and Pacing Horse Assn. (past pres.), Ind. Roentgen Soc. (past pres., Gold medal 1997). Office: AMA 515 N State St Chicago IL 60610-4325

KNOTT, JOHN RAY, JR. language professional, educator; b. Memphis, July 9, 1937; s. John Ray and Wilma (Henshaw) K.; m. Anne Percy, Dec. 5, 1959; children: Catherine, Ellen, Walker, Anne. A.B., Yale U., 1959, Carnegie fellow, 1960; Ph.D., Harvard U., 1965. Instr. Harvard U., 1965-67; mem. faculty U. Mich., Ann Arbor, 1967—, prof. English, 1976—, chmn. dept., 1982-87, assoc. dean Coll. Arts and Scis., 1977-80, acting dean Coll. Arts and Scis., 1980-81, interim dir. Inst. for Humanities, 1987-88, interim dir. Program in the Environment, 2001—02. Dir. region IV Mellon Fellowship Selection Com., 1989-94, interim dir. Program in the Environment, 2001-02. Author: Milton's Pastoral Vision, 1971, The Sword of the Spirit, 1980, Discourses of Martyrdom in English Literature, 1563-1694, 1993, Imagining Wild America, 2002; editor: The Triumph of Style, 1967, Mirrors: An Introduction to Literature, rev. edit., 1987, The Huron River: Voices From the Watershed, 2000, Reimagining Place, 2001, Imagining Wild America, 2002; contbr. articles on Abbey, Berry, Browne, Bunyan, Fox, Foxe, Milton, and Spenser to scholarly jours. Woodrow Wilson fellow, 1960-61; NEH fellow, 1974 Mem. MLA, Milton Soc., Renaissance Soc. Am., Sierra Club. Office: Univ Mich Dept English Ann Arbor MI 48109

KNOTTS, FRANK BARRY, physician, surgeon; b. St. Louis, Jan. 27, 1948; s. Frank Louis and Anna Lee (Amerman) K.; m. Wendy Diane Lautz Horton (div.); children: Ryan Matthew, Kara Luan; m. Denise Marie Stern, Aug. 26, 1984. BA in Physics, Johns Hopkins U., 1969; PhD in Molecular Biology, UCLA, 1974, MD, 1975. Diplomate Am. Bd. Surgery with subspecialties in gen. surgery and surg. crit. care. Mem. Rotary. Avocations: flying, scuba, skiing, software devel. Home: 26029 Edinborough Cir Perrysburg OH 43551-9545 Office: St Vincent Mercy Med Ctr 2409 Cherry St MOB 303 Toledo OH 43608

KNOUS, PAMELA K. wholesale distribution executive; Student, Carleton Coll.; Degree in Math., Bus. Adminstrn., Acctg., U. Ariz. Ptnr. KPMG Peat Marwick, L.A.; exec. v.p., CFO, treas. The Vons Cos., Inc., 1991; exec. v.p., CFO Supervalu Inc., Mpls. Office: Supervalu Inc 11840 Valley View Rd Eden Prairie MN 55344

KNOWLES, RICHARD ALAN JOHN, English language educator; b. Southbridge, Mass., May 17, 1935; s. Clarence Fay and Mildred Elizabeth (Branniff) K.; m. Jane Marie Boyle, Sept. 1, 1958; children: Jonathan Edwards, Katherine Mary. BA magna cum laude, Tufts U., 1956; MA, U. Pa., 1958, PhD, 1963. Physics asst. Tufts U., Medford, Mass., 1954-56; asst. instr. English U. Pa., Phila., 1956-60; from asst. prof. to prof. U. Wis., Madison, 1962-90, Dickson-Bascom prof. humanities, 1990—. Vis. lectr. U. Pa., 1967, George Washington U., Am. U., 1969, Cath. U., Washington, 1985; manuscript reader various univs., 1965—; cons. Am. Players Theater, Spring Green, Wis., 1980-83; poetry judge Brittingham Poetry Prize, Madison, 1986—, NEH referee, panelist, Washington, 1988—. Author: (with others) Shakespeare Variorum Handbook, 1971; editor: (with others) English Renaissance Drama, 1978; editor: New Variorum As You Like It, 1977; co-editor New Variorum Shakespeare, 1978—; mem. editl. bd. Shakespeare Notes, 1996—. Officer, producer Madison Savoyards, Wis., 1978—; pres. Friends U. Wis. Librs., Madison, 1982-84. Folger Libr. fellow, Washington, 1968, Guggenheim fellow, N.Y., 1976-77; NEH fellow 1983-87; Rsch. fellow Humanities Rsch. Inst., Madison, 1990. Mem. MLA, Shakespeare Assn. Am., Internat. Assn. Univ. Profs. English, Assn. Lit. Critics and Scholars, Nakoma Country Club. Democrat. Avocations: theater, chamber music, opera, gardening, carpentry. Home: 2226 Commonwealth Ave Madison WI 53705-5302 Office: U Wis Dept English 600 N Park St Madison WI 53706-1403 E-mail: rknowles@facstaff.wisc.edu.

KNOX, DOUGLASS RICHARD, publishing executive; b. Springfield, Mass., Nov. 13, 1951; s. Richard Arnold and Marjory (Hazel) K.; m. Cheryl R. Ford; children: Sara, Stephen. BS, No. Ill. U., 1973, MBA, 1976. Salesman Tyndale House Pubs., Carol Stream, Ill., asst. dir. mktg., dir. mktg., v.p. mktg. and sales. Chmn. CBA/Exhibitors Assn., Colorado Springs, Colo., 1987—. Mem. Am. Mktg. Assn. (exec.).

KNOX, JAMES EDWIN, lawyer; b. Evanston, Ill., July 2, 1937; s. James Edwin and Marjorie Eleanor (Williams) K.; m. Rita Lucille Torres, June 30, 1973; children: James Edwin III, Kirsten M., Katherine E., Miranda G. BA in Polit. Sci., State U. Iowa, 1959; JD, Drake U., 1961. Bar: Iowa 1961, Ill. 1962, Tex. 1982. Law clk. to Justice Tom C. Clark, U.S. Supreme Ct., Washington, 1961-62; assoc., then ptnr. Isham, Lincoln & Beale, Chgo., 1962-70; v.p. law N.W. Industries, Inc., 1970-80; exec. v.p., gen. counsel Lone Star Steel Co., Dallas, 1980-86; sr. v.p. law Anixter Internat. Inc., Chgo., 1986—. Instr. contracts and labor law Chgo. Kent Coll. Law, 1964—69; arbitrator Nat. Ry. Adjustment Bd., 1967—68; ptnr. Mayer, Brown & Platt, Chgo., 1992—96; gen. counsel Arris Group, Inc., 1996—. Mem. ABA, Ill. Bar Assn., Order of Coif, Phi Beta Kappa. Office: Anixter Internat Inc 676 N Michigan Ave Ste 2800 Chicago IL 60611-2861 E-mail: jeknoxie@aol.com.

KNOX, LANCE LETHBRIDGE, venture capital executive; b. Hartford, Conn., Sept. 25, 1944; s. Robert Chester and Leonice Katherine (Merrels) K.; children: Michele Merrels, Elizabeth McVarish; m. Mary E. Lambert, 1981. BA, Williams Coll., 1966; MBA, NYU, 1970. Asst. cashier Citibank, N.C., N.Y.C., 1968-70, asst. v.p., 1970-72, v.p., 1972-74, sr. credit officer, 1973-74; v.p. fin. GATX Corp., Chgo., 1974-77; pvt. investor venture capital, 1978—. Pres. Bistrot Zinc, Chgo. Bd. dirs. Better Govt. Assn.; trustee Kingswood-Oxford Sch., West Hartford.

KNOX, WILLIAM ARTHUR, judge; b. Fargo, N.D., Jan. 8, 1945; BS, N.D. State U., 1966; JD, U. Minn., 1968. Law specialist USCG, Boston and Juneau, Alaska, 1968-72; prof. U. Mo. Sch. Law, Columbia, 1972-85; magistrate judge U.S. Cts., Jefferson City, Mo., 1985—. Author: (books) Federal Criminal Forms, 1993, Missouri Criminal Practice, 1995. Office: 131 W High St Jefferson City MO 65101-1557

KNOX, WILLIAM DAVID, publishing company executive; b. Sault Ste. Marie, Mich., June 9, 1920; s. Victor A. and Bertha V. (Byers) K.; m. Jane Edith Shaw, June 15, 1941; children: Georgia Knox Mode, William David II, Randall S., Brian V. BS, Mich. State U., 1941; postgrad., Harvard U., 1943-44; LLD (hon.), U. Wis., 1973. Youth editor Hoard's Dairyman mag., W.D. Hoard & Sons Co., Fort Atkinson, Wis., 1941-42, asso. editor, 1946-49, editor, 1949—, pres., treas., gen. mgr., 1972—. Pres. Nat. Brucellosis Com., 1955-66, chmn. Wis. com., 1951-60; mem. nat. agrl. adv. com., 1961-62, nat. adv. com. on trade negotiations, 1976-82; bd. dirs. First Am. Bank and Trust, D.C.I. Mktg., Inc. Pres. Fort Atkinson Bd. Edn., 1948-59; bd. visitors U. Wis., 1979-84; trustee Univ. Rsch. Park, Inc., 1984-93; bd. dirs. Wis. Taxpayers Alliance, 1976-98. Lt. USNR, 1942-46. Recipient Disting. Svc. award Nat. Brucellosis Com., 1957, Pure Milk Assn., 1966, Am. Dairy Sci. Assn., 1970, Wis. Farm Bur. Fedn., 1974, Nat. Assn. Animal Breeders, 1981, Nat. Assn. Livestock Records, 1983, Wis. Agri-Bus. Coun., 1992, Nat. Agri-Mktg. Assn., 1992, Outstandin ANR Patriarch award Alumni assn. Coll. of Agr. and Natural Resources, Mich. State U., 1992; service citations Fla. Dairy Farmers Fedn., 1962, Wis. Farm Bur. Fedn., 1956, Nat. Plant Food Coun., 1963, Dairy Coun. Ctrl. Ga., 1967, Mid-Am. Dairymen Salute award, 1977, Nat. 4-H Alumni award, 1965, Mich. State U. Disting. Alumnus award, 1966; named Tri-State Man of Yr., 1966, Milw. Milk Prodrs. Assn. Man of Yr., 1976. Fellow Am. Dairy Sci. Assn.; mem. Agrl. Publs. Assn. (pres. 1979-81), Am. Newspaper Pubs. Assn., Am. Vet. Med. Assn. (hon.), Am. Jersey Cattle Club (hon.), Am. Agrl. Econs. Assn., Wis. Vet. Med. Assn. (hon.), Rotary (Internat. Svc. citation 1956), Alpha Gamma Rho, Alpha Zeta (Centennial Honor Roll award 1997). Republican. Episcopalian. Home: 703 Robert St Fort Atkinson WI 53538-1150 Office: Hoard's Dairyman W D Hoard & Sons Co PO Box 801 Fort Atkinson WI 53538-0801

KNUE, PAUL FREDERICK, newspaper editor; b. Lawrenceburg, Ind., July 11, 1947; s. Paul F. and Neil (Beadel) K.; m. Elizabeth Wegner, Sept. 6, 1969; children: Amy, Katherine BS in Journalism and English, Murray State U., 1969. Mng. editor Evansville Press, Ind., 1975-79; editor Ky. Post, Covington, 1979-83, Cin. Post., 1983—. Trustee Scripps Howard Found. Mem. Am. Soc. Newspaper Editors, AP Mng. Editors Assn., AP Soc. Ohio (trustee). Office: E W Scripps Co 125 E Court St Cincinnati OH 45202-1212 Home: 7 White Water Way Milford OH 45150-5813

KNUTH, RUSS, histologist, radio personality; Grad. Atmospheric Scis., St. Cloud State U. With Digital Cyclone; meteorologist Sta. WCCO-Radio, Mpls. Office: WCCO 625 2nd Ave S Minneapolis MN 55402*

KNUTSEN, ALAN PAUL, pediatrician, allergist, immunologist; b. Mpls., July 21, 1948; s. Donald Richard and Shirley Marie (Erickson) K.; children: Laura Joelle, Brian A., Benjamin C., Elizabeth G., Katherine M., Amy S. BA, U. Calif., Riverside, 1971; MD, St. Louis U., 1975. Resident pediatrics St. Louis U. Med. Ctr., 1975-78; fellow allergy Duke U. Med. Ctr., Durham, N.C., 1978-80;, 1980-93; dir. dept. allergy and immunology St. Louis U. Med. Ctr., 1985—; prof. St. Louis U., 1993—, 1993—. Mem. credentials com. St. Louis U. Med. Ctr., 1980—, infectious disease com., 1980—; dir. diagnostic pediatric immunology lab, 1983—; cons. NIOSH, 1984. Contbr. articles to profl. jours. Mem. Am. Acad. Allergy/Immunology, Southwestern Allergy Assn., Clin. Immunology Soc., Mo. State Allergy Assn., So. Pediatric Rsch., Phi Beta Kappa, Alpha Omega Alpha. Democrat. Presbyterian. Home: 10 Orchard Way Saint Louis MO 63122-6920 Office: St Louis U Pediatric Rsch Inst 1465 S Grand Blvd Saint Louis MO 63104-1003 E-mail: knutsenm@slu.edu.

KNUTSON, DAVID LEE, state legislator, lawyer; b. Mpls., Nov. 24, 1959; s. Howard Arthur and Jerroldine Margo (Sundby) K.; m. Laurie Sjoquist, June 25, 1983; children: Ann Marie, Timothy David. BA, St. Olaf Coll., 1982; JD, William Mitchell Coll. Law, 1986. Bar: Minn. 1986, U.S. Dist. Ct. Minn. 1986, U.S. Ct. Appeals (8th cir.) 1987, U.S. Tax Ct. 1989. Pvt. practice, Burnsville, Minn., 1986—; mem. Minn. State Senate Dist. 36, 1993—, asst. minority leader, 1995—. Bd. dirs. Our Saviour's Shelter for Homeless, Mpls., 1988-90, City Task Force on Arts, Burnsville, 1988, Legal Assistance Dakota County, Ltd., 1994—, Dakota County Tech. Coll.

Found., 1994—; bd. dirs. Minn. Valley YMCA, 1988-2000, chmn., 1991-93, 99-00. Named one of Ten Outstanding Young Minnesotans, Minn. Jaycees, 1993; recipient Lake Conf. Disting. Alumni award, 1996, Pro Bono Publico award Legal Svcs. Coalition, 1998, YMCA Disting. Vol. award, 1999, Outstanding Achievement award Burnsville H.S., 2001. Mem. Minn. Bar Assn., Dakota County Bar Assn., Burnsville Jaycees (bd. dirs. 1988-90), Apple Valley C. of C., Burnsville C. of C. (bd. dirs. 1990-92), Burnsville Breakfast Rotary. Republican. Avocation: reading, travel, sports. Office: Severson Sheldon Dougherty & Molenda PA Ste 600 7300 W 147th St Apple Valley MN 55124 E-mail: knutsond@seversonsheldon.com.

KO, WEN-HSIUNG, electrical engineering educator; b. Shang-Hong, Fukien, China, Apr. 12, 1923; came to U.S., 1954, naturalized, 1963; s. Sing-Ming and Sou-Yu (Kao) K.; m. Christina Chen, Oct. 12, 1957; children: Kathleen, Janet, Linda, Alexander. BSEE, Nat. Amoy U., Fukien, China, 1946; MS, Case Inst. Tech., 1956, PhD, 1959. Engr., then sr. engr. Taiwan Telecommunication Adminstrn., 1946-54; mem. faculty Case Inst. Tech., Cleve., 1956-93; prof. elec. and biomed. engring. Case Western Res. U., 1967-93, prof. emeritus, 1994—, dir. engring. design center, 1970-82; pres., prin. Wen H. Ko & Assocs., 1996—. Cons. NSF, N.Am. Mfg. Co., NIH, 1966-82; pres. Transducer Rsch. Found., 1986—; rschr. in med. implant electronics, telemetry and stimulation, microsensors and microactuators, micro-electro-mech.-sys. Recipient career achievement award Transducer Internat. Conf., Chgo., 1997. Fellow IEEE, AIMBE; mem. Instrument Soc. Am., Bio-Med. Engring. Soc., Sigma Xi, Eta Kappa Nu. Home: 1356 Forest Hills Blvd Cleveland OH 44118-1359 Office: Case Western Res U Electronics Design Ctr Cleveland OH 44106

KOBS, JAMES FRED, advertising agency executive; b. Chgo., June 27, 1938; s. Fred Charles and Ann (Ganser) K.; m. Nadine Schumacher, May 18, 1963; children: Karen, Kathleen, Kenneth. B.S. in Journalism, U. Ill., 1960. Copywriter Rylander Co., Chgo., 1960-62; mng. dir. Success Mag., 1963-65; mail order mgr. Am. Peoples Press, Westmont, Ill., 1966-67; exec. v.p. Stone & Adler Advt., Chgo., 1967-78; chmn. Kobs & Brady Advt., Inc. (now Draft Direct Worldwide), 1978-88; vice chmn. Kobs & Brady Advt., Inc. (now Draft Worldwide), 1988; chmn. Kobs Gregory & Passavant, 1989—. Guest lectr. U. Wis., U. Ill., NYU; adj. prof. direct mktg. Northwestern U. Medill Sch. Journalism Grad. Program; internat. lectr. in field. Author: Profitable Direct Marketing, 2d edit., 1991, 24 Ways to Improve Your Direct Mail Results, 99 Proven Direct Response Offers; contbr. articles to periodicals. Vice-chmn. Direct Mktg. Ednl. Found. Recipient numerous local and nat. advt. awards; named to Direct Mktg. Hall of Fame. Mem. Direct Mktg. Assn. (dir., sec., mem. exec. com., recipient Silver and Gold Mailbox, Gold Medallion, Gold Echo, Ed Mayer award), Chgo. Assn. Direct Mktg. (past pres., Direct Marketer of Yr.), Boys and Girls Clubs of Chgo. (corp. bd.), Alpha Delta Sigma. Office: Kobs Gregory Passavant 205 N Michigan Ave Chicago IL 60601-5927

KOCH, CHARLES DE GANAHL, manufacturing executive; b. Wichita, Kans., Nov. 1, 1935; s. Fred Chase and Mary Clementine (Robinson) K. B.S. in Gen. Engring, MIT, 1957, M.S. in Mech. Engring., 1958, M.S. in Chem. Engring., 1959. Engr. Arthur D. Little, Inc., Cambridge, Mass., 1959-61; v.p. Koch Engring. Co., Inc., Wichita, 1961-63, pres., 63-71, chmn., 1967-78; pres. Koch Industries, Inc., 1966-74, chmn., CEO, 1967—. Bd. dirs. Intrust Bank, N.A. Chmn. Inst. Humane Studies Mercatus Ctr. Mem.: Mt. Pelerin Soc., The Vintage Club, Wichita Country Club. Office: Koch Industries PO Box 2256 4111 E 37th St N Wichita KS 67220-3298

KOCH, CHARLES JOHN, credit agency executive; Pres., COO, CEO Charter One Bank FSB, 1976—; pres. Charter One Fin. Inc., Cleve., First Fed. Savings Ball. Office: Charter One Fin Inc 1215 Superior Ave E Cleveland OH 44114-3249

KOCH, DAVID VICTOR, librarian, administrator; b. Highland, Ill., Feb. 19, 1937; s. Victor Hugo and Eunice Louise (Matter) K.; m. Noel Janet Wyandt, July 15, 1959 (div. 1968); 1 child, John David; m. Carolyn Melvin, Mar. 21, 1970 (div. 1979); 1 child, Victor Louis; m. Loretta Marie Peterson, Aug. 25, 1979; 1 child, Elizabeth Louise. BA in Lit., DePauw U., 1959; MA in English and Modern Lit., So. Ill. U., 1963, postgrad., U. Cin. Reporter, columnist Dayton (Ohio) Jour. Herald newspaper, 1959-61; instr. dept. English Wright State U., Dayton, 1964-69; asst. rare books libr. Morris Libr., So. Ill. U., Carbondale, 1961-64, rare books libr., 1970-80, curator spl. collections, univ. archivist, 1980-91, dir. spl. collections and devel., 1991-96, assoc. dean spl. collections and devel. svcs., 1997—. Mem. Midwest Archives Conf., 1980—; mem. Conf. of Editors of Learned Jours., 1974—; mem. univ. acad./student affairs com. So. Ill. U., Carbondale, 1984-86, univ. rsch. com., 1980-82, 97—, libr. affairs mgmt. com., 1991—, libr. affairs exec. com., 1991—, univ. libr. of the future com., 1992—; mem. adv. bd. Ill. State Archives, 1997—, Ill. State Hist. Records, 1997-99, internal rev. com., Internat. Edn. Assn., 1999—. Editor: (with Joseph Katz and Dick Allen) The Mad River Review, 1965-68, (with Alan Cohn and Kenneth Duckett) ICarbS; contbr. articles to profl. jours. Home: 2800 W Sunset Dr Carbondale IL 62901-2046 Office: So Ill U Spl Collections Morris Libr Carbondale IL 62901-6632

KOCH, DONALD LEROY, geologist, state agency administrator; b. Dubuque, Iowa, June 3, 1937; s. Gregory John and Josephine Elizabeth (Young) K.; m. Celia Jean Swede, July 5, 1962; children: Kyle Benjamin, Amy Suzanne, Nathan Gregory. BS, U. Iowa, 1959, MS in Geology, 1967, postgrad., 1971-73. Research geologist Iowa Geol. Survey, Iowa City, 1959-71, chief subsurface geology, 1971-75, asst. state geologist, 1975-80, state geologist and dir., 1980-86; state geologist and bur. chief Geol. Survey Bur., 1986. Contbr. articles to profl. jours. Fellow Iowa Acad. Sci. (bd. dirs. 1986-89); mem. Geol. Soc. Iowa (pres. 1969), Iowa Groundwater Assn. (pres. 1986), Sigma Xi. Lodge: Rotary. Avocations: bicycling, camping, chess, numismatics. Home: 1431 Prairie Du Chien Rd Iowa City IA 52245-5615 Office: Geol Survey Bur 109 Trowbridge Hall Iowa City IA 52242-1319 E-mail: don.koch@dnr.state.ia.us.

KOCH, LORETTA PETERSON, librarian, educator; b. Anna, Ill., Mar. 5, 1951; d. Vance G. and Dorothy M. (Cline) Peterson; m. David Victor Koch, Aug. 25, 1979; 1 child, Elizabeth; stepchildren: John, Victor. AB in English with high honors, U. Ill., 1973, MS in LS, 1974; postgrad., So. Ill. U., Carbondale, 1976. Adult svcs. libr. Carbondale Pub. Libr., 1974-81; owner, operator L. Koch-Words, editing and word processing, Carbondale, 1981-85; rsch. asst. So. Ill. U., 1973, asst. humanities libr., 1985-86, libr. tech. asst. III humanities div., 1986-89, asst. humanities libr., 1989-92, acting humanities libr., 1992-93, humanities libr., 1993—, asst. prof. libr. affairs, 1989-95, assoc. prof. libr. affairs, 1995—, mem. faculty exec. bd., 1989-91. Participant confs. and workshops; presenter in field; field reader grant proposals Ill. Coop. Collection Mgmt. Coordinating Com., 1993. Contbr. articles to profl. publs. Divsn. coord. fund drive United Way, 1989, 90; room parent Lakeland Sch., 1993-94, Parrish Sch., 1994-95, 95-96, 96-97, Thomas Sch., 1998-99, 99-2000; asst. leader troop 813, Girl Scouts U.S.A., 1993-94. Mem. ALA (chmn. poster session abstracts booklet com. 1993-94), Assn. of Coll. and Rsch. Libr. (comm. com. women's studies sect. 1993-95), Libr. Adminstrn. and Mgmt. Assn. (using stats. for libr. evaluation com.), Reference and adult svcs. divsn. Ill. Libr. Assn. (nominations com. resources and tech. svcs. forum 1993-94), Margaret Atwood Soc., Midwest Assn. for Can. Studies, Assn. for Can. Studies in U.S., Beta Phi Mu. Home: 2800 W Sunset Dr Carbondale IL 62901-2046 Office: So Ill U Humanities Div Morris Libr Carbondale IL 62901 E-mail: lkoch@lib.siu.edu.

KOCH, ROBERT LOUIS, II, manufacturing company executive, mechanical engineer; b. Evansville, Ind., Jan. 6, 1939; s. Robert Louis and Mary L. (Bray) K.; m. Cynthia Ross, Oct. 17, 1964; children: David, Kevin, Kristen, Jennifer. BSME, U. Notre Dame, 1960; MBA, U. Pitts., 1962; D of Tech. (hon.), Vincennes U., 1992. Registered profl. engr., Ind. V.p. Ashdee Corp., Evansville, 1962-68, pres., 1968-82; ptnr. Fesk Partnership, 1964—; chmn., CEO Gibbs Die Casting Corp., Henderson, Ky., 1976—; pres., CEO Koch Enterprises, Inc., Evansville, 1982—; chmn., dir. UNISEAL, Inc., 1984—; v.p., dir. Brake Supply Co., 1986—; chmn. bd. Marco Sales, Inc., St. Louis, 1997—. Exec. in residence U. So. Ind., Evansville, 1967; bd. dirs. Fifth-Third Bacnorp, Cincinnati, Ohio, Bindley Western Industries, Indpls., So. Ind. Properties, Inc., Evansville, So. Ind. Minerals, Inc., N.Am. Green, Inc., Audubon Metals LLC, Vectren Corp.; chmn. bd. dirs. Uniseal Rubber Products, Inc., Arnold, Mo., 1988-95. Inventor, patentee water purifier, drying oven, powder coating booth, electro painting system. Contr., dep. mayor City of Evansville, 1976-80; active Gov.'s Fiscal Policy Adv. Com., Indpls., 1978-89, Pres. Adv. Coun. Indiana Univ., 1992—, Purdue U., 1992—, parents exec. com., West Lafayette, 1985-88, sch. bd. nominating com., 1987-89; vice-chmn. bd. trustees U. Evansville, 1985-92, chmn. bd. trustees, 1993-96; pres. Signature Learning Ctr. Inc., Evansville, 1994—; vice-chmn. bd. trustees Evansville Mus. Arts and Scis., 1982-92; bd. dirs. SW Ind. Pub. Broadcasting, 1985-89, Pub. Edn. Found., Evansville, 1986-88, Hoosiers for Higher Edn., 1991-98, Commit, Inc., Cmty. Alliance Found., 1991—, Ind. Colls. Ind., 1992—, Found. for Ind. Higher Edn., 1996—, Project E, 2000; treas. Vanderburgh County Rep. Com., Evansville, 1984-88; pres. Cath. Edn. Found., Evansville, 1978-82; chmn. Ind. Econ. Devel. Coun., 1991-92, Ind. Humanities Coun. Bus. Forum, 1999, United Way of Southwestern Ind. Campaign, 1998; co-chmn. Ind. Bus. Higher Edn. Forum, 1991-96; pres. Cath. Found. Southwestern Ind., 1992—; v.p. Ind. Acad., Indpls., 1999--; pres. Evansville Regional Bus. Com., 2002--. 1st lt. USAR, 1961-67. Recipient Challenger award Nat. Assn. Woodworking Machinery Mfrs., Louisville, 1980, Boy Scout's Disting. Citizen's award, 1991, Rotary Club Citizenship award, 1991, Sagamore of the Wabash, 1999; named Exec. of Yr. Profl. Secs. Assn., 1984, Knight of the Order of the Holy Sepulchre, 1996, Entrepreneur of Yr., Ind. Mfg., 1998. Mem. Metro Evansville C. of C. (bd. dirs. Met. 1983-96, named Bus. Person of Yr. 1998), Ind. C. of C. (bd. dirs., chmn. 1991—), Young Pres. Orgn., World Pres. Orgn., Evansville Country Club, Victoria Nat. Golf Club. Avocations: golf, tennis, snow skiing. Office: Koch Enterprises Inc 10 S 11th Ave Evansville IN 47744-0001

KOCHAR, MAHENDR SINGH, physician, educator, administrator, scientist, writer, consultant; b. Jabalpur, India, Nov. 30, 1943; arrived in U.S., 1967, naturalized, 1978; s. Harnam Singh and Chanan Kaur (Khaturia) K.; m. Arvind Kaur, 1968; children: Baltej (Baj), Ajay (Jay). MB, BS, All India Inst. Med. Scis., New Delhi, 1965; MSc, Med. Coll. Wis., 1972; MBA, U. Wis., Milw., 1987. Diplomate Am. Bd. Internal Medicine, Nephrology and Geriat., Am. Bd. Family Practice, Am. Bd. Mgmt., Am. Bd. Clin. Pharmacology. Intern All India Inst. Med. Scis. Hosp., New Delhi, 1966-67, Passaic (N.J.) Gen. Hosp., 1967-68; resident in medicine Allegheny Gen. Hosp., Pitts., 1968-70; fellow in clin. pharmacology Milw. VA Med. Ctr., 1970-71, attending physician, 1973; fellow in nephrology and hypertension Milw. County Gen. Hosp., 1971-73, attending physician, 1973-95, St. Michael Hosp., Milw., 1974—, dir. hemodialysis unit, 1975-80; clin. asst. prof. medicine and pharmacology and toxicology Med. Coll. Wis., 1973-75, asst. prof., 1975-78, assoc. prof., 1978-84, prof., 1984—, assoc. dean continuing med. edn., 1985-86, assoc. dean grad. med. edn., 1987-99, sr. assoc. dean acad. affairs, 1994-95, sr. assoc. dean grad. med. edn., 1999—. Attending physician St. Joseph's Hosp., Milw., 1975—; chmn. medicine Northpoint Med. Group, Milw., 1974-75; dir. Milw. Blood Pressure Program, 1975-78; dir. Hypertension Clinic, Milwaukee County Downtown Med. and Health Services, 1975-79; chief hypertension. VA Med. Ctr., Milw., 1978-2000, assoc. chief staff for edn., 1979-2000; exec. dir. Med. Coll. Wis. Affiliated Hosps. Inc., Milw., 1987—. Author: Hypertension Control, 1978, 2nd rev. edit., 1985; editor: Textbook of General Medicine, 1983, Concise Textbook of Medicine, 2d edit., 1990, 3d edit., 1998. Recipient Grad. of Last Decade award U. Wis., Milw., 1998. Fellow ACP/Am. Soc. Internal Medicine (pres., gov. Wis. chpt. 1994-98, mem. bd. regents 1997—, chmn. bd. govs. 1998-99, Laureate award 2000, Key Contact award 2001), Am. Coll. Cardiology (gov. Am. Coll. Cardiology dept. vets. affair, 1999-2000), Am. Acad. Family Physicians, Royal Coll. Physicians Can., Am. Coll. Clin. Pharmacology, Am. Heart Assn. (high blood pressure coun.), Royal Coll. Physicians (London), Am. Coll. Physician Execs.; mem. AMA (alt. del. Wis.), Am. Assn. Physicians from India (pres. Wis. chpt. 1995-97), Am. Fedn. Med. Rsch., Milw. Acad. Medicine (pres. 1996-97, trustee 1997—, pres.'s award 1998), Milw. County Med. Soc. (bd. dirs. 2000-2002, pres.-elect 2002-), Wis. Med. Soc. (alt. del. ho. dels. AMA, Disting. Svc. award 2001), Mensa, Highlander Elite Tennis Club, Univ. Club Milw. Home: 18630 Le Chateau Dr Brookfield WI 53045-4924 Office: Med Coll Wis 8701 Watertown Plank Rd Milwaukee WI 53226 E-mail: kochar@mcw.edu.

KOCHER, JUANITA FAY, retired auditor; b. Falmouth, Ky., Aug. 9, 1933; d. William Birgest and Lula (Gillespie) Vickroy; m. Donald Edward Kocher, Nov. 18, 1953. Grad. high sch., Bright, Ind. Cert. internal auditor and compliance officer. Bookkeeper Mchts. Bank and Trust Co., West Harrison, Ind., 1952-56, teller, asst. cashier, 1962-87, br. mgr., 1979-87, internal auditor, 1987-96, ret., 1996; bookkeeper Progressive Bank, New Orleans, 1956-58; with proof dept. 1st Nat. Bank, Cin., 1958-59, teller Harrison, 1959-62. Bookkeeper Donald E. Kocher Constrn., Harrison, 1981—. Mem. Am. Bankers Assn., Ind. Bankers Assn. Home: 11277 Biddinger Rd Harrison OH 45030

KOCORAS, CHARLES PETROS, federal judge; b. Chgo., Mar. 12, 1938; s. Petros K. and Constantina (Cordonis) K.; m. Grace L. Finlay, Sept. 22, 1968; children: Peter, John, Paul. Student, Wilson Jr. Coll., 1956-58; BS, DePaul U., 1961, JD, 1969. Bar: Ill. 1969. Various positions IRS, Chgo., 1962-69; assoc. Bishop & Crawford, 1969-71; asst. atty. Office of U.S. Atty. U.S. Dist. Ct. (no. dist.) Ill., Chgo., 1971-77, judge, 1980—; chmn. Ill. Commerce Commn., 1977-79; ptnr. Stone, McGuire, Benjamin and Kocoras, 1979-80. Adj. prof. trial practice, evening divsn. John Marshall Law Sch., 1975—. With Army N.G., 1961-67. Mem. Chgo. Bar Assn., Fed. Criminal Jury Instrn. Com. 7th Cir., Beta Alpha Psi. Greek Orthodox. Office: US Courthouse 2588 Dirksen Bldg 219 S Dearborn St Chicago IL 60604-1702

KOEBEL, SISTER CELESTIA, health care system executive; b. Chillicothe, Ohio, Jan. 12, 1928; BS, Coll. of Mount St. Joseph, 1958; MHA, St. Louis U., 1964; D, U. Albuquerque, 1976. Asst. dir. nursing svcs. Good Samaritan Hosp. & Health Ctr., Dayton, Ohio, 1961-62; adminstrv. resident Providence Med. Ctr., Seattle, 1963-64; pres. St. Joseph Healthcare Corp., Albuquerque, 1964-85, Sisters of Charity Health Care Systems, Cin., 1985-96; hon. offcl. Cath. Health Initiatives, Denver, 1996—. Mem. Am. Hosp. Assn. (adv. coun., 1987-88), N.Mex. Hosp. Assn. (treas. 1968-69, v.p. 1970, pres. 1972). Office: 345 Neeb Rd Cincinnati OH 45233-5102

KOEHLER, JIM, electronics executive; CFO Micro Electronics Inc., Columbus, Ohio. Office: Micro Electronics Inc PO Box 1143 Hilliard OH 43026-6143

KOENEMANN, CARL F. electronics company executive; CFO Motorola, Inc., Schaumburg, Ill., exec. v.p., CFO. Office: Motorola Inc 1303 E Algonquin Rd Schaumburg IL 60196-1079

KOENIG, JACK L. chemist, educator; b. Cody, Nebr., Feb. 12, 1933; s. John and Lucille (Ewart) K.; m. Jeanus Brosz, July 5, 1953; children: John, Robert, Stan, Lori. BS, Yankton Coll., 1955; MS, U. Nebr., 1957, PhD, 1959. Chemist E. I. DuPont, Wilmington, Del., 1959-63; prof. Case Western Res. U., Cleve., 1963—. Program officer NSF, Washington, 1972-74. Author: Chemical Microstructure of Polymer Chains, 1982, Spectroscopy of Polymers, 1992; co-author: Physical Chemistry of Polymers, 1985, Theory of Vibrational Spectroscopy of Polymers, 1987. With U.S. Army, 1953-55. Recipient Disting. Lectr. award BASF, 1990, Internat. Rsch. award Soc. Plastics Engrs., 1991, Disting. Svc. award Cleve. Tech. Socs. Coun., 1991, Pioneer in Polymer Sci. award Polymer New Mag., 1991, ACS award in applied polymer sci. Am. Chem. Soc., 1997. Fellow Am. Physics Soc.; mem. NAE, Am. Chem. Soc. (award in applied polymer sci. 1997), Soc. Applied Spectroscopy. Achievements include research in characterization of polymers by spectroscopic methods. Office: Case Western Res U 10900 Euclid Ave # 7202 Cleveland OH 44106-1712

KOENIG, MICHAEL EDWARD DAVISON, information science educator; b. Rochester, N.Y., Nov. 1, 1941; s. Claremont Judson and Mary Fletcher (Davison) K.; m. Nancy Crane Packard, 1966 (div. 1976); children: Christopher Wells Bowen, Davison Packard; m. Luciana Marulli, Feb. 2, 1980. BA in Psychology, Yale U., 1963; MLS, U. Chgo., 1968, MBA, 1970; PhD in Information Sci., Drexel U., 1982. Info. svcs. mgr. Pfizer, Inc., Groton, Conn., 1970-74; info. ops. dir. Inst. Scientific Info., Phila., 1974-77, devel. dir., 1977-78; v.p. ops. Swets N.Am., Berwyn, Pa., 1978-80; assoc. prof. Columbia U., N.Y.C., 1980-85; v.p. info. mgmt. Tradenet, Inc., 1985-88; prof., dean sch. libr. and info. sci. Dominican U., River Forest, Ill., 1988-96, prof., dean emeritus, 1996-99; dean, prof. Coll. Info. and Computer Sci. Long Island U., Brookville, N.Y., 1999—. Chmn. editl. bd. Third World Librs., 1991-96. Contbr. more than 100 articles to profl. jours. Lt. USNR, 1963-65. Mem. ALA (councilor 1993-97, 2001—), Am. Soc. Info. Sci., Internat. Soc. Scientometrics and Informetrics (pres. 1995-97), Assn. Computing Machinery, Spl. Librs. Assn., Grolier Club, Caxton Club, Elizabethan Club. Home: 16 Buckwalter Farm Ln Phoenixville PA 19460-2317

KOENIGSKNECHT, ROY A. education administrator; b. Fowler, Mich., Dec. 27, 1942; s. Joseph I. and Katherine (Zimmermann) K.; m. Marilie A. Dani, Aug. 20, 1966; children: John, Adam, Amanda. AB in Psychology, Central Mich. U., 1964; MA in Speech and Lang. Pathology, Northwestern U., 1965, PhD in Communicative Disorders, 1968. Head speech and lang. pathology Northwestern U., Evanston, Ill., 1973-78, prof. speech and lang. pathology, 1975-85, chair communicative disorders, 1978-81, assoc. dean Grad. Sch., 1981-85; dean Grad. Sch. Ohio State U., Columbus, 1985-95; v.p. Ohio State U. Rsch. Found., 1985-95. Mem. Grad. Record Exams. Bd., 1991-95, NIH adv. bd. on deafness and other communicative disorders, 1990-95; cons. evaluator Commn. on Instns. Higher Edn., 1996—. Author: Developmental Sentence Analysis, 1974; Interactive Language Development, 1975. Contbr. articles to profl. jours. Mem. adv. coun. on grad. study Ohio Bd. Regents, Columbus, 1985-95; bd. dirs. Friends of Evanston Pub. Libr., 1984, Evanston Pub. Libr., 1985. Recipient Disting. Alumni award Central Mich. U., 1977; Fulbright fellow, 1982. Fellow Am. Speech-Lang. Hearing Assn. (exec. bd. 1986-91, pres. 1990), AAU Assn. Grad. Schs.), Com. on Instnl. Cooperation Grad. Deans (chair 1985-86), Nat. Assn. State U. and Land Grant Colls.- Coun. Rsch. Pol. and Grad. Edn. (exec. com. 1995-96). Avocations: golf; skiing. Home: 720 Gatehouse Ln Columbus OH 43235-1732 Office: Ohio State U 105 Pressey Hall Columbus OH 43210-1335

KOENKER, DIANE P. history educator; b. Chgo., July 29, 1947; m. Roger Koenker; 1 child. AB in History, Grinnell Coll., 1969; AM in Comparative Studies in History, U. Mich., 1971, PhD in History, 1976. From asst. prof. to assoc. prof. in history Temple U., Phila., 1976-83; asst. prof. history U. Ill., Urbana-Champaign, 1983-86, assoc. prof., 1986-88, prof. history, 1988—, dir. Russian and East European Ctr., 1990-96, editor Slavic Rev., 1996—. Vis. lectr. history U. Ill., Urbana-Champaign, 1975; vis. fellow Australian Nat. U., 1989; Fulbright-Hays Faculty Rsch. Abroad, 1993; active Study Group on Russian Revolution, Study Group on Internat. Labor and Working-Class History; lectr. in field. Author: Moscow Workers and the 1917 Revolution, 1981, paperback edit., 1986, (with William G. Rosenberg) Strikes and Revolution in Russia 1917, 1989, editor: Tret'ya Vserossiiskaya Konferentsiya Professional'nykh Soyuzov 1917, 1982, (with William G. Rosenberg and Ronald Grigor Suny) Party, State and Society in the Russian Civil War: Explorations in Social History, 1989, (with Ronald D. Bachman) Revelations from the Russian Archives, 1997; editor, translator: (with S.A. Smith) Notes of a Red Guard, 1993; mem. editl. bd. Cambridge Soviet Paperbacks; mem. adv. bd. Soviet Studies in History, 1986-89; book reviewer to numerous jours.; contbr. articles to profl. jours. Rsch. fellow Temple U., 1977, 82, Sr. fellow Russian Inst.-Columbia U., 1977-78, Individual fellow NEH, 1983-84, Rsch. fellow NEH, 1984-85, 94-95, MUCIA Exch. fellow Moscow State U., 1991; grantee Am. Coun. Learned Socs.-Social Sci. Rsch. Coun., 1977-78, Temple U., 1979-81, 82-83, William and Flora Hewlett Internat. Rsch. grantee, 1986, 91, Nat. Coun. for Soviet and East European Rsch. grantee, 1989, IREX Travel grantee, 1993; recipient Fulbright-Hays Faculty Rsch. award for USSR, 1989, Arnold O. Beckman Rsch. Bd. award, 1990-91, 2002-. Mem. Am. Hist. Assn. (mem. membership com. 1996-98, European History sect. chair 2001), Am. Assn. Advancement Slavic Studies (bd. dirs. 1996—), Midwest Workshop of Russian and Soviet Historians, Assn. Women in Slavic Studies. Office: U Ill Slav Rev 57 E Armory Ave Champaign IL 61820-6601 also: U Ill Dept History 309 Gregory Hall 810 S Wright St Urbana IL 61801-3644

KOEPP, DONNA PAULINE PETERSEN, librarian; b. Clinton, Iowa, Oct. 8, 1941; d. Leo August and Pauline Sena (Outzen) Petersen; m. David Ward Koepp, June 5, 1960 (div. June 1984). BS in Edn., U. Colo., 1967; MA in Libr., U. Denver, 1974; postgrad., U. Colo., 1984-85. Subject specialist govt. publs., map dept. Denver Pub. Libr., 1967-85; head govt. documents, map libr. U. Kans., Lawrence, 1985-2000, map and geomedia svcs. libr., 2000—. Apptd. Fed. Depository Libr. Coun. to Pub. Printer, 1998-2001; head govt. document, microforms, reference instrn. Soc. Sci. Program Harvard U., 2002-. Prodn. mgr. Meridian Jour., 1988-93, 96-99; editor: Index and Carto-Bibliography of Maps, 1789-1969, 1995. Recipient Documents to the People award Congl. Info. Svc./Govt. Documents Round Table/ALA, 1999. Mem. Map & Geography Round Table of Am. Libr. Assn. (chmn. 1986-87, Outstanding Contbn. to Map Librarianship 1991), Govt. Documents Round Table of Am. Libr. Assn., Western Assn. Map Librs. (sec. 1983-84). Office: Govt Documents Microforms Libr Lamont Libr Lower Level U Harvard College Libr Cambridge MA 02138- E-mail: koepp@fas.harvard.edu.

KOEPPEN, RAYMOND BRADLEY, lawyer; b. Valparaiso, Ind., July 9, 1954; s. Raymond Carl August and Thelma Gleda (Moore) K.; m. Debra Gail Ray, Dec. 21, 1985. BS, Ball State U., 1976; MA, Kent (Ohio) State U., 1983; JD, Valparaiso U., 1983. Bar: Ind. 1984, Fla. 1984. Assoc. Sachs & Hess, P.C., Hammond, Ind., 1984-85, Lucas Holcomb Medrea, Merrillville, 1985; city atty. City of Valparaiso, 1985-88; ptnr. Clifford, Clauden, Alexa & Koeppen, Valparaiso, 1988-90, Douglas, Alexa, Koeppen and Hurley, Valparaiso, 1991—. Mem. com. Valparaiso Popcorn Festival, 1985-97; mem. Valparaiso Econ. Devel. Corp., 1986, 87; mem. Valparaiso C. of C.; bd. dirs. Boys and Girls Club of Porter County, 1986—, chmn. bd. dirs., 1995-97. Greek Ministry of Culture and Sci. scholar, 1975; Fulbright scholar U.S. Ednl. Found., 1976. Mem. ABA, Ind. State Bar Assn., Porter County Bar Assn., Fla. Bar Assn., Phi Alpha Theta, Pi Gamma Mu, Beta Theta Pi. Presbyterian. Avocations: golf, basketball, reading, running, community volunteering. Home: 2005 Beulah Vista Blvd Valparaiso IN 46383-2950 Office: Douglas Alexa et al PO Box 209 14 Indiana Ave Valparaiso IN 46383-5634

KOETZLE, GIL, state legislator, fire fighter, professional association administrator; b. Sioux Falls, S.D., May 22, 1952; s. Donald John Sr. and Elizabeth Odilla (Lefebvre) K.; m. Debra Anne Phelps, Aug. 26, 1972; children: Jesse John, Stephanie Michael. Student, N.D. State Sch. Sci., 1970-72. Fire fighter, 1976-82; operator fire apparatus, 1982—; mem. S.D. Senate from 15th dist., Pierre, 1992—. Treas. Fire Fighters Local 814, Sioux Falls, 1980-81, sec., 1981-84, pres., 1984-85; state rep. Internat. Assn. Fire Fighters, 1985—; sec. Profl. Fire Fighters S.D., 1987-93, lobbyist, 1987-92. Ch. commentator and lector Roman Catholic Ch., mem. parish coun., leader parish youth group, head diocese social justice com. Named Outstanding Young Leader, S.d. Jaycees, 1992, Future Leader, Sioux Falls Argus Leader, 1990. Democrat. Avocations: golf, coaching sports, family, politics. Home: 705 N Prairie Ave Sioux Falls SD 57104-2220

KOFF, ROBERT HESS, foundation administrator; b. Chgo., June 5, 1938; s. Arthur Karl and Dorothy (Hess) K. BA, U. Mich., 1961; MA, U. Chgo., 1962, PhD, 1966. Lic. psychologist, Calif. Instr., counselor S. Shankman Orthogenic Sch. U. Chgo., 1961-64; tchr. U. Chgo. Lab. Sch., 1963-64; instr. U. Ill., Champaign, 1964, U. Chgo., 1964-66; vis. scientist, Lab. for Hypnosis Rsch., asst. prof. Stanford (Calif.) U., 1966-72; prof., dean Roosevelt U., Chgo., 1972-79; univ. dean SUNY, Albany, 1979-92; program dir., v.p. Danforth Found., St. Louis, 1992—. Vis. scholar Oxford U., Eng., 1965; chmn. N.Y. State Ednl. Conf. Bd., Albany, 1981-92. Mem. Nat. Adv. Coun. on Edn. of Disadvantaged Children, Washington, 1979-82, Gov.'s Adv. Commn. on Children and Youth, Albany, 1981-92. Mem. APA (com. chmn.), Am. Ednl. Rsch. Assn., Nat. Register Health Svc. Providers in Psychology. Office: 211 N Broadway Saint Louis MO 63102-2733

KOGER, FRANK WILLIAMS, federal judge; b. Kansas City, Mo., Mar. 20, 1930; s. C.H. and Lelia D. (Williams) K.; m. Jeanine E. Strawhacker, Mar. 19, 1954; children: Lelia Jane, Mary Courtney. AB, Kansas City U., 1951, LLB, 1953; LLM, U. Mo., Kansas City, 1966. Staff judge adv. USAF, Rapid City, S.D., 1953-56; ptnr. Reid, Koger & Reid, Kansas City, 1956-61, Shockley, Reid & Koger, Kansas City, 1961-86; U.S. bankruptcy judge U.S. Dept. Judiciary, 1986—; chief judge 8th Cir. Bankruptcy Appellate Panel, 1997—. Adj. prof. law sch. U. Mo., Columbia, 1990—, U. Mo.-Kansas City, 1992—. Author: (manual) Foreclosure Law in Missouri, 1982, Missouri Collection Law, 1983; author, co-editor: Bankruptcy Handbook, 1992; editor: Bankruptcy Law, 1990. Bd. dirs. Jackson County Pub. Hosp., Kansas City, 1974-79, St. Lukes Hosp., Kansas City, 1970—; chair subcom. Jackson County Charter Transition Com., Kansas City, 1978-79. Capt. USAF, 1953-56. Recipient Shelley Peters Meml. award Am. Inst. Banking, Kansas City, 1986. Fellow Am. Coll. Bankruptcy Judges; mem. Nat. Conf. Bankruptcy Judges (dir. 1990-93, sec. 1994-95, pres.-elect 1995-96, pres. 1996-97), Comml. Law League Am. (pres. 1983-84). Avocations: contract bridge, gardening. Office: US Bankruptcy Ct 400 E 9th St Kansas City MO 64106-2607

KOGGE, PETER MICHAEL, computer scientist, educator; b. Washington, Dec. 3, 1946; s. Roy and Louise (McGrath) K.; m. Mary Ellen Clarke, June 12, 1971; children: Peter Michael, Mary Elizabeth, Timothy McGrath. BSEE, U. Notre Dame, 1968; MS in Systems Info. Scis., Syracuse U., 1970; PhDEE, Stanford U., 1973. Jr. engr. IBM, Owego, N.Y., 1968-72, staff engr., 1972-74, adv. engr., 1974-76, sr. engr., 1976-81, mem. sr. tech. staff, 1981-93; IBM fellow, 1993; McCourtney prof. computer sci. U. Notre Dame, Ind., 1994—2001, interim dept. chair computer sci. dept., 2000—01, assoc. dean rsch. Coll. Engring, 2001—. Adj. prof. computer scis. SUNY, Binghamton, 1977—94; past mem. rev. com. NSF Computing Divsn.; program chair 6th Symposium on Frontiers of Massively Parallel Computation, 1996; disting. vis. scientist NASA Jet Propulsion Lab., 1997; program com. Supercomputing, 1998, 99, 2000, 02, Internat. Symposium on Computer Arch., 1999; program vice chair 7th Symposium on Frontiers of Massively Parallel Computation, 1999; program co-chmn. Great Lakes Conf. on VLSI, 2002. Author: Architecture of Pipelined Computers, 1980, Architecture of Symbolic Computers, 1991; editor conf. proc. Internat. Conf. on Parallel Processing, 1988. Recipient IBM Outstanding Innovation awards for Space Shuttle, IOP, 3838 Array Processor, AI Parallel Processor, Pres.'s award for patents, Daniel L. Slotnick award for most original paper Internat. Conf. Parallel Processing, 1994, Outstanding Computer Sci. and Engring. Dept. Instrn., 1999. Fellow IEEE; mem. Assn. for Computing Machinery, Am. Assn. Artificial Intelligence, IBM Acad. Tech. Roman Catholic. Office: U Notre Dame Dept Computer Sci and Engring 384 Fitzpatrick Hl Engrng Notre Dame IN 46556-5637 E-mail: kogge@cse.nd.edu.

KOGUT, JOHN ANTHONY, retail/wholesale executive; b. Lackawanna, N.Y., Dec. 8, 1942; s. John J. and Rose J. (Gaj) K.; m. Deborah A. Hillman; children: David J., Robert J., Katherine A., Lindsey A., Kimberly M. B.S. in Pharmacy, U. Buffalo, 1965; M.B.A., Syracuse U., 1978. Pharmacist, mgr. Fay's Drug Co., Liverpool, N.Y., 1969-75, v.p., 1975-82, sr. v.p., 1982-89, pres., 1989-95; pres. Health Mart divsn., v.p. Franchise Svcs. FoxMeyer Corp., 1995-96; pres. Health Mart Divsn., v.p. mktg. McKesson Corp., 1996-99; pres. pharmac ops. Cmty. Health Svcs., Inc., Chgo., 1999—. Mem. N.Y. State Bd. Pharmacy, 1987-95. Served to capt. U.S. Army, 1966-69 Mem. Am. Pharm. Assn., Pharm. Soc. of State N.Y., Am. Mgmt. Assn., Nat. Assn. Chain Drug Stores (pharmacy affairs com. chmn. 1982-83), N.Y. State Bd. Pharmacy. Republican. Roman Catholic

KOHL, DAVID, dean, librarian; b. Grand Island, Nebr., July 31, 1942; s. D. Franklin and La Vern Harriet (De Long) K; m. Marilyn L. Kohl, Sept. 28, 1969 (div. 1986); 1 child: Nathaniel F. BA cum laude, Carleton Coll., 1965; ThM Divinity Sch., U. Chgo., 1967, DMn, 1969, MA, 1972. Asst. dir. Admission and Aid U. Chgo., 1969-72; Social Scis. reference librarian Washington State U., Pullman, 1972-77, head ctrl. circulation, 1977-80; undergrad librarian U. Ill., Urbana, 1980-86; asst. dir. Pub. Svcs. U. Colo., Boulder, 1986-91, head Norlin Libr., 1989-91; dean, univ. libr. U. Cin., 1991—; dir. U. Cin. Digital Press, 1996—. Assoc. prof. U. Ill. Urbana Libr. Sch., 1984-86, Emporia State U., 1991-92, Ind. U., Bloomington, 1992, U. Ky., 1994—. Author: Handbooks for Library Management (6 vols.), 1984-86, 12 Years 'Til 2000, 1990; review editor RQ Reference Tools, 1988—; contbr. articles to profl. jours. Relief houseparent for Learning Disabled Student Whitman County Mental Health, Pullman, Wash., 1973-75; Koinonia House Bd. (pres. 1979-80), Pullman, 1975-81; mem. bd. Mental Health Found., Boulder County, 1986-91. Rockefeller fellow Rockefeller Found., 1965-66; Disciples House scholar Disciples Divinity House, Chgo., 1965-69. Mem. ALA (v.p., pres. reference and adult svc. divsn. 1993—), Libr. Guild. Presbyterian. Avocation: jogging. Home: 2929 Courtropes Ln Cincinnati OH 45244-3807 Office: Univ of Cincinnati Langsam Libr Mail Location 33 Cincinnati OH 45221-0001 E-mail: david.kohl@uc.edu.

KOHL, HERBERT, senator, professional sports team executive; b. Milw., Feb. 7, 1935; BA, U. Wis., 1956; MBA, Harvard U., 1956. Owner Milw. Bucks (NBA) Milw. Brewers; U.S. senator from Wis., 1989—; pres. Herbert Kohl Investments. State chmn. Dem. Party, Wis., 1975-77; mem. com. on aging, Appropriations Com., Senate Dem. Steering & Coordination Com., Com. on Judiciary, 1989; ranking minority mem. Jud. subcom. on Terrorism, Tech. & Govt. Info. With USAR, 1958-64. Office: US Senate 330 Hart Senate Office Bldg Washington DC 20510-0001 also: Milw Bucks Bradley Ctr 1001 N 4th St Milwaukee WI 53203-1314

KOHLER, HERBERT VOLLRATH, JR. diversified manufacturing company executive; b. Sheboygan, Wis., Feb. 20, 1939; s. Herbert Vollrath and Ruth Miriam (DeYoung) K.; children: Laura Elizabeth, Rachel DeYoung, Karger David; m. Natalie Black. Grad., The Choate Sch., 1957; B.S., Yale U., 1965. With Kohler Co., Wis., 1965—, gen. supr. warehouse div., 1965-67, factory systems mgr., 1967-68, v.p. operations, 1968-71, exec. v.p., 1971-72, chmn. bd., chief exec. officer, 1972—, pres., 1974—, dir., 1967—. Ret. chmn. Kohler Found.; dir. emeritus Harnischfeger Corp. Served with U.S. Army, 1957-58. Inductee Nat. Kitchen and Bath Hall of Fame, 1989, Nat. Housing Hall of Fame, 1993, Morgan Horse Hall of Fame, 1996. Mem. Am. Horse Show Assn., Am. Morgan Horse Assn. Republican. Episcopalian. Club: Sheboygan Economic (pres. 1973-74). Office: Kohler Co 444 Highland Dr Kohler WI 53044

KOHLER, KENNETH JAMES, lawyer; b. Redwood Falls, Minn., Sept. 18, 1956; s. James Claire and Blanche (Genevieve) K.; m. Gail Ann Buldhaupt, May 21, 1983; children: Benjamin Thomas, Rebecca Erin. BA, U. Minn., Morris; JD, Hamline U. Asst. Redwood County Atty., Redwood Falls, Minn., 1983-85, Nobles County Atty., Worthington, 1985—; ptnr. Mork, Darling, Hagemann & Kohler, 1985—. Bd. dirs. S.W. Women's Shelter, Marshall, Minn., 1985—. Served to cpt. Minn. N.G., 1984—. Mem. ABA, Minn. Bar Assn., Assn. Trial Lawyers Am., County Atty.'s Assn., Dist. Attys.' Assn., Nobles County Child Protection Team. Lutheran. Lodge: Kiwanis. Home: 1505 Park Ave Worthington MN 56187-1149 Office: Nobles County Attorneys Office PO Box 607 Worthington MN 56187-0607

KOHLER, LAURA E. human resources executive; married; 2 children. Grad., Duke U., 1984; MFA, Cath. U., 1987. Past tchr. Chgo. Pub. Schs.; past corp. team facilitator; past mgr. Nat. Players, Washington; past residence mgr. Olney (Md.) Theatre; founder Address Unknown, Chgo.; past exec. dir. Kohler Found., Inc.; v.p. human resources Kohler Co., 1994—. Office: Kohler Co 444 Highland Dr Kohler WI 53044-1500

KOHLHEPP, ROBERT J. diversified services executive; Pres., COO Cintas Corp., Cin., 1984-95, pres., CEO, 1995—. Office: Cintas Corp 6800 Cintas Blvd Mason OH 45040

KOHLS, WILLIAM RICHARD, bank executive; b. St. Johns, Mich., Apr. 17, 1957; s. Richard William and Helen A. (Arndt) K.; m. Susan Marie Matbick, Mar. 12, 1983. BBA, Northwood Inst., 1979. Controller Pacesetter Bank and Trust, Owosso, Mich., 1979-82; asst. v.p., controller First Nat. Bank, Howell, 1982-85; v.p., sec. and treas. Ind. Bank Corp., Ionia, 1985—. Bd. dirs. IBC Services Corp., Belding, Mich., 1986—. Home: 600 Covered Vlg Belding MI 48809-1667 Office: Ind Bank Corp 230 W Main St PO Box 491 Ionia MI 48846

KOHLSTEDT, JAMES AUGUST, lawyer; b. Evanston, Ill., June 1, 1949; s. August Lewis and Deloris (Weichelt) K.; m. Patricia Ann Lang, Oct. 8, 1977; children: Katherine, Matthew, Lindsey, Kevin. BA, Northwestern U., 1971; JD, MBA, Ind. U., 1976. Bar: U.S. Dist. Ct. (no. dist.) Ill. 1976, U.S. Tax Ct. 1978. Tax specialist Peat Marwick, Mitchell & Co., Chgo., 1976-77; assoc. Bishop & Crawford Ltd., Oak Brook, Ill., 1977-83, 1984-85; ptnr. Arnstein, Gluck, Lehr & Milligan, 1985-87, Keck, Mahin and Cate, Oak Brook, 1987-96, McBride Baker & Coles, 1996-2001, mem. mgmt. com., 1997; chair McBride Baker & Coles Trade and Profl. Assn. Practice Group; sr. ptnr. Kohlstedt and Teske LLC, 2001—. Bd. dirs. Nat. Entrepreneurship Found., Bloomington, Ind., 1981-92, Camp New Hope Devel. Bd., Oak Brook, 1983; mem. sch. bd. Lyons Twp. H.S. Dist. 204, La Grange , Ill., 1985-2001, Hinsdale (Ill.) Cmty. House Coun., 1991-94; mem. area leadership com. Superconducting Super Collider, 1987-88; mem. citizens adv. com. on edn. to U.S. Congressman Harris Fawell, 1986-93; bd. dirs. Ill. Corridor Partnership for Excellence in Edn., 1988-94; mem. planned giving com. Elmhurst Coll., 1986—; mem. citizens adv. panel U.S. Army ROTC Cadet Command, 1991-94; bd. dirs. Ill. Math and Sci. Acad. Alliance, 1989—; del. White House Conf. Travel and Tourism, 1995; mem. allied adv. bd. midwest chpt. Am. Soc. Travel Agents, 1995; Collegiate Edn. adv. com. Dept. Def., 1995. Recipient Outstanding Young Citizen of Chgo. award 1987. Mem. ABA, Ill. Travel and Tourism Assn., Ill. Bar Assn., DuPage Estate Planning Coun., Oak Brook Jaycees (pres. 1984—, chmn. bd. 1985, trustee 1985-86), Beta Gamma Sigma. Republican. Lutheran.

KOHLSTEDT, SALLY GREGORY, history educator; b. Ypsilanti, Mich., Jan. 30, 1943; BA, Valparaiso U., 1965; MA, Mich. State U., 1966; PhD, U. Ill., Urbana, 1972. Asst. prof. Simmons Coll., Boston, 1971-75; assoc. prof. to prof. Syracuse (N.Y.) U., 1975-89; prof. history of sci. U. Minn., Mpls., 1989—; dir. Ctr. for Advanced Feminist Studies, 1997-98. Vis. prof. history of sci. Cornell U., 1989, Amerika Inst. U. Munich, 1997; lect. univs. in U.S. and abroad; mem. nat. panels. Author: The Formation of the American Scientific Community: AAAS, 1848-1860, 1976; editor: (with Margaret Rossiter) Historical Writing on American Science, Osiris, 2d Series, 1, 1985, (with R.W. Home) International Science and National Scientific Identity: Australia between Britain and America, 1991, The Origins of Natural Science in the United States: The Essays of George Brown Goode, 1991, (with Barbara Haslett et al.) Gender and Scientific Authority, 1996, (with Helen Lonino) The Women, Gender, and Science Question, 1997, (with Bruce Lewenstein and Michael Sokal) The Establishment of American Science, 1999, The History of Women in Science: An Isis Reader, 1999, (with Bruce Leavenstein and Michael Sokal) The Establishment of Science in America: The American Association for the Advancement of Science, 1999; contbr. articles to profl. jours.; mem. editl. bd. Signs, 1980-88, 90-93, Sci., 1980-81, News and Views: History of Am. Sci. Newsletter, 1980-86, Sci., Tech. and Human Values, 1983-90, Syracuse Scholar, 1985-88, chair, 1988, Isis, 2002-; assoc. editor Am. Nat. Biography, 2d edit., 1988-98, consulting edit., 1993—; Gruphon Press Reprints in the History of Science, 1993-98; reviewer books, articles, proposals for NSDF, NEH, U. Chgo. Press, numerous other pub. cos.; editor sci. biography series Cambridge U., 1997—. NSF grantee, 1969, 78-79, 84, 93-95, Smithsonian Instn. predoctoral fellow, 1970-71, Danforth Assoc., 1975-82, Syracuse U. grantee, 1976, 82, Am. Philos. Soc. rsch. grantee, 1977, Haven fellow Am. Antiquarian Soc., 1982, Fulbright Sr. fellow U. Melbourne, Australia, 1983, Woodrow Wilson Ctr. fellow, 1986, Smithsonian Instn. Sr. fellow, 1987. Fellow AAAS (nominating com. 1980-83, 96-98, sect. chair 1986, bd. dirs. 1998—2002), Am. Hist. Assn. (profl. com. 1974-76, rep. U.S. Nat. Archives Adv. Coun. 1974-76), Berkshire Conf. Women Historians (program com. 1974), Forum on the History Sci. in Am. (coord. com. 1980-86, chair 1985, 86), History of Sci. Soc. (sec. 1978-81, coun. 1982-84, 89-91, 94-96, com. on publs. 1982-87, chair nominating com. 1985, women's com. 1972-74, vis. lectr. 1988-89, chair edn. com. 1989, pres. 1992, 93), Internat. Congress for History of Sci. (U.S. del. 1977, 81, vice chair 1985) Orgn. Am. Historians (chair com. on status of women 1983-85, endowment fund drive, auction subcom. 1990-91). Lutheran. Home: 4140 Edmund Blvd Minneapolis MN 55406-3646 E-mail: sgk@tc.umn.edu.

KOHN, JAMES PAUL, engineering educator; b. Dubuque, Iowa, Oct. 31, 1924; s. Harry Theodore and Kathryn (Piepel) K.; m. Mary Louise McGovern, Aug. 30, 1958; children: Kathleen, Kevin, Mary Louise. B.S. in Chem. Engring, U. Notre Dame, 1951; M.S., U. Mich., 1952; Ph.D., U. Kans., 1956. Chem. engr. Reilly Tar & Chem. Corp., Indpls., 1946-51; mem. faculty U. Notre Dame, 1955—, prof., 1964-95, prof. emeritus, 1995—; dir. Solar Lab. for Thermal Applications, 1973—. Cons. Am. Oil Co., summer 1958, Imagineering Interprises, 1957-65, Hills-Morrow, 1966-70, Frito Lay Corp., 1982—, South Bend Energy Conservation Commn., 1983—, sec. 1986—. Patentee removal acidic gaseous components from natural gas. Served with U.S. Army, 1943-46. Decorated Bronze star, Purple Heart; recipient Faculty award U. Notre Dame, 1983, Outstanding Tchr. of Yr. award, 1987, Outstanding Faculty mem. minority engring. program, 1995, Spl. Presdl. award Notre Dame, 1995; Donald L. Katz award Gas Processors Assn., 1988. Fellow AIChE; mem. AAAS, Am. Chem. Soc., Sigma Xi. Republican. Roman Catholic. Home: 17684 Waxwing Ln South Bend IN 46635-1387

KOHN, SHALOM L. lawyer; b. Nov. 18, 1949; s. Pincus and Helen (Roth) K.; m. Barbara Segal, June 30, 1974; children: David, Jeremy, Daniel. BS in Acctg. summa cum laude, CUNY, 1970; JD magna cum laude, MBA, Harvard U., 1974. Bar: Ill. 1975, U.S. Dist. Ct. (no. dist.) Ill. 1975, U.S. Ct. Appeals (7th cir.) 1976, U.S. Supreme Ct. 1980, N.Y. 1988, U.S. Dist. Ct. (so. dist.) N.Y. 1988. Law clk. to chief judge U.S. Ct. Appeals (2d cir.), N.Y.C., 1974-75; assoc. Sidley & Austin, Chgo., 1975-80, ptnr., 1980—. Exec. com. Adv. Coun. Religious Rights in Eastern Europe and Soviet Union, Washington, 1984-86; bd. dirs. Brisk Rabbinical Coll., Chgo. Contbr. articles to profl. jours. Mem. ABA, Chgo. Bar Assn. Office: Sidley & Austin Bank One Plz 10 South Dearborn Chicago IL 60603 also: 875 3rd Ave New York NY 10022-6225

KOHN, WILLIAM IRWIN, lawyer; b. Bronx, N.Y., June 27, 1951; s. Arthur Oscar and Frances (Hoffman) K.; m. Karen Mindlin, Aug. 29, 1974; children: Shira, Kinneret, Asher. Student, U. Del., 1969-71; BA with honors, U. Cin., 1973; JD, Ohio State U., 1976. Bar: Ohio 1976, U.S. Dist. Ct. (no. dist.) Ohio 1982, Ind. 1982, U. S. Dist. Ct. (no. and so. dists.) Ind. 1982, D.C. 1992, U.S. Supreme Ct., 1992, Ill. 1994; cert. Bus. Bankruptcy Law Am. Bankruptcy Bd. Cert. Ptnr. Krugliak, Wilkins, Griffith & Dougherty, Canton, Ohio, 1976-82, Barnes & Thornburg, Chgo., 1982—. Adj. prof. law U. Notre Dame, Ind., 1984-90. Author: West's Indiana Business Forms, West's Indiana Uniform Commercial Code Forms; contbr. articles to profl. jours. Bd. dirs. Family Svcs., South Bend, 1985-94, Jewish Fedn., Highland Park United Way. Mem. ABA (bus. bankruptcy subcom.), Am. Bankruptcy Inst. (insolvency sect., bd. dirs.), Ill. Bar Assn., Chgo. Bar Assn., Comml. Law League, Am. Bd. Certification (dir., std. com.). Office: Sachmoff & Weaver Ltd Ste 2900 305 Wacker Dr Chicago IL 60606 E-mail: wkohn@sachmoff.com.

KOHRMAN, ARTHUR FISHER, pediatrics educator; b. Cleve., Dec. 19, 1934; s. Benjamin Myron and Leah (Fisher) K.; m. Claire Hoffenberg, Nov. 10, 1955; children: Deborah, Benjamin, Ellen, Rachel. BA, BS, U. Chgo., 1955; MD, Western Res. U., 1959. Diplomate Am. Bd. Pediatrics. Lic. Ill., Mich., Ind. Intern Cleve. Met. Gen. Hosp., 1959-60; resident in pediatrics Western Res. U., Cleve., 1960-62; post doctoral fellow Stanford U., Palo Alto, Calif., 1965-68; asst. prof. to prof. Mich. State U., East Lansing, 1968-81, assoc. chmn. dept. human devel., 1968-78, assoc. dean Coll. Human Medicine, 1977-81; prof., assoc. chmn. dept. pediatrics U. Chgo., 1981-96; pres. La Rabida Children's Hosp. and Research Ctr., Chgo., 1981-96; prof. pediatrics, assoc. chmn. Northwestern U. Sch. Medicine and Children's Meml. Hosp., 1997—. Congl. fellow Office Tech. Assessment, U.S. Congress, 1980-81; pres. Children's Hospice Internat., 1983-86; chmn. instl. rev. bd. U. Chgo., 1986-96. Contbr. numerous scholarly articles to profl. jours. Served to capt. USAF, 1962-65. Recipient Outstanding Service award Am. Diabetes Assn. Mich. chpt., 1977. Fellow Am. Acad. Pediatrics (chmn. com. on bioethics 1990-94); mem. Am. Pediatric Soc., Ambulatory Pediatric Assn., Soc. Pediatric Rsch., Lawson Wilkins Pediatric Endocrine Soc., Alpha Omega Alpha. Office: Childrens Meml Hosp 2300 N Childrens Plz Chicago IL 60614-3394

KOIVISTO, DON, state legislator; married. BS, Ctrl. Mich. U., 1971. Mem. Mich. Ho. of Reps. from 110th dist., Lansing, 1980-86; chmn. Agrl. & Forestry Com.; mem. Conservation, Tourism, Econ. Devel., Mil. & Vets. Affairs Com., Mich. Senate from 38th dist., Lansing, 1990—; mem. appropriations com.; mem. agr. com., higher edn. com., natural resources com.; mem. joint capital outlay com.; mem. gaming and casino oversight com. Mem. Agriculture and Forestry, Health Policy, Joint Adminstrv. Rules & Natural Resources & Environ. coms. Mich. State Senate. Home: 735 Van Buskirk Rd Ironwood MI 49938-3140 Also: PO Box 30036 Lansing MI 48909-7536

KOLA, ARTHUR ANTHONY, lawyer; b. New Brunswick, N.J., Feb. 16, 1939; s. Arthur Aloysius and Blanche (Raym) K.; m. Jacquelin Lou Draper, Sept. 3, 1960; children— Jill, Jean, Jennifer; m. Anna Molnar, Apr. 15, 1977 AB, Dartmouth Coll., 1961; LLB, Duke U., 1964. Bar: Ohio 1964, U.S. Dist. Ct. (no. dist.) Ohio 1969, U.S. Ct. Appeals (6th cir.) 1971, U.S. Supreme Ct. 1972. Assoc. Squire, Sanders & Dempsey, Cleve., 1964-65, assoc., 1968-74, ptnr., 1974-94; pvt. practice Kola Law Office, 1994—. Asst. prof. law Ind. U., Bloomington, 1967-68; instr. labor law Case Western Res. U., Cleve., 1976 Bd. visitors Duke U. Sch. Law, 1985—. Served to capt. U.S. Army, 1965-67 Mem. Ohio Bar Assn., Cleve. Bar Assn. (chmn. labor and employment law sect. 1993-94), Am. Arbitration Assn. (bd. dirs. 1991-97). Office: Kola Law Office Corp Plz I Ste 100 6450 Rockside Woods Blvd S Cleveland OH 44131

KOLAKOWSKI, DIANA JEAN, county commissioner; b. Detroit, Aug. 28, 1943; d. Leo and Genevieve (Bosh) Zyskowski; m. William Francis Kolakowski, Jr., Oct. 22, 1966; children: Wiliam Francis III, John. BS, U. Detroit, 1965. Lab. asst. chemistry dept. U. Detroit, 1961-65; rsch. chemist Detroit Inst. Cancer Rsch., Mich. Cancer Found., 1965-70; substitute tchr. Warren (Mich.) Consol. Schs., 1979-81; mem. Macomb County Bd. Commrs., Mt. Clemens, Mich., 1983—, vice chmn., 1993-95, chmn., 1995-97. Dir. S.E. Mich. Transp. Authority, Detroit, 1983—85; trustee Macomb County Ret. System, Mt. Clemens, 1988—91, 1992—95; chmn. Regional Transit Coord. Coun., 1995—97; del. S.E. Mich. Coun. Govts., Detroit, 1987—, vice chmn., 1995—99, chmn., 1999—2000, Regional Transit Coord. Coun., 1995—97; bd. dirs. Creating a Healthier Macomb, 1996—2001, Macomb Bar Found., 1996—. Contbr. articles to sci. jours. Trustee Myasthenia Gravis Found., Southfield, Mich., 1964-71; dir. Otsikita coun. Girl Scouts Am., 1995-96; mem., sec. Sterling Heights (Mich.) Bd. Zoning Appeals, 1978-83; mem. Macomb County Dem. Exec. Com., Mt. Clemens, 1982—, 10th and 12th Dem. Congl. Dist. Exec. Com., Warren, 1982—, del. 1996 Dem. Nat. Conv.; mem. behavioral medicine adv. coun. St. Joseph Hosp. GM scholar U. Detroit, 1961-65; named Woman of Distinction Macomb County Girl Scouts U.S.A., 1996; recipient Leadership award Cath. Social Svcs. Macomb, 1997, Polish Pride award Polish Am. Citizens for Equity, 1997, Excellence in County Govt. award, 1997, others. Mem. Nat. Assn. Counties, Mich. Assn. Counties, Mich. Assn. Planning Ofcls., Am. Polish Cultural Ctr., Polish Am. Congress, Alpha Sigma Nu. Roman Catholic. Avocations: singing, piano, crossword and jigsaw puzzles. Home: 33488 Breckenridge Dr Sterling Heights MI 48310-6082 Office: Office Bd Commrs Macomb Co Adminstrn Bldg 1 S Main St Fl 9 Mount Clemens MI 48043-2306 E-mail: dianakolakowski1@comcast.net.

KOLATTUKUDY, PAPPACHAN ETTOOP, biochemist, educator; b. Cochin, Kerala, India, Aug. 27, 1937; came to the U.S., 1960; m. Marie M. Paul. BS, U. Madras, 1957; B in Edn., U. Kerala, 1959; PhD, Oreg. State U., 1964. Prin. jr. high sch., India, 1957-58; high sch. chemistry tchr. India, 1959-60; asst. biochemist Conn. Agrl. Experiment Sta., New Haven, 1964-69; assoc. prof. Wash. State U., Pullman, 1969-73, prof. biochemistry, 1973-80, dir. inst. biol. chemistry, 1980-86; dir. Ohio State Biotech. Ctr., Columbus, 1986-95, dir. neurobiotech. ctr., dir. med. biotech., 1995—. Cons. Analabs, New Haven, Allied Chem. Corp., Solvay, N.Y., Genencor Corp., South San Francisco, Calif., Monsanto Co., St. Louis; mem. Overseas Adv. Com., India; mem. Edison Bio-Tech. Ctr., Cleve., trustee; mem. adv. com. to MUCIA on Sci. and Tech., Nat. Agrl. Biotech.

Consortium; Ohio rep. to Midwest Plant Biotech. Consortium. Contbr. over 300 articles to profl. jours.; patentee in field. Recipient Golden Apple award Wash. State Apple Commn., President's Faculty Excellence award Wash. State U.; grantee NIH, NSF, Am. Heart Assn., Am. Cancer Soc., DOE. Mem. Fedn. Am. Socs. for Exptl. Biology, Am. Soc. Plant Physiologists, Am. Soc. Microbiology. Home: 2301 Hoxton Ct Columbus OH 43220-4739 Office: Ohio State Neurobiotech Ctr 1060 Carmack Rd Columbus OH 43210-1002

KOLB, DAVID ALLEN, psychology educator; b. Moline, Ill., Dec. 12, 1939; s. John August and Ethel May (Petherbridge) K.; m. Alice Yoko; 1 son, Jonathan Demian. AB cum laude, Knox Coll., 1961; PhD, Harvard U., 1967; ScD (h.c.), U. N.H., 1984; PhD (h.c.), Internat. Mgmt. Ctr., Buckingham, 1988; LittD (h.c.), Franklin U., 1994; DHL (h.c.), SUNY, 1996. Asst. prof. organizational psychology MIT, Cambridge, 1965-70, assoc. prof., 1970-75; prof. organizational behavior and mgmt. Case Western Res. U., Cleve., 1976—, deWindt Prof. Leadership and Enterprise Devel. Weatherhead Sch. Mgmt., 1992-97, chmn. dept., 1984-90. Vis. prof. mgmt. London Grad. Sch. Bus., 1971; dir. Devel. Research Assos., 1966-80; mgmt. cons., U.S., Australia, N.Z., Indonesia, Singapore, Malaysia, Thailand, Japan. Author: Experiential Learning: Experience as the source of learning and development, 1984, Conversational Learning: An Experimental Approach to Knowledge Creation, 2002; co-author: Organizational Behavior: An Experiential Approach, 7th edit, 2001, Organizational Behavior: A Book of Readings, 7th edit, 2001, Changing Human Behavior: Principles of Planned Intervention, 1974, Innovation in Professional Education: Steps on Journey from Teaching to Learning, 1995, Conversational Learning: An Experiential Approach to Knowledge Creation, 2002. Woodrow Wilson fellow, 1962 Mem. Internat. Assn. Applied Social Scientists (charter), Soc. Intercultural Edn., Tng. and Rsch. (charter), Coun.l Advancement of Experiential Learning (Research Excellence award 1984, Morris T. Keaton Adult and Experiental Learning award 1991). Office: Case Western Res U Dept of Orgn Behavior Cleveland OH 44106 E-mail: dak5@msn.com.

KOLB, VERA M. chemistry educator; b. Belgrade, Yugoslavia, Feb. 5, 1948; came to U.S., 1973; d. Martin A. Dobrila (Lopicic) K.; m. Cal Y. Meyers, 1976 (div. 1986); m. Michael S. Gregory, 1997 (div. 1999). BS, Belgrade U., 1971, MS, 1973; PhD, So. Ill. U., 1976. Fellow So. Ill. U., Carbondale, 1977-78, faculty, 1978-85; assoc. prof. chemistry U. Wis., Parkside, 1985-90, prof. chemistry, 1990—, dept. chair, 1995-97. Faculty San Francisco State U., 1997; vis. scientist The Salk Inst. for Biol. Studies, U. Calif., San Diego, 1992-94. Editor: Teratogens, Chemicals Which Cause Birth Defects, 1988, 2d edit., 1993; contbr. articles to profl. jours.; patentee in field. Violinist Racine (Wis.) Symphony Orch.; assoc. dir. higher edn. Wis. Space Grant Consortium, 1995-97. Fulbright grantee, 1973-76, grantee NIH, 1984-87, Am. Soc. Biochemistry and Molecular Biology, 1988; NASA fellow, 1992-94; named to hall of fame Wis. Ed., 2002. Mem. Am. Chem. Soc. (task force on occupational safety and health 1980-94). Office: Univ Wis Parkside Dept Chemistry PO Box 2000 Kenosha WI 53141-2000 E-mail: kolb@uwp.edu.

KOLEHMAINEN, JAN WALDROY, professional association administrator; b. Virginia, Minn., July 8, 1940; s. John Ilmari and Astrid Irene (Petrell) K.; m. Katherine Lorene MacDanel, June 18, 1966; children: Lynn Kristine, Mark Daven. BA, Heidelberg Coll., 1962; MA, Bowling Green U., 1965. Asst. dir. admissions Syracuse U., N.Y., 1965-68; dir. admissions St. Xavier Coll., Chgo., 1968-72; dir. med. soc. rels. AMA, 1972-80; dir. intersplty. affairs Minn. Med. Assn., Mpls., 1980-82; exec. dir. Am. Acad. Neurology, 1982-99; ret., 1999. Mem. Am. Soc. Assn. Execs., Minn. Soc. Assn. Execs. (bd. dirs. 1989-93, sec.-treas. 1991-93), Am. Assn. Med. Soc. Execs. (bd. dirs. 1984-88), Profl. Conv. Mgrs. Assn. (bd. dirs. 1992-93). Avocations: tennis; fishing; reading. Office: Am Acad Neurology 1080 Montreal Ave Saint Paul MN 55116-2386

KOLEK, ROBERT EDWARD, lawyer; b. Chgo., June 1, 1943; s. Joseph and Mary Kolek; m. Linda L. Bernicchi, Aug. 27, 1966; children: Kimberley M., Robert E. Jr. BBA, Loyola U., Chgo., 1965, JD, 1968. Bar: Ill. 1968. Law clk. to Hon. Thomas Kluczynski, Ill. Supreme Ct., Chgo., 1968-70. Mem. ABA, Chgo. Bar Assn. Roman Catholic. Avocation: photography. Office: Schiff Hardin & Waite 6600 Sears Tower Chicago IL 60606 E-mail: rKolek@schiffhardin.com.

KOLESON, DONALD RALPH, retired college dean, educator; b. Eldon, Mo., June 30, 1935; s. Ralph A. and Fern M. (Beanland) K.; children— Anne, David, Janet. B.S. in Edn., Central Mo. State U., 1959; M.Ed., So. Ill. U., 1973. Mem. faculty So. Ill. U., Carbondale, 1968-73; dean tech. edn. Belleville (Ill.) Area Coll., 1982-93; ret. 1993. Mem. Am. Vocat. Edn. Assn., Am. Welding Assn., Nat. Assn. Two-Year Schs. of Constrn. (pres. 1984-85). Clubs: Masons; Shriners, Jesters.

KOLK, FRITZ D. retail executive; CFO Meijer Inc., Grand Rapids, Mich. Office: Meijer Inc 2629 Walker Ave NW Grand Rapids MI 49544-1305

KOLKER, ALLAN ERWIN, ophthalmologist; b. St. Louis, Nov. 2, 1933; s. Paul P. and Jean Kolker; m. Jacquelyn Krupin, Dec. 8, 1957; children: Robin, Marci, David, Scott. AB, Washington U., St. Louis, 1953, MD, 1957. Diplomate Am. Bd. Ophthalmology (dir. 1994-98). Intern St. Louis Children's Hosp., 1957-58; resident in ophthalmology Washington U./Barnes Hosp., St. Louis, 1960-65; glaucoma fellow Washington U., 1963—64, staff, faculty, 1964—, prof. ophthalmology, 1974-96, clin. prof. ophthalmology, 1996—; ophthalmologist Eye Health Care Assocs., 1996—. Med. dir. The Glaucoma Inst., St. Louis; mem. glaucoma com. Prevent Blindness Am. Author: (with J. Hetherington) Becker and Shaffer's Diagnosis and Therapy of the Glaucomas, 3d, 4th, 5th edit., 1983, (with T. Krupin) Complications in Ophthalmic Surgery, 1999; contbr. numerous articles to profl. jours., chpts. to books. Served with USPHS, 1958-60. NIH spl. fellow, 1963-65; grantee, 1969-80; 1st Disting. Eye Alumni award Washington U., 1990, Alumni/Faculty award Washington U. Sch. Medicine, 2002. Mem. AMA, Assn. Rsch. in Vision and Ophthalmology, Am. Acad. Ophthalmology (mem. coun. 1986-92, trustee 1994-98), Am. Bd. Ophthalmology (dir. 1994-98), Am. Ophthal. Soc., Am. Glaucoma Soc. (founding mem., pres. 1992-94, Spl. Honor award 2002), Mo. Ophthal. Soc. (pres. 1986-87), St. Louis Med. Soc. Home: 176 Plantation Dr Saint Louis MO 63141-8352 Office: 12601 Olive Blvd Saint Louis MO 63141-6313 E-mail: akolker@novamed.com.

KOLKEY, ERIC SAMUEL, customer service representative; b. Chgo., Sept. 30, 1960; s. Eugene Louis and Gilda P. (Cowan) K. Student, Columbia Coll., 1979-82. Booking agt. C.O.D. Club, Chgo., 1979—83; mgr. Video Plus, 1984—90; freelance screenwriter, 1991—96; customer comm. specialist MCSI, Bensenville, Ill., 1997—. Lectr. Northwestern U., Evanston, Ill., 1982. Contbr. articles to profl. jours. Active Presdl. Trust, Washington, 1992, Nat. Rep. Senatorial Com., Washington, 1992, Rep. Party Platform Planning Com., Washington, 1992. Recipient Cert. of Recognition Rep. Nat. Com., 1991, Cert. of Award Rep. Presdl. Adv. Com., 1992. Avocation: weightlifting. Home: 750 N Dearborn St Apt 2302 Chicago IL 60610-5379 Office: MCSI 621 Busse Hwy Bensenville IL E-mail: eric.kolkey@mcsinet.com.

KOLKEY, GILDA, artist; b. Chgo. d. David and Evelyn (Jacobson) Cowan; m. Gene Kolkey (dec.); children: Daniel, Sandor, Eric. BA in Painting, U. Ill., Champaign; postgrad., Art Inst. Chgo., 1978-79. Art tchr. Highland Park (Ill.) Recreational Ctr., 1976. Exhibited in group shows at Art Inst. Chgo. and vicinity, 1949, 1950, 1956, Thompson Ctr., Chgo., 1998, 1999, ArtLink Gallery, Ft. Wayne, Ind., 1998, Art Ho., 2001, Mars Gallery, 2001, Jettsett Gallery, 2002, Chgo. Anthenaeum, Shamburg, Ill., 2002; contbr. paintings. Recipient award of Excellence, North Shore Art League, 1965—66, Painting award, New Horizons Painting, 1959, Scan Members Show, 1992, San Juried Show, 1992—2000, Hon. Mention, Women's Club Evanston, 1972. Mem.: Chgo. Soc. Artists, Arts Club Chgo., Mid-Am. Club. Republican. Home: 1100 N Lake Shore Dr Apt 21B Chicago IL 60611-1088

KOLLER, DON, state legislator; b. Granite City, Ill., Dec. 3, 1942; Mo. state rep. Dist. 153, 1985—. Owner grocery store. Home: PO Box 135 Summersville MO 65571-0135 Office: 201 W Capitol Ave Jefferson City MO 65101-1556

KOLLER, MARITA ANN, accountant; b. Chgo., June 6, 1955; d. Frank J. and Jean J. Koller. BA, Western Ill. U., 1976; MPA, Am. U., 1980; AAS, Oakton Coll., 1989. Legis. asst. U.S. Congress, 1977-81; acct. UOP, Des Plaines, Ill., 1986—; UOP group leader Document Control-UOP Modular Tech. Ctr.; computer specialist Baxter Labs., Deerfield, Ill., 1985-86; actuarial asst. Towers, Perrin, Foster and Crosby, Chgo., 1981-85; instr. computer tech. Oakton Coll., Des Plaines, 1985—. U. Ill. scholar. Mem. Am. Mgmt. Assn., Am. Soc. Profl. and Women Execs., Nat. Soc. Pub. Accts. Home: 934 E Forest Ave Des Plaines IL 60018-1476

KOLODZIEJ, EDWARD ALBERT, political scientist, educator; b. Chgo., Jan. 4, 1935; s. Albert Stanley and Anna Caroline (Chudzik) K.; m. Antje Heberle, Aug. 15, 1959; children: Peter, Andrew, Matthew, Daniel. BS summa cum laude, Loyola U., Chgo., 1956; MA, U. Chgo., 1957, PhD, 1961. Analyst nat. security fgn. affairs div. Congl. Research Service, Library of Congress, Washington, 1960-62; asst. prof. polit. sci. U. Va., Charlottesville, 1962-67, assoc. prof., 1967-73, chmn. dept. govt. and fgn. affairs, 1967-69, prof. polit. sci., 1973-83; head dept. U. Ill., Urbana, 1973-77, dir. Office Arms Control, Disarmament and Internat. Security, 1983-86, research prof. polit. sci., 1983—, elected univ. scholar, 1988. Cons. in field Author: The Uncommon Defense and Congress, 1966, French International Policy under de Gaulle and Pompidou: The Politics of Grandeur, 1974, Making and Marketing Arms: The French Experience and Its Implications for the International System, 1987; editor: American Security Policy, 1979, Security Policies of Developing States, 1981, Limits of Soviet Power in the Developing World, 1987, Security and Arms Control: Guide to National and International Policy-Making, 2 vols., 1989, Cold War as Cooperation, 1991, Coping with Conflict After the Cold War, 1996; mem. editl. bd. Internat. Studies Quar., Defence and Peace Econs., Contemporary Security Policy, European Security; contbr. articles on fgn. and security policy and decision-making to profl. jours., U.S., Europe; also contbg. author books. Mershon Postdoctoral fellow nat. security Ohio State U., 1964-65, Rockefeller Postdoctoral fellow in internat. rels., Paris, 1965-66, Ford Found. fellow in social sci., 1969-71, Fulbright Rsch. fellow, 1986; NSF grantee, 1971, Deutscher Akademischer Austauschdienst grantee, 1975, Ford Found. Internat. Arms Control Competition grantee, 1976, Ctr. for Advanced Study, U. Ill., 1979, 95—, Rockefeller Found. grantee, 1980, grantee NEH, 1981, Woodrow Wilson Ctr., 1987, U.S. Inst. Peace grantee, 1987, 91, grantee Ford Found., 1993; recipient Burlington award for outstanding tchg. and scholarship, 1985. Mem. Internat. Inst. Strategic Studies London, Council Fgn. Relations N.Y., Am., Midwest internat. polit. sci. assns., Internat. Studies Assn. Home: 711 W University Ave Champaign IL 61820-3919 Office: U Ill Dept Polit Sci Urbana IL 61801

KOMIVES, PAUL J. federal judge; b. 1932; AB, U. Detroit, 1954; JD, U. Mich., 1958. Bar: Mich. 1958, D.C. 1958, U.S. Ct. Appeals (6th cir.) 1961, U.S. Ct. Appeals (D.C. cir.) 1961, U.S. Supreme Ct. 1963. Asst. U.S. atty. U.S. Dist. Ct. (ea. dist.) Mich., 1961-66; spl. prosecutor Mich. Cir. Ct., Detroit, 1966-67; pvt. practice, 1967-71; magistrate judge U.S. Dist. Ct. (ea. dist.) Mich., Detroit, 1971—. Adj. prof. Detroit Coll. Law, 1972-2000; adj. prof. Wayne State U. Law Sch., Detroit, 1998—. Office: US Dist Ct Ea Dist Mich 629 US Courthouse 231 W Lafayette Blvd Detroit MI 48226-2700 Fax: 313-234-5497.

KOMMEDAHL, THOR, plant pathology educator; b. Mpls., Apr. 1, 1920; s. Thorbjørn and Martha (Blegen) K.; m. Faye Lillian Jensen, June 2, 1924; children: Kris Alan, Siri Lynn, Lori Anne. B.S., U. Minn., 1945, M.S., 1947, Ph.D., 1951. Instr. U. Minn., St. Paul, 1946-51, asst. prof. plant pathology, 1953-57, assoc. prof., 1957-63, prof., 1963-90, prof. emeritus, 1990—; asst. prof. plant pathology Ohio Agrl. Research and Devel. Ctr., Wooster, 1951-53, Ohio State U., Columbus, 1951-53; prof. Univ. Coll., U. Minn., St. Paul, 1990—. Cons. botanist and taxonomist Minn. Dept. Agr., 1954-60, Sci. Mus. Minn., 1990—; 7th A.W. Dimock lectr. Cornell U., 1979; external assessor U. Pertanian Malaysia, 1994-97. Author: Pesky Plants, 1989; co-author: Scientific Style and Format, 1994; editor Minn. Fulbright newsletter, 1995—, Procs. IX Internat. Congress Plant Protection, 2 vols., 1981, Corn Disease newsletter, 1970-76; assoc. editor The Boghopper, 1996—; cons. editor McGraw Hill Ency. Sci. and Tech., 1972-78; editor-in-chief Phytopathology, 1964-67; sr. editor: Challenging Problems in Plant Health, 1982, Plant Disease Reporter, 1979; contbr. articles to profl. jours. Bd. mem. Park Bugle, 1998—. Recipient Elvin Charles Stakman award, 1990, Award of Merit, Gamma Sigma Delta, 1994; Guggenheim fellow, 1961, Fulbright scholar, 1968. Fellow AAAS, Am. Phytopathol. Soc. (councilor 1958-60, pres. 1971, publs. coord. 1978-84, Disting. Svc. award 1984, 93, sci. adv. 1984—, mem. adv. bd. office internat. programs 1987-93, editor Focus 1981—); mem. Am. Inst. Biol. Scis., Bot. Soc. Am., Coun. Sci. Editors, Internat. Soc. Plant Pathology (councilor 1971-78, sec.-gen. and treas. 1983-88, treas. 1988-93, editor newsletter 1983-93), Mycol. Soc. Am., Minn. Acad. Sci., N.Y. Acad. Scis., Weed Sci. Soc. Am. (award of excellence 1968), Fulbright Assn. (Minn. chpt., editor newsletter 1995—). Baptist. Home: 1666 Coffman St Apt 322 Saint Paul MN 55108-1340 Office: U Minn Dept Plant Pathology 495 Borlaug Hall 1991 Upper Buford Cir Saint Paul MN 55108-6030 Office Fax: 612-625-9728. E-mail: thork@puccini.crl.umn.edu.

KONECK, JOHN MICHAEL, lawyer; b. Mpls., Aug. 16, 1953; s. Robert W. and Bernice V.; m. Debra K. Plotz, Aug. 16, 1980; 1 child, Robert John. BS, N.D. State U., 1975; J.D., Yale Law Sch., Mpls., 1978. Bar: N.D. 1978, Minn. 1979. Jud. law clk. N.D. Supreme Ct., Bismarck, 1978-79; ptnr. Fredrikson & Byron, Mpls., 1979—. Real property law specialist, mem. Minn. Bd. Legal Cert., Supreme Ct. Minn., 1994-99, chmn., 1996-99; mem. Vol. Lawyers Network; assoc. prof. William Mitchell Coll. Law, 1997—. Mem. ABA (chair litigation and dispute resolution, com. of sect. real property, probate and trust law 1995-98, chief editor newsletter of litigation and dispute resolution com. 1991-93, vice chair 1991-95), Minn. State Bar Assn. (co-chair real property cert. coun. 1990—, mem. rules of profl. conduct com.), State Bar Assn. N.D., Hennepin County Bar Assn. (co-chair rules of profl. conduct com. 1994-96). Office: Fredrikson & Byron 4000 Pillsbury Ctr 200 South 6th St Minneapolis MN 55402-1425 E-mail: jkoneck@fredlaw.com.

KONENKAMP, JOHN K. state supreme court justice; b. Oct. 20, 1944; m. Geri Konenkamp; children: Kathryn, Matthew. JD, U. S.D., 1974. Dep. state's atty., Rapid City; pvt. practice, 1977-84; former and presiding judge S.D. Cir Ct. (7th cir.), 1988-94; assoc. justice S.D. Supreme Ct., Pierre, 1994—. Bd. dirs. Alt. Dispute Resolution Com., Adv. Bd. for Casey Family Program. With USN. Mem. Am. Judicature Soc., State Bar S.D., Pennington County Bar Assn., Nat. CASA Assn., Am. Legion. Office: SD Supreme Ct 500 E Capitol Ave Pierre SD 57501-5070*

KONERKO, PAUL, baseball player; b. Providence, Mar. 2, 1976; 1st baseman Chgo. White Sox, 1999—. Host Starlight Children's Found., Comiskey Park. Office: Chgo White Sox 333 W 35th St Chicago IL 60616*

KONICEK, MICHAEL, city official; b. Cleve., Oct. 5, 1943; m. Paula Lauracella; children: David, John. B Chem. Engring., MSChemE, Ohio State U., 1966. Rsch. engr. Sohio, Cleve., 1966-69; sr. rsch. engr. Monsanto Rsch. Corp., Dayton, Ohio, 1969-72; R & D group leader, tech. supt., staff engr. Diamond Shamrock, Cleve., mgr. R & D and market devel., mgr. bus. devel., 1972-82; mgr. bus. devel. Eltech Sys. Corp., Chardon, Ohio, 1982-84; v.p., ptnr. Lectranator Corp., 1984-87; tech. mgr. Lectranator Corp. subs. Olin Corp., 1987-90; dir. pub. utilities City of Cleve., 1990—. Bd. dirs. N.E. Ohio Regional Sewer Dist., 1994—. Office: Cleve Dept Pub Utilities 1201 Lakeside Ave Cleveland OH 44114-1132

KÖNIG, PETER, pediatrician, educator; b. Cluj, Romania, Feb. 14, 1938; came to U.S., 1976; s. Rudolf and Irina (Grünwald) K.; m. Lea Schiffer, Sept. 30, 1965; 1 child, Orly. Graduate, Timisoara Med. Sch., Romania, 1959; MD, Hebrew U., Jerusalem, 1966; PhD, U. London, 1974. Resident Bikur Cholim Hosp., Jerusalem, 1970-71, staff, 1974-76; fellow in pulmonary diseases Brompton Hosp., London, 1971-74; asst. prof. child health U. Mo., Columbia, 1976-80, assoc. prof. child health, 1980-84, prof. in child health, 1984—. Fellow Am. Acad. Allergy; mem. Am. Thoracic Soc., Acad. Allergy, Soc. Pediatric Research, Chilean Asthma Found., Sigma Xi. Home: 1310 Vintage Dr Columbia MO 65203-4878 Office: U Mo Child Health 1 Hospital Dr Columbia MO 65212-5276 E-mail: KonigP@health.missouri.edu.

KONOPINSKI, VIRGIL JAMES, industrial hygienist; b. Toledo, July 11, 1935; BSChemE, U. Toledo, 1956; MSChemE, Pratt Inst., 1960; MBA, Bowling Green State U., 1971. Registered profl. engr., Ohio, Ind., Calif.; cert. indsl. hygienist; cert. safety profl. Assoc. engr. Owens Illinois, Toledo, 1956, 60; real estate developer Grand Rapids, 1961; chem. engr. USPHS, Cin., 1961-64; sr. environ. engr. Vistron Corp., Lima, 1964-67; environ. specialist, asst. to dir. environ. control Owens Corning Fiberglas, Toledo, 1967-72; gen. mgr. Midwest Environ. Mgmt., Maumee, 1972-73; staff specialist, indl. hygienist Williams Bros. Waste Control, Tulsa, Okla., 1973-75; dir. divsn. indsl. hygiene and radiol. health Ind. State Bd. Health, Indpls., 1975-87; exec. v.p. ACT of Ind., 1987-89; sr. cons. Occusafe, Chgo., 1990-91; regional safety engr., human resources analyst/safety U.S. Postal Svc., Bloomingdale, Ind., 1991—. Bd. dir. IOSHA indsl. hygiene, 1975-83; cons. indoor air, radon, occupational health, Zionsville, 1987-91, Cary, 1991—; lectr. Contbr. articles to profl. jours. With USNR, 1956-59. Mem.: Ret. Oficers Assn., Naval Res. Assn., Am. Soc. Safety Engrs., Am. Indsl. Hygiene Assn. Republican. Roman Catholic. Home: 14 Fairfield Ln Cary IL 60013-1946 Office: 4th Flr 244 Knollwood Dr Fl 4 Bloomingdale IL 60108-2208

KONZ, GERALD KEITH, retired manufacturing company executive; b. Racine, Wis., Apr. 3, 1932; m. Marianne Bubolz; children: Richard C., Brenda S. BS in Econs., U. Wis., 1957, LLB, 1960. V.p. in charge corp. tax dept. S.C. Johnson & Son, Inc., Racine, 1982-98, chmn. bd. trustees pension trust, employee profit sharing and savs. plan, 1982-98. Bd. dirs. Johnson Family Funds, Inc., Racine; mem. adv. bd. Venture Investors, Inc., Madison, Wis., 1997—. Treas. St. Catherines H.S. Found., Racine, 1994—97, pres., 1997—2001; bd. dirs. YMCA, 1988—98. Mem. ABA, Tax Execs. Inst. (pres. Wis. chpt. 1972), Wis. Bar Assn., Racine-Kenosha Estate Planning Coun. (pres. 1980). Office: 3515 Taylor Ave Racine WI 53405-4727 E-mail: gkkonz@execpc.com.

KOOB, ROBERT DUANE, chemistry educator, educational administrator; b. Graetinger, Iowa, Oct. 14, 1941; s. Emil John and Rose Mary (Slinger) Koob; m. E. Yvonne Ervin, June 9, 1960; children: Monique, Gregory, Michael, Eric, David; children: Angela, Julie. BA in Edn., U. No. Iowa, 1962; PhD in Chemistry, U. Kans., 1967. From asst. prof. to prof. chemistry N.D. State U., Fargo, 1967—90, chmn. dept. chemistry, 1974—78, 1979—81, dir. Water Inst., 1975—85, dean Coll. Sci. and Math., 1981—84, v.p., 1985—90, interim pres., 1987—88; v.p. for acad. affairs, sr. v.p. Calif. Poly. State U., San Luis Obispo, 1990—95; pres. U. No. Iowa, Cedar Falls, 1995—, prof., 1995—. Cons. TransAlta, Edmondton, Alta., Canada, Alta. Rsch. Coun., Mitre Corp., Washington; bd. dirs. State Bank Fargo, Fargo Cass County Econ. Devel. Corp.; chair bd. dirs. Cal Poly Found.; chair Iowa Coordinating Coun. for Post-H.S. Edn., 1996—97. Contbr. articles to profl. jours. V.p. Crookston Diocesan Sch. Bd., Minn., 1982; pres. elem. sch. bd., St. Joseph's Ch., Moorhead, 1982, parish coun., Moorhead, 1983; pres. bd. Shanley H.S., Fargo, 1985. Grantee in field. Mem.: Iowa Assn. Coll. Pres. (pres. 1996—). Roman Catholic. Avocations: reading, flying, sailing, racquet sports, water skiing . Office: Univ of Northern Iowa 1227 W 27th St Cedar Falls IA 50614-0001

KOOISTRA, WILLIAM HENRY, clinical psychologist; b. Grand Rapids, Mich., May 20, 1936; s. Henry P. and Marguerite (Brinks) K.; m. Jean Heynen, Aug. 24, 1957 (div. Dec. 1984); children: Kimberly Lynn, William Peter, Kristin Jean, Allison Carol; m. Carol Sue Smitter, Mar. 9, 1985. BA, Calvin Coll., 1957; PhD, Wayne (Mich.) State U., 1963. Diplomate Am. Bd. Profl. Psychology, Am. Bd. Forensic Examiners. Intern psychology Lafayette Clinic, Detroit, 1961-62; chief psychologist Pine Rest Christian Hosp., Grand Rapids, Mich., 1964-67; clin. psychologist Kooistra, Jansma, Teitsma, DiNallo & Van Hoek, 1967—. Instr. Wayne State U., 1959-63, Hope Coll., Holland, Mich., 1964, Calvin Coll., Grand Rapids, 1964-81, Grand Valley State U., 1987-92. Founder Project Rehab., Grand Rapids, 1968, bd. dirs., 1969—, pres., 1972-74; mem. Kent County Dem. Exec. Com., 1969-73, 79-82, 86—, mem. governing bd. Fountain Street Ch., 1989-95, pres. 1994; rep. 3d dist. Presl. Electoral Coll., 1992. Mem. Am. Psychol. Assn. (council rep. 1982-85), Am. Soc. Psychologists in Pvt. Practice (sec. 1973-75), Mich. Psychol. Assn.(pres. 1979), Mich. Soc. Forensic Psychology, Grand Rapids Area Psychol. Assn (pres. 1968). Avocations: golf, tennis, sailing. Home: 2946 Cascade Rd SE Grand Rapids MI 49506-1965 Office: 3330 Claystone St SE Grand Rapids MI 49546-7716

KOONTZ, FRANK P. microbiology educator, research administrator; Prof. U. Iowa; dir. clin. microbiology lab. U. Iowa Hosps. and Clinics, Iowa City. Recipient Sonnenwirth Meml. award Am. Soc. Microbiology, 1995. Office: U Iowa Hosps and Clinics Dept Pathology Iowa City IA 52242 E-mail: franklin-koontz@viowa.edu.

KOOP, CHARLES HUBERT, lawyer; b. Plymouth, Wis., Feb. 23, 1950; s. Chester S. and G. Windred (Smith) K.; m. Christine A. Blue, Aug. 7, 1971; children: Haley, Sally, Charles II. BA, Eastern Mich. U., 1973; JD, Detroit Coll. Law, 1976. Bar: Mich. 1977, U.S. Dist. Ct. (ea. dist.) Mich. 1977, U.S. Dist. Ct. (we. dist.) Mich. 1979, U.S. Ct. Appeals (6th cir.) 1985, U.S. Supreme Ct. 1986, U.S. Ct. Claims 1987. Atty. Eastern Mich. Legal Service, Flint, 1977; sole practice Traverse City, Mich., 1977-80; chief trial prosecutor, office pros. atty. Grand Traverse County, 1980-84; ptnr. Thompson, Zirnhelt, Koop, Seaman, Bruce & Gurnst, P.C. and predecessor firm, 1984—. Spl. pros. Benize County, 1988—, Manister County, 1989—. Grantee Nat. Dist. Attys. Assn., 1973, Pros. Attys. Assn. Mich., 1973. Mem. ABA, Mich. Bar Assn., Grand Traverse, Leelanau & Antrim Bar Assn. (pres. 1984-85, v.p. 1983, sec., treas. 1982, bd. govs. 1986). Episcopalian. Club: Exchange (Traverse City). Lodge: Rotary. Home: PO Box 411 Kewadin MI 49648

KOPELOW, ERIC, food service executive; b. Phila., Jan. 6, 1959; two children. Grad., Culinary Inst. Am. Extern Montauk (N.Y.) Yacht Club, 1979; exec. chef Ramadas Downington (Pa.) Inn and Resort, 1980-81, Indian River Plantation Hotel and Resort, Hutchenson Island, Stuart, Fla., 1981; exec. sous chef/garde mgr. chef Washington Hilton Hotel and Towers, Washington, 1981-83; exec. chef gourmet restaurants Trumps Castle Hotel and Casino, Atlantic City, 1985; exec. chef United Airlines-Phila. Internat. Airport, 1983-94; corp. exec. chef R&D United Airlines Corp., Elk Grove Village, Ill., 1994—. Recipient Grand Champion gold medal award Am. Culinary Fedn., 1996. Avocations: motorcycling, collecting pinball and slot machines, collecting Planet Hollywood pins. Office: United Airlines PO Box 66100 Chicago IL 60666-0100 E-mail: cheferic7006555@aol.com.

KOPF, GEORGE MICHAEL, retired ophthalmologist; b. Chilton, Wis., Oct. 20, 1935; s. George and Mary (Schmid) K.; m. Sandra Mary Nolte, Dec. 29, 1962; children: Karen, Jennifer, Nancy. BS, U. Wis., 1958, MD, 1961. Diplomate Am. Bd. Ophthalmology. Intern Luther Hosp., Eau Claire, Wis., 1961-62; resident Milw. County Hosp., 1962-63, Detroit Gen. Hosp., 1965-68; ophthalmologist pvt. practice, Zanesville, Ohio, 1968—; ret., 1999. Mem. med. staff Bethesda Hosp., Zanesville; mem. med. Staff Good Samaritan Med. Ctr., Zanesville, pres., 1978, sec. bd. dirs., 1986-96. Capt. USAF, 1963-65. Fellow ACS, Am. Acad. Ophthalmology; mem. Ohio Ophthalmology Soc. (pres. 1976-77), Muskigum County Acad. Medicine (pres. 1983), Ohio State Med. Assn., Rotary. Republican. Roman Catholic. Avocations: tennis, swimming, hiking, reading, travel. Home: 2950 Ash Meadows Blvd Zanesville OH 43701-9081

KOPF, RICHARD G. federal judge; b. 1946; BA, U. Nebr., Kearney, 1969; JD, U. Nebr., Lincoln, 1972. Law clk. to Hon. Donald R. Ross U.S. Ct. Appeals (8th cir.), 1972-74; ptnr. Cook, Kopf & Doyle, Lexington, Neb., 1974-87; U.S. magistrate judge, 1987-92; fed. judge U.S. Dist. Ct. (Nebr. dist.), 1992—, chief judge, 1999—. Mem. ABA, ABA Found., Nebr. State Bar, Nebr. State Bar Found. Office: US Dist Ct 586 US Courthouse 100 Centennial Mall N Lincoln NE 68508-3859

KOPRIVICA, DOROTHY MARY, management consultant, real estate and insurance broker; b. St. Louis, May 27, 1921; d. Mitar and Fema (Kuzmic) K. BS, Washington U., St. Louis, 1962. cert. in def. inventory mgmt. Dept. Def., 1968. Mgmt. analyst Transp. Supply and Maintenance Command, St. Louis, 1954-57, Dept. Army Transp. Material Command, St. Louis, 1957-62; program analyst Dept. Army Aviation System Command, 1962-74, spl. asst. to comdr., 1974-78; ins. broker D. Koprivica, Ins., 1978-81; real estate broker, 1978-81. Mem. Bus. and Profl. Women (pres. 1974-75), Order Ea. Star. Eastern Orthodox.

KORANDO, DONNA KAY, journalist; b. Chester, Ill., Mar. 31, 1950; d. Samuel L. and Dorothy L. (Meyer) K.; m. James J. Heidenry, Nov. 28, 1981; children: Reid Samuel, Rachel. BA, So. Ill. U., 1972; MSL, Yale U., 1980. Tchr. journalism Lincoln H.S., Manitowoc, Wis., 1972-73; copy editor St. Louis Post-Dispatch, 1973-77, editorial writer, 1977-86, editor commentary page, 1986—. Mem. Lafayette Square Restoration Com., St. Louis, 1981—. Mem. Assn. Opinion Page Editors (bd. dirs.). Roman Catholic. Avocations: children, literature. Office: St Louis Post Dispatch 900 N Tucker Blvd Saint Louis MO 63101-1099

KORBITZ, BERNARD CARL, retired oncologist, hematologist, educator, consultant; b. Lewistown, Mont., Feb. 18, 1935; s. Fredrick William and Rose Eleanore (Ackmann) K.; m. Constance Kay Bolz, June 22, 1957; children: Paul Bernard, Guy Karl. B.S. in Med. Sci., U. Wis.-Madison, 1957, M.D., 1960, M.S. in Oncology, 1962; LL.B., LaSalle U., 1972. Asst. prof. medicine and clin. oncology, U. Wis. Med. Sch., Madison, 1967-71; dir. medicine Presbyn. Med. Ctr., Denver, 1971-73; practice medicine specializing in oncology, hematology, Madison, 1973-76; med. oncologist, hematologist Radiologic Ctr. Meth. Hosp., Omaha, 1976-82; practice medicine specializing in oncology, hematology, Omaha, 1982-95, ret., 1995; sci. advisor Citizen's Environ. Com., Denver, 1972-73; mem. Meth. Hosp., Omaha, 1977—; dir. Bernard C. Korbitz, P.C., Omaha, 1983-96; bd. dirs., pres. B.C. Korbitz P.C., ret., 1996. Contbr. articles to profl. jours. Webelos leader Denver area Council, Mid. Am. Council of Nebr. Boy Scouts Am.; bd. elders King of Kings Luth. Ch., Omaha, 1979-80; bd. elders St. Mark Luth. Ch., Omaha, 1993-98; mem. People to People Del. Cancer Update to People's Republic China, 1986, Eastern Europe and USSR, 1987; mem. U.S. Senatorial Club, 1984, Republican Presdl. Task Force, 1984. Served to capt. USAF, 1962-64. Named Medford (Wis.) H.S. Athletic Hall of Fame, 1997. Fellow ACP, Royal Soc. Health; mem. Am. Soc. Clin. Oncology, Am. Soc. Internal Medicine, AMA, Nebr. Med. Assn., Omaha Med. Society, Omaha Clin. Soc., Phi Eta Sigma, Phi Beta Kappa, Phi Kappa Phi, Alpha Omega Alpha. Avocations: photography, fishing, travel. Home: 9024 Leavenworth St Omaha NE 68114-5150

KORDONS, ULDIS, lawyer; b. Riga, Latvia, July 9, 1941; came to U.S., 1949; s. Evalds and Zenta Alide (Apenits) K.; m. Virginia Lee Knowles, July 16, 1966. AB, Princeton U., 1963; JD, Georgetown U., 1970. Bar: N.Y. 1970, Ohio 1978, Ind. 1989. Assoc. Whitman, Breed, Abbott & Morgan, N.Y.C., 1970-77, Anderson, Mori & Rabinowitz, Tokyo, 1973-75; counsel Armco Inc., Parsippany, N.J., 1977-84; v.p., gen. counsel, sec. Sybron Corp., Saddle Brook, 1984-88, Hillenbrand Industries Inc., Batesville, Ind., 1989-92; pres. Plover Enterprises, Cin., 1992-95, Kordons & Co., LPA, Cin., 1996—. Lt. USN, 1963-67. Mem. N.Y. Bar Assn., Ohio Bar Assn., Ind. Bar Assn. Office: 8238 Wooster Pike Cincinnati OH 45227-4010 E-mail: ukordlaw@aol.com.

KOREN, YORAM, mechanical engineering educator; b. Tel Aviv, Aug. 1, 1938; came to U.S., 1985; s. Shlomo and Bathia (Rabinowitz) Shterwzis; m. Aliza Halina Palyard, Apr. 3, 1963; children: Shlomik, Esther. Prof. U. Mich., Ann Arbor. Cons. Ford, Coldy Internat., Cybernet System, Metcut, SKF, Frat, 1980—. Author: Computer Control of Manufacturing Systems, 1983, Robotics for Engineers, 1985, Numerical Control of Machine Tools, 1978; contbr. articles to profl. jours.; patentee in field. Sgt. maj. USAF, 1957-61. Fellow SME, ASME; mem. IEEE (sr.), CIRP. Home: 4101 Thornoaks Dr Ann Arbor MI 48104-4255 Office: U Mich 2250 GG Brown Bldg Ann Arbor MI 48109-2125

KORENIC, LYNETTE MARIE, librarian; b. Berwyn, Ill., Mar. 29, 1950; d. Emil Walter and Donna Marie (Harbutt) K. m. Jerome Dennis Reif, Dec. 31, 1988. BS in Art, U. Wis., 1977, MFA, 1979, MA in LS, 1981, MA in Art History, 1984. Asst. art libr. Ind. U., Bloomington, 1982-84; art libr. U. Calif., Santa Barbara, 1984-88, head Arts Libr., 1988-99; art libr. U. Wis., Madison, 1999—. Author articles. Mem. Art Librs. Soc. N.Am. (sec. 1983-84, v.p. 1989, pres. 1990), Beta Phi Mu. Office: U Wis Kohler Art Libr Madison WI 53706 E-mail: lkorenic@library.wisc.edu.

KORHONEN, KAI ANTERO, paper products executive; Pres., CEO Consolidated Papers (now Stora Enso), Wisconsin Rapids, Wis., 2000—. Office: Stora Enso 231 1st Ave N Wisconsin Rapids WI 54495

KORNFELD, STUART A. hematology educator; b. St. Louis, Oct. 4, 1936; AB, Dartmouth Coll., 1958; MD, Washington U., 1962. Rsch. asst. biochemistry dept. sch. medicine Washington U., St. Louis, 1958-62, from instr. to asst. prof. medicine, 1966-70, from asst. to assoc. prof. biochemistry, 1968-72, prof. medicine dept. internal medicine, 1972—, prof. biochemistry, co-dir. divsn. hematology and oncology, 1976—, dir. divsn. oncology, 1973-76; intern med. ward Barnes Hosp., 1962-63, asst. resident, 1965-66; rsch. assoc. nat. inst. arthritis and metabolic disease NIH, 1963-65. Faculty rsch. assoc. Am. Cancer Soc., 1966-71; mem. cell biology study sect. NIH, 1974-77; mem. bd. sci. counselors Nat. Inst. Arthritis, Diabetes & Digestive & Kidney Disease, 1983-87; mem. sci. rev. bd. Howard Hughes Med. Inst., 1986—; mem. bd. sci. advisers Jane Coffin Childs Meml. Fund. Res., 1987—; Jubilee lectr. Biochemistry Soc., 1989. Assoc. editor Jour. Clin. Investigation, 1977-81, editor, 1981-82; assoc. editor Jour. Biol. Chemistry, 1982-87; author 145 publs. Recipient Borden award, 1962, Rsch. Career Devel. award NIH, 1971-76; named Harden Medallist, Biochemistry Soc., 1989, Passano Found. laureate, 1991. Mem. NAS (mem. inst. medicine), Am. Soc. Clin. Investigation (counselor 1972-75), Am. Soc. Hematology, Am. Soc. Biol. Chemists, Assn. Am. Physicians (sec. 1986—), Am. Acad. Arts and Sci., Am. Chem. Soc., Sigma Xi. Achievements include research in the structure, biosynthesis and function of glycoproteins, especially those which are found on the surface of normal and malignant cells, targeting of newly synthesized acid hydroloses to lysosomes. Office: 8826 Clin Scis Res Bldg PO Box 8125 Saint Louis MO 63156-8125

KORNGOLD, GERALD, law educator; BA, U. Pa., 1974, JD, 1977. Bar: Pa. Atty. Wolf, Block, Schorr & Solis-Cohen, Phila., 1977-79; asst. prof. to prof. N.Y. Law Sch., N.Y.C., 1979-87, assoc. dean for acad. affairs, 1984-86; prof. Case Western Res. U. Sch. Law, Cleve., 1987—, Everett D. and Eugenia S. McCurdy prof., 1994—, dean, 1997—. Author: Private Land Use Arrangements: Easements, Covenants, and Equitable Servitudes, 1990, (with Paul Goldstein) Real Estate Transactions, 1993. Mem. Am. Law Inst. Office: Case Western Res U Sch Law 11075 East Blvd Cleveland OH 44106-5409

KORNICK, MICHAEL, chef; Grad., Culinary Inst. Am., 1982. Chef Quilted Giraffe, NY, Windsor Ct. Hotel, New Orleans; mng. ptnr. KDK Restaurant Group; exec. chef Gordon, 1985, Lettuce Entertain You Enterprises, Four Seasons Hotel Aujord'hui, Boston, 1991, Marche, Red Light; owner, chef MK the Restaurant, Chgo., 1998—. Named Best New Chef de Cuisine, Boston mag., 1992; recipient award, James Beard Found., 2001. Office: 868 N Franklin Chicago IL 60610

KORNMANN, CHARLES BRUNO, lawyer; b. Watertown, S.D., Sept. 14, 1937; BA, Coll. St. Thomas, 1959; LLB, Georgetown U., 1962. Bar: S.D. 1962. Ptnr. Richardson, Groseclose, Kornmann & Wyly, Aberdeen, S.D.; dist. judge U.S. Dist. Ct., 1995—. Mem. S.D. Constnl. Revision Commn., 1974-77, S.D. Bd. Charities and Corrections, 1973-80, pres. 1978. Mem. Brown County Bar Assn., The State Bar of S.D. (bd. commrs. 1978-81, pres. 1988-89), Assn. Ins. Attys., S.D. Trial Lawyers Assn., Phi Delta Phi. Office: District of SD Ctrl and Northern Divsn Kornmann & Wyly 102 4th Ave SE Ste 408 Aberdeen SD 57401-4309

KORSCHOT, BENJAMIN CALVIN, investment executive; b. LaFayette , Ind., Mar. 22, 1921; s. Benjamin G. and Myrtle P. (Goodman) K.; m. Marian Marie Schelle, Oct. 31, 1941; children: Barbara E. Korschot Haehlen, Lynne D. Korschot Gooding, John Calvin. BS, Purdue U., 1942; MBA, U. Chgo., 1947. V.p. No. Trust Co., Chgo., 1947-64; sr. v.p. St. Louis Union Trust Co., 1964-73; exec. v.p. Waddell and Reed Co., Kansas City, Mo., 1973-74, pres., 1974-79, vice-chmn. bd., 1979-85; pres. Waddell & Reed Investment Mgmt. Co., 1985-86; chmn. bd. Waddell & Reed Asset Mgmt. Co., 1973-86. Pres. United Group of Mut. Funds, Inc., Kansas City, Mo., 1974-85, chmn., 1985-86; vice-chmn. Roosevelt Fin. Group, St. Louis, 1968-91, chmn. adv. bd., 1991-92; treas. Helping Hand of Goodwill Industries, 1993-95, chmn. investment com., 1995—; bd. dirs. Mo. United Meth. Found., 1995—, chmn. investment com., 2001—; chmn. bd. govs. Investment Co. Inst., 1980-82; chmn. bd. Fin. Analyst Fedn., 1978-79; chmn. investment comt., 2001-. Contbr. articles on investment fin. to profl. publs.; author autobiography, 1997. Mem. Civic Coun. Greater Kansas City, Mo., 1974-85; chmn. fin. com. ARC Retirement Sys., 1986-87. With USN, 1942-45, 50-52. Mem. Inst. CFAs, Fin. Execs. Inst., Kansas City Soc. Fin. Analysts, Lakewood Oaks Golf Club. Republican. Home: 101 NW Hackberry St Lees Summit MO 64064-1477 E-mail: bckorschot@yahoo.com.

KORT, BETTY, secondary education educator; English tchr. Hastings (Nebr.) Sr. High Sch., 1979—. Named Nebr. State English Tchr. of Yr., 1993. Office: Hastings Sen High Sch 1100 W 14th St Hastings NE 68901-3064

KOSKAN, JOHN M. state legislator; b. Winner, S.D., Sept. 27, 1955; s. Milo Harlan and Juanita Mae (Mitchell) K.; m. Verna Gale Heying, 1973; children: Fawn Michelle, Tracy Michael, Joel Mathew, Joni Melissa. BS, S.D. Sch. Mines & Tech., 1977. Mem. Sch. Bd., Wood, S.D., 1984-90, S.D. Ho. of Reps., 1991-2000, mem. taxation and transp. coms.; design engr. Boeing Aircraft, Wichita, Kans., 1977-79, Cessna Aircraft Co., Wichita, 1979-80; design cons., mfr. Piper Advanced Technologies, 1980-81; farmer, rancher Wood, S.D., 1980—; mem. S.D. Senate from 26th dist., Pierre, 2001—. Home: HC 1 Box 117A Wood SD 57585-9611 Office: State Capitol Senate 500 E Capitol Ave Pierre SD 57501-5070

KOSMAHL, HENRY GOTTFRIED, electron physicist; b. Wartha, Germany, Dec. 14, 1919; came to U.S., 1956, naturalized, 1962; m. Gisela Zelder; children: Monika, Beatrix, Ronald. Student, U. Dresden, Germany, 1940-43; D.S., U. Darmstadt, Germany, 1949. Asst. prof. U. Darmstadt, 1949-50; research physicist Telefunken-AEG, Ulm, Germany, 1950-56; head microwave amplifiers NASA Lewis Research Ctr., Cleve., 1956-84; disting. rsch. assoc. NASA Le R Ctr., 1984—; cons. NASA, Westlake, Ohio; co-owner, founder AWT Co. Cons. Aero. Systems and Space divs. USAF., Westinghouse E.D.D.; sci. cons. Hughes AC, Electron Dynamics div., 1984-89 Co-author 2 books; past assoc. editor: Transactions on Electronic Devices; contbr. sci. articles to profl. jours. Recipient Sci. Achievement medal NASA, 1973, Inventor of Yr. award, 1987, Disting. Rsch. Assoc., 1994, LauraLs award Aviation Week, 1983; grantee NASA. Fellow IEEE (Tech. Advancement award 1977, Maj. Inventor award 1980, Cecon Centennial award 1983) Achievements include patents in U.S. and abroad. also: 30087 Persimmon Dr Westlake OH 44145

KOSS, JOHN CHARLES, consumer electronics products manufacturing company executive; b. Milw., Feb. 22, 1930; s. Earl L. and Eda K.; m. Nancy Weeks, Apr. 19, 1952; children: Michael, Debra, John Charles, Linda, Pamela. Student, U. Wis., Milw., 1952; D.Eng. (hon.), Milw. Sch. Engring. Founder Koss Corp., TV leasing co., Milw., 1953; owner, operator Koss Corp., 1953-58, pres., 1972-81, chmn. bd., 1974—, chief exec. officer, 1974-91; creator home-stereophone, 1958. Bd. dirs. Milw. Hearing Soc.; bd. dirs., past pres. Jr. Achievement S.E. Wis. With Air Force Band USAF, 1950-52. Named Entrepreneur of Yr. Research Dirs. Assn. Chgo., 1972, Mktg. Man of Yr. Milw. chpt., 1972; named to Audio Hall Fame, 1979; Mktg. Exec. of Yr. Sales and Mktg. Execs., 1976; recipient Debby award Soc. Audio Cons.'s, 1975 Mem. Chief Execs. Orgn., Inst. High Fidelity (pres. 1968), Wis. Pres.'s Orgn., World Bus. Coun. Republican. Baptist. Clubs: Milw. Country, University; Les Ambassadeurs (London). Office: Koss Corp 4129 N Port Washington Rd Milwaukee WI 53212-1029

KOSTECKI, MARY ANN, financial tax consultant, small business consultant; b. St. Louis, Jan. 6, 1941; 4 children. Student, Forest Park Jr. Coll., 1969-72, Washington U., 1973-77. Dem. candidate for U.S House 2nd Dist., Mo., 1996. Office: 7446 Sieloff Dr Ste G Hazelwood MO 63042-2250

KOSTKA, RONALD WAYNE, marketing consultant; b. Chgo., Sept. 13, 1931; s. James V. and Marie (Zvolanek) K.; m. Madonna Lou Miller, June 8, 1957 (div. Dec. 1980); children: Paul, Daniel, Jane; m. Irene Mary Harnett, Sept. 14, 1991. BS in journalism, U. Ill., Urbana, 1957. Reporter Champaign News Gazette, Champaign, Ill., 1956-57; copy editor Mpls. Tribune, Mpls., 1957-58; pub. rels. mgr. 3M Co., St. Paul, 1958-92; cons. mktg. Pub. Rel., Minnetonka, 1992—. Contbr. articles to profl. jours. Firearms safety instr. State of Minn., Minnetonka, 1967-77. Staff Sgt. USAF, 1951-55, Korea. Decorated Air medal (4 OLC), Purple Heart, Hwarang (Republic of Korea). Mem. DAV, Nat. Muzzle Loading Rifle Assn., NRA, Soc. of Profl. Jours. (cert 1957), Minnetonka Game & Fish Club. Avocations: canoeing, hunting, competitive skeet shooting. Home: 1004 Sunset Dr S Minnetonka MN 55305-1164

KOSTYO, JACK LAWRENCE, physiology educator; b. Elyria, Ohio, Oct. 1, 1931; s. Louis and Matilda (Thomasko) K.; m. Shirlianne Guth, June 10, 1953; children: Cecile A., Louis C. AB, Oberlin Coll., 1953; PhD, Cornell U., 1957; MD (hon.), U. Göteborg, 1978. NRC fellow Harvard Med. Sch., Boston, 1957-59; asst. prof., then prof. physiology Duke U., 1959-68; prof., chmn. dept. physiology Emory U., Atlanta, 1968-79; prof. physiology U. Mich. Med. Sch., Ann Arbor, 1979-94, chmn. dept. physiology, 1979-85, active prof. emeritus in internal medicine, 1995—; assoc. dir. Mich. Diabetes Rsch. and Tng. Ctr., 1986-97, dir. grants program, 1997—. Mem. endocrinology study sect. NIH/USPHS, 1967-71, internat. and coop. projects study sect., 1992-96; mem. physiology test com. Nat. Bd. Med. Examiners, 1974-77, mem. comprehensive part II com., 1986-91, U.S. Med. Licensure Examination Step 2 Com., 1990-91. Editor in chief Endocrinology, 1978-82; sect. editor Ann. Rev. Physiology, 1982-86; mem. editorial bd. Growth Regulation, 1990-97; contbr. articles to profl. jours. Mem. adv. bd. Searle Scholars. Recipient Lederle Med. Faculty award, 1961, Ernst Oppenheimer Meml. award Endocrine Soc., 1969 Mem. Endocrine Soc. (editl. bd., coun., chmn. awards com.), Am. Physiol. Soc. (editl. bd., coun., chmn. standing com. on edn., mem. coun. of endocrinology and metabolism sect., chmn. endocrinology and metabolism sect. 1990-91, rep. to Coun. Acad. Socs. of Assn. Am. Med. Colls., mem. AAAS sect. on med. scis., editor Handbook of Physiology sect. 7, Endocrinology, vol. 5), Soc. for Exptl. Biology and Medicine (editl. bd.), Internat. Union Physiol. Scis. (commn. on med. edn.), Assn. Chmn. Depts. Physiology (pres. 1979, coun.), Am. Diabetes Assn., Coun. Acad. Socs. (adminstrv. bd. 1983-86), Sigma Xi. Home: 1100 Highway 98 E Unit B304 Destin FL 32541-8516 Office: Mich Diabetes Rsch-Tng Ctr U Mich Med Sch 1331 E Ann St 0580 Ann Arbor MI 48109 E-mail: jkostyo@umich.edu.

KOTEN, JOHN A. retired communications executive; b. Indpls., May 21, 1929; s. Roy Y. and Margaret (Neerman) K.; m. Catherine M. Hruska, Nov. 22, 1952; children: John, Mark, Sarah. BA, North Cen. Coll., Naperville, Ill., 1951, LLD (hon.), 1991; postgrad., Northwestern U., 1953; LLD (hon.), Quincy Coll., 1990. Supr. field advt. Montgomery Ward, Chgo., 1951-52; asst. dir. pub. rels. Am. Osteo. Assn., 1952-53; editorial asst. Ill. Bell Tel. Co., 1955-56, editor Telebriefs newsletter, 1956-57, supr. info., 1957-59, supr. comml. staff, 1959-60, supr. news svc. and advt. Springfield, 1960-62, dist. comml. mgr., 1962-63; supr. pub. info. AT&T, N.Y.C., 1963, supr. customer rels., 1963-64; mgr. div. traffic Ill. Bell Tel. Co., Chgo., 1965-66, mgr. pub. rels., 1966-68, asst. v.p. civic affairs, 1968-69, asst. v.p. Chgo. ops., 1969-70, gen. mgr. upstate area Joliet, 1970-71; dir. state regulatory matters AT&T, Lisle, Ill., 1971-72; asst. v.p. pub. rels. Ill. Bell Tel. Co., Chgo., 1972-74; dir. pub. rels. AT&T, N.Y.C., 1974-75; v.p. pub. rels. N.J. Bell Telephone Co., Newark, 1975-77, Ill. Bell Telephone Co., Chgo., 1977-80, v.p. corp. communications, 1980-87; sr. v.p. corp. communications Ameritech Corp., Chgo., 1987-92, ret., 1992; pres. The Wordsworth Group, Barrington Hills, Ill. Trustee Chgo. Symphony Orch., 1985-97, life trustee, 1997—; trustee Joint Coun. on Econ. Edn., N.Y.C.; trustee Am. Coun. Arts, 1987-98, treas., 1991-93; v.p. Ill. Arts Alliance, Chgo., 1986-91; trustee Arthur W. Page Soc., 1985—, pres., 1985-87; pres. Ameritech Found., Chgo., 1987-94; vice chmn. Am. Arts Alliance, Washington, 1983-92; bd. dirs. Am. Symphony Orch. League, Washington, 1982-94, Gt. Books Found., Chgo., 1991—, chmn. exec. com.; trustee SOS Children's Internat. Villages, Ill., 1996-00; trustee Assoc. Colls. Ill., Chgo., 1986-96, life trustee, 1997—; trustee Nat. Cultural Alliance, 1990-98; bd. visitors Medill Sch. Journalism, Northwestern U., 1988-94; assoc. trustee Wordsworth Trust, Eng., 1988; mem. corp. coun. Bus. Com. for Arts, 1988-96; mem. bd. overseers Curtis Inst. Music, Phila., 1997—; life trustee North Ctrl. Coll., Ill., 1997—; bd. trustees Dist. 220 Edn. Found., vice chmn., 1999—. Mem. Pub. Rels. Soc. Am., Conf. Bd. Corp. Communications Coun., Chgo. Advt. Club (bd. dirs. 1978-82), Ind. Soc., Pub. Affairs Coun., Brookings Coun., Chgo. Club, Tavern Club, Econs. Club, Chgo. Yacht Club. Home and Office: The Wordsworth Group 271 Otis Rd Barrington IL 60010-5123

KOTLOWITZ, ALEX, writer, journalist; Student, Wesleyan U. Former prodr. segments TV series MacNeil/ Lehrer NewsHour; former reporter The Wall Street Jour.; former contbr. NPR. Author: There Are No Children Here: The Story of Two Boys Growing Up In the Other America, 1991 (Helen Bernstein award Excellence Journalism N.Y. Pub. Libr. 1992), The Other Side of the River: A Story of Two Towns, a Death and America's Dilemma, 1998 (Heartland prize for nonfiction Chgo. Triune 1998); contbr. various mags., including The New Yorker, The N.Y. Times Mag., This Am. Life. Recipient George Polk award TV reporting Long Island U. Journalism dept. work on MacNeil/Lehrer NewsHour, 1984, Robert F. Kennedy award Coverage of Disadvantaged.

KOTOWICZ, WILLIAM E. dean, dental educator; Acting dean U. Mich., Ann Arbor. Office: U Mich Sch Dentistry 1011 N University Ave Ann Arbor MI 48109-1078

KOTULAK, RONALD, newspaper science writer; b. Detroit, July 31, 1935; s. John and Mary (Roman) K.; m. Jean Bond, May 6, 1961 (dec. July 1974); chidren: Jeffrey, Kerry, Christopher; m. Donna Clausonthue, July 19, 1980; stepchildren: Paul, Lisa. Student, Wayne State U., 1953-54; BJ, U. Mich., 1959. Mem. staff Chgo. Tribune, 1959—, sch. bd. reporter, 1961-63, writer, 1965—. Recipient 1st pl. sci. writing award ADA, 1966, 1st pl. med. writing award AMA, 1968, 1st pl. Howard Blakeslee sci. writing award Am. Heart Assn., 1968, 1st prize Russell L. Cecil award Arthritis Found., 1969, 1st pl. Claude Bernard Sci. Journalism award Nat. Soc. Med. Rsch., 1971, James T. Brady award Am. Chem. Soc., 1974, Lifeline award Am. Health Found., 1976, Edward Scott Beck award Chgo. Tribune, 1965, 76, 91, 93, Outstanding Achievement award U. Mich., 1978, Robert T. Morse Writers award Am. Psychiat. Assn., 1982, 89, Helen Carringer Nat. Mental Health Journalism award Nat. Mental Health Assn., 1988, Excellence in Journalism award Am. Aging Assn., 1992, Pulitzer Prize for explanatory journalism, 1994, others. Mem. Nat. Assn. Sci. Writers (pres. 1972-73). Home: 737 N Oak Park Ave Oak Park IL 60302-1536 Office: The Chicago Tribune 435 N Michigan Ave Chicago IL 60611-4066

KOUCHOUKOS, NICHOLAS THOMAS, surgeon; b. Grand Rapids, Mich., Dec. 26, 1936; s. Thomas Paul and Antoinette (Karver) K.; m. Judith Buell, Aug. 24, 1966; children— Nicholas Thomas, Robert Buell, Thomas Paul. Student (James B. Angell scholar), U. Mich., 1954-57; MD cum laude, Washington U., 1961. Diplomate Am. Bd. Thoracic Surgery (bd. dirs. 1989-96). Intern Barnes Hosp., Washington U. Med. Ctr., St. Louis, 1961-62, asst. resident in surgery, 1962-65, chief adminstrv. resident, 1965-66; sr. clin. trainee in surgery USPHS, 1966-67; asst. in surgery Sch. Medicine Washington U., St. Louis, 1961-65, instr. surgery, 1965-67, John M. Shoenberg prof. cardiovascular surgery, 1984-96, vice chmn. dept. surgery, 1993-96; research fellow surgery Sch. Medicine, U. Ala., Birmingham, 1967-68, instr. surgery, 1967-69, advanced trainee thoracic and cardiovascular surgery, 1968-70, asst. prof. surgery, 1969-71, assoc. prof., 1971-74, prof., vice-dir. div. thoracic and cardiovascular surgery, 1974-81, John W. Kirkin prof. cardiovascular surgery, 1981, clin. prof., 1981-84; cardiovascular surgeon-in-chief Jewish Hosp. of St. Louis, 1984-96, surgeon in chief, 1988-96; mem. cardiovascular research study com. Am. Heart Assn., 1977-79; surgery study sect. USPHS, Bethesda, Md., 1977-80; vice chmn. dept. surgery Washington U. Sch. Medicine, St. Louis, 1991-96. Ad hoc cons. Specialized Centers in Research Arteriosclerosis, Nat. Heart and Lung Inst., Bethesda, 1971-72, mem. ad hoc rev. com. for collaborative studies on coronary artery surgery, 1973-75, surgery A study sect., 1976-77; mem. merit rev. bd. in cardiovascular studies VA, Washington, 1976-78 Editorial bd. Jour. Cardiac Rehab., 1979-84, Current Topics in Cardiology, 1977-92, Circulation, 1978-81, 86-88, Cardiology Update, 1979-92, Annals Thoracic Surgery, 1980-89, Cardiosat, 1984-92; assoc. editor Jour. Thoracic and Cardiovascular Surgery, 1994-98. Fellow: ACS, Am. Coll. Cardiology (asst. treas. 1997—99, sec. 1999—2000, finalist Young Investigators award 1962); mem.: AAUP, AMA, Internat. Cardiovascular Soc., Soc. Vascular Surgery, Soc. Univ. Surgeons, So. Surg. Assn., So. Thoracic Surg. Assn., St. Louis Thoracic Surg. Soc. (pres. 1993—95), Soc. Thoracic Surgeons (treas. 1992—97, v.p. 1998, pres. 1999—2000), John Kirklin Soc., St. Louis Met. Med. Soc., Internat. Surg. Soc., Assn. Acad. Surgery, Assn. Clin. Cardiac Surgeons, Am. Surg. Assn., Am. Assn. Thoracic Surgery, ALpha Omega Alpha, Phi Beta Kappa. Home: 25 Picardy Ln Saint Louis MO 63124-1606 Office: Mo Bapt Hosp 3009 N Ballas Rd Ste 266C Saint Louis MO 63131-2308 E-mail: htkouch@aol.com.

KOUCKY, JOHN RICHARD, metallurgical engineer, manufacturing executive; b. Chgo., Sept. 21, 1934; s. Frank Louis and Ella (Harshman) K.; m. Beverly Irene O'Dell, Aug. 16, 1958 (dec. May 1990); children: Deborah, Diane; m. Beverly Kay Cummins, Apr. 27, 1991 (dec. Jan. 1996); m. Mary Ann Hubbard, Jan. 4, 1997. BS in MetE., U. Ill., 1957; MBA, Northwestern U., 1959. Metallurgist, asst. plant mgr. Fansteel Metall. Corp., North Chicago, Ill., 1957-64; supr. production engring. cen. foundry div. Gen. Motors Corp., Saginaw, Mich., 1964-67; asst. gen. mgr. Marion (Ind.) Malleable Iron, 1967-68; mgr. production engring. tech., plant mgr., v.p. engr. Wagner Castings Co., Decatur, Ill., 1968-79, 83-91; v.p., gen. mgr. Pa. mall iron div. Gulf & Western, Lancaster, 1979-82; v.p. tech. Wagner Laser Techs., 1989-94; v.p. Decatur Mfg. Co., 1993-95, 300 Below, Inc., Decatur, 1993—. Served to 1st lt. U.S. Army, 1957-58. Mem. Am. Soc. Metals (local chmn. 1976—), Am. Foundrymans Soc. (local vice chmn. 1968—), Ductile Iron Soc. (nat. bd. dirs. 1983—), Iron Castings Soc., Soc. Automotive Engrs., U. Ill. Dept. Materials Sci. Alumni Assn. (bd. dirs. 1983-98, Loyalty award 1986), Gray Iron Founders Assn., Soc. for Advancement Material and Process Engring., Country Club Decatur, Decatur Tennis Club (pres. 1976-78), Decatur Racquet Club. Republican. Avocations: tennis, golf, bridge, gardening. Home: 510 Greenway Ln Decatur IL 62521-2533 Office: 300 Below Inc 2999 Parkway Dr Decatur IL 62526

KOUTSKY, DEAN ROGER, advertising executive; b. Omaha, Nov. 17, 1935; s. John Lewis and Ann Helen (Swan) K.; m. Kathryn Junette Strand; children: Linda, Lisa. BFA, Mpls. Coll. Art and Design, 1957. Art dir. Knox Reeves Advt., Inc., Mpls., 1958-65; v.p., exec. art dir. BBDO, Inc., 1965-70; v.p., assoc. creative dir. Campbell-Mithun, Inc., 1970-80, sr. v.p., creative dir., 1980-83, exec. v.p., exec. creative dir., 1983-85, vice chmn., 1985-89; exec. cons. Campbell-Mithun Esty, Inc., 1989-90; ptnr., mgr. Harmon Ct., 1991-97. Bd. trustees Mpls. Coll. Art and Design, 1982-90, chmn., bd. trustees, 1985-89, adj. prof. advt./design divsn., 1995—. Office: 2005 James Ave S Minneapolis MN 55405-2404

KOUVEL, JAMES SPYROS, physicist, educator; b. Jersey City, May 23, 1926; s. Spyros and Ifegenia (Cassianos) K.; m. Audrey Lumsden, June 26, 1953; children: Diana, Alexander. B.Engring., Yale U., 1946, Ph.D., 1951. Research fellow U. Leeds, Eng., 1951-53, Harvard, 1953-55; physicist Gen. Electric Co. Research and Devel. Center, 1955-69; prof. physics U. Ill.-Chgo., 1969—. Vis. scientist Atomic Energy Rsch. Establishment, Harwell, Eng., 1967-68; vis. prof. U. Paris, Orsay, France, 1981; cons. Argonne (Ill.) Nat. Lab., 1969-89, mem. rev. com., 1970-72, vis. scientist, 1973-74; mem. materials rsch. adv. com. NSF, 1980-82, mem. materials rsch. groups spl. emphasis panel, 1993; mem. evaluation panel NRC, 1981-85. Author papers in field.; Editor: Magnetism Conf. proc, 1965-67; editorial bd.: Jour. Magnetism and Magnetic Materials, 1975— . Served with USNR, 1944-46. Guggenheim fellow, 1967-68; NSF rsch. grantee, 1973-96. Fellow Am. Phys. Soc., AAAS Home: 223 N Euclid Ave Oak Park IL 60302-2107 Office: U Ill Physics Dept Chicago IL 60607-7059 E-mail: kouvel@uic.edu.

KOUYOUMJIAN, ROBERT G. electrical engineering educator; b. Apr. 26, 1923; BS in Physics, Ohio State U., 1948, PhD in Physics, 1953. Prof. emeritus dept. elec. engring. Ohio State U. Mem. URSI Commn. B. Fellow IEEE (Fellow award, Disting. Lectr., Centennial medal 1984); mem. Sigma Xi, Eta Kappa Nu, Sigma Pi Sigma. Office: Ohio State U Dept of Elec Engring Rm 256 2015 Neil Ave Dept Of Columbus OH 43210-1210

KOVAC, F. PETER, advertising executive; Pres., CEO NKH&W, Inc., Kansas City, Mo. Office: NKH&W Inc 5th Fl 600 Broadway Kansas City MO 64105

KOVACIK, THOMAS L. chief operating officer and safety director; b. Toledo, Aug. 9, 1947; BS in Chemistry, Bowling Green State U., 1969, MA, 1971. Chemist water treatment City of Toledo, 1967-69, chief chemist water plant, chief chemist, dir. pollution control, dir. pub. utilities, 1982-89; pres. Envirosafe, Toledo, 1989-92, Great Lakes N-Viro, 1992-94; cons. Toledo, 1994-96; COO, safety dir. City of Toledo, 1996—. Office: City of Toledo Ste 2200 1 Govt Ctr Toledo OH 43604

KOVACS, ROSEMARY, newpaper editor; BS in Journalism, Bowling Green State U., 1968. Mng. editor prodn. The Plain Dealer, Cleve., 1990—. Named to Bowling Green State U. Journalism Hall of Fame, 1988. Mem. Press Club of Cleve. (pres.). Office: Plain Dealer Pub Co 1801 Superior Ave Cleveland OH 44114-2198

KOVANDA, GARY, computer wholesale distributing executive; BS in Acctg., U. Ill., 1979. CPA, Ill. Controler Xetel Corp.; controller Comark, Bloomingdale, Ill., 1993-97, CFO, 1997—. Office: Comark 444 Scott Dr Bloomingdale IL 60108

KOWALSKI, KENNETH LAWRENCE, physicist, educator; b. Chgo., July 24, 1932; s. Florian Lawrence and Emily Helen (Sinoga) K.; m. Audrey Bellin; children— Eric Clifford, Claudia Gail. B.S., Ill. Inst. Tech., 1954; Ph.D. (Universal Match Found. fellow), Brown U., 1963. Aero. research scientist Lewis Research Center, NACA, 1954-57; research asso. in physics Brown U., summer 1962, Case Inst. Tech., Cleve., 1962-63, asst. prof. physics, 1963-67, asso. prof., 1967-73, Case Western Res. U., 1967-73, prof., 1973—, exec. officer dept. physics, 1970-71, chmn. dept. physics, 1971-76. Vis. prof. Inst. Theoretical Physics U. Louvain, Belgium, 1968-69; scientist-in-residence Argonne Nat. Lab., 1986-87, User Fermilab, 1993—. Author: (with S.K. Adhikari) Dynamical Collision Theory and It's Applications, 1991; editor: (with W.J. Fickinger) Modern Physics in America, 1988; contbr. articles to profl. jours. NSF grantee, 1972-96. Mem. Am. Phys. Soc. Achievements include rsch. on theoretical physics. Home: 2275 S Overlook Rd Cleveland Heights OH 44106-3141 Office: Case Western Res U Dept Physics 10900 Euclid Ave Dept Physics Cleveland OH 44106-1712

KOWALSKI, RICHARD SHELDON, hospital administrator; b. Detroit, Feb. 18, 1944; s. Richard Joseph and Margaret Lucile (Sheldon) K.; m. Doris Kay Smith, Nov. 20, 1982; children: Renée Marie, Jerrod Patrick, Sterling Prescott. BBA, Ea. Mich. U., 1966; MS in Health Adminstrn., Trinity U., San Antonio, 1971. Adminstrv. asst. Univ. Hosp.-U. Wash., Seattle, 1969-70; med. facilities cons. Ill. Dept. Health, Des Moines, 1970-72; asst. adminstr. Mercy Hosp., Cedar Rapids, Iowa, 1972-79; chief exec. officer St. Mary Med. Ctr., Galesburg, Ill., 1979—. Mem. coun. for govt. rev. Crescent Counties Found. for Med. Care, Naperville, Ill., 1986—; bd. dirs. Assn. Venture Corp., Naperville; chmn. bd. dirs. United Health Properties, Galesburg, 1985—; mem. adv. bd. Physician Hosp. Inst.; mem. comty. bd. Wells Fargo. Mem. strategic planning steering com. City of Galesburg, 1986—; bd. dirs. Econ. Devel. Coun., Galesburg, 1986—, Knox County Devel. Corp., 1986, Civic Ctr. Authority, 2001—. Named hon. alumnus Grad. Program in Hosp. and Health Adminstrn., U. Iowa, 1990. Fellow Am. Coll. Healthcare Execs. (regent Ctrl. Ill.); mem. Ill. Hosp. Assn. (pres. region 1-B, bd. dirs. 1987—, Disting. Leadership award 1986), Galesburg Area C. of C. (chmn. 1990), Soangetaha Country Club (bd. dirs. 1990), Rotary. Avocations: golf, tennis. Office: St Mary Med Ctr 3333 N Seminary St Galesburg IL 61401-1251

KOZAK, JOHN W. bank executive; b. Zanesville; With Mut. Fed. Savs. Bank (now named Century Nat. Bank), Park Nat. Corp. (formerly Mut. Fed. Savs. Bank), 1990, Park Nat. Bank, Newark, 1991-98, CFO, 1998, sr. v.p., 1998—. Office: Park Nat Bank 50 N 3d St Newark OH 43055 Fax: 740-349-3787.

KOZITZA, WILLIAM, printing company executive; CFO Taylor, North Mankato, Minn. Office: Taylor 1725 Roe Crest Dr North Mankato MN 56003 Office Fax: (507) 625-2988.

KOZMA, ADAM, electrical engineer; b. Cleve., Feb. 2, 1928; s. Desire and Vera (Nagy) K.; m. Eileen Marie Somogyi, Oct. 24, 1956 (dec. Jan. 1978); children: Paul A. (dec.), Peter A.; m. Rebecca Chelius, Feb. 6, 1993. BSME, U. Mich., 1952, MS in Engring.-Instrumentation Engring., 1964; MS in Engring. Mechanics., Wayne State U., 1961; PhDEE, U. London, 1968. Design engr. US Broach Co., Detroit, 1951-57; rsch. engr. Inst. Sci. & Tech., Willow Run Labs. U. Mich., Ann Arbor, 1958-69; gen. mgr. Electro Optics Ctr. Harris, Inc., 1969-73; sr. rsch. engr. radar div. Environ. Rsch. Inst. Mich., 1973-75, mgr. elec. and electromagnetics dept., 1975-76, mgr. tech. staff, 1976-77, v.p., dir. radar div., 1977-85, v.p., corp. devel., 1985-86; v.p., dir. def. electronics engring. div. Syracuse (N.Y.) Rsch. Corp., 1986-88; head intelligence systems dept. MITRE Corp., Bedford, Mass., 1988-89, head advanced systems dept., 1990-93; adj. prof. Coll. Engring. U. Mich., Ann Arbor, 1993—. Cons. Conductron Corp., Ann Arbor, 1966, IBM, Endicott, N.Y., 1967-68, U.S. Army Missile Command, Huntsville, Ala., 1974-76, MITRE Corp., 1993-2001, Veridian-ERIM-Internat., Inc., 1998-2001; lectr. various univs.; engring. cons., 1993—. Co-author: Hologram Visual Displays (Motion Picture TV Engrs. honorable mention 1977); patentee in field. With U.S. Army, 1946-47. Fellow IEEE (life), Optical Soc. Am.; mem. Aero. and Electronics Systems Soc. of IEEE (radar systems panel 1984—, bd. govs. 91-93), Geoscience and Remote Sensing Soc. of IEEE, Am. Def. Preparedness Assn. (chmn. various coms. avionics sect. 1975-88, Ordnance medal 1984), Soc. Photo-Optical Instrumentation Engrs., Sigma Xi. Lutheran. Avocations: tennis, skiing, bicycling. Home and Office: 2996 Appleway Ann Arbor MI 48104-1808 E-mail: akozma@cmcast.net.

KRAEMER, HARRY M. JANSEN, JR. medical products company executive; BA in Math. and Econs. summa cum laude, Lawrence U., 1977; M Mgmt. in Fin. and Acctg., Northwestern U., 1979. CPA, Ill. With N.W. Industries, Bank of Am.; dir. corp. devel. Baxter Internat. Inc., Deerfield, Ill., from 1982, various positions in domestic and internat. ops., sr. v.p., CFO, 1993-97, pres., 1997—, CEO, 1998—, mem. Office Chief Exec., 1995—, also bd. dirs. Bd. dirs. Comdisco, Inc., MedPtnrs., Inc., Sci. Applications Internat. Corp.; mem. coun. fin. execs. Conf. Bd. Bd. dirs. Highland Park (Ill.) Hosp.; mem. alumni adv. bd. Northwestern U. J.L. Kellogg Grad. Sch. Mgmt.; former mem. alumni bd. dirs. Lawrence U. Recipient Schaffner award Northwestern U. J.L. Kellogg Grad. Sch. Mgmt., 1996. Mem. Fin. Execs. Inst., Chgo. Club, Comml. Club Chgo., Mid-Am. Club, Execs. Club Chgo. Office: Baxter Internat Inc One Baxter Pky Deerfield IL 60015-4633

KRAFT, BURNELL D. agricultural products company executive; b. Chester, Ill., July 24, 1931; s. Herman F. and Ella Kraft; m. Shirley Ann Huch, Dec. 30, 1950; children: Jon B., Julie Ann Kraft Schwalbe. BS, So. Ill. U., 1956. Acct., mcht. Tabor and Co., Decatur, Ill., 1956-59, v.p., 1959-61, exec. v.p., 1961-70, pres., 1970-75; with Archer Daniels Midland Co. (merged with Tabor and Co.), 1975-84, corp. v.p., 1984-94, group v.p., 1994-97, sr. v.p., 1997—, pres. ADM/GROWMARK River System div., 1985—, pres. Collingwood Grain div., 1989-94. Bd. dirs. Alfred C. Toepfer Internat., United Grain Growers. Trustee Millikin U., Decatur, 1983-95, chmn. trustees, 1990-94; bd. dirs. Decatur Meml. Hosp., 1970-80. With U.S. Army, 1952-53, Korea. Mem. N.Am. Export Grain Assn., Nat. Feed Grains Council, Nat. Grain and Feed Assn., St. Louis Mchts. Exchange, Chgo. Bd. Trade, Decatur C. of C. (past bd. dirs.), Phi Kappa Phi, Beta Gamma Sigma. Republican. Lutheran. Clubs: Decatur, Country Club Decatur (bd. dirs. 1974-78). Avocations: aviation, golf, boating, tennis. Office: Archer Daniels Midland Co 4666 Faries Pkwy PO Box 1470 Decatur IL 62525-1820

KRALEWSKI, JOHN EDWARD, health service administration educator; b. Durand, Wis., May 20, 1932; s. Joseph and Esther (Hetrick) K.; m. Marjorie L. Gustafson; Apr. 22, 1957; children: Judy, Ann, Sara. BS in Pharmacy, U. Minn., 1956, MHA, 1962, PhD, 1969. Asst. prof. U. Minn., Mpls., 1965-69, prof., 1978—, U. Colo., Denver, 1969-78. Contbr. articles to profl. jours. 1st lt. USAF, 1957-60. Kellogg fellow Kellogg Found., 1962-65, Valencia (Spain) Acad. Medicine fellow, 1993. Mem. APHA, Assn. Health Svcs. Rsch. Avocation: oenology. Office: U Minn Health Svc Rsch 420 Delaware St SE Box 729 Minneapolis MN 55455-0374

KRAMER, CAROL GERTRUDE, marriage and family counselor; b. Grand Rapids, Mich., Jan. 14, 1939; d. Wilson John and Katherine Joanne (Wasdyke) Rottschafer; m. Peter William Kramer, July 1, 1960; children: Connie R. Kramer Sattler, Paul Wilson Kramer. AB, Calvin Coll., 1960; MA, U. Mich., 1969; PhD, Holy Cross Coll., 1973; MSW, Grand Valley State U., 1985. Diplomate Internat. Acad. Behavioral Medicine, Counseling and Psychotherapy, cert. addictions/substance abuse counselor Mich., hypnotherapist/psychotherapist, clin. certified forensic counselor 2001. Elem. tchr. Jenison (Mich.) Pub. Sch., 1960-65; sch. social worker Grand Rapids Pub. Sch., 1964-81; pvt. practice marriage and family counselor Grand Rapids, 1973—; v.p. Human Resource Assocs., 1983-88; pres. bd. dirs. Telecounseling, 1996-99. Guest lectr. Calvin Coll., Mich. State U., Grand Valley State U., 1975-85. Co-author: Parent Involvement Program, 1993, Stop Sexual Abuse for Everyone, 1996. Ruling elder 1st Presbyn. Ch., Grand Rapids, 1975-78; mem. Gerald R. Ford Rep. Women, Grand Rapids, 1980-87; co-chair pastoral rels. com. Gun Lake Community Ch., 1989-91, v.p. consistory, 1991-93; apptd. fellow State Mich. Bd. Marriage Counselors, 1985-87; pres. bd. dirs. Stop Sexual Abuse for Everyone. Named one of Outstanding Young Women in Am., 1974; recipient Meritorious Svc. award Kent County Family Life Coun., 1983. Fellow Am. Assn. Marriage and Family Therapist; mem. NASW, Mich. Assn. Marriage Counselors (awards com. 1988, chmn. 1991, nominations com. 1992-95), Kent County Family Life Coun. (pres. 1975), Voters Against Sexual Abuse (pres., bd. dirs. 1992—). Home: 12622 Park Dr Wayland MI 49348-9085 Office: 1251 Century Ave SW Ste 107 Grand Rapids MI 49503-8047

KRAMER, DALE VERNON, retired English language educator; b. Mitchell, S.D., July 13, 1936; s. Dwight Lyman and Frances Elizabeth (Corbin) K.; m. Cheris Gamble Kramarae, Dec. 21, 1960; children: Brinlee, Jana. B.S., S.D. State U., 1958; M.A., Case Western Res. U., 1960, Ph.D., 1963. Instr. English Ohio U., Athens, 1962-63, asst. prof., 1963-65, U. Ill., Urbana, 1965-67, assoc. prof., 1967-71, prof. English, 1971-96; prof. emeritus, 1997—; acting head English dept. U. Ill., Urbana, 1982, 86-87, assoc. dean Coll. of Arts & Scis., 1992-95. Chmn. bd. editors Jour. English and Germanic Philology, 1972-95; assoc. vice provost, prof. English, U. Oreg., 1990. Author: Charles Robert Maturin, 1973, Thomas Hardy: The Forms of Tragedy, 1975, Thomas Hardy: Tess of the d'Urbervilles, 1991; editor: Critical Approaches to the Fiction of Thomas Hardy, 1979, Thomas Hardy, The Woodlanders, 1981, 85, Thomas Hardy, The Mayor of Casterbridge, 1987, Critical Essays on Thomas Hardy: The Novels, 1990, The Cambridge Companion to Thomas Hardy, 1999. Served to capt. U.S. Army, 1958-66. Mem. Center for Advanced Study, 1971; Am. Philos. Soc. grantee, 1969, 86, NEH grantee, 1986. Congregationalist.

KRAMER, EUGENE LEO, lawyer; b. Barberton, Ohio, Nov. 7, 1939; s. Frank L. and Portia I. (Acker) Kramer; m. JoAnn Stockhausen, Sept. 17, 1970; children: Martin, Caroline, Michael. AB, John Carroll U., 1961; JD, U. Notre Dame, 1964. Bar: Ohio 1964. Law clk. U.S. Ct. Appeals (7th cir.), Chgo., 1964-65; ptnr. Squire, Sanders & Dempsey, Cleve., 1965-91, Roetzel & Andress, A Legal Profl. Assn., Cleve. and Akron, 1992-97. Cons. Ohio Constl. Revision Commn., Columbus, 1970—74. Trustee Regina Health Ctr., 1997—, pres., 2001—; past pres. HELP Found., Inc., HELP, Inc., Cleve., 1981—92, Playhouse Sq. Assn., Cleve., 1980—84; pres. N.E. Ohio Transit Coalition, 1992—; mem. policy com. Build-Up Greater Cleve. Program, 1982—98; mem. Greater Cleve. Growth Assn.; trustee Consultation Ctr. Diocese Cleve., 1990—96, Citizens League Greater Cleve., 1984—90, 1993—, Citizens League Rsch. Inst., 1995—97, St. Ann Found., 1990—92, Lyric Opera Cleve., 1995—. Recipient Disting. Leadership award, HELP, Inc., 1986, Pioneer Achievement award, HELP-Six Chimneys, Inc., 1986, Disting. Svc. award, Assn. Retarded Citizens, 1990, Vol. Svc. award, City of Lakewood, 2001. Mem.: ABA, Cleve. Bar Assn., Ohio State Bar Assn. (chmn. local govt. law com. 1986—90), Club Key Tower, Clifton Club (Lakewood, Ohio) (bd. dirs. 1986—89). Democrat. Roman Catholic. Avocations: music, theater , sports, travel. Home and Office: 1422 Euclid Ave Ste 706 Cleveland OH 44115-2001

KRAMER, FERDINAND, mortgage banker; b. Chgo., Aug. 10, 1901; s. Adolph F. and Ray (Friedberg) K.; m. Stephanie Shambaugh, Dec. 22, 1932 (dec. Feb. 1973); children: Barbara Shambaugh Kramer Bailey, Douglas, Anthony; m. Julia Wood McDermott, Aug. 19, 1975. PhB, U. Chgo., 1922. Engaged in real estate bus. and mortgage banker, Chgo., 1922—; with Draper & Kramer, Inc., 1922—, chmn. bd., 1944-95, chmn. emeritus, 1995—. Dir., mem. exec. com. Chgo. 21 Corp.; Program supr. Div. Def. Housing Coordination (and successor Nat. Housing Agy.), Washington, 1941-42; past pres. Met. Housing and Planning Council, Chgo., Actions, Inc.; past mem. Pres.'s Com. Equal Opportunity in Housing. Past chmn. steering com. United Negro Fund; mem. vis. com. dept. design and visual arts Harvard, 1963-64; life trustee U. Chgo. Recipient citation of merit U. Chgo. Alumni Assn., 1947, Individual Disting. Housing and Redevel. Svc. award Nat. Assn. Housing Ofcls., 1952, Disting. Alumnus award, 1982, Alumni Svc. medal, 1997, Disting. Pub. Svc. award Union League Club, Chgo., 1994. Mem. Chgo. Mortgage Bankers Assn. (past pres.), Mortgage Bankers Assn. Am., Nat. Assn. Housing Ofcls., Chgo. Assn. Commerce and Industry. Clubs: Chicago, Quadrangle, Standard, Tavern, Mid-Town Tennis, Commercial (Chgo.). Home: 1115 S Plymouth Ct Apt 511 Chicago IL 60605-2038

KRAMER, JOEL ROY, journalist, newspaper executive; b. Bklyn., May 21, 1948; s. Archie and Rae (Abramowitz) K.; m. Laurie Maloff, 1969; children— Matthew, Elias, Adam B.A., Harvard U., Cambridge, 1969. Editor-in-chief Harvard Crimson; reporter Sci. Mag., Washington, 1969-70; free lance writer, 1970-72; from copy editor to news editor, exec. news editor, asst. mng. editor Newsday, L.I., N.Y., 1972-80; exec. editor Buffalo Courier-Express, 1981-82, Star Tribune, Mpls., St. Paul, 1983-91, pub., pres., 1992-98; sr. fellow Sch. Journalism and Mass Comms., U. Minn., Mpls., 1998—. Bd. dirs. Harvard Crimson Inc., 1969—, World Press Inst. Chmn. bd. Mpls. Children's Theatre Co., 1994-96. Co-recipient Pulitzer prize for Pub. Service, Newsday (The Heroin Trail), 1973; Best Legal Writing on Large Daily award N.Y. Bar Assn., 1974. Address: Sch Journalism U Minn 111 Murphy Hall 206 Church St SE Minneapolis MN 55455-0488

KRAMER, MARY ELIZABETH, state legislator, health services executive; b. Burlington, Iowa, June 14, 1935; d. Ross L. and Geneva M. (McElhinney) Barnett; m. Kay Frederick Kramer, June 13, 1958; children: Kent, Krista. BA, U. Iowa, 1957, MA, 1971. Cert. tchr., Iowa. Tchr. Newton (Iowa) Pub. Schs., 1957-61, Iowa City Pub. Schs., 1961-67, tchr., asst. supt., 1971-75; dir. pers. Younkers, Inc., Des Moines, 1975-81; v.p. Wellmark, Inc., 1981-99; mem. Iowa Senate from 37th dist., 1990—; pres. of the senate, 1997—. Mem. Olympic adv. com. Blue Cross and Blue Shield Assn., Chgo., 1988—92; presdl. appointee White House Commn. on Presdl. Scholars, 2001, now chmn.; Bd. dirs. Polk County Child Care Rsch. Ctr., Des Moines, 1986—96, YWCA, Des Moines, 1989—94. Named Mgr. of Yr. Iowa Mgmt. Assocs., 1985, Woman of Achievement YWCA, 1986, Woman of Vision Young Women's Resource Ctr., 1989. Mem. Soc. Human Resource Mgmt. (Profl. of Yr. 1996), Iowa Mgmt. Assn. (pres. 1988), Greater Des Moines C. of C. (bd. dirs. 1986-96), Nexus, Rotary Internat. Republican. Presbyterian. Avocations: music, public speaking. Home: 13598 Village Ct Clive IA 50325 also: Iowa State Senate State Capitol Des Moines IA 50319-0001 E-mail: mkramer@legis.state.ia.us., kaynmary@aol.com.

KRAMER, WEEZIE CRAWFORD, former broadcast executive; Student, U. Ky., 1977, Wheaton Coll. Sales/local sales mgr. WKQQ, Lexington, Ky., 1977-80; local sales mgr. WHBQ, Memphis, 1980-81; gen. sales mgr. KBPI/KNUS, Denver, 1981-85, WFYR, Chgo., 1985-88, WMAQ All News 67, Chgo., 1988-94, sta. mgr., 1994, v.p., gen. mgr., 1994-99. Office: WMAQ-AM 455 N Cityfront Plaza Dr Chicago IL 60611-5503

KRANITZ, THEODORE MITCHELL, lawyer; b. St. Joseph, Mo., May 27, 1922; s. Louis and Miriam (Saferstein) K.; m. Elaine Shirley Kaufman, June 11, 1944; children: Hugh David, Karen Gail and Kathy Jane (twins). Student, St. Joseph Jr. Coll., 1940-41; BS in Fgn. Svc., Georgetown U., 1948, JD, 1950. Bar: Mo. 1950, U.S. Supreme Ct. 1955. Pres., sr. ptnr. Kranitz & Kranitz, PC, St. Joseph, 1950—. Author articles in field Pres. St. Joseph Comty. Theatre, Inc., 1958-60; bd. dirs. United Jewish Fund St. Joseph, 1957—, pres., 1958-63; sec. Boys' Baseball St. Joseph, 1964-68; trustee Temple Adath Joseph, 1970-74, 77-80; bd. dirs. B'nai Sholem Temple, 1976—, Lyric Opera Guild Kansas City, 1980-91; founder, pres. St. Joseph Light Opera Co., Inc., 1989-90; mem. St. Joseph Postal Customers Adv. Coun., 1993—, chmn., 1993-95; mem., sec. St. Joseph Downtown Assn., 1995-97. Mem. Mo. Bar, St. Joseph Bar Assn. (pres. 1977-78), Am. Legion, Air Force Assn., B'nai B'rith (dist. bd. govs.

1958-61). Home: 2609 Gene Field Rd Saint Joseph MO 64506-1615 Office: Kranitz & Kranitz PC Boder Bldg 107 S 4th St PO Box 968 Saint Joseph MO 64502-0968 Fax: (816) 232-8558. E-mail: kranitz@ponyexpress.net.

KRANTZ, KERMIT EDWARD, physician, educator; b. Oak Park, Ill., June 4, 1923; s. Andrew Stanley and Beatrice H. (Cibrowski) K.; m. Doris Cole Krantz, Sep. 7, 1946; children: Pamela (Mrs. Richard Huffstutter), Sarah Elizabeth, Kermit Tripler. BS, Northwestern U., 1945, BM, MS in Anatomy, Northwestern U., 1947, MD, 1948; LittD (hon.), William Woods Coll., 1971. Diplomate Am. Bd. Ob-Gyn. Intern ob-gyn. N.Y. Lying-In Hosp., 1947-48; asst. resident, asst. ob-gyn. Cornell U. Med. Coll., N.Y. Lying-In Hosp., N.Y. Hosp., 1948-50; fellow, resident in ob-gyn Mary Fletcher Hosp., Burlington, Vt., 1950-51; dir. Durfee Clinic, 1952-55; instr., then asst. prof. U. Vt. Coll. Medicine, 1951-55; asst. prof. U. Ark. Med. Sch., 1955-59; prof., chmn. dept. ob-gyn. U. Kans. Med. Ctr., 1959-90, Univ. Disting. prof., 1990-94, prof. anatomy, 1963—, lectr. history medicine, 1959—, dean clin. affairs, 1972-74, chief staff, 1972-74, obstetrician and gynecologist in chief, 1959-90, assoc. to exec. vice chancellor for facilities devel., 1974-83; univ. disting. prof. emeritus ob/gyn. and anatomy U. Kans., 1994—. Cons. in field. Author numerous articles in field. Mem. Nat. Adv. Child Health and Human Devel. Council, NIH, 1974-76. Bowen-Brooks fellow N.Y. Acad. Medicine, 1948-50; recipient Found. award South Atlantic Assn. Obstetricians and Gynecologists, 1950, Found. award Am. Assn. Obstetricians and Gynecologists, 1950, Wyeth-Ayerst Pub. Recognition award 1st Am. Assn. Prof. of Gynecology and Obstetrics, 1988; named Outstanding Prof. in Coll. of Medicine Nu Sigma Nu, 1955; Robert A. Ross lectureship award Armed Forces Dist. meeting Am. Coll. Obstetricians and Gynecologists, 1972, Outstanding Civilian Service medal U.S. Army-Dept. Def., 1985; Charles A. Durham Meml. lectr. Ann. Session Tex. Med. Assn., 1978; Markle scholar med. sci., 1957-62; Kermit E. Krantz Soc. established at U. Kans. Med. Ctr., 1982. Founding fellow Am. Coll. Obstetricians and Gynecologists (Kermit E. Krantz Lectureship award established 1973, Outstanding Dist. Services award 1978, 82); fellow ACS, Am. Coll. Ob-Gyn (life); mem. Am. Assn. Anatomists, Am. Fedn. Clin. Research, AMA, Am. Med. Writers Assn., Am. Fertility Soc., AAUP, Soc. Exptl. Biology and Medicine, Aerosopace Med. Assn., Endocrine Soc., Soc. Gynecologic Investigation, Central Assn. Obstetricians and Gynecologists, N.Y. Acad. Medicine, N.Y. Acad. Sci., Kans. Med. Soc., Assn. Mil. Surgeons U.S. (sustaining), Kans. Obstet. Soc., Sigma Xi, Alpha Omega Alpha. Home: 6711 Overhill Rd Shawnee Mission KS 66208-2263 Office: U Kans Med Ctr Kansas City KS 66160-0001

KRANTZ, STEVEN GEORGE, mathematics educator, writer; b. San Francisco, Feb. 3, 1951; s. Henry Alfred and Norma Oliva (Crisafulli) K.; m. Randi Diane Ruden, Sept. 7, 1974. BA, U. Calif., Santa Cruz, 1971; PhD, Princeton U, 1974. Asst. prof. UCLA, 1974-81; assoc. prof. Pa. State U., University Park, 1981-84, prof., 1984-86; prof. dept. math. Washington U., St. Louis, 1986—, chmn. dept. math., 1999—. Adv. bd. Am. Inst. Math., Am. Math. Soc. book series; mng. editor Jour. Math. Analysis and Applications. Founder, mng. editor Jour. Geometric Analysis; editor-in-chief Jour. of Math. Analysis and Apps.; Author: Function Theory of Several Complex Variables (monograph), 1982, 2d edition, 1992, Complex Analysis: The Geometric Viewpoint, 1990, Real Analysis and Foundations, 1991, Partial Differential Equations and Complex Analysis, 1992, A Primer of Real Analytic Functions, 1992, Geometric Analysis and Function Spaces, 1993, How to Teach Mathematics, 1993, 2nd edit., 1999, A Tex Primer for Scientists, 1995, The Elements of Advanced Mathematics, 1995, 2d edit., 2002, Techniques of Problem Solving, 1996, Function Theory of One Complex Variable, 1997, A Primer of Mathematical Writing, 1996; (with H. R. Parks) The Geometry of Domains in Space, 1999, Contemporary Issues in Mathmatics Education, 1999, A Handbook of Complex Variables, 1999, A Panorama of Harmonic Analysis, 1999, Handbook of Typography for the Mathematical Sciences, 2000, The Implicit Function Theory, 2002, Mathematical Aporypha, 2002; cons. editor Birkhäuser Pub., 2002-, McGraw-Hill, 2002-; contbr. numerous rsch. articles to profl. publs. Recipient Disting. Tchg. award, UCLA Alumni Found., 1979;NSF rsch. grantee, 1975—, Kemper grantee, 1994. Richardson fellow Australian Nat. U., 1995; mem. Am. Math. Soc. (prin. organizer summer rsch. inst. 1989), Math. Assn. Am. (Chauvenet prize, Beckenbach prize 1994), Textbook Authors Assn. E-mail: sk@math.wustl.edu.

KRANZ, KENNETH LOUIS, human resources company executive, entrepreneur; b. Evanston, Ill., July 7, 1946; s. Kenneth Louis Sr. and Florence A. (Knapton) K.; m. Susan Emilie Mueller, Apr. 3, 1976. BA, Tarkio Coll., 1969. Cert. compensation profl.; lic. IRS enrolled agt., adminstrv. svc. mgr., life and health agt. Cost acct. Fluid Power, Wheeling, Ill., 1969-71, Wells Lamont Corp., Chgo., 1971-74, sr. cost acct., 1974-76, asst. mgr. cost, audit, 1977-80, asst. mgr. taxes, employee benefits, 1980-81, mgr. taxes, employee benefits, 1981-84; benefits mgr. Keeler Brass Co., Grand Rapids, Mich., 1984-86, employee benefits and compensation mgr., 1986-90; human resources mgr. GRM Industries, 1990-92; co-owner Profl. Benefits Svcs., Inc., 1992-95; pres. MagnaCare Group Inc., 1995—. Mem. Home Health Svcs. (treas. 1986-90), Internat. Soc. Pre-Retirement Planners, West Mich. Compensation Assn., Am. Compensation Assn., Human Resource Mgmt. Assn., Life Underwriters Assn. Republican. Reformed Church American. Avocations: numismatics, all sports. Office: MagnaCare Group Inc 6140 28th St SE Ste 14 Grand Rapids MI 49546-6934

KRASNY, MICHAEL P. computer company executive; BS in Fin., U. Ill., 1975. Founder, chmn., CEO, sec. CDW Computer Ctrs., Vernon Hills, Ill., 1984—. Office: CDW 200 N Milwaukee Ave Vernon Hills IL 60061-1577

KRATT, PETER GEORGE, lawyer; b. Lorain, Ohio, Mar. 7, 1940; s. Arthur Leroy and Edith Ida (Dietz) K.; m. Sharon Amy Maruska, June 15, 1968; children: Kevin George, Jennifer Ivy. BA, Miami U., Oxford, Ohio, 1962; JD, Case Western Res. U., 1966. Bar: Ohio 1966. Atty. Cleve. Trust Co., 1966-74; assoc. counsel AmeriTrust Co., 1974-84, sec., assoc. counsel, 1985-87, sed., sr. assoc. counsel, 1987-92; ret. v.p., mgr. personal trust adminstrn. Huntington Trust Co., 1993-99. Mem. Am. Soc. Corp. Secs., Ohio Bar Assn., Rotary, Lions. Methodist. Avocations: hiking, gardening.

KRAUSE, ARTHUR B. telecommunications industry executive; BBA in Acctg., Marquette U. Various positions in acctg. and contr. depts. Gen. Tel. and Electronics; asst. contr. United Tel. Co. Sprint, 1971-75, contr., 1975, v.p. fin., 1977, sr. v.p. adminstrn. tel. hdqrs., 1980, pres. United Tel.-Ea. Group, 1986; exec. v.p., CFO Sprint Corp., 1990—. Office: Sprint Corp 2330 Shawnee Mission Pkwy Shawnee Mission KS 66205

KRAUSE, CAROLYN H. state legislator, lawyer; m. David Krause. BA, U. Wis.; JD, IIT. Assoc. Foss, Schuman & Drake, Chgo., 1966-73; lawyer, solo practice Mt. Prospect, Ill., 1973-76; pvt. practice Krause & Krause, 1976—; mayor Mt. Prospect, 1973-76; Dist. 56 rep. Ill. Ho. Reps., Springfield, 1993—. Spokesman appropriations, gen. svcs., cities and villages, fin. instns., healthcare, and human svcs. coms., Ill. Ho. Reps. Apptd. by Gov. James Thompson (Ill.) to local govt. fin. study commn., 1980, criminal justice info. authority, 1985-87; past dir. Clearbrook Ctr.; chair Mcpl. Conf.; dir. Pub. Action to Deliver Shelter of Northwest Cook County. Mem. Ill. and Chgo. Bar Assns. Home: 204 S George St Mount Prospect IL 60056-3430 Office: Ill Ho of Reps State Capitol Springfield IL 62706-0001 Also: 111 E Busse Ave Ste 605 Mount Prospect IL 60056-3249

KRAUSE, CHARLES JOSEPH, otolaryngologist; b. Des Moines, Apr. 21, 1937; s. William H. and Ruby I. (Hitz) Krause; m. Barbara Ann Steelman, June 14, 1962; children: Sharon, John, Ann. B.A., State U. Iowa, 1959, M.D., 1962. Diplomate Am. Bd. Otolaryngology. Intern Phila. Gen. Hosp., 1962—63; resident in surgery U. Iowa, 1965—66, resident in otolaryngology, 1966—69; fellow dept. plastic surgery Marien Hosp., Stuttgart, Germany, 1970; asst. prof. otolaryngology U. Iowa, 1969—72, asso. prof., 1972—75, vice chmn. dept. otolaryngology, 1973—77, prof., 1975—77; prof., chmn. dept. otolaryngology U. Mich. Med. Sch., Ann Arbor, 1977—92; pres. Am. Bd. Otolaryngology, Houston. Chief clin. affairs U. Mich. Hosps., Ann Arbor, 1986—89; asst. dean for clin. affairs U. Mich., 1986—89, sr. assoc. dean med. sch., 1992—96, chief clin. affairs, 1992—95, sr. assoc. hosp. dir., 1995—96, prof. dept. otolaryngology, 1996—. Author: book in field; contbr. chapters to books, articles. Capt. USAF, 1963—65. Fellow: Am. Soc. Head and Neck Surgery (coun. 1980—83, chmn. rsch. com. 1980—83, pres. 1987—88); mem.: Am. Bd. Otolaryngology (bd. dirs. 1984—, exam. com. chair 1993—, pres.-elect 1996—98, pres. 1998—2000), Centurions of Deafness Rsch. Found., Am. Laryngol. Assn., Am. Laryngol., Rhinol. and Otol. Soc., Am. Cancer Soc. (med. adv. com. Washtenaw County unit), Walter P. Work Soc. (pres. 1987), Soc. United Otolaryngologists, Am. Acad. Depts. Otolaryngology, Mich. Otolaryngol. Soc., Mich. State Med. Soc., Washtenaw County Med. Soc. (exec. com. 1979—82), Assn. Rsch. in Otolaryngology, Am. Asssn. Cosmetic Surgeons, Assn. Head and Neck Oncologists, ACS (adv. coun. otolaryngology 1979—83), Am. Acad. Facial Plastic and Reconstructive Surgery (regional v.p. 1977—80, chmn. rsch. com. 1977—80, pres. 1981—82), Am. Acad. Otolaryngology Head and Neck Surgery (bd. dirs. 1987—93, sec.-treas. 1987—93, pres.-elect 1995, pres. 1996), AMA. Republican. Presbyterian. Home and Office: 880 Sea Dune Ln Marco Island FL 34145-1840 Office: U Mich 1904 Taubman Ctr 1500 E Medical Center Dr Ann Arbor MI 48109-0005 E-mail: ckrause@umich.edu.

KRAUSE, CHESTER LEE, publishing company executive; b. Iola, Wis., Dec. 16, 1923; s. Carl and Cora E. (Neil) K. Grad. high sch., Iola. Ind. contractor, 1946-52; chmn. bd. Krause Publs., Inc., Iola, 1952-95. Co-editor: Standard Catalog of World Coins. Chmn. bldg. fund drive Iola Hosp., 1975-80; active Village Bd., 1963-72, Assay Commn., 1961, Marshfield Clinic Nat. Adv. Coun., 1992-96. With AUS, 1943-46. Named Wis. Small Businessman of Yr. Wis. Small Bus. Adminstrn. Adv. Coun., 1990; Melvin Jones fellow, 1989; recipient Meguiar award, 1995, Friend of Automotive History award Soc. Automotive Historians, 1995, Marshfield Clinic Heritage Found. award, 2001. Mem. Soc. of Automobile Historians (Friends of Automobile Historians 1995), Am. Numis. Assn. (medal of merit, Farren Zerbe award, Hall of Fame, Lifetime Achievement award), Can. Numis. Assn. Home: 290 E Iola St Iola WI 54945-9620 Office: 700 E State St Iola WI 54945-9642 E-mail: krausec@krause.com.

KRAUSE, HARRY DIETER, law educator; b. Görlitz, Germany, Apr. 23, 1932; came to U.S., 1951, naturalized, 1954; s. Renatus and Ellen (Abel-Musgrave) K.; m. Eva Maria Disselnkötter, Aug. 30, 1957; children: Philip Renatus, Thomas Walther, Peter Herbert. Student, Freie U., Berlin, 1950-51; B.A., U. Mich., 1954, J.D., 1958. Bar: Mich. 1959, D.C. 1959, Ill. 1963, U.S. Supreme Ct. 1963. With firm Covington & Burling, 1958-60; with Ford Motor Co., Dearborn, Mich., 1960-63; asst. prof. to prof. law U. Ill., Champaign, 1963-82, Alumni Disting. prof. law, 1982-89, Max L. Rowe prof. law, 1989-94, tchg. prof. emeritus, 1994—. Fulbright prof. U. Bonn, Germany 1976-77; vis. assoc. Ctr. Socio-Legal studies, 1977; vis. fellow Wolfson Coll. Oxford (Eng.) U., 1984; U.S. Del. to Hague Conf. on Pvt. Internat. Law Treaty on Internat. Adoptions, 1990-93; commr. Uniform State Laws, Ill., 1991-97; reporter Uniform Parentage Act, 1969-73, Rev. Uniform Adoption Act, 1979-84, Uniform Putative Fathers Act, 1985, Nat. Conf. Commrs. on Uniform State Laws; mem. Internat. Acad. Comparative Law Rapporteur U.S., Uppsala, 1966, Teheran, 1974, Budapest, 1978, Caracas, 1983, Sydney, 1986, gen. rep. Athens, 1994; cons. on family law and social legis. to fed. and state legis., jud. and exec. commns.; vis. prof. law U. Mich., 1981, U. Miami, 1987; Culverhouse prof. Stetson U., 1991. Author: Illegitimacy: Law and Social Policy, 1971, Family Law: Cases and Materials, 1976, 4th edit., 1998, Kinship Relations, 1976, Family Law in a Nutshell, 1977, 3d edit., 1995, Child Support in America: The Legal Perspective, 1981; law editor: (with R. Walker et. al.) Inclusion Probabilities in Parentage Testing, 1983, Family Law (West's Blackletter Series), 1988, 2d edit., 1996, International Library of Essays in Law and Legal Theory: Family Law I: Society and Family, 1992, Family Law II: Cohabitation, Marriage and Divorce, 1992, Child Law: Parent, Child and State, 1992; bd. editors Mich. Law Rev., 1957-58, Family Law Quar., 1971—, Jour. Legal Edn., 1988-91, Am. Jour. Comparative Law, 1991—, and others. With U.S. Army, 1954-56. Recipient von Humboldt Found. rsch. prize, 1992; Guggenheim fellow, 1969-70; assoc. Ctr. Advanced Study U. Ill., 1970, 79; German Marshall Fund U.S. fellow, 1977-78; Hewlett fellow, Australia, 1984; German Acad. Exch. Svc. fellow, 1985. Mem. ABA (past mem. coun. sect. family law, com. chmn.), Am. Law Inst. (adviser family law project 1990—), Ill. Bar Assn. (past mem. coun. sect. on family law, internat. law), Am. Assn. Comparative Study of Law (dir. 1980—), Internat. Soc. Family Law (v.p. 1973-77, exec. coun. 1977-97), Order of Coif. Office: U Ill Coll Law Champaign IL 61820 Home: 965 Roland Miller Dr Vero Beach FL 32963-3403

KRAUSE, JERRY (JEROME RICHARD KRAUSE), professional basketball team executive; b. Chgo., Apr. 6, 1939; s. Paul and Gertrude (Sherman) K.; m. Sharon Bergofsky, Oct. 16, 1969 (div. 1971); m. Thelma Frankel, July 1, 1979; children: Stacy, David. Student, Bradley U., 1957-61. Dir. scouting Balt. Bullets Basketball Club, 1962-65, 67-69, Chgo. Bulls Basketball Club, 1969-72, v.p. basketball ops., 1985—; dir. scouting Phoenix Suns Basketball Club, 1972-75; gen. mgr. Portland Baseball Club, Pacific Coast League, 1966; scout Cleve. Indians Baseball Club, 1967-72, Oakland (Calif.) Athletics Baseball Club, 1973-75; dir. scouting Los Angeles Lakers Basketball Club, 1977-79; supr. Midwestern scouting Seattle Mariners Baseball Club, 1977-79; spl. assignment scout Chgo. White Sox Baseball Club, 1979-85. Contbr. articles to profl. jours. Named Exec. of Yr. NBA, 1988, named to Bradley U. Athletic Hall of Fame, 1992. Mem. Nat. Basketball Assn. (competition com., Exec. of Yr. 1988). Office: Chgo Bulls 1901 W Madison St Chicago IL 60612-2459

KRAUSS, CARL F. lawyer; b. St. Louis, Mar. 22, 1936; s. Frederick Emanuel and Jewell Edith (Bell) K.; m. Gladys Weber, July 27, 1972; children: Kenneth F., Stephen W. AB in Econs./Bus. Adminstrn., Knox Coll., 1958; JD, U. Mo., 1961. Bar: Mo. 1961, Kansas 1981, Tex. 1989. Assoc. Morrison & Hecker, Kansas City, Mo., 1961-67, ptnr., 1967-81, Morrison & Hecker, L.L.P, Overland Park, Kans., 1981—. Bd. editors Mo. Law Review. Founding mem. Overland Park Econ. Devel. Coun., 1986. Mem. ABA, Mo. Bar Assn., Kansas Bar Assn., Tex. Bar Assn., Johnson County Bar Assn., Johnson County Farm Bur. (dir. 2002--), Kansas City Met. Bar Assn., Overland Park C. of C. (dir. 1991-97). Avocation: farming. Home: 1608 E Frontier Ln Olathe KS 66062-2243 Office: Morrison & Hecker LLP 9 Corporate Woods 450 9200 Indian Creek Pkwy Overland Park KS 66210-2002

KRAUTER, AARON JOSEPH, state legislator, farmer; b. Dickinson, N.D., July 21, 1956; s. Adam Robert and Ann Christine (Grundhauser) K.; m. Cynthia Marie Nordquist, June 28, 1986; children: Emily Christine, Mitchell Aaron, Hannah Marie. BSEd., U. Mary, Bismarck, 1978, BSBA, 1981. Music instr. Cooperstown (N.D.) High Sch., 1978-79; store mgr. Best Product, Inc., Bismarck, 1979-85, ops. mgr. Richmond, Va., 1985-87; farmer Regent, N.D., 1987—; mem. N.D. Senate, 1990—. Mem. N.D. Gov.'s Coun. on Children and Youth, Bismarck, 1989-94, N.D. Gov.'s Coun. on Phys. Fitness and Health, 1992-94; mem. agronomy seed adv. bd. N.D. State U., 1991—, mem. ext. adv. coun., 1991—; chair N.D. Senate Dem. Caucus, 1993-97; asst. minority leader, 1997—. Recipient Know Your State award N.D. Bar Assn., 1974, Excellence in Govt. award Assn. Counties, 1993, Flemming Fellow Leadership award Ctr. for Policy Alternatives, Washington, 1995. Mem. KC, Elks. Democrat. Roman Catholic. Home and Office: HC 1 Box 27 Regent ND 58650-9721

KRAVITT, JASON HARRIS PAPERNO, lawyer; b. Chgo., Jan. 19, 1948; s. Jerome Julius and Shirley (Paperno) K.; m. Beverly Ray Niemeier, May 11, 1974; children: Nikola Wedding, Justin Taylor Paperno. AB, Johns Hopkins U., 1969; JD, Harvard U., 1972; diploma in comparative legal studies, Cambridge U., Eng., 1973. Bar: Ill., U.S. Dist. Ct. (no. dist.) Ill. Assoc. Mayer, Brown & Platt, Chgo., 1973-78, ptnr., 1979—, co-chmn., 1998-2001. Adj. prof. law Northwestern U., Evanston, Ill., 1994—, adj. prof. fin. Kellogg Sch. Mgmt., 1998—. Editor: Securitization of Financial Assets, 2d edit., 1996. Bd. dirs. Chgo. Met. YMCA, 1998-2001, Mus. Contemporary Art, Chgo., 1974-75; dir., chmn. The Cameron Kravitt Found., 1984—. Fellow Am. Coll. Comml. Lawyers; mem. ABA, Chgo. Coun. Lawyers, Chgo. Bar Assn., Econ. Club of Chgo., Execs. Club Chgo. Home: 250 Sheridan Rd Glencoe IL 60022-1948 Office: Mayer Brown Rowe & Maw 190 S La Salle St Ste 3100 Chicago IL 60603-3441 E-mail: jkravitt@mayerbrownrowe.com.

KRAWETZ, STEPHEN ANDREW, molecular medicine and genetics scientist; b. Fort Frances, Ont., Can., Sept. 17, 1955; s. Stephen and Michaelene (Medynski) K.; m. Lorraine Ruth St. John, Aug. 19, 1977; children: Rhochelle Tairaesa, Alexandra Renée. BSc, U. Toronto, Ont., 1977, PhD, 1983. Tchr. Scarborough Bd. Edn., Ont., 1976-77; Alberta Heritage Found. Med. Rsch. postdoc. fellow U. Calgary, Alta., Can., 1983-89; asst. prof. rsch. ctr. for molecular biology Wayne State U., Detroit, 1989, asst. prof. molecular biology and genetics, 1989-92, asst. prof. obstetrics and gynecology and molecular biology and genetics, 1992-94, assoc. prof. ob/gyn. and molecular medicine and genetics, 1994-2000; prof. ob-gyn. and molecular medicine and genetics Inst. Scientific Computing, 2000-01; Charlotte B. Failing prof. ob-gyn. and molecular medicine and genetics and Inst. Sci. Computing, Wayne State U., 2001—. Biotech. cons., Calgary, 1985-89, Grosse Pointe Woods, Mich., 1989—; co-founder Genetic Imaging, Inc., 1988; mem. gene therapy group DMC, Detroit, 1997—. Mem. editl. bd. BioTechniques, Ag Biotech News and Info.; contbr. numerous articles to scholarly jours. Recipient B.C. Childrens Hosp. Rsch. award, Vancouver, 1984, Computer Applications in Molecular Biology award, IntelliGenetics Inc., Mountain View, Calif., 1988; Alta. Heritage Found. Med. Rsch. fellow, 1985-88. Mem. AAAS, Am. Soc. Human Genetics, Soc. for the Study of Reproduction, Internat. Soc. for Matrix Biology (founding mem.). Achievements include development of splinkers for sequencing DNA, of a computer-based imaging system for biological data, of VPCS cloning vectors, of the basis of biological sequence alignment algorithm; one of the first to describe overlapping reading frames in eucaryotes; first detailed analysis of a mammalian protamine gene; first definition of sequence interpretation errors in the GenBank database; first to define a genic domain in human sperm; research in gene therapy targeted to the amelioration of human disease; showed that selective potentiation of our genome mediates cell-phenotype. Home: 805 Canterbury Rd Grosse Pointe Woods MI 48236-1285 Office: Dept Ob-Gyn Ctr Molecular Med Genetics Detroit MI 48201 E-mail: steve@compbio.med.wayne.edu.

KREBS, EUGENE KEHM, II, state legislator; b. Hamilton, Ohio, Aug. 4, 1953; s. Eugene Kehm and Martha Logan (Magaw) K.; m. Janet Lynn Krepp, Dec. 27, 1975; children: Kindra, Alaina. BS, Bowling Green State U., 1975. Farmer, Camden, Ohio, 1975—; mem. Ohio Ho. of Reps., Columbus, 1993—. Contbr. article to Wall St. Jour. Mem. Sch. Bd., Eaton (Ohio) City Schs., 1990-92. Republican. Methodist. Avocations: writing children's books, tree plantations, epée fencing. Home: 12173 State Route 732 Camden OH 45311-9642 Office: Ohio Ho of Reps 77 S High St Columbus OH 43215-6108

KREBS, WILLIAM HOYT, company executive, industrial hygienist; b. Detroit, Apr. 6, 1938; s. William Thomas and Mary Louise (Hoyt) K.; m. Susan Kathryn Bartholomew, Aug. 8, 1964 (div. July 1976); children: Elizabeth Louise, William Thomas II; m. Jane Germer Meikle, June 18, 1983; stepchildren: David Andrew, Sarah Elizabeth. BS, U. Mich., 1960, MPH (IH), 1963, MS, 1965, PhD, 1970. Rsch. asst. U. Mich., Ann Arbor, 1962-63; indsl. hygienist Lumbermens Mut. Casualty Co., Chgo., 1963-64, GM Corp., Detroit, 1970-77, mgr. toxic materials control activity, 1977-81, dir. toxic materials control activity, 1981-90, dir. indsl. hygiene activity, 1990-93; v.p. Indsl. Health Scis., Inc., Grosse Pointe Park, Mich., 1993—. Mem. asbestos adv. com. Mich. Occupational Health Standards Commn., Lansing, 1984—. Contbr. articles to profl. jours. Mem. Grosse Pointe Meml. Ch., Grosse Pointe Farms, 1954; mem. health and safety com. Detroit Area coun. Boy Scouts Am., 1980; mem. environment and energy com. Detroit Regional Chamber. Fellow Am. Indsl. Hygiene Assn. (hon. mem.; bd. dirs. 1976-79, v.p. 1986-87, pres. 1988-89); mem. AAAS, APHA, Mich. Indsl. Hygiene Soc. (pres. 1980-81), Brit. Occupational Hygiene Soc., Internat. Occupational Hygiene Assn. (v.p. 1990-91, pres. 1992-93), Internat. Commn. on Occpl. Health, Soc. Automotive Engrs. Presbyterian. Home: 1014 Bishop Rd Grosse Pointe Park MI 48230-1421 Office: Indsl Health Scis Inc 1014 Bishop Rd Grosse Pointe Park MI 48230-1421

KREBSBACH, KAREN K. state legislator; m. Paul Krebsbach; 2 children. BS, Minot State U. Corp. sec. Krebsbach's, Inc.; mem. N.D. State Senate from 40th and 50th dists., 1989-. Mem. adv. bd. SBA. Bd. dirs. Trinity Med. Ctr. Mem. Minot (N.D.) C. of C., Kiwanis Club, Trinity Med. Ctr. Republican. Home: PO Box 1767 Minot ND 58702-1767

KREDIT, KENNETH E. former state legislator, automobile dealership executive; Mem. S.D. Ho. of Reps., Pierre, 1995-98, mem. appropriations com., 1995-98. Republican.

KREER, IRENE OVERMAN, association and meeting management executive; b. McGrawsville, Ind., Nov. 11, 1926; d. Ralph and Laura Edith (Sharp) Overman; m. Henry Blackstone Kreer, Dec. 22, 1946; children: Laurene (dec.), Linda Kreer Witt. BS in Speech Pathology, Northwestern U., 1948. Speech pathologist Ill. pub. schs., 1947-49; staff asst., lectr. Art Inst. Chgo., 1962—; pres. Irene Overman Kreer & Assocs., Inc., Chgo., 1962—. Frequent lectr. on art, arch., Chgo. area; TV appearances representing Art Inst. edn. programs. Past bd. dirs. Glenview (Ill.) Pub. Libr.; mem. The Art Inst. Chgo., Glenview Cmty. Ch., Field Mus., Chgo. Architecture Found., Smithsonian Assocs. Mem. Nat. Trust Hist. Preservation, Assn. Alumnae Northwestern U. (bd. dirs. 1975—), Delta Delta Delta. Republican. Avocations: travel, archaeology, tennis (ranked in women's singles and doubles, Chgo.).

KREGEL, JAMES R. publishing executive; b. Grand Rapids, Mich., Apr. 18, 1950; BA, Mich. State U., 1972. Pres. Kregel Publs., Grand Rapids, Mich., 1989—. Office: Kregel Publs Box 2607 733 Wealthy St SE Grand Rapids MI 49503-5553

KREHBIEL, FREDERICK AUGUST, II, electronics company executive; b. Chgo., June 2, 1941; s. John Hammond and Margaret Ann (Veeck) K.; m. Kay Kirby, Dec. 20, 1973; children: William Veeck, Jay Frederick. B.A., Lake Forest Coll., 1963. Export mgr., then v.p. internat. Molex Inc., Lisle, Ill., 1970-75, exec. v.p., dir., from 1976; vice chmn., CEO Molex Co., 1988-93; chmn., CEO Molex, Inc., Lisle, Ill., 1993—, co-chmn., CEO,

2001—. Bd. dirs. Tellabs Inc., Mollex, Inc., No. Trust Bank, DeVry, Inc., Grainger Inc. Trustee Rush Med. Ctr., Chgo., Lyric Opera, Chgo., Chgo. Zool. Soc., Chgo. Hist. Soc., Mus. Sci. and Industry, Chgo., Chgo. Orch. Assn., Sch. of Art Inst., Chgo., Tenna Mus. Mem. Hinsdale (Ill.) Golf Club, Chgo. Club, Casino Club (Chgo.), Chgo. Yacht Club, Racquet Club Chgo., Everglades Club (Palm Beach). Home: 505 S County Line Rd Hinsdale IL 60521-4725 Office: Molex Inc 2222 Wellington Ave Lisle IL 60532-3820

KREHBIEL, ROBERT JOHN, lawyer; b. Waukegan, Ill., Dec. 8, 1948; BA magna cum laude, Knox Coll., 1971; JD, Washington U., 1980. Bar: Mo. 1980, U.S. Dist. Ct. (ea. dist.) Mo. 1980, U.S. Dist. Ct. (we. dist.) Mo. 1992, Ill. 1981, U.S. Ct. Appeals (8th cir.) 1981, U.S. Supreme Ct. 1987. Mem. Evans & Dixon, St. Louis. Mem. Mo. Bar, Bar Assn. Met. St. Louis, Order of Coif, Phi Beta Kappa. Office: Evans & Dixon 1200 St Louis Pl 200 N Broadway Ste 1200 Saint Louis MO 63102-2749

KREIBICH, ROBIN G. state legislator; b. June 4, 1959; BA, U. Minn.; postgrad., Brown Inst. Broadcasting. Former TV anchorman; former media specialist U. Wis., Eau Claire; mem. from dist. 93 Wis. State Assembly, Madison, 1992—. Address: 3437 Nimitz St Dr Eau Claire WI 54701-7200

KREIDER, JIM, state legislator, farmer; b. Nurnburg, Germany, June 24, 1955; (parents Am. citizens); m. Debbie Kreider; children: Lacey, Neeley. Student, S.W. Mo. State U. Farmer, Nixa, Mo.; mem. Mo. Ho. of Reps., Jefferson City, 1992—, spkr. pro tem, 1997—2001, spkr., 2001—. Mem. agr.-bus. com., agr. com., edn. com., energy environ. com. Mem. com. Am. Soil Conservation Svc. Named Farm Family of Yr., 1992. Mem. Christian County Farm Bur. (v.p., legis. chmn.). Democrat. Home and Office: PO Box 1980 Nixa MO 65714-1980 Office: Capitol Bldg Rm 308 Jefferson City MO 65101

KREIDER, LEONARD EMIL, economics educator; b. Newton, Kans., Feb. 25, 1938; s. Leonard C. and Rachel (Weaver) K.; m. Louise Ann Pankratz, June 10, 1963; children: Brent Emil, Todd Alan, Ryan Eric. Student, Bluffton Coll., 1956-58; BA, Bethel Coll., 1960; student, Princeton U., 1960-61; MA, Ohio State U., 1962, PhD, 1968. Economist So. Ill. U., Carbondale, 1965-70; asst. prof. Beloit (Wis.) Coll., 1970—, prof., 1978, chmn. dept. econs. and mgmt., 1984-89, acting v.p. acad. affairs, 1987-88, Allen Bradley prof. econs., 1991—. Chief of party Devel. Assocs., Asuncion, Paraguay, 1970; economist Deere and Co., 1973, Castle and Cooke, San Francisco, 1975-76, AmCore, Rockford, Ill., 1984, Rockford Meml. Hosp., 1990-91, Stone Container, San Jose, Costa Rica, 1996; cons. corps. and attys. Author: Development and Utilization of Managerial Talent, 1968; contbr. numerous articles, reports to profl. jours. Mem. Nat. Assn. Bus. Economists, Am. Econs. Assn., Am. Assn. Higher Edn., Soc. Internat. Devel. (pres. So. Ill. chpt. 1969), Indsl. Relations Research Assn. (elections com. 1974). Presbyterian. Home: 820 Milwaukee Rd Beloit WI 53511-5636 Office: Beloit Coll Dept Econ Mgmt Beloit WI 53511

KREININ, MORDECHAI ELIAHU, economics educator; b. Tel Aviv, Jan. 20, 1930; came to U.S., 1951, naturalized, 1960; m. Marlene Miller, Aug. 29, 1956; children: Tamara, Elana, Miriam. B.A., U. Tel Aviv, 1951; M.A., U. Mich., 1952, Ph.D., 1954. Asst. prof. econs. Mich. State U., East Lansing, 1957-59, assoc. prof., 1959-61, prof., 1961-90, univ. disting. prof. econs., 1990—. Vis. prof. econs. UCLA, 1969, UN, Geneva, 1971-73, NYU, 1975, 93, 96, U. Toronto, 1978, others; vis. scholar Inst. Internat. Econs. Studies, U. Stockholm, 1978-80, U. B.C., summer, 1983, Monash U., Melbourne, Australia, 1987-94, 2002, NYU, 1993, 96, Copenhagen Bus. Sch., Denmark, 1994-95, Kobe (Japan) U., 1997, Ctr. Southeast Asian Studies, U. Singapore, 1998; adj. rsch. assoc. East-West Ctr., Honolulu, 1990—; world lectr. tours on behalf of U.S. Info. Svc., 1974-96; cons. to Dept. Commerce, 1964-66, Dept. State, 1972-74, UN Coun. Fgn. Rels, N.Y.C., 1965-67, Brockings Instn., 1972-75, C. Am. Common Market, 1972-75, Internat. Monetary Fund, 1976, East-West Ctr., Honolulu, 1987—; mem. internat. econs. rev. bd. NSF, 1981, 85; bd. dirs. Internat. Trade and Fin. Assn., 1990—, pres. 1993; sr. Fulbright specialist, 2001--. Author: Israel and Africa: A Study in Technical Cooperation, 1964, Alternative Commercial Policies*Their Effects on the American Economy, 1967, International Economics-A Policy Approach, 9th edit., 2002, Trade Relations of the EEC*An Empirical Investigation, 1974, International Commercial Policy: Issues for the 1990's, 1993, Contemporary Issues in Trade Policy, 1995, (with L. Officer) The Monetary Approach to the Balance of Payments: A Survey, 1978, Economics, 1983, 3d edit., 1999; editor: Can Australia Adjust?, 1988, International Commercial Policy: Issues for the 90's, 1993, Contemporary Issues in Trade Policy, 1995, The U.S.-Canada Free Trade Agreement, 1999; co-editor: Asia-Pacific Economic Linkages, 1997; contbr. articles to profl. jours. NSF fellow, 1964-73, Ford Found. fellow, 1960-61; recipient Disting. Faculty award Mich. State U., 1968, State of Mich. Collegiate award, 1984, Whitefield Winslow Faculty award, 1994. Mem. AAUP, Am. Econ. Assn., Midwest Econ. Assn., Western Econ. Assn., Royal Econ. Assn., Internat. Trade and Fin. Assn. (bd. dirs. 1991-94). Jewish. Home: 1431 Sherwood Ave East Lansing MI 48823-1851 Office: Mich State U Dept Econs East Lansing MI 48824 E-mail: kreinin@pilot.msu.edu.

KREIS, JASON, professional soccer player; b. Omaha, Dec. 29, 1972; Student, Duke U. Midfielder Dallas Burn, 1998—, U.S. Nat. Team, 1999—. U.S. Nat. Soccer Team debut 1996; finished 9th in MLS scoring, 1996, scored goal in all-star game; 3-time All-Am., Duke U. Office: US Soccer Fedn 1801-1811 S Prairie Ave Chicago IL 60616 and: Dallas Burn 2602 Mckinney Ave Ste 200 Dallas TX 75204-8543

KREITLOW, PAT, newscaster; m. Sharry Kreitlow; 2 children. Degree in journalism, U. Wis., Eau Claire. News dir. radio stas., Rice Lake and West Bend, Wis.; mem. staff WAXX-WAYY radio, Eau Claire; prodr., reporter, co-anchor, weekend anchor NewsCenter 13 WEAU-TV, 1996—. Bd. dirs. Chippewa Valley chpt. Literacy Vols. Am. Office: WEAU-TV PO Box 47 Eau Claire WI 54702

KREITZER, MELVYN, II, optical designer; b. Cape Town, South Africa, Oct. 21, 1945; came to U.S., 1973; s. Charles and Lucy (Faktor) K.; m. Sharon Meyerowitz, Apr. 6, 1971; children: Jason, David. BS, U. Cape Town, South Africa, 1964, BS (hon.), 1966; MS, Rochester Inst. Tech., 1968; MS, PhD, U. Ariz., 1976. Co-author chpt. to book; patentee in field. Mem. Optical Soc. Am. (Engring. Excellence award 1995). Avocations: reading, movies, golf. Home: 3681 Carpenters Creek Dr Cincinnati OH 45241-3824 Office: Opcon Assocs Inc 3997 Mcmann Rd Cincinnati OH 45245-2307

KREMER, EUGENE R. architecture educator; b. N.Y.C., Jan. 4, 1938; s. John and Ida (Applegreen) K.; m. Sara Lillian Kimmel, June 26, 1960; children: Michael, Ian. BArch, Rensselaer Poly. Inst., 1960; postgrad., U. Pa., 1960-61; MArch, U. Calif., 1967; grad. coll. mgmt. program, Carnegie Mellon U., 1991. Registered architect, N.Y., Kans. Architect Ulrich Franzen Assoc., N.Y.C., 1963-66; asst. prof. Washington U., St. Louis, 1967-70; lectr. Portsmouth (Eng.) Poly. Inst., 1970-71, Poly. Ctrl. London, 1971-72; dir. Inst. Environ. Design, Washington, 1972-73; prof., head dept. architecture Kans. State U., Manhattan, 1973-85, 92-95, dir. program devel. Coll. Architecture and Design, 1985-92, asst. dean, 1988-90. Dir. Boston Architecture and Design, summer, 1983—90; vis. faculty mem. Czech Tech U., Prague, 1999; scholar in residence AIA, Washington, 2002; mem. State Bldg. Adv. Bd., Topeka, 1984—86, Topeka, 1992—95; mem. editl. bd. Jour. Arch. and Planning Rsch., College Station, Tex., 1983—. Author: Careers in Architecture, 1967, Leadership Meetings in Environmental Design, 1973; author/editor newsletter Architecture Update, 1984-86, 92—; editor Architecture and Design News, 1990-92; contbr. Architects Handbook of Professional Practice, 13th edit., also articles to profl publs. Chmn. Adv. Bd. Gifted, Talented, Creative, Manhattan, 1974-75; mem. Convocations Com., Manhattan, 1974-93, chn., 1984-88, 90-93; mem. Truman Scholarship Com., Manhattan, 1980—; pres. Friends Kans. State U. Librs., Manhattan, 1985-86. Fellow AIA (Spl. Svc. award Kans. 1984, 88, 91, 94, 98, 99, Presdl. citation Kansas City 1993); mem. Environ. Design Rsch. Assn., Assn. Collegiate Schs. Architecture (treas. 1976-80, pres. 1981-82, Svc. award 1983), AIA Kans. (sec. 1989, v.p./pres.-elect 1990, pres. 1991, past pres. 1992, univ. liaison 1993—), AIA Flint Hills (pres. 1998), Golden Key (hon.), Tau Sigma Delta, Tau Beta Pi, SCARAB (hon.), Tau Epsilon Phi (pres. 1959-60). Avocations: reading, photography. Office: Kans State U Coll Architecture Planning and Design 211 Seaton Hall Manhattan KS 66506-2900

KREMER, ROBERT M. state legislator; b. Aurora, Nebr., Dec. 8, 1936; m. Beverly Jackson, July 19, 1958; children: Mark Kremer, Sheila Miller, Sherri Holm, Shauna Moody. BS, Northwestern Coll., 1958. Farmer, cattle feeder; mem. Nebr. Legislature from 34th dist., Lincoln, 1998—. County pres., state bd. dirs., mem. state edn. adv. com., mem. state policy devel. com. Nebr. Farm Bur.; county pres., state bd. dirs., mem. nat. com. Nebr. Cattlemen; bd. dirs. Edgerton Explorit Ctr., Nebr. Energy Coop.; chmn., youth leader Pleasant View Bible Ch.; mem. Ag Builders Nebr.; former mem. Aurora Dist 4-R Bd. Edn. Mem. Nebr. Corn Growers Assn. (bd. dirs.), Aurora C. of C. (mem. agr. com.), Rotary, 4-H Club (leader). Office: State Capitol Dist 34 PO Box 94604 Rm 1529 Lincoln NE 68509-4604 Home: 186 Donegal Rd Aurora NE 68818-1430

KREMKAU, PAUL, principal; Prin. Highland Middle Sch. (formerly Highland Upper Grade Ctrl. Sch.), Libertyville, Ill., 1984—. Recipient Blue Ribbon Sch. award U.S. Dept. Edn., 1990-91. Office: Highland Mid Sch 310 W Rockland Rd Libertyville IL 60048-2739

KRENDL, KATHY, dean; Dean Ohio U. Coll. Comms., Athens, 1996—. Office: Ohio U Coll Comm 9 S College St Rm 483B Athens OH 45701-2905

KRENTZ, EUGENE LEO, university president, educator, minister; b. Edmonton, Alta., Can., June 16, 1932; came to U.S., 1958; s. Emil and Natalie (Martin) K.; m. Joyce Ann Triolet, Feb. 1, 1958; children— Paul, Cynthia, Tamara B.Th., Concordia Theol. Sem., Springfield, Ill., 1958, B.D., 1971, M.Div., 1973; M.A., Eastern Mich. U., 1973; Ph.D., U. Mich., 1980; LHD (hon.), Dominican U., River Forest, Ill., 1995. Ordained to ministry Lutheran Ch. 1958. Pastor St. Paul Luth. Ch., Susanville, Calif., 1958-61; pastor Trinity Luth. Ch., St. Joseph, Mich., 1961-65; prof. Concordia Coll., Ann Arbor, 1965-83; pres. Concordia U., River Forest, Ill., 1983-95; exec. dir. Concordia Mission Soc., 2000. Contbg. author: Concordia Pulpit, 1974, 78, 80, 83, 85; contbg. editor: Luth. Edn., 1983-95. Chmn. coll. divsn. United Way, Ann Arbor; mem. troop com. Boy Scouts Am., Ann Arbor; peer reviewer U.S. Dept. Edn.; bd. dirs. Fedn. Ind. Ill. Colls. and Univs.; mem., past pres. Luth. Edn. Conf. N.Am. Recipient Servus Ecclaesiae Christi, Concordia Theol. Sem., Ft. Wayne, Ind., 1978, Servant of Christ award Condordia Coll., Bronxville, N.Y., 1995. Mem. Luth. Edn. Assn., Phi Delta Kappa Avocations: tennis; sailing; skiing; reading; travel. Home: 36395 N Tara Ct Ingleside IL 60041-8576

KRENTZ, JANE, state legislator, elementary education educator; b. Mpls., Dec. 24, 1952; children: Leah, Sarah, Jeremy. BA, Hamline U., 1971; MEd, U. Minn., 1996. Elem. sch. tchr.; mem. Minn. Senate from 51st dist., St. Paul, 1993—. Mem. C. of C. Stillwater, Forest Lake, Anoka County (all Minn.). Home: 14177 Paris Ave N Stillwater MN 55082-8523 Office: Minn State Senate 234 State Capitol Saint Paul MN 55155-0001

KRETSCHMAR, WILLIAM EDWARD, state legislator, lawyer; b. St. Paul, Aug. 21, 1933; s. William Emanuel and Frances Jane (Peterson) K. BS, Coll. St. Thomas, 1954; LLB, U. Minn., 1961. Bar: N.D. 1961, U.S. Dist. Ct. N.D. 1961. Pvt. practice Kretschmar Law Office, Ashley, ND, 1962—98; mem. N.D. Ho. of Reps., Bismarck, 1972-98, speaker, 1988-90, 2000—. Mem. N.D. Commn. Uniform State Laws, 1987—; bd. dirs. N.W. G.F. Mut. Ins. Co., Eureka, S.D.; del. N.D. Constl. Conv., Bismarck, 1971-72. Mem. ABA, State Bar Assn. N.D., Lions (pres. local club 1972-73, 93-94), Elks. Republican. Roman Catholic. Avocations: hunting, swimming, hiking, bicycling, skiing. Home: 201 E 3d St Venturia ND 58489-4015 Office: Kretschmar Law Office 117 1st Ave NW Ashley ND 58413-7037

KRETSCHMER, CHARLES J. electronics executive; b. 1956; V.p. ESCO, St. Louis, 1999, v.p., CFO, 1999-00, sr. v.p., CFO, 2000—. Office: ESCO Electronics Corp 8888 Ladue Rd Ste 200 Saint Louis MO 63124-2090

KREUSER, JAMES E. state legislator; b. Kenosha, Wis., May 20, 1961; s. Harold Floyd and LaVerne Kreuser; m. Jane, 1990; children: Justin, James Jr. BA, U. Wis.-Parkside, 1983, MPA, 1986. Adminstrv. asst. Kenosha County Exec. Bd., Wis.; assemblyman Wis. State Assembly Dist. 64, 1993—. Elections & constnl. law com. Wis. State Assembly, hwy. & transp. com., mandates com., spl. com. on electronic benefit transfer sys., legal council com. on Indian affairs. Past exec. bd. ARC. Mem. Kenosha Area Devel. Corp., Sr. Action Coun., Rotary, Masons, Danish Brotherhood, Kenosha Sport Fishing and Conservation Assn. Office: PO Box 8952 Madison WI 53708-8952

KREUTER, GRETCHEN V. academic administrator; b. Mpls., May 7, 1934; d. Sigmund and Marvyl (Larson) von Loewe; m. Robert L. Sutton, 1993; children: David Karl, Betsy Ruth Rymes. BA, Rockford Coll., 1955; MA, U. Wis., 1958, PhD, 1961; LLD (hon.), Rockford Coll., 1992, Coll. St. Mary, 1994. Lectr. in Am. Studies Colgate U., Hamilton, N.Y., 1962-67; lectr. in history Coll. St. Catherine, St. Paul, 1969-71, Hamline U., St. Paul, 1971-72; prof. of history Macalester Coll., 1972-73, St. Olaf Coll., Northfield, Minn., 1975-80; asst. to pres. Coll. St. Catherine, St. Paul, 1980-84; asst. to v.p. acad. affairs U. Minn., Mpls., 1984-87; pres. Rockford Coll., Ill., 1987-92, Olivet (Mich.) Coll., 1992-93; sr. fellow Am. Coun. Edn., Washington, 1993-94; hon. fellow Inst. for Rsch. in Humanities U. Wis., Madison, 1994—; interim pres. Coll. of St. Mary, Omaha, 1995-96. Mem., chmn. Minn. Humanities Coun., St. Paul, 1974-83; mem. Mich. Humanities Coun., 1993; bd. dirs. Nat. Assn. State Humanities Commn., Washington, 1984-86. Author: An American Dissenter, 1969 (McKnight prize 1978), Running the Twin Cities: editor: Women of Minnesota, 1977, 2d edit., 1998, Two Career Family, 1978, Forgotton Promise: Race and Gender Conflict on a Small College Campus: A Memoir, 1996. Bd. dirs. Kobe Coll. Corp., Rockford Mus. Ctr., ACE Commn. on Minorities in Higher Edn., 1991-92, Mich. Humanities Coun., 1993-94. Address: 2402 Kendall Ave Madison WI 53705-3845 E-mail: gkreuter@facstaff.wisc.edu.

KREUZE, CALVIN, office products company executive; CFO Haworth Inc., Holland, Mich. Office: Haworth Inc One Haworth Ctr Holland MI 49423

KRIEGEL, DAVID L. retail executive; b. 1946; Grad., Bliss Bus. Coll., 1968. With Lake End Sales, Inc. subs. of Scot Lad Foods, Inc., Fort Wayne, Ind., 1968-73; pres. Am. Merchandising Assocs., Inc., Van Wert, Ohio, 1973-88; chmn., pres., CEO Diamond Distributing, Inc., Lima, 1978—, Kriegel Holding Co., Inc., Van Wert, 1978—; corp. v.p. Roundy's, Inc., 1988-90; v.p. Cardinal Health and Mktg. Group, divsn. of Cardinal Distribution, Inc., 1990-93; CEO Drug Emporium, Inc., Powell, Ohio, 1993—. Office: Drug Emporium Inc 14525 Highway 7 Minnetonka MN 55345-3734

KRIEGER, IRVIN MITCHELL, chemistry educator, consultant; b. Cleve., May 14, 1923; s. William I. and Rose (Brodsky) K.; m. Theresa Melamed, June 9, 1965; 1 dau., Laura. B.S., Case Inst. Tech., 1944, M.S., 1948; Ph.D., Cornell, 1951. Rsch. asst. Case Inst. Tech., Cleve., 1946-47; teaching fellow Cornell U., Ithaca, N.Y., 1947-49; instr. Case Western Res. U., 1949-51, asst. prof., 1951-55, assoc. prof., 1955-68, prof., 1968-88, prof. emeritus, 1988—; dir. Center for Adhesives, Sealants and Coatings, 1983-88. Vis. prof. U. Bristol, 1977-78; cons. for chem. firms; prof. invité Ecole Nat. Supérieure de Chimie de Mulhouse, 1987, Louis Pasteur U., Strasbourg, France, 1989. Contbr. articles to profl. jours. Served as ensign USNR, 1943-46. NSF fellow Université Libre De Bruxelles, 1959-60; sr. fellow Weizmann Inst., 1970 Mem. Am. Chem. Soc., Am. Inst. Chem. Engrs., AAUP, Soc. Rheology (pres. 1977-79, Bingham medalist 1989). Home: 3460 Green Rd Apt 101 Beachwood OH 44122-4076 Office: Case Western Reserve U Cleveland OH 44106 E-mail: imk@po.cwru.edu.

KRIEGER, MARK H. food products executive; Various positions corp. planning Anheuser-Busch Cos., Inc., 1980-83; mgr. bus. planning Earthgrains Co. (formerly Campbell Taggart, Inc.), 1983-86, dir. corp. planning, 1986-89, v.p. corp. planning, 1989-93, v.p., CFO, 1994—. Office: The Earthgrains Co 8400 Maryland Ave Saint Louis MO 63105

KRIER, HERMAN, mechanical and industrial engineering educator; b. Maribor, Yugoslavia, Feb. 15, 1942; came to U.S., 1950; s. Jacob and Katherine (Kless) K.; m. Marion Puleio, June 12, 1965; children: Melissa, Daniel Herman. BS, U. Pitts., 1964; MA, Princeton (N.J.) U., 1966, PhD, 1968. Asst. prof. mechanical and indsl. engring. U. Ill., Urbana, 1969-73, assoc. prof., 1973-78, prof., 1978—. Chief scientist Combustion Scis., Inc., Champaign, Ill., 1977-92. Editor: Proceedings of the 18th Combustion Symposium, 1980, Proceedings of the 19th Combustion Symposium, 1982; co-editor: Progress in Aeronautics and Astronautics, 1979; contbr. articles to profl. jours. Fellow AIAA, mem. ASME, The Combustion Inst. Achievements include being author or co-author of more than 100 publications in the field of combustion. Office: U Ill Dept Medh and Ind Engring 1206 W Green St Urbana IL 61801-2906

KRIER, JAMES EDWARD, law educator, writer; b. Milw., Oct. 19, 1939; s. Ambrose Edward and Genevieve Ida (Behling) Krier; m. Gayle Marian Grimsrud, Mar. 22, 1962 (div.); children: Jennifer, Amy; m. Wendy Louise Wilkes, Apr. 20, 1974; children: Andrew Wilkes-Krier, Patrick Wilkes-Krier. BS, U. Wis., 1961, JD, 1966. Bar: Wis. 1966, U.S. Ct. Claims 1968. Law clk. to chief justice Calif. Supreme Ct., San Francisco, 1966-67; assoc. Arnold & Porter, Washington, 1967-69; acting prof., then prof. law UCLA, 1969-78, 80-83; prof. law Stanford U., 1978-80, U. Mich. Law Sch., Ann Arbor, 1983—, Earl Warren DeLano prof., 1988—. Cons. Calif. Inst. Tech., EPA; mem. pesticide panel NAS, 1972—75, mem. com. energy and the environment, 1975—77. Author: (book) Environmental Law and Policy, 1971; author: (with Stewart) Environmental Law and Policy, 2d edit., 1978; author: (with Ursin) Pollution and Policy, 1977; author: (with Dukeminier) Property, 1981, Property, 5th edit., 2002; contbr. articles to profl. jours. Served to lt. U.S. Army, 1961—63. Mem.: Order of Coif, Artus, Phi Kappa Phi. Office: U Mich Law Sch 625 S State St Ann Arbor MI 48109-1215 E-mail: jkrier@umich.edn.

KRIMM, SAMUEL, physicist, educator; b. Morristown, N.J., Oct. 19, 1925; s. Irving and Ethel (Stein) K.; m. Marilyn Marcy Neveloff, June 26, 1949; children: David Robert, Daniel Joseph. B.S., Poly. Inst. Bklyn., 1947; M.A., Princeton U., 1949, Ph.D., 1950. Postdoctoral fellow U. Mich., Ann Arbor, 1950-52, mem. faculty, 1952—, prof. physics, 1963-2001, prof. emeritus, 2001—, mem. Macromolecular Rsch. Ctr., 1968—, mem. biophysics rsch. divsn., 1962—, chmn. biophysics rsch. div., 1976-86, dir. program in protein structure and design, 1985-94, assoc. dean research Coll. Lit., Sci. and Arts, 1972-75. Chmn. infrared spectroscopy Gordon Rsch. Conf., 1968; mem. NAS/NRC NBS Polymers divsn. Evaluation Panel, 1973-76, chmn., 1975-76; mem. materials rsch. adv. com. NSF, 1981-86, chmn., 1984; mem. DOE Coun. on Material Scis., 1986-89; mem. program adv. com. Internat. Conf. on Raman Spectroscopy, 1984-86, mem. exec. com., 1988-90; Fraser Price Meml. lectr., 1988; disting. lectr. Inst. Materials Sci. U. Conn., 1995; mem. com. on promoting rsch. collaboration NAS/IOM, 1987-89; cons. B.F. Goodrich, 1956-86, Allied 1963-93, Monsanto, 1987-92; vis. prof. U. Mainz, 1983, U. Paris, 1991. Author papers on vibrational spectroscopy, x-ray diffraction studies of natural and synthetic polymers, potential energy function devel.; mem. editorial bd. Jour. Polymer Sci. Polymer Physics Edn., 1967-99; Biopolymers, 1973—; Macromolecules, 1968-71; Jour. Macromolecular Sci.-Rev. Macromolecular Chemistry, 1983-92. Served with USNR, 1944-46. Recipient Humboldt award, 1983; U. Mich. Disting. Faculty Achievement award, 1986; Textile Research Inst. fellow, 1947-50; NSF sr. postdoctoral fellow, 1962-63; sr. fellow U. Mich. Soc. Fellows, 1971-76 Fellow AAAS, Am. Phys. Soc. (High Polymer Physics prize 1977, chmn. div. biol. physics 1979, div. councilor 1981, exec. com. 1983, planning com. 1992); mem. Am. Chem. Soc., Am. Crystallographic Assn., Biophys. Soc., Coblentz Soc. (hon., bd. mgr. 1967-70). Office: U Mich Dept Physics 930 N University Ave Ann Arbor MI 48109-1001 E-mail: skrimm@umich.edu.

KRINGEL, JEROME HOWARD, lawyer; b. Milw., Apr. 2, 1940; s. Lester E. and Irene A. (Kreutzer) K.; m. Mary Kathleen McAuliffe, Sept. 8, 1962; children: Anne, Mary Karen, Jennifer, Elisabeth, Katherine. AB, Marquette U., 1962; postgrad., U. Heidelberg, Germany, 1963; LLB, Yale U., 1966. Bar: Wis. 1966, U.S. Dist. Ct. (ea. dist.) Wis. 1966, U.S. Ct. Appeals (7th cir.) 1966. Ptnr., coord. bus. practice Michael, Best & Friedrich, Milw., 1966—. Trustee Shorewood (Wis.) Village Bd., 1974-80. Mem. ABA, Wis. Bar Assn. (chmn. bus. law sect. 1990-91), Milw. Bar Assn. Office: Michael Best & Friedrich LLP 100 E Wisconsin Ave Ste 3300 Milwaukee WI 53202-4108 E-mail: jhkringel@mbf-law.com.

KRINGEN, DALE ELDON, state legislator, trasportation executive; b. Chester, S.D., May 8, 1935; s. Palmer and Madeline (Amundson) K.; children from previous marriage: Brian, Brad, Kevin, Kane; m. Katherine T. Krinteh, Aug. 27, 1990; 1 child, Anne. BS, S.D. State U., 1967, MEd, 1960. Tchr., coach, Ruthton, Minn.; prin.; supt. schs. Alexandria, S.D.; rep. Scott, Foresman Pub. Co., Glenview, Ill.; dir. S.D. Job Svc., Pierre, S.D.; owner Allied Transp. Svcs., Inc., 1983—, Continental Transp. Svcs., Inc., 1983—, Truck Bonding, USA, 1983—, Truck Process Agents Am., Inc., 1983—, Assist Fin. Svcs., 1986—. Home: RR 1 Box 86H Wentworth SD 57075-9602

KRINGSTAD, EDROY, state legislator; m. Faye Kringstad; 3 children. BS, Valley City State U.; MS, U. N.D. Senator Dist. 49 N.D. Senate, mem. natural resources com., appropriations com., vice chmn. fin. and taxation com. Named to Hall of Fame, Valley City State U., Nat. Wrestling Hall of Fame; named Nat. Coach of Yr. Nat. Jr. Coll. Athletic Assn., Athletic Dir. and Dance Tchr. of Yr. N.D. Health, Phys. Edn. Recreation and Dance. Mem. Amvets, Am. Legion, Nat. Coaches Assn. (past pres.), Am. Fedn. Tchrs., Elks, Eagles. Republican.

KRINKIE, PHILIP B. state legislator, business executive; b. St. Paul, Feb. 3, 1950; s. Frederic W. and Helen (Trieglaff) K.; m. Mary Ramsey, 1984. BA, Coe Coll., Cedar Rapids, Iowa, 1975. Pres. Shelling Co., 1981—; Dist. 53A rep. Minn. Ho. of Reps., St. Paul, 1991—. Mem. govt.

op. and gaming-state govt. fin. divsn., local govt. and met. affairs, and transp. and transit coms., Minn. Ho. of Reps. Chmn. 4th Congrl. Dist. Rep. Com., 1983-84. Recipient spl. achievement award, Army Corps of Engrs., 1976. Mem. Sigma Nu. Office: 100 Constitution Ave Saint Paul MN 55155-1232

KRISCH, ALAN DAVID, physics educator; b. Phila., Apr. 19, 1939; s. Kube and Jeanne (Freiberg) K.; m. Jean Peck, Aug. 27, 1961; 1 child, Kathleen Susan. AB, U. Pa., 1960; PhD, Cornell U., 1964. Instr. Cornell U., 1964; mem. faculty U. Mich., Ann Arbor, 1964—, assoc. prof. high energy physics, 1966-68, prof., 1968—. Vis. prof. Niels Bohr Inst., Copenhagen, 1975-76; trustee Argonne Nat. Lab., 1972-73, 80-82, chmn. zero gradient syncrotron users group, 1973-75, 78-79, chmn. internat. com. for high energy spin physics symposia, 1977-94, past chmn., 1995—, chmn. organizing com. conf. on particle and nuclear physics intersections, 1983-86, mem., 1987-91, hon. mem., 1994—; chmn.-elect, chmn. IUCF Users Group, 1997—; spokesperson NEPTUN-A Expt. at 400 GeV UNK accelerator in Russia, 1989-99, SPIN collaboration Fermilab, 1991-95, SPIN at HERA collaboration DESY in Germany, 1996-99, SPINatU-70 Exp. at 70 Gev IHEP accelerator in Protvino, Russia, 2000—. Trustee Ann Arbor Hands On Mus., 1999-02. Fellow NSF, 1963, Guggenheim Found., 1971-72, Denmark Nat. Bank, 1975-76. Fellow Am. Phys. Soc.; mem. AAAS. Achievements include discovery of heavy elementary particles, of structure within the proton, of scaling in inclusive reations, of spinning core within proton, of large spin forces in violent proton collisions, of precise confirmation of large spin forces; invention of inclusive reactions; development of first high energy spin-polarized proton beam, of first strong focusing spin-polarized proton beam; demonstration of "Siberian snake" technique for accelerating spin-polarized beams. Office: U Mich Randall Lab Ann Arbor MI 48109-1120

KRISS, GARY W(AYNE), Episcopal priest; b. Balt., Dec. 29, 1946; s. Warren B. and Margaret L. (Austin) K. AB cum laude, Dartmouth Coll., 1968; MDiv, Yale U. Divinity Sch., 1972; postgrad. studies, The Gen. Theol. Sem., N.Y.C., 1972, St. George Coll., Jerusalem, 1978; DD, Nashotah House, 2001. Ordained to ministry Episcopal Ch. as deacon, 1972, as priest 1972. Chaplain to the congregation Cathedral Ch. of St. Paul, Burlington, Vt., 1972-74; coord. Rock Point (Vt.) Summer Confs., 1973-77; vicar St. Mark's, St. Luke's Parishes, Castleton and Fair Haven, Vt., 1974-78; asst. to dean The Cathedral of All Saints, Albany, N.Y., 1978-79, canon precentor, 1979-84, dir. inst. Christian studies, 1979-84; dean Cathedral of All Saints, 1984-91; dean and pres. Nashotah (Wis.) House, 1992—2001; interim rector St. Paul's Epis. Ch., Troy, NY, 2001—. Bd. dirs. Brookhaven Home for Boys, Chelsea, Vt., 1975-79, Albany Collegiate Interfaith Ctr., 1982-90, pres. 1984-90; Episcopal campus priest, SUNY, Albany, 1980-84; bd. dirs. Capital Area Coun. of Chs., Albany, N.Y., 1989-91, chmn. of Faith and Learning Commn.; The Living Ch. Found., 1994—. Bd. dirs. Samaritan Shelters, Glenmont, N.Y., 1979-91, The Child's Hosp., Albany, 1986-90, Child's Nursing Home, Albany, 1987-91, pres. 1990-91. Home and Office: PO Box 26 Cambridge NY 12816

KRISS, ROBERT J. lawyer; b. Cleve., Dec. 15, 1953; BA summa cum laude, Cornell U., 1975; JD cum laude, Harvard U., 1978. Bar: Ill. 1978, U.S. Dist. Ct. (no. dist.) Ill. 1978, U.S. Ct. Appeals (7th cir.) 1983, U.S. Dist. Ct. (no. dist. trial bar) Ill. 1982, U.S. Ct. Appeals (5th cir.) 1984. Ptnr. Mayer, Brown, Rowe & Man, Chgo. Presenter in field; adj. prof. trial practice Northwestern U. Law Sch. Author short story. Chmn. consent degree task force Chgo. Park Dist., 1986-87; bd. dirs. Chgo. Legal Assistance Found., 1996—. Mem. Nat. Inst. Trial Advocacy (faculty midwest regional program 1988-91, 94), Winnetka Caucus (chmn. schs. candidate selection com. 1997). Office: Mayer Brown Rowe & Man 190 S La Salle St Ste 3100 Chicago IL 60603-3441

KRISTENSEN, DOUGLAS ALLAN, state legislator; b. Kearney, Nebr., Jan. 4, 1955; s. Donald M. and Mary Lou (Martin) K.; m. Terri S. Harder; 2 children. BA, U. Nebr., 1977; JD, Drake U., 1980. Ptnr. Lieske & Kristensen, 1981—; atty. Kearney County, 1982-88; mem. Nebr. Legislature from 37th dist., Lincoln, 1988—; chmn. transp. com. Nebr. Legislature, 1991-98, mem. intergovtl. coop. and revenue coms., mem. exec. bd., chair transp. com., 1991-97, speaker of the legislature, 1998—. Bd. dirs. young lawyers ssect. Nebr. Bar, 1984-88, Nebr. CLE Inc., 1986-90. Henry Toll fellow, 1991; recipient Pres.' award Nebr. Assn. County Ofcls., 1987. Mem. Nebr. Bar Assn., Iowa Bar Assn., Nebr. County Atty.'s Assn. (bd. dirs. 1985—), Rotary Internat., Optimists Club. Office: Nebr State Senate State Capitol Rm 2103 Lincoln NE 68509 Home: 219 N Brown Ave Minden NE 68959-1524

KRITZER, PAUL ERIC, media executive, communications lawyer; b. Buffalo, May 5, 1942; s. James Cyril and Bessie May (Biddlecombe) K.; m. Frances Jean McCallum, June 20, 1970; children: Caroline Frances, Erica Hopkins. BA, Williams Coll., 1964; MS in Journalism, Columbia U., 1965; JD, Georgetown U., 1972. Bar: U.S. Supreme Ct. 1978, Wis. 1980. Reporter, copy editor Buffalo Evening News, 1964, 69, 70; instr. English Augusta (Ga.) Coll., 1968-69; law clk. Office of FCC Commr., Washington, 1971, MCI, Washington, 1972; counsel U.S. Ho. of Reps., 1972-77; assoc. counsel Des Moines Register & Tribune, 1977-80; editor, pub. Waukesha (Wis.) Freeman, 1980-83; legal v.p., sec. Jour. Communications Inc., Milw., 1983—. Trustee Carroll Co., Waukesha, 1981-89; producer Waukesha Film Festival, 1982; bd. dirs. Des Moines Metro Opera, Inc., 1979-80; bd. dirs. Milw. Youth Symphony Orch., 1992-2001, pres. 1994-97; bd. dirs. Milw. Symphony Orch., 1997—; bd. dirs. United Performing Arts Fund, 1994-97. With U.S. Army, 1965-68. Presbyterian. Avocations: bridge, gardening. Home: 211 Oxford Rd Waukesha WI 53186-6263 Office: Jour Communications Inc 333 W State St PO Box 661 Milwaukee WI 53201-0661 Business E-Mail: pkritzer@jc.com.

KRIVIT, JEFFREY SCOT, surgeon; b. Aug. 15, 1955; m. Mary Hoyme, July 6, 1986; children: Bradley, Alex, Elyse, Hanna. BS, U. Ill., 1977, MD, 1981. Resident Ill. Eye & Ear Infirmary, Chgo., 1982-86; physician Carle Clinic Assoc., Urbana, Ill., 1986-89, Linn Head & Neck Surgery, Cedar Rapids, Iowa, 1989-92, Cedar Rapids ENT, 1992-96, Ea. Iowa ENT, Cedar Rapids, 1996—. Chief surgery St. Luke's Hosp., Cedar Rapids, 1995-96. Fellow Am. Rhinol. Soc., Am. Acad. Otolaryngology Head & Neck Surgery, Am. Soc. Head & Neck Surgery, Am. Acad. Facial Plastic & Reconstructive Surgery, Am. Coll. Surgeons; mem. AMA, Linn County Med. Soc., Iowa Med. Soc. Office: PCI ENT Dept 2d Fl 600 7th St SE Fl 2D Cedar Rapids IA 52401-2112

KRIVKOVICH, PETER GEORGE, advertising executive; b. Bad Ischl, Austria, Oct. 25, 1946; came to U.S., 1953; s. George M. Krivkovich and Ada (Kalenkiewicz) Bajor; m. Linda J. Monken, Aug. 30, 1970; children: Peter A., Alexis C. BS, U. Ill., 1969; postgrad., Loyola U., Chgo., 1972-73. Advt. asst. Kemper Ins. Co., Chgo., 1969-71; account exec. Nader-Lief, 1971-72; account mgr. Leo Burnett, 1972-73; ptnr. Hackenberg, Normann, Krivkovich, 1973-80; pres. Cramer-Krasselt, 1981-86, pres., COO Chgo./Milw./Orland, Phx., 1987-98, pres., CEO, chmn. bd. Chgo./Milw./Orland, 1999—. Mem. Nat. Advt. Rev. Bd. Bd. dir. Mfg. Bank, Off The Street Club, Prentice Hosp., Chgo. Humanities Festival. Named One of 100 Best and Brightest Advt. Execs. of Yr. Advt. Age mag., 1986, Midwest Advt. Exec. of Yr. Adweek mag., 1987. Mem. Am. Assn. Advt. Agys. (chmn. Chgo. chpt. 1992, 93, regional bd. govs. 1996, 97, nat. bd. govs. 1998, 99, 2000, 2001), Direct Mktg. Assn., Chgo. Assn. Direct Mktg., Chgo. Advt. Club, Glenview (Ill.) C. of C., Tavern Club, Exec. Club. Office: Cramer-Krasselt 225 N Michigan Ave Ste 800 Chicago IL 60601-7690 E-mail: pkrivkov@c-k.com.

KRIZAN, KELLY JOE, physician, leather craftsman; b. Winner, S.D., Jan. 16, 1951; s. Miles Woodrow and Sadie Mae (DeSmet) K.; m. Susan Barker, Aug. 21, 1971 (div. Aug. 1983); children: Jennifer Rebecca, Nicholas Miles; m. Cynthia Lydia Obras, Aug. 6, 1983. BS, S.D. State U., 1973; BS in Medicine, U. S.D., 1976; MD, Tufts U., 1978. Diplomate Am. Bd. Family Practice. Commd., Am. Bd. Radiology. (first active duty capt. U.S. Air Force, 1978, advanced through grades to lt. col., 1984. Intern USAF Med. Ctr., Scott AFB, Ill., 1978-79, resident, 1979-81; staff physicain USAF Hosp., Hill AFB, Utah, 1981-83; chief emergency svcs., chief family practice USAF Hosp., Hill AFB, Utah, Incirlik AB, Turkey, 1983-84, chmn. dept. family practice, 1985-86; resident radiology U. Wash., 1986-90, clin. asst. prof., 1990—; chmn. dept. radiology 13th AF Med. Ctr., Clark AB, Philippines, 1990-91, St. Mary's Health Care Ctr., Pierre, S.D., 1993—, chmn. radiology, 1993—, chief of staff, 1997, St. Mary's Healthcare Ctr. . Artist leather goods, winner various awards. U. S.D. Presdl. scholar, 1969. Fellow Am. Acad. Family Physicians; mem. Am. Coll. Radiology, Am. Roentgen Ray Soc., Radiological Soc. N.Am., Phi Kappa Phi. Roman Catholic.

KRIZEK, RAYMOND JOHN, civil engineering educator, consultant; b. Balt., June 5, 1932; s. John James and Louise (Polak) K.; m. Claudia Stricker, Aug. 1964; children— Robert A., Kevin J. BE, Johns Hopkins U., 1954; MS, U. Md., 1961; PhD, Northwestern U., 1963. Instr. U. Md., College Park, 1957-61; rsch. asst. civil engring. Northwestern U., Evanston, Ill., 1961-63, asst. prof. civil engring., 1963-66, assoc. prof. civil engring., 1966-70, prof. civil engring., 1970, chmn. dept. civil engring., 1980-92, dir. Master of Project Mgmt. program, 1994—, Stanley F. Pepper chair prof., 1987—. Cons. to industry Editor books; contbr. numerous articles to profl. jours. Served to lt. U.S. Army, 1955-57 Decorated Palmes Academiques (France), 1993; recipient Hogentogler award ASTM, 1970; named disting. vis. scholar NSF, 1972. Mem.: ASCE (hon.; pres. GEO Inst. 1997—98, Huber Rsch prize 1971, Karl Teraghi award 1997, Ill. sect. Civil Engr. of Yr. 1999, Hon. mem. 2002), Internat. Soc. Soil Mechanics and Geotech. Engring., Nat. Acad. Engring., Spanish Acad. Engring. (corr.). Roman Catholic Home: 1366 Sanford Ln Glenview IL 60025-3165 Office: Dept Civil Engring Northwestern U 2145 Sheridan Rd Evanston IL 60208-0834

KROCK, CURTIS JOSSELYN, pulmonologist; b. Fort Smith, Ark., Oct. 11, 1935; s. Frederick Henry and Hazel Armiger (Josselyn) Krock; m. Ruth Leone Johnson, Apr. 27, 1968; children: Eric Gregory, Lynn Alyson. BA, Stanford U., 1957; MD, Johns Hopkins U. Sch. Medicine, 1961. Diplomate Am. Bd. Internal Medicine, Am. Bd. Pulmonary Medicine. Intern Barnes Hosp., St. Louis, 1961-62, resident in internal medicine, 1963-65; resident in pathology Johns Hopkins U. Sch. Medicine, Balt., 1962-63; pulmonary fellow Duke U., Durham, N.C., 1965-66; pvt. practice Holt-Krock Clinic, Ft. Smith, Ark., 1968-72, Carle Clinic, Urbana, Ill., 1972-2001, also bd. dirs., 1978-80, chief medicine dept., 1996-99; clin. asst. prof. U. Ill., 1976-99, clin. assoc. prof., 2000—; assoc. program dir. med. residency program UICOM-UC. Capt. U.S. Army, 1966—68. Fellow: ACP; mem.: Sierra Club, Sigma Xi. Avocations: violin, reading. Home: 2125 Lynwood Dr Champaign IL 61821-6606 Office: Carle Clin Edn Ctr Forum Bldg 611 W Park Urbana IL 61801-2530 E-mail: curtis.krock@carle.com.

KROENERT, ROBERT MORGAN, lawyer; b. Kansas City, Mo., July 19, 1939; s. Robert Andrew and Marion Leona (Morgan) K.; m. Susan Aldrich, Aug. 18, 1962; children: Kathleen Susan, Ann Elizabeth, Robert Aldrich. BS, U. Kans., 1961; JD, U. Mich., 1964. Bar: Mo. 1964, U.S. Dist. Ct. (we. dist.) Mo. 1965, U.S. Ct. Appeals (8th cir.) 1984, U.S. Ct. Appeals (5th, 10th and D.C. cirs.) 1986, U.S. Supreme Ct. 1991. Assoc. Morrison & Hecker L.L.P., Kansas City, 1964-69; ptnr. Morrison & Hecker, 1969—2002. Bd. dirs. Guadalupe Ctr., Inc., Kansas City, 1978-87; mem. adv. bd. greater univ. fund, U. Kans., Lawrence, 1985-88; Mem. fin. com. Johnson County Rep. Com., 1987-90, Mo. Supreme Ct. Disciplinary Com. for Jackson County, 1992-2000, divsn. chair, 1995-97; mem. coun. Colonial Congregtional Ch., 1990-93, moderator, 1991-93. Mem. Mo. Bar, Kansas City Met. Bar Assn., Internat. Assn. Def. Counsel, Mo. Orgn. Def. Lawyers, Lawyers Assn. Kansas City (bd. dirs., pres. 1998-99, past pres., past pres. found.), Kansas City Club, Mission Hills Country Club, Rotary. Avocation: golf. Office: Morrison & Hecker LLP 2600 Grand Blvd Ste 1200 Kansas City MO 64108-4606

KROEPLIN, KENNETH, state legislator; b. Grand Forks, N.D., Jan. 15, 1952; m. Sharon; 3 children. Farmer; supr. Township, N.D., Edendale; mem. House of Rep., N.D. Senate from 23rd dist., Bismark, 1996—. Bd. dirs. Steele County Farmers Union, Steele County Mut. Ins.; mem. Hope Rural Fire Protection Dist. With N. D. Nat. Guard, 1970-76; Hope Am. Legion (vice cmdr.) Democrat. Lutheran. Office: Dist 23 Rt 1 Box 39 Hope ND 58046 E-mail: kkroepli@state.nd.us.

KROGSTAD, JACK LYNN, accounting educator, dean; b. Harlan, Iowa, Jan. 27, 1944; s. Chester Milo and Geraldine Elizabeth (Archibald) K.; m. Nancy Ellen Coffin, June 18, 1967; children: Kristine Ellen, Brian Lynn. BS, Union Coll., 1967; MBA, U. Nebr., 1971, PhD, 1975. Staff acct. Trachtenberg & Grant CPAs, Lincoln, Nebr., 1967-68; asst. prof. U. Tex., Austin, 1975-78; assoc. prof. Kans. State U., Manhattan, 1978-80; John P. Begley prof. acctg. Creighton U., Omaha, 1980-96, prof. acctg., 1997—, assoc. dean, 2000—. Vis. assoc. prof. U. Mich., Ann Arbor, 1980; vis. prof. U. Ill.; dir. rsch. Nat. Commn. Fraudulent Fin. Reporting, 1985-87. Editor: Auditing: A Journal of Practice and Theory; contbr. articles to profl. jours. With U.S. Army, 1968-70. Recipient Disting. Faculty Svc. award Creighton U., 1988; Arthur Anderson & Co. doctoral fellow, 1974-75, Paton Acctg. Ctr. rsch. fellow, 1980. Mem. AICPA, Nebr. Soc. CPAs (Acctg. Educator of Yr. award 1983), Am. Acctg. Assn. (regional v.p. 1984-85, auditing sect. chmn. 1984-85, Outstanding Auditing Educator award 1994), Beta Gamma Sigma, Beta Alpha Psi. Republican. Seventh-Day-Adventist. Home: 56717 Deacon Rd Pacific Junction IA 51561-4169 E-mail: jkrogstad@creighton..edu.

KROHNKE, DUANE W. retired lawyer; b. Keokuk, Iowa, June 29, 1939; s. Ward Glenn and Marian Frances (Brown) K.; m. Mary Alyce Luschen, June 25, 1963; children: Alan Duane, Brian Douglas. BA, Grinnell (Iowa) Coll., 1961, Oxford U., 1963, MA, 1970; JD, U. Chgo., 1966; DHL, Grinnell Coll., 1999. Bar: N.Y. 1967, Minn. 1970, U.S. Supreme Ct. 1970, U.S. Ct. Appeals (2d cir.) 1967, U.S. Ct. Appeals (8th cir.) 1970, U.S. Ct. Appeals (D.C.) 1974, U.S. Dist. Ct. (so., ea. dists.) N.Y. 1967, U.S. Dist. Ct. Minn. 1970. Assoc. atty. Cravath, Swaine, Moore, N.Y.C., 1966-70, Faegre & Benson, Mpls., 1970-73, ptnr., 1974-2000, of counsel, 2001; ret., 2001. Editl. bd.: U. Chgo., 1964—66. Co-chair Bicentennial com. U.S. Dist. Ct. Minn. dist., Mpls., 1986-88; elder Westminster Presbyn. Ch., Mpls., 1985-91; trustee United Theol. Seminary, New Brighton, Minn., 1988-98. Recipient Alumni award Grinnell Coll., 1982; Rhodes scholar Rhodes Trustees, Oxford, Eng., 1961-63; Mecham scholar U. Chgo., 1963-66. Mem. Minn. State Bar Assn. (co-chair antitrust sect. 1982-84, co-chair ethics/standards of practice com. of ADR sect. 1995-96, chair elect ADR sect. 1996-97, chair ADR sect. 1997-98), Minn. Human Rights Advocates (vol. award 1991, 99, 2002), Order of Coif, Phi Beta Kappa. Avocations: reading, cultural events, exercise.

KROLL, BARRY LEWIS, lawyer; b. Chgo., June 8, 1934; s. Harry M. and Hannah (Lewis) K.; m. Jayna Vivian Leibovitz, June 20, 1956; children: Steven Lee, Joan Lois Kroll Dolgin, Nancy Maxine Kroll Richardson. A.B. in Psychology with distinction, U. Mich., 1955, J.D. with distinction, 1958. Bar: Ill. 1958. Assoc. firm Jacobs & McKenna, Chgo., 1958-66, Epstein, Manilow & Sachnoff, Chgo., 1966-68, Schiff, Hardin, Waite Dorschel & Britton, Chgo., 1968-69; ptnr. Wolfberg & Kroll, 1970-74, Kirshbaum & Kroll, Chgo., 1972-74; of counsel Jacobs, Williams & Montgomery, Ltd., 1973-74; ptnr. Jacobs, Williams & Montgomery Ltd., 1974-85, Williams & Montgomery Ltd., Chgo., 1985—. Faculty John Marshall Law Sch., Chgo., 1969-73; atty. for petitioner in U.S. Supreme Ct. decision Escobedo vs Ill., 1964, guest lectr. before groups, 1964— ; mem. legal and legis. com. Internat. Franchise Assn., 1976-80 Asst. editor: Mich. Law Rev, 1957-58. Chmn. Park Forest Bd. Zoning Appeals, 1971-78. Served to capt. AUS, 1959-62. Named Outstanding Young Man Park Forest Jr. C. of C., 1966. Mem. Ill. Bar Assn., Chgo. Bar Assn. (chmn. legis. com. 1974-75), Ill. Appellate Lawyers Assn. (treas. 1978-79, sec. 1979-80, pres. 1981-82), Bar Assn. 7th Fed. Circuit, Order of Coif, Tau Epsilon Rho, Alpha Epsilon Pi. Jewish (trustee congregation 1966-70, 72-75, 90—, pres. men's club 1965-66). Home: 1440 N State Pky Chicago IL 60610-1564 Office: Williams Montgomery & John Ltd 20 N Wacker Dr Ste 2100 Chicago IL 60606-3005 E-mail: blk@willmont.com.

KROMKOWSKI, THOMAS S. state legislator; b. South Bend, Ind., Sept. 2, 1942; m. Janeen Kromkowski, 1963; 2 children. With A M Gen. Corp.; rep. Dist. 7 Ind. Ho. of Reps., 1980—, chmn. elec. and apportionment com., ranking minority mem., mem. labor and employment com., mem. pub. health, aged and aging com. Mem. Westside Dem. and Civic Club, South Bend; vice chmn. United Auto Workers; mem. St. Joseph County Coun. Mem. VFW, Polish Falcons Am. Club.

KRON, RANDY, farmer, agricultural association administrator; m. Joyce Kron; children: Victoria, Benjamin. B Agrl. Econs., Purdue U., 1983. Dir. Ind. Farm Bur, Indpls., 1995—, now v.p.; owner farm Evansville, Ill. Chmn. polit. action com. Ind. Farm Bur., mem. state young farmer com., 1986—87. Mem. Vanderburgh County Soil and Water Conservation Bd.; past pres. county extension bd.; rep. agrl. adv. com. Rep. John Hostettler; sr. youth sponsor Salem United Ch. of Christ, Darmstadt, Ill. Recipient Young Farmer Achievement Bd., Ind. Farm Bur., 1989. Office: Ind Farm Bur Inc PO Box 1290 Indianapolis IN 46206

KRONEGGER, MARIA ELISABETH, French and comparative literature educator; b. Graz, Austria, Sept. 23, 1932; came to U.S., 1962, naturalized, 1968; d. Karl and Josefine (Sparovitz) K. Grad., Karl-Franzens U., Austria, 1960; postgrad., U. Sorbonne, Paris, 1953-55; MA in English and Am. Lit., Kans. U., 1958; PhD in French and Humanities, Fla. State U., 1960. Instr. French, German and Humanities Fla. State U., 1958-60; mem. faculty Internat. Coll., St. Gallen, Switzerland, 1961-62; asst. prof. Hollins Coll., Va., 1962-64; asst. prof. French and comparative lit. Mich. State U., East Lansing, 1964-67, assoc. prof., 1967-70, prof., 1970—. Author: James Joyce and Associate Image Makers, 1968, Impressionist Literature, 1973, The Life Significance of French Baroque Poetry, 1988; editor: Phénoménologie et Littérature: L'origine de l'oeuvre d'art, Hommages à A.-T. Tymieniecka, 1986, Phenomenology and Aesthetics: Approaches to Comparative Literature and the Other Arts, 1990, Dordrecht (Kluwer) vol. XXXIII of book series Analecta Husserliana, 1990; editor: Esthétique Baroque et Imagination Créatrice, 1997, Allegory Old and New in Literature, the Fine Arts, Music and Theatre, and its Continuity in Culture, 1994; co-editor: Life, The Human Quest for an Ideal, 1996, Life Differentiation and Harmony: Vegetal, Animal, Human, Analecta Husseliana LVII, 1998; contbr. more than 135 articles on 17th and 20th century French and English lit., lit. and the fine arts, lit. and phenomenology to scholarly publs., anelecta Husserliana LVII, 1998. Bd. dirs. World Inst. Phenomenology, 1980—; pres. Internat. Soc. Phenomenology and Lit., Internat. Soc. Phenomenology, Fine Arts and Aesthetics; exec. v.p. World Inst. for Advanced Phenomenological Rsch. and Learning. Fulbright scholar, 1957-60; Ford Found. grantee, 1965-66 Mem. MLA, AAUP, Am. Soc. Aesthetics, Am. Comparative Lit. Assn., Semiotic Soc. Am., Chinese Comparative Lit. Assn., Internat. Soc. for Phenomenology and Lit. (pres. 1985—), Internat. Comparative Lit. Assn., Internat. Soc. Civilization, Internat. Semiotic Soc., South Atlantic MLA, Société Paul Claudel, Am. Assn. Tchrs. French, Fédération Internationale de Langues et Littératures Modernes, Golden Key Soc. (hon., Rsch. award). Roman Catholic. Home: 1324 Chartwell Carriage Way N Stonelake East Lansing MI 48823 Office: Mich State U Old Horticulture East Lansing MI 48824 E-mail: kronegger@pilot.mus.edu.

KRSUL, JOHN ALOYSIUS, JR. lawyer; b. Highland Park, Mich., Mar. 24, 1938; s. John A. and Ann M. (Sepich) K.; m. Justine Oliver, Sept. 12, 1958; children: Ann Lisa, Mary Justine. BA, Albion Coll., 1959; JD, U. Mich., 1963. Bar: Mich. 1963. Assoc. Dickinson Wright PLLP, 1963-71, ptnr., 1971-99, consulting ptnr., 2000—. Asst. editor: U. Mich. Law Rev, 1962-63. Recipient Disting. Alumnus award Albion Coll., 1984; Sloan scholar, 1958-59; Fulbright scholar, 1959-60; Ford. Found. grantee, 1964 Fellow: Am. Bar Found. (life; chmn. Mich. chpt. 1988—89); mem.: ABA (ho. of dels. 1979—2002, chmn. standing com. on membership 1983—89, exec. coun. 1984—91, chmn. sect. gen. practice 1989—90, tort and ins. practice sect., exec. coun. 1991—94, bd. govs. 1991—99, chmn. fin. com. 1993—94, exec. com. 1993—94, 1996—99, editl. bd. ABA Jour. 1996—99, treas. 1996—99, audit com. 2001—), Am. Bar Ins. Cons. Inc. (bd. dirs. sec. 1988—95), Am. Bar Endowment (bd. dirs. 1996—99), Nat. Conf. Bar Pres. (exec. coun. 1986—89), Am. Judicature Soc. (dir. 1971—79, exec. com. 1973—74), Fellows of Young Lawyers Am. Bar (bd. dirs. 1977—86, pres. 1983—84, chmn. bd. 1984—86), Mich. State Bar Found. (trustee 1982—83, 1985—99, chmn. fellows 1986—87), State Bar Mich. (commr. 1973—83, pres. 1982—83), Detroit Bar Assn. Found. (dir. 1971—84, pres. 1979—80), Detroit Bar Assn. (dir. 1971—80, pres. 1979—80), Am. Bar Retirement Assn. (bd. dirs. 1999—), Sixth Cir. Jud. Conf. (life), Detroit Club, Orchard Lake Country Club, Delta Tau Delta, Phi Eta Sigma, Omicron Delta Kappa, Phi Beta Kappa. Home: 7094 Huntington Dr Sawyer MI 49125-9319 Office: Dickinson Wright PLLC 500 Woodward Ave Ste 4000 Detroit MI 48226-3416

KRUEGER, BONNIE LEE, editor, writer; b. Chgo., Feb. 3, 1950; d. Harry Bernard and Lillian (Soyak) Krueger; m. James Lawrence Spurlock, Mar. 8, 1972. Student, Morraine Valley Coll., 1970. Adminstrv. asst. Carson Pirie Scott & Co., Chgo., 1969-72; traffic coord. Tatham Laird & Kudner, 1973-74, J. Walter Thompson, Chgo., 1974-76, prodn. coord., 1976-78; editor-in-chief Assoc. Pubs., 1978—, Sophisticate's Hairstyle Guide, 1978—, Sophisticate's Beauty Guide, 1978—, Complete Woman, 1981—; pub., editorial svcs. dir. Sophisticate's Black Hair Guide, 1983—, Sophisticate's Soap Star Styles, 1994-95. Mem. Statue of Liberty Restoration Com., N.Y.C., 1983; campaign worker Cook County State's Atty., Chgo., 1982; poll watcher Cook County Dem. Orgn., 1983; mem. Chgo. Architecture Found. Recipient Exceptional Woman in Pub. award, Women in Periocical Pub., 2000. Mem. Soc. Profl. Journalists, Am. Health and Beauty Aids Inst. (assoc. mem.), Lincoln Park Zool. Soc., Landmarks Preservation Coun. of Ill., Art Inst. Chgo., Chgo. Hist. Soc., Mus. Contemporary Art, Peta, Headline Club, Sigma Delta Chi. Lutheran. Office: Complete Woman 875 N Michigan Ave Chicago IL 60611-1803

KRUEGER, DARRELL WILLIAM, university president; b. Salt Lake City, Feb. 9, 1943; s. William T. and E. Marie (Nelson) K.; m. Verlene Terry, July 1, 1965 (dec. Jan., 1969); 1 child, William; m. Nancy Leane Jones, Sept. 2, 1969; children: Tonya, Amy, Susan. BA summa cum laude, So. Utah State Coll., 1967; MA in Govt., U. Ariz., 1969, PhD in Govt., 1971. Asst. prof. polit. sci. N.E. Mo. State U., Kirksville, 1971-73, v.p. acad. affairs, dean of instrn., 1973-89; pres. Winona State U., Minn., 1989—. Facilitator The 7 Habits of Highly Effective People, 1993; mem. adv. bd. U.S. Bank, Rochester, Minn., 1989—. Mem. Gamehaven Coun. Boy Scouts Am., 1989—. Recipient Outstanding Alumnus award, So. Utah State, 1992. Mem. Am. Assn. State Colls. and Univs., Am. Assn. Higher

Edn., Rotary, Phi Beta Kappa. Mem. LDS Ch. Avocations: running, golf. Home: 1411 Heights Blvd Winona MN 55987-2519 Office: Winona State U Somsen 201 8th & Johnson Winona MN 55987

KRUEGER, JAMES H. social service association executive; With Aid Assn. for Luths., Appleton, Wis., 1965—, from dist. reps. to gen. agt., 1965-83, gen. agt., dir. of agys. Agy. and Sales Wis., 1987—, mem. mktg. and strategy couns. Instr. CLU. Recipient Jack Nussbaum Disting. Svc. award Wis. Assn. Life Underwriters, 1989. Mem. Chartered Life Underwriters, Chartered Fin. cons., Gen. Agts. and Mgrs. Assn. (chmn. internat. mktg. com.), Nat. Assn. Life Underwriters, Life Underwriting Tng. Coun. (bd. dirs.), Golden Key Soc. Office: Aid Assn for Lutherans 4321 N Ballard Rd Appleton WI 54919-0001

KRUEGER, RAYMOND ROBERT, lawyer; b. Portage, Wis., Aug. 29, 1947; s. Earl Andrew and Catherine Virginia (Klenert) K.; m. Barbara Bowen, June 21, 1969; children: Lindsey, Michael. BA in Econs., U. Wis., 1969, JD, 1972. Bar: Wis. 1972. Assoc. Charne, Glassner, Tehan, Clancy & Taitelman S.C., Milw., 1973-79, shareholder, 1979-91, Charne Clancy Krueger Pollack & Corris S.C., Milw., 1991-92; ptnr. Michael, Best & Friedrich, 1992—. Presenter numerous seminars. Chmn. Georgia O'Keeffe Found., Abiquiu, N.Mex., 1989—; trustee Village of Whitefish Bay, Wis., 1989—; mem. Milwaukee River Revitalization Coun., 1988—, vice chair, 1989—96, chair, 1996—; dir. River Revitalization Found., Inc., 1998—, chair, 2001—; mem. Milw. Art Mus. Bldg. Com., 1996—. Capt. USAF, 1969—78. Mem. ABA (natural resources sect.), State Bar Wis. (environ. law sect.), Milw. Bar Assn. (environ. law sect.), Environ. Law Inst. Avocation: visual arts. Office: Michael Best & Friedrich 100 E Wisconsin Ave Ste 3300 Milwaukee WI 53202-4108 E-mail: rrkrueger@mbf-law.com.

KRUEGER, RICHARD ARNOLD, technology executive; b. St. Paul, Feb. 13, 1949; s. Richard Earnest and Shirley Mae (Popp) K.; m. Diane Susan Schiller, Apr. 14, 1973; children: Melissa, Ryan, Alisha. BA, Winona State Coll., 1971; MA in Teaching, Coll. of St. Thomas, 1973; MPA, Harvard U., 1992; PhD, U. Minn., 1997. Program dir. Midway YMCA, St. Paul, 1971-72; tchr. Lakeville (Minn.) Pub. Schs., 1973-79; dir. Staples (Minn.) Tchr. Ctr., 1979-82; owner Computer Networx, Inc., Staples, 1983-89; mem. Minn. Ho. of Reps., St. Paul, 1983-94, asst. majority leader, 1987-90, chair internat. trade and tech. com., 1989-90, speaker pro tempore, 1991-92, chair state govt. fin., 1993-94; info. mgmt. cons., Staples, 1990-94; pres. Minn. High Tech. Assn., Inc., Eagan, 1994-99; CEO, pres. KeyTech, Inc., 1999-2000; v.p. Key Investment, Inc., Mpls., 2000-01, JLT Group, Inc., 2001—. Contbr. articles to profl. publs. Named Outstanding Alumnus, Winona State U., 1990; recipient Top Tech. Legis. Group award Am. Electronic Assn., 1992, Top Pub. Sector award Med. Alley, 1993, Chairs award Minn. High Tech. Assn., 1999. Mem. Democrat Farm Labor Party. Lutheran. Avocations: swimming, reading. Home: 11605 177th St W Lakeville MN 55044-7676 Office: 601 2nd Ave S Ste 5200 Minneapolis MN 55402-4317

KRUEGER-HORN, CHERYL, apparel executive; B in Home Econs. and Bus., Bowling Green State U., 1974. Buyer Burdine's Dept. Store, 1974-76; mdse. mgr. The Limited, 1976; v.p. sale Chaus Sportswear, CEO, until 1985; owner Cheryl's Cookies; pres., CEO Cheryl & Co. Bd. dirs. Bob Evans. Recipient Columbus Area Small Bus. Person of Yr. award Small Bus. Adminstrn., 1986, Woman of Achievement award YWCA, 1992, Outstanding Innovation Achievement award Innovation Alliance, 1992, Ctrl. Ohio Entrepreneur of Yr. award Inc. Mag. and Ernest & Young, 1994, Salesperson of Yr. award Columbus C. of C. Sales Exec. Club, Businessperson of Yr. award Ohio State U., Rosabeth Moss Kantor Excellence in Enterprise award Ohio Dept. Devel., 1996. Mem. Young Pres. Orgn. Office: 646 Mccorkle Blvd Westerville OH 43082-8778

KRUG, SHIRLEY, state legislator; b. Milw., Jan. 29, 1958; BS, U. Wis., Milw., 1981, MA, 1983. Mem. from dist. 13 Wis. State Assembly, Madison, 1984-96, mem. from dist. 12, 1984—. Former adj. prof. econs. U. Wis., Parkside. Commr. Mils. Met. Sewerage Dist.; former v.p. Jobs with Peace. Address: 6105 W Hope Ave Milwaukee WI 53216-1226 Office: Wis State Assembly State Capitol PO Box 8952 Madison WI 53708-8952

KRUIDENIER, DAVID, newspaper executive; b. Des Moines, July 18, 1921; s. David S. and Florence (Cowles) K.; m. Elizabeth Stuart, Dec. 29, 1948; 1 child, Lisa. BA, Yale U., 1946; MBA, Harvard U., 1948; LLD, Buena Vista Coll., 1960, Simpson Coll., 1963; LittD, Luther Coll., 1990; DHL, Drake U., 1990. With Mpls. Star and Tribune, 1948-52; with Des Moines Register and Tribune, 1952-85, pres., pub., 1971-78, chief exec. officer, 1971-85, chmn., chief exec. officer, 1982-85; with Cowles Media Co., 1983-93, pres., chief exec. officer, 1983-84, chmn., chief exec. officer, 1984-85, chmn., 1985-97. Chmn. Gardner and Florence Call Cowles Found.; trustee Drake U., Des Moines Art Ctr., Grinnell Coll. Greater Des Moines Found. With USAAF, 1942-45. Decorated Air medal with three clusters, D.F.C. Mem. Coun. on Fgn. Rels. , Des Moines Club, Mpls. Club, Sigma Delta Chi, Beta Theta Pi, Beta Gamma Sigma. Home: 3409 Southern Hills Dr Des Moines IA 50321-1318 Office: 715 Locust St Des Moines IA 50309-3703

KRUKOWSKI, LUCIAN, philosophy educator, artist; b. N.Y.C., Nov. 22, 1929; s. Stefan and Anna (Belcarz) Krukowski; m. Marilyn Denmark, Jan. 14, 1955; 1 child Samantha. BA, CUNY, 1952; BFA, Yale U., 1955; MS, Pratt Inst., 1958; PhD, Wash. U., St. Louis, 1977. Faculty mem. Pratt Inst., N.Y.C., 1955-69; dean Sch. Fine Arts Wash. U., St. Louis, 1969-77, prof. philosophy, 1977-96, chmn. dept. philosophy, 1986-89, prof. philosophy emeritus, 1996—. Author: Art and Concept, 1987, Aesthetic Legacies, 1992; contbr. articles to publs.; artist 10 one-person shows, 1960-92, outdoor murals for copr. bldgs., 1972, 83. Cpl. USMC, 1952—54. Mem.: Am. Philos. Assn., Am. Soc. Aesthetics. Avocations: climbing, hiking. Home: 6003 Kingsbury Blvd Saint Louis MO 63112 Office: Washington U Dept of Philosophy 1 Brookings Dr Dept Of Saint Louis MO 63130-4899 E-mail: LucianK@swbell.net.

KRULITZ, LEO MORRION, financial executive; b. Wallace, Idaho, June 15, 1938; s. John Morrion and Myrtle (Parker) K.; m. Donna Eileen Ristau, June 18, 1960; children— Cynthia, Pamela. B.A., Stanford U., 1960; J.D. cum laude, Harvard U., 1963; M.B.A., Stanford U., 1969. Bar: Idaho bar 1963, Ind. bar 1969, D.C. bar 1978, U.S. Supreme Ct. bar 1978. Ptnr. firm Moffatt, Thomas, Barrett & Blanton, Boise, Idaho, 1963-67; v.p., treas. Irwin Mgmt. Co., Columbus, Ind., 1969-77; solicitor Dept. of the Interior, Washington, 1977-79; gen. counsel Cummins Engine Co., Columbus, Ind., 1979-80, v.p., 1980-92; pres. Cummins Fin., Inc., 1984-92, Cummins Cash and Info. Svcs., Inc., 1988-92; pres., CEO Saunders, Inc., Birmingham, Ala., 1992-93; pres., CEO, dir. Parkland Mgmt. Co., Cleve., 1994—; endowment trustee Euclid Ave. Christian Ch., 1995-2001; dir. Horvitz Newspapers, Inc., Bellevue, Wash., 1994—. Trutee Lois U. Horvitz Found., 1998—; exec. dir. H.R.H. Family Found., 1994-98; treas. Irwin-Sweeney-Miller Found., Columbus, 1976-77; dir. L'Enfant Plaza Properties, Washington, 1974-77; mem. U.S. delegation Soviet Union Conf. on Environ. Law, 1978 Mem. Bartholomew Consol. Sch. Bd., 1982-88. Mem. Idaho Bar Assn., Ind. Bar Assn., D.C. Bar Assn., Harvard Club (N.Y.C.), Union Club (Cleve.). Democrat. Home: 20900 Colby Rd Shaker Heights OH 44122-1906 Office: 1001 Lakeside Ave E Ste 900 Cleveland OH 44114-1172

KRULL, DOUGLAS ARTHUR, lawyer; b. Grundy Center, Iowa, Oct. 11, 1958; s. Harm Henry and Esther S. (Schipper) K.; m. Jennifer Jo Shuldhiess, Aug. 23, 1986. BA, Upper Iowa U., 1981; JD, U. Iowa, 1984. Bar: Iowa 1985, U.S. Dist. Ct. (no. dist.) Iowa 1986. Assoc. Law Office John H. Greve, Northwood, Iowa, 1985-86; ptnr. Greve & Krull, 1986—; county atty. Worth County, 1986—. Chmn. Worth County Repub. Cen. Com., 1988—. Mem. Iowa Bar Assn., 2A Bar Assn., Worth County Bar Assn., Masons (Iowa Young Mason Yr. Award 1990), Northwood Area C. of C. Home: 401 11th St S Northwood IA 50459-1817 Office: Greve & Krull 736 Central Ave # 167 Northwood IA 50459-1518

KRULL, JEFFREY ROBERT, library director; b. North Tonawanda, N.Y., Aug. 29, 1948; s. Robert George and Ruth Otilie (Fels) K.; m. Alice Marie Hart, Apr. 12, 1969; children: Robert, Marla. BA, Williams Coll., Williamstown, Mass., 1970; MLS, SUNY, Buffalo, 1974. Cert. profl. libr., N.Y., Ohio, Ind. Traffic mgr. New England Tel. Co., Burlington, Vt., 1970-71; tchr. Harrisburg (Pa.) Acad., 1971-72; reference libr. Buffalo and Erie County Pub. Libr., 1973-76; head libr. Ohio U., Chillicothe, 1976-78; dir. Mansfield-Richland County Pub. Libr., Ohio, 1978-86, Allen County Pub. Libr., Ft. Wayne, Ind., 1986—. Mem. exec. com. Ft. Wayne Area Libr. Svc. Authority, 1986-90, v.p., 1989; mem. exec. com. Ind. Coop. Libr. Svcs. Authority, 1992—, pres., 1994-95; mem. Online Computer Libr. Ctr. Pub. Libr. Adv. Coun., 1994-97; pres. Ft. Wayne Area INFONET, 1995—. Pres. Three Rivers Literary Alliance, 1997—; trustee Ohionet, Columbus, 1984—86. Named Sagamore of the Wabash, Gov. Ind., 2001. Mem. ALA, Pub. Libr. Assn. (pres. met. librs. sect. 1990-91, statistical report adv. com.), Libr. Adminstrn. and Mgmt. Assn. (sec. libr. orgn. and mgmt. assn. 1996-97), Ohio Libr. Assn. (bd. dirs. 1985-86), Ind. Libr. Fedn. (vice chmn. legis. com. 1987—), Beta Phi Mu. Home: 3017 Oak Borough Run Fort Wayne IN 46804-7808 Office: Allen County Pub Libr PO Box 2270 900 Webster St Fort Wayne IN 46801-2270 E-mail: jkrull@acpl.lib.in.us.

KRUPANSKY, ROBERT BAZIL, federal judge; b. Cleve., Aug. 15, 1921; s. Frank A. and Anna (Lawrence) K.; m. Marjorie Blaser, Nov. 13, 1952. BA, Western Res. U., 1946, LLB, 1948, JD, 1968. Bar: Ohio 1948, Supreme Ct. Ohio 1948, Supreme Ct. U.S. 1948, U.S. Dist. Ct. (no. dist.) Ohio 1948, U.S. Ct. Appeals (6th cir.) 1948, U.S. Ct. Customs and Patent Appeals 1948, U.S. Customs Ct. 1948, ICC 1948. Pvt. practice law, Cleve., 1948—52; asst. atty. gen. State of Ohio, 1951—57; mem. Gov. of Ohio cabinet and dir. Ohio Dept. Liquor Control, 1957—58; judge Common Pleas Ct. of Cuyahoga County, 1958—60; sr. ptnr. Metzenbaum, Gaines, Krupansky, Finley & Stern, 1960—69; U.S. atty. U.S. Dist. Ct. (no. dist.) Ohio, Cleve., 1969—70, U.S. dist. judge, 1970—82; judge, now sr. judge U.S. Ct. Appeals (6th cir.), Ohio, 1982—. Spl. counsel Atty. Gen. Ohio, 1964—68; adj. prof. law Case Western Res. U. Sch. Law, 1969—70. 2d lt. U.S. Army. Mem.: FBA, ABA, Assn. Asst. Attys. Gen. State Ohio, Am. Judicature Soc., Cuyahoga County Bar Assn., Cleve. Bar Assn. Office: 127 Public Square Rm 5110 Cleveland OH 44114-1201

KRUPINSKI, JERRY W. state legislator; b. Feb. 27, 1941; m. Eileen Krupinski; children: Scott, Erin, Todd. Commr. Jefferson County, Ohio, 1981-86; state rep. Dist. 98 Ohio State Congress, 1987—. Recipient Caritas medal Diocese of Steubenville, Excellence in Govt. award Steubenville C. of C., Consumer of Yr. award Ohio Consumer Coun., 1991. Mem. Polish Nat. Alliance, Gen. George Custer Com., Farm Bur., Indian Club, KC, Moose.

KRUPKA, ROBERT GEORGE, lawyer; b. Rochester, N.Y., Oct. 21, 1949; s. Joseph Anton and Marjorie Clara (Meteyer) Krupka; m. Pamela Banner Krupka; children: Kristin Nicole, Kerry Melissa. BS, Georgetown U., 1971; JD, U. Chgo., 1974. Bar: Ill. 1974, Colo. 1991, D.C., 1991, Calif. 1998, U.S. Dist. Ct. (no. dist.) Ill. 1974, U.S. Dist. Ct. (ea. dist.) Wis. 1974, U.S. Ct. Appeals (7th cir.) 1976, U.S. Supreme Ct. 1978, U.S. Dist. Ct. (cen. dist.) Ill. 1980, U.S. Dist. Ct. (no. dist.) Calif. 1980, U.S. Dist. Ct. (ctrl. and so. dists.) Calif. 1999, U.S. Ct. Appeals (4th and fed. cirs.) 1982, U.S. Ct. Appeals (6th cir.) 1985, U.S. Ct. Appeals (1st, 2d, 3d, 5th, 8th, 9th, 10th and 11th dists.) 1999. Assoc. Kirkland & Ellis, Chgo., 1974-79, ptnr., 1979—. Author: Infringement Litigation Computer Software and Database, 1984, Computer Software, Semiconductor Design, Video Game and Database Protection and Enforcement, 1984. Mem. bd. trustees Francis W. Parker Sch., 1987-98, pres., 1994-97. Mem. ABA (chmn. sec. com. 1982-88, chmn. div. 1988-90, 98—, coun. 1994-97), Computer Law Assn., U.S. Patent Quar. Adv. Bd., Am. Intellectual Property Law Assn. (chmn. subcom. 1988—), Mid-Am. Club, Chgo. Club. Roman Catholic. Office: Kirkland & Ellis 200 E Randolph St Fl 54 Chicago IL 60601-6636 E-mail: bob_krupka@kirkland.com.

KRUSE, DENNIS K. state legislator; b. Auburn, Ind., Oct. 7, 1946; s. Russell Wayne and Luella Marie (Boger) K.; m. Kay Adele Yerden, 1968; children: Dennis K. II, John Mark, Timothy James, Daniel Webster. Student, Anderson U., 1967—68; BS, Ind. U., 1970; postgrad., Purdue U. Auctioneer Kruse Auctioneers, 1964—; realtor Kruse Realtors, 1968—; asst. to corp. officer Ambassador Steel Corp., 1981—95; rep. Dist. 51 Ind. Ho. of Reps., 1990—, ranking mem. county and twp. com., interstate coop. and pub. safety com., mem. ways and means com. Precinct committeeman Jackson Twp. S. DeKalb County, 1968—72; mem. U.S. Electoral Com., Ind., 1972—; trustee Jackson Twp., 1983—89; del. Ind. Rep. State Conv., 1990—; chmn. Ind. Conservative Assembly, Legis. Coalition to Reduce Underage Drinking; parade marshall Gradili County Fair, Ind., 1990—; mem. DeKalb County Right to Life; adv. bd. DeKalb County Am. Family Assn., 1988—; mem. Child Evangelism Fellowship N.E. Ind., DeKalb Coun. Pregnancy, Right-to-Life, Ind. Family Inst.; bd. dirs. Northeastern Ind. Child Evangelism, 1986—96.

KRUSE, JOHN ALPHONSE, lawyer; b. Detroit, Sept. 11, 1926; s. Frank R. and Ann (Nestor) K.; m. Mary Louise Dalton, July 14, 1951; children: Gerard, Mary Louise, Terence, Kathleen, Joanne, Francis, John, Patrick. BS, U. Detroit, 1950, JD cum laude, 1952. Bar: Mich. bar 1952. Ptnr. Alexander, Buchanan & Conklin, Detroit, 1952-69, Harvey, Kruse, PC, Detroit, 1969—. Guest lectr. U. Mich., U. Detroit, Inst. Continuing Legal Edn.; city atty. Allen Park, Mich., 1954-59; twp. atty., Van Buren Twp., Mich., 1959-61. Co-founder Detroit and Mich. Cath. Radio. Past pres. Palmer Woods Assn.; mem. pres.'s cabinet U. Detroit; bd. dirs. Providence Hosp. Found.; trustee Ave Maria Coll. Named one of 5 Outstanding Young Men in Mich., 1959, Outstanding Alumnus, U. Detroit Sch. Law, 1989, Humanitarian award Neuromuscular Inst. 1988. Mem. Detroit Bar Assn., State Bar Mich. (past chmn. negligence sect.), Assn. Def. Trial Counsel (bd. dirs. 1966-67), Am. Judicature Soc., Internat. Assn. Def. Counsel, Equestrian Order of the Holy Sepulchre, Cath. Campaign for Am., Gabriel Richard Hist. Soc. (bd. of dirs.) Roman Catholic. Club: Detroit Golf (past pres.). Home: 5569 Hunters Gate Dr Troy MI 48098-2342 Office: 1050 Wilshire Dr Ste 320 Troy MI 48084-1526 E-mail: jkruse@harveykruse.com, johnakruse@comcast.com.

KRUSE, LOWEN V. state legislator; b. Boelus, Nebr., 1929; BA, Wesleyan U., 1951; M, Northwestern U., 1955. Pastor Buffalo, Custer and Douglas Counties, Nebr.; supt. chs. N.E. Nebr., 1972; dir. ministries Nebr. Meth. Chs., 1974; exec. min. Omaha 1st United Meth. Ch., 1979; supt. Omaha dist. United Meth. Ch., 1988; mem. Nebr. Legislature from 13th dist., Lincoln, 2001—. Author: 3 Nebr. history books. Mem. Kiwanis, Lions, North Omaha Comml. Club. Home: 5404 N 50th Ave Omaha NE 68104-1836 Office: Rm 1117 State Capitol Lincoln NE 68509

KRUSE, WILBUR FERDINAND, architect; b. Selden, Kans., Nov. 4, 1922; s. John Arnold and Kathryn (Zimmerman) K.; m. Mary Teresa Armstrong, Sept. 5, 1949; children: William, Karen, Katherine, Teresa, Peter, Thomas, Ann, Joan. Elem. tchr. cert., Fort Hays Tchrs. Coll., 1942; student, Tex. A&M Mil. Coll., 1943; BS in Arch., Kans. State U., 1949. Assoc. architect Glen H. Thomas & A.B. Harris Architects, Wichita, Kans., 1948-57; owner Wilbur F. Kruse Architects and Assocs., 1957-67, Kruse Architects and Cons., Wichita, 1967—, K Industries. Patentee screened veneer vent for masonry, 1986; prin. works include Kans. Vocat. Correctional Tng. Ctr., Topeka, 1983, also numerous jails, detention ctrs, chs., and schs., Wichita Century II Auditorium Complex. Bd. dirs. Cmty. Corrections Wch/Sedgwick Co., Wichita, 1979-83, Kans. chpt. Arthritis Found., 1985-89; advisor to Arthritis Water Exercise Club Inc. Lt. USAF, 1942-45, ETO. Decorated 3 battle stars, pres. unit citation, air medal, 3 clusters; recipient Cert. Appreciation Kans. Dept. Corrections, Topeka, 1983, Honor award for Marshall County govt. complex State Soc. Engrs. Mem. Assn. Prin. Architects, Serra Internat. Club, Wichita Club (pres. 1988, gov. Dist. 12, 1993, reg. dir. #9, US and Canada Counc., 1995-97, sec., US and Canada Counc., 1997-99), Sierra Internat. Found. (trustee 1998—). Roman Catholic. Avocation: travel. Home: 1641 Womer St Wichita KS 67203-1537 Office: Kruse Architects and Cons 1337 N Meridian Ave Wichita KS 67203-4641

KRUSICK, MARGARET ANN, state legislator; b. Milw., Oct. 26, 1956; d. Ronald J. and Maxine C. K. BA, U. Wis., 1978; postgrad., U. Wis., Madison, 1979-82. Legal asst. Milw. Law Office, 1973-78; teaching asst. U. Wis., Milw., 1978-79; staff mem. Govs. Ombudsman Program for the Aging & Disabled, Madison, Wis., 1980; administrv. asst. Wis. Higher Edn. Aids Bd., 1981; legis. aide Wis. Assembly, 1982-83, state rep., 1983—. Author: Wisconsin Youth Suicide Prevention Act, 1985, Wisconsin Nursing Home Reform Act, 1987, Wisconsin Truancy Reform Act, 1988, Elder Abuse Fund, 1989, Stolen Goods Recovery Act, 1990, Fair Prescription Drug Pricing Act, 1994, Anti-Graffiti Act, 1996, Caregiver Criminal Background Checks and Abuse Prevention Act, 1997, Child Abuse Prosecution Act, 1998, Nursing Home Resident Protection Act, 1998. Mem. St. Gregory Great Cath. Ch., Milw., 1960—, Dem. Party, Milw., 1980—; bd. dirs. Alzheimer's Assn., 1986-88. Named Legislator of Yr. award Wis. Sch. Counselors, Madison, 1986, Wis. County Constnl. Officers Legislator of Yr., 1999; recipient Sr. Citizen Appreciation Allied Coun. for Sr. Milw., 1987, Crime Prevention award Milw. Police Dept., Milw., 1988, Cert. Appreciation, Milw. Pub. Sch., 1989, Friends of Homecare award, 1989, Environ. Decades' Clean 16 award, 1986-90, 95-96, Badger State Sheriff's Law and Order award, 1993, Appreciation award Coalition of Wis. Aging Groups, 1998. Mem. Jackson Park Neighborhood Assn., U. Milw. Alumni Assn. (trustee 1986-90). Home: 3426 S 69th St Milwaukee WI 53219-4037 Office: Wis Assembly State Capitol Madison WI 53702-0001

KRUTSCH, PHYLLIS, academic administrator; MS, U. Wis. Regent U. Wis., 1990—97, 2000—, chmn. edn. com., 1994—97, chmn. com. bd. effectiveness. Grantee, Bradley Found. Mailing: 727 Superior Ave Washburn WI 54891

KRUTTER, FORREST NATHAN, lawyer; b. Boston, Dec. 17, 1954; s. Irving and Shirley Krutter. BS in Econs., MS in Civil Engring., MIT, 1976; JD cum laude, Harvard U., 1978. Bar: Nebr. 1978, U.S. Supreme Ct. 1986, N.Y. 1991. Antitrust counsel Union Pacific R.R., Omaha, 1978-86; sr. v.p. law, sec. Berkshire Hathaway Group, 1986—; pres. Republic Ins., Dallas, 2000—. Co-author: Impact of Railroad Abandonments, 1976, Railroad Development in the Third World, 1978; author: Judicial Enforcement of Competition in Regulated Industries, 1979; contbr. articles Creighton Law Rev. Mem. ABA, Phi Beta Kappa, Sigma Xi. Office: Berkshire Hathaway Group 4016 Farnam St Omaha NE 68131-3016 E-mail: qedqedfak@aol.com.

KRUZAN, MARK R. state legislator; b. Hammond, Ind., Apr. 11, 1960; BA, Ind. U., 1982, JD, 1985. Pvt. practice law; state rep. Dist. 61 Ind. Ho. of Reps., 1986—, mem. pub. policy, ethics, vet. affairs and judiciary coms., vice chmn. environ. affairs com., ranking minority mem., mem. ways and means and caucus campaign com., legis coun., chmn. environ. policy com. Adj. prof. Ind. U. Mem. Cmty. Svc. Coun. Mem. Ind. U. Alumni Assn. (life), Ind. State Bar Assn., Greater Bloomington C. of C., Bloomington Press Club, Sigma Delta Chi. Home: 111 E 6th St Bloomington IN 47408-3303

KSIENSKI, AHARON ARTHUR, electrical engineer; b. Warsaw, Poland, June 23, 1924; came to U.S., 1951, naturalized, 1959; s. Isreal and Rebecca K.; married; children: David, Ruth. B.E. in Mech. Engring, Inst. Mech. Engring., London, 1947; M.Sc. in Elec. Engring, U. So. Calif., 1952, Ph.D., 1958. Sr. staff engr., head antenna dept. research staff Hughes Aircraft Co., Culver City, Calif., 1958-67; prof. elec. engring., tech. dir. communication systems electrosci. lab. Ohio State U., 1967-76, prof. elec. engring., chmn. communication and propagation com. electrosci. lab., 1976-87, prof. emeritus, 1987—. Bd. dirs. Ohio State U. Research Found., 1975-79; cons. in field. Editor trans., revs. in field. Recipient Brabazon award Inst. Electronic and Radio Engrs., London, 1967, 76 Fellow IEEE; mem. Internat. Union Radio Sci. (chmn. commns. B and C 1972-75) Home: 1780 Lynnhaven Dr Columbus OH 43221-1410 Office: 1320 Kinnear Rd Columbus OH 43212-1156 E-mail: a-arthur@worldnet.att.net.

KUBALE, BERNARD STEPHEN, lawyer; b. Reedsville, Wis., Sept. 5, 1928; s. Joseph and Josephine (Novak) K.; m. Mary Thomas, Apr. 21, 1956; children: Caroline, Catherine, Anne. BBA, U. Wis., 1950, LLB, 1955; LLD (hon.), St. Norbert Coll., 1985. Bar: Wis. 1955; CPA, Wis. Acct. John D. Morrison and Co., Marquette, Mich., 1950-51; atty., ptnr. Foley and Lardner, Milw., 1955—, chmn. mgmt. com., 1985-94. Bd. dirs. Green Bay Packers, Wis. E.R. Wagner Mfg. Co., Milw., Wausau, Homes, Wis. Chmn. bd. dirs. St. Norbert Coll., DePere, Wis., 1980-84, Children's Hosp. Wis., Milw., 1982-91. 1st lt. USAF, 1951-53. Mem. ABA, AICPAs, Wis. Inst. CPAs, Wis. Bar Assn., Milw. Bar Assn., Cheneque Country Club, Milw. Country Club, The Milw. Club. Republican. Roman Catholic. Avocations: fishing, skiing, baseball. Home: 5935 Monclaire Rd Hartland WI 53029 Office: Foley & Lardner 1st Wisconsin Ctr 777 E Wisconsin Ave Ste 3800 Milwaukee WI 53202-5367

KUBIDA, JUDITH ANN, museum administrator; b. Chgo., Aug. 29, 1948; d. William and Julia Ann (Kun) K.; m. Benjamin Kocolowski, Nov. 22, 1980. Attended, Southeast Coll. Adminstrn. asst. in vis. svcs. and sci. and edn. depts. Mus. Sci. and Industry, Chgo. Columnist monthly community newspaper Pullman Flyer. Vice-pres. pub. rels. Hist. Pullman Found., Hist. Pullman Dist., Chgo., editor quarterly newsletter Update, create publicity brochures, liaison with Ill., Chgo. Film Offices, publ. chmn., mem. annual house tour com., prodr. commemorative plate. Democrat. Home: 11334 S Langley Ave Chicago IL 60628-5126 Office: Hist Pullman Found Hotel Florence 11111 S Forrestville Ave Chicago IL 60628-4649

KUBO, GARY MICHAEL, advertising executive; b. Chgo., Aug. 15, 1952; s. Robert S. and Hideko (Nishimura) Kubo; m. Harriet Davenport, June 14, 1975; children: Michael J., R. Scott. BS, Ill. State U., 1974. Rsch. project dir. Foote, Cone & Belding Comms., Chgo., 1974—76, account rsch. supr., 1976—79, rsch. mgr., 1979—80; assoc. rsch. dir. Young & Rubicam, Chgo., 1980—83; ptnr., group rsch. dir. Tatham, Laird & Kudner Advt., 1983—89; v.p. dir. strategic planning and rsch./Midwest Bozell, Inc., 1989—91, sr. v.p., dir. strategic planning and rsch./Midwest, 1991—93; sr. v.p. dir. strategic planning rsch. Ogilvy & Mather, Chgo.,

1993—95; prin. The KUBO Group, Ltd., 1995—2001; exec. v.p. mktg. 141 Communicator, 2001—. Bd. dirs. Chgo. Coun. Urban Affairs, 1992—, Prevent Child Abuse Am.-Chgo. Mem.: Am. Mktg. Assn. (speaker 1983—84, exec. bd.), Advt. Rsch. Found. Avocations: racquet sports, running, music. Home: 2129 Scarlet Oak Ln Lisle IL 60532-2855 Office: 54 W Hubbard St Chicago IL 60610

KUCERA, DANIEL WILLIAM, retired bishop; b. Chgo., May 7, 1923; s. Joseph F. and Lillian C. (Petrzelka) K. BA, St. Procopius Coll., 1945; MA, Catholic U. Am., 1950, PhD, 1954. Joined Order of St. Benedict, 1944, ordained priest Roman Cath. Ch., 1949. Registrar St. Procopius Coll. and Acad., Lisle, Ill., 1945-49, St. Procopius Coll., Lisle, 1954-56, acad. dean, head dept. edn., 1956-59, pres., 1959-65; abbot St. Procopius Abbey, Lisle, 1964-71; pres. Ill. Benedictine Coll. (formerly St. Procopius Coll.), 1971-76, chmn. bd. trustees, 1976-78; aux. bishop of Joliet, 1977-80; bishop of Salina Kans., 1980-83; archbishop of Dubuque Iowa, 1983-95; ret., 1995. Mem. KC (4 degree).

KUCEY, REGINALD MATTHEW, research scientist, microbiology researcher; b. Yorkton, Sask., Can., May 31, 1954; s. Theodore Eddie and Eleanor Marie (Dumanski) K.; m. Jamie Darlene Chizmazia, Nov. 7, 1981; 1 child, Justin James Matthew. BSc with honors, U. Sask., Saskatoon, 1976, PhD, 1980. Rsch. scientist Agrl. Agri-Food Can., Lethbridge, Alta., Can., 1980-89, rsch. coord. Ottawa, Ont., Can., 1989-92, dir. rsch. sta. Morden, Man., Can., 1992-96, Brandon, Can., 1996—. Microbiology researcher IAEA, South Korea, 1984, Brazil, 1984, Internat. Devel. Rsch. Ctr., Thailand, 1986-88. Contbr. more than 40 articles to profl. jours.; inventor phosphate Solubilizing fungus. Recipient Cert. of Recognition, Govt. of Can., 1992. Avocations: reading, camping, carving.

KUCINICH, DENNIS J. congressman; b. Oct. 8, 1946; 1 child, Jackie. Student, Cleveland State U.; BA, MA, Case Western Reserve U. Pres. K Comm., Cleve.; v. pres. sales and mktg. Town and Country Printing; councilman City of Cleve., 1969-73, clk. of mcpl. ct., 1975-77, mayor, 1977-79; senator State of Ohio; mem. U.S. Congress from 10th Ohio dist., 1997—; mem. edn. and the workforce, govt. reform coms.; chair. Congress. Prog. Caucus. Named Outstanding Pub. Official, Internat. Eagles. Office: US Ho of Reps 1730 Longworth Ho Office Bldg Washington DC 20515-3510*

KUDISH, DAVID J. financial executive; b. N.Y.C., Aug. 10, 1943; s. L. Ben and Nellie D. (Kaufman) K.; children: Lisa, Seth, Debra. BS, U. Rochester, 1965; MS, U. Minn., 1967; postgrad., Harvard. U., 1996. With Dean Witter & Co., Inc., N.Y.C., 1968-73; with Oppenheimer & Co., 1973-74; ptnr., dir. investment services Hewitt Assocs., Lincolnshire, Ill., 1974-82; pres., mng. dir. Stratford Adv. Group, Inc., Chgo., 1982—; pres. Stratford Investment Group, Inc., 1983-2000. Investment cons. pension, endowment and charitable funds. Editor Benefits Quar. Mem. Mayor's Energy Task Force, City of Chgo.; gov. mem. Sustaining Fellows, Art Inst. Chgo., Contemporary Art Ctr. of Mus. Contemporary Art; benefactor Lyric Opera of Chgo.; mem. gala com. Chgo. Abused Women's Coalition; bd. dirs. Com. for Accuracy in Mid. East Reporting in Am., Aspen Cmty. Campaign; mem. Jewish Cmty. Rels. Coun., Jewish Fedn. Met. Chgo.; mem. exec. bd. Chgo. chpt. Am. Jewish Com.; bd. govs. The Investigative Project. With USAF, 1968, Air NG, 1968-73. Minn. Mining and Mgr. fellow U. Minn., 1967; NSF grantee, 1967 Mem. Tau Beta Pi, Sigma Alpha Mu. Republican. Jewish. Clubs: Standard. Home: 1325 N Astor St Chicago IL 60610-2113

KUDO, IRMA SETSUKO, not-for-profit executive director; b. Ica, Peru, Feb. 25, 1939; arrived in U.S., 1944; d. Seiichi and Angelica (Yoshinaga) Higashide. Asst. dir. coun. annual session ADA, Chgo., 1971-80; exec. dir. Am. Assn. of Endodontists, 1980—. Recipient Warren Wakai medal Japan Endodontic Assn., 1992. Mem. ADA Alumni Assn. Student Clinicians (hon.), Am. Assn. Endodontists (hon.), Am. Soc. of Assn. Execs., Profl. Conv. Mgmt. Assn., Assn. Forum Chicagoland. Office: Am Assn of Endodontists 211 E Chicago Ave Ste 1100 Chicago IL 60611-2687 E-mail: ikudo@aae.org.

KUEHN, GEORGE E. lawyer, former beverage company executive; b. N.Y.C., June 19, 1946; m. Mary Kuehn; children: Kristin, Rob, Geoff. BBA, U. Mich., 1968, JD, 1973. Bar: Mich. 1974. Assoc. Hill, Lewis et al, Detroit, 1974-78; ptnr. Butzel, Long et al, 1978-81; exec. v.p., gen. counsel, sec. The Stroh Brewery Co., 1981-99—; shareholder Butzel Long, 2000—. With U.S. Army, 1969-71. Office: Butzel Long Ste 900 150 W Jefferson Ave Detroit MI 48226 E-mail: Kuehn@butzel.com.

KUEHNE, CARL W. food products executive; CEO, pres. Am. Foods Group, Dakota Pork Industries. Office: Am Foods Group PO Box 8547 544 Acme St Green Bay WI 54308-8547

KUEHNLE, KENTON LEE, lawyer; b. Chgo., Nov. 10, 1945; s. Robert Louis and Mary Caroline (Recktenwald) K.; m. Sherry L. Esposito, June 6, 1970; children: Robert, Amanda, Matthew. BA, Augustana Coll., 1967; JD, Duke U., 1970. Bar: Ohio 1970, U.S. Dist. Ct. (so. dist.) Ohio 1971. Assoc. Dunbar, Kienzle & Murphey, Columbus, Ohio, 1970-77; ptnr. Loveland, Callard & Clapham, 1977-80, Scott, Walker & Kuehnle, Columbus, 1980-86, Thompson, Hine & Flory, Columbus, 1986—2001, Roetzel & Andress, Columbus, 2001—. Mem., lectr. standard forms com. Columbus Bd. Realtors; instr. paralegal program Capital U. Law Sch. Co-author: (seminar book) Foreclosure Law, 1989-98, Title Insurance Endorsements, 1991-97, Commercial Leasing, 1994-97, Condominium Law, 1981-97, Use of Internet for Real Estate Lawyer, 1997; contbr. articles to profl. jours. Mem. Augustana Coll. Alumni Bd., Rock Island, Ill., 1986-89; trustee Madison Plains Scholarship Found., Madison County, Ohio, 1986—; elder First Presbyn. Ch., Grove City, Ohio, 1990-93; pres. Computer Users Group, Columbus, 1985-86. Mem. ABA (sect. real property, probate and trust law 1973—, com. on condominium and coop. housing 1977—), Columbus Bar Assn. (chmn. real property com. 1976-78, chmn. micro computer subcom. 1986-87, 92-94, lectr. for bar assn. seminars), Ohio State Bar Assn. (bd. govs. real property sect. 1979-82, 90—, chmn. 1997-99, editor state real property sect. newsletter 1995-99, chmn. subcom. to rev. condominium statute 1980-81, lectr. continuing legal edn. programs), Am. Coll. Real Estate Lawyers, Coun. Ethics in Econs., Honesty in Bus., Legal Profession Task Force, Joseph Fletcher Lawyers Conf. (ann. ethics conf., spkr. selection chair). Avocations: computer programming, baseball, theology. Home: 11325 Big Plain Circleville Rd Orient OH 43146-9301 Office: Roetzel & Andress 155 E Broad St Ste 1200 Columbus OH 43215-3609 E-mail: kkuehnle@prodigy.net.

KUENNEN, THOMAS GERARD, journalist; b. St. Louis, June 30, 1953; s. George Glennon and Earline (Doherty) K.; m. Anne L. Gillette, Sept. 10, 1988; 1 child, Madeline Livingston. BJ, U. Mo., 1975. Copy editor Macon (Ga.) Telegraph & News, 1976-77; news editor Mascoutah (Ill.) Herald, and related newspapers, 1977-79; pub. rels. assoc. Booker Assocs., Inc., St. Louis, 1979-80, Fru Con Corp., St. Louis, 1980-81; assoc. editor Rock Products Mag., Chgo., 1981-84; editor Roads & Bridges Mag., Des Plaines, Ill., 1984-95; prin., editor Expresswaysonline.com, Wheeling, 1995—. Mem. editl. com. Am. Bus. Press, N.Y.C., 1984-85. Recipient Jesse H. Neal award Am. Bus. Press, 1983, Svc. award La. Associated Gen. Contractors, 1990, Editl. Excellence award Am. Soc. Bus. Press Editors, 1998. Mem. Constrn. Writers Assn. (bd. dirs. 1985-86, 95-99, Robert F. Boger award 1985, 93, 95, 98), Nat. Asphalt Pavement Assn. (Hot Mix Hall of Fame), Women in Comm. (treas. 1983-84, Cub's Cup 1985). Roman Catholic. Office: Expwys Publishing 925 N Milwaukee Ave Ste 224B Wheeling IL 60090-1869

KUENSTER, JOHN JOSEPH, magazine editor; b. Chgo., June 18, 1924; s. Roy Jacob and Katheryn (Holechek) K.; m. Mary Virginia Maher, Feb. 15, 1947 (dec. Feb. 1983); m. Suely Brazão, July 1, 1995. Editor The Columbian, Chgo., 1948-57; staff writer Chgo. Daily News, 1957-65; dir. devel. and pub. relations Mercy Hosp., 1965-66; sr. writer The Claretians, 1966—; editor Baseball Digest, Evanston, Ill., 1969—; exec. editor Century Pub. Co. Author: Cobb to Catfish, Heartbreakers, (booklets) The Police, Money, Mission in Guatemala, Honesty, Is it the Best Policy?; co-author: To Sleep with the Angels. Mem. Baseball Writers' Assn. Am. Roman Catholic. Office: Baseball Digest Century Publishing Co 990 Grove St Evanston IL 60201-6510 E-mail: jkuenster@centurysports.net.

KUFFEL, EDMUND, electrical engineering educator; b. Poland, Oct. 28, 1924; s. Franciszek and Marta (Glodowska) K.; m. Alicja, Oct. 4, 1952; children: Anna, John, Richard, Peter. BSc, U. Coll., Dublin, 1953, MSc, 1954, PhD, 1959; DSc, U. Manchester, 1967. Rsch. engr. Met. Vickers Electric Co., Manchester, Eng., 1954-60; mem. faculty elec. engring. U. Manchester Inst. Sci. and Tech., 1960-68; head of elect. engring. U. Windsor, Ont., Can., 1970-78; prof. elec. engring. U. Man., Winnipeg, Can., 1968-70, head of elec. engring. Can., 1978-79, dean of engring. Can., 1979-89, prof. elec. engring., dean emeritus, 1989—. Cons. various mfrs. high voltage cables; bd. dirs. Man. Hydro Elec. Bd., 1978-96; cons. prof. Xi'an Jiaotong U., People's Rep. China, 1986—. Author or co-author 4 textbooks and more than 200 pub. tech. papers on high voltage engring. Fellow IEEE, Can. Acad. Engring. Home: 2661 Knowles Ave Winnipeg MB Canada R2G 2K7 Office: U Manitoba Fac Engring Winnipeg MB Canada R3T 2N2

KUFFNER, GEORGE HENRY, dermatologist, educator; b. S.I., N.Y., Aug. 22, 1949; s. George Henry and Wilmouth Anne (Clendenin) K.; m. Lynne Diane Blakeslee, May 17, 1975; children: Kevin, Todd A. BA, Johns Hopkins U., 1971, MD, 1975. Intern U. Hosps. Cleve., 1975-78, resident, 1978-81; staff dermatologist Cleve. Clinic Found. (formerly The Wooster Clinic), Wooster, Ohio, 1981—. Asst. clin. prof. dermatology U. Hosps. Cleve., 1981—. Contbr. articles to profl. jours. Fellow Am. Acad. Dermatology; mem. Ohio Med. Assn., Ohio Dermatology Assn., Ohio Soc. Dermatologic Surgery (mem. Akron dermatology staff), Cleve. Dermatology Soc. Methodist. Avocations: swimming, piano, reading, video/stero electronics, travel. Office: Wooster Clin LLC Cleve Clinic Reg Practice 1740 Cleveland Rd Wooster OH 44691-2204

KUHI, LEONARD VELLO, astronomer, university administrator; b. Hamilton, Ont., Can., Oct. 22, 1936; came to U.S., 1958; s. John and Sinaida (Rose) K.; m. Patricia Suzanne Brown, Sept. 3, 1960 (div.); children: Alison Diane, Christopher Paul; m. Mary Ellen Murphy, July 15, 1989. BS, U. Toronto, 1958; PhD, U. Calif., Berkeley, 1964. Carnegie postdoctoral fellow Hale Obs., Pasadena, Calif., 1963-65; asst. prof. U. Calif., Berkeley, 1965-69, assoc. prof., 1969-74, prof., 1974-89, chmn. dept. astronomy, 1975-76, dean phys. scis. Coll. Letters and Sci., 1976-81, provost, 1983-89; sr. v.p. for acad. affairs, provost U. Minn., Mpls., 1989-91, prof. astronomy, 1989—, chmn. dept. astronomy, 1997—. Vis. prof. U. Colo., 1969, Coll. de France, Paris, 1972-73, U. Heidelberg, 1978, 80-81; bd. dirs. Am. Inst. Physics. Contbr. articles to profl. jours. Recipient Alexander von Humboldt Sr. Scientist award, 1980-81; NSF research grantee, 1966—. Fellow AAAS; mem. Am. Astron. Soc. (treas. 1987, 96—), Astron. Soc. Pacific (pres. 1978-80), Internat. Astron. Union, Assn. Univ. for Rsch. Astronomy (chair bd. dirs.), Sigma Xi. Office: U Minn Dept Astronomy 116 Church St SE Minneapolis MN 55455-0149 E-mail: kuhi@astro.umn.edu.

KUHL, DAVID EDMUND, physician, nuclear medicine educator; b. St. Louis, Oct. 27, 1929; s. Robert Joseph and Caroline Bertha (Waldemar) Kuhl; m. Eleanor Dell Kasales, Aug. 7, 1954; 1 child David Stephen. AB, Temple U., Phila., 1951; MD, U. Pa., 1955; LHD (hon.) , Loyola U. Chgo., 1992. Diplomate Am. Bd. Radiology, Am. Bd. Nuc. Medicine (a founder; life trustee 1977-). Intern, then resident in radiology Sch. Medicine and Hosp. U. Pa., 1955—56, 1958—63, mem. faculty, 1963—76, prof. radiology, 1970—76, vice chmn. dept., 1975—76, chief div. nuc. medicine, 1963—76; prof. radiol. scis. UCLA Sch. Medicine and Hosp., 1976—86, chief div. nuc. medicine, 1976—84, vice-chmn. dept., 1977—86; prof. internal medicine and radiology U. Mich. Sch. Medicine, Ann Arbor, 1986—2000, prof. radiology, 2000—, chief divsn. nuc. medicine, dir. PET Ctr., 1986—. Disting. faculty lectr. in biomed. rsch. U. Mich. Med. Sch., 1992, Henry Russel lectr., 98; mem. adv. com. Dept. Energy, NIH, Internat. Commn. on Radiation Units and Measures, Max Planck Soc. Mem. editl. bd.: various jours.; contbr. articles to med. jours. Served as officer M.C. USNR, 1956—58. Recipient Rsch. Career Devel. award, USPHS, 1961—71, Ernst Jung prize for medicine, Jung Found., Hamburg, 1981, Emil H. Grubbe gold medal, Chgo. Med. Soc., 1983, Berman Found. award peaceful uses atomic energy, 1985, Steven C. Beering award for advancement med. sci., Ind. U., 1987, Disting. Grad. award, U. Pa. Sch. Medicine, 1988, William C. Menninger Meml. award, ACP, 1989, Javits Neurosci. Investigator award, NIH, 1989, Charles F. Kettering prize, GM Cancer Rsch. Found., 2001, Hon. Lifetime Mem. award, Einstein Soc. , Nat. Atomic Mus. Found., 2001. Fellow: Nat. Inst. for Med. and Biol. Engring., Am. Coll. Nuc. Physicians, Am. Coll. Radiology; mem.: Inst. Medicine Nat. Aad. Scis., Soc. Neurosci., Rocky Mountain Radiol. Soc., Am. Neurol. Assn. (Foster Elting Bennett Meml. lectr. 1981), Am. Heart Assn. (fellow coun. circulation), Soc. Nuc. Medicine (ann. lectr. 1991, Nuc. Pioneer citation 1976, Herman L. Blumgart, M.D. Pioneer award 1995, Disting. Scientist award 1981, George Charles de Hevesy Nuc. Medicine Pioneer award 1995, Benedict Cassen prize for rsch. 1996), Radiol. Soc. N.Am. (ann. orator 1982, Outstanding Rschr. award 1996), Assn. Univ. Radiologists, Am. Epilepsy Soc., Assn. Am. Physicians, Alpha Omega Alpha, Sigma Xi. Office: U Mich Hosp Divsn Nuc Medicine 1500 E Medical Center Dr Ann Arbor MI 48109-0005 E-mail: dkuhl@umich.edu.

KUHLER, DEBORAH GAIL, grief therapist, former state legislator; b. Moorhead, Minn., Oct. 12, 1952; d. Robert Edgar and Beverly Maxine (Buechler) Ecker; m. George Henry Kuhler, Dec. 28, 1973; children: Karen Elizabeth, Ellen Christine. BA, Dakota Wesleyan U., 1974; MA, U. N.D., 1977. Cert, grief therapist; lic. profl. counselor, S.D. Outpatient therapist Ctr. for Human Devel., Grand Forks, N.D., 1975-77; mental health counselor Community Counseling Services, Huron, S.D., 1978-88, 91-93; owner, dir. bereavement svcs. Kuhler Funeral Home, 1978—; adj. prof. Huron U., 1979-83, 90—; mem. from dist. 23 S.D. Ho. Reps., Pierre, 1987-90; mem. House Judiciary com., chair House Health and Welfare Com., 1990. Active 1st United Meth. Ch. Named Young Alumnus of the Yr., Dakota Wesleyan U., 1989, Bus. and Profl. Women, 1989. Mem. ACA, AAUW (Achievement in Politics award 1987), PEO, Am. Mental Health Counselors Assn., Assn. for Death Edn. and Counseling, Phi Kappa Phi. Avocations: reading, breadmaking, sewing, piano. Home: 1360 Dakota Ave S Huron SD 57350-3660

KUHLMAN, JAMES WELDON, retired county extension education director; b. Amarillo, Tex., Feb. 13, 1937; s. Herman and Alma Marie (Gerdsen) K.; m. Ann Bullock Davis, Dec. 23, 1967; children: Lisa Ann, Jennifer Shawn. BS, West Tex. State U., Canyon, 1959; MS, U. Nebr., 1962. Tchg. West Tex. State U., Canyon, 1958-59; grad. asst. U. Nebr., Lincoln, 1959-62, county ext. agt. Kearney, 1962-67, Buffalo County ext. agt., chair, 1967-72; Worth County ext. dir. Iowa State U., Northwood, 1972-81, Cerro Gordo County ext. edn. dir. Mason City, 1981-97; ret., 1997; farmer, Randall County, Tex., 1955—, Buffalo County, Nebr., 1955-97. Spkr. various civic clubs, 1980—, flower garden Buchart Gardens in Victoria, Can., 1990-2001. Author: The History of the Nance Hereford Ranch, 1996, The Block Pasture, 1998, From Kirchhatten to Canyon, 2001. Mem., past pres., past treas. No. Iowa Figure Skating Club, Mason City, 1984-98; active Mason City Iowa Conv. and Visitors Bur., chair grants com., 1998-2000; treas. River City Trees, 1998—. With U.S. Army Res., 1961-67. Recipient Disting. Pres. award Sertoma Club Internat., Kearney, Nebr., 1966, Top award Lions Club Internat., Northwood, Iowa, 1979. Mem. Nat. Assn. County Agrl. Agts. (mem. nat. com., voting dir. 1984, 90, Disting. Svc. award 1984), Nat. Assn. Ret. Fed. Employees (pres. local chpt. 1998-1999), State Conv. of Nat. Assn. Ret. Fed. Employees (co-chair 2001), Am. Hereford Assn., Iowa Hereford Assn. (dir. 1991-99), Nebr. Hereford Assn., Holstein Assn. Am., North Ctrl. Geneology Club (past vice chair, pres. 1999-2000), Rotary Club Mason City (com. chair 1988, 97—, bd. dirs. 2000—), Mason City C. of C. (agr. com. 1981—, chmn. regional issues com. 1990-91), Iowa State U. Ext. Assn. (dir. 1980s), Iowa State U. Coun. Ex Profls. (chair retiree sect. 1999-2000), Rotary (bd. dirs. 2000—), Epsilon Sigma Phi (dir. 1999—). Presbyterian. Avocations: cattle breeding and cattle history of Hereford breed, genealogy research, writing, art, photography. Home: 722 N Hampshire Ave Mason City IA 50401-2440

KUHLMANN, FRED MARK, lawyer, business executive; b. St. Louis, Apr. 9, 1948; s. Frederick Louis and Mildred (Southworth) K.; m. Barbara Jane Nierman, Dec. 30, 1970; children: F. Matthew, Sarah Ann. AB summa cum laude, Washington U., St. Louis, 1970; JD cum laude, Harvard U., 1973. Bar: Mo. 1973. Assoc. atty. Stolar, Heitzmann & Eder, St. Louis, 1973-75; from tax counsel to sr. v.p. McDonnell Douglas Corp., 1975—95, sr. v.p., gen. counsel, 1995—97; of counsel Bryan Cave, 1997-98; pres. Sys. Svc. Enterprises, 1998—. Bd. dirs. Republic Health Corp., Dallas, 1988-90; mem. governing bd. Luth. Med. Ctr., 1989-95, chmn., 1990-92. Bd. dirs. Luth. Charities Assn., 1982-91, sec. 1984-86, chmn. 1986-89; elder Lutheran Ch. of Resurrection, 1977-80; mem. Regents Coun. Concordia Sem., 1981-84; chmn. cub scout pack 459 Boy Scouts Am., 1984-86; bd. dirs. Luth. High Sch. Assn., 1978-84, 91-97, pres. 1992-97, long range planning com. 1990-92, chmn. alumni assn. 1981; chmn. north star dist. Boy Scouts Am., 1990-93; bd. dirs. Mcpl. Theatre Assn., St. Louis, 1991—; chmn. long range planning com. St. Paul's Luth. Ch., 1988-91, 98-2001, pres., 1996-97, 2002-; bd. dirs., mem. exec. com. United Way of Greater St. Louis, 1994-97, chmn. Vanguard divsn., 1994-97; mem. amb. coun. Luth. Family and Children's Svcs. of St. Louis, 1998—; bd. dirs. Luth. Charities Found., 1998—; mem. adv. bd. Webster U. Bus. and Tech. Sch., 1999-2001; mem. bd mgrs. worker benefit plans Luth Ch.-Mo. Synod, 2001—. Recipient Disting. Leadership award Luth. Assn. for Higher Edn., 1981. Mem. ABA, Mo. Bar Assn., Bar Assn. Met. St. Louis, Bellerive Country Club, Phi Beta Kappa, Omicron Delta Kappa. Republican. Avocations: tennis, golf, racquetball. Home: 1711 Stone Ridge Trails Dr Saint Louis MO 63122-3546 Office: Sys Svc Enterprises 77 Westport Plz Ste 500 Saint Louis MO 63146-3126 E-mail: fmkuhlmann@sseinc.com.

KUHN, EDWIN P. travel company executive; Pres., CEO TravelCenters of Am, 1992—. Mem. Nat. Assn. Truck Stop Operators (chmn. long-range planning com.). Office: TravelCenters of Am Inc 24601 Center Ridge Rd Ste 200 Westlake OH 44145-5677

KUHN, ROBERT MITCHELL, retired rubber company executive; b. N.Y.C., May 9, 1942; s. Robert M. and Marie (Mildenberger) K.; m. Edda Clorinda Barsotti, Sept. 7, 1968; children— Marisa A., Michele T. B.A. in Psychology, Alfred U., 1964; M.B.A., NYU, 1970. Various fin. and operational positions Singer Co., Stamford, Conn., 1970-75, United Techs., Hartford, 1975-82; exec. v.p., dir. Armstrong Rubber Co., New Haven, 1982; pres. Dayco Products, Inc., Dayton, Ohio, 1986-98; ret., 1998. Bd. dirs. Copolymer Rubber & Chem. Corp., Baton Rouge. Served to capt. USMC, 1964-68, Vietnam Republican. Roman Catholic Home: 9 Christmas Tree Ln Southport CT 06490-1313 Office: Goss Graphics Systems 700 Oakmont Ln Westmont IL 60559-5551

KUHN, ROSEANN, sports association administrator; Staff mem. Women's Internat. Bowling Congress, Greendale, Wis., 1974-96, exec. dir., 1996—. Office: Womens Internat Bowling Congress (WIBC) 5301 S 76th St Greendale WI 53129-1128

KUHN, RYAN ANTHONY, information industry investment banker; b. Framingham, Mass., Sept. 15, 1947; s. Robert Anthony Kuhn and Julia (Scott) McMillan; m. Cynthia Lynn DeVore, June 4, 1988; 1 child, Ryan R. BA in Psychology, Trinity Coll., Hartford, Conn., 1970; MBA, Harvard U., 1979. Mgr. corp. acquisitions McGraw-Hill, N.Y.C., 1979-85; sr. assoc. venture capital Golder Thoma Cressey, Chgo., 1985-86; pres. Reid Psychol. Systems, 1986-90, Lilly Pulitzer, Chgo., 1990-93; prin. Kuhn Capital, 1990—. Contbr. articles to profl. publs. and mags.; guest spkr. TV and radio talk show. Bd. dirs. Infant Welfare Soc. Chgo., Harvard Bus. Sch. of Chgo. Republican. Episcopalian. Office: Kuhn Capital 440 N Wells Ste 650 Chicago IL 60610

KUHN, WHITEY, advertising executive; Pres. Kuhn & Wittenborn Advt., Kansas City, Mo., 1978—. Office: Kuhn & Wittenborn Advt Ste 600 2405 Grand Blvd Kansas City MO 64108

KUHRMEYER, CARL ALBERT, manufacturing company executive; b. St. Paul, May 12, 1928; s. Carl and Irma Luella (Lindeke) K.; m. Janet E. Pedersen, Oct. 31, 1953; children: Karen Graden, John, Paul. BSME, U. Minn., 1949. Registered profl. engr., Minn. Design engr. Magney, Tusler & Setter, St. Paul, 1950-51; with 3M Co., 1951-93, successively product devel. engr., machine devel. engr., project leader, copy machine prodn. supr., process engring. and contracting supr., process engring. mgr., project mgr., until 1964, tech. dir., 1964-66, div. v.p., 1967-70, corp. group v.p., 1970-80, corp. v.p., 1980-93. Bd. dirs., chmn. bd. Product Level Control, Eagan, Minn., 1995—; bd. dirs. 1-800-TAKE-OFF, North Palm Beach, Fla. Patentee in field. Mem. nat. adv. coun. Nat. Multiple Sclerosis Soc., 1973—; trustee United Theol. Sem., St. Paul, 1986—; bd. dirs. Minn. Protestant Found., St. Paul, 1987—, pres., 1997—; bd. dirs. Minn. Pvt. Coll. Fund, St. Paul, 1986-95, St. Paul Winter Carnival Assn., 1987-93, chmn., dir., 1990-91; bd. dirs., v.p. Family Resources Devel. Inc., St. Paul. Mem. St. Paul C. of C. (bd. dirs. 1988-95, chmn. bd. 1993), Minn. Club (bd. dirs. 1994—), White Bear Yacht Club (bd. dirs. 1995-97), North Oaks Country Club (bd. dirs. 1981-83, pres. 1983), Osman Temple. Mem. United Church of Christ. Office: 3050 Minnesota World Trade Ctr 30 7th St E Saint Paul MN 55101-4914 E-mail: cakuhrmeyer@mmm.com .

KUJALA, WALFRID EUGENE, musician, educator; b. Warren, Ohio, Feb. 19, 1925; s. Arvo August and Elsie Fannie (Ojajarvi) K.; m. Sherry Henry, Dec. 29, 1989; children by previous marriage: Stephen, Gwen, Daniel. MusB, Eastman Sch. Music, 1948, MusM, 1950. Flutist Rochester Philharm. Orch., 1948—54; soloist, flutist, piccoloist Chgo. Symphony Orch., 1954—2001; prof. flute Northwestern U., Evanston, 1962—. Vis. prof. of flute Shepherd Sch. Music, Rice U., 1995-97. Author: The Flutist's Progress, 1970, The Flutist's Vade Mecum of Scales, Arpeggios, Trills and Fingering Technique, 1995; consulting editor Flute Talk Mag., 1991—; contbr. articles to profl. jours.; performed world premiere of Concerto for Flute by Gunther Schuller with Chgo. Symphony Orch., conducted by Sir Georg Solti, 1988. Served with AUS, 1943-45, ETO, PTO. Recipient

Exemplar of Music Tchg. award, Northwestern U., 1992. Mem.: Nat. Flute Assn. (past pres., Lifetime Achievement award 1997). Office: Sch Music Northwestern U Evanston IL 60208-0001 E-mail: wkujala222@cs.com.

KULCINSKI, GERALD LAVERNE, nuclear engineer, educator; b. La Crosse, Wis., Oct. 27, 1939; s. Harold Franklin and June Kramer K.; m. Janet Noreen Berg, Nov. 25, 1961; children: Kathryn, Brian, Karen. BS in Chem. Engring., U. Wis., 1961, MS in Nuclear Engring., 1962, PhD in Nuclear Engring., 1965. Rschr. Los Alamos (N.Mex.) Nuclear Lab., 1963; lectr. Ctr. Grad. Study, Richland, Wash., 1965-71; sr. rsch. sci. Battelle Northwest Lab., 1965-71; prof. U. Wis., Madison, 1972—, dir. Fusion Tech. Inst., 1973-75, 79—, Grainger Prof. Nuclear Engring., 1984—, assoc. dean rsch. Coll. Engring., 2001—. Vis. sci. Karlsruhe (Germany) Nuclear Rsch. Ctr., 1977, Bechtel Corp., San Francisco, 1989, 95; active Gov. Energy Policy Task Force, Wis., 1980; U.S. del. to Internat. Tokamak Reactor Project, Vienna, Austria, 1979-81; mem. adv. panel INTOR, 1987; mem. numerous review panels, including Los Alamos Nat. lab., Sandia Nat. Lab., Argonne Nat. Lab. Assoc. editor: Fusion Engring. and Design. Recipient Curtis W. McGraw Rsch. award Engring. Rsch. Com. Am. Assn. Engring. Edn., 1978, John Randle Grumman Achievement award Grumman Aircraft Corp., 1987, Leadership Fusion award Fusion Power Assocs., 1992, NASA Pub. Svc. medal, 1993, Disting. Faculty award Wis. Alumni Assn., 1994, Big 10 Centennial award, 1995. Fellow Am. Nuclear Soc. (sec. Richland sect. 1970, student advisor Wis. chpt. 1972-73, chmn. 2nd topical meeting on fusion tech. 1976, bd. dirs. 1987-90, Outstanding Achievement award 1980); mem. Nat. Acad. Engring. Home: 6013 Greentree Rd Madison WI 53711-3125 Office: U Wis 1500 Johnson Dr Madison WI 53706-1609 E-mail: kulcinski@engr.wisc.edu.

KULLBERG, DUANE REUBEN, accounting firm executive; b. Red Wing, Minn., Oct. 6, 1932; s. Carl Reuben and Hazel Norma (Swanson) K.; m. Sina Nell Turner, Oct. 19, 1958 (dec. Sept. 1989); children: Malissa Ryan, Caroline Godellas; m. Susan Turley, Dec. 30, 1992; stepchildren: Betsy Lucas, Jane Holtzermann. BBA, U. Minn., 1954. With Andersen Worldwide, 1954-89, ptnr., 1967-89, mng. ptnr., Mpls., 1970-74, dep. mng. ptnr., Chgo., 1975-78, vice chmn. acctg. and audit practice worldwide, 1978-80, mng. ptnr., CEO, 1980-89, ret., 1989. Bd. dirs. John Nuveen Co., Carlson Cos., Inc., Chgo. Bd. Options Exch. Life trustee Northwestern U., Art Inst. Chgo., U. Minn. Found., chmn. bd. trustees, 1993-95; chair Swedish Coun. Am. Found., 1999-2001. With U.S. Army, 1956-58. Decorated comdr. Royal Order of Polar Star (Sweden), 1989; recipient Legend in Leadership award Emory U., 1992, Regents award U. Minn., 1995, Outstanding Achievement award U. Minn., 1990. Mem. Chgo. Club, Comml. Club, Mpls. Club. Home: 179 E Lake Shore Dr Apt 1001 Chicago IL 60611-1306 also: 6444 N 79th St Scottsdale AZ 85250-7919

KUMAR, PANGANAMALA RAMANA, electrical and computer engineering educator; b. Nagpur, Maharashtra, India, Apr. 21, 1952; came to U.S., 1973; s. Panganamala Bhavanarayana and Panganamala Kamala (Avasarala) Murthy; m. Devarakonda Jayashree Sundaram, Jan. 22, 1982; children: P. Ashwin, Shilpa P. BTech., Indian Inst. Tech., Madras, India, 1973; MS, Washington U., 1975, DSc, 1977. Asst. prof. dept. math. and computer sci. U. Md., Baltimore County, 1977-82, assoc. prof. dept. math. and computer sci., 1982-84; assoc. prof. dept. elec. and computer engring. and coordinated sci. lab. U. Ill., Urbana, 1985-87, prof. dept. elec. and computer engring., 1987—, rsch. prof. coordinated sci. lab., 1987—, Franklin Woeltge prof. elec. and computer engring., 2000—. Co-author: Stochastic Systems, 1986; assoc. editor: Systems and Control Letters, 1984-93, Math. of Control, Signals and Systems, 1986—, SIAM Jour. on Control and Optimization, 1989-93, Jour. of Discrete Event Dynamic Systems: Theory and Application, 1993—; assoc. editor-at-large IEEE Trans. on Automatic Control, 1989-97; mem. editl. bd. Jour. on Adaptive Control and Signal Processing, 1986-99, Math. Problems in Engring., 1995—; contbr. articles to profl. jours. Recipient Donald P. Eckman award Am. Automatic Control Coun., 1985. Fellow IEEE. Avocation: table tennis. Office: U Ill Coordinated Sci Lab 1308 W Main St Urbana IL 61801-2307 E-mail: prkumar@uiuc.edu.

KUMAR, ROMESH, chemical engineer; b. Rajpura, India, Oct. 18, 1944; came to U.S., 1966; s. Kundan Lal and Pushpa (Wati) Agarwal; m. Kumkum Khanna, Feb. 22, 1976. B.S., Panjab U., India, 1965; M.S., U. Calif., Berkeley, 1968, Ph.D., 1972. Postdoctoral appointee Argonne (Ill.) Nat. Lab., 1972-73, asst. chem. engr., 1973-76, chem. engr., 1976—; also head Fuel All Dept. Chem. Tech. divsn. Argonne Nat. Lab. Tchr. fuel cell power sys. design and analysis for transp. applications. Contbr. to Weissberger's Techniques in Chemistry, 1975; patentee in field. Recipient Silver medal Panjab U., 1965 Hindu. Home: 1549 Ceals Ct Naperville IL 60565-6148 Office: 9700 Cass Ave Argonne IL 60439-4803 E-mail: kumar@cmt.anl.gov.

KUMMER, FRED S. construction company executive; b. 1929; BS, U. Mo., 1952. Engr. William Ittner & Co., 1952-56; with Buckley Constrn. Co., Inc., 1957-59, Kummer Constrn. Co., Inc., from 1959; now pres., treas. HBE Corp., St. Louis. Address: HBE PO Box 419039 Saint Louis MO 63141-9039 Office: Adam's Mark Hotels 11330 Olive St Rd Box 27339 Saint Louis MO 63141

KUMMEROW, ARNOLD A. superintendent of schools; b. Framingham, Mass., Mar. 25, 1945; s. Arnold A. Sr. and Elizabeth Patricia (Westfield) K.; m. Constance Booth, July 10, 1971. BME, Eastern Mich. U., 1968, MA, 1975; PhD, U. Mich., 1989. Cert. adminstrn., Mich. Instrumental music dir. Vandercook Lake Pub. Schs., Jackson, Mich., 1968-74; instrumental music dir., asst. prin., prin. L'Anse Creuse Pub. Schs., Mt. Clemens, 1975-89; asst. supt. curriculum and pers. Lincoln Consol. Schs., Ypsilanti, 1989-91; asst. supt. Ypsilanti Pub. Schs., 1991-93; mem. curriculum devel. staff Mich. Dept. Edn., 1993-94; supt. Carsonville-Port Sanilac (Mich.) Schs., 1994-97, Armada (Mich.) Area Schs., 1997—. Named Exemplary Sch. Prin., Mich. Dept. Edn. and U.S. Dept. Edn. Mem. AASA, MASA, ASCD. Home: 17201 Knollwood Dr Clinton Township MI 48038-2833 Office: Armada Area Schs 74500 Burk St Armada MI 48005-3314

KUMMLER, RALPH H. chemical engineer, educator, dean; b. Jersey City, Nov. 1, 1940; m. Jean Evelyn Helge, Aug. 25, 1962; children: Randolph Henry, Bradley Rolf, Jeffrey Ralf. BSChemE, Rensselaer Poly. Inst., 1962; PhD, Johns Hopkins U., 1966. Chem. engr. GE Space Scientist Lab., Valley Forge, Pa., 1965-69; assoc. prof. chem. engring. Wayne State U., Detroit, 1970-75, prof., 1975—, chmn. dept., 1974-93, dir. hazardous waste mgmt. programs, 1986—, assoc. dean rsch., 1997-2001, interim dean, 2001—. Contbr. articles to publs. Bd. dirs., past pres. Kirkwood Lake Assn. Fellow: Engr. Soc. Detroit (Young Engr. of Yr. award 1975, Gold award 1990, Disting. Svc. award 1994, Horace Rackham Humanitarian award 1999), Am. Inst. Chemists; mem.: AIChE (past pres. Detroit chpt.), Svc. award 1981, Chem. Engr. of Yr. award 1981), Mich. Air and Waste Mgmt. Assn. ((past pres.), Waste Mgmt. award 2002), Am. Chem. Soc., Tau Beta Pi, Sigma Xi. Achievements include co-patentee in chem. innovations. Office: Wayne State U Coll Engring Detroit MI 48202

KUMP, WARREN LEE, retired diagnostic radiologist; b. Jennings, Kans., June 30, 1926; s. Lee Robert and Hazel Jessie (Bobbitt) K.; m. Patricia Jeanne Burke, Oct. 16, 1950; children: Theresa, Lee, Mary, John. BA, U. Kans., 1947, MD, 1950. Diplomate Am. Bd. Radiology. Intern U. Ill., Chgo., 1950-51; med. officer USN/USMC, 1951-53; resident U. Minn., Mpls., 1953-56; staff radiologist North Meml. Med. Ctr., 1957-96. Chief radiology North Meml. Med. Ctr., 1965-91, chief of staff, 1974-75, trustee, 1982-2001, chmn. bd. dirs., 1993-2000; pres. Mpls. Radiology Assocs., 1965-91. Bd. dirs. Newman Found., 1955-60, St. Therese Found., New Hope, Minn., 1962-94; pres. St. Therese Charitable Svcs., New Hope, 1991-94. Fellow Am. Coll. Radiology; mem. AMA, Radiol. Soc. N.Am., Am. Roentgen Ray Soc., Minn. Radiol. Soc. (pres. 1974-75), Minn. Med. Assn. Roman Catholic. Avocations: reading, traveling, historical research. Office: Mpls Rad Assocs 604 Oakdale Med Bldg Minneapolis MN 55422 E-mail: Wlkump@aol.com.

KUN, JOYCE ANNE, secondary education educator, small business owner; b. Salem, Ohio, Oct. 20, 1946; d. Robert Malvern Slutz and Helen Roberta (Williams) Short; m. James Joseph Kun, June 10, 1978; 1 child, Jessica Erin. BS in Edn., Ohio U., 1969; MA in Tech., Kent State U., 1980. Cert. tchr., Ohio. Tchr. Ridgewood Local, West Lafayette, Ohio, 1970-71, Norton (Ohio) High Sch., 1971—; owner The Norton Pub, Norton, 1992—. Mem. NEA, Canton chpt. DAR, Ohio Edn. Assn., Ohio Tech. Edn. Assn., N.E. Ohio Tech. Edn. Assn. (officer 1972-78), Norton Classroom Tchrs. Assn. (exec. bd.), Norton Grange, Barberton Moose Lodge, Epsilon Pi Tau. Lutheran. Avocations: bowling, golf, flower gardening. Office: The Norton Pub 4020 Cleve Mass Rd Norton OH 44203-5601 Home: 3500 Greenwich Rd Norton OH 44203-5567 Office: Norton High Sch 4128 Cleve Mass Rd Norton OH 44203-5633 E-mail: joycekun@aol.com.

KUNDERT, ALICE E. retired state legislator; b. Java, S.D., July 23, 1920; d. Otto J. and Maria (Rieger) K. elem. tchr.'s cert., state tchr. cert., No. State Coll. Tchr. elem. grades, 1939-43, 48-54; clk., mgr., buyer Gates Dept. Store, Beverly Hills, Calif., Clifton Dress Shop, Hollywood, 1943-48; dep. supt. schs. Campbell County, S.D., 1954; county cts. clk., 1955-60; register deeds, 1955-69; town treas. Mound City, 1965-69; auditor State of S.D., Pierre, 1969-79; sec. of state, 1980-87; dir. sch. programs S.D. Dept. Edn. and Cultural Affairs, 1987-89; state rep. State of S.D., 1991-93, ret., 1993. Nat. adv. coun. bd. mem. Ctr. for Western Studies, Augustana Coll., Sioux Falls, S.D., 1996-97, mem. adv. bd. Boe Forum on Nat. and Internat. Affairs, 1994—. Leader 4-H Club, 1949-53, county project leader in citizenship, 1963-64; sec. Greater Campbell County Assn., 1955-57; organizer, leader Mound City Craft and Recreation Club, 1955-60; chmn. Heart Fund, March Dimes, Red Cross, Mental Health drs.; mem. S.D. Gov.'s Study Commn., 1968— ; mem. state and local adv. com. region VIII Office Econ. Opportunity; bd. mem., chmn. Black Hills Recreation Lab., 1956-61; exec. sec. Internat. Leaders Lab., Ireland, 1963; Polit. co. vice chmn. Rep. Com., 1964-69, sec-treas. fin. chmn., 1968; mem. State Rep. Adv. Com., 1966-68; state and nat. counselor Teen Age Rep. Club Campbell County, 1964— . Named Outstanding Teenage Rep. adv. in nation, 1970, 71, 76; Recipient Disting. Alumni award No. State Coll., 1975 Home: PO Box 67 Mound City SD 57646-0067 Office: Office Sec of State State Capital Bldg Pierre SD 57501

KUNDERT, JOHN F. state finance administrator; Sec. Wis. Fin. Instn. Dept., Madison. Office: Wis Fin Instn Dept PO Box 8861 Madison WI 53708-8861

KUNDTZ, JOHN ANDREW, lawyer; b. Cleve., June 23, 1933; s. Ewald E. and Elizabeth (O'Neill) K.; m. Helen Margaret Luckiesh, Aug. 31, 1957; children— John M., Helen E., Margaret L. B.S. in Social Studies, Georgetown U., 1955; J.D., Case Western Reserve U., 1958. Bar: Ohio 1958, U.S. Dist. Ct. (no. dist.) Ohio 1961. Ptnr. Falsgraf, Kundtz, Reidy & Shoup, Cleve., 1961-69; ptnr. Thompson Hine and Flory, 1970-90; pvt. practice, 1990—. Dir. Investment Advisors Internat., Inc., Cleve. Trustee Hathaway Brown Sch., Shaker Heights, Ohio, Chagrin River Land Conservancy, Chagrin Falls, Ohio, Cleve. Soc. for the Blind. 1st lt. USAF, 1958-60. Mem. ABA, Ohio State Bar Assn., Assn. Transp. Practitioners. Republican. Roman Catholic. Home: 32540 Creekside Dr Pepper Pike OH 44124-5224 Office: 3550 Lander Rd Ste 140 Cleveland OH 44124-5727

KUNG, HAROLD HING-CHUEN, engineering educator; b. Hong Kong, Oct. 12, 1949; s. Shien C. and Kai Sau (Wong) K.; m. Mayfair Chu, June 12, 1971; children: Alexander, Benjamin. BS in chem. engring., U. Wis., 1971; PhD in chemistry, Northwestern U., 1974. Rsch. sci. ctrl. rsch. and devel. dept. E.I. duPont de Nemours & Co., Wilmington, Del., 1974-76; asst. prof. chem. engring. Northwestern U., 1976, asst. prof. chem. engring. and chemistry, 1977, assoc. prof., 1981, prof. chem. engring. and chemistry, 1985-97, chmn. chemical engring., 1986-92; dir. Ctr. for Catalysis and Surface Sci., 1993-97. Chmn. Gordon rsch. Conf. on Catalysis, 1995; tech. advisor UNIDO Mission, 1995; John McClanahan Henske Disting. lectr. Yale U., 1996; mem. com. to rev. PNGV program Nat. Rsch. Coun., 1996-2000; Olaf Hongen vis. prof. U. Wis., Madison, 1999. Author: Transition Metal Oxides, Surface Chemistry and Catalysis, 1989, Catalyst Modificaton-Selective Oxidation Processes, 1991; editor: Methanol Production and Use, 1994, Applied Catalysis A = General, 1996—; patents include Photolysis of Water Using Rhodate Semiconductive Electrodes, and Oxidative Dehydrogenation of Alkanes to Unsaturated Hydrocarbons. Japanese Soc. for Promotion of Sci. fellow, 1996. Mem. AIChE, Am. Chem. Soc., Chgo. Catalysis Club (program chair 1992, pres. 1993, Herman Pines award 1999), N.Am. Catalysis Soc. (Paul H. Emmett award 1991, Robert L. Barwell lectr. 1999), Phi Lambda Epsilon. Office: Dept of Chem Engring Northwestern University 2145 Sheridan Rd Evanston IL 60208-0834 E-mail: hkung@northwestern.edu.

KUNKEL, RICHARD W. state legislator; BS, Minot State; MEd, EdD, U. N.D.; PhD, Columbia U. Retired supt. of schs.; mem. N.D. Ho. of Reps., 1991-98, vice chmn. appropriations com., vice chmn. edn. com., vice chmn. environ. divsn. com. Past pres. United Way; exec. coun. Boy Scouts Am.; bd. dirs. N.D. Bd. Higher Edn., 1999—. Mem. Elks, Rotary (past pres.), Eagles, Cmty. Concert Assn. (past pres.). Home: 1312 6th St Devils Lake ND 58301-2812

KUNKLE, WILLIAM JOSEPH, JR. lawyer; b. Lakewood, Ohio, Sept. 3, 1941; s. William Joseph and Georgia (Howe) K.; m. Sarah Florence Nesti, July 11, 1964; children: Kathleen Margaret, Susan Mary. BA, Northwestern U., Evanston, Ill., 1963; Jd, Northwestern U., 1969. Bar: Ohio 1969, U.S. Dist. Ct. (no. dist.) Ill. 1969, Ill. 1969, U.S. Ct. Appeals (7th cir.) 1991, U.S. Supreme Ct. 1991. Process control engr. Union Carbide Corp., Cleve., 1964-65, prodn. supr. Greenville, S.C., 1965-66; assoc. Hauxhurst, Sharp, Mollison & Gallagher, Cleve., 1969-70; asst. pub. defender Cook County Pub. Defender, Chgo., 1970-73; asst. states atty. Cook County States Atty., 1973-85; ptnr. Phelan, Cahill & Quinlan, Ltd., 1985-96, Cahill, Christian & Kunkle, LTD., Chgo., 1996—. Chmn. The Ill. Gaming Bd., 1990-93; dep. spl. outside counsel U.S. Ho. Reps., Washington, 1988-89; adj. prof. I.I.T. Chgo. Kent Sch. Law, 1980-84; instr. Nat. Inst. for Trial Advocacy, Chgo., 1978-82, 86; lectr. Nat. Coll. Dist. Attys., Houston, Denver, Chgo., Atlanta, Louisville, 1978-85, Nat. Law Enforcement Inst., San Francisco, Portland, Atlanta, Pitts., Boston, St. Louis, Chgo., 1983-85; 1st asst. states atty. of Cook County, 1983-85; spl. state's atty. 18th Jud. Cir., DuPage County, 1995-99. Contbg. author: Punishment Prosecutor's Viewpoint, 1983, 1989, Trial Techniques Compendium, Nat. College of Dist. Attys. (2d, 3rd, 4th, 5th, 6th eds.). Recipient Disting. Faculty award Nat. Coll. Dist. Attys., 1980, Award for Prosecution Svc. Chgo. Assn. Commerce & Industry, 1981. Fellow Am. Coll. Trial Lawyers, ABA; mem. Internat. Soc. Barristers, Nat. Dist. Attys. Assn. (bd. dirs. 1984-85), Assn. Govt. Attys. in Capital Litigation (pres. 1983-84), Chgo. Bar Assn. (bd. mgrs. 1983-84), Ill. State Bar Assn. (LAWPAC trustee 1989-95), Internat. Assn. Gaming Attys., Chgo. Crime Commn. (bd. dirs.). Republican. Avocations: golf, softball, carpentry, motorcycling. Office: Cahill Christian & Kunkle Ltd 224 S Michigan Ave Ste 1300 Chicago IL 60604-2583

KUNTZ, WILLIAM HENRY, lawyer, mediator; b. Indpls., Feb. 27, 1954; s. Herman William and Ethel Cleora (Stangle) K. BA in Chemistry, Purdue U. at Indpls., 1984; MS in Chemistry, Purdue U., Indpls., 1986; JD, Ind. U., Indpls., 1989. Bar: Ind. 1989, U.S. Dist. Ct. (so. and no. dists.) Ind. 1989, U.S. Patent Office 1992, U.S. Supreme Ct. 1993. Assoc. Urdal, Tarvin and Alexander, P.C., Connersville, Ind., 1989-90; dep. prosecutor County of Fayette, 1990, chief dep. prosecutor, 1991-92; pvt. practice Indpls., 1992-94; chief dep. prosecutor Fayette County, Connersville, 1995-98; with Baker and Bodwell, P.C., Ind., 1999—. Mem. ABA, Nat. Bar Assn., Ind. State Bar Assn. (bd. dirs. ADR sect. 1997—), Indpls. Bar Assn. (chmn. legal awareness com. 1996, chmn. law student liaison com. 1996), Fayette County Bar Assn. (sec.-treas. 1989-90), Marion County Bar Assn., Ind. Trial Lawyers Assn., Ind. Assn. Mediators (sec. 1993-94, 97—, pres.-elect 1994-95, pres. 1995-96), Soc. Profls. in Dispute Resolution, Acad. Family Mediators, Purdue U. Indpls. Sch. Sci. Alumni Bd. (v.p. 1998—). Home: 2065 Lick Creek Dr Indianapolis IN 46203-4922 Office: Bader and Bodwell PC County of Fayette 621 N Central Ave Ste 1 Connersville IN 47331-2012

KUNZE, RALPH CARL, retired savings and loan executive; b. Buffalo, Oct. 31, 1925; s. Bruno E. and Esther (Graubman) K.; m. Helen Hites Sutton, Apr. 1978; children by previous marriage: Bradley, Diane Kunze Cowgill, James. BBA, U. Cin., 1950, postgrad., 1962-63; grad., Ind. U. Grad. Sch. Savs. and Loan, 1956, U. Calif., 1973. With Mt. Lookout Savs. & Loan Co., Cin., 1951-63, sec., mng. officer, 1958-63; with Buckeye Fed. Savs. & Loan Assn., Columbus, Ohio, 1963-77, exec. v.p., sec., 1967-70, pres., sec., vice chmn. bd. dirs., 1970-77; pres., chief operating officer, dir. Gate City Savs. and Loan Assn., Fargo, N.D., 1977-81; chief exec. officer, dir. United Home Fed., Toledo, 1981-91, also chmn. bd. dirs., 1985-91; ret., 1991. Former trustee Ohio Savs. and Loan League, Toledo C. of C.; mem. investment adv. com. City of Toledo; mem. media contact group and legis. com. U.S. Savs. League. Mem. Toledo Com. 100, Toledo Zool. Soc., St. Vincent Hosp. Found.; past pres. Toledo Zoo; past pres. coun. Hope Luth. Ch.; pres. Toledo Neighborhood Housing Svcs., 1981-83; pres., chmn. pers. com. United Way Franklin County, Ohio; past pres. Ohio Soc. Prevention Blindness; bd. dirs. Revitalization Corp. Toledo, 1983-84, Bittersweet Farms, Autistic Cmty. of N.W. Ohio, Inc.; past mem., trustee Kidney Found. Northwestern Ohio and Luth. Social Svcs., Wesley Glen Retirement Meth. Ctr., Columbus, 1974-77. Served with USNR, 1944-45. Mem. Lambda Chi Alpha. Home: 2606 Emmick Dr Toledo OH 43606-2701

KUNZEL, ERICH, JR. conductor, arranger, educator; b. N.Y.C., Mar. 21, 1935; s. Erich and Elisabeth (Enz) K.; m. Brunhilde Gertrud Strodl, Sept. 5, 1965. AB with distinction in Music, Dartmouth, 1957; postgrad., Harvard, 1957-58; AM, Brown U., 1960; LittD, No. Ky. State U., 1973; DA, Coll. Mt. St. Joseph, 1996; D in musical Arts, U. Cin., 2000. Condr. Sante Fe Opera, 1957, 64, 65; music faculty Brown U., 1958-65; asst. condr. R.I. Philharmonic, 1963-65; resident condr. Cin. Symphony Orch., 1965-77; condr. Cin. Summer Opera, 1966, 73, Cin. Ballet Co., 1966-68; asso. prof. U. Cin. Coll.-Conservatory Music, 1965-71, chmn. opera dept., 1968-70; music dir. Philharmonia Orch., 1967-71, New Haven Symphony Orch., 1974-77, San Francisco Art Commn. Pops, 1981-83; condr. Cin. Pops Orch., 1977—; prin. pops condr. Naples Philharm. Orch., 1993—. Guest condr. Boston Symphony, Cleve. Orch., Boston Pops, Phila. Orch., San Francisco Symphony, Buffalo Philharmonic, Rochester Philharmonic, Pitts. Symphony, Atlanta Symphony, Pitts. Symphony Orch., Chgo. Symphony Orch., Interlochen Arts Festival, Dallas Symphony, Detroit Symphony, Toronto Symphony, Montreal Symphony, St. Louis Symphony, Nat. Symphony, London Symphony, China Nat. Symphony, Can. Opera Co., others. Editor, arranger choral works; recs. for Decca Gold Label, Atlantic Records, Telarc Internat., Vox Records, Caedmon Records, Pro Arte Records, Fanfare, MMG, MCA Classics Gold. Vice pres. Pierre Monteux Meml. Found., Met. Opera Guild; chmn. Greater Cin. Arts and Edn. Ctr., 1998—. Recipient Grand Prix du Disque, 1989, Sony Tiffany award, 1989, Classical Record of Yr. award Japan, 1989, Grammy nomination, 1989, 91, 93, 95, Grammy award, 198, Presdl. medal, Dartmouth Coll., 1991, The Salvation Army "Others" award, 1995, Disting. Alumnus award Phi Delta Theta Internat. Fraternity, 1996, Ohioana Pegasus award, 2000; named to Hon. Order Ky. Cols.; named Billboard Crossover Artist of Yr., 1988, 89, 90, 91. Mem. Am. Symphony Orch. League, Phi Delta Theta, Phi Mu Alpha Sinfonia, Delta Omicron. Office: Music Hall 1241 Elm St Cincinnati OH 45210-2231

KUPCHELLA, CHARLES EDWARD, academic administrator, author, educator; b. Nanty Glo, Pa., July 7, 1942; s. Charles Francis and Margaret (Bouite) K.; m. R. Adele Kiel, July 20, 1963; children: Richard Charles, Michele Louise, Jason Charles. BS in Edn., Indiana U. of Pa., 1964; PhD, St. Bonaventure U., 1968. Asst. prof. Bellarmine Coll., Louisville, 1968-72, assoc. prof., 1972-73; assoc. dir. cancer rsch. ctr. Sch. of Medicine, assoc. prof. U. Louisville, 1973-79; prof., chmn. dept. biology Murray (Ky.) State U., 1979-85; dean Ogden Coll. Western Ky. U., Bowling Green, 1985-93; provost S. E. Mo. State U., Cape Girardeau, 1993—. Author: Sights/Sounds: Special Senses, 1976, Environmental Science, 1986, 3rd rev. edit., 1993, Dimensions of Cancer, 1987; contbr. chpts. to books, over 50 articles to profl. jours. Bd. dirs. Ky. Ctr. for Pub. Issues, Lexington, 1990-93; mem. cancer edn. rev. com. NIH/Nat. Cancer Inst., 1993-97; mem. inst. rsch. grant rev. com. Am. Cancer Soc., 1993-96. NDEA fellow, 1964-68. Mem. AAAS (nominating com. sect. on sci. and engring. 1995-97), Ky. Acad. Sci. (pres. 1977), Ky. Sci. and Tech. Coun. (sec., treas. Lexington 1988-93), Am. Assn. Cancer Edn. (chairperson fin. com. 1990-93, treas. 1993-, pres. elect 1998—, exec. coun.). Office: U of North Dakota Office of Pres Grand Forks ND 58202

KUPCINET, IRV, columnist; b. Chgo., July 31, 1912; s. Max and Anna (Paswell) K.; m. Essee Joan Solomon, Feb. 12, 1939; children: Karyn (dec.), Jerry Solomon. AB, Northwestern U., 1930-32; A.B., U. N.D., 1935. Columnist Chgo. Daily Times, 1935-43, Kup's Column, Chgo. Sun Times, 1943—; host TV program Kup's Show, Chgo., 1959—; commentator WBBM-TV; former commentator Chgo. Bears football broadcasts. Spl. cons. in charge of columnists for War Fin. Divsn., drives U.S. Treasury Dept. V.p. Dr. Jerome D. Solomon Meml. Found.; originator, host Purple Heart Cruise. Recipient Emmy award, Peabody award, moderator TV show, numerous civic and profl. awards; Wabash Ave. Bridge, Chgo. renamed Irv Kupcinet Bridge, 1986. Mem. Newspaper Guild, Nat. Press Club (Washington), Chgo. Press Club, Tau Delta Phi. Office: Chgo Sun-Times 401 N Wabash Ave Chicago IL 60611-5642

KUPPER, BRUCE DAVID, advertising executive; b. Geneva, Nov. 17, 1952; s. Alan D. and Leila (Winograd) K.; m. Karen Ryan Kupper, Sept. 12, 1976; children: David, Laura. BA, Bates Coll., 1975. Account exec. Lieberman Advt., St. Louis, 1976-77; account supr. Young & Rubicam, Detroit, 1977-78; sr. ptnr., chief exec. officer Kupper Advt., Inc., St. Louis, 1978—; pres. Kupnic, Inc., 1991—; sr. ptnr. Kupper Parker Communications Inc., 1992—. Author: (Book) French Canadians in Am., 1975. Fellow: Coro Found.; mem. St. Louis Advt. Club, Am. Assn. Advt. Agys. (regional bd. mem.), Westborough Country Club.

KUPST, MARY JO, psychologist, researcher; b. Chgo., Oct. 4, 1945; d. George Eugene and Winifred Mary (Hughes) K.; m. Alfred Procter Stresen-Reuter Jr., Aug. 21, 1977. BS, Loyola U., 1967, MA, 1969, PhD, 1972. Lic. psychologist, Ill., Wis. Postdoctoral fellow U. Ill. Med. Ctr., Chgo., 1971—72; rsch. psychologist Children's Meml. Hosp., 1972—89; assoc. prof. psychiatry and pediatrics Northwestern U. Med. Sch., 1981—89; prof. pediatrics Med. Coll. Wis., Milw., 1989—, dir. pediatric psychology, 1995—2001, vice-chair childrens oncology group psychology com., 2001—. Practice clin. psychology, Chgo., 1975-89, McHenry, Ill., 1987-89; co-chair pediat. oncology group psychology com., 1995-2001, vice-chair children's oncology group psychology com., 2001—. Editor: (with others) The Child with Cancer, 1980; contbr. articles to profl. jours. V.p. McHenry County Mental Health Bd., 1997—2001. Fellow APA; mem. Wis. Psychol. Assn., Soc. Pediatric Psychology. Office: Med Coll Wis Dept Pediats 8701 W Watertown Plank Rd Milwaukee WI 53226-3548 E-mail: mkupst@mcw.edu.

KURIT, NEIL, lawyer; b. Cleve., Aug. 31, 1940; s. Jay and Rose (Rainin) K.; m. Doris Tannenbaum, Aug. 9, 1964 (div.); m. Donna Chernin, Aug. 24, 1986. BS, Miami U., Oxford, Ohio, 1961; JD, Case Western Res. U., 1964. Bar: Ohio 1964. Prin. Kahn, Kleinman, Yanowitz & Arnson Co., L.P.A., Cleve., 1964—. Co-author Handbook for Attys. and Accts., Jewish Cmty. Fedn. Endowment Fund. Trustee, v.p. Montefiore Home, 1983-87; trustee Jewish Cmty. Fedn. Cleve., 1983-86, 90-95. Mem. ABA, Ohio State Bar Assn. E-mail: nkurit@kkya.com Home: 2870 Courtland Blvd Cleveland OH 44122-2802 Office: Kahn Kleinman Yanowitz & Arnson Co LPA 2600 Tower at Erieview Cleveland OH 44114

KURTH, RONALD JAMES, university president, retired naval officer; b. Madison, Wis., July 1, 1931; s. Peter James and Celia (Kuehn) K.; m. Esther Charlene Schaefer, Dec. 21, 1954; children: Steven, Audrey, John, Douglas. BS, U.S. Naval Acad., 1954; MPA, Harvard U., 1961, PhD, 1970. Commd. ensign U.S. Navy, 1954, advanced through grades to rear adm., 1981; U.S. naval attache Moscow, 1975-77; comdg. officer NAS, Memphis at Millington, Tenn., 1977-79; mil. fellow Council Fgn. Relations, N.Y.C., 1979-80; exec. asst. to dep. chief naval ops. Dept. Navy, Washington, 1980-81, dir. Pol-Mil Policy and Current Plans, 1981-83, dir. Long Range Planning Group, 1983-84; U.S. def. attache Moscow, 1985-87; pres. U.S. Naval War Coll., Newport, R.I., 1987-90, Murray (Ky.) State U., 1990-94; dean acad. affairs Air War Coll., Maxwell AFB, Ala., 1994-98; pres. St. John's Northwestern Mil. Acad., Delafield, Wis., 1998—. Teaching fellow Harvard U., Cambridge, Mass., 1969-70. Author: The Politics of Technological Innovation in the Navy, 1970. Mem. nat. adv. bd. Boy Scouts Am. Decorated Def. D.S.M., Navy D.S.M., Legion of Merit with 2 gold stars, Meritorious Svc. medal with gold star. Mem. Am. Acad. Polit. Sci., U.S. Naval Inst. (life), Naval War Coll. Found. (life), U.S. Naval Acad. Alumni, Harvard U. Alumni, Rotary. Episcopalian. Home: 505 Saint Johns Rd Delafield WI 53018-1440 Office: St John's Northwestern Mil Acad Delafield WI 53018 E-mail: rkurth@sjnma.org.

KURTICH, JOHN WILLIAM, architect, film-maker, educator; b. Salinas, Calif., Oct. 18, 1935; s. John Joseph and Elizabeth (Lyons) K. BA in Theatre and Cinematography, UCLA, 1957; BArch, U. Calif., Berkeley, 1966; MS in Architecture and Urban Design, Columbia U., 1968. Film-maker SMP Architects, San Francisco, 1960-61; film-maker, archtl. draftsman McCue & Assocs., 1962-66; freelance film-maker, designer Friedberg, N.Y., 1968; instr. Sch. of Art Inst., Chgo., 1968-70, asst. prof., 1970-74, assoc. prof., 1974-82, prof., 1982—, chmn. dept. design and communication, 1981-85, area head interior arch., 1987-94, chmn. undergrad. divsn. Staff arch. Am. Excavations, Samothrace, Greece, 1970—; archtl. cons. Fed. Res. Bank Chgo., 1978; William Bronson Mitchell and Grayce Slovet Mitchell endowed chair in Interior Architecture, 1995—. Multi-media prodns. include: Hellas, Columbia U., N.Y.C., 1968, Art Inst. Chgo., 1971, 79, Muncie: Microsm of America (NEA grante), Muncie, Ind., 1972, Legend of the Minotaur, Art Inst. Chgo., 1973, The Seasons, Shapes, Contrasts, Art Inst. Chgo., 1977, 83, 84, Canal du Midi, Art Inst. Chgo., 1987, Light: A History of Architecture from Stonehenge to the Fall Of Western Civilization, Graham Found., 1988, The Desert of Rets, Graham Found., 1989, The Mysteries of Samothrace, Art Inst. Chgo., 1989, Echoes of Eternity, Art Inst. Chgo., 1989, Porno Versailles, Graham Found., 1990, Monuments and Memorials, State Ill. Art Gallery, 1990, The Art Institute of Chicago: The Corporation, Art Inst. Chgo., 1990, The Seven Wonders of the World, Mus. Contemporary Art, 1991, Design in the Fourth Dimension Space-Time, Neo Con/Chgo. Architecture Found., 1993, The Ancient World, Art Inst. Chgo., 1994, Ilumine: The Architecture of Light, Graham Found., 1995, Recent Excavations at Samothrace, Graham Found., 1996. Served with USNR, 1957-60. Recipient Architecture medal Alpha Rho Chi, 1966; William Kinne fellow Columbia U., Fgn. Travelling fellow; grantee NEA, 1972, Woman's Bd. Art Inst. Chgo., 1973, Union Ind. Colls. Art, 1974, Fulbright-Hays (Eng.), 1976, Fulbright-Hays (Jordan), 1981, Ford Foun./Art Inst Chgo. Faculty Enrichment, 1982, 87, 91, 93, 2000, Graham Found. for Advanced Studies in Fine Arts, 1988. Fellow Royal Soc. Arts (London); mem. AIA (corp. mem.), Soc. Archtl. Historians, Nat. Com. for Interiors, Chgo. Archtl. Club. Home: 4737 S Ellis Ave Chicago IL 60615-1807 Office: Sch of Art Inst Chgo Office of Interior Arch 37 S Wabash Ave Chicago IL 60603-3103 E-mail: jkurtich@artic.edu.

KURTZ, CHARLES JEWETT, III, lawyer; b. Columbus, Ohio, May 13, 1940; s. Charles Jewett, Jr. and Elizabeth Virginia (Gill) K.; m. Linda Rhoads, Mar. 18, 1983. BA, Williams Coll., 1962; JD, Ohio State U., 1965. Bar: Ohio 1965, D.C. 1967, U.S. Dist. Ct. (so. dist.) Ohio 1967, U.S. Dist. Ct. (no. dist.) Ohio 1976, U.S. Ct. Appeals (6th cir.) 1992. Law clk. to justice Ohio State Supreme Ct., Columbus, 1965-67; assoc. Porter, Wright, Morris & Arthur, 1967-71, ptnr., 1972—, mng. ptnr. litigation dept., 1988-91, mem. directing ptnrs. com., 1988-89. Mem. faculty Ohio Legal Ctr. Inst. Trustee Ballet Met., Columbus, 1990-94; mem. vestry St. Albans Episcopal Ch., 1986-89. Mem. ABA, Am. Arbitration Assn. (mem. panel comml. arbitrators), Ohio Bar Assn. (mem. workers compensation com.), Columbus Bar Assn. (sustaining mem.), Columbus Bar Found., Columbus Def. Assn. (pres. 1976), Athletic Club, Columbus Country Club, Capital Club. Office: Porter Wright Morris & Arthur 41 S High St Ste 2900 Columbus OH 43215-6194 E-mail: ckurtz@porterwright.com.

KURTZ, HARVEY A. lawyer; b. Baraboo, Wis., July 9, 1950; s. Walter R. and Henrietta M. (Hinze) K.; m. Yvonne Larme, Jan. 28, 1978; children: Benjamin L., Leah L. BA, U. Wis., 1972; JD, U. Chgo., 1975. Bar: Wis. 1975, U.S. Dist. Ct. (ea. dist.) Wis. 1980. Atty. Whyte & Hirschboeck S.C., Milw., 1975-89, shareholder, 1981-89; ptnr. Foley & Lardner, 1989—. Mem. ABA, State Bar of Wis. Assn., Milw. Bar Assn. (chmn. employee benefits sect. 1993-94), Greater Milw. Employee Benefit Coun., Wis. Retirement Plan Profls. (pres. 1987-88), Internat. Pension and Employee Benefits Lawyers Assn., Kiwanis, Phi Beta Kappa. Home: 3927 N Stowell Ave Milwaukee WI 53211-2461 Office: Foley & Lardner Ste 3800 777 E Wisc Ave Milwaukee WI 53202 E-mail: hkurtz@foleylaw.com.

KURTZ, SHELDON FRANCIS, lawyer, educator; b. Syracuse, N.Y., May 18, 1943; s. Abraham Kurtz and Rosalyn (Bronstein) Stern; m. Alice Kaufman, June 22, 1968; children: Andrea, Emily. AB, Syracuse U., 1964, JD, 1967. Bar: N.Y. 1967, Iowa 1973. Assoc. Nixon, Mudge, Guthrie, Alexander & Mitchell, N.Y.C., 1967-69, Cleary, Gottlieb, Steen & Hamilton, N.Y.C., 1970-73; prof. U. Iowa Coll. Law, Iowa City, 1973-89, U. Va. Sch. Law, Charlottesville, 1979-80; dean Coll. Law, Fla. State U., Tallahassee, 1989-91; prof. Coll. Law U. Iowa, Iowa City, 1991—, prof. Coll. Med. Author: Kurtz on Iowa Estates, 3 vols., 1981, 2d edit., 2 vols., 1989, Problems, Cases and Materials on Family Estate Planning, 1983, (with Hood and Shors) Estate Planning for Shareholders of a Closely Held Corporation, 2 vols. and supplement, 1986, (with Hovenkamp) American Property Law, 1987, 3d edit., 1999, (with McGovern) Wills, Trusts and Estates, 2d edit., 2001, (with Hovenkamp) The Law of Property, 2001 (with Moynihan) Introduction to the Law of Real Property, 3d edit., 2002; also articles. Recipient Burlington No. tchg. award U. Iowa, 1987, Michael J. Brody Disting. Svc. award, 2001. Mem. Iowa Bar Assn. (commr. Uniform State Laws), Am. Law Inst. Avocations: cooking, hiking. Office: U Iowa Coll Law Rm 446 Iowa City IA 52242 E-mail: sheldon-kurtz@uiowa.edu.

KURTZMAN, CLETUS PAUL, microbiologist, researcher; b. Mansfield, Ohio, July 19, 1938; s. Paul A. and Marjorie M. (Gartner) K.; m. Mary Ann Dombrink, Aug. 4, 1962; children: Mary, Mark, Michael. BS, Ohio U., 1960; MS, Purdue U., 1962; PhD, W.Va. U., 1967. Microbiologist Nat. Ctr. Agrl. Utilization Rsch./USDA, Peoria, Ill., 1967-85, rsch. leader, 1985—. U.S. rep. Internat. Commn. on Yeasts, 1980—, World Fedn. Culture Collections, 1988—. Editor: Yeasts in Biotechnology, 1988, The Yeasts, A Taxonomic Study, 4th edit., 1998; contbr. papers to sci. jours. 1st lt. U.S. Army, 1962-64. Named Midwest Area Outstanding Scientist USDA, 1986; recipient Medal of Merit award Ohio U., 1992. Fellow Am. Acad. Microbiology; mem. AAAS, Internat. Mycol. Assn. (sec.-gen. 1990-94, v.p. 1994—), Mycol. Soc. Am., Am. Soc. Microbiology (divsn. chair 1991-92, J. Roger Porter award 1990), U.S. Fedn. Culture Collections (pres. 1976-78), Soc. Gen. Microbiology. Achievements include patent for Xylose Fermentation in Yeasts; research in the correlation of DNA relatedness and fertility in yeasts, correlation of ribosomal RNA divergence. Office: Nat Ctr Agrl Utilization Rsch 1815 N University St Peoria IL 61604-3902

KUSHNER, JEFFREY L. manufacturing company executive; b. Wilmington, Del., Apr. 7, 1948; s. William and Selma (Kreger) K.; m. Carolyn Patricia Hypes, May 2, 1975; children: Tawnya Lynne. BBA summa cum laude, U. Hawaii, 1970; MBA, Columbia U., 1972. Sr. fin. analyst Black & Decker, Towson, Md., 1972-73, div. controller Solon, Ohio, 1973-74; asst. div. controller Rockwell Internat., Pitts., 1974-75; div. contr. Carborundum Corp., Niagara Falls, N.Y., 1975-77; mgr. fin. planning United Techs. Corp., Hartford, Conn., 1977-80, corp. v.p. fin. planning, 1986-88, corp. v.p. asset mgmt., 1989-92; asst. contr. Sikorsky Aircraft, Stratford, 1980-82, div. controller, 1982-83, v.p. fin., chief fin. officer, 1983-85; v.p. fin. and adminstrn. MasterBrand Industries Inc., Deerfield, Ill., 1993-98; sr. v.p. fin. and CFO Lorillard Tobacco Co., 1998; exec. v.p., CFO Cookson Electronics, 1999—. Bd. dirs. ACR, Hartford. 1987-88. Recipient Bronfman Found. fellowship, 1970-71. Mem. Conf. Bd. (coun. 1987-88), Fin. Execs. Inst. Home: 195 Woodland Rd Westwood MA 02090-2631 E-mail: jeffkushner@hotmail.com.

KUSHNER, MARK JAY, physics and engineering educator; b. L.A., Dec. 21, 1952; s. Leonard Harry and Muriel (Chelin) K. BA, BS, UCLA, 1976; MS, Calif. Inst. Tech., 1977, PhD, 1979. Postdoctoral Calif. Inst. Tech., Pasadena, 1979-80; physicist Sandia Nat. Labs, Albuquerque, 1980-81, Lawrence Livermore (Calif.) Nat. Labs, 1981-83; dir. electron, atomic and molecular physics Spectra Tech., Bellevue, Wash., 1983-86; prof., Founder prof. engring. U. Ill., Urbana, 1986—. Chairperson Gaseous Electronics Conf., 1996-98. Assoc. editor Transactions Plasma Sci., 1989—; editl. bd. Plasma Sources Sci. and Tech., 1991—, Jour. Vacuum Sci. & Tech. A, 1998—; contbr. over 170 articles to tech. jours. Fellow IEEE (Plasma Sci. and Applications award 2000), Am. Phys. Soc., Optical Soc. Am., Am. Vacuum Soc. (Plasma Sci. and Tech. award 1999); mem. Materials Rsch. Soc., Nat. Rsch. Coun.-Plasma Sci. Com., 1998—. Office: U Ill 1406 W Green St Urbana IL 61801-2918 E-mail: mjk@uiuc.edu.

KUTA, JEFFREY THEODORE, lawyer; b. Oak Park, Ill., Aug. 30, 1947; s. Stanley Joseph and Helen Mary (Terpin) K.; m. Diane LaVerne Jancovic, June 22, 1969; children: Jonathan Paul, Joseph Anthony. BA with honors, U. Chgo., 1969, JD, 1972. Bar: Ill. 1972, U.S. Dist. Ct. (no. dist.) Ill. 1972. Assoc. Hopkins & Sutter, Chgo., 1972-76; assoc. to ptnr. Newman, Stahl & Shadur, 1976-80; ptnr. Holleb & Coff, 1981—. Instr. Chgo. Kent Coll. Law, 1978-79; adj. prof. John Marshall Law Sch., 1996—. Sec. Chgo. Equity Fund, Inc., 1985—; sec. Nat. Equity Fund, Inc., 1987-89, sec. Cmty. Reinvestment Fund, Inc., 1997—. Mng. editor U. Chgo. Law Rev., 1971-72. Mem. ABA (mem. spl. com. on housing and urban devel. law 1987-91, editor ABA Jour. Affordable Housing and Cmty. Devel. Law 1991-93, mem. governing com. of forum on affordable housing and cmty. devel. law 1992-95, chmn. 1993-94), Chgo. Bar Assn. (chmn. mag. 1982-83), Chgo. Coun. Lawyers, U. Chgo. Alumni Assn. (v.p. 1973-76, chmn. law jour. 1973-76), Cliff Dwellers Club, Lambda Alpha Internat. Home: 442 W Melrose St Chicago IL 60657-3834 Office: Holleb & Coff 55 E Monroe St Ste 4100 Chicago IL 60603-5896

KUTLER, STANLEY IRA, history and law educator, author; b. Cleve., Aug. 10, 1934; s. Robert P. and Zelda R. (Coffman) K.; m. Sandra J. Sachs, June 24, 1956; children: Jeffrey, David, Susan, Andrew. BA, Bowling Green State U., 1956; PhD, Ohio State U., 1960. Instr. history Pa. State U., State College, 1960-62; asst. prof. San Diego State U., 1962-64; from asst. prof. to prof. U. Wis., Madison, 1964-80, E. Gordon Fox prof. Am. instns., law and history, 1980—. Disting. exchange scholar to China Nat. Acad. Scis., 1982; Kenneth Keating lectr. Tel Aviv U., 1984; sr. Fulbright lectr. to Japan, 1977, to Israel, 1985, China, 1986; disting. vis. Fulbright scholar, Peru, 1987; Bicentennial prof. Tel Aviv U., 1985; cons. NEH, 1975—, The Constitution Project, 1985—; disting. chair Polit. Sci., U. Bologna, 1991; hist. cons. BBC/Discovery series Watergate, 1994. Author: Judicial Power and Reconstruction, 1968, Privilege and Creative Destruction, 1971, 2d edit., 1990, The American Inquisition, 1983, The Wars of Watergate: The Last Crisis of Richard Nixon, 1990, 92, Abuse of Power: The New Nixon Tapes, 1997; editor: Supreme Court and the Constitution, 1969, 3d edit., 1984, Looking for America, 1975, 80, The Encyclopedia of the Vietnam War, 1995, Encyclopedia of 20th Century America, 1995, American Perspectives: Historians on Historians, 1996, Watergate: The Fall of Richards Nixon, 1996, Dictionary of American History, 10 vols., 1996—; founding editor Rev. in Am. History, 1972-97; mem. adv. editor Greenwood Pub., 1968-73, Johns Hopkins U. Press, 1982—. Recipient Silver Gavel award ABA; fellow Sage Found., 1967-68, Emmy award, 1994, Peabody award, 1994, Best Reference Work award, Am. Assn. Pubs., 1996; fellow Guggenheim Found., 1971-72, Rockefeller Found., 1979-80. Jewish. Office: U Wis Dept History Madison WI 53706

KUTZ, KENNETH L. district attorney; b. Hibbing, Minn., Oct. 20, 1953; s. Leroy Dennis and Rosemary Helen (Marold) K.; m. Mary Patricia McConnell, July 18, 1981; children: Brian, Sean, Brendan. BA, U. Minn., Duluth, 1976; JD, Marquette U. Law Sch., Milw., 1979. Bar: Wis. 1979, U.S. Dist. Ct. (ea. dist., we. dist.) Wis. 1979. Assoc. atty. Sorenson Law Office, Ripon, Wis., 1979-83; asst. dist. atty. Burnett Cty. Dist. Atty., Siren, 1983-86, dist. atty., 1987—. Mem., past chmn. Burnett Cty. Dem. Party, Siren, 1983—; dir. Cmty. Referral Agy., Milltown, 1986-90;, bd. pres., dir. Burnett Med. Ctr., Grantsburg, Wis., 1993—. Recipient Integrity award U.S. Inspector Gen's. Office, Chgo., 1993. Mem. Wis. Bar Assn., Wis. Dist. Atty's. Assn. Democrat. Roman Catholic. Home: PO Box 231 Grantsburg WI 54840-0231 Office: Burnett Cty Dist Atty 7410 County Road K Ste 113 Siren WI 54872-9067

KUWAYAMA, S. PAUL, physician, allergist, immunologist; b. Sapporo, Hokkaido, Japan, Nov. 8, 1932; s. Satoru and Chiyoko (Nishikawa) K.; m. Barbara Ann Dresback, June 29, 1974; children: David, Steven, Jason. BS, Hokkaido U., Sapporo, 1955, MD, 1959. Diplomate Am. Bd. Pediatrics, 1965, Am. Bd. Allergy & Immunology, 1972, Am. Bd. Pediatric Allergy, 1970; lic. Nat. Bd. Med. Examiners of Japan, 1960, Wis. State Bd. Med. Examiners, 1968, Ariz. State Bd. Med. Examiners, 1987, N.Mex. State Bd. Med. Examiners, 1987, Tenn. State Bd. Med. Examiners, 1992. Intern U.S. Naval Hosp., Seattle, 1959-60, St. Mary's Hosp., Milw., 1960-61; jr. resident in pediatrics Temple U. Sch. of Medicine, Phila., 1961-62; chief pediat. resident W.Va. U. Sch. of Medicine, Morgantown, 1962-63; postdoctoral fellow in immunology, jr. fellow in pediatric allergy The Children's Mercy Hosp.-U. Kans. Sch. of Medicine, Kansas City, 1964-65; staff pediatrician Atomic Bomb Casualty Commn. in Hiroshima, U.S. Nat. Acad. of Scis.-U.S. Atomic Energy Commn., 1966-67; sr. pediatric allergist, dept. immunobiology U. Kans. Sch. of Medicine, 1967-68. Asst. clin. prof. pediatric allergy and immunology Med. Coll. Wis., Milw., 1970—. Contbg. author texts and forward to books. Fulbright scholar, 1960-63. Fellow Am. Acad. Pediatrics (sect. on allergy and immunology), Am. Coll. Allergy, Asthma and Immunology, Am. Assn. Cert. Allergists, Am. Acad. Allergy, Asthma and Immunology, Am. Assn. Clin. Immunology and Allergy; mem. AMA, Fulbright Scholarship Grantee Alumni Assn., State Med. Soc. of Wis., Milw. Pediatric Soc. Office: 11035 W Forest Home Ave Hales Corners WI 53130-2541

KUZNESOF, ELIZABETH ANNE, history educator; BA, U. Wash., 1961, MA, 1968; PhD, U. Calif., Berkeley, 1976. Vis. prof. history U. Kans., Lawrence, 1976-77, asst. prof. history, 1977-80, assoc. prof., 1980-85, prof., 1985—, asst. prof. history, 1977-80, assoc. prof., 1981-87, prof., 1987—, dir. L.Am. Studies, 1992—. Author: Household Economy and Urban Development in Sao Paulo 1765 to 1836, 1986; guest editor, author Jour. Family History, 1985; contbr. articles to profl. jours. Numerous fellowships and grants NEH, 1980, 91, Social Sci. Rsch. Coun., 1991-92, Fulbright/S.Am. Today Grant, 1986, Fulbright Tchg. Rsch. Grant to Brazil, 1988; Tinker fellow, 1981-82; John Carter Brown Libr., Hall Found. for Humanities, 1985-86, Utah Eccles Fellowship, 1991-92. Office: Univ of Kansas Ctr Latin Am Studies Lawrence KS 66045-0001

KVALSETH, TARALD ODDVAR, mechanical engineer, educator; b. Brunkeberg, Telemark, Norway, Nov. 7, 1938; married; 3 children. B.S., U. Durham, King's Coll., Eng., 1963; M.S., U. Calif.-Berkeley, 1966, Ph.D., 1971. Research asst. engring. expt. sta. U. Colo., Boulder, 1963-64, teaching asst. dept. mech. engring.; mech. engr. Williams & Lane Inc., Berkeley, 1964-65; research asst. dept. indsl. engring. and ops. research U. Calif.-Berkeley, 1965-71, research fellow, 1973; asst. prof. Sch. Indsl. and Systems Engring. Ga. Inst. Tech., Atlanta, 1971-74; sr. lectr. indsl. mgmt. div. Norwegian Inst. Tech. U. Trondheim, 1974-79, head indsl. mgmt. div., 1975-79; assoc. prof. dept. mech. engring. U. Minn., Mpls., 1979-82, prof., 1982—. Guest worker NASA Ames Research Ctr., Calif., 1973; mem. organizing com. 1st Berkeley-Monterey Conf. Timespan, Pay and Discretionary Capacity, 1973; mem. steering com. Internat. Conf. Human Factors in Design and Op. Ships, Gothenburg, Sweden, 1977; mem. bd. Norwegian Ergonomics Com., 1977-80; gen. session chmn. Conf. Work Place Design and Work Environ. Problems, Trondheim, 1978 Author book chpts., articles, presentations, reports in field; editor text books; mem. editl. bd., reviewer for numerous profl. jours., patentee in field. Fellow AAAS; mem. IEEE, Inst. Indsl. Engrs. (sr.), Human Factors and Ergonomics Soc. (pres. upper Midwest chpt.), Nordic Ergonomics Soc. (coun. 1977-80), Internat. Ergonomics Assn. (gen. coun. 1977-80, v.p. 1982-85), Ergonomics Soc., Psychonomic Soc., Am. Psychol. Soc., Am. Statis. Assn., Sigma Xi. Lutheran. Home: 4980 Shady Island Cir Mound MN 55364 Office: U Minn Dept Mech Engring Minneapolis MN 55455 E-mail: kvals001@umn.edu.

KWAN, NESITA, newscaster; b. Canada; , U.S. BA English, U. Va. Reporter Sta. WINA-AM, Charlottesville, Va., 1986; anchor, reporter Sta. WDBJ-TV, Roanoke, 1987—90; co-anchor, reporter Sta. WVEC-TV, Norfolk, 1990—92; co-anchor weekend news Sta. KHOU-TV, Houston, 1992—94; co-anchor weekend evening edition NBC 5 Chgo. News, 1994, co-anchor weekday morning show, anchor late night news. Office: NBC 454 N Columbus Dr Chicago IL 60611*

KWON, OJOUNG, computer scientist, educator, consultant; b. Taegu, South Korea, Apr. 18, 1955; came to U.S., 1982; s. Hun Sul Kwon and Suk Han Kim; m. Myounghie Kim, July 4, 1986; children: Eunice M., Daniel M., Ruth C.M. BSEE, Yeungnam U., Taegu, South Korea, 1978, MSEE, 1982; MBA, N.H. Coll., 1985; PhD, U. Ala., Tuscaloosa, 1991. Instr. Yeungnam Jr. Coll. of Tech., Taegu, 1982; grad. asst. N.H. Coll., Manchester, 1983-85; systems analyst Info. Resource Group, Inc., Contoocook, N.H., 1985; rsch. asst. Ala. Productivity Ctr. U. Ala., Tuscaloosa, 1989, rsch. asst. Artificial Intelligence Lab., 1985-90; asst. prof. mgmt. info. systems Univ. Ill. at Springfield, 1991-96, assoc. prof. mgmt. info. sys., 1996—. Contbr. articles to profl. jours. and procs. With Korean Army, 1978-80. Recipient Competitive Scholarly Rsch. award, 1992, 93, 95, 96, 97, 98; U. Ala. Grad. Coun. rsch. fellow, 1988, Disting. Achievement award U. Ill., Springfield, 1993. Mem. Decision Sci. Inst., Korean Scientists and Engrs. Assn., Am. Assn. for Artificial Intelligence, Soc. of Computer Simulation, Internat. Assn. Knowledge Engrs., Inst. Mgmt. Sci., Beta Gamma Sigma, Mu Sigma Rho. Avocations: table tennis, tennis, audio systems, classical music. Office: Univ Ill Springfield Dept MIS L-109 Springfield IL 62794-9243

KWONG, EVA, artist, educator; b. Hong Kong, Feb. 9, 1954; came to the U.S., 1967; d. Tony and Ivory K.; m. Kirk S. Mangus, 1976; children: Una K., Jasper M. BFA, RISD, 1975; MFA, Tyler Sch. Art/Temple U., Phila., 1977. Vis. artist, 1977—; vis. faculty Cleve. (Ohio) Inst. Art, 1982-83; part-time faculty U. Akron, Ohio, 1987, 89, 95, Kent (Ohio) State U., 1990—. Lectr. in field. Works in over 180 exhbns. Visual Arts Regional fellow Arts Midwest, Mpls., 1987, Visual Arts fellow Nat. Endowment for the Arts, Washington, 1988, Ohio Arts Coun., Columbus, 1988, 94, 99. Mem. Nat. Coun. on Edn. for the Ceramic Arts (dir.-at-large 1995-97). Office: Kent State Univ Art Dept Main St Kent OH 44242-0001

KYLE, RICHARD HOUSE, federal judge; b. St. Paul, Apr. 30, 1937; s. Richard E. and Geraldine (House) K.; m. Jane Foley, Dec. 22, 1959; children: Richard H. Jr., Michael F., D'Arcy, Patrick G., Kathleen. BA, U. Minn., 1959, LLB, 1962. Bar: Minn. 1962, U.S. Dist. Ct. Minn. 1992. Atty. Briggs & Morgan, St. Paul, 1963-68, 1970-92; solicitor gen. Minn. Atty. Gen. Office, 1968-70; judge U.S. Dist. Ct., 1992—. Pres. Minn. Law Rev., Mpls., 1962. Mem. Minn. State Bar Assn., Ramsey County Bar Assn. Republican. Episcopal. Office: US Dist Ct Federal Courts Bldg 316 Robert St N Saint Paul MN 55101-1495

KYLE, ROBERT ARTHUR, medical educator, oncologist; b. Bottineau, N.D., Mar. 17, 1928; s. Arthur Nichol and Mabel Caroline (Crandall) K.; m. Charlene Mae Showalter, Sept. 11, 1954; children: John, Mary, Barbara, Jean. AA, N.D Sch. Forestry, 1946; BS, U. N.D., 1948; MD, Northwestern U., 1952; MS, U. Minn., 1958. Diplomate Am. Bd. Internal Medicine; subsplty. Hematology. Fellow Mayo Grad. Sch., Rochester, Minn., 1953-59; clin. asst. Tufts U. Sch. Medicine, Boston, 1960-61; cons. internal medicine Mayo Clinic, Rochester, 1961—; prof. medicine and lab. medicine Mayo Med. Sch., 1975—. Pres. med. subjects unit Am. Topical Assn., Johnstown, Pa., 1976-81; chmn. standards, ethics and peer rev. orgn. Cancer & Acute Leukemia Group B, Scarsdale, N.Y., 1978-82; Robert A. Hettig lectr. in hematology Baylor U. Coll. of Medicine, Houston, 1984; Waldenström lectr., Stockholm, 1988; Redlich Meml. lectr Cedars-Sinai Med. Ctr., U. Calif., L.A.; vis. prof. St. Elizabeth's Med. Ctr., Tufts U. Sch. Medicine, Boston, 1998; bd. dirs. Waldenstrom's Macroglobulinemia Support Group. Author: The Monoclonal Gammopathies, 1976, Medicine and Stamps, vols. 1 and 2, 1980; author/editor: Neoplastic Disease of the Blood, 3rd edit., Myeloma: Biology and Management, 1995, 2nd edit. 1998. Chmn. bd. trustees First Presbyn. Ch., Rochester, Minn., 1967; chmn. Rochester Med. Ctr. Ministry, 1979-86. Capt. USAF, 1955-57. Named Disting. Topicl Philatelest, Am. Topical Soc., 1982; Recipient Waldenström award Internat. Workshop for Myeloma, Italy, 1991, Henry S. Plummer Distinguished Internist award Mayo Clin., 1995, Mayo Distinguished Clinician award 1996, Sioux award U. N.D., 1998; Bruce Wiseman lectr. Ohio State U., 1991, Kauffman Meml. lectr. Meml. Sloan Kettering Med. Ctr., N.Y.C., 1997; Clement Finch prof. U. Wash., 1993. Master ACP; mem. N.Y. Acad. Scis., Am. Soc. Hematology, Internat. Soc. Hematology (sec.-gen. Inter-Am. divsn. 1990), Am. Assn. Cancer Rsch., Internat. Myeloma Found. (chmn. scientific adv. bd. 1995), Phi Beta Kappa. Republican. Avocation: philately. Home: 1207 6th St SW Rochester MN

55902-1918 Office: Mayo Clinic 200 1st St SW Rochester MN 55905-0002 also: 920 Hilton Rochester MN 55905-0001

KYLE, ROBERT CAMPBELL, II, publishing executive; b. Cleve., Jan. 6, 1935; s. Charles Donald and Mary Alice (King) K.; children: Peter F., Kit C., Scott G. BS, U. Colo., 1956; MA, Case Western Res. U., 1958; MBA, Harvard U., 1963, DBA, 1966. Ptnr. McLagan & Co., Chgo., 1966-67; founder, pres. Devel. Sys. Corp. (subs. Longman Group USA), 1967-82; pres. Longman Group USA, 1982-89; chmn., CEO Dearborn Pub. Group, Inc. (formerly Longman Group USA), 1989-98. Chmn. CTS Fin. Pub., 1997-2000. Author: Property Management, 1979; co-author: Modern Real Estate Practice, 1967, How to Profit From Real Estate, 1988 (Chgo. Book Clinic Lifetime Achievement award 1998). Mem. dean's adv. coun. Coll. Bus. U. Colo., 1992-98, Ctr. for Entrepreneurship Adv. Bd., U. Colo., 1996—; trustee Mystic Seaport Mus., 1989—, exec. com., 1999—; dir. Chgo. Maritime Soc., pres. 1999-2000. Mem. Real Estate Educators Assn. (pres. 1981), Internat. Assn. Fin. Planning, Chgo. Book Clinic (dir.), Harvard Club N.Y., Econs. Club, Chgo. Yacht Club, San Diego Yacht Club, N.Y. Yacht Club. Avocations: yacht racing, tennis. Home: 2910 Owens St San Diego CA 92106 E-mail: rckyle@aol.com.

LABAN, MYRON MILES, physician, administrator; b. Detroit, Mar. 9, 1936; s. Larry Max and Mary Marsha (Harris) LaB.; m. Rita Joyce Hochman, Aug. 17, 1958; children: Terry, Amy, Craig B.A., U. Mich., Ann Arbor, 1957, M.D., 1967; M.Med. Sci., Ohio State U., Columbus, 1965. Diplomate Am. Bd. Phys. Medicine and Rehab. Intern Sinai Hosp., Detroit, 1961-62; resident Ohio State U. Hosp., 1962-65; assoc. dir. phys. medicine and rehab. Letterman Gen. Hosp., San Francisco, 1965-67; dir. phys. medicine and rehab. William Beaumont Hosp., Royal Oak, Mich., 1967—; Licht lecturer Ohio State U., 1986, clin. prof., 1993. Clin. prof. Wayne State U., Detroit, 1990, clin. prof. Oakland U., Rochester, Mich., 1983, Ohio State U., Columbus, 1992; bd. dirs. Oakland County Med. Bd., Birmingham, Mich., 1982-87; rep. to Commn. on Phys. Medicine and Rehab., Mich. State Med. Soc. Contbr. chpts. in books, articles to profl. publs. Med. dir. Oakland County March of Dimes, Mich., 1969-83. Served to capt. U.S. Army, 1965-67 Fellow Am. Acad. Phys. Medicine and Rehab. (bd. dirs. 1980, pres. 1985-86, Bernard Baruch Rsch. award 1961, R. Rosenthal Rsch. award 1982, Zeiter lectureship, Disting. Clinician award 1991, "Top Doc" PM&R Detroit Monthly 1993, 96, Frank H. Krusen award 1997); mem. AMA, Am. Congress Rehab. Medicine, Am. Assn. Electromyography and Electrodiagnosis (program dir. 1972), Oakland County Med. Soc. (treas. 1983, pres.-elect 1987, pres. 1988-89), Mich. State Med. Soc., Mich. Acad. Phys. Med. and Rehab. (pres. 1982-84, jud. commr. 1991-95, mem. editl. bd. Jour. Phys. Med. and Rehab.). Republican. Jewish Avocations: gardening; ship modeling. Office: LMT Rehabilitation Assocs 3535 W 13 Mile Rd Rm 703 Royal Oak MI 48073-6710 E-mail: myjoy@comcast.net.

LABSVIRS, JANIS, economist, educator; b. Bilska, Latvia, Mar. 13, 1907; s. Karlis and Kristina L.; Mag.Oec., Latvian State U., 1930; MS, Butler U., 1956; PhD, Ind. U., 1959; Dr. hist. (hon.), Latvian Acad. Scis., 1994. Tchr., Latvia, 1930-36; dir. dept. edn. Fedn. Latvian Trade Unions, 1936-37; v.p. Kr. Baron's U., Extension, Riga, Latvia, 1938-40, also exec. v.p. Filma, Inc., 1939-40; with UNRRA and Internat. Refugee Orgn., Esslingen, Germany, 1945-50; asst. prof. econs. Ind. State U., Terre Haute, 1959-62, assoc. prof., 1963-68, prof., 1969-73, prof. emeritus, 1973—; head dept. pub. and social affairs Latvian Ministry for Social Affairs, 1938-40; dir. Sch. of Commerce and Gymnasium, Tukums, Latvia, 1941-44. Danforth grantee, 1961; Ind. State U. research grantee, 1966; Mem. Am. Latvian Assn., Am. Assn. Advancement Slavic Studies, Assn. Advancement Baltic Studies, Am. Econ. Assn., Royal Econ. Soc. Lutheran. Author: Local Government's Accounting and Management Practices, 1947, 2d edit. 1992; A Case Study in the Sovietization of the Baltic States: Collectivization of Latvian Agriculture 1944-1956, 1959, 2d & 3d edit., 1988, 4th edit. 1989; Atminas un Pardomas, 1984, reprinted in Latvia, 3d edit., 1993, Kurp Ejam ?, 1996, reprinted in Latvia, 1997; Karlis Ulmanis, 1987, reprinted in Latvia, 2d edit., 1991, Kam Drosme Ir, 1990, reprinted in Latvia, 5th edit., 1992; contbr. articles profl. jours. Recipient Triju Zvaigznu Ordenis highest civilan medal President of Latvia, 1995. Home: 2617 Bridgeview Way Apt 1A Indianapolis IN 46220-1438

LABUDDE, ROY CHRISTIAN, lawyer; b. Milw., July 21, 1921; s. Roy Lewis and Thea (Otteson) LaB.; m. Anne P. Held, June 7, 1952; children: Jack, Peter, Michael, Susan, Sarah. AB, Carleton Coll., 1943; JD, Harvard U., 1949. Bar: Wis. 1949, U.S. Dist. Ct. (ea. and we. dists.) Wis. 1950, U.S. Ct. Appeals (7th cir.) 1950, U.S. Supreme Ct. 1957. Assoc. Michael, Best & Friedrich, Milw., 1949-57, ptnr., 1958—. Dir. DEC-Inter, Inc., Aunt Nellie's Farm Kitchens, Inc. Bd. dirs. Wis. Hist. Soc. Found.; chmn., bd. dirs. Milw. div. Am. Cancer Soc. Served to lt. j.g. USNR, 1943-46. Mem. Milw. Estate Planning Coun. (past pres.), Wis. Bar Assn., Wis. State Bar Attys. (chmn. tax sch., bd. dirs. taxation sect.), Univ. Club, Milw. Club, Milw. Country Club. Republican. Episcopalian. Home: 4201 W Stonefield Rd Mequon WI 53092-2771 Office: Michael Best & Friedrich 100 E Wisconsin Ave Ste 3300 Milwaukee WI 53202-4108

LACEY, GARY EUGENE, lawyer; b. Scottsbluff, Nebr., Oct. 2, 1942; s. Harold Kenneth and Chelsa (Hiatt) L.; m. Carol Leitschuck, June 6, 1965 (div. Nov. 1992); children: David, Anne; m. Janet England, July, 1993. BA, U. Nebr., 1965, JD, 1971. Bar: Nebr. 1972, U.S. Dist. Ct. Nebr. 1972, U.S. Ct. Appeals (8th cir.) 1980. Econ. reporter So. Ill., Carbondale, 1965-66; staff atty. Centel Corp., Lincoln, Nebr., 1971-75; dep. county atty. Lancaster County, 1975-90, county atty., 1991—. Prosecutor Lancaster County, Lincoln, 1990—; bd. dirs. YMCA, Lincoln, 1989—. 1st lt. U.S. Army, 1967-69. Mem. Nebr. County Atty. Assn. (bd. dirs. 1985—), Nebr. Bar Assn. (Ho. of Dels. 1986-90), Univ. Club, Shriners, Masons. Republican. Methodist. Avocations: reading, writing, politics, cooking. Office: Lancaster County Atty 555 S 10th St Lincoln NE 68508-2810

LACH, JOSEPH THEODORE, physicist; b. Chgo., May 12, 1934; s. Joseph and Kate (Ziemba) L.; m. Barbara Ryan, June 26, 1965; children—Michael, Elizabeth A.B., U. Chgo., 1953, M.S., 1956; Ph.D., U. Calif.-Berkeley, 1963. Rsch. assoc. in physics Yale U., New Haven, 1963-65, asst. prof. physics, 1966-69; physicist Fermi Nat. Accelerator Lab., Batavia, Ill, 1969—, chmn. dept. physics, 1974-75; chmn. Gordon Rsch. Conf. in Elem. Particle Physics, 1975. Mem. joint rsch. program with USSR and People's Republic of China. Fellow Am. Phys. Soc., Physicians for Social Responsibility, Ill. Geol. Survey (rsch. affiliate). Home: 28w364 Indian Knoll Trl West Chicago IL 60185-3013 Office: Fermilab PO Box 500 Batavia IL 60510-0500 E-mail: lach@fnal.gov.

LA COUR, LOUIS BERNARD, lawyer; b. Columbus, Ohio, Aug. 12, 1926; s. Louis and Cleo (Carter) La C.; m. Jane Lee McFarland, Mar. 24, 1950; children: Lynne Denise, Avril Rose, Cheryl Celeste. BA, Ohio State U., 1951; LLB, Franklin U., 1961; JD, Capital U., Columbus, 1967. Bar: Ohio 1962. Land commr. U.S. Dist. Ct. (so. dist.) Ohio, Columbus, 1981, spl. master, 1983-87; spl. counsel City of Columbus Atty.'s Office, 1986—. Contbr. articles to profl. jours. Cons. NAACP, N.Y.C., 1975-80; mem. Greater Columbus Arts Coun., Model State Legis. Com.; sec. Mid-Ohio Regional Planning Commn., Columbus, 1978; vice-chmn. Columbus Civic Ctr. Commn., 1979; mem. rural zoning commn. Franklin County, 1994; mem. Ohio Elected Ofcls. Commn.; mem. Franklin Soil and Water Conservation Dist. Mem. ABA, Columbus Bar Assn., Am. Planning Assn. (task force), Ohio Elected Ofcls. Commn., New Albany C.C., Franklin Soil and Water Conservation, Sigma Pi Phi, Lambda Boulé. Democrat. Roman Catholic. Avocations: tennis, cooking, theatre, jazz. Home: 1809 N Cassady Ave Columbus OH 43219-1520 Office: 500 S Front St Ste 1140 Columbus OH 43215-7628

LACY, ALAN JASPER, retail executive; b. Cleveland, Tenn., Oct. 19, 1953; BSIM, Ga. Inst. Tech., 1975; MBA, Emory U., 1977. CFA. Fin. analyst Holiday Inns, Inc., Memphis, 1977-79; mgr. investor rels. Tiger Internat., L.A., 1979-80, Dart Industries, L.A., 1980-81; dir. corp. fin. Dart & Kraft, Northbrook, Ill., 1981-82, asst. treas., 1982-83, treas., v.p., 1984-86, v.p. fin. and adminstrn. internat., 1987-88; v.p., treas., CFO Minnetonka Corp., Bloomington, Minn., 1988-89; sr. v.p. strategy and devel. Kraft Gen. Foods, Glenview, Ill., 1989-90, sr. v.p. fin., 1990-92, sr. v.p. fin., strategy, sys., 1992-93; v.p. fin. svcs. and sys. Philip Morris Cos., 1993-95; exec. v.p., CFO Sears, Roebuck & Co., 1995-97, pres., credit svcs., 1997-99, CEO, pres., chmn., 2000—. Mem. Econ. Club (Chgo.). Office: Sears Roebuck 3333 Beverly Rd Hoffman Estates IL 60179

LACY, ANDRE BALZ, industrial executive; b. Indpls., Sept. 12, 1939; s. Howard J. II and Edna B. (Balz) L.; m. Julia Lello, Feb. 23, 1963; children: John Andre, Mark William, Peter Lello. BA Econs., Denison U.; DEng (hon.), Rose-Hulman Inst. Various mgmt. positions U.S. Corrugated, Indpls., 1961-69, exec. v.p., 1969-72; exec. v.p., chief ops. officer Lacy Diversified Industries, 1972-78, chmn. bd. subs., 1973-78, pres., chief ops. officer, 1978-83; pres., chief exec. officer Lacy Diversified Industries, now LDI, Ltd., 1983—, chmn., 1992. Bd. dirs. Herff Jones, Inc., Indpls., Patterson Dental Co., Mpls., Finish Master, Inc., Nat. Bank Indpls. Mem. bd. mgrs. Rose-Hulman Inst., Terre Haute, Ind.; pres. Indpls. Bd. Sch. Commn., Indpls., 1985-86; hon. mem. 500 Festival Assocs., Inc., Indpls.; chmn. United Way Greater Indpls., 1989-91; bd. dirs. Hudson Inst., Indpls. Conv. and Visitors Assn., 1996; dir. Ctrl. Ind. Corp. Partnership, Indpls. Downtown, Inc. Mem. Nat. Assn. Wholesaler Distbrs. (dir.), Young Pres. Orgn., Ind. C. of C. (bd. dirs. 1989), Ind. Pres. Orgn., Kiwanis Club of Indpls., Skyline Club, Columbia Club, Meridian Hills Golf and Country Club (Indpls.), Lost Tree Club. Republican. Episcopalian. Avocation: sailing. Home: 450 E Vermont St Indianapolis IN 46202-3680 Office: LDI Ltd 54 Monument Cir Ste 800 Indianapolis IN 46204-2928

LACY, PAUL ESTON, pathologist; b. Trinway, Ohio, Feb. 7, 1924; s. Benjamin Lemmert and Amy Cass (Cox) Lacy; m. Emelyn Ellen Talbot, June 7, 1945; children: Paul Eston Jr., Steven T. BA cum laude, Ohio State U., 1945, MD cum laude, MSc in Anatomy, 1948; PhD in Pathology, U. Minn.-Mayo Found., 1955; Doctor of Medicine (honoris causa), Uppsala (Sweden) U., 1977. Asst. instr. anatomy Ohio State U., Columbus, 1944—48; intern White Cross Hosp., 1948—49; fellow in pathology Mayo Clinic, Rochester, Minn., 1951—55; postdoctoral fellow Washington U. Med. Sch., St. Louis, 1955—56, instr. pathology, 1956—57, asst. prof. pathology, 1957—61, asst. dean, 1959—61, assoc. prof. pathology, 1961, Mallinckrodt prof., chmn. dept. pathology, 1961—85, Robert L. Kroc prof. of pathology, 1985—95, prof. emeritus pathology, 1995—; pathologist-in-chief Barnes & Allied Hosps., 1985—95, pathologist, 1985—95, prof. emeritus pathology, 1995—. Capt. U.S. Army, 1949—51. Recipient Banting award, Brit. Diabetes Assn., 1963, Am. Diabetes Assn., 1970, 3M Life Scis. award, FASEB, 1981, Rous-Whipple award, Am. Assn. Pathologists, 1984. Fellow: Am. Acad. Arts and Sci., AAAS; mem.: Inst. of Medicine of NAS. Avocations: horticulture, literature. Office: Washington Univ Med Sch Dept of Pathology 660 S Euclid Ave Saint Louis MO 63110-1010

LADD, JEFFREY RAYMOND, lawyer; b. Mpls., Apr. 10, 1941; s. Jasper Raymond and Florence Marguerite (DeMarce) L.; m. Kathleen Anne Crosby, Aug. 24, 1963; children: Jeffrey Raymond, John Henry, Mark Jasper, Matthew Crosby. Student, U. Vienna, Austria; BA, Loras Coll.; postgrad., U. Denver; JD, Ill. Inst. Tech. Bar: Ill. 1973, U.S. Dist. Ct. 1973. V.p. mktg. Ladd Enterprises, Des Plaines, Ill., 1963-66, v.p. mktg. and fin. Crystal Lake, 1966-70; ptnr. Ross & Hardies, Chgo., 1973-81, Boodell, Sears, et al., 1981-86, Bell, Boyd & Lloyd, Chgo., 1986—. Spl. asst. atty. gen. for condemnation State of Ill., 1977-82; chmn. Metra, 1984—. Named Chgo. City Club's 1995 Citizen of Yr. Mem. ABA, Chgo. Bar Assn., Nat. Assn. Bond Lawyers, Ill. Assn. Hosp. Attys., Am. Acad. Hosp. Attys., Crystal Lake Jaycees (Disting. Svc. award), Crystal Lake C. of C. (past pres.), Econ. Club, Legal Club, Union League Club, Bull Valley Golf Club, Woodstock Country Club, Alpha Lambda. Roman Catholic. Avocations: golf, hunting, fishing, tennis, skiing. Office: Bell Boyd & Lloyd 3 First National Pla 70 W Madison St Ste 3300 Chicago IL 60602-4284

LADEHOFF, LEO WILLIAM, metal products manufacturing executive; b. Gladbrook, Iowa, May 4, 1932; s. Wendell Leo and Lillian A. L.; m. Beverly Joan Dreessen, Aug. 1, 1951; children: Debra K., Lance A. BS, U. Iowa, 1957. Supt. ops. Square D Co., 1957-61; mfg. mgr. Fed. Pacific Electric Co., 1961; v.p. ops. Avis Indsl. Corp., 1961-67; pres. energy products Group Gulf & Western Industries, Inc., 1967-78; chmn. bd., pres., chief exec. officer, dir. Amcast Indsl. Corp., Ohio, 1978-95, chmn. bd. dirs., 1995—97, 2001—. With USAF, 1951—54, Korea. Mem. Soc. Automotive Engrs., U. Iowa Alumni Assn., Forest Highlands Country Club, The Estancia Club. Republican. Home: 27276 N 103d Way Scottsdale AZ 85255 Office: Amcast Indsl Corp PO Box 98 Dayton OH 45401-0098 also: Elkhart Products Corp 1255 Oak St Elkhart IN 46514-2277 E-mail: lladehoff@aol.com.

LADISCH, MICHAEL R. biochemical engineering educator; b. Upper Darby, Pa., Jan. 15, 1950; s. Rolf Karl and Brigitte M. (Gareis) L.; m. christine Schmitz, July 26, 1975; children: Sarah, Mark. BSChemE, Drexel U., Phila., 1973; MSChemE, Purdue U., 1974, PhD in Chem. Engring., 1977. Rsch. engr. Lab. Renewable Resources Engring. and dept. chem. engring. Purdue U., West Lafayette, Ind., 1977-78, asst. prof. food and agrl. engring., 1978-81, assoc. prof., 1981-85, prof., 1985-2000, disting. prof., 2000—. Dir. Lab Renewable Resources, Eng., 1999—. Contbr. articles to profl. jours.; patentee in field. Chmn. com. on bioprocess engring. Nat. Rsch. Coun., 1991—. Recipient U.S. Presdl. Young Investigator award NSF, 1984. Fellow Am. Inst. Med. and Biol. Engrs.; mem. U.s. Nat. Acad. Engring., Am. Chem. Soc. (librarian 1982-84, chmn.-elect 1985—, program chmn. 1985-86, past chmn. 1986—, coord. long range program 1990—, Van Lanen award BIOT div. 1990, W.H. Peterson award Microbiol. div. 1977, Agrl. Rsch. award from Purdue U. 1985), Am. Inst. Chem. Engring., Am. Soc. Agrl. Engrs. Office: Purdue U LORRE West Lafayette IN 47907 E-mail: landisch@ecn.purdue.edu.

LA DU, BERT NICHOLS, JR. pharmacology educator, physician; b. Lansing, Mich., Nov. 13, 1920; s. Bert Nichols and Natalie (Kerr) La D.; m. Catherine Shilson, June 14, 1947; children: Elizabeth, Mary, Anne, Jane. B.S., Mich. State Coll., 1943; M.D., U. Mich., 1945; Ph.D. in Biochemistry, U. Calif., Berkeley, 1952. Intern Rochester (N.Y.) Gen. Hosp., 1945-46; research asso. N.Y.U. Research Service, Goldwater Meml. Hosp., N.Y.C., 1950-53; sr. asst. surgeon USPHS, Nat. Heart Inst., 1954-57; surgeon, later sr. surgeon, med. dir. Nat. Inst. Arthritis and Metabolic Disease, 1957-63; prof., chmn. dept. pharmacology N.Y.U. Med. Sch., 1963-74; prof. pharmacology U. Mich. Med. Sch., Ann Arbor, 1974-89, prof. emeritus, 1989—, chmn. dept., 1974-81. Contbr. articles to profl. jours. Served with AUS, 1943-45. Mem. AAAS, Am. Chem. Soc., N.Y. Acad. Sci. (pres.), Am. Soc. Biol. Chemistry, Am. Soc. Pharmacol. Therapeutics (pres.), Am. Soc. Human Genetics, Biochem. Soc. (Gt. Britain). Home: 505 E Huron St Apt 702 Ann Arbor MI 48104-1541 Office: U Mich Med Sch 7422 MSRB3 Ann Arbor MI 48109-0632 E-mail: bladu@umich.edu.

LADUKE, NANCIE, lawyer, corporate executive; b. Mayfield, Ky. m. Daniel E. LaDuke, 1978. BA, Wayne State U., 1962; JD, U. Detroit, 1976. Pvt. practice, Detroit, 1976; atty. Kmart Corp., Troy, Mich., 1977-84, comml. law counsel, 1984-90, v.p., sec., 1991-2001; ret. Office: Kmart Corp 3100 W Big Beaver Rd Troy MI 48084-3163

LADWIG, BONNIE L. state legislator; b. Dec. 11, 1939; married. Student, U. Wis. Mem. from dist. 63 Wis. State Assembly, Madison, 1992—. Mem. Racine County and Coastal Mgmt. Coun.; mem. County Human Svc. Bd., past chmn. Office: 6437 Norfolk Ln Racine WI 53406-1859

LAESSIG, RONALD HAROLD, preventive medicine and pathology educator, state official; b. Marshfield, Wis., Apr. 4, 1940; s. Harold John and Ella Louise L.; m. Joan Margaret Spreda, Jan. 29, 1966; 1 child, Elizabeth Susan. BS, U. Wis., Stevens Point, 1962; PhD, U. Wis., 1965. Jr. faculty Princeton (N.J.) U., 1966; chief clin. chemistry Wis. State Lab. Hygiene, Madison, 1966-80, dir., 1980—; asst. prof. preventive medicine U. Wis., 1966-72, assoc. prof., 1972-76, prof., 1976—, prof. pathology, 1980—. Cons. Ctr. Disease Control, Atlanta; dir. Nat. Com. for Clin. Lab. Stds., Villanova, Pa., 1977-80; chmn. invitro diagnostic products adv. com. FDA, 1974-75; mem. rev. com. Nat. Bur. Stds., 1983-86 Mem. editl. bd. Med. Electronics, 1970—, Analytical Chemistry, 1970-76, Health Lab. Sci., 1970—; contbr. articles to profl. jours. Mem. State of Wis. Tech. Com. Alcohol and Traffic Safety, 1970-88. Sloan Found. grantee, 1966; recipient numerous grants Mem. APHA (Difco award 1974), Am. Assn. Clin. Chemistry (chmn. safety com. 1984-86, bd. dirs. 1986-89, Natelson award 1989, Contbns. Svc. to Profession award 1990, Reiner award 1998, Eiler award 1999), Am. Soc. for Med. Tech., Nat. Com. Clin. Lab. Stds. (pres. 1980-82, bd. dirs. 1984-87), Sigma Xi Avocation: woodworking. Office: State Lab Hygiene 465 Henry Mall Madison WI 53706-1578 E-mail: rhl@mail.slh.wisc.edu.

LAFAVE, ARTHUR J., JR. financial executive, lawyer; b. Cleve., Mar. 28, 1933; s. Arthur J. and Florence (Carr) L.; m. Carolyn Bone; children: Arthur III, Charles, Lisa, Anne, William, Evelyn. BA, Williams Coll., 1955; LLB, Yale U., 1958. Bar: Ohio. Assoc. Black & Apicella, Portland, Oreg., 1958-60, Arter & Hamen, Cleve., 1960-62; sr. group v.p., CFO Internat. Mgmt. Group, 1982—. Home: 19900 Shaker Blvd Cleveland OH 44122-1871 Office: Internat Mgmt Group IMG Center 1360 E 9th St Ste 100 Cleveland OH 44114

LAFAVE, JOHN, state legislator; Mem. Wis. St. Assembly, 1993—. Address: 7237 W Wabash Ave Milwaukee WI 53223-2608

LAFLEY, ALAN G. consumer products company executive; b. Keene, N.H., June 13, 1947; AB, Hamilton Coll., 1969; MBA, Harvard Bus. Sch., 1977. Brand asst. Joy Procter & Gamble, 1977-78, sales tng. Denver Sales Dist., 1978-80, asst. brand mgr. Tide, 1978-80, brand mgr. Dawn & Ivory Snow, 1980-81, brand mgr. spl. assignment and Ivory Snow, 1981-82, brand mgr. Cheer, 1982-83, assoc. advt. mgr. PS&D Divsn. to advt. mgr., 1983-86, 86-88, gen. mgr. laundry products PS&D Divsn., 1988-91, v.p. laundry and cleaning products, 1991-92, group v.p., pres. laundry and cleaning products, 1992-94, group v.p., pres. Far East Divsn., 1994-95, exec. v.p., pres. Asia Divsn., 1995-98, exec. v.p., pres. N.Am. Divsn., 1998-99, pres. Global Beauty Care and North Am., 1999-2000; pres. & CEO Proctor & Gamble, 2000—. Trustee Hamilton Coll., Cin. Playhouse in the Park, Cin. Symphony Orchestra, Cin. Inst. of Fine Arts, The Seven Hills Sch.; past mem. Am. C. of C. in Japan, adv. coun. Schulich Sch. of Bus., York U., Toronto. With USN, 1970-75. Mem. Hamilton Club of So. Ohio, Harvard Club of Cin., Met. Club, Commonwealth Club of Cin. Office: The Proctor & Gamble Co 1 Procter And Gamble Plz Cincinnati OH 45202-3315

LA FOLLETTE, DOUGLAS J. secretary of state; b. Des Moines, June 6, 1940; s. Joseph Henry and Frances (Van der Wilt) LaF. B.S., Marietta Coll., 1963; M.S., Stanford U., 1964; Ph.D., Columbia U., 1967. Asst. prof. chemistry and ecology U. Wis.-Parkside, 1969-72; mem. Wis. Senate, 1973-75; sec. state State of Wis., Madison, 1975-79, 83—. Author: Wisconsin's Survival Handbook, 1971, The Survival Handbook, 1991. Mem. Council Econ. Priorities; mem. Lake Michigan Fed., Wis. Environ. Decade, 1971, S.E. Wis. Coalition for Clean Air, Dem. candidate for U.S. Congress, 1970, for Wis. lt. gov., 1978, for U.S. Senate, 1988. Recipient Environ. Quality EPA, 1976 Mem. Am. Fedn. Tchrs., Fedn. Am. Scientists, Phi Beta Kappa Office: Office Sec State of Wis PO Box 7848 Madison WI 53707-7848

LAFORGE, EDWARD, state legislator; b. Nov. 22, 1935; Grad., Bronson Hosp. Sch. Nursing. Rep. Mich. State Dist. 60, 1995—. Minority vice chair Family and Children Svcs., Agrl. and Resource Mgmt., Employment Rels., Tng. and Safety. Address: PO Box 30014 Lansing MI 48909-7514

LAGALLY, MAX GUNTER, physics educator; b. Darmstadt, Germany, May 23, 1942; came to U.S., 1953, naturalized, 1960; s. Paul and Herta (Rudow) L.; m. Shelley Meserow, Feb. 15, 1969; children: Eric, Douglas, Karsten BS in Physics, Pa. State U., 1963; MS in Physics, U. Wis.-Madison, 1965, PhD in Physics, 1968. Registered profl. engr., Wis. Instr. physics U. Wis., Madison, 1970-71, asst. prof. materials sci., 1971-74, assoc. prof., 1974-77, prof. materials sci. and physics, 1977—, dir. thin-film deposition and applications ctr., 1982-93, John Bascom Prof. materials sci., 1986—, E.W. Mueller Prof. materials sci. and physics, 1993—. Gordon Godfrey vis. prof. physics, U. New South Wales, Sydney, Australia, 1987; cons. in thin films, 1977—; vis. scientist Sandia Nat. Lab., Albuquerque, 1975; pres. Piezomax Techs., Inc., 1997—. Editor: Kinetics of Ordering and Growth at Surfaces, 1990, (with others) Methods of Experimental Physics, 1985, Evolution of Surface and Thin-Film Microstructure, 1993, Morphological Organization in Epitaxial Growth and Removal, 1998; mem. editorial bd., also editor spl. issue Jour. Vacuum Sci. and Tech., 1978-81; prin. editor Jour. Materials Rsch., 1990-93; mem. editorial bd. Surface Sci., 1994-2001, Revs. Sci. Instruments, 1997-2000, Diffusion and Defect Data, 1997—; contbr. articles to profl. jours.; patentee in field. Max Planck Gesellschaft fellow, 1968, Alfred P. Sloan Found. fellow, 1972, H.I. Romnes fellow, 1976, Humboldt Sr. Rsch. fellow, 1992, 93; grantee fed. agys. and industry; recipient Outstanding Sci. Alumnus award Pa. State U., 1996. Fellow AAAS, Am. Phys. Soc. (D. Adler award 1994, Davisson-Germer prize 1995), Australian Inst. Physics, Am. Vacuum Soc. (M.W. Welch prize 1991, trustee 1995-97); mem. Materials Rsch. Soc. (medal 1994), Leopoldina-German Acad. Scis., Nat. Acad. Engring. Home: 5110 Juneau Rd Madison WI 53705-4744 Office: U Wis Materials Sci & Engring 1509 University Ave Madison WI 53706-1538 E-mail: lagally@engr.wisc.edu., lagally@piezomax.com.

LAGARDE, CHRISTINE, lawyer; b. Paris, Jan. 1, 1956; d. Lallouette Robert and Carre Nicole; m. Wilfrid Lagarde, June 17, 1982 (div. Apr. 1992); children: Pierre-Henri, Thomas. BA, U. Avignon, France, 1979; M of Law, U. Paris, 1979; M Polit. Scientist, Polit. Scis. Inst., 1977. Assoc. Baker McKenzie, Paris, 1981-87, ptnr., 1987-91, mng. ptnr., 1991-95, chmn. Chicago, IL, 1999—. Author: Breaking New Ground, 1991, Into France, 1993. Mem. Cercle Foch. Office: Baker McKenzie 1 Prudential Plaza 130 E Randolph St Fl 2500 Chicago IL 60601-6306

LAGRAND, KENNETH, technology products company executive; b. 1941; married. BS in Mech. Engring., Mich. State U., 1964. Dir. mktg. Grayson Divsn. Robertshaw Controls Co., 1975-79; v.p., gen. mgr.

Simicon Divsn. Robertshaw Controls Co., Holland, Mich., 1979-87; exec. v.p., dir. Gentex, 1987—. Mem. Soc. Automotive Engrs. Office: Gentex Corp 600 N Centennial St Zeeland MI 49464-1318

LAGUNOFF, DAVID, physician, educator; b. N.Y.C., N.Y., Mar. 14, 1932; s. Robert and Cicele (Lipman) L.; m. Susan P. Powers, Mar. 8, 1958; children: Rachel, Liza, Michael. MD, U. Chgo., 1957. Rsch. asst. microbiology U. Miami, Coral Gables, Fla., 1951-53; intern U. Calif. San Francisco Hosp., 1957-58; postdoctoral fellow dept. pathology U. Wash., Seattle, 1958-59, trainee in pathology, 1959-60, instr. pathology, 1960-62, asst. prof., 1962-65, assoc. prof., 1965-69, prof., 1969-79; prof. dept. pathology St. Louis U., 1979—, chmn. dept. pathology, 1979-89, 91-96, asst. v.p., 1989-93. Assoc. dean rsch. St. Louis U. Sch. Medicine, 1989—96; vis. lectr. dept. pathology Sackler Sch. Medicine, Tel Aviv, 1988; vis. prof. dept. pathology U. Wash., Seattle, 2001—02. Nat. Heart Inst. fellow Carlsberg Laboratorium, Copenhagen, 1962-64, Nat. Cancer Inst. fellow Sir William Dunn Sch. Pathology, Oxford, Eng., 1970. Mem.: AAUP, AAAS, Am. Soc. Investigative Pathologists, Am. Soc. Cell Biology. Office: St Louis Univ Sch Medicine Dept Pathology 1402 S Grand Blvd Saint Louis MO 63104-1004 E-mail: lagunofd@slucare1.sluh.edu.

LAHAIE, PERRY, radio director; m. Teresa LaHaie, 1985; children: Kali, Taylor. Asst. mgr. Family Life Radio WUGN, Midland, Mich., 1989—. Performer: 4 CDs of original songs. Avocations: basketball, mountain biking. Office: 510 E Isabella Rd Midland MI 48640

LAHAINE, GILBERT EUGENE, retail lumber company executive; b. Owosso, Mich., Jan. 30, 1926; s. Eric Eugene and Martha Dorothy (Wetzel) LaH.; m. Dorothy Jean Williams, July 1, 1945; children: Gilbert Eugene Jr., Susan, Karen, David, Barbara, Ruth, Marianne, Steven, Eric. BA, Mich. State U., 1949. Acct. Hazen Lumber Co., Lansing, Mich., 1949-56; pres., mgr. Gilbert Lumber Co., 1956-94, also bd. dirs., sec., 1994—. Sec. bd. dirs. Duane Bone Builder, Inc., East Lansing, Mich. Bd. dirs. Mo. Synod, Luth. Ch., St. Louis, 1987-95. With USN, 1944-46. Avocations: fishing, softball, reading, hunting. Home: 2401 Stirling Ave Lansing MI 48910-2755 Office: Gilbert Lumber Co 3501 S Pennsylvania Ave Lansing MI 48910-4734

LAHOOD H. RAY, congressman; b. Peoria, Ill., Dec. 6, 1945; m. Kathleen (Kathy) Dunk LaHood; children: Darin, Amy, Sam, Sara. Student, Canton Jr. Coll., Ill.; BS in Edn. and Sociology, Bradley U., 1971. Tchr. Catholic and pub. jr. high schs., 1971-77; dist. administrv. asst. to congressman Tom Railsback, 1977; mem. Ill. Ho. of Reps., 1982; Chief of Staff Ho. of Reps.; mem. 106th Congress from 18th Ill. dist., 1995—. Mem. Intelligence Com., Appropriations Com., Budget Com. Bd. dirs. Economic Devel. Coun.; pres. sch. bd. Spalding and Notre Dame H.Schs., Bradley U. Nat. Alumni Bd.; svc. to Children's Hosp. Bd., Peoria Area Retarded Citizens Bd.; dir. Rock Island County Youth Svcs. Bur. Mem. ITOO Soc., Downtown Rotary Club, Holy Family Ch. (Peoria), Peoria Area C. of C. Roman Catholic. Office: US House Reps 1424 Longworth HOB Washington DC 20515-0001 also: US Rep Ray LaHood 100 NE Monroe St Ste 100 Peoria IL 61602-1047*

LAIDIG, GARY W. state legislator; b. York, Pa., Aug. 15, 1948; s. Robert Vance and Daisy (Harvey) L.; m. Paula Jane Kinney, 1972; two children. Student, Morningside Coll., 1966-67, U. Wis., River Falls. Dist. 51A rep. Minn. Ho. of Reps., St. Paul, 1972-82; Dist. 56 senator Minn. State Senate, 1982—. Mem. ethics and campaign reform, crime prevention fin. divsn., environ. and natural resources and fin. divsn., and fin. and rules and adminstrn. coms., Minn. State Senate. Decorated Nat. Defense Medal, two Vietnamese Svc. ribbons. Named Outstanding Young Man of Stillwater, Minn., 1974; recipient Disting. Svc. awared Stillwater Jaycees, 1975. Mem. VFW, Am. Legion, Jaycees. Office: 855 Eagle Ridge Ln Stillwater MN 55082-9171 also: State Senate 100 Constitution Ave Saint Paul MN 55155-1232

LAIDLAW, ANDREW R. lawyer; b. Durham, N.C., Aug. 28, 1946; BA, Northwestern U., 1969; JD, U. N.C., 1972. Bar: Ill. 1972. Chair exec com., mem. Seyfarth, Shaw, Chgo., CEO Chicago. Contbr. articles to profl. jours. Mem. ABA (antitrust and securities law coms. 1982—), Barristers. Office: Seyfarth Shaw Mid Continental Plz 55 E Monroe St Ste 4200 Chicago IL 60603-5863

LAIKIN, ROBERT J. electronics company executive; V.p. Centruy Cellular Network, 1986-87; pres., 1988-93; v.p., treas. Brightpoint, Inc., Indpls., 1989-92; pres., 1992-96; CEO, 1994—; also chmn. Office: Brightpoint Inc # 575 600 E 96th St Indianapolis IN 46240-3788

LAING, KAREL ANN, magazine publishing executive; b. Mpls., July 5, 1939; d. Edward Francis and Elizabeth Jane Karel (Templeton) Hannon; m. G. R. Cheesebrough, Dec. 19, 1959 (div. 1969); 1 child, Jennifer Read; m. Ronald Harris Laing, Jan. 6, 1973; 1 child, Christopher Harris Grad., U. Minn., 1960. With Guthrie Symphony Opera Program, Mpls., 1969-71; account supr. Colle & McVoy Advt. Agy., Richfield, Minn., 1971-74; owner The Cottage, Edina, 1974-75; salespromotion rep. Robert Meyers & Assocs., St. Louis Park, 1975-76; cons. Webb Co., St. Paul, 1976-77, custom pub. dir., 1977-89; pres. K.L. Publs., Inc., Bloomington, Minn., 1989—. Contbr. articles to profl. jours. Community vol. Am. Heart Assn., Am. Cancer Soc., Edina PTA; charter sponsor Walk Around Am., St. Paul, 1985 Mem. Bank Mktg. Assn., Fin. Instn. Mktg. Assn., Advt. Fedn. Am., Am. Bankers Assn., Direct Mail Mktg. Assn., Minn. Mag. Pub. Assn. (founder, bd. govs.), St. Andrews Soc. Republican. Presbyterian Avocations: painting; gardening; reading; traveling. Office: KL Publs 2001 Killebrew Dr Minneapolis MN 55425-1865

LAKE, ROBERT D. transportation executive; BS in Mfg. Tech., MS in Indsl. Adminstrn., Purdue U. With Ryder Sys., Inc., N.Am. Van Lines, Inc., Internat. Harvester; pres. Caliber Logistics (formerly Roadway Logistics Sys.), 1989-95; CEO, NFC Ams. & Asia Pacific, Naperville, Ill., 1995—. Mem. Coun. Logistics Mgmt., Nat. Def. Transp. Assn. Office: Am & Asia Pacific NFC plc 215 W Diehl Rd Naperville IL 60563-1278

LAKIN, JAMES DENNIS, allergist, immunologist, director; b. Harvey, Ill., Oct. 4, 1945; s. Ora Austin and Annie Pitranella (Johnson) L.; m. Sally A. Stuteville, July 22, 1972; children: Margaret K., Matthew A. PhD, Northwestern U., 1968, MD, 1969; MBA in Med. Group Mgmt., U. St. Thomas, 1996. Diplomate Am. Bd. Internal Medicine, Am. Bd. Allergy and Immunology. Dir. allergy rsch. Naval Med. Rsch. Inst., Bethesda, Md., 1974-76; clin. prof. U. Okla., Oklahoma City, 1976-89; dir. lab., chmn. allergy and immunology dept. Oxboro Clinics, Bloomington, Minn., 1989—; dir. Fairview Allergy and Asthma Svcs., 1995-2001; mng. ptnr. Minn. Allergy and Asthma Consultants, LLP, 2001—. Bd. dirs. Okla. Med. Rsch. Found., Oklahoma City, 1980-89; regional cons. Diver Alert Network, Duke U., Chapel Hill, N.C., 1987—; cert. diving med. officer NOAA, 1988. Co-author: Allergic Diseases, 1971, 3d edit., 1986; contbr. articles, revs. to profl. publs. Councilperson Our Lord's Luth. Ch., Oklahoma City, 1978-88, Faith Luth. Ch., Lakeville, Minn., 1990-91. Lt. comdr. USN, 1970-76. Fellow ACP, Am. Acad. Allergy and Immunology, Am. Coll. Chest Physicians, Am. Coll. Med. Practice Execs. (E.B. Stevens Article of Yr. award 1998); mem. Am. Assn. Immunologists, Med. Group Mgmt. Assn., Am. Coll. Physician Execs. Achievements include research in characterization of the immunoglobulin system of the rhesus monkey, alterations in allergic reactivity during immunosuppression. Office: Minn Allergy and Asthma Cons LLP 600 W 98th St Bloomington MN 55420-4773

LAKIN, SCOTT BRADLEY, insurance agent; b. Kansas City, Mo., Dec. 28, 1957; s. John Bradley and Marilyn (Marr) L.; m. Cynthia Kay Wohlgemuth, May 26, 1979; children: Kyle, Caroline, Christopher. BS, William Jewell Coll., 1980. Congl. aide Congressman Richard Bolling, Kansas City, Mo., 1979-83; mem. Mo. State Legislature, 1992-2000. Gov. apptd. dir. Mo. Dept. Ins., 2001—. Bd. dirs. Safe Haven Domestic Violence Shelter. Mem. Sertoma (bd. dirs. 1989-92), Kansas City C. of C., Gladstone C. of C., Northland Regional C. of C. Democrat. Baptist. Avocations: jogging, tennis, reading. Home: 6020 N Chelsea Ave Kansas City MO 64119-3059 E-mail: slakin@services.state.mo.us., xrep33@hotmail.com.

LALIBERTE, GARLAND EVERETT, agricultural engineering educator; b. Walkerburn, Man., Can., Dec. 28, 1936; m. Audry Whitlock; 2 children: Tracy, Marnie. BS in Agrl. Engring., U. Sask., Can., 1956, MS, 1961; PhD, Colo. State U., 1966. Prof. biosys. engring. U. Man., Winnipeg, 1967—. Mem. Man. Econ. Innovation and Tech. Coun., 1992-94. Recipient Achievement in Academe award Colo. State U., 1994. Fellow Agrl. Inst. Can. (nat. coun. 1980-82), Can. Soc. Agrl. Engring. (charter, sr., v.p. tech. 1971-73, pres. 1978-79, Maple Leaf award 1981); mem. Assn. Faculties Agr. in Can. (charter, bd. dirs. 1974-78, sec.-treas. 1974-75, pres. 1976-78), Assn. Profl. Engrs. Man. (coun. 1984-90, pres. 1988-89, Outstanding Svc. award 1994), Can. Coun. Profl. Engrs. (bd. dirs. 1989-90, exec. com. 1991-96, pres. 1994-95), Am. Soc. Agrl. Engrs., Man. Inst. Agrologists, Prairie Agrl. Machinery Inst. (coun. 1983-85). Office: Univ Man Pfo Biosys Engring 438 Engring Bldg Winnipeg MB Canada R3V 5V6

LALONDE, BERNARD JOSEPH, educator; b. Detroit, June 3, 1933; s. John Bernard and Fannie (Napier) LaL.; m. Barbara Elaine Eggenberger, Sept. 6, 1958; children— Lisa Renee, Michell Ann, Christopher John. A.B., U. Notre Dame, 1955; M.B.A., U. Detroit, 1957; Ph.D., Mich. State U., 1961. Asst. prof. mktg. U. Colo., Boulder, 1961-65; assoc. prof. Mich. State U., East Lansing, 1965-69; James R. Riley prof. mktg. and logistics Ohio State U., Columbus, 1969-85, Raymond E. Mason prof. transp. and logistics, 1985-95, prof. emeritus, 1995. Author: Physical Distribution Management, 2d edit, 1968, Customer Service: A Management Perspective, 1988; Editor: Jour. Bus. Logistics; Jour. book and monographs editor, Am. Mktg. Assn.; Contbr. articles to profl. jours. Pres. Transp. Research Found. Recipient John Drury Sheehan award, 1976; Formerly Ford scholar; Gen. Electric fellow. Mem. Am. Marketing Assn., Regional Sci. Assn., Council Logistic Mgmt., Soc. Logistics Engrs., Beta Gamma Sigma, Alpha Kappa Psi. Roman Catholic. Home: 8538 Pitlochry Ct Dublin OH 43017-9770 Office: Ohio State U Coll Bus Supply Chain Mgmt Rsch Grp 421 Hagerty Hall Columbus OH 43210

LAMB, GORDON HOWARD, music educator; b. Eldora, Iowa, Nov. 6, 1934; s. Capp and Ethel (Hayden) L; m. Nancy Ann Painter; children: Kirk, Jon, Phillip. B in Music Edn., Simpson Coll., 1956; M of Music, U. Nebr., 1962; PhD, U. Iowa, 1973. Choral dir. Iowa pub. schs., Tama/Paullina, Sac City, 1957-68; asst. prof. music U. Wis., Stevens Point, 1969-70, U. Tex., Austin, 1970-74, prof., dir. divsn. music San Antonio, 1974-79, prof., v.p. acad. affairs, 1979-86; pres. Northeastern Ill. U., Chgo., 1986-95, pres. emeritus, 1996—; sr. v.p. EFL Assocs./TranSearch, Overland Park, Kans., 2000—. Vis. prof. music dept. Western Ill. U., 1996-97; interim chancellor U. Wis., Parkside, 1997-98, U. Mo., Kansas City Author: Choral Techniques, 1974, 3d edit. 1988; editor: Guide for the Beginning Choral Director; contbr. articles to scholarly and profl. jours.; composer numerous pieces choral music. Served with U.S. Army, 1957-58. Recipient Most Supportive Pres. or Chancellor award Am. Assn. Colls. for Tchr. Edn., 1992. Mem. Am. Assn. Higher Edn., Am. Assn. State Colls. and Univs., Am. Choral Dirs. Assn. (life, chmn. nat. com. 1970-72). Office: EFL Assocs/TranSearch 7101 College Blvd Ste 550 Overland Park KS 66210

LAMB, RONALD M. convenience stores executive; Store mgr. Casey' Gen. Stores, Inc., v.p., 1976-88, pres., CEO Iowa, 1988—, also bd. dirs. Office: Casey's Gen Stores Inc 1 Convenience Blvd Ankeny IA 50021-8045

LAMB, STEVEN G. financial executive; BSEE, U.S. Mil. Acad.; MBA, Harvard U. Mgmt. and operational positions Internat. Paper, 1988-92; exec. asst. to pres. Tenneco Inc.; mng. dir. Europe Case Corp., Racine, Wis., 1993-95, exec. v.p., COO, 1995-97, pres., COO, 1997—. Office: 700 State St Racine WI 53404-3343

LAMBERT, DANIEL MICHAEL, academic administrator; b. Kansas City, Mo., Jan. 16, 1941; s. Paul McKinley and Della Mae (Rogers) L.; m. Carolyn Faye Bright, Dec. 27, 1969; children: Kristian Paige, Dennis McKinley. AB, William Jewell Coll., 1963; MA, Northwestern U., 1965; postgrad., Harvard U., 1965-66; PhD, U. Mo., Columbia, 1977. Dean student affairs William Jewell Coll., Liberty, Mo., 1970-77, exec. asst. to pres., 1977-80, v.p., 1980-85; pres. College Hill Investments Inc., 1985-87, Baker U., Baldwin City, Kans., 1987—. Bd. dirs. Ferrell Co., Liberty; dir. Kansas City Bd. of Trade, 1988-90; hon. trustee Dohto U., Japan. Bd. dirs. Nat. Assn. Intercollegiate Athletics, The Barstow Sch., Kans. Ind. Colls. Assn.; trustee Midwest Rsch. Inst. Capt. U.S. Army, 1966-70, Vietnam. Recipient Civic Leadership award Mo. Mcpl. League, 1986. Mem. KC. Home: 505 E 8th St Baldwin City KS 66006 Office: Baker U Office of Pres PO Box 65 Baldwin City KS 66006-0065

LAMBERT, GEORGE ROBERT, lawyer, real estate broker; b. Muncie, Ind., Feb. 21, 1933; s. George Russell and Velma Lou (Jones) L.; m. Mary Virginia Alling, June 16, 1956; children: Robert Allen, Ann Holt, James William. BS, Ind. U., Bloomington, 1955; JD, IIT Chgo., 1962. Bar: Ill. 1962, U.S. Dist. Ct. (no. dist.) Ill. 1962, Iowa 1984, Pa. 1988, Ind. 1999. V.p., gen. counsel, sec. Washington Nat. Ins. Co., Evanston, Ill., 1970-82; v.p., gen. counsel Washington Nat. Corp., 1979-82; sr. v.p., sec., gen. counsel Life Investors Inc., Cedar Rapids, Iowa, 1982-88; v.p., gen. counsel Provident Mut. Life Ins. Co., Phila., 1988-95; pres. Lambert Legal Consulting, Inc., Wilmington, Del., 1995—; realtor Coldwell Banker, North Palm Beach, Fla., 1996—2001, Cressy and Everett GMAC Real Estate, South Bend, Ind., 1999-2000; owner, broker Lambert Realty, Granger, 2001—. Alderman Evanston City Coun., 1980-82. Served to lt. USAF, 1955-57. Mem. Ill. State Bar Assn., Ind. Bar Assn., Iowa Bar Assn., Assn. of Life Ins. Counsel (past pres.), Nat. Assn. Realtors, Ind. Assn. Realtors, Greater South Bend-Mishawaka Assn. Realtors, Inc. Home: 51702 Stoneham Way Granger IN 46530-8493

LAMBERT, JOHN BOYD, chemical engineer, consultant; b. Billings, Mont., July 5, 1929; s. Jean Arthur and Gail (Boyd) L.; m. Jean Wilson Bullard, June 20, 1953 (dec. 1958); children: William, Thomas, Patricia, Cathy, Karen; m. Ilse Crager, Sept. 20, 1980 (dec. 1995). BS in Engring., Princeton U., 1951; PhD, U. Wis., 1956. Rsch. engr. E.I. DuPont de Nemours Co., Wilmington, Del., 1956-69; sr. rsch. engr. Fansteel, Inc., Balt., 1969, mktg. mgr., plant mgr. North Chicago, Ill., 1970-73, mgr. mfg. engring. Waukegan, 1974-80, corp. tech. dir. North Chicago, 1980-86, gen. mgr. metals, 1987-90, v.p., corp. tech. dir., 1990-91. IESC vol., Brazil, 1995; ind. cons., Lake Forest, Ill., 1991—. Contbr. articles to profl. jours. Recipient Charles Hatchett medal Inst. Metals, London, 1986. Mem. AIChE, Am. Chem. Soc., Am. Soc. Metals, Sigma Xi. Episcopalian. Achievements include patents in field of dispersion-strengthened metals, refractory metals, chemical vapor deposition, both products and processes. Home and Office: 617 Greenbriar Ln Lake Forest IL 60045-3214 Fax: 847-234-7649. E-mail: drjbl@aol.com.

LAMBERT, JOSEPH BUCKLEY, chemistry educator; b. Ft. Sheridan, Ill., July 4, 1940; s. Joseph Idus and Elizabeth Dorothy (Kirwan) L.; m. Mary Wakefield Pulliam, June 27, 1967; children: Laura Kirwan, Alice Pulliam, Joseph Cannon. BS, Yale U., 1962; Ph.D. (Woodrow Wilson fellow 1962-63, NSF fellow 1962-65), Calif. Inst. Tech., 1965. Asst. prof. chemistry Northwestern U., Evanston, Ill., 1965-69, assoc. prof., 1969-74, prof. chemistry, 1974-91, Clare Hamilton Hall prof. chemistry, 1991—, Charles Deering McCormick prof., 1999—, chmn. dept., 1986-89, dir. integrated sci. program, 1982-85. Vis. assoc. Brit. Mus., 1973, Polish Acad. Scis., 1981, Chinese Acad. Scis., 1988. Author: Organic Structural Analysis, 1976, Physical Organic Chemistry through Solved Problems, 1978, The Multinuclear Approach to NMR Spectroscopy, 1983, Archaeological Chemistry III, 1984, Introduction to Organic Spectroscopy, 1987, Recent Advances in Organic NMR Spectroscopy, 1987, Acyclic Organonitrogen Stereodynamics, 1992, Cyclic Organonitrogen Stereodynamics, 1992, Prehistoric Human Bone, 1993, Traces of the Past, 1997, Organic Structural Spectroscopy, 1998; audio course Intermediate NMR Spectroscopy, 1973; editor in chief Journal of Physical Organic Chemistry; contbr. articles to sci. jours. Recipient Nat. Fresenius award, 1976, James Flack Norris award, 1987, Fryxell award, 1989, Nat. Catalyst award, 1993; Alfred P. Sloan fellow, 1968-70, Guggenheim fellow, 1973, Interacad. exch. fellow (U.S.-Poland), 1985, Air Force Office sci. rsch. fellow, 1990. Fellow AAAS, Japan Soc. for Promotion of Sci., Brit. Interplanetary Soc., Ill. Acad. Sci. (life); mem. Am. Chem. Soc. (chmn. history of chemistry divsn., 1996, F.S. Kipping award 1998), Royal Soc. Chemistry, Soc. Archaeol. Scis. (pres. 1986-87), Phi Beta Kappa, Sigma Xi (hon. lectr. 1997-98). Home: 1956 Linneman St Glenview IL 60025-4264 Office: Northwestern University Dept of Chemistry 2145 Sheridan Rd Evanston IL 60208-3113

LAMBERT, ROBERT FRANK, electrical engineer, consultant; b. Warroad, Minn., Mar. 14, 1924; s. Fred Joseph and Nutah (Gibson) L.; m. June Darlene Flatten, June 30, 1951; children: Cynthia Marie, Susan Ann, Katherine Cheryl. B.E.E., U. Minn., 1948, M.S. in Elec. Engring, 1949, Ph.D., 1953. Asst. prof. U. Minn. Inst. Tech., Mpls., 1953-54, assoc. prof., 1955-59, prof. elec. engring., 1959-94, prof. emeritus, 1994; dir. propagation research lab. U. Minn., 1968-87; assoc. dean U. Minn. (Inst. Tech.), 1967-68; asst. prof. Mass. Inst. Tech., 1954-55. Cons. elec. engr., also in acoustics, 1953—; guest scientist Third Phys. Inst., Göttingen, Fed. Republic Germany, 1964; vis. scientist NASA, Hampton, Va., 1979; dir. Inst. Noise Control Engring., Washington, 1972-75 Contbr. numerous articles to tech. jours. Served with USNR, 1943-46. Fellow IEEE, Acoustical Soc. Am. (assoc. editor jour. 1985-93); mem. Am. Soc. Engring. Edn., Am. Soc. Engring. Sci., AAAS, Inst. Noise Control Engring. (dir., John C. Johnson Meml. award), Sigma Xi, Tau Beta Pi, Eta Kappa Nu, Gamma Alpha. Lutheran. Achievements include rsch. in acoustics, communication tech. random vibrations. Home: 2503 Snelling Curv N Saint Paul MN 55113 Office: U Minn Inst Tech Dept Elec Engring Minneapolis MN 55455

LAMBERTI, DONALD, convenience store executive; Chmn., CEO, co-founder Casey's Gen. Stores, Inc., Ankeny, Iowa, chmn., 1998—. Office: Casey's Gen Stores Inc 1 Convenience Blvd Ankeny IA 50021-8045

LAMBERTI, JEFF, state legislator, lawyer; b. Des Moines, Oct. 21, 1962; m. Shannon Lamberti; 2 children. BA, Drake U., 1985, MBA, JD, Drake U., 1989. Assoc. Ahlers, Cooney, Dorweiler, Haynie, Smith & Albee, P.C., 1989-94; prin. Jeffrey M. Lamberti Law Firm, 1995—; shareholder Handley, Gocke, Block, Lamberti, Barnes and Moore, P.C., 1998—; mem. Iowa Ho. of Reps., Des Moines, 1994-98, Iowa Senate from 33rd dist., Des Moines, 1998—; vice chair state govt. com., mem. ways and means com.; vice chair jud. com., mem. commerce com. Iowa Senate, Des Moines, mem. appropriations com. Bd. dirs. Polk County Health Svcs.; chair, bd. dirs. On with Life; mem. Neveln Cmty. Resource Ctr.; bd. dirs. Family Futures Network, Homeless Child Day Care and Family Suppot Ctr.; mem. Ankeny Area Hist. Soc. Mem. ABA, Nat. Assn. Bond Lawyers, Iowa State Bar Assn., Polk County Bar Assn., Ankeny C. of C., Polk City C. of C., KC, Vittoria Lodge. Republican. Roman Catholic. Office: State Capitol 9th And Grand Ave Des Moines IA 50319-0001 E-mail: jeff_lamberti@legis.state.ia.us.

LAMBORN, LEROY LESLIE, law educator; b. Marion, Ohio, May 12, 1937; s. LeRoy Leslie and Lola Fern (Grant) Lamborn. AB, Oberlin Coll., 1959; LLB, Western Res. U., 1962; LLM, Yale U., 1963; JSD, Columbia U., 1973. Bar: N.Y. 1965, Mich. 1974. Asst. prof. law U. Fla., 1965-69; prof. Wayne State U., Detroit, 1970-97, prof. emeritus, 1997—. Vis. prof. State U., Utrecht, 1981. Author: (book) Legal Ethics and Professional Responsibility, 1963; contbr. articles on victimology to profl. jours. Mem.: World Soc. Victimology, Nat. Orgn. Victim Assistance (exec. com. 1982—94, bd. dirs. 1979—88), Am. Law Inst. Home: Apt 2502 1300 E Lafayette St Detroit MI 48207-2924 Office: Wayne State U Law Sch Detroit MI 48202

LAMBRIGHT, STEPHEN KIRK, brewing company executive; b. Kansas City, Mo., Dec. 3, 1942; s. Ray B. and Janet Lambright; m. Gail T. Tabler; children: Stephen K. Jr., James H., Sarah E., Catherine L. BS in Acctg., U. Mo., 1965; JD cum laude, St. Louis U., 1968, MBA in Fin., 1977. Bar: Mo., 1968, Va. 1979, D.C. 1979; CPA, Mo. Tax acct. Arthur Andersen & Co., 1965-69; atty. Lashly, Caruthers, Thies, Rava & Hamel, 1970-77; asst. gen. counsel Anheuser-Busch Cos., St. Louis, 1977-78, exec. asst. chmn. bd., 1978-79, v.p., nat. affairs Washington, 1979-81, v.p., industry and govt. affairs St. Louis, 1981-83, mem. corp. policy com., 1981—, v.p. group exec., 1983—, group v.p., gen. counsel, 1998. Bd. dirs. St. Louis U.; chmn. legal and legis. com. C. of C. of U.S.; mem. exec. com., treas. Shriner's Hosp. for Crippled Children; mem. Keep Am. Beautiful. Mem. Beer Inst., Northwestern U. Traffic Inst., Alcoholic Beverage Med. Rsch. Found. Presbyterian. Home: 415 Sheffield Estate Dr Saint Louis MO 63141-8523 Office: Anheuser-Busch Cos Inc 1 Busch Pl Saint Louis MO 63118-1852

LAMM, MICHAEL EMANUEL, pathologist, immunologist, educator; b. Bklyn., May 19, 1934; s. Stanley S. and Rose (Lieberman) L.; m. Ruth Audrey Kumin, Dec. 16, 1961; children— Jocelyn, Margaret Student, Amherst Coll., 1951-54; M.D., U. Rochester, 1959; M.S. in Chemistry, Western Res. U., 1962. Diplomate Am. Bd. Pathology. Intern, asst. resident in pathology Inst. Pathology Western Res. U. and Univ. Hosps. of Cleve., 1959-62; research assoc. NIMH, Bethesda, Md., 1962-64; asst. prof. pathology NYU Sch. Medicine, N.Y.C., 1964-68, assoc. prof., 1968-73, prof., 1973-81; prof. dept. pathology Case We. Res. U. Sch. Medicine, 1981—; chmn. dept. Case Western Res. U. Sch. Medicine, 1981-2001. Vis. sci. dept. biochemistry U. Oxford, 1968; vis. prof. dept. pathology U. Geneva, 1976-77; mem. cancer spl. program adv. com. Nat. Cancer Inst., Bethesda, 1976-79, mem. bd. sci. counselors divsn. cancer biology, diagnosis and ctrs., 1993-95; mem. sci. adv. com. Damon Runyon-Walter Winchell Cancer Fund, N.Y.C., 1978-82; mem. immunol. sci. study sect. NIH, Bethesda, 1988-92; mem. immunotoxicology subcom. NRC, 1989-90; mem. toxin peer rev. panel Am. Inst. Biol. Sci., 1990—; bd. dirs. Univ. Associated for Rsch. and Edn. Pathology. Mem. editl. bd. Procs. Soc. Exptl. Biology and Medicine, 1973-82, Molecular Immunology, 1979-83, Jour. Immunol. Methods, 1980—, Jour. Immunology, 1981-85, Am. Jour. Pathology, 1982-92, Regional Immunology, 1988-95, Modern Pathology, 1989-96; contbr. articles to profl. jours. Recipient for excellence in teaching NYU Sch. Medicine, 1974; named Career Scientist Health Research Council, City of N.Y., 1966-75; NIH grantee, 1965— Fellow N.Y. Acad. Scis.; mem. Am. Assn. Pathologists (councilor 1986-88, sec. treas. 1988-

90, v.p. 1990-91, pres. 1991-92), Am. Assn. Immunologists, Am. Soc. Biochemistry and Molecular Biology, Coll. Am. Pathologists, U.S. and Can. Acad. Pathology, Soc. for Exptl. Biol. Medicine, Clin. Immunology Soc., Soc. Mucosal Immunology, Am. Soc. Clin. Pathologists, Harvey Soc., Sigma Xi, Alpha Omega Alpha. Home: Apt 6B 13515 Shaker Blvd Cleveland OH 44120-5602

LAMP, BENSON J. tractor company executive; b. Cardington, Ohio, Oct. 7, 1925; m. Martha Jane Motz, Aug. 21, 1948; children: Elaine, Marlene, Linda, David. BS in Agr. and B in Agrl. Engring., Ohio State U., 1949, MS in Agrl. Engring., 1952; PhD in Agrl. Engring., Mich. State U., 1960. Registered profl. engr., Ohio. Prof. agrl. engring. Ohio State U., Columbus, 1949-61, 87-91, prof. emeritus, 1991—; product mgr. Massey Ferguson Ltd., Toronto, Can., 1961-66; product planning mgr. Ford Tractor Ops. div. Ford Motor Co., Troy, Mich., 1966-71, mktg. mgr., 1971-76, bus. planning mgr., 1978-87; v.p. mktg. and devel. Ford Aerospace div. Ford Motor Co., Dearborn, 1976-78. Author: Corn Harvesting, 1962. Served to 2d lt. USAF, 1943-45. Fellow Am. Soc. Agrl. Engrs. (pres. 1985-86, Gold medal 1993); mem. Nat. Acad. Engring., Country Club at Muirfield Village (Dublin, Ohio). Avocations: golf, tennis, bridge. Office: BJM Company Inc 6128 Inverurie Dr E Dublin OH 43017-9472

LAMPERT, LEONARD FRANKLIN, mechanical engineer; b. Mpls., Nov. 13, 1919; s. Arthur John Lampert and Irma (Potter) Smith. BME, U. Minn., 1943, B in Chem. Engring., 1959, MS in Biochemistry, 1964, PhD in Biochemistry, 1969. Registered profl. engr., Minn. With flight measurement rsch. dept. Douglas Aircraft Corp., El Segundo, Calif., 1943-47; researcher, tchr. U. Minn., Mpls., 1947-83; with rsch. engring. dept. Mpls. Honeywell Corp., 1950-55; info. scientist Control Data Corp., Mpls., 1982-88; mech. engr. Leonard Lampert Co., White Bear Lake, Minn., 1988—. Scientist Eurasion Watermilfoil Control, White Bear Lake, 1989—; stockholder rep. Lampert Lumber Co., St. Paul, 1988—. Contbr. articles to profl. jours. Mem. Am. Inst. Chem. Engrs. (award 1959), Am. Chem. Soc., U. Minn. Alumni Assn. (advisor) MIT Alumni Assn. (advisor), Phi Gamma Delta (advisor), Gamma Alpha, Phi Lambda Upsilon. Republican. Avocations: Ballroom dancing competitions, snow and water skiing, biking, geography, travel. Home and Office: 2467 S Shore Blvd Saint Paul MN 55110-3820

LAMPERT, STEVEN A. lawyer; b. Chgo., Nov. 11, 1944; BS, U. Ill., 1966; JD cum laude, Northwestern U., 1969. Bar: Ill. 1969. Ptnr. Neal, Gerber & Eisenberg, Chgo. Mem. editorial bd. Northwestern U. Law Rev., 1968-69. Mem. ABA, Ill. State Bar Assn., Chgo. Bar Assn., Chgo. Estate Planning Coun. Office: Neal Gerber & Eisenberg 2 N La Salle St Ste 2200 Chicago IL 60602-3801

LAMPINEN, JOHN A. newspaper editor; b. Waukegan, Ill., Nov. 26, 1951; s. Walter Valentine and Patricia Mae Irene (Pruess) L.; m. Belinda Walter, Oct. 20, 1973; children: Amanda Michelle, Heidi Elizabeth. BS in Comm., U. Ill., 1973. Staff writer Paddock Cir. Newspapers, Libertyville, Ill., 1973-75; regional editor The Jour., New Ulm, Minn., 1975-76; various positions Daily Herald, Arlington Heights, Ill., 1976-90, asst. v.p., mng. editor, 1990-97, asst. v.p., exec. editor, 1997-99, v.p., exec. editor, 1999—. Adj. prof. Medill Sch. Journalism, Northwestern U., Evanston, Ill., 1995-98. Mem. Assoc. Press Mng. Editors, Soc. Profl. Journalists, Am. Soc. Newspaper Editors. Avocations: baseball, long-distance running, coaching girls softball, sports memorabilia. Office: Daily Herald 155 E Algonquin Rd Arlington Heights IL 60005-4617

LAMPING, KATHRYN G. medical educator, medical researcher; BS in Biology, U. Ill., 1976; MS in Pharmacology, Med. Coll. Wis., 1982, PhD in Pharmacology, 1983. Postdoctoral rsch. fellow Dept. Internal Medicine, U. Iowa, Iowa City, 1983-86, asst. rsch. scientist, 1986-89, adj. asst. prof., 1989-95, asst. prof., 1995—. Contbr. articles to profl. jours. Mem. Am. Heart Assn. (Established Investigator award 1995), Am. Physiol. Soc., Microcirculatory Soc. Office: U Iowa Ctr on Agin 2159 Westlawn S Iowa City IA 52242-1100

LAMSON, GEORGE HERBERT, economics educator; b. Hartford, Conn., Feb. 21, 1940; s. Arroll Liscomb and Marguerite (Brechbuhler) L.; m. Susan Kathryn Lippert, Sept. 7, 1968; children: Scott, Brandon. A.B., Princeton U., 1963; M.A., Northwestern U., 1966, Ph.D., 1971. Research asst. Northwestern U. Econ. Survery of Liberia, Monrovia, 1962-63; instr. dept. econs. Loyola U., Chgo., 1967-68, U. Conn., Storrs, 1968-69; asst. prof. then assoc. prof. dept. econs. Carleton Coll., Northfield, Minn., 1969-80, Williams prof., 1981—, chmn. dept., 1978-84, 99-00. Cons. Minn. Higher Edn. Coordinating Com., St. Paul, 1971-72; textbook reviewer John Wiley & Sons, N.Y.C., 1979-82; reviewer NSF grad. fellowship program, 1988-90; vis. prof. U. Internat. Bus. and Econs., Beijing, China, 1994, 98; dir. Carleton Oversees seminar in econs. Cambridge, U.K., 1986, 91, 97, 2002; vis. scholar Chinese Acad. Social Scis., Beijing, 2001. Intersocietal studies fellow Northwestern U., 1966-67; recipient Faculty Devel. awards 1979, 90-91. Mem. Am. Econ. Assn., Midwest Econ. Assn., Minn. Econ. Assn. (bd. dirs. 1981-83, pres. 1984) Home: 4485 Detelemark Rd Dundas MN 55019-4050 Office: Carleton Coll Dept Econs Northfield MN 55057 E-mail: glamson@carleton.edu.

LANANE, TIMOTHY S. state legislator, lawyer; m. Cynthia Lanane; children: Angelique Boyle, Katie, Meaghan. BS, Ball State U.; JD, Ind. U. Atty. City of Anderson, Ind.; mem. Ind. Senate from 25th dist., Indpls., 1997—; ranking minority mem. commerce and consumer affairs; mem. ins. and fin. instns. com.; mem. jud. com., mem. natural resources com. Mem. East Ctrl. Legal Svcs. Bd., Anderson City Sister Cities Com., Madison County Urban League. Mem. ABA, Madison County Bar Assn., Ind. Trial Lawyers Assn. Democrat. Avocations: reading, golf, running. Office: 200 W Washington St Indianapolis IN 46204-2728

LANCASTER, JOAN ERICKSEN, state supreme court justice; b. 1954; BA magna cum laude, St. Olaf Coll., Northfield, Minn., 1977; spl. diploma in social studies, Oxford U., 1976; JD cum laude, U. Minn., 1981. Atty. LeFevere, Lefler, Kennedy, O'Brien & Drawz, Mpls., 1981-83; asst. U.S. atty. Dist. Minn., 1983-93; shareholder Leonard, Street and Deinard, 1993-95; dist. ct. judge 4th Jud. Dist., 1995-98; assoc. justice Minn. Supreme Ct., 1998—. Office: Minn Supreme Ct 25 Constitution Ave Saint Paul MN 55155-1500

LANDAU, BERNARD ROBERT, biochemistry educator, physician; b. Newark, June 24, 1926; s. Morris Harry and Estelle (Kirsch) L.; m. Lucille Slosberg, Jan. 11, 1956; children: Steven Brian, Deborah Louise (dec.), Rodger Martin. S.B., MIT, 1947; Ph.D., Harvard U., 1950, M.D., 1954; MD (hon.), Karolinska Inst., 1993. Diplomate: Am. Bd. Internal Medicine. Intern Peter Bent Brigham Hosp., Boston, 1954-55; clin. assoc. Nat. Cancer Inst., Bethesda, Md., 1955-57; fellow in biochemistry Harvard U., 1957-58; sr. resident Peter Bent Brigham Hosp., 1958-59; asst. prof. medicine Case Western Res. U., 1959-62, assoc. prof., 1962-67, prof., 1969—, prof. biochemistry, 1979—, physician Univ. Hosps., 1969—. Dir. dept. biochemistry Merck and Co., Rahway, N.J., 1967-69 Contbr. articles to profl. jours. Fellow Commonwealth fund, 1965-66, Fogarty Sr. Internat. fellow 1986-87, 93-94; grantee Am. Heart Assn., 1959-64; recipient William B. Peck Postgrad. Research award, 1961 Fellow AAAS; mem. Am. Fedn. Clin. Research, Am. Soc. Clin. Investigation, Assn. Am. Physicians, Am. soc. Biol. Chemists, Am. Physiol. Soc., Endocrine Soc., Central Soc. Clin. Research, Am. Diabetes Assn., Sigma Xi, Alpha Omega Alpha Home: 19501 S Woodland Rd Cleveland OH 44122-2834 Office: University Hosps Cleveland 11100 Euclid Ave Cleveland OH 44106-1736 E-mail: brl@po.cwru.edu.

LANDAU, WILLIAM MILTON, neurologist, department chairman; b. St. Louis, Oct. 10, 1924; s. Milton S. and Amelia (Rich) L.; m. Roberta Anne Hornbein, Apr. 3, 1947; children: David, John, Julia, George. Student, U. Chgo., 1941-43; M.D. cum laude, Washington U., St. Louis, 1947. Diplomate: Am. Bd. Psychiatry and Neurology (dir. 1967, pres. 1975). Intern U. Chgo. Clinics, 1947; resident St. Louis City Hosp., 1948; fellow Washington U., St. Louis, 1949-52, NIH, Bethesda, Md., 1952-54; instr. neurology Washington U., 1952-54, asst. prof., 1954-58, assoc. prof., 1958-63, prof., 1963—, dept. head, 1970-91, co-head dept. neurology and neur. surgery, 1975. Chmn. Nat. Com. for Research in Neurol. and Communicative Disorders, 1980 Editorial bd.: Neurology, 1963, A.M.A. Archives Neurology, 1965, Annals Neurology, 1977. Mem. ACLU (trustee East Mo. 1956—), Am. Neurol. Assn. (pres. 1977), Am. Acad. Neurology, Assn. U. Profs. Neurology (pres. 1978), Soc. Neurosci., Am. Physiol. Soc., Am. Electro-encephalography Soc. Rsch. in neurophysiology. Office: Washington U Sch Med Dept Neurology 660 S Euclid Ave Saint Louis MO 63110-1010 E-mail: landauw@neuro.wustl.edu.

LANDER, JOYCE ANN, nursing educator, medical/surgical nurse; b. Benton Harbor, Mich., July 27, 1942; d. James E. and Anna Mae Remus LPN, Kalamazoo Practical Nursing, Ctr., 1967; AAS, Kalamazoo Valley C.C., 1981, Grad. Massage Therapy Program, 1995. LPN-RN Bronson Meth. Hosp., Kalamazoo, 1972-82; RN med./surg. unit Borgess Med. Ctr., 1982-84; RN pediatrics Upjohn Home Health Care, 1984-88; supr. nursing lab Kalamazoo Valley Community Coll., 1982—. Therapeutic massage therapist in client homes with Business Kneading Peace Therapeutic Massage, Kalamazoo, 1995—; nursing asst., instr. State of Mich. Observer, 1990-96. Author: What Is A Nurse, 1980. Address: 3300 Woodstone Dr E Apt 108 Kalamazoo MI 49008-2548

LANDES, WILLIAM M. law educator; b. 1939. AB, Columbia U., 1960, PhD in Econs., 1966. Asst. prof. econs. Stanford U., 1965-66; asst. prof. U. Chgo., 1966-69; asst. prof. Columbia U., 1969-72; assoc. prof. Grad. Ctr., CUNY, 1972-73; now prof. U. Chgo. Law Sch.; founder, chmn. Lexecon Inc., 1977-98, chmn. emeritus, 1998—; mem. bd. examiners GRE in Econs., ETS, 1967-74. Mem. Am. Econ. Assn., Am. Law and Econ. Assn. (v.p. 1991-92, pres. 1992-93), Mont Pelerin Soc. Author: (with Richard Posner) The Economic Structure of Tort Law, 1987; editor: (with Gary Becker) Essays in the Economics of Crime and Punishment, 1974; editor Jour. Law and Econs., 1975-91, Jour. Legal Studies, 1991—. Office: U Chgo Sch Law 1111 E 60th St Chicago IL 60637-2776 also: Lexecon Inc 332 S Michigan Ave Ste 1300 Chicago IL 60604-4406

LANDGREBE, DAVID ALLEN, electrical engineer; b. Huntingburg, Ind., Apr. 12, 1934; s. Albert E. and Sarah A. L.; m. Margaret Ann Swank, June 7, 1959; children: James David, Carole Ann, Mary Jane. BSEE, Purdue U., 1956, MSEE, 1958, PhD, 1962. Mem. tech. staff Bell Telephone Labs., Murray Hill, N.J., 1956; electronics engr. Interstate Electronics Corp., Anaheim, Calif., 1958, 59, 62; mem. faculty Purdue U., West Lafayette, Ind., 1962—, dir. lab. for applications of remote sensing, 1969-81, prof. elec. engring., 1970—, assoc. dean engring., 1981-84, acting head sch. elec. and computer engring., 1995-96. Rsch. scientist Douglas Aircraft Co., Newport Beach, Calif., 1964; dir. Univ. Space Rsch. Assn., 1975-78. Author: (with others) Remote Sensing: The Quantitative Approach, 1978. Recipient medal for exceptional sci. achievement NASA, 1973, William T. Pecora award NASA/U.S. Dept. Interior, 1990. Fellow IEEE (pres. Geosci. and Remote Sensing Soc. 1986-87, Sci. Achievement award 1992), AAAS, Am. Soc. Photogrammetry and Remote Sensing; mem. Am. Soc. for Engring. Edn., Sigma Xi, Tau Beta Pi, Eta Kappa Nu. Office: Purdue U Dept Elec Engring West Lafayette IN 47907-1285 E-mail: landgreb@ecn.purdue.edu.

LANDGREBE, JOHN ALLAN, chemistry educator; b. San Francisco, May 6, 1937; s. Herbert Frederick and Janet Miller (Allan) L.; m. Carolyn Jean Thomson, Dec. 23, 1961; children— Carolyn Janet, John Frederick B.S., U. Calif.-Berkeley, 1959; Ph.D., U. Ill., 1962. Asst. prof. U. Kans., Lawrence, 1962—67, assoc. prof., 1967—71, prof., 1971—2002, prof. emeritus, 2002—, dept. chmn., 1970—80. Vis. prof. U. Calif.-Berkeley, 1974 Author: Theory and Practice in the Organic Laboratory, 1973, 4th edit., 1993. NSF fellow, 1960-62; E. Watkins Faculty fellow U. Kans., 1963; recipient Career Tchg. award Chancellors Club, 1999. Mem. Am. Chem. Soc., Royal Soc. of Chemistry, Phi Lambda Upsilon Republican. Lutheran. Avocations: shade and water gardening, camping, hiking. Home: 1125 Highland Dr Lawrence KS 66044-4523 Office: U Kansas Dept Chemistry Lawrence KS 66045-0001

LANDINI, RICHARD GEORGE, university president, emeritus English educator; b. Pitts., June 4, 1929; s. George R. and Alice (Hoy) L.; m. Phyllis Lesnick, Nov. 26, 1952 (dec. Mar. 1992); children: Richard, Gregory, Matthew, Cynthia, Vincent; m. Barbara Lee Shockley, Oct. 5, 1996. A.B., U. Miami, 1954, M.A., 1956; Ph.D., U. Fla., 1959; D in Civil Law, Quincy Coll., 1985; LLD, U. Miami, 1980, Baiko Jo Gakuin Coll., Japan, 1987, Ind. State U., 1996. From asst. prof. to prof. English Ariz. State U., 1959-70, dean, 1968-70; prof. English, acad. v.p. U. Mont., 1970-75; pres. Ind. State U., 1975-92, prof. English, 1975—. Author: Owls and Sycamores, 2000; contbr. articles on lit. and higher edn. to profl. jours. Served with U.S. Army, 1948-51. Decorated Sagamore of the Wabash, 1977; comdr. Knight of the Holy Sepulchre Jerusalem, 1996. Mem. Phi Beta Kappa, Phi Delta Kappa, Phi Alpha Theta, Phi Kappa Phi, Sigma Tau Delta. Roman Catholic. Office: Ind State Univ Dept English Root Hl # A-288 Terre Haute IN 47809-0001 E-mail: ejlandi@root.indstate.edu.

LANDIS, DAVID MORRISON, state legislator; b. Lincoln, Nebr., June 10, 1948; m. Melodee Ann McPherson, June 6, 1969; children: Matthew, Melissa. BA, U. Nebr., 1970, JD, 1971, M. in Cmty. Regional Planning, 1995; MPA, U. Nebr., Omaha, 1984. Bar: Nebr. 1972. Practice law, Lincoln, 1972-74; mem. Nebr. Legislature from 46th dist., 1978—; chmn. govt. mil. and vets. affairs com. Nebr. Legislature, 1983-87, chmn. banking, commerce and ins., 1988—. Instr. Coll. Law U. Nebr., 1990—; adj. faculty mem. dept. pub. adminstrn. U. Nebr., Omaha, 1984—; adj. faculty mem. N.E. Wesleyan U., 1995-96, 99—; adj. mem. bus. faculty Doane Coll., 1985-95. Bd. dirs. Lower Platte S. Natural Resources Dist., 1971-78; officer PTA, 1979-80; adminstrv. law judge Dept. Labor, 1977-78; mem. Nebr. Humanities Coun., 1990-96; mem. N.E. Repertory Theatre. Named Doane Coll. Tchr. of the Yr., 1987, 88, 92; recipient Purple Mask theater honorary, 2002. Mem. Innocents Soc. (hon.), Golden Key Soc. (hon., U. Nebr.), Pi Alpha Alpha (hon. U. Nebr. at Omaha), Tau Sigma Delta (hon. U. Nebr., Lincoln). Office: Nebr State Legislature Rm 1116 State Capitol Lincoln NE 68509 E-mail: dlandis@unicam.state.ne.us.

LANDIS, FRED, mechanical engineering educator; b. Munich, Mar. 21, 1923; came to U.S., 1947, naturalized, 1954; s. Julius and Elsie (Schulhoff) L.; m. Billie H. Schiff, Aug. 26, 1951 (dec. Jan. 10, 1985); children: John David, Deborah Ellen, Mark Edward. B.Eng., McGill U., 1945; S.M., MIT, 1949, Sc.D., 1950. Design engr. Canadian Vickers, Ltd., Montreal, Can., 1945-47; asst. prof. mech. engring. Stanford U., 1950-52; research engr. Northrop Aircraft, Inc., Hawthorne, Calif., 1952-53; asst. prof. NYU, 1953-56, assoc. prof., 1956-61, prof., 1961-73, chmn. dept. mech. engring., 1963-73; dean, prof. mech. engring. Poly. U., Bklyn., 1973-74; dean Coll. Engring. and Applied Sci., U. Wis., Milw., 1974-83, prof. mech. engring., 1984-94; emeritus prof. U. Wis., 1994—. Staff cons. Pratt & Whitney Aircraft Co., 1957-88. Cons. editor, Macmillan Co., 1960-68; cons. editorial bd.: Funk & Wagnalls Ency., 1969-90 , Compton's Ency., 1984-94; contbr. numerous rsch. articles to profl. jours. and encys., including Ency. Britannica. Mem. Dobbs Ferry (N.Y.) Bd. Edn., 1965-71, v.p. 1966-67, 70-71, pres., 1967-68; bd. dirs. Westchester County Sch. Bds. Assn., 1969-70, v.p., 1970, pres., 1970-71; bd. dirs. Engring. Found., 1988-94. Fellow AIAA (assoc.), ASME (hon. mem., divsn. exec. com. 1965-73, policy bd. 1973-89, v.p. 1985-89, 92-95, bd. govts. 1989-91), Am. Soc. Engring. Edn.; mem. Sigma Tau, Tau Beta Pi, Pi Tau Sigma. Home: 2420 W Acacia Rd Milwaukee WI 53209-3306

LANDO, JEROME BURTON, macromolecular science educator; b. Bklyn., May 23, 1932; s. Irving and Ruth (Schwartz) L.; m. Geula Ahroni, Dec. 2, 1962; children: Jeffrey, Daniel, Avital. A.B., Cornell U., 1953; Ph.D., Poly. Inst. Bklyn., 1963. Chemist Camille Dreyfus Lab., Research Triangle Inst., Durham, N.C., 1963-65; asst. prof. macromolecular sci. Case Western U., Cleve., 1965-68, assoc. prof., 1968-74, prof., 1974—; chmn. dept. Case Western, 1978-85; pres., CEO Edison Polymer Inovation Corp., 2000—. Erna and Jakob Michael vis. prof. Weizmann Inst. Sci., Rehovot, Israel, 1987; Lady Davis vis. prof. Technion, Haifa, Israel, 1992-93. Author: (with S. Maron) Fundamentals of Physical Chemistry, 1974; mem. editl. adv. bd. Polymers for Advanced Techs. Served to lt. U.S. Army, 1953-55. Named Alexander Von Humboldt Sr. Am. Scientist U. Mainz, Germany, 1974, disting. alumnus Poly. U., 1990. Fellow Am. Phys. Soc.; mem. Am. Chem. Soc., Am. Crystallographic Assn., Soc. Plastics Engrs. (rsch. award 1994, edn. award 1999), Sigma Xi. Jewish. Home: 21925 Byron Rd Cleveland OH 44122-2942 Office: Case Western Res U Dept Macromolecular Sci Kent Hale Smith Bldg 321 Cleveland OH 44106

LANDON, ROBERT GRAY, retired manufacturing company executive; b. Portsmouth, Ohio, Dec. 22, 1928; s. Herman Robert and Hazel Ruth Landon; m. Carole A. Beaumont, Aug. 30, 2001; children: Geoffrey, Suzanne. Student, Cornell U., 1947-49; BA in Econs., U. Pa., 1955; grad. advanced mgmt. program, Harvard Sch. Bus., 1978. Loan officer Nat. City Bank, Cleve., 1955-60; SEC adminstr. Smith Kline Corp., 1960-64; controller, treas. Grumman Allied Industries, Inc., Garden City, N.Y., 1964-76, v.p., 1977-82; v.p. investment mgmt. Grumman Corp., Bethpage, N.Y., 1978-79; pres. Grumman Ohio Corp., Worthington, Ohio, 1979-88. Served with AC, USN, 1949-53. Mem. The Oaks Club.

LANDOW-ESSER, JANINE MARISE, lawyer; b. Omaha, Sept. 23, 1951; d. Erwin Landow and Beatrice (Hart) Appel; m. Jeffrey L. Esser, June 2, 1974; children: Erica, Caroline. BA, U. Wis., 1973, JD with honors, George Washington U., 1976. Bar: Va. 1976, DC 1977, Ill. 1985. Atty. U.S. Dept. Energy, Washington, 1976-83, Bell, Boyd & Lloyd, Chgo., 1985-86, Seyfarth, Shaw, Fairweather & Geraldson, Chgo., 1986-88, Holleb & Coff, Chgo., 1988-2000, Quarles & Brady, Chgo., 2000—. Contbr. articles to profl. jours. Bd. dirs. Bernard Zell Anshe Emet Day Sch. Parent-Tchr. Orgn., 1991-95. Mem. ABA, Chgo. Bar Assn. (vice chmn. environ. law com. 1990-91, chmn. 1991-92), Am. Jewish Congress (bd. dirs., pres. Midwest Region 2001--). Office: Quarles & Brady 500 W Madison St Ste 3700 Chicago IL 60661-2592 E-mail: je3@quarles.com.

LANDRY, MARK EDWARD, podiatrist, researcher; b. Washington, May 24, 1950; s. John Edward and Daphne (Fay) L.; m. Mary Ann Kotey, Sept. 7, 1974; children: John Ryan, Christopher John, Jessica Marie. D in Podiatry, Ohio Coll. Podiatric Medicine, 1975; MS in Edn., U. Kans., 1982. Diplomate Am. Bd. Podiatric Surgery, Am. Bd. Podiatric Orthopedics and Primary Podiatric Medicine. Gen. practice podiatry, Kansas City, Mo., 1977—, Overland Park, Kans., 1980—; clin. asst. prof. U. Health Scis., Kansas City, 1985-98; clin. assoc. prof. Coll. Podiatric Medicine and Surgery U. Osteo. Medicine and Health Scis., Des Moines, 1985-92; clin. instr. Sch. Medicine U. Mo., Kansas City, 1987-95. Founder, bd. dirs. Kansas City Podiatric Residency Program, Kansas City, 1982-91; adv. bd. Rockport Shoe Co.; chmn. podiatry dept. Park Lane Med. Ctr., Kansas City, Mo., 1995-97; dir. continuing edn. Kans. Podiatric Med. Assn., 1997—. Contbr. articles to profl. jours. Cons. Mid-Am. Track and Field Assn., Lenexa, Kans., 1978-88; com. chmn. Boy Scouts Am., Overland Park, Kans.; coach Johnson County Soccer League, 1987-90; head coach 6th and 7th grade girls' Cath. Youth Orgn. Basketball, 1995-96, 97; sponsor 8 & 11 Baseball League, 1987-90. 1st lt. USAF, 1975-77. Recipient Pres.'s award Ohio Sch. Podiatric Medicine, 1975; USAF scholar Armed Forces Health Professions, 1973-75. Fellow Am. Coll. Foot Surgeons, Acad. Podiatric Sports Medicine, Am. Coll. Primary Podiatric Medicine & Podiatric Orthopedics; mem. Kans. Podiatric Med Assn. (bd. dirs. 1997—), Brit. Podiatry Assn. (hon.), Am. Bd. Primary Podiatric Medicine (founding dir., bd. examiner 1994—), Holy Cross Social Club (pres. 1983-84), Prairie Life Club, Leukemia Assn. of Am. (team in tng. 1997-2000, team capt. 1999, K.C. corp. challenge participant 1997-99), K.C. (4th degree 1995—, chancellor 1998, 99), KC Ski Club (trip capt. 1999). Republican. Roman Catholic. Avocations: triathlon training (completed Grand Floridian Ironman competition, 1998, Ironman Fla., 1999), skiing. Home: 8120 W 99th St Overland Park KS 66212-3444 Office: 10550 Quivira Rd Ste 260 Overland Park KS 66215-2375 E-mail: mlandry398@aol.com.

LANDRY, PAUL LEONARD, lawyer; b. Mpls., Nov. 23, 1950; s. LeRoy Robert Landry and Alice Ruth (Swain) Stephens; m. Lisa Yvonne Yeo, Dec. 13, 1984; children: Marc, Lauren, Matthew. BA, Macalester Coll., 1974; postgrad., Georgetown U., 1976-77; JD, Boston U., 1977. Bar: Va. 1977, D.C. 1978, Minn. 1984, U.S. Dist. Ct. D.C., U.S. Dsit. Ct. Va., U.S. Dist. Ct. Minn., U.S. Ct. Appeals (D.C., 2d, 4th and 8th cirs.). Dancer Dance Theater Harlem, N.Y.C., 1971-72; prin. dancer Dance Theatre Boston, 1972-75; atty. EPA, Washington, 1976-77; assoc. Reed, Smith, Shaw & McClay, 1977-83; officer, shareholder Fredrikson & Byron, P.A., Mpls., 1984—. Adj. prof. law William Mitchell Coll. Law, St. Paul, 1985-89. Bd. dirs. Ind. Sch. Dist. 284, Wayzata, Minn., 1989-96, 2002-, chmn., 1992-93; bd. dirs. Walker Art Ctr., Mpls., 1992—; bd. dirs., vice chair Greater Twin Cities Youth Symphonies, 1999-2001; advisor Kevin McCary Scholarship Fund. Mem. ABA (conf. of minority ptnrs. adv. com.), Nat. Bar Assn., Minn. State Bar Assn. (art and entertainment sect., labor and employment sect.), D.C. Bar, Hennepin County Bar Assn., Black Entertainment and Sports Lawyers Assn., Barristers. Avocations: golf, music, basketball. Office: Fredrikson & Byron PA 900 2nd Ave S Ste 1100 Minneapolis MN 55402-3328 E-mail: plandry@fredlaw.com.

LANDSBERG, LEWIS, endocrinologist, medical researcher; b. N.Y.C., Nov. 23, 1938; AB, Williams Coll., 1960; MD, Yale U., 1964. From instr. to asst. prof. medicine Sch. Medicine Yale U., 1969-72; from asst. prof. to assoc. prof. Harvard Med. Sch., 1972-77, from assoc. prof. to prof., 1977-86; Irving S. Cutter prof., chmn. dept. medicine Med. Sch. Northwestern U. Med. Sch., 1990—; dir. Ctr. Endocrinology, Metabolism & Nutrition Northwestern U., 1990-93. Assoc. physician Yale-New Haven Hosp., 1969-71, attending physician, 1971-72, Beth Israel Hosp., 1974-79, physician, 1979-88, sr. physician, 1988-90; attending physician West Haven VA Hosp., 1970-72; assisting physician Boston City Hosp., 1972-73, assoc. vis. physician, 1973-74; physician-in-chief dept. medicine Northwestern Meml. Hosp., 1990—. Fellow ACP, AAAS; mem. Am. Fedn. Clin. Rsch., Endocrine Soc., N.Y. Acad. Scis., AHA, Am. Soc. Pharmacology and Exptl. Therapeutics, Am. Physiology Soc., Am. Soc. Clin. Investigators, Am. Clin. and Climatological Assn., Assn. Am. Physicians. Achievements include rsch. in catecholamines and the sympathoadrendal system, nutrition and the sympathetic nervous system, obesity and hypertension. Office: Northwestern Univ Med Sch Wesley Pavilion 296 250 E Superior St Chicago IL 60611-2958

LANDSKE, DOROTHY SUZANNE (SUE LANDSKE), state legislator; b. Evanston, Ill., Sept. 3, 1937; d. William Gerald and Dorothy Marie (Drewes) Martin; m. William Steve Landske, June 1, 1957; children: Catherine Suzanne Jones, Jacqueline Marie Basilotta, Pamela Florence Snyder, Cheryl Lynn Boisson, Eric Thomas. Student, St. Joseph Coll., Ind. U., U. Chgo. Owner, operator Sues Bridal House, 1967-75; dep. clk.-treas. Cedar Lake, 1975; chief dep. twp. assessor Center Twp., Crown Point, Ind., 1976-78, twp. assessor, 1979-84; mem. Ind. Senate, 1984—. Asst. pres., chair elections protem-senate. Vice chair Lake County Rep. Cen. Com., 1978-89, 97—. Maj. NG Res. Mem. LWV, Coun. State Govts., Nat. Order Women Legislators, Nat. Coun. State Legislators, Bus. and Profl. Women, Grange Ind. Farm Bur. Roman Catholic. Office: Ind Senate Dist 6 200 W Washington St Indianapolis IN 46204-2728

LANDWEHR, BRENDA, state legislator, financial executive; Mem. Kans. Ho. of Reps. Address: 1927 N Gow St Wichita KS 67203-1106

LANE, AL, state legislator; m. Peggy Lane. Grad. Ohio State U. Kans. state rep. Dist. 25, 1989—; internat. airline capt., ret., 1964-88. Home: 6529 Sagamore Rd Shawnee Mission KS 66208-1946

LANE, KENNETH EDWIN, retired advertising agency executive; b. Orange, N.J., Sept. 30, 1928; s. Clarence Edwin and Erma Catherine (Kinser) L.; children by previous marriage— Kenneth, Laura, Linda, Katherine; m. Susan Spafford Zimmer, Sept. 13, 1980; stepchildren— Todd and Margaret Zimmer. B.A., U. Chgo., 1947, M.A., 1950. Mgr. media Toni div. Gillette Co., 1953-63; media dir. MacParland-Aveyard Co., 1963-64; assoc. media dir. Leo Burnett Co., Chgo., 1964-71, mgr. media dept., 1971-75, sr. v.p. media services, 1975-84. Bd. dirs. Traffic Audit Bur. Maj. USAR, ret. Mem. Am. Assn. Advt. Agys., Media Dirs. Council., Phi Beta Kappa Office: Leo Burnett Agy 35 W Wacker Dr Chicago IL 60601-1614

LANE, MEREDITH ANNE, botany educator, museum curator; b. Mesa, Ariz., Aug. 4, 1951; d. Robert Ernest and Elva Jewell (Shilling) L.; m. Donald W. Longstreth, Apr. 6, 1974 (div. Feb. 1985). BS, Ariz. State U., 1974, MS, 1976; PhD, U. Tex., 1980. Asst. prof. U. Colo., Boulder, 1980-88, assoc. prof., 1988-89; assoc. prof., curator div. botany Natural History Mus., U. Kans., Lawrence, 1989-96, prof., 1997—. Vis. asst. prof. U. Wyo., Laramie, 1985-86; vis. scholar U. Conn., Storrs, 1989; cons. editor McGraw-Hill Ency. of Sci. and Tech., N.Y.C., 1985-92; program dir. Nat. Sci. Found., 1995-97; rsch. assoc. Smithsonian Inst., 1995—; agy. rep. Nat. Sci. and Tech. Coun., 1997. Editor Plant Sci. Bull., 1990-94; contbr. over 25 articles to profl. jours. Mem. Am. Soc. Plant Taxonomists (sec. 1986-88, program dir. 1986-90, councillor 1993-96, Cooley award 1982), Bot. Soc. Am. (sect. chmn. 1984-86, sect. sec. 1986-90), Internat. Orgn. for Plant Biosystematics (councillor 1989-92), Internat. Assn. Plant Taxonomists, Calif. Bot. Soc. Avocations: reading, conversation, country dance, hiking, furniture refinishing. Office: R L McGregor Herbarium 2045 Constant Ave Lawrence KS 66047-3729

LANE, MICHAEL HARRY, steel company executive; b. St. Louis, Jan. 8, 1943; s. Harry T. and Margaret (Cody) L.; m. Karen Numi, June 13, 1964; children: Michael P., Kelly, Richard. B.S. in Commerce, St. Louis U., 1964. C.P.A., Mo., Fla. Mgr. Price Waterhouse, Miami, Fla., 1964-72, St. Louis, 1964-72; v.p. fin. Laclede Steel Co., 1972—. Mem. Fin. Execs. Inst., Am. Inst. C.P.A.s, Mo. Soc. C.P.A.s Club: Mo. Athletic. Office: Laclede Steel Co 440 N. FOURTH St Saint Louis MO 63102

LANE, N. GARY, retired paleontologist; Emeritus prof. of paleontology Ind. U. Recipient Raymond C. Moor Paleontology medal Soc. for Sedimentary Geology, 1995. Office: Geology Dept Ind U Bloomington IN 47401

LANE, ROBERT W. farm equipment manufacturing executive; b. Washington D.C. BA (high honors), Wheaton (Ill.) Coll., 1972; MBA, U. Chgo. Grad. Sch. Bus., 1974. First Nat. Bank Chgo., Europe; various positions Deere & Co., Moline, Ill., 1982—, CFO, sr. v.p. fin./tax/acctg., 1996—, sr. v.p., mng. dir. mfg. mktg. Europe, Africa, Middle East, 1998—, pres. worldwide agrl. equip. divn., 1999, COO, pres., 2000—, chmn. bd., CEO, 2000—. Office: Deere & Co 1 John Deere Rd Moline IL 61265-8098

LANE, RONALD ALAN, lawyer; b. Ames, Iowa, July 15, 1950; s. Raymond Oscar and Beverly (Burdge) L.; m. Eileen Smietana, June 17, 1972; children: Andrew, Audrey. AB, Miami U., Oxford, Ohio, 1972; JD, Northwestern U., 1975; MBA, U. Chgo., 1987. Bar: U.S. Dist. Ct. (no. dist.) Ill. 1975, U.S. Ct. Appeals (7th cir.) 1975, U.S. Supreme Ct. 1980. Atty. Atchison, Topeka & Santa Fe Ry. Co., Chgo., 1975-78; from asst. gen. atty. to gen. atty. Santa Fe So. Pacific Corp., 1979-86, gen. corp. atty., 1986-87; asst. v.p. pers. and labor rels. Atchison, Topeka & Santa Fe Ry. Co., 1987-90; v.p., gen. counsel Ill. Ctrl. R.R. Co., Chgo., 1990-99; of counsel Franczek Sullivan, P.C., 1999—. Dir. Chgo. Ctrl. Area Com., 1995-99, Transp. Tech. Ctr., Inc., 1997-99; mem. railroad shipper trans. adv. coun. Surface Transp. Bd., 1996-99. Office: Franczek Sullivan PC 300 S Wacker Dr Ste 3400 Chicago IL 60606-6708

LANE, WILLIAM NOBLE, III, financial executive; b. Evanston, Ill., Aug. 2, 1943; s. William Noble and Marjorie Elizabeth (Hamilton) L.; children: Campbell, Heather, Carl. A.B., Princeton U., 1965. Salesman, Wallace Press, Inc., 1965-66; mgr. corp. planning Gen. Binding Corp., Northbrook, Ill., 1966-72, vice chmn., 1978-82, chmn., 1983—; pres. Northwestco, Inc., Chgo., 1972-78; chmn. bd., pres., CEO Lane Industries, Inc., Northbrook, 1978—. Chmn. bd. Lake View Trust & Savs. Bank, Chgo., N.W. Nat. Bank Chgo., Pioneer Bank & Trust Co., Northbrook Trust & Savs. Bank; dir. Hydraulic Component Services, Inc., Otis Assos. (architects), Schwaab, Inc. Trustee Rush Presbyn. St. Luke's Med. Center, Chgo., Lake Forest (Ill.) Acad., Chgo. Zool. Soc.; bd. govs. United Republican Fund Ill.; mem. Northwestern U. Assos.; econ. adv. council Princeton U.; bd. dirs. Irving Park YMCA, Chgo. Mem. Explorers Club. Episcopalian. Clubs: Winter (Lake Forest), Onwentsia (Lake Forest); Princeton (N.Y.C.); Port Royal Beach (Naples, Fla.); Commonwealth (Chgo.), Univ. (Chgo.), Econ. (Chgo.); Adventurers. Office: Lane Industries 1200 Shermer Rd Ste 400 Northbrook IL 60062-4561 also: Gen Binding Corp 1 Gbc Plz Northbrook IL 60062-4104 also: 4747 W Irving Park Rd Chicago IL 60641-2764

LANER, RICHARD WARREN, lawyer; b. Chgo., July 12, 1933; s. Jack E. and Esther G. (Cohon) L.; m. Barbara Lee Shless, Aug. 15, 1954 (dec. Oct. 1997); children: Lynn, Kenneth; m. Daryl Lynn Homer, Sept. 17, 1998. Student, U. Ill., 1951-54; BS, Northwestern U., 1955, LLB, 1956. Bar: Ill. 1956. Assoc. Laner, Muchin, Dombrow, Becker, Levin & Tominberg, Ltd., Chgo., 1956-62, ptnr., 1962-99, of counsel, 1999. Editor Northwestern Law Rev., 1954-56; contbr. articles to profl. jours. Mem. Chgo. Bar Assn. (chmn. com. labor law 1972-73), Chgo. Assn. Commerce and Industry, Order of Coif. Home: 161 E Chicago Ave Unit 41de Chicago IL 60611-2601 Office: Laner Muchin Dombrow Becker Levin & Tominberg Ltd 515 N State St Fl 28 Chicago IL 60610-4325 E-mail: rlaner@lmdblt.com.

LANEY, SANDRA EILEEN, service company executive; b. Cin., Sept. 17, 1943; d. Raymond Oliver and Henrietta Rose (Huber) H.; m. Dennis Michael Laney, Sept. 30, 1968; children: Geoffrey Michael, Melissa Ann. AS in Bus. Adminstrn., Thomas More Coll., 1988, BA in Bus. Adminstrn., 1993. Adminstrv. asst. to chief exec. officer Chemed Corp., Cin., 1982, asst. v.p., 1982-84, v.p., 1984-91, v.p., chief adminstrv. officer, 1991-93, sr. v.p., chief adminstrv. officer, 1993-2001, bd. dirs., 1986—, exec. v.p. chief adminstrn. officer, 2001—. Bd. dirs. Omnicare Inc., Covington, Ky. Mem. bd. advisors Sch. Nursing U. Cin., 1992—; bd. overseers Cin. Symphony Orch., 1998; trustee Lower Price Hill Cmty. Sch., Cmty. Land Coop. of Cin. Mem. AAUW, NOW, Internat. Platform Assn., Amnesty Internat., World Affairs Coun., Women's Action Coun. Roman Catholic. Office: Chemed Corp 2600 Chemed Ctr 255 E 5th St Cincinnati OH 45202-4700

LANFORD, LUKE DEAN, retired electronics company executive; b. Greer, S.C., Aug. 4, 1922; s. John D. and Ethel W. (Ballenger) L.; m. Donna Marie Cellar, Dec. 20, 1945 (dec. Apr. 29, 1984); 1 dau., Cynthia Lea Lanford Brown; m. Jacquelyn Sue Carr Bussell, Feb. 14, 1986 B.S.E.E., Va. Poly. Inst., 1943. With Western Electric Co., Inc., 1946-78, asst. mgr. tng., 1957-60, mgr. engring. Kansas City, 1960-63, asst. works mgr. Allentown, Pa., 1963-65; plant mgr. Reading, 1965-69; gen. mgr. Indpls., 1969-78. Dir. Met. Indpls. Television Assn., Inc., Sta. WFYI-TV, 1970— , pres., 1975-79 Served with U.S. Army, 1943-46. Mem. IEEE, Telephone Pioneers Am., Jacaranda West Country Club, Eta Kappa Nu, Tau Beta Pi, Phi Kappa Phi. Republican. Presbyterian. Home: 1935 Pebble Beach Ct Venice FL 34293-3830

LANG, CRAIG, farmer, farm association officer; m. Mary Lang; 4 children. Grad., Iowa State U. Co-owner dairy operation, Iowa; pres. Iowa Farm Bur., West Des Moines, 2001—. Mem. polit. action com., dairy adv. com. Iowa Farm Bur., mem. state bd., 1992, v.p.; bd. dirs. Am. Farm Bur. Sunday sch. tchr. Madison Ch. of Christ. Office: Iowa Farm Bur 5400 University Ave West Des Moines IA 50266

LANG, DANIEL W. trust company executive; BSBA, U. Colo.; MBA, U. Mo., Kansas City. With trust dept. Commerce Bank, 1982, NationsBank; exec. v.p., personal trust mgr. The Midwest Trust Co., Overland Park, Kans. Mem. planned gift coun. Children's Mercy Hosp. Mem.: Estate Planning Soc. Kansas City. Office: The Midwest Trust Co 10740 Nall Ave Ste 100 Overland Park KS 66211*

LANG, LOUIS I. state legislator, lawyer; b. Chgo., Nov. 26, 1949; s. Eugene and Shirley (Busel) L.; m. Teri Rosenbaum, 1987; children: David, Adam, Matthew Paul, Chad Paul, Rebecca. BA with high honors in Polit. Sci., U. Ill., 1971; JD with honors, DePaul U., 1974. Litigation ptnr. Feingold, Lang & Levy, 1977-93; attorney Niles Twp. Govt., Ill., 1977-87; Dist. 16 rep. Ill. Ho. Reps., Springfield, 1987—; of counsel Baker & Miller, 1993-95; chief counsel Cook County Emergency Telephone Svc. Bd., 1994—; of counsel Goldberg Weisman & Cairo Ltd., Chgo., 1995—. Ill. Ho. Reps. Dem. fl. rep., vice chmn. state govt. adminstrn. com. and judiciary I com., mem. appropriations II, cities and villages, human svcs., higher edn., children, aging coms.; chmn. mental health select, health care, real estate law, and rules coms., and spl. com. on flicts of interest. Mem. Mayor's Task Force on Traffic, Skokie; campaign mgr. Samuel Berger for State Senate, Ill., 1980; bd. dirs. Holocaust Meml. Found., 1987—; bd. dirs. Jewish Cmty. Ctr., 1987—, North Ctrl. Skokie Homeowners Assn.; mgr. Little League Baseball. Named Citizen of the Month, Lerner Newspapers, 1986, Legislator of the Yr. Ill. Hosp. Assn., Ill. Pub. Action Coun., Ill. Social Workers Assn., Chgo. Tchrs. Union, Ill. Coun. on Sr. citizens, Suburban Area Agy. on Aging, Nat. Assn. Social Workers, Ill. Assn. Social Workers, Svc. Employees Union, Ind. Voters of Ill., Ethel Parker award Ind. Voters of Ill., 1993 Maccabean award Zionist Orgn. Chgo., Kit Pfau Voters Rights award Ind. Voters of Ill., Best Legis. Voting Record award, 1995 Activator Friend of Agr. award Ill. Farm Bur., Statesman of the Yr. award Internat. Union Operating Engrs., 1996. Mem. Niles Twp. Dem. Orgn., Decalogue Soc. of Lawyers, Ill. Bar Assn., Chgo. Bar Assn., Hillel Found., Pi Lambda Phi. Home: 5123 Jerome Ave Skokie IL 60077-3359

LANG, OTTO, industry executive, former Canadian cabinet minister; b. Handel, Sask., Can., May 14, 1932; s. Otto T. and Maria (Wurm) L.; m. Adrian Ann Merchant, 1963-88; children: Maria (dec.), Timothy, Gregory, Andrew, Elisabeth, Amanda, Adrian; m. Deborah McCawley, 1989; stepchildren: Andrew, Rebecca. BA, U. Sask., 1951, LLB, 1953; BCL (Rhodes scholar), Oxford (Eng.) U., 1955; LLD (hon.), U. Man., 1987. Bar: Sask. 1956, Ont., Yukon and N.W.T 1972, Man. 1988; created Queen's counsel 1972. Mem. faculty Law Sch., U. Sask., 1956-68, assoc. prof. law, 1958-61, prof., dean law, 1961-68; M.P. for Sask.-Humboldt, 1968-79; Canadian min. without portfolio, 1968-69; min. for energy and water, 1969; min. of manpower and immigration, 1970-72; min. of justice, 1972-75, 78-79; min. transport, 1975-79; min.-in-charge Canadian Wheat Bd., 1969-79; exec. v.p. Pioneer Grain Co. Ltd., James Richardson & Sons Ltd., Winnipeg, Manitoba, Can., 1979-88; chmn. Transp. Inst., U. Man., 1988-93; mng. dir. Winnipeg Airports Authority, Inc., 1992-93, vice chmn., 1993—; pres., CEO Centra Gas Manitoba, Inc., Winnipeg, 1993-99; cons., 1999—; sr. counsel G.P.C., 2000—. Mem. Queen's Privy Coun. for Can.; hon. consul gen. for Japan, 1993-97; bd. dirs. Investors Group Trust Co., London Life Trust Co. Editor: Contemporary Problems in Public Law, 1967. V.P. Sask. Liberal Assn., 1956-62, fed. campaign chmn., Sask., 1963-64; campaign chmn. Winnipeg United Way, 1983; chmn. Royal Winnipeg Ballet Captial Campaign, 1996-99. Decorated officer Order of Can. Mem.: St. Charles Golf Club. Roman Catholic. Office: GPC 6 Liss Rd Saint Andrews MB Canada R1A 2X2 Fax: 204-338-1524. E-mail: olang@mb.sympatico.ca.

LANG, THOMPSON HUGHES, publishing company executive; b. Albuquerque, Dec. 12, 1946; s. Cornelius Thompson and Margaret Miller (Hughes) L. Student, U. N.Mex., 1965-68, U. Americas, Mexico City, 1968-69. Advt. salesman Albuquerque Pub. Co., 1969-70, pres., 1971—; pub., pres., treas., dir. Jour. Pub. Co., 1971—; pres., dir. Masthead, Internat., 1971—; pres. Magnum Systems, Inc., 1973—; pres., treas., dir. Jour. Ctr. Corp., 1979—; chmn. bd., dir. Starline Printing, Inc., 1985—. Chmn. bd. dirs. Corp. Security and Investigation, Inc., 1986—; pres., bd. dirs. Eagle Systems, Inc., 1986—. Mem. HOW Orgn., Sigma Delta Chi. Home: 8643 Rio Grande Blvd NW Albuquerque NM 87114-1301 Office: Albuquerque Pub Co PO Drawer JT 87103 7777 Jefferson St NE Albuquerque NM 87109-4343

LANGBO, ARNOLD GORDON, food company executive; b. Richmond, B.C., Can., Apr. 13, 1937; s. Osbjourn and Laura Marie (Hagen) L.; m. Martha Marie Miller, May 30, 1959; children: Sharon Anne, Maureen Bernice, Susan Colleen, Roderick Arnold, Robert Wayne, Gary Thomas, Craig Peter, Keith Edward. Student, U. B.C. Retail salesman Kellogg Co., Vancouver, 1956-57, dist. mgr. Prince George, B.C., 1957-60, supermarket salesman Vancouver, 1960, dist mgr. Winnipeg, Man., 1964-65; acct. mgr. Kellog Co. of Can., Ltd., Toronto, 1965-67; sales staff asst. Kellogg Co., Battle Creek, Mich., 1967-69, adminstrv. asst. to pres., 1969; exec. v.p. Kellogg Co. of Can. Ltd., London, 1970; v.p. sales and mktg. Kellogg Salada Can. Ltd., Toronto, 1971-74, sr. v.p. sales and mktg., 1974-76, pres., chief exec. officer, 1976-78; pres. food products div. Kellogg U.S., Battle Creek, 1978-81; past exec. v.p. Kellogg Co., group exec. v.p., 1983-86, exec. v.p., 1986—; pres. Kellogg Internat., 1986—, Mrs. Smith's Frozen Foods Co. subs. Kellogg Co., Battle Creek, 1983-85, chmn., CEO, 1985—; pres. Kellogg Internat., 1986—, pres., COO, internat. bd. dirs., 1990-99; chmn., CEO, pres. Kellogg Co., Battle Creek, 1992-99, also bd. dirs., retired, 1999. Bd. dirs. Johnson & Johnson, Atlantic Richfield Co., Whirlpool Corp.; chmn. Grocery Mfrs. Am. Co-trustee W.K. Kellogg Found. Trust; chmn. trustee Albion Coll. Bd.; bd. dirs. Internat. Youth Found., America's Promise; adv. bd. J.K. Kellogg Grad. Sch. of Mgmt., Northwestern U. Mem. The Bus. Roundtable. Office: Kellogg Co Box 3599 1 Kellogg Sq Battle Creek MI 49016-0075

LANGDON, HERSCHEL GARRETT, lawyer, director; b. Lowry City, Mo., Oct. 6, 1905; s. Isaac Garrett and Della (Park) L.; m. Ethel Virginia Waterson, May 26, 1931 (dec. Apr. 1979); children: Richard G., Ann Virginia (Mrs. Charles Eugene Willoughby Ward); m. Miriam Pickett, May 17, 1982. B.A., U. Iowa, 1930, J.D., 1931. Bar: Iowa 1931. Atty. Herrick, Langdon & Langdon (and predecessors), 1935—. Fellow Am. Coll. Trial Lawyers, Am. Bar Found.; mem. Am., Iowa, Polk County bar assns., Phi Beta Kappa, Delta Sigma Rho, Phi Delta Pi. Congressionalist. Club: Mason. Office: 1800 Financial Ctr 7th and Walnut Des Moines IA 50309 Home: 612 Glenview Dr Des Moines IA 50312-2528

LANGE, CRYSTAL MARIE, university official, nursing educator; b. Snover, Mich., Aug. 22, 1927; d. Bazil H. and Crystal S. (Hilborn) Morse; m. Elmer William Lange, June 10, 1961; children: Gregory, Frederick, Helen, Charles, G. Benson, Robert, Larry. BSN, U. Mich., 1949; MSN, Wayne State U., 1961; PhD, Mich. State U., 1972. Pvt. duty nurse, Richmond, Ind., 1949-50; asst. DON, nursing supr., instr. St. Mary's Hosp., Tucson, 1950-58; night supr. Pima County Hosp., 1958-59; asst. dir. Sch. Nursing, Saginaw (Mich.) Gen. Hosp., 1959-60; from instr. to prof., chmn. divsn. Delta Coll., University Center, Mich., 1962-76; dean Sch. Nursing and Allied Health Scis., prof. nursing Saginaw Valley State U., 1976-96, asst. to v.p. acad. affairs, 1976-96, assoc. v.p. acad. affairs, 1996—. Mem. vis. com. U. Mich. Med. Ctr., Ann Arbor, 1978-81. Author: Leadership for Quality, 1966, Instructor's Guide—Nursing Skills and Techniques, 1969, The Use of the Auto-Tutorial Laboratory and the Mobile Tutorial Unit in Teaching, 1969, Instructor's Guide—Nursing Skills and Techniques—Films 76-126, 1972, Films 127-151, 1971, Auto-Tutorial Techniques in Nursing Education, 1971, Future Education: Diagnosis Prescriptions Evaluation, 1971; contbr. articles to profl. jours. Bd. dirs. Saginaw chpt. ARC, 1982—, Saginaw Vis. Nurse Assn., 1980—. Recipient award Mich. Acad. Sci., Arts and Letters, 1970, Monsour Found. lectureship award Health Edn. Media Assn., 1977; named Woman of Distinction Bay Area coun. Girl Scouts U.S.A., 1997; fellow NEH, 1983. Fellow Am. Acad. Nursing (governing coun., sec. 1978-80); mem. ANA, Am. Acad. Arts and Scis., AAUP (chpt. v.p. 1975, award citation 1970), Am. Ednl. Scis., Mich. Nurses Assn., Saginaw Dist. Nurses Assn. (bd. dirs. 1976—), U. Mich. Alumnae Assn., Wayne State U. Alumnae Assn., Phi Kappa Phi, Sigma Theta Tau. Home: 4135 Kochville Rd Saginaw MI 48604-9750 Office: Saginaw Valley State U Office Vice Pres University Center MI 48710-0001

LANGE, DAVID CHARLES, journalist; b. Natrona Hts., Pa., Oct. 14, 1949; s. Charles Manfred Lange and Helga (Hingst) Faverty; m. Linda Gaiduk, June 29, 1974; children: Erik David, Anthony Charles. BA in Journalism, Kent State U., 1975; postgrad., Akron U., 1980-83. Placement specialist Goodwill Industries Cleve., 1976-77; mng. editor, sports editor Chagrin Valley Times, Chagrin Falls, Ohio, 1977-82; editor Chagrin Valley Times/Solon Times, 1988—; features editor, Sunday editor Lake County Telegraph, Painesville, Ohio, 1982-83; editor Geauga Times Leader, Chardon, 1983-84; editor-in-chief Habitat, Cleve., 1984-88. Asst. swim coach Lake Erie Silver Dolphins/Kenston H.S., 1999—. With USN, 1968-71, Vietnam. Recipient Democracy in Housing award Cleve. Assn. Real Estate Brokers, 1988. Mem. Soc. Profl. Journalists (Excellence in Journalism award human interest reporting 1981, Best Columnist in Ohio 2000), Ohio Newspaper Assn. (Hooper award for editl. writing 1991-92, 94, 96-2002, 2d place 1990, 93, Hooper award for column writing 1993, 97, 2001-02), Chagrin Valley C. of C., Solon C. of C., Cleve. Press Club, Nat. Newspaper Assn., VFW, Am. Legion, Vietnam Vets. Am. Avocations: swimming, skiing, tennis, basketball. Home: 8353 Chagrin Rd Chagrin Falls OH 44023-4757 Office: Chagrin Valley Times PO Box 150 Chagrin Falls OH 44022-0150

LANGE, GERALD F. state legislator; b. Devils Lake, N.D., Sept. 19, 1928; m. Alice Lange; 4 children. B.A. Philosophy, U. N.D., 1951; student, Georgetown U., 1957, U. Navarra, Pampaloma, Spain, 1964. High school teacher, 1954-62; prof. of history & govt. Dakota State U., 1964-90; mem. S.D. Senate, 1990—, mem. transp. retirement laws and taxation coms., chmn. local govt. com.; farmer. With US Army Signal Corps, 1946-47, with Army of Occupation, Japan, 1946-47.n Home: RR 3 Box 109 Madison SD 57042-9342

LANGE, MARILYN, social worker; b. Milw., Dec. 6, 1936; d. Edward F. and Erna E. (Karstaedt) L.; divorced; children: Lara Cash, Gregory Cash. B of Social Work, U. Wis., Milw., 1962, MSW, 1974. Cert. ind. clin. social worker. Recreation specialist Dept. Army, Europe, 1962-63; social worker Family Svc. Milw., 1967-75, dir. homecare divsn., 1975-85; nat. field rep. Alzheimers Assn., Chgo., 1986-90; exec. dir. Village Adult Svcs., Milw., 1991—. Mem. Nat. Coun. Aging, Wis. Adult Daysvcs. Assn. (past pres.), Dementia Care Network, Older Adult Svc. Providers Consortium, U. Wis.-Milw. Alumni Assn. Home: 8959 Woodbridge Dr Greendale WI 53129 Office: Village Adult Svcs 336 W Walnut St Milwaukee WI 53212-3811 E-mail: marilyn_lange@aurora.org.

LANGER, EDWARD L. trade association administrator; b. Cleve., May 8, 1936; s. Edward L. and Evelyn (Palmer) L.; m. Sheila Mary Fitzpatrick, Nov. 5, 1957 (div. Sept. 1976); children— Dennis, Edward, Michael, Thomas, Michele; m. Carol E. Stower, Aug. 4, 1979; children— Tamara, Troy BS, John Carroll U., 1958, MA, 1964; postgrad., Ohio U., 1962, 63, Cleve. State U., 1967-68. Asst. dean admissions and records John Carroll U., University Heights, Ohio, 1964-65; head guidance Wickliffe City Schs., 1965-67; successively dir. mem. relations, mktg., planning, asst. mng. dir. Am. Soc. for Metals, Materials Park, 1967-84, mng. dir., 1984-96; bd. dirs., vice-chmn. Kolene Corp, 1997—. Bd. dirs. Kolene Corp. Author: Solid State Structures and Reactions, 1968 Bd. dirs., vice chmn. Cleve. Conv. Bur., 1984-98. Mem. Am. Soc. Assn. Execs. (bd. dirs., vice chmn. 1988-92), Coun. Engring. and Sci. Soc. Execs. (bd. dirs. 1987-93, pres. 1992), numerous other engring. and sci. socs. Avocations: fishing, golf.

LANGER, RICHARD J. lawyer; b. Rockford, Ill., June 10, 1944; s. John W. and Dorothy E. (Brunn) Langrehr; m. Audrey A. Russo, Jan. 28, 1967; children: Kathleen M., Michael R. BS, U. Ill., 1967; JD, U. Wis., 1974. Bar: Wis. 1974, U.S. Dist. Ct. (we. dist.) Wis. 1974. Assoc. Ela, Esch, Hart & Clark, Madison, Wis., 1974-76; ptnr. Stolper, Koritzinsky, Brewster & Neider, 1976-91, Michael, Best & Friedrich, Madison, 1991—. Pres. Hospice Care Found., Inc. Author: The Marital Property Classification Handbook, 1986, 2d edit., 1998, Workbook For Wisconsin Estate Planners, 1997, Family Estate Planning in Wisconsin, 1996, also articles. Sec. Combat Blindness Found., Madison, 1988—. Fellow Am. Coll. Trust and Estate Coun.; mem. ABA, State Bar Wis., Madison Estate Coun. Avocations: scuba diving, traveling, bicycling. Home: 1502 Windfield Way Madison WI 53562-3808 Office: Michael Best & Friedrich 1 S Pinckney St Madison WI 53703-2892

LANGER, STEVEN, human resources management consultant and industrial psychologist; b. N.Y.C., June 4, 1926; s. Israel and Anna (Glaisner) L.; m. Jacqueline White, Oct. 11, 1954 (dec. Dec. 1969); children: Bruce, Diana, Geoffrey; m. Elaine Catherine Brewer, Dec. 29, 1979 (dec. Feb. 1992). BA in Psychology, Calif. State U., Sacramento, 1950; MS in Pers. Svcs., U. Colo., 1958; PhD, Walden U., 1972. Lic. psychologist, Ill. Asst. to pers. dir. City and County of Denver, 1956-59; pres. dir. City of Pueblo (Colo.), 1959-60; pers. cons. J.L. JAcobs & Co., Chgo., 1961-64, adminstrv. mgr., 1966-67; sales selection mgr. Reuben H. Donnelly Corp., 1964-66; pres. Abbott, Langer & Assocs., Crete, Ill., 1967—. Vis. prof. mgmt. Loyola U., Chgo., 1969-71; community prof. behavioral scis. Purdue U., Calumet campus, Hammond, Ind., 1973-75. Contbr. articles on indsl. psychology and human resources mgmt. to profl. publs. Mem. Ill.

Psychol. Assn. (chmn. sect. indsl. psychologists 1971-72), Chgo. Psychol. Assn. (pres. 1974-75, 94-95), Chgo. Indsl./Orgnl. Psychologists, Soc. Human Resources Mgmt. (accredited, chmn. rsch. award com. 1966-69), World at Work, Chgo. Compensation Assn. (sec. 1976-77), Mensa (pres. Chgo. chpt. 1972-74). Unitarian. Home: 309 Herndon St Park Forest IL 60466-1132 Office: Abbott Langer & Assoc 548 1st St Crete IL 60417-2199 E-mail: slanger@abbott-langer.com.

LANGHOLZ, ARMIN PAUL, communications educator; b. St. Paul, June 25, 1929; s. Christian Theodore and Selma Cora (Kamholz) L.; m. Mary Ann Green, Aug. 13, 1955; children: Kevin Dean, Lori Lee Langholz West. BS in Edn., Capital U., 1951; MA, Ohio State U., 1955, PhD, 1965. Instr. Capital U., Columbus, Ohio, 1954-57, asst. prof., 1957-66, assoc. prof., 1966-71, prof., 1971-94, dept. chmn., 1970-75, 80-93, prof. emeritus, 1994—. Dir. comm. Met. Area Ch. Bd., Columbus, 1959-70; cons. Luth. Edn. Conf. of North Am., Washington, 1980-94. Prodr.: (children's TV program) Wonderbox, 1959-70, (religious news program) We Want to Know. Bd. dirs., chmn. Luth. Sr. City, Columbus, 1985-90; bd. dirs. cen. Ohio Luth. Social Svcs., 1990-97. Sgt. 1st class U.S. Army, 1952-54, Korea. Recipient Stellhorn award, Capital U., 1985, Praestantia award for Disting. Teaching, Capital U., 1986. Mem. NATAS (bd. dirs. Columbus/Dayton/Cin. chpt., Disting. Svc. award Ohio Valley chpt. 1994), Speech Comm. Assn., Ohio Speech Comm. Assn., Broadcast Edn. Assn., Nat. Collegiate Players, Tau Kappa Alpha. Avocations: golf, gardening. Home: 1348 Haddon Rd Columbus OH 43209-3101

LANGLEY, GRANT F. municipal lawyer; b. Worcester, Mass., July 20, 1945; BA, U. Wis., 1967. Asst. city atty. City of Milw., 1971-84, city atty., 1984—. Mem. Internat. Mcpl. Lawyers Assn. Office: Office of City Atty City Hall Rm 800 200 E Wells St Milwaukee WI 53202-3515

LANGSETH, KEITH, state legislator, farmer; b. Moorhead, Minn., Jan. 20, 1938; s. Norman Clifford and Ruth (Rosenquist) L.; m. Lorraine Mae Ersland, 1957; children: Danny, Gayle, Joy. Farmer; Dist. 9B rep. Minn. Ho. of Reps., St. Paul, 1975-78; mem. Minn. Senate from 9th dist., 1980—. Chmn. agr., transp. and semi-states divsn., Minn. State Senate; mem. Edn., Edn. Funding, Fin., Transp., and Met. Affairs coms. Chmn. Dist. 9 Dem.-Farmer-Labor party, Minn., 1973-74, chmn. Clay County Dem.-Farmer-Labor party, 1974. Office: RR 2 Box 81 Glyndon MN 56547-9631 also: State Senate State Capital Building Saint Paul MN 55155-0001

LANGSLEY, DONALD GENE, psychiatrist, medical board executive; b. Topeka, Oct. 5, 1925; s. Morris J. and Ruth (Pressman) L.; m. Pauline R. Langsley, Sept. 9, 1955; children: Karen Jean, Dorothy Ruth, Susan Louise. B.A., SUNY, Albany, 1949; M.D., U. Rochester, 1953. Diplomate: Am. Bd. Psychiatry and Neurology (dir. 1976-80), Nat. Bd. Med. Examiners. Intern USPHS Hosp., San Francisco, 1953-54; resident psychiatry U. Calif., 1954-59, NIMH career tchr. in psychiatry, 1959-61; candidate San Francisco and Chgo. insts. for psychoanalysis, 1958-67; asst. prof., assoc. prof. psychiatry U. Colo. Sch. Medicine, 1961-68; prof., chmn. dept. psychiatry U. Calif., Davis, 1968-77, U. Cin., 1977-81; prof. dept. psychiatry Northwestern U. Sch. Medicine, Chgo., 1981—. Mem. psychiatry edn. com. NIMH, 1969-75; exec. v.p. Am. Bd. Med. Spltys., 1981-91; trustee Ednl. Commn. for Fgn. Med. Graduates, 1983-91; mem. adv. com. on Grad. Med. Edn. Dept. Def., 1986-87; bd. govs. EcuMed, 1983-85; bd. dirs. Nat. Resident Matching Program, 1982, sec. 1984-87, 89-91, pres. 1987-89; mem. Ill. Med. Disciplinary Bd., 2000—. Author: The Treatment of Families in Crisis, 1968, Mental Health Education in the New Medical Schools, 1973, Peer Review Manual for Psychiatry, 1976, Handbook of Community Mental Health, 1981, Evaluating the Skills of Medical Specialists, 1983, Legal Aspects of Certification & Accreditation, 1983, Trends in Specialization, 1985, Hospital Privileges & Specialty Medicine, 1986, Hospital Privileges & Specialty Medicine, 2d edit., 1991, How to Evaluate Residents, 1986, How to Select Residents, 1988, Health Policy Issues in Graduate Medicine Education, 1992, Ethics Primer of American Psychiatric Association, 2000; contbr. articles to med. jours. Served with AUS, 1943-46; med. officer USPHS, 1953-54. Recipient Spl. awards Colo. Assn. for Mental Health, 1968, Spl. awards Sacramento Area Mental Health Assn., 1973 Fellow Am. Psychiat. Assn. (Hofheimer award 1971, pres. 1980-81, chmn. peer rev. com. 1975-77, Kiewit lectr. 1990, Adminstrv. Psychiatry award 1993, ethics appeals bd. 1993-99, ethics com. 2000-03), Am. Coll. Psychiatrists; mem. Ctrl. Calif. Psychiat. Soc. (pres. 1973-74), Colo. Psychiat. Soc. (pres.-elect 1967-68), Soc. Med. Adminstrs. Home and Office: 9445 Monticello Ave Evanston IL 60203-1117 E-mail: langsley@northwestern.edu.

LANGSLEY, PAULINE ROYAL, psychiatrist; b. Lincoln, Nebr., July 2, 1927; d. Paul Ambrose and Dorothy (Sibley) Royal; m. Donald G. Langsley, Sept. 9, 1955; children: Karen Jean, Dorothy Ruth Langsley Runman, Susan Louise. BA, Mills Coll., 1949; MD, U. Nebr., 1953. Cert. psychiatrist, Am. Bd. Psychiatry and Neurology. Intern Mt. Zion Hosp., San Francisco, 1954; resident U. Calif., 1954-57, student health psychiatrist Berkeley, 1957-61, U. Colo., Boulder, 1961-68; assoc. clin. prof. psychiatry U. Calif. Med. Sch., Davis, 1968-76; student health psychiatrist U. Calif., 1968-76; assoc. clin. prof. psychiatry U. Cin., 1976-82; pvt. practice psychiatry Cin., 1976-82; cons. psychiatrist Federated States of Micronesia, Pohnpei, 1984-87; fellow in geriatric psychiatry Rush-Presbyn./St. Luke Hosp., Chgo., 1989-91. Mem. accreditation rev. com. Accreditation Coun. for Continuing Med. Edn., 1996-98. Trustee Mills Coll., Oakland, 1974-78, 2001—; bd. dirs. Evanston Women's Club. Fellow Am. Psychiat. Assn. (chair continuing med. edn. 1990-96); mem. AMA, Am. Med. Womens Assn., Ohio State Med. Assn., Ill. Psychiat. Assn. (sec. 1993-95, pres.-elect 1995-96, pres. 1996-97, accreditation coun. 1996-98). Home and Office: 9445 Monticello Ave Evanston IL 60203-1117

LANGWORTHY, AUDREY HANSEN, state legislator; b. Grand Forks, N.D., Apr. 1, 1938; d. Edward H. and Arla (Kuhlman) Hansen; m. Asher C. Langworthy Jr., Sept. 8, 1962; children: Kristin Langworthy McLaughlin, Julia Langworthy Steinberg. BS, U. Kans., 1960, MS, 1962; postgrad., Harvard U., 1989. Tchr. jr. high sch. Shawnee Mission Sch. Dist., Johnson County, Kans., 1963-65; councilperson City of Prairie Village, 1981-85; mem. Kans. Senate from 7th dist., Topeka, 1985-2001. Alt. del. Nat. Conf. State Legislatures, 1985-87, del., 1987—, nominating com., 1990-92, vice chair fed. budget and taxation com., 1994, chair fed. budget and taxation com., 1995-96, vice chair assembly on federal issues, 1996-97, mem. exec. com., 1997-2000; del. Midwestern Conf. State Legislatures, 1989-98; mem. strategic planning com. Coun. State Govts., 1997-98; bd. dirs. St. Luke's/Shawnee Mission Med. Ctr. Found., 1997—. City co-chmn. Kassebaum for U.S. Senate, Prairie Village, 1978; pres. Jr. League Kansas City, Mo., 1977, Kansas City Eye Bank, 1980-82, chmn., 1983-85, bd. mem., 1977-98; mem. bd. Greater Kansas City ARC, 1975—, pres., 1984, chmn. midwestern adv. coun., 1985-86, nat. bd. govs., 1987-93; mem. Johnson County C.C. Found., 1999—; mem. Leadership Kans., Germany Today Program, 1991; bd. dirs. Kans. Wildlife & Parks Fund; trustee Found. on Aging, 1992-96; hon. co-chair Shawnee Mission Edn. Found. Benefit Showtime 99, 1999; mem. Johnson County adv. com. Met. Orgn. to Counter Sexual Assault, 1999—; bd. dirs. Cmty. Found. of Johnson County, 1999—, Heart of Am. United Way, 2000—; chair Kans. 3rd dist. George W. Bush-Pres., 2000; elected precinct committeewoman, 2000—; del. Rep. Nat. Conv., 2000, mem. platform com. Recipient Outstanding Vol. award Cmty. Svcs. Award Found., 1983, Confidence in Edn. award Friends of Edn., 1984, Pub. Svc. award as Kans. Legislator of Yr., Hallmark Polit. Action Com., 1991, Clara Barton Honor award Greater Kans. City ARC, Intergovtl. Leadership award League Kans. Mcpls., 1994, Disting. Pub. Svc. award United Cmty. Svcs. of Johnson County, 1995, Outstanding Achievement in Hist. Preservation award Alexander Majors Hist. House, 1995, Kansas City Spirit award, 1996, disting. pub. svc. award Prairie Village, 1995, Audrey Langworthy award Univ. Mo-Kansas City Women's Coun. Grad. Asst. Fund, 1997, Audrey Langworthy award Outstanding Youth Vol. Work Greater Kansas City ARC, 1996, Regional Leadership award Mid-Am. Regional Coun., 1999, award of appreciation Kans. Rep. Party, 2000, Cmty. Svc. award Greater Kansas City Women's Polit. Caucus, 2000, Recognition for Leadership and Svc., Greater Kansas City C. of C., 2000; named 1st hon. chair The Genevieve Byrn Series, Greater Kansas City ARC, 2000. Mem. LWV, Women's Pub. Svc. Network, U. Kans. Alumni Assn. Episcopalian. Avocations: hunting, running, family. Home: 6324 Ash St Prairie Village KS 66208-1369 E-mail: alangwo622@aol.com.

LANGWORTHY, ROBERT BURTON, lawyer; b. Kansas City, Mo., Dec. 24, 1918; s. Herman Moore and Minnie (Leach) L.; m. Elizabeth Ann Miles, Jan. 2, 1942; children: David Robert, Joan Elizabeth Langworthy Tomek, Mark Burton. AB, Princeton U., 1940; JD, Harvard U., 1943. Bar: Mo. 1943, U.S. Supreme Ct. 1960. Practiced in, Kansas City, 1943—; assoc., then mem. and v.p. Linde, Thomson, Langworthy, Kohn & Van Dyke, P.C., 1943-91; pres., mng. shareholder Blackwood, Langworthy & Schmelzer, P.C., Kansas City, Mo., 1991-96; mng. mem. Blackwood & Langworthy, LC, 1996—. Lectr. on probate, law sch. CLE courses U. Mo., Kansas City. Mem. bd. editors Harvard Law Rev., 1941-43; contbr. chpts. to Guardian and Trust, Powers, Conservatorships and Nonprobate Desk Books of Mo. Bar. Mem. edn. appeal bd. U.S. Dept. Edn., 1982-86; commr. Housing Authority Kansas City, 1963-71, chmn., 1969-71; chmn. Bd. Election Commrs. Kansas City, 1973-77; chmn. bd. West Ctrl. area YMCA, 1969—; mem. bd. Mid-Am. region YMCA, 1970-83, vice chmn., 1970-73, chmn., 1973-78; pres. Met. Bd. Kansas City (Mo.) YMCA (now YMCA of Greater Kansas City), 1965, bd. dirs., 1965—, mem. nat. bd. 1971-78, 79-83; bd. dirs. YMCA of the Rockies, 1974—, bd. sec., 1994-99; chmn. bd. trustees Sioux Indian YMCAs, 1983—; bd. dirs. Armed Svcs. YMCA, 1984-85; pres. Met. Area Citizens Edn., 1969-72; chmn. Citizens Assn. Kansas City (Mo.), 1967, bd. dirs., 1995-96; bd. dirs. Project Equality Kans.-Mo., 1967-80, pres., 1970-72, treas., 1972-73, sec., 1973-76; 1st v.p. Human Resources Corp. Kansas City, 1969-71, 72-73, bd. dirs., 1965-73; hon. v.p. Am. Sunday Sch. Union (now Am. Missionary Fellowship), 1965—; vice chmn. bd. trustees Kemper Mil. Sch., 1966-73; U.S. del. YMCA World Coun., Buenos Aires, 1977, Estes Park, Colo., 1981, Nyborg, Denmark, 1985; bd. dirs. Mo. Rep. Club, 1960—; del., mem. platform com. Rep. Nat. Conv., 1960; Rep. nominee for U.S. Congress, 1964; mem. gen. assembly Com. on Representation Presbyn., 1991-97, moderator, 1993-94; commr. to gen. assembly Presbyn. Ch., 1984, mem. gen. assembly com. on location of hdqs. 1984-87; moderator Heartland Presbyn., 1984. Lt. (j.g.) USNR, 1943-46, capt. Res. ret. Mem.: ABA, Harvard Law Sch. Assn. Mo. (v.p. 1973—74, pres. 1974—75, 1985—87), Lawyers Assn. Kansas City, Mo. State Bar (chmn. probate and trust com. 1983—85, chmn. sr. lawyers com. 1991—93), Kansas City Bar Assn. (chmn. probate law com. 1988—90, 1999—2000, living will com. 1989—91), Kansas City Club. Presbyterian (Elder). Home: Claridge Ct Apt 305 8101 Mission Rd Prairie Village KS 66208-5238 Office: 1220 Washington St Ste 300 Kansas City MO 64105-1439 E-mail: Robertlangworthy@aol.com.

LANGWORTHY, THOMAS ALLAN, microbiologist, educator; b. Oak Park, Ill., Aug. 7, 1943; s. Thomas Earl and Jean Carolyn (Hruby) L.; m. Pamela Joyce Tanis, May 15, 1965 (div. 1985); children: Jocelyn Ann, Jennifer Elise; m. Jane Rae Heckenlively, Sept. 15, 1988. AB, Grinnell Coll., 1965; PhD, U. Kans., 1971. Asst. prof. U. S.D., Vermillion, 1973-78, assoc. prof., 1978-82, prof., 1982-91, prof., chair, 1991-95, prof., 1995—. Alexander von Humboldt preistrager and guest prof. U. Regensburg, Germany, 1984-85; cons. EG&G Idaho, Idaho Falls, 1984—. Contbr. articles to profl. jours. and chpts. to books; mem. editl. bd. Applied and Environ. Microbiology, 1987-96. Fellow Am. Acad. Microbiology; mem. Am. Soc. for Microbiology, AAAS, Internat. Orgn. for Mycoplasmology, Sigma Xi. Office: U SD Sch Medicine 414 E Clark St Vermillion SD 57069-5166 E-mail: tlangwor@usd.edu.

LANIGAN, JOHN, radio personality; b. Pgallala, Nebr. With WGAR, 1970—83; radio host WMJI, Cleve., 1985—. Office: 6200 Oak Tree Blvd 4th Fl Cleveland OH 44131*

LANKFORD, RAYMOND LEWIS, baseball player; b. Modesto, Calif., June 5, 1967; Student, Modesto Jr. Coll. Selected 3d round free-agt. draft Chgo. Cubs, 1986, St. Louis Cardinals, 1987; outfielder Appalachian League, 1987, Midwest League, 1988, St. Louis Cardinals, 1990—. Office: care St Louis Cardinals Busch Stadium 250 Stadium Plz Saint Louis MO 63102-1722*

LANNERT, ROBERT CORNELIUS, manufacturing company executive; b. Chgo., Mar. 14, 1940; s. Robert Carl and Anna Martha (Cornelius) L.; children: Jacqueline, Krista, Kevin, Meredith. B.S. in Indsl. Mgmt., Purdue U., 1963; M.B.A., Northwestern U., 1967; grad. Advanced Mgmt. Program, Harvard U., 1978. With Navistar Internat. Corp. (formerly Internat. Harvester), Chgo., 1963—; staff asst. overseas fin. Navistar Internat. Transp. Corp. (formerly Internat. Harvester), 1967-70; asst. mgr., treas. and contr. IH Finanz AG, Zurich, Switzerland, 1970-72; mgr. overseas fin. corp. hdqrs. Internat. Truck & Engine Co., Chgo., 1972—76, asst. treas., 1976—79, v.p., treas., 1979—90; exec. v.p., chief fin. officer Navistar Internat. Corp., 1990—2002, vice chmn., CFO, 2002—, also bd. dirs. Bd. dirs. NITC, Harbour Assurance Co., Bermuda, Navistar Fin. Corp., Chgo. Mem. Fin. Execs. Inst. Home: 130 N Grant St Hinsdale IL 60521-3334 Office: Navistar Internat Corp 4201 Winfield Rd PO Box 1488 Warrenville IL 60555

LANPHEAR, BRUCE PERRIN, health facility administrator, educator; BA in Biology, U. Mo., Kansas City, 1985, MD, 1986; MPH, Tulane Sch., 1988. Diplomate Am. Bd. Gen. Preventive Medicine and Pub. Health. Resident in gen. preventive medicine and pub. health Tulane Sch. of Pub. Health and Tropical Medicine, 1989; fellowship in gen. acad. pediatric rsch. U. Rochester Sch. Medicine and Dentistry, 1995; assoc. prof. pediatrics; dir. children's environtl. health ctr. Cin. Children's Hosp. Med. Ctr. Sci. and rsch. work group EPA's Office of Children's Environtl. Health Protection; scientific cons. Nat. Ctr. for Lead-Safe Housing, Columbia, Md.

LANSAW, JUDY W. public utility executive; b. Dayton, Ohio, July 12, 1951; d. Edwin Columbus and Stella Sabra (Roark) Wyatt; m. James L. Schaefer, Oct. 16, 1971 (div. 1975); m. Charles Edward Lansaw, Dec. 30, 1982; 1 child, Eric. BA in Organizational Communications, Wright State U., Dayton, 1988. Legal sec. Robert Abrahamson, atty., Dayton, 1970-78; exec. adminstrv. asst. Dayton Power & Light Co., 1978-81, mktg. rsch. energy specialist, 1981-84, exec. asst. to chief exec. officer, 1984-88, corp. sec., 1988—, v.p., 1989—; corp. sec. DPL Inc., Dayton, 1988—, v.p., 1989—. Trustee Jobs for Grads., Inc., Dayton, 1989-92, Victoria Theatre Assn., Dayton, 1990—. Mem. Am. Soc. Corp. Secs., Dayton Club, Racquet Club. Republican. Avocations: tennis, skiing, golf, sailing. Home: PO Box 750130 Dayton OH 45475-0130 Office: DPL Inc 1065 Woodman Dr Dayton OH 45432-1438

LANTZ, JOANNE BALDWIN, academic administrator emeritus; b. Defiance, Ohio, Jan. 26, 1932; d. Hiram J. and Ethel A. (Smith) Baldwin; m. Wayne E. Lantz. BS in Physics and Math., U. Indpls., 1953; MS in Counseling and Guidance, Ind. U., 1957; PhD in Counseling and Psychology, Mich. State U., 1969; LittD (hon.), U. Indpls., 1985; LHD (hon.), Purdue U., 1994; LLD (hon.), Manchester Coll., 1994. Tchr. physics and math. Arcola (Ind.) High Sch., 1953-57; guidance dir. New Haven (Ind.) Sr. High Sch., 1957-65; with Ind. U.-Purdue U., Fort Wayne, 1965—, interim chancellor, 1988-89, chancellor, 1989-94, chancellor emeritus, 1994—. Bd. dirs., hon. dir. Ft. Wayne Nat. Corp.; bd. dirs. Foellinger Found. Contbr. articles to profl. jours. Mem. Ft. Wayne Econ. Devel. Adv. Bd. and Task Force, 1988-91, Corp. Coun., 1988-94; bd. advisors Leadership Ft. Wayne, 1988-94; mem. adv. bd. Ind. Sml. Bus. Devel. Ctr., 1988-90; trustee Ancilla System, Inc., 1984-89, chmn. human resources com., 1985-89, exec. com., 1985-89; trustee St. Joseph's Med. Ctr., 1983-84, pers. adv. com. to bd. dirs., 1978-84, chmn., 1980-84; bd. dirs. United Way Allen County, sec., 1979-80; bd. dirs. Anthony Wayne Vocat. Rehab. Ctr., 1969-75. Mem.: AAUW (internat. fellowship com. 1986—88, program com. 1981—83, Am. women fellowship com. 1978—83, chmn. 1981—83, trust rsch. grantee 1980), APA, Southeastern Psychol. Assn. (referee conv. papers 1987, 1988), Ft. Wayne Ind.-Purdue Alumni Soc. (hon. mem. 1987), Ind. Sch. Women's Club (v.p. program chair 1979—81), Delta Kappa Gamma (editl. bd. 1986—88, gen. chair conv. 1985—86, dir. N.E. region 1982—84, adminstrv. bd. 1982—84, exec. bd. 1982—84, leadership devel. com. 1978—82, bd. trustees ednl. found. 1996—2002), Sigma Xi, Pi Lambda Theta. Avocations: swimming, reading, knitting, boating. E-mail: joalantz@aol.com.

LANZINGER, KLAUS, language educator, educator; b. Woergl, Tyrol, Austria, Feb. 16, 1928; came to U.S., 1971, naturalized, 1979; m. Aida Schuessl, June, 1954; children: Franz, Christine. BA, Bowdoin Coll., 1951; PhD, U. Innsbruck, Austria, 1952. Rsch. asst. U. Innsbruck, 1957-67; assoc. prof. modern langs. U. Notre Dame, Ind., 1967-77, prof., 1977-97, prof. emeritus, 1997—. Resident dir. fgn. study program, Innsbruck, 1969-71, 76-78, 82-85; acting chmn. dept. Modern and Classical Languages, U. Notre Dame, fall 1987, chmn. dept. German and Russian, 1989-96. Author: Epik im amerikanischen Roman, 1965, Jason's Voyage: The Search for the Old World in American Literature, 1989; editor: Americana-Austriaca, 5 vols., 1966-83; contbr. numerous articles to profl. jours. Bowdoin Coll. fgn. student scholar, 1950-51; Fulbright rsch. grantee U. Pa., 1961; U. Notre Dame summer rsch. grantee Houghton Libr., Harvard U., 1975, 81; named to Internat. Order of Merit, 2001. Mem. MLA, Deutsche Gesellschaft für Amerikastudien, Thomas Wolfe Soc. (Zelda Gitlin Lit. prize 1993). Home: 52703 Helvie Dr South Bend IN 46635-1215 Office: Dept German Russian Langs & Lits U Notre Dame Notre Dame IN 46556

LAPACZ, STEVEN P. social services association executive; b. Green Bay, Wis. Former tchr. jr. h.s.; sr. programmer Aid Assn. for Luths., Appleton, Wis., 1974-79, sr. programmer analyst, 1979-87, dir. micro-devel. svcs., 1987-88, asst. v.p., 1988-95, 2d v.p. micro-devel. svcs., 1995, 2d v.p. application devel. svcs., 1995—. Mem. Ops. Coun., Soc. for Info. Mgmt. Office: Aid Assn for Luths 4321 N Ballard Rd Appleton WI 54919-0001

LAPHEN, JAMES A. investment company executive; Pres., COO Comml. Fed. Bank, Omaha, 1988-2000; CEO 1st Fed. Lincoln (Nebr.) Bank, 2000—. Office: 1st Fed Lincoln Bank 1235 North St Lincoln NE 58508

LAPIDUS, DENNIS, real estate developer; b. Chgo., Oct. 21, 1942; s. Sidney and Mildred (Karlin) L. BSME, Northwestern U., 1964; MBA, Roosevelt U., 1967. Pres., founder Productive Computer Sys., Chgo., 1980-86, MBI Leasing, Chgo., 1986—. Bd. dirs. Anti-Cruelty Soc., New Century Bank. Productive Computer Sys. named to Inc. Mag. 500 Fastest Growing Privately Held Cos., 1986. Mem. Ravisloe Country Club, Medinah Country Club. Avocations: golf, basketball. Home: 1941 N Fremont St Chicago IL 60614-5016 Office: MBI Leasing PO Box 146522 Chicago IL 60614-6400 E-mail: dlap268244@aol.com.

LAPIN, HARVEY I. lawyer; b. St. Louis, Nov. 23, 1937; s. Lazarus L. and Lillie L.; m. Cheryl A. Lapin; children: Jeffrey, Gregg. BS, Northwestern U., 1960, JD, 1963. Bar: Ill. 1963, Fla. 1980, Wis. 1985; cert. tax lawyer, Fla.; CPA, Ill. Atty. Office Chief Counsel, IRS, Washington, 1963-65; trial atty. Office Regional Counsel, IRS, 1965-68; assoc., then ptnr. Fiffer & D'Angelo, Chgo., 1968-75; pres. Harvey I. Lapin, P.C., 1975-83; mng. ptnr. Lapin, Hoff, Spangler & Greenberg, 1983-88, Lapin, Hoff, Slaw & Laffey, Chgo., 1989-91; ptnr. Gottlieb and Schwartz, 1992-93; prin. Harvey I. Lapin & Assocs., P.C., Northbrook, Ill., 1993—. Instr. John Marshall Law Sch., 1969—; facility adv. lawyers asst. program Roosevelt U., Chgo.; mem. cemetery adv. bd. Ill. Comptroller, 1974-96, 99—; mem. IRS Great Lakes TE/EO Coun., 2001—. Asst. editor Fed. Bar Jour., 1965-67; contbg. editor Cemetery and Funeral Service Business and Legal Guide; contbr. articles to profl. jours. Mem. ABA, Fla. Bar Assn., Wis. Bar Assn., Ill. Bar Assn., Chgo. Bar Assn., (mem. tax exempt orgns. subcom., sect. taxation 1988-90). Jewish. Office: Harvey I Lapin & Assocs PC PO Box 1327 Northbrook IL 60065-1327

LAPIN, JEFFRY MARK, magazine publisher; b. Pawtucket, R.I., Mar. 18, 1953; s. Nathan and Jeannette Mildred (Rose) L.; m. Lynne Miller, June 7, 1975. BA, Bethany Coll., 1975; MBA, Xavier U., 1984. Fashion illustrator, copywriter L.S. Good & Co., Wheeling, W.Va, 1975; mgr. mktg. Writer's Digest Books, Cin., 1976-80; dir. circulation Harvest Pub. Co., Cleve., 1980-82, bus. mgr., 1982-84; dir. circulation F&W Pubs., Inc., Cin., 1984-85, v.p., gen. mgr. mag. div., 1986—; pub. Artist's Mag., 1985—. Cons. copy/design, Cleve., 1980-84. Author Circulation Mgmt., 1987—. Mem. Mag. Pubs. Assn., Hobby Industries Am., Nat. Art Materials Trade Assn., Cin. Art Club, Cin. Direct. Mktg. Club. Avocations: music, art, home remodeling. Office: F&W Pubs 1507 Dana Ave Cincinnati OH 45207-1000

LAPINSKY, JOSEPH F. manufacturing company executive; married; 2 daughters. MS in Indsl. Rels., W.Va. U., 1973; MBA in Mgmt., Youngstown State U., 1984. Early career positions include conditioning foreman Copperweld Steel Co., then ops., mgr. human resources, v.p. human resources, 1974-91, also exec. v.p.; ind. industry cons., 1991-95; gen. mgr. hot rolled bar ops. Republic Techs. Internat., Akron, Ohio, 1995-97, pres. Hot Rolled Bar divsn., 1997-98; pres., COO Republic Engrineered Steels and Bar Techs., 1998—; COO Republic Techs. Internat., 1999—.

LA PLATA, GEORGE, federal judge; b. 1924; m. Frances Hoyt; children: Anita J. La Plata Rard, Marshall. AB, Wayne State U., 1951; LLB, Detroit Coll. Law, 1956. Pvt. practice law, 1956-79; judge Oakland County (Mich.) Cir. Ct., Pontiac, 1979-85, U.S. Dist. Ct. (ea. dist.) Mich., Ann Arbor, 1985-96; spl. litigation counsel Allan Miller, P.C., Mich., 1996—. Prof. Detroit Coll. Law, 1985-86. Trustee William Beaumont Hosp., 1979—, United Found., 1983—. Served to col. USMC, 1943-46, 52-54. Mem. ABA, Oakland County Bar Assn., Hispanic Bar Assn. Lodge: Optimists. Office: Allan Miller PC 370 E Maple Rd Fl 4 Birmingham MI 48009-6303

LAPTEWICZ, JOSEPH E., JR. medical products executive; married; 3 children. MS in Biochem. Engring., Cornell U., 1972; BSChemE, Worcester Polytechnic Inst., 1971; MBA in Mktg. and Fin., U. New Haven, 1978. Prodn. supr. Pfizer Chem. Divsn., Southport and Groton, 1972-77; project leader fermentation recovery Pfizer Ctrl. Rsch. Divsn., Groton, 1977-80; contr. Howmedica R&D Pfizer Hosp. Products Group, 1981-83, dir. ventures, 1984-86, dir. corp. R&D, 1987-89; v.p., gen. mgr. Schneider U.S. Stent Divsn., Plymouth, Minn., 1990-91; pres., exec. v.p. Schneider (USA) Inc., 1991-94; pres., CEO, Empi, Inc., St. Paul, 1994—; dir. Angiodynamics, Inc. Patentee in field. Key account exec. Mpls. chpt. United Way; bd. advisors Coll. of St. Catherine. Mem. AIChE, Worcester Polytechnic Inst. Alumni Assn. Avocations: sailing, golfing. Office: EMPI,Inc 599 Cardigan Rd Saint Paul MN 55126-4099

LARBALESTIER, DAVID CHISTOPHER, materials scientist; b. Castle Carey, U.K., May 22, 1943; came to U.S., 1976; s. Basil Douglas and Anna (Felder) L.; m. Karen Anne Williams, May 6, 1967; children: Nikolai David, Laura Jane, Eleanor Lucy. BS, U. London, 1965, PhD, 1970. Staff scientist Battelle Lab., Geneva, 1970-72; sr. sci. officer Rutherford Lab., Chilton Didcot, U.K., 1973-76; asst. prof. U. Wis., Madison, 1976-78, assoc. prof., 1978-81, prof., 1981—, L.V. Shubnikov prof., 1990—, dir. Applied Superconductivity Ctr., 1991—, Grainger prof., 1996. Panel mem. NAS, Washington, 1987. Recipient Matthey prize U. London, 1970, IEEE particle Accelerator Conf. award, 1991, Byron award U. Wis., 1992, others. Fellow Am. Phys. Soc.; mem. Materials Rsch. Soc., Metall. Soc. Office: U Wis Appl Superconductivity Ctr Rm 915 ERB 1500 Engineering Dr Madison WI 53706-1609

LARDAKIS, MOIRA GAMBRILL, insurance executive, lawyer; b. Cleve., Sept. 14, 1951; d. Merle LC. and Ellen K. (Moore) Gambrill; m. Tony E. Lardakis, Aug. 31, 1985; children: Christopher E., Michael A. BA, Cleve. State U., 1972; JD, Cleveland Marshall Coll. Law, 1981. Bar: Ohio 1981. Child care supr. Lake County Comprehensive Ctr., Cleve., 1973-75, work adjustment counselor, 1975-78; with Progressive Casualty Ins. Co., Mayfield Village, Ohio, 1978—, gen. mgr., 1985-87, div. pres., 1987—. Mem. Ohio Bar Assn.

LARDNER, HENRY PETERSEN (PETER LARDNER), insurance company executive; b. Davenport, Iowa, Apr. 5, 1932; s. James Francis and Mary Catharine (Decker) L.; m. Marion Cleaveland White, Dec. 28, 1954; children: Elisabeth, Emily Decker, David, Peter, Sarah (dec.). B.S.E. (Indsl. Engring.), U. Mich., 1954; M.A., Augustana Coll., 1982. C.P.C.U. Indsl. engr. Cutler-Hammer, Milw., 1954; Agt. H.H. Cleaveland Agy., Rock Island, Ill., 1956-60; with Bituminous Ins. Cos., 1960—, exec. v.p., 1968-72, pres., 1972-95, chmn. and CEO, 1984-2000, chmn., 2000—01; pres. Bitco Corp., Rock Island, 1973-95, chmn. bd. dirs., 1973—2001. Bd. dirs. Old Republic Internat.; trustee Underwriters Lab., Inc., 1997—. Bd. govs. State Colls. and Univs., 1971-80; trustee Black Hawk Coll., 1964-72; mem. Ill. Bd. Higher Edn., 1976-77; chmn. Ill. State Scholarship, 1982-85. Served with AUS, 1954-56. Home: 3227 29th Ave Rock Island IL 61201-5568 E-mail: peter.lardner@verizon.net.

LARDY, HENRY A(RNOLD), biochemistry educator; b. Roslyn, S.D., Aug. 19, 1917; s. Nicholas and Elizabeth (Gebetsreiter) L.; m. Annrita Dresselhuys, Jan. 21, 1943; children; Nicholas, Diana, Jeffrey, Michael. BS, S.D. State U., 1939, DSc (hon.), 1979; MS, U. Wis., 1941, PhD, 1943. Asst. prof. U. Wis., Madison, 1945-47, assoc. prof., 1947-50, prof., 1950-88, Vilas prof. biol. sci., 1966-88, prof. emeritus, 1988—. Henry Lardy annual lectr. S.D. State U., Brookings, 1985. Edtl. bd. Archives Biochemistry and Biophysics, 1957-60, Jour. Biol. Chemistry, 1958-64, 80-85, Biochem. Preparations, Methods of Biochem. Analysis, Biochemistry, 1962-73, 75-81; contbr. over 450 articles to profl. jours. Pres. Citizens vs McCarthy, Wis., 1950. Recipient Neuberg medal Am. Soc. European Chemists, 1956, Wolf Found. award in Agr., 1981, Nat. award Agrl. Excellence, 1982. Fellow Wis. Acad. Arts and Scis.; mem. Am. Chem. Soc. (chmn. biol. divsn. 1958, Paul-Lewis Labs. award 1949), Am. Soc. Biol. Chemists (pres. 1964, William Rose award 1988), Am. Acad. Arts and Scis. (Amory prize 1984), Am. Philos. Soc., Am. Diabetes Assn., Nat. Acad. Scis., Biochem. Soc. Great Britain, Harvey Soc., Soc. for Study of Reprodn. (Carl Hartman award 1984), The Endocrine Soc., Japanese Biochem. Soc. (hon.), Golden Retriever Club Am. (pres. 1964). Democrat. Achievements include patents for steroid compounds and lab. apparatus. Home: 1829 Thorstrand Rd Madison WI 53705-1052 Office: U Wis 1710 University Ave Madison WI 53705-4087

LARDY, SISTER SUSAN MARIE, academic administrator; b. Sentinel Butte, N.D., Nov. 9, 1937; d. Peter Aloysius and Elizabeth Julia (Dietz) L. BS in Edn., U. Mary, Bismarck, N.D., 1965; MEd, U. N.D., 1972. Entered Order of St. Benedict, Bismarck, 1957. Elem. tchr. Cathedral Grade Sch., Bismarck, 1958-67, Christ the King Sch., Mandan, N.D., 1967-68, 70-72, St. Joseph's Sch., Mandan, 1968-70; asst. prof. edn. U. Mary, Bismarck, 1972-80; adminstr., asst. prioress Annunciation Priory, 1980-84, prioress, major superior, 1984-96; dir. U. Mary-Fargo (N.D.) Ctr., 1997—. Dir. Fargo Ctr. U. Mary, 1997—. Mem. Delta Kappa Gamma. Home: 1101 32nd Ave S Fargo ND 58103-6036 Office: U Mary Fargo Ctr 3001 25th St S Fargo ND 58103-5055

LARKIN, BARRY LOUIS, professional baseball player; b. Cin., Apr. 28, 1964; m. Lisa Davis. Student, U. Mich., 1982-85. Baseball player Cincinnati Reds, 1985—. First baseball player twice named MVP of Big Ten Athletic Conf.; two-time All-Am. honors; named MVP of National League, 1995, Rookie of Yr. and to All-Star team, 1988-95, to Topps' Triple-A All-Star team, 1986, All-Star teams by Sporting News, 1988-92, 94-95, AP, 1990, UPI, 1990, Maj. League Baseball, 1988-91, 93, to N.L. Silver Slugger team Sporting News, 1988-92, 95; recipient Gold Glove award, 1994-96. Achievements include mem. U.S. Olympic Baseball Team, 1984, World Series Team, 1990. Office: Cin Reds 100 Cinergy Fld Cincinnati OH 45202-3543*

LARKIN, BRUCE F. state legislator; m. Judy Larkin. Kans. state rep. Dist. 63; farmer.

LAROCCA, PATRICIA DARLENE MCALEER, middle school mathematics educator; b. Aurora, Ill., July 12, 1951; d. Theodore Austin and Lorraine Mae (Robbins) McAleer; m. Edward Daniel LaRocca, June 28, 1975; children: Elizabeth S., Mark E. BS in Edn./Math., No. Ill. U., 1973, postgrad., 1975. Tchr. elem. sch. Roselle (Ill) Sch. Dist., 1973-80; instr. math. Coll. DuPage, Glen Ellyn, Ill., 1988-90; tchr. math. O'Neill Mid. Sch., Downers Grove, 1995—. Pvt. cons., math. tutor, Downers Grove, Ill., 1980-88, 90-95. Bd. dirs. PTA, Hillcrest Elem. Sch., Downers Grove; active Boy Scouts Am.; mem. 1st United Meth. Ch. Ill. teaching scholar, 1969. Methodist. Avocations: antiques, softball, organ, dance. Home and Office: 5648 Dunham Rd Downers Grove IL 60516-1246

LARRICK, MONTE, radio personality; b. Chgo., Oct. 26; Sr. news corr. Sta. WMBI Radio, Chgo. Avocations: swimming, softball, reading, music. Office: WMBI 820 N LaSalle Blvd Chicago IL 60610*

LARRIMORE, RANDALL WALTER, wholesale company executive; b. Lewes, Del., Apr. 27, 1947; s. Randall A. and Irene Larrimore; m. Judith Cutright, Aug. 29, 1970; children: Jacob, Alex. BS, Swarthmore (Pa.) Coll., 1969; MBA, Harvard U., 1971. Product mgr. Richardson-Vick, Wilton, Conn., 1971-75; sr. engagement mgr. McKinsey & Co., N.Y.C., 1975-80; pres. Pepsi-Cola Italia, Rome, 1980-83, Beatrice Home Specialties, Inc. (later acquired by Am. Brands), Skokie, Ill., 1983-87; pres., CEO, MasterBrand Industries, Inc. (subs. of Am. Brands, Inc.), 1988-97; v.p. Am. Brands, Inc., 1988-95; chmn. Moen Inc., 1990-97, chief exec. officer, 1990-94; chmn., chief exec. officer Master Lock Co., 1996-97; pres., CEO United Stationers, Des Plaines, Ill., 1997—, also bd. dirs., 1997—. Bd. dirs. Winnetka Congl. Ch., 1989-90; exec. com. hardware/home improvement coun. City of Hope, 1991-97, pres. 1991-93; exec. com. office products coun. City of Hope, 1997, pres., 2000—; commr. Landmark Preservation Coun., Winnetka, 1992-98; bd. dirs. Olin Corp., 1998—, Evanston Hosp. Corp., 1996—, Students In Free Enterprise, 1998—; trustee Lake Forest Acad., 2002--. Capt. USAR, 1971-79. Named Exec. of Yr., Office Products Internat., 1999. Mem. Plumbing Mfg. Inst. (bd. dirs. 1991-93), Nat. Assn. of Wholesalers (adv. bd. 1999—). Office: United Stationers 2200 E Golf Rd Des Plaines IL 60016-1257 E-mail: rlarrimore@ussco.com.

LARSEN, EDWARD WILLIAM, mathematician, nuclear engineering educator; b. Flushing, N.Y., Nov. 12, 1944; BS, Rensselaer Polytech Inst., 1966, PhD in Math., 1971. Asst. prof. math. NYU, 1971-76; assoc. prof. U. Del., 1976-77; mem. staff math. Los Alamos (N.Mex.) Nat. Lab., 1977; prof. dept. nuc. engring. U. Mich., Ann Arbor. Editor Transport Theory and Stats. Physics, 1975—, Jour. Applied Math., 1976—; contbr. articles to profl. jours. Recipient Ernest Orlando Lawrence Meml. award U.S. Dept. Energy, 1994. Mem. Am. Nuc. Soc. (Arthur Holly Compton award 1996), Soc. Indsl. and Applied Math. Office: U Mich Dept Nuc Engring & Radiol Scis 1906 Cooley Bldg Ann Arbor MI 48109-0001

LARSEN, PAUL EMANUEL, religious organization administrator; b. Mpls., Oct. 5, 1933; s. David Paul and Myrtle (Grunnet) L.; m. Elizabeth Helen Taylor, Mar. 19, 1966; children: Kristin, Kathleen (dec.). BA, Stanford U., 1955; MDiv, Fuller Theol. Sem., 1958; STD, San Francisco Theol. Sem., 1978; DD, North Park U., 1998. Ordained to ministry Evang. Ch., 1963. Asst. pastor Evang. Ch., Eagle Rock, Calif., 1958-59; pastor Pasadena, 1963-70, Peninsula Covenant Ch., Redwood City, 1971-86; pres. Evang. Covenant Chs., Chgo., 1986—. Chmn. meeting U.S. ch. leaders, 1992—. Author: Wise Up and Live, Mission of a Covenant. Mem. Internat. Fedn. of Free Evang. Chs. (pres. 1996—). Home: 36125 Avenida De Las Montana Cathedral City CA 92234-1516 Office: Evang Covenant Ch 5101 N Francisco Ave Chicago IL 60625-3611

LARSEN, PEG, state legislator; b. Aug. 10, 1949; m. Thomas Larsen; 4 children. BA, U. Slippery Rock. Minn. state rep. Dist. 56B, 1994—. Former ednl. asst. spl. needs. Address: 409 Quixote Ave N Lakeland MN 55043-9645 Also: 100 Constitution Ave Saint Paul MN 55155-1232

LARSEN, ROBERT EMMETT, federal judge; b. Queens, N.Y., Sept. 9, 1946; s. Robert Ludwig and Elizabeth Catherine (Colgan) L.; m. Roberta Barclay, Sept. 22, 1973; children: Matthew Robert, Thomas Barclay, Paige Barclay. BA, Rockhurst Coll., 1969; JD, U. Mo., Kansas City, 1973. Bar: Mo. 1973, U.S. Dist. Ct. (we. dist.) Mo. 1973, U.S. Ct. Appeals (D.C. cir.) 1974, U.S. Ct. Appeals (8th cir.) 1977, U.S. Supreme Ct. 1977. Staff atty. criminal div. U.S. Dept. Justice, Washington, 1974-76; asst. U.S. atty. U.S. Atty.'s Office, Kansas City, 1976-81, chief criminal div., 1981-83, atty.-in-charge organized crime drug enforcement task force, 1983-88, 1st asst. U.S. atty., 1988-90, sr. litigation counsel, 1990-91; U.S. magistrate judge U.S. Cts., 1991—. Commr. Mental Health Commn., Mo., 1990—; chmn. Metro. Kansas City Task Force on Alcohol and Drug Abuse, 1986-90; chmn., adv. bd. Mo. Fedn. of Parents for Drug Free Youth, Springfield, Mo., 1987-88; bd. trustees Nat. Coun. Alcoholism for Drug Free Youth, Kansas City, 1988-90; bd. dirs. YouthNet, Good Samaritan Project, Kansas City Consensus, Della Lamb Community Svcs.; bd. regents Rockhurst Coll. Regents, 1994—; mem. adv. bd. drug awareness Park Hill Sch. Dist., 1988-90; mem. steering com. Coalition for Positive Family Relationships, 1992—; mem. divsn. alcohol and drug abuse States Adv. Coun., 1987-88. Author: Pretrial Preparation, 1985; contbr.: 8th Circuit Criminal Institute, 1992. Co-chmn. Harmony in World of Difference, Kansas City, 1989—; mem., bd. dirs. Life Edn. Ctr., Kansas City, 1990—, Genesis, Kansas City, 1992; active Northland Citizen's Crusade Coun., Inc., 1989—, Ad Hoc Group Against Crime, 1986—. Recipient Community Svc. award Nat. Coun. Alcohol and Drug Abuse, 1988, Cert. Appreciation, 1988, Pub. Adv. award Dept. Mental Health, State of Mo., 1988, Law Enforcement award Ad Hoc Group Against Crime, 1989, GEICO Pub. Svc. award, 1990. Mem. ABA, Mo. Bar Assn., D.C. Bar Assn., Kansas City, Mo. Bar Assn. Roman Catholic. Home: 420 NW Briarcliff Pky Kansas City MO 64116-1670 Office: US Dist Ct 231 US Courthouse 811 Grand Blvd Ste 201 Kansas City MO 64106-1904

LARSEN, ROBERT LEROY, artistic director; b. Walnut, Iowa, Nov. 28, 1934; s. George Dewey and Maine M. (Mickel) L. MusB, Simpson Coll., Indianola, Iowa, 1956; MusM, U. Mich., 1958; MusD, Ind. U., 1972. Music prof. Simpson Coll., 1957—, chmn. music dept., 1965-99. Founder, artistic dir. Des Moines Met. Opera, 1973—. Mus. coach Tanglewood, Lenox, Mass., 1963, Oglebay Pk. (W.Va.) Opera, 1965, Chgo., N.Y. studios; condr., stage dir. Simpson Coll., Des Moines Met. Opera, Miss. Opera, U. Ariz.; solo pianist, song recital coach and accompanist; adjudicator Met. auditions and competitions, Mpls., Chgo., Kansas City, Mo., Tulsa, San Antonio; stage dir., condr. operas, Simpson Coll., Des Moines Met. Opera, 1973—; editor Opera Anthologies by G. Schirmer; piano rec. artist for G. Schirmer Libr. Recipient Gov's. award State of Iowa, 1974, Iowa Arts award for long term commitment to excellence in the arts, 1998. Mem. Am. Choral Dir. Assn., Nat. Opera Assn., Music Tchrs. Nat. Assn., Pi Kappa Lambda, Phi Kappa Phi, Phi Mu Alpha Sinfonia (faculty advisor). Presbyterian. Avocations: reading, theatre, coaching students. Office: Des Moines Metro Opera 106 W Boston Ave Indianola IA 50125-1836

LARSEN, STEVEN, orchestra conductor; b. Oak Park, Ill., Feb. 10, 1951; s. Edwin Earnest and Sylvia Nila Larsen; divorced; children: Vanessa, Krista; m. Martha Jane Bein, Mar. 21, 1993. MusB, Am. Conservatory Music, Chgo., 1975; MusM, Northwestern U., 1976. Cert. Nederlandse Dirigenten Kursus. Instr. music theory, chair instrumental dept Am. Conservatory Music, Chgo., 1976-82, orch. dir., 1978; music dir. Opera Theatre of San Antonio, 1987-90; orch. dir. Rockford (Ill.) Symphony Orch., 1991—. Music dir., acting artistic dir. Chgo. Opera Theater, 1981-92; interim artistic dir. Dayton (Ohio) Opera, 1996; music dir. Champaign-Urbana (Ill.) Symphony, 1996—; lectr. opera performance Chgo. Mus. Coll., 1989-96. Recipient Disting. Svc. award Rockford Park Dist., 1997, Condr. of Yr., Ill. Coun. of Orchs., 1998-99, Mayor's Arts award Rockford Area Arts Coun., 1999. Mem. Rockford Downtown Rotary. Office: Rockford Symphony Orch 711 N Main St Rockford IL 61103-7204 E-mail: steve@larsenbein.com.

LARSEN, WILLIAM LAWRENCE, materials science and engineering educator; b. Crookston, Minn., July 16, 1926; s. Clarence M. and Luverne (Carlisle) L.; m. Gracie Lee Richey, June 19, 1954; children— Eric W., Thomas R. B.M.E., Marquette U., 1948; M.S., Ohio State U., 1950, Ph.D., 1956; postgrad., U. Chgo., 1950-51. Registered profl. engr., Iowa. Research assoc. Ohio State U., Columbus, 1951-56; research metallurgist E. I. duPont de Nemours & Co., Wilmington, Del., 1956-58; metallurgist Ames Lab., AEC, Iowa, 1958-73; assoc. prof. Iowa State U., Ames, 1958-73, prof. materials sci. and engring., 1973-93; prof. emeritus, 1993—. Cons. metallurgical engring., 1960—. Contbr. articles to profl. jours. Served with USNR, 1944-46. Mem.: NSPE, NACE Internat. (cert.), ASTM, ASM Internat. (life). Home and Office: 2332 Hamilton Dr Ames IA 50014-8201

LARSON, ALLAN LOUIS, political scientist, educator, lay church worker; b. Chetek, Wis., Mar. 31, 1932; s. Leonard Andrew and Mabel (Marek) L. BA magna cum laude, U. Wis., Eau Claire, 1954; PhD, Northwestern U., 1964. Instr. Evanston Twp. (Ill.) High Sch., 1958-61; asst. prof. polit. sci. U. Wis., 1963-64; asst. prof. Loyola U., Chgo., 1964-68, assoc. prof., 1968-74, prof., 1974—. Author: Comparative Political Analysis, 1980, Soviet Society in Historical Perspective: Polity, Ideology and Economy, 2000, (essay) The Human Triad: An Introductory Essay on Politics, Society, and Culture, 1988; (with others) Progress and the Crisis of Man, 1976; contbr. articles to profl. jours. Assoc. mem. Paul Galvin Chapel, Evanston, Ill. Norman Wait Harris fellow in polit. sci. Northwestern U., 1954-56 Mem. AAAS, ASPCA, AAUP, Humane Soc. U.S., Northwestern U. Alumni Assn., Am. Polit. Sci. Assn., Am. Acad. Polit. and Social Sci., Acad. Polit. Sci., Midwest Polit. Sci. Assn., Spiritual Life Inst., Anti-Cruelty Soc., Nat. Wildlife Fedn., N.Am. Butterfly Assn., Acad. of Am. Poets (assoc.), Policy Studies Orgn., Noetic Scis. Inst., Humane Soc. U.S., Kappa Delta Pi, Pi Sigma Epsilon. Roman Catholic. Home: 4169 112th St Chippewa Falls WI 54729-6626 Office: Loyola U 6525 N Sheridan Rd Damen Hall Rm 915 Chicago IL 60626

LARSON, BRIAN FOIX, architect; b. Eau Claire, Wis., July 6, 1935; s. Albert Foix and Dorothy Jean (Thompson) L.; m. Mildred Anne Nightswander, Feb. 13, 1961; children: Urban Alexander, Soren Federick. BArch, U. Ill., 1959. Registered architect, Wis., Minn., Colo., Mass., N.H., Fla. Architect-in-tng. Geometrics, Inc., Cambridge, Mass., 1959-60, Bastille Halsey Assoc., Boston, 1960-62; ptnr. Larson, Playter, Smith, Eau Claire, 1962-72; v.p. Larson, Hestekins, Smith, Ltd., 1962-80, Ayres Assocs., Eau Claire, 1980—. Sec. Wis. Bd. Archtl. Examiners, 1985-88, chmn., 1988-89; master juror Nat. Coun. Archtl. Reg. Bd. Bldg. Design Exam, 1987-96. Prin. works include One Mill Plaza, Laconia, N.H. (Honor award New Eng. Regional Council AIA 1974), Eau Claire County Courthouse, Wis., (Honor award Wis. Soc. Architects 1978), St. Croix County Courthouse, Wis., Dunn County Jud. Ctr. Mem. Hist. Bldg. Code Adv. Com., Wis., 1985. Mem. AIA (bd. dirs. 1996-98), Wis. Soc. Architects (pres. 1983), Wis. Architects Found. (bd. dirs. 1992-98), Soc. Archtl. Historians. Home: 215 Roosevelt Ave Eau Claire WI 54701-4065 Office: Ayres Assocs PO Box 1590 Eau Claire WI 54702-1590 E-mail: larsonb@ayresassociates.com.

LARSON, CAL, state legislator; b. Aug. 10, 1930; m. Loretta Larson; two children. BA, Concordia Coll., Moorhead, Minn. Formerly real estate/ins. broker; mem. Minn. Ho. of Reps., St. Paul, 1967-74, Minn. Senate from 10th dist., St. Paul, 1986—. Mem. edn.-higher edn. divsn. and edn. funding, fin., commerce, elections, and rules and adminstrn. Minn. State Senate. Address: 153 State Office Bldg Saint Paul MN 55155-0001

LARSON, CHARLES W. prosecutor; Grad., Kans. State U., U. Iowa Sch. Law. Magistrate Iowa 5th Judicial Ct., 1973; commr. Iowa Dept. Public Safety, 1973—79; mgr. law enforcement Sanders and Assocs., 1979—82; ptnr. Walker, Larson and Billingsley, Newton, Iowa, 1982—86; U.S. atty. No. dist. Iowa, Cedar Rapids , 1986—93, 2001—. Office: PO Box 74950 Cedar Rapids IA 52407-4950

LARSON, CHUCK, JR. state representative; m. Jennifer Eileen Larson. Doctorate, Uinv. Iowa, 1996; BA in Econ. with hon., Univ. Iowa, 1992. State chmn. Rep. Party of Iowa, 2001—; coun. ESCO Group, Cedar Rapids, Iowa, 1999—; asst. atty. Jones County, 1997—99; state rep. Iowa House Dist. 55, 1992—. State vice chair George W. Bush for Pres., 1999—2000; chmn. House Judiciary Com., 1992—; chair Economic Devel. Com.; mem. Res. Officers Assn. Bd. dirs. Salvation Army. Capt. USAR, 1987—. Mem.: Iowa State Bar Assn., Am. Legion, Rotary, Phi Beta Kappa. Republican. Office: 521 E Locust Ste 200 Des Moines IA 50309*

LARSON, DAVID J. religious organization executive; b. Mpls., 1937; m. Caryl Larson; 2 children. BA, Wesleyan U.; JD, LLB, NYU. Bar: ABA. Mem. law dept. Lutheran Brotherhood, Mpls., 1968—, sr. v.p., sec., gen. counsel. Pres. Nat. Fraternal Congress of Am., 1999-00, bd. dirs., mem. marshal program com., mem., past pres. Assn. Fraternal Benefit Counsel, mem., past pres. law sect., chair and mem. law com., chair fed. issues subcom.; active Minn. Fraternal Congress, Am. Coun. Life Ins., Ins. Fedn. Minn. Mem. Luth. Social Svcs. of Minn. Found.; bd. regents Augsburg Coll., Mpls.; bd. dirs. Luther Inst., Washington. Office: 625 4th Ave S Minneapolis MN 55415-1624

LARSON, DAVID LEE, surgeon; b. Kansas City, Mo., Dec. 9, 1943; s. Leonard Nathaniel and Mary Elizabeth (Stuck) L.; m. Sherrill Ankli, Apr. 16, 1977; children: Jeffrey David, Dawn Elizabeth, Bradley Jesse. BS, Bowling Green State U., 1965; MD, La. State U., 1969. Diplomate Am. Bd. Plastic Surgery (bd. dirs. 1996—, sec.-treas. 1998—). Intern Charity Hosp. of La., New Orleans, 1969-70; resident otolaryngology Baylor Coll. Medicine, Houston, 1972-76; plastic surgery resident Ind. U., Indpls., 1976-78; surgeon M.D. Anderson Cancer Ctr., Houston, 1978-85; prof., chmn. dept. plastic and reconstructive surgery Med. Coll Wis., Milw., 1986—. Alano J. Ballantyne prof. in head and neck surgery, M.D. Anderson Cancer Ctr., Houston, 1985; sec.-treas. Am. Bd. Plastic Surgery, 1996-2002. Editor: Cancer in the Neck, 1987, Essentials of Head and Neck Oncology, 1998. Capt. USNR, 1991—. Mem. Am. Assn. Plastic Surgeons, Nat. Inst. Healthcare Rsch. (chmn. bd. dirs. 1995-2000), Plastic Surgery Ednl. Found. (pres. 2001—). Avocations: reading, family, exercise. Home: 13510 Braemar Dr Elm Grove WI 53122-2509 Office: Med Coll Wis 9200 W Wisconsin Ave Milwaukee WI 53226-3522 E-mail: dlarson@mcw.edu.

LARSON, EDWARD, state supreme court justice; m. Mary Loretta Thompson; children: Sarah, John, Mary Elizabeth. BS, Kans. State U., 1954; JD, Kans. U., 1960. Pvt. practice, Hays, Kans., 1960—87; judge Kans. Ct. Appeals, 1987—95; justice Kans. Supreme Ct., Topeka, 1995—. Mcpl. judge City of Hays, 1965—72. 2nd lt. USAF. Office: Kans Supreme Ct 301 W 10th Rm 388 Topeka KS 66612*

LARSON, GARY, cartoonist; b. Tacoma, Aug. 14, 1950; s. Vern and Doris Larson; married. BA in Communications, Wash. State U., 1972. Jazz musician, 1973-76; with music store, Seattle, 1976-77, Humane Soc., Seattle, 1978-80; cartoonist Seattle Times, 1978-79; syndicated cartoonist The Far Side Chronicle Features Syndicate, San Francisco, 1979-84; syndicated cartoonist The Far Side cartoon panel Universal Press Syndicate, Kansas City, Mo., 1984-94; cartoonist, 1994—. Prodr. books, calendars, greeting cars, t-shirts, day runner organizers, computer calendars, screen savers, coffee mugs.; since The Far Side was retired in 1994, it still appears syndicated in over 200 newspapers in fgn. market by Creators Syndicate Internat. Exhbns. include The Far Side of Sci. (exhibited at Calif. Acad. Scis., 1987, Smithsonian Instn., 1987, Denver Mus. Natural History, L.A. County Mus., Shedd Aquarium, Chgo., other mus.), The Far Side of the Zoo, Washington Park Zoo, Portland, Oreg., 1987; author: (cartoon collections) The Far Side, 1982, Beyond The Far Side, 1983, In Search of The Far Side, 1984, Bride of The Far Side, 1985, Valley of the Far Side, 1985, It Came from The Far Side, 1986, The Far Side Observer, 1987, Hound of the Far Side, 1984, Night of the Crash-Test Dummies, 1988, Wildlife Preserves, 1989, The Prehistory of the Far Side: A 10th Anniversary Exhibit, 1989, Weiner Dog Art, 1990, Unnatural Selections, 1991, Cows of Our Planet, 1992, The Chickens are Restless, 1993, The Curse of Madame "C", 1994, Last Chapter and Worse, 1996, (cartoon anthologies) The Far Side Gallery, 1984, The Far Side Gallery II, 1986, The Far Side Gallery III, 1988, The Far Side Gallery IV, 1993, The Far Side Gallery V, 1995, There's A Hair in My Dirt! A Worm's Story, 1998; animated film and CBS TV Halloween spl. Gary Larson's Tales from The Far Side, 1994 (Grand prix Annecy Film Festival, 1995), 2d animated film Gary Lason's Tales from The Far Side II, 1997. Recipient award for Best Humor Panel, Nat. Cartoonists Soc., 1986, Reuben award for Outsdanding Cartoonist of Yr. Nat. Cartoonists Soc., 1991, 94, Max and Moritz prize for best internat. comic strip panel Internat. Comics Salon, 1993, other awards. Avocation: jazz music. Address: Creators Syndicated Internat 5777 W Century Blvd Ste 700 Los Angeles CA 90045 also: care Andrews McMeel Pub 4520 Main St Ste 700 Kansas City MO 64111-7701

LARSON, GREGORY DANE, lawyer; b. Mpls., Mar. 11, 1947; s. Allen L. and Lohma (Rogers) L.; m. Susan K. Strand, Sept. 8, 1973; children: Jennifer, Dane, Kyle, Kathleen. BA, Bemidji State Coll., 1969; JD, William Mitchell Coll. of Law, 1976. County atty. Hubbard County, Park Rapids, Minn., 1986—. With U.S. Army, 1970-72. Mem. Minn. State Bar Assn. (15th dist. pres.), Am. Legion (judge advocate 1982—). Democrat. Roman Catholic. Home: RR 1 Box 186 Park Rapids MN 56470-9018 Office: PO Box 486 Park Rapids MN 56470-0486

LARSON, JERRY LEROY, state supreme court justice; b. Harlan, Iowa, May 17, 1936; s. Gerald L. and Mary Eleanor (Patterson) L.; m. Debra L. Christensen; children: Rebecca, Jeffrey, Susan, David. BA, State U. Iowa, 1958, JD, 1960. Bar: Iowa. Partner firm Larson & Larson, 1961-75; dist. judge 4th Jud. Dist. Ct. of Iowa, 1975-78; justice Iowa Supreme Ct., 1978—. Office: Supreme Ct Iowa PO Box 109 Des Moines IA 50319-0001*

LARSON, JOHN DAVID, insurance company executive, lawyer; b. Madison, Wis., July 6, 1941; s. Lawrence John and Anna Mathilda (Furseth) Larson; m. Evelyn Vie Smith, Jan. 22, 1966 (div. Apr. 1980); children: Eric John, Karen Annette; m. Nancy Jay With, Nov. 29, 1980 (div. Dec. 1998); stepchildren: Andrew Zachary With, Anne Elizabeth With, Christopher Allen With. BBA, U. Wis., 1964, JD, 1965, MBA, 1966. CPA Wis.; CLU; bar: Wis. 1965, U.S. Ct. Mil. Appeals 1966; chartered fin. cons. With Nat. Guardian Life Ins. Co., Madison, 1969—, exec. v.p., treas., 1973, pres., dir., 1974—, pres., chief exec. officer, 1989—. Bd. advisors U.S. Bank, Madison; bd. dirs. TV Wis., Inc., KELAB, Inc. Chmn. Madison chpt. ARC, 1974—75; pres. United Way Dane County, 1975, Wis. N.G. Assn., 1992—96; trustee Village of Maple Bluff, 1997—. With U.S. Army, 1966—69. Named Disting. Bus. Alumnus, U. Wis.-Madison, 1996; recipient Know Your Madisonian award, Wis. State Jour., 1973. Mem.: ABA, Am. Soc. Fin. Svc. Profls., State Bar Wis., U. Wis. Bus. Alumni (bd. dirs. 1986—90), Madison C. of C. (dir. 1976—80), Maple Bluff Club (bd. dirs. 1974—80), Rotary. Lutheran. Home: 401 New Castle Way Madison WI 53704-6070 Office: PO Box 1191 Madison WI 53701-1191

LARSON, LARRY GENE, financial planner; b. Sioux Falls, S.D., July 9, 1948; s. L. Dale and Doris L. (Iverson) L.; m. Mary Kemppainen, Aug. 13, 1977; children: Kay, Lynn, Bret. BA, Augustana Coll., 1970. Republican. Lutheran. Avocations: fishing, golf. Home: 2172 Center St Marquette MI 49855-1302 Office: Am Express 2400 Us Highway 41 W Marquette MI 49855-2261

LARSON, MICHAEL LEN, newspaper editor, hospital administrator; b. St. James, Minn., Feb. 3, 1944; s. Leonard O. and Lois O. (Holte) L.; m. Kay M. Monahan, June 18, 1966; children: Christopher, David, Molly. BA, U. Minn., 1966; MBA, Mankato State U., 1986. Mng. editor Paddock Circle Inc., Libertyville, Ill., 1972-74, New Ulm (Minn.) Journal, 1974-76, Republican-Eagle, Red Wing, Minn., 1976-79, Mankato (Minn.) Free Press, 1979-84, editor, 1984-95, editor of editl. page, 1995-97; editor Minot (N.D.) Daily News, 1997-2000; bus. editor St. Cloud (Minn.) Times, 2000—01; asst. adminstr. Melrose Area Hosp. Complex, 2001—. Bd. dirs. Minot Area Devel. Corp. D. dirs. Valley Indsl. Devel. Corp., Mankato, 1985-95, also treas.; adv. bd. Mankato State U. Bus. Sch. With U.S. Army, 1966-68, Vietnam. Recipient First Place award for investigative reporting Minn. Newspaper Assn., 1969, 71, 72, 76, 78, First Place award for feature writing, Suburban Newspapers Am., 1974. Mem. Minn. AP (pres. 1988—), Kiwanis. Roman Catholic. Avocation: bicycling. Home: 1808 N Eighth St Sartell MN 56377-1697 Office: Melrose Area Hosp Complex 111 N 5th Ave W Melrose MN 56352

LARSON, PAUL WILLIAM, public relations executive; b. Wilmington, N.C., May 28, 1956; s. Robert WIlliam and Helen Joyce (Hillen) L. BA, U. Calif., Berkeley, 1981; MS in Journalism Medill Sch. of Journalism, Northwestern U., Evanston, Ill., 1991. Reporter Turlock (Calif.) Daily Jour., 1982-84; writer, editor Paul Larson Commns., Modesto, Calif., 1984-90; dir. external affairs and publs. Medill Sch. Journalism, Northwestern U., Evanston, Ill., 1991-96; mgr. strategic com. AMA, Chgo., 1996-98, dir. membership com., 1998-2000, v.p. mem. and bus. comms., 2000—. Adj. lectr. Medill Sch. Journalism, Evanston, 1991-97; assoc. master Commns. Residential Coll., Northwestern U., Evanston, 1993-96. Bd. dirs. Housing Options for Mentally Ill, Evanston, 1993-2000, chmn. comm. com. 1995-2000; docent Evanston Hist. Soc., 1992-95. Recipient Rotary Group Study Exchg. award Rotary Internat., 1986, Rotary Found. Dist. Svc. award, 1995, Leadership Evanston Evanston Cmty. Rels., 1995-96, Vol. of the Yr. award Evanston McGaw YMCA, 1995. Mem. Rotary (bd. dirs. Evanston 1991-95). Office: AMA 515 N State St Chicago IL 60610-4325

LARSON, PETER N. company executive; b. 1939; BS, Oreg. State U.; JD, Seton Hall U. With Johnson & Johnson, N.J., 1967-78, 91-95, Kimberly Clark; chmn. bd., CEO Brunswick Corp., Lake Forest, Ill., 1995—. Office: Brunswick Corp One Northfield Ct Lake Forest IL 60045

LARSON, ROBERT FREDERICK, communications production company executive; b. Detroit, Mar. 24, 1930; s. Trygve and Solveig Johanna (Larsen) L.; m. Shirley Ann Burch, Aug. 20, 1955; children: Robb Jonathan, Peer Christopher. B.A., Muskingum Coll., 1953; M.Div., Pitts. Theol. Sem., 1956, Th.M, 1960; M.A. in Communications, U. Mich, 1964, Ph.D., 1969. Ordained to ministry Presbyterian Ch. Producer, dir. WITF-TV, Harrisburg, Pa., 1964-68, asst. mgr. program devel., 1968-70, pres., gen. mgr., 1970-83; exec. sec. radio/TV Pa. Council Chs., 1967-70; pres., gen. mgr. WTVS-TV, Detroit, 1983-95, pres. emeritus, 1995—; pres. The Larson Comms. Group, Inc., 1996—. Bd. dirs. Am's. Pub. TV Stas., Mich. Pub. Broadcasting, Interlochen Ctr. Arts, Mich's Children, New Detroit Inc., Community Telecom. Network, Neighborhood Renaissance, Inc., Ctrl. Bus. Dist. Assn., New Ctr. Area Coun., William Tyndale Coll.; former vice chmn. bd. dirs. PBS. Producer, dir. (TV program) Sons and Daughters, 1967, A Time to Act, 1968, Is Religion Obsolete?, 1969; exec. producer: All About Welfare, No Time To Be A Child, Act Against Violence: Help Wanted; producer: So Where Are You, God?. Mem. Detroit Coun. of Chs., Detroit Presbytery. Mem. Detroit Athletic Club. E-mail: larscomm@aol.com.

LARSON, ROY, journalist, publisher; b. Moline, Ill., July 27, 1929; s. Roy W. and Jane (Beall) L.; m. Dorothy Jennisch, June 7, 1950; children: Mark, Bruce, Jodie, Bradley. A.B., Augustana Coll., Rock Island, Ill., 1951; M.Div., Garrett Theol. Sem., 1955. Ordained to ministry Methodist Ch., 1956; min. Covenant United Meth. Ch., Evanston, Ill., 1963-68, First United Meth. Ch., Elmhurst, 1968-69; religion editor Chgo. Sun-Times, 1969-85; pub. The Chgo. Reporter, 1985-94; exec. dir. Garrett-Medill Ctr. for Religion and News Media, Evanston, Ill., 1995—. Home: 1508 Hinman Ave Evanston IL 60201-4664 Office: Garrett-Medill Ctr 2121 Sheridan Rd Evanston IL 60201-2926

LARSON, RUSSELL GEORGE, magazine publisher; b. Waukesha, Wis., May 4, 1942; s. George Arthur and Dorothy Edna (Hanneman) L.; m. Barbara Kay Krsek, Aug. 1, 1964; children— Eric, Craig, Denise AAS, Milw. Sch. Engring., 1962. Tech. writer various publs., 1962-69; assoc. editor Model Railroader Mag., Milw., 1969-75, mng. editor, 1975-77, editor, 1977-93, v.p. editorial, 1989-93, sr. v.p. editorial, 1993—. Pub. Model Railroader Mag., Classic Toy Trains Mag., The Writer, Plays, Garden Railways Mag., Milw. Author: N Scale Primer, 1973, Beginner's Guide to N Scale Model Railroading, 1990, Beginner's Guide to Large Scale Model Railroading, 1994. Lutheran. Avocations: golf, model railroading, reading, travel. Office: Kalmbach Pub Co PO Box 1612 21027 Crossroads Cir Waukesha WI 53186-4055

LARSON, SIDNEY, art educator, artist, writer, painting conservator; b. Sterling, Colo., June 16, 1923; s. Harry and Ann Levin; m. George Ann Madden, Aug. 30, 1947; children: Sara Catherine, Nancy Louise. BA, U. Mo., 1949, MA in Art, 1950. Prof. art Columbia Coll., Mo., 1951—; art curator State Hist. Soc. Mo., 1962—; painting conservator, Columbia, 1960—. Exhibited paintings and drawings in group shows in Midwest, Washington, N.Y. and Japan; executed murals Daily News, Rolla, Mo., Shelter Ins., Columbia, Mo., Guitar Bldg., Columbia, Mcpl. Bldg., Jefferson City, Mo., Centerre Bank, Columbia, chs. in Okla. and Ark. Adv. Mo. State Council on Arts, 1960, Boone County Courthouse, Columbia. Served with USN, 1943-46, PTO. Fellow Huntington Hartford Found., 1962; rRecipient Commendation award Senate of State of Mo., 1977, 87, Nat. Prof. of Yr. award, Bronze medalist, Mo. State Prof. of Yr. award Coun. for Advancement and Support Edn., 1987, Disting. Svc. award State Hist. Soc. Mo., Mo. State Arts Coun. award, 1991. Mem. Am. Inst. Conservation of Hist. and Artistic Works (assoc. mem.), Nat. Assn. Mural Painters. Avocations: world travel, reading. Home: 1408 Whitburn Dr Columbia MO 65203-5172 Office: Columbia Coll Dept Art Columbia MO 65216-0001

LARSON, VERN L. state agency administrator; Grad., No. State U. Aide to Rep. Jim Abdnor, SD, 1974—78; state auditor State of S.D., Pierre, 1978—. Republican. Office: Office of State Auditor Capitol Bldg 2d Fl 500 E Capitol Pierre SD 57501-5070

LARSON, VICKI LORD, communication disorders; b. Prentice, Wis., Sept. 21, 1944; d. Edward A. and Stella Mae (Hilton) Lord; m. James Roy Larson, Sept. 3, 1966. BSEd, U. Wis., Madison, 1966, MS, 1968, PhD, 1974. Speech-lang. pathologist Coop. Ednl. Svc. Agy. 2, Minoqua, Wis., 1967—69; instr. U. Wis., Whitewater, 1969—71, rsch. asst. Madison, 1971—73, asst. prof. Eau Claire, 1973-77, assoc. prof., 1977—81, prof. communication disorders, 1981—91, dept. chair, 1978—83, asst. dean grad. studies and univ. rsch., 1984—89, assoc. dean grad. studies and univ. rsch., 1989—91, prof. comm. Oshkosh, 1991—2000, dean Grad. Sch. Rsch., 1991—94; provost, vice chancellor acad. affairs, 1994—2000. Acquistions editor Thinking Publs., Eau Claire, 2001—. Author: Adolescents: Communication Development and Disorder, 1983, Communication Assessment and Intervention Strategies for Adolescents, 1987; contbr. Handbook of Speech-Language Pathology and Audiology, 1988, Language Disorders in Older Students, 1995. Fellow: Am. Speech, Lang., Hearing Assn. (councilor); mem.: Wis. Speech, Lang., Hearing Assn. (pres. 1976, honors 1991), Phi Kappa Phi, Omicron Delta Kappa. Avocations: traveling, quilting, reading. E-mail: larsonvl@northnet.net.

LARUE, PAUL HUBERT, lawyer; b. Somerville, Mass., Nov. 16, 1922; s. Lucien H. and Germaine (Choquet) LaR.; m. Helen Finnegan, July 20, 1946; children: Paul Hubert, Patricia Seward, Mary Hogan. PhB, U. Wis., 1947, JD, 1949. Bar: Ill. 1955, Wis. 1949, U.S. Supreme Ct. 1972. Grad. asst. instr. polit. sci. dept. U. Wis., 1947-48; mem. staff Wis. Atty. Gen., 1949-50; trial atty., legal advisor to commr. FTC, 1950-55; pvt. practice Chgo.; mem. Chadwell & Kayser, Ltd., 1958-90; ptnr. Vedder, Price, Kaufman & Kammholz, 1990-93; of counsel, 1993-99. Spkr. profl. meetings; mem. Com. Modern Cts. in Ill., 1964; mem. Ill. Com. Constl. Conv., 1968, Better Govt. Assn., 1966-70 Contbr. articles to profl. jours. Mem. lawyers com. Met. Crusade of Mercy, 1967-68, United Settlement Appeal, 1966-68; apptd. pub. mem. Ill. Conflict of Interest Laws Commn., 1965-67. With AUS, 1943-45, ETO; capt. JAGC, USAFR, 1950-55. Fellow Ill. Bar Found. (life); mem. ABA (mem. coun. sect. antitrust law 1980-83, chmn. Robinson-Patman Act com. 1975-78), Ill. State Bar Assn., Chgo. Bar Assn. (chmn. antitrust com. 1970-71), Wis. State Bar, Rotary. Roman Catholic. Home: 250 Cuttriss Pl Park Ridge IL 60068 E-mail: phlarue@aol.com.

LA RUSSA, TONY, JR. (ANTHONY LA RUSSA JR.), professional baseball manager; b. Tampa, Fla., Oct. 4, 1944; m. Elaine Coker, Dec. 31, 1973; 2 daus.: Bianca, Devon. Student, U. Tampa; BA, U. So. Fla., 1969; LLB, Fla. State U., 1978. Bar: Fla., 1979. Player numerous major league and minor league baseball teams, 1962-77; coach St. Louis Cardinals orgn., 1977; mgr. minor league team Knoxville, 1978, Iowa, 1979; coach Chgo. White Sox, 1978, mgr., 1979-86, Oakland A's, 1986-95, St. Louis Cardinals, 1996—. Mgr. A.L. champion Oakland A's, 1988, 89, 90, World champions, 1989; mgr. All-Star team, 1988, coach, 1984, 87. Named Am. League Mgr. of Yr. Baseball Writers' Assn. Am., 1983, 88, 92, AP, 1983, Sporting News, 1983, Am. League Mgr. of Yr., 1988, 92. Office: St Louis Cardinals Busch Stadium 250 Stadium Plz Saint Louis MO 63102-1722*

LARUSSO, NICHOLAS F. gastroenterologist, educator, scientist; Prof., chmn. dept. internal medicine Mayo Med. Sch. Clin. & Found., Rochester, Minn., 1977—, dir. Ctr. Basic Rsch. Digestive Disorders, 1977—. Office: Mayo Clinic Ctr Basic Rsch Digestive Disease Guggenheim 17 Rochester MN 55905-0001

LASEE, ALAN J. state legislator; b. Rockland, Wis., July 30, 1937; Mem. Wis. Senate from 1st dist, Madison, 1977—. Office: 2259 Lasee Rd De Pere WI 54115-9663 also: RR 2 De Pere WI 54115-9802 also: State Senate State Capitol Madison WI 53702-0001

LASEE, FRANK G. state legislator; b. Dec. 11, 1961; BA, U. Wis., Green Bay. Chmn. Town of Ledgeview, 1993-97. Wis. state assemblyman, Dist. 2, 1994—. Home: 1601 Riverbend Terrace Green Bay WI 54311-5687 Office: PO Box 8952 Madison WI 53708-8952

LASHBROOKE, ELVIN CARROLL, JR. law educator, consultant; b. Dec. 14, 1939; s. Elvin Carroll Sr. and Lois Lenora (Weger) L.; m. Margaret Ann Jones, Dec. 19, 1964; children: Michelle Ann, David C. BA, U. Tex., 1967, MA, 1968, JD, 1972, LLM, 1977; PhD, Mich. State U., 1993. Bar: Tex. 1972, Fla. 1973. Legis. counsel Tex. Legis. Coun., Austin, 1972-75; pvt. practice law, 1975-77; asst. prof. coll. of law DePaul U., Chgo., 1977-79, Stetson U., St. Petersburg, Fla., 1979-80; assoc. prof. sch. law Notre Dame, Ind., 1981-85; prof., chmn. bus. law dept. Mich. State U., East Lansing, 1985-95; assoc. dean adminstrn. Eli Broad Coll. Bus., 1993-97; pvt. practice cons., 1986-97; dean Coll. Bus. U. Nev., Las Vegas, 1997-99; assoc. dean Broad Grad. Sch. of Mgmt., Mich. State U., East Lansing, 1999—2001, dir. study abroad and e-learning initiatives, 2001—. Instr. St. Edward's U., Austin, 1975-76. Author: Tax Exempt Organizations, 1985, The Legal Handbook of Business Transactions, 1987; contbr. articles to profl. jours. Mem. Tex. Bar Assn., Fla. Bar Assn. Avocation: computers. Home: 6405 Ridgepond Pl East Lansing MI 48823-9777 Office: Mich State Univ Broad Grad Sch of Mgmt East Lansing MI 48824-1122

LASHUTKA, GREGORY S. mayor, lawyer; b. N.Y.C., 1944; m. Catherine Adams; children: Stephanie, Michael, Nicholas, Lara. BS, Ohio State U., 1967; JD, Capital U., 1974. Bar: Ohio, 1974, Fla., D.C., 1975. Former ptnr. Squire, Sanders & Dempsey, Columbus, Ohio; elected mayor City of Columbus, 1991-99; former Columbus City Atty.; sr. v.p. corp. rels. Nationwide, Columbus, 2000—. Past chmn. Columbus-Area Sports Devel. Corp.; pres. Nat. League of Cities; comentator of the Ohio State U. Football Color, 1983-90; active civic and charitable orgns.; bd. dirs Simon Kenton coun. Boy Scouts Am.; bd. dirs. Columbus Assn. of Performing Arts, Cath. Social Svcs., Columbus chpt. Am. Heart Assn. Served to lt., USN. Named Mcpl. Leader of the Yr., Am. City and County mag., 1993. Mem. Nat. Acad. Pub. Adminstrs. Office: Nationwide One Nationwide Plz Columbus OH 43215-2220

LASKER, GABRIEL WARD, anthropologist, educator; b. York, Eng., Apr. 29, 1912; s. Bruno and Margaret Naomi (Ward) L.; m. Bernice Kaplan, July 31, 1949; children: Robert Alexander, Edward Meyer, Ann Titania. Student, U. Wis., 1928-30; A.B., U. Mich., 1934; A.M., Harvard U., 1940, Ph.D., 1945; DSC (hon.), U. Turin, Italy, 2000. Instr. English Chiao T'ung U., Peking, China, 1936-37; teaching fellow in anatomy Harvard Med. Sch., 1941-42; mem. faculty dept. anatomy Wayne State U. Sch. Medicine, Detroit, 1946—, asst. prof., 1947-55, assoc. prof., 1955-64, prof., 1964-82, prof. emeritus, 1982—; fellow commoner Churchill Coll., Cambridge U., 1983-84. Conducted Wayne U.-Viking Fund field trip to Mexico to study effects of migration on phys. characteristics of Mexicans, 1948 Author: Physical Anthropology, The Evolution of Man, Surnames and Genetic Structure, Happenings and Hearsay: Experiences of a Biological Anthropologist, 1999; editor: Yearbook of Phys. Anthropology, 1945-51, Human Biology, 1953-87, Research Strategies in Human Biology: Field and Survey Studies, 1993; contbr. articles to profl. jours. Fellow Am. Anthrop. Assn., AAAS (v.p 1968); mem. Am. Assn. Phys. Anthropologists (sec.-treas. 1947-51, v.p. 1960-62, pres. 1963-65, Charles Darwin award 1993), Am. Assn. Anatomists, Human Biology Assn., (pres. 1982-84, First Franz Boas Prize, 1996), Soc. Study Human Biology (U.K.), Asociación Mexicana de Antropología Biológica, Sigma Xi. Office: 540 E Canfield St Detroit MI 48201-1928

LASKOWSKI, LEONARD FRANCIS, JR. microbiologist; b. Milw., Nov. 16, 1919; s. Leonard Francis and Frances (Cyborowski) L.; m. Frances Bielinski, June 1, 1946; children— Leonard Francis III, James, Thomas. B.S., Marquette U., 1941, M.S., 1948; Ph.D., St. Louis U., 1951. Diplomate: Am. Bd. Microbiology. Instr. bacteriology Marquette U., 1946-48; mem. faculty St. Louis U., 1951—, prof. pathology and internal medicine, Div. Infectious Diseases, 1969-90, prof. emeritus, 1990—, assoc. prof. internal medicine, 1977-90—. Dir. clin. microbiology sect. St. Louis U. Hosps. Labs., 1965— ; cons. clin microbiology Firmin Desloge Hosp., St. Louis U. Group Hosps., St. Marys Group Hosps.; cons. bacteriology VA Hosp.; asst. dept. chief Pub. Health Lab., St. Louis Civil Def., 1958— ; cons. St. Elizabeths Hosp., St. Louis County Hosp., St. Francis Hosp. Contbr. articles to profl. jours. Health and tech. tng. coordinator for Latin Am. projects Peace Corps, 1962-66. Served with M.C. AUS, 1942-46. Fellow Am. Acad. Microbiology; mem. Soc. Am. Bacteriologists, N.Y. Acad. Scis., Am., Mo. pub. health assns., AAUP, Med. Mycol. Soc. Am., Alpha Omega Alpha. Home: 6229 Robertsville Rd Villa Ridge MO 63089-2617 Office: 1402 S Grand Blvd Saint Louis MO 63104-1004

LASKOWSKI, MICHAEL, JR. chemist, educator; b. Warsaw, Poland, Mar. 13, 1930; came to U.S., 1947, naturalized, 1955; s. Michael and Maria (Dabrowska) L.; m. Joan Claire Heyer, Nov. 29, 1957; children: Michael Christopher, Marta Joan. B.S. magna cum laude, Lawrence Coll., 1950; Ph.D. (NIH fellow), Cornell U., 1954, postgrad., 1954-55, Yale U., 1955-56. Research asst. Marquette U., 1949-50; instr. Cornell U., 1956-57; asst. prof. chemistry Purdue U., 1957-61, asso. prof., 1961-65, prof., 1965—. Chmn. Gordon Rsch. Conf. Physics and Phys. Chemistry Biopolymers, 1966, Proteolytic Enzymes and Their Inhibitors, 1982; mem. study sect. NIH, 1967-71, NSF, 1989, sci. adv. bd. Receptor, Inc., 1993-94, Khepri Pharms., Inc., 1993-95, BioNoma Dynamics, 2002-. Mem. editorial bd. Archives Biochemistry and Biophysics, 1972-90, Biochemistry, 1973-78, Jour. Protein Chemistry, 1981-97, Jour. Biol. Chemistry, 1983-88; mem. expert sci. coun. Protein Identification Resource, 2000—; contbr. articles to profl. jours. Recipient McCoy award Purdue U., 1975; co-recipient award in biol. scis. Alfred Jurzykowski Found., 1977 Mem. Am. Chem. Soc. (chmn. sect. 1968-69, treas. div. biol. chemistry 1981-84, councillor 1985-88), Am. Soc. Biol. Chemists, Biophys. Soc., Protein Soc., AAAS, AAUP, Polish Acad. Arts, Sci. Am., ACLU, Sigma Xi. Home: 222 E Navajo St West Lafayette IN 47906-2155 Office: Purdue U Dept Chemistry West Lafayette IN 47907 Office Fax: 765-494-0239. E-mail: michael.laskowski.1@purdue.edu.

LASKOWSKI, RICHARD E. retail hardware company executive; b. 1941; With Ace Hardware Corp., Oak Brook, Ill., 1962-98, now chmn. bd. dirs., also pres. subs., ret. from bd. dirs., 1998; now mgr., owner Ace Hardware Stores, Round Lake, 1998—. Office: Ace Hardware Corp 659 Railroad Ave Round Lake IL 60073-3299

LASSAR, SCOTT R. prosecutor; b. Evanston, Ill., Apr. 5, 1950; s. Richard Ernest and Jo (Ladenson) L.; m. Elizabeth Levine, May 22, 1977; children: Margaret, Kate. B.A., Oberlin Coll., 1972; J.D., Northwestern U., 1975. Bar: Ill. 1975. Former dep. chief spl. prosecutions divsn. no. dist. Office U.S. Atty., Chgo.; former ptnr. Keck, Mahin & Cate, Chgo.; now U.S. atty. North Dist. Dept. Justice, Chgo. Office U.S. Atty., Chgo. Office: US Attys Office 219 S Dearborn St Ste 1500 Chicago IL 60604-1700

LASSETER, ROBERT HAYGOOD, electrical engineering educator, consultant; b. Miami, Fla., Apr. 4, 1938; s. J. Haygood and Elsiemae (Davis) L.; m. Lucy Taylor, Sept. 2, 1979; children: Courtney M., Malahn P., Robert M., Lauren L. BS in Physics, N.C. State U., 1963, MS in Physics, 1967; PhD in Physics, U. Pa., 1971; postdoctoral work, U. Pa., Phila., 1971-73. Cons. engr. GE Co., Phila., 1973-80; from asst. prof. to assoc. prof. U. Wis., Madison, 1980-85, assoc. chmn., 1984-85, prof., 1985—. Dir. power sys. Engring. Rsch. Ctr.- Wis., 1994—; cons. engr. Siemens AG, Germany, 1985-86; cons. Elec. Power Rsch. Inst., Palo Alto, Calif., 1990—, others; expert advisor Conf. Internat. des Grands Réseaux Electriques, 1982—. Contbr. numerous papers to profl. socs. Fellow IEEE. Achievements include pioneering work in application of digital methods to the design of high voltage direct current power systems; basic development of analytical methods for design and study of power electronic controllers in power systems; creating a concept of Microgrids as applied to distributed resources in power systems. Office: Univ Wisconsin Electrical & Computer Engineering 1415 Engineering Dr Madison WI 53706-1607

LASTER, DANNY BRUCE, animal scientist; b. Scotts Hill, Tenn., Nov. 29, 1942; married 1960; 2 children. BS, U. Tenn., 1963; MS, U. Ky., 1964; PhD in Animal Breeding, Okla. State U., 1970. Rsch. specialist U. Ky., Lexington, 1965-68; asst. prof. endocrinology Iowa State U., 1970-71; rsch. leader reproduction rsch. unit, Clay Ctr. Agr. Rsch. Svc. USDA, Nebr., 1971-78, nat. program leader, assoc. dep. adminstr. Agrl. Rsch. Svc., 1981-88; dir. Roman L. Hruska U.S. Meat Animal Rsch. Ctr. Clay Ctr., Nebr., 1998-2000. Mem. Am. Soc. Animal Sci.

LATELL, ANTHONY A., JR. state legislator; m. Dorothy Kreeger; children: Jacqueline, Kurt, Tod. BS, U. Dayton; postgrad., Wright State U., Youngstown State U. Councilman-at-large, coun. pres., Girard City, Ohio, 1976-80; state senator Dist. 32 Ohio Senate, 1992-2000; state rep. Ohio Ho. of Reps., 2001—. Ranking minority mem. Ohio Senate, mem. finance and fin. instns. com., hwys. and transp. com., ins., commerce and labor com., state and local govt. and vets. affairs com., joint com. agy. rule rev.; precinct com. person, mem. Trumbull County Dems., 1970—; commr. Trumbull County, 1980—. Active United Way, Big Brothers/Big Sisters, Leadership Geauga County, Geauga County Libr.; trustee Found. Extended. Mem. Internat. Narcotics Enforcement Offices Assn., Sons of Italy, Elks, KC Office: 862 Krehl Ave Girard OH 44420-1903 also: Rm # 050, Ground Fl Senate Bldg Columbus OH 43215

LATHAM, TOM, congressman; b. Hampton, Iowa, July 14, 1948; s. Willard and Evelyn L.; m. Kathy Swinson, 1975; children: Justin, Jennifer, Jill. Student, Watrburg Coll., Iowa State U. Bank teller, bookkeeper, Brush, Colo., 1970-72; ind. ins. agent Fort Lupton, 1972-74; mktg. rep. Hartford Ins. Co., Des Moines, 1974-76; with Latham Seed Co., Alexander, Iowa, 1976—, now v.p., co-owner; mem. 104th-106th Congress from 5th Iowa dist., 1994—. Sec. Republican Party of Iowa; rep. 5th dist. Republican State Ctrl. com.; co-chair Francklin County Republican Ctrl. com.; whip Iowa del. Republican Nat. Conv., 1992. Past chair Franklin County Extension Coun.; mem. Nazareth Lutheran Ch., past pres.; citizens adv. coun. Iowa State U. Mem. Am. Soybean Assn., Am. Seed Trade Assn., Iowa Farm Bur. Fedn., Iowa Soybean Assn., Iowa Corn Growers Assn., Iowa Seed Assn., Agribusiness Assn. of Iowa. Lutheran. Office: US House Reps 440 Cannon Hob Washington DC 20515-1505*

LATIMER, KENNETH ALAN, lawyer; b. Chgo., Oct. 26, 1943; s. Edward and Mary (Schiller) L.; m. Carole Ross, June 23, 1968; children: Cary, Darren, Wendy. BS, U. Wis., 1966; JD with honors, George Washington U., 1969. Bar: D.C. 1969, Ill. 1970. Atty. U.S. Office of Comptroller, Washington, 1969-70; assoc. Berger, Newmark & Fenchel, Chgo., 1970-74, ptnr., 1975-86, Holleb & Coff, Chgo., 1986-99, Duane, Morris & Heckscher LLP, Chgo., 1999—. Guest speaker Ill. Inst. for Continuing Legal Edn., Chgo., 1975-87; lectr. Banking Law Inst., 1996—. Pres. North Suburban Jewish Cmty. Ctr., Highland Park, Ill., 1985; bd. dirs. Jewish Cmty. Ctrs. Chgo., 1985-95. Mem. ABA Fellows, Ill. Bar Assn. (chmn. sect. coun. on comml. banking and bankruptcy 1990-91), ABA (com. on banking and comml. finance), Chgo. Bar Assn. (com. on fin. instns.), Comml. Fin. Assn. Edn. Found. (founders coun.), Assn. Comml. Fin. Attys. (bd. regents), Am Coll. Comml. Fin Attys., Standard Club. Avocations: jogging, travel. Office: Duane Morris LLC 227 W Monroe St Ste 3400 Chicago IL 60606-5098 E-mail: kalatmer@duane.morris.com.

LA TOURETTE, JOHN ERNEST, academic administrator; b. Perth Amboy, N.J., Nov. 5, 1932; s. John Crater and Charlotte Ruth (Jones) LaT.; m. Lillie M. Drum, Aug. 10, 1957; children— Marc Andrew, Yanique Renee. B.A., Rutgers U., 1954, M.A., 1955, Ph.D., 1962. From asst. prof. to prof. Rutgers U., New Brunswick, N.J., 1960-61, SUNY, Binghamton, 1961-76, chair dept. econs., 1967-75, provost grad. studies, 1975-76; dean grad. sch., vice provost grad. studies Bowling Green (Ohio) State U., 1976-79; v.p., provost No. Ill. U., DeKalb, 1979-86, acting pres., 1984-85, pres., 1986—. Vis. prof. Karlsruhe (W. Ger.) U., 1974; research prof. Brookings Inst., 1966-67; vis. scholar Ariz. State U., 1969, 70; lectr. Econs. Inst., U. Colo., 1966; dir. NSF Departmental Sci. Devel. Grant, 1970-75, First Am. Bank, DeKalb, 1985—, Higher Edn. Stategic Planning Inst., Washington, 1984-88; cons. North Cen. Assn., 1983—. Contbr. articles to profl. jours. Served to capt. USAF, 1955-58. Ford Found. grantee, 1963; SUNY Found. grantee, 1963, 65, 70 Mem. Am. Econ. Assn., Can. Econ. Assn. (fin. acctg. adv. standards coun. 1991-94). Office: No Ill U Office of Pres Dekalb IL 60115

LATOURETTE, STEVEN C. congressman; b. Cleve., July 22, 1954; married; 4 children. BA in Hist., U. Mich., 1976; JD, Cleve. State U., 1979. Asst. pub. defender Lake County Pub. Defender's Office, 1980-83; assoc. Cannon, Stern, Aveni & Krivok, Painesville, 1983-86; with Baker, Hackenberg & Collins, 1986-88; prosecuting atty. Lake County Prosecutor Office, 1988-93; mem. U.S. Ho. of Reps., Washington, 1994—, mem. Com. on Transp. & Infrastructure, subcom. pub. bldgs. & econ. devel., hwys. and transit, & water resources and environ., mem. govt. reform and oversight com., mem. fin. svcs. com., mem. U.S. Holocaust Meml. Coun., trans. & infrastructure, 1995—. Office: US House Reps 2453 Rayburn HOB Washington DC 20515-3519*

LATSHAW, JOHN, entrepreneur, director; b. Kansas City, Dec. 10, 1921; s. Ross W. and Edna (Parker) L.; m. Barbara Haynes, Nov. 13, 1954 (div. Dec. 1975); children: Constance Haynes, Elizabeth Albright. Student, Kansas City Jr. Coll., 1938-40; BS, Mo. U., 1942. Mgr. trading dept. Harris, Upham & Co., 1943-49; ptnr. Uhlmann & Latshaw, 1949-53, E.F. Hutton & Co. (merger with Uhlmann & Latshaw), 1954-87, exec. v.p., mgn. dir., 1987—. Chmn. bd. dirs., chief exec. officer B.C. Christopher & Co., 1987-89, chmn. emeritus, 1989-90; chmn., chief exec. officer Conchemco Inc.; chmn., chief exec. officer, mng. dir. Latshaw Enterprises, 1990—; chmn. bd. dirs. Bus. Communications, Inc., Install, Maintain and Repair, Inc., Interior Designs, Inc.; mem. Kansas City Bd. Trade; gov. Midwest Stock Exchange, 1966-68; moderator, opening speaker Plenary Panel on Needs and Opportunities in Key Bus. Sectors, Miami Conf. on the Caribbean, 1980; pres. World Cable Ltd. Past Chmn. Key Men's Council; past pres. Friends of Zoo, 1970; mem. exec. com. Religious Heritage Am., Starlight Theatre, Performing Arts Kansas City; v.p., mem. exec. bd. Am. Cancer Soc., 1970, 71; mem. Jackson County and Crusade Adv. Com., Gov.'s Com. on Higher Edn.; bd. dirs. Kansas City Theatre Guild Council, The Curry Found., Am. Urban Devel. Found., Kansas City Crime Commn.; trustee City Employees Pension Plan, St. Andrew's Episcopal Ch. Meml. and Res. Trust Fund, U. Mo., Kansas City; bd. govs. Am. Royal, Agrl. Hall of Fame, 1976-77; exec. bd. Kansas City Area council Boy Scouts Am., 1970-72, adv. bd., 1973, chmn. patriotism program, 1970; hon. bd. dirs. Rockhurst Coll.; past pres. Kansas City Soccer Club, Inc.; mem. exec. com. N.Am. Soccer League, 1968, 69; bd. govs. Invest-In-Am. Nat. Council; mem. Central Region exec. com.; regional chmn. Invest-in-Am. Week Liaison, 1958— ; mem. fin. com. Mayor's Profl. Theater; mem. Univ. Assos. of U. Mo. of Kansas City; chmn. hon. trustees YWCA, 1968-69; trustee Midwest Research Inst.; mem. chancellor's adv. council Met. Community Colls., 1976-77; mem. pres.'s council bd. hon. trustees Kansas City Art Inst.; mem. Pres.' Scholarship Club Avila Coll.; bd. dirs., mem. fin. com. Mayor's Christmas Tree Assn.; chmn. bd. trustee Conservatory of Music; community adv. com. U. Mo. Kansas City Sch. Nursing; mem. Civic Council Greater Kansas City; chmn. Brotherhood Citation Dinner for NCCJ, 1980; trustee Westminster Coll., 1981; hon. bd. govs. Hyman Brand Hebrew Acad.; adv. com. Metro Energy Ctr., 1982; mem. NASA adv. bd. to Pres. U.S., 1983-86. Recipient citation of merit U. Mo., 1957, Golden Eagle award Nat. Invest in Am. Coun., 1970, Chaturathabhorn of Most Exalted Order of White Elephant award, Thailand, 1983; named hon. consul Thailand, Royal Consulate Gen., 1986, The Knight Comdr. of the Most Noble Order of the Crown of Thailand, 1993; decorated Knight Hospitaller of Malta Sovereign Order St. John Jerusalem. Mem. Internat. Trade Assn. (chmn. bd.), Kansas City C. of C. (dir., past pres.), Bus. and Profl. Assn. Western Mo. (mem. adv. bd.), Kansas City Security Traders Assn. (past pres.), Nat. Security Traders Assn. (past exec. v.p.), Wine Soc. of World, Order Jim Daisy, Sigma Nu. Episcopalian (trustee). Clubs: Carriage, Mission Hills Country. Home: 5049 Wornall Apt 2C Kansas City MO 64112-2409 also: 4530 Gulf Shore Blvd N unit 152 Naples FL 34103 Office: 800 W 47th St Ste 716 Kansas City MO 64112-1249

LATTA, ROBERT E. state representative; b. Bluffton, Ohio, Apr. 18, 1956; m. Marcia Sloan; 2 children. BA, Bowling Green State U., 1978; JD, U. Toledo, 1981. Bar: Ohio 1981. Commr. Wood County, Ohio, 1990-98; mem. 2d dist. Ohio Senate, Columbus, 1997-2001; rep. 4th dist. Ho. of Reps., 2001—. Recipient Legislator's award Ohio Assn. Alcohol Drug Addiction & Mental Health Svcs., Maj. Gen. Charles Dick award Ohio N.G. Assn. Watchdog of Treas. award, United Conservatives of Ohio, 1998, 2000; named Outstanding Freshman Legislator, 1998, Legislator of Yr., Ohio Farmers Union, League of Ohio Sportsmen, 2000; cert. Appreciation Ohio Supts. Edl. Svc. Ctr. Assoc. Mem. Wood County Farm Bur., Wood County Bar Assn., Bowling Green C. of C. E-mail: rep04@ohr.state.oh.us Office: 77 S High St 13th Fl Columbus OH 43215

LATTO, LEWIS M. broadcasting company executive; b. Duluth, Minn., Jan. 21, 1940; s. Lewis M. and Ethel S. L.; divorced; children: Aaron, Caroline. B.A., U. Minn., 1963. Owner, mgr. Sta. KXTP, Duluth, 1965-94, Sta. WAKX-FM, 1974-94; owner Sta. KRBT-AM, WEVE-FM, Eveleth, Minn., 1978—, Sta. KGPZ-FM, Grand Rapids, 1995—. Mem. Duluth City Council, 1969-75, pres., 1974. Mem. Nat. Radio Broadcasters Assn. (dir.), Minn. Broadcasters Assn. (pres. 1992-93). Republican. Methodist. Office: Northland Radio Stas 5732 Eagle View Dr Duluth MN 55803-9498 E-mail: lewlatto@aol.com.

LAU, MICHELE DENISE, advertising consultant, sales trainer, television personality; b. St. Paul, Dec. 6, 1960; d. Dwyane Udell and Patricia Ann (Yri) L. Student, U. Minn., 1979-82. Pub. rels. coord. Stillwater (Minn.) C. of C., 1977-79; asst. mgr. Salkin & Linoff, Mpls., 1982, store merchandiser, sales trainer, 1982-83; rental agt. Sentinel Mgmt. Co., St. Paul, 1983-84; account exec. Community Svc. Publs., Mpls., 1984-85, frwy. news supr., 1985, asst. sales mgr., 1985-86, St. Paul Pioneer Press Dispatch, 1986-91; pres. Promotional Ptnrs., Eden Prairie, Minn., 1991-96; on-air show host Home Shopping Network, 1996—. On-air personality Sta. WCCO II Cable TV Mpls., 1988-89, co-host Afternoon Midwest, 1989-93; co-host Home Shopping Show, host Minn. Voices, Fox 29, 1995; cons. U. Minn. Alumni mag., 1986-89. Author mechandising and sales tng. manuals. Fund-raiser sustaining program YMCA, Mpls., 1986, Jr. Achievement, St. Paul, 1988; cons. Muscular Dystrophy Assn., St. Paul, 1988-89; bd. dirs. St. Paul Jaycees. Mem. NAFE, Nat. Assn. Home Builders, Mpls. Builder Assn. (amb.), Metro-East Profl. Builders Assn. (spl. events com.), Advt. Fedn., The Newspaper Guild, Internat. Platform Assn., Speakeasy Club. Lutheran. Avocations: tennis, golf, aerobics. Home: 4961 Bacopa Ln S Unit 102 Saint Petersburg FL 33715-2621 E-mail: michelelau@aol.com.

LAU, PAULINE YOUNG, chemist; b. Harbin, China, June 18, 1943; d. Ching-ju and Chuan-erh (Fu) Young; m. Roland Lau, Sept. 16, 1967 (div. 1990); 1 child, Joan Mann. BS in Med. Tech., Nat. Taiwan U., 1964; MS in Chemistry, Wayne State U., Detroit, 1967; PhD in Chemistry, 1984. Med. technologist Detroit Gen. Hosp., 1967-68; adminstrv. asst. in rsch. Purdue U., W. Lafayette, Ind., 1970-72; supr. chemistry dept. Raritan Valley Hosp., Greenbrook, N.J., 1973-75; head chemistry dept. Princeton (N.J.) Med. Ctr., 1975-80; mgr. S.E. region RIA Ctr., Columbia, S.C., 1980-82; rsch. chemist Med. Product dept. DuPont Co., Wilmington, Del., 1984-88; mgr. rsch./devel. Boehringer Mannheim Diagnostics, Indpls., 1988—. Com. mem. Nat. Com. on Clin. Lab. Stds., 1989—. Author: Clinical Chemistry Laboratory Procedures, 1977. Recipient Outstanding Product Devel. award, Boehringer Mannheim Co., 1990. Mem. Chinese Acad. and Profl. Assn. in Mid-Am. (bd. dirs. 1990—), Ind. Assn. Chinese Ams. (pres. 1993), Mt. Jade Assn. (chmn. biomed. div. 1990—), Ctrl. Ind. Clin. Biochemistry Forum (pres. 1993—), Am. Assn. Clin. Chemistry (chpt. treas. 1989-92, divsn. sec. 1992-93), Am. Chem. Soc. (chpt. bd. dirs. 1990-91), Ind. Chinese Profl. Assn. (v.p. 1990-91, pres. 1992-93), N.Am. Chinese Clin. Chemists Assn. (bd. dirs. 1988-91, pres. 1992—). Office: Roche Diagnostic Corp 9115 Hague Rd Indianapolis IN 46256-1025

LAUDERDALE, KATHERINE SUE, lawyer; b. Wright-Patterson AFB, Ohio, May 30, 1954; d. Azo and Helen Ceola (Davis) L. BS in Polit. Sci., Ohio State U., 1975; JD, NYU, 1978. Bar: Ill. 1978, U.S. Dist. Ct. (no. dist.) Ill. 1978, Calif. 1987. Assoc. Schiff, Hardin & Waite, Chgo., 1978-82; dir. bus. and legal affairs Sta. WTTW-TV, 1982-83, gen. counsel, 1983—, also v.p., sr. v.p., gen. counsel legal and bus. affairs, 1993—, acting sr. v.p. Prodn. Ctr., 1994, sr. v.p. new ventures, 1995-99, sr. v.p. network Chgo. implementation, 1999—, sr. v.p. strategic partnerships and gen. counsel, 2000—. Mem. Lawyers Com. for Harold Washington, Chgo. 1983; bd. dirs. Midwest Women's Ctr., Chgo., 1985-94; active Chgo. Coun. Fgn. Rels., 1981—, mem. fgn. affairs com., 1985—; mem. adv. bd. Malcolm X Coll. Sch. Bus., 1996-99. Mem. ABA, Chgo. Bar Assn. (bd. dirs. TV Prodns., Inc. 1986—), Lawyers for Creative Arts (bd. dir. 1984—, v.p. 1998—), ACLU (bd. dirs. 1987-94), Nat. Acad. TV Arts and Scis., NYU Law Alumni Assn. Midwest (mem. exec. bd. 1982—), The Ohio State U. Pres.'s Nat. Adv. Coun. on Pub. Affairs (Chgo. com., 1994—), The U. Chicago Women's Bd., 1996—. Democrat. Office: Sta WTTW-TV 5400 N Saint Louis Ave Chicago IL 60625-4680

LAUER, RONALD MARTIN, pediatric cardiologist, researcher; b. Winnipeg, Man., Can., Feb. 18, 1930; m. Eileen Pearson, Jan. 12, 1959; children: Geoffrey, Judith Lauer. BS, U. Man., 1953, MD, 1954. Diplomate Am. Bd. Pediatrics. Asst. prof. pediatrics U. Pitts., 1960-61; asst. prof. pediatrics U. Kans., 1961-67, assoc. prof. pediatrics, 1967-68; prof. pediatrics, dir. pediatrics cardiology U. Iowa, 1968-95 , vice chmn. pediatrics, 1974-82, prof. pediatrics and preventive medicine 1980— . Office: U Iowa Coll Medicine Divsn Pediat Cardiology 200 Hawkins Dr Iowa City IA 52242-1009

LAUFF, GEORGE HOWARD, biologist; b. Milan, Mar. 23, 1927; s. George John and Mary Anna (Klein) L. B.S., Mich. State U., 1949, M.S., 1951; postgrad., U. Mont., 1951, U. Wash., 1952; Ph.D., Cornell U., 1953. Fisheries research technician Mich. Dept. Conservation, 1950; teaching asst. Cornell U., 1952-53; instr. U. Mich., 1953-57, asst. prof., 1957-61, asso. prof., 1961-62; research asso. Gt. Lakes Research Inst., U. Mich., 1954-59; dir. U. Ga. Marine Inst., 1960-62; asso. prof. U. Ga., 1960-62; research coord. Sapelo Island Research Found., 1962-64; dir. Kellogg Biol. Sta., 1964-90; prof. dept. fisheries and wildlife and zoology Mich. State U., East Lansing, 1964-91, prof. emeritus, 1991—. Mem. cons. and rev. panels for Smithsonian Inst., Nat. Water Commn., NSF, Nat. Acad. Sci., Am. Inst. Biol. Sci., U.S. AEC, Inst. Ecology, others. Editor: Estuaries, 1967, Experimental Ecological Reserves, 1977. Served with inf. U.S. Army, 1944-46. Office of Naval Research grantee; U.S. Dept. Interior grantee; NSF grantee; others. Fellow AAAS; mem. Am. Inst. Biol. Sci., Am. Soc. Limnology and Oceanography (pres. 1972-73), Ecol. Soc. Am., Freshwater Biology Assn., INTECOL, Societas Internationalis Limnologiae, Orgn. Biol. Field Stas., Sigma Xi, Phi Kappa Phi. Home: 3818 Heights Dr Hickory Corners MI 49060-9504 Office: 3700 E Gull Lake Dr Hickory Corners MI 49060-9505

LAUFMAN, LESLIE RODGERS, hematologist, oncologist; b. Pitts., Dec. 13, 1946; d. Marshall Charles and Ruth Rodgers; m. Harry B. Laufman, Apr. 25, 1970 (div. Apr. 1984); children: Hal, Holly; m. Rodger Mitchell, Oct. 9, 1987. BA in Chemistry, Ohio Wesleyan U., 1968; MD, U. Pitts., 1972. Diplomate Am. Bd. Internal Medicine and Hematology. Intern Montefiore Hosp., Pitts., 1972-73, resident in internal medicine, 1973-74; fellow in hemotology and oncology Ohio State Hosp., Columbus, 1974-76; dir. med. oncology Grant Med. Ctr., 1977-92; practice medicine specializing in hematology and oncology, 1977—. Bd. dirs. Columbus Cancer Clinic; prin. investigator Columbus Cmty. Clin. Oncology Program, 1989-98. Contbr. articles to profl. jours. Mem. AMA, Am. Women Med. Assn. (sec./treas. 1985-86, pres. 1986-87), Am. Soc. Clin. Oncology, Southwest Oncology Group, Nat. Surg. Adjuvant Project for Breast and Bowel Cancers. Avocations: tennis, piano, sailing, hiking, travel. also: 8100 Ravines Edge Ct Columbus OH 43235-5426 Office: 8100 Ravines Edge Ct Columbus OH 43235-5426

LAUGHLIN, NANCY, newspaper editor; Nation/world editor Detroit Free Press, 1992—. Office: Detroit Free Press Inc 600 W Fort St Detroit MI 48226-2706

LAUGHLIN, STEVEN L. advertising executive; b. 1948; Copy writer Fuller Biety Connell Agy., Milw., 1968-74, Cramer Krusselt Co., Milw., 1974-75; with Laughlin/Constable Inc., 1975—, pres., ptnr., creative dir., writer, ptnr. Office: Laughlin/Constable Inc 207 E Michigan St Milwaukee WI 53202-4996

LAUGHREY, NANETTE KAY, judge, federal; b. Cheyenne, Wyo., Feb. 11, 1946; m. Christopher Sexton Kelly; children: Hugh, Jessica Katherine. BA, UCLA, 1967; JD, U. Mo. Columbia, 1975. Bar: Mo. 1975, U.S. Dist. Ct. (we. dist.) Mo. 1975, U.S. Ct. Appeals (8th cir.) 1976, U.S. Supreme Ct. 1978. Asst. atty. gen. Mo. Atty. Gen.'s Office, Kansas City, 1975-79; assoc. Craig Van Matre, P.C., Columbia, 1980-83; assoc. prof. law U. Mo. Columbia, 1983-87, prof. law, 1987-89, William H. Pittman prof. law, 1989-96; judge U.S. Dist. Ct. (we. dist.) Mo., Kansas City, 1996—. Mcpl. judge City of Columbia, 1979-83; vis. prof. law U. Iowa, 1990; dep. atty. gen. Mo. Atty. Gen.'s Office, 1992-93. Contbr. articles to profl. jours. Bd. dirs. Columbia Housing Authority. Mem.: ABA, Mo. Bar Assn., Am. Law Inst., U. Mo. Alumni Assn., Am. Whitewater Assn., Mo. Whitewater Assn. Office: US Dist Ct 400 E 9th St Ste 7452 Kansas City MO 64106-2670

LAUMANN, EDWARD OTTO, sociology educator; b. Youngstown, Ohio, Aug. 31, 1938; m. Anne Elizabeth Solomon, June 21, 1980; children: Christopher, Timothy; children by previous marriage: Eric, Lisa. AB summa cum laude, Oberlin Coll., 1960; MA, Harvard U., 1962, PhD, 1964. Asst. prof. sociology U. Mich., Ann Arbor, 1964-69, assoc. prof., 1969-72; prof. sociology U. Chgo., 1973—, George Herbert Mead Disting. Service prof., 1985—, chmn. dept., 1981-84, 97-99, dean div. of social scis., 1984-92, provost, 1992-93. Bd. govs. Argonne Nat. Lab., 1992-93. Author: Prestige and Associations in an Urban Community, 1966, Bonds of Pluralism, 1973, (with Franz U. Pappi) Networks of Collective Action, 1976, (with John P. Heinz) Chicago Lawyers, 1982, (with David Knoke) The Organizational State, 1987, (with John P. Heinz, Robert Nelson and Robert Salisbury) The Hollow Core, 1993, (with John Gagnon, Robert Michael, Stuart Michaels) The Social Organization of Sexuality, 1994, (with Robert Michael, John Gagnon, Gina Kolata) Sex in America, 1994, (with Robert T. Michael) Sex, Love and Health, 2001; editor Am. Jour. Sociology, 1978-84, 95-97. Mem. sociology panel NSF, Washington, 1972-74; commr. CBASSE, NRC, 1986-91; v.p., trustee NORC; trustee U. Chgo. Hosps., 1992-93. Fellow AAAS (chmn. sect. K 2001—); mem. Internat. Acad. Sex Rsch., Sociol. Rsch. Assn., Am. Sociol. Assn., Population Assn. Am. Office: U Chgo 5848 S University Ave Chicago IL 60637-1515 E-mail: ob01@midway.uchicago.edu.

LAURENCE, MICHAEL MARSHALL, magazine publisher, writer; b. N.Y.C., May 22, 1940; s. Frank Marshall and Edna Ann (Roeder) L.; m. Patricia Ann McDonald, Mar. 1, 1969; children: Elizabeth Sarah, John Marshall. AB cum laude, Harvard U., 1963. From sr. editor to asst. pub. Playboy mag., Chgo., 1967—77, asst. pub., 1977—82; mng. editor Oui mag., 1973-77; editor, pub. Linn's Stamp News, Sidney, Ohio, 1982—2002, also columnist Editor's Choice; sr. v.p., editl. dir. Amos Hobby Pub., 2002—. Co-founder, dir. U.S. 1869 Pictorial Rsch. Assocs., 1975-82. Author: Playboy's Investment Guide, 1971; editor: U.S. Mail and Post Office Assistant, 1975; author articles. Recipient G.M. Loeb award for disting. mag. writing U. Conn., 1968; named to Writers Hall of Fame, Am. Philatelic Soc., 1994. Mem. U.S. Philat. Classics Soc. (life, Elliott Perry award 1975, bd. dir. 1975-81), Harvard Club (N.Y.C.), Collectors Club Chgo. (bd. dires. 1978-82), Collectors Club N.Y.C. Avocations: stamp collecting, gardening. Office: Linn's Stamp News 911 S Vandemark Rd Sidney OH 45365-8974

LAURIE, WILLIAM, sports team executive; b. Versailles, Mo. m. Nancy, 1974; 1 child. B in Secondary Edn., Memphis State Coll., 1974. Tchr., basketball coach Christian Bros. Coll. High Sch., Memphis, 1974-78, Rock Bridge High Sch., Columbia, Mo., 1978-83; exec. Crown Ctr. Farms, 1983-99; chmn., owner St. Louis Blues Hockey Team, 1999—; onwer Kiel Ctr., St. Louis. Booster U. Mo. Tiger Sport. Office: Kiel Ctr 1401 Clark Ave Saint Louis MO 63103-2709

LAURITZEN, BRUCE RONNOW, banker; b. Omaha, June 21, 1943; s. John Ronnow and Elizabeth Ann (Davis) L.; m. Kimball McKay Bowles, Nov. 26, 1965; children: Margaret, Blair, Clarkson. AB, Princeton U., 1965; MBA, U. Va., 1967. With First Nat. Bank Omaha, 1967—, 2d v.p., 1972, v.p., 1972-83, exec. v.p., 1983-87, pres., 1987—, chmn., 1999, also bd. dirs., mem. exec. com., 1968—. Pres. Farmers Savs. Bank, Shelby, Iowa, 1969-82, Harlan County Bank, Alma, Nebr., 1972-96, Landmands Nat. Bank, Audubon, Iowa, 1972—, Sibley (Iowa) Ins. Agy., 1972-98, Sibley State Bank, 1972-91, First Nat. Bank, Elm Creek, Nebr., 1974-77, Landmands Ins. Agy., Kimballton, Iowa, 1974-98, K.B.J. Enterprises, Iowa, 1975—, Viking Corp., Iowa, 1975—, Lauritzen Corp., Nebr. and Iowa, 1985—, Emerson (Iowa) State Bank, 1980-84; chmn. Crawford County Bank, Denison, Iowa, 1976-98, MCV Acceptance Corp., Omaha, 1986—, Sibley State Bank, 1991—; bd. dirs. York State Bank. Chmn. Charlson Regional Health Svcs.; bd. dirs. Creighton U., Omaha; trustee Joslyn Art Mus., Omaha, Nebr.; bd. govs. Ak-Sar-Ben ; trustee, regional rep. St. Paul's Sch.; pres., dir. Omaha Riverfront Devel. Corp. Recipient Bus. Leadership award UNL Coll. Bus. Adminstrn., 1989. Mem. Young Pres. Orgn. (chpt. chmn. 1988-89), Omaha C. of C. (chmn. 1989, named Outstanding Young Omahan, 1978). Republican. Episcopalian. Clubs: Omaha Country, Omaha, Omaha Press; Univ. Cottage (Princeton, N.J.); Minnesouri Angling (Alexandria, Minn.), Roaring Fork (Basalt, Colo.). Avocations: skiing, golf, hunting. Home: 608 Fairacres Rd Omaha NE 68132-1806 Office: One First National Ctr 1 First National Ctr Omaha NE 68102

LAUSE, MICHAEL FRANCIS, lawyer; b. Washington, Aug. 3, 1948; s. Walter Francis and Junilla Rose (Marquart) L.; m. Ann G. Hellman, Aug. 29, 1981; children: Andrew Edward, Scott Michael. BA, St. Benedict's Coll., 1970; JD, U. Ill., 1973. Bar: Mo. 1973. Ptnr. Thompson Coburn LLP, St. Louis, 1973—. Mem. mgmt. com. Thompson Coburn LLP, St. Louis, 1988-90. Gen. counsel Mo. Health and Ednl. Facilities Authority, 1986—, St. Louis Zoo, 1992—. Mem. ABA, Mo. Bar Assn., St. Louis Bar Assn., Nat. Assn. Bond Lawyers, Bellerive Country Club. Roman Catholic. Home: 9822 Old Warson Rd Saint Louis MO 63124-1066 Office: Thompson Coburn LLP One US Bank Plz Saint Louis MO 63101

LAUTERBUR, PAUL C(HRISTIAN), chemistry educator; b. Sidney, Ohio, May 6, 1929; BS, Case Inst. Tech., 1951; PhD, U. Pitts., 1962; PhD (hon.), U. Liege, Belgium, 1984; DSc (hon.), Carnegie Mellon U., 1987; DEng (hon.), Copernicus Med. Acad., Cracow, Poland, 1988; DSc (hon.), Wesleyan U., 1989, SUNY, Stony Brook, 1990; DEng (hon.), Rensselaer Poly. Inst., 1991, U. Mons, Hainaut, Belgium, 1996. Rsch. asst. and assoc. Mellon Inst., Pitts., 1951—54, fellow, 1955—63; 1assoc. prof. chemistry SUNY, Stony Brook, 1963—69, prof. chemistry, 1969—84, rsch. prof. radiology, 1978—85, univ. prof., 1984—85; prof. (4) depts. U. Ill., Urbana, 1985—, Disting. Univ. prof. Coll. Medicine Chgo., 1990—. Mem. sci. couns. Contbr. articles; mem. editl. bds. Cpl. U.S. Army, 1953—55. Recipient Clin. Rsch. award, Lasker Found., 1984, Nat. Medal of Sci., U.S.A., 1987, Fiuggi Internat. prize, Fondazione Fiuggi, 1987, Roentgen medal, 1987, Gold medal, Radiol. Soc. N.Am., 1987, Nat. Medal of Tech., 1988, Gold medal, Soc. Computed Body Tomography, 1989, The Amsterdam (Alfred Heineken) prize in medicine, 1989, Laufman-Greatbatch award, Assn. for Advancement Med. Instrumentation, 1989, Leadership Tech. award, Nat. Elec. Mfrs. Assn., 1990, Bower award and prize for achievement in sci., Benjamin Franklin Nat. Meml. Commn. of the Franklin Inst., 1990, Internat. Soc. Magnetic Resonance award, 1992, Kyoto prize, Inamori Found., 1994. Fellow: Am. Inst. Med. and Biol.

Engring., Am. Phys. Soc. (Biol. Physics prize 1983), AAAS; mem.: Internat. Soc. Magnetic Resonance in Medicine (Gold medal 1982), IEEE (sr.), Am. Chem. Soc., NAS. Office: U Ill Dept Chemistry 600 S Mathews CLSL 51-6 Urbana IL 61801 E-mail: pcl@uiuc.edu.

LAUZEN, CHRISTOPHER J. state legislator; b. Aurora, Ill., Dec. 30, 1952; MBA, Harvard U. Owner Comprehensive Acct. Svcs., Geneva; mem. Ill. Senate from dist. 21, Springfield, 1992—. Office: 613B Capitol Bldg Springfield IL 62706

LAVELLE, ARTHUR, anatomy educator; b. Fargo, N.D., Nov. 29, 1921; s. Frank and Lillie (Hanson) LaV.; m. Faith Evelyn Wilson, 1947; 1 dau., Audrey Anne. B.S., U. Wash., 1946; M.A., Johns Hopkins, 1948; Ph.D., U. Pa., 1951. USPHS postdoctoral fellow U. Pa., Phila., 1951-52; mem. faculty dept. anatomy U. Ill. Coll. Medicine, Chgo., 1952—, assoc. prof., 1958-65, prof., 1965-87, prof. emeritus, 1987—. Vis. prof. UCLA, 1968-69; cons. Galesburg (Ill.) State Rsch. Hosp., 1965-68; mem. Biol. Stain Commn., 1953-93, trustee, 1978-93, pres., 1981-86, v.p., 1991-92. Mem. editorial bd. Biotechnic and Histochemistry, 1989-93; contbr. articles to profl. jours. USPHS research grantee, 1953-70; Cerebral Palsy Found. grantee, 1964-68; Guggenheim fellow, 1968-69 Mem. Am. Assn. Anatomists, Am. Soc. Cell Biology, Soc. Developmental Biology, AAAS, Soc. Neurosci., Sigma Xi. Office: 1853 W Polk St Chicago IL 60612-4316

LAVENGOOD, LAWRENCE GENE, management educator, historian; b. Tulsa, June 30, 1924; s. Lawrence Wilbur and Elizabeth (Gardner) L.; m. Gloria M. deLeon, Aug. 27, 1947; children: Jessica, Abigail, Timothy, Rachel. M.A., U. Chgo., 1947, Ph.D., 1953. Asst. prof. bus. history Northwestern U., Evanston, Ill., 1953-59, assoc. prof., 1959-69, chmn. dept. policy and environ., 1980-82, prof. bus. history and policy and environ., 1970-94, prof. emeritus, 1994—. Mem. Com. on Ethics in Bus. Edn., 1977-79; cons. on mgmt. devel. edn. U.S. and European corps.; U.S. faculty coord. Sasin Grad. Inst. Bus. Arminstrn., Chulalongkorn U., Bangkok, 1983-95; chmn. bd. dirs. ctr. for ethics Garrett-Evang. Theol. Sem., Evanston, 1995—. Editor, contbr.: Moral Man and Economic Enterprise, 1967. Mem. Bd. Edn. Ill. elem. dist. 65, Evanston, 1967-72, 75-78; bd. dirs. Evanston Comm. Found., 1996—. Recipient Ann. Kellogg Alumni Choice award, 1992. Democrat. Presbyterian.

LAVIN, BERNICE E. cosmetics executive; b. 1925; m. Leonard H. Lavin, Oct. 30, 1947; children: Scott Jay (dec.), Carol Marie, Karen Sue. Student, Northwestern U. Vice chairperson of bd., sec.- treas. Alberto-Culver Co.; dir., v.p., sec.- treas. Alberto-Culver U.S.A., Inc. Sec.-treas., dir. Alberto-Culver Internat., Inc.; sec.-treas. Sally Beauty Co., Inc. Office: Alberto-Culver Co 2525 Armitage Ave Melrose Park IL 60160-1163 E-mail: blavin@alberto.com.

LAVORATO, LOUIS A. state supreme court chief justice; s. Charles Lavorato; m. Janis M. Lavorato; children: Cindy, Natalie, Anthony, Dominic. BS in Bus. Adminstrn., Drake U., 1959, JD, 1962. Judge Iowa Supreme Ct., Des Moines, 1986—; sole practice, 1962-79; judge Iowa Dist. Ct., 1979-86; justice Iowa Supreme Ct., 1986—2000, chief justice, 2000—. Office: Iowa Supreme Ct St Capitol Bldg Des Moines IA 50319-0001*

LAW, GERALD H. state legislator; b. May 20, 1944; m. Chris; children: Jenney, Katie. MBA, U. Detroit, 1969; MD, Wayne State U. Sch. Law, 1974. Rep. Mich. State Dist. 36, 1983-91, Mich. State Dist. 20, 1995—. Trustee Plymouth Twp., Mich.; past Rep. precinct del.; fin. analyst Ford Motor Credit Co. Mem. Kiwanis, K. of C., YMCA, Libr. Soc. Address: PO Box 30014 Lansing MI 48909-7514

LAW, VELDON LEE, college administrator; b. Ft. Eustis, Va., Dec. 12, 1952; s. Vernon and VaNita (McGuire) L.; m. D. Lorraine Schultz, Apr. 21, 1974; children: Allison, Garrett, Jesse, Lindsay, Blake. BS, Brigham Young U., 1976, MREA, 1977; EdD, U. Nev., Las Vegas, 1988. Asst. dir. community svcs. Snow Coll., Ephraim, Utah, 1976-78; extended svcs. coord. N.Mex. Jr. Coll., Hobbs, 1978-79, dir. community devel., 1979-82; asst. dean continuing edn. Santa Barbara (Calif.) City Coll., 1982-84; exec. dir. community edn. Clark County Community Coll., Las Vegas, 1984-88; dean instrn. John Wood Community Coll., Quincy, Ill., 1988-96; pres. Barton County C.C., Great Bend, Kans., 1996—. First counselor Ch. Jesus Christ of Latter-day Saints, Quincy, 1989—. Mem. Exchange Club, Ill. Community Coll. Coun. Adminstrs. (chair 1989, instrnl. svcs. commn. 1990). Avocations: camping, golf. Office: Barton County Community College 245 NE 30 Rd Great Bend KS 67530-9107

LAWFER, I. RONALD, state legislator; BA, U. Ill. Dir. Kent Bank; Dist. 74 rep. Ill. Ho. Reps. Mem. Jo Daviess County bd.; bd. dirs. Northwestern Ill. Cmty. Action Agy., Jo Daviess Farm Bur., Jo Daviess Agrl. Extension Coun. Address: 14123 Burr Oak Ln Stockton IL 61085-9514 Also: 19 S Chicago Ave Freeport IL 61032-4229

LAWLER, JAMES EDWARD, physics educator; b. St. Louis, June 29, 1951; s. James Austin and Dolores Catherine Lawler; m. Katherine Ann Moffatt, July 21, 1973; children: Emily Christine, Katie Marie. BS in Physics summa cum laude, U. Mo., Rolla, 1973; MS in Physics, U. Wis., 1974, PhD in Physics, 1978. Rsch. assoc. Stanford (Calif.) U., 1978-80; asst. prof. U. Wis., Madison, 1980-85, assoc. prof., 1985-89, prof., 1989—, Arthur & Aurelia Schawlow prof., 1999—. Product devel. cons. Nat. Rsch. Group, Inc., Madison, 1977-78; cons. GE, Schenectady, N.Y., 1985-96, Teltech, Inc., 1990—; exec. com. Gaseous Electronics Conf., 1987-89, treas., 1992-94, DAMOP program com., 1993-95. Editor: (with R.S. Stewart) Optogalvanic Spectroscopy, 1991; contbr. articles to profl. jours. Recipient Penning award Internat. Conf. on Phenomena in Ionized Gases, 1995; Schumberger scholar U. Mo., 1971-72; grad. fellow U. Wis. Alumni Rsch. Found., 1973-74, NSF, 1974-76, H.I. Romnes faculty fellow U. Wis., 1987. Fellow Am. Phys. Soc. (Will Allis prize 1992), Optical Soc. Am.; mem. Sigma Xi. Achievements include patent for Echelle Sine Bar for dye laser cavity; development of laser diagnostics for glow discharge plasmas, of methods for measuring accurate atomic transition probabilities and radiative lifetimes. Office: U Wis Dept Physics 1150 University Ave Madison WI 53706-1302

LAWLER, JAMES F. state senator; b. Howard, S.D., Dec. 14, 1935; m. Christine A. Lawler; children: Jeff, James, Lisa. BS in Math., Sci., Dakota State U., Madison, S.D., 1958; MPH, U. Minn., 1962. Dist. environ. sanitarian S.D. Dept. of Health, Sioux Falls, 1959-62; mild and food cons. USPHS Bur. of State Svcs., Washington, 1962-64; radiation surveillance officer USPHS, DHHS, Kansas City, Mo., 1964-67, spl. asst. to area dir., chief tng. svcs. Aberdeen Area Indian Health Svc. Aberdeen, 1964-67, chief tng. ops. Desert Willow Tng. Ctr. Tucson, 1972-77, spl. asst. to area dir. Aberdeen Area Indian Health Svc. Aberdeen, 1977-79, area instnl. environ. control officer Aberdeen Area Indian Health Svc., 1979-85, spl. project dir. Aberdeen Area Indian Health Svc., 1985-92, retire, 1992; rep. for dist. 3 S.D. State Senate, 1992—. Guest speaker numerous colls. and univs.; prof. No. State U., Aberdeen. Contbr. articles to mags. and newsletters. Mem. PTA, Aberdeen Conv. and Visitors Bur.; bd. dirs. Boys and Girls Club Aberdeen, Salvation Army, Am. Lung Assn. S.D.; past pres. adv. coun. Foster Grandparent Program, Kiwanis Club Aberdeen; past mem., bd. dirs. Adjustment Tng. Ctr., Aberdeen. With S.D. N.G., 1954-62, capt. USPHS, 1962-92. Recipient Acad. scholarship 1954-58, Exemplary Performance award U. S.D. Sch. Medicine, 1989, Surgeon Gen.'s Exemplary Svc. medal, 1992; named Vol. Family Yr., S.D. Spl. Olympics, 1989. Mem. Nat. Environ. Health Assn., Internat. Assn. Milk, Food and Environ. Sanitarians, S.D. Pub. Health Assn. (pres. 1988-89, G.J. Van Heuvelen award 1990), S.D. Environ. Health Assn. (pres. 1983-84, Sanitarian Of Yr. 1988), Commd. Officers Assn. USPHS (Aberdeen area past pres.), Nat. Assn. Retarded Children, Nat. Coun. Exceptional Children, Elks, Moose, Kappa Sigma Iota. Office: 13084 385th Ave Aberdeen SD 57401-8447 Address: SD Senate 602 W 5th St Pierre SD 57501-1413

LAWLER, JAMES RONALD, French language educator; b. Melbourne, Australia, Aug. 15, 1929; married, 1954; 2 children. BA, U. Melbourne, 1950, MA, 1952; DUniv., U. Paris, 1954. Lectr. French U. Queensland, Australia, 1955-56; sr. lectr. U. Melbourne, 1957-62; prof., head dept. U. Western Australia, 1963-71; prof., chmn. dept. UCLA, 1971-74; McCulloch prof. Dalhousie U., Halifax, N.S., Can., 1974-79; prof. French U. Chgo., 1979—, Edward Carson Waller Disting. Svc. prof., 1983-97, prof. emeritus, 1998. Vis. prof. Coll. de France, 1985, Tokyo, 1996, 98, 99; chmn. vis. com. Romance Langs. and Lits. Harvard U., 1991-94, Soc. Amis U. Paris cons. Author: Form and Meaning in Valery's Le Cimetiere Marin, 1959, Lecture de Valery: Une Etude de Charmes, 1963, The Language of French Symbolism, 1969, The Poet as Analyst, 1974, Rene Char: The Myth and the Poem, 1978, Edgar Poe et les Poetes Francais, 1989, Rimbaud's Theatre of the Self, 1992, Poetry and Moral Dialectic: Baudelaire's Secret Architecture, 1997; co-author: Paul Valery; Poems, 1971, Paul Valery: Leonardo, Poe, Mallarme, 1972; editor: An Anthology of French Poetry, 1960, Paul Valery: An Anthology, 1977, Paul Valery, 1991; founding editor Essays in French Literature, 1964, Dalhousie French Studies, 1980. Decorated officier Palmes Academiques; recipient Prix Internat. Amities Françaises, Prix du rayonnement de la langue francaise Academie Francaise, 1999; Brit. Coun. interchange scholar, 1967; Australian Acad. Humanities fellow, 1970, Guggenheim Found. fellow, 1974, NEH fellow, 1985. Mem. MLA (coun. 1978-82), Am. Assn. Tchrs. French, Internat. Assn. French Studies (pres. 1998—). Achievements include rsch. in modern French poetry, poetics, 20th century novel. Office: U Chgo Dept Romance Langs & Lit 1050 E 59th St Chicago IL 60637-1559

LAWNICZAK, JAMES MICHAEL, lawyer; b. Toledo, Sept. 11, 1951; m. Christine Nielsen, Dec. 31, 1979; children: Mara Katharine, Rachel Anne, Amy Elizabeth. BA, U. Mich., 1974, JD, 1977. Bar: Mich. 1977, Ill. 1979, Ohio 1989. Law clk. to the Honorable Robert E. DeMascio U.S. Dist. Ct. (ea. dist.) Mich., Detroit, 1977-79; assoc. Levy and Erens, Chgo., 1979-83; assoc. then ptnr. Mayer, Brown & Platt, 1983-88; ptnr. Calfee, Halter & Griswold, LLP, Cleve., 1988—. Contbg. author: Collier on Bankruptcy, 15th rev. edit., 1997—. Mem. Chgo. Bar Assn. (subcom. on bankruptcy 1983-88), Cleve. Bar Assn. (bankruptcy com.). Home: 14039 Fox Hollow Dr Novelty OH 44072-9773 Office: Calfee Halter & Griswold 800 Superior Ave E Ste 1400 Cleveland OH 44114-2601 E-mail: jlawniczak@calfee.com.

LAWRENCE, BARBARA, state legislator; m. Richard Lawrence. Grad., Coll. Emporia. Kans. state rep. Dist. 30, 1993—; tchr. Office: Kans State Senate State Capital Topeka KS 66612

LAWRENCE, DAVID, radio personality; b. Denver, Sept. 08; m. Deanna Joy Utrecht, Mar. 16, 1985; children: Dan, Bailey. Radio host WDAF/61 Country, Westwood, Kans., 1973—. Avocations: collecting 45rmp records, gardening. Office: WDAF/61 Country 4935 Belinder Rd Westwood KS 66205

LAWRENCE, JAMES A. food products executive; m. Mary G. Lawrence; 3 children. BA, Yale U., 1974; MBA with distinction, Harvard U., 1976. With Fidelity Funds, Boston Cons. Group; ptnr. Bain & Co.; co-founder, ptnr. The LEK Partnership; pres., CEO The Pepsi-Cola co.; exec. v.p., CFO Northwest Airlines, St. Paul, 1996—, General Mills, Inc., Mpls. Bd. dirs. Am. Re-Ins. Corp., TransTech., Inc., TWA. Bd. dirs. U.S. China Bus. Coun., Computer Mus.; chair U.S. South Africa Bus. Devel. Com. Office: Gen Mills 1 General Mills Blvd Minneapolis MN 55426

LAWRENCE, JAMES KAUFMAN LEBENSBURGER, lawyer; b. New Rochelle, N.Y., Oct. 8, 1940; s. Michael Monet and Edna (Billings) L.; m. George-Ann Adams, Apr. 5, 1969; children: David Michael, Catherine Robin. AB, Ohio State U., 1962, JD, 1965; postgrad., Otterbein Coll., 2002—. Bar: Ohio. 1965, U.S. Dist. Ct. (so. dist.) Ohio 1971, U.S. Ct. Appeals (6th cir.) 1971, U.S. Ct. Appeals (4th cir.) 1978. Field atty. NLRB, Cin., 1965-70; ptnr. Frost Brown Todd LLC, 1970—. Adj. prof. econs. dept. and Coll. Law U. Cin., 1975—, Ohio State U. Coll. Law, 1995—, Xavier U., 1995—, McGregor Sch., Antioch U., 1993—98; adj. prof. MBA program Otterbein Coll., 2002; treas. Potter Stewart Inn of Ct., Cin., 1988—90; tchg. fellow Harvard Negotiation Project, 1991; chmn. adv. panel on appointment of magistrate judges U.S. Dist. Ct. for So. Dist. Ohio, 1993—. Contbr. articles to profl. jours. Mem. nat. coun. Ohio State U. Coll. Law, 1974—; mem. steering com. Leadership Cin., 1985-89; mem. Seven Hills Neighborhood Houses, Cin., 1973-95, pres., 1992-94; bd. dirs. Beechwood Home, Cin., 1973-85; mem. adv. bd. Emerson Behavioral Health Svcs., 1990-95, chmn., 1995; chmn. Labor Dept., 1978-89, Franciscan Hosp. Devel. Coun., 1995-99, chmn., 1996-97; trustee Ctr. for Resolution of Disputes, Inc., 1988-91, treas., 1990-91; mem. Ohio Gov.'s Ops. Improvement Task Force, 1991. Recipient Outstanding Adj. Faculty award, U. Cin., 1998. Fellow Coll. Labor and Employment Lawyers; mem. ABA, Cin. Bar Assn. (chmn. labor law com. 1979-82, comm. adv. com. 1994-96, alternative dispute resolution com. 1996—), Ohio Bar Assn. (vice chmn. labor and employment law sect. 1987-90, chmn. 1990-92), Indsl. Rels. Rsch. Assn. (bd. govs. 1977-80), Alumni Assn. Coll. Law Ohio State U. (pres. 1984-85), Assn. for Conflict Resolution, Cincinnatus Assn. (pres. 1985-86), Collaborative Law Ctr. (steering com. 1996—), Univ. Club; master Potter Stewart Inn of Ct. Avocations: collecting movie posters, biking. Home: 3300 Columbia Pkwy Cincinnati OH 45226-1044 Office: Frost Brown Todd LLC 2500 PNC Ctr 201 E 5th St Cincinnati OH 45202-4182 E-mail: jlawrence@fbtlaw.com.

LAWRENCE, JEREMY, radio director; m. Jennifer Lawrence, 1997; 1 child Alexander. Cmty. rels. dir WUGN, Midland, Mich., 1998—. Avocation: golf. Office: WUGN 510 E Isabella Rd Midland MI 48640

LAWRENCE, JOAN WIPF, former state legislator; m. Wayman; children: Wayman, Anne, David. RN, L.I. Coll. Hosp. Sch. Nursing, 1952; student, Douglass Coll., 1952-53, Rutgers U., 1953, Ohio State U., 1968-70. Rep. Dist. 87 Ohio Ho. Dist., 1983-92, rep. Dist. 80, 1993-99; dir. Ohio Dept. Aging, 1999—. Mem. Big Walnut Bd. Edn., 1970-73. Mem. LWV (Ohio pres. 1975-77), YWCA, Women's Polit. Caucus, Ohio Reps. for Choice, Farm Bur. Office: Ohio Dept Aging 9th Fl 50 W Broad St Fl 9 Columbus OH 43215-3301

LAWRENCE, JOHN KIDDER, lawyer; b. Detroit, Nov. 18, 1949; s. Luther Ernest and Mary Anna (Kidder) L.; m. Jeanine Ann DeLay, June 20, 1981. AB, U. Mich., 1971; JD, Harvard U., 1974. Bar: Mich. 1974, U.S. Supreme Ct. 1977, D.C. 1978. Assoc. Dickinson, Wright, McKean & Cudlip, Detroit, 1973-74; staff atty. Office of Judge Adv. Gen., Washington, 1975-78; assoc. Dickinson, Wright, McKean, Cudlip & Moon, Detroit, 1978-81; ptnr. Dickinson, Wright, Moon, VanDusen & Freeman, 1981-98, Dickinson Wright PLLC, Detroit, 1998—. Exec. sec. Detroit Com. on Fgn. Rels., 1988—; trustee Ann Arbor (Mich.) Summer Festival, Inc., 1990—; patron Founders Soc. Detroit Inst. Arts, 1979—. With USN, 1975-78. Mem. AAAS, ABA, Am. Law Inst., State Bar Mich., D.C. Bar Assn., Am. Judicature Soc., Internat. Bar Assn., Am. Hist. Assn., Detroit Athletic Club, Econ. Club Detroit, Phi Eta Sigma, Phi Beta Kappa. Democrat. Episcopalian. Office: Dickinson Wright PLLC 500 Woodward Ave Ste 4000 Detroit MI 48226-3416

LAWRENCE, WALTER THOMAS, plastic surgeon; b. Balt., Sept. 5, 1950; s. Walter Jr. and Susan (Shryock) L.; m. Marsha Blake, May 30, 1987. BS, Yale U., 1972; MPH, Harvard U., 1976; MD, U. Va., 1976. Diplomate Am. Bd. Surgery. Diplomate Am. Bd. Plastic Surgery. Intern and resident in gen. surgery U. N.C., Chapel Hill, 1976-78; resident gen. surgery Med. Coll. Va., Richmond, 1978-81; resident plastic surgery U. Chgo., 1981-83; expert NIH, Bethesda, Md., 1983-85; asst. prof. U. N.C., Chapel Hill, 1985-92, assoc. prof., div. chmn., 1992-95; prof., divsn. chmn. U. Mass. Med. Ctr., 1995-99, U. Kans. Med. Ctr., Kansas City, 1999—. Fellow Am. Coll. Surgeons; mem. Am. Assn. Plastic Surgeons, Am. Soc. Plastic and Reconstructive Surgeons, Plastic Surgery Rsch. Coun., Humera Soc., Womack Soc. Avocations: skiing, sailing, tennis. Office: U Kans Med Ctr Sutherland Inst/Pl Surgery 3901 Rainbow Blvd Kansas City KS 66160-0001 E-mail: tlawrence@kumc.edu.

LAWRENCE, WAYNE ALLEN, publisher; b. Cin., Dec. 11, 1938; s. Clarence E. and Edna M. (Newman) L.; m. Carol SueAnn Wisecup, July 28, 1959; children: Jeffrey Thomas, Jon Christopher, Jeremy Wayne. Student public schs., Seaman, Ohio. Advt. salesman Amos Press, Inc., Sidney, Ohio, 1957-61, v.p., 1973-83, sr. v.p., 1983-92, ret., 1992, also bd. dirs. Pub. Stamp World, Linns Stamp News, 1977-82; v.p. advt. Coin World, Sidney, 1973-78; advt. mgr. World Coins, Sidney, 1964-68, advt. dir., 1968-73, v.p., 1973-77; adv. mgr. Numis. Scrapbook, Sidney, 1967-68, advt. dir., 1968-73, v.p. advt., 1973-78; pub. Cars & Parts, Sidney, 1978-85; propr., dir. Sidney Camera, 1981-87; pres. Scott Pub. Co., 1984-92. Contbr. articles and editorials on coins, stamps and cars to Amos publs. Bd. dirs. Shelby County (Ohio) United Way, 1970-76, 1st United Meth. Ch., Sidney, 1982— ; bd. dirs. Sidney-Shelby County C. of C., 1982-85, sec., 1985; mem. U.S. Assay Commn., 1975. Mem. Am. Mgmt. Assn., Am. Numis. Assn., Am. Philatelic Assn., Numis. Lit. Guild, Am. Stamp Dealers Assn., Mag. Pubs. Assn., Am. Motorcycle Assn., Soc. Automotive Historians. Home: 1444 Double D Dr Sevierville TN 37876-0287 Office: 911 S Vandemark Rd Sidney OH 45365-8974 E-mail: shadowace1100@earthlink.net.

LAWRENCE, WILLIAM JOSEPH, JR. retired corporate executive; b. Kalamazoo, Feb. 1, 1918; s. William J. and Borgia M. (Wheeler) L.; m. Doris Luella Fitzgerald, Aug. 19, 1955; children: Aaron Frances, Cleve Moren, Julie Anne, William III. A.B., Kalamazoo Coll., 1941. Engaged in personal investments; dir. emeritus Superior Pine Products Co.; dir. LPI. Trustee emeritus, mem. fin. and adminstrn. com. Kalamazoo Found.; trustee emeritus Kalamazoo Coll., Borgess Med. Ctr. With AUS, 1942-46. Mem. Kalamazoo C. of C., Kiwanis, Com. of Twenty-Five (Palm Springs, Calif.), O'Donnell Golf Club (Palm Springs), Gull Lake Country Club, Park Club. Roman Catholic. Home: PO Box 37 Richland MI 49083-0037 Office: 136 E Michigan Ave Ste 1000 Kalamazoo MI 49007

LAWRIE, DUNCAN H. computer science educator, consultant; b. Chgo., Apr. 26, 1943; s. John Lawrie and Annabel (Harwood) McKenna; m. Linda K. Zapf, June 1, 1974. BA, De Pauw U., 1966; BSEE, Purdue U., 1966; MS, U. Ill., 1969, PhD, 1973. Asst. prof. U. Ill., Urbana, 1973-79, assoc. prof., 1979-84, prof., 1984—, head dept. computer sci., 1990-96. Contbr. numerous articles to profl. jours.; patentee computer memory. Fellow IEEE (editor-in-chief transp. parallel and distributed systems); mem. IEEE Computer Soc. (pres. 1991), Assn. Computing Machinery. Office: U Ill Dept Computer Sci 1304 W Springfield Ave Urbana IL 61801-2910

LAWSON, A. PETER, lawyer; AB, Dartmouth Coll., 1968; JD, Columbia U., 1971. Bar: N.Y. 1971, Ill. 1979. Assoc. Sullivan & Cromwell, 1971-78; sr. counsel Baxter Internat., 1978-79; various positions Motorola Corp., 1979-89, corp. v.p., asst. gen. counsel, 1989-95, sr. v.p., asst. gen. counsel, 1995-96, sr. v.p., sec., gen. counsel, 1996-98, exec. v.p., gen. counsel, sec., 1998—. Office: Motorola Inc 1303 E Algonquin Rd Schaumburg IL 60196-1079

LAWSON, CONNIE, state legislator; b. Indpls., Apr. 20, 1949; m. Jack Lawson; 2 children: Brandon, Kylie. Diploma, Assn. Ind. Counties, 1996. Owner Lawson Bros. Auctioneers, Jack Lawson Realtors; mem. Ind. Senate from 24th dist., Indpls., 1996—; mem. agr. and small bus. com., mem. elections com. Ind. Senate. Mem. liaison com. Nat. Election Ctr. Recipient Outstanding Election Admistr. award Ind. State Election Bd., 1994, Cir. Ct. Clk. of Yr., 1993, Cert. Appreciation Hendricks County Bar Assn., 1996. Mem. Assn. Cir. Ct. Clks. Ind. (pres.), Ind. Supreme Ct. Records (mgmt. com.), Assn. Ind. Counties (legis. com., bd. dirs., Clk. of Yr. 1996). Republican. Office: 200 W Washington St Indianapolis IN 46204-2728

LAWSON, ROBERT DAVIS, theoretical nuclear physicist; b. Sydney, Australia, July 14, 1926; came to U.S., 1949; s. Carl Herman and Angeline Elizabeth (Davis) L.; m. Mary Grace Lunn, Dec. 16, 1950 (div. 1976); children: Dorothy, Katherine, Victoria; m. Sarah Virginia Roney, Mar. 13, 1976 (dec. 1994). B.S., U. B.C., Can., 1948; M.S., U. B.C., 1949; Ph.D., Stanford U., 1953. Research assoc. U. Calif., Berkeley, 1953-57; research assoc. Fermi Inst. U. Chgo., 1957-59; assoc. physicist Argonne (Ill.) Nat. Lab., 1959-65; sr. physicist Argonne Nat. Lab., 1965—. Vis. scientist U.K. Atomic Energy Authority, Harwell, Eng., 1962-63, Oxford U., Eng., 1970, 85; vis. prof. SUNY, Stony Brook, 1972-73; vis. fellow Australian Nat. U., Canberra, 1982; vis. prof. U. Groningen, 1973, U. Utrecht, 1974, Technische Hochschule, Darmstadt, 1975, 78, Free U., Amsterdam, 1976, 81, others; TRIUMF, U. B.C., Vancouver, Can., 1984. Author: Theory of the Nuclear Shell Model, 1980. Contbr. articles to sci. jours. Fellow Weizmann Inst. Sci., 1967-68, Niels Bohr Inst., 1976-77; Sir Thomas Lyle fellow U. Melbourne, Australia, 1987. Fellow Am. Phys. Soc. Home: 1590 Raven Hl Wheaton IL 60187-7109 Office: Argonne Nat Lab Bldg 203 Argonne IL 60439

LAWSON, WILLIAM HOGAN, III, electrical motor manufacturing executive; b. Lexington, Ky., Feb. 3, 1937; s. Otto Kirsky and Gladys (McWhorter) L.; div.; children: Elizabeth, Cynthia; m. Ruth Stanat, 1995. BSME, Purdue U., 1959; MBA, Harvard U., 1961. Gen. mgr. svc. divsn. Toledo Scale Corp., 1964-68; exec. v.p., COO Skyline Corp., Elkhart, Ind., 1968-85; chmn. bd. dirs., CEO Franklin Elec. Co., Inc., Bluffton, 1985—, also bd. dirs. Bd. dirs. JSJ Corp., Skyline Corp., Sentry Ins. (a Mut. Ins. Co.); instr. U. Toledo, 1966-67. With U.S. Army, 1961-63. Mem. Harvard U. Bus. Sch. Assn., Ft. Wayne Country Club, Summit Club Ft. Wayne, Harvard Club N.Y.C., Bird Key Yacht Club. Republican. Presbyterian. Home: 7126 Blue Creek Dr Fort Wayne IN 46804-1483 also: 232 Bird Key Dr Sarasota FL 34236-1602 Office: Franklin Electric Co Inc 400 E Spring St Bluffton IN 46714-3798

LAWTON, FLORIAN KENNETH, artist, educator; b. Cleve., June 20, 1921; m. Lois Mari Ondrey, June 19, 1948; children: Kenneth R., David F., Dawn M., Patricia A. Student, Cleve. Sch. Art, 1941-43, Cleve. Inst. Art, 1948-51, John Huntington Polytech. Inst., 1946-50. Instr. Cooper Sch. Art, Cleve., 1976-80, Cleve. Sch. Art, 1980-82. Cons., instr. Orange Art Ctr., Pepper Pike, Ohio, 1978—; cons. in field, juror, 1968—. Exhbns. include Am. Watercolor Soc., N.Y., Cleve. Mus. Art, Butler Mus., Youngstown, Ohio, Canton (Ohio) Mus., Massillon (Ohio) Mus., Nat. Arts Club, N.Y.C., Pitts. Watercolor Soc., Audubon Artists, N.Y.C., Salmagundi Club, N.Y.C., Parkersburg (W.Va.) Art Ctr., Boston Mills Arts Festival, Peninsula, Ohio,

Marietta (Ohio) Coll., Nat. Pks. Assn. Exhbn., 1996, 97, 2000, many others; 25 yrs. retrospective exhbn. Amish paintings, Butler Inst. Am. Art, 1989; represented in collections including Am. Soc. Metals, Ctrl. Nat. Bank, Diamond-Shamrock, Diocese Cleve., Kaiser Found., Ohio Conservation Found., Nat. City Bank Ohio, TRW, Standard Oil Co., Huntington Bank, Nat. Mennonite Mus., Lancaster, Pa., Ohio Bell Telephone Co., Day-Glo Corp., Soc. Bank Corp., The White House Collection, Washington, numerous others U.S. and internat., also pvt. collections; featured mags., calendars; Mill Pond Press; cons., artist (documentary) Amish Romance, 1979; official Coast Guard artist; artist Amish Documentary-PBS, 1996. Cons. Aurora (Ohio) Community Libr., 1990—. Cpl. USAF, 1943-46, PTO. Recipient Disting. Alumni award Garfield Hgts. (Ohio) High Sch., 1990, 1st place award Grand Invitational Exhbn., Akron, Ohio, 1996, numerous others. Mem. Ohio Watercolor Soc. (signature, charter, Grand Buckeye award 1983), Am. Watercolor Soc. (signature, Strathmore award 1977), Nat. Watercolor Soc. (signature), Akron Soc. Artists, Assoc. Audubon Artists, Artists Fellowships Inc. (N.Y.), Ky. Watercolor Soc. (signature), Midwest Watercolor Soc., Pa. Watercolor Soc. (signature), Ga. Watercolor Soc., Whiskey Painters Am., Rotary Club Chagrin Valley (Paul Harris fellow 1989). Office: 410-29 Willow Cir Aurora OH 44202-9131 Fax: 330-562-4102.

LAWTON, MATT, professional baseball player; b. Gulfport, Miss., Nov. 3, 1971; Baseball player Minn. Twins, 1995—. Office: 34 Kirby Puckett Pl Minneapolis MN 55415*

LAWYER, VIVIAN JURY, retired lawyer; b. Farmington, Iowa, Jan. 7, 1932; d. Jewell Everett Jury and Ruby Mae (Schumaker) Brewer; m. Berne Lawyer, Oct. 25, 1959; children: Michael Jury, Steven Verne. BS with honors, Iowa State U., 1953; JD with Honors, Drake U., 1968. Bar: Iowa 1968, U.S. Supreme Ct. 1986; cert. tchr. Tchr. home econs. Waukee High Sch., Iowa, 1953-55, Jr. High and High Sch., Des Moines, 1955-61; atty. pvt. practice, 1972-95; chmn. juvenile code tng. sessions Iowa Crime Commn., 1978-79. Coord. workshops, 1980; assoc. Lawyer, Lawyer & Assocs., Des Moines, 1981-98; co-founder, bd. dirs. Youth Law Center, Des Moines, 1977-93; mem. com. rules of juvenile procedure Supreme Ct. Iowa, 1981-87, adv. com. on costs of ct. appointed counsel Supreme Ct. Iowa, 1985-88; trustee Polk County Legal Aid Svcs., Des Moines, 1980-82; mem. Iowa Dept. Human Svcs. and Supreme Ct. Juvenile Justice County Base Joint Study Com., 1984—. Editor: Iowa Juvenile Code Manual, 1979, Iowa Juvenile Vode Workshop Manual, 1980; co-editor: 1987 Cumulative Supplement, 1993, supplement, Iowa Academy of Trial Lawyers Trial Handbook; author booklet in field. Mem. Iowa Task Force permanent families project Nat. Coun. Juvenile and Family Ct. Judges, 1984-88; mem. substance avuse com. Commn. children, Youth and Families, 1985—; co-chair Polk County Juvenile Detention Task Force, 1988; mem. Polk County Citizens Commn. Corrections, 1977. Iowa Dept. Social Svcs. grantee, 1980. Mem. Purple Arrow, Phi Kappa Phi, Omicron Nu. Democrat. Home: 5831 N Waterbury Rd Des Moines IA 50312-1339

LAY, DONALD POMEROY, federal judge; b. Princeton, Ill., Aug. 24, 1926; s. Hardy W. and Ruth (Cushing) L.; m. Miriam Elaine Gustafson, Aug. 6, 1949; children: Stephen Pomeroy(dec.) , Catherine Sue, Cynthia Lynn, Elizabeth Ann, Deborah Jean, Susan Elaine. Student, U.S. Naval Acad., 1945—46; BA, U. Iowa, 1948, JD, 1951; LLD (hon.) (hon.) , Mitchell Coll. Law, 1985. Bar: Nebr. 1951, Iowa 1951, Wis. 1953. Assoc. Kennedy, Holland, DeLacy & Svoboda, Omaha, 1951—53, Quarles, Spence & Quarles, Milw., 1953—54, Eisenstatt, Lay, Higgins & Miller, 1954—66; judge U.S. Ct. Appeals (8th cir.), 1966—, chief judge, 1980—92, senior judge, 1992—. Faculty mem. on evidence Nat. Coll. Trial Judges, 1964—65, U. Minn. Law Sch., William Mitchell Law Sch.; mem. U.S. Jud. Conf., 1980—92. Mem. editl. bd.: Iowa Law Rev., 1950—51; contbr. With USNR, 1944—46. Recipient Hancher-Finkbine medal, U. Iowa, 1980, Disting. Alumni award, 2000. Mem.: ATLA (bd. govs. 1963—65, Jud. Achievement award), ABA, Am. Judicature Soc., Wis. Bar Assn., Iowa Bar Assn., Nebr. Bar Assn., Internat. Acad. Trial Lawyers, Order of Coif, Sigma Chi, Phi Delta Phi, Delta Sigma Rho (Significant Sig award 1986, Herbert Harley award 1988). Presbyterian. Office: US Ct Appeals 8th Cir 316 Robert St N Ste 560 Saint Paul MN 55101-1461

LAYMAN, DALE PIERRE, medical educator, author, researcher; b. Niles, Mich., July 3, 1948; s. Pierre Andre and Delphine Lucille (Lenke) L.; m. Kathleen Ann Jackowiak, Aug. 8, 1970; children: Andrew Michael, Alexis Kathryn, Allison Victoria, Amanda Elizabeth. AS in Life Sci., Lake Mich. Coll., 1968; BS in Anthropology and Zoology with distinction, U. Mich., 1971, MS in Physiology, 1974; EdS in Physiology and Health Sci., Ball State U., 1979; PhD in Health and Safety Studies, U. Ill., 1986. Histological technician in neuropathology U. Mich. Med. Sch., Ann Arbor, 1971-72, tchg. fellow in human physiology, 1972-74; instr. in human anatomy, physiology, and histology Lake Superior State U., Sault Ste. Marie, Mich., 1974-75; prof. med. terminology, human anatomy and physiology Joliet (Ill.) Jr. Coll., 1975—. Author: The Terminology of Anatomy and Physiology, 1983, The Medical Language: A Programmed Body-Systems Approach, 1995; contbr. articles to profl. jours. Founder Robowatch. Named Notable Author, Text and Acad. Authors, Inc., Internat. Intellectual of Yr., Contributions to Medicine, 2001; recipient Presdl. Seal Honor for 2001, 2001. Fellow Soc. of Leading Intellectuals of the World; mem. Human Anatomy and Physiology Soc., Text and Acad. Authors Assn., Inc. (coun. mem.), Ill. Cmty. Coll. Faculty Assn. (campus coord.), Am. Biog. Inst. (continental gov., dep. gov., world laureate, rsch. bd. of advisors, sec. gen. United Cultural Conv.), London Diplomatic Acad. (mem. acad. coun.), Phi Kappa Phi, Kappa Delta Pi. Avocations: running, swimming, reading motivational literature. Home: 509 Westridge Ln Joliet IL 60431-4883 Office: Joliet Jr Coll 1215 Houbolt Rd Joliet IL 60431-8938

LAZAR, JILL SUE, home healthcare company executive; b. Oak Park, Ill., June 15, 1954; d. Norton David and Carol Ellen (Kaufmann) Freyer; m. Bruce Horwich, Aug. 21, 1976 (div. Sept. 1982); 1 child, Mathew Freyer Horwich; m. Neil Lazar, Nov. 23, 1986. BS in Mktg., No. Ill. U., 1975. Mktg. rsch. assoc. McDonald's Corp., Oak Brook, Ill., 1976-80; renewal coord. Time, Inc., Chgo., 1984-87; product mgr. Macmillan Directory Div., Wilmette, Ill., 1987-92; with DependiCare, Broadview, 1992—. Mem. provider adv. panels Chad Therapeutics, Aradigm Corp., others. Mem. Chgo. Health Execs. Forum. Avocations: swimming, reading. Office phone: (708) 345-7599 ext. 202. Office: DependiCare 1815 Gardner Rd Broadview IL 60155-4401

LAZAR, KATHY PITTAK, lawyer; b. Lorain, Ohio, Nov. 12, 1955; BA summa cum laude, Kent State U., 1978; JD, Case Western Res. U., 1982. Bar: Ohio 1982. Sr. counsel TRW Inc. Rsch. editor Case Western Res. U. Law Rev., 1981-82. Mem. ABA, Ohio State Bar Assn., Cleve. Bar Assn., Order of Coif, Phi Beta Kappa. Office: TRW Inc 1900 Richmond Rd Cleveland OH 44124-3760

LAZAR, RAYMOND MICHAEL, lawyer, educator; b. Mpls., July 16, 1939; s. Simon and Hessie (Teplin) L; children: Mark, Deborah. BBA, U. Minn., 1961, JD, 1964. Bar: Minn. 1964, U.S. Dist. Ct. Minn. 1964. Spl. asst. atty. gen. State of Minn., St. Paul, 1964-66; pvt. practice Mpls., 1966-72; ptnr. Lapp, Lazar, Laurie & Smith, 1972-86; ptnr., officer Fredrikson & Byron P.A., 1986—. Lectr. various continuing edn. programs, 1972—; adj. prof. law U. Minn., Mpls., 1983-99. Fellow Am. Acad. Matrimonial Lawyers; mem. ABA (chair divorce laws and procedures com. family law sect. 1993-94), Minn. Bar Assn., Hennepin County Bar Assn. (chair family law sect. 1978-79). Home: 400 River St Minneapolis MN 55401 Office: Fredrikson & Byron PA 4000 Pillsbury Ctr Minneapolis MN 55402-3314 E-mail: rlazar@fredlaw.com.

LAZERSON, EARL EDWIN, academic administrator emeritus; b. Detroit, Dec. 10, 1930; s. Nathan and Ceil (Stashefsky) L.; m. Ann May Harper, June 11, 1966; children from previous marriage: Joshua, Paul. BS, Wayne State U., Detroit, 1953; postgrad., U. Leiden, Netherlands, 1957-58; MA, U. Mich., 1954, PhD, 1982. Mathematician Inst. Def. Analyses, Princeton, N.J., 1960-62; asst. prof. math. Washington U., St. Louis, 1962-65, 66-69; vis. asso. prof. Brandeis U., 1965-66; mem. faculty So. Ill. U., Edwardsville, 1969—, prof. math., 1973—, chmn. dept. math. studies, 1972-73, dean Sch. Sci. and Tech., 1973-76, univ. v.p., provost, 1977-79, pres., 1980-93; pres. emeritus, 1994—. Chmn. Southwestern Ill. Devel. Authority, City of East St. Louis Fin. Adv. Authority; active Leadership Coun. Southwestern Ill., Gateway Ctr. Met. St. Louis, Inc., St. Louis Symphony Soc.; trustee Jefferson Nat. Expansion Meml. Assn., Ill. Econ. Devel. Bd. Recipient Sr. Teaching Excellence award Standard Oil Found., 1970-71 Mem. Am. Math. Soc., Math. Assn. Am., European Math. Soc., London Math. Soc., Soc. Mathematique France, Fulbright Alumni Assn., Sigma Xi. Home: 122 Forest Grove Dr Glen Carbon IL 62034 E-mail: laze@charter.net.

LAZICH, MARY A. state legislator; Mem Wis. Senate Dist. 28, Madison, 1998—.

LAZO, JOHN, JR. physician; b. Passaic, N.J., Nov. 29, 1946; s. John and Mary (Beley) Lazo; m. Donnalynn Margaret Materna, July 22, 1972; children: Jonathan Christopher, Ashley Jude. BS, Fairleigh Dickinson U., 1974; MD, Univ. Autonoma de Guadalajara, Mex., 1978. Diplomate Am. Bd. Emergency Medicine, Am. Bd. Forensic Examiners, Am. Bd. Forensic Medicine. Intern Akron (Ohio) City Hosp., 1980-81, resident in emergency medicine, 1981-83, chief resident in emergency medicine, 1982-83; med. dir. emergency svcs. Parma (Ohio) Cmty. Gen. Hosp., 1986-93, chmn. emergency dept., 1994-95, vice-chmn. emergency dept., 1995-99, chmn. emergency dept., 2000—. Dir. Paramedic Edn. Program, Parma, 1986—93; med. dir. Emergeny Medicine Physicians - Cuyahoga County, LLC, 2002—; bd. dirs. Cmty. Emergency Physicians, Inc. Sgt. USAF, 1966—70. Fellow: Am. Coll. Emergency Physicians; mem.: Cleve. Acad. Medicine, Ohio Am. Coll. Emergency. Republican. Russian Orthodox. Avocations: photography, cooking. Home: 545 Eastwood Dr Hinckley OH 44233-9496 Office: Parma Cmty Gen Hosp 7007 Powers Blvd Parma OH 44129-5437

LAZZARA, DENNIS JOSEPH, orthodontist; b. Chgo., Mar. 14, 1948; s. Joseph James and Jacqueline Joan (Antonini) L.; m. Nancy Ann Pirhofer, Dec. 18, 1971; children: Kristin Lynn, Bryan Matthew, Matthew Dennis, Kathryn Marie, David Brady. BS, U. Dayton, 1970; DDS, Loyola U., 1974, MS in Oral Biology, cert. orthodontics, Loyola U., 1976. Practice dentistry specializing in orthodontics, Geneva, 1976—. Mem. dental staff Delnor Cmty. Hosp., Geneva and St. Charles, Ill., 1976—; sec. dental staff, Geneva, 1978-80, v.p., 1980-82, pres., 1982-84, exec. com., 1982-84. Leader Boy Scouts Am., 1988-90. Recipient award of merit Am. Coll. Dentists, 1974. Mem. ADA, Am. Assn. Orthodontists (presenter ann. meeting 1997, Harry Sicher hon. mention award 1977), Midwestern Soc. Orthodontists, Ill. Soc. Orthodontists, Fox River Valley Dental Soc. (bd. dirs. 1983-86), Blue Key Nat. Honor Soc. Roman Catholic. Avocations: sailing, golf. Office: PO Box 431 Geneva IL 60134-0431

LEA, LORENZO BATES, lawyer; b. St. Louis, Apr. 12, 1925; s. Lorenzo Bates and Ursula Agnes (Gibson) L.; m. Marcia Gwendolyn Wood, Mar. 21, 1953; children— Victoria, Jennifer, Christopher. BS, MIT, 1946; JD, U. Mich., 1949; grad. Advanced Mgmt. Program, Harvard U., 1964. Bar: Ill. 1950. With Amoco Corp. (formerly Standard Oil Co. Ind.), Chgo., 1949—, asst. gen. counsel, 1963-71, assoc. gen. counsel, 1971-72, gen. counsel, 1972-78, v.p., gen. counsel, 1978-89. Trustee Village of Glenview (Ill.) Zoning Bd., 1961-63, Cmty. Found. Collier Country; bd. dirs. Chgo. Crime Commn., 1978— , Midwest Council for Internat. Econ. Policy, 1973— , Chgo. Bar Found., 1981— , Chgo. Area Found. for Legal Services, 1981— ; bd. dirs. United Charities of Chgo., 1973—, chmn., 1985—; bd. dirs. Cmty. Foun. of Collier County, 1997—, Naples Bot. Garden, 2000—. Served with USNR, 1943-46. Mem. ABA, Am. Petroleum Inst., Am. Arbitration Assn. (dir. 1980—), Ill. Bar Assn., Chgo. Bar Assn., Assn. Gen. Counsel, Order of Coif, Law Club, Econs. Club, Legal, Mid-Am. (Chgo.), Glen View, Wyndemere, Hole-In-The-Wall, Sigma Xi. Republican. Mem. United Ch. of Christ.

LEACH, JAMES ALBERT SMITH, congressman; b. Davenport, Iowa, Oct. 15, 1942; s. James Albert and Lois (Hill) L.; m. Elisabeth Foxley, Dec. 6, 1975; 1 child, Gallagher BA, Princeton U., 1964; MA, Johns Hopkins U., 1966; postgrad., London Sch. Econs., 1966-68. Mem. staff Congressman Donald Rumsfeld, 1965-66; U.S. fgn. svc. officer, 1968-69, 70-73; spl. asst. to dir. OEO, 1969-70; mem. U.S. del. Geneva Disarmament Conf., 1971-72, UN Gen. Assembly, 1972, UN Natural Resources Conf., 1975; pres. Flamegas Companies Inc., Bettendorf, Iowa, 1973-76; chmn. bd. Adel Wholesalers, Inc., 1973-76; mem. 95th-106th Congresses from 1st Iowa dist., 1977—; chmn. banking and fin. svcs. com., mem. internat. rels. com.; mem. U.S. Adv. Commn. Internat. Ednl. and Cultural Affairs, 1975-76, mem. com. govt. reform & oversight, transp. & infrastructure. Chmn. Iowa Rep. Directions '76 Com. Episcopalian. Office: 2186 Rayburn Bldg Washington DC 20515-1501*

LEACH, JANET C. publishing executive; Mng. editor The Cin. Enquirer, until 1998; editor Akron Beacon Jour., 1998—. Office: Akron Beacon Jour 44 East Exchange St PO Box 640 Akron OH 44328

LEACH, MICHAEL, financial executive; Degree in acctg., Miami (Ohio) U. CPA, Ohio. With Ernst & Young; contr. Drug Emporium, Powell, Ohio, 1993-98, CFO, 1998—. Pres. DrugEmporium.com.; CFO Healthcite.com. Office: Drug Emporium Inc 14525 Highway 7 Minnetonka MN 55345-3734

LEACH, RALPH F. banker; b. Elgin, Ill., June 24, 1917; s. Harry A. and Edith (Sanders) L.; m. Harriet C. Scheuerman, Nov. 18, 1944; children: C. David, H. Randall, Barbara E. A.B., U. Chgo., 1938. Investment analyst Harris Trust & Savs. Bank, Chgo., 1940-48, Valley Nat. Bank, Phoenix, 1948-50; chief govt. finance sect. Fed. Res. Bd., Washington, 1950-53; treas. Guaranty Trust Co., N.Y.C., 1953-59, v.p., 1958-59; v.p., treas. Morgan Guaranty Trust Co., N.Y.C., 1959-62, sr. v.p., treas., 1962-64, exec. v.p., treas., 1964-68, vice chmn. bd. dirs., 1968-71, chmn. exec. com., 1971-77. Chmn. emeritus Energy Conversion Devices Inc. Served to capt. USMCR, 1940-45. Mem. Coral Ridge Country Club, Phi Kappa Psi. Home: 4211 NE 25th Ave Fort Lauderdale FL 33308-5706

LEACH, RONALD GEORGE, educational administration educator; b. Monroe, Mich., Feb. 22, 1938; s. Garnet William and Erma (Erbadine) L.; m. Joy Adeline Moore, Dec. 21, 1956; children— Ronald George, Debra Mabel, Catherine Louise, Shane John. B.S. in Secondary Edn, Central Mich. U., 1966; M.A. in L.S. (U.S. Office Edn. fellow 1968-69), U. Mich., 1969; Ph.D. in Higher Edn. Adminstrn, Mich. State U., 1980. Head libr. Ohio State U., Mansfield, 1969-70; asst. dir., then acting dir. libr. Lake Superior State Coll., Sault Ste. Marie, Mich., 1970-76; assoc. dir. librs. Central Mich. U., 1976-80; dean libr. svcs. Ind. State U., Terre Haute, 1980-93, assoc. v.p. info. svcs., dean of librs., 1994-97, prof. higher ednl. adminstrn., 1997—. Prof. edn., mem. accreditation teams North Ctrl. Assn. Author articles in field. Served with N.G., 1955-61. Mem. ALA, INFORMA (steering com. 1990—), Assn. Coll. and Rsch. Librs., Libr. Info. and Tech. Assn., Ind. Libr. Assn., Am. Soc. Info. Sci., Libr. Adminstrn. and Mgmt. Assn. (pres. 1985-86), Online Computer Libr. Ctr. User Council (exec. com. 1986, 88). Home: 4815 E Wolf Tree Ave Terre Haute IN 47805-9414 Office: Ind State U Dept Leadership Admin Found Terre Haute IN 47809-0001

LEACH, RUSSELL, judge; b. Columbus, Ohio, Aug. 1, 1922; s. Charles Albert and Hazel Kirk (Thatcher) L.; m. Helen M. Sharpe, Feb. 17, 1945; children: Susan Sharpe Snyder, Terry Donnell, Ann Dunham Samuelson. B.A., Ohio State U., 1946, J.D., 1949. Bar: Ohio 1949. Clk. U.S. Geol. Survey, Columbus, 1948-49; reference and teaching asst. Coll. Law, Ohio State U., 1949-51; asst. city atty. City of Columbus, 1951, 53-57, city atty., 1957-63, presiding judge mcpl. ct., 1964-66; ptnr. Bricker & Eckler, 1966-88, chmn. exec. com., 1982-87; judge Ohio Ct. Claims, 1988—. Commr., Columbus Met. Housing Authority, 1968-74; chmn. Franklin County Republican Com., 1974-78. Served with AUS, 1942-46, 51-53 Named One of 10 Outstanding Young Men of Columbus, Columbus Jaycees, 1956, 57 Mem. ABA, FBA, Ohio Bar Assn. (coun. of dels. 1970-75), Columbus Bar Assn. (pres. 1973-74, Svc. medal 1993), Am. Judicature Soc., Pres.' Club Ohio State U., Am. Legion, Delta Theta Phi, Chi Phi. Presbyterian. Home: 1232 Kenbrook Hills Dr Columbus OH 43220-4968 Office: Ohio Ct Claims 65 E State St Ste 1100 Columbus OH 43215-4213

LEAGUE, DAVID, hardware company executive; V.p., gen. counsel Ace Hardware Corp., Oak Brook, Ill. Office: Ace Hardware Corp 2200 Kensington Ct Hinsdale IL 60523-2100

LEAKE, SAM, former state legislator, farmer; b. Ralls County, Mo., Feb. 19, 1945; m. Sharon K. Day, 1964; children: Jeff, Scott, Terri, Kevin. Student, Moler Barbar Coll. Farmer, Laddonia, Mo.; mem. Mo. Ho. of Reps., Jefferson City, until 2000. Mem. agr. com., edn. com., social svcs. and medicaid, state parks com., recreation and natural resources com. Del. state and dist. Dem. convs., 1988—. Recipient farm mgmt. award U. Mo., 1982. Mem. Twain Lake Assn. Home: RR 2 Box 2706 Center MO 63436-9506

LEASE, ROBERT K. lawyer; b. Cleve., 1948; AB magna cum laude, Dartmouth Coll., 1970; JD cum laude, U. Conn., 1976. Bar: Ohio. Ptnr. Baker & Hostetler LLP, Cleve. Mem. Phi Beta Kappa. Office: Baker & Hostetler LLP 3200 Nat City Ctr 1900 E 9th St Ste 3200 Cleveland OH 44114-3485 E-mail: rlease@bakerlaw.com.

LEATHERDALE, DOUGLAS WEST, insurance company executive; b. Morden, Man., Can., Dec. 6, 1936; came to U.S., 1968; s. Walter West and Lena Elizabeth (Gilligan) L.; children: Mary Jo, Christopher B.A., United Coll., Winnipeg, Man., 1957. Investment analyst, officer Gt. West Life Assurance Co., Winnipeg, 1957-68; assoc. exec. sec. Bd. Pensions, Luth. Ch., Mpls., 1968-72; exec. v.p., then v.p. St. Paul Investment Mgmt. Co., subs. St. Paul Cos., Inc., 1972-77; v.p.-fin. St. Paul Cos., Inc., 1974-81, sr. v.p.-fin., 1981-82, exec. v.p., 1982-89, also dir., pres., chief oper. officer, 1989-90, chmn.,ceo and pres., 1990—. Bd. dirs. St. Paul Fire and Marine Ins. Co., St. Paul Land Resources, Inc., St. Paul Real Estate of Ill., Inc., John Nuveen & Co. Inc., St. Paul Properties, Inc., St. Paul Oil and Gas Corp., St. Paul Fire & Marine Ins. Co. (U.K.) Ltd., St. Paul Mercury Ins. Co., St. Paul Guardian Ins. Co., St. Paul Surplus Lines Ins. Co., Nat. Ins. Wholesalers, Atwater McMillian, 77 Water St., Inc., Ramsey Ins. Co., St. Paul Risk Services, Inc., St. Paul Plymouth Ctr., Inc. Athena Assurance Co., St. Paul Fin. Group, Inc., Graham Resources, Inc., Carlyle Capital, L.P., United HealthCare Corp. Mem. Twin Cities Soc. Security Analysts, Fin. Execs. Inst. Club: Minnesota (St. Paul) Avocation: horses.

LEAVITT, JEFFREY STUART, lawyer; b. Cleve., July 13, 1946; s. Sol and Esther (Dolinsky) L.; m. Ellen Fern Sugerman, Dec. 21, 1968; children: Matthew Adam, Joshua Aaron. AB, Cornell U., 1968; JD, Case Western Res. U., 1973. Bar: Ohio 1973. Assoc. Jones, Day, Reavis & Pogue, Cleve., 1973-80, ptnr., 1981—. Contbr. articles to profl. jours. Trustee Bur. Jewish Edn., Cleve., 1981-93, v.p., 1985-87; trustee Fairmount Temple, Cleve., 1982-2002, v.p., 1985-90, pres., 1990-93; trustee Citizens League Greater Cleve., 1982-89, 92-94, pres., 1987-89; trustee Citizens League Rsch. Inst., Cleve., 1989-98, Great Lakes Region of Union Am. Hebrew Congregations, 1990-93; mem. bd. govs. Case Western Res. Law Sch. Alumni Assn., 1989-92; sec. Kulas Found., 1986-88, 93-99, asst. treas., 1989-92. Mem. ABA (employee benefits coms. 1976—), Nat. Assn. Pub. Pension Attys., Midwest Pension Conf. Jewish. Home: 7935 Sunrise Ln Novelty OH 44072-9404 Office: Jones Day Reavis & Pogue N Point 901 Lakeside Ave E Cleveland OH 44114-1190

LEAVITT, JUDITH WALZER, history of medicine educator; b. N.Y.C., July 22, 1940; d. Joseph Phillip and Sally (Hochman) Walzer; m. Lewis Arger Leavitt, July 2, 1966; children: Sarah Abigail, David Isaac. BA, Antioch Coll., 1963; MA, U. Chgo., 1966, PhD, 1975. Asst. prof. history of medicine U. Wis., Madison, 1975-81, assoc. prof., 1981-86, prof., 1986—, Evjue-Bascom prof., 1990-95, chmn. dept., 1981-93, assoc. dean for faculty, 1996-99, Ruth Bleier prof., 1997—. Author: The Healthiest City, 1982, Brought to Bed, 1986, Typhoid Mary, 1996; editor: Women and Health, 1984, 2d edit., 1999, Sickness and Health in America, 1985, 3d edit., 1998. Office: U Wis Dept History Medicine 1300 University Ave Madison WI 53706-1510

LEAVITT, MARTIN JACK, lawyer; b. Detroit, Mar. 30, 1940; s. Benjamin and Annette (Cohen) L.; m. Janice C. McCreary; children: Michael J., Paul J., David A., Dean N., Keleigh R. LLB, Wayne State U., 1964. Bar: Mich. 1965, Fla. 1967. Assoc. Robert A. Sullivan, Detroit, 1968-70; officer, bd. dirs. Law Office Sullivan & Leavitt, Northville, Mich., 1970—, pres., 1979—. Bd. dirs. Tyrone Hills of Mich., Premiere Video, Inc., others. Lt. comdr. USNR, 1965-68. Detroit Edison upper class scholar, 1958-64. Mem. ABA, Mich. Bar Assn., Fla. Bar Assn., Transp. Lawyers Assn., ICC Practitioners, Meadowbrook Country Club, Huron River Hunting and Fishing Club (past pres.), Rolls Royce Owners Club (bd. dirs.). Jewish. Office: Sullivan and Leavitt PC PO Box 5490 Northville MI 48167-5490 E-mail: mjl@sullivanleavitt.com.

LEB, ARTHUR STERN, lawyer; b. Cleve., June 26, 1930; s. Ernest A. and Bertha (Stern) L.; m. Lois Shafron, Jan. 31, 1954; children: Gerald P., Judith A., Robert B. AB, Columbia Coll., 1952; JD, Case Western Res. U., 1955. Bar: Ohio 1955, U.S. Supreme Ct. 1965. Ptnr. Leb & Halm, Canton, Ohio, 1961-84, Amerman, Bert & Jones, L.P.A., Canton, 1985-90; of counsel Buckingham, Doolittle & Burroughs, L.L.P., 1991—. Founding mem., exec. com. Ohio Coun. Sch. Bd. Attys., 1976-84, pres. 1983. Served to 1st lt. JAGC, USAF, 1955-57. Recipient Merit award Ohio Legal Ctr. Inst., 1964. Fellow Ohio Bar Found.; mem. ABA, Ohio Bar Assn., Stark County Bar Assn. (pres. 1985-86). E-mail: asleb@bdblaw.com.

LEBAMOFF, IVAN ARGIRE, lawyer; b. Ft. Wayne, Ind., July 20, 1932; s. Argire V. and Helen A. (Kachandov) L.; m. Katherine S. Lebamoff, June 9, 1963; children— Damian I., Jordan I., Justin A. A.B. in History, Ind. U., 1954, J.D., 1957. Bar: Ind. 1957, U.S. Ct. Dist. Ct. (no. and so. dists.) 1958, U.S. Supreme Ct. 1963. Sole practice, Ft. Wayne, Ind., 1957-68; ptnr. Lebamoff, Ver Wiebe & Snow, 1968-71; mayor City of Ft. Wayne, 1972-75; sole practice Lebamoff Law Offices, Ft. Wayne, 1975—. U.S. commr. No. Dist. Ind., 1957-62; fgn. service officer USIA Dept. Commerce, Bulgaria, 1964; vis. prof. dept. urban affairs Ind. U.-Purdue, Ft. Wayne, 1976-77 Chmn. Allen County Democratic Com., 1968-75, Ft. Wayne Dept. Parks and Recreation, 1984-88; nat. pres. Macedonian Patriotic Orgn. of U.S. and Can., 1983-94. Served with USAF, 1958-64

Mem. ABA, Allen County Bar Assn., Ind. Bar Assn., Am. Trial Lawyers Assn., Ind. Trial Lawyers Assn. Eastern Orthodox. Lodge: Kiwanis. Home: 205 E Packard Ave Fort Wayne IN 46806-1014 Office: Lebamoff Law Offices 918 S Calhoun St Fort Wayne IN 46802-2502

LEBEAU, DICK, professional football coach, retired football player; b. , Ohio, Sept. 9, 1937; m. Nancy LeBeau; 1 child Brandon Grant. Attended, Ohio State Univ., 1955—58. Head coach Cin. Bengals, 2000—, asst. head coach & defensive coord., 1997—2000; defensive coord. Pitts. Steelers, 1995—96, asst. coach, 1992—94; defensive coord. Cin. Bengals, 1984—91, asst. coach, Green Bay Packers, 1976—79, Phila. Eagles, 1976—79; cornerback Detroit Linos, 1959—72. Office: Cin Bengels 1 Paul Brown Stadium Cincinnati OH 45202*

LEBEDOFF, DAVID M. lawyer, writer, investment advisor; b. Mpls., Apr. 29, 1938; s. Martin David and Mary Louise (Galanter) L.; m. Randy Louise Miller, Feb. 7, 1981; children: Caroline, Jonathan, Nicholas. BA magna cum laude, U. Minn., 1960; JD, Harvard U., 1963. Bar: Minn. 1963. Spl. asst. atty. gen. Atty. Gen. of Minn., St. Paul, 1963-65; pvt. practice law Mpls., 1967-81; ptnr. Lindquist & Vennum, 1981-91, Briggs & Morgan, Mpls., 1991-95; sr. v.p. Voyageur Asset Mgmt., 1995—; of counsel Gray, Plant, Mooty, Mooty & Bennett, 1995—. Spl. master U.S. Dist. Ct., Mpls., 1974-75. Author: The 21st Ballot, 1969, Ward Number Six, 1972, The New Elite, 1981, Cleaning Up, 1997; contbr. articles to profl. and gen. jours. Bd. regents U. Minn. , Mpls and St. Paul, 1977-89, chmn. bd. 1987-89; chmn. Mpls. Inst. Arts, 1989-91, bd. dirs. 1975—, life trustee, 1997—; bd. dirs. Coun. on Crime and Justice, 1999—; bd. dirs. Ctr. of the Am. Experiment, 1997-2001; former bd. dirs. Guthrie Theatre U. Minn. Found., The Blake Sch., Mpls. Club. Recipient Outstanding Achievement award U. Minn., 1991, Minn. Book award, 1998. Mem. Mpls. Club, Minikahda Club, Phi Beta Kappa. Home: 1738 Oliver Ave S Minneapolis MN 55405-2222

LEBEDOFF, JONATHAN GALANTER, federal judge; b. Mpls., Apr. 29, 1938; s. Martin David and Mary (Galanter) L.; m. Sarah Sargent Mitchell, June 10, 1979; children: David Shevlin, Ann McNair. BA, U. Minn., 1960, LLB, 1963. Bar: Minn. 1963, U.S. Dist. Ct. Minn. 1964, U.S. Ct. Appeals (8th cir.) 1968. Pvt. practice, Mpls., 1963-71; judge Hennepin County Mcpl. Ct., State Minn., 1971-74; dist. ct. judge State of Minn., 1974-91; U.S. magistrate judge U.S. Dist. Ct., 1991—. Mem. Gov.'s Commn. on Crime Prevention, 1971-75; mem. State Bd. Continuing Legal Edn.; mem. Minn. Supreme Ct. Task Force for Gender Fairness in Cts., mem. implementation com. of gender fairness in cts.. Jewish. Avocations; reading (biographies, history), family, bridge. Office: 300 S 4th St Minneapolis MN 55415-1320

LEBEDOFF, RANDY MILLER, lawyer; b. Washington, Oct. 16, 1949; m. David Lebedoff; children: Caroline, Jonathan, Nicholas. BA, Smith Coll., 1971; JD magna cum laude, Ind. U., 1975. Assoc. Faegre & Benson, Mpls., 1975-82, ptnr., 1983-86; v.p., gen. counsel Star Tribune, 1989—2001; asst. sec. Star Tribune Cowles Media Co., 1990—98; pvt. practice, 2001—. Bd. dirs. Milkweed Editions, 1989-96. Bd. dirs. Minn. Opera, 1986-90, YWCA, 1984-90, Planned Parenthood Minn., 1985-90, Fund for Legal Aid Soc., 1988-96—, Abbott-Northwestern Hosp., 1990-94. Mem. Newspaper Assn. Am. (legal affairs com. 1991—), Minn. Newspapers Assn. (bd. dirs. 1995—, pres. 2002). Home: 1738 Oliver Ave S Minneapolis MN 55405-2222 Office: 3112 Hennepin Ave S Minneapolis MN 55488

LEBEDOW, AARON LOUIS, consulting company executive; b. Chgo., Aug. 19, 1935; s. Isidor and Fannie (Perchikoff) L.; m. Madeleine Hellman; children: Ellen, Francine, Sheri, Sherri Michaels, Tracey Michaels. B.S. in Indsl. Engring, Ill. Inst. Tech., 1957; M.B.A., U. Mich., 1958. Cert. mgmt. cons. Asst. marketing mgr. Imperial-Eastman, Chgo., 1960-61; mgr. Corplan Assos., 1961-66; chmn. bd. Technomic, Inc., 1966-87, Technomic Consultants Internat., Deerfield, 1987-93, Global Marketactics Inc., Chgo., 1993—, Global Devel. Network, Inc., 1993—, Hoganson Venture Group Inc., Hinsdale, IL, 1998-2000, Bus. Search Ltd., 2000—. Bd. dirs. Coun. for Jewish Elderly. Served to 1st lt. USAF, 1958-60. Mem. Am. Mgmt. Assn., Am. Mktg. Assn., Tau Epsilon Phi. Mem. B'nai B'rith. Office: Global Devel Network Inc 6540 N Kilbourn Ste A100 Lincolnwood IL 60712-3437 E-mail: lebedowa@aol.com.

LEBLOND, RICHARD FOARD, internist, educator; b. Seattle, July 17, 1947; s. Donald E. and Ruth Elizabeth (Foard) LeB.; m. Anita Caraig Garcia, Dec. 28, 1994; children: Sueno Emmeline, Edgardo Alan. AB, Princeton U., 1969; MD, U. Wash., 1972. Diplomate Am. Bd. Internal Medicine (bd. dirs. 1993-98, sec.-treas. 1996-98). Intern Harlem Hosp., N.Y.C., 1972-73; resident in medicine, clin. fellow in oncology U. Wash., Seattle, 1975-78; pvt. practice, Livingston, Mont., 1978-96; dir. Livingston Meml. Hosp., 1979-91, 93-96, chmn. bd. dirs., 1984-91. Clin. asst. prof. medicine Mont. State U., Bozeman, 1979-96, U. Wash., 1991-96, U. Calif., San Francisco, 1991-92; acting instr. Makerere U., Kampala, 1991-92; prof. clin. medicine U. Iowa, Iowa City, 1996—, med. dir. U. Iowa Hosps. and Clinics Family Care Ctr., 1997—; bd. dirs. Am. Bd. Family Practice, RRC-1M, Inst. for Clinical Evaluation, treas., 1999-2001. Bd. dir. Park County Friends of the Arts, Livingston, Iowa, 1981—87, Livingston Cmty. Trust, 1986—91. Named Regional Trustee of Yr., Am. Hosp. Assn., 1989; recipient med. achievement award Deaconess Found., 1995, Mont. ACP Laureate award, 1996. Fellow ACP; mem. AMA, Am. Soc. for Internal Medicine, Iowa Med. Soc. Avocations: fishing, hunting, hiking, reading, gardening. Home: 2023 Laurence Ct NE Iowa City IA 52240-9150 Office: Univ of Iowa Hosps and Clinics 200 Hawkins Dr Iowa City IA 52242-1009 E-mail: richard-leblond@uiowa.edu.

LEBOWITZ, ALBERT, lawyer, writer; b. St. Louis, June 18, 1922; s. Jacob and Lena (Zemmel) L.; m. Naomi Gordon, Nov. 26, 1953; children— Joel Aaron, Judith Leah. A.B., Washington U., St. Louis, 1945; LL.B., Harvard U., 1948. Bar: Mo. bar 1948. Assoc. Frank E. Morris, St. Louis, 1948-55; partner firm Morris, Schneider & Lebowitz, 1955-58, Crowe, Schneider, Shanahan & Lebowitz, St. Louis, 1958-66; counsel firm Murphy & Roche, 1966-67, Murphy & Schlapprizzi, St. Louis, 1967-81; partner firm Murphy, Schlapprizzi & Lebowitz, 1981-86; editor lit. quar. Perspective, 1961-80; of counsel Donald L. Schlapprizzi, P.C., 1986—, John T. Murphy, Jr., 1986-88. Author: novel Laban's Will, 1966, The Man Who Wouldn't Say No, 1969, A Matter of Days, 1989; also short stories. Served as combat navigator USAAF, 1943-45, ETO. Decorated Air medal with 3 oak leaf clusters. Mem. ABA, Mo., St. Louis bar assns., Phi Beta Kappa. Home: 743 Yale Ave Saint Louis MO 63130-3120 Office: Gateway One On The Mall 701 Market St Ste 1550 Saint Louis MO 63101-1897

LECHTENBERG, VICTOR L. agricultural studies educator; b. Butte, Nebr., Apr. 14, 1945; m. Grayce Lechtenberg; 4 children. BS, U. Nebr., 1967; PhD in Agronomy, Purdue U., 1971. Prof. agronomy Purdue U., West Lafayette, Ind., 1971—, assoc. dir. Agrl. Experiment Sta., 1982-89, exec. assoc. dean agr., 1989-93, dean agr., 1994—. Chmn. adv. bd. USDA nat. Agrl. Rsch. Ext., Edn. and Econs., 1996—. Contbr. articles to profl. jours., chpts. to books. Scoutmaster Boy Scouts Am., 1983-85. Recipient Nebr. 4-H Dist. Alumni award, 1981. Fellow Am. Soc. Agronomy (Ciba-Geigy award), Crop Sci. Soc. Am. (past pres.); mem. Crop Sci. Soc. Agrnomy, Coun. Agrl. Sci. and Tech. (past pres., bd. dirs.), USDA (mem., chmn. nat. agrl. rsch., extension, edn. and econs. adv. bd.). Sigma Xi, Alpha Zeta, Gamma Sigma Delta. Roman Catholic. Avocation: woodworking. Office: Purdue Univ 1140 Ag Ad Bldg West Lafayette IN 47907 E-mail: vll@purdue.edu.

LECKEY, ANDREW A. financial columnist; b. Chgo., Sept. 22, 1949; s. Alexander and Ellen (Martin) L. B.A., Trinity Coll., Deerfield, Ill., 1971; M.A. in Journalism, U. Mo., 1975; postgrad., Columbia U., 1978-79, Rutgers U., 1981. Fin. editor Oreg. Statesman, Salem, 1975-76; statehouse reporter Phoenix Gazette, 1976-78; fin. columnist Chgo. Sun-Times, 1979-85, Chgo. Tribune and N.Y. Daily News, 1985—; fin. commentator Sta. WBEZ, Chgo., 1981-83, Sta. WLS-TV, Chgo., 1983—; syndicated fin. columnist Los Angeles Times Syndicate, 1983-85, Tribune Media Services, 1985—. Author: Make Money with the New Tax Laws, 1987. Office: Tribune Media Svcs 435 N Michigan Ave Ste 1500 Chicago IL 60611-4012

LEDERMAN, LEON MAX, physicist, educator; b. N.Y.C., July 15, 1922; s. Morris and Minna (Rosenberg) Lederman; m. Florence Gordon, Sept. 19, 1945; children: Rena S., Jesse A., Heidi R.; m. Ellen Carr, Sept. 17, 1981. BS, CCNY, 1943, DSc (hon.) , 1980; AM, Columbia U., 1948, PhD, 1951; DSc (hon.) , No. Ill. U., 1984, U. Chgo., 1985, Ill. Inst. Tech., 1987; 35 additional hon. degrees. Assoc. in physics Columbia U., N.Y.C., 1951, asst. prof., 1952—54, assoc. prof., 1954—58, prof., 1958—89, Eugene Higgins prof. physics, 1972—79; Frank L. Sulzberger prof. physics U. Chgo., 1989—92; dir. Fermi Nat. Accelerator Lab., Batavia, Ill., 1979—89, dir. emeritus, 1989—; Pritzker prof. sci. Ill. Inst. Tech., Chgo., 1992—; resident scholar Ill. Math. and Sci. Acad., 1998—. Dir. Nevis Labs., Irvington, NY, 1962—79; guest scientist Brookhaven Nat. Labs., 1955; cons. Nat. Accelerator Lab., European Orgn. for Nuc. Rsch. (CERN), 1970—; mem. high energy physics adv. panel AEC, 1966—70; mem. adv. com. to divsn. math. and phys. scis. NSF, 1970—72; sci. advisor to gov. State of Ill., 1989—93; chmn. XXIV Internat. Physics Olympiad, 1991—93; co-chair com. on capacity bldg. in sci. Internat. Sci. Unions, 1994—2001; pres. bd. sponsors Bull. Atomic Scientists, 2000—; mem. adv. com. to dean U. Chgo., 2000—; pres.'s coun. The Cooper Union, 2002—. Author: Quarks to the Cosmos, 1989, The God Particle, 1993; editor, contbr.: Portraits of Great American Scientists, 2001; contbr. over 200 articles to profl. jours. Commr. White House Fellows Program, 1997—2000; Univ. Rsch. Assocs., 1967—71, 1992—; mem. sci. adv. bd. Sec. of Energy, 1991—2001; bd. dirs. Mus. Sci. and Industry, Chgo., 1989—, Weizmann Inst. Sci., Israel, 1988—; pres. bd. sponsors Bull. Atomic Scientists, 2001—. Named Hon. Prof., Beijing Normal U.; recipient Nat. medal of Sci., 1965, Townsend Harris medal, CUNY, 1973, Elliot Cresson medal, Franklin Inst., 1976, Wolf prize, 1982, Nobel prize in Physics, 1988, Enrico Fermi prize, 1992, Rosenblith lectr. in Sci. and Tech., NAS, Joseph Priestly award, Dickinson Coll., 1996, Pres.'s medal, CCNY, 1993, Heald prize, Ill. Inst. Tech., 2000, Pupin Med. award, Columbia U., 2000, Faraday award, NSTA, Discover, 2002; fellow Guggenheim, 1958—59, Ford Found., European Ctr. for Nuc. Rsch., Geneva, 1958—59, NSF, 1967, Presdl., World Bank, 1996—99; scholar Great Minds program, Ill. Math. Sci. Acad. Fellow: AAAS (pres. 1990—91, chmn. 1991—92, Abelson award 2001), Am. Phys. Soc. (mem. coun.); mem.: IEEE, NAS (U.S., Argentina, Finland, Mex.), Coun. Advancement of Sci. Writing, Tchrs. Acad. for Math. and Sci. in Chgo. (co-chmn. 1990—), Italian Phys. Soc. (hon.), Ill. Math. Sci. Acad. (vice chmn. 1985—98), Aspen Inst. Physics (pres. 1990—92). E-mail: Lederman@fnal.gov.

LEDWIDGE, PATRICK JOSEPH, lawyer; b. Detroit, Mar. 17, 1928; s. Patrick Liam and Mary Josephine (Hooley) L.; m. Rosemary Lahey Mervenne, Aug. 3, 1974; stepchildren: Anne Marie, Mary Clare, John, David, Sara Mervenne. A.B., Coll. Holy Cross, 1949; J.D., U. Mich., 1952. Bar: Mich. 1952. Assoc. firm Dickinson, Wright, Moon, Van Dusen & Freeman, Detroit, 1956-63; ptnr. Dickinson Wright PLLC, Bloomfield Hills, Mich., 1964—. Served to lt. j.g. U.S. Navy, 1952-55. Mem. Mich. Bar Assn., Detroit Bar Assn., Am. Law Inst. Roman Catholic. Clubs: Detroit Athletic, Detroit Golf. Office: Dickinson Wright PLLC 38525 Woodward Ave Ste 2000 Bloomfield Hills MI 48304-5092 E-mail: pledwidge@dickinson-wright.com.

LEE, BERNARD SHING-SHU, research company executive; b. Nanking, People's Republic of China, Dec. 14, 1934; came to U.S., 1949; s. Wei-Kuo and Pei-fen (Tang) L.; m. Pauline Pan; children: Karen, Lesley, Tania. BSc, Poly. Inst. Bklyn., 1956, DSc in Chem. Engring., 1960. Registered profl. engr., N.Y., Ill. With Arthur D. Little, Inc., Cambridge, Mass., 1960-65, Inst. Gas Tech., Chgo., 1965-78, pres., 1978—. Chmn. M-C Power Corp., Burr Ridge, Ill., Shanghai Zhihai Gasification Tech. Devel.; chmn. steering com. LNG-13; bd. dirs. NUI corp., Bedminster, N.J., Nat. Fuel Gas Co., Buffalo, Peerless Mfg. Co., Dallas. Contbr. over 60 articles to profl. jours. Recipient Outstanding Personal Achievement in Chem. Engring. award Chem. Engring. mag., 1978. Fellow AAAS, Am. Inst. Chem. Engrs. (33d inst. lectr. 1981); mem. Am. Chem. Soc., Am. Gas Assn. (Gas Industry Rsch. award 1984, Disting. Svc. award 1998). Office: Inst Gas Tech 1700 S Mount Prospect Rd Des Plaines IL 60018-1800

LEE, BRANT THOMAS, lawyer, federal official, educator; b. San Francisco, Feb. 17, 1962; s. Ford and Patricia (Leong) L.; m. Marie Bernadette Curry, Sept. 20, 1991. BA in Philosophy, U. Calif., Berkeley, 1985; JD, Harvard U., 1990, M in Pub. Policy, 1994. Bar: Calif. 1992. Counsel subcom. on Constitution, U.S. Senate Judiciary Com., Washington, 1990-92; assoc. Breon, O'Donnell, Miller, Brown & Dannis, San Francisco, 1992-96; dep. staff sec., spl. asst. to Pres. (acting) The White House, Washington, 1993; vis. asst. prof. Syracuse (N.Y.) U. Coll. Law, 1996-97; asst. prof. U. Akron (Ohio) Sch. Law, 1997-2001, assoc. prof., 2001—. Commr. San Francisco Ethics Commn., 1995-96. Bd. dirs., Asian Svcs. in Action, Inc., Akron, 1998—; trustee Chinese for Affirmative Action, San Francisco, 1992-96; bd. dirs. Conf. Asian Pacific Am. Leadership, Washington, 1990-92; staff mem. Dukakis for Pres., Boston, 1988. Mem. ABA, Nat. Asian Pacfic Am. Bar Assn. E-mial. Office: U Akron Sch Law Akron OH 44325-0001 E-mail: btlee@uakron.edu.

LEE, CATHERINE M. business owner, educator; b. Grand Rapids, Mich., Aug. 21, 1941; m. Gordon Timothy Lee; 4 children. BA, Aquinas Coll., 1963; MA, U. Mich., 1964; postgrad., Wayne State U., 1965-67. Pres. CDL & Assocs., Barrington, Ill., 1988—. Mem. Unit Dist. 220 Bd. Edn., 1984-93; Dem. candidate Ill. Ho. of Reps., 1992; Dem. candidate 16th dist. Ill. U.S. Ho. of Reps., 1996. Roman Catholic. Office: CDL & Assocs 445 Shady Ln Barrington IL 60010-4141

LEE, DAVE, radio personality; m. Julie Lee; 3 children. Grad., U. N.D. With Sta. KFGO-Radio, Fargo, ND, program dir.; with morning show Sta. WCCO Radio, Mpls. PA announcer Minn. Gopher Football Games; vol. Children's Heartlink, Mt. Olivet Rolling Acres for the Develop. Disabled, Pennies for Patients for Leukemia Soc. Recipient 3 Minn. Play by Play Broadcaster of Yr. awards, AP. Office: WCCO 625 2nd Ave S Minneapolis MN 55402*

LEE, DER-TSAI, electrical engineering and computer science educator, researcher, consultant; b. Taipei, Taiwan, Apr. 5, 1949; BSEE, Nat. Taiwan U., 1971; MS in Computer Sci., U. Ill., 1976, PhD in Computer Sci., 1978. Asst. prof. elec. engring. and computer sci. Northwestern U., Evanston, Ill., 1978-81, assoc. prof. elec. engring. and computer sci., 1981-86, prof. elec. engring. and computer sci., 1986—; adj. prof. Nat. Taiwan U., 1984-85; program dir. NSF, Washington, 1989-90. Vis. rsch. prof. Inst. Info. Sci., Academia Sinica, Taipei, 1984-85; cons., IBM, Yorktown Heights, N.Y., 1982, USDA, New Orleans, 1985-89. Editor: Algorithmic Aspects of VLSI Layout, 1994, Internat. Jour. Computational Geometry and Applications, 1991—. Fellow IEEE, Assn. for Computing Machinery; mem. Soc. Indsl. and Applied Math. Achievements include copyright for Geosheet: A Distributed Visualization Tool for Geometrics Algorithms; patent pending on nonlinear muscle-like controller. Office: Northwestern U ECE Dept Elec and Comp Engring 2145 Sheridan Rd Dept Elecand Evanston IL 60208-0834

LEE, DICK, radio director; Sta. mgr. WCRF-FM, Cleve. Office: 9756 Barr Rd Cleveland OH 44141

LEE, DON YOON, publisher, academic researcher and writer; b. Seoul, Korea, Apr. 7, 1936; came to U.S., 1957; s. Yoo-ehn and Ch'i-ho (Kim) L. BA, U. Wash., 1963; MA, St. John's U., Jamaica, N.Y., 1967; MS, Georgetown U., 1971; MA, Ind. U., 1975, 90. Founder, pub. Eastern Press, Inc., Bloomington, Ind., 1981—. Author: History of Early Relation Between China and Tibet, 1981, An Introduction to East Asian and Tibetan Linguistics and Culture, 1981, Learning Standard Arabic, 1988, An Annotated Bibliography of Selected Works on China, 1981, Light Literature and Philosophy of East Asia, 1982, An Annotated Bibliography on Inner Asia, 1983, An Annotated Archaeological Bibliography of Selected Works on Norther and Central Asia, 1983, Traditional Chinese Thoughts: The Four Schools, 1990, others. Office: Eastern Press Inc PO Box 881 Bloomington IN 47402-0881

LEE, E. BRUCE, electrical engineering educator; b. Brainerd, Minn., Feb. 1, 1932; s. Ernest R. and Hazel B. Lee; m. Judith P. Paine, Apr., 1954; children: Brian, Kevin, Timothy, Joel, Cara, Elizabeth. AA, Brainerd State Coll., 1952; BSME, U. N.D., 1955, MSME, 1956; PhD, U. Minn., 1960. Rsch. engr. Honeywell, Inc., Mpls., 1955-63; assoc. prof. U. Minn., 1963-65, prof., 1966—, head dept. elec. engring., 1976-82, acting head elec. engring. dept., 1983-84, assoc. dir. Ctr. for Control Sci., 1984—. Cons. Nat. Sci. Found., Washington, 1978-80, Fulbright (CIES), Washington, 1980-82. Author: Foundations of Optimal Control Theory, 1986. Recipient medal of distinction Tech. U. Warsaw, Gold medal ASME. Fellow: IEEE; mem. Polish Acad. Scis. (fgn.). Home: 1705 Innsbruck Pky Minneapolis MN 55421-2003 Office: U Minn Elec Engring Dept 200 Union St SE Minneapolis MN 55455-0154

LEE, EDWARD L. bishop; b. Fort Washington, Pa., 1934; m. Kathryn Fligg, 1961; 1 child, Kathryn E. Grad. cum laude, Brown U., 1956; MDiv, Gen. Theol. Seminary, 1959. Ordained diaconate, priesthood Episc. Ch., 1959. Curate Ch. Holy Trinity, Phila., 1959-64; Episc. advisor Univ. Christian Movement Temple Univ., 1964-73; rector St. James Ch., Florence, Italy, 1973-82, St. John's Ch., Washington, 1982-89; bishop Episcopal Diocese We. Mich., 1989—. Sunday, pastoral asst. Ch. Annunciation, Phila.; parish cons. St. Peters Ch., Germantown; lectr. homiletics Phila. Divinity Sch.; nat. chair Episc. Peace Fellowship, 1970-73; with Convocation of Am. Chs. Europe, pres. coun. advice; dep. Gen. Conv., 1976, 79; chair Coun. Coll. Preachers; active Washington Diocesan Coun., chmn. exec. com.; com. inquiry on the nuclear issues Diocesan Peace Commn. Former chair bd. advisors Am. Internat. Sch. Florence. Office: Episcopal Diocese Western Mich 2600 Vincent Ave Portage MI 49024-5600

LEE, E(UGENE) STANLEY, engineer, mathematician, educator; b. Hopeh, China, Sept. 7, 1930; came to U.S., 1955, naturalized, 1961; s. Ing Yah and Lindy (Hsieng) L.; m. Mayanne Lee, Dec. 21, 1957 (dec. June 1980); children: Linda J., Margaret H.; m. Yuan Lee, Mar. 8, 1983; children— Lynn Hua Lee, Jin Hua Lee, Ming Hua Lee. BS, Chung Cheng Inst. Tech., Taiwan, Republic of China, 1953; MS, N.C. State U., 1957; PhDChemE, Princeton U., 1962. Rsch. engr Phillips Petroleum Co., Bartlesville, Okla., 1960-66; asst. prof. chem. engring. Kans. State U., Manhattan, 1966-67, assoc. prof. indsl. engring., 1967-69, prof. indsl. engring., 1969—; prof. chem. and elec. engring. U. So. Calif., 1972-76. Hon. prof. Chinese Acad. Sci., 1987—; chaired prof. Yuan-ze Inst. Tech., Taiwan, Republic of China, 1993—; cons. govt. and industry. Author: Quasilinearization and Invariant Imbedding, 1968, Coal Conversion Technnology, 1979, Operations Research, 1981, Fuzzy and Evidence Reasoning, 1996, Fuzzy and Multi-level Decision Making, 2000; editor: Energy Sci. and Tech., 1975; assoc. editor: Jour. Math. Analysis and Applications, 1974—, assoc. editor: Computers and Mathematics with Applications, 1974, editl. bd.: Jour. Engring. Chemistry and Metallurgy, 1989—, editl. bd.: Jour. of Nonlinear Differential Equations, 1992—, editl. bd.: Jour. Chinese Fuzzy Sys. Assn., 1995—, editl. bd.: Fuzzy Optimization and Decision Making, 2000—, editl. bd.: Internat. Jour. Modeling and Optimization, 2001—, editl. bd.: Math. Scis. Rsch. Hot-line, An Internat. Jour. Rapid Publ., 2001—. Grantee Dept. Def., 1967-72, Office Water Resources, 1968-75, EPA, 1969-71, NSF, 1971—, USDA, 1978-90, Dept. Energy, 1979-84, USAF, 1984-88. Mem. Soc. Indsl. and Applied Math., Ops. Rsch. Soc. Am., N. Am. Fuzzy Info. Processing Soc., Internat. Neural Network Soc., Sigma Xi, Tau Beta Pi, Phi Kappa Phi. Office: Kans State U Dept Indsl Engring Manhattan KS 66506

LEE, HOWARD D. academic administrator; B, M, U. Wis.; PhD Edn., U. Minn., 1981. Grad. program dir. master's program vocat. and tech. edn. U. Wis., exec. dir. Stout Solutions, 2002—. Office: U Wis Stout Solutions 140 Vocat Rehab Bldg Menomonie WI 54751-0790*

LEE, HWA-WEI, librarian, educator, consultant; b. Guangdong, China, Dec. 7, 1933; came to U.S., 1957, naturalized, 1962; s. Luther Kan-Chun and Mary Hsiao-Wei (Wang) L.; m. Mary F. Kratochvil, Mar. 14, 1959; children: Shirley, James, Pamela, Edward, Charles, Robert. BEd, Nat. Taiwan Normal U., 1954; MEd, U. Pitts., 1959, PhD, 1964; MLS, Carnegie Mellon U., 1961. Asst. libr. U. Pitts. Librs., 1959-62; head tech. svcs. Duquesne U. Libr., Pitts., 1962-65; head libr. U. Pa., Edinboro, 1965-68; dir. libr. and info. ctr. Asian Inst. Tech., Bangkok, 1968-75; assoc. dir. librs., prof. libr. adminstrn. Colo. State U., Fort Collins, 1975-78; dean librs., prof. Ohio U., Athens, 1978-99, dean emeritus, librs., 1999—; disting. vis. scholar OCLC, 2000—. Fulbright sr. specialist, 2001; cons. FAO, UNESCO, U.S. AID, World Bank, Internat. Devel. Rsch. Ctr., Asia Found., OCLC; del.-at-large White House Conf. Libr. and Info. Svcs., 1991. Author: Librarianship in World Perspectives, 1991, Fundraising for the 1990s: The Challenge Ahead, 1992, Modern Library Management, 1996, Knowledge Management: Theory and Practice, 2002; exec. editor Jour. Ednl. Media and Libr. Sci., 1982—; mem. editl. bd. Internat. Comm. in Libr. Automation, 1975-76, Jour. Libr. and Info. Sci., 1975-78, Libr. Acquisition: Practice and Theory, 1976-83; adv. bd. Jour. Info., Comm. and Libr. Sci., 1994—; contbr. articles to profl. jours. Recipient Disting. Svc. award Libr. Assn. of China (Taiwan), 1989; new bldg. on Ohio U. campus named in his honor: Hwa-wei Lee Libr. Annex, and 1st flr. of the main libr.: Hwa-wei Lee Ctr. for Internat. Collections, 1999. Mem. ALA (councilor 1988-92, 93-97, John Ames Humphry/Forest Press award 1991), Acad. Libr. Assn. Ohio, Am. Soc. Info. Sci., Asian-Pacific Am. Librs. Assn. (Disting. Svc. award 1991), Internat. Fedn. Libr. Assns. and Instns. (standing com. univ. librs. and other gen. rsch. librs. 1989-93), Assn. Coll. and Rsch. Librs. Chinese-Am. Librs. Assn. (Disting. Svc. award 1983), Internat. Assn. Orientalist Librs., Ohio Libr. Coun. (bd. dirs. 1991-92, Libr. of the Yr. 1987, Hall of Fame Libr. 1999), Online Computer Libr. Ctr. (users coun. 1987-91), Ohio Chinese Acad. and Profl. Assn. (founding pres. 1988-90). Home: 19 Mulligan Rd Athens OH 45701-3734 Office: Ohio U Hwa-Wei Lee Libr Annex Athens OH 45701 E-mail: leeh@ohio.edu.

LEE, JACK (JIM SANDERS BEASLEY), broadcast executive; b. Buffalo Valley, Tenn., Apr. 14, 1936; s. Jesse McDonald and Nelle Viola (Sanders) Beasley; m. Barbara Sue Looper, Sept. 1, 1961; children: Laura Ann, Elizabeth Jane, Sarah Kathleen. Student, Wayne State U., 1955-57; BA, Albion Coll., 1959. Announcer Sta. WHUB-AM, Cookeville, Tenn., 1956; news dir., program dir. Sta. WALM-AM, Albion, Mich., 1957-59;

radio-TV personality WKZO-Radio-TV, Kalamazoo, 1960-62; prodn. dir. Stas. WKMH-WKNR, Detroit, 1962-63; gen. mgr. Sta. WAUK-AM-FM, Waukesha, Wis., 1963-65; asst. program mgr. Sta. WOKY, Milw., 1965-70; program mgr. Sta. WTMJ-WKTI, 1970-76; gen. mgr. Sta. WEMP-WMYX, 1976-88; pres. Jack Lee Enterprises Ltd., 1977—; pres., CEO, Milw. Area Radio Stas., 1989—. Instr. dept. mass comm. U. Wis.-Milw., 1972-81. With U.S. Army, 1959, 61-62; maj. CAP, 1964-01, ret. Decorated Army Commendation medal; cert. radio mktg. cons., Broadcasters Hall of Fame, 1999. Mem. AFTRA, Actors Equity, Milw. Advt. Club, Omicron Delta Kappa, Alpha Epsilon Rho. Home and Office: W277 W N Chicory Ln # 2793 Pewaukee WI 53072 E-mail: jleemars@msn.com.

LEE, JANIS K. state legislator; b. Kensington, Kans., July 11, 1945; m. Lyn Lee; children: David, Brian, Daniel. BA, Kans. State U., 1970. Mem. from dist. 36 Kans. State Senate, 1988—. Mem. Kappa Delta Pi, Phi Kappa Phi. Democrat. Home: RR 1 Box 145 Kensington KS 66951-9801 Office: Kansas Senate State Capitol Rm 402-S Topeka KS 66612

LEE, JUDITH, state legislator; b. Redding, Calif., Mar. 7, 1942; m. Duane Lee, 1964; 2 children. BS, U. N.D., 1964. Real estate broker; mem. N.D. Senate from 13th dist., Bismark, 1994—; human svcs., chair human svcs. com., mem. polit. subdivsn. coms. N.D. Senate. Mem. West Fargo (N.D.) Planning and Zoning Com., 1982—94; bd. dirs. United Way of Cass-Clay, 1987—93, Hospice of Red River Valley, 1997—2002, Fargo-Moorhead Symphony, 2000—. Named Realtor of Yr., Fargo-Moorhead Area Assn. Realtors, 1988, YWCA Woman of the Yr. in Vol. Category, 1994, Legislator of Yr., N.D. Assn. Township Officers, 1998; recipient Guardian of Sm. Bus. award, Nat. Fedn. Ind. Businesses, 1998. Mem.: LWV, Park Co. County Realtors/GMAC, Fargo C. of C. (bd. dirs. 1993—99), West Fargo C. of C. 1985—88. Office: PO Box 89 Fargo ND 58107-0089

LEE, KAREN, art appraiser; B Polit. Sci., Tung-hai U., Taiwan; JD, Washburn U., 1983. Ind. art dealer, Topeka. Bd. regents Washburn U., 1999—. Home and Office: 132 SW Fairlawn Rd Topeka KS 66606

LEE, KRISTI, broadcast executive, reporter; b. Indpls., July 17, 1960; d. Sammy Cecil Gibson and Mary Scott (Pounds) Crawley. Student, Ind. U., 1978—. T.v. engr. WRTV-Channel 6, Indpls., 1980-86; t.v. engr., dir. KOAT-TV, Albuquerque, 1986-88; radio news dir. Bob and Tom Show WFBQ-095, Indpls., 1988—; sports reporter ESPN, ESPN 2, 1993—. Dir. Musicians Against Child Abuse, Indpls., 1995—; fundraiser, vol. Hope Lodge. Mem. Am. Women in Radio and TV (95 Radio Personality of the Yr. award). Avocations: movies, golf, sports events, gardening, travel. Office: WFBQ-Q95 6161 Fall Creek Rd Indianapolis IN 46220-5032

LEE, MARGARET BURKE, college president, English educator; b. San Diego, Dec. 28, 1943; d. Peter John and Margaret Mary (Brown) Burke; m. Donald Harry Lee, June 30, 1973; children: Katherine Louise, Kristopher Donald. BA summa cum laude, Regis Coll., 1966; MA with honors, U. Chgo., 1970, PhD, 1978; IEM Cert., Harvard U., 1992, Seminar for New Pres., 1996. Asst. to humanities MIT, Cambridge, 1969; instr. Dover-Sherborn H.S., Dover, 1973-75, Alpena (Mich.) C.C., 1975-80, dean liberal arts, 1980-82; dean instrn. Kalamazoo Valley C.C., 1982-85; v.p. Oakton C.C., Des Plaines, Ill., 1985-95, pres., 1995—. Cons. evaluator North Ctrl. Assn., Chgo., 1982—, commr.-at-large, 1988-92, commn. on inst. of higher edn. bd. dirs., 1992—, vice chair, 1996-98, chair, 1998, now v.p.; vice chair Am. Coun. on Internat. Intercultural Edn.; cons., field faculty Vt. Coll., Montpelier, 1982-85; mem. admissions com. Ill. Math and Sci. Acad., 1988—; bd. govs. North Cook Ednl. Svc. Ctr., 1988—, bd. dirs., 1989—, vice chair, 1990-91, chair, 1992-94. Mem. Bd. Edn. Dist. 39, Wilmette, Ill., 1990-92, Des Plaines Sister Cities, 1995—; bd. dirs. Ill. C.C. Atty.'s Assn., 1994—; mem. Career Edn. Planning Dist., Kalamazoo, 1982, Kalamazoo Forum/Kalamazoo Network, 1982, Needs Assessment Task Force, 1984. Ford Found. fellow, 1969-73, Woodrow Wilson Found. fellow, 1975; fed. grantee, 1978-84. Mem. Am. Assn. of C.C.'s (bd. dirs.), Am. Assn. Cmty. and Jr. Colls., Mich. Assn. C.C. Instrnl. Adminstrs. (pres. 1983-85), Mich. Occupl. Deans Adminstrs. Coun. (exec. bd. 1983-85), Mich. Women's Studies Assn. (hons. selection com. 1984), North Ctrl. Assn. Acad. Deans (pres. 1988-90), Kalamazoo Consortium Higher Edn. (pres.'s coun. coord. com. 1982-85), Kalamazoo C. of C. (vocat. edn. subcom. indsl. coun. 1982), North Ctrl. Assn. Acad. Deans (v.p., pres. 1985-87), Des Plaines C. of C. (mem. bd. dirs. 1995—). Democrat. Lutheran. Avocations: quilt collecting, reading, listening to classical music, sports spectating, theatre-going. Home: 2247 Lake Ave Wilmette IL 60091-1410 Office: Oakton CC 1600 E Golf Rd Des Plaines IL 60016-1234

LEE, MICHAEL, leasing company executive, real estate company executive; b. Chgo., Nov. 26, 1953; s. Joseph A. and Mildred M. Kathrein; m. Victoria Lee; children: Jane Emily, Joseph Andrew, Theodore Michael, Elizabeth Grace, Fay Golda. BS in Acctg., U. Nebr., 1978; M in Mgmt., Northwestern U., 1985. CPA, Ill.; lic. real estate broker, pilot. Tax mgr. Touche Ross & Co., Chgo., 1978-84; corp. contr., v.p. Lettuce Entertain You Enterprises, 1984-86; pres., CEO Kathrein Leasing Co., 1983—; also bd. dirs.; pres., chief exec. officer Empire Real Estate Investment Co., Chgo., 1986—. Bd. dirs., speaker Nat. Speakers Bur., N.Y.C., 1985-94; cons. Fla. Investor, Inc., Cocoa, 1986—. Author: (how-to book) Real Estate Comparative Analysis, 1986. Bd. dirs. Revenue Crusade of Mercy, United Way, Chgo., 1980. Mem. AICPA, Cert. Mgmt. Accts. Assn. (cert.), Cert. Internal Auditors Assn. (cert.), Nat. Assn. Realtors, Young Pres.'s Orgn., Northwestern U. Alumni Assn., Mensa. Avocations: aviation, lecturing. Home: 7601 N Eastlake Ter Chicago IL 60626-1421

LEE, MORDECAI, political scientist, educator; b. Milw., Aug. 27, 1948; s. Jack Harold and Bernice (Kamesar) L.; 1 child, Ethan. BA, U. Wis., 1970; MPA, Syracuse U., 1972, PhD, 1975. Guest scholar Brookings Instn., Washington, 1972-74; legis. asst. to Congressman Henry Reuss, 1975; asst. prof. polit. sci. U. Wis.-Whitewater and Parkside, 1976; mem. Wis. Ho. Reps., 1977-82, Wis. Senate, 1982-89; exec. dir. Milw. Jewish Coun. Cmty. Rels., 1990-97; asst. prof. govt. U. Wis.-Milw., 1997—2002, assoc. prof., 2002—.

LEE, ROBERT LLOYD, pastor, religious association executive; b. Escanaba, Mich., Jan. 3, 1943; s. Lloyd Benjamin and Eleanor Mae (Leece) L.; m. Gloria Jeanne James, June 3, 1967; children: Adam Robert, Amy Vicary Lee Skogerboe. BA, Augsburg Coll., 1965; MDiv, Free Luth. Sem., 1968; ThM, Bethel Theol. Sem., 1988. Ordained min. Luth. Ch., 1968. Pastor Tioga (N.D.) Luth. Parish, 1966-72, Grace & Zion Luth. Chs., Valley City, N.D., 1972-79, Helmar Luth. Ch., Newark, 1990-92; prof. hist. theology Free Luth. Schs., Mpls., 1979-89; pres. Assn. Free Luth. Congregations, 1992—. Author: Fever Saga, 1987, A New Springtime, 1997; editor: Do the Work of An Evangelist, 1990; editor The Luth. Ambassador, 1990-93. Co-chmn. Luth. Estonian Am. Friends, 1992—. Mem. Valdres Samband, Norwegian-Am. Hist. Assn., N.Am. Manx Assn. Office: Assn Free Luth Congregations 3110 E Medicine Lake Blvd Minneapolis MN 55441-3008

LEE, SHUISHIH SAGE, pathologist; b. Soo-chow, Kiang su, China, Jan. 5, 1948; came to U.S., 1972, naturalized, 1979; m. Chung Seng Lee; children: Yvonne Claire, Michael Chung. MD, Nat. Taiwan U., 1972; PhD, U. Rochester, 1976. Resident in pathology Strong Meml. Hosp., Rochester, N.Y., 1976-78, Northwestern Meml. Hosp., Chgo., 1978-79; dir. cytology and electron microscopy Parkview Meml. Hosp., Ft. Wayne, Ind., 1979—. Clin. prof. Ind. U. Med. Sch. Contbr. articles to profl. jours. Fellow: Am. Soc. Clin. Pathologists, Coll. Am. Pathologists; mem.: AMA, Internat. Assn. Chinese Pathologists (pres. 1999—2001, 1999—2001), Ft. Wayne Acad. Physicians and Surgeons 1990, Ft. Wayne Med. Soc. 2001—02, Electron Microscopy Soc. Am., Internat. Acad. Cytology, Internat. Acad. Pathology, Am. Soc. Cytology, Am. Assn. Pathologists, N.Y. Acad. Scis., Ind. Assn. Pathologists, N.E. Ind. Pathologists Assn. (sec. 1984), Ind. Med. Assn. Home: 5728 The Prophets Pass Fort Wayne IN 46845-9659 Office: Parkview Meml Hosp 2200 Randallia Dr Fort Wayne IN 46805-4699

LEE, STEPHEN W. lawyer; b. New Castle, Ind., Oct. 25, 1949; s. Delmer W. Lee and Loma F. (Thurston) McCall; m. Pamela A. Summers, Aug. 2, 1969; children: Erin E., Stephanie M. BS, Ball State U., 1971; JD summa cum laude, Ind. U., 1977. Bar: Ind. 1977, U.S. Dist. Ct. (so. dist.) Ind. 1977, U.S. Ct. Appeals (7th cir.) 1977, U.S. Supreme Ct. 1982. Officer, lt.(j.g.) USNR, Phila., 1971-74; law clk. U.S. Dist. Ct. (no. dist.) Ind., Ft. Wayne, 1977-78; assoc. Barnes, Hickam, Pantzer & Boyd, Indpls., 1978-82, Barnes & Thornburg, Indpls., 1982-83, ptnr., 1984—. Dir. The Julian Ctr., Indpls., 1999—; mem. Ind. U. Sch. of Law Bd. of Visitors, 1999—. Editor-in-chief: Indiana Law Jour., 1976-77. Dir. Ind. Repertory Theatre, Indpls., 1986-91; exec. coun. Ind. U. Alumni Assn., Bloomington, 1989; dir. Ind. U. Sch. of Law Alumni Assn., Bloomington, 1984-90, pres., 1991-92; mem. Ball State U. Coll. Bus. Alumni Bd., 1991-2000, Ball State U. Entrepreneurship Adv. Bd., 1994—. Mem. Ind. State Bar Assn., Indpls. Bar Assn. (chmn. bus. sect. 1985), Highland Golf & Country Club. Republican. Avocation: golf. Office: Barnes & Thornburg 11 S Meridian St Ste 1313 Indianapolis IN 46204-3535 E-mail: slee@btlaw.com.

LEE, WILLIAM CHARLES, judge; b. Ft. Wayne, Ind., Feb. 2, 1938; s. Russell and Catherine (Zwick) L.; m. Judith Anne Bash, Sept. 19, 1959; children: Catherine L., Mark R., Richard R. AB, Yale U., 1959; JD, U. Chgo., 1962; LLD (hon.), Huntington Coll., 1999. Bar: Ind. 1962. Ptnr. Parry, Krueckeberg & Lee, Ft. Wayne, 1963-69, chief dep., 1966-69; U.S. atty. No. Dist. Ind., 1970-73; ptnr. Hunt, Suedhoff, Borror, Eilbacher & Lee, 1973-81; U.S. dist. judge U.S. Dist. Ct. (no. dist.) Ind., 1981—. Instr. Nat. Inst. Trial Advocacy; lectr. in field. Co-author: Business and Commercial Litigation in Federal Courts, 1998; author: Volume I Federal Jury Practice and Instructions, 1999; contbr. to numerous publs. in field. Co-chmn. Fort Wayne Fine Arts Operating Fund Drive, 1978; past bd. dirs., v.p., pres. Fort Wayne Philharm. Orch.; past bd. dirs., v.p. Hospice of Fort Wayne, inc.; past bd. dirs. Fort Wayne Fine Arts Found., Fort Wayne Civic Theatre, Neighbors, Inc., Embassy Theatre Found.; past bd. dirs., pres. Legal Aid of fort Wayne, Inc.; past mem. chm. coun., v.p. Trinity English Lutheran Ch. Coun.; past trustee, pres. Fort Wayne Cmty. Schs., 1978-81, pres., 1980-81; trustee Fort Wayne Mus. Art, 1984-90; past bd. dirs., pres. Fort Wayne-Allen County Hist. Soc. Griffin Scholar, 1955-59; chmn. Fort Wayne Cmty. Schs. Scholarship Com.; bd. dirs. Arts United of Greater Fort Wayne, Fort Wayne Ballet. Weymouth Kirkland scholar, 1959-62; named Ind. Trial Judge of Yr., 1988. Fellow Am. Coll. Trial Lawyers, Ind. Bar Found.; mem. ABA, Allen County Bar Assn., Ind. State Bar Assn., Fed. Bar Assn., Seventh Cir. Bar Assn., Benjamin Harrison Am. Inn of Ct., North Side High Alumni Assn. (bd. dirs., pres.), Fort Wayne Rotary Club (bd. dirs.), Phi Delta Phi (past bd. dirs., 1st pres.). Republican. Lutheran. Office: US Dist Ct 2145 Fed Bldg 1300 S Harrison St Fort Wayne IN 46802-3495

LEE, WILLIAM MARSHALL, lawyer; b. N.Y.C., Feb. 23, 1922; s. Marshall McLean and Marguerite (Letts) L.; m. Lois Kathryn Plain, Oct. 10, 1942; children: Marsha (Mrs. Stephen Derynck), William Marshall Jr., Victoria C. (Mrs. Larry Nelson). Student, U. Wis., 1939-40; BS, Aero. U., Chgo., 1942; postgrad., UCLA, 1946-48, Loyola U. Law Sch., L.A., 1948-49; JD, Loyola U., Chgo., 1952. Bar: Ill. 1952, U.S. Supreme Ct., 1972. Thermodynamicist Northrop Aircraft Co., Hawthorne, Calif., 1947-49; patent agt. Hill, Sherman, Meroni, Gross & Simpson, Chgo., 1949-51, Borg-Warner Corp., Chgo., 1951-53; ptnr. Hume, Clement, Hume & Lee, 1953-72; pvt. practice, 1973-74; ptnr. Lee and Smith (and predecessors), 1974-89, Lee, Mann, Smith, McWilliams, Sweeney & Ohlson, Chgo., 1989—; ind. expert intellectual property Barrington, Ill., 1999—. Cons. Power Packaging, Inc. Speaker and contbr. articles on legal topics. Pres. Glenview (Ill.) Citizens Sch. Com., 1953-57; v.p. Glenbrook High Sch. Bd., 1957-63. Lt. USNR, 1942-46, CBI. Recipient Pub. Svc. award Glenbrook High Sch. Bd., 1963 Mem. ABA (chmn. sect. intellectual property law 1986-87, sect. fin. officer 1976-77, sect. sec. 1977-80, sect. governing coun. 1980-84, 87-88), Ill. Bar Assn., Chgo. Bar Assn., 7th Fed. Cir. Bar Assn., Am. Intellectual Property Law Assn., Intellectual Property Law Assn. Chgo., Licensing Execs. Soc. (pres. 1981-82, treas. 1977-80, trustee 1974-77, 80-81, 82-83, internat. del. 1980—), Phi Delta Theta, Phi Alpha Delta. Republican. Office: 84 Otis Rd Barrington IL 60010-5128

LEEGE, DAVID CALHOUN, political scientist, educator; b. Elkhart, Ind., May 18, 1937; s. Harold Martin and Nellie Josephine (Bliss) L.; m. Patricia Ann Schad, June 8, 1963; children— David McChesney, Lissa Maria, Kurt Johannes B.A., Valparaiso U., 1959; postgrad., U. Chgo., 1959-60; Ph.D., Ind. U., 1965. Instr. social sci. Concordia Coll., River Forest, Ill., 1962-64; asst. prof. polit. sci., dir. pub. opinion survey unit U. Mo., Columbia, 1964-68; assoc. prof., dir. survey research center SUNY, Buffalo, 1968-70; assoc. prof. U. Ill., Chgo., 1970-72, prof., 1972-76, head dept., 1972-73; prof. govt. and internat. studies U. Notre Dame, Ind., 1976—, dir. center for study of contemporary society, 1976-85, dir. London program, 1982, dir. program for research on religion, church and society, 1984—; dir. Hesburgh Program in Pub. Service, 1987-92. Program dir. for polit. sci. NSF, 1974-76; mem. vis. faculty York U., Toronto, Ont., Can., 1970, U. Mich., 1971, 73, U. Leuven, Belgium, 1980, Cath. U. Am., 1985-86, U. Ariz., 2001, 02. Author: (with Wayne Francis) Political Research, 1974, (with Lyman Kellstedt) Rediscovering the Religious Factor in American Politics, 1993, (with K. Wald, B. Krueger and P. Mueller) The Politics of Cultural Differences, 2002; editor: The Missouri Poll, 1965-68, (with Joseph Gremillion) The Notre Dame Study of Catholic Parish Life Report Series, 1984-89; contbr. articles to profl. jours. Mem. bd. overseers Am. Nat. Election Studies, 1991-99, chair, 1994-97; mem. coun. ICPSR, 1966-69; bd. dirs. Luth. Music Program, Inc. Recipient numerous profl. prizes. Mem.: Midwest Polit. Sci. Assn. (chair nominating com., coun., program co-chair), Am. Polit. Sci. Assn. (sect. officer, program com., chmn. task force). Lutheran. Office: U Notre Dame Dept Govt Notre Dame IN 46556-0368 Home: 2155 W Via Nuevo Leon Green Valley AZ 85614

LEEKLEY, JOHN ROBERT, lawyer; b. Phila., Aug. 27, 1943; s. Thomas Briggs and Dorothy (O'Hora) L.; m. Karen Kristin Myers, Aug. 28, 1965 (dec. Mar. 1997); children: John Thomas, Michael Dennis; m. Gerry Lee Gildner, June 5, 1999. BA, Boston Coll., 1965; LLB, Columbia U., 1968. Bar: N.Y. 1968, Mich. 1976. Assoc. Curtis, Mallet-Prevost, Colt & Mosle, N.Y.C., 1968-69, Davis Polk & Wardwell, N.Y.C., 1969-76; asst. corp. counsel Masco Corp., Taylor, Mich., 1976-77, corp. counsel, 1977-79, v.p., corp. counsel, 1979-88, v.p., gen. counsel, 1988-96, sr. v.p., gen. counsel, 1996—. Bd. visitors Columbia U. Law Sch., N.Y.C., 1994-96; mem. Freedom Twp. Bd. Tax Appeals, 1984-85. Mem. ABA (com. long range issues affecting bus. practice 1976-96), Mich. State Bar Assn. Democrat. Roman Catholic. Avocations: Percheron horse breeding, hunting, fishing, outdoor activities. Office: Masco Corp 21001 Van Born Rd Taylor MI 48180-1300

LEEPA, ALLEN, artist, educator; b. N.Y.C., Jan. 9, 1919; s. Harvey and Esther (Gentle) L. Student (scholar), The New Bauhaus Sch., 1937-38; scholar, Hans Hofmann Sch., 1938-39; B.S., Columbia U., 1942, M.A. (scholar), 1948, Ed.D., 1960. Art instr. Hull Sch., Chgo., 1937-38, Bklyn. Art Ctr., 1939-40, 99, Met. Mus., N.Y.C., 1940-41, St. Marks Center, N.Y.C., 1941-42; draftsman Acrotorque Co., Conn., 1942, Glen Martin Aircraft, N.Y.C., 1942-44; prof. art Mich. State U., 1945-84, ret. prof. emeritus. Mem. Leepa Gallery of Fine Art, Tarpon Springs, Fla., 1987-90. Author: The Challenge of Modern Art, 1949, 95, Abraham Rattner, 1974; contbr.: (anthologies) The New Art, 1966, 68, The Humanitites in Contemporary Life, 1960, Minimal Art; art editor: The Centennial Rev. Arts and Scis. Jour., 1959-62; one man shows Artists Gallery, N.Y.C., 1953, La Cours D'Ingres, Paris, 1961, Artists Mart, Detroit, 1969, Duke U., 1981; group shows include Mus. Modern Art, N.Y.C., 1953, VII Bienal, São Paulo, Brazil, 1963, Prado Mus., Madrid, Spain, 1956, Detroit Inst. Arts, 1948, 50, 56, 80, Pa. Acad. Fine Arts, 1951, 63; represented in permanent collections Mich. State U., Grand Rapids (Mich.) Mus., South Bend (Ind.) Mus.; lifetime work Tampa Mus. Fine Art, Leepa/Rattner Mus. Fine Arts St. Petersburg (Fla.) Jr. Coll. Fulbright award to Paris, 1950-51; Ford Found. grantee Brazil, 1970; recipient numerous prizes for paintings including: 1st prize statewide mural competition, Mich., 1983; 1st prize abstract painting Guild Hall Mus., East Hampton, N.Y., 1985 Mem. Mich. Acad. Arts, Scis., Letters. E-mail: lpwac@aol.com.

LEFAVRE, HADIA, human resources executive; Various human resources positions Bull, Paris, Compaq Computer, Regie Renault, France; sr. v.p. human resources worldwide Rhône-Poulenc Rorer, Inc., The Scott Co., 1999—. Office: 41 S High St Ste 3500 Columbus OH 43215-6110

LEFF, ALAN RICHARD, medical educator, researcher; b. May 23, 1945; s. Maurice D. and Grace Ruth (Schwarz) Leff, Maurice D. and Grace Ruth (Schwarz) Leff; m. Donna Rae Rosene, Feb. 14, 1975; children: Marni, Karen, Alison; m. Donna Rae Rosene, Feb. 14, 1975. AB cum laude, Oberlin Coll., 1967; MD, U. Rochester, 1971. Diplomate Am. Bd. Internal Medicine, Am. Bd. Pulmonary Disease. Intern U. Mich. Hosp., Ann Arbor, 1971-72, resident, 1974-76; fellow U. Calif., San Francisco, 1976-77, postdoctoral fellow, 1977-79; asst. prof. medicine U. Chgo., 1979-85, assoc. prof. medicine and clin. pharm., 1985-89, prof. medicine, anesthesia, critical care and clin. pharm., 1989—, prof. cell physiology, 1992—, prof. pediats., pharm. and phys. scis., 1993—, dir. pulmonary medicine svc., 1984-87, dir. Pulmonary Function Lab., 1979-87, chief sect. pulmonary and critical care medicine, 1987-2000, sr. dir. R&D biol. scis., 2000—. Dir. NIAID Asthma and Allergic Disease Coop. Rsch. Ctr., Chgo., 1993—97; co-chair asthma sect. NIAID Task Force on Immunology, 1996—98; advisor San Francisco Dept. Pub. Health, 1977—79, Chgo Dept. Health, 1979—; dir. Ctr. of Excellence in Asthma Glaxo Smith Kline, 2000—. Editor: Am. Jour. Respiratory Critical Care Medicine, 1994—99; contbr. Bd. dirs. Chgo. Lung Assn., 1984—93. Recipient Citation of Merit, Chgo. Lung Assn., 1974, Am. Lung Assn., 1998; fellow, Leopold Schepp Found., 1967—69. Fellow: Am. Coll. Chest Physicians; mem.: Am. Assn. Immunologists, Ctrl. Soc. for Clin. Investigation, Am. Thoracic Soc. (Spl. Citation 1999), Assn. Am. Physicians, Am. Physiol. Soc., Am. Soc. Clin. Investigation, Am. Fedn. Clin. Rsch. (councilor 1983—86), Sigma Xi. Avocation: music. Home: 5730 S Kimbark Ave Chicago IL 60637-1615 Office: U Chgo Pritzker Sch Medicine Div Biological Scis MC 6076 5841 S Maryland Ave Chicago IL 60637-1463 E-mail: aleff@medicine.bsd.uchicago.edu.

LEFFERTS, WILLIAM GEOFFREY, physician, educator; b. Towanda, Pa., Mar. 24, 1943; s. William LeRoy and Beatrice (Smith) L.; m. Susan Lynn Hiles, Oct. 31, 1970. B.A., Hamilton Coll., 1965; M.D., Hahnemann Med. Coll., 1969. Intern Hahnemann Hosp., 1969-70; resident in internal medicine Cleve. Clinic Hosp., 1970-73, chief med. resident, 1972-73; asst. prof. internal medicine Hahnemann Med. Coll., 1973-77; assoc. prof. Med. Coll. Pa., 1978-82, dir. primary care unit, 1978-82, dir. div. gen. internal medicine, 1979-82; staff physician Cleve. Clinic Found., 1982—. Fellow ACP. Office: 9500 Euclid Ave Cleveland OH 44195-0001

LEFFLER, CAROLE ELIZABETH, mental health nurse, women's health nurse; b. Sidney, Ohio, Feb. 18, 1942; d. August B. and Delores K. Aselage; children: Veronica, Christopher. ADN, Sinclair Community Coll., Dayton, Ohio, 1975. Cert. psychiat. nurse supr. Nurse Grandview Hosp, Dayton, 1961-76; substitute sch. nurse Fairborn (Ohio) City Schs., 1981-82; dir. nursing Fairborn Nursing Home, 1983; psychiat. nurse supr. Twin Valley Behavioral Health Ctr., 1984—. Mem. exec. bd. 1199; chmn. disaster mental health com. ARC Ohio. Vol., instr., disaster health nurse ARC, chmn. State of Ohio disaster mental health com.; officer, leader, camp nurse for Girl Scouts, Boy Scouts; Ch. Parish Coun. Recipient Fleur de Lis award Girl and Boy Scouts, Svc. award ARC, Fairborn Mayor's Cert. of Merit for Civic Pride, State of Ohio Govs. award Innovation Ohio. Mem. ANA, Ohio Nurses Assn. Home: 3020 N Dayton Lakeview Rd New Carlisle OH 45344-8505

LEFKOWITZ, IRVING, engineering educator; b. N.Y.C., July 8, 1921; s. Adolph and Celia (Berko) L.; m. Madelyn I. Moinester, July 3, 1955; children: Deborah, Daniel. B.S. in Chem. Engring., Cooper Union, 1943; M.S. in Instrumentation Engring., Case Inst. Tech., 1955, Ph.D., 1958. With J.E. Seagram & Sons, 1943-53, dir. instrumentation research, 1951-53; faculty Case Inst. Tech., 1953-87, prof. engring., 1965-87, prof. emeritus, 1987—, dir. research group in control of complex systems, 1960-85; acting chmn. systems engring. dept. Case Western Res. U., 1972-76, chmn., 1980-83; v.p. techs. devel. Control Soft, Inc., Cleve., 1994—. Mem. sci. staff Internat. Inst. Applied Systems Analysis, Austria, 1974-75; Cons. in field, 1959— Contbr. papers to profl. lit.; Editorial adv. bd.: Jour. Dynamic Systems, Measurement and Control, 1972-77. NATO postdoctoral fellow, 1962-63 Fellow IEEE, AAAS; mem. Systems Sci. and Cybernetics Soc. (adminstr. com. 1969-72), Am. Automatic Control Council (chmn. systems engring. com. 1968-69, Control Heritage award 1982), IFAC (vice-chmn. systems engring. com. 1975-78, chmn. com. 1978-81, vice chmn. tech. bd. 1981-84), IEEE Control Systems Soc. (chmn. control of indsl. systems tech. com. 1983-87 , bd. govs. 1985-86). Office: Case Western Res U Sys Engring Dept 706 Olin Bldg Cleveland OH 44106 Home: Apt 301 3330 Warrensville Center Rd Shaker Heights OH 44122-3790 E-mail: ixl@po.cwru.edu.

LEGAN, KENNETH, state legislator, farmer; b. Halfway, Mo., Aug. 3, 1946; s. Adolphus J. and June (Jones) L.; m. Rebecca M. Bodenhamer, 1969; children: Brock Alan, Stephanie Kaye. BS, U. Mo., 1969. Owner, mgr. Legan Farms, Halfway, 1971—; mem. Mo. Ho. of Reps., Jefferson City, 1981—, sr. rep., 1992—. Mem. Polk County (Mo.) Rep. Ctrl. Com., 1971—, chmn., 1976-80, vice chmn., 1980-86. Recipient Farm Mgmt. award Kansas City C. of C., 1976, Disting. Legislator award MCCA, 1992; named hon. chpt. farmer Halfway Future Farmers Am., 1978. Mem. Farm Bur., Legis. Exch., Lions, Masons, Shriners. Home: 1901 E 487th Rd Half Way MO 65663-9281

LEGER, JAMES ROBERT, engineering educator; BS in Applied Physics, Calif. Inst. Tech., 1974; PhD in Elec. Engring., U. Calif., San Diego, 1980. With 3M; mem. rsch. staff Lincoln Lab. MIT, 1984-91; mem. faculty U. Minn., 1991, prof. electrical and computer engineering. Contbr. articles to profl. jours., chpt. to book. Achievements include application of new techniques in Fourier optics and holography to modern electrooptic devices, leading to new applications ranging from optical pattern recognition to novel laser systems; first application of multi-level diffractive micro-optics to diode laser arrays; development of the Talbot caivty and Dammann grating techniques; application of diffractive optics in laser reesonators. Home: 19000 31st Ave N Plymouth MN 55447-1085 Office: U Minn Dept Elec & Computer Engring 200 Union St SE Minneapolis MN 55455-0154 Fax: (612) 625-4583. E-mail: leger@ece.umn.edu.

LEGGE KEMP, DIANE, architect, landscape architect; b. Englewood, N.J., Dec. 4, 1949; d. Richard Claude and Patricia (Roney) L.; m. Kevin A. Kemp; children: Alloy Hudson, McClelland Beebe, Logan Roney. BA,

Stanford U., 1972; M in Architecture, Princeton U., 1975. Architect Northrop, Kaelber & Kopf, Rochester, N.Y., 1971, Michael Graves, Architect, Princeton, 1972-75, The Ehrenkrantz Group, N.Y.C., 1975-77; ptnr. Skidmore Owings & Merrill, Chgo., 1977-89; prin. Diane Legge Kemp Architecture and Landscape Consulting, Riverside, Ill., 1989-93, pres., 1993—, DLK Architecture, 1993—. Chair Princeton U. adv. bd. Sch. Architecture, 1991—; dir. Newhouse Archtl. Found., Chgo., 1991—. Designer, architect: Boston Globe Satellite Printing Plant, 1984, Mfrs. Hanover Plaza, Wilmington, 1987, Herman Miller Showroom, Chgo., 1988, Arlington Internat. Racecourse, 1989, Phila. Newspapers Espansion and Retrofit, 1989, Navy Pier R constrn., 1990, McCormick Place Retrofit and Expansion, 1991, L.A. Times Master Plan, 1992, CRSS capital project mgmt. Chgo. Park Dist., 1993, Chgo. Hist. Blvds. Restoration, 1993, Roosevelt Rd. Reconstruction, Chgo., 1993, Field, Shedd, Adler Mus. Campus, Goodman Theater, Chgo., 1995, Job Corps Tng. Campus, 1995, Chgo. area Circulator Urban Design, 1995, Cook County Hosp., 1996, Ft. Sherman Base, 1997, Girl Scouts Svc. Ctr., 1997, Michigan Ave. Renovation, 1997. Mem. bd. govs. Sch. of Art Inst., Chgo., 1991—; dir., past pres. Soc. for Contemporary Art, Chgo., 1991—. Recipient 40 under 40 award N.Y. Archtl. League, 1986; Urban Design award Progressive Architecture, 1984; named one of 100 Most Influential Women in Chgo., Crain's, 1996. Fellow AIA (Disting. Bldg. award 1983, Interiors award 1988, Nat. Urban Design award 1996); mem. NCARB, Am. Soc. Landscape Architects, Urban Land. Inst. Avocations: piano, flute, skiing, sailing, gardens. Office: DLK Architecture 410 S Michigan Ave Chicago IL 60605-1308

LEGGETT, ANTHONY J. education educator; b. London, 1938; Student, Balliol Coll., Oxford, Eng.; degree in physics, PhD in Theoretical Physics, Merton Coll. Mem. faculty U. Sussex (UK), 1967-71, reader, 1971-78, prof., 1978-83; John D. and Catherine T. Macarthur prof. U. Ill., Urbana-Champaign, 1983—. Rschr. Urbana, Ill., Kyoto, Japan; lectr. in field. Author: The Problems of Physics, 1987, Quantum Tunnelling in Condensed Media, 1992; contbr. articles to profl. jours. Achievements include research in condensed matter physics, high-temperature superconductivity, foundations of quantum mechanics. Office: U Ill 1110 W Green St Urbana IL 61801-9013

LE GRAND, CLAY, lawyer, former state justice; b. St. Louis, Feb. 26, 1911; s. Nicholas and Mary Margaret (Leifield) Le G.; m. Suzanne Wilcox, Dec. 30, 1935, (wid.); children: Mary Suzanne Le Grand Murray, Julie A. Le Grand Ekstrand, Nicholas W.; m. Margaret Morris Burrows, Dec. 11, 1993. Student, St. Ambrose Coll., Davenport, Iowa, 1928-31; LL.B., Catholic U. Am., 1934. Bar: Iowa 1934. Practice law, Davenport, 1934-57; judge Dist. Ct., 1957-67; justice Supreme Ct. Iowa, Davenport, 1967-83; of counsel Stanley, Rehling, Lande & Van Der Kamp, 1983-92, Noyes, O'Brien, Gosma and Brooke, Davenport, 1992-95, Noyes & Gosma, Davenport, 1995-98, Gosma & Gallagher, Davenport, 1998—. Lectr. St. Ambrose Coll., 1957-67 Recipient award for outstanding achievement in field of law and the cts. Cath. U. Am., 1969; award of merit for profl. achievement St. Ambrose Coll., 1976 Mem. Am., Iowa, Scott County bar assns., Am. Judicature Soc., Inst. Jud. Adminstrn. Home: 4130 Northwest Blvd Apt 32 Davenport IA 52806-4234 Office: Gosma & Gallagher 4301 E 53rd St # 300 Davenport IA 52807-3040

LEHMAN, GEORGE MORGAN, food sales executive; b. Chgo., Apr. 28, 1938; s. George Daniel and Margaret Marie (Cunningham) L.; m. Kathleen Marie Loftus, June 30, 1962; children: Robert Patrick, Daniel Joseph, Kathleen Marie, Michael Francis, William Terrance, Marilyn Elizabeth. BS, Marquette U., 1960; postgrad., Marquette Law Sch., 1962. Salesman, area mgr., city mgr. Am. Dist. Telegram Co., Chgo., 1964-79; security cons. A.I.C. Security Systesm, 1981-83; exec. acct. mgr. Murphy Butter & Egg Co., 1984-90; acct. exec. Badger/Murphy Food Svc., 1990—. Assoc. mem. Chef's De Cuisine, Chgo., 1985-97. V.p. Sch. Dist. 126, Oak Lawn, Ill.; coach, umpire, v.p. Oak Lawn Little League; coach YMCA Basketball, Oak Lawn Pk. Dist. Basketball. Recipient Those Who Excell in Edn. award Ill. Assn. Sch. Bds., 1991, Cert. of Achievement, 1992. Mem. Roosevelt Stamp Club, Beverly Stamp Club, Delta Sigma Pi. Roman Catholic. Avocations: stamps, basketball, darts. Home: 10733 Lawler Ave Oak Lawn IL 60453-5113 Office: Badger/Murphy Food Svc 700 N Western Ave Chicago IL 60612-1218 also: PO Box 228 Oak Lawn IL 60454-0228

LEHMAN, HARRY JAC, lawyer; b. Dayton, Ohio, Aug. 29, 1935; s. H. Jacques and Mildred (Benas) L.; m. Linda L. Rocker, June 7, 1964 (div. Mar. 1977); children: Sara Beth, Adam Henry, Matthew Daniel; m. Patricia L. Steele, Aug. 30, 1980; 1 child, Alexandra Steele. BA, Amherst Coll., 1957; JD, Harvard U., 1960. Bar: Ohio 1960. Assoc. Burke, Haber & Berick, Cleve., 1960-61, Falsgraf, Kundtz, Reidy & Shoup, Cleve., 1961-66, ptnr., 1967-70; of counsel Benesch, Friedlander, Coplan & Aronoff, 1971-80; ptnr. Jones, Day, Reavis & Pogue, Columbus, 1980-99. Adj. prof. law Ohio State U., Columbus, 1980-84, 86-87; mem. Bd. Bar Examiners, State of Ohio, Columbus, 1983-85. Contbr. articles to profl. jours. Mem. Ohio Ho. of Reps., Columbus, 1971-80; chmn. House Judiciary Com., 1975-80; mem. Ohio Elections Com., Columbus, 1983-88, State Underground Parking Com., Columbus, 1983-87, chmn., 1984-86. Served with USAR, 1960-66. Named one of Ten Outstanding Young Men, Cleve. Jaycees, 1968-69; recipient Disting. Service award NAACP, 1968, Outstanding Freshman Legislator award Ohio Legis. Correspondents Assn., 1971-72, Disting. Service award Ohio Edn. Assn., 1972, Most Effective Legislator award Ohio Legis. Correspondents Assn., 1973-74, Pub. Service award Ohio Pub. Defender Assn., 1974, Outstanding Pub. Service award Ohio Pub. Transit Assn., 1978, Disting. Service award ACLU Ohio Found., 1978, Most Effective Legislator 112th Gen. Assembly Ohio award Columbus Monthly Mag., 1980, Most Effective Legislator 113th Gen. Assembly Ohio award Columbus Monthly Mag. Mem. Ohio Bar Assn., Columbus Bar Assn., Cleve. Bar Assn., Columbus Athletic Club, New Albany Country Club. Democrat. Jewish. Avocations: reading, golf, family. Home: 2642 Charing Rd Columbus OH 43221-3628 Office: Jones Day Reavis & Pogue 41 S High St Ste 1900 Columbus OH 43215-6196

LEHMAN, JEFFREY SEAN, dean, law educator; b. Bronxville, N.Y., Aug. 1, 1956; s. Leonard and Imogene (McAuliffe) L.; m. Diane Celeste Becker, May 20, 1979; children: Rebecca Colleen, Jacob Keegan, Benjamin Emil. AB, Cornell U., 1977; M of Pub. Policy, JD, U. Mich., 1981. Bar: D.C. 1983, U.S. Ct. Appeals (fed. cir.) 1984, U.S. Ct. Appeals (D.C. cir.) 1987, U.S. Supreme Ct. 1987. Law clk. to chief judge U.S. Ct. Appeals (1st cir.), Portland, Maine, 1981-82; law clk. to assoc. justice U.S. Supreme Ct., Washington, 1982-83; assoc. Caplin & Drysdale, Chartered, 1983-87; asst. prof. U. Mich. Law Sch., Ann Arbor, 1987-92, prof., 1992-93, prof. law and pub. policy, 1993—, dean, 1994—. Vis. prof. Yale U., 1993, U. Paris II, 1994. Co-author: Corporate Income Taxation, 1994; editor-in-chief: Mich. Law Rev., 1979-80. Foster parent Arlington County Dept. Human Svcs., 1983-87; trustee Skadden Fellowship Found., 1995—. Henry Bates fellow, 1981. Mem. ABA, Am. Law Inst., Order of Coif. Democrat. Jewish. Office: U Mich Law Sch 324 Hutchins Hall 625 S State St Ann Arbor MI 48109-1215 E-mail: jlehman@umich.edu.

LEHMAN, MICHAEL A. state legislator; Mem. Wis. State Assembly Dist. 58, 1988—. Home: 1317 Honeysuckle Rd Hartford WI 53027-2614 Office: State Capitol Rm 103 West Madison WI 53708-0952

LEHMAN, RICHARD LEROY, lawyer; b. Johnstown, Pa., Feb. 4, 1930; s. John S. and Deliah E. (Chase) L.; m. Lucia M. Ragnone; children: Ann Laurie, Leslie Ann, Lucia Marie. AB in Social Work, U. Ky., 1957; LLB, U. Detroit, 1960. Bar: Mich. 1961, U.S. Dist. Ct. (ea. dist.) Mich. 1961, U.S. Ct. Appeals (6th cir.) 1961. Pvt. practice, Detroit; ptnr. Garan, Lucow, Miller, Lehman, Seward & Cooper, 1961-79; pres. Home Bldg. Plan Svc., Inc., Portland, Oreg., 1979-82; pres., gen. counsel Matvest Inc., Farmington Hills, Mich., 1980-86; pres. Xi Industries, Flint, 1982-86; ptnr. Lehman & Valentino, P.C., Bloomfield Hills, 1986—; pres. Premiere Packaging, Inc., Flint, 1987-91, chmn., CEO, 1990-98. Vis. lectr. U. Detroit Law Sch., 1970-74, also Inst. Continuing Legal Edn. Mem. exec. com. pres.'s cabinet U. Detroit, 1975-79; mem. Old Newsboys Goodfellow Fund Detroit, 1966—, bd. dirs., 1975-78. 1st lt. AUS, 1947-53. Recipient Algernon Sydney Sullivan Medallion U. Ky., 1957; fellow U. Ky. Mem. SAR, Mich. Bar Assn., Genesee County Bar Assn. (mem. bench and bar com. 1975-78), U. Ky. Alumni Assn., U. Detroit Law Sch. Alumni Assn. (dir. 1970-77, pres. 1974-75), U. Detroit Alumni Assn., 6th Cir. Jud. Conf. (life), Pine Lake Country Club (bd. dirs. 1991-96, pres. 1994-95), K.C., Am. Legion, VFW. Roman Catholic. Avocations: golf, downhill skiing, carpentry. Home: 6790 Telegraph Rd Bloomfield Township MI 48301 Office: Lehman & Valentino PC 43996 S Woodward Ave Bloomfield Hills MI 48302-0546

LEHMANN, RICHARD J. former banker; b. Portland, OR, 1944; BA, U. Wash., 1967, MBA, 1969. Trainee European div. Citibank, 1969-70, planning officer, 1970-71, sr. asst. mgr., 1971-72, gen. mgr. German ops., 1972-74, sr. rep., 1974-76, sr. officer ops. European div., 1976; pres., chief exec. officer Citicorp, 1977-85, sr. corp officer Europe, Africa, Mid. East, from 1985; pres. Valley Nat. Bank of Ariz. and Valley Nat. Corp., from 1988, now chmn. bd., chief exec. officer; vice-chmn. Bank One Corp., Columbus, 1998-99. Office: Bank One Corp 100 E Broad St Ste 1 Columbus OH 43215-3607

LEIBOWITZ, DAVID PERRY, lawyer; b. Bronx, N.Y., Jan. 21, 1950; s. Bernard B. and Annette (Friedman) L.; m. Teri H. Bandala, Aug. 22, 1971; children: Rachel, Saryn. BA in Econs., Northwestern U., 1970; JD cum laude, Loyola U., 1974. Bar: Ill. 1974, U.S. Dist. Ct. (no. dist) Ill. 1974, U.S. Ct. Appeals (7th cir.) 1974, U.S. Supreme Ct. 1982, U.S. Ct. Appeals (11th cir.) 1985. Assoc. Goebel & Kal, Chgo., 1974-75; judicial clerk Ill. Appellate Ct., 1975-76; ptnr. Schwartz, Cooper, Kolb & Gaynor, 1976-91, Freeborn & Peters, Chgo., 1992-99; pvt. practice Highland Park, 1999—. Adj. prof. John Marshall Law Sch., 1997—. Mem. bd. edn. Highland Park (Ill.) Sch. Dist., 1987-92; pres. bd. edn. North Shore Sch. Dist. 112, Highland Park, 1992-98; pres. bd. trustees Highland Park Pub. Libr., 1991-92. Mem. Am. Bankruptcy Inst., Ill. Bar Assn., Chgo. Bar Assn., Lake County Bar Assn. Office: Law Offices David P Leibowitz 222 Washington St Waukegan IL 60085-5618 E-mail: dpl@lakelaw.com.

LEICHTMAN, MARIA LUISA, mental health services professional; b. Philippines; B, Assumption Coll.; D of Clin. Psychology, U. Kans. With Irving Schwartz Inst. Children, Phila. Psychiat. Ctr., until 1979, Menninger, Topeka, 1979—, dir. child & adolscent residential treatment program, 1999—. Fulbright scholar. Office: Menninger PO Box 829 Topeka KS 66601-0829

LEIER, CARL VICTOR, internist, cardiologist; b. Bismarck, N.D., Oct. 20, 1944; married; 3 children. Grad., Creighton U., 1965, MD cum laude, 1969. Diplomate Am. Bd. Internal Medicine, Cardiovascular Medicine, Critical Care Medicine, Geriatric Medicine, Electrocardiography, Nat. Bd. Med. Examiners; lic. med., surgical Nebr., med. Ohio. Intern Ohio State U. Coll. Medicine, Columbus, 1969-70, med. resident (instr.) dept. medicine, 1971-73, chief resident (instr.), 1973-74, fellowship divsn. cardiology, 1974-76; pathology resident dept. pathology St. Vincent Hosp., Worcester, Mass., 1970-71; trainee NIH Tng. Grant, 1974-75; asst. prof. medicine cardiology dept., Ohio State U. Coll. Medicine, Columbus, 1976-80, asst. prof. pharmacology, 1976-80, assoc. prof., 1980-84, faculty mem. grad. sch., 1980—, dir. rsch. divsn. cardiology, 1980-83, James W. Overstreet prof. of medicine, 1983—, prof. of medicine divsn. cardiology, 1984—, prof. pharmacology, dept. pharmacology, 1984—, dir. divsn. cardiology, 1986-98. Hosp. procedures com. Ohio State U. Hosps., 1973-74; mem. pharmacology and therapeutics com. Ohio State U. Hosps., 1976-80; mem. rsch. com. ctrl. Ohio chpt. Am. Heart Assn., 1977-84, bd. trustees, 1979-88, exec. rsch. com., 1979-84, vice chmn. rsch. com., 1980-82, chmn. rsch. peer rev. com., 1982-84, v.p., 1984-86, pres. elect, 1986-88; numerous other coms.; cons. cardiorenal adv. bd. Smith-Kline Labs., 1982-85, com. on cardio-vascular rsch. and devel., 1982-85., AMA on Drugs and Tech., 1985—, FDA Cardiorenal adv. com. 1986-92, Lilly-Elanco devel. ractopamine, 1989; mem. ad hoc adv. com. on carvedilol in congestive heart failure, Smith, Kline and Beacham Pharms., 1991, ad hoc adv. com. on PDEI devel., McNeil Pharms., 1991, ad hoc adv. com. for clin. trials on Ibopamine, Zambon Pharms., 1993, sci. adv. com. Ohio State Univ. Brain Tumor Rsch. Ctr., 1993—, data safety monitoring bd., Otsuka Vesnarinone Trials, 1993— mem. chmn. Annual Sci. Sessions of the Am. Coll. of Cardiolog, 1996-97; vis. prof., lectr. and presenter at numerous sci. confs., insts. in U.S. and internationally. Editor: (book) Cardiotonic Drugs, 1986, 2d rev. edit., 1991; co-author: (with H. Boudoulas) CardioRenal Disorders and Diseases, 1986, 2d edit., 1992 (with J. Vincent) Critical Care Medicine: Recent Advances in Cardiovascular Medicine, 1990; contbr. more than 40 chpts. to other medical books and almost 200 articles to peer reviewed jours. including: Vascular Surgery, Archives of Internal Medicine, Circulation, Brit. Heart Jour., Jour. Electrocardiology, Clinical Pharmacologic Therapy, Chest, Am. Jour. Medicine, Jour. Cardiovascular Pharmacology, Am. Heart Jour., Geriatrics, Annals of Internal Medicine and others; editor in chief Congestive Heart Failure: Index and Revs., 1988—; mem. editorial bds. of ten medical jours. concerned with heart diseases, the review bds. of others including New Eng. Jour. Medicine, Internat. Jour. Cardiology, Jour. of Lab. and Clin. Medicine. Recipient Upjohn award, 1969, Lange Scholar award, 1969, Golden Apple Student Tchg. award, 1973, 75, Young Investigator award Ctrl. Ohio Heart Chpt., Am. Heart Assn., 1976-78, Rsch. Recognition award, 1978; named One of Best Doctors of Columbus, Columbus Monthly, 1992. Fellow Am. Coll. Clin. Pharmacology, Coun. on Clin. Pharmacology, Am. Heart Assn., Am. Coll. Cardiology, Am. Coll. Physicians, Coun. on Geriatric Cardiology; mem. AAAS, Ohio State Med. Assn., Am. Fedn. for Clin. Rsch., Ctrl. Soc. for Clin. Rsch., Am. Soc. Clin. Investigation, Assn. Univ. Cardiologists, Internat. Soc. for Heart Rsch., Internat. Soc. Cardiovascular Pharmacotherapy, Assn. Profs. of Cardiology. Office: Ohio State U Med Ctr Divsn Cardiology 1654 Upham Dr Columbus OH 43210-1250

LEIGH, SHERREN, communications executive, editor, publisher; b. Cleve., Dec. 22, 1942; d. Walter Carl Maurushat and Treva Eldora (Burke) Morris; m. Norman J. Hickey Jr., Aug. 23, 1969 (div. 1985). BS, Ohio U., 1965. Communications dir. Metal Lath Assn., Cleve., 1965-67; creative dir. O'Toole Inc., Chgo., 1967-69; sr. v.p. RLC Inc., 1969-77; pres. Leigh Communications Inc., 1978—; chmn. Today's Chgo. Woman mag., 1982—. Pres. Ill. Ambassadors, Chgo., 1985-86; bd. dirs. Chgo. Fin. Exchange, 1985-87. Author: How to Write a Winning Resume, How to Negotiate for Top Dollar, How to Find, Get and Keep the Job You Want. Bd. dirs. Midwest Women's Ctr., Chgo., 1984-86, Girl Scouts Chgo., 1985-87, Black Women's Hall of Fame Found., Chgo., 1986—, Apparel Industry Bd., Chgo., 1988, Auditorium Theater of Roosevelt U.; pres. Today's Chgo. Woman Found., 1998; mem. adv. bd. Salvation Army, 1998. Recipient Corp. Leadership award YWCA Met. Chgo., 1979, Entrepreneurship award, 1988, Media Advocate of Yr. award U.S. SBA, 1994, Achievement award Network of Women Entrepreneurs, 1998, Golden Heart award Ill Assn. Non-Profit Orgns., 1998, Women with A Vision award Women's Bar Assn. Ill., 1998; named one of 10 Women of Achievement Midwest Women's Ctr., Chgo., 1987, Advt. Woman of Yr. Women's Advt. Club, Chgo., 1988; inducted City of Chgo. Women's Hall of Fame, 1988. Mem. Chgo. Network, Econ. Club Chgo., Execs. Club Chgo., Com. of 200 (founding mem.). Office: Leigh Communications Inc 150 E Huron St Ste 1225 Chicago IL 60611-2872 E-mail: sleigh@todayschicagowomen.com.

LEIGHTON, GEORGE NEVES, retired federal judge; b. New Bedford, Mass., Oct. 22, 1912; s. Antonio N. and Anna Sylvia (Garcia) Leitao; m. Virginia Berry Quivers, June 21, 1942; children: Virginia Anne, Barbara Elaine. AB, Howard U., 1940; LLB, Harvard U., 1946; LLD, Elmhurst Coll., 1964; LLD., John Marshall Law Sch., 1973; LLD, Southeastern Mass. U., 1975, New Eng. U. Sch. Law, 1978, R.I. Coll., 1992, So. New Eng. Sch. Law, 2000; LLD (hon.), Loyola U., Chgo., 1989. Bar: Mass. 1946, Ill. 1947, U.S. Supreme Ct. 1958. Ptnr. Moore, Ming & Leighton, Chgo., 1951-59, McCoy, Ming & Leighton, Chgo., 1959-64; judge Cook County Circuit Ct., 1964-69, Ill. Appeals Ct. (1st cir.), 1969-76; U.S. dist. judge U.S. Dist. Ct. (no. dist.) Ill., 1976-86, sr. dist. judge, 1986-87; ret.; of counsel Earl L. Neal & Assocs., 1987—. Adj. prof. John Marshall Law Sch., Chgo., 1965—; commr., mem. character and fitness com. for 1st Appellate Dist., Supreme Ct. Ill., 1955-63, chmn. character and fitness com., 1961-62; joint com. for revision Ill. Criminal Code, 1959-63; chmn. Ill. adv. com. U.S. Commn. on Civil Rights, 1964; mem. pub. rev. bd. UAW, AFL-CIO, 1961-70; Asst. atty. gen. State of Ill., 1950-51; pres. 3d Ward Regular Democratic Orgn., Cook County, Ill., 1951-53; v.p. 21st Ward, 1964; spl. counsel to chmn. bd. Chgo. Transit Authority, 1988. Contbr. articles to legal jours. Bd. dirs. United Ch. Bd. for Homeland Ministries, United Ch. of Christ, Grant Hosp., Chgo.; trustee U. Notre Dame, 1979-83, trustee emeritus, 1983—; bd. overseers Harvard Coll., 1983-89. Capt., inf. AUS, 1942-45. Decorated Bronze Star; recipient Civil Liberties award Ill. div. ACLU, 1961, U.S. Supreme Ct. Justice John Paul Stevens award, 2000, Father Agustus Tolton awardCath. Archdioceses Chgo., 2000; named Chicagoan of Year in Law and Judiciary Jr. Assn. Commerce and Industry, 1964, Laureate, Acad. Ill. Lawyers, 2000. Fellow ABA (chmn. coun. 1976, mem. coun. sect. legal edn. and admissions to bar), Am. Coll. Trial Lawyers; mem. NAACP (chmn. legal redress com. Chgo. br.), John Howard Assn. (bd. dirs.), Chgo. Bar Assn., Ill. Bar Assn. (joint com. mem. for revision jud. article 1959-62, sr. counselor 1996), Nat. Harvard Law Sch. Assn. (mem. coun.), Howard U. Chgo. Alumni Club (chmn. bd. dirs.), Phi Beta Kappa. Office: Earl L Neal & Assocs 111 W Washington St Ste 1700 Chicago IL 60602-2711

LEIGHTON, ROBERT JOSEPH, state legislator; b. Austin, Minn., July 7, 1965; s. Robert Joseph Sr. and JoAnn (Mulvihill) L. BA, U. Minn., 1988; JD, U. Calif., Berkeley, 1991. Minn. state rep. Dist. 27B, 1995—. Presdl. and Waller scholar U. Minn., 1988. Mem. ABA, Minn. Bar Assn., Minn. Trial Lawyers Assn., Phi Beta Kappa. Home: 900 4th St NW Austin MN 55912-2001 Office: Leighton Meany Cotter & Enger 601 N Main St Austin MN 55912-3319

LEIKEN, EARL MURRAY, lawyer; b. Cleve., Jan. 19, 1942; s. Manny and Betty G. L.; m. Ellen Kay Miner, Mar. 26, 1970; children: Jonathan, Brian. BA magna cum laude, Harvard U., 1964, JD cum laude, 1967. Asst. dean, assoc. prof. law Case Western Res. U., Cleve., 1967-71; ptnr. Hahn, Loeser, Freedheim, Dean & Wellman, 1971-86, Baker & Hostetler, Cleve., 1986—. Adj. faculty, lectr. law Case Western Res. U., 1971-86. Pres. Shaker Heights (Ohio) Bd. Edn., 1986-88, Jewish Community Ctr., Cleve., 1988-91, Shaker Heights Family Ctr., 1994-97; mem. Shaker Heights City Coun., 2000—. Named one of Greater Cleve.'s 10 Outstanding Young Leaders, Cleve. Jaycees, 1972; recipient Kane award Cleve. Jewish Community Fedn., 1982. Mem. ABA, Greater Cleve. Bar Assn. (chmn. labor law sect. 1978). Home: 20815 Colby Rd Cleveland OH 44122-1903 Office: Baker & Hostetler 3200 Nat City Ctr 1900 E 9th St Ste 3200 Cleveland OH 44114-3475

LEINENWEBER, HARRY D. federal judge; b. Joliet, Ill., June 3, 1937; s. Harry Dean and Emily (Lennon) L.; m. Lynn Morley Martin, Jan. 7, 1987; 5 children; 2 stepchildren. AB cum laude, U. Notre Dame, 1959; JD, U. Chgo., 1962. Bar: Ill. 1962, U.S. Dist. Ct. (no. dist.) Ill. 1967. Assoc. Dunn, Stefanich, McGarry & Kennedy, Joliet, Ill., 1962-65, ptnr., 1965-79; city atty. City of Joliet, 1963-67; spl. counsel Village of Park Forest, Ill., 1967-74; spl. prosecutor County of Will, 1968-70; spl. counsel Village of Bolingbrook, 1975-77, Will County Forest Preserve, 1977; mem. Ill. Ho. of Reps., Springfield, 1973-83, chmn. judiciary I com., 1981-83; ptnr. Dunn, Leinenweber & Dunn, Joliet, 1979-86; fed. judge U.S. Dist. Ct. (no. dist.) Ill., Chgo., 1986—. Bd. dirs. Will County Bar Assn., 1984-86, State Jud. Adv. Coun., 1973-85, sec. 1975-76; tchr. legis. process seminar U. Ill., Chgo., 1988-2001; coord. U. Ill. Disting. Lecture Series, 2002--; mem. U. Ill. Inst. Govt. and Pub. Affairs Nat. Adv. Com., 1998—. Bd. dirs. Will County Legal Assistance Found., 1982-86, Good Shepard Manor, 1981—, Am. Cancer Soc., 1981-85, Joliet (Ill.) Montessori Sch., 1966-74; del. Rep. Nat. Conv., 1980; precinct committeeman, 1966-86; mem. nat. adv. com. U. Ill. Inst. Govt. and Pub. Affairs, 1998-2001. Recipient Environ. Legislator Golden award. Mem. Will County Bar Assn. (mem. jud. adv. coun., 1973-85, sec. 1975-76, bd. dirs. 1984-86), Nat. Conf. Commrs. on Uniform State Laws (exec. com. 1991-93, elected life mem. 1996), The Law Club of Chgo. (bd. dirs. 1996-98). Roman Catholic. Office: US Dist Ct 219 S Dearborn St Ste 1946 Chicago IL 60604-1801

LEINIEKS, VALDIS, classicist, educator; b. Liepaja, Latvia, Apr. 15, 1932; came to U.S., 1949, naturalized, 1954; s. Arvid Ansis and Valia Leontine (Brunaus) L. BA, Cornell U., 1955, MA, 1956; PhD, Princeton U., 1962. Instr. classics Cornell Coll., Mount Vernon, Iowa, 1959-62, asst. prof. classics, 1962-64; assoc. prof. classics Ohio State U., 1964-66, U. Nebr., Lincoln, 1966-71, prof. classics, 1971—, chmn. dept. classics, 1967-95, chmn. program comparative lit., 1970-86, interim chmn. dept. modern langs., 1982-83. Author: Morphosyntax of the Homeric Greek Verb, 1964; The Structure of Latin, 1975; Index Nepotianus, 1976; The Plays of Sophokles, 1982, The City of Dionysos, 1996. Contbr. articles to profl. jours. Mem. AAUP, Am. Classical League, Classical Assn. Middle West and South, Am. Philol. Assn. Home: 2505 A St Lincoln NE 68502-1841 Office: U Nebr Dept Classics Lincoln NE 68588-0337

LEININGER, MADELEINE MONICA, nursing educator, editor, writer; b. Sutton, Nebr., July 13, 1925; d. George M. S. and D. Irene (Sheedy) L. BS in Biology, Scholastic Coll., 1950, LHD, 1976; MS in Nursing, Cath. U. Am., 1953; PhD in Anthropology, U. Wash., 1965; DSc (hon.), U. Indpls., 1990; PhDN (hon.), 1990, U. Kuopio, Finland, 1991. RN; cert. transcultural nurse FAAN/Am. Acad. Nursing. Instr., mem. staff, head nurse med.-surg. unit, supr. psychiat. unit St. Joseph's Hosp., Omaha, 1950-54; assoc. prof. nursing, dir. grad. program in psychiat. nursing U. Cin. Coll. Nursing, 1954-60; research fellow Nat. League Nursing, Eastern Highlands of New Guinea, 1960-62, 78, 92; research assoc. U. Wash. Dept. Anthropology, Seattle, 1964-65; prof. nursing and anthropology, dir. nurse-scientist PhD program U. Colo., Boulder and Denver, 1966-69; dean sch. nursing, prof. nursing, lectr. anthropology U. Wash., Seattle, 1969-74; dean coll. nursing, prof. nursing and anthropology U. Utah, Salt Lake City, 1974-80; Anise J. Sorell prof. nursing Troy (Ala.) State U., 1981; prof. nursing, adj. prof. anthropology, dir. Ctr. for Health Research, dir. transcultural nursing offerings Wayne State U., Detroit, 1981-95, prof. emeritus, 1995—; prof. Coll. Nursing U. Nebr. Med. Ctr., 1997—2001; ret., 2001—. Adj. prof. anthropology U. Utah, 1974-81; adj. prof. nursing U. Nebr., 1997—; disting. vis. prof. over 85 univs., U.S. and overseas, 1970—; transcultural nursing cons. Saudi Arabia, Brazil, Europe, Japan, China, Burnei, Indonesia, South Africa, Sweden, The Netherlands, New Guinea, Australia, Jordan, Thailand, Russia, Iran, Africa, Taiwan, Portugal, Switzerland, Puerto Rico, Norway, Phuket, 60 health instns. in U.S., numerous others. Author: 28 books including Nursing and Anthropology:

Two Worlds to Blend, 1970, Contemporary Issues in Mental Health Nursing, 1973, Caring: An Essential Human Need, 1981, Reference Sources for Transcultural Health and Nursing, 1984, Basic Psychiatric Concepts in Nursing, 1960, Care: The Essence of Nursing and Health, 1984, Qualitative Research Methods in Nursing, 1985, Care: Discovery and Clinical-Community Uses, 1988, Ethical and Moral Dimensions of Caring, 1990, Culture Care, Diversity and Universality: A Theory of Nursing, 1991, 2002, Care: The Compassionate Healer, 1991, Caring Imperative for Nursing Education, 1991, Transcultural Nursing 2d edit., 1995, Transcultural Nursing Concepts, Theories, Research and Practice, 3d edit., 2002; editor, founder Jour. of Transcultural Nursing, 1988-2000; contbr. over 210 articles to profl. jours., chpts. to books. Recipient Outstanding Alumni award Cath. U. Am., 1969, hon. award Am. Assn. Colls. of Nursing, 1976, 96, Nurse of Yr. award Dist. 1 Utah Nurses Assn., 1976, Lit. award Utah Nurses Assn., 1978, Trotter Disting. Pub. Lectr. award U. Tex., 1985, Disting. Faculty Tchg. Recognition award Wayne State U., 1985, Outstanding Faculty Rsch. scholar award Wayne State U. and Gerontology Inst., 1985, Gershenson Rsch. award Wayne State U., 1985, Pace Inst. Rsch. award, 1992, Hewlett Packard Rsch. award, 1992, award for Acad. Excellence AAUW-Detroit, 1986, Disting. award Bd. Govs., 1987, Pres. Excellence in Tchg. award, 1988, Women of Sci. award U. Calif. at Fullerton, 1990, Outstanding Univ. Grad. Mentor award Wayne State U., 1995, Nightingale Rsch. award Oakland U., 1995, outstanding nursing leader Russell Sage Coll, Sigma Theta Tau Intl. Disting. scholar award Russell Sage Coll., 1995, Nobel prize nominee, 1999; Leininger Learning and Transcultural Nursing Collection libr. and reading sects. at Madonna U., Livonia, Mich. named in her honor, 1996; Leininger Archival Room at Trinity Coll., Moline, Ill. named in her honor, 2002; Mary Boynton Disting. lectr., 1998; Disting. vis. scholar Jimmy Crockett Lectr. Series, Disting. Vis. scholar U. Nebr., 1999; named Disting. scholar U. Wis., 2001, 2002; Worldwide Transcultural Nursing Ctr. named in her honor, 2001. Fellow ANA, Am. Anthropol. Soc. for Applied Anthropology (exec. com. 1980-84), Am. Acad. Nursing (Living Legend award 1998), Royal Coll. Nursing Australia (First Internat. Achievement award 2000); mem. Am. Assn. Humanities, Am. Applied Anthropol. Soc., Royal Coll. Nursing Australia, Mich. Nurses Assn. (Bertha Culp Human Rights award 1994), Ctrl. States Anthropology, Amnesty Internat., Transcultural Nursing Soc. (founder, bd. dirs., pres. 1974-80), Cultural Cmty. Group Assn. (ethics, humanities heritage study group), Nat. Rsch. Care Confs. (leader human care rsch.), Internat. Assn. Human Caring (founder, pres., bd. dirs.), Nordic Caring Soc. Sweden (hon.), Sigma Xi, Pi Gamma Mu, Sigma Theta Tau (Lectr. of Yr. 1987—), Delta Kappa Gamma, Alpha Tau Delta. Office: 11211 Woolworth Plz Omaha NE 68144-1875

LEISTEN, ARTHUR GAYNOR, lawyer; b. Chgo., Oct. 17, 1941; s. Arthur Edward Leisten and Mary (Francis) Gaynor; m. Florence T. Kelly, May 11, 1968; children: Thomas, Hillary. AB magna cum laude, Loyola U., Chgo., 1963; JD, Harvard U., 1966; grad. exec. mgmt. program, Northwestern U., Chgo., 1983 and 1986, Pa. State U., 1985. Bar: Ill. 1966, U.S. Dist. Ct. (no. dist.) Ill. 1967, U.S. Ct. Appeals 1967. Assoc. prof. Sch. Law Loyola U., 1966-69; assoc. Chadwell & Kayser, Ltd., Chgo., 1969-74; staff atty. Texaco, Inc., 1974-75; atty. USG Corp., 1975-78, sr. atty., 1978-82, sr. gen. atty., 1982-85, assoc. gen. counsel, 1985, v.p., assoc. gen. counsel, 1985-86, v.p., gen. counsel, 1986-90, sr. v.p., gen. counsel, 1990-93, sr. v.p., gen. counsel, sec., 1993—. Mem. ABA (corp. counsel com.), Chgo. Bar Assn., Am. Corp. Counsel Assn., Univ. Club, Law Club (Chgo.), Mich. Shores Club (Wilmette, Ill.), Westmoreland Country Club. Office: USG Corp PO Box 6721 125 S Franklin St Fl 2 Chicago IL 60606-4678

LEITCH, DAVID R. state legislator; b. Three Rivers, Mich., Aug. 22, 1948; m. Marlene Leitch; three children. BA, Kalamazoo Coll., 1970. Dist. 47 senator Ill. Senate, Springfield, 1986-87; Dist. 93 rep. Ill. Ho. Reps., 1988—. Asst. majority leader, mem. appropriations II, utilities, environ. and energy, rules, Medicaid, labor and commerce, reapportionment, and legis. rsch. unit coms., Ill. Ho. Reps. Mem. Rep. ctrl. and fin. coms., Peoria County, Ill., 1975—; v.p. First of Am.-Ill. Named Outstanding Young Man in Peoria; recipient Disting. Svc. award, 1981. Mem. Inst. Physical Medicine, Heartland Health Clinic, United Way, Komen Found., Rotary. Address: 5921 N Cypress Dr Apt 1602 Peoria IL 61615-2627 Also: 3114 N University St Peoria IL 61604-1317

LEITH, EMMETT NORMAN, b. Detroit, Mar. 12, 1927; s. Albert Donald and Dorothy Marie (Emmett) Leith; m. Lois June Neswold, Feb. 17, 1956; children: Kim Ellen, Pam Elizabeth. BS, Wayne State U., 1950, MS, 1952, PhD, 1978; DSc (hon.) , U. Aberdeen, Scotland, 1996. Mem. rsch. staff U. Mich., 1952—, prof. elec. engring., 1968—. Cons. several indsl. corps. Contbr. articles to profl. jours. With USNR, 1945—46. Named Man of Yr., Indsl. Rsch. mag., 1966; recipient Gordon Meml. award, SPIE, 1965, citation, Am. Soc. Mag. Photographers, 1966, Achievement award, U.S. Camera and Travel mag., 1967, Excellence of Paper award, Soc. Motion Picture and TV Engrs., 1967, Daedalion award, 1968, Stuart Ballantine medal, Franklin Inst., 1969, Alumni award, Wayne State U., 1974, cited by Nobel Prize Commn. for contbns. to holography, 1971, Holley medal, ASME, 1976, Nat. medal of Sci., 1979, Russel lecture award, U. Mich., 1981, Denins Gabor medal, Soc. Photo-Instrumentation Engrs., 1983, Gold medal, 1990, Mich. Trailblazer award, 1986. Fellow: IEEE (Liebmann award 1967, Inventor of Yr. award 1976), Optical Soc. Am. (Wood medal 1975, Herbert Ives medal 1985), The Royal Photographic Soc. of Great Britain (hon.), Engring. Soc. Detroit (hon.); mem.: NAE, Sigma Pi Sigma, Sigma Xi. Achievements include patents in field;first demonstrating (with colleague) capability of holography to form high-quality 3-dimensional image. Home: 51325 Murray Hill Dr Canton MI 48187-1030 Office: Univ Mich Inst Sci and Tech PO Box 618 Ann Arbor MI 48106-0618 E-mail: leith@umich.edu.

LEIWEKE, TOD, professional sports team executive; m. Tara Leiweke; children: Tyler, Tori. Prin. Leiweke & Co., Kansas City, 1982—87; v.p. mktg. and broadcasting Golden State Warriors, NBA, 1987—91, pres. arena devel. co., 1994; exec. v.p. Orca Bay Sports and Entertainment; exec. dir. First Tee, World Golf Found.; pres. Minn. Wild Minn. Hockey Ventures Group LP, St. Paul, 1999—2001, COO, 2001—. Office: 317 Washington St Saint Paul MN 55102

LELAND, BURTON, state legislator; b. Detroit, Nov. 24, 1948; s. Morris Leland and Beatrice (Bernstein) L.; m. Rosanne Letvin; children: Zachary Levi, Gabriel Daniel. BS, Wayne State U., 1971; MSW, U. Mich., 1977. Social worker Wayne County Dept. Social Svc., 1972-80; state rep. Dist. 13 Mich. Ho. of Reps., 1981-98; mem. Mich. Senate from 5th dist., Lansing, 1999—. Mem. Joint Com. on Adminstrv. Rules, Elec. Consumers, Pub. Health & Transp. Coms. Mich. Ho. of Reps.; vice-chmn. Tourism, Fisheries & Wildlife Com. Mem. NASW, Nat. Conf. State Legislators, Alpha Epsilon Pi. Home: 17254 Bentler St Detroit MI 48219-4746 Office: 315 Farnum Bldg PO Box 30036 Lansing MI 48909-7536

LELAND, DAVID J. political association executive; m. Cindy Leland; children: Ben, Maria. BA, Ohio State U., 1975; JD, Capital U., 1978. Committeeman 19th ward Dem. Com., 1972—; vice-chmn. Franklin County Dem. Com., 1972-77; state assemblyman dist. 28 Ohio State Assembly, 1983-84; alt. del. Nat. Dem. Conv., 1988; fin. dir. polit. campaigns Mayor candidate Ben Epsy, Columbus, 1991-94, Coun. Pres. Cynthia Lazarus, 1991-94, Atty. Gen. Lee Fisher, 1991-94; rep. State of Ohio Nat. Dem. Conv. Platform com., 1992; chmn. Dem. Nat. Conv., 1996, mem. Rules & By-Laws com., 1996—; del. State of Ohio Dem. State Party, 1996—; chmn. Ohio Dem. State Party, 1996—; staff coun. Ohio Civil Svc. Employees Assn., 1980-82. Instr. bus. and govt. law Columbus Tech. Inst., 1983-84; atty. Gibson and Robbins-Penniman, 1985-86, Schwartz, Warren and Ramirez, 1991-96; dir. transp. dept. Pub. Utilities Commn., Ohio, 1986-90. Named one of Ten Outstanding Young Citizens, Columbus Jaycees, 1975, 79, Dem. of Yr. Franklin County Dem. Party, 1982, Outstanding Freshman State Rep. Columbus Monthly Mag., 1983-84. Office: OH Democratic Party 271 E State St Columbus OH 43215-4330

LEMAIRE, JACQUES, professional hockey coach; b. Lasalle, Que., Can., Sept. 7, 1945; Player Montreal Canadiens, 1967-79, head coach, 1983-85; head coach, player Sierre Hockey Club, Switzerland, 1979-81; asst. coach SUNY Coll., Plattsburgh, 1981-82; coach Longueuil Chevaliers, maj. jr. league, Que., 1982-83; dir. of hockey pers. Montreal Canadiens, 1985-87, asst. to mng. dir., 1987-93; head coach N.J. Devils, 1993-98; cons. to gen. mgr. Montreal Canadiens, 1998-00; head coach Minnesota Wild, Saint Paul, 2000—. Mem. Stanley Cup Championship teams, 1968, 69, 71, 73, 76-79. Named NHL Coach of Yr., Sporting News, 1993, 94. Address: Minn Wild Piper Jaffray Tower 444 Cedar St Ste 900 Saint Paul MN 55101-2126

LEMAN, EUGENE D. meat industry executive; b. Peoria, Ill., Dec. 1, 1942; s. Vernon L. and Viola L. (Beer) L.; m. Carolyn Leman, June 14, 1964; children— Jill C., Jennifer A. B.S., U. Ill., 1964. Dir. various depts. Wilson Foods, Oklahoma City, 1964-78, v.p. fresh and processed pork, 1978-80, v.p. fresh meat group, 1980-81; group v.p. IBP, Inc., Dakota City, Nebr., 1981-86, exec. v.p., 1986—, also bd. dirs., CEO. Mem. Am. Meat Inst. (chmn. pork com. 1980-81), Nat. Pork Producers Council (packer rep. Pork Value Task Force 1981-82, 88, pork export com. 1985) Republican. Club: Sioux City Country (Iowa) Office: IBP Inc Ste 820 800 Stevens Port Dr Dakota Dunes SD 57049-5005

LEMANSKE, ROBERT F., JR. allergist, immunologist; b. Milw., 1948; MD, U. Wis., 1975. Diplomate Am. Bd. Pediats., Am. Bd. Allergy and Immunology. Intern U. Wis. Hosp., Madison, 1975-76, resident in pediats., 1976-78, prof. pediats. medicine, divsn. head pediat. allergy, immunology & rheumatology. Fellow: Am. Acad. Allergy and Immunology, Am. Acad. Pediat. Office: Clin Sci Ctr Rm K4/916 600 Highland Ave Madison WI 53792-0001

LE MASTER, DENNIS CLYDE, natural resource economics and policy educator; b. Startup, Wash., Apr. 22, 1939; s. Franklin Clyde and Delores Ilene (Schwartz) Le M.; m. Kathleen Ruth Dennis, Apr. 4, 1961; children: Paul, Matthew. BA, Wash. State U., 1961, MA, 1970, PhD, 1974. Asst. prof. dept. forestry and range mgmt. Wash. State U., Pullman, 1972-74, assoc. prof., 1978-80, prof., chair dept., 1980-88; prof., head dept. forestry and natural resources Purdue U., West Lafayette, Ind., 1988—; dir. resource policy Soc. Am. Foresters, Bethesda, Md., 1974-76; staff counsel subcom. on forests Ho. of Reps., Washington, 1977-78. Cons. USDA Forest Svc., Washington, 1978, Com. on Agr., Ho. of Reps., 1979-80, Forest History Soc., Durham, N.C., 1979-83, The Conservation Found., 1989-90, Office Tech. Assessment, Washington, 1989-91, Consultative Group on Biol. Diversity, 1991. Author: Decade of Change, 1984; co-editor 8 books; contbr. articles to profl. jours. Bd. dirs. Pinchot Inst. for Conservation, treas., 1996-97, vice-chair, 1998-99, chair, 2000-01. Mem. AAAS, Soc. Am. Foresters (coun. 1988, chair house of soc. dels. 1982), Inland Empire Soc. of Soc. Am. Foresters (chair 1980-81, Forester of Yr. award 1982, fellow 2000), Soc. for Range Mgmt., Forest Products Soc., Omicron Delta Epsilon, Beta Gamma Sigma, Epsilon Sigma Phi, Xi Sigma Pi. Democrat. Episcopalian. Avocation: fishing. Home: 824 Lazy Ln Lafayette IN 47904-2722 Office: Purdue U Dept Forestry and Natural Resources West Lafayette IN 47907

LEMAY, RONALD T. telecommunications industry executive; Pres., chief oper. officer long distance div. U.S. Sprint, Westwood, Kans. Office: US Sprint 2330 Shawnee Mission Pkwy Shawnee Mission KS 66205

LEMBERGER, LOUIS, pharmacologist, physician; b. Monticello, N.Y., May 8, 1937; s. Max and Ida (Siegel) L.; m. Myrna Sue Diamond, 1959; children: Harriet Felice Schor, Margo Beth. BS magna cum laude, Bklyn. Coll. Pharmacy, L.I. U., 1960; PhD in Pharmacology, Albert Einstein Coll. Medicine, 1964, MD, 1968; Doctorate (hon.), L.I. U., 1994. Pharmacy intern VA Regional Office, Newark, summer 1960; postdoctoral fellow Albert Einstein Coll. Medicine, 1964-68; intern in medicine Met. Hosp. Center, N.Y. Med. Coll., N.Y.C., 1968-69; rsch. assoc. NIH, Bethesda, Md., 1969-71; clin. pharmacologist Lilly Lab. for Clin. Rsch., Eli Lilly & Co., Indpls., 1971-75, chief clin. pharmacology, 1975-78, dir. clin. pharmacology, 1978-89, clin. rsch. fellow, 1982-93; asst. prof. pharmacology Ind. U., 1972-73, asst. prof. medicine, 1972-73, assoc. prof. pharmacology, 1973-77, assoc. prof. medicine, 1973-77, prof. pharmacology, 1977—, prof. medicine, prof. psychiatry, 1977—, mem. grad. faculty, 1975—; adj. prof. clin. pharmacology Ohio State U., 1975-86; physician Wishard Meml. Hosp., 1976-98. Cons. U.S. Nat. Commn. on Marijuana and Drug Abuse, 1971-73, Can. Commn. Inquiry into Non-Med. Use of Drugs, 1971-73; mem. Pharm. Mfrs. Assn. Commn. on Medicines for Drug Dependence and Abuse, 1990-93, Ind. Optometric Legend Drug Adv. Com., 1991-96; guest lectr. various univs., 1968—; lectr. U. Minn., 1993—; mem. adv. com. Faseb Life Scis. Rsch. Office, 1993-96. Author: (with A. Rubin) Physiologic Disposition of Drugs of Abuse, 1976; contbr. numerous articles on biochemistry and pharmacology to sci. jours.; editorial bd.: Excerpta Medica, 1972-96, Clin. Pharmacology and Therapeutics, 1976-96, Communications in Psychopharmacology, 1975-91, Pharmacology, Interant. Jour. Exptl. and Clin. Pharmacology, 1978-94, Drug and Alcohol Abuse Rsch., 1979-86, Drug Devel. Rsch., 1980-87, Trends in Pharmcol. Scis., 1980-85. Post adviser Crossroads of Am. coun. Boy Scouts Am., 1972-77. With USPHS, 1969-71. Recipient Disting. Alumnus award Albert Einstein Coll. Medicine, 1989, Disting. Alumnus award L.I. U., 1990, Pres. award L.I. U., 1998, Cornerstone award for Oustanding Lifetime Achievement in Health Scis., Am. Drugstore Mus., 2000. Fellow ACP, AAAS, Am. Coll. Neuropsychopharmacology (chmn. credentials com. 1993) , Am. Coll. Clin. Pharmacology; mem. Am. Soc. Pharmacology and Exptl. Therapeutics (com. div. clin. pharmacology 1972-78, chmn. com. 1978-83, coun. 1980-83, chmn. long-range planning com. 1984-86, pres. 1987-88, ASPET award in Therapeutics, 1985, Harry Gold award for rsch. and teaching excellence in clin. pharmacology 1993), Am. Soc. Clin. Pharmacology and Therapeutics (chmn. sect. neuropsychopharmacology 1973-80, chmn. fin. com. 1976-83, 89-92, v.p. 1981-82, pres. 1983-84, dir. 1975-81, 84-87, Rawls-Palmer award 1986, Henry Elliot Disting. Svc. award 1992), Am. Soc. Clin. Investigation, Collegium Internat. Neuro-Psychopharmacologicum, Am. Fedn. Clin. Rsch. Ctrl. Soc. Clin. Rsch., Soc. Neuroscis., Sigma Xi, Alpha Omega Alpha, Rho Chi. Jewish. Achievements include being first person to administer and study the actions in humans of the antidepressant drug Prozac (fluoxetine), Permax (pergolide) the drug used to treat Parkinson's disease, and the cannabinoid drug Cesamet (nabilone) utilized for the treatment of nausea and vomiting secondary to cancer chemotherapy and Zyprexa (Olanzepine) the drug utilized in schizophrenia; responsible for directing and spearheading the clinical development of Prozac, Permax and Cesamet through clinical trials, regulatory approval and eventually into the marketplace. Home: 3315 Walnut Creek Dr N Carmel IN 46032-9038 Office: Ind Univ Sch Medicine Dept Pharmacology and Medicine Indianapolis IN 46202

LE MENAGER, LOIS M. incentive merchandise and travel company executive; b. Cleve., Apr. 25, 1934; d. Lawrence M. and Lillian C. (Simicek) Stanek; m. Charles J. Blabolil (dec. 1982); children: Sherry L., Richard A.; m. Spencer H. Le Menager, Mar. 23, 1984. Grad. high sch. Travel counselor Mktg. Innovators, Rosemont, Ill., 1978-80, mktg. dir., 1980-82, chmn., CEO, owner, 1982—. Dir. Northwest Commerce Bank, Rosemont. Recipient Entrepreneurial Success award U.S. Small Bus. Adminstrn., 1999; named Supplier of Yr., J.C. Penney Co., Inc. Mem. NAFE, Am. Inst. Entrepreneurs (Entrepreneur of Yr. 1988), Am. Mktg. Assn., Internat. Soc. Mktg. Planners, Soc. Incentive Travel Execs., Am. Soc. Travel Agts., Nat. Fedn. Ind. Bus., Nat. Assn. Women Bus. Owners, Des Plaines C. of C., Rosemont C. of C., Chicagoland C. of C. (dir.), The Chgo. Network, Exec. Club (Chgo.). Congregationalist. Office: Mktg Innovators Internat Inc 9701 W Higgins Rd Des Plaines IL 60018-4703

LEMIEUX, JOSEPH HENRY, manufacturing company executive; b. Providence, Mar. 2, 1931; s. Mildred L. Lemieux; m. Frances Joanne Schmidt, Aug. 11, 1956; children: Gerald Joseph, Craig Joseph, Kimberly Mae Lemieux Wolff, Allison Jo. Student, Stonehill Coll., 1949-50, U. R.I., 1950-51; BBA summa cum laude, Bryant Coll., 1957. With Owens-Ill., Toledo, 1957—, various positions with glass container div. and closure and metal container group; exec. v.p. Owens-Ill. Owens-Ill., Inc., 1984, pres. pkg. ops., 1984, pres., COO, 1986-90, pres., CEO, 1990-91, chmn. bd., CEO, 1991—, also bd. dirs. Bd. dirs. Nat. City Bank Northwest, Toledo, Nat. City Corp., Cleve. Trustee Bryant Coll.; vice-chmn. bd. govs. Edison Indsl. Systems Ctr. U. Toledo, 1986. Staff sgt. USAF, 1951-55. Named one of Outstanding Young Men Am., Jaycees, 1965, Recipient glass industry's Phoenix award, 1997. Mem. Glass Packaging Inst. (chmn. 1984-86), Inverness Club (Toledo). Roman Catholic. Avocations: golf, tennis. Office: Owens-Illinois Inc 1 Seagate Toledo OH 43666-0001

LEMKE, ALAN JAMES, environmental specialist; b. Appleton, Wis., May 22, 1945; s. Edwin R. and Ethel Mae (Noe) L.; m. Joyce Eileen Kruse, May 24, 1975; 1 child, David Edwin. BS in chemistry, Coll. Idaho, 1968. Rsch. chemist Am. Med. Ctr., Denver, 1972-74; chemist U.S. Geol. Survey, 1975-77; chemist II Occupl. Health Lab., Portland, Oreg., 1977-80, State Hygienic Labs., Des Moines, 1980-82; indsl. hygienist Iowa Divsn. Labor, 1982-88; environ. specialist Iowa Dept. Natural Resources, Spencer, 1988—. Small bus. owner Al's Stamps and Collectables. Author: The Noe Family's Involvement in the Civil War: A History of Wisconsin's 19th Volunteer Infantry Regiment, 1994. Republican. Evangelical. Avocations: camping, hiking, fishing, history, reading. Home: 1110 15th Ave W Spencer IA 51301-2943 Office: Iowa Dept Natural Resources 1900 N Grand Ave Spencer IA 51301-2200

LEMMON, JEAN MARIE, editor-in-chief; b. Duluth, Minn., Nov. 11, 1932; d. Lawrence Howard and Marie Julien (Gunderson) H.; m. Richard LuVerne LemMon, Apr. 17, 1965 (div. 1976); 1 child, Rebecca Jean. BA, U. Minn., 1954. Editor Better Homes and Gardens Mag., Des Moines, 1961-63, dept. head crafts, 1985-86, editor-in-chief, 1993—; women's editor Successful Farming, 1963-68; pres. Jean LemMon & Assocs., 1968-84; project editor Meredith Pub. Svcs., 1984-85; editor-in-chief Country Home Mag., 1986-93. Adv. bd. Drake U. Journalism Sch., 1991—. Mem. ASCAP, Mensa Internat., Am. Soc. Interior Designers. Office: Better Homes and Gardens 1716 Locust St Des Moines IA 50309-3038

LEMPERT, RICHARD OWEN, lawyer, educator; b. Hartford, Conn., June 2, 1942; s. Philip Leonard and Mary (Steinberg) L.; m. Cynthia Ruth Willey, Sept. 10, 1967 (div.); 1 child, Leah Rose; m. Lisa Ann Kahn, May 26, 2002. AB, Oberlin Coll., 1964; JD, U. Mich., 1968, PhD in Sociology, 1971. Bar: Mich. 1978. Asst. prof. law U. Mich., Ann Arbor, 1968-72, assoc. prof., 1972-74, prof. law, 1974—, prof. sociology, 1985—, Francis A. Allen collegiate prof. law, 1990—2001, acting chair dept. sociology, 1993-94, chair dept. sociology, 1995-98, dir. life scis., values and soc. program, 2000—, Eric Stein Disting. Univ. prof. law and sociology, 2001—; dir. divsn. social and econ. scis. NSF, 2002—. Mason Ladd disting. vis. prof. U. Iowa Law Sch., 1981; vis. fellow Centre for Socio-Legal Rsch., Wolfson Coll., Oxford (Eng.) U., 1982; mem. adv. panel for law and social sci. div. NSF, 1976-79, mem. exec. com. adv. com. for social sci., 1979; mem. com. law enforcement and adminstrn. of justice NRC, vice chmn., 1984-87, chmn., 1987-89; mem. adv. panel NSF program on Human Dimensions of Global Change, 1989, 92-94; mem. com. on DNA technology in forensic sci. NRC, 1989-92, com. on drug testing in workplace, 1991-93; vis. scholar Russell Sage Found., 1998-99; vis. scholar Russell Sage Found., 1998-99. Author: (with Stepehn Saltzburg) A Modern Approach to Evidence, 1977, 2d edit., 1983, 3d edit. (with Sam Gross and James Liebman), 2000; (with Joseph Sanders) An Invitation to Law and Social Science, 1986, Under the Influence, 1993; editor: (with Jacques Normand and Charles O'Brien) Under the Influence? Drugs and the American Work Force, 1994; editorial bd. Law and Soc. Rev., 1972-77, 89-92, 98—, editor, 1982-85; mem. editl. bd. Evaluation Rev., 1979-82, Violence and Victims, 1985—, Jour. Law and Human Behavior, 1980-82; contbr. articles to profl. jours. Fellow Ctr. for Advanced Study in Behavioral Scis., 1994-95; vis. scholar Russell Sage Found., 1998-99. Fellow Am. Acad. Arts and Scis.; mem. Am. Sociol. Assn. (chair sect. sociology of law 1995-96), Law and Society Assn. (trustee 1977-80, 90-93, exec. com. 1979-80, 82-87), Order of Coif, Phi Beta Kappa, Phi Kappa Phi. Office: U Mich Law Sch 625 S State St Ann Arbor MI 48109-1215 E-mail: rol25@hotmail.com.

LEMPKE, MICHAEL R. treasurer; Sr. v.p., treas. Fort James Corp., Deerfield, Ill., 1998—. Office: Fort James Corp 1919 S Broadway Green Bay WI 54304-4905

LENGA, J. THOMAS, lawyer; b. Toledo, Dec. 16, 1942; s. Casimir M. and Rose C. (Sturniolo) L.; children by previous marriage: Christina M., John Thomas Jr., Peter M. BA, U. Toledo, 1965, JD, 1968. Bar: Mich. 1968, Ohio 1968. Capt. JAGC U.S. Army, 1968—72; mem. Dykema Gossett PLLC, Detroit, 1972-96, Clark Hill P.L.C., Detroit, 1996—, CEO, 2001—. Mem. com. on std. jury instrns. Mich. Supreme Ct.; advocate Am. Bd. of Trial Advocates. Named Disting. Alumnus, Coll. Law, U. Toledo, 1987. Fellow: Am. Coll. Trial Lawyers, Internat. Acad. Trial Lawyers; mem.: Internat. Assn. Def. Counsel, State Bar Mich. (bd. commrs. 1992—, treas. 1995—96, v.p. 1996—97, pres.-elect 1997—98, pres. 1998—99), Detroit Bar Assn. 1989—90. Office: Clark Hill PLC 500 Woodward Ave Ste 3500 Detroit MI 48226-3435 E-mail: tlenga@clarkhill.com.

LENKOSKI, LEO DOUGLAS, psychiatrist, educator; b. Northampton, Mass., May 13, 1925; s. Leo L. and Mary Agnes (Lee) L.; m. Jeannette Teare, July 12, 1952; children— Jan Ellen, Mark Teare, Lisa Marie, Joanne Lee. A.B., Harvard, 1948, spl. student, 1948-49; M.D., Western Res. U., 1953; grad., Cleve. Psychoanalytic Inst., 1964. Intern Univ. Hosps., Cleve., 1953-54, resident in psychiatry, 1956-57, dir. psychiatry, 1970-86, chief of staff, 1982-90; dir. profl. services Horizon Ctr. Hosp., 1980; asst. resident in psychiatry Yale U., New Haven, 1954-56; teaching fellow Case Western Res. U., Cleve., 1957-60, from instr. to prof. psychiatry, 1960-93; prof. emeritus, 1993—; assoc. dean Sch. Medicine Case Western Res. U., Cleve., 1982-93, dir. Substance Abuse Ctr., 1990-93. Cons. Cleve. Ctr. on Alcoholism, DePaul Maternity and Infant Home, St. Ann's Hosp., Def. Dept., Cleve. VA Hosp., Psychiat. Edn. br. NIMH; mem. Cuyahoga County Mental Health and Retardation Bd., 1967-73, 94—, Health Planning and Devel. Commn., 1967-73, Ohio Mental Health and Retardation Commn., 1976-78. Contbr. articles to profl. jours. Bd. dirs. Hough-Norwood Health Ctr., Hitchcock Ctr., Hopewell Inn, Woodruff Found, 2001—. 1st lt. USAAF, 1943-46. Decorated D.F.C., Air medal with oak leaf cluster.; Career Tchr. grantee NIMH, 1958-60 Fellow Am. Psychiat. Assn. (life), Am. Coll. Psychiatrists, Am. Coll. Psychoanalysts (pres. 1988-89); mem. AMA, AAAS, Ohio Psychiat. Assn. (pres. 1974—), Am. Psychoanalytic Assn., Assn. Am. Med. Colls., Cleve. Acad. Medicine (bd. dirs. 1987-90), Ohio Med. Assn., Pasteur Club, Am. Assn. Chairmen Depts. Psychiatry (pres. 1978-79), Alpha Omega Alpha. Home: 1 Bratenahl Pl Apt 1010 Cleveland OH 44108-1155 Office: 11000 Euclid Ave Cleveland OH 44106-1714

LENN, STEPHEN ANDREW, lawyer; b. Ft. Lauderdale, Fla., Jan. 6, 1946; s. Joseph A. and Ruth (Kreis) L.; 1 child, Daniel Lenn. BA, Tufts U., 1967; JD, Columbia U., 1970. Assoc. Kronish, Lieb, Shainswit, Weiner & Hellman, N.Y.C., 1970-72, Shereff, Friedman, Hoffman & Goodman, N.Y.C., 1972-75; exec. v.p., gen. counsel Union Commerce Bank, Union Commerce Corp., Cleve., 1975-83; ptnr., mng. ptnr. Porter, Wright, Morris & Arthur, 1983-88; ptnr. Baker & Hostetler, 1988-97; CEO Capital Strategies Inc., 1997—. Trustee Gt. Lakes Sci. Ctr. Mem. ABA, Oakwood Club. Office: Capital Strategies Inc 1801 E 9th St 1350 Cleveland OH 44114

LENNES, GREGORY, manufacturing and financing company executive; b. Chgo., Aug. 5, 1947; s. Lawrence Dominic and Genevieve (Karoll) L.; m. Kathie Lennes; children: Robert, Sandra, Ryan, Bonnie. BA, U. Ill., 1969, MA, 1971, postgrad., 1971-73. Corp. archivist Navistar Internat. Corp. (formerly Internat. Harvester Co.), Chgo., 1973-80, records mgr., 1980—, asst. sec., 1980—; dir. document mgmt., 1997—; sec. Navistar Fin. Corp., Schaumburg, Ill., 1980—, Internat. Truck and Engine Corp., 1987—. Editor: Historical Records in the Farm Equipment Industry, 1977. Mem. Am. Soc. Corp Secs., Assn. Records Mgrs. and Adminstrs., Soc. Am. Archivists, Midwest Archives Conf., Assn. Info. and Image Mgmt., Nat. Assn. Stock Plan Profls. Home: 6412 S Knox Ave Chicago IL 60629-5522 Office: Internat Truck and Engine Corp 4201 Winfield Rd Warrenville IL 60555

LENON, RICHARD ALLEN, chemical corporation executive; b. Lansing, Mich., Aug. 4, 1920; s. Theo and Elizabeth (Amon) L.; m. Helen Johnson, Sept. 13, 1941; children: Richard Allen, Pamela A., Lisa A. BA, Western Mich. Coll., 1941; postgrad., Northwestern U., 1941-42. Mgr. fin. div. Montgomery Ward & Co., Chgo., 1947-56; v.p. fin. Westinghouse Air Brake Co., 1963-67, treas., 1965-67; v.p., treas. Internat. Minerals & Chem. Corp., Skokie, Ill., 1956-63, group v.p. fin. and adminstrn., 1967-68, exec. v.p., 1968-70, pres., 1970-78, chmn., 1977-86, chmn. exec. com., 1986-88, IMC Global Inc., 1989-96. Lt. comdr. USNR, 1942-47. Clubs: University (Chgo.); Glen View (Ill.) Home: 803 Solar Ln Glenview IL 60025-4464 Office: 100 Saunders Rd Ste 300 Lake Forest IL 60045-2502

LENSKI, RICHARD EIMER, evolutionary biologist, educator; b. Ann Arbor, Mich., Aug. 13, 1956; AB in Biology, Oberlin Coll., 1977; PhD in Zoology, U. N.C., 1982. Postdoctoral rsch. assoc. dept. zoology U. Mass., Amherst, 1982-85; asst. prof. dept. ecology and evolutionary biology U. Calif., Irvine, 1984-88, assoc. prof., 1988-91; Hannah prof. Ctr. for Microbial Ecology Mich. State U., East Lansing, 1991—. Vis. asst. prof. dept. biol. scis. Dartmouth Coll., Hanover, N.H., 1984; mem. NRC Commn. on Life Scis., 1990-96, NRC Bd. Biology, 1990-96. Assoc. editor Evolution, 1990-93; editorial bd. Microbial Ecology, 1991-93; contbg. author: Coevolution, 1983; contbr. articles to Sci., Nature, Ecology, Am. Naturalist. NSF fellow, 1977-81; Presdl. Young Investigator NSF, 1988-93; rsch. fellow Guggenheim Found., 1992-93; vis. fellow All Souls Coll., Oxford U., 1992-93; McArthur fellow, 1996. Fellow Am. Acad. Arts Sci.; mem. Am. Soc. Microbiology, Am. Soc. Naturalists, Ecol. Soc. Am.(com. on environ. applications genetically engineered organisms 1988), Genetics Soc. Am., Soc. Study Evolution, Sigma Xi. Achievements include research on ecology, genetics and evolution of microbial populations including studies on coevolution of bacteria, viruses and plasmids, causes of mutation. Office: Ctr Microbial Ecology Mich State U 288 Plant And Soil Science East Lansing MI 48824-1325

LENZMEIER, ALLEN U. consumer products company executive; CFO, Best Buy Co., Inc., Mpls., pres., Best Buy Retail Stores divsn, 2001—. Office: Best Buy Co Inc PO Box 9312 Minneapolis MN 55440-9312

LEON, ARTHUR SOL, research cardiologist, exercise physiologist; b. Bklyn., Apr. 26, 1931; s. Alex and Anne (Schrek) L.; m. Gloria Rakita, Dec. 23, 1956; children: Denise, Harmon, Michelle. BS in Chemistry with high honors, U. Fla., 1952; MS in Biochemistry, U. Wis., 1954, MD, 1957. Intern Henry Ford Hosp., Detroit, 1957-58; fellow in internal medicine Lahey Clinic, Boston, 1958-60; fellow in cardiology Jackson Meml. Hosp.-U. Miami (Fla.) Med. Sch., 1960-61; dir. clin. pharmacology research unit Hoffmann-La Roche Inc.-Newark Beth Israel Med. Ctr., 1969-73; from instr. to assoc. prof. medicine Coll. Medicine and Dentistry N.J., Newark, 1967-73; from assoc. prof. to prof. div. epidemiology U. Minn., Mpls., 1973—, H.L. Taylor prof. exercise sci. and health enhancement, dir. lab. physiol. hygiene and exercise sci., div. kinesiology, Coll. Edn., 1991—, dir. applied physiology and nutrition, 1973-91. Mem. med. eval. team Gemini and Apollo projects NASA, 1964-67. Editor Procs. of the NIH Consensus Conf. on Phys. Activity and Cardiovasc. Health, 1997; assoc. editor Surgeon Gen.'s Report on Health Benefits of Exercise, 1996; contbr. numerous articles to profl. publs. Trustee Vinland Nat. Sports Health Ctr. for Disabled, 1978—; mem. gov.'s coun. physical fitness sports, 1979—. Served as officer M.C. U.S. Army, 1961-67, 90-91, col. Res. 1978-92, ret. Recipient Anderson award AAHPER, 1981, Presdl. award for exercise sci. rsch. Internat. Olympic Com., 1999; Am. Heart Assn. fellow, 1960-61 Fellow Am. Coll. Cardiology, Am. Coll. Chest Physicians, Am. Coll. Clin. Pharmacology, N.Y. Acad. Scis., Am. Coll. Sports Medicine (trustee 1976-78, 82-83, v.p. 1977-79, pres. Northland chpt. 1975-76, Citation award 1995), Am. Assn. Cardiovasc. and Pulmonary Rehab. (trustee 1989-90), Am. Acad. Kinesiology and Phys. Edn.; mem. Am. Physiol. Soc., Am. Soc. Pharmacology and Exptl. Therapeutics, Am. Inst. Nutrition, Am. Heart Assn. (v.p. Hennepin County divsn. 1980-81, pres. 1982-83), Am. Coll. Nutrition, Am. Fedn. Clin. Rsch., Minn. Lung Assn. (trustee 1978-81), Phi Beta Kappa, Phi Kappa Phi. Jewish. Home: 5628 Glen Ave Minnetonka MN 55345-6610 Office: U Minn Sch Kinesiology & Leisure Studies 202 Cooke Hall Minneapolis MN 55455-0136 E-mail: leonx002@tc.umn.edu.

LEONARD, EUGENE ALBERT, banker; b. St. Louis, Aug. 27, 1935; s. Albert Hiram and Mary (Crowson) L.; m. Mary Ann Sampson, Aug. 31, 1956 (div. 1994); children: Charles, James, Susan; m. Constance Anne Deschamps, June 3, 1995. BS, U. Mo., 1957, MS, 1958, PhD, 1962; postgrad., Stonier Grad. Sch. Banking, Rutgers U., 1964-66. Instr. agrl. econs. U. Mo. at Columbia, 1959-60; with Fed. Res. Bank St. Louis, 1961-77; v.p., mgr. Fed. Res. Bank St. Louis (Memphis br.), 1967-70, sr. v.p., 1970-71, 1st v.p., 1971-77; on loan to bd. govs. FRS as asst. sec., Washington, 1970-71; sr. v.p. Merc. Bancorp. Inc., St. Louis, 1977-87; pres. Corp. for Fin. Risk Mgmt., 1987—. Instr. econs. Central States Sch. Banking, 1962-69, Ill. Bankers Sch., 1962-74, Sch. Banking South, 1970-83, Stonier Grad. Sch. Banking, 1975-80, bd. regents, 1978-81; adj. assoc. prof. econs. Memphis State U., 1969-70; bd. dirs. Ctrl. West End Bank, St. Louis, 1997—. Bd. dirs. Logos Sch., St. Louis, 1977-85, chmn., 1985; bd. dirs. Repertory Theater of St. Louis, 1981-87. Mem. Mo. Bankers Assn. (treas. 1984-85, pres. 1986-87), U. Mo. Columbia Alumni Assn. (nat. pres. 1980-81, bd. dirs. devel. fund 1981-89, Faculty Alumni award 1986), Gamma Sigma Delta, Kappa Sigma. Unitarian. Home: 30 Portland Pl Saint Louis MO 63108-1204 Office: Corp for Fin Risk Mgmt 1829 Belt Way Dr Saint Louis MO 63114-5815

LEONARD, GEORGE EDMUND, real estate, bank, high tech and consulting executive; b. Phoenix, Nov. 20, 1940; s. George Edmund and Marion Elizabeth (Fink) L.; m. Gloria Jean Henry, Mar. 26, 1965 (div. Feb. 1981); children: Tracy Lynn McKinney, Amy Theresa Blanchard, Kristin Jean Steel; m. Mary C. Short, Sept. 22, 1990. Student, Ariz. State U., 1958-60; BS, U.S. Naval Acad., 1964; postgrad., Pa. State U., 1969-70; MBA, U. Chgo., 1973. Commd. ensign USN, 1964, advanced through grades to lt. comdr., 1975; v.p. 1st Nat. Bank Chgo., 1970-75; exec. v.p., chief banking, CFO, chief lending officer Mera Bank, Phoenix, 1975-90, also bd. dirs., 1982-90; pres., CEO Ctrl. Savs., San Diego, 1985-87; chmn., CEO AmBank Holding Co. of Colo., Scottsdale, Ariz., 1990-91, Consumer Guarantee Corp., Phoenix, 1996; pres., CEO Diversified Mgmt. Svcs., Inc., 1991-96, GEL Mgmt. Inc., Phoenix, 1991—; CFO Western Pacific Airlines, Colorado Springs, 1996-98, bd. dirs., 1996-98; exec. v.p., CFO, treas., sec., dir. fin. Radi Sys. Microwave Sys. Corp., Des Moines, 1998—, COO, bd. dirs., 2000—01. Active Phoenix Thunderbirds, 1979—; bd. dirs. Maricopa C.C.s Found., treas., 2nd v.p., 1991-93, 1st v.p., 1993-94, pres., 1994-95, past pres., 1995-96, Camelback Charitable Trust, 1991-92, The Samaritan Found., 1993-96, chmn. fin. com., 1994-96, vice chmn., 1996. Mem. Phoenix Met. C. of C. (bd. dirs. 1975-82), Inst. Fin. Edn. (bd. dirs. 1980-87, nat. chmn. 1985-86), Ariz. State U. Coll. of Bus. Deans Coun. of 100, Paradise Valley Country Club (bd. dirs. 1991-98, treas. 1992-95, pres. 1995-97), White Mountain Country Club, Glen Oaks Country Club, Kiwanis. Republican. Roman Catholic. Home: 409 Silverado Pt Waukee IA 50263-8150 Office: Radi Sys Microware Sys Corp 1500 NW 118th St Des Moines IA 50325-8242

LEONARD, KURT JOHN, plant pathologist, retired university program director; b. Holstein, Iowa, Dec. 6, 1939; s. Elvin Elsworth and Irene Marie (Helkenn) L.; m. Maren Jane Simonsen, May 28, 1961; children: Maria Catherine, Mary Alice, Benjamin Andrew. BS, Iowa State U., 1962; PhD, Cornell U., 1968. Plant pathologist Agrl. Rsch. Svc. USDA, Raleigh, N.C., 1968-88, dir. Cereal Disease Lab. U. Minn. St. Paul, 1988—2001. Author: (with others) Annual Review of Phytopathology, 1980; co-editor: Plant Disease Epidemiology, vol. 1, 1986, vol. 2, 1989; editor-in-chief: Phytopathology, 1981-84, Am. Phytopathol. Soc. Press, 1994-97; contbr. numerous articles to profl. jours. Fellow Am. Phytopathol. Soc. (coun. 1981-84, 94-97); mem. Am. Mycol. Soc., Internat. Soc. Plant Pathology (councilor 1982-93), Brit. Soc. Plant Pathology, Phi Kappa Phi, Sigma Xi, Gamma Sigma Delta. Achievements include description of new species and genera of plant pathogenic fungi; research on spread of disease through crop mixtures, on relationships between virulence and fitness in plant pathogenic fungi. Office: U Minn USDA ARS Cereal Disease Lab Saint Paul MN 55108

LEONARD, LAURA L. lawyer; AB, U. Calif., Davis, 1978; JD, Loyola U., Chgo., 1983. Bar: Ill. 1983. Assoc. Sidley & Austin, Chgo., ptnr. Lectr. on environ. aspects of bus. trans., including Northwestern U. Kellogg Grad. Sch. Mgmt.; mem. adv. bd. BNA's Environ. Due Digigence Guide. Office: Sidley & Austin 1 S First National Plz Chicago IL 60603-2000 Fax: 323-853-7620. E-mail: lleonard@sidley.com.

LEONARD, MICHAEL A. automotive executive; b. Cadillac, Mich., Aug. 3, 1937; s. Hugel A. and Mildred (Johnson) L.; m. Frances Erickson, June 18, 1960; children: Kristin, Anne. MA, Alma Coll., 1959; MBA, Wayne State U., 1964; MS, MIT, 1971. Exec. Chrysler Corp., Highland Park, Mich., 1959-75; group v.p. Bendix Corp., Southfield, 1975-83; v.p., group exec. Allied Signal Automotive, Bloomfield Hills, 1983-91; pres. Harman, Inc., Southfield, 1991-94; mng. ptnr. Exec. Resources Inc., Bloomfield Hills, 1994—. Bd. dirs. Kalyani Brake Co., Pune, India, Bendix France, Paris, Bendix Italy, and fgn. subs. Trustee Alma (Mich.) Coll.; chmn. Presbyn. Villages of Mich. Sloan fellow, MIT. Mem. Soc. Automotive Engrs., Delta Sigma Phi (pres. 1958-59). Presbyterian. Avocations: swimming, golf, boating. Home: 4375 Barchester Dr Bloomfield Hills MI 48302-2116 Office: Executive Resources Inc PO Box 625 Bloomfield Hills MI 48303-0625

LEPPARD, RAYMOND JOHN, conductor, harpsichordist; b. London, Aug. 11, 1927; came to U.S., 1976; s. Albert Victor and Bertha May (Beck) L. MA, U. Cambridge, Eng., 1955; DLitt (hon.), U. Bath, Eng., 1973; PhD (hon.), U. Indpls., 1991, Purdue U., 1992, Butler U., 1994, Wabash Coll., 1995; DMusic (hon.), Ind. U., 2001. Fellow Trinity Coll., Cambridge; lectr. music U. Cambridge, 1958-68; condr. Indpls. Symphony Orch., 1987-2001. Mus. dir. English Chamber Orch., London, 1959-77; prin. condr. BBC Philharm., Manchester, Eng., 1972-80; condr. symphony orchs. in Am. and Europe, Met. Opera, N.Y.C., Santa Fe Opera, San Francisco Opera, Covent Garden, Glyndebourne, Paris Opera; prin. guest condr. St. Louis Symphony Orch., 1984-90, music dir. Indpls. Symphony Orch., 1987-2001, European tours, 1993, 97; rec. artist, composer numerous film scores; author: Authenticity in Music, 1989, Raymond Leppard on Music/An Anthology of Critical and Personal Writings, 1993. Decorated Commendatore Della Republica Italiana; comdr. Order Brit. Empire

LEPPIK, MARGARET WHITE, state legislator; b. Newark, June 5, 1943; d. John Underhill and Laura Schaefer White; m. Ilo Elmar Leppik, June 18, 1967; children: Peter, David, Karina. BA, Smith Coll., 1965. Rsch. asst. Wistar Inst., U. Pa., Phila., 1967-68, U. Wis., Madison, 1968-69; mem. Minn. Ho. Reps., St. Paul, 1990—, chair higher edn. fin. com. Mem. Golden Valley (Minn.) Planning Commn., 1982—90, Golden Valley Bd. Zoning Appeals, 1985—87; bd. dirs. Partnership for Action Against Tobacco, 1998—. Recipient Citizen of Distinction award Hennepin County Human Svcs. Planning Bd. 1992; named Legislator of Yr., U. Minn. Alumni Assn., 1995, 98-99, Legislator of Yr., Minn. State U. Student assn., 1999. Mem. LWV (v.p., dir. 1984-90), Minn. Opera Assn. (pres. 1986-88), Rotary Internat., Optimists Internat. Republican. Avocations: gardening, biking, canoeing. Home: 7500 Western Ave Golden Valley MN 55427-4849 Office: 485 State Office Bldg Saint Paul MN 55155-0001 E-mail: rep.peggy.leppik@house.leg.state.mn.us.

LERNER, ALFRED, professional sports team executive, real estate and financial executive; b. N.Y.C., May 8, 1933; s. Abraham and Clara (Abrahmson) Lerner; m. Norma Wokloff, Aug. 7, 1955; children: Nancy Faith, Randolph David. BA, Columbia U., 1965. Chmn. bd., chief exec. officer Multi-Amp Corp., Dallas, 1970—80, Realty Refund Trust, Cleve., 1971—90; pres., chief exec. officer Refund Advisers, Inc., 1971—, Town & Country Mgmt. Corp., 1979—93; chmn., dir. Equitable Bancorp., Balt., 1981—90; chmn., bd. dirs. Prog. Corp., Cleve., 1988—93; chmn., CEO, pres. MBNA Corp., Newark, 1991—; chmn., CEO Town & Country Trust, 1993—; owner, chair Cleveland Browns, 1998—. Chmn., bd. dirs. MNC Corp., Balt., 1991—93. Trustee Columbia U., Case Western Res. U.; pres. Cleve. Clin. 1st lt. Res. USMC, 1955—57. Mem.: Young Pres. Orgn., Harmonie Club (N.Y.C.), Beechmont Club (Cleve.). Jewish. Home: 19000 S Park Blvd Cleveland OH 44122-1853 Office: MBNA Corporation 1100 N King St Wilmington DE 19884-0001 also: Cleveland Browns 76 Lou Groza Blvd. Berea OH 44017

LERNER, HARRY JONAS, publishing company executive; b. Mpls., Mar. 5, 1932; s. Morris and Lena (Liederschneider) L.; m. Sharon Ruth Goldman, June 25, 1961 (dec. 1982); children: Adam Morris, Mia Carol, Daniel Aryeh, Leah Anne; m. Sandra Karon Davis, Aug. 24, 1996. Student, U. Mich., 1952, Hebrew U., Jerusalem, 1953-54; B.A., U. Minn., 1957. Founder Lerner Publs. Co., Mpls., 1959, chief exec. officer, 1959—; founder Muscle Bound Bindery, Inc., 1967, chief exec. officer, 1967—; founder Carolrhoda Books, Inc., 1969; gen. mgr. Interface Graphics Inc., 1969—, CEO, 1993—. Bd. visitors U. Minn. Press; del. White House Conf. on Libr. and Info. Svcs., 1979; chmn. North Loop Bus. Assn., Mpls., 1972-79, Minn. Book Pubs. Roundtable, 1974; bd. overseers Hill Monastic Manuscript Libr., St. John's U., Collegeville, Minn., 1986-89; bd. dirs., libr. dir. Jewish Community Ctr. Pres. Twin City chpt. Am. Jewish Com., 1980-85; bd. dirs. Fgn. Policy Assn. Minn., 1970-71, bd. dirs. Children's Book Coun., N.Y.C., 1991-94, Minn. Libr. Assn. Found., 1997; bd. advisors Books for Africa, 1996. Recipient Brotherhood award, NCCJ, 1961, Kay Sexton award, 2002, numerous graphic arts awards. Mem. ACLU, Mpls. Inst. Art, Walker Art Ctr, St. Paul-Mpls. Com. on Fgn. Affairs, Jewish Hist. Soc. Upper Midwest, Ampersand Club, Daybreakers Breakfast Club (Mpls.). E-mail: lernerbooks.com. Home: 2215 Willow Ln N Minneapolis MN 55416-3862 Office: Lerner Pub Group 241 1st Ave N Minneapolis MN 55401-1676

LESEWSKI, ARLENE, state legislator, insurance agent; b. Apr. 12, 1936; m. Thomas Lesewski; three children. Student, Southwest State U., Minn. Ins. agent; mem. Minn. Senate from 21st dist., St. Paul, 1993—. Home: PO Box 341-b Marshall MN 56258-0690 Office: Minn State Senate State Capital Building Saint Paul MN 55155-0001 Also: 807 Columbine Dr Marshall MN 56258-2406

LESNIK, STEVEN HARRIS, public relations and sports marketing executive; b. Newark, May 1, 1940; s. Seymour J. and Ida (Rosenblatt) L.; m. Madeline Sigfried, June 1, 1963; children: Blaine R., Joshua W. BA, Brown U., 1962; postgrad., Am. U., 1969. Reporter, columnist The Stamford (Conn.) Advocate, 1963-65; press rels. rep. Ins. Info. Inst., N.Y.C., 1966, asst. mgr. Chgo., 1967; ea. corp. rels. mgr. Kemper Ins. Cos., Washington, 1968-72, asst. to pres. for corp. affairs Long Grove, Ill., 1972; dir. communications and pub. affairs Kemper Group, 1973, v.p., 1977; pres. Kemper Sports Mgmt., Northbrook, Ill., 1977; chmn., chief exec. officer Kemper Lesnik Orgn., 1977—. Chief exec. officer Sioux Falls Skyforce; mem. Conf. Bds. Pub. Affairs Rsch. Coun., 1975-79; pres. Insurers Pub. Rels. Coun., 1975-79. Vice-chmn. Community Action Com., Montgomery County, Md., 1969-72; mem. Winnetka (Ill.) Caucus Com., 1979; pres. Met. Chgo. Housing Corp., 1974-79; mem. Ill. Econ. Bd., 1990—. Mem. Internat. Pub. Rels. Assn., Pub. Rels. Soc. Am., Nat. Press Club, Publicity Club Chgo., N.Y. Publicity Club, Ill. Profl. Golfers Assn. (adv. com.), Ill. Math. and Sci. Acad. Fund for Advancement of Edn., Internat. Assn. Bus. Communicators. Office: Kemper Lesnik Orgn 500 Skokie Blvd Ste 444 Northbrook IL 60062-2867

LESSARD, ROBERT BERNARD, state legislator, recreational facility executive; b. International Falls, Minn., May 18, 1931; s. William O. and Beatrice (Miller) L.; m. Toni Ballon; children: Wendy Jo, Kelly Jo, Brett, Shawn. Owner Spawn Inlet Lodge, Rainy Lake, Minn., 1954-64; mgr. Great Bear Lodge, Can., 1964-67; owner Viking Cruiser, Inc., Rainy Lake, 1970—; mem. Minn. Senate from 3rd dist., St. Paul, 1976—. Chmn. environ. and natural resources com., mem. fin., local and urban govt., rules and adminstrn., and vet. and mil. affairs coms., Minn. State Senate. Office: State Senate 111 State Capitol Saint Paul MN 55155-0001

LESSEN, LARRY LEE, federal judge; b. Lincoln, Ill., Dec. 25, 1939; s. William G. and Grace L. (Plunkett) L.; m. Susan Marian Vaughn, Dec. 5, 1964; children: Laura, Lynn, William. BA, U. Ill., 1960, JD, 1962. Bar: Ill. 1962, U.S. Dist. Ct. (ctrl. dist.) Ill. 1964, U.S. Bankruptcy Ct. 1964, U.S. Tax Ct. 1982, U.S. Ct. Appeals (7th cir.) 1981, U.S. Supreme Ct. 1981. Law clk. to presiding justice U.S. Dist. Ct., 1962-64; asst. state's atty. State of Ill., Danville, 1964-67; mng. ptnr. Sebat, Swanson, Banks and Lessen, 1967-85; judge U.S. Bankruptcy Ct., 1973-85, U.S. Magistrate, Danville, 1973-84; chief judge U.S. Bankruptcy Ct., Springfield, Ill., 1985-93; U.S. bankruptcy judge Springfield divsn., 1993—. Mem. ABA, FBA, Sangamon County Bar Assn., Vermilion County Bar Assn, Nat. Conf. Bankruptcy Judges (bd. govs. 1994-97), Am. Bankruptcy Inst., Lincoln-Douglas Inn of Cts. Office: US Bankruptcy Ct 235 U S Courthouse 600 E Monroe St Springfield IL 62701-1626

LESSICK, MIRA LEE, nursing educator; b. Hazleton, Pa., Jan. 25, 1949; d. Jack H. and Shirley E. (Frumkin) L. Diploma in nursing, Albany (N.Y.) Med. Ctr., 1969; BSN, Boston U., 1972; MS, U. Colo., 1973; PhD, U. Tex., 1986. Staff nurse Boston City Hosp. and Mass. Gen. Hosp., 1969-72; instr. to asst. prof. nursing, genetics clinician U. Rochester, N.Y., 1973-79; asst. prof. nursing, practitioner Rush U. Coll. Nursing, Chgo., 1986-91, assoc. prof. nursing, 1992—2001, project dir. genetic health nursing program, 1993—2001; assoc. prof. U. Toledo, 2001—. Mem. human genome rsch. initial rev. group, ethical, legal, and social implications subcom. Nat. Human Genome Rsch. Inst., NIH, 1996-99; peer reviewer Bur. Health Professions, HHS, 2001—. Mem. editl. adv. bd. AWHONN Lifelines, 1999—; genetics column editor Medsurg Nursing: The Jour. of Adult Health; contbr. articles to profl. jours. Recipient Bd. of Govs. award, Excellence in Pediatric Nursing award Albany Med. Ctr., 1969, Outstanding Nurse Recognition award March of Dimes Birth Defects Found., 1991, Recognition award for Individual Contbn. to Maternal-Child Health Nat. Perinatal Assn., 1993, Founders Award in Edn., Internat. Soc. Nurses in Genetics, 1997. Mem. AAAS, ANA, APHA, Internat. Soc. Nurses in Genetics (chair rsch. com. 1993—, Founders award in Edn. 1997), Assn. Women's Health, Obstetric, and Neonatal Nurses, Am. Soc. Human Genetics, Chgo. Nurses Assn. (legis. com. 1990-91), N.Y. Acad. Scis., Midwest Nursing Rsch. Soc., Sigma Theta Tau (Luther Christman award for excellence in published writing 1993, Luther Christmas award Excellence Pub. Writing, 1998), Phi Kappa Phi. Achievements include development of a genetic health area of concentration within a graduate level nursing program. Office: U Toledo Coll Health and Human Svcs Scott Park Campus Toledo OH 43606-3390 E-mail: mlessic@utnet.utoledo.edu.

LESTER, SUSAN E. former bank executive; CFO U.S. Bancorp, Mpls., to 2000. Office: US Bancorp First Bank Pl 601 2nd Ave S Minneapolis MN 55402-4303

LESTINA, GERALD F. wholesale grocery executive; Pres., CEO Roundy's Inc., Pewaukee, Wis. Office: Roundy's Inc 23000 Roundy Dr Pewaukee WI 53072

LESTON, PATRICK JOHN, judge; b. Maywood, Ill., May 2, 1948; s. John R. and Lorraine (McQueen) L.; m. Kristine Brzezinski; children: Alison, Adam. BS in Communications, U. Ill., 1970; JD cum laude, Northwestern U., Chgo., 1973. Bar: Ill. 1973, U.S. Dist. Ct. (no. dist.) Ill. 1973, U.S. Ct. Appeals (7th cir.) 1973. Ptnr. Jacobs & Leston, Villa Park, Ill., 1973-79; pvt. practice Glen Ellyn, 1979-89; ptnr. Keck, Mahin & Cate, Oakbrook Terrace, 1989-95; judge 18th Cir. Ct., DuPage County, 1995—. Presenter at profl. confs. Editor Ill. State Bar Assn./Young Lawyers Divsn. Jour., 1983-85. Class rep. Northwestern U. Law Sch. Fund, 1982-88; organizer DuPage County (Ill.) Law Explorers. Fellow ABA (Ill. del. to ABA/Young Lawyers divsn. assembly 1982-85), Ill. Bar Assn. (chmn. fellows 1991-92, mem. bd. govs. 1990-97, chmn. young lawyers divsn. 1985, chmn. agenda com. 1986, del. to 18th jud. cir. assembly 1982-88), Ill. Judges Assn. (bd. dirs. 1997—), Ill. Bar Found. (charter), Am. Bar Found.; mem. DuPage County Bar Assn. (pres. 1987, bd. dirs. 1979-84, chmn. judiciary com. 1988, gen. counsel 1989), Lions, Chi Psi. Avocations: volleyball, skiing, scuba diving, travel, golf. Office: 18th Jud Cir Ct 505 N County Farm Rd Wheaton IL 60187-3907

LESZINSKE, WILLIAM O. bank executive; Pres., chief investment officer Harris Investment Mgmt. Inc., Harris Bankcorp., Inc., Chgo., 1996—. Office: Harris Bankcorp Inc 190 S Lasalle St Chicago IL 60603-3410

LETARTE, CLYDE, state legislator; BA, Muskegon C.C., Hope Coll.; MA, Mich. State U. Pres. Jackson C.C.; state rep. Mich., until 1998; mem. appropriations com.; cons. New Horizons Tour and Travel, Jackson, Mich., 1999—. Office: New Horizons Tour and Travel 2727 Springharbor Rd Jackson MI 49201

LETHAM, DENNIS J. wholesale company executive; CFO, sr. v.p. fin. Anixter Internat. Inc., Skokie, Ill. Office: Anixter Internat Inc 4711 Golf Rd Skokie IL 60076-1224

LETSINGER, ROBERT LEWIS, chemistry educator; b. Bloomfield, Ind., July 31, 1921; s. Reed A. and Etna (Phillips) L.; m. Dorothy C. Thompson, Feb. 6, 1943; children: Louise, Reed, Sue. Student, Ind. U., 1939-41; B.S., Mass. Inst. Tech., 1943, Ph.D., 1945; DSc (hon.), Acadia U., Can., 1993. Research assoc. MIT, 1945-46; research chemist Tenn. Eastman Corp., 1946; faculty Northwestern U., 1946—, prof. chemistry, 1959—, chmn. dept., 1972-75, joint prof. biochemistry and molecular biology, 1974—, Clare Hamilton Hall prof. chemistry, 1986-92, Clare Hamilton Hall prof. emeritus chemistry, 1992—; founder Nanosphere Inc., 2000—. Mem. med. and organic chemistry fellowship panel NIH, 1966-69, medicinal chem. A study sect., 1971-75; bd. on chem. scis. and tech. NRC, 1987-90. Mem. bd. editors Nucleic Acids Research, 1974-80; contbr. articles to profl. jours. Guggenheim fellow, 1956; JSPS fellow Japan, 1978; recipient Rosenstiel Medallion, 1985, Humboldt Sr. US Scientist award, 1988, NIH merit award, 1988, Arthur C. Cope scholar award, 1993, B.F. Goodrich Collegiate Inventors award, 1997. Fellow Am. Acad. Arts and Scis., Nat. Acad. Scis., Am. Assn. Arts and Scis.; mem. Am. Chem. Soc. (bd. editors 1969-72, bioconjugate chemistry 1992—), Internat. Union Pure and Applied Chemistry, Sigma Xi, Phi Lambda Upsilon (hon. mem.). Home: 1034 Sassafras Cir Bloomington IN 47408 Office: Northwestern U Chemistry Dept 2145 Sheridan Rd Evanston IL 60208-0834 E-mail: r-letsinger@chem.northwestern.edu.

LETT, PHILIP WOOD, JR. defense consultant; b. Newton, Ala., May 4, 1922; s. Philip Wood Sr. and Lily Octavia (Kennedy) L.; m. Katy Lee Howell, June 26, 1948; children: Kathy, Warren, Lisa. B MechE, Ala. Poly. Inst., 1943; MS in Engring., U. Ala., 1947; PhD MechE, U. Mich., 1950; MS in Indsl. Mgmt., MIT, 1960. Registered profl. engr., Mich. Lab. engr., engring. div. Chrysler Corp., 1950-52, project engr., def. engring. div., 1952-54, chief engr., def. engring. div., 1954-61, operating mgr., def. engring. div., 1961-73, head XM1 Tank task force Mich., 1973-76; gen. mgr. Sterling Def. div. Chrysler Corp., 1976-79; v.p. engring. Chrysler Def. Inc., Center Line, Mich., 1980-82; v.p. research & engring. Gen. Dynamics Land Systems Div., 1982-86, v.p., asst. to gen. mgr., 1986-87; pres. PWL Inc., 1987—. Mem. U.S. delegation to NATO Indsl. Adv. Group. Contbr. articles to tech. jours. and to Internat. Def. Rev. Trustee Judson Ctr., 1989—. Capt. U.S. Army, 1943-46. Decorated Cheonsu medal Republic of Korea; awarded membership U.S. Nat. Acad. Engring., 1984; recipient Outstanding Engr. award Auburn U., 1984, Ben S. Gilmer award, 1991, Gold medal Am. Def. Preparedness Assn., 1997; named Disting. Engring. fellow U. Ala. Coll. Engring., 1992; elected to Ala. Engring. Hall of Fame, 1992; Sloan fellow MIT, 1960-61. Mem. Orchard Lake Country Club. Baptist. Home: 1330 Oxford Rd Bloomfield Hills MI 48304-3952 Office: PO Box 2074 Warren MI 48090-2074

LEUCK, CLAIRE M. state legislator; m. Richard Leuck. Student, Ind. Vo-Tech. Coll., Ind. State U. Clk. Benton County Cir. Ct., Ind., 1974-82, bailiff, sec., 1984-86; state rep. Dist. 25 Ind. Ho. of Reps., 1986—, chmn. agr. com., mem. natural resources, rds. and transp. com., mem. county and twp. elec., agr. and rural devel. com., ranking minority mem. Farmer. Bd. dirs. Coun. for Acad. Excellence-Dollars for Scholars; mem. St. Anne Soc.; mem. dean's adv. coun. Purdue U. Agr. Mem. Am. Legion Aux., No. Dist. Cir. Ct. Clks., Kappa Kappa Kappa. Home: RR 1 Box 203 Fowler IN 47944-9772 Office: Ind Ho of Reps State Capitol Indianapolis IN 46204 Also: 2816 N 400 E Fowler IN 47944-8081

LEUTHOLD, RAYMOND MARTIN, agricultural economics educator; b. Billings, Mont., Oct. 13, 1940; s. John Henry and Grace Irene L.; m. Jane Hornaday, Aug. 20, 1966; children— Kevin, Gregory. Student, Colo. U., 1958-59; B.S., Mont. State U., 1962; M.S., U. Wis., 1966, Ph.D., 1968. Faculty U. Ill., Urbana-Champaign, 1967—, now prof. emeritus dept. agrl. econs., T.A. Hieronymus disting. prof. Vis. scholar Stanford U., 1974, Chgo. Mercantile Exch., 1990, 91. Co-author: The Theory and Practice of Futures Markets, 1989; editor: Commodity Markets and Futures Prices, 1979; co-editor: Livestock Futures Research Symposium, 1980. Served with U.S. Army, 1962-64. Fulbright research scholar Institute de Gestion Internationale Agro-Alimentaire, Cergy, France, 1981 Mem. Am. Econ. Assn., Am. Agrl. Econs. Assn. (Disting. Policy award 1980, Outstanding Instr. award 1986, 88, 90, 92, College Funk award 1993). Office: 305 Mumford Hall 1301 W Gregory Dr Urbana IL 61801-9015

LEVCO, STANLEY M. lawyer; BA in English, U. Mass., 1968; JD, Ind. U., 1971. Bar: Ind. 1972. Chief dep. prosecutor, Posey County, Ind., 1972-75; judge Posey and Gibson County, 1976-80; dep. prosecutor, pvt. practice Vanderburgh County, 1981-90; prosecutor, 1991—. Tchr. English jr. h.s., Cleve., 1969-71; lectr. Ind. Prosecutor's Assn., Ind. Coroner's Assn. Author: The Best of Stan Levco, 1986, Problems with Documentary Evidence, 1989, Impeachment: A Practical and Tactical Approach, National College of District Attorneys, 1996; weekly columnist Evansville Press and Evansville Courier, 1981-90. Mem. Nat. Dist. Attys. Assn., Ind. State Bar Assn. (lectr.), Assn. Govt. Attys. in Capital Litigation. Office: Vanderburgh County Prosecuting Atty 1 NW Martin Luther King Jr Blv Evansville IN 47708-1831

LEVEN, CHARLES LOUIS, economics educator; b. Chgo., May 2, 1928; s. Elie H. and Ruth (Reinach) R.; m. Judith Danoff, 1950 (div. 1970); m. Dorothy Wish, 1970 (div. 1999); children: Ronald L., Robert M., Carol E., Philip W., Alice S. Student, Ill. Inst. Tech., 1945-46, U. Ill., 1947; B.S., Northwestern U., 1950, M.A., 1957, Ph.D., 1958. Economist Fed. Res. Bank of Chgo., 1950-56; asst. prof. Iowa State U., 1957-59, U. Pa., 1959-62; asso. prof. U. Pitts., 1962-65; prof. econs. Washington U., St. Louis, 1965-91, chmn. dept. econs., 1975-80, prof. emeritus, 1991—; dir. Inst. Urban and Regional Studies, 1965-85. Disting. prof. U. Mo., St. Louis, 1991-99; cons. EEC, Ill. Auditor Gen., Polish Ministry of Planning and Constrn., St. Louis Sch. Bd., Ukrainian Ctr. for Markets and Entrepreneurship, Joel Popkin & Co. Author: Theory and Method of Income and Product Accounts for Metropolitan Areas, 1963, Development Benefits of Water Resource Investment, 1969, An Analytical Framework for Regional Development Policy, 1970, Neighborhood Change, 1976, The Mature Metropolis, 1978. Served with USNR, 1945-46. Ford Found. fellow, 1956; grantee Social Sci. Rsch. Coun., 1960; grantee Com. Urban Econ., 1965; grantee NSF, 1968, 73, Merc. Bancorp., 1976, HUD, 1978, NIH, 1985, 2001. Mem. Am. Econ. Assn., Regional Sci. Assn. (pres. 1964-65, Walter Isard award for distig. scholarship 1995), Western Regional Sci. Assn. (pres. 1974-75, Disting. fellow 1999), So. Regional Sci. Assn. (disting. fellow 1991). Home: 151 Marigold Ln Milford PA 18337-7322 Office: Washington U Box 1208 1 Brookings Dr Saint Louis MO 63130-4899

LEVENFELD, MILTON ARTHUR, lawyer; b. Chgo., Mar. 18, 1927; s. Mitchell A. and Florence B. (Berman) L.; m. Iona R. Wishner, Dec. 18, 1949; children— Barry, David, Judith Ph.B., U. Chgo., 1947, J.D., 1950. Bar: Ill. 1950. Ptnr. Altman, Levenfeld & Kanter, Chgo., 1961-64, Levenfeld and Kanter, Chgo., 1964-80, Levenfeld, Eisenberg, Janger & Glassberg, Chgo., 1980-99; of counsel Levenfeld Pearlstein, 1999—. Former dir. Bank of Chgo., Garfield Ridge Trust & Savs. Bank; lectr. in fed. taxation Contbr. articles to profl. jours. Bd. dirs. Spertus Coll. Judaica, Jewish Fedn. Chgo., 1975-84, Am. Israel C. of C., 1st nat. v.p.; chmn. legacies and endowments com., 1982-84; co-gen. chmn. Chgo. Jewish United Fund, 1977, vice chmn. campaign, 1979; gov. mem. Orchestral Assn. Chgo. Symphony Orch.; vis. com. U. Chgo. Law Sch., 1989-91; pres. Am. Israel C. of C. of Met. Chgo., 1993-95, 96-98. With USNR, 1944-45. Recipient Keter Shem Tov award Jewish Nat. Fund, 1978 Mem. ABA, Ill. Bar Assn., Chgo. Bar Assn., Am.-Israel C. of C. (past pres.). Home: 866 Stonegate Dr Highland Park IL 60035-5145 Office: 33 W Monroe St Chicago IL 60603-5300 E-mail: mlevenfeld@lplegal.com.

LEVENS, DORSEY (HERBERT LEVENS), professional football player; b. Syracuse, N.Y., May 21, 1970; Student, U. Notre Dame, Ga. Poly. U. Running back Green Bay (Wis.) Packers, 1994—; mem. Super Bowl 31 Championship team, 1996; lost Super Bowl 32 to New Eng. Patriots, 1997; mem. Pro Bowl team, 1997. Office: c/o Green Bay Packers PO Box 10628 Green Bay WI 54307-0628

LEVENTHAL, BENNETT LEE, psychiatry and pediatrics educator, administrator; b. Chgo., July 6, 1949; s. Howard Leonard and Florence Ruth (Albert) L.; m. Celia G. Goodman, June 11, 1972; children: Matthew G., Andrew G., Julia G. Student, Emory U., 1967-68, La. State U., 1968-70, BS, 1972, postgrad., 1970-74, MD, 1974. Diplomate Am. Bd. Psychiatry and Neurology in Psychiatry, Am. Bd. Psychiatry and Neurology, Child Psychiatry; lic. physician N.C., La., Ill., Va. Undergrad. rsch. assoc. Lab. Prof. William A. Pryor dept. chemistry, La. State U., 1968-70; house officer I Charity Hosp. at New Orleans, 1974; resident in psychiatry Duke U. Med. Ctr., Durham, N.C., 1974-78, chief fellow divsn. dept. psychiatry, 1976-77, chief resident dept. psychiatry, 1977-78, clin. assoc. dept. psychiatry, 1978-80; staff psychiatrist, head psychiatry dept. Joel T. Boone Clinic, Virginia Beach, Va., 1978-80; staff psychiatrist, faculty mem. dept. psychiatry Naval Regional Med. Ctr., Portsmouth, 1978-80; asst. prof. psychiatry and pediats. U. Chgo., 1978-85, dir. Child Psychiatry Clinic, 1978-85, dir. Child and Adolescent Psychiatry Fellowship tng. program, 1979-88; Irving B. Harris prof. child and adolescent psychiatry Irving B. Harris, 1998—; dir. Sonia Shankman Orthogenic Sch., 2002—. Psychiat. cons. Caledonia State Prision/Halifax Mental Health Ctr., Tillery, N.C., 1976-77, Fed. Correctional Inst., Butner, N.C., 1977-78; cons. Norfolk Cmty. Mental health Ctr., 1978-80; adj. prof. psychology, biopsychology, and devel. psychology U. Chgo., 1990, adj. assoc. prof. dept. psychology and com. on biopsychology, 1987-90; meed. dir. Child Life and Family Edn. program Wyler Children's Hosp. of U. Chgo., 1983-95; dir. child and adolescent programs Chgo. Lakeshore Hosp., 1986—; Pfizer vis. prof. dept. psychiatry U. P.R., 1992; examiner Am. Bd. Psychiatry and Neurology in Gen. Psychiatry and Child Psychiatry, 1982—; mem. steering com. Harris Ctr. for Devel. Studies, U. Chgo., 1983—; mem. com. on evaluation of GAPS project AMA, 1993—; treas. Chgo. Consortium for Psychiat. Rsch., 1994; pres. Ill. Coun. Child and Adolescent Psychiatry, 1992-94; vis. scholar Hunter Inst. Mental Health and U. New Castle, NSW, Australia, 1995; mem. Gov.'s Panel on Health Svcs., 1993-94; prof. psychiatry & pediats. U. Chgo., 1990—, chmn. dept. psychiatry, 1991-98, Irving B. Harris prof. child & adolescent psychiatry, 1998—; presenter in field. Mem. editl. bd. Univ. Chgo. Better Health Letter, 1994-96; cons. editor: Jour. Emo tional and Behavioral Disorders, 1992-96; reviewer: Archives of Gen. Psychiatry, 1983—, Biol. Psychiatry, 1983—, Am. Jour. Psychiatry, 1983—, Jour. AMA, 1983—, Jour. Am. Acad. Child and Adolescent Psychiatry, 1983—, Sci., 1983—; book rev. editor Jour. Neuropsychiatry and Clin. Neuroscis., 1989-92, mem. editl. bd., 1989-92; contbr. articles to profl. jours. Lt. comdr. M.C., USNR, 1978-80. Recipient Crystal Plate award Little Friends, 1994, Individual Achievement award Autism Soc. Am., 1991, Merit award Duke U. Psychiat. Resident's Assn., 1976, Bick award La. Psychiat. Assn., 1974; Andrew W. Mellon Found. faculty fellow U. Chgo., 1983-84; John Dewey lectr. U. Chgo., 1982. Fellow Am. Acad. Child and Adolescent Psychiatry (Outstanding Mentor 1988, dep. chmn. program com. 1979—, chmn. arrangements com. 1979—, new rsch. subcom. for ann. meeting 1986—, mem. work group on rsch. 1989—), Am. Psychiat. Assn. (Falk fellow, mem. Ittleson Award Bd. 1994-97, mem. Am. Psychiat. Assn./Wisniewski Young Psychiatrists Rsch. Award Panel 1994—), Am. Acad. Pediats., Am. Orthopsychiat. Assn.; mem. AAAS, Am. Coll. Psychiatrists, Brain Rsch. Inst., Ill. Coun. Child and Adolescent Psychiatry, Ill. Psychiat. Soc., Soc. for Rsch. in Child Devel., Soc. of Profs. of Child and Adolescent Psychiatry, Soc. Biol. Psychiatry, Nat. Bd. Med. Examiners, Mental Health Assn. Ill. (profl. adv. bd. 1991—), Sigma Xi. Office: U of Chgo Pritzker Sch of Medicine 5841 S Maryland Ave Chicago IL 60637-1463 E-mail: b-leventhal@uchicago.edu.

LEVER, ALVIN, health science association administrator; b. St. Louis, Jan. 27, 1939; s. Jack I. and Sabina (Vogel) L.; m. Norine Sue Schwedt, Jan. 27, 1963; children: Daniel Jay, Michael Leonard. BS in Archtl. Scis., Washington U., St. Louis, 1961, BArch, 1963; MA in Applied Psychology, U. Santa Monica, 1992. Registered architect, Mo., Ill. Project designer Sir Basil Spence, Architects, Edinburgh, Scotland, 1963-65; sr. project designer Hellmuth, Obata & Kassabaum, St. Louis, 1965-68, v.p., project mgr., 1968-72; v.p. facility devel. Michael Reese Med. Ctr., Chgo., 1972-74; v.p., gen. mgr. Apelco Internat., Ltd., Northbrook, Ill., 1974-90; dir. membership and fin. Am. Coll. Chest Physicians, 1990-92, exec. dir., 1992-95, exec. v.p., CEO, 1995—. Pub. jour. Chest. Pub. Chest. Bd. dirs. Chest Found., 1997; v.p. Congregation B'nai Tikvah, 1987-91, pres., 1993-95. Mem. Profl. Conv. Mgmt. Assn., Am. Soc. Med. Soc. Execs., Am. Soc. Assn. Execs., Chgo. Soc. Assn. Execs., Chgo. Assn. Healthcare Execs., Alliance for Continuing Med. Edn., Mission Hills Country Club. Avocations: scuba diving, bicycling, travel., golf. Office: Am Coll Chest Physicians 3300 Dundee Rd Northbrook IL 60062-2303

LEVI, JOHN G. lawyer; b. Chgo., Oct. 9, 1948; s. Edward H. and Kate (Sulzberger) L.; m. Jill Felsenthal, Oct. 7, 1979; children: Benjamin E., Daniel F., Sarah K.H. AB, U. Rochester, 1969; JD, Harvard U., 1972, LLM, 1973. Bar: Ill. 1973. Ptnr. Sidley & Austin, Chgo. Vice chmn. bd. Weiss Mem. Hosp., Chgo.; pres. bd. Francis W. Parker Sch., Chgo.; bd. dirs. Chgo. Child Care Sco.; vis. com. U. Chgo. Coll.; mem. Citizens Com. Juvenile Ct., Chgo. Mem. ABA, Ill. Bar Assn., Chgo. Bar Assn., Law Club Chgo. Office: Sidley & Austin Bank One Plz 425 W Surf St Apt 605 Chicago IL 60657-6139

LEVI, PETER STEVEN, municipal official, lawyer; b. Washington, June 3, 1944; s. Kurt and Ruth (Neumann) L.; m. Enid Goldberg, Jan. 26, 1969; children: Joshua, Jeff. BA, Northwestern U., 1966; JD, U. Mo., Kansas City, 1969, LLM in Urban Legal Affairs, 1971. Bar: Mo. 1969. Gen. counsel Mid Am. Regional Coun., Kansas City, 1971-77, exec. dir., 1977-90; pres. Greater Kansas City C. of C., 1990—. Participant internat. local govt. mgmt. exch. program with Israel, Internat. City Mgmt. Assn., 1985-86. Author: Model Subdivision Regulations, 1975; contbr. numerous articles to legal and pub. adminstrn. jours. Bd. dirs. Downtown Coun., Full Employment Coun., City of Fountains; past pres. Kehilath Israel Synagogue. Recipient Pub. Adminstr. of Yr. award Am. Soc. Pub. Adminstrn., 1985, L.P. Cookingham Pub. Adminstrn. award, 1989; Walter Scheiber Regional Leadership award Nat. Assn. Regional Couns., 1990; fellow U.S. Dept. Transp., 1975. Mem. Assn. C.C. Execs., Rotary. Home: 3720 W 119th Ter Leawood KS 66209-1046 Office: Greater Kans City C of C 911 Main St Ste 2600 Kansas City MO 64105-5303 E-mail: levi@kcchamber.com.

LEVIN, ARNOLD MURRAY, social worker, psychotherapist; b. Bklyn., Dec. 26, 1924; s. William and Pauline Levin; m. Elaine M. Zimmerman, Dec. 19, 1946 (dec. Aug. 1971); children: Michael, Nancy Jo Noteman, Amy Louise. BA, U. Mass., 1948; MA, U. Chgo., 1950, PhD, 1975; Cert., Chgo. Inst. Psychoanalysis, 1955. ACSW, LCSW, BCD. Case worker Jewish Family Svcs., Chgo., 1950-53; group therapist Portal House Clinic Alcoholism, 1952-55; exec. dir. Family Svc., Mental Health Ctr. So. Cook County, Park Forest, Ill., 1953-60; pvt. practice in social work Chgo., 1960—. Founder, pres. Inst. Clin. Social Work, Chgo., 1979—; bd. dirs. Jewish Childrens Bur., Chgo., 1987—; founder, pres., Ill. Soc. Clin. Social Workers, Chgo., 1971-76; mem. 90 for the 90's, Ill. Author: Private Practice of Psychotherapy, 1983. Sgt. U.S. Army, 1943-46. NIMH grantee, 1971; recipient Gov.'s award, Chgo., 1975, Alumnus of Yr. award U. Chgo., 1976. Mem. Nat. Registry of Health Care Providers in Clin. Social Wk. (bd. dirs. 1985-88), Nat. Fedn. Socs. for Clin. Social Work (founder 1971-75), Am. Acad. of Practice (diplomate, disting. practitioner). Avocations: acting, theatre, biking. Home: 3180 N Lake Shore Dr Apt 11G Chicago IL 60657-4865 Office: 151 N Michigan Ave Apt 809 Chicago IL 60601-7543 E-mail: arnielev@aol.com.

LEVIN, BURTON, diplomat; b. N.Y.C., Sept. 28, 1930; s. Benjamin and Ida (Geller) L.; m. Lily Lee, Jan. 4, 1960; children: Clifton, Alicia. BA, CUNY, 1952; M Internat. Affairs, Columbia U., 1954; postgrad., Harvard U., 1964; LLD (hon.), Carleton Coll., 1993. Commd. fgn. service officer Dept. State, 1954; counselor/econ. officer Am. Embassy, Taipei, Taiwan, 1954-56, polit. officer Taiwan, 1969-74; intelligence research specialist Dept. State, Washington, 1956-58, dir. Republic China affairs, 1974-77; polit. officer Am. Embassy, Jakarta, Indonesia, 1959-63, Am. Consulate Gen. Hong Kong, 1965-69, dep. chief mission, 1977-78, consul gen., 1981-86; dep. chief mission Am. Embassy, Bangkok, Thailand, 1978-81; amb. to Burma, 1987-90; dir. Asia Soc. Hong Kong Ctr., 1990-95. Vis. prof. Carleton Coll., 1995; vis. fellow Stanford U., 1974; vis. lectr. Harvard U., 1986, Carleton Coll., 1994; bd. dirs. Mansfield Found., China Fund; mem. coun., co-chmn. Hopkins-Nanjing U. Ctr. for Chinese and Am. Studies Johns Hopkins U. Mem. Am. Fgn. Service Assn. Clubs: Am., Hong Kong Country. Home: 314 2nd St E Northfield MN 55057-2204

LEVIN, CARL, senator; b. Detroit, June 28, 1934; m. Barbara Halpern, 1961; children: Kate, Laura, Erica. BA, Swarthmore Coll., 1956; JD, Harvard U., 1959. Ptnr. Grossman, Hyman & Grossman, Detroit, 1959-64; asst. atty. gen., gen. counsel Mich. CRC, 1964-67; chief appellate defender City of Detroit, 1968-69, mem. coun., 1970-73, pres. coun., 1974-77; ptnr. Schlussel, Lifton, Simon, Rands & Kaufman, 1971-73, Jaffe, Snider, Raitt, Garratt & Heuer, 1978-79; U.S. senator from Mich., 1979—. Past instr. Wayne State U., U. Detroit; chmn. Armed Svcs. Com., Govtl. Affairs Com., Com. on Small Bus., Senate Dem. Steering & Coordination Com., Senate Select Com. on Intelligence. Mem. Mich. Bar Assn., D.C. Bar. Democrat. Office: US Senate 269 Russell Senate Ofc Washington DC 20510-2202*

LEVIN, CHARLES EDWARD, lawyer; b. Chgo., Oct. 6, 1946; m. Barbara Serwer, Dec. 28, 1975. BA with high honor, DePaul U., 1968; JD cum laude, Northwestern U., Chgo., 1971. Bar: Ill. 1971. Asst. instr. legal writing and rsch. Northwestern U. Law Sch., 1970-71; assoc. D'Ancona & Pflaum, Chgo., 1971-76, ptnr., 1977-90, Jenner & Block, Chgo., 1990-2000, McDermott, Will & Emery, Chgo., 2000—. Mem. governing bd. Comml. Fin. Assn. Edn. Found., 1990—; asst. instr. legal writing, rsch. Northwestern U., 1970-71. Mem. bd. editors Northwestern U. Law Rev., 1970-71. Mem. aux. bd. Chgo. Architecture Found., 1989-99; mem. founders leadership coun. C omml. Fin. Assn. Edn. Found., N.Y. Mem. ABA (bus. sect. 1992—), Chgo. Bar Assn. (vice chmn. architecture and law com. 1974-75, vice chmn. divsn. D, mem. exec. com. fed. tax com. 1983-84, comml. fin. and trans. com. 1990—, Article 9 drafting subcom.), East Bank Club Chgo., Met. Club. Avocations: acquisition fine arts, support arts organizations, jogging. Office: McDermott Will & Emery 227 W Monroe St Ste 4400 Chicago IL 60606-5016

LEVIN, CHARLES LEONARD, state supreme court justice; b. Detroit, Apr. 28, 1926; s. Theodore and Rhoda (Katzin) L.; children: Arthur, Amy, Fredrick. B.A., U. Mich., 1946, LL.B., 1947; LL.D. (hon.), Detroit Coll. of Law, 1980. Bar: Mich. 1947, N.Y. 1949, U.S. Supreme Ct. 1953, D.C. 1954. Pvt. practice law, N.Y.C., 1948-50, Detroit, 1950-66; ptnr. Levin, Levin, Garvett & Dill, 1951-66; judge Mich. Ct. Appeals, 1966-73; assoc. justice Mich. Supreme Ct., 1973-96. Mem. Mich. Law Revision Commn., 1966 Trustee Marygrove Coll., 1971-77, chmn., 1971-74; mem. vis. coms. to Law Schs., U. Mich., U. Chgo., 1977-80, Wayne State U. Mem. Am. Law Inst. Office: Mich Supreme Ct 500 Woodward Ave Fl 20 Detroit MI 48226-5498

LEVIN, DAVID L. state legislator; m. Valerie Levin; children: Kimberly, Shawn. Mem. dist. 82 Mo. Ho. of Reps., 1994—. Mem. appropriations, edn. and pub. safety com., comsumer protection and housing com., edn., elementary and secondary com., mcpl. corps. com., critical issues com., civil and administrv. law com., interim joint com. on immigration, interim joint com. on St. Louis downtown revitalization. Office: 11208 Sherwood Oak Ct Rm 116-3 Saint Louis MO 63146-5520

LEVIN, GEOFFREY ARTHUR, botanist; b. Los Alamos, N.Mex., Dec. 7, 1955; s. Jules Samuel and Jane Walden (Settle) L.; children: Tobias, Madeline; m. Lori E. Davis, 2001. BA, Pomona Coll., 1977; MS, U. Calif., Davis, 1980, PhD, 1984. Asst. prof. Ripon (Wis.) Coll., 1982-84; curator, chmn. botany dept. San Diego Natural History Mus., 1984-93; lectr. U. San Diego, 1984-90; asst. profl. scientist Ill. Natural History Survey, Champaign, 1994-96, assoc. profl. scientist, dir. Ctr. for Biodiversity, 1996—. Adj. asst. prof. dept. plant biology U. Ill., 1995—; rsch. assoc. Mo. Bot. Garden, 1994—. Contbr. articles to jours. in field. Bd. dirs. Fond du Lac Audubon Soc., 1983-84, San Diego Audubon Soc., 1986-87; pres. Summit Unitarian Universalist Fellowship, El Cajon, Calif., 1989-91; treas. Unitarian Universalist Ch., Urbana, Ill., 1996-98, moderator, 1998-2000. Recipient Jesse M. Greenman award. Mo. Bot. Garden, 1987; NSF grad. fellow, 1977-81. Mem. Am. Inst. Biol. Scis., Am. Soc. Plant Taxonomists, Bot. Soc. Am., Soc. Systematic Biologists, Calif. Bot. Soc. (bd. editors 1992-95), Phi Beta Kappa, Sigma Xi. Democrat. Office: Ill Natural History Survey Ctr for Biodiversity 607 E Peabody Dr Champaign IL 61820-6970

LEVIN, JACK S. lawyer; b. Chgo., May 1, 1936; s. Frank J. and Judy G. (Skerball) L.; m. Sandra Sternberg, Aug. 24, 1958; children: Lisa, Laura, Leslie, Linda. B.S. summa cum laude, Northwestern U., 1958; LL.B. summa cum laude, Harvard U., 1961. Bar: Ill. 1961; C.P.A. (gold medalist), Ill., 1958. Law clk. to chief judge U.S. Ct. of Appeals 2d Circuit, N.Y.C., 1961-62; asst. for tax matters to Solicitor Gen. of U.S., Washington, 1965-67; assoc. law firm Kirkland & Ellis, Chgo., 1962-65, ptnr., 1967—. Frequent lectr. on legal aspects of venture capital transactions, mergers, acquisitions, buyouts, workouts, fed. income tax matters; vis. com. Harvard Law Sch., 1987-93, lectr., 1997—; lectr. Law Sch. U. Chgo., 1988—. Author book on structuring venture capital, pvt. equity and entrepreneurial transactions; co-author multi-volume treatise on mergers, acquisitions and buyouts; case editor Harvard Law Rev., 1959-61; contbr. numerous articles to legal jours. and chpts. to law books. Parliamentarian Winnetka (Ill.) Town Meetings, 1974-83, 89, 93-96; chmn. nat. fundraising drives Harvard Law Sch., 1985-86, 90-91, 95-96, 2001, chmn. lawyer's divsn. Jewish United Fund Chgo., 1993-95. Mem. ABA (chmn. subcom. 1968-79), Fed. Bar Assn., Chgo. Bar Assn. (exec. com. 1985—), Am. Coll. Tax Counsel. Clubs: Mid-Am. (bd. dirs. 1985-88), Birchwood (Highland Park, Ill.) (pres. 1980-82). Home: 985 Sheridan Rd Winnetka IL 60093-1558 Office: Kirkland & Ellis 200 E Randolph St 57th Fl Chicago IL 60601-6608 Business E-Mail: jack.levin@kirkland.com.

LEVIN, MARVIN EDGAR, physician; b. Terre Haute, Ind., Aug. 11, 1924; s. Benjamin A. and Bertha Levin; m. Barbara Yvonne Symes; 3 children. BA, Washington U., St. Louis, 1947, MD, 1951. Diplomate Am. Bd. Internal Medicine. Intern Barnes Hosp., St. Louis, 1951-52, asst. resident in internal medicine, 1952-53; Nat. Polio Found. fellow in metabolism and endocrinology Sch. Medicine, Washington U., 1953-55; prof. clin. medicine, assoc. dir. Endocrine, Diabetes and Metabolism Clinic, Washington U. Vis. prof. endocrinology and diabetes People's Republic of China, 1982, Jakarta, Indonesia, Cairo, 92, Taipei, 94, Malvern, England, 96; med. dir. Harry and Flora D. Freund Meml. Found. Author: Levin and O'Neal's The Diabetic Foot, 6th edit., 2001; contbr. numerous articles to profl. jours., book chpts. Recipient Disting. Alumni award, Washington U., 1989, Arts and Scis. Disting. award, 1998. Fellow ACP, Soc. Vascular Medicine and Biology; mem. AMA, Am. Diabetes Assn. (nat. bd. dirs. 1984-86, chmn. publ. com. 1986-87, bd. dirs. Mo. chpt. 1987-93, editor in chief Clin. Diabetes 1988-93, co-editor Diabetes Spectrum 1988-93, Outstanding Clinician award 1979, Outstanding Physician Educator award 1991), Am. Dietetic Assn. (hon., Marvin E. Levin, MD Scholarship Program for rsch. in diabetic lower extremity disease named in his honor), St. Louis Clin. Diabetes Assn. (pres. 1965-66), Am. Thyroid Assn., Endocrine Soc., St. Louis Soc. Internal Medicine, St. Louis Internist Club (pres. 1972), Sigma Xi, Alpha Omega Alpha. Avocations: golf, collecting Belle Epoque French prints. Office: 732 Fairfield Lake Dr Town And Country MO 63017-5928 E-mail: blevin0001@aol.com.

LEVIN, MICHAEL DAVID, lawyer; b. Chgo., Oct. 11, 1942; s. Joseph F. and Libbie (Landman) L.; children: Victoria, David, Elizabeth, Emma, Madeline; m. Carol A. McErlean, Oct. 10, 1993. AB, U. Mich., 1964, JD, 1967. Bar: Ill. 1967. Assoc. Arnstein, Gluck, Weitzenfeld & Minow, Chgo., 1967-73, ptnr., 1973-81, Latham & Watkins, Chgo., 1982-95; sr. v.p., sec. & gen. counsel Sears Roebuck & Co., Hoffman Estates, Ill., 1996-98; ptnr. Latham & Watkins, 1998—. Mem. ABA, Chgo. Bar Assn. (chmn. securities law 1982-83), Met. Club. Republican. Jewish. Office: Sears Roebuck & Co 5800 Sears Tower Chicago IL 60684-0001

LEVIN, RONALD MARK, law educator; b. St. Louis, May 11, 1950; s. Marvin S. and Lois (Cohn) L.; m. Anne Carol Goldberg, July 29, 1989. BA magna cum laude, Yale U., 1972; JD, U. Chgo., 1975. Bar: Mo. 1975, D.C. 1977. Law clk. to Hon. John C. Godbold U.S. Ct. Appeals, 5th cir., 1975-76; assoc. Sutherland, Asbill & Brennan, Washington, 1976-79; asst. prof. law Washington U., St. Louis, 1979-80, assoc. prof. law, 1980-85, prof. law, 1985-2000, assoc. dean, 1990-93, Henry Hitchcock prof. law, 2000—. Cons. Adminstrv. Conf. U.S., 1979-81, 93-95. Co-author: Administrative Law and Process, 4th edit., 1997, State and Federal Administrative Law, 2d edit., 1998. Chair senate coun. Washington U., 1988-90. Mem.: ABA (chair sect. adminstrv. law and regulatory practice 2000—01), Assn. Am. Law Sch. (chair sect. adminstrv. law 1993, chair sect. legis. 1995). Home: 7352 Kingsbury Blvd Saint Louis MO 63130-4142 Office: PO Box 1120 Saint Louis MO 63188-1120

LEVIN, SANDER M. congressman; b. Detroit, Sept. 6, 1931; s. Saul R. and Bess (Levinson) L.; m. Victoria Schlafer, 1957 B.A., U. Chgo., 1952; M.A., Columbia U., 1954; LL.B., Harvard U., 1957. Supr. Oakland County Bd. Suprs., Mich., 1961-64; mem. Mich. Senate, 1965-70; fellow Kennedy Sch. Govt., Inst. Politics, Harvard U., Cambridge, Mass., 1975; asst. adminstr. AID, Washington, 1977-81; mem. U.S. Congresses from 12th (formerly 17th) Mich dist., 1983—; mem. ways and means com. Adj. prof. law Wayne State U., Detroit, 1971-74 Chmn. Mich. Dem. Com., 1968-69; Dem. Candidate for Gov., 1970, 74. Office: US Ho of Reps 2300 Rayburn House Office Bldg Washington DC 20515-0001*

LEVINE, DONALD NATHAN, sociologist, educator; b. New Castle, Pa., June 16, 1931; s. Abe and Rose (Gusky) L.; m. Joanna Bull, Nov. 6, 1955 (div. 1967); children: Theodore, William; m. Ruth Weinstein, Aug. 26, 1967; 1 child, Rachel. AB, U. Chgo., 1950, MA, 1954, PhD, 1957; postgrad., U. Frankfurt, Germany, 1952-53. Asst. prof. sociology U. Chgo., 1962-65, assoc. prof., 1965-73, prof., 1973-86, dean of Coll., 1982-87, Peter B. Ritzma prof., 1986—. Founder, pres. Aiki Exts., Inc., 1998—. Author: Wax and Gold: Tradition and Innovation in Ethiopian Culture, 1965, Georg Simmel on Individuality and Social Forms, 1971, Greater Ethiopia: The Evolution of a Multiethnic Society, 1974, Simmel and Parsons: Two Approaches to the Study of Society, 1980, The Flight from Ambiguity: Essays in Social and Cultural Theory, 1985, Visions of the Sociological Tradition, 1995; editor: The Heritage of Sociology series, 1988—. Mem. adv. bd. Ethiopian Cmty. Assn. Chgo., 1993—. Recipient Quantrell award U. Chgo., 1971, Cert. of award Ethiopian Rsch. Coun., 1993, Amoco Found. award for disting. contbn. to undergrad. tchg., 1996, Outstanding Cmty. Support award Ethiopian Cmty. Assn. of Chgo., 2000; Guggenheim fellow, 1980; fellow Ctr. for Advanced Study in Behavioral Scis., 1980-81. Mem. Internat. Soc. Comparative Study Civilization, Am. Sociol. Assn. (chair theory sect. 1996-97). Jewish. Office: U Chgo 1126 E 59th St Chicago IL 60637-1580 E-mail: dlok@midway.uchicago.edu.

LEVINE, LAURENCE HARVEY, lawyer; b. Cleve., Aug. 23, 1946; s. Theodore and Celia (Chaikin) Levine; m. Mary M. Conway, May 13, 1978; children: Abigail, Adam, Sarah. BA cum laude, Case Western Res. U., 1968; JD, Northwestern U., 1971. Bar: Ill. 1971, U.S. Dist. Ct. (no. dist.) Ill. 1972, U.S. Ct. Appeals (6th, 7th, 10th, 11th and D.C. cirs.), U.S. Ct. Claims 1997, U.S. Ct. Appeals (fed. cir.) 2000. Law clk. to presiding judge U.S. Ct. Appeals (6th cir.), Detroit, 1971-72; assoc. Kirkland & Ellis, Chgo., 1972-76; ptnr. Latham & Watkins, 1976—. Bd. editors Northwestern Law Rev., 1968-71. Mem. ABA, Chgo. Bar Assn., Mid-Am. Club. Office: Latham & Watkins Sears Tower Ste 5800 Chicago IL 60606-6306 E-mail: laurence.levine@lw.com.

LEVINE, NORMAN M. academic administrator; b. Chgo., 1943; BS Engring., Ill. Inst. Tech., 1964; MBA, Marquette U., 1969. Sr. v.p., CFO DeVry Inc., Oakbrook Terrace, 2001—. Mem. Fin. Execs. Internat. Office: DeVry Inc Ste 1000 One Tower Ln Oakbrook Terrace IL 60181 Fax: 630-571-0317.

LEVINE, PETER S. corporate lawyer; b. Cleve., Jan. 15, 1959; BA with honors, Northwestern U., 1981; JD, U. Mich., 1984. Bar: Ohio 1984. Assoc. Benesch, Friedlander, Coplan & Aronoff, 1984-85; trial atty. Equal Employment Opportunity Commn., 1985-88; law instr. Case We. Res. U., 1988-90; trustee Cleve. Legal Aid Soc., 1988-90; counsel TRW Inc., Washington, 1990-93, sr. counsel, 1993-99, v.p., asst. gen. counsel, 1999—. Mem.: ABA, Ohio State Bar Assn., Cleve. Bar Assn. Office: TRW Inc 4505 26 Mile Rd Washington MI 48094-2600

LE VINE, VICTOR THEODORE, political science educator; b. Berlin, Dec. 6, 1928; came to U.S., 1938; s. Maurice and Hildegard (Hirschberg) LeV.; m. Nathalie Jeanne Christian, July 19, 1958; children: Theodore, Nicole. BA, UCLA, 1950, MA, 1958, PhD, 1961. Research assoc. UCLA, 1958-60; prof., head dept. polit. sci. U. Ghana, Legon, 1969-71; vis. prof. Hebrew U., Jerusalem, 1978, U. Tex., Austin, 1980; Fulbright prof. U. Yaounde, Cameroon, 1981-82; prof. polit. sci. Washington U., St. Louis, 1961—. Cons. U.S. Dept. State, Dept. Def., 1971—; lectr. USIA, 1981—; mem. U.S. Nat. Commn. UNESCO, 1964; dir. Office Internat. Studies, Washington U., 1975-76; vis. lectr. Fudan U., U. Nanjing (China), 1987, Ibn Saud and King Abdulazziz Univs., Saudi Arabia, 1990; mem. Carter Ctr. Internat. monitoring team to Ghana nat. elections, 1992. Author: Cameroons: Mandate to Independence, 1964, 70, Cameroon Federal Republic, 1971, Political Corruption: Ghana, 1975, (with Timothy Luke) Arab-African Connection, 1979; (with Heidenheimer and Johnston) Political Corruption: A Handbook, 1990; Conceptualizing Ethnicity and Ethnic Conflict: A Controversy Revisited, 1997Parapolitics: Mapping The Terrain of Informal Politics, 2002. Mem., dir. UN Assn., St. Louis, 1964-74; mem. Coun. on World Affairs, 1969-2000; pres. Ctr. for Internat. Understanding, 1988-2000. With U.S. Army, 1951-54. Ford. Found. fellow Cameroon, 1960-61; Hoover Instn. fellow, 1974; Lester Martin fellow Truman Instn., Jerusalem, 1978; Fulbright lectr. U.S. Fulbright Commn., Yaounde, Cameroon, 1981-82 Mem. Am. Polit. Sci. Assn., African Studies Assn., Mideast Studies Assn., Midwest Polit. Sci. Assn., Mo. Polit. Sci. Assn. Office: Washington U Dept Polit Sci Saint Louis MO 63130 E-mail: vlevine@artsci.wustl.edu.

LEVINGS, THERESA LAWRENCE, lawyer; b. Kansas City, Mo., Oct. 24, 1952; d. William Youngs and Dorothy (Neer) Frick; m. Darryl Wayne Levings, May 25, 1974; children: Leslie Page, Kerry Dillon. BJ, U. Mo., 1973; JD, U. Mo., Kansas City, 1979. Bar: Mo. 1979, U.S. Dist. Ct. (we. dist.) Mo. 1979, U.S. Ct. Appeals (8th cir.) 1982, U.S. Ct. Appeals (10th cir.) 1986, U.S. Dist. Ct. (ea. dist.) Mo. 1989. Copy editor Kansas City Star, 1975-78; law clk. to judge Mo. Supreme Ct., Jefferson City, 1979-80; from assoc. to ptnr. Morrison & Hecker, Kansas City, 1980-94; founding ptnr. Badger & Levings, L.C., 1994—. Mem. fed. practice com. U.S. Dist. Ct. (we. dist.), 1990-95; mem. fed. adv. com. U.S. Ct. Appeals (8th cir.), 1994-97. Leadership grad. Kansas City Tomorrow; account exec. United Way; bd. dirs. Jr. League, Housing Info. Ctr. Mem. Mo. Bar (bd. govs. 1990—, pres. 2001-, young lawyers coun. 1982-89, chair 1988-89, Pres. award 1989, Outstanding Svc. award young lawyers coun. 1985, 86), Assn. Women Lawyers Greater Kansas City (pres. 1986-87, Woman of Yr. 1993), Lawyers Assn. Greater Kansas City (bd. dirs. young lawyers sect. 1982-83), Kansas City Met. Bar Assn. (chair civil practice and procedure com. 1988-89, chair fed. practice com. 1990-91). Avocations: antiques, history, cooking. Office: Badger & Levings LC 1101 Walnut St Kansas City MO 64106-2134

LEVI-SETTI, RICCARDO, physicist, director; b. Milan, July 11, 1927; married; 2 children. Doctor Degree in Physics, U. Pavia, Italy, 1949; Libera Docenza in Physics, U. Rome, 1955. Asst. prof. U. Pavia, Italy, 1949-51; rsch. mem. Nat. Inst. for Nuclear Rsch. U. Milan, 1951-56; rsch. assoc. Enrico Fermi Inst. U. Chgo., 1956-57, asst. prof., 1957-62, assoc. prof., 1962-65, prof. physics, 1965—, emeritus prof. physics, 1992—; Guggenheim fellow CERN, Geneva, 1963. Hon. rsch. assoc. Field Mus. Natural History, Chgo., 1976—. Decorated Commendatore dell'Ordine al Merito (Italy); John Simon Guggenheim fellow, 1963, Angelo della Riccia fellow Italian Phys. Soc., 1954. Fellow Am. Phys. Soc.; mem. Phi Beta Kappa. Office: U Chgo Enrico Fermi Inst 5640 S Ellis Ave Chicago IL 60637-1433

LEVIT, WILLIAM HAROLD, JR. lawyer; b. San Francisco, Feb. 8, 1938; s. William Harold and Barbara Janis Kaiser L.; m. Mary Elizabeth Webster, Feb. 13, 1971; children: Alison Jones Baumler, Alexandra Bradley Kovacevich, Laura Elizabeth Fletcher, Amalia Elizabeth Webster Todryk, William Harold, III. BA magna cum laude, Yale U., 1960; MA Internat. Rels., U. Calif., Berkeley, 1962; LLB, Harvard U., 1967. Bar: N.Y. 1968, Calif. 1974, Wis. 1979. Fgn. service officer Dept. State, 1962-64; assoc. Davis Polk & Wardwell, N.Y.C., 1967-73; assoc. ptnr. Hughes Hubbard & Reed, N.Y.C., L.A., 1973-79; sec. and gen. counsel Rexnord Inc., Milw., 1979-83; ptnr., dir., chair internat. practice group Godfrey & Kahn, 1983—. Substitute arbitrator Iran-U.S. Claims Tribunal, The Hague, 1984-88; lectr. Practicing Law Inst., ABA, Calif. Continuing Edn. of Bar, State Bar of Wis. Contbr. to: Mergers and the Private Antitrust Suit: The Private Enforcement of Section 7 of the Clayton Act, 1977. Bd. dirs. Wis. Humane Soc., 1980-90, pres., 1986-88; bd. dirs. Vis. Nurse Corp., Milw., 1980-90, chmn., 1985-87; bd. dirs. Vis. Nurse Found., 1986-95, chmn., 1989-91; bd. dirs. Aurora Health Care Inc., 1988-93, Wis. Soc. to Prevent Blindness, 1981-91, Columbia Coll. Nursing, 1992—, chair, 2002—, Aurora Health Care Ventures, 1993—, chair, 1998-2000, 2002-; adv. bd. Med. Coll. Wis. Cardiovasc. Ctr., 1994—, chmn., 1999-2002, chmn. Bd. Ad Oversight Supreme Ct. Wis. Office Lawyer Regulation, 2000—; rep. Assn. Yale Alumni, 1976-79, 81-84, 90-93; pres. Yale Club So. Calif., 1977-79; mem. neutral advisor panel and franchise, and ins. panels CPR Inst. for Dispute Resolution. Ford Found. fellow U. Pa., 1960-61, NDEA fellow U. Calif., Berkeley, 1961-62. Mem.: ABA, Am. Arbitration Assn. (comml. panel 1977—, internat. panel 1997—), Inst. Jud. Adminstrn., Am. Soc. Internat. Law, N.Am. Coun. London Ct. of Internat. Arbitration, N.Y. Stock Exch. (panel arbitrators 1988—), Chartered Inst. Arbitrators (London), Nat. Assn. Security Dealers (panel arbitrators 1988—), Am. Br. Internat. Law Assn., Bar Assn. 7th Cir. (pres. 2002—), State Bar Wis. (dir. internat. bus. transactions sect. 1985—92, dist. 2 Wis. Supreme Ct. bd. attys. profl. responsbility com. 1985—94, chmn. 1993—94), L.A. County Bar Assn. (ethics com. 1976—79), State Bar Calif. (com. on continuing edn. of bar 1977—79), Assn. Bar City N.Y., Am. Soc. Corp. Secs. (dir. 1981—92, pres. Wis. chpt. 1982—83), Am. Law Inst., Town Club, Milw. Athletic Club, Milw. Club, Phi Beta Kappa. Office: 780 N Water St Ste 1500 Milwaukee WI 53202-3512 E-mail: walevit@gklaw.com.

LEVITT, SEYMOUR HERBERT, physician, radiology educator; b. Chgo., July 18, 1928; s. Nathan E. Levitt and Margaret (Chizever) D.; m. Phillis Jeanne Martin, Oct. 31, 1952 (div. Oct. 1981); children: Mary Jeanne, Jennifer Gaye, Scott Hayden; m. Solveig I. Ostberg, Feb. 6, 1983. BA, U. Colo., 1950, MD, 1954, DSc (hon.), 1997. Diplomate Am. Bd. Radiology. Intern Phila. Gen. Hosp., 1954-55; resident in radiology U. Calif. at San Francisco Med. Center, 1957-61; instr. radiation therapy U. Mich., Ann Arbor, 1961-62, U. Rochester, N.Y., 1962-63; asso. prof. radiology U. Okla., Oklahoma City, 1963-66; prof. radiology, chmn. div. radiotherapy Med. Coll. Va., Richmond, 1966-70; prof., head dept. therapeutic radiology U. Minn., Mpls., 1970-99. Cons. in field. Exec. bd. Am. Joint Com. for End Result Reporting and Cancer Staging; com. radiation oncology studies Nat. Cancer Inst.; trustee Am. Bd. Radiology, 1977-89; bd. dirs. Found. for Rsch. and Edn. Bd. dirs., mem. exec. com. Am. Cancer Soc., 1990-95. With M.C., AUS, 1955-57. Recipient Disting. Svc. award U. Colo., 1988. Fellow: Am. Coll. Radiology (bd. chancellors, Gold medal 1995); mem.: Am. Soc. Therapeutic Radiologists (exec. bd. 1974—78, pres. 1978—79, chmn. bd. 1979—80, Gold medal 1991), Am. Soc. Clin. Oncology, Soc. Nuclear Medicine, Internat. Soc. Radiation Oncology (pres. 1981—85), Soc. Chmn. Acad. Radiation Oncology Programs 1974—76, German Soc. Radiation (hon.), European Coun. Radiology (hon.), German Soc. Radiology (hon.), Am. Roentgen Ray Soc., Am. Cancer Soc. (pres. Minn. divsn. 1979—80, nat. bd., exec. com.), Am. Assn. Cancer Rsch., Radiol. Soc. N.Am. (bd. dirs. 1991—2000, chmn. bd. dirs. 1997—98, pres.-elect 1998, pres. 1999—2000), Am. Radium Soc. (sec. 1981—83, pres. 1983—84, Janeway medal 1989), Alpha Omega Alpha, Sigma Xi, Phi Beta Kappa. Home: 7233 Lewis Ridge Pkwy Minneapolis MN 55439-1933 Office: U Minn Med Sch PO MMC 436 Minneapolis MN 55455

LEVY, DEBORAH, security company executive; m. Barry W. Levy (dec.). Student, So. Ill. U. Exec. v.p., sec., officer, dir. Levy Security Corp., Chgo., until 1994, chair, CEO, 1994—. Mem. Women Bus. Enterprise Initiative (Mem. of Yr. award 1997), Nat. Assn. Women Bus. Owners, Am. Soc. Indsl. Security. Office: Levy Security Corp 230 E Ohio St Ste 700 Chicago IL 60611-3258

LEVY, EDWARD CHARLES, JR. manufacturing company executive; b. Detroit, Nov. 14, 1931; s. Edward Charles and Pauline (Birndorf) Levy; 2 children. SB, MIT, 1952. From staff to exec. v.p. Edward C. Levy Co., Detroit, 1952-70, pres., 1970—. Bd. dirs. Edward C. Levy Found., Karmanos Cancer Inst., Detroit, Round Table of Christians and Jews, Mackinac Ctr. for Pub. Policy; trustee Children's Hosp. of Mich., Citizens Rsch. Coun. Mich., Washington Inst. for Near East Policy; officer Am. Israel Pub. Affairs Com. Mem. ASTM, Am. Concrete Inst., Engring. Soc. Detroit, Detroit Club, Renaissance Club, Franklin Hills Country Club. Jewish. Office: Edward C Levy Co Inc 8800 Dix St Detroit MI 48209-1096

LEVY, NELSON LOUIS, physician, scientist, corporate executive; b. Somerville, N.J., June 19, 1941; s. Myron L. and Sylvia (Cohen) L.; m. Joanne Barnett, Dec. 21, 1963 (div. 1972); children: Scott, Erik, Jonathan; m. Louisa Douglas Stiles, Dec. 21, 1974; children: Michael, Andrew, David. BA/BS summa cum laude, Yale U., 1963; MD, Columbia U., 1967; PhD, Duke U., 1972. Diplomate Am. Bd. Allergy and Immunology. Intern U. Colo. Med. Ctr., Denver, 1967-68; resident Duke U. Med. Ctr., Durham, N.C., 1970-73; rsch. assoc. NIH, Bethesda, Md., 1968-70; asst. prof. immunology Duke U. Med. Ctr., Durham, 1972-75, assoc. prof. immunology and neurology, 1975-80, prof., 1980-81; dir. biol. rsch. Abbott Labs., Abbott Park, Ill., 1981, v.p. rsch., 1981-84; pres. Nelson L. Levy Assocs. Inc., 984-87; CEO The CoreTechs Corp., Lake Forest, Ill., 1987-92; pres. Fujisawa Pharm., Deerfield, 1992-93; CEO Ill. Tech. Devel. Corp., 1993-95; chmn. bd. dirs., CEO The Core Techs Corp., Lake Forest, Ill., 1995-99. Chmn. bd. dirs. Horizon Quest Inc., Laguna Hills, Calif., 1996-97, ColesCraft Corp., 1997—, IMM UVA Corp., New Orleans, 1997—; bd. dirs. ChemBridge Corp., San Diego, Targeted Genetics Corp., Seattle, Biona PTY Ltd., Laguna Beach, Internat. Med. Rsch/, Inc., Brea, Calif., Cary Pharm. Co., Bethesda, Md.; chmn. sci. adv. bd. Neoprobe Corp.; mem. sci. adv. bd. Ligand Pharms. Inc., First Horizon Pharmaceuticals, Inc.; cons. Upjohn Co. Inc., Kalamazoo, 1976-77, G.D. Searle Inc., Skokie, Ill., 1984-87, Erbamont Inc., Stamford, Conn., 1984-90, Eastman Kodak, Rochester, N.Y., LyphoMed Inc., Rosemont, Ill., 1985-89, The Nutrasweet Co., Skokie, 1985-88, Bayer AG, 1987-89, Fujisawa Pharm. Co., 1988-92, Alcide Corp., 1991—, Ameritech, 1993—, several venture cos., U.S. Dept. treasury, 1999—. Editor several books; contbr. articles to profl. publs., chpts. to books. Coach Little League, Am. Youth Soccer Orgn.; corp. adv. bd. Family Svc. of South Lake County, 1991—. Surgeon USPHS, 1968-70. Grantee Am. Cancer Soc., 1970-75, NIH, 1971-81, Nat. Multiple Sclerosis Soc., 1974-81, Ill. Dept. Commerce and Cmty. Affairs, 1993—. Mem. Am. Assn. Immunologists, Am. Assn. Cancer Rsch., Licensing Execs. Soc., Rotary, Phi Beta Kappa, Sigma Xi, Alpha Omega Alpha, Phi Gamma Delta. Avocations: triathlons, biking, rock 'n roll. Office: 1391 Concord Rd Lake Forest IL 60045-1506

LEVY, RICHARD PHILIP, physician, educator; b. Hempstead, N.Y., Nov. 3, 1923; s. Edward I. and Elma (Nathan) L.; m. Barbara Quint, Sept. 15, 1945 (div.); children: Donald Martin, Ellen Susan, Charles Edward B.S., Yale U., 1944, M.D., 1947. Intern, resident Univ. Hosps. of Cleve., 1947-53; faculty Case Western Res. Med. Sch., Cleve., 1953—, prof. medicine, 1977-78, clin. prof. medicine, 1978—, prof. internal medicine, 1978—, chmn. dept. internal medicine, 1983-89; prof. internal medicine endocrinology Coll. Medicine Northeastern Ohio U., Akron, Ohio, 1978—; svc. chief endocrinology St. Thomas Med. Ctr., 1985-92. Med. editor Webster's New World Dictionary, 1970 Contbr. articles to profl. jours. Served with USNR, 1949-51 Fellow ACP; mem. Thyroid Assn., Endocrine Soc., Am. Diabetes Assn., Am. Coll. Clin. Endocrinology, Sigma Xi. Office: 444 N Main St Akron OH 44310-3110

LEWAND, F. THOMAS, lawyer; b. San Diego, July 24, 1946; s. Barbara (Boening) L.; m. Kathleen Sullivan, Aug. 3, 1968; children: Thomas, Kevin, Kristen, Carrie. BA, U. Detroit, 1968; JD, Wayne State U., 1970. Bar: Mich. 1970, U.S. Dist. Ct. (ea. dist.) 1970. Law clk. to judge U.S. Ct. Appeals (6th cir.), Detroit, 1970; commr. Oakland County, Pontiac, 1978-80; chief of staff to Gov. J. Blanchard Lansing, 1982-83; ptnr. Jaffe, Raitt & Heuer, Detroit, 1970-92, Bodman, Longley & Dahling, Detroit, 1992—. Trustee Gov. Blanchard Found., Lansing, 1982—; dir. Wayne County Econ. Devel. Corp., 1997—, Nat. Conf. on Cmty. and Justice, 1999—; trustee U. Detroit Mercy., 1996—, chmn., 2001—. Campaign mgr. Gov. James J. Blanchard, MIch., 1978; chmn. Mich. Dems., 1989-91. Mem. State Bar Mich., Nat. Assn. Bond Lawyers. Office: Bodman Longley & Dahling 100 Renaissance Ctr Fl 34 Detroit MI 48243-1001

LEWELLEN, WILBUR GARRETT, management educator, consultant; b. Charleroi, Pa., Jan. 21, 1938; s. Anthony Garrett and Cozie Harriett (Watson) L.; m. Jean Carolyn Vanderlip, Dec. 8, 1962 (div. 1982); children— Stephen G., Jocelyn A., Jonathan W., Robyn E.; m. Eloise Evelyn Vincent, Mar. 5, 1983 B.S., Pa. State U., University Park, 1959; M.S., MIT, Cambridge, 1961, Ph.D., 1967; LhD (hon.), Budapest U. of Econ. Scis., 1996. Asst. prof. mgmt. Purdue U., West Lafayette, Ind., 1964-68, assoc. prof. mgmt., 1968-72, prof., 1972-83, Loeb prof. mgmt., 1983-88, Krannert disting. prof. mgmt., 1988—, dir. exec. edn. programs, 1985—. Cons. Bank Am., San Francisco, 1975—90, Ind. Bell Tel. Co., Indpls., 1976—90, Am. Water Works Co., Wilmington, Del., 1978—94, Indpls. Power and Light Co., 1993—99, NiSource, Inc., 2000—; bd. dirs. Indsl. Dielectrics, Inc. Author: Executive Compensation in Large Industrial Corporations, 1968, Ownership Income of Management, 1971, The Cost of Capital, 1981, Financial Management: An Introduction to Principles and Practice, 2000. Recipient Salgo-Noren award as Outstanding Tchr. in Grad. Profl. Programs, Salgo-Noren Found., 1973, 77, 79, 84. Mem. Fin. Mgmt. Assn. (v.p. 1973-74), Am. Fin. Assn., Strategic Mgmt. Soc., AAUP, Western Fin. Assn., Lafayette Country Club. Methodist. Office: Purdue Univ Grad Sch Mgmt West Lafayette IN 47907

LEWIS, ANDRÉ LEON, artistic director; b. Hull, Que., Can., Jan. 16, 1955; s. Raymond Lincoln and Theresa L. Student, Classical Ballet Studio, Ottawa, Royal Winnipeg (Man.) Ballet Sch., 1975; studies with David Moroni, Arnold Spohr, Rudi van Dantzig, Jiri Kylian, Peter Wright, Hans van Manen, and Alicia Markova, among others. Mem. corps de ballet Royal Winnipeg (Man.) Ballet, 1979-82, soloist, artistic coord., 1984-89, interim artistic dir., 1989-90, assoc. artistic dir., 1990-96, artistic dir., 1996—. Staged Danzig's Romeo and Juliet, Teatro Comunale, Florence, Italy, Greek Nat. Opera, Athens. Dancer, soloist (ballets) Song of a Wayfarer, Fall River Legend, Nuages Pas de Deux, Lento A Tempo E Appassionatto, Nutcracker, Four Last Songs, Romeo and Juliet, Belong Pas de Deux, Ecstasy of Rita Joe, (TV and films) Fall River Legend, Giselle, Heartland, Romeo and Juliet, The Big Top, Firebird; performed at many events including the opening Gala performance of the Internat. Ballet competition in Jackson, Miss., Le Don Des Etoiles, Montreal, a spl. gala honoring Queen Beatrix of Holland and at a Gala performance in Tchaikovsky Hall, Moscow; appeared as a guest artist throughout N.Am., the Orient and USSR. Avocation: listening to opera. Office: Can Royal Winnipeg Ballet 380 Graham Ave Winnipeg MB Canada R3C 4K2 E-mail: ballet@rwb.org.

LEWIS, CALVIN FRED, architect, educator; b. Chgo., Mar. 27, 1946; s. Howard George and Fern Teresa (Voelsch) L.; m. L. Diane Johnson, Aug. 24, 1968; children: Nathan, Miller, Cooper, Wilson. BArch, Iowa State U., 1969. Architect Charles Herbert and Assocs., Des Moines, 1970-86; prin. Herbert Lewis Kruse Blunck Architecture, 1987—; prof., dept. arch chair Iowa State U., 2000—. Arch. nat. lectr.; AIA awards juror. More tha 50 projects published in profl. jours. Recipient Best in Design award Time mag.; named one of Top Young Architects in Country, Met. Home mag.; firm named Nat. AIA Firm of Yr., 2001. Fellow AIA (more than 70 Design awards 1972—, 3 Nat. Honor awards 1997, 2002, Internat Design award Bus. Week/Archtl. Record 1998, Internat. Design mag. awards 1998, 99, Nat. Design award AIA-AISC 1999). Avocations: sports, photography. Office: Herbert Lewis Kruse Blunk Architecture 202 Fleming Bldg Des Moines IA 50309-4081

LEWIS, CHARLES A. investment company executive; b. Orange, N.J., Oct. 23, 1942; s. F. Donald and Edna H. L.; m. Gretchen Smith, July 1967 (div.); m. Penny Bender Sebring, June 9, 1984. BA, Amherst Coll., 1964; MBA, U. Pa., 1966. Asst. to pres. Computer Tech., Inc., Skokie, Ill., 1969-70; 1st v.p. White, Weld, & Co., 1970-78; vice chmn. investment banking Merrill Lynch & Co., Chgo., 1978—. Life trustee Amherst Coll., Folger Shakespear Libr., 1989—, Chgo. Symphony Orch., 1989—; life dir. Juvenile Diabetes Rsch. Found. Greater Chgo.; vis. com. divsn. social scis. U. Chgo.; trustee Ravinia Festival, 1995—98; leadership coun. Chgo. Pub. Edn. Fund, 2000—; governing bd. North Kenwood/Oakland Charter Sch.,

2000—; bd. dirs. Juvenile Diabetes Rsch. Found. Internat., 1994—95. Mem. Chgo.Club, Glen View Club, Econ. Club Chgo., Fisher Island Club. Office: Merrill Lynch & Co 5500 Sears Tower Chicago IL 60606 E-mail: calewis@exchange.ml.com.

LEWIS, DAN ALBERT, education educator; b. Chgo., Feb. 14, 1946; s. Milton and Diane (Sabath) L.; m. Stephanie Riger, Jan. 3, 1982; children: Matthew, Jake. BA cum laude, Stanford U., 1968; PhD, U. Calif., Santa Cruz, 1980. Rsch. assoc. Arthur Bolton Assocs., Sacramento, 1969-70; survey contr. Sci. Analysis Corp., San Francisco, 1971; dir. Stanford Workshops on Polit. and Social Issues Stanford (Calif.) U., 1971-74; projects adminstr. Ctr. Urban Affairs and Policy Rsch., Northwestern U., Evanston, Ill., 1975-80, asst. prof. edn., 1980-86, assoc. prof. edn., 1986-90, assoc. dir., chair grad. program human devel./social policy, 1987-90, prof. edn., 1990—. Vis. scholar Sch. Edn., Stanford U., 1990-91; mem. task force on restructuring mental health svcs. Chgo. Dept. Health, 1982; mem. human rights authority Ill. Guardianship and Advocacy Commn., 1980-82; adv. mem. com. on planning and inter-agy. coordination Commn. Mental Health and Devel. Disabilities, 1979; interim adv. com. on mental health City of Chgo., 1978; adv. mem. Gov.'s Commn. to Revise Mental Health Code Ill., 1975-77; presenter at profl. confs.; presenter workshops. Editor: Reactions to Crime, 1981; co-author: Fear of Crime: Incivility and the Production of a Social Problem, 1986, The Social Construction of Reform: Crime Prevention and Community Organizations, 1988, The Worlds of the Mentally Ill, 1991, The State Mental Patient in Urban Life, 1994, Race and Educational Reform, 1995; contbr. articles, book revs. to profl. publs. Bd. dirs. Designs for Change, Ill. Mental Health Assn.; rsch. adv. com. Chgo. Urban League, Chgo. Panel Pub. Sch. Finances, 1989-91; needs assessment tech. com. United Way Chgo., 1989-90; ednl. coun. Francis W. Parker Sch., Chgo., 1988-90; task force on restructuring mental health svcs. Chgo. Dept. Health, 1982; com. on mentally disabled Ill. State Bar Assn., 1983-89; rsch. policy com. Ill. Dept. Mental Health, 1978; bd. dirs. Mental Health Assn. Greater Chgo., 1977-84, v.p. pub. policy, 1979-83 Recipient Excellence in Tchg. award Northwestern U. Alumni Assn., 1998. Office: Northwestern Univ 2040 Sheridan Rd Evanston IL 60208-0855 E-mail: dlewis@northwestern.edu.

LEWIS, DARRELL L. retail executive; b. Mason City, Iowa, Nov. 20, 1931; s. Milton Loren and Blanche Ione (Wilson) L.; m. Mary Jo Bahnsen, Oct. 22, 1950; children— John L., Lonnette Ann, Sherri Jo. MBA, Stanford U., 1970. With Osco Drug, Inc. subsidiary Jewel Cos., Inc., 1949-62; with Jewel Turn-Style, 1962; pres. Turn-Style Family Centers, Franklin Park, Ill., 1967-74, head Jewel Hypermarket, 1974; pres. Osco Drug, Inc., 1974-75, v.p. store and sales devel., 1976-77; pres. D.L. Lewis Drug Co. Inc., Bensenville, Ill., 1978—, chmn. bd., 1987—. Home: 12338 Sunset Dr Three Rivers MI 49093-9580 Office: DL Lewis Drug Co 12338 Sunset Dr Three Rivers MI 49093-9580

LEWIS, EDWARD ALAN, religious organization adminstrator; b. Brazil, Ind., July 22, 1946; s. Edward and Ruth Margaret (Eberwein) L. B in Music Edn., Grace Coll., 1969; M in Divinity, Grace Sem., 1973. Asst. to pastor, youth dir. Grace Brethren Ch., Winona Lake, Ind., 1969-73; nat. dir. youth ministries Grace Brethren Ch. Christian Edn., 1973-85; dir. candidate personnel Grace Brethren Fgn. Missions, 1982-88; exec. dir. Grace Brethren Ch. Christian Edn., 1985—. Mem. Grace Brethren Ch., Winona Lake, 1969—, exec. mem. denominational youth com., 1984—; moderator Nat. Fellowship of Grace Brethren Chs., 1994-95. Mem. Grace Sem. Alumni Assn. (pres. 1984-85), Ind. Dist. Ministerium, Nat. Ministerium Assn. Avocations: music, piano, singing, jogging, travel. Home and Office: PO Box 365 Winona Lake IN 46590-0365

LEWIS, FRANK RUSSELL, JR. surgeon; b. Willards, Md., Feb. 23, 1941; m. Janet Christensen, 1996. AB in Physics, Princeton U., 1961; MD, U. Md., 1965; postgrad. in med. physics, U. Calif., Berkeley, 1970. Surg. dir. M/SICU San Francisco Gen. Hosp., 1973-80, dir. emergency dept., 1980-83, chief of staff, 1983-85, asst. chief of surgery, 1981-86, chief of surgery, 1986-92; prof. surgery Case Western Res. U., Cleve., 1994—; chmn. dept. surgery Henry Ford Hosp., Detroit, 1992—. Fellow ACS (1st v.p. 1995-96, gov. 1988-93); mem. Cen. Surg. Soc., Western Surg. Soc., Am. Surg. Assn., Shock Soc. (pres., coun. mem. 1978—), Am. Assn. for Surgery Trauma (pres. 1999—). Office: Henry Ford Hosp Dept Surg E 837 2799 W Grand Blvd Detroit MI 48202-2689 E-mail: flewis1@hfhs.org., frlewis@mediaone.net.

LEWIS, GENE DALE, historian, educator; b. Globe, Ariz., Feb. 20, 1931; s. Abner E. and May J. (Hyatt) L.; m. Dottie Ladd Bidlingmeyer, Aug. 3, 1963. BA, Ariz. State U., 1951, MA, 1952; PhD, U. Ill., 1957. Lectr. Ariz. State U., 1953, So. Ill. U., 1957-58; vis. assoc. prof. history U. Ill., Urbana, 1965, Case Western Res. U., Cleve., 1966; prof. history U. Cin., 1958—, acting head dept., 1981-82, dir. grad. studies, 1989, head dept., 1989-98. Sr. v.p., provost, 1973-76 Author: Charles Ellet Jr., Engineer as Individualist, 1968; editor: New Historical Perspectives: Essays on the Black Experience in Antebellum America, 1984; co-editor Greater Cincinnati Bicentennial History Series, 1988—. Recipient Barbour award for excellence U. Cin., 1969, Nat. award Omicron Delta Kappa, 1968 Mem. AAUP, So. Hist. Assn., Am. Hist. Assn., Orgn. Am. Historians. Home: 444 Rawson Woods Ln Cincinnati OH 45220-1142 Office: U Cin Dept History Cincinnati OH 45221-0001

LEWIS, JAMES A. state legislator; b. Highland, Ky., Dec. 26, 1930; m. Anna Mae Spencer; children: David, Thomas, Charles. Student, Purdue U. Bldg. contr.; mem. Ind. Ho. of Rep., 1970-72, Ind. Senate from 45th dist., 1974—; minority caucus chmn.; mem. natural resources, fin., agr. and small bus. coms.; mem. labor and pensions com.; ranking minority mem.; mem. appointments and claims com.; mem. consumer affairs com. Mem. City Council, 1960-68; mem. Clark County, Ind. coun., 1981-82; precinct committeeman; scoutmaster Boy Scouts Am. Recipient Best Citizen award Jaycees, 1959. Mem. So. Home Bldrs. Assn., Clark County Conservation Club, Masons, Scottish Rite, Moose.

LEWIS, JEFF, construction company executive; CFO Huber, Hunt & Nichols, Indpls., until 1999. Office: Huber Hunt & Nichols 250 E 96th St Ste 415 Indianapolis IN 46240-3730

LEWIS, JOHN BRUCE, lawyer; b. Poplar Bluff, Mo., Aug. 12, 1947; s. Evan Bruce and Hilda Kathryn (Kassebaum) L.; m. Diane F. Grossman, July 23, 1977; children: Samantha Brooking, Ashley Denning. BA, U. Mo., 1969, JD, 1972; LLM in Labor and Employment Law, Columbia U., 1978; diploma, Nat. Inst. Trial Advocacy, 1982. Bar: Mo. 1972, U.S. Ct. Appeals (8th cir.) 1973, U.S. Dist. Ct. (ea. dist.) Mo. 1974, U.S. Dist. Ct. (no. dist.) Ohio 1979, Ohio 1980, U.S. Ct. Appeals (6th cir.) 1982, U.S. Dist. Ct. (ea. dist.) Mich. 1983, U.S. Ct. Appeals (3d cir.) 1987, U.S. Supreme Ct. 1987, U.S. Dist. Ct. (no. dist.) Calif. 1987, U.S. Ct. Appeals (7th cir.) 1990. Assoc. Millar, Schaefer & Ebling, St. Louis, 1972-77, Squire, Sanders & Dempsey, Cleve., 1979-85; ptnr. Arter & Hadden, 1985-2001, Baker & Hostetler, Cleve., 2001—. Lectr. in field. Author: Employment Practices Self-Assessment Guide, 2d edit., 2000; contbr. articles to legal jours. Mem. Cleve. Council on World Affairs. Mem. ABA (sec. labor and employment law, com. EEO law, comm. law forum), Ohio State Bar Assn. (sec. labor and employment law), Greater Cleve. Bar Assn. (sec. labor law), St. Louis Met. Bar Assn., Am. Law Inst., Selden Soc., Ohio C. of C. (labor adv. com.), William K. Thomas Inn of Ct. (master bencher). Office: Baker & Hostetler 3200 Nat City Ctr 1900 E 9th St Cleveland OH 44114-3485 Business E-Mail: jlewis@bakerlaw.com.

LEWIS, JOHN D. banking official; Various mgmt. positions with Comerica, Inc., Detroit, 1970-95, vice-chmn., 1995—, also bd. dirs. Office: Comerica Inc Comerica Twr/500 Woodward A Detroit MI 48226

LEWIS, JOHN FRANCIS, lawyer; b. Oberlin, Ohio, Oct. 25, 1932; s. Ben W. and Gertrude D. Lewis; m. Catharine Monroe, June 15, 1957; children: Ben M., Ian A., Catharine G., William H. B.A., Amherst Coll., 1955; J.D., U. Mich., 1958. Bar: Ohio 1958, U.S. Dist. Ct. (no dist.) Ohio 1959, U.S. Supreme Ct. 1973. Assoc. firm Squire, Sanders & Dempsey, Cleve., 1958-67; ptnr. Squire, Sanders & Dempsey LLP, 1967—, mng. ptnr. Cleve. office, 1985—. Co-author: Baldwin's Ohio School Law, 1980-91, Ohio Collective Bargaining Law, 1983. Trustee Ohio Found. Ind. Colls., Case Western Res. U., chmn., 1995-2001; trustee Playhouse Sq. Found., chmn., 1980-85; trustee, chmn. Ohio Aerospace Coun., 2001—; former mem. exec. com. Greater Cleve. Growth Assn.; trustee Musical Arts Assn., Univ. Circle, Inc., Ohio Foundn. Independent Coll.; hon. trustee Found. for Sch. Bus. Mgmt., Leadership Cleve., 1977-78; chmn. Cleanland Cleve., 1992-95. Recipient Malcolm Daisley Labor-Mgmt. Rels. award, 1991, Tree of Life award Jewish Nat. Fund, 1993, Nat. Conf. award, 1995, Franklin D. Roosevelt March of Dimes award, 1999. Mem. Cleve. Bar Assn., Ohio Bar Assn., ABA, Nat. Sch. Bd. Assn., Edn. Law Assn. (past pres.), Ohio Assn. Sch. Bus. Ofcls. (hon. life, Marion McGehey Edn. Law award 1998), Fifty Club of Cleve., Ohio Council Sch. Bd. Attys. (founding chair). Episcopalian. Home: 2 Bratenahl Pl Ste 7ef Bratenahl OH 44108-1183 Office: Squire Sanders & Dempsey 4900 Key Tower 127 Public Sq Ste 4900 Cleveland OH 44114-1304 E-mail: capeoceans@aol.com., Jlewis@ssd.com.

LEWIS, JORDAN D. federal judge; b. 1932; JD, Ind. U., 1959. Atty. Lewis & Lewis, 1959-96; part-time magistrate judge U.S. Dist. Ct. (so. dist.) Ind., Terre Haute, 1979—. Served with U.S. Army, 1952-55. Office: 207 Federal Bldg Terre Haute IN 47808

LEWIS, LISA, psychologist, administrator; B of Psychology and Biology, Pa. State U.; M of Clin. Psychology, Conn. Coll.; D of Clin. Psychology, Miami U., Oxford, Ohio. Intern Fla. Med. Sch.; dir. clin. psychology Menninger, Topeka. Presenter in field. Contbr. articles to profl. jours. Recipient David Rappaport Excellence in Teaching award; postdoctoral fellow Menninger. Office: Menninger PO Box 829 Topeka KS 66601-0829

LEWIS, MARTIN EDWARD, shipping company executive, foreign government concessionary; b. Chgo., Dec. 27, 1958; s. Martin Luther and Anna Adlene (Gaines) L. BA, Johns Hopkins U., 1981; postgrad., Rush Med. Coll., 1983-85. Chmn. bd., chief exec. officer Internat. Financier Inc., Chgo., 1987—; co. rep. Assn. S.E. Asia Nations Secretariat Gen., Jakarta, Indonesia, 1995—. Co. rep. OPEC, Vienna, 1988—, Supreme Coun. States of Cooperation Coun., Summit Confs. Countries of Cooperation Coun. for Arab States of Gulf, Secretariat Gen., Riyadh, Saudi Arabia, 1989—; corp. amb. plenipotentiary GM Overseas Ops., N.Y.C., 1977, Adam Opel, Russelsheim, Fed. Republic Germany, 1977. Mem. Asia Soc., Japan Soc. Republican. Avocations: golf, tennis, yachting, scuba diving. E-mail: info@ifiworld.com.

LEWIS, MERLE DEAN, electric and gas utility executive; b. Madison, S.D., Nov. 21, 1947; s. Elmer and Fern (Runestad) L.; m. Barbara K. Minnaert, Aug. 9, 1969; children: Eric, Robin, Amy. BS, Dakota State U., 1970; JD, U. S.D., 1973. Bar: S.D. Assoc. law Lassegard & Lewis, Mitchell, S.D., 1973-75; corp. atty. Northwestern Pub. Svc. Co., Huron, 1975-82, corp. atty., asst. corp. sec., 1982-85, asst. v.p. corp. svcs., 1985-87, v.p. corp. svcs., 1987—; chmn., CEO Northwestern Corp., Sioux Falls. Bd. dirs. Huron Regional Med. Ctr., Norwest Bank, Huron. Mayor City of Huron, 1990—; chmn. James River Water Devel. Dist., Huron, 1986-90, Huron Area C. of C., 1988-89; bd. dirs. S.D. Water Congress, Pierre, 1988-90. Named Jaycee Internat. Senator, Jaycees Internat., 1980, Outstanding Young Citizen, S.D. Jaycees, 1980. Mem. ABA, S.D. Bar Assn., Res. Officer Assn. Lutheran. Avocations: golf, fishing, hunting. Home: 2000 Cardinal Ln Huron SD 57350-3493 Office: Northwestern Corp 125 S Dakota Ave Sioux Falls SD 57104

LEWIS, PETER BENJAMIN, insurance company executive; b. Cleve., Nov. 11, 1933; s. Joseph M. and Helen (Rosenfeld) L.; married, June 19, 1955 (div. 1980); children: Ivy, Jonathan, Adam. AB, Princeton U., 1955. With Progressive Ins. Cos., 1955—; exec. trainee Progressive Casualty Ins. Co.; pres., CEO The Progressive Corp., Ohio, 1965-2000, Mayfield Village, 1965-94; chmn. bd. The Progressive Corp., 2000—. Mem. Soc. C.P.C.U., Cleve. Racquet Club. Office: Progressive Corp 6300 Wilson Mills Rd Cleveland OH 44143-2109

LEWIS, PHILLIP HAROLD, museum curator; b. Chgo., July 31, 1922; s. Bernard and Sonia (Pimstein) L.; m. Sally Leah Rappaport, Aug. 25, 1949; children— David Bernard, Betty Alice and Emily Ruth (twins). B.F.A., Art Inst. Chgo., 1947; M.A., U. Chgo., 1953, Ph.D., 1966; postgrad. (Fulbright ednl. grant), Australian Nat. U., Canberra, 1953-54. Conducted field research projects on art and soc. of New Ireland, 1953-54, 70, 81; asst. curator primitive art Field Mus. Natural History, Chgo., 1957-59, asso. curator, 1960, curator, 1961-67, curator primitive art and Melanesian ethnology, 1968-92, ret., 1992, chmn. dept. anthropology, 1975-79, co-chmn. dept., 1980-81, acting chmn. dept., 1987; curator emeritus, 1994—. Served with USAAF, 1942-45. Fellow Royal Anthrop. Inst. Gt. Britain and Ireland, Am. Anthrop. Assn. Home: 1222 Chicago Ave Apt 303b Evanston IL 60202-1338

LEWIS, RICHARD PHELPS, physician, educator; b. Portland, Oreg., Oct. 26, 1936; s. Howard Phelps and Wava Irene (Brown) L.; m. Penny A. Brown, Oct. 12, 1982; children: Richard Phelps, Heather Brown. BA, Yale U., 1957; MD, U. Oreg., 1961. Intern Peter Bent Brigham Hosp., Boston, 1961-62, resident, 1962-63; Howard Irwin fellow in cardiology U. Oreg., Portland, 1963-65; sr. resident Stanford U., 1965-66, instr. dept. medicine, 1968-69; asst. chief cardiology Madigan Gen. Hosp., Tacoma, 1966-68; asst. prof. medicine div. cardiology Ohio State U., 1969-71, assoc. prof., 1971-75, prof., 1975-2000, dir. Divsn. Cardiology, 1972-86, dir., 1972-86, assoc. chmn. for hosp. and clin. affairs, 1980-86, prof. emeritus, 2000—. Mem. cardiovascular sect. Am. Bd. Internal Medicine, 1981-87, critical care medicine, 1988-92. Contbr. articles to profl. jours. Served with M.C. U.S. Army, 1966-68, col. res. Decorated Army Commendation medal Fellow ACP (gov. Ohio chpt. 1976-80, chmn. MKSAP cardiovascular sect. 1989-82), Am. Heart Assn. (coun. on clin. cardiology), Am. Coll. Cardiology (Ohio gov. 1988-91, chmn. bd. govs. 1990-91, trustee 1991-2000; editor self assessment program, 1991-96, 2000—, v.p. 1994-95, pres.-elect 1995-96, pres. 1996-97), Am. Clin. and Climatological Assn.; mem. Am. Fedn. Clin. Rsch., Ctrl. Soc. Clin. Rsch., Laennec Soc., Am. Heart Assn., Assn. U. Cardiologists, Alpha Omega Alpha. Republican. Episcopalian. Home: 5088 Stratford Ave Powell OH 43065-8771 Office: 473 W 12th Ave Columbus OH 43210-1240

LEWIS, ROBERT ENZER, lexicographer, educator, editor; b. Windber, Pa., Aug. 12, 1934; s. Robert Enzer and Katharine Torrence (Blair) L.; m. Julie Fatt Cureton, May 14, 1977; children: Perrin Lewis Rubin, Torrence Evans Lewis; stepchildren: Sarah Cureton Kaufman, James S. Cureton. BA, Princeton U., 1959; MA, U. Pa., 1962, PhD, 1964. Tchr. English Mercersburg (Pa.) Acad., 1959-60; teaching fellow U. Pa., Phila., 1961-63; lectr. Ind. U., Bloomington, 1963-64, asst. prof., 1964-68, assoc. prof., 1968-75, prof. English, 1975-82, U. Mich., Ann Arbor, 1982—. Author: (with A. McIntosh) Descriptive Guide to the Manuscripts of the Prick of Conscience, 1982, (with others) Index of Printed Middle English Prose, 1985; editor: De Miseria Condicionis Humane (Lotario dei Segni), 1978; co-editor: Middle English Dictionary, 1982-83, editor-in-chief: vols. 8, 9, 10, 11, 12, 13, 1984-2001; gen. editor: Chaucer Libr., 1970—, chmn. editl. com., 1978-89, 97—. Bd. regents Mercersburg Acad., 1975-87. U.S. Army, 1954-56. Vis. rsch. fellow Inst. Advanced Studies in the Humanities, U. Edinburgh, 1973-74; Am. Coun. Learned Socs. fellow, 1979-80. Mem. Medieval Acad. Am. (mem. publs. com. 1987-92), Dictionary Soc. N.Am., New Chaucer Soc. Episcopalian. Office: U Mich Dept English 3187 Angell Hall Ann Arbor MI 48109-1003 E-mail: relewis@umich.edu.

LEWIS, ROBERT LAWRENCE, lawyer, educator; b. N.Y.C., Sept. 25, 1919; s. Isador and Sadie (Holzinger) L.; m. Frieda Friedman, Nov. 24, 1940 (dec. 1961); children— Brian S., Paul E., David N.; m. Joanne Marcia Waxman, June 16, 1963; children— Pavia S., Eraclea S. A.B., Hamilton Coll., 1940; LL.B., Case Western Res. U., 1948. With firm Ulmer & Berne, Cleve., 1948-64, ptnr., 1956-64; ret., 1964. Prof. law, dir. grad. div. Cleve.-Marshall Law Sch. (now Cleve. State U.), 1948-53; bd. dirs. Banner Industries, Inc., Cleve.; scholar-in-residence, prof. classics Cuayhoga C.C.; adj. prof. nonprofit governance Case Western Res. U., Cleve. Author: Five Angry Women, 1990, Agatharcus, 1993. Cons., evaluator North Central Assn. Colls. and Schs., Middle States Assn. Mem. Cleve. Area Arts Council, 1971-73; pres. Fairmount Center for Creative and Performing Arts, 1973-75; trustee, chmn. bd. Cuyahoga Community Coll.; trustee Cuyahoga Community Coll. Found., Playhouse Sq. Found., Cleve., Cleve. Commn. Higher Edn., Lake Erie Coll., Council for Interinstnl. Leadership, Pace Assn., New Orgn. for Visual Arts; bd. dirs. Assn. Governing Bds. Univs. and Colls.; bd. advisers Cleve. Ballet; trustee, v.p. New Cleve. Opera Co. Served to 1st lt., arty. and ordnance corps AUS, 1942-46, NATOUSA. Decorated Legion of Merit, Purple Heart Mem. Exec. Order Ohio Commodore, Phi Beta Kappa. Home: 2425 N Park Blvd Apt 4 Cleveland OH 44106-3154 Office: 900 Bond Ct Bldg Cleveland OH 44114

LEWIS, STEPHEN RICHMOND, JR. economist, educator, academic administrator; b. Englewood, N.J., Feb. 11, 1939; s. Stephen Richmond Lewis and Esther (Magan) Lewish; m. Judith Frost, 1996; children from previous marriage: Virginia, Deborah, Mark. BA, Williams Coll., 1960, LLD, 1987; MA, Stanford U., 1962, PhD, 1963; LHD, Doshisha U., 1993. Instr. Stanford U., 1962—63; research advisor Pakistan Inst. Devel. Econs., Karachi, 1963—65; asst. prof. econs. Harvard U., 1965—66, Williams Coll., 1966—68, assoc. prof., 1968—73, prof., 1973—76, Herbert H. Lehman prof., 1976—87, provost of coll., 1968—71, 1973—77, spl. asst. to pres., 1979—80, dir. Williams-Botswana Project, 1982—88, chmn. dept. econs., 1984—86; vis. sr. research fellow Inst. Devel. Studies, Nairobi, Kenya, 1971—73; econ. cons. to Ministry of Finance and Devel. Planning, Govt. of Botswana, 1975—; vis. fellow Inst. Devel. Studies, Sussex, England, 1986—87; pres., prof. econs. Carleton Coll., Northfield, Minn., 1987—. Cons. econs. Ford Found., Edna McConnell Clark Found., World Bank, Orgn. Econ. Coop. and Devel., Govts. of Kenya, Philippines, Botswana; trustee Carnegie Endowment for Internat. Peace, 1988—. Author (with others): Relative Price Changes and Industrialization in Pakistan, 1969; author: Economic Policy and Industrial Growth in Pakistan, 1969, Pakistan: Industrialization and Trade Policy, 1970, Williams in the Eighties, 1980, Taxation for Development, 1983, South Africa: Has Time Run Out?, 1986, Policy Choice and Development Performance in Botswana, 1989, The Economics of Apartheid, 1989; mem. editl. bd.: Jour. Econ. Lit., 1985—87; contbr. chapters to books, articles to profl. jours. Exec. com. Indianhead coun. Boy Scouts Am., 1989—. Decorated Presdl. Order of Meritorious Svc. Botswana; recipient Disting. Eagle Scout award, 1993; fellow, Danforth Found., 1960—63, dissertation, Ford Found., 1962—63. Mem.: Am. Econ. Assn., Nat. Tax Assn., Coun. on Fgn. Rels., Phi Beta Kappa. Office: Carleton Coll Office Pres 1 N College St Ofc Pres Northfield MN 55057-4001

LEX, WILLIAM JOSEPH, college official; b. Temple, Tex., Sept. 3, 1944; s. Henry Joseph and Mary Dorothy (Jeske) L.; m. Diane Chostner, Nov. 25, 1967; 1 child, Carolyn Kimberly. AA, San Francisco City Coll., 1965; BA, U. Calif., Santa Barbara, 1967; MS, Oreg. State U., 1973; PhD, U. Tex., 1984. Head resident Oreg. State U., Corvallis, 1971-73; head resident edn. and programs U. Alaska, Fairbanks, 1973-76; dir. vocat. and tech. studies Tanana Valley C.C., 1976-86; assoc. dean, dir. North Campus Pa. Coll. Tech., Wellsboro, 1986-91; dean Mendocino Coast Campus, Ft. Bragg, Calif., 1991-96; pres. Frontier C.C., Fairfield, Ill., 1996—. Chmn. community devel. com. Mendocino Pvt. Industry Coun.; mem. coastal com. Mendocino County Econ. Summit Steering Com.; mem. adv. com. Ft. Bragg Police Dept., Mendocino County Arts Coun. Mem. Nat. Coun. Instrnl. Adminstrs., Wellsboro Area C. of C. (bd. dirs. 1987-91), Mendocino Coast C. of C. (chmn. community devel. com.), Rotary (bd. dirs. GAleton, Pa. chpt. 1988-89, active Ft. Bragg chpt.), Phi Kappa Phi, Kappa Delta Pi. Democrat. Avocations: reading, gardening, music, outdoor sports. Office: Apt 118 2300 Overlook Rd Cleveland OH 44106-2346

LEYDA, JAMES PERKINS, retired pharmaceutical company executive; b. Youngstown, Ohio, Oct. 2, 1935; s. Walter Cletus and Dorothy Eleanor (Perkins) L.; m. Barbara Marie Dykstra, Sept. 9, 1967; children: Jason Walter, Jeffrey Albert, Justin Michael. BS in Pharmacy, Ohio No. U., 1957; MSc in Pharmacy, Ohio State U., 1959, PhD in Pharmacy, 1962. Registered pharmacist, Ohio. Devel. chemist Lederle Labs., Pearl River, N.Y., 1962-66; mgr. new product devel. Cyanaid Internat., 1966-69; dir. new product devel. Merrell Internat., N.Y.C. also Westport, Conn., 1969-81; dir. pharmacy rsch. Merrell Dow Pharm., Cin., 1981-84, dir. comml. devel., 1984-89; assoc. dir. product approval Marion Merrell Dow Inc. (name changed to Hoechst Marion Rousssel, Inc.), 1992-98; pres. Nova Cell Biotech., 1997-2000, Emerging Concepts, Inc., Cin., 1998—, Emerging Concepts Inc., Cin. Author: Pharmaceutical Chemistry, 1964; contbr. articles to profl. jours. Recipient Ohio No. U./Bristol Labs. Bristol award, 1957, Richardson Merrell Inc. Lunsford Richardson award, 1960, NIH Predoctoral Fellowship award, 1960. Mem. AAAS, Am. Pharm. Assn., Acad. Pharm. Scis., N.Y. Acad. Scis., Sigma Xi Avocations: tennis, golf. Home: 10597 Tanagerhills Dr Cincinnati OH 45249-3634 Office: Emerging Concepts Inc 3130 Highland Ave Fl 3 Cincinnati OH 45219-2374 E-mail: jleyda@aol.com., jleyda.ECI@biostart.org.

LEYH, GEORGE FRANCIS, retired association executive; b. Utica, N.Y., Oct. 1, 1931; s. George Robert and Mary Kathleen (Haley) L.; m. Mary Alice Mosher, Sept. 17, 1955; children: Timothy George, Kristin Ann. B.C.E., Cornell U., 1954; M.S. (Univ. fellow), 1956. Structural engr. Eckerlin and Klepper, Syracuse, N.Y., 1956-59; assoc. dir. engring. Martin Marietta Corp., Chgo., 1959-63; structural engr. Portland Cement Assn., 1963-67; dir. mktg. Concrete Reinforcing Steel Inst., 1967-75; exec. v.p. Am. Concrete Inst., Detroit, 1975—, editor jour., 1975—. Mem. Planning Commn., Streamwood, Ill., 1960-68; chmn. Lake Bluff (Ill.) Citizens Com. for Conservation, 1972. Recipient Bloem Disting. Service award Am. Concrete Inst., 1972 Mem. ASCE, Am. Soc. Assn. Execs. (chmn. key profl. assns. com. 1989-90), Nat. Inst. Bldg. Scis., Am. Ry. Engring. Assn., Am. Nat. Standards Inst. (bd. dirs. 1986—), Am. Soc. for Concrete Constrn. (bd. dirs. 1984—), Phi Kappa Phi. Clubs: North Cape Yacht, Lake Bluff Yacht (dir. 1969-74, commodore 1973). Home: 30405 Oakview Way Bingham Farms MI 48025-4631 Office: Am Concrete Inst PO Box 9094 Farmington Hills MI 48333-9094

LHOTA, WILLIAM J. electric company executive; Exec. v.p. Am. Electric Power Svc. Corp., Columbus, Ohio. Office: Am Electric Power Svc Corp 1 Riverside Plz Columbus OH 43215-2355

LI, CHU-TSING, art history educator; b. Canton, China, 1920; came to U.S., 1947; m. Yao-wen; children: Ulysses, Amy. BA, U. Nanking, 1943;

MA in English Lit., U. Iowa, 1949, PhD in Art History, 1955. Instr. U. Iowa, 1954-55, 56-58, asst. prof., 1958-62, assoc. prof., 1962-65, prof., 1965-66; prof. art history U. Kans., Lawrence, 1966-78, dept. chmn., 1972-78, Judith Harris Murphy Disting. prof., 1978-90, prof. emeritus, 1990—, dir. NEH summer seminar on Chinese art history, 1975, 78, coordinator Mellon faculty seminar, 1979; acting asst. prof. Oberlin Coll., 1955-56; asst. prof. Ind. U., summer 1956; coordinator N.Y. state faculty seminar on Chinese Art History, SUNY, 1965; research curator Nelson Gallery of Art, Kansas City, 1966—. Vis. prof. fine arts Chinese U., Hong Kong, 1972-73, summer 1971, leader China visit group, 1973; vis. prof. Grad. Inst. Art History, Nat Taiwan U., 1990; vis. Andrew W. Mellon prof. U. Pitts., 1995; dir. NEH Summer Inst. Modern Chinese Art and Culture, 1991; participant Internat. Symposiums on Chinese Painting, Nat. Palace Mus., Taipei, 1970, Cleve. Mus. Art, 1981, Huangshan Sch. Painters, Hefei, Ahnui, Rep. China, 1984, on Words and Images in Chinese Painting, Met. Mus. Art, N.Y.C., 1985, on the Elegant Brush: Chinese Painting under the Qianlong Emperor, Phoenix Art Mus., 1985, to celebrate 60th anniversary Nat. Palace Mus., Taipei, Taiwan, 1985, on History of Yuan Dynasty, Nanjing U., China, 1986, on art of Badashanren (Chu Ta), Nanchang, China, 1986; on Dunhuang Grottoes, China, 1987; on the Four Monk Painters, Shanghai Mus., 1987; on art of Chang Dai-chien, Nat. Mus. History, Taipei, 1988; Symposium on Contemporary Artistic Development, Nanjing, 1988; Symposium on Chinese Painting of Ming Dynasty Chinese U. Hong Kong, 1988; Symposium on Chinese Painting of the Ming and Qing Dynasties from the Forbidden City, Cleve. Mus. Art, 1989, Symposium on Hist. Studies, since 1911, Nat. Taiwan U., 1989, Symposium on 40th Anniversary of Founding of Liaoning Provincial Mus., Shenyang, China, 1989, Symposium on Painting of Wu Sch., Palace Mus., Beijing, 1990; Internat. Colloquium on Chinese Art History, Nat. Palace Mus. Taipei, 1991, Internat. Symposium on Art of Four Wangs, Shanghai, 1992, VIIeme Colloque Internat. de Sinologie, Chantilly, France, 1992, Symposium Painting at Close Qing Empire, Phoenix, 1992, Symposium on Ming & Qing Painting, Beijing, 1994, Symposium on Art of Zhao Meng-fu, Shanghai, 1995, Symposium on 20th Century Chinese Painting, Hong Kong Mus. Art, 1995, Symposium on Contemporary Chinese Painting, Biennale of Shanghai Art Mus., 1998; spl. cons. Chinese U., Hong Kong, 1971, Symposium on Painting and Calligraphy by Ming Loyalists, Early Ch'ing Period, 1975. Author: books and exhbn. catalogues including The Autumn Colors on the Ch'iao and Hua Mountains, A Painting by Chao Meng-fu, 1254-1322, 1965, Liu Kuo-sung: The Development of a Modern Chinese Artist, 1970, A Thousand Peaks and Myriad Ravines: Chinese Paintings in the Charles A Drenowatz Collection, 2 vols., 1974, Trends in Modern Chinese Painting, 1979; co-author: History of Modern Chinese Painting, Part 1: Late Qing, 1998, Part 2: Republican China, 2001; editor: Artists and Patrons: Some Social and Economic Aspects of Chinese Painting, 1990; co-editor: Chinese Scholar's Studio: Artistic Life in Late Ming, Asia Soc., 1987; contbr. , articles to books and catalogues. Ford Found. Fgn. Area Tng. fellow, 1959-60; grantee Am. Council Learned Socs. and Social Sci. Research Council, 1963-64, NEH, 1975, 78, 91, Com. for Scholarly Communication with People's Republic of China Nat. Acad. Scis., 1979, Am. Council Learned Socs., 1980, Asian Cultural Council, N.Y., 1981, Kans. U., summers 1966-80; U. Iowa research prof., 1963-64; Fulbright-Hayes faculty fellow, 1968-69 Mem. Coll. Art Assn. Am., Assn. for Asian Studies, Midwest Art History Soc., Internat. House of Japan, Min-chiu Soc. Hong Kong, Phi Tau Phi, Phi Beta Kappa (hon.), Phi Beta Delta. Home: 1108 Avalon Rd Lawrence KS 66044-2506 Office: Univ Kans Kress Found Dept Art History Lawrence KS 66045-0001 E-mail: ctsli@ku.edu., ctsli@juno.com.

LI, NORMAN N. chemicals executive; b. Shanghai, China, Jan. 14, 1933; came to U.S.; naturalized, 1969. s. Lieh-wen and Amy H. Li; m. Jane C. Li, Aug. 17, 1963; children: Rebecca H., David H. BSChemE, Nat. Taiwan U., Taipei, 1955; MS, Wayne State U., 1957; PhD, Stevens Inst. Tech., 1963. Sr. scientist Exxon Rsch. and Engring. Co., Linden, N.J., 1963-81; dir. separation sci. and tech. UOP, Des Plaines, Ill., 1981-88; dir. engineered products and process tech. Allied-Signal Inc., 1988-92, dir. rsch. and tech., 1993-95; pres., CEO NL Chem. Technology, Inc., 1995—. Mem. NRC, 1985-89; lectr. AIChE, 1975-86. Editor 13 books on separation sci. and tech.; contbr. articles to jours. in field; patentee in field. Fellow: AIChE (dir. divsn. food, pharms. and bioengring. 1988—91, bd. dirs. 1992—94, Alpha Chi Sigma rsch. award 1988, Ernest Thiele award 1995, Chem. Engring. Practice award 2000, Lifetime Achievement award 2001); mem.: Acad. Sinica, Chinese Acad. Scis., N.Am. Membrane Soc. (pres. 1991—93, Perkin medalist 2000), Am. Chem. Soc. (Separation Sci. and Tech. award 1988), NAE. Home: 620 N Rolling Ln Arlington Heights IL 60004-5820 E-mail: nlchem@aol.com.

LI, TING-KAI, medical educator, researcher; BA in Chemistry and Biology, Northwestern U.; MD, Harvard U.; DSc (hon.), Northeastern Ohio U. Dep. dir. biochemistry divsn. Walter Reed Army Inst. Rsch.; Disting. Prof. Medicine and Biochemistry Ind. U., assoc. dead rsch.; dir. Ind. Alcohol Rsch. Ctr. Contbr. articles to profl. jours. Recipient Markle Scholar award in Academic Medicine, Disting. Rsch. award Rsch. Soc. on Alcoholism, James B. Isaacson award for Rsch. Excellence in Chem. Dependency, Jellinek award, W. George Pinnell award for Outstanding Svc., R. Brinkley Smithers Disting. Scientist award, Irwin Rsch. Scholar award, Mark Keller Hon. Lecture award Nat. Inst. on Alcohol Abuse and Alcoholism NIH. Fellow Soc. for Study of Addiction (hon.). Office: Ind U Sch Medicine 545 Barnhill Dr # 421 Indianapolis IN 46202-5112

LI, TZE-CHUNG, lawyer, educator; b. Shanghai, China, Feb. 17, 1927; came to U.S., 1956; s. Ken-hsiang Li and Yun-hsien (Chang) Li; m. Dorothy In-lan Wang, Oct. 21, 1961; children— Lily, Rose LL.B., Soochow U., Shanghai, 1948; Diploma, Nat. Chengchi U., Nanking, 1949, China Research Inst. of Land Econs., Taipei, 1952; M.C.L., So. Meth. U., Dallas, 1956; LL.M., Harvard U., Cambridge, 1958; M.S., Columbia U., N.Y.C., 1965; Ph.D., New Sch. for Social Research, N.Y.C., 1963. Judge Hwa-lien Dist. Ct., Hwa-lien, Taiwan, Republic of China, 1949-51; dist. atty. Ministry of Justice, Taipei, 1951-52; chief law sect. Ministry of Nat. Def., 1952-56; asst. prof. library sci. Ill. State U., Normal, 1965-66; asst. prof. polit. sci., library sci. Rosary Coll., River Forest, Ill., 1966-69, assoc. prof. library sci., 1969-70, 72-74, prof. library sci., 1974-82, dean, prof. Grad. Sch. Library and Info. Sci., 1982-88; prof. Dominican U., 1988-99, dean, prof. emeritus, 2000—; vis. assoc. prof. law Nat. Taiwan U., 1969; vis. assoc. prof. polit. sci. Soochow U., Taipei, 1969; dir. Nat. Central Library, 1970-72. Chmn. Grad. Inst. Library Sci., Nat. Central Library, Taipei, 1970-72; commr. Ministry of Examination, Examination Yuan, Taipei, 1971; chmn. com. on library standards, Ministry of Edn., Taipei, 1972; library cons. Soochow U., Nat. Chengchi U., Dr. Sun Yat-sen Meml. Library; mem. library adv. com. Ency. Britannica, 1982-95; hon. prof. library and info. sci. Jiangxi U., People's Republic of China, 1985—; vis. prof. law Suzhou U., Peking U., 1991, Nat. Taiwan U., 1991; hon. cons. univ. library, 1985—; hon. cons. Jiangxi Med. Coll., 1985—; adv. prof. East China Normal U., 1987—; cons. Nova U., 1987-88; mem. ad hoc adv. com. Chgo. Pub. Library Bldg. Planning, 1987-88; CEO LLD Group, 1972—; bd. chmn. Li Ednl. Found., 1977—. Author books including: Social Science Reference Sources, 1980, 2d edit., 1990, Mah Jong, 1982, 2d edit., 1991, An Introduction to Online Searching, 1985; also numerous articles in profl., scholarly jours.; editor Third World Librs., 1996—; founding editor Jour. Library and Info. Sci., 1975-80, mem. editl. bd. 1986-90; founding chmn., mem. editl. bd. Internat. Jour. of Revs., 1984-89; editor: World Libraries, 1996-99. Pres. Chinese Am. Ednl. Found., Chgo., 1968-70. Recipient Govt. Citation Republic of China, 1956, 1972, Philip D. Sang Excellence in Teaching award Rosary Coll., 1971, Disting. Service award Phi Tau Phi, Chgo., 1982, Service award HUD, Chgo. region, 1985, Disting. Service award Chinese Am. Librarians Assn., 1988. Mem. Chinese Am. Librarians Assn. (founding pres. 1976-80), Library Assn. China (Taipei), Phi Tau Phi (pres. 1985-87) Roman Catholic Home: PO Box 444 Oak Park IL 60303-0444 Office: Dominican U 7900 Division St River Forest IL 60305-1066

LIAO, SHUTSUNG, biochemist, oncologist; b. Tainan, Taiwan, Jan. 1, 1931; s. Chi-Chun Liao and Chin-Shen Lin; m. Shuching Liao, Mar. 19, 1960; children: Jane, Tzufen, Tzuming, May. BS in Agrl. Chemistry, Nat. Taiwan U., 1953, MS in Biochemistry, 1956; PhD in Biochemistry, U. Chgo., 1961. Rsch. assoc., 1960-63; asst. prof. U. Chgo., 1964-69; assoc. prof. dept. biochemistry and molecular biology Ben May Lab. Cancer Rsch., U. Chgo., 1969-71; prof. depts. biochemistry, molecular and cancer biology Ben May Inst. for Cancer Rsch., 1972—; dir. Tang Ctr. Herbal Medicine Rsch., 2000—. Cons. in field. Mem. editl. bd. Jour. Steroid Biochemistry and Molecular Biology, The Prostate, Receptors, Signal Transduction; assoc. editor Cancer Rsch., 1982-89; contbr. over 200 articles to profl jours. V.p. Chgo. Formosan Fed. Credit Union, 1977-79; trustee Taiwanese United Fund in U.S., 1981-85; mem. adv. com. Taiwan-U.S. Cultural Exch. Ctr., 1984-87. Recipient Sci-Tech. Achievement prize Taiwanese-Am. Found., 1983, Pfizer Lecture fellow award Clin. Rsch. Inst. Montreal, 1972, Gregory Pincus medal and award Worcester Found. for Exptl. Biology, 1992, Tzongming Tu award Formosan Med. Assn., 1993, C.H. Li Meml. Lecture award, 1994; NIH grantee, 1962—; Am. Cancer Soc. grantee, 1971-81. Fellow Am. Acad. Art and Scis.; mem. Am. Soc. Biochemistry and Molecular Biology, Am. Assn. Cancer Rsch., Endocrine Soc., N.Am.-Taiwanese Profs. Assn. (pres. 1980-81, exec. dir. 1981—), Nat. Acad. Taiwan. Achievements include discovery of androgen activation mechanism and androgen receptors; cloning and structural determination of androgen receptors and other novel nuclear receptors, and their genes, and receptor gene mutation in hereditary abnormalities and cancers; rsch. on regulation of hormone-dependent gene expression and cell growth, molecular bases of cancer cell growth and progression, chemoprevention, and therapeutic treatment of hormone-sensitive and insensitive cancers and diseases, molecular bases of cholestoral accumulation and control. Home: 5632 S Woodlawn Ave Chicago IL 60637-1623 Office: U Chgo Ben May Inst Cancer Rsch 5841 S Maryland Ave Chicago IL 60637-1463

LIBA, HON. PETER MICHAEL, Canadian provincial government official; b. Winnipeg, Man., Can., May 10, 1940; s. Theodore and Rose Liba; m. Shirley Ann Collett, May 4, 1963; children: Jennifer Lacombe, Jeffrey, Christopher. DHL(hon.) , U. Manitoba, 2001. Reporter, news editor The Daily Graphic, The Neepawa Press, Portage la Prairie, Man., 1957-59; reporter The Winnipeg Tribune, 1959-67, city editor, 1967-68; ind. communications cons. Winnipeg, 1968-73; v.p. pub. affairs CanWest Broadcasting Ltd., 1974-75, exec. v.p., 1979-97; asst. gen. mgr. Sta. CKND-TV, 1975-79, mgr., 1980-87, gen. mgr., 1987-92; pres., CEO CKND TV Inc./SaskWest TV Inc., 1988-94; exec. v.p. CanWest Global Comm. Corp., 1993-97, exec. dir. corp. affairs, 1997-99; lt. gov. Province of Man., Can., 1999—. Bd. dirs. Global Comm. Ltd., Toronto, CanWest Broadcasting Ltd., Winnipeg, CanWest TV, Inc., Winnipeg, CanWest Prodns., Ltd., Winnipeg, CanWest Properties Ltd., Winnipeg, CanWest Maritime TV, Inc., Halifax, TV 3 Network, New Zealand, Network Ten (alternate), Australia; pres. Peli Ventures, Inc., 1975—. Trustee Transcona-Springfield Sch. divsn., Winnipeg, Canada, 1964—67; founding chmn. Variety Club Telethon, Canada; chmn. Winnipeg Conv. Ctr/; bd. dirs. Conv. Ctr. Corp. , Winnipeg, 1976—86, chmn. bd. dirs., 1981—84; bd. dirs. Atomic Energy of Can., Ltd., Ottawa, 1981—86, St. Boniface Gen. Hosp., Winnipeg, 1987—99. Decorated Order of Can., chancellor and 1st mem. Order of Manitoba; named Manitoban of Month, Mid Can. Commerce Mag., 1982, Knight of Justice, vice prior Order of St. John, 1999, citizen of yr., Manitoba Chinese Cmty., 2001; recipient Presidl. citation, Variety Clubs Internat., 1983, Internat. Media award, 1986, Commemorative medal, 125th Anniversary Can., 1992, Golden Dragon Citizen of Yr. award, 2001. Mem. Broadcasters Assn. Man. (pres. 1981-82), Western Assn. Broadcasters (pres. 1984-85, Broadcaster of Yr. award 1991, Broadcaster of Decade award 1994), Can. Assn. Broadcasters (chmn. bd. 1990-92, Spl. Gold Ribbon award 1999 named to Can. Broadcasters Hall of Fame, 1998), St. Charles Cluntry Club, Man. Club, Variety Club Man. (chief barker 1984-85). Office: Lieutenant Governor Ste 235 Legislative Bldg Winnipeg MB Canada R3C 0V8

LIBERT, DONALD JOSEPH, lawyer; b. Sioux Falls, S.D., Mar. 23, 1928; s. Bernard Joseph and Eleanor Monica (Sutton) L.; m. Jo Anne Murray, May 16, 1953; children: Cathleen, Thomas, Kevin, Richard, Stephanie. B.S. magna cum laude in Social Scis., Georgetown U., 1950, LL.B., 1956. Bar: Ohio. From assoc. to ptnr. Manchester, Bennett, Powers & Ullman, Youngstown, Ohio, 1956-65; various positions to v.p., gen. counsel and sec. Youngstown Sheet & Tube Co., 1965-78; assoc. group counsel LTV Corp., Youngstown and Pitts., 1979; v.p. and gen. counsel Anchor Hocking Corp., Lancaster, Ohio, 1979-87; pvt. practice, 1987—. Served to lt. (j.g.) USN, 1951-54. Mem. Ohio Bar Assn. (former chmn. sr. lawyers com.), Fairfield County Bar Assn. (mem. alt. dispute resolution com.), Lancaster Country Club, Rotary. Republican. Roman Catholic. Office: 127 W Wheeling St Lancaster OH 43130-3737

LICHTER, ALLEN S. oncology educator, university dean; BS, U. Mich., 1968, MD, 1972. Intern St. Joseph Hosp., Denver; resident U. Calif., San Francisco, 1976; former dir. radiation therapy sect. radiation oncology br. Nat. Cancer Inst.; dir. breast oncology program Comprehensive Cancer Ctr., U. Mich., Ann Arbor, 1984-91, chmn. dept. radiation oncology, 1984-97, interim dean Med. Sch., 1998-99, prof. radiation oncology, 1999—, dean Med. sch., 1999—. Assoc. editor Jour. Clin. Oncology; editl. bd. Jour. Nat. Cancer Inst., Internat. Jour. Radiation Oncology; co-editor Clinical Oncology, 1995, 2d edit., 1999. Mem. Am. Soc. Clin. Oncology (past pres.), Am. Soc. Therapeutic Radiology and Oncology (bd. dirs.). Office: U Mich M4101 Med Science Bldg I-C Wing 1301 Catherine St Ann Arbor MI 48109-0600

LICHTER, PAUL RICHARD, ophthalmology educator; b. Detroit, Mar. 7, 1939; s. Max D. and Buena (Epstein) L.; m. Carolyn Goode, 1960; children: Laurie, Susan. BA, U. Mich., 1960, MD, 1964, MS, 1968. Diplomate Am. Bd. Ophthalmology. Asst. to assoc. prof. ophthalmology U. Mich., Ann Arbor, 1971-78, prof., chmn. dept. ophthalmology and visual scis., 1978—. Chmn. Am. Bd. Ophthalmology, 1987. Editor-in-chief Ophthalmology jour., 1986-94. Served to lt. comdr. USN, 1969-71. Fellow: Am. Acad. Ophthalmology (bd. dirs. 1981—97, pres. 1996, sr. hon. award 1986, Lifetime Achievement award 2001); mem.: Acad. Ophthalmologica Internat., Internat. Coun. Ophthalmology, Assn. Univ. Profs. Ophthalmology (trustee 1986—93, pres. 1991—92), Mich. Ophthalmol. Soc. 1993—95, Washtenaw County Med. Soc., Mich. State Med. Soc., Pan Am. Assn.Ophthalmology (bd. dirs. 1988—, sec.-treas. English-speaking countries 1991—95, pres. 1999—2001), Am. Ophthalmol. Soc. 2000—01, AMA, Alpha Omega Alpha. Office: U Mich Med Sch Kellogg Eye Ctr 1000 Wall St Ann Arbor MI 48105-1912 E-mail: Plichter@umich.edu.

LICHTWARDT, ROBERT WILLIAM, mycologist; b. Rio de Janeiro, Nov. 27, 1924; s. Henry Herman and Ruth Moyer Lichtwardt; m. Elizabeth Thomas, Jan. 27, 1951; children: Ruth Elizabeth, Robert Thomas. AB, Oberlin Coll., 1949; MS, U. Ill., 1951, PhD, 1954. Postdoctoral fellow NSF, Panama, Brazil, 1954-55; postdoctoral rsch. assoc. Iowa State U., Ames, 1955-57; asst. prof. U. Kans., Lawrence, 1957-60, assoc. prof., 1960-65; sr. postdoctoral fellow NSF, Hawaii, Japan, 1963-64; prof. U. Kans., Lawrence, 1965-94, prof. emeritus, 1994—. Author: The Trichomycetes, Fungal Associates of Arthropods, 1986; contbr. 100 articles to profl. jours. Mem. Mycological Soc. Am. (life, pres. 1971-72, editor-in-chief 1965-70, William H. Weston award for tchg. excellence in mycology 1982, Disting. Mycologist award 1991), Brit. Mycological Soc. (hon.), Japan Mycological Soc. (hon.). Office: U Kans Dept Ecology Evol Biology Lawrence KS 66045-2106 E-mail: licht@ku.edu.

LICKHALTER, MERLIN EUGENE, architect; b. St. Louis, May 4, 1934; s. Frank E. and Sophia (Geller) L.; m. Harriet Braen, June 9, 1957; children: Debra, Barbara. BArch, MIT, 1957. Registered arch., Mo., Ill., Calif., Fla., Mich., Wis., Nev., Tex., Ala., Okla., Va., Conn., La., Ga., B.C., Man. Ptnr. Drake Partnership, Architects, St. Louis, 1961-77; pres. JRB Architects, Inc., 1977-81; sr. v.p., mng. dir. Stone, Marraccini & Patterson, 1981-93; sr. v.p., dir. Cannon, 1993—. Owner, pres. mgmt. program Harvard U. Bus. Sch., 1992; cons. Dept. Def., Washington, 1977-78; lectr. Washington U. Sch. Medicine, 1989—. Prin. projects include The Mayo Clinic, Jacksonville, Fla., Washington U. Med. Ctr., St. Louis, U.S. Army Hosp., Frankfurt, Germany, Nat. AIDS Rsch. Ctr., NIH, Washington, Evanston (Ill.) Hosp., Loma Linda (Calif.) U. Med. Ctr., U. Mo. Health Scis. Ctr., Columbia, St. Louis U. Health Scis. Ctr., Children's Hosp. Rsch. Inst., New Orleans, U. Ala. Birmingham Sch. Medicine, U. Ala. Sch. Optometry. Trustee United Hebrew Cong., St. Louis, 1980-88, 93-98, 2000—; exec. com. bd. dirs. Arts & Edn. Coun. St. Louis, 1991—; pres. Acad. Architecture for Health Found. Capt. U.S. Army, 1957-59. Recipient Renovation Design award St. Louis Producers Coun., 1976, USAF Europe Design Award, 1990. Fellow: Am. Coll. Healthcare Architects; mem.: AIA (chmn. nat. acad. architect for health 1993), Acad. Arch. for Health Found. (pres. 2000—), Am. Assn. Health Planning, Am. Hosp. Assn., Hawthorne Found., St. Louis Regional Growth Assn., Frontenac Racquet Club, St. Louis Ambs., St. Louis Club, Masons. Jewish. Home: 160 N Brentwood Blvd Clayton MO 63105-3741 Office: Cannon Design One City Ctr Saint Louis MO 63101

LIDDY, BRIAN, food products executive; CFO Schreiber Foods, Inc., Green Bay, Wis. Office: Schreiber Foods Inc PO Box 19010 Green Bay WI 54307 Office Fax: (920) 437-1617.

LIDDY, EDWARD M. insurance company executive; b. 1945; married. Student, Cath. U., 1966; MBA, George Washington U., 1968. With Internat. Harvester Co., Ford Motor Co., Ryder Systems Inc., 1968-79; sr. v.p. G.D. Searle & Co., Skokie, Ill., 1979-85; with ADT Inc., N.Y.C., 1985-88, CFO, exec. v.p., dir., 1986-88; CFO Sears, 1988-94; pres., COO Allstate Ins Co., Northbrook, Ill., 1994-98, chmn., pres., CEO, 1999—. Office: Allstate Insurance Co 2775 Sanders Rd Northbrook IL 60062-6127

LIDDY, RICHARD A. insurance company executive; b. 1935; BS, Iowa State U., 1957. V.p. ops. Conn. Gen. Life, Hartford, 1957-82; exec. v.p. Continental Corp., 1982-88; pres., COO, now pres., CEO, Gen. Am. Life Ins. Co., St. Louis, 1988-95; chmn. Gen. Am. Fin. Corp., 1995—, pres., CEO. Office: Gen Am Life Ins Co POBox 396 700 Market St Saint Louis MO 63101

LIEB, MICHAEL, English educator, humanities educator; AB in Eng. Lit., Rutgers U., 1962, AM in Eng. Lit., 1964, PhD in Eng. Lit., 1967; student, U. Iowa, 1962-63, U. Chgo. Divinity Sch., 1974-75, Spertus Coll. of Judaica, 1987-92. Asst. prof. Eng. Coll. of William and Mary, Williamsburg, Va., 1967-70; assoc. prof. Eng. U. Ill., Chgo., 1970-75, prof. Eng., 1975-88, rsch. prof. humanities, 1988—. Vis. professorial lectr. U. Chgo. Divinity Sch., 1979; bd. dirs. Friends of Milton's Cottage; mem. exec. com. U. Chgo. Renaissance Seminar, 1977—; mem. exec. com. Divsn. 17th Century Eng. Lit. MLA, 1982-86, Divsn. Religious Approaches to Lit., 1987-91; mem. exec. com. Ctr. Renaissance Studies Newberry Libr., 1979—, mem. com. Brit. Acad. Fellowships, 1982-83, mem. search com. for dir., 1984; mem. adv. com. 2d Internat. Milton Symposium, 1983, 4th, 1990; campus rep. Woodrow Wilson Found., 1982-83; mem. numerous coms. U. Ill. Author: The Dialectics of Creation: Patterns of Birth and Regeneration in Paradise Lost, 1970, Poetics of the Holy: A Reading of Paradise Lost, 1981 (James Holly Hanford award Milton Soc. Am.), The Sinews of Ulysses: Form and Convention in Milton's Works, 1989, The Visionary Mode: Biblical Prophecy, Hermeneutics and Cultural Change, 1991, Milton and the Culture of Violence, 1994; co-editor, contbg. author: Achievements of the Left hand: Essays on the Prose of John Milton, 1974, Eyes Fast Fixt: Current Perspectives in Milton Methodology, 1975, Literary Milton: Text, Pretext, Context, 1994, The Miltonic Samson, 1996; contbr. articles to profl. jours.; symposia speaker in field; panelist; invited speaker; cons. edit. bds., univ. presses, profl. jours., librs., depts. Eng., Comparative Lit., Divinity. Pres., co-founder Oak Park Housing Ctr., 1971-73, Advocate award 1992; mem. hon. com. Ill. Humanities Coun., 1986; mem. Am. Jewish Com. Academicians Seminar, Israel, 1986. NEH U. Tchrs. fellow, 1991-92, John Simon Guggenheim Meml. Found. fellow 1987-88, U. Ill. Chgo. Inst. for Humanities sr. fellow 1983, Newberry Libr. Nat. Endowment for Humanities sr. fellow 1981-82, NEH Younger Humanist Study fellow 1974-75; recipient Am. Coun. Learned Societies Grant-in-Aid, 1985, Am. Philosophical Soc. Grant-in-Aid, 1983, Folger Shakespeare Libr. fellow, 1970, 74; Honors Coll. U. Ill. Chgo. fellow 1986—; others. Mem. Milton Soc. Am. (chair James Holly Hanford awards com. 1991-93, treas. 1973-77, v.p. 1980, pres. 1981, honored scholar 1992), Modern Lang. Assn., Milton Soc. of Japan, Southeastern Renaissance Conf., Renaissance Soc. of Am., Calif. Renaissance Conf., Northeastern Modern Lang. Assn., Newberry Libr. Milton Seminar (co-founder, co-chair 1986—), Newberry Libr. Dante Lectures. Home: 212 S Ridgeland Ave Oak Park IL 60302-3226 Office: U Ill Chgo Coll Liberal ARts & Scis Dept Eng M/C 162 601 S Morgan St Chicago IL 60607-7100

LIEBERMAN, ARCHIE, photographer, writer; b. Chgo., July 17, 1926; s. Sol and Rose (Schiff) L.; m. Esther Kraus, Jan. 11, 1948; children: Eric Joseph, Robert Charles Vories, Kurt Murrow Student, Inst. Design, Chgo., 1946-48; HHD (hon.), U. Dubuque, 1996. Contract photographer Time Mag., Chgo., 1950-51; staff photographer Black Star Pub. Co., N.Y.C., 1951-61. Adj. prof. Chgo. Theol. Sem., 1976-74; instr. Columbia Coll., Chgo., 1968-74; prof. art Knox Coll., Galesburg, Ill., U. Dubuque, Iowa. One man shows include Presbyn.-St. Luke's Hosp., Chgo., Chapel Hill Shopping Ctr., Akron, Ohio Mchts. Assn., Flint, Mich., Arie Crown Theater, Chgo., Carson Pirie Scott & Co., Chgo., Prudential Bldg., Chgo., Agr. U.S.A., Soviet Union, U. Ill., Lake Forest Coll., Kodak Gallery, Grand Central Sta., N.Y.C., Rizzoli Gallery, Chgo., U. Dubuque (retrospective), 1987, Dubuque Mus. Art, Lands End Gallery, Dodgeville, Wis., 1991, Ford Ctr. Fine Art-Knox Coll., 1993, Elveahjem Mus., Madison, Wis., 1994, Freeport Art Mus., 1994, Lake Forest Coll., 1995; group shows include Jewish Mus., N.Y.C., Tower Gallery, Chgo., Garrett Bible Inst., Evanston, Met. Mus. Art, N.Y.C., Expo '67, Montreal, Art Inst. Chgo., 1986, Photography in Fine Arts, N.Y.C., San Diego Mus. Photographic Arts, 1986, Mitchell Mus., Mt. Vernon, Ill., 1987, 88, The Art Inst. of Chgo., 1986, 92, numerous others; author, photographer: The Israelis, 1965 (One of Best 50 Books award), Farm Boy (Friends of Lit. award), Neighbors, 1993; photographer books: Shalom, A Solitary Life, The Future of Religions, The Eternal Life, Holy Holy Land, The Story of Israel, Chicago In Color, Chicago, God Make Me Brave For Life, (with Ray Bradbury) The Mummies of Guanajuato, Chicago: A Celebration, 1990; photojournalist for mags. including: Look, Life, Saturday Evening Post, Collier's, Ladies Home Jour., Fortune, London Illustrated, Redbook, Farm Jour., Pageant, Parade, Bus. Week, Am. Weekly, Venture, U.S. News & World Report, Newsweek, Paris Match, Chgo. Mag.; indsl. photographer for corps. including Inland Steel, Acme Steel, Lands' End, Harvester, Gould Inc., McDonald's, Motorola, Grumman Corp., Internat. Minerals & Chem. Corp.; advt. photographs for: Allstate Ins., Phillip Morris, Schlitz, United Airlines, Jack Daniel, others Trustee Dubuque Mus. Art. Recipient Peter Lisagor award Headline Club of Sigma Delta Chi, 1980; Sinai Health

Service award Mt. Sinai Hosp. Med. ctr., Chgo., 1985; various award U. Mo. Sch. Journalism Mem.: Galena Artists Guild, Dubuque Shooting Soc., Tavern Club, Chgo. Press Club, Arts Club of Chgo. Office: PO Box 61 Scales Mound IL 61075-0061

LIEBERMAN, EDWARD JAY, lawyer; b. Evansville, Ind., Apr. 8, 1946; s. Heiman George and Anna Sharp (Blacker) L.; m. Ellen Ackerman Wequsen, June 1, 1969; 1 child: Laura Amy. BSBA, Washington U., St. Louis, 1968, JD, 1971. Bar: Mo. 1971. Jr. ptnr. Bryan Cave, St. Louis, 1972-76; assoc. counsel 1st Nat. Bank in St. Louis, 1976-80; ptnr. Lowenhaupt, Chasnoff, Armstrong & Mellitz, St. Louis, 1980-84, Husch & Eppenberger, LLC, St. Louis, 1984—. Mem. ABA, Mo. Bar, Bar Assn. Met. St. Louis, Am. Coll. Mortgage Attys., Nat. Health Care Lawyers Assn. Office: Husch & Eppenberger, LLC 190 Carondelet Plz Ste 600 Saint Louis MO 63105 E-mail: ed.lieberman@husch.com.

LIEBERMAN, EUGENE, lawyer; b. Chgo., May 17, 1918; s. Harry and Eva (Goldman) L.; m. Pearl Naomi Feldman, Aug. 3, 1947; children: Mark, Robert, Steven. LLB, DePaul U., 1940, JD, 1941. Bar: Ill. 1941, U.S. Supreme Ct. 1963. Mem. firm Jacobs and Lieberman, 1954-60; sr. ptnr. Jacobs, Lieberman and Aling, 1960-74; spl. hearing officer U.S. Dept. Justice, 1967-78; hearing officer Ill. Pollution Control Bd., 1973—; pvt. practice Chgo. Contbr. articles to profl. jours. With U.S. Army, 1942-45. Recipient 1st in State award Moot Ct. Championship, 1940, gold award Philatelic Exhbn., Taipei, 1981, gold award World Philatelic Exhbn., Melbourne, 1984, Meritorious Svc. medal, bronze arrowhead award, others. Mem. Ill. State Bar Assn. (sr. counselor 1991), Chgo. Bar Assn., Appellate Lawyers Assn., Chgo. Philatelic Soc. (pres. 1964-68), Ill. Athletic Club. Home: 801 Leclaire Ave Wilmette IL 60091-2065

LIEBERMAN, LAURENCE, poet, educator; b. Detroit, Feb. 16, 1935; s. Nathan and Anita (Cohen) L.; m. Bernice Clair Braun, June 17, 1956; children— Carla, Deborah, Isaac. BA, U. Mich., 1956, MA in English, 1958; postgrad., U. Calif.-Berkeley. Prof. English Coll. V.I., 1964-68; prof. English and creative writing U. Ill., Urbana, 1968—. U. Ill. Ctr. for Advanced Study Creative Writing fellow, Japan, 1971-72 Author: The Unblinding, 1968, The Achievement of James Dickey, 1969, The Osprey Suicides, 1973, Unassigned Frequencies: American Poetry in Review (1964-77), 1977, God's Measurements, 1980, Eros At the World Kite Pageant, 1983, The Mural of Wakeful Sleep, 1985, (poems) The Creole Mephistopheles, 1989, The Best American Poetry, 1991 (award), New and Selected Poems (1962-92), 1993, The St. Kitts. Monkey Feuds, 1995, Beyond the Muse of Memory: Essays on Contemporary Poets, 1995, Dark Songs: Slave House and Synagogue, 1996, Compass of the Dying, 1998, The Regatta in the Skies: Selected Long Poems, 1999, Flight From the Mother Stone, 2000; poetry editor poetry books program U. Ill. Press, 1970—; contbr. poetry to lit. jours., popular mags. Recipient award for Best Poems of 1968, Nat. Endowment for Arts, 1969, Jerome P. Shestack award Am. Poetry Rev., 1986; creative writing fellow U. Ill. Ctr. for Advanced Study, 2000—, Nat. Endowment Arts, 1986-87. Office: U Ill English Dept 608 S Wright St Urbana IL 61801-3630

LIEBERMAN-CLINE, NANCY, professional basketball coach, former player; b. July 1, 1958; m. Tim Cline, 1988; 1 child, Timothy Joseph. Grad., Old Dominion U., 1981. Guard WBL's Dallas Diamonds, 1980-86, USBL's L.I. Knights, 1986-87, Washington Generals, 1987-88, Athletes in Action, 1996-97, WNBA - Phoenix Mercury, 1997-97; head coach, gen. mgr. WNBA - Detroit Shock, 1998—. Women's basketball analyst NBA Broadcasting, ESPN, ABC, ESPN 2, Fox Sports NEtwork, NBC. Recipient Broderick Cup, 1979, 80, Wade Trophy (2), U.S. Olympic Silver medal, 1976; named All- Am., 1978-80, ODU Outstanding Female Athlete of Yr., 1977-80; mem. Women's Am. Basketball Championship team, 1985; Named to Basketball Hall of Fame, 1996. Office: Detroit Shock 2 Championship Dr Auburn Hills MI 48326-1753

LIEBLER, ARTHUR C. automotive executive; b. Pitts., June 19, 1942; s. Arthur Cyril and Frances (Coyle) L.; m. Nancy Elizabeth Cullen, Sept. 19, 1964; children: Molly, Katie, Patrick. AB in Journalism, Marquette U., 1964; postgrad., Wayne State U. Reporter WRJN Radio Racine Journal Times, Wis., 1964; jr. acct. exec. The Selz Orgn., Chgo., 1965-66; staff reporter, employer Ford Motor Co., Dearborn, Mich., 1966-67, corporate pub. rels. staff, 1967-76; sr. v.p. acct. mgmt. and supv. Ross Roy Inc., Detroit, 1976-80; dir. corp. mdse. Chrysler Corp., 1980-82, dir. communications programs, 1982, gen. mktg. mgr., 1983-87, dir. mktg. svcs., 1987-98, v.p. mktg., 1998—; sr. v.p. mktg. Daimler Chrysler, Auburn Hills, Mich., 1998-2000, sr. v.p. global brand mktg., 2000—. Bd. dirs. Common Ground (Drug Prevention) Birmingham Mich., 1966-70; committeeman Dem. Party Chectenham Township Pa., 1971-72; miscellaneous Sch. Bd. Activities, Birmingham Mich., 1974-77. Mem. Detroit Adcraft Club (accredited, bd. dirs.), Pub. Rels. Soc. Am. (bd. dirs.), Am Advt. Fedn. (bd. dirs.), Detroit Golf Club.

LIEDER, BERNARD L. state legislator, civil engineer; m. Shirley B. Lieder; three children. Student, U. Ill., Purdue U. Engineer; Dist. 2A rep. Minn. Ho. of Reps., St. Paul, 1984—. Vice chmn. agr., transp. and semi-state divsn. appropriations com., chmn. transp. fin. divsn. appropriations Minn. Ho. of Reps.; mem. local govt. and met. affairs and transp. coms.; former chmn. ethics com.; mem. capital investments, econ. devel., infrastructure and regulation fin. coms. Home: 911 Thorndale Ave Crookston MN 56716-1150

LIEGEL, CRAIG A. meat packing company executive; CFO Packerland Packing Co., Green Bay, Wis. Office: Packerland Packing Co PO Box 23000 Green Bay WI 54305-3000

LIEM, KHIAN KIOE, medical entomologist; b. Semarang, Java, Indonesia, Jan. 11, 1942; came to U.S., 1969; s. Coen Ing T and Marie Soei-Nio (Goei) L.; m. Anita Tumewu, Apr. 3, 1980; children: Brian Dexter, Tiffany Marie, Jennifer Amanda, Ashley Elizabeth. BS, Bandung Inst. Tech., Bandung, Indonesia, 1964; MS, Bandung Inst. Tech., 1966, Eastern Ill. U., 1970; PhD, U. Ill., 1975. Registered profl. entomologist, vector ecologist. Grad. teaching asst. Bandung Inst. Tech., 1964-66, grad. instr., 1966-68; grad. rsch./teaching asst. Eastern Ill. U., 1969-70; grad. teaching asst. U. Ill., 1970-74; med. entomologist South Cook County Mosquito Abatement Dist., Harvey, Ill., 1974-76, mgr./dir. med. entomologist, 1977—. Cons. U.S. AID, Washington, 1979--. Recipient Community Svc. award Asian Am. Coalition, 1993. Mem. Am. Mosquito Control Assn. (chmn. resolution com. 1977-78, mem. editorial bd. 1980-83, mem. worldwide com. 1987—), Ill. Mosquito Control Assn. (pres. 1979-81), Entomol. Soc. Am. (com. on book revs.), Am. Tropical Medicine and Hygiene Assn., Am. Registry of Profl. Entomologists, Scientists Inst. Pub. Info., Soc. Vector Ecology, Sigma Xi, Phi Sigma. Roman Catholic. Avocations: soccer, tennis, martial arts, camping, classical music. Home: 8012 Binford Dr Orland Park IL 60462-2300 Office: Mosquito Abatement Dist 15440 Dixie Hwy Harvey IL 60426-2801 E-mail: sccmad@aol.com.

LIEN, BRUCE HAWKINS, minerals and oil company executive; b. Waubay, S.D., Apr. 7, 1927; s. Peter Calmer and LaRece Catherine (Holm) L.; m. Deanna Jean Browning, May 4, 1978. BS in Bus., Wyo. U., 1953; D in Bus. (hon.), S.D. Sch. Mines & Tech., 1996; hon. doctorate, SDSMT, 1996. Corp. exec. Pete Lien & Sons, Inc., Rapid City, S.D., 1944-60, bd. chmn., 1960—, Concorde Gaming Corp., 1990—, Browning Resources U.S., 1989—. Chmn. Cmty. Chest, Rapid City, S.D., 1956; pres. U. Wyo. Found., 1989-90; life bd. dirs. Salvation Army. 1st lt. U.S. Army, 1945-47, 50-52. Recipient Disting. Svc. award S.D. Sch. Mines, Rapid City, 1972, Disting. Svc. award Cosmopolitan Internat., Rapid City, 1983; named Disting. Alumnus, Wyo. U., Laramie, 1982, 1996. Mem. Internat. Lime Assn. (pres. 1973-75), Nat. Lime Assn. (pres. 1973-75, Merit award 1973, bd. dirs.), VFW, Am. Legion, Cosmopolitan Club, Masons, Elks. Republican. Lutheran. Home: PO Box 440 Rapid City SD 57709-0440 Office: Pete Lien & Sons Inc I 90 & Deadwood Ave PO Box 440 Rapid City SD 57709-0440

LIENEMANN, DELMAR ARTHUR, SR. accountant, real estate developer; b. Papillion, Nebr., May 17, 1920; s. Arthur Herman and Dorothea M. (Marth) L.; m. Charlotte Peck, Jun 17, 1944 (dec. Mar. 1995); children: Delmar Arthur Jr., David (dec.), Diane, Douglas, Dorothy, Daniel, Denise. BS, U. Nebr., 1941. CPA, Nebr. Acct. Wickstrom Supply, Lincoln, Nebr., 1941, L.L. Coryell & Sons, Lincoln, 1942, Lester Buckley, CPA, Lincoln, 1943-45; pvt. practice, 1945—. Pres., v.p., sec., treas., bldg. chmn., charter mem. Christ Luth. Ch., Lincoln, 1949-70; co-commr. Lancaster County, Lincoln, 1954-58; pres. Lincoln Symphony Orch. Found., 1984—, Ethel S. Abbott Charitable Found. Mem. AICPA, N.E. Soc. CPA, Colo. Soc. CPA, Tex. Soc. CPA, Sertoma (sec.-treas. Lincoln chpt. 1952-68, Internat. Sertoman of Yr. 1962), Hillcrest Country Club, Nebr. Club, Nebr. Chancelors Club, Nebr. Touchdown Club, Nebr. Power Club, Nebr. Rebounders Club. Republican. Avocation: travel. Office: PO Box 81407 Lincoln NE 68501-1407

LIESE, CHRISTOPHER A. benefits and financial consulting company owner, state legislator; b. St. Louis, Mar. 24, 1963; s. Albert Joseph and Rose Clare (Kaufmann) L.; m. Sheila Marie Bercier, May 8, 1993. BA, St. Louis U., 1985. CFP. Owner Liese & Assocs., St. Louis; mem. Mo. Ho. of Reps. Dist. 85, Jefferson City, 1992—. Legal intern Legal Svcs. for Ea. Mo., Inc., 1984-85; vol. athletic instr. Mo. Athletic Club, 1983—; mem. St. John Bosco Ch., St. Blaise Alumni Com., Mo. River Twp. Dem. Club, N.W. River Twp. Dem. Club, Young Dems. Greater St. Louis. Mem. Mo. Assn. Life Underwriters, Maryland Heights/Westport C. of C. (econ. devel. com. 1990, 91), Jaycees, Delta Sigma Phi (pres. 1983-84). Home: 12230 Foxpoint Dr Maryland Heights MO 63043-2110 Office: House Post Office State Capitol 201 W Capitol Ave Jefferson City MO 65101-1556

LIFKA, MARY LAURANNE, history educator; b. Oak Park, Ill., Oct. 31, 1937; d. Aloysius William and Loretta Catherine (Juric) L. B.A., Mundelein Coll., 1960; M.A., Loyola U., Los Angeles, 1965; Ph.D., U. Mich., 1974; postdoctoral student London U., 1975. Life teaching cert. Prof. history Mundelein Coll., Chgo., 1976-84, coordinator acad. computer, 1983-84, prof. history Coll. St. Teresa, Winona, Minn., 1984-89, Lewis U., Romeoville, Ill., 1989—; chief reader in history Ednl. Testing Service, Princeton, N.J., 1980-84; cons. world history project Longman, Inc., 1983— ; cons. in European history Coll. Bd., Evanston, Ill., 1983— ; mem. Com. on History in the Classroom. Author: Instructor's Guide to European History, 1983; contbr. articles to publs. Recipient Br. Miguel Febres Cordero award for scholarship, 1998. Mem. Am. Hist. Assn., Ednl. Testing Service Devel. Com. of History. Democrat. Roman Catholic. Office: Lewis U RR 53 Romeoville IL 60446

LIGGETT, HIRAM SHAW, JR. retired diversified industry financial executive; b. St. Louis, Jan. 12, 1932; s. Hiram Shaw and Lucille (Gardner) L.; m. Margaret McGinness, Jan. 21, 1961; children: Lucille Gardner, Frances Shelby. BA, Colo. Coll., 1953; LLD (hon.), Maryville U., 1991. Cashier Brown Group, Inc., St. Louis, 1957-64, asst. treas., 1964-68, treas., 1968—, v.p., 1983-86 (ret.). Bd. dirs. Roosevelt Fed. Savs. and Loan, St. Louis Past trustee, vice chmn. bd. dirs. McKendree Coll., Lebanon, Ill., 1980-88; trustee, past chmn. bd. trustees Maryville U., St. Louis, 1982-91; past chmn. Provident Counseling, 1983; past v.p., bd. dirs. Jr. Achievement Miss. Valley, 1983; past dir. bi-state chpt. ARC, 1983; bd. dirs., pres. Cardinal Ritter Inst.; bd. dirs., chmn. devel. bd. Paraquad. Capt. USNR, 1953-79. Mem. Fin. Execs. Inst. (pres., dir. 1983—), St. Louis Coun. Navy League (bd. councilors 1982), Univ. Club (St. Louis, chmn. house com. 1975-78), Strathalbyn Farms Club (chmn. house com., pres. bd. dirs.), Alpha Kappa Psi, Tau Kappa Alpha. Republican. Presbyterian. E-mail: hligg498aol.com. Home: 64 Chesterfield Lakes Rd Chesterfield MO 63005-5400 Office: Liggett-Black & Co 8000 Bonhomme Ave #320 Saint Louis MO 63105

LIGGETT, RONALD DAVID, state legislator; m. Frances Liggett. Student, Ball State U., Muncie, Ind., 1963-65. Owner/contr. Liggett Constrn. Co.; rep. Dist. 33 Ind. Ho. of Reps., 1992—, mem. cities and towns, elec. and apportionment coms., mem. labor and employment com.; vice chmn. agr. and rural devel. com. Mem. Pvt. Industry Coun. Mem. Lions, Moose, Masons. Address: RR 1 Box 482 Redkey IN 47373-9797 Also: 7483 S 1000 W Redkey IN 47373-9398

LIGGIO, CARL DONALD, lawyer; b. N.Y.C., Sept. 5, 1943; AB, Georgetown U., 1963; JD, NYU, 1967. Bar: N.Y. 1967, D.C. 1967, Wis. 1983, Ill. 1998. Cons. Arent, Fox, Kintner, Plotkin & Kahn, Washington, 1968-69; assoc. White & Case, N.Y.C., 1969-72; gen. counsel Arthur Young & Co., 1972-89, Ernst & Young, N.Y.C., 1989-94; ptnr. Dickinson, Wright, Moon, Van Dusen & Freeman, Chgo., 1995-97, of counsel, 1998-99; CFO, gen. counsel, dir. Tempico, Inc., 1998—; of counsel McCullough, Campbell & Lane, 1999—. Bd. dirs. Fios, Inc., WZ.com; mem. Brookings Civil Justice Reform Task Force, 1988—. Mem. editl. bd. Rsch. in Acctg. Jour.; contbr. articles to profl. jours. Trustee Fordham Prep. Sch. Mem. ABA, Am. Corp. Counsel Assn. (chmn. bd. dirs. 1984, mem. exec. com. 1982-95), Am. Judicature Soc. (bd. dirs. 1988-92), Coll. Law Mgmt., N.Y. State Bar Assn., Wis. Bar Assn., Ill. Bar Assn., D.C. Bar Assn. Home: 233 E Walton St Chicago IL 60611-1510 Office: 401 N Michigan Ave Chicago IL 60611-4255

LIGHT, TERRY RICHARD, orthopedic hand surgeon; b. Chgo., June 22, 1947; BA, Yale U., 1969; MD, Chgo. Med. Sch., 1973. Asst. prof. Yale U., New Haven, 1977-80, Loyola U., Maywood, Ill., 1980-82, assoc. prof., 1982-88, prof., 1988-90, Dr. William M. Scholl prof., chmn. orthop. surgery and rehab, 1991—. Attending surgeon Hines (Ill.) VA Hosp., 1980—, Shriner's Hosp., Chgo., 1981—, Foster McGaw Hosp., Maywood, 1981—; hand cons. Chgo. White Sox, 1986—; bus. mgr. Jour. Hand Surgery, 1995-99. Editor Am. Acad. Orthop. Surgeons Hand Surgery Update, 1999, 2d edit. V.p. Frank Lloyd Wright Home and Studio Found., Oak Park, Ill., 1985-88, pres., 1988-90; chmn. bd. Fairfield Pub. Gallery, Sturgeon Bay, Wis., 1998-99; bd. dirs. Loyola U. Health Sys., 1999—. Fellow: ACS, Am. Acad. Orthop. Surgeons (chair Jour. Hand Surgery com.95 1995—99); mem.: Ill. Orthop. Soc. (v.p. 1995, pres.-elect. 1996, pres. 1997), Twenty-First Century Orthop. Soc. 1979—, Acad. Orthopaedic Soc. (second pres.-elect 1999—2000, first pres.-elect 2000—01, pres. 2001—02), Chgo. Soc. for Surgery of Hand (sec. 1985—87, pres.-elect 1987—88, pres. 1988), Am. Assn. Hand Surgery (bd. dirs. 1989—91), Am. Soc. for Surgery of Hand (treas.-elect 1998—99, treas. 1999—2002), Alpha Omega Alpha. Avocation: collecting American arts and crafts and pottery. Office: Loyola U Med Ctr 2160 S 1st Ave Maywood IL 60153-3304 E-mail: tlight@lumc.edu.

LIGHTFOOT, EDWIN NIBLOCK, JR. retired chemical engineering educator; b. Milw., Sept. 25, 1925; married 1949, 5 children. BS, Cornell U., 1947, PhD in Chem. Engring., 1951. Asst prof., prof. biochem engr. U. Wis., Madison, 1953-80, prof. chem. engr., 1980-95, prof. emeritus, 1995—. Vis. prof. Tech. U. Norway, 1962, Stanford U., 1971, U. Canterbury, New Zealand , 1972. Author 14 books; contbr. articles to profl. jours. Recipient William H. Walker award Am. Inst. Chem. Engrs, 1975, Food, Pharm. and Bioeng award, 1979, Warren K. Lewis award, 1991. Mem. NAS, AAAS, Nat. Acad. Engr., Royal Norwegian Soc. Sci. & Letter, Am. Inst. Chem. Engr., Am. Chem. Soc. (E.V. Murphree award, 1994). Achievements include research on physical separation tech. mass transfer, biomedical engring. Office: U Wis 3639 Engineering Bldg 1415 Engineering Dr Madison WI 53706-1607 E-mail: lightfoot@engr.wisc.edu.

LIGHTFORD, KIMBERLY A. state legislator; BA in Pub. Comm., Western Ill. U.; MPA, U. Ill., Springfield. Mem. Ill. Senate, Springfield, 1998—. Elected chair Ill. Senate Black Caucus; trustee Village of Maywood, chair recreation youth & sr. svcs. com.; chair adv. coun. Boys & Girls Club. Democrat. Office: State Capitol 311 Capitol Bldg Springfield IL 62706-0001 also: 5943 W Chicago Ave Chicago IL 60651-2524

LILEY, PETER EDWARD, mechanical engineering educator; b. Barnstaple, North Devon, Eng., Apr. 22, 1927; came to U.S., 1957; s. Stanley E. and Rosa (Ellery) L.; m. Elaine Elizabeth Kull, Aug. 16, 1963; children: Elizabeth Ellen, Rebecca Ann. BSc, U. London, 1951, PhD in Physics, DIC, U. London, 1957. With Brit. Oxygen Engring., London, 1955-57; asst. prof. mech. engring. Purdue U., West Lafayette, Ind., 1957-61, assoc. prof., 1961-72; assoc. sr. researcher Thermophys. Properties Research Ctr., Purdue U., 1961-72, prof. mech. engring., 1972-98; prof. emeritus, 1998—; sr. rschr. Ctr. for Info. and Numerical Data Analysis and Synthesis, Purdue U., West Lafayette, Ind., 1972-92. Cons. in field. Author: Sect. 2 Perry's Chemical Engineers Handbook, 7th edit., 1997, (with Hartnett et al.) Handbook of Heat Transfer Fundamentals, 2d edit., 1985, (with others) Marks Mechanical Engineers Handbook, 10th edit., 1996, Schaums 2000 Solved Problems in Mechanical Engineering Thermodynamics, 1988, Tables and Charts for Thermodynamics, 1995, Kutz Mechanical Engineers Handbook, 1998; co-author: Steam and Gas Tables with Computer Equations, 1985, Thermal Conductivity of Nonmetallic Liquids and Gases, 1970, Properties of Nonmetallic Fluid Elements, 1981, Properties of Inorganic and Organic Fluids, 1988; editor, mem. editl. bd. Internat. Jour. Thermophysics, 1980-96; contbr. chpts. to handbooks in field; contbr. articles to profl. jours.; reviewer profl. jours. Served with Royal Corps Signals, Brit. Army, 1945-48. Lutheran. Home: 3608 Mulberry Dr Lafayette IN 47905-3937 Office: Purdue U Dept Mech Engring Lafayette IN 47907 E-mail: eandpliley@insightbb.com.

LILJEGREN, FRANK SIGFRID, artist, art association official; b. N.Y.C., Feb. 23, 1930; s. Josef Sigfrid and Ester (Davidsson) L.; m. Donna Kathryn Hallam, Oct. 12, 1957. Student, Art Students League, N.Y.C., 1950-55. Instr. painting, drawing, composition Westchester County Ctr., White Plains, N.Y., 1967-77, Art Students League, 1974-75, Wassenberg Art Ctr., Van Wert, Ohio, 1978-80, Wright State U. Br. Western Ohio Campus, Celina, 1981—. Corr. sec. Allied Artists Am., N.Y.C., 1967, exhbn. chmn., 1968— , pres., 1970-72, also bd. dirs. Exhibited at Suffolk Mus., Stonybrook, N.Y., Springfield (Mass.) Mus., Marion Kugler McNay Art Inst., San Antonio, Philbrook Mus., Tulsa, NAD, N.Y.C., New Britain (Conn.) Mus. Art, Ft. Wayne (Ind.) Mus. Art; represented in permanent collections Art Students League, Univ. Mus., S.E. Mo. State U., Cape Girardeau, Manhattan Savs. Bank, N.Y.C., Am. Ednl. Pubs. Inst., N.Y.C., New Britain Mus. Am. Art, Conn. With AUS, 1951. Recipient numerous awards for still life oil paintings. Mem. Fine Arts fedn. N.Y, Art Students League (life), Acad. Artists Assn., Coun. Am. Artists Socs., Artists Fellowship, Salmagundi.

LILLEHAUG, DAVID LEE, lawyer; b. Waverly, Iowa, May 22, 1954; s. Leland Arthur and Ardis Elsie (Scheel) L.; m. Winifred Sarah Smith, May 29, 1982; 1 child, Kara Marie. BA summa cum laude, Augustana Coll., Sioux Falls, S.D., 1976; JD cum laude, Harvard U., 1979. Bar: Minn. 1979, U.S. Dist. Ct. Minn. 1979, D.C. 1981, U.S. Ct. Appeals (8th cir.) 1981, U.S. Dist. Ct. D.C. 1982. Law clk. to presiding judge U.S. Dist. Ct. Minn., Mpls., 1979-81; assoc. Hogan & Hartson, Washington, 1981-83, 84-85; issues aide, exec. asst. to Walter Mondale, 1983-84; assoc. Leonard, Street & Deinard, Mpls., 1985-87, ptnr., 1988-93, 98-99; U.S. atty. Dist. of Minn., 1994-98. Candidate U.S. Senate, 1999—. Mondale Policy Forum fellow U. Minn., 1990-91. Mem. ABA, Minn. Bar Assn. (past chair constrn. law sect., Author's award 1990). Lutheran. Avocations: fishing, golf. Home: 6701 Parkwood Ln Edina MN 55436-1735 Office: Lillehaug Law Office 1515 One Financial Plaza Minneapolis MN 55402 E-mail: DLL6701@cs.com.

LILLESAND, THOMAS MARTIN, remote sensing educator; b. Laurium, Mich., Oct. 1, 1946; m. Theresa Hofmeister, 1968; children: Mark, Kari, Michael. BS, U. Wis., 1969, MS, 1970, PhD in Civil Engring., 1973. Prof. remote sensing SUNY, Syracuse, 1973-78, U. Minn., 1978-82, U. Wis., Madison, 1982—. Cons., 1973—. Mem. ASCE (pres.), Am. Soc. Photogrammetry and Remote Sensing (Alan Gordon award 1979, 93, Talbert Abrams award 1984, Fennell award 1988), Soc. Am. Foresters, Am. Congress on Surveying and Mapping. Office: U Wis Environ Remote Sensing Ctr 1225 W Dayton St Rm 1239B Madison WI 53706-1612

LILLESTOL, JANE BRUSH, development consultant; b. Jamestown, N.D., July 20, 1936; d. Harper J. and Doris (Mikkelson) Brush; m. Harvey Lillestol, Sept. 29, 1956; children: Kim, Kevin, Erik. BS, U. Minn., 1969, MS, 1973, PhD, 1977; grad. Inst. Ednl. Mgmt., Harvard U., 1984. Dir. placement, asst. to dean U. Minn., St. Paul, 1975-77; assoc. dean, dir. student acad. affairs N.D. State U., Fargo, 1977-80; dean Coll. Human Devel. Syracuse (N.Y.) U., 1980-89, v.p. for alumni rels., 1989-95, project dir. IBM Computer Aided Design Lab., 1989-92; prin. Lillestol Assocs. Charter mem. Mayor's Commn. on Women, 1986-90; NAFTA White House Conf. for Women Leaders, 1993. Bd. dirs. Univ. Hill Corp. Syracuse, 1983-93; mem. steering com. Consortium for Cultural Founds. of Medicine, 1980-89; trustee Pebble Hill Sch., 1990-94, Archbold Theatre, 1990-95, N.D. State U., 1992—. Recipient award U.S. Consumer Product Safety Commn., 1983, Woman of Yr. award AAUW, 1984, svc. award Syracuse U., 1992; named among 100 Outstanding Alumni Over Past 100 Yrs., U. Minn. Coll. Human Ecology, 2001. Roman Catholic. Office: 8046 E Via De Los Libros Scottsdale AZ 85258-3056 E-mail: lillestol@bigfoot.com.

LILLY, AIMEE, radio personality; b. Wheaton, Ill., Dec. 09; m. Scott Lilly. Radio host Sta. WMBI , Chgo. Office: WMBI 820 N LaSalle Rd Chicago IL 60610*

LILLY, GEORGE DAVID, broadcasting executive; b. Winchester, Mass., Nov. 4, 1934; s. George M. and Eleanor (Hamlin) L.; children: Brian, Kevin, Kristin. BS in Communication Arts, Boston U., 1956. Mgr. Sta. WGAN-TV, Portland, Maine, 1960-69, Sta. WIVB-TV, Buffalo, 1969-80; v.p. TV ops. Park TV, Ithaca, N.Y., 1980-83; prin., pres. BK&K, Inc., Syracuse, 1986—, SJL Broadcast Mgmt. Corp., Billings, Mont. and Montecito, Calif., 1984-95, owner Kans., 1988-95; prin., dir. Fayetteville, N.C., 1985—; owner Sta. KTVQ-TV, Billings, 1984—, Sta. WKFT-TV, Fayetteville, 1985—, Sta. WSTM-TV, Syracuse, 1986—; pres., CEO SJL Mgmt., Santa Barbara, Calif. Mem. CBS Affiliates Govt. Relations com., 1986; owner Sta. KSNW-TV, Wichita, Sta. KSNC-TV, Great Bend, Kans., Sta. KSNG-TV, Garden City, Kans., Sta. KSNK-TV, Overlin, Nebr., Sta. KSNT-TV, Topeka, Sta. WJRT-TV, Flint, Mich., 1989, SJL Comms., Inc., 1996—, KSBY-TV, San Luis Obispo, Calif., 1996—, WICU-TV, Erie, Pa., 1996—, WFXP-TV (LMA), Erie, Pa., 1996—. With U.S. Army, 1957-59. Mem. Nat. Assn. Broadcasters. Avocations: skiing, pvt. pilot. Office: SJL Mgmt 633 Picacho Ln Santa Barbara CA 93108-1224 also: KSNW 833 N Main St Wichita KS 67203-3606

LILLY, KRISTINE MARIE, soccer player; b. Wilton, Conn., July 27, 1971; Grad., U. N.C., 1993. Midfielder Washington Warthog, Landover, Md., 1995—, U.S. Women's Nat. Soccer Team, Chgo., 1987. Recipient Hemann Trophy, 1991; named Most Valuable Offensive Player NCAA Championship, 1989, 91, U.S. Soccer's Female Athlete of the Yr., 1993, U.S. Nat. Team All-Time Appearance Leader (more than 90 games); mem. FIFA Women's World Championship Team, 1991; mem. World Cup Team, 1999. Office: US Soccer Fedn 1801 S Prairie Ave Chicago IL 60616-1319

LIM, HENRY WAN-PENG, physician; b. Bandung, Indonesia, July 19, 1949; s. Budiman Ruslim and Nietje Tedjasuryani; m. Mamie Wong-Lim, July 20, 1975; children: Christopher T., Kevin T. BS in Biochemistry with honors, McGill U., 1971; MD cum laude, SUNY, Bklyn., 1975. Diplomate in dermatology, dermatol. immunology/diagnostic and lab. immunology Am. Bd. Dermatology; diplomate Nat. Bd. Med. Examiners. Intern Albert Einstein Coll. Medicine, Bronx, N.Y., 1975-76; resident dept. dermatology NYU Sch. Medicine, 1976-79, NIH fellow in dermatology, 1979, Dermatology Found. fellow, 1979-80, from instr. to assoc. prof. dermatology, 1979-93, prof. dermatology, 1993-97, asst. dean for vet. affairs, 1993-97; chmn. and Clarence S. Livingood chair dermatology Henry Ford Health Sys., Detroit, 1997—. Chief dermatology svc. N.Y. VA Med. Ctr., N.Y.C., 1985-94, chief staff, 1993-97, staff physician dermatology svc., 1994-97. Editor Photodermatology, Photoimmunology & Photomedicine, 2000—; mem. editl. bd. Jour. Am. Acad. Dermatology, 1993—; mem. editl. bd. Jour. Cut Med. Surg., 2000—. Recipient numerous awards; McGill U. scholar, 1968-70. Mem.: AMA, AAAS, Photomedicine Soc. (pres. 1992—99), Am. Assn. Immunologists, Am. Soc. for Photobiology (councilor 1998—2001, pres. 2002—), Am. Fedn. for Clin. Rsch., Assn. Profs. Dermatology (bd. dirs. 2000—), Am. Dermatology Assn. (chair membership com. 2002—), Dermatology Found., Soc. for Investigative Dermatology, Am. Acad. Dermatology (chair environ. com. 2000—, bd. dirs. 2002—), Alpha Omega Alpha. Avocations: travel. Office: Henry Ford Hosp Dept Dermatology 2799 W Grand Blvd Dept Detroit MI 48202-2689

LIMBACK, E(DNA) REBECCA, vocational education educator; b. Higginsville, Mo., Mar. 23, 1945; d. Henry Shobe and Martha Pauline Rebecca (Willard) Ernstmeyer; m. Duane Paul Limback, Nov. 9, 1963; children: Lisa Christine, Derek Duane. BE, Cen. Mo. State U., 1968, MEd, 1969, EdS, 1976; EdD, U. Mo., 1981. Cert. bus., English and vocat. tchr. Supervising tchr. Lab. Sch. Cen. Mo. State U., Warrensburg, 1969-76, asst. to grad. dean, 1977-79, asst. prof., asst. to bus. dean, 1981-83, assoc. prof. computer and office info. systems, 1984-95, 1986-95, prof. computer and office info. sys., 1996—. Mem. manual editing/revision staff State of Mo., Jefferson City, 1989-90; textbook reviewer Prentice-Hall, Englewood Cliffs, N.J., 1990-91. Author various curriculum guides; mem. editl. bd. Cen. Mo. State U. Rsch., 1982-92. Active Warrensburg Band Aides, 1989-93. Recipient Mo. Gov.'s Excellence in Tchg. award, 2001; grantee, RightSoft Corp., 1988. Mem. DAR, Nat. Bus. Edn. Assn. (mem. conf. profl. opportunities com. 1989-99, info. processing editor Bus. Edn. Forum 1991), Assn. Career and Tech. Edn., North Cen. Bus. Edn. Assn. (Mo. rep., Collegiate Disting. Svc. award 1993), Mo. Bus. Edn. Assn. (all-chpt. pres. 1988-89, chair strategic planning com. 1999—, Postsecondary Tchr. of Yr. 1992), Assn. Bus. Comms., Warrensburg Athletic Booster Club, Phi Delta Kappa (all-chpt. pres. 1985), Delta Pi Epsilon (rsch. rep. 1989-92, nat. publs. com. 1993—). Lutheran. Avocations: archaeology, oil painting. Home: 1102 Tyler Ave Warrensburg MO 64093-2049 Office: Dockery 200-B/COIS Dept Cen Mo State U Warrensburg MO 64093 E-mail: limback@CMSU1.cmsu.edu.

LIMBAUGH, STEPHEN NATHANIEL, JR. state supreme court chief justice; b. Cape Girardeau, Mo., Jan. 25, 1952; s. Stephen N. and Anne (Mesplay) L.; m. Marsha Dee Moore, July 21, 1973; children: Stephen III, Christopher K. BA, So. Meth. U., 1973, JD, 1976; LLM, U. Va., 1998. Bar: Tex. 1977, Mo. 1977. Assoc. Limbaugh, Limbaugh & Russell, Cape Girardeau, 1977-78; pros. atty. Cape Girardeau County, 1979-82; shareholder, ptnr. Limbaugh, Limbaugh, Russell & Syler, 1983-87; cir. judge 32d Jud. Cir., 1987-92; judge Supreme Ct. Mo., Jefferson City, 1992—. Mem. ABA, State Bar Tex., Mo. Bar. Office: Supreme Ct Mo 207 W High St Jefferson City MO 65101-1516

LIMBAUGH, STEPHEN NATHANIEL, federal judge; b. Cape Girardeau, Mo., Nov. 17, 1927; s. Rush Hudson and Bea (Seabaugh) L.; m. DeVaughn Anne Mesplay, Dec. 27, 1950; children— Stephen Nathaniel Jr., James Pennington, Andrew Thomas. BA, S.E. Mo. State U., Cape Girardeau, 1950; JD, U. Mo., Columbia, 1951. Bar: Mo. 1951. Prosecuting atty. Cape Girardeau County, Mo., 1954-58; judge U.S. Dist. Ct. (ea. and we. dists.) Mo., St. Louis, 1983—. With USN, 1945-46. Recipient Citation of Merit for Outstanding Achievement and Meritorious Service in Law, U. Mo., 1982 Fellow Am. Coll. Probate Counsel, Am. Bar Found.; mem. ABA (ho. of dels. 1987-90), Mo. Bar Assn. (pres. 1982-83). Republican. Methodist. E-mail: stephen. Office: US Dist Ct Thomas F Eagleton Courthous 111 S Tenth St Ste 3.125 Saint Louis MO 63102 E-mail: limbaugh@moed.uscourts.gov.

LIMMER, WARREN E. state legislator, real estate broker; m. Lori Limmer; two children. BA, Cloud State U. Real estate broker; Dist. 33B rep. Minn. Ho. of Reps., St. Paul, 1988-95; mem. Minn. Senate from 33rd dist., 1995—. Former mem. govt. op., labor-mgmt. rels., judiciary, edn.-higher edn. fin. divsn., and environ. and natural resources coms., Minn. Ho. of Reps. Home: 12888 73rd Ave N Maple Grove MN 55369-5247

LIN, CHUN CHIA, research physicist, educator; b. Canton, China, Mar. 7, 1930; s. Yue Hang Lam and Kin Ng. BS, U. Calif., Berkeley, 1951, MA, 1952; PhD, Harvard U., 1955. Asst. prof. physics U. Okla., Norman, 1955-59, assoc. prof. physics, 1959-63, prof. physics, 1963-68, U. Wis., Madison, 1968—. Cons., univ. retainee Tex. Instruments Inc., 1960-68; cons. Sandia Labs., 1976-81; sec. Gaseous Electronics Conf., 1972-73, chmn., 1990-92. Contbr. articles ot profl. jours. Sloan Found. fellow, 1962-66; rsch. grantee NSF and Aif Force Office Sci. Rsch. Fellow Am. Phys. Soc. (sec. divsn. electron and atomic physics 1974-77, chair divsn. atomic molecular and optical physics 1994-95, Will Allis prize 1996). Home: 1652 Monroe St Apt C Madison WI 53711-2046 Office: U Wis Dept Physics Madison WI 53706

LIN, JAMES CHIH-I, biomedical and electrical engineer, educator; b. Dec. 29, 1942; m. Mei Fei, Mar. 21, 1970; children: Janet, Theodore, Erik. BS, U. Wash., 1966, MS, 1968, PhD, 1971. Engr. Crown Zellerbach Corp., Seattle, 1966-67; asst. prof. U. Wash., 1971-74; prof. Wayne State U., Detroit, 1974-80, U. Ill., Chgo., 1980—, head dept. bioengring., 1980-92, dir. robotics and automation lab., 1982-89, dir. spl. projects Coll. Engring., 1992-94, rsch. chair NSC, 1993-97, dir. Ctr. Wireless Tech. and Bioelectromagnetics, 1997—. Vis. prof., Beijing, Rome, Shan Dong, Taiwan Univs.; lectr. short courses, 1974—; cons. Battelle Meml. Inst., Columbus, Ohio, 1973-75, SRI Internat., palo Alto, Calif., 1978-79, Arthur D. Little Inc., Cambridge, Mass., 1980-83, Ga. Tech. Rsch. Inst., Atlanta, 1984-86, Walter Reed Army Inst. Rsch., 1973, 87, 88, Naval Aerospace Med. Rsch. Labs., Pensacola, 1982-83, U.R.S. Corp., San Francisco, 1985-87, CBS Inc., N.Y., 1988, U. Va., 1991-92, ACS Inc., Santa Clara Calif., 1989-90, Luxtron Corp., Mountainview, Calif., 1991-92, Commonwealth Edison, Chgo., 1991-95, Lucent Tech./Bell Labs., 1998-2000; program chmn. Frontiers of Engring. and Computing Conf., Chgo., 1985; chmn., convener URSI Jt. Symposium Electromagnetic Waves in Biol. Sys., Tel Aviv, 1987, Internat. Conf. on Sci. and Tech., 1989-91; chmn. Chinese-Am. Acad. and Profl. Conv., 1993; mem. Congrl. Health Care Adv. Coun., 13th dist., Ill., 1987-99; panelist NSF Presdl. Young Investigator award com., Washington, 1984, 89; mem. NIH diagnostic radiology, 1981-85, chmn. spl. study sect., 1986—; mem. U.S. Nat. Commn. for URSI, NAS, 1980-82, 90-99, chair Commn. K., 1990-99, Extremely Low Frequency Field monitoring com., 1995-97; mem. Pres. Com. Nat. Medal of Sci., 1992-93; mem. Nat. Coun. Radiation Protection and Measurement, 1992—, chmn. radio frequency sci. com., 1995—; chmn. Internat. Union of Radio Scis. Commn., Electromagnetics in Biology and Medicine, 1996-99; chmn. Internat. Sci. Meeting on Electromagnetics in Medicine, 1997; mem. citizen's adv. coun. Hinsdale Cen. H.S., 1988-93. Author: Microwave Auditory Effects and Applications, 1978, Biological Effects and Health Implications of Radiofrequency Radiation, 1987, Electromagnetic Interaction with Biological Systems, 1989, Mobile Comm. Safety, 1996; editor: Advances in Electromagnetic Fields in Living Systems, 1994—; columnist: ACM Mobile Computing and Comms. Rev., 1999—, columnist: IEEE Antennas and Propagation Mag., 1999—, columnist: IEEE Microwave Mag., 2000—, columnist: Radio Sci. Bull., 2001—, guest editor: EMB Mag., 1997—99, guest editor: Wireless Networks, 1996—97; contbr. articles to profl. jours. Recipient Nat. Rsch. Svcs. award 1982, Disting. Svc. award, Outstanding Leadership award Chinese Am. Acad. and Profl. Assn. MidAm., 1989. Fellow AAAS, AIMBE, IEEE (tech. policy coun. 1990-91, chmn. com. on man and radiation, 1990-91, assoc. and guest editor transactions on biomed. engring., guest editor transaction on microwave theory and techniques, disting. lectr. engring. in medicine and biology 1991—, Transaction Best Paper award 1975); mem. Biomed. Engring. Soc. (sr. mem.), Robotics Internat. (sr. mem.), Am. Soc. Engring. Edn., Bioelectromagnetics Soc. (charter, pres.-elect 1993-94, pres. 1994-95, chmn. ann. meeting 1994), Electromagnetics Acad., Marconi Found. (sci. com. 1996—), Golden Key, Sigma Xi, Phi Tau Phi (v.p.), Tau Beta Pi. Office: U Ill Coll Engring 1030 SEO MC/154 851 S Morgan St Chicago IL 60607-7042 E-mail: lin@uic.edu.

LIN, PEN-MIN, electrical engineer, educator; b. Liaoning, China, Oct. 17, 1928; came to U.S., 1954; s. Tai-sui and Tse-san (Tang) Lin; m. Louise Shou Yuen Lee, Dec. 29, 1962; children: Marian, Margaret, Janice. B.S.E.E., Taiwan U., 1950; M.S.E.E., N.C. State U., 1956; Ph.D. in Elec. Engring., Purdue U., 1960. Asst. prof. Purdue U., West Lafayette, Ind., 1961-66, assoc. prof., 1966-74, prof. elec. engring., 1974-94, prof. emeritus, 1994—. Author: (with L.O. Chua) Computer Aided Analysis of Electronic Circuits, 1975, Symbolic Network Analysis, 1991, (with R.A. DeCarlo) Linear Circuit Analysis, 1995, 2d edit., 2001. Fellow IEEE (life). Home: 3029 Covington St West Lafayette IN 47906-1107 Office: Purdue Univ Sch Of Elec Engring West Lafayette IN 47907

LIND, JON ROBERT, lawyer; b. Evanston, Ill., July 4, 1935; s. Robert A. and Ruth (Anderson) L.; m. Jane Langfitt, Aug. 29, 1959; children: Jon Robert Jr., Elizabeth Neal, Susan Porter. AB, Harvard U., 1957, LLB, 1960; diploma in comparative law, Cambridge (Eng.) U., 1961. Bar: Ill. 1961. Assoc. Isham, Lincoln & Beale, Chgo., 1961-68, ptnr., 1968-88, McDermott, Will & Emory, Chgo., 1988-96, of counsel, 1997—. Atty. Winnetka (Ill.) Park Dist., 1973-78; bd. dirs. Swedish-Am. Mus. Ctr., 1988-96. Mem. ABA, Chgo. Bar Assn., Harvard U. Alumni Assn. (sec. 1970-73), Econ. Club Chgo., Law Club Chgo. Home: 644 Walden Rd Winnetka IL 60093-2035 Office: McDermott Will & Emery 227 W Monroe St Ste 3100 Chicago IL 60606-5096

LINDA, GERALD, advertising and marketing executive; b. Boston, Nov. 25, 1946; s. Edward Linda and Anne Beatrice (Lipofsky) Coburn; m. Claudia Wollack, Sept. 24, 1978; children— Jonathan Daniel Rezny, Jessica Simone. BS in Bus. Adminstrn., Northeastern U., 1969, MBA, 1971; postgrad., U. Mich., 1971-75. Faculty U. Ky., Lexington, 1975-77; ptnr. Tatham-Laird & Kudner, Chgo., 1977-80; v.p. Marsteller, 1980-84; sr. v.p. HCM, 1984-86; pres. Gerald Linda & Assocs., 1986-89; prin. Kurtzman/Slavin/Linda, Inc., 1990-93, Kapuler Mkgt. Rsch., Chgo., 1993-94; pres. Gerald Linda & Assocs., Glenview, Ill., 1994—. Mem. editorial review bd. Jour. Current Issues and Rsch. in Advt., 1984—. E-mail: glamktg@aol.com.

LINDAAS, ELROY NEIL, state legislator; b. Mayville, N.D., Aug. 10, 1937; m. Janice Roberta Pederson; 7 children. 3d generation farmer; mem. N.D. Senate from 20th dist., Bismark, 1991—; mem. appropriations com. N.D. Senate. Past mem. agrl. stblzn. and conservation com. Trail Co.; mem. Farmers Home Adminstrn. Com.; past emergency coord. N.D. Radio; mem. Amateur Civil Emergency Svc.

LINDAHL, DENNIS, retail executive; CFO Holiday Cos., Mpls. Office: Holiday Cos PO Box 1224 Minneapolis MN 55440-1224

LINDAU, PHILIP, commodities trader; b. 1936; With Pillsbury Co., 1964-93; pres. Pillsbury Flour Milling & Spl. Commodities Ops., Mpls.; pres., CEO Commodity Specialists Co. Office: Commodity Specialists Co 301 4th Ave S Minneapolis MN 55415-1015

LINDBERG, CHARLES DAVID, lawyer; b. Moline, Ill., Sept. 11, 1928; s. Victor Samuel and Alice Christine (Johnson) L.; m. Marian J. Wagner, June 14, 1953; children: Christine, Breta, John, Eric. AB, Augustana Coll., Rock Island, Ill., 1950; JD, Yale U., 1953; DHL, Augustana Coll., 2000. Bar: Ohio 1954. Assoc. Taft, Stettinius & Hollister, Cin., 1953-61, ptnr., 1961-85, mng. ptnr., 1985-98, of counsel, 1999—. Dir. Cin. Bengals Profl. Football Team; chmn. bd. dirs. Schonstedt Instrument Co., 1994—97. Editor Nat. Law Jour., 1979-90. Bd. dirs. Taft Broadcasting Co., Cin., 1973-87, Dayton Walther Corp., 1986-87, Gibson Greeting, Inc., 1991-2000; bd. dirs. Augustana Coll., 1978-87, 91-99, 2000—, sec., 1981-82, vice-chmn., 1982-83, chmn., 1983-86; pres. Cin. Bd. Edn., 1971, 74, Zion Luth. Ch., Cin., 1966-69; chmn. policy com. Hamilton County Rep. Com., 1981-90; mem. exec. com. Ohio Rep. Fin. Com., 1989-90; trustee Greater Cin. Ctr. Econ. Edn., 1976-91, pres., 1987-89, chmn., 1989-91; chmn. law firm divsn. Fine Arts Fund, 1985; trustee Pub. Libr. Cin. and Hamilton County, 1982—, pres., 1989, 96, 01. Mem. Cin. Bar Assn., Greater Cin. C. of C. (trustee 1985, exec. com., vice chmn. govt. and cmty. affairs com. 1989-91), Ohio Libr. Trustees Assn. (bd. dirs. 1986-87), Ohio C. of C. (bd. dirs. 1988-89), Queen City Club (sec. 1989-91), Commonwealth Club, Comml. Club (sec. 1994-96), Cin. Country Club, Optimists. Office: 1800 Firstar Tower 425 Walnut St Cincinnati OH 45202-3923 E-mail: lindberg@taftlaw.com.

LINDBERG, DUANE R. bishop, historian; b. Thief River Falls, Minn., Apr. 16, 1933; s. Edgar and Alice (Amundson) L.; m. E. Mardell Kvitne, June 6, 1954; children: Erik Duane, Karen Kristin Kelle, Karl Stephen, Martha Alice Stone, Kristian John. BS in Chemistry, U. N.D., 1954; MDiv in Theology, Luther Sem., St. Paul, 1961; MA in Am. Studies, U. Minn., 1969, PhD in Am. Studies, 1975. Rsch. chemist DuPont Co., 1954; tchg. asst. chemistry dept. U. Wis., Madison, 1956-57; chemist Minn. Farm Bur. Lab., St. Paul, 1957-59; pastor Epping and Wheelock (N.D.) Luth. Chs., 1961-68; rsch. historian Minn. State Hist. Soc., St. Paul, 1969-71; pastor Zion Luth. Ch., West Union, Iowa, 1971-78; sr. pastor Trinity Luth. Ch., Waterloo, 1978-87, Acension Luth. Ch., Waterloo, 1987—; nat. ch. body founder, presiding pastor Am. Assn. Luth. Chs., Mpls., 1987-99, presiding pastor emeritus, 1999—. Vis. prof. Upper Iowa U., Fayette, 1976-77; adj. prof. Am. Luth. Theol. Sem., St. Paul, 1996-2000. Author: Uniting Word, 1969, Men of the Cloth, 1980; contbr. articles to profl. jours. Bd. dirs. Palmer Meml. Hosp., West Union, Iowa, 1972-78, Allen Meml. Hosp., Waterloo, 1979—; founder, bd. mem. Buffalo Trails Mus., Epping, N.D., 1964-68; founder, bd. mem. Fayette County Hist. Soc., West Union, 1975-78; dean Decorah Conf. Am. Luth. Ch., 1976-78, exec. com. Iowa Dist., 1976-78; bd. dirs. Great Plains Inst. Theology, 1965-68; pres. Eastern Iowa Luth. H.S. Assn., 1997-. With U.S. Army, 1954-56. Recipient award of commendation Concordia Hist. Inst., St. Louis, 1980, Nehemiah award Abiding Word Ministries, Mpls., 1990, award of excellence Allen Meml. Hosp., Waterloo, 1995. Mem. numerous profl. ministerial groups and ch. bds., Rotary, Sons of Norway. Address: Valley Lutheran High School 1024 W 8th St Waterloo IA 50702

LINDBERG, GEORGE W. federal judge; b. Crystal Lake, Ill., June 21, 1932; s. Alger Victor and Rilla (Wakem) L. BS, Northwestern U., 1954, JD, 1957. V.p., legal counsel John E. Reid & Assocs., Chgo., 1955-68; ptnr. Franz, Franz, Wardell & Lindberg, Crystal Lake, 1968-73; comptr. State of Ill., Springfield, 1973-77, dep. atty. gen. Chgo., 1977-78; justice Ill. Appellate Ct., Elgin, 1978-89; dist. judge U.S. Dist. Ct. (no. dist.) Ill., Chgo., 1989—. Chmn. Ill. House Com. on Judiciary, Com. on Ethics, Springfield, 1970-73. Holder numerous govt. offices, 1966—. Office: US Dist Ct 219 S Dearborn St Ste 1472 Chicago IL 60604-1705

LINDE, MAXINE HELEN, lawyer, business executive, private investor; b. Chgo., Sept. 2, 1939; d. Jack and Lottie (Kroll) Stern; B.A. summa cum laude, UCLA, 1961; J.D., Stanford U., 1967; m. Ronald K. Linde, June 12, 1960. Bar: Calif. 1968. Applied mathematician, reseach engr. Jet Propulsion Lab., Pasadena, Calif., 1961-64; law clk. U.S. Dist. Ct. No. Calif., 1967-68; mem. firm Long & Levit, San Francisco, 1968-69, Swerdlow, Glikbarg & Shimer, Beverly Hills, Calif., 1969-72; sec., gen. counsel Envirodyne Industries, Inc., Chgo., 1972-89; pres. The Ronald and Maxine Linde Found., 1989—; vice chmn. bd., gen. counsel Titan Fin. Group, LLC, Chgo., 1994-98. Mem. bd. visitors Stanford Law Sch., 1989-92, law and bus. adv. coun., 1991-94, dean's adv. coun. 1992-94. Mem. Order of Coif, Phi Beta Kappa, Pi Mu Epsilon, Alpha Lambda Delta.

LINDE, RONALD KEITH, corporate executive, private investor; b. L.A., Jan. 31, 1940; s. Morris and Sonia Doreen (Hayman) L.; m. Maxine Helen Stern, June 12, 1960. BS with honors, UCLA, 1961; MS (Inst. scholar), Calif. Inst. Tech., 1962, PhD (ARCS scholar, Rutherford scholar), 1964. Cons. Litton Industries, L.A., 1961-63, engr., 1961; materials scientist Poulter Labs., Stanford Rsch. Inst., Menlo Park, Calif., 1964; head solid state rsch. Stanford Rsch. Inst., 1965-67; chmn. shock wave physics dept., mgr. tech. svcs. Poulter Labs., 1967, dir. shock and high pressure physics div., 1967-68, chief exec. labs., 1968-69; dir. phys. scis. Stanford Rsch. Inst., 1968-69; chmn. bd., CEO Envirodyne Industries, Inc., Chgo., 1969-89; chmn. bd. The Ronald and Maxine Linde Found., 1989—. Co-chmn. bd. Titan Fin. Group, LLC, Chgo., 1994-98; law and bus. adv. coun. Stanford Law Sch., 1991-94, dean's adv. coun. 1992-94. Contbr. articles to various publs.; patentee in field. Mem. adv. bd. ARCS Found., Chgo., 1993-98; mem. Northwestern U. Assocs., 1978—; trustee Calif. Inst. Tech., 1989—, Harvey Mudd Coll., 1989-98, vice chmn., bd. trustees, 1993-98, vice chmn. emeritus, 1998—. Mem. Sigma Xi, Tau Beta Pi, Phi Eta Sigma. Office: Linde Found 180 E Pearson St Ste 5801 Chicago IL 60611-2182

LINDELL, ANDREA REGINA, dean, nurse; b. Warren, Pa., Aug., 21, 1943; d. Andrew D. and Irene M. (Fabry) Lefik; m. Warner E. Lindell, May 7, 1966; children: Jennifer I., Jason M. B.S., Villa Maria Coll., 1970; M.S.N. Catholic U., 1975, D.N.Sc., 1976; diploma R.N., St. Vincent's Hosp., Erie, Pa. Instr. St. Vincent Hosp. Sch. Nursing, 1964-66; dir. Rouse Hosp., Youngsville, Pa., 1966-69; supr. Vis. Nurses Assn., Warren, Pa., 1969-70; dir. grad. program Cath. U., Washington, 1975-77; chmn., assoc. dean U. N.H., Durham, 1977-81; dean, prof. Oakland U., Rochester, Mich., 1981-90, dean, Schmidlapp prof. nursing U. Cin., 1990—; bd. dirs. CHEMED Corp.; cons. Moorehead U., Ky., 1983. Editor; Jour. Profl. Nursing, 1985; contbr. articles to profl. jours. Mem. sch. bd. Strafford Sch. Dist., N.H., 1977-80; Gov.'s Blue Ribbon Commn. Direct Health Policies, Concord, N.H., 1979-81; vice chmn. New England Commn. Higher Edn. in Nursing, 1977-81; mem. Mich. Assn. Colls. Nursing, 1981— . Named Outstanding Young Woman Am., 1980. Mem. Nat. League Nursing, Am. Assn. Colls. Nursing (pres. 1996—), Sigma Theta Tau. Democrat. Roman Catholic. Avocations: water skiing, roller skating, reading, fishing, camping. Office: College of Nursing & Health 3110 Vine St Cincinnati OH 45221-0001

LINDELL, EDWARD ALBERT, former college president, religious organization administrator; b. Denver, Nov. 30, 1928; s. Edward Gustaf and Estelle (Lundin) L.; m. Patricia Clare Eckert, Sept. 2, 1965; children: Edward Paul, Erik Adam. B.A., U. Denver, 1950, M.A., 1956, Ed.D., 1960, L.H.D. (hon.), 1975; Litt.D. (hon.), Tusculum Coll., 1979; D.H.L. (hon.), Roanoke Coll., 1981; Litt.D (hon.), Christ Coll., Irvine, 1992. Tchr. N. Denver High Sch., 1952-61; asst. dean Coll. Arts and Scis., U. Denver, 1961-65, dean, 1965-75; pres. Gustavus Adolphus Coll., St. Peter, Minn., 1975-80, Luth. Brotherhood Mut. Funds, Mpls., 1980—. V.p. Lutheran Brotherhood Found., 1980—, exec. dir. Mem. exec. bd. Rocky Mountain Synod Lutheran Ch. Am., 1968—, also pres. bd. coll. edn. and ch. vocations; trustee Midland Luth. Coll., Fremont, Nebr., Kans. Wesleyan U., Colo. Assn. Ind. Colls. and Univs., Luth. Med. Center, Wheatridge, Colo., Luth. Sch. Theology, Chgo., 1975—, St. John's U., Minn., 1978—; bd. dirs. Pacific Luth. Theol. Sem., 1978-80, Loretto Heights Coll., Colo., 1978-86, Swedish Coun. Am., 1978—, pres., chmn.-elect, 2001; bd. dirs. Gettysburg Theol. Sem., 1981-83; exec. bd. Luth. Coun. U.S.A., v.p., 1975—; mem. adv. bd. Royal Swedish Acad. Scis., 1980; v.p. Am.-Swedish Inst., 1980; exec. v.p. for external affairs Luth. Brotherhood, 1981—; pres. Nat. Fraternal Congress Am., 1988—; bd. dirs. Wittenberg U., 1988, Bethany Coll., 1991—, Minn. Orch., 1983—, Am. Scandinavian Found., 1982—, Fairview Hosp., 1982—, U.S. Swedish Found. Internat. Sci. Rsch., 1981— (v.p. 1986—), Habitat for Humanity Internat., 1992—; pres. U.S. Wittenberg Found., 1996—. Named Outstanding Faculty Mem. Coll. Arts and Scis., U. Denver, 1964; decorated knight King of Sweden, 1976; recipient Suomi Disting. Svc. award, 1989. Mem. Good Samaritan Soc. (bd. dirs. 1997—, vice-chmn. 98-99, chmn.-elect 1999, chmn. 2000—), Swedish Pioneer Hist. Soc. (dir. 1979—), U. Denver Alumni Assn. (Career Alumni Achievement award 1994), Phi Beta Kappa. Office: Swedish Coun Am 2600 Park Ave S Minneapolis MN 55407 E-mail: edlindell@swedishcouncil.org.

LINDEN, HENRY ROBERT, chemical engineering research executive; b. Vienna, Austria, Feb. 21, 1922; arrived in U.S., 1939, naturalized, 1945; s. Fred and Edith (Lermer) L.; m. Natalie Govedarica, 1967; children by previous marriage: Robert, Debra. BS, Ga. Inst. Tech., 1944; MChemE, Poly. U., 1947; PhD, Ill. Inst. Tech., 1952. Chem. engr. Socony Vacuum Labs., 1944-47; with Inst. of Gas Tech., 1947-78, various rsch. mgmt. positions, 1947-61, dir., 1961-69, exec. v.p., dir., 1969-74, pres., trustee, 1974-78; various acad. appointments Ill. Inst. Tech., Chgo, 1954-86, Frank W. Gunsaulus Disting. Prof. chem. engring., 1987-90, McGraw prof. energy and power engring. and mgmt., 1990—, interim pres., CEO, 1989-90, interim chmn., CEO Ill. Inst. Tech. Rsch. Inst., 1989-90; COO, GDC, Inc., Chgo., 1965-73; CEO Gas Devel. Corp. subs. Inst. Gas Tech., 1973-78, also bd. dirs.; pres., dir. Gas Rsch. Inst., 1976-87, exec. advisor, 1987-2000. Author tech. articles; holder U.S. and fgn. patents in fuel tech. Recipient award of merit oper. sect. Am. Gas Assn., 1956, Disting. Svc. award, 1974, Gas Industry Rsch. award, 1982, R&D award Nat. Energy Resources Orgn., 1986, Homer H. Lowry award for excellence in fossil energy rsch. U.S. Dept. Energy, 1991, award U.S. Energy Assn., 1993, Walton Clark medal Franklin Inst., 1972, Bunsen-Pettenkofer-Ehrentafel medal Deutscher Verein des Gas und Wasserfaches, 1978, Alumni medal Ill. Inst. Tech., 1995, Lifetime Achievement award The Energy Daily jour., 1996; named to Hall of Fame, Ill. Inst. Tech., 1982, Engring. Hall of Fame Ga. Tech., 1996. Fellow AIChE (Ernest W. Thiele award 2000), Inst.

Energy; mem. NAE, AAAS, Am. Chem. Soc. (recipient H.H. Storch award, chmn. divsn. fuel chemistry 1967, councilor 1969-77), So. Gas Assn. (hon. life). Office: Ill Inst Tech PH 135 10 W 33rd St Chicago IL 60616-3730

LINDENBAUM, SHARON, publishing executive; V.p. fin. Kansas City (Mo.) Star. Office: Kansas City Star 1729 Grand Blvd Kansas City MO 64108-1458

LINDENLAUB, JOHN CHARLES, electrical engineer, educator; b. Milw., Sept. 10, 1933; m. Deborah Hart, 1957; children: Brian, Mark, Anne, David. BS, MIT, 1955, MS, 1957; PhD in Elec. Engring., Purdue U., 1961. From asst. prof. to prof. Purdue U., West Lafayette, Ind., 1961-72, prof. elec. engring., 1972—, dir. Ctr. Instrnl. Devel. Engring., 1977-81. Mem. tech. staff Bell Telephone Labs., 1968-69; cons. Western Elec., N.Y. State Bd. Regents, Control Data Corp., J. Warren Rsch. in Higher Edn., Nat. Technol. U. Contbr. articles to profl. jours. Recipient Helen Plants award Frontiers in Edn. Conf., 1980, 87, 93; Danforth Found. assoc., 1966. Fellow IEEE (Edn. Soc. Achievement award 1984, Schmitz award FIE Conf.), Fellow Am. Soc. Engring. Edn. (Chester F. Carlson award 1988, Disting. Svc. citation 1993, E.R.M. Disting. Svc. award 1999). Office: Purdue Univ Elec Engring Bldg Lafayette IN 47907 E-mail: john.c.lindenlaub.1@purdue.edu.

LINDER, CARL H., III, diversified financial services company executive; BBA, U. Cinn., 1975. Co-pres. Am. Fin. Group, Inc., 1995—. Office: Am Fin Group Inc 1 E 4th St Cincinnati OH 45202-3717

LINDGREN, A(LAN) BRUCE, church administrator; b. Grand Rapids, Mich., July 1, 1948; m. Carole Coonce; children: Stacey, Michael, David (dec.). BS in Sociology, Mich. State U., 1970; MDiv, St. Paul Sch. Theology, 1975. Ordained high priest. Campus minister Park Coll., 1975-77; dir. ministerial edn. Temple Sch., 1986-92; exec. min., World Ch. sec., exec. asst. to 1st presidency Cmty. of Christ, 1992—. Dir. devel. basic leadership curriculum Temple Sch., 1977-86. Editor: Leaders Handbook, 1985-92. Office: Cmty of Christ 1001 W Walnut Independence MO 64050

LINDLEY, MARALEE IRWIN, county official, consultant, speaker; b. Springfield, Ill., June 30, 1925; d. Oramel Blackstone and Rachel Virginia (Elliott) Irwin; m. Joseph Perry Lindley, Sept. 18, 1948; children: Joseph Perry, Richard Fleetwood. BS Psychology, Northwestern U., 1947; MA in Counseling, U. Ill., Springfield, 1973, MA in Comm., 1979. Cert. tchr., Ill. Bookkeeper, acct. Ill. State Bar Assn., Springfield, 1947-48; curriculum coord., tchr. Sch. Dist. 186, 1966-80; auditor, trustee Woodside Twp., 1977-81; county auditor Sangamon County, Ill., 1980-86, county clk., 1986—. Dir. Ill. Dept. on Aging, Springfield, 1992-99; co-author/developer Ill. Elem. Gifted Program, 1977-80 (exemplary citation 1978); rep. Internat. Fedn. on Aging of UN; vice chair U.S. Com. for Celebration of UN Internat. Yr. of Older Persons, 1999; chair Nat. Effort for Global Embrace Walk, 1999; adv. com. Nat. Silver Haired Congress; charter mem. Internat. Conf. Intergenerational Programs to Promote Social Change. Mem. Mayor's Commn. on Internat. Visitors, Springfield, 1964—; sec. Sangamon State U. Found., 1984-86, Symphony Guild, Springfield, 1983-86; treas. Springfield Women's Polit. Caucus, 1983-85; pres. Capitol City Rep. Women's Club, Springfield, 1985-87. Recipient hon. Thanks award Land of Lincoln coun. Girl Scouts U.S., 1958, Appreciation award City of Springfield, 1964, Disting. Citizen award Sch. Dist. 1986, Elizabeth Cady Stanton award Springfield Women's Polit. Caucus, 1987; named to Women of Achievement in Govt., Sangamon State U., 1985, One of 5 Rep. County Ofciles. of Yr., 1985. Mem. Ill. Assn. County Auditors (sec. 1982-84, treas. 1984-86, v.p. 1986), Assn. Govt. Accts. (pres. 1984-85), Am. Soc. Pub. Adminstrn., Nat. Assn. Govt. Accts. (regional v.p.), Ill. Women in Govt. (treas.), Women in Mgmt. (Woman of Achievement award 1985), LWV. Lodge: Zonta. Avocations: dulcimer, folk singing, sports, reading, public speaking. Home: 2332 S Noble Ave Springfield IL 62704-4344

LINDNER, ARLON, state legislator; b. Aug. 3, 1935; m. Shirlee Lindner; 4 children. BA, Tex. State U.; MDiv, Cen. Bapt. Theol. Sem., Mpls. Minn. state rep. Dist. 33A, 1993—. Self-employed businessman. Address: 19508 Country Cir E Rogers MN 55374-9709

LINDNER, CARL HENRY , JR. sports team executive, insurance company executive; b. Dayton, Ohio, Apr. 22, 1919; s. Carl Henry and Clara (Serrer) L.; m. Edith Bailey, Dec. 31, 1953; children: Carl Henry III, Stephen Craig, Keith Edward. Co-founder United Dairy Farmers, 1940; pres. Am. Fin. Corp., Cin., 1959-84, chmn., 1959—, CEO, 1984—; owner, CEO Cincinnati Reds, 1999—. Bd. advs. Bus. Adminstrn. Coll., U. Cin. Republican. Baptist.

LINDNER, CRAIG, financial services company executive; Co-pres. Am. Fin. Group, Inc., Cin., 1999—. Office: Am Fin Group Inc One E 4th St Cincinnati OH 45202

LINDNER, KEITH E. food company executive; Sr. exec. v.p. United Brands Co., Cincinnati; pres., chief oper. officer Chiquita Brands Internat. Inc. (formerly United Brands Co.), vice chmn. of bd., 1997—. Office: Chiquita Brands Internat Inc One E 4th St Cincinnati OH 45202

LINDNER, ROBERT DAVID, finance company executive; b. Dayton, Ohio, Aug. 5, 1920; s. Carl Henry and Clara (Serrer) L.; m. Betty Ruth Johnston, Mar. 29, 1947; children: Robert David, Jeffrey Scott, Alan Bradford, David Clark. Chmn. bd. United Dairy Farmers, Cin., 1940—; With Am. Financial Corp., 1950-95, former v.p., vice chmn. bd., now vice chmn. bd. dirs.; chmn. bd. United Dairy Farmers. Trustee No. Bapt. Theol. Sem. Served with U.S. Army, 1942-45. Mem. Masons (33 degree). Home: 6950 Given Rd Cincinnati OH 45243-2840 Office: United Dairy Farmers 3955 Montgomery Rd Cincinnati OH 45212-3798

LINDQUIST, SUSAN LEE, biology and microbiology educator; b. June 5, 1949; BA in Microbiology with honors, U. Ill., 1971; PhD in Biology, Harvard U., 1976. Asst. prof. dept. biology U. Chgo., 1978-84, assoc. prof., 1984-88, prof. dept. molecular genetics & cell biology, 1988—, investigator Howard Hughes Med. Inst., 1988—. Mem. com. genetics, com. devel. biology U. Chgo., 1999—; cons. Mus. Sci. & Industry, Chgo., 1983-87; vis. scholar Cambridge U., 1983; cons., prin. in film Lights Breaking, 1985; mem. sci. adv. com. Helen Hay Whitney Found., 1997—; lectr. in field. Co-editor: The Stress Induced Proteins, 1988, Heat Shock, 1990; assoc. editor The New Biologist, 1991-93; mem. editl. bd. Cell Regulation, 1989—, Molecular and Cell Biology, 1984—, Gene Expression, 1994-95, Cell Stress and Chaperones, 1995—, Current Biology, 1996—, Molecular Biology of the Cell, 1996—; monitoring editor Jour. Cell Biology, 1993—; contbr. articles to profl. jours. Teaching fellow Harvard U., 1973-74, Postdoctoral fellow Am. Cancer Soc., 1976-78. Fellow Am. Acad. Microbiology, AAAS, NAS, Am. Acad. Arts and Sci.; mem. Am. Soc. Cell Biology, Am. Soc. Microbiology, Fedn. Am. Scientists for Exptl. Biology, Genetics Soc. Am. (elected sec. 1998—), Molecular Medicine Soc. Home: 1200 E Madison Park Chicago IL 60615-2961 Office: U Chgo 5841 S Maryland Ave Chicago IL 60637-1463

LINDSAY, DIANNA MARIE, educational administrator; b. Boston, Dec. 7, 1948; d. Albert Joseph and June Hazelton Raggi; m. James William Lindsay III, Feb. 14, 1981. BA in Anthropology, Ea. Nazarene Coll., 1971; MEd in Curriculum and Instrn., Wright State U., 1973, MA in Social Studies Edn., 1974, MEd in Edn. Adminstrn., 1977; EdD in Urban History, Ball State U., 1976; MA in Counseling, U. Dayton, 2000. Supr. social edn. Ohio Dept. Edn., Columbus, 1976-77; asst. prin. Orange City Schs., Pepper Pike, Ohio, 1977-79; prin. North Olmsted (Ohio) Jr. High Sch., 1979-81; dir. secondary edn. North Olmsted City SChs., 1981-82; supt. Copley (Ohio)-Fairlawn City Schs., 1982-85; prin. North Olmsted High Sch., 1985-89, New Trier High Sch., Winnetka, Ill., 1989-96, Worthington Kilbourne H.S., Columbus, Ohio, 1996-2001; headmaster Columbus Jewish Day Sch., New Albany, 2001—. Bd. dirs. Harvard Prins. Ctr., Cambridge, Mass. Contbr. articles to profl. jours. Bd. dirs. Nat. PTA, Chgo., 1987-89 (Educator of Yr. 1989), Found. Human Potential, Chgo.,; bd. trustee Columbus Jewish Country Day Sch. Named Prin. of Yr. Ohio Art Tchrs., 1989, one of 100 Up and Coming Educators, Exec. Educator Mag., 1988, Milken Educator of the Yr. Ohio, 1999; recipient John Vaughn Achievements in Edn. North Cen. Assn., 1988; named Ohio Prin. of Yr, 2000. Mem. AAUW, Ill. Tchrs. Fgn. Lang., Rotary Internat., Phi Delta Kappa. Methodist. Avocations: stained glass, reading, travel, biking, harpist. Office: Columbus Jewish Day Sch 79 N High St New Albany OH 43054

LINDSAY, JAMES WILEY, retired agricultural company executive; b. Des Moines, Sept. 13, 1934; s. Worthington U. Lindsay and Marsha E. (Wiley) Asher; m. Shirley L. Shutt, July 2, 1953 (div. May 1985, dec. 1990); children: Elizabeth Lindsay Foster, James W. II, Jennifer, Lindsay; m. Jean M. Baumann, Aug. 2, 1986; 1 child, Amanda Marie. Mgr. ops. Archer, Daniels, Midland, Fredonia, Kans., 1968-70, Lincoln, Nebr., 1970-72, mgr. export Decatur, Ill., 1972-74, v.p. western region Lincoln, 1974-76, v.p. ops. Cedar Rapids, Iowa, 1979-80, ops. mgr. Decatur, 1980-83; pres. Brazil ops. T.V.P., Inc., Campinas, Brazil, 1976-79; chief exec. officer AG Processing Inc., Omaha, 1983-2000; ret. Bd. dirs. ABC Ins., Des Moines; mem. adv. bd. U.S.Bank; pres., bd. dirs. Proagro and Protinal, Caracas, Venezuela. Mem. trade and environ. policy adv. com. U.S. Trade Rep.; bd. dirs. United Way, Elkhorn Sch. Found. Mem. Nat. Soybean Processors Assn. (chmn. 1987-91), Jaycees (pres. Fredonia chpt. 1963-64, bd. dirs. Des Moines chpt. 1960). Republican. Roman Catholic. Lodge: Masons.

LINDSAY, JOHN CONAL, state legislator; b. Omaha, June 27, 1959; m. Mary Beth Barbina, 1988; children: John, Patrick, Robert. BA, Creighton U., 1981, JD cum laude, 1984; postgrad., U. Nebr., 1981-82. Bar: Nebr., 1984. Ptnr. Lindsay & Lindsay, 1985-97; mem. from dist. 9 Nebr. State Senate, Lincoln, mem. govt., mil. and vet. affairs coms., 1989-97, mem. banking, commerce and ins. coms., com. on coms., chmn. judiciary com.; lobbyist O'Hara & Assocs., 1997—. Vis. asst. prof. bus. law Nebr. Wesleyan U., 1985-86; del. Dem. Nat. Conv., 1992, 96. Mem. Archdiocesan Social Min. Commn., 1997—. Named One of Ten Outstanding Young Omahans, 1990. Mem. Nebr. Bar Assn., Omaha Bar Assn., KC, Rotary Club, Omaha Barristers Club (v.p. 1986-87, pres. 1987-88). Home: 120 S 51st St Omaha NE 68132-3524

LINDSEY, ADA MARIE, dean, nursing educator; b. Dayton, Ohio, May 8, 1937; m. George T. Lindsey. BS in Nursing, Ohio State U., 1959, MS, 1960; PhD, U. Md., 1977. RN. Staff nurse Ohio State U. Hosp., Columbus, 1960; instr. Mt. Carmel Sch. Nursing., 1960-65, asst. dir., 1965-68; asst. prof. U. Md., Balt., 1968-77, assoc. prof., asst. dean, 1977-78; assoc. prof. U. Calif., San Francisco, 1979-83, chmn., 1979-86, prof., 1983-86; prof., dean Sch. Nursing UCLA, 1986-95; dean coll. nursing U. Nebr. Med. Ctr., 1995—. Co-editor: Pathophysiological Phenomena in Nursing, 1993 (Book of Yr. award 1986); contbr. articles to profl. jours. Fellow Am. Acad. Nursing; mem. Am. Nurses Assn., Nebr. Nurses Assn., Oncology Nursing Soc., Sigma Theta Tau. Office: U Nebraska Med Ctr 98-5330 Coll Nursing Omaha NE 68198-0001

LINDSEY, DAVID HOSFORD, lawyer; b. Kingsville, Tex., July 25, 1950; s. Ernest Truman and Helen Elizabeth (Hosford) L.; m. Marilyn Kay Williams, June 8, 1974; children: Seth Williams, Brooks Daniel. BS in Bus. Adminstrn., U. Mo., 1972; JD, Washburn U., 1975. Bar: Mo. 1975. With trust dept. Commerce Bank, Kansas City, Mo., 1974-75, asst. v.p., 1979-83, v.p., 1983-85, sr. v.p., 1985-94, chief credit officer, 1989—, exec. v.p., 2000—; mgr., sales dept. Pioneer Pallet, Inc., North Kansas City, 1976; asst. cashier Nat. Bank, 1977, asst. v.p., 1977-78, v.p., 1978-79. Vice chmn. planning and zoning com. City of Liberty, Mo., 1981-93; bd. dirs. Kansas City Met. YMCA. Mem. Mo. Bar Assn., Lawyers Assn. Kansas City, Kansas City Met. Bar Assn., Robert Morris Assn. (bd. dirs. Kansas City chpt.), Kansas City C. of C., Kansas City Alumni Assn. (bd. dirs.), Clayview Country Club, Phi Gamma Delta, Omicron Delta Kappa. Baptist. Home: 602 Camelot Dr Liberty MO 64068-1176 Office: Commerce Bank 1000 Walnut St Ste 730 Kansas City MO 64106-2123

LINDSEY, SUSAN LYNDAKER, zoologist; b. Valley Forge, Pa., Aug. 23, 1956; d. Howard Paul and Lillian Irene (Whitman) Lyndaker; m. Kevin Arthur Lindsey, July 17, 1982; children: Ryan Howard, Shannon Marie. BS in Biology, St. Lawrence U., 1978; MA in Zoology, So. Ill. U., Carbondale, 1980; PhD in Zoology, Colo. State U., 1987. Rschr. St. Lawrence U., Kenya, East Africa, 1978; tchr. Beth Jacob H.S., Denver, 1986-87; rschr. mammal dept. Dallas Zoo, 1988-93; exec. dir. Wild Canid Survival and Rsch. Ctr., Eureka, Mo., 1993—. Adj. prof. Cedar Valley Coll., 1992-93, So. Ill. U., Carbondale, 1996—; mgmt. group mem. Red Wolf Species Survival Plan, Tacoma, Wash., 1994—, Mexican Gray Wolf Species Survival Plan, Albuquerque, 1993—, Maned Wolf Species Survival Plan, Washington, 1999—. Author: (with others) The Okapi: Mysterious Animal of Congo-Zaire, 1999; contbr. articles to profl. jours. Docent Denver Zool. Found., Denver Zoo, 1985-88. Mem. Acad. Sci. St. Louis, Am. Zoo and Aquarium Assn., Am. Behavior Soc., Am. Soc. of Mammalogists, Beta Beta Beta, Phi Beta Kappa, Psi Chi. Avocations: horseback riding, canoeing, gardening, photography, travel. Office: Wild Canid Survival Rsch Ctr Wash U PO Box 760 Eureka MO 63025-0760

LING, TA-YUNG, physicist; b. Shanghai, Feb. 2, 1943; married, 1969; 3 children. BS, Tunghai U., Taiwan, 1964; MS, U. Waterloo, Ont., Can., 1966; PhD in Physics, U. Wis., 1971. Rsch. asst. U. Wis., 1967-71; rsch. assoc. physics U. Pa., Phila., 1972-75, asst. prof., 1975-77; from asst. prof. to assoc. prof. Ohio State U., Columbus, 1977-83, prof. physics, 1983—. Recipient Outstanding Jr. Investigator award Dept. of Energy, 1977. Mem. Am. Phys. Soc. Achievements include research in experimental high energy physics; deep inelastic neutrino-nucleon scattering, neutrino masses and mixing, neutrino oscillations, deep inelastic electron-proton scattering, high energy proton-proton collisions. Office: Ohio State U High Energy Physics Lab Physics Dept/Smith Lab 174 W 18th Ave Columbus OH 43210-1106 E-mail: ling@mps.ohio-state.edu.

LINHARDT, ROBERT JOHN J, medicinal chemistry educator; b. Passaic, N.J., Oct. 18, 1953; s. Robert J. and Barbara A. (Kelley) L.; m. Kathryn F. Burns, May 31, 1975; children: Kelley, Barbara. BS in Chemistry, Marquette U., 1975; MA in Chemistry, Johns Hopkins U., 1977, PhD in Organic Chemistry, 1979; postgrad., Mass. Inst. Tech., 1979-82. Rsch. assoc. Mass. Inst. Tech., Cambridge, 1979-82; asst. prof. U. Iowa, Iowa City, 1982-86, assoc. prof., 1986-90, prof. medicinal and natural products chemistry, 1990—, prof. chem. and biochem. engring., 1996—, F. Wendell Miller Disting. prof., 1996, prof. chemistry, 1999—. Cons. in field.; interacad. exchange scientist to USSR NAS, 1988. Mem. editl. bd. Applied Biochemistry and Biotech., 1985—, Carbohydrate Rsch., 1990—, Jour. Carbohydrate Chemistry, 1995—, Jour. Biol. Chem., 1995-2000, Analytical Biochemistry, 1991-97, 2001—; contbr. numerous articles to profl. jours. Johnson and Johnson fellow MIT, 1981; NIH grantee, 1982—. Mem. AAAS, AACP (Volwiler award 1999), Am. Chem. Soc. (Horace S. Isbell award Carbohydrate Chemistry 1994), Soc. Glycobiology. Office: U Iowa Coll Pharmacy Phar # 303A Iowa City IA 52240 E-mail: robert-linhardt@uiowa.edu.

LINK, DAVID THOMAS, lawyer, university administrator; b. 1936. B.S. magna cum laude, U. of Notre Dame, 1958, J.D., 1961; postgrad., Georgetown U., 1965-66. Bar: Ohio 1961, Ill. 1966, Ind. 1975, U.S. Supreme Ct. Trial atty., Office of Chief Counsel, IRS, 1961-66; ptnr., Winston, Strawn, Smith & Patterson, Chgo., 1966-70; prof., U. Notre Dame Law Sch., Notre Dame, Ind., 1970—, dean, 1975—; cons. to GAO; mem. Ind. Gov's Com. on Individual Privacy; mem. pres.' task force on New Methods for Improving the Quality of Lawyers' Services to Clients; chair Ind. State Ethics Commn., 1988-90; acad. coun., provost's adv. com., athletic affairs, acad. affairs, faculty affairs coms. of bd. of trustees U. Notre Dame; founding pres., vice chancellor U. Notre Dame, Perth, Aus., 1990-92, bd. trustees, bd. govs. Iterim dir. U. Notre Dame Ctr. for Civil and Human Rights; chair World Law Inst. Served to lt. comdr. USN. Mem. Soc. for Values in Higher Edn., ABA (council on sci. and tech., com. on advt., sect. on legal edn., com. on professionalism 1993-97). Author: (with Soderquist) Law of Federal Estate and Gift Taxation, Vol. 1, 1978, Vol. 2, 1980. Office: U Notre Dame Law Sch Notre Dame IN 46556

LINK, TERRY, state legislator; b. Waukegan, Ill., Mar. 20, 1947; m. Susan McCall; 4 children. Student, Stout State U. Ptnr. Lake County Indsl. Equipment; mem. Ill. Senate, Springfield, 1997—, mem. commerce & industry, exec. appts., state govt. ops. com. Democrat. Office: State Capitol 119-b Capitol Bldg Springfield IL 62706-0001 also: 425 Sheridan Rd Ste B Highwood IL 60040-1308

LINKLATER, WILLIAM JOSEPH, lawyer; b. Chgo., June 3, 1942; s. William John and Jean (Connell) L.; m. Dorothea D. Ash, Apr. 4, 1986; children: Erin, Emily. BA, U. Notre Dame, 1964; JD, Loyola U., 1968. Bar: Ill. 1968, U.S. Dist. Ct. (no. dist.) Ill. 1968, U.S. Ct. Appeals (7th cir.) 1971, U.S. Supreme Ct. 1971, U.S. Ct. Appeals Washington, 1978, U.S. Ct. Appeals Washington 1978, Calif. 1981, U.S. Dist. Ct. (cen. dist.) Calif. 1981, U.S. Tax Ct. 1982, U.S. Dist. Ct. (no. dist.) Calif. 1983, U.S. Dist. Ct. (ea. dist.) Mich. 1989, U.S. Ct. Appeals (6th cir.) 1990, U.S. Dist. Ct. Hawaii, 1992. Atty. Fed. Defender Project, Chgo.; assoc. Baker & McKenzie, 1968-75, ptnr., 1975—. Contbr. articles to profl. jours. Mem.: Wong Sun Soc. San Francisco (internat. proctor), Chgo. Inn of Ct., Am. Bd. Criminal Lawyers, ACTL, Colo. Bar Assn., Calif. Bar Assn., Internat. inst., Chgo. Bar Assn. (pres. 2000—01, bd. mgrs. 1997—2002, past v.p. jud. candidates evaluation com., chmn. large law firm com.), 7th Cir. Bar Assn., Ill. Bar Assn., FBA, ABA (past co-chmn. com. on internat. criminal law criminal justice sect. , mem. criminal practice and procedure com. antitrust sect., others), Alpha Sigma Nu. Office: Baker & McKenzie 1 Prudential Plz Ste 3000 Chicago IL 60601

LINOWES, DAVID FRANCIS, political economist, educator, corporate executive; b. N.J., Mar. 16, 1917; m. Dorothy Lee Wolf, Mar. 25, 1946; children: Joanne Linowes Alinsky, Richard Gary, Susan Linowes Allen (dec.), Jonathan Scott. Founder, ptnr. Leopold & Linowes (now BDO Siedman), Washington, 1946-62; cons. sr. ptnr. Leopold & Linowes, 1962-82; nat. founding ptnr. Laventhol & Horwath, 1965-76; chmn. bd, CEO Mickleberry Comm. Corp., 1970-73; chmn., CEO Perpetual Investment Co., Inc., 1950-88; dir. Horn & Hardart Co., 1971-77, Piper Aircraft, 1972-77, Saturday Rev./World Mag., Inc., 1972-77, Chris Craft Industries, Inc., 1958—, Work in Am. Inst., Inc.; prof. polit. economy, pub. policy, bus. adminstrn. U. Ill., Urbana, 1976—, Boeschensten prof. emeritus, 1987—. Cons. DATA Internat. Assistance Corps., 1962-68, U.S. Dept. State, UN, Sec. HEW, Dept. Interior; chmn. Fed. Privacy Protection Commn., Washington, 1975-77, U.S. Commn. Fair Market Value Policy for Fed. Coal Leasing, 1983-84, Pres.'s Commn. on Fiscal Accountability of Nation's Energy Resources, 1981-82; chmn. Pres.' Commn. on Privatization, 1987-88; mem. Council on Fgn. Relations; cons. panel GAO; adj. prof. mgmt. NYU, 1965-73; Disting. Arthur Young Prof. U. Ill., 1973-74; emeritus chmn. internat. adv. com. Tel Aviv U.; headed U.S. State Dept. Mission to Turkey, 1967, to India, 1970, to Pakistan, 1968, to Greece, 1971 ; U.S. rep. on privacy to Orgn. Econ. Devel. Intergovtl. Bur. for Informatics, 1977-81, cons., N.Y.C., 1977-81; U.S. State Dept. mission to Chile, Argentina and Uruguay, July, 1988, Yugoslavia, May, 1991. Author: Managing Growth Through Acquistion, Strategies for Survival, Corporate Conscience; commn. report Personal Privacy in Information Society, Fiscal Accountablility of Nation's Energy Resources; editor: The Impact of the Communication and Computer Revolution on Society, Privacy in America, 1989, Creating Public Policy, 1998, Living Through 50 Years of Economic Progress with 10 Presidents-The Most Productive Generation in History 1946-1996, 2000; contbr. articles to profl. jours. Trustee Boy's Club Greater Washington, 1955-62, Am. Inst. Found., 1962-68; assoc. YM-YWHA's Greater N.Y., 1970-76; chmn. Charities Adv. Com. of D.C., 1958-62; emeritus bd. dirs. Religion in Am. Life, Inc.; former chmn. U.S. People for UN; chmn. citizens com. Combat Charity Rackets, 1953-58. 1st lt. Signal Corps, AUS, 1942-46. Recipient 1970 Human Relations award Am. Jewish Com., U.S. Pub. Service award, 1982, Alumni Achievement award U. Ill., 1989, CPA Distinguished Pub. Svc. award, Washington, 1989. Mem. AICPA (v.p. 1962-63), U. Ill. Found. (emeritus bd. dirs. 1), Coun. Fgn. Rels., Cosmos Club (Washington), Phi Kappa Phi (nat. bd. dirs.), Beta Gamma Sigma. Office: U Ill 308 Lincoln Hall Urbana IL 61801 also: 9 Wayside Ln Scarsdale NY 10583-2907 Home: # 524 120 SE 5th Ave Boca Raton FL 33432-5072

LINSEY, NATHANIEL L. bishop; b. Atlanta, July 24, 1926; s. Samuel and L. E. (Forney) L.; m. Mae Cannon Mills, June 8, 1951; children: Nathaniel Jr., Ricardlo Mills, Julius Wayne, Angela Elise. BS, Paine Coll., 1948, LLD (hon.), 1990; BD, Howard U., 1951; MA in Evangelism, Scarritt Coll., 1974; DD (hon.), Miles Coll., 1975, Tex. Coll., 1985. Ordained to ministry Christian M.E.Ch., 1948. Nat. dir. youth Christian M.E.Ch., 1951-52; pastor Rock of Ages Christian M.E.Ch., 1952-53; presiding elder Columbia (S.C.) dist. Christian M.E.Ch., 1953-55; pastor Vanderhorst Christian M.E.Ch., 1955-56, Mattie E. Coleman Christian M.E.Ch., 1956-62, Thirgood Christian M.E.Ch., 1962-66; gen. sec. evangelism Christian M.E.Ch., 1966-78, chmn. bd. lay activities, 1978-82, chmn. fin. com., 1982-86, elected 39th bishop, 1978—, sr. bishop, CEO, presiding bishop 2d dist., 1994, founder Congress on Evangelism, chmn. dept. fin., 1982-86, chmn. bd. evangelism, missions and human concerns, chmn. Coll. of Bishops, 1980, 92; v.p. Interfaith Christian Coun., Washington, 1979-82. Mem. presidium World Meth. Coun.; regional sec. N.Am. sect. world evangelism com. World Methodist Coun. Pres. local chpt. NAACP, Knoxville, Tenn., 1957; trustee Miles Coll., Birmingham, Ala.; mem. World Coun. of Chs., Nat. Coun. of Chs., Ky. Coun. of Chs.; patron bishop women's missionary coun. CME Ch., 1994—. Recipient Disting. Alumni award Paine Coll., 1978, Presdl. citation Nat. Assn. for Equal Opportunities in Higher Edn., 1979, Disting. Svc. award Govt. D.C., 1984, Pub. Svc. award Tex. Coll., 1984, Disting. Missionary award Calif. conf. M.E.Ch., 1985; chieftancy of Obong Uwanna Ibibio Tribe, Nigeria, 1992—. Mem. World Meth. Coun. (founding mem. Hon. Order Jerusalem), So. Calif. Ecumenical Coun. Chs. (pres. L.A. chpt. 1984). Democrat. Home: 5115 Rollman Estate Dr Cincinnati OH 45236-1457 E-mail: nlml@aol.com.

LINSON, ROBERT EDWARD, university administrator emeritus; b. Indpls., Dec. 10, 1922; s. William Albert and Anne Charlotte (Karstedt) L.; m. Nancy Sue Hughes, June 6, 1948; children: Cynthia, Lawrence, LuAnn. BS, Ball State U., Muncie, Ind., 1947; MS, Ball State U., 1948; EdD, U. Denver, 1957. Prin., acting supt. Jonesboro (Ind.) pub. schs., 1948-49; prin

J.C. Knight Sch., Jonesboro, 1949-50, 51-52, Spiceland (Ind.) pub. schs., 1952-55; dir. alumni rels. Ball State Tchrs. Coll., Muncie, 1955-75; exec. dir. alumni and devel. Ball State U., 1975-80, v.p. univ. relations, 1980-87, v.p. univ. relations emeritus, 1987—. Cons. in field. Contbr. articles to profl. jours. Bd. dirs. Planned Parenthood of East Ctrl. Ind., 1988-91, United Way of Delaware County, Muncie, 1982-86, Muncie YMCA, 1980-84; mem. task force on govtl. rels. United Way of Ind., Indpls., 1985-91; founder Coun. Advancement and Support of Edn., 1974; bd. dirs. Ind. Basketball Hall of Fame. With USAF, 1943-46, 50-51. Named Outstanding U.S. Advancement Officer, Coun. for Advancement & Support of Edn., 1986; Alumni Disting. Svc. award, Ball State U., 1980, Ball State U. Athletic Hall of Fame, others. Mem. Am. Alumni Coun. (chmn. bd. dirs. 1972-73), Sagamore of the Wabash, Rotary. Democrat. Presbyterian. Avocations: travel, reading, intercollegiate athletics. Home: 909 N Meadow Ln Muncie IN 47304-3326

LINSTROTH, TOD BRIAN, lawyer; b. Racine, Wis., Feb. 19, 1947; s. Eugene and Gloria L.; m. Jane Kathryn Zedler, June 23, 1972; children: Kathryn, Krista, Kassandre, Kyle. BBA in Acctg., U. Wis., 1970, JD, 1973. Bar: Wis. Assoc. Michael, Best & Friedrich, Madison, Wis., 1973-79, ptnr., mem. firm mgmt. com., 1980—. Chmn. Wis. Tech. Coun., Inc., 2001—. Bd. visitors Univ. Wis. Sch. Bus., 1991-94; mem. Wis. Gov.'s Sci. and Tech. Coun., Madison, 1993-95; pres. Madison Repertory Theatre. Mem. Greater Madison Area C. of C., Wis. Venture Fair (chair Steering Com. 1997—), Wis. Tech. Coun. (chair 2001—). Republican. Avocations: skiing, sailing, reading. Office: Michael Best & Friedrich 1 S Pinckney St Ste 700 Madison WI 53703-4236

LINTON, WILLIAM CARL, state legislator; b. Ft. Worth, Nov. 26, 1929; s. Carl Gustav and Mary Zola (Delashamit) L.; m. Lois Anne Reeder, Dec. 16, 1935; children: David, Rebecca, Angela, Steven. BS in Indsl. Engring., Washington U., 1951; MS in Engring. Mgmt., U. Mo., Rolla, 1974. Registered profl. engr., Mo. Indsl. engr. Laclede Steel, Alton, Mo., 1953-54; sales engr. Nooter Corp., St. Louis, 1954-84; sales rep. Hill Equip. Co., 1984-86; state rep. Mo. Ho. of Reps., Jefferson City, 1986—. Mem. Rockwood Bd. of Edn., St. Louis County, 1976-82, pres., 1981. With U.S. Army, 1951-53. Mem. Nat. Assn. Corrosion Engrs. (chmn. 1964), Eureka C. of C., West St. Louis C. of C. Republican. Presbyterian. Avocation: sports. Office: Ho of Reps State Capitol Building Jefferson City MO 65101-1556 Home: 16709 Marcross Ct Chesterfield MO 63005-4822

LINTZ, ROBERT CARROLL, financial holding company executive; b. Cin., Oct. 2, 1933; s. Frank George and Carolyn Martha (Dickhaus) L.; m. Mary Agnes Mott, Feb. 1, 1964; children— Lesa, Robert, Laura, Michael. B.B.A., U. Cin., 1956. Staff accountant Alexander Grant, Cin., 1958-60; dist. mgr. Uniroyal, Memphis, 1960-65; v.p. Am. Fin. Corp., Cin., 1965— ; dir. Rapid-American Corp., McGregor Corp., Faberge Inc., all N.Y.C., H.R.T. Industries Inc., Los Angeles. Fisher Foods Inc., Cleve., Am. Agronomics, Tampa, Fla. Trustee, St. Francis-St. George Hosp., Cin., 1974-81. Served to capt. U.S. Army, 1956-58, 61-62. Republican. Roman Catholic. Home: 5524 Palisades Dr Cincinnati OH 45238-5620 Office: Am Fin Corp 1 E 4th St Cincinnati OH 45202-3717

LINVILLE, RANDAL L. agricultural company executive; married; 1 child. B in Bus. and Agrl. Econs., Kans. State U., 1976, M in Agrl. Econs., 1977. Merchandise mgr. Scoular, Omaha, 1984, v.p., gen. mgr. grain divsn., 1992, CEO, 1999—. Office: Scoular 2027 Dodge St Omaha NE 68102

LIPFORD, ROCQUE EDWARD, lawyer, corporate executive; b. Monroe, Mich., Aug. 16, 1938; s. Frank G. and Mary A. (Mastromarco) L.; m. Marcia A. Griffin, Aug. 5, 1966; children: Lisa, Rocque Edward, Jennifer, Katherine. BS, U. Mich., 1960, MS, 1961, JD with distinction, 1964. Bar: Mich. 1964, Ohio 1964. Instr. mech. engring. U. Mich., 1961-63; atty. Miller, Canfield, Paddock & Stone, Detroit, 1965-66; asst. gen. counsel Monroe Auto Equipment Co., 1966-70, gen. counsel, 1970-72, v.p., gen. counsel, 1973-77, Tenneco Automotive, 1977-78; ptnr. firm Miller, Canfield, Paddock & Stone, Detroit, 1978—, mng. ptnr., 1988-91. Bd. dirs. La-Z-Boy Inc., Monroe Bank & Trust. Mem.: Knights of Malta, Legatus, Mich. Bar Assn., Mariner Sands Golf and Country Club, Monroe Golf and Country Club, North Cape Yacht Club, Otsego Ski Club, Pi Tau Sigma, Tau Beta Pi. Home: 1065 Hollywood Dr Monroe MI 48162-3045 Office: Miller Canfield Paddock & Stone 214 E Elm Ave Ste 100 Monroe MI 48162-2682 E-mail: lipford@mcps.com.

LIPINSKI, ANN MARIE, newspaper editor; Assoc. mng. editor for met. news. Chgo. Tribune, now dep. mng. editor, now mng. editor, 1995—. Recipient Pulitzer prize for series on politics and conflicts of interest Chgo. City Coun., 1988. Office: Chgo Tribune 435 N Michigan Ave Chicago IL 60611-4066

LIPINSKI, WILLIAM OLIVER, congressman; b. Chgo., Dec. 22, 1937; s. Oliver and Madeline (Collins) L.; m. Rose Marie Lapinski, Aug. 29, 1962; children: Laura, Daniel. Student, Loras Coll., Dubuque, Iowa, 1957-58. Various positions to area supr. Chgo. Parks, 1958-75; alderman Chgo. City Coun., 1975-83; mem. 98th-107th Congresses from 5th (now 3rd) Dist. Ill., 1983—, mem. transp. and infrastructure com. Dem. ward committeeman, Chgo., 1975—; del. Dem. Nat. Midterm Conv., 1974, Dem. Nat. Conv., 1976, 84, 88; pres. Greater Midway Econ. and Community Devel. Com.; mem. Chgo. Hist. Soc., Art Inst., Chgo., pres.'s coun. St. Xavier Coll.; mem. Congl. Competitive Caucus, Congl. Caucus for Women's Issues, Congl. Hispanic Caucus, Congl. Human Rights Caucus, Congl. Populist Caucus, Dem. Study Group, Export Task Force, Inst. for Ill., Maritime Caucus, N.E.-Midwest Congl. Coalition, Urban Caucus. Named Man of Yr. Chgo. Park Dist. 4, 1983; recipient Archer Heights Civic Assn. award 1979, 23d Ward Businessmen and Mchts. award Chgo., 1977, Garfield Ridge Hebrew Congregation award Chgo., 1975-77, Installing Officer award Vittum Park Civic Assn., 23d Ward Minuteman award, Friends of Vittum Park Polish award, Nathan Hale Grand award from S.W. Liberty Soc., S.W. Am. Edn. and Recreation program award, Sentry of Yr. award Stars & Stripes Soc., Ill. State Minuteman award 1991. Mem. Polish Nat. Alliance, Kiwanis (Disting. Svc. award, pres., Peace Through Strength Leadership award 1991). Democrat. Roman Catholic. Office: US Ho of Reps 2470 Rayburn House Office Bldg Washington DC 20515-0001 also: 5832 S Archer Ave Chicago IL 60638-1637*

LIPKIN, DAVID, chemist; b. Phila., Jan. 30, 1913; s. William and Ida (Zipin) L.; m. Silvia Stantic Alvarez, Nov. 10, 1973; children— Jeffrey Alan, Edward Walter. B.S., U. Pa., 1934; Ph.D., U. Calif., Berkeley, 1939. Research chemist Atlantic Refining Co., Phila., 1934-36; research fellow U. Calif., Berkeley, 1939-42; research chemist Manhattan Project, 1942-43; research chemist, group leader Los Alamos Sci. Lab., 1943-46; mem. faculty Washington U., St. Louis, 1946—81, prof. chemistry, 1948-66, chmn. dept., 1964-70, William Greenleaf Eliot prof., 1966-81, emeritus, 1981—. Sr. vis. fellow Agrl. Research Council, Cambridge, Eng., 1960; vis. research scientist John Innes Inst., Norwich, Eng., 1971, 78; trustee Argonne Univs. Assn., 1969-71; cons. in field. Author; patentee in field. Guggenheim fellow, 1955-56 Mem. Am. Chem. Soc. (St. Louis award 1970), AAUP, Sigma Xi, Tau Beta Pi, Pi Mu Epsilon. Office: Washington Univ Chemistry Dept Saint Louis MO 63130

LIPMAN, DAVID, retired journalist, multimedia consultant; b. Springfield, Mo., Feb. 13, 1931; s. Benjamin and Rose (Mack) L.; m. Marilyn Lee Vittert, Dec. 10, 1961; children: Gay Ilene, Benjamin Alan. BJ, U. Mo., 1953, LHD (hon.), 1997. Sports editor Jefferson City (Mo.) Post-Tribune, 1953, Springfield Daily News, 1953-54; gen. assignment reporter Springfield Leader and Press, 1956-57; reporter, copy editor Kansas City (Mo.) Star, 1957-60; sports reporter St. Louis Post-Dispatch, 1960-66, asst. sports editor, 1966-68, news editor, 1968-71, asst. mng. editor, 1971-78, mng. editor, 1979-92; chmn. Pulitzer 2000 Pulitzer Pub. Co., St. Louis, 1992-96, multimedia cons., 1997-2000. Guest lectr. Am. Press Inst., Columbia U. Journalism Sch., 1967-70; chmn. bd. advisors U. Mo. Sch. Journalism, 1989-2001, chmn. bd. dirs. multi-cultural mgmt. program, 1995-97; bd. dirs. Columbia Missourian, 1989—, chmn. task force, 2001-2002. Author: Maybe I'll Pitch Forever, The Autobiography of LeRoy (Satchel) Paige, 1962, reissued, 1993, Mr. Baseball, The Story of Branch Rickey, 1966, Ken Boyer, 1967, Joe Namath, 1968; co-author: The Speed King, The Story of Bob Hayes, 1971, Bob Gibson Pitching Ace, 1975, Jim Hart Underrated Quarterback, 1977. Bd. dirs. Mid-Am. Press Inst., 1973-97, chmn., 1975-77; mem.-at-large nat. coun., bd. dirs. Am. Jewish Com. St. Louis, 1997—; bd. dirs. Rabbi Samuel Thurman Ednl. Found., 1997—; trustee United Hebrew Congregation, 1975-77; bd. dirs. Parkview Housing Corp.; chmn. com. 21st Century, U. Mo., 1993-94; vice chair Mo. Gov.'s Commn. on Info. Tech., 1994-95; chmn. ethics commn. City of Creve Coeur, 2001—, chair new tech. com., 1997-2001; mem. Creve Coeur Charter Commn., 2000-2001; cons. Mo. Press-Bar Commn., 1995—; mem. adv. bd. Jewish Light, 2001—. 1st lt. USAF, 1954-56. Recipient Univ. Mo. Faculty and Alumni award, 1988, Univ. Mo. Disting. Svc. in Journalism medal, 1989, St. Louis Jermiah award, 1991; named to Writers Hall of Fame of Am., Springfield, Mo., 2002. Mem. Am. Soc. Newspaper Editors, Newspaper Assn. Am. (mem. industry devel. com. 1993-96), Mo. Editors and Pubs. Assn. (pres. 1990-91), Mo. Soc. Newspaper Editors (bd. dirs. 1990-97, vice chmn. 1992-93, chmn. 1993), Mo. Press Assn. (1st v.p. 1994-95, pres. 1997, bd. dirs. 1998—), Mo. AP Mng. Editors Assn. (pres. 1990), U. Mo. Sch. Journalism Nat. Alumni Assn. (chmn. 1980-83), Press Club of St. Louis (chmn. 1987-94), Soc. Profl. Journalists (pres. St. Louis chpt. 1976-77), Kappa Tau Alpha, Omicron Delta Kappa. Jewish.

LIPO, THOMAS A. electrical engineer, educator; b. Milw., Feb. 1, 1938; married; 4 children. BEE, Marquette U., 1962, MSEE, 1964; PhD, U. Wis., 1968. Grad. trainee Allis-Chalmers Mfg. Co., Milw., 1962-64, engring. analyst, 1964; instr. U. Wis., 1964-66; NRC rsch. fellow U. Manchester (Eng.) Inst. Sci. and Tech., 1968-69; elec. engr. Gen. Electric Co., Schenectady, 1969-79; prof. Purdue U., West Lafayette, Ind., 1979-80, U. Wis., Madison, 1981-90, W.W. Grainger prof. pwoer electronics and elec. machines, 1990—. Co-dir. Wis. Elec. Machines and Power Electronics Consortium, 1981—. Fellow IEEE, IEEE Power Engring. Soc., IEEE Indsl. Applications Soc., IEEE Power Electronics Soc. Office: U Wis Dept Elec & Comp Eng 1415 Engineering Dr Dept Elec& Madison WI 53706-1607

LIPOVSKY, ROBERT P. marketing executive; b. Chgo., Apr. 15, 1950; s. Rudolph John and Anna Mary (Nemec) L.; m. Sharon Sue Zelienka, July 1, 1972; children: Katherine Michelle, Robert Paul. BS, Western Ill. U., 1972. Dist. mgr. W.R. Grace and Co., Peoria, Ill., 1972-78; mktg. mgr. Doane Agrl. Svc., St. Louis, 1978-82; v.p., div. mgr. Maritz Mktg. Rsch. Inc., 1982—, pres., Maritz Performance Improvement Co., Fenton, Mo. Mem. Nat. Agrl. Mktg. Assn. Republican. Lutheran. Avocations: golfing, hunting, sports, trap and skeet shooting. Office: Maritz Performance Improvement Co 14 S Hwy Dr Fenton MO 63099-0001

LIPP, SUSAN, company executive; Pres. Full Compass Sys. Ltd., 1980—. Office: 8001 Terrace Ave Middleton WI 53562-3192 E-mail: slipp@fullcompass.com.

LIPPE, MELVIN KARL, lawyer; b. Chgo., Oct. 21, 1933; s. Melvin M. and Myrtle (Karlsberg) L.; children: Suzanne, Michael S., Deanna; m. Sandra M. Bauer, Jan. 5, 1974. BS, Northwestern U., 1955, JD, 1958; grad. cert., Grad. Sch. Banking, U. Wis., 1965; cert., Sr. Bank Officers Seminar, Harvard U., 1966. Bar: Ill. 1958; CPA, Ill. Assoc. D'Ancona, Pflaum, Wyatt & Riskind, Chgo., 1958-61; asst. to chmn. bd. Exchange Nat. Bank of Chgo., 1961-62, asst. v.p., 1962-64, v.p., 1964-66, sr. v.p., sec. to bd. dirs., 1966-69, exec. v.p., dir., 1969-74, vice chmn. bd., dir., 1974-76; dir. Am.-Israel Bank, Ltd., 1974-76; ptnr. Antonow & Fink, Chgo., 1977-88, Altheimer and Gray, Chgo., 1988—. Instr. Ill. Inst. Tech., 1960-63 Bd. dirs. Jewish Cmty. Ctrs. Chgo., 1972—, pres., 1980-82; bd. dirs. Chgo. chpt. Am. Jewish Com., 1974-78; life bd. dirs. Jewish Coun. for Youth Svcs., Chgo., pres., 1971; bd. dirs. Family Focus, 1992-98. With Ill. N.G., 1959. Mem. ABA, Chgo. Bar Assn., Phi Epsilon Pi, Beta Gamma Sigma. Jewish. Office: Altheimer & Gray 10 S Wacker Dr Ste 4000 Chicago IL 60606-7407 E-mail: lippem@altheimer.com.

LIPPINCOTT, JAMES ANDREW, biochemistry and biological sciences educator; b. Cumberland County, Ill., Sept. 13, 1930; s. Marion Andrew and Esther Oral (Meeker) L.; m. Barbara Sue Barnes, June 2, 1956; children— Jeanne Marie, Thomas Russell, John James A.B., Earlham Coll., 1954; A.M., Washington U., St. Louis, 1956, Ph.D., 1958. Lectr. botany Washington U., 1958-59; Jane Coffin Childs Meml. fellow Centre Nat. de la Recherche Scientifique, France, 1959-60; asst. prof. biol. scis. Northwestern U., Evanston, Ill., 1960-66, assoc. prof., 1966-73, prof., 1973-81, prof. biochemistry, molecular biology and cell biology, 1981-94, prof. emeritus Ill., 1994—, assoc. dean biol. scis., 1980-83. Vis. assoc. prof. U. Calif., Berkeley, 1970-71; vis. prof. Inst. Botany U. Heidelberg (Germany), 1974. Contbr. articles to profl. jours. Grantee NIH, NSF, Am. Cancer Soc., USDA Mem. Am. Soc. Biol. Chemists, Am. Soc. Plant Physiologists, Bot. Soc. Am., Am. Soc. Microbiology

LIPSCHUTZ, MICHAEL ELAZAR, chemistry educator, consultant, researcher; b. Phila., May 24, 1937; s. Maurice and Anna (Kaplan) L.; m. Linda Jane Lowenthal, June 21, 1959; children: Joshua Henry, Mark David, Jonathan Mayer B.S., Pa. State U., 1958; S.M., U. Chgo., 1960, Ph.D., 1962. Gastdocent U. Bern, Switzerland, 1964-65; from asst. prof. chemistry to assoc. head dept. Purdue U., West Lafayette, Ind., 1965—93, assoc. head dept. of chemistry, 1993—2001; dir. chemistry ops. Purdue Rare Isotope Measurement Lab. (PRIME), 1990—2002. Vis. assoc. prof. Tel Aviv U., 1971-72; vis. prof. Max-Planck Inst. fuer Chemie, Mainz, Fed. Republic Germany, 1987; mem. panel space sci. experts Com. on Space Rsch., Space Agy. Forum of the Internat. Space Yr., Internat. Coun. Sci. Unions, 1990-92; cons. in field. Assoc. editor 11th Lunar and Planetary Sci. Conf., 3 vols., 1980; fin. editor Meteoritics and Planetary Sci., 1992-2000; contbr. numerous articles to profl. jours. Served to 1st lt. USAR, 1958-64 Recipient Cert. of Recognition, NASA, 1979, Cert. of Spl. Recognition, 1979, Group Achievement award, 1983, Cert. Appreciation, Nat. Commn. on Space, 1986; postdoctoral fellow NSF, 1964-65, NATO, 1964-65; Fulbright fellow, 1971-72 Fellow Meteoritical Soc. (treas. 1978-84, mem. joint com. on pubs. of Geochem. and Meteoritical Socs. 1985-93, fin. officer 1985-93, chmn. 1988-90); mem. AAAS, Am. Chem. Soc., Am. Geophys. Union, Planetary Soc., Internat. Astron. Union (U.S. rep. 1988—), Sigma Xi. Achievements include having minor planet named in honor of Lipschutz by Internat. Astronomical Union, 1987. Office: Purdue U Dept Chemistry West Lafayette IN 47907

LIPTON, LOIS JEAN, lawyer; b. Chgo., Jan. 14, 1946; d. Harold and Bernice (Reiter) Farber L.; m. Peter Carey, May 30, 1978; children: Rachel, Sara. BA, U. Mich., 1966; JD summa cum laude, DePaul Coll. Law, Chgo., 1974; postgrad., Sheffield (Eng.) U., 1966. Bar: Ky. 1974, U.S. Dist. Ct. (we. dist.) Ky. 1974, U.S. Ct. Appeals (6th cir.) 1974, Ill. 1975, U.S. Dist. Ct. (no. dist.) Ill. 1975, U.S. Ct. Appeals (7th cir.) 1976. Staff counsel Roger Baldwin Found. of ACLU, Inc., Chgo., 1975-79, dir. reproductive rights project, 1979-83; atty. McDermott, Will & Emergy, 1984-86, G.D. Searle, Skokie, Ill., 1988-90; sr. atty. AT&T, Chgo., 1990—. Del. White House Conf. on Families, Mpls., 1980. Recipient Durfee award, 1984. Mem. ACLU (v.p.), ABA, Chgo. Coun. Lawyers. Office: AT&T # R15 222 W Adams St Chicago IL 60606-5017 E-mail: llipton@att.com.

LIPTON, RICHARD M. lawyer; b. Youngstown, Ohio, Feb. 25, 1952; s. Sanford Y. Lipton and Sarah (Kentor) Goldman; m. Jane Brennan, May 24, 1981; children— Thomas, Anne, Martin, Patricia. B.A., Amherst Coll., 1974; J.D., U. Chgo., 1977. Bar: Ill. 1977, D.C. 1978, U.S. Dist. Ct. (no. dist.) Ill. 1979, U.S. Ct. Appeals (D.C. and 7th cirs.) 1979, U.S. Tax Ct. 1977, U.S. Ct. Claims 1979. Law clk. to judge Hall, U.S. Tax Ct., Washington, 1977-79; assoc. Isham, Lincoln & Beale, Chgo., 1979-83; ptnr. Ross & Hardies, Chgo., 1983-86; v.p. Pegasus Broadcasting, Chgo., 1986-88; ptnr. Sonnenschein Nath & Rosenthal, Chgo., 1988—. Contbr. articles to profl. jours. Recipient Order of Coif award U. Chgo. Law Sch., 1977. Fellow Am. Coll. Tax Counsel (regent 1998—); mem. ABA (coun. dir. 1990-93, vice chair taxation sect. 1993-96), Chgo. Bar Assn. (subcom. chair, chair fed. taxation com. 1991-92), Union League Club, Michigan Shores Club, Conway Farms Club. Republican. Office: Sonnenschein Nath Rosenthal 233 S Wacker Dr Ste 8000 Chicago IL 60606-6491

LISHER, JAMES RICHARD, lawyer; b. Aug. 28, 1947; s. Leonard B. and Mary Jane (Rafferty) L.; m. Martha Gettelfinger, June 16, 1973; children: Jennifer, James Richard II. AB, Ind. U., 1969, JD, 1975. Bar: Ind. 1975, U.S. Dist. Ct. (so. dist.) Ind. 1975, U.S. Supreme Ct. 2000. Assoc. Rafferty & Wood, Shelbyville, Ind., 1976, Rafferty & Lisher, Shelbyville, 1976-77; dep. prosecutor Shelby County Prosecutor's Office, 1976-78; ptnr. Yeager, Lisher & Baldwin, 1977-96; pvt. practice, 1996—. Pros. atty. Shelby County, Shelbyville, 1983-95, pub. defender, 1995—, chief pub. defender, 2000—. Speaker, faculty advisor Ind. Pros. Sch., 1986. Editor: (manual) Traffic Case Defenses, 1982, First Law Office, 1998. Bd. dirs. Girls Club of Shelbyville, 1979-84, Bears of Blue River Festival, Shelbyville, 1982-2002; pres. Shelby County Internat. Rels. Coun., 1997-2002. Recipient Citation of Merit, Young Lawyers Assn. Mem. ATLA, Nat. Assn. Criminal Def. Lawyers, Ind. Pub. Defender Assn., Ind. State Bar Assn. (bd. dirs. young lawyer sect. 1979-83, bd. dirs. gen. practice sect. 1996-98, treas. 1997-98, vice-chmn. 1998-99, chmn. 2000-01), Shelby County Bar Assn. (sec.-treas. 1986, v.p. 1987, pres. 1988), Ind. Prosecuting Attys. Assn. (bd. dirs. 1985-95, sec.-treas. 1987, v.p. 1988, pres. 1990), Masons, Elks, Lions. Home: 106 Western Trce Shelbyville IN 46176-9765 Office: 407 S Harrison St Shelbyville IN 46176-2170

LISHER, JOHN LEONARD, lawyer; b. Indpls., Sept. 19, 1950; s. Leonard Boyd and Mary Jane (Rafferty) L.; m. Mary Katherine Sturmon, Aug. 17, 1974. BA in History with honors, JD, Ind. U., 1975. Bar: Ind. 1975. Dep. atty. gen. State of Ind., Indpls., 1975-78; asst. corp. counsel City of Indpls., 1978-81; assoc. Osborn & Hiner, Indpls., 1981-86; ptnr. Osborn, Hiner & Lischer, P.C., 1986—. Vol. Mayflower Classic, Indpls., 1981-86; pres. Brendonwood Common Inc.; asst. vol. coord. Marion County Rep. Com., Indpls., 1979-80; vol. Don. Bogard for Atty. Gen., Indpls., 1980, Steve Goldsmith for Prosecutor, Indpls., 1979-83, Sheila Suess for Congress, Indpls., 1980. Recipient Outstanding Young Man of Am. award Jaycees, 1979, 85, Indpls. Jaycees, 1980. Mem. ABA, Ind. Bar Assn., Indpls. Bar Assn. (membership com.), Assn. Trial Lawyers Am., Ind. U. Alumni Assn., Hoosier Alumni Assn. (charter, founder, pres.), Ind. Trial Lawyers Assn., Ind. Def. Lawyers Assn., Ind. U. Coll. Arts and Scis. (bd. dirs. 1983-92, pres. 1986-87), Wabash Valley Alumni Assn. (charter), Founders Club, Pres. Club, Phi Beta Kappa, Eta Sigma Phi, Phi Eta Sigma, Delta Xi Alumni Assn. (Outstanding Alumnus award 1975, 76, 79, 83), Delta Xi Housing Corp. (pres.), Pi Kappa Alpha (midwest regional pres. 1977-86, parliamentarian nat. conv. 1982, del. convs. 1978-80, 82, 84, 86, trustee Meml. Found. 1986-91. Presbyterian. Avocations: reading, golf, jogging, Roman coin collecting. Home: 5725 Hunterglen Rd Indianapolis IN 46226-1019 Office: Osborn Hiner & Lisher PC 8500 Keystone Xing Ste 480 Indianapolis IN 46240-2460

LISHKA, EDWARD JOSEPH, insurance underwriter; b. Chgo., Oct. 8, 1949; s. Edward John and Virginia Nelly (Powers) L.; m. Marie Ann Slawniak, June 7, 1975 (dec. Dec. 1993); 1 child, Ann. BS, Bradley U., 1971, MA, 1972. CPCU. Design engr. Forest Electric Co., Melrose Park, Ill., 1972-73; tech. writer Advance Schs. Inc., Des Plaines, 1973-74; design engr. Universal Oil Products, 1974-75; account engr. Oil Ins. Assn., Chgo., 1975-81; policy cons. CNA Ins. Co., 1981-85; underwriter Service Ins. Agy., Mount Prospect, Ill., 1985-86; sr. acct. underwriter Arkwright Mut. Inst. Co., Schaumburg Village, 1986-92; acct. analyst Mack & Parker, Chgo., 1992—. Mem. Schaumburg Village Ins. Com., 1983—. Mem. Soc. CPCUs (speaker 1987—, chmn. candidate devel. 1987-88, Profl. Devel. award 1986, 88, 89, 90, 92), Accredited Advisers in Ins. (assoc. in risk mgmt., assoc. in marine ins. mgmt.), Four Winds Ski Club (Itasca, Ill.). Republican. Roman Catholic. Avocations: skiing, golf, bicycling, fishing. Home: 100 Idlestone Ln Schaumburg IL 60194-4044 Office: Mack & Parker 55 E Jackson Blvd Ste 600 Chicago IL 60604-4187 E-mail: EdLishka@aol.com., elishka@mackparker.com.

LISIO, DONALD JOHN, historian, educator; b. Oak Park, Ill., May 27, 1934; s. Anthony and Dorothy (LoCelso) Lisio; m. Susznne Marie Swanson, Apr. 22, 1958; children: Denise Anne, Stephen Anthony. BA, Knox Coll., 1956; MA, Ohio U., 1958; PhD, U. Wis., 1965. Mem. faculty overseas div. U. Md., 1958-60; from asst. prof. history to prof. emeritus Coe Coll., Cedar Rapids, Iowa, 1964—2002, prof. emeritus, 2002—. Author: (book) The President and Protest: Hoover, Conspiracy, and the Bonus Riot, 1974, Hoover, Blacks, and Lily-Whites: A Study of Southern Strategies, 1985; contbg. author: book The War Generation, 1975; contbr. articles to hist. jours. Mem. exec. com. Cedar Rapids Com. Hist. Preservation, 1975—77. With U.S. Army, 1958—60. Fellow William F. Vilas Rsch., U. Wis., 1963—64, NEH, 1969—70, Rsch., 1984—85, Am. Coun. Learned Socs., 1977—78; grantee, 1971—72, Rsch., U.S. Inst. Peace, 1990. Mem.: ACLU, AAUP, Am. Hist. Assn., Orgn. Am. Historians. Roman Catholic. Home: 4203 Twin Ridge Ct SE Cedar Rapids IA 52403-3950 Office: Coe Coll Cedar Rapids IA 52402

LISKA, PAUL J. insurance company executive; married; 3 children. Grad., U. Notre Dame, 1977; Masters, Northwestern U. CPA. With Price Waterhouse & Co., Am. Hosp. Supply Corp., Quaker Oats Co.; CFO Kraft Gen. Foods, 1988-94; pres., CEO Specialty Foods Corp., 1994-96; exec. v.p., CFO The St. Paul Cos., 1997-2001. Office: The St Paul Cos 385 Washington St Saint Paul MN 55102-1309

LISS, HERBERT MYRON, communications executive, educator, journalist; b. Mpls., Mar. 23, 1931; s. Joseph Milton and Libby Diane (Kramer) L.; m. Barbara Lipson, Sept. 19, 1954; children: Lori-Ellen, Kenneth Allen, Michael David. BS in Econs., U. Pa., 1952. With mktg. mgmt. Procter & Gamble Co., Cin., 1954-63, Procter & Gamble Internat., various countries, 1963-74; gen. mgr. Procter & Gamble Comml. Co., San Juan, P.R., 1974-78; v.p., mgr. internat. ops. InterAm. Orange Crush Co. subs. Procter & Gamble Co., Cin., 1981-84; pres. River Cities (Ohio) Communications Inc, 1985—; pub. The Downtowner newspaper and others, Cin., 1985-96. Lectr. MBA and undergrad. bus. program Xavier U., Ohio, 1998—. Bd. dirs. Charter Com., Cin., 1958-63, Promotion and Mktg. Assn. U.S., 1978-81, Jr. Achievement, Cin., 1980-87, Inst. for Learning in Retirement, 1998—, Downtown Coun., Cin., 1985-94, treas., 1991-92; bd. dirs. Downtown Cin. Inc., 1995-98, mem. DCI retail mktg. com., 1995-98. Mem. Manila Yacht Club, Manila Polo, Club Escuela de Equitación De Somos Aquas (Madrid), Rotary Club. (Cin.), Cin. Racquet Club. Home: 8564 Wyoming Club Dr Cincinnati OH 45215-4243

LISSKA, ANTHONY JOSEPH, humanities educator, philosopher; b. Columbus, Ohio, July 23, 1940; s. Joseph Anthony and Florence (Wolfel) L.; m. Marianne Hedstrom, Mar. 16, 1968; children: Megan Catherine, Elin Elizabeth. BA in Philosophy cum laude, Providence Coll., 1963; AM in Philosophy, St. Stephen's Coll., Dover, Mass., 1967; PhD in Philosophy, Ohio State U., 1971; Cert., Harvard U., Cambridge, 1979. Asst. prof. Denison U., Granville, Ohio, 1969-76, assoc. prof., 1976-81, dean of coll., 1978-83, prof. philosophy, 1981—, dir. honors program, 1987—2002, Charles and Nancy Brickman disting. svc. chair, 1998-2001. Vis. scholar U. Oxford, Eng., 1984; project reviewer NEH, Washington, 1979-90, evaluator; adv. bd. Midwest Faculty Seminar, Chgo., 1981-90; mem. scholarship com. Sherex Chem. Co., Dublin, Ohio, 1984-92; cons. Franklin Pierce Coll., Ringe, N.H., 1991, Hampden-Sydney (Va.) Coll., 1998; referee various philosophy jours. Author: Philosophy Matters, 1977, Aquinas's Theory of Natural Law, 1996, paperback edit. 1997; co-editor: The Historical Times, 1988-2002; contbr. numerous articles to profl. jours., chpts. to books. Bd. mgmt. Granville Hist. Soc., 1987-2002; precinct rep. Dem. Party, Granville, 1994—; convener Civil War Roundtable, Granville, 1989-95. Named Carnegie Prof. of Yr., Carnegie Found., 1994, Sears Found. Teaching award, 1990; NEH grantee, 1973, 77, 85. Mem. Am. Philos. Assn. (Teaching award 1994), Am. Cath. Philos. Assn., Nat. Collegiate Honors Coun., Soc. for Ancient Greek Philosophy, Soc. for Medieval and Renaissance Philosophy, Internat. Thomas Aquinas Soc. Democrat. Roman Catholic. Avocations: local history, photography. Home: 285 Burtridge Rd Granville OH 43023-1214 Office: Denison U Dept Philosophy Gilpatrick House Granville OH 43023 E-mail: lisska@denison.edu.

LISZT, HOWARD PAUL, advertising executive; b. Mpls., Aug. 12, 1946; s. Melvin Sherman and Evalyn (Chapman) Schwartz; m. Roberta Jean Bregman, Feb. 14, 1970; children: Andrew Charles, Daniel Mark. BA, U. Minn., 1968, MBA, 1970. From market rsch. mgr. to sr. product mgr. Green Giant Co., Mpls., 1970-76; from. account exec. to exec. v.p., gen. mgr. Campbell-Mithun, 1976-88, pres., chief oper. officer, 1988-94, CEO, 1995-2000; sr. fellow U. Minn., 2000—; cons. Campbell-Mithun-Esty Advt., Mpls., 2000—. Lectr. Augsburg Coll., Mpls., 1981-86. Chmn. bd. Coleman Natural Products, 2000—; dir. Zomax, Inc., 1997—. Bd. dirs. St. Paul Chamber Orch., 1984—, Minn. Children's Mus., St. Paul, 1979-86, Greater Mpls. C. of C., 1988-94, Blake Schs. 1990—, Boys and Girls Club 1996—. Mem. Am. Mktg. Assn., Am. Assn. Advt. Agys. (mem. client svc. com.), Oakridge Club. Jewish. Avocations: golfing, traveling, theater. Office: Campbell-Mithun-Esty Advt 222 S 9th St Fl 26 Minneapolis MN 55402-3389 E-mail: liszt002@umn.edu.

LITCHFIELD, JEAN ANNE, nurse; b. Gary, Ind., Oct. 6, 1942; d. Donald Kleine and Helen Louise (Sweet) Eller; m. Norman E. Stone, Dec. 27, 1965 (div. Aug. 1973); children: Diana, David, Julie; m. Frank Litchfield, Jan. 26, 1974. Lic. practical nurse, Ind. U. Vocat. Tech. Coll., 1973; AS in Biology, Richland C.C., 1991; BSN, Millikin U., 1993; MSN, Ind. State U., 1995. RN, Ind., Ill. Nurse asst. St. Anthony Hosp., Terre Haute, Ind., 1960-73, nurse, 1973-93; charge nurse psychiatric ward St. Mary's Hosp., Decatur, Ill., 1993-99; asst. prof. AD Nursing program Richland C.C., 1995—. Mem. student welfare com. Millikin U., Decatur, 1991-92. Recipient 1st place art award 1984, 85, 86, 2d place art award 1984, 85, 2d place County Fair, 1985, Gold Poet award World of Poetry, 1989, Silver Poet award, 1990, Outstanding Innovations in Tchg. and Learning award Richland C.C., 1997, 98, Excellence in Nursing Edn. award Decatur Area Task Force Nursing Edn., 2000; named Most Caring Nurse St. Mary's Hosp. 1990, Clara Compton scholar, St. Mary's Hosp., 1993, 94, scholar Am. Legion, 1992. Mem. Internat. Platform Assn., Barn Colony Artists (treas. 1986-88), Phi Theta Kappa, Beta Sigma Phi (treas. 1976-78), Alpha Tau Delta (treas. 1991-92, pres. 1992-93), Sigma Theta Tau Internat. Home: 1680 N 30th St Decatur IL 62526-5416

LITT, MORTON HERBERT, macromolecular science educator, researcher; b. N.Y.C., Apr. 10, 1926; s. Samuel Bernard and Minnie (Hertz) L.; m. Lola Natalie Abrahamson, July 7, 1957; children: Jonathan S., Jennifer A. B.S., CCNY, 1947; M.S., Bklyn. Poly. Inst., 1953, Ph.D., 1956. Turner and Newall fellow U. Manchester, Eng., 1956-57; sr. research fellow N.Y. State Coll. Forestry, Syracuse, N.Y., 1958-59; sr. scientist Allied Chem. Corp., Morristown, N.J., 1960-64, assoc. dir. research, 1965-67; assoc. prof. Case Western Res. U., Cleve., 1967-76, prof. macromolecular sci., 1976—. Cons. in industry and govt. Mem. adv. bd. Jour. Polymer Sci. and Polymer Chemistry; patentee in field. Fellow Am. Inst. Physics; mem. AAAS, Materials Rsch. Soc., Am. Chem. Soc., Chem. Soc. London, Electrochem. Soc. Home: 2575 Charney Rd Cleveland OH 44118-4402 Office: Case Western Res U Kent H Smith Bldg Cleveland OH 44106-7202 E-mail: MHL2@pop.cwru.edu.

LITTLE, BRUCE WASHINGTON, professional society administrator; b. Feb. 22, 1936; m. Nancy J. Mains; children: Elizabeth, Thomas, David. BS, Kans. State U., 1963, DVM, 1965. Pvt. practice assoc., Normal, Ill., 1965-69; pvt. practice Americana Animal Hosp., Bloomington, 1969-85; asst. exec. v.p. AVMA, Schaumburg, 1986-96, exec. v.p., 1996—. Rabies control officer McLean County, Ill., 1968-72; instr. U. Ill. Extension Svc., 1974, adv. Mclean County Bd. of Health, 1980-85; pres., ops. mgr. Blooming Grove Farm, Inc., Bloomington, 1983-86; spkr. in field. Contbr. articles to profl. jours. Coach, Ill. 4-H Equine Judging Teams, 1974-76; bd. dirs. Mclean County Assn. Commerce Industry, 1983-85; v.p. Ill. State U. Athletic Booster Club, 1980-82, pres., 1982-84. With U.S. Army, 1955-57. Mem. AVMA, Ill. State Vet. Med. Assn., Chgo. Vet. Med. Assn., Rotary (Paul Harris Fellow), Alpha Zeta. Avocations: sports, golfing, reading, horse breeding. Office: Am Vet Med Assn 1931 N Meacham Rd Schaumburg IL 60173-4364

LITTLE, CHARLES L. retired labor union administrator; b. Burnet, Tex., May 5, 1936; m. Mary Ann Little, 1963; 6 children. Student, U. Houston. With Houston Belt & Terminal Rd. Co., 1955—, gen. chairperson, 1979; sec., treas. local 1524 United Transp. Union, Houston, 192-78, gen. chmn., 1978-84, del., 1979, 83, v.p., 1984, 87, gen. sec., treas., 1991, internat. pres. Cleve., 1995-2001. Cpl. USMC, 1953-55, USMCR, 1955-61. Office: United Transp Union 14600 Detroit Ave Ste 200 Cleveland OH 44107-4250

LITTLE, DANIEL EASTMAN, philosophy educator, university program director; b. Rock Island, Ill., Apr. 7, 1949; s. William Charles and Emma Lou (Eastman) L.; m. Ronnie Alice Friedland, Sept. 12, 1976 (div. May 1995); children: Joshua Friedland-Little, Rebecca Friedland-Little. BS in Math. with highest honors, AB in Philosophy with high honors, U. Ill., 1971; PhD in Philosophy, Harvard U., 1977. Asst. prof. U. Wis.-Parkside, Kenosha, 1976-79; vis. assoc. prof. Wellesley (Mass.) Coll., 1985-87; vis. scholar Ctr. Internat. Affairs Harvard U., 1989-91, assoc. Ctr. Internat. Affairs, 1991-95; asst. prof. Colgate U., Hamilton, N.Y., 1979-85, assoc. prof., 1985-92, prof., 1992-96, chmn. dept. philosophy and religion, 1992-93, assoc. dean faculty, 1993-96; v.p. academic affairs Bucknell U., Lewisburg, Pa., 1996-2000, prof. philosophy, 1996-2000; chancellor U. Mich., Dearborn, 2000—, prof. philosophy, 2000—. Teaching fellow Harvard U., 1973-76; participant internat. confs. Ctr. Asian and Pacific Studies, U. Oreg., 1992, Social Sci. Rsch. Coun./McArthur Found., U. Calif., San Diego, 1991, Budapest, Hungary, 1990, Morelos, Mex., 1989, Rockefeller Found., Bellagio, Italy, 1990, U. Manchester, Eng., 1986; mem. screening com. on internat. peace and security Social Sci. Rsch. Coun./MacArthur Found., 1991-94; manuscript reviewer Yale U. Press, Cambridge U. Press, Princeton U. Press, Oxford U. Press, Westview Press, Harvard U. Press, Can. Jour. Philosophy, Philosophy Social Scis., Synthese, Am. Polit. Sci. Rev.; grant proposal reviewer NSF, Social Sci. Rsch. Coun., Nat. Endowment for Humanities; tenure and promotion reviewer U. Tenn., Bowdoin Coll., Duke U., U. Wis.; faculty assoc. Inter-Univ. Consortium for Social and Polit. Rsch., 2000—. Author: The Scientific Marx, 1986, Understanding Peasant China: Case Studies in the Philosophy of Social Science, 1989, Varieties of Social Explanation: An Introduction to the Philosophy of Social Science, 1991 (Outstanding Book award Choice 1992), On the Reliability of Economic Models, 1995, Microfoundations Method and Causation: On the Philosophy of the Social Sciences, 1998; contbr. articles to profl. jours., books. Social Sci. Rsch. Postdoctoral fellow MacArthur Found., 1989-91, Rsch. grantee NSF, 1987, Woodrow Wilson Grad. fellow, 1971-72. Mem. Am. Philos. Assn., Assn. Asian Studies, Internat. Devel. Ethics Assn., Social Sci. History Assn., Soc. for the History of Tech., Phi Beta Kappa. Office: Chancellor U Mich Dearborn 4901 Evergreen Rd Dearborn MI 48128 E-mail: delittle@umich.edu.

LITTLE, ROBERT ANDREWS, architect, designer, painter; b. Brookline, Mass., Sept. 9, 1915; s. Clarence Cook and Katherine Day (Andrews) L.; m. Ann Murphy Halle, Dec., 27, 1940; children: Sam Robertson, Revere (dec.). A.B. cum laude, Harvard U., 1937, M.Arch., 1939. Designer G.H. Perkins, Cambridge, Mass., 1939-41; architect U.S. Navy, Washington, 1941-43; ops. analyst Air Staff Intelligence, 1943-45; prin. Robert A. Little & Assos., Cleve., 1946-58, 67-69; partner Little & Dalton, 1958-67; dir. design Dalton-Dalton-Little-Newport, 1969-78; owner Robert A. Little, Design and Architecture, 1978—. Tchr., lectr. Harvard, U. Pa., Carnegie Inst. Tech., U. Mich., Smith Coll., U. Notre Dame, Kent State U. Exhibited art and graphics in Cleve., Phila., Boston., since 1970; works include Air Force Mus., Dayton, Ohio; one-person shows in Ohio, Maine, Mass. Trustee Cleve. Mus. Sci., 1952-56, Cleve. Inst. Music, 1956-58; mem. Cleve. Fine Arts Com. Served with U.S. Army, 1940. Fellow AIA (pres. Cleve. chpt. 1966-68, nat. and state design awards), Harvard Sch. of Design Alumni Assn. (past pres., internat. dir. of devel.) Home: 5 Pepper Ridge Rd Cleveland OH 44124-4904 Office: Robert A Little FAIA Design 5 Pepper Ridge Rd Cleveland OH 44124-4904

LITTLE, ROBERT EUGENE, mechanical engineering educator, materials behavior researcher, consultant; b. Enfield, Ill., May 24, 1933; s. John Henry and Mary (Stephens) L.; m. Barbara Louina Farrell, Feb. 4, 1961; children: Susan Elizabeth, James Robert, Richard Roy, John William. BSME, U. Mich., 1959; MSME, Ohio State U., 1960; PhDME, U. Mich., 1963. Asst. prof. mech. engring. Okla. State U., Stillwater, 1963-65; assoc. prof. U. Mich., Dearborn, 1965-68, prof., 1968—. Author: Statistical Design of Fatigue Experiments, 1975, Probability and Statistics for Engineers, 1978 Mershon fellow Ohio State U., 1960 Mem. ASTM, Am. Statis. Assn. Home: 3230 Pine Lake Rd West Bloomfield MI 48324-1951 Office: U Mich 4901 Evergreen Rd Dearborn MI 48128-2406

LITTLE, WILLIAM G. manufacturing executive; m. Corinne Little. Grad., U. Mo. Sales exec. Lathe divsn. Amsted Industries, South Bend, Ind.; distbr. sales mgr. Quam-Nichols Co., 1970, pres., CEO. Co-chair U.S. del. U.S.-Japanese Electronic Industries Plenary Session, Tokyo, 1988; participant Dept. of Def. Joint Civilian Orientation Conf., 1990; bd. dirs. Ohmite Mfg. Co., Skokie, Ill., Aerovox, Inc., New Bedford, Mass. Inductee Hall of Fame, Electronic Distbrs. Rsch. Inst., 1981. Mem. Electronic Industries Assn. (chmn., chmn. distbr. products divsn.), Electronic Industry Show Corp. (officer), U.S. C. of C. (dir. 1994—, vice chmn. 1997-98). Office: Quam-Nichols Co 234 E Marquette Rd Chicago IL 60637-4090

LITTLEFIELD, ROBERT STEPHEN, communication educator, training consultant; b. Moorhead, Minn., June 21, 1952; s. Harry Jr. and LeVoyne Irene (Berg) L.; m. Kathy Mae Soleim, May 24, 1974; children: Lindsay Jane, Brady Robert. BS in Edn., Moorhead State U., 1974; MA, N.D. State U., 1979; PhD, U. Minn., 1983. Tchr. Barnesville (Minn.) Pub. Schs., 1974-78; teaching asst. N.D. State U., Fargo, 1978-79, lectr., 1979-81; teaching assoc. U. Minn., Mpls., 1981-82; instr. N.D. State U., Fargo, 1982-83, asst. prof., chmn., 1983-89, assoc. prof., chmn., 1989-90, interim dean, 1990-92, assoc. prof., chmn., 1992-94, prof., 1994—; dir. Inst. for Study of Cultural Diversity, 1992-97. Owner KIDSPEAK Co., Moorhead, 1987-97. Author/co-author: (series) KIDSPEAK, 1989-92; lyricist (centennial hymn) Built on a Triangle with Faith in the Triune, 1989; contbr. more than 50 articles to profl. jours. Vol. forensic coach Fargo Cath. Schs. Network, 1992—; mem. N.D. dist. com. Nat. Forensic League, 1995—; advisor to exec. coun. Nat. Jr. Forensic League, 1995—. Recipient Burlington No. award N.D. State U., 1988-89; named Outstanding Speech Educator, Nat. Fedn. High Sch. Activities Assn., 1990-91. Mem. Am. Forensic Assn. (sec. 1990-92), N.D. Speech and Theatre Assn. (historian 1989—, pres. 1985-87, Hall of Fame 1989, Scholar of Yr. 1989), N.D. Multicultural Assn., Speech Comm. Assn., Pi Kappa Delta (nat. coun. 1983—, nat. pres. 1991-93, nat. sec.-treas. 1993—), Fargo Lions Club (pres. 1990-91). Democrat. Lutheran. Office: ND State U 321G Minard Hall Fargo ND 58105

LITTLEFIELD, VIVIAN MOORE, nursing educator, administrator; b. Princeton, Ky., Jan. 24, 1938; children: Darrell, Virginia. BS magna cum laude, Tex. Christian U., 1960; MS, U. Colo., 1964; PhD, U. Denver, 1979. Staff nurse USPHS Hosp., Ft. Worth, 1960-61; instr. nursing Tex. Christian U., 1961-62; nursing supr. Colo. Gen. Hosp., Denver, 1964-65; pvt. patient practitioner, 1974-78; asst. prof. nursing U. Colo., Denver, 1965-69, asst. prof., clin. instr., 1974-76, acting asst. dean, assoc. prof. continuing edn. regional perinatal project, 1976-78; assoc. prof., chair dept. women's health care nursing U. Rochester Sch. Nursing, N.Y., 1979-84; clin. chief ob-gyn., nursing U. Rochester Strong Meml. Hosp., 1979-84; prof., dean U. Wis. Sch. Nursing, Madison, 1984-99, prof., 2000—. Cons. and lectr. in field. Author: Maternity Nursing Today, 1973, 76, Health Education for Women: A Guide for Nurses and Other Health Professionals, 1986; mem. editl. bd. Jour. Profl. Nursing; contbr. articles to profl. jours. Bur. Health Professions Fed. trainee, 1963-64. Recipient Nat. Sci. Service award, 1976-79. Mem. MAIN, AACN (bd. dirs.), NLN (bd. dirs.), Am. Acad. Nursing, Am. Nurses Assn., Consortium Prime Care Wis. (chair), Health Care for Women Internat., Midwest Nursing Research Soc., Sigma Theta Tau (pres. Beta Eta chpt., co-chair coun. nursing practice and edn. 1995). Avocations: golf, biking. Office: U Wis Sch Nursing 600 Highland Ave # H6150 Madison WI 53792-3284

LITWIN, BURTON HOWARD, lawyer; b. Chgo., July 26, 1944; s. Manuel and Rose (Boehm) L.; m. Nancy Iris Stein, Aug. 25, 1968; children: Robin Meredith Litwin Levine, Keith Harris, Jill Stacy. BBA with honors, Roosevelt U., 1966; JD cum laude, Northwestern U., 1970. Bar: Ill. 1970, U.S. Dist. Ct. (no. dist.) Ill. 1970, U.S. Tax Ct. 1971, U.S. Ct. Fed. Claims 1983; CPA, Ill. Of counsel Neal, Gerber & Eisenberg, Chgo., 2002—. Author chpts. of books; contbr. articles to profl. jours. Recipient Gold Watch award Fin. Execs. Inst., Chgo., 1965. Mem. ABA (chmn. nonfiler task force for No. Ill. 1992-94), Chgo. bar Assn. (chmn. adminstrv. practice subcom., fed. taxation subcom. 1982-83) Avocations: roses, painting, photography. Office: Neal Gerber & Eisenberg Two N LaSalle St Ste 2200 Chicago IL 60602-3801 E-mail: burtl@attbi.com, blitwin@ngelaw.com.

LIU, BEN-CHIEH, economist; b. Chungking, China, Nov. 17, 1938; came to U.S., 1965, naturalized, 1973; s. Pei-juang and Chung-su L.; m. Jill Jyh-huey, Oct. 2, 1965; children— Tina Won-ting, Roger Won-jung, Milton Won-ming. B.A., Nat. Taiwan U., 1961; M.A., Meml. U. Nfld., 1965, Washington U., St. Louis, 1968, Ph.D., 1971. Economist Chinese Air Force and Central Customs, Taiwan, 1961-63; resource economist Canadian Land Inventory and Forest Services, Nfld., 1963-65; research project dir. St. Louis Regional Indsl. Devel. Corp., 1968-72; prin. econs. Midwest Research Inst., Kansas City, Mo., 1972-80; mgr. Energy and Environ. Systems Div., Argonne (Ill.) Nat. Lab., 1980-81. Prof. econs., assoc. dir. rsch. Oklahoma City U., 1981-82; prof. mgmt., mktg. and info. systems Chgo. State U., 1982—; pres. Liu & Assocs., Inc., 1982—; vis. prof. econs. U. Mo., 1970-78, Nat. Taiwan U., 1991-92; Fulbright prof., dir. Internat. Enterprises Inst., Nat. Dong-Hwa U., Taiwan, 1997-98; dean Coll. Bus., Chung-Yuan Christian U., Taiwan, 2000—; cons. UN, NSF; mem. Gov. Thompson's Adv. Com. on Agrl. Export, 1985-87, Congressman Fawell's Adv. Com. on Sci. and Tech., 1985-98; commr. Nat. Commn. on Librs. and Info. Svcs., 1991-94. Author: Interindustrial Structure Analysis: An Input-Output Study for St. Louis Region, 1968, The Quality of Life in the United States, 1970, Rating, Index and Statistics, 1973, Quality of Life Indicators in U.S. Metropolitan Areas, 1975, Physical and Economic Damage Functions for Air Pollutants by Receptors, 1976, Earthquake Risk and Damage Functions, An Integrated Model, 1981, Income, Energy and Quality of Life: An Information Systems Approach to Decisions, 1988; mem. editorial bd.: Internat. Jour. Math. Social Sci, Am. Jour. Econs. and Sociology, Hong Kong Jour. Bus. Mgmt., Internat. Jour. of Bus.; Internat. Jour. Mgmt.; contbr. articles to profl. jours. Recipient rsch. study award Am. Indsl. Devel. Coun., 1969—, Fulbright Scholar awards, 1992, 96, Faculty Meritorious awards Chgo. State U., 1983, 86, 89, 90, Disting. Prof. Advancement Increase awards, 1990, 96, Outstanding Rsch. award Nat. Sci. Coun., 1997-98; U.S. Econ. Devel. Adminstrn. fellow, 1967-68; Korean Govt. scholar, 1963-65; Fulbright scholar Mgmt. Devel. Inst., Delhi U., 1992. Fellow Am. Statis. Assn. (com. mem.); mem. Am. Econ. Assn. (com. mem.), Econometric Soc., Royal Econ. Soc., Internat. Statis. Instn., Assn. for Social Econs. (com. mem.), Tax Inst. Am., Chinese Acad. and Profl. Assn. (pres. 1984-85), Chinese Econ. Assn. in N.Am. (pres. 1988-90), Chinese Am. Profs. Assn. (pres. 1996—). Home: 5360 Pennywood Dr Lisle IL 60532-2032 Office: Chgo State U Chicago IL 60628 E-mail: benclin678@hotmail.com.

LIU, BENJAMIN YOUNG-HWAI, engineering educator; b. Shanghai, China, Aug. 15, 1934; s. Wilson Wan-su and Dorothy Pao-ning (Cheng) L.; m. Helen Hai-ling Cheng, June 14, 1958; 1 son, Lawrence A.S. Student, Nat. Taiwan U., 1951-54; B.S. in Mech. Engring., U. Nebr., 1956; Ph.D., U. Minn., 1960; doctorate (hon.), U. Kupio, Finland, 1991. Asso. engr. Honeywell Co., Mpls., 1956; research asst., instr. U. Minn., 1956-60, asst. prof., 1960-67, asso. prof., 1967-69, prof., 1969-93, regent's prof., 1993—, dir. Particle Tech. Lab., 1973-95; dir. Ctr. for Filtration Rsch., 1995—. Vis. prof. U. Paris, 1968-69; patentee in field. Contbg. author: Aerosol Science, 1966; editor: Fine Particles, 1976, Application of Solar Energy for Heating and Cooling Buildings, 1977, Aerosols in the Mining and Industrial Work Environment, 1983, Aerosols: Science, Technology and Industrial Application of Airborne Particles, 1984; editor-in-chief: Aerosol Sci. and Tech., 1983-93; contbr. articles to Ency. Chem. Tech., Ency. Applied Physics. Guggenheim fellow, 1968-69; recipient Sr. U.S. Scientist award Alexander von Humboldt Found., 1982-83. Mem. ASME, ASHRAE, Inst. Environ. Scis. (v.p. 1993-95), Air and Waste Mgmt. Assn., Am. Assn. for Aerosol Rsch. (pres. 1986-88), Chinese Am. Assn. Minn. (pres. 1971-72), NAE (Fuchs' prize 1994), Am. Filtration and Separation Soc. Home: 1 N Deep Lake Rd North Oaks MN 55127-6504 Office: U Minn Particle Tech Lab 111 Church St SE Minneapolis MN 55455-0150

LIU, GANG-YU, chemist, educator; b. Zhengzhou, Henan, China, Apr. 19, 1964; came to U.S., 1986; parents Zhen Kun and Quan Xian (Guo) L.; m. Xiaoyuan Li, Dec. 1, 1987. BS, Peking (China) U., 1988; MS, Princeton U., 1990, PhD, 1992. Postdoctoral assoc. U. Calif., Berkeley, 1992-94; asst. prof. chemistry Wayne State U., Detroit, 1994—. Camille & Henry Dreyfus fellow, 1994—, Miller Rsch. fellow The Miller Inst. for Basic Rsch. in Sci., 1992-94, Harold W. Dodds Honorific fellow Princeton U., 1991-92, CGP fellow Ministry of Edn., China, 1986-87. Mem. AAAS, Am. Chem. Soc., Am. Phys. Soc., Am. Vacuum Soc. Office: U Cal Dept Chem 1 Shields Ave Davis CA 95616

LIU, LEE, utility company executive; b. Hunan, People's Republic of China, Mar. 30, 1933; came to U.S., 1953; s. Z. Liang and Swai Chin (Chan) L.; m. Andrea Pavageau, Dec. 19, 1959; children: Monica, Christine BS, Iowa State U. With Iowa Electric Light & Power Co., Cedar Rapids, 1957—; pres., CEO IES Industries, 1991—; chmn., chief exec. officer Iowa Electric Light & Power Co., Iowa so. Utilities Co., 1983—; also bd. dirs. Iowa Electric Light & Power Co.; pres., chief exec. officer IES Industries Inc., 1991—. Bd. dirs. Firstar Bank Cedar Rapids, N.A., Edison Electric Inst., Hon Industries, Muscatine, Iowa, Prin. Fin., Des Moines; bd. visitors Univ. Iowa Coll. Bus.; bd. trustees U. No. Iowa; mem. Iowa State U. Pres.'s Coun. Trustee Mercy Med. Ctr., Iowa Natural Heritage Found., Hoover Presdl. Libr. Assn. Recipient Prof. Achievement citation Iowa State Univ., 1984; named Iowa Bus. Leader of Yr., Des Moines Register, 1990. Mem. Iowa Utility Assn., Iowa Bus. Coun., Iowa Group for Econ. Devel., Cedar Rapids Country Club. Republican. Roman Catholic. Office: 222 W Washington Ave Madison WI 53703-2719

LIU, MING-TSAN, computer engineering educator; b. Peikang, Taiwan, Aug. 30, 1934; BSEE, Nat. Cheng Kung U., Tainan, Taiwan, 1957; MSEE, U. Pa., 1961, PhD, 1964. Prof. dept. computer and info. sci. Ohio State U. Recipient Engring. Rsch. award Ohio State U., 1982, Best Paper award Computer Network Symposium 1984, Disting. Achievement award Nat. Cheng Kung U., 1987, Disting. Scholar award Ohio State U., 1991, Ameritech prize for excellence in telecom. Ameritech Found., 1991. Fellow IEEE (chmn. tech. com. on distbtd. processing Computer Soc. 1982-84, editor IEEE Transactions on Computers 1982-86, chmn. Eckert-Mauchly award com. 1984-85, 91-92, bd. govs. Computer Soc. 1984-90, chmn. tutorials com. 1982, program chmn. 1985, gen. chmn. 1986, chmn. steering com. 1989, gen. co-chmn. Internat. Conf. on Distbtd. Computing Sys. 1992, chmn. steering com. Symposium on Reliable Distbtd. Sys. 1986-89, v.p. membership and info. Computer Soc. 1984, mem. fellow com. 1986-88, editor-in-chief IEEE Transactions on Computers 1986-90, program chmn. IEEE Internat. Conf. on Data Engring. 1990, mem. TAB awards and recognition com. 1990-91, program chmn. Internat. Symposium on Comm. 1991, Internat. Phoenix Conf. on Computers and Comm. 1992, mem. TAB new tech. directions com. 1992-93, gen. co-chmn. Internat. Conf. on Parallel and Distbtd. Sys. 1992, Meritorious Svc. award Computer Soc. 1985, 87, 90, Outstanding Mem. Columbus sect. 1986-87). Office: Ohio State U 279 Dreese Labs 2015 Neil Ave Columbus OH 43210-1210

LIU, RUEY-WEN, electrical engineering educator; b. Kiang-en, China, Mar. 18, 1930; came to U.S., 1951, naturalized, 1956; s. Yen-sun and Wei-en (Chang) L.; m. Nancy Shao-lan Lee, Aug. 18, 1957; children—Alexander, Theodore B.S., U. Ill., 1954, M.S., 1955, Ph.D., 1960. Asst. prof. elec. engring. U. Notre Dame, Ind., 1960-63, assoc. prof., 1963-66, prof., 1966—, Frank M. Freimann prof elec. and computer engring., 1989—. Vis. prof. U. Calif.-Berkeley, 1965-66, Nat. Taiwan U., Taipei, spring 1969, U. Chile, Santiago, summer 1970; hon. prof. Fu-dan U., Shanghai, 1986, Inst. Electronics, Academia Sinica, Beijing, China, 1989. Trustee Calif. Buddhism Assn., 1974-76 U. Ill. fellow, 1954; Gen. Electric fellow, 1958; NSF grantee, 1962 Fellow IEEE (editor transaction on circuits and systems jours. 1989—, pres. circuits and sys. soc., 1995); mem. N.Y. Acad. Scis., Am. Math. Soc., Soc. Indsl. and Applied Math., Chinese Acad. Sci., Beijing (hon.), Inst. Electronics, Info. and Communications Engrs. (overseas adv. com. transactions in fundamentals of electronics, communications and computer scis., 1991—), Sigma Xi, Tau Beta Pi, Pi Mu Epsilon Home: 1929 Dorwood Dr South Bend IN 46617-1818 Office: Notre Dame Univ Dept Elec Engring Notre Dame IN 46556

LIU, WING KAM, mechanical and civil engineering educator; b. Hong Kong, May 15, 1952; came to U.S., 1973, naturalized, 1990; s. Yin Lam and Siu Lin (Chan) L.; m. Betty Hsia, Dec. 12, 1986; children: Melissa Margaret, Michael Kevin. BSc with highest honors, U. Ill., Chgo., 1976; MSc, Calif. Inst. Tech., 1977, PhD, 1981. Registered profl. engr., Ill. Asst. prof. mech. and civil engring. Northwestern U., Evanston, Ill., 1980-83, assoc. prof., 1983-88, prof., 1988—. Prin. cons. reactor analysis and safety div. Argonne (Ill.) Nat. Lab., 1981—. Co-author: Nonlinear Finite Elements for Continua and Structures, 2000; co-editor: Innovative Methods for Nonlinear Problems, 1984, Impact-Effects of Fasts Transient Loadings, 1988; musician: Computational Mechanics of Probabilistic and Reliability Analysis, 1989. Recipient Thomas J. Jaeger prize Internat. Assn. for Structural Mechanics in Reactor Tech., 1989, Ralph R. Teetor award Soc. Automotive Engrs., 1983; named among 93 most highly cited rschrs. in engring. Inst. for Sci. Info., 2001; grantee USF, Army Rsch. Office, NASA, AFSOR, ONR, GE, Ford Motor, Chrysler. Fellow ASCE, ASME (exec. mem. applied mechanics divsn. 2001, Melville medal 1979, Pi Tau Sigma gold medal 1985, Gustus L. Larson Meml. award 1995), U.S. Assn. Computational Mechanics (pres. 2000—, Computational Structural Mechs. award 2001), Am. Acad. Mechanics. Office: Northwestern U Dept Mech Engring 2145 Sheridan Rd Evanston IL 60208-0834 E-mail: w-liu@northwestern.edu.

LIU, YUAN HSIUNG, drafting and design educator; b. Tainan, Taiwan, Feb. 24, 1938; came to U.S., 1970; s. Chun Chang and Kong (Wong) L.; m. Ho Pe Tung, July 27, 1973; children: Joan Anshen, Joseph Pinyang. BEd, Nat. Taiwan Normal U., Taipei, 1961; MEd, Nat. Chengchi U., Taipei, 1967, U. Alta., Edmonton, 1970; PhD, Iowa State U., 1975. Cert. tchr. Tchr. indsl. arts and math. Nan Ning Jr. H.S., Tainan, Taiwan, 1961-64; tech. math. instr. Chung-Cheng Inst. Tech., Taipei, 1967-68; drafter Sundstrand Hydro-Transmission Corp., Ames, Iowa, 1973-75; assoc. prof. Fairmont (W.Va.) State Coll., 1975-80; per course instr. Sinclair C.C., Dayton, Ohio, 1985; assoc. prof. Miami U., Hamilton, 1980-85, Southwest Mo. State U., Springfield, 1985—. Cons. Monarch Indsl. Precision Co., Springfield, 1986, Gen. Electric Co., Springfield, 1988, Fasco Industries, Inc., Ozark, Mo., 1989, 95, Springfield Remfg. Corp., 1990, 92, Ctrl. States Indsl., Intercont Products, Inc., L&W Industries, Inc., ZERCO Mfg. Co., 1994-95, Paul Mueller Co., 1996. 2d lt. R.O.C. Army, 1962-63. Recipient Excellent Teaching in Drafting award Charvoz-Carsen Corp., Fairfield, N.J., 1978. Mem. Am. Design Drafting Assn. Avocations: walking, TV. Office: SW Mo State U Dept Indsl Mgmt 901 S National Ave Springfield MO 65804-0094 E-mail: yhl045f@smsu.edu.

LIUZZI, ROBERT C. chemical company executive; b. Boston, 1944; married. AB, Coll. of Holy Cross, 1965; LLB, U. Va., 1968. V.p., gen. counsel U.S. Fin., Inc., 1969-74; with CF Industries, Inc., Long Grove, Ill., 1975—, exec. v.p., CFO, 1977-80, exec. v.p., operating officer, 1980-84, pres., CEO, 1985—. Chmn. ad hoc com. Domestic Nitrogen Prodrs., Washington; chmn. bd. dirs. Can. Fertilizers Ltd.; bd. dirs. The Fertilizer Inst., Nat. Coun. Farmer Coops., Fla. Phosphate Coun., Tallahassee; mem. Nat. Forum Nonpoint Source Pollution sponsored by Nat. Geographic Soc. and Conservation Fund of Washington. Mem. coun. Internat. Exec. Svc. Corps, Stamford, Conn.; mem. bus. adv. coun. Law Sch. U. Va., Charlottesville. Mem. Ill. Bus. Roundtable, Northwestern U. Assocs., Coun. of 100, Tampa Fla., Internat. Fertilizer Industry Assn. (mem. coun.). Office: CF Industries Inc One Salem Lake Dr Long Grove IL 60047-8402

LIVINGSTON, HOMER J., JR. stock exchange executive; b. Chgo., 1935; BA in Econs., Princeton U., 1957; JD, Chgo. Kent Coll. Law, 1966. With First Nat Bank, Chgo., 1963-79, Lehman Bros. Kuhn Loeb, Chgo., 1979-82, William Blair & Co., Chgo., 1982-84, Algemene Bank Nederland, Chgo., 1984-88, H. Livingston & Co., L.P., Chgo., 1988-92, Livingston Co. Southwest, L.P., Chgo., 1988-92, Midwest Securities Trust Co., Chgo., 1992-95. Bd. dirs. Peoples Energy Co., Am. Nat. Can Corp. Office: Peoples Energy Corp 130 E Randolph Dr Fl 24 Chicago IL 60601-6207

LLEWELLYN, JOHN T. state legislator; m. Becky; children: Evan, Elizabeth, Matthew. BA, Alma Coll. Commr. Newago County, Mich., 1989-92; mem. Pub. Health Bd., 1990-92; mem. Newago County Zoning & Planning Bd., 1990-92; state rep. Dist. 100 Mich. Ho. of Reps., 1993-98; owner, operator family orchard Fremont, Mich., 1996—; dep. dir. Rep. caucus svcs. Mich. Ho. Reps., 1998—. Chair Consumers Com. Mich. Ho. of Reps., vice-chair Ins. Com., 1993—, mem. Conservation, Edn. Great Lakes & Higher Edn. Coms., 1993—, mem. task force to study advt. impact, house oversight ethics com., 1996—, chmn. Ins. Com., 1996—, vice chmn. Human Resources & Labor Com., 1996—, co-chair. Mem. Mich. Agrl. Coop. Mktg. Assn. Home: 5588 W 32nd St Fremont MI 49412-7723 Office: 720 House Office Bldg Lansing MI 48909

LLOYD, JOHN RAYMOND, mechanical engineering educator; b. Mpls., Aug. 1, 1942; s. Raymond Joseph and Wilma Mable (Epple) L.; m. Mary Jane Whiteside, Dec. 20, 1963; children: Jay William, Stephanie Christine. BS in Engring., U. Minn., 1964, MSME, 1966, PhDME, 1971; D in Tech. Sci. (hon.), Russian Acad. Scis., 2000. Devel. engr. Procter & Gamble Co., Cin., 1966-67; prof. mech. engring. U. Notre Dame, South Bend, Ind., 1970-83; disting. prof. Mich. State U., East Lansing, 1983—, chmn. dept. mech. engring., 1983-91, dir. Inst. Global Engring. Edn., 1997—2001. Cons. LeRoy Troyer & Assocs., Mishawaka, Ind., 1980—90, Azdel Inc., Shelby, NC, 1987—90; advisor NSF, Washington, 1987—90; Nat. Bur. Stds. assessment panel NRC, Washington, 1987—93; sci. coun. Internat. Ctr. Heat and Mass Transfer, Yugoslavia, 1986—; chmn. Midwest Energy Consortium, 1993—2000; adv. editor McGraw Hill, Inc., 1990—. Adv. editor Internat. Jour. Heat and Fluid Flow, 1985—, Jour. Engring. Physics and Thermodynamics, 1993—; contbr. over 100 articles to profl. jours., chpts. to books. Recipient Outstanding Faculty award U. Notre Dame, 1975, 82, Ralph R. Teetor Ednl. award Soc. Automotive Engrs., 1986. Fellow: ASME (nat. bd. comm. 1983—90, rsch. and tech. devel. bd. 1985—99, editor Jour. Heat Transfer 1989—95, coun. on edn., critical techs. com. 1991—93, sr. v.p. engring. 1999—2002, v.p. rsch. 1995—98, Outstanding Paper award 1977, Melville medal 1978, Heat Transfer Meml. award 1995, Dedicated Svc. award 1999). Office: Mich State U Dept Mech Engring 2242 Engring Bldg East Lansing MI 48824 E-mail: lloyd@egr.msu.edu.

LLOYD, WILLIAM F. lawyer; b. Youngstown, Ohio, Dec. 27, 1947; AB magna cum laude, Brown U., 1969; JD cum laude, U. Chgo., 1975. Bar: Ill. 1975, U.S. Supreme Ct. 1980. Ptnr. Sidley & Austin, Chgo. Mem. ABA (mem. litigation and bus. sects.), Chgo. Bar Assn., Legal Club Chgo. Office: Sidley & Austin Bank One Plz 425 W Surf St Apt 605 Chicago IL 60657-6139

LO, KWOK-YUNG, astronomer, educator, astronomer, researcher; b. Nanking, Jiangsu, China, Oct. 19, 1947; came to U.S., 1965; s. Pao-Chi and Ju-Hwa (Hsu) Lu; m. Helen Bo Kwan Chen Lo, Jan. 1, 1973; children: Jan Hsin, Derek. BS in Physics, MIT, 1969, PhD in Physics, 1974. Rsch. fellow Calif. Inst. Tech., Pasadena, 1974-76, sr. rsch. fellow, 1978-80, asst. prof., 1980-86; prof. U. Ill., Urbana, 1986-2000, assoc. Ctr. for Advanced Study, 1991-92, chmn. astronomy dept., 1995-97; dir., disting. fellow Inst. Astronomy and Astrophysics, Academia Sinica, Taipei, Taiwan, 1997—, disting. rsch. fellow Taiwan, 1997—, elected academician Taiwan, 1998; prof. physics Nat. Taiwan U., 1998—. Chmn. vis. com. to Haystack Obs., Westford, Mass., 1991—92; mem. adv. panel Academic Sinica Inst. Astronomy and Astrophysics, Taipei, Taiwan, 1993—; mem. AUI vis. com. for Nat. Radio Astronomy Obs., 1993—97; mem. steering com. Australia Telescope Nat. Facility, 1999—2001. Recipient Alexander von Humboldt award, 1995; grantee NSF, 1977-96; Miller fellow U. Calif., Berkeley, 1976-78, James Clerk Maxwell telescope fellow U. Hawaii, 1991. Mem. Am. Astron. Soc., Internat. Astron. Union, Acad. Sinica. Achievements include identification of accretion of ionized gas in center of Galaxy, size measurement of compact radio source at Galactic Center, first suggestion of circumnuclear H2O masers in active galaxies, and conditions of star formation in galaxies; observation of cosmic microwave background. Office: ASIAA PO Box 23-141 Taipei 106 Taiwan E-mail: kyl@asiaa.sinica.edu.tw.

LOBBIA, JOHN E. retired utility company executive; b. 1941; married BSEE, U. Detroit, 1964. Asst. primary svc. engr. sales dept. Detroit Edison Co., 1964-68, acting asst. dist. mgr., 1968-69, dir. svc. planning, 1969-72, project mgr. constrn., 1972-74, dir. generation constrn. dept., 1974-75, mgr. Ann Arbor div., 1975-76, asst. mgr. Detroit div., 1976-78, mgr. Oakland div., 1978-80, asst. vice chmn., 1980-81, asst. v.p., mgr. fuel support, 1981-82, v.p. fin. svcs., 1982-87, exec. v.p., 1987-88, pres., COO, 1988-94, chmn., CEO, 1990-98, also bd. dirs. Bd. dirs. Nat. Bank of Detroit, NBD Bancorp, Inc., DTE Energy Co., Detroit Investment Fund

LOCH, JOHN ROBERT, university administrator; b. Aug. 25, 1940; s. Robert Addison and Mary Virginia (Beck) L. Student, Waynesburg Coll., 1958; AB, Grove City Coll., 1962; postgrad., Pitts. Theol. Sem., 1962; MEd, U. Pitts., 1966, PhD, 1972, Harvard U., 1984. Cert. program planner. Asst. to dean of men, program planner U. Pitts., 1963-64, dir. student union, 1964-70, dir. student affairs rsch., 1970-71, dir. suburban ednl. svcs. Sch. Gen. Studies, 1971-75; dir. continuing edn. and pub. svc. Youngstown (Ohio) State U., 1975-82, dir. univ. outreach, 1990—. Chief adminstrv. officer Metro Coll., 1996-98; assoc. mem. grad. faculty, 1980-95; rsch. assoc. Pres.'s Commn. on Campus Unrest, 1970; chmn. program com. Park Vista Retirement Cmty., 1994-95, vice chair bd. dirs., 1995-96, mktg. com., 1999—; trustee Ohio Presbyn. Retirement Cmtys., 1993-99, program com., 1993-99. Trustee Mahoning Shenango Area Health Edn. Network, 1976-91, Career Devel. Ctr. for Women, 1978-80; trustee Youngstown Area Arts Coun., 1980-85, pres., 1981-83; bd. dirs. Protestant Family Svcs., 1981-83; active Older Adults Task Force, Mahoning County, 1992-96; trustee Mahoning County RSVP, 1983-89, chmn. evaluation com., 1983-84, chmn. pers. com., 1984-85, chmn. bd. trustees, 1986-87; coord. fund raising Nat. Unity Campaign, Mahoning County, 1980; state chmn. Young Rep. Coll. Coun. Pa., 1960. Mem. AAUW, Assn. Continuing Higher Edn. (chair-elect region VI 1997-98, chair 1998-99), Adult Edn. Assn. USA, Nat. U. Continuing Edn. Assn., Ohio Coun. Higher Continuing Edn. (pres. 1979-80), Ohio Continuing Higher Edn. Assn. (hon. life mem., co-chmn. constn. com. 1982, v.p. state univs. 1984-85, pres.-elect 1985-86, pres. 1986-87, historian 1988-96, chmn. awards and honors com. 1989-92, editor Voluntary Continuing Edn. Requirements 1993-95, Spl. Svc. award 1989), Ohio-Pa. Higher Edn. Network (chmn. 1989-90), Learning Resources Network (Univ. Coun. Gt. Lakes rep. 1996—), Youngstown Traffic Club (hon. life mem.), Youngstown Club, Kiwanis (dir. 1981-82), Youngstown Dist., Purchasing Mgrs. Assn., Omicron Delta Kappa, Kappa Kappa Psi, Phi Kappa Phi (pres. 1980-81, pres. 1994-95, 96-97, Disting. Mem. award 2000), Alpha Phi Omega, Alpha Sigma Lambda, Phi Delta Kappa. Presbyterian. Home: 242 Upland Ave Youngstown OH 44504-1849 Office: Met Coll Southwoods Commons 100 De Bartolo Pl Youngstown OH 44512 E-mail: jrloch@cc.ysu.edu.

LOCHNER, JAMES V. food products executive; Exec. v.p. mfg. fresh meats IBP, Inc., Dakota Dunes, S.D., 1998—, pres. mfg. fresh meats. Office: IBD Inc 800 Stevens Port Dr Dakota Dunes SD 57049-5005

LOCIGNO, PAUL ROBERT, public affairs executive; b. Cleve., Sept. 17, 1948; s. Paul Robert and Anna Mae (Zingale) L.; m. Ki Cho Rim; children: Paul III, Tammy, Robert. AA, Cuyahoga C.C., Parma, Ohio, 1974; BA, Case Western Res. U., 1976; postgrad., Cleve. State U., 1977-78. Part-time faculty Cuyahoga Community Coll., 1979-83; vice-chmn. Presdl. Inaugural Labor Com., Washington, 1980-81; vice-chmn. labor com. Presdl. Inaugural Com., 1984-85; legis. agt. Internat. Brotherhood of Teamsters, 1977-90, dir. govt. internat. affairs, 1983-89, dir. Asian/Pacific br. Taipei, Taiwan, 1985-88; spl. rep. of chmn. Hill & Knowlton Pub. Affairs Worldwide, Washington, 1989-91; pres., founding ptnr. Rollins Internat. Ltd., Alexandria, Va., 1997—; CEO Ganeden Biotech Inc., San Diego. Bd. dirs. Nanjing Ya Dong Corp. Mem. Pres.'s Export Coun., 1988-89; mem. Asia adv. com. Bicentennial of U.S. Constitution, 1990; bd. govs. Am. League for Exports and Security Assistance, 1989; mem. Nat. Commn. for Employment Policy, Washington, 1981-86; bd. dirs. Children's Right Coun., Washington, 1997—. With USMC, 1968-70, Vietnam. Republican. Roman Catholic. Avocations: archery, golf, fishing. Home: 15100 Hawksbill Ct Woodbridge VA 22193-5831 Office: Ganeden Biotech Inc 1228 Euclid Ave Ste 900 Cleveland OH 44115-1845

LOCK, RICHARD WILLIAM, packaging company executive; b. N.Y.C., Oct. 5, 1931; s. Albert and Catherine Dorothy (Magnus) L.; m. Elizabeth Louise Kenney, Nov. 2, 1957; children— Albert William, Dorothy Louise Lock Kuhl, John David. B.S., Rutgers U., 1953; M.B.A., N.Y. U., 1958. Acct. Gen. Electric Co., 1953-54, Union Carbide Co., N.Y.C., 1956-58; div. controller St. Regis Paper Co., Houston, 1959-62, Owens-Illinois, Inc., Toledo, 1962-64, supr. programmer office methods and data processing, 1964-65, asst. mgr. data processing procedures, 1965-67, mgr. systems analysis and devel., 1967-68, mgr. corp. systems analysis and devel., 1968-70, dir. corp. systems and data processing, 1970-72, gen. mgr. electro/optical display, 1972-75, treas., 1975-80, v.p., dir. corp. planning, 1980-84, v.p., asst. chief fin. officer, treas., 1984-88; mng. dir. Magnus Assocs., 1989—. Mem. adv. bd. Toledo Salvation Army, 1973—, chmn., 1974-77; pres. Toledo Area Govtl. Research Assn., 1978-79; bd. dirs. Riverside Hosp. Found., Toledo, 1982—. Served with USAF, 1954-56. Mem. Fin. Execs. Inst., Am. Soc. Corp. Secs., Phi Beta Kappa. Republican. Lutheran. Club: Toledo. Home: 5831 Monroe St Apt 406 Sylvania OH 43560-2256

LOCKE, CARL EDWIN, JR. academic administrator, engineering educator; b. Palo Pinto County, Tex., Jan. 11, 1936; s. Carl Edwin Sr. and Caroline Jane (Brown) L.; m. Sammie Rhae Batchelor, Aug. 25, 1956; children: Stephen Curtis, Carlene Rhae. BSChemE, U. Tex., 1958, MSChemE, 1960, PhDChemE, 1972. Rsch. engr. Continental Oil Co., Ponca City, Okla., 1959-65; prodn. engr. R.L. Stone Co., Austin, Tex., 1965-66; prodn. rsch. engr. Tracor Inc., 1966-71; vis. assoc. prof. U. Tex., 1971-73; from asst. prof. to prof., dir. chem. engring. U. Okla., Norman, 1973-86; dean engring. U. Kans., Lawrence, 1986—. Co-author: Anodic Protection, 1981; contbr. articles to profl. jours. Disting. Engring. grad. U. Tex., 1993, Kansas Engr. of Yr. Kansas Engring. Soc., 1996. Fellow Am. Inst. Chem. Engrs.; mem. ASTM, Nat. Assn. Corrosion Engrs. (regional chair 1988-89, Eben Junkin award South Cen. region 1990), Am. Soc. Engring. Edn. (vice-chair engring. deans coun. 1999-2001, chair 2001—), Lawrence C. of C., Rotary (pres. 2001—). Democrat. Presbyterian. Office: U Kans Sch Engring Rm 4010 1530 W 15th St Lawrence KS 66045-7526 E-mail: lok@ku.edu.

LOCKETT, TYLER CHARLES, state supreme court justice; b. Corpus Christi, Tex., Dec. 7, 1932; s. Tyler Coleman and Evelyn (Lemond) L.; m. Sue W. Lockett, Nov. 3, 1961; children: Charles, Patrick. AB, Washburn U., 1955; JD, 1962. Bar: Kans. 1962. Pvt. practice law, Wichita, 1962—; judge Ct. Common Pleas, 1971-77, Kans. Dist. Ct. 18th Dist., 1977-83; justice Supreme Court Kans., Topeka, 1983—. Methodist. Office: Kans Supreme Ct 374 Kansas Judicial Ctr Topeka KS 66612-1502*

LOCKHART, GREGORY GORDON, prosecutor; b. Dayton, Ohio, Sept. 2, 1946; s. Lloyd Douglas and Evelyn (Gordon) L.; m. Paula Louise Jewett, May 20, 1978; children: David H., Sarah L. BS, Wright State U., 1973; JD, Ohio State U., 1976. Bar: Ohio 1976, U.S. Dist. Ct. (so. dist.) Ohio 1977, U.S. Ct. Appeals (6th cir.) 1988, U.S. Supreme Ct. 1993. Legal advisor Xenia and Fairborn (Ohio) Police Dept., 1977-78; asst. pros. atty. Greene County Prosecutor, Xenia, 1978-87; ptnr. DeWine & Schenck, 1978-82, Schenck, Schmidt & Lockhart , Xenia, 1982-85, Ried & Lockhart, Beavercreek, Ohio, 1985-87; asst. U.S. atty. So. Dist. of Ohio, Columbus, 1987-2001, U.S. atty. Dayton, 2001—. Adj. prof. Coll. Law U. Dayton, 1990—, Wright State U., Dayton, 1979—. Co-author: Federal Grand Jury Practice, 1996. Pres. Greene County Young Reps., Xenia, 1977-79. With USAF, 1966-70; Vietnam. Mem. Fed. Bar Assn. (chpt. pres. 1994-95), Dayton Bar Assn., Kiwanis (pres. 1983-84, lt. gov. 1986-87), Jaycees (pres. 1976-79), Am. Inns of Ct. (master of bench emeritus). Methodist. Avocations: golf, tennis, hiking, camping. Office: US Attorney Federal Bldg 200 W 2d St Rm 602 Dayton OH 45402 E-mail: gregory.lockhart@usdoj.gov.

LOCKHART, JOHN MALLERY, management consultant; b. Mellen, Wis., May 17, 1911; s. Carl Wright and Gladys (Gale) L.; m. Judith Anne Wood, Feb. 26, 1938 (dec. June 1991); children: Wood Alexander, Gale, Thomas; m. Frances Whittaker, Jan. 7, 1993. BS, Northwestern U., 1931; JD, IIT, 1938. CPA, Ill. Teaching fellow Northwestern U., 1931; asst. v.p. Welsh, Davis & Co. (investment bankers), Chgo., 1935-41; treas. Transcontinental & Western Air, Inc., Kansas City, Mo., 1941-47; exec. v.p., CEO TACA Airways, S.A., 1944-45; v.p., dir. The Kroger Co., 1947-71, exec. v.p., 1961-71; pres. Kroger Family Ctr. Stores, 1969-71, Lockhart Co. (mgmt. cons.), 1971—; v.p. corp. fin. Gradison & Co., 1973-86. Chmn. bd. dirs., CEO Ohio Real Estate Investment Co., Ohio Real Estate Equity Corp., 1974-76; bd. dirs. Employers Mut. Cos., Des Moines, Witt Co.; chmn. bd. dirs. Autotronics Systems, Inc., 1976-78; bd. dirs. Vectra Internat., Inc., Hamilton Mut. Ins. Co. Chmn. Hamilton County Hosp. Commn., 1965-84; mem. adv. bd. Greater Cin. Airport, 1961-86. Mem. Comml. Club, Cin. Country Club, Conquistadores del Cielo Club. Home and Office: 2770 Walsh Rd Cincinnati OH 45208-3425

LOCKINGTON, DAVID, conductor; b. Eng. arrived in U.S., 1978; m. Dylana Jenson; 3 children. BA, U. Cambridge, Eng.; MA in cello performance, Yale U. Prin. cellist Nat. Youth Orch. Great Britain; cellist New Haven Symphony Orch.; asst. prin. cellist Denver Symphony Orch., asst. conductor; music dir. Cheyenne Symphony Orch., Denver Young Artist's Orch., Boulder Bach. Festival; founder, conductor Acad. Wilderness Chamber Orch.; asst. conductor Opera Colo., Balt. Symphony Orch., 1992, assoc. conductor, 1993-95; music dir. Ohio Chamber Orch., N.Mex. Symphony Orch., 1995—, Grand Rapids Symphony, Grand Rapids, Mich. Guest conductor St. Louis Symphony, Colo. Symphony, Grand Rapids (Mich.) Symphony, Pacific Symphony, Wichita (Kans.) Symphony, Honolulu Symphony, Harrisburg (Pa.) Symphony, Fla. Orch., Dayton (Ohio) Philharmonic, La. Philharmonic, World Youth Symphony, Interlochen Arts Acad. Office: Grand Rapids Symphony Ste 1 169 Louis Campau Promenade NW 1 Grand Rapids MI 49503-2629

LOCKMAN, STUART M. lawyer; b. Jersey City, July 18, 1949; s. Albert Korey and Edna Sally (Easton) L.; m. Deena Laurel Young, Dec. 27, 1970; children: Jeffrey, Susan, Karen. BA, U. Mich., 1971, JD, 1974. Bar: Mich. 1974, Fla. 1991; bd. cert. health law specialist, Fla. Ptnr. Honigman Miller Schwartz and Cohn, Detroit, 1974—. Office: Honigman Miller Schwartz & Cohn 2290 1st National Bldg Detroit MI 48226 E-mail: sml@honigman.com.

LOCKNER, VERA JOANNE, farmer, rancher, legislator; b. St. Lawrence, S.D., May 19, 1937; d. Leonard and Zona R. (Ford) Verdugt; m. Frank O. Lockner, Aug. 7, 1955; children: Dean M., Clifford A. Grad., St. Lawrence (S.D.) High Sch., 1955. Bank teller/bookkeeper First Nat. Bank, Miller, S.D., 1963-66, Bank of Wessington, 1968-74; farmer/rancher Wessington, 1955-2000. Sunday sch. tchr. Trinity Luth. Ch., Miller, 1968-72; treas. PTO, Wessington, 1969-70; treas., vice chmn., chmn., state com. woman Hand County Dems., Miller, 1978—; mem. S.D. Dem. Exec. Bd., 1997-2000. Named one of Outstanding Young Women of Am., Women's Study Club, Wessington, 1970. Mem. Order of Ea. Star (warder, marshall, chaplain 1970—). Avocations: oil painting, crafts, gardening, photography. Home and Office: 301 3rd St NW Saint Lawrence SD 57373-2324

LOCKWOOD, DEAN H. physician, pharmaceutical executive; b. Milford, Conn., June 17, 1937; s. Horace Musson and Lucille Ruth (Fengler) L.; m. Carol Hay, June 21, 1958 (div. Mar. 1979); children: Andrew Brooks, Craig Stewart, Wendy Susan; m. Elizabeth East, July 19, 1980. AB, Wesleyan U., 1959; MD, John Hopkin's U., 1963. Intern in medicine Olser Medical Svc., The John Hopkins Hosp., Balt., 1963-64, asst. resident in medicine, 1964-65; staff assoc. sect. of intermediary metabolism Nat. Inst. Arthritis and Metabolic Diseases, NIH, Bethesda, Md., 1965-67; fellow dept pharmacology and experimental therapeutics and of medicine The John Hopkins U., Balt., 1967-69, asst. prof. medicine Sch. Medicine, 1969-74, asst. prof. pharm. and exptl. therapeutics, 1971-76, assoc. prof. medicine, 1974-76; staff physician The John Hopkins Hosp., 1969-76; dir. Diabetes Mgmt. Clin., The John Hopkins Hosp., 1971-76; prof. medicine Sch. Medicine U. Rochester, N.Y., 1976-92, head endocrine metabolism unit, dept. medicine, Sch. Medicine, 1976-91, assoc. chair medicine, 1991; v.p. clin. rsch. Warner Lambert Co., Ann Arbor, Mich., 1991-92, 93-94, acting sr. v.p. clin. rsch., 1992-93. Staff physician Balt. City Hosp., 1969-76, Strong Meml. Hosp., 1976-91; med. cons. Highland Hospital of Rochester, 1977-91, attending cons. Park Ridge Hosp., 1989-91; assoc. chmn. rsch. dept. medicine U. Rochester, 1991; adj. prof. medicine Sch. Medicine U. Rochester, 1992-93; lectr. in the field. Editorial bd. mem.: Internat. Jour. Obesity, 1975-84, Endocrinology, 1981-85, Am. Jour. Physiology, 1982-88; cons. editor: Jour. Clin. Investigation, 1992-97. Recipient Bordon Undergrad. Rsch. award, 1963, NIH Rsch. Career Devel. award, 1969-74; Henry Strong Denison scholar, 1962-63; Am. Diabetes Assn. grantee, 1986-91, NIH grantee, 1969-92. Mem. Am. Diabetes Assn., Am. Fedn. for Rsch., The Endocrine Soc., Am. Soc. Biol. Chemists, Am. Soc. Clin. Investigation, Sigma Xi, Alpha Omega Alpha, Phi Beta Kappa. Office: Warner Lambert 2800 Plymouth Rd Ann Arbor MI 48105-2430 Home: 205 Royal Vw Pittsford NY 14534-9635

LOCKWOOD, FRANK JAMES, manufacturing company executive; b. San Bernadino, Calif., Oct. 30, 1931; s. John Ellis and Sarah Grace (Roberts) L.; children from previous marraige: Fay, Frank, Hedy, Jonnie, George, Katherine, Bill, Dena; m. 2d. Crystal Marie Miller, 1986. Student, Southeast City Coll., Chgo., 1955, Ill. Inst. Tech., 1963-64, Bogan Jr. Coll., Chgo., 1966. Foreman Hupp Aviation, Chgo., 1951-60; dept. head UARCO, Inc., 1960-68; pres. XACT Machine & Engring., 1968—. Chmn. bd., pres., bd. dirs. Lockwood Engring., Inc., Chgo.; Ill. Nat. Corp., Chgo., and cons. engr., Chgo. Patentee printing equipment, beverage cans, gasoline pump dispenser "Super Pin", bus. forms equipment. Participant Forest Land Mgmt. Program; mem. Ill. Ambassadors; commr. Econ. Devel. Commn., Mt. Vernon, Ill., 1985; mem. bd. County of Jefferson, Ill., 1992—; mem. exec. com., legis. com. Ill. County Bds. Coun. Named Chgo. Ridge Father of the Yr., 1964. Mem. Ill. Divers' Assn. (pres. 1961-62). Lodge: Masons (32 degree), Shriners (past master 2). Home: RR 1 Texico IL 62889-9801 Office: 7011 W Archer Ave Chicago IL 60638-2201

LOCKWOOD, GARY LEE, lawyer; b. Woodstock, Ill., Dec. 3, 1946; s. Howard and Luella Mae (Behrens) L.; m. Cheryl Lynn Wittrock, Jan. 5, 1967; children: Jennifer, Lee, Cynthia. BA magna cum laude, Iowa

Wesleyan Coll., 1969; student, Albert Ludwig U., Freiburg in Breisgau, Fed. Republic Germany, 1968-69; JD, Northwestern U., 1976. Bar: Ill. 1976, U.S. Dist. Ct. (no. dist.) Ill. 1976, U.S. Ct. Appeals (7th cir.) 2000. Assoc. Lord, Bissell & Brook, Chgo., 1976-85, ptnr., 1985—. Bd. dirs. McHenry Sch. Dist. 15, Ill., 1974-85, pres., 1979-80. Served to sgt. U.S. Army, 1970-72. Mem. ABA (bus. and ins. com. 1985—). Methodist. Avocations: sports. Home: 175 N Harbor Dr Chicago IL 60601-7344 Office: Lord Bissel & Brook 115 S La Salle St Fl 3600 Chicago IL 60603-3902 E-mail: glockwoo@lordbissell.com.'

LOCKWOOD, JOHN LEBARON, plant pathologist, educator; b. Ann Arbor, Mich., May 28, 1924; s. George LeBaron and Mary Bonita (Leininger) L.; m. Jean Elizabeth Springborg, Mar. 21, 1959; children: James L., Laura A. Student, Western Mich. Coll., 1941-43; BA, Mich. State Coll., 1948, MS, 1950; PhD, U. Wis., 1953. Asst. prof. Ohio Agrl. Expt. Sta., Wooster, 1953-55, Mich. State U., East Lansing, 1955-61, assoc. prof., 1961-67, prof., 1967-90, prof. emeritus, 1990—. Served with U.S. Army, 1943-46 NSF research fellow, 1970-71. Fellow Am. Phytopathol. Soc. (pres. 1984-85).

LOEB, DEANN JEAN, nurse; b. West Union, Iowa, Aug. 1, 1960; d. Dale Alfred and Annagene Helen (Suhr) Ungerer; m. Thomas Allan Loeb, Sept. 1, 1985; children: Ryan, Jennifer, Andrea, Cody. Diploma in nursing, NE Iowa Tech. Inst., 1982. Lic. practical nurse, Iowa. Laundry aide Good Samaritan Ctr., West Union, 1977, kitchen aide, cook, 1977-79, nurses asst., 1979-81, practical nurse, 1982-84, Ind. (Ind.) Care Ctr., 1985-89, Dr. Jose C. Aguiar, Waterloo, Iowa, 1989-93, Dr. John Musgrave-Dr. Mary O'Connell, Waterloo, 1993-94; nurse Waterloo Asthma and Allergy Clinic, 1994—; on call nurse Interim Health, 2001—. Leader Brownies, asst. leader Girl Scouts U.S.; tchr. Bible, Sunday sch., mem. parish bd. edn., mem. parish life com. Zion Jubilee Luth. Ch., Jesup, Iowa, altar com., worship com., chair altar guild; mem. Cub Scout Com. Republican. Home: 7144 Spring Creek Rd Jesup IA 50648-9568

LOEB, JANE RUPLEY, university administrator, educator; b. Chgo., Feb. 22, 1938; d. John Edwards and Virginia Pentland (Marthens) Watkins; m. Peter Albert Loeb, June 14, 1958; children: Eric Peter, Gwendolyn Lisl, Aaron John. BA, Rider Coll., 1961; PhD, U. So. Calif., 1969. Clin. psychology intern Univ. Hosp., Seattle, 1966-67; asst. prof. ednl. psychology U. Ill., Urbana, 1968-69, asst. coord. rsch. and testing, 1968-69, coord. rsch. and testing, 1969-72, asst. to vice chancellor acad. affairs, 1971-72, dir. admissions and records, 1972-81, assoc. prof. ednl. psychology, 1973-82, assoc. vice chancellor acad. affairs, 1981-94, prof. edn. psychology, 1982—. Author: College Board Project: the Future of College Admissions, 1989; co-editor: Academic Couples: Problems and Promises, 1997. Chmn. Coll. Bd. Coun. on Entrance Svcs., 1977-82; bd. govs. Alliance for Undergrad. Edn., 1988-93; active charter com. Coll. Bd. Acad. Assembly, 1992-93. HEW grantee, 1975-76. Mem. APA, Am. Ednl. Rsch. Assn., Nat. Coun. Measurement in Edn., Harvard Inst. Ednl. Mgmt. Avocation: the french horn. Home: 1405 N Coler Ave Urbana IL 61801-1625 Office: U Ill 1310 S 6th St Champaign IL 61820-6925

LOEB, JEROME THOMAS, retail executive; b. Sept. 13, 1940; s. Harry W. and Marjorie T. Loeb; m. Carol Bodenheimer, June 15, 1963; children: Daniel W., Kelly E. BS, Tufts U., 1962; MA, Washington U., St. Louis, 1964. Asst. dir. rsch., dir. EDP, div. v.p., dir. mgmt. info. svc. Famous-Barr div. May Dept. Stores Co., St. Louis, 1964-74, v.p. mgmt. info. svcs./EDP parent co., 1974-77; sr. v.p., CFO Hecht's div., Washington, 1977-79; exec. v.p. devel. May Dept. Stores Co., St. Louis, 1979-81, exec. v.p., CFO, 1981-86, vice-chmn., CFO, 1986-93, pres., 1993-98, chmn. bd. dirs., 1998—. Bd. dirs. Jr. Achievement of Mississippi Valley, 1980—, chmn., 1993-95; bd. dirs. Jr. Achievement Nat. Bd., 1988—, chmn., 1999—; bd. trustees, St. Louis Sci. Ctr., 1991—, chmn., 1994-98; bd. dirs. Barnes-Jewish Hosp., 1984—, vice-chmn., 1988, bd. dirs. BJC Health Sys., 1992—, OASIS, 1999—, Nat. Retail Fedn., 1996—, United Way of Greater St. Louis, 1998—; mem. pres. cabinet Am. Jewish Com., 1994—. Mem. Westwood Country Club, Boone Valley Golf Club, Persimmon Woods Golf Club. Office: May Dept Stores Co 611 Olive St Saint Louis MO 63101-1721

LOEB, LEONARD L. lawyer; b. Chgo., Mar. 30, 1929; BBA, U. Wis., 1950, JD, 1952. Bar: Wis. 1952, U.S. Supreme Ct. 1960. Sole practice, Milw., 1952—; ptnr. Loeb & Herman. Faculty family mediation inst. Harvard Law Sch.; lectr. family law Marquette U., U. Wis., Madison; cons. revisions Wis. Family Code Wis. Legislature; mem. com. for review of initiatives in child support State of Wis.; Concordia Coll. (Wis.) Paralegal Adv. Bd. Author: Systems Book for Family Law; contbr. articles to profl. jours. Served to col. JAGC, USAF, 1952-53. Fellow Am. Bar Found., Am. Acad. Matrimonial Lawyers (past charter pres. Wis. chpt., pres. nat. chpt.); mem. ABA (past chmn. family law sect., del. to ho. of dels.), Wis. Bar Assn. (pres. 1999-2000), Wis. Bar Found. (bd. dirs.), Milw. Bar Assn. (past chmn. family law sect., past pres.). Office: Loeb & Herman Ste 1125 111 E Wisconsin Ave Milwaukee WI 53202-4868 E-mail: lloeb@loebherman.com.

LOEB, VIRGIL, JR. oncologist, hematologist; b. St. Louis, Sept. 21, 1921; s. Virgil and Therese (Meltzer) Loeb; m. Lenore Harlow, Sept. 8, 1950 (dec. Nov. 1987); children: Katherine Loeb Doumas, Elizabeth Loeb McCane, David, Mark; m. Elizabeth Moore, Dec. 1990. Student, Swarthmore Coll., 1938—41; MD, Washington U., St. Louis, 1944. Diplomate Am. Bd. Internal Medicine. Intern Barnes and Jewish Hosps., St. Louis, 1944—45; resident in internal medicine, research fellow in hematology Barnes Hosp., 1947—52; med. faculty Washington U., 1951—, prof. clin. medicine, 1978—96, prof. emeritus clin. medicine, 1996—; practice medicine specializing in oncology and hematology, 1956—96. Cons., clin. rschr.; dir. Ctrl. Diagnostic Labs. Barnes Hosp., 1952—68; staff numerous hosps., 1951—96; cons. Nat. Cancer Inst., 1966—96, chmn. cancer clin. investigation rev. com., 1966—69, mem. diagnostic rsch. adv. com., 1972—9715, bd. sci. counselors, DCPC, 1983—87; mem. oncology merit rev. bd. VA, 1971—75. Contbr. books, articles to profl. jours. Bd. dirs. Am. Cancer Soc., mem. nat. adv. com., 1969—, pres. Mo. divsn., 1983—85, nat. pres., 1986—87; trustee John Burroughts Sch., 1966—69; bd. dirs. St. Louis Blue Cross and Blue Shield, Bi-State Red Cross. Served with M.C. U.S. Army, 1945—47. Fellow: ACP; mem.: Am. Assn. for Cancer Edn., Am. Soc. Clin. Oncology, St. Louis Soc. Internal Medicine (pres. 1974), Am. Soc. Hematology, Internat. Soc. Hematology, Am. Assn. Cancer Rsch., Inst. Medicine of NAS, Ctrl. Soc. Clin. Rsch., St. Louis Met. Med. Soc. (hon.), Alpha Omega Alpha, Sigma Xi. Home: 24 Deerfield Rd Saint Louis MO 63124-1412 Office: Barnes Hosp 1 Barnes Hospital Plz Saint Louis MO 63110-1036

LOEFFLER, FRANK JOSEPH, physicist, educator; b. Ballston Spa, N.Y., Sept. 5, 1928; s. Frank Joseph and Florence (Farrell) L.; m. Eleanor Jane Chisholm, Sept. 8, 1951; children: Peter, James, Margaret, Anne Marie. B.S. in Engring. Physics, Cornell U., 1951, Ph.D. in Physics, 1957. Research asso. Princeton U., 1957-58; mem. faculty Purdue U., Lafayette, Ind., 1958-97, prof. physics, 1962-97; prof. emeritus, 1997—; vis. prof. Hamburg U., Germany, 1963-64, Heidelberg U., Germany, CERN, Switzerland, 1971, Stanford U. Linear Accelerator Ctr., 1980-83. Trustee, mem. exec. com., chmn. high energy com. Argonne Univs. Assn., 1972-76, 78-79, mem. com. on fusion programs, 1979-80; vis. prof. U. Hawaii, 1985-86. Contbr. to profl. publs. Recipient Antarctic Svc. medal NSF/USN, 1990, Ruth and Joel Spira award for outstanding tchg., 1992. Fellow Am. Phys. Soc., Sigma Xi, Tau Beta Pi. Achievements include developing and manufacturing undergraduate physics laboratory experiments and lecture demonstration apparatus. Exptl. research in astrophysics, high energy gamma ray astronomy, high energy particle interactions and on-line data acquisition-processing systems. Established gamma ray astronomy lab. at South Pole, Antarctica, 1989, 91, 92. Home: 341 Hokulani St Makawao HI 96768-8612 Office: Purdue U Dept Physics Lafayette IN 47907

LOEHR, MARLA, spiritual care coordinator; b. Cleve., Oct. 7, 1937; d. Joseph Richard and Eleanore Edith (Rothschuh) L. BS, Notre Dame Coll., South Euclid, Ohio, 1960; MAT, Ind. U., 1969; PhD, Boston Coll., 1988; Degree (hon.), Notre Dame Coll. Ohio, 1995. Cert. high sch. tchr., counselor, Ohio; cert. spiritual dir., pastoral min. Math and sci. educator, 1960-66; adminstrn. asst., dir. residence halls Notre Dame Acad., Chardon, Ohio, 1966-72; dean students Notre Dame Coll., South Euclid, 1972-85, acting acad. dean, 1988, pres., 1988-95; spiritual care coord. Hospice of Western Res., Cleve., 1995—. Author: Mentor Handbook, 1985; co-author: Notre Dame College Model for Student Development, 1980. Hon. mem. Leadership Cleve. Class of 1990; v.p., trustee SJ Wellness Ctr., 1999; mem. leadership coun. Future Ch., Diocese of Cleve. Recipient Career Woman of Achievement award YWCA, 1992; named One of 100 Cleve.'s Most Powerful Women, New Cleve. Woman. Mem. Spiritual Dirs. Internat., Nat. Hospice Assn., Alpha Sigma Nu, Kappa Gamma Pi. Avocations: photography, hiking, reading, sports. E-mali. Office: Hospice Western Res 29101 Health Campus Dr Ste 400 Westlake OH 44145-5268 E-mail: marlajlo@cs.com.

LOESCH, KATHARINE TAYLOR (MRS. JOHN GEORGE LOESCH), communication and theatre educator; b. Berkeley, Calif., Apr. 13, 1922; d. Paul Schuster and Katharine (Whiteside) Taylor; m. John George Loesch, Aug. 28, 1948; 1 child, William Ross. Student, Swarthmore Coll., 1939-41, U. Wash., 1942; BS, Columbia U., 1944, MA, 1949; grad., Neighborhood Playhouse Sch., 1946; postgrad., Ind. U., 1953; PhD, Northwestern U., 1961. Instr. speech Wellesley (Mass.) Coll., 1949-52, Loyola U., Chgo., 1956; asst. prof. English and speech Roosevelt U., 1957, 62-65; assoc. prof. comm. and theatre U. Ill., 1968-87, assoc. prof. emeritus, 1987—. Contbr. articles to profl. jours.; author numerous poems; performer of poetry. Active ERA, Ill., 1975-76. Am. Philos. Soc. grant, 1970. Mem. MLA, Am. Soc. for Aesthetics, Linguistic Soc. Am., Chgo. Linguistic Soc. (co-chmn. 1954-56), Nat. Comm. Assn. (chair interpretation divsn. 1979-80, Golden Ann. award 1969), Celtic Studies Assn. N.Am., Pi Beta Phi. Episcopalian. Home: 2129 N Sedgwick St Chicago IL 60614-4619 Office: U Ill Dept Performing Arts M/C 255 1040 W Harrison St Chicago IL 60607-7130 E-mail: dpa@uic.edu.

LOEWENBERG, GERHARD, political science educator; b. Berlin, Germany, Oct. 2, 1928; came to U.S., 1936, naturalized, 1943; s. Walter and Anne Marie (Cassirer) L.; m. Ina Perlstein, Aug. 22, 1950; children: Deborah, Michael. A.B., Cornell U., 1949, A.M., 1950, Ph.D., 1955. Mem. faculty Mount Holyoke Coll., 1953-69, chmn. dept. polit. sci., 1963-69, acting academic dean, 1968-69; prof. polit. sci. U. Iowa, Iowa City, 1970—, chmn. dept., 1982-84, dean Coll. Liberal Arts, 1984-92, dir. Comparative Legis. Research Center, 1971-82, 92—; vice chair East-West Parliamentary Practice Project, 1990-2000. Vis. assoc. prof. Columbia, UCLA, 1966, U. Mass. summer session at Bologna, Italy, 1967, Cornell U., 1968; mem. council Inter-Univ. Consortium for Polit. Research, 1971-74, chmn., 1973-74 Author: Parliament in the German Political System, 1967, Parlamentarismus im politischen System der Bundesrepublik Deutschland, 1969, Modern Parliaments: Change or Decline, 1971; co-author: Comparing Legislatures, 1979; co-editor: Handbook of Legislative Research, 1985, Legis. Studies Quar., Legislatures: Comparative Perspectives on Representative Assemblies, 2002; contbr. articles to profl. jours. Trustee Mt. Holyoke Coll., 1971-84, chmn., 1979-84. Fulbright fellow, 1957-58; Rockefeller fellow, 1961-62; Social Sci. Research Council faculty research fellow, 1964-65; Guggenheim fellow, 1969-70 Mem. Am. Polit. Sci. Assn. (coun. 1971-73, v.p. 1990-91), Midwest Polit. Sci. Assn., Phi Beta Kappa, Phi Kappa Phi, Pi Sigma Alpha. Office: U Iowa 336 Schaeffer Hall Iowa City IA 52242-1409

LOFGREN, KARL ADOLPH, surgeon, educator; b. Killeberg, Sweden, Apr. 1, 1915; s. Hokan Albin and Teckla Elizabeth (Carlsson) L.; m. Jean Frances Taylor, Sept. 12, 1942; children: Karl Edward, Anne Elizabeth. Student, Northwestern U., 1934-37; M.D., Harvard U., 1941; M.S. in Surgery, U. Minn., 1947. Diplomate Am. Bd. Surgery. Intern U. Minn. Hosps., Mpls., 1941-42; Mayo Found. fellow in surgery, 1942-44, 46-48; asst. surgeon Royal Acad. Hosp., Uppsala, Sweden, 1949; asst. to surg. staff Mayo Clinic, Rochester, Minn., 1949-50, cons. sect. peripheral vein surgery, 1950-81; instr. in surgery Mayo Grad. Sch. Medicine, 1951-60, asst. prof. surgery, 1960-74; comdg. officer USNR Med. Co. Mayo Clinic, 1963-67, head sect. peripheral vein surgery, dept. surgery, 1966-79, sr. cons., 1980-81. Assoc. prof. surgery Mayo Med. Sch., 1974-79, prof., 1979-81, emeritus prof., 1982— ; cons. surg. staff Rochester Meth. Hosp., St. Mary's Hosp. Contbr. chpts. to textbooks, articles to profl. jours. Mem. adv. bd. Salvation Army, Rochester, 1959-81, 82— , pres., 1962-63. Served to capt. M.C. USNR, 1944-46. Decorated Bronze Star Fellow ACS; mem. Soc. Vascular Surgery, Midwestern Vascular Surgery Soc., Internat. Cardiovascular Soc., Minn. Surg. Soc., Swedish Surg. Soc. (hon.), Swiss Soc. Phlebology (co-worker), So. Minn. Med. Assn. (pres. 1972-73), Scandinavian Soc. Phlebology (hon.), Am. Venous Forum, Rotary Club, Sigma Xi. Baptist. Office: Mayo Clin Rochester MN 55905-0001 Home: 211 2nd St NW Apt 1916 Rochester MN 55901

LOFTON, KENNETH, professional baseball player; b. East Chicago, Ind., May 31, 1967; Student, U. Ariz. Baseball player Houston Astros, 1988-91, Cleveland Indians, 1991-96, Atlanta Braves, 1996-97, Cleve. Indians, 1997—2001, Chicago White Sox, 2002, San Francisco Giants, 2002—. Ranked 1st in Am. League for stolen bases, 1992; recipient Am. League Gold Glove award, 1993-96; named to All-Star Team, 1994-96. Office: San Francisco Giants Pacific Bell Park 24 Willie Mays Plaza San Francisco CA 94107*

LOFTON, THOMAS MILTON, lawyer; b. Indpls., May 12, 1929; s. Milton Alexander and Jane (Routzong) L.; m. Betty Louise Blades, June 20, 1954; children: Stephanie Louise, Melissa Jane. BS, Ind. U., 1951, JD, 1954, LLD (hon.), 2000, Wabash Coll., 2001. Bar: Ind. 1954, U.S. Ct. Appeals (7th cir.) 1959, U.S. Supreme Ct. 1958. Law clk. to justice U.S. Supreme Ct., Washington, 1954-55; ptnr. Baker & Daniels, Indpls., 1958-91. Dir. Ind. U. Found., Bloomington, 1978-91, Clowes Fund, 1980-2001; chmn. bd. Lilly Endowment, Indpls., 1991—; mem. bd. visitors Ind. U. Law, Bloomington, 1976—. Editor-in-chief Ind. Law Jour., 1953. Trustee Earlham Coll., 1988—91; dir. Allen Whitehill Clowes Charitable Found., 1990—. 1st lt. U.S. Army, 1955—58. Recipient Peck award Wabash Coll., 1982, Disting. Alumni Svc. award Ind. U., 1997. Mem.: Ind. Acad., Masons, Order of Coif, Sigma Nu, Beta Gamma Sigma. Republican. Presbyterian. Home: 9060 Pickwick Dr Indianapolis IN 46260-1714 Office: Lilly Endowment 2800 N Meridian St Indianapolis IN 46208-4713

LOGA, SANDA, physicist, educator; b. Bucharest, Romania, June 13, 1932; came to U.S., 1968; d. Stelian and Georgeta (Popescu) L.; m. Karl Heinz Werther, Mar. 1968 (div. 1970); m. Radu Zaciu, 1996. MS in Physics, U. Bucharest, 1955; PhD in Biophysics, U. Pitts., 1978. Asst. prof. faculty medicine and pharmacy, Bucharest, 1963-67; rsch. asst. Presbyn./St. Luke's Hosp., Chgo., 1968-69; assoc. rsch. scientist Miles Labs., Elkhart, Ind., 1969-70; rsch. asst. U. Pitts., 1971-78; rsch. assoc. Carnegie-Mellon U., Pitts., 1978-80; health physicist VA Med. Ctr., Westside, Chgo., 1980; med. physicist, VA Med. Ctr. N. Chgo, 1980-97. Assoc. prof. Chgo. Med. Sch., N. Chgo., 1985-98. Mem. Am. Assn. Physicists in Medicine, Health Physics Soc. Office: Chgo Med Sch U Health Scis 3333 Green Bay Rd North Chicago IL 60064-3037

LOGAN, HENRY VINCENT, retired transportation executive; b. Phila., Nov. 7, 1942; s. Edward Roger and Alberta L.; m. Mary Genzano, Sept. 28, 1963; children: Michele Leah, Maureen Laura, Monica Lynn. BS in Commerce, DePaul U., 1975; M in Mgmt., Northwestern U., 1984. Successively supr. corp. acctg., asst. mgr. gen. acctg., mgr. gen. acctg., dir. corp. acctg. and taxes TTX Co., Chgo., 1962-70, contr., 1970-78, dir. fin. planning, 1978-83, mng. dir., fin. adminstr., 1983-85, CFO, v.p., 1985-88, sr. v.p. fleet mgmt., 1988-97. Bd. dirs. Calpro, Co., Mira Loma, Calif., RailGon Co., Chgo. Treas. TTX Co. Polit. Action Com., Chgo., 1980; vol Sch. Dist. 87 Task Force, Glen Ellyn, Ill., 1986. Hon. fellow U. Denver Intermodal Transp. Inst., 1999. Mem. Nat. Freight Transp. Assn., Intermodal Assn. N.Am. (chmn. legis. com. 1992-94), Rlwy. Supply Assn. (bd. dirs., treas., sec., v.p., chmn. fin. com., pres. 2001), Union League Club (mem. reception com. 1987-92, fin. com. 1993-95), Medinah (Ill.) Country Club, Willoughby Golf Club, Fla. Republican. Roman Catholic. Avocations: golf, music, reading, bicycling. Home: 4522 SE Waterford Dr Stuart FL 34997

LOGAN, JAMES KENNETH, lawyer, former federal judge; b. Quenemo, Kans., Aug. 21, 1929; s. John Lysle and Esther Maurine (Price) Logan; m. Beverly Jo Jennings, June 8, 1952; children: Daniel Jennings, Amy Logan Sliva, Sarah Logan Sherard, Samuel Price. AB, U. Kans., 1952; LLB magna cum laude, Harvard U., 1955. Bar: Kans. 1955, Calif. 1956. Law clk. U.S. Cir. Judge Huxman, 1955—56; with firm Gibson, Dunn & Crutcher, LA, 1956—57; asst. prof. law U. Kans., 1957—61, prof., dean Law Sch., 1961—68; ptnr. Payne and Jones, Olathe, 1968—77; judge U.S. Ct. Appeals (10th cir.), 1977—98; pvt. practice Logan Law Firm LLC, Olathe, 1998—2001, Foulston Siefkin LLP, Overland Park, 2002—. Ezra Ripley Thayer tchg. fellow Harvard Law Sch., 1961—62; vis. prof. U. Tex., 1964, Stanford U., 1969, U. Mich., 1976; sr. lectr. Duke U., 1987, 91, 93; commr. U.S. Dist. Ct., 1964—67; mem. U.S. Jud. Conf. Adv. Com. Fed. Rules of Appellate Procedure, 1990—97, chair, 1993—97. Author (with W.B. Leach): Future Interests and Estate Planning, 1961; author: Kansas Estate Administration, 5th edit., 1986; author: (with A.R. Martin) Kansas Corporate Law and Practice, 2d edit., 1979; author: The Federal Courts of the Tenth Circuit: A History, 1992, also articles. Candidate for U.S. Senate, 1968. Served with U.S. Army, 1947—48. Recipient Disting. Svc. citation, U. Kans., 1986, Francis Rawle award, ABA-ALI, 1990; scholar Rhodes, 1952. Mem.: ABA, Kans. Bar Assn., Order of Coif, Phi Delta Phi, Alpha Kappa Psi, Pi Sigma Alpha, Omicron Delta Kappa, Beta Gamma Sigma, Phi Beta Kappa. Democrat. Presbyterian. E-mail: jlogan@foulston.com.

LOGAN, JOSEPH PRESCOTT, lawyer; b. Topeka, Jan. 21, 1921; s. Joseph Glenn and Corinne (Ripley) L.; m. Yvonne Marie Westrate, July 17, 1943; children: John Daniel, Kathleen Elisabeth, Laurie Prescott. AB, Dartmouth Coll., 1942; LLB, Harvard U., 1948. Bar: Mo. 1948, U.S. Dist. Ct. Mo. 1948. Ptnr. Thompson Coburn, St. Louis, 1958—. Pres., chmn. bd. Ranken Jordan Home for Convalescent Crippled Children, St. Louis, 1968-93. Lt. USNR, 1942-46. Mem. ACLU (bd. mem. 1988, civil liberties award 1982), Noonday Club. Democrat. Congregationalist. Avocations: hiking, mountain climbing, sailing. Home: 36 S Gore Ave Saint Louis MO 63119-2910 Office: Thompson Coburn 1 Firstar Plz Saint Louis MO 63101-1643 E-mail: jlogan@thompsoncoburn.com.

LOGAN, SEAN D. state legislator; b. Salem, Ohio, Feb. 11, 1966; s. Robert C. and Dorothy (Hall) L.; m. Melissa Logan. BA, Muskingum Coll., 1988. Intern Legis. Svc. Commn., 1988; legis. aide Ho. Rep. Ohio State Congress, 1989-90, state reg. Dist. 3, 1990—. Recipient Friendship Pin Beaver Creek Lodge N FOP, Svc. award Columbiana County Fedn. Conservation Club, 1993, Ohio/W.Va. Pub. Svc. award Am. Heart Assn., 1996; named Regional Pub. Servant of Yr. Nat. Soc. Social Workers, 1993. Mem. Nat. Conf. State Legislators, Ohio Farm Bur. (hon.), Sons of Am. Legion (hon.), Ruritan Internat., Columbiana County Twp. Trustees and Clks. Assn. (hon.).

LOGGIE, JENNIFER MARY HILDRETH, medical educator, physician; b. Lusaka, Zambia, Feb. 4, 1936; arrived in U.S., 1964, naturalized, 1972; d. John and Jenny (Beattie). M.B., B.Ch., U. Witwatersrand, Johannesburg, South Africa, 1959. Intern Harare Hosp., Salisbury, Rhodesia, 1960-61; gen. practice medicine Lusaka, 1961-62; sr. pediatric house officer Derby Children's Hosp., also St. John's Hosp., Chelmsford, Eng., 1962-64; resident in pediatrics Children's Hosp., Louisville, 1964, Cin., 1964-65; fellow clin. pharmacology Cin. Coll. Medicine, 1965-67; mem. faculty U. Cin. Med. Sch., 1967—, prof. pediatrics, 1975-98, assoc. prof. pharmacology, 1972-77, prof. emeritus pediatrics, 1998—. Contbr. articles to med. publs.; editor Pediatric and Adolescent Hypertension, 1991. Grantee Am. Heart Assn., 1970-72, 89-90 Mem. Am. Pediatric Soc. (elected; Founder's award 1996), Midwest Soc. Pediatric Rsch. Episcopalian. Home: 1133 Herschel Ave Cincinnati OH 45208-3112

LOGIE, JOHN HOULT, mayor, lawyer; b. Ann Arbor, Mich., Aug. 11, 1939; s. James Wallace and Elizabeth (Hoult) L.; m. Susan G. Duerr, Aug. 15, 1964; children: John Hoult Jr., Susannah, Margaret Elizabeth. Student, Williams Coll., 1957-59; BA, U. Mich., 1961, JD, 1968; MS, George Washington U., 1966. Bar: Mich. 1969, U.S. Dist. Ct. (we. and ea. dists.) Mich. 1969, U.S. Ct. Appeals (6th cir.) 1987. Assoc. Warner, Norcross & Judd, Grand Rapids, Mich., 1969-74, ptnr., 1974—2001, of counsel, 2002—; mayor City of Grand Rapids, 1992—. Chmn. civil justice adv. group U.S. Dist. Ct. (we. dist.) Mich. 1995-99; program coord. condemnation law sect. Inst. CLE; guest lectr. Grand Rapids C.C., Grand Valley State U., Western Mich. U., Mich. State U.; bd. vis. Sch. Bus. and Pub. Mgmt. George Washington U, 1995—; instr. U.S. Naval Acad., 1964-66. Trustee Grand Valley State U. Found., 1998—; chmn. Clarke Hist. Libr./Ctrl. Mich. U., 2000—; pres. Grand Rapids PTA Coun., 1971-73, Heritage Hill Assn., 1976, pres., trustee, 1971-84; chmn. Grand Rapids Urban Homesteading Commn., 1975-80, Grand Rapids Hist. Commn., 1985-90, Grand Rapids/Kent County Sesquicentennial Com., 1986-88; mem. Headlee Blue Ribbon Commn., 1993-94, Mich. Workforce Investment Bd., 2002; v.p., bd. dirs. Goodwill Industries, Grand Rapids, 1973-79, Am. Cancer Soc., Grand Rapids, 1970-81; pres., trustee Hist. Soc. Mich., 1984-90. Lt. USN, 1961-66. Recipient Lifetime Achievement award Mich. Hist. Preservation Network, 2000. Mem. ABA (forum com. on healthlaw 1980—), Am. Health Lawyers Assn., Mich. Bar Assn. (chmn. condemnation com. real property sect. 1985-88), Grand Rapids Bar Assn. (dir. young lawyers sect. 1970), Mich. Soc. Hosp. Attys. (pres. 1976-77), Univ. Club (dir. 1979-82, pres. 1980-82), Peninsular Club, Williams Club (N.Y.C.). Avocations: motor cruising, hunting, fishing. Home: 601 Cherry St SE Grand Rapids MI 49503-4726 Office: Warner Norcross and Judd 111 Lyon St NW Ste 900 Grand Rapids MI 49503-2487 also: Office of Mayor 300 Monroe Ave NW Grand Rapids MI 49503-2206 E-mail: logiejh@wnj.com.

LOGRASSO, DON, state legislator, lawyer; b. Kansas City, Mo., May 31, 1951; m. Leelah Lograsso; children: Chad, Scott. BA, MA, JD, U. Mo. Bar: Mo. Mem. Mo. Ho. of Reps. Dist. 54, Jefferson City, 1991—. Mem. civil and criminal law, ethics, judiciary and state instn. and property coms. Address: 404 NE Stonewall Dr Blue Springs MO 64014-1759 Office: Mo Ho Rep House Post Office 201 W Capitol Ave Jefferson City MO 65101-1556

LOH, HORACE H. pharmacology educator; b. Canton, Republic China, May 28, 1936; BS, Nat. Taiwan U., Taipei, Republic China, 1958; PhD, U. Iowa, 1965. Lectr. dept. pharmacology U. Calif. Sch. Medicine, San Francisco, 1967; assoc. prof. biochem. Wayne State U., Detroit, 1968-70; lectr., rsch. assoc. depts. psychiatry, pharmacology Langley Porter Neuropsychiatric Inst. U. Calif. Sch. Medicine, San Francisco, 1970-72, assoc. prof. depts. psychiatry, pharmacology Langley Porter Neuropsychiatric Inst., 1972-75, prof. depts. psychiatry, pharmacology Langley Porter Neuropsychiatric Inst., 1975-88; prof., head dept. pharmacology U. Minn. Med. Sch., Mpls., 1989—, Frederick and Alice Stark prof., head dept. pharmacology, 1990—. Chmn. ann. meeting theme com. on receptors Fedn. Am. Socs. for Exptl. Biology, 1984; mem. exec. com. Internat. Narcotic Rsch. Conf., 1984—87, chair sci. program ann. meeting, 1986; mem. adv. com. Nat. Tsing Hua U. Inst. Life Scis., Taiwan, China, 1985—89; mem. exec. com. Com. on Problems of Drug Dependence, Inc., 1985—88; mem. sci. adv. coun. Nat. Found. for Addictive Diseases, 1987—; cons. U.S. Army R & D Dept. Def., 1980—84. Contbr. ; , editor (1 book) ; contbr. Recipient Career Devel. award, USPHS, 1973—78, 1978—83, Rsch. Scientist award, 1983—88, 1989—94, Humboldt award for sr. U.S. scientists, 1977. Mem.: We. Pharmacology Soc. (councilor 1980—83, pres. 1984—85), Soc. Chinese Bioscientists in Am. 1985—86, Am. Soc. Pharmacology and Exptl. Therapeutics (program com. 1976—86, trustee bd. publs. 1987—93, com. on confs. 1990—93), Am. Coll. Neuropsychopharmacology (honorific awards com. 1988—). Office: U Minn Med Sch Dept Pharm 6-120 Jackson Ha 321 Church St SE Minneapolis MN 55455-0250

LOH, ROBERT N. K. academic administrator, engineering educator; b. Lumut, Malaysia; arrived in Can., 1962, came to U.S., 1968; m. Annie Loh; children: John, Peter, Jennifer. BSc in Engring., Nat. Taiwan U., Taipei, 1961; MSc in Engring., U. Waterloo, Ont., Can., 1964, PhD, 1968. Asst. prof. U. Iowa, Iowa City, 1968-72, assoc. prof., 1973-78; prof. Oakland U., Rochester, Mich., 1978—, John F. Dodge prof., 1984—, assoc. dean, 1985-98, dir. Ctr. for Robotics and Advanced Automation, 1984—. Mem. editorial bd. Info. Systems, 1975—, Jour. of Intelligent and Robotic Systems, 1987—, Asia-Pacific Engring. Jour., 1990—; contbr. over 190 jour. publs. and tech. reports. Recipient numerous research grants and contracts from Dept. Def., NSF and pvt. industry. Mem. IEEE, Soc. Machine Intelligence (bd. dirs. 1985—), Assn. Unmanned Vehicle Systems, 1987—, Sigma Xi, Tau Beta Pi. Office: Oakland U Ctr for Robotics and Advanced Automation Dodge Hall Engring Rochester MI 48309-4401

LOKEN, JAMES BURTON, federal judge; b. Madison, Wis., May 21, 1940; s. Burton Dwight and Anita (Nelson) Loken; m. Caroline Brevard Hester, July 30, 1966; children: Kathryn Brevard, Kristina Ayres. BS, U. Wis., 1962; LLB magna cum laude, Harvard U., 1965. Law clk. to chief judge Lumbard U.S. Ct. Appeals (2d Cir.), N.Y.C., 1965—66; law clk. to assoc. justice Byron White U.S. Supreme Ct., Washington, 1966—67; assoc. atty. Faegre & Benson, Mpls., 1967—70, ptnr., 1973—90; gen. counsel Pres.'s Com. on Consumer Interests, Office of Pres. of U.S., Washington, 1970; staff asst. Office of Pres. of U.S., 1970—72; judge U.S. Ct. Appeals (8th cir.), St. Paul, 1991—. Editor: Harvard Law Rev., 1964—65. Mem.: Minn. State Bar Assn., Phi Kappa Phi, Phi Beta Kappa. Avocations: golf, running. Office: US Courthouse 300 S 4th St Ste 11W Minneapolis MN 55415-0848

LOMAS, LYLE WAYNE, agricultural research administrator, educator; b. Monett, Mo., June 8, 1953; s. John Junior and Helen Irene Lomas; m. Connie Gail Frey, Sept. 4, 1976; children: Amy Lynn, Eric Wayne. BS, U. Mo., 1975, MS, 1976; PhD, Mich. State U., 1979. Asst. prof., animal scientist S.E. Agrl. Rsch. Ctr., Kans. State U., Parsons, 1979-85, assoc. prof., 1985-92, prof., 1992—, head, 1985—. Contbr. articles to refereed sci. jours. Mem. Am. Soc. Animal Sci., Am. Registry Profl. Animal Scientists, Am. Forage and Grassland Coun., Rsch. Ctr. Adminstrs. Soc. (bd. dirs. 1993—, sec. 1999-2000, 2d v.p. 2000-01, v.p. 2001-02, pres. 2002-03), Rotary (bd. dirs. Parsons 1992—96 v.p. 1994-95, pres. 1995-96), Phi Kappa Phi, Gamma Sigma Delta. Presbyterian. Achievements include research in ruminant nutrition, forage utilization by grazing stocker cattle. Home: 24052 Douglas Rd Dennis KS 67341-9014 Office: Kans State U SE Agrl Rsch Ctr PO Box 316 Parsons KS 67357-0316 E-mail: llomas@oznet.ksu.edu.

LOMBARD, ARTHUR J. judge; b. N.Y.C., Nov. 30, 1941; s. Maurice and Martha (Simons) L.; m. Frederica Koller, Aug. 18, 1968; children: David, Lisa. BS in Acctg. magna cum laude, Columbia U., 1961; JD, Harvard U., 1964. Bar: N.Y. 1964, U.S. Ct. Appeals (2d cir.) 1965, U.S. Supreme Ct. 1970, U.S. Ct. Appeals (6th cir.) 1972, Mich. 1976. Law clk. to J. Edward Lumbard chief judge U.S. Ct. Appeals (2d cir.), N.Y.C., 1964-65; teaching fellow law sch. Harvard U., Cambridge, Mass., 1965-66; instr. Orientation Program in Am. Law, Assn. Am. Law Schs., Princeton, N.J., 1966; prof. law Wayne State U., Detroit, 1966-87, assoc. dean law, 1978-85; prof. Detroit Coll. Law, 1987-94, dean, chief adminstrv. officer, 1987-93; judge Wayne County (Mich.) Cir. Ct., 1994—. Chmn. revision of Mich. class action rule com. Mich. Supreme Ct., 1980-83; reporter rules com. U.S. Dist. Ct. (ea. dist.) Mich., 1978-94. Contbr. articles to profl. jours. Mem. Mich. Civil Rights Comm., 1990-94, co-chmn., 1992-93, chmn. 1993-94. Office: 1913 City County Bldg Detroit MI 48226

LOMBARDI, CORNELIUS ENNIS, JR. lawyer; b. Portland, Oreg., Feb. 12, 1926; s. Cornelius Ennis and Adele (Volk) L.; m. Ann Vivian Foster, Nov. 24, 1954; children— Cornelius Ennis, Gregg Foster, Matthew Volk. BA, Yale, 1949; JD, U. Mich., 1952. Bar: Mo. Since practiced in, Kansas City, Mo.; mem. firm Blackwell, Sanders, Matheny, Weary & Lombardi, 1957-92, of counsel. Former pres. Kansas City Mus. Assn., Estate Planning Coun. of Kansas City; trustee Pembroke Country Day Sch.; chmn. soc. of fellows Nelson Gallery Found.; bd. dirs., Mo. Parks Assn. Mem.: Kansas City Country Club, Order of Coif, Phi Alpha Delta. Home: 5049 Wornall Rd Kansas City MO 64112-2423 Office: 2 Pershing Sq 2300 Main St Ste 1100 Kansas City MO 64108-2416

LOMBARDI, FREDERICK MCKEAN, lawyer; b. Akron, Ohio, Apr. 1, 1937; s. Leonard Anthony and Dorothy (McKean) L.; m. Margaret J. Gessler, Mar. 31, 1962; children: Marcus M., David G., John A., Joseph F. BA, U. Akron, 1960; LLB, Case Western Res., 1962. Bar: Ohio 1962, U.S. Dist. Ct. (no. and so. dists.) Ohio 1964, U.S. Ct. Appeals (6th cir.) 1966. Prin., shareholder Buckingham, Doolittle & Burroughs, Akron, 1962—, chmn. comml. law and litigation dept., 1989-99. Bd. editors Western Res. Law Rev., 1961-62. Trustee, mem. exec. com., v.p. Ohio Ballet, 1985-93; trustee Walsh Jesuit H.S., 1987-90; life trustee Akron Golf Charities, NEC World Series of Golf; bd. mem. Summa Health Sys. Found., Downtown Akron Partnership, St. Hilary Parish Found. Mem. Ohio Bar Assn. (coun. of dels. 1995-97), Akron Bar Assn. (trustee 1991-94, 97-2000, v.p., pres.-elect 1997-98, pres. 1998-99), Case Western Res. U. Law Alumni Assn. (bd. govs. 1995-98), Case Western Res. Soc. Benchers, Fairlawn Swim and Tennis Club (past pres.), Portage Country Club, Pi Sigma Alpha. Democrat. Roman Catholic. Office: Buckingham Doolittle & Burroughs 50 S Main St Akron OH 44308-1828 E-mail: flombardi@bdblaw.com.

LOMBARDO, PHILIP JOSEPH, broadcasting company executive; b. Chgo., June 13, 1935; s. Joseph Pete and Josephine (Franco) L.; m. Marilyn Ann Tellefsen, June 22, 1963; children: Dean, Jeffrey. Student, U. Ill., 1953-55; BA in Speech, Journalism and Radio/TV, postgrad. speech, U. Mo., 1958; grad. advanced mgmt. program, Harvard U., 1976. Account exec. Sta. WWCA, Ind., 1959-60; producer-dir. Sta. WBBM-TV, Chgo., 1960-65; program mgr., acting gen. mgr. Sta. WLWT, Cin., 1965-67; v.p., gen. mgr. Sta. WGHP-TV, N.C., 1968-73; pres., chief exec. officer Corinthian Broadcasting Corp., N.Y.C., 1973-82; chmn., pres., chief exec. officer Champlain Communications Corp., 1982-84; mng. gen. ptnr. Citadel Communications Co. Ltd., 1982—; chmn., pres., chief exec. officer Citadel Communications, Co. Ltd., C.C.C. Communications Corp., Lombardo Communications II, Inc., P.J.L. Investments, Inc., 1984—; mng. gen. ptnr., nat. sales rep. U.S. and Can. TV stas. Can. Communications Co., Toronto, 1985—; mng. gen. ptnr. Coronet Communications Co., N.Y.C., 1985—, Capital Comm. Co., Inc., 1994—, Citadel Comm., LLC, 1995—. Bd. dirs. The Gabelli Group, The Lynch Corp., N.Y.C. Mem. adv. bd. Salvation Army; com. budget, bd. dirs. United Fund; mem. com. High Point (N.C.) United Schs.; 1st vice chmn. Central Carolina chpt. Nat. Multiple Sclerosis Soc., 1968-73; bd. dirs. High Point Arts Council, 1968-73. Served with AUS, 1959, 62. Recipient Disting. Svc. award Freedom Found., Am. Legion, High Point (N.C.) Youth Coun. Mem. Dirs. Guild Am., Internat. Radio and TV Soc. (bd. govs.). Clubs: Winged Foot Golf, Marco Polo, Board Room, Bronxville Field, Chgo. Press. Lodges: Rotary, Kiwanis. Home: 24 Masterton Rd Bronxville NY 10708-4804 Office: Citadel Comm Co 99 Pondfield Rd Bronxville NY 10708-3902 E-mail: citnyltd@aol.com.

LONDON, TERRY, former state legislator; b. Apr. 15, 1940; married 1980. Rep. Mich. Ho. of Rep., 1985-86, state rep. Dist. 81, 1988-98; chmn. St. Clair County Rep. Com. Home: 1020 Illinois St Marysville MI 48040-1575

LONERGAN, ROBERT C. financial executive; b. Conn., 1943; BSBA in Fin., Georgetown U.; MBA, Case Western Res. U. Mgmt. positions GE Plastics; pres. Reb Plastics; pres. window group Owens Corning, 1993, pres. sci. and tech. ops., 1995, v.p., pres. bldg. materials Europe and Africa, 1998, sr. v.p. strategic resources. Office: Owens Corning One Owens Corning Pkwy Toledo OH 43659

LONEY, MARY ROSE, airport administrator; Planning svcs. mgr. McCarran Internat. Airport, Las Vegas, Nev., 1979-84; asst. aviation dir. Albuquerque Internat. Airport, 1984-86; asst. dir. aviation San Jose (Calif.) Internat. Airport, 1986-89; first dep. commr. aviation Chgo. Airport Sys., 1989-92; dep. exec. dir. fin. and adminstrn. Dallas/Ft. Worth Internat. Airport, 1992-93; dir. aviation Phila. Internat. Airport, 1993-96; commr. avication Chgo. Midway Airport, 1996—. Lectr. in field. Named Santa Clara County Woman of Achievement, 1988, Woman of Yr., Phila. Customs Brokers and Freight Forwarders Assn., 1994, one of State Pa. Honor Roll of Women, 1996; recipient YWCA's Tribute to Women in Industry award, 1989, Bus. Woman of Yr. award Great Valley Regional C. of C., 1994, Transp. award March of Dimes, 1995. Mem. FAA (appointed rsch. engring. and devel. adv. com.), Am. Assn. Airport Execs. (nat. bd. dirs., chmns. award 1994), St. Joseph's U. (bd. trustees). Office: Chgo Midway Airport Mgr's Office 5700 S Cicero Ave Chicago IL 60638-3831

LONG, CLARENCE WILLIAM, accountant; b. Hartford City, Ind., Apr. 17, 1917; s. Adam and Alice (Weschke) L.; m. Mildred Bernhardt, Aug. 8, 1940; children: William Randall, David John, Bruce Allen. B.S., Ind. U., 1939. With Ernst & Young, Indpls., 1939-78, ptnr., 1953-78, ret., 1978. Mem. econ. exec. com. Gov. Ind., 1968-73. Mem. nat. budget and consultation com. United Way of Am., 1968-70; bd. dirs. United Fund Greater Indpls., 1966—, treas., 1968—; bd. dirs. Jr. Achievement, Ind., 1966-67; mem. exec. com. Nat. Jr. Achievement, 1966-67; mem. fin. com. Indpls. Hosp. Devel. Assn., 1966-67; trustee Ind. U., 1975-84; trustee Art Assn. Indpls., pres., 1977-86; mem. adv. com. to dir. NIH, 1986-92. Mem. Am. Inst. C.P.A.'s (council 1959-62), Ind. Assn. C.P.A.'s, Nat. Assn. Accountants, Ind. C. of C. (dir.), Delta Chi, Beta Alpha Psi, Alpha Kappa Psi. Republican. Lutheran. Clubs: Woodstock (Indpls.) (dir. 1958-60), Columbia (Indpls.) (dir. 1971-77, pres. 1976), Royal Poinciana Golf Club (Naples, Fla.). Home: 607 Somerset Dr W Indianapolis IN 46260-2924 Office: 1 Indiana Sq Indianapolis IN 46204-2004

LONG, DAVID C. state legislator, lawyer; m. Melissa Long; children: Adam, Erik. BA, U. Calif.-Davis; JD, U. Santa Clara. Gen. counsel Pizza Hut of Ft. Wayne, Inc.; mem. Ind. Senate, Indpls., 1996—, ranking mem. commerce and consumer affairs com., mem. corrections, criminal and civil procedures com., former mem. jud. com., mem. pensions and labor com. Mem. Ft. Wayne Plan Commn., Urban Enterprise Zone Bd., Ft. Wayne; former mem. cable TV negotiation team City of Ft. Wayne; former mem. Ft. Wayne City Coun., 1988-95; mem. Utility Privatization Study Com.; bd. dirs. Arts United. Office: 200 W Washington St Indianapolis IN 46204-2728

LONG, EDWIN TUTT, surgeon; b. St. Louis, July 23, 1925; s. Forrest Edwin and Hazel (Tutt) L.; m. Mary M. Hull, Apr. 16, 1955; children: Jennifer Ann, Laura Ann, Peter Edwin. AB, Columbia U., 1944, MD, 1947. Diplomate Am. Bd. Surgery, Am. Bd. Thoracic Surgery. Rotating intern Meth. Hosp., Bklyn., 1947-478; surg. intern U. Chgo. Clinics, 1948-49, resident in gen. surgery, 1952-55, resident in thoracic surgery, 1955-57; asst. prof. surgery U. Chgo., 1957-59; thoracic and cardiovasc. surgeon, chief surgery dept. Watson Clinic, Lakeland, Fla., 1960-69; assoc. prof. surgery U. Pa., Phila., 1970-73; thoracic and cardiovasc. surgeon Allegheny Cardiovasc. Surg. Assocs., Pitts., 1973-88; exec. v.p. Mailings Clearing House and Roxbury Press, Inc., 1988-90, pres., 1990-96, chmn. bd. dirs., 1991—. Dir. Watson Clinic Rsch. Found., 1965-69; with Physicians Nat. Health Program, 1999—; bd. dirs. Roxbury Press, Inc., Cardiac Telecom, Inc., Pitts.; Disting. lectr., curriculum advisor healthcare leadership program Herzberg Sch. Mgmt., Rockhurst U., 2001—. Patentee gas sterilizer, 1969. Mem. bd. regents Rockhurst U., 2000—. Capt. USAF, 1950-52. Pressure Vectorography rsch. grantee Alfred P. Sloan Found., 1963; Nelson-Atkins Mus. fellow, 1997—. Mem. ACS, Am. Coll. Cardiology, Internat. Soc. for Cardiovasc. Surgery, Nat. Assn. Pacing and Electrophysiology (charter), Allegheny Vascular Soc. (pres. 1987), Ea. Vascular Soc. (founding mem.), Soc. Thoracic Surgery (founding mem.), Midwest Bioethics Ctr., Kansas City Concensus, Woodside Club, Rotary, Sigma Xi, Beta Theta Pi. Home: 4550 Warwick Blvd # 1204 Kansas City MO 64111-7725 Office: 4550 Warwick Blvd # 1209 Kansas City MO 64111 also: Roxbury Press Inc 601 E Marshall St Sweet Springs MO 65351-0295 E-mail: elongmd@kc.rr.com.

LONG, ELIZABETH L. state legislator, small business owner; m. Kent Long; children: Amie, Dana, Sarah. Student, Drury Coll. County clk. Laclede County, Mo., 1982-90; owner, mgr. retail gift shop, Lebanon; mem. Mo. Ho. of Reps. Dist. 146, Jefferson City, 1991—. Mem. election fed.-state rels. and vet. affairs, fees and salaries, state parks, recreation and natural resources and tourism, recreation and cultural affairs coms. Mem. Lebanon Area Found. Mem. Lebanon C. of C. Republican. Office: Rm 201E State Capitol Jefferson City MO 65101

LONG, GARY, former insurance company executive; CFO Northwestern Mutual Life, Milw. Office: Northwestern Mutual Life 720 E Wisconsin Ave Milwaukee WI 53202-4703

LONG, HELEN HALTER, writer, educator; b. St. Louis, Nov. 19, 1906; d. Charles C. and Ida (May) Halter; m. Forrest E. Long, June 22, 1944. AB, Washington U., St. Louis, 1927, AM, 1928; PhD, NYU, 1937. Grad. fellow Washington U., 1927-28; tchr. social studies Venice, Ill., 1928-30; asst. prof. social sci. N.Y. State Coll. for Tchrs., Albany, 1930-38; tchr. pub. schs. Mamaroneck, N.Y., 1938-42; prin. elem. and jr. high schs., 1942-54; asst. supt. schs., 1954-61; dir. Inst. Instructional Improvement, N.Y.C., 1962-88; pres. Books of World, Sweet Springs, Mo., 1962-86, Roxbury Press, Sweet Springs, 1988-93, also bd. dirs., 1963-96, bd. dirs. emeritus, 1997—. Teaching fellow, instr. Sch. Edn. NYU, 1936-43; assoc. editor Clearing House, 1935-55. Author: Society in Action, 1936, National Safety Council Lesson Units, 1944-52, (with Forrest E. Long) Social Studies Skills, 8th edit, 1976 (with Forrest E. Long). Mem. Phi Beta Kappa, Pi Gamma Mu, Kappa Delta Pi, Alpha Xi Delta (Diamond Jubilee Outstanding Women award 1968) Home: The Gatesworth One McKnight Pl Apt 155 Saint Louis MO 63124 Office: Roxbury Press Inc 601 E Marshall Sweet Springs MO 65351-0295

LONG, JAN MICHAEL, judge; b. Pomeroy, Ohio, May 31, 1952; s. Lewis Franklin and Dorothy (Clatworthy) L.; m. Susan Louise Custer, May 12, 1978; children: John D., Justin M., Jason M. BA, Ohio State U., 1974; JD, Capital U., 1979. Adminstrv. asst. Congressman Doug Applegate, Washington, 1974-77; asst. prosecuting atty. Pickaway County, Circleville, Ohio, 1979-80; mem. Ohio State Senate, Columbus, 1987-97; asst. minority whip Ohio Senate, 1995-97; juvenile/probate judge for Pickaway County Circleville, Ohio, 1997—. Named one of Outstanding Young Men Am. U.S. Jaycees, 1987. Mem. Pickaway County Bar Assn. (treas. 1985-86, sec. 1986-87). Democrat. Home: 522 Glenmont Dr Circleville OH 43113-1523 Office: Juvenile Ct 207 S Court St Circleville OH 43113-1648

LONG, JOHN PAUL, pharmacologist, educator; b. Albia, Iowa, Oct. 4, 1926; s. John Edward and Bessie May L.; m. Marilyn Joy Stookesberry, June 11, 1950; children: Jeff, John, Jane. B.S., U. Iowa, 1950, M.S., 1952, Ph.D., 1954. Research scientist Sterling Winthrop Co., Albany, N.Y., 1954-56; asst. prof. U. Iowa, Iowa City, 1956-58, asso. prof., 1958-63, prof. pharmacology, 1963—, head dept., 1970-83. Author 315 research publs. in field. Served with U.S. Army, 1945-46. Recipient Abel award Am. Pharm. Assn., 1958; Ebert award Pharmacology Soc., 1962 Mem. Am. Soc. Pharm. Exptl. Therapy, Soc. Exptl. Biol. Medicine. Republican. Home: 1817 Kathlin Dr Iowa City IA 52246-4617 Office: U Iowa Coll Medicine Dept Pharmacology Iowa City IA 52242

LONG, ROBERT EUGENE, banker; b. Yankton, S.D., Dec. 5, 1931; s. George Joseph and Malinda Ann (Hanson) L.; m. Patricia Louise Glass, June 19, 1959; children: Malinda Ann, Robert Eugene, Jennifer Lynn, Michael Joseph. B.S. in Acctg., U. S.D., 1956; M.B.A., U. Mich., 1965; grad., Madison Grad. Sch. Banking, 1973, Nat. Comml. Lending Grad. Sch., U. Okla., 1977. Cert. comml. lender. Financial analyst Chrysler Corp., 1958-59; supr. finance Ford Motor Co., 1966-67; with First Wis. Bankshares Corp., Milw., 1967—, v.p. fin., 1973—; exec. v.p. 1st Wis. Fond du Lac, 1978—; dir. 1st Wis. Nat. Bank of, Southgate, Waukesha and Fond du Lac; exec. v.p., dir. West Allis State Bank, 1979-81, pres., dir., 1981—, chief exec. officer, 1983—; sr. v.p. adminstrn. Park Banks, 1987—; chmn., pres., CEO Robert E. Long & Assoc., L.L.C., 2002—. Speaker/chmn. banking seminars Am. Mgmt. Assn., 1970— Pres. local br. Aid Assn. Luth., 1970—, corp. bd. dirs., 1982—, vice chmn. bd., 1989—; pres. Mt. Carmel Luth. Ch., Milw., 1972; team capt. Re-elect Nixon campaign, 1972; bd. dirs. Luth. Social Svcs. of Wis. and Upper Mich., 1978—, chmn. bd., 1983—; bd. dirs. Luther Manor, 1981, Luther Manor Found., 1984, pres. bd. dirs. United Luth. Program for Aging, 1986—; bd. dirs. Wis. Inst. Family Medicine, 1985, pres., 1992—, elected corp. adv. coun., 1996; vice chmn. adv. coun. West Allis Meml. Hosp., 1993—; bd. dirs. Luth. Sem. Theology at Chgo., 1997. With USAF, 1951-52. Recipient Good Citizenship award Am. Legion, 1948 Mem. Wis. Assn. Family Practice (bd. dirs. 1992—), Wauwatosa C. of C. (bd. dirs. 1992—), Alpha Tau Omega. Lutheran. Clubs: Western Racquet (Elm Grove, Wis.) (dir. 1976—); Bluemound Golf and Country; Elmbrook Swim (pres. 1977-78). Lodges: Masons, Shriners, Jesters, Scottish Rite. Home and Office: N21w24052 Dorchester Dr Unit 6D Pewaukee WI 53072-4692 E-mail: PattyLou4@aol.com.

LONG, ROBERT M. newspaper publishing executive; m. June Long; children: Shannon, Bob. BBA, Dyke Coll. CPA, Ohio. From acct. to treas. and contr. Plain Dealer Pub. Co., Cleve., 1965-92, exec. v.p., 1992—. V.p. Plain Dealer Charities, Inc., Delcom, Inc. Trustee Dyke Coll., Cleve. Ballet, St. Vincent Quadrangle, Inc.; bd. dirs. Jr. Achievement; active Leadership Cleve., 1993. Mem. Internat. Newspaper Fin. Execs. (bd. dirs.), Ohio Soc. CPAs, Cleve. Treas. Club. Office: The Plain Dealer Pub Co 1801 Superior Ave E Cleveland OH 44114-2198

LONG, SARAH ANN, librarian; b. Atlanta, May 20, 1943; d. Jones Lloyd and Lelia Maria (Mitchell) Sanders; m. James Allen Long, 1961 (div. 1985); children: Andrew C., James Allen IV; m. Donald J. Sager, May 23, 1987. BA, Oglethorpe U., 1966; M in Librarianship, Emory U., 1967. Asst. libr. Coll. of St. Matthias, Bristol, Eng., 1970-74; cons. State Libr. Ohio, Columbus, 1975-77; coord. Pub. Libr. of Columbus and Franklin County, 1977-79; dir. Fairfield County Dist. Libr., Lancaster, Ohio, 1979-82, Dauphin County Libr. Sys., Harrisburg, Pa., 1982-85, Multnomah County Libr., Portland, Oreg., 1985-89; sys. dir. North Suburban Libr. Sys., Wheeling, Ill., 1989—. Chmn. Portland State U. Libr. Adv. Coun., 1987-89. Contbr. articles to profl. jours. Bd. dirs. Dauphin County Hist. Soc., Harrisburg, 1983-85, ARC, Harrisbiry, 1984-85; pres. Lancaster-Fairfield County YWCA, Lancaster, 1981-82; vice chmn. govt. and ednl. divsn. Lancaster-Fairfield County United, Lancaster, 1981-82; sec. Fairfield County Arts Coun., 1981-82; adv. bd. Portland State U., 1987-89; mentor Ohio Libr. Leadership Inst., 1993, 95. Recipient Dir.'s award Ohio Program in Humanities, columbus, 1982; Sarah Long Day established in her honor Fairfield County, Lancaster, Bd. Commrs., 1982. Mem. ALA (pres. 1999-2000, elected coun. 1993-97, chair Spectrum fund faising com. 2001—), Pub. Libr. Assn. (pres. 1989-90, chair legis. com. 1991-95, chair 1998, nat. conf. com. 1995-98), Ill. Libr. Assn. (pub. policy com. 1991-97, Librarian of Yr. award 1999), Ill. Libr. Sys. Dirs. Orgn. (pres. 2000—), North Suburban Libr. Found. (bd. dirs. 1995—). Office: N Suburban Libr Systems 200 W Dundee Rd Wheeling IL 60090-4750

LONG, SARAH ELIZABETH BRACKNEY, physician; b. Sidney, Ohio, Dec. 5, 1926; d. Robert LeRoy and Caroline Josephine (Shue) Brackney; m. John Frederick Long, June 15, 1948; children: George Lynas, Helen Lucille Corcoran, Harold Roy, Clara Alice Lawrence, Nancy Carol Sieber. BA, Ohio State U., 1948, MD, 1952. Intern Grant Hosp., Columbus, Ohio, 1952-53; resident internal medicine Mt. Carmel Med. Ctr., 1966-69, chief resident internal medicine, 1968-69; med. cons. Ohio Bur. Disability Determination, 1970—. Physician student health Ohio State U., Columbus, 1970-73; sch. physician Bexley (Ohio) City Schs., 1973-83; physician advisor to peer rev. Mt. Carmel East Hosp., Columbus, 1979-86, med. dir. employee health, 1981-96; physician cons. Fed. Black Lung program U.S. Dept. Labor, Columbus, 1979-98. Mem. AMA, Gerontol. Soc. Am., Ohio Hist. Soc., Ohio State Med. Assn., Franklin County Acad. Medicine, Alpha Epsilon Delta, Phi Beta Kappa. Home: 2765 Bexley Park Rd Columbus OH 43209-2231

LONG, THOMAS LESLIE, lawyer; b. Mansfield, Ohio, May 30, 1951; s. Ralph Waldo and Rose Ann (Cloud) L.; m. Peggy L. Bryant, Apr. 24, 1982. AB in Govt., U. Notre Dame, 1973; JD, Ohio State U., 1976. Bar: Ohio 1976, U.S. Dist. Ct. (so. dist.) Ohio 1976, U.S. Dist. Ct. (no. dist.) Ohio 1977, U.S. Ct. Appeals (6th cir.) 1978. Assoc. Alexander, Ebinger, Fisher, McAlister & Lawrence, Columbus, Ohio, 1976-82, ptnr., 1982-85, Baker & Hostetler, Columbus, 1985—. Mem. ABA, Ohio Bar Assn., Columbus Bar Assn., Fed. Bar Assn., Assn. Trial Lawyer Am. Democrat. Roman Catholic. Club: Capitol (Columbus). Home: 2565 Leeds Rd Columbus OH 43221-3613 Office: Baker & Hostetler 65 E State St Ste 2100 Columbus OH 43215-4260

LONG, WILLIS FRANKLIN, electrical engineering educator, researcher; b. Lima, Ohio, Jan. 30, 1934; s. Jesse Raymond and Cerelda Elizabeth (Stepleton) L.; m. Ginger Carol Miller; children: Andrew Mark, Kristin Kay, David Franklin. BS in Engrng. Physics, U. Toledo, 1957, MSEE, 1962; PhD, U. Wis., 1970. Registered profl. engr., Wis. Project engr. Doehler Jarvis div. Nat. Lead Co., Toledo, 1957, 59-60; instr. U. Toledo, 1962-66; mem. tech. staff Hughes Rsch. Labs., Malibu, Calif., 1969-73; asst., then assoc. prof. depts. extension engrng. and elec. engrng. U. Wis., Madison, 1973-80, prof., chair dept. extension engrng., 1980-83, prof. depts. engrng., profl devel. and elec. and computer engrng., 1985—, prof. emeritus, 2001—; dir. ASEA Power System Ctr., New Berlin, Wis., 1983-85. Prin. Long Assocs., Madison, 1973—; cons. Dept. Energy, Washington, 1978—, ABB Power Systems, Raleigh, N.C., 1985—. Editor EMTP Rev., 1987-91; contbr. articles to profl. jours.; patentee power switching. Mem. adv. com. energy conservation Wis. Dept. Labor, Industry and Human Rels., 1976-77; mem. rural energy mgmt. coun. Wis. Dept. Agrl., Trade and Comsumer Protection, 1999-2001; chmn. Wis. chpt. Sierra Club, 1977; pres. bd. dirs. Madison Urban Ministry, 1993-95. 2d lt. Signal Corps., U.S. Army, 1958. Recipient Disting. Engrng. Alumnus award U. Toledo, 1983, award of excellence U. Wis.-Extension, 1987; Sci. Faculty fellow NSF, 1966. Fellow IEEE (life, Meritorious Achievement in Continuing Edn. award 1991); mem. Internat. Conf. on Large High Voltage Electric Systems (expert advisor 1979—). Mem. United Ch. of Christ. Avocation: canoeing. Home: 125 N Hamilton St #9D Madison WI 53703 Office: U Wis 432 N Lake St Rm 737 Madison WI 53706-1415

LONGABERGER, TAMI, home decor accessories company executive; BBA in Mktg., Ohio State U., 1984. Joined Longaberger Co., Newark, 1984, pres., 1994, CEO. Trustee Ohio State U.; bd. dirs. John Glenn Inst. for Pub. Svc. and Pub. Policy. Named to Ohio Women's Hall of Fame; recipient Women Mean Business award. Mem. Direct Selling Assn. (chmn. bd. dirs.), Ohio Fed. Bus. and Profl. Women.

LONGENECKER, MARK HERSHEY, JR. lawyer; b. Akron, Ohio, Feb. 16, 1951; s. Mark Hershey and Katrina (Hetzner) L.; m. Ruth Rounding, June 17, 1978 (div.); children: Emily Irene, Mark Hershey III. BA, Denison U., 1973; JD, Harvard U., 1976. Bar: Ill. 1976, Ohio 1979. Atty. Lord, Bissell & Brook, Chgo., 1976-79; ptnr. Frost Brown Todd LLC (and predecessor firms), Cin., 1979—, chmn. bus.-corp. dept., 1996—2002. Dir. ST Publ. Inc. Bd. govs. Ohio Fair Plan Underwriting Assn., Columbus, 1989-92; dir. Seven Hills Neighborhood Houses, Cin., 1990-2001, Salvation Army, Cin., 2000—. Mem. Cin. Country Club, Queen City Club, Gyro Club, Harvard Club (Cin. pres. 1993-94). Office: Frost Brown Todd LLC 2500 PNC Ct 201 E 5th St Ste 2500 Cincinnati OH 45202-4182 E-mail: mlongenecker@fbtlaw.com.

LONGHOFER, RONALD STEPHEN, lawyer; b. Junction City, Kans., June 30, 1946; s. Oscar William and Anna Mathilda (Krause) L.; m. Elizabeth Norma McKenna; children: Adam, Nathan, Stefanie. BMus, U. Mich., 1968, JD, 1975. Bar: Mich. 1975, U.S. Dist. Ct. (ea. dist.) Mich., U.S. Ct. Appeals (6th cir.), U.S. Supreme Ct.; cert. chartered fin. analyst. Law clk. to judge U.S. Dist. Ct. (ea. dist.) Mich., Detroit, 1975-76; ptnr. Honigman, Miller, Schwartz & Cohn, 1976—, chmn. litigation dept., 1993-96. Co-author: Mich. Court Rules Practice-Evidence, 1998, Courtroom Handbook on Michigan Evidence, 2001, Michigan Court Rules Practice, 1998, Courtroom Handbook on Michigan Civil Procedure, 2001; editor Mich. Law Rev., 1974-75. Served with U.S. Army, 1968-72. Mem. ABA, Detroit Bar Assn., Fed. Bar Assn., U. Mich. Pres.' Club, Order of Coif, Phi Beta Kappa, Phi Kappa Phi, Pi Kappa Lambda. Home: 974 Penniman Ave Plymouth MI 48170 Office: Honigman Miller Schwartz & Cohn 2290 1st National Bldg Detroit MI 48226 E-mail: rsl@honigman.com.

LONGO, AMY L. lawyer; BSN, Creighton U., 1970, JD, 1979. Bar: Nebr. 1979. Ptnr. Ellick, Jones, Buelt, Blazek & Longo, Omaha. Mem. moot ct. bd., adj. asst. prof. law Coll. Medicine, U. Nebr., 1987—. Fellow Am. Bar Found.; mem. ABA (del. 1993), Nebr. State Bar Assn. (pres.-elect, ho. dels. 1984—, chair 1996), Omaha Bar Assn. Office: Ellick Jones Buelt Blazek & Longo 8805 Indian Hills Dr Ste 280 Omaha NE 68114-4077

LONGONE, DANIEL THOMAS, chemistry educator emeritus; b. Worcester, Mass., Sept. 16, 1932; s. Daniel Edward and Anne (Novick) L.; m. Janice B. Bluestein, June 13, 1954. B.S., Worcester Poly. Inst., 1954; Ph.D., Cornell U., 1958. Research fellow chemistry U. Ill., Urbana, 1958-59; mem. faculty dept. chemistry U. Mich., Ann Arbor, 1959—, assoc. prof., 1966-71, prof., 1971-87, emertius prof., 1988—. Cons. Gen. Motors Research Co., 1965-77 Am. Chem. Soc.-Petroleum Research Fund internat. fellow, 1967-68; Fulbright scholar, 1970-71 Mem. Am. Chem. Soc., Sigma Xi, Tau Beta Pi, Phi Lambda Upsilon. Home: 1207 W Madison St Ann Arbor MI 48103-4729 Office: U Mich 3533 Chemistry Ann Arbor MI 48109 E-mail: dtlongwfl@netscape.com.

LONGSTAFF, RONALD E. federal judge; b. 1941; BA, Kans. State Coll., 1962; JD, U. Iowa, 1965. Law clk. to Hon. Roy L. Stephenson U.S. Dist. Ct. (so. dist.) Iowa, 1965-67, clk. of ct., 1968-76, U.S. magistrate judge, 1976-91, fed. judge, 1991—; assoc. McWilliams, Gross and Kirtley, 1967-68. Adj. prof. law Drake U., 1973-76. Mem. Iowa State Bar Assn. (chmn. spl. commn. to revise Iowa exemption law 1968-70, mem. adv. com. 8th cir. ct. appeals 1988—). Office: US Dist Ct 422 US Courthouse 123 E Walnut St Des Moines IA 50309-2035

LONGWORTH, RICHARD COLE, journalist; b. Des Moines, Mar. 13, 1935; s. Wallace Harlan and Helen (Cole) L.; m. Barbara Bem, July 19, 1958; children: Peter, Susan. BJ, Northwestern U., 1957; postgrad., Harvard U., 1968-69. Reporter UPI, Chgo., 1958-60, parliamentary corr. London, 1960-65, corr. Moscow, 1965-68, Vienna, 1969-72, diplomatic corr. Brussels, 1972-76; econ. and internat. affairs reporter Chgo. Tribune, 1976-86, bus. editor, econ. columnist, 1987-88, chief European corr., 1988-91, sr. writer, 1991—2002, sr. corr., 2002—; internat. affairs commentator Sta. WBEZ-FM, Chgo., 1984—. Adj. prof. Northwestern U., 1998—, guest scholar, 2001. Author: Global Squeeze: The Coming Crisis for First-World Nations, 1998, Global Chicago, 2000. With U.S. Army, 1957-58. Nieman fellow, 1968-69; recipient award for econ. reporting U. Mo., 1978, 80, John Hancock, 1978, 79, 82, Gerald Loeb award for econ. reporting, 1979, Media award for econ. understanding Dartmouth Coll., 1979, award Inter-Am. Press Assn., 1979, Peter Lisagor award Sigma Delta Chi, 1979, Sidney Hillman award, 1985, Lowell Thomas award for travel writing, 1985, Beck award for fgn. corr., 1986, Domestic Reporting award, 1987, Overseas Press Club award, 1994, 97, Alumni Merit award Northwestern U., 2000. Mem. Coun. Fgn. Rels. N.Y., Chgo. Com. of Council Fgn. Rels., Assn. Am. Corrs. in London, Internat. Music Found. (dir.), Ednl. Found. for Nuclear Sci. (dir.). Office: Chicago Tribune 435 N Michigan Ave Chicago IL 60611-4066 E-mail: rlongworth@tribune.com.

LONNGREN, KARL ERIK, electrical and computer engineering educator; b. Milw., Aug. 8, 1938; s. Bruno Leonard and Edith Irene (Osterlund) L.; m. Vicki Anne Mason, Feb. 16, 1963; children: Sondra Lyn, Jon Erik. B.S. in Elec. Engring., U. Wis., 1960, M.S., 1962, Ph.D., 1964. Postdoctoral appointment Royal Inst. Tech., Stockholm, 1964-65; asst. prof. elec. engring. U. Iowa, Iowa City, 1965-67, assoc. prof., 1967-72, prof., 1972—. Vis. scientist Inst. Plasma Physics, Nagoya, Japan, 1972, Math Rsch. Ctr., Madison, 1976, Los Alamos (N.Mex.) Sci. Labs., 1979, 80, Inst. Space and Astron. Sci., Tokyo, 1981, Danish Atomic Energy, Riso, 1982, others. Author: Introduction to Physical Electronics, 1988, Electromagnetics with MATLAB, 1997; co-author: Introduction to Wave Phenomena, 1985; co-editor: Solitons in Action, 1978. Recipient Disting. Svc. citation U. Wis. Madison, 1992. Fellow Am. Phys. Soc., IEEE Presbyterian. Home: 21 Prospect Pl Iowa City IA 52246-1932 Office: U Iowa Dept Elec & Computer Engring Iowa City IA 52242 E-mail: lonngren@eng.uiowa.edu.

LOOK, DONA JEAN, artist; b. Port Washington, Wis., Mar. 30, 1948; m. Kenneth W. Loeber. BA, U. Wis., Oshkosh, 1970. Art tchr. Dept. Edn., NSW, Australia, 1976-78; ptnr. Look and Heaney Studio, Byron Bay, 1978-80; studio artist Algoma, Wis., 1980—. One person shows include Perimeter Gallery, Chgo., 1991; exhibited in group shows Perimeter Gallery, Chgo., 1983, 93, 94, Phila. Mus. Art, 1984, Civic Fine Arts Mus., Sioux Falls, S.D., 1985, Dacotah Prairie Mus., Aberdeen, S.D., 1985, Bergstrom-Mahler Mus., Neenah, Wis., 1985, Lawton Gallery, U. Wis.-Green Bay, 1985, J. B. Speed Art Mus., Louisville, 1986, Laguna (Calif.) Art Mus., Am. Craft Mus., N.Y.C., 1985, 86, 87, 89, Ark. Arts Ctr. Decorative Arts Mus., Little Rock, 1987, Cultural Ctr., Chgo., 1988, Erie (Pa.) Art Mus., 1988, Maine Crafts Assn., Colby Coll. Mus. Art, 1989, Ft. Wayne (Ind.) Mus. Art, 1989, The Forum, St. Louis, 1990, Palo Alto (Calif.) Cultural Ctr., 1990, Neville Pub. Mus., Green Bay, Wis., 1992, Waterloo (Iowa) Mus. Art, 1993, Sybaris Gallery, Royal Oak, Mich., 1993, 95, Sun Valley Ctr. for Arts and Humanities, Ketchum, Idaho, 1995, Nat. Mus. Am. Art, Smithsonian Instn., Washington, 1995; represented in permanent collections The White House Collection, Phila. Mus. Art, MCI Telecomms. Corp., Inc., Washington, Am. Craft Mus., N.Y.C., Ark. Arts Ctr., Little Rock, C. A. Wustum Mus. Fine Arts, Racine, Erie Art Mus.; works included in publs. The White House Collection of American Crafts, 1995, Craft Today: Poetry of the Physical, 1986, International Crafts, 1991, FIBERARTS Design Book Four, 1991, The Tactile Vessel, 1989, Creative Ideas for Living, 1988, The Basketmaker's Art: Contemporary Baskets and Their Makers, 1986. Recipient 1st prize award Phila. Craft Show, 1984, 2d prize award, 1985, Design award Am. Craft Mus., 1985, Craftsmen's award Phila. Craft Show, 1986; Nat. Endowment for Arts/Arts Midwest fellow, 1987, Nat. Endowment for Arts Fellowship grantee, 1988. Office: Perimeter Gallery 210 W Superior St Chicago IL 60610-3508

LOOMAN, JAMES R. lawyer; b. Vallejo, Calif., June 5, 1952; s. Alfred R. and Jane M. (Halter) L.; m. Donna G. Craven, Dec. 18, 1976; children: Alison Marie, Mark Andrew, Zachary Michael. BA, Valparaiso U., 1974; JD, U. Chgo., 1978. Bar: Ill, 1978, U.S. Dist. Ct. (no dist.) Ill. 1978, U.S. Claims Ct. 1979. Ptnr. Sidley Austin Brown & Wood, Chgo., 1986—. Fellow Am. Coll. Comml. Fin. Lawyers; mem. ABA, Chgo. Bar Assn., Chgo. Athletic Assn., Skokie Country Club, Mid-Day Club. Lutheran. Office: Sidley Austin Brown & Wood Bank One Plz Chicago IL 60603-2003 E-mail: jlooman@sidley.com.

LOOMIS, SALORA DALE, psychiatrist; b. Peru, Ind., Oct. 21, 1930; s. S. Dale Sr. and Rhea Pearl (Davis) L.; m. Carol Marie Davis, Jan 3, 1959; children: Stephen Dale, Patricia Marie. AB in Zoology, Ind. U., 1953, MS in Human Anatomy, 1955, MD, 1958. Diplomate Am. Bd. Psychiatry and Neurology. Intern Cook County Hosp., Chgo., 1958-59; resident in psychiatry Logansport (Ind.) State Hosp., 1959-60, Ill. State Psychiat. Inst., Chgo., 1960-62; staff psychiatrist Katharine Wright Psychiat. Clinic, 1962-65, dir., 1965-92. Cons. Ill. Youth Commn. 1962-64; instr. psychiatry Northwestern U. Med. Sch., Chgo., 1962-64, assoc. 1964-67; asst. dir. Northwestern U. Psychiat. Clinics, Chgo., 1963-65; attending psychiatrist St. Joseph Hosp., Chgo., 1964—; lectr. psychiatry and neurology Loyola U. Med. Sch. Chgo., 1964-65, assoc. 1965, asst. prof. 1965-73, lect. 1980-89, clin. assoc. prof., 1989—; psychiat. cons. Ill. Dept. Pub. Health, 1967—; sr. attending psychiatrist, chmn. dept. psychiatry Ill. Masonic Med. Ctr., Chgo. 1970-92, chmn. emeritus, 1992—; assoc. prof. psychiatry U. Ill. Coll. Medicine, Chgo., 1973—. Fellow Am. Coll. Psychiatrists, Am. Psychiat. Assn. (life), Acad. Psychosomatic Medicine; mem. AMA, Ill. State Med. Soc. (chmn. council on mental health and addiction 1974-75, chmn. joint peer rev. com. 1975-76), Ill. Psychiat. Soc. (chmn. ethics com. 1974-75, chmn. peer rev. com. 1976-78), Chgo. Med. Socs. Fax: 630-845-9145.

LOOP, FLOYD D. health, medical executive; b. Lafayette, Ind., Dec. 17, 1936; s. Floyd Addison and Marie D. L.; m. Bernadine P. Healy, Aug. 17, 1985; children: Alison, Frederick, Kendall, Bartlett, Marie. BS, Purdue U., 1958; MD, George Washington U., 1962. Diplomate: Am. Bd. Surgery, Am. Bd. Thoracic Surgery. Intern, resident in gen. surgery George Washington U., 1962-64, chief resident, 1967-68; fellow in cardiac surgery Cleve. Clinic Found., 1968-70, staff surgeon thoracic and cardiovascular surgery, 1971-75, chmn. dept. thoracic and cardiovascular surgery, 1975-89, chmn. bd. govs., chief exec. officer, 1990—; bd. dirs. Tenet Healthcare, Santa Barbara, 1999—. Trustee Healthcare Leadership Coun. Mem. Editorial bd. Jour. Thoracic and Cardiovascular Surgery, 1979-85, Am. Jour. Cardiology, 1978-83, Am. Heart Jour, 1980— , Clin. Cardiology, 1979— , Jour. Cardiac Surgery, 1986— , Jour. Cardiothoracic Anesthesia, 1986— , Cleve. Clinic Jour. Medicine, Perfusion. With M.C. USAF, 1964-66. Decorated Brazilian Order of Merit Fellow ACS (adv. council for cardiothoracic surgery 1986—), Am. Coll. Cardiology (Theodore and Susan B. Cummings Humanitarian award 1975); mem. Am. Assn. Thoracic Surgery (treas. 1984—, mem. council 1984—), Am. Surg. Assn., Soc. Thoracic Surgeons, Am. Coll. Chest Physicians (bd. regents 1986—), Thoracic Surgery Dirs. Assn., Am. Heart Assn. (exec. com. of council on cardiovascular surgery 1985—, Paul Dudley White citation for internat. service 1980), Am. Soc. Artificial Internal Organs Soc. Vascular Surgery. Office: Cleve Clinic Found 1 Clinic Ctr 9500 Euclid Ave Cleveland OH 44195-0001

LOORY, STUART HUGH, journalist; b. Wilson, Pa., May 22, 1932; s. Harry and Eva (Holland) L.; m. Marjorie Helene Dretel, June 19, 1955 (div. July 1995); children: Joshua Alan, Adam Edward, Miriam Beth; m. Nina Nikolaevna Kudriavtseva, Aug. 17, 1995. B.A., Cornell U., 1954; M.S. with honors, Columbia U., 1958; postgrad., U. Vienna, Austria, 1958. Reporter Newark News, 1955-58, N.Y. Herald Tribune, 1959-61, sci. writer, 1961-63, Washington corr., 1963-64, fgn. corr., 1964-66; sci. editor Metromedia Radio Stas., 1962-64, Moscow corr., 1964-66; sci. writer N.Y. Times, 1966; White House corr. Los Angeles Times, 1967-71; fellow Woodrow Wilson Internat. Center for Scholars, Washington, 1971-72; exec. editor WNBC-TV News, 1973; Kiplinger prof. pub. affairs reporting Ohio State U., Columbus, 1973-75; assoc. editor Chgo. Sun-Times, 1975-76, mng. editor, 1976-80; v.p., mng. editor Washington bur. Cable News Network, 1980-82, Moscow bur. chief, 1983-86, sr. correspondent, 1986, exec. producer, 1987-90; exec. dir. internat. rels. Turner Broadcasting System, Inc., Atlanta, 1988—; editor-in-chief CNN World Report, 1990-91; v.p. CNN, 1990-95; exec. v.p. Turner Internat. Broadcasting, Russia, 1993-97; v.p., supervising prodr. Turner Original Prodns., 1995. Lee Hills chair of free press studies U. Mo., Columbia, 1997—; lectr. in field. Author: (with David Kraslow) The Secret Search for Peace in Vietnam, 1968, Defeated: Inside America's Military Machine, 1973, (with Ann Imse) Seven Days That Shook the World: The Collapse of Soviet Communism, 1991; Editor IPI Report (Internat. Press Inst.), 1998—, IPI Global Journalist, 1999—; contbr. articles mags. and encys. Recipient citation Overseas Press Club, 1966; Raymond Clapper award Congl. Press Gallery, 1968; George Polk award L.I.U., 1968; Du Mont award U. Calif. at Los Angeles, 1968; Distinguished Alumni award Columbia, 1969; 50th Anniversary medal Columbia Sch. Journalism, 1963; Edwin Hood award for diplomatic corr. Nat. Press Club, 1987; Pulitzer traveling scholar, 1958. Jewish. Office: U Mo Sch Journalism 132A Neff Annex Columbia MO 65211-1200 E-mail: loorys@missouri.edu.

LOPATIN, DENNIS EDWARD, immunologist, educator; b. Chgo., Oct. 26, 1948; s. Leonard Harold and Cynthia (Shifrin) L.; m. Marie S. Ludmer, June 6, 1971 (div. 1983); 1 child, Jeremy; m. Constance Maxine McLeod, July 24, 1983. BS, U. Ill., 1970, MS, 1972, PhD, 1974. Postdoctoral fellow Northwestern U. Med. Sch., Chgo., 1974-75; rsch. scientist U. Mich., Ann Arbor, 1976-90, prof., 1982—. Contbr. articles to sci. jours. Mem. Am. Assn. Immunologists, Am. Soc. Microbiology, Internat. Assn. Dental Rsch., Sigma Xi. Office: U Mich Sch Dentistry 1011 N University Ave # 1078 Ann Arbor MI 48109-1078 Error in get_biog_sketch for2197371ORA-20101: in exception SELECT EXTRACT2.MEMBERSHIP(2197371) FROM DUAL ORA-06502: PL/SQL: numeric or value error: character string buffer too small

LOPES, DAVEY, professional baseball manager; b. Providence, May 3, 1946; 1 child, Vanessa Lin. Grad., Washburn U., Topeka, 1969. Profl. baseball player Dodgers, Athletics, Cubs, Astros, 1972-87; dugout and first base coach Tex. Rangers, 1988-91; mgr. Ariz. Fall League; first base coach Balt. Orioles, 1992-94, San Diego Padres, 1995-99; mgr., head coach Milw. Brewers Baseball Club, 1999—. Office: Milw Brewers County Stadium PO Box 3099 Milwaukee WI 53201-3099*

LOPEZ-COBOS, JESUS, conductor; b. Toro, Spain, Feb. 25, 1940; m. Brigitte Elm, Aug. 13, 1998; 3 children. PhD in philosophy and music, U. Madrid, 1964; diploma composition, Madrid Conservatory, 1966; diploma conducting, Viennna (Austria) Acad., 1969. Gen. music dir. Deutsche Oper Berlin, 1981-90; prin. guest condr. London Philharm., 1981-86; prin. condr., artistic dir. Spanish Nat. Orch., 1984-89; music dir. Cin. Orch., 1986—2001, Orchestre de Chambre de Lausanne, Switzerland, 1990—2000, condr. Switzerland. Also condr. concerts Edinburgh Festival, London Symphony, Royal Philharm., N.Y. Philharm., L.A. Philharm., Chgo. Symphony, Cleve. Orch., Phila. Orch., Berlin Philharm., Berlin Radio Orch., Amsterdam Concertgebouw, Vienna Philharm., Swiss Romande, Muncih Philharm., Hamburg NDR, Oslo Philharm., Zurich Tonhalle, Israel Philharm., opera prodns. at Royal Opera House, Covent Garden, London, La Scala, Milan, Italy, Met. Opera, N.Y.C., Paris Opera, others; recs. include Lucia di Lammermoor New Philham. Orch., Otello, recital and operatic disc with José Carrera and London Symphony Orch., Liszt's Dante Symphony with Swiss Romande, Falla's Three-Cornered Hat, R-K Capricio Espangnole, Chiabrier's Espana with L.A. Philharm., others. Decorated iffucer Arts and Letters (France); recipient 1st prize Besancon Internat. Condr.'s Competition, 1969, Prince of Astrurias award Spanish Govt., 1981, 1st Class Disting. Svc. medal Fed. Republic of Germany, 1989, medalla Bellas Artes (Spain), 2001. Address: 8 Chemin Bellerive 1007 Lausanne Switzerland

LOPICCOLO, JOSEPH, psychologist, educator, author; b. L.A., Sept. 13, 1943; s. Joseph E. and Adeline C. (Russo) Lo P.; m. Leslie Joan Matlen, June 20, 1964 (div. 1978); 1 child, Joseph Townsend; m. Cathryn Gail Pridal, Dec. 20, 1980; 1 child, Michael James. BA with highest honors, UCLA, 1965; MS, Yale U., 1968, PhD, 1969. Lic. psychologist, Mo. Asst. prof. U. Oreg., Eugene, 1969-73; assoc. prof. U. Houston, 1973-74; prof. SUNY, Stony Brook, 1974-84, Tex. A&M U., College Station, 1984-87; prof. psychology U. Mo., Columbia, 1987—, chmn. dept., 1987-90. Vis. scholar Cambridge (Eng.) U., 1991. Author: Becoming Orgasmic, 1976, 2d edit., 1988, also book chpts.; editor: Handbook of Sex Therapy, 1978; contbr. numerous articles to profl. jours. Woodrow Wilson Found. fellow; NIH rsch. grantee, 1973-84 Fellow Am. Psychol. Assn.; mem. Internat. Acad. Sex Rsch., Soc. for Sci. Study of Sex (pres. 1983-84, Alfred Kinsey Meml. Rsch. award), Soc. for Sex Therapy and Rsch. (Masters and Johnson Rsch. award 1997), Phi Beta Kappa, Sigma Xi. Office: U Mo Dept Psychology 210 Mcalester Hall Columbia MO 65211-2500 E-mail: LoPiccoloJ@missouri.edu.

LOPRETE, JAMES HUGH, lawyer; b. Detroit, Sept. 17, 1929; s. James Victor and Effie Hannah (Brown) LoP.; m. Marion Ann Garrison, Sept. 11, 1952; children: James Scott, Kimberly Anne, Kent Garrison, Robert Drew. AB, U. Mich., 1951, JD with Distinction, 1953. Bar: Mich. 1954. Practiced law, Detroit, 1954—; atty. Chrysler Corp., 1953; assoc. firm Monaghan, LoPrete, McDonald, Yakima & Grenke, P.C. and predecessor firms, from 1954, mem. firm, 1966—, pres., 1979—. Bd. dirs. Drake's Batter Mix Co.; instr. legal writing Wayne State U., Detroit, 1955-57 Trustee U. Mich. Club of Detroit Scholarship Fund, 1967, pres., 1982—; trustee Samuel Westerman Found., 1971—, pres., 1984; trustee John R. & M. Margrite Davis Found.; pres. Louis & Nellie Sieg Found., 2000—, Frank G. and Gertrude Dunlap Found., 2001—. Fellow Am. Coll. Trust and Estate Counsel, Internat. Acad. Estate and Trust Law; mem. ABA, Oakland County bar assns., State Bar Mich., Detroit Athletic Club (dir. 1983-88, sec. 1986-88), Orchard Lake Country Club, U. Mich. of Greater Detroit (pres. 1966). Home: 2829 Warner Dr Orchard Lake MI 48324-2449 Office: Monaghan LoPrete McDonald et al 40700 Woodward Ave Ste A Bloomfield Hills MI 48304-5110 E-mail: monaghan@bignet.net.

LORCH, KENNETH F. lawyer; b. Indpls., July 24, 1951; BSBA, Washington U., 1973; JD, John Marshall Sch. Law, 1976. Bar: Ill. 1976, U.S. Dist. Ct. (no. dist.) Ill. 1977; CPA, Ill. Ptnr. Wildman, Harrold, Allen & Dixon, Chgo. Mem. planned giving adv. coun. Chgo. Symphony Orch.; pres. Chgo. bd. Am. Technion Soc.; mem. planned giving steering com. City of Hope; bd. dirs. Chgo. Coun. on Planned Giving, Coun. for Jewish Elderly; mem. profl. adv. com. Chgo. Cmty. Trust. Mem. Chgo. Bar Assn. (exec. com., Cook County Probate Ct. rules and forms com., mem. legis. com., mem. probate practice com. 1991, mem. trust law com., chmn. estate planning com., mem. young lawyers sect. 1983-85), Chgo. Estate Planning Coun., Jewish Fedn. Chgo. (past chair profl. adv. com.). Office: Wildman Harrold Allen & Dixon 225 W Wacker Dr Ste 3000 Chicago IL 60606-1224

LORENZ, JOHN DOUGLAS, college official; b. Talmage, Nebr., July 2, 1942; s. Orville George and Twila Lucille (Larson) L.; m. Alice Louise Hentzen, Aug. 26, 1967; 1 child, Christian Douglas. BS, U. Nebr., 1965, MS, 1967, PhD, 1973. Systems analyst U. Nebr., Lincoln, 1967-73; asst. prof. Kettering U., Flint, Mich., 1973-74, assoc. prof., 1974-78, prof., 1978—, dept. head, 1984-87, asst. dean, 1986-88, provost, dean faculty, 1988-92, Richard L. Terrell prof. acad. leadership, 1990—, v.p. for acad. affairs, provost, 1992—. Cons. GM, Detroit, 1973-82, various orgns. Contbr. articles to profl. jours. Judge Internat. Sci. and Engring. Fair, various locations, 1989—. Mem. NSPE, Soc. Mfg. Engrs. (sr.), So. Automotive Engrs., Accreditation Bd. for Engring. and Tech., Am. Soc. Engring. Edn., Antique Auto Racing Assn., Model Engine Collectors Assn., Antique Model Race Car Club. Home: 8165 Shady Brook Ln Flushing MI 48433-3007 Office: Kettering U 1700 W 3rd Ave Flint MI 48504-4898 E-mail: jlorenz@kettering.edu.

LORENZ, KATHERINE MARY, banker; b. Barrington, Ill., May 1, 1946; d. David George and Mary (Hogan) L. BA cum laude, Trinity Coll., 1968; MBA, Northwestern U., 1971; grad., Grad. Sch. for Bank Adminstrn., 1977. Ops. analyst Continental Bank, Chgo., 1968-69, supr. ops. analysis, 1969-71, asst. mgr. customer profitability analysis, 1971-73, acctg. officer, mgr. customer profitability analysis, 1973-77, 2d v.p., 1976, asst. gen. mgr. contr.'s dept., 1977-80, v.p., 1980, contr. ops. and mgmt. svcs. dept., 1981-84, v.p., sr. sector contr. retail banking, corp. staff and ops. depts., 1984-88, v.p., sr. sector contr. pvt. banking, centralized ops. and corp. staff, 1988-90, v.p., sr. sector contr. bus. analysis group/mgmt. acctg., 1990-94, mgr. contrs. dept. adminstrn. and tng., 1990-94; v.p., chief of staff to chief adminstrv. officer Bank Am. Ill., 1994-96, sr. v.p., mgr. adminstrv. svcs., 1996-97, mng. dir., mgr. adminstrv. svcs., 1998-99; sr. v.p., Chgo. adminstrn. exec. Bank Am., 1999—. Mem. Execs. Club Chgo., Trinity Coll. Alumnae Assn. (bd. dirs.). Office: Bank of Am 231 S La Salle St Rm 1320 Chicago IL 60604-1407

LORENZO, ALBERT L. academic administrator; BS, U. Detroit, 1965, MBA, 1966; LLD (hon.), Walsh Coll. Accountancy and Bus. Adminstrn., 1987. Asst. dir. housing U. Detroit, 1964-65; staff acct. McManus, McGraw and Co., Detroit, 1964-66; asst. prof. acctg. Macomb Community Coll., Warren, Mich., 1966-68, bus. mgr., 1968-74, contr., 1974-75, v.p. bus., 1975-79, pres., 1979—. Lectr., pub. speaker, presenter in field. Dir. rsch. SBA, 1966; mem. Mayor's Adv. Com. Small Bus., Detroit, 1967-70, base-community coun. Selfridge Air NG, 1978-86, steering com. March of Dimes, 1980-86, adv. coun. Met. Affairs Corp., 1982—, Mich. Competitive Enterprise Task Force, 1988-90, adv. bd. Nat. Inst. Leadership Devel., 1988—, Community Growth Alliance Macomb County, 1982—, selection panel Heart of Gold ann. awards Southeastern Mich. United Way, 1990; chair div. II United Found., 1981; apptd. commr. State Mich. High Edn. Facilties Authority, 1988-90; bd. dirs. N.E. Guidance Community Mental Health Ctr., 1976-79, Mich. Nat. Bank Macomb, 1981-87, Indsl. Tech. Inst., 1982—; trustee Nat. Commn. Coop. Edn., 1985—; trustee St. Joseph Hosp., 1984-87, sec. 1985-87, mem. adv. bd. 1981-83. Recipient Resolution of Tribute Mich. State Senate, 1979, Italian-Am. Citizen Recognition award, 1980, Volkswagen Am. Recognition award, 1982, Excellence in Speech Writing award Internat. Assn. Bus. Communicators, 1988, Nat. Leadership award U. Tex., 1989, Thomas J. Peters Nat. Leadership award, 1989; named Pres. of Yr. Am. Assn. Women in Community and Jr. Colls., 1985. Mem. Am. Assn. Community and Jr. Colls., World Future Soc., Met. Mus. Art, Mich. Community Coll. Assn., Econ. Club Detroit. Office: 14500 E 12 Mile Rd Warren MI 48088-3870

LORIE, JAMES HIRSCH, business administration educator; b. Kansas City, Feb. 23, 1922; s. Alvin J. and Adele (Hirsch) L.; m. Sally Rosen, June 16, 1948 (div. 1953); 1 child Susan; m. Nancy A. Wexler, June 19, 1958 (dec. 1966); stepchildren: Katherine Wexler, Jeffrey Wexler; m. Vanna Metzenberg Lautman, Aug. 27, 1967; stepchildren: Erika Lautman, Victoria Lautman, Karl Lautman. A.B., Cornell U., 1942, A.M., 1945; Ph.D., U. Chgo., 1947. Research asst. Cornell U., Ithaca, N.Y., 1944-45; mem. staff seminar Am. civilization Salzburg, Austria, 1947; mem. faculty U. Chgo. Grad. Sch. Bus., 1947-92, prof. bus. adminstrn., asso. dean, 1956-61; dir. Center Research in Security Prices, 1960-75. Cons. divsn. rsch. and statistics bd. govs. Fed. Res. Sys., 1950-52; cons. U.S. Treas. Dept., 1973-74; bd. dirs. Thornburg Mortgage Co., Inc., Chgo.; mem. Nat. Market Adv. Bd., 1975-77. Author: (with Harry V. Roberts) Basic Methods of Marketing Research, 1951, (with Richard A. Brealey) Modern Developments in Investment Management, 1972, (with Mary T. Hamilton) The Stock Market: Theories and Evidence, 1973; Contbr. articles to profl. jours. Served with USCGR, 1942-44. Mem. Am. Econ. Assn., Mont Pelerin Soc., Nat. Assn. Securities Dealers (dir. 1972-75), Phi Beta Kappa. Clubs: Arts (Chgo.); Quadrangle (U. Chgo.). Home: 2314 N Lincoln Park W Chicago IL 60614-3455

LOSEE, JOHN FREDERICK, JR. manufacturing executive; b. Milw., Apr. 27, 1951; s. John Frederick and Helen (Joslyn) L.; m. Jane Agnes Trawicki, Aug. 25, 1973; children: Nicole Marie, John Michael. BSME, Marquette U., 1973, MS in Indsl. Engring., 1982. Registered profl. engr., Wis.; cert. numerical control mgr., Wis. Mfg. engr. OMC-Evinrude div. Outboard Marine Corp., Milw., 1975-78, mfg. engr. supr., 1978-80, mgr. tool engring., 1980-85, mgr. process and tool engring., 1985-86, dir. mfg. engring., 1986-88; v.p. ops. Rytec Corp., Jackson, Wis., 1988-90; v.p. adminstrn. Custom Products Corp., 1990-91; part-owner Nat. Mfg. Co. Inc., Milw., 1991-96; owner JFL Mfg., Inc., Sussex, Wis., 1996—. Mem. Numerical Control Soc., Soc. Mfg. Engrs., Computer and Automated Systems Assn. Republican. Roman Catholic. Home: W264 N6565 Hillview Dr Sussex WI 53089-3452 E-mail: jflmfg27@aol.com.

LOSH, J. MICHAEL, automotive company executive; b. 1946; BSME, Gen. Motors Inst., 1970; MBA, Harvard U., 1970. With GM, Detroit, 1964—, v.p., gen. mgr., 1984—; exec. dir. fin. GM do Brasil SA, 1980-82; dep. mng. dir. GM de Mexico, 1982-84; exec. v.p., CFO GM. Office: GM Global Headquarters 482A 39 B 12 100 Renaissance Ctr Detroit MI 48243-1001 also: General Motors Accept Corp (GMAC) 3044 W Grand Blvd Detroit MI 48202-3037

LOTVEN, HOWARD LEE, lawyer; b. Springfield, Mo., Apr. 8, 1959; s. Isadore and Gytel (Tuchmeier) L.; m. Charlotte Lotven. BA, Drake U., 1981; JD, U. Mo., Kansas City, 1984. Bar: Mo. 1984, U.S. Dist. Ct. (we. dist.) Mo. 1984. Pvt. practice, Kansas City, 1984—; asst. prosecutor City of Kansas City, 1985. Prosecutor City of Harrisonville (Mo.), 1989-91, atty., 1989-91; prosecutor City of Napoleon, Mo., 2001—. Mem. Hyde Park Crime Patrol, 1985—91, Hyde Park Assn. Zoning and Planning Commn., 1993—97; vol. Heartland United Way, 1995; trustee Pilgrim Chapel, 2001—, Heart of Am. Stand Down, 2001; judge Mo. Sta H.S. Moot Ct. Competition, 1992. Mem. ABA, Mo. Bar Assn. (young lawyers coun. 1986-88, lectr. 1987-90, criminal law com. 1989—, gen. practice law com. 1990—, co-chair criminal law com. 1991-92, exec. coun. gen. practice law com. 1993-99, Law Day spkr. 1986, 96, lectr. 1987-90, 92, 97), Kansas City Bar Assn. (chmn. mcpl. cts. com. 2002, Vol. Atty. Project, 1992—, Vol. Atty. Project award winner 1994, continuing edn. spkr. 2000—), House Rabbit Soc., Delta Theta Phi, Omicron Delta Kappa, others. Democrat. Jewish. Avocation: sports. Office: 1125 Grand Blvd Ste 915 Kansas City MO 64106

LOUCKS, VERNON R., JR. retired medical technologies executive; b. Evanston, Ill., Oct. 24, 1934; s. Vernon Reece and Sue (Burton) L.; m. Linda Kay Olson, May 12, 1972; 6 children. B.A. in History, Yale U., 1957; M.B.A., Harvard U., 1963. Sr. mgmt. cons. George Fry & Assos., Chgo., 1963-65; with Baxter Travenol Labs., Inc. (now Baxter Internat. Inc.), Deerfield, 1966—99, exec. v.p., 1976, also bd. dirs., chmn., 1980, CEO, 1990—99. Bd. dirs. Dun & Bradstreet Corp., Emerson Electric Co., Quaker Oats Co., Anheuser-Busch Cos.; bd. advisors Nestlē U.S.A. Trustee Rush-Presbyn.-St. Luke's Med. Ctr.; assoc. Northwestern U. 1st lt. USMC, 1957-60. Recipient Citizen Fellowship award Chgo. Inst. Medicine, 1982, Nat. Health Care award B'nai B'rith Youth Svcs., 1986, William McCormick Blair award Yale U., 1989, Yale medal, 1997, Semper Fidelis award USMC, 1989, Disting. Humanitarian award St. Barnabas Found., 1992, Alexis de Tocqueville award for community svc. United Way Lake County, 1993, Industrialist of Yr. award Am. Israel C. of C., 1996; named 1983's Outstanding Exec. Officer in the healthcare industry Fin. World; elected to Chgo.'s Bus. Hall of Fame, Jr. Achievement, 1987. Mem.: Bus. Coun., Bus. Roundtable (conf. bd., mem. policy com.), Health Industry Mfrs. Assn. (chmn. 1983), Chgo. Club.

LOUGHEAD, JEFFREY LEE, physician; b. Mystic, Conn., May 11, 1957; s. Lawrence L. and Alice M. L.; m. Melinda K., Apr. 29, 1995; children: Brittany, Molly, Connor. BA, Miami U., 1979; MD, U. Cin., 1983; postgrad. in bus. adminstrn., Wright State U., 1997-98. Intern Children's Hosp. Med. Ctr., Cin., 1983-84, resident, 1984-86, chief resident, 1986-87; fellow in neonatal-perinatal medicine U. Cin., 1987-90; med. dir. spl. care unit Good Samaritan Hosp., Dayton, 1991-95; dir. quality assurance Children's MEd. Ctr., 1991-97, physician advisor nursing rsch. com., 1993-97; clin. dir. Children's Med. Ctr., 1995-97; dir. neonatal intensive care unit Ctrl. Dupage Hosp.; dir. strategic ops. Midwest Neoped Assocs. Ltd., 1998—. Author: (chpts.) Principles of Perinatal and Neonatal Metabolism, 1991, 2d edit., 1998, Current Pediatric Therapy, 1996; nutrition editor: Neonatal Network, 2000—. Fellow Am. Coll. Nutrition (Young Investigator award 1988), Am. Acad. Pediatrics (diplomate pediatrics, neonatal perinatal medicine); mem. PHi Beta Kappa, Alpha Omega Alpha, Beta Gamma Sigma. Avocation: amateur and profl. auto racing driver. Office: 900 Jorie Blvd Ste 186 Oak Brook IL 60523-3808

LOUGHNANE, DAVID J. lawyer; b. Chgo., Sept. 3, 1947; BA, U. Wis., 1969; student, U. So. Calif.; JD, Loyola U., 1972. Bar: Ill. 1972, Wis. 1972, U.S. Dist. Ct. (no. dist.) Ill., 1972. With Johnson & Bell, Chgo., 1996—. Author: Institutional Negligence, 1989. Mem. Am. Acad. Hosp. Attys., Def. Rsch. Inst. Office: Johnson & Bell Ste 4100 55 E Monroe Chicago IL 60603-5896

LOUGHREY, F. JOSEPH, manufacturing executive; b. Holyoke, Mass., Oct. 27, 1949; s. F. Joseph and Helen T. (Barrett) Loughrey; m. Deborah Jane Welsh, July 23, 1988; 1 stepchild Blair Edward Welsh. BA in Econs., African Studies, U. Notre Dame, 1971. Pres. AIESEC-U.S. Inc., N.Y.C., 1971-73; mgr. corp. employment Cummins Engine Co., Columbus, Ind., 1974-75, mgr. internat. personnel, 1975-79, dir. personnel (mktg.), 1979-81, dir. personnel (mktg. and subs.), 1981-83, dir. internal mgmt., 1983-84; mng. dir. Holset Engring. Co. Ltd., Huddersfield, Eng., 1984-86; v.p. employee rels. Cummins Engine Co., Columbus, Ind., 1986-87, from. v.p. So. Ind. ops. to v.p. heavy duty engines, 1988-90, group v.p. worldwide ops., 1990-95, exec. v.p., group pres. indsl. and chief tech. officer, 1996-99, pres., 1999—. Sr. mem. nat. adv. bd. Tauber Mfg. Inst. U. Mich.; mem. adv. coun. coll. arts and letters U. Notre Dame; pres. bd. dir. Developmental Svcs., Inc.; bd. dir. Tower Automotive, Inc., Sauer-Danfoss, Inc., Cummins Found. Trustee Columbus Child Care Ctr. Fellow: Brit. Inst. Mgmt.; mem.: AIESEC Internat. (sr.), Jr. Achievement (bd. dir.). Democrat. Roman Catholic. Office: Cummins Engine Co PO Box 3005 Columbus IN 47202-3005 E-mail: Joe.Loughrey@Cummins.com.

LOUREY, BECKY J. state legislator; b. 1943; m. Gene Lourey; 11 children. Student, Asbury Coll., U. Minn. Mem. Minn. Ho. of Reps., St. Paul, 1990-96, mem. various coms., vice-chair health and housing fin. divsn., mem. internat. trade, tech. and econ. devel. divsn., mem. Legis. Commn. Health Care Access; mem. Minn. Senate from 8th dist., St. Paul, 1996—. Democrat. Home: Box 100 Star Rte Kerrick MN 55756 Office: G-9 Capitol 75 Constitution Ave Saint Paul MN 55155-1601

LOUSBERG, PETER HERMAN, former lawyer; b. Des Moines, Aug. 19, 1931; s. Peter J. and Otillia M. (Vogel) L.; m. JoAnn Beimer, Jan. 20, 1962; children: Macara Lynn, Mark, Stephen. AB, Yale U., 1953; JD cum laude, U. Notre Dame, 1956. Bar: Ill. 1956, Fla. 1972, Iowa 1985; cert. mediator, Iowa. Law clk. to presiding justice Ill. Appellate Ct., 1956-57; asst. states atty. Rock Island County, Ill., 1959-60; ptnr. Lousberg, Kopp, Kutsunis and Weng, P.C., Rock Island; opinion commentator Sta. WHBF, 1973-74. Lectr., chmn. Ill. Inst. Continuing Edn.; lectr. Ill. Trial Lawyers seminars; chmn. crime and juvenile delinquency Rock Island Model Cities Task Force, 1969; chmn. Rock Island Youth Guidance Coun., 1964-69; mem. adv. bd. Ill. Dept. Corrections Juvenile Divsn., 1976; Ill. commr. Nat. Conf. Commrs. Uniform State Laws, 1976-78; treas. Greater Quad City Close-up Program, 1976-80; mem. nominations commn. U.S. Senate Judicial Nominations Commn. Ctrl. Dist., Ill., 1995; bd. visitors No. Ill. U. Coll. Law. Contbr. articles to profl. jours. Bd. dirs. Rock Island Indsl.-Comml. Devel. Corp., 1977-80; bd. govs. Rock Island Cmty. Found., 1977-82. 1st lt. USMC, 1957-59. Fellow Am. Bar Found. (rsch. adv. com., chair 1993-96, Ill. chair of fellows 1995—), Am. Coll. Trial Lawyers, Ill. Bar Found. (bd. dirs. 1986-93, chmn. fellows 1987-88); mem. ABA (ho. of dels. 1990-93, com. on client protection 1997—), Am. Law Inst., Ill. State Bar Assn. (bd. govs. 1969-74, 88-94, chmn. spl. survey com. 1974-75, com. on mentally disabled 1979-80, spl. com. on professionalism 1986-87, task force on professionalism 1987-89, atty.'s fees 1988, bd. dirs. 1989—, pres. 1992-93, pres./chair bd. Mutual Ins. Co. 1993-94), Rock Island Bar Assn., Assn. Trial Lawyers Am., Ill. Trial Lawyers Assn. (bd. mgrs. 1974-78), Am. Judicature Soc., Nat. Legal Aid and Defenders Assn. (regional coord. 1989-90), Ill. Inst. Continuing Legal Edn. (bd. dirs. 1980-83, chmn. 1981-82), Lawyers Trust Fund Ill. (bd. dirs. 1984-88), Fla. Bar Assn. (chmn. out-of-state practitioners com. 1985-86), Rock Island C. of C. (treas. 1975, pres. 1978), Quad Cities Coun. of C. of C. (1st chmn. 1979-80), Notre Dame Club, Quad Cities Club, Rotary (bd. dirs. Quad Cities). Roman Catholic. Home: 5281 Isla Key Blvd S Apt 404 Saint Petersburg FL 33715-1683 Office: 322 16th St Rock Island IL 61201-8626

LOUX, P. OGDEN, distribution company executive; CFO, sr. v.p. W.W. Grainger, Inc., Lincolnshire, Ill. Office: WW Grainger Inc 100 Grainger Pkwy Lake Forest IL 60045-5201

LOVE, JOSEPH L. history educator, former cultural studies center administrator; b. Austin, Tex., Feb. 28, 1938; s. Joseph L. Sr. and Virginia (Ellis) L.; m. Laurie Reynolds, Dec. 23, 1978; children: Catherine R., David A.; children from previous marriage: James A., Stephen N. AB in Econs. with honors, Harvard U., 1960; MA in History, Stanford U., 1963; PhD in History with distinction, Columbia U., 1967. From instr. to prof. U. Ill., Urbana-Champaign, 1966—, dir. ctr. Latin Am. and Caribbean studies, 1993-99. Rsch. assoc. St. Antony's Coll. Oxford U.; vis. prof. Pontifical Cath. U., Rio de Janeiro, 1987; presenter in field. Author: Rio Grande do Sul and Brazilian Regionalism, 1882-1930, 1971, Sao Paulo in the Brazilian Federation, 1889-1937, 1980, Crafting the Third World: Theorizing Underdevelopment in Rumania and Brazil, 1996; editor: (with Robert S. Byars) Quantitative Social Science Research on Latin America, 1973, (with Nils Jacobsen) Guiding the Invisible Hand: Economic Liberalism and the State in Latin American History, 1988, (with Werner Baer) Liberalization and its Consequences: A Comparative Perspective on Latin America and Eastern Europe, 2000; bd. editors Latin Am. Rsch. Rev., 1974-78, Hispanic Am. Hist. Rev., 1984-89, The Americas, 1995-99; contbr. articles to profl. jours. Fulbright-Hays Rsch. grantee; fellow Social Sci. Rsch. Coun., IREX, Guggenheim; vis. fellow U. São Paulo, Inst. Ortega y Gasset, Madrid; sr. rsch. fellow NEH, others; sr. univ. scholar U. Ill., 1993-96. Mem. Am. Hist. Assn., Conf. Latin Am. History (chair Brazilian studies com. 1973, mem. gen. com. 1983, Conf. prize 1971), Latin Am. Studies Assn. Unitarian. Office: U Ill Dept History 309 Gregory Hall 810 S Wright St Urbana IL 61801-3644 E-mail: j-love2@uiuc.edu.

LOVEDAY, WILLIAM JOHN, hospital administrator; b. Lynn, Mass., Nov. 4, 1943; married. B, Colby Coll., 1967; MHA, U. Chgo., 1970. Adminstrv. asst. Meml. Med. Ctr., Long Beach, Calif., 1970—71, asst. adminstr., 1971—74, v.p., 1974—82, exec. v.p., 1982—88; pres., chief exec. officer Meth. Hosp. Ind., Inc., Indpls., 1988—97; pres., CEO Clarian Health Ptnrs., Inc., Indpsl., 1997—. Office: Clarian Health PO Box 1367 Indianapolis IN 46206-1367

LOVELL, EDWARD GEORGE, mechanical engineering educator; b. Windsor, Ont., Can., May 25, 1939; s. George Andrew and Julia Anne (Kopacz) L.; m. Roxann Engelstad; children: Elise, Ethan B.S., Wayne State U., 1960, M.S., 1961; Ph.D., U. Mich., 1967. Registered profl. engr., Wis. Project engr. Bur. Naval Weapons, Washington, 1959, Boeing Co., Seattle, 1962; test engr. Ford Motor Co., Troy, Mich., 1960; instr. U. Mich., Ann Arbor, 1963-67; design engr. United Tech., Hartford, Conn., 1970; prof. engring. U. Wis., Madison, 1968—, chmn. dept. engring. mechanics and astronautics, 1992-95. Cons. structural engring. to govt. labs., indsl. orgns., maj. textbook pubs., 1968— Contbr. numerous articles to profl. jours. Postdoctoral research fellow Nat. Acad. Sci., 1967; NATO Sci. fellow, 1973; NSF fellow, 1961 Mem. Wis. Fusion Tech. Inst., Wis. Ctr. for Applied Microelectronics, Sigma Xi, Tau Beta Pi, Phi Kappa Phi Office: U Wis Dept Mech Engring 1513 University Ave Madison WI 53706-1539

LOVIN, KEITH HAROLD, university administrator, philosophy educator; b. Clayton, N.Mex., Apr. 1, 1943; s. Buddie and Wanda (Smith) L.; m. Marsha Kay Gunn, June 11, 1966; children: Camille Jenay, Lauren Kay B.A., Baylor U., 1965; postgrad., Yale U., 1965-66; Ph.D., Rice U., 1971. Prof. philosophy Southwest Tex. State U., San Marcos, 1970-77, chmn. dept. philosophy, 1977-78, dean liberal arts, 1978-81; provost, v.p. acad. affairs Millersville U., Pa., 1981-86; provost, v.p. acad. and student affairs U. So. Colo., Pueblo, 1986-92; pres. Maryville U. St. Louis, 1992—. Contbr. articles on philosophy of law, philosophy of religion to profl. publs.; mem. adv. bd. Southwest Studies in Philosophy, 1981-90. Bd. dirs. St. Louis Symphony Orch., Boys Hope, Jr. Achievement Mississippi Valley, Inc., St. Luke's Hosp., Nat. Coun. Alcohol and Drug Abuse Adv. Bd., St. Louis Intercollegiate Athletic Conf., Higher Edn. Coun.; bd. dirs., pres. Ind. Colls. and Univs. of Mo. Mem. Chesterfield C. of C., Univ. Club, Media Club. Avocation: fly fishing. Home: 13664 Conway Rd Saint Louis MO 63141-7234 Office: Maryville U 13550 Conway Rd Saint Louis MO 63141-7299 E-mail: klovin@maryville.edu.

LOW, ROBERT E. transportation executive; Student, U. Mo. Founder, pres. Prime, Inc., Urbana, Mo., 1970-80, Springfield, 1980—. Avocations: golf, horse racing, basketball, gaming. Office: Prime Inc 2740 N Mayfair Ave Springfield MO 65803-5084

LOWE, ALLEN, state legislator; Rep. Dist. 105 Mich. Ho. of Rep., 1993-98; city mgr. Grayling, Mich., 2000—. Home: 1101 Ottawa St Grayling MI 49738-1323

LOWE, FLORA LESTER, librarian; b. Richmond, Va., Feb. 22, 1948; d. Gerald Kennedy and Mary Opal (Booth) Stith; m. William Curtis Lowe, June 14, 1969; 1 child, Elizabeth Nell. AB, Coll. William & Mary, 1969; M.Libr., Emory U., 1977. Libr. paraprofl. Emory U., Atlanta, 1969-77; libr. asst. Marshall U. Med. Sch. Libr., Huntington, W.Va., 1978-79; retrospective conversion cataloger Deere & Co., Moline, Ill., 1979-80; libr. dir. Mt. St. Clare Coll., Clinton, Iowa, 1980—, instr. ESL, 1980-91. Chairperson, co-founder River Cities Libr. consortium, Clinton, 1988-90, 95—. Mem. ALA, AAUW (scholarship chairperson 1990-91), Iowa Libr. Assn., Iowa Pvt. Acad. Librs., Assn. Coll. and Rsch. Librs., Assn. Coll. and Libr. Rsch., Beatrix Potter Soc., Arnold Bennett Soc., Midwest Archives Conf., Jr. C. of C. (Outstanding Young Woman Am. 1979), Brontë Soc., Kappa Delta Pi, Pi Delta Phi, Beta Phi Mu. Episcopalian. Home: 717 S 15th St Clinton IA 52732-5311 Office: Mt St Clare Coll Coll Libr 400 N Bluff Blvd Clinton IA 52732-3997

LOWE, JOHN BURTON, molecular biology educator, pathologist; b. Sheridan, Wyo., June 13, 1953; s. Burton G. and Eunice D. Lowe. BA, U. Wyo., 1976; MD, U. Utah, 1980. Diplomate Am. Bd. Pathology. Asst. med. dir. Barnes Hosp. Blood Bank, St. Louis, 1985-86; instr. Sch. of Medicine Washington U., 1985, asst. prof. Sch. of Medicine, 1985-86; asst. investigator Howard Hughes Med. Inst., Ann Arbor, Mich., 1986-92, assoc. investigator, 1992-96, investigator, 1997—; asst. prof. Med. Sch. U. Mich., 1986-91, assoc. prof. Med. Sch., 1991-95, prof. Med. Sch., 1995—. Dep. editor Jour. Clin. Investigation, 1997—2002, mem. editl. bd. European Jour. Biochemistry, 2001—; contbr. articles. Fellow: AAAS; mem.: Am. Assn. Physicians, Am. Soc. Clin. Investigation. Office: U Mich Howard Hughes Med 1150 W Medical Center Dr Ann Arbor MI 48109-0726

LOWE, MARVIN, artist, educator; b. Bklyn., May 19, 1922; m. Juel Watkins, Apr. 1, 1949; 1 dau., Melissa. Student, Julliard Sch. Music, 1952-54; BA, Bklyn. Coll., 1956; MFA, U. Iowa, 1961. Prof. fine arts Ind. U., Bloomington, 1968-92, prof. emeritus, 1992—. Vis. artist-lectr., 1970-91. Exhibited in 64 one-person shows; over 200 group and invitational exhbns.; participated in U.S. info. exhbns. in Latin Am., Japan, USSR, and most European countries; represented in 84 permanent collections including Phila. Mus. Art, Bklyn. Mus., Smithsonian Instn., Brit. Mus., Japan Print Assn., N.Y.C. Pub. Libr., Calif. Palace Legion of Honor, San Francidso, Boston Pub. Libr., Columbia U., Libr. of Congress, Indpls. Mus. Art, Ringling Mus., Honolulu Acad. Art, Ft. Wayne Mus. Art, Purdue U. Mus. Fine Art, Springfield, Mass, Retrospective exhbn. Ind. U. Art Mus., 1998 Served with USNR, 1942-45. Fellow Nat. Endowment for Arts, 1975; fellow Ford Found., 1979, Ind. Arts Commn., 1987; recipient numerous Purchase awards, 1960—; grantee: Ind. Arts. Commn., 1997, Florsheim, 1997. Office: Ind U Sch Fine Arts Bloomington IN 47405

LOWE, PETER, electric power industry executive; BS in Commerce, U. Melbourne, Australia; MBA, U. Melbourne. Mgmt. Price Waterhouse, 1974-82, Foster's Brewing Group, Ltd., 1982-94; CFO, group mgr. bus. svcs. United Energy Limited, 1994-99, v.p. fin. mgmt. and acctg. svcs., 1999-00, sr. v.p., CFO, 2000—. Office: Utilicorp United 20 W 9th St Kansas City MO 64105

LOWE, RONALD, SR. chief of police; b. Dayton, Ohio; Student, U. Dayton, Wright State U., Ohio State U., Sinclair C.C.; grad., FBI Acad., 1988; grad. Sr. Exec. Inst., U. Va. Police officer Dayton Police Dept., 1974-83, sgt., 1983-87, police maj., supt. profl. stds., 1987-90, police maj., supt. ops., 1990-83; chief of police Chatham, Ga., 1993-95; dir., chief of police Dayton Police Dept., 1995—. Recipient Police medal of honor, Masonic Comty. Svc. award, Soc. Bank Officer of Yr. award, Legis. awards for outstanding svc. U.S. Congress, Ohio House and Senate, Ga. House and Senate, numerous comty. svc. awards and honors; named Police Officer of Yr. Mem. Internat. Assn. Chiefs of Police, Pub. Mgmt. Assn., Profl. Exec. Leadership Coll. Assn., Nat. Orgn. Black Law Enforcement Execs., Am. Colls. Criminal Justice Scis., FBI Nat. Acad., FBI Law Enforcement Exec. Devel. Assn., U.S. Secret Svc. Dignitary Protection Affiliate, Ohio Assn. Chiefs of Police, Montgomery County Chiefs of Police Assn. Avocations: computers, music, reading, weight lifting. Office: Dayton Police Dept Rm 164 335 W 3rd St Dayton OH 45402-1424

LOWRIE, WILLIAM G. former oil company executive; b. Painesville, Ohio, Nov. 17, 1943; s. Kenneth W. and Florence H. (Strickler) L.; m. Ernestine R. Rogers, Feb. 1, 1969; children: Kristen, Kimberly. BChemE, Ohio State U., 1966. Engr. Amoco Prodn. Co. subs. Standard Oil Co. (Ind.), New Orleans, 1966-74, area supt., Lake Charles, La., 1974-75, div. engr., Denver, 1975-78, div. prodn. mgr., Denver, 1978-79, v.p. prodn., Chgo., 1979-83; v.p. supply and marine transp. Standard Oil Co. (Ind.), Chgo., 1983-85; pres., Amoco Can., 1985-86; sr. v.p. prodn., Amoco Prodn. Co., 1986-87, exec. v.p. USA, 1987-88; exec. v.p. Amoco Oil Co., Chgo., 1989-90, pres., 1990-92; pres. Amoco Prodn. Co., 1992-94; exec. v.p. E&P sector Amoco Corp., 1994-95, pres. 1996-98, dep. CEO BP Amoco. Bd. dirs. Jr. Achievement, Northwestern Meml. Corp.; trustee, bd. dirs. Nat. 4-H Coun. Named Outstanding Engring. Alumnus, Ohio State U., 1979, Disting. Alumnis Ohio State U., 1985. Mem. Am. Petroleum Inst., Soc. Petroleum Engrs., Mid-Am. Club (Chgo.). Republican. Presbyterian.

LOWRY, DONALD MICHAEL, retired lawyer; b. Milw., 1929; LLB, Marquette U., 1953, PhB. Bar: Wis. 1953, Ill. 1961. Underwriter CNA Lloyd's of Tex.; sr. v.p., gen. counsel Am. Casualty Co., Reading, Pa., CNA Life & Annuity Co., Continental Assurance Co., Nat. Fire Ins. Co., Hartford, Conn., Transcontinental Ins., Transportation Ins. Co., Valley Forge Ins. Co., Valley Forge Life Ins. Co., Continental Casualty Co. Inc.; v.p., sec. CNA Fin. Corp., 1958-98, ret., 1998. Office: CNA Fin Corp CNA Plaza Chicago IL 60685

LOWTHER, GERALD HALBERT, lawyer; b. Slagle, La., Feb. 18, 1924; s. Fred B. and Beatrice (Halbert) L.; children by previous marriage: Teresa, Craig, Natalie, Lisa. AB, Pepperdine Coll., 1951; JD, U. Mo., 1951. Bar: Mo. 1951. Since practiced in, Springfield; ptnr. firm Lowther, Johnson, Joyner, Lowther, Cully & Housley. Mem. Savs. and Loan Commn. Mo., 1965-68, Commerce and Indsl. Commn. Mo., 1967-73; lectr. U. Tex., 1955-57, Crested Butte, Colo., 1958-59 Contbr. articles law jours.

Past pres. Ozarks Regional Heart Assn.; Del., mem. rules com. Democratic Nat. Conv., 1968; treas. Dem. Party Mo., 1968-72, mem. platform com., 1965, 67, mem. bi-partisan commn. to reapportion Mo. senate, 1966; Bd. dirs. Greene County Guidance Clinic, Ozark Christian Counseling Service, Greene County, Mo.; past pres. Cox Med. Center. Served with AUS, 1946-47; Col. staff of Gov. Hearnes 1964, 68, Mo. Mem. ABA, Mo. Bar Assn., Greene County Bar Assn., Def. Orientation Conf. Assn., Internat. Assn. Ins. Counsel, Def. Rsch. Inst., Springfield C. of C. Clubs: Kiwanian (pres. 1962), Quarterback (pres. 1958), Tip Off (pres. 1960). Office: 901 E Saint Louis St Fl 20 Springfield MO 65806-2540 Home: 350 S John Q Hammons Pkwy Springfield MO 65806-2505

LOWTHIAN, PETRENA, college president; b. Feb. 10, 1931; d. Leslie Irton and Petrena Lowthian; m. Clyde Hennies (div.); children: David L. Hennies, Geoffrey L. Hennies; m. Nisson Mandel, 1987. Grad., Royal Acad. Dramatic Art, London, 1952. Retail career with various orgns., London and Paris, 1949-57; founder, pres. Lowthian Coll. divsn. Lowthian Inc., Mpls., 1964-97. Mem. adv. coun. Minn. State Dept. Edn., Mpls. 1974-82; mem. adv. bd. Mpls. Comty. Devel. Agy., Mpls., 1983-85; mem. Downtown Coun. Mpls., 1972, chmn. retail bd., 1984-92; mem. Bd. Bus. Indsl. Advisors U. Wis.-Stout, Menomonie, 1983-89. Mem. Fashion Group, Inc. (regional bd. dirs. 1980), Rotary (mem. career and econ. edn. 1988—). Home and Office: 10 Creekside Dr Long Lake MN 55356-9431

LOY, RICHARD FRANKLIN, civil engineer; b. Dubuque, Iowa, July 6, 1950; s. Wayne Richard and Evelyn Mae (Dikeman) L.; m. Monica Lou Roberts, Sept. 2, 1972 (div.); children: Taneha Eve, Spencer Charles. BSCE, U. Wis., Platteville, 1973. Registered profl. engr., Wis., Ohio. Engr. aid Wis. Dept. of Transp., Superior, 1969; asst. assayer Am. Lead & Zinc Co., Shullsburg, Wis., 1970; asst. grade foreman Radandt Construction Co., Eau Claire, 1970; air quality technician U. Wis., Platteville, 1972-73; asst. city engr. City of Kaukauna, Wis., 1973-77, City of Fairborn, Ohio, 1977-89, city engr., 1989-93, pub. works dir., 1993—. Bd. dirs. YMCA Fairborn, 1990-95; mem. coun. Trinity United Ch. of Christ, Fairborn, 1989-98; chmn. Chillicothe dist. Tecumseh coun. Boy Scouts Am., 1991-93. Recipient Blue Coat award, 1983; named to Exec. Hall of Fame, N.Y., 1990. Mem. ASCE, NSPE, Am. Pub. Works Assn., Am. Water Works Assn., Inst. Transp. Engrs., Street Maintenance and Sanitation Ofcls. E-mail: GATV10.erinet.com.

LOYND, RICHARD BIRKETT, consumer products company executive; b. Norristown, Pa., Dec. 1, 1927; s. James B. and Elizabeth (Geigus) L.; m. Jacqueline Ann Seubert, Feb. 3, 1951; children: Constance, John, Cynthia, William, James, Michael. B.S. in Elec. Engring., Cornell U., 1950. Sales engr. Lincoln Electric Co., Cleve., 1950-55; with Emerson Electric Co., St. Louis, 1955-68, pres. Builder Products div., 1965-68, v.p. Electronics and Space div., 1961-65; v.p. ops. Gould, Inc., Chgo., 1968-71; exec. v.p. Eltra Corp., N.Y.C., 1971-74, pres., 1974-81; chmn. Converse, Inc., 1982-88; CEO Furniture Brands Internat., Inc (formerly Interco Inc.), St. Louis, 1989-96; chmn. Interco Inc., 1989-98; chmn. exec. com. Furniture Brands Internat. Inc., 1998—. Home: 19 Randall Dr Short Hills NJ 07078-1957 Office: Furniture Brands Internat Inc 101 S Hanley Rd Saint Louis MO 63105-3406

LOZANO, RUDOLPHO, federal judge; b. 1942; BS in Bus., Ind. U., 1963, LLB, 1966. Mem. firm Spangler, Jennings, Spangler & Dougherty. P.C., Merrillville, Ind., 1966-88; judge U.S. Dist. Ct. (no. dist.) Ind., Hammond, 1988—. With USAR, 1966-73. Mem. ABA, Ind. State Bar Assn., Def. Rsch. Inst. Office: US Dist Ct 205 Fed Bldg 507 State St Hammond IN 46320-1533

LOZOFF, BETSY, pediatrician; b. Milw., Dec. 19, 1943; d. Milton and Marjorie (Morse) L.; 1 child, Claudia Brittenham. BA, Radcliffe Coll., 1965; MD, Case Western Res. U., 1971, MS, 1981. Diplomate Am. Bd. Pediat. From asst. prof. to prof. pediatrics Case Western Res. U., Cleve., 1974-93; prof. pediatrics U. Mich., Ann Arbor, 1993—, dir. Ctr. for Human Growth and Devel., 1993—. Recipient Rsch. Career Devel. award Nat. Inst. Child Health and Human Devel., 1984-88. Fellow Am. Acad. Pediatrics; mem. Soc. for Pediatric Rsch., Soc. Rsch. in Child Devel. (program com. 1991-97), Soc. Behavioral Pediatrics (exec. com. 1985-88), Ambulatory Pediatric Soc. Office: Univ Mich Ctr Human Growth and Devel 300 N Ingalls St Ann Arbor MI 48109-2007

LUBAWSKI, JAMES LAWRENCE, health care consultant; b. Chgo., June 4, 1946; s. Harry James and Stella Agnes (Pokorny) L.; m. Kathleen Felicity Donnellan, June 1, 1974; children: Kathleen N., James Lawrence, Kevin D., Edward H. BA, Northwestern U., 1968, MBA, 1969, MA, 1980. Asst. prof. U. Northern Iowa, Cedar Falls, 1969-72; instr. Loyola U., Chgo., 1974-76; dir., market planning Midwest Stock Exchange, 1976-77; dir. mktg. Gambro Inc., Barrington, 1977-79; mktg. mgr. Travenol Labs., Deerfield, 1979-82; dir. mktg. Hollister Inc., Libertyville, 1982-84; pres., chief exec. officer Neomedica Inc., Chgo., 1984-86; v.p. bus. devel. Evangl. Health Svcs., Oak Brook, 1986-87; pres., chief exec. officer Cath. Health Alliance Met. Chgo., 1987-95; mng. dir. Ward Howell Internat., Chgo., 1995-98; v.p. A.T. Kearney, 1998-2000; pres. Zwell Internat., 2000—02; founder Lubawski & Assocs., Northfield, 2002—. Author: Food and Man, 1974, Food and People, 1979; co-editor: Consumer Behavior in Theory and in Action, 1970. Am. Assn. Advt. Acys. Faculty fellow, 1973. Mem. Evanston Golf Club (pres.), Equestrian Order of Knights of Holy Sepulchre. Avocation: golf, fishing. Office: 1765 Maple St Ste 15 Northfield IL 60093 E-mail: Jim@Lubawski.com.

LUBBEN, DAVID J. lawyer; b. Cedar Rapids, Iowa, 1951; BA, Luther Coll., 1974; JD, U. Iowa, 1977. Bar: Minn. 1977. Ptnr. Dorsey & Whitney, Mpls., to 1993; gen. counsel UnitedHealth Group, Minnetonka, Minn., 1993—. Office: UnitedHealth Group 9900 Bren Rd E Minnetonka MN 55343-9664

LUBBERS, AREND DONSELAAR, retired academic administrator; b. Milw., July 23, 1931; s. Irwin Jacob and Margaret (Van Donselaar) L.; m. Eunice L. Mayo, June 19, 1953 (div.); children— Arend Donselaar, John Irwin Darrow, Mary Elizabeth; m. Nancy Vanderpol, Dec. 21, 1968; children— Robert Andrew, Caroline Jayne. AB, Hope Coll., 1953; AM, Rutgers U., 1956; LittD, Central Coll., 1977; DSc, U. Sarajevo, Yugoslavia, 1987; LHD, Hope Coll., 1988; DSc, Akademia Ekonomiczna, Krakow, Poland, 1989, U. Kingston Univ., Eng., 1995. Rsch. asst. Rutgers U., 1954-55; rsch. fellow Reformed Ch. in Am., 1955-56; instr. history and polit. sci. Wittenberg U., 1956-58; v.p. devel. Central Coll., Iowa, 1959-60, pres., 1960-69, Grand Valley State U., Allendale, Mich., 1969-2001; ret., 2001. Mem. Am. Assn. State Colls. and Univs. seminar in India, 1971, Fed. Commn. Orgn. Govt. for Conduct Fgn. Policy, 1972; USIA insp., Netherlands, 1976; mem. pres.'s commn. NCAA, 1984-87, 89—, chmn. pres.'s commn., 1998-2002; bd. dirs. Grand Bank, Grand Rapids, Mich. Sutdent Cmty. amb. from Holland (Mich.) to Yugoslavia, 1951; bd. dirs. Grand Rapids Symphony, 1976-82, 99, Butterworth Hosp., 1988; chmn. divsn. II NCAA Pres.'s Commn., 1992-95, 98-99, mem. pres.'s coun., 1997; mem. Michigan Cmty. Svc. Commn., 2001--. Recipient Golden Plate award San Diego Acad. Achievement, 1962, Golden-Emblem Order of Merit Polish Peoples Republic, 1988, trustee's award cmty. leadership Aquinas Coll., 1998; named 1 of top 100 young men in U.S. Life mag., 1962. Mem. Mich. Coun. State Univs. Pres. (chmn. 1988, 2000—), Grand Rapids World Affairs Council (pres. 1971-73), Phi Alpha Theta, Pi Kappa Delta, Pi Kappa Phi. Home: 4195 N Oak Pointe Ct Grand Rapids MI 49525 E-mail: njdelta@aol.com.

LUBBERS, TERESA S. state legislator, public relations executive; b. Indpls., July 5, 1951; d. Richard and Evelyn (Ent) Smith; m. R. Mark Lubbers, Oct. 7, 1978; children: Elizabeth Stone, Margaret Smith. AB, Ind. U., 1973; MPA, Harvard U., 1981. Tchr. English Warren Ctrl. High Sch., 1973-74; pub. info. officer Office of Mayor Richard Lugar, 1974-75; dep. press sec., legis. asst. Office of U.S. Senator Richard Lugar, 1976-78; legis. rep. Nat. Fedn. Ind. Bus., 1978-80; dir. info. INC. Mag., 1981-82; press sec. Dielmann for Congress, 1982-83; pres. pub. rels. firm Capitol Communications, 1983—; mem. Ind. Senate from 30th dist., Indpls., 1992—. Co-founder, v.p. Richard G. Lugar Excellence in Pub. Svc. Series, 1990—; bd. dirs. Young Audiences Ind., Nat. Policy Forum. Bd. deacons Tabernacle Presbyn. Ch.; mem. cultural enrichment com. Immaculate Heart Sch., Meridian Kessler Neighborhood Assn., Rep. Profl. Women's Roundtable; mem. steering com. Forum Series, Girls Inc.; bus. mem. Broad Ripple Village Assn.; vol. Dick Lugar's 1974 Senate Campaign; pub. info. officer Mayor's Office, 1974-75; office mgr., Friends of Dick Lugar, 1976; senate staff Office of Senator Richard Lugar, 1976-78; adv. com. Ind. Sch. for Blind; bd. dirs. Brebeuf Prep. Sch., St. Vincent New Hope; cmty. adv. bd. Jr. League of Indpls.; exec. bd., crossroads coun. Boy Scouts of Am.; mem. devel. commn. White River State Park. Republican. Office: Ind Senate Dist 30 200 W Washington St Indianapolis IN 46204-2728

LUBIN, BERNARD, psychologist, educator; b. Washington, Oct. 15, 1923; s. Israel Harry and Anne (Cohen) L.; m. Alice Weisbord, Aug. 5, 1957. B.A., George Washington U., 1952, M.A., 1953; Ph.D., Pa. State U., 1958. Diplomate: Am. Bd. Profl. Psychology, Am. Bd. Psychol. Hypnosis; lic. psychologist, Mo., Tex. Intern St. Elizabeths Hosp., 1952-53, Roanoke (Va.) VA Hosp., 1954-55, Wilkes-Barre (Pa.) VA Hosp., 1955; USPHS postdoctoral fellow, postdoctoral residency in psychotherapy U. Wis. Sch. Medicine, 1957-58; staff psychologist, instr. dept. psychiatry Ind. U. Sch. Medicine, Indpls., 1958-59, chief psychologist adult outpatient service, 1960-62, assoc. prof., 1964-67; dir. psychol. services Dept. Mental Health, Indpls., 1962-63, dir. div. research and tng., 1963-67; dir. div. psychology Greater Kansas City (Mo.) Mental Health Found., 1967-74; prof. dept. psychiatry U. Mo. Sch. Medicine, Kansas City, 1967-74, 76—; prof., dir. clin. tng. program dept. psychology U. Houston, 1974-76; prof., chmn. dept. psychology U. Mo. at Kansas City, 1976-83, Curators' prof., 1988; trustees' faculty fellow, 1994. Cons. Am. Nurses Assn., Panhandle Eastern Pipeline Co., Eli Lilly Pharm. Co., U.S. Sprint, Am. Mgmt. Assn., Inst. Psychiat. Research, Ind. U. Med. Center, Ind. U. Sch. Dentistry, Goodwill Industries, USPHS Bur. Health Services, mental retardation div., (univ.-affiliated facilities br.), U.S. VA, Baylor U. Med. Sch., U. Tex. Health Scis. Center, Houston, 1974-76; Mem. tng. staff Nat. Tng. Labs. Inst.; dean or faculty mem. numerous confs., 1960— ; exec. sec. Ind. Assn. for Advancement Mental Health Research and Edn., 1962-67 Author: (with M. Zuckerman) Multiple Affect Adjective Check List: Manual, 1965, 2d edit., 1985, 3d edit., 1999, (with E.E. Levitt) The Clinical Psychologist: Background, Roles and Functions, 1967, Depression: Concepts, Controversies, and Some New Facts, 1975, 2d edit., 1983, Depression Adjective Check Lists: Manual, 1967, rev. edit., 1994, (with L.D. Goodstein and A.W. Lubin) Organizational Development Sourcebooks I and II, 1979; (with W.A. O'Connor) Ecological Approaches to Clinical and Community Psychology, 1984, (with Alice W. Lubin) Comprehensive Index to the Group Psychotherapy Literature: 1906-1980, 1987, (with A.W. Lubin) Family Therapy: A Bibliography, 1937-86, 1988, (with R. Gist) Psychosocial Aspects of Disaster, 1989 (with R.V. Whitlock) Homelessness in America: A Bibliography with Selective Annotations, 1894-1994, 1994, (with D. Wilson, S. Petren and A. Polk) Research on Group Methods of Treatment: 1970-1996, 1996, (with D. Wilson) Annotated Bibliography on Organizational Consultation, 1997, (with P. G. Hanson) Answers to the Most Frequently Asked Questions About Organization Development, 1995, (with R. Gist) Ecological and Community Approaches to Disaster Response, 1999, (with R.V. Whitlock) Mental Health Services in Criminal Justice Settings, 1999, also articles; editorial bd. Jour. Community Psychology; mem. editorial bd. Internat. Jour. Group Psychotherapy, Profl. Psychology: Research and Practice; cons. reader, bd. dirs. Jour. Cons. and Clin. Psychology. Pres. Midwest Group for Human Resources, Inc., 1965-69, trustee, 1965. Recipient N.T. Veatch award for disting. rsch. and creative activity, 1983; faculty fellow U. Kansas City, 1994. Mem. APA (chmn. sponsor approval com., exec. bd. dirs. cons. psychology, coun. rep., Disting. Sr. Contbr. to Counseling Psychology award 1995, Harry Levinson award for excellence in consultation 1996), AAAS, Mo. Psychol. Assn. (exec. bd., Richard Wilkinson Lifetime Achievement award 1997), Am. Group Psychotherapy Assn. (edit. com.); mem. Midwestern Psychol. Assn., Ind. Psychol. Assn. (pres. 1967), World Fedn. for Mental Health, Conf. Psychologist Dirs. and cons. in State, Fed. and Territorial Mental Health Programs (editor conf. procs. 1966-68, Perspective 1966-68, mem. exec. com. 1946-68), Inter-Am. Congress Psychology, Cert. Cons. Internat. (charter), NTL Inst. (bd. dirs. 1986-92), Sigma Xi, Phi Kappa Phi, Psi Chi (v.p. for midwest, mem. nat. coun. 1986-90, pres.-elect 1991-92, pres. 1992-93, past pres. 1993-94). Office: U Mo Kansas City Dept Psychology 5307 Holmes St Kansas City MO 64110-2437

LUBIN, DONALD G. lawyer; b. N.Y.C., Jan. 10, 1934; s. Harry and Edith (Tannenbaum) L.; m. Amy Schwartz, Feb. 2, 1956; children: Peter, Richard, Thomas, Alice Lubin Spahr. BS in Econs., U. Pa., 1954; LLB, Harvard U., 1957. Bar: Ill. 1957. Ptnr. Sonnenschein Nath & Rosenthal, Chgo., 1957—, chmn. exec. com., 1991-96. Bd. dirs., mem. exec. com., sec. audit com., nominating and corp. governance com. McDonald's Corp., Molex, Inc.; chmn. audit com. Daubert Industries Inc., Charles Levy Co., Tennis Corp. Am. Former mem. Navy Pier Redevel. Corp., Highland Park Cultural Arts Commn.; life trustee, former chmn. bd. Highland Park Hosp., Ravinia Festival Assn.; chmn. Chgo. Metropolis 2020, Anchor Cross Soc.; trustee, mem. exec. com. Rush-Presbyn.-St. Luke's Med. Ctr.; life trustee Chgo. Symphony Orch.; bd. dirs., v.p. Ronald McDonald House Charities, Inc., Chgo. Found. for Edn.; former dir. Smithsonian Inst., Washington; pres., bd. dir. The Barr Fund; former bd. dirs., v.p., sec. Ragdale Found.; bd. govs. Art Inst. Chgo.; former mem. Chgo. Lighthouse for the Blind; mem. citizens bd. U. Chgo.; mem. coun. Children's Meml. Hosp.; former bd. overseers Coll. Arts and Sci., U. Pa.; dir. Nat. Mus. Am. History, Washington. Woodrow Wilson vis. fellow Fellow Am. Bar Found., Ill. Bar Found., Chgo. Bar Found.; mem. ABA, Ill. Bar Assn., Chgo. Bar Assn., Lawyers Club Chgo., Chgo. Hort. Soc. (past bd. dirs.), Econ. Club (civic com.), Comml. Club (mem. exec. com.), Std. Club, Lakeshore Club, Beta Gamma Sigma. Home: 2269 Egandale Rd Highland Park IL 60035-2501 Office: Sonnenschein Nath & Rosenthal 233 S Wacker Dr Ste 8000 Chicago IL 60606-6491 E-mail: dlubin@sonnenschein.com.

LUCAS, ALEXANDER RALPH, child psychiatrist, educator, writer; b. Vienna, Austria, July 30, 1931; came to U.S., 1940, naturalized, 1945; s. Eugene Hans and Margaret Ann (Weiss) L.; m. Margaret Alice Thompson, July 6, 1956; children: Thomas Alexander, Nancy Elizabeth Watson, Alexander Eugene, Peter Clayton. B.S., Mich. State U., 1953; M.D., U. Mich., 1957. Diplomate Am. Bd. Psychiatry and Neurology (psychiatry and child and adolescent psychiatry), Am. Bd. of Med. Specialties. Intern U. Mich. Hosp., 1957-58; resident in child psychiatry Hawthorn Ctr., Northville, Mich., 1958-59, 61-62, staff psychiatrist, 1963-65, sr. psychiatrist, 1965-67; resident in psychiatry Lafayette Clinic, Detroit, 1959-61, rsch. child psychiatrist, 1967-71, rsch. coord., 1969-71; asst. prof. psychiatry Wayne State U., 1967-69, assoc. prof., 1969-71; cons. child and adolescent psychiatry Mayo Clinic, 1971-97; assoc. prof. Mayo Med Sch., 1973-76, prof., 1976-97; emeritus prof., 1998—; head sect. child and adolescent psychiatry Mayo Clinic, Rochester, Minn., 1971-80, emeritus cons., 1998—. Dir. com. on certification in child and adolescent psychiatry Am. Bd. Psychiatry and Neurology, 1997-2001; mem. residency rev. com. Accreditation Coun. for Grad. Med. Edn., 1999-2001. Author: (with C. R. Shaw) The Psychiatric Disorders of Childhood, 1970. Recipient Eating Disorders Scientific Achievement award, 1998. Fellow Am. Acad. Child and Adolescent Psychiatry (life, editl. bd. jour. 1976-82), Am. Orthopsychiat. Assn. (life), Am. Psychiat. Assn. (life); mem. Minn. Soc. Child and Adolescent Psychiatry (pres. 1993-95), Soc. Profs. Child and Adolescent Psychiatry (pres. 2000-2002), Sigma Xi. Achievements include research in biol. aspects of child psychiatry, psychopathology, psychopharmacology, eating disorders, psychiat. treatment of children, adolescents, and young adults. Office: Mayo Clinic 200 1st St SW Rochester MN 55905-0002

LUCAS, BERT ALBERT, pastor, social services administrator, consultant; b. Hammond, Ind., Mar. 26, 1933; s. John William and Norma (Gladys) Graham; m. Nanci Dai Hindman, Sept. 10, 1960; children: Bradley Scott, Traci Dai. BA, Wheaton Coll., 1956; BD, No. Bapt. Theol. Sem., 1960, ThM, 1965; MSW, U. Mich., 1971; D in Marriage and Family, Ea. Bapt. Theol. Sem., 1988. Lic. social worker, Ohio; ordained clergyman Am. Baptist Conv.; cert. family life educator. Chaplain Miami Children's Ctr., Maumee, Ohio, 1967-83; assoc. pastor First Bapt. Ch., La Porte, Ind., 1959-62; pastor Maumee Bapt. Ch., 1963-67; adminstrv. social work supr. Lucas County (Ohio) Children Svcs., 1967-97; pastor Holland (Ohio) United Meth. Ch., 1979-90, Broadway United Meth. Ch., 1994-97, Bono Bapt. Ch., Toledo, 1997-99. Adj. prof. Bowling Green (Ohio) State U., 1972-79; family life cons. New Horizon's Acad., Holland, 1984-86, co-dir. family svcs. 1985-86; cons. parenting, marriage enrichment, Toledo, 1986—. Rep. precinct capt., Toledo, 1984. Bert A. Lucas Day proclaimed City of Holland, 1984. Mem. AACD, Am. Assn. Marriage and Family Therapy (assoc.), Assn. for Couples in Marriage Enrichment, Hist. Preservations of Am. (Community Leader and Noteworthy Ams. award 1976-77), Council Family Rels. E-mail: bert.lucas@worldnet.att.net.

LUCAS, BONNIE, radio personality; Radio host morning show Sta. WHO-AM, Des Moines. Office: WHO Radio 1801 Grand Ave Des Moines IA 50309*

LUCAS, JOHN HARDING , JR. professional basketball coach; b. Durham, N.C., Oct. 31, 1953; s. John and Blondola L.; m. Debbie Fozard, 1978; children Tarvia, John III, Jai. BA, U. Md., 1976. Profl. basketball player Houston Rockets, 1976-78, 84-86, 89-90, Golden State Warriors, 1978-81, Washington Bullets, 1981-83, San Antonio Spurs, 1983-84, Milw. Bucks, 1986-88, Seattle Supersonics, 1988-89; owner Miami Tropics; head coach San Antonio Spurs, 1993-94; head coach, gen. mgr., v.p. basketball ops. Philadelphia 76ers, 1994—. Mem. Jr. Davis Cup Team. Named to NBA All-Rookie team, 1977, NBA All-Star, 1977-78. First pick in NBA draft, 1976; placed # 10 NBA all-time assist leader. Office: Cleveland Cavaliers Gund Arena One Center Court Cleveland OH 44115*

LUCAS, LARRY JAMES, state legislator; b. Jan. 10, 1951; m. Debera Lucas; 4 children. Student, S.D. State U., 1969-74. Mem. S.D. Ho. of Reps., 1991—, mem. edn. and state affairs coms.; tchr. Todd County Sch. Dist., 1975—. Democrat. Home: PO Box 182 Mission SD 57555-0182

LUCAS, ROBERT ELMER, soil scientist, researcher; b. Malolos, The Philippines, June 27, 1916; (parents Am. citizens); s. Charles Edmund and Harriet Grace (Deardorff) L.; m. Norma Emma Schultz, Apr. 27, 1941; children: Raymond and Richard (twins), Milton, Keith, Charles. BSA, Purdue U., 1939, MS, 1941; PhD, Mich. State U., 1947. Research asst. Va. Agrl. Research Sta., Norfolk, 1941-43; farmer Culver, Ind., 1943-44; grad. asst. Mich. State U., East Lansing, 1945, assoc. prof. soil sci., 1951-57, prof., 1957-77, prof. emeritus, 1977—; agronomist William Gehring, Inc., Rensselaer, Ind., 1946-50, 77-78. Vis. prof. Everglades Research Sta. U. Fla., Belle Glade, 1979-80. Author chpts. in books, research reports. Leader Boy Scouts Am., Lansing, Mich., 1961-72, dist. chmn. Chief Okemos (Mich.) Coun. Boy Scouts Am., 1965-66; pres. Okemos Cmty. Sr. citizens, 1987-88, pres. Lansing Area Farmers Agrl. Club, 1992, sec.-treas., 1994-99. Named Outstanding Specialist Mich. Coop. Extension Specialist Assn., 1967. Fellow Soil Sci. Soc. Am., Am. Soc. Agronomy (contbr. articles to jour.); mem. Internat. Peat Soc. (del. 1963—), U.S. Peat Soc., Mich. Onion Growers Assn. (sec. 1953-72), Mich. Muck Farmers Assn. (sec. 1953-72, Assoc. Master-Farmers award 1966), Mich. Mint Growers Assn. (sec. 1953-60). Republican. Lutheran. Avocations: traveling, gardening, sports, genealogy. Home: 3827 Dobie Rd Okemos MI 48864-3703 Office: Mich State Univ Dept Of Crop & Soil Sci East Lansing MI 48824

LUCAS, ROBERT EMERSON, JR. economist, educator; b. Yakima, Wash., 1937; BA, U. Chgo., 1959, PhD, 1964. Lectr. U. Chgo., 1962-63; asst. prof., economics Carnegie-Mellon U., Pittsburgh, 1963-67; assoc. prof., 1967-70; prof., 1970-75; prof., economics U. Chicago, 1975-80, John Dewey Disting. Svc. prof., 1980—. Ford Found. vis. rsch. prof. U. Chgo., 1974-75; vis. prof. econ. Northwestern U., Chgo., 1981-82. Author: Studies in Business-Cycle Theory, 1981, Models of Business Cycles, 1987; co-editor: Rational Expectations and Econometric Practice, 1981; assoc. editor Jour. Econ. Theory, 1972-78, Jour. Monetary Econs., 1977—; editor Jour. Polit. Theory, 1978-81; contbr. articles to profl. jours. Woodrow Wilson fellow, 1959-60, Brookings fellow, 1961-62, Woodrow Wilson Dissertation fellow, 1963, Ford Found. Faculty fellow, 1966-67, Guggenheim Found. fellow, 1981-82; Proctor and Gamble scholar, 1955-59; recipient Nobel Prize in Econ., 1995. Fellow AAAS; mem. NAS, Econometric Soc. (2nd v.p.). Office: U Chgo Dept Econs 1126 E 59th St Chicago IL 60637-1580

LUCAS, STANLEY JEROME, retired radiologist, physician; b. Cin., Mar. 23, 1929; s. Morris and Ruby (Schaen) L.; m. Judith Esther Schulzinger, May 14, 1953; children— Barbara Ellen, Daniel Nathan, Betsy Diane, Marvin Howard, Ronna Sue BS, U. Cin., 1948, MD, 1951. Diplomate Am. Bd. Radiology. Intern Cin. Gen Hosp., 1951-52, resident, 1952-53, 55-57; practice medicine specializing in radiology Cin., 1957-2000; mem. staff William Booth Meml. Hosp., 1957-61, Speer Meml. Hosp., 1957-61, Jewish Hosp., Cin., 1961-94. Past chmn. bd. Iona, Inc.; bd. dirs. Physician Ins. Co. Ohio. Chmn. med. div. United Appeal, 1978, Jewish Welfare Fund, 1980; bd. dirs., treas. Midwest Found. Med. Care; founder Choicecare, Inc., 1978-86; mem. policy devel. com. Local Health Planning Agy., 1978-82; trustee Cin. Med. Found., 1995—, also pres., 1999, trustee Health Found. Cin., 1999—. Capt. USAF, 1953-55. Honoree, Jewish Nat. Fund, 1994. Fellow Emeritus Am. Coll. Radiology; mem. Radiol. Soc. N.Am., AMA (alt. del. 1982-87, del. 1987-99), Ohio Med. Assn. (del. 1975-85, 94—, 1st dist. councilor 1985-90, pres.-elect 1991, pres. 1992-93), Cin. Acad. Medicine (pres. 1976-77, co-chmn. 140th anniversary 1997), Radiol. Soc. Cin. (pres. 1967), Ohio State Radiol. Soc. (Silver medal 2000), Am. Roentgen Ray Soc., Phi Beta Kappa, Phi Eta Sigma. Club: Losantiville Country. Jewish Home: 6760 E Beechlands Dr Cincinnati OH 45237-3728

LUCAS, WAYNE LEE, sociologist, educator; b. Joliet, Ill., Jan. 6, 1947; s. Cecil Elmer and Mabel (Torkelson) L.; m. Nancy Jean Floyd, Aug. 23, 1969; children: Jeffrey, Keri. BS, Ill. State U., 1969, MS, 1972; PhD, Iowa State U., 1976. Assoc. prof. U. Mo. Kansas City, 1976—. Contbr. articles to profl. jours. Mem. Acad. Criminal Justice Scis., Am. Soc. Criminology, Soc. for Study of Social Problems, Midwestern Criminal Justice Assn. Democrat. Presbyterian. Avocations: fishing, guitar, woodworking. E-mail: lucasw@umkc.edu.

LUCCHESI, LIONEL LOUIS, lawyer; b. St. Louis, Sept. 17, 1939; s. Lionel Louis and Theresa Lucchesi; m. Mary Ann Wheeler, July 30, 1966; children: Lionel Louis III, Marisa Pilar. BSEE, Ill. Inst. Tech., 1961; JD, St. Louis U., 1969. Bar: Mo. 1969. With Emerson Electric Co., 1965-69;

assoc. Polster, Polster & Lucchesi, St. Louis, 1969-74, ptnr., 1974—. City atty. City of Ballwin, Mo., 1979—85, 1992—. Mem. Zoning Commn., 1971—77; alderman City of Ballwin, 1977—79. Recipient Am. Jurisprudence award, St. Louis U., 1968—69; scholar NROTC, 1957—61. Mem.: ATLA, ABA, Newcomen Soc. N.Am., St. Louis Met. Bar Assn. (exec. com., pres.-elect 1984, pres. 1985—86), Am. Patent Law Assn., Forest Hills Club, Rotary (pres.-elect St. Louis 1991—92, pres. 1992—93). Republican. Roman Catholic. Office: 763 S New Ballas Rd Saint Louis MO 63141-8704 E-mail: llucchesi@patpro.com.

LUCK, JAMES I. foundation executive; b. Akron, Ohio, Aug. 28, 1945; s. Milton William and Gertrude (Winer) L.; children: Andrew Brewer, Edward Aldrich, L. BA, Ohio State U., 1967; MA, U. Ga., 1970. Caseworker Franklin County Welfare Dept., Columbus, Ohio, 1967-69; dir. forensics Tex. Christian U., Ft. Worth, 1970-74; assoc. dir. Bicentennial Youth Debates, Washington, 1974-76; exec. dir. Nat. Congress on Volunteerism and Citizenship, 1976-77; fellow Acad. Contemporary Problems, Columbus, Ohio, 1977-79; exec. dir. Battelle Meml. Inst. Found., 1980-82; pres. Columbus Found., 1981—; exec. dir. Columbus Youth Found. and Ingram-White Castle Funds, 1981—. Co-chmn. Task Force on Citizen Edn., Washington, 1977; mediator Negotiated Investment Strategy, Columbus, 1979; chmn. Ohio Founds. Conf., 1985; cons. HEW, Peace Corps., U. Va. Author: Ohio-The Next 25 Years, 1978, Bicentennial Issue Analysis, 1975; editor: Proceedings of the Nat. Conf. on Argumentation, 1973; contbr. articles to profl. jours. Trustee Godman Guild Settlement House, Columbus, 1979-81, Am. Diabetes Assn., Ohio, 1984-88; chmn. spl. com. on displacement Columbus City Coun., 1978-80; bd. dirs. Commn. on the Future of the Professions in Soc., 1979. Mem. Donors Forum Ohio. Clubs: Capital, Columbus Club, Columbus Met., Kit-Kat. Lodge: Rotary. Avocations: travel, reading. Home: 1318 Hickory Ridge Ln Columbus OH 43235-1131 Office: The Columbus Found 17 S High St Ste 799 Columbus OH 43215

LUCK, RICHARD EARLE, astronomy educator; b. Mar. 9, 1950; BA, U. Va., 1972; MA, U. Tex., 1975, PhD in Astronomy, 1977. Chmn., Warner prof. astronomy Case Western Res. U., Cleve. Mem. Am. Astron. Soc., Royal Astron. Soc. Office: Dept Astronomy Case Western Res Univ University Circle Cleveland OH 44106

LUCKE, ROBERT VITO, merger and acquisition executive; b. Kingston, Pa., July 26, 1930; s. Vito Frank and Edith Ann (Adders) L.; m. Jane Ann Rushin, Aug. 16, 1952; children: Thomas, Mark, Carl. BS in Chemistry, Pa. State U., 1952; MS in Mgmt., Rensselaer Polytech Inst., 1956. Polymer chemist Uniroyal Naugatuck (Conn.) Chem. Div., 1954-60; comml. devel. engr. Exxon Enjay Div., Elizabeth, N.J., 1960-66; gen. mgr. Celanese Advanced Composites, Summit, 1966-70; bus. mgr. polymer div. Hooker Chem., Burlington, 1970-74; gen. mgr. Oxy Metal Industries Environ. Equipment. Divs., Warren, Mich., 1974-79; v.p., gen. mgr. Hoover Universal Plastic Machinery Divs., Manchester, 1979-84; pres. Egan Machinery, Somerville, N.J., 1984-87; pres., chief exec. officer Krauss Maffei Corp., Cin., 1987-93; pres. Dubuc, Lucke, Koring Co., Inc., 1990—. Instr., Chem. Market Rsch. Assn., 1974. Author: (with others) Plastics Handbook, 1972; inventor, patentee in field. 1st lt. Corp Engrs., 1952-54, Korea. Senatorial scholar, Pa. State U., 1948-52. Mem. Am. Chem. Soc., Soc. Plastics Engrs. (sect. engr. STDS com. 1969), Tech. Assn. Pulp Paper Industry, Comml. Devel. Assn., Assn. Corp. Growth. Avocations: golf, skiing, travel, gardening. Office: Adventa Global LLC 414 Walnut St Ste 607 Cincinnati OH 45202-3913 E-mail: wiseowl726@aol.net., AdventaGlobal@fuse.net.

LUCKETT, BYRON EDWARD, JR. chaplain, career officer; b. Mineral Wells, Tex., Feb. 2, 1951; s. Byron Edward and Helen Alma (Hart) L.; m. Kathryn Louise Lambertson, Dec. 30, 1979; children: Florence Louise, Byron Edward III, Barbara Elizabeth, Stephanie Hart. BS, U.S. Mil. Acad., 1973; MDiv, Princeton Theol. Sem., 1982; MA, Claremont Grad. Sch., 1987. Commd. 2d lt. U.S. Army, 1973, advanced through grades to lt. col.; stationed at Camp Edwards E., Korea, 1974-75; bn. supply officer 563rd Engr. Bn., Kornwestheim, Germany, 1975-76; platoon leader, exec. officer 275th Engr. Co., Ludwigsburg, Germany, 1976-77; boy scout project officer Hdqrs., VII Corps, Stuttgart, Germany, 1977-78; student intern Moshannon Valley Larger Parish, Winburne, Penn., 1980-81; Protestant chaplain Philmont Scout Ranch, Cimarron, N.Mex., 1982; asst. pastor Immanuel Presbyn. Ch., Albuquerque, 1982-83, assoc. pastor, 1983-84; tchr. Claremont High Sch., 1985-86; Protestant chaplain 92nd Combat Support Group, Fairchild AFB, Wash., 1986-90; installation staff chaplain Pirinclik Air Station, Turkey, 1990-91; Protestant chaplain Davis-Monthan AFB, Ariz., 1991-95; dir. readiness ministries Offutt AFB, Nebr., 1995-96, sr. Protestant chaplain, 1996-98, Elmendorf AFB, AK, 1998-2000; wing chaplain Minot AFB, N.D., 2000—. Mem. intern program coun. Claremont (Calif.) Grad. Sch. Contbr. articles to profl. jours. Bd. dirs. Parentcraft, Inc., Albuquerque, 1984, United Campus Ministries, Albuquerque, 1984, Proclaim Liberty, Inc., Spokane, 1987-90; bd. dirs. western region Nat. Assn. Presbyn. Scouters, Irving, Tex., 1986-89, chaplain, 1991-93; mem. N.Mex. Employer Co, in Support of the Guard and Reserve, Albuquerque, 1984, Old Baldy coun. Boy Scouts Am., 1986; chmn. Fairchild Parent Coop., Fairchild AFB, 1986-87; pres. Co. Grade Officers Coun., Fairchild AFB, 1987-88. Capt. U.S. Army Reserve; chaplain USAF Res., 1983-86; lt. col. 1998. Recipient Dist. Award of Merit for Disting. Svc. Boy Scouts Am., 1977. Mem. Soc. Cin. Md., Mil. Order Fgn. Wars U.S., Civil Affairs Assn. Presbyterian. Office: 5 BW/HC 230 Missile Ave Minot AFB ND 58705-5026 E-mail: byron.luckett@minot.af.mil.

LUCKNER, HERMAN RICHARD, III, interior designer; b. Newark, Mar. 14, 1933; s. Herman Richard and Helen (Friednour) L. BS, U. Cin., 1957. Cert. interior designer and appraiser. Interior designer Greiwe Inc., Cin., 1957-64; owner, internat. designer Designers Loft Interiors, 1964—; owner Designer Accents, 1991—. Mem. bd. adv. Ohio Valley Organ Procurement Ctr., Cin., 1987—, U. Cin. Fine Arts Collection and Hist. Southwest Ohio, 1987-97; bd. dirs. Cin. Club Travelers, 1997-2000. Mem. Am. Soc. Interior Designers, Appraisers Assn. Am., Metropolitan Club. Republican. Avocations: needlepoint, collecting 18th century Chinese porcelain. Home and Office: 555 Compton Rd Cincinnati OH 45231-5005

LUCKY, ANNE WEISSMAN, dermatologist; b. N.Y.C., May 11, 1944; d. Jacob and Gertrude (Tetelman) Weissman; m. Paul A. Lucky, May 19, 1972; children: Jennifer, Andrea. BA, Brown U., 1966; MD, Yale U., 1970. Diplomate Nat. Bd. Med. Examiners, Am. Bd. Pediatrics/subspecialty of pediatric endocrinology, Am. Bd. Dermatology (pres. 1998—). Intern and resident in pediatrics The Children's Hosp. Med. Ctr., Boston, 1970-73; fellow in human genetics and pediatrics Yale U. Sch. Medicine, New Haven, 1973-74, resident in dermatology, 1979-81, instr. pediatrics, 1980-81, assoc. prof. dermatology and pediatrics, 1981-83; clin. assoc. Reprodn. Rsch. Br./Nat. Inst. Child Health/NIH, Bethesda, Md., 1974-76; asst. prof. pediatrics Wyler Children's Hosp./Pritzker Sch. Med./U. Chgo. Hosps., 1976-79; assoc. prof. dermatology, pediatrics U. Cin. Coll. Medicine, 1983-88; pvt. practice Dermatology Assocs. of Cin, Inc., 1988—; pres. Dermatology Rsch. Assocs., Inc., Cin., 1988—; dir. Dermatology Clinic Children's Hosp. Med. Ctr., 1989—. Vol. prof. dermatology and pediatrics U. Cin. Coll. Medicine, 1988-94. Editorial bd. Pediatric Dermatology, 1992—, Archives of Dermatology, 1983-94; contbr. numerous articles to profl. jours., publs. Recipient the Janet M. Glasgow Meml. Scholarship, Am. Women's Med. Assn., 1970, the Ramsey Meml. Scholarship award Yale U. Sch. Medicine, 1968, others; grantee USPHS, 1964-66, 67, 68-70, NIH, 1977-79, 79-82, 82-87, 84-87, 87-93, others. Mem. Lawson Wilkins Pediatric Endocrine Soc., Soc. for Pediatric Endocrinology (bd. dirs. 1984-87, pres. 1990-91), Am. Acad. Dermatology, Soc. Investigative Dermatology, Soc. for Dermatologic Genetics of the Am. Acad. Dermatology, Endocrine Soc., Acad. Medicine/Cin. Women's Faculty Assn./The Children's Hosp. Med. Ctr., Women's Derm. Soc. (bd. dirs. 1993—), Ohio State Med. Assn., Soc. Pediatric Rsch., Cin. Derm. Soc. (pres. elect 1995-96), Phi Beta Kappa, Sigma Xi, Alpha Omega Alpha. Office: Derm Assocs of Cin 7691 5 Mile Rd Cincinnati OH 45230-4348

LUDEMA, KENNETH C. mechanical engineer, educator; b. Dorr, Mich., Apr. 30, 1928; BS, Calvin Coll., 1955, U. Mich., 1955, MS, 1956, PhD in Mechanical Engring., 1963; PhD in Physics, Cambridge U., 1965. Instr. mechanical engring. U. Mich., 1955-62, from asst. prof. to assoc. prof., 1964-72, prof. mechanical engring., 1972—. Mem. ASME (Mayo D. Hersey award 1995), Am. Soc. Testing & Mat. Achievements include research in sliding friction and wear behavior of solids, steels, plastics and rubbers; fundamental adhesion mechanisms between dissimilar materials; skid resistance properties of tires and roads. Office: U Mich Dept Mechanical Engring 2250GGBL 2350 Hayward St Ann Arbor MI 48109-2125

LUDES, JOHN T. financial executive; Pres., CEO Acushnet Co., 1982-94; group v.p. Fortune Brands, 1988-94; chmn. bd., CEO Fortune Brands Internat. Corp., 1990-94; pres., COO Fortune Brands, Inc., Lincolnshire, Ill., 1995-98, vice-chmn., 1999—. Bd dirs. Fortune Brands, Inc., mem. exec. com., conflicts of interest com., capital appropriations com. Dir. New Eng. Zenith Fund. Office: Fortune Brands Inc 300 Tower Pkwy Lincolnshire IL 60069-3640

LUDWIG, RICHARD JOSEPH, ski resort executive; b. Lakewood, Ohio, July 28, 1937; s. Mathew Joseph and Catherine Elizabeth (Sepich) L.; m. Erleen Catherine Halambeck Ramus, July 22, 1977; children: Charleen, Tracey, Charles. Cassandra. Student, Ohio State U., 1955-59; BBA Fenn Coll., Cleve. State U, 1963. C.P.A., Ohio. Sr. acct. Ernst & Whinney, Cleve., 1964-66; supervising acct. Ernst & Young, 1966-70; asst. treas. Midland Ross Corp., Cleve., 1970-71, treas., 1971-76; v.p. fin., treas. U.S. Realty Investments, 1976-78, v.p.-fin., chief fin. officer, 1978-79; owner Boston Mills Ski Resort, Inc., Peninsula, Ohio, 1979—, Brandywine Ski Resort, Inc., Sagamore Hills, 1990—. Mem. Firestone Country Club (Akron, Ohio), Saddlebrook Club (Wesley Chapel, Fla.), Black Diamond Ranch Club (Lecanto, Fla.), Walden Country Club (Aurora, Ohio), Mediterra Country Club (Naples, Fla.), Mayacama Golf Club (Santa Rosa, Calif.), The Club at Mediterra (Naples), Stonewater Golf Club (Highland Heights, Ohio). Home: 15659 Villoresi Way Naples FL 34110 Office: PO Box 175 7100 Riverview Rd Peninsula OH 44264

LUDWIG, WILLIAM JOHN, advertising executive; b. Detroit, Apr. 7, 1955; s. Albert Donald and Vivian Delores (Bantle) L.; m. Karen Sue Ward, Sept. 25, 1981; children: Adam, Gunnar. BA, Western Mich. U., 1978. Writer, producer Patten Corp., Southfield, Mich., 1978-80; writer D'Arcy, MacManus & Masius, Bloomfield Hills, 1980-82; sr. writer Campbell-Ewald, Warren, 1982-83, v.p., group head, 1983-85, sr. v.p., group supr., 1985, sr. v.p., creative dir., 1985-87, group sr. v.p., creative dir., 1987-89; exec. v.p., creative dir. Lintas: Campbell-Ewald, 1989; vice chmn., chief creative officer Lintas: Campbell-Ewald (now Campbell Ewald), 1998—. Recipient numerous awards. Mem. Adcraft, Bloomfield Open Hunt Club. Office: Campbell Ewald 30400 Van Dyke Ave Warren MI 48093-2368

LUEBBERS, JAMES, gas utility company executive; With Peoples Energy Corp., Chgo., v.p. corp. planning, CFO, contr., 1998—. Office: Peoples Energy Corp 130 E Randolph Dr 24th Fl Chicago IL 60601-6207

LUEBBERS, JEROME F. state legislator; m. Judy Luebbers; children: Joe, Jerry, Jim, Julie, Jill, Jesse. Student, Quincy Coll. State rep. Dist. 21 Ohio State Congress, 1979-92, state rep. Dist. 33, 1993-2000. Trustee Delhi Twp., 1970-78; pres. Cin. Newsmonth Inc. Recipient Certificate Support Ohio Farmers Union, 1990, Appreciation award Boy Scouts Am. Troop 483, 1991, Things Keep Looking Up award Downs Syndrome Assn. Greater Cin., 1991, Jack Wolf Meml. award Ohio Sec. State, 1991, Legis. Appreciation award Ohio Right to Life, 1991, Guardian of Small Bus. Nat. Fedn. Ind. Bus., 1992; named Legislator of Yr. Hamilton County Assn. Trustees and Clks., 1985, Hamilton County Twp. Assn., 1990. Mem. Delhi Twp. Civic Assn., Prince Hill Civic Assn., Easter Seals (Mary Schloss award selection com.), Oak Hills Local Sch. Dist. (Hall Honor selection com.), Cath. Soc. Svc. Bd. Cin. Archdiocese, Delhi/Riverview Kiwanis, Diamond Oaks Adv. Com. Office: 417 Anderson Ferry Rd Cincinnati OH 45238-5228

LUECHTEFELD, DAVID, state legislator; b. Lively Grove, Ill., Nov. 8, 1940; m. Flo; 4 children. B, St. Louis U., 1962; M, So. Ill. U., Edwardsville, 1970. Tchr., athletic dir., coach, basketball, baseball; mem. Ill. Senate, Springfield, 1995—, mem. agrl. & conservation, state govt. ops. coms. Republican. Office: State Capitol Capitol Bldg M122 Springfield IL 62706-0001 also: 700 E North St Frnt Okawville IL 62271-1178

LUECKE, ELEANOR VIRGINIA ROHRBACHER, civic volunteer; b. St. Paul, Mar. 10, 1918; d. Adolph and Bertha (Lehman) Rohrbacher; m. Richard William Luecke, Nov. 1, 1941; children: Glenn Richard, Joan Eleanor Ratliff, Ruth Ann (dec.). Student, Macalester Coll., St. Paul, 1936-38, St. Paul Bus. U., 1938-40. Author lit. candidate and ballot issues, 1970—; producer TV local issues, 1981—; contbr. articles to profl. jours. Founder, officer, dir., pres. Liaison for Inter-Neighborhood Coop., Okemos, Mich., 1972—; chair countrywide special edn. millage proposals, 1958, 1969; trustee, v.p., pres. Ingham Intermediate Bd. Edn., 1959-83; sec., dir. Tri-County Cmty. Mental Health Bd., Lansing, 1964-72; founder, treas., pres. Concerned Citizens for Meridian Twp., Okemos, 1970-86; mental health rep. Partners of the Americas, Belize, Brit. Honduras, 1971; trustee Capital Area Comprehensive Health Planning, 1973-76; v.p., dir. Assn. Retarded Citizens Greater Lansing, 1973-83; chair, mem. Cmty. Svcs. for Developmentally Disabled Adv. Coun., 1973—; dir., founder, treas. Tacoma Hills Homeowners Assn. Bd., Okemos, 1985-97; facilitator of mergers Lansing Child Guidance Clinic, Clinton and Easton counties Tri-County Cmty. Mental Health Bd., Lansing Adult Mental Health Clinic, founder. Recipient Greater Lansing Cmty. Svcs. Coun. "Oscar," United Way, 1955, state grant Mich. Devel. Disabilities Coun., Lansing, 1983, Disting. award Mich. Assn. Sch. Bds., Lansing, 1983, Pub. Svc. award C.A.R.E.ing, Okemos, 1988, Earth Angel award WKAR-TV 23, Mich. State U., East Lansing, 1990, Cert. for Cmty. Betterment People for Meridian, Okemos, 1990, 2nd pl. video competition East Lansing/Meridian Twp. Cable Comm. Commn., 1990, 1st pl. award video competition, 1992, Outstanding Sr. Citizen award Charter Twp. of Meridian, Okemos, Mich., 2001; Ingham Med. Hosp. Commons Area named in her honor, Lansing, 1971. Mem. Advocacy Orgn. for Patients and Providers (dir. 1994-99). Avocations: reading, interior design, landscaping, gardening. Home: 1893 Birchwood Dr Okemos MI 48864-2766

LUEDERS, WAYNE RICHARD, lawyer; b. Milw., Sept. 23, 1947; s. Warren E. and Marjorie L. (Schramek) L.; m. Patricia L. Rasmus, Aug. 1, 1970 (div. Nov. 1990); children: Laurel, Daniel, Kristin. BBA with honors, U. Wis., 1969; JD, Yale U., 1973, Yale Law Sch. Bar: Wis. 1973. Acct. Arthur Andersen & Co., Milw., 1969-70; atty. Foley & Lardner, 1973-80, ptnr., 1980—. Bd. dirs. numerous cos. Bd. dirs. Riveredge Nature Ctr., Milw., 1983-92, 96-99, Wis. Pro Soccer, 1986—, Milw. Art Mus., 1992-2001, Child Abuse Prevention Fund, Milw., 1989—, Michael Fields Agrl. Inst., 1991—, Florentine Opera Co., 1992—; class agt. Yale Law Sch., 1978—. With U.S. Army, 1969-75. Mem. ABA, AICPA (Wisc.), Wis. Bar Assn., Milw. Bar Assn., Estate Counselors Forum, Univ. Club (Milw.), Phi Kappa Phi. Avocations: theater, racquetball, violin. Office: Foley & Lardner 777 E Wisconsin Ave Ste 3800 Milwaukee WI 53202-5367 E-mail: wlueders@foleylaw.com.

LUE-HING, CECIL, civil engineer; Dir. R&D Met. Water Reclamation Dist. Gtr. Chgo. V.p. Environ. and Water Resources Inst. Mem. NAE. Office: Metro Water Reclamation Dist Gtr Chgo 100 E Erie St Chicago IL 60611

LUENING, ROBERT ADAMI, agricultural economics educator emeritus; b. Milw., Apr. 20, 1924; s. Edwin Garfield and Irma Barbara (Adami) L.; m. Dorothy Ellen Hodgskiss, Aug. 27, 1966. B.S., U. Wis., 1961, M.S., 1968. Dairy farmer, Hartland, Wis., 1942-58; fieldman Waukesha County Dairy Herd Improvement Assn., Waukesha, 1958; adult agr. instr. Blair Sch. Dist., Wis., 1961-63; extension farm mgmt. agt. U. Wis.-Racine, 1963-69; extension farm record specialist Dept. Agrl. Econs. U. Wis.-Madison, 1969-88; free-lance work, 1988—. Author: (with others) The Farm Management Handbook, 1972, 7th edit., 1991, Teacher's Manual, 1991, Managing Your Financial Future Farm Record Book Series, 1980, 4th edit., 1987, USDA Yearbook of Agriculture, 1989, Beef, Sheep and Forage Production in Northern Wisconsin, 1992, Dairy Farm Business Management, 1996, Poultry Farm Business Management, 1999, 2d edit., 2000; writer mag. column: Agri-Vision, 1970-88. Founder, exec. pres. Lüning Family Orgns. U.S.A., Inc.; bd. dirs. Friends of the Max Kade Inst. for German-Am. Studies. Recipient John S. Donald Excellence in Teaching award U. Wis.-Madison, 1980; recipient Wis. State Farmer award Vocat. Agr. Inst. Wis., 1980, Second Mile award Wis. County Agts. Assn., 1980, Outstanding Svc. to Wis. Agr. award Farm and Industry Short Course, 1989. Mem. Wis. Soc. Farm Mgrs. and Rural Appraisers (coll. v.p. 1976, chmn. editl. com. 1978-80, sec.-treas. 1968-80, pres. 1982, Silver Plow award 1988), Wis. State Geneal. Soc. (pres. S.C. chpt. 1995-96, pres. PAF Users group 1995), Epsilon Sigma Phi (Disting. Service award 1988), Alpha Gamma Rho, Kiwanis. Presbyterian. Lodge: Masons. Home: 5313 Fairway Dr Madison WI 53711-1038 Office: U Wis Dept Agrl and Applied Econs 427 Lorch St Rm 216 Madison WI 53706-1513 E-mail: rluening@facstaff.wisc.edu.

LUEPKER, RUSSELL VINCENT, epidemiology educator; b. Chgo., Oct. 1, 1942; s. Fred Joeseph and Anita Louise (Thornton) L.; m. Ellen Louise Thompson, Dec. 22, 1966; children: Ian, Carl. BA, Grinnell Coll., 1964; MD with distinction, U. Rochester, 1969; MS, Harvard U., 1976; PhD (hon.), U. Lund, Sweden, 1996. Intern U. Calif., San Diego, 1969-70; resident Peter Bent Brigham Hosp., Boston, 1973-74; cardiology fellow Peter Bent Brigham Hosp./Med., 1974-76; asst. prof. divsn. epidemiology med. lab. physiol. hygiene U. Minn., Mpls., 1976-80, assoc. prof., 1980-87, prof. divsn. epidemiology and medicine, 1987—, dir. divsn. epidemiology, 1991—. Cons. NIH, Bethesda, Md., 1980—, U. So. Calif., L.A., 1985—, Armed Forces Epidemiology Bd., 1993-97; vis. prof. U. Goteborg, Sweden, 1986, Ninewells Med. Sch., Dundee, Scotland, 1995. With USPHS, 1970-73. Harvard U. fellow, 1974-76, Bush Leadership fellow, 1990; recipient Prize for Med. Rsch. Am. Coll. Chest Physicians, 1970, Nat. Rsch. Svc. award Nat. Heart, Lung and Blood Inst., Bethesda, 1975-77, Disting. Alumni award Grinnell Coll., 1989. Fellow ACP, Am. Coll. Cardiology, Am. Heart Assn. (chmn. coun. on epidemiology 1992-94, chair program com. sci. sessions 1995-97, award of merit 1997), Am. Coll. Epidemiology; mem. Am. Epidemiol. Soc., Am. Soc. Preventive Cardiology (Joseph Stokes award 1999), Delta Omega Soc. (Nat. Merit award 1988). Office: Univ Minn Sch Pub Health Div Epidemiology 1300 S 2nd St Minneapolis MN 55454-1087 E-mail: luepker@epi.umn.edu.

LUERSSEN, FRANK WONSON, retired steel company executive; b. Reading, Pa., Aug. 14, 1927; s. George V. and Mary Ann (Swoyer) L.; m. Joan M. Schlosser, June 17, 1950; children: Thomas, Mary Ellen, Catherine, Susan, Ann. BS in Physics, Pa., State U., 1950; MSMetE, Lehigh U., 1951; LLD (hon.), Calumet Coll.; DPS (hon.), Xavier U. Metallurgist research and devel. div. Inland Steel Co., East Chicago, Ind., 1952-54, mgr. various positions, 1954-64, mgr. research, 1964-68, v.p. research, 1968-77, v.p. steel mfg., 1977-78, pres., 1978-85, chmn., 1983-92. Contbr. articles on steelmaking tech. to various publs. Trustee Northwestern U., 1980—; trustee, sec., treas. Munster Sch. Bd., 1957-66; trustee Mus. Sci. & Industry. With USNR, 1945-47. Named disting. alumnus Pa. State U. Fellow Am. Soc. Metals; mem. AIME (Disting. life mem., B.F. Fairless award, Howe meml. lectr. 1988-91), Am. Iron and Steel Inst. (Gary medal, chmn. 1989-90), Nat. Acad. Eng. Home and Office: 8226 Parkview Ave Munster IN 46321-1419

LUETKENHAUS, WILLIAM JOSEPH, state legislator; b. Josephville, Mo., Sept. 15, 1962; s. Elmer William and Marilyn (Jenkins) L.; m. Patricia Ann Schulte; children: Katie, Andrew. Attended, Ranken Tech Coll., 1982-84. Lic. real estate broker, Mo. Plumber Lic. Journeymen, 1984—; owner, pres. Luetkenhaus Properties, Inc.; village trustee Town Bd., Josephville, 1989-90; county commr. St. Charles County, 1991-92; mem. Mo. Ho. of Reps. 12th Dist., Jefferson City, 1992—. Active St. Joseph Ch., Josephville. Mem. Plumbers and Pipefitters Local 567, Ranken Alumni Club, Lions. Catholic. Avocations: hunting, family, travel. Home: 742 Hancock Rd Wentzville MO 63385-3104 Office: Ho of Reps State Capital Jefferson City MO 65101

LUGAR, RICHARD GREEN, senator; b. Indpls., Apr. 4, 1932; s. Marvin L. and Bertha (Green) L.; m. Charlene Smeltzer, Sept. 8, 1956; children: Mark, Robert, John, David. BA, Denison U., 1954; BA, MA (Rhodes scholar), Oxford (Eng.) U., 1956. Mayor, Indpls., 1968-75; vis. prof. polit. sci. U. Indpls., 1976; mem. from Ind. U.S. Senate, 1977—, chmn. com. fgn. rels., 1985-86, chmn. com. on agr., nutrition and forestry, 1995-2001; chmn. Nat. Rep. Senatorial Com., 1983-84. Pres. Lugar Stock Farm, Inc.; mem. Indpls. Sch. Bd., 1964-67, v.p., 1965-66; vice chmn. Adv. Commn. on Intergovtl. Relations, 1969-75; pres. Nat. League of Cities, 1970-71; mem. Nat. Commn. Standards and Goals of Criminal Justice System, 1971-73; Del., mem. resolutions com. Republican Nat. Conv., 1968, del., mem. resolutions com., 1992, Keynote speaker, 1972, del., speaker, 1980., 88, 92, 96. Author: Letters to the Next President, 1988. Trustee Denison U., U. Indpls., 1970-2002; bd. dirs. Nat. Endowment for Democracy, 1992-2000. Served to lt. (j.g.) USNR, 1957-60. Pembroke Coll., Oxford U. hon. fellow. Mem. Rotary, Blue Key, Phi Beta Kappa, Omicron Delta Kappa, Pi Delta Epsilon, Pi Sigma Alpha, Beta Theta Pi. Methodist. Office: US Senate 306 Hart Senate Bldg Washington DC 20510-0001

LUHMAN, GARY LEE, lawyer; b. Milford, Ill., July 13, 1957; s. Edgar C. and Ruth A. (Schuldt) L.; m. Beth Luhman, Aug. 25, 1984; children: Christopher, Ethan. BA, U. Ill., 1979; JD, U. Wis., Madison, 1982. Asst. dist. atty. County of Green, Monroe, Wis., 1983-88, County of Lafayette, Darlington, 1988-89; assoc. Ewald Law Offices, Monroe, 1989—. Village atty. Village of Browntown, Wis., 1989—; asst. city atty. City of Monroe, 1989—. Rep. candidate for Green County Dist. Atty., Monroe, 1989-90; pres. Jordan Luth. Ch., 1985-90. Mem. Kiwanis, Phi Beta Kappa. Home: 9440W Coon Creek Rd Browntown WI 53522-9765 Office: Ewald Law Offices 1112 17th Ave Monroe WI 53566-2007

LUHMAN, WILLIAM SIMON, community development administrator; b. Belvidere, Ill., May 15, 1934; s. Donald R. and H. Elizabeth (Rudberg) L. AB, Park Coll., 1956; MA, Fla. State U., 1957. City planner City of Moline, Ill., 1959-64; planning dir. Rock Island County, 1964-66; exec. dir. Bi-State Met. Planning Commn., Rock Island, 1966-71; dir. regional devel. Northeastern Ill. Planning Commn., Chgo., 1971-74, assoc. dir., 1975-76, dep. dir., 1977-79, acting exec. dir., 1979-80, asst. dir., 1980-81; v.p. Pub. Mgmt. Info. Svc., 1981; asst. dir. No. Ill. U. Ctr. Govt. Studies, DeKalb, 1981-91, program coord., 1991; exec. dir. Growth Dimensions for Belvidere-Boone County, Ill., 1991—2001, pres., 1982-86, asst. dir., 2002—. Vis. instr. Augustana Coll., Rock Island, 1967, 69. Bd. dirs. Rockford Area Coun. of 100, 1983-86; Boone County Regional Planning Commn., 1986—, chmn., 1986-90; mem. Belvidere-Boone County Regional Planning Commn., 1986—, chmn., 1990-92; bd. dirs. Sch. Dist. 100 Found. for Excellence in Edn., 1992-99; mem. Sch. Dist. 100 Citizens Adv. Coun., 1999—, Sch. Dist. 100 Com. Strat. Planning, 1999; bd. dirs. Boone County United Way, 1999—, No. Ill. Cmty. Found.; ; trustee Cmty. Foun. No. Ill., 2002; active Boone County Arts Coun., Friends of Ida Pub. Libr., Belvidere Sister Cities Assn.; Ill. Regional Pub. Libr. Svc. Planning Panelist, 1996. Mem. Am. Soc. Pub. Adminstrn., Am. Planning Assn., Internat. City Mgmt. Assn., Ill. Devel. Coun. Home: 1538 Fremont St Belvidere IL 61008-5939 Office: 200 S State St Belvidere IL 61008-3687 E-mail: bluhman@growthdimensions.org., bluhman@aol.com.

LUKE, RANDALL DAN, retired tire and rubber company executive, lawyer; b. New Castle, Pa., June 4, 1935; s. Randall Beamer and Blanche Wilhelmina (Fisher) L.; m. Patricia Arlene Moody, Aug. 4, 1962 (div. Jan. 1977); children: Lisa Elin, Randall Sargent; m. Saralee Frances Krow, Mar. 1, 1979; 1 stepchild, Stephanie Sogg. BA in Econs. with honors, U. Pa., 1957, JD, 1960. Bar: Ohio 1960, Calif. 1962, Ill. 1989. Assoc., ptnr. Daus, Schwenger & Kottler, Cleve., 1965-70; ptnr. Kottler & Danzig, 1970-75, Hahn, Loeser, Freedheim, Dean & Wellman, Cleve., 1975-81; assoc. gen. counsel The Firestone Tire & Rubber Co., Akron, Ohio, 1981-82, v.p., assoc. gen. counsel and sec., 1982-88, Bridgestone/Firestone, Inc., Akron, 1988-91; of counsel Hahn Loeser & Parks, Cleve., 1991-2000. Trustee, Akron Art Mus., 1982-87, Akron Symphony Orch., 1986-87, Cleve. Opera League, 1992-98. Served to Capt. USNR, 1960-81; ret. 1981. Mem.: Ill. Bar Assn., Ohio Bar Assn., Calif. Bar Assn., Union Internat. Avocats, Union Club (Cleve.)., Mayfield Country Club (S. Euclid, Ohio), Cleve. Skating Club. Republican. Avocations: tennis, jogging, golf, squash, skiing. Home: 13901 Shaker Blvd Cleveland OH 44120-1582

LUMENG, LAWRENCE, physician, educator; b. Manila, Aug. 10, 1939; came to U.S., 1958; s. Ming and Lucia (Lim) Lu; m. Pauline Lumeng, Nov. 26, 1966; children: Carey, Emily. AB, Ind. U., 1960, MD, 1964, MS, 1969. Intern U. Chgo., 1964-65; resident Ind. U. Hosps., Indpls., 1965-67, fellow, 1967-69, asst. prof. Sch. of Medicine, 1971-73, assoc. prof. Sch. of Medicine, 1974-79, prof. Sch. of Medicine, 1979—, dir. div. gastroenterology and hepatology Sch. of Medeine, 1984—; chief gastroenterology sect. VA Med. Ctr., 1979—. Mem. merit rev. bd. VA. Cen. Office, Washington, 1981-84; mem. alcohol biomed. res. rev. com. NIAAA, Washington, 1982-86; mem. grant rev. panel USDA, Washington, 1985—. Contbr. over 250 articles to profl. jours. Maj. U.S. Army, 1969-71. Fellow ACP; mem. Am. Soc. Clin. Investigation, Am. Soc. Biol. Chemists, Rsch. Soc. on Alcoholism (treas. 1985-87, sec. 1987-89), Am. Gastroenterological Assn., Am. Assn. for the Study of Liver Diseases, Am. Assn. Physicians. Avocations: painting, music. Office: Ind U Med Ctr 975 W Walnut St Indianapolis IN 46202-5181

LUMPE, SHEILA, state commissioner, former state legislator; b. Apr. 17, 1935; m. Gustav H. Lumpe, 1958. AB, Ind. U.; postgrad., Johns Hopkins U.; MA, U. Mo. Formerly mem. Mo. Ho. of Reps.; now . Mo. Pub. Svc. Commn. Active Women's Polit. Caucus; bd. dirs. Mo. Humanities Coun., Partnership for Outstanding Schs. Democrat. Home: 320 Washington St Apt 201 Jefferson City MO 65101-1570 Office: Pub Svc Commn PO Box 360 Jefferson City MO 65102-0360

LUMPKIN, JOHN ROBERT, public health physician, state official; b. Chgo., July 28, 1951; s. Frank and Beatrice (Shapiro) L.; m. Mary S. Blanks, Jan. 28, 1984; children: Alia, John R. Jr. BS, Northwestern U., Evanston, Ill., 1973; MD, Northwestern U., Chgo., 1974; MPH, U. Ill., Chgo., 1985. Diplomate Am. Bd. Emergency Medicine. Intern U. Chgo. Hosps., 1975, resident in anesthesiology, 1976-78, vice-chmn. emergency medicine, 1981-84; asst. prof. U. Chgo., 1978-84; asst. dir. emergency medicine South Chgo. Hosp., 1984-85; staff physician St. Mary of Nazareth Hosp., Chgo., 1985; assoc. dir. Ill. Dept. Pub. Health, Springfield and Chgo., 1985-90, dir., 1990—. Cons. Egyptian Ministry Health, Cairo, 1986-90; mem. sec.'s adv. com. on injury control Ctrs. for Dis. Control, Atlanta, 1989-93. Fellow Am. Coll. Emergency Physicians (bd. dirs. 1987-93); mem. Soc. Tchrs. Emergency Medicine (pres. 1981-82), Ill. Coll. Emergency Physicians (pres. 1982-83, Bill B. Smiley award 1986), Assn. State and Territorial Health Ofcls. (pres. 1995-96). Avocations: racquetball, model trains, football, computers. Office: Ill Dept Pub Health 100 W Randolph St Ste 6-600 Chicago IL 60601-3229

LUMPKINS, ROBERT L. food products executive; b. Lawrenceburg, Tenn., Jan. 25, 1944; s. Robert L. and Maude (Holthouse) L.; m. Sara Jane O'Connell, Dec. 29, 1966; 1 child, Christine Jane. BS in Math. magna cum laude, U. Notre Dame, 1966; MBA, Stanford U., 1968. Fin. analyst Cargill Inc., Mpls., 1968-70, mgr. fin. info. svcs. dept., 1970-73, gen. mgr. Cargill Leasing corp., 1973-75, group contr., 1975-82, sec., fin. com., 1975-82, pres. fin. svcs. divsn., 1983-88, chief fin. offficer Cargill Europe London, 1988-89, CFO Mpls., 1989-95, vice chmn., 1995—, CFO, 1998—. Bd. dirs. Ecolab Inc., Wherenet Corp. Mem. sci. adv. coun. U. Notre Dame, 1994-99; bd. dirs. Minn. Orch. Assn., Mpls., 1993-2000; trustee Minn. Med. Found., Mpls., 1992—; bd. dirs. Greater Mpls. Met. Housing Corp., 1996-99, Technoserve Inc., 1997—; trustee Howard U., 1998—; mem. adv. coun. Stanford Bus. Sch., 2000—. Mem. Minikahda Club. Roman Catholic. Office: Cargill Inc PO Box 9300 Minneapolis MN 55440-9300

LUND, DORIS HIBBS, retired dietitian; b. Des Moines, Nov. 10, 1923; d. Loyal Burchard and Catharine Mae (McClymond) Hibbs; m. Richard Bodholdt Lund, Nov. 9, 1946; children: Laurel Anne, Richard Douglas, Kristi Jane Lund Lozier. Student, Duchesne Coll., Omaha, 1941-42; BS, Iowa State U., 1946; postgrad., Grand View Coll., Des Moines, 1965; MS in Mgmt., Iowa State U., 1968. Registered dietitian, lic. dietitian. Clk. Russell Stover Candies, Omaha, 1940-42; chemist Martin Bomber Plant, 1942-43; dietitian Grand Lake (Colo.) Lodge, 1946; tailoring instr. Ottumwa Pub. Schs., 1952-53; cookery instr. Des Moines Pub. Schs., 1958-62; dietitian Calvin Manor, Des Moines, 1963; home economist Am. Wool Coun./Am. Lamb Coun., Denver, 1963-65, The Merchandising Group of N.Y., 1965-68, Thomas Wolff, Pub. Rels., 1968-70; home economist weekly TV program Iowa Power Co., 1968-70; cons. in child nutrition programs Iowa Dept. Edn., Des Moines, 1970-95; ret. Nutritioneering, Ltd., 1995. Mem. Iowa Home Economists in Bus. (pres. 1962-63), PEO, Pi Beta Phi (Iowa Gamma chpt. pres. 1945-46). Pres. Callanan Jr. H.S. PTA, 1964, Roosevelt H.S. PTA, 1966; amb. Friendship Force Internat., 1982—; alliance mem. Des Moines Symphony; guild mem. Civic Music Des Moines Met. Opera; mem. Civic Music Guild, Des Moines Symphony Alliance, Bot. Ctr. Des Moines, Des Moines Art Ctr., Des Moines Civic Ctr.; chmn. Met. Opera Previews; pres., mem. Ctrl. Presbyn. Mariners, Des Moines; ruling elder, clk. of session Ctrl. Presbyn. Session, 1972—78; bd. dirs. Ctrl. Found., Ctrl. Pastor Seeking Nomination Com., 1996; chair cmty. concers Calvin Cmty. Found., 1998, chair support and edn., 1999—. Duchesne Coll. 4 yr. scholar. Mem. Am. Dietetic Assn., Iowa Home Economists in Bus. (pres. 1962-63), PEO, Pi Beta Phi (pres. 1945-46). Republican. Avocations: international travel, writing, sailing, sewing, cooking. Home: 105 34th St Des Moines IA 50312-4526

LUNDBERG, GEORGE DAVID, II, medical editor in chief, pathologist; b. Pensacola, Fla., Mar. 21, 1933; s. George David and Esther Louise (Johnson) L.; m. Nancy Ware Sharp, Aug. 18, 1956 (div.); children: George David III, Charles William, Carol Jean; m. Patricia Blacklidge Lorimer, Mar. 6, 1983; children: Christopher Leif, Melinda Suzanne AA, North Park Coll., Chgo., 1950; BS, U. Ala., Tuscaloosa, 1952; MS, Baylor U., Waco, Tex., 1963; MD, Med. Coll. Ala., Birmingham, 1957; ScD (hon.), SUNY, Syracuse, 1988, Thomas Jefferson U., 1993, U. Ala., Birmingham, 1994, Med. Coll. Ohio, 1995. Intern Tripler Hosp., Hawaii; resident Brooke Hosp., San Antonio; assoc. prof. pathology U. So. Calif., Los Angeles, 1967-72, prof., 1972-77; assoc. dir. labs. Los Angeles County-U. So. Calif. Med. Ctr., 1968-77; prof., chmn. dept. pathology U. Calif.-Davis, Sacramento, 1977-82; v.p. scientific info., editor Jour. AMA, Chgo., 1982-99, editor in chief scientific publ., 1991-95; editor in chief AMA Sci. Info. and Multimedia, 1995-99; editor-in-chief Medscape, 1999—; editor Medscape Gen. Medicine, 1999—; editor-in-chief and exec. v.p. Medicalogic/Medscape, 2000—. Vis. prof. U. London, 1976, Lund U., Sweden, 1976; prof. clin. pathology Northwestern U., Chgo., 1982—; adj. prof. health policy Harvard U., Boston, 1993—; vis. prof. pathology, 1994-96; sr. fellow Northwestern U., 1999—. Author, editor: Managing the Patient Focused Laboratory, 1975, Using the Clinical Laboratory in Medical Decision Making, 1983, 51 Landmark Articles in Medicine, 1984, AIDS From the Beginning, 1986, Caring for the Uninsured and Underinsured, 1991, Violence, 1992, 100 Years of JAMA Landmark Articles, 1997, Severed Trust: Why American Medicine Hasn't Been Fixed, 2001; contbr. articles to profl. jours. Served to lt. col. M.C., U.S. Army, 1956-67. Fellow Am. Soc. Clin. Pathologists (past pres.), Am. Acad. Forensic Sci.; mem. N.Y. Acad. Scis., Inst. Medicine, Alpha Omega Alpha. Democrat. Episcopalian. Office: Medscape 224 W 30th St New York NY 10001

LUNDBERG, JOE, meteorologist, radio personality; Meteorologist Sta. WMBI Radio, Chgo. Avocations: bowling, softball, golf, singing, playing games. Office: WMBI 820 N LaSalle Blvd Chicago IL 60610*

LUNDBERG, SUSAN ONA, musical organization administrator; b. Mandan, N.D., Mar. 15, 1947; d. Robert Henry and Evelyn (Olson) L.; m. Paul R. Wick, July 2, 1972 (div. May 1976); 1 child, Melissa. BA, Stephens Coll., 1969; MLS, Western Mich. U., 1970; MPA, Calif. State U., Fullerton, 1980. Children's and reference libr. Bismarck (N.D.) Pub. Libr., 1970-71; reference libr. U. Tenn., Knoxville, 1971-72; coord. children's svcs. Orange County (Calif.) Pub. Libr., 1972-75; exec. dir. Bismarck-Manda Orch. Assn., 1992—. Exec. dir., founder Sleepy Hollow Summer Theatre, Bismarck, 1990—; trustee Gabriel J. Brown Trust, Bismarck, 1989—. Chair Nat. Music Week N.D., 1990—, Friends of the Belle, 1994—. Named Outstanding Leaders of Yr. Bismarck Tribune, 1995. Mem. Calif. Libr. Assn. (pres. children's svcs. 1971-72), Bismarck Art Assn. (pres. 1982-84), Bismarck Art and Galleries Assn. (bd. dirs. 1985—, pres. 1986-88, Honor Citation award 1992), Jr. Svc. League. Lutheran. Avocations: painting, singing. Home: 112 Ave E W Bismarck ND 58501

LUNDBY, MARY A. state legislator; b. Carroll County, Feb. 2, 1948; d. Edward A. and Elizabeth Hoehl; m. Michael Lundby, 1971; 1 child, Daniel. BA in History, Upper Iowa U., 1971. Former staff asst. Senator Roger Jepsen; mem. Iowa Senate from 26th dist., Des Moines, 1994—. Active Solid Waste Adv. Com. Republican. Home: PO Box 563 Marion IA 52302-0563 Office: Iowa State Senate State Capitol Des Moines IA 50319-0001

LUNDE, HAROLD IRVING, management educator; b. Austin, Minn., Apr. 18, 1929; s. Peter Oliver and Emma (Stoa) L.; m. Sarah Jeanette Lysne, June 25, 1955; children: Paul, James, John, Thomas. B.A., St. Olaf Coll., 1952; M.A., U. Minn., 1954, Ph.D., 1966. Assoc. prof. econs. Macalester Coll., St. Paul, 1957-64; fin. staff economist Gen. Motors Corp., N.Y.C., 1965-67; corp. sec. Dayton Hudson Corp., Mpls., 1967-70; mgr. planning and gen. research May Dept. Stores Co., St. Louis, 1970-72, v.p. planning and research, 1972-78; exec. v.p. adminstrn. Kobacker Stores, Inc., Columbus, Ohio, 1979; prof. mgmt. Bowling Green (Ohio) State U., 1980-98, emeritus, 1998—. Mem. Acad. Mgmt., Am. Econ. Assn., Nat. Assn. Bus. Economists, Decision Scis. Inst., Phi Beta Kappa, Phi Kappa Phi, Omicron Delta Kappa, Beta Gamma Sigma. Home: 880 Country Club Dr Bowling Green OH 43402-1602

LUNDERGAN, BARBARA KEOUGH, lawyer; b. Chgo., Nov. 6, 1938; d. Edward E. and Eleanor A. (Erickson) Keough; children: Matthew K., Mary Alice BA, U. Ill., 1960; JD, Loyola U., Chgo., 1964. Bar: Ill. 1964, Ga. 1997, U.S. Dist. Ct. (no. dist.) Ill. 1964, U.S. Tax Ct. 1974. With Seyfarth Shaw, Chgo., 1964—, ptnr., 1971-98, of counsel, 1998—. Fellow Am. Coll. Trust and Estate Counsel; mem. ABA (com. on fed. taxation), Ill. Bar Assn. (coun. sect. on fed. taxation 1983-91, chair 1989, coun. sect. on trusts and estates sect. coun. 1992-97, sec. 1996-97, editl. bd. Ill. Bar Jour. 1993-96), Chgo. Bar Assn. (chmn. trust law com. 1982-83, com. on fed. taxation). Office: Seyfarth Shaw 55 E Monroe St Ste 4200 Chicago IL 60603-5863

LUNDSTEDT, SVEN BERTIL, behavioral and social scientist, educator; b. N.Y.C., May 6, 1926; s. Sven David and Edith Maria L.; m. Jean Elizabeth Sanford, June 16, 1951; children: Margaret, Peter, Janet. AB, U. Chgo., 1952, PhD, 1955; SM, Harvard U., 1960. Lic. in psychology, N.Y., Ohio; cert. Council for Nat. Register of Health Services. Asst. dir. Found. for Research on Human Behavior, 1960-62; asst. prof. Case-Western Res. U., Cleve., 1962-64, assoc. prof., 1964-68; assoc. prof. adminstrv. sci. Ohio State U., Columbus, 1968-69, prof. pub. policy and mgmt., 1969—, Ameritech Research prof., 1987-89, prof. internat. bus. and pub. policy, 1988—, prof. mgmt. and human resources, 1990—, mem. John Glenn Inst. for Pub. Svc. and Pub. Policy, 1999—. Affiliate scientist Battelle PNL, 1994—; chmn. Battelle endowment program for tech. and human affairs, 1976-80, mem. Univ. Senate; dir. project on edn. of chief exec. officer Aspen Inst., 1978-80; advisor Task Force on Innovation, U.S. Ho. of Reps., 1983-84, Citizens Network for Fgn. Affairs, 1988—; mem. Am. Com. on U.S. Soviet Relations, 1985—, chair trade and negotiation project; cons. E.I. duPont de Nemours & Co., B.F. Goodrich Co., Bell Telephone Labs., Battelle Meml. Inst., Nat. Fulbright Award Com.; invited speaker Royal Swedish Acad. Scis., 1989. Author: Higher Education in Social Psychology, 1968; co-author: Managing Innovation, 1982, Managing Innovation and Change, 1989; author, editor: Telecommunications, Values and the Public Interest, 1990; contbr. articles to profl. jours. Pres., Cleve. Mental Health Assn., 1966-68; mem. Ohio Citizen's Task Force on Corrections, 1971-72. Served with U.S. Army, 1944-46 Harvard U. fellow, 1960; grantee Bell Telephone Labs., 1964-65, NSF, 1965-67, Kettering Found., 1978-80, Atlantic Richfield Found., 1980-82, German Marshall Fund of U.S. to conduct internat. ednl. joint ventures on econ. negotiations, Budapest, Hungary, 1990; recipient Ohio Ho. of Reps. award, 1986. Mem.: Internat. Soc. Panetics (mem., sec. bd. govs., founding mem.), Am. Soc. for Pub. Adminstrn. (pres. Central Ohio chpt. 1975—77, founder, chmn. com. on bus. govt. relations 1977—79, editl. bd. Pub. Adminstrn. Rev. 1978—82), Am. Acad. Arts and Scis. (chmn. PIN com. on east/west trade negotiation), Internat. Inst. for Applied Systems Analysis (innovation task force, nat. adv. com. project. internat. negotiation with AAAS, founder, chmn. U.S. Midwest Assn. for IIASA 1986—, sr. social sci. advisor 1994—), Am. Psychol. Assn. Unitarian Home: 197 Riverview Park Dr Columbus OH 43214-2023 Office: Ohio State U Sch Pub Policy and Mgmt 2100 Neil Ave Columbus OH 43210-1144 E-mail: lundstedt.1@osu.edu.

LUNDY, SHERMAN PERRY, secondary school educator; b. Kansas City, Mo., July 26, 1939; s. Loren F. and O. Metta (Brown) L.; m. Beverly J., Feb. 25, 1960; children: Paul, Carolyn. BA, U. Okla., 1963; MA, So. Meth. U., 1966; EdS, U. Iowa, 1975. Cert. tchr., Iowa. Tchr. Platte Canyon High Sch., Bailey, Colo., 1964-65, Lone Grove (Okla.) High Sch., 1966-68, Ardmore (Okla.) High Sch., 1968-69; tchr., sci. dept. chair Burlington (Iowa) High Sch., 1969—. Geologist Basic Materials Corp., Waterloo, Iowa, 1983—, Raid Quarries, Burlington, 1975-80. Contbr. articles to profl. jours.; author curriculum guide: Environmental Activities, 1975. Mem., commr. Regional Solid Waste Commn., Des Moines County, 1990—; mem., pres. Conservation Bd., Des Moines County, 1978-88; bd. dirs. Iowa Conservation Bd. Assn., 1984-85; mem. Civil Rights Commn., City of Burlington, 1970-76; pres. Burlington Trees Forever, 1998-99. With USMC, 1960-64. Recipient Silver Beaver Boy Scouts Am., 1975, Service Recognition, Des Moines County Conservation Bd., 1988, Project ES-TEEM agt., Harvard/Smithsonian, 1992, Soil Conservation Water Shed Achievement award State of Iowa, 1998, DAR Award for Conservation, 1998, Environ. Educator of Yr. award U.S. EPA, Region 7, Iowa, 1998. Mem. Geol. Soc. Am. (North Cen. edn. com. 1989—), Iowa Acad. Sci. (edn. com. 1990-91, chair earth sci. tchrs. sect. 1993-94, exec. bd. 1992-94), Nat. Assn. Geology Tchrs. (Outstanding Earth Sci. Tchr. 1992, v.p. ctrl. sect. 1994-95, pres. ctrl. sect. 1996-98), Soc. Econ. and Sedimentary Geology, Geol. Soc. Iowa, Am. Chem. Soc. (Excellence in Sci. Tchg. award consortiums 1996, Chem. Cos. award), Unitarian Fellowship, Sons of Confederate Vets. (comdr. Camp 1759 1998—), SE Iowa Civil War Round Table (chair 1992-94). Unitarian. Avocations: civil war, stamp collecting, fossil collecting. Home: 4668 Summer St Burlington IA 52601-8985

LUNDY, WALKER, newspaper editor; b. St. Petersburg, Fla. m. Saralyn Lundy; 2 children. BSJ, U. Fla. Reporter Atlanta Jour.-Constitution; reporter, city editor Detroit Free Press; mng. editor, exec. editor Tallahassee Democrat; mng. editor Ft. Worth Star-Telegram; editor Arkansas Gazette, Little Rock; gen. editor, sr. v.p. St. Paul Pioneer Press, 1990—, exec. editor, sr. v.p., 1990—. Office: Northwest Publishing Inc 345 Cedar St Saint Paul MN 55101-1004

LUNGSTRUM, JOHN W. federal judge; b. Topeka, Nov. 2, 1945; s. Jack Edward and Helen Alice (Watson) L.; m. Linda Eileen Ewing, June 21, 1969; children: Justin Matthew, Jordan Elizabeth, Alison Paige. BA magna cum laude, Yale Coll., 1967; JD, U. Kans., 1970. Bar: Kans. 1970, Calif. 1970, U.S. Dist. Ct. (ctrl. dist.) Calif., U.S. Ct. Appeals (10th crct.). Assoc. Latham & Watkins, L.A., 1970-71; ptnr. Stevens, Brand, Lungstrum, Golden & Winter, Lawrence, Kans., 1972-91; U.S. Dist. judge Dist. of Kans., Kansas City, 1991—, chief judge, 2001—. Lectr. law U. Kans. Law Sch., 1973—; mem. faculty Kans. Bar Assn. Coll. Advocacy , Trial Tactics and Techniques Inst., 1983-86; chmn. Douglas County Rep. Ctrl. Com., 1975-81; mem. Rep. State Com.; del. State Rep. Convention, 1968, 76, 80; chair com. on ct. adminstrn. and case mgmt. Jud. Conf. of the U.S., 2000—. Chmn. bd. dirs. Lawrence C. of C., 1990-91; pres. Lawrence United Fund, 1979; pres. Independence Days Lawrence, Inc., 1984, 85, Seem-to-be-Players, Inc., Lawrence Rotary Club, 1978-79; bd. dirs. Lawrence Soc. Chamber Music, Swarthout Soc. (corp. fund-raising chmn.); mem. Lawrence Art Commn., Williams Scholarship Fund, Lawrence League Women Voters, Douglas County Hist. Soc.; bd. trustees, stewardship chmn. Plymouth Congl. Ch.; pres. Lawrence Round Ball Club; coach Lawrence Summertime Basketball; Vice chmn. U. Kans. Disciplinary Bd.; bd. govs. Kans Sch. Religion; bd. dirs. Kans. Day Club, 1980, 81. National Merit scholar, Yale Nat. scholar. Fellow Am. Bar Found.; mem. ABA (past mem. litigation and ins. sect.), Douglas County Bar Assn., Johnson County Bar Assn., Wyandotte County Bar Assn., Kans. Bar Assn. (vice chair legislative com., subcom. litigation, mem. continuing legal edn. com.), U Kans. Alumni Assn. (life), Phi Beta Kappa, Phi Gamma Delta, Phi Delta Phi. Avocations: basketball, hiking, skiing. Office: Robt J Dole US Courthouse Ste 517 500 State Ave Rm 517 Kansas City KS 66101-2400

LUNING, THOMAS P. lawyer; b. St. Louis, Oct. 11, 1942; AB magna cum laude, Xavier U., 1964; JD, Georgetown U., 1967. Bar: D.C. 1968, Ill. 1968. Law clk. to Hon. Spottswood W. Robinson III and to ct. U.S. Ct. Appeals (D.C. cir.), 1967-68; atty. Schiff Hardin & Waite, Chgo. Mng. editor Georgetown Law Jour., 1966-67. Mem. ABA, Ill. State Bar Assn., Chgo. Bar Assn., 7th Cir. Bar Assn., Chgo. Coun. Lawyers. Office: Schiff Hardin & Waite 6600 Sears Tower Chicago IL 60606 E-mail: tluning@schiffhardin.com.

LUOMA, JUDY, ranching executive; Office: Luoma Egg Ranch Inc 2535 Highway 18 Finlayson MN 55735-8700

LUPULESCU, AUREL PETER, medical educator, researcher, physician; b. Manastiur, Banat, Romania, Jan. 1, 1923; came to U.S., 1967, naturalized, 1973; s. Peter Vichentie and Maria Ann (Dragan) L. MD magna cum laude, Sch. Medicine, Bucharest, Romania, 1950; MS in Endocrinology, U. Bucharest, 1965; PhD in Biology, U. Windsor, Ont., Can., 1976. Diplomate Am. Bd. Internal Medicine. Chief lab. investigations Inst. Endocrinology, Bucharest, 1950-67; rsch. assoc. SUNY Downstate Med. Ctr., 1968-69; asst. prof. medicine Wayne State U., 1969-72, assoc. prof., 1973—. Vis. prof. Inst. Med. Pathology, Rome, 1967; cons. VA Hosp., Allen Park, Mich., 1971-73. Author: Steroid Hormones, 1958, Advances in Endocrinology and Metabolism, 1962, Experimental Pathophysiology of Thyroid Gland, 1963, Ultrastructure of Thyroid Gland, 1968, Effect of Calcitonin on Epidermal Cells and Collagen Synthesis in Experimental Wounds As Revealed by Electron Microscopy Autoradiography and Scanning Electron Microscopy, 1976, Hormones and Carcinogenesis, 1983, Hormones and Vitamins in Cancer Treatment, 1990, Cancer Cell Metabolism and Cancer Treatment, 2001; reviewer various sci. jours.; contbr. chpts., numerous articles to profl. publs. Fellow Fedn. Am. Socs. for Exptl. Biology; mem. AMA, AAAS, Electron Microscopy Soc. Am., Soc. for Investigative Dermatology, N.Y. Acad. Scis., Am. Soc. Cell Biology, Soc. Exptl. Biology and Medicine. Republican. Achievements include research on hormones and tumor biology; studies regarding role of hormones and vitamins in carcinogenesis. Home: 21480 Mahon Dr Southfield MI 48075-7525 Office: Wayne State U Sch Medicine 540 E Canfield St Detroit MI 48201-1928

LURAIN, JOHN ROBERT, III, gynecologic oncologist; b. Princeton, Ill., Oct. 27, 1946; s. John Robert Jr. and Elizabeth Helen (Grampp) L.; m. Nell Lee Snavely, June 14, 1969; children: Alice Elizabeth, Kathryn Anne. BA, Oberlin Coll., 1968; MD, U. N.C., 1972. Diplomate Am. Bd. Ob-Gyn., Am. Bd. Gynecologic Oncology. Resident in ob-gyn. U. Pitts./Magee-Womens Hosp., 1972-75; fellow in gynecologic oncology Roswell Park Cancer Inst., Buffalo, 1977-79; prof. ob-gyn. Northwestern U. Med. Sch., Chgo., 1979—, John and Ruth Brewer prof. gynecology and cancer rsch., 1985—. Head sect. gynecol. oncology, chief gynecologic oncology svc. Northwestern Meml. Hosp./Prentice Women's Hosp., Chgo., 1985—. Contbr. over 130 articles to profl. jours., chpts. to books. Lt. comdr. USN, 1975-77. Fellow Am. Coll. Ob-Gyn.; mem. Soc. Gynecologic Oncologists, Am. Soc. Clin. Oncology, Ctrl. Assn. Ob-Gyn., Am. Soc. for Colposcopy and Cervical Pathology, Chgo. Gynecol. Soc. Avocations: golf, tennis. Office: Northwestern U Med Sch 333 E Superior St Chicago IL 60611-3015 E-mail: jlurain@nmh.org.

LUSHER, JEANNE MARIE, pediatric hematologist, educator; b. Toledo, June 9, 1935; d. Arnold Christian and Violet Cecilia (French) L. BS summa cum laude, U. Cin., 1956, MD, 1960. Resident in pediat. Tulane divsn. Charity Hosp. La., New Orleans, 1961-64; fellow in pediat. hematology-oncology Child Rsch. Ctr. Mich., Detroit, 1964-65, St. Louis Children's Hosp./Washington U., 1965-66; instr. pediat. Washington U., St. Louis, 1965-66; from instr. to assoc. prof. Sch. Medicine Wayne State U., Detroit, 1966-74, prof., 1974-97, disting. prof., 1997—; dir. divsn. hematology-oncology Children's Hosp. Mich., 1976—. Marion I. Barnhart prof. hemostasis rsch. Sch. Medicine Wayne State U., Detroit, 1989—; med. dir. Nat. Hemophilia Found., N.Y.C., 1987—94, chmn. med. and sci. adv. coun., 1994—2001, bd. dirs., 1997—2001, co-chmn. gene therapy working group, 2000—. Author, editor: Treatment of Bleeding Disorders with Blood Components, 1980, Sickle Cell, 1974, 76, 81, Hemophilia and von Willebrand Disease in the 1990's, 1991, Acquired Bleeding Disorders in Children, 1981, F VIII/von Willebrand Factor and Platelets in Health and Disease, 1987, Inhibitors to Factor VIII, 1994, Blood Coagulation Innhibitors, 1996. Mem. Citizens Info. Com., Pontiac Township, Mich., 1980-82; apptd. mem. Hazardous Waste Incinerator Commn., Oakland County, Mich., 1981. Recipient Disting. Alumnus award U. Cin. Alumni Assn., 1990, Lawrence Weiner award Wayne State U. Sch. Medicine Alumni Assn., 1991. Mem. Am. Bd. Pediat. (chmn. sub-bd. on hematology-oncology 1988-90), Am. Soc. Hematology (chmn. sci. com. pediat. 1991-92, sci. com. hemostasis 1998—), Am. Pediat. Soc., Soc. Pediat. Rsch., Internat. Soc. Thrombosis-Hemostasis (chmn. factor VIII/IX sub-com. 1985-90, chmn. sci. and standardization com. 1996-98), Mich. Humane Soc. Avocations: nature, wildlife. Office: Children's Hosp Mich 3901 Beaubien Blvd Detroit MI 48201-2119 E-mail: jlusher@med.wayne.edu.

LUSK, WILLIAM EDWARD, real estate and oil company executive; b. Medicine Lodge, Kans., May 16, 1916; s. William Edward and Teresa (Rhoades) L.; m. Anita Ballard, Feb. 1, 1942; children— William Edward, Janet Kathryn and James Raymond (twins). BS in Edn; AB in Econs., Ft. Hays State Coll., 1939; student, Washburn U., 1936; postgrad., Kans. U., 1940-41. Tchr. Protection (Kans.) High Sch., 1939-41; mgr. real estate dept. Wheeler, Kelly & Hagny Investment Co., Wichita, Kans., 1946-63; co-founder, exec. v.p., treas., dir. Clinton Oil Co., 1963-73; pres. Lusk Real Estate Co., 1963—, Lusk Investment Co., 1973—. Pres. Wichita Real Estate Bd., 1961 Founder Lusk Found., 1968, William E. Lusk Scholarship, Ft. Hays State Coll., 1969; bd. dirs. Jr. Achievement Wichita. Served with USNR, 1942-46; comdr. Res. Named Kans. Realtor of Year Kans. Assn. Real Estate Bds., 1962; recipient Alumni Achievement award Ft. Hays Kan. State Coll., 1971 Mem. VFW, Sojourners, Res. Officers Assn., Naval Res. Officers Assn., Navy League, Phi Alpha Delta, Alpha Kappa Psi (hon.) Methodist (bd. dirs. 1965-70, fin. chmn. 1969—). Clubs: Wichita Country, Wichita (bd. dirs. 1969-72, pres. 1972), McConnell AFB Officers. Lodge: Masons (32 degree). Home: 6 West Pkwy N Wichita KS 67206-2446 Office: 1608 E Lewis St Wichita KS 67211-1823 E-mail: William.lusksr@gte.net.

LUSSEN, JOHN FREDERICK, pharmaceutical laboratory executive; b. N.Y.C., Jan. 5, 1942; s. Frederick Maurice and Kathleen (Herlihy) L.; m. Kathleen Elizabeth Sheppard; children: Tara, Eric, Gregory. BS in Fin., Fordham U., 1963, JD, 1967; LLM in Tax, NYU, 1971. Bar: N.Y. 1967. Tax atty. Pfizer Inc., N.Y.C., 1971-74; mgr. taxes SCM Corp., 1974-79; v.p. taxes Abbott Labs., Abbott Park, Ill., 1979—. PhRMA tax com. Fin. Execs. Inst. Capt. U.S. Army, 1968-70. Mem. ABA, Tax Execs. Inst., Bus. Roundtable (mem. tax subcom.), P.R. USA Found. (pres.). Avocations: tennis, golf. Home: 1055 Westleigh Rd Lake Forest IL 60045 Office: Abbott Labs D367 AP6D 100 Abbott Park Rd Abbott Park IL 60064-6057 E-mail: john.lussen@Abbott.com.

LUSTER, JORY F. president of manufacturing company; Prin., owner Luster Products, Inc., Chgo., 1991—. Office: Luster Products Inc 1104 W 43rd St Chicago IL 60609-3342

LUSTREA, ANITA, radio personality; b. Blue Hill, Maine, May 28; m. Bob Lustrea; 1 child John. Radio host Sta. WMBI , Chgo. Office: WMBI 820 LaSalle Blvd Chicago IL 60610*

LUTHER, ROBERT K. college president; BA, MA, Eastern Ill. U.; PhD, U. Mich. V.p. Carl Sandburg Coll., Galesburg, Ill.; pres. Columbia-Greene Cmty. Coll., Hudson, N.Y., Lake Land Coll., Mattoon, Ill., 1988—. Pres. East Ctrl. Ill. Dev. Corp., Coles Together; v.p. Ill. Council Cmty. Coll. Pres.; mem. Ill. Human Resource Investment Council (chmn. employment opportunities com.), Ill. Cmty. Coll. Bd., Ill. Bd. Higher Edn. Workforce Dev. Task Force. Office: Lake Land College 5001 Lake Land Bvld Mattoon IL 61938-9366

LUTHER, WILLIAM P. congressman; b. Fergus Falls, Minn., June 27, 1945; s. Leonard and Eleanor L.; m. Darlene Luther, Dec. 16, 1967; children: Alexander, Alicia. BS in Elec. Engring. with high distinction, U. Minn., 1967; JD cum laude, U. Minn. Law Sch., 1970. Judicial clerkship 8th cir. U.S. Ct. Appeals, 1970-71; atty. Dorsey & Whitney Law Firm, Mpls., 1971-74, William P. Luther Law Office, Mpls., 1974-83; founder, sr. ptnr. Luther, Ballenthin & Carruthers Law Firm, 1983-92; state sen. 47th dist. State of Minn., 1977-94, asst. maj. leader, 1983-94; mem. U.S. Congress from 6th Minn. dist., 1995—; mem. commerce com., telecomm., trade & consumer protection , fin., hazardous materials subcoms. Home: 6375 Saint Croix Trl N Apt 147 Stillwater MN 55082-6932 Office: US House Reps 117 Cannon House Office Bldg Washington DC 20515-2306 also: 1811 Weir Dr Ste 150 Woodbury MN 55125-2291*

LUTHRINGSHAUSEN, WAYNE, brokerage house executive; b. 1945; Commodities sys. analyst Howard, Weil, Labouesse, Friedricks, Inc., New Orleans, 1968-70; planning specialist Chgo. Bd. Trade, 1970-72; with Options Clearing Corp., Chgo., chmn., CEO. Office: Options Clearing Corp 440 S La Salle St Ste 2400 Chicago IL 60605-1028

LUTHRINGSHAUSER, DANIEL RENE, manufacturing company executive; b. Fontainebleau, France, July 23, 1935; came to U.S., 1937; s. Ernest Henri and Jeanne (Guerville) L.; m. Carol King; children: Mark Ernest, Heidi Elizabeth. BS, NYU, 1956, MBA, 1970. With exec. tng. program, internat. pub. relations Merck & Co. Inc., Rahway, N.J. and N.Y.C., 1962-65; dep. mktg. dir. Merck Sharp & Dohme Internat., Brussels, 1965-66; mktg. service dir. Paris, 1966-69; gen. mgr. Merck Sharp & Dohme/Chibret, 1970-74; v.p. mktg. Merrell (France), 1974-78; v.p. gen. mgr. Revlon Devel. Corp., 1978-82, Medtronic Europe, Paris, Africa, Middle East, 1982-86; v.p. internat. Medtronic Inc., Mpls., 1986-98; prin. DRL Internat. Cons., 1998—. Bd. dirs. Medtronic Found., Mpls., 1986-91; chmn. Internat. Assn. of Prosthesis Mfrs., Paris, 1983-85. Bd. dirs. Am. Hosp. Paris, 1983-86, 94-95, Minn. Internat. Ctr., 1990—; mem. Am. Club Paris, 1970-80, Medtronic Found., Mpls., 1986-91. Served to capt. USAF, 1956-62. Recipient Gold medal Am. Mktg. Assn., 1956. Club: Ausable (Keene Valley, N.Y.). Avocations: gardening, golf, squash, skiing. Home: 480 Peavey Rd Wayzata MN 55391-1529 Office: PO Box 286 Wayzata MN 55391

LUTTER, PAUL ALLEN, lawyer; b. Chgo., Feb. 28, 1946; s. Herbert W. and Lois (Muller) L. BA, Carleton Coll., 1968; JD, Yale U., 1971. Bar: Ill. 1971, U.S. Tax Ct. 1986. Assoc. Ross & Hardies, Chgo., 1971-77, ptnr., 1978—. Co-author: Illinois Estate Administration, 1993. Dir. Howard Brown Health Ctr.; chmn.'s coun. Design Industries Found. Fighting AIDS, Chgo. Mem. ABA, Chgo. Bar Assn. Home: 2214 N Magnolia Ave Chicago IL 60614-3104 Office: Ross & Hardies 150 N Michigan Ave Ste 2500 Chicago IL 60601-7567

LUTZ, LARRY EDWARD, state legislator; b. Evansville, Ind., Oct. 28, 1938; s. Edward George and Bertha (Eberhardt) L.; m. Mary Lotus Toelle, 1961; 1 child, Chris Edward. Student, Lockyears Bus. Coll., Evansville, Ind., 1963, U. so. Ind., 1985. Lt. Evansville Fire Dept., 1963-65, inspector, 1966-68, dist. chief, 1979-83; master firefighter State of Ind., 1979; assessor Perry Twp., Vanderburgh County, Ind., 1979-82; mem. Ind. Ho. of Reps. from 76th dist., 1982-96; chmn. environ. affairs com.; mem. ins. corp. and sml. bus. com.; mem. pub. safety com., labor com., rds. and transp. com.; mem. Ind. Senate from 49th dist., 1999—. Named Hon. State Fire Marshal, 1980-83, Firfighter of Yr., Kiwanis, Ind., 1980. Mem. Ind. Firefighters Assn. (pres. 1976-77), Ind. Assessors Assn. (v.p. 1981), Kiwanis. Home: 5530 Whippoorwill Dr Evansville IN 47712-7120

LUTZ, ROBERT ANTHONY, automotive company executive; b. Zurich, Switzerland, Feb. 12, 1932; came to U.S., 1939; s. Robert H. and Marguerite (Schmid) L.; m. Betty D. Lutz, Dec. 12, 1956 (div. 1979); children: Jacqueline, Carolyn, Catherine, Alexandra; m. Heide Marie Schmid, Mar. 3, 1980 (div. Dec. 1992); m. Denise Ford, Apr. 17, 1994; 2 stepchildren. BS in Prodn. Mgmt., U. Calif., Berkeley, 1961, MBA in Mktg. with highest honors, 1962; LLD, Boston U., 1985. Research assoc., sr. analyst IMEDE, Lausanne, Switzerland, 1962-63; sr. analyst forward planning GM, N.Y.C., 1963-65, mgr. vehicle div. Paris, 1966-69; staff asst., mng. dir. Adam Opel, Russelsheim, Germany, 1965-66, asst. mgr. domestic sales Germany, 1969, dir. sales Vorstand Germany, 1969-70; v.p. Vorstand BMW, Munich, 1972-74; gen. mgr. Ford of Germany, Cologne, Germany, 1974-76; v.p. truck ops. Ford of Europe, Brentwood, Eng., 1976-77, pres. Eng., 1977-79, chmn. Eng., 1979-82, also bd. dirs. Eng.; exec. v.p. Ford Internat., Dearborn, Mich., 1982-84, Chrysler Motors Corp., Highland Park, 1986-88; pres. ops., pres., COO Chrysler Corp., 1988-96, vice chmn.; chmn., CEO, pres. Exide Corp., 1998—. Bd. dirs. Northrop-Grumman, Kepner-Tregoe, Silicon Graphics, Northrop-Grumman, ASCOM, Switzerland; mem., former chmn. Hwy. Users Fedn. for Safety and Mobility. Trustee Mich. Cancer Found.; bd. dirs. United Way of Southeastern Mich., USMC Command and Staff Coll. Found.; mem. adv. bd. Walter A. Haas Sch. Bus., U. Calif., Berkeley, 1979—. Capt. USMC, 1954-59. Named Alumnus of Yr., Sch. Bus., U. Calif., 1983; Kaiser Found. grantee, 1962. Mem. NAM (exec. com.), Phi Beta Kappa. Republican. Avocations: skiing, motorcycling, bicycling, helicopter flying, vintage cars, fixed-wing flying. Office: 2901 Hubbard St Ann Arbor MI 48109-2435 also: Exide Corp 645 Penn St Reading PA 19601

LYALL, KATHARINE C(ULBERT), academic administrator, economics educator; b. Lancaster, Pa., Apr. 26, 1941; d. John D. and Eleanor G. Lyall. BA in Econs., Cornell U., 1963, PhD in Econs., 1969; MBA, NYU, 1965. Economist Chase Manhattan Bank, N.Y.C., 1963-65; asst. prof. econs. Syracuse U., 1969-72; prof. econs. Johns Hopkins U., Balt., 1972-77, dir. grad. program in pub. policy, 1979-81; dep. asst. sec. for econs. Office Econ. Affairs, HUD, Washington, 1977-79; v.p. acad. affairs U. Wis. Sys., 1981-85; prof. of econ. U. Wis., Madison, 1982—; acting pres. U. Wis. Sys., 1985-86, 91-92, exec. v.p., 1986-91, pres., 1992—. Bd. dirs. Kemper Ins. Cos., Marshall & Ilsley Bank, Wis. Power & Light, Alliant; pres., bd. dirs. Carnegie Found. for Advancement of Teaching. Author: Reforming Public Welfare, 1976, Microeconomic Issues of the 70s, 1978. Mem. Mcpl. Securities Rulemaking Bd., Washington, 1990-93. Mem. Am. Econ. Assn., Assn. Am. Univs., Phi Beta Kappa. Home: 6021 S Highlands Ave Madison WI 53705-1110 Office: U Wis Sys Office of Pres 1720 Van Hise Hall 1220 Linden Dr Madison WI 53706-1559

LYALL, LYNN, consumer products company executive; Sr. v.p. fin., info. svcs. & tech. Cadbury Schweppes, PLC; exec. v.p., CFO Blockbuster Entertainment, Inc.; v.p., CFO Amway Corp., 1999—. Office: Amway Corp 7575 Fulton St E Ada MI 49355

LYBYER, MIKE JOSEPH, former state legislator, farmer; b. Waynesville, Mo., Feb. 23, 1947; m. Mary Jane Rockill, 1981. BS, U. Mo., 1969. Farmer, Huggins, Mo., 1969—; mem. Mo. Senate, Jefferson City, 1976-98. Mem. edn. and transp. bill coms., chmn. agr., conservation and parks com.; govt. cons. Mem. Masons, Shriners, Odd Fellows. Democrat. Address: 12743 Highway 38 Huggins MO 65484-9108

LYDECKER, ANN MARIE, college administrator; B, Oberlin (Ohio) Coll., 1966, MAT, 1972; PhD, U. Mich., 1982. Prof., chair curriculum and instrn. dept. Mankato (Minn.) State U., 1987-92; dean Sch. Edn. and Allied Studies Bridgewater (Mass.) State Coll., 1992-95, acting v.p. acad. affairs, 1995-96, provost, v.p. acad. affairs, 1995-2000; chancellor U. Wisc., River Falls, 2000—. Office: U Wisc River Falls 116 North Hall 410 S 3d St River Falls WI 54022 E-mail: ann.m.lydecker@uwrf.edu.

LYNCH, DANIEL C. state legislator; b. Omaha, Aug. 9, 1929; m. Jane Lynch, 1950; children: Debby, Julia, Marrianne, Maureen, Dan Jr. Student, Loras Coll. Pres. Lynch Plumbing & Heating Co.; mem. from 13th dist. Nebr. State Senate, Lincoln, 1984—, chmn. rules com., past mem. com. on coms., appropriations com., past mem. Nebr. retirement sys. com.; v.p. consumer and govt. affairs Blue Cross/Blue Shield, Omaha, 1984—. V.p. consumer and govt. affairs Blue Cross/Blue Shield, Nebr. Commr. Douglas County, 1960-81; mem. Pres.' Coun. on Intergovtl. Affairs; mem. adv. com. Ea. Nebr. Office on Aging. Mem. Assn. Counties, Omaha Comml. Club. Office: Nebr State Senate Nebr Unicameral Dist 13 PO Box 94604 Lincoln NE 68509-4604 also: Blue Cross/Blue Shield 7261 Mercy Rd Omaha NE 68124-2349

LYNCH, DAVID WILLIAM, physicist, educator; b. Rochester, N.Y., July 14, 1932; s. William J. and Eleanor (Fouratt) L.; m. Joan N. Hill, Aug. 29, 1954 (dec. Nov. 1989); children: Jean Louise, Richard William, David Allan; m. Glenys R. Bittick, Nov. 14, 1992. BS, Rensselaer Poly. Inst., 1954; MS, U. Ill., 1955, PhD, 1958. Asst. prof. physics Iowa State U., 1959-63, assoc. prof., 1963-66, prof., 1966—, chmn. dept., 1985-90, disting. prof. liberal arts and scis., 1985—; on leave at U. Hamburg, Germany; and U. Rome, Italy, 1968-69; sr. physicist Ames Lab. of Dept. of Energy; acting assoc. dir. Synchrotron Radiation Ctr., Stoughton, Wis., 1984. Vis. prof. U. Hamburg, summer 1974; dir. Microelectronics Rsch. Ctr., Iowa State U., 1995-99. Fulbright scholar U. Pavia, Italy, 1958-59. Fellow Am. Phys. Soc.; mem. AAAS, Optical Soc. Am. Achievements include research on solid state physics. Home: 2020 Elm Cir West Des Moines IA 50265-4294 E-mail: dwl@ameslab.gov.

LYNCH, EDWARD FRANCIS, professional sports team executive; b. Bklyn., Feb. 25, 1956; m. Kristin Kacer; children: Meghan, James. BA in Fin., U. S.C., 1977; JD, U. Miami, 1990. Pitcher Chgo. Cubs, 1977-80, 86-87, gen. mgr., v.p., 1994—; spl. asst. to exec. v.p. baseball ops. N.Y. Mets, 1980-86; dir. minor leagues San Diego Padres, 1990-93; pitcher Tex. Rangers, 1977-79, N.Y. Mets, 1980-86, dir. ops., 1993. Office: Chicago Cubs 1060 W Addison St Chicago IL 60613-4397

LYNCH, GEORGE MICHAEL, auto parts manufacturing executive; b. Ft. Lauderdale, Fla., Apr. 7, 1943; s. Jack Traverse and Ruth Margarite (Koehler) L.; m. Carol Rollins, June 18, 1966; children: Kristin Ruth, Michael Scott. BSEE, Cornell U., 1965, MEE, 1966; MS in Indsl. Adminstrn., Carnegie-Mellon U., 1968. Fin. analyst, various supervisory positions Ford Motor Co., Dearborn, Mich., 1968-73, mgr. car product analysis, 1973-76, mgr. N.Am. ops. N.Am. contrs. analysis dept. office, 1976-77, mgr. programming and capacity dept., 1977-81, mgr. facilities and fin. staff mgmt. svcs., 1981-83, dir. fin. Ford of Australia, 1983-86, contr. Ford Tractor div. Troy, Mich., 1986-87; exec. v.p., chief fin. officer Ford New Holland, Inc., New Holland, Pa., 1987-97; v.p., contr. Dow Chem. Co., 1997-2000; exec. v.p., CFO Fed.-Mogul Corp., Southfield, Mich., 2000—. Mem. Lancaster C. of C. (dir. 1988—), Lancaster Country Club, Birmingham Athletic Club (tennis chmn. 1977—), Phi Kappa Phi, Tau Beta Pi. Avocations: tennis, biking. Office: Fed Mogul Corp 26555 Northwestern Hwy Southfield MI 48034 Home: 2566 Kent Ridge Ct Bloomfield Hills MI 48301-2276

LYNCH, HENRY THOMSON, medical educator; b. Lawrence, Mass., Jan. 4, 1928; s. Henry F. and Eleanor (Thomson) L.; m. Jane Smith, Nov. 9, 1951; children— Patrick, Kathleen, Ann. B.S., Okla., 1951; M.A., Denver U., 1952; M.D., U. Tex., Galveston, 1960. Intern St. Mary's Hosp., Evansville, Ind., 1960; resident U. Nebr. Sch. Medicine, 1961-64, sr. clin. cancer trainee, 1964-66; practice medicine specializing in internal medicine and medical oncology Omaha, 1967—; asst. prof. medicine U. Tex. M.D. Anderson Hosp., Houston, 1966-67; assoc. prof. Creighton U. Sch. Medicine, Omaha, 1967-70, prof., chmn. dept. preventive medicine and pub. health, 1970—, prof. medicine, 1982—. Editor: Hereditary Factors in Carcinoma, 1967, Dynamic Genetic Counseling for Clinicians, 1969, Cancer and You, 1971, Skin, Heredity and Malignant Neoplasms, 1972, Cancer Genetics, 1975, Genetics and Breast Cancer, 1981, Cancer Associated Genodermatoses, 1982, Colon Cancer Genetics, 1985, Biomarkers, Genetics and Cancer, 1985; contbr. over 550 sci. articles. Served with USNR, 1944-46. Recipient Bristol-Myers Squibb Co. unrestricted cancer rsch. grantee, 1996. Office: Creighton U Sch Med Dept Preventive Med Criss Ii Omaha NE 68178-0001

LYNCH, JOHN PETER, lawyer; b. Chgo., June 5, 1942; s. Charles Joseph and Anne Mae (Loughlin) L.; m. Judy Godvin, Sept. 21, 1968; children: Julie, Jennifer. AB, Marquette U., 1964; JD, Northwestern U., 1967. Bar: Ill. 1967, U.S. Ct. Appeals (7th cir.) 1979, U.S. Ct. Appeals (5th cir.) 1976, U.S. Supreme Ct. 1979. Ptnr. Kirkland & Ellis, Chgo., 1973-76, Hedlund, Hunter & Lynch, Chgo., 1976-82, Latham, Watkins, Hedlund, Hunter & Lynch, Chgo., 1982-85, Latham & Watkins, Chgo., 1985—. Mem. vis. com. Northwestern U. Law Sch. Served as lt. USN, 1968-71. Mem. ABA, Ill. Bar Assn., Assn. Trial Lawyers Am., Order of Coif, City Club, Exec. Club, Met. Club. Notes and Comments editor Northwestern U. Law Rev., 1967. Home: 439 Sheridan Rd Kenilworth IL 60043-1220 Office: Latham & Watkins Ste 5800 Sears Tower Chicago IL 60606

LYNCH, LELAND T. advertising executive; Co-founder, chmn., CEO Carmichael Lynch, Mpls., 1962—. Co-founder Leading Ind. Agy. Network. Bd. dis. Planned Parenthood Minn., Minn. Pub. Radio; chair-elect Mpls. Downtown Coun., 1996—. Mem. Am. Assn. Advt. Agys. (regional pres., nat. sec./treas.). Office: Carmichael Lynch Inc 800 Hennepin Ave Minneapolis MN 55403-1817

LYNCH, MIKE, meteorologist, radio personality; Instr. astronomy Wood Lake Nature Ctr., Richfield, Minn., 1973; instr., 1973—, Wis., 1973—; broadcast meteorologist Sta. WCCO Radio, Mpls., 1981—. Office: WCCO 602 2nd Ave S Minneapolis MN 55402*

LYNCH, PRISCILLA A. nursing educator, therapist; b. Joliet, Ill., Jan. 8, 1949; d. LaVerne L. and Ann M. (Zamkovitz) L. BS, U. Wyo., 1973; MS, St. Xavier Coll., Coll., 1981. RN, Ill. Staff nurse Rush-Presbyn.-St. Luke's Med. Ctr., Chgo., 1977-81, psychiat.-liaison cons., 1981-83, asst. prof. nursing, unit dir., 1985—. Mgr. and therapist Oakside Clinic, Kankakee, Ill., 1987—; mem. adv. bd. Depressive and Manic Depression Assn., Chgo., 1986—; mem. consultation and mental health unit Riverside Med. Ctr., Kankakee, 1987—; speaker numerous nat. orgns. Contbr. numerous abstracts to profl. jours., chpts. to books. Bd. dirs. Cornerstone Svcs., ARC of Ill. Recipient total quality mgmt. award Rush-Presbyn.-St. Luke's Med. Ctr., 1991, named mgr. of the quarter, 1997, Wayne Lerner Leadership award, 1998. Mem. ANA, Ill. Nurses Assn. (coms.), Coun. Clin. Nurse Specialists, Profl. Nursing Staff (sec. 1985-87, mem. coms.). Presbyterian. Home: 606 Darcy Ave Joliet IL 60436-1673

LYNCH, RICHARD GREGORY, medical educator; b. Apr. 9, 1934; BA, U. Mo., 1961; MD, U. Rochester, 1966. Resident Washington U., St. Louis, 1966-69, from asst. prof. to assoc. prof. pathology, 1972-80; dir. NIH Tng. Program, 1980-81, 84-87; prof., head dept. pathology U. Iowa, Iowa City, 1981-99, prof. microbiology, 1982-99, Hanson prof. immunology, 1992—. Chmn. pathology B study sect. NIH, 1983-86. Postdoctoral immunology fellow Washington U., St. Louis, 1969-72; recipient Rous-Whipple award, 1997. Office: U Iowa Dept Pathology 200 Hawkins Dr Rm 1117 ML Iowa City IA 52242-1009 E-mail: Richard-Lynch@uiowa.edu.

LYNCH, THOMAS JOSEPH, museum and historic house manager; b. Omaha, Feb. 15, 1960; s. James Humphery and Patricia Mae (Gaughan) L. BA in History, U. Nebr., 1984. Mus. asst. Father Flanagan's Boys' Home, Boys Town, Nebr., 1986-88, mus. assoc., 1988-93; CEO, mgr. Boys Town Hall of History and Fr. Flanagan's House, 1993—. Bd. dirs. Union Pacific R.R. Mus. Mem. Am. Assn. for State and Local History, Am. Mus. Assn., Nebr. Mus. Assn. (bd. dirs., v.p.), Nat. Hist. Landmark Stewards Assn. Office: Boys Town Hall of History 14057 Flanagan Blvd Boys Town NE 68010-7509

LYNCH, WILLIAM THOMAS, JR. advertising agency executive; b. Evergreen Park, Ill., Dec. 3, 1942; s. William T. and Loretta J. L.; children: Kelly, Maureen, Kim, Meagan, Molly. BA, Loras Coll., 1964; MBA, U. Iowa, 1966. Media trainee Leo Burnett Co. Inc., chgo., 1966-68, asst. account exec., 1968-76, v.p., 1976-79, sr. v.p., 1979-82, exec. v.p., 1981-85; vice chmn. Leo Burnett USA, 1985-89, chmn., CEO Chgo., 1987-91; pres. Leo Burnett Co., Inc., 1992-93; pres., CEO Leo Burnett Worldwide, 1993; CEO, pres. Leo Burnett Worldwide, Leo Burnett Co. Inc., 1993-97; pres., CEO Liam Holdings, Prospect Heights, Ill., 1997—. Bd. dirs. Pella Corp., Krispy Creme Doughnut Corp., SEI Info. Tech. Mem. coun. U. Chgo. Grad. Sch. Bus.; bd. dirs. Northwestern Meml. Found., Northwestern Meml. Hosp., Chgo.; bd. dirs., exec. com. Big Shoulders Archdiocese of Chgo.; bd. regents Loras Coll. Mem. Econ. Club Chgo., Comml. Club Chgo. Roman Catholic. Avocations: running, skiing, gardening, golf. Office: Liam Holdings 206 N Pine St Prospect Heights IL 60070-1524

LYNETT, WILLIAM RUDDY, publishing, broadcasting company executive; b. Scranton, Pa., Jan. 18, 1947; s. Edward James and Jean O'Hara Lynett; m. Mary Jean Foley; children: Scott, Jennifer, Christopher P., Brigid P., Jean O. B.S., U. Scranton, 1972. Pub. Scranton Times, 1966—; pres., chief exec. officer Shamrock Communications, Inc., 1971—; pres. Towanda Daily Rev., 1977-81, Owego Pennysaver Press, Inc., 1977-81. Owner, Pres. Mgmt. Program, Harvard U., 1990; vice-chmn. bd. dirs. WVIA TV. Bd. dirs. Cmty. Med. Ctr., Scranton, 1974—96; pres. Scranton Cultural Ctr.; chmn. Mayor's Libr. Fund Drive, 1974; chmn. spl. gifts divsn. Heart Fund, 1975; bd. govs. Scranton Area Found., chmn., 1996—97; trustee U. Scranton, 1990—96; chmn. Steamtown Nat. Pk. Grand Opening Com.; mem. exec. com. N.E. coun. Boy Scouts Am. Mem. Nat. Assn. Broadcasters, Pa. Assn. Broadcasters, Am. Newspaper Pubs. Assn., Pa. Newspaper Pubs. Assn., Greater Scranton C. of C. (chmn. membership drive 1980-81) Democrat. Roman Catholic. Clubs: Scranton Country, Elks, K.C. Office: 149 Penn Ave Scranton PA 18503-2022

LYNHAM, C(HARLES) RICHARD, foundry company executive; b. Easton, Md., Feb. 24, 1942; s. John Cameron and Anna Louise (Lynch) L.; m. Elizabeth Joy Card, Sept. 19, 1964; children: Jennifer Beth, Thomas Richard. BME, Cornell U., 1965; MBA with distinction, Harvard U., 1969. Sales mgr. Nat. Carbide Die Co., McKeesport, Pa., 1969-71; v.p. sales Sinter-Met Corp., North Brunswick, N.J., 1971-72; sr. mgmt. analyst Am. Cyanamid Co., Wayne, 1972-74; gen. mgr. ceramics and additives div. Foseco Inc., Cleve., 1974-77, dir. mktg. steel mill products group, 1977-79; pres., chief exec. officer Exomet, Inc. subs. Foseco, Inc., Conneaut, Ohio, 1979-81, Fosbel Inc. subs. Foseco, Inc., Cleve., 1981-82; gen. mgr. splty. ceramics group Ferro Corp., 1982-84, group v.p. splty. ceramics, 1984-92; owner, pres. Harbor Castings, Inc., North Canton, Ohio, 1992—, Island

Castings, Inc., Muskegan, Mich., 2000—; owner, CEO Blue Ridge Castings, Inc., Piney Flats, Tenn., 2000—. Bd. dirs. Corrpro Cos., Inc., Western Res. Bancorp., Inc. Patentee foundry casting ladle, desulphurization of metals. Past pres. bd. trustees Hospice of Medina County; treas., past pres. bd. trustees BridgesHome Health Care. Capt. C.E., U.S. Army, 1965-67. Decorated Bronze Star with one oak leaf cluster; recipient Frank H.T. Rhodes Exemplary Alumni Svc. award, Cornell U., 1999. Mem. Am. Foundrymen's Soc., Cornell U. Alumni Coun., Cornell U. Alumni Class 1963 (past v.p., past pres.), Cornell U. Alumni Fedn. (past pres., bd. dirs., past v.p.), Chippewa Yacht Club (commodore 1982), Cornell Club of N.E. Ohio (past pres., bd. dirs.), Harbor Bay Yacht Club. Republican. Congregationalist. Avocations: sailing, genealogy. bus. Home: 970 Hickory Grove Ave Medina OH 44256-1616 Office: Harbor Castings Inc 4321 Strausser St NW North Canton OH 44720-7144 E-mail: lynhamcr@ohio.net., harborci@raex.com.

LYNN, EMERSON ELWOOD, JR. retired newspaper editor/publisher; b. Boulder, Colo., Aug. 18, 1924; s. Emerson Elwood and Ruth Merriman (Scott) L.; m. Mickey June Killough, Jan. 27, 1950; children: Emerson Killough, Michael Jay, Angelo Scott, Susan. BS, U. Chgo., 1947. Editor/pub. The Humboldt (Kans.) Union, 1951-58, The Bowie (Tex.) News, 1958-65, The Iola (Kans.) Register, 1965-2001. Chmn. Iola Industries, Inc.; mem. SEK, Inc.; chmn. bd. dirs. Huck Boyd Found., Manhattan, Kans., 2001—. Chmn. Allen County Hosp. Bd., Iola, 1970-77, adv. bd. Kans. Dept. Transp., Topeka, 1992-93; mem. panels on reform of probate code, Kans. Jud. Coun., others; mem. Pulitzer Prize Nominating Jury, 2000-20001. Sgt. USAF, 1942-46. Rotary Internat. fellow U. Melbourne, 1948-49. Mem. Rotary Internat. (pres.), Kans. Press Assn. (pres. 1979, Clyde Reed Master Editor award 1995), William Allen White Found. (pres. 1978). Republican. Presbyterian. Home: 821 S Buckeye St Iola KS 66749-3807 Office: The Iola Register 302 S Washington St Iola KS 66749-3255

LYNN, LAURENCE EDWIN, JR. university administrator, educator; b. Long Beach, Calif., June 10, 1937; s. Laurence Edwin and Marjorie Louise (Hart) L.; m. Patricia Ramsey Lynn; 1 dau., Katherine Bell; children from previous marriage— Stephen Louis, Daniel Laurence, Diana Jane, Julia Suzanne. A.B., U. Calif., 1959; Ph.D. (Ford Found. fellow), Yale, 1966. Dir., dep. asst. sec. def. (OASD/SA) Dept. Def., Washington, 1965-69; asst. for program analysis NSC, 1969-70; assoc. prof. bus. Grad. Sch. Bus., Stanford (Calif.) U., 1970-71, vis. prof. pub. policy, 1982-83; asst. sec. planning and evaluation HEW, Washington, 1971-73; asst. sec. program devel. and budget U.S. Dept. Interior, 1973-74; sr. fellow Brookings Instn., 1974-75; prof. pub. policy John Fitzgerald Kennedy Sch. Govt. Harvard U., Cambridge, Mass., 1975-83; dean Sch. Social Service Adminstrn. U. Chgo., 1983-88, prof., sch. of social svc. adminstrn. and Harris grad. sch. pub. policy studies, 1983—, dir. Ctr. for Urban Rsch. and Policy Studies, 1986—; dir. Mgmt. Inst., 1992-99; Sydney Stein, Jr. prof., 1997—2002; Buch chair and prof. Bush Sch. Govt. and Pub. Svc. , Tex A&M U., 2002—. Author: Designing Public Policy, 1980, The State and Human Services, 1980, Managing the Public's Business, 1981, Managing Public Policy, 1987, Public Management as Art, Science and Profession, 1996, Teaching and Learning with Cases: A Guide; co-author: The President as Policymaker, 1981, Improving Governance: A New Logic for Empirical Research, 2001; contbr. articles to profl. jours. Bd. dirs. Chgo. Met. Planning Coun., 1984-89, Leadership Greater Chgo., 1989-92; mem. coun. of scholars Libr. of Congress, 1989-93. 1st lt. AUS, 1963-65. Recipient Sec. Def. Meritorious Civilian Svc. medal, Presdl. Cert. of Disting. Achievment, Vernon prize, best book award Acad. Mgmt., 1996. Fellow Nat. Acad. Public Adminstrn.; mem. ASPA, U. Calif. Alumni Assn., Coun. on Fgn. Rels., Assn. Pub. Policy Analysis and Mgmt. (past pres.), Phi Beta Kappa. Office: 22129 Academic West 4220 TAMU Coll College Station TX 77843-4220 E-mail: llynn@bushschool.tamu.edu.

LYNN, NAOMI B. academic administrator; b. N.Y.C., Apr. 16, 1933; d. Carmelo Burgos and Maria (Lebron) Berly; m. Robert A. Lynn, Aug. 28, 1954; children: Mary Louise, Nancy Lynn Francis, Judy Lynn Chance, Jo-An Lynn Cooper. BA, Maryville (Tenn.) Coll., 1954; MA, U. Ill., 1958; PhD, U. Kans., 1970. Instr. polit. sci. Cen. Mo. State Coll., Warrensburg, Mo., 1966-68; asst. prof. Kans. State U., Manhattan, 1970-75, assoc. prof., 1975-80, acting dept. head, prof., 1980-81, head polit. sci. dept., prof., 1982-84; dean Coll. Pub. and Urban Affairs, prof. Ga. State U., Atlanta, 1984-91; chancellor U. Ill., Springfield, 1991-2001, chancellor emerita, 2001—. Cons. fed., state and local govts., Manhattan, Topeka, Altanta, 1981-91; bd. dirs. Bank One Springfield. Author: The Fulbright Premise, 1973; editor: Public Administration, The State of Discipline, 1990, Women, Politics and the Constitution, 1990; contbr. articles and textbook chpts. to profl. pubs. Bd. dirs. United Way of Sangamon County, 1991—, Ill. Symphony Orch., 1992-95; bd. dirs. Urban League, 1993—. Recipient Disting. Alumni award Maryville Coll., 1986; fellow Nat. Acad. Pub. Adminstrn. Mem. Nat. Assn. Schs. Pub. Affairs and Adminstrn. (nat. pres.), Am. Soc. Pub. Adminstrn. (nat. pres. 1985-86), Am. Polit. Sci. Assn. (mem. exec. coun. 1981-83, trustee 1993—), Am. Assn. State Colls. and Univs. (bd. dirs.), Midwest Polit. Sci. Assn. (mem. exec. coun. 1976-79), Women's Caucus Polit. Sci. (pres. 1975-76), Greater Springfield C. of C. (bd. dirs. 1991—, accreditation task force 1992), Pi Sigma Alpha (nat. pres.). Presbyterian.

LYNNES, R. MILTON, advertising executive; b. Chgo., Apr. 16, 1934; s. Roy Milton and Ethel (Wolfe) L.; m. Carol Rinehart, Aug. 30, 1958; children: Christopher, Katherine, Jeffrey, Jennifer. BS, Iowa State U., 1957. Advt. sales promotion supr. Interlake Steel, Chgo., 1961-62; copywriter Garfield-Linn, 1963; account exec. Biddle Co., Appleton, Wis., 1964-66; exec. v.p. Marsteller HCM, Chgo., 1966-84, bd. dirs., 1978-84; prin. Grant, Jacoby Inc., Chgo., 1985-89, pres., 1989-94, chmn. CEO, 1994—. Bd. dirs. Worldwide Ptnrs., Denver, chmn. N.Am. region, 1996-97. Bd. dirs. MTW/WWP Media Venture, 1995, Better Bus. Bur., Chgo., 1984-87. Mem. Am. Assn. Advt. Agys. (vice chmn. ctrl. region, bd. dirs. 1981-82), Chicagoland C. of C. (bd. dirs. 1999), Chgo. Advt. Club (bd. dirs. 1985-86), Exmoor Country Club (pres. 1998-99), Bob O Link Golf Club, Pelican Bay Golf Club, Econs. Club, Tavern Club, Chicago Club. Republican. Congregationalist. Office: Grant/Jacoby Inc 737 N Michigan Ave Ste 2200 Chicago IL 60611-2615

LYON, BOB, state legislator; m. Rita Lyon. Mem. Kans. State Senate, 2001—, mem. membership fed. and state affairs com., mem. state bldg. constrn. com., mem. transp. com., mem. utilities com. Republican. Address: 14431 Saline Rd Winchester KS 66097 Office: 1201 Walnut St Kansas City MO 64106-2149 E-mail: lyon@senate.state.ks.us., blyon55@hotmail.com.

LYON, JEFFREY, journalist, author; b. Chgo., Nov. 28, 1943; s. Herbert Theodore and Lyle (Hoffenberg) L.; m. Bonita S. Brodt, June, 20, 1981; children: Lindsay, Derek. BS in Journalism, Northwestern U., 1965. Reporter Miami (Fla.) Herald, 1964-66, Chgo. Today, 1966-74, Chgo. Tribune, 1974-76, columnist, 1976-80, 94—, feature writer specializing in sci., 1980—, editor Tempo sect., 1997. Creative writing adj. prof.; coord. joint sci. and journalism programs Columbia Coll., Chgo., 1987—, dir., 1988—. Author: Playing God in the Nursery, 1985, Altered Fates: Gene Therapy and the Retooling of Human Life, 1995; also newspaper series Altered Fates, 1986 (Pulitzer Prize 1987). Mem. State of Ill. Perinatal Adv. Com., Springfield, 1986-90; mem. pediat. ethics com. U. Chgo. Hosps., 1985-90; bd. dirs. Shore Cmty. Svcs. to Retarded Citizens, Evanston, Ill., 1985-90; mem. bd. Little City, Palatine, Ill., 1979—. Recipient Nat. Headliner award Atlantic City Press Club, 1984, Citizen Fellow award Inst. Medicine of Chgo., 1987, Peter Lisagor award, 1990. Office: The Chgo Tribune 435 N Michigan Ave Chicago IL 60611-4066 E-mail: jlyon@tribune.com.

LYON, STERLING RUFUS WEBSTER, justice; b. Windsor, Ont., Can., Jan. 30, 1927; s. David Rufus and Ella Mae (Cuthbert) L.; m. Barbara Jean Mayers, Sept. 26, 1953; children: Nancy, Andrea, Peter, Jennifer, Jonathan. B.A., U. Winnipeg, 1948; LL.B., U. Man., 1953. Bar: Man. 1953, created Queen's Counsel 1960. Crown atty., Man., 1953-57; mem. Man. Legis. Assembly, 1958-69, 76-86; atty. gen. Man., 1958-63, 66-69; minister of mcpl. affairs, 1960-61; of pub. utilities, 1961-63; of mines and natural resources, 1963-66; of tourism and recreation, 1966-68; commr. No. affairs, 1966-68; leader Man. Progressive Conservative Party, 1975-83; premier of Man., 1977-81; leader of the opposition, 1976-77, 81-83; mem. Her Majesty's Privy Council for Can., 1982; apptd. justice Man. Ct. of Appeal, Winnipeg, 1986—. Chmn. 1st Can. Conf. on Pollution, Montreal, 1966, Can. Premier's Conf., 1980-81; pres. Can. Coun. Resource Ministers, 1965-66. Former trustee Ducks Unltd., Delta Waterfowl Found.; bd. regents U. Winnipeg, 1972-76; dir. Can. Royal Heritage Trust. With RCAF Res., 1950-53. Recipient U. Winnipeg Alumni Assn. Jubilee award, 1973; U. Man. scholar, 1945. Office: Law Cts 408 York Ave Winnipeg MB Canada R3C 0P9

LYON, THOMAS L. agricultural organization administrator; b. Toledo, Sept. 12, 1940; m. Barbara Lyon; children: Jeff, Melissa, Scott. BS in Dairy Sci., Iowa State U., 1962. Exec. sec. Iowa State Dairy Assn.; with 21st Century Genetics, gen. mgr., 1976-93; pres. Coop. Resources Internat., Shawano, Wis., 1993—, now CEO. Bd. dirs. Am. Farmland Trust, Coop. Bus. Internat., Coop. Devel. Found.; chmn. Nat. Coop. Bus. Assn.; mem. Nat. Rural Devel. Task Force & Coop. 2000 com., Dairy Shrine Club, steering com. Wis. Dairy Inititative 2020, Kellogg Found. Food Systems; bd. advisors U. Wis., Eau Claire; bd. visitors U. Wis., Madison; trustee Grad. Inst. Coop. Leadership, Coop. Found.; cons. U. Wis. Bus. Schs. Review. Recipient Friend of Extension award U. Wis., 1981, Wis. Friend of County Agents award, 1984, Dairy Industry Person of Yr. award World Dairy Expo, 1985, Nat. Coop. Pub. Svc. award, 1991, Disting. Citizen Shawano award, 1993, Agribus. award Iowa State U. Coll. Agr. Alumni Soc., 1995. Office: Coop Resources Internat 100 NBC Dr PO Boox 469 Shawano WI 54166

LYONS, DUDLEY E. business executive; Sr. v.p. Brunswick Corp., Lake Forest, Ill., 1999—. Office: Brunswick Corp 1 N Field Ct Lake Forest IL 60045-4811

LYONS, EILEEN, state legislator; b. N.Y.C., July 3, 1941; Ill. state rep. Dist. 47, 1995—. Office: 1030 S La Grange Rd La Grange IL 60525-2800

LYONS, GORDON, marketing executive; V.p. supermarket devel. Schnuck Market Inc., St. Louis. Office: Schnuck Market Inc 11420 Lackland Rd Saint Louis MO 63146-3559

LYSON, STANLEY W. state legialator; b. Porshall, N.D., Mar. 5, 1956; m. Shirley; 3 children. , MInot STate U. Sheriff; retired; mem. N.D. Senate from 1st dist., Bismark, 1999—. With U.S. Army. REcipient Lone Eagle award. Mem. N.D. Assn. Counties (pres.), N.D. Peace Officers Assn. (pres.), Am. Legion, VFW, Elks. Office: Dist 1 1608 4th Ave W Williston ND 58801-4127 E-mail: sysonstate@nd.us.

LYST, JOHN HENRY, newspaper editor; b. Princeton, Ind., Mar. 28, 1933; s. John Henry and Marguerite (McQuinn) L.; m. Sharon Long, Dec. 29, 1956; children: Shannon M., Bettina A., Audrey K., Ellen K. AB, Ind. U., 1955. Reporter Indpls. Star, 1956-67, bus. columnist, from 1967, editor editl. page, 1979—. Corr. N.Y. Times, from 1964. Served with AUS, 1956-59. Mem. Indpls. Press Club (pres. 1968, bd. dirs. 1969), Sigma Delta Chi. Office: Indpls Newspapers Inc PO Box 145 Indianapolis IN 46206-0145

LYTHCOTT, MARCIA A. newspaper editor; Op-ed editor Chicago Tribune, Ill., 1991—. Office: Chicago Tribune 435 N Michigan Ave Chicago IL 60611-4066

LYTLE, L(ARRY) BEN, insurance company executive, lawyer; b. Greenville, Tex., Sept. 30, 1946; children: Hugh, Larry. BS in Mgmt. Sci. and Indsl. Psychology, East Tex. State U., 1970; JD, Ind. U., 1980. Computer operator/programmer U.S. Govt., Ft. Smith, Ark., 1964-65; customer engr. Olivetti Corp., San Antonio, 1965-66; mgr. computer ops. and computer software LTV Electrosystems, Greenville, 1966-70; project mgr. electronic fin. system, dir. systems planning Assocs. Corp. N.Am., South Bend, Ind., 1970-75; asst. v.p. systems Am. Fletcher Nat. Bank, Indpls., 1975-76; with Anaheim Ins. Cos., Inc., 1976-99; pres. Assoc. Ins. Cos., Inc., 1987-99, COO, 1987-89, CEO, 1989-99; chmn. Anthem Ins. Cos., Inc.; retired. Chmn. bd. dirs. Anthem Cos., Inc., Acordia, Inc.; chmn. bd. dirs. AdminaStar, Inc., Health Networks Am., Inc., Novalis, Inc., Robinson-Conner Nev., Inc.; bd. dirs. The Shelby Ins. Group, Raffensperger, Hughes & Co., Inc., Indpls. Power and Light Co. Enterprises; mem. adv. bd. CID Venture Ptnrs., Ltd. Partnership; rschr., cons. state and fed. govt. orgns., including, Adv. Coun. on Social Security, Pepper Commn. of U.S. Congress, others. Chmn. health policy commn. State of Ind., Indpls., 1990-92; active various civic orgns., including United Negro Coll. Fund, Indpls. Mus. Art. Mem. ABA, Ind. Bar Assn., Indpls. Bar Assn., Ind. State C. of C. (bd. dirs.), Indpls. C. of C. (bd. dirs.). Home: PO Box 441830 Indianapolis IN 46244-1830 Office: Anthem Ins Cos Inc 120 Monument Cir Indianapolis IN 46204-4906

LYTLE, MARKT L. state legislator; Student, Oakland City Coll., Ball State U., Muncie, Ind.; grad., Ky. Sch. Mortuary Sci. Mng. dir. Lytle-Gans-Andrew Funeral Home; state rep. Dist. 69 Ind. Ho. of Reps., 1992—, mem. county and twp. ways and means com., vice chmn. natural resources com. Mem. agriculture, natural resources and rural devel. com. (chmn.), evniron. affairs com., local govt. com. Mayor, City of Madison Ind.; recorder Jefferson County, Ind.; precinct committeeman; mem. Southeastern Ind. Regional Planning Commn. Mem. Sons of Legion, Elks. Home: 423 W Main St Madison IN 47250-3736

MAAS, DUANE HARRIS, distilling company executive; b. Tilleda, Wis., Aug. 26, 1927; s. John William and Adela (Giessel) M.; m. Sonja Johnson, Mar. 11, 1950; children: Jon Kermit, Duane Arthur, Thomas Ervin. B.S., U. Wis., 1951. With Shell Chem. Corp., 1951-59; plant mgr. Fleischmann Distilling Corp., Owensboro, Ky., 1959-63, Plainfield, Ill., 1963-65; asst. to v.p. Barton Distilling Co., Chgo., 1965-68, exec. asst. to pres., 1968, v.p. adminstrn., 1968; v.p., gen. mgr. Barton Brands, Inc., Chgo., 1968— 72; pres. Leaf Confectionery div. W.R. Grace, 1972-74; v.p., gen. mgr. Romano Bros., 1974-79; v.p., sec.-treas. Marketing Directions Inc., 1974-77; pres. Associated Wine Producers, Inc., 1979-80; exec. v.p., chief exec. officer Mohawk Liqueur, Detroit, 1980-86; v.p. McKesson Wine & Spirits Group of N.Y., 1982-86; pres. Mgmt. Cons. Services Co., Chgo., 1986—, U.S. Distilled Products Co., Princeton, Minn., 1996-99. Chmn. Qingdao Johnson Distiller Co. Ltd., Qingdao, China, 1996-99; past pres. Bart on Distilling (Can.), Ltd.; past mng. dir. Barton Distilling (Scotland), Ltd.; past dir. Barton Distillers Europe, Barton Internat., Ltd. Sec.-treas. Plainfield Twp. Park Dist., 1967-70; chmn. Plainfield Planning and Zoning Commn., 1965-70. Served with USAAF, 1945-47. Mem.: Wis. Alumni Assn. Lutheran. Home and Office: 13264 W Highway 29 Bowler WI 54416 E-mail: dhm@mcservices.com.

MAATMAN, GERALD LEONARD, insurance company executive; b. Chgo., Mar. 11, 1930; s. Leonard Raymond and Cora Mae (Van Der Laag) M.; children: Gerald L. Jr., Mary Ellen; m. Bernice Catherine Brummer, June 3, 1971. BS, Ill. Inst. Tech., 1951. Asst. chief engineer Ill. Inspection & Rating Bur., Chgo., 1951-58; prof., dept. chmn. Ill. Inst. Tech., 1959-65; v.p. engring. Kemper Group, 1966-68, pres. Nat. Loss Control Svc. Corp., 1969-74, v.p. corp. planning Long Grove, Ill., 1974-79, sr. v.p. info. svcs. group, 1979-85, exec. v.p. ins. ops., 1985-87; pres. Kemper Nat. Ins. Co., 1987-92, CEO, 1989-95, also bd. dirs., chmn. bd. dirs., 1991-95. Bd. dirs. Advs. for Auto and Hwy. Safety, 1992-98; chmn. bd. trustees Underwriters Labs., 1991-2002. Lt. (j.g.) USCGR, 1952-54. Mem. Knollwood Golf Club, Springs Club, Tau Beta Pi. Republican. Roman Catholic.

MABEE, KEITH V. communications/investor relations executive; BS in Journalism, Bowling Green State U., 1969; MEd in Sociology, Wayne State U., 1972; MBA, Pepperdine U., 1980. Comm. specialist Internat. Paper Co., N.Y.C., 1969-70, 73; pub. affairs officer, U.S. Army NATO, Europe, 1970-72; sr. lectr. Coll. Mgmt., Queensland U. Tech., Australia, 1973-77; organizational/effectiveness officer U.S. Army, Pacific, 1978-80; sr. v.p., corp. comm. AMFAC, Inc., San Francisco, 1980-89; v.p. comm. Indsl. Indemnity, 1989-93; v.p. corp. rels. Figgie Internat. Inc., 1993-98; sr. exec. v.p. Dix & Eaton, 1997-98, pres., 1998—2001, pres. & CEO, 2001—. Former pres. San Francisco chpt. Nat. Investor Rels. Inst., former officer, former dir. nat. bd., mem. sr. roundtable steering com.; founding trustee, lectr. San Francisco Acad.; bd. dirs. Citizens League Rsch. Inst., Ohio Tuition Trust Authority. Mem. Pub. Rels. Soc. Am. Office: The Galleria and Tower at Erieview 1301 E 9th St Ste 1300 Cleveland OH 44114-1882 Fax: 216-241-3070.

MABLEY, JACK, newspaper columnist, communications consultant; b. Binghamton, N.Y., Oct. 26, 1915; s. Clarence Ware and Mabelle (Howe) M.; m. Frances Habeck, Aug. 29, 1940; children: Mike, Jill, Ann, Pat, Robert. B.S., U. Ill., 1938. With Chgo. Daily News, 1938-61, reporter, writer, columnist, 1957-61; columnist Chgo.'s Am., 1961-69, asst. mng. editor, 1966-69; asso. editor Chgo. Today, 1969-73; columnist Chgo. Today, Chgo. Tribune, 1973-74, Chgo. Tribune, 1974-82; pres. Mabley & Assocs., Corp. Communications, Glenview, Ill., 1982; columnist Daily Herald, Arlington Heights, 1987—. Lectr. journalism Northwestern U., 1949-50 Pres. Village of Glenview, Ill., 1957-61, Skokie Valley Community Hosp., Skokie, Ill., 1977-79. Served from ensign to lt. USNR, 1941-45. Recipient Media award Nat. Assn. for Retarded Citizens, 1977 Home and Office: 2275 Winnetka Rd Glenview IL 60025-1825 E-mail: jmabley@dailyherald.com.

MACAULEY, EDWARD C. retired company executive; b. St. Louis, Mar. 22, 1928; s. Charles J. and Josephine (Durkin) M.; m. Jacqueline Combs, July 12, 1952; children: Mary Ann, Robert, Teresa, Michael, Kathleen, Margaret. BS, St. Louis U., 1949. Basketball player Boston Celtics, 1950-56, St. Louis Hawks, 1957-58, coach, 1959-60; sports dir. Stas. KTVI-TV and KSDK-TV, St. Louis, 1960-70; stockbroker A.G. Edwards-Shearson Lehman, 1970-81; pres. Macauley Kremjet, 1981—, Eagle Communications, St. Louis, 1982-86. Bd. dirs. Color Art Printing Co., St. Louis. Trustee Basketball Hall of Fame, Springfield, Mass., 1980—, Mo. Basketball Hall of Fame, Columbia, 1988—, Marianist Apostolic Ctr., St. Louis, 1988—; mem. St. Liborius Food Pantry, St. Louis, 1988-89; organizer St. Nicholas Food Pantry, St. Louis, 1989; ordained deacon Archdiocese of St. Louis, Roman Cath. Ch., 1989—. Named to All Am. Basketball Team, AP, UP, Life, Colliers mag., 1948, 49, All Pro Team, NBA, 1951, 52, 53; inducted into Basketball Hall of Fame, 1961. Avocations: golf, travel, preaching. Home and Office: 1455 Reauville Dr Saint Louis MO 63122-1441

MACCARTHY, TERENCE FRANCIS, lawyer; b. Chgo., Feb. 5, 1934; s. Frank E. and Catherine (McIntyre) MacC.; m. Marian Fulton, Nov. 25, 1961; children— Daniel Fulton, Sean Patrick, Terence Fulton, Megan Catherine B.A. in Philosophy, St. Joseph's Coll., 1955; J.D., DePaul U., 1960. Bar: Ill. 1960, U.S. Dist. Ct. (no. dist.) Ill. 1961, U.S. Ct. Appeals (7th cir.) 1961, U.S. Supreme Ct. 1966. Assoc. prof. law Chase Coll. Law, Cin., 1960-61; law clk. to chief judge U.S. Dist. Ct., 1961-66; spl. asst. atty. gen. Ill., 1965-67; exec. dir. Fed. Defender Program, U.S. Dist. Ct. (no. dist.) Ill., Chgo., 1966—. Mem. nat. adv. com. on criminal rules; 7th cir. criminal jury instrn. com.; chmn. Nat. Defender Com.; chmn. bd. regents Nat. Coll. Criminal Def.; faculty Fed. Jud. Ctr., Nat. Coll. Criminal Def., Nat. Inst. Trial Advocacy, U. Va. Trial Advocacy Inst., Harvard Law Sch. Trial Advocacy Program, Western Trial Advocacy Inst., Northwestern U., U. Ill. Defender Trial Advocacy course, Nat. Criminal Def. Coll., Loyola U. Trial Advocacy Program; lectr. in field Contbr. articles on criminal law to profl. jours. Bd. dirs. U.S.O. Served as 1st lt. USMC, 1955-57 Recipient Nat. Legal Aid and Defender Assn./ABA Reginald Heber Smith award, 1986, Alumni Merit award St. Joseph Coll., 1970, Cert. of Distinction USO, 1977, Harrison Tweed Spl. Merit award Am. Law Inst./ABA, 1987, Bill of Rights award Ga. chpt. ACLU, 1986, William J. Brennan award U. Va., 1989, Alumni Svc. award DePaul U. Coll. Law, 1994, Ann. Significant Contbns. award Calif. Attys. for Criminal Justice, Defender of the Century Fed. Defenders Assn., Inns of Ct. and Ct. of Appeals (7th cir.) Professionalism award; named to Outstanding Young Men of Am., 1970. Mem. ABA (past chmn. criminal justice sect., ho. of dels., bd. govs., Charles English award criminal justice sect.), Ill. Bar Assn., Chgo. Bar Assn., 7th Cir. Bar Assn., Nat. Assn. Criminal Def. Lawyers (Disting. Svc. award 1993), Nat. Legal Aid and Defender Assn., Nat. Coll. Criminal Def. (chair), Union League of Chgo. (pres.). Democrat. Roman Catholic. Office: US Dist Ct No Dist Ill 55 E Monroe St Ste 2800 Chicago IL 60603-5802

MACDONALD, JOHN, marketing executive; V.p. mktg. Chrysler Corp., Auburn Hills, Mich., 1996-98, v.p. sales and svc., 1997-99; sr. v.p. sales and svc. DaimlerChrysler Corp., 1999—. Office: DaimlerChrysler Corp 1000 Chrysler Dr Auburn Hills MI 48326-2766

MACDOUGAL, GARY EDWARD, corporate director, foundation trustee; b. Chgo., July 3, 1936; s. Thomas William and Lorna Lee (McDougall) MacD.; children: Gary Edward, Michael Scott; m. Charlene Gehm, June 15, 1992. BS in Engring., UCLA, 1958; MBA with distinction, Harvard U., 1962. Cons. McKinsey & Co., L.A., 1963-68, ptnr., 1968-69; chmn. bd., chief exec. officer Mark Controls Corp. (formerly Clayton Mark & Co.), Evanston, Ill., 1969-87; gen. dir. N.Y.C. Ballet, 1993-94; chmn. Gov. Task Force on Human Svcs. Reform State of Ill., 1993-97. Sr. advisor and asst. campaign mgr. George Bush for Pres., Washington, 1988; chmn. Bulgarian-Am. Enterprise Fund, Chgo. and Sophia, Bulgaria, 1991-93; bd. dirs., 1991—; apptd. to U.S. Commn. on Effectiveness of UN, 1992-93; bd. dirs. United Parcel Svc. Am., Inc., Atlanta; adv. dir. Saratoga Ptnrs., N.Y.; instr. UCLA, 1969. Author: Make a Difference: How One Man Helped Solve America's Poverty Problem, 2000; contbr. articles to Harvard Bus. Rev., Wall St. Jour., N.Y. Times, Chgo. Tribune, other publs., chpts. to books. Trustee Annie E. Casey Found., UCLA Found., 1973-79, W.T. Grant Found., 1992-94, Russell Sage Found., 1981-91, chair, 1987-90; apptd. by Pres. Bush as pub. del., alt. rep., U.S. Del. UN 44th Gen. Assembly, 1989-90; commr. Sec. Labor's Commn. on Workforce Quality and Productivity, Washington, 1988-89. Lt. USN, 1958-61. Mem. Coun. Fgn. Rels., Author's Guild, Harvard Club, Kappa Sigma. Episcopalian. Home: 505 N Lake Shore Dr Apt 2711 Chicago IL 60611-3406*

MACE, GEORGIA MAE, insurance company administrator; b. Pisgah, Iowa, June 7, 1949; d. George and Lois Mae (Rife) Stevens; m. Ronald Eugene Mace, May 14, 1971; children: Brandi Lynn, Dana Lynn. AA, Iowa Western Community Coll., 1987; BA in Acctg., Buena Vista Coll., 1989. Acctg. clk. U.S. Fidelity & Guaranty, Omaha, 1967-72; supr. Cornhusker

Casualty Co. (subs. Berkshire-Hathaway Group), 1973-77, treas., 1977-79; asst. comptroller Drum Fin. Corp., 1979-80; treas. Acceptance Ins. Holding Inc., 1980—. Mem. Ins. Acctg. and Systems Assn. Avocations: tennis, running, school. Home: 706 Maple St Missouri Valley IA 51555-1100 Office: Acceptance Ins Holding Inc Ste 600 N 222 S 15th St Omaha NE 68102-1400

MACE, JERILEE MARIE, opera company executive; BA in Speech Comm. and Mgmt. magna cum l, Simpson Coll., 1991. Mem. adminstrv. staff Des Moines Metro Opera, 1976, dir. mktg., exec. dir., 1988—. Developer OPERA Iowa, Des Moines Metro Opera; cons. various opera cos. On-site evaluator NEA; grad., bd. dirs. Greater Des Moines Leadership Inst.; founding mem. Warren County Leadership Com. Named Iowa Arts Orgn. of Yr., 2000; recipient Outstanding Achiever award, Ft. Dodge C. of C., 1994, Best Kept Secret award for bus. excellence, Greater Des Moines Partnership 2001, Women of Influence award, Des Moines Bus. Record, 2001; fellow exec., OPERA Am., 1993. Office: Des Moines Metro Opera 106 W Boston Ave Indianola IA 50125-1836 E-mail: jerimace@aol.com.

MACFARLANE, ALASTAIR IAIN ROBERT, business executive; b. Sydney, Australia, Mar. 7, 1940; came to U.S., 1978; s. Alexander Dunlop and Margaret Elizabeth (Swan) M.; m. Madge McCleary, Sept. 24, 1966; children: Douglas, Dennis, Robert, Jeffrey. B in Econs. with honours, U. Sydney, 1961; MBA, U. Hawaii, 1964; postgrad., Columbia U., 1964; AMP, Harvard U., 1977. Comml. cadet B.H.P. Ltd., Australia, 1958-62; product mgr. H.J. Heinz Co., Pitts., 1965-66, gen. mgr. new products div. Melbourne, Australia, 1967-72; ptnr., dir., gen. mgr. Singleton, Palmer & Strauss McAllan Pty. Ltd., Sydney, 1972-73; dir., gen. mgr. successor co. Doyle Dane Bernbach Internat. Inc., 1973-77, group sr. v.p. N.Y.C., 1978-84; pres., chief exec. officer PowerBase Systems, Inc., 1984-85, Productivity Software Internat. L.P., N.Y.C., 1985-86; div. pres., pub. Whittle Comm. L.P., Knoxville, Tenn., 1987-88; chmn., CEO Phyton Techs. Inc., 1988-94; pres., CEO Knox Internat. Corp., 1988-94; chmn., CEO Mich. Bulb Co., Grand Rapids, 1988-94; dir. Univ. of Sydney USA Found., 1994—; chmn., CEO Creative Pub. Internat., Inc., Minnetonka, Minn., 1997-99; sr. v.p. Pleasant Co., Middleton, Wis., 2000-2001; CEO Centric Strategies Internat., Inc., Mpls., 2001—. Chmn., CEO Lansinoh, Labs., Inc., Oak Ridge, Tenn., 1994—96; lectr. Monash U., Melbourne, 1970—71; ind. mgmt. cons., Melbourne, 1970—72. Author papers in field. V.p. Waverley Dist. Cricket Club, 1975-77. East-West Ctr. fellow, 1962-64; Australian Commonwealth scholar, Australian Steel Industry scholar, 1958-61. Fellow Australian Inst. Mgmt. (assoc.); mem. Australian Soc. Accts. (assoc.), Harvard Club N.Y.C., Blackhawk Country Club (Madison). Home and Office: Centric Strategies Internat Inc 6219 S Highlands Ave Madison WI 53705

MACFARLANE, JOHN CHARLES, utility company executive; b. Hallock, Minn., Nov. 8, 1939; s. Ernest Edward and Mary Bell (Yates) MacF.; m. Eunice Darlene Axvig, Apr. 13, 1963; children: Charles, James, William. BSEE, U. N.D., 1961. Staff engr. Otter Tail Power Co., Fergus Falls, Mn., 1961-64, div. engr. Jamestown, N.D., 1964-71, div. mgr. Langdon, 1972-78, v.p. planning and control Fergus Falls, 1978-80, exec. v.p., 1981-82, pres. and chief exec. officer, 1982—, also bd. dirs., now chmn. Bd. dirs. Wells Fargo, Fergus Falls, Pioneer Mut. Ins. Co. Pres. Langdon City Commn., 1974-78; chmn. Fergus Falls Port Authority, 1985-86; bd. dirs. Minn. Assn. Commerce and Industry, Minn. Safety Coun., Edison Electric Inst., Village Family Svcs., Fargo; bd. dirs. U. N.D. Energy Rsch. Adv. Coun. Served with U.S. Army, 1962-64. Mem. Am. Mgmt. Assn., IEEE (chmn. Red River chpt.), U. N.D. Alumni Assn., Fergus Falls C. of C. Republican. Presbyterian. Lodges: Rotary, Masons. Office: Otter Tail Power Co 215 S Cascade St Fergus Falls MN 56537-2897

MACGREGOR, DAVID LEE, lawyer; b. Cedar Rapids, Iowa, Sept. 17, 1932; s. John H. and Beulah A. (Morris) MacG.; m. Helen Jean Kolberg, Aug. 7, 1954; children— Scott J., William M., Brian K., Thomas D. B.B.A., U. Wis., 1954, LL.B., 1956. Assoc. Quarles & Brady and predecessor firms, Milw., 1959-64, ptnr., 1964-99, retired, 1999—. Pres. Nat. Assn. Estate Planning Coun., 1979-80, pres. Milw. chpt. 1972-73; mem. adv. bd. CCH Fin. and Estate Planning, N.Y.C., 1982-87 Mem. State Bar Wis. (chmn. taxation sect. 1977-78), Regency House Condominium Assn. (treas., dir.), Stackner Family Found. Inc. (asst. sec., dir.). Home: 929 N Astor St Unit 1608 Milwaukee WI 53202-3486 Office: Quarles & Brady 411 E Wisconsin Ave Ste 2550 Milwaukee WI 53202-4497

MACH, RUTH, principal; m. Stan Mach; 2 children. Grad., Truman State U., 1958; M, U. Mo.; PhD, St. Louis U. Cert. elem. sch. adminstr., reading specialist, tchr. of learning disabled, tchr. behaviorally disturbed. Tchr. Affton Sch. Dist., Lindbergh Sch. Dist.; elem. sch. prin. Mehlville Sch. Dist.; prin. Meramec Elem. Sch., Clayton, Mo. Bd. dirs. Truman State U. Found.; apptd. bd. govs. Truman State U., 1995—. Mem.: ASCD, St. Louis Suburban Prins. Assn. (past pres., Disting. Prin. award), Conf. on Edn., Mo. Assn. Elem. Sch. Prins. (Disting. Elem. Prin. award), Nat. Assn. Elem. Sch. Prins. Office: Meramec Elem Sch 400 S Meramec Clayton MO 63105*

MACHASKEE, ALEX, newspaper publishing company executive; b. Warren, Ohio; m. Carol Machaskee. BA in Mktg., Cleve. State U., 1972, LHD (hon.), 1995, U. Akron, 1998. Sports reporter The Warren (Ohio) Tribune; promo dir. to dir. labor rels. & pers. to v.p., gen. mgr. The Plain Dealer, Cleve., 1985-90, pres., pub., 1990—. V.p. Mus. Arts Assn. (Cleve. Orch.); chmn. United Way Campaign; mem. bd. governance, fin. and adminstrn. com. Cleve. Found.; bd. dirs. Ohio Arts Coun., Univ. Cir. Inc., Greater Cleve. Growth Assn., Cleve. Tomorrow, Gt. Lakes Sci. Mus., United Way Svcs., Mus. Coun. of Cleve. Mus. Art, St. Vladimir's Orthodox Theol. Sem.; vis. com. Weatherhead Sch. Mgmt., Case Western Res. U.; adv. com. Newspaper Mgmt. Ctr., Northwestern U.; trustee WVIZ/PBS and 90.3 WCPN ideastream; nat. bd. dirs. IOCC. Mem. Newspaper Assn. Am. (mem. labor rels. subcom.), Am. Soc. Newspaper Editors, Greater Cleve. Roundtable (past chmn.). Office: Plain Dealer Pub Co 1801 Superior Ave E Cleveland OH 44114-2198

MACHIN, BARBARA E. lawyer; b. Kansas City, Mo., Mar. 26, 1947; d. Roger H. and Doris D. (Dunkel) Elliott; m. Peter A. Machin, June 1, 1969; 1 child, Andrew D. BS in Sec. Edn., U. Kans., 1969, MA in Curriculum Devel./Anthropology, 1973; JD, U. Toledo Coll., 1978. Bar: Ohio 1978, U.S. Dist. Ct. (no. dist.) Ohio 1978, U.S. Ct. Appeals (6th cir.) 1981, U.S. Supreme Ct. 1987. Instr. rsch. and writing U. Toledo Coll. of Law, 1978-79; law clerk Lucas County Ct. of Common Pleas, Toledo, 1979-80; assoc., ptnr. Doyle, Lewis & Warner, 1980-87; assoc. Shumaker, Loop & Kendrick, 1987-92; gen. counsel U. Toledo, 1993—. Pres., v.p., mem. bd. trustees Toledo Legal Aid Soc., 1983-93; pres. Toledo Civil Trial Attys., 1990-93; trustee Esworth Found., 1993-96. Contbr. articles to profl. jours. Mem. house corp. bd. Gamma Phi Beta Sorority, 1985—; mem. bd. trustees Epworth Found., 1993—, St. Luke's Hosp., 1994—. Mem. Ohio State Bar Assn., Toledo Bar Assn., Toledo Women's Bar Assn., Toledo Civil Trial Attys. (pres. 1983-92). Home: 414 Grenelefe Ct Holland OH 43528-9232 Office: U of Toledo Office of the Gen Counsel 3620 University Hall 2801 W Bancroft Toledo OH 43606

MACIAS, EDWARD S. chemistry educator, university official and dean; b. Milw., Feb. 21, 1944; s. Arturo C. Macias and Minette (Schwenger) Wiederhold; m. Paula Wiederhold, June 17, 1967; children: Matthew Edward, Julia Katherine. AB, Colgate U., 1966; PhD, MIT, 1970. Asst. prof. Washington U., St. Louis, 1970-76, assoc. prof., 1976-84, prof. chemistry, 1984—, chmn. dept., 1984-88, provost, 1988-95, interim dean Faculty Arts and Scis., 1994-95, exec. vice chancellor and dean Faculty Arts and Scis., 1995—. Cons. Meteorology Rsch., Inc., Altadina, Calif., 1978-81, Salt River Project, Phoenix, 1980-83, Santa Fe Rsch., Bloomington, Minn., 1985-88, AeroVironment, Inc., Monrovia, Calif., 1986-88. Author: Nuclear and Radiochemistry, 1981; editor: Atmospheric Aerosol, 1981; contbr. numerous articles to profl. jours. Bd. dirs. Mark Twain Summer Inst., St. Louis, 1984-87, 88-90, The Coll. Sch., St. Louis, 1984-88, Colgate U., 1997—. Grantee NSF, EPA, Electric Power Rsch. Inst., So. Calif. Edison Co., Dept. Energy, AEC. Mem. Am. Chem. Soc., Am. Assn. Aerosol Rsch. (editorial bd.), Am. Phys. Soc., AAAS. Home: 6907 Waterman Ave Saint Louis MO 63130-4333 Office: Washington U Campus Box 1094 One Brookings Dr Saint Louis MO 63130

MACINNIS, AL, professional hockey player; b. Inverness, N.S., Can., July 11, 1963; Hockey player Calgary (Can.) Flames, 1981-94, St. Louis Blues, 1994—. Recipient Max Kaminsky trophy, 1982-83, Conn Smythe trophy, 1988-89; played in NHL All-Star Game, 1985, 88, 90-92, 94; named to The Sporting News All-Star first team, 1989-90, 90-91, NHL All-Star first team, 1989-90, 90-91, Stanley Cup championship team, 1989. Office: care St Louis Blues Kiel Ctr 1401 Clark Ave Saint Louis MO 63103-2700

MACIUSZKO, KATHLEEN LYNN, librarian, educator; b. Nogales, Ariz., Apr. 8, 1947; d. Thomas and Stephanie (Horowski) Mart; m. Jerzy Janusz Maciuszko, Dec. 11, 1976; 1 child, Christinia Alexsandra. BA, Ea. Mich. U., 1969; MLS, Kent State U., 1974; PhD, Case Western Res. U., 1987. Reference libr. Baldwin-Wallace Coll. Libr., Berea, Ohio, 1974-77, dir. Conservatory of Music Libr., 1977-85; dir. bus. info. svcs. Harcourt Brace Jovanovich, Inc., Cleve., 1985-89; staff asst. to exec. dir. Cuyahoga County Pub. Libr., 1989-90; dir. Cleve. Area Met. Library System, Beachwood, Ohio, 1990; media specialist Cleve. Pub. Schs., 1991-93, Berea (Ohio) City Sch. Dist., 1993—. Author: OCLC: A Decade of Development, 1967-77, 1984; contbr. articles to profl. jours. Named Plenum Pub. scholar, 1986. Mem. Spl. Librs. Assn. (pres. Cleve. chpt. 1989-90, v.p. 1988-89, editor newsletter 1988-89), Baldwin-Wallace Coll. Faculty Women's Club (pres. 1975), Avocation: piano. Office: Midpark HS 7000 Paula Dr Middleburg Heights OH 44130

MACIVER, JOHN KENNETH, lawyer; b. Milw., Mar. 22, 1931; s. Wallace and Elizabeth (MacRae) MacI.; m. Margaret J. Vail, Sept. 4, 1954; children: Douglas B., Carolyn V., Kenneth D., Laura E. BS, U. Wisc., 1953, LLB, 1955; D Laws & Econ. Devel. (hon.), Milw. Sch. Engring., 1997. Bar: Wisc. 1955. Sr. ptnr. Michael Best & Friedrich LLP, Milw., 1955—. Mem. various bds. dirs. Chmn. Thompson for Gov. steering coms., 1986, 90, 94, 98; state chmn. Wisc. Bush for Pres. coms., 1980, 88, 92; chmn. Wis. Nixon for Pres. com., 1968, 72, Olson for Gov. com., 1970; co-chmn. Wis. George W. Bush for Pres., state co-chair, 2000; vice chmn. Knowles for Gov. com., 1964, 66; bd. dirs. Milw. Symphony Orch., 1968-96, pres. 1981-82; trustee Milw. Symphony Endowment Trust, 1988—; chmn. exec. com., bd. govs. East-West Ctr., 1970-76 (Disting. svc. award Honolulu 1976); pres., chmn. bd. dirs. Nat. Coun. Alcoholism, 1974-77, bd. dirs. 1968-78 (Silver Key award N.Y. 1975); pres., campaign co-chmn. United Performing Arts Fund Greater Milw., 1974-76 (Stiemke award Arts 1988); bd. dirs., exec. com. Greater Milw. Edn. Trust, 1988-97, Project New Hope, 1991—; sec., gen. counsel Wisc. Mfrs. and Commerce, 1980—; regent, sec., gen. counsel Milw. Sch. Engring., 1987—; bd. dirs., sec. Pettit Nat. Ice Tng. Ctr., 1992—; bd. dirs. Milw. Nat. Heart Project; bd. dirs., exec. com., founding mem., sec. Competitive Wisc. Inc., 1982—; bd. dirs., vice-chair Met. Milw. Assn. Commerce, 1987—; mem. Greater Milw. Com. 1985—; trustee Milw. County Pub. Mus., 1989-92. Recipient Wisc. Gov's. awards in Support of Arts, 1989, cmty. svc. award Assoc. Gen. Contractors of Greater Milw. Mem. Wis. Bar Assn. (chmn. commn. litigation costs and delay, past chmn. labor law sect., commn. on jud. elections and ethics), Milw. Bar Assn. (chmn. jud. selection and qualifications com.), Milw. Club, Town Club. Republican. Avocations: Am. history, tennis, charities, politics. Home: 959 E Circle Dr Milwaukee WI 53217-5362 Office: Michael Best & Friedich 100 E Wisconsin Ave Ste 3300 Milwaukee WI 53202-4108

MACK, ALAN WAYNE, interior designer; b. Cleve., Oct. 30, 1947; s. Edmund B. and Florence I. (Oleksa) M. BS in Interior Design, Case Western Res. U., 1969. Designer interior design dept. Halle's, Cleve., 1969, 71-73; designer Nahan Co., New Orleans, 1973-75, Hemenway's Contract Design, New Orleans, 1975-76; ptnr. Hewlett-Mack Design Assocs., 1976-85; prin., dir. interior design HLM Design, Inc., 1985—2001; prin., ptnr. Proteus Group, Chgo., 2001—. Mem. adv. com. interior design dept. Delgado Jr. Coll., New Orlean s; mktg./merchandising adv. coun. St. Mary's Dominican Coll., New Orleans; mem. friends devel. coun. U. Iowa Mus. Art, 1986-91, chair, 1990-91; chmn. adv. com. interior design program Iowa State U., 1991-96; mem. design review com., City of Iowa City, 1992-93. Co-author: audiovisual presentation Nat. Home Improvement COun. Conf., 1981. Bd. dirs. Johnson County United Way, 1991-96. Served with U.S. Army, 1969-71. Mem. ASID (profl. mem., presdl. citation 1980, treas. La. dist. chpt. 1984), Vis. Nurses Assn. (bd. dirs. 1991-96), Found. for Interior Design Edn. Rsch. (standards com. 1972-76, bd. visitors 1977-80, accreditation com. 1981-95, trustee 1996-99, chmn. bd. dirs. 1998, pres. 1999). Home: 3800 N Lake Shore Dr Ste 2G Chicago IL 60613-3313 E-mail: amack@proteusgroup.net.

MACK, JIM, advertising executive; With Frankel & Co., Chgo., 1979-89, pres., 1989-98, pres., CEO, 1998—. Office: Frankel and Co 111 E Wacker Dr Chicago IL 60601-3713

MACK, ROBERT EMMET, hospital administrator; b. Morris, Ill., 1924; M.D., St. Louis U., 1948. Diplomate: Am. Bd. Internal Medicine. Intern St. Marys Hosp. Group, 1948-49; asst. resident, then resident internal medicine St. Louis U., 1949-52; asst. chief radioisope clinic Walter Reed Army Med. Center, 1954-56; chief med. service, chief radioisotope service St. Louis VA Hosp., 1956-61; vis. physician St. Louis City Hosp., 1957-61; chmn. dept. medicine Womans Hosp., Detroit, 1961-66; dir. Hutzel Hosp., 1966-71, pres., 1971-80; v.p. for academic affairs Detroit Med. Center Corp., 1980-96. Asst. prof. medicine St. Louis U., 1957-61; assoc. prof. medicine, Wayne State U., Detroit, 1961-66, prof., 1966-96, emeritus prof. internal medicine, 1996—, dir. admissions, 1978-81, asst./assoc. dean Med. Ctr. Rels., 1981-96. Fellow ACP, Am. Coll. Hosp. Adminstrs., Soc. Med. Adminstrs. (pres. 1987-89); mem. AMA, Am. Fedn. Clin. Rsch., Cen. Soc. Clin. Rsch., Am. Endocrine Soc., Am. Physiol. Soc. Home: 3020 S Westview Ct Bloomfield Hills MI 48304-2472 Office: Detroit Medical Ctr 4201 Saint Antoine St Detroit MI 48201-2153 E-mail: vmack@intmed.wsu.edu.

MACK, STEPHEN W. financial planner; b. Chgo., Mar. 4, 1954; s. Walter M. and Suzanne (Charbonneau) M.; m. Dayle A. Rothermel, Nov. 19, 1983; children: Michael, Veronica, Kevin. BBA in Fin., U. Mich., 1976; cert., Coll. Fin. Planning, Denver, 1987. NASD Lic. Series 63 Uniform Securities Agent State Law Exam., Series 7 Gen. Securities Rep., Series 5 Interest Rate Options, Series 8 Gen. Securities Sales Supr., Series 15 Fgn. Currency Options, Series 24 Gen. Securities Prin., Series 4 Registered Options Prin., Series 53 Municipal Securities Prin. Gen. sales mgr. Mack Cadillac Corp., Mt. Prospect, Ill., 1976-81; sales rep. Merrill Lynch Co., Chgo., 1981-84, resident mgr. Rockford, Ill., 1984-85, asst. v.p. Skokie, 1985-86; pres., chief exec. officer Mack Investment Securities, Inc., Glenview, 1986—. Editor, distributor Mack Tracks (trademark), monthly newsletter; creator, developer Money Mgrs. Plus Program and Website. Bdi. dirs. Glenview Youth Baseball, 1994-99, pres., 1999-2001. Mem. Inst. Cert. Fin. Planners, Internat. Assn. registered Fin. Planners, Nat. Assn. Securities Dealers, Internat. Assn. Fin. Planners, Am. Assn. Cert. Fin. Planners, Am. Assn. Registered Fin. Planners, Am. Assn. Registered Investment Advisers, Soc. Asset Allocation and Fund Timers, Mensa. Avocations: skiing, tennis, running. Office: Mack Investment Securities Inc 1939 Waukegan Rd Glenview IL 60025-1715

MACKAY, ALFRED F. dean, philosophy educator; b. Ocala, Fla., Oct. 1, 1938; s. Kenneth Hood and Julia Horsey (Farnum) MacK.; m. Ann Nadine Wilson, Feb. 4, 1962; children: Douglas Kevin, Robert Wilson. AB, Davidson Coll., 1960; PhD, U. N.C., 1967. Prof. philosophy Oberlin (Ohio) Coll., 1967-84, 96—, dean Coll. Arts and Scis., 1984-95, acting pres., 1991. Vis. asst. prof. philosophy dept. U. Ill., Urbana/Champaign, 1970-71; vis. prof. philosophy dept. Wayne State U., Detroit, 1983. Author: Arrow's Theorem: The Paradox of Social Choice, 1980; editor: Society: Revolution and Reform, 1971, Issues in the Philosophy of Language, 1976. Campaign cons. Buddy MacKay for U.S. Senate, Fla., 1988. 1st lt. U.S. Army, Airborne, 1961-63. Fellow Woodrow Wilson Found., 1963-66, Am. Coun. of Learned Socs., 1973, Humanities fellow Rockefeller Found., 1981. Democrat. Avocations: choral singing, automobiles. Office: Oberlin Coll Dept Philosophy King Bldg Oberlin OH 44074

MACKENZIE, GEORGE ALLAN, diversified company executive; b. Kingston, Jamaica, Dec. 15, 1931; s. George Adam and Annette Louise (Maduro) MacK.; m. Valerie Ann Marchand, June 30, 1971; children from previous marriage: Richard Michael, Barbara Wynne. Student, Jamaica Coll., Kingston, 1944-48. Commd. flying officer Canadian Air Force, 1951, advanced through grades to lt. gen., 1978; comdr. Canadian Forces Air Command, Winnipeg, Man., 1978-80, resigned, 1980; exec. v.p., COO Gendis Inc., 1980-89, pres., COO, 1989-99, pres., CEO, 1999—, also bd. dirs.; bd. dirs. Sony of Can. Ltd., Willowdale, Ont., Can.; chmn., CEO SAAN Stores Ltd., 1999—. Chmn. exec. com. SAAN Stores Ltd.; bd. dirs. Gendis Inc., Boltons Capital Corp., Fort Chicago Energy Mgmt. Ltd., Gendis Realty, Inc. Mem. regional adv. bd. Carleton U.; mem. jud. coun. Province of Manitoba; mem. Bus. Coun. Manitoba; bd. trustees Victoria Gen. Hosp. Decorated comdr. Order of Mil. Merit, Order St. Johns, Can. Decoration, Knight of St. Lazarus of Jerusalem. Mem. United Services Inst. Can. (hon. v.p.), Canadian Corps Commissionaires (gov.), Police Chiefs Research Found. (co-chmn.), Lakewood Country Club (Delta), Manitoba Club, St. Charles Golf and Country Club. Home: 383 Christie Rd Winnipeg MB Canada R2N 4A5 Office: Gendis Inc 1370 Sony Pl Winnipeg MB Canada R3T 1N5

MACKENZIE, RONALD ALEXANDER, anesthesiologist; b. Detroit, Mar. 31, 1938; s. James and Elizabeth Mackenzie; m. Nancy Lee Vogan, Aug. 25, 1962; children: Margaret, James. BS, Alma Coll., 1961; DO, Kansas City Coll., 1967. Diplomate Am. Bd. Anesthesiology. Resident in anesthesiology Detroit Osteo. Hosp., 1970-72, Cleve. Clinic, 1972-73, Mayo Clinic, Rochester, Minn., 1973-74, cons. in anesthesia, 1974—; pres. ceo Am. Soc. Anesthesiologists. Vice-chmn. dept. anesthesiology Mayo Clinic, 1988-98. Pres. Minn. Orch., Rochester, 1987-89. Fellow Am. Coll. Anesthesiologists; mem. Am. Soc. Anesthesiologists (bd. dirs. 1983-87, sec. 1991-97, 1st v.p. 1998, pres.-elect 1999), Sigma Xi. Avocations: sailing, photography. Office: Mayo Clinic 200 1st St SW Rochester MN 55905-0002

MACKEY, MAURICE CECIL, university president, economist, lawyer; b. Montgomery, Ala., Jan. 23, 1929; s. M. Cecil and Annie Laurie (Kimrey) M.; m. Clare Siewert, Aug. 29, 1953; children: Carol, John, Ann. B.A., U. Ala., 1949, M.A., 1953, LL.B., 1958; Ph.D., U. Ill., 1955; postgrad., Harvard U., 1958-59. Bar: Ala. 1958. Asst. prof. econs. U. Ill., 1955-56; assoc. prof. econs. U.S. Air Force Acad., 1956-57; asst. prof. law U. Ala., 1959-62; with FAA, 1963-65, U.S. Dept. Commerce, 1965-67; asst. sec. U.S. Dept. Transp., 1967-69; exec. v.p., prof. law Fla. State U., Tallahassee, 1969-71; pres. U. South Fla., Tampa, 1971-76; pres., prof. law Tex. Tech U., Lubbock, 1976-79; pres., prof. econs. Mich. State U., East Lansing, 1979-85, prof. econs., 1985—. Asst. counsel Subcom. on Antitrust and Monopoly, U.S. Senate, 1962-63; bd. dirs. Community First Bank, Lansing, Mich.; mem. adv. com. U.S. Coast Guard Acad., 1969-71; chmn. Fla. Gov.'s Adv. Com. on Transp., 1975, Nat. Boating Safety Adv. Council, 1975— ; mem. adv. council NSF, 1978-81; assoc. China Council, 1979—; Disting. vis. prof. United Arab Emirates U., 1990, 91, 92, 93; bd. dirs. Summit Holding Corp., Lansing. Bd. dirs. Gulf Ridge council Boy Scouts Am.; pres. Chief Okemos council, 1981-82; bd. dirs. Tampa United Fund, Lubbock United Way; chmn., bd. dirs. Debt for Devel. Coalition, 1989—. Served with USAF, 1956-57. Recipient Arthur S. Flemming award Washington Jaycees, 1967 Mem. Fla. Council 100, Tampa C. of C. (bd. govs.), Am. Assn. State Colls. and Univs. (pres., dir.), Artus, Chi Alpha Phi. Office: Mich State U Dept Econs 101 Marshall Hall East Lansing MI 48824-1038

MACKIE, RICHARD H. orchestra executive; married; 3 children. Grad., Tulane U.; M in Arts Adminstrn., U. Wis., Madison. Jazz musician New Hyperion Oriental Foxtrot Orch.; pres. Friends of WHA-TV; dir. devel. Edgewood Coll.; exec. dir. Madison (Wis.) Symphony Orch., 1999—. Office: Madison Symphony Orch 6314 Odana Rd Madison WI 53719

MACKIEWICZ, LAURA, advertising agency executive; Formerly with D'Arcy Advt.; with BBDO, Chgo., 1973—, now sr. v.p., dir. broadcast and print svcs. Office: BBDO Chgo 410 N Michigan Ave Ste 8 Chicago IL 60611-4273

MACKINNEY, ARCHIE ALLEN, JR. physician; b. St. Paul, Aug. 16, 1929; s. Archie Allen and Doris (Hoops) MacK.; m. Shirley Schaefer, Apr. 9, 1955; children— Julianne, Theodore, John. B.A., Wheaton (Ill.) Coll., 1951; M.D., U. Rochester, 1955. Intern, resident in medicine U. Wis. Hosp., 1955-59; clin. assoc. NIH, 1959-61; clin. investigator VA, 1961-64; asst. prof. medicine U. Wis., Madison, 1964-68, assoc. prof., 1968-74, prof., 1974-98, med. alumni prof., 1987. Mentor class of '03 U. Wis. Med. Sch.; chief hematology VA Hosp., Madison, 1964-98, chief nuclear medicine, 1964-73, 78-79 Author, editor Pathophysiology of Blood, 1984. Contbr. articles to med. jours. Trustee Intervarsity Christian Fellowship, 1985-88. Served with USPHS, 1959-61. Danforth assoc., 1962 Mem. Am. Soc. Hematology, Am. Fedn. Clin. Research, Central Soc. Clin. Research. Republican. Baptist. Home: 190 N Prospect Ave Madison WI 53705-4071 Office: 2500 Overlook Ter Madison WI 53705-2254

MACKINNON, CATHARINE ALICE, lawyer, law educator, legal scholar, writer; d. George E. and Elizabeth V. (Davis) MacKinnon. BA in Govt. magna cum laude with distinction, Smith Coll., 1969; JD, Yale U., 1977, PhD in Polit. Sci., 1987. Vis. prof. Harvard U., Stanford U., Yale U., others, Osgoode Hall, York U., Canada, U. Basel, Switzerland; prof. of law U. Mich., 1990—. Long term vis. prof. U. Chgo., 1997—. Author: Sexual Harassment of Working Women, 1979, Feminism Unmodified, 1987, Toward a Feminist Theory of the State, 1989, Only Words, 1993, Sex Equality, 2001; co-author: In Harm's Way, 1997. Office: U Michigan Law School Ann Arbor MI 48109-1215

MACKLIN, CROFFORD JOHNSON, JR. lawyer; b. Columbus, Ohio, Sept. 10, 1947; S. Crofford Johnson, Sr. and Dorothy Ann (Stevens) M.; m. Mary Carole Ward, July 5, 1969; children: Carrie E., David J. BA, Ohio State U., 1969; BA summa cum laude, U. West Fla., 1974; JD cum laude, Ohio State U., 1976. Bar: Ohio 1977, U.S. Tax Ct. 1978. Acct. Touche Ross, Columbus, 1976-77; assoc. Smith & Schnacke, Dayton, 1977-81; ptnr. Porter, Wright, Morris & Arthur, 1983-88; shareholder Smith & Schnacke, 1988-89; ptnr. Thompson, Hine LLP, 1989—; practice group leader personnel and succession planning Thompson, Hine & Flory,

2001—; sole practice Dayton, 1981-82. Adj. faculty Franklin U., 1977; adj. prof. U. Dayton Law Sch., 1981. Contbr. articles to profl. jours. Bd. dirs. Great Lakes Nat. Bank Ohio, 1997, Easter Seals, 1984-86. Served to capt. USMCR, 1969-74. Fellow Am. Coll. Trust and Estate Counsel; mem. ABA, Dayton Bar Assn. (chmn. probate com. 1981-83), Dayton Trust & Estate Planning (pres. 1983-84), Ohio Bar Assn. Presbyterian. Home: 3 Forest Pl Glendale OH 45246-4407 Office: Thompson Hine LLP 2000 Courthouse Pla NE PO Box 8801 Dayton OH 45401-8801

MACKLIN, MARTIN RODBELL, psychiatrist; b. Raleigh, N.C., Aug. 27, 1934; s. Albert A. and Mitzi (Robdell) M.; m. Ruth Chimacoff (div.); children: Meryl, Shelley; m. Anne Elizabet Warren, May 25; children: Alicia, Aaron. BME, Cornell U., 1957, M in Indsl. Engring., 1958; PhD in Biomed. Engring., Case Western Res. U., 1967, MD, 1977. Diplomate Am. Bd. Psychiatry and Neurology; cert. in alcoholism and other drug dependencies Am. Soc. Addiction Medicine. Investigator Am. Heart Assn., Cleve., 1969-74; vis. fellow U. Sussex, Brighton, England, 1970; assoc. prof. biomed. engring. Case Western Res. U., 1972-81, asst. prof. psychiatry, 1981—; clin. dir. Horizon Ctr. Hosp., Warrensville Township, Ohio, 1981-83; adminstrv. dir. Riverview Psychiat. Assocs., 1983-94; med. dir. Woodside Hosp., 1989-94; v.p. med. affairs UHHS Geauga Regional Hosp., Chardon, Ohio, 1994—; 27. Psychiat. cons. Glenbeigh Hosp., Ohio and Fla.; cons. various indsl. cos.; chair quality intervention panel Ohio State Med. Bd. Contbr. articles to profl. jours; patentee in field. NIH rsch. grantee Kellogg Found., Cleve., 1967-81; Laughlin fellow Am. Coll. Psychiatry, 1980. Mem. Am. Psychiat. Assn., Am. Coll. Physician Execs., Cleve. Acad. Medicine, Cleve. Psychiat. Soc. Avocations: woodworking, gardening. Home: 348 N Chestnut St Jefferson OH 44047-1103 E-mail: martin.macklin@uhhs.com.

MACKLIN, PHILIP ALAN, physics educator; b. Richmond Hill, N.Y., Apr. 13, 1925; s. Egbert Chalmer and Margaret Griswold (Collins) M.; m. Cora Baldwin Galindo, Sept. 5, 1953; children: Susan, Steven, Peter. B.S. cum laude, Yale U., 1944; M.A., Columbia U., 1949, Ph.D., 1956. Physicist Carbide & Carbon Chems. Corp., Oak Ridge, 1946-47; research scientist AEC, Columbia U., 1949-51; instr. physics Middlebury Coll., Vt., 1951-54, acting chmn. dept., 1953-54; mem. faculty Miami U., Oxford, Ohio, 1954—, prof. physics, 1961-93, chmn. dept., 1972-85, prof. emeritus, 1993—. Research scientist Armco Steel Co., summers 1955-56; vis. prof. U. N.Mex., summers 1957-68, Boston U., fall 1985-86; physicist Los Alamos Sci. Labs., summers 1960-62; participant NSF summer insts., 1970-71; vis. scientist MIT, 1985-86 Author publs. in field; patentee in field. Vestryman Holy Trinity Episcopal Ch., Oxford , 1959-61, 67, 71-73, 75-77, mem. fin. com., chmn. blood assurance program, 1980—, lector, 1989—. With USN, 1944-46. Mem. AAAS, AAUP, LWV of Oxford (treas. 1986-88, dir. governance 1997—), Am. Phys. soc., Forum Physics and Soc., Am. Assn. Physics Tchrs., Kiwanis (bd. dirs. 1994-97), Torch Club of Butler County (pres. 1982-83, 96-97, mem. editl. adv. com. The Torch), 1809 Club (pres. 1964-65), Campus Ministry Ctr. (trustee 1994-2002), Union of Concerned Scientists, Ctr. for Voting and Democracy (charter), Membership Assn. Miami U. Art Mus. (exec. com. 1999-2002), Phi Beta Kappa (pres. Iota of Ohio chpt. 1987-88), Sigma Xi, Sigma Pi Sigma, Omicron Delta Kappa. Democrat. Home: 211 Oakhill Dr Oxford OH 45056-2710 Office: 117 Culler Hall Miami Univ Oxford OH 45056 E-mail: macklipa@muohio.edu.

MACKUS, ELOISE L. food products company executive; Asst. gen. counsel J.M. Smucker Co., Orrville, Ohio, 1994-99, dir. internat., 1999, v.p., gen. mgr. internat. market, 2000—. Office: 1 Strawberry Ln Orrville OH 44667-1241

MACLAUGHLIN, HARRY HUNTER, federal judge; b. Breckenridge, Minn., Aug. 9, 1927; s. Harry Hunter and Grace (Swank) MacL.; m. Mary Jean Shaffer, June 25, 1958; children: David, Douglas. BBA with distinction, U. Minn., 1949, JD, 1956. Bar: Minn. 1956. Law clk. to justice Minn. Supreme Ct.; ptnr. MacLaughlin & Mondale, MacLaughlin & Harstad, Mpls., 1956-72; assoc. justice Minn. Supreme Ct., 1972-77; U.S. sr. dist. judge Dist. of Minn., Mpls., 1977—. Part-time instr. William Mitchell Coll. Law, St. Paul, 1958-63; lectr. U. Minn. Law Sch., 1973-86; mem. 8th Cir. Jud. Council, 1981-83. Bd. editors: Minn. Law Rev, 1954-55. Mem. Mpls. Charter Commn., 1967-72, Minn. State Coll. Bd., 1971-72, Minn. Jud. Council, 1972; mem. nat. adv. council Small Bus. Adminstrn., 1967-69. Served with USNR, 1945-46. Recipient U. Minn. Outstanding Achievement award, 1995; named Best Fed. Dist. Ct. Judge in 8th Cir., Am. Lawyer mag., 1983. Mem. ABA, Minn. Bar Assn., Hennepin County Bar Assn., Beta Gamma Sigma, Phi Delta Phi. Congregational. Office: US Dist Ct 684 US Courthouse 110 S 4th St Minneapolis MN 55401-2205

MACLEAN, DOUG, hockey coach; b. Summerside, P.E.I., Can., Apr. 12, 1954; Student, P.E.I.; M in Ednl. Psychology, We. Ont. Asst. coach London Knights of OHL, 1984-85, St. Louis Blues, 1986-87, 87-88, Washington Capitals, 1988-89, 89-90, Detroit Red Wings, 1990-91, asst. gen. mgr., 1992-93, 93-94; gen. mgr. Adirondack, Red Wing orgn., 1992-93, 93-94; dir. player devel., scout Fla. Panthers, 1994-95, head coach, 1995-98. Office: 200 W Nationwide Blvd Ste Level Columbus OH 43215-2563

MACLIN, ALAN HALL, lawyer; b. DuQuoin, Ill., Dec. 22, 1949; s. John E. and Nora (Hall) M.; m. Joan Davidson (div. Dec. 1981); children: Molly, Tess, Anne; m. Jeanne Sittlow, Nov. 17, 1984. BA magna cum laude, Vanderbilt U., 1971; JD, U. Chgo., 1974. Bar: Minn. 1974, U.S. Dist. Ct. Minn. 1974, U.S. Ct. Appeals (8th cir.) 1974, U.S. Ct. Appeals (5th cir.) 1975. U.S. Supreme Ct. 1978. Asst. atty. gen. Minn. Atty. Gen., St. Paul, 1974-80; chief anti-trust divsn. Briggs & Morgan, 1980—, mem. bd. dirs., 1993-96. Mem. Minn. State Bar Assn. (treas. anti-trust sect. 1978-80, 96-98, chair 1998—), Ramsey County Bar Assn. (sec. jud. com. 1980-82), Phi Beta Kappa. Unitarian. Office: Briggs & Morgan 2200 1st St N Saint Paul MN 55109-3210 E-mail: amaclin@briggs.com.

MACMILLAN, SHANNON ANN, soccer player; b. Syosset, N.Y., Oct. 7, 1974; Student in social work, U. Portland. Mem. U.S. Nat. Women's Soccer Team, 1993—, including silver medal World Univ. Games team, Buffalo, N.Y., 1993, gold medal U.S. Olympic Team, 1996; mem. U.S. Women's Under-20 Nat. Team, 1993-94, including championship Internat. Women's Tournament, Montricoux, France, 1993; mem. La Jolla (Calif.) Nomads club soccer team, winning state club championship, 1991, 92; mem. Japanese women's profl. league, 1996, 97. Recipient Mo. Athletic Club award, 1995, Hermann award, U. Portland, 1995; naemd 1995 Soccer Am. Player of Yr.; recipient Bill Hayward award 1995; named Female Athlete of Yr., 1993, 95, U. Portland; named to San Diego Union Tribune All-Acad. team. Office: US Soccer Fedn 1801-1811 S Prairie Ave Chicago IL 60616

MACMILLAN, WHITNEY, food products and import/export company executive; Chmn., CEO Cargill, Wayzata, Minn., chmn. emeritus, 1996—. Mem. bd. dirs. Deluxe Corp., Minn. Office: Cargill PO Box 9300 Minneapolis MN 55440-9300

MACPHAIL, ANDREW B. professional sports team executive; b. Bronxville, N.Y., Apr. 5, 1953; m. Lark MacPhail; children: William Reed, Andrew Hamilton. Grad., Dickinson Coll., 1976. Bus. mgr. Cubs' orgn., Bradenton Rookie affiliate Gulf Coast League, 1976-77; asst. parks ops. Cubs' Orgn., 1977, with dept. player devel., 1978, asst. dir. dept. player devel., asst. dir. scouting; asst. gen. mgr. Houston Astros, 1982-85; v.p. player personnel Minn. Twins, 1985-86, exec. v.p., gen. mgr., 1986-94; pres., CEO Chgo. Cubs., 1994—. Named Maj. League Exec. of Yr., The Sporting News, 1991, Am. League Exec. of Yr., United Press Internat., 1991; winner World Series Championship, 1987, 91. Office: Chgo Cubs 1060 W Addison St Chicago IL 60613-4383

MACPHERSON, COLIN R(OBERTSON), pathologist, educator; b. Aberdeen, Scotland, Sept. 2, 1924; came to U.S., 1956; s. Donald J.R. and Nora (Tait) M.; m. Margaret E. Mitchell, Dec. 21, 1949; children: Shelagh, Catherine, Janet, Mary. MBChB, U. Cape Town, Union South Africa, 1946, M.Med., MD in Pathology, 1954. Diplomate Anatomic and Clinical Pathology, Blood Banking. Resident, instr. U. Cape Town, 1948-54; fellow Postgrad. Med. Sch., London, 1955-56; asst., assoc. then prof. pathology Ohio State U., Columbus, 1956-75, vice chmn. lab. med., 1961-75; dir. lab. medicine U. Cin., 1975-87, dep. dir. Hoxworth Blood Ctr., 1988-90, prof. dept. pathology and lab. medicine, 1991-95, prof. emeritus, 1995—. Contbr. articles to profl. jours. Chmn. bd. schs., rev. bd. Nat. Accrediting Agy. for Clin. Lab. Scis., 1968-74. Mem. Am. Assn. Blood Banks. Presbyterian. Avocations: music, color photography. Office: U Cin Med Ctr Goodman St Cincinnati OH 45267-0714

MAC WATTERS, VIRGINIA ELIZABETH, singer, music educator, actress; b. Phila. d. Frederick-Kennedy and Idoleein (Hallowell) Mac W.; m. Paul Abée, June 10, 1960. Grad., Phila. Normal Sch. for Tchrs., 1933; student, Curtis Inst. Music, Phila., 1936. With New Opera Co., N.Y.C., 1941-42; artist-in-residence Ind. U. Sch. Music, 1957-58; assoc. prof. U. Ind. Sch. Music, 1958-68, prof. voice, 1968-82, prof. emeritus, 1982—. Singer: leading roles Broadway mus. Rosalinda, 1942-44, Mr. Strauss Goes to Boston, 1945, leading opera roles New Opera Co., N.Y.C., 1941-42, San Francisco, 1944, N.Y.C. Ctr., 1946-51; leading soprano for reopening of Royal Opera House, Covent Garden, London, 1947-48, Guatemala, El Salvador, Cen. Am., 1948-49; debut at Met. Opera, N.Y.C., 1952; TV spls. on NBC include Menotti's Old Maid and the Thief, 1949, Would-be Gentleman (R. Strauss), 1955; leading singer with Met. Opera Co. on coast to coast tour of Die Fledermaus, 1951-52,, Met. Opera debut, N.Y.C., 1952, leading soprano Cen. City Opera Festival, Colo., 1952-56; performed with symphony orchs. in U.S., Can., S.Am.; concert recitalist U.S., Can., 1950-62; opened N.Y. Empire State Music Festival in Ariadne auf Naxos (Strauss), 1959; soloist Mozart Festival, Ann Arbor, Mich. Recipient Mile award Album Familiar Music, 1949, Ind. U. Disting. Tchg. award, 1979; named One of 10 Outstanding Women of the Yr.; Zeckwer Hahn Phila. Mus. Acad. scholar, 1941-42; MacWatters chair donated by New Auer Grand Concert Hall, U. Ind. Sch. Music. Mem. Nat. Fedn. of Music Clubs, Nat. Soc. Arts and Letters, Nat. Soc. Lit. and Arts, Soc. Am. Musicians, Nat. Assn. Tchrs. of Singing, Internat. Platform Assn., Sigma Alpha Iota. Club: Matinee Musical (hon. mem. Phila., Indpls. chpts.). Achievements include having only original recorded version of Zerbinetta aria from Ariadne auf Naxos (Strauss). Home: 3800 Arlington Rd Bloomington IN 47404-1347 Office: Ind U Sch Music Bloomington IN 47405

MACY, JOHN PATRICK, lawyer; b. Menomonee Falls, Wis., June 26, 1955; s. Leland Francis and Joan Marie (LaValle) M. BA, Carroll Coll., 1977; JD, Marquette U., 1980. Bar: Wis. 1980, U.S. Dist. Ct. (we. and ea. dists.) Wis. 1980, U. S. Ct. Appeals (7th cir.) 1980. Assoc. Hippenmeyer Reilly Arenz Molter Bode & Gross, Waukesha, Wis., 1980-83; ptnr. Arenz Molter Macy & Riffle, S.C., 1983--. Lectr. in field. Mem. ABA, Waukesha County Bar Assn. (chair 1995-96). Republican. Roman Catholic. Home: 4839 Hewitts Point Rd Oconomowoc WI 53066-3320 Office: Arenz Molter Macy & Riffle SC 720 N East Ave Waukesha WI 53186-4800

MADANSKY, ALBERT, statistics educator; b. Chgo., May 16, 1934; s. Harry and Anna (Meidenberg) M.; m. Paula Barkan, June 10, 1990; children from previous marriage: Susan, Cynthia, Noreen, Michele. AB, U. Chgo., 1952, MS, 1955, PhD, 1958. Mathematician Rand Corp., Santa Monica, Calif., 1957-65; sr. v.p. Interpub. Group of Companies, N.Y.C., 1965-68; pres. Dataplan Inc, 1968-70; prof. computer scis. CCNY, 1970-74; prof. bus. adminstrn. grad. sch. U. Chgo., 1974—, assoc. dean, 1985-90, dep. dean, 1990-93, H.G.B. Alexander prof. bus. adminstrn., 1996-99, H.G.B. Alexander emeritus bus. adminstrn., 1999—. Bd. dirs. Analytic Services, Washington, 1975—. Author: Foundations of Econometrics, 1975, Prescriptions for Working Statisticians, 1988. Fellow: Ctr. for Advanced Study in Behavioral Scis., Am. Statis. Assn., Inst. Math. Stats., Econometric Soc. Home: 200 E Delaware Pl Apt 23F Chicago IL 60611-5799 Office: U of Chicago Grad Sch Business Chicago IL 60637 E-mail: albert.madansky@gsb.uchicago.edu.

MADDEN, CHERYL BETH, state legislator; b. Burke, S.D., Nov. 15, 1948; d. Herman and Ida Denker; m. Michael K. Madden, 1977; children: Pamela, Jessica, Rachel. Grad. high sch. Mem. S.D. Ho. of Reps., Pierre, 1992-98, mem. edn., health and human svc. coms.; mem. S.D. Senate from 35th dist., Pierre, 1999—. Chaplain, chmn. Fedn. Rep. Women. Address: 4955 Enchanted Pines Dr Rapid City SD 57701-9252

MADDEN, LAURENCE VINCENT, plant pathology educator; b. Ashland, Pa., Oct. 10, 1953; s. Lawrence Vincent and Janet Elizabeth (Wewer) M.; m. Susan Elizabeth Heady, July 7, 1984. BS, Pa. State U., 1975, MS, 1977, PhD, 1980. Research scientist Ohio State U., Wooster, 1980-82, asst. prof., 1983-86, assoc. prof., 1986-91, prof., 1991—. Invited univ. lectr. on plant disease epidemiology in more than 10 countries. Author: Introduction to Plant Disease Epidemiology; sr. editor Phytopathology, 1988-90, APS Press, 1988-90; editor-in-chief Phytopathology, 1991-93; contbr. 140articles to profl. jours. U.S. Dept. Rsch. grantee, 1984, 85, 86, 87, 89, 90, 91, 95, 99, 2000; Disting. scholar Ohio State U., 1991,; recipient Outstanding Alumni award Pa. State U. Coll. Agrl. Scis. Fellow AAAS, The Linnean Soc. of London, Am. Phytopathol. Soc. (chmn. com. 1983, 86, coun. 1991-93, Ciba Geigy Agrl. Achievement award 1990, v.p. 1994-95, pres.-elect 1995-96, pres. 1996-97); mem. Biometric Soc., Brit. Soc. Plant Pathology, Sigma Xi (chpt. pres. 1985). Achievements include development of statistical and mathematical models for understanding, predicting and comparing botanical epidemics and assessing crop losses. Home: 1295 Briarcrest Cir Wooster OH 44691 Office: Ohio State U OARDC Dept Plant Pathology Wooster OH 44691 E-mail: madden.1@osu.edu.

MADDEN, THOMAS A. automotive parts manufacturing executive; BBA, U. Pa.; MBA, U. Pitts. CPA, Mich. Mgr. Coopers & Lybrand; asst. corp. contr. Meritor/Rockwell, 1981-82, dir. fin. reports and policies, mgr. external reports, 1982-87, asst. corp. contr., 1987; sr. v.p. Meritor Automotive, Inc.; sr. v.p., CFO ArvinMeritor, Inc., Troy, Mich., 2000—. Trustee Mich. Colls. Found.; bd. dirs. Leadership Coun. Pitts. Family Hospice. Mem. Fin. Execs. Inst. (bd. dirs. Pitts. chpt.), U. Pitts. Alumni Assn. (bd. dirs.). Office: Arvin Meritox Inc 2135 W Maple Rd Troy MI 48084-7186

MADDOX, O. GENE, state legislator, lawyer; b. Peoria, Ill., Aug. 23, 1938; BS, Northwestern U., 1960, JD, 1963. Pvt. practice, Des Moines, 1963—; gen. counsel, employee rels. v.p. Mid-Continent Industries, 1987—; mem. Iowa Senate from 38th dist., 1992—; vice chair commerce com., mem. appropriations com.; mem. jud. com., mem. state govt. com.; mem. ways and means com. Mayor City of Clive, 1978-93; mem. Grace United Meth. Ch.; v.p. Iowa Affiliate, Am. Diabetes Assn.; mem. Iowa Natural Heritage Found.; vol. reader Visually Impaired Persons; mem. Iowa Hist. Soc., Polk-Des Moines Taxpayers. Mem. ABA, Iowa Bar Assn., Polk County Bar Assn., Iowa Jaycees (pres.), Iowa League of Cities (pres. 1987-88), Iowa Municipalities (bd. dirs. 1983-89, pres. 1987-88), Greater Des Moines C. of C., Rotary (N.W. Des Moines chpt.), Lions. Republican. Office: State Capitol 9th And Grand Ave Des Moines IA 50319-0001 E-mail: gene_maddos@legis.state.ia.us.

MADDOX, WILMA, health facility administrator; Grad., Truman State U., 1979. Bus. mgr. Vision Care Assocs., Macon, Maine. Bd. govs. Truman State U., 1994—; mem. Ko. K-16 Coalition; mem. bd. edn. Macon County R-I Sch. Dist.; vol. aftersch. program Macon United Meth. Ch. Mem.: Am. Found. for Vision Awareness (past pres. Mo. affiliate). Office: Vision Care Assocs 1402 N Rutherford St Macon MO 63552

MADGETT, NAOMI LONG, poet, editor, publisher, educator; b. Norfolk, Va., July 5, 1923; d. Clarence Marcellus and Maude Selena (Hilton) Long; m. Julian F. Witherspoon, Mar. 31, 1946 (div. Apr. 1949); 1 child, Jill Witherspoon Boyer; m. William H. Madgett, July 29, 1954 (div. Dec. 1960); m. Leonard P. Andrews, Mar. 31, 1972 (dec. May 1996). BA, Va. State Coll., 1945; MEd, Wayne State U., 1956; PhD, Internat. Inst. for Advanced Studies, 1980; LHD (hon.), Siena Heights Coll., 1991, Loyola U., 1993; DFA (hon.), Mich. State U., 1994. Reporter, copyreader Mich. Chronicle, Detroit, 1946; svc. rep. Mich. Bell Telephone Co., 1948-54; tchr. English pub. high schs., 1955-65, 66-68; rsch. assoc. Oakland U., Rochester, Mich., 1965-66; mem. staff Detroit Women Writers Conf. Ann. Writers Conf., 1968—; lectr. English U. Mich., 1970-71; assoc. prof. English Eastern Mich. U., Ypsilanti, 1968-73, prof., 1973-84, prof. emeritus, 1984—; editor-pub. Lotus Press, 1974—. Editor Lotus Poetry Series, Mich. State U. Press, 1993-98. Author: (poetry) Songs to a Phantom Nightingale (under name Naomi Cornelia Long), 1941, One and the Many, 1956, Star by Star, 1965, 70, Pink Ladies in the Afternoon, 1972, 90, Exits and Entrances, 1978, Phantom Nightingale: Juvenilia, 1981, Octavia and other Poems (Creative Achievement award Coll. Lang. Assn.), 1988, Remembrances of Spring: Collected Early Poems, 1993; (textbook) (with Ethel Tincher and Henry B. Maloney) Success in Language and Literature B, 1967, A Student's Guide to Creative Writing, 1980; editor: (anthology) A Milestone Sampler: 15th Anniversary Anthology, 1988, Adam of Ife: Black Women in Praise of Black Men, 1992; In Her Lifetime tribute Afrikan Poets Theatre, 1989. Participant Creative Writers in Schs. program. Recipient Esther R. Beer Poetry award Nat. Writers Club, 1957, Disting. English Tchr. of Yr. award, 1967; Josephine Nevins Keal award, 1979; Mott fellow in English, 1965, Robert Hayden Runagate award, 1985, Creative Artist award Mich. Coun. for the Arts, 1987, award Nat. Coalition 100 Black Women, 1984, award Nat. Coun. Tchrs. English Black Caucus, 1984, award Chesapeake/Virginia Beach chpt. Links, Inc., 1981, Arts Found. Mich. award, 1990, Creative Achievement award Coll. Lang. Assn., 1988; Arts Achievement award Wayne State U., 1985, The Black Scholar Award of Excellence, 1992; Am. Book award, 1993, Mich. Artist award, 1993; Creative Contbrs. award Gwendolyn Brooks Ctr. Black Lit. and Creative Writing Chgo. State U., 1993, George Kent award, 1995; Naomi Long Madgett Poetry award named for her, 1993—; inducted Sumner H.S. Hall of Fame, St. Louis, 1997, Nat. Lit. Hall Fame for Writers African Descent, Chgo. State U., 1999; named Poet Laureate, City of Detroit, 2001—. Mem. NAACP, Coll. Lang. Assn., So. Poetry Law Ctr., Langston Hughes Soc., Detroit Women Writers, Charles H. Wright Mus. African Am. History, Fred Hart Williams Geneal. Soc., Alpha Kappa Alpha. Congregationalist. Home: 18080 Santa Barbara Dr Detroit MI 48221-2531 Office: PO Box 21607 Detroit MI 48221-0607 E-mail: nlmadgett@aol.com.

MADIGAN, JOHN WILLIAM, publishing executive; b. Chgo., June 7, 1937; s. Edward P. and Olive D. Madigan; m. Holly Williams, Nov. 24, 1962; children: Mark W., Griffith E., Melanie L. BBA, U. Mich., 1958, MBA, 1959. Fin. analyst Duff & Phelps, Chgo., 1960-62; audit mgr. Arthur Andersen & Co., 1962-67; v.p. investment banking Paine, Webber, Jackson & Curtis, 1967-69; v.p. corp. fin. Salomon Bros., Chgo., 1969-74; v.p., CFO, dir. Tribune Co., Chgo., 1975-81, exec. v.p., 1981-91; pub. Chgo. Tribune, 1990-94; pres., CEO Tribune Pub. Co., Chgo., 1991-94; pres., COO Tribune Co., 1994-5, pres., CEO, 1995—, chmn., pres., CEO, 1996—. Bd. dirs. AP. Trustee Rush-Presbyn.-St. Luke's Med. Ctr., Mus. TV & Radio in N.Y., Northwestern U., Ill. Inst. Tech. Mem. Chgo. Coun. on Fgn. Rels. (bd. dirs.), Robert R. McCormick Tribune Found. (bd. dirs.), Newspaper Assn. Am. (bd. dirs.), Econ. Club Chgo., Comml. Club Chgo. (chmn.). Office: Tribune Co 435 N Michigan Ave Chicago IL 60611-4066

MADIGAN, LISA, state legislator; Grad., Georgetown U., Loyola U. Asst. dean adult, continuing edn. Wilbur Wright Coll.; mem. Ill. Senate, Springfield, 1999—, mem. appropriations, local govt. coms. Bd. dirs. AIDS Living Rememberance Com. Mem. Ill. Bar Assn., Women's Bar Assn. Ill., Chgo. Bar Assn. Office: State Capitol Capitol Bldg 105C Springfield IL 62706-0001 also: 2006 W Addison St Chicago IL 60618-6102

MADIGAN, MICHAEL JOSEPH, state legislator; b. Chgo., Apr. 19, 1942; m. Shirley Roumagoux; children: Lisa, Tiffany, Nicole, Andrew. Ed., U. Notre Dame, Loyola U., Chgo. Mem. Ill. Ho. of Reps., 1971—, majority leader, 1977-80, minority leader, 1981-82, house spkr., 1983-94, Dem. leader, 1995-96, ho. spkr., 1997—; lawyer. Sec. to Alderman David W. Healey; hearing officer Ill. Commerce Commn.; del. 6th Ill. Constnl. Conv.; trustee Holy Cross Hosp.; ex officio mem. adv. com. to pres. Richard J. Daley Coll.; adv. com. Fernley Harris Sch. for Handicapped; committeeman 13th Ward Democratic Orgn.; chmn. Ill. Dem. Party. Mem. Council Fgn. Relations, City Club Chgo. Office: House Reps 300 State Capital Bldg Springfield IL 62706-0001*

MADIGAN, ROBERT A. state legislator; b. Lincoln, Ill., Nov. 28, 1942; m. to Connie Madigan; two children. BS, Millikin U., 1966. Dist. 45 senator Ill. Senate, Springfield, 1987—. Mem. agr. and conservation, labor and commerce, elem. and secondary edn., pensions and licensed activities, welfare and corrections, pub. health, welfare and corrections coms., Ill. Senate; mem. joint coms. on intergovernmental cooperation, regulation of professions and occupations, consumer banks, Ill. pension funds in Northern Ireland; bd. dirs. Comprehensive Health Ins. Plan, Geologic Map Task Force. Home: 618 N Chicago St Lincoln IL 62656-2131

MADISON, GEORGE W. lawyer, company executive; b. 1953; BS, NYU; MBA, JD, Columbia U. Law clk. to Hon. Nathaniel R. Jones U.S. Ct. Appeals (6th cir.) Ohio, Cin., 1980-81; assoc. Shearman & Sterling, N.Y.C., 1981-87; with Mayer, Brown & Platt, 1987-89, ptnr., 1989-96; exec. v.p., corp. sec., gen. counsel Comerica Inc., Detroit, 1996—. Dir. Legal Svcs. of N.Y.C., Inc., Assn. of Bar of City of N.Y. Fund, Inc. Mem. ABA, Assn. of Bar of City of N.Y., Met. Black Bar Assn. Office: PO Box 75000 Detroit MI 48275-0001

MADISON, ROBERT PRINCE, architect; b. Cleve., July 28, 1923; s. Robert J. and Nettie (Brown) M.; m. Leatrice L. Branch, Apr. 16, 1949; children: Jeanne Marie, Juliette Branch. Student, Howard U., 1940-43, HHD, 1987; B.Arch., Western Res. U., 1946-48; M.Arch., Harvard, 1952; DFA (hon.), Cleveland State U., 2000. Mem. various archtl. firms, 1948-52; instr. Howard U., Washington, 1952-54; chmn., CEO Robert P. Madison Internat., architects, engrs. and planners, Cleve., 1954—. Trustee Am. Automobile Assn.; vis. prof. Howard U., 1961-62; lectr. Western Res. U., 1964-65; mem. U.S. architects del. Peoples Repub. China, 1974 Prin. works include U.S. Embassy Dakar, Senegal, West Africa, 1966, State of Ohio Computer Ctr., 1988, Cuyahoga County Jail, 1990, Continental Airlines Hub Concourse, Cleve. Internat. Airport, 1991. Mem. tech. adv. com. Cleve. Bd. Edn., 1960—; mem. adv. com. Cleve. Urban Renewal, 1963—; mem. fine arts adv. com. to mayor, Cleve.; mem. archtl. adv. coun. Cornell U.; trustee Case Western Res. U., Cleve. Opera, 1990, NCCJ, 1990, Commn. on Higher Edn., 1990; bd. dirs. Jr. Achievement Greater Cleve.; trustee Cuyahoga County Hosp. Found., 1983—, Univ. Circle Inc., Midtown Corridor Inc.; mem. Ohio Bd. Bldg. Standards, 1986, Cleveland Heights City Planning Commn., 1987. 1st lt., inf. AUS, 1943-46. Decorated Purple Heart; Fulbright fellow, 1952-53; recipient Disting. Svc. award Case Western Res. U., 1989, Disting. Archtl. Firm award Howard

U., 1989, Entrepreneur of Yt. award Ernst Young, Inc., Merrill Lynch, 1991, Arch. of Yr. Nat. Tech. Assn., 1996, Martin Luther King Jr. Corp. award African-Am. Archives Aux. Western Res. Hist. Soc., 1997, Disting. Alumni award Case We. Res. U., 1997; named to Corp. Hall of Fame, Ohio Assembly of Couns., 1991, Pres. award Kent State U., 1999. Fellow AIA (chpt. pres., nat. task force for creative econs. 1976, mem. jury of fellows 1983-85, mem. nat. judicial coun. 1993, Gold Medal Firm award Ohio 1994, Gold Medal award Ohio 1997); mem. Architects Soc. Ohio, Epsilon Delta Rho, Alpha Phi Alpha, Sigma Pi Phi. Home: 13600 Shaker Blvd Apt 206 Cleveland OH 44120-1591 Office: Robert P Madison Internat Inc 2930 Euclid Ave Cleveland OH 44115-2416

MADORI, JAN, art gallery director; Pres. Personal Preference Inc., Bolingbrook, IL, 1979—. Office: Personal Preference Inc 800 Remington Blvd Bolingbrook IL 60440-4800

MADSEN, H(ENRY) STEPHEN, retired lawyer; b. Momence, Ill., Feb. 5, 1924; s. Frederick and Christine (Landgren) Madsen; m. Carol Ruth Olmstead, Dec. 30, 1967; children: Stephen Stewart, Christie Morgan, Kelly Ann. MBA, U. Chgo., 1948; LLB, Yale U., 1951. Bar: Wash. 1951, Ohio 1953, U.S. Supreme Ct. 1975. Rsch. asst. Wash. Water Power Co., Spokane, 1951; assoc. Baker, Hostetler & Paterson, Cleve., 1952-59, ptnr., 1960-88, sr. ptnr., 1989-92; ret., 1992. Danish consul for Ohio, 1973—98. Active Bus. Advisers Cleve.; trustee Breckenridge Ret. Cmty., Ohio Presbyn. Ret. Svcs. With AC U.S. Army, 1943—46. Decorated Knight Queen of Denmark. Fellow: ABA (life); mem.: Cleve. Bar Assn., Am. Law Inst., Am. Coll. Trial Lawyers (life), Country Club Cleve. Office: 17409 Wildoak Pl Chagrin Falls OH 44023-1414

MADURA, JAMES ANTHONY, surgical educator; b. Campbell, Ohio, June 10, 1938; s. Anthony Peter and Margaret Ethel (Sebest) M.; m. Loretta Jayne Sovak, Aug. 8, 1959; children: Debra Jean, James Anthony II, Vikki Sue. BA, Cogate U., 1959; MD, Western Res. U., 1963. Diplomate Am. Bd. Surgery. Intern in surgery Ohio State U., Columbus, 1963—64, resident in surgery, 1966—71; asst. prof. surgery Ind. U., Indpls., 1971—76, assoc. prof. Surgery, 1976—80, prof. Surgery, 1980—, J.S. Battersby prof. surgery, 2001—. Dir. gen. surgery Ind. U. Sch. Medicine, Indpls., 1985—, vice-chmn., 1985—. Contbr. articles to profl. jours. Capt. U.S. Army, 1964-66, Vietnam. Fellow Am. Coll. Surgeons; mem. Cen. Surg. Assn., Western Surg. Assn., Soc. Surgery Alimentary Tract, Midwest Surg. Assn., Internal Biliary Assn., Assn. Acad. Surgeons, The Columbia Club. Republican. Roman Catholic. Home: 9525 Copley Dr Indianapolis IN 46260-1422 Office: Ind U Dept of Surgery 545 Barnhill Dr # 244 Indianapolis IN 46202-5112 Personal E-mail: jmadura1@comcast.net. Business E-Mail: jmadura@iupui.edu.

MAEHR, MARTIN LOUIS, psychology educator; b. Guthrie, Okla., June 25, 1932; s. Martin J. and Regina (Meier) M.; m. Jane M. Pfeil, Aug. 9, 1959; children— Martin, Michael, Katherine B.A., Concordia Coll., 1953, M.A., 1959; Ph.D., U. Nebr., 1960. Counselor U. Nebr., Lincoln, 1959-60; asst. prof. to assoc. prof. Concordia Sr. Coll., Fort Wayne, Ind., 1960-67; assoc. prof. ednl. psychology U. Ill., Urbana, 1967-70, prof., 1970—, chmn. dept. ednl. psychology, 1970-75, assoc. dean grad. and internat. programs prof., 1975-77, research prof., dir. Inst. Research on Human Devel., prof. ednl. psychology, 1977-88, assoc. dir. Office Gerontology and Aging Studies, 1980-82; prof. edn. and psychology U. Mich., Ann Arbor, 1988—, chair combined program edn. and psychology, 1988-92. Vis. prof. U. Queensland, Australia, 1981; vis. prof., cons. to dean Faculty Edn. U. Tehran, Iran, 1973-74 Author: Sociocultural Origins of Achievement, 1974, (with Jane Maehr) Being a Parent in Today's World, 1980, (with L.A. Braskamp) The Motivation Factor, 1986, (with Carol Midgley) Transforming School Cultures, 1996; editor: Advancement in Motivation and Achievement series; contbr. articles to profl. jours. Lutheran

MAGARO, PETER ANTHONY, psychology educator; b. Harrisburg, Pa., Jan. 24, 1935; s. Peter A. and Mildred (Alexis) M.; m. Geneva L. Watts, Aug. 22, 1964; children— Lisa, Jennie, Elizabeth, Peter B.S., Pa. State U., 1959; Ph.D., U. Ill., 1965. Mem. faculty No. Ill. U., DeKalb, 1965-68; mem. faculty U. Main, Orono, 1968-80, prof., until 1980; prof. psychology Ohio State U., Columbus, 1980—. Cons. State of Maine, U.S. Govt. Author: Construction of Madness, 1976, The Mental Health Industry, 1978, Cognition in Schizophrenia and Paranoia, 1980 Fulbright fellow, Florence, Italy, 1976; Inst. for Indian Studies scholar, India, 1982 Fellow Am. Psychol. Assn. Office: Ohio State U Dept Psychology Columbus OH 43210

MAGEE, MARK E. lawyer, financial executive; b. 1948; BA, Miami U.; JD, U. Cin. Bar: Ohio 1975. V.p., gen. counsel, sec. Provident Bancorp, Inc., Cin. Office: 1 E 4th St Cincinnati OH 45202-3717

MAGEE, PAUL TERRY, geneticist and molecular biologist, college dean; b. Los Angeles, Oct. 26, 1937; s. John Paul and Lois Lorene (Cowgill) M.; m. Beatrice Buten, Aug. 6, 1964; children: Alexander John, Amos Hart. B.S., Yale U., 1959; Ph.D., U. Calif., Berkeley, 1964. Am. Cancer Soc. postdoctoral fellow Lab. Enzymologie, Gif-sur-Yvette, France, 1964-66; mem. faculty Yale U., 1966-77, asst. prof. microbiology, 1966-72, assoc. prof. microbiology and human genetics, 1972-75, assoc. prof. human genetics, 1975-77; dean Trumbull Coll., 1969-72; prof. microbiology, chmn. dept. microbiology and pub. health Mich. State U., East Lansing, 1977-87, dir. Biotech. Research Ctr., 1985-87; dean Coll. Biol. Scis. U. Minn., 1987-95, prof. genetics and cell biology, 1987—. Mem. genetics adv. panel NSF, 1978-83, mem. adv. com. biology directorate, 1992-97, chair, 1995-96; chmn. BBS task force looking to 21st century, 1991; cons. Corning Glass Works, 1978-80, Pillsbury Rsch., 1990-96; mem. pers. com. Am. Cancer Soc., 1983-87; mem. microbial genetics and physiology study sect. NIH, 1984-88; co-chmn. com. grad. record exam. biochemistry cell and molecular biology Ednl. Testing Svc., 1988-98; co-chair Gordon Rsch. Conf. on Cellular and Molecular Mycology, 1996; mem. microbiology and infectious disease rsch. com. NIH, 1994-99, chair, 1996-99; chair Burroughs Wellcome Fund Award Com. in Molecular Pathogenic Mycology, 1995—; traveling fellow Japanese Soc. for Promotion of Sci., 1995—; divsn. F lectr. annual meeting Am. Soc. Microbiology, 1998. Mem. editorial bd. Jour. Bacteriology, 1975-80, Molecular and Cell Biology, 1981-92, Fungal Genetics and Biology, 1996—. Named Mich. champion masters swimming, 1978-84, 86, Minn. champion masters swimming, 1988, 89, 91-99, nat. YMCA swimming champion, 1990, nat. Can. swimming champion, 1999. Mem. AAAS, Am. Soc. Microbiologists, Genetics Soc. Am. Jewish. Office: U Minn Coll Biol Scis Dept Genetics and Cell Biol Saint Paul MN 55108-1095

MAGEN, MYRON SHIMIN, osteopathic physician, educator, university dean; b. Bklyn., Mar. 1, 1926; s. Barney and Gertrude Beatrice (Cohen) M.; m. Ruth Sherman, July 6, 1952; children— Jed, Ned, Randy D.O., Coll. Osteo. Medicine and Surgery, 1951; Sc.D. (hon.), U. Osteo. Medicine and Health Scis., Des Moines, 1981. Rotating intern Coll. Hosp., Des Moines, 1951-52, resident in pediatrics, 1953-54; chmn. dept. pediatrics Coll. Osteo. Medicine and Surgery, 1958-62, Riverside Osteo. Hosp., Trenton, Mich., 1962-68, Detroit Osteo. Hosp., 1965-67; med. dir., dir. med. edn. Zieger-Botsford Hosps., Farmington, Mich., 1968-70; prof. pediatrics Mich. State Coll. Osteo. Medicine, East Lansing, 1970—, dean, 1970-98, dean emeritus, 1998—. Mem. spl. med. adv. group to chief med. dir. VA, 1973-77; mem. grad med. edn. nat. div. com. HHS, Washington, 1978-80; James Watson disting. lectr. Ohio Ostio Assn., 1974, Grad. Med. Edn. Nat. Adv. Com.; Watson Meml. lectr. Am. Coll. Osteo. Pediatricians, 1987; chair Mich. Med. Schs. Coun. Deans, 1979-84, 90-91; mem. PEW Health Professions Com., 1991—. Contbr. articles to profl. jours. Served with USN, 1943-45 Recipient Disting. Service award Okla. Coll. Osteo. Medicine and Surgery, 1975; Founder's medal Tex. Coll. Osteo. Medicine, 1978 Mem. NAS, Am. Assn. Colls. Osteo. Medicine (pres. 1977), Am. Osteo. Assn. (com. edn., chair com. on colls. 1987-90, La. Burns lectr. 1977, chair bur. profl. edn. 1990-92), Am. Coll. Osteo. Pediats. (pres. 1965-66), Inst. of Medicine, Mich. Assn. Osteo. Physicians and Surgeons. Home: 1251 Farwood Dr East Lansing MI 48823-1831 Office: Mich State Univ Coll Osteopathic Medicine 541 W Fee Hall East Lansing MI 48824-1315

MAGGS, PETER BLOUNT, lawyer, educator; b. Durham, N.C., July 24, 1936; s. Douglas Blount and Dorothy (Mackay) M.; m. Barbara Ann Widenor, Feb. 27, 1960; children: Bruce MacDowell, Gregory Eaton, Stephanie Ann, Katherine Ellen. AB, Harvard U., 1957, JD, 1961; postgrad. (exchange student), Leningrad (USSR) State U., 1961-62. Bar: D.C. 1962. Research assoc. Law Sch. Harvard U., 1963-64; asst. prof. law U. Ill., 1964-67, assoc. prof., 1967-69, prof., 1969-88, William and Marie Corman prof., 1988-98, Peer & Sarah Pedersen prof., 1998—2002, acting dean, 1990, Clifford M. and Bette A. Carney chair in law, 2002—; dir. Rule of Law program Washington, 1994. Fulbright lectr. Moscow State U., 1977; reporter Uniform Simplification of Land Transfers Act.; vis. prof. George Washington U., 1998. Author: (with others) The Mandelstam File, 1996; translator: Civil Code of the Russian Federation, 1998, Civil Code of the Republic of Armenia, 1999, (in Russian) Intellectual Property, 2000, Internet and Computer Law, 2001, Trademark and Unfair Competition, 2002; designer talking computers for the blind. Fulbright rsch. scholar, Yugoslavia, 1967; East-West Ctr. fellow, 1972, Guggenheim fellow, 1979. Mem. ABA, D.C. Bar, Am. Assn. Advancement Slavic Studies, Assn. Am. Law Schs., Am. Law Inst. (consultative group, UCC Article 2), Internat. Acad. Comparative Law. Office: U Ill Coll Law 504 E Pennsylvania Ave Champaign IL 61820-6909 E-mail: p-maggs@uiuc.edu.

MAGILL, FRANK JOHN, federal judge; b. Verona, N.D., June 3, 1927; s. Thomas Charles and Viola Magill; m. Mary Louise Timlin, Nov. 22, 1955; children: Frank Jr., Marguerite Connolly, R. Daniel, Mary Elizabeth, Robert, John. BS in Fgn. Svc., Georgetown U., 1951, LLB, 1955; MA, Columbia U., 1952. Ptnr. Nilles, Hansen, Magill & Davies, Ltd., Fargo, ND, 1955—86; judge U.S. Ct. Appeals (8th cir.), 1986—. Chmn. fin. disclosure com. U.S. Jud. Conf., 1993—98. Fellow: Am. Coll. Trial Lawyers; mem.: Cass County Bar Assn. (Pres. 1970). Republican. Avocations: tennis, sailing, skiing. Home: 501 7th St S Apt 301 Fargo ND 58103-2761 Office: Quentin N Burdick US Courthouse 655 1st Ave N Ste 320 Fargo ND 58102-4932 Fax: 701 297-7255. E-mail: frank_magill@ca8.uscourts.gov.

MAGLIOCHETTI, JOSEPH M. automotive executive; BA, U. Ill. With Victor Mfg. Co. subs. Dana Corp., Chgo., 1967-78; gen. mgr. spicer clutch divsn. Dana Corp., Toledo, 1978-80, pres. London, 1980-85, group v.p. N.Am. ops. Toledo, 1985-90, pres. automotive N.Am. ops., 1990-92, pres. N.Am. ops., 1992-96, pres., 1996-97, pres., COO, 1997-99, pres., CEO & chmn., 1999—. Office: Dana Corp PO Box 1000 Toledo OH 43697-1000

MAGNUS, KATHY JO, religious organization executive; b. Brainerd, Minn., Oct. 22, 1946; d. Fred L. and Doris K. (Anderson) Kunkel; m. Richard A. Magnus, Dec. 17, 1966; children: Erica Jo, Cory Allan. BS, U. Minn., 1968. Tchr. St. Paul Schs., 1968-69, Denver Pub. Schs., 1969-75; dir. comm. St. Paul Luth. Ch., Denver, 1979-81; adminstrv. asst. to bishop Rocky Mountain Synod Luth. Ch. Am., 1981-87; exec. staff Rocky Mountain Synod Evang. Luth. Ch. Am., 1988—; v.p. Evangel. Luth. Ch. in Am., 1991-97, assoc. dir. for missionary support svcs./candidate screening, 1997—, assoc. dir. internat. personnel, 1997—. Mem. ctrl. com. World Coun. Chs., Geneva, 1995—. Named exemplar of univ. Calif. Luth. U., 1992. Avocations: writing, reading. Office: Evang Luthern Ch in Am 8765 W Higgins Rd Chicago IL 60631-4101

MAGNUSON, JOHN JOSEPH, zoology educator; b. Evanston, Ill., Mar. 8, 1934; BS, U. Minn., 1956, MS, 1958; PhD in Zoology, U. B.C., 1961. Chief tuna behavior program Biol. Lab. Bur. Comml. Fisheries U.S. Fish and Wildlife Svc., Honolulu, 1961-67; program dir. ecology NSF, Washington, 1975-76; asst. prof. to assoc. prof. U. Wis., Madison, 1968-74, chmn. oceanography and limnology grad. program, 1978-83, 86, prof. zoology, limnology, ecology fishes, dir. Trout Lake Biol. Sta., 1974-82, prof. zoology, 1982-2000, prof. emeritus, 2000—, dir. Ctr. Limnology, 1982-2000. Lead investigator North Temperate Lakes Long Term Ecol. Rsch. site, NSF, U. Wis., 1981-99; chmn. Aquatic Ecol. sect. Ecol. Soc. Am., 1975-76; chair Com. Fisheries, Nat. Rsch. Coun., 1981-83, 93-94; chmn. Com. Sea Turtle Conservancy, 1989-90, chmn. Com. Protection & Mgmt. Pacific N.W. Anadromous Salmonids, 1992-94; chmn. com. Assessment Atlantic Bluefin, 1994; mem. Ocean Studies Bd., 1995-97, com. Sustainable Fisheries, 1995-99; working group on hydrology and aquatic ecology Intergovernmental Panel on Climate Change, 1993-95, and Ecosystems, 1998-2000. Recipient Wis. Idea award in Natural Policy, 1990; NSF midcareer fellow U. Wash., 1992. Fellow AAAS; mem. Am. Fisheries Soc. (pres. 1981, Disting. Svc. award 1980, award of excellence 2000), Am. Soc. Limnology and Oceanography (at large 2000—), Ecol. Soc. Am., Soc. Internat. Limnology. Office: Univ Wisconsin Madison Ctr Limnology 680 N Park St Madison WI 53706-1413

MAGNUSON, PAUL ARTHUR, federal judge; b. Carthage, S.D., Feb. 9, 1937; s. Arthur and Emma Elleda (Paulson) Magnuson; m. Sharon Schultz Magnuson, Dec. 21, 1959; children: Marlene Peterson, Margaret(dec.), Kevin, Kara Berger. BA, Gustavus Adolphus Coll, 1959; JD, William Mitchell Coll., 1963; DLL (hon.), Wm. Mitchell Coll., 1991. Bar: Minn. 1963, U.S. Dist. Ct. Minn. 1968. Asst. registrar William Mitchell Coll. of Law, 1959-60; claim adjuster Agrl. Ins. Co., 1960-62; clk. Bertie & Bettenberg, 1962-63; ptnr. LeVander, Gillen, Miller & Magnuson, South St. Paul, Minn., 1963-81; judge U.S. Dist. Ct. Minn., St. Paul, 1981—, chief judge, 1994—2001. Jurist-in-residence Hamline U., 1985, Augsberg Coll., 1986, Bethel Coll., 1986, Concordia Coll., St. Paul, 1987, U. Minn., Morris, 1987; instr. William Mitchell Coll. Law, 1984-92, Corcordia Coll., Moorhead, 1988, St. John's U., 1988, Coll. of St. Benedict, 1988; mem. judicial conf. com. on adminstrn. of Bankruptcy System, 1987-96, chmn. 1993-96; mem. judicial conf. com. on Internat. Judicial Rels., 1996—, chair, 1999—; mem. com. on dist. judges edn. Fed. Judicial Ctr., 1998—. Mem. Met. Health Bd., St. Paul, 1970-72; legal counsel Ind. Republican Party Minn., St. Paul, 1979-81 Recipient Disting. Alumnus award Gustavus Adolphus Coll., 1982, First Disting. Svc. award William Mitchell Coll. Law, 1999. Mem. Minn. State Bar Assn., 1st Dist. Bar Assn. (pres. 1974-75), Dakota County Bar Assn., Am. Judicature Soc., Fed. Judges Assn. (bd. dirs. 1993—, treas. 1997-2001, v.p. 2001—). E-mail: PAMagnuson@mnd.uscourts.gov.

MAGNUSON, ROGER JAMES, lawyer; b. St. Paul, Jan. 25, 1945; s. Roy Gustaf and Ruth Lily (Edlund) M.; m. Elizabeth Cunningham Shaw, Sept. 11, 1982; children: James Roger, Peter Cunningham, Mary Kerstin, Sarah Ruth, Elizabeth Camilla, Anna Clara, John Edlund, Britta Kristina. BA, Stanford U., 1967; JD, Harvard U., 1971; BCL, Oxford U., 1972. Bar: Minn. 1973, U.S. Dist. Ct. Minn. 1973, U.S Ct. Appeals (8th, 9th, 10th cirs.) 1974, U.S. Supreme Ct. 1978. Chief pub. defender Hennepin County Pub. Defender's Office, Mpls., 1973; ptnr. Dorsey & Whitney, 1972—. Dean Oak Brook Coll. of Law and Govt. Policy, 1995—; chancellor Magdalen Coll., 1999—. Author: Shareholder Litigation, 1981, Are Gay Rights Right, The White-Collar Crime Explosion, 1992, Informed Answers to Gay Rights Questions, 1994; contbr. articles to profl. jours. Elder, Straitgate Ch., Mpls., 1980—. Mem. Christian Legal Soc., The Am. Soc. Writers of Legal Subjects, Mpls. Club, White Bear Yacht Club. Republican. Home: 625 Park Ave Saint Paul MN 55115-1663 Office: Dorsey & Whitney LLP 50 S 6th St Ste 1500 Minneapolis MN 55402-1498 Business E-Mail: magnuson.roger@dorseylaw.com.

MAGOON, PATRICK M. healthcare executive; MS, U. Ill., 1978. Pres., CEO Children's, 1998. Mem. Nat. Assn. of Children Hosp., Ill. Health Sys. Assn., Near North Health Svc. Corp. (bd. dirs.). Office: 2300 N Childrens Plz Chicago IL 60614-3363

MAGORIAN, JAMES, writer, poet; b. Palisade, Nebr., Apr. 24, 1942; s. Jack and Dorothy (Gorthey) M. BS, U. Nebr., 1965; MS, Ill. State U., 1969; postgrad., Oxford U., 1972, Harvard U., 1973. Author children's books: School Daze, 1978, 17%, 1978, The Magic Pretzel, 1979, Ketchup Bottles, 1979, Imaginary Radishes, 1980, Plucked Chickens, 1980, Fimperings and Torples, 1981, The Witches' Olympics, 1983, At the City Limits, 1987, The Beautiful Music, 1988, Magic Spell #207, 1988; author numerous books of poetry, including: Ideas for a Bridal Shower, 1980, The Edge of the Forest, 1980, Spiritual Rodeo, 1980, Tap Dancing on a Tight Rope, 1981, Training at Home to Be A Locksmith, 1981, The Emily Dickinson Jogging Book, 1984, Keeper of Fire, 1984, Weighing the Sun's Light, 1985, Summer Snow, 1985, The Magician's Handbook, 1986, Squall Line, 1986, The Hideout of the Sigmund Freud Gang, 1987, Haymarket Square, 1998, Dragon Bones, 1999, Millennial Journal, 2000, (novels) America First, 1992, Hearts of Gold, 1996; contbr. poems and stories to numerous publs. Home and Office: 1225 N 46th St Lincoln NE 68503-2308

MAGRUDER, JACK, academic administrator; m. Sue Brimer; children: Julie Magruder Lochbaum, Kerry, Laura Magruder Mann. BS in Chemistry and Math., Truman State U.; MA in Chemistry and Sci. Edn., U. No. Iowa; postgrad., La. State U.; grad., Harvard U. Inst. Ednl. Mgmt., 1992. Asst. prof. chemistry Truman State U., Kirksville, Mo., 1964—86, prof., head divsn. sci., 1986—89, acting dean instrn., 1989—91, v.p. acad. affairs, 1991—94, pres., 1994—. Cons.-evaluator Higher Learning Commn. North Ctrl. Assn. Colls. and Schs.; chmn. com. on transfer and articulation Mo. Coord. Bd. for Higher Edn.; past pres. Coun. of Pub. Liberal Arts Colls., Coun. Pub. Higher Edn. for Mo. Mem.: Sci. Tchrs. Mo., Am. Chem. Soc., Sigma Beta Delta, Phi Kappa Phi, Phi Delta Kappa, Beta Gamma Sigma, Phi Beta Kappa. Office: Truman State U Pres' Office MC200 100 E Normal St Kirksville MO 63501

MAGUIRE, JOHN PATRICK, investment company executive; b. New Britain, Conn., Apr. 1, 1917; s. John Patrick and Edna Frances (Cashen) M.; m. Mary-Emily Jones, Sept. 8, 1945; children: Peter Dunbar (dec.), Joan Guilford. Student, Holy Cross Coll., 1933-34; degree in bus. adminstrn. with distinction, Babson Inst., 1936; A.B. cum laude, Princeton U., 1941; BS (hon.), Babson Inst., 1995, Babson Coll., 1995; J.D., Yale U., 1943; PhD (hon.), St. Bonaventure U., 1965. Bar: Conn. 1943, N.Y. 1944. Assoc. Cravath, Swaine & Moore (and predecessor), N.Y.C., 1943-50, 52-54; v.p., dir. Forbes, Inc.; also mng. editor Investors Adv. Inst., 1951-52; asst. counsel Gen. Dynamics Corp., 1954-60, sec., 1962-87, v.p., 1981-87; sec., gen. counsel Tex. Butadiene and Chem. Corp., 1960-62; with J.P. Maguire Investment Advisors, 1987-95; exec. v.p. Fiduciary Asset Mgmt. Co., 1995—2002. Mem. bd. govs. N.Y. Young Rep. Club, 1951-52; chmn. fin. and investment coms. St. Louis Art Mus., 1984-94; trustee St. Bonaventure U., 1965-71, Webster U., 1983-85, John Burroughs Sch. (chmn. investment com.) 1976-85. Mem. ABA. Clubs: Piping Rock (Locust Valley, L.I.); Yale (St. Louis); St. Louis Country; Princeton (St. Louis); Tiger Inn (Princeton). Home: PO Box 1088 Boca Grande FL 33921-1088 E-mail: jmaguire@sbcglobal.net.

MAHAFFEY, MARYANN, councilwoman; b. Burlington, Iowa, Jan. 18, 1925; m. Herman Dooha; 1 child, Susan. BA, Cornell Coll., 1946, LHD (hon.), 1995; MSW, U. So. Calif., 1951. Legis. rep., chair Mich. Social Work Coun., 1965-68; founder, chair City of Detroit Task Force on Hunger & Malnutrition, 1969-74; council member, pres. pro tem City of Detroit, 1974—; emeritus prof. Wayne State U., Detroit, 1990—. Pres. Detroit City Coun., 1991-98. Del. founding conv. Nat. Women's Polit. Caucus, 1971-73; chair, founder Mich. Statewide Nutrition Commn., 1973-83; designer, initiator Detroit Police Dept. Rape Crisis Ctr. and Family Trouble Clinic of Detroit, Family Svc. and Police, 1974-75; del. IWY, Mexico City, 1975, Houston, 1978; dep. chair U.S. Conf. on Families, 1979-81; chair human devel. com. Nat. League of Cities, 1992, chair Mich. del. to UN Conf. Women, Beijing, 1995; summer recreation dir. Nat. Intercollegiate Christian Coun. in Concentration Camp for Japanese Ams., 1945; trainer, integrator Brownie Troop Indpls. Girl Scouts, 1951-52; organizer Welfare Rights, Detroit, 1961; founder Nat. Peace and Disarmament Com. NASW, 1962-69, pres., 1975-77; founder Women in Social Welfare, 1972-74; author policy of women's rights, Internat. Fedn. Social Workers, 1987; mem. exec. com. Internat. Fedn. Social Workers, 1984-86. Mem. NAACP (life), Am. Orthopsychiat. Assn. (pres. 1984-85), Japanese Am. Citizens League , Women in Mcpl. Govt. (pres. 1995, adv. bd. 1996—, mem. NLC policy adv. coun. 1997—), Nat. Coun. Negro Women (life). Office: 1340 City County Bldg Detroit MI 48226

MAHAR, WILLIAM F., JR. state legislator; b. Chicago Heights, Ill., Feb. 13, 1947; m. Elizabeth Mahar; two children. BA, So. Ill. U.; MS, Purdue U. Trustee Village of Homewood, Ill., 1979-85; Dist. 19 senator Ill. Senate, Springfield, 1985—. Mem. election and reapportionment, local govt., appropriations I, energy and environment, econ. devel., fin. and credit regulations, pub. health, welfare and corrections, and state govt. orgn. and adminstrn. coms., Ill. Senate. Office: State Senate State Capital Springfield IL 62706-0001 Also: 14700 S Ravinia Ave Orland Park IL 60462-3134

MAHER, DAVID WILLARD, lawyer; b. Chgo., Aug. 14, 1934; s. Chauncey Carter and Martha (Peppers) M.; m. Jill Waid Armagnac, Dec. 20, 1954; children: Philip Armagnac, Julia Armagnac. BA, Harvard, 1955, LLB, 1959. Bar: N.Y. 1960, Ill. 1961, Wis. 1996, U.S. Patent Office 1961. Pvt. practice, Boston, N.Y.C., 1958-60; assoc. Kirkland & Ellis, and predecessor firm, 1960-65, ptnr., 1966-78, Reuben & Proctor, 1978-86, Isham, Lincoln and Beale, 1986-88, Sonnenschein, Nath & Rosenthal, Chgo., 1988—. Gen. counsel BBB Chgo. and No. Ill.; lectr. DePaul U. Sch. Law, 1973—79, Loyola U. Law Sch., Chgo., 1980—84. Vis. com. U. Chgo. Div. Sch., 1986—. 2d lt. USAF, 1955-56. Fellow Am. Bar Found. (life); mem. ABA, Am. Law Inst., Ill. Bar Assn., Wis. State Bar, Chgo. Bar Assn., Internet Soc. (v.p. pub. policy), Chgo. Lit. Club, Union League Club, Tavern Club. Roman Catholic. Home: 501 N Clinton St Apt 1503 Chicago IL 60610-8886 Office: Sonnenschein Nath & Rosenthal 233 S Wacker Dr Ste 8000 Chicago IL 60606-6491 E-mail: dwm@sonnenschein.com.

MAHER, FRANCESCA MARCINIAK, lawyer, air transportation executive; b. 1957; BA, Loyola U., 1978, JD, 1981. Ptnr. Mayer, Brown & Platt, Chgo., 1981-93; v.p. law, corp. sec. UAL Corp., Elk Grove Village, Ill., 1993-97, v.p., gen. counsel, sec., 1997-98, sr. v.p., gen. counsel, sec., 1998—. Bd. dirs. YMCA Met. Chgo., Lincoln Park Zool. Soc. Mem. Ill. Humane Soc. (pres. 1996-98). Office: UAL Corp PO Box 66100 Chicago IL 60666-0100

MAHER, FRANK ALOYSIUS, research and development executive, psychologist; b. Jamaica, N.Y., Mar. 31, 1941; s. Frank A. and Gertrude F. (Peterson) M.; m. Barbara A. Eggers, Aug. 14, 1965 (div. 1978); children: B. Kelly, F. Scott, Erin K.; m. Karen S. Adcock, June 28, 1980. BA, U. Dayton, 1966, MS, 1971. Lic. psychologist, Ohio. Research psychologist Ritchie Inc., Dayton, Ohio, 1965-68, Bunker Ramo, Dayton, 1968-70;

lectr., research assoc. Wright State U., 1970-71; research psychologist USAF, Wright Patterson AFB, Ohio, 1971-84; dir. Perceptronics, Inc., Dayton, 1984-87; rsch. and devel. exec. Unisys, 1987-92, bus. devel. cons., 1992-94; dir. Gibson Fisher Ltd, 1997—. Counseling psychologist Eastway Mental Health Ctr., Dayton, 1974-75, Good Samaritan Mental Health Ctr., Dayton, 1979. Conbtg. author: Perceptions in Information Sciences; editor: Developmental Learning Handbook. Bd. dirs. Miami Valley Mental Health Assn., Dayton, 1974-77, Greene Mental Health Assn., Xenia, Ohio, 1977. Roman Catholic. Avocations: tennis, skiing, sailing, sports car racing. Office: Gibson Fisher 3070 Riverside Dr Columbus OH 43221 E-mail: frankamaher@aol.com.

MAHER, L. JAMES, III, molecular biologist; b. Mpls., Nov. 28, 1960; s. Louis James and Elizabeth Jane (Crawford) M.; m. Laura Lee Moseng, July 2, 1983; children: Elizabeth Lillian, Christina Ailene. BS in Molecular Biology, U. Wis., 1983, PhD in Molecular Biology, 1988. Fellow U. Wis., Madison, 1983-84, rsch. asst., 1984-88; postdoctoral fellow Calif. Inst. Tech., Pasadena, 1988-91; asst. prof. molecular biology Eppley Inst., U. Nebr. Med. Ctr., Omaha, 1991-95; assoc. prof. biochem. molecular biology Mayo Found., Rochester, Minn., 1995-2000, prof., 2000—. Editorial bd. Antisense and Nuclear Acid Drug Design, 1991—, Nucleic Acids Rsch. Jour., 1988—; contbr. articles to profl. jours. Musician, Madison Symphony Orch., 1983-88, Calif. Inst. Tech. Symphony Orch., L.A., 1988-91. Gosney fellow, 1988; Am. Cancer Soc. postdoctoral fellow, 1988. Mem. AAAS, Phi Beta Kappa. Evangelical Christian Ch. Achievements include research in chemical and biochemical agents designed to artificially regulate the flow of genetic information in biological systems. Office: Mayo Found Dept Biochem and Molec Biol 200 1st St SW Rochester MN 55905-0001

MAHER, LOUIS JAMES, JR. geologist, educator; b. Iowa City, Dec. 18, 1933; s. Louis James and Edith Marie (Ham) M.; m. Elizabeth Jane Crawford, June 7, 1956; children: Louis James, Robert Crawford, Barbara Ruth. BA, U. Iowa, 1955, MS, 1959; PhD, U. Minn., 1961. Mem. faculty dept. geology and geophysics U. Wis.-Madison, 1962—, prof., 1970—, chmn. dept., 1980-84. Contbr. articles to profl. jours. Served with U.S. Army, 1956-58. Danforth fellow, 1955-61; NSF fellow, 1959-61; NATO fellow, 1961-62 Fellow AAAS, Geol. Soc. Am.; mem. Am. Quaternary Assn., Ecol. Soc. Am., Wis. Acad. Sci., Arts and Letters, Sigma Xi. Episcopalian. Office: U Wis Dept Geology and Geoph 1215 W Dayton St Madison WI 53706-1600 E-mail: maher@geology.wisc.edu.

MAHNKE, KURT LUTHER, psychotherapist, clergyman; b. Milw., Feb. 18, 1945; s. Jonathan Henry and Lydia Ann (Pickron) M.; m. Dana Moore, Mar. 19, 1971; children: Rachel Lee, Timothy Kurt, Jonathan Roy. BA, Northwestern Coll., Watertown, Wis., 1967; MDiv, Wis. Luth. Sem., 1971; MA, No. Ariz. U., 1984. Cert. profl. counselor, marriage and family therapist, ind. clin. social worker, trauma counselor. Pastor Redeemer/Grace Luth. Chs., Phoenix & Casa Grande, Ariz., 1971-75, St. Philips Luth. Ch., Milw., 1975-78, 1st Luth. Ch., Prescott, Ariz., 1978-82; counselor NAU Counseling/Testing Ctr., Flagstaff, 1983-84, Wis. Luth. Child & Family Svc., Wausau, Wis., 1984-86, area adminstr. Appleton, 1986-89; founder, psychotherapist Family Therapy & Anxiety Ctr., Menasha, 1989—. Part-time min. St. Paul Luth. Ch., Appleton, 1993-94; presenter Nat. Police Week, Washington, 1995—, 13th Nat. Conf. on Anxiety Disorders, Charleston, S,C., 1993; cons. editor Northwestern Pub. House, Milw., 1990—; adj. faculty Fox Valley Tech. Coll., Appleton, 1993—; on-call critical incident stress debriefer, U.S. Marshall's Svc., 1999—; critical incident stress cons., Appleton Police Dept., Bri llion Police Dept., Menasha Police Dept., Neenah Police Dept., Two Rivers Police Dept., Outagamie County Sheriff's Dept., 1999—, New London Police Dept., Winnebago County Sheriff's Dept., 2000—. Cons. editor Counseling at the Cross, 1990; contbr. articles to profl. publs. Cons. Wis. Evang. Luth. Synod, Milw., 1986—; cons. crisis counselor Fox Valley Luth. H.S., Appleton, Appleton Police Dept., Menasha Police Dept., Brillion Police Dept. Outagamie County Sheriff's Dept., 1998—, New London Police Dept., Winnegago County Sheriff's Dept., U.S. Marshall's Office, 1999—; crisis counselor, clin. dir. Critical Incident Stress Debriefing Team, Fox Cities, 1991—, U.S. Atty.'s Office, 1995-99; victim crisis response coord. Appleton Police Dept., 1996-99, Neenah Police Dept., Menasha Police Dept., Town of Menasha Police Dept., 1997-99. Mem. Internat. Critical Stress Found., Nat. Anxiety Found., Obsessive Compulsive Found. Republican. Lutheran. Office: Family Therapy/Anxiety Ctr 1477 Kenwood Ctr Menasha WI 54952-1160 E-mail: klmahnke@aol.com.

MAHONE, BARBARA JEAN, automotive company executive; b. Notasulga, Ala., Apr. 19, 1946; BS, Ohio State U., 1968; MBA, U. Mich., 1972; program for mgmt. devel., Harvard U., 1981. Sys. analyst GM, Detroit, 1968-71, sr. staff asst., 1972-74, mgr. career planning, 1975-78, dir. pers. adminstrn. Rochester, N.Y., 1979-81, mgr. indsl. rels. Warren, Ohio, 1982-83, dir. human resources mgmt. Chevrolet-Pontiac-Can. group, 1984-86, dir. gen. pers. and pub. affairs Inland divsn. Ohio, 1986-88, gen. dir. pers. Indland Fisher Guide divsn. Detroit, 1989-91, gen. dir. employee benefits, 1991-93, dir. human resources truck group Pontiac, 1994—2000, exec. dir. human resources, 2001—. Chmn. Fed. Labor Rels. Authority, Washington, 1983-84, Spl. Panel on Appeals; dir. Metro Youth; mem. bd. govs. U. Mich. Alumni. Bd. dirs. ARC, Rochester, 1979-82, Urban League Rochester, 1979-82, Rochester Aea Multiple Sclerosis; mem. human resources com. YMCA, Rochester, 1980-82; mem. exec. bd. Nat. Coun. Negro Women; mem. allocations com. United Way Greater Rochester. Recipient Pub. Rels. award Nat. Assn. Bus. and Profl. Women, 1976, Mary McLeod Bethune award Nat. Coun. Negro Women, 1977, Senate resolution Mich. State Legislature, 1980; named Outstanding Woman, Mich. Chronicle, 1975, Woman of Yr., Nat. Assn. Bus. and Profl. Women, 1978, Disting. Bus. Person, U. Mich., 1978, one of 11 Mich. Women, Redbook mag., 1978. Mem. Nat. Black MBA Assn. (bd. dirs., nat. pres. Disting. Svc. award, bd. dirs., nat. pres. Outstanding MBA), Women Econ. Club (bd. dirs.), Indsl. Rels. Rsch. Assn., Internat. Assn. for Pers. Women, Engring. Soc. Detroit. Republican. Home: 175 Kirkwood Ct Bloomfield Hills MI 48304-2927 Office: MC 483-585-227 585 South Blvd Pontiac MI 48341-3146

MAHONEY, JOAN, law educator; AB, AM, U. Chgo.; JD, Wayne State U.; PhD, Cambridge U. Assoc. Honigman Miller Schwartz and Cohn, Detroit; mem. law faculty U. Mo., Kansas City, 1980—94; mem. faculty, dean Western New Eng. Coll. Law, 1994—96; mem. faculty Wayne State U. Law Sch., Detroit, 1994—, dean, 1996—. Contbr. articles to profl. jours., chpts. to books. Office: Wayne U Law Sch 471 W Palmer Detroit MI 48202

MAHONEY, JOHN JEREMY, state legislator; m. Ann Christianson; 4 children. BS, U. N.D., 1975, JD, 1978. Atty. Center City, N.D., 1979—; ptnr. Mahoney & Mahoney, Center City, 1979—; mem. N.D. Ho. of Reps., 1991—, mem. indsl., bus. and labor com., mem. transp. com., mem. judiciary com., chmn. interim criminal justice com. Oliver County States Atty., 1979—. Mem. KC, Elks, Oliver County Gun Club. Home: PO Box 355 Center ND 58530-0355

MAHONEY, PATRICK MICHAEL, federal judge; b. 1946; BA, St. Ambrose Coll., 1968; JD, U. Ill., 1971. Magistrate judge U.S. Dist. Ct. (no. dist.) Ill., We. Divsn., 1976—. Office: US Dist Ct 211 S Court St Ste 204 Rockford IL 61101-1226

MAHONEY, ROBERT WILLIAM, electronic and security systems manufacturing executive; b. N.Y.C., Sept. 10, 1936; s. Francis Joseph and Margaret (Colleton) M.; m. Joan Marie Sheraton, Oct. 3, 1959; children: Linda Marie, Stephen Francis, Brian Michael. BS, Villanova U., 1958, MBA, Roosevelt U., Chgo., 1961. With sales dept. NCR, Inc., Phila., 1961-70, sales mgr., Allentown, Pa. and Atlanta, 1971-76, v.p., Dayton, Ohio, 1977-80; pres. NCR Can. Ltd., Toronto, 1981-82; sr. v.p. Diebold, Inc., Canton, Ohio, 1983-84, pres., chief op. officer, 1984-85, pres., chief exec. officer, 1985-88, chmn. bd., chief exec. officer, 1988—, also bd. dirs.; bd. dirs. Timken Co. Bd. dirs. Timken Mercy Med. Ctr., Canton, 1983—, Northeast Ohio Council, Cleve., 1986—, Profl. Football Hall of Fame, Canton, 1987—, Stark County Devel. Bd., Canton, 1986—, Canton Symphony Orch., 1985, Jr. Achievement, Canton, 1984, Akron (Ohio) U. Econ. Devel. Bd., 1982; trustee Canton City Schs., 1986, Mount Union Coll., 1988—, Ohio Found. Ind. Colls., 1988—; mem. adv. bd. C. of C. Leadership Canton, 1987. Served with USN, 1958-61. Republican. Roman Catholic. Clubs: Firestone Country (Akron); Brookside Country (Canton). Office: Diebold Inc PO Box 8230 Canton OH 44711-8230

MAHOWALD, ANTHONY PETER, geneticist, developmental biologist, educator; b. Albany, Minn., Nov. 24, 1932; s. Aloys and Cecilia (Maus) Mahowald; m. Mary Lou Briody, Apr. 11, 1971; children: Maureen, Lisa, Michael. BS, Spring Hill Coll., 1958; PhD, Johns Hopkins U., 1962. Asst. prof. Marquette U., Milw., 1966-70; asst. staff mem. Inst. Cancer Rsch., Phila., 1970-72; assoc. prof. Ind. U., Bloomington, 1972-76, prof., 1976-82; Henry Willson Payne prof. Case Western Res. U., Cleve., 1982-90, chmn. dept. anatomy, 1982-88, chmn. dept. genetics, 1988-90; Louis Block prof., chmn. dept molecular genetics and cell biology U. Chgo., 1990—2002, Louis Block prof. emeritus, 2002—. Chmn. Com. Devel. Biology U. Chgo., 1991-99. Woodrow Wilson Found. fellow, 1958, NSF fellow, 1958-62. Fellow AAAS, Am. Acad. Arts and Scis., Soc. Scholars Johns Hopkins U.; mem. Nat. Acad. Scis., Genetics Soc. Am. (sec. 1986-88), Soc. Devel. Biology (pres. 1989, editor-in-chief jour. 1980-85), Am. Soc. Cell Biology (coun. mem. 1996-98). Office: U Chgo Dept Molec Genet/Cell Biol 920 E 58th St Chicago IL 60637-5415

MAHSMAN, DAVID LAWRENCE, religious publications editor; b. Quincy, Ill., Aug. 16, 1950; s. Alvin Henry and Dorothy Marie (Schnack) M.; m. Lois Jean Mohn, July 27, 1975. BS in Journalism, So. Ill. U., 1972; MDiv, Concordia Theol. Seminary, Fort Wayne, Ind., 1983; STM, Concordia Sem., St. Louis, 1995. Staff writer Paddock Publs., Arlington Heights, Ill., 1972-73, Decatur (Ill.) Herald & Rev., 1973-76; press asst. Hon. Tom Railsback U.S. Ho. Reps., Washington, 1976-79, campaign press sec. Hon. Dan Coats Ft. Wayne, Ind., 1979-80, 82; pastor Trinity Luth. Ch., Glen Cove, N.Y., 1983-85; dir. news and info. Luth. Ch.-Mo. Synod, St. Louis, 1985—; exec. editor, contbr. Luth. Witness, 1985—; exec. editor Reporter, 1985—. Mem. Inter-Luth. task force on pornography Luth. Coun. U.S.A., 1986; mem. Washington adv. coun. Mo. Synod, Office of Govt. Info., Washington, 1987-2000. Editor: Augsburg Today: This We Believe, Teach and Confess, 1997. Recipient Jacob Scher Investigative Reporting award Women in Comm., 1974, Commendation award Concordia Hist. Inst., 1988, 98. Mem. Concordia Hist. Inst. (life). Republican. Avocations: travel, photography. Office: Luth Ch-Mo Synod 1333 S Kirkwood Rd Saint Louis MO 63122-7226 E-mail: david.mahsman@lcms.org.

MAIBACH, BEN C., JR. service executive; b. Bay City, Mich., 1920; With Barton-Malow Co., Detroit, 1938—, v.p., dir.-in-charge field ops., 1949-53, exec. v.p., 1953-60, pres., 1960-76, chmn. bd., 1976; chmn. and dir. Barton-Malow Ent.; chmn. bd. Cloverdale Equipment Co. Trustee Barton-Malow Found, Maibach Found., 1967—; chmn. Apostolic Christian Woodhaven, Detroit; bishop Apostolic Christian Ch., Mich., Ont., Fla.; bd. dirs. S.E. Mich. chpt. ARC, Rural Gospel and Med. Missions of India. Home: 29711 Wentworth St Apt 207 Livonia MI 48154-3887 also: 5525 Azure Way Sarasota FL 34242-1857

MAIBACH, BEN C., III, construction company executive; b. May 5, 1946; BS, Mich. State U., 1969. With Barton-Malow Corp., Oak Park, Mich., 1964—, v.p field ops., 1964-68, systems analyst, programmer, 1968-70, project adminstr., 1970-72, officer mgr., purchasing agt., 1972-73, v.p., 1973-76, exec. v.p., 1976-81, pres., 1981—. Office: Barton-Malow Co 27777 Franklin Rd Ste 800 Southfield MI 48034-8258

MAICKI, G. CAROL, former state senator, consultant; b. Holden, Mass., July 16, 1936; d. John Arne and Mary Emily (Bumpus) Mannisto; m. Henry J. Maicki, May 4, 1957; children: Henry III, Matthew, Scott, Julia, Mary. BA, U. Mich., 1978. Exec. dir. Sweetwater County Task Force/Sexual Assault, Rocksprings, Wyo., 1978-81; program mgr. Family Violence/Sexual Assault, Cheyenne, 1981-85; coord. S.D. Coalition Against Domestic Violence and Sexual Assault, Black Hawk, 1985-90; state senator S.D. Legislature, Pierre, 1990-92. Cons. Black Hawk, 1990—, Nat. Coalition Against Domestic Violence, 1987; spkr. Nat. Coalition Against Sexual Assault, Portland, Oreg., 1987, 96, Rutger Ctr. for Women in Politics, San Diego, 1991, Gov.'s Conf., Las Vegas, Nev., 1997; mem. planning com. Office for Victims of Crime, U.S. Justice, Phoenix, 1989; expert witness state and fed. cts., 1990—. Author: (manuals) Operating Standards, 1984, Rules and Regulations, 1986, Shelter Procedures, 1987, Administrative Procedures, 1995, Responders to Rope, 1996, Cultural Competency, 2001. Com. mem. Health and Human Svc. State Legislature, Pierre, 1990-92, local govt., 1990-92; commn. mem. local govt. study commn., Pierre, 1990-92; bd. dirs. Crisis Intervention Svcs., 1991-99, Dakotah territory, 1996—; apptd. def. adv. com. on women in svcs. Sec. of Def., 1995-97; apptd. exec. com. def. adv. com. on women in the svcs., 1996-97; founder Women's Connection, Inc., 1996; mem. Dacotah Terr. Youth Devel., Inc. Recipient award Gov. Wyo., 1985, Spirit of Peace award Women Against Violence, Rapid City, 1993, U.S. Dept. of Justice award, 1994, fellowship Share Our Strength, 1996-98, Equity award S.D. chpt. AAUW, 1996, Failure is Impossible award Rapid City, 1998. Mem. S.D. Alliance for Mentally Ill, Rapid City Womens Network, S.D. Advocacy Network for Women. Democrat. Avocations: reading, crosswords, gardening. Home: PO Box 375 Black Hawk SD 57718-0375 E-mail: gcarol@starband.net.

MAIDA, CARDINAL ADAM JOSEPH, cardinal; b. East Vandergrift, Pa., Mar. 18, 1930; Student, St. Vincent Coll., Latrobe, Pa., St. Mary's U., Balt., Lateran U., Rome, Duquesne U. Ordained priest Roman Cath. Ch., 1956, consecrated bishop, 1984. Bishop Green Bay, Wis., 1984-89; archbishop Detroit, 1990—; elevated to Cardinal, 1994—. Home: 75 E Boston Blvd Detroit MI 48202-1318 Office: Archdiocese of Detroit 1234 Washington Blvd Ste 1 Detroit MI 48226-1800

MAIER, DONNA JANE-ELLEN, history educator; b. St. Louis, Feb. 20, 1948; d. A. Russell and Mary Virginia Maier; m. Stephen J. Rapp, Jan. 3, 1981; children: Alexander John, Stephanie Jane-Ellen. BA, Coll. of Wooster, 1969; MA, Northwestern U., 1972, PhD, 1975. Asst. prof. U. Tex. at Dallas, Richardson, 1975-78; asst. prof. history U. No. Iowa, Cedar Falls, 1978-81, assoc. prof., 1981-86, prof., 1986—. Cons. Scott, Foresman Pub., Glenview, Ill., 1975-94; editl. cons. Children's Press, 1975-76, Macmillan Pubs., 1989-90, Harper-Collins Pubs., 1994. Co-author: History and Life, 1976, 4th edit., 1990; author: Priests and Power, 1983; co-editor African Economic History, 1992—; contbr. articles to profl. jours, Encyclopedia Britannica. Mem. Iowa Dem. Cen. Com., 1982-90, chmn. budget com., 1986-90; chmn. 3d Congl. Dist. Cen. Com., 1986-88. Fulbright-Hays fellow, Ghana, 1972, Arab Republic Egypt, 1987; fellow Am. Philos. Soc., London, 1978; recipient Iowa Bd. Regents Faculty Excellence award, 1996. Mem. African Studies Assn., AAUW (fellow Ghana 1973), pres. Quota Internat. of Waterloo, 1999-2000, Quota Club. Home: 219 Highland Blvd Waterloo IA 50703-4229 Office: U No Iowa Dept History Cedar Falls IA 50614-0001

MAIER, JACK C. food products company executive; Chmn. Frisch's Restaurants, Inc., Cin. Office: Frisch's Restaurants Inc 2800 Gilbert Ave Cincinnati OH 45206-1206

MAIESE, KENNETH, neurologist; b. Audubon, N.J., Dec. 5, 1958; s. Charles and Margaret (Fioretti) M. BA summa cum laude, U. Pa., 1981; MD, Cornell U., 1985. Intern N.Y. Hosp., 1985-86, resident in neurology, 1986-89, asst. attending physician, 1989-94; asst. prof. Cornell U. Med. Coll., N.Y.C., 1989-94; assoc. prof. dept. neurology, anatomy and cell biology Wayne State U. Ctr. for Molecular Toxicology & Medicine, Detroit, 1994—; dir. lab. molecular and cellular cerebral ischemia Wayne State U. Ctr. for Molecular Toxicology, 1994—, prof. dept. neurology, anatomy, cell biology, 1999—. Dir. neurol. diagnosis N.Y. Hosp., 1991-94. Author: Neurology and General Medicine, 1989, Neurological and Neurosurgical ICU Medicine, 1988; contbr. articles to Neurology, Jour. Cerebral Blood Flow and Metabolism, Jour. Intensive Care Medicine, Jour. Neurosci., Jour. Neurosci. Rsch., Neurosci. Lett., Jour. Brain Rsch., Jour. Neurochem. Joseph Collins scholar, 1981-85, Grupe Found. scholar, 1985; grantee NIH, 1990—, Nat. Stroke Assn., 1992-94, Alzheimer's Assn., 1994—, Am. Heart Assn., 1995—, United Cerebral Palsy Found., 1995—, Janssen Found., 1995—; recipient Young Scientist award Jours. Cerebral Blood Flow, 1991, Hoechst Investigator award, 1993, Robert G. Siekert award in stroke, 1994, Johnson and Johnson Disting. Investigator award, 1996-98, Maiese Lab. Neurosci. Tng. award J & J/Janssen, 1998, Boehringer Investigator award, 1999, NIH/NIEHS award. Mem. Am. Acad. Neurology, N.Y. Acad. Scis., Assn. for Rsch. in Nervous and Mental Diseases, Am. Neurol. Assn. (elected), Soc. Neurosci. Roman Catholic. Achievements include rsch. in imidazole receptors, cerebral ischemia, nitric oxide toxicity, growth factor neuroprotection, signal cellular transduction mechanisms, metabotropic glutamate receptors, gene regulation, and gene therapy. Office: Wayne State U Sch Medicine 8C-1 U Health Ctr Dept Neur 4201 Saint Antoine St Detroit MI 48201-2153

MAIR, DOUGLAS DEAN, medical educator, consultant; b. Mpls., May 29, 1937; s. Lester Alexander and Irene Clare (Fisher) M.; m. Joanne Mary Elliott, Aug. 18, 1963; children: Scott, Michele, Todd. BA, U. Minn., 1959, MD, 1962. Bd. cert. pediats. and pediat. cardiology. Cons. Mayo Clinic, Rochester, Minn., 1971—; from asst. prof. pediats. to assoc. prof. pediats. Mayo Med. Sch., 1972-80, prof. pediats., 1980—, assoc. prof. internal medicine, 1978—. Contbr. numerous articles and book chpts. to profl. publs. Capt. USAF, 1966-67.

MAITLAND, JOHN W., JR. state legislator; b. Normal, Ill., July 19, 1936; m. Joanne Sieg; three children. Student, Ill. State U. Grain farmer; Dist. 44 senator Ill. Senate, Springfield, 1979—. Asst. majority leader, Ill. Senate; mem. elem. and secondary edn. appropriations I, energy and environment, and appropriations II coms.; minority spokesman; mem. commn. intergovernmental cooperation, con. and fiscal commn., task force on sch. fin. Office: 525 N East St Bloomington IL 61701-4087

MAJERUS, PHILIP WARREN, physician; b. Chgo., July 10, 1936; s. Clarence Nicholas and Helen Louise (Mathis) Majerus; m. Janet Sue Brakensiek, Dec. 28, 1957; children: Suzanne, David, Juliet, Karen; m. Elaine Michelle Flansburg, 1996. BS, Notre Dame U., 1958; MD, Washington U., 1961. Resident in Medicine Mass. Gen. Hosp., Boston, 1961—63; research assoc. NIH, Bethesda, Md., 1963—66; asst. prof. biochemistry Washington U., St. Louis, 1966—75, asst. prof. medicine, 1966—69, assoc. prof. medicine, 1969—71, prof. medicine, 1971—, dir. div. hematology, 1973—, prof. biochemistry, 1976—. Mem. editl. bd. numerous jours. and profl. mags.; contbr. articles. Recipient Faculty Rsch. Assoc. award, Am. Cancer Soc., 1966—75, Disting. Career award for contbns. to hemostasis, Internat. Soc. for Thrombosis and Hemostasis, 1985, Alumni Faculty award, Washington U. Sch. Medicine, 1986, The Robert J.. and Claire Pasarow Found. award, 1994, Bristol-Myers Squibb prize for cardiovascular rsch., 1998, numerous others. Fellow: ACP; mem.: Inst. of Medicine of NAS, Am. Soc. Clin. Investigation (pres. 1981—82), Am. Soc. Biol. Chemists, Am. Fedn. Clin. Rsch., Am. Soc. Hematology 1991, Assn. Am. Physicians, Am. Acad. Arts and Scis., Alpha Omega Alpha, Sigma Xi. Home: 7220 Pershing Ave Saint Louis MO 63130-4248 Office: Wash Univ Sch of Med Dept Int Med Saint Louis MO 63110

MAKI, DENNIS G. medical educator, researcher, clinician; b. River Falls, Wis., May 8, 1940; m. Gail Dawson, 1962; children: Kimberly, Sarah, Daniel. BS in Physics with honors, U. Wis., 1962, MS in Physics, 1964, MD, 1967. Diplomate Am. Bd. Internal Medicine, Am. Bd. Infectious Diseases, Am. Bd. Critical Care Medicine. Physicist, computer programmer Lawrence Radiation Lab., AEC, Livermore, Calif., 1962; intern, asst. resident Harvard Med. unit Boston City Hosp., 1967-69, chief resident, 1972-73; with Hosp. Infections sect. Ctrs. for Disease Control, USPHS, Atlanta, 1969-71; acting chief nat. nosocomial infections study Ctr. for Disease Control, USPHS, 1970-71; sr. resident dept. medicine Mass. Gen. Hosp., 1971-72, clin. and research fellow infectious disease unit, 1973-74; asst. prof. medicine U. Wis., Madison, 1974-78, assoc. prof., 1978-82, prof., 1982—; hosp. epidemiologist, U. Wis. Hosp. and Clinic, 1974—; Ovid O. Meyer chair in medicine U. Wis., 1975—, head sec. infectious diseases, 1979—, attending physician Ctr. for Trauma and Life Support, 1976—. Clinician, rschr., educator in field; mem. program com. Intersci. Conf. on Antimicrobial Agts. and Chemotherapy, 1987-94; mem. Am. Bd. Critical Care Medicine, 1989-95. Sr. assoc. editor Infection Control and Hosp. Epidemiology, 1979-93; mem. editl. bd. Jour. Lab. and Clin. Investigation, 1980-86, Jour. Critical Care, 1985-96, Jour. Infectious Diseases, 1988-90, Critical Care Medicine, 1989-94, 97—; contbr. articles to med. jours. Recipient 1st award for disting. rsch. in Antibiotic Rev., 1980, Internat. CIPI award, 1994, SHEA lectr., 1999, numerous tchg. awards and hon. lectrs. Master ACP; fellow Infectious Diseases Soc. Am. (coun. 1993-96), Am. Acad. Microbiology, Soc. for Critical Care Medicine, Surg. Infection Soc.; mem. Soc. Hosp. Epidemiologists Am. (pres. 1990), Ctrl. Soc. for Clin. Rsch., Am. Soc. Microbiology, Am. Fedn. Clin. Rsch., Alpha Omega Alpha (nat. bd. dirs. 1983-89). Office: U Wis Hosp and Clinics H4/574 Madison WI 53792 Fax: 608-231-3896. E-mail: dgmaki@facstaff.wisc.edu.

MAKINEN, MARVIN WILLIAM, biophysicist, educator; b. Chassell, Mich., Aug. 19, 1939; s. William John and Milga Katarina (Myllyla) M.; m. Michele de Groot, July 30, 1966; children: Eric William, Stephen Matthew. AB, U. Pa., 1961; postgrad., Free U. Berlin, 1960-61; MD, U. Pa., 1968; DPhil, U. Oxford, Eng., 1976. Diplomate Am. Bd. Med. Examiners. Intern Columbia-Presbyn. Med. Ctr., N.Y.C., 1968-69; rsch. assoc. NIH, Bethesda, Md., 1969-71; vis. fellow U. Oxford, Eng., 1971-74; asst. prof. biophysics U. Chgo., 1974-80, assoc. prof., 1980-86, prof. biochemistry and molecular biology, 1986—, chmn. dept., 1988-93. Established investigator Am. Heart Assn., 1975-80; lectr. in field. Contbr. numerous articles to profl. jours. Sr. surgeon USPHS, 1969-71. John Simon Guggenheim fellow 1997-98, John E. Fogarty Sr. Internat. fellow, 1984-85, European Molecular Biology Orgn. sr. fellow, 1984-85, NIH spl. fellow, 1971-74, Berquist fellow Am. Scandinavian Found., 1970. Fellow Am. Inst. Chemists; mem. Am. Chem. Soc., Biophys. Soc., Am. Soc. Biochemistry and Molecular Biology, The Protein Soc., AAAS. Office: U Chgo Dept Biochemistry/Mol Biol 920 E 58th St Chicago IL 60637-5415 E-mail: makinen@uchicago.edu.

MAKRI, NANCY, chemistry educator; b. Athens, Greece, Sept. 5, 1962; came to the U.S., 1985; d. John and Vallie (Tsakona) M.; m. Martin Gruebele, July 9, 1992; children: Alexander Makris Gruebele, Valerie Gruebele Makri. BS, U. Athens, 1985; PhD, U. Calif., Berkeley, 1989. Jr. fellow Harvard U., Cambridge, Mass., 1989-91; from asst. prof. to assoc. prof. U. Ill., Urbana, 1992-99, prof., 1999—. Recipient Beckman Young Investigator award Arnold & Mabel Beckman Found., 1993, Ann. medal Internat. Acad. Quantum Molecular Sci., 1995, Camille Dreyfus Tchr.-Scholar award The Camille and Henry Dreyfus Found., 1997, Agnes Fay Morgan award Iota Sigma Pi, 1999, physics prize Bodossaki Found., 1999; named NSF Young Investigator, 1993; Packard fellow for sci. and engring. David and Lucile Packard Found., 1993, Sloan Rsch. fellow Alfred Sloan Found., 1994, Cottrell scholar Rsch. Corp., 1994; univ. scholar U. Ill., 1999. Fellow: APS, AAAS. Home: 2722 Valley Brook Dr Champaign IL 61822-7634 Office: U Ill Urbana Dept Chem 601 S Goodwin Ave Urbana IL 61801-3709 E-mail: nancy@makri.scs.uiuc.edu.

MAKUPSON, AMYRE PORTER, television station executive; b. River Rouge, Mich., Sept. 30, 1947; d. Rudolph Hannibal and Amyre Ann (Porche) Porter; m. Walter H. Makupson, Nov. 1, 1975; children: Rudolph Porter, Amyre Nisi. BA, Fisk U., 1970; MA, Am. U., Washington, 1972. Asst. dir. news Sta. WGPR-TV, Detroit, 1975-76; dir. pub. rels. Mich. Health Maintenance Orgn., 1976-77; mgr. pub. affairs, news anchor Sta. WKBD-TV, Southfield, Mich., 1977—, Children's Miracle Network Telethon, 1989—. Mem. Co-Ette Club, Inc., Met. Detroit Teen Conf. Coalition; mem. adv. com., bd. dirs. Alzheimers Assn.; bd. dirs. com. March of Dimes; pres. bd. dirs. Detroit Wheelchair Athletic Assn.; bd. dirs. Providence Hosp. Found., Sickle Cell Assn., Kids In Need of Direction, Drop-out Prevention Collaborative, Merrill Palmer Inst., Skillman Found. Recipient 5 Emmy awards 3 Best Commentary/Best Anchor, Best Interview/Discussion Show, 24 Emmy nominations NATAS, Editl. Best Feature award AP, Media award UPI, Oakland County Bar Assn., TV Documentary award, Detroit Press Club, Bishop Gallagher award Mental Illness Rsch. Assn., Svc. award Arthritis Found. Mich., Mich. Mchts. Assn., DAV, Jr. Achievement, City of Detroit, Salvation Army, Spirit award City of Detroit, Spirit award City of Pontiac, Golden Heritage award Little Rock Bapt. Ch., 1993, Neal Shine award outstanding contbn. Nat. Soc. Fund-raising Execs., Virginia Merrick award outstanding contbn. Christ Child Soc., Outstanding Achievement award Tuskegee Airmen, Best Feature Story award Mich. Assn. Broadcasters; named Media Person of the Yr., So. Christian Leadership Conf., 1994, Humanitarian of the Yr., March of Dimes, 1995. Mem. Pub. Rels. Soc. Am., Am. Women in Radio and TV (Outstanding Achievement award 1981, Outstanding Woman in TV Top Mgmt. 1993, Mentor award 1993), Women in Comm., Nat. Acad. TV Arts and Scis., Detroit Press Club, Ad-Craft, Howard U. Nat. Gold Key Honor Soc. (hon.). Roman Catholic. Office: 26955 W 11 Mile Rd Southfield MI 48034-2292

MALACARNE, C. JOHN, insurance company executive, lawyer; b. St. Louis, Dec. 26, 1941; s. Claude John and Virginia E. (Miller) M.; m. Kathleen M. Morris, Aug. 27, 1966; children: Tracy, Kristen, Lisa. AA, Harris-Stowe State Coll., 1962; BS in Pub. Adminstrn., U. Mo., 1964, JD, 1967. Bar: Mo. 1967. Asst. counsel Kansas City (Mo.) Life, 1967-71, assoc. counsel, 1971-74, asst. gen. counsel, 1974-76, assoc. gen. counsel, 1976-80, gen. counsel, 1980-81, v.p., gen. counsel, sec., 1981—. Bd. dirs. Kansas City Life Ins. Co., Sunset Life Ins. Co. Am., Alaska Life & Health Guarangy Assn., Calif. Life and Health Ins. Guaranty Assn., Mo. Life and Health Guaranty Assn.; sec., bd. dirs. Old Am. Ins. Co. Sec., bd. dirs. Mid-Continent coun. Girl Scouts U.S.A., Kansas City, 1986-88; v.p., bd. dirs. Kansas City Eye Bank, 1986-91; pres., bd. dirs. Shepherd's Ctr., Kansas City, 1982-84; bd. dirs. Shepherd's Ctr. Internat., 1986-92, Community Mental Health Svcs. Found., sec. rsch., 1992-94, v.p., 1995—; mem. Bd. Edn. Consolidated Sch. Dist. #4, Jackson County, Mo., 1989-91. Mem. ABA, Kansas City Met. Bar Assn. (vice chmn. corp. counsel com. 1986-87, vice chmn. corp. law 1993-94, chmn. corp. law com. 1994-95), Lawyers Assn. Kansas City (bd. dirs. 1976), Internat. Assn. Def. Counsel (chmn. accident health and life sect. 1982-84, ins. exec. com. 1986, v.p., mem. exec. com. 1988-90), Jr. C. of C. (bd. dirs. 1972), Kiwanis (pres. Kansas City 1975-76). Home: 604 Tam O Shanter Dr Kansas City MO 64145-1240 Office: Kansas City Life Ins Co PO Box 219139 Kansas City MO 64121-9139

MALEY, WAYNE ALLEN, engineering consultant; b. Stanley, Iowa, Mar. 9, 1927; s. Neil Gordon and Flossie Amelia (Wharram) M.; m. Marianne Nelson, Aug. 2, 1959; children: James G., Mary E., Mark A. BS in Agrl. Engring., Iowa State U., 1949; postgrad., Purdue U., Ga. Tech., IIT. Cert. mediator. Power use advisor Southwestern Electric, Greenville, Ill., 1949-53; field agt. Am. Zinc Inst., Lafayette, Ind., 1953-59; mktg. devel. specialist U.S. Steel, Des Moines, 1959-65, mktg. rep. Pitts., 1965-71, bar products rep., 1972-76; assoc. Taylor Equipment, 1977-81; mgr. pub. rels. Am. Soc. Agrl. Engrs., St. Joseph, Mich., 1981-84, dir. mem. svcs., 1984-92; cons. Tech. Tours, 1992—. Author: Iowa Really Isn't Boring, 1993, (textbook) Farm Structures, 1957, (computer program/workbook) Rim Lift Material Handling, 1970 (Blue Ribbon award 1971); editor: Agriculture's Contract with Society, 1991. Pres. Ednl. Concerns for Hunger Orgn., Ft. Myers, Fla., 1979-81; dist. activity dir. Boy Scouts Am., Moon Twp., 1969-70. With USN, 1945-46. Named Hon. Star Farmer, FFA Ill., 1958. Fellow Am. Soc. Agrl. Engrs. (bd. dirs. 1979-81 hon. for forum leadership 1991); mem. Agrl. Editors Assn., Coun. Engring. Soc. Execs. (bd. dirs. 1984-85), Sigma Xi (pres./del. Whirlpool chpt. 1993-94). Presbyterian. Achievements include patents for fence building machine, for material handling system; design of cable fences; design and installation of steel beverage can recycling center. Home and Office: Tech Tours 2592 Stratford Dr Saint Joseph MI 49085-2714 E-mail: wamaley@juno.com.

MALICKY, NEAL, college president; b. Sour Lake, Tex., Sept. 14, 1934; s. George and Ethel L. (Reed) M.; m. Margaret A. Wilson, Sept. 2, 1956; children: Michael Neal, Eric Scott, David Matthew. A.B., Baker U., 1956; B.D., So. Meth. U., 1959; Ph.D., Columbia U., 1968; postgrad., Harvard U., 1978. Ordained to ministry Meth. Ch., 1959, pastor Kans., 1959-62, Van Cortlandtville, N.Y., 1962-66; asst. prof., dir. semester on UN Drew U., 1966-69; prof. polit. sci., dean Coll., Baker U., Baldwin City, Kans., 1969-75, acting pres., 1973-75; v.p. acad. affairs, also dean Baldwin-Wallace Coll., Berea, Ohio, 1975-81, pres., 1981-99; ret., 2000. Author: To Keep the Peace, 1965, Non-Governmental Organizations at the United Nations, 1968; contbr. articles to profl. jours. Mem. Leadership Cleve., Nat. Conf. Christian and Jews, Cleve. Commn. Higher Edn., Cleve. Coun. World Affairs, Greater Cleve. Roundtable (chmn. edn. com.), Cleve. Initiative Edn. (vice chmn.), Summit on Edn. (co-convenor), Assn. Independent Colls. Ohio (chmn.). Mem. UN Assn. Clubs: Union of Cleve., Fifty of Cleve. Office: Baldwin-Wallace Coll Office of Pres 275 Eastland Rd Berea OH 44017-2005

MALKASIAN, GEORGE DURAND, JR. physician, educator; b. Springfield, Mass., Oct. 26, 1927; s. George Dur and Gladys Mildred (Trombley) M.; m. Mary Ellen Koch, Oct. 16, 1954; children: Linda Jeanne, Karen Diane, Martha Ellen. AB, Yale U., 1950; MD, Boston U., 1954; MS, U. Minn., 1963. Diplomate Am. Bd. Ob-Gyn. Intern Worcester (Mass.) City Hosp., 1954-55; resident in ob-gyn Mayo Grad. Sch. Hosp., Rochester, Minn., 1955-58, 60-61; mem. faculty Mayo Med. Sch., 1962—, prof. ob-gyn, 1976—, chmn. dept. ob-gyn, 1976-86. Author articles in field. Served to lt. comdr. M.C., USNR, 1958-60. Named Tchr. of Yr., Mayo Grad. Sch. Medicine, 1973, 77, Alumnus of Yr., Boston U. Sch. Med., 1990. Fellow Royal Coll. Obstetricians and Gynecologists (ad eundum); mem. ACS, Am. Coll. Ob-Gyn (pres. 1989-90), Am. Ob-Gyn Soc., Am. Radium Soc., Soc. Ob-Gyn, Assn. Profs. Ob-Gyn., N.Am. Ob-Gyn. Soc., Ctrl. Assn. Ob-Gyn, Minn. Soc. Ob-Gyn, Internat. Fedn. Ob-Gyn (v.p. 1997—), Zumbro Valley Med. Soc. (exec. dir. 1996—). Home: 1750 11th Ave NE Rochester MN 55906-4215 Office: Mayo Clinic 200 1st St SW Rochester MN 55905-0001

MALKIN, CARY JAY, lawyer; b. Chgo., Oct. 6, 1949; s. Arthur D. and Perle (Slavin) M.; m. Lisa Klimley, Oct. 27, 1976; children: Dorothy R., Victoria S., Lydia R. BA, George Washington U., 1971; JD, Northwestern U., 1974. Bar: Ill. 1974, U.S. Dist. Ct. (no. dist.) Ill. 1974, N.Y. 2001. Assoc. Mayer, Brown & Platt, Chgo., 1974-80, ptnr., 1991—2002, Mayer, Brown, Rowe & Maw, Chgo., 2002—. Chmn. spl. events com. Mental Health Assn., 1984-85; mem. steering com. Endowment Campaign of the Latin Sch. of Chgo., 1990-91, trustee, 1991-2000, v.p., 1992-98, chmn. capital campaign, 1995-98, nat. trustee, 2000-2002, sr. trustee, 2002—; mem. exec. com. Friends of Prentice Women's Hosp., 1991-92; bd. dirs. SOS Children's Village Ill., 1992-96; mem. M.S. Weiss fund bd. Children's Meml. Hosp., 1989-93; mem. Graziano Fund bd. Children's Meml. Hosp., 1993-96; mem. steering com. Founder's Coun. Field Mus., 1995—, chmn. steering com., 1999—, trustee, 1999—. Mem. Chgo. Club, Saddle and Cycle Club, Arts Club, Standard Club, Order of the Coif, Phi Beta Kappa. Home: 233 E Walton St Chicago IL 60611-1526 Office: Mayer Brown Rowe & Maw 190 S La Salle St Ste 3100 Chicago IL 60603-3441

MALKUS, DAVID STARR, mechanics educator, applied mathematician; b. Chgo., June 30, 1945; s. Willem V.R. Malkus and Joanne (Gerould) Simpson; m. Evelyn R. (div.); children: Christopher, Annelise, Byron, Renata. AB, Yale U., 1968; PhD, Boston U., 1976. Mathematician U.S. Nat. Bur. Standards, Gaithersburg, Md., 1975-77; asst. prof. math. Ill. Inst. Tech., Chgo., 1977-83, assoc. prof., 1983-84; assoc. prof. mechanics U. Wis., Madison, 1984-87, prof., 1987—, chmn. Rheology Rsch. Ctr., 1991-94. Chair prof. Nanjing (People's Republic China) Aero. Inst., 1986. Co-author: Concepts and Applications of Finite Element Analysis, 1989; contbr. articles to Computer Methods Applied Mech. Engring., Jour. Computational Physics. Mem. Soc. Rheology. Achievements include research on finite element methods--reduced and selective integration techniques, a unification of concepts. Home: 2710 Mason St Madison WI 53705-3716 Office: U Wis Dept Engring Physics 1500 Engineering Dr Madison WI 53706-1609 E-mail: malkus@cms.wisc.edu.

MALLETT, CONRAD LEROY, JR. state supreme court chief justice; b. Detroit, Oct. 12, 1953; s. Conrad LeRoy and Claudia Gwendolyn (Jones) M.; m. Barbara Straughn, Dec. 22, 1984; children: Alex Conrad, Mio Thomas, Kristan Claudia. BA, UCLA, 1975; MPA, JD, U. So. Calif., 1979. Bar: Mich. 1979. Legal asst. to congressman, Detroit, 1979-80; dep. pol. div. Dem. Nat. Com., Washington, 1980-81; assoc. Miller, Canfield, Paddock & Stone, Detroit, 1981-82; legal counsel, dir. to gov. State of Mich., Lansing, 1983-84; sr. exec. asst. to Mayor City of Detroit, 1985-86; ptnr. Jaffe, Raitt, Heuer & Weiss, Detroit, 1987-90; justice Mich. Supreme Ct., Lansing, 1990—, chief justice, 1997-98; gen. counsel and chief adminstrv. officer Detroit Med. Ctr., 1998—. Mem. NAACP, Kappa Alpha Psi. Democrat. Roman Catholic. Avocations: writing, fiction. Office: Detroit Med Ctr Office Gen Counsel 3663 Woodward Detroit MI 48201

MALLORY, MARK L. state legislator, librarian; b. Cincinnati, Apr. 2, 1962; Student, Cin. Acad. Math. & Sci.; BS, U. Cin. Dept. mgr. Hamilton County Pub. Libr. Graphic Prodn., Cin.; rep. dist. 31 Ohio Ho. Reps., Columbus, 1994-98; mem. Ohio State Senate Dist. 9, 1998—. Mem. NAACP, Libr. Staff Assn., Black Male Coalition, Friends of Pub. Libr., Urban League of Cin., Pub. Libr. Staff Assn., Internat. TV Assn. Office: State House Senate Rm 226 Columbus OH 43215

MALLORY, ROBERT MARK, controller, finance executive; b. Mattoon, Ill., Apr. 15, 1950; s. Robert Monroe and Betty Ann (Mudd) M.; m. Diana Marie Burde, Aug. 19, 1972; 1 child, Laura Elizabeth. BS in Accountancy, U. Ill., 1972; MBA, Northwestern U., 1985. CPA, Ill. Staff acct. Price Waterhouse, Chgo., 1972-74, sr. acct., 1974-77, mgr., 1977-79; dir. internal audit Mark Controls Corp., Skokie, Ill., 1979-81, corp. contr., 1981-86, v.p., contr., 1986-88; contr., dir. planning Tribune Co., Chgo., 1988-91, v.p., contr., 1991—. Bd. dirs. Met. Family Svcs. Mem. AICPA (Elijah Watts Sells award 1972), Ill. CPA Soc., Fin. Execs. Inst., Internat. Newspaper Fin. Execs. (bd. dirs.), Beta Gamma Sigma. Methodist. Home: 3312 Lakewood Ct Glenview IL 60025-2505 Office: Tribune Co 435 N Michigan Ave Chicago IL 60611-4066 E-mail: mallory435@aol.com.

MALLOY, EDWARD ALOYSIUS, priest, university administrator, educator; b. Washington, May 3, 1941; s. Edward Aloysius and Elizabeth (Clark) M. BA, U. Notre Dame, 1963, MA, 1967, ThM, 1969; PhD, Vanderbilt U., 1975. Joine Congregation Holy Cross, 1963, ordained priest Roman Cath. Ch., 1970. Instr. U. Notre Dame, Ind., 1974-75, asst. prof., 1975-81, assoc. prof., 1981-88, prof. theology, 1988—, assoc. provost, 1982-86, pres. elect, 1986, pres., 1987—. Bd. regents U. Portland, Oreg., 1985—. Author: Homosexuality and the Christian Way of Life, 1981, The Ethics of Law Enforcement and Criminal Punishment, 1982, Culture and Commitment: The Challenge of Today's University, 1992, Monk's Reflections: A View from the Dome, 1999; co-author: Colleges and Universities as Citizens, 1999; contbr. articles to profl. jours. Chmn. Am. Coun. on Edn.; bd. dirs. NCAA Found., 1989—; mem. Bishops and Pres.' com. Assn. Cath. Colls. and Univs., 1988—; bd. dirs. Internat. Fedn. Cath. Univs., 1988—; mem. Pres.'s Adv. Coun. on Drugs, 1989—; mem. adv. bd. AmeriCorps and Nat. Civilian Community Corps, 1994-97; interim chmn. Ind. Commn. on Community Svc., 1994-97; mem. Boys and Girls Clubs Am., 1997—; trustee St. Thomas U., 1997—, Vanderbilt U., 1999; bd. advisors Bernardin Ctr., 1997—; bd. dirs. Points of Light; past chmn. Campus Compact. Established chair Cath. Studies in the name of Edward A. Malloy, Vanderbilt U., 1997. Mem. Cath. Theol. Soc., Am. Soc. Christian Ethics, Bus.-Higher Edn. Forum, Assn. Governing Bds. of Univs. and Colls. (vice chair 1996—), The Conf. Bd., Nat. Assn. of Ind. Colls. and Univs. (bd. dirs. 1997). Office: U Notre Dame Office Pres Notre Dame IN 46556

MALMBERG, AL, radio personality; m. Kathy Malmberg, 1971; 2 children. Grad. h.s., Richfield, 1969. Gen. mgr., corp. program dir., network anchorman, syndicated talk show host; corr. Triple M Network, Sidney, Ind. Radio Network, London; radio host late night show Sta. WCCO, Mpls. Office: WCCO 625 2nd Ave S Minneapolis MN 55402*

MALONE, JIMMY, radio personality; Radio host WMJI, Cleve. Stand-up comedian. Active Cleve. Scholar Program, Providence House, Greater Cleve. Hunger Task Force. Named Radio and TV Coun. Students' Boradcaster of Yr.; named to, Shaker Heights Alumni Hall of Fame. Office: WMJI 6200 Oak Tree Blvd 4th Fl Cleveland OH 44131*

MALONE, MICHAEL W. manufacturing executive; Grad., St. John's U. CPA. With Arthur Andersen & Co., Polaris Industries Inc., Medima, Minn., 1984—, asst. treas., CFO, treas., 1993—. Office: Polaris Industries Inc 2100 Highway 55 Medina MN 55340-9100

MALONE, ROBERT ROY, artist, art educator; b. McColl, S.C., Aug. 8, 1933; s. Robert Roy and Anne (Matthews) M.; m. Cynthia Enid Taylor, Feb. 26, 1956; 1 child, Brendan Trevor. BA, U. N.C., 1955; MFA, U. Chgo., 1958; postgrad., U. Iowa, 1959. Instr. art Union U., Jackson, Tenn., 1959-60, Lambuth Coll., 1959-61; asst. prof. art Wesleyan Coll., Macon, Ga., 1961-67, assoc. prof., 1967-68, W.Va. U., 1968-70, So. Ill. U., Edwardsville, 1970-75, prof., 1975—. One-man shows at Gallery Illien, Atlanta, 1969, De Cinque Gallery, Miami, 1968, 71, Ill. State Mus., Springfield, 1974, U. Del., Newark, 1978, Elliot Smith Gallery, St. Louis, 1985, Merida Galleries, Louisville, 1985, Yvonne Rapp Gallery, Louisville, 1990, 92, 93, 96, 98, 2000, St. John's Coll., Santa Fe, 1991, Uzelac Gallery, Pontiac, Mich., 1997, others; group shows include Bklyn. Mus., 1966, Assoc. Am. Artists Gallery, N.Y.C., 1968, Musée d'Art Modern, Paris, 1970, DeCordova Mus., 1973, 74, St. Louis Art Mus., 1985, Wake Forest U., 1985, New Orleans Mus. Art, 1990, Dakota Internat., Vermillion, 1994; represented in numerous permanent collections including Smithsonian Instn., Washington, USIA, Washington, Library of Congress, Calif. Palace of Legion of Honor, San Francisco, N.Y. Pub. Library, N.Y.C., Victoria and Albert Mus., London, Chgo. Art Inst., Indpls. Mus. Art, Humana Inc., Louisville, State of Ill. Ctr., Chgo., Speed Mus., Louisville, N. Ill. Univ., Capital Devel. Bd., Ill.; co-editor: Contemporary American Printmakers, 1999 (English and Chinese edits.). Recipient numerous regional, nat. awards in competitive exhbns.; Ford fellow, 1977; So. Ill. U. at Edwardsville sr. research scholar, 1976, 84 Home: 600 Chapman St Edwardsville IL 62025-1260 Office: So Ill U Dept Art and Design Edwardsville IL 62025 E-mail: rmalone@sive.edu.

MALONEY, RITA, radio personality; With Sta. WBVP, Pitts., news dir.; radio host Sta. WCCO radio, Mpls. Named one of Pitts. 50 Finest Young Profls.; recipient Best Regularly Scheduled Newscast award, 3 AIR awards for Best Traffic Reporter, Best Spot News Coverage award, Pa. AP. Office: WCCO 625 2nd Ave S Minneapolis MN 55402*

MALOON, JERRY L. trial lawyer, physician, medicolegal consultant; b. Union City, Ind., June 23, 1938; s. Charles Elias and Bertha Lucille (Creviston) M.; children: Jeffrey Lee, Jerry Lee II. BS, Ohio State U., 1960, MD, 1964; JD, Capital U. Law Sch., 1974. Intern Santa Monica (Calif.) Hosp., 1964-65; tng. psychiatry Ctrl. Ohio Psychiat. HOsp., 1969, Menninger Clinic, Topeka, 1970; clin. dir. Orient (Ohio) Devel. Ctr., 1967-69, med. dir., 1971-83; assoc. med. dir. Western Electric, Inc., Columbus, 1969-71; cons. State Med. Bd. Ohio, 1974-80; pvt. practice law Columbus, 1978—; pres. Jerry L. Maloon Co., L.P.A., 1981—. Medicolegal cons., 1972—; pres. Maloon, Maloon & Barclay Co., L.P.A., 1990-95; guest lectr. law and medicine Orient Devel. Ctr. and Columbus Devel. Ctr., 1969-71; dep. coroner Franklin County (Ohio), 1978-84. Dean's coun. Capital U. Law Sch. Capt. M.C., AUS, 1965-67. Fellow: Columbus Bar Found., Am. Coll. Legal Medicine; mem.: ATLA, AMA, ABA, Am. Profl. Practice Assn., Columbus Trial Lawyers Assn., Ohio Trial Lawyers Assn., Columbus Bar Assn., Ohio Bar Assn., Ohio State U. Alumni Assn., U.S. Trotting Assn., The Country Club at Muirfield Village, Ohio State U. Pres.'s Buckeye Club. Home: 2140 Cambridge Blvd Upper Arlington OH 43221-4104 Office: 9155 Moors Pl North Dublin OH 43017 Office Fax: 614-798-8747.

MALTER, JAMES SAMUEL, pathologist, educator; b. Tooele, Utah, May 18, 1956; s. Robert Henry Malter and Evvajean (Harris) Mintz; m. Elaine Gadzicki, May 26, 1988. AB, Dartmouth Coll., 1979; MD, Washington U., 1983. Diplomate Am. Bd. Clin. Pathology. Resident in pathology U. Pa., Phila., 1983-88, chief resident, 1987-88; asst. prof. pathology Tulane U., New Orleans, 1988-91; dir. exptl. pathology Tulane Med. Ctr., 1988-91, dir. Blood Ctr., 1989-91; asst. prof. pathology Sch. Medicine U. Wis., Madison, 1991-97; med. dir. Blood Bank U. Wis. Hosp. & Clinic, 1991—; prof. pathology Sch. Medicine U. Wis., 1997—. Mem. editl. bd. Hepatology jour., 1991—. Recipient Nat. Rsch. Svc. award NIH, 1986-88, Clin. Investigator award NCI-NIH, 1988-91, Ind. Investigator award NIH, 1991—. Mem. Am. Assn. Blood Banks, Am. Assn. Pathologists, Am. Coll. Pathologists (diplomate). Office: U Wis Hosp & Clinic Dept of Pathology 600 Highland Ave # B4 263 Madison WI 53792-0001

MALTZ, ROBERT, surgeon; b. Cin., July 21, 1935; s. William and Sarah (Goldberg) M.; m. Sylvia Moskowitz, Aug. 24, 1958; children: Mark Edward, Deborah Lynn, Steven Alan, David Stuart. BS in Zoology, U. Cin., 1958, MD, 1962. Diplomate Am. Bd. Otolaryngology, 1970. Intern Cin. Gen. Hosp., 1962-63; resident Barnes Hosp., St. Louis, 1965-69; asst. prof. surgery Stanford U. Med. Ctr., Palo Alto, Calif., 1969-71; asst. prof. otolaryngology U. Cin. Med. Ctr., 1971-75, assoc. prof. otolaryngology, 1975—; dir. dept. otolaryngology Jewish Hosp., Cin., 1992—. Chief, divsn. head and neck surgery, dept. otolaryngology and maxillofacial surgery U. Cin. Med. Ctr., 1972-76; bd. dirs. Cancer Control Council, U. Cin. Med. Cntr.; cons. Bur. Crippled Children's Svcs., State of Ohio; on staff Univ. Hosp., Cin., Jewish Hosp., Cin., Children's Hosp. Med. Ctr., Bethesda Hosp., Cin., Christ Hosp., Our Lady of Mercy Hosp.; del. to numerous profl. confs.; mem. health affairs adv. com. Cmty. Mut. Ins. Co.; mem. mng. bd. PIE Mut. Ins. Co.; bd. dirs. UCATS, 1995-98; trustee Health Found. Greater Cin., 1997—, vice-chmn., 2000-01, chmn. 2001—, chmn. program com., 2000-01; instr. short term courses in field; pres.-elect alulmni exec. coun. U. Cin. Coll. Medicine, 1998-2000, pres., 2000-2002. Contbr. articles to profl. jours. Bd. dirs. Jewish Cmty. Rels. Coun.; bd. trustees Cin. Art Acad., 1998—; faculty adv. com. U. Cinn. Capt. USAF, 1963-65, PTO. USPHS fellow, 1968-69; grantee Eli Lilly Co. grantee, 1971-76, Burroughs Wellcome Co., 1972. Fellow ACS, Am. Acad. Facial and Reconstructive Surgery (edn. com. 1972, future plans com. 1973-75, sci. program com., budget and fin. com. 1975, chmn. credentials com., no. sect. 1980-85), Royal Soc. Health, Internat. Cosmetic Surgeons, Am. Acad. Cosmetic Surgeons, Am. Assn. Cosmetic Surgeons (sec.-treas. 1976-81); mem. Am. Acad. Otolaryngology and Head and Neck Surgery, Am. Coun. Otolaryngology, Soc. Univ. Otolaryngologists, Pan-Am. Assn. Oto-Rhino-Laryngology and Broncho-Esophagology, Ohio State Med. Assn., Cin. Acad. Medicine (trustee 1992-95, treas. 1993-95, pres. 1996-97, chmn. pub. rels. com. 1980, chmn. comm. com. 1994-96, chmn. sply. soc. com. 1995, legis. com. 1985, editl. bd. 1994-96, jud. com. 1995—, chmn. managed care med. dirs. com. 1997—), U. Cin. Alumni Assn. (bd. govs., sec. 1994, fin. v.p. 1995, 1st v.p. 1996, pres. 1997-98), Acad. Medicine Found. (bd. dirs., v.p., pres. 2002--), Cin. Ear, Nose and Throat Soc., Losantiville Country Club (bd. govs. 1996—, pres. 1999-2001), Omicron Delta Kappa, Sigma Sigma, Sigma Alpha Mu. Avocations: tennis, golf, traveling. Home: 2601 Willowbrook Dr Cincinnati OH 45237-3725 Office: 10496 Montgomery Rd Cincinnati OH 45242-5223

MAMAT, FRANK TRUSTICK, lawyer; b. Syracuse, N.Y., Sept. 4, 1949; s. Harvey Sanford and Annette (Trustick) M.; m. Kathy Lou Winters, June 23, 1975; children: Jonathan Adam, Steven Kenneth. BA, U. Rochester, 1971; JD, Syracuse U., 1974. Bar: D.C. 1976, U.S. Ct. Appeals (D.C. cir.) 1976, Fla. 1977, U.S. Supreme Ct. 1979, US. Dist. Ct. (ea. dist.) 1983, U.S. Ct. Appeals (6th cir.) 1983, Mich. 1984, U.S. Dist. Ct. (no. dist.) Ind. 1984. Atty. NLRB, Washington, 1975—79; assoc. Proskauer, Rose, Goetz & Mendelsohn, Washington, N.Y.C. and L.A., 1979—83, Fishman Group, Bloomfield Hills, Mich., 1983—85, ptnr., 0985—1987; sr. ptnr. Honigman, Miller, Schwartz and Cohn, 1987—94; pres., CEO Morgan Daniels Co., Inc., West Bloomfield, Mich., 1994—; ptnr. Clark Klein & Beaumont, P.L.C., Detroit, 1995—96, Clark Hill, P.L.C., Detroit, 1996—, mem. exec. com., 1999—2001. Bd. dirs. Mich. Food and Beverage Assn., Air Conditioning Contractors of Am., Air Conditioning Contractors of Mich., Am. Subcontractors Assn., Mich. Mfrs. Assn. Labor Counsel, Jewish Vocat. Svcs., Constrn. Fin. Mgmt. Assn., Mich. Assn. Home Bldg. Gen. counsel Rep. Com. of Oakland County, 1986—; chmn. Constrn. Code Commn. Mich., 1993—; bd. dirs. 300 Club, Mich., 1984-90; pres. 400 Club, 1990-93, chmn., 1993—; mem. Associated Gen. Contractors Labor Lawyers Coun.; mem. Rep. Nat. Com. Nat. Rep. Senatorial Com., Presdl. Task Force, Rep. Labor Coun., Washington; city dir. West Bloomfield, 1985-87; pres. West Bloomfield Rep. CLub, 1985-87; fin. com. Rep. Com. of Oakland County, 1984-93; pres. Oakland County Lincoln Rep. Club, 1989-90; bd. dirs. camping svcs. and human resources com. YMCA, 1989-93, Anti-Defamation League, 1989—; vice chmn. Lawyers for

Reagan-Bush, 1984; v.p. Fruehauf Farms, West Bloomfield, Mich., 1985-88; mem. staff Exec. Office of Pres. of U.S. Inquiries/Comments, Washington, 1981-83. Fellow Coll. Labor and Employment Attys.; mem. ABA, FBA, Mich. Bar Assn., Fla. Bar Assn. (labor com. 1977—), Rep. Nat. Lawyers Assn., Mich. Bus. and Profl. Assn., Am. Acad. Constrn. and Labor Attys. (exec. dir. 1998—), Am. Subcontractors Assn. (Southeastern Mich., bd. dirs.), Founders Soc. Detroit Bar Assn., Oakland County Bar Assn., B'nai B'rith (v.p. 1982-83, trustee 1987-88, bd. dirs. Detroit Barristers unit 1983-91, pres. 1985-87), Am. Soc. Employers (vice chmn. 2002-), Oakpointe Country Club, Detroit Soc. Clubs, Skyline Club, Fairlane Club, Detroit Athletic Club, Renaissance Club, Econ. Club Detroit. Office: Clark Hill PLC 500 Woodward Ave Ste 3500 Detroit MI 48226-3435 also: Morgan Daniels Co Inc 5484 Crispin Way Rd West Bloomfield MI 48323-3402 E-mail: fmamat@aol.com., fmamat@clarkhill.com.

MAMAYEK, TELLY, radio personality; married; children: Emily, Nathan. BA Journalism, U. Wis., 1985. With Stas. WBIZ/WJJK Radio, Eau Claire, Wis., Stas. KZIO/WDSM Radio, Duluth, Minn., Sta. WNIU Pub. Radio, DeKalb, Ill., Sta. WCKY Radio, Cin., Sta. WCCO Radio, Mpls., 1991—, morning news editor, anchor. Mem.: Minn. AP Broadcast Bd., Minn. Chpt. Profl. Journalists (pres.). Avocation: bicycling. Office: WCCO 625 2nd Ave S Minneapolis MN 55402*

MAMER, STUART MIES, lawyer; b. East Hardin, Ill., Feb. 23, 1921; s. Louis H. and Anna (Mies) M.; m. Donna E. Jordan, Sept. 10, 1944; children: Richard A., John S., Bruce J. A.B., U. Ill., 1942, J.D., 1947. Bar: Ill. bar 1947. Assoc. Thomas & Mulliken, Champaign, 1947-55; partner firm Thomas, Mamer & Haughey, 1955—. Lectr. U. Ill. Coll. Law, Urbana, 1965-85; Mem. Atty. Registration and Disciplinary Commn. Ill., 1976-82 Chmn. fund drive Champaign County Community Chest, 1955; 1st pres. Champaign County United Fund, 1957; Pres., dir. U. Ill. McKinley Found., Champaign, 1957-69; trustee Children's Home and Aid Soc. of Ill., v.p., 1977-96. Served as pilot USAAF, 1943-45. Mem. Am. Coll. Trust and Estate Counsel (bd. regents 1984-90), Phi Beta Kappa, Phi Gamma Delta. Republican. Presbyterian. Home: 101 W Windsor Rd # 3105 Urbana IL 61802-6663 Office: Thomas Mamer & Haughey 30 E Main St Fl 5 Champaign IL 61820-3629 E-mail: smamer@tmh-law.com.

MANCOFF, NEAL ALAN, lawyer; b. Chgo., May 7, 1939; s. Isadore and Sarah (Leviton) M.; m. Alys Belofsky, June 26, 1966; children: Wesley, Frederick, Daniel. BBA, U. Wis., l961; JD, Northwestern U., 1965. Bar: Ill. l965, U.S. Dist. Ct. (no. dist.) Ill. l965. Assoc. Aaron Aaron Schimberg & Hess, Chgo., 1965-72, ptnr., 1972-80, Schiff Hardin & Waite, Chgo., 1980—. Author: Qualified Deferred Compensation Plans, l983, Nonqualified Deferred Compensation Agreements, 1987. Lst lt. U.S. Army, l961-62. Mem. Chgo. Bar Assn. (chmn. employee benefits com. 1984). Office: Schiff Hardin & Waite 7500 Sears Tower Chicago IL 60606

MANCUSO, JOHN H. lawyer, bank executive; b. Utica, N.Y., June 5, 1944; s. Sam A. and Frances H. (Nelson) M.; m. Etel Tumma, July 18, 1970; children: Christa E., John A. BA in English magna cum laude, Boston Coll., 1968; MA in English, Lehigh U., 1970; MS in Higher Edn. Adminstrn., Syracuse U., 1973, PhD in Higher Edn. Adminstrn., 1978, JD, 1975. Bar: N.Y. 1976, Ohio 1976; U.S. Dist. Ct. (no. dist.) Ohio 1994. Assoc. Hiscock & Barclay, Syracuse, 1976-80, ptnr., 1981-90; gen. counsel Key Bank of N.Y., Albany, 1992-94; sr. v.p., dep. gen. counsel KeyCorp, Cleve. and Albany, NY, 1990—2001, exec. v.p., gen. coun., 2001—; dir., gen. counsel, sec. Key Bank Nat. Assn., Cleve., 1994—, vice chmn., 2001—. Mem. U.S.Seante Banking Com. Task Force on Fin. Modernization Bill, 1998; adj. prof. law Syracuse U., 1976-87, tchr. higher edn. adminstrn. grad. sch.; English tchr. at various colls., secondary schs., 1968-73; spkr. in field; bd. dirs. Key Bank Nat. Assn., Key Corporate Capital Inc., KeyCorp Ins. Co. Ltd. Author: Home Equity Update: A Manual for Lenders and Lawyers, 1989; co-author: Compliance Examinations Update for Financial Institutions, 1985—, The Law of Truth in Lending: 1989, Supplement, Reporting to Bank Regulators: Requirements and Forms Manual, 1990, Bank Regulatory Update: Beyond Consumer Issues, 1995-97; contbr. numerous articles to profl. publs. Chmn. planning bd. Village of Manlius, N.Y., 1983-86; bd. trustees Cleve. Hearing and Speech Ctr., 2000—. Mem. ABA (chair housing fin. subcom., consumer fin. svcs. com., bus. law sect. 1990-92), Am. Bankers Assn. (bank counsel com. 1996-98), Am. Coll. Consumer Fin. Svcs. Lawyers (founding mem.), N.Y. State Bar Assn. (chair bus. law sect. 1994-95, chmn. cinsumer fin. svcs. com. bus. law sect. 1988-91, chmn. subcom. on equal credit opportunity/truth-in-lending 1985-86, chmn. subcom. on credit cards/fair credit billing 1982-83), N.Y. State Bankers Assn. (mem. lawyers retail legis. com. 1992-94, ops. and payments sys. com. 1988-90, legal advisor to residential mortgage com. of consumer banking divsn. 1986-87, mem. lawyers adv. com. 1994—), Consumer Bankers Assn. (mem. ad hoc com. on bank investment products 1993-97, mem. lawyers com. 1987-97), Justinian Soc., Order of Coif. Republican. Avocations: skiing, golf, tennis, reading, chess. Office: KeyCorp 127 Public Sq Cleveland OH 44114-1306 E-mail: john_mancuso@keybank.com.

MANDEL, JACK N. manufacturing company executive; b. Austria, July 16, 1911; s. Sam and Rose M.; m. Lilyan, Aug. 14, 1938 (dec.) Student, Fenn Coll., 1930-33. Founder, former pres., chmn. Premier Indsl. Corp., Cleve.; chmn., pres. Manbro Corp.; exec. dir. Parkwood Corp.; gen. ptnr. Courtland Assocs. Former mem. exec. com. NCCJ; former life trustee Wood Hosp.; trustee Fla. Soc. for Blind; life trustee South Broward Jewish Fedn., Cleve. Jewish Welfare Fedn.; former pres., life trustee Montefiore Home for Aged; pres. adv. bd. Barry U.; hon. trustee Hebrew U.; trustee Tel Aviv U. Mus. of the Diaspora; life trustee The Temple, Woodruff Found.; trustee Cleve. Play House. Mem. Beachmont Country Club, Commede Club, Union Club, Club at Williams Island. Office: Parkwood Corp 2829 Euclid Ave Cleveland OH 44115-2413

MANDEL, KARYL LYNN, accountant; b. Chgo., Dec. 14, 1935; d. Isador J. and Eve (Gellar) Karzen; m. Fredric H. Mandel, Sept. 29, 1956; children: David Scott, Douglas Jay, Jennifer Ann. Student, U. Mich., 1954-56, Roosevelt U., 1956-57; AA summa cum laude, Oakton Community Coll., 1979. CPA, Ill; registered investment advisor; lic. life ins. provider. Pres. Excel Transp. Service Co., Elk Grove, Ill., 1958-78; tax mgr. Chunowitz, Teitelbaum & Baerson, CPA's, Northbrook, 1981-83, tax ptnr., 1984—. Sec-treas. Lednam, Inc., Coffee Break, Inc.; mem. acctg. curriculum adv. bd. Oakton C.C., Des Plaines, Ill., 1987—; pres. Lednam Enterprises, LLC, 2001—. Contbg. author: Ill. CPA's News Jour., Acctg. Today. Recipient State of Israel Solidarity award, 1976. Mem. AICPA, Am. Soc. Women CPA, Women's Am. ORT (pres. Chgo. region 1972-74, v.p. midwest dist. 1975-76, nat. endowment com., nat investment adv. com.), Ill. CPA Soc. (chmn. estate and gift tax com. 1987-89, legis. contact com. 1981-82, pres. North Shore chpt., award for Excellence in Acctg. Edn., Bd. dirs. 1989-91), Chgo. Soc. Women CPA, Chgo. Estate Planning Coun., Nat. Assn. Women Bus. Owners, Lake County Estate Planning, Coun., Greater North Shore Estate Planning Coun. Office: 401 Huehl Rd Northbrook IL 60062-2300 E-mail: KLM@CTBLTD.COM.

MANDEL, SHELDON LLOYD, dermatologist, educator; b. Mpls., Dec. 6, 1922; s. Maurice and Stelle R. M.; m. Patricia E., Oct. 15, 1978; 1 child, Melissa A. BA, U. Minn., Mpls., 1943, BS, 1944, BM, MD, U. Minn., 1946. Diplomate Am. Bd. Dermatology, 1953. Intern U. Okla., 1946-47; resident Valley Forge (Pa.) Gen. Hosp., 1947—49, VA Hosp., Mpls., 1949—51, VA Hosp. and U. Minn., Mpls., 1949—51; pvt. practice dermatology, 1951—; prof. clin. dermatology U. Minn., 1970—. Contbr. articles to profl. jours. Capt. MC, U.S. Army, 1947-49. Fellow Royal Soc. Medicine (Britain), Am. Acad. Dermatology (life); mem. AMA, Minn. Med. Soc., Noah Worcester Dermatol. Soc. (bd. dirs. 1988-91), Internat. Dermatol. Soc. Address: Downtown Dermatology PA 825 Nicollet Mall Ste 1629 Minneapolis MN 55402-2705

MANDELKER, DANIEL ROBERT, law educator; b. Milw., July 18, 1926; s. Adolph Irwin and Marie (Manner) M.; divorced; children: Amy Jo, John David. BA, U. Wis., 1947, LLB, 1949; JSD, Yale U., 1956. Bar: Wis. 1949. Asst. prof. law Drake U., 1949-51; atty. HHFA, Washington, 1952-53; asst. prof., then assoc. prof. law Ind. U., 1953-62; mem. faculty Washington U., St. Louis, 1962—, prof. law, 1963-74, Howard A. Stamper prof. law, 1974—. Walter E. Meyer rsch. prof. law Columbia U., 1971-72; Ford Found. law faculty fellow, London, 1959-60; cons. State of Hawaii Dept. Planning and Econ. Devel., 1972-78, State of Hawaii Office of State Planning, 1993-94; legal resources adv. group Transp. Rsch. Bd., 1991-94; mem. local govt. adv. bd. intergovtl. rels. U.S. Adv. Commn., 1985-88; mem. devel. regulations coun. Urban Land Inst., 1980-96; cons. housing subcom., banking and currency com. U.S. Ho. of Reps., 1970-71, cons. policy studies, ins. subcom., banking, fin., urban affairs coms., 1989-91; mem. commn. on environ. law World Conservation Union, 1997—; cons. state and local govts. on land use regulation; Nat. Disting. lectr. Fla. State Jour. Land Use and Environ. Law, 1992; 15th Denman lectr. U. Cambridge, Eng., 1992, Inaugural Robert E. Boden lectr. Marquette U. Sch. Law, 1997; cons. Master Plan Coalition, New Orleans, 2001--; frequ.nt spkr. at nat. confs. on land use law. Author: Green Belts and Urban Growth: English Town and Country Planning in Action, 1962, Controlling Planned Residential Developments, 1966, Managing Our Urban Environment-Cases, Text and Problems, 1966, 2d edit., 1971, Case Studies in Land Planning and Development, 1968, The Zoning Dilemma, 1971, (with W.R. Ewald) Street Graphics and the Law, 1971, 2d edit., 1988, (with R. Montgomery) Housing in America: Problems and Perspectives, 1973, 2d edit., 1979, Housing Subsidies in the United States and England, 1973, New Developments in Land and Environmental Controls, 1974, Environmental and Land Controls Legislation, 1976, supplement, 1982, (with D. Netsch) State and Local Government in a Federal System, 1977, (with D. Netsch and P. Salsich) 2d edit., 1983, (with Netsch, Salsich and Wegner) 3rd edit., 1990, 5th edit., 2002, (with R. Cunningham) Planning and Control of Land Development, 1979, 3d edit., 1990, (with R. Cunningham and J. Payne) 4th edit., 1995, (with J. Payne) 5th edit., 2001, Environment and Equity, 1981, (with others) Cases and Materials on Housing and Urban Development, 1981, 2d edit., 1989, 3rd edit., 1999, Land Use Law, 1982, 4th edit., 1997, supplement 2001 (with F. Anderson, D. Tarlock and R. Glicksman) Environmental Protection Law and Policy, 2d edit., 1990, 3d edit., 1999, NEPA Law and Litigation, 2d edit., 1992, supplement, 2001, (with J. Gerard and T. Sullivan) Federal Land Use Law, 1986, supplement, 2000, (with others) Property Law and the Public Interest, 1998; mem. editl. adv. bd. various land use jours. Mem. nat. adv. com. on outdoor advt. and motorist info. Dept. Transp., 1980-81; mem. adv. com. on housing Dem. Caucus, U.S. Ho. of Reps., 1981-82; pres. Nat. Coalition for Scenic Beauty, 1987-88; sr. fellow Urban Land Inst., 1989-95; mem. law sch. editl. bd. Lexis Law Pub., 1989-97. Mem. NAS (com. social and behavioral urban rsch. 1967-68), Am. Planning Assn. (bd. dirs. 1981-84, Housing Policy Task Force 1990-93, property rights task force 1994-95, amicus curiae com. 1995—, prin. cons. growing smart model legislation project 1996-2001), Nat. Assn. Environ. Profls. (chair legal issues com. NEPA working group 1999-01), Order of Coif, Phi Beta Kappa, Phi Kappa Phi. Office: PO Box 1120 Saint Louis MO 63188-1120 E-mail: mandelker@wulaw.wustl.edu.

MANDELSTAMM, JEROME ROBERT, lawyer; b. St. Louis, Apr. 3, 1932; s. Henry and Estelle (London) M.; m. Carolyn A. White; stepchildren: John M. Gagliardi, Maria A. Amundson, Amy E. Gagliardi. A.B., U. Pa., 1954; LL.B., Harvard U., 1957. Bar: Mo. 1957. Since practiced in, St. Louis; partner Greenfield, Davidson, Mandelstamm & Voorhees, 1969-81, Schmitz, Mandelstamm, Hawker & Fischer, 1981-82; sole practice, 1982—. Bd. dirs. Legal Aid Soc. City and County St. Louis, 1967-75, pres., 1969-70; bd. dirs. Lawyers Reference Service Met. St. Louis, 1976-83, chmn., 1978-83; bd. dirs. Mo. Legal Aid Soc., 1977-82; mem. 22d Jud. Cir. Bar Com., 1983-85, gen. chmn., 1984-85 Mem. St. Louis County Bd. Election Commrs., 1973-77. Served with AUS, 1957. Mem. ABA, Mo. Bar Assn., Am. Arbitration Assn. (panel of arbitrators 1984—), Bar Assn. Met. St. Louis (v.p. 1974-75, treas. 1975-76). Home: 7217 Princeton Saint Louis MO 63130-3000 Office: 1010 Market St Ste 1600 Saint Louis MO 63101-2032

MANDERS, KARL LEE, neurosurgeon; b. Rochester, N.Y., Jan. 21, 1927; s. David Bert and Frances Edna (Cohan) Mendelson; m. Ann Laprell, July 28, 1969; children: Karlanna, Maidena; children by previous marriage; Karl, Kerry, Kristine. Student, Cornell U., 1946; MD, U. Buffalo, 1950. Diplomate Am. Bd. Neurol. Surgery, Am. Bd. Clin. Biofeedback, Am. Bd. Hyperbaric Medicine, Am. Bd. Pain Medicine, Nat. Bd. Med. Examiners. Intern U. Va. Hosp., Charlottesville, 1950-51, resident in neurol. surgery, 1951-52, Henry Ford Hosp., Detroit, 1954-56; pvt. practice Indpls., 1956—. Med. dir. Cmty. Hosp. Rehab. Ctr. for Pain, 1973—; chief hosp. med. and surg. neurology Cmty. Hosp., 1983, 93; coroner Marion County, Ind., 1977-85, 92-96. With USN, 1952-54, Korea. Recipient Cert. achievement Dept. Army, 1969, Disting. Physician award Comm. Hosp., 1997. Fellow ACS, Internat. Coll Surgeons, Am. Acad. Neurology; mem. Congress Neurol. Surgery, Internat. Assn. Study of Pain, Am. Assn. Study of Headache, N.Y. Acad. Sci., Am. Coll. Angiology, Am. Soc. Contemporary Medicine and Surgery, Am. Holistic Med. Assn. (co-founder), Undersea Med. Soc., Am. Acad. Forensic Sci., Am. Asssn. Biofeedback Clinicians, Soc. Cryosurgery, Pan Pacific Surg. Assn., Biofeedback Soc. Am., Acad. Psychosomatic Medicine, Pan Am. Med. Assn., Internat. Back Pain Soc., North Am. Spine Soc., Am. Soc. Stereotaxic and Functional Neurosurgery, Soc. for Computerized Tomography and Neuroimaging, Ind. Coroners Assn. (pres. 1979), Royal Soc. Medicine, Nat. Assn. Med. Examiners, Am. Pain Soc., Midwest Pain Soc. (pres. 1988), Am. Acad. Pain Medicine, Cen. Neurol. Soc., Interurban Neurosurg. Soc., Internat. Soc. Aquatic Medicine, James A. Gibson Anat. Soc., Am. Bd. Med. Psychotherapists (mem. profl. adv. council), James McClure Surg. Soc., Brendonwood Country Club, Highland Country Club. Home: 5845 High Fall Rd Indianapolis IN 46226-1017 Office: 7369 Shadeland Sta Ste 100 Indianapolis IN 46256-3958

MANDERSCHEID, LESTER VINCENT, agricultural economics educator; b. Andrew, Iowa, Oct. 9, 1930; s. Vincent John and Alma (Sprank) M.; m. Dorothy Helen Varnum, Aug. 29, 1953; children: David, Paul, Laura, Jane. BS, Iowa State U., 1951, MS, 1952; PhD, Stanford U., 1961. Grad. asst. Iowa State U., Ames, 1951-52, Stanford (Calif.) U., 1952-56; asst. prof. Mich. State U., East Lansing, 1956-65, assoc. prof., 1965-70, prof., 1970-73, prof., assoc. chmn., 1973-87, prof., chmn., 1987-92, prof., 1992-95, prof. emeritus, 1996—, coord. Grad. Sch., 1993—. Reviewer Tex. A&M Agrl. Econ. Program, College Station, 1989; cons. Consortium Internat. Earth Sci. Info. Network, Ann Arbor, 1990. Co-author: Improving Undergraduate Education, 1967; contbr. articles to jours. in field. Pres. parish coun. St. Thomas, East Lansing, 1984-87; coll. coord. United Way, East Lansing, 1983-84; pres. bd. dirs. Cristo Rey Cmty. Ctr., 1998-2001. Recipient Disting. Faculty award Mich. State U., 1977. Mem. Am. Agrl. Econ. Assn. (pres. 1988-89, bd. dirs. 1982-85, excellence in teaching award 1974), Am. Statis. Assn., Am. Evaluation Assn., Am. Econ. Assn., University Club, Sigma Xi (pres. 1986-87), Phi Kappa Phi (pres. 1979-80). Roman Catholic. Home: 2372 Burcham Dr East Lansing MI 48823-3885 Office: Mich State U Dept of Agrl Econs Circle Dr East Lansing MI 48824-1039 E-mail: mandersc@msu.edu.

MANELLI, DONALD DEAN, screenwriter, film producer; b. Burlington, Iowa, Oct. 20, 1936; s. Daniel Anthony and Mignon Marie (Dean) M.; m. Susan Linda Allen, June 16, 1964 (div. Aug. 1973); children: Daniel, Lisa. BA, U. Notre Dame, 1959. Communications specialist Jewel Cos., Melrose Park, Ill., 1959; script writer Coronet Films, Chgo., 1960-62; freelance writer, 1962-63; creative dir. Fred A. Niles Communications Ctrs., 1963-67; sr. writer Wild Kingdom NBC-TV, 1967-70; freelance film writer, producer, 1970-76; pres. Donald Manelli & Assocs., Inc., Chgo. and Paris, 1976—. Screenwriter, prodr. more than 225 documentary films, 1970—, numerous episodes Wild Kingdom, 1967-82 (Emmy award 1969, 70). Recipient numerous awards various orgns. including N.Y. Internat. Film Festival, Houston Internat. Film Festival, Berlin, Paris, Venice Internat. Film Festivals, CINE, 1976—. Mem. Writers Guild Am. Roman Catholic. Avocations: photography, traveling, tennis. Office: 1 E Delaware Pl Chicago IL 60611-1449 also: 1 Rue Goethe 75116 Paris France E-mail: dmanelli@earthlink.net.

MANERI, REMO R. management consultant; b. Cleve., Aug. 16, 1928; s. Quinto Peter and Lucia (Massenzi) M.; m. Camille Ann Caranna, Aug. 26, 1950; children: Peter, Alisa, Leonard, Celia. B.S. in Chem. Engring., Case Inst. Tech., 1950; grad., Advanced Mgmt. Program, Harvard U., 1969. Devel. engr. Dow Corning, 1950-53, market researcher, 1956, comml. devel. mgr., 1957-63, chief engr., 1964-66, unit mfg. mgr., 1967-69, dir. tech. service and devel., 1970-72, bus. mgr., v.p., 1973-74, mgr. bus., group v.p., 1975-76; pres. Dow Corning U.S.A., 1977-80; exec. v.p. Dow Corning Corp., 1981-82, also bd. dirs.; chmn. bd. Quantum Composites, 1982-85, pres., chmn. bd., 1985-87, chmn. bd., 1987-89, also bd. dirs.; mgmt. cons., 1989—. Bd. dirs. Comerica Bank-Midland, Duro-Last Roofing, Inc., Quantum Composites, Inc.; cons. in field. Contbr. articles to profl. jours.; patentee in field. Bd. dirs. Midland Hosp. Assn. Served with Signal Corps, U.S. Army, 1954-56. Named Man of Year Adhesives and Sealants Coun., 1988. Mem. AAAS, Chem. Spltys. Mfg. Assn. (dir.), Am. Chem. Soc., Sigma Xi, Tau Beta Pi, Alpha Chi Sigma. Roman Catholic. Club: Midland Country. Home and Office: 5808 Siebert St Midland MI 48640-2753

MANGIERI, PAUL L. lawyer; b. Galesburg, Ill., Jan. 17, 1959; s. Joseph L. and Dorothy Fern (McKinley) M.; m. Lori A. Armstrong, Nov. 17, 1979 (div. Oct. 1990); children: Regina A., Joseph P., Amy E., Michael T.; m. Felicia E. Hunt, Feb. 14, 1991; children: Jessica E. Fredrickson, Rudena J. Fredrickson, Dorothy D., Allison L. BA, Coe Coll., 1981; JD, St. Louis U., 1984. Bar: Ill. 1984, Mo. 1985, U.S. Dist. Ct. (ctrl. dist.) Ill. 1988. Judge adv. gen. USN-USS Saratoga, 1984-88; ptnr. Barash & Stoerzbach, Galesburg, Ill., 1988—. Lt. comdr. USN, 1984-88. Mem. KC. Democrat. Roman Catholic. Avocations: farming, hunting. Home: 1987 N Broad St Galesburg IL 61401-1448 Office: Barash & Stoerzbach 139 S Cherry St Galesburg IL 61401-4511

MANGLER, ROBERT JAMES, lawyer, judge; b. Chgo., Aug. 15, 1930; s. Robert H. and Agnes E. (Sugrue) M.; m. Geraldine M. Delich, May 2, 1959; children: Robert Jr., Paul, John, Barbara. BS, Loyola U., Chgo., 1952, MA, 1983; JD, Northwestern U., 1955. Bar: Ill. 1958, U.S. Dist. Ct. (no. dist.) Ill. 1959, U.S. Supreme Ct. 1976, U.S. Ct. Appeals (7th cir.) 1980. Author: (with others) Illinois Land Use Law, Illinois Municipal Law. Village atty., prosecutor Village of Wilmette, 1965-93; mcpl. prosecutor City of Evanston, 1963-65, adminstrv. law judge, 2000—; chmn. Ill. Traffic Ct. Conf., 1977—; pres. Ill. Inst. Local Govt. Law; mem. home rule attys. com. Ill. Mcpl. League. Mem. ABA (chmn. adv. com. traffic ct. program), Nat. Inst. Mcpl. Law Officers (past pres.), Ill. Bar Assn. (former chmn. traffic laws and ct. com.), Chgo. Bar Assn. (former chmn. traffic ct. seminar, former chmn. traffic laws com.), Caxton Club, Phi Alpha Delta.

MANGUN, CLARKE WILSON , JR. public health physician, consultant; b. Iowa Falls, Iowa, Feb. 12, 1919; s. Clarke Wilson and Vallie Hazel (Hoffman) M.; m. Edith Lauretta DuBois, May 13, 1945; children: Edith Ann, Nancy June, Laura Jane. BS, U. Iowa, 1940, MD, 1943; MPH, Columbia U., 1947. Diplomate Am. Bd. Preventive Medicine. Commd. officer USPHS, 1945-66; med. adminstr. Am. Hosp. Assn., Chgo., 1966-67, Chgo. Heart Assn., 1967-68, AMA, Chgo., 1969-80; long-term cons. Abbott Labs., North Chicago, Ill., 1980—. Recipient award Nat. Bd. Med. Examiners, 1944. Fellow APHA, Am. Coll. Preventive Medicine; mem. AMA (Physician's Recognition award, 1970—), Ill. State Med. Soc., Chgo. Med. Soc. Avocations: photography, travel, gardening. Home and Office: 733 S Greenwood Ave Park Ridge IL 60068-4539

MANION, DANIEL ANTHONY, federal judge; b. South Bend, Ind., Feb. 1, 1942; s. Clarence E. and Virginia (O'Brien) Manion; m. Ann Murphy Manion, June 29, 1984. BA, U. Notre Dame, 1964; JD, Ind. U., 1973. Bar: Ind., U.S. Dist. Ct. (no. dist.) Ind., U.S. Dist. Ct. (so. dist.) Ind. Dep. atty. gen. State of Ind., 1973—74; from assoc. to ptnr. Doran, Manion, Boynton, Kamm & Esmont, South Bend, 1974—86; judge U.S. Ct. Appeals (7th cir.), 1986—. Mem. Ind. State Senate, Indpls., 1978—82. Office: US Ct Appeals US Courthouse & Federal Bldg 204 S Main St Rm 301 South Bend IN 46601-2122 Home: 20725 Riverlan Rd South Bend IN 46637-1029

MANION, THOMAS A. chancellor; b. Aug. 10, 1934; m. Maureen O'Mara; children: Gregory, Marcy, Andrew, Margaret, Vicki, Tina, Thomas. B.B.A., St. Bonaventure U., 1959; M.B.A., Boston Coll., 1962; Ph.D., Clark U., 1968; D.Pedagogy, Bryant Coll., 1973. Chmn. econs. dept., dean grad. sch., acad. provost v.p. Bryant Coll., Smithfield, R.I.; pres. Coll. Saint Rose, Albany, N.Y., 1973-83, St. Nobert Coll., De Pere, Wis., 1983-2000, chancellor, 2000—. Bd. dirs. Associated Kellogg Bank, Green Bay, Wis. Bd. dirs. Higher Edn. Aids Coun., State of Wis. Mem. NCAA, Nat. Assn. Ind. Colls. and Univs. (mem. commn. on campus concerns), Am. Assn. Higher Edn., Am. Coun. Edn., Nat. Cath. Edn. Assn., Assn. Cath. Colls. and Univs., Coun. Ind. Colls. (bd. dirs.), Wis. Assn. Ind. Colls. and Univs. (pres.), Wis. Found. Ind. Colls., Delta Epsilon, Delta Mu Delta. Office: St Norbert Coll 100 Grant St De Pere WI 54115-2002

MANKA, RONALD EUGENE, lawyer; b. Wichita, Kans., Dec. 12, 1944; s. James Ashford and Jane Bunn (Meeks) M.; m. Frances Ann Patterson, Aug. 7, 19665 (dec. Dec. 1985); children: Kimberly Ann, Lora Christine; m. Linda I. Bailey, Mar. 11, 1995. BBA cum laude, U. Kans., 1967; JD cum laude, U. Mich., 1970. Bar: Conn. 1970, Mo. 1974, Kans. 1985, Colo. 2001. Assoc. Day, Barry & Howard, Hartford, Conn., 1970-73, Lathrop & Gage L.C., Kansas City, Mo., 1973-78, mem., 1979-82, 85—; group counsel Butler Mfg. Co., 1982-83, div. gen. mgr., 1983-84. Bd. dir. Colo. Lawyers for Arts; legal com. Boulder County Cmty. Found., Colo., 2002—. Trustee, clk., elder Village Presbyn. Ch., Prairie Village, Kans.; dir., treas. Lyric Opera of Kansas City, 1995—; pres. Genesis Sch., Kansas City, 1987-89; devel. chmn. Kansas City Friends of Alvin Ailey, 1987-89; chmn. Kansas City Mus., 1988-92, gen. counsel, 1994—; gen. counsel Spirit Festival, Kansas City, 1985-87, Kansas City C. of C., 1989-96; pres. Ctr. for Mgmt. Assistance, Kansas City, 1991-93; dir. Colo. Music Festival, 2002-. Mem. ABA, Mo. Bar Assn. (alt. dispute resolution com. 1986—), Lawyers Assn. Kansas City, Silicon Prairie Tech. Assn. (bd. dirs. 1990-92), Homestead Country Club (pres. 1984-85). Republican. Avocations: bicycling, swimming. Home: 812 Walnut Apt F Boulder CO 80302 Office: 4845 Pearl East Cir Ste 300 Boulder CO 80301 Fax: 816-292-2001. E-mail: RManka@LathropGage.com.

MANLEY, ROBERT EDWARD, lawyer, economist; b. Cin., Nov. 24, 1935; s. John M. and Helen Catherine (McCarthy) M.; m. Roberta L. Anzinger, Oct. 21, 1971 (div. 1980); 1 child, Robert Edward. ScB in Econs, Xavier U., 1956; AM in Econ. Theory, U. Cin., 1957; JD, Harvard U.,

1960; postgrad., London Sch. Econs. and Polit. Sci., 1960, MIT, 1972. Bar: Ohio 1960, U.S. Supreme Ct. 1970. Pvt. practice law, Cin., 1960—; chmn. Manley Burke, 1977. Taft teaching fellow econs. U. Cin., 1956-57, vis. lectr. community planning law Coll. Design, Architecture and Art, 1967-73, adj. assoc. prof. urban planning Coll. Design, Architecture, Art and Planning, 1972-81, adj. prof., 1981—, adj. prof. law, 1980—. Author: Metropolitan School Desegregation, 1978, (with Robert N. Cook) Management of Land and Environment, 1981, others; chmn. editl. adv. bd. Urban Lawyer, 1986-95. Mem. Hamilton County Pub. Defender Commn., 1976-79; trustee HOPE, Cin., Albert J. Ryan Found.; counsel, co-founder Action Housing for Greater Cin.; mem. Spl. Commn. on Formation U. Cin. Health Maintenance Orgn., Mayor Cin. Spl. Com. on Housing; chmn. Cin. Environ. Adv. Coun., 1975-76; trustee The Americas Fund for Ind. Univs., 1987-2000; trustee Ohio Planning Conf., 1982-91, pres., 1987-89, trustee, 1987-90; sec. Cin. Mounted Patrol Com., 1993—; active Bd. Cin. Downtown Coun., 1991-98. Mem. ABA (coun. sect. local govt. law 1976-80, 81-85, 88-92), Ohio Bar Assn., Cin. Bar Assn., Am. Judicature Soc., Law and Soc. Assn., Nat. Coun. Crime and Delinquency, Harvard U. Law Sch. Assn. Cin. (pres. 1970-71), Am. Econ. Assn., Am. Acad. Polit. and Social Sci., Queen City Club, Explorers Club (N.Y.C.) (trustee, sec. Clark chpt. 1992—), Athenaeum Club (Phila.), S.Am. Explorers Club (Lima, Peru). Republican. Roman Catholic. Office: Manley Burke 225 W Court St Cincinnati OH 45202-1052 E-mail: info@manleyburke.com.

MANN, BENJAMIN HOWARD, management consultant; b. Ashland, Ky., July 10, 1958; s. James Edward and Nancy Ann (Riddle) M. BSBA, Ohio State U., 1980. Fin. analyst Bison Mfg. and Fabrication, Buffalo, 1980-82; fin. contr. Bush Plastics, Inc., Salamanca, N.Y., 1982-83; pres. Bison Leasing Co., Inc., Cleve., 1983-94; CFO golf course devel. and mgmt. The Van Cleef Cos., Beachwood, 1994, CFO Cleve., 1994-95; COO, CFO Secured Paper Solutions, Ltd., 1995; mgmt. cons. Deloitte & Touche LLP, 1996-97; sr. mgr. Veritus Cons., Solon, 1997—2000; sr. mgr. financial recovery svcs. BDO Seidman LLP, Phila., 2000—. Vice chmn. Buffalo Holdings, Inc., 1985-94. Mem. NRA, Buffalo Club, Canterbury Golf Club, Crag Burn Golf Club, Sand Hills Golf Club, Racquet Club of Phila., Univ. Club of N.Y. Republican. Episcopalian. Avocations: skiing, golf, squash. E-mail: benjamin.mann@worldnet.att.net.

MANN, DAVID SCOTT, lawyer; b. Cin., Sept. 25, 1939; s. Henry M. and Helen Faye M.; m. Elizabeth Taliaferro, Oct. 5, 1963; children: Michael, Deborah, Marshall. AB cum laude, Harvard Coll., 1961, LLB magna cum laude, 1968. Bar: Ohio 1968. Assoc. Dinsmore & Shohl, Cin., 1968-74, ptnr., 1974-83, Taliaferro and Mann, Cin., 1983-92; councilman City of Cin., 1974-92, mayor, 1980-82, 91; mem. 103d Congress 1st Ohio dist., Washington, 1993-94; mem. armed svcs. com., mem. jud. com.; of counsel Thompson, Hine and Flory, Cin., 1995-96; pvt. practice Mann & Mann, LLC, 1997—. Adj. prof. Coll. of Law, U. Cin., 1995—. Editor Harvard Law Rev., 1966-68, notes editor, 1967-68; contbr. articles to profl. jours. Mem., chmn. Cin. Bd. Health, 1972-74. With USN, 1961-65. Mem. Cin. Bar Assn. Democrat. Methodist. Home: 568 Evanswood Pl Cincinnati OH 45220-1527

MANN, DAVID WILLIAM, minister; b. Elkhart, Ind., Apr. 17, 1947; s. Herbert Richard and Kathryn (Bontrager) M.; m. Brenda Marie Frantz, June 7, 1969; children: Troy, Todd, Erika. BA, Bethel Coll., 1969; MS, Nat. Louis U., 1986. Ordained to ministry Missionary Ch., 1978. Campus life dir. Youth for Christ, Elkhart, 1969-77; denominational youth dir. Missionary Ch., Ft. Wayne, Ind., 1977-81, Christian edn. dir., 1981-88, U.S. dir. missions, 1990—; assoc. dir. World Ptnrs., 1988-90. Dir. Missionary Ch. Vol. Svc., Ft. Wayne, 1983—, World Ptnrs. USA, 1998—. Author: (with others) Youth Leaders Source Book, 1985; contbr. articles to profl. jour. Mgr. Little League, Ft. Wayne, 1981-89, bd. dirs. 1986. Mem. Nat. Assn. Evangelicals, Evangelical Fellowship of Mission Agys. (nat. bd. dirs. 1999—), Denominational Execs. in Christian Edn. (chmn. 1988), Aldersgate Pub. Assn. (bd. dirs. 1985, 87), Nat. Christian Edn. Assn. (exec. com. 1987-89). Avocations: baseball, skiing, fishing, woodworking. Office: Missionary Ch PO Box 9127 Fort Wayne IN 46899-9127

MANN, HENRY DEAN, accountant; b. El Dorado, Ark., Feb. 8, 1943; s. Paul L. and Mary Louise (Capps) M.; m. Rebecca Balch, Aug. 14, 1965; children: Julie Elizabeth, Betsey Sawyer Mann. BSBA, U. Ark., 1965. CPA, Mo., Tex. Staff acct., mgr. Ernst & Whinney, Houston, 1967-76, ptnr., 1976-77; regional personnel ptnr. Ernst & Whinney (now Ernst & Young), St. Louis, 1977-78, mng. ptnr., 1978-88; pres. Mann Industries, Inc., 1988-89; pres., dir. 1st Capital Corp., Ft. Scott, Kans., 1989—, chmn., CEO, dir., 1989—, Citizens Bank, N.A., Fort Scott, 1989—. CEO, chmn. bd. dirs. Humble (Tex.) Nat. Bank, 1992-98; adv. bd. U. Mo. Sch. Accountancy, Columbia, 1979-82; bd. dirs. Cupples Co. Mfrs., St. Louis. Treas. Jr. Achievement, St. Louis, 1984-98, bd. dirs., 1986-98; treas., bd. dirs. United Way, St. Louis, 1986-92, Art and Edn. Coun., St. Louis, 1986-91; bd. dirs. St. Louis Symphony, 1988-89, Mercy Hosp. Found., Ft. Scott, Kans., 2000—, Bankers Bank of Kans., Wichita, 2000—; bd. dirs. Kammergild Chamber Orch., St. Louis, 1986, pres., 1983-85. Mem. AICPA, Mo. Soc. CPAs, Ft. Scott C. of C. (bd. dirs., pres.2001—), Bellerive Country Club (treas. 1986-87, v.p. 1988-89), Beta Gamma Sigma, Beta Alpha Psi. Presbyterian. Office: Citizens Bank NA 200 S Main St Fort Scott KS 66701-2045

MANN, PHILLIP LYNN, data processing company executive; b. Charleston, W.Va., July 26, 1944; s. Clarence Edward and Virginia Charlotte (Rupe) M.; m. Edith Jane Dewell, Dec. 28, 1966 (div. 1977); 1 child, Cynthia Lynn; m. Phyllis Anita Berg, May 18, 1979; children: Stacia Lynn, Brandon Granville. BSEE, Purdue U., 1970; MBA, U. Chgo., 1975. Devel. engr. Western Electric Co., Inc., Lisle, Ill., 1970-77; v.p. Uniq Digital Techs., Inc., Batavia, 1977-88; pres. ProTech Computer Group, Inc., 1988—. Served with USN, 1962-66. Avocations: radio control helicopters, fishing. Home: 428 Meadowrue Ln Batavia IL 60510-2815 Office: ProTech Computer Group Inc 428 Meadowrue Ln Batavia IL 60510-2815

MANNA, JOHN S. fraternal organization administrator; Office: Woodmen of the World 1700 Farnam St Ste 2200 Omaha NE 68102-2007

MANNING, BLANCHE M. federal judge; b. 1934; BEd, Chgo. Tchrs. Coll., 1961; JD, John Marshall Law Sch., 1967; MA, Roosevelt Univ., 1972; LLM, Univ. of Va. Law Sch., 1992; DHL (hon.), Chgo. State U., 1998. Asst. states atty. State's Atty.'s Office (Cook County), Ill., 1968-73; supervisory trial atty. U.S. EEOC, Chgo., 1973-77; gen. atty. United Airlines, 1977-78; asst. U.S. atty. U.S. Dist. Ct. (no. dist.) Ill., 1978-79; assoc. judge Cir. Ct. of Cook County, 1979-86, circuit judge, 1986-87; appellate court judge Ct. of Review Ill. Appellate Ct., 1987-94; district judge U.S. Dist. Ct. (no. dist.) Ill., Chgo., 1994—. Tchr. A. O. Sexton Elem. Sch. James Wadsworth Elem. Sch., Wendell Phillips H.S. Adult Program, Morgan Park H.S. Summer Sch. Program, South Shore H.S. Summer Sch. Program, Carver H.S. Adult Edn. Program; lectr. Malcolm X C.C., 1970-71; adj. prof. NCBL C.C. of Law, 1978-79, DePaul Univ. Law Sch., 1992—; tchg. team mem. Trial Advocacy Workshop, Harvard Law Sch., U. Chgo. Law Sch., 1991—; chmn. Com. on Recent Devels. in Evidence, Ill. Judicial Conf., 1991; faculty mem. New Judges Seminar, Ill. Judicial Conf.; past faculty mem. Profl. Devel. Seminar for New Assoc. Judges, Cook County Cir. Ct.; past mem. bd. dirs., trained intervenor Lawyers' Assistance Program, Inc.; past mem. adv. coun. Lawyer's Asst. Program, Roosevelt U. Former trustee Sherwood Music Conservatory Bd.; clarinetist Cmty. Concert band Chgo. State U.; saxophonist Jazz ensemble, Chgo. State U. Jazz Band, jazz band Diversity. Mem. Cook County Bar Assn. (second v-p 1974), Nat. Bar Assn., Nat. Judicial Coun., Ill. Judicial Coun. (treas. 1982-85, chmn. 1988, chmn. judiciary com. 1992), Ill. State Bar Assn. (past mem. bd. dirs. Lawyers Assistance Program Inc.), Am. Bar Assn. (fellow 1991), Chgo. Bar Assn. (clarinetist Symphony Orch., saxophonist), John Marshall Law Sch. Alumni Assn. (bd. dirs.), Chgo. State Univ. Alumni Assn. (bd. dirs.). Office: US Dist Ct 2156 US Courthouse 219 S Dearborn St Ste 2050 Chicago IL 60604-1800

MANNING, DANIEL RICARDO, professional basketball player; b. Hattiesburg, Miss., May 17, 1966; s. Ed Manning. Student, U. Kans. Forward L.A. Clippers, 1988-93, Atlanta Hawks, 1993-94, Phoenix Suns, 1994-99, Milw. Bucks, 1999—. Recipient Bronze medal U.S. Olympic Basketball Team, 1988; named Most Outstanding Player NCAA Divsn. I Tournament, 1988, Naismith award, 1988, Wooden award, 1988; named to Sporting News NCAA All-Am. first team, 1987, 88, NBA All-Star Team, 1993-94. Achievements include first pick overall NCAA draft, 1988; mem. NCAA Divsn. I Championship team, 1988. Office: Milw Bucks 1001 N 4th St Milwaukee WI 53203-1314

MANNING, JOHN WARREN, III, retired surgeon, medical educator; b. Phila., Nov. 24, 1919; s. John Warren Jr. and Edith Margaret (Reagan) M.; m. Muriel Elizabeth Johnson, Oct. 11, 1944; children: John, Melissa, Susan. BS in Chemistry with honors, Ursinus Coll., 1940; MD, U. Pa., 1943; postgrad., 1978. Diplomate Am. Bd. Surgery. Naval intern Pa. Naval Hosp., 1946; resident Saginaw (Mich.) Gen. Hosp., 1947-50; preceptor Dr. H.M. Bishop, 1950-52; pvt. practice Saginaw, 1950—. Sr. staff mem. Saginaw Gen. Hosp., St. Luke's Hosp., Saginaw; past chief of surgery, chmn. tissue com. St. Mary's Hosp., Saginaw; cons. VA Hosp., Saginaw; assoc. clin. prof. surgery Mich. State U., assoc. prof. surgery, 1976-92, prof. emeritus, 1992—; mem. search com. Saginaw Coop. Hosp. Contbr. articles to profl. publs. Lt. USN, 1942-46, PTO. Fellow ACS; mem. AMA, Mich. State Med. Soc., Saginaw Surg. Soc., Soc. Abdominal Surgeons, Am. Coll. Angiology, Soc. Am. Gastrointestinal Endoscopic Surgeons. Office: 4515 Gratiot Rd Saginaw MI 48603-6261

MANNING, KENNETH PAUL, technologies company executive; b. N.Y.C., Jan. 18, 1942; s. John Joseph and Edith Helen (Hoffmann) M.; m. Maureen Lambert, Sept. 12, 1964; children: Kenneth J., John J., Elise, Paul, Carolyn, Jacqueline. BME, Rensselaer Poly. Inst., 1963; postgrad., George Washington U., 1965-66; MBA in Ops. Rsch., Am. U., 1968. With W.R. Grace & Co., N.Y.C., 1973-87, v.p. European consumer divsn., 1975-76, pres. ednl. products divsn., 1976-79, pres. real estate divsn., 1979-81, v.p. corp. tech. group, 1981-83, pres., CEO, Ambrosia Chocolate Co. divsn. Milw., 1983-87; group v.p. Sensient Techs. Corp., 1987-89, exec. v.p., dir., 1989-92, pres., COO, dir., 1992-96; pres., CEO, dir. Universal Foods Corp., 1996—, chmn., CEO, 1997—. Bd. dirs. Firstar Corp., Milw., Badger Meter, Inc., Milw. Vice chmn. Greater Milw. Com.; bd. dirs. Milw. Harbor Commn. Served as lt. USN, 1963-67; rear adm. USNR, ret. Decorated Legion of Merit, Nat. Def. medal, others. Mem. Am. Chem. Soc., Navy League, U.S. Naval Inst., Naval Res. Assn., Milw. Metro Assn. Commerce (bd. dirs.), Union League (N.Y.C.), Milw. Club, Knights of Malta. Republican. Roman Catholic. Home: 5240 N Lake Dr Milwaukee WI 53217-5369 Office: Sensient Techs Corp 777 E Wisconsin Ave Milwaukee WI 53202-5304

MANNING, PETER KIRBY, sociology educator; b. Salem, Oreg., Sept. 27, 1940; s. Kenneth Gilbert and Esther Amelia (Gibbard) M.; m. Victoria Francis Shaughnessy, Sept. 1, 1961 (div. 1981); children— Kerry Patricia, Sean Peter, Merry Kathleen; m. Betsy Cullum-Swan, Aug. 4, 1991 (div. 1997). BA, Willamette U., 1961; MA, Duke U., 1963, PhD, 1966; MA (hon.), Oxford U., Eng., 1983. Instr. sociology Duke U., 1964-65; asst. prof. sociology U. Mo., 1965-66, Mich. State U., East Lansing, 1966-70, assoc. prof. sociology and psychiatry, 1970-74, prof., 1974—; prof. criminal justice, 1993—. Beto chair lectr. Sam Houston State U., 1990; Ameritech lectr. E. Ky. U., 1983; vis. prof. U. Victoria, 1968, MIT, 1982, SUNY, Albany, 1982, U. Mich., 1990—91, York U., Toronto, 1999; vis. sr. scholar Northeastern U. Coll. Criminal Justice, 2001, E.V. and E.M. Brooks chair; cons. Nat. Inst. Law Enforcement and Criminal Justice (later Nat. Inst. Justice), U.S. Dept. Justice, Rsch. Triangle Inst., NSF, Nat. Health and Med. Rsch. Coun., Australia, 1980—, Social Sci. Rsch. Coun. Eng., AID, Jamaica, 1991, Sheehy com. Police Pay and Performance, England, 1993. Author: Sociology of Mental Health and Illness, 1975, Police Work, 1977, 2d edit., 1997, The Narcs' Game, 1980, 2d edit., 2002, Semiotics and Fieldwork, 1987, Symbolic Communication, 1988, Organizational Communication, 1992, Private Policing, 1999, other books; also book chpts., articles in profl. jours.; cons. editor series: Principal Themes in Sociology; co-editor Sage Series in Qualitative Methods; mem. editorial bd. numerous jours. in social scis. Recipient Bruce Smith Sr. award Acad. Criminal Justice Scis., 1993, O.W. Wilson award, 1997, Charles H. Cooley award Mich. Sociol. Assn., 1994; NDEA fellow, 1962-64, NSF fellow, 1965, fellow Balliol Coll., Oxford U., 1982-83, vis. fellow Wolfson Coll., Oxford U., 1981, 82-83, fellow, 1984-86; Am. Bar Found. rsch. fellow, 1998; Rockefeller resident, Bellagio, Italy, 2000. Mem. Am. Soc. Criminology, Am. Sociol. Assn., Brit. Soc. Criminology, Internat. Sociol. Assn., Midwest Sociol. Soc., Soc. Study of Social Problems, Soc. for the Study of Symbolic Interaction (spl. recognition award 1990, v.p. 1992-93, program chair 1993), Internat. Soc. for Semiotics and Law. Office: Northeastern U Coll Criminal Justice Boston MA 02115 E-mail: manningpk@hotmail.com.

MANNING, PEYTON, professional football player; b. Mar. 24, 1976; Grad., U. Tenn. Quarterback Indpls. Colts, 1998—. Office: Indianapolis Colts PO Box 535000 Indianapolis IN 46253-5000 also: Indianapolis Colts 7001 West 56th Strreet Indianapolis IN 46254

MANNING, RONALD LEE, banker; b. Hillsboro, Ohio, Jan. 15, 1951; s. George Charles and Margaret Alice (Hail) M. BSBA, Bowling Green State U., 1973; Cert., U. Okla., 1984. Teller, collection coordinator Bank of Wood County, Bowling Green, Ohio, 1972-73; mgr. Park Nat. Bank, Newark, 1973-76; mgr., asst. v.p. BancOhio Nat. Bank, Cin., 1976-78, br. adminstr., 1978-81, mgr. comsumer credit, 1981-83, v.p., dist. lending mgr. Newark, 1983-88, pres. Bellefontaine and Kenton, 1988-92, Nat. City Bank, Newark-Licking, Perry, 1993-96, regional mgr. Newark/Lancaster region, 1996-99, area exec. Toledo/N.W. area, 1999-2000; regional sales mgr., head pvt. banking Unizan Bank, N.A., Columbus, Ohio, 2000—. Mem. adv. com. Ctrl. Ohio Tech. Coll., Newark, 1983-90; lectr. U. Cin., 1978-85, Camp Enterprise, Newark, 1993-99; chmn. Manningstead Farms, Howard, Ohio, 1986—. Mem. adv. com. Am. Cancer Soc., Newark, 1976—, lay trustee Ohio div., 1990; mem. United Way of Licking County, 1993-99, United Way of Lucas County, 1999-2000; pres. Mann, Inc., 1990—; bd. dirs. Par Excellence Sch., 1995-99; bd. dirs. Licking County Indsl. Growth Corp., 1994-99; mem. fin. com. Inst. Indsl. Tech., 1995-99; mem. governing com. Licking County Found., 1993-2000; mem. bus. and industry coun. Licking Meml. Hosp., 1993-99. Named to Hon. Order of Ky. Col., 1972. Mem. Mental Health Assn., Newark Area C. of C. (dir. 1993-99), Am. Inst. Banking, Ohio Oil & Gas Assn., Rotary, Valley of Cin., Masons. Avocations: sports, hunting. Home: 1440 Sedgefield Dr New Albany OH 43054 Office: Unizan Bank 66 S 3rd St Columbus OH 43215-4201

MANNING, SYLVIA, English studies educator; b. Montreal, Que., Can., Dec. 2, 1943; came to U.S., 1967; d. Bruno and Lea Bank; m. Peter J. Manning, Aug. 20, 1967; children— Bruce David, Jason Maurice B.A., McGill U., 1963; M.A., Yale U., 1964, Ph.D. in English, 1967. Asst. prof. English Calif. State U.-Hayward, 1967-71, assoc. prof., 1971-75, assoc. dean, 1972-75; assoc. prof. U. So. Calif., 1975-94, prof., assoc. dir. Ctr. for Humanities, 1975-77, assoc. dir. Ctr. for Humanities, 1975-77, chmn. freshman writing, 1977-80, chmn. dept. English, 1980-83, vice provost, exec. v.p., 1984-94; prof. English U. Ill., Champaign, 1994—, v.p. for acad. affairs, prof. English, 1994—, interim chancellor Chgo., 1999-2000, chancellor, 2000—. Author: Dickens as Satirist, 1971; Hard Times: An Annotated Bibliography, 1984. Contbr. essays to mags. Woodrow Wilson fellow, 1963-64, 66-67 Mem. MLA, Dickens Soc. Office: U of Ill Office of Chancellor 2833 University Hall 601 S Morgan St Chicago IL 60607-7100

MANNING, WILLIAM DUDLEY, JR. retired specialty chemical company executive; b. Tampa, Fla., Mar. 7, 1934; s. William Dudley and Rebecca (Reid) M.; m. Carol Randolph Gillis, June 30, 1962; children: Carol Randolph, Rebecca Barrett, Anne Gillis. BA in Chemistry, Fla. State U., 1957. Sales rep. Amoco Chem. Co., St. Louis and Cleve., 1959-63; sales engr. The Lubrizol Corp., Tulsa, 1963-64, southwestern regional sales mgr., 1964-66, mgr. chem. product sales Wickliffe, Ohio, 1966-72, sales mgr., western U.S., 1972, gen. sales mgr., asst. div. head-sales, 1972-79, mktg. mgr., asst. div. head-sales, 1979-80, v.p. mktg., 1980-81, v.p., bus. devel. div., 1981-85, sr. v.p. sales and mktg., 1985-87; pres. Lubrizol Petroleum Chems. Co., 1987-94; sr. v.p., asst. to pres. The Lubrizol Corp., 1994; cons., investor, 1994—. Bd. dirs. NYCO Am. LLC, Paterson, N.J., Robbins and Myers, Dayton, Ohio, UNIFRAX Corp., Niagara Falls, N.Y. Trustee Vocat. Guidance Svcs., Cleve., 1991-2000, Borromeo Sem., 2000—. With USAR, 1957-63. Mem. Soc. Automotive Engrs. (assoc.), Kirtland Country Club (v.p. 1986-88, pres. 1988-89), Tavern Club (trustee 1986-91), Chagrin Valley Hunt Club, Sand Ridge Golf Club. Republican. Roman Catholic. Office: 2550 S0M Center Rd Ste 120 Willoughby OH 44094 E-mail: wdmann@compuserve.com.

MANNING, WILLIAM HENRY, lawyer; b. Dallas, Feb. 5, 1951; BA, Creighton U., 1973; JD, Hamline U., 1978. Bar: Minn. 1978, U.S. Dist. Ct. Minn. 1978, U.S. Ct. Appeals (8th cir.) 1979; cert. civil trial specialist. Spl. asst. atty. gen. Minn. Atty. Gen.'s Office, St. Paul, 1980-83, dir. tort litigation div., 1984-86; ptnr. Robins, Kaplan, Miller & Ciresi, Mpls., 1986—. Office: Robins Kaplan Miller & Ciresi 800 Lasalle Ave Ste 2800 Minneapolis MN 55402-2015

MANNIX, PATRICK C. manufacturing company executive; Various positions Ralston Purina, Co. (formerly part of Union Carbide), Sydney, Australia, 1963-85; chmn. Eveready Battery Co. Asia Pacific, Hong Kong, 1985-91; exec. v.p. to corp. v.p. Ralston Purina, 1991, 92-95, pres. Eveready Specialty Bus., 1995-98; v.p., pres. Eveready Battery Co., Inc. Ralston Purina, Co., St. Louis, 1998—. Office: Ralston Purina Co Checkerboard Sq Saint Louis MO 63164-0001

MANOOGIAN, RICHARD ALEXANDER, manufacturing company executive; b. Long Branch, N.J., July 30, 1936; s. Alex and Marie (Tatian) M.; children: James, Richard, Bridget. B.A. in Econs, Yale U., 1958. Asst. to pres. Masco Corp., Taylor, Mich., 1958-62, exec. v.p., 1962-68, pres., 1968-85, chmn. bd., CEO, 1985—. Chmn., dir. Mascotech, Inc., Trimas Corp.; dir. First Chgo. NBD Corp., Detroit Renaissance, Am. Bus. Conf. Trustee U. Liggett Sch., State Dept. Fine Arts Comsn., Founder's Soc., Detroit Inst. Arts, Center for Creative Studies; trustee coun. Nat. Gallery Art. Mem. Yale Alumni Assn. Clubs: Grosse Pointe Yacht, Grosse Pointe Hunt, Country Club Detroit, Detroit Athletic. Office: Masco Corp 21001 Van Born Rd Taylor MI 48180-1300

MANOS, JOHN, editor-in-chief; Editor-in-chief Consumer's Digest, Chgo., 1987—. Office: Consumer Digest 8001 Lincoln Ave Skokie IL 60077-3695

MANOS, JOHN M. federal judge; b. Cleve., Dec. 8, 1922; m. Viola Manos; 4 children. BS, Case Inst. Tech., 1944; JD, Cleve.-Marshall Coll. Law, 1950. Bar: Ohio 1950. Asst. plant mgr. Lake City Malleable Iron Co., Cleve., 1946-50; atty. Manos & Manos, 1950-63; law dir. City of Bay Village, 1954-56; industries rep. Cleve. Regional Bd. of Rev., 1957-59; judge Ohio Ct. Common Pleas, Cuyahoga County, 1963-69, Ohio Ct. Appeals, Cuyahoga County, 1969-76; sr. judge U.S. Dist. Ct. (no. dist.) Ohio, Cleve., 1976-91, 1991—. With USN, 1942-45. Named Phi Alpha Delta Man of Yr., 1972, Outstanding Alumnus Cleve.- Marshall Law Alumni Assn., 1976. Mem. ABA, Fed. Bar Assn., Ohio State Bar Assn., Nat. Lawyers Club (hon.), Bar Assn. Greater Cleve., Cuyahoga County Bar Assn., Delta Theta Phi (Man of Yr. 1970). Office: US Dist Ct 201 Superior Ave E Cleveland OH 44114-1201

MANOUS, PETER J. lawyer; m. Susan Severtson Manous. BS in pub. adminstrn. & mgmt., Ind. Univ., 1984; law degree, Valparaiso U. , 1987. Bar: Ind. State Bar Assn. Pvt. atty., 1994—; coord. Frank O'Bannon's Campaign , 1996—2000; adv. Governor Residence Commn. Bd. dirs. Lake Area United Way; past pres. Millennium Housing Found.; Lake County Welfare to Work Coun.; mem. N.W. Ind. Quality Life Coun.; bd. dirs. Tradewinds; mem. Ind. Dem. Party Deputy Chairmen; regional coord. Evan Bayh U.S. Senate; vol. Kennedy for Pres. Campaign, 1980; mem. St. George Greek Orthodox Ch. Mem.: Am. Bar Assn., Lake County Bar Assn. Democrat. Office: 9111 Broadway Ste GG Merrillville IN 46410*

MANSELL, KEVIN B. retail executive; Sr. exec. v.p. merchandising and mktg. Kohl's Corp., Menomonee Falls, Wis., pres., also bd. dirs. Office: Kohl's Corp N 56 W 17000 Ridgewood Dr Menomonee Falls WI 53051

MANSFIELD, KAREN LEE, lawyer; b. Chgo., Mar. 17, 1942; d. Ralph and Hilda (Blum) Mansfield; children: Nicole Rafaela, Lori Michele. BA in Polit. Sci., Roosevelt U., 1963; JD, DePaul U., 1971; student U. Chgo., 1959-60. Bar: Ill. 1972, U.S. Dist. Ct. (no. dist.) Ill. 1972. Legis. intern Ill. State Senate, Springfield, 1966-67; tchr. Chgo. Pub. Schs., 1967-70; atty. CNA Ins., Chgo., 1971-73; law clk. Ill. Apellate Ct., Chgo., 1973-75; sr. trial atty. U.S. Dept. Labor, Chgo., 1975—, mentor Adopt-a-Sch. Program, 1992-95. Contbr. articles to profl. jours. Vol. Big Sister, 1975-81; bd. dirs. Altgeld Nursery Sch., 1963-66, Ill. div. UN Assn., 1966-72, Hull House Jane Addams Ctr., 1977-82, Broadway Children's Ctr., 1986-90, Acorn Family Entertainment, 1993-95; mem. Oak Park Farmers' Market Commn., 1996—; rsch. asst. Citizens for Gov. Otto Kerner, Chgo., 1964; com. mem. Ill. Commn. on Status of Women, Chgo., 1964-70; del. Nat. Conf. on Status of Women, 1968; candidate for del. Ill. Constl. Conv., 1969. Mem. Chgo. Council Lawyers, Women's Bar Assn. Ill., Lawyer Pilots Bar Assn., Fed. Bar Assn. Unitarian. Clubs: Friends of Gamelan (performer), 99's Internat. Orgn. Women Pilots (legis. chmn. Chgo. area chpt. 1983-86, legis. chmn. North Cen. sect. 1986-88, legis. award 1983, 85). Home: 204 S Taylor Ave Oak Park IL 60302-3307 Office: US Dept Labor Office Solicitor 230 S Dearborn St Fl 8 Chicago IL 60604-1505

MANSKE, PAUL ROBERT, orthopedic hand surgeon, educator; b. Ft. Wayne, Ind., Apr. 29, 1938; s. Alfred R. and Elsa E. (Streufert) M.; m. Sandra H. Henricks, Nov. 29, 1975; children: Ethan Paul, Claire Bruch, Louisa Hendricks. BA, Valparaiso U., 1960, DSc (hon.), 1985; MD, Washington U., St. Louis, 1964. Diplomate Am. Bd. Surgery. Intern U. Wash., Seattle, 1964-65, resident in surgery, 1965-66; resident in orthopedic surg. Washington U., St. Louis, 1969-72; hand surgery fellow U. Louisville, 1971; instr. orthopedic surgery Washington U. Med. Sch., St. Louis, 1972-76, asst. prof. orthopedic surgery, 1976-83, prof., 1983—, chmn. dept., 1983-95. Editor-in-chief Jour. Hand Surgery, 1996—; contbr. over 215 articles to profl. jours. Lt. comdr. USN, 1966-69, Vietnam. Fellow AMA, Am. Acad. Orthopaedic Surgery, Am. Orthopaedic Assn.; mem. Am. Soc. Surgery of the Hand, Alpha Omega Alpha. Lutheran. Office: Washington Univ Dept Orthop Surgery 1 Barnes Hospital Plz Saint Louis MO 63110-1036

MANSON, ANNE, music director; Grad., Harvard U.; postgrad., King's Coll., London, Royal Coll. Music, Royal Northern Coll. Music; studied with Norman Del Mar, James Lockhart. Music dir. Kansas City (Mo.) Symphony, 1998—. Condr. Mecklenburgh Opera, 1991, Endymion Ensemble, 1992-93, London Mozart Players, 1993-94, BBC Scottish Symphony and Iceland Symphony Orch., 1994-95, Northern Sinfonia, Resedentie Orch. in The Hague, Ensemble Inter Contemporain, Paris, 1996-97, Bournemouth Symphony Orch., Royal Scottish Nat. Orch., 1997-98. Dir. operas The Emperor of Atlantis, Die Weisse Rose, Manekiny, Hansel and Gretel, Marriage of Figaro, Cosi fan Tutte, The Magic Flute, Il Combattimento, Echoes, Royal Opera House, Don Pasquale, Don Giovanni, English Touring Opera, House of the Dead, Salzburg Festival, Lohengrin, Blood Wedding, 1992-93, Petrified, The Place Theatre, London, 1992, Brundibar, Queen Elizabeth Hall, London, 1993, Craig's Progress, 1994, Boris Godunov, Vienna State Opera, 1994, Vanessa, 1994-95, Rise and Fall of the City of Mahagonny, Netherlands Touring Opera, 1996, Dangerous Liaisons, Washington Opera, 1997, Voices, Berlin Biennale, 1997-98. Marshall scholar Royal Coll. Music; Conducting fellow Royal Northern Coll. Music. Office: Kansas City Symphony 1020 Central St Ste 300 Kansas City MO 64105-1663

MANSOORI, G. ALI, chemical engineer, educator; b. Naragh, Iran, Oct. 8, 1940; came to the U.S., 1964; s. Abbas and Khanam (Eslami) M.; m. Manijeh Mansoori, Jan. 10, 1992; 1 child, :Rana Mariam. BSChE, U. Tehran, 1963; MSChE, U. Minn., 1967; PhD, U. Okla., 1969; postdoctoral fellow, Rice U., 1969-70. Prof. U. Ill., Chgo., 1970—. Vis. scientist Argonne (Ill.) Nat. Lab., 1974-80, Nat. Inst. Standards and Tech., Boulder, Colo., 1983, 87, CRN-Pisa, Italy, 1985, 86; vis. prof. Bandug (Indonesia) Inst. Tech., 1992, 94; cons. numerous orgns. including Chevron, ARCO, Pertamina, NIOC, PEMEX, IMP, PETROBAS. Editor several jours.; series editor: Advances in Thermodynamics, 1987—; contbr. over 170 articles to profl. jours. Mem. AIChE, SPE, Internat. Non-Renewable Energy Source Conf. (tech. program chair 1993—), Internat. Fluid and Thermal Energy Conf. (tech. program co-chair 1994—). Avocations: mountain climbing, tennis, racquetball, swimming. Home: 1530 N Dearborn Pkwy Apt 23S Chicago IL 60610-1496

MANSOUR, GEORGE P. Spanish language and literature educator; b. Huntington, W.Va., Sept. 4, 1939; s. Elia and Marie (Yazbek) M.; m. Mary Ann Rogers, Dec. 27, 1961; children: Alicia, Philip. AB, Marshall U., 1961; MA, Mich. State U., 1963, PhD, 1965. Assoc. prof. Mich. State U., East Lansing, 1968-77, prof., 1977—, chmn. dept. Romance and Classical langs., 1982—. Cons. Mich. Dept. Edn., Lansing, 1984-85. Contbr. articles to profl. jours., including Hispania, Revista de estudias, hispanicos, also chpts. to books. Mem. Am. Assn. Tchrs. Spanish and Portuguese (v.p. 1969-71), Mich. Fgn. Lang. Assn. (pres. 1982-84). Democrat. Mem. Eastern Orthodox Ch. Avocations: Pysanky, golf. Home: 1303 Lucerne Dr Dewitt MI 48820-9528 Office: Mich State U Dept Romance & Classical Langs East Lansing MI 48824

MANTHEY, THOMAS RICHARD, lawyer; b. St. Cloud, Minn., May 5, 1942; s. Richard Jesse and Dolores Theresa (Terhaar) M.; m. Janet S. Barth, Dec. 18, 1965; children: Molly, Andrew, Luke. BA cum laude, St. John's U., Collegeville, Minn., 1964; JD cum laude, Harvard U., 1967. Bar: Minn. 1967. Assoc. Dorsey & Whitney, Mpls., 1967-73, ptnr. real estate dept., 1974—, also mem. Indian and gaming law practice group, chmn. real estate workout practice group. Contbr. articles to profl. jours. Capt. U.S. Army, 1968-70. Mem. Minn. State Bar Assn. (real estate sect.), Hennepin County Bar Assn. (real estate sect.). Roman Catholic. Avocations: volleyball, golf, fishing. Home: 9958 Wellington Ln Woodbury MN 55125-8459 Office: Dorsey & Whitney 220 S 6th St Ste 2200 Minneapolis MN 55402-1498

MANTIL, JOSEPH CHACKO, nuclear medicine physician, researcher; b. Kottayam, Kerala, India, Apr. 22, 1937; came to U.S., 1958; s. Chacko C. and Mary C. Manthuruthil; m. Joan J. Cunningham, June 18, 1966; children: Ann Marie, Lisa Susan. BS in Physics, Chemistry and Math. with distinction, Poona U., India, 1956; MS, U. Detroit, 1960; PhD, Ind. U., 1965; MS in Biological Scis., Wright State U., 1975; MD, U. Autonoma de Ciudad Juarez, Mex., 1977. Diplomate Am. Bd. Internal Medicine, Am. Bd. Nuclear Medicine; lic. physician, Ohio, Ind., Ky. Rsch. physicist Aerospace Rsch. Lab, Wright Patterson AFB, Ohio, 1964-75; chief resident, resident in internal medicine Good Samaritan Hosp., Dayton, 1977-80; chief resident, resident in nuclear medicine Cin. Med. Ctr., 1980-82; assoc. dir., divsn. nuclear med. Kettering (Ohio) Med. Ctr., 1982-86, dir. dept. nuclear medicine/PET, 1986—; dir. Kettering-Scott Magnetic Resonance Lab., Kettering Med. Ctr. Wright State U. Sch. Medicine, Kettering, 1985—, clin. prof. medicine, chief divsn. nuclear medicine, dept. medicine, 1988—. Served as session chmn., speaker, amd co-organizer for five internat. confs. Author: Radioactivity in Nuclear Spectroscopy Vol. I and II, 1972; contbr. 38 articles to profl. jours. Mem. ACP, Am. Physical Soc., Soc. Nuclear Medicine, Soc. Magnetic Resonance in Medicine, Soc. Magnetic Resonance Imaging. Achievements include research in proton and phosphorous NMR spectroscopy and glucose metabolism (using PET) in various types of dementia; use of NMR spectroscopy (both proton and phosphorous) and positron emission tomography (measurement of glucose and protein metabolism) in the study of tumors and assessment of thier reponse to chemotherapy and radiation therapy; positron emission tomography in the study of myocardial viabilty; PET in the diagnosis of coronary artery disease; PET in seizire disorders; PET in solid tumors, devel. of positron probe as an aid in the surgical vesection of tumors, gene therapy of glioblastoma mustiforme. Home: 6040 Mad River Rd Dayton OH 45459-1508 Office: Kettering Med Ctr 3535 Southern Blvd Kettering OH 45429-1221

MANTONYA, JOHN BUTCHER, lawyer; b. Columbus, Ohio, May 26, 1922; s. Elroy Letts and Blanche (Butcher) M.; m. Mary E. Reynolds, June 14, 1947 (dec. 1987); children: Elizabeth Claire, Mary Kay, Lee Ann; m. Carole L. Lugar, Sept. 28, 1989. A.B. cum laude, Washington and Jefferson Coll., 1943; postgrad., U. Mich. Law Sch., 1946-47; J.D., Ohio State U., 1949. Bar: Ohio 1949. Assoc. A.S. Mitchell (Atty.), Newark, 1949-50, C.D. Lindrooth, Newark, 1950-57; partner firm Lindrooth & Mantonya, 1957-74; firm John B. Mantonya, 1974-81, John B. Mantonya, L.P.A., 1981—. Mem. North Fork Local Bd. Edn., 1962-69; adv. com. Salvation Army, Licking County, 1965— , Mayor of, Utica, Ohio, 1953-59. Served with AUS, 1943-45. Mem. Am. Bar Assn., Ohio Bar Assn., Licking County Bar Assn. (pres. 1967), Phi Delta Phi, Beta Theta Pi. Home: 11055 Reynolds Rd Utica OH 43080-9549 Office: 3 N 3rd St Newark OH 43055-5506

MANTSCH, HENRY HORST, chemistry educator; b. Mediasch, Transylvania, Romania, July 30, 1935; emigrated to Can., 1968; s. Heinrich Johann and Olga Augusta (Gondosch) M.; m. Amy Emilia Kory, Nov. 2, 1959; children: Monica, Marietta. BSc, U. Cluj, Transylvania, 1958, PhD, 1964. Rsch. scientist Romanian Acad. Sci., Cluj, 1958-65, Tech. U. Munich, Germany, 1966-68; with NRC, Ottawa, Can., 1968-72; prof. biochemistry U. Cluj, 1973-74, Liebig U., Giessen, Germany, 1975-76; head molecular spectroscopy NRC, Ottawa, 1977—; mem. Can. Rsch. Coun., 1977-91, Winnipeg, Can., 1992—. Adj. prof. Carleton U., Ottawa, 1978-90, U. Ottawa, 1990-92, U. Manitoba, Winnipeg, 1992—. Contbr. articles to profl. jours.; patentee in field. Recipient medal Ministry of Edn., Bucharest, 1972, Humboldt Found. medal Bonn, 1980, Herzberg award, 1984, Marcus Marci medal, 1998; Chem. Inst. Can. fellow, 1979, Royal Soc. Can. fellow, 1982. Mem. Am. Biophys. Soc., Soc. Applied Spectroscopy, Chem. Inst. Can. (chmn. biol. chem. divsn. 1980-81), Can. Spectroscopy Soc. (nat. exec. com. 1981-90), Can. Biophys. Soc. (sec. 1999—). Home: 2222 W Taylor Blvd R3P 2J5 Winnipeg MB Canada R3P 2J5 Office: NRC Can 435 Ellice Ave Winnipeg MB Canada R3B 1Y6 E-mail: henry.mantsch@nrc.ca.

MANTULIN, WILLIAM W. biophysicist, laboratory director; b. Munich, Germany, Apr. 5, 1946; came to U.S., 1950; BS, U. Rochester, 1968; PhD, Northeastern U., 1972. Postdoctoral fellow Tex. Tech U., Lubbock, 1972-74, U. Ill., Urbana, 1975-77, adj. assoc. prof., 1986—, dir. Lab. Fluorescence Dynamics, 1986—; instr. Baylor Coll. Medicine, Houston, 1978-83, asst. prof., 1984-86. Cons. Exxon Corp., Houston, 1980-84. Author: (book chpt.) Fluorescent Biomolecules, 1989; contbr. articles to Bioimaging, Biochemistry. Recipient Paul Naney award Am. Heart Assn., 1987. Mem. Am. Chem. Soc., Am. Assn. Biochemistry and Molecular Biologists, Biophys. Soc. Achievements include patent for near infrared optical imaging. Office: U Ill Lab Fluorescence Dynamics 1110 W Green St Urbana IL 61801-3080 E-mail: lfd@uiuc.edu.

MANUEL, CHARLIE FUQUA, JR. professional baseball manager; children: Charles Jr., Julie. Outfielder Minn. Twins, 1963-74; with Bklyn. Dodgers, 1974-75, Yakult Swallows and Kintetsu Buffaloes, Japan, 1976-81; scout Minn. Twins, 1982; mgr. class A Wisconsin Rapids, 1983; various coaching and mgr. positions, 1983-99; mgr. Cleve. Indians, 1999—. Inducted Salem-Roanoke Baseball Hall of Fame, 1995. Office: Cleve Indians 2401 Ontario St Cleveland OH 44115-4003*

MANUEL, JERRY, professional sports team manager; b. Hahira, Ga., Dec. 23, 1953; m. Renette Caldwell; children: Angela, Jerry, Anthony, Natalie. Switch-hitting infielder Detroit Tigers, 1972, Class A Lakeland, Class AAA Toledo, 1973, Class AAA Evansville, 1974-75, Detroit Tigers, 1975-76, Montreal, Can., 1980-81, San Diego, 1982, Class AAA Iowa, 1983, Class AAA Denver, 1984; scout White Sox, 1985; player, coach Indpls. orgn., 1986, infield instr., 1987; minor-league fielding coord. Expos orgn., 1988-89; mgr. Class AAA Indpls. Montreal Expos Sys., 1991; coach maj. league baseball Montreal Expos, 1991-96; mgr. Chgo. White Sox, 1997—. Bench coach Fla. Marlins, 1997. Named So. League Mgr. of Yr., 1992. Office: Chgo White Sox 333 W 35th St Chicago IL 60616-3651*

MANUEL, RALPH NIXON, former private school executive; b. Frederick, Md., Apr. 21, 1936; s. Ralph Walter and Frances Rebecca (Nixon) M.; m. Sarah Jane Warner, July 22, 1960; children: Mark, David, Stephen, Bradley. A.B., Dartmouth Coll., 1958; M.Ed., Boston U., 1967; Ph.D., U. Ill., 1971. Assoc. dean Dartmouth Coll., Hanover, N.H., 1971-72, dean of freshmen, 1972-75, dean, 1975-82; pres. Culver (Ind.) Acad. and Culver Edn. Found., 1982-99. Bd. dirs. Ind. Sch. Cen. States, 1986-99, chair, 1993-95. Mem. Assn. Mil. Colls. and Schs. of U.S. (pres., bd. dirs.), Nat. Assn. Ind. Schs. (bd. dirs. 1995-99). E-mail: ralph.n.manuel@valley.net.

MANWARING, STEVE R. mechanical engineer; b. Conneaut, Ohio, Feb. 4, 1959; m. Rebecca Manwaring; children: Jonathan, Alyssa. BSME, Ohio U., 1982, MSME, 1984; PhD, Purdue U., 1989. Mech. engr. GE Aircraft Engines, Cin., 1989—. Recipient Gas Turbine award ASME, 1994. Mem. Internat. Gas Turbine Inst. Office: GE Aircraft Engines 1 Neumann Way Cincinnati OH 45215-1915

MANZ, JOHN R. bishop; Consecrated aux. bishop, 1996; aux. bishop Archdiocese of Chgo., 1996—. Office: 1820 S Leavitt St Chicago IL 60608-2518

MANZULLO, DONALD A, congressman, lawyer; b. Rockford, Ill., 1944; s. Frank A. Sr. and Catherine M.; m. Freda Teslik; children: Neil, Noel, Katie. BA in Polit. Sci./Internat. Rels., American U., 1967; JD, Marquette U. Law Sch. Atty., 1970—; mem. U.S. Congress from 16th Ill. Dist., 1993—. Mem. House Com. on Internat. Rels., subcom. internat. econ. policy and trade, subcom. on Asia and the Pacific, House Com. on small bus., chmn. on subcom. on tax, fin. and exports, Banking Com. and its capital markets, securities and govt.-sponsored enterprises subcom. Mem. No. Ill. Alliance for Arts, Friends of Severson Dells, Citizens Against Govt. Waste, Rep. Nat. Com. Recipient George Washington honor medal for excellence in pub. comm. Freedoms Found., Valley Forge, Pa., 1991. Mem. ABA, Ill. Bar Assn., Ogle County Bar Assn. (pres. 1971, 73), Nat. Legal Found., Acad. Polit. Sci., Ill. Press Assn., Ill. C. of C., Oregon City C. of C., Nat. Land Inst., Nat. Fedn. Ind. Bus., Ogle County Hist. Soc., Aircraft Owners and Pilots Assn., Ogle County Pilots Assn., Ill. Farm Bur., Ogle County Farm Bur. Office: US Ho of Reps 409 Cannon Bldg Ofcbld Washington DC 20515-0001*

MAPOTHER, DILLON EDWARD, physicist, university official; b. Louisville, Aug. 22, 1921; s. Dillon Edward and Edith (Rubel) M.; m. Elizabeth Beck, June 29, 1946; children: Ellen, Susan, Anne. B.S. in Mech. Engring, U. Louisville, 1943; D.Sc. in Physics, Carnegie-Mellon U., 1949. Engr. Westinghouse Research Labs., East Pittsburgh, Pa., 1943-46; instr. Carnegie Inst. Tech., Pitts., 1946; mem. faculty U. Ill., Urbana, 1949-94, prof. physics, 1959-94, dir. acad. computing services, 1971-76, assoc. vice chancellor for research, 1976-94, acting dean grad. coll., vice chancellor research, 1977-78, assoc. dean grad. coll., 1979-94, assoc. vice chancellor rsch. emeritus, 1995—, assoc. dean emertus grad. coll., prof. emeritus physics, 1995—. Cons. in field. DuPont fellow, 1947-49; Alfred P. Sloan fellow, 1958-61; Guggenheim fellow, 1960-61 Fellow Am. Phys. Soc.; mem. AAAS, Assn. Univ. Tech. Mgrs., Am. Assn. Physics Tchrs., Sigma Xi. Achievements include research on ionic mobility in alkali halides, thermodynamic properties of superconductors, calorimetric study of critical points, administration of university research, commercialization of academic research technology. Home: 1013 Ross Dr Champaign IL 61821-6631 Office: U Ill Physics Dept Loomis Lab 1110 W Green St Urbana IL 61801-9013 E-mail: mapother@staff.uiuc.edu.

MARA, JOHN LAWRENCE, retired veterinarian, consultant; b. Whitesboro, N.Y., May 17, 1924; s. William Edward and Olive Pearl (Brakefield) M.; m. Kathleen Keefe, 1946 (div. 1958); children: William, Michael, Daniel, Patrick; m. Patricia Louise Paulk, 1970 (div. 1994); children: Jennifer Lee, Kennon. DVM, Cornell U., 1951. Diplomate Am. Coll. Vet. Nutrition. Intern N.Y. State Coll. Vet. Medicine, Cornell U., Ithaca, 1951-52; assoc. veterinarian L.W. Goodman Animal Hosp., Manhasset, N.Y., 1952-55; owner, pres. Mara Animal Hosp., Huntington, 1955-79; profl. rep. Hills Pet Products, Topeka, 1979-80, mgr. profl. rels., 1980-81, dir. profl. affairs, 1981-88, dir. vet. affairs, 1988-94, sr. fellow profl. and acad. affairs, 1994-97, sr. fellow global vet. bus. devel., 1997-2000; ret., 2000. V.p. Huntington United Fund; chmn. Huntington Taxpayers Party, 1968-78, Ch. in the Garden, Garden City, N.Y., 1975-77, trustee, 1975-77; trustee, v.p. vet. divsn. Morris Animal Found. Sgt. U.S. Army, 1943-45, ETO. Recipient Disting. Svc. award We. Vet. Conf., 1988; named hon. alumnus Coll. Vet. Medicine, Wash. State U.; Jack L. Deans scholarship named in his honor Sch. Vet. Medicine U. Pa. Mem. AVMA (Pres.'s award, Jack L. Mara vet. technician program), L.I. Vet. Medicine Assn., N.Y. State Vet. Medicine Assn. (Outstanding Svc. award 2001), Am. Animal Hosp. Assn. (disting. life, Outstanding Svc. award 1996-97), Kans. Vet. Medicine Assn., Am. Coll. Vet. Nutrition (hon. diplomate). Republican. Baptist. Avocations: gardening, swimming, reading. Home: 6439 SW Castle Ln Topeka KS 66614-4392 E-mail: jmara@kscable.com.

MARANS, ROBERT WARREN, architect, planner; b. Detroit, Aug. 3, 1934; s. Albert and Anne Rose (Siegel) M.; m. Judith Ann Bloomfield, Jan. 24, 1956; children: Gayl Elizabeth, Pamela Jo. BArch, U. Mich., 1957; M in Urban Planning, Wayne State U., 1961; PhD, U. Mich., 1971. Reg. architect, Mich. Archtl. engr., planner Detroit City Planning Comn., 1957-61; planning cons. Blair & Stein Assocs., Providence, 1961-64; architect-urban designer Artur Glikson, Architect, Tel Aviv, Israel, 1964-65; regional planner Detroit Area Transp. Land Use Study, 1965-67; asst. prof. Fla. State U., Talahassee, 1967; rsch. assoc., sr. study dir. Inst. Social Rsch., Ann Arbor, Mich., 1968-74, sr. rsch. scientist, 1974—; from lectr. to assoc. prof. Coll. Architecture Urban Planning, 1971-78; prof. architecture and urban planning U. Mich., 1978—. Cons. TVA, 1972, UN, 1974; chmn. urban and regional planning program, 1987-98. Co-author: Planned Residential Environments, 1970, Quality of NonMetropolitan Living, 1978, Evaluating Built Environments, 1981, Retirement Communities: An American Original, 1984; co-editor: Methods of Environmental and Behavioral Research, 1987, Environmental Stimulation: Research and Policy Perspectives, 1993, Advances in Environment, Behavior and Design, vol. IV, 1997; contbr. articles to profl. jours. and tech. reports. Sec. Washtenaw County Parks Recreation Commn., Ann Arbor, 1972—; chmn. Huron-Clinton Met. Parks Authority, Brighton, Mich., 1986—. Recipient fellow Social Sci. Rsch. Coun., 1969-70; Fulbright Rsch. award Coun. Internat. Exchange Scholars, Israel, 1977; Progressive Architecture Applied Rsch. award Progressive Architecture Mag., 1982; Design Rsch. Recognition award Nat. Endowment for Arts, 1983. Mem. Am. Planning Assn., Nat. Recreation Pk. Assn., Environ. Design Rsch. Assn. Avocations: swimming, stamp collecting. Office: U Mich Coll Arch and Urban Planning Ann Arbor MI 48109 E-mail: marans@umich.edu.

MARBLE, DUANE FRANCIS, geography educator, researcher; b. Seattle, Dec. 10, 1931; s. Francis Augustus and Beulah Belle (Simmons) M.; m. Jacquelynne Hardester, Aug. 18, 1957; children: Kimberley Eileen Beauclair, Douglas Craig. BA, U. Wash., 1953, MA, 1956, PhD, 1959. Asst. prof. real estate U. Oreg., Eugene, 1959; asst. prof. regional sci. U. Pa., Phila., 1960-63; from assoc. prof. geography to prof. geography Northwestern U., Evanston, Ill., 1963-73, assoc. dir. Transp. Ctr., 1966-73; prof. geography and computer sci. SUNY at Buffalo, Amherst, N.Y., 1973-87; prof. geography and natural resources Ohio State U., Columbus, 1987-98, prof. emeritus, 1998—. Chmn. com. on geog. data sensing and processing Internat. Geog. Union, 1980-88; bd. dirs. Castlereagh Enterprises, Phoenix; founder Internat. Symposium Spatial Data Handling; cons. on geog. info. systems to U.S. Bur. Census, UN, also pvt. orgns. Editor: Intro Readings in GIS, 1990, Taylor & Francis, 1990-95; author computer program (best software award Assn. Am. Geogs. 1990); mem. editl. bd. Annals of Assn. Am. Geography, 2000—. Recipient Legend in Leadership award Environ. Sys. Rsch. Inst., 1997. Mem.: IEEE Computer Soc., AAAS, Assn. Am. Geographers (honors 1993). Home: 1310 Langston Dr Upper Arlington OH 43220-3900 Office: Ohio State U Ctr for Mapping Columbus OH 43212

MARBLE, GARY, state legislator; Mem. dist. 130 Mo. Ho. of Reps., 1994—. Home: 1616 Ridgewood Neosho MO 64850-6821 Office: State Capitol Bldg Rm 203A Jefferson City MO 65101

MARCDANTE, KAREN JEAN, associate dean; b. Milw., Sept. 15, 1955; d. Willard Karl and Beth Elaine (Maule) Kohn; m. Mark Wendelberger, Aug. 5, 1978 (div. Sept. 1985); m. Anthony Marcdante, Oct. 17, 1998. Student, Marquette U., 1973-76; MD, Med. Coll. Wis., 1980. Diplomate Am. Bd. Pediat. Resident in pediat. Med. Coll. Wis. affiliated hosps., Milw., 1980-83; instr. pediat. Med. Coll. Wis., 1983-85, asst. prof. pediat., 1987-94, assoc. prof. pediat., 1994-2000, prof. pediat., 2000—, assoc. dean curriculum, 1997—, vice-chair edn. dept. pediat., 1994—; fellow in pediatric critical care U. Calif., San Francisco, 1985-87; vice chief staff Children's Hosp. Wis., Milw., 1995-97. Dir. Respiratory Care Svcs., 1992-98, Transport Program, 1998—; chief dept. pediat. Children's Hosp. Wis., 1991-95, dept. critical care 1993-95, mem. numerous coms., including care mgmt. steering com., 1994—, critical care com., 1991—. Contbr. numerous articles to profl. jours. Recipient New Investigator award Assn. Am. Med. Colls., 1992, Cert. Leadership award YWCA and Marquette Electronics Found., 1992; grantee Dept. HHS, 1996—. Mem. Am. Acad. Pediat. (pub. rels. chair Wis. chpt. 1988-91, sec.-treas. 1990-95, v.p. 1995-96, chair careers and opportunities 1996—), Soc. Critical Care Medicine (chair task force on quality improvement pediat. 1994—, quality indicator devel. work group 1997—, Presdl. citation 1996, 97), Coun. on Med. Student Edn. in Pediat. (co-chair task force on tchg. methods 1991—, nominating com. 1993—, exec. com. 1996—, sec.-treas. 1997—). E-mail: kwendel@mail.mcw.edu.

MARCHESE, RONALD THOMAS, ancient history and archaeology educator; b. Fresno, Calif., Mar. 17, 1947; s. John Anthony and Julie Rita (Ferrarese) M.; m. Marcia Lynn Schneider, Apr. 6, 1974 (div. Apr. 1980); 1 child, Stephanie Jo; m. K. Werdin, 1988; children: Alexander Joseph, Kayla Marie. BA summa cum laude, Calif. State U., Fresno, 1970; MA, N.Y.U., 1972, PhD with distinction, 1976; postgrad., Columbia U., 1972-73. Asst. prof. Va. Poly. Inst., Blacksburg, 1976-77; asst. to assoc. prof. ancient history and archaeology U. Minn., Duluth, 1977-87, prof., 1987—. Rsch. assoc. dept. classics NYU, 1972-74; evaluator grant proposals NEH, HSF; excavator numerous sites in Israel, Turkey, and Greece; lectr. in field. Author, editor 7 books; author articles on nomadic material culture and religious textiles. Recipient Fulbright-Hays Sr. Research fellowship, Turkey, 1984-85, 91-92, The Am. Council Learned Socs. fellowship, 1977-78, NDEA Title VI Fgn. Languages fellowship, 1972-75, Spl. Commendation for Excellence award Phi Alpha Theta, 1979; grantee NEH, 1978, 80, nat. Geographic Soc., 1974, Andrew Mellon Found., NSF, Ford Found., 1971-72, U. Minn., others. Mem. NEH, Nat. Assn. Scholars, Coun. for Internat. Exchange, Am. Coun. Learned Socs., Fulbright Alumni Assn., Phi Alpha Theta, Sigma Xi, Alpha Phi Omega. Roman Catholic. Avocations: tennis, golf, dressage. Home: 5789 220th St N Forest Lake MN 55025-9677 E-mail: ronmarchese@hotmail.com.

MARCIL, WILLIAM CHRIST, SR. publisher, broadcast executive; b. Rolette, N.D., Mar. 9, 1936; s. Max L. and Ida (Fuerst) M.; m. Jane Black, Oct. 15, 1960; children: Debora Jane, William Christ Jr. BSBA, U. N.D., 1958. Br. mgr. Community Credit Co., Mpls., 1959-61; with Forum Comms. Co., Fargo, N.D., 1961—, pres., pub., CEO, 1969—. Pres. Forum Comm. Found.; past bd. dirs. North Ctrl. region Boy Scouts Am. With U.S. Army, 1958-59. Mem. Inland Newspaper Press Assn., N.D. Press Assn., Am. Newspaper Pubs. Assn. (past dir., chmn.), Fargo and Morehead C. of C., N.D. State C. of C. (past pres.), U.S. C. of C. (past chmn.), Sigma Delta Chi, Lambda Chi Alpha. Republican. Lodges: Masons, Shriners, Elks, Rotary. Office: Forum Comm Co 101 5th St N Fargo ND 58102-4826 Home: 7770 E Vaquero Dr Scottsdale AZ 85258-2101

MARCOUX, WILLIAM JOSEPH, lawyer; b. Detroit, Jan. 20, 1927; s. Lona J. and Anna (Ransom) C.; m. Kae Marie Sanborn, Aug. 23, 1952; children: Ann K., William C. BA, U. Mich., 1949, JD, 1952. Bar: Mich. 1953. Pvt. practice, Pontiac, Mich., 1953; assoc. McKone, Badgley, Domke and Kline, Jackson, 1953-65, ptnr., 1965-75; dir. Marcoux, Allen, Abbott, Schomer & Bower, P.C., 1975—. Mem. exec. bd. Great Sauk Trail council Boy Scouts Am., pres., 1965-66; bd. dirs. Jackson County United Way, pres., 1983-84. Served with USNR, 1945-46. Recipient Silver Beaver award Boy Scouts Am., 1969, Disting. Citizen award Land O'Lakes coun. Boy Scouts Am., 1991. Fellow Am. Coll. Trial Lawyers, Mich. State Bar Found.; mem. Mich. State Bar Assn., Jackson County Bar Assn. (pres. 1979-80), Jackson Rotary Club (pres. 1963-64), Country Club of Jackson, Clark Lake Yacht Club (hon., commodore 1959). Methodist. Home: 1745 Malvern Dr Jackson MI 49203-5378 Office: Marcoux Allen Abbott Schomer & Bower PC PO Box 787 Jackson MI 49204-0787 E-mail: wmarcoux@marcouxallen.com.

MARCOVICH, TOBY, lawyer; BS, JD, U. Wis. Instr. sociology U. Minn., Duluth, 1978—83; instr. trial practice U. Wis., Madison, Wis., 1987—88. Mem. bd. regents U. Wis., Wis., former mem. found. bd. Mem.: ATLA, Lawyer Pilots Bar Assn., Wis. Acad. Trial Lawyers (former bd. dirs.). Office: Marcovich Cochrane & Milliken 1214 Belknap St Superior WI 54880

MARCUM, JOSEPH LARUE, insurance company executive; b. Hamilton, Ohio, July 2, 1923; s. Glen F. and Helen A. (Stout) M.; m. Sarah Jane Sloneker, Mar. 7, 1944; children: Catharine Ann Marcum Lowe, Joseph Timothy (dec.), Mary Christina Marcum Manchester, Sarah Jennifer Marcum Shuffield, Stephen Sloneker. B.A., Antioch Coll., 1947; M.B.A. in Fin, Miami U., 1965. With Ohio Casualty Ins. Co. and affiliates, 1947—, now chmn. bd., also bd. dirs. Capt., inf. U.S. Army. Mem. Soc. CPCU, Queen City Club, Bankers Club, Princeton Club N.Y., Little Harbor club, Walloon Lake Country Club, Mill Reef Club. Presbyterian. Office: Ohio Casualty Corp 136 N 3rd St Hamilton OH 45011-2726 Home: 1278 Stephanie Dr Hamilton OH 45013-1290

MARCUS, DONALD HOWARD, advertising executive; b. Cleve., May 16, 1916; s. Joseph and Sarah (Schmitman) Marcus; m. Helen Olen Weiss, Feb. 12, 1959; children: Laurel Kathy Heifetz, Carol Susan, James Randall(dec.) , Jonathan Anthony. BA, Cleve. State U., 1996. Mem. publicity dept. Warner Bros. Pictures, Cleve., 1935-37; mem. advt. dept. RKO Pictures, 1937-40; mem. sales dept. Monogram Pictures, 1940-42; pres. Marcus Advt. Inc., 1946-85, chmn., 1986-2000; chmn. emeritus Marcus Thomas, 2001—. Vice-chmn. comm. divsn. Jewish Welfare Fund Appeal Cleve., 1964—70, chmn., 1971—72; trustee Cleve. Jewish News, 1974—96, v.p., 1983—85; mem. Ohio Dem. Exec. Com., 1969—70, del. nat. conv., 1968; trustee Jewish Cmty. Fedn., 1973—74, No. Ohio regional office Anti-Defamation League of B'nai B'rith, 1986—, Jewish Cmty. Ctr., 1988—90; bd. dirs. Cuyahoga County unit Am. Cancer Soc., 1979—, Cleve. State U. Devel. Found., 1987—. Recipient Disting. Alumnus award, Cleve. State U., 2001. Mem.: NATAS (Silver Cir. award 1994), Cleve. Advt. Club (elected to Hall of Fame), Mensa, Clee. Growth Assn., Beechmont Country Club (past pres.), Union Club Cleve., Ohio Commodores. Jewish. Home: 22449 Shelburne Rd Cleveland OH 44122-2053 Office: Marcus Thomas 25700 Science Park Dr Cleveland OH 44122-7319

MARCUS, JOHN, wholesale distribution executive; b. N.Y.C., Oct. 18, 1941; s. Sam and Margaret (McCoy) M.; m. Helen S. Bondurant, Aug. 14, 1965; children: Lisa Marie, Lynn Michelle. AA, Wentworth Mil. Acad., Lexington, Mo., 1961. Buyer Foley Bros. Dept. Stores, Houston, 1963-65; owner JOMARC, 1965-66; sales mgr. Firestone Tire & Rubber Co., 1966-67; distbn. mgr. Matthews Book Co., St. Louis, 1967-69, office mgr., 1969, gen. mgr., 1970, v.p. ops., 1971, pres., 1972, chmn., CEO, 1974—. Pres., CEO McCoy Collegiate Svcs., St. Louis, 1969—, NACSCORP Inc., Oberlin, Ohio, 1983, Coll. Stores Rsch. and Edn. Found., 1984-85, chmn., CEO Founders Bookstore Svcs.; CEO Coll. Bookstores of Am., St. Louis, 1986—. Contbr. articles to publs. Bd. dirs. YMCA, Wentworth Mil. Acad. Mem. Nat. Assn. Coll. Stores (pres. 1981-82), The Employee Stock Ownership Plans Assn. Office: Matthews Book Co 11559 Rock Island Ct Maryland Heights MO 63043-3596

MARCUS, JOSEPH, child psychiatrist; b. Cleve., Feb. 27, 1928; s. William and Sarah (Marcus) Schwartz; m. Cilla Furmanovitz, Oct. 3, 1951; children: Oren, Alon. B.Sc., Western Res. U., 1963; M.D., Hebrew U., 1958. Intern Tel Hashomer Govt. Hosp., Israel, 1956-57; resident in psychiatry and child psychiatry Ministry of Health, Govt. of Israel, 1958-61; acting head dept. child psychiatry Ness Ziona Rehab. Ctr., 1961-62; sr. psychiatrist Lasker dept. child psychiatry Hadassah U. Hosp., 1962-64; research asso. Israel Inst. Applied Social Research, 1966-69; practice medicine specializing in psychiatry Jerusalem, 1966-72; assoc. dir. devel. neuropsychiatry Jerusalem Infant and Child Devel. Ctr., 1969-70; dept. head Eytanim Hosp., 1970-72; cons. child psychiatrist for Jerusalem Ministry of Health, 1970-72; dir. dept. child psychiatry and devel. Jerusalem Mental Health Ctr., 1972-75; prof. child psychiatry, dir. unit for research in child psychiatry and devel. U. Chgo., 1975-85, prof. emeritus, co-dir. unit for research in child psychiatry and devel., 1986—; vis. research psychiatrist UCLA Dept. Psychiatry, 1987—. Chief editor: Early Child Devel. and Care, 1972-76; mem. editorial bd.: Israel Annals of Psychiatry and Related Disciplines, 1965-70, Internat. Yearbook of Child Psychiatry and Allied Professions, 1968-74; contbr. articles to med. jours. Mem. Am. Acad. Child Psychiatry (com. on research, com. on psychiat. aspects of infancy), Soc. Research in Child Devel., Internat. Assn. Child Psychiatry and Allied Professions (asst. gen. sec. 1966-74), European Union Paedopsychiatry (hon.), World, Israel psychiat. assns., Internat. Coll. Psychosomatic Medicine, Israel Center Psychobiology. Home: 910 Chelham Way Santa Barbara CA 93108-1049 Office: # MC 3077 5841 S Maryland Ave Chicago IL 60637-1463 E-mail: jmarcusmd@cox.net.

MARCUS, JOYCE, anthropology educator; Prof. of anthropology, mus. anthropology U. Mich., Ann Arbor.

MARCUS, LARRY DAVID, broadcast executive; b. N.Y.C., Jan. 27, 1949; s. Oscar Moses and Sylvia (Ackerman) Marcus; children from previous marriage: Julia Ilene, Barbara Maureen. BBA, CUNY, 1970, postgrad. studies Bus. Admistrn., 1970-72. Acctg. mgr. Sta. WPLG-TV, Miami, Fla., 1974-75; v.p., bus. mgr. Sta. KPLR-TV-Koplar Comm., Inc., St. Louis, 1976-82; chief fin. officer Koplar Comm., Inc., 1982-88, River City Broadcasting Co., St. Louis, 1988-96; gen. ptnr. Marcus Investments, L.P., 1996—; CEO Peak Media Holdings LLC, Clayton, Mo., 1997—. Bd. dirs. Radio One, Inc. Bd. dirs. Kids in the Mid., St. Louis Nat. Pub. Radio. Mem.: Broadcast Cable Fin. Mgmt. Assn. (bd. dirs. 1976—89, treas. 1989—90, sec. 1990—91, v.p 1991—92, pres. 1992—93). Jewish. Avocations: sports, skiing, golf, scuba diving. Office: Peak Media LLC 248 Gay Ave Clayton MO 63105-3622 E-mail: ldmarcus@aol.com.

MARCUS, RICHARD STEVEN, lawyer; b. Cin., May 26, 1950; s. Bernard Benjamin and Norma (Ginsberg) M.; m. Jane Iris Schreiber, Sept. 12, 1971; children: Rebecca, Sarah. BA in English, U. Wis., 1972; JD, Harvard U., 1975. Bar: Wis. 1975, U.S. Tax Ct. 1976, U.S. Ct. Appeals (7th cir.) 1977, U.S. Dist. Ct. (ea. dist.) Wis. 1979, U.S. Ct. Claims 1979. Assoc. Godfrey & Kahn, S.C., Milw., 1975—. Pres., Milw. Assn. for Jewish Edn., 1992; bd. dirs. Milw. Jewish Fedn., 1992, Milw. chpt. Jewish Nat. Fund, 1992. Office: Godfrey & Kahn SC 780 N Water St Ste 1500 Milwaukee WI 53202-3590

MARCUS, STEPHEN HOWARD, hospitality and entertainment company executive; b. Mpls., May 31, 1935; s. Ben D. and Celia Marcus; m. Joan Glasspiegel, Nov. 3, 1962; children: Greg, David, Andrew. B.B.A., U. Wis., Madison, 1957; LL.B., U. Mich., 1960. Bar: Wis. 1960. V.p. Pfister Hotel Corp., Milw., 1963-69, exec. v.p., 1969-75; pres. Marcus Hotel Corp., 1975-91; chmn., COO Marcus Corp., 1980—, COO, dir., 1988; exec. v.p. Marc Plaza Corp.; v.p. Wis. Big Boy Corp., Marcus Theatres Corp., Milw.; dir. Med. Coll. Wis., 1986—; chmn., CEO Marcus Corp. Dir. Preferred Hotels Assn., 1972—, chmn. bd., 1979; dir. Bank One N.A. Pres. Milw. Conv. and Visitors Bur., 1970-71, bd. dirs., mem. exec. com., 1968—; chmn. Wis. Gov.'s Adv. Council on Tourism, 1976-81; bd. dirs. Multiple Sclerosis Soc. Milw., 1965-67, Milw. Jewish Fedn., 1968-76, Milw. Jewish Chronicle, 1973-76, Children's Hosp. Found., Inc., Competitive Wis.; asso. chmn. bus. div. United Fund Campaign, Milw., 1971; co-chmn. spl. gifts com. United Performing Arts Fund, Milw., 1972-74, bd. dirs., 1973-81, chmn. maj. gifts, 1982, co-chmn., 1983— ; bd. dirs. Friends of Art, Milw., 1973-74; pres. Summerfest, 1975; bd. dirs. MECCA, Milw., 1975-82, mem. exec. com., 1977; bd. dirs. Jr. Achievement, Milw., 1976— ; trustee Mt. Sinai Med. Center, 1977— , Nat. Symphony Orchestra, 1985; bd. govs. Jewish Community Campus; co-chmn. Ann. Freedom Fund Dinner, NAACP, 1980-81; chmn. Icebreaker Festival, 1989. Served with U.S. Army, 1960-61. Recipient Ben Nickoll award Milw. Jewish Fedn., 1969, Headliner award Milw. Press Club, 1986, Humanitarian award NCCJ, 1988, Lamplighter award Greater Milw. Conv. and Visitors Bur., 1991. Mem. Am. Hotel and Motel Assn. (dir. 1976-79, exec. com. 1978-79), Greater Milw. Hotel and Motel Assn. (pres. 1967-68), Wis. Innkeepers Assn. (pres. 1972-73), Variety Club, Milw. Assn. Commerce (bd. dirs. 1982-85), Downtown Assn., Young Pres.'s Orgn., Wis. Assn. Mfrs. and Commerce (dir. 1978-82), Greater Milw. Com. (dir. 1981) Office: The Marcus Corporation 250 E Wisconsin Ave Ste 1700 Milwaukee WI 53202-4217

MARELLI, SISTER MARY ANTHONY, secondary school principal; Prin. Boylan Ctrl. Cath. High Sch., Rockford, Ill. Recipient Blue Ribbon Sch. award U.S. Dept. Edn., 1986-87, 90-91. Office: Boylan Ctrl Cath High Sch 4000 Saint Francis Dr Rockford IL 61103-1661

MARENDT, CANDACE L. state legislator; Student, Ind. U. Mem. Ind. State Ho. of Reps. Dist. 94, mem. commerce and econ. devel. com., mem. judiciary and pub. safety com., vice-chmn. families, children and human affairs com. Mem. MIBOR, Circle City Child Care Assn., N.W. Roundtable, Pike, Wayne, Washington and Eagle Creek GOP Clubs. also: Electronics Divsn 302 W Washington St Rm 204 Indianapolis IN 46204

MARES, HARRY, state legislator; b. Dec. 21, 1938; m. Geri Mares; 7 children. BA, Loras Coll., Dubuque, Iowa; MS, Winona State U. Minn. state rep. Dist. 55A, 1994—. Former tchr. Address: 2592 Crown Hill Ct White Bear Lake MN 55110-4974

MARGERUM, DALE WILLIAM, chemistry educator; b. St. Louis, Oct. 20, 1929; s. Donald C. and Ida Lee (Nunley) M.; m. Sonya Lora Pedersen, May 16, 1953; children: Lawrence Donald, Eric William, Richard Dale. BA, S.E. Mo. State U., 1950; PhD, Iowa State U., 1955. Research chemist Ames Lab., AEC, Iowa, 1952-53; instr. Purdue U., West Lafayette, Ind., 1954-57, asst. prof., 1957-61, assoc. prof., 1961-65, prof., 1965-97, disting. prof. chemistry, 1997—, head dept. chemistry, 1978-83. Inorganic-analytical chemist, vis. scientist Max Planck Inst., 1963, 70; vis. prof. U. Kent, Canterbury, Eng., 1970; mem. med. chem. study sect. NIH, 1965-69; mem. adv. com. Research Corp., 1973-78; mem. chemistry evaluation panel Air Force Office Sci. Research, 1978-82 Cons. editor McGraw Hill, 1962-72; mem. editorial bd. Jour. Coordination Chemistry, 1971-81, Analytical Chemistry, 1967-69, Inorganic Chemistry, 1985-88. Recipient Grad. Rsch. award Phi Lambda Upsilon, 1954, Alumni Merit award S.E. Mo. State U., 1991, Sagamore of the Wabash, State of Ind., 1994; NSF sr. postdoctoral fellow, 1963-64. Fellow AAAS; mem. AAUP, Am. Chem. Soc. (chmn. Purdue sect. 1965-66, com. on profl. tng. 1993—, Disting. Svc. award in advancement of inorganic chemistry 1996), Sigma Xi (Monie A. Ferst award 2000), Phi Lambda Upsilon. Office: Dept Chemistry Purdue U West Lafayette IN 47907

MARGOLIASH, EMANUEL, biochemist, educator; b. Cairo, Feb. 10, 1920; s. Wolf and Bertha (Kotler) M.; m. Sima Beshkin, Aug. 22, 1944; children: Reuben, Daniel. BA, Am. U., Beirut, 1940, MA, 1942, MD, 1945. Rsch. fellow, lectr., acting head cancer rsch. labs. Hebrew U., Jerusalem, 1945-58; rsch. fellow Molteno Inst. Cambridge (Eng.) U., 1951-53; Dazian fellow Nobel Inst., 1958; rsch. assoc. U. Utah, Salt Lake City, 1958-60, McGill U., Montreal, Que., Can., 1960-62; rsch. fellow Abbott Labs., North Chicago, Ill., 1962-69, sr. rsch. fellow, 1969-71, head protein sect., 1962-71; prof. biochemistry and molecular biology Northwestern U., Evanston, Ill., 1971-90, prof. chemistry, 1985-90, Owen L. Coon prof. molecular biology, 1988-90, Owen L. Coon prof. molecular biology emeritus, 1990—; prof. biol. scis. U. Ill., Chgo., 1989—, coord. lab. for molecular biology, 1990-93. Mem. com. on cytochrome nomenclature Internat. Union Biochemistry, 1962-75 ; mem. adv. com. Plant Research Lab., Mich. State U./AEC, 1967-72; co-chmn. Gordon Research Conf. on Proteins, 1967 Editl. bd. Jour. Biol. Chemistry, 1966-72, Biochem. Genetics, 1966-80, Jour. Molecular Evolution, 1971-82, Biochemistry and Molecular Biology Internat., 1981-99, Jour. Protein Chemistry, 1982-86, Chemtracts, Biochem. Molecular Biology, 1990-99; contbr. over 280 articles and revs. to sci. jours. Rudi Lemberg fellow Australian Acad. Sci., 1981; Guggenheim fellow, 1983 Fellow Am. Acad. Arts and Scis., Am. Acad. Microbiology, Am. Inst. Chemists; mem. Nat. Acad. Scis., Biochem. Soc. (Keilin Meml. lectr. 1970), Harvey Soc. (lectr. 1970-71), Am. Soc. Biochem. Molecular Biology (publs. com. 1973-76), Am. Chem. Soc., Am. Soc. Microbiology, Can. Biochem. Soc., Soc. Devel. Biology, Biophys. Soc. (exec. com. U.S. bioenergetics group 1980-83), N.Y. Acad. Sci., Ill. Acad. Sci., Am. Soc. Naturalists, Sigma Xi (nat. lectr. 1972-73, 74-77). Home: 353 Madison Ave Glencoe IL 60022-1809 Office: Univ Ill Chgo Dept Bio-Scis MC 066 845 W Taylor St Dept Bio Chicago IL 60607-7056

MARGOLIS, PHILIP MARCUS, psychiatrist, educator; b. Lima, Ohio, July 7, 1925; s. Harry Sterling and Clara (Brunner) M.; m. Nancy Nupuf, July 26, 1959; children: Cynthia, Marc, David, Laurence. B.A. magna cum laude, U. Minn., 1945, M.D., 1948. Diplomate Am. Bd. Psychiatry and Neurology (examiner 1973—). Intern Milw. County Hosp., 1948-49; resident VA Hosp. and U. Minn., 1949-52, Mass. Gen. Hosp. and Harvard U., Boston, 1952-54; instr. U. Minn., Milw., 1953-55; asst. prof. dept. psychiatry Med. Sch., U. Chgo., 1955-60, assoc. prof., 1960-66; prof. psychiatry Med. Sch. U. Mich., 1966—, prof. cmty. mental health, 1968—; prof. psychiatry emeritus L.S.A., 1997—, instr., 1977-97; mem. civil liberties bd. U. Mich., 1995—, chair civil liberties bd., 1996—; chief psychiat. inpatient service U. Chgo. Hosps. and Clinics, 1956-66; dir. Civil Forensic Tng. Program, 1997—. Cons. Forensic Psychiat. Ctr., State of Mich., 1972—, coord. med. student edn. program, 1975-78, dir., 1978-82; cons. Turner Geriatric Clin., 1978-86, cons. Breast Cancer Clinic, 1988, Powertrain subs. Gen. Motors, 1984—, Dept. Mental Health, U.S. Dept. Justice; assoc. chief clin. affairs U. Mich. Hosps., 1981-85, chair legis. govt. com., 1996—, chmn. ethics com.; bd. dirs., mem. profl. rev. com. PSRO Area VII, 1982-86; mem. Mich. State Bd. Medicine, 1986-94, chmn. 1992-94, senate adv. com. Univ. Affairs., 1986-89; bd. dirs. Fedn. of State Med. Bds., 1994-98, spl. com. on profl. conduct and ethics, 1998—, Mich. del., 1988-96, FLEX Com. Nat. Bd. Med. Examiners, 1988-98. Author: Guide for Mental Health Workers, 1970, Patient Power: The Development of a Therapeutic Community in a General Hospital, 1974; also articles.; cons. editor: Community Mental Health jour, 1967— . Recipient Commonwealth Fund fellow award, 1964, Career Svc. award, 1992, Resident Appreciation award, 1991. Fellow: Am. Coll. Psychiatrists (chmn. bylaws com. 1997—), Am. Psychiat. Assn. (life; chmn. membership com. 1979—83, cons. ethics com. 1983—86, trustee 1985—88, sec. 1989—91, chmn. ethics appeals bd. 1989—, cons. steering com. on practical guidelines 1991—, budget com. 1991—, mem. assembly 1992, coun. med. edn. and career devel. 1993—, pres. Lifers 1994—, recertification com. 1998—, annual Lifers award 1999); mem.: Am. Acad. Psychiatry and Law (com. on psychoanalytic edn. 1995—, edn. com. 1998, treas. midwest chpt. 1998—2000, pres. 2001—02), Am. Acad. Psychoanalysis, Mich. State Med. Soc. (bioethics com. 1989—, com. on med. licensure and discipline 1995—, mental health liaison com. 1995—, legis. and regulations com. 1995—, liaison com. Gen. Motors 1998—, chair 2000—), Mich. Psychiat. Soc. (pres. 1980—81, chmn. ethics com. 1983—86, resolutions officer student rights responsibilities 1996—, chmn. legislation and govt. com. 1996—, v.p. 2000—, Career Achievement award 2000), Washtenaw County Med. Soc. (exec. coun. 1982—, chmn. ethics com. 1983—87, pres. 1987—88, editl. bd. 1995—, chair legis. commn. 1999—). Home: 228 Riverview Dr Ann Arbor MI 48104-1846 Office: 900 Wall St Ann Arbor MI 48105-1910

MARGOLIS, ROB, publisher; m. Alycia Margolis; children: Zachary, Noah. Acct. mgr. TV Guide, 1982, assoc. publ., 1992-97, v.p., publ., 1997-98; sr. v.p. bus. devel. New Am. Mktg., Chgo., 1998—. Office: News Am Mktg 303 E Wacker Dr Fl 21 Chicago IL 60601-5212

MARIANI, CARLOS, state legislator; b. July 13, 1957; m. Maritza Mariani; two children. Student, Macalester Coll.; postgrad., UJ. Miami. Social issues program dir.; Dist. 65B rep. Minn. Ho. of Reps., St. Paul, 1990—. Former vice chmn. econ. devel., infrastructure and regulations fin. com., Minn. Ho. of Reps.; asst majority leader; mem. edn.-higher edn., and housing and transp. and transit coms. Office: 187 Congress St W Saint Paul MN 55107-2114 Also: 100 Constitution Ave Saint Paul MN 55155-1232

MARINE, CLYDE LOCKWOOD, agricultural business consultant; b. Knoxville, Tenn., Dec. 25, 1936; s. Harry H. and Idelle (Larue) M.; m. Eleanor Harb, Aug. 9, 1958; children: Cathleen, Sharon. B.S. in Agr., U. Tenn., 1958; M.S. in Agrl. Econs., U. Ill., 1959; Ph.D. in Agrl. Econs., Mich. State U., 1963. Sr. market analyst Pet Milk Co., St. Louis, 1963-64; mgr. market planning agr. chems. div. Mobile Chem. Co., Richmond, Va., 1964-67; mgr. ingredient purchasing Central Soya Co., Ft. Wayne, Ind., 1970-73, corp. economist, 1967-70, v.p. ingredient purchasing, 1973-75, sr. v.p., 1975-90; pres. Marine Assocs., 1991—; bd. dirs. SCAN, 1992—. Mem. agrl. policy adv. com. U.S.D.A. Bd. dirs. Ft. Wayne Fine Arts Found., 1976-79; bd. dirs. Ft. Wayne Pub. Transp. Corp., 1975-83; v.p. Ft. Wayne Philharm., 1974-76. Served with U.S. Army, 1959-60. Mem. Nat. Soybean Processors Assn. (chmn.), U.S. C. of C., Am. Agrl. Econs. Assn., Am. Feed Mfrs. Assn. (chmn. purchasing coun.). Episcopalian. Club: Ft. Wayne Country. Office: Marine Assocs 4646 W Jefferson Blvd Fort Wayne IN 46804-6842 E-mail: lmarine@attglobal.net.

MARING, MARY MUEHLEN, state supreme court justice; b. Devils Lake, N.D., July 27, 1951; d. Joseph Edward and Charlotte Rose (Schorr) Muehlen: m. David Scott Maring, Aug. 30, 1975; children: Christopher David, Andrew Joseph. BA in Polit. Sci. summa cum laude, Moorhead State U., 1972; JD, U. N.D., 1975. Bar: Minn., N.D. Law clk. Hon. Bruce Stone, Mpls, 1975-76; assoc. Stefanson, Landberg & Alm, Ltd., Moorhead, Minn., 1976-82, Ohnstad, Twichell, Breitling, Rosenvold, Wanner, Nelson, Neugebauer & Maring, P.C., West Fargo, N.D., 1982-88, Lee Hagan Law Office, Fargo, 1988-91; pvt. practice Maring Law Office, 1991-96; assoc. justice N.D. State Supreme Ct., Bismarck, N.D., 1996—. Women's bd. mem. 1st Nat. Bank, Fargo, 1977-82; career day speaker Moorhead Rotarians, 1980-83. Contbr. note to legal rev.; note editor N.D. Law Rev., 1975. Mem. ABA (del. ann. conv. young lawyers sect. 1981-82, bd. govs. 1982-83), Minn. Women Lawyers, N.D. State Bar Assn. (bd. govs. 1991-93), Minn. Trial Lawyers Assn., Clay County Bar Assn. (v.p. 1983-84), N.D. Trial Lawyers Assn. (pres. 1992-93), Roman Catholic. Office: ND Supreme Ct 600 E Boulevard Ave Dept 180 Bismarck ND 58505-0530

MARITZ, W. STEPHEN, marketing professional, service executive; BA, Princeton U. CEO Maritz, Fenton, Mo., 1998—. Office: Maritz 1375 N Highway Dr Fenton MO 63099

MARK, JAMES EDWARD, physical chemist, department chairman; b. Wilkes-Barre, Pa., Dec. 14, 1934; married, 1964; married, 1990; 2 children. BS, Wilkes Coll., 1957; PhD in Physical Chemistry, U. Pa., 1962. Rsch. chemist Rohm & Haas Co., 1955-56; rsch. asst. Stanford U., 1962-64; asst. prof. chemistry Polytechnic Inst. Brooklyn, N.Y., 1964-67; from asst. prof. to prof. chemistry U. Mich., Ann Arbor, 1967-77; disting. prof. polymer chemistry U. Cincinnati, 1977—. Cons. various industries, 1963—; vis. prof. Stanford U., 1973-74; spl. rsch. fellow NIH, 1975-76; lectr. short course program Am. Chem. Soc., 1973—. Recipient Am. Chem. Soc. award in Applied Polymer Sci., 1995. Mem. AAAS, Am. Chem. Soc. (Am. Chem. Soc. award in applied polymer sci. 1994), Am. Phys. Soc., N.Y. Acad. Sci. Research in statistical properties of chain molecules; elastic properties of polymer networks. Office: U Cincinnati Dept Chemistry Cincinnati OH 45221-0001

MARKEE, DAVID JAMES, university official, education educator; b. Madison, Wis., Oct. 26, 1942; s. Richard L. and Cathrine Ann (Whalen) M.; m. Lou Ann Markee, Aug. 14, 1965; children: Jeffrey, Gregory. BS in English and Geography, U. Wis., Platteville, 1964, MEd in Counseling and Guidance, 1968; PhD in Counseling Psychology, U. Mo., 1974. Tchr. English, Platteville High Sch., 1964-67; asst. dir. residence halls U. Wis., 1967-69; asst. dir. student life U. Mo., Columbia, 1970-71, assoc. dir., 1971-72, dir., 1972-75; prof. edn. U. Wis., Whitewater, 1973-80, asst. chancellor student affairs, 1975-80; prof., v.p. for student svcs. No. Ariz. U., Flagstaff, 1980-94; v.p. instl. advancement, 1994-96; chancellor U. Wis., Platteville, 1996—. Contbr. articles to profl. jours. Pres., bd. dirs. Cath. Social Svcs., Flagstaff, 1983—; bd. dirs. Citizens Against Drug Abuse, Flagstaff, 1987-89, Flagstaff Arboretum, 1988—; chmn. Flagstaff Beautification Commn., 1988-93; co-chair Flagstaff United Way. Recipient Person of Yr. award U. Wis.-Whitewater Student Govt., 1975, Chief Manueleto award Navajo Nation, 1990. Mem. Nat. Assn. Student Pers. Adminstrs. (bd. dirs. 1989-90), Ariz. Assn. Student Pers. Adminstrs. (pres. 1986-87), Kiwanis (Outstanding Mem. award Flagstaff 1983-85), Kappa Delta Pi. Democrat. Office: U Wis One Univ Plz Platteville WI 53818 E-mail: markee@uwplatt.edu.

MARKEL, HOWARD, medical educator; b. Detroit, Apr. 23, 1960; s. Samuel and Bernice Markel; m. Marcia Deborah Gordin, Sept. 20, 1987 (div. Oct. 1988); m. Kate Gelya Levin, Aug. 17, 1997. AB in English Lit. summa cum laude, U. Mich., 1982, MD cum laude, 1986; PhD in History of Sci., Medicine & Tech., Johns Hopkins U., 1994. Intern, resident Johns Hopkins Hosp. & Sch. Medicine, Balt., 1986-89; asst. prof. pediatrics, communicable diseases U. Mich., Ann Arbor, 1993-98, assoc. prof. pedicatrics, communicable diseases, 1998—2002, George E. Wantz prof. history medicine, 2000—, prof. pediat. and communicable diseases, 2002—. Dir. Hist. Ctr. Health Scis. U. Mich., 1996—. Author: The H.L. Mencken Baby Book, 1990, The Portable Pediatrician, 1992, The Portable Pediatrician, 2nd edit., 2000, The Practical Pediatrician, 1996 (Child Mag. Book of Yr., 1997), Quarantine! East European Jewish Immigrants and the New York City, 1997. Recipient Nat. Rsch. Svc. award, NIH, 1991, James A. Shannon Dirs. award, 1996, Burroughs Wellcome Fund 40th Ann. History Medicine award, 1996; fellow Clin., Adolescent Medicine & Gen. Pediat. Johns Hopkins Hosp. & Sch. Medicine, 1989—91, History Medicine, 1991—93; scholar Robert Wood Johnson Found., 1996—2000. Fellow: Am. Acad. Pediat.; mem.: Am. Pediat. Soc., Soc. Pediat. Rsch., Am. Assn. History Medicine (exec. coun. 1994—97), Am. Hist. Assn. Democrat. Jewish. Office: U Mich Hist Ctr Health Scis 100 Simpson Meml Inst 102 Obs Ann Arbor MI 48109-0725

MARKEL, LYNN, retired oil industry executive; CFO Koch Industries Inc., Wichita, Kans. Office: Koch Industries Inc PO Box 2256 Wichita KS 67201-2256

MARKEY, JAMES KEVIN, lawyer; b. Springfield, Ill., July 15, 1956; s. James Owen and Marjorie Jean (Diesness) M.; m. Allison Markey; children: Lauren, Katherine. BBA with highest honors, U. Notre Dame, 1977; JD cum laude, U. Mich., 1980; MBA, U. Chgo., 1987; LLM in

Taxation, DePaul U., 1993. Bar: Ill. 1980; CPA, Ill. Assoc. Chapman & Cutler, Chgo., 1980-81; atty. Quaker Oats Co., 1981-84; corp. counsel Baxter Healthcare Corp., Deerfield, Ill., 1984-90; v.p. law and other positions Motorola, Inc., Schaumburg, 1990-2000; v.p., chief counsel-securities and internat. Kellogg Co., Battle Creek, Mich., 2000—. Mem. ABA, Beta Alpha Psi, Beta Gamma Sigma. Avocations: racquetball, running, bridge. Home: 3541 Sandhill Ln Portage MI 49024 Office: 1 Kellogg Sq Battle Creek MI 49017-3534 E-mail: jim.markey@kellogg.com.

MARKEY, ROBERT GUY, lawyer; b. Cleveland, Ohio, Feb. 25, 1939; s. Nate and Rhoda (Gross) Markey; m. Nanci Louise Brooks, Aug. 25, 1990; children: Robert Guy, Randolph. AB, Brown U., 1961; JD, Case Western Res., 1964. Bar: Ohio 1964. Ptnr. Baker & Hostetler, Cleve., 1983—. Office: Baker & Hostetler 3200 National City Ctr 1900 E 9th St Ste 3200 Cleveland OH 44114-3475

MARKIN, DAVID ROBERT, motor company executive; b. N.Y.C., Feb. 16, 1931; s. Morris and Bessie (Markham) M.; children: Sara, John, Christopher, Meredith. B.S., Bradley U., 1953. Foreman Checker Motors Corp., Kalamazoo, 1955-57, factory mgr., 1957-62, v.p. sales, 1962-70, pres., 1970—, dir. Bd. dirs. Jackpot Inc. Trustee Kalamazoo Coll. Served to 1st lt. USAF, 1953-55. Mem. Alpha Epsilon Pi Clubs: Standard (Chgo.); Park (Kalamazoo). Home: 2121 Winchell Ave Kalamazoo MI 49008-2205 Office: Checker Motors Corp 2016 N Pitcher St Kalamazoo MI 49007-1894

MARKLE, SANDRA, publishing company executive; 7th grade sci. tchr., Ohio; pres. CompuQuest, Inc., Bartlett, Ill. Office: CompuQuest Inc 366 S Main St Bartlett IL 60103-4423

MARKMAN, RONALD, artist, educator; b. Bronx, N.Y., May 29, 1931; s. Julius and Mildred (Berkowitz) M.; m. Barbara Miller, Sept. 12, 1959; 1 dau., Ericka Elizabeth. B.F.A., Yale U., 1957, M.F.A., 1959. Instr. Art Inst. Chgo., 1960-64; prof. fine arts Ind. U., 1964—. Color cons. Hallmark Card Co., 1959-60 One-man shows Kanegis Gallery, 1959, Reed Coll., 1966, Terry Dintenfass Gallery, 1965, 66, 68, 70, 76, 79, 82, 85, The Gallery, Bloomington, Ind., 1972, 79, Indpls. Mus., 1974, Tyler Sch. Art, Phila., 1976, Franklin Coll., 1980, Dart Gallery, Chgo., 1981, Patrick King Gallery, Indpls., 1983, 86, John Heron Gallery, Indpls., 1985, New Harmony Gallery, 1985; two-man show Dintenfass Gallery, 1984; group shows include Kanegis Gallery, Boston, 1958, 60, 61, Boston Arts Festival, 1959, 60, Mus. Modern Art, 1959, 66, Whitney Mus., N.Y.C., 1960, Art Inst. Chgo., 1964, Gallery 99, Miami, Fla., 1966, Ball State Coll., 1966, Butler Inst., 1967, Indpls. Mus., 1968, 69, 72, 74, Phoenix Gallery, N.Y.C., 1970, Harvard U., 1974, Skidmore Coll., 1975, Am. Acad. Arts and Letters, 1977, 89, Tuthill-Gimprich Gallery, N.Y.C., 1980, Patrick King Gallery, 1988, numerous others; represented in permanent collections Met. Mus. Art, Mus. Modern Art, Art Inst. Chgo., Library of Congress, Cin. Art Mus., Bklyn. Mus., Ark. Art Center, others; commns. include 5 murals Riley Children's Hosp., Indpls., 1986; installation Evanston (Ill.) Art Ctr., 1989, 2-part installation Ortho Child Care Ctr., Raritan, N.J., 1991; illustrator Acid and Basics-A Guide to Acid-Base Physiology, 1992. Served with U.S. Army, 1952-54. Recipient Ind. Arts Commn. award, 1990, 93; Fulbright grantee, Italy, 1962, grantee Ctr. for New TV, Chgo., 1992; Lilly Endowment fellow, 1989, honorable mention, Ohio Film Festival, 1995. Home and Office: 1623 Saint Margarets Rd Annapolis MD 21401-5540 Office: Ind U Dept Fine Arts Bloomington IN 47401

MARKMAN, STEPHEN J. Supreme Ct. judge; b. Detroit, June 4, 1949; s. Julius and Pauline Markman; m. Mary Kathleen Sites, Aug. 25, 1974; children: James, Charles. BA, Duke U., 1971; JD, U. Cin., 1974. Asst. to Rep. Edward Hutchinson, Mich., 1975; legis. asst. to Rep. Tom Hagedorn, Minn., 1976-78; chief counsel, staff dir. subcom. on constn. Senate Com. on Judiciary, 1978-85, dep. chief counsel, 1983; asst. atty. gen. Office Legal Policy, Dept. Justice, Washington, 1985-89; U.S. atty. U.S. Dept. Justice, Detroit, 1989-93; mem. Miller, Canfield, Paddock & Stone, 1993-99; justice Mich. Supreme Ct., Lansing, 1999—. Office: Mich Supreme Ct G Mennen Williams Bldg 525 W Ottawa St Fl 2 Lansing MI 48933-1067

MARKO, SHARON, state legislator; b. Mar. 2, 1953; BS, Ind. U.; postgrad., U. Minn. Minn. state rep. Dist. 57B, 1994—. Comms. cons. Address: 1401 2nd Ave Newport MN 55055-1118

MARKOS, CHRIS, retired real estate company executive; b. Cleve., Nov. 25, 1926; s. George and Bessie (Papathatou) Markos; m. Alice Zaharopoulos, Dec. 11, 1949 (dec.); children: Marilyn Martin, Irene Matthews, Betsy Fierabend. BA, Case Western Reserve, Cleve., 1960; LLB, LaSalle U., Chgo., 1964. Cert. gen. real estate appraiser, Ohio. Vice-pres. Herbert Laronge Inc., Cleve., 1963-76; v.p. Calabrese, Racek and Markos Inc., 1976-83, Herbert Laronge Inc., Cleve., 1983-87, pres., 1987-88; v.p. Cragin Lang, Inc., 1989-91; sr. cons. Grubb & Ellis, 1991-93; sr. v.p. Realty One Appraisal Divsn., Independence, Ohio, 1993-98. Pres. Alcrimar Inc., 1989-98. Co-author: Ohio Supplement to Modern Real Estate Practice, 5th-7th edits.; cons. editor, co-author: Modern Real Estate Practice in Ohio, 1st-3rd edits. Bd. dirs. David N. Meyers Coll., Cleve., 1984-97. With U.S. Army, 1945-46. Mem. Am. Soc. Appraisers (sr., pres. 1973, state dir. 1976), Cleve. Bd. Realtors (hon. life mem., pres. 1974, Realtor of Yr. award 1976). Republican. Greek Orthodox. Home: Ocean Monarch Condominium Unit 811 133 N Pompano Beach Blvd Pompano Beach FL 33062-5732 E-mail: alcrimar@webtv.net.

MARKOVITS, ANDREI STEVEN, political science educator; b. Timisoara, Romania, Oct. 6, 1948; came to U.S., 1960, naturalized, 1971; s. Ludwig and Ida (Ritter) M. BA, Columbia U., 1969, MBA, 1971, MA, 1973, MPhil, 1974, PhD, 1976. Mem. faculty NYU, 1974, John Jay Coll. Criminal Justice, CUNY, 1974, Columbia U., 1975; rsch. assoc. Inst. Advanced Studies, Vienna, Austria, 1973-74, Wirtschafts und Sozialwissenschaftliches Inst., German Trade U. Fedn., Düsseldorf, Germany, 1979, Internat. Inst. Comparative Social Rsch., Sci. Ctr. Berlin, 1980; asst. prof. govt. Wesleyan U., Middletown, Conn., 1977-83; assoc. prof. polit. sci. Boston U., 1983-92; prof., chair dept. politics U. Calif., Santa Cruz, 1992-99; prof. dept. Germanic langs. and lit. U. Mich., Ann Arbor, Mich., 1999—; Fulbright prof. U. Innsbruck, Austria, 1996. Vis. prof. Tel Aviv U., 1986, Osnabruck U., 1987, Bochum U., 1991; sr. rsch. assoc. Ctr. for European Studies, Harvard U., 1975-99. Author, editor books and papers in field; TV and radio commentator. Univ. Pres.'s fellow Columbia U., 1969, B'nai B'rith Found. fellow, 1976-77, Kalmus Found. fellow, 1976-77, Ford Found. fellow, 1979, Hans Boeckler Found. fellow, 1982 Inst. for Advanced Study Berlin fellow, 1998-99; N.Y. State scholar Columbia U., 1969. Mem. N.Y. Acad. Scis., Am. Polit. Sci. Assn., Internat. Polit. Sci. Assn., AAUP. Home: 718 Onondaga St Ann Arbor MI 48104-2611 Office: Univ Mich 3110 Modern Lang Bldg 812 E Washington St Ann Arbor MI 48109-1275 also: Harvard U Ctr European Studies 27 Kirkland St Cambridge MA 02138-2043 E-mail: andymark@umich.edu., andreimarkovits@cs.com.

MARKOWSKY, JAMES J. retired utilities executive; BS, Pratt Inst.; MS, PhD, Cornell U. Lic. profl. engr. Ind., Ky., Mich., N.Y., Ohio, Tenn., Va., W.Va. Sr. engr. mech. engring. divsn. Am. Electric Power Co., Inc., Columbus, Ohio, 1971-77, program mgr., 1977-84, head mech. engring. divsn., asst. v.p., 1984-87, v.p. mech. engring., 1987-88, sr. v.p., chief engr., 1988-93, exec. v.p. engring. and constrn., 1993-96, exec. v.p. power generation, 1996-00; ret., 2000. Adj. assoc. prof. CUNY, 1975-77. Fellow ASME; mem. Nat. Acad. Engring., Nat. Rsch. Coun. (chmn. com. R & D opportunities for coal fired energy complexes), Assn. Edison Illuminating Cos.' (power generation com.), Coal Utilization Rsch. Coun. (chmn.), Office: Am Electric Power Co Inc 1 Riverside Plz Columbus OH 43215-2355

MARKS, ESTHER L. metals company executive; b. Canton, Ohio, Oct. 3, 1927; d. Jacob and Ella (Wisman) Rosky; m. Irwin Alfred Marks, June 29, 1947; children: Jules, Howard, Marilyn. Student, Ohio State U., 1945-46, Youngstown State U., 1946-47. V.p. Steel City Iron & Metal, Inc., Youngstown, Ohio. Pres. Jr. Hadassah, Youngstown, 1943-45, Pioneer Women, Youngstown, 1951, Anshe Emeth Sisterhood, Youngstown, Broadway Theatre League, Youngstown, 1958, B'nai B'rith Women, Youngstown, 1962, Dist. 2 B'nai B'rith Women, Cleve., 1969-70, Jewish Cmty. Ctr., Youngstown, Youngstown Area Jewish Fedn., 1988-90; v.p. United Way, Youngstown, 1991, chmn., 1996; grad. Leadership Youngstown, 1991; bd. Akiva Acad. Commn. for Jewish Edn., Temple El Emeth, Stambaugh Auditorium. Named Guardian of the Menorah B'nai B'rith, Youngstown, 1978; recipient B'nai B'rith Girls Alumda award, Washington, 1989, Woman of Valor award Jewish Fedn., 1996. Mem. LMV, YWCA, Ohio Hist. Soc. Democrat. Jewish. Avocations: knitting, organizational work. Home: 1295 Virginia Trl Youngstown OH 44505-1637 Office: 703 Wilson Ave Youngstown OH 44506-1445

MARKS, MARTHA ALFORD, writer; b. Oxford, Miss., July 27, 1946; d. Truman and Margaret Alford; m. Bernard L. Marks, Jan. 27, 1968. BA, Centenary Coll., 1968; MA, Northwestern U., 1972, PhD, 1978. Tchr. Notre Dame High Sch. for Boys, Niles, Ill., 1969-74; teaching asst. Northwestern U., Evanston, 1974-78, lectr., lang. coord., 1978-83; asst. prof. Kalamazoo (Mich.) Coll., 1983-85; writer Riverwoods, Ill., 1985—. Cons. WGBH Edn. Found., Boston, 1988-91, Am. Coun. on the Tchg. of Fgn. Langs., 1981-92, Ednl. Testing Svcs., 1988-90, Peace Corps., 1993. Co-author: Destinos: An Introduction to Spanish, 1991, 96, Al corriente, 1989, 93, 97, Que tal?, 1986, 90; author: (workbook) Al corriente, 1989, 93; contbr. articles to profl. jours. Mem. Lake County (Ill.) Bd., Forest Preserve Commn., 1992—, Lake County Conservation Alliance; vice chmn. Friends of Ryerson Conservation Area Bd.; co-founder, pres. Rep Am., Reps. for Environ. Protection. Home: 2940 Cherokee Ln Riverwoods IL 60015-1609 Office: County Bd Office 18 N County St Waukegan IL 60085-4351

MARKUS, KENT RICHARD, lawyer; b. Cleve., Feb. 1, 1959; s. Richard and Carol (Slater) M.; m. Susan Mary Gilles, Apr. 15, 1987. BS, Northwestern U., 1981; JD with honors, Harvard U., 1984. Bar: Ohio 1984, U.S. Dist. Ct. (no. dist.) Ohio 1984, U.S. Ct. Appeals (6th cir.) 1986. Jud. clk. to Hon. Alvin I. Krenzler U.S. Dist. Ct. (no. dist.) Ohio, Cleve., 1984-86; litigation assoc. Gold, Rotatori, Schwartz & Gibbons, 1986-89; transition dir. Ohio Atty. Gen. Office, Columbus, Ohio, 1990-91, first asst. atty. gen., chief of staff, 1991-93; counsel to dep. atty. gen. U.S. Dept. Justice, Washington, 1994, dep. assoc. atty. gen., 1994-95, acting asst. atty. gen. legis affairs, 1995, counselor to atty. gen., 1996-98, dep. chief of staff, 1997-98; prof., dir. Dave Thomas Ctr. for Adoption Law, Capitol U. Law Sch., 1998—. Adj. prof. law Cleveland-Marshall Coll. Law, 1987-88. Co-editor: Trial Handbook for Ohio Lawyers, 2nd edit., 1988; contbn. editor for law Webster's New World Dictionary, 4th edit., 1999. Former bd. dirs., former legis. chair Handgun Control Fedn. of Ohio, 1984-93; mem. adv. coun. Northwestern U. Sch. Speech, 1985—; spl. projects dir. Celeste for Gov. Com., Cleve., 1986; campaign mgr. Lee Fisher for Atty. Gen., Cleve. and Columbus, 1989-90; bd. dirs., former trustee, life mem. Cleve. NAACP, 1986-87; chief of staff Dem. Nat. Com., Washington, 1993-94. Named Rising Star of Dem. Party, Campaigns and Elections mag., 1991. Mem. ABA, Ohio State Bar Assn. (former chair young lawyers divsn.), Columbus Bar Assn. Home: 5636 Indian Hill Rd Dublin OH 43017-8209 Office: Capital Univ Law Sch 303 E Broad St Columbus OH 43215-3201 E-mail: kmarkus@law.capital.edu.

MARKUS, LAWRENCE, retired mathematics educator; b. Hibbing, Minn., Oct. 13, 1922; s. Benjamin and Ruby (Friedman) M.; m. Lois Shoemaker, Dec. 9, 1950; children: Sylvia, Andrew. BS, U. Chgo., 1942, MS, 1946; PhD, Harvard U., 1951. Instr. meteorology U. Chgo., 1942-44; rsch. meteorologist Atomic Project, Hanford, 1944; instr. math. Harvard U., 1951-52; instr. Yale U., 1952-55; lectr. Princeton U., 1955-57; asst. prof. U. Minn., Mpls., 1957-58, assoc. prof., 1958-60, prof. math., 1960-93, assoc. chmn. dept. math., 1961-63, dir. control scis., 1964-73, Regents' prof. math., 1980-93, Regents' prof. emeritus, 1993—, dir. Control Sci. and Dynamical Sys. Ctr., 1980-89. Leverhulme prof. control theory, dir. control theory ctr. U. Warwick, Eng., 1970-73, Nuffield prof. math., 1970-85, hon. prof., 1985—; regional conf. lectr. NSF, 1969; vis. prof. Yale U., Columbia U., U. Calif., U. Warsaw, 1980, Tech. Inst. Zurich, 1983, Peking U. (China), 1983; dir. conf. Internat. Ctr. Math., Trieste, 1974; lectr. Internat. Math. Congress, 1974, Iranian Math. Soc., 1975, Brit. Math. Soc., 1976, Japan Soc. for Promotion Sci., 1976, Royal Instn., London, 1982, U. Beer Sheva, Israel, 1983; vis. prof. U. Tokyo, 1976, Tech. U., Denmark, 1979; mem. panel Internat. Congress Mathematicians, Helsinki, 1978; sr. vis. fellow Sci. Rsch. Coun., Imperial Coll., London, 1978; mem. UNESCO sci. adv. com. Control Symposium, U. Strasbourg, France, 1980; IEEE Plenary lectr., Orlando, Fla., 1982; Sci. and Engring. Rsch. Coun. vis. prof. U. Warwick, Eng., 1982-90; Neustadt Meml. lectr. U. So. Calif., 1985, prin. lectr. symposium U. Minn., 1988, dir. NSF workshop, 1989, prin. lectr. symposium in honor of his 75th birthday, 1997; Tate lectr. U. Cin., 1998; mem. adv. bd. Office Naval Rsch., Air Force Office Sci. Rsch. Author: Flat Lorentz Manifolds, 1959, Flows on Homogeneous Spaces, 1963, Foundations of Optimal Control Theory, 1967, rev. edit., 1985, Lectures on Differentiable Dynamics, 1971, rev. edit., 1980, Generic Hamiltonian Dynamical Systems, 1974, Distributed Parameter Control Systems, 1991, Boundary Value Problems and Symplectic Algebra, 1998, Multi-Interval Linear Ordinary Boundary Value Problems and Complex Symplectic Algebra, 2001; editor Internat. Jour. Nonlinear Mechanics, 1965-73, Jour. Control, 1963-67; mem. editl. bd. Proc. Georgian Acad. Sci. Math., 1993—; contbr. articles to profl. jours. Lt. (j.g.) USNR, 1944-46. Recipient Rsch. prize Internat. Conf. Nonlinear Oscillations, Ukrainian Acad. Sci., Kiev, 1969, Festschrift volume, 1993; Fulbright fellow Paris, 1950; Guggenheim fellow Lausanne, Switzerland, 1963. Fellow Royal Soc. of Edinburgh (hon.); mem. Am. Math. Soc. (past mem. nat. coun.), Am. Geophys. Soc., Soc. Indsl. and Applied Math. (past nat. lectr.), Phi Beta Kappa, Sigma Xi. Office: U Minn Math Dept 127 Vincent Hall Minneapolis MN 55455 E-mail: markus@math.umn.edu.

MARKUS, RICHARD M. judge, mediator; b. Evanston, Ill., Apr. 16, 1930; s. Benjamin and Ruby M.; m. Carol Joanne Slater, July 26, 1952; children: Linda, Scott, Kent. BS magna cum laude, Northwestern U., 1951; JD cum laude, Harvard U., 1954. Bar: D.C. 1954, Ohio 1956, Fla. 1994. Appellate atty., civil div. Dept. Justice, Washington, 1954-56; ptnr. civil litigation law firms Cleve., 1956-76, 89-98; judge Cuyahoga County (Ohio) Common Pleas Ct., 1976-80, Ohio Ct. Appeals, 1981-88. Instr. M.I.T., 1952-54; adj. prof. Case Western Res. U. Law Sch., 1972-78, 84-87, Cleve. State U. Law Sch., 1960-80, prof. 1999-2000; prof. Harvard Law Sch., 1980-81; mem. Nat. Commn. on Med. Malpractice, 1971-73; chmn. Nat. Inst. Trial Advocacy, 1978-81, trustee 1971—. Author: Trial Handbook for Ohio Lawyers, 5th edit., 2002, Ohio Evidence Rules with Commentary, 1999; contbr. articles to profl. jours.; editor Harvard U. Law Rev, 1952-54. Republican nominee Justice of Ohio Supreme Ct., 1978; bd. dirs. Luth. Metro Ministry, 1988—, Fairview Luth. Hosp., 1985—. Mem. Ohio State Bar Assn. (pres. 1991-92), Cuyahoga County Bar Assn., Greater Cleve. Bar Assn. (trustee 1967-70, 85-90), Assn. Trial Lawyers Am. (nat. pres. 1970-71), Ohio Acad. Trial Lawyers (pres. 1965-66), Phi Beta Kappa, Pi Mu Epsilon, Delta Sigma Rho, Phi Alpha Delta. Home and Office: Pvt Judicial Svcs Inc 3903 N Valley Dr Cleveland OH 44126-1716

MARLETT, JUDITH ANN, nutritional sciences educator, researcher; b. Toledo; BS, Miami U., Oxford, Ohio, 1965; PhD, U. Minn., 1972; postgrad., Harvard U., 1973-74. Registered dietitian. Therapeutic and metabolic unit dietitian VA Hosp., Mpls., 1966-67; spl. instr. in nutrition Simmons Coll., Boston, 1973-74; asst. prof. U. Wis., Madison, 1975-80, assoc. prof. dept. nutritional scis., 1981-84, prof. dept. nutritional scis., 1984—. Cons. U.S. AID, Leyte, Philippines, 1983; acting dir. dietetic program dept. Nutritional Scis. U. Wis., 1977-78, dir., 1985-89; cons. grain, drug and food cos., 1985—, adv. bd. U. Ariz. Clin. Cancer Ctr., 1987-95; sci. bd. advisors Am. Health Found., 1988—; reviewer NIH, 1982—. Mem. editl. bd. Jour. Sci. of Food and Agrl., 1989—, Jour. Food Composition and Analysis, 1994-2000; contbr. articles to profl. jours. Mem. AAAS, NIH (Diabetes and Digestive and Kidney Disease spl. grant rev. com. 1992-96), Am. Soc. Nutritional Scis., Am. Dietetic Assn., Am. Soc. Clin. Nutrition, Inst. Food Technologists, Am. Assn. Cereal Chemists. Achievements include research and international speaker on human nutrition and disease, dietary fiber and gastrointestinal function. Office: U Wis Dept Nutritional Sci 1415 Linden Dr Madison WI 53706-1527 E-mail: jmarlett@nutrisci.wisc.edu.

MARLETTA, MICHAEL, biochemistry educator, researcher, protein chemist; b. Rochester, N.Y., Feb. 12, 1951; m. Margaret Gutowski, 1991. BA, SUNY, 1973; PhD in Pharm. Chemistry, U. Calif., 1978. Fellow MIT, Cambridge, 1978-80, from asst. prof. to assoc. prof. toxicology, 1980-87; assoc. prof. med. chemistry U. Mich., Ann Arbor, 1987-91, assoc. prof. biol. chemistry, 1989-91, John G. Searle prof. med. chemistry, prof. biol. chemistry, 1991—. Investigator Howard Hughes Med. Inst., 1997. John D. and Catherine T. MacArthur fellow, 1995. Mem. AAAS, Am. Soc. Biochem. and Molecular Biology, Am. Chem. Soc. Achievements include research in protein/structure function with a particular interest in enzyme reaction mechanisms and molecular mechanisms of signal transduction, study of nitric oxide synthase, guanylate cyclase and related enzymes in this signaling system. Office: U Mich Howard Hughes Med Inst Dept Biol Chemistry 1150 W Medical Center Dr Ann Arbor MI 48109-0726

MARLING, KARAL ANN, art history and social sciences educator, curator; b. Rochester, N.Y., Nov. 5, 1943; d. Raymond J. and Marjorie (Karal) M. PhD, Bryn Mawr Coll., 1971. Prof. art history and Am. studies U. Minn., Mpls., 1977—. Author: Federal Art in Cleveland, 1933-1943: An Exhibition, 1974, Wall-to-Wall America: A Cultural History of Post-Office Murals in the Great Depression, 1982, 2d edit., 2000, The Colossus of the Roads: Myth and Symbol along the American Highway, 1984, 2d edit., 2000, Tom Benton and His Drawings: A Biographical Essay and a Collection of His Sketches, Studies, and Mural Cartoons, 1985, Frederick C. Knight (1898-1979), 1987, George Washington Slept Here: Colonial Revivals and American Culture, 1876-1986, 1988, Looking Back: A Perspective on the 1913 Inaugural Exhibition, 1988, Blue Ribbon: A Social and Pictorial History of the Minnesota State Fair, 1990, (with John Wetenhall) Iwo Jima: Monuments, Memories, and the American Hero, 1991, Edward Hopper, 1992, As Seen on T.V.: The Visual Culture of Everyday Life in the 1950's, 1994, Graceland: Going Home with Elvis, 1995; editor (with Jessica H. Foy) The Arts and the American Home, 1890-1930, 1994, Norman Rockwell, 1997, Designing the Disney Theme Parks: The Architecture of Reassurance, 1997, Merry Christmas! Celebrating America's Greatest Holiday, 2000; contbr. essays to exhbn. catalogs. Recipient Minn. Humanities Commn. award 1986, Minn. Book award History, 1994, Robert C. Smith award Decorative Arts Soc., 1994, Internat. Assn. of Art Critics award, 1998. Office: 1920 S 1st St Ste 1301 Minneapolis MN 55454-1190

MAROVICH, GEORGE M. federal judge; b. 1931; AA, Thornton Community Coll., 1950; BS, U. Ill., 1952, JD, 1954. Atty. Chgo. Title & Trust Co., 1954-59; mem. firm Jacobs & Marovich, South Holland, Ill., 1959-66; v.p., trust officer South Holland Trust & Savs. Bank, 1966-76; judge Cir. Ct. Cook County, Ill., 1976-88; dist. judge U.S. Dist. Ct. (no. dist.) Ill., Chgo., 1988—. Adj. instr. Thornton Community Coll., 1977-88. Mem. Ill. Judges Assn., Ill. Jud. Conf., Chgo. Bar Assn., South Suburban Bar Assn. Office: US Dist Ct Chambers 1956 219 S Dearborn St Ste 2050 Chicago IL 60604-1800

MAROVITZ, JAMES LEE, lawyer; b. Chgo., Feb. 21, 1939; s. Harold and Gertrude (Luster) M.; m. Gail Helene Florsheim, June 17, 1962; children: Andrew, Scott. BS, Northwestern U., 1960, JD, 1963. Bar: Ill. 1963, U.S. Dist. Ct. (no. dist.) Ill. 1963, U.S. Ct. Appeals (7th cir.) 1990. Assoc. Leibman, Williams, Bennett, Baird & Minow, Chgo., 1963-70, ptnr., 1970-72, Sidley & Austin, Chgo., 1972-99, sr. counsel, 2000—. Bd. dirs. Cobra Elec. Corp., Chgo. Plan commr. Village of Deerfield, Ill., 1972-79, trustee, 1983-93, police commr. 1995—. Mem. ABA, Ill. Bar Assn., Chgo. Bar Assn. Club: Univ. (Chgo.). Office: Sidley & Austin 1 Bank One Plz 425 W Surf St Apt 605 Chicago IL 60657-6139 E-mail: jmarovit@sidley.com.

MAROZSAN, JOHN ROBERT, retired publishing company executive; b. Trenton, N.J., Oct. 25, 1941; s. John Nichols and Anna Mary (Lacko) M.; m. Anne Marie Gousha, Mar. 18, 1983; children— Andre J., Marc J., Carl B. A.S., Trenton Jr. Coll., 1965; B.A., Trenton State Coll., 1967; M.A., Harvard U., 1969. Tchr. Princeton Pub. Sch., N.J., 1967-68; coordinator secondary pub. Ginn and Co., Boston, 1969-72, program mgr. Lexington, Mass., 1972-75; v.p., editor-in-chief Aspen Publishers, Inc., Rockville, Md., 1975-80, sr. v.p. pub., 1980-85; pres. Aspen Pubs., Inc., Gaithersburg, 1986-96; COO Commerce Clearing House, Riverwoods, Ill., 1996-97; pres., CEO Commerce Clearinghouse; ret., 1999. Bd. dirs. Innodata. Bd. dirs. Hospice Caring, Wolters Klumen, U.S. Bd.; bd. examiners Henry B. Betts Found.; bd. govs. WUSA One and Only Award. With USAF, 1959-63. Recipient Sci. award NSF, 1968. Mem. Newsletter Assn. Am., Rotary, North Star Owners Assn. (pres. 1998-2001). Home: 220 E Prospect Ave Lake Bluff IL 60044 E-mail: jmarozsan@aol.com.

MARQUARDT, CHRISTEL ELISABETH, judge; b. Chgo., Aug. 26, 1935; d. Herman Albert and Christine Marie (Geringer) Trolenberg; children: Eric, Philip, Andrew, Joel. BS in Edn., Mo. Western Coll., 1970; JD with honors, Washburn U., 1974. Bar: Kans. 1974, Mo. 1992, U.S. Dist. Ct. Kans. 1974, U.S. Dist. Ct. (we. dist.) Mo. 1992. Tchr. St. John's Ch., Tigerton, Wis., 1955-56; pers. asst. Columbia Records, L.A., 1958-59; ptnr. Cosgrove, Webb & Oman, Topeka, 1974-86, Palmer & Marquardt, Topeka, 1986-91, Levy and Craig P.C., Overland Park, Kans., 1991-94; sr. ptnr. Marquardt and Assocs., L.L.C., Fairway, 1994-95; judge Kans. Ct. Appeals, 1995—. Mem. atty. bd. discipline Kans. Supreme Ct., 1984—86. Mem. editorial adv. bd. Kans. Lawyers Weekly, 1992-96; contbr. articles to legal jours. Bd. dirs. Topeka Symphony, 1983-92, 95-2002, Arts and Humanities Assn. Johnson County, 1992-95, Brown Found., 1988-90; hearing examiner Human Rels. Com., Topeka, 1974-76; local advisor Boy Scouts Am., 1973-74; bd. dirs., mem. nominating com. YWCA, Topeka, 1979-81; bd. govs. Washburn U. Law Sch., 1987-2002, v.p., 1996-98, pres., 1998-2000; mem. dist. bd. adjudication Mo. Synod Luth. Ch., Kans., 1982-88. Named Woman of Yr., Mayor, City of Topeka, 1982; Obee scholar Washburn U., 1972-74; recipient Jennie Mitchell Kellogg Atty. of Achievement award, 1999, Phil Leives medal of Distinction, 2000, Atty. of Achievement award Kans. Women Attys. Assn., Disting. Svc. award Washburn U. Law Sch., 2002. Fellow: Kans. Bar Found. (trustee 1987—89), Am. Bar Found.; mem.: ABA (specialization com. 1987—93, mem. ho. dels. 1988—, chmn. 1989—93, lawyer referral com. 1993—95, state del. 1995—99, bar svcs. and activities 1995—99, bd. govs., program and planning com. 1999—2002, bd. govs. 1999—, ctrl. and ea. European law initiative 2001—), Law and Organizational Econ. Ctr. (bd. dirs. 2000—02), Am. Bus. Women's Assn. (lectr., corr. sec. 1983—84, pres. career chpt. 1986—87, named one of Top 10 Bus. Women of Yr. 1985), Topeka Bar Assn., Kans. Trial Lawyers Assn. (bd. govs. 1982—86, lectr.), Kans. Bar Assn. (sec., treas. 1981—85, bd. dirs. 1983—, v.p. 1985—86, pres. 1987—88). Home: 3408 SW Alameda Dr Topeka KS 66614-5108 Office: 301 SW 10th Ave Topeka KS 66612-1502 E-mail: marquardt@kscourts.org.

MARQUARDT, STEVE ROBERT, library director; b. St. Paul, Sept. 7, 1943; s. Robert Thomas and Dorothy Jean (Kane) M.; m. Judy G. Brown, Aug. 4, 1968; 1 child, Sarah. BA in History, Macalester Coll., 1966; MA in History, U. Minn., 1970, MLS, 1973, PhD in History, 1978. History instr. Macalester Coll., St. Paul, 1968-69; cataloger N.Mex. State U. Libr., Las Cruces, 1973-75; acting univ. archivist, acting dir. Rio Grande Hist. Collections N. Mex. State U. Libr., 1973-74; acquisitions librarian Western Ill. U. Libr., Macomb, 1976-77, head cataloger, Online Computer Libr. Ctr. coord., 1977-79; asst. dir. resources & tech. svcs. Ohio U. Libr., Athens, 1979-81; dir. librs. U. Wis., Eau Claire, 1981-89; dir. univ. librs. No. Ill. U., DeKalb, 1989-90; dir. librs. U. Wis., Eau Claire, 1990-96; dean of librs. S.D. State U., Brookings, 1996—. Editor Jour. Rio Grande History, 1974; contbg. editor: Library Issues, 1994-99; contbr. articles to profl. jours. Coord. Amnesty Internat. Adoption Group 275, Eau Claire, 1985-88; pres. Chippewa Valley Free-net, 1994-96. Mem. ALA, Assn. Coll. and Rsch. Librs. (chmn. performance measures in acad. librs. com. 1985-89). Lutheran. Avocations: tennis, bicycling. Office: SD State U Briggs Libr PO Box 2115 Brookings SD 57007-0001 E-mail: steve_marquardt@sdstate.edu.

MARQUETTE, I. EDWARD, lawyer; b. Hannibal, Mo., Oct. 15, 1950; s. Clifford M. and Doris Elizabeth (McLane) M.; m. Ansie S. Goodrich, May 20, 1972; children: Brandeis, Brooks. BA in Econs., U. Mo., 1973; JD, Harvard U., 1976. Bar: Mo. 1976. Ptnr. Spencer, Fane, Britt & Browne LLP, Kansas City, Mo., 1976—. Contbr. articles to profl. jours., chpts. to books. Bd. dirs. Midwest Christian Counseling Combined Health Appeal, Kansas City, 1988-95. Mem. ABA (new info. tech. com.), Mo. Bar Assn. (tech. com.), Kansas City Bar Assn. (chmn. antitrust study group 1984, chmn. computer law com. 1989, 90, 95, 99), Silicon Prairie Tech. Assn. Democrat. Baptist. Avocation: computer programming. Office: Spencer Fane Britt & Browne LLP 1000 Walnut St Ste 1400 Kansas City MO 64106-2140

MARRA, SAMUEL PATRICK, retired pharmacist, small business owner; b. Sault Ste Marie, Mich., Apr. 15, 1927; s. Leonard and Nancy (Clement); m. Jeanette L. Rohr, Sept. 2, 1949; children: Rebecca, Nancy, David, Dana, Janet. BS in Pharmacy, Ferris State Coll., 1949. Ret. Bd. dirs. Chem. Bank, No. States Bancshares, Chem. Bank North. Bd. dirs. Houghton Lake Edn. Found.; pres. Houghton Lake Grenadier Band; co-chmn. Scheutte for Congress, Roscommon County, 1984, 86. Mem. Nat. Assn. Retail Druggists. Republican. Avocations: music, photography. Home: 10672 Westshore Dr Houghton Lake MI 48629-8636

MARSH, BENJAMIN FRANKLIN, lawyer; b. Toledo, Apr. 30, 1927; s. Lester Randall and Alice (Smith) M.; m. Martha Kirkpatrick, July 12, 1952; children: Samuel, Elizabeth. BA, Ohio Wesleyan U., 1950; JD, George Washington U., 1954. Bar: Ohio 1955. Pvt. practice law, Toledo, 1955-88, Maumee, 1988—; assoc., ptnr. Doyle, Lewis & Warner, Toledo, 1955-71; ptnr. Ritter, Boesel, Robinson & Marsh, 1971-88, Marsh & McAdams, Maumee, 1988-98; personnel officer AEC, 1950-54; asst. atty. gen. State of Ohio, 1969-71; asst. solicitor City of Maumee, 1959-63, solicitor, 1963-92; ptnr. Marsh McAdams Scharty Brogan & Schaefer, Ltd., 1999—. Mem. U.S. Fgn. Claims Settlement Commn., Washington, 1990-94; counsel N.W. Ohio Mayors and Mgrs. Assn., 1990-2000; mem. regional bd. rev. Indsl. Commn. Ohio, Toledo, 1993-94; mem. Ohio Dental Bd., 1995-2000; trustee Corp. for Effective Govt., 1998—; mem. Ohio Elections Commn., 2001—. U.S. rep. with rank spl. amb. to 10th Anniversary Independence of Botswana, 1976; past pres. Toledo and Lucas County Tb Soc., citizens for metro pks.; past mem. Judges Com. Notaries Pub.; formerly mem. Lucas County Bd. Elections; former chmn. bldg. commn. Riverside Hosp., Toledo; past trustee Com. on Rels. with Toledo, Spain; past chmn. bd. trustee Med. Coll., Ohio; past treas. Coglin Meml. Inst.; chmn. Lucas County Rep. Exec. Com., 1973-74; precinct commiteeman, Maumee, 1959-73; legal counsel, bd. dirs. Nat. Coun. Rep. Workshops, 1960-65; pres. Rep. Workshops, Ohio, 1960-64; alt. del. Rep. Nat. Conv., 1964; candidate 9th dist. U.S. Ho. of Reps., 1968; adminstrv. asst. to Rep. state chmn. Ray C. Bliss, 1954; chmn. Lucas County Bush for Pres., 1980; co-chmn. Reagan-Bush Com. for Northwestern Ohio, 1980, vice chmn. fin. com. Bush-Quayle, 1992; co-chmn. Ohio steering com. Bush for Pres., mem. nat. steering com., 1988; del. Rep. Nat. Conv., 1988; past bd. dirs. Ohio Tb and Respiratory Disease Assn.; apptd. Ohio chmn. UN Day, 1980, 81, 82; adminstrv. asst. Legis. Svc. Commn., Columbus, 1954-55; mem. Lucas County Charter Commn., Toledo, 1959-60; vice-chmn. U.S. Nat. Commn. for UNESCO, mem. legal com., del. 17th gen. conf., Paris, 1972, U.S. observer meeting of nat. commns., Africa, 1974, Addis Ababa, Ethiopia; past mem. industry functional adv. com. on standards trade policy matters; mem. nat. def. exec. res. Dept. Commerce; active Am. Bicentennial Presdl. Inauguration, Diplomatic Adv. Com. With USNR, 1945-46. Named Outstanding Young Man of Toledo, 1962. Mem. ABA, Maumee C. of C. (past pres.), Ohio State Bar Assn., Toledo Bar Assn., Ohio Mpcl. League (past pres.), Am. Legion, Lucas County Maumee Valley Hist. Soc. (trustee, past pres.) George Washington Law Assn., Internat. Inst. Toledo, Ohio Mcpl. Attys. Assn. (past pres.), Orgn. Security and Cooperation in Europe (registration supr., adjudicator, elections supr. in Bosnia), Ohio Hist. Soc., Canal Soc. Ohio, Toledo Mus. Art, Ohio Wesleyan U. Alumni Assn. (past pres.), Toledo C. of C., Ohio State Bar Found., Toledo Bar Found., Rotary, Faculty Club Med. Coll., Toledo Country Club, Omicron Delta Kappa, Delta Sigma Rho, Theta Alpha Phi, Phi Delta Phi. Presbyterian. Home: 124 W Harrison St Maumee OH 43537-2119 Office: 204 W Wayne St Maumee OH 43537-2125 E-mail: bmarsh124@aol.com.

MARSH, JAMES C., JR. secondary school principal; Headmaster Westminster Christian Acad., St. Louis, 1985—. Recipient Blue Ribbon Sch. award U.S. Dept. of Edn., 1990-91. Office: Westminster Christian Acad 10900 Ladue Rd Saint Louis MO 63141-8496

MARSH, MILES L. paper company executive; b. 1947; With various divsns. Dart & Kraft Inc., Gen. Foods USA; chmn., CEO, Pet Inc., St. Louis, until 1995; pres., CEO, Ft. James Corp., Richmond, 1995—, chmn. bd., 1996—, chmn., CEO Deerfield, Ill. Office: Ft James Corp PO Box 89 Deerfield IL 60015-0089

MARSH, RICHARD H. utilities company executive; CFO, v.p. First Energy Corp., Akron, Ohio. Office: First Energy Corp 76 Simain St Akron OH 44308-1890

MARSHAK, MARVIN LLOYD, physicist, educator; b. Mar. 11, 1946; s. Kalman and Goldie (Hait) M.; m. Anita Sue Kolman, Sept. 24, 1972; children: Rachel Kolman, Adam Kolman. AB in Physics, Cornell U., 1967; MS in Physics, U. Mich., PhD in Physics, 1970. Rsch. assoc. U. Minn., Mpls., 1970-74, from asst. prof. to assoc. prof., 1974-83, prof. physics, 1983-96, dir. grad. studies in physics, 1983-86, prin. investigator high energy physics, 1982-86, head Sch. Physics and Astronomy, 1986-96, sr. v.p. for acad. affairs, 1996-97, Morse-Alumni disting. tchg. prof. physics, 1996—, dir. residential coll., 1997—, faculty legis. liason, 1997—2001. Contbr. articles to profl. jours. Trustee Children's Theater Co., 1989-94. Mem. Am. Phys. Soc. Home: 2855 Ottawa Ave S Minneapolis MN 55416-1946 E-mail: marshak@umn.edu.

MARSHALEK, EUGENE RICHARD, physics educator, researcher; b. N.Y.C., Jan. 17, 1936; s. Frank M. and Sophie (Weg) M.; m. Sonja E. M. Lennhart, Dec. 8, 1962; children: Thomas, Frank. BS, Queens Coll., 1957; PhD, U. Calif., Berkeley, 1962. NSF postdoctoral fellow Niels Bohr Inst., Copenhagen, 1962-63; rsch. assoc. Brookhaven Nat. Lab., Upton, N.Y., 1963-65; asst. prof. physics U. Notre Dame, Ind., 1965-69, assoc. prof., 1969-78, prof., 1978—. Contbr. articles to profl. jours. Recipient Alexander von Humboldt sr. scientist award, 1985. Fellow Am. Phys. Soc.; mem. AAAS, Sigma Xi. Office: U Notre Dame Dept Physics Notre Dame IN 46556

MARSHALL, CAROLYN ANN M. church official, executive; b. Springfield, Ill., July 18, 1935; d. Hayward Thomas and Isabelle Bernice (Hayer) McMurray; m. John Alan Marshall, July 14, 1956 (dec. Sept. 1990); children: Margaret Marshall Bushman, Cynthia Marshall Kyrouac, Clinton, Carol Bentler. Student, De Pauw U., 1952-54; BSBA, Drake U., 1956; D of Pub. Svc. (hon.), De Pauw U., 1983; LHD (hon.), U. Indpls., 1990. Corp. sec. Marshall Studios, Inc., Veedersburg, Ind., 1956-89, exec. cons., 1989-93; sec. Gen. Conf., lay leader South Ind. conf. United Meth. Ch., 1988-96; exec. dir. Lucille Raines Residence, Inc., Indianapolis, 1996—. Carolyn M. Marshall chair in women studies Bennett Coll., Greensboro, N.C., 1988; fin. cons. Lucille Raines Residence, Inpls., 1977-95. Pres. Fountain Ctrl. Band Boosters, Veedersburg, 1975-77; del. Gen. Conf., United Meth. Ch., 1980, 84, 88, 92, 96, 2000, pres. women's divsn. gen. bd. global ministries, 1984-88; bd. dirs. Franklin (Ind.) United Meth. Ch. Home: 204 N Newlin St Veedersburg IN 47987-1358 Office: Lucille Raines Residence Inc 947 N Pennsylvania St Indianapolis IN 46204-1070 E-mail: cmarshall@sprintmail.com.

MARSHALL, CODY, bishop; Bishop No. Ill. Ch. of God in Christ, Chgo. Office: Freedom Temple Church of God in Christ 6028 S Champlain Ave Chicago IL 60637-2512

MARSHALL, DONALD GLENN, English language and literature educator; b. Long Beach, Calif., Sept. 9, 1943; s. Albert Louis and Margaret Corinne (Morrison) M.; m. Kathleen Bonann, June 21, 1975; children: Stephanie Deborah, Zachary Louis AB summa cum laude, Harvard U., 1965; MPhil, Yale U., 1969, PhD, 1971. Asst. prof. English UCLA, 1969-75; from assoc. prof. to prof. English U. Iowa, Iowa City, 1975-90; honors dir. U. Iowa Coll Liberal Arts, 1981-85; prof., head English dept. U. Ill., Chgo., 1990—. Editor: Philosophy as Literature/Literature as Philosophy, 1986; compiler: Contemporary Critical Theory: A Selective Bibliography, 1993; translator: (with Joel Weinsheimer) Truth and Method by Hans-Georg Gadamer, 1989; contbr. articles and revs. to profl. jours. Recipient Bell prize Harvard U., 1965, Webster prize Yale U., 1967; NEH Younger Humanist fellow, 1973-74; grantee UCLA, U. Iowa Mem.: MLA, Ill. Humanities Coun. (bd. dirs. 1994—2000, Chgo. Humanities Festival 1997—), Modern Poetry Assn. (pres. 1998—2000), Conf. Christianity and Lit. (bd. dirs. 2000—). Democrat. Roman Catholic. Office: U Ill Dept English Univ Hall 601 S Morgan St Chicago IL 60607-7120 E-mail: marshall@uic.edu.

MARSHALL, FRANCIS JOSEPH, aerospace engineer; b. N.Y.C., Sept. 5, 1923; s. Francis Joseph and Mary Gertrude (Leary) M.; m. Joan Eager, June 14, 1952; children— Peter, Colin, Stephen, Dana. B.S. in Mech. Engring, CCNY, 1948; M.S., Rensselaer Poly. Inst., 1950; Dr. Eng. Sci., N.Y. U., 1955. Engr. Western Union Co., N.Y.C., 1948, Gen. Electric Co., Schenectady, 1948-50; engr. Wright-Aero Corp., Woodridge, N.J., 1950-52; group leader Lab. for Applied Scis., U. Chgo., 1955-60; instr. Ill. Inst. Tech., 1957-59; prof. Sch. Aeros. and Astronautics, Purdue U., West Lafayette, Ind., 1960—. Engr. U.S. Naval Underseas Warfare Center, Pasadena, Calif., 1966-68; faculty fellow NASA-Langley, 1969-70; vis. prof. Inst. Tech. Mara-Midwest Univs. Consortium for Internat. Activities, Malayasia, 1989. Contbr. articles to profl. jours. Served with U.S. Army, 1943-46. Decorated Combat Inf. badge.; NASA research grantee, 1970-76; Fulbright scholar, Turkey, 1988-89. Asso. fellow AIAA; mem. Am. Soc. Engring. Edn., AAUP. Home: 120 Leslie Ave West Lafayette IN 47906-2410 Office: Sch Aeros and Astronautics Purdue U West Lafayette IN 47907

MARSHALL, GARLAND ROSS, biochemist, biophysicist, medical educator; b. San Angelo, Tex., Apr. 16, 1940; s. Garland Ross and Jewel Wayne (Gray) M.; m. Suzanne Russell, Dec. 26, 1959; children: Chris, Keith, Melissa, Lee. BS, Calif. Inst. Tech., 1962; PhD, Rockefeller U., 1966; DSc (hon.), Politechnika, Lodz, Poland, 1993. Instr. Washington U., St. Louis, 1966-67, asst. prof., 1967-72, assoc. prof., 1972-76, prof. biochemistry, 1976—, prof. pharmacology, 1985-2000, dir. Ctr. for Molecular Design, 1988-2000; pres. MetaPhore Pharm. Inc., 1995—. Vis. prof. Massey U., Palmerston North, New Zealand, 1975; vis. prof. chemistry U. Florence, Italy, 1991; pres. Tripos Assocs., Inc., St. Louis, 1979-87; chmn. 10th Am. Peptide Symposium, St. Louis, 1986-88; councilor Am. Peptide Soc., 1990-93; established investigator Am. Heart Assn., Washington, 1970-75. Editor: Peptides: Chemistry and Biology, 1988, Peptides: Chemistry, Structure and Biology, 1990; editor-in-chief Jour. Computer-Aided Molecular Design, 1986-98. Recipient medal L-Lecia Tech. U., Lodz, Poland, 1987, Vincent de Vigneaud award Am. Peptide Soc., 1994, Sci. and Tech. award St. Louis Regl. Commerce and Growth Assn., 1996. Mem. Am. Chem. Soc. (Medicinal Chemistry award 1988, Midwest award 1996), Am. Soc. for Biochemistry and Molecular Biology, Am. Soc. for Pharmacology and Exptl. Therapeutics, Biophys. Soc., Am. Peptide Soc. (Vincent du Vigneaud award 1994, Merrifield award 2001), Chinese Peptide Soc. (Cathay award 2000). Office: Washington U Ctr for Computational Biol 700 S Euclid Ave Saint Louis MO 63110-1012 E-mail: garland@pcg.wustl.edu.

MARSHALL, GERALD FRANCIS, physicist; b. Seven Kings, Eng., Feb. 26, 1929; BSc in Physics, London U., 1952. Physicist Morganite Internat., London, 1954—59; sr. rsch. devel. engr. Ferranti Ltd., Edinburgh, Scotland, 1959—67; project mgr. Diffraction Limited Inc., Bedford, Mass., 1967—69; dir. engring. Medical Lasers, Inc., Burlington, 1969—71; staff cons. Speedring Systems, Troy, Mich., 1971—76; dir. optical engring. Energy Conversion Devices, Inc., 1976—87; sr. tech. staff specialist Kaiser Electronics, San Jose, Calif., 1987—89; cons. in optics design and engring., 1989—. Editor(contbg. author): Laser Beam Scanning, 1985, Optical Scanning, 1991. Fellow: Optical Soc. Am. (program chair 1979—80, pres. Detroit sect. 1980—81, bd. dirs. No. Calif. sect. 1990—92), Internat. Soc. Optical Engring. (symposia chair 1990, bd. dirs. 1991—93, exec. chair Internat. Symposium on Electronic Imaging Device Engring., 1993), Inst. Physics. Achievements include patents in field. E-mail: marshallgf@aol.com.

MARSHALL, IRL HOUSTON, JR. franchise company executive; b. Evanston, Ill., Feb. 28, 1929; s. Irl H. and Marjorie (Greenleaf) M.; m. Barbara Favill, Nov. 5, 1949; children: Alice Marshall Vogler, Irl Houston III, Carol Marshall Allen. AB, Dartmouth Coll., 1949; MBA, U. Chgo., 1968; cert. franchise exec., La. State U., 1991. Gen. mgr. Duraclean Internat., Deerfield, Ill., 1949-61; mgr. Montgomery Ward, Chgo., 1961-77; pres., chief exec. officer Duraclean Internat., 1977-98; pres. Franchise Cons. Svcs., 1998—. Cons. Exec. Svc. Corps., 1999—. Inventor/patentee in field. Pres. Cliff Dwellers, Chgo., 1977; exec. com., treas., dir. Highland Park Hosp., 1971-80; bd. dirs. Better Bus. Bur. Chgo. & No. Ill., Chgo., 1988—. Mem. Internat. Franchise Assn. (bd. dirs. 1981-90, pres. 1985, chmn. 1985-86, bd. dirs. Ednl. Found. 1984—), Inst. Cert. Franchise Execs. (bd. govs. 1995—), Econ. Club Chgo., Exmoor Country Club, Univ. Club Chgo. Presbyterian. Home: 1248 Ridgewood Dr Northbrook IL 60062-3725

MARSHALL, JEFFREY SCOTT, mechanical engineer, educator; b. Cin., Feb. 10, 1961; s. James C. and Norma E. (Everett) M.; m. Marilyn Jane Patterson, July 16, 1983; children: Judith K., Eric G., Emily J., Paul E. BS summa cum laude, UCLA, 1983, MS, 1984; PhD, U. Calif., Berkeley, 1987. Asst. rsch. engr. U. Calif., Berkeley, 1988; engr. Creare, Inc., Hanover, N.H., 1988-89; from asst. to assoc. prof. dept. ocean engring. Fla. Atlantic U., 1989-93; from assoc. prof. to prof. dept. mech. engring. U. Iowa, Iowa City, 1993—2001, prof., chair dept. mech. and indsl. engring., 2001—. Assoc. editor Jour. Fluids Engring.; contbr. articles to profl. jours.; textbook author. Recipient Young Investigator award, 1992-95. Mem. ASME (assoc. editor jour. Fluids Engring. 2001-03, Henry Hess award 1992), Am. Phys. Soc., Tau Beta Pi. Achievements include research in fluid mechanics, three-dimensional vortex dynamics and vortex-structure interaction and thin film flows. Office: U Iowa Dept Mech & Indsl Engring Iowa City IA 52242 E-mail: jeffrey-marshall@uiowa.edu.

MARSHALL, JOHN DAVID, lawyer; b. Chgo., May 19, 1940; s. John Howard and Sophie (Brezenk) M.; m. Marcia A. Podlasinski, Aug. 26, 1961; children: Jacquelyn, David, Jason, Patricia, Brian, Denise, Michael, Catherine. BS in Acctg., U. Ill., 1961; JD, Ill. Inst. Tech., 1965. Bar: Ill. 1965, U.S. Tax Ct. 1968, U.S. Dist. Ct. (no. dist.) Ill. 1971; CPA, Ill. Ptnr. Mayer, Brown & Platt, Chgo., 1961—. Bd. dirs. Levinson Ctr. for Handicapped Children, Chgo., 1970-75. Fellow Am. Coll. Probate Counsel; mem. Ill. Bar Assn., Chgo. Bar Assn. (agribus. com. 1978—, trust law com. 1969—, probate practice com. 1969—, com. on coms. 1983—, vice chmn. 1988-89, chmn. 1989-90, legis. com. of probate practice com. 1983—, chmn. and vice chmn. legis. com. of probate practice com. 1983-84, chmn. exec. com. probate practice com. 1982-83, vice chmn. exec. com. 1981-82, sec. exec. com. 1980-81, div. chmn. 78-79, div. vice chmn. 1977-78, div. sec. 1976-77, Appreciation award 1982-83), Chgo. Estate Planning Council. Roman Catholic. Club: Union League (Chgo.). Office: Mayer Brown & Platt 190 S La Salle St Ste 3100 Chicago IL 60603-3441 Home: 429 N Willow Wood Dr Palatine IL 60074-3831

MARSHALL, JOHN ELBERT, III, foundation executive; b. Providence, July 2, 1942; s. John Elbert Jr. and Millicent Edna (Paige) M.; m. Diana M. Healy, Aug. 16, 1968; children: Nelson John, Priscilla Anne. B.A., Brown U., 1964. Advt. mgr. U.N. Alloy Steel Corp., Boston, 1968-70; assoc. dir. devel. Brown U., 1970-74; exec. dir. R.I. Found., Providence, 1974-79; v.p. Kresge Found., Troy, Mich., 1979-82, exec. v.p., 1982-87, pres., 1987—, trustee, 1991—; CEO, 1993—. Bd. dirs. Ind. Sector; former chmn. Mich. Cmty. Found. Youth Project. Bd. dirs. United Way Cmty. Svcs., Detroit Symphony Orch. Hall, Greater Downtown Partnership, Schs. for 21st Century; former bd. dirs. Mich. Campus Compact; former bd. dirs., vice chmn. Family Svc. Detroit and Wayne County; past pres. Bloomfield Village Assn.; former trustee Coun. on Founds., Washington. Office: Kresge Found PO Box 3151 Troy MI 48007-3151

MARSHALL, MARK F. lawyer; b. 1954; BS, U. S.D., 1977, JD, 1981. Bar: S.D. 1981, U.S. Dist. Ct. S.D. 1981, U.S. Ct. Appeals (8th cir.) 1981, U.S. Supreme Ct. 1984. Law clk. hon. Fred J. Nichol, 1981-83; assoc. Bangs, McCullen, Butler, Foye & Simmons, Rapid City, SD, 1983-96; of counsel Johnson, Heidepriem, Miner, Marlow & Janklow, Sioux Falls, 1996—2000; magistrate judge U.S. Dist. Ct. S.D., 1996-2000; ptnr. Davenport Law Firm, 2000—. Office: 513 S Main Ave # 1030 Sioux Falls SD 57104-6813

MARSHALL, RON, company executive; BS with honors, Wright State U. V.p., CFO Barnes & Noble Bookstores; sr. v.p., CFO Dart Group Corp., Md., 1991-94; exec. v.p., CFO, Pathmark Stores, N.J., 1994-98; pres., CEO, Nash Finch Co., Mpls., 1998—. Mem. Food Mktg. Inst. (bd. dirs.). Office: Nash Finch Co 7600 France Ave S Ste 200 Minneapolis MN 55435-5920

MARSHALL, SHERRIE, newspaper editor; Metro editor Star Tribune, Mpls., to 1998, editor news content, 1995—, dep. managing editor, 1999—. Office: Star Tribune 425 Portland Ave Minneapolis MN 55488-0002

MARSHALL, SIRI SWENSON, corporate lawyer; BA, Harvard U., 1970; JD, Yale U., 1974. Bar: N.Y. 1975. Assoc. Debevoise & Plimpton, 1974-79; atty., sr. atty., asst. gen. counsel Avon Products, Inc., N.Y.C., 1979-85, v.p. legal affairs, 1985-89, sr. v.p., gen. counsel, 1990-94, Gen. Mills, Inc., Mpls., 1994-99, sr. v.p. corp. affairs, gen. counsel, sec., 1999—. Bd. dirs. Jafra Cosmetics, Am. Arbitration Assn.; mem. exec. com. Ctr. Pub. Resources. Trustee Mpls. Inst. Arts. Office: Gen Mills Inc Number One Gen Mills Blvd Minneapolis MN 55426

MARSHALL, VINCENT DE PAUL, industrial microbiologist, researcher; b. Washington, Apr. 5, 1943; s. Vincent de Paul Sr. and Mary Frances (Bach) M.; m. Sylvia Ann Kieffer, Nov. 15, 1986; children from previous marriage: Vincent de Paul III, Amy. BS, Northeastern State Coll., Tahlequah, Okla., 1965; MS, U. Okla. Health Sci. Ctr., Oklahoma City, 1967, PhD, 1970. Rsch. assoc. U. Ill., Urbana, 1970, postdoctoral fellow, 1971-73; rsch. scientist The Upjohn Co., Kalamazoo, 1973-74, rsch. head, 1975, sr. rsch. scientist, 1976-91, sr. scientist, 1991-2000; cons., 2000—. Mem. editl. bd. Jour. of Antibiotics, 1990-2001, Jour. Indsl. Microbiology, 1989-2001, Devels. in Indsl. Microbiology, 1990; contbr. numerous articles to profl. jours., chpts. to books; patentee in field. Served with U.S. Army Nat. Guard, 1960-65. NIH predoctoral fellow, 1967-70; NIH postdoctoral fellow, 1971-73. Fellow Am. Acad. Microbiology; mem. Soc. for Indsl. Microbiology (membership com. 1988-90, co-chair edn. com. 1989-93, local sects. com. 1991-96, chair nominating com. 1993-94, mem. nominating com. 1999-2000, co-chair program com. 1993-94, dir. 1994-96, pres. So. Great Lakes sect. 1992-95), Am. Soc. Microbiology, Am. Soc. Biochemistry and Molecular Biology, Internat. Soc. for Antimicrobial Activity of Non-Antibiotics (sci. adv. bd.), Sigma Xi. Republican. Lutheran. Home and Office: 203 Paisley Ct Kalamazoo MI 49006-4359 E-mail: vince3795@aol.com.

MARTEL, WILLIAM, radiologist, educator; b. N.Y.C., Oct. 1, 1927; s. Hyman and Fanny M.; m. Rhoda Kaplan, Oct. 9, 1956; children: Lisa, Pamela, Caryn, Jonathan, David. M.D., NYU, 1953. Intern, Kings County Hosp., N.Y., 1953-54; resident in radiology Mt. Sinai Hosp., N.Y.C., 1954-57; instr. radiology U. Mich., Ann Arbor, 1957-60, asst. prof., 1960-63, asso. prof., 1963-67, prof., 1967—, Fred Jenner Hodges prof., 1984—, chmn. dept. radiology, 1981-92, dir. skeletal radiology, 1970-81, Fred Jenner Hodges prof. emeritus radiology, 1997—. Contbr. articles to Radiol. Diagnoses of Arthritic Diseases. Served with USAAF, 1945-46. Recipient Amoco U. Mich. Outstanding Teaching award, 1980; established William Martel professorship in radiology U. Mich., 1997. Mem. Radiol. Soc. N.Am., Am. Roentgen Ray Soc., Assn. Univ. Radiologists. Home: 2972 Parkridge Dr Ann Arbor MI 48103-1737 Office: Univ Mich Hosps Dept Radiology 1500 E Med Ctr Dr Ann Arbor MI 48109 E-mail: wmartel@umich.edu.

MARTEN, J. THOMAS, judge; BA, Washburn U., 1973, JD, 1976. Judge U.S. Dist. Ct. Kans., 1996—. Office: US Courthouse 401 N Market St Wichita KS 67202-2089

MARTEN, RANDOLPH L. transportation executive; Pres., chmn. Marten Transport, Ltd., Mondovi, Wis., 1974—. Office: Marten Transport Ltd 129 Marten St Mondovi WI 54755-1700

MARTH, MARY ELLEN (KIM MARTIN), entertainer; b. Atkinson, Minn., July 15, 1936; d. Sigvard B. Kanikkeberg and Beatrice M. (Lundberg) Wangen; m. T.A. Martinez (div.); m. Luther H. Marth (div.); children: Mitzie, Leslie, Tina, Allen. Entertainer The Kim Martin Show, 1960—. Band leader Kim Martin Show, 1960—; real estate owner Marth Properties, Mpls., 1972—. Author of poems, songs, articles, short stories, childrens books, historian, humanitarian. Sec. Hennepin County Adult Foster Care, Mpls, 1983—; mem. Summit Ministries, Colo, 1995, Columbia Heights Owners Assn., 1990—, Multi-Housing Assn., Mpls, 1993—, Vesterheim Geneal. Mus., 1990, Norwegian Am. Mus., 1988—. Named Queen of Country Music, Country Entertainers Assn., Mpls., 1977, Entertainer of Yr. 1978, Female Vocalist of Yr., 1978, Best Band of Yr., 1979, Songwriter of Yr., 1980. Mem. Winnesheik Geneal. Soc., Filmore County Hist. Soc., Vesterheim Geneal. Soc., Minn. Historical Soc. Lutheran. E-mail: Kimtonem@aol.com.

MARTIN, ARTHUR MEAD, lawyer; b. Cleveland Heights, Ohio, Mar. 29, 1942; s. Bernard P. and Winifred (Mead) M. AB, Princeton U., 1963; LLB, Harvard U., 1966. Bar: Ill. 1966, U.S. Dist. Ct. (no. dist.) Ill. 1969, U.S. Ct. Appeals (7th cir.) 1970, U.S. Supreme Ct. 1980, U.S. Ct. Appeals (fed. cir.) 2000. Instr. law U. Wis., Madison, 1966-68; assoc. Jenner & Block, Chgo., 1968-74, ptnr., 1975—. Co-trustee Dille Family Trust, 1982—; bd. dirs. Sleepeck Printing Co. Author: Historical and Practice Notes to the Illinois Civil Practice Act and Illinois Supreme Court Rules, 1968-88. Trustee 4th Presbyn. Ch., Chgo., sec. 1997-99, exec. com. 1997-99; bd. dirs. Stop Colon/Rectal Cancer Found., 1998—. Mem. ABA, Am. Law Inst., Ill. Bar Assn., Chgo. Bar Assn. (bd. editors 1972-86), Ill. State Hist. Soc. (adv. bd. 1998-99, bd. dirs. 1999—, exec. com. 1999—, fin. com. 1999—, treas. 2002--), Ill. Centennial Bus. Com., Lake Mich. Fedn. (bd. dirs. 1993—, exec. com. 1994—, treas. 1994-99, 2001--, sec. 1999-2001), Law Club Chgo., Legal Club Chgo. Office: Jenner & Block 1 IBM Plz Fl 4400 Chicago IL 60611-7603 E-mail: amartin@jenner.com.

MARTIN, BRUCE JAMES, newspaper editor; b. Pontiac, Mich., Sept. 2, 1956; s. James Patrick and Patricia Ann (Taylor) M.; m. Elizabeth Hartley Nutting, July 30, 1988. BJ, U. Mo., 1982. Reporter Spinal Col. Newsweekly, Union Lake, Mich., 1982; sports editor Northville (Mich.) Record/Novi News, 1982-85; news editor Novi News, Northville, 1984-85; copy editor Kalamazoo Gazette, 1985-89, Ann Arbor (Mich.) News, 1989-91, homes editor, 1991, arts and entertainment editor, 1991—. Recipient 1st Place in Sports Writing in Circulation Category, Mich. Press Assn., 1993. Avocations: songwriting, playing piano and guitar. Office: Ann Arbor News 340 E Huron St Ann Arbor MI 48104-1900

MARTIN, GARY JOSEPH, medical educator; b. Chgo., Mar. 12, 1952; m. Helen Gartner; children: Daniel T., David G. BA in Psychology, U. Ill., 1974, MD, 1978. Diplomate Am. Bd. Internal Medicine, Am. Bd. Cardiovascular Disease, Nat. Bd. Med. Examiners; lic. physician, Ill. Intern, resident internal medicine Northwestern U. Med. Sch., Chgo., 1978-81, instr. medicine, 1981-82, asst. prof. medicine, 1984-90, assoc. prof., 1990-96, prof., 1996—, divsn. chief, divsn. gen. internal medicine, 1988-2001, assoc. chmn. dept. medicine, 1998-2000, vice chmn. dept. medicine, 2001—; cardiology fellow Loyola U. Med. Ctr., 1982-84; attending physician Northwestern Meml. Hosp./Northwestern Med. Faculty Found., Chgo., 1984—; chief med. resident, attending physician Northwestern Meml. Hosp., 1981-82; dir. primary care clerkship Nat. Ctr. for Advanced Med. Edn., 1984—. Chmn. outpatient utilization rev. and quality assurance com., 1985-93; chmn. Northwestern Meml. Hosp./Lakeside VA Rsch. Com., 1988-91; dir. tng. gen. internal medicine residency program, 1985—; bd. dirs. com. Northwestern Med. Faculty Found., 1993—; cons. health care divsn. Ernst & Young, 1991—; peer reviewer Faculty Devel. Rev. Com. Panel 1, 1994. Contbr. articles to profl. jours. Fellow Buehler Ctr. on Aging. Fellow Am. Coll. Cardiology; mem. ACP, Soc. Gen. Internal Medicine, Am. Heart Assn. Office: Northwestern U Med Sch Divsn Gen Internal Medicine 675 N Saint Clair St Ste 18-200 Chicago IL 60611-5929

MARTIN, J(OSEPH) PATRICK, lawyer; b. Detroit, Apr. 19, 1938; s. Joseph A. and Kathleen G. (Rich) M.; m. Denise Taylor, June 27, 1964; children: Timothy J., Julie D. AB magna cum laude, U. Notre Dame, 1960; JD with distinction, U. Mich., 1963; postgrad., London Sch. Econs., 1964. Bar: Mich. 1963, U.S. Dist. Ct. (ea. dist.) Mich. 1963, U.S. Ct. Appeals (6th cir.) 1967, U.S. Supreme Ct. 1979, U.S. Dist. Ct. (we. dist.) Mich. 1981, U.S. Ct. Fed. Claims 1999. Spl. asst. to gen. counsel Ford Motor Co., Dearborn, Mich., 1962; assoc. Dykema, Wheat, Spencer et al, Detroit, 1963-66; assoc., then ptnr. Poole Littell Sutherland, 1966-76; sr. atty., ptnr., shareholder Butzel Long, Detroit and Birmingham, Mich., 1976-94; sr. atty., shareholder Vlcko, Lane, Payne & Broder PC, Bingham Farms, 1994-96; sr. atty. Gourwitz and Barr PC, Southfield, 1996-99; pvt. practice, 2000—. Adj. prof. remedies and alternative dispute resolution U. Detroit Law Sch., 1989—, Wayne State U. Law Sch., 1996—, Cooley Law Sch., 2001--; arbitrator Am. Arbitration Assn., Southfield, Mich., 1968—, Nat. Assn. Security Dealers, 1988—, N.Y. Stock Exch., 1991—; state court adminstrv. office approved mediator all Mich. Cts. under new ADR rules; case evaluator, discovery master Oak County Cir. Ct., Pontiac, Mich., 1985—; mediator Lex Mundi, Coll. of Mediators, 1992—; case evaluator Mediation Tribunal Assn. for Wayne County Cir. Ct., 1992—; moderator Mich. State Ct. Appeals, 1995—; case evaluator Oakland County Dist. Cts., 1998—. Author, editor: Laches-Oak County Bar Assn. Legal Jour., 1984, 92, 96, Real Property Rev., 1989-90, Mich. Law Weekly, 1990; ADR Newsletter, 2000. Scholar Cook Found., Ford Found., London, 1963-64. Mem. ABA, State Bar Mich. (chair alternative dispute sect.), Oakland County Bar Assn. (chair fed. ct. com., chair Mich. dist. ct. com.), Mich. State Bar Found. Roman Catholic. Avocations: gardening, golf, walking. Home and Office: 1663 Hoit Tower Dr Bloomfield Hills MI 48302-2630 Fax: 248-932-0368. E-mail: jpatrickmartin@aol.com.

MARTIN, KATHRYN A. academic administrator; Dean Sch. Fine and Performing Arts Wayne State U., Detroit; chancellor U Minn, Duluth, 1995—. Office: University of Minnesota-Duluth Office of the Chancellor Admin Bldng 10 University Dr Duluth MN 55812-2496

MARTIN, KEVIN JOHN, nephrologist, educator; b. Dublin, Ireland, Jan. 18, 1948; came to U.S., 1973; s. John Martin and Maura Martin; m. Grania E. O'Connor, Nov. 16, 1972; children: Alan, John, Ciara, Audrey. MB BCh, Univ. Coll. Dublin, 1971. Diplomate Am. Bd. Internal Medicine, Am. Bd. Nephrology. Intern St. Vincent's Hosp., Dublin, 1971-72, resident, 1972-73, Barnes Hosp., St. Louis, 1973-74, fellow, 1974-77; asst. prof. Washington U., 1977-84, assoc. prof., 1984-89; prof., dir. div. nephrology St. Louis U., 1989—. Contbr. numerous articles to med. jours. Office: Saint Louis Univ Med Ctr 3635 Vista Ave Saint Louis MO 63110-2539

MARTIN, KIM See MARTH, MARY ELLEN

MARTIN, LAURA BELLE, real estate and farm land owner and manager; b. Jackson County, Minn., Nov. 3, 1915; d. Eugene Wellington and Mary Christina (Hanson) M. BS, Mankato State U., 1968. Tchr. rural schs., Renville County, Minn., 1936-41, 45-50, Wabasso (Minn.) Pub. Sch., 1963-81; pres. Renville Farms and Feed Lots, 1982-86. Author: Historical Biography of Joseph Renville, 1996; published poet Nat. Libr. Poetry. Pres. Wabasso (Minn.) Edn. Assn., 1974-75, publicity chmn., 1968-74; sec. and publicity agt. Hist. Renville Preservation Com., 1978-86; publicity chmn., sec. Town and Country Boosters, Renville, 1982-83. Mem. Genealogy Soc. Renville County, Am. Legion Aux. Democrat. Lutheran. Avocations: antique furniture, travel, sewing, writing poetry. Home and Office: 334 NW 1201st Rd Holden MO 64040-9378

MARTIN, MARY, secondary education educator; b. Detroit, May 17, 1954; d. Enos and Sara (Evans) M. AS, Highland Park C.C., 1975; BA, Wayne State U., 1975, MA in Teaching, 1981; postgrad., So. Calif. Sch. Ministry, Detroit, 1992—. Dietary aide Allan Dee Nursing Home, Detroit, 1972, Harper Hosp., Detroit, 1973, 74, nurse aide, 1974-75, respiratory technician, 1975-80, Dr.'s Hosp., Detroit, 1980; head cook, supr. Focus Hope, 1981; substitute tchr. Detroit Bd. Edn., 1984-90, tchr. adult edn., 1990-93, tchr., 1993—. Interim advisor student coun. Wayne State U., Detroit, 1985. Sunday sch. teaching trainer People's Missionary Bapt. Ch., Detroit, 1986, del., 1984-87, mem. All Aid, 1984-87, mem. choir, 1984, usher, 1984; precinct del. 13th Congl. Dist., 1986-88, 90-92, model, 1985. Recipient Spirit of Detroit award Detroit City Coun., 1993, Spl. Congl. cert. Hon. Barbara Rose Collins, 1994, Proclamation, Wayne County Commr. George Cushingberry, 1994. Mem. Nat. Sociol. Honor Soc. Democrat. Avocations: reading, shopping, movies, golf, driving.

MARTIN, NOEL, graphic design consultant, educator; b. Syracuse, Ohio, Apr. 19, 1922; s. Harry Ross and Lula (Van Meter) M.; m. Coletta Ruchty, Aug. 29, 1942; children— Dana, Reid Cert. in Fine Arts, Art Acad. Cin., Doctorate (hon.), 1994. Designer Cin. Art Mus., 1947-93, asst. to dir., 1947-55; freelance designer for various ednl., cultural and indsl. orgns., 1947—; instr. Art Acad. Cin., 1951-57, artist-in-residence, 1993—. Design cons. Champion Internat., 1959-82, Xomox Corp., 1961—, Federated Dept. Stores, 1962-83, Hebrew Union Coll., 1969—; designer-in-residence U. Cin., 1968-71, adj. prof., 1968-73; mem. adv. bd. Carnegie-Mellon U., R.I. Sch. Design, Cin. Symphony Orch., Am. Inst. Graphic Arts; lectr. Smithsonian Instn., Libr. of Congress, Am. Inst. Graphic Arts, Aspen Design Conf., various additional schs. and orgns. nationally. One man shows include Contemporary Arts Ctr., Cin., 1954, 71, Addison Gallery Am. Art, 1955, R.I. Sch. Design, 1955, Soc. Typographic Arts, Chgo., 1956, White Mus. of Cornell U., 1956, Cooper & Beatty, Toronto, Ont., Can., 1958, Am. Inst. Graphic Arts, 1958, Ind. U., 1958, Ohio State U., 1971; exhibited in group shows at Mus. Modern Art, N.Y.C., Library of Congress, Musee d'Art Moderne, Paris, Grafiska Inst., Stockholm, Carpenter Ctr., Cambridge, Gutenberg Mus., Mainz, U.S. info. exhbns. In Europe, South America and USSR; represented in permanent collections Mus. Modern Art, Stedelijk Mus., Amsterdam, Cin. Art Mus., Boston Mus. Fine Arts, Cin. Hist. Soc., Library of Congress; contbr. to various publs. Served to sgt. U.S. Air Force, 1942-45 Recipient Art Directors medal, Phila., 1957, Sachs award, Cin., 1973, Lifetime Achievement award Cin. Art Dirs., 1989.

MARTIN, PATRICIA, dean, nursing educator; BSN, U. Cin.; MS, Wright State U.; PhD, Case Western Res. U. Dir. nursing rsch., interim dean, assoc. prof. Wright State U. Contbr. articles to profl. jours. Office: Wright State U 168 University Hall Dayton OH 45435-0001

MARTIN, PHILLIP HAMMOND, lawyer; b. Tucson, Jan. 4, 1940; s. William P. and Harriet (Hammond) M.; m. Sandra S. Chandler, June 17, 1961 (div. Mar. 1989); children: Lisa, Craig, Wade, Ryan; m. Erika Zetty, May 9, 1990. BA, U. Minn., 1961, JD, 1964. Bar: Minn. 1964, U.S. Tax Ct. 1967, U.S. Dist. Ct. Minn. 1968, U.S. Ct. Appeals (8th cir.) 1973, U.S. Supreme Ct. 1981, U.S. Claims Ct. 1983, U.S. Ct. Appeals (fed. cir.) 1988, U.S. Ct. Appeals (7th cir.) 1989. Assoc. Dorsey & Whitney, Mpls., 1964-69, ptnr., 1970—. Home: 487 Portland Ave Saint Paul MN 55102-2216 Office: Dorsey & Whitney Ste 1500 50 S 6th St Minneapolis MN 55402-1498 E-mail: martin.phil@dorseylaw.com.

MARTIN, QUINN WILLIAM, lawyer; b. Fond du Lac, Wis., Mar. 12, 1948; s. Quinn W. and Marcia E. Martin; m. Jane E. Nehmer; children: Quinn W., William J. BSME, Purdue U., 1969; postgrad., U. Santa Clara, 1969-70; JD, U. Mich., 1973. Bar: Wis. 1973, U.S. Dist. Ct. (ea. dist.) Wis. 1973, U.S. Ct. Appeals (7th cir.) 1973. Sales support mgr. Hewlett-Packard, Palo Alto, Calif., 1969-70; assoc. Quarles & Brady, Milw., 1973-80, ptnr., 1980—. Bd. dirs. Associated Bank Milw., U-Line Corp., Gen. Timber and Land, Inc., Fond du Lac. Chmn. gov. McCallum Trans Com., Wis., U. Mich. Law Sch. Fund; bd. dirs. Milw. Zool. Soc., Found. for Wildlife Conservation. Mem. ABA, Wis. Bar Assn., Milw. Club, Ozaukee Country Club, Chaine des Rottiseurs, Delta Upsilon (sec.), Milw. Alumni Club, Rotary. Office: Quarles & Brady 411 E Wisconsin Ave Ste 2550 Milwaukee WI 53202-4497

MARTIN, REX, manufacturing executive; Chmn, pres., CEO Nibco, Elkhart, Ind. Office: Nibco Inc 1516 Middleberry St PO Box 1167 Elkhart IN 46515-1167

MARTIN, ROBERT DAVID, judge, educator; b. Iowa City, Oct. 7, 1944; s. Murray and G'Ann (Holmgren) M.; m. Ruth A. Haberman, Aug. 21, 1966; children: Jacob, Matthew, David. AB, Cornell Coll., Mt. Vernon, Iowa, 1966; JD, U. Chgo., 1969. Bar: Wis. 1969, U.S. Dist. Ct. (we. dist.) Wis. 1969, U.S. Dist. Ct. (ea. dist.) Wis. 1974, U.S. Supreme Ct. 1973. Assoc. Ross & Stevens, S.C., Madison, Wis., 1969-72, ptnr., 1973-78; chief judge U.S. Bankruptcy Ct. We. Dist. Wis., 1978—. Instr. gen. practice course U. Wis. Law Sch., 1974, 76, 77, 80, lectr. debtor/creditor course, 1981-82, 83, 85, 87, 2001, farm credit seminar, 1985, advanced bankruptcy problems, 1989, 91, 96; co-chmn. faculty Am. Law Inst.-ABA Fin. and Bus. Planning for Agr., Stanford U., 1979; faculty mem. Fed. Jud. Ctr. Schs. for New Bankruptcy Judges, 1985-96; chmn. Ann. Continuing Legal Edn. Wis. Debtor Creditor Conf., 1981—. Author: Bankruptcy: Annotated Forms, 1989; co-author: Secured Transactions Handbook for Wisconsin Lawyers and Lenders, Bankruptcy-Text Statutes Rules and Forms, 1992, Ginsberg and Martin on Bankruptcy, 4th edit., 1996. Chmn., bd. dirs., mem. exec. com. Luth. Social Svc. Wis. and Upper Mich.; bd. dirs., mem. exec. com. Turnaround Mgmt. Assn., 1997—. Mem. Wis. State Bar, Am. Coll. Bankruptcy, Am. Judicature Soc., Nat. Conf. Bankruptcy Judges (bd. govs. 1989-91, sec. 1993-94, v.p. 1994-95, pres. 1995-96), Nat. Bankruptcy Conf. Office: 120 N Henry Rm 340 PO Box 548 Madison WI 53701-0548

MARTIN, ROBERT EDWARD, architect; b. Dodge City, Kans., Mar. 17, 1928; s. Emry and Alice Jane (Boyce) M.; m. Billie Jo Lange, Aug. 16, 1952 (div. Feb. 1970); m. Kathryn M. Arvanitis, June 26, 1971; children: Lynn, Amy, Blaine. Student, McPherson Coll., 1946-48; BArch, U. Cin., 1954. Registered architect, Ohio. Architect Samborn, Steketee, Otis & Evans, Inc., Toledo, 1956-58; prin. Schauder & Martin, 1958-72, The Collaborative, Inc., Toledo, 1972-93. Mem. Bd. Examiners Archs., Ohio, 1985-95, pres., 1989-94; bd. examiners Nat. Coun. Archtl. Registration Bds., 1986-95, edn. com., 1992; chmn. site design divsn. Archtl. Registration Exam., 1989, 90, 91; mem. Nat. Coun. Archtl. Registration Bds. Grading, 1987-94; chmn. study of Toledo Fire & Rescue Dept., Corp. for Effective Govt., 1994. Artist numerous paintings. Mem. Toledo Planning Commn., 1971-74, Toledo Zoning Appeals Bd., 1973, Toledo Bd. Bldg. Stds., 1967-84, Citizens Fire Adv. Commn., 1974-80, Citizens Urban Area Adv. Commn., 1962, Toledo Area Coun. Govts., 1977-80, Com. of 100, Toledo, 1987-89, Spectrum Friends Fine Arts, Inc., Toledo; chmn. bd. Toledo Area Govtl. Rsch. Assn., 1981-90; chmn. Corp. for Effective Govt., Study of Toledo Fire and Rescue Dept., 1994; chmn. Cystic Fibrosis, Toledo. 1985. Served to capt. USAF, 1954-56. Recipient numerous watercolor awards. Fellow AIA (pres. Toledo chpt. 1966, Arch. of Yr. 1993), Archs. Soc. Ohio (pres. 1975), Ohio Watercolor Soc. (trustee 1999—), N.W. Ohio Watercolor Soc., Toledo Fedn. Art Socs. (pres. 1989, 90), Spectrum, Tile Club (v.p.), Toledo Artists Club, Sylvania Country Club, Rotary, Masons, Shriners, Jesters. Mem. Ch. of Brethren. Avocation: painting. Home: 5119 Regency Dr Toledo OH 43615-2946 Office: 1700 N Reynolds Rd Toledo OH 43615-3628

MARTIN, ROGER BOND, landscape architect, educator; b. Virginia, Minn., Nov. 23, 1936; s. Thomas George and Audrey (Bond) M.; m. Janis Ann Kloss, Aug. 11, 1962; children: Thomas, Stephen, Jonathan. BS with high distinction, U. Minn., 1958; M. Landscape Arch., Harvard U., 1961. Asst. prof. U. Calif.-Berkeley, 1964-66; from assoc. prof. to prof. emeritus U. Minn., Mpls., 1966—99, prof. emeritus, 1999—; owner Roger Martin & Assoc., site planners and landscape architects, 1966-68, 99—; prin. InterDesign, Inc., 1968-84, Martin & Pitz Assocs., Inc., 1984-98; vis. prof. U. Melbourne, 1979-80. Vis. prof. coll. architecture, 2000—02. Prin. works include Minn. Zool. Gardens, 1978 (merit award Am. Soc. Landscape Archs., 1978), Mpls. Pkwy. Restorations, 1972—87 (merit award, 1978, Minn. Classic award Am. Soc. Landscape Archs., 1994), South St. Paul Ctrl. Sq., 1978 (merit award, 1978), Festival Park, Chisholm, Minn., 1986 (merit award, 1986), Miss. Wildlife Refuge Visual Image assessment (merit award, 1989), Nicollet Island Park, Hennepin Avenue Master Plan, 1995 (merit award, 1995). Recipient Fredrick Mann award for svc. to edn. U. Minn., 1990, Disting. Educator award Sigma Lambda Alpha, 1990, Bradford Williams medals for outstanding articles in landscape Architecture mag., 1968, 69, Minn. chpt. Lob Pine award for outstanding svc. to landscape architecture, 1988, Mpls. Com. on Urban Environ. award for design of Whittier Park, 1997; fellow Am. Acad. in Rome, 1962-64. Fellow Am. Soc. Landscape Archs. (pres. Minn. chpt. 1970-72, trustee 1980-84, nat. pres. 1987, chmn.-elect coun. fellows 1991, chmn. 1992-94, past chmn. 1994-96, Pub. Svc. award 1985, Minn. chpt. Classic award 1994); mem. Nat. Coun. Instrs. Landscape Architecture (pres. 1973-74), Can. Soc. Landscape Archs. (hon.). Home and Office: 2912 45th Ave S Minneapolis MN 55406-1829 E-mail: marti009@tc.umn.edu.

MARTIN, TERENCE D. food products executive; CFO Am. Cyanamid Co.; exec. v.p., CFO Gen. Signal Corp.; sr. v.p. fin., CFO Quaker Oats Co., Chgo., 1998—. Office: Quaker Oats Quaker Tower 321 N Clark St Ste 27-8 Chicago IL 60610-4714

MARTIN, VINCENT LIONEL, manufacturing company executive; b. Los Angles, June 29, 1939; s. Arthur Seymon and Alice Maria (Miller) M.; m. Janet Ann Dowler, Mar. 25, 1961; children: Jennifer Lynn, Karen Arlene, Timothy Paul. BS, Stanford U., 1960; MBA, Harvard U., 1963. Various staff positions FMC Corp, Chgo, 1966-74, gen. mgr. Crane and Excavator div. Cedar Rapids, Iowa, 1974-79; pres. Equipment Systems div. AMCA Internat. Corp., Houston, 1979-81, group v.p. Brookfield, Wis., 1981-85; CEO, pres. Jason Inc., Milw., 1986-96, chmn. CEO, 1996-99, chmn., 1999—. Mem. Phi Beta Kappa, Tau Beta Pi Republican. Presbyterian. Home: 2601 W Cedar Ln Milwaukee WI 53217-1138 Office: Jason Inc 411 E Wisconsin Ave Milwaukee WI 53202-4461 E-mail: Vmartin@jasoninc.com.

MARTIN, WILLIAM BRYAN, chancellor, lawyer, minister; b. Lexington, Ky., Apr. 11, 1938; s. William Stone and Alice Bryan (Spiers) Martin; m. Mary Ellen Matson, Aug. 11, 1973; children: Chanley Morgan, Matson Bryan, Evan Andrew. AB, Transylvania U., 1960; JD, U. Ky., 1964; LLM, Georgetown U., Washington, 1965; MDiv summa cum laude, Emory U., 1979. Bar: Ky. 1964, D.C. 1964; ordained to ministry Christian Ch. (Disciples of Christ), 1981. Legal intern Pub. Defender, Washingotn, 1964-65; asst. U.S. atty. Western Dist. Ky., 1965-67; assoc. McElwain, Denning, Clarke and Winstead, Louisville, 1967-69; asst. atty. gen. Commonwealth of Ky., 1969-70; prof. U. Louisville Sch. Law, 1970-81; dean Oklahoma City U. Sch. Law, 1982-83; pres. Franklin Coll. Ind., 1983-97. Bd. dirs. Coun. Ind. Colls., Washington, 1990-94; mem. Commn. on Pub. Rels. Nat. Assn. Ind. Colls. and Univs., 1992-99 (chmn. 1998-99); bd. dirs. Ind. Colls. Ind. Found., 1983-97, 1st vice chmn., 1992—, chmn., 1993-94, mem. spl. study com. and strategic planning com., mem. transition task force, 1991-92; mem. Ind. Colls. Ind., Ind. Conf. Higher Edn., 1983—; sec. Am. Bapt. Assn. Colls. and Univs., 1989-97; cons.-evaluator North Ctrl. Assn., Commn. on Instns. Higher Edn., 1985. Columnist Scripps Howard News Svc., 1991-97; contbr. articles to profl. jours. Mem. adv. bd. Heartland Film Festival, 1995—; bd. regents Ind. Acad., 1988-97, v.p. bd. 1986-98; bd. trustees Christian Theol. Sem., 1986-98, past mem. investment com., chair ednl. policies com.; bd. dirs., exec. com. Historic Landmarks Found. Ind., 1987-91, adv. coun., 1991—; first chmn. coun. pres. Ind. Collegiate Athletic Conf., 1987-90; elder Tabernacle Christian Ch., Franklin, 1983-91, North Christian Ch., Columbus, 1994-98; mem. Progress Forum Johnson County, 1987-92; mem. adv. bd. Greater Johnson County Cmty. Found., Inc., 1992-94; mem. Historic Preservation Task Force, Divsn. Historic Preservation and Archaeology, Ind. Dept. Natural Resources; mem. Nat. Environ. Task Force.ship com., tchr. family life class Douglass Blvd. Christian Ch.; deacon Crown Heights Christian Ch., Okla. Recipient Svc. award Franklin Heritage, 1986, Man of Yr. award Franklin C. of C., 1986, Disting. Svc. cert. Transylvania U., 1987, Assoc. Alumnus award Franklin Coll., 1998. Mem. Ben Franklin Soc., Ind. Soc. Chgo., Econ. Club Indpls., Junto Club Indpls., Columbia Club Indpls., Rotary of Franklin, Hillview Country Club, Alpha Soc. Home: Pres Residence & Reception Chancellors House 550 Davis Dr Franklin IN 46131 Office: Franklin Coll Ind 501 E Monroe St Franklin IN 46131-2512

MARTIN, WILLIAM F. transportation company legal executive; V.p., legal and asst. sec. Yellow Freight System, Inc., Overland Park, Kans. Office: Yellow Freight System IncDel 10777 Barkley St Overland Park KS 66211-1161

MARTIN, WILLIAM GIESE, lawyer; b. Canton, Ohio, Nov. 4, 1934; s. George Denman and Emily (Giese) M.; m. Martha Justice, June 14, 1958; children: William E.J., Peter J.D., George F.D. BA, Yale U., 1956; LLB, Harvard U., 1959. Bar: Ohio 1959, U.S. Dist. Ct. (so. dist.) Ohio 1963. Assoc. Porter, Stanley, Treffinger & Platt, Columbus, Ohio, 1963-68; ptnr. Porter, Wright, Morris & Arthur, 1968-97, of counsel, 1997—. Trustee Coun. for Ethics in Econs., 1997—. Lt. USNR, 1959-63. Mem. ABA, Ohio State Bar Assn., Capital Club, Rocky Fork Hunt and Country Club, Yale Club of N.Y. Home: 6169 Havens Corners Rd Blacklick OH 43004-9676 Office: Porter Wright Morris & Arthur 41 S High St Ste 3100 Columbus OH 43215-6101

MARTIN, WILLIAM RUSSELL, nuclear engineering educator; b. Flint, Mich., June 2, 1945; s. Carl Marcus and Audrey Winifred (Rosene) M.; m. Patricia Ann Williams, Aug. 13, 1967; children: Amy Leigh, Jonathn William. B.S.E. in Engring. Physics, U. Mich., 1967; MS in Physics, U. Wis., 1968; M.S.E. in Nuclear Engring., U. Mich., 1975, PhD in Nuclear Engring., 1976. Prin. physicist Combustion Engring., Inc., Windsor, Conn., 1976-77; asst. prof. nuclear engring. U. Mich., Ann Arbor, 1977-81, assoc. prof. nuclear engring., 1981-88, prof. nuclear engring., 1988—, dir. lab. for sci. computation, 1986—2001, chmn. nuclear engring., 1990-94, assoc. dean for acad. affairs Coll. Engring., 1994-99, dir. Ctr. for Advanced Computing, 2002—. Cons. Lawrence Livermore Nat. Lab., Livermore, Calif., 1982—, Los Alamos (N.Mex.) Nat. Lab., 1980-89, 2001—, IBM, Inc., Kingston, N.Y., 1984, Rockwell Internat., Pitts., 1985. Author:

Transport Theory, 1979; author tech. and conf. papers. Recipient Glenn Murphy award Am. Soc. for Engring. Edn., 1993; Disting. scholar U. Mich. Coll. Engring., 1967; vis. fellow Royal Soc., London, 1989. Fellow Am. Nuclear Soc.; mem. Am. Phys. Soc., Soc. for Indsl. and Applied Math., IEEE. Avocations: running, reading, skiing, sailing. Home: 1701 Crestland St Ann Arbor MI 48104-6329 Office: U Mich Dept Nuclear Engring Ann Arbor MI 48109 E-mail: wrm@umich.edu.

MARTINEZ, ARTHUR C. retail company executive; b. N.Y.C., Sept. 25, 1939; s. Arthur F. and Agnes (Caulfield) M.; m. Elizabeth Rusch, July 30, 1966; children: Lauren, Gregory. BSME, Polytech. U., 1960; MBA, Harvard U., 1965; JD (hon.), U. Notre Dame, 1997. Dir. planning Internat. Paper Co., N.Y.C., 1967-69; asst. to pres. Talley Industries, Mesa, Ariz., 1969-70; dir. fin. RCA Corp., N.Y.C., 1970-73, v.p., 1973-80; sr. v.p., CFO Saks Fifth Ave., 1980-84, exec. v.p., 1984-87, vice chmn., dir., 1990-92; sr. v.p. and group chief exec. Batus Inc., Louisville, 1987-90; vice chmn., dir. Saks Fifth Ave., 1990-92; chmn., CEO Sears Merchandise Group, Chgo., 1992-95, Sears, Roebuck and Co., 1995—. Bd. dirs. Sears, Roebuck and Co., Ameritech, Pepsico, Inc.; dep. chmn. Fed. Res. Bank, Chgo.; former chmn. Nat. Minority Supplier Devel. Coun., Inc. Bd. dirs. Defenders of Wildlife, 1992—, Nat. Urban League; chmn. bd. trustees Polytech. U., 1990—; trustee Art Inst., Orch. Assn. Chgo. Symphony Orch.; bd. dirs. Northestern Meml. Hosp., Chgo. 1st lt. U.S. Army, 1961-63. Named CEO of Yr., Fin. World Mag., 1996; recipient T.C. and Elizabeth Clarke medallion Sch. of Bus., Coll. William and Mary, 1997, Olin Sch. of Bus. Excellence in Bus. award, Washington U., St. Louis, 1997. Mem. Nat. Retail Fedn. (chmn. bd. dirs.). Avocations: tennis, golf, gardening. Office: Sears Roebuck and Co 3333 Beverly Rd Hoffman Estates IL 60179

MARTINEZ, JIM, communications executive; Degree in Econ., Northwestern U., 1977. Editor Los Vecinos sect. Sun-Times, with Washington bur.; met. editor Chgo. Sun-Times, asst. editor; with Ogilvy Adams & Rinehart; leader Chgo. Advanced Tech. Team Hill & Knowlton Martinez; pres. pub. rels. KemperLesnik Comm., Chgo. Mem. adv. bd. multicultural journalism edn. Roosevelt U.; instr. grad. media mgmt. students Medill Sch. Journalism, Northwestern U. Office: Ste 1500 455 N Cityfront Plaza Dr Chicago IL 60611-5313 Fax: 312-755-0274.

MARTING, MICHAEL G. lawyer; b. Cleve., Nov. 5, 1948; BA summa cum laude, Yale U., 1971, JD, 1974. Bar: Ohio 1974. Assoc. Jones, Day, Reavis & Pogue, Cleve., 1974-83, ptnr., 1984—. Mem.: Tavern Club (treas., sec., trustee local chpt. 1985—88), Cleve. Racquet Club, Union Club. Avocations: fly fishing, bird shooting, big game hunting, squash. Office: Jones Day Reavis & Pogue N Point 901 Lakeside Ave E Cleveland OH 44114-1190

MARTINO, FRANK DOMINIC, union executive; b. Albany, N.Y., Apr. 9, 1919; s. Benedetto and Rosina (Esposita) M.; m. Phyllis E. Higgins, June 15, 1963; children— Michael M., Lisa R. Student, Rutgers U., Cornell U., Oxford U. Timekeeper N.Y.C. R.R., 1937-41; chem. operator Sterling Drug Co., 1946-56; internat. rep. Internat. Chem. Workers Union, Akron, Ohio, 1956-70, internat. v.p., 1970-72, sec.-treas., 1972-75; internat. pres. Internat. Chem. Workers Union Coun./United Food Comml. Workers/UFCW, 1975—; Washington rep., dir. Internat. Chem. Workers Union Coun./USCW, 1962-70. Served with USAF, 1941-45. Democrat. Roman Catholic. Office: Internat Chem Workers Union Coun/UFCW 1655 W Market St Akron OH 44313-7004

MARTINO, ROBERT SALVATORE, orthopedic surgeon; b. Clarksburg, W.Va., May 31, 1931; s. Leonard L. and Sarafina (Foglia) M.; m. Lenora Cappellanti, May 22, 1954; children: Robert S. Jr., Leslie F. Reckziegal. AB, W.Va. U., 1953, postgrad., 1955-56, BS in Medicine, 1958; MD, Northwestern U., 1960. Diplomate Am. Bd. Orthopaedic Surgery; lic. Ill., Calif., Ind. Intern Chgo. Wesley, 1960-61; resident dept. orthopaedic surgery Northwestern U., 1961-65, Chgo. Wesley Meml., 1961-62, Am. Legion Hosp. for Crippled Children, 1962-63, Cook County Hosp., Chgo., 1964, 64-65; orthopaedic surgeon Gary, Ind., 1965-67; orthopaedic surgeon Merrillville, 1967—. Fellow Nat. Found. Infantile Paralysis, 1956, Office of Vocat. Rehab., Hand Surgery, 1965; chief of staff St. Mary Med. Ctr., 1976, chief of surgery, 1974-85; chief of staff Gary Treatment Ctr./Ind. Crippled Children's Svcs., 1974-84; adj. asst. prof. anatomy Ind. U., 1978, clin. asst. prof. orthopaedic surgery, 1980, others; mem. Zoning Bd., 1989-90. Chmn. Planning Bd. Town of Dune Acres, 1992-96; bd. dirs. United Steel Workers Union Health Plan, 1994—, St. Mary's Med. Ctr., Hobart, Ind.; com. on Health Care Reform. Capt. U.S. Army, 1953-56. Fellow ACS (emeritus)mem. AMA, Ind. Med. Soc., Ill. Med. Soc., Chgo. Med. Soc., Ill. Orthopaedic Soc., Ind. Orthopaedic Soc., Mid-Am. Orthopaedic Assn., Tri-State Orthopedic Soc., Clin. Orthopaedic Soc. Home: Dune Acres 22 Oak Dr Chesterton IN 46304-1016

MARTINS, HEITOR MIRANDA, foreign language educator; b. Belo Horizonte, Brazil, July 22, 1933; came to U.S., 1960; s. Joaquim Pedro and Emilia (Miranda) M.; m. Teresomja Alves Pereira, Nov. 1, 1958 (div. 1977); children— Luzia Pereira, Emilia Pereira; m. Marlene Andrade, Jan. 11, 1984 A.B., U. Federal de Minas Gerais, 1959; Ph.D., U. Federal de Minas Gerais, 1962. Instr. U. N.M., Albuquerque, 1960-62; asst. prof. Tulane U., New Orleans, 1962-66, assoc. prof., 1966-68; prof. dept. Spanish and Portuguese Ind. U., Bloomington, 1968—, chmn. dept., 1972-76. Vis. prof. U. Tex., Austin, 1963, Stanford U. 1968 Author: poetry Sirgo nos Cabelos, 1961; essay Manuel de Galhegos, 1964; essays Oswald de Andrade e Outros, 1973; critical anthology Neoclassicismo, 1982; Essays Do Barroco a Guimarães Rosa, 1983; editor: essays Luso-Brazilian Literary Studies. Social Sci. Research Council grantee, 1965; Fulbright-Hays Commn. grantee, 1966; Ford Found. grantee, 1970, 71 Mem. MLA, Renaissance Soc. Am., Am. Comparative Lit. Assn., Am. Assn. for 18th Century Studies. Home: 1316 S Nancy St Bloomington IN 47401-6050 Office: Indiana U Dept Spanish and Portuguese Bloomington IN 47405 E-mail: martins@indiana.edu.

MARTON, LAURENCE JAY, researcher, educator, clinical pathologist; b. Bklyn., Jan. 14, 1944; s. Bernard Dov and Sylvia (Silberstein) M.; m. Marlene Lesser, June 27, 1967; 1 child, Eric Nolan BA, Yeshiva U., 1965, DSc (hon.), 1993; MD, Albert Einstein Coll. Medicine, 1969. Intern Los Angeles County-Harbor Gen. Hosp., 1969-70; resident in neurosurgery U. Calif.-San Francisco, 1970-71, resident in lab. medicine, 1973-75, asst. research biochemist, 1973-74, asst. clin. prof. depts. lab. medicine and neurosurgery, 1974-75, asst. prof., 1975-78, assoc. prof., 1978-79, prof., 1979-92, asst. dir. div. clin. chemistry, dept. lab. medicine, 1974-75, dir. divsn., 1975-79, acting chmn. dept., 1978-79, chmn. dept., 1979-92; dean med. sch. U. Wis., 1992-95, prof. pathology and lab. medicine and oncology, 1992-2000, prof. dept. human oncology, 1993-95. Interim vice chancellor Ctr. Health Scis., U. Wis., 1993-94; adj. prof. dept. lab medicine U. Calif., San Francisco, 1992—; pres., CEO SLIL Biomed. Corp., 1998-2000, chief sci. and med. officer, 2000—. Co-editor: Polyamines in Biology and Medicine, 1981; Liquid Chromatography in Clinical Analysis, 1981; Clinical Liquid Chromatography, vol. 1, 1984, vol. 2, 1984 Served with USPHS, NIH, 1971-73 Recipient Rsch. Career Devel. award Nat. Cancer Inst., Disting. Alumnus award Albert Einstein Coll. Medicine, 1992. Mem. Am. Assn. Cancer Rsch., AAAS, Acad. Clin. Lab. Physicians and Scientists, Am. Soc. Investigative Pathology, Alpha Omega Alpha. Jewish Avocations: photography, art, music, travel. Home: 5810 Tree Line Dr Fitchburg WI 53711-5826 Office: SLIL Biomed Corp 37 Kessel Ct Madison WI 53711-6233

MARTY, JOHN, state legislator, writer; b. Evanston, Ill., Nov. 1, 1956; s. Martin E. and Elsa Louise (Schumacher) M.; m. Connie Jaarsma, Nov. 29, 1980; children: Elsa, Micah. BA in Ethics, St. Olaf Coll., 1978. Rschr. Minn. Ho. of Reps., St. Paul, 1980-82, com. adminstr. com. criminal justice, 1982-84; corp. found. grant adminstr., 1984-86; mem. Minn. Senate from 54th dist., St. Paul, 1987—. Author Minn. Govt. Ethics Law, campaign fin. reform, DWI (driving while intoxicated) laws. Dem. Farm Labor gubernatorial candidate, 1994. Office: 325 Capitol 75 Constitution Ave Saint Paul MN 55155-1601

MARTY, MARTIN EMIL, religion educator, editor; b. West Point, Nebr., Feb. 5, 1928; s. Emil A. and Anne Louise (Wuerdemann) Marty; m. Elsa Schumacher Marty, 1952 (dec. 1981); children: Frances, Joel, John, Peter, James, Micah, Ursula; m. Harriet Lindemann Marty, 1982. MDiv, Concordia Sem., 1952; STM, Luth. Sch. Theology, Chgo., 1954; PhD in Am. Religious and Intellectual History, U. Chgo., 1956; LittD (hon.) , Thiel Coll., 1964; LHD (hon.) , W.Va. Wesleyan Coll., 1967, Marian Coll., 1967, Providence Coll., 1967; DD (hon.) , Muhlenberg Coll., 1967; LittD (hon.) , Thomas More Coll., 1968; DD (hon.) , Bethany Sem., 1969; LLD (hon.) , Keuka Coll., 1972; LHD (hon.) , Willamette U., 1974; DD (hon.) , Wabash Coll., 1977; LLD (hon.) , U. So. Calif., 1977, Valparaiso U., 1978; LHD (hon.) , St. Olaf Coll., 1978, De Paul U., 1979; DD (hon.) , Christ Sem.-Seminex, 1979, Capital U., 1980; LHD (hon.) , Colo. Coll., 1980; DD (hon.) , Maryville Coll., 1980, North Park Coll. Sem., 1982; LittD (hon.) , Wittenberg U., 1983; LHD, Rosary Coll., 1984, Rockford Coll., 1984; DD (hon.) , Va. Theol. Sem., 1984; LHD (hon.) , Hamilton Coll., 1985, Loyola U., 1986; LLD (hon.) , U. Notre Dame, 1987; LHD (hon.) , Roanoke Coll., 1987, Mercer U., 1987, Ill. Wesleyan Coll., 1987, Roosevelt U., 1988, Aquinas Coll., 1988; LittD (hon.) , Franklin Coll., 1988, U. Nebr., 1993; LHD (hon.) , No. Mich. U., 1989, Muskingum Coll., Coe Coll., Lehigh U., 1989, Hebrew Union Coll. and Governors State U., 1990, Whittier Coll., 1991, Calif. Luth. U., 1993; DD (hon.) , St. Xavier Coll. and Colgate U., 1990, Mt. Union Coll., 1991, Tex. Luth. Coll., 1991, Aurora U., 1991, Baker U., 1992; LHD (hon.) , Luth. U., 1993, Calif. Luth. U., 1993, Midland Luth. Coll., 1995; DD, Hope Coll., 1993, Northwestern Coll., 1993; LHD (hon.) , George Fox Coll., 1994, Drake U., 1994, Centre Coll., 1994, Fontbonne Coll., 1996; DD, Yale U., 1995; LHD (hon.) , Otterbein Coll., 1996; ThD (hon.) , Lycoming Coll., 1997; LHD, Dana Coll., 1998; LittD (hon.) , Alma Coll., 1998, Concordia U. Portland, 1998, Niagara U., 1998; LHD (hon.) , Kalamazoo Coll., 1999, William Jewell Coll., 1999; LittD (hon.) , U. Miami, 1999; DD, DD, Trinity Coll., 2001; DHum, DHum, Westminster Choir Coll., 2001; LHD, LHD, U. Scranton, 2001. Ordained to ministry Luth. Ch., 1952. Pastor, Washington, 1950—51; asst. pastor River Forest, Ill., 1952—56; pastor Elk Grove Village, 1956—63; prof. history of modern Christianity Div. Sch. U. Chgo., 1963—, Fairfax M. Cone Disting. Svc. prof., 1978—98, prof. emeritus, 1998—; assoc. editor Christian Century mag., Chgo., 1956—85, sr. editor, 1985—98; co-editor Ch. History mag., 1963—97. Pres. Park Ridge (Ill.) Ctr., 1989—, sr. scholar, 1989—; pres. Am. Inst. for Study of Health, Faith and Ethics, 1985—89; dir. fundamentalism project Am. Acad. Arts and Scis., 1988—; dir. The Pub. Religion Project, 1996—99; interim pres. St. Olaf Coll., 2000—01; sr. scholar Park Ridge Ctr., 1989—. Author: A Short History of Christianity, 1959, The New Shape of American Religion, 1959, The Improper Opinion, 1961, The Infidel, 1961, Baptism, 1962, The Hidden Discipline, 1963, Second Chance for American Protestants, 1963, Church Unity and Church Mission, 1964, Varieties of Unbelief, 1964, The Search for a Usable Future, 1969, The Modern Schism, 1969, Righteous Empire, 1970, Protestantism, 1972, You Are Promise, 1973, The Fire We Can Light, 1973, The Pro and Con Book of Religious America, 1975, A Nation of Behavers, 1976, Religion, Awakening and Revolution, 1978, Friendship, 1980, By Way of Response, 1981, The Public Church, 1981, A Cry of Absence, 1983, Health and Medicine in the Lutheran Tradition, 1983, Pilgrims in Their Own Land, 1984, Protestantism in the United States, 1985, Modern American Religion, The Irony of it All, Vol. 1, 1986, An Invitation to American Catholic History, 1986, Religion and Republic, 1987, Modern American Religion: The Noise of Conflict, Vol. 2, 1991; author: (with R. Scott Appleby) The Glory and the Power, 1992; editor (with Jerald C. Brauer): The Unrelieved Paradox: Studies in the Theology of Franz Bibfeldt, 1994; editor: (with Micah Marty) Places Along the Way, 1994; editor: Our Hope for Years to Come, 1995, Modern American Religion, Under God, Indivisible, Vol. 3, 1996, The One and the Many, 1997, The Promise of Winter, 1997, When True Simplicity is Gained, 1998, Politics, Religion, and the Common Good, 2000, Education, Religion, and the Common Good, 2001; editor: (jours.) Context, 1969—; editor: Second Opinion; sr. editor: The Christian Century, 1956—98; contbr. articles to religious publs. Chmn. bd. regents St. Olaf Coll., 1996—2001; dir. The Pub. Religion Project, 1996—; sr. regents St. Olaf Coll., 2002—. Recipient Nat. Medal Humanities, 1997, Alumni medal, U. Chgo., 1998; scholar Sr. scholar-in-residence, The Park Ridge Ctr., 1989—. Fellow: Soc. Am. Historians, Am. Acad. Arts and Scis. (dir. fundamentalism project 1988—94); mem.: Am. Antiquarian Soc., Am. Acad. Religion (pres. 1987—88), Am. Cath. Hist. Assn. 1981, Am. Soc. Ch. History 1971, Am. Phil. Soc. Office: 239 Scottswood Rd Riverside IL 60546-2223 E-mail: memarty@aol.com.

MARTZ, MIKE, professional football coach; b. Sioux Falls, S.D., May 13, 1951; BS summa cum laude, Fresno State. Asst. coach Los Angeles Rams, 1992—99, Washington Redskins, 1997-98; offensive coord. St. Louis Rams, 1999—2000, head coach, 2000—. Office: Saint Louis One Rams Way Saint Louis MO 63045

MARUSKA, EDWARD JOSEPH, zoo administrator; b. Chgo., Feb. 19, 1934; s. Edward M.; m. Nancy; children— Donna, Linda. Student, Wright Coll., Chgo., 1959-61; D.Sc. (hon.), Xavier U., 1986, U. Cin., 1989. Keeper hoofed animals Lincoln Park Zoo, Chgo., 1956-62; head keeper Children's Zoo, 1959-62; gen. curator Cin. Zoo, 1962-68, dir., 1968—. Lectr. biol. sci. U. Can.; numerous TV appearances. Recipient Cin. Conservation Man of Year award, 1973, Ambassador award Cin. Conv. and Visitors Bur., 1974 Fellow Am. Assn. Zool. Parks and Aquariums (pres. 1978-79); mem. Am. Soc. Ichthyologists and Herpetologists, Whooping Crane Conservation Assn., Internat. Union Zoo Dirs., Langdon Club, Cin. Naturalists Soc. Office: Zool Society of Cin 3400 Vine St Cincinnati OH 45220-1333

MARVIN, JAMES CONWAY, librarian, consultant; b. Warroad, Minn., Aug. 3, 1927; s. William C. and Isabel (Carlquist) M.; m. Patricia Katharine Moe, Sept. 8, 1947; children: James Conway, Jill C., Jack C. B.A., U. Minn., 1950, M.A., 1966. City librarian, Kaukauna, Wis., 1952-54; chief librarian Eau Claire, 1954-56; dir. Cedar Rapids (Iowa) Pub. Library, 1956-67, Topeka Pub. Library, 1967-92. ALA-Rockefeller Found. vis. prof. Inst. Libr. Sci., U. Philippines, 1964-65; vis. lectr. dept. librarianship Emporia (Kans.) State U., 1970-80; chmn. Kans. del. to White House Conf. on Librs. and Info. Svcs., Gov.'s Com. on Libr. Resources, 1980-81; mem. Kans. Libr. Adv. Commn., 1992—, chmn., 1998—. Served with USNR, 1945-46. Mem. ALA, Iowa Libr. Assn. (past pres.), Kans. Libr. Assn., Philippine Libr. Assn. (life), Mountain Plains Libr. Assn. Home: 40 SW Pepper Tree Ln Topeka KS 66611-2055

MARWEDEL, WARREN JOHN, lawyer; b. Chgo., July 3, 1944; s. August Frank and Eleanor (Wolgamot) M.; m. Marilyn Baran, Apr. 12, 1975. BS in Marine Engring., U.S. Merchant Marine Acad., 1966; JD, Loyola U., Chgo., 1972. Bar: Ill. 1972, U.S. Dist. Ct. (no. dist.) Ill. 1972, U.S. Supreme Ct. 1974. With U.S. Merchant Marines, 1966-70. Mem. ABA (Ho. of Dels. 1989-96), Ill. Bar Assn., Chgo. Bar Assn., Maritime Law Assn.(sec.), Propeller Club (Chgo. pres. 1982). Avocations: boating, reading, history. Office: Marwedel Minichello & Reeb PC 10 S Riverside Plz Chicago IL 60606-3708

MARX, DAVID, JR. lawyer; b. Chgo., Nov. 15, 1950; BA cum laude, Amherst Coll., 1972; JD, Syracuse U., 1975. Bar: N.Y. 1976, Ill. 1986. Ptnr. McDermott, Will & Emery, Chgo. Mem. ABA, Chgo. Bar Assn. Office: McDermott Will & Emery 227 W Monroe St Fl 31 Chicago IL 60606-5016

MARX, THOMAS GEORGE, economist; b. Trenton, N.J., Oct. 25, 1943; s. George Thomas and Ann (Szymanski) Marx; m. Arlene May Varga, Aug. 23, 1969; children: Melissa Ann, Thomas Jeffrey, Jeffrey Alan. BS summa cum laude, Rider Coll., 1969; PhD, U. Pa., 1973. Fin. analyst Am. Cyanamid Co., Trenton, 1968; economist FTC, Washington, 1973; econ. cons. Foster Assocs. Inc., 1974-77; sr. economist GM, Detroit, 1977-79, mgr. indsl. econs., 1980-81, dir. econs. policy studies, 1981-83, dir. corp. strategic planning group, 1984-86, gen. dir. market analysis and forecasting, 1986-88, gen. dir. econ. analysis, 1988-90, gen. dir. issues mgmt. on industry govt. rels. staff, 1990-96, dir. econ. issues and analysis corp. affairs staff, 1996-97, dir. global climate issue, 1997—. Mem. faculty Temple U., Phila., 1972—73, U. Pa., Phila., 1972—73; adj. prof. Wayne State U., 1981—89, U. Detroit, 1988—. Assoc. editor: Bus. Econs., 1980—98, mem. editl. bd.: Akron Jour. Bus. and Econs., 1981—90; contbr. articles to profl. jours. With USAF, 1961—65. Mem.: Assn. Pub. Policy Analysts, Planning Forum, Western Econ. Assn., So. Econ. Assn., Econ. Soc. Mich., Detroit Area Bus. Economists (v.p.), Nat. Assn. Bus. Economists, Am. Econ. Assn., Nat. Econs. Club, Beta Gamma Sigma, Pi Gamma Mu. Roman Catholic. Home: 3312 Bloomfield Park Dr West Bloomfield MI 48323-3514 Office: GM Corp MC 482-C27-C22 PO Box 300 300 Renaissance Ctr Detroit MI 48265-3000 E-mail: tom.marx@gm.com.

MARZLUF, GEORGE AUSTIN, biochemistry educator; b. Columbus, Ohio, Sept. 29, 1935; s. Paul Bayhan and Opal Faun (Simmons) M.; m. Zarife Sahenk; children: Bruce, Julie, Philip, Glenn. BS, Ohio State U., 1957, MS, 1960; PhD, Johns Hopkins U., 1964. Postdoctoral fellow U. Wis., Madison, 1964-66; asst. prof. biochemistry Marquette U., Milw., 1966-70; assoc. prof. Ohio State U., Columbus, 1970-75, prof., 1975—, chmn. dept. biochemistry, 1985-2000. Contbr. articles to profl. jours. Mem. Genetics Soc. Am., Am. Soc. Microbiology, AAAS, Am. Soc. Biochemists and Molecular Biologists. E-mail: Marzluf.1@osu.edu. Office: Ohio State U Dept of Biochemistry 484 W 12th Ave Columbus OH 43210-1214

MARZULLO, LARRY A. transportation executive; Chmn., CEO The Bekins Co., Inc., Hillside, Ill., 1995—. Avocations: 708-547-2246. Office: The Bekins Co Inc 330 S Mannheim Rd Hillside IL 60162-1833

MASBACK, CRAIG, executive director United States track and field; BA, Princeton U.; JD, Yale U. Track and field broadcaster various television stations, 1982; asst. to dir. Olympic Mus., Lausanne, Switzerland, 1982-84; attorney Wash.; exec. dir. U.S.A. Track & Field, Indpls., 1997—. Creator Foot Locker Slam Fest. Keasbey scholar Trinity Coll., NCAA scholar Oxford U; runner, 1980 U.S. indoor mile champion, U.S. record holder 2000 meters, 1985 U.S. team World Cup Champion. Mem. TAC/USA (bd. dirs., athletes adv. com., internat. competition com., mktg. media com.). Office: USA Track & Field 1 Rca Dome Ste 140 Indianapolis IN 46225-1023

MASEK, MARK JOSEPH, writer; b. Joliet, Ill., June 13, 1957; s. Glenn James and Helen Margaret (Gleason) M.; m. Theresa Marie Norton, Oct. 24, 1987. BJ, U. Ill., 1979. Reporter The Daily Illini, Champaign, 1976-79, Joliet Herald-News, 1978-79; columnist, editor Elgin (Ill.) Daily Courier-News, 1979-88; editor The Daily Herald, Arlington Heights, Ill., 1988-90; publs. mgr. Argonne (Ill.) Nat. Lab., 1990-98. V.p. Recycle Now-Joliet, 1991—; active City of Joliet Environ. Commn., 1993-96; bd. dirs. Will County Habitat for Humanity, 1994-99, pres., 1997-99. Recipient 1st pl. pub. svc. award Ill. AP Editor's Assn., 3d pl. pub. svc. award, 1980, 2d pl. columns award No. Ill. Newspaper Assn., 1982, 1st pl. columns award Nat. Newspaper Assn., 1982. Mem. Soc. Profl. Journalists, Mensa. Democrat. Roman Catholic.

MASH, DONALD J. college president; b. Oct. 12, 1942; children: Maria, Christina, Donnie (dec.). BS in Edn., Ind. U. Pa., 1960; MA in Geography, U. Pitts., 1966; PhD, Ohio State U., 1974. Teaching fellow U. Pitts., 1964-65; instr. geography U. Pitts.-Bradford, 1965-68; dean for student svcs. Ohio Dominican Coll., 1968-75; v.p. for student affairs George Mason U., Fairfax, Va., 1975-85, exec. v.p. adminstrn., 1985-88; pres. Wayne (Nebr.) State Coll., 1988-98; chancellor U. Wis.-Eau Claire, 1998—. Office: Univ of Wisconsin-Eau Claire Office of Chancellor PO Box 4004 Eau Claire WI 54702-4004

MASON, EARL LEONARD, food products executive; b. Jersey City, July 12, 1947; s. Herman E. and Marguerite (Rondeau) M.; m. Patricia Fladung (div. 1976); children: Holly Ann, Wendy Lynn; m. Bonita L. Blair, Dec. 11, 1976. BS, Fairleigh Dickinson U., 1969, MBA, 1984. With AT&T, N.J., 1969-79, dir. mktg., 1979-81; corp. contr. ATT Info. Systems, 1981-85; dir. fin. mgmt. and planning AT&T, N.J., 1985-87; controller mfg. Digital Equipment Corp., Maynard, Mass., 1987-91, European CFO Geneva, 1990-91; v.p. fin., CFO Inland Steel Industries, Chgo., 1991-96, sr. v.p., 1995-96; sr. v.p., CFO Compaq Computer Corp., Houston, 1996-99; pres. CEO Alliant Foodservice, Chgo, 1999-2001. Dir. Family Inn, Boston, 1992—. Dir. Family Inn, Boston, 1992—, State of Ill. Mem. Am. Iron and Steel Inst., Fin. Execs. Inst., Univ. Club, East Bank Club, City of Chgo. C. of C. (bd. dirs.). Avocations: squash, racquetball, tennis, golf, boating. Office: Alliant Foodservice One Parkway North Deerfield IL 60015

MASON, EDWARD EATON, surgeon; b. Boise, Idaho, Oct. 16, 1920; s. Edward Files and Dora Bell (Eaton) M.; m. Dordana Fairman, June 18, 1944; children— Daniel Edward, Rose Mary, Richard Eaton, Charles Henry. B.A., U. Iowa, 1943, M.D., 1945; Ph.D. in Surgery, U. Minn., 1953. Intern, resident in surgery Univ. Hosps., Mpls., 1945-52; asst. prof. surgery U. Iowa, 1953-55, asso. prof., 1956-60, prof., 1961-91, prof. emeritus, 1991—, chmn. gen. surgery, 1978-91. Cons. VA Hosp.; trainee Nat. Cancer Inst., 1949-52 Author: Computer Applications in Medicine, 1964, Fluid, Electrolyte and Nutrient Therapy in Surgery, 1974, Surgical Treatment of Obesity, 1981; developer gastric bypass and gastroplasty for treatment of obesity; contbr. articles profl. jours. Served to lt. (j.g.) USNR, 1945-47. Fellow ACS; mem. AMA, Am. Surg. Assn., Western Surg. Assn., Soc. Univ. Surgeons, Internat. Soc. Surgery, Ctrl. Surg. Assn., Soc. Surgery Alimentary Tract, Am. Thyroid Assn., Am. Soc. Bariatric Surgery, Sigma Xi, Alpha Omega Alpha. Republican. Presbyterian. Home: 5 Melrose Cir Iowa City IA 52246-2013 Office: University Hosp Dept of Surgery Iowa City IA 52242

MASON, JOHN MILTON (JACK MASON), judge; b. Mankato, Minn., Oct. 31, 1938; s. Milton Donald and Marion (Dailey) M.; m. Vivian McFerran, Aug. 25, 1962; children: Kathleen, Peter, Michael. BA cum laude, Macalester Coll., 1960; JD, Harvard U., 1963. Bar: Minn. 1963, U.S. Supreme Ct. 1970. Assoc. Dorsey & Whitney, Mpls., 1963-68, ptnr., 1969-71, 73-95; solicitor gen. State of Minn., St. Paul, 1971, chief dep. atty. gen., 1972-73; U.S. magistrate judge Dist. of Minn., 1995—. Bd. dirs. Macalester Coll., St. Paul, 1971-77, St. Paul Chamber Orch., 1979-88, U. Minn. Hosps. and Clinics, St. Paul, 1979-83, Mpls. Bd. Edn., 1973-80, Minn. Chorale, 1990-95, MacPhail Ctr. for Arts, 1990-96, Ordway Music

Theatre, 1990-99, 2000—; mem. nat. adv. bd. Concordia U. Lang. Villages, 1996—, Theatre de la Jeune Lune, 1998-2001. With USAF, 1957, with Res., 1957-65. Mem. Harvard Law Sch. Assn. (pres. Minn. sect. 1980-81) Avocations: classical piano, bicycling, accordion, foreign languages. Home: 2849 Burnham Blvd Minneapolis MN 55416-4331 Office: 610 Federal Cts Bldg 316 Robert St N Saint Paul MN 55101-1495 E-mail: jmmason@mnd.uscourts.gov.

MASON, LINDA, physical education educator, softball and basketball coach; b. Indpls., Jan. 29, 1946; d. Harrison Linn and Hazel Marie (Bledsoe) Crouch; divorced; children: Cassandra, Andrew. BS, Ind. U., 1968, MS, 1977. Cert. phys. edn. tchr., K-12, Ind. Tchr. phys. edn. Woodview Jr. H.S., Indpls., 1968-71; tchr. phys. edn., coach Ind. U.-Purdue U. of Indpls., 1972-76; basketball coach Butler U., Indpls., 1976-84; head softball coach, asst. basketball coach Westfield Washington High Sch., Westfield, Ind., 1985; tchr. phys. edn., basketball coach Orchard Park Elementary Sch., Carmel, 1985—; elem. physical edn. tchr. Carmel-Clay Schs., 1985—; asst. varsity coach softball Carmel H.S., 1993-95, head varsity softball coach, 1996-99. Head coach Ind. Girls' H.S. All-Stars Basketball Team, Indpls., 1980. Named Coach of Yr. Dist. 4, Nat. Collegiate Athletic Assn., 1983, Coach of Yr. for softball ICGSA, 1997, coach ICGSA Girls All Stars, 1998. Mem. Delta Psi Kappa. E-mail: lmason@ccs.k12.in.us.

MASON, PERRY CARTER, philosophy educator; b. Houston, Sept. 24, 1939; s. Lloyd Vernon and Lorraine (Carter) M.; m. Judith Jane Fredrick, June 11, 1960; children— Gregory Charles, Nicole Elizabeth B.A., Baylor U., Waco, Tex., 1961; B.D., Harvard U., 1964; M.A., Yale U., 1966, Ph.D., 1968. Asst. prof. philosophy Carleton Coll., Northfield, Minn., 1968-73, assoc. prof. philosophy, 1973-80, prof. philosophy, 1980—, v.p. for planning and devel., 1988-89, v.p. for external rels., 1989-91. Contbr. articles to profl. publs. Mem. Minn. Philos. Soc., Am. Philos. Assn. Democrat Home: 8629 Hall Ave Northfield MN 55057-4884 Office: Carleton College 1 N College St Northfield MN 55057-4044 E-mail: pmason@carleton.edu.

MASON, RICHARD J. lawyer; b. Syracuse, N.Y., June 16, 1951; BA with high honors, U. Ill., 1973; MBA, U. Chgo., 1980; JD, U. Notre Dame, 1977. Bar: Ill. 1977. Ptnr., mem. exec. com. Ross & Hardies, Chgo., 1995—. Adj. prof. law Kent Coll. Law, Inst. Tech., Chgo., 1984—. Bd. dirs. Ill. Farm Legal Assistance Found., 1985-88. Mem. ABA (chmn. bus. bankruptcy subcom. on use and disposition of property under the bankruptcy code 1989—), Am. Bankruptcy Inst., Ill. State Bar Assn. (mem. banking and bankruptcy law sect. coun. 1986-88), Chgo. Bar Assn. (mem. bankrupcty and reorgn. com. 1978—), Comml. Law League. Office: Ross & Hardies 150 N Michigan Ave Ste 2500 Chicago IL 60601-7567

MASON, THOMAS ALBERT, lawyer; b. Cleve., May 4, 1936; s. Victor Lewis and Frances (Speidel) M.; m. Elisabeth Gun Sward, Sept. 25, 1965; children: Thomas Lewis, Robert Albert. AB, Kenyon Coll., 1958; LLB, Case-Western Res. U., 1961. Bar: Ohio 1961. Assoc. Thompson, Hine and Flory, Cleve., 1965-73, ptnr., 1973—. Trustee Cleve. YMCA, 1975-94. Capt. USMCR, 1962-65. Mem. ABA, Am. Coll. Real Estate Lawyers, Am. Land Title Assn. (lender's counsel group), Mortgage Bankers Assn. of Met. Cleve., Ohio Bar Assn., Cleve. Bar Assn., Am. Coll. Mortgage Attys., The Country Club. Republican. Episcopalian. Avocations: tennis; golf. Home: 23375 Duffield Rd Cleveland OH 44122-3101 Office: Thompson Hine LLP 3900 Key Ctr 127 Public Sq Cleveland OH 44114-1216 E-mail: tom.mason@thompsonhine.com.

MASSENGALE, MARTIN ANDREW, agronomist, university president; b. Monticello, Ky., Oct. 25, 1933; s. Elbert G. and Orpha (Conn) M.; m. Ruth Audrey Klingelhofer, July 11, 1959; children: Alan Ross, Jennifer Lynn. BS, Western Ky. U., 1952; MS, U. Wis., 1954, PhD, 1956; LHD (hon.), Nebr. Wesleyan U., 1987; DS (hon.), Senshu U., Tokyo, 1995. Cert. profl. agronomist, profl. crop scientist. Research asst. agronomy U. Wis., 1952-56; asst. prof., asst. agronomist U. Ariz., 1958-62, assoc. prof., assoc. agronomist, 1962-65, prof., agronomist, 1965-76, head dept., 1966-74, assoc. dean Coll. Agr. assoc. dir. Ariz. Agr. Expt. Sta., 1974-76; vice chancellor for agr. and natural resources U. Nebr., 1976-81; chancellor U. Nebr.-Lincoln, 1981-91, interim pres., 1989-91; pres. U. Nebr., 1991-94, pres. emeritus, 1994, found. disting. prof. and dir., 1994—. Chmn. pure seed adv. com. Ariz. Agrl. Expt. Sta.; past chmn. bd., pres. Mid-Am. Internat. Agrl. Consortium; coord. com. environ. quality EPA-Dept. Agrl. Land Grand U.; past chmn. bd. dirs. Am. Registry Cert. Profls. in Agronomy, Crops and Soils; bd. dirs. Ctr. for Human Nutrition; bd. dirs., trustee U. Nebr. Found.; chair bd. dirs. Agronomic Sci. Found., chmn. selection com; dir. devel. Secretariat, Filippo Maseri Florio World Prize for Disting. Rsch. in Agr.; exec. com. U. Nebr. Tech. Park, LLC; bd. dirs. Lincoln Ins. Group., Woodmen Accident & Life Co., LIG, Inc., Am. First, LLC; mem. adv. bd. Nat. Agrl. Rsch., Ext., Edn. and Econs., 1998—, mem. exec. com.; mem. nat. adv. bd. Trees Am., 1998—. Chmn. NCAA Pres.'s Commn., 1988-91; distbn. revenue com., standing com. on appointments North Ctrl. Assn. Commn. on Insts. Higher Edn., 1991; trustee Nebr. Hist. Soc. Found.; bd. dirs. Nebr. Hist. Soc.; bd. govs. Nebr. Sci. and Math. Initiative; mem. Knight Found. Commn. on Intercollegiate Athletics; bd. dirs. Great Plains Funds, IBP; hon. life trustee Nebr. Coun. on Econ. Edn.; hon. lifetime trustee Nebr. Coun. on Econ. Edn. With U.S. Army, 1956-58. Named Midlands Man of Yr., 1982, to We. Ky. U. Hall of Disting. Alumni, 1992, DeKalb Crop Sci. Disting. Career award, 1996, Outstanding Educator Am., 1970; recipient faculty recognition award Tucson Trade Bur., 1971, Ak-Sar-Ben Agrl. Achievement award, 1986, Agrl. Builders Nebr. award, 1986, Walter K. Beggs award, 1986, Vol. of Yr. award for disting. svc. Nebr. Coun. on Econ. Edn., IANR Team Initiation award, Agri award Triumph of Agr. Expn., 1999, Exemplary Svc. to Agr. award Nebr. AgRels. Coun., 2000, Friend of LEAD award Nat. LEAD Alumni Assn., 2001, Outstanding Pres. award All-Am. Football Found., 2001; hon. state farmer degrees Ky., Ariz., Nebr. Future Farmers Am. Assns. Fellow AAAS (sect. chmn.), Crop Sci. Soc. Am. (past dir., pres. 1972-73, past assoc. editor, pres. western soc., disting. career award 1996), Am. Soc. Agronomy (past dir., vis. scientist program, past assoc. editor Agronomy Jour., Disting. Svc. award 1984); mem. Am. Grassland Coun., Ariz. Crop Improvement Assn. (bd. dirs.), Am. Soc. Plant Physiology, Nat. Assn. Colls. and Tchrs. Agr., Soil and Water Conservation Soc. Am., Ariz. Acad. Sci., Nebr. Acad. Sci., Agrl. Coun. Am. (bd. dirs., issues com.), Coun. Agrl. Sci. and Tech. (bd. dirs. budget and fin. 1979-82, 94—, treas., exec. com. 1997—), Nat. Assn. State Colls. and Land Grant Univs. (chmn. com. on info. tech. 1987-94, exec. com. 1990-92, bd. dirs. 1992-94), Edn. Engring. Professions (mem. commn.), Coll. Football Assn. (chmn., bd. dirs. 1986-88), Am. Assn. State Coll. and Univs. (task force instl. resource allocation), Assn. Am. Univs. Rsch. Librs. (steering com. 1992-94), Nebr. Crop Improvement Assn. (disting. svc. award), Grazing Lands Forum (pres.), Nebr. C. of C. and Industry, Nebr. Diplomats Inc. (hon. diplomate), Nebr. Vet. Med. Assn. (hon.), Sigma Xi, Phi Kappa Phi, Gamma Sigma Delta (Award of Merit), Alpha Zeta, Phi Sigma, Gamma Alpha, Alpha Gamma Rho, Phi Beta Delta, Golden Key Nat. Honor Soc., Innocents Soc. Office: U Nebr 220 Keim Hall Lincoln NE 68583-0953 E-mail: mmassengale1@unl.edu.

MASSEY, ANDREW JOHN, conductor, composer; b. Nottingham, Eng., May 1, 1946; came to U.S., 1978; s. Henry Louis Johnson and Margaret (Park) M.; m. Sabra Ann Todd, May 29, 1982; children: Colin Sebastian, Robin Elizabeth. BA, Oxford U., 1968, MA, 1981, Nottingham U., 1969. Asst. condr. The Cleve. Orch., 1978-80; assoc. condr. New Orleans Symphony, 1980-86, San Francisco Symphony, 1985-88; music dir. Fresno (Calif.) Philharmonic, 1986-93, R.I. Philharmonic, Providence, 1986-91, Toledo Symphony Orch., 1991—, also condr. Vis. scholar Brown U., Providence, 1986-91; music dir. Oreg. Mozart Players, 1998—. Composer incidental music (stage prodns.) Murder in the Cathedral, 1968, King Lear, 1971, A Midsummer Night's Dream, 1972. Avocations: trees, computers, astrology, philosophy of Karl Popper. Office: Toledo Symphony Two Maritime Plz Toledo OH 43604-1868

MASSEY, DONALD E. automotive executive; CEO Don Massey Cadillac. Office: Don Massey Cadillac Inc 40475 Ann Arbor Rd E Plymouth MI 48170-4576

MASSEY, RAYMOND LEE, lawyer; b. Macon, Ga., Sept. 25, 1948; s. Ford B. and Juanita (Sapp) M.; m. Lynn Ann Thielmeier, Aug. 23, 1967; children: Daniel, Caroline. BA, U. Mo., St. Louis, 1971; JD, U. Louisville, 1974. Bar: Mo. 1974, Ill. 1976, U.S. Dist. Ct. (ea. and we. dists.) Mo. 1974, U.S. Dist. Ct. (so. dist.) Ill. 1976. Assoc. Thompson & Mitchell, St. Louis, 1974-79; ptnr. Thompson & Mitchell (now Thompson & Coburn), 1979—. Mem. Maritime Law Assn. of U.S. (bd. dirs., chmn. ocean and river towing). Home: 3 Wild Rose Dr Saint Louis MO 63124-1465 Office: Thompson Coburn Firstar Plazq Ste 3400 Saint Louis MO 63101-1643

MASSEY, ROBERT JOHN, telecommunications executive; b. Montclair, N.J., July 12, 1945; s. William A. and Elizabeth (Grissing) M.; m. Sue A. Lavallee, July 26, 1968; children: Mary Beth, Michelle, Megan. BA, Holy Cross Coll., Worcester, Mass., 1967; MBA, Syracuse U., 1969. Mktg. rep. IBM, Washington, 1969-70, Boston, 1971-73; mktg. rep. Control Data Corp., Greenwich, Conn., 1974-75, mktg. mgr., N.Y.C., 1975-76; area mgr. CompuServe Inc., Eastern area, 1976-78, v.p. sales, Stamford, Conn., 1979-83, exec. v.p. bus. svcs., Columbus, Ohio, 1984-86, exec. v.p. software products, 1987-90, exec. v.p. network svcs., 1990, pres., until 1997; exec. v.p. bus. devel. Calltech Comm., Columbus, 1997-98; pres. Massey & Assocs., 1997-99; chmn. Calltech Comm. LLC, Columbus, 1999—. Bd. dirs. CompuServe. Coach Dublin (Ohio) Youth Athletics, 1978-85; parents coun. St. Mary's Coll., Notre Dame, Ind., 1988—. Mem. Dublin C. of C., Ohio State Fastbreakers, Holy Cross Alumni Assn., Syracuse U. Bus. Alumni Assn., Country Club of Muirfield Village (golf. com.). Avocations: golf, tennis. Office: Calltech Comm LLC 4335 Equity Dr Columbus OH 43228-3842

MASSEY, VINCENT, biochemist, educator; b. Berkeley, NSW, Australia, Nov. 28, 1926; s. Walter and Mary Ann (Mark) M.; m. Margot Grunewald, Mar. 4, 1950; children: Charlotte, Andrew, Rachel. BSc with honors, U. Sydney, Australia, 1947; PhD, U. Cambridge, Eng., 1953; DSc (hon.), U. Tokushima, 1994. Mem. research staff Henry Ford Hosp., Detroit, 1955-57; lectr. to sr. lectr. U. Sheffield, 1957-63; prof. Med. Sch. U. Mich., Ann Arbor, 1963-95, J. Lawrence Oncley Disting. U. prof., 1995—. Permanent guest prof. U. Konstanz, 1975—; mem. fellowship rev. panel NIH, 1965-69, mem. biochemistry study sect., 1972-76, chmn. 1974-76; mem. biochemistry and biophysics rev. panel NSF, 1980-84. Contbg. author numerous books.; co-editor Flavins and Flavoproteins, 1982, 96; contbr. numerous articles, chiefly on oxidative enzymology, to profl. jours. Recipient Alexander von Humboldt U.S. Sr. Scientist award, 1973-74, 86; Imperial Chem. Industries Research fellow, 1953-55. Fellow Royal Soc. London; mem. NAS, Biochem. Soc., Am. Soc. Biochemistry and Molecular Biology (membership com. 1970, nominating com. 1978-80, chmn. 1979-80, chmn. program com. 1992-93), Am. Chem. Soc. (exec. bd. divsn. biol. chemistry 1975-77). Home: 2536 Bedford Rd Ann Arbor MI 48104-4008 Office: U Mich Med Sch Dept Biol Chemistry Ann Arbor MI 48109 E-mail: massey@umich.edu.

MASSIE, MICHAEL EARL, lawyer; b. Stambaugh, Mich., Aug. 12, 1947; s. Glen E. and Bernice L. (Lambert) M.; m. Vicki L. Colmark, June 11, 1977; children: Christopher, Adam. BA, U. Ill., 1969, JD, 1972. Bar: Ill. 1972, U.S. Dist. Ct. (cen. dist.) Ill. 1989, U.S. Ct. Appeals (7th cir.) 1989. Pvt. practice, Galva, Ill., 1972—. Dir., sec. Community State Bank Galva, 1980—. Fellow Am. Bar Found., Ill. Bar Found.; mem. ABA (chair, coun. mem. gen. practice sect. 1989—), Ill. State Bar Assn. (chmn. gen. practice sect. 1980, chmn. agrl. law com. 1980), Ill. Farm Legal Assistance Found. (chmn. bd. 1985-98). Republican. Avocations: tennis, handball. Office: 115 NW 3rd Ave Galva IL 61434-1325

MASSIE, ROBERT JOSEPH, publishing company executive; b. N.Y.C., Mar. 19, 1949; BA, Yale U., 1970; MBA, JD, Columbia U., 1974; diploma, U. d'Aix en Provence, France, 1969. Bar: D.C. 1974. Assoc. Covington & Burling, Washington, 1975-79; mgmt. cons. McKinsey & Co., N.Y.C., 1979-82; v.p. Harlequin Enterprises, Toronto, Ont., Can., 1982-90; pres., CEO Gale Rsch., Inc., Detroit, 1990-92; dir. Chem. Abstracts Svc., Columbus, Ohio, 1992—. Chmn. bd. dirs. Harlequin Mondadori, Milan, Italy, 1985-88; bd. dirs. Harlequin Hachette, Paris, Cora Verlag, Hamburg, Fed. Republic Germany, Mills & Boon, Sydney, Australia. Contbr. articles to law jours. Bd. dirs. Mindleaders.com. Harlan Fiske Stone scholar, 1974. Office: Am Chem Soc Chem Abstracts Svcs PO Box 3012 Columbus OH 43210-0012

MASSURA, EDWARD ANTHONY, accountant; b. Chgo., July 1, 1938; s. Edward Matthew and Wilma C. (Kussy) M.; m. Carol A. Barber, June 23, 1962; children: Edward J., Beth Ann, John B. BS, St. Joseph's Coll., Rensselaer, Ind., 1960; JD, DePaul U., 1963. Bar. Ill. 1963; CPA, Mich., Ill., others. Tax acct. Arthur Andersen LLP, Chgo., 1963-98, ptnr., 1973-98, dir. tax div. Detroit, 1974-84; dep., co-dir. internat. tax Arthur Andersen & Co., 1983-84, ptnr.-in-charge internat. trade customs practice, 1983-88. Co-author: West's Legal Forms, 2d. edit., 1984; contbr. numerous articles to bus. jours. Bd. dirs. Arts Found. of Mich., Detroit, 1982-95, treas., 1982-93; bd. dirs. Ctr. for Internat. Bus. Edn. and Rsch., Wayne State U.; bd. trustees St. Joseph's Coll., Rensselaer, Ind. Mem. AICPA, Internat. Fiscal Assn. (v.p. Eastern Gt. Lakes region), Assn. for Corp. Growth, Mich. Assn. CPAs, Mich. Dist. Export Coun. (chmn. 1985-92), Detroit Internat. Tax Group (founder,co-moderator), Licensing Exec. Soc., World Trade Club of Detroit, Bus. Assn. Mexico and Mich, Inc., Orchard Lake Country Club, Butterfield Country Club, Lely Golf & Country Club.

MASTERS, ARLENE ELIZABETH, singer; b. Freeport, Ill., Oct. 6, 1960; d. Elmer and Mary (Green) Masters; m. Douglas Dewayne Burck (div.); 1 child, Douglas. Singer classic rock and blues; with The Blues Transit Band, A. Masters Publishing. Home: PO Box 8221 Rockford IL 61126-8221

MASTERS, DAVID ALLEN, lawyer; b. Cape Girardeau, Mo., May 23, 1952; s. Elmo and Mary Louise (Davis) M.; m. Ginger N. Lloyd, May 28, 1977; children: Cecily, Phillip, Spencer, Rachel, Samuel. BA with honors, U. Ill., 1974; JD, U. Mo., 1984. Bar: Mo. 1984, U.S. Dist. Ct. (ea. dist.) Mo. 1985, U.S. Dist. Ct. (we. dist.) Mo. 1986, U.S. Ct. Appeals (8th cir.) 1987. Assoc. Oswald & Cottey, P.C., Kirksville, Mo., 1984-90; pvt. practice Macon; prosecuting atty. County of Macon, 1990—. Instr. Peoples Law Sch. Program, Mo. Assn. Trial Attys., Kirksville, 1987-88. Mem. Assn. Trial Lawyers Am., Macon County Bar Assn. (pres.), Mo. Assn. Trial Attys. Avocations: hiking, camping. Office: 108 Vine St Macon MO 63552-1655

MATASAR, ANN B. former dean, business and political science educator; b. N.Y.C., June 27, 1940; d. Harry and Tillie (Simon) Bergman; m. Robert Matasar, June 9, 1962; children— Seth Gideon, Toby Rachel AB, Vassar Coll., 1962; MA, Columbia U., 1964, PhD, 1968; M of Mgmt. in Fin., Northwestern U., 1977. Assoc. prof. Mundelein Coll., Chgo., 1965-78; prof., dir. Ctr. for Bus. and Econ. Elmhurst Coll., Elmhurst, Ill., 1978-84; dean Roosevelt U., Chgo., 1984-92; prof. Internat. Bus. and Fin. Walter E. Heller Coll. Bus. Adminstrn. Roosevelt U., 1992—. Dir. Corp. Responsibility Group, Chgo., 1978-84; chmn. long range planning Ill. Bar Assn., 1982-83; mem. edn. com. Ill. Commn. on the Status of Women, 1978-81 Author: Corporate PACS and Federal Campaign Financing Laws: Use or Abuse of Power?, 1986; (with others) Research Guide to Women's Studies, 1974, (with others) The Impact of Geographic Deregulation on the American Banking Industry, 2002; contbr. articles to profl. jours. Dem. candidate 1st legis. dist. Ill. State Senate, no. suburbs Chgo., 1972; mem. Dem. exec. com. New Trier Twp., Ill., 1972-76; rsch. dir., acad. advisor Congressman Abner Mikva, Ill., 1974-76; bd. dirs. Ctr. Ethics and Corp. Policy, 1985-90. Named Chgo. Woman of Achievement Mayor of Chgo., 1978. Fellow AAUW (trustee ednl. found. 1992-97, v.p. fin. 1993-97); mem. Am. Polit. Sci. Assn., Midwest Bus. Adminstrn. Assn., Acad. Mgmt., Women's Caucus for Polit. Sci. (pres. 1980-81), John Howard Assn. (bd. dirs. 1986-90), Am. Assembly of Coll. Schs. of Bus. (bd. dirs. 1989-92, chair com. on diversity in mgmt. edn. 1991-92), North Ctrl. Assn. (commr. 1994-97), Beta Gamma Sigma. Democrat. Jewish Avocations: jogging, biking, tennis, opera, crosswords. Office: Roosevelt U Coll Bus Adminstrn Dept Fin 430 S Michigan Ave Chicago IL 60605-1394 E-mail: amatasar@roosevelt.edu.

MATASOVIC, MARILYN ESTELLE, business executive; b. Chgo., Jan. 7, 1946; d. John Lewis and Stella (Butkauskas) M. Student, U. Colo. Sch. Bus., 1963-69. Owner, pres. UTE Trail Ranch, Ridgway, Colo., 1967—; pres. MEM Equipment Co., Mokena, Ill., 1979—; sec./treas. Marlin Corp., Ridgway, 1991—, v.p., sec.-treas., 1991—, pres., 1994—; sec.-treas. Linmar Corp., Mokena, 1991-93, pres., 1994—; ptnr. Universal Welding Supply Co., New Lenox, Ill., 1964-90; v.p. OXO Welding Equipment Co, Inc., 1964-90; ptnr. Universal Internat., Mokena, Ill., 1990—; ind. travel agt. Ideal Travel Concepts, 1994—; mgr. Hereford Works Warehouse, 1997—, owner, 2001—, Barnyardblvd.com, 2001—. Co-editor newsletters. U.S. rep. World Hereford Conf., 1964, 68, 76, 80, 84, 96. Recipient Outstanding Hereford Woman award, 1999. Mem. Am. Hereford Aux. (charter, bd. dirs. 1989-94, historian 1990-92, v.p. 1992, pres.-elect 1993, pres. 1994), Am. Hereford Women (charter, pres. 1994, bd. dirs. 1994-96, award 1999), Am. Agri-Women, Colo. Hereford Aux., Ill. Hereford Aux. (sec. 1969-70, publicity 1970-72), U. Colo. Alumni Assn., Ill. Agri-Women, Las Vegas Social Register. Avocations: showing cattle, computers, travel. E-mail: herefordworks@usa.net.

MATCHETT, ANDREW JAMES, mathematics educator; b. Chgo., Jan. 30, 1950; s. Gerald James and Margaret Ellen (Stump) M.; m. Nancy Valentine Stasack, Aug. 7, 1976; children: Gerald Albert, Philip Joseph, Melanie Jeanne. BS, U. Chgo., 1971; PhD, U. Ill., 1976. Grad. teaching asst. U. Ill., Urbana, 1971-76; asst. prof. Tex. A&M U., College Station, 1976-82, U. Wis., La Crosse, 1982-86, assoc. prof., 1986—; grad. teaching asst. U. Ill., Urbana, 1971-76. Dir. Consortium for Core Math. Curriculum, Wis., 1987-88. Contbr. articles to profl. jours. Chmn. troop 18 com. Boy Scouts Am., La Crosse, 1990, charter rep. troop 18, 1992-94, scoutmaster, 1994-97, mem. com., 1997—. Mem. AAAS, Am. Math. Soc., Am. Statis. Assn., Math. Assn. Am. (sec.-treas. Wis. sect. 1989—, admin. 1999—). Unitarian. Achievements include development of a theory of class group homomorphisms. Avocations: astronomy, skiing, ice skating, backpacking. Home: 327 24th St N La Crosse WI 54601-3850 Office: U Wis Dept Math 1725 State St La Crosse WI 54601 E-mail: matchett@math.uwlax.edu.

MATELES, RICHARD ISAAC, biotechnologist; b. N.Y.C., Sept. 11, 1935; s. Simon and Jean (Phillips) M.; m. Roslyn C. Fish, Sept. 2, 1956; children: Naomi, Susan, Sarah. BS, MIT, 1956, MS, 1957, DSc, 1959. USPHS fellow Laboratorium voor Microbiologie, Technische Hogeschool, Delft, The Netherlands, 1959-60; mem. faculty MIT, 1960-70, assoc. prof. biochem. engring., 1965-68; dir. fermentation unit Jerusalem, 1968-77; prof. applied microbiology Hebrew U., Hadassah Med. Sch., 1968-80; vis. prof. dept. chem. engring. U. Pa., Phila., 1978-79; asst. dir. rsch. Stauffer Chem. Co., Westport, Conn., 1980, dir. rsch., 1980-81, v.p. rsch., 1981-88; sr. v.p. applied scis. IIT Rsch. Inst., Chgo., 1988-90; proprietor Candida Corp., 1990—. Editor: Jour. Chem. Tech. and Biotech., 1972—; editor: (N.Am. edit.) Biotech., 2001—; editor: Directory of Toll Fermentation and Cell Culture Facilities, 2001—, Penicillin: A Paradigm for Biotechnology, 1998—; contbr. articles to profl. jours. Mem. Conn. Acad. Sci. Engring., 1981—; mem. vis. com., dept. applied biol. sci. MIT, 1980-88; mem. exec. com. Coun. on Chem. Rsch., 1981-85. Fellow Am. Inst. Med. and Biol. Engring.; mem. AICE, AAAS, SAR, Am. Chem. Soc., Am. Soc. Microbiology, Soc. for Gen. Microbiology U.K., Inst. Food Technologists, Soc. Chem. Ind. (U.K.) Union League, Sigma Xi. Home: 150 W Eugenie St Apt 46 Chicago IL 60614-5843 Office: Candida Corp Ste 1310 220 S State St Chicago IL 60604 E-mail: rmateles@candida.com.

MATERNA, JAMES M. business executive; CFO OM Group, Inc., Cleve., 1989—. Office: OM Group Inc 3300 Terminal Tower 50 Public Sq Cleveland OH 44113-2201

MATHENY, EDWARD TAYLOR, JR. lawyer; b. Chgo., July 15, 1923; s. Edward Taylor and Lina (Pinnell) Matheny; m. Marion Elizabeth Shields, Sept. 10, 1947; children: Nancy Elizabeth, Edward Taylor III; m. Ann Spears, Jan. 14, 1984. B.A., U. Mo., 1944; J.D., Harvard, 1949. Bar: Mo. 1949. Pvt. practice, Kansas City, 1949-91; ptnr. firm Blackwell, Sanders, Matheny, Weary & Lombardi, 1954-91. Pres. St. Luke's Hosp., Kansas City, 1980-95; bd. dirs. Dunn Industries, Inc., Tnemec Co., Inc. Author: The Presence of Care (History of St. Luke's Hospital, Kansas City), 1997, A Long and Constant Courtship (The History of a Law Firm), 1998, The Rise and Fall of Excellence, 2000, The Pursuit of a Ruptured Duck (When Kansas Citians Went to War), 2001. Pres. Cmty. Svc. Broadcasting of Mid-Am., Inc., 1971-72; chmn. Citizens Assn. Kansas City, 1958; chmn. bd. dirs. St. Luke's Found., Kansas City, 1980-95; trustee U. Kansas City, 1980-96, Kansas City Cmty. Found., 1983-94, Eye Found., Kansas City, 1990-2000, H&R Block Found., Kansas City, 1996—, Jacob L. and Ella C. Loose Found., Kansas City, 1996—. Mem. Kansas City Bar Assn., Mo. Bar, River Club, Mission Hills Country Club, Phi Beta Kappa, Sigma Chi (Balfour Nat. award 1944) Episcopalian (chancellor emeritus Diocese West Mo.). Home: 2510 Grand Blvd Kansas City MO 64108-2678 Office: 2300 Main St Kansas City MO 64108-2416

MATHENY, RUTH ANN, editor; b. Fargo, N.D., Jan. 17, 1918; d. Jasper Gordon and Mary Elizabeth (Carey) Wheelock; m. Charles Edward Matheny, Oct. 24, 1960. BE, Mankato State Coll., 1938; MA, U. Minn., 1955; postgrad., Universidad Autonoma de Guadalajara, Mex., summer 1956, Georgetown U., summer, 1960. Tchr., U.S. and S.Am., 1938-61; assoc. editor Charles E. Merrill Pub. Co., Columbus, Ohio, 1963-66; tchr. Confraternity Christian Doctrine, Washington Court House, 1969-70; assoc. editor Jr. Cath. Messenger, Dayton, 1966-68; editor Witness Intermediate, 1968-70; editor in chief, assoc. pub. Today's Cath. Tchr., 1970—; editor in chief Catechist, 1976-89, Ednl. Dealer, Dayton, 1976-80; v.p. Peter Li, Inc., 1980—. Editorial collaborator: Dimensions of Personality series, 1969— ; co-author: At Ease in the Classroom; author: Why a Catholic School?, Scripture Stories for Today: Why Religious Education? Bd. dirs. Friends Ormond Beach Library. Mem.: 3d Order St. Francis (eucharistic min. 1990—), Cath. Press Assn., Nat. Coun. Cath. Women. Home: 26 Reynolds Ave Ormond Beach FL 32174-7043 Office: Peter Li Ednl Group 2621 Dryden Rd Ste 300 Dayton OH 45439 E-mail: chilermat@aol.com.

MATHER, GEORGE ROSS, clergy member; b. Trenton, N.J., June 1, 1930; s. Samuel Wooley and Henrietta Elizabeth (Deardorff) M.; m. Doris Christine Anderson, June 28, 1958; children: Catherine Anne Mather-Grimes, Geoffrey Thomas. BA, Princeton U., 1952; MDiv, Princeton

Theol. Sem., 1955; DD, Hanover Coll., 1986. Ordained to Ministry, 1955. Asst. pastor Abington (Pa.) Presbyn., 1955-58; pastor 1st Presbyn. Ch. Ewing, Trenton, 1958-71; sr. pastor 1st Presbyn. Ch. Ft. Wayne, Ind., 1971-86; pastor 3d Presbyn. Ch. Ft. Wayne, 1987-95. Author: Frontier Faith: The Story of the Pioneer Congregations, 1992, The Best of Fort Wayne, vol. 1, 2000, vol. 2, 2001; co-editor: On the Heritage Trail, 1994; contbr. articles to profl. jours. Pres. Allen County Libr. Trustees, Ft. Wayne, Allen County Libr. Found., Ft. Wayne, Clergy United for Action, Ft. Wayne; trustee Hanover (Ind.) Coll.; chmn. Bicentennial Religious Heritage Commn., 1994; bd. dirs. Smock Found., 1971-85. Mem. Ind. Religious History Assn. (bd. dirs.), Allen County Ft. Wayne Hist. Soc. (bd. dirs.), The Quest Club (pres.). Avocations: tennis, travel, hiking, canoeing. Home: 6726 Quail Ridge Ln Fort Wayne IN 46804-2874

MATHERN, DEB, state legislator; 2 children. , N.D. State Coll. of Sc.; grad. Credit Union mgmt., U. Wis. Mem. N.D. Senate from 45th dist., Bismark, 1999—. Bd. dirs. N. D. Credit Union League, 1999—. Recipient Profl. of the Year, 1997. Mem. Fargo C. of C., NDCUL and affiliates. Office: Dist 45 3228 2nd St N Fargo ND 58102-1109 E-mail: dmathern@state.nd.us.

MATHERN, TIM, state legislator; b. Edgeley, N.D., Apr. 19, 1950; s. John J. and Christina Mathern; m. Lorene Mathern, Feb. 12, 1971; children: Reba, Tonya, Josh, Zach. BA, N.D. State U., 1971; MSW, U. Nebr., Omaha, 1980; MPA, Harvard U., 2000. Staff Cath. Family Svc., Fargo, N.D., 1973-99; mem. N.D. Senate, Bismarck, 1986—; parish adminstr. Fargo, N.D., 2000—; mem. legis. mgmt. com. N.D. Senate, Bismarck, 1993-99, asst. majority leader, 1991, senate minority leader, 1995-99, also mem. jud. stds. com. Mem. polit. subdivsn. com., N.D., 1995-97, intergovtl. com., 1999—, human svcs. com, 2000—, govt. and veterans com., 2000 chmn. Budget Com. on Govt. Adminstrn., 2001—; mem. Kennedy Sch. Student Govt., Cambridge, Mass., 1999-2000. Mem. Fargo-Cass County Econ. Devel. Corp., 1993-99; bd. dirs. Prairieland Home Care, 1993-99, Charism Cmty. Ctr., 1997—; pres., bd. dirs. Kaleidoscope, 2001—; mem. exec. com. N.D. Dem. Nonpartisan League Party, 1995-99; chmn. Budget Com. on Human Svcs., 1997-99; mem. Garrison Diversion Overview Com., 93-99; sch. coun., Martin Luther King Jr., Cambridge, Mass., 1999-00. Recipient N.D. Prairie Peacemaker award, 2000, Pub. Svc. award U. Nebr. Alumni Assn., 2002; named Legislator of Yr., Red River Valley Mental Health Assn., 1989, 91, Legislator of Yr., N.D. Children's Caucus, 1993, 98; Bush Leadership fellow, 1999. Mem. NASW (Social Worker of Yr. award 1987, Lifetime Achievement award 1998), Mental Health Assn. Democrat. Roman Catholic. Home: 406 Elmwood Fargo ND 58103-4315 E-mail: tmathern@state.nd.us.

MATHEWS, DAVID, foundation executive; b. Grove Hill, Ala., Dec. 6, 1935; s. Forrest Lee and Doris (Pearson) M.; m. Mary Chapman, Jan. 24, 1960; children: Lee Ann Mathews Hester, Lucy Mathews Heegaard. A.B., U. Ala., 1958; Ph.D., Columbia U., 1965; LL.D., U. Ala., 1969, Mercer U., 1976; L.H.D., William and Mary Coll., 1976, Med. U. S.C., 1976, Samford U., 1978, Transylvania U., 1978, Stillman Coll., 1980, Miami U., 1982; H.H.D., Birmingham-So. Coll., 1976, Wash. U., St. Louis, 1984; L.H.D., Ctr. Coll., 1985; L.L.D., Ohio Wesleyan U., 1987, Lynchburg Coll., 1987; L.H.D., U. New Eng., 1988. Exec. v.p. U. Ala., 1968-69, pres., 1969-80, prof. history, 1977-81; pres., chief exec. officer Charles F. Kettering Found., Dayton, Ohio, 1981—. Sec. HEW, Washington, 1975-77; dir. Birmingham br. Fed. Res. Bank of Atlanta, 1970-72, chmn., 1973-75; mem. council SRI Internat., 1978-85; chmn. Council Public Policy Edn., 1980— Contbr. articles to profl. jours. Trustee Judson Coll., 1968-75, Am. Univs. Field Staff, 1969-80; bd. dirs. Birmingham Festival of Arts Assn., Inc., 1969-75; mem. Nat. Programming Council for Public TV, 1970-73, So. Regional Edn. Bd., 1969-75, Ala. Council on Humanities, 1973-75; vice chmn. Commn. on Future of South, 1974; mem. So. Growth Policies Bd., 1974-75; mem. nat. adv. council Am. Revolution Bicentennial Adminstrn., 1975; mem. Ala. State Oil and Gas Bd., 1975, 77-79; bd. dirs. Acad. Ednl. Devel., 1975— , Ind. Sector, 1982-88, ; chmn. Pres.'s Com. on Mental Retardation, 1975-77; chmn. income security com. aging com. Health Ins. Com. of Domestic Council, 1975-77; bd. govs. nat. ARC, 1975-77; bd. govs., bd. visitors Washington Coll., 1982-86 ; trustee John F. Kennedy Center for Performing Arts, 1975-77, Woodrow Wilson Internat. Center for Scholars, 1975-77; fed. trustee Fed. City Council, 1975-77; bd. dirs. A Presdl. Classroom for Young Americans, Inc., 1975-76; trustee Tchrs. Coll., Columbia U., 1977— , Nat. Found. March of Dimes, 1977-83, Coun. om Learning, 1977-84, Miles Coll., 1978— ; mem. nat. adv. bd. Nat. Inst. on Mgmt. Lifelong Edn., 1979-84; mem. Ala. 2000, 1980— ; spl. adviser Aspen Inst., 1980-84; mem. bd. trustees Gerald R. Ford Found., 1988—, bd. visitors Mershon Ctr. Ohio State U., 1988-91. Served with U.S. Army, 1959-60. Recipient Nicholas Murray Butler medal Columbia U., 1976, Ala. Adminstr. of Year award Am. Assn. Univ. Adminstrs., 1976, Educator of Year award Ala. Conf. Black Mayors, 1977, Brotherhood award NCCJ, 1979 Mem. Newcomen Soc. Am., Phi Beta Kappa, Phi Alpha Theta, Omicron Delta Kappa, Delta Theta Phi. Home: 6050 Mad River Rd Dayton OH 45459-1508 Office: Charles F Kettering Found 200 Commons Rd Dayton OH 45459-2788 E-mail: jenkyn@kettering.org.

MATHEWSON, JAMES L. state legislator; b. Warsaw, Mar. 16, 1938; m. Doris Angel Mathewson, 1964; 3 children. Student, Redding Jr. Coll., Calif. State U. Real estate appraiser, Sedalia, Mo.; mem. Mo. Ho. of Reps., Jefferson City, 1974-80, Mo. Senate, Jefferson City, 1980—, majority floor leader, 1984-88, pres. pro tem, 1989-96. Mem. Sedalia C. of C., Am. Legion, Masons, Elks, Moose. Democrat. Office: 301 S Ohio Ave Sedalia MO 65301-4431 also: Rm 319 State Capitol Jefferson City MO 65101

MATHEWSON, MARK STUART, lawyer, editor; b. Pana, Ill., Mar. 6, 1950; s. Raymond Glenn and Frances (King) M.; m. Barbara Jean Siegert, Oct. 30, 1980; children: Margie, Molly. BA, U. Wis., Madison, 1978; JD, U. Ill., 1984; MA, U. Iowa, 1985. Bar: Ill. 1985. Reporter Ill. Times, Springfield, 1985; asst. prof. Culver Stockton Coll., Canton, Mo., 1986-87; pvt. practice Pana, Ill., 1987-88; mng. editor Ill. State Bar Assn., Springfield, 1988—. Mem. adv. bd. West Pub. Editors Exchange, Eagan, Minn., 1993-95. Home: RR 1 Box 2 Athens IL 62613-9787 Office: Ill State Bar Assn Ill Bar Journal Ill Bar Ctr Springfield IL 62701

MATHILE, CLAYTON LEE, pet food company executive; b. Portage, Ohio, Jan. 11, 1941; s. Wilbert and Helen (Good) M.; m. Mary Ann Maas, July 7, 1962; children: Cathy, Tim, Mike, Tina, Jennie. BA, Ohio No. U., 1962, DBA (hon.), 1991; postgrad., Bowling Green State U., 1964. Acct. GM, Napoleon, Ohio, 1962-63, Campbell Soup Co., Napoleon, 1963-65, buyer, 1965-67, purchasing agt., 1967-70; gen. mgr. The Iams Co., Dayton, Ohio, 1970-75, v.p., 1975-80, chief exec. officer, 1980-90, chmn., 1990-99, also dir.; ret., 1999. Mem. Pet Food Inst.; bd. dirs. Midwest Group, Cin., Bush Bros. Co., Knoxville, Tenn., The Iams Co., 1999—. Author: A Business Owner's Perspective on Outside Boards. Trustee Chaminade-Julienne High Sch., Dayton, 1987—, U. Dayton; mem. adv. bd. coll. bus. Ohio No. U., Ada, 1987—, also trustee. Named Best of Best Ctr. for Values Rsch., Houston, 1987. Mem. Am. Mgmt. Assn., Am. Agt. Assn. Roman Catholic. Avocations: traveling, swimming, golf. Office: The Iams Company PO Box 13615 Dayton OH 45413-0615

MATHIS, DAVID B. insurance company executive; b. Atlanta; BA, Lake Forest Coll., 1960. Chmn. Kemper Corp., Long Grove, Ill., 1992-96, also bd. dirs.; chmn., pres., CEO, Kemper Ins. Cos., 1996-97. Office: Kemper Ins Cos 1 Kemper Dr Long Grove IL 60049-0001 E-mail: DMathis@Kemperinsurance.com.

MATHIS, GREG, judge, radio personality; Mem. staff Councilman Clyde Cleveland, 1983; civil rights activitist Operation P.U.S.H.; mgr. Detroit Neighborhood City Halls Mayor Coleman A. Young, 1986—93, campaign coord., 1988; judge 36th dist. Mich. Superior Ct.; host Judgement Call WCIU-TV, Chgo., 1995—. Performer: (musical stage play) Been There Done That, 2000. Mem.: So. Christian Leadership Conf. (nat. bd. dirs.), NAACP (life). Office: 36th Dist Ct 421 Madison Ave Detroit MI 48226

MATHIS, LOIS RENO, retired elementary education educator; b. Vinson, Okla., June 10, 1915; d. William Dodson and Trudie Frances (Brady) Reno; m. Harold Fletcher Mathis, June 6, 1942 (dec.); children: Robert F., Betty Mathis Sproule. BS, Southwestern Okla. U., 1939; MA, U. Pitts., 1945; PhD, Ohio State U., 1965. Cert. elem. tchr.; cert. elem. supr. Tchr. Okla. Pub. Schs., Tea Cross, 1936-39, Tipton, 1939-42, Ohio County Schs., Wheeling, W.Va., 1944-45, Norman (Okla.) Pub. Schs., 1951-52, Kent (Ohio) State U., 1954-60, Ohio State U., Columbus, 1961-62, Columbus (Ohio) Pub. Schs., 1967-80; ret., 1980. Ednl. cons. in field, 1965—. Mem. Women's Round Table, Columbus, 1986-88; mem. data collection com. 100 Good Schs., Columbus, 1982-84. Mem. AAUW (pres. 1986-88), Ohio State Univ. Women's Club, Phi Delta Gamma (pres. 1980-82), Pi Lambda Theta, Alpha Delta Kappa, Kappa Delta Pi (counselor 1976—, alumni counselor exec. coun. internat. 1990-92, Honor Key 1991). Democrat. Baptist. Avocations: reading, bell collecting and research, entertaining friends, church activities. Home: 4590 Knightsbridge Blvd Apt 242 Columbus OH 43214-4353

MATHISEN-REID, RHODA SHARON, international communications consultant; b. Portland, Oreg., June 25, 1942; d. Daniel and Mildred Elizabeth Annette (Peterson) Hager; m. James Albert Mathisen, July 17, 1964 (div. 1977); m. James Albert Mathisen, July 17, 164 (div. 1977); m. James A. Reid Sr., Jan. 1, 1991. BA in Edn., Music, Bible Coll., Mich., 1964. Cmty. rels. officer Gary-Wheaton Bank, Wheaton, Ill., 1971-75; br. mgr. Stiver Temporary Personnel, Chgo., 1975-79; v.p. sales Exec. Technique, 1980-83; prin. Mathisen Assocs., Clarendon Hill., Ill., 1983—. Presenter seminars; featured speaker Women in Mgmt. Oak Brook Chpt., 1988.; cons. Haggai Inst., Atlanta; adv. mem. Nat. Bd. Success Group, 1986. Newsletter editor/publisher: 90th Divsn. Assn. (WWII Vets) 2001—. Mem. Downers Grove Twp. Precinct # 87 Rep. Com., 1998—; pres. chancel choir Christ Ch. Oak Brook, 1985—87; bd. dirs. Career Devel. Inst., Oak Brook, 1992—99, chair operational fin. com., 1997—98; bd. dirs. Crossroads Ministry Internat., 2000—; chmn. 1st Profl. Women's Seminar, 1995; judge Mrs. Ill., USI Pageant, 1994; exec. sec., treas. 90th Divsn. Assn., 2001—. Recipient Denby Steel award, 90th Divsn. Assn., 2001. Mem. Bus. and Profl. Women (charter mem., Woodfield chpt.), Execs. Club Oak Brook, Assn. Commerce and Industry (named Ambassdor of Month N.W. suuburban chpt. 1979), Oak Brook Assn. Commerce and Industry (membership com.), Women Entrepreneurs of DuPage County (membership chmn., featured speaker Ja 1988), Art. Inst., Willowbrook/Burr Ridge C. of C., 90th Divsn. Assn. (asst. sec., treas., 2001 Denby Steel award, editor newsletter), US Army WWII Vets. Orgn. (newsletter editor 2001-). Office: Mathisen Assocs 17 Lake Shore Dr Hinsdale IL 60527-2221

MATHISON, IAN WILLIAM, chemistry educator, academic dean; b. Liverpool, Eng., Apr. 17, 1938; came to U.S., 1963; s. William and Grace (Almond) M.; m. Mary Ann Gordon, July 20, 1968; children: Mark W., Lisa A. B. Pharm., U. London, 1960, Ph.D., 1963, D. Sci., 1976. Lic. pharmacist, Gt. Britain. Research assoc. U. Tenn. Ctr. for Health Scis., Memphis, 1963-65, asst. prof., 1965-68, assoc. prof., 1968-72, prof., 1972-76; medicinal chemistry prof. Ferris State U., Big Rapids, Mich., 1977—, dean, prof., 1977—. External examiner U. Sci., Malaysia, 1978-79; mem. Mich. dept. Mental Health Pharmacy Facilities Rev. Panel, Lansing, 1978-90, Quality Assurance Commn., 1979-90; cons. WHO, 1999; cons. in field. Mem. editorial bd.: Jour. Pharm. Sci., 1981-86 ; contbr. articles to profl. jours.; sr. inventor, patentee in field. Marion Labs. awardee, 1965-74; NSF grantee, 1968-72; Beecham Co. grantee, 1974-79 Fellow Royal Inst. Chemistry, Royal Soc. Chemistry; mem. Am. Pharm. Soc., Am. Chem. Soc., Am. Assn. Coll. Pharmacy (bd. dirs. 1988-90), Nat. Assn. Retail Druggists (edn. adv. com. 1989-94), Royal Pharm. Soc. Gt. Britain, Nat. Assn. Chain Drug Stores (ednl. adv. com. 1993—). Home: 820 Osborn Cir Big Rapids MI 49307-2536 Office: Ferris State U 220 Ferris Dr Big Rapids MI 49307-2295

MATHOG, ROBERT HENRY, otolaryngologist, educator; b. New Haven, Apr. 13, 1939; s. William and Tiby (Gans) M.; m. Deena Jane Rabinowitz, June 14, 1964; children: Tiby, Heather, Lauren, Jason. AB, Dartmouth Coll., 1960; MD, NYU, 1964. Diplomate Am. Bd. Facial Plastic and Reconstructive Surgery. Intern Duke Hosp., Durham, N.C., 1964-65, resident surgery, 1965-66, resident otolaryngology, 1966-69; practice medicine, specializing in otolaryngology Mpls., 1971-77, Detroit, 1977—; chief of otolaryngology Hennepin County Med. Center, Mpls., 1972-77; asst. prof. U. Minn., 1971-74, asso. prof., 1974-77; prof., chmn. dept. otolaryngology Wayne State U. Sch. Medicine, 1977—. Chief otolaryngology Hennepin County Hosp., Mpls., 1972-77, Harper-Grace Hosps., Detroit, 1977—, Detroit Receiving Hosp., 1977-92; cons. staff VA Hosp., Allen Park, Minn., 1977—, Children's Hosp., Detroit, 1977—, Hutzel Hosp., Detroit, 1966, St. Joseph Mercy Hosp., Oakland, Mich., 2001; mem. adv. coun. Nat. Inst. Deaf and Other Communicable Disorders NIH, 1992-96; chief otolaryngology, head and neck surgery June Hosp., 1994-95. Author: Otolaryngology Clinics of North America, 1976, Textbook of Maxillofacial Trauma, 1983; editor in chief Videomed. Edn. Systems, 1972-75; editor: Atlas of Craniofacial Trauma, 1992; contbr. articles to med. jours. Bd. dirs. Bexer County Hearing Soc., 1969-71; adv. coun. WIDCB, 1993. Maj. USAF, 1969-71; chmn. Lens Hearing Ctr. of S.E. Mich. Recipient Valentine Mott medal for proficiency in anatomy, 1961, Recognition award Wayne State Bd. Govs. Faculty, 1993; Deafness Rsch. Found. grantee, 1979-81, NIH grantee, 1986, 92, 96, Lawrence M. Weiner Alumni award Wayne State U. Sch. Med., 1999. Fellow ACS, Am. Acad. Otolaryngology, Head and Neck Surgery (Cert. award 1976, Cert. of Appreciation 1978), Am. Soc. Head and Neck Surgery, Triological Soc. (v.p. 1995-96, mtg. guest of honor 2002), Am. Otol. Soc., Am. Acad. Facial Plastic and Reconstructive Surgery (v.p. 1980), Am. Neurotology Soc.; mem. AMA, Am. Laryngol. Soc. (coun. 1994—), Am. Laryngol. Assn., Mich. Med. Soc., Am. Head and Neck Soc., Soc. Univ. Otolaryngologists (pres. 1995), Assn. Acad. Depts. Otolaryngology, Assn. Rsch. Otolaryngology (pres. 1981). Home: 27115 Wellington Rd Franklin MI 48025-1329 Office: 27177 Lahser Rd Ste 203 Southfield MI 48034-8468 Also: Wayne State U Sch Med 540 E Canfield St Detroit MI 48201-1928

MATIA, PAUL RAMON, federal judge; b. Cleve., Oct. 2, 1937; s. Leo Clemens and Irene Elizabeth (Linkert) M.; m. Nancy Arch Van Meter, Jan. 2, 1993. BA, Case Western Res. U., 1959; JD, Harvard U., 1962. Bar: Ohio 1962, U.S. Dist. Ct. (no. dist.) Ohio 1969. Law clk. Common Pleas Ct. of Cuyahoga County, Cleve., 1963-66, judge, 1985-91; asst. atty. gen. State of Ohio, 1966-69, adminstrv. ast. to atty. gen. Columbus, 1969-70; senator Ohio State Senate, 1971-75, 79-83; ptnr. Hadley, Matia, Mills & MacLean Co., L.P.A., Cleve., 1975-84; judge U.S. Dist. Ct. (no. dist.) Ohio, 1991-99, chief dist. judge, 1999—; mem. 6th Cir. Jud. Coun., 1999—. Candidate Lt. Gov. Rep. Primary, 1982, Ohio Supreme Ct., 1988. Named Outstanding Legislator, Ohio Assn. for Retarded Citizens, 1974, Watchdog of Ohio Treasury, United Conservatives of Ohio, 1979; recipient Heritage award Polonia Found., 1988. Mem. Fed. Bar Assn., Club at Key Ctr. Avocations: skiing, gardening, travel. Office: US Dist Ct 201 Superior Ave E Cleveland OH 44114-1201

MATIS, JIMMY, radio personality; married; 5 children. Radio host Sta. WFBQ-FM, Indpls. Office: WFBQ 6161 Fall Creek Rd Indianapolis IN 46220*

MATKOWSKY, BERNARD JUDAH, applied mathematician, educator; b. N.Y.C., Aug. 19, 1939; s. Morris N. and Ethel H. M.; m. Florence Knobel, Apr. 11, 1965; children: David, Daniel, Devorah. B.S., CCNY, 1960; M.E.E., NYU, 1961, M.S., 1963, Ph.D., 1966. Fellow Courant Inst. Math. Scis., NYU, 1961-66; mem. faculty dept. math. Rensselaer Poly. Inst., 1966-77; John Evans prof. applied math., mech. engring. & math. Northwestern U., Evanston, Ill., 1977—, chmn. engring. sci. and applied math. dept., 1993-99. Vis. prof. Tel Aviv U., 1972-73; vis. scientist Weizmann Inst. Sci., Israel, summer 1976, summer 1980, Tel Aviv U., summer 1980; cons. Argonne Nat. Lab., Sandia Labs., Lawrence Livermore Nat. Lab., Exxon Research and Engring. Co. Editor Wave Motion—An Internat. Jour., 1979-99, Applied Math. Letters, 1987—, SIAM Jour. Applied Math., 1976-95, European Jour. Applied Math., 1990-96, Random and Computational Dynamics, 1991-97, Internat. Jour. SHS, 1992—, Jour. Materials Synthesis and Processing, 1992—; mem. editl. adv. bd. Springer Verlag Applied Math. Scis. Series; contbr. chpts. to books, articles to profl. jours. Fulbright grantee, 1972-73; Guggenheim fellow, 1982-83 Fellow: AAAS, Am. Acad. Mechs.; mem.: Soc. Natural Philosophy, Com. Concerned Scientists, Conf. Bd. Math. Scis. (coun., com. human rights math. scientists), Am. Assn. Combustion Synthesis, Am. Physics Soc., Combustion Inst., Am. Math. Soc., Soc. Indsl. and Applied Math., Eta Kappa Nu, Sigma Xi. Home: 3704 Davis St Skokie IL 60076-1745 Office: Northwestern U Technological Institute Evanston IL 60208-0001 E-mail: b-matkowsky@northwestern.edu.

MATLAK, JOHN, radio personality; Degree magna cum laude, U. Dayton, 1975. Radio host, sports dir. Grand Rapids First News Wood 1300, Grand Rapids, Mich. Recipient numerous awards, Mich. Assn. Broadcasters, AP. Office: Newsradio Wood 1300 77 Monroe Center Ste 100 Grand Rapids MI 49503

MATSLER, FRANKLIN GILES, retired education educator; b. Glendive, Mont., Dec. 27, 1922; s. Edmund Russell and Florence Edna (Giles) M.; m. Lois Josephine Hoyt, June 12, 1949; children— Linda, Jeanne, David, Winfield. B.S., Mont. State U., Bozeman, 1948; M.A., U. Mont., Missoula, 1952; Ph.D., U. Calif. at Berkeley, 1959. Tchr. Missoula County (Mont.) High Sch., 1949-51, Tracy (Calif.) Sr. Elem. Schs., 1952-53, San Benito County (Calif.) High Sch. and Jr. Coll., 1953-55; grad. asst. U. Calif. at Berkeley, 1955-58; asst. prof. Humboldt State Coll., Arcata, Calif., 1958-62, assoc. prof., 1962-63, asst. exec. dean, 1958-63; chief specialist higher edn. Calif. Coordinating Council for Higher Edn., Sacramento, 1963-68; exec. dir. Ill. Bd. Regents, Springfield, 1968-84; prof. higher edn. Ill. State U., Normal, 1968-96, Regency prof. higher edn., 1984-96; ret., 1996. Chancellor Ill. Bd. Regents, 1995-96. Bd. dirs. Ill. Edn. Consortium, 1972-76; bd. dirs. Central Ill. Health Planning Agy., 1970-76, Springfield Symphony Orch. Assn.; pres. Bloomington/Normal Symphony Soc., 1988-90. Served to 1st lt. AUS, 1943-46. Mem. Nat. Assn. Sys. Heads (exec. v.p. 1985-92), Am. Assn. State Colls. and Univs. Assn. for Instl. Rsch., Phi Delta Kappa, Lambda Chi Alpha. Home: 31 Arbor Ct Bloomington IL 61704-2452 Office: Illinois State U 539 DeGarmo Hall Normal IL 61761 E-mail: fmatsler@ilstu.edu.

MATSON, WESLEY JENNINGS, educational administrator; b. Svea, Minn., June 25, 1924; s. James and Ettie (Mattson) Matson; m. Doris Cragg; 1 child James Jennings. BS with distinction, U. Minn., 1948; MA, U. Calif., Berkeley, 1954; EdD, Columbia U., 1960. High sch. tchr. Santa Barbara County Pub. Schs., Santa Maria, Calif., 1948-50; instr. U. Calif., Berkeley, 1950-54, Columbia U., N.Y.C., 1954-55; lectr. Fordham U., 1955-56; asst. prof. U. Md., College Park, 1956-59; prof., asst. dean U. Wis., Milw., 1959-72; dean, prof. Winona (Minn.) State U., 1972-88, emeritus, 1989—. Vis. prof. U. P.R., Rio Peidras, We. Wash. U., Bellingham, San Diego State U., U. Minn., Mpls., U. Hawaii; adj. faculty St. Olaf Coll., Northfield, Minn.; cons. U.S. Dept. Edn., Washington, Ill. State U.; bd. regents Wis. Dept. Pub. Instrn.; examiner Nat. Coun. Accreditation Tchr. Edn. North Ctrl. assn., Chgo. Contbr. Exec. com. Minn. Alliance of Arts, Mpls.; mem. Minn. com. Certification Stds., St. Paul; cons. ARC; bd. dirs. Ft. Snelling Meml. Chapel Found.; apptd. by Minn. Supreme Ct. to Minn. Bd. CLE. Capt. USAF. Decorated Bronze Star; recipient Disting. Svc. award, Wis. Assn. Tchr. Edn., 1972. Mem.: NEA (life), VFW, Minn. edn. Assn., Assn. Higher Edn., Nat. Assn. Tchr. Educators (exec. com.), Minn. Assn. Colls. for Tchr. Edn. (pres. 1983—85, Hon. life Award of Merit), U. Minn. Alumni Soc. (Outstanding Educator award 1984), Am. Legion, Minn. Hist. Soc., Rotary Club, Alpha Sigma Phi, Kappa Delta Pi, Phi Delta Kappa. Home: 6615 Lake Shore Dr S Minneapolis MN 55423-2218

MATTHEI, EDWARD HODGE, architect; b. Chgo., Dec. 21, 1927; s. Henry Reinhard and Myra Beth (Hodge) M.; m. Mary Nina Hoffmann, June 30, 1951; children: Edward Hodge, Suzanne Marie, Christie Ann, Laura Jean, John William. B.S. in Archtl. Engring, U. Ill., 1951. Registered arch. 17 states, including Ariz., Fla., Ill., Mich., N.Y., Wis., Calif.; cert. NCARB. Dir. health facilities planning and constrn. Child & Smith (architects and engrs.), Chgo., 1951-60; sr. v.p. health facilities planning Perkins & Will, 1960-74; ptnr. firm Matthei & Colin Assoc., 1974-96; planning and archtl. design cons., 1996—. Com. chmn. Am. Nat. Standards Inst., 1983-89; lectr. 1st Internat. Conf. on Rehab. of Handicapped, Beijing, 1986, Design USA, Novosbirsk and Moscow, USSR, 1990. Editor: Inland Architect, 1956-58; prin. works health facilities projects, med. ctr. master plans including Akron (Ohio) Gen. Hosp., Heritage Hosp., Taylor, Mich., Rose Meml., Denver, Silver Cross Hosp., Joliet, Ill., Shands Tchg. Hosp. & Med. Sch., U. Fla., Gainesville, Mercy Hosp., Davenport, Iowa, Westlake Cmty. Hosp., Chgo., Highland Park (Ill.) Hosp., Ctrl. DuPage Hosp., Winfield, Ill., Nebr. Meth. Hosp., Omaha, Rockford (Ill.) Meml. Hosp., U. Ala. Med. Ctr., Birmingham, U. Calif. Sch. Medicine, Irvine, Kent Hall, U. Chgo., Holy Cross Hosp., Md., West Mich. Cancer Ctr. Second v.p. Nat. Easter Seal Soc., 1978; mem. bd. dirs. St. Scholastica H.S., Chgo., 1973-83, 86-96; mem. Welfare Coun. Greater Met. Chgo., 1965-72; chair profl. adv. coun. Nat. Easter Seal Soc., 1988-89. With AUS, 1946-47. Recipient Leon Chatelain award for barrier-free environ. Nat. Easter Seals Soc., 1979, Disting. Svc. award, 1990, 99, Meritorious Svc. award Am. Nat. Standards Inst., 1987, Speedy award Paralyzed Vets. Am., 1993. Fellow AIA (Disting. Svc. award Chgo. chpt. 1988); mem. Am. Hosp. Assn., Am. Assn. Hosp. Planning, Internat. Hosp. Fedn., Nat. Center Barrier Free Environ. (dir.), Builders Assn. Chgo., Chgo. Assn. Commerce and Industry. Home: 1437 W Glenlake Ave Chicago IL 60660-1801 Office: Matthei & Colin Assocs 332 S Michigan Ave Chicago IL 60604-4434

MATTHEWS, C(HARLES) DAVID, real estate appraiser, consultant; b. Anniston, Ala., June 15, 1946; s. James Boyd and Emma Grace (McCullough) M.; m. Stephanie Ann Woods, Dec. 28, 1968; children: Alison Paige, Dylan McCullough. BS, U. Tenn., 1968. County appraiser Assessor's Office, Freeport, Ill., 1969-71; staff appraiser Ill. Dept. Highways, Springfield, 1971-72; appraiser, dir. counseling Norman Benedict Assocs., Hamden, Conn., 1972-76; mgr. appraisal dept. Citizens Realty & Ins., Evansville, Ind., 1976-80; owner, mgr. David Matthews Assocs., 1980—. Adj. real estate faculty U. Conn., 1974-76, U. Evansville, 1978-87, Appraisal Inst., 1989—; citizen amb. to Russia on Urban Valuation Team, 1993. Tympanist Chattanooga Symphony; drummer Templeaires Big Band; author: (with others) Downtown Master Plan of Evansville, Indiana, 1984, The Appraisal of Real Estate, 10th edit. Mem. Leadership Evansville, 1982; arbitrator Am. Arbitration Assn., 1986-91; chmn. bd. trustees Meth. Temple, 1994-98, 2001. Recipient merit award Willard Libr. Photog.

Contest, 1988. Mem. Am. Inst. Real Estate Appraisers (vice chmn. nat. admissions 1990, state pres. 1987, governing councillor 1989-90), Appraisal Inst. (chmn. gen. appraiser bd. 1991-92, exec. com. 1991-92, 95-96, chmn. pub. rels. 1993, chmn. comm. 1995-96, Percy Wagner award 1992, Y.T. Lum award 1997), Soc. Real Estate Appraisers (local pres. 1981), Evansville Bd. Realtors (pres. 1986, Realtor of Yr. award 1987), Counselors of Real Estate, Evansville C. of C. (chair govt. affairs 1998-99), Mensa, Rotary. Avocations: cinematographer, jazz drummer, travel, golf. Home: 430 S Boeke Rd Evansville IN 47714-1616 Office: 123 NW 4th St Rm 711 Evansville IN 47708-1719 E-mail: dma@evansville.net.

MATTHEWS, ELIZABETH WOODFIN, law librarian, law educator; b. Ashland, Va., July 30, 1927; d. Edwin Clifton and Elizabeth Frances (Luck) Woodfin; m. Sidney E. Matthews, Dec. 20, 1947; 1 child, Sarah Elizabeth Matthews Wiley. BA, Randolph-Macon Coll., 1948, LLD (hon.), 1989; MS in Libr. Sci., U. Ill., 1952; PhD, So. Ill. U., 1972; LLD, Randolph-Macon Coll., 1989. Cert. law libr., med. libr., med. libr. III. Libr. Ohio State U., Columbus, 1952-59; libr., instr. U. Ill., Urbana, 1962-63; lectr. U. Ill. Grad. Sch. Libr. Sci., 1964; libr., instr. Morris Libr. So. Ill. U., Carbondale, 1964-67; classroom instr. So. Ill. U. Coll Edn., 1967-70; med. libr., asst. prof. Morris Libr. So. Ill. U., 1972-74, law libr., asst. prof., 1974-79, law libr., assoc. prof., 1979-85, law libr., prof., 1985-92, prof. emerita, 1993—. Author: Access Points to Law Libraries, 1984, 17th Century English Law Reports, 1986, Law Library Reference Shelf, 1988, 4th edit., 1999, Pages and Missing Pages, 1983, 2d edit., 1989, Lincoln as a Lawyer: An Annotated Bibliography, 1991. Mem. AAUW (pres. 1976-78, corp. rep. 1978-88), Am. Assn. Law Librs., Beta Phi Mu, Phi Kappa Phi. Methodist. Home: 811 S Skyline Dr Carbondale IL 62901-2405 Office: So Ill U Law Libr Carbondale IL 62901

MATTHEWS, JACK (JOHN HAROLD MATTHEWS), English educator, writer; b. Columbus, Ohio, July 22, 1925; s. John Harold and Lulu Emma (Grover) M.; m. Barbara Jane Reese, Sept. 16, 1947; children: Cynthia Ann Matthews Warnock, Barbara Ellen Matthews Saunders, John HHarold. B.A., Ohio State U., 1949, M.A., 1954. Clk. U.S. Post Office, Columbus, 1950-59; prof. English Urbana Coll., Ohio, 1959-64, Ohio U., Athens, 1964-77, disting. prof., 1977—. Author: Bitter Knowledge, 1964 (Ohioana fiction award 1964), Hanger Stout, Awake!, 1967, The Charisma Campaigns, 1972 (nominee NBA Fiction award), Sassafras, 1983, Crazy Women, 1985, Booking in the Heartland, 1986 (Ohioana non-fiction award 1986), Ghostly Populations, 1986, Memoirs of a Bookman, 1989, Dirty Tricks, 1990, On The Shore of That Beautiful Shore (play), 1991, An Interview with the Sphinx (play), 1992, Storyhood As We Know It and Other Tales (stories), 1993, Booking Pleasures, 1996, (essays) Reading Matter, 2000, others. Served with USCG, 1943-45. Recipient numerous ind. artist awards Ohio Art Council, Major Artist award, 1989-90; Guggenheim fellow, 1974-75 Mem. Phi Beta Kappa E=mail. Home: 4314 Fisher Rd Athens OH 45701-9333 Office: Ohio U Dept English Athens OH 45701 E-mail: matthej1@ohio.edu.

MATTHEWS, JAMES SHADLEY, lawyer; b. Omaha, Nov. 24, 1951; s. Donald E. and Lois Jean (Shadley) M.; m. Mary Kvaal, May 3, 1991; 1 child, Katherine. BA cum laude, St. Olaf Coll., 1973; JD, U. Ill., 1976; MBA, U. Denver, 1977. Bar: Minn. 1976, U.S. Dist. Ct. Minn. 1978. With Northwestern Nat. Life Ins. Co., Mpls., 1978-89, v.p., asst. gen. counsel, 1985-89; ptnr. Lindquist & Venum, Mpls., 1990—. Sr. v.p., gen. counsel Washington Square Capital, Inc., 1989; bd. dirs., sec. NWNL Health Network, Inc., St. Paul, 1987-89; pub. dir. Minn. Health Reins. Assn., 1992-94; spkr. to profl. orgns., 1984—; bd. dirs. Northstar Life Ins. Co. Mem. ABA, Am. Health Lawyers Assn., Minn. Bar Assn. (chmn. health law sect. 1986-87). Office: Lindquist & Vennum IDS Ctr 80 S 8th St Ste 4200 Minneapolis MN 55402-2274 E-mail: jmatthews@lindquist.com.

MATTHEWS, L. WHITE, III, railroad executive; b. Ashland, Ky., Oct. 5, 1945; s. L. White and Virginia Carolyn (Chandler) M.; m. Mary Jane Hanser, Dec. 30, 1972; children: Courtney Chandler, Brian Whittlesey. BS in Econs, Hampden-Sydney Coll., 1967; MBA in Fin. and Gen. Mgmt, U. Va., 1970. Corp. fin. Chem. Bank, N.Y.C., 1970-72, asst. sec., 1972-74, asst. v.p., 1974-75, v.p., 1976-77; treas. Mo. Pacific Corp., St. Louis, 1977-82; v.p. fin. Mo. Pacific R.R. Co. subs. Mo. Pacific Corp., 1979-82; v.p., treas. Union Pacific Corp. and Union Pacific R.R. Co., N.Y.C., 1982-87; sr. v.p. fin. Union Pacific Corp., Bethlehem, Pa., 1987-92, exec. v.p. fin., 1992-98; exec. v.p., CFO Ecolab Inc., 1999—. Bd. dirs. Union Pacific Corp., 1995, 98, Ecolab Inc., Lexent Inc., Nortrax Inc., 2000—.

MATTHIAS, JOHN EDWARD, English literature educator; b. Columbus, Ohio, Sept. 5, 1941; s. John Marshall and Lois (Kirkpatrick) M.; m. Diana Clare Jocelyn, Dec. 27, 1967; children— Cynouai, Laura. BA, Ohio State U., 1963; MA, Stanford U., 1966; postgrad., U. London, 1967. Asst. prof. dept. English U. Notre Dame, Ind., 1966-73, assoc. prof., 1973-80, prof., 1980—. Vis. fellow Clare Hall, Cambridge U., 1966-77, assoc., 1977— ; vis. prof. dept. English, Skidmore Coll., Saratoga Springs, N.Y., 1975, U. Chgo., 1980. Author: Bucyrus, 1971, Turns, 1975, Crossing, 1979, Five American Poets, 1980, Introducing David Jones, 1980, Contemporary Swedish Poetry, 1980, Bathory and Lermontov, 1980, Northern Summer, New and Selected Poems, 1984, The Battle of Kosovo, 1987, David Jones: Man and Poet: A Gathering of Ways, 1991, Reading Old Friends, 1991, Swimming at Midnight, 1995, Beltane at Aphelion, 1995, Pages: New Poems and Cuttings, 2000. Recipient Columbia U. Transl. award, 1978, Swedish Inst. award, 1981, Poetry award Soc. Midland Authors, 1984, Ingram Merrill Found. award, 1984, 90; Woodrow Wilson fellow, 1963, Lily Endowment fellow, 1993; Fulbright grantee, 1966. Mem. AAUP, PEN, Poets and Writers, Poetry Soc. Am. (George Bogin Meml. award 1990). Office: U Notre Dame Dept English Notre Dame IN 46556

MATTHIES, FREDERICK JOHN, architectural engineer; b. Omaha, Oct. 4, 1925; s. Fred. J. and Charlotte Leota (Metz) M.; m. Carol Mae Dean, Sept. 14, 1947; children— John Frederick, Jane Carolyn Matthies Goding BSCE, Cornell U., 1947; postgrad., U. Nebr., 1952-53. Diplomate Am. Acad. Environ. Engrs.; registered profl. engr., Iowa, Nebr. Civil engr. Henningson, Durham & Richardson, Omaha, 1947-50, 52-54; sr. v.p. devel. Leo A. Daly Co., 1954-90; cons. engr., 1990—. Lectr. in field; mem. dist. export coun. U.S. Dept. Commerce, 1981-83. Contbr. articles to profl. publs. Mem. Douglas County Rep. Cen. Com., Nebr., 1968-72; bd. regents Augustana Coll., Sioux Falls., S.D., 1976-89; bd. dirs. Orange County Luth. Hosp. Assn., Anaheim, Calif., 1961-62, Nebr. Humanities Coun., 1988-94, Omaha-Shizuoka City (Japan) Sister City Orgn.; trustee Luth. Med. Ctr., Omaha, 1978-82; mem. adv. bd. Marine Mil. Acad., Harlingen, Tex. 1st lt. USMCR, 1943-46, 50-52, Korea. Fellow ASCE, Instn. Civil Engrs. (London, Euro Engr. European Econ. Commn.); mem. NSPE, Am. Water Works Assn. (life), Air Force Assn., Am. Legion, VFW, The Omaha Club. Lutheran. Home: 337 S 127th St Omaha NE 68154-2309

MATTSON, STEPHEN JOSEPH, lawyer; b. Abilene, Tex., Oct. 11, 1943; s. Joseph Martin and Dorothy Irene (Doyle) M.; m. Lynn Louise Mitchell, Mar. 13, 1965; children: Eric, Laura. BA (hon.), U. Ill., 1965, JD (hon.), 1970. Bar: Ill., 1970, U.S. Dist. Ct. (no. dist.) Ill. 1970. Assoc. Mayer, Brown, Rowe & Maw, Chgo., 1970—77, ptnr., 1978—. Mem. ABA, Ill. State Bar Assn., Chgo. Bar Assn., Fed. Energy Bar Assn., Order of Coif. Office: Mayer Brown Rowe & Maw 190 S La Salle St Ste 3100 Chicago IL 60603-3441

MATUNE, FRANK JOSEPH, lawyer; b. Youngstown, Ohio, Jan. 11, 1948; s. Walter John and Eve (Skiljo) M.; m. Doreen Mary Dolan, June 1, 1974; children: Molly Catherine, John Walter, Kelly Dolan. BA, Ill. Benedictine Coll., 1970; JD, Thomas M. Cooley Law Sch., Lansing, Mich., 1979; LLM, Georgetown U., 1980. Bar: Pa. 1979, Ohio, 1998, U.S. Dist. Ct. (western dist.) Pa. 1982, U.S. Tax Ct. 1980. Tax clk. Bd. Tax Appeals State Mich. Dept. Revenue, Lansing, 1978-79; ptnr. Routman, Moore, Goldstone & Valentino, Sharon, Pa., 1981-98, Nadler, Nadler & Burdman Co., LPA, Youngstown, Ohio, 1998—. Author: Pennsylvania Tax Service, 1987, Federal Tax Service, 1988. Mem. ABA, Ohio Ba Assn., Pa. Bar Assn., Mercer County Bar Assn. (treas. 1983-86). Republican. Roman Catholic. Avocations: sports, classical music. Home: 798 Lillian Dr Hermitage PA 16148-1571 Office: Nadler Nadler & Burdman Co 20 Federal Plz W Ste 600 Youngstown OH 44503-1424

MATZICK, KENNETH JOHN, hospital administrator; b. Chgo., May 31, 1943; married. B, U. Iowa, 1965, MHA, 1967. Adminstrv. resident VA Med. Ctr., Iowa City, 1966, Morristown (N.J.) Meml. Hosp., 1967-68, asst. to exec. v.p., 1968-69; asst. dir. William Beaumont Hosp., Royal Oak, Mich., 1969-76, dir. Troy, 1976-83, v.p., COO Royal Oak, 1983-97, exec. v.p., COO, 1997—. Home: 22500 Lavon St Saint Clair Shores MI 48081-2076 Office: William Beaumont Hosp 3601 W 13 Mile Rd Royal Oak MI 48073-6712

MATZKE, JAY, internist; b. Sidney, Nebr., Oct. 2, 1956; m. Ann Matzke, Feb. 13, 1982; children: Alex, Jered, Sloan. B Medicine, U. Nebr. Med. Ctr., 1979, MD, 1983. Diplomate Am. Acad. Family Physicians. Resident in family practice U. Nebr. Med. Ctr., Nebr., 1984—86; ptnr. Martin Med. Clinic/Sidney Meml. Hosp., 1987—90; med. dir. Sidney Meml. Hosp. Addiction Ctr., 1987—89; staff physician Omaha Family Practice, 1990—96; ptnr. Immanuel Clinic/Immanuel Med. Ctr., 1990—96; med. dir. Immanuel/Alegent Health Sports Medicine, 1995—96; staff physician Meml. Health Care Sys., Seward, Nebr., 1997—, chief med. staff, 1999; med. dir. S.W. Rural Fire Dept., 1998—; med. advisor Lancaster County Red Cross, 1999—. Chmn. emergency cardiac care com. for Nebr. Am. Heart Assn., 1995—, instr. ACLS, 1984—; instr. ATLS ACS, 1986—. Dist. chmn. Boy Scouts Am., 2000—, pack com. chmn., 1997—98; trustee Nebr. Children's Home Soc., Nebr., 1999—; bd. dirs. Emergency Med. Svcs., 1998—; mem. pres.' adv. com. U. Nebr., 1997—2000; den leader Boy Scouts Am., 1985—87; chmn. ACLS Task Force, Nebr., 1992—95; pres., v.p., treas. Millard Sch. Bd., 1993—97; mem. Sidney City Coun., 1988—90; pres., charter mem. Cheyenne County Cmty. Ctr. Found., Inc., 1988—90; mem. bd. mission outreach, trustee Faith Luth. Ch., 1997—. Named Outstanding Young Nebraskan, Nebr. Jaycees, 1989, Outstanding Chamber Mem., Cheyenne County C. of C., 1988; recipient award of achievement, Nebr. Assn. Sch. Bds., 1995, 1996. Mem.: Am. Med. Soc. Sports Medicine. Mailing: 1423 N 8th St Seward NE 68434

MAULE, THERESA MOORE, lawyer; b. Winner, S.D., Jan. 20, 1966; d. Robert James and Serrilyn Rae (Belmer) M.; m. Brian Lee Kramer, Nov. 25, 1996. BA summa cum laude, Dakota Wesleyan U., 1988; MA, U. S.D., 1990, JD, 1994. Bar: S.D., U.S. Dist. Ct. S.D., Lower Brule Sioux Tribal Ct., Rosebud Sioux Tribal Ct. Prosecutor Rosebud (S.D.) Sioux Tribal Ct., 1994-96; ptnr. Maule & Maule Law Offices, Winner, S.D., 1995—; prosecutor Lower Brule (S.D.) Sioux Tribal Ct., 1996—; states atty Tripp County, Winner, 1997—. Mem. Tripp County Child Protection Team, Winner, S.D., 1997—. Mem. ABA, S.D. Bar Assn., Nat. Dist. Attys. Assn., S.D. Trial Lawyers Assn., Bus. and Profl. Women (Young Careerist 1996), Phi Kappa Phi, Phi Alpha Theta. Republican. Episcopalian. Avocations: camping, ceramics. Office: Maule & Maule Law Offices PO Box 1831 Winner SD 57580-1031

MAURER, DAVID LEO, lawyer; b. Evansville, Ind., Oct. 31, 1945; s. John G. Jr. and Mildred M. (Lintzenich) M.; m. Diane M. Kaput, Aug. 11, 1973; children: Eric W., Kathryn A. BA magna cum laude, U. Detroit, 1967, Cert. in Teaching, 1971; JD, Wayne State U., 1975. Bar: Mich., U.S. Dist. Ct. (ea. and we. dist.) Mich., U.S. Ct. Appeals (6th cir.) Cin. Law clk. Mich. Ct. Appeals, Detroit, 1976, Supreme Ct. Mich., Lansing, 1977-78; asst. U.S. atty. civil div. U.S. Dept. Justice, Detroit, 1978-81; assoc. to ptnr. Butzel, Long, Gust, Klein & Van Zile, 1981-85; ptnr. Pepper, Hamilton & Scheetz (now Pepper Hamilton LLP), 1985—. Guest lectr. Practicing Law Inst., 1988—, Nat. Bus. Inst., 1989—, U. Mich. Law Sch., U. Detroit Law Sch., 1990, Hazardous Waste Super Conf., 1986-87. Co-author: Michigan Environmental Law Deskbook, 1992; contbr. articles to profl. jours. and chpts. in books. Mem. Energy & Environ. Policy Com., 1988—, chairperson, 1989-90; mem. Great Lakes Water Resources Commn., 1986. Mem. State Bar Mich. (environ. couns. 1986-91, sec., treas., chairperson-elect, chairperson 1991-93). Office: Pepper Hamilton LLP 100 Renaissance Ctr Ste 3600 Detroit MI 48243-1101

MAURER, EDWARD LANCE, chiropractor, radiologist; b. Rahway, N.J., June 4, 1937; s. Frank Eugene and Charlotte Marian (Crook) Maurer; m. Jean Carol Outten, Feb. 14, 1960 (dec. Dec. 1995); children: Lance P., Terry L. D of Chiropractic, Lincoln Chiropractic Coll., Indpls., 1958; student, Western Mich. U., 1970-72, Upper Iowa U., 1974-76. Diplomate Am. Chiropractic Bd. Radiology. Pvt. practice, Kalamazoo, 1961—. Past pres. Chiro/Net Ltd., Chiropractic IPA; chmn. Valhalla Enterprises; mem. postgrad. faculty in radiology Nat. coll. Chiropractice; hon. bd., adv. com. Coll. Human Svcs. Fla. State U.; exec. v.p. Mich. Chiro/Net Corp. Editor (-in-chief): ACA Press Pub.; mem. editl. bd. Jour. Manipulative and Physiol. Therapeutics, Am. Jour. Chiropractic Medicine, D.C. Tracts Periodical, chmn. editl. bd. Jour. Am. Chiropractic Assn.; author: (book) Practical Applied Roentgenology, 1983, Selected Ethics and Protocols in Chiropractic, 1991; contbr. articles to profl. jours., chapters to books. Bd. dirs., chmn. Lincoln Coll. Edn. and Rsch. Fund, others. Fellow: Internat. Coll. Chiropractic, Can. Chiropractic Coll. Radiologists; mem.: Am. Chiropractic Registry Radiol. Techs. (exec. v.p.), Am. Chiropractic Coun. Diagnostic Imaging (past dist bd. dirs. and pres.), Mich. Chiropractic Assn. (past dist. v.p.), Mich. Chiropractic Assn. (past dist. v.p.) (Chiropractor of Yr. 1981), Kalamazoo county Chiropractic Assn. (past pres.), Am.. Chiropractic Assn. (chmn. bd. govs., exec. com., radiol. health cons., state del. (Chiropractor of Yr. 2001). Republican. Office: Kalamazoo Chiropractic Ctr 2330 Gull Rd Kalamazoo MI 49048-1432

MAURER, HAROLD MAURICE, pediatrician; b. N.Y.C., Sept. 10, 1936; s. Isador and Sarah (Rothkowitz) M.; m. Beverly Bennett, June 12, 1960; children: Ann Maurer Rosenbach, Wendy Maurer Rausch. AB, NYU, 1957; MD, SUNY, Bklyn., 1961. Diplomate Am. Bd. Pediatrics, Am. Bd. Pediatric Hematology-Oncology. Intern pediatrics Kings County Hosp., N.Y.C., 1961-62; resident in pediatrics Babies Hosp., Columbia-Presbyn. Med. Center, 1962-64; fellow in pediatric hematology/oncology Columbia-Presbyn. Med. Center, 1966-68; asst. prof. pediatrics Med. Coll. Va., Richmond, 1968-71, asso. prof., 1971-75, prof., 1975—, chmn. dept. pediatrics, 1976-93; dean U. Nebr. Coll. Medicine, Omaha, 1993-98; chancellor U. Nebr. Med. Ctr., 1998—. Chmn. Intergroup Rhabdomyosarcoma Study, 1972-98; exec. com. Pediatric Oncology Group; mem. cancer clin. investigation rev. com. NIH, Gov.'s Homeland Security Policy Group. Editor: pediatrics, 1983, Rhabdomyosarcoma and Related Tumors in Children and Adolescence, 1991; mem. editorial bd. Am. Jour. Hematology, Journal Pediatric Hematology and Oncology, Medical and Pediatric Oncology, 1984-99; contbr. articles to profl. jours. Mem. Youth Health Task Force, City of Richmond., Gov.'s Adv. Com. on Handicapped., Gov.'s Homeland Security Policy Group, Nebr., 2002-; mem. nat. com. on childhood cancer Am. Cancer Soc., bd. dirs. Va. div. Served to lt. comdr. USPHS, 1964-66. NIH grantee, 1974-98. Mem. Am. Acad. Pediatrics (com. oncology-hematology), Am. Soc. Hematology, Soc. Pediatric Rsch., Am. Pediatric Soc., Va. Pediatric Sic. (exec. com.), Assn. Med. Sch. Pediatric Dept. Chmn., Internat. Soc. Pediatric Oncology, Am. Soc. Clin. Oncology, Va. Hematology Soc., Am. Assn. Cancer Rsch., Am. Cancer Soc., Am. Soc. Pediatric Hematology-Oncology (v.p. 1990-91, pres. 1991-93), Sigma Xi, Coun. Deans AAMC, Gov.'s Blue Ribbon Commn., Alpha Omega Alpha. Republican. Jewish. Home: 9822 Ascot Dr Omaha NE 68114-3848 Office: U Nebr Med Ctr 986605 Nebraska Med Ctr Omaha NE 68198-0001 E-mail: hmmaurer@unmc.edu.

MAURSTAD, DAVID INGOLF, federal agency administrator, insurance company executive; b. North Platte, Nebr., Aug. 25, 1953; s. Ingolf Byron and Marilyn Sophia (Gimble) M.; m. Karen Sue Micek, Sept. 7, 1974; children: Ingolf, Derek, Laura. A. in Fine Arts, Platte Community Coll., Columbus, Nebr., 1973; BSBA, U. Nebr., 1989, MBA, 2000. Asst. golf profl. Country Club of Lincoln (Nebr.), 1973-76; head golf profl. Westward Ho Country Club, Sioux Falls, S.D., 1977; ins. agt. Maurstad/Zimmerman Ins., Beatrice, Nebr., 1978-84; ins. agy. mgr. Maurstad Ins. Svcs., Inc., 1984-90, pres., 1990—; mayor City of Beatrice, 1991-94; mem. Nebr. Senate from dist. 30, 1995—99; lt. gov. State of Nebr., 1998—2001; regional dir. FEMA, 2001—. Pres. Beatrice YMCA, 1982-83, Gage County United Way, Beatrice, 1985, founding trustee, 1st pres. Beatrice Ednl. Found., 1988-96; mem. Nebr. Rep. State Cen. Com., Lincoln, 1985-90, 95-97, elected Bd. Edn. Sch. Dist. #15, Beatrice, 1988-90; candidate Nebr. Legislature, Lincoln, 1986; chmn. Highway 77 Improvement Assn., 1991-94; chair Nebr. Info. Tech. Commn., 1999—; trustee Beatrice Libr. Found., 1996—; bd. dirs. Madonna Found., 1997—. Named Outstanding Young Man of Am., Beatrice Jaycees, 1985, Citizen of Yr. Beatrice C. of C., 1993, Outstanding Amateur Golfer Nebr. Golf Assn., 1981, Harold Sieck Pub. Ofcl. of Yr., Arc of Nebr., 1998; recipient Young Alumnus award U. Nebr. Alumni Assn., 1993, Disting. Svc. award Nat. Fedn. Interscholastic Ofcls. Assn., 1989, Disting. Svc. award League of Nebr. Municipalities, 1998, Outstanding Alumnus award Ctrl. C.C. Platte Campus, Coll. Alumni Assn., 1998, Disting. Alumni award Nebr. C.C. System, 2000. Mem. Ind. Ins. Agts. Nebr. (Young Agt. of Yr. 1985), Blue Valley Life Underwriters (bd. dirs. 1988-94), Beatrice C. of C. (bd. dirs. 1985-87), U. Nebr.-Lincoln Coll. Bus. Adminstrn. Alumni Bd. (bd. dirs. 1989-96, pres. 1994-95, Leadership award 1994), Nebr. Diplomate, Shriners, Rotary, Eagles, Mason. Lutheran. Avocations: golf, reading, spectator sports.

MAUST, JOSEPH J. agricultural products supplier; Pres. Active Feed Co., Pigeon, Mich., 1984—. Office: Active Feed Co 7564 Pigeon Rd Pigeon MI 48755-9701

MAUTINO, FRANK J. state legislator; b. Spring Valley, Ill., Aug. 7, 1962; BS, Ill. State U. Dist. 76 rep. Ill. Ho. Reps., Springfield, 1991—. Mem. housing ins., pub. safety,and infrastructure appropriations coms., Ill. Ho. Reps.

MAWARDI, OSMAN KAMEL, plasma physicist; b. Cairo, Dec. 12, 1917; came to U.S., 1946, naturalized, 1952; s. Kamel Ibrahim and Marie (Wiennig) M.; m. Betty Louise Hosmer, Nov. 23, 1950. B.S., Cairo U., 1940, M.S., 1945; A.M., Harvard U., 1947, Ph.D., 1948. Lectr. physics Cairo U., 1940-45; asst. prof. Mass Inst. Tech., 1951-56, asso. prof., 1956-60; prof. engring., dir. plasma research program Case Inst. Tech., Cleve., 1960-88; dir. Energy Research Office, Case Western Res. U., 1977-82. Pres. Collaborative Planners, Inc.; mem. Inst. Advanced Study, 1969-70; also cons. Contbr. articles to profl. jours. Past trustee Print Club Cleve., Cleve. Inst. Art. Recipient Biennial award Acoustical Soc. Am., 1952; CECON medal of achievement, 1979 Fellow AAAS, Acoustical Soc. Am., Am. Phys. Soc., IEEE (Edison lectr. 1968-69, Centennial award 1984, Cleve. sect. Engr. of Yr. 1994); mem. N.Y. Acad. Scis., Sigma Xi, Eta Kappa Nu. Home: 15 Mornington Ln Cleveland OH 44106 Office: 2490 Lee Rd Cleveland OH 44118-4125 E-mail: okm@po.cwru.edu.

MAWBY, RUSSELL GEORGE, retired foundation executive; b. Grand Rapids, Mich., Feb. 23, 1928; s. Wesley G. and Ruby (Finch) M.; m. Ruth E. Edison, Dec. 16, 1950 (dec. 2000); children: Douglas, David, Karen. B.S. in Horticulture, Mich. State U., 1949, Ph.D. in Agrl. Econs., 1959, LL.D. (hon.), 1972; M.S. in Agrl. Econs, Purdue U., 1951, D.Agr. (hon.), 1973; L.H.D. (hon.), Luther Coll., Decorah, Iowa, 1972, Alma (Mich.) Coll., 1975, Nazareth Coll., 1976, Madonna Coll., 1983, N.C. Central U., 1986; LL.D. (hon.), N.C. A&T State U., Greensboro, 1974, Tuskegee Inst., 1978, Kalamazoo Coll., 1980; D.P.A. (hon.), Albion Coll., 1976; D.C.L. (hon.), U. Newcastle, Eng., 1977; D.Sc. (hon.), Nat. U. Ireland, 1980; D.Pub. Service (hon.), No. Mich. U., 1981; D.H.L. (hon.), So. Utah State Coll., 1983; HHD (hon.), Grand Valley State U., 1988; ScD (hon.), Calif. State U., 1989; LLD (hon.), Adrian Coll., 1990; LittD (hon.), Olivet Coll., 1991. Ext. specialist Mich. State U., East Lansing, 1952-56, asst. dir. coop. ext. svc., 1956-65; dir. div. agr. W.K. Kellogg Found., Battle Creek, Mich., 1965-66, mem., trustee, 1967—, v.p. programs, 1966-70, pres., 1970-82, chmn., CEO, 1982-95, chmn. emeritus, 1995—. Bd. dirs. Detroit br. Fed. Res. Bank Chgo., 1980-85, J.M. Smucker Co., 1983—; fellow Inst. for Children, Youth and Families Mich. State U., 1993; hon. fellow Kellog Coll., U. Oxford, Eng., 1990; mem. chancellor's ct. of benefactors U. Oxford, Eng., 1991; Disting. Vis. Prof. Inst. for Children, Youth and Families and Coll. of Edn., Mich. State U., 1996—. Trustee Youth for Understanding, 1973-79, Mich. State U. Coll. of Agr. and Natural Resources Alumni Assn., 1977-80, pres. 1978-79; trustee Arabian Horse Trust, 1978-90 (emeritus 1990—), Starr Commonwealth, 1987-97, 98—, (chmn. bd. trustees 1993-95), Found. Ctr., 1988-94 (chmn. bd. trustees 1989-94), Mich. Non-profit Assn., 1990-94 (chmn. bd. trustees 1990-94, emeritus 1994—), Mich. State U., 1992-96 (chmn. bd. trustees 1995); founding chmn. Coun. of Mich. Founds., 1972-74, chmn. emeritus 1994—; bd. dirs. Coun. on Founds., 1978-84, Mich.'s Children, 1995-98, emeritus 1998—; mem. Joint Coun. on Food and Agrl. Scis., USDA, 1984-88; mem. Com. on Agrl. Edn. in Secondary Schs., NRC, 1985-88, Gov.'s Task Force on Revitalization of Agr. Through Rsch. and Edn., 1986; mem. rural bus. partnership adv. bd. Mich. Dept. Commerce, 1989-90, Mich. Coop. Ext. Svc. Study Com., 1989; mem. pres.'s adv. coun. Clemson U., 1987-95; vis. com. Med. U. of S.C., 1990-95; steering com. Econ. Devel. Forum of Calhoun County, Mich., 1991—; mem. policy bd. Calhoun County Cmtys. in Schs., 1995-98; mem. Lt. Gov.'s Children's Commn., State of Mich., 1995-96; mem. leadership adv. coun. Olivet Coll., 1995—; trustee Battle Creek Community Found., 1996—, Mich. 4-H Found., 1996—, hon. trustee, 1996—; scholar-in-residence Ind. U. Ctr. on Philanthropy, 1996—; mem. State Officers compensation Commn., State of Mich., 1996-98; mem. bd. govs. Ind. U. Ctr. on Philanthropy, 2000—; bd. visitors Coll. of Nursing Mich. State U., 1997—; bd. dirs. Mich. State U. Found., 1998—. With AUS, 1953-55. Decorated knight 1st class Royal Order St. Olaf Norway, 1974; knight's cross Order of Dannebrog 1st class Denmark, 1976; comdr.'s medal Order of Finnish Lion Finland, 1981; recipient Disting. Service award U.S. Dept. Agr., 1963, Disting. Alumni award Mich. State U., 1971, Nat. Alumni award 4-H Clubs, 1972, Disting. Eagle Scout award Boy Scouts Am., 1973, Meritorious Achievement award Fla. A&M U., 1973, Nat. Ptnr. in 4-H award Dept. Agr. Ext. Svc., 1976; named hon. fellow Spring Arbor (Mich.) Coll., 1972; recipient Walter F. Patenge medal for pub. service Coll. Osteo. Medicine, Mich. State U., 1977, Disting. Service award Coll. Agr. and Natural Resources, 1980, Seaman A. Knapp Meml. lectr. U.S. Dept. Agr., 1983; recipient George award for cmty. svc. City of Battle Creek, 1986, Disting. Service award Rural Sociol. Soc., 1986, Centennial Alumnus award for Mich. State U. Nat. Assn. State Univs. and Land Grant Colls., 1988, Pres.'s award Clemson U., 1989, Disting. Citizen award Southwest Mich. Coun. Boy Scouts Am., 1989, Disting. Svc. award 1890 Land-Grant Colls. and Univs., 1990, Vol. of Yr. award Clemson U., 1990, Disting. Grantmaker award Coun. on Founds., 1992, Disting. Svc. award Nat. Assn. Homes and Svcs. for Children, 1992,

Merit award Nat. Soc. Fund Raising Execs. West Mich. chpt., 1992, Red Rose award Rotary Club of Battle Creek, 1993, George W. Romney award Nat. Soc. Fund Raising Execs. Greater Detroit chpt., 1993, Director's award Arabian Horse Assn. of Mich., 1994, Disting. Svc. award Mich. Hort. Soc., 1994, Michiganian of Yr. The Detroit News, 1995, Gerald G. Hicks Child Welfare Leadership award Mich. Fedn. Private Child and Family Agys., 1995, Leon Bradley Humanitarian for Youth award No. Area Assn., Detroit, 1995, award of Honor Am. Hosp. Assn., 1995, Spirit of the Drum award, Nat. Youth Leadership Coun., 1996, Crystal Apple award Featherstone Soc. Coll. Edn. Mich. State U., 1996, Nat. Govs. Assn. award for disting. svc. to state govt., 1997, Nat. Interfraternity Conf. Gold Medal award, 1998, Govs. award for stewardship State of Mich., 1999; named Friend of the Coll., Mich. State U. Coll. Human Ecology, 1996, Internat. Adult and Continuing Edn. Hall of Fame, 1996, Owner of Yr. Mich. Harness Horsemen's Assn., 1999; Louis Harris fellow Rotary Club Battle Creek, 1998. Mem. Mich. Soc. Architects (hon.), Am. Agrl. Econ. Assn., Mich. State U. Alumni Assn. (bd. dirs. 1984-88), Alpha Gamma Rho (dir. 1976-82, grand pres. 1980-82, Man of Year Chgo. Alumni chpt. 1976, Hall of Fame 1986), Alpha Zeta, Phi Kappa Phi (Disting. Mem. award Mich. State U. 1978), Epsilon Sigma Phi (certificate of recognition 1974, Nat. Friend of Ext. 1982), Gamma Sigma Delta, Delta Sigma Pi (hon. mem., 1995). Home: 8400 N 39th St Augusta MI 49012-9713 Office: Heritage Tower 25 Michigan Ave W Ste 1701 Battle Creek MI 49017-7023

MAXSON, LINDA ELLEN, biologist, educator; b. N.Y.C., Apr. 24, 1943; d. Albert and Ruth (Rosenfeld) Resnick; m. Richard Dey Maxson, June 13, 1964; 1 child, Kevin. BS in Zoology, San Diego State U., 1964, MA in Biology, 1966; PhD in Genetics, San Diego State U./U. Calif., Berkeley, 1973. Instr. biology San Diego State U., 1966-68; tchr. gen. sci. San Diego Unified Sch. Dist., 1968-69; instr. biochemistry U. Calif., Berkeley, 1974; asst. prof. zoology, dept. genetics and devel. U. Ill., Urbana-Champaign, 1974-76, asst. prof. dept. genetics, devel. and ecology, ethology & evolution, 1976-79, assoc. prof., 1979-84, prof., 1984-87, prof. ecology, ethology and evolution, 1987-88; prof., head dept. biology Pa. State U., State College, 1988-94; assoc. vice-chancellor acad. affairs/dean undergrad. acad. affairs, prof. ecology and evolutionary biology U. Tenn., Knoxville, 1995-97; dean Coll. Liberal Arts & Scis., prof. biol. scis. U. Iowa, Iowa City, 1997—. Exec. officer biology programs Sch. Life Scis., U. Ill., 1981-86, assoc. dir. acad. affairs, 1984-86, dir. campus honors program, 1985-88; vis. prof. ecology and evolutionary biology U. Calif., Irvine, 1988; mem. adv. panel rsch. tng. groups behavioral biol. scis. NSF, 1990-94. Author: Genetics: A Human Perspective, 3d edit., 1992; mem. editl. bd. Molecular Biology Evolution; exec. editor Biochem. Sys. & Ecology, 1993-2001; contbr. numerous articles to scientific jours. Recipient Disting. Alumni award San Diego State U., 1989, Disting. Herpetologist award Herpetologists' League, 1993. Fellow: AAAS; mem.: Herpetologists League, Soc. Molecular Biology and Evolution (treas. 1992—94, sec. 1992—95), Soc. Study Evolution, Soc. for Study of Amphibians and Reptiles (pres. 1991), Am. Men and Women in Sci., Phi Beta Kappa. Office: U Iowa 240 Schaeffer Hall Iowa City IA 52242-1409 E-mail: linda-maxson@uiowa.edu.

MAXWELL, CHIP, state legislature; b. Omaha, Aug. 10, 1962; m. Pam Maxwell; children: Tomas, Oto. B in Polit. Sci., Boston Coll., 1984; M in Am. History, Oxford U., 1987; JD, U. Nebr., 1992. Law clk. Nebr. Ct. Appeals; editl. writer Omaha World-Herald; spl. asst. to U.S. Senater Chuck Hagel; devel. dir. Jesuit Mid. Sch., Our Lady Guadalupe & St. Agnes Mission Sch.; mem. Nebr. Legislature from 9th dist., 2001—. Mem. Nebr. BAr Assn. Home: 3835 California St Omaha NE 68131 Office: Rm 1115 State Capitol Lincoln NE 68509

MAXWELL, DAVID E. academic executive, educator; b. N.Y.C., Dec. 2, 1944; s. James Kendrick and Gertrude Sarah (Bernstein) M.; children: Justin Kendrick, Stephen Edward. BA, Grinnell Coll., 1966; MA, Brown U., 1968, PhD, 1974. Instr. Tufts U., Medford, Mass., 1971-74, asst. prof., 1974-78, assoc. prof. Russian lang. and lit., 1978-89, dean undergrad. studies, 1981-89; pres. Whitman Coll., Walla Walla, Wash., 1989-93; dir. Nat. Fgn. Lang. Ctr., Washington, 1993-99; pres. Drake U., Des Moines, 1999—. Chmn. steering com. Coop. Russian Lang. Program, Leningrad, USSR, 1981-86, chmn. 1986-90; cons. Coun. Internat. Ednl. Exch., 1974-94, bd. dirs., 1988-92, 93-94, vice chair, 1991-92, cons. Internat. Rsch. Exchs., 1976—; mem. adv. bd. Israeli Lang. Policy Inst. Contbr. articles to scholarly jours. Bd. mem. Iowa Rsch. Coun.; cmty. bd. dirs. Wells Fargo; bd. dirs. Des Moines Devel. Corp., Iowa Wellness Coun.; v.p. Greater Des Moines Partnership. Fulbright fellow, 1970-71, Brown U., 1966-67, NDEA Title IV, 1967-70; recipient Lillian Leibner award Tufts U., 1970; citation Grad. Sch. Arts and Scis., Brown U., 1991. Mem. MLA, Am. Coun. Edn. (commn. on internat. edn., pres.'s coun. on internat. edn.), Am. Assn. Advancement of Slavic Studies, Am. Assn. Tchrs. Slavic and E. European Langs., Assn. Am. Colls., Am. Assn. Higher Edn., Am. Coun. Tchg. Fgn. Langs., Brown U. Alumni Assn., Phi Beta Kappa. Democrat. Avocations: tennis, running, music. Office: Drake Univ Office of the Pres 2507 University Ave Des Moines IA 50311-4505

MAXWELL, JOE EDWIN, lieutenant governor, lawyer; b. Kirksville, Mo., Mar. 17, 1957; s. Robert E. and Molly B. Maxwell; m. Sarah Baker; children: Megan, Shannen. BS in Secondary Edn., Social Studies, U. Mo., 1986, JD, 1990. Farmer, Rush Hill, Mo., 1976-78; ptnr., operator Maxwell Svcs., Laddonia, 1978-84; rural mail carrier U.S. Postal Svc., Rush Hill, 1980-84; outstate field coord. Travis Morrison's Campaign for State Auditor, Mo., 1986; Mo. state field coord. Richard Gephardt for Pres., 1986-87; atty. Mexico, Mo., 1992—; mem. Mo. House, 1990-94, Mo. Senate, 1995—. Mem. Senate Appropriations, Judiciary, Labor and Indsl. Rels., Pub. Health and Welfare coms.; vice chair Elections, Corrections, and Vet.'s Affairs coms.; chair Commerce and Environment Com. Assoc. editor-in-chief Mo. Jour. of Dispute Resolution, 1989. Mem. Am. Legion, 1982—, adj. Post 510, 1982-84; mem. Young Dem. Clubs Mo., 1982—, jud. coun. Young Dems. Am., 1985, pres., 1984-87, 9th Congl. Dist. chmn., 1982; mem. Laddonia Bapt. Ch., 1975—, Sunday Sch. tchr., 1990-91, pulpit com.; bd. dirs. Handi-Shop Inc., Mexico, 1981-84, chmn. mfg. and mktg. com., 1982-84; bd. dirs. Boy Scouts Am. Troop 94, 1980-82. Recipient St. Louis Globe Dem. award for outstanding achievement, 1979, Cert. of Appreciation, Troop 94, Boy Scouts Am., 1982, Mo.'s Outstanding Male Young Dem. award, 1987, George B. Freeman award for outstanding svc., 1987, Appreciation award Mo. Bar, 1992, Mo. Ho. of Reps. Resolution # 624 for exceptional svc. Mo., 1987, Mo. State Senate Resolution # 382 for exceptional svc. Mo., 1987; named one of Outstanding Young Men of Am., 1983, 85. Mem. Moose, Jaycees (Laddonia chpt. pres. 1978-79, coord. Laddonia Area Blood Drive, coord. Laddonia City Clean-up Day, chmn. Mexico Soybean Festival 1989, chmn. Lenten Breakfast 1990, Presdl. award of honor 1979), Kappa Delta Pi, Golden Key Nat. Honor Soc. Office: Office of Lt Gov Rm 121 Capitol Bldg Jefferson City MO 65101

MAXWELL, ROBERT WALLACE, II, lawyer; b. Sept. 6, 1943; s. Robert Wallace and Margaret Maxwell; m. Mamie Lee Payne, June 18, 1966; children: Virginia, Robert, William. BS magna cum laude, Hampden-Sydney Coll., 1965; JD with hons., Duke U., 1968. Bar: Ohio 1968. Assoc. Taft, Stettinius & Hollister, Cin., 1968—75, ptnr., 1975—88, Keating, Muething & Klekamp, Cin., 1988—. Instr. U. Cin. Sch. Law, 1975—76. Elder Wyoming Presbyn. Ch.; bd. dir. Contemporary Arts Ctr. of Cin., Cin. Ballet Co. Mem.: ABA, Am. Assn. Mus. Trustees. Republican. Home: 535 Larchmont Dr Cincinnati OH 45215-4215 Office: Keating Muething & Klekamp 1 E 4th St Ste 1800 Cincinnati OH 45202-3752

MAY, ALAN ALFRED, lawyer; b. Detroit, Apr. 7, 1942; s. Alfred Albert and Sylvia (Sheer) M.; m. Elizabeth Miller; children: Stacy Ann, Julie Beth. BA, U. Mich., 1963, JD cum laude, 1966. Bar: Mich. 1967, D.C. 1976; former reg. nursing home adminstr., Mich. Ptnr. Map and Map, PC, Detroit, 1979—2001, Kemp Klein, Umphrey and May, 2001—. Spl. asst. atty. gen. State of Mich., 1970—; pres., instr. Med-Leg Seminars, Inc., 1978; lectr. Wayne State U., 1974; instr. Oakland U., 1969. Chmn. Rep. 18th Congressional Dist. Com., 1983-87, now chmn. emeritus; chmn. 19th Congressional Dist. Com., 1981-83; mem. Mich. Rep. Com., 1976-84; del. Rep. Nat. Conv., 1984, rules com., 1984; del. Rep. Nat. Conv., 1988, platform com., 1988; former chmn. Mich. Civil Rights Commn.; former mem. Mich. Civil Svc. Commn., 1984-88; former trustee, mem. exec. bd., vice chmn. nat conf. for cmty. and justice NCCJ; trustee Temple Beth El Birmingham, Mich., pres. exec. bd.; mem. Electoral Coll.; bd. dirs. ADL, Mich.; bd. dirs. exec. bd., pres., Detroit Region/Nat. Conf. Cmty. and Justice, Charfoos Charitable Found. Mem. Nat. Conf. Cmty. and Justice (exec. bd., vice chmn.), Detroit Bar Assn., Oakland County Bar Assn., Victors Club, Franklin Hills Country Club (past pres., bd. dirs.), President's Club (trustee). Home: 4140 Echo Rd Bloomfield Hills MI 48302-1941 Office: May & May PC 3000 Town Ctr Ste 2600 Southfield MI 48075-1375

MAY, BRIAN HENRY, state legislator; b. St. Louis, Nov. 22, 1962; BS in Edn. summa cum laude, Harris-Stowe State Coll., 1986; JD, St. Louis U., 1989. Mem. dist. 108 Mo. Ho. of Reps.; with firm Casserly, Jones & Brittingham, P.C., St. Louis, 1990-95, Larsen, Feist & Bedell, P.C., St. Louis, 1995—. Office: 692 Meramec View Dr Eureka MO 63025-3716

MAY, GEORGIANA, biologist, educator; PhD, U. Calif., Berkeley, 1987. Assoc. prof. dept. plant biology U. Minn., St. Paul. Contbr. articles to profl. jours. Recipient Alexopoulos prize Mycological Soc. Am., 1997. Achievements include research on the interactions of fungi with plants, evolution of fungal populations and their interactions with other organisms, evolution of gene structure and function in mating compatibility loci, determining the genetic basis of smut resistance in maize, the impact of agricultural practice on host/pathogen interactions. Office: U Minn Dept Plant Biology 220 Biological Sci Ctr 1445 Gortner Ave Saint Paul MN 55108 Fax: 612-625-1738. E-mail: gmay@maroon.tc.umn.edu.

MAY, J. PETER, mathematics educator; b. N.Y.C., Sept. 16, 1939; s. Siegmund Henry and Jane (Polachek) M.; m. Maija Bajars, June 8, 1963; children: Anthony D., Andrew D. BA, Swarthmore Coll., 1960; PhD, Princeton U., 1964. Instr. Yale U., New Haven, 1964-65, asst. prof., 1965-67; assoc. prof. U. Chgo., 1967-70, prof., 1970—, chmn. dept. math., 1985-91, chmn. coun. on teaching, 1991-96. Mem. Inst. Advanced Study, Princeton, 1966; vis. prof. Cambridge U., Eng., 1971-72, 1977. Author: Simplicial Objects in Algebraic Topology, 1967, The Geometry of Iterated Loop Spaces, 1972, E-infinity Ring Spaces and E-infinity Ring Spectra, 1977, Equivariant Homotopy and Cohomology Theory, 1996, A Concise Course in Algebraic Topology, 1999; co-author: The Homology of Iterated Loop Spaces, 1976, H-infinity Ring Spectra and Their Applications, 1986, Equivariant Stable Homotopy Theory, 1987, Rings Modules and Algebras in Stable Homotopy Theory, 1997, A Concise Course in Algebraic Topology, 1999; also numerous articles and monographs. NSF grantee, 1967—; Fulbright fellow, 1971-72; fellow Nat. Research Council, Eng., 1977. Mem. AAUP, Am. Math. Soc. Office: U Chgo Dept Math 5734 S University Ave Chicago IL 60637-1514

MAY, WALTER GRANT, chemical engineer, educator; b. Saskatoon, Sask., Can., Nov. 28, 1918; came to U.S., 1946, naturalized, 1954; s. George Alfred and Abigail Almira (Robson) M.; m. Mary Louise Stockan, Sept. 26, 1945 (dec. 1977); children: John R., Douglas W., Caroline O; m. Helen Dickerson, 1988. B.Sc., U. Sask., Saskatoon, 1939, M.Sc., 1942; Sc.D., M.I.T., 1948. Registered profl. engr., Ill. Chemist British Am. Oil Co., Moose Jaw, Sask., 1939-40; asst. prof. U. Sask., 1943-46; with Exxon Research & Engring. Co., Linden, N.J., 1948-83; sr. sci. adv., 1976-83; prof. U. Ill., 1983-90, prof. emeritus, 1990—. With Advanced Research Projects Agy., Dept. Def., 1959-60; industry based prof. Stevens Inst. Tech., 1968-74, Rensselaer Poly. Inst., 1975-77 Recipient Process Indsl. Div. award ASME, 1972 Fellow Am. Inst. Chem. Engrs.; mem. Am. Inst. Chem. Engrs. (Chem. Engring. Practice award 1989), Nat. Acad. Engring. Home: 916 W Clark St Champaign IL 61821-3328 Office: U Ill Dept Chem Engring 1209 W California Ave Urbana IL 61801-3705 E-mail: w-may@uiuc.edu.

MAYANS, CARLOS, state legislator; m. Linda K. Mayans. Kans. state rep. Dist. 100, 1993—; chmn. health and human svcs. com.; owner ins. agy. Home: 1842 N Valleyview St Wichita KS 67212-6738

MAYBERRY, ALAN REED, lawyer; b. Akron, Ohio, Mar. 15, 1954; s. Franklin Reed Mayberry and Mark K. (Kissane) Mayberry Alexander Botten; m. Lisa Renee Rush, Dec. 19, 1981; children: Reed Alan, Mason Rush, Clark Carroll. BS in Edn., Bowling Green State U., 1975; JD, U. Toledo, 1978; postgrad., Nat. Coll. Dist. Attys., Nat. Law Inst. Faculty Nat. Advocacy Ctr. Office: Wood County Prosecuting Attys Office 1 Court House Sq Bowling Green OH 43402-2427 E-mail: amayberry@co.wood.oh.us.

MAYER, FRANK D., JR. lawyer; b. Dec. 23, 1933; BA, Amherst Coll., 1955; student, Cambridge U.; JD, U. Chgo., 1959. Bar: Ill. 1959. Ptnr. Mayer, Brown & Platt, Chgo. Mem. ABA, Chgo. Bar Assn., Order of Coif, Phi Beta Kappa. Office: Mayer Brown Rowe and Maw 190 S La Salle St Ste 3100 Chicago IL 60603-3441 E-mail: fmayer@mayerbrown.com.

MAYER, RAYMOND RICHARD, business administration educator; b. Chgo., Aug. 31, 1924; s. Adam and Mary (Bogdala) M.; m. Helen Lakowski, Jan. 30, 1954; children: Mark, John, Mary, Jane. B.S., Ill. Inst. Tech., 1948, M.S., 1954, Ph.D., 1957. Indsl. engr. Standard Oil Co., Whiting, Ind., 1948-51; orgn. analyst Ford Motor Co., Chgo., 1951-53; instr. Ill. Inst. Tech., 1953-56, asso. prof., 1958-60; asst. prof. U. Chgo., 1956-58; Walter F. Mullady prof. bus. adminstrn. Loyola U., Chgo., 1960—. Author: Financial Analysis of Investment Alternatives, 1966, Production Management, 1962, rev. edit., 1968, Production and Operations Management, 1975, rev. edit., 1982, Capital Expenditure Analysis, 1978. Served with USNR, 1944-46. Ingersoll Found. fellow, 1955-56; Machinery and Allied Products Inst. fellow, 1954-55; Ford Found. fellow, 1962 Mem. Acad. Mgmt., Am. Econ. Assn., Am. Statis. Assn., Am. Inst. for Decision Scis., Nat. Assn. Purchasing Mgmt., Polish Inst. Arts and Scis. in Am., Alpha Iota Delta, Alpha Kappa Psi, Beta Gamma Sigma. Home: 730 Green Bay Rd Winnetka IL 60093-1912 Office: 820 N Michigan Ave Chicago IL 60611-2147

MAYER, ROBERT ANTHONY, retired college president; b. N.Y.C., Oct. 30, 1933; s. Ernest John and Theresa Margaret (Mazura) M.; m. Laura Wiley Christ, Apr. 30, 1960. BA magna cum laude, Fairleigh Dickinson U., 1955; MA, NYU, 1967. With N.J. Bank and Trust Co., Paterson, 1955-61, mgr. advt. dept., 1959-61; program supr. advt. dept. Mobil Oil Co., N.Y.C., 1961-62; asst. to dir. Latin Am. program Ford Found., 1963-65, asst. rep. Brazil, 1965-67; asst. to v.p. adminstrn., 1967-73; officer in charge logistical services Ford Found., 1968-73; asst. dir. programs N.Y. Community Trust, N.Y.C., 1973-76; exec. dir. N.Y. State Council on the Arts, 1976-79; mgmt. cons., 1979-80; dir. Internat. Mus. Photography, George Eastman House, Rochester, N.Y., 1980-89, mgmt. cons., 1989-90; pres. Cleve. Inst. of Art, 1990-97; ret., 1997. Mem. editorial adv. bd.: Grants mag., 1978-80; author: (plays) La Borgia, 1971; Alijandru, 1971, They'll Grow No Roses, 1975. Mem. state program adv. panel NEA, 1977-80; mem. Mayor's Com. on Cultural Policy, N.Y.C., 1974-75; mem. pres.'s adv. com. Bklyn. campus, L.I. U., 1978-79; bd. dirs. Fedn. Protestant Welfare Agys., N.Y.C., 1977-79, Arts for Greater Rochester, 1981-83, Garth Fagan's Dance Theatre, 1982-86; trustee Internat. Mus. Photography, 1981-89, Lacoste Sch. Arts, France, 1991-96, sec., 1994-96; mem. dean's adv. com. Grad. Sch. Social Welfare, Fordham U., 1976; mem. N.Y. State Motion Picure and TV Devel. Adv. Bd., 1984-87, N.Y. State Martin Luther King Jr. Commn., 1985-90, Cleve. Coun. Cultural Affairs, 1992-94; chmn. Greater Cleve. Regional Transit Authority Arts in Transit Com., 1992-95; bd. dirs. Friends of Ariz. State U. Ctr. for Latin Am. Studies, 1997-99; pres. bd. dirs. Villa Solana Townhouse Assn., 2000. Recipient Nat. award on advocacy for girls Girls Clubs Am., 1976 Mem. Nat. Assembly State Art Agys. (bd. dirs. 1977-79, 1st vice chmn. 1978-79), Alliance Ind. Colls. Art (bd. dirs. 1983-91, vice chmn. 1986-87, sec. 1987-89), N.Y. State Assn. Museums (bd. councilors 1983-86, pres. 1986-89), Assn. Ind. Colls. Art and Design (bd. dirs. 1991-97, exec. com. 1991-93, 96-97). Home: 2704 N 60th St Scottsdale AZ 85257-1012

MAYER, VICTOR JAMES, geologist, educator; b. Mayville, Wis., Mar. 25, 1933; s. Victor Charles and Phyllis (Bachhuber) M.; m. Mary Jo Anne White, Nov. 25, 1965; children: Gregory, Maribeth. BS in Geology, U. Wis., 1956; MS in Geology, U. Colo., 1960, PhD in Sci. Edn., 1966. Tchr. Colo. Pub. Schs., 1961-65; asst. prof. SUNY Coll., Oneonta, 1965-67, Ohio State U., Columbus, 1967-70, assoc. prof., 1970-75, prof. ednl. studies, geol. scis. and natural resources, 1975-95, prof. emeritus, 1995—. Co-organizer symposa at 29th and 31st Internat. Geol. Congresses; internat. sci. edn. assistance to individuals and orgns. in Japan, Korea, Taiwan, Russia, and Venezuela; dir. NSF Insts., program for leadership Earth Sys. Edn., 1990-95; dir. Korean Sci. Tchrs. Insts., 1986-88, 95; keynote spkr. U.S.A. rep. Internat. Conf. on Geoscis. Edn., Southampton, Eng., 1993; co-convenor Second Internat. conf. on Geosci. Edn., Hilo, Hawaii, 1997; disting. vis. prof. SUNY, Plattsburg, 1994; vis. rsch. scholar Hyogo U., Japan, 1996; sr. Fulbright rschr. Shizuoka U., Japan, 1998; vis. prof. Korea Nat. U. of Edn., 2000. Contbr. articles to profl. jours. Served with USAR. Recipient Lifetime Disting. Svc. award to the Internat. Earth Sci. Edn. Cmty., 1997; named Disting. Investigator, Ohio Sea Grant Program, 1983. Fellow AAAS (chmn. edn. 1988-89), Ohio Acad. Sci. (v.p. 1978-79, exec. com. 1993-94, outstanding univ. educator 1995); mem. Nat. Sci. Tchrs. Assn. (bd. dirs. 1984-86), Sci. Edn. Coun. Ohio (pres. 1987-88), Sigma Xi, Phi Delta Kappa. Roman Catholic. Avocation: photography. Home: 111 W Dominion Blvd Columbus OH 43214-2607 Office: Ohio State U Dept Geol Scis 125 S Oval Mall Columbus OH 43210-1308 E-mail: mayer.4@osu.edu.

MAYES, PAUL EUGENE, engineering educator, technical consultant; b. Frederick, Okla., Dec. 21, 1928; s. Robert Franklin and Bertha Ellen (Walter) M.; m. Lola Mae Davis, June 4, 1950; children: Gwynne Ellen, Linda Kay, Stuart Franklin, Patricia Gail, Steven Lee, David Thomas. BS in Elec. Engring., U. Okla., 1950; MS in Elec. Engring., Northwestern U., 1952, PhD, 1955. Rsch. asst. Northwestern U., Evanston, Ill., 1950-54; asst. prof. U. Ill., Urbana, 1954-58, assoc. prof., 1958-63, prof., 1963-93, prof. emeritus, 1994—. Tech. cons. Walter Gee and Assocs., San Jose, Calif. Author: Electromagnetics for Engineers, 1965; contbr. articles to profl. jours.; inventor in field. Fellow IEEE. Avocations: woodworking, hiking, camping. Home: 1508 Waverly Dr Champaign IL 61821-5002 Office: U Ill 1406 W Green St Urbana IL 61801-2918 E-mail: pemayes@ix.netcom.com.

MAYLAND, KENNETH THEODORE, economist; b. Miami, Fla., Nov. 17, 1951; s. Herbert and Vera (Bob) M; m. Gail Fern Bassok, Apr. 14, 1984. BS, MIT, 1973; MS, U. Pa., 1976, PhD, 1979. Cons. economist Data Resources, Inc., Lexington, Mass., 1973; economist, then chief economist First Pa. Bank, Phila., 1973-89; sr. v.p., chief economist Soc. Nat. Bank, Cleve., 1989-94; sr. v.p., chief fin. economist Key Corp., 1994-96, sr. v.p., chief economist, 1996-2000; pres. ClearView Econs., LLC, 2000—. Econs. instr., Chartered Fin. Aanalysts Assn., Phila, 1984—; econ. adv. com. Phila. Econ. Devel. Coalition, 1984-86; chmn. econ. adv. com. Pa. Bankers Assn., Harrisburg, 1982-84; mem. Gov.'s Econ. Adv. Com., Ohio, 1989—. Contbr. semi-monthly periodical Money Markets, 1981-85, quar. periodical Regional Report, 1980-89, EconViewpoint/KeyViewpoint biweekly periodical, 1989—, Regional Rev. quar. periodical, 1989-94/ Mem. curriculum adv. com. Widener U., 1986-89. Mem. Am. Bankers Assn. (econ. adv. com. 1990-93), Internat. Econ. Roundtable (vice chmn. 1987-88, chmn. 1988-90), Nat. Assn. Bus. Economists (New Face for the Eighties award 1979), Phila. Coun. Bus. Economists (pres. 1982-84), Cleve. Bus. Economist Club (sec.-treas. 1990-91, v.p. 1991-92, pres. 1992-93). Avocations: fishing, badminton, gardening, camping. Home: 3237 Fox Hollow Dr Cleveland OH 44124-5426 Office: Key Corp 127 Public Sq Cleveland OH 44114-1306

MAYNARD, JOHN RALPH, lawyer; b. Mar. 5, 1942; s. John R. and Frances Jane (Mitchell) Maynard Kendryk; m. Meridee J. Sagadin, Sept. 10, 1995; children: Bryce James, Pamela Ann. BA, U. Wash., 1964; JD, Calif. Western U., San Diego, 1972; LLM, Harvard U., 1973. Bar: Calif. 1972, Wis. 1973. Assoc. Whyte & Hirschboeck, Milw., 1973-78, Minahan & Peterson, Milw., 1979-91, Quarles & Brady, Milw., 1991-2000, Davis & Kuelthau, Milw., 2000—. Bd. dirs. Am. Heart Assn., 1979—82, Transitional Living Svcs., Inc., 1999—2001; pres. Milw. Chamber Orch., 2000—01; mem. Wis. Adv. Coun. to U.S. SBA, 1987—89. Mem.: ABA, Milw. Yacht Club, Harvard Club (Wis.). Home: 809 E Lake Forest Ave Milwaukee WI 53217-5377 Office: Davis & Kuelthau 111 E Kilbourn Ste 1400 Milwaukee WI 53202

MAYNARD, OLIVIA P. foundation administrator; m. S. Olof Karlstrom. BA, Geroge Washington U., 1959; MSW, U. Mich., 1971. Dir. Mich. Office Svcs. to Aging, 1983—90; tchr. Sch. Social Work U. Mich., Mich. State U.; tchr. Ctr. for Aging Edn. Lansing (Mich.) C.C.; pres. Mich. Prospect for Renewed Citizenship, Flint. Del. White House Conf. on Aging, 1995. Regent U. Mich., Ann Arbor; chmn. Mich. Dem. Party, 1973—82; candidate Lt. Gov. of Mich., 1990. Democrat. Office: Northbank Ctr Ste 406 432 N Saginaw St Flint MI 48502

MAYNARD, ROBERT HOWELL, retired lawyer; b. San Antonio, Feb. 15, 1938; s. William Simpson Sr. and Lillian Isabel (Tappan) M.; m. Joan Marie Pearson, Jan. 6, 1962; children: Gregory Scott, Patricia Kathryn, Alicia Joan, Elizabeth Simms. BA, Baylor U., 1959, LLB, 1961; LLM, Georgetown U., 1965. Bar: Tex. 1961, D.C. 1969, Ohio 1973. Trial atty. gen. litigation sect. lands div. U.S. Dept. Justice, Washington, 1964-65; spl. asst. to solicitor U.S. Dept. Interior, 1965-69; legis. asst. U.S. Senate, 1969-73; ptnr., dept. head Smith & Schnacke, Dayton, Ohio, 1973-83; dir. Ohio EPA, Columbus, 1983-85; ptnr., environ. policy and strategy devel., tech. law Vorys, Sater, Seymour and Pease, 1985-2000; ret., 2000; pres. Tappan Woods LLC, 2001—. Trustee Ohio Found. for Entrepren. Edn., Business Technology Ctr., 1994-2000, Episcopal Cmty. Svcs. Found., 1990-96, Industry & Tech. Coun. Ctrl. Ohio, Johnson's Island Preservation Soc. USNR, 1962-65. Episcopalian. Office: Vorys Sater Seymour & Pease PO Box 1008 52 E Gay St Columbus OH 43215-1008

MAYNE, LUCILLE STRINGER, finance educator, educator; b. Washington, June 6, 1924; d. Henry Edmond and Hattie Benham (Benson) Stringer; children: Patricia Anne, Christine Gail, Barbara Marie. BS, U. Md., 1946; MBA, Ohio State U., 1949; PhD, Northwestern U., 1966. Instr. fin. Utica Coll., 1949-50; lectr. fin. Roosevelt U., 1961-64, Pa. State U., 1965-66, asst. prof., 1966-69, assoc. prof., 1969-70; assoc. prof. banking and fin. Case-Western Res. U., 1971-76, prof., 1976-94, prof. emerita, 1994—, grad. dean Sch. Grad. Studies, 1980-84. Sr. economist, cons.

FDIC, 1977-78; cons. Nat. Commn. Electronic Fund Transfer Sys., 1976; rsch. cons. Am. Bankers Assn., 1975, Fed. Res. Bank of Cleve., 1968-70, 73; cons. Pres.'s Commn. Fin. Structure and Regulation, 1971, staff economist, 1970-71; analytical statistician Air Materiel Command, Dayton, Ohio, 1950-52; asst. to promotion mgr. NBC, Washington, 1946-48; expert witness cases involving fin. instns. Assoc. editor: Jour. Money, Credit and Banking, 1980-83, Bus. Econs., 1980-85; contbr. articles to profl. jours. Vol. Cleve. Soc. for Blind, 1979—, Benjamin Rose Inst., 1995—; mem. policyholders nominating com. Tchrs. Ins. and Annuity Assn./Coll. Retirement Equities Fund, 1982-84, chairperson com., 1984; bd. dirs. Women's Cmty. Found., 1994-96. Grad. scholar Ohio State U., 1949; doctoral fellow Northwestern U., 1963-65. Mem. LWV (bd. dirs. Shaker Heights chpt. 1999--), Midwest Fin. Assn. (pres. 1991-92, bd. dirs. 1975-79, officer 1988-93), Phi Kappa Phi, Beta Gamma Sigma. Episcopalian. Home: 3723 Normandy Rd Cleveland OH 44120-5246 Office: Case Western Res U Weatherhead Sch Mgmt U Circle Cleveland OH 44106-7235 E-mail: lsm5@po.cwru.edu.

MAYNE, WILEY EDWARD, lawyer; b. Sanborn, Iowa, Jan. 19, 1917; s. Earl W. and Gladys (Wiley) M.; m. Elizabeth Dodson, Jan. 5, 1942; children— Martha (Mrs. F.K. Smith), Wiley Edward, John. S.B. cum laude, Harvard, 1938; student, Law Sch., 1938-39; J.D., State U. Iowa, 1939-41. Bar: Iowa bar 1941, U.S. Supreme Ct. 1950. Practiced in, Sioux City, 1946-66, 75—; mem. Shull, Marshall, Mayne, Marks & Vizintos, 1946-66, Mayne and Berenstein, 1975-87, Mayne & Mayne, 1988-99, Mayne, Marks, Madsen and Hirschbach, 1999—. Spl. agt. FBI, 1941-43; Mem. 90th-93d Congresses, 6th Dist. Iowa; mem. judiciary com., agr. com. Commr. from Iowa Nat. Conf. Commrs. Uniform State Laws, 1956-60; chmn. grievance commn. Iowa Supreme Ct., 1964-66; del. FAO, 1973; chmn. Woodbury County Compensation Bd., 1975-80 Chmn. Midwest Rhodes Scholar Selection Com., 1964-66; pres. Sioux City Symphony Orch. Assn., 1947-54, Sioux City Concert Course, 1982-85; vice chmn. Young Republican Nat. Fedn., 1948-50; bd. dirs. Iowa Bar Found., 1962-68. Served to lt. (j.g.) USNR, 1943-46. Fellow Am. Coll. Trial Lawyers; mem. ABA (ho. of dels. 1966-68), Iowa Bar Assn. (pres. 1963-64), Sioux City Bar Assn., Internat. Assn. Def. Counsel (exec. com. 1961-64), Harvard Club (N.Y.C.), Sioux City Country Club, Masons (Scottish Rite/33 deg.). Home: 2728 Jackson St Sioux City IA 51104 Office: Pioneer Bank Bldg 701 Pierce St Ste 300 Sioux City IA 51101 Fax: 712-252-1535. E-mail: maynelaw@pionet.net.

MAYR, JAMES JEROME, fertilizer company executive; b. Beaver Dam, Wis., Aug. 19, 1942; s. Alfred A. and Maxine E. (Kuehl) M.; m. Carol Ann Kaufman, Sept. 4, 1965; children: Christin and Carin (twins), Cathy, Conni. BS in Agrl. Econs., U. Wis., 1964. Mgr. trainee Oscar Mayer, Madison, Wis., 1964-65; v.p. Mayr's Seed and Feed, Beaver Dam, 1966-78; product mgr. Chem. Enterprises, Houston, 1978-80; gen. mgr. Coash, Inc., Bassett, Nebr., 1981-88, v.p., 1989; mgr. Blicks Agri-Farm Ctr., Inc., Scott City, Kans., 1990-91; area mgr. Rosen's Inc., Fairmont, Minn., 1992-95, Helena Chem. Co., Rochester, 1995—. Cons. Beaver Dam, 1971-75; speaker fertilizer orgns., Wis. Advisor U. Wis. Coll. Agriculture; mem. com. Upper Elk Horn Natural Resources Dist., Oneill, Nebr., 1985-86. Mem. Wis. Fertilizer Assn. (bd. dirs. 1970-74), Nat. Fertilizer and Solutions Assn., Nebr. Fertilizer and Chem. Assn. Republican. Roman Catholic. Lodge: KC (dep. grand knight 1978-80, 81-85, Man of Yr. 1982). Avocations: target shooting, hunting, fishing, teaching target shooting. Home: 2550 Oak Hills Dr SW Rochester MN 55902-1263 E-mail: jmayrusa@aol.com.

MAYS, CAROL JEAN, state legislator; b. Independence, Mo., July 16, 1933; m. Ronald H. Mays; children: Terri, Melanie, Hugh. Student, Baker U. State rep., chmn. consumer protection edn. appropriations com., mem. transp., ways & means & comm. coms. Mo. Ho. of Reps., Jefferson City. Restaurant owner. Mem. Mo. Restaurant Assn., Independence C. of C., Fairmount Comml. Club, Alpha Chi Omega. Democrat. Methodist. Home: 3603 S Hedges Ave Independence MO 64052-1167 Office: Mo Ho of Reps State Capitol Bldg 201 W Capitol Ave Rm 206A Jefferson City MO 65101-1556

MAYS, M. DOUGLAS, state legislator, financial consultant; b. Pittsburg, Kans., Aug. 18, 1950; s. Marion Edmund and Lilliemae Ruth (Norris) M.; m. Lena M. Krog, June 10, 1971; children: Jessica, Aaron. BFA, Pittsburg State U., 1972; postgrad., Washburn U., 1973—. Registered rep. Waddell & Reed, Inc., Topeka, 1981-83, Paine Webber Jackson & Curtis, Topeka, 1983-85, Columbian Securities, Topeka, 1985-87; commr. securities State of Kans., 1987-91; pres. Mays & Assocs., 1991—; mem. Kans. Ho. Reps., 1993—, asst. majority leader, 1997-99, spkr. pro tem, 1999—. Adminstrv. law judge various securities proceedings, 1987—; with securities and commodities fraud working group U.S. Dept. Justice, 1988-90; with penny stock task force SEC, 1988-90; del. Commonwealth Secretariat Symposium Comml. Crime, Cambridge, Eng., 1989; securities arbitrator, 1991—. Rep. precinct committeeman Shawnee County, Kans., 1976—, county chmn., 1978-82; mem. 2d Dist. Rep. State Com., Kans., 1976-86, 92—; mem. Kans. Rep. State Com., 1976-87; Senate steering com. Kassebaum for Senate campaign, 1978; chmn., mgr. Hoferer for Senate campaign, 1984; campaign coord., dir. fin. Hayden for Gov., 1986; mem. pub. bldg. commn. City of Topeka, 1985-86, bldg. and fire appeals bd. , 1986-89, dep. mayor, 1987-88; mem. Topeka City Coun., 1985-89; exec. bd. Topeka/Shawnee County Interngovtl. Coun., 1986-89; adv. bd. Topeka Performing Arts Ctr., 1989-90; active Topeka/Shawnee County Met. Planning Commn., 1992—, chmn., 1994-97. Mem. North Am. Securities Adminstrs. Assn. (chmn. enforcement sect. 1988-89, pres.-elect, bd. dirs. 1989-90, pres. 1990-91), Nat. Assn. Securities Dealers, Nat. Futures Assn. (bd. arbitrators), Internat. Orgn. Securites Commns. (inter-Am. activities consultative com. 1990, pres.'s com. 1990, del. 1990). Methodist. Home: 1920 SW Damon Ct Topeka KS 66611-1926 Office: Kans Ho Reps State Capitol Topeka KS 66612

MAYS, WILLIAM G. chemical company executive; MBA, Ind. U. Test chemist Linkbelt Facility, Indpls.; acct. mgr. Procter & Gamble; market planning Eli Lilly and Co.; asst. to pres. Cummins Engine Co.; founder, pres. Mays Chem. Co., Indpls., 1980—. Bd. dirs. NBD-Inc. Mem. exec. com., bd. dirs. United Way Ctrl. Ind., Ind. Conv. and Visitors Assn.; bd. dirs. Associated Group, Corp. Cmty. Coun., Ind. Univ. Found., Cmty. Leaders Allied for Superior Schs.; mem. dean's adv. coun. Ind. U. Sch. Bus.; mem. pres.'s coun. Ind. U.; co-chmn. Coca-Cola Circle City Classic; elder Witherspoon Presbyn. Ch. Recipient Man of Yr. award B'Nai B'Rith Isidora Feibleman award, 1990, Elder Watson Diggs Achievement award Kappa Alpha Psi, 1991, Ind. Minority Small Bus. Advocate of Yr. award, 1991, Sagamore of Wabash award Gov. Ind., 1991, Ind. Enterprise award, 1992, Ind. Christian Leadership Conf. Businessman of Yr. award, 1992, Disting. Hooser, 1992, 13th in Black Enterprise Mag. Top 100 Indsl./Svc Cos., 'Above and Beyond' award Ind. Black Expo, 1992, Pres.'s award Black Pres.'s Roundtable Assn., 1992, Vol. Fund Raiser award, 1992, Anti-Defamation League Americanizm award, 1993, Charles Whistler award, 1993, Indpls. Edn. Assn.'s Human Rights award, 1994, Ind. State Conf. NAACP Labor and Industry award, 1994, Robert W. Briggs Humanitarian award, 1995, and numerous others; carried Olympic flame during trip through Indpls., 1995. Mem. Ind. C. of C. (bd. dirs.), Indpls. C. of C. (exec. com., bd. dirs.). Office: Mays Chemical Co Inc PO Box 50915 Indianapolis IN 46250-0915

MAYSENT, HAROLD WAYNE, hospital administrator; b. Tacoma, June 26, 1923; s. Wayne L. Shivley and Esther Pierce M.; m. Marjorie Ellen Hodges, June 13, 1953; children: Jeffrey, Nancy, Brian, Gregory. BA, U. Wash., 1950; MS in Hosp. Adminstrn. with distinction, Northwestern U., 1954. Adminstrv. resident Passavant Meml. Hosp., 1953-54, adminstrv. asst., 1954-55; research asso. hosp. adminstrn. Northwestern U., Evanston, Ill., 1954-55; with Lankenau Hosp., Phila., 1955-72, dir., 1963-67, exec. dir., 1967-72; exec. v.p. Rockford (Ill.) Meml. Hosp., 1972-75, pres., 1975-91, Rockford Meml. Corp., 1983-91, pres. emeritus, 1991—; pres. The Rockford Group, 1983-91. Tchg. assoc. Rockford Sch. Medicine, U. Ill., 1974-89, adj. assoc. prof., 1989-92; mem. Ill. Health Facility Planning Bd., 1980-92; chmn. bd. Ill. Hosp. Joint Ventures, Inc., 1977-78, Vol. Hosps. Am. Midwest Partnership, 1985-89. Contbr. articles to profl. jours. Chmn.-elect Coll. Healthcare Execs., 1988-89, chmn., 1989; coach, adminstr. Broomal (Pa.) Little League, 1962-72; bd. dirs. Community Health Assn., 1964-70, Rockford Med. Edn. Found., 1972-87, Tri State Hosp. Assembly, 1978-80, Rockford Coun. 100, 1987-91, exec. com. 1987-91. With AUS, 1942-46. Recipient Malcolm T. MacEachern award Northwestern U., 1954, Laura G. Jackson Alumni Assn. award, 198, Disting. Svc. award Ill. Hosp. Assn., 1989. Fellow Am. Coll. Hosp. Adminstrs. (life, Ill. regent 1979-84, dist. bd. govs. 1984-88, gov. 1984-88, chmn. elect 1988-89, chmn. 1989-90, past chmn. 1990-91); mem. Am. Hosp. Assn. (com. on vols. 1976-80, coun. patient svcs. 1980-82, ho. of dels. 1977-84, rep. Am. Acad. Pediatrics com. on hosp. care 1983-85), Pa. Hosp. Assn. (bd. dirs. 1965-68), Ill. Hosp. Assn. (trustee 1973-79, sec. 1974-76, chmn. elect 1977, chmn. bd. trustees 1978, named Outstanding Leader in Hosp. Industry 1978, Disting. Svc. award 1989). Office: Rockford Meml 2400 N Rockton Ave Rockford IL 61103-3681

MAZE, THOMAS H. engineering educator; b. St. Paul, June 1, 1952; s. Robert O. and Viola A.E. (Schultz) M.; m. Leslie Foster Smith, Aug. 2, 1979; children: Lauren L. Simonds, Julie W. Simonds. BS in Civil Engring., Iowa State U., 1975; M of Engring., Urban and Pub. Systems, U. Calif., Berkeley, 1977; PhD in Civil Engring., Mich. State U., 1982. Asst. prof. dept. civil engring. Wayne State U., 1979-82; assoc. prof. sch. civil engring. and environ. sci. U. Okla., Norman, 1982-87; prof. dept. civil and construction engring. Iowa State U., Ames, 1988—, prof. in-charge transp. planning program, 1987—, dir. ctr. for transp. rsch. and edn., ext. and applied rsch., 1988-99; v.p. H.R. Green Corp., St. Paul, 1999—. Assoc. dir. inst. urban transp., transp. rsch. ctr. Ind. U., Bloomington, 1987—; dir. Midwest Transp. Ctr., U.S. Dept. Transp.'s Univ. Transp. Ctr. Fed. Region VII, 1990-96. Mem. ASCE, Am. Pub. Transit Assn., Its Am. (founding, instl. issues com., CVO com.), Am. Pub. Works Assn. (adj. workshop faculty mem. 1986-91, exec. coun. inst. equipment svcs. 1991—), Coun. Univ. Transp., Transp. Rsch. Bd. (mem. various coms., chair 8th equipment mgmt. conf. 1990), Inst. Transp. Engrs. (assoc. mem. dept. 6 standing com., chmn. various coms., pres. U. Fla. student chpt. 1976-79), Chi Epsilon (faculty advisor U. Okla. 1985-87), Sigma Xi. Office: HR Green Co 1326 Energy Park Dr Saint Paul MN 55108-5202

MAZZE, ROGER STEVEN, medical educator, researcher; b. N.Y.C., May 14, 1943; s. Harry Alan and Mollie (Schneider) M.; m. Rochelle Linda March, Dec. 28, 1969; children— Aaron, Rebekkah BA, Queens Coll., 1965, MA, 1967; PhD, U. Ill., 1971. Fellow in social psychiatry Brandeis U., Waltham, Mass., 1971; chmn. urban studies Fordham U., N.Y.C., 1970-75; from assoc. to full prof. epidemiololgy and social medicine Einstein Coll. Medicine, 1975-87, exec. dir. Diabetes Research and Tng. Ctr., 1980-88; sr. v.p. research and devel. Internat. Diabetes Ctr., Mpls., 1988—; clin. prof. U. Minn. Med. Sch., 1988—; v.p. Inst. for Rsch. and Edn., Health Sys. Minn., Mpls., 1993—. Adv. bd. Nat. Diabetes Info. Clearinghouse, Washington, 1980-84, Pa. Diabetes Acad., Harrisburg, 1982—; co-dir. WHO Coll. Ctr. in Diabetes Care, Edn. and Computer Sci., Mpls., 1988—. Author: Narcotics, Knowledge and Nonsense, 1977, Professional Education in Diabetes, 1983, Frontiers of Diabetes Research, 1990, Staged Diabetes Management, 1995, Stage Diabetes Management: A Systemic Approach, 2000; editor: Practical Diabetes, 1987-89; contbr. articles to profl. jours. Active Internat. Diabetes Fedn., European Assn. for Study of Diabetes; chmn. Am. Diabetes Assn. Named Disting. vis. Scientist CDC, 1983-84; Hoechst lectr. Australian Diabetes Soc., 1985, 87, Japanese Diabetes Assn., 1983, 88, 93, 94, 99, Polish Diabetes Assn., 1993, 94, 95, 96, 99; named Best Spkr. of Yr., Soc. for Clin. Chemistry, 1991, Minn. Med. Alley award for excellence in rsch. and devel., 1995; grantee NIH, 1977—, ADA, 1991—, Juvenile Diabetes Found., 1992—; recipient Rschr. of Yr. award Inst. for Rsch. and Edn., 2000. Mem. Am. Diabetes Assn. (chmn.), Internat. Diabetes Fedn., European Assn. for Study Diabetes. Home: 5870 Boulder Bridge Ln Excelsior MN 55331-7969 Office: Internat Diabetes Ctr 3800 Park Nicollet Blvd Minneapolis MN 55416-2527 E-mail: mazzer@hsmnet.com.

MCALISTER, ROBERT BEATON, lawyer; b. N.Y.C., Oct. 5, 1932; s. Richard Charles and Martha Olive (Weisenbarger) McA.; widowed; children: Michael, Peter, Betsy. AB, Kenyon Coll., 1954; JD, U. Mich., 1957. Ptnr. Alexander, Ebinger, Fisher, McAlister & Lawrence, Columbus, Ohio, 1957-85; supt. Ohio Div. Savs. & Loan Assns., 1985; ptnr. Baker & Hostetler, 1985—, chmn. litigation dept., 1988-93. Exec. com. mem. Ohio Dem. Party, Columbus, 1967-74; active Dem. Nat. Com., Washington, 1972-76; counsel Gov. Richard F. Celeste, Columbus, 1982-90, Senator John Glenn, Washington, 1986-98. With USAF, 1968-64. Fellow Ohio Bar Found., Columbus Bar Found. Democrat. Episcopalian. Home: 77 E Nationwide Blvd Columbus OH 43215-2539 Office: Baker & Hostetler 65 E State St Ste 2100 Columbus OH 43215-4260

MCARDLE, RICHARD JOSEPH, academic administrator, retired; b. Omaha, Mar. 10, 1934; s. William James and Abby Marie (Menzies) McA.; m. Katherine Ann McAndrew, Dec. 27, 1958; children: Bernard, Constance, Nancy, Susan, Richard. B.A., Creighton U., 1955, M.A., 1961; Ph.D., U. Nebr., 1969. Tchr. pub. high schs., Nebr., 1955-65; grad. asst. romance langs. U. Nebr., 1965-66, instr. fgn. lang. methods, 1966-69; chmn. dept. edn. Cleve. State U., 1969-70; chmn. dept. elem. and secondary edn. U. North Fla., 1971-75; dean Coll. Edn. Cleve. State U., 1975-87, prof. edn., 1987-89, spl. asst. to pres. for campus planning, 1989-91, vice provost for strategic planning, 1991-92, acting provost, v.p. for acad. affairs, 1992-94, vice provost for strategic planning, 1994-96, prof. edn., 1996-2001, ret., 2001. Cons. in field. Author articles related to issues in tchr. edn. Mem. World Future Soc., Am. Assn. Higher Edn., Am. Assn. Adult and Continuing Edn., Phi Delta Kappa. Office: CASAL Dept Cleve State U Cleveland OH 44115

MCAULIFFE, RICHARD L. church official; m. Janet Bettinghaus; children: Brian, Andrea Stephenson. Student, Carleton Coll.; MBA, Harvard U. Exec. v.p., treas., CFO Harris Bankcorp, Harris Trust and Savs. Bank, 1960-90; mng. agt. Resolution Trust Corp., 1990-92; treas. Evang. Luth. Ch. in Am., Chgo., 1992—. Pres. Grace Luth. Ch., Glen Ellyn, Ill., Evang. Luth. Ch. Am. Ch. Coun.; treas. English Synod and Christ Sem.-Seminex, AELC; bd. dirs./com. mem. Christian Century Found., Luth. Gen. Healthcare Sys.; active Luth. Social Svcs. Ill. Office: Evang Luth Ch Am 8765 W Higgins Rd Chicago IL 60631-4101

MCBEATH, ANDREW ALAN, orthopedic surgery educator; b. Milw., Mar. 4, 1936; s. Ivor Charles and Lida McBeath; m. Margaret McBeath; children: Craig Matthew, Drew Alan. BS, U. Wis., 1958, MD, 1961. Diplomate Am. Bd. Orthopaedic Surgery (oral examiner). Intern, resident Hartford (Conn.) Hosp., 1961-63; resident in orthopedic surgery U. Iowa, Iowa City, 1963-66; asst. prof. div. orthopedic surgery div. surgery U. Wis., Madison, 1968-72, assoc. prof., 1972-79, prof., 1979—, Frederick J. Gaenslen prof., 1980, acting chmn. div., 1972-75, chmn. div., 1975-2000. Contbr. over 75 articles, chpt. to books. Capt. M.C., USAF, 1966-68. Mem. AMA, Am. Acad. Orthopaedic Surgeons, Orthopaedic Rsch. Soc., Am. Orthopaedic Assn., Hip Soc., Wis. Orthopaedic Soc., Rotary, Alpha Omega Alpha. Avocations: bicycling, skiing, reading. Office: U Wis Div Orthopedic Surg 600 Highland Ave # G5361 Madison WI 53792-0001

MCBRIDE, ANGELA BARRON, nursing educator; b. Balt., Jan. 16, 1941; d. John Stanley and Mary C. (Szcpepanska) Barron; m. William Leon McBride, June 12, 1965; children: Catherine, Kara. BS in Nursing, Georgetown U., 1962, LHD (hon.), 1993; MS in Nursing, Yale U., 1964; PhD, Purdue U., 1978; D of Pub. Svc. (hon.), U. Cin., 1983; LittD (hon.), Purdue U., 1998; LLD (hon.), Ea. Ky. U., 1991; DSc(hon.), Med. Coll. of Ohio, 1995; LHD (hon.), U. Akron, 1997. Asst. prof., rsch. asst. inst. Yale U., New Haven, 1964-73; assoc. prof., chairperson Ind. U. Sch. Nursing, Indpls., 1978-81, 80-84, prof., 1981-92, assoc. dean rsch., 1985—91, interim dean, 1991—92, univ dean, 1992—, disting. prof., 1992—; sr. v.p. acad. affairs, nursing Clarian Health Ptnrs., 1997—. Mem. Nat. Adv. Mental Health Coun., 1987—91; mem. adv. com. NIH Office of Women's Health Rsch., 1997—2001; mem. Yale U. Coun., 2000—; ext. acad. advisor dept. nursing Hong Kong Polytechnic U., 2000—. Author: The Growth and Development of Mothers, 1973 (Best Book award 1973), Living with Contradictions, A Married Feminist, 1976, How to Enjoy A Good Life With Your Teenager, 1987; editor: Psychiatric-Mental Health Nursing: Integrating the Behavioral and Biological Sciences, 1996 (Best Book award 1996); compiler: Nursing and Philanthropy, 2000. Recipient Disting. Alumna award Yale U., Disting. Alumna award Purdue U., Univ. Medallion, U. San Francisco, 1993, Hoosier Heritage award, 2000; named Influential Woman in Indpls., Indpls. Bus. Jour./Ind. Lawyer, 1999, Disting. Nurse Educator award Coll. Mt. St. Joseph, Cin., 2000; Kellog nat. fellow; Am. Nurses Found. scholar, Salute to Women award Indpls. YMCA, 1999, Sagamore of Wabash, 1999. Fellow: Nat. Acads. Practice, Am. Acad. Nursing (past pres.), APA (nursing and health psychology award divsn. 38 1995); mem.: Nat. Acad. Scis., Inst. of Medicine, Soc. for Rsch. in Child Devel., Midwest Nursing Rsch. Soc. (Disting. Rsch. award 1985), Sigma Theta Tau (mentor award 1993, disting. lectr 1995—99, Melanie Dreher award for contbns. as a dean 2001), Chi Eta Phi (hon.). Home: 744 Cherokee Ave Lafayette IN 47905-1872 E-mail: amcbride@iupui.edu.

MCBRIDE, BEVERLY JEAN, lawyer; b. Greenville, Ohio, Apr. 5, 1941; d. Kenneth Birt and Glenna Louise (Ashman) Whited; m. Benjamin Gary McBride, Nov. 28, 1964; children: John David, Elizabeth Ann. BA magna cum laude, Wittenberg U., 1963; JD cum laude, U. Toledo, 1966. Bar: Ohio 1966. Intern Ohio Gov.'s Office, Columbus, 1962; asst. dean women U. Toledo, 1963-65; assoc. Title Guarantee and Trust Co., Toledo, 1966-69; spl. counsel Ohio Atty. Gen.'s Office, 1975; assoc. Cobourn, Smith, Rohrbacher and Gibson, 1969-76; v.p., gen. counsel, sec. The Andersons, Maumee, Ohio, 1976—. Exec. trustee, bd. dirs. Wittenberg U., Springfield, Ohio, 1980-83; trustee Anderson Found., Maumee, 1981-93; mem. Ohio Supreme Ct. Task Force on Gender Fairness, 1991-94, Regional Growth Partnership, 1994—; chmn. Sylvania Twp. Zoning Commn., Ohio, 1970-80; candidate for judge Sylvania Mcpl. Ct., 1975; trustee Goodwill Industries, Toledo, 1976-82, Sylvania Cmty. Svcs. Ctr., 1976-78, Toledo-Lucas County Port Authority, 1992-99, vice chair Fla. CPA; chair St. Vincent Med. Ctr., 1992-99; founder Sylvania YWCA Program, 1973; active membership drives Toledo Mus. Art, 1977-87. Recipient Toledo Women in Industry award YWCA, 1979, Outstanding Alumnus award Wittenberg U., 1981. Fellow Am. Bar Found.; mem. ABA, AAUW, Ohio Bar Assn., Toledo Bar Assn. (pres., treas., chmn., sec. various coms.), Toledo Women Attys. Forum (exec. com. 1978-82), Pres. Club (U. Toledo exec. com.). Home: 5274 Cambrian Rd Toledo OH 43623-2626 Office: The Andersons 480 W Dussel Dr Maumee OH 43537-1690

MCBRIDE, BRIAN, soccer player; b. Arlington Heights, Ill., June 19, 1972; Student, St. Louis U. Player Vfl Wolfsburg, German 2nd Divsn., 1994-95, Columbus Crew, 1996—, U.S. Nat. Team, 1996—. Named to Eastern Conf. All Star Team, 1996, 97. Office: c/o Columbus Crew 77 E Nationwide Blvd Columbus OH 43215-2539 also: US Soccer Fedn 1801 S Prairie Ave # 1811 Chicago IL 60616-1319

MCBRIDE, JERRY E. state legislator; b. Licking, Mo., May 20, 1939; m. Deloris Pearl Harris, 1971; children: Heather, Jarrett, Ginger Dee. Grad. high sch., Rolla, Mo. Mem. Mo. Ho. of Reps., Jefferson City, 1974-76, 78-80, 1982—. Chmn. state parks, recreation and natural resources com., mem. agribus., rules and joint rules and appropriations, natural and econ. resources com. Mem. SAR, Mo. Sch. Mines-U. Mo. Rolla Alumni Assn. (life), Order of Stars and Bars. Democrat. Home: PO Box 292 Edgar Springs MO 65462-0292

MCBRIDE, TED, prosecutor; Clk. Chief Judge Fred J. Nichol U.S. Dist. Ct. S.D.; fed. prosecutor Rapid City (S.D.) Office, 1980—; asst. U.S. atty. S.D.; asst. dir. Atty. Gen.'s Advocacy Inst., Washington, 1992-93; U.S. atty. S.D. dist. U.S. Dept. Justice. Office: 230 S Phillips Ave Ste 600 Sioux Falls SD 57104-6325

MC BRIDE, WILLIAM LEON, philosopher, educator; b. N.Y.C., Jan. 19, 1938; s. William Joseph and Irene May (Choffin) McB.; m. Angela Barron, July 12, 1965; children: Catherine, Kara. A.B., Georgetown U., 1959; postgrad. (Fulbright fellow), U. Lille, 1959-60; M.A. (Woodrow Wilson fellow), Yale U., 1962, PhD (Social Sci. Rsch. Coun. fellow), 1964. Instr. philosophy Yale U., New Haven, 1964-66, asst. prof., 1966-70, assoc. prof., 1970-73; lectr. Northwestern U., Evanston, Ill., summer 1972; assoc. prof. Purdue U., West Lafayette, Ind., 1973-76, prof., 1976-2001, Arthur G. Hansen disting. prof., 2001—. Lectr. Korcula Summer Sch., Yugoslavia, 1971, 73; Fulbright lectr. Sofia U., St. Kliment Ohridski, Bulgaria, fall 1997. Author: Fundamental Change in Law and Society, 1970, The Philosophy of Marx, 1977, Social Theory at a Crossroads, 1980, (with R.A. Dahl) Demokrati og Autoritet, 1980, Sartre's Political Theory, 1991, Social and Political Philosophy, 1994, Philosophical Reflections on the Changes in Eastern Europe, 1999, From Yugoslav Praxis to Global Pathos, 2001; editor: (with C.O. Schrag) Phenomenology in a Pluralistic Context, 1983, Sartre and Existentialism, 8 vols., 1997. Decorated chevalier Ordre des Palmes Académiques. Mem. AAUP (pres. Purdue chpt. 1983-86, pres. Ind. conf. 1988-89), Am. Philos. Assn. (chmn. com. on internat. coop. 1992-95, bd. dirs. 1992-95), N.Am. Soc. Social and Polit. Philosophy (v.p. 1997-2000, pres. 2000—), Am. Soc. Polit. and Legal Philosophy, Soc. Phenemenology and Existential Philosophy (exec. co-sec. 1977-80), Sartre Soc. N.Am. (chmn. bd. dirs. 1985-88, 91-93), Am. Soc. Philosophy in the French Lang. (pres. 1994-96), Fed. Internat. Soc. Philosophie (mem. steering com. 1998—). Home: 744 Cherokee Ave Lafayette IN 47905-1872 Office: Purdue U Dept Philosophy West Lafayette IN 47907-1360

MCBRIEN, RICHARD PETER, theology educator; b. Hartford, Conn., Aug. 19, 1936; s. Thomas Henry and Catherine Ann (Botticelli) McB. AA, St. Thomas Sem., 1956; BA, St. John Sem., 1958, MA, 1962; STD, Gregorian U., 1967. Assoc. pastor Our Lady of Victory Ch., West Haven, Conn., 1962-63; prof., dean of studies Pope John XXIII Nat. Sem., Weston, Mass., 1965-70; prof. theology Boston Coll., Newton, 1970-80, dir. inst. of religious edn. and pastoral ministry, 1975-80; prof. theology U. Notre Dame, Ind., 1980—, chmn. dept., 1980-91. Cons. various dioceses and religious communities in the U.S. and Can., 1965—; vis. fellow John F. Kennedy Sch. Govt. Harvard U., Cambridge, 1976-77; mem. Council on Theol. Scholarship and Research Assn. of Theol. Schs., 1987-91. Author: Do We Need Church?, 1969, Catholicism, 2 vols., 1980, rev. edit., 1994 (Christopher award 1981), Caesar's Coin: Religion and Politics in America, 1987, Report on the Church: Catholicism after Vatican II, 1992, Responses to 101 Questions on the Church, 1996, Inside Catholicism, 1996; editor: Encyclopedia of Religion, 1987, HarperCollins Encyclopedia of Catholicism, 1995, Lives of the Popes: The Pontiffs from St. Peter to

John Paul II, 1997, Lives of the Saints: from Mary and St. Francis of Assisi to John XXIII and Mother Teresa. Recipient Best Syndicated Weekly Column award Cath. Press Assn. of U.S. and Can., 1975, 77, 78, 84. Mem. Cath. Theol. Soc. of Am. (pres. 1973-74, John Courtney Murray award 1976), Coll. Theology Soc., Am. Acad. Religion. Office: U of Notre Dame Dept Theology 327 O'Shaughnessy Hall Notre Dame IN 46556

MCCABE, MICHAEL J. insurance executive; b. Denver, June 19, 1945; s. Joseph J. and Mary J. (Kane) McC.; m. Catherine Corrine Marquette, July 21, 1978; children: Brian Michael, Shannon Marquette. BS, U. No. Colo., 1967; JD, Cath. U. Am., 1971. Bar: D.C. Air transport econ. analyst U.S. Civil Aeronautics Bd., Washington, 1967-71; Washington counsel Allstate Ins. Co., 1971-74, of counsel Ill., 1974-82, asst. v.p. bus. planning, 1982-84, v.p. corp. planning, 1984-89, group v.p., gen. atty., 1989-95; v.p., gen. counsel Allstate Corp.; sr. v.p., gen. counsel Allstate Ins. Co., 1999—. Bd. advisors No. Ill. U. Sch. Bus., DeKalb, 1986—. Chmn. Gateway Found. Mem. ABA, Fed. Bar Assn., D.C. Bar Assn., Planning Forum, Sigma Chi, Pi Alpha Delta. Democrat. Roman Catholic. Office: Allstate Ins Co 2775 Sanders Rd Northbrook IL 60062

MCCAFFERTY, MICHAEL, corporate executive; CEO TTC Illinois, Kankakee, Ill. Office: TTC Illinois 50 Meadowview Ctr Kankakee IL 60901-2041

MCCAFFERTY, OWEN EDWARD, accountant, dental-veterinary practice consultant; b. Cleve., Sept. 5, 1952; s. Owen James and Ann Theresa (Barrett) McC.; m. Colleen Maura Mullen, Aug. 3, 1974; children: Owen Michael, Hugh Anthony, Maura Kathleen, Bridget Colleen. AB, Xavier U., 1974. CPA, Ohio, Ga., S.C., Tex., Nev.; diplomate Am. Coll. Forensic Acctg.; cert. vet. practice mgr. Mem. staff to sr. accountant Deloitte, Haskins, & Sells, Cleve., 1974-78; ptnr., pres. Douglas, McCafferty & Co., Inc., Rocky River, Ohio, 1978-86; pres. Owen E. McCafferty, CPA, Inc., North Olmsted, 1986—, McCafferty/Beach Devel., Inc., North Olmsted, 1989—, Anicare N.Am., Inc., 1994—, McCafferty/Beach Devel., Inc., North Olmsted, 1989—, Anicare N.Am., Inc., 1994—. Lectr. various vet. and dental assns.; cons. in field; mng. ptnr. McCafferty/Beach Real Estate Ventures, 1988—; pres. Virtual Profl. Publ. Inc., 1997—; mng. unit holder Prescott/McCafferty Initiative, LLC; asst. treas. Vet. Study Groups, Inc. Co-author: The Business of Veterinary Practice, 1993; mem. editl. adv. bd. Vet. Econs. Mag., 1977-97, Vet. Bus., 1999—; contbr. articles to acctg. and vet. jours.; co-author audiotape vet. practice mgmt. series, 1997; mem. editl. bd. Vet. Bus. Jour., 1999—. Mem. fin. com. St. Richard Parish, 1987-95, chmn. budgeting com., 1991-95. Recipient Meritorius Service award Ohio Vet. Med. Assn., 1986, Am. Animal Hosp. Assn. award, 1988. Mem. AICPA (pvt. cos. practice sect., mgmt. cons. divsn., tax divsn.), Ohio Soc. CPAs (chmn. mgmt. adv. svcs. com. Cleve. chpt. 1987-89), mem. liaison com.), Vet. Hosp. Mgrs. Assn. (pres. 1993), Vet. Practice Mgrs. Assn. Gt. Britain and Republic of Ireland (hon. life), Am. Soc. Appraisers (candidate), Am. Coll. Forensic Examiners. Democrat. Roman Catholic. Office: PO Box 819 North Olmsted OH 44070-0819 E-mail: omccaffert@aol.com.

MCCALEB, MALCOLM, JR. lawyer; b. Evanston, Ill., June 4, 1945; BA, Colgate U., 1967; JD, Northwestern U., 1971. Bar: Ill. 1971. Atty. McCaleb, Lucas & Brugman, Chgo., 1970—85; ptnr. Keck, Mahin & Cate, 1985—95, Foley & Lardner, Chgo., 1995—2000, Barack Ferrazzano Kirschbaum Perlman & Nagelberg, LLC, Chgo., 2000—. Chmn. Northfield (Ill.) Village Caucus, 1981-82, active, 1977-82, Northfield Zoning Commn., 1985-88; pres. bd. dirs. Vols. Am., 1977-79; active Northfield Sch. and Park Bd. Caucus, 1980-87. Mem. Chgo. Bar Assn., Bar Assn. 7th Fed. Cir., Patent Law Assn. Chgo., Internat. Trademark Assn. Office: Barack Ferrazzano Kirschbaum Perlman & Nagelberg LLC 333 W Wacker Dr Chicago IL 60606 Business E-Mail: mac.mccaleb@bfkpn.com.

MC CALL, JULIEN LACHICOTTE, banker; b. Florence, S.C., Apr. 1, 1921; s. Arthur M. and Julia (Lachicotte) McC.; m. Janet Jones, Sept. 30, 1950; children: Melissa, Alison Gregg, Julien Lachicotte Jr. BS, Davidson Coll., 1942, LLD (hon.), 1983; MBA, Harvard U., 1947. With First Nat. City Bank, N.Y.C., 1948-71, asst. mgr. bond dept., 1952-53, asst. cashier, 1953-55, asst. v.p., 1955-57, v.p., 1957-71; 1st v.p. Nat. City Bank, Cleve., 1971-72, pres., 1972-79, chmn., 1979-85, chief exec. officer, from 1979, also bd. dirs.; pres. Nat. City Corp., 1973-80, chmn., chief exec. officer, 1980-86, also bd. dirs., cons. Mem. fed. adv. coun. Fed. Res. Bd., 1984-87. Trustee St. Luke's Found., United Way Services, Boy Scouts Am., Playhouse Sq. Found., Cleve. Mus. Natural History. Served with AUS, 1942-46, Africa, ETO. Mem. Pepper Pike Club, Chagrin Valley Hunt Club, Mountain Lake Club (Lake Wales, Fla.), Rolling Rock Club (Ligonier, Pa.). Home: Arrowhead 115 Quail Ln Chagrin Falls OH 44022 Office: 30195 Chagrin Blvd Ste 104W Pepper Pike OH 44124-5703

MCCALLUM, LAURIE RIACH, lawyer, state government; b. Virginia, Minn., Aug. 19, 1950; d. Keith Kelvin and Maybelle Louella (Hanson) Riach; m. J. Scott McCallum, June 19, 1979; children: Zachary, Rory, Cara. BA, U. Ariz., 1972; JD, So. Meth. U., 1977. Bar: Wis. 1977. Consumer atty. Office of Commr. of Ins., Madison, Wis., 1977-79; asst. legal counsel Gov. of Wis., 1979-82; mng. ptnr. Petri and McCallum Law Firm, Fond du Lac, 1979-80; exec. dir. Wis. Coun. on Criminal Justice, Madison, 1981-82; commr. Wis. Pers. Commn., 1982—, chairperson, 1988—. Mem. gov.'s jud. selection com. Supreme Ct., 1993; dir. State Bar Labor Law Sect., Madison, 1988-91; faculty U. Wis. Law Sch., Madison, 1992, 93. Chair vol. com. Wis. Spl. Olympics, Madison, 1981; dir. Off-the-Square Club, Madison, 1981, Met. Madison YMCA, Madison, 1982-88. Republican. Avocations: piano, tennis, youth sports. Office: State Pers Commn Ste 1004 131 West Wilson St Madison WI 53703-3233

MCCALLUM, RICHARD WARWICK, medical researcher, clinician, educator; b. Brisbane, Australia, Jan. 21, 1945; came to U.S., 1969; MD, BS, Queensland U., Australia, 1968. Rotating intern Charity Hosp. La., New Orleans, 1969-70; resident in internal medicine Barnes Hosp., Washington, 1970-72; fellow in gastroenterology Wadsworth VA Hosp., L.A., 1972-74, chief endoscopic unit, dept gastroenterology, 1974-76; dir. gastrointestinal diagnostic svcs. Yale-New Haven Med. Ctr., New Haven, 1979-85; asst. prof. medicine UCLA, 1974-76, Yale U., New Haven, 1977-82, assoc. prof., 1982-85; prof., chief div. gastroenterology, hepatology and nutrition U. Va., Charlottesville, 1985-95; dir. GI Motility Ctr. U. Va. Health Sci. Ctr., 1990-96; Paul Janssen prof. medicine U. Va., 1987-96; prof. medicine and physiology U. Kans. Med. Ctr., Kansas City, 1996—, chief div. gastroenterology and hepatology, 1996—, dir. Ctr. for Gastrointestinal Motility Disorders, 1996—. Patentee catheter for esophageal perfusion, gastrointestinal pacemaker haveing phased multipoint stimulation, esophageal protection by mastication. Fellow ACP, Am. Coll. Gastroenterology (gov. Kans. 1998—), Royal Australasian Coll. Physicians, Royal Australian Coll. Surgeons; mem. Australian Gastroenterology Soc., Am. Fedn. Clin. Rsch., Am. Assn. Study Liver Diseases, Am. Soc. Gastrointestinal Endoscopy, Am. Soc. for Clin. Investigation, Am. Gastroenterology Assn., Am. Motility Soc. (host-organizer 11th biennial meeting Kansas City 2000), So. Soc. for Clin. Investigation (pres. 1997-98), Internat. Electrogastrography Soc. (pres. 1998-2000), So. Med. Assn. (chmn. gastrointestinal 1996-97). Office: U Kans Med Ctr Dept Internal Medicine 3901 Rainbow Blvd Kansas City KS 66160-0001 E-mail: rmccallu@kumc.edu.

MCCALLUM, SCOTT, governor; b. Fond du Lac, Wis., May 2, 1950; m. Laurie McCallum; children: Zachary, Rory, Cara. BA, Macalester Coll., 1972; MA in Internat. Studies, Johns Hopkins U., 1974. Property developer, Fond du Lac; mem. Wis. State Senate, 1976-87; lt. gov. State of Wis., 1987-2001, gov., 2001—. Dir. Workplace Child Care Clearinghouse; chair Repeat Offenders Task Force State of Wis., Trauma and Injury Prevention Task Force; coord. Gov.'s Conf. on Small Bus.; presdl. appointee to Internat. Trade Policy Adv. Com.; past chair Nat. Conf. of Lt. Govs.; gov.'s appointee to Nat. Aerospace States Assn. Office: 115 E State Capitol PO Box 7863 Madison WI 53702*

MCCAMPBELL, ROBERT GARNER, prosecutor; b. Oklahoma City, Nov. 23, 1957; s. Stanley Reid and Joan Fontaine (Garner) McC. BA in History with honors, Vanderbilt U., 1980; JD, Yale U., 1983. Bar: Okla. 1983. Assoc. Crowe & Dunlevy, Oklahoma City, 1983-87; asst. U.S. atty. Western Dist. Okla. , 1987-94; chief fin. fraud unit Western Dist. Okla., 1990-94, interim U.S. atty., 2001—; dir. Crowe & Dunlevy , 1994—2001. Dir. Ctr. for Advancement of Sci. and Tech., 1995, chmn., 1999—. Mem. ABA, Phi Beta Kappa. Republican. Episcopalian. Office: US Atty 210 W Park Ave Ste 400 Oklahoma City OK 73102

MCCANLES, MICHAEL FREDERICK, English language educator; b. Kansas City, Mo., Mar. 8, 1936; s. Martin and Dorothy (Kaysing) McC.; m. Penelope A. Mitchell, May 27, 1967; children— Christopher, Stephanie, Jocelyn. BS, Rockhurst Coll., 1957; MA, U. Kans., 1959, PhD, 1964. Instr. dept. English U. Cin., 1962-64; asst. prof. Marquette U., 1964-68, assoc. prof., 1968-76, prof., 1976—. Author: Dialectical Criticism and Renaissance Literature, 1975, The Discourse of Il Principe, 1983, The Text of Sidney's Arcadian World, 1989, Jonsonian Discriminations: The Humanist Poet and the Praise of True Nobility, 1992; contbr. articles to profl. jours. Guggenheim fellow, 1978-79 Office: Dept English Marquette U Milwaukee WI 53233

MCCANN, DENNIS JOHN, columnist; b. Janesville, Wis., July 25, 1950; s. Thomas G. and Jean E. (Skelly) McC.; m. Barbara Jo Bunker, Sept. 11, 1971. BA, U. Wis., 1974. Reporter WMIR Radio, Lake Geneva, Wis., 1974, Janesville (Wis.) Gazette, 1975-83; reporter, columnist Milw. Jour. Sentinel, 1983—. Reporter Daily Herald, Arlington Heights, Ill., 1978. Author: The Wisconsin Story: 150 Stories, 150 Years, 1998, Dennis McCann Takes You for a Ride, 1999; contbg. author: Best of the Rest, 1993. Recipient Writing awards Milw. Press Club, Wis. Newspaper Assn., Newspaper Farm Editors. Avocations: golf, running. Office: The Milw Jour Sentinel 333 W State St Milwaukee WI 53203-1305

MCCANN, E. MICHAEL, lawyer; b. Chgo., 1936; BA, U. Detroit, 1959; LLB, Georgetown U., 1962; LLM, Harvard U., 1963; LLD honoris causa, Marquette U., 1997. Dist. atty. Milwaukee County, Wis. Lectr. Nat. Coll. Dist. Attys., Wis. Law Sch., Marquette Law Sch., Wis. Bar Continuing Legal Edn. Programs, State Prosecutor Edn. and Tng. Program, various state dist. atty. assns. Contbr. articles to law revs. Fellow Am. Bar Found., Am. Coll. Trial Lawyers; mem. ABA (resource team for high profile trials, past chair com. on victims, past chair criminal justice sect.), Nat. Dist. Attys. Assn. (lectr., bd. dirs.), Wis. Dist. Attys. Assn. (pres.), Pretrial Svcs. Resource Ctr. (bd. dirs.). Office: Milwaukee County Dist Atty's Office 821 W State St Rm 412 Milwaukee WI 53233-1427

MCCARNEY, DAN, football coach; b. Iowa City, July 28, 1953; m. Margy McCarney; children: Shane, Jillian, Melanie. BS, Univ. Iowa, 1975. Coach Iowa U., 1977-89; defensive coord. Wis. U., 1990-94; head football coach Iowa State Univ., 1995—. Mem. Am. Football Coaches Assn. Home: 2000 Michael Lane Ames IA 50010 Office: Iowa State Univ 1800 S 4th St Ames IA 50011-0001

MCCARRON, JOHN FRANCIS, editor; b. Providence, Jan. 20, 1949; s. Hugh Francis and Katherine Anne (Brooks) McC.; m. Janet Ann Velsor, Sept. 3, 1971; children: Veronica, Catherine. BS in Journalism, Northwestern U., 1970, MS in Journalism, 1973. Gen. assignment reporter Chgo. Tribune, 1973-80, urban affairs writer, 1980-91, fin. editor, 1991-92, editorial bd. columnist, 1992-2000; v.p. strategy and comms. Met. Planning Coun. Chgo., 2000—02; vis. prof. Roosevelt U., 2002—. Contbr. to Planning mag., World Book Ency., Preservation mag. Lt. USNR, 1970-72. Recipient Editors award AP, 1983, 84, Ann. Journalism award Am. Planning Assn., 1983, Heywood Broun award Am. Newspaper Guild, Washington, 1989, Peter Lisagor award Soc. Profl. Journalists, 1994. Home: 1425 Noyes St Evanston IL 60201-2639 Office: MPC 25 E Washington St Ste 1600 Chicago IL 60602 E-mail: j.mccarron@att.net.

MC CARTAN, PATRICK FRANCIS, lawyer; b. Cleve., Aug. 3, 1934; s. Patrick Francis and Stella Mercedes (Ashton) Mc Cartan; m. Lois Ann Buchman, Aug. 30, 1958; children: M. Karen, Patrick Francis III. AB magna cum laude, U. Notre Dame, 1956, JD, 1959. Bar: Ohio 1960, U.S. Ct. Appeals (6th cir.) 1961, U.S. Ct. Appeals (3rd cir.) 1965, U.S. Ct. Appeals (DC cir.) 1980, U.S. Ct. Appeals (5th cir.) 1981, U.S. Ct. Appeals (4th cir.) 1989, U.S. Ct. Appeals (7th cir.) 1992, U.S. Supreme Ct. 1970. Law clk. to Hon. Charles Evans Whittaker, U.S. Supreme Ct., 1959; assoc. Jones, Day, Reavis & Pogue, Cleve., 1961—65, ptnr., 1966—93, mng. ptnr., 1993—. Trustee U. Notre Dame, 2000—, chair, 2000—; trustee Cleve. Clinic Found.; chair Greater Cleve. Roundtable; mem. standing com. on rules of practice and procedure Jud. Conf. of U.S. Fellow: Internat. Acad. Trial Lawyers, Am. Coll. Trial Lawyers; mem.: ABA, Bar Assn. Greater Cleve. (pres. 1977—78), Ohio Bar Assn., 6th Cir. Jud. Conf. (life), U.S.-Japan Bus. Coun., Coun. on Fgn. Rels., Greater Cleve. Growth Assn. (chmn. 1997—2000), Musical Arts Assn. (trustee). Roman Catholic. Office: Jones Day Reavis & Pogue North Point 901 Lakeside Ave E Cleveland OH 44114-1190 E-mail: pmccartan@jonesday.com.

MCCARTER, CHARLES CHASE, lawyer; b. Pleasanton, Kans., Mar. 17, 1926; s. Charles Nelson and Donna (Chase) McC.; m. Clarice Blanchard, June 25, 1950; children— Charles Kevin, Cheryl Ann. BA, Principia Coll., 1950; JD, Washburn U., 1953; LLM, Yale U., 1954. Bar: Kans. 1953, U.S. Supreme Ct. 1962, Mo. 1968. Asst. atty. gen. State of Kans., 1954-57; lectr. law sch. Washburn U., 1956-57; appellate counsel FCC, Washington, 1957-58; assoc. Weigand, Curfman, Brainerd, Harris & Kaufman, Wichita, 1958-61; gen. counsel Kans. Corp. Commn., 1961-63; ptnr. McCarter, Frizzel & Wettig, Wichita, 1963-68, McCarter & Badger, Wichita, 1968-73; pvt. practice law St. Louis, 1968-76; ptnr. McCarter & Greenley, 1976-85; mng. ptnr. Gage & Tucker, 1985-87, Husch and Eppenberger, St. Louis, 1987-89, McCarter & Greenley, LLC, St. Louis, 1990—. Prof. law, assoc. dir. law sch. Nat. Energy Law and Policy Inst. Tulsa U., 1977-79; prof. law, coach nat. moot ct. coll. of law Stetson U. Coll., St. Petersburg, Fla., 1980-84; mem. govtl. adv. coun. Gulf Oil Corp., 1977-81 ; legal com. Interstate Oil Compact Commn.; mem. adv. bd. Allegiant Bank Trust Divsn., 1997—. Co-author: Missouri Lawyers Guide; assoc. editor Washburn U. Law Rev., 1952-53; contbr. articles to profl. jours. Chmn. Wichita Human Rels. Devel. Adv. Bd., 1967-68; bd. dirs. Peace Haven Assn.; active St. Louis estate planning coun., 1987—, bequests and endowment com. Salvation Army, 1995—, YMCA endowment com., 1996—. With USNR, 1944-46. Recipient Excellent Prof. award U. Tulsa , 1979; vis. scholar Yale U., 1980 Mem. ABA (sect. real property, probate and trust law, bus. law sect.), Kans. Bar Assn., Mo. Bar Assn. (probate and trust com., tax com.), Am. Legion, VFW, Native Sons and Daus. Kans (pres. 1957-58), Kappa Sigma, Delta Theta Phi, Principia Dads Club (bd. dirs.) Republican. Office: One Metropolitan Sq 1 Metropolitan Sq Ste 2100 Saint Louis MO 63102-2797 E-mail: cmccarter@mccartergreenley.com.

MC CARTER, JOHN WILBUR, JR. museum executive; b. Oak Park, Ill., Mar. 2, 1938; s. John Wilbur and Ruth Rebecca McC.; m. Judith Field West, May 1, 1965; children: James Philip, Jeffrey John, Katherine Field. A.B., Princeton U., 1960; postgrad., London Sch. Econs., 1961; M.B.A., Harvard U., 1963. Cons., assoc., v.p. Booz Allen and Hamilton, Inc., Chgo., 1963-69; White House fellow Washington, 1966-67; dir. Bur. Budget and Dept. Fin., State of Ill., Springfield, 1969-73; v.p. DeKalb AgResearch, Ill., 1973-78, dir., 1975-86, exec. v.p., 1978-80, pres., 1981-82; pres., chief exec. officer DeKalb-Pfizer Genetics, 1982-86; pres. DeKalb Corp., 1985-86; sr. v.p. Booz Allen & Hamilton Inc., 1987-97; pres., CEO Field Mus., Chgo., 1996—. Bd. dirs. A.M. Castle & Co., Divergence LLC, W.W. Grainger, Inc., Harris Insight Funds. Trustee Chgo. Pub. Television, 1973—, chmn., 1989-96, trustee Princeton U., 1983-87, U. Chgo., 1993—. Office: Field Museum 1400 S Lake Shore Dr Chicago IL 60605-2496

MCCARTER, W. DUDLEY, lawyer; b. St. Louis, Dec. 20, 1950; s. Willard Dudley and Vera Katherine (Schneider) McC.; m. Elizabeth Dunlop, June 14, 1986; children: Katherine, Elizabeth, Emily. BA, Knox Coll., 1972; JD, U. Mo., 1975. Bar: Mo. 1975, U.S. Dist. Ct. (ea. dist.) Mo. 1976, U.S. Ct. Appeals (8th cir.) Mo. 1977. Assoc. Mann & Poger, St. Louis, 1975-76, Suelthaus & Krueger, St. Louis, 1976-80; ptnr. Suelthaus & Kaplan, P.C., 1980-92, Behr, McCarter & Potter P.C., St. Louis, 1992—. Atty. for the City of Creve Coeur, Mo., 1992—. Author editor: Missouri Civil Litigation Handbook, 1992; author Jour. of the Mo. Bar, St. Louis Bar Jour. and Mo. Law Rev. Recipient W. Oliver Rasch award, 1985, 1989, Outstanding Young Lawyer award St. Louis County Bar Assn. 1983. Fellow ABA; mem. The Missouri Bar (pres. 1993-94). Office: Behr McCarter & Potter PC 7777 Bonhomme Ave Ste 1810 Saint Louis MO 63105-1911

MCCARTHY, HAROLD CHARLES, retired insurance company executive; b. Madelia, Minn., Dec. 5, 1926; s. Charles and Merle (Humphry) McC.; m. Barbara Kaercher, June 24, 1949; children: David, Susan. B.A., Carleton Coll., Northfield, Minn., 1950; postgrad. With Federated Mut. Ins. Co., Owatonna, Minn., 1950-67; with Meridian Mut. Ins. Co., Indpls., 1967-91, exec. v.p., then exec. v.p., gen. mgr., 1972-75, pres., 1975-90, bd. dirs., past chmn. bd., 1990-91; past pres. North Meridian Bus. Group; past pres., chmn. bd. Meridian Ins. Group, Inc. Chmn. bd., dir. Meridian Life Ins. Co.; past chmn., exec. com., bd. dirs. Ind. Ins. Inst.; mem. adv. bd. Harbor Fed. Savs. Bank. Former mem. Met. Devel. Commn., Corp. Community Council; bd. dirs. Meth. Health Found., Family Services Assn., Boy Scouts Am.; trustee Butler U.; mem. adv. bd. Harbor Fed. Bank. With USNR, 1944-46. Named Sagamore of the Wabash. Mem. Govs. Club of the Palm Beaches, Indian River Golf Club. Republican. Congregationalist. Office: 2955 N Meridian St Indianapolis IN 46208-4714

MCCARTHY, KAREN P. congresswoman, former state representative; b. Mass., Mar. 18, 1947; BS in English, Biology, U. Kans., 1969, MBA, 1985; MEd in English, U. Mo., Kansas City, 1976. Tchr. Shawnee Mission (Kans.) South High Sch., 1969-75, The Sunset Hill (Kans.) Sch., 1975-76; mem. Mo. House of Reps., Jefferson City, 1977-94; cons. govt. affairs Marion Labs., Kansas City, Mo., 1986-93; mem. U.S. Congress from 5th Mo. dist., Washington, 1995—; mem. commerce com. Rsch. analyst pub. fin. dept. Stearn Bros. & Co., 1984-85, Kansas City, Mo.; rsch. analyst Midwest Rsch. Inst., econs. and mgmt. scis. dept., Kansas City, 1985-86. Del. Dem. Nat. Conv., 1992, Dem. Nat. Party Conf., 1982, Dem. Nat. Policy Com. Policy Commn., 1985-86; mem. Ho. Commerce Com. Energy and Power, Telecom., Trade and Consumer Protection; co-chair Dem. Caucus Task Health Care Reform. Recipient Outstanding Young Woman Am. award, 1977, Outstanding Woman Mo. award Phi Chi Theta, Woman of Achievement award Mid-Continent Coun. Girl Scouts U.S., 1983, 87, Annie Baxter Leadership award, 1993; named Conservation Legislator of Yr., Conservation Fed. Mo., 1987. Fellow Inst. of Politics; mem. Nat. Inst. of Politics; mem. Nat. Conf. on State Legis. (del. on trade and econ. devel. to Fed. Republic of Germany, Bulgaria, Japan, France and Italy, mem. energy com. 1978-84, fed. taxation, trade and econ. devel. com. 1986, chmn. fed. budget and taxation com. 1987, vice chmn. state fed. assembly 1988, pres.-elect 1993, pres. 1994), Nat. Dem. Inst. for Internat. Affairs (instr. No. Ireland 1988, Baltic Republics 1992, Hungary 1993). Office: US House Reps 1330 Longworth H OB Washington DC 20515-0001*

MCCARTHY, MARK FRANCIS, lawyer; b. Boston, July 8, 1951; s. William Alfred and Martha Louise (Blodgett) McC.; m. Karen Marie Umerley; children: Kevin Francis, Daniel Henry. AB in Theology, Georgetown U., 1973, JD, 1976. Bar: Ohio 1976. Assoc. Sweeney, Mahon, & Vlad, Cleve., 1976-80; ptnr. Arter & Hadden, 1980—. Atty. asst. to bd. pres. Bd. Cuyahoga County Commrs., Cleve., 1976-80; adj. prof. Case Western Reserve Law Ctr., Cleve., 1986—. Active Greater Cleve. Growth Assn. Leadership Cleve., 1979-80; trustee Parmadale, Parma, Ohio, Western Res. Hist. Soc., 1978-80, Cath. Charities Found.; chmn. Cath. Charities Svcs. Corp. Mem. Ohio Assn. Civil Trial Attys. (chmn. product liability sect. 1989—), Fedn. Ins. & Corp. Counsel, Ct. of Nisi Prius, Rowfant Club. Democrat. Roman Catholic. Avocations: book collecting, fly fishing, upland shooting. Home: 363 Britannia Pky Avon Lake OH 44012-2180 Office: Arter & Hadden 1100 Huntington Bldg 925 Euclid Ave Ste 1100 Cleveland OH 44115-1475 E-mail: mark.mccarth@arterhadden.com.

MCCARTHY, MICHAEL M. construction executive; CEO McCarthy, St. Louis, chmn., 1976—. Office: McCarthy Bldg Cos 1341 N Rock Hill Rd Saint Louis MO 63124-1441

MCCARTHY, MICHAEL SHAWN, health care company executive, lawyer; b. Evergreen Park, Ill., May 16, 1953; s. Martin J. and Margaret Anne (McNeill) McC.; m. Jane F. Alberding, Oct. 28, 1988; children: Caroline Margaret, Nicholas Michael, Claire Patricia. BA, Georgetown U., 1975; MS, U. Ill., 1976; JD, Loyola U., 1980. Bar: Ill. 1980, U.S. Dist. Ct. (no. dist.) Ill. 1980. V.p., sec., gen. counsel Luth. Gen. Health Care System, Park Ridge, Ill., 1980-85, sr. v.p., sec., gen. counsel, 1985-91, sr. v.p. corp. svcs., sec., gen. counsel, 1990-93; chmn., CEO Parkside Sr. Svcs., LLC, Skokie, 1993—. Chmn. bd. trustees Lake Forest Acad., 1995-98. Mem. ABA, ASHA (exec. bd.), Ill. Hosp. Assn., Ill. Pub. Health Assn., Chgo. Bar Assn., ALFA Leadership Coun. Roman Catholic. Avocations: golf, travel. Home: 1026 Pine St Winnetka IL 60093-2024 Office: Parkside Sr Svcs LLC 5215 Old Orchard Rd Skokie IL 60077-1035 E-mail: McCarthy@parkside-sr.com.

MCCARTHY, PAUL FENTON, aerospace executive, former naval officer; b. Boston, Mar. 3, 1934; s. Paul Fenton and Jane Gertrude (O'Connor) McC.; m. Sandra Williams, June 20, 1959; children: Paul Fenton III, Susan Stacy. B.S. in Marine and Elec. Engring., Mass. Maritime Acad., 1954; M.S. in Mgmt., U.S. Naval Postgrad. Sch., 1964; D of Pub. Adminstrn. (hon.), Mass. Maritime Acad., 1987. Commd. ensign U.S. Navy, 1954, advanced through grades to vice adm., 1985; 7 command tours have included Aircraft Carrier USS Constellation, Carrier Group One, Task Force Seventy; commdr. U.S. 7th Fleet, 1980-82; dir. R & D USN, Washington, 1980-83; negotiator Naval Air, Incidents at Sea Agreement, Moscow, 1980; ret., 1990; cons. in field Alexandria, Va., 1990-92; pres. McCarthy and McCarthy, Ltd.; v.p., chief engr., dep. gen.mgr. McDonnell Douglas Aerospace/Boeing, St. Louis, 1992-95; v.p. processes and sys. integration McDonnell Douglas Aerospace, 1995-97, dir. naval systems integration, 1997-2000; vis. disting. prof. Peter Conrad Chair Naval Post Grad. Sch., 2000-02. Mem. engring adv. coun. Fla. State U. Trustee Naval Mus., 1990; bd. visitors Mass. Maritime Acad., 1993. Decorated D.S.M., Legion of Merit, D.F.C., also by govts. of South Vietnam, Korea, Japan. Mem. Mass. Maritime Acad. Alumni Assn., Soc. Exptl. Test Pilots, Naval

Inst., Nat. Soc. Profl. Engrs. (mem. industry adv. group). Episcopalian. Avocations: research, development and acquisition, aircraft and missile systems, financial management. E-mail: mcandmc@aol.com.

MC CARTHY, WALTER JOHN, JR. retired utility executive; b. N.Y.C., Apr. 20, 1925; s. Walter John and Irene (Trumbl) McC.; m. Linda Lyon, May 6, 1988; children by previous marriage: Walter, David, Sharon, James, William. B.M.E., Cornell U., 1949; grad., Oak Ridge Sch. Reactor Tech., 1952; D.Eng. (hon.), Lawrence Inst. Tech., 1981; D.Sc. (hon.), Eastern Mich. U., 1983; LHD, Wayne State U., 1984; LLD, Alma (Mich.) Coll., 1985. Engr. Public Service Electric & Gas Co., Newark, 1949-56; sect. head Atomic Power Devel. Assos., Detroit, 1956-61; gen. mgr. Power Reactor Devel. Co., 1961-68; with Detroit Edison Co., 1968-90, exec. v.p. ops., 1975-77, exec. v.p. divs., 1977-79, pres., chief operating officer, 1979-81, chmn., chief exec. officer, 1981-90. Bd. dirs. Energy Conversion Devices Inc. Author papers in field. Past chmn., bd. dirs. Inst. Nuclear Power Ops.; past pres. Monterey County Symphony Orch. Fellow Am. Nuc. Soc., Engring. Soc. Detroit; mem. ASME, NAE. Methodist.

MCCARTNEY, N. L. investment banker; b. Jameson, Mo., Oct. 12, 1923; m. Helen M. Walsh, Feb. 11, 1950; children: Patricia, Deborah, Patrick. BS, U. Md., 1956; MBA, Syracuse U., 1959; MPA, George Washington U., 1963. Enlisted U.S. Army, 1944, advanced through grades to col., ret., 1972; dir. S.W. Mo. Health Care Foun., Springfield, 1974-88; pres. Resource Mgmt. Co., 1988-96; exec. v.p. Spencer and Assocs., 1990-94, Mo. Adv. Capital, 1995-99; pres. DMS, Inc., 1999—. Instr. Southwest Mo. State U., Springfield, 1972-82, Crescent Capital, 1999-2000. Pres. S.W. Mo. Adv. Coun. Govts., Ozarks Crime Prevention Coun., 1983-93, Vis. Nurse Assn.; mayor of Springfield, 1993-95. Mem. Rotary. Methodist. Home: 1233 E Loren St Springfield MO 65804-0041 Office: 330 N Jefferson Springfield MO 65806

MCCASKEY, MICHAEL B. professional football team executive; b. Lancaster, Pa., Dec. 11, 1943; s. Edward B. and Virginia (Halas) McCaskey; m. Nancy McCaskey; children: John, Kathryn. Grad., Yale U., 1965; PhD, Case Western Res. U. Tchr. UCLA, 1972-75, Harvard U. Sch. Bus., Cambridge, Mass., 1975-82; pres., chief exec. officer Chgo. Bears (NFL), 1983-99, chmn. bd., 1999—. Author: The Executive Challenge: Managing Change and Ambiguity. Named Exec. of Yr. Sporting News, 1985. Office: Chgo Bears Halas Hall 250 Washington Rd Lake Forest IL 60045-2459 also: 1000 Football Dr Lake Forest IL 60045-4829

MC CASKEY, RAYMOND F. insurance company executive; b. 1942; With Continental Assurance Co., Chgo., 1963-73, Health Care Svc. Corp., Chgo., 1976—, now pres., CEO. Office: Health Care Service Corp 300 E Randolph St Chicago IL 60601-5014

MCCASKILL, CLAIRE, auditor; Auditor State of Mo., Jefferson City. Office: Mo State Auditors Off PO Box 869 Jefferson City MO 65102-0869 Fax: 573-751-6539.

MCCASLIN, W.C. products and packaging executive; Owner, CEO Douglas Products and Packaging. Office: Douglas Products & Packaging 1550 E Old 210 Hwy Liberty MO 64068

MCCAULEY, MATTHEW D. lawyer; b. 1942; AB, Harvard U.; JD, U. Mich. V.p., assoc. gen. counsel Gen. Am. Corp., St. Louis, 1994—. Office: Gen Am Corp Ste H6-02 H2-2 700 Market St Saint Louis MO 63101-1829

MCCAUSLAND, THOMAS JAMES, JR. brokerage house executive; b. Cleve., Nov. 27, 1934; s. Thomas James and Jean Anna (Hanna) McC.; m. Kathryn Margaret Schacht, Feb. 9, 1957; children: Thomas James III, Andrew John, Theodore Scott. BA in Econs., Beloit (Wis.) Coll., 1956. V.p. A.G. Becker & Co., Inc., Chgo., 1959-74; v.p. The Chgo. Corp., 1974-76, sr. v.p., dir., 1976-83, exec. v.p., 1983-90, vice chmn., 1991-96; pres. The Chgo. Corp. Internat., 1990-96; also bd. dirs. ABN AMRO, Inc. (formerly Cgo. Corp.). Bd. dirs. The Founders Fund, Naples, Fla.; treas. The LaSalle St. Coun., Chgo. V.p. Hospice the North Shore, Evanston, Ill., 1986-90; bd. dirs. McCormick Theol. Sem., Chgo., 1971-79, Presbyn. Home, Evanston, 1968-74; trustee Beloit Coll., 1987-90. Lt. USN, 1956-59. Mem. Union League, United Presbyn. Found. (trustee, vice-chmn. 1980-86), Skokie Country Club (bd. dirs. 1983-85, pres. 1993), Pelican Bay Club (Naples, Fla.), Royal Poinciana Golf Club (Naples). Republican. Avocations: travel, Am. history, golf. Office: ABN AMRO Inc 208 S La Salle St Ste 300 Chicago IL 60604-1065

MCCLAIN, RICHARD WARNER, state legislator; m. Barrie L. McClain. BS, Purdue U., 1970. Sales mgr. east coast CTS Microelectronics; owner, mgr. The Spogge Shoppe, The Capt. Logan Hotel and Office Bldg.; sales and mktg. mgr. Controls, Inc.; trustee Jefferson Twp., 1978-80; city engr. Logansport, 1980-84; mem. Ind. Ho. Reps. Dist. 24. Me. roads and transp. com., ways and means com. Active Boy Scouts Am., Red Cross, United Way, Farm Bur. Mem. Am. Legion, C. of C.

MCCLAIN, WILLIAM ANDREW, lawyer; b. Sanford, N.C., Jan. 11, 1913; s. Frank and Blanche (Leslie) McC.; m. Roberta White, Nov. 11, 1944. AB, Wittenberg U., 1934; JD, U. Mich., 1937; LLD (hon.), Wilberforce U., 1963, U. Cin., 1971; LHD, Wittenberg U., 1972. Bar: Ohio 1938, U.S. Dist. Ct. (so. dist.) Ohio 1940, U.S. Ct. Appeals (6th cir.) 1946, U.S. Supreme Ct. 1946. Mem. Berry, McClain & White, 1937-58; dep. solicitor, City of Cin., 1957-63, city solicitor, 1963-72; mem. Keating, Muething & Klekamp, Cin., 1972-73; gen. counsel Cin. br. SBA, 1973-75; judge Hamilton County Common Pleas Ct., 1975-76; judge Mcpl. Ct., 1976-80; of counsel Manley, Burke, Lipton & Cook, Cin., 1980—; adj. prof. U. Cin., 1963-72, Salmon P. Chase Law Sch., 1965-72. Mem. exec. com. ARC, Cin., 1978—; bd. dirs. NCCJ, 1975—. Served to 1st lt. JAG, U.S. Army, 1943-46. Decorated Army Commendation award; recipient Nat. Layman award, A.M.E. Ch., 1963; Alumni award Wittenberg U., 1966; Nat. Inst. Mcpl. Law Officers award, 1971, Ellis Island Medal of Honor, 1997. Fellow Am. Bar Found.; mem. ABA, FBA, Am. Judicature Soc., Cin. Bar Assn., Ohio Bar Assn., Nat. Bar Assn., Friendly Sons St. Patrick, Bankers Club, Masons (33d degree), Alpha Phi Alpha, Sigma Pi Phi. Republican. Methodist. Home: 2101 Grandin Rd Apt 904 Cincinnati OH 45208-3346

MCCLAMROCH, N. HARRIS, aerospace engineering educator, consultant, researcher; b. Houston, Oct. 7, 1942; s. Nathaniel Harris and Dorthy Jean (Orand) McC.; m. Margaret Susan Hobart, Aug. 10, 1963; 1 child, Kristin Jean B.S., U. Tex., 1963, M.S., 1965, Ph.D., 1967. Prof. dept. elec. engring. and computer sci. U. Mich., Ann Arbor, 1967—, chair dept. aerospace engring., 1992-95. Research engr. Cambridge U., Eng., 1975, Delft U., Netherlands, 1976, Sandia Labs., Albuquerque, 1977, C.S. Draper Lab., Cambridge, Mass., 1982 Author: State Models of Dynamic Systems, 1980; contbr. numerous articles to profl. jours. Chmn. U. Mich. Faculty Senate, 1987-88. Fellow IEEE (v.p. Control Sys. Soc. 1998, editor Transactions on Automatic Control 1989-92, Millennium medal 2000); mem. AAAS. Home: 4056 Thornoaks Dr Ann Arbor MI 48104-4254 Office: U Mich Dept Aerospace Engring Ann Arbor MI 48109 E-mail: nhm@umich.edu.

MC CLARREN, ROBERT ROYCE, librarian; b. Delta, Ohio, Mar. 15, 1921; s. Dresden William Howard and Norma Leona (Whiteman) Mc Clarren; m. Margaret Aileen Weed (dec. Oct. 2001); children: Mark Robert(dec.) , Todd Adams. Student, Antioch Coll., 1938-40; AB, Muskingum Coll., 1942; MA in English, Ohio State U., 1951; MS in L.S., Columbia, 1954; DLitt (hon.), Rosary Coll. (now Dominican U., 1989. Registration officer VA, Cin., 1946-47; instr. English Gen. Motors Inst., 1949-50; head circulation dept. Oak Park (Ill.) Pub. Libr., 1954-55, acting head librarian, 1955; head librarian Crawfordsville (Ind.) Pub. Libr., 1955-58, Huntington Pub. Libr., Western Counties Regional Pub. Libr., W.Va., 1958-62; dir. Ind. State Libr., 1962-67; system dir. North Suburban Libr. System, 1967-89, system dir. emeritus, 1990—; cons. libr. Chgo. Pub. Libr. Found., 1990. Del. White House Conf. on Librs., 1979; instr. U. Wis., summer 1964, Rosary Coll., 1968-80, U. Tex., summer 1979, 82, No. Ill. U., 1980; pres. W.Va. Libr. Assn., 1960, Ill. Libr. Assn., 1975; mem. Gov. Ind. Commn. Arts, 1964-65, Ill. State Libr. Adv. Com., 1972-79, 87-89, chmn., 1975-79, vice chmn., 1988-89; bd. dirs. Ill. Regional Libr. Coun., 1972-82, pres., 1977; chmn. adv. commn. Nat. Periodical System, Nat. Commn. on Librs. and Info. Sci., 1978-81; treas. Ill. Coalition Libr. Advs., 1982-89. Contbr. articles to profl. jours. Served to 1st lt. AUS, 1942-46, 51-52; maj. Res. Named Ill. Librarian of Yr., 1978; recipient Sagamore of Wabash (Ind.), 1966. Mem. ALA (councilor 1966-68, 74-78, treas. 1968-72, endowment trustee 1972-78, mem. publ. bd. 1972-75, pres. reference and adult svc. div. 1975-76, Joseph Towne Wheeler award 1954, Melville Dewey award 1989, Nat. Libr. Advocacy Honor Roll 2000), Assn. State and Coop. Libr. Agys. (prs. 1972), Beta Phi Mu. Home: 1560 Oakwood Pl Deerfield IL 60015-2014 Office: 200 W Dundee Rd Wheeling IL 60090-4750

MCCLATCHEY, KENNETH D. pathology educator; degree, DDS, MD, degree in medicine, U. Mich. Dir. clin. microbiology and virology lab. U. Mich. Med. Ctr., 1978-96, assoc. chmn., dir. labs., 1981-91; Helen M. & Raymond M. Galvin prof., chmn. dept. pathology Loyola U. Chgo. Stritch Sch. Medicine, Maywood, Ill., 1991—. Mem. Nat. Com. for Clin. Lab. Stds. Author: Clinical Laboratory Medicine; editor Archives of Pathology and Lab. Medicine; mem. editl. bd. jour. AMA; contbr. over 150 articles to profl. jours., chpts. to books. Mem. Coll. Am. Pathologists, Am. Soc. Clin. Pathologists, World Assn. Socs. Pathology. Office: Loyola U Med Ctr Stritch Sch Medicine 2160 S 1st Ave Maywood IL 60153-3304

MCCLELLAN, LARRY ALLEN, educator, writer, minister; b. Buffalo, Nov. 3, 1944; s. Edward Lurelle McClellan and Helen (Denison) Greenlee; m. Diane Eunice Bonfoey, Aug. 19, 1973; children: Kara E., Seth C. Student, U. Ghana, 1964-65; BA in Psychology, Occidental Coll., 1966; MTh, U. Chgo., 1969, D Ministry, 1970. Ordained to ministry Presbyn. Ch. (U.S.A.), 1970. Prof. of sociology and community studies Govs. State U., University Park, Ill., 1970-86; interim pastor Presbyn. Ch. (U.S.A.), Chgo. area, 1980-86; sr. pastor St. Paul Community Ch., Homewood, Ill., 1986-96; adj. prof. Govs. State U., University Park, 1987-96; dir. South Met. Regional Leadership Ctr., Govs. State U., 1996—2001; cmty. rels. dir. Northeastern Ill. Planning Commn., 2001—. Newspaper columnist Star Publs. Chgo., 1993—; trustee Internat. Coun. Community Chs., 1989-91, pres., 1991-93. Author: Local History South of Chicago, 1988; developer social simulation games; contbr. articles to profl. publs. Mayor Village of Park Forest South (name now University Park), Ill., 1975-79; co-organizer S. Region Habitat for Humanity, Chgo. area, 1989; pres. S. Suburban Heritage Assn., Chgo. area, 1988-91. Fellow Layne Found., 1966-70, NEH, 1979. Mem. Urban Affairs Assn., Assn. for Sociology of Religion, Am. Assn. State and Local History, Ill. State Hist. Soc. (Spl. Achievement award 1989). E-mail: larryamcclel@msn.com.

MCCLELLAND, EMMA L. state legislator; b. Springfield, Mo., Feb. 26, 1940; m. Alan McClelland; children: Mike, Karen. BA, U. Mo., 1962. mem. appropriations, natural and econ. resources com., budget com., elem. and secondary edn. com., mcpl. corps. com., rules, joint rules and bills perfected and printed com., social services com., medicaid and elderly com. Dir. field office, corp. divsn. Mo. Sec. of State, St. Louis; committeewoman Gravois Twp.; mem. St. Louis County Rep. Cent. Com., Mo. Rep. State Com., Mo. Ho. of Reps., Jefferson City, 1991—; mem. appropriations, budget, edn., mcpl. corps., rules, joint rules and bills perfected and printed, social svcs., medicaid and the elderly coms. Bd. dirs. Ct. Apptd. Spl. Advocates, Family Support Network; elder Webster Groves Presbyn. Ch.; mem. Leadership St. Louis. Recipient Leadership award for govt. YWCA of St. Louis, Spirit of Enterprise award Mo. C. of C., Mental Health Assn. award for legis. svc., 1998, Mo. Child Adv. of Yr. award Mo. Child Care Assn., 1998. Mem. Webster Groves C. of C., Pi Lambda Theta. Republican. Presbyterian. Home: 455 Pasadena Ave Webster Groves MO 63119-3126 Office: Mo Ho of Reps State Capitol Building Jefferson City MO 65101-1556

MCCLENDON, EDWIN JAMES, health science educator; b. Troy, Okla., Dec. 3, 1921; s. Charles Wesley and Mattie (Reed) McClendon; m. Ruby Wynona Scott, May 5, 1950 (dec. Apr. 8, 2001); children: Edwin James Jr., Melody Jan, Joy Renee. BS, Okla. East Ctrl. State U., 1946; MEd, U. Okla., 1954; EdD, Wayne State U., 1964; hon. DrPH, Seoul Nat. U., 1989. Instr. U. Okla., Norman, 1946-47; head speech dept., tchr. Wewoka High Sch., Okla., 1947-49; assoc. dir. Tb Control, Oklahoma City, 1949-51; dir. sch health project Okla. Dept. Health and Edn., 1951-54; assoc. dir. Tb Control, Wayne County, Mich., 1954-56; dir. sch. health, 1956-63; dir. secondary edn. Wayne County Intermediate Sch., Detroit, 1963-67; supt. schs. Highland Park, Mich., 1967-68; v.p. Highland Park Coll., 1968-69; asst. supt. health Mich. Dept. Edn., Lansing, 1969-71; prof., chmn. health edn. U. Mich., Ann Arbor, 1971-88, prof. health behavior and pub. health, 1971-88, prof. emeritus, 1988—; cons. pub. health care WHO, 1985—. Cons. WHO, 1978-89, dir. field study for Western Pacific, 1981; health field study of Arabic states, 1979-80; cons., Papua, New Guinea, Japan, Korea, Philippines, 1983-84, Fiji and Malaysia, 1987-88; vis. prof. U. Okla., 1965, Okla U. Liberal Arts, 1966, U. Wis., Madison, Kent U., Ohio, Wayne State U., Mich. State U., U. Mich., Flint and Dearborn, 1979-97. Author: Drug Education-A Teacher's Guide, 1969, Maxi Minds in Mini Cages, The Gifted, 1972, Healthful Living for Today and Tomorrow, 1981, Health and Wellness, 1987, Evaluation Study of Growing Healthy, 1993; contbg. author: Practical Stress Management, 2000; editor: Michigan Tenth Largest, A History of Plymouth-Canton Schools, 1986; contbr. 60 articles to profl. publs. Chmn. bd. dirs. Am. Cancer Soc., Detroit, 1977-78, mem. nat. pub. edn. com., 1969-83, hon. life mem., 1980—; mem. adv. coun. alcohol abuse NIH, 1976-80; pres. Plymouth-Canton Sch. Bd., 1974-78, 82-91; Tax Rev. Bd., Plymouth, Mich., 1980-85; chmn. Jr. Red Cross S.E. Mich., 1969-73; chmn., cons. Polio Plus immunization campaign, WHO, Rotary Internat; bd. dirs. ARC S.E. Mich., 1992-98, exec. com., 1993—, mem. health, safety, youth and internat. coms, chair HIV/AIDS com.; Choctaw Tribal rep. Served with USN, 1942-46. Decorated Bronze Star with V for Valor, others; recipient Disting. Health Edn. award Cen. Mich. U., 1978; adminstrn. bldg. Plymouth-Canton (Mich.) schs. dedicated E.J. McClendon Edn. Ctr., 1992, Inductee Hon. Hall of Fame Plymouth Culture Ctr., 2002. Fellow APHA, Am. Sch. Health Assn. (pres. 1970-71, Disting. Service award 1962, William A. Howe award 1976), Am. Cancer Soc. (hon. life mem., bd. dirs.), Am. Social Health Assn. (dir. 1978-86), Royal Soc. Health (London); mem. NEA (hon. life), AAUP, VFW (life), Mich. Sch. Health Assn. (hon. life mem., Disting. service award 1967, Golden Anniversary award 1985), Nat. Assn. Curriculum and Devel., Am. Venereal Disease Assn., Alliance Advancement Health Edn., Soc. Pub. Health Edn., Soc. Sex Educators and Counselors, Nat. Coun. for Internat. Health, Am. Assn. for WHO, Tcgh. Prof. Alumni Wewoka and Seminole (life, disting. svc. award, 50 Yr. Svc. award), Soc. Native Am. Indians, Rotary (pres. 1989-91, chair dist. polio plus campaign, elected to Plymouth Hall of Fame), Phi Delta Kappa. Democrat. Methodist. Home and Office: 40664 Newport Dr Plymouth MI 48170-4704

MCCLURE, ALVIN BRUCE, technical consultant; b. Cin., Mar. 2, 1953; s. Alphonso Bruce McClure and Jewel Lee (Smith) Yates; m. Katherine Shenkar, Nov. 7, 1979; children: Jaina, Randi; m. Penny Bliss, July 7, 2000. Student, U. Mich., 1971-73, 76-77, Fanshawe Coll., London, Ont., Can., 1974-75, Coll. of St. Thomas, 1989-91. Programmer Mfg. Data Systems, Ann Arbor, Mich., 1978-79; systems software specialist Mpls. Star and Tribune, 1979-81; systems analyst NCR COMTEN, Inc., Roseville, Minn., 1981-84; software systems support programmer INTRAN Corp., Bloomington, 1984-85; programmer/analyst Minn. Dept. Natural Resources, St. Paul, 1985-97; local area network adminstr. Minn. Pollution Control Agy., 1997-98; network mgr. Minn. Dept. Health, Mpls., 1998; info. sys. mgr. Van Wageneon Co., Eden Prairie, 1998-99; sr. tech. cons. Database/Network/WEB Lawson Software, St. Paul, 1999-2000; tech. cons. Productive Solutions Group, Mpls., 2000—01; pres. Reality Bytes, Inc., Elk River, 2001—. Mem. mgmt. info. services tech. com., St. Paul, 1987-97. Community adv. bd. Sta. WCAL-FM, 1988-90. Mem. IEEE, Am. Inst. Physics, Audio Engring. Soc., Internat. Platform Assn., Mgmt. Info. Svcs., Aikido Yoshinkai Mpls.-St. Paul (5th degree black belt, head instr.). Avocations: chess, photography, audiophile, sailing, aquaria. Home: 14348 96th St NE Elk River MN 55330-7376 Office: Reality Bytes Inc 14348 96th St NE Elk River MN 55330-7376 E-mail: alvin@heisei.com.

MCCLURE, CHARLES G. automotive executive; BS in Mech. Engring., Cornell U.; MBA, U. Mich. Heavy truck sales engr., product engr. Ford Motor Co.; v.p., gen. mgr. automotive sys. groups for the Ams. Johnson Controls, Inc., pres., Detroit Diesel Corp., 1997—, CEO, 1999—, also bd. dirs. Office: Federal Mogul Corp 26555 Northwestern Hwy Southfield MI 48034

MCCLURE, JAMES JULIUS, JR. lawyer, former city official; b. Oak Park, Ill., Sept. 23, 1920; s. James J. and Ada Leslie (Baker) McC.; m. Margaret Carolyn Phelps, Apr. 9, 1949; children: John Phelps, Julia Jean, Donald Stewart. BA, U. Chgo., 1942, JD, 1949. Bar: Ill. 1950. Ptnr. Gardner, Carton & Douglas, Chgo., 1962-91, of counsel, 1991—; mem. Oak Park Plan Commn., 1966-73, Northeastern Ill. Planning Commn., 1973-77, pres., 1975-77, Village of Oak Park, 1973-81, Oak Park Exch. Congress Inc., 1978—2002. Mem. Bus. Leaders for Transp., 1998—. Pres. United Christian Cmty. Svcs., 1967-69, 71-73, Erie Neighborhood House, 1953-55, Oak Park-River Forest Cmty. Chest, 1967; moderator Presbytery Chgo., 1969; mem. Gov.'s Spl. Com. on MPO, 1978-79; bd. dirs. Leadership Coun. of Met. Open Cmtys., 1981-2002, sec., 1990-98; bd. dirs. Met. Planning Coun., 1982-93, hon. dir., 1993—; bd. dirs. Cmty. Renewal Soc., 1982-91, v.p., 1984-88, treas. 1988-91; chmn. Christian Century Found., 1981—; bd. trustees McCormick Theol. Sem., 1981—, chmn. bd. 1987-90. hon. trustee, 1990—; mem. ch. vocations unit, 1987-91, vice chair 1990; mem. gen. assembly coun. Presbyn. Ch. U.S.A., 1987-90, mem. gen. assembly Permanent Jud. Commn., 1997—; bd. dirs. Oak Park Edn. Found., 1991-96, Oak Park River Forest Cmty. Found., 1991-2002; mem. Vision 2000 (Oak Park) Coordinating Com., 1995. With USNR, 1942-46. Recipient Disting. Citizen award Oak Park, 1976; Silver Beaver award; Disting. Eagle Scout award Boy Scouts Am., Carl Winters Cmty. Svc. award Oak Park Rotary Club, 1996, William Staczak award Oak Park Edn. Found., 1997, Rita Johnson award Oak Park Family Svc. and Mental Health Ctr., 1997, Public Svc. award U. Chgo. Alumni Assn., 1997, Tradition of Excellence award Oak Pk. River Forest H.S., 1998. Mem. ABA, Am. Coll. Trust and Estate Counsel, Ill. State Bar Assn., Chgo. Bar Assn., Am. Law Inst., Order of the Coif, Lambda Alpha. Clubs: Univ. (Chgo.). Home: One Calvin Cir # C 309 Evanston IL 60201 Office: Gardner Carton & Douglas 321 N Clark St Ste 3200 Chicago IL 60610-4719

MCCLURE, LAURA, state legislator; m. John D. McClure. Kans. state rep. Dist. 119, 1993—. Office: Kans Ho of Reps State Capitol Topeka KS 66612

MCCLURE, WALTER F. risk management marketing company executive; b. 1934; Head retail brokerage network Arthur J. Gallagher & Co., Itasca, Ill., sr. v.p., dir., chmn., 1993—. Office: Arthur J Gallagher & Co 2 Pierce Pl Itasca IL 60143-3141 Fax: (630) 285-4000.

MCCLURG, JAMES EDWARD, research laboratory executive; b. Bassett, Nebr., Mar. 23, 1945; s. Warren James and Delia Emma (Allyn) McC. B.S., N.E. Wesleyan U., 1967; Ph.D., U. Nebr., 1973. Instr., U. Nebr. Coll. Medicine, Omaha, 1973-76, research instr., 1973-76, clin. asst. prof. Med. Ctr., 1984—; v.p., tech, dir. Harris Labs., Inc., Lincoln, Nebr., 1976-82, exec. v.p., 1982-84, pres., chief exec. officer, 1984— ; bd. dirs. Lincoln Mut. Life Ins. Co., Lincoln Gen. Hosp. (chmn.), Unemed Corp., Lincoln, Harris Labs. Ltd, Belfast No. Ireland. Mem. editorial bd. Clin. Rsch. Practices and Drug Regulatory Affairs, 1984. Contbr. articles to profl. jours. Trustee Univ. Nebr. Found.; mem. Commn. on Human Rights, Lincoln, 1982-85; com. mem. Nebr. Citizens for Study Higher Edn., Lincoln, 1984; chmn. U. Nebr. Found. Recipient ann. research award Central Assn. Obstetricians and Gynecologists, 1982. Mem. Am. Assn. Lab. Accreditation (bd. dirs.). Republican. Clubs: Century (pres. Nebr. Wesleyan U. 1983-84), Nebraska (Lincoln). Lodge: Rotary. Avocation: boating. Office: Harris Labs Inc PO Box 80837 Lincoln NE 68501-0837

MCCOLLEY, ROBERT MCNAIR, history educator; b. Salina, Kans., Feb. 2, 1933; s. Grant and Alice Elizabeth (McNair) McC.; m. Diane Laurene Kelsey, Aug. 30, 1958; children: Rebecca, Susanna, Teresa, Margaret, Carolyn, Robert Lauren. B.A., Harvard U., 1954, M.A., 1955; Ph.D., U Calif.-Berkeley, 1960. Instr. to prof. history U. Ill., Urbana, 1960-97. Mem. Com. for Advanced Placement Test in Am. History, 1987-90, chmn. 1988-90. Author: Slavery and Jeffersonian Virginia, 1964 (Dickerson award 1964); editor: Federalists, Republicans and Foreign Entanglements, 1969; editor: Henry Adams, John Randolph, 1995; co-editor: Refracting America, 1993; mem. editorial bd. Jour. Early Republic, 1981-85, Va. Mag. of History and Biography, 1994-98; editor Jour. Ill. State Hist. Soc., 1998—; classical recs. reviewer Fanfare mag., 1989—. Mem. Soc. Historians of Early Republic (pres. 1982), Orgn. Am. Historians, Va. Hist. Soc., Ill. Hist. Soc. (bd. dirs. 1978-81, 92-95, pres. 1997-99), Chgo. Hist. Soc., Cliff Dwellers. Episcopalian. Home: 503 W Illinois St Urbana IL 61801-3927 Office: U Ill Dept History 810 S Wright St Urbana IL 61801-3644 E-mail: rmccolle@uiuc.edu.

MCCOLLUM, BETTY, congresswoman; b. July 12, 1954; m. Douglas McCollum; 2 children. BS in Edn., Coll. St. Catherine. Retail store mgr., Minn.; mem. Minn. Ho. Reps., 1992-2000, mem. edn. com., environ. and natural resources com., mem. gen. legis. com., vet. affairs and elections com., mem. transportation and transit com., asst. majority leader, chair legis. commn. on econ. status of women, mem. rules and adminstrv. legis. com.; mem. U.S. Congress from Minn. 4th Dist., Washington, 2001—; mem. edn. and workforce com., resources com. Mem. St. Croix Valley Coun. Girl Scouts. Mem. VFW Aux., Am. Legion Aux. Democrat. Office: US Ho of Reps 1029 Longworth HOB Washington DC 20515 Home: Ste 17 165 Western Ave N Saint Paul MN 55102-4613*

MCCOLLUM, W. LEE, chemical company executive; CFO SC Johnson & Son, Inc., Racine, Wis. Office: SC Johnson & Son Inc 1525 Howe St Racine WI 53403

MCCOMBS, BILLY JOE (RED MCCOMBS), professional football team executive; m. Charlene McCombs; 3 daughters. Former owner, chmn. bd. Denver Nuggets; founder, dir. Clear Channel Communications, Inc;

former owner, chmn. bd. San Antonio Spurs; chair. bd of trustees Southwestern Univ.; owner, chair., pres. Minnesota Vikings, Eden Prairie, 1998-. Chmn. bd. trustees Southwestern U.; former chmn. United Way of San Antonio, HemisFair World's Fair '68. Named to Bus. Hall of Fame. Mem. San Antonio C. of C. (former chmn.), Nat. Ford Dealers, U. Tex. Longhorn Club. Office: Minnesota Vikings 9520 Viking Dr Eden Prairie MN 55344-3898

MCCOMBS, CHARLINE, professional sports team executive; m. Red McCombs, 1950; children: Lynda, Marsha, Connie. DH(hon.) , Southwestern U. Owner Minn. Vikings, Inc. Co-host Tex. Tuxedo fundraiser U. Minn., 1999; vol. Salvation Army, Cris Carter Viking Super Challenge; mentor San Antonio elem. schs.; mem. adv. bd. Friends of Ronald McDonald; bd. dirs. Las Casas Found., San Antonio, Susan G. Komen Breast Cancer Found., nat. adv. bd.; bd. dirs. Cancer Ctr. Coun.; former bd. dirs. Friends of Ronald McDonald, San Antonio; bd. dirs. McNay Art Mus., mem. art and edn. coms. Named Mother of Yr., Advance orgn.; recipient Trfoil award, Girl Scouts U.S., 1999, Spirit of Youth award, Boys Town, Sch. Arch. and Design award, U. Tex., Outstanding Philanthropist award, NAFE, Civic Virtue award, Freedom of Info. Found., Spirit of Philanthropy award, Non-Profit Resource Ctr. Office: 9520 Vikings Dr Eden Prairie MN 55344

MCCONAHEY, STEPHEN GEORGE, retired securities company executive; b. Fond du Lac, Wis., Nov. 8, 1943; s. George and Charlotte McC.; m. Kathleen Louise Litten, Aug. 19, 1967; children: Heather, Benjamin. BS, U. Wis., 1966; MBA, Harvard U., 1968. Assoc. McKinsey & Co., Washington, 1968-72; White House fellow, 1972-73; program adminstr. Dept. Transp., 1973-75; spl. asst. to Pres. Gerald Ford The White House, 1975-77; underwriter, ptnr. Boettcher & Co., Inc., Denver, 1977-80, mgr. pub. fin., 1980-82, mgr. corp. fin., 1982-84, pres., chief exec. officer, 1984-86, chmn. bd., 1986-87, Boettcher Investment Corp., Denver, 1987-90; sr. v.p. for corp. and internat. devel. Kemper Corp., Chgo., 1991—; exec. v.p. Kemper Fin. Svcs., Inc., 1991—; pres., COO EVEREN Capital Corp., from 1994. Chmn. oper. com. EVEREN Securities, Chgo., 1994—; trustee Amli Properties, Ill. Inst. Tech. Trustee Denver Symphony Assn., 1986, Ill. Inst. Tech., Chgo. Field Mus., U.S. Ski Team Found.; chmn. Greater Denver Corp., 1987; bd. dirs. The Denver Partnership; bd. fellows U. Denver; nat. trustee Boys and Girls Clubs Am. Mem. Young Presidents Orgn., Greater Denver C. of C. (bd. dirs.), Denver Club, Colo. Harvard Bus. Sch. Club (Denver), Cherry Hills Country Club (Englewood, Colo.), Castle Pines Country Club (Castle Rock, Colo.), Chgo. Club, Econ. Club Chgo. Home: 100 E Huron St Chicago IL 60611-2932 Office: EVEREN Securities Inc 77 W Wacker Dr Chicago IL 60601-1651

MCCONKIE, GEORGE WILSON, educational psychology educator; b. Holden, Utah, July 15, 1937; s. G. Wilson and Mabel (Stephenson) McC.; m. Orlene Carol Johnson, Sept. 6, 1962; children: Lynnette Mooth, Heather Usevitch, April Rhiner, Faline Coffelt, George Wilson, Bryce Johnson, Camille Howard, Elissa, Esther, Bryna, Ruth, Anna May Cox, Cynthia, Thomas Oscar. AA, Dixie Jr. Coll., 1957; BS, Brigham Young U., 1960, MS, 1961; PhD, Stanford U., 1966. Missionary LDS Ch., 1957-59; asst. prof. edn. Cornell U., 1964-70, asso. prof., 1970-75, prof., 1975-78, chmn. dept. edn., 1977-78; prof. U. Ill., Champaign, 1978—, chmn. dept. ednl. psychology, 1993-94, 95-97. Sr. scientist Ctr. for Study of Reading, 1978-95, Beckman Inst., 1989—; rsch. fellow Cath. U. Louvain, Belgium, 1991-92; vis. prof. Nat. Yang Ming U., Taiwan, 1998, Beijing Normal U., 1999. Contbr. articles to profl. jours. Recipient Outstanding Sci. Contbn. award Soc. for Sci. Study of Reading, 1995; NIMH spl. fellow, 1971-72, NIH Fogarty Internat. fellow, 1991-92; grantee U.S. Office Edn., 1970-73, Nat. Inst. Edn., 1974-77, NIMH, 1974-84, NICHHD, 1983-89, 91-95, AT&T, 1986-89, NSF, 1989-91, 2000—, CIA, 1991-97, Army Rsch. Lab., 1996-2001, Yamaha Motor Corp., 1997-99, GM, 2002-; Fulbright scholar, Taiwan, 1998, Sr. scholar Chiang Chung Kuo Found., 1998-99. Fellow APA; mem. Am. Ednl. Rsch. Assn., Psychonomic Soc., Cognitive Sci. Soc. Mem. LDS Ch. Home: 2605 Berniece Dr Champaign IL 61822-7225 Office: Beckman Inst for Advanced Sci and Tech 405 N Mathews Ave Urbana IL 61801-2300 E-mail: gmcconk@uiuc.edu.

MCCONNAUGHEY, GEORGE CARLTON, JR. retired lawyer; b. Hillsboro, Ohio, Aug. 9, 1925; s. George Carlton and Nelle (Morse) McC.; m. Carolyn Schlieper, June 16, 1951; children: Elizabeth, Susan, Nancy. B.A., Denison U., 1949; LL.B., Ohio State U., 1951, J.D., 1967. Bar: Ohio 1951. Sole practice, Columbus; ptnr. McConnaughey & McConnaughey, 1954-57, McConnaughey, McConnaughey & Stradley, 1957-62, Laylin, McConnaughey & Stradley, 1962-67, George, Greek, King, McMahon & McConnaughey, 1967-79, McConnaughey, Stradley, Mone & Moul, 1979-81, Thompson, Hine & Flory (merger McConnaughey, Stradley, Mone & Moul with Thompson, Hine & Flory), Cleve., Columbus, Cin., Dayton and Washington, 1981-93; ret. ptnr. Thompson Hine LLP, Columbus, 1993—. Bd. dirs. N.Am. Broadcasting Co. (Sta. WMNI, WBZX and WEGE Radio); asst. atty. gen. State of Ohio, 1951-54. Pres. Upper Arlington (Ohio) Bd. Edn., 1967-69, Columbus Town Meeting Assn., 1974-76; chmn. Ohio Young Reps., 1956; U.S. presdl. elector, 1956; trustee Buckeye Boys Ranch, Columbus, 1967-73, 75-81, Upper Arlington Edn. Found., 1987-93; elder Covenant Presbyn. Ch., Columbus. With U.S. Army, 1943-45, ETO. Fellow Am. Bar Found., Ohio Bar Found., Columbus Bar Found.; mem. ABA, Ohio Bar Assn., Columbus Bar Assn., Am. Judicature Soc., Scioto Country Club, Athletic Club, Rotary, Masons. Home: 1993 Collingswood Rd Columbus OH 43221-3741 Office: Thompson Hine LLP One Columbus 10 W Broad St Ste 700 Columbus OH 43215-3435

MCCONNELL, E. HOY, II, advertising/public policy executive; b. Syracuse, N.Y., May 14, 1941; s. E. Hoy and Dorothy R. (Schmitt) McC.; m. Patricia Irwin, June 26, 1965; children: E. Hoy, III, Courtney. BA in Am. Studies magna cum laude, Yale U., 1963; MBA in Mktg, Harvard Bus. Sch., 1965. With Foote, Cone & Belding, 1965-76, v.p. account supr., 1971-72, 74-76, Phoenix, 1972-74; with D'Arcy-MacManus & Masius, Chgo., 1976-85, sr. v.p., dir. client services, then vice chmn., 1978-80, pres., 1980-84, chmn., 1984-85; mng. dir. D'Arcy Masius Benton & Bowles, 1986-96, also bd. dirs.; sr. v.p., account dir. Leo Burnett Co., 1996-98; exec. dir. Bus. and Profl. People for the Pub. Interest, 1999—. Bd. dirs. Evanston (Ill.) United Way, 1980-83, Evanston Youth Hockey Assn., 1980-89, pres. 1981-83; bd. dirs. Off-the-Street Club, 1980-90, Bus. Profl. People for Pub. Interest, 1981-83, 96—, v.p. 1984-89, pres. 1990-95; bd. dirs. Harvard Bus. Sch. Club, 1990-92, The Cradle Soc., 2000—; mem. Chgo. Coun. on Fgn. Rels., 1989-95. Mem. Am. Assn. Advt. Agys. (gov.-at-large Chgo. coun. 1984, sec. 1986, vice chmn. 1987, chmn. 1988-89), BBB Chgo. (mem. advt. rev. bd.), Glen View Country Club (bd. dirs. 1992-96), Dairymen's Country Club, Chgo. Club (membership comm. 1994-96), Yale Club Chgo. (bd. dirs. 1996-99). Democrat. Unitarian. Home: 2703 Colfax St Evanston IL 60201-2035 Office: BPI 25 E Washington St Ste 1515 Chicago IL 60602-1804 E-mail: hmcconnell@bpichicago.org.

MCCONNELL, JOHN HENDERSON, metal and plastic products manufacturing executive, professional sports team executive; b. New Manchester, W.Va., May 10, 1923; s. Paul Alexander and Mary Louise (Mayhew) McC.; m. Margaret Jane Rardin, Feb. 8, 1946; children—Margaret Louise, John Porter B.A. in Bus., Mich. State U., 1949; Dr. Law (hon.), Ohio U., 1981. Sales trainee Weirton Steel Co., W.Va., 1950-52; sales mgmt. Shenango-Steel Co., Farrell, Pa., 1952-54; founder, chmn. bd. Worthington Industries, Inc., Columbus, Ohio, 1955—, also past CEO; bd. dirs. Pitts. Pirates; owner, NHL Franchise Columbus Blue Jackets, Worthington, Ohio, 1998—. Dir. Alltel Corp., Hudson, Ohio, Anchor Hocking, Lancaster, Ohio, Nat. City Corp., Cleve. Bd. dirs. Children's Hosp., Columbus; trustee Ashland Coll., Ohio. Served with USN, 1943-46 Recipient Ohio Gov.'s award Gov. State of Ohio, 1980; Horatio Alger award Horatio Alger Assn., 1983; named Outstanding Chief Exec. Officer, Fin. World Mag., 1981 Mem. Columbus Area C. of C. (chmn. 1978) Republican. Presbyterian. Clubs: Golf (New Albany, Ohio) (pres. 1983—); Brookside Country (Columbus) (pres. 1964-65). Lodge: Masons Avocations: flying; golf. Address: Columbus Blue Jackets 150 E Wilson Bridge Rd Ste 235 Columbus OH 43085-2328 Office: Worthington Industries Inc 1205 Dearborn Dr Columbus OH 43085-4769

MCCONNELL, JOHN P. metal and plastics products executive; Gen. laborer Worthington Industries, Columbus, Ohio, 1975; with sales, ops., personnel; vice chmn. bd., 1992; CEO, 1993—; chmn., 1996—. Office: Worthington Industries 1205 Dearborn Dr Columbus OH 43085

MCCONNELL, JOHN THOMAS, newspaper executive, publisher; b. Peoria, Ill., May 1, 1945; s. Golden A. and Margaret (Lyon) McC.; 1 child, Justin. B.A., U. Ariz., 1967. Mgr. Fast Printing Co., Peoria, 1970-71; mgmt. trainee Quad-Cities Times, Davenport, Iowa, 1972-73; asst. gen. mgr., then v.p., gen. mgr. Peoria Jour. Star, 1973-81, pub., 1981—, pres., 1987—; v.p. The Copley Press, Inc., Peoria, 1997—. Bd. dirs. Peoria Downtown Devel. Council, Peoria Devel. Corp.; past trustee Methodist Hosp., Peoria. Served with USAR, 1967-69. Named Young Man of Year Peoria Jaycees, 1979 Mem. Peoria Advt. and Selling Club, Peoria C. of C. Congregationalist. Club: Peoria Country. Office: Peoria Jour Star Inc 1 News Plz Peoria IL 61643-0001 E-mail: mac@pjstar.com.

MCCONNELL, MIKE, radio personality; b. Media, Pa. Radio host 700 WLW, Cin., 1983—. Office: 700 WLW 1111 St Gregory St Cincinnati OH 45202*

MCCONNELL, WILLIAM THOMPSON, commercial banker; b. Zanesville, Ohio, Aug. 8, 1933; s. William Gerald and Mary Gladys McC.; m. Jane Charlotte Cook, Aug. 25, 1956; children: Jennifer Wynne, William Gerald. BA, Denison U., 1955; MBA, Northwestern U., 1959. Pres. Park Nat. Bank, Newark, 1979-83, pres., chief exec. officer, 1983-93, chmn., chief exec. officer, 1993-98, also bd. dirs., chmn., 1999—; pres., chief exec. officer Park Nat. Corp., 1987-94, chmn., CEO, 1994-98, chmn., 1999—. Mem. Newark Area C. of C. (past pres., dir. 1977-83), Ohio Bankers Assn. (pres., chmn. 1981-83), Am. Bankers Assn. (pres. 1997-98). Office: Park Nat Bank PO Box 3500 Newark OH 43058-3500

MCCONNELL SERIO, SUZIE THERESA, basketball player; b. Pitts., July 29, 1966; married; 4 children. BA, Pa. State U., 1988. Coach Oakland Cath. High Sch., Pitts.; guard Cleve. Rockers, WNBA, 1998—. Recipient Gold medal Olympic Games, Barcelona, 1988, Bronze medal Olympic Games, Seoul, 1992, Sportsmanship award WNBA, 1998, Newcomer award, 1998; named to All-WNBA 1st team, 1988. Office: Cleveland Rockers 1 Center Ct Cleveland OH 44115-4001

MCCONVILLE, RITA JEAN, finance executive; b. Chgo., July 7, 1958; d. Daniel Joseph and Rosemary (Smolinski) McC. BA, Northwestern U., 1979; MBA, U. Chgo., 1982. CPA, Ill. Fin. analyst Miami Valley Hosp., Dayton, Ohio, 1982-85; sr. cons. Health Facilities Corp., Northfield, Ill., 1985-87; sr. fin. analyst Lyphomed, Inc., Rosemont, 1987-88, mgr. fin. planning, 1988-90; controller Videocart, Inc., Chgo., 1990-93, OptionCare, Inc., Bannockburn, Ill., 1993-97; v.p., CFO, sec. Akorn, Inc., Buffalo Grove, 1997—. Mem. Ill. CPA Soc. Office: Akorn Inc 2500 Millbrook Dr Buffalo Grove IL 60089-4694

MCCOOLE, ROBERT F. construction company executive; b. St. Louis, Mar. 26, 1950; BS, St. Louis U., 1972. Project mgr. J.S. Alberici Constrn. Co. Inc., St. Louis, 1981-84, v.p. bus. devel., 1987-93, sr. v.p. bus. devel., 1993-96, pres., 1996—. Mem. Assoc. Gen. Contractors (chair 1997—). Office: JS Alberici Constrn Co Inc 2150 Kienlen Ave Saint Louis MO 63121-5505

MCCORMACK, MARK HUME, advertising executive, lawyer; b. Chgo., Nov. 6, 1930; s. Ned and Grace (Wolfe) McC.; m. Nancy Ann Breckenridge, Oct. 9, 1954 (div.); children: Breck, Todd, Leslie; m. Betsy Nagelsen, 1986; 1 child, Maggie. BA, William and Mary Coll., 1951; LLB, Yale U., 1954; PhD (hon.), St. Lawrence U., 1991; LHD, Coll. William and Mary, 1997. Assoc. Arter and Hadden, Cleve., 1957-63, ptnr., 1963—; pres., CEO IMG, The Mark McCormack Group of Cos., Cleve., 1964—. Editor: The World of Professional Golf, 1967-2000; author: Arnie, The Evolution of a Legend, 1967, Arnie, The Man and the Legend, 1967 (British edit.), Arnie, What They Don't Teach You at Harvard Business School, 1984, The Terrible Truth About Lawyers, 1987, What They Still Don't Teach You at Harvard Business School, 1989, The 110% Solution, 1991, Hit the Ground Running, 1993, Getting Results for Dummies, 2000, Staying Street Smart in the Internet Age, 2000. With U.S. Army, 1955-56. Decorated Order of the Polar Star (Sweden). Mem. Cleve. Bar Assn., Author's Guild, Royal and Ancient Club (St. Andrews, Scotland), Union Club, Pepper Pike Club, The Club (Cleve.), Isleworth Club, Deepdale Club, All England Club, Theta Delta Chi. Office: IMG 1360 E 9th St Ste 100 Cleveland OH 44114-1730

MCCORMACK, MICHAEL, state supreme court justice; b. Omaha, July 20, 1939; JD, Creighton U., 1963. Asst. pub. defender, Douglas County, Nebr., 1963-66; pvt. practice Omaha, 1966-97; justice Nebr. Supreme Ct., 1997—. Office: State Capitol Bldg Rm 2218 Lincoln NE 68509 also: PO Box 98910 Lincoln NE 68509*

MCCORMACK, MICHAEL JOSEPH, foundation administrator; b. St. Ignatius, Mont., July 19, 1952; s. Richard Joseph and Leona Julianna (Wasinger) McC.; m. Eileen Marie Turro, June 21, 1997. BA, Harvard U., 1974. Co-founder World Hello Day, 1973—. Author: Senti and Pigasso, 1997, Farewell Fillmore High, 1999; actor (play) My Antonia, 1994, Glory Years, 1995, Tony 'n Tina's Wedding, 1998-99, Farewell Fillmore High, 1999; (film) The Chess Murders, 1996, What Happened to Tully?, 1999; represented in permanent collections Internat. Mus. Peace and Solidarity, Samarkand, Uzbekistan, 1993. Recipient Freedoms Found. award Freedoms Found. Valley Forge, 1970. Mem. Signet Soc., Theatre Arts Guild, Alleged Perpetrators Improv, Nebr. Film, Video and TV Assn. Roman Catholic. Avocations: song writing, reading, violin, art, history. Office: World Hello Day PO Box 993 Omaha NE 68101-0993

MCCORMACK, ROBERT CORNELIUS, investment banker; b. N.Y.C., Nov. 7, 1939; m. Mary Lester, Dec. 14, 1963; children: Robert Cornelius Jr., Walter, Scott. BA, U. N.C., 1962; MBA, U. Chgo., 1968. V.p. Dillon Read & Co. Inc., 1968-81; mng. dir. Morgan Stanley & Co., Inc., Chgo., 1981-87; dep. asst sec. def. prodn. support U.S. Dept. Def., Washington, 1987-88, dep. under sec. def. indsl. and internat. programs, 1988-89, acting dep. under sec. of def. acquisition, 1989-90, asst. sec. Navy fin. mgmt., 1990-93; founding ptnr. Trident Capital L.P., Chgo., 1993—. Served to lt. USNR, 1963-66. Office: Trident Capital LP 272 E Deerpath Rd Ste 304 Lake Forest IL 60045-1947

MCCORMICK, EDWARD JAMES, JR. lawyer; b. Toledo, May 11, 1921; s. Edward James and Josephine (Beck) McC.; m. Mary Jane Blank, Jan. 27, 1951; children: Mary McCormick Krueger, Edward James III, Patrick William, Michael J. B.S., John Carroll U., 1943; J.D., Western Res. U., 1948. Bar: Ohio 1948, U.S. Supreme Ct. 1980. Mem. teaching staff St. Vincent Hosp. Sch. Nursing, 1951-67. Pvt. practice 1948—; Trustee Toledo Small Bus. Assn., 1950-75, pres., 1954-55, 56-58, 67-68; trustee Goodwill Industries Toledo, 1961-74, chmn. meml. gifts com., mem. exec. com., 1965-70; trustee Lucas County unit Am. Cancer Soc., 1950-61, sec., 1953, v.p., 1954-56, pres., 1957-58; founder, incorporator, sec., trustee Cancer Cytology Research Fund Toledo, Inc., 1956-79; trustee Ohio Cerebral Palsy Assn., 1963-70; incorporator, sec., trustee N.W. Ohio Clin. Engring. Ctr., 1972-74; trustee Friendly Ctr., 1973-83, Ohio Blind Assn., 1970-79; founder-incorporator, trustee, sec. Western Lake Erie Hist. Soc., 1978-85; mem. Toledo Deanery Diocesan Coun. Cath. Men; asst. gen. counsel U.S. Power and Sail Squadrons; life mem. China, Burma and India Vets. Assn., Inc. 1st lt. U.S. Army, 1942-46, USAR, 1946-52. Named Outstanding Young Man of Yr., Toledo Jr. C. of C., 1951; Man of Nation, Woodmen of World, Omaha, 1952. Fellow Ohio State Assn.; mem. ABA, Ohio Bar Assn. (chmn. Am. citizenship com. 1958-67, mem. pub. rels. com. 1967-72, estate planning, probate and trust law com.), Toledo Bar Assn. (chmn. pub. rels. com. 1979, mem. grievance com. 1974-92, chmn. probate, estate planning and trust law com. 1986-90, Disting. Svc. award in memory Robert A. Kelb, Esq. 1993), Lucas County Bar Assn. (chmn. Am. citizenship com.), Assn. Trial Lawyers Am., Am. Judicature Soc., Am. Arbitration Assn., Conf. Pvt. Orgns. (sec.-treas.), Toledo C. of C., Toledo Yacht Club (mem. com. 1970-71), Toledo Torch Club, Blue Gavel, Elks (grand esteemed leading knight 1964-65, mem. grand forum 1965-70), Lions (trustee, legal advisor Ohio Eye Research Found. 1956-70; pres. 1957-58, chmn. permanent membership com. 1961-85, hon. mem. 1984, pres. 1957, A.B. Snyder award 1979), Ky. Col. Deceased. Office: 2828 W Central Ave Ste 10 Toledo OH 43606-3078

MCCORMICK, MICHAEL D. lawyer; b. Vincennes, Ind., Mar. 18, 1948; m. Margaret A. McCormick; children: Claire E., Brooks R. AB, Duke U., 1970; JD, Ind. U., 1980. V.p. I & S McDaniel Inc., Vincennes, 1970-77; ptnr. Scopelitis & Garvin, Indpls., 1980-83; pres. Wales Transp. Co., Dallas, 1983-85; v.p., gen. counsel Overland Express Inc., Indpls., 1985-87, Bindley Western Industries Inc., Indpls., 1987—. Mem. ABA, Ind. Bar Assn., Indpls. Bar Assn.

MCCORMICK, WILLIAM THOMAS, JR. electric and gas company executive; b. Washington, Sept. 12, 1944; s. William Thomas and Lucy Valentine (Offutt) McC.; m. Ann Loretta du Mais, June 13, 1969; children: Christopher, Patrick. B.S., Cornell U., 1966; Ph.D., M.I.T., 1969. Mem. staff Inst. for Def. Analysis, Arlington, Va., 1969-72; mem. staff Office of Sci. and Tech., Exec. office of the Pres., Washington, 1972-73; sr. staff mem. Energy Policy Office, The White House, 1973-74; chief sci. and energy tech. br. Office Mgmt. and Budget, Exec. Office of the Pres., 1974-75; dir. commercialization U.S. Energy Research and Devel. Adminstrn., 1975-76; v.p. policy and govt. relations Am. Gas Assn., 1976-78; v.p., asst. to chmn. Am. Natural Resources Co., Detroit, 1978-80; exec. v.p. Mich. Wis. Pipeline Co., Am. Natural Resources System, 1980-82; pres. Am. Natural Resources Co., 1982-85; chmn., chief exec. officer Consumers Power Co., Jackson, Mich., 1985-92, chmn., 1992—; chmn., CEO CMS Energy Corp. Bd. dirs. Bank One Corp., Rockwell Inst., Schlumberger Ltd. Prin. author, editor: Commercialization of Synthetic Fuels in the U.S, 1975. Bd. dirs. McGregor Fund, St. John Hosp. Alfred P. Sloan scholar, 1962-66 Mem. Econ. Club Detroit (bd. dirs.), Detroit Athletic Club, Country Club Detroit, Detroit Club. Roman Catholic. Office: CMS Energy Corporation Fairlane Plaza South Suite 1100 330 Town Center Dr Dearborn MI 48126-2738 also: CMS Energy Corp 330 Town Center Dr Ste 1100 Dearborn MI 48126-2711

MCCOTTER, THADDEUS G. state legislator; b. Livonia, Mich., Aug. 22, 1965; s. Dennis and Joan McCotter; m . Rita Michel; children: George, Timothy, Emilia. BA summa cum laude, U. Detroit, 1987, JD, 1990. Bar: Mich. 1991. Trustee Schoolcraft C.C., 1989; commr. Wayne County, Mich., 1992-98; mem. 9th dist. Mich. Senate, Lansing, 1998—. Rep. precinct del., 1986; chair Wayne County Rep. com. Republican. Office: Farnum Bldg PO Box 30036 Lansing MI 48909-7536

MCCOY, BERNARD ROGERS, television anchor; b. Cortland, N.Y., Dec. 24, 1955; s. Donald Richard and Vivian Alicia (Rogers) McC.; m. Joanne Louise Lohr, Apr. 29, 1989; children: Emily Louise, Marian Alicia. BS in Journalism, U. Kans., 1979; M in Telecomm. Mgmt., Mich. State U., 1996. Mgmt. trainee Garney Constrn. Co., Kansas City, Mo., 1979-80; reporter, anchor Sta. WIBW-AM-FM-TV, Topeka, 1979-80, Sta. KCTV-TV, Kansas City, 1980-89; anchor Sta. WKBD-TV, Detroit, 1989-93, Sta. WILX-TV, NBC, Lansing, Mich., 1993-99, Sta. WBNS-TV, CBS, Columbus, Ohio, 1999—. Chmn. Earthwork Environ. Adv. Bd., Southfield, Mich., 1989—. Bd. dirs. Judson Ctr.; celebrity fundraiser Salvation Army, Detroit, 1989, March of Dimes, Detroit, 1989, hon. co-chair Mid-Mich. WalkAmerica, 1996; celebrity fundraiser Cancer Soc., Detroit, 1989, The Sanctuary, Royal Oak, Mich., 1989; mem. YMCA, 1991—; mem. Sparrow Hosp. Children's Miracle Network Com., 1996, Mid-Mich. Environ. Action Coun., 1996; project coord. News-10 Computer Edn., 1996. Recipient Spot News awards Mo. Broadcasters Assn., 1987, Kansas City Press Club, 1987, Kans. Broadcasters Assn., 1987, Disting. Environ. Reporting awards Detroit Audubon Soc., 1991, Mich. Audubon Soc., 1992, Ben East award Mich. United Conservation Clubs, 1991, 93, Mich. Outstanding Individual Reporting award UPI, 1991, Emmy award for Outstanding Reporting in Mich., 1994, Gen. Excellence in TV Reporting award Mich. AP, 1999, Disting. Svc. medal Mich. Dept. Mil. Affairs, Wolverine Guard award for media excelence Mich. N.G. Mem. Nat. Acad. of TV Arts and Scis. (bd. dirs. Mich. chpt., Dising. Svc. award 1997), Nat. Geo. Soc., Soc. Environ. Journalists (charter, planner nat. conf.). Avocations: back-packing, golf, fishing, tennis, running. Office: WBNS-TV 770 Twin Rivers Dr Columbus OH 43215 E-mail: rmc@wbnslotv.com.

MCCOY, FREDERICK JOHN, retired plastic surgeon; b. McPherson, Kans., Jan. 17, 1916; s. Merle D. and Mae (Tennis) McC.; m. Mary Bock, May 17, 1972; children: Judith, Frederick John, Patricia, Melissa, Steven. BS, U. Kans., 1938, MD, 1942. Diplomate Am. Bd. Plastic Surgery (dir. 1973-79, chmn. 1979). Intern Lucas County Hosp., Toledo, 1942-43; resident in plastic surgery U. Tex. Med. Sch., Galveston, 1946; preceptorship in surgery Grand Rapids, Mich., 1947-50; practice medicine specializing in plastic and reconstructive surgery Kansas City, Mo., 1950-93; staff St. Mary's Hosp., 1950-83, St. Joseph's Hosp., 1950—, N. Kansas City Meml. Hosp., 1955—; mem. staff, chief plastic surgery Kansas City Gen. Hosp. and Med. Center, 1952-72, Children's Mercy Hosp., 1954-93, Research Hosp., 1950—, St. Luke's Hosp., 1951—, Baptist Hosp., 1958—, Menorah Hosp., 1950—; chief div. plastic surgery Truman Med. Ctr., 1972-91; chmn. maxillo-facial surgery U. Kansas City Sch. Dentistry, 1950-57; assoc. prof. surgery U. Mo. Med. Sch., Kansas City, 1964-69, clin. prof. surgery, 1969—; pres. McCoy Enterprises, Kansas City, Mo. Contbr. articles to profl. jours.; editor: Year Book of Plastic and Reconstructive Surgery, 1971-88. Bd. govs. Kansas City Mus., 1959-93, pres., 1973-74. Served to maj. M.C. U.S. Army, 1943-46. Mem. ACS (pres. Mo. chpt. 1973), AMA, Am. Acad. Pediatrics, Am. Soc. Plastic and Reconstructive Surgeons (sec. 1969-73, dir. 1973-76, pres. 1976, chmn. bd. 1977, Spl. Achievement award 1988), Am. Soc. Pediat. Plastic Surgeons, Pan Pacific Surg. Soc., Singleton Surg. Soc. (v.p. 1965), Am. Assn. Plastic Surgeons (founder plastic surgery rsch. coun.), Internat. Soc. Aesthetic Plastic Surgery, Am. Soc. Aesthetic Plastic Surgery, Jackson County Med. Soc. (pres. 1964-65), Kansas City Southwest Clin. Soc. (pres. 1971), Mo. Med. Assn. (v.p. 1975), Internat. Coll. Surgeons (v.p. 1969), Royal Soc. Medicine (London), U. Tex. Sys. Chancellors Coun., Kansas City C. of C., Conservation Fedn. Mo., Natural Sci. Soc. (founder, chmn. 1973), Citizens Assn. Kansas City, Explorer's Club, Mission Hills Country Club, Boone and Crocket Club, Phi Delta Theta, Nu Sigma Nu. Republican. Mem. Christian Ch. Home: 5814 Mission Dr Shawnee Mission KS 66208-1139 Office: 801 W 47th St Ste 421 Kansas City MO 64112-1253

MCCOY, JOHN BONNET, retired banker; b. Columbus, Ohio, June 11, 1943; s. John Gardner and Jeanne Newlove (Bonnet) McC.; m. Jane Deborah Taylor, Apr. 21, 1968; children: Tracy Bonnet, Paige Taylor, John Taylor. BA, Williams Coll., 1965; MBA, Stanford U., 1967; LLD (hon.), Williams Coll., 1991; D of Bus. Adminstrn. (hon.), Ohio State U., 1993; LLD (hon.), Kenyon Coll., 1994. With Banc One Corp., Columbus NA, Columbus, Ohio, 1970—, banking officer, 1970-73, v.p., 1973-77, pres., 1977-83; pres., COO Banc One Corp., 1983-84, pres., CEO, 1984-87, chmn., CEO, 1987-99, also bd. dirs., now chmn., CEO Chgo., 1999. Pres., COO Banc One Corp., Columbus, Ohio, 1983-84, pres., CEO, 1984-87, chmn. CEO, 1987—, also bd. dirs.; pres. Bank One Trust Co., 1979-81; bd. dirs. Cardinal Health, Inc., Fed. Nat. Mortgage Assn., Ameritech Corp., Tenneco Inc.; fed. adv. coun. Fed. Res. Sys., 1991-93. Active Boy Scouts Am.; trustee, chmn. bd. dirs. Kenyon Coll.; trustee Stanford U., Battelle Meml. Inst.; bd. dirs. Sr. PGA Tour; pres. Columbus Area Growth Found.; chmn. Capitol South Urban Redevel. Corp. Capt. USAF, 1967-70. Recipient Ernest C. Arbuckle award Stanford U., 1994. Mem. Columbus C. of C. (past chmn., trustee), Am. Bankers Assn., Bankers Roundtable (bd. dirs. 1989-94), Assn. Bank Holding Cos., Young Pres. Orgn. (chmn. Columbus chpt. 1982-83), Cypress Point Club, Seminole Golf Club, Links Club N.Y.C. Episcopalian. Office: Banc One Corp 1st National Plz Ste 0895 Chicago IL 60670-0001

MCCOY, JOHN JOSEPH, lawyer; b. Cin., Mar. 15, 1952; s. Raymond F. and Margaret T. (Hohmann) McC. BS in Math. summa cum laude, Xavier U., 1974; JD, U. Chgo., 1977. Bar: Ohio 1977, D.C. 1980. Ptnr. Taft, Stettinius & Hollister, Cin., 1977—. Lectr. Greater Cin. C. of C., 1984. Pro bono rep. Jr. Achievement Greater Cin., 1978; fund raiser Dan Beard coun. Boy Scouts Am., 1983; fund raising team leader Cin. Regatta, Cin. Ctr. Devel. Disorders, 1983; account mgr. United Appeal, Cin., 1984; mem. green areas trust adv. com. Village of Indian Hill, 1994-98. Mem. ABA, Ohio State Bar Assn. (banking, comml. and bankruptcy law com., corp. law com., fed. ct. practice com.), Cin. Bar Assn. (fed. cts., common pleas cts. and negligence law coms., trustee Vol. Lawyers for the Poor Found. 1994—, chmn. 1996-97), Cin. Inn. of Ct. (barrister 1984-86), Cin. Athletic Club (pres. bd. trustees 1986-89, nominating com. 1989—), Rhodesian Ridgeback Club of the U.S. (bd. dirs. 2000—).

MCCOY, MARILYN, university official; b. Providence, Mar. 18, 1948; d. James Francis and Eleanor (Regan) McC.; m. Charles R. Thomas, Jan. 28, 1983. BA in Econs. cum laude, Smith Coll., 1970; M in Pub. Policy, U. Mich., 1972. Dir. Nat. Ctr. for Higher Edn. Mgmt. Systems, Boulder, Colo., 1972-80; dir. planning and policy devel. U. Colo., 1981-85; v.p. adminstrn. and planning Northwestern U., Evanston, Ill., 1985—. Trustee One Group Funds. Co-author: Financing Higher Education in the Fifty States, 1976, 3d edit., 1982. Bd. dirs. Evanston Northwestern HealthCare, 1988—, Mather Found., 1995—. Mem. Am. Assn. for Higher Edn., Soc. for Coll. and Univ. Planning (pres., v.p., sec., bd. dirs. 1980—), Assn. for Instnl. Rsch. (pres., v.p., exec. com., publs. bd. 1978-87), Chgo. Network (chmn. 1992-93), Chgo. Econ. Club. Home: 1100 N Lake Shore Dr Chicago IL 60611-1070 Office: Northwestern U 633 Clark St Evanston IL 60208-0001

MCCOY, MATTHEW WILLIAM, state legislator, human resource manager; b. Des Moines, Mar. 29, 1966; s. William Paul and Mary Ann (Kenneally) McC.; m. Jennifer Ann Stitt, May 29, 1993; 1 son, Jack William. BA in History and Polit. Sci., Briar Cliff Coll., 1988. V.p. industry rels. Ruan Transp. Mgmt. Systems, Des Moines, 1989-92; mem. Iowa Ho. of Reps., 1992-96, Iowa Senate from 34th dist., Des Moines, 1996—. Bd. dirs. Polk County (Iowa) Conservation Bd.; vice chair YMCA Bd. Mgrs.; mem. Youth Emergency Svcs. & Shelter Bd.; fundraising chair, Boy Scouts of Am. Democrat. Roman Catholic. E-mail: mmccoy@ruan.com. Also: mmcoy@mccoyfor congress.com. E-mail: mmccoy@ruan.com.

MCCOY, MICHAEL J. food products company executive; BS in Acctg., Loras Coll., 1969. With Hormel Foods Corp., Austin, Minn., 1992—, mem. staff treas.' office, co. treas., 1996-97, v.p., 1997-2000, sr. v.p. adminstrn., CFO, 2000—. Office: Hormel Foods 1 Hormel Pl Austin MN 55912-3680

MCCRACKEN, ELLIS W., JR. lawyer, corporation executive; B.A., Lebanon Valley Coll., 1963; LL.B., St. John's U., 1967. Bar: N.Y. 1967, N.J. 1969, Ohio 1972, Mo. 1993. Primary contract atty. foods div. Borden, Inc., 1970-74; assoc. Milbank, Tweed, Hadley & McCloy, 1967-70; v.p., gen. counsel Campbell Taggart, Inc., Dallas, 1980-92, v.p. gen. coun. Anheuser-Busch Co., Saint Louis, 1992—. Office: Anheuser-Busch Co One Busch Pl Saint Louis MO 63118

MCCRACKEN, THOMAS JAMES, JR. lawyer; b. Chgo., Oct. 27, 1952; s. Thomas J. Sr. and Eileen (Brophy) McC.; m. Peggy A. Jamrok; children: Catherine, Michael, Amanda, Quinn. BA, Marquette U., 1974; JD, Loyola U., 1977. Bar: Ill. 1977, U.S. Dist. Ct. (no. dist.) Ill., U.S. Ct. Appeals (7th cir.) 1984. Asst. state's atty. DuPage County State's Atty.'s Office, Wheaton, Ill., 1977-81; assoc. atty. McCracken & Walsh, Chgo., 1981-84; ptnr. McCracken, Walsh deLaVan & Hetler, 1984—. Commr. Nat. Conf. of Commns. on Uniform State Laws, 1989—; bd. dirs. Oak Trust and Savs. Bank, Chgo. Contbr. articles to profl. jours. State rep. Ill. Gen. Assembly, Springfield, Ill., 1983-93, state senator, 1993; chmn. Regional Trans. Authority, Chgo., 1993—. Named Top Ten Legislators Chgo. Mag., 1990. Mem. Chgo. Bar Assn., Ill. State Bar Assn. Avocations: skiing, fishing, hunting, coaching children's sports. Office: McCracken Walsh deLaVan & Hetler 134 N La Salle St Ste 600 Chicago IL 60602-1079

MCCRAE, KEITH R. medical educator, researcher; b. Springfield, Mass., Dec. 4, 1956; m. Jo Ann; children: Brett, Kristen Ann. BA in Biochemistry summa cum laude, Dartmouth Coll., 1978; MD, Duke U., 1982. Diplomate Am. Bd. Internal Medicine, Am. Bd. Med. Oncology, Am. Bd. Hematology. Resident in internal medicine Duke U. Med. Ctr., Durham, N.C., 1982-85; fellow in hematology and oncology U. Pa., Phila., 1985-89, postdoctoral fellow, 1986-88, co-dir. clin. coagulation lab., 1991-93, dir. clin. coagulation course, 1992-93; rsch. assoc. U. Pa. Sch. Medicine, 1989, lectr. bridge curriculum, 1989-93, asst. prof. medicine, 1990-93, asst. prof. pathology and lab. medicine, 1991-93; lectr. basic curriculum U. Pa. Dental Sch., 1989-92; attending physician Hosp. of U. Pa., 1989-93, Phila. VA Hosp., 1990-93, Temple U. Hosp., 1993—; asst. prof. medicine Temple U. Sch. Medicine, 1993-96, lectr. bridge curriculum, 1993—, assoc. prof. medicine, 1996—. Tchg. attending hematology consult svc. U. Pa., 1989-93, tchg. attending hematology oncology inpatient unit, 1992-93; with hematology/oncology outpatient clinic, 1989-93; attending staff mem. hematology consult svc. Temple U. Sch. Medicine, 1993—, attendin staff mem. hematology sickle cell outpatient clinic, 1993—, attending staff mem. gen. internal medicine svc., 1993. Co-author (with M.D. Feldman) Blood: Hemostasis, Transfusion and Alternatives in the Perioperative Period, 1995; jour. reviewer Blood, 1990—, Thrombosis and Haemostasis, 1991—, Annals of Internal Medicine, 1991—, Jour. Biol. Chem., 1992—, Placenta, 1992—, Jour. Exptl. Medicine, 1992—, Platelets, 1992—, Jour. Allergy and Clin. Immunology, 1992—, Cancer Rsch., 1993—, Am. Jour. Hematology, 1993—, Jour. Clin. Oncology, 1994—, Jour. Histochemistry and Cytochemistry, 1994—, Am. Jour. Physiol., 1995—, Thrombosis Rsch., 1995—; contbr. articles to profl. jours., chpts. to books; lectr. in field. Recipient Rsch. award Am. Diabetes Assn., 1995. Mem. AAAS, Am. Heart Assn. (mem. thrombosis coun. 1994—, mem. arteriosclerosclerosis coun. 1994—, mem. southeastern Pa. peer rev. com. B 1995—), Am. Soc. Hematology, Am. Fedn. Clin. Rsch., Phi Beta Kappa. Office: Case Western Res U Sch Med 2109 Adelbert Rd Cleveland OH 44106-2624

MCCRAY, CURTIS LEE, university president; b. Wheatland, Ind., Jan. 29, 1938; s. Bert and Susan McCray; m. Mary Joyce Macdonald, Sept. 10, 1960; children: Leslie, Jennifer, Meredith. BA, Knox Coll., Galesburg, Ill., 1960; postgrad., U. Pa., 1960-61; PhD, U. Nebr., 1968. Chmn. dept. English Saginaw Valley Coll., University Center, Mich., 1972-73, dean arts and scis., 1973-75, v.p. acad. affairs, 1975-77; provost, v.p. acad. affairs Govs. State U., Chgo., 1977-82; pres. U. North Fla., Jacksonville, 1982-88, Calif. State U., Long Beach, 1988-93, Millikin U., Decatur, Ill., 1993-98, Nat. Lewis U., Chgo., 1998—. Bd. dirs. Jacksonville United Way, 1982-88, campaign chmn., 1987; bd. dirs. Sta. WJCT Channel 7 and Stereo 90, Jacksonville, 1982-88, Jacksonville Art Mus., 1983-88, Meml. Med. Ctr., Jacksonville, 1983-88, Jacksonville Cmty. Coun. Inc., 1982-88, Arts Assembly Jacksonville, 1984-88, Jacksonville Urban League, 1985-88; hon. dir. Jacksonville Symphony Assn., 1983; mem. Dame Point Bridge Commn., Jacksonville, 1982; mem. Jacksonville High Tech. Task Force, 1982; chmn. SUS High Tech. and Industry Coun., 1986-88; mem. state rels. and undergrad. edn. com. Am. Assn. State Colls. and Univs., 1985-88. Woodrow Wilson fellow, 1960; Johnson fellow, 1966; George F. Baker scholar, 1956; Ford Found. grantee, 1969; recipient Landee award for excellence in tchg. Saginaw State Coll., 1972. Mem. AAUP, Torch Club. Office: 122 S Michigan Ave Chicago IL 60603-6191

MCCUE, JUDITH W. lawyer; b. Phila., Apr. 7, 1948; d. Emanuel Leo and Rebecca (Raffel) Weiss; m. Howard M. McCue III, Apr. 3, 1971; children: Howard, Leigh. BA cum laude, U. Pa., 1969; JD, Harvard U., 1972. Bar: Ill. 1972, U.S. Tax Ct. 1984. Ptnr. McDermott, Will & Emery, Chgo., 1995—. Dir. Schawk, Inc., Des Plaines, Ill.; past pres. Chgo. Estate Planning Coun. Trustee Chgo. Symphony Orch., 1995—, vice chair, 1998—2001. Fellow Am. Coll. Trust and Estate Counsel (com. chair 1991-94, 98—, regent 1992-2000, treas. 2002—); mem. Chgo. Bar Assn. (chmn. probate practice com. 1984-85, chmn. fed. estate and gift tax divsn. fed. tax com. 1988-89). Office: McDermott Will & Emery 227 W Monroe St Ste 3100 Chicago IL 60606-5096 E-mail: jmccue@mwe.com.

MCCUEN, JOHN FRANCIS, JR. lawyer; b. N.Y.C., Mar. 11, 1944; s. John Francis and Elizabeth Agnes McCuen; m. Christine McCuen; children: Sarah, Mary, John. AB, U. Notre Dame, 1966; JD, U. Detroit, 1969. Bar: Mich. 1970, Fla. 1970, Ohio 1978. Legal counsel Kelsey-Hayes Co., Romulus, Mich., 1970-77; corp. counsel Sheller-Globe Corp., Toledo, 1977-79, v.p., gen. counsel, 1979-86, sec., 1982-87, sr. v.p. gen. counsel, 1986-89; ptnr. Marshall & Melhorn, Toledo, 1989-92; pvt. practice Law Offices John F. McCuen, 1992-93; counsel Butzel Long, Ann Arbor, Mich., 1994; v.p. legal Kelsey Hayes Co., Livonia, 1994-98, v.p., gen. counsel, 1998-99; of counsel Butzel Long, 1999—2001. Trustee Kidney Found. N.W. Ohio, 1979-88, pres., 1984-86. Mem. ABA, Fla. Bar, Mich. Bar, Forest Lake Country Club. Home: 1668 Trading Post Ln Bloomfield Hills MI 48302-1868

MCCULLOH, JUDITH MARIE, editor; b. Spring Valley, Ill., Aug. 16, 1935; d. Henry A. and Edna Mae (Traub) Binkele; m. Leon Royce McCulloh, Aug. 26, 1961. BA, Ohio Wesleyan U., 1956; MA, Ohio State U., 1957; PhD, Ind. U., 1970. Asst. to dir. Archives of Traditional Music, Bloomington, Ind., 1964-65; asst. editor U. Ill. Press, Champaign, 1972-77, assoc. editor, 1977-82, sr. editor, 1982-85, exec. editor, 1985—, dir. devel., 1992—; asst. dir., 1997—. Advisor John Edwards Meml. Forum, Los Angeles, 1973—. Mem. Editorial Bd. Jour. Am. Folklore, Washington, 1986-90; co-editor Stars of Country Music, 1975; editor (LP) Green Fields of Ill., 1963, (LP) Hell-Bound Train, 1964, Ethnic Recordings in America, 1982; gen. editor Music in American Life series. Trustee Am. Folklife Ctr., Libr. of Congress, Washington, 1986-2004, chair, 1990-92, 96-98. Fulbright grantee, 1958-59; NDEA grantee, 1961, 62-63; grantee Nat. Endowment for the Humanities, 1978; recipient Disting. Achievement citation Ohio Wesleyan U. Alumni Assn., Disting. Svc. award Soc. for Am. Music. Fellow: Am. Folklore Soc. (exec. bd. 1974—79, pres. 1986—87, exec. bd. 2001—); mem.: Am. Anthropol. Assn., Women in Scholarly Pub., Soc. Am. Music (1st v.p. 1989—93), Soc. for Ethnomusicology (treas. 1982—86). Democrat. Office: U Ill Press 1325 S Oak St Champaign IL 61820-6903 E-mail: jmmccull@uillinois.edu.

MCCULLOUGH, RICHARD LAWRENCE, advertising agency executive; b. Chgo., Dec. 1, 1937; s. Francis John and Sadie Beatrice McCullough; m. Julia Louise Kreimer, May 6, 1961; children: Stephen, Jeffery, Julie. BS, Marquette U., 1959. Commd. U.S. Army, 1959, advance through grades to sgt., 1966; account exec. Edward H. Weiss Advt., Chgo., 1960-66; account supr. Doyle Dane Bernbach, N.Y.C., 1966-68; sr. v.p. J. Walter Thompson Co., Chgo., 1969-86; pres. E.H. Brown Advt., 1986-97; exec. v.p. Space-Time Media Mgmt., 1997—; ptnr. Callahan Group, 2000—. Developer Mktg. with Country Music nat. seminar, 1996. Author: Building Country Radio, 1986, A New Look at Country Music Audiences, 1988, (video) Country Music Marketing, 1989. Bd. dirs. Gateway Found., Chgo., 1976—, chmn., 1988-91; bd. dirs., chmn. mktg. com. Cath. Charities, Chgo. Mem. Country Music Assn. (Nashville bd. dirs. 1979—, pres. 1983-85, Pres.'s award 1987, elector Country Music Hall of Fame), NARAS (Nashville chpt.), North Shore Country Club (Glenview, Ill.), Dairymen's Country Club (Boulder Junction, Wis.), Quail Creek Country Club (Naples, Fla.). Roman Catholic. Home: 2720 Lincoln St Evanston IL 60201-2043 Office: Space-Time Media Mgmt Inc 35 E Wacker Dr Chicago IL 60601-2103 Home: 2720 Lincoln St Evanston IL 60201-2043 E-mail: dick@spacetimemedia.com., relchar@aol.com.

MCCUNE, THOMAS, construction executive contractor; CEO M. A. Mortenson, Mpls., 1996—. Office: M A Mortenson PO Box 710 Minneapolis MN 55440-0710

MCCURRY, MARGARET IRENE, architect, interior and furniture designer, educator; b. Chgo., Sept. 26, 1942; d. Paul D. and Irene B. McC.; m. Stanley Tigerman, Mar. 17, 1979. BA, Vassar Coll., 1964. Registered architect, Ill., Mass., Mich., Tex., Wis., Pa., Ind., Fla.; registered interior designer, Ill. Design coord. Quaker Oats Co., Chgo., 1964-66; sr. interior designer Skidmore, Owings & Merrill, 1966-77; pvt. practice architect Margaret I, 1977-82; ptnr. Tigerman, McCurry, 1982—. Vis. studio critic Art Inst. Chgo., 1985-86, 88, 98, lectr., 1988, 98; vis. studio critic U. Ill., Chgo., Miami U., Oxford, Ohio, 1990; juror Internat. furniture awards Progressive Architecture mag., N.Y.C., 1986, advt. awards, 1988; juror design grants Nat. Endowment for Arts, Washington, 1983; NEA Challenge Design Rev., 1992; peer reviewer design excellence program Gen. Svcs. Adminstrn., 1992—; juror, Wis., Minn., Calif., Va., Washington, Pitts., Ky., Ga. Conn. Soc. Architects, Detroit, N.Y.C., Memphis, Austin, L.A. chpts. AIA, Am. Wood Coun., AIA Students Design Competition, 1993. Author: Margaret McCurry: Constructing 25 Short Stories, 2000; contbr. Chgo. Archtl. Club Jour.; designer, contbr. archtl. exhibit Art Inst. Chgo., 1983-85, 93, 99, Chgo. Hist. Soc., 1984, Gulbenkian Found., Lisbon Portugal, 1989, Chgo. Athenaeum, 1990, Gwenda Jay Gallery, 1992, Women of Design Traveling Exhbn., 1992-96; archtl. drawings and models in permanent collection Art Inst. Chgo. and Deutsches Architektur Mus., Frankfurt. Chmn. furniture sect. fundraising auction Sta. WTTW-TV, PBS, Chgo., 1975-76; mem. Chgo. Beautiful Com., 1968-70; pres. alumni coun. Grad. Sch. Design, Harvard U., 1997-2000; bd. dirs. Architecture and Design Soc. Art Inst. Chgo., 1988-97, mem. textile adv. bd. textile dept. Loeb fellow Harvard U., 1986-87; recipient Builders Choice Grand award Builders Mag., 1985, Interior Design award Interiors Mag., 1983, Dean of Architecture award Chgo. Design Source and the Merchandise Mart, 1989; inducted into Interior Design Hall of Fame, Interior Design Mag., 1990. Fellow AIA (v.p. bd. dirs. Chgo. chpt. 1984-89, chair 1993, nat. design com., lectr. Colo. chpt. 1985, nat. conv. 1988, 97, 98, Monterey Design Conf. 1989, Washington Design Ctr. 1989, Nat. Honor award 1984, Nat. Interior Architecture award 1992, 98, Disting. Bldg. award Chgo. chpt. 1984, 86, 91, 94, 99, 2000, Disting. Interior Architecture award 1981, 83, 88, 91, 97; product display Neocon award 1985, 88, gold award best of Neocon 1998), Coll. of Fellows AIA, Internat. Interior Design Assn., Chgo. Network, Am. Soc. Interior Designers (Nat. Design award 1992, 94, Ill. chpt. Design award 1994, Ill. chpt. Merit award 1994,v.p. bd. dirs. Chgo. chpt.), Chgo. Archtl. Club, Arts Club Chgo., Womens Athletic Club, Harvard Alumni Assn. (dir. 2000—). Episcopalian. Avocations: drawing, writing, travel, golf, gardening. Office: Tigerman McCurry Archs 444 N Wells St Chicago IL 60610-4501 E-mail: mimccurry@tigerman-mccurry.com.

MCCUSKER, THOMAS J. corporate lawyer, insurance company executive; b. 1943; BA, JD, U. Notre Dame. Bar: Nebr. 1970. Exec. v.p., gen. counsel Mutual of Omaha Ins. Co. Mem. ABA. Office: Mutual of Omaha Ins Co Mutual Of Omaha Plz Omaha NE 68175-0001

MCCUSKEY, MICHAEL PATRICK, judge; b. Peoria, Ill., June 30, 1948; s. Frank Morgan and Margaret Gertrude (Watkins) McC.; m. Linda A. Weers, July 1, 1978 (div. July 1985); 1 child, Melinda; m. Brenda Huber, Dec. 3, 1990; 1 child, Ryan Michael. BSEd, Ill. State U., 1970; JD, St. Louis U., 1975. Tchr. Ottawa (Ill.) Twp. High Sch., 1970-72; ptnr. Pace, McCuskey and Galley, Lacon, Ill., 1975-88; pub. defender Marshall County State of Ill., 1976-88; judge 10th Jud. Circuit of Ill., Peoria, 1988-90; justice 3d Dist. Appellate Ct., Ottawa, 1990—. Bd. dirs. Cen. Ill. chpt. ARC, Peoria, 1989-95, Ill. State U. Alumni Assn., Normal, 1995—. Mem. Ill. Judges Assn., Ill. State Bar Assn. (gen. practice sect. coun. 1991—, assembly 1992—, criminal justice sect. coun. 1994—, family law sect. coun. 1997—), Peoria County Bar Assn., Rotary (Paul Harris fellow 1985—). Democrat. Methodist. Avocations: spectator sports. Home: 4010 N Brandywine Dr Peoria IL 61614-6866 Office: Third Dist Appellate Ct 124 SW Adams St Ste 595 Peoria IL 61602-1392

MCCUTCHAN, GORDON EUGENE, retired lawyer, insurance company executive; b. Buffalo, Sept. 30, 1935; s. George Lawrence and Mary Esther (De Puy) McC.; m. Linda Brown; children: Lindsey, Elizabeth. BA, Cornell U., 1956, MBA, 1958, LLB, 1959. Bar: N.Y. 1959, Ohio 1964. Pvt. practice, Rome, 1959-61; atty., advisor SEC, Washington, 1961-64; ptnr. McCutchan, Druen, Maynard, Rath & Dietrich, 1964-94; mem. office of gen. counsel Nationwide Mut. Ins. Co., Columbus, Ohio, 1964-94, sr. v.p., gen. counsel, 1982-89, exec. v.p., gen. counsel, 1989-94; exec. v.p. Law and Corp. Svcs., Nationwide Ins. Enterprise, 1994-98; ret., 1998. Trustee, bd. govs. Franklin U., 1992-97; trustee Ohio Tuition Trust Authority, 1992-97. Mem. Columbus Bar Assn., Ohio Bar Assn., Am. Corp. Counsel Assn., Assn. Life Inst. Counsel (bd. govs. 1990-94), Fedn. Ins. and Corp. Counsel, Am. Coun. Life Ins. (chair legal sect. 1992-93). Home: 2376 Oxford Rd Columbus OH 43221-4011 E-mail: tunkpa@columbus.rr.com.

MC CUTCHEON, JOHN TINNEY, JR. retired journalist; b. Chgo., Nov. 8, 1917; s. John Tinney and Evelyn (Shaw) McC.; m. Susan Dart, Feb. 1, 1943; children: Anne McCutcheon Lewis, Mary, John Tinney III. BS, Harvard U., 1939. Reporter City News Bur., Chgo., 1939-40, Chgo. Tribune, 1940-51, editor column A Line O' Type or Two, 1951-57, editorial writer, 1957-71, editor editorial page, 1971-82, columnist, 1967-70. Pres. Lake Forest (Ill.) Libr., 1970-72. Served with USNR, 1941-46. Mem. Soc. Midland Authors, Am. Soc. Newspaper Editors, Nat. Conf. Editorial Writers, Geog. Soc. Chgo. (pres. 1955-57), Chgo. Zool. Soc. (hon. trustee), Chgo. Hist. Soc. (life trustee), Inter Am. Press Assn. (dir., freedom of press com. 1978-87), Sigma Delta Chi. Clubs: Tavern (Chgo.), Wayfarers (Chgo.), Tryon (N.C.) Country. Home: 10 Fox Paw Ln Saluda NC 28773-9527

MCDADE, JOE BILLY, federal judge; b. 1937; BS, Bradley U., 1959, MA, 1960; JD, U. Mich., 1963. Staff atty. antitrust divsn. U.S. Dept. Justice, 1963-65; exec. trainee First Fed. Savs. and Loan Assn., 1965; exec. dir. Greater Peoria (Ill.) Legal Aid Soc., 1965-69; ptnr. Hafele & McDade, Peoria, Ill., 1968-77; pvt. practice, 1977-82; assoc. cir. judge State of Ill., 1982-88; cir. judge Cir. Ct. Ill., 1988-91; fed. judge U.S. Dist. Ct. (ctrl. dist.) Ill., 1991—. Bd. dirs. Peoria (Ill.) Pub. Libr., 1965-77, Peoria YMCA, ARC, Peoria Tri-Centennial; fin. chmn. St. Peters Cath. Ch.; active Peoria Civic Ctr. Authority, 1976-82; pres. Ill. Health Systems Agy., 1978-80, bd. dirs., 1975-82. Mem. Ill. State Bar Assn., Peoria County Bar Assn. (bd. dirs. 1980-82). Office: US Dist Ct 100 NE Monroe St Peoria IL 61602-1003

MCDANIEL, CHARLES-GENE, journalism educator, writer; b. Luxora, Ark., Jan. 11, 1931; s. Charles Waite and Edith Estelle (Kelly) McD. B.S., Northwestern U., 1954, M.S. in Journalism, 1955. Reporter Gazette and Daily, York, Pa., 1955-58; sci. writer Chgo. bur. A.P., 1958-79; assoc. prof. journalism dept. Roosevelt U., Chgo., 1979-83, prof., 1984-96, chmn. dept., 1979-93, head faculty of journalism and communication studies, 1993-95, prof. emeritus, 1996—. Contbg. editor Libido; contbr. to anthologies, poems, Ency. Britannica, World Book Ency.; contbr. articles to profl. jours.; Chgo. corr. The Med. Post, Toronto, 1979-2000; columnist www.libidomag.com. Trustee Roosevelt U., 1985-94; bd. dirs. Internat. Press Ctr. Chgo., 1993-96. Recipient writing awards Erikson Inst. for Early Edn., 1972, writing award AMA, 1974, writing awards Chgo. Inst. for Psychoanalysis, 1971, 73, writing awards Ill. Med Soc., 1972, 73, writing awards ADA, 1975, Am. Psychol. Assn., 1982. Mem. ACLU, Fellowship of Reconciliation, War Resisters League, Art Inst. Chgo. (life), Mus. Contemporary Art (charter), Nat. Lesbian and Gay Journalists Assn., Ill. Arts Alliance, Handgun Control Inc., Hemlock Soc., Ptnrship in Caring. Home and Office: 5109 S Cornell Ave Chicago IL 60615-4215

MCDANIEL, JAMES EDWIN, lawyer; b. Dexter, Mo., Nov. 22, 1931; s. William H. and Gertie M. (Woods) McD.; m. Mary Jane Crawford, Jan. 22, 1955; children: John William, Barbara Anne. AB, Washington U., St. Louis, 1957, JD, 1959. Bar: Mo. 1959. Assoc. firm Walther, Barnard, Cloyd & Timm, 1959-60, McDonald, Barnard, Wright & Timm, 1960-63, ptnr., 1963-65; ptnr. firm Barnard, Timm & McDaniel, St. Louis, 1965-73, Barnard & Baer, St. Louis, 1973-82; ptnr. Lashly & Baer, 1982—2002, of counsel, 2002—, prosecuting atty., 1968—. City atty. City of Glendale, Mo., 1996—; bd. dirs. Eden. Theol. Sem.; lectr. Latvian U., Riga, Inst. Fgn. Rels., Banking in Am., 1992-93. Leader legal del. Chinese-Am. Comparative Law Study, People's Republic China, 1988, Russian-Am. Comparative Law Study, USSR, 1990; trustee, past chmn., past treas. 1st Congl. Ch. St. Louis. With USAF, 1951-55. Fellow Am. Bar Found. (life), St. Louis Bar Found. (life); mem. ABA (bd. govs. 1997-2000, ho. of dels. 1976-80, 84-92, 97-2000, state del. 1986-92, chmn. lawyers conf., jud. adminstrn. divsn. 1992-95, 8th cir. rep. standing com. on fed. jud. 1995-98, mem. standing com. on jud. qualification, tenure and compensation 1996-97), The Mo. Bar (pres. 1981-82, bd. govs. 1974-83), Mo. Assn. Def. Counsel, Bar Assn. Met. St. Louis (pres. 1972), Internat. Assn. Ins. Counsel, Assn. Def. Counsel St. Louis (past pres.), Phi Delta Phi. Home: 767 Elmwood Ave Saint Louis MO 63122-3216 Office: Lashly & Baer 714 Locust St Saint Louis MO 63101-1699

MCDANIEL, JAN, television station executive; b. St. Louis, June 27, 1951; BA in Journalism, U. Mo., 1973. Pres., gen. mgr. Sta. KAKE-TV, 1991-96; gen. mgr. Sta. WCCO-TV, Mpls., 1996—. Mem. Women in Comm. Office: Sta WCCO-TV 90 S 11th St Minneapolis MN 55403-2414

MCDANIEL, MIKE, political association executive; b. Muncie, Ind., Feb. 11, 1951; m. Gail McDaniel, 1978. BS, Ball State U., 1973, MPA, 1979. Legis. intern Rep. Caucus Ind. State Senate, 98th Session, Ind. Gen.

Assemply; rsch. dir. City County Coun., Indpls., 1974-75; adminstrv. asst. to Pres. ProTem Ind. State Senate, 1975-76, minority caucus adminstr., 1977-78, spl. asst. to majority caucus, 1978-79; campaign dir. Rep. State Senate Campaign com., 1978; campaign mgr. John Mutz for Lt. Gov. campaign, 1980, 87-88; asst. to gov.-elect Hon. Judge Robert D. Orr, Ind.; chief of staff Lt. Gov. Ind., Hon. John M. Mutz, 1981-87; chmn. Ind. State Rep. Party; pub. rels. account exec. Caldwell Van Riper, Indpls. Instr. polit. sci. Ball State U., 1984—; exec. asst. to v.p. for bus. affairs, 1988-94, dir. govt. rels., 1994-95; exec. dir. Ind. State Election Bd., 1988; writer, producer, dir., editor video module series Ind. Gen. Assemply, 1990; bd. dirs. Bowen Inst. for Practical Politics. Recipient Sagamore of Wabash prize Gov. Otis R. Bowen, 1979, Gov. Robert D. Orr, 1981.

MCDERMOTT, ALAN, newspaper editor; b. Kansas City, Mo., Sept. 5, 1951; Sr. editor Universal Press Syndicate, Kansas City, Mo., 1996—. Office: Universal Press Syndicate 4520 Main St Ste 700 Kansas City MO 64111-7701

MCDERMOTT, JOHN H(ENRY), lawyer; b. Evanston, Ill., June 23, 1931; s. Edward Henry and Goldie Lucile (Boso) McD.; m. Ann Elizabeth Pickard, Feb. 19, 1966; children: Elizabeth A., Mary L., Edward H. BA, Williams Coll., 1953; JD, U. Mich., 1956. Bar: Mich. 1955, Ill. 1956. Assoc. McDermott, Will & Emery, Chgo., 1958-64, ptnr., 1964-99, of counsel, 2000—. Bd. dirs. Patrick Industries Inc. 1st lt. USAF, 1956-58. Mem. ABA, Chgo. Bar Assn. Clubs: Commerical of Chgo., Econ. of Chgo., Legal Chgo. (pres. 1981-82), Law Chgo. (pres. 1986-87). Home: 330 Willow Rd Winnetka IL 60093-4130 Office: McDermott Will & Emery 227 W Monroe St Ste 3100 Chicago IL 60606-5096 E-mail: mcdermott330@cs.com.

MCDERMOTT, KEVIN R. lawyer; b. Youngstown, Ohio, Jan. 26, 1952; s. Robert J. and Marion D. (McKeown) McD.; m. Cindy J. Darling, Dec. 11, 1976; children: Ciara, Kelly. AB, Miami U., Oxford, Ohio, 1974; JD, Ohio State U., 1977. Bar: Ohio 1977, U.S. Dist. Ct. (so. dist.) Ohio 1978, U.S. Dist. Ct. (no. dist.) Ohio 1988, U.S. Dist. Ct. (we. dist.) Mich. 1993, U.S. Supreme Ct. 1990, U.S. Ct. Appeals (3rd cir.) 1996, U.S. Ct. Appeals (6th cir.) 1988. Assoc. ptnr. Murphey Young & Smith, Columbus, Ohio, 1977-88; ptnr. Squire Sanders & Dempsey, 1988-90, Schottenstein Zox & Dunn, Columbus, 1990—. Adv. bd. mem. Capital U. Legal Asst. Program, Columbus, Ohio, 1988—. Bd. pres. Easter Seal Soc. Ctrl. Ohio, Columbus, 1992-94, bd. mem. 1988-92; pres. Upper Arlington Civic Svc. Commn., Columbus, Ohio, 1988-93. Office: Schottenstein Zox & Dunn 41 S High St Ste 2600 Columbus OH 43215-6109

MCDILL, THOMAS ALLISON, minister; b. Cicero, Ill., June 4, 1926; s. Samuel and Agnes (Lindsay) McD.; m. Ruth Catherine Starr, June 4, 1949; children: Karen Joyce, Jane Alison, Steven Thomas. Th.B., No. Baptist Sem., Oakbrook, Ill., 1951; B.A., Trinity Coll., 1954; M.Div., Trinity Evang. Div. Sch., 1955, DD, 1989; D.Ministries, Bethel Theol. Sem., 1975. Ordained to ministry Evang. Free Ch. Am., 1949. Pastor Community Bible Ch., Berwyn, Ill., 1947-51, Grace Evang. Free Ch., Chgo., 1951-58, Liberty Bible Ch., Valparaiso, Ind., 1959-67, Crystal Evang. Free Ch., Mpls., 1967-76; v.p., moderator Evang. Free Ch. of Am., 1973-74, chmn. home missions bd., 1968-72, chmn. exec. bd., 1973-90, pres., 1976-90, ret., 1990; min. at large Evang. Free Ch. Am., 1991—. Contbr. articles to publs. Chmn. bd. Trinity Coll., Deerfield, Ill., 1974-76; bd. govs. Trinity Western U.; bd. dirs. Trinity Evang. Divinity Sch. Mem. Evang. Free Ch. Ministerial Assn., Evang. Ministers Assn., Nat. Assn. Evangelicals (bd. adminstrn. 1976—, mem. exec. com. 1981-88), Greater Mpls. Assn. Evangelicals (bd. dirs., sec. bd. 1969-73) Home: 3790 Lawndale Ln #313 Plymouth MN 55446 Office: 901 E 78th St Bloomington MN 55420-1334

MC DONAGH, EDWARD CHARLES, sociologist, university administrator; b. Edmonton, Alta., Can., Jan. 23, 1915; came to U.S., 1922, naturalized, 1936; s. Henry Fry and Aletta (Bowles) McD.; m. Louise Lucille Lorenzi, Aug. 14, 1940 (dec.); children: Eileen, Patricia. A.B., U. So. Calif., 1937, A.M., 1938, Ph.D., 1942. Asst. prof. So. Ill. U., Carbondale, 1940-46, asst. to pres., 1942-44; asst. prof. U. Okla., Norman, 1946-47, U. So. Calif., L.A., 1947-49, assoc. prof., 1949-56, prof., 1956-69, head dept., 1958-62, chmn., acad. univ. affairs com., 1963, assoc. dean divsn. social scis. and comms., 1960-63; head dept. sociology U. Ala., 1969-71; chmn. dept. sociology Ohio State U., Columbus, 1971-74, acting dean Coll. Social and Behavioral Scis., 1974—, dean Coll. Social and Behavioral Scis., 1975-78, chmn. coordinating coun. deans Colls. Arts and Scis., 1977-78, prof. emeritus Colls. Arts and Scis., 1981—. Smith-Mundt prof., Sweden, 1956-57; vis. prof. U. Hawaii, summer 1965; cons. Los Angeles and related sch. dists.; mem. Region XV Woodrow Wilson Selection Com., 1961-62 Author: (with E.S. Richards) Ethnic Relations in the U.S, 1953, (with J.E. Nordskog, M.J. Vincent) Analyzing Social Problems, 1956, (with Jon Simpson) Social Problems: Persistent Challenges, 1965, rev., 1969; Assoc. editor: Sociology and Social Research, 1947-69; editorial cons.: Sociometry, 1962-65; Contbr. articles to profl. publs. Served with AUS, 1944-46. Fellow Am. Sociol. Assn. (co-chmn. nat. conf. com. 1963, budget and exec. office com. 1975-78); mem. AAUP, AAAS, Am. Assn. Pub. Opinion Rsch., Alpha Kappa Delta (pres. united chtps. 1965-66), Phi Beta Kappa (chpt. pres. 1959-60), Humanist, Blue Key, Skull and Dagger. Democrat. Home: 201 Spencer Dr Amherst MA 01002-3362

MCDONALD, DAVID EUGENE, package car driver; b. Decatur, Ill., July 6, 1956; s. Robert Alexander McDonald and Ida Jane (Varvil) Crowell; m. Lynda Jean Christensen McDonald, Apr. 23, 1983; children: Melanie Ann, Joshua Glen and Jordan David (twins). BS in History, Ill. State U., Normal; student, Parkland C.C., Champaign, Ill. Asst. mgr. Gen. Cinema Corp., Decatur, Champaign, Chgo., 1978-81; mgr. Classic Cinemas, Elmhurst, Ill., 1981-83, World Mgmt. Inc., Downers Grove, 1983-87; driver UPS, Addison, 1987—. Active Jr. Achievement, 1971-75, Dupage County Rep., Wheaton, Ill., 1993—; treas. Local Luth. Laymans League, 2000—. Named Mr. Exec. Jr. Achievement, Decatur, Ill., 1975; recipient Internat. Literary award Manuscripts Internat., Dayton, Wash., 1988. Republican. Lutheran. Avocations: politics, photography, reading, writing. Home: 841 Prospect Ave Elmhurst IL 60126-4862 Office: UPS 150 S Lombard Rd Addison IL 60101-3020

MCDONALD, JESS, state official; BA, Ill. State U.; MA in Social Svc. Adminstrn., U. Chgo.; postgrad., Harvard U. With Ill. Dept. Children and Family Svcs., Bloomington, acting dir., 1990-94; exec. dir. Ill. Assn. Cmty. Mental Health Agys., 1991; dir. Dept. Mental Health and Devel. Disabilities, 1992, Ill. Dept. Children and Family Svcs., Bloomington, 1994—. Recipient award of excellence in pub. child welfare adminstrn. Nat. Assn. Pub. Child Welfare Adminstrs., 1996, Motorola award for excellence in pub. svc., 1997. Mem. Nat. Assn. Pub. Child Welfare Adminstrs. (exec. com.), Am. Pub. Welfare Assn. (chair children and family svcs. com.). Office: Children and Family Svcs Dept 406 E Monroe St Springfield IL 62701-1411

MCDONALD, JOHN CECIL, lawyer; b. Lorimor, Iowa, Feb. 19, 1924; s. Cecil F. and Mary Elsie (Fletcher) McD.; m. Barbara Joan Berry, May 8, 1943; children: Mary Elisabeth (Mrs. Dell Richard), Joan Frances (Mrs. Andrew Ackerman), Jean Maurine. Student, Simpson Coll., 1942, So. Ill. U., 1943; J.D., Drake U., 1948. Bar: Iowa 1948, U.S. Ct. Mil. Appeals 1956, U.S. Supreme Ct. 1956. Practiced in, Dallas Center, Iowa, 1948—; sr. ptnr. McDonald, Brown & Fagen and predecessor firms, 1971—; county atty. Dallas County, 1958-62; asst. county atty., 1963-69; city atty. Dallas Center, 1956-80. Mem. Simpson Coll. Alumni Council, pres., 1977-80; legal adviser Dallas Community Bd. Edn., 1953-69, pres., mem., 1968-76; nat. adv. com. Cen. Coll.; alt. del. Iowa Coordinating Council for Post-High Sch. Edn.; finance chmn. Dallas County Rep.Cen. Com., 1954-63, chmn., 1963-68; chmn. Iowa 7th Congl. Dist. Rep. Cen. Com., 1968-69, Iowa Rep. Cen. Com., 1969-75; mem. Rep. Nat. Com., 1969-88, mem. exec. com., 1973— ; mem. Rule 29 com., com. on reform; mem. Gov. Iowa's inaugural com., 1969, 71, 73, 75, 79; del. Rep. Nat. Conv., 1964, 72, 76, 80, 84, chmn. com. on contests, 1976, 80, 84, 88, chmn. com. on credentials, 1976, 80, 88, mem. com. on arrangements and exec. com. of com. on arrangements, 1976, 80, 84, mem. rules rev. com., 1977-84; chmn. Midwest Rep. State Chairmen's Assn., 1973-75, Nat. Rep. State Chairmen's Adv. Com., 1973-75; hon. co-chmn. Vice Pres.'s Inaugural, 1981; trustee Dallas County Hosp., Perry, Iowa; bd. visitors U.S. Air Force Acad., 1975-78, chmn., 1977-78; trustee Simpson Coll., 1978— ; bd. dirs. Iowa Student Loan Liquidity Corp., 1987-99; mem. Iowa Coll. Aid Commn., 1989—; mem. Iowa Bd. Regents, 1981-87, pres., 1985-87; bd. dirs. Iowa Public Broadcasting Network, 1981-85; U.S. commr. Am. Battle Monuments Commn., 1982-94. Served with USAAF, 1942-46; Col. USAF, 1951-52, ret. Recipient Alumni Achievement award Simpson Coll., 1974; Disting. Service award Drake U., 1978 Mem. ABA, Iowa Bar Assn. (past chmn. spl. com. on mil. affairs, mem. mil. affairs com.), Dallas County Bar Assn. (past pres.), Am. Legion, Farm Bur., Blackfriars, Drake U. Law Sch. Alumni Assn. (class officer), Comml. Club (past pres.) (Dallas Ctr.), Hillcrest Country Club (past pres.) (Adel, Iowa), Des Moines Club, Masons (32 degree), Shriners, Rotary (past pres. Dallas Ctr.), Alpha Tau Omega, Delta Theta Phi, Alpha Psi Omega. Presbyterian. Club: Des Moines. Lodges: Masons (32 deg.), Shriners, Rotary (pas pres. Dallas Ctr.). Home: 1006 13th St PO Box 250 Dallas Center IA 50063-0250 Office: McDonald Brown Fagen & Flanders PO Box 250 Dallas Center IA 50063-0250 E-mail: dalctlaw@miindspring.com.

MCDONALD, MALCOLM WILLIS, real estate company executive; b. Mpls., Nov. 17, 1936; s. Malcolm Blanchard and Ruth Virginia (Stees) McD.; m. Judy Glynn Ballard, Aug. 22, 1959; children: Malcolm Scott, Margaret Alice, Philip Brian. BA magna cum laude with high honors and high orations, Yale Coll., 1958; MBA, Harvard U., 1960. V.p. First Nat. Bank of St. Paul, 1960-77; dir., sr. v.p., trustee Space Center, Inc., St. Paul, 1977—. Adj. prof. grad. programs in mgmt. U. St. Thomas, St. Paul, 1975—94; mem. adv. bd. Firstar Bank of Minn., St. Paul, 1999—2001; bd. dirs. Scherer Bros. Lumber Co., Mpls.; vice chair adv. coun. Minn. State Bd. of Investment, St. Paul, 1982—; mem. adv. bd. Sherbrooke Capital, 2002—, Hill Monastic Manuscript Libr., St. John's U., Collegeville, Minn., 1980—97; bd. dirs. Minntech, Inc., Plymouth, 1998—2001. Mem. North Oaks Home Owners Assn., 1996; trustee, sec., chmn. audit com., investment com. Amherst H. Wilder Found., St. Paul, 1971—; trustee Bigelow & FR Bigelow Found., St. Paul, 1967-98, Lee and Rose Warner Found., 1990—, Manitou Fund, 1990—, Adelaide and Harry G. McNeely Found., St. Paul, 1980-98, Minn. State Fair Found., 2002; trustee, treas. mem., Grotto Found., St. Paul, 1980—; pres. Minn. Taxpayers Assn., 1994-96; former bd. dirs. Guthrie Theater, Minn. Orchestral Assn.; bd. dirs. Minn. State Fair Found., 2002- Mem. Mpls. Club (bd. ogvs. 2002-), Minn. Landmarks, North Oaks Golf Club, White Bear Racquet & Swim Club, Yale Club of N.Y.C., St. Paul C. of C. (Bravo awards), Colony Found., U. Club of St. Paul, Mpls. Club (bd. govs.), Phi Beta Kappa, Phi Beta Kappa Assocs., Phi Gamma Delta. Republican. Episcopalian. Avocations: physical fitness, gardening, travel, encouraging 3rd graders to read. Home: 21 E Oaks Rd North Oaks MN 55127-2527 Office: Space Center Inc 2501 Rosegate Saint Paul MN 55113-2717 E-mail: mmcdonald@spacecenterinc.com.

MCDONALD, PATRICK ALLEN, lawyer, arbitrator, educator; b. Detroit, May 11, 1936; s. Lawrence John and Estelle (Maks) Mc D.; m. Margaret Mercier, Aug. 10, 1963; children: Michael Lawrence, Colleen Marie, Patrick Joseph, Timothy, Margaret, Thomas, Maureen. PhB cum laude, U. Detroit, 1958, JD magna cum laude, 1961; LLM (E. Barrett Prettyman Trial scholar, Hugh J. Fegan fellow), Georgetown U., 1962. Bar: D.C. 1961, Mich. 1961, Colo. 1993. Case worker Dept. Pub. Welfare, Detroit, 1958; field examiner NLRB, 1961; practiced in Washington, 1961-62; trial cons. NIH, Bethesda, Md., 1962; staff judge adv. USAF, France, 1962-65; ptnr. Monagham, LoPrete, Mc Donald, Yakima & Grenke, Detroit, 1965—. Bd. dirs., past chmn. Delta Dental Plan of Mich.; past chmn. Delta Dental Plan of Ohio; bd. dirs., v.p. Guest House, Lake Orion, Mich., Rochester, Minn., Detroit Athletic Club, Brighton Hosp.; instr. polit. sci. and law U. Md., 1963-65, U. Detroit Law Sch., adj. prof., 1965—. Co-author: Law and Tactics in Federal Criminal Cases, 1963. Mem. Detroit Bd. Edn., 1966-76, pres.; sec., trustee Mt. Elliott Cemetary Assn.; mem. U. Detroit Sports Hall of Fame; mem. adv. bd. Providence Hosp., Southfield, Mich.; exec. bd. U. Detroit Pres.'s Cabinet. Named one of Five Outstanding Young Men of Mich., Outstanding Young Man of Detroit. Mem. ABA, Detroit Bar Assn., State Bar Mich. (commr.), U. Detroit Alumni Assn. (bd. dirs.), Mensa, Blue Key, Alpha Phi Omega (pres. Eta Pi chpt. 1955), Alpha Sigma Nu (v.p. 1960). Home: 13066 Lashbrook Ln E Brighton MI 48114-6002 Office: 40700 Woodward Ave Bloomfield Hills MI 48304-2211

MCDONALD, THOMAS ALEXANDER, lawyer; b. Chgo., Aug. 20, 1942; s. Owen Gerard and Lois (Gray) McD.; m. Sharon Diane Hirk, Nov. 25, 1967; children: Cristin, Katie, Courtney, Thomas Jr. AB, Georgetown U., 1965; JD, Loyola U., Chgo., 1968. Bar: Ill. 1969, U.S. Dist. Ct. (no. dist.) Ill. 1969. Ptnr. Clausen Miller, PC, Chgo., 1969—. Mem. ABA, Ill. Bar Assn., Chgo. Bar Assn. Office: Clausen Miller PC 10 S La Salle St Ste 1600 Chicago IL 60603-1098 Fax: 312-606-7777. E-mail: tmcdonald@clausen.com.

MCDONALD, WILLIAM HENRY, lawyer; b. Niangua, Mo., Feb. 27, 1946; s. Milburn and Fannie M. McDonald; m. Janice E. Robinson, July 13, 1968; children: Melissa L., Meghan M. BS in Pub. Adminstrn., Southwest Mo. State U., 1968; JD, U. Mo., 1971. Bar: Mo. 1971, U.S. Dist. Ct. (we. dist.) Mo. 1973, U.S. Supreme Ct. 1978, U.S. Ct. Appeals (8th cir.) 1982. Ptnr., pres. Woolsey, Fisher, Whiteaker & McDonald, PC, 1973-95; pres. William H. McDonald & Assocs., PC, Springfield, Mo., 1995—. Chmn. blue ribbon task force on Delivery of Mental Health Services to Southwest Mo., Mo. Commn. Continuing Legal Edn.; pres. Tan Oaks Homeowners Assn.; mem. fin. com. Child Adv. Council, Rep. Nat. Com., Mo. Rep. Com., Greene County Nat. Com.; active various Southwest Mo. State U. Clubs; bd. dirs. Greene County div. Am. Heart Assn., Ozarks regional Am. Athletic Union Jr. Olympics; pres., bd. dirs. Springfield Little Theatre; v.p. pub. affairs Springfield Area C. of C., bd. dirs., 1995-98. Capt. U.S. Army, 1971-73. Named one of Outstanding Young Men Am., 1978, 81, Outstanding Young Men Springfield, 1980. Fellow ABA (life, antitrust and litigation and torts and ins. sects.); mem. ATLA, Fed. Bar Assn., Mo. Bar Assn. (chmn. spol. com. on mandatory continuing edn., various coms., Pres.'s award 1986), Mo. Assn. Trial Attys. (bd. govs. 1998-2001), Springfield Met. Bar Assn. (bd. dirs., chmn. pub. edn. speakers bur.), Met. Bar Assn. St. Louis, Def. Rsch. Inst., Am. Judicature Soc., Am. Bd. Trial Advs. (state coord.), Nat. Bd. Trial Advs., Am. Coll. Barristers, Million Dollar Forum, 31st Jud. Cir. Bar Com. (chmn.), Supreme Ct. Hist. Soc., U. Mo.-Kansas City Sch. Law Found., Springfield Claims Assn. (pres.), U.S. Cavalry Assn., Am. Legion, 1st Inf. Divsn. Soc., K.T., Beta Omega Tau, Kappa Epsilon. Presbyterian. Home: 4857 E Royal Dr Springfield MO 65809-2425

MCDONELL, EDWIN DOUGLAS, information systems executive, consultant, writer; b. Johnson City, N.Y., Aug. 16, 1953; s. Alexander Edwin and Loretta Arlene (Terry) McD; m. Katherine A. Mandusic (div. 1994); m. Lizabeth L. Marks, Feb. 14, 1998; children: Elizabeth Ashley, Stephanie Allyn. BA in English Lit., U. Cin., 1976; MSLS in Info. Sci., Case Western Reserve U., 1978; MBA in Mgmt. Info. Systems, Ind. U., 1983. Assoc. Crowe Chizek & Co., CPAs, Indpls., 1983-88, prin., 1989-92; dir. office automation USA Group, Fishers, Ind., 1992-95; ind. cons. and writer, 1995—. Com. chairperson Fin. Mgrs. Soc., Chgo., 1989-92; cons., spkr. Lafferty Group Confs., London, 1992-2000; writer Trade Press Svcs., Thousand Oaks, Calif., 2000—. Author: (books) Creating a Customer-Driven Retail Bank, 1991, Rebuilding the Retail Bank, 1992, Document Imaging Technology, 1993; contbg. author procs., reports in field; contbg. editor Bank Adminstrn. Inst., Chgo., 1989-91; contbr. articles to profl. jours. Trustee Sunrise United Meth. Ch. at Geist, 1998—. Mem. Inst. Mgmt. Cons. (cert.), Beta Gamma Sigma, Sigma Iota Epsilon. Home and Office: 8403 La Habra Ln Indianapolis IN 46236-8832 E-mail: edmcdonnell@juno.com.

MCDONNELL, JOHN FINNEY, former aerospace and aircraft manufacturing executive; b. Mar. 18, 1938; s. James Smith and Mary Elizabeth (Finney) McD.; m. Anne Marbury, June 16, 1961. BS in Aero. Engring., Princeton U., 1960, MS in Aero. Engring., 1962; postgrad. in bus. adminstrn., Washington U., St. Louis, 1962-66. Strength engr. McDonnell Aircraft Co. (subs. McDonnell Douglas Corp.), St. Louis, 1962, corp. analyst, 1963-65, contract coord., adminstr., 1965-68; asst. to v.p. fin. Douglas Aircraft Co. (subs. McDonnell Douglas Corp.), 1968; v.p. McDonnell Douglas Fin. Corp. (subs. McDonnell Douglas Corp.), 1968-71; staff v.p. fiscal McDonnell Douglas Corp., 1971-75, corp. v.p. fin. and devel., 1975-77, corp. exec. v.p., 1977-80, pres., 1980—, mem. exec. com., 1975—, chmn., 1988-97; past CEO, also bd. dirs. Bd. dirs. Ralston Purina Co. Mem. bd. commrs. St. Louis Sci. Ctr.; trustee KETC, Washington U., also chmn. nat. coun. faculty arts and scis. com.

MCDONNELL, SANFORD NOYES, aircraft company executive; b. Little Rock, Oct. 12, 1922; s. William Archie and Carolyn (Cherry) McD.; m. Priscilla Robb, Sept. 3, 1946; children: Robbin McDonnell MacVittie, William Randall. BA in Econs., Princeton U., 1945; BS in Mech. Engring., U. Colo., 1948; MS in Applied Mechanics, Washington U., St. Louis, 1954. With McDonnell Douglas Corp. (formerly McDonnell Aircraft Corp.), St. Louis, 1948—, v.p., 1959-66, pres. McDonnell Aircraft div., 1966-71, corp. exec. v.p., 1971, corp. pres., from 1971, chief exec. officer, from 1972, chmn., 1980-88, chmn. emeritus, 1988—. Active St. Louis United Way; mem. exec. bd. St. Louis and nat. councils Boy Scouts Am.; trustee, elder Presbyn. Ch.; chmn. bd. Character Edn. Partnership, Washington, 1993—. Fellow AIAA; mem. Navy League U.S. (life), Tau Beta Pi. Office: McDonnell Douglas Corp PO Box 516 Saint Louis MO 63166-0516

MCDONOUGH, BRIDGET ANN, music theatre company director; b. Milw., June 19, 1956; d. James and Lois (Hunzinger) McD.; m. Gregory Paul Opelka, Sept. 20, 1986 (div. Aug. 1993); m. Robert Markey, Feb. 29, 2000. BS, Northwestern U., 1978. Bus. mgr. Organic Theater Co., Chgo., 1979-80; mng. dir., founder Light Opera Works, Evanston, Ill., 1980—. U.S. rep. European Congress Musical Theatre, 1995. Founder, mem. Chgo. Music Alliance, 1984—, pres., 1995-98; mem. Ill. Arts Alliance; bd. dirs., Nat. Alliance for Musical Theatre, 2001—; bd. dirs. Evanston Convention Visitors Bur.; mem. alumni adv. bd. Northwestern U. Sch. Speech. Recipient Women on the Move award Evanston YWCA, 1991. Mem. Evanston C. of C. (bd. dirs., 1993-99), Rotary (pres. Evanston chpt. 1999-2000). Avocation: birding. Office: Light Opera Works 927 Noyes St Evanston IL 60201-6206

MCDONOUGH, JOHN J. household products company executive; V.p. fin. Litton med. products Litton Industries; v.p., treas. Am. TV and Comm., Denver; CFO, v.p. Blount, Inc., Montgomery, Ala.; sr. v.p. fin. Newell, 1981-83; founder, pres. GENDEX Corp. (merger with Dentsply Internat. 1993), 1983-93; vice chmn., CEO Dentsply Internat., 1993-95; CEO, vice chmn. bd. Newell Rubbermaid Inc., Freeport, Ill., 1997-2000, also bd. dirs. Chmn. bd. dirs. Juvenile Diabetes Found., 1998—, former mem. exec. and fin. coms., chmn. planned giving and vice chmn. $200 million internat. initiative. Named Man of Yr. Chgo. chpt. Juvenile Diabetes Found., 2000, Office: Newell Rubbermaid Inc 29 E Stephenson St Freeport IL 61032-4235

MCDONOUGH, JOHN MICHAEL, lawyer; b. Evanston, Ill., Dec. 30, 1944; s. John Justin and Anne Elizabeth (O'Brien) McD.; m. Susan J. Moran, Sept. 19, 1981; children: John E., Catherine Anne. AB, Princeton U., 1966; LLB, Yale U., 1969. Bar: Ill. 1969, Fla. 1991. Assoc. Sidley & Austin, Chgo., 1969-75, ptnr., 1975—. Bd. dirs. Met. Planning Coun., 1978—, pres., 1982-84; bd. dirs. Ctr. Am. Archeology, 1980-85, chmn., 1982-84; bd. dirs. Leadership Greater Chgo., 1984-90, sec.-treas., 1987-90; bd. dis. Brian Rsch. Found., 1985—, pres., 1989-94. With JAGC, USAR, 1969-75. Mem. ABA, Ill. Bar Assn., Chgo. Bar Assn., Racquet Club, Saddle & Cycle Club, Commonwealth Club, Econ. Club, Phi Beta Kappa. Democrat. Episcopalian. Home: 1407 N Dearborn St Chicago IL 60610-1505 Office: Sidley & Austin 425 W Surf St Apt 605 Chicago IL 60657-6139

MCDOUGAL, ALFRED LEROY, publishing executive; b. Evanston, Ill., Feb. 12, 1931; s. Alfred L. and Mary (Gillett) McD.; m. Gudrun Fenger, May 7, 1960 (div. 1982); children: Thomas, Stephen; m. Nancy A. Lauter, Mar. 1, 1986. BA, Yale U., 1953; MBA, Harvard U., 1957. Asst. to pres. Rand McNally & Co., Skokie, Ill., 1962-65, mgr. sch. dept., 1965-69; pres. McDougal, Littell & Co., Evanston, 1969-91, chmn., CEO, 1991-94; dir. Houghton Mifflin Co., Boston, 1994-2001; CEO Alm Corp., 1994—. Chmn. McDougal Family Found.; gov. Yale U. Press, 1995—. Trustee Hadley Sch. for Blind, Winnetka, Ill., 1980-83; chmn. budget com. Evanston United Fund, 1974-76, bd. dirs.; bd. dirs. Evanston YMCA, 1988-94, Youth Job Ctr., 1987-93, chmn., 1989-91, Opportunity Internat., 1994-2000, Literacy Chgo., 1992-98, treas., 1994-96, Hubbard St. Dance, Chgo., 1995—. With U.S. Army, 1953-55. Mem. Assn. Am. Pubs. (exec. com. sch. divsn. 1981-94, chmn. 1988-89, 92-94, dir. 1987-89), No. Ill. Assn. (1st v.p. 1984, chmn. 1985). Office: ALM Corp 400 N Michigan Ave Ste 300 Chicago IL 60611-4130 E-mail: alfredmcdougal@yahoo.com.

MCDOUGAL, MARIE PATRICIA, retired educator, freelance writer and editor; b. Mt. Clemens, Mich., Apr. 10, 1946; d. Allan Charles and Dorothy Nadine (Berger) Ling; m. Douglas Stevens McDougal, Aug. 23, 1969. BA, Cen. Mich. U., 1968; MA, Antioch U., 1997. Lic. tchr., Mich. Tchr. L'Anse Creuse High Sch., Harrison Twp., Mich., 1969-97; retired, 1997. Mem. L'Anse Creuse High Crisis Team, 1988-93, S.A.F.E. Task Force, Harrison Twp., 1996-98; spkr. in field. Author: Mount Clemens: Bath City U.S.A. in Vintage Post Cards, 2000; columnist: The Jour. Newspaper, 1983—90, writer: Interospective Mag., 1996—98, writer, editor : Antiquities Guide, 1997—98; author: Harrison Township, Michigan, 2002. Mem. L'Anse Creuse Athletic Boosters; chair Harrison Twp. Hist. Commn. Recipient Appreciation award Macomb County Hist. Soc., 1989, Pres. award for lit. excellence The Nat. Authors Registry, 1994. Mem. Soc. Children's Book Writers and Illustrators, Romance Writers Am., Venice Shores Property Owners (bd. dirs. 1994-2000, corr. sec. 1994-98), Detroit Women Writers, L'Anse Creuse Public Schs. Alumni Assn. (steering com. 1996-98), Am. Auto Immune-Related Diseases Assn. Lutheran. Avocations: boating, crafts, reading. E-mail: ratisboat@aol.com.

MCDOUGAL, STUART YEATMAN, comparative literature educator, author; b. L.A., Apr. 10, 1942; s. Murray and Marian (Yeatman) McD.; m. Menakka Weerasinghe, Apr. 29, 1967 (div. 1977); children— Dyanthe Rose, Gavin Rohan; m. Nora Gunneng, Aug. 4, 1979; children— Angus Gunneng, Tobias Yeatman B.A., Haverford Coll., 1964; M.A., U. Pa.,

1965, Ph.D., 1970. Lectr. U. Lausanne, Switzerland, 1965-66; asst. prof. Mich. State U., East Lansing, 1970-72; from asst. prof. to prof. English, comparative lit. and film /video U. Mich., Ann Arbor, 1972-85; dir. program in comparative lit. U. Mich., 1981-97, asst. to dean spl. projects, 1997-98; Dewitt Wallace prof. English, chair English Dept. Macalester Coll., St. Paul, 1998—. Vis. prof. film Aegean Inst., Greece, 1994; vis. scholar Senapulli, Brazil, 1996. Author: Ezra Pound and the Troubadour Tradition, 1972 (Bredvold prize 1973), 1973; Made into Movies: From Literature to Film, 1985,; editor: Dante Among the Moderns, 1985; co-editor: Play It Again, Sam: Retakes on Remakes, 1998; contbr. articles to profl. jours. Am. Council of Learned Socs. fellow, 1974-75; U. Mich. Rackham Research grantee, 1975-76; Fulbright Assn. sr. lectr., Italy, 1978; recipient Faculty Recognition award, U. Mich., 1987. Fellow Dirs. Guild Am. (summr workshop, 1993); mem. MLA, Am. Comparative Lit. Assn. (sec.-treas. 1983-89, v.p. 1989-91, pres. 1991-93), Internat. Comparative Lit. Assn., Soc. Cinema Studies. Democrat Office: Macalester Coll English Dept 1600 Grand Ave Saint Paul MN 55105-1801

MCDOWELL, JOHN EUGENE, lawyer; b. Toledo, Nov. 22, 1927; s. Glenn Hugh and Evelyn (Millspaugh) McD.; m. Jean Ann Hepler, June 18, 1950; children: Jane Lynn McDowell Thummel, Sheila Lorraine McDowell Laing. BS, Miami U., Oxford, Ohio, 1949; JD, U. Mich., 1952. Bar: Ohio 1952. Assoc. Dinsmore & Shohl, Cin., 1952-59, ptnr., 1959-97, of counsel, 1997—. Bd. dirs. Structural Dynamics Rsch. Corp., Milford, Ohio. Mem. solicitation coms. United Appeal, Cin., NCCJ, Cin., Boy Scouts Am., Cin. Mem. ABA, Ohio Bar Assn., Cin. Bar Assn., Cin. Country Club, Queen City Club, Order of Coif. Democrat. Episcopalian. Office: Dinsmore & Shohl 1900 Chemed Ctr 255 E 5th St Cincinnati OH 45202-4700

MCDOWELL, RICHARD WILLIAM, college president; b. McDonald, Pa., Aug. 20, 1936; s. William Murdock and Cora Josephine (Brackman) McD.; m. Ann Brammer, May 27, 1961; children: Susan, Kathleen, Karen. BS, Indiana U. of Pa., 1960, MEd, 1962; MS, Purdue U., 1967, PhD, 1969. Cert. tchr., Pa. Tchr. Penn Hills Sch. Dist., Pa., 1960-67; divsn. chmn. Cmty. Coll. Allegheny County, West Mifflin, 1969-71; dean, acting pres. C.C. Beaver County, Monaca, 1971-72; exec. dean C.C. Allegheny County, Monroeville, 1972-80, v.p. strategic planning Pitts., 1980-81; pres. Schoolcraft Coll., Livonia, Mich., 1981—. Mgmt. cons., Pa. and Ill., 1975-80; chmn., mem. evaluation team Middle States Assn., Phila., 1972-80; trainer workshop leaders Higher Edn. Mgmt. Inst., Washington, 1976-77. With USMC, 1954-56. Recipient Outstanding Tchr. award Spectroscopy Soc., Pitts., 1966, Edn. award Plymouth C. of C., Mich., 1982. Mem. Am. Assn. Cmty. and Jr. Colls., Mich. C.C. Assn. (bd. dirs. exec. com.), W.E. Mich. League C.C. (chmn.), North Central Assn., Assn. C.C. Trustees. Office: Schoolcraft Coll 18600 Haggerty Rd Livonia MI 48152-3932

MCEACHEN, RICHARD EDWARD, banker, lawyer; b. Omaha, Sept. 24, 1933; s. Howard D. and Ada Carolyn Helen (Baumann) McE.; m. Judith Ann Gray, June 28, 1969; children: Mark E., Neil H. BS, U. Kans., Lawrence, 1955; JD, U. Mich., 1961. Bar: Mo. 1961, Kans. 1982. Assoc. Hillix, Hall, Hasburgh, Brown & Hoffhaus, Kansas City, Mo., 1961-62; sr. v.p. First Nat. Bank, 1962-75; exec. v.p. Commerce Bank Kansas City, 1975-85, Centerre Bank of Kansas City N.A., 1985-87, Security Bank Kansas City, Kans., 1987-88; exec. v.p., trust officer UMB Overland Park Bank, 1988-93; atty. Ferree, Bunn, O'Grady & Rundberg, Chartered, Overland Park, 1994—. Gov. Am. Royal Assn., Kansas City, Mo., 1970—, amb., 1980—, com. mem., 1995—; bd. dirs. Harry S. Truman Med. Ctr., Kansas City, 1974-86, mem. fin. com., 1975-86, treas., 1979-84, bd. govs., 1986—, mem. bldg. and grounds com., 1993—, mem. pension com., 1976-93, 96-2000; trustee Clearinghouse for Midcontinent Founds., 1980-87; bd. dirs. Greater Kansas City Mental Health Found., 1963-69, treas., 1964-69, v.p., 1967-69; adv. bd. urban svcs. YMCA, Kansas City, 1976-83; cubmaster Kanza dist. Boy Scouts Am., 1982-83, dist. vice chmn., 1982-83, troop com., 1983-90, treas., 1986-88; bd. dirs. Scout Booster Club, Inc., 1989-94; mem. planned gift com. William Rockhill Nelson Gallery Art, Children's Mercy Hosp. Planned Gift Coun., 1991; mem. adv. com. Legal Assistance Program Avila Coll., 1978-80, adv. coun. Future Farmers Am., 1972-82; mgr. Oppenstein Bros. Found., 1979-85; trustee Village Presbyn. Ch., 1987-90, chmn., 1989-90, elder, 1994-97; found. com. Am. Royal Charitable Found., 1995—; bd. dirs. Village Presbyn. Ch. Found., 1987-89, 94-97, chmn., 1996-97, mem. adv. bd., 1997-2001; bd. dirs. Estate Planning Coun., 1984-86; mem. Kansas City Fed. Estate Planning Symposium Com., 1992-98; bd. dirs. Shawnee Mission Med. Ctr. Found., 1988—, fin. com., 1989-92, mem. planned giving com., 1996-, mem. investment com. Mem. Nat. Assn. Securities Dealers Inc. (bd. arbitrators 1994—), Am. Arbitration Assn. (panel arbitrators 1994-96), Estate Planning Soc. Kansas City, Mo. Bar Assn., Kans. Bar Assn., Johnson County Bar Assn., Estate Planning Assn. (pres. 1974-75), Kansas City Jr. C. of C. (v.p. 1964-66), Ea. Kans. Estate Planning Coun., 40-Yrs. Ago Column Club (program com. 1999-2000, pres. 2001, bd. trustees 2001-), Indian Hills Club, Delta Tau Delta Alumni (v.p. Kansas City chpt. 1978-80). Republican. Home: 9100 El Monte St Shawnee Mission KS 66207-2627 Office: One Glenwood Pl 9300 Metcalf Ave Ste 300 Shawnee Mission KS 66212-6319

MCELHANEY, JAMES WILLSON, lawyer, educator; b. N.Y.C., Dec. 10, 1937; s. Lewis Keck and Sara Jane (Hess) McE.; m. Maxine Dennis Jones, Aug. 17, 1961; children: David, Benjamin. AB, Duke U., 1960; LLB, 1962. Bar: Wis. 1962. Assoc. Wickham, Borgelt, Skogstad & Powell, 1966; asst. prof. U. Md. Law Sch., 1966-69, assoc. prof., 1969-72; vis. prof. So. Meth. U. Sch. of Law, Dallas, 1973-74, prof., 1974-76; Joseph C. Hostetler prof. trial practice and advocacy Case Western Res. U. Sch. of Law, Cleve., 1976—; mem. faculty Nat. Inst. Trial Advocacy, Boulder, Colo., 1975—. Vis. prof. U. Tulsa Coll. Law, summer 1977, 79, Ind. U. Law Sch., summer 1980; cons. to U.S. Atty. Gen. on Justice Dept. Advocacy Tng. Programs, 1979— ; lectr. in field; litigation cons.; spl. cons. U. S.C. Sch. of Law Nat. Advocacy Ctr., 1998. Author: Effective Litigation: Trials, Problems and Materials, 1974, Trial Notebook, 1981, 3rd edit., 1994, Trial Notebook on Tape: The Basics, 1989, Mc Elhaney's Trial Notebook on Tape: Advanced Techniques, 1991, Mc Elhaney's Trial Notebook on Tape: Evidence, Foundations and Objections, 1992, Mc Elhaney's Trial Notebook on Tape: Winning Tactics, 1994, Mc Elhaney's Litigation, 1995, Mc Elhaney on Cross-Examination on Tape, 1997, Mc Elhaney on Depositions and Trial Preparation on Tape, 1999; editor-in-chief Litigation mag., 1984-86, sr. editor, 1986—; columnist Trial Notebook, Litigation; contbr. articles to profl. jours. Mem. ABA (mem. coun. on litigation 1987—, author jour. column Litigation), Assn. Am. Law Schs. (chmn. sect. on trial advocacy 1974-76, chmn. sect. on evidence 1978). Office: Case Western Res U 11075 East Blvd Cleveland OH 44106-5409

MCELROY, DAN, state legislator; b. July 15, 1948; m. Mary McElroy. BA, U. Notre Dame. Minn. state rep. Dist. 36B, 1994—. Former mgmt. cons. Address: 12805 Welcome Ln Burnsville MN 55337-3623

MCELWREATH, SALLY CHIN, public relations executive; b. N.Y.C., Oct. 15, 1940; d. Toon Guey and Jean B. (Wong) Chin; m. Joseph F. Callo, Mar. 17, 1979; 1 child, R.J. McElwreath III. BA, Pace Coll., 1963; MBA, Pace U., 1969. Copywriter O.E. McIntyre, N.Y.C., 1963-65; editorial asst. Sinclair Oil Corp., 1966-70; account exec. Muller, Jordan & Herrick, 1970-71; regional mgr. pub. relations United Airlines, 1971-79; dir. corp. communications Trans World Airlines, 1979-86; v.p. pub. rels. TWA Mktg. Svcs., Inc., 1986-88; ptnr. The Communications Group, N.Y., 1988-90; gen. mgr. corp. comms. Official Airline Guides, 1990-91; v.p. corp. comms. Macmillan, Inc., 1991-93; cons. N.Y.C., 1993-94; sr. v.p. corp. comms Utilicorp United, Inc., Kansas City, 1994—. Capt. USNR, 1973-2000. Named Woman of Yr., YWCA, 1980, Alumnus of Yr., Pace U., 1976. Mem. N.Y. Airline Pub. Rels. Assn. (chmn. 1978-79), Wings Club (N.Y.C.), The Navnd Club (London). Clubs: Wings (N.Y.C.), Naval and Mil. (London), Ski Club Great Britain. Avocations: riding, sailing, skiing, harpsichord. Office: Utilicorp United Inc 20 W 9th St Kansas City MO 64105-1704 E-mail: sallymc79@aol.com.

MCENIRY, ROBERT FRANCIS, education educator, researcher; b. Milw., Feb. 22, 1918; s. Frank Michael and Mary (Brown) McE. BA, St. Louis U., 1941, Philosophiae Licentiatus cum laude, 1944, Theologiae Licentiatus cum laude, PhL, ThL cum laude, St. Louis U., 1953; PhD, Ohio State U., 1972. Elem. sch. inst., 1938-40; tchr. Howdershell Grade Sch., 1939-40; radio announcer Sta. WOW, St. Louis, 1941-43; instr. classics St. Louis U. High Sch., 1944-47, Creighton Prep. Sch., Omaha, 1947-48; asst. prof., chmn. classics Rockhurst Coll., Kansas City, Mo., 1953-58; retreat dir. White House Retreat, St. Louis, 1958-68; assoc. research prof. Creighton U., Omaha, 1972-89; ret., 1989. Dir., facilitator Growth for Couples, 1975-89; lectr. Creighton Natural Family Planning Ctr.; facilitator groups Adult Children of Alcoholism and Dysfunctional Families, 1989-93; vis. lectr. San Francisco Sch. Theology, San Anselmo, Calif., 1985; more than 800 presentations (lectrs., papers, workshops and seminars) in 175 cities, 22 states and 12 fgn. countries on value decisions during high anxiety and stress in marriage, family, teaching and learning; exec. dir. Studies Adult Survivors of Abuse, 1993—; tchr., counselor in marriage and family issues. Editor and pub. Interaction Review, 1982-89; editor Scholar and Educator, 1974-76; mem. editorial bd. Counseling and Values, 1976-82; editor (book) Pastoral Counseling, 1977, Premarriage Counseling, 1978; contbr. over 180 articles to profl. jours.; literary agent, 1992-98. Mem. Bd. of Pastoral Ministry, Omaha, 1972-78. Research grantee Council for Theol. Reflection, 1975-77; recipient Research award Creighton U., 1977; 1st prize for "Pro and Con" in Queen's Work Play contest, 1945. Fellow Nat. Acad. Counselors and Family Therapists (editor book rev. 1979-91); mem. APA, Am. Assn. for Religious Values in Counseling (editor newsletter 1982-89, Outstanding Svc. award 1985, Meritorious Svc. award 1989, Edgar Dale award 1995), Phi Delta Kappa (exec. com. 1977-83, del. 1981-83). Avocations: barbershop quartets, photography, Civil War sites, yoga. Home: 3030 S 60 St #231 Omaha NE 68124-3263

MCENROE, PAUL, reporter; Gen. assignment reporter, National writer Mpls. Star Tribune, Mpls, to 1996, investigative reporter in projects unit, 1996—. Office: Star Tribune 425 Portland Ave Minneapolis MN 55488-0002

MCFADDEN, JOHN VOLNEY, retired manufacturing company executive; b. N.Y.C., Oct. 3, 1931; s. Volney and Mary Lucile (McConkie) McF.; m. Marie Linstead, June 27, 1953; children— Deborah, John Scott, David. B.S. in Commerce and Fin, Bucknell U., 1953; J.D., Detroit Coll. Law, 1960. Pres., vice chmn. MTD Products, Inc., Cleve., 1960-92; pres. MTD Products Inc., 1980-91, vice chmn., 1990-92; gen. ptnr. Camelot Ptnrs.; owner, mgr. Parkside Acquisition Ptnrs. Ltd., 1997—. Vice chmn. C.E. White Co.; bd. dirs. Fusion Inc., Flambeau Corp., West Roofing Supply Inc.; chmn. bd. dirs. Guarantee Spltys. Inc.; past chmn. financing adv. bd. State of Ohio Devel.; past pres. Cleve. World Trade Assn.; chmn. Parkside Acquisition Ptnrs. Ltd.; vice chair Chemitrol Chem. Co., Inc. Trustee Fairview Health Svcs, Cleve. Clinic. Lt. Supply Corps, USN. Mem. Cleve. Yachting Club. Office: Parkside Acq Ptnrs Ltd 20160 Parkside Dr Cleveland OH 44116-1347

MCFARLAND, KAY ELEANOR, state supreme court chief justice; b. Coffeyville, Kans., July 20, 1935; d. Kenneth W. and Margaret E. (Thrall) McF. BA magna cum laude, Washburn U., Topeka, 1957, JD, 1964. Bar: Kans. 1964. Sole practice, Topeka, 1964-71; probate and juvenile judge Shawnee County, 1971-73; dist. judge, 1973-77; assoc. justice Kans. Supreme Ct., 1977-95, chief justice, 1995—. Mem. Kans. Bar Assn., Women Attys. Assn. Topeka. Office: Kans Supreme Ct Kans Jud Ctr 301 W 10th St Topeka KS 66612 Fax: (785) 291-3274.

MC FARLAND, ROBERT HAROLD, physicist, educator; b. Severy, Kans., Jan. 10, 1918; s. Robert Eugene and Georgia (Simpson) McF.; m. Twilah Mae Seefeld, Aug. 28, 1940; children: Robert Alan, Rodney Jon. B.S. and B.A., Kans. State Tchrs. Coll., Emporia, 1940; Ph.M. (Mendenhall fellow), U. Wis., 1943, Ph.D., 1947. Sci. instr., coach high sch., Chase, Kans., 1940-41; instr. navy radio sch. U. Wis., Madison, 1943-44; sr. engr. Sylvania Elec. Corp., 1944-46; faculty Kans. State U., 1947-60, prof. physics, 1954-60, dir. nuclear lab., 1958-60; physicist U. Calif. Lawrence Radiation Lab., 1960-69; dean Grad. Sch., U. Mo., Rolla, 1969-79, dir. instnl. analysis and planning, 1979-82; prof. physics U. Mo., 1969-84, prof. emeritus physics dept., 1985—; v.p. acad. affairs U. Mo. System, 1974-75; Intergovtl. Personnel Act appointee Dept. Energy, Washington, 1982-84; vis. prof. U. Calif., Berkeley, 1980-81. Mem. Grad. Record Exams. Bd., 1971-75, chmn. steering com., 1972-73; cons. Well Surveys, Inc., Tulsa, 1953-54, Argonne Nat. Lab., Chgo., 1955-59, Kans. Dept. Pub. Health, 1956-57, cons. in residence Lawrence Radiation Lab., U. Calif., 1957, 58, 59, med. physics U. Okla. Med. Sch., 1971, grad. schs., PhD physics program, Utah State U., 1972; physicist, regional counselor Office Ordnance Research, Durham, N.C., 1955. Contbr. over 110 articles to profl. jours.; patentee in field of light prodn., vacuum prodn., controlled thermonuclear reactions. Active Boy Scouts Am., 1952—, mem. exec. bd. San Francisco Bay Area council, 1964-68, Ozark Council, 1986—; chmn. Livermore (Calif.) Library Bond drive, 1964. Mem. Kans. N.G., 1936-40. Recipient Silver Beaver award Boy Scouts Am., 1968, Community Service award C. of C., 1965, Disting. Alumnus award Kans. State Tchrs. Coll., 1969. Fellow AAAS, Am. Phys. Soc., Kiwanis Internat.; mem. AAUP (chpt. pres. 1956-57), Am. Assn. Physics Tchrs., Mo. Acad. Sci., Mo. Assn. Phys. Sci. Tchrs., Am. Soc. Engring. Edn., Kiwanis (lt. gov. Mo.-Ark. dist. 1984-85, internat. accredited rep. 1985-92, Disting. Lt. Gov. 1985, Tablet of honor award 1997), Sigma Xi, Lambda Delta Lambda, Xi Phi, Kappa Mu Epsilon, Kappa Delta Pi, Pi Mu Epsilon, Gamma Sigma Delta, Phi Kappa Phi. Home: 309 Christy Dr Rolla MO 65401-4073 Office: U Mo Dept Physics Rolla MO 65401

MC FARLANE, KAREN ELIZABETH, concert artists manager; b. St. Louis, Jan. 2, 1942; d. Nicholas and Bonita Margaret (Fults) Walz; m. Ralph Leo McFarlane, Nov. 30, 1968 (div.); children: Sarah Louise.; m. Walter Holtkamp, June 19, 1982. B.Mus.Ed. (Presser Music Found. scholar), Lindenwood Coll., 1964. Public sch. music tchr., St. Louis County, 1964-66; music asst. Riverside Ch., N.Y.C., 1966-70; dir. music Park Ave. Christian Ch., 1974-81; also pres. Murtagh/McFarlane Artists, Inc., Cleve., 1976-88; pres. Karen McFarlane Artists, 1989-2000. Mem. Am. Guild Organists, Nat. Assn. Performing Arts Mgrs. and Agts., Inc., Internat. Soc. Performing Arts Adminstrn. Democrat. Presbyterian. Office: 2385 Fenwood Rd Cleveland OH 44118 E-mail: karen@concertorganists.com.

MCFARREN, FREDDY E. military career officer; b. Cleburne, Tex., Oct. 13, 1943; s. Aubrey McFarren; children: Preston, William. BS, U.S. Mil. Acad., 1966; MEd, Duke U.; grad., Armed Forces Staff Coll., U.S. Army War Coll. Commd. 2d lt. U.S. Army, 1966, advanced through grades to maj. gen., various positions, comdr. 18th Field Artillary Brigade, XVIII Airborne Corps, bn. comdr. 1st Bn. 319th Airborne Field Artillery 82d Divsn., exec. officer 155mm bn. 8th Inf. Divsn. Europe; tactical officer U.S. Mil. Acad.; advisor to Vietnamese Rangers U.S. Army, Vietnam, field arty. battery comdr. XVIII Airborne Corps Arty., asst. chief staff ops. G3 XVIII Airborne Corps N.C., asst. divsn. comdr. 24th Inf. Divsn. (Mechanized) Ft. Stewart, Ga.; comdt. of cadets U.S. Mil. Acad., West Point, N.Y.; dir. tng. Office of the Dep. Chief Staff for Ops. and Plans U.S. Army, Washington, chief Office Mil. Cooperation Cairo, commdg. gen. Ft. Riley Kans., 1998—. Decorated Silver Star, Def. Superior Svc. medal, Legion of Merit with four oak leaf clusters, Bronze Star with V device and three oak leaf clusters, Purple Heart, Meritorious Svc. medal with two oak leaf clusters, Air medal, Army Commendation medal with oak leaf cluster, French Croix de Guerre with Gold Star, The Republic of Vietnam Cross of Gallantry with two Palms and the Honor medal first class. Office: Fort Riley-US Army Fort Riley KS 66442

MCFATE, KENNETH LEVERNE, trade association administrator; b. LeClaire, Iowa, Feb. 5, 1924; s. Samuel Albert and Margaret (Spear) McF.; m. Imogene Grace Kness, Jan. 27, 1951; children: Daniel Elliott, Kathryn Margaret, Sharon Ann. BS in Agrl. Engring., Iowa State U., 1950; MS in Agrl. Engring., U. Mo., 1959. Registered profl. engr., Mo. Agrl. sales engr. Ill. No. Utility Co., Aledo, 1950-51; extension agrl. engr. Iowa State U., Ames, 1951-53, rsch. agrl. engr., 1953-56; prof. agrl. engr. U. Mo., Columbia, 1956-86, prof. emeritus, 1986; dir. Mo. Farm Electric Coun., 1956-75; exec. mgr. Nat. Farm Electric Coun., 1975-86; pres. Nat. Food and Energy Coun., 1986-91, pres. emeritus, 1991; mgr. Electrotechnology Rsch., 1991-93. Bd. dirs. Internat. Congress Agrl. Engrs., Brussels, 1989-94. Editor, author: (with others) Handbook for Elsevier Science, Electrical Energy in World Agriculture, 1989; mem. editl. bd. Energy in Agriculture for Elsevier Sci., Amsterdam, The Netherlands, 1981-88. 2d lt. USAAF, 1943-45. Recipient Outstanding Svc. awards Nat. Safety Coun., 1975, MOFEC, 1976, Nat. 4-H Coun., 1982, Nat. Hon. Extension Frat., 1984, Hon. Am. Future Farmers Assn. degree, 1991. Fellow Am. Soc. Agrl. Engrs. (George Kable elec. award 1974, Spl. Svc. award, 2000); mem. Alpha Epsilon, Gamma Sigma Delta. Republican. Presbyterian. Avocations: technical writing, gardening, woodworking.

MCFEE, WILLIAM WARREN, soil scientist; b. Concord, Tenn., Jan. 8, 1935; s. Fred Thomas and Ellen Belle (Russell) McF.; m. Barbara Anella Steelman, June 23, 1957; children— Sabra Anne, Patricia Lynn, Thomas Hallie. B.S., U. Tenn., 1957; M.S., Cornell U., 1963, Ph.D., 1966. Mem. faculty Purdue U., 1965—, prof. soil sci., 1973—, dir. natural resources and environ. sci. program, 1975-91, head dept. agronomy, 1991-2001. Vis. prof. U. Fla., 1986-87; cons. U.S. Forest Svc., Desert Rsch. Inst. Author articles in field, chpts. in books. Served with USAR, 1958-61. Alpha Zeta scholar, 1957; named Outstanding Agr. Tchr. Purdue U., 1972; recipient Am. Educator award Soil Sci. Soc., 1987. Fellow: Soil Sci. Soc. Am. (pres. 1991—92), Am. Soc. Agronomy 1996—97, (resident edn. award 1989); mem.: Purdue Agrl. Alumni Assn. (cert. of distinction 2002), Ind. Seed Trade Assn. (hon.), Sigma Xi. Presbyterian. Home: 708 Mccormick Rd West Lafayette IN 47906-4915 Office: Purdue U Dept Agronomy West Lafayette IN 47907 E-mail: wmcfee@purdue.edu.

MCFEETORS, RAYMOND L. insurance company executive; b. May 23, 1944; m. Lynne-Anne; children: Leah, Marshall, Holly, Drew. BA, U. Winnipeg, Man., Can., 1968. CFA. Trainee group divsn. Great-West Life Assurance Co., Winnipeg, 1968-71, with bond investments dept., 1971-76, mgr. bond investments, 1976-78, bond investment officer, 1978-80, investment officer, pvt. placements, 1980-84, v.p. bond and pvt. placement investments, 1984-86, sr. v.p. pvt. placement investments Can., 1986-91, sr. v.p., CFO, 1991-92, pres., chief investment officer, 1992—; pres., CEO London Life, 1997. Avocation: boating. Office: Gt-West Life Assurance Co 100 Osborne St N Winnipeg MB Canada R3C 1C3

MCFERSON, DIMON RICHARD, insurance company executive; b. 1937; m. Darlene Moss; 7 children. BA, UCLA, 1959; MA, U. So. Calif., 1972. CPA, CLU. With Ernst & Young; sr. v.p. finance Surety Life Ins. Co., Salt Lake City, New Eng. Life, until 1979; sr. v.p. fin., then exec. v.p. Nationwide Mut. Ins. Co., 1978-88, pres., dir., 1988-96, CEO, 1996—, also chmn. bd. dirs.; also pres. Nationwide Mut. Fire Ins., Nationwide Gen. Ins. Co.; sr. v.p. fin., dir. Nationwide Fin. Svcs. Inc.; sr. v.p. Nationwide Devel. Co.; CEO Nationwide Ins. Enterprise, Columbus, Ohio, 1992-2000, chmn., 1996-2000. Office: Nationwide Life Insurance Co 1 Nationwide Plz Columbus OH 43215-2239

MCGAFFEY, JERE D. lawyer; b. Lincoln, Nebr., Oct. 6, 1935; s. Don Larsen and Doris McG.; m. Ruth S. Michelsen, Aug. 19, 1956; children: Beth, Karen. BA, BSc with high distinction, U. Nebr., 1957; LLB magna cum laude, Harvard U., 1961. Bar: Wis. 1961. Mem. firm Foley & Lardner, Milw., 1961—, ptnr., 1968—. Dir. Smith Investment Co., Northwestern Mut. Trust Co., Lord Balt. Corp., Wis. Gas Co., 1978-2000. Author works in field. Chmn. bd. dirs. Helen Bader Found.; vice chmn. legis. Milw. Met. Assn. Commerce; former chmn. Wis. Taxpayers Alliance, sec.-treas., 1994—; former chmn. bd. dirs. Aurora Health Care, 1986—; chmn. bd. advisors U. Wis. Nursing Sch., Milw. Mem. ABA (chmn. tax sect. 1990-91, ho. dels. 1995-2000), AICPA, Wis. Bar Assn., Wis. Inst. CPAs, Am. Coll. Tax Counsel (chmn. 1996-98), Am. Coll. Trust and Estate Counsel (chmn. bus. planning com. 1994-97, regent 2000—), Am. Law Inst., Univ. Club (Milw.), Milw. Club, Milw. Country Club, Harvard Club N.Y.C., Univ. Club Washington, Phi Beta Kappa, Beta Gamma Sigma, Delta Sigma Rho. Home: 12852 NW Shoreland Dr Mequon WI 53097-2304 Office: Foley & Lardner 777 E Wisconsin Ave Ste 3600 Milwaukee WI 53202-5302 E-mail: jkmcgaffey@foleylaw.com.

MCGANNON, JOHN BARRY, university chancellor; b. Humboldt, Kans., Apr. 18, 1924; s. Patrick Joseph and Jane Clare (Barry) McG. AB magna cum laude, St. Louis U., 1947, MA, 1952, PhD, 1963. Joined Soc. of Jesus, 1942, ordained priest Roman Catholic Ch., 1955. Dean Coll. Arts and Scis. St. Louis U., 1963-73; v.p. Rockhurst Coll., Kansas City, 1973-77; v.p. for devel. St. Louis U., 1977-90, chancellor, 1990—. Cons., examiner North Ctrl. Accrediting Assn., Chgo., 1958-80. Trustee Loyola U., New Orleans, 1988-94, St. Peter's Coll., Jersey City, 1991-97, U. San Francisco, 1991—. Mem. Jesuit Advancement Adminstrs. (pres. 1985-87), Coun. for Advancement and Support of Edn., Nat. Soc. Fund Raising Execs., Nat. Coun. for Planned Giving, Rotary. Office: St Louis U 221 N Grand Blvd Saint Louis MO 63103-2006

MCGARITY, MARGARET DEE, federal judge; b. 1948; BA, Emory U., 1969; JD, U. Wis., 1974. Bar: Wis. 1974. Pvt. practice, 1974-87; bankruptcy judge U.S. Dist. Ct. (ea. dist.) Wis., 1987—. Lectr. on marital property, bankruptcy and family law Fed. Judicial Ctr., Nat. Conf. Bankruptcy Judges, State Bar Wis., Nat. Child Support Enforcement Assn., others. Co-author: Marital Property Law in Wisconsin, 2d edit. 1986, Collier Family Law and the Bankruptcy Code, 1991. Mem. Nat. Conf. Bankruptcy Judges, State Bar Wis., Nat. Assn. Women Judges, Milw. Bar Assn., Assn. Women Lawyers, Thomas E. Fairild Inn, Am. Coll. Bankruptcy, Am. Bankruptcy Inst. Office: 162 US Courthouse 517 E Wisconsin Ave Milwaukee WI 53202-4500

MCGARR, FRANK JAMES, retired federal judge, dispute resolution consultant; b. Feb. 25, 1921; married; 6 children. BA cum laude in Philosophy, Loyola U., Chgo., 1942; JD, Loyola U., 1950. Bar: Ill. 1950. Assoc. Dallstream Schiff Stern & Hardin, Chgo., 1952—54; asst. U.S. atty., chief criminal divsn. No. dist. of Ill., 1954—55, first asst. U.S. atty., 1955—58; ptnr. McKay Solum & McGarr, Chgo., 1958—68; first asst. atty. gen. State of Ill., 1969—70; judge U.S. Dist. Ct. for No. Ill., 1970—88, chief judge, 1981—86, sr. judge, 1986—88; of counsel Phelan Cahill & Quinlan, Chgo., 1988—96, Foley & Lardner, Chgo., 1996—2001; pvt. practice, 2001—. Instr. Eng. and pub. speaking Loyola U., 1946—48, administrv. asst. to pres., 1948—52; instr. law Loyola U. Law Sch., 1950—52, instr. criminal law, 1953—57, prof. admiralty and maritime law, 1953—57; instr. legal ethics John Marshal Law Sch., 1985—86. Chmn.

law observance com. Chgo. Crime Comm., v.p., bd. dirs.; chmn. Law Enforcement Week Com.; pres. Constl. Rights Found., 1994; chmn. Ill Gov.'s Comm. on Death Penalty, 2000. With USN, 1942—45, Pacific Fleet. Named Man of Yr., Cath. Lawyers Guild Chgo., 1985; recipient Alumni Medal of Excellence, Loyola Law Alumni, 1964, Mother Cabrini award, Columbus-Cuneo-Cabrini Med. Ctr., 1978, Dei Gloriam award, St. Ignatius Coll. Prep, 1984. Fellow: Am. Coll. Trial Lawyers; mem.: Soc. Trial Lawyers, Chgo. Bar Assn., Fed. Bar Assn. (pres. chgo. chpt. 1962—63, mem. exec. com.), 7th Cir. Bar Assn. Office: 4146 Venard Rd Downers Grove IL 60515-1908

MCGARR, JOSEPH W. paper company executive; Dir. strategy, consumer products bus. James River Corp., 1982-96; v.p. cost and sys. effectiveness, 1996-97; sr. v.p. planning and strategy Ft. James Corp. (merger Ft. Howard Corp. and James River), Deerfield, 1997-2000; exec. v.p., CFO Ill., 2000—. Office: Fort James Corp 1919 S Broadway Green Bay WI 54304-4905

MCGAVRAN, FREDERICK JAEGER, lawyer; b. Columbus, Ohio, Apr. 24, 1943; s. James Holt and Marion (Jaeger) McG.; m. Elizabeth Dowlig, Jan. 5, 1980; children: Sarah Ann, Marian Katherine. BA, Kenyon Coll., 1965; JD, Harvard U., 1972. Bar: Ohio 1972, U.S. Supreme Ct. 1984, Ky. 1992. Assoc. Kyte, Conlan, Wulsin & Vogeler, Cin., 1972-78, Frost & Jacobs, Cin., 1978-2000, Frost, Brown & Todd, LLC, Cin., 2000—. Editor-in-chief Sixth Circuit Federal Practice Manual, 1999. Lt. USN, 1965-69. Mem. Fed. Bar Assn. (pres. Cin. chpt. 1984-85, mem. exec. com. Cin. chpt. 1985—), Ohio State Bar Assn. (chmn. com. on fed. cts. 1982-85), Univ. Club of Cin., The Literary Club. Home: 2560 Perkins Ln Cincinnati OH 45208-2723 Office: Frost Brown & Todd LLC 2200 PNC Ctr Cincinnati OH 45202 E-mail: fmcgavran@fbtlaw.com.

MCGEE, CHICK, radio personality; Radio host morning show Sta. WFBQ-FM, Indpls. Office: WFBQ 6161 Fall Creek Rd Indianapolis IN 46220*

MCGEE, HOWARD, radio personality; Weekend radio host Sta. WGCI-FM, Chgo., midday radio host, afternoon radio host, 1996—98, morning show radio host, 1998—. Office: WGCI 332 S Michigan Ave Ste 600 Chicago IL 60604*

MC GEE, JOSEPH JOHN, JR. former insurance company executive; b. Kansas City, Mo., Dec. 2, 1919; s. Joseph J. and Margaret (Cronin) McG.; m. Anne Cunningham, Apr. 30, 1949; children: Sally, Peter, Mary, John, David, Julie, Simon. Attended, Rockhurst Coll., Kansas City, Georgetown U. Asst. sec. Old Am. Ins. Co., Kansas City, Mo., 1939-45, v.p., 1946-51, exec. v.p., 1952-55, pres., 1956-87; ins. cons. Kansas City, Mo., 1987-91. Bd. dirs. Truman Med. Ctr., Truman Libr. Inst. for Nat. and Internat. Affairs; trustee emeritus Rockhurst Coll.; pres. McGee Found. Office: 1045 W 54th St Kansas City MO 64112

MCGEE, PATRICK EDGAR, postal service clerk; b. Chgo., Jan. 13, 1944; s. Ralph and Minnie Odelia (Crutcher) McG. Machine clk. U.S. Postal Svc., Chgo., 1977—. Author of poems. Mem. The Art Inst. Chgo., Mus. Sci. & Industry, Chgo. Mem. Internat. Soc. Poets. Democrat. Roman Catholic. Avocations: painting, jazz, walking, jogging.

MCGEE, SHERRY, retail executive; b. Honolulu, Nov. 16, 1957; d. Winnie R. Johnson; 1 child, Michael L. BS, Wayne State U., 1987, MBA, 1991. Divsn. sales mgr. CDI Corp., 1978-89; sales tng. cons. McGee & Co., 1990-92; dir. mktg. Bartech, Inc., 1992-97; founder, pres. Apple Book Ctr., 1996—. Vol. Jr. Achievement. Office: Apple Book Ctr 7900 W Outer Dr Detroit MI 48235 E-mail: apple001@aol.com.

MCGEE, WILLIAM DEAN (WILLIE MCGEE), professional baseball player; b. San Francisco, Nov. 2, 1958; Student, Diablo Valley Coll., Pleasant Hill, Calif. Baseball player N.Y. Yankees, 1977-81, St. Louis Cardinals, 1981-90, 95—, Oakland Athletics, 1990, San Francisco Giants, 1990-95. Mem. Nat. League All-Star Team, 1983, 85, 87-88; recipient Gold Glove Award, 1983, 85-86; named Nat. League Most Valuable Player, Basball Writers Assoc. of Am., 1985; Sporting News Nat. League Player of the Year, 1985; recipient Silver Slugger award, 1985; Nat. League Batting Champion, 1985, 90. Achievements include playing in the World Series, 1982, 85, 87, 90. Office: St Louis Cardinals Busch Stadium 250 Stadium Plz Saint Louis MO 63102-1722

MC GEHEE, H(ARRY) COLEMAN, JR. bishop; b. Richmond, Va., July 7, 1923; s. Harry Coleman and Ann Lee (Cheatwood) McG.; m. June Stewart, Feb. 1, 1946; children: Lesley, Alexander, Harry III, Donald, Cary. BS, Va. Poly. Inst., 1947; JD, U. Richmond, 1949; MDiv, Va. Theol. Sem., 1957, DD, 1973. Bar: Va. 1949, U.S. Supreme Ct. 1954; ordained to ministry Episcopal Ch., 1957. Spl. counsel dept. hwys. State of Va., 1949-51, gen. counsel employment svc., 1951, asst. atty. gen., 1951-54; rector Immanuel Ch.-on-the-Hill, Va. Sem., 1960-71; bishop Diocese of Mich., Detroit, 1971-90. Adv. bd. Nicaraguan Network, Ctr. for Peace and Conflict Studies, Wayne State U.; bd. dirs. Mich. Religious Coalition for Abortion Rights, 1976-84; trustee Va. Theol. Sem., 1978-93; pres. Episc. Ch. Pub. Co., 1978-85. Columnist: Detroit News, 1979-85; weekly commentator pub. radio sta. WDET-AM, Detroit, 1984-90. Mem. Gov.'s Commn. on Status of Women, 1965-66, Mayor's Civic Com., Alexandria, 1967-68; sponsor Nat. Assn. for ERA, 1977-85; pres. Alexandria Legal Aid Soc., 1969-71; bd. dirs. No. Va. Fairhousing Corp., 1963-67; pres. Mich. Coalition for Human Rights, 1980-89; chmn. Citizens' Com. for Justice in Mich., 1983-84; sponsor Farm Labor Orgn. for Children, 1983-85; bd. dirs. Pub. Benefit Corp., Detroit, 1988-90, Mich. Citizens for Personal Freedom, 1989-92, Poverty and Social Reform Inst., Detroit, 1989—, Bread for the World, 1990-94, Ams. United for Separation of Ch. and State, 1990, ACLU Oakland County, Mich., 1991-94; co-chair Lesbian-Gay Found. Mich., 1991—. 1st lt. C.E., U.S. Army, 1943-46. Named Feminist of Yr., Detroit NOW, 1978, Person of Yr., Econ. Justice Commn. Mich., 1997; recipient Humanitarian award Detroit ACLU, 1984, Phillip Hart medal Mich. Women's Studies Assn., 1984, Sayre award for justice and peace Episc. Peace Fellowship, 1988, Spirit of Detroit award, 1989, Archbishop Romero award Mich. Labor Com., 1990, Brotherhood award AME Ch., Detroit, 1993, Ira Jayne award Detroit br. NAACP, 1993, Martin Luther King, Jr. award United Ch. of Christ, 1995, William Scarlett award Episc. Ch. Pub. Co., 1997. Mem.: Detroit Econ. Club (bd. dirs.). Home: 1496 Ashover Dr Bloomfield Hills MI 48304-1215 Office: Diocese of Mich 4800 Woodward Ave Detroit MI 48201-1399

MCGILLEY, SISTER MARY JANET, nun, educator, writer, academic administrator; b. Kansas City, Mo., Dec. 4, 1924; d. James P. and Peg (Ryan) McG. BA, St. Mary Coll., 1945; MA, Boston Coll., 1951; PhD, Fordham U., 1956; postgrad., U. Notre Dame, 1960, Columbia U., 1964. Joined Sisters of Charity, Roman Catholic Ch., 1946. Social worker, Kansas City, 1945-46; tchr. English Hayden H.S., Topeka, 1948-50, Billings (Mont.) Central H.S., 1951-53; faculty dept. English St. Mary Coll., Leavenworth, Kans., 1956-64, pres., 1964-89, disting. prof. English and Liberal Studies, 1990-96, pres. emeritus, 1989—. Contbr. articles, fiction and poetry to various jours. Bd. dirs. United Way of Leavenworth, 1966-85; mem. Mayor's Adv. Coun., 1967-72; bd. dirs. Kans. Ind. Coll. Fund, 1964-89, exec. com., 1985-86, vice chmn., 1984-85, chmn., 1985-86. Recipient Alumnae award St. Mary Coll., 1969; Disting. Service award Baker U., 1981, Leavenworth Bus. Woman of Yr. Athena award, 1986. Mem. Nat. Coun. Tchrs. of English, Nat. Assn. Ind. Colls. and Univs. (bd. dirs. 1982-85), Kans. Ind. Coll. Assn. (bd. dirs. 1964-89, treas. 1982-84, v.p. 1984-85, chmn. exec. com. 1985-86), Am. Coun. Edn. (com. on women in higher edn. 1980-85), Am. Assn. Higher Edn., Kansas City Regional Coun. for Higher Edn. (bd. dirs. 1965-89, treas. 1984-85, v.p. 1986-88), Ind. Coll. Funds Am. (exec. com. 1974-77, trustee-at-large 1975-76), North Cen. Assn. Colls. and Schs. (exec. commr. Com. on Insts. Higher Edn. 1980-88, vice chair 1985-86, chair 1987-88), Leavenworth C. of C. (bd. dirs. 1964-89), Assn. Am. Colls. (commn. liberal learning 1970-73, com. on curriculum and faculty devel. 1979-82) St. Mary Alumni Assn. (hon. pres. 1964-89), Delta Epsilon Sigma. Democrat. Office: St Mary Coll 4100 S 4th St Leavenworth KS 66048-5082

MCGILLIVRAY, DONALD DEAN, seed company executive, agronomist; b. Muscatine, Iowa, Aug. 28, 1928; s. Walter C. and Pearl E. (Potter) McG.; m. Betty J. Anderson, June 24, 1951; children: Ann E., Jean M. BS in Agronomy, Iowa State U., 1950. Asst. mgr. Iowa, Minn., Wis. sect. Funk Seeds Internat., Belle Plaine, Iowa, 1965-69, mgr., 1969-70, mgr. hybrid corn ops. Bloomington, Ill., 1970-75, v.p. ops., 1976-82, pres., 1982-88; assoc. Smart Seeds, Inc., 1989—. Dir. U.S. Grains Coun., Washington, 1984-87. Bd. dirs. Ill. Agrl. Leadership Found., Macomb, 1985—, chmn. bd., 1990-2000; bd. dirs. Ill. Wesleyan Assocs., 1986-89, Ill. 4-H Found., 1996—; mem. adv. bd. Bro-Menn Hosp., 1985—, pres., 1989-90. Sgt. U.S. Army, 1951-53. Mem. Am. Seed Trade Assn. (bd. dirs. 1986-, divsn. chmn. 1978-79, 2d v.p. 1986-87, 1st v.p. 1987-88, pres. 1988-89), Am. Seed Rsch. Found. (bd. dirs. 1982-95, pres. 1984-87), Exch. Club, Masons.

MC GIMPSEY, RONALD ALAN, oil company executive; b. Cleve., June 7, 1944; s. John E. and Muriel N. McGimpsey; m. Linda V. Tiffany, Apr. 20, 1974. BS, Case Inst. Tech., 1966; MS, Case Western Res. U., 1974; grad. exec. program, Stanford U., 1987. With BP Amoco Corp. (formerly Standard Oil Co.), Ohio, 1966—; treas. BP Am. Inc. (formerly Standard Oil Co.), 1977-81, v.p. fin., 1981-82, sr. v.p. crude trading and transp., 1982-86, sr. v.p. petroleum products and refining, 1986-89; group contr. BP-London, 1989-91; regional sr. v.p., CFO BP America, Cleve., 1991-92, sr. v.p., fin. officer, 1992-93; CEO BP Australia, Melbourne, 1994-98; chief adminstrv. officer USA BP Amoco Corp., 1999—. Chmn. bd. trustees Marymount Hosp., Cleve., 1986-88; adv. bd. Case Inst. Tech. Mem. Bus. Coun. Australia, Australia Inst. of Petroleum (chmn. 1995-97). Office: BP Amoco Corp 545 Lincoln Ave Winnetka IL 60093-2349

MCGINLEY, JACK L. healthcare company executive; B in Mktg. Adminstrn., U. N.D. With Baxter Healthcare, 1970—, various sales and mktg. positions, v.p. Baxter Can., 1982, gen. mgr. Baxter U.K., 1984, v.p. mktg. and mfg. Baxter's World Trade Corp., pres. Baxter Japan, pres. drug adminstn. divsn., corp. v.p., pres. IV systems divsn., group v.p., group v.p. IV systems/med. products. Office: Baxter Healthcare One Baxter Parkway Deerfield IL 60015-4633

MCGINN, BERNARD JOHN, religious educator; b. Yonkers, N.Y., Aug. 19, 1937; s. Bernard John and Catherine Ann (Faulds) McG.; m. Patricia Ann Ferris, July 10, 1971; children: Daniel, John. BA, St. Joseph's Sem., Yonkers, N.Y., 1959; Licentiate in Sacred Theology, Gregorian U., Rome, 1963; PhD, Brandeis U., 1970. Diocesan priest Archdiocese N.Y., N.Y.C., 1963-71; prof. U. Chgo., 1969—, Naomi Shenstone Donnelly Prof., 1992—. Program coord. Inst. for Advanced Study of Religion, Divinity Sch., U. Chgo., 1980-92. Author: The Calabrian Abbott, 1985, Meister Eckhart, 1986, Foundations of Mysticism, 1991, Growth of Mysticism, 1994, Antichrist, 1994, Flowering of Mysticism, 1998; editor: (series) Classics of Western Spirituality, 1978, (book) God and Creation, 1990. Fellow Medieval Acad. Am. Home: 5701 S Kenwood Ave Chicago IL 60637-1718 Office: U Chgo Divinity Sch 1025 E 58th St Chicago IL 60637-1509 E-mail: bmcginn@midway.uchicago.edu.

MCGINN, MARY J. lawyer, insurance company executive; b. St. Louis, Apr. 9, 1947; d. Martin J. and Janet McGinn; m. Bernard H. Shapiro, Sept. 6, 1971; children: Sara, Colleen, Molly, Daniel. BA, Dominican U., River Forest, Ill., 1967; JD, St. Louis U., 1970. Bar: Mo. 1970, Ill. 1971. Atty. tax div. U.S. Dept. Justice, Washington, 1970-73; atty. Allstate Ins. Co., Northbrook, Ill., 1973—, v.p., dep. gen. counsel, 1980—. Mem. ABA, Am. Coll. Investment Counsel, Assn. Life Ins. Counsel. Roman Catholic. Home: 155 N Buckley Rd Barrington IL 60010-2607 Office: Allstate Ins Co 3075 Sanders Rd Ste G5A Northbrook IL 60062-7127 E-mail: mmcginn@allstate.com.

MCGINNIS, GARY DAVID, chemist, science educator; b. Everett, Wash., Oct. 1, 1940; BS, Pacific Lutheran U., 1962; MS, U. Wash., 1968; PhD in Organic Chem., U. Mont., 1970. Prodn. chemist Am. Cyanamid Co., 1964-67; fellow U. Mont., 1970-71; from asst. prof. wood chemistry to assoc. prof. wood sci. Forest Products Utilization Lab. Mich. State U., 1971—. Mem. Am. Chem. Soc., Forest Products Rsch. Soc., Sigma Xi. Office: Michigan Technology University Forestry Bldg Rm 150 Houghton MI 49931

MCGINNIS, KENNETH L. former state official; Dir. Corrections Dept., Lansing, Mich., til 1999. Office: Corrections Dept Grandview Plz PO Box 30003 Lansing MI 48909-7503

MCGINNIS, W. PATRICK, diversified company executive; V.p. Ralston Purina Co., St. Louis, pres. branded foods group, now pres., CEO. Office: Ralston Purina Co Checkerboard Sq Saint Louis MO 63164-0001

MCGIVERIN, ARTHUR A. former state supreme court chief justice; b. Iowa City, Nov. 10, 1928; s. Joseph J. and Mary B. McG.; m. Mary Joan McGiverin, Apr. 20, 1951; children: Teresa, Thomas, Bruce, Nancy. BSC with high honors, U. Iowa, 1951, JD, 1956. Bar: Iowa 1956. Pvt. practice law, Ottumwa, Iowa, 1956; alt. mcpl. judge, 1960-65; judge Iowa Dist. Ct. 8th Jud. Dist., 1965-78; assoc. justice Iowa Supreme Ct., Des Moines, 1978-87, chief justice, 1987-2000, sr. judge, 2000—. Mem. Iowa Supreme Ct. Commn. on Continuing Legal Edn., 1975. Served to 1st lt. U.S. Army, 1946-48, 51-53. Mem. Iowa State Bar Assn., Am. Law Inst. Roman Catholic. Avocation: golf. Office: Iowa Supreme Court State Capitol Building Des Moines IA 50319-0001*

MC GLAMERY, MARSHAL DEAN, crop scientist, weed science educator; b. Mooreland, Okla., July 29, 1932; s. Walter Gaiford and Bernice (Gardner) McG.; m. Marilyn Hudson, June 2, 1957; children: Paul, Steve. B.S., Okla. State U., 1956, M.S., 1958; Ph.D., U. Ill., 1965. Instr. Panhandle A. and M. Coll., 1958-60; agronomist Agribus. Co., Lawrence, Kans., 1960-61; teaching asst. U. Ill., 1961-63, research fellow, 1963-65, asst. prof. weed sci., 1965-70, assoc. prof., 1970-76, prof., 1976-2000, ext. crop scientist, 1965-2000; ret., 2000. Served with U.S. Army, 1953-55. NSF fellow, 1963 Mem. Weed Sci. Soc. Am., Coun. Agr. and Tech. Baptist. Home: 35 Lange Ave Savoy IL 61874-9705 Office: 1102 S Goodwin Ave Urbana IL 61801-4730 E-mail: mmcglame@uiuc.edu.

MCGLAUCHLIN, TOM, artist; b. Turtle, Wis., Sept. 14, 1934; s. Charles Orion and Frances Lenore (Cadman) McG.; m. Patricia Ann Smith, Aug. 5, 1961; children: Christopher, Jennifer (dec.), Patrick (dec.). BS in Art, U. Wis., 1959, MS in Art, 1960; studied pottery with James McKinnell, 1962. Instr. dept. art and art edn. U. Wis., Madison, 1960-61; instr. art dept. Cornell Coll., Mt. Vernon, Iowa, 1961-64, asst. prof. art dept., 1964-68, assoc. prof., chmn. art dept. N.Y., 1968-71; instr. Toledo Mus. Art, 1971-82, prof., dir. glass program, 1982-84. One-man exhbns. include Habatat Gallery, Dearborn, Mich., 1979, Glass Art Gallery, Toronto, 1981, 85, Glass Gallery, Bethesda, Md., 1981, 85, 87, 91, Heller Gallery, N.Y.C., 1983, B.Z. Wagman Gallery, St. Louis, 1983, Running Ridge Gallery, Santa Fe, 1990; selected group exhbns. include Toledo Mus. Art, 1972, 88, Glasmuseum Frauenau, Franenau, Germany, 1977, Habatat Gallery, 1980, 84, The Hand and the Spirit Gallery, Scottsdale, Ariz., 1980, Gallery of Contemporary Crafts, Detroit, 1980, The Naples (Fla.) Art Gallery, 1981, The Craftsman's Gallery, Scarsdale, N.Y., 1981, 84, The Nat. Mus. Modern Art, Kyoto and Tokyo, 1981, Perception Gallery, Houston, 1985, The AirLoft Gallery, Honolulu, 1986, The Corning (N.Y.) Mus. Glass, 1987; selected competitive exhbns. include Everson Mus. Art, Syracuse, N.Y., 1961, 62, Mus. Contemporary Crafts, N.Y.C., 1962, Corning Glass Mus., Met. Mus. Art, N.Y.C., Victoria and Albert Mus., London, Musee Ars Decoratif, Paris; public collections include Toledo Mus. Art, The Smithsonian Collection, Washington, Portland (Oreg.) Art Mus., New Orleans Mus. Art, Mus. Contemporary Crafts, Musee des arts decoratifs de la Ville de Lausanne, Switzerland, Minn. Mus. Art, St. Paul, Kunstmuseum, Dusseldorf, Germany, Corning Glass Mus. Grantee Associated Colls. Midwest, 1966-67; recipient First Jury award Toledo Glass Nat. II, 1968. Mem. Am. Crafts Coun., Internat. Sculpture Soc., Ohio Designer-Craftsmen, Glass Art Soc. Office: The Glass Studio 1940 W Central Ave Toledo OH 43606-3944 E-mail: meglauc@accesstoledo.com.

MCGLOCKTON, CHESTER, professional football player; b. Whiteville, N.C., Sept. 16, 1969; Student, Clemson U. Defensive tackle Oakland Raiders, 1992-97, Kansas City Chiefs, 1998—. Named to Sporting News NFL All-Pro Team, 1994, to NFL Pro Bowl Team, 1994. Office: Kansas City Chiefs One Arrowhead Dr Kansas City MO 64129

MCGRATH, BARBARA GATES, city manager; m. Pat McGrath; 1 child, Caitlin. BS summa cum laude, Ohio State U., 1976; JD magna cum laude, Capital U., 1979. Bar: Ohio 1979. Asst. city atty. Columbus (Ohio) City Atty.'s Office, 1979-85; dep. dir. Civil Svc. Commn. City of Columbus, 1985-90, exec. dir. Civil Svc. Commn., 1990—. Past chair bd. dirs. Lifescapes, Inc., A Place to Grow; grad. Columbus Area Leadership Program, 1989. Mem. Columbus Bar Assn. Office: City of Columbus Civil Svc Commn 50 W Gay St Fl 5 Columbus OH 43215-2821

MCGRATH, MARY HELENA, plastic surgeon, educator; b. N.Y.C., Apr. 12, 1945; d. Vincent J. and Mary M. (Manning) McG.; children: Margaret E. Simon, Richard M. Simon. BA, Coll. New Rochelle, 1966; MD, St. Louis U., 1970; MPH, George Washington U., 1994. Lic. surgeon, Ill. Resident in surg. pathology U. Colo. Med. Ctr., Denver, 1970-71, intern in gen. surgery, 1971-72, resident in gen. surgery, 1971-75, chief resident in gen. surgery, 1975-76; resident in plastic and reconstructive surgery Yale U. Sch. Medicine, New Haven, 1976-77, chief resident plastic and reconstructive surgery, 1977-78; fellow in hand surgery U. Conn.-Yale U., 1978; instr. in surgery divsn. plastic and reconstructive surgery Yale U. Sch. Medicine, 1977-78, asst. prof. plastic surgery, 1978-80; attending in plastic and reconstructive surgery Yale-New Haven Hosp., 1978-80, Columbia-Presbyn. Hosp., N.Y.C., 1980-84, George Washington U. Med. Ctr., Washington, 1984-2000, Children's Nat. Med. Ctr., Washington, 1985-2000, Loyola U. Med. Ctr., 2000—, Hines Veterans Adminstrn. Hosp., 2001—; asst. prof. plastic surgery Columbia U., N.Y.C., 1980-84; assoc. prof. plastic surgery Sch. Medicine, George Washington U., Washington, 1984-87, prof. plastic surgery, 1987-2000, Loyola U. Med. Ctr., 2000—. Attending physician VA Hosp., West Haven, Conn., 1978-80; attending in surgery Hosp. Albert Schweitzer, Deschapelles, Haiti, 1980; prin. investigator various rsch. grants, 1978-89; historian., bd. dirs. Am. Bd. Plastic Surgery, 1991-95; guest examiner certifying exam., 1986-88, 95-2001; specialist site visitor Residency Rev. Com. for Plastic Surgery, 1985, 87, 91, 94; presenter in field; cons. in field; senator med. faculty senate George Washington U., bd. govs. Med. Faculty Assocs. Co-editor: (with M.L. Turner) Dermatology for Plastic Surgeons, 1993; assoc. editor: The Jour. of Hand Surgery, 1984-89, Annals of Plastic Surgery, 1984-87, Plastic and Reconstructive Surgery, 1989-95, Contemporary Surgery, 1999—; contbr. book chpts.: Problems in General Surgery, 1985, Human and Ethical Issues in the Surgical Care of Patients with Life-Threatening Disease, 1986, Problems in Aesthetic Surgery, Biological Causes and Clinical Solutions, 1986; guest reviewer numerous jours.; contbr. articles, abstracts to profl. jours. Fellow ACS (bd. govs. 1995-98, exec. com. 1996-97, chmn. adv. coun. for plastic surgery 1995-98, chmn. adv. coun. chmns. surgical specialists 1996-98, regent 1997—); mem. AAAS, Am. Surg. Assn., Am. Assn. Hand Surgery (exec. sec. 1988-90, rsch. grants com. 1983-86, chmn. edn. com. 1983-88, 1st prize ann. resident contest 1978, numerous other coms., D.C. chpt. program ann. meeting chmn. 1992, pres. 1994-95), Am. Assn. Plastic Surgeons (trustee 1997-2000), Am. Burn Assn., Am. Soc. for Aesthetic Plastic Surgery, Am. Soc. Maxillofacial Surgeons, Am. Soc. Plastic and Reconstructive Surgery (chmn. ethics com. 1985-87, chmn. device/tech. evaluation com. 1993-94, chmn. workforce task force 1997-2000, bd. dirs. 1994-96, chmn. endowment bd. dirs. 2000—, mem. ednl. found. bd. dirs. 1985-96, treas. 1989-92, v.p. 1992-93, pres.-elect 1993-94, pres. 1994-95), Am. Soc. Reconstructive Microsurgery (mem. edn. com. 1992-94), Am. Soc. Surgery of Hand (chmn. 1987 ann. residents' and fellows conf. 1986-87, mem. rsch. com. 1988-90), Assn. Acad. Chmn. Plastic Surgery (bd. dirs. 1999—), Assn. Acad. Surgery, Chgo. Soc. Plastic Surgeons (treas. 2001-), Midwestern Soc. Plastic Surgeons, Chgo. Surgical Soc., Internat. Soc. Reconstructive Surgery, Met. D.C. Soc. Surgery Hand (pres. 1995-97), N.Y. Surg. Soc., Northeastern Soc. Plastic Surgeons (chmn. sci. program com. 1991, chmn. fin. com. 1992-93, treas. 1993-96, pres. 1997-98), Plastic Surgery Rsch. Coun. (chmn. 1990), Surg. Biology Club III, The Wound Healing Soc. Office: Loyola U Med Ctr Divsn Plastic Surgery 2160 S 1st Ave Maywood IL 60153-3304 E-mail: mmcgra4@lumc.edu.

MCGRATH, MICHAEL G. finance company executive; CFO, mng. ptnr. Accenture, Chgo. Office: One Accenture 100 S Wacker Dr Ste 1059 Chicago IL 60606

MCGREGOR, DOUGLAS HUGH, pathologist, educator; b. Temple, Tex., Aug. 28, 1939; s. Harleigh Heath and Joyce Ellen (Lambert) McG.; m. Mizuki Kitani, July 6, 1969; children: Michelle Sakuya, David Kenji. BA, Duke U., 1961, MD, 1966; postgrad., U. Edinburgh, Scotland, 1961-62. Diplomate Am. Bd. Pathology. Intern, chief resident in pathology UCLA Med. Ctr., 1966-68; surgeon, lt. comdr. Atomic Bomb Casualty Commn., Hiroshima, Japan, 1968-71; chief resident in pathology Queens Med. Ctr., Honolulu, 1971-73; asst., assoc. prof. pathology U. Kans. Med. Ctr., Kansas City, 1973-82, prof., 1982—. Dir. anat. pathology VA Med. Ctr., Kansas City, Mo., 1975-94, chief pathology and lab. medicine, 1994—. Contbr. numerous articles to profl. jours., chpts. to books. Leader YMCA Indian Princess Program, Overland Park, Kans., 1977-79, Indian Guide Program, 1978-80, Cub Scout Am., Overland Park, 1980-82, Boy Scouts Am., Leawood, Kans., 1982—. Lt. comdr. USPHS, 1968-71, Japan. Grantee Merck, Sharp and Dohme, 1980. Fellow Coll. Am. Pathologists, Am. Soc. Clin. Pathologists; mem. Am. Assn. Pathologists, Internat. Acad. Pathologists, Soc. Exptl. Biology and Medicine, N.Y. Acad. Scis., AAAS, Kansas City Soc. Pathologists (sec.-treas. 1982-83, pres. 1983-84), Leawood Country Club. Achievements include research in ultrastructure and pathobiology of neoplasms, radiation carcinogenesis, and morphogenesis of atherosclerosis. Home: 9400 Lee Blvd Shawnee Mission KS 66206-1826 Office: VA Med Ctr 4801 E Linwood Blvd Kansas City MO 64128-2226

MCGUFF, JOSEPH THOMAS, professional sports team executive; m. Mary Heard; children: Nanch Thomas, Mike, Marianne, John, Elaine, Bill. Sportwriter Kansas City (Mo.) Star, 1948-66, sports editor, 1966-86, v.p., editor, 1986-92, ret., 1992; bd. dirs. Kansas City Royals, 1994—. Author: Winning It All, Why Me? Why Not Joe McGuff. Recipient 6 Outstanding Sports Writer in Mo. awards Sportswriters and Sportscasters Assn.; named

Mr. Baseball, Kansas City Baseball Awards Dinner, 1983; named to writers wing Baseball Hall of Fame, 1986. Mem. Baseball Writers and AP Sports Editors (past nat. pres.), Mo. Sports Hall of Fame. Office: Kansas City Royals PO Box 419969 Kansas City MO 64141-6969

MCGUIRE, JOHN C. state legislator; b. Joliet, Ill. m. Marilyn McGuire; four children. Student, Joliet (Ill.) Jr. Coll.; BA, Colo. State Coll. Trustee, supr. Joliet Twp.; tchr., coach; Dist. 86 rep. Ill. Ho. Reps., Springfield, 1991—. Mem. labor and commerce, transp. and motor vehicles, econ. and urban devel., elem. and secondary edn., gen. svc. appropriations, and aging coms., Ill. Ho. Reps. Mem. VFW, Irish Am. Soc. Address: 1510 Glenwood Ave Joliet IL 60435-5832 Also: 121 Springfield Ave Joliet IL 60435-6561

MCGUIRE, JOHN W., SR. advertising executive, marketing professional, author; b. Chgo., May 12, 1952; s. Eugene H. Sr. and Marjorie (Bolger) McG.; m. Mary Sue Roper, June 17, 1972 (div. 1977); 1 child, John William Jr.; m. Lynn L. Rembos, June 21, 1984 (div. April 1991); children: Kelly Lynn, Ryan Michael. AA, Chgo. City Colls., 1972; BA, Northeastern Ill., Chgo., 1974. Janitor Bd. of Edn., Chgo., 1970-74; sales rep. Motorola Comms., Inc., Schaumburg, Ill., 1974-76, Pattis Group, Chgo., 1976-77; midwest sales mgr. Harcourt Brace Jovanovich Pub. Co., N.Y.C., 1977-79; account sales mgr. Cosmopolitan Mag. Hearst Pub. Co., 1979-81; midwest acct. mgr. Psychology Today Mag. Ziff-Davis Pub. Co., 1981-82; midwest regional mgr. Pennwell Pub. Co., Tulsa, Okla., 1982-84; western regional sales mgr. Nursing Mgmt. Mag. SN Pub. Co., West Dundee, Ill., 1984-91; western regional sales mgr., midwest regional sales mgr. U.S. Pharmacist Mag. Jobson Pub. Co., N.Y.C., 1991-98; v.p. SK&A Info. Svcs., Irvine, Calif., 1998-99; assoc. pub. Health Mgmt. Technology Mag. Nelson Pub., Nokomis, Fla., 1999; pres., CEO Blossom Pub. Co., Wasco, Ill., 2000—. Author: (book) One Man's Life: A Poetic Review, 1995, singer (cassette tapes), designer (creative posters). With USN, 1970. Mem. VFW, Midwest Healthcare Mktg., Arlington Poetry Project. Republican. Roman Catholic. Avocations: writer, scuba, horsemanship, traveling, skydiving.

MCGUIRE, MARY JO, state legislator; b. Mpls., 1956; BA in Bus. Adminstrn., Coll. of St. Catherine, 1978; JD, Hamline U., 1988; postgrad., Harvard U., 1995-97. Mem. Minn. Ho. of Reps., 1988—, mem. judiciary com., judiciary fin. divsn., vice chair family and early childhood edn. fin. divsn., mem. govt. ops., chair data practices subcom., lead minor mem. Democrat. Home: 1529 Iowa Ave W Saint Paul MN 55108-2128 Office: Minn Ho of Reps State Ho Office Bldg Saint Paul MN 55155-0001

MCGUIRE, TIM, editor; Editor, sr. v.p. Star Tribune, Mpls., 1993—. Office: Star Tribune 425 Portland Ave Minneapolis MN 55488-0002

MCGUIRE, TIMOTHY JAMES, lawyer, editor; b. Mount Pleasant, Mich., Mar. 24, 1949; s. James Edward and Anita Matilda (Starr) McGuire; m. T. Jean Fannin, May 10, 1975; children: Tracy, Jason, Jeffrey. BA, Aquinas Coll., Grand Rapids, Mich., 1971; JD cum laude, William Mitchell Coll. Law, St. Paul, 1987. Bar: Minn. 1987. Mng. editor Ypsilanti Press, Mich., 1973—75, Corpus Christi Caller, Tex., 1975—77, Lakeland Ledger, Fla., 1977—79, Mpls. Star, 1979—82; mng. editor features and sports Mpls. Star and Tribune, 1982—84, mng. editor, 1984—91, exec. editor, 1991—93, editor, sr. v.p., 1993—2002. Pulitzer Prize juror, 1988—89, 1995—2002. Lay preacher at St. Joseph Roman Cath. Ch., Mpls., 1995—. Mem.: Minn. State Bar Assn., Am. Soc. Newspaper Editors (bd. dirs. 1992—, chmn. change com. 1994—95, chmn. program com. 1996—97, treas. 1998—99, sec. 1999—2000, v.p. 2000—01, pres. 2001—02). Roman Catholic. Home: 3645 Rosewood Ln N Minneapolis MN 55441-1127

MCGUIRE, WILLIAM W. medical association administrator; b. Troy, N.Y., 1948; Grad., U. Tex., 1970, grad., 1974. Exec. v.p. United Healthcare Corp., Minnetonka, Minn., 1988—89, pres., CEO, 1989—, chmn., 1991—; pres., CEO, chmn., dir. UnitedHealth Group, 1991—2000, CEO, chmn., dir., 2000—. Bd. dirs. Minn. Bus. Partnership. Trustee Mpls. Inst. Arts; dir. Minn. Orch. Assn. Office: United Health Group 9900 Bren Rd E Minnetonka MN 55343-9664

MCGUIRE-RIGGS, SHEILA, Democrat.*

MCGUNNIGLE, GEORGE FRANCIS, judge; b. Rochester, N.Y., Feb. 22, 1942; s. George Francis and Mary Elizabeth (Curran) McG.; m. Priscilla Ann Lappin, July 13, 1968; children: Cynthia A., Brian P. AB, Boston Coll., 1963; LLB, Georgetown U., 1966; LLM, George Wash. U., 1967. Bar: Conn. 1971, Minn. 1972, U.S. Dist. Ct. D.C. 1967, U.S. Dist. Ct. Conn. 1971, U.S. Dist. Ct. Minn. 1972, U.S. Ct. Appeals (2d cir.) 1971, U.S. Ct. Appeals (8th cir.) 1977, U.S. Supreme Ct. 1986. Asst. U.S. atty. Office of U.S. Atty., Bridgeport, Conn., 1971—72; assoc. Leonard, Street and Deinard, Mpls., 1972—73, ptnr., 1974—2000; judge Fourth Jud. Dist., 2000—. Editor: Business Torts Litigation, 1992. Bd. dirs. Cath. Charities, 1997—, Minn. chpt. Arthritis Found., Mpls., 1986-92, 94—, mem. exec. com., 1988-92, 2001—. Lt. JAGC, USN, 1967-71. Recipient Nat. Vol. Svc. citation Arthritis Found., 1992. Mem. ABA (litigation sect., chmn. bus. torts litigation com. 1988-91, divsn. dir. 1991-92, 97-98, coun. 1992-95, sect. of dispute resolution coun. 2000-01). Avocations: reading, boating. E-mail. Office: Fourth Judicial Dist C-1251 Hennepin County Govt Ctr Minneapolis MN 55487-0422 E-mail: george.mcgunnigle@co.hennepin.mn.us.

MCGWIRE, MARK DAVID, professional baseball player; b. Pomona, Calif., Oct. 1, 1963; s. John and Ginger McGwire; m. Kathy McGwire; 1 child, Matthew. Student, U. So. Calif. With Oakland Athletics, 1984-97, St. Louis Cardinals, 1997—. Player World Series, 1988, 89, 90. Named Am. League Rookie of Yr. Baseball Writers' Assn. Am., 1987, Sporting News, 1987; recipient Gold Glove award, 1990; named to All-Star team, 1987-92, 95-96, 1999; recipient Silver Slugger Award, 1992; Am. League Home Run Leader, 1987; mem. U.S. Olympic Baseball Team, 1984, Player of the Month, 1999, Player of the Yr. AP, 1999, Baseball Am., 1999. Office: St Louis Cardinals Busch Stadium 250 Stadium Plz Saint Louis MO 63102-1722*

MCHALE, JOHN, JR. professional sports team executive; b. Detroit; s. John J. and Patricia (Cameron) McH.; m. Sally McHale; children: Duncan, William, Frances. Grad., U. Notre Dame, 1971; degree in Law, Boston Coll., 1975; master's in Law, Georgetown U., 1982. Lawyer, Denver, 1981-91; chmn. bd. dirs. Denver Maj. League Baseball Stadium Dist., 1989-91; exec. v.p. baseball ops. Colo. Rockies, 1991-93, exec. v.p. ops., 1993; pres., CEO Detroit Tigers, 1995—. Dir. Maj. League Baseball Enterprises; mem. baseball ops. com. Maj. League Baseball. Chmn. Southeast Mich. WalkAm., March of Dimes, 1996, 97; mem. pres. adv. coun. Henry Ford Mus., Greenfield Village; bd. dirs. caring athletes team Children's Hosp., Henry Ford Hosp. Office: Detroit Tigers 2100 Woodward Ave Detroit MI 48201-3474 Fax: 313-965-2138.

MCHALE, KEVIN EDWARD, former professional basketball player, sports team executive; b. Hibbing, Minn., Dec. 19, 1957; m. Lynn McHale; children: Kristyn, Michael. Student, U. Minn., 1976-80. Basketball player Boston Celtics, 1980-93; v.p. basketball ops. Minn. Timberwolves, 1995—. Named to NBA All Rookie Team, 1981, NBA All-Defensive First Team, 1986-88, All-NBA First Team, 1987, NBA All-Star Game, 1984, 86-91; recipient NBA Sixth Man award, 1984, 85. Achievements include playing on NBA Championship Team, 1981, 84, 86. Office: Minn Timberwolves 600 1st Ave N Minneapolis MN 55403-1416

MCHALE, VINCENT EDWARD, political science educator; b. Jenkins Twp., Pa., Apr. 17, 1939; m. Ann Barbara Cotner, Nov. 8, 1963; 1 child, Patrick James. A.B., Wilkes Coll., 1964; M.A., Pa. State U., 1966, Ph.D. in Polit. Sci., 1969. Asst. prof. polit. sci. U. Pa., Phila., 1969-75, dir. grad. studies, 1971-73; assoc. prof. Case Western Res. U., Cleve., 1975-84, prof., 1984—, chmn. dept. polit. sci., 1978—; vis. lectr. John Carroll U., summer 1980, Beaver Coll., spring 1975. Author: (with A.P. Frognier and D. Paranzino) Vote, Clivages Socio-politiques et Developpement Regional en Belgique, 1974. Co-editor; contbr.: Evaluating Transnational Programs in Government and Business, 1980; Political Parties of Europe, 1983; edtl. adv. bd. Worldmark Ency. of Nations, 1994—. Contbr. chpts. to books, articles to profl. jours. Project cons. Council Econ Opportunity in Greater Cleve., 1978-81; mem. Morris Abrams Award Com., 1977—. Recipient Outstanding Prof. award Lux chpt. Mortar Bd., 1989, 90; named one of Most Interesting People of 1988, Cleve. Mag.; NSF grantee, 1971-72; HEW grantee, 1976-78; Woodrow Wilson fellow, 1968, Ruth Young Boucke fellow, 1967-68; All-Univ. fellow, 1967-68. Mem. Phi Kappa Phi. Home: 3070 Coleridge Rd Cleveland OH 44118-3556 Office: Case Western Res U Cleveland OH 44106

MCHENRY, MARTIN CHRISTOPHER, physician, educator; b. Feb. 9, 1932; s. Merl and Marcella (Bricca) McH.; m. Patricia Grace Hughes, Apr. 27, 1957; children: Michael, Christopher, Timothy, Mary Ann, Jeffrey, Paul, Kevin, William, Monica, Martin Christopher. Student, U. Santa Clara, 1950-53; MD, U. Cin., 1957; MS in Medicine, U. Minn., 1966. Diplomate Am. Bd. Internal Medicine. Intern Highland Alameda County (Calif.) Hosp., Oakland, 1957-58; resident, internal medicine fellow Mayo Clinic, Rochester, Minn., 1958-61, spl. appointee in infectious diseases, 1963-64; staff physician Henry Ford Hosp., Detroit, 1964-67, Cleve. Clinic, 1967-72, chmn. dept. infectious diseases, 1972-92, sr. physician infectious diseases, 1992-98. Cons. infectious diseases, 1998—; asst. clin. prof. Case Western Res. U., 1970-77, assoc. clin. prof. medicine, 1977-91, clin. prof. medicine, 1991—; assoc. vis. physician Cleve. Met. Gen. Hosp., 1970-00; cons. VA Hosp., Cleve., 1973-74. Contbr. more than 100 articles to profl. jours., also chpts. to books. Chmn. manpower com. Swine Influenza Program, Cleve., 1976. With USNR, 1961-63. Named Disting. Tchr. in Medicine, Cleve. Clinic, 1972, 90; recipient 1st ann. Bruce Hubbard Stewart award Cleve. Clinic Found. for Humanities in Medicine, 1985, Nightingale Physician Collaboration award Cleve. Clinic Found. Divsn. Nursing, 1995, Clinician of Yr. award Acad. Medicine of Cleve./No. Ohio Med. Assn., 2002. Fellow ACP, Infectious Diseases Soc. Am. (Clinician award 2000), Am. Coll. Chest Physicians (chmn. com. cardiopulmonary infections 1975-77, 81-83), Royal Soc. Medicine of Gt. Britain; mem. Am. Soc. Clin. Pharmacology and Therapeutics (chmn. sect. infectious diseases and antimicrobial agts. 1970-77, 80-85, dir.), Am. Thoracic Soc., Am. Soc. Clin. Pathologists, Am. Fedn. Clin. Rsch., Am. Soc. Tropical Medicine and Hygiene, Am. Soc. Microbiology, N.Y. Acad. Scis., Assn. for Profls. in Infection Control and Epidemiology, So. Med. Assn. Home: 2779 Belgrave Rd Pepper Pike OH 44124-4601 Office: 9500 Euclid Ave Cleveland OH 44195-0001

MC HENRY, POWELL, lawyer; b. Cinn., May 14, 1926; s. L. Lee McHenry and Marguerite L. (Powell) Heinz; m. Venna Mae Guerrea, Aug. 27, 1948; children: Scott, Marshall, Jody Lee, Gale Lynn. AB, U. Cinn., 1949; LLB, Harvard U., 1951, JD, 1969. Bar: Ohio 1951, U.S. Ct. Appeals (6th cir.) 1964, U.S. Supreme Ct. 1966. Assoc. Dinsmore, Shohl, Sawyer & Dinsmore, Cinn., 1951-57; ptnr. Dinsmore, Shohl, Coates & Deupree (and predecessors), 1958-75; gen. counsel Federated Dept. Stores, Inc., 1971-75; assoc. gen. counsel Procter & Gamble Co., 1975-76, v.p., gen. counsel, 1976-83, sr. v.p., gen. counsel, 1983-91; counsel Dinsmore & Shohl, Cin., 1991—; bd. dirs. Eagle Picher Industries, Inc., 1991-97. Mem. com. Hamilton County Pub. Defender, Cin., chmn., 1996-2000. With USNR, 1944-46. Recipient award of merit Ohio Legal Center Inst., 1969. Mem. ABA, Ohio Bar Assn., Cin. Bar Assn. (pres. 1979-80, exec. com. 1975-81), Harvard U. Law Sch. Assn. Cin. (pres. 1960-61), Am. Law Inst., Assn. Gen. Counsel (pres. 1986-88), Harvard Club, Western Hill Country Club (bd. dirs. 1964-70, sec. 1966-69, 87-89, treas. 1969-70, 89-90), Queen City Club, Commonwealth Club (pres. 1996-97). Republican. Methodist. Office: Dimsmore & Shohl 1900 Chemed Ctr 255 E 5th St Cincinnati OH 45202-4700

MCHENRY, ROBERT (DALE), editor; b. St. Louis, Apr. 30, 1945; s. Robert Dale and Pearl Lenna (Nalley) McH.; m. Carolyn F. Amundson, Oct. 2, 1971; children: Curran, Zachary. BA in English Lit., Northwestern U., 1966; MA in English Lit., U. Mich., 1967; MBA in Mgmt., Northwestern U., 1987. Proofreader, prodn. editor Ency. Britannica, Inc., Chgo., 1967-69, editor, 1974-75, dir. yearbooks, 1985-86, mng. editor, 1986-90, gen. editor, v.p., 1990-92, editor-in-chief, 1992-97, editor-at-large, 1997—. Editor: Documentary History of Conservation in America, 1972, Webster's American Military Biographies, 1978, Liberty's Women, 1980, Webster's New Biographical Dictionary, 1983. Mem. United Ch. of Christ.

MCHUGH, MIKE E. news executive; Bur. chief Chgo. Dow Jones Newswires, 1997—. Office: 21st Fl One S Wacker Dr Chicago IL 60606

MCHUGH, RICHARD WALKER, lawyer; b. Sullivan, Ind., Dec. 9, 1952; s. Richard Harrison and Virginia Ann (Robinson) McH.; m. Marsha J. Marshall, May 24, 1975; children: Walker, Cora. BA, Wabash Coll., 1975; JD, U. Mich., 1978. Bar: Mich. 1984, Ky. 1979, U.S. Supreme Ct. 1987. Assoc. Youngdahl Law Firm, Little Rock, 1978-79; staff atty. Legal Aid Soc., Louisville, 1979-84; assoc. gen. counsel Internat. Union UAW, Detroit, 1984-95; pvt. practice, Ann Arbor, Mich., 1995-98; staff atty. Mich. Poverty Law Prgm., 1998-2000, Nat. Employment Law Project, Dexter, Mich., 2000—. Dir. Mich. Legal Svcs., Detroit, 1986-91. Mem. Nat. Acad. Social Ins. Democrat. Avocations: fishing, backpacking. Office: Nat Employment Law Project PO Box 369 Dexter MI 48130-0369

MCILROY, ALAN F. manufacturing company executive; b. 1950; Internat. contr. Wheelabrator Corp., 1983-87; bus. unit contr. Gen. Chem., 1987-90; sr. v.p. Harris Chem.; head Greenock Group; CFO Dayton Superior Corp., Miamisburg, Ohio, 1997—. Office: Dayton Superior Corp Ste 130 7777 Washington Village Dr Dayton OH 45459

MCINERNY, RALPH MATTHEW, philosophy educator, writer; b. Mpls., Feb. 24, 1929; s. Austin Clifford and Vivian Gertrude (Rush) McI.; m. Constance Terrill Kunert, Jan. 3, 1953; children: Cathleen, Mary, Anne, David, Elizabeth, Daniel. BA, St. Paul Sem., 1951; MA, U. Minn., 1952; PhD summa cum laude, Laval U., 1954; LittD (hon.), St. Benedict Coll., 1978, U. Steubenville, 1984; DHL (hon.), St. Francis Coll., Joliet, Ill., 1986; DHL, St. John Fisher Coll., 1994, St. Anselm Coll., 1995; DHS (hon.) , Our Lady Holy Cross, New Orleans. Instr. Creighton U., 1954-55; prof. U. Notre Dame, Ind., 1955—, Michael P. Grace prof. medieval studies, 1988—, dir. dept., 1978-85. Vis. prof. Cornell U., 1988, Cath. U., 1971, Louvain, 1983, 95; founder Internat. Catholic Univ.; disting. vis. prof. Truman State U., Mo., 1999. Author: (philos. works) The Logic of Analogy, 1961, History of Western Philosophy, vol. 1, 1963, vol. 2, 1968, Thomism in an Age of Renewal, 1966, Studies in Analogy, 1967, New Themes in Christian Philosophy, 1967, St. Thomas Aquinas, 1976, Ethica Thomistica, 1982, History of the Ambrosiana, 1983, Being and Predication, 1986, Miracles, 1986, Art and Prudence, 1988, A First Glance at St. Thomas: Handbook for Peeping Thomists, 1989, Boethius and Aquinas, 1989, Aquinas on Human Action, 1991, The Question of Christian Ethics, 1993, Aquinas Against the Averroists, 1993, The God of Philosophers, 1994, Aquinas and Analogy, 1996, Ethica Thomistica, 1997, Vernunftgemässes Leben, 2000, Characters in Search of Their Authors, 2001, Conversion of Edith Stein, 2001, John of St. Thomas, Summa Theologiae, 2001; (novels) Jolly Rogerson, 1967, A Narrow Time, 1969, The Priest, 1973, Gate of Heaven, 1975, Rogerson at Bay, 1976, Her Death of Cold, 1977, The Seventh Station, 1977, Romanesque, 1977, Spinnaker, 1977, Quick as a Dodo, 1978, Bishop as Pawn, 1978, La Cavalcade Romaine, 1979, Lying Three, 1979, Abecedary, 1979, Second Vespers, 1980, Rhyme and Reason, 1981, Thicker than Water, 1981, A Loss of Patients, 1982, The Grass Widow, 1983, Connolly's Life, 1983, Getting Away with Murder, 1984, And Then There Were Nun, 1984, The Noonday Devil, 1985, Sine Qua Nun, 1986, Leave of Absence, 1986, Rest in Pieces, 1985, Cause and Effect, 1987, The Basket Case, 1987, Veil of Ignorance, 1988, Abracadaver, 1989, Body and Soil, 1989, Four on the Floor, 1989, Frigor Mortis, 1989, Savings and Loan, 1990, The Search Committee, 1991, The Nominative Case, 1991, Sister Hood, 1991, Judas Priest, 1991, Easeful Death, 1991, Infra Dig, 1992, Desert Sinner, 1992, Seed of Doubt, 1993, The Basket Case, 1993, Nun Plussed, 1993, Mom and Dead, 1994, The Cardinal Offense, Law and Ardor, 1995, Let's Read Latin, 1995, Aguinas and Analogy, 1996, The Tears of Things, 1995, Half Past Nun, 1997, On This Rockne, 1997, Penguin Classic Aquinas, 1997, The Red Hat, 1998, What Went Wrong With Vatican II, 1998, Lack of the Irish, 1998, Irish Tenure, 1999, Grave Undertakings, 1999, Student Guide to Philosophy, 1999, Heirs and Parents, 2000, Shakespearean Variations, 2000, Defamation of Pius XII, 2001, Book of Kills, 2001, Triple Pursuit, 2001, Still Life, 2001, Sub Rosa, 2001, Emerald Aisle, 2001; John of St. Thomas, Summa Theologiae, 2001, Conversion of Edith Stein, 2001, editor The New Scholasticism, 1967-89; editor, pub. Crisis, 1982-96; pub. Catholic Dossier, 1995—. Exec. dir. Wethersfield Inst., 1989-92; bd. govs. Thomas Aquinas Coll., Santa Paula, Calif., 1993-2001; bd. dirs. Southern Cross Found., 1999—. With USMCR, 1946-47. Fulbright rsch. fellow, Belgium, 1959-60, NEH fellow, 1977-78, NEA fellow, 1983, Catholic Scholars fellow; Fulbright scholar, Argentina, 1986, 87, Outstanding Philosophical scholar Delta Epsilon Sigma, 1990; recipient Thomas Aquinas medal U. Dallas, 1990, Thomas Aquinas Coll., 1991, Maritain medal Am. Maritain Assn., 1994, P.G. Wodehouse award CRISIS Mag., 1995; Gifford lectr. Glasgow U., Scotland, 1999-2000. Fellow Pontifical Roman Acad. St. Thomas Aquinas; mem. Am. Philos. Assn., Am. Cath. Philos. Assn. (past pres., St. Thomas Aquinas medal 1993), Cath. Acad. Scis., Am. Metaphys. Soc. (pres. 1992), Internat. Soc. for Study Medieval Philosophy, Medieval Acad., Mystery Writers Am. (Lifetime Achievement award 1993), Authors Guild, Fellowship Cath. Scholars (pres. 1992-95, Cardinal Wright award 1996). Home: 51236 Golfview Ct Granger IN 46530-6500 Office: U of Notre Dame Jacques Maritain Ctr 714 Hesburgh Notre Dame IN 46556-5677

MCINTOSH, DAVID M. former congressman; b. June 8, 1958; m. Ruthie McIntosh. Grad., Yale Coll., 1980, U. Chgo., 1983. Bar: Ind., U.S. Supreme Ct. Spl. asst. domestic affairs to Pres. Reagan; spl. asst. to Atty. Gen. Meese; liaison Pres.'s Commn. on Privatization; spl. asst. to V.P. Quayle, dep. legal counsel to; exec. dir. Pres.'s Coun. on Competitiveness; sr. fellow Citizens for a Sound Economy; founder Federalist Soc. for Law & Pub. Policy, now co-chmn.; mem. U.S. Congress from Ind., Washington, 1995-2001. Mem. State Bar of Ind. Republican. Office: PO Box 3300 Muncie IN 47307 also: Mayer Brown & Platt 1909 K St NW Washington DC 20006 E-mail: dmcintosh@mayerbrown.com.

MCINTOSH, ELAINE VIRGINIA, nutrition educator; b. Webster, S.D., Jan. 30, 1924; d. Louis James and Cora Boletta (Bakke) Nelson; m. Thomas Henry McIntosh, Aug. 28, 1955; children: James George, Ronald Thomas, Charles Nelson. BA magna cum laude, Augustana Coll., Sioux Falls, S.D., 1945; MA, U. S.D., 1949; PhD, Iowa State U., 1954. Registered dietitian. Instr., asst. prof. Sioux Falls Coll., 1945-48; instr. Iowa State U., Ames, 1949-53, rsch. assoc., 1955-62; postdoctoral rsch. assoc. U. Ill., Urbana, 1954-55; asst. prof. human biology U. Wis., Green Bay, 1968-72, assoc. prof., 1972-85, prof., 1985-90, emeritus prof., 1990—, writer, cons., 1990—, chmn. human biology dept., 1975-80, asst. to vice chancellor, asst. to chancellor, 1974-76. Author 2 books including American Food Habits in Historical Perspective, 1995; contbr. numerous articles on bacterial metabolism, meat biochemistry and nutrition edn. to profl. jours. Fellow USPHS, 1948-49. Mem. Am. Dietetic Assn., Inst. Food Technologists, Wis. Dietetics Assn. Avocation: traveling. Office: U Wis Green Bay ES 301 Human Biology 2420 Nicolet Dr Green Bay WI 54311-7001

MCINTURFF, FLOYD M. retired state agency administrator; b. Greenback, Tenn., May 1, 1923; s. Samuel Floyd and Hazel Agnes (Vaden) M.; m. Merle Celeste Sosna, May 27, 1950; children: Judith Margaret, Laura Ellen, Melissa Ann. BS, U. Tenn., Knoxville, 1950. Asst. to the chief engr., missiles Rockwell Internat., Columbus, 1957-73; chief, targeted jobs tax credit program Ohio Bur. Employment Svcs., 1974-88; ret., 1988. Commd. officer U.S. Army Signal Corps., 1942-46, 51-52. Mem. Opera Columbus, Columbus Astron. Soc., Am. Atheists, Sons of Revolution, First Families of Tenn. Avocations: music, astronomy, photography, elderhostel. Home: 4985 Beatrice Dr Columbus OH 43227-2114

MCINTYRE, EDWARD J. power company executive; BBA, Minot State U., 1973. Jr. acct. No. States Power Co., Minot, N.D., 1973, rate analyst Mpls., 1975, gen. mgr. revenue requirements, 1983, dir. gas supply and storage, dir. gas supply and bus. ops., pres., CEO Wis. subs., v.p., CFO, 1993-2000; with Xcel Energy Inc. Bd. dirs. Greater Mpls. Met. Housing Corp., Jr. Achievement, Como Zoo & Conservatory Soc. Office: Xcel Energy Inc 800 Nicollet Mall #3000 Minneapolis MN 55402-2023

MCINTYRE, MICHAEL JOHN, lawyer, educator; b. Attleboro, Mass., Mar. 12, 1942; sd. John W. and Margaret E. (McBrien) McI.; m. May Ping Soo Hoo; children: Devin J., Colin J. AB, Providence Coll., 1964; JD, Harvard U., 1969. Bar: Mass. 1969, D.C. 1970. Vol. Peace Corps, Bhopal, India, 1964-66; assoc. Ivins, Phillips and Barker, Washington, 1969-71; dir. tng. Internat. Tax Program, Harvard U., Cambridge, Mass., 1971-75; prof. law Wayne State U., Detroit, 1975—. Cons. govt. of Egypt, State of N.Y., Navaho Tribe, govts. of Spain, Australia, 1975—; cons. UN Ctr. Transnat. Cooperation, 1975-82. Author: Readings in Federal Taxation, 1983, International Income Tax Rules of United States, 1989, 91, (with Arnold) International Tax Primer, 1995; editor-in-chief Tax Notes Internat., 1989-91; contbr. articles to numerous publs. Mem. Nassau Suffolk Horseman's Assn. (bd. dirs.). Office: Wayne State Univ Law Sch Detroit MI 48202

MCKAY, MARK, radio personality; m. Marcia McKay; 3 children. Program dir. WRKO/FM, Boston, Y106, Orlando, Fla., KCMO-FM, Kansas City; radio host KFRC, San Francisco, KMEL, Oldies 95, Mission, Kans. Named one of Am.'s Most Influential Air Personalities of the Top 40 Era, Radio & Recs. Pub., 1998. Avocations: golf, baseball, travel. Office: Oldies 95 5800 Foxridge Dr 6th Fl Mission KS 66202

MCKAY, NEIL, banker; b. East Tawas, Mich., Aug. 9, 1917; s. Lloyd G. and Rose (McDonald) McK.; m. Olive D. Baird, Nov. 11, 1950; children: Julia B., Lynn B., Hunter L. A.B., U. Mich., 1939, J.D. with distinction, 1946. Bar: Mich. 1946, Ill. 1947. With firm Winston & Strawn, Chgo., 1946-63, partner, 1954-63, mem. mgmt. com., 1958-63; with First Nat. Bank of Chgo., 1963-83, from v.p. charge heavy industry lending div., gen. mgr. London br., to exec. v.p., cashier, 1970-75, vice chmn. bd., 1976-83, also dir. Exec. v.p., sec. First Chgo. Corp., 1970-75, vice chmn. bd., 1976-83; also bd. dirs.; bd. dirs. Baird & Warner, Inc., Chgo.; founding dir. Student Loan Mktg. Assn. Mem.: U. Mich. Law Rev; assoc. editor-in-chief: U. Mich. Law Rev., 1942, sr. editor, 1946. Trustee Morton Arboretum; former trustee Kalamazoo Coll. and Ill. Inst. Tech. Served with USNR, 1942-46. Mem. ABA, Ill. Bar Assn., Dunham Woods Riding Club, Chgo. Hort. Soc. (bd. dirs.), Chgo. Club, Mid-Day Club, Geneva Golf Club. Office: 21 S Clark St Ste 2590 Chicago IL 60603

MCKEACHIE, WILBERT JAMES, psychologist, educator; b. Clarkston, Mich., Aug. 24, 1921; s. Bert A. and Edith E. (Welberry) McK.; m. Virginia Mae Mack, Oct. 30, 1942; children: Linda, Karen. BA, Mich. State Normal Coll., 1942; MA, U. Mich., 1946, PhD, 1949; LLD, Ea. Mich. U., 1957, U. Cin.; ScD, Northwestern U., 1973, Denison U., 1975, Nat. Acad. Edn., 1977, Alma Coll., 1995; DLitt (hon.), Hope Coll., 1985; LHD (hon.), Shawnee State U., 1994. Faculty U. Mich., 1946—, chmn. dept., 1961-71, dir. Center for Research in Learning and Teaching, 1975-83. Mem. nat. adv. mental health council NIMH, 1976-80; mem. spl. med. adv. group VA, 1967-72 Author: (with J.E. Milholland) Undergraduate Curricula in Psychology, 1961, (with Charlotte Doyle and Mary Margaret Moffett) Psychology, 1966, 3d edit., 1977 (also Spanish edit. and instr.'s manual), Teaching Tips, 11th edit., 2002. Trustee Kalamazoo Coll., 1964-77; trustee-at-large Am. Psychol. Found., 1974-84, 92-96, pres., 1979-82. Officer USNR, 1943-45. Recipient Outstanding Tchr. award U. Mich. Alumni Assn., Am. Coll. Testing-Am. Ednl. Rsch. Assn. award for outstanding rsch. on coll. students, 1973, career contbns. award, 1990, award for disting. teaching in psychology Am. Psychol. Found., 1985, Gold medal award Am. Psychol. Found., others. Mem. APA (sec., dir., pres. 1976-77, Disting. Career Contbn. to Edn. and Tng. in Psychology award 1987, E.L. Thorndike award for outstanding rsch., 1988), Internat. Assn. Applied Psychology (pres. div. ednl. instrn. and sch. psychology 1982-86), Am. Assn. Higher Edn. (dir. 1974-80, pres. 1978), AAUP (pres. U. Mich. chpt. 1970-71), AAAS (chmn. sect. on psychology 1976-77), Sigma Xi. American Baptist. Home: 4660 Joy Rd Dexter MI 48130-9706 Office: U Mich Dept Psychology 525 E University Ave Ann Arbor MI 48109-1109 E-mail: billmck@umich.edu.

MCKEAGUE, DAVID WILLIAM, judge; b. Pitts., Nov. 5, 1946; s. Herbert William and Phyllis (Forsyth) McK.; m. Nancy L. Palmer, May 20, 1989; children: Mike, Melissa, Sarah, Laura, Elizabeth, Adam. BBA, U. Mich., 1968, JD, 1971. Bar: Mich. 1971, U.S. Dist. Ct. (we. dist.) Mich. 1972, U.S. Dist. Ct. (ea. dist.) 1978, U.S. Ct. Appeals (6th cir.) 1988. Assoc. Foster, Swift, Collins & Smith, Lansing, Mich., 1971-76, ptnr., 1976-92, sec.-treas., 1990-92; judge U.S. Dist. Ct., Western Dist. Mich., Lansing, 1992—. Adj. prof. Thomas M. Cooley Law Sch., Mich. State U. Detroit Coll. Law. Nat. com. U. Mich. Law Sch. Fund, 1980-92; gen. counsel Mich. Rep. Com., 1989-92; adv. coun. Wharton Ctr., Mich. State U., 1996—. Mem. FBA (bd. dirs. Western Mich. chpt. 1991—), Mich. Bar Assn., Am. Inns of Ct. (pres. Mich. State U. Detroit Coll. of Law chpt. 1999-01), Country Club Lansing (bd. govs. 1988-92, 96—), The Federalist Soc. for Law and Pub. Studies (lawyers divsn. Mich. chpt. 1996—). Roman Catholic. Office: US Dist Ct 315 W Allegan St Lansing MI 48933-1500

MCKEAN, ANDY, state legislator; b. June 23, 1949; m. Constance Hoefer. BS, SUNY, 1974; JD, U. Iowa, 1977. Lawyer; owner, operator Shaw Haw Bed and Breakfast; mem. Iowa Senate from 28th dist., Des Moines, 1992—; mem. ethics com., mem. local govt. com., mem. transp. com.; chair jud. com. Grad. sch. instr. U. Iowa. Square Dance caller Scotch Grove Pioneers; mem. Martella Christian Ch.; m. Jones County Hist. Soc. Mem. Jones County Bar Assn. Republican. Office: State Capitol 9th And Grand Ave Des Moines IA 50319-0001 E-mail: andy_mckean@legis.state.ia.us.

MCKECHNIE, ED, state legislator; b. July 31, 1963; m. Kristy McKechnie. Kans. state rep. Dist. 3. Mem. Lions. Address: 224 W Jefferson St Pittsburg KS 66762-5140

MCKEE, CHRISTOPHER FULTON, librarian, historian, educator; b. Bklyn., June 14, 1935; s. William Ralph and Frances (Manning) M.; m. Ann Adamczyk, 1993; children: Sharon, David B. AB, U. St. Thomas, Houston, 1957; AMLS, U. Mich., 1960. Catalogue libr. Washington and Lee U., Lexington, Va., 1958-62; social sci. libr. So. Ill. U., Edwardsville, 1962-66, book selection officer, 1967-69, asst. dir., 1969-72; libr. of coll. Grinnell Coll., Iowa, 1972—, Samuel R. and Marie-Louise Rosenthal prof. Sec. of Navy rsch. chair in naval history Naval Hist. Ctr., Washington, 1990-91; trustee Bibliog. Ctr. Rsch., Denver, 1984-88; scholar-in residence Obermann Ctr. for Advanced Studies, U. Iowa, 1997-98. Author: Edward Preble, 1972, A Gentlemanly and Honorable Profession: The Creation of the U.S. Naval Officer Corps 1794-1815, 1991, Sober Men and True: Sailor Lives in the Royal Navy 1900-1945, 2002. NEH-Newberry Libr. fellow, 1978-79, Newberry Libr.-Brit. Acad. fellow, 1995-96; recipient U.S. Naval History prize for best pub. article, 1985, John Lyman book award N.Am. Soc. Oceanic History, 1991, Samuel Eliot Morison Disting. Svc. award USS Constitution Mus., Boston, 1992. Mem. Can. Nautical Rsch. Soc., Navy Records Soc., Soc. for Mil. History, Orgn. Am. Historians, Soc. Historians of Early Am. Republic, U.S. Naval Inst. Home: 2382 Willowbrooke Ln Iowa City IA 52246-1834 Office: Grinnell Coll Burling Libr 1111 6th Ave Grinnell IA 50112-1690

MCKEE, GEORGE MOFFITT, JR. civil engineer, consultant; b. Valparaiso, Nebr., Mar. 27, 1924; s. George Moffitt and Iva (Santrock) McK.; m. Mary Lee Taylor, Aug. 11, 1945; children: Michael Craig, Thomas Lee, Mary Kathleen, Marsha Coleen, Charlotte Anne. Student, Kans. State Coll. Agr. and Applied Sci., 1942-43, Bowling Green State U., 1943; BSE in Civil Engring., U. Mich., 1947. Registered profl. civil engr., Kans., Okla., land surveyor, Kans. Draftsman Jackson Constrn. Co., Colby, Kans., 1945-46; asst. engr. Thomas County, 1946; engr. Sherman County, Goodland, Kans., 1947-51; salesman Oehlert Tractor & Equipment Co., Colby, 1951-52; owner, operator George M. McKee, Jr.; cons. engrs. Colby, 1952-72; sr. v.p. engring. Contract Surety Cons., Wichita, Kans., 1974-2000; engring. cons., 2000—. Adv. rep. Kans State U., Manhattan, 1957-62; mem. adv. com. N.W. Kans. Area Vocat. Tech. Sch., Goodland, 1967-71; chmn. ofcl. bd. Meth. Ch., 1966-67. With USMCR, 1942-45. Mem. Kans. Soc. Profl. Engrs. (pres. N.W. profl. engrs. chpt. 1962-63, treas. cons. engrs. sect. 1961-63), Kans. County Engr.'s Assn. (dist. v.p. 1950-51), N.W. Kans. Hwy. Ofcls. Assn. (sec. 1948-49), Nat. Soc. Profl. Engrs., Kans. State U. Alumni Assn. (life, pres. Thomas County 1956-57), Am. Legion (Goodland 1st vice comdr. 1948-49), The Alumni Assn. U. Mich. (life), Colby C. of C. (v.p. 1963-64), Goodland Jr. C. of C. (pres. 1951-52), Masons (32 degree, Shriner), Order of the Ea. Star. Home: 8930 Suncrest St Apt 502 Wichita KS 67212-4069

MCKEE, JAMES STANLEY COLTON (JASPER MCKEE), physics educator; b. Belfast, Northern Ireland; m. Christine McKee (dec. May 1995); children: Conor, Siobhan. BS in Physics with honors, Queen's U., Belfast, 1952, PhD in Theoretical Physics, 1956; DSc in Physics, Birmingham U., Eng., 1968. Asst. lectr. dept. physics Queen's U., Belfast, 1954-56; lectr. dept. physics U. Birmingham, 1956-64, sr. lectr. dept. physics, 1964-74; prof. physics U. Man., Winnipeg, Can., 1974-96, prof. emeritus, 1996—, acting dir. Cyclotron Lab. Can., 1975, dir. Cyclotron Lab./Accelerator Ctr. Can., 1975—. Mem. senate U. Manitoba, 1975-95, mem. senate exec. com., 1982-86, corp. rep. to Can. Nuclear Assn., 1979-85, mem. senate planning and priorities com., 1981-86, chmn. senate planning and priorities com., 1983-85, mem. bd. govs., 1984-94, exec. com. mem., 1985-88, fin. com., 1988-93; mem. evaluation com. Sci. Culture Can., 1988—; hon. mem. adv. com. on sci. and tech. CBC, 1985-88; mem. Manitoba Fusion Power Com., 1980—; mem. NSERC Nuclear Physics Grant Selection Com., 1978-81; corr. Info. Radio, Manitoba, 1980-88; adv. bd. Energy Sources, 1988-93; invited presenter papers at 18 internat. confs. Author: Random Recollections of a Peripatetic Physicist, 1998, Physics in the Real World, 1999, The View From Below Cashel Hill, 2000; editor: Physics in Can., 1990—; sci. columnist CBC Newsworld TV, 1988-91; referee Phys. Rev., Phys. Rev. Letters, Jour. Physics G.; contbr. over 200 articles profl. jours., 5 chpts. to books and conf. proceedings. Dep. chmn. United Way Campaign, 1992-93; univ. divsn. chmn. United Way of Winnipeg, 1990-92; mem. Nat. Adv. Bd. on Sci. and Tech., 1994-95; bd. dirs. Atomic Energy of Can., 1995—, Smart Park at U. Man., 1999—. Recipient Local Actra award, 1972, Outreach award U. Man., 1986, McNeil medal Royal Soc. Can., 1995, Kirkby medal for outstanding contbns. to physics in Can., 1998; Kitchener scholar Queen's U., 1948-52, Univ. grad. scholar, 1952-55, Fulbright scholar, 1965-66. Mem. Can. Assn. Physicists (v.p.-elect 1985-86, pres. 1986-87, past pres. 1987-88), ACSTP (chair action com. of sci. and tech. pres. 1987), Rotary Club of Winnipeg West (bd. dirs. 1992-93). Achievements include research in high energy proton PIXE; nuclear few body problems, polarisation transfer studies. Office: U Manitoba-Dept Physics 223 Allen Bldg Winnipeg MB Canada R3T 2N2 E-mail: mckee@physics.umanitoba.ca.

MCKEE, KEITH EARL, manufacturing technology executive; b. Chgo., Sept. 9, 1928; s. Charles Richard and Maude Alice (Hamlin) McK.; m. Lorraine Marie Celichowski, Oct. 26, 1951; children: Pamela Ann Houser, Paul Earl. BS, Ill. Inst. Tech., 1950, MS, 1956, PhD, 1962. Engr. Swift & Co., Chgo., 1953-54; rsch. engr. Armour Rsch. Found., 1954-62; dir. design and product assurance Andrew Corp., Orland Park, Ill., 1962-67; dir. engring. Rsch. Ctr. Ill. Inst. Tech., Chgo., 1967-80, dir. mfg. prodn. ctr., 1977—. Prof. Ill. Inst. Tech., Chgo., 1979—; coord. Nat. Conf. on Fluid Power, Chgo., 1983-88; mem. com. on materials and processing Dept. Def., Washington, 1986-92. Author: Productivity and Technology, 1988; editor: Automated Inspection and Process Control, 1987; co-editor: Manufacturing High Technology Handbook, 1987; mng. editor: Manufacturing Competitiveness Frontier, 1977-97. Capt. USMC, 1950-54. Recipient oustanding presentation award Am. Soc. of Quality Control, Milw., 1983. Fellow World Acad. Productivity Scis.; mem. ASCE, Am. Def. Preparedness Assn. (pres. Chgo. chpt. 1972-95), Am. Assn. Engring. Soc. (Washington) (coor. com. on productivity 1978-88), Inst. of Indsl. Engrs., Soc. Mfg. Engrs. (Gold medal 1991), Am. Assn. for Artificial Intelligence, Robotic Industry Assn. (bd. dir. 1978-81), Assn. for Mfg. Excellence, Soc. for Computer Simulation. Democrat. Roman Catholic. Home: Ste 504 3115 S Michigan Ave Chicago IL 60616 Office: Illinois Inst Tech Mfg Productivity Ctr 10 W 32d St Chicago IL 60616-3793 E-mail: mckee@iit.edu.

MCKEE, PETER B. healthcare services executive; BBA, Northwestern U.; studnet, NYU Grad. Sch. Bus. Sr. fin. positions Ford Motor Co., Cooper Industries; CFO, Metro Airlines, Swift Ind. Packaging; sr. v.p., CFO, FoxMeyer Health Corp., Dallas, 1993-96; CFO, Allegiance Healthcare Corp., McGraw Parl, Ill., 1996—, cons. Office: Allegiance Healthcare Corp 1430 Waukegan Rd Mc Gaw Park IL 60085-6787

MCKEE, RICHARD MILES, animal studies educator; b. Cottonwood Falls, Kans., Oct. 8, 1929; m. Marjorie Fisk, June 22, 1952; children: Dave, Richard, Annell, John. BS in Agriculture, Kans. State Coll. Agriculture and Applied Sci., 1951; MS in Animal Husbandry, Kans. State U., 1963; PhD in Animal Science, U. Ky., 1968. Herdsman Moxley Hall Hereford Ranch, Coun. Grove, Kans., 1951-52, 54-55, Luckhardt Farms, Tarkio, Mo., 1955-58; asst. mgr. L&J Crusoe Ranch, Cheboygan, Mich., 1958-59; asst. instr., cattle herdsman Kans. State U., Manhattan, 1959-65, from asst. prof. to assoc. prof., 1959-65, prof., departmental teaching coord., 1976-99. Program participant and/or official judge numerous shows, field days including Kans. Jr. Hereford Field Day, Kans. Jr. Shorthorn Field Day, Better Livestock Day, Kans. Jr. Livestock Assn., Am. Jr. Hereford Assn. Field Day, Cheyenne, Wyo., 1973, Kans. Jr. Polled Hereford Field Day, Am. Jr. Shorthorn Assn., Kans. City, Mo., 1965, Am. Internat. Jr. Charolais Assn. Show, Lincoln, Nebr., 1976, Am. Royal 4-H Livestock Judging Contest, Kans. City, 1975, Jr. Livestock Activities various cattle breed assns. nationwide, 1977-81; served on many breed assn. coms.; judge County Fairs; official judge 14 different Nat. Beef Breed Shows U.S. and Can.; conducted 60 livestock judging and showmanship schs. at county level. Contbr. articles to profl. jours. Deacon 1st Presbyn. Ch., Manhattan, 1969-75, Sunday Sch. tchr., Chancel choir, elder; project leader com. mem. 4-H; foster parent Kans. State U. Football Program. Lt. USMC, 1952-54, Korea. Named Hon. State Farmer of Kans.; Hall of Merit Honoree for Edn. by Am. Polled Hereford Assn., 1985; NDEA scholar U. Ky., 1966-67; Miles McKee Student Enrichment Fund established at Kans. State U. Mem. Am. Soc. Animal Sci., Kans. Livestock Assn. (beef cattle improvement com. 1970-78, cow-calf clinic com. 1973, 74, 75, 76, 77, 78), Nat. Assn. Colls. and Tchrs. Agriculture, Block and Bridle Club, Am. Jr. Hereford Assn. (hon.), FarmHouse, Sigma Xi, Phi Kappa Phi, Alpha Zeta, Gamma Sigma Delta, Alpha Tau Alpha (hon.). Home: 901 Juniper Dr Manhattan KS 66502-3148 Office: Dept of Animal Scis & Industry Kansas State U Manhattan KS 66506

MCKEE, THOMAS FREDERICK, lawyer; b. Cleve., Oct. 27, 1948; s. Harry Wilbert and Virginia (Light) McK. BA with high distinction, U. Mich., 1970; JD, Case Western Rs. U., 1975. Bar: Ohio 1975, U.S. Dist. Ct. (no. dist.) Ohio 1975, U.S. Supreme Ct. 1979. Assoc. firm Calfee, Halter & Griswold, Cleve., 1975-81, ptnr., 1982—, also mem. exec. com., chmn. operating com.; sec. McDonald & Co. Investments, Inc., Chart Industries, Inc., Heathometer Products, Inc., Collaborative Clin. Rsch., Inc.; bd. dirs. Mr. Coffee, Inc. Contbg. editor Going Public, 1985. Mem. ABA (com. fed. regulation securities law sect.), Bar Assn. Greater Cleve., Order of Coif., Union Club, Tavern Club, Country Club, Hillbrook Club. Home: 210 Pheasant Run Dr Chagrin Falls OH 44022-2968 Office: Calfee Halter & Griswold 800 Superior Ave E Ste 1400 Cleveland OH 44114-2601

MCKEEN, ALEXANDER C. retired engineering executive, foundation administrator; b. Albion, Mich., Oct. 10, 1927; s. John Nisbet and Janet (Callander) McK.; m. Evelyn Mae Feldkamp, Aug. 18, 1951; Jeffrey, Brian, Andrew. BSME, U. Mich., 1950; MBA, Mich. State U., 1968. Registered profl. engr., Mich. From asst. supt. maintenance to supt. final assembly Cadillac Motor Car divsn. GM, Detroit, 1961-69; asst. dir. reliability cadillac motor car divsn. GM, 1969-72, exec. engr. product assurance Warren, 1972-75, from asst. dir. to dir engring. analysis, 1975-87; pres., owner Engring. Analysis Assocs., Inc., Bingham Farms, 1987-99; cons. Detroit Exec. Svc. Corps, 1999—; pres. McKeen Found., 2002—. Pres. Dells of Bloomfield Home Owners Assn., Bloomfield Hills, Mich., 1987-88; trustee Kirk in Hills, Bloomfield Hills, 1990-93, elder, 1995-97. Mem. Soc. Auto. Engrs., Am. Soc. Quality Control, Econ. Club Detroit, Detroit Athletic Club, Stonycroft Hills Golf Club, Pelican Nest Golf Club, Beta Gamma Sigma. Avocations: tennis, golf, photography, travel, gardening. Home: 5071 Champlain Cir West Bloomfield MI 48323-3530 Office: Detroit Executive Service Corps 23815 Northwestern Hwy Southfield MI 48075-7713

MC KELVEY, JOHN CLIFFORD, retired research institute executive; b. Decatur, Ill., Jan. 25, 1934; s. Clifford Venice and Pauline Lytton (Runkel) McK.; m. Carolyn Tenney, May 23, 1980; children: Sean, Kerry, Tara, Evelyn, Aaron. B.A., Stanford U., 1956, M.B.A., 1958. Research analyst Stanford Research Inst., Palo Alto, Calif., 1959-60, indsl. economist, 1960-64; with Midwest Research Inst., Kansas City, Mo., 1964—, v.p. econs. and mgmt. sci., 1970-73, exec. v.p., 1973-75, pres., chief exec. officer, 1975—. Trustee Rockhurst Coll., 1993, Hoover Presdl. Libr. Assn., West Branch, Iowa, 1997; mem. Civic Coun. of Greater Kansas City; bd. dirs. Yellow Corp., Mid-Am. Mfg. Tech. Ctr., 1991; trustee The Menninger Found., 1975. Clubs: Carriage, Mission Hills. Home: 1156 W 103d St # 232 Kansas City MO 64114-4511 Office: Midwest Rsch Inst 425 Volker Blvd Kansas City MO 64110-2299

MCKENDRY, JOHN H., JR. lawyer, educator; b. Grand Rapids, Mich., Mar. 24, 1950; s. John H. and Lois R. (Brandel) McK.; m. Linda A. Schmalzer, Aug. 11, 1973; children: Heather Lynn, Shannon Dawn, Sean William. BA cum laude, Albion Coll., 1972; JD cum laude, U. Mich., 1975. Bar: Mich. 1975. Assoc., then ptnr. Landman, Latimer, Clink & Robb, Muskegon, Mich., 1976-85; ptnr. Warner, Norcross & Judd, 1985—. Dir. debate Mona Shores High Sch., Muskegon, 1979-90; adj. prof. of taxation (employee benefits), Grand Valley State U., 1988—; debate instr. Muskegon C.C., 1999-2001. Pres. local chpt. Am. Cancer Soc., 1979; bd. dirs. West Shore Symphony, 1993-2000, v.p. 1995-97, pres., 1997-99; bd. dirs. Cath. Social Svcs., 1998—; chair profl. divsn. United Way, 1994, 98. Recipient Disting. Service award Muskegon Jaycees, 1981; named 1 of 5 Outstanding Young Men in Mich., Mich. Jaycees. 1982; named to Hall of Fame, Mich. Speech Coaches, 1986, Diamond Key Coach Nat. Forensic League, 1987. Mem. ABA, Mich. Bar Assn., Muskegon County Bar Assn. (dir. 1992-98, pres. 1996-97), Muskegon C. of C. (bd. dirs. 1982-88), Mich. Interscholastic Forensic Assn. (treas. 1979-86), Optimists (pres. 1992). Republican. Roman Catholic. Home: 1575 Brookwood Dr Muskegon MI 49441-5276 Office: Warner Norcross & Judd LLP PO Box 900 400 Terrace Pla Muskegon MI 49443-0900 E-mail: mckendjh@wnj.com.

MCKENNA, ALVIN JAMES, lawyer; b. New Orleans, Aug. 17, 1943; s. Dixon N. Sr. and Mabel (Duplantier) McK.; m. Carol Jean Windheim, 1963; children: Sara, Alvin James Jr., Martha, Andrea, Erin, Rebecca. AB, Canisius Coll., 1963; JD, Notre Dame U., 1966. Bar: N.Y. 1966, Ohio 1967, U.S. Dist. Ct. (so. dist.) Ohio 1968, U.S. Dist. Ct. (no. dist.) Ohio 1978, U.S. Ct. Appeals (6th cir.) 1969, U.S. Supreme Ct. 1977. Law clk. to judge of U.S. Dist. Ct. (so. dist.), Columbus, Ohio, 1966-68; asst. U.S. atty., 1968-70; ptnr. Porter, Wright, Morris & Arthur, 1970—. Mem. Gahanna (Ohio) City Council, 1972-80, 82-84; chmn. Gahanna Charter Rev. Commn., 1981; pres. Community Urban Redevel. Corp., Gahanna, 1984—. Named one of Ten Outstanding Young Persons in Columbus, Jaycees, 1974. Mem. ABA, Ohio Bar Assn., Fed. Bar Assn. (pres. Columbus chpt. 1973-74), Columbus Bar Assn. (chair fed. cts. com. 1972-74). Home: 202 Academy Ct Columbus OH 43230-2104 Office: Porter Wright Morris & Arthur 41 S High St Ste 2800 Columbus OH 43215-6194 E-mail: amckenna@porterwright.com.

MCKENNA, ANDREW JAMES, paper distribution and printing company executive, baseball club executive; b. Chgo., Sept. 17, 1929; s. Andrew James and Anita (Fruin) McK.; m. Mary Joan Pickett, June 20, 1953; children: Suzanne, Karen, Andrew, William, Joan, Kathleen, Margaret. B.S., U. Notre Dame, 1951; J.D., DePaul U., 1954. Bar: Ill. Chmn., CEO Schwarz Paper Co. (name now Schwarz), Morton Grove, Ill., 1964—; dir. Chgo. Nat. League Ball Club Inc., Chgo. Bears. Bd. dirs. Skyline Corp., Tribune Co., AON Corp., Click Commerce, Inc., McDonald's Corp. Chmn. trustees, emeritus U. Notre Dame; trustee Mus. Sci. & Industry, Chgo.; bd. dirs. Cath. Charities of Chgo., Children's Meml. Med. Ctr. Chgo. Mem. Chgo. Athletic Assn., Econ. Club Chgo., Lyric Opera (bd. dirs.), Chgo. Club, Comml. Club Chgo. (chmn.), Execs. Club Chgo., Glenview Golf Club, Old Elm Club, Merit Club, Casino Club, The Island Club, Chgo. Metropolis 2020 (chmn.). Home: 60 Locust Rd Winnetka IL 60093-3751 Office: Schwarz 8338 Austin Ave Morton Grove IL 60053-3288

MCKENNA, GEORGE LAVERNE, art museum curator; b. Detroit, Dec. 7, 1924; s. John LaVerne and Carolyn Georgia (Schwab) McK.; m. Janice Ballinger, July 22, 1966. Student, U. Oreg., 1943-44, U. Calif., Berkeley, 1948-49, U. Chgo., 1950; AB, Wayne State U., 1948, MA, 1951. Curator prints, drawings and photographs Nelson-Atkins Mus. Art, Kansas City, Mo., 1952-96, cons, 1997—. Cons. Hallmark Cards, Inc., Kansas City, 1974-76. Curator, author exhbn. and coll. catalogues. With U.S. Army, 1943-46. Mem. Am. Assn. Mus., Print Coun. Am. Office: Nelson-Atkins Mus Art 4525 Oak St Kansas City MO 64111-1873

MCKENNA, WILLIAM JOHN, textile products executive; b. N.Y.C., Oct. 11, 1926; s. William T. and Florence (Valis) McK.; m. Jean T. McNulty, Aug. 27, 1949 (dec. Nov. 1984); children: Kevin, Marybeth, Peter, Dawn; m. Karen Lynne Hilgert, Aug. 6, 1988; children: Katherine Lynne, William John IV. BBA, Iona Coll., 1949; M.S. (Univ. Store Service scholar), NYU, 1950. V.p. Hat Corp. Am., N.Y.C., 1961-63, v.p. mktg., 1961-63, exec. v.p., 1963-67; pres. Manhattan Shirt Co., 1967-74; pres., dir. Lee Co., Inc., Shawnee Mission, Kans., 1974-82, Kellwood Co., St. Louis, 1982—, chief exec. officer, 1984—, also bd. dirs., chmn., CEO, 1991-97, chmn., 1991-99, chmn. emeritus, 1999—. Dir. United Mo. Bancshares, Kansas City, Mo., United Mo. Bank of St. Louis. Trustee emeritus St. Louis U., Boys Hope, St. Louis U. H.S.; permanent deacon Archdiocese St. Louis. With USN, 1944-46, PTO. Mem. Sovereign Mil. Order Malta, St. Louis Club, Bellerive Country Club. Roman Catholic. Office: Kellwood Co PO Box 14374 Saint Louis MO 63178-4374 E-mail: william_mckenna@kellwood.com.

MCKENZIE, LLOYD W. real estate development executive; V.p. Indpls. divsn. Crossman Cmtys., Inc., 1992—. Office: Crossman Cmtys Inc 9202 N Meridian St Ste 300 Indianapolis IN 46260-1833

MCKENZIE, ROBERT ERNEST, lawyer; b. Cheboygan, Mich., Dec. 7, 1947; s. Alexander Orlando and Edna Jean (Burt) McK.; m. Theresia Wolf, Apr. 26, 1975; 1 child, Robert A. BA in Personnel Adminstrn., Mich. State U., 1970; JD with high honors, Ill. Inst. Tech., 1979. Bar: Ill. 1979, U.S. Dist. Ct. (no. dist.) Ill. 1979, U.S. Tax Ct. 1979, U.S. Ct. Appeals (7th cir.) 1979, U.S. Supreme Ct. 1984; lic. pvt. pilot. Revenue officer IRS, Chgo., 1972-78; ptnr. McKenzie & McKenzie, 1979-2000, Arnstein & Lehr, 2000—. Lectr. Tax Seminars Inst., Chgo., 1984—. Author: Representation Before the Collection Divison of the IRS, 1989; co-author: Representing the Audited Taxpayer Before the IRS, 1990; contbr. articles to profl. jours. Mem. tax adv. com. Nat. Bankruptcy Rev. Commn., 1997; del. Rep. Nat. Conv., Detroit, 1980, Ill. State Rep. Conv., Peoria, 1980. Served with U.S. Army, 1970. Recipient scholarship Mich. State U., 1966-70, State of Mich., 1966-70, Silas Strawn scholarship ITT, 1977. Fellow Am. Bar Found., N.W. Suburban Bar Assn; mem. ABA (chmn. employment tax com. tax sect. 1992-94, co-chmn. bankruptcy task force 1997-98, coun. tax sect. 1998-2001), Chgo. Bar Assn. (chmn. com. devel. tax com. 1996-97), Fed. Bar Assn. (tax com.), Rotary (pres. Norridge club 1985-86). Office: Ste 1200 120 S Riverside Plz Chicago IL 60606 E-mail: remckenzie@arnstein.com.

MCKEON, JOHN ALOYSIUS (JACK) (JACK MCKEON), professional baseball manager; b. South Amboy, N.J., Nov. 23, 1930; m. Carol McKeon; children: Kelly, Kasey, Kristi, Kori. BA in Phys. Edn. and Sci., Elon Coll. Baseball mgr. in 13 maj. and minor league cities; mgr. Kansas City Royals, Am. League, 1973-75, Oakland A's, 1977-78; v.p. baseball ops. San Diego Padres, Nat. League, 1980-93, mgr., 1988-90, Cincinnati Reds, 1997—. Bd. dirs. San Diego Make-a-Wish Found. NL Mgr. of The Year, 1999. Office: Cincinnati Reds Cinergy Field 100 Cinergy Fld Cincinnati OH 45202-3543

MCKEON, THOMAS JOSEPH, lawyer; b. Feb. 3, 1955; s. Thomas Michael and Mary Rose (Luzar) McKeon. BA, Ind. U., 1974; JD cum laude, U. Ind., Indpls., 1977. Bar: Ind. 1977, U.S. Dist. Ct. (so. dist.) Ind. 1977, U.S. Supreme Ct. 1979. Assoc. Nisenbaum & Brown, Inpls., 1977, Osborn & Hiner, Inpls., 1977; counsel Am. Family Ins., 1982—; asst. counsel Radio Earth Internat., Inc., Radio Earth Curacao, Netherlands Antilles, 1985—. Author: (book) Post Traumatic Stress Disorder: Real or Imagined, 1986, Repetition Strain as a Compensable Injury, 1987; contbr. articles to profl. jours. Mem.: ABA, ATLA (assoc.), Ind. Arson and Crime Assn., Ind. Assn. Pvt. Detectives, Am. Corp. Counsel Assn., Def. Rsch. &

Trial Lawyers Assn., Indpls. Bar Assn., Ind. Trial Lawyers Assn., Ind. Def. Lawyers Assn., Ind. Bar Assn., San Diego Turtle and Tortoise Soc. Office: 7330 Shadeland Sta Indianapolis IN 46256-3919

MCKIBBEN, LARRY, state legislator, lawyer; b. Marshalltown, Iowa, Jan. 5, 1947; m. Marki McKibben; 2 children. BA, U. No. Iowa; JD, U. Iowa. Atty.; mem. Iowa Senate from 32nd dist., Des Moines, 1996—; chair bus. and labor rels. com.; mem. jud. com., mem. local govt. com.; mem. transp. com., vice chair ways and means com. Republican. Office: State Capitol 9th And Grand Ave Des Moines IA 50319-0001 E-mail: larry_mckibben@legis.state.ia.us.

MCKIM, SAMUEL JOHN, III, lawyer; b. Pitts., Dec. 31, 1938; s. Samuel John and Harriet Frieda (Roehl) McK; children: David Hunt, Andrew John; m. Eugenia A. Leverich. AA cum laude, Port Huron Jr. Coll., 1959; BA cum laude, U. Mich., 1961, JD cum laude, 1964. Bar: Mich. 1965, U.S. Dist. Ct. (so. dist.) Mich. 1965, U.S. Ct. Appeals (6th cir.) 1969, U.S. Supreme Ct. 1994. Assoc. Miller, Canfield, Paddock and Stone, PLC, Detroit, Bloomfield Hills, 1964-71, sr. mem., 1971—, head state and local tax sect., 1985—, chmn. tax dept., 1989-94, mng. ptnr., 1979-85, chmn., mng. ptnr., 1984-85. Mem. tax coun. State Bar Mich., 1981-94, chmn. state and local tax com. real property sect., 1982-90; adj. prof. law sch. Wayne State U., 1993-99. Assoc. editor Mich. Law Rev. Bd. dirs., past chmn. Goodwill Industries of Greater Detroit, 1970-2000; dir. Goodwill Industries Found., 1982-95; elder Presbyn. Ch., Stevens min.; coun. mem. at large Detroit area coun. Boy Scouts Am., 1987—. Fellow Am Coll. Tax Counselors; mem. ABA, Mich. Bar Assn., Detroit Bar Assn., Barrister's Soc., Ostego Ski Club, Port Huron Golf Club, Order of Coif, Nomads Club, Phi Delta Phi. Home: 32778 Friar Tuck Ln Beverly Hills MI 48025-2500 Office: Miller Canfield Paddock & Stone 150 W Jefferson Ave Ste 2500 Detroit MI 48226-4416

MCKINNELL, ROBERT GILMORE, zoology, genetics and cell biology educator; b. Springfield, Mo., Aug. 9, 1926; s. William Parks and Mary Catherine (Gilmore) McK.; m. Beverly Walton Kerr, Jan. 24, 1964; children: Nancy Elizabeth, Robert Gilmore, Susan Kerr. AB, U. Mo., 1948; BS, Drury Coll., 1949, DSc (hon.), 1993; PhD, U. Minn., 1959. Research assoc. Inst. Cancer Research, Phila., 1958-61; asst. prof. biology Tulane U., New Orleans, 1961-65, assoc. prof., 1965-69, prof., 1969-70; prof. zoology U. Minn., Mpls., 1970—, prof. genetics and cell biology St. Paul, 1976—, prof. emeritus, 1999—; NATO sr. sci. fellow St. Andrews U., Scotland. Vis. scientist Dow Chem. Co., Freeport, Tex., 1976; guest dept. zoology U. Calif., Berkeley, 1979; Royal Soc. guest rsch. fellow Nuffield dept. pathology John Radcliffe Hosp., Oxford U., 1981-82; NATO vis. scientist Akademisch Ziekenhuis, Ghent, Belgium, 1984; faculty rsch. assoc. Naval Med. Rsch. Inst., Bethesda, Md., 1988; secretariat Third Internat. Conf. Differentiation, 1978; organizer, secretariat 6th Internat. Conf. on Pathology of Reptiles and Amphibians, 2001; mem. amphibian com. Inst. Lab. Animal Resources, NRC, 1970-73, mem. adv. coun., 1974; mem. panel genetic and cellular resources program NIH, 1981-82, spl. study sect., Bethesda, 1990. Author: Cloning: Amphibian Nuclear Transplantation, 1978, Cloning, A Biologist Reports, 1979; sr. editor: Differentiation and Neoplasia, 1980, Cloning: Leben aus der Retorte, 1981, Cloning, of Frogs, Mice, and other Animals, 1985, (with others) The Biological Basis of Cancer, 1998; mem. editl. bd. Differentiation, 1973—; assoc. editor: Gamete Research, 1980-86; mem. bd. advisors Marquis Who's Who; contbr. articles to profl. jours. Served to lt. USNR, 1944-47, 51-53. Recipient Outstanding Teaching award Newcomb Coll., Tulane U., 1970; Disting. Alumni award Drury Coll., 1979, Morse Alumni Teaching award U. Minn., 1992; Research fellow Nat. Cancer Inst., 1957-58, Prince Hitachi award Japanese Found. Cancer Rsch., 1998; Sr. Sci. fellow NATO, 1974 Fellow AAAS, Linnean Soc. (London); mem. Am. Assn. Cancer Rsch. (emeritus), Am. Assn. Cancer Edn. (sr.), Am. Inst. Biol. Scis., Indian Soc. Devel. Biology (lifetime emeritus mem.), Internat. Soc. Differentiation (exec. com., sec.-treas. 1975-92, pres. elect 1992-94, pres. 1994-96), Gown-in-Town Club, Sigma Xi. Home: 2124 Hoyt Ave W Saint Paul MN 55108-1315 Office: U Minn Dept Genetics Cell Bio Saint Paul MN 55108-1095 E-mail: mckin002@tc.umn.edu.

MCKINNEY, DENNIS, state legislator; m. Jean McKinney. Farmer, stockman, Greensburg, Kans.; mem. from dist. 108 Kans. State Ho. of Reps., Topeka, 1993—. Address: 612 S Spruce St Greensburg KS 67054-1944

MCKINNEY, DENNIS KEITH, lawyer; b. Ottawa, Ill., May 12, 1952; s. Robert Keith and Delroy Louise (Clayton) McK.; m. Patricia Jean Boyle, Oct. 4, 1986; 1 child, Geoffrey Edward. BS, Ball State U., 1973; JD, Ill. Inst. Tech., 1976. Bar: Ind. 1977, U.S. Dist. Ct. (so. dist.) Ind. 1977, U.S. Supreme Ct. 1993. Appellate dep. Ind. Atty. Gen, Indpls., 1977-78, trial dep., 1978-79, sr. trial dep., 1979-81, chief real estate litigation sect., 1981-94; clk. to Hon. James S. Kirsch Ind. Ct. Appeals, 1994-95; staff atty. Ind. Supreme Ct. Disciplinary Commn., 1995—. Author: Eminent Domain, Practice and Procedure in Indiana, 1991, A Guide to Indiana Easement Law, 1995, A Railroad Ran Through It, 1996; contbg. author: Indiana Real Estate Transactions, 1996; contbr. articles to profl. jours. Active Indpls.-Scarborough Peace Games, 1983-84. Avocations: reading, volleyball, wargaming. Office: Ind Supreme Ct Disciplinary 115 W Washington St Indianapolis IN 46204-3420

MCKINNEY, E. KIRK, JR. retired insurance company executive; b. Indpls., Mar. 27, 1923; s. E. Kirk and Irene M. (Hurley) McK.; m. Alice Hollenbeck Greene, June 18, 1949; children: Kirk Ashley, Alan Brooks, Nora Claire McKinney Hiatt, Margot Knight. A.B., U. Mich., 1948. Asst. treas. Jefferson Nat. Life Ins. Co., Indpls., 1949-52, asst. to pres., asst. treas., 1952-53, treas., asst. to pres., 1953-55, v.p., treas., 1955-59, pres., 1959-90, chmn. bd., 1970-90, ret., 1990; vice chmn. bd. Somerset Group Inc., 1986-89, ret., 1990. Corp. relations com. U. Mich.; former pres., former chief exec. officer, bd. govs. , treas., bd. dirs., exec. com. Indpls. Mus. Art; past bd. dirs. (hon.) Greater Indpls. Progress Com.; former vice chmn. Indpls.-Marion County Bd. Ethics; former dir. Park Tudor Sch., Community Svc. Coun. Indpls., Hosp. Devel. Corp., Ind. Repertory Theater; past adv. com. Indpls. Retirement Home; former bd. dirs., and pres. Episcopal Community Services, Inc.; former vice chmn., life trustee Nature Conservancy; mem. adv. bd. Ind. U., Purdue U.; active Indpls. Symphony Orch.; former bd. dirs. Ind. Pub. Broadcasting Soc.; bd. dirs. Indpls. Civic Theater, 2001—. Mem. Life Office Mgmt. Assn. (bd. dirs. 1981-83), Am. Council Life Ins. (state v.p. 1973-75, dir., exec. com. 1976-79), Assn. Ind. Life Ins. Cos. (pres. 1969-71), Indpls. C. of C., Sigma Chi. Democrat. Club: Economic of Indpls. (bd. dirs.) Home: 250 W 77th St Indianapolis IN 46260-3608 Office: 1330 W 38th St #100 Indianapolis IN 46208-4103 E-mail: ekirkjr@aol.com.

MCKINNEY, JEFF, radio personality; b. Charlottesville, Va. married; 2 children. Student, Vanderbilt U.; BA English Lit., Washington U., St. Louis. With CBS Broadcasting, 1983; broadcast journalist Sta. WCCO radio, Mpls., 1994—. Recipient award, L.A. Press Club, Northwest Broadcasters Assn. Office: WCCO 625 2nd St S Minneapolis MN 55402*

MCKINNEY, LARRY, religious organization administrator; m. Debra Ann Dillworth; 2 children. BS in Bible, Phila. Coll. Bible, Langhorne, Pa., 1972; MA in Ednl. Ministries, Wheaton (Ill.) Coll., 1974; EdD in Ednl. Adminstrn., Temple U., 1986. Ordained to ministry Evang. Free Ch., 1974. Former pastor local chs., N.J., Pa.; exec. dir. Fay-West Youth for Christ, Uniontown, Pa., 1972-73, 74-80; dean students, v.p. for student devel. Phila. Coll. Bible, 1980-93; pres. Providence Coll. and Sem., 1993—, Assn. Can. Bible Colls., 1994—. Former instr. numerous grad. and postgrad. ednl.-related fields; frequent spkr. for chs., confs., seminars; former mem. or chmn. 6 evaluation teams Accrediting Assn. Bible Colls.; mem. coun. Evang. Fellowship Can. Contbr. numerous articles to mags. and ednl. jours. Avocations: reading, history, running, weightlifting, watching sports. Office: Providence Coll & Sem Otterburne MB Canada R0D 1G0

MCKINNEY, LARRY J. federal judge; b. South Bend, Ind., July 4, 1944; s. Lawrence E. and Helen (Byers) McK.; m. Carole Jean Marie Lyon, Aug. 19, 1966; children: Joshua E., Andrew G. BA, MacMurray Coll., Jacksonville, Ill., 1966; JD, Ind. U., 1969. Bar: Ind. 1970, U.S. Dist. Ct. (so. dist.) Ind. 1970. Law clk. to atty. gen. State of Ind., Indpls., 1969-70, dep. atty. gen., 1970-71; ptnr. Rodgers and McKinney, Edinburgh, Ind., 1971-75, James F.T. Sargent, Greenwood, 1975-79; judge Johnson County Cir. Ct., Franklin, 1979-87, U.S. Dist. Ct. (so. dist.) Ind., Indpls., 1987—, chief judge, 2001—. Presbyterian. Avocations: reading, jogging. Office: US Dist Ct 204 US Courthouse 46 E Ohio St Indianapolis IN 46204-1903

MCKINNEY, MYRON W. electronic company executive; b. Bolivar, Mo., 1945; m. Janet M.; children: Shannon Bowman, Rebecca McKinney. B in Bus. Adminstrn., SW Mo. State U., 1967. Sales cons. Empire Dist. Elec. Co., Joplin, Mo., 1967-82, v.p. commercial ops., 1982-94, v.p., 1994-95, exec. v.p. commercial ops., 1995-97, pres., CEO, 1997—. Mem. Mo. Valley Elec. Assn. Bd. dirs., Joplin Bus. and Indsl. Devel. Corp.; mem. Ozarks Pub. Telecomms., Joplin So. Corp., Rotary, Joplin C. of C., United Way. Office: Emprie Dist Electric Co PO Box 127 Joplin MO 64802-0127

MC KINNEY, ROBERT HURLEY, lawyer, business executive; b. Indpls., Nov. 7, 1925; s. E. Kirk and Irene (Hurley) McK.; m. Arlene Frances Allsopp, Nov. 28, 1951; children: Robert, Marni, Kevin, Kent, Lisa. BS, U.S. Naval Acad., 1946; JD, Ind. U., 1951. Bar: Ind. 1951. Since practiced in, Indpls.; sr. ptnr. Bose McKinney & Evans, 1963—; chmn., chief exec. officer The Somerset Group, Inc. and subs., Indpls., 1961-77, 79—, First & Loan Bank, Indpls., 1961—; chmn. Fed. Home Loan Bank Bd., 1977-79. Bd. dirs. Fed. Nat. Mortgage Assn., Wholesale Club, Inc., Lily Industries Coatings, Inc.; mem. adv. com. on internat. investment Dept. State. Chmn. Urban Reinvestment Task Force, Indpls.; bd. dirs. Children's Mus. Indpls., Ind. State Symphony Soc.; bd. dirs., mem. exec. com. Brebeuf Prep. Sch., 1970— ; trustee Ind. U., U.S. Naval Coll.; del. Dem. Nat. Conv., 1968, 76, 80, 84. Lt. comdr. USNR, 1946-49, 51-53. Mem. Am., Ind., Indpls. bar assns., Com. for Econ. Devel., Young Pres. Orgn. (nat. chmn. for econ. edn. 1968-69, pres. Ind. chpt. 1973-74), Chief Exec. Orgn., Inc., Ind. C. of C. (bd. dirs.), Indpls. C. of C. (bd. dirs.), Knights of Malta. Office: First Ind Bank 2800 First Indiana Pla 135 N Pennsylvania St Fl 28 Indianapolis IN 46204-2400

MCKINNEY, WILLIAM T. psychiatrist, educator; b. Rome, Sept. 20, 1937; BA cum laude, Baylor U., 1959; MD, Vanderbilt U., 1963. Diplomate Nat. Bd. Med. Examiners (mem. psychiatry test com. 1982-87, chmn. 1984-87); cert. Am. Bd. Psychiatry and Neurology (sr. examiner 1979-90, bd. dirs. 1991—, mem. rsch. com., co-chair part I test com., chair added qualifications in geriatric psychiatry test com., mem. part II audio visual com., mem. disability accomodations com., rep. to residency rev. com.). Intern in medicine Bowman Gray Sch. Medicine, Wake Forest U., Winston-Salem, N.C., 1963-64; resident dept. psychiatry Sch. Medicine, U. N.C., Chapel Hill., 1964-66, Sch. Medicine, Stanford (Calif.) U., 1966-67; clin. assoc. psychosomatic sect. adult psychiatry br., tng. specialist, asst. br. chief NIMH, Bethesda, Md., 1967-69; asst. prof. psychiatry dept. psychiatry Sch. Medicine, U. Wis., Madison, 1969-72, assoc. prof. psychiatry, 1972-74, prof. psychiatry, 1974-93; Asher prof. of psychiatry dept. psychiatry and behavioral scis., dir. Asher Ctr. for Study and Treatment of Depressive Disorders Med. Sch., Northwestern U., Chgo., 1993—. Part-time clin. pvt. practice, Bethesda, 1967-69; NIMH rsch. career investigator Sch. Medicine, U. Wis., Madison, 1970-75, rsch. psychiatrist Primate Lab., 1974-93, affiliate sci. Wis. Regional Primate Rsch. Ctr., 1974-93, affiliate prof. psychology dept. psychology, 1974-93, chmn. dept. psychiatry, 1975-80, dir. Wis. Psychiat. Rsch. Inst. Ctr. Health Scis., 1975-80; sr. staff psychiatrist William S. Middleton Meml. VA Hosp., Madison, Wis., 1974-93; rschr. sub dept. animal behaviour U. Cambridge, Eng., 1974; mem. rsch. rev. com. VA Behavioral Scis., 1976-79; Abbott Sigma XI Club lectr., 1976; Milw. Psychiat. Hosp. lectr., 1977; mem. program adv. com. and workshop chmn. Dahlem Found. Internat. Conf. on Depression, Berlin, 1982; U. Minn. lectr. at Festshrift, 1982; cons. grad. sch. U. Minn., 1982; fellow Ctr. Advanced Study in Behavioral Scis., Stanford, Calif., 1983-84; mem. external adv. bd. Clin. Rsch. Ctr. Dept. Psychiatry U. N.C., Chapel Hill, 1984—, cons., bd. advisors clin. rsch. fellow tng. program dept. psychology, 1988—; William F. Orr lectr. Vanderbilt U., 1985; vis. prof. dept. psychiatry U. Tex. Health Scis. Ctr., Dallas, 1986, U. Utah Sch. Medicine, Salt Lake City, 1987, U. Minn. Sch. Medicine, Mpls., 1988; cons. biol. scis. tng. br. divsn. manpower and tng. programs NIMH, 1975-76, mem. psychiatry spl. tng. com. 1983, plenary lectr., Clearwater, Fla., 1987, co-chairperson Workshop on Non-Human Primate Models of Psychopathology, 1987, mem. biol. psychopathology spl. rev. com., 1992—; mem. sci. core group MacArthur Found. Mental Health Rsch. Network I: The Psychobiology of Depression and Other Affective Disorders, 1988-93; vis. spkr. So. Calif. Psychiat. Soc., L.A., 1988; plenary lectr. Soc. Biol. Psychiatry ann. meeting, Montreal, 1988; vis. prof. Dalhousie U. Sch. Medicine, N.S., 1989, HCA Riveredge Hosp., Chgo., 1989, U. Pa., Phila., 1991, U. N.Mex., Albuquerque, 1992, Northwestern U., Chgo., 1992; invited spkr. Animal Models in Psychopharmacology Symposium, Duphar, Amsterdam, 1990; vis. spkr., cons. CIBA-GEIGY, Basel, Switzerland, 1990; mem. minority instns. rsch. devel. rev. com. Alcohol, Drug Abuse and Mental Health Adminstrn., 1990; guest spkr. Inst. Pa. Hosp., Phila., 1991; reviewer Human Frontier Sci. Program, 1992—; external cons. dept. psychiatry Mental Health Clin. Rsch. Ctr. U. Tex. Southwestern Med. Ctr., Dallas, 1992—; presenter in field. Author: Animal Models of Mental Disorders: A New Comparative Psychiatry, 1988; co-author: Mood Disorders: Towards a New Psychobiology, 1984; mem. editl. bd. Archives of Psychiatry and Neurol. Scis., Contemporary Psychiatry, 1981-82, Ethology and Sociobiology, Experientia, 1982-89, Trends in Neurosciences, 1982-86, Neuropsychopharmacology, 1987-90; manuscript and book reviewer numerous sci. jours.; contbr. articles to profl. jours. USHPS fellow in biostats. Vanderbilt U., 1962; recipient Beauchamp award Vanderbilt U. Med. Sch., 1963, Rsch. Career Devel. award NIMH, 1975, Rsch. Leave award U. Wis., 1983-84, Am. Acad. Pediats. award, 1991. Fellow Am. Psychiat. Assn. (cons. psychiat. edn. consultation svc. 1983—), Am. Coll. Psychiatrists, Am. Coll. Neuropsychopharmacology (mem. constn. and rules com. 1985-87, mem. ethics com. 1987-89, mem. fin. com. 1990-92, panel chair San Juan, P.R. 1992, panel presenter 1992); mem. Am. Soc. Primatologists, Am. Psychosomatic Soc. (mem. program com. 1975-76), Internat. Primatology Soc., Internat. Coll. Neurobiology, Biol. Psychiatry and Psychopharmacology (lectr. Zurich 1985), Internat. Soc. Devel. Psychobiology, Internat. Soc. Ethological and Behavioral Pharmacology (bd. advisors 1983—), Collegium Internat. Neuro-Psychopharmacologicum, Psychiat. Rsch. Soc., Soc. Neuroscience, Wis. Psychiat. Assn. (chmn. program com. 1972, co-chairperson task force on sexual misconduct and membership edn. 1986-88, pres.-elect 1989-91, pres. 1991-93). Office: Northwestern U Med Sch Dept Psychiatry and Behavioral Scis 303 E Chicago Ave Bldg 9-176 Chicago IL 60611-3072

MCKINNIS, MICHAEL B. lawyer; b. St. Louis, May 31, 1945; s. Bayard O. and Doris (Lammert) McK.; m. Patricia Butow, Aug. 24, 1968; children: Scott, Christopher, Elizabeth. BS, Drake U., 1967; JD, U. Mo., 1970. Bar: Mo. 1970, U.S. Dist. Ct. (ea. dist.) Mo. Ptnr. Bryan Cave, St. Louis, leader firm litigation practice, mem. firm operating group. Editor U. Mo. Law Rev., 1969-70. Mem. ABA, Mo. Bar Assn., Order of Coif, Phi Delta Phi. Office: Bryan Cave 1 Met Sq 211 N Broadway Saint Louis MO 63102-2733

MCKITRICK, JAMES THOMAS, retail executive; b. Cin., Sept. 14, 1945; s. Harry J. and L. May (Buck) McK.; m. Margaret J. Haynes, Sept. 6, 1975; children: Angela, Greg, Randal, Paul, Sheri, Richard, Mike. Student, Salem Coll., 1963-64. Dir. mdse. K Mart Corp., Troy, Mich., 1965-84; exec. v.p., gen. mgr. T.G. & Y. Stores, Oklahoma City, 1984-86, exec. v.p. merchandising and mktg., 1986; pres., chief exec. officer Warehouse Club, Skokie, Ill., 1986-87; pres., chief operating officer G.C. Murphy Co. subs. Ames, Rocky Hill, Conn., 1987-89; chmn. Zayre Discount, 1988-89; pres. & CEO Builders Emporium, Irvine, CA, 1989-92, Quality Stores Inc. (formerly Central Tractor Farm & Country), Muskegon, MI, 1992—. Republican. Methodist. Office: Quality Stores Inc 455 E Ellis Rd Muskegon MI 49441-5676 Home: 409 Torrey Rd Cadillac MI 49601-9395

MCLAREN, DERRYL, state legislator; b. Shenandoah, Iowa, Mar. 22, 1949; m. Carma Herrig. BS in Agr. Bus., Iowa State U., 1971, postgrad. Farmer; mem. Iowa Senate from 43rd dist., Des Moines, 1990—; chair appropriations com.; mem. state govt. com., mem. ways and means com. Mem. Iowa Corn Promotion Bd., 1985-87, Asia market com.; past chair Fremont County Reps. Mem. Nat. Corn Growers, Iowa Soybeans Assn., Iowa Farm Bur., Iowa Corn Growers, Nat. Corn Devel. Found., U.S. Feed Grains Coun., Farm Credit Task Force, Gamma Gamma Rho, Phi Kappa Phi, Alpha Zeta, Phi Eta Sigma. Office: State Capitol 9th And Grand Des Moines IA 50319-0001 E-mail: derryl_mclaren@legis.state.ia.us.

MCLAREN, KAREN LYNN, advertising executive; b. Flint, Mich., Feb. 14, 1955; m. Michael L. McLaren, June 18, 1974. AA, Mott Community Coll., Flint, 1976; BA, Mich. State U., 1978. Writer Sta. WGMZ-FM, Flint, 1979-84; writer, producer Tracy-Stephens Advt., 1984-87; pres. McLaren Advt., Troy, Mich., 1987—. Contbr. articles to profl. jours. Mem. centennial com. Wolverine region ARC, 1981, pub. rels. com., 1981-84; vol. coord., pub. rels. tour guide Whaley Hist. Ho., Flint, 1980-91; home designer, tour guide Romeo (Mich.) Hist. Home Tour, 1992; mem. Nat. Trust for Hist. Preservation, 1991-95; com. chair Crim Festival of Races, Flint, 1992, 93, 94, 95; active Sta. WFUM-Pub. TV, Flint, 1980-91; panelist career fair Modona U., Livonia, Mich., 1994, 95, 96, 97; ad book chair Juvenile Diabetes Found./Detroit Evening of Brilliance, 1997; mem. Oakland Regional Bd. Barbara Ann Karmanos Cancer Instn., 1999. Recipient 3 awards, 2 Nat. Health Care Mktg. Competition awards, Women's Adv. Club Detroit Pres.'s award, 1994. Mem. NAFE, Women's Advt. Club Detroit (scholar chmn. 1988-88, bd. dirs. 1989, 92-93, chmn. scholarship fundraiser 1991, co-chmn. career fair 1989, 90, 92, career fair panelist 1993, v.p. 1990, pres. 1991, amb. 1992, chmn. woman of yr. award 1994-96, by-laws chmn. 1994), Women's Econ. Club Detroit (progam com. 1996, workplace of tomorrow com. 1996, vice chair 1997, chair 1999). Office: 3001 W Big Beaver Rd Ste 306 Troy MI 48084-3104

MCLAREN, RICHARD WELLINGTON, JR. lawyer; b. Cin., May 15, 1945; s. Richard Wellington and Edith (Gillett) McL.; m. Ann Lynn Zachrich, Sept. 4, 1971; children: Christine, Richard, Charles. BA, Yale U., 1967; JD, Northwestern U., 1973. Bar: Ohio 1973, Ill. 1997, U.S. Dist. Ct. (no. dist.) Ohio 1973, U.S. Dist. Ct. (no. dist.) Ill. 1997, U.S. Ct. Appeals (6th cir.) 1978, U.S. Ct. Appeals (7th cir.) 1997, U.S. Ct. Appeals (fed. cir.) 1997, U.S. Supreme Ct. 1981. Assoc. Squire, Sanders & Dempsey, Cleve., 1973-82, ptnr., 1983-87; prin., counsel Ernst & Whinney, 1988-89; assoc. gen. counsel Ernst & Young, 1989-93; prin. counsel Centerior Energy Corp., 1994-96; prin. Welsh & Katz, Ltd., Chgo., 1997—. 1st lt. U.S. Army, 1967-70. Mem. ABA (litigation, intellectual property and corp. law), FBA, Am. Judicature Soc., Ohio Bar Assn., Ill. Bar Assn. Home: 638 S Monroe St Hinsdale IL 60521-3926 Office: 120 S Riverside Plz Fl 22D Chicago IL 60606-3913 E-mail: rwmclaren@welshkatz.com.

MCLAUGHLIN, HARRY ROLL, architect; b. Indpls., Nov. 29, 1922; s. William T. and Ruth E. (Roll) McL.; m. Linda Hamilton, Oct. 23, 1954. Registered architect, Ind., Ohio, Ill., Nat. Coun. Archtl. Registration Bds. Past pres. James Assocs. Inc., Indpls. Specializing in restoration of historic bldgs. and domestic architecture. Restorations include Old State Bank State Meml, Vincennes, Ind., Andrew Wylie House, Bloomington, Ind., Old Opera House State Meml, New Harmony, Ind., Old Morris-Butler House, Indpls. (Merit award 1972), Market St. Restoration and Maria Creek Baptist Ch., Vincennes, Benjamin Harrison House, Old James Ball Residence, Lafayette, Ind. (1st Design award 1972), Lockerbie Sq. Master Plan Park Sch., Indpls., Knox County Ct. House, Vincennes, 1972, J.K. Lilly House, Indpls., 1972, Waiting Station and Chapel, Crown Hill Cemetery, Indpls., 1972, Blackford-Condit House Ind. State U., Terre Haute, several Indian houses Angel Mounds Archaeol. Site and Interpretative Ctr. near Evansville, Ind.; architect: Glenn A. Black Mus. Archaeology, Ind. U., Bloomington; Restoration Morgan County Ct. House, Indpls. City Market, Hist. Schofield House, Madison, Ind., Ernie Pyle Birthplace, Dana, Ind., Phi Kappa Psi Nat. Hdqrs, Indpls., 1980 (Design award), East Coll. Bldg, DePauw U., Greencastle, Ind., Pres.'s House Restoration, DePauw U., 1992; contbr. articles to profl. jours.; Illustrator: Harmonist Construction. Past chmn. bd., past pres., now chmn. emeritus Historic Landmarks Found., Ind.; bd. dirs., archtl. adviser, bd. advisers Historic Madison, Inc.; mem. adv. coun. Historic Am. Bldgs. Survey, Nat. Park Svc., 1967-73; past mem. Ind. profl. rev. com. for Nat. Register nominations, 1967-81; past adv. bd. Conner Prarie Mus., Patrick Henry Sullivan Found.; past adviser Indpls. Historic Preservation Commn.; past mem. preservation com. Ind. U.; architect mem. Meridian St. Preservation Commn., Indpls., 1971-2001; hon. mem. Ind. Bicentennial Commn.; bd. dirs. Park-Tudor Sch., 1972-85; past nat. bd. dirs. Preservation Action; bd. dirs. Historic New Harmony; trustee Masonic Heritage Found.; bd. dirs. Masonic Home, 1984-91, Inpls. Pub. Libr. Found., treas. 1988, 95—, v.p., 1989, pres. 1990-97; past trustee Eiteljorg Mus. Western Art, mem. adv. and planning com., 1999; past mem. Hamilton County Tourism Commn., 1989-91. Recipient numerous award including gov.'s citation State of Ind., 1967, Sagamore of Wabash award, 1967, 80, 82; Mayor's citation for svcs. in preservation archtl. heritage City of Indpls., sec.'s citation U.S. Dept. Interior, design and environ. citation for work in preservation, 1975. Fellow AIA (nat. com. historic bldgs., chmn. historic resources com. 1970); mem. Ind. Soc. Architects (state preservation coord. 1960—, Biennial award 1972, Design award 1978), Nat. Trust Historic Preservation (past trustee, bd. advisers), Soc. Archtl. Historians (Wilbur D. Peat award Ctrl. Ind. chpt. outstanding contbns. to understanding and appreciation of archtl. heritage 1993, past bd. dirs.), Ind. Com. for Preservation of Archtl. Records, Indpls. Mus. Art. (trustee, chmn. bldgs. com., bd. govs. 1986-95), Assn. Preservation Tech., Zionsville C. of C. (hon. bd. dirs.), U.S. Capitol (hon. trustee), Ind. Hist. Soc. (pres. 1999, trustee, bldg. com.), Marion County Hist. Soc. (past v.p., bd. dirs.), Zionsville Hist. Soc. (hon. life), Navy League U.S. (life), Ind. State Mus. Soc. (life), English Speaking Union (bd. dirs. Indpls.), Hamilton County Hist. Soc. (life), Woodstock Club (bd. dirs. 1982-86, pres. 1985, ex-officio 1986), Literary Club Found. (trustee), Amateur Movie Club, Skyline Club (life), Packard Club, Masons (33 deg.). Home and Office: 950 W 116th St Carmel IN 46032-8864

MCLAUGHLIN, PATRICK MICHAEL, lawyer; b. Monahans, Tex., July 23, 1946; s. Patrick John and Ann (Donnelly) M.; m. Christine Manos, Aug. 21, 1970; children— Brian Patrick, Christopher Michael, Conor Andrew B.Gen. Studies, Ohio U., 1972; J.D., Case Western Res. U., 1976. Bar: Ohio 1976, U.S. Dist. Ct. (no. dist.) Ohio 1978, U.S. Ct. Appeals (6th cir.) 1979, U.S. Supreme Ct. 1980; U.S. Dist. Ct. (so. dist.) Ohio 1989, U.S.

Ct. Appeals (5th cir.). Dir. vets. edn. project. Am. Assn. Community and Jr. Colls., Washington, 1972-73; law clk. Common Pleas Ct., Cleve., 1976-77; law clk. to judge 8th Jud. Dist. Ct. of Appeals, 1977-78; asst. U.S. atty. No. Dist. Ohio, 1978-82, chief civil div., 1982-84, U.S. atty., 1984-88; ptnr. Janik & McLaughlin, 1988-89, Mansour, Gavin, Gerlack & Manos Co., L.P.A., Cleve., 1989-97; apptd ind. spl. prosecutor Ohio Attorneys General, 1993-96; mng. ptnr. McLaughlin & McCaffrey, LLP, Cleve., 1997—. Cons. Nat. League of Cities, U.S. Conf. Mayors, 1971-72; co-creator Opportunity Fair for Veterans Concept, 1971 Editor-in-chief Case Western Res. Jour. Internat. Law, 1975-76 Chmn. North Ohio Drug Abuse Task Force, 1986-88; chmn. Law Enforcement Coordinating Commn., North Ohio, 1985-88; chmn. civil issues subcom. Atty. Gen.'s Adv. Com., 1986-88; exec. v.p. Greater Cleve. Vets. Meml., Inc., 1993, pres., 1994—. Decorated Silver Star, Bronze Star, Purple Heart, Army Commendation medal, Vietnamese Cross of Gallantry with Silver and Bronze Stars Mem. ABA, FBA, Ohio Bar Assn., Cleve. Bar Assn., Nat. Assn. Former U.S. Attys., Soc. 1st Divsn., 18th Inf. Regiment Assn., Order of Ahepa, Vietnam Vets. Am., Nat. Vietnam Vets. Network (Disting. Vietnam Vet. award 1985), Nat. Assn. Concerned Vets. (nat. v.p. external affairs 1971-72, exec. dir. 1972-73), Cuyahoga County Vets. (award 1985), Nat. Soc. SAR (law enforcement commendation medal 1989). Republican. Roman Catholic Office: McLaughlin & McCaffrey LLP Eaton Ctr 1111 Superior Ave Ste 1350 Cleveland OH 44114-2500

MCLAUGHLIN, T. MARK, lawyer; b. Salem, Mass., Apr. 20, 1953; s. Terrence E. and Mary E. (Donlon) McL.; m. Sandra L. Roman, Oct. 16, 1982; children: Daniel, Kathleen, Eileen. BA in Econs., U. Notre Dame, 1975, JD, 1978. Bar: Ill. 1978, U.S. Dist. Ct. (no. dist.) Ill. 1978, U.S. Dist. Ct. (cen. dist.) Ill. 1992, U.S. Dist. Ct. (ea. dist.) Wis. 1992, U.S. Ct. Appeals (7th cir.) 1982, U.S. Ct. Appeals (11th cir.) 1982, U.S. Ct. Appeals (8th cir.) 1998. Assoc. Mayer Brown Rowe & Maw, Chgo., 1978-84, ptnr., 1985—. Adj. faculty law Loyola U., Chgo., 1983, 86-90. Bd. dirs. no. Ill. affiliate Am. Diabetes Assn., Chgo., 1985-94. Mem. ABA (franchising forum com. antitrust law sect.), Phi Beta Kappa. Office: Mayer Brown Rowe & Maw 190 S La Salle Street Ste 3100 Chicago IL 60603-3441 E-mail: mmclaughlin@mayerbrownrowe.com.

MCLEAN, JAMES, retail merchandise/grocery executive; Pres., CEO Meijer, Grand Rapids, Mich. Office: Meijer 2929 Walker St NW Grand Rapids MI 49544 Office Fax: (616) 791-2572.

MCLEOD, PHILIP ROBERT, publishing executive; b. Winnipeg, Man., Can., May 4, 1943; s. Donald G. and Phyllis (Brown) McL.; m. Cheryl Amy Stewart, Sept. 25, 1965 (div. 1992); children: Shawn Robert, Erin Dawn; m. Virginia Mary Corner, Nov. 6, 1992. Journalist Bowes Pub., Grande Prairie, Alta Truro, N.S., 1962-76; journalist, dep. mng. editor Toronto (Ont., Can.) Star, 1976-87; editor-in-chief London (Ont.) Free Press, 1987-98; pub. Brockville (Ont.) Recorder & Times, 1998—. Southam fellow Southam Newspapers, 1970. Mem. The Brockville Country Club. Avocations: canoeing, skiing. Office: Brockville Recorder & Times 23 King St W PO Box 10 Brockville ON Canada K6V 5T8

MCLEVISH, TIMOTHY, financial professional; Various mgmt. positions Mead Corp, Dayton, Ohio, 1987-99, v.p., CFO, 1999—. Office: Mead Corp World Hdqrs Courthouse Plz NE Dayton OH 45463-0001

MCLIN, RHINE LANA, state legislator, funeral service executive, educator; b. Dayton, Ohio, Oct. 3, 1948; d. C. Josef, Jr. and Bernice (Cottman) McL. BA in Sociology, Parsons Coll., 1969; MEd. Xavier U., 1972; postgrad. in law, U. Dayton, 1974-76; AA in Mortuary Sci., Cin. Coll., 1988. Lic. funeral dir. Tchr. Dayton Bd. Edn., 1970-72; divorce counselor Domestic Rels. Ct., Dayton, 1972-73; law clk. Montgomery Common Pleas Ct., 1973-74; v.p., dir., embalmer McLin Funeral Homes, 1972—; mem. Ohio Ho. of Reps. from 36th & 38th dists., Columbus, 1988-94, Ohio Senate from 5th dist., Columbus, 1994—; mem. Ways & Means Com.; controlling bd. , ins. commerce comn. ranking mem.; state and local govt. com.; minority whip Ohio Senate. Instr. Central State U., Wilberforce, Ohio, 1982-97; mem. Ohio Tuition Trust Authority. Mem. Dem. Nat. Com., Children's Def. Fund. Toll fellow; Paul Harris fellow; Flemming fellow; BLLD fellow; named Ohio Legislator of Yr., Ohio Social Workers Assn., 1999. Mem. Nat. Funeral Dirs. Assn., Ohio Funeral Dirs. Assn., Montgomery County Hist. Soc., NAACP (life), Nat. Coun. Negro Women (life), Delta Sigma Theta. Home: 1130 Germantown St Dayton OH 45408-1465 Office: Ohio State Senate State House Columbus OH 43215

MCLUCKIE, STEVE, state legislator; b. Midland, Mich., July 17, 1956; s. Robert Frost and Gladys (Wilson) McL.; married. BSW cum laude, Western Mich. U., 1978. Field rep. Mo. Fedn. Tchrs., 1985—; mem. Mo. Ho. of Reps., Jefferson City, 1993—. Bd. dirs. Mo. Citizen Action, 1981—, Com. for County Progress, 1988—, Kansas City Progress, 1989—; former mem. transition team for Marsha Murphy for County Exec.; Mo. labor coord. Mondale for Pres., 1984. Democrat. Office: 201 W Capitol Ave Jefferson City MO 65101-1556

MCMAHON, JOHN PATRICK, lawyer; b. Monroeville, Ohio, Feb. 8, 1919; s. George James and Eleanor Helene (Ruffing) McM.; m. Patricia Patterson McDanel, May 6, 1950 (dec. July 1983); children: Colleen, Kevin, Patricia, Brian, Barry, Michael; m. Mary Echard, Mar. 7, 1987. B.A. cum laude, Ohio State U., 1940, J.D. summa cum laude, 1942. Bar: Ohio 1942, U.S. Supreme Ct. 1949, U.S. Dist. Ct. Ohio 1949, U.S. Ct. Appeals (6th cir.) 1959, U.S. Ct. Appeals (D.C. cir.) 1975. Ptnr. George, Greek, King, McMahon, Columbus, Ohio, 1954-79, Baker & Hostetler, Columbus, 1979-85; with nat. coun. Ohio State U. Coll. Law, 1980—. Capt. USAAF, 1943-46, PTO. Mem. ABA, Ohio Bar Assn., Columbus Bar Assn., Transp. Lawyers Assn., Pres.' Club of Ohio State U. (Columbus), Athletic Club (Columbus), Home: 2880 Halstead Rd Columbus OH 43221-2916 Office: Baker & Hostetler 65 E State St Ste 2100 Columbus OH 43215-4260 E-mail: jmemahon@columbus.rr.com.

MCMAHON, THOMAS MICHAEL, lawyer; b. Evanston, Ill., May 11, 1941; s. Robert C. and Kathryn D. (Dwyer) McM.; m. M. Ann Kaufman, July 11, 1964; children— Michael, Patrick. Student, U. Notre Dame, 1959-61; BA, Marquette U., 1963; JD magna cum laude, Northwestern U., 1970. Bar: Ill. 1970. Mgr. legal adv. sect. Ill. EPA, Springfield, 1970-72; assoc. Sidley & Austin, Chgo., 1972-75, ptnr., founder nat. environ. group, 1975-2000, sr. counsel, 2001—. Lectr. in field; mem. City of Evanston Environ. Control Bd., 1981-83. Author: The Superfund Handbook, 1989, International Environmental Law and Regulation, 1992, Legal Guide to Working with Environmental Consultants, 1992, The Environmental Manual, 1992. Lt. USN, 1963-67. Decorated Republic of Vietnam Campaign medal. Mem. ABA (vice-chmn. alternative dispute resolution com., past vice-chmn. environ. quality com., environ. aspects of bus. trans. com., internat. environ. law com., lectr. confs., teleconfs. and satellite seminars), Order of Coif. Office: Sidley Austin Brown & Wood Bank One Plz Chicago IL 60603-2000 E-mail: tmcmahon@sidley.com.

MCMAINS, MELVIN L(EE), administrative executive; b. Oskaloosa, Iowa, Aug. 1, 1941; m. Kathryn Elaine Murphy; children: Kimberly, Lindsay. BA, U. Northern Iowa, 1966, MA, 1968. CPA, Iowa; CMA. V.p. adminstrv. svcs. HON Industries, Inc., Muscatine, Iowa, 1979—. Mem. AICPA, Fin. Execs. Inst., Iowa Soc. CPA's, Inst. Mgmt. Accts., Geneva Golf and Country Club. Office: HON Industries PO Box 1109 Muscatine IA 52761-0071

MC MANUS, EDWARD JOSEPH, federal judge; b. Keokuk, Iowa, Feb. 9, 1920; s. Edward W. and Kathleen (O'Connor) McM.; m. Sally A. Hassett, June 30, 1948 (dec.); children: David P., Edward W., John N., Thomas J., Dennis Q.; m. Esther Y. Kanealy, Sept. 15, 1987. Student, St. Ambrose Coll., 1936-38; B.A., U. Iowa, 1940, J.D., 1942. Bar: Iowa 1941. Gen. practice of law, Keokuk, 1946-62; city atty., 1946-55; mem. Iowa Senate, 1955-59; lt. gov. Iowa, 1959-61; chief U.S. judge No. Dist. Iowa, 1962-85, sr. U.S. judge, 1985—. Del Democratic Nat. Conv., 1956, 60. Served as lt. AC USNR, 1942-46. Office: US Dist Ct 329 US Courthouse 101 1st St SE Cedar Rapids IA 52401-1202

MCMANUS, GEORGE ALVIN, JR. state legislator, cherry farmer; b. Traverse City, Mich., Dec. 12, 1930; s. George Alvin and Frieda Anna (Fromholz) McM.; m. Clara Belle Kratochvil, Aug. 16, 1949; children: Eliza J. Saints, Molly S. Agostinelli, Margaret L. Egelus, Kathleen E. Nurohammed, Kerry E. Canellos, George A., John K., Bridgett E. Popp,Matthew R. BS, Mich. State U., 1952, MS, 1953. Fruit grower pvt. practice, Traverse City, Mich., 1953—; coop. extension agt. Mich. State U., 1956-82; mem. Mich. Senate from 36th dist., Lansing, 1991—. Trustee Northwestern Mich. Coll., Traverse City, 1970-90; pres. Traverse City C.of C., 1982, Traverse City Rotary, 1993. Named Citizen of Yr. Traverse City C. of C., 1984. Mem. KC, Elks Club, Rotary Club. Republican. Roman Catholic. Avocation: golf. Office: Mich State Senate 52 Capital Bldg Lansing MI 48913-0001

MCMANUS, JAMES WILLIAM, lawyer; b. Kansas City, Mo., Aug. 1, 1945; s. Gerald B. and Mary M. (Hagan) McM.; m. Julie C. Waters, Feb. 17, 1973. BA, Rockhurst Coll., 1967; JD, St. Louis U., 1971. Bar: Mo. 1971, U.S. Dist. Ct. (we. dist.) Mo. 1972, U.S. Ct. Appeals (8th cir.) 1974, U.S. Supreme Ct. 1979, U.S. Ct. Appeals (10th cir.) 1984, U.S. Dist. Ct. Kans., 1995. Law clk. to presiding justice U.S. Dist. Ct. (we. dist.) Mo., 1971-73; assoc. Shughart, Thomson & Kilroy, P.C., Kansas City, 1973-76, dir., 1977-94; counsel Dysart, Taylor, Lay, Cotter & McMonigle, P.C., 1994—2002, DeWitt & Zeldin, L.L.C., Kansas City, 2002—. Course lectr. med. jurisprudence U. Health Scis., Coll. Osteo. Medicine, Kansas City, 1994. Mem. adv. coun. St. Joseph Health Ctr., 1989—. Mem. ABA, Mo. Bar Assn., Kansas City Lawyers Assn., Kansas City Met. Bar Assn. (chmn. alternate dispute resolution com. 1996-97, vice chmn. 1994-95, chmn. med. malpractice com. 1989), St. Louis Alumni Assn. (pres. 1984-92), St. Louis U. Law Sch. Alumni Assn. Home: 6824 Valley Rd Kansas City MO 64113-1929 Office: DeWitt & Zeldin LLC Harzfeld Bldg Ste 700 Town Pavilion 1111 Main St Kansas City MO 64105 E-mail: jamesmcmanus@justice.com.

MCMANUS, JOHN FRANCIS, association executive, writer; b. Bklyn., Jan. 24, 1935; s. V. Paul and Dorothy F. (Devenport) McM.; m. Mary Helen O'Reilly, Oct. 19, 1957; children: John G., Margaret A. Strauss, Paul J., Mary Anne Power. BS in Physics, Holy Cross Coll., 1957. Elec. engr. Transitron Corp., Wakefield, Mass., 1960-66; field coord. The John Birch Soc., Belmont, 1966-68, projects mgr., 1968-73, dir. pub. rels., 1973-91, pres. Appleton, Wis., 1991—. Author: An Overview of Our World, 1971, The Insiders: Architects of the New World Order, 1992, 4th edit., 1995, Financial Terrorism: Hijacking America Under the Threat of Bankruptcy, 1993, Changing Commands: The Betrayal of America's Military, 1995; author weekly column, 1973-96. Lt. USMC, 1957-60, capt., USMCR, 1960-68. Avocations: reading, outdoor sports, family. Home: PO Box 3076 Wakefield MA 01880-0772 Office: John Birch Society PO Box 8040 Appleton WI 54912-8040 E-mail: jfm@jbs.org.

MCMEEKIN, DOROTHY, botany, plant pathology educator; b. Boston, Feb. 24, 1932; d. Thomas LeRoy and Vera (Crockatt) McM. BA, Wilson Coll., 1953; MA, Wellesley Coll., 1955; PhD, Cornell U., 1959. Asst. prof. Upsala Coll., East Orange, N.J., 1959-64, Bowling Green State U., Ohio, 1964-66; prof. natural sci. Mich. State U., East Lansing, 1966-89, prof. botany, plant pathology, 1989—. Author: Diego Rivera: Science and Creativity, 1985; contbr. articles to profl. jours. Mem. Am. Phytopath. Soc., Mycol. Soc. Am., Soc. Econ. Bot., Mich. Bot. Soc. (former bd. dirs.), Mich. Women's Studies Assn., Sigma Xi, Phi Kappa Phi. Avocations: gardening, sewing, travel, drawing. Home: 1055 Marigold Ave East Lansing MI 48823-5128 Office: Mich State U Dept Botany-Plant Pathology 221 N Kedzie Hall East Lansing MI 48824-1031 E-mail: mcmeekin@msu.edu.

MC MEEL, JOHN PAUL, newspaper syndicate and publishing executive; b. South Bend, Ind., Jan. 26, 1936; s. James E. and Naomi R. (Reilly) McM.; m. Susan S. Sykes, Apr. 16, 1966; children: Maureen, Suzanne, Bridget. BS, U. Notre Dame, 1957. Sales dir. Hall Syndicate, 1960-67; asst. gen. mgr., sales dir. Publishers-Hall Syndicate, 1968-70; co-founder Universal Press Syndicate, Kansas City, Mo., 1970; pres. Andrews McMeel Universal, 1970—. Bd. dirs. Newspaper Features Coun.; chmn. bd. Andrews McMeel Pub., 1973—; mem. arts and letters U. Notre Dame. Co-founder Christmas in October, Kansas City, 1984—, James F. Andrews fellowship program, U. Notre Dame, 1981, adv. com. program in journalism; trustee Nelson-Atkins Mus. Art, The Civic Coun. Greater Kansas City. Mem. Fed. Assn. USA, Sovereign Mil. Order Malta, Internat. Press Inst. (chmn. Am. com., mem. internat. bd. dirs.). Home: Three Sunset Pl 5300 Sunset Dr Kansas City MO 64112-2358 Office: Andrews McMeel Universal 4520 Main St Kansas City MO 64111-1816

MCMENAMIN, JOHN ROBERT, lawyer; b. Evanston, Ill., Sept. 30, 1946; BA, U. Notre Dame, 1968, JD, 1971. Bar: Ill. 1971. Law clk. to presiding judge U.S. Ct. Appeals (7th cir.), 1971-72; ptnr. Mayer, Brown & Platt, Chgo., 1978-89, McDermott, Will & Emery, Chgo., 1989—. Chmn. adv. bd. Holy Trinity High Sch., Chgo., 1986-88. Mem. ABA, Mid-Am. Com. Roman Catholic. Clubs: Law, Legal, University (Chgo.), Econ. (Chgo.). Office: McDermott Will & Emery 227 W Monroe St Ste 3100 Chicago IL 60606-5096

MCMILLAN, C. STEVEN, food products executive; b. Tyler, Tex., Dec. 10, 1945; s. Charles and Faye (Mills) McM.; children: Mandy, Megan BS, Auburn U., 1968; MBA, Harvard U., 1973. Mgmt. cons. McKinsey & Co., Chgo., 1973-76; pres., CEO Aqualux Water Processing Co., Ft. Lauderdale, Fla., 1976—79; pres. Electrolux Corp., Toronto, Ont., Can., 1979-82, CEO Canada, 1982—86; sr. v.p. strategy devel. Sara Lee Corp., Chgo., 1986-90; sr. v.p., CEO SaraLee Bakery-Worldwide, 1990-97; pres., COO SaraLee Corp., 1997-2000, chmn., pres., CEO. Bd. dirs. Sara Lee/DE, Pharmacia, Monsanto, Bank of Am. Active Joffrey Ballet, Chgo., Chgo. Symphony Orch., Chgo.; mem. adv. bd. Stedman Nutrition Ctr. Duke U. Med. Sch., J.L. Kellogg Grad. Sch. Mgmt. Mem. Harvard Bus. Sch. Club of Chgo. (v.p.) Office: Sara Lee Corp 3 First National Plz Chicago IL 60602

MCMILLAN, CARY D. food products executive; Grad. Coll. Commerce and Bus. Adminstrn., U. Ill., 1980. Mgr. Arthur Andersen, Chgo., 1985—, mng. ptnr., 1992—; exec. v.p., CFO Sara Lee Corp., 2000—. Office: SARA LEE CORP 3 1st Nat Plz Chicago IL 60602-4260

MC MILLAN, R(OBERT) BRUCE, museum executive, anthropologist; b. Springfield, Mo., Dec. 3, 1937; s. George Glassey and Winnie Mae (Booth) McM.; m. Virginia Kay Moore, Sept. 30, 1961; children: Robert Gregory, Michael David, Lynn Kathryn. BS in Edn, S.W. Mo. State U., 1960; MA in Anthropology, U. Mo., Columbia, 1963; PhD in Anthropology (NSF fellow), U. Colo., Boulder, 1971. Rsch. assoc. in archaeology U. Mo., 1963-65, 68-69; assoc. curator anthropology Ill. State Mus., Springfield, 1969-72, curator anthropology, 1972-73, asst. mus. dir., 1973-76, mus. dir., 1977—; exec. sec. Ill. State Mus. Soc., 1977—. Lectr. anthropology Northwestern U., 1973. Editor: (with W. Raymond Wood) Prehistoric Man and His Environments, 1976. Mem. Ill. Spl. Events Commn., 1977-79, program chmn., 1977-78; commr. Ill. and Mich. Canal Nat. Heritage Corridor Commn., 1988—; bd. dirs. Found. Ill. Archaeology, 1978-83. Grantee NSF, 1971-72, 80, Nat. Endowment for Humanities, 1978. Fellow AAAS, Am. Anthrop. Assn.; mem. Am. Assn. Mus. (council 1982-86), Midwest Mus. Conf. (pres.), Soc. Am. Archaeology, Current Anthropology (asso.), Am. Quaternary Assn., Sigma Xi. Office: Ill State Mus Spring And Edwards Sts Springfield IL 62706-0001 also: Dickson Mounds Museum Lewistown IL 61542 E-mail: rbm@museum.state.il.ul.

MCMILLIAN, THEODORE, federal judge; b. St. Louis, Jan. 28, 1919; m. Minnie E. Foster, Dec. 8, 1941. BS, Lincoln U., 1941, HHD (hon.), 1981; LLD, St. Louis U., 1949; HHD (hon.), U. Mo., St. Louis, 1978. Mem. firm Lynch & McMillian, St. Louis, 1949-53; asst. circuit atty. City of St. Louis, 1953-56; judge U.S. Ct. Appeals (8th cir.), 1978—. Judge Circuit Ct. for City St. Louis, 1956-72, Mo. Ct. Appeals eastern div., 1972-78; asso. prof. adminstrn. justice U. Mo., St. Louis, 1970— ; asso. prof. Webster Coll. Grad. Program, 1977; mem. faculty Nat. Coll. Juvenile Justice, U. Nev., 1972— Served to 1st lt. Signal Corps U.S. Army, 1942-46. Recipient Alumni Merit award St. Louis U., 1965, ACLU Civil Liberties award, 1995, Disting. Lawyer award Bar Assn. Met. St. Louis, 1996, Salute to Excellence Civil Rights award St. Louis Am., 1997; named Disting. Non-Alumnus U. Mo.-Columbia Law Sch., 1999. Mem. Am. Judicature Soc., Am. Bd. Trial Advs. (hon. diplomate), Lawyers Assn. Mo., Mound City Bar Assn., Phi Beta Kappa, Alpha Sigma Nu. Office: Thomas F Eagleton Court House Ste 25 162 111 S 10th St Saint Louis MO 63102

MCMILLIN, DAVID ROBERT, chemistry educator; b. East St. Louis, Ill., Jan. 1, 1948; s. Robert Cecil and Clara Rose McMillin; m. Nicole Wilson, Nov. 3, 1974; children: Robert Stephen, Andrew Wilson. BA, Knox Coll., 1969; PhD, U. Ill., 1973. Postdoctoral fellow Calif. Inst. Tech., Pasadena, 1974; asst. prof. chemistry Purdue U., West Lafayette, Ind., 1975-80, assoc. prof., 1980-85, prof., 1985—. Contbr. articles to profl. jours. Recipient F.D. Martin Teaching award Purdue U., 1975. Mem. Am. Chem. Soc., Inter-Am. Photochem. Soc. (sec. 1986-90, v.p. 1994-96, pres. 1996-98), Phi Beta Kappa, Sigma Xi. Presbyterian. Avocations: sports, reading. Office: Purdue U Dept Chemistry West Lafayette IN 47907-1393 E-mail: mcmillin@purdue.edu.

MCMORROW, MARY ANN G. state supreme court justice; b. Chgo., Jan. 16, 1930; m. Emmett J. McMorrow, May 5, 1962; 1 dau., Mary Ann. Student, Rosary Coll., 1948-50; JD, Loyola U., 1953. Bar: Ill. 1953, U.S. Dist. Ct. (no. dist.) Ill. 1960, U.S. Supreme Ct. 1976. Atty. Riordan & Linklater Law Offices, Chgo., 1954-56; asst. state's atty. Cook County, 1956-63; sole practice, 1963-76; judge Cir. Ct. Cook County, 1976-85, Ill. Appellate Ct., 1985-92, Supreme Ct. Ill., 1992—. Faculty adv. Nat. Jud. Coll., U. Nev., 1984. Contbr. articles to profl. jours. Mem. Chgo. Bar Assn., Ill. State Bar Assn., Women's Bar Assn. of Ill. (pres. 1975-76, bd. dirs. 1970-78), Am. Judicature Soc., Northwestern U. Assocs., Ill. Judges Assn., Nat. Assn. Women Judges, Advocates Soc., Northwest Suburban Bar Assn., West Suburban Bar Assn., Loyola Law Alumni Assn. (bd. govs. 1985—), Ill. Judges Assn. (bd. dirs.), Cath. Lawyers Guild (v.p.), The Law Club of the City of Chgo., Inns of Ct. Office: Supreme Ct of Ill 160 N La Salle St Chicago IL 60601-3103

MCMULLEN, W. RODNEY, financial officer; b. Pineville, Ky., July 25, 1960; s. William C. and Henrietta (Helton) McM.; m. Kathryn King, Feb. 15, 1986. BS in Acct., BBA in Fin., U. Ky., 1981, MS in Acctg., 1982. CPA. Fin. analyst The Kroger Co., Cin., 1985-88, asst. treas., 1988-90, v.p. planning and capital mgmt., 1990-93, v.p. fin. svcs. and control, 1993-95, group v.p., chief fin. officer, 1995-97, chief fin. officer, sr. v.p., 1997-2000, exec. v.p. strategy, planning and fin., 2000—. Office: The Kroger Co 1014 Vine St Cincinnati OH 45202-1100

MCMULLIN, RUTH RONEY, publishing executive, trustee, management fellow; b. N.Y.C., Feb. 9, 1942; d. Richard Thomas and Virginia (Goodwin) Roney; m. Thomas Ryan McMullin, Apr. 27, 1968; 1 child, David Patrick. BA, Conn. Coll., 1963; M Pub. and Pvt. Mgmt., Yale U., 1979. Market rschr. Aviation Week Mag., McGraw-Hill Co., N.Y.C., 1962-64; assoc. editor, bus. mgr. Doubleday & Co., 1964-66; mgr. Natural History Press, 1967-70; v.p., treas. Weston (Conn.) Woods, Inc., 1970-71; staff assoc. GE, Fairfield, Conn., 1979-82; mng. fin. analyst, credit analyst corp. GECC Transp., Stamford, 1982-85; credit analyst corp. fin. dept. GECC, 1984-85; sr. v.p. GECC Capital Markets Group, Inc., N.Y.C., 1985-87; exec. v.p., COO John Wiley & Sons, 1987-89, pres., CEO, 1989-90, Harvard Bus. Sch. Pub. Corp., Boston, 1991-94; mem. chmn.'s com., acting CEO UNR Industries Inc., Chgo., 1991-92, also bd. dirs.; mgmt. fellow, vis. prof. Sch. Mgmt. Yale U., New Haven, 1994-95; chairperson trustees Eagle-Picher Personal Injury Settlement Trust, 1996—; chairperson Claims Procesing Facility, Inc., 1998—. Bd. dirs. Bausch & Lomb, Rochester, N.Y.; vis. prof. Sch. Mgmt., Yale U., New Haven, 1994-95; chair bd. trustees Eagle Picher Personal Injury Settlement Trust, 1996—. Mem. dean's adv. bd. Sch. Mgmt. Yale U., 1985—92; bd. dirs. Yale U. Alumni fund, 1986—92, Yale U. Press, 1988—99, Math. Scis. Edn. Bd., 1990—93; bd. dirs., treas. Mighty Eighth Air Force Heritage Mus., 2000—; bd. dirs. Savanna Symphony, 1999—, The Landings Club, 2002—. Mem. N.Y. Yacht Club, Stamford Yacht Club. Avocations: sailing, skiing, golf, tennis. Home: 8 Breckenridge Ln Savannah GA 31411-1701 Office: Eagle Picher Trust P O box 206 652 Main St Cincinnati OH 45202-2542 E-mail: RRmcmullin@att.net., rrmcmullin@aya.yale.edu.

MCNALLY, ALAN G. bank executive; b. Quebec, Can., Nov. 3, 1945; m. Ruth; 2 children. BSc., M Eng., Cornell U., 1967; Internat. MBA, York U., Can. With Aluminum Co. of Can.; vice chmn. personal and commercial fin. svcs. Bank of Montreal Group, 1975-93; CEO, vice chmn. Harris Bank and Haris Bankcorp Inc., 1993-1995, chmn. bd., CEO, 1995—. Trustee DePaul U., adv. bd. mem. Northwestern U. J.L. Kellogg Grad. Sch. Mgmt., bd. mem. Evenston Northwestern Healthcare, mem. bd. govs. York U., dir. Canadian Coun. for Aboriginal Bus. Gen. chair United Way/Crusade of Mercy fundraising campaign, 1996, dir. Chgo. Youth Ctrs., treas. Queen Elizabeth Hosp. Found., dir. Kid's Help Phone. Recipient Americanism award Anti-Defamation League, Community Builder award Christian Insudtrial League, Outstanding Exec. Leadership award York U. Schulich Sch. Bus., Toronto, Prime Movers award. Bd. dirs. Econ. Club Chgo., Chgo. Club, civic com. Commercial Club Chgo., Executive's Club Chgo., Glen View Club. Office: Harris Bank 111 W Monroe St Chicago IL 60603-4096

MCNALLY, ANDREW, IV, publishing executive, director; b. Chgo., Nov. 11, 1939; s. Andrew and Margaret C. (MacMillin) McN.; m. Jeanine Sanchez, July 3, 1966; children: Andrew, Carrie, Ward. BA, U. N.C., 1963; MBA, U. Chgo., 1969. Bus. mgr. edn. divsn. Rand McNally & Co., Chgo., 1967-70, exec. v.p., sec., 1970-74, pres., 1974-97, CEO, 1978-97, also chmn. bd. dirs., 1993-97; prin. Hammond Kennedy Whitney, 1998—; chmn. River Rd. Ptnrs., 1998—. Bd. dir. Hubbell Inc., Reinhold Industries, Seneca Inc. Trustee Newberry Libr.; bd. dirs. Children's Meml. Hosp.; active vis. com. of libr. U. Chgo. With Air Force N.G., 1963-69. Mem. Chgo. Club, Saddle and Cycle Club, Commonwealth Club, Glen View Golf Club, Racquet Club, Links (N.Y.C.). Office: Hammond Kennedy Whitney 333 N Michigan Ave Ste 501 Chicago IL 60601-3903

MCNAMARA, DAVID JOSEPH, financial and tax planning executive; b. Osceola, Iowa, Feb. 6, 1951; s. Loras Emmett and Nadine Evelyn (DeLancey) McN.; m. Ruth Ellen Hanken, Oct. 4,1974; children: Benjamin, Shawna, Heather. BGS, U. Iowa, 1974. Cert. fin. planner Coll. Fin.

Planning, 1985; registered prin. Nat. Assn. Securities Dealers. Pres. The Planners, 1985; ptnr. VF Realty Ptnrs., West Desmoines, Iowa, 1987—. Mem. Fin. Planning Assn. (bd. dirs. Iowa chpt. 1984-850. Republican. Office: Integrated Tax/Fin Planning Svc 1012 Grand Ave West Des Moines IA 50265-3255

MCNAMARA, EDWARD HOWARD, county official, former mayor; b. Detroit, Sept. 21, 1926; s. Andrew Kursina and Ellen Gertrude (Bennett) McN.; m. Lucille Yvonne Martin, June 26, 1948; children— Colleen, Michael, Nancy, Kevin, Terence Ph.B., U. Detroit, 1959; Ph.D. (hon.), Madonna Coll., 1982. Mgr. Mich. Bell Telephone Co., Detroit, 1948-70; mayor City of Livonia, Mich., 1970-86; county exec. Wayne County, Detroit, 1987—. Served with USN, 1944-46 Democrat. Roman Catholic Home: 16501 Park St Livonia MI 48154-2203 Office: Office of the County Exec 600 Randolph St Detroit MI 48226-2817

MCNAMARA, JOHN D. food products executive; Student, Ryerson U., Toronto. Various mgmt. positions Procter & Gamble Can.; dir. Maple Leaf Monarch Co.; merchandising mgr. Arthur Daniels Midlands Co., 1985-92, pres. ADM Agri-Industries (Canadian subs.), 1992-97, group v.p., prs. N.Am. Oilseed Processing Divsn., 1997, pres. Mem. Nat. Oilseed Processors Assn., Canadian Oilseed Processors Assn. (chmn.), Canola Coun. Can. (bd. dirs.), Can. Inst. Edible Oils (bd. dirs.). Office: 4666 E Faries Pkwy Decatur IL 62526-5666

MCNEALEY, J. JEFFREY, lawyer, corporate executive; b. Cin., Feb. 8, 1944; s. J. Lawrence and Louise McNealey; m. Sara Wilson, Sept. 24, 1988; children: Anne Elizabeth, John Alexander. BA, Cornell U., 1966; JD, Ohio State U., 1969. Ptnr. Porter, Wright, Morris & Arthur, Columbus, Ohio, 1969—. Bd. dirs. TRC Cos., Windsor, Conn., 1985—; sec., bd. dirs. The Smoot Corp., Columbus, 1972—. Trustee Columbus Cancer Clinic, 1972—, past pres.; trustee German Village Soc., Columbus, 1986—, past pres.; bd. dirs. Columbus chpt. ARC, 1983-86, Columbus Urban League, 1984-90; active Union League Chgo., 1981—, Columbus/Dresden Sister City, Inc., 1996—; mem. vestry Trinity Episcopal Ch., 2000—. Mem. ABA, Ohio State Bar Assn. (past chmn. environ. com. 1978-84), Columbus Bar Assn., Columbus Country Club, Capital Club of Columbus, Cornell Club of Ctrl. Ohio (trustee 1978—, past pres.). Episcopalian. Avocations: flying, racquet sports, wood working, flyfishing. Office: Porter Wright Morris & Arthur 41 S High St Ste 30 Columbus OH 43215-6101

MCNEELY, JAMES LEE, lawyer; b. Shelbyville, Ind., May 4, 1940; s. Carl R. and Elizabeth J. (Orebaugh) McN.; m. Rose M. Wisker, Sept. 5, 1977; children: Angela, Susan, Meg, Matt. AB, Wabash Coll., 1962; JD, Ind. U., 1965. Bar: Ind. 1965, U.S. Dist. Ct. (so. dist.) Ind. 1965, U.S. Ct. Appeals (7th cir.) 1970. Assoc. Pell & Matchett, Shelbyville, 1965-70; ptnr. Matchett & McNeely, 1970-74; sole practice, 1974-76; sr. ptnr. McNeely & Sanders, 1976-86, McNeely, Sanders & Stephenson, Shelbyville, 1986-89, McNeely, Sanders, Stephenson & Thopy, Shelbyville, 1989-96, McNeely, Stephenson, Thopy & Harrold, Shelbyville, 1997—. Guest lectr. Franklin Coll., Ind., 1965-72; judge Shelbyville City Ct., 1967-71. Chmn. Shelbyville County Rep. Cen. Com., 1968-88; bd. dirs. Ind. Lung Assn., 1972-75, Crossroads Council Boy Scouts Am., 1982; bd. dirs., pres. Shelbyville Girls Club. Named Sagamore of the Wabash, gov. Otis Bowen, 1977, gov. Robert Orr, 1986, 88, gov. Evan Bayh, 1996. Fellow Ind. Bar Found. (patron, sec. 1999-2000, chair elect 2000-01); mem. ABA, Ind. Bar Assn. (sec. 1985-87, bd. dirs. 1976-78, chair-elect Ho. Dels. 1994-95, chair 1995-96, v.p. 1996-97, pres.-elect 1997-98, pres. 1998-99), Shelby County Bar Assn. (pres. 1975), Ind. Lawyers Commn. (pres., dir.), Fed. Merit Selection Commn. (adv. mem. 1988-92, chmn. 2001—), Shelbyville Jaycees (Distinguished Service award 1969, Good Govt. award 1970), Wabash Coll. Nat. Assn. Wabash Men (dir. 1983-89, sec. 1989-91, v.p. 1991-93, pres. 1993-95, Man of Yr. 1995), Kappa Sigma Alpha Pi chpt. (Hall of Fame 1995). Methodist. Lodges: Lions, Elks, Eagles. Avocations: golf, travel. Home: 1902 E Old Rushville Rd Shelbyville IN 46176-9569

MCNEELY, JOHN J. lawyer; b. Mpls., Oct. 8, 1931; s. John J. Sr. and Mae (Carlin) McN.; children: Mary Ann, John J. Jr., Michael F., Patricia C., David C. BS, Georgetown U., 1955, JD, 1958. Bar: Minn. 1958. Law clk. Minn. Supreme Ct., St. Paul, 1958-59; ptnr. Briggs & Morgan, 1959—. Sgt. USMC, 1950-52. Fellow Am. Coll. Trust and Estate Counsel; mem. ABA, Minn. State Bar Assn., Ramsey County Bar Assn., Prestwick Country Club. Home: 1183 Ivy Hill Dr Saint Paul MN 55118-1827

MCNEIL, JOHN W. lawyer; b. Detroit, July 18, 1942; BA, Mich. State U., 1964; JD, U. Mich., 1967. Bar: Mich. 1968. Ptnr. Miller, Johnson, Snell & Cummiskey, PLC, Grand Rapids, Mich. Chmn. Goodwill Inds. Internat., Inc., 1992-94; bd. dirs. Goodwill Industries of Greater Grand Rapids, 1973-97, Goodwill Inds. Internat., Inc., 1988-97. Mem. State Bar Mich. (coun. of taxation sect. 1975-82, chmn. taxation sect. 1980-81), Grand Rapids Bar Assn. Office: Miller Johnson Snell & Cummiskey 250 Monroe Ave NW Ste 800 Grand Rapids MI 49503-2250

MCNEIL, SUE, engineering educator; b. Newcastle, Australia, June 17, 1955; d. George Peers and Norma (Avard) McGeachie; m. John Franklin McNeil, Dec. 4, 1976; children: Sarah, Emily. BS, U. Newcastle, Newcastle, Australia, 1976; B.E., U. Newcastle, 1978; MS, Carnegie Mellon U., 1981, PhD, 1983. Registered profl. engr., N.J. Asst. works engr. N.S.W. Dept. Main Rds., Singleton, Australia, 1977-79; transp. engr. Garmen Assocs., Montville, N.J., 1983-84; vis. lectr. Princeton U., Princeton, 1984-85; asst. prof. MIT, Cambridge, Mass., 1985-87, Carnegie Mellon U., Pitts., 1988-90, assoc. prof. to prof., 1990—2000; dir. The Brownfields Ctr., Mellon U. Carnegie, 1998—2000; dir. Urban Transp. Ctr. U. Ill., Chgo.; prof. Coll. Urban Planning and Pub. Affairs, 2000—. Assoc. editor Jour. of Infrastructive Systems. Contbr. articles to profl. jours. Doctoral dissertation fellow AAUW, 1982-83; named Presdl. Young Investigator, NSF, 1987-92. Mem.: ASCE (chmn. facilities mgmt. com. 1988—94), Transp. Rsch. Bd. (assoc.), INFORMS (assoc.), Inst. Transp. Engrs. (assoc.). Office: U Ill Urban Transp Ctr MC357 412 S Peoria St Ste 340 Chicago IL 60607-7063

MCNEILL, G. DAVID, psycholinguist, educator; b. Santa Rosa, Calif., Dec. 21, 1931; s. Glenn H. and Ethel G. (Little) McN.; m. Nobuko Baba, Dec. 17, 1957; children: Cheryl, Randall L.B.. AB, U. Calif. at Berkeley, 1953, PhD, 1962. Research fellow Harvard U., 1962-65; asst. prof. psychology U. Mich., 1965-66, assoc. prof., 1966-68; prof. psychology and linguistics U. Chgo., 1969—, chmn. dept. psychology, 1991-97. Vis. fellow Ctr. for Humanities, Wesleyan U., Middletown, Conn., 1970; mem. Inst. Advanced Study, Princeton, 1973-75; fellow Netherlands Inst. for Advanced Studies, 1983-84; visitor Max Planck Inst. for Psycholinguistics, Nijmegen, Germany, 1998-99. Author: The Acquisition of Language, 1970, The Conceptual Basis of Language, 1979, Psycholinguistics: A New Approach, 1987, Gengo Shinrigaku, 1991, Hand and Mind: What Gestures Reveal about Thought, 1992; editor: Language and Gesture. Recipient Faculty Achievement award, 1991, Ann. Excellence in Pub. award Assn. Am. Pubs., Gordon G. Laing prize U. Chgo. Press, 1995; Guggenheim fellow, 1973-74; grantee NSF, 1983-89, 97—, Spencer Found., 1979-82, 89-92, 95-99, NIDCD, 1992-96. Fellow AAAS, Am. Psychol. Soc.; mem. Cognitive Sci. Soc., Linguistic Soc. Am., Violoncello Soc., Phi Beta Kappa, Sigma Xi. Office: U Chgo Dept Psychology 5848 S University Ave Chicago IL 60637-1515 E-mail: dmcn@ccp.uchicago.edu.

MCNEILL, ROBERT PATRICK, investment counselor; b. Chgo., Mar. 17, 1941; s. Donald Thomas and Katherine (Bennett) McN.; m. Martha Stephan, Sept. 12, 1964; children— Jennifer, Donald, Victoria, Stephan, Elizabeth B.A. summa cum laude (valedictorian), U. Notre Dame, 1963; M.Letters, Oxford U., 1967. Chartered investment counselor. Assoc. Stein Roe & Farnham, Chgo., 1967-72, gen. ptnr., 1972-77, sr. ptnr., 1977-86, exec. v.p., 1986-89; pres., mng. dir. Stein Roe Internat., 1989—. Underwriting mem. Lloyds of London, 1980— ; dir. Comml. Chgo. Corp.; vice chmn. bd. Hill Internat. Prodn. Co., Houston, 1982— ; dir., adv. bd. Touche Remnant Investment Counselors, London, 1983— ; dir. TR Worldwide Strategy Fund, Luxembourg, Konrad Adenauer Fund for European Policy Studies, Fed. Republic Germany. Voting mem., sec Ill. Rhodes Scholarship Selection Com.; voting mem. Ill. rep. Great Lakes Dist. Rhodes Scholarship Selection Com.; bd. dirs. Kennedy Sch. for Retarded Children, Palos Park, Ill., 1972— , Winnetka United Way, Ill., 1984— , Division St. YMCA, Chgo., 1972— ; assoc. Rush-Presbyterian-St. Lukes Med. Ctr., Chgo., 1975—; mem. leadership com. Rush Alzheimer's Disease Ctr. Rhodes scholar, 1963 Fellow Fin. Analysts Fedn.; mem. Chgo. Council on Fgn. Relations (bd. dirs., treas. 1975—), Inst. European Studies (bd. govs., vice-chmn. 1981—), Investment Analysts Soc. Chgo. (chgo. com., com. on fgn. affairs, com. on internat. and domestic issues), Assn. for Investment Mgmt. and Rsch., Chgo. Soc. Clubs, Econ. Club of Chgo, Sunset Ridge Country (bd. dirs. Northfield, Ill., 1983—). Avocations: coin collecting; bridge; golf; skiing; art.

MCNEILL, THOMAS B. retired lawyer; b. Chgo., Oct. 28, 1934; s. Donald T. and Katherine M. (Bennett) McN.; m. Ingrid Sieder, May 11, 1963; children: Christine, Thomas, Stephanie. B.A., U. Notre Dame, 1956, J.D., 1958. Ptnr. Mayer, Brown & Platt, Chgo., 1962-99. Dir. Deltona Corp., Ocala, Fla. Served to capt. JAGC USAF, 1959-62. Fellow Am. Coll. Trial Lawyers; mem. Chgo. Bar Assn., Chgo. Council Lawyers, The Lawyers Club (Chgo. chpt.). Club: Indian Hill (Winnetka, Ill.). Home: 2418 Iroquois Rd Wilmette IL 60091-1335 E-mail: tomingrid@aol.com.

MCNENNY, KENNETH G. state legislator; m. Herrietta; 4 children. Mem. S.D. Ho. of Reps., 1993—, vice chmn. agr. and natural resources, mem. appropriations com.; rancher. Home: HC 75 Box 192 Sturgis SD 57785-8909

MCNERNEY, W. JAMES, manufacturing executive; BA, Yale U.; MBA, Harvard U. Pres. GE Info. Svcs.; exec. v.p. GE Capital; pres., CEO GE Elec. Distribution and Control; pres. GE Asia-Pacific; pres., CEO GE Aircraft Engines; chmn., CEO 3M Co, St. Paul. Office: 3M Co 3M Ctr Saint Paul MN 55144

MCNOWN, CADE, professional football player; b. Oreg., Jan. 12, 1977; Student, UCLA. Football player Chgo. Bears, 1999—. Office: Chgo Bears Halas Hall at Conway Park 1000 Football Dr Lake Forest IL 60045

MCPHEE, MARK STEVEN, medical educator, physician, gastroenterologist; b. Kansas City, Mo., Nov. 8, 1951; s. William Robert and Mary Kay (Paige) McP.; m. Christina Marie Luebke, July 14, 1974; children: Molly Amanda, Ian Andrew. BA magna cum laude, Pomona Coll., Claremont, Calif., 1973; MD summa cum laude, U. Kans., Kansas City, 1976. Diplomate Nat. Bd. Med. Examiners; diplomate in internal medicine and gastroenterology Am. Bd. Internal Medicine. Intern, resident, fellow Harvard U. Med. Sch., Boston, 1976-80; dir. gastrointestinal endoscopy unit Kans. U. Med. Ctr., Kansas City, 1980-85; chief sect. gastroenterology St. Luke's Hosp., Mo., 1988-93, chair dept. medicine, 1992-97, assoc. dir. med. edn., 1995-97, dir. med. edn., 1997—; assoc. dean U. Mo.-Kansas City Med. Sch., 1997—. Asst. prof. medicine U. Kans., KansasCity, 1980-85, assoc. prof., 1985; clin. prof. medicine U. Mo., Kansas City, 1970-97, prof. medicine, 1997—. Author: Annotated Key References in Gastroenterology, 1982; contbr. chpts. to textbook, articles to profl. jours. Bd. dirs. St. Luke's Hosp., Kansas City,Mo., 1993—, Am. Digestive Health Found., Bethesda, Md., 1996—. Fellow ACP, Am. Coll. Gastroenterology; mem. Am. Gastroent. Assn. (mem. governing bd., treas.), St. Lukes Hosp. Physicians Assn. (bd. dirs.), HealthNet Physician Ptnrs. (bd. dirs.), Alpha Omega Alpha. Episcopalian. Avocations: poetry, hiking/camping, golf, tennis, sporting clay target shooting. Office: St Lukes Hosp Dept Med Edn 44th and Wornall Rd Kansas City MO 64111

MCPHEETERS, F. LYNN, manufacturing executive; B in Acctg., So. Ill. U.; grad., Duke U. Adv. Mgmt. Program, Stafrod U. Adv. Fin. Mgmt. Trainee in acctg. Caterpillar, 1964, exec. v.p. fin. svcs. corp., 1990-96, corp. treas., 1996-98, v.p., 1998—. Office: Caterpillar Inc 100 NE Adams St Peoria IL 61629

MCPHERSON, MELVILLE PETER, academic administrator, former government official; b. Grand Rapids, Mich., Oct. 27, 1940; s. Donald and Ellura E. (Frost) McP.; m. Joanne McPherson; 4 children. JD, Am. U., 1969; MBA, Western Mich. U., 1967; BA, Mich. State U., 1963. Peace Corps vol., Peru, 1965-66; with IRS, Washington, 1969-75; spl. asst. to pres. and dep. dir. Presdl. Pers. White Ho., 1975-77; mng. ptnr. Washington office Vorys, Sater, Seymour & Pease, 1977-81; adminstr. AID, Washington, 1981-87; dep. sec. Dept. Treasury, 1987-89; group exec. v.p. Bank of Am., San Francisco, 1989-93; pres. Mich. State U., East Lansing, 1993—. Mem. D.C. Bar Assn., Mich. Bar Assn. Republican. Methodist. Office: Office of the Pres Mich State U 450 Administration East Lansing MI 48824-1046

MCPHERSON, MICHAEL STEVEN, academic administrator, economics educator; b. June 6, 1947; married; two children. BA in Math., U. Chgo., 1967, MA in Econs., 1970, PhD in Econs., 1974. Instr. econs. dept. U. Ill., Chgo., 1971-74; asst. prof. econs. Williams Coll., 1974-81, assoc. prof. econs., 1981-84, prof. econs., 1984-96, chmn. econs. dept., then dean of faculty, 1986-91; pres. Macalester Coll., St. Paul, 1996—. Cons. Data Resources, Inc., 1979, Nat. Research Coun. Commn. Human Resources, 1979, Modern Lang. Assn., 1980, Nat. Acad. of Edn., 1980, Smith Coll., 1982, The Coll. Bd., 1983, Rand Corp., 1985-86, U.S. Dept. Edn. Ctr. for Statistics, 1986. Author: (with M.O. Shapiro) Keeping College Affordable: Government and Educational Opportunity, 1991, The Student Aid Game: Meeting Need and Rewarding Talent in American Higher Education, 1998, (with D. Hausman) Economic Analysis and Moral Philosophy, 1996; editor: The Demand for New Faculty in Science and Engineering, 1980, Democracy, Development, and the Art of Trespassing: Essays in Honor of Albert O. Hirschman, 1986; contbr. articles to profl. jours. Trustee Coll. Bd., 1997—. Ford Found. grantee 1981-83, Mellon Found grantee 1984-86; Am. Coun. Learned Socs. Study fellow, 1977-78, vis. fellow Princeton U., 1977-78, sr. fellow Brookings Instn., 1984-86. Home: 1750 Summit Ave Saint Paul MN 55105-1834 Office: Macalester Coll 1600 Grand Ave Saint Paul MN 55105-1801

MC PHERSON, PETER, university president; BA in Polit. Sci., Mich. State U., 1963; MBA, Western Mich. U., 1967; JD, Am. U., 1969; LHD (hon.), Va. State U., 1984, Mt. St. Mary;s Coll., 1986; LLD (hon.), Mich. State U., 1984. Tax law specialist IRS, 1969-75; spl. asst. to Pres. Ford, deputy dir. presdl. personnel The White House, Washington, 1975-77; ptnr. Vorys, Sater, Seymour & Pease, 1977-80; adminstr. Agy. for Internat. Devel., 1981-87; deputy sec. Treasury Dept., Washington, 1987-89; group exec. v.p. Bank Am., 1989-93; pres. Mich. State U., East Lansing, 1993—. Chmn. bd. Overseas Pvt. Investment Corp., 1981-87. Gen. counsel Reagan-Bush Transition, 1980-81; vol. Peace Corps, Peru, 1964-65. Recipient Humanitarian of Yr. award Am. Lebanese League, 1983, UNICEF award.

MCQUARRIE, DONALD GRAY, surgeon, educator; b. Richfield, Utah, Apr. 17, 1931; s. John Gray and LoRetta (Smith) McQ.; m. Dolores Jean Dietrich, July 16, 1956; children— William Gray, Michelle Dolores Colton. BS, U. Utah, 1952, MD, 1956; PhD, U. Minn., 1964. Diplomate Am. Bd. Surgery, Am. Bd. Thoracic and Cardiovascular Surgery. Intern U. Minn. Hosps., 1956-57; resident in surgery U. Minn., Mpls., 1957-59, resident, 1961-65, asst. prof. surgery, 1964-68, assoc. prof. surgery, 1968-72, prof. surgery, 1972—99; prof. emeritus Mpls. VA Hosp., 1999—; vice chmn. dept. surgery U. Minn., 1993—99; mem. surg. staff Mpls. VA Hosp., 1964-99, chief surgical svc., 1993-99, resident in thoracic surgery, 1965-66, dir. surg. research lab., 1964-78. Vis. prof. U. Tex.-San Antonio, 1974, U. Ind. and Indpls. VA, 1977, affiliated program U. Ariz., Phoenix, 1982, Case Western Res. U., 1986. Editor, contbg. author: Head and Neck Cancer, 1986, Reoperations in General Surgery, 1991, 2d edit., 1996; contbr. articles on surg. and basic med. scis. to profl. publs., 1955— Served to lt. M.C., USN, 1959-61 USPHS postdoctoral fellow, 1962-65 Fellow ACS (commn. on cancer 1980-89, exec. council commn. on operating room environ. 1985-91, pres. Minn. chpt. 1983-84, liaison to Assn. Oper. Rm. Nurses 1985-97, gov. 1990-96); mem. Minn. Surg. Soc. (pres. 1980-81), Assn. Acad. Surgery, Mpls. Surg. Soc. (pres. 1978-79), Soc. Head and Neck Surgeons, Central Surg. Assn., Western Surg. Soc., Soc. Univ. Surgeons, Société Internationale de Chirurgie, Am. Surg. Assn., Royal Soc. Medicine, Assn. VA Surgeons (pres. 1987), Soc. Surg. Oncology, Hennepin County Med. Soc., Minn. Med. Assn., Am. Soc. Clin. Oncology, Phi Beta Kappa, Phi Kappa Phi Clubs: Minneapolis, Interlachen Country (Mpls.) Avocations: computer applications to medicine, jewelry design, lapidary work. Home: 6625 Mohawk Trl Minneapolis MN 55439-1029 Office: Dept Surgery Medical Sch Box 195 D VA 698 Mayo 420 Delaware St SE Minneapolis MN 55455-0390 Fax: 612-625-8496.

MCQUEEN, PATRICK M. bank executive; BBA, U. Mich., Dearborn; MBA, Mich. State U. Commr. Mich. Fin. Instns. Bur., 1993—; acting commr. Mich. Ins. Bur., 1995; pres., CEO Bank of Bloomfield Hills, Mich., 1999—. Mem. Conf. State Bank Suprs. (bd. dirs., legis. svcs. coun., internat. task force, strategic planinng coun.). Avocations: hunting, fishing. Office: Bank of Bloomfield Hills 38505 Woodward Ave Bloomfield Hills MI 48304

MCREYNOLDS, ALLEN, JR. retired investment company executive; b. Carthage, Mo., Dec. 25, 1909; s. Allen and Maude (Clark) McR.; m. Virginia Madeliene Hensley, Jan. 17, 1946; children: Sharron Anne, Amy Elizabeth, Mary Armilda, Allen IV. Student, N.Mex. Mil. Inst., 1926-29, U. Mo., 1929-31. Pres. Joplin (Mo.) Stockyards, Inc., 1945-83; v.p., dir. First Nat. Bank, Monett, Mo., 1943-80, v.p., cashier Golden City, 1950-56; dir. First Nat. Bancorp, Joplin, 1982-87; asst. adminstr. Mo. State Coun. Civil Defence, 1941-44. Pres. Jasper County Assn. for Soc. Services, 1976-78, Mo. State Southern Coll. Found., Joplin, 1984-85. Mem. Sigma Nu. Democrat. Episcopalian. Avocation: farming. Home: 1202 Mississippi Ave Joplin MO 64801-5344 Office: Lower Level LLS Bancorp Bldg Rm 021 Joplin MO 64801

MCSPADDEN, KATHERINE FRANCES, English language educator; b. Niagara Falls, N.Y., Nov. 13, 1941; d. John Hehir and Mildred Lorraine (Allen) M. BA, Niagara U., 1963; MA, Loyola U., Chgo., 1967, PhD, 1985. Tchr. Madonna H.S., Niagara Falls, 1962-63; tchg. asst. Loyola U., 1964-68; English educator Truman Coll., Chgo., 1968—, asst. chair dept. comm., 1992-2000, pres. faculty coun., 1991-92, 98-99, interim asst. dean arts and humanities, 2001—. Bd. dirs. Chgo. Area Women's Studies Assn., 1977-79; mem. exec. com. Midwest Women's Caucus for Modern Langs., 1982-83; mem. alumni adv. bd. grad. sch. Loyola U., Chgo., 1996-98; mem. nat. screening coms. for Fulbright U.S. Grad. Student Program, 1997-99. Contbr. articles to profl. jours. Leader Girl Scouts Am., Chgo., 1982-83; bd. dirs. Friends of Northtown Libr. br. of Chgo. Pub. Libr. Fulbright Tchr. Exch. Program scholar, United Kingdom, 1986-87. Mem. Nat. Coun. Tchrs. English, Conf. on Coll. Composition and Communication, Two-Yr. Coll. English Assn., Tchrs. English Spkrs. Other Langs., Am. Assn. Women in Cmty. Colls. (pres. Truman Coll. chpt. 1995-96, chosen for Nat. Inst. Leadership Devel. 1997, Ruth Burgos-Sasscer Leadership award Truman chpt. 1998, sec. Truman Coll. chpt., 2001-02), Fulbright Assn., Ill. TESOL/Bilingual Educators. Avocations: traveling, outdoor activities, photography, folk music and dancing. E-mail: kmcspadden@ccc.edu.

MCSPADDEN, LETTIE, political science educator; b. Battle Creek, Mich., Apr. 9, 1937; d. John Dean and Isma Doolie (Sullivan) McSpadden; m. Manfred Wilhelm Wenner, Apr. 3, 1962; children: Eric Alexis, Adrian Edward. AB, U. Chgo., 1959; MA, U. Calif., Berkeley, 1962; PhD, U. Wis., 1972. Fgn. svc. officer Dept. State, Washington, 1961-63; rsch. assoc. Dept. HEW, 1965-67; asst. prof. polit. sci. U. Ill., Chgo., 1972-79, assoc. prof. polit. sci., 1979-88; prof. and chair dept. polit. sci. No. Ill. U., De Kalb, 1988-94, prof. dept. polit. sci., 1994—. Author: One Environment Under Law, 1976, The Environmental Decade in Court, 1982, United States Energy and Environmental Interest Groups, 1990. Mem. Am. Polit. Sci. Assn., Midwest Polit. Sci. Assn., Law and Society Assn., Pub. Policy Assn., Audubon Soc., Sierra Club. Democrat. Office: No Ill U Dept Polit Sci Dekalb IL 60115 Home: Apt 812A 901 S Ashland Ave Chicago IL 60607-4089

MCSWEENEY, MAURICE J. (MARC), lawyer; b. Chgo., July 3, 1938; s. Thomas J. and Margaret F. (Ahern) McS.; m. Sandra A. Panosh, Sept. 30, 1967; children: Erin, Sean. BS, DePaul U., 1960; JD, U. Chgo., 1963. Ptnr. Foley and Lardner, Milw., 1963—. Bd. dirs. Harambee Elem. Sch., Internat. Clown Hall of Fame. Bd. dirs. Milw. Pub. Schs., 1973-79, Milw. chpt. ARC, 1979-85, Alverno Coll., Milw., 1984—, Health Edn. Ctr. of Wis., 1987-96. Fellow Am. Coll. Trial Lawyers; mem. ABA, Wis. Bar Assn., Milw. Bar Assn., Am. Judicature Soc. (bd. dirs. 1988-93), Milw. Area Tech. Coll. Found., Rotary (bd. dirs. Milw. 1986-88). Avocations: skiing, tennis, karate. Office: Foley & Lardner 777 E Wisconsin Ave Ste 3800 Milwaukee WI 53202-5367

MCSWINEY, CHARLES RONALD, lawyer; b. Nashville, Apr. 23, 1943; s. James W. and Jewell (Bellar) Mc.; m. Jane Detrick McSwiney, Jan. 2, 1970. BA, Kenyon Coll., Gambier, Ohio, 1965; JD, U. Cin., 1968. Assoc. Smith & Schnacke, Dayton, Ohio, 1968-72, ptnr., 1972-89, pres. and mng. ptnr., 1984-89; sr. v.p., gen. counsel The Danis Cos., 1989-92, 99-2000; vice chmn. Carillon Capital, Inc., 1992-99. Chmn., CEO Crysteco, Inc., Wilmington, Ohio, 1995-99; pres. interchange exec. Presdl. Commn. on Pers. Interchange, Washington, 1972-73. Chmn., pres. bd. trustees Dayton Ballet Assn., 1985-88; trustee Columbus (Ohio) Symphony Orch., 1981-84; chmn. Dayton Performing Arts Fund, 1989-92, Dayton Devel. Coun., 1987-90, Wright State U. Found., Dayton, 1988-94, Miami Valley Sch., Dayton, 1988-94, Arts Ctr. Found., 1986—; mem. bd. advisors Wright State U. Coll. Bus. Adminstrn., 1988-98; bd. vis. U. Cin. Coll. Law, 1987-89. Recipient Bronze Medal for Performance U.S. EPA, 1973. Mem. ABA, Ohio Bar Assn., Dayton Bar Assn., Dayton Area C. of C. (trustee 1987-90). Republican. Presbyterian. Home: 5916 C Rayton Rd Naples FL 34103 Office: McSwiney & Co Ltd 2 River Pl Ste 400 Dayton OH 45405-4936 E-mail: ron.mcswiney@worldnet.att.net.

MC SWINEY, JAMES WILMER, retired pulp and paper manufacturing company executive; b. McEwen, Tenn., Nov. 13, 1915; s. James S. and Delia (Conroy) McS.; m. Jewel Bellar, 1940; children: Charles Ronald, Margaret Ann. Grad., Harvard Advanced Mgmt. Program, 1954. Lab. technician, shipping clk. Nashville div. The Mead Corp., 1934-39; asst. office mgr. Harriman div., 1939; plant mgr. Rockport, Ind., 1940; asst. office mgr. Kingsport (Tenn.) div.), 1941-44; exec. asst. to pres. Dayton,

Ohio, 1954-57; v.p. devel., 1957-59; adminstrv v.p. Harriman div. (Kingsport (Tenn.) div.), 1959; group v.p., gen. mgr. Mead Bd. div., 1961-63, exec. v.p. corp., 1963-67, pres., chief exec. officer, 1968-71, chmn. bd., chief exec. officer, 1971-78, chmn. bd., 1978-82, also dir. Acct., office mgr., asst. sec.-treas. Brunswick Pulp & Paper Co., Ga., 1944-45; bd. dirs. Ultra-Met, Gosinger, Inc., Sea Island Co. Trustee Com. for Econ. Devel. Aviation cadet USAAF, 1942-44. Home: PO Box 30604 401 Ocean Rd Sea Island GA 31561 E-mail: jwmcs@technonet.com.

MCVISK, WILLIAM KILBURN, lawyer; b. Chgo., Oct. 8, 1953; s. Felix Kilburn and June (DePear) Visk; m. Marlaine Joyce McDonough, June 20, 1975. BA, U. Ill, 1974; JD, Northwestern U., 1977. Bar: Ill. 1977, Ind. 1999, U.S. Dist. Ct. (no. dist.) Ill. 1977, U.S. Ct. Appeals (7th cir.) 1978, U.S. Dist. Ct. (no. and so. dists.) Ind. 1999. Assoc. Jerome H. Torshen, Ltd., Chgo., 1977-80, Silets & Martin, Chgo., 1980-81, Peterson & Ross, Chgo., 1981-85, ptnr., 1985-95, Johnson & Bell Ltd., Chgo., 1995—. Contbr. articles to profl. jours. Mem.: ABA, Ill. Assn. Def. Trial Lawyers (chmn. ins. coverage com.), Ill. Assn. Hosp. Attys. (pres., bd. dirs.), Am. Health Lawyers Assn., Def. Rsch. Inst., Chgo. Bar Assn. Office: Johnson & Bell 55 E Monroe St Fl 41 Chicago IL 60603-5713 E-mail: mcviskw@jbltd.com.

MCVOY, KIRK WARREN, physicist, educator; b. Mpls., Feb. 22, 1928; s. Kirk Warren and Phyllis (Farmer) McV.; m. Hilda A. Van Der Laan, Aug. 15, 1953; children— Christopher, Lawrence, Annelies. B.A., Carleton Coll., 1950; B.A. (Rhodes scholar), Oxford U., Eng., 1952; Dipl., U. Gottingen, Germany, 1953; Ph.D., Cornell U, 1956. Rsch. assoc. Brookhaven Nat. Lab., Upton, N.Y., 1956-58; asst. prof. Brandeis U., 1958-62; assoc. prof. physics U. Wis., Madison, 1963-67, prof., 1967-93, prof. emeritus, 1993—. Vis. disting. prof. physics Bklyn. Coll., 1970-71; vis. prof. Ind. U., 1971-72. Fulbright rsch. grantee U. Utrecht, Netherlands, 1960-61; sr. scientist awardee A. von Humboldt Found., Max-Planck-Institut für Kernphysik, Heidelberg, W. Ger., 1980-81. Fellow Am. Phys. Soc.; mem. Mex. Acad. Scis. (corr.). Achievements include rsch. and publs. on nuclear reaction theory. Office: U Wis Dept Physics 1150 University Ave Madison WI 53706-1302

MCWEENY, PHILIP, corporate lawyer; BS, Holy Cross Coll., 1961; JD, U. Mich., 1964. Bar: Ohio 1965. Asst. gen. counsel-antitrust Owens-Illinois, Inc., 1980-88, v.p., gen. counsel-corp., asst. sec., 1988—. Office: Owens-Illinois Inc 1 Seagate Toledo OH 43604-1558

MCWHIRTER, BRUCE J. lawyer; b. Chgo., Sept. 11, 1931; s. Sydney and Martha McWhirter; m. Judith Hallett, Apr. 14, 1960; children: Cameron, Andrew. BS, Northwestern U., 1952; LLB, Harvard U., 1955. Bar: DC 1955, Ill 1955, US Ct Appeals (7th cir) 1963, US Supreme Ct. Assoc. Lord, Bissell & Brook, Chgo., 1958-62; from assoc. to sr. ptnr. Ross & Hardies, 1962-95, of counsel, 1996—. Editor: Donnelley SEC Handbook, 1972—87; contbr. articles to profl jours. With U.S. Army, 1955—57. Mem.: ABA, Harvard Law Soc Ill, Chicago Bar Asn, Harvard Club (New York City), Lawyers Club Chicago, Phi Beta Kappa. Democrat. Home: 111 Sheridan Rd Winnetka IL 60093-4223 Office: Ross & Hardies 150 N Michigan Ave Ste 2500 Chicago IL 60601-7567 E-mail: jbmcw@aol.com.

MEAD, JOHN STANLEY, university administrator; b. Indpls., Dec. 9, 1953; s. Judson and Jane (Stanley) M.; m. Virginia Potter, Aug. 11, 1979; children: Christopher, Carolyn. BA, Ind. U., 1976; JD, U. Ill., 1979. Bar: Ill. Staff atty. Ill. Energy Resources Commn., Springfield, 1979-82, staff dir., 1982-85; mgr. coal rsch. Ill. Dept. Energy Natural Resources, 1985-87, dir. office of coal devel. and mktg., 1987-89; dir. coal rsch. ctr. So. Ill. U., Carbondale, 1989—. B. dirs. Mid-West Univ. Energy Consortium Inc., Chgo.; mem., past chair Ill. Clean Coal Inst., 1986—. Mem. Ill. Bd. Natural Resources and Conservation, 1997—, sec., 2000—; mem. dist. com., scoutmaster Boy Scouts Am. Recipient gold medal Tech. Univ. Ostrava, Czech Republic, 1992, Georgius Agricola medal, 1994. Mem. Am. Radio Relay League, Ill. State Bar Assn., Carbondale Rotary Breakfast (pres. 2000-2001). Lutheran. Home: 78 Magnolia Ln Carbondale IL 62901-7665 Office: So Ill U Coal Rsch Ctr Mail Code 4623 Carbondale IL 62901 E-mail: jmead@siu.edu.

MEAD, PRISCILLA, state legislator; b. Columbus, OH, Feb. 7, 1944; m. John L. Mead; children: John, Willian, Neel, Sarah. Student, Ohio State U. Councilwoman, Upper Arlington, Ohio, 1982-90; mayor, 1986-90; mem. Ohio Ho. of Reps. from 28th dist., Columbus, 1992-2000, Ohio Senate from 16th dist., Columbus, 2001—. Mem. Franklin County Child Abuse and Neglect Found., Coun. for Ethics and Econs. Recipient Svc. award Northwest Kiwanis, Woman of Yr. award Upper Arlington Rotary, Citizen of Yr. award U.S. C. of C. Mem. LWV, Upper Arlington Edn. Found., Jr. League Columbus, Upper Arlington C. of C., Delta Gamma. Republican. Home: 2281 Brixton Rd Columbus OH 43221-3117 Office: Ohio Ho of Reps State House Columbus OH 43215

MEADOR, RON, newspaper editor, writer; b. Buffalo, Nov. 24, 1952; s. Meril E. and Evelyn (Lyons) M.; divorced; 1 child, Benjamin Brian. BA, Ind. U., 1975. Copy editor The Courier-Journal, Louisville, 1975-78, The New York Times, 1978-80; reporter, state editor, city editor, asst. mng. editor Star Tribune, Mpls., 1980-96, mem. editl. bd., editl. writer, 1996—. Mem. Investigative Reporters and Editors, Inc., Nat. Conf. Editl. Writers, Soc. Environ. Journalists. Office: Star Tribune 425 Portland Ave Minneapolis MN 55488-0002

MEAL, LARIE, chemistry educator, researcher, consultant; b. Cin., June 15, 1939; d. George Lawrence Meal and Dorothy Louise (Heileman) Fitzpatrick. BS in Chemistry, U. Cin., 1961, PhD in Chemistry, 1966. Rsch. chemist U.S. Indsl. Chems., Cin., 1966-67; instr. chemistry U. Cin., 1968-69, asst. prof., 1969-75, assoc. prof., 1975-90, prof., 1990—, rschr., 1980—. Cons. in field. Contbr. articles to profl. jours. Mem. AAAS, N.Y. Acad. Scis., Am. Chem. Soc., NOW, Planned Parenthood, Iota Sigma Pi. Democrat. Avocations: gardening, yard work. Home: 2231 Slane Ave Norwood OH 45212-3615 Office: U Cin 2220 Victory Pky Cincinnati OH 45206-2822

MEALMAN, GLENN, corporate marketing executive; b. Prescott, Kans., June 10, 1934; s. Edgar R. and Mary E. (Holstein) M.; m. Gloria Gail Proch, June 12, 1955; children: Michael Edward, Cathy Gail. BS in Bus., Kans. State Coll., Emporia, 1957; postgrad., Harvard U., 1970. With Fleming Cos., Topeka, 1957—, sr. v.p. mktg., 1981-82, exec. v.p. mktg., 1982-86, exec. v.p. Mid-Am. region, 1986-93, exec. v.p. nat. accts., 1994-96. Dir. PBI-Gordon Co., Furrs Supermarkets. Pres. bd. Topeka YMCA, 1981; trustee Ottawa U., Kans., 1980. Served with USNR, 1954-56. Mem. Kans. State C. of C. and Industry (bd. dirs. 1991—), Blue Hills Country Club, Gainey Ranch Country Club, Keystone Ranch Country Club, Rotary, Sigma Phi Epsilon (Kans. chpt.). Presbyterian. Office: PO Box 7448 Shawnee Mission KS 66207-0448

MEBUST, WINSTON KEITH, surgeon, educator; b. Malta, Mont., July 2, 1933; s. Hans G. and Anna C. (Leiseth) M.; m. Lora June Peterson, Sept. 15, 1955; children— Leanne, Kevin, Kreg, Kari. Student, U. Wash., 1951-54, M.D., 1958. Diplomate: Am. Bd. Urology (trustee 1983-89, pres. 1988-89). Intern King County Hosp., Seattle, 1958-59; resident Virginia Mason Hosp., 1959-63, Kans. U. Med. Center, 1963-66; practice medicine, specializing in urology, 1966—; instr. surgery and urology U. Kans. Med. Center, Kansas City, 1966-69, asst. prof., 1969-72, asso. prof., 1972-76, chmn. urology sect., 1974—, prof., 1977—; chief urology service VA Hosp., Kansas City, Mo., 1966-75. Contbr. articles, chpts. to med. jours. and texts. Served with U.S. Army, 1961-63. Mem. ACS, Am. Cancer Soc., Am. Bd. Surgery, Kansas City Urol. Assn., Assn. for Acad. Surgery, Am. Urol. Assn. (pres. S. Ctrl. sect. 1983, exec. com. 1992—, treas. 1996—, pres. elect 2001—), Wyandotte Med. Soc., Kans. Med. Assn., Soc. Univ. Urologists, Am. Assn. Genitourinary Surgeons, Sigma Xi, Alpha Omega Alpha. Republican. Home: 422 Lansbrook Dr Venice FL 34292-4620 Office: 39th and Rainbow Blvd Kansas City MO 66103 E-mail: wmebust@comcast.net.

MECHEM, CHARLES STANLEY, JR. former broadcasting executive, former golf association executive; b. Nelsonville, Ohio, Sept. 12, 1930; s. Charles Stanley and Helen (Hall) Mechem; m. Marilyn Brown, Aug. 31, 1952; children: Melissa, Daniel, Allison. A.B., Miami U., Oxford, Ohio, 1952; LL.B., Yale U., 1955. Bar: Ohio 1955. Practice in, Cin., 1955-67; partner Taft, Stettinius & Hollister, 1965-67; chmn. bd. Taft Broadcasting Co., Cin., 1967-90; commr. LPGA, Daytona Beach, Fla., 1990-95, commr. emeritus, 1995—; chmn. U.S. Shoe, 1993-95; chmn. Cin. Bell, Inc., 1996-98, Convergys Corp., 1998-2000; cons. Arnold Palmer Enterprises, Cin., 1996—. Bd. dir. Myers Y. Cooper Co., J.M. Smucker Co., Royal Precision, Inc., Molecular Circuitry, Inc., Messer Cons. Capt. JAGC U.S. Army, 1956—59. Mem.: Cin. C. of C. (pres. 1977), Comml. Club. Office: Taft Stettinius & Hollister LLP 425 Walnut St Ste 1800 Cincinnati OH 45202-4122

MECKLENBURG, GARY ALAN, hospital executive; m. Lynn Kraemer; children: John, Sarah. BA, Northwestern U., 1968; MBA, U. Chgo., 1970. Adminstrv. resident Presbyn.-St. Luke's Hosp., Chgo., 1969-70, adminstrv. asst., 1970-71, asst. supt., 1971-76, assoc. supt., 1976-77, U. Wis. Hosps., Madison, 1977-80; adminstr. Stanford U. Hosp. Clinics, Calif.; pres., CEO St. Joseph's Hosp., Milw., 1980-85; pres., dir. Franciscan Health Care Inc., 1985; pres., CEO Northwestern Meml. HealthCare, Chgo., 1985—. Preceptor, guest lectr., mem. adv. bd. Kellogg Sch. Mgmt., chgo., 1986—; pres., chief exec. officer, dir. Northwestern Healthcare Network, 1990-92. Recipient Todd Scout award Boy Scouts Am., 1998, Chgo. Bus. Hall of Fame award Jr. Achievement, 2000, GSB Disting. Pub. Svc./Pub. Sector Alumnus award U. Chgo., 2000. Mem. Am. Hosp. Assn. (sect. met. hosps., governing coun. 1984-92, chmn. 1991, 2001, trustee 1996—, exec. com. 1997—, mem. regional policy bd., #5 1984, 87-89, 91-93, 95-99, chmn. 1996-99, 2001, mem. ho. dels. 1984, 87-89, 91—, mem. com. on med. edn. 1976-80), Ill. Hosp. Assn. (bd. dirs. 1988-95, chmn. 1994, mem. adv. panel coun. tchg. hosps. 1997—), U. Chgo. Hosp. Adminstrn. Alumni Assn. (pres. 1985-86), Econ. Club Chgo., Comml. Club Chgo. Office: Northwestern Meml Hosp 251 E Huron St Ste 3-708 Chicago IL 60611-2908

MEDALIE, JACK HARVEY, physician; b. Buhl, Minn., Jan. 8, 1922; married; 3 children. BSc, Witwatersrand U., Johannesburg, 1941, MD, BChir, 1945; MPH cum laude, Harvard U., 1958. Instr. dept. anatomy U. Witwatersrand, 1942—43; resident Johannesburg, 1945—47; rural family physician, 1948—53; sr. lectr. dept. social medicine Hebrew U., Hadassah, Jerusalem, 1962—66; from assoc. prof. to prof., chmn. dept. family medicine Tel Aviv U., 1966—74; chmn. dept. family medicine Case Western Res. U., 1975—87, prof. cmty. health, 1976—87, prof. family medicine, 1976—, prof. med. and pediat., 1978—87, prof. emeritus, 1992—; med. dir. Family and Cmty. Health Ctr., Jerusalem, 1953—62. Prin. investigator Israel Ischemic Heart Disease Study, 1962—75; co-prin. investigator congenital abnormality study NIH, 1972—74; Robert Wood Johnson Found. fellowship program Case Western Res. U., 1978—88; vis. prof. family medicine and epidemiology U. N.C., Chapel Hill, 1973—74; vis. sr. rsch. scientist Nat. Heart, Blood and Lung Inst., Bethesda, Md., 1974, Bethesda, 1990—91; med. coun. U. Hosps., Cleve., 1975—87; com. impaired physicians U. Hosps. , Cleve., 1980—87; med. edn. com. Case Western Res. U., 1980—85, chmn. ambulatory and primary care clerkship com., 1981—83; task force health consequences bereavement NAS, 1982—85, membership com., 1984—88; dir. dept. family practice U. Hosps., Cleve., 1982—87; rsch. cons. Mt. Sinai Med. Ctr., Cleve., 1991—99. Contbr. articles. With U.S. Army, 1942—45. Recipient Lifetime Achievement award in medicine, Golden Age Ctrs., 1997. Fellow: Royal Soc. Med. Found., Am. Heart Assn., Am. Acad. Family Physicians; mem.: Soc. Behavioral Medicine, Soc. Tchrs. Family Medicine (chmn. task force 1985—87, Curtis Hames Career Rsch. award 1988, Cert. Excellence 1988, Maurice Saltzman award 1988), Inst. Medicine-NAS. Office: Case Western Res Univ Dept of Family Medicine 10900 Euclid Ave Cleveland OH 44106-4901

MEDH, JHEEM D. medical educator, biochemistry researcher; BS in Chemistry and Biochemistry, U. Bombay, India, 1982; MS in Biochemistry, U. Bombay, 1984; PhD in Biochemistry, U. Tex. Med. Br., Galveston, 1990. Jr. rsch. fellow, dept. physiology L.T.M. Med. Coll., Bombay, 1984-86; rsch. asst., dept. human biol. chemistry and genetics U. Tex. Med. Br., 1986-90; postgrad. rsch. biochemist, dept. medicine U. Calif., San Diego, 1991-93; asst. rsch. scientist, adj. asst. prof., dept. medicine U. Iowa Coll. Medicine, Iowa City, 1993—. Presenter in field of role of LDL receptor-related protein, receptor-associated protein and lipoprotein lipase on the regulation of lipoprotein metabolism. Juvenile Diabetes Internat. Found. fellow 1992-93; recipient nat. grand-in-aid award Am. Heart Assn., 1995-98; recipient Gip Hudson award Nat. Student Rsch. Forum, 1989, Stephen C. Silverthorne award Grad. Sch. Biomed. Scis., U. Tex. Med. Br. Mem. Am. Heart Assn. (coun. for basic science), Am. Soc. Cell Biology, Juvenile Diabetes Found. Internat. Office: U Iowa Coll Med 200 CMAB Iowa City IA 52242

MEDLAND, WILLIAM JAMES, college president; b. Logansport, Ind., Jan. 1, 1944; s. Thomas Gallagher and Mary Elizabeth (Hassett) M.; m. Donna Lee Bahnaman, Mar. 12, 1977; children: Bridget Marie, Mark David, Jeanne Nicole. BA, U. Notre Dame, 1966; student, St. Louis U., 1972-74; MA in History, Ball State U., 1967, MA in Edn., 1979, PhD in History, 1980; postgrad., Inst. for Mgmt. Lifelong Edn., Harvard U., 1985, Ctr. Internat. Cooperation and Security Studies, U. Wis., 1988, Ctr. Internat. Studies, MIT, 1989, Freie Universitat, Berlin, 1991. Instr. history and philosophy Donnelly coll., Kansas City, Kans., 1967-70; curricular advisor Ball State U., Muncie, Ind., 1970-71, teaching fellow, 1977-80; asst. dean St. Louis (Mo.) U., 1971-75; employee supr. Wilson, Inc., Logansport, 1975-76; ops. mgr. Watson-Jenkins, Inc., Indpls., 1976-77; dean of coll., asst. prof. history Springfield (Ill.) Coll., 1980-81; acad. dean, assoc. prof. history and edn. Marymount Coll., Salina, Kans., 1981-86; exec. v.p., provost, prof. history St. Mary's U., Winona, Minn., 1986-91; pres., prof. history Viterbo U., LaCrosse, Wis., 1991—, also bd. dirs., CEO, 1991—. Edn. cons. Am. Inst. Banking, Springfield, 1980-81; advisor Adv. Com. to Sch. Bd., Salina, 1984, Salina Diocesan Bd. Edn., 1981-83; evaluator North Ctrl. Assn., Chgo., 1987-2000. Author: Cuban Missile Crisis of 1962-Needless or Necessary?, 1988, reprint, 1990, A Guide to Writing College Research Papers, 1989, The Catholic School: A Bibliographical Resource Guide, 1990; editor: Ind. Acad. Social Scis. jour., 1979, Perspectives: A Liberal Arts Exchange (faculty jour.), 1988. Coll. solicitor United Way, St. Louis, 1973; coord. Coll./Cmty. Artist Series, Salina, 1981—84; chair Franciscan-Skemp Healthcare Cmty. Bd., 2002—; bd. dirs. Immaculate Heart of Mary Sem., Winona, 1987—91, La Crosse Med. Health Sci. Consortium, 1993—; Wis. Found. for Ind. Colls., 1994—98; Assn. Franciscan Colls. and Univs., 1999—; chair La Crosse Diocesan Edn. Commn., 1994—2001. Fellow Ctr. Internat. Studies, MIT/Harvard U., 1989. Mem.: KC, Wis. Assn. Ind. Colls. and Univs. (bd. dirs. 1991—), Am. Assn. Ind. Coll. Pres., Am. Assn. Coll. Pres., Am. Assn. Higher Edn., La Crosse C. of C. 2000—, (exec. com. 2001—), Rotary, Phi Delta Kappa, Phi Alpha Theta (rsch. award Ball State U. 1979). Roman Catholic. Avocations: reading, research. Home: 119 Calla Ct Onalaska WI 54650-8317 Office: Viterbo Univ Office of Pres 815 9th St S La Crosse WI 54601-4777 E-mail: wjmedland@viterbo.edu.

MEDLER, MARY ANN L. federal judge; JD, St. Louis U., 1983. Atty. Thompson Coburn, St. Louis, 1983-85; asst. cir. atty. Office of Cir. Atty. of City of St. Louis, 1985-92; atty. Union Pacific R.R., St. Louis, 1992-93; magistrate judge U.S. Dist. Ct. (ea. dist.) Mo. Office: 111 S 10th St Rm 13S Saint Louis MO 63102 E-mail: Mary_Ann_Medler@MOED.USCOURTS.gov.

MEDNICK, ROBERT, accountant; b. Chgo., Apr. 1, 1940; s. Harry and Nettie (Brenner) M.; m. Susan Lee Levinson, Oct. 28, 1962; children: Michael Jon, Julie Eden, Adam Charles. BSBA, Roosevelt U., Chgo., 1962. CPA Ill. Staff asst. Arthur Andersen, Chgo., 1962-63, sr. acct., 1963-66, mgr., 1966-71, ptnr., 1971-98, mng. dir. SEC policies, 1973-76, mng. dir. auditing procedures, 1976-79. Vice chmn. com. on profl. stds. Andersen Worldwide, 1979-82, chmn. com., 1982-98, mng. ptnr. profl. and regulatory matters, 1993-98; mem. faculty Northwestern U. Kellogg Grad. Sch. Mgmt., 1999. Contbr. articles to profl. jours. Bd. dirs. Roosevelt U., Chgo., 1977—, vice chmn., 1986-94, sr. vice chmn., 1994—, life trustee, 1999—; bd. dirs. Auditorium Theatre Coun., 1990-96, Lake Shore Drive Synagogue, 1992—; co-chmn. adv. coun. Chgo. Action for Soviet Jewry, Highland Park, Ill., 1983-87; bd. dirs., mem. exec. com. Am. Judicature Soc., 1990-95, vice chmn., 1993-95; bd. overseers Rand Corp. Inst. Civil Justice, 1994-98; bd. dirs. Nat. Bur. of Econ. Rsch., 1998—, treas., 1999—. Sgt. USAFR, 1965-69. Recipient Silver medal Ill. CPA Soc., 1962; named One of Ten Outstanding Young Men in Chgo., Chgo. Jr. C. of C., 1973-74; recipient Rolf A. Weil Disting. Service award, Roosevelt U., Chgo., 1983; Max Block award N.Y. State C.P.A. Soc., 1984; Ann. Literary award Jour. Accountancy, 1986, 88; Andrew D. Bradin award for distinctive contbns. to discipline of accountancy Case Western Res. U., Cleve., 1996; Disting. Alumni award Roosevelt U. Walter E. Heller Coll. Bus. Adminstrn., 1997; Disting. Vis. scholar Hebrew U., Jerusalem, 1999, 2000. Mem. AICPA (bd. dirs. 1986-87, 92-94, 95-98, vice chmn. 1995-96, chmn. 1996-97, numerous coms., Elijah Watt Sells award 1962, Gold Medal for Disting. Svc. 1998), Ill. CPA Soc. (acctg. prins. com. 1973, legal liability com. 1986-89, mgmt. of acctg. practice com. 1991-94, regulation and legis. com. 1998—). Jewish. Avocations: collecting art, travel. E-mail: robert.mednick@awo.com.

MEDVED, PAUL STANLEY, lawyer; b. Milw., May 6, 1956; s. Frank F. and Evelyn F. (Poplawski) M.; m. Danita C. Cole, Aug. 27, 1988. BA with honors, Marquette U., 1978; JD, Columbia U., 1981. Bar: Wis. 1981, U.S. Dist. Ct. (ea. dist.) Wis. 1981, U.S. Dist. Ct. (we. dist.) Wis. 1984, U.S. Ct. Appeals (7th cir.) 1984. Assoc. Michael, Best & Friedrich, Milw., 1981-88, ptnr., 1988-97; shareholder Mallery & Zimmerman, S.C., 1997—. Office: Mallery & Zimmerman SC 731 N Jackson St Ste 900 Milwaukee WI 53202-4697 E-mail: pmedved@mzmilw.com.

MEDVIN, HARVEY NORMAN, diversified financial services company executive, treasurer; b. Chgo., Sept. 6, 1936; s. Benjamin and Clara (Edelstein) M.; m. Sheila S. Spitzner, July 5, 1965; children: Arla Risa, Steven Merrill. BS in Acctg., U. Ill., 1958. CPA, Ill. Mem. audit staff Coopers & Lybrand, 1958-63; treas., v.p. The Martin Brower Co., Des Plaines, Ill., 1963-73, Ryan Ins. Group, Inc., Chgo., 1983—; sr. v.p., chief fin. officer Combined Internat. Corp. Chgo., 1983—; exec. v.p., CFO, treas. Aon Corp., 1987—, also bd. dirs. all subs. Bd. dirs. Schwarz Paper Co., Morton Grove, Ill., La Salle Bank Corp., La Salle Nat. Bank Chgo. Bd. dirs. Highland Park (Ill.) Hosp.; bd. govs. Chgo. Lighthouse for Blind; trustee Ravina Festival Highland Park, Ill., La Salla Nat. Bank, La Salle Nat. Corp., Chgo. With U.S. Army, 1958-59. Mem. AICPA. Office: Aon Corp 123 N Wacker Dr Chicago IL 60606-1700

MEEHL, PAUL EVERETT, psychologist, educator; b. Mpls., Jan. 3, 1920; s. Otto John and Blanche Edna (Duncan) Swedal; m. Alyce M. Roworth, Sept. 6, 1941 (dec. 1972); children: Karen, Erik; m. Leslie Jane Yonce, Nov. 17, 1973. A.B., U. Minn., 1941, Ph.D., 1945; Sc.D., Adelphi U., 1984. Diplomate Am. Bd. Profl. Psychology (clin. psychology, bd. dirs.1957-62, Disting. Svc. and Outstanding Contbns. award 1989). Instr., asst., assoc. prof., chmn. dept. psychology U. Minn., 1951-57, prof., 1952—, prof. dept. psychiatry Med. Sch., 1952-90, regents' prof. psychology, 1968-89, Hathaway-Meehl prof. psychology, 1990-93, regent's prof. psychology emeritus, 1993—; prof. Minn. Ctr. for Philosophy of Sci., 1953-56, 69—, prof. philosophy, 1971—; acting chief clin. psychology VA Hosp., Mpls., 1947-49; participant Dartmouth Conf. on Behavior Theory, 1950; mem. panel on criminal deterrence Nat. Acad. Sci., 1975-77; practice psychotherapy, 1951-94; staff Nicollet Clinic, 1970-80. Author: (with S.R. Hathaway) Atlas for Clinical Use of MMPI, 1951, (with others) Modern Learning Theory, 1954, Clinical Versus Statistical Prediction, 1954, What, Then, Is Man?, 1958, Psychodiagnosis, 1973, Selected Philosophical and Methodological Papers, 1991, (with N. Waller) Multivariate Taxometric Procedures, 1998; contbr. articles to profl., legal and philos. jours. Recipient Ednl. Testing Svc. award for contbns. to measurement, 1994, Clin. Psychology Centennial prize for lifetime achievement APA, Bruno Klopfer disting. contbn. award, 1979, Gold medal for life achievement application of psychology Am. Psychol. Found., 1989, Disting. Svc. award Am. Bd. Profl. Psychologists, 1989, Joseph Zubin prize lifetime contbns. to psychopathology, 1993; William James fellow Am. Psychol. Soc., 1989. Fellow Am. Psychol. Soc. (James McKeen Cattell fellow 1998), Inst. for Advanced Study in Rational Psychotherapy; mem. APA (pres. 1961-62, Disting. Contbr. award clin. divsn. 1967, Disting. Sci. Contr. award 1958, Disting. Scientist award 1976, Disting. Contbn. to Knowledge award 1993, award for Outstanding Lifetime Contbn. to Psychology 1996), Am. Acad. Arts and Scis., Nat. Acad. Sci., Philosophy of Sci. Assn., Phi Beta Kappa, Sigma Xi, Psi Chi. Home: 1544 E River Ter Minneapolis MN 55414-3646 Office: U Minn N218 Elliott Hall 75 E River Rd Minneapolis MN 55455-0280 E-mail: pemeehl@umn.edu.

MEEK, VIOLET IMHOF, dean; b. Geneva, June 12, 1939; d. John and Violet (Krepel) Imhof; m. Devon W. Meek, Aug. 21, 1965 (dec. 1988); children: Brian, Karen; m. Don M. Dell, Jan. 4, 1992. BA summa cum laude, St. Olaf Coll., 1960; MS, U. Ill., 1962, PhD in Chemistry, 1964. Instr. chemistry Mount Holyoke Coll., South Hadley, Mass., 1964-65; asst. prof. to prof. Ohio Wesleyan U., Delaware, Ohio, 1965-84, dean for ednl. svcs., 1980-84; dir. annual programs Coun. Ind. Colls., Washington, 1984-86; assoc. dir. sponsored programs Rsch. Found. Ohio State U., Columbus, 1986-91, dean, dir. Lima, 1992—. Vis. dean U. Calif., Berkeley, 1982, Stanford U., Palo Alto, Calif., 1982, reviewer GTE Sci. and Tech. Program, Princeton, N.J., 1986-92, Goldwater Nat. Fellowships, Princeton, 1990-98. Co-author: Experimental General Chemistry, 1984; contbr. articles to profl. jours. Bd. dirs. Luth. Campus Ministries, Columbus, 1988-91, Luth. Social Svcs., 1988-91, Americom Bank, Lima, 1992-98, Art Space, Lima, 1993—, Allen Lima Leadership, 1993—, Am. House, 1992—, Lima Vets. Meml. Civic Ctr. Found., 1992—; chmn. synodical coms. Evang. Luth. Ch. Am., Columbus, 1982; bd. trustees Trinity Luth. Sem., Columbus, 1996—; chmn. Allen County C. of C., 1995—, chair bd. dirs., 1999; bd. dirs. Lima Syphomy Orch., 1993—, pres. bd. dirs., 1997— Recipient Woodrow Wilson Fellowship, 1960. Mem. Nat. Coun. Rsch. Adminstrs. (named Outstanding New Profl. midwest region 1990), Am. Assn. Higher Edn., Phi Beta Kappa. Avocations: music, skiing, woodworking, Civil War history, travel. Home: 209 W Beechwold Blvd Columbus OH 43214-2012 Office: Ohio State U 4240 Campus Dr Lima OH 45804-3576

MEEKS, CAROL JEAN, educator; b. Columbus, Ohio, Mar. 9, 1946; d. Clarence Eugene and Clara Johanna (Schwartz) B.; m. Joseph Meeks, Aug. 17, 1968 (div. 1981); children: Catherine Rachael, Tiffany Johannah. BS, Ohio State U., Mex., 1968; MS, Ohio State U., 1969, PhD, 1972. Rsch. asst., assoc. Ohio State U., Columbus, 1968-71; internship Columbus Area C. of C., Ohio, 1970; lectr. Ohio State U., Columbus, 1970, 72; asst. prof. U. Mass., Amherst, 1972-74, Cornell U., Ithaca, N.Y., 1974-78, assoc. prof., 1978-80; legis. fellow Senate Com. Banking, 1984; supr. economist, head housing section USDA, Washington, 1980-85; assoc. prof. housing and consumer econs. U. Ga., Athens, 1985-90, prof., 1990-97, head housing and consumer econs., 1992-97; dean Coll. Family and Consumer Scis. Iowa State U., Ames, 1997—. Rsch. fellow Nat. Inst. for Consumer Rsch., Oslo, Norway, 1992; cons. Yale U., 1976-77, HUD, Cambridge, Mass., 1978, MIT Ctr. for Real Estate Devel. Ford Found. Project on Housing Policy; del. N.E. Ctr. for Rural Devel. Housing Policy Conf. Reviewer Home Econ. Rsch. Jour., 1987—, ACCI conf., 1987—; contbr. articles to profl. mags. Mem. panel town of Amherst Landlord Tenant Bd.; bd. dirs. Am. Coun. Consumer Interests; mem. adv. coun. HUD Nat. Mfg. Housing, 1978-80, 91-93; chair Housing Mfg. Inst. Consensus Commn. on Fed. Standards. Recipient Leader award AAFCS, 1996, Disting. Alumni award Ohio State U., 1999; named one of Outstanding Young Women of Am., 1979; Columbus Womens Chpt. Nat. Assn. Real Estate Bds. scholar, Gen. Foods fellow, 1971-72, HEW grantee, 1978, travel grantee NSF bldg. rsch. bd., AID grantee, USDA Challenge grant, 1995-98. Mem. Am. Assn. Housing Educators (pres. 1983-84), Nat. Inst. Bldg. Sci. (bd. sec. 1984, 85, 89-92, bd. dirs. 1981-83, 85, 87-93), Internat. Assn. Housing Sci., Com. on Status on Women in Econs., Nat. Assn. Home Builders (Smart House contract 1989, treas. bd. human sci. 2001-), Epsilon Sigma Phi, Phi Upsilon Omicron, Gamma Sigma Delta, Phi Beta Delta, Kappa Omicron Nu (v.p. of programs 1995-96), Phi Kappa Phi, others. Office: Iowa State U 122 Mackay Hl Ames IA 50011-0001

MEEKS, CHARLES B. state legislator; m. Marjorie Meeks; 1 son. Student, FBI Acad., Quantico, Va., 1978, Nat. Sheriff's Inst., UCLA, 1975. Enlisted USAF, 1967, ret., 1990; with USN, 1954-58; ret. businessman; ret. law enforcement officer; mem. Ind. Senate from 14th dist., Indpls., 1998—; mem. ins. and fin. instns. com., mem. pension and labor com. Ind. Senate, mem. planning and econ. devel. com., mem. pub. policy com. Bd. dirs. McMillen Ctr. for Health Edn., 1980-89, Ind. Correctional Code, 1980-82, Jail Stds. Com., 1978-82; mem. jail accreditatio program com. AMA, 1975-82. Named Outstanding Dep. Sheriff Jaycees, 1972, Am. Legion, 1973; recipient Cert. Accreditation AMA, 1978, Silver Star Allen County Sheriff's Office. Mem. Nat. Sheriffs Assn. Republican. Office: 200 W Washington St Indianapolis IN 46204-2728

MEEKS, ROBERT L. state legislator; b. Ft. Wayne, Ind., Feb. 3, 1934; m. Carol Meeks; children: Denise Schrock, Kevin, Layne, Kent. Mem. Ind. Senate from 13th dist., 1988—; sen. finance, nat. resources, local govt. issues coms.; chair budget sub-com. Past trustee Lakeland Sch. Bd. Recipient Maddox award FOP Life Savers Club, Allen County. Mem. Am. Legion, C. of C., Masons (Shriner). Home: 5840 E 025 N Lagrange IN 46761-9519

MEERS, BILL M. news executive; News bur. chief Met. Network News, 1999—. Office: # 910 Plymouth Bldg 12 S 6th St Minneapolis MN 55402-1508

MEERSCHAERT, JOSEPH RICHARD, physician; b. Detroit, Mar. 4, 1941; s. Hector Achiel and Marie Terese (Campbell) M.; m. Jeanette Marie Ancerewicz, Sept. 14, 1963; children: Eric, Amy, Adam. BA, Wayne State U., 1965, MD, 1967. Diplomate Am. Bd. Phys. Medicine and Rehab., Am. Bd. Pain Medicine. Intern Harper Hosp., Detroit, 1967-68; resident in phys. medicine and rehab. Wayne State U. Rehab. Inst., 1968-71; chief divsn. phys. medicine Naval Hosp., Chelsea, Mass., 1971-73; attending physician William Beaumont Hosp., Royal Oak, Mich., 1973—, med. dir. rehab. unit, 1979-87; pvt. practice medicine specializing in phys. medicine and rehab., 1973—; pvt. practice specializing in pain medicine, 1990—. Mem. med. adv. bd. Nat. Wheelchair Athletic Assn., 1973—, U.S. team physician VII World Wheelchair Games, Stoke Mandeville, Eng.; clin. instr. Wayne State U., 1973-83, clin. asst. prof. phys. medicine and rehab., 1983— ; mem. Mich. Dept. Licensing and Regulation State Bd. Phys. Therapy, 1978-81. Contbr. articles to profl. jours. With M.C. USN, 1971-73. Recipient John Hussey award Mich. Wheelchair Athletic Assn., 1981. Fellow Am. Coll. Pain Medicine; mem. Am. Acad. Phys. Medicine and Rehab. (reviewer, presenter) Am. Congress Rehab. Medicine, Mich. Phys. Medicine and Rehab. Soc., Am. Geriatrics Soc., Am. Assn. Electromyography and Electrodiagnosis, Mich. Rheumatism Soc., Mich. Acad. Phys. Medicine and REhab. (pres. 1986-87, chmn. program com. 1977-78, trustee 1980—, pres. bd. dirs. 1994-97), Oakland County Med. Soc. (bd. dirs. 1991, 97), Alpha Omega Alpha. Roman Catholic. Office: 44199 Dequindre Rd Troy MI 48085-1128

MEHLER, BARRY ALAN, humanities educator, journalist, consultant; b. Bklyn., Mar. 18, 1947; s. Harry and Esther Mehler; m. Jennifer Sue Leghorn, June 2, 1982; 1 child, Isaac Alan. BA, Yeshiva U., 1970; MA, CCNY, 1972; PhD, U. Ill., 1988. Rsch. assoc. Washington U., St. Louis, 1976-80, instr. history, 1977; NIMH trainee racism program U. Ill., Champaign, 1981-85, rsch. asst. IBM EXCEL project, 1986-88; asst. prof. humanities Ferris State U., Big Rapids, Mich., 1988-93, assoc. prof., 1993-99, prof., 1999—. Media cons. Scientist's Inst. for Pub. Info., N.Y.C., 1980-98; cons. Calif. Humanities Coun., 1995, ZDF/arte (Zweite Deutsches Fernshen--German pub. TV), 1995, House Subcom. on Consumer Protection, 1994, McIntosh Commn. for Fair Play in Student-Athlete Admissions, 1994, Can. Broadcast Svc., Toronto, Ont., 1985-92; judge Women's Caucus Awards for Excellence, St. Louis, 1989-91, 93; dir. Inst. for Study of Acad. Racism, 1993—; mem. Pres.'s. Initiative on Race, 1998, One Am. initiative, named Promising Practices; presenter Performance Art in the Classroom, Minority Equity Conf. XI, 2001. Contbg. editor: Encyclopedia of Genocide, 1997; contbr. more than 100 articles and revs. to profl. jours. Mem. vol. com. parents A Different Look at DARE, 1995; mem. adv. bd. Homes for the Homeless, Austin, Tex., 2000-01, Internat. Inst. for Study of Psychiatry and Psychology Washington, 1999—; founder, sec.-treas. Internat. Com. to Free Russell Smith, 1977-79; co-founder Gay Peoples Alliance, St. Louis, 1978; mem. adv. bd. Stop Prison Rape, 2001. Recipient cert. of recognition Ferris State Bd. of Control, 1994, Hesburgh award for excellence in undergrad. edn., TIAA-CREFF and Am. Coun. on Edn., 2000; NSF rsch. fellow, 1976-80, Babcock fellow U. Ill., 1985-86; grantee Rockefeller Found., 1977; structured learning assistance program grantee Office of Minority Affairs, Lansing, Mich., 1994-97. Mem. Am. Hist. Soc., Behavior-Genetics Assn., NAACP, Ctr. for Dem. Renewal, History of Sci. Soc., Internat. Behavioral and Neural Geneteics Soc., Orgn. Am. Historians, B'nai B'rith (Anti-Defamation League), Coalition for Human Dignity, Facing History. Jewish. Avocations: hiking, camping. Home: 216 Rust Ave Big Rapids MI 49307-1726 Office: Ferris State U 901 S State St Big Rapids MI 49307-2295 E-mail: bmehler@netonecom.net.

MEHLMAN, MARK FRANKLIN, lawyer; b. L.A., Dec. 18, 1947; s. Jack and Elaine Pearl (Lopater) M.; m. Barbara Ann Novak, Aug. 20, 1972; children: David, Jennifer, Ilyse. BA, U. Ill., 1969; LLB, U. Mich., 1973. Bar: Ill. 1973; U.S. Dist. Ct. (no. dist.) Ill. 1973. Assoc. Sonnenschein, Nath & Rosenthal, Chgo., 1973-80, mem. policy and planning com., 1989—. Trustee Groveland Health Svcs., Highland Park (Ill.) Hosp., 1991-97; trustee, treas., exec. com. Spertus Inst. Jewish Studies, Chgo., 1992-97, vice chmn. bd. trustees, 1996—; vice-chmn. regional bd. Anti-Defamation League, 1987-89, hon. life mem. nat. commn., 1993—. Fellow Am. Bar Found.; mem. ABA (chmn. mortgages and other debt financing subcom. 1991-95, supervisory coun. 1997—), Am. Coll. Real Estate Lawyers (bd. govs. 2000—, chmn. MDP com. 2000—, chmn. mem. selection com. 2000-01), Nat. Conf. Lawyers and CPAs, Ango-Am. Real Property Inst., Legal Club of Chgo., Lake Shore Country Club, Standard Club, Exec. Club of Chgo. Office: Sonnenschein Nath & Rosenthal 233 S Wacker Dr Ste 8000 Chicago IL 60606-6491

MEHLMAN, MAXWELL JONATHAN, law educator; b. Washington, Nov. 4, 1948; s. Jacob and Betty (Hoffman) M.; m. Cheryl A. Stone, Sept. 15, 1979; children: Aurora, Gabriel. BA, Reed Coll., 1970, Oxford U., England, 1972; JD, Yale U., 1975. Bar: D.C. 1976, Ohio 1988. Assoc. Arnold & Porter, Washington, 1975-84; asst. prof. Case Western Res. U., Cleve., 1984-87, assoc. prof., 1987-90, prof. law, 1990-96, Arthur E. Petersilge prof., 1996—, prof. biomed. ethics, 1998—. Spl. counsel N.Y. State Bar, N.Y.C., 1988-94, Nat. Kidney Found., 1991; cons. Am. Assn. Ret. Persons, Washington, 1992. Editor: High Tech Home Care, 1991, (with T. Murray) Encyclopedia of Ethical, Legal and Policy Issues in Biotechnology; author: (with J. Botkin) Access to the Genome: The Challenge to Equality, 1998, (with Andrews and Rothstein) Genetics: Ethics, Law and Policy, 2002; contbr. articles to profl. jours. Active steering com. AIDS Commn. Greater Cleve., 1986-90. Rhodes scholar, 1970; Rsch. grantee NIH, 1992-94, 97—. Mem. Am. Assn. Law Schs. (chmn. sect. on law, medicine and health care 1990), Phi Beta Kappa. Avocations: skiing, choral music, sea kayaking. Office: Case Western Reserve U Sch Law-Law Medicine Ctr Gund Hall 11075 E Blvd Cleveland OH 44106

MEHTA, ZARIN, music festival administrator; b. Bombay, India, Oct. 28, 1938; came to Can., 1962, naturalized, 1969; s. Mehli and Tehmina Mehta; m. Carmen Lasky, July 1, 1966; children— Rohanna, Rustom. Chartered acct., London, 1957. Acct. Frederic B. Smart & Co., London, 1957-62, Coopers & Lybrand, Montreal, Que., Can., 1962-81; mng. dir. Orchestre Symphonique de Montreal, 1981-90, dir., 1973-81; exec. dir., chief oper. officer Ravinia Festival, 1990-99, pres., CEO, 1999—. Fellow Inst. Chartered Accts. in Eng. and Wales; mem. Ordre des Comptables Agrees du Que. Office: Ravinia Festival 400 Iris Ln Highland Park IL 60035-5208

MEIER, ARLENE, retail executive; CFO, exec. v.p.,& sec Kohl's Corp., Menomonee Falls, Wis., 1994-. Office: Kohls Corp N56 W 17000 Ridgewood Dr Menomonee Falls WI 53051

MEIER, JOHN F. consumer products company executive; With Libbey Inc., Toledo, 1970-90, gen. mgr., 1990-93, CEO, 1993—, also chmn. bd. dirs.; pres. Owens-Ill., Inc., 1990. Bd. dirs. Tire & Rubber Co. Office: Libbey Inc 300 Madison Ave Fl 4 Toledo OH 43604-2634

MEIJER, DOUGLAS, retail company executive; b. 1954; With Meijer Inc., 1967—, co-chmn., 1990—. Office: Meijer Inc 2929 Walker Ave NW Grand Rapids MI 49544-9428

MEIJER, FREDERIK, retail company executive; b. 1919; married. Former pres. Meijer, Inc., then chmn. bd., CEO, 1975-90, chmn. exec. com., CEO, 1990-97, chmn. exec. com., 1997—, also bd. dirs. Office: Meijer Inc 2929 Walker Ave NW Grand Rapids MI 49544-9428

MEIJER, MARK, retail executive; With Bud's Ambulance Svc., Grand Rapids, Mich., 1977-79; pres. Life EMS Inc., 1979—; bd. dirs. Meijer Cos. Ltd. Office: Meijer Companies LTD 2929 Walker Ave NW Grand Rapids MI 49544-9428

MEINERT, JOHN RAYMOND, investment banker, clothing manufacturing and retailing executive; b. White Cloud, Mich., Aug. 11, 1927; m. Joyce Macdonell, Nov. 5, 1955; children: Elizabeth Tinsman, Pamela Martin. Student, U. Mich., 1944-45; B.S., Northwestern U., 1949. C.P.A., Ill., 1952. With Hart Schaffner & Marx/Hartmarx Corp., Chgo., 1950-90, exec. v.p., 1975-80, vice chmn., 1981-85, sr. vice chmn., 1985-86, chmn., 1987-90, chmn. emeritus, 1990—, also bd. dirs.; prin. investment banking J.H. Chapman Group, LLC, Rosemont, Ill., 1990—, chmn., 1995—. Bd. dirs. County Seat Stores, Inc., N.Y.C., 1998-99, The John Evans Club, BBB, Chgo. C.of C.; trustee Amalgamated Ins. Fund, 1980-90, Rotary Internat. Retirement Fund, 2000—; dir. Evanston Hosp., 1988-94, Clothing Mfrs. Assn., pres., 1982-87, chmn. 1987-90; instr. acctg. Northwestern U., 1949; faculty Lake Forest Grad. Sch. Mgmt., 1994-95; arbitrator Am. Arbitration Assn., 1993—. Chmn. bus. adv. coun. U. Ill., 1989-90; mem. Fin. Acctg. Stds. Adv. Coun., 1989-92, Chgo. Coun. Fgn. Rels., Sisters City Com.; mem. adv. coun. Northwestern U. Kellogg Grad. Sch. Recipient Alumni Merit award Northwestern U. Kellogg Grad. Sch., 1989; named Humanitarian of Yr., Five Hosp. Found., 1995. Mem. AICPA (v.p. 1985-86, bd. dirs. 1975-78, coun. 1971-93, trustee benevolent fund 1992-95, gold medal 1987), Ill. CPA Soc. (pub. svc. award 1996, pres. 1982-83, bd. dirs. 1966-68, 81-84, hon. award), Chicagoland C. of C. (bd. dirs.), Rotary (pres. Chgo. 1989-90, trustee found. 1991-95, asst. dist. gov. 1997-2000), Univ. Club, Execs. Club, Rolling Green Country Club. Presbyterian (elder). Home: 634 N Ironwood Dr Arlington Heights IL 60004-5818 Office: J H Chapman Group LLC 9700 W Higgins Rd Rosemont IL 60018-4796

MEISEL, DAN, chemist; b. Tel Aviv, July 4, 1943; s. Arie and Mariasha Miriam (Ribak) M.; m. Osnat Meisel, Dec. 30, 1965; children: Einat, Omer. BSc, Hebrew U., 1967, MSc, 1969, PhD, 1974. Dir. radiation lab., prof. chemistry U. Notre Dame, Ind., 1998—. Adv. bd.: Jour. Phys. Chem., 1993—2002; editor: Photochem. Energy Conversion, 1989, Semiconductors Nanoclusters, 1997. Mem. AAAS, Am. Chem. Soc., Am. Nuclear Soc. Office: U Notre Dame Radiation Lab Notre Dame IN 46556-0579 E-mail: dani@nd.edu.

MEISEL, GEORGE VINCENT, lawyer; b. St. Louis, Sept. 24, 1933; s. Leo Otto and Margaret (Duggan) M.; m. Joy C. Cassin, May 18, 1963 B.S. summa cum laude, St. Louis U., 1956, J.D. cum laude, 1958. Bar: Mo. 1958. Assoc. Grand Peper & Martin, St. Louis, 1961-64, ptnr., 1965; jr. ptnr. Bryan Cave McPheeters & McRoberts, St. Louis, 1966-69; ptnr. Bryan Cave, LLP, 1970-2000, of counsel, 2000—. Served to 1st lt. USAF, 1958-61 Mem. ABA, Bar Assn. Met. St. Louis, Mo. Bar Assn. Roman Catholic. Clubs: Saint Louis, Mo. Athletic (St. Louis). Home: 2029 S Warson Rd Saint Louis MO 63124-1151 E-mail: gvmeisel@bryancavellp.com.

MEISENHELDER, ROBERT JOHN, II, pharmaceutical company executive; b. 1943; BS, U.S. Air Force Acad.; JD, Harvard U. Bar: Mich., 1975. V.p., assoc. gen. coun. Pharmacia & Upjohn, Inc., Kalamazoo. Office: Pharmacia & Upjohn Inc 7000 Portage Rd Kalamazoo MI 49001-0102

MEISNER, GARY WAYNE, landscape architect; b. Terre Haute, Ind., Oct. 19, 1949; s. Ervin Gustav and Mary Lou (Marett) M.; children: Christopher Wayne, Kira Valora. BS in Landscape Architecture, Mich. State U., 1972. Lic. landscape architect, Ohio, Mich., Ind., Ill., Ky., W.Va. Designer Huron Clinton Metro Parks, Detroit, 1969, City of East Lansing, Mich., 1970, Fairfax County Park Authority, Annandale, Va., 1971; city design adminstr. Akron (Ohio) Dept. Planning and Urban Devel., 1972-79; prin. Bentley Meisner Assocs., Inc, Cin., 1979-94, Myers, Schmalenberger, Meisner Inc., Cin. and Columbus, Ohio, 1994-99, Meisner & Assocs., Cincinnati, 1999—. Designer Akron Downtown Plan, 1978, King Sch. Plan, 1980 (honor award 1982), master plan Toyota Regional Office, 1983 (honor award 1987), Falls at Cumberland Hill, 1987 (honor award 1989), Cin. Mus. Ctr., 1990 (honor award 1990), Walk Across Am. Garden, 1990 (honor award 1991), Dayton Nat. Cemetery, 1993 (honor award 1994), Piatt Park on Garfield Place, 1990 (honor award OPWA grand award 1992), Dayton Plaza of Flight (honor award 1995), Taylor Park Historic Riverwalk, 1995 (Ky. Gov.'s award 1996), Walnut Hills H.S. Master Plan (honor award 1999), Ea. Corridor Land Use Vision Plan (AIA award 2000). Trustee Cin. Hillside Trust, 1987—, Capitol Square Renovation Found., Columbus, Ohio, 1987—93, cin. Sculpture Coun., 1989—94, Hubbard Ednl. Trust, 1988—, Ohio Gov.'s Residence Commn., 2000—. Recipient gov.'s commendation State of Ohio, 1985, Ohio Arts Coun. fellow, 1992-93, Apple award Architecture Found. of Cin., 1995. Fellow Am. Soc. Landscape Architects (nat. trustee 1982-89, chmn. nat. cmty. assistance team program 1983-86, chmn. editorial bd. Garden Design mag. 1986-90, mem. nat. publs. bd. 1988-92, 96-98, Nat. Com. Assistance Team commendation 1986, Trustee commendation 1989); mem. Am. Soc. Botanic Garden and Arboretum, Urban Land Inst., Am. Underground Space Assn, Scenic Ohio (treas. 1985—). Mem. Unity Ch. Home: 4137 Jora Ln Cincinnati OH 45209-1406 Office: Meisner & Assocs 2043 Madison Rd Cincinnati OH 45208-3218

MEISSNER, ALAN PAUL, research engineer; b. Marshfield, Wis., Dec. 22, 1968; s. Arnold John and Viva Irene (Erickson) M.; m. Staci G. Olson, Oct. 8, 1994. Student, U. Wis., Eau Claire, 1987-89; BSME, U. Wis., Platteville, 1993. Registered profl. engr., Wis. Lab. technician Omni Engrs., Appleton, Wis., summers 1989-91; project engr. Pella (Iowa) Corp., 1992; rsch. engr. Modine Mfg. Co., Racine, Wis., 1993—. Mem. Tau Beta Pi, Phi Eta Sigma, Pi Tau Sigma. Avocations: reading, computers, football, basketball, cross-training. Home: 7803 Briarwood Dr Franklin WI 53132-8843 Office: Modine Mfg Co 1500 De Koven Ave Racine WI 53403-2552

MEISSNER, EDWIN BENJAMIN, JR. retired real estate broker; b. St. Louis, Dec. 27, 1918; s. Edwin B. and Edna (Rice) Meissner; m. Nina Renard, Dec. 17, 1946; children: Edwin Benjamin III, Wallace, Robert;1 child Donald. B.S., U. Pa., 1940. Joined St. Louis Car Co., 1934, asst. to pres., v.p., exec. v.p., 1950-56, pres., gen. mgr., 1956-61; pres. St. Louis Car div. Gen. Steel Industries, Inc., 1961-67; sr. v.p., dir. Gen. Steel Industries, Inc., 1968-74; v.p. Bakewell Corp., 1974-85; real estate broker, v.p. Hilliker Corp., St. Louis, 1985-96. Mem. pres.' coun. St. Louis U.; bd. dirs. Washington U. Med. Ctr. Redevel. Corp., Barnard Free Skin and Cancer Hosp.; past bd. dirs. James S. McDonnell USO; outreach com. St. Louis Symphony Soc.; hon. dir. Humane Soc. Mo.; v.p. Gateway Ctr. Met. St. Louis; chmn. Ladue (Mo.) Police and Fire Commn.; mem. Jefferson Nat. Expansion Meml. Commn.; mil. affairs com. Regional Commerce. Mem. Am. Ordnance Assn. (life), Internat. Assn. Chiefs of Police (assoc.), Mo. Athletics Club, Westwood Country Club, Bridlespur Hunt Club, St. Louis Club, Beta Gamma Sigma. Office: 509 Olive St Ste 608 Saint Louis MO 63101-1855 Home: Ste 608 509 Olive St Saint Louis MO 63101-1855

MEISSNER, SUZANNE BANKS, pastoral associate; b. Flint, Mich., July 12, 1943; d. Leon J. and Eunice Alberta (Conners) Banks; m. Edward J. Meissner, Aug. 20, 1966 (div. Sept. 1975). BA, North Park Coll., 1965; MA, Ea. Mich. U., 1979; M in Pastoral Studies, Loyola U., New Orleans, 1991. Cert. secondary educator, spiritual dir., Hypnotist, Mich.; commd. min. Diocese of Lansing, 1997. Tchr. Flint (Mich.) Cmty. Schs., 1965-94; pastoral assoc. St. Michael Ch., Flint, 1985—2002, Holy Redeemer Parish , Burton, Mich., 2002—. Mem. adv. bd. New Covenant Initiative, Diocese of Lansing, Mich., 1994—98; co-chmn. Profl. Pastoral Mins. Assn., 1994—98, chmn. diocesan pastoral coun., 1986—88, mem. docesan strategic pastoral planning commn.; mem. pastoral planning adv. com. Hurley Med. Ctr.; adj. faculty Siena Heights U., Adrian, Mich. Mem. presdl. search com. Mott C.C.; core team leader for Healing Min., Gerholz Christian Counseling Ctr. Mem. Internat. Assn. Counselors and Therapists, Rotary Internat., Phi Kappa Phi, Phi Delta Kappa. Democrat. Avocations: theatre, Audi owners, opera, travel. Home: 7217 N Mckinley Rd Flushing MI 48433-9046 Office: St Michael Church 609 E 5th Ave Flint MI 48503-1597 E-mail: suzmeis@aol.com., meissnersuzanne@hotmail.com.

MEISTER, BERNARD JOHN, chemical engineer; b. Maynard, Mass., Feb. 27, 1941; s. Benjamin C. and Gertrude M. (Meister); m. Janet M. White, Dec. 31, 1971; children: Mark, Martin, Kay Ellen. BSChemE, Worcester Poly. Inst., 1962; PhD in Chem. Engring., Cornell U., 1966. Engring. rschr. Dow Chem. Co., Midland, Mich., 1966—, sr. rsch. specialist, 1978-81, assoc. scientist, 1981-85, sr. assoc. scientist, 1985-92, rsch. scientist, 1992—. Contbr. articles to profl. jours. Mem. United Meth. Ch. Mem. Am. Inst. Chem. Engrs., Am. Chem. Soc., Soc. Plastics Engrs., Soc. Rheology, Sigma Xi. Methodist. Home: 2925 Chippewa Ln Midland MI 48640-4181 Office: Dow Chem Co 438 Bldg Midland MI 48667-0001

MEISTER, MARK JAY, museum director, professional society administrator; b. Balt., June 26, 1953; s. Michael Aaron and Yetta (Haransky) M.; m. Carla Steiger, Aug. 7, 1977; children: Rachel, Kaitlin. AB, Washington U., St. Louis, 1974; MA, U. Minn., 1976; cert. mus. mgmt., U. Calif., Berkeley, 1983. Asst. lectr. St. Louis Art Mus., 1974; asst. coord. young people's program Mpls. Inst. Arts, 1975-76, coord. mobile program, 1976, coord. tchrs. resource svcs., 1976-77; dir. Mus. Art and History, Port Huron, Mich., 1978-79, Midwest Mus. Am. Art, Elkhart, Ind., 1979-81; exec. dir. Children's Mus., St. Paul, 1981-86; dir. Mus. Art, Sci. and Industry, Bridgeport, Conn., 1986-89; exec. dir. Archaeol. Inst. of Am., Boston, 1989-99; exec. dir. Archl. Inst. Am. Inst. Archeologique d'Amerique, Boston and Toronto, 1994-99; exec. dir. Dayton Soc. Natural History, 2000—. Adj. lectr. museology Kenyon Coll., Gambier, Ohio, 1977; adj. lectr. art history Ind. U., South Bend, 1980—81; regional reviewer Inst. Mus. Svcs., Washington, 1985—86, Washington, 1989; treas., vice chmn. Minn. Assn. Mus., St. Paul, 1983—86; ex-officio trustee U.S. com. Internat. Coun. on Monuments and Sites, 1995—99. Bd. dirs. Seaway Arts Coun., St. Clair County, Mich., 1978-79, Dayton Sister Cities Com., 2000—, Dayton Peace Accords Project, 2000—; mem. Mayor's Arts Adv. Com., Elkhart, 1981; mem. projects with industry bus. adv. coun. Goodwill Industries of Southwestern Conn., 1988-89; mem. exec. com., Conf. Adminstrv. Officers, Am. Coun. Learned Socs., 1994-97; pres. Asian Arts Ctr., Dayton, 2002. NEH museology fellow, Mpls. Inst. Arts, 1976-77, Kress fellow U. Minn. 1977-78, Bush leadership summer fellow, Bush Found., St. Paul, 1983; named One of Outstanding Young Men Am., 1981. Mem.: Assn. Children's Mus., Ohio Mus. Assn., Assn. Sci. and Tech. Ctrs., Am. Zoo and Aquarium Assn., Assn. Sci. Mus. Dirs., Archeol. Inst. Am., Soc. for Am. Archaeology, Am. Coun. Learned Socs. (chair nominating com. 1997, mem. exec. com. conf. of adminstrv. officers 1994—97), Am. Assn. Mus. Office: Dayton Soc Natural History 2600 Deweese Pkwy Dayton OH 45414-5400

MEITES, SAMUEL, clinical chemist, educator; b. St. Joseph, Mo., Jan. 3, 1921; s. Benjamin and Frieda (Kaminsky) M.; m. Lois Pauline Maranville, Mar. 11, 1945; 1 child, David Russell. AS, St. Joseph Jr. Coll., 1940; AB, U. Mo., 1942; PhD, Ohio State U., 1950. Diplomate Am. Bd. Clin. Chemistry. Clin. biochemist VA Hosp., Poplar Bluff, Mo., 1950-52, Toledo Hosp., 1953-54; Children's Hosp. Columbus, Ohio, 1954-91; prof. dept pediatrics Coll. Medicine Ohio State U., Columbus, 1972-91, prof. dept. pathology, 1974-91, prof. emeritus, 1991—. Prof. dept. pediats. Ohio State U. Coll. Medicine, Columbus, 1972-91, prof. emeritus, 1991—, prof. dept. pathology, 1974-91; cons. Brown Labs., Columbus, 1968-83, VA, Chillicothe, Ohio, 1980-84. Co-author: Manual of Practical Micro and General Procedures in Clinical Chemistry, 1962; editor: Standard Methods of Clinical Chemistry, Vol. 5, 1965, Pediatric Clinical Chemistry, 1st edit., 1977, 3d edit., 1989; co-editor: Selected Methods for the Small Clinical Chemistry Laboratory, 1982, Biography of Otto Folin, 1989; assoc. editor Geriatric Clin. Chemistry, 1994; contbr. articles to profl. jours. 1st lt. U.S. Army, 1942-46. Fellow AAAS; mem. Am. Chem. Soc., Am. Assn. Clin. Chemistry (Bernard Katchman award Ohio Valley sect. 1971, Fisher award

1981, Miles-Ames award 1990, sec. 1975-77, chmn. com. on archives, 1982-86, history divsn., 1992-99), Nat. Acad. Clin. Biochemists (hon., Johnson & Johnson award 1996), Midwest Assn. Toxicology (hon., award 1998). Democrat. Jewish. Avocations: gardening, history of clinical chemistry. Office: Childrens Hosp Dept Clin Biochemistry 700 Childrens Dr Columbus OH 43205-2696

MELAMED, LEO, investment company executive; b. Bialystok, Poland, Mar. 20, 1932; came to U.S., 1941, naturalized, 1950. s. Isaac M. and Fayga (Barakin) M.; m. Betty Sattler, Dec. 26, 1953; children: Idelle Sharon, Jordan Norman, David Jeffrey. Student, U. Ill., 1950-52; JD, John Marshall Law Sch., Chgo., 1955. Bar: Ill. 1955. Sr. ptnr. Melamed, Kravitz & Verson, Chgo., 1956-66; chmn., CEO Sakura Dellsher, Inc., 1965—2000, Melamed & Assoc., Inc., Chgo., 1993—. Mem. Chgo. Merc. Exch., 1953—, mem. bd. govs., 1967—91, chmn. emeritus, 1991—, chmn. bd., 1969—71, 1975—77, chmn. exec. com., 1985—91, also spl. counsel, apptd. sr. policy advisor, 1997—; chmn. bd. Internat. Monetary Market, 1972—75, spl. counsel, 1976—91; mem. Chgo. Bd. Trade, 1969—; mem. corp. adv. bd. U. Ill., Chgo., 1991—; mayor Chgo. Coun. Manpower and Econ. Advisors, 1972; adv. coun. mem. Grad. Sch. Bus. U. Chgo., 1980—. Author: (sci. fiction novel) The Tenth Planet, 1987, Leo Melamed on the Markets, 1993, Escape to the Futures, 1996; editor: The Merits of Flexible Exchange Rates, 1989. Trustee Trustee John Marshall Law Sch., 1991—; coun. mem. U.S. Holocaust Meml. Mus., 1992—, dir. Named Man of Yr., Israel Bonds, 1975; recipient Am. Jewish Com. Human Rights medallion, 1991. Fellow: Internat. Assn. Fin. Engrs. (sr.); mem.: ABA, Nat. Bur. Econ. Rsch. (bd. dirs.), Chgo. Bar Assn., Ill. Bar Assn., Am. Judicature Soc., Nat. Futures Assn. (chmn. 1982—89, spl. advisor 1989—), Am. Contract Bridge League (life master), Standard Club, Chgo. Club, Union League Club, Econs. Club Chgo. Avocations: writing, jogging. Office: Melamed & Assocs Inc 10 S Wacker Dr Ste 3275 Chicago IL 60606-7442

MELDMAN, ROBERT EDWARD, lawyer; b. Milw., Aug. 5, 2000; s. Louis Leo and Lillian (Gollusch) M.; m. Sandra Jane Setlick, July 24, 1960; children: Saree Beth, Richard Samuel. B.S., U. Wis., 1959; LL.B., Marquette U., 1962; LL.M. in Taxation, NYU, 1963. Bar: Wis. 1962, Fla. 1987, Colo. 1990, U.S. Ct. Fed. Claims, U.S. Tax Ct. 1963, U.S. Supreme Ct. 1970. Practice tax law, Milw., 1963—; pres. Meldman, Case & Weine, Ltd., 1975-85; dir. tax div. Mulcahy & Wherry, S.C., 1985-90; shareholder Reinhart, Boerner, Van Deuren, S.C., 1991—. Adj. prof. taxation U. Wis., Milw., 1970—2000, mem. tax adv. coun., 1978—2000; adj. prof. Marquette U. Sch. Law, Milw., 2001—, The U. of Queensland TeBeirne Sch. Law, 2002; mem. Internat. Revenue Svc. Midwest Citizen Adv. Panel, 2001—; sec. Profl. Inst. Tax Study, Inc., 1978—; bd. dirs. Wis. Bar Found., 1988—94; exec. in residence Deloitte & Touche Ctr. for Multistate Taxation, U. Wis., Milw., 1996—2000. Co-author: Federal Taxation Practice and Procedure, 1983, 1986, 1988, 1992, 1998, Practical Tactics for Dealing with the IRS, 1994, A Practical Guide to U.S. Taxation of International Transactions, 1996, 1997, 2000, Federal Taxation Practice and Procedure Study Guide/Quizzes, 1998; editor: Jour. Property Taxation, 1996—2002; mem. editl. bd.: Tax Litigation Alert, 1995—2000; contbr. articles to legal jours. Mem. IRS Taxpayer Advocacy Panel, 2001—. Recipient Adj. Taxation Faculty award UWM Tax Assn., 1987; named Outstanding Tax Profl. 1992 Corp. Reports Wis. Mag. and UWM Tax Assn. Fellow Am. Coll. Tax Coun.; mem. ABA, Fed. Bar Assn. (pres. Milw. chpt. 1966-67), Milw. Bar Assn. (chmn. tax sect. 1970-71), Wis. Bar Assn. (bd. dirs. tax sect. 1964-78, chmn. 1973-74), Internat. Bar Assn., The Law Assn. for Asia and the Pacific (chair tax sect. 2000—, dep. chair bus. law sect.), Marquette U. Law Alumni Assn. (bd. dirs. 1972-77), Milw. Athletic Club, Wis. Club, B'nai B'rith (trustee, Ralph Harris Meml. award Century Lodge 1969-70), Phi Delta Phi, Tau Epsilon Rho (chancellor Milw. chpt. 1969-71, supreme nat. chancellor 1975-76, v.p. Wis. chpt., tech. 1992-2000). Jewish (trustee congregation 1972-77). Home: 7455 N Skyline Ln Milwaukee WI 53217-3327 Office: 1000 N Water St Ste 2100 Milwaukee WI 53202-3197 E-mail: rmeldman@reinhartlaw.com.

MELE, JOANNE THERESA, dentist; b. Chgo., Dec. 5, 1943; d. Andrew and Josephine Jeanette (Calabrese)./ Diploma, St. Elizabeth's Sch. Nursing, Chgo., 1964; diploma in dental hygiene, Northwestern U., 1977; AS, Triton Coll., 1979; DDS, Loyola U., 1983. RN, dental hygienist. Staff nurse medicine/surgery St. Elizabeth's Hosp., Chgo., 1964-66, oper. room nurse, 1966-67; head nurse oper. room Cook County Hosp., 1967-76, head nurse ICU, 1976-77; dental hybienist Mele Dental Assocs., Ltd., Oakbrook, Ill., 1977-79, practice dentistry, 1983—. Clinical asst. prof. Loyola U., Chgo., 1988. Recipient Northwestern U. Dental Hygiene Clinic award, 1977; Dr. Duxler Humanitarian award scholar Loyola U., 1982. Mem. Chgo. Dental Soc., Ill. State Dental Soc., Acad. Gen. Dentistry, Am. Assn. Women Dentists, Acad. operative Dentistry, Am. Prosthodontic Soc., Psu Omege (Kappa chpt.). Roman Catholic. Avocations: reading, music, golfing, jogging, skiing. Home: 3 N Tower Rd Oak Brook IL 60523

MELHORN, WILTON NEWTON, geosciences educator; b. Sistersville, W.Va., July 8, 1921; s. Ralph Wilton and Pauline (Jones) M.; m. Agnes Leigh Beck, Aug. 25, 1961; children— Kristina L., Kimberly M. B.S., Mich. State U., 1942, M.S., 1951, N.Y. U., 1943; Ph.D., U. Mich., 1955. Hydrogeologist Mich. Geol. Survey, Lansing, 1946-49; hydrologist U.S. Weather Bur., Indpls., 1949-50; asst., then asso. prof. engring. geology Purdue U., Lafayette, Ind., 1954-70, head dept. geoscis., 1967-70, prof., 1970-91, prof. emeritus, 1991—. Vis. prof. U. Ill. at Urbana, 1960-61, U. Nev., Reno, 1971-72, adj. prof., 1973-82; geol. cons. Cook County Hwy Commn., Chgo., 1955-56, Martin-Marietta Corp., Balt., 1964-66, Calif. Nuclear, Inc., Lafayette, 1966-68; hydrology cons. Town of Shadelund, Ind., 1998-99. Editor 3 books; contbr. articles to tech. jours. Served to maj. USAAF, 1942-46. Fellow Geol. Soc. Am., AAAS, Ind. Acad. Scis. (pres. 1988, exec. officer 1992-94), Explorers Club; mem. Am. Assn. Petroleum Geologists, Soc. Econ. Geologists and Paleontologists, Speleological Soc., Mich. Acad. Arts, Sci. and Letters, Am. Meteorol. Soc., Sigma Xi, Sigma Gamma Epsilon. Office: Purdue Univ Dept Earth & Atmospheric Sc West Lafayette IN 47907 Home: 6500 W Hazelrigg Rd Thorntown IN 46071-9245

MELLEMA, DONALD EUGENE, retired radio news reporter and anchor; b. Chgo., Mar. 30, 1937; s. Raymond Cornelius and Dorothy Sofia (Miller) M.; m. Freda Dieterlen Mellema, Sept. 23, 1961; children: Darryl Emerson, Duane Edward. BA in Speech, Beloit (Wis.) Coll., 1959. News dir. WGEZ Radio, Beloit, 1959; evening host, newsman WOSH Radio, Oshkosh, Wis., 1959-63; morning host, newsman WANE Radio, Ft. Wayne, Ind., 1963-65; news dir. WATI Radio, Indpls., 1965-67; news writer WGN Radio, Chgo., 1967-69; news reporter, anchor WBBM Radio, 1969-96; ret., 1996. Mem. publs. adv. bd., pres's adv. coun., cons. Beloit Coll., 1996-2000, also profl.-in-residence. Speaker, motivator Chgo. Pub. Sch. Youth Motivation Program, 1993-96; advisor, cons. media rels. to various police and civic orgns.; commr., unit leader Boy Scouts Am., 1971-81; ch. deacon Park Ridge (Ill.) Presbyn. Ch., 1980-83. Recipient regional award Radio TV News Dirs. Assn., 1994, Newsfinder award AP, 1995, career recognition award Chgo. Police Dept., 1997, Mark Twain award Ill. AP, 1997; named to Taft H.S. Hall of Fame, 1995. Mem. Ill. News Broadcasters Assn. (Silver Dome 1st Place award 1994), Soc. Profl. Journalists (Peter Lisagor award 1991, 96), Am. Legion. Republican. Avocations: woodworking, reading, photography, birding, travel. E-mail: DONMELLEMA@NETSCAPE.NET.

MELLI, MARYGOLD SHIRE, law educator; b. Rhinelander, Wis., Feb. 8, 1926; d. Osborne and May (Bonnie) Shire; m. Joseph Alexander Melli, Apr. 8, 1950; children: Joseph, Sarah Bonnie, Sylvia Anne, James Alexander. BA, U. Wis., 1947, LLB, 1950. Bar: Wis. 1950. Dir. children's code revision Wis. Legis. Coun., Madison, 1950-53; exec. dir. Wis. Jud. Coun., 1955-59; asst. prof. law U. Wis., 1959-66, assoc. prof., 1966-67, prof., 1967-84, Voss-Bascom prof., 1985-93, emerita, 1993—. Assoc. dean U. Wis., 1970-72, rsch. affiliate Inst. for Rsch. on Poverty, 1980—; mem. spl. rev. bd. Dept. Health and Social Svcs., State of Wis., Madison, 1973—. Author: (pamphlet) The Legal Status of Women in Wisconsin, 1977, (book) Wisconsin Juvenile Court Practice, 1978, rev. edit., 1983, (with others) Child Support & Alimony, 1988, The Case for Transracial Adoption, 1994; co-editor: Child Support: The Next Frontier, 1999; contbr. articles to profl. jours. Bd. dirs. Am. Humane Assn., 1985-95; chair A Fund for Women, Madison, Wis., 2002. Named one of five Outstanding Young Women in Wis., Jaycees, 1961; rsch. grantee NSF, 1983; recipient Belle Case LaFollette award for outstanding svc. to the profession, 1994, award for Outstanding Contbn. to Advancement of Women in Higher Edn., 1991, award for Lifelong Contbn. to Advancement of Women in the Legal Prof., 1994, Rotary Sr. Svc. award, Madison, Wis., 2002. Fellow Am. Acad. Matrimonial Lawyers (exec. editor jour. 1985-90); mem. Am. Law Inst. (cons. project on law of family dissolution), Internat. Soc. Family Law (v.p. 1994-2000, mem. exec. coun.), Wis. State Bar Assn. (reporter family law sect.), Nat. Conf. Bar Examiners (chmn. bd. mgrs. 1989). Democrat. Roman Catholic. Avocations: jogging, swimming, collecting art. Home: 2904 Waunona Way Madison WI 53713-2238 Office: U Wis Law Sch Madison WI 53706 E-mail: msmelli@facstaff.wisc.edu.

MELLOY, MICHAEL J. federal judge; b. 1948; m. Jane Anne Melloy; children: Jennifer, Katherine, Bridget. BA, Loras Coll., 1970; JD, U. Iowa, 1974. With O'Conner & Thomas P.C. (formerly O'Conner, Thomas, Wright, Hammer, Bertsch & Norby, Dubuque, Iowa, 1974-86; judge U.S. Bankruptcy Ct. (no. dist.) Iowa, 1986-92, U.S. Dist. Ct. (no. dist.) Iowa, Cedar Rapids, 1992—. With U.S. Army, 1970-72, USAR, 1972-76. Mem. ABA, Comml. Law League Am., Nat. Conf. Bankruptcy Judges, Eighth Cir. Judicial Coun. (bankruptcy judge rep., bankruptcy com.), Iowa State Bar Assn. (coun. mem. bankruptcy and comml. law sect.), Ill. State Bar Assn., Dubuque County Bar Assn., Linn County Bar Assn., Mason L. Ladd Inn of Ct., Rotary. Office: US Dist Ct 101 1st St SE Ste 304 Cedar Rapids IA 52401-1202

MELLUM, GALE ROBERT, lawyer; b. Duluth, Minn., July 5, 1942; s. Lester Andrew and Doris Esther (Smith) M.; m. Julie Murdoch Swanstrom, July 23, 1966; children: Eric Scott, Wendy Jane. BA summa cum laude, U. Minn., 1964, JD magna cum laude, 1968. Bar: Minn. 1968. Assoc. Faegre & Benson, Mpls., 1968-75, ptnr., 1976—, mem. mgmt. com., 1986-98. Planning com. Garret Corp. and Securities Law Inst., Northwestern U. Law Sch., 1984—; adv. bd. Quali Tech Inc., Chaska, Minn., 1985-98, bd. dirs.; bd. dirs. The Tesseract Group, Inc., Mpls.; corp. sec. Excelsior-Henderson Motorcycle Mfg. Co., Belle Plaine, Minn., 1997-2000. Hockey chmn. LARC Bd., Mpls., 1980—85. Mem. ABA (fed. securities regulation com.), Minn. Bar Assn., Hennepin County Bar Assn. (securities regulation com.). Republican. Lutheran. Avocations: tennis, golf, snow and water skiing, handball, boating. Home: 3833 Thomas Ave S Minneapolis MN 55410 Office: Faegre & Benson 2200 Wells Fargo Ctr 90 S 7th St Ste 2200 Minneapolis MN 55402-3901 E-mail: gmellum@faegre.com.

MELSHER, GARY WILLIAM, lawyer; b. Cleve., Mar. 8, 1939; BS, Ohio State U., 1961; JD, Case Western Reserve U., 1964. Bar: Ohio 1964. Ptnr. Jones, Day, Reavis & Pogue, Cleve. Mem. Order of Coif. Office: Jones Day Reavis & Pogue North Point 901 Lakeside Ave E Cleveland OH 44114-1190

MELSOP, JAMES WILLIAM, architect; b. Columbus, Ohio, June 2, 1939; s. James Brendan and Juanita Kathryn (Van Scoy) M.; m. Sandra Lee Minnich, Sept. 21, 1957; children: Deborah Lee, Susan Elizabeth, Kathryn Anne. BArch, Ohio State U., 1964; MArch, Harvard U., 1965; MBA, U. Chgo., 1975. Reg. architect, profl. engr. Architect The Austin Co., Chgo., 1967-69, mgr. bus. devel., 1969-74, asst. dist. mgr., 1974-75; pres., mng. dir. Austin Brasil, Sao Paulo, 1975-78; asst. dist. mgr. The Austin Co., Roselle, N.J., 1978-80, dist. mgr. Detroit, 1980-81, v.p., dist. mgr. Cleve., 1986, group v.p., dir., 1986—, exec. v.p. chief oper. officer, 1992, pres., CEO, 1992—, also chmn., bd. dirs.; founder, prin. owner Austin Holdings, Inc., 1997—. Named E&Y Entrepreneur of Yr., 1999. Mem. Am. Inst. Architects., Harvard Club N.Y.C., Presidents' Club, Ohio State U. (Disting. Alumnus award 1989). Home: 3165 Trillium Trail Cleveland OH 44124-5205 Office: Austin Co 3650 Mayfield Rd Cleveland OH 44121-1791

MELTON, DAVID REUBEN, lawyer; b. Milw., Apr. 4, 1952; s. Howard and Evelyn Frances (Cohen) M.; m. Nancy Hillary Segal, May 22, 1981; children: Michelle, Hannah. BA, U. Wis., 1974; JD, U. Chgo., 1977. Bar: Ill. 1977, U.S. Dist. Ct. (no. dist.) Ill. 1977, U.S. Ct. Appeals (7th cir.) 1981, U.S. Supreme Ct. 1982, U.S. Fed. Cir. Ct. Appeals, 1991. Assoc. Karon, Morrison & Savikas, Ltd., Chgo., 1977-83; ptnr. Karon, Morrison & Saviskas, Ltd., 1983-87, Karon, Savikas & Horn, Ltd., Chgo., 1987-88, Keck, Mahin & Cate, Chgo., 1988-96; counsel Mayer, Brown & Platt 1996-99, ptnr., 2000—. Office: Mayer Brown & Platt 190 S Lasalle St Ste 3900 Chicago IL 60603-3410 E-mail: dmelton@mayerbrown.com.

MELTON, EMORY LEON, lawyer, state legislator, publisher; b. McDowell, Mo., June 20, 1923; s. Columbus Right and Pearly Susan (Wise) M; m. Jean Sanders, June 19, 1949; children: Stanley Emory, John Russell. Student, Monett Jr. Coll., 1940-41, S.W. Mo. State U., 1941-42; LLB, U. Mo., 1945. Bar: Mo. 1944. Pvt. practice, Cassville, Mo., 1947—; pres. Melton Publs., Inc., 1959—; pros. atty. Barry County (Mo.), 1947-51; mem. Mo. Senate, 1973-97. Chmn. Barry County republican Com., 1964-68. Served with AUS, 1945-46. Recipient Meritorious Pub. Svc. award St. Lousi Globe-Democrat, 1976. Mem. Mo. Bar Assn., Lions, Masons. Office: PO Box 488 Cassville MO 65625-0488

MELTON, OWEN B., JR. banking company executive; b. 1946; BS, Indiana U., 1973. Chief adminstrv. officer Fed. Home Loan Bank Bd., Washington, 1977-79; exec. v.p. Skokie (Ill.) Fed. Savs. and Loan, 1979-81; chmn. bd. dirs., pres., chief exec. officer Diamond Savs. and Loan Co., 1981-83; with First Ind. Bank, Indpls., 1972—; now pres., CEO, also bd. dirs. First Ind. Fed. Savs. Bank. Served with USAF, 1967-70. Office: 1st Ind Bank 135 N Pennsylvania St Indianapolis IN 46204-2400

MELTZER, BERNARD DAVID, law educator; b. Phila., Nov. 21, 1914; s. Julius and Rose (Welkov) M.; m. Jean Sulzberger, Jan. 17, 1947; children: Joan, Daniel, Susan. A.B., U. Chgo., 1935, J.D., 1937; LL.M., Harvard U., 1938. Bar: Ill. 1938. Atty., spl. asst. to chmn. SEC, 1938-40; assoc. firm Mayer, Meyer, Austrian & Platt, Chgo., 1940; spl. asst. to asst. sec. state, also acting chief fgn. funds control div. State 1941-43; asst. trial counsel U.S. prosecution Internat. Nuremberg War Trials, 1945-46; from professorial lectr. to disting. svc. prof. law emeritus U. Chgo. Law Sch., 1946—; counsel Vedder, Price, Kaufman & Kamnholz, Chgo., 1954-55, Sidley and Austin, Chgo., 1987-89. Hearing commr. NPA, 1952-53; labor arbitrator; spl. master U.S. Ct. Appeals for D.C., 1963-64; bd. publs. U. Chgo., 1965-67, chmn., 1967-68; mem. Gov. Ill. Adv. Commn. Labor-Mgmt. Policy for Pub. Employees in Ill., 1966-67, Ill. Civil Service Commn., 1968-69; cons. U.S. Dept. Labor, 1969-70 Author: Supplementary Materials on International Organizations, 1948, (with W.G. Katz) Cases and Materials on Business Corporations, 1949, Labor Law Cases, Materials and Problems, 1970, supplement, 1972, 75, 2d edit., 1977, supplements, 1980, 82 (with S. Henderson), 3d edit. (with S. Henderson), 1985, supplement, 1988; also articles. Bd. dirs. Hyde Park Community Conf., 1954-56, S.E. Chgo. Commn., 1956-57. Served to lt. (j.g.) USNR, 1943-46. Mem. ABA (co-chmn. com. devel. law under NLRA 1959-60, mem. spl. com. transp. strikes), Ill. Bar Assn., Chgo. Bar Assn. (bd. mgrs. 1972-73), Am. Law Inst., Coll. Labor and Employment Lawyers, Am. Acad. Arts and Scis., Order of Coif, Phi Beta Kappa Home: 1219 E 50th St Chicago IL 60615-2908 Office: U Chgo Law Sch 1111 E 60th St Chicago IL 60637-2776

MELTZER, BRIAN, lawyer; b. Chgo., Apr. 15, 1944; s. Maurice and Ethel (Goldstein) M.; m. Rosemary Labriola, Sept. 11, 1982; children: Stuart Joseph, Alan Phillip, Martin Angelo. BA in Math., Cornell U., 1966; JD, Harvard U., 1969. Bar: Ill. 1969. Assoc. atty. D'ancona & Pflaum, Chgo., 1969-72; assoc. then ptnr. Schwartz & Freeman, 1972-88; ptnr. Keck, Mahin & Cate, 1988-95, Meltzer, Purtill & Stelle, Schaumburg, Ill., 1996—. Office: 1515 E Woodfield Rd Schaumburg IL 60173-6046

MELTZER, DAVID BRIAN, retail executive; b. Phila., Apr. 15, 1929; s. Abraham L. and Minerva M. (Manko) M.; student U. Chgo., 1946-49; B.S., N.Y. U., 1950; children— Robert K., Jeffrey K. Mem. Mandels Tng. Squad, 1947-49; with Evans, Inc., Chgo., 1951— , mdse. mgr., 1956-58, v.p., 1958-63, exec. v.p., 1963-64, pres., 1964-88, chief exec. officer, 1968-88, chmn. bd., 1976— . Chmn. FICA, Internat., Info. Coun. Am., Fur Am.; bd. dirs., exec. com. State St. Council; bd. trustees Lincoln Acad. of Ill. Served to lt. Q.M.C., AUS, 1949-51. Named Man of Year in fur industry, Fur Trade Found., 1993; recipient Prime Minister's medal State of Israel, 1977. Mem. Nat. Retail Mchts. Assn. (dir. Jewish Clubs: Standard, Mid Am., Shriners. Office: Evans Inc 36 S State St Ste 600 Chicago IL 60603-2604

MELVIN, STEWART WAYNE, engineering educator; BS in Agrl. Engring., Iowa State U., 1964, MS in Agrl. Engring., 1967, PhD, 1970. Registered agrl. engr., Iowa. With Soil Conservation Svc., USDA, 1963—67; asst. prof. Colo. State U., 1969-70, Iowa State U., Ames, 1970-74, assoc. prof. agrl. engring., 1974-79, prof. agrl. engring., 1979—, head agrl. engring., 1994—2001. Vis. prof. Silsoe Coll., Eng., 1985-86. Contbr. numerous articles to profl. jours. Fellow Am. Soc. Agrl. Engrs.; mem. Internat. Soil and Tillage Rsch. Orgn., Soil and Water Conservation Soc. Am., Am. Soc. Engring. Edn., Phi Kappa Phi, Tau Beta Pi, Gamma Sigma Delta, Sigma Xi, Epsilon Sigma Phi, Alpha Epsilon. Office: Iowa State U Agrl-Biosys Engring Dept 104 Davidson Hl Ames IA 50011-0001 Fax: (515) 294-4250. E-mail: swmelvin@iastate.edu.

MENARD, JOHN R. lumber company/homeimprovement retailer executive; b. 1940; Pres., ceo Menard Inc., Eau Claire, Wis., 1960—; owner Menard Racing, 1979—. Office: Menard Inc 4777 Menard Dr Eau Claire WI 54703-9625

MENCER, JETTA, lawyer; b. Coshocton, Ohio, Apr. 7, 1959; d. William J. and Virginia M. (Fry) M. BS, Ohio State U., 1980, JD, 1983. Bar: Ohio, U.S. Dist. Ct. (so. dist.) Ohio. Assoc. Berry, Owens & Manning, Coshocton, 1983-86; asst. pros. atty. Coshocton County, 1983-86, Licking County, Newark, 1986-88, asst. atty. gen., 1988-95; pvt. practice Coshocton, 1995-96; prosecuting atty. Coshocton County (Ohio) Prosecutor's Office, 1997-2001; atty. Lee Smith & Assocs., Columbus, Ohio, 2001—. Treas. Coshocton County Dem. Cen. & Exec. Coms., 1984-86; chmn., 1986-88; sec., bd. dirs. Heart Ohio Girl Scout Council, Inc., Zanesville, Ohio, 1985-87; fin. chmn., bd. dirs. YMCA, Coshocton, 1985-87. Mem. Ohio State Bar Assn., Coshocton County Bar Assn., Lions Club. Democrat. Methodist. Office: 929 Harrison St Columbus OH 43215 E-mail: jmencer@clover.net.

MENCHIK, PAUL LEONARD, economist, educator; b. N.Y.C., Sept. 16, 1947; s. Irving and Eleanor (Swedlow) M.; m. Bettie Ann Landauer, May 28, 1972; children: Daniel Aron, Jeremy Matthew. BA, SUNY, Binghamton, 1969; AM, U. Pa., 1971, PhD, 1976. Lectr. Rutgers Coll., New Brunswick, N.J., 1974-76; rsch. assoc. Inst. for Rsch. on Poverty, U. Wis., Madison, 1976-79; prof. dept. econs. Mich. State U., East Lansing, 1979—, chairperson dept. econs., 1992-96; sr. economist, econ. policy Office Mgmt. & Budget, Washington, 1990-91. Acad. visitor Stanford (Calif.) U., 1980, London Sch. Econs., 1987-88; vis. assoc. prof. U. Pa., Phila., 1982-83; vis. scholar Congrl. Budget Office, 1997-98; cons., advisor in field. Mem. editl. bd. Jour. Income Distbn., Amsterdam, 1992—; contbr. articles to profl. jours. Grantee NSF, Social Security Adminstrn., U.S. Dept. Health and Human Svcs.; recipient Best Article of Yr. award Econ. Inquiry, 1987. Mem. Am. Econ. Assn., Nat. Tax Assn., Nat. Bur. Econ. Rsch. Conf. on Income & Wealth. Avocations: bowling, racquetball, golf, travel, camping. Office: Mich State U 101 Marshall Hall E Circle Dr East Lansing MI 48824

MENDELSOHN, ZEHAVAH WHITNEY, data processing executive; b. Houston, Nov. 22, 1956; d. Alfred Peter and Sarah (Carsey) Whitney. AA, College of DuPage, 1988; BA, Nat. Louis U., 1989. Cert. quality analyst, cert. software test engr. Mgmt. analyst U. Ill., Abraham Lincoln Sch. Medicine, Chgo., 1976-83; sr. analyst quality assurance Ofcl. Airline Guides, Oak Brook, Ill., 1983-95; dir. application quality mgmt U.S. Cellular, 1995—. Mem. Quality Assurance Inst., Am. Soc. for Quality Control, Chgo. Quality Assurance Assn., Chicagoland Handicapped Skiers (pres. 1986-87, 89-91), Profl. Ski Instrs. Am. Avocations: skiing, roses, golf, birdwatching. Office: US Cellular 1101 Tower Ln Bensenville IL 60106

MENEFEE, FREDERICK LEWIS, advertising executive; b. Arkansas City, Kans., Oct. 22, 1932; s. Arthur LeRoy and Vera Mae (Rather) M.; m. Margot Leuze, Sept. 16, 1955; children: Gregory S., Christina Menefee-Anderson. AA, Arkansas City Jr. Coll., 1952; BA, U. Wichita, 1958. Sports editor, bus. mgr. Ark. Light and Tiger Tales, 1949-52; sports reporter Arkansas City Daily Traveler, 1950-52; advt. mgr. Derby Star, Haysville Herald and Sedgwick County News, 1956-57; v.p., account exec. Associated Advt. Agy., 1958-64; with McCormick-Armstrong Adv. Agy. (now Menefee and Ptnrs., Inc.), Wichita, 1964—, agy. mgr., 1964—, account supr., 1965—, gen. mgr., 1972—, pres., CEO, 1979—, chmn. bd., 1989-96. Vol. Wichita River Festival, 1974-98; pub. rels. chmn. Wichita Centennial Nat. Art Show and Exhibit, 1969-70. With AUS, 1953-55. Named Advt. Man of Yr., Advt. Club of Wichita, 1964, Advt. Man of Yr., 9th Dist. Am. Advt. Fedn. Colo., Nebr., Iowa, Mo., Kans., 1965, Adm. Windwagon Smith III Wichita Festivals Inc., 1976. Mem. Am. Advt. Fedn. (nat. bd. dirs. 1969-70, dist. gov. 1968-69, chmn. nat. coun. govs. 1969-70), Wichita Wagonmasters (founding mem., capt. 1974-75, dir., charter, founder, commodore 1999), Wichita Advt. Club (bd. dirs. 1958-68), v.p. awards 1961-62, v.p. membership 1962, v.p. programs 1963, pres. 1964-65), PAWS Inc. (founder, 1st pres. 1978-86), Alpha Delta Sigma (pres. 1957-58, Outstanding Svc. award 1958), Quill & Scroll. Home: 2235 Red Bud Ln Wichita KS 67204-5346 Office: Menefee & Ptnrs Inc 1065 N Topeka St Wichita KS 67214-2913

MENG, JOHN C. food service executive; b. 1944; BA, Wabash Coll., 1966; MBA, Washington U., 1967. From supr. to plant mgr. Schreiber Foods, Green Bay, Wis., 1968-74, v.p., sec. treas., 1974-77, sr. v.p. fin., 1977-81, exec. v.p., 1981-85, pres., COO, 1985-89, CEO, 1989-99. Bd. dirs. WPS Resources, Corp., Green Bay. Office: 700 N Adams St Green Bay WI 54301-5145

MENGEDOTH, DONALD ROY, commercial banker; b. Naperville, Ill., Aug. 10, 1944; s. Orville Gustav and Bernice Lydia (Fries) M.; m. Stacy K. Halverson; children: Paul Bernard, Daniel Lawrence, Mary Bernice. BS, Marquette U., 1968, MBA, 1973. Ops. officer 1st Bank, N.A.-Milw., 1968-69, asst. v.p., 1969-71, v.p., 1971-73, sr. v.p., 1973-79; v.p. 1st Bank

System, Inc., Mpls., 1979-82, sr. v.p., 1983-87, pres., CEO, 1987—2000; chmn. Cmty. First Bankshares Inc., Fargo, ND, 1987—. Bd. dirs. Treasure Enterprises, Inc., Vail Banks Inc. Adv. bd. United Way Cass-Clay Campaign, Fargo, 1988-89; chmn. Cmty. 1st Polit. Action Com., Fargo, 1988-89; bd. dirs. Fargo Cath. Schs. Network Found., 1989-92; bd. dirs., vice chmn. Red River Zool. Soc., 1993-96; chmn. Diocesan God's Gift Appeals, Fargo, 1989. Mem. Am. Bankers Assn. (govt. rels. coun., pres. 2000-2001), Am. Mgmt. Assn., N.D. Bankers Assn., S.D. Bankers Assn., Greater N.D. Assn., Fargo Country Club. Avocations: tennis, golf, hunting, reading. Office: Cmty 1st Bankshares 520 Main Ave Fargo ND 58124-0001 E-mail: don_mengedoth@cfbx.com.

MENGEL, DAVID BRUCE, agronomy and soil science educator; b. East Chicago, Ind., May 1, 1948; s. Bill M. and Thelma Lee (Miller) M.; m. Susan Kay Haverstock, Aug. 30, 1968; children: David, Erin. BS in Agricultural Edn., Purdue U., 1970, MS in Agronomy, 1972; PhD in Soil Sci., N.C. State U., 1975. Cert. profl. agronomist, soil scientist. Asst. prof. agronomy La. State U., Crowley, 1975-79, Purdue U., West Lafayette, Ind., 1979-82, assoc. prof., 1982-86, prof. agronomy, 1986-98; prof., head agronomy Kans. State U., Manhattan, Kans., 1998—. Mem. Am Soc. Agronomy, Soil Sci. Soc. Am., Internat. Soil Sci. Soc., Sigma Xi, Gamma Sigma Delta, Epsilon Sigma Phi, Delta Tau Delta. Avocations: fishing, woodworking. Office: Plant Sci Ctr Dept Agronomy Kans State U 2004 Throckmorton Manhattan KS 66506-5501 E-mail: dmengel@ksu.edu.

MENGELING, CARL F. bishop; b. Oct. 22, 1930; Ordained priest Roman Cath. Ch., 1957. Priest Archdiocese of Gary, Ind., 1957; consecrated bishop, 1995; bishop Archdiocese of Lansing, Mich., 1996—. Office: 300 W Ottawa St Lansing MI 48933-1530

MENGLER, THOMAS M. dean; b. May 18, 1953; BA in Philosophy magna cum laude, Carleton Coll., 1975; MA in Philosophy, U. Tex., 1977, JD, 1981. Bar: Ill., Tex., D.C., U.S. Ct. Appeals (5th, 7th and 10th cirs.), U.S. Dist. Ct. (we. dist.) Tex. Law clk. to Hon. James K. Logan U.S. Ct. Appeals for 10thCir., Olathe, Kans., 1980-81; assoc. atty. Arnold & Porter, Washington, 1982-83; asst. atty. gen. Office of Atty. Gen. of Tex., Austin, 1983-85; asst. prof. law U. Ill. Coll. Law, Champaign, 1985-89, assoc. prof., 1989-91, prof. law, 1991—, assoc. dean for acad. affairs, 1992-93, dean, 1993—2002; dean, prof. law U. St. Thomas Sch. Law, Mpls., 2002—. Contbr. numerous articles to profl. jours. Mem. ABA, Ill. State Bar Assn., Order of Coif, Phi Beta Kappa. Office: Univ St Thomas Sch Law Mail TMH 440 1000 LaSalle Ave Minneapolis MN 55403-2005

MENNINGER, ROY WRIGHT, medical foundation executive, psychiatrist; b. Topeka, Oct. 27, 1926; s. William Claire and Catharine (Wright) M.; m. Beverly Joan Miller, Mar. 4, 1973; children: Heather, Ariel, Bonar, Eric, Brent, Frederick, Elizabeth. AB, Swarthmore (Pa.) Coll., 1947; MD, Cornell U., 1951; DHL, Ottawa (Kans.) U., 1977; LittD, William Jewell Coll., Liberty Mo., 1985. Diplomate Am. Bd. Psychiatry and Neurology, 1959. Intern N.Y. Hosp., 1951-52; resident in psychiatry Boston State Hosp., 1952-53, Boston Psychopathic Hosp., 1953-56; from resident psychiatrist to assoc. med. psychiatrist Peter Bent Brigham Hosp., Boston, 1956-61; teaching and rsch. fellow Harvard U. Med. Sch., 1956-61; staff psychiatrist Menninger Found., Topeka, 1961-63, dir. dept. preventive psychiatry, 1963-67, pres., CEO, 1967-93, chmn. trustees, 1991—. Bd. dirs. Bank IV Topeka N.A., CML Corp., The New Eng., U.S. Behavioral Health; mem. Karl Menninger Sch. Psychiatry, Topeka, 1972—, Ind. Sector, 1990—; clin. prof. psychiatry U. Kans. Med. Ctr., Wichita, 1977—; cons. Colmery-O'Neil VA Med. Ctr., Topeka, 1979—. Author: Trends in American Psychiatry: Implication for Psychiatry in Japan; co-author: The Medical Marriage, 1988, The Psychology of Postponement in the Medical Marriage; cons. editor Jour. Medical Aspects Human Sexuality, 1967-90; editor adv. bd. Parents mag., 1966-80, Clin. Psychiatry News, 1973—; reviewer Am. Jour. Psychiatry, 1980—. Mem. sponsoring com. Inst. Am. Democracy, 1967-70; mem. adv. group Horizons '76 Am. Revolution Bicentennial Commn.; adv. bd., steering com. Topeka Inst. Urban Affairs, 1967-70; adv. bd. Highland Park-Pierce Neighborhood House, Topeka, 1967-70; bd. dirs. Shawnee council Campfire Girls, Topeka, 1962-69, A.K. Rice Inst., Washington, Sex Info. and Edn. Council U.S., 1972-73, mem. edn. com., long range planning com., 1972-73; bd. dirs. Goals for Topeka, Topeka Inst. Urban Affairs, 1969-74, v.p., 1973; med. adv. com. VA Hosp., 1972-78; mem. Gov.'s Com. on Criminal Adminstrn., 1971-74; trustee People-to-People, Kansas City, Mo., 1967-69, Baker U., 1968-72, Midwest Research Inst., 1967-1986, 86—, mem. exec. com., 1970-86; vis. lectr. Fgn. Service Inst., State Dept., 1963-66; chmn. social issues com. Group Advancement Psychiatry, 1972-82; community adv. bd. Kans. Health Workers Union, 1968-70; adv. com. to bd. dirs. New Eng. Mut. Life Ins. Co., 1968-70. With U.S. Army, 1953-55. Recipient Disting. Svs. citation U. Kans., 1985; Pacific Rim Coll. Psychiatry fellow. Fellow Am. Psychiat. Assn. (life), Joint Info. Svc. (exec. com.), Am. Coll. Psychiatry, Am. Orthopsychiat. Assn., Am. Coll. Mental Health Adminstrs.; mem. AAAS, Northeastern Group Psychotherapy (hon.), Physicians Social Responsibility, Kans. Psychiat. Soc., Greater Topeka C. of C. (dir.). Episcopalian. Avocations: stamp collecting, chamber music, microcomputers. Office: Menninger Found PO Box 829 Topeka KS 66601-0829

MENNINGER, WILLIAM WALTER, psychiatrist; b. Topeka, Oct. 23, 1931; s. William Claire and Catharine Louisa (Wright) M.; m. Constance Arnold Libbey, June 15, 1953; children: Frederick Prince, John Alexander, Eliza Wright, Marian Stuart, William Libbey, David Henry. AB, Stanford U., 1953; MD, Cornell U., 1957; LittD (hon.), Middlebury Coll., 1982; DSc (hon.), Washburn U., 1982; LHD (hon.), Ottawa U., 1986; LLD (hon.), Heidelberg Coll., 1993. Diplomate Am. Bd. Psychiatry and Neurology, Am. Bd. Forensic Psychiatry. Intern Harvard Med. Service, Boston City Hosp., 1957-58; resident in psychiatry Menninger Sch. Psychiatry, 1958-61; chief med. officer, psychiatrist Fed. Reformatory, El Reno, Okla., 1961-63; assoc. psychiatrist Peace Corps, 1963-64; staff psychiatrist Menninger Found., Topeka, 1965—, coordinator for devel., 1967-69, dir. law and psychiatry, 1981-85, dir. dept. edn., dean Karl Menninger Sch. Psychiatry and Mental Health Scis., 1984-90, exec. v.p., chief of staff, 1984-93, CEO, 1993—2001, pres., 1993—96, 1999—2001, chmn. trustees, 2001—; clin. supr. Topeka State Hosp., 1969-70, sect. dir., 1970-72, asst. supt., clin., dir. residency tng., 1972-81; pres. Menninger Clinic, Topeka, 1991-96; staff Stormont-Vail Hosp., 1984-94, assoc., 1994—. Clin. prof. Kans. U. Med. Coll.; adj. prof. Washburn U.; mem. adv. bd. Nat. Inst. Corrections, 1975-88 , chmn., 1980-84; cons. U.S. Bur. Prisons; mem. Fed. Prison Facilities Planning Council, 1970-73; mem. adv. bd. FirstStar Bank, Topeka, 1999—. : syndicated columnist In-Sights, 1975—83; author: Happiness Without Sex an dOther Things Too Good to Miss, 1976, Caution: Living May Be Hazardous, 1978, Behavioral Science and the Secret Service, 1981, Chronic Mental Patient II, 1987; editor: Psychiatry Digest, 1971—74, Bull. of Menninger Clinic, 2001—; contbr. articles to profl. jours., chpts. to books. Mem. nat. adv. coun. Boy Scouts Am., 1970—, chmn., 1980—85, mem. nat. exec. bd., 1980—90, mem. nat. adv. coun., 1990—; bd. dirs. Nat. Com. Prevention Child Abuse, 1975—83; mem. nat. adv. health coun. HEW, 1967—71; mem. Nat. Commn. Causes and Prevention Violence, 1968—69; rsch. adv. com. U.S. Secret Svc., 1990—; pres. Jayhawk coun. Boy Scouts Am., 1998—2001; mem. Kans. Gov.'s Adv. Commn. Mental Health, Mental Retardation an dCmty. Mental Health Svcs., 1983—90, Kans. Gov.'s Penal Planning Coun., 1970; chmn. Kans. Gov.'s Criminal Justice Coun., 1970; trustee Kenworthy-Swift Found., 1980—; active Kans. Gov.'s Commn. on Crime Reduction and Prevention/Koch Commn., 1994—98; dir. Police Found., Washington, 1996—, Koch Crime Inst., 1998—2000; trustee Midwest Rsch. Inst., Kansas City, Mo., 1996—; ruling elder 1st Presbyn. Ch., Topeka, 1992—95. Fellow ACP, Am. Psychiat. Assn. (chmn. com. on chronically mentally ill 1984-86, chmn. Guttmacher award bd. 1990-96), Am. Coll. Psychiatrists; mem. AAAS, AMA, Group for Advancement of Psychiatry (chmn. com. mental health svcs. 1974-77, 91—), Inst. Medicine NAS, Am. Psychoanalytic Assn. (chmn. com. on psychoanalysis, community and society 1984-93), Am. Acad. Psychiatry and Law, Stanford (Univ.) Assocs. Office: Menninger Found PO Box 829 Topeka KS 66601-0829

MENZNER, DONALD, food products executive; CEO Marathon (Wis.) Cheese. Office: Marathon Cheese 304 East St Marathon WI 54448

MEOLA, TONY, professional soccer player, actor; b. Belleville, N.J., Feb. 21, 1969; s. Vincent and Maria Meola; m. Colleen Meola; 1 child, Jonathan. Student, U. Virginia, 1986-89. Goalkeeper CONCACAF World Cup Qualifying Games, 1989, U.S. World Cup Team, 1990, Brighton Football Club, England, 1990, Fort Lauderdale Strikers, Amer. Prof. Soccer League, 1991, U.S. Nat. Team, 1992-94, Long Island Roughriders, 1994-95, U.S. World Cup Team, 1994, NY-NJ MetroStars, Secaucus, 1996-98, Kansas City (Mo.) Wizards, 1998—. Drafted ctr. fielder N.Y. Yankees; tried out as placekicker for N.Y. Jets, 1994. Appeared in play Tony N' Tina's Wedding, 1995. Named Hermann Trophy winner, Mo. Athletic Club Player of Yr., 1989, MVP U.S. Cup, 1993. Achievements include being a mem. N.J. State H.S. Soccer Champions, 1986, NCAA Division I Co-Champions, 1989. Office: care Kansas City Wizards Two Arrowhead Dr Kansas City MO 64129

MERANUS, LEONARD STANLEY, lawyer; b. Newark, Jan. 7, 1928; s. Norman and Ada (Binstock) M.; m. Jane B. Holzman, Sept. 20, 1989; children: Norman, James M., David. LittB, Rutgers U., 1948; LLB, Harvard U., 1954. Bar: Ohio 1954. Assoc. Paxton & Seasongood, cin., 1954-59, ptnr., 1959-85, pres., 1985-89; ptnr. Thompson, Hine and Flory, 1989-96, ptnr.-in-charge Cin. office, 1989-91, mem. firm mgmt. com., 1991-93, of counsel, 1998—; adj. prof. law U. Cin. Coll. Law, 1998-2000. Chmn. bd. dirs. Jewish Hosp., 1982-86; trustee Andrew Jergens Found., 1962-97. Mem. ABA, Ohio Bar Assn., Cin. Bar Assn., Am. Arbitration Assn. (chmn. comml. arbitration adv. com., Ohio panel large, complex arbitration cases). Office: Thompson Hine LLP 312 Walnut St Ste 14 Cincinnati OH 45202-4089

MERCER, DAVID ROBINSON, cultural organization administrator; b. Van Nuys, Calif., Aug. 14, 1938; s. Samuel Robinson and Dorothy (Lenox) M.; m. Joyce Elaine Dahl, Aug. 23, 1958; children: Steven, Michael, Kimberly. BA, Calif. State U., L.A., 1961. Exec. dir. YMCA of L.A., 1963-69, sr. v.p., 1969-80; reg. mgr. Am. City Bur., Hoffman Estates, Ill., 1980-82; pres. YMCA of San Francisco, 1982-90; nat. exec. dir. YMCA of USA, Chgo., 1990—. Cons. fin. devel. YMCAs throughout U.S., 1975—. Mem. The Family, Rotary (bd. dirs. 1987-89). Republican. Methodist. Avocations: golf, bridge, flying, back packing. Office: YMCA of USA 101 N Wacker Dr Chicago IL 60606-7386

MERCER, RON, professional basketball player; b. May 18, 1976; Student, U. Ky. Guard Boston Celtics, 1997-99, Denver Nuggets, 1999-00, Orlando Magic, 2000, Chgo. Bulls, 2000—. Named SEC Player of the Yr., 1997. Office: Indiana Pacers Market Street Arena 300 E Market St Fl 1 Indianapolis IN 46204-2603

MERCHANT, JAMES A. medical educator; MD, U. Iowa; PhD in Epidimiology, U. N.C. Resident Cleve. Metro. Gen. Hosp.; fellow Duke U.; Trudeau fellow Brompton Hosp., London; mem. faculty U. N.C., 1973-75; adj. prof. W.Va. U., 1985-81; mem. faculty Coll. Medicine U. Iowa, 1981—. Contbr. articles to profl. jours. Mem. APHA, Am. Coll. Radiology, Am. Lung Assn., Am. Occupl. Medicine Assn., Am. Thoracic Soc., Internat. Assn. Occupl. Health, Nat. Inst. Occupl. Safety and Health (mem. bd. sci. counselors), Alpha Omega Alpha. Office: U Iowa Coll Medicine 2707 Steindler Building Iowa City IA 52242-1008

MERCHANT, MYLON EUGENE, physicist, engineer; b. Springfield, Mass., May 6, 1913; s. Mylon Dickinson and Rebecca Chase (Currier) M.; m. Helen Silver Bennett, Aug. 4, 1937; children: Mylon David (dec.), Leslie Ann Merchant Alexander, Frances Sue Merchant Jacobson. BS magna cum laude, U. Vt., 1936, DSc (hon.), 1973; DSc, U. Cinn., 1941; DSc (hon.), U. Salford, Eng., 1980; D of Engring (hon.), Kettering U., 1994. Research physicist Milacron, Inc., 1940-48, sr. research physicist, 1948-51, asst. dir. research, 1951-57, dir. phys. research, 1957-63, dir. sci. research, 1963-69, dir. research planning, 1969-81, prin. scientist, mfg. research, 1981-83; dir. advanced mfg. research Metcut Research Assocs., Inc., 1983-90; sr. cons. TechSolve, Cinn., 1990—. Adj. prof. mech. engring. U. Cin., 1964-69, mfg. engring., 2001-; vis. prof. mech. engring. U. Salford, Eng., 1973—; hon. prof. U. Hong Kong, 1995—. Bd. dirs. Dan Beard council Boy Scouts Am., 1967-80, pres.'s council, 1980— . Recipient Georg Schlesinger prize City of Berlin, 1980; Otto Benedikt prize Hungarian Acad. Scis., 1981, 1st Japan Soc. Precision Engring. prize, 1997; named to Automation Hall of Fame, 1995. Fellow Soc. Tribologists and Lubrication Engrs. (pres. 1952-53), Am. Soc. Metals Internat., Ohio Acad. Sci., Soc. Mfg. Engrs. (hon. mem., pres. 1976-77); mem. NAE, ASME (hon., mfg. medal 1988), Internat. Instn. Prodn. Engring. Rsch. (hon., pres. 1968-69), Engrs. and Scientists of Cin. (pres. 1961-62), Fedn. Materials Socs. (pres. 1974), Phi Beta Kappa, Sigma Xi, Tau Beta Pi. Achievements include research on machining process and systems approach to manufacturing. Home: 3939 Erie Ave Apt 105 Cincinnati OH 45208-1913 Office: TechSolve 1111 Edison Dr Cincinnati OH 45216-2265 E-mail: merchant@techsolve.org., gmerchant@fuse.net.

MERCURI, JOAN B. foundation executive; b. N.Y.C. BA, Va. Commonwealth U., 1984. Mgmt. positions various corps., Ill., 1986-96; exec. dir. Frank Lloyd Wright Home and Studio Found., Oak Park, 1996—; pres., CEO Frank Lloyd Wright Preservation Trust, 2000—. Mem. Am. Assn. Museums, Nat. Trust for Hist. Preservation, Frank Lloyd Wright Bldg. Conservatory, Am. Soc. Assn. Execs., Assn. Fundraising Profls., Board Source.

MEREDITH, EDWIN THOMAS, III, media executive; b. Chgo., Feb. 7, 1933; s. Edwin Thomas, Jr. and Anna (Kauffman) M.; m. Katherine Comfort, Sept. 4, 1953; children: Mildred K. (dec.), Dianna M., Edwin Thomas. Student, U. Ariz., 1950-53. With Meredith Corp., Des Moines, 1956—, varied mgmt. positions in mag., book and printing groups, 1956-65, asst. sec., bd. dirs., 1966-68, v.p., 1968-69, v.p., asst. to gen. mgr. mag. div., 1969-71, pres., chief exec. officer, 1971-73, chmn. bd., chief exec. officer, 1973-77, chmn. bd., 1977-88, chmn. exec. com., 1988—, also bd. dirs. Bd. dirs. Nat. Merit Scholarship Corp., Evanston, Ill., Iowa Natural Heritage Found, Des Moines; trustee Iowa Methodist Med. Ctr., Iowa 4-H Found., Ames; bd. govs. Drake U., Des Moines. With U.S. Army, 1953-56. Mem. Des Moines Club, Wakonda Club. Office: Meredith Corp 1716 Locust St Des Moines IA 50309-3023

MERIDEN, TERRY, physician; b. Damascus, Syria, Oct. 12, 1946; came to U.S., 1975; s. Izzat and Omayma (Aidi) M.; m. Lena Kahal, Nov. 17, 1975; children: Zina, Lana. BS, Sch. Sci., Damascus, 1968; MD, Sch. Medicine, Damascus, 1972, doctorate cum laude, 1973. Diplomate Am. Bd. Internal Medicine. Resident in infectious diseases Rush Green Hosp., Romford, Eng., 1973; house officer in internal medicine and cardiology Ashford (Eng.) Group Univ. Hosps., 1973-74; sr. house officer in internal medicine and neurology Grimsby (Eng.) Group Univ. Hosps., 1974; registrar in internal medicine and rheumatology St. Annes Hosp., London, 1974-75; jr. resident in internal medicine Shadyside Hosp., Pitts., 1975-76, sr. resident in internal medicine, 1976-77; fellow in endocrinology and metabolism Shadyside Hosp. and Grad. Inst., 1976-77; clin. asst. prof. U. Ill., Peoria, 1979; pres. Am. Diabetes Assn., 1982-84; dir. Proctor Diabetes Unit, 1984—, 1984—. Adviser to the Gov. of Ill. on Diabetes. Mem. editorial bd. Diabetes Forecast mag., Clin. Diabetes, 1990; contbr. articles to profl. jours. Fellow ACP, FACE, Am. Coll. Endocrinology; mem. AMA (Recognition award 1985, ADA (chmn. profl. edn. and rsch. 1980—, mem. editl. bd. and Spanish lit. bd. nat. bd. dirs. 1986—, vice chmn. nat. com. on diabetes edn. and affiliate svcs. 1986—, Outstanding Svc. award 1984, Outstanding Diabetes Educator award 1986), Am. Cancer Soc. (Life Line award 1983), Am. Assn. Clin. Endocrinology (founding), Am. Coll. Endocrinology, The Obesity Found. (Century award 1984, Recognition award 1985). Home: 115 E Coventry Ln Peoria IL 61614-2103 Office: 900 Main St Ste 300 Peoria IL 61602-1049

MERIWETHER, HEATH J. newspaper publisher; b. Columbia, Mo., Jan. 20, 1944; s. Nelson Heath and Mary Agnes (Immele) M.; m. Patricia Hughes, May 4, 1979; children: Graham, Elizabeth. BA in History, BJ, U. Mo., 1966; MA in Teaching, Harvard U., 1967. Reporter Miami (Fla.) Herald, 1970-72, editor Broward and Palm Beach burs., 1972-77, exec. city editor, 1977-79, asst. mgr. editor news, 1979-80, mng. editor, 1981-83, exec. editor, 1983-87, Detroit Free Press, 1987-95, publisher, 1996—. Trustee Greenhills Sch., 1995—; bd. dirs. Detroit Symphony Orch., 1996—. Served to lt. USNR, 1967-70. Journalism fellow Stanford U., 1980. Roman Catholic. Avocation: tennis. Office: Detroit Free Press 600 W Fort St Detroit MI 48226-2706

MERRIGAN, WILLIAM A. food services company executive; Dir. distbn. Grand Union Co.; corp. dir. warehouse & transportation A&P Corp.; v.p. transportation & logistics Wakefern Food Corp.; sr. v.p. distbn. & logistics Nash Finch Co., Mpls. Office: Nash Finch Co 7600 France Ave S Minneapolis MN 55435-5924

MERRILL, CHARLES EUGENE, lawyer; b. San Antonio, Aug. 26, 1952; s. Charles Perry and Florence Elizabeth Merrill; m. Carol Ann Rutter, Apr. 28, 1984; children: Elizabeth C., Charles C. AB, Stanford U., 1974; JD, U. Calif., Berkeley, 1977. Bar: Mo. 1977, Calif. 1983, Ill. 1993. Mem. Husch & Eppenberger, LLC, St. Louis, 1977—. Mem. ABA, Bar Assn. of Met. St. Louis. Office: Husch & Eppenberger LLC 190 Carondelet Plz Ste 600 Saint Louis MO 63105-3441 E-mail: charlie.merrill@husch.com.

MERRILL, THOMAS WENDELL, lawyer, law educator; b. Bartlesville, Okla., May 3, 1949; s. William McGill and Dorothy (Glasener) M.; m. Kimberly Ann Evans, Sept. 8, 1973; children: Jessica, Margaret, Elizabeth. BA, Grinnell Coll., 1971, Oxford U., 1973; JD, U. Chgo., 1977. Bar: Ill. 1980, U.S. Dist Ct. (no. dist.) Ill. 1980, U.S. Ct. Appeals (5th cir.) 1982, U.S. Ct. Appeals (7th cir.) 1983, U.S. Ct. Appeals (9th and D.C. cirs.) 1984, U.S. Supreme Ct. 1985. Clk. U.S. Ct. Appeals (D.C. cir.), Washington, 1977-78, U.S. Supreme Ct., Washington, 1978-79; assoc. Sidley & Austin, Chgo., 1979-81, counsel, 1981-87, 90—; dep. solicitor gen. U.S. Dept. Justice, 1987-90; prof. law Northwestern U., Chgo., 1981—, John Paul Stevens prof., 1993—. Contbr. articles to profl. jours. Rhodes scholar Oxford U., 1971; Danforth fellow, 1971. Home: 939 Maple Ave Evanston IL 60202-1717 Office: Northwestern U Sch Law 357 E Chicago Ave Chicago IL 60611-3059

MERRITT, JAMES W., JR. state legislator, real estate developer; b. Indpls., July 28, 1959; s. James Warner and Marion Jane (Brown) M.; m. Kelley A. McCloskey, May 10, 1985. BS in Arts & Sci., Ind. State U., 1981. Candidate asst. Merchert for Congress, Indpls., 1981-82; campaign mgr. Hillis for Congress, Kokomo, 1982-83; dist. asst. U.S. Rep. Bud Hillis, 1983; property mgr. Circle Fin. Corp., Indpls.; mem. Ind. Senate from 31st dist., Indianapolis, 1990—. Mem. ward chmn. Marion County Rep. Party Lawrence Twp. 1987—. Mem. Jr. Achievement, Toastmasters. Republican. Office: Circle Fin Corp 9102 N Meridian St Indianapolis IN 46260-1860 Address: Ind Senate Dist 31 200 W Washington St Indianapolis IN 46204-2728

MERRYMAN, GEORGE, automotive executive; CFO Jordan Motors Inc., Mishawaka, Ind. Office: Jordan Motors Inc 609 E Jefferson Blvd Mishawaka IN 46545-6524

MERSEREAU, JOHN, JR. Slavic languages and literatures educator; b. San Jose, Calif., Apr. 16, 1925; s. John Joshua and Winona Beth (Roberts) M.; m. Nanine Landell, July 11, 1953; children: Daryl Landell, John Coates. AB, U. Calif., 1945, MA, 1950, PhD, 1957. Teaching fellow, Slavic dept. U. Calif., Berkeley, 1950-52, research asst., 1953-54; instr. Slavic dept. U. Mich., Ann Arbor, 1956-59, asst. prof., 1959-61, assoc. prof., 1961-63, prof., 1963—, chmn. dept., 1961-71, 85-89, prof. emeritus, 1990—, dir. Residential Coll., 1977-85. Mem. Joint Com. Eastern Europe of Am. Council Learned Socs./Social Sci. Research Council, 1971-74, chmn., 1973-74. Author: Mikhail Lermontov, 1962, Baron Delvig's Literary Almanac: Northern Flowers, 1967, Translating Russian, 1968, Russian Romantic Fiction, 1983, Orest Somov, 1989, How to Grill a Gourmet, 2000; assoc. editor Mich. Slavic Publs., 1962—; contbr. articles to profl. jours. Served to lt. (j.g.) USNR, 1943-46, PTO. Calmerton Slavic scholar U. Calif., Berkeley, 1954-55; Ford Found. fellow, London and Paris, 1955-56, Guggenheim fellow, 1972-73; recipient Disting. Service award U. Mich., Ann Arbor, 1961. Mem. Am. Assn. Advancement Slavic Studies, U. Mich. Research Club. Club: Waterloo Hunt (Grass Lake, Mich., sec. 1970-80); Commanderie de Bordeaux (Detroit). Avocations: flying, gourmet cuisine, raising horses. Office: U of Mich Slavic Dept Ann Arbor MI 48109 E-mail: mersereа@umich.edu.

MERSHAD, FREDERICK J. retail executive; b. 1943; Exec. merchandising Rich's, McRae's, Millers; exec. v.p. Proffitt's, Inc., 1994-95, pres., CEO, 1995, Elder-Beerman, 1995—. Office: Elder-Beerman Stores Corp PO Box 1448 Dayton OH 45401-1448

MERTENS, THOMAS ROBERT, biology educator; b. Fort Wayne, Ind., May 22, 1930; s. Herbert F. and Hulda (Burg) M.; m. Beatrice Janet Abair, Apr. 1, 1953; children: Julia Ann, David Gerhard B.S., Ball State U., 1952; M.S., Purdue U., 1954, Ph.D., 1956. Research assoc. dept. genetics U. Wis.-Madison, 1956-57; asst. prof. biology Ball State U., Muncie, Ind., 1957-62, assoc. prof., 1962-66, prof., 1966-93, dir. doctoral programs in biology, 1974-93, disting. prof. biology edn., 1988-93, prof. emeritus, 1993—. Author: (with A. M. Winchester) Human Genetics, 1983 (with R.L. Hammersmith) Genetics Laboratory Investigations, 9th edit., 1991, 12th edit., 2001 (co-recipient William Holmes McGuffey Longevity award Text and Acad. Authors Assn. 1998); contbr. numerous articles to profl. jours. Co-recipient Gustav Ohaus award for innovative coll. sci. tchg. NSTA, 1986, recipient Disting. Svc. to Sci. Edn. citation, 1987; fellow NSF, 1963-64, Ind. Acad. Scis., 1969. Fellow AAAS; mem. Nat. Assn. Biology Tchrs. (pres. 1985, hon. mem. 1988), Am. Genetic Assn., Genetics Soc. Am. Episcopalian. Home: 4501 N Wheeling 9B-4 Muncie IN 47304-1277 Office: Ball State U Dept Biology Muncie IN 47306-0001

MERTINS, JAMES WALTER, entomologist; b. Milw., Feb. 18, 1943; s. Walter Edwin and Harriet Ellen (Sockett) M.; m. Marilee Eloise Joeckel, Dec. 8, 1979. BS in Zoology, U. Wis., Milw., 1965; MS in Entomology, U. Wis., 1967, PhD in Entomology, 1971. Project assoc. dept. entomology U. Wis., Madison, 1971-75, rsch. assoc. dept. entomology, 1975-77; asst. prof. dept. entomology Iowa State U., Ames, 1977-84; entomol. cons., 1984-89; entomologist Nat. Vet. Svcs. Labs. USDA Animal and Plant Health Inspection Svc., 1989—. Co-author: (textbook) Biological Insect Pest Suppression, 1977, Russian edit., 1980, Chinese edit., 1988; contbr. articles to profl. jours. NSF Grad. fellow, 1970. Mem. Entomol. Soc. Am. (Insect Photography award 1984, 86), Entomol. Soc. Can., Mich. Entomol. Soc., Wis. Entomol. Soc. (pres., sec., treas., bd. dirs.), Cyclone Corvettes, Inc. (co-founder, pres. 1978, 79, sec., treas., bd. dirs., Mem. of Yr. 1982), Am. Mensa. Avocations: insect photography, Corvette automobile activities, gardening, movies, insect collecting. Office: USDA Animal and Plant Health Inspection Svc PO Box 844 Ames IA 50010-0844 E-mail: James.W.Mertins@aphis.usda.gov.

MERTZ, DOLORES MARY, farmer, state legislator; b. Bancroft, Iowa, May 30, 1928; d. John Francis and Gertrude (Erickson) Shay; m. H. Peter Mertz (dec. 1983), Dec. 27, 1951; children: Peter, Mary Simpson, David, Ann Cornicelli, Helen Powell, Janice, Carol. AA, Briar Cliff Coll., 1948. Pres. Coun. Cath. Women, Sioux City, Iowa, 1986-88; state regent Cath. Daus. Am., 1988-94; county supr. Kossuth County, 1983-89; mem. Iowa Ho. of Reps., Des Moines, 1989—. Dem. precinct com. person, Kossuth County, Iowa, sec. 1975—. Recipient Womens Leadership award Iowa Lakes Community Coll., 1988; named Woman of Yr. Beta Sigma Phi Internat., West Bend, Iowa, 1989; recipient Iowa Lakes Community Coll. Disting. Svc. award, 1992, Guardian of Small Businsess award. Mem. Soroptomist Internat. (Woman of Distinction award 1987), Drama Club (pres. 1970's). Roman Catholic. Office: Iowa Ho of Reps State Capitol Des Moines IA 50319-0001 Home: 607 110th St Ottosen IA 50570-8504

MERVIS, LOUIS, school system administrator; Chmn. Ill. Bd. Edn., Springfield, 1991-93, 97-99; owner Mervis Industries, Danville, Ill. Office: Mervis Industries 3295 E Main St Danville IL 61834-9382

MERWIN, DAVIS UNDERWOOD, newspaper executive; b. Chgo., June 22, 1928; s. Davis and Josephine (Underwood) M.; m. Nancy Snowden Smith Tailer, Nov. 14, 1958 (dec. Feb. 1995); children: Davis Fell, Laura Howell; m. Sharon Adkins Todd, May 12, 1998. AB, Harvard U., 1950; LLD (hon.), Ill. Wesleyan U., 1991. Pres. Evergreen Comm., Inc., Bloomington, Ill., 1969-80; pub. Daily Pantagraph, 1968-80; pres. Wood Canyon Corp., Tucson, 1989-93; vice-chmn. Bloomington Broadcasting Corp., 1993-99. Dir. State Farm Growth, Balanced Mcpl. Bond and Interim Funds, State Farm Variable Products Funds. Trustee emeritus Ill. Wesleyan U.; trustee Ill. Nature Conservancy. Recipient Disting. Svc. award U.S. Jaycees, 1959 Mem. Am. Newspaper Pubs. Assn., Inland Daily Press Assn. (pres. 1977, chmn. bd. dirs. 1978), Harvard Club (Chgo.), Phoenix-SK Club, Hasty Pudding Club, Bloomington Country Club, Ristigouche Salmon Club. Republican. Unitarian. Office: 2422 E Washington St Bloomington IL 61704-4478 Mailing: PO Box 1665 Bloomington IL 61702-1665 E-mail: DUMerwin@aol.com.

MERZ, JAMES LOGAN, electrical engineering and materials educator, researcher; b. Jersey City, Apr. 14, 1936; s. Albert Joseph and Anne Elizabeth (Farrell) M.; m. Rose-Marie Weibel, June 30, 1962; children: Kathleen, James, Michael, Kimarie. BS in Physics, U. Notre Dame, 1959; postgrad., U. Göttingen, Fed. Republic Germany, 1959-60; MA, Harvard U., 1961, PhD in Applied Physics, 1967; PhD (hon.), Lingköping U., Sweden, 1993. Mem. tech. staff Bell Labs., Murray Hill, N.J., 1966-78; prof. elec. engring. U. Calif., Santa Barbara, 1978-94, prof. materials, 1986-94, chmn. dept. elec. and computer engring., 1982-84, assoc. dean for rsch. devel. Coll. Engring., 1984-86, acting assoc. vice chancellor, 1988, dir. semiconductor rsch. corp. core program on GaAs digital ICs, 1984-89, dir. Compound Semiconductor Rsch. Labs., 1986-92, dir. NSF Ctr. for Quantized Electronic Structures, 1989-94; Freimann prof. elec. engring. U. Notre Dame (Ind.), 1994—, v.p. for grad. studies and rsch., dean Grad. Sch., 1996-2001. Mem. exec. com. Calif. Microelectronics Innovation and Computer Rsch. Opportunities Program, 1986-92; mem. NRC com. on Japan, NAS/NAE, 1988-90; mem. internat. adv. com. Internat. Symposium on Physics of Semiconductors and Applications, Seoul, Republic of Korea, 1990, Conf. on Superlattices and Microstructures, Xi'an, China, 1992; participant, mem. coms. other profl. confs. and meetings. Contbr. over 400 articles to profl. jours.; patentee in field. Fulbright fellow, Danforth Found. fellow, Woodrow Wilson Found. fellow. Fellow IEEE, Am. Phys. Soc.; mem. IEEE Lasers and Electro-Optics Soc. (program com. annual mtg. 1980), IEEE Electron Device Soc. (sec. 1994, 95), Am. Vacuum Soc. (exec. com. electronic materials and processing divsn. 1988-89), Electrochem. Soc., Materials Rsch. Soc. (editl. bd. jour. 1984-87), Soc. for Values in Higher Edn., Inst. Electronics, Info. and Comm. Engrs. (overseas adv. com.), Sigma Xi, Eta Kappa Nu. Achievements include research in field of optoelectronic materials and devices: semiconductors and ionic materials; optical and electrical properties of implanted ions, rapid annealing; semiconductor lasers, detectors, solar cells, other optoelectronic devices; low-dimensional quantum structures, nanostructures. Office: U Notre Dame Grad Sch 416 Main Bldg Notre Dame IN 46556-5602 E-mail: jmerz@nd.edu.

MERZ, MICHAEL, federal judge; b. Dayton, Ohio, Mar. 29, 1945; s. Robert Louis and Hazel (Appleton) M.; m. Marguerite Logan LeBreton, Sept. 7, 1968; children: Peter Henry, Nicholas George. AB cum laude, Harvard U., 1967, JD, 1970. Bar: Ohio 1970, U.S. Dist. Ct. (so. dist.) Ohio 1971, U.S Supreme Ct. 1974, U.S. Ct. Appeals (6th cir.) 1975. Assoc. Smith & Schnacke, Dayton, Ohio, 1970-75, ptnr., 1976-77; judge Dayton Mcpl. Ct., 1977-84; magistrate U.S. Dist. Ct. (so. dist.) Ohio, 1984—. Adj. prof. U. Dayton Law Sch., 1979—; mem. rules adv. com. Ohio Supreme Ct., 1989-96. Bd. dirs. United Way, Dayton, 1981-95; trustee Dayton and Montgomery County Pub. Libr., 1991—, Montgomery County Hist. Soc., 1995—, Ohio Libr. Coun., 1997-2000. Fellow Am. Bar Found.; mem. ABA, Fed. Bar Assn., Am. Judicature Soc., Fed. Magistrate Judges Assn. (trustee 1997-2000), Ohio State Bar Assn., Dayton Bar Assn. Republican. Roman Catholic. Office: US Dist Ct 902 Federal Bldg 200 W 2nd St Dayton OH 45402-1430

MESCHKE, HERBERT LEONARD, retired state supreme court justice; b. Belfield, N.D., Mar. 18, 1928; s. G.E. and Dorothy E. Meschke; m. Shirley Ruth McNeil; children: Marie, Jean, Michael, Jill. BA, Jamestown Coll., 1950; JD, U. Mich., 1953. Bar: N.D. Law clk. U.S. Dist. Ct. N.D., 1953-54; practice law Minot, N.D., 1954-85; mem. N.D. Ho. of Reps., 1965-66, N.D. Senate, 1967-70; justice N.D. State Supreme Ct., 1985-98; of counsel Pringle & Herigstad Law Firm, Minot, 1999—. Mem. ABA, Am. Law Inst., Am. Judicature Soc., N.D. Bar Assn.

MESHEL, HARRY, state senator, political party official; b. Youngstown, Ohio, June 13, 1924; s. Angelo and Rubena (Markakis) Michelakis; children: Barry, Melanie. BSBA, Youngstown Coll., 1949; MS, Columbia U., 1950; LLD (hon.), Ohio U., Youngstown State U., Ohio Coll. Podiatric Medicine; LHD (hon.), Youngstown State U. Exec. asst. to mayor City of Youngstown, Ohio, 1964-68, urban renewal dir. Ohio, 1969; mem. 33d district Ohio Senate, Columbus, 1971-93, Dem. minority leader, 1981-82, 85-90, pres. and majority leader, 1983-84, com. mem. econ. develop., sci. & tech., state & local govt., ways & means, commerce & labor, controlling bd., state employment compensation bd., fin. chmn., 1974-81, rules chmn., 1983-84, com. mem. rules, reference & oversight, 1985-90; state chair Ohio Dem. Party, 1993-95. Real estate broker; adj. prof. polit. sci. Ohio U.; faculty mem. (limited svc.) Youngstown State U.; div. mgr. investment firm; Ohio Senate special com. mem. Task Force on Drug Strategies, Ohio Acad. Sci. Centennial Celebration Commn., Motor Vehicle Inspection & Maintenance Program, Legis. Oversight Com., Ohio Boxing Commn., Correctional Inst. Inspection Com., Ohio Small Bus. & Entrepreneurship Coun., Gov.'s Adv. Coun. Travel & Tourism, Legis. Svc. Commn., Capital Sq. Rev. & Adv. Bd., others. Past pres., past lt. gov. Am. Hellenic Ednl. Prog. Assn. (AHEPA); precinct committeeman Mahoning County Dem. Party, ward captain, mem. exec. com.; campaign mgr. local candidates, county campaign mgr. presdl. candidates; del. Dem. Mid-Term Conv., 1981; founder Great Lakes/N.E. Legis. Coalition; chmn., founder Nat. Dem. State Legis. Leaders Assn.; dir. State Legis. Leaders Found.; state/fed. assembly, mem. communications com. Nat. Conf. State Legis., legis. mgmt. com., govt. opers. com.; chair fiscal affairs com. Midwest Conf. Coun. State Govts., task force on econs. & fiscal affairs; del., exec. com. Dem. Nat. Com.; mem. Dem. Leadership Coun., State Dem. Exec. Com.; exec. com. Assn. State Dem. Chairs; bd. trustees Nat. Hall of Fame for Persons with Disabilities; mem. St. Nicholas Greek Orthodox Ch.; mem. Mill Creek Metro Park Bd. Commrs. With USN, 1943-46. Decorated two Bronze Battle Stars; recipient Dist. Svc. award Office of Pres., Top Legislator award Ohio Union Patrolmen Assn., Dist. Citizen award Med. Coll. Ohio, City of Hope Leadership award, 1993, Legis. Leadership award Ohio Coalition for Edn. of Handicapped Children, Phillips Medal of Pub. Svc., Ohio U., John E. Fogarty award Gov.'s Com. of Employment of Handicapped, Gov.'s award, 1992, U. Cin. Award for Excellence, Lamp of Learning award Ohio Edn. Assn., Black Cultural Soc. award East Liverpool, Mahoning Valley Man of Yr. award, Mahoning Valley Econ. Devel. Corp., Office Holder of Yr. award Truman-Johnson Dem. Women, Best Interest of Children award Fathers of Equal Rights, Founders Day award Circle of Friends Found., Helping Hand award Easter Seal Soc., Honorary Riverboat Captain award Mahoning County Dem. Party, Community Svc. and Special Svcs. awards Eastern Orthodox Men's Soc., Periclean award AHEPA, Academy of Achievement award Nat. AHEPA Ednl. Found., Nat. Svc. Dem. award AHEPA, 1994, Disting. Citizen award Youngstown State U. Alumni Assn., numerous appreciation and recognition awards; recipient Outstanding Legislator awards Ohio Acad. Trial Lawyers, Ohio Assn. Pub. Sch. Employees, Ohio Rehab. Assn., League Ohio Sportsmen; recipient Dist. Svc. awards Youngstown State U., Ohio Edn. Assn., Ohio Union Patrolmen Assn., Ohio Disabled Vets., AFL-CIO Ohio Barbers Union, AFL-CIO Nat. Assn. of Theatre Owners of Ohio; named Guardian of the Menorah, Youngstown B'nai B'rith, Outstanding Dem., Fairfield Dem. Club, 1993; named to Ohio Vets. Hall of Fame. Mem. (life) NAACP, ACLU, AMVETS (Legislator of Yr. 1993), VFW, Am. Legion, Cath. War Vets (Dist. Legislator award), Vet. Boxers Assn. Mercer County, Pa., Trumbull County Boxers' Legends of Leather (Man of Yr. award Hall of Fame), William Holmes McGuffey Hist. Soc., Buckeye Elks Lodge (hon.); mem. Kiwanis Internat., Urban League, Alliance C. of C., Southern Community Jaycees (hon.), Soc. for Preservation of Greek Heritage, Greek Am. Progressive Assn., Pan Cretan Assn., Arms Hist. Mus. Soc., Eagles, Moose, The Stambaugh Pillars.

MESHII, MASAHIRO, materials science educator; b. Amagasaki, Japan, Oct. 6, 1931; came to U.S., 1956; s. Masataro and Kazuyo M.; m. Eiko Kumagai, May 21, 1959; children: Alisa, Erica. BS, Osaka (Japan) U., 1954, MS, 1956; PhD, Northwestern U., 1959. Lectr., rsch. assoc. dept. materials sci. and engring. Northwestern U., Evanston, Ill., 1959-60, asst. prof., assoc. prof., then prof., 1960-88, chmn. dept. materials sci. and engring., 1978-82, John Evans prof., 1988—. Vis. scientist Nat. Rsch. Inst. Metals, Tokyo, 1970-71; NSF summer faculty rsch. participant Argonne (Ill.) Nat. Lab., 1975; guest prof. Osaka U., 1985; Acta/Scripta Metallurgica lectr., 1993-95. Co-editor: Lattice Defects in Quenched Metals, 1965, Martensitic Transformation, 1978, Science of Advanced Materials, 1990; editor: Fatigue and Microstructures, 1979, Mechanical Properties of BCC Metals, 1982; contbr. over 245 articles to tech. publs. and internat. jours. Recipient Founders award Midwest Soc. Electron Microscopists, 1987. Fellow ASM (Henry Marion Howe medal 1968), Japan Soc. Promotion of Sci.; mem. AIME, Metallurgical Soc., Japan Inst. Metals (Achievement award 1972, hon. mem. 2000). Home: 3051 Centennial Ln Highland Park IL 60035-1017 Office: Northwestern U Dept Materials Sci Eng Evanston IL 60208-3108 E-mail: m-meshii@northwestern.edu.

MESSER, RANDY KEITH, graphic designer, illustrator; b. Des Moines, Sept. 10, 1960; s. Delmar Keith and Thelma Darlene (Myers) M.; m. Jennifer Rae Harmeling, June 12, 1982; children: Joanna, Andrew. BA, Ctrl. Coll., Pella, Iowa, 1982; Assoc. in Applied Arts, Des Moines Area C.C., Ankeny, Iowa, 1984. Designer Eagle Sign and Advt., Des Moines, 1983-84, Perfection Form Co., Des Moines, 1984-90; asst. design dir. Perfection Learning Co., 1990-93, design dir., 1993—. Mem. adv. bd. Des Moines Area C.C., Ankeny, 1987—. Illustrator: Great Eagle and Small One, 1997. Elder Calvary Reformed Ch., Des Moines, 1989—. Recipient Silver awards Iowa Art Dirs. Exhbn., Des Moines, 1989, 91, Highest award Dale Carnegie Leadership, Des Moines, 1996; Art Dirs. Assn. Iowa scholar Iowa Art Dirs. Assn., Des Moines, 1984. Mem. Art Dirs. Assn. Iowa (treas. 1988-89, v.p. programs 1989-90, v.p. exhbn. 1990-91, pres. 1991-92, Gold award 1992). Avocations: hunting, fishing, photography, gardening, traveling. Home: 9319 Lakewood Pointe Dr Norwalk IA 50211-1769 Office: Perfection Learning Corp 10520 New York Ave Des Moines IA 50322-3775

MESSIN, MARLENE ANN, plastics company executive; b. St. Paul, Oct. 6, 1935; d. Edgar Leander and Luella Johanna (Rahn) Johnson; m. Eugene Carlson (div. 1972); children: Rick, Debora, Ronald, Lori; m.. Willard Smith (dec. 1975); m. Frank Messin, Sept. 24, 1982; 5 stepchildren. Bookkeeper Jeans Implement Co., Forest Lake, Minn., 1952-53, part-time bookkeeper, 1953-57; bookkeeper Great Plains Supply, St. Paul, 1960-62, Plastic Products Co., Inc., Lindstrom, Minn., 1962-75, pres., 1975—; co-owner, treas. Gustaf's Fine Gifts, 1985—. Bookkeeper Trinity Luth. Ch., Lindstrom, 1976-81. Mem. Soc. Plastic Engrs., Swedish Inst., Soc. Plastic Industry, Minn. State Hist. Soc., Chgo. County Hist. Soc. Home: 28968 Olinda Trl Lindstrom MN 55045-9429 Office: 30355 Akerson St Lindstrom MN 55045-9456

MESSNER, JAMES W. advertising executive; b. 1939; Attended, 1959-61. With Sta. WCSM, Celina, Ohio, 1961-63, Sta. WTOD, Toledo, 1961-63, Detroit Advt. Agy., 1965-68, Norman, Navan, Moore & Bard, 1968-77; CEO J.W. Messner Inc., Grand Rapids, Mich., 1977—. Office: JW Messner Inc 161 Ottawa Ave NW Ste 403 Grand Rapids MI 49503-2760

METCALF, CHARLES DAVID, museum director, retired military officer; b. Anamosa, Iowa, June 18, 1933; m. Patricia (Sedlacek) M.; children: Christin, Karen. BA, Coe Coll., 1955; MBA, Mich. State U., 1964. Commd. 2d lt. USAF, 1955; advanced through grades to maj. gen., 1986; various fin. mgmt. duties USAF; asst. dir. Defense Security Assistance Agy.; commdr. Air Force Acctg. and Fin. Ctr.; ret., 1991; dir. USAF Mus., Wright-Patterson AFB, Ohio, 1996—. Decorated D.S.M. with one oak leaf cluster, Def. Superior Svc. medal, Legion of Merit. Office: USAF Mus 1100 Spaatz St Wright Patterson AFB OH 45433-7102

METCALF, DEAN, radio personality; Radio host morning show Sta. WFBQ-FM, Indpls. Office: WFBQ 6161 Fall Creek Rd Indianapolis IN 46220*

METCALF, ROBERT CLARENCE, architect, educator; b. Nashville, Nov. 7, 1923; s. George and Helen May (Drake) M.; m. Bettie Jane Sponseller, Sept. 15, 1943. Student, Johns Hopkins U., 1943; B.Arch., U. Mich., 1950. Draftsman G.B. Brigham, Jr., Architect, Ann Arbor, Mich., 1948-52; pvt. practice architecture, 1953—; lectr. architecture U. Mich., 1955-58, asst. prof., 1958-63, asso. prof., 1963-68, prof., 1968-91, chmn. dept., 1968-74; dean U. Mich. (Coll. Architecture and Urban Planning), 1974-86; Emil Lorch prof. emeritus U. Mich., 1991—, dean emeritus, 1991—; pvt. practice, 1991—. Sec. Mich. Bd. Registration for Architects, 1975-79, chmn., 1980-82 Designer more than 140 bldgs., Ann Arbor, 1953—. Served with U.S. Army, 1943-46, ETO. Decorated Silver Star; recipient Sol King award for excellent teaching in architecture U. Mich., 1974; named Emil Lorch Professor of Architecture, 1989. Fellow AIA (Pres.'s award 1999); mem. AIA Mich., Assn. Collegiate Schs. Architecture, Phi Kappa Phi, Tau Sigma Delta. Home: 1052 Arlington Blvd Ann Arbor MI 48104-2816 Office: U Mich 2150 Art Architecture Bldg Ann Arbor MI 48109 also: Metcalf Architect 2211 Medford Rd Ann Arbor MI 48104-5004

METCALFE, WALTER LEE, JR. lawyer; b. St. Louis, Dec. 19, 1938; s. Walter Lee and Carol (Crowe) Metcalfe; m. Cynthia Williamson, Aug. 26, 1965; children: Carol, Edward. AB, Washington U., St. Louis, 1960; JD, U. Va., 1964. Bar: Mo. 1964. Ptnr. Armstrong, Teasdale, Kramer & Vaughan, St. Louis, 1964—81; sr. ptnr. Bryan Cave LLP, 1982—, now chmn. Dep. chmn. Fed. Res. Bd. St. Louis; bd. dirs. Washington U., Danforth Found., St. Louis RCGA, Pulitzer Found. for Arts. Mem.: ABA, St. Louis Bar Assn., Mo. Bar Assn., Noonday Club, Bogey Club (pres.). Episcopalian. Home: 26 Upper Ladue Rd Saint Louis MO 63124-1675 Office: Bryan Cave 211 N Broadway 1 Metropolitan Sq Ste 3600 Saint Louis MO 63102-2750

METTE, VIRGIL LOUIS, publishing executive, biology educator; b. Moscow Mills, Mo., Jan. 8, 1942; s. Louis Charles Mette and Virginia Frances (Hustedde) Williams; m. Sharon Ann Werr, Aug. 15, 1964; children— Keith Douglas, Jeffrey Alan B.S., U. Mo., 1964. Gen. mgr. Sci. Research Assocs., Chgo., 1976-78; mktg. mgr. C. V. Mosby Co., St. Louis, 1978-79, editor-in-chief, 1979-80, v.p., 1980-83, sr. v.p., 1983-85. Teaching asst. U. Mo., Columbia, 1961-64 Sec. sch. bd. Zion Luth. Sch., Harvester, Mo., 1982-84 Avocations: boating; golf; reading. Office: C V Mosby Co 11830 Westline Industrial Dr Saint Louis MO 63146-3318

METTERS, THOMAS WADDELL, sports writer; b. Columbus, Ohio, Apr. 17, 1939; s. Thomas Hammond and Charlotte Ann (Waddell) M. BS in Journalism, Ohio U., 1965. Sports editor The Traveller, Ft. Lee, Va., 1960-62; sports writer The Athens (Ohio) Messenger, 1965—. Asst. to officials Legion Baseball, Athens, 1962—. Contbr.: Ohio Interscholastic Athletic Media Guide, 1985. Bd. dirs. Athens H.S. Booster Club, 1975—, Athens H.S. Athletic Hall of Fame, 2000; ofcl. scorekeeper Am. Legion World Series, Millington, Tenn., 1989. With U.S. Army, 1959-62. Named to Ohio H.S. Basketball Coaches Assn. Hall of Fame, 1993; recipient Contributor award Ohio H.S. Track & Field Coaches Assn., 1995, Ohio H.S. Athletic Assn. Media Svc. award, 1998. Mem. Soc. Profl. Journalists (Recognition plaque 1973), Ohio Associated Press Sports Writers Assn. (pres. 1984), Green & White Club (sec. 1983—, Jonesy Sams award 1987), Ohio Prep Sports Writers Assn. (Hall of Fame 1990), Ky. Colonels, Am. Legion. Republican. Avocation: bowling. Home: 71 Sunnyside Dr Athens OH 45701-1921 Office: The Athens Messenger 9300 Johnson Rd Athens OH 45701

METZ, ADAM S. real estate executive; Bachelor, Cornell U.; M of Mgmt., Northwestern U. Corp. lending officer 1st Nat. Bank Chgo., 1983-87; v.p. Capital Markets Group, JMB Realty, 1987-93; treas., CFO, exec. v.p, dir. acquisitions Urban Shopping Ctrs., Inc., 1993-2000, pres., 2000—. Mem. Internat. Coun. Shopping Ctrs. Office: Urban Shopping Ctrs Inc 900 N Michigan Ave Chicago IL 60611-1542

METZ, ANTHONY J., III, federal judge; Bankruptcy judge U.S. Dist. Ct. (so. dist.) Ind., Indpls., 1997—. Office: 317 US Courthouse 46 E Ohio St Indianapolis IN 46204-1903 E-mail: anthony_metz@insb.uscourts.gov.

METZ, CHARLES EDGAR, radiology educator; b. Bayshore, N.Y., Sept. 11, 1942; s. Clinton Edgar and Grace Muriel (Schienke) M.; m. Maryanne Theresa Bahr, July, 1967 (div. 1988); children: Rebecca, Molly. BA, Bowdoin Coll., 1964; MS, U. Pa., 1966, PhD, 1969. Instr. radiology U. Chgo., 1969-71, asst. prof., 1971-75, assoc. prof., 1976-80, dir. grad. programs in med. physics, 1979-85, prof., 1980—, prof. structural biology, 1984-86. Mem. diagnostic rsch. adv. group Nat. Cancer Inst., 1980-81; mem. sci. com. Nat. Coun. on Radiation Protection and Measurements, 1982-95, Internat. Commn. on Radiation Units and Measurements, 1988-96, chmn. sci. com., 1992-99; cons. and lectr. in field. Assoc. editor: Radiology Jour., 1986—91, assoc. editor: Med. Physics Jour., 1992—95, mem. editl. bd.: Med. Decision Making, 1980—84; contbr. over 200 articles to sci. jours. and chpts. to books, software analysis used in more than 4500 labs. worldwide. Mem. Radiol. Soc. N.Am., Am. Assn. Physicists in Medicine, Soc. Med. Decision Making, Assn. Univ. Radiologists, Soc. for Health Svcs. Rsch. in Radiology, Phi Beta Kappa, Sigma Xi. Office: U Chgo Dept Radiology MC2026 5841 S Maryland Ave Chicago IL 60637-1463 E-mail: c-metz@uchicago.edu.

METZ, PHILIP STEVEN, surgeon, educator; b. Omaha, May 12, 1945; s. Roman A. and Gwanetha (Hamilton) M.; m. Dianne Pearson, July 11, 1970; children: Amy Michelle, Wendy Marie, Stephanie Joy, Philip Robb. BS, Loras Coll., 1965; MD, U. Nebr., 1969. Diplomate Am. Bd. Surgery and Bd. Plastic Surgery with spl. qualification in hand surgery. Commd. USN, 1969; intern Nat. Naval Med. Ctr., Bethesda, Md., 1969-70; resident gen. surgery Oakland (Calif.) Naval Hosp., 1970-74; resident plastic and reconstructive surgery U. Utah, 1974-76; fellow hand surgery Derbyshire Royal Infirmary, Derby, Eng., 1980; dir. cleft palate team Nat. Naval Med. Ctr., Bethesda, 1977-79, chmn. plastic surgery, 1978-79, Bethesda Naval Hosp., Washington, 1979-80; pvt. practice Denver, 1980-82, Lincoln, Nebr., 1982—. Chmn. surgery Lincoln Gen. Hosp., 1986-87; mem. bd. med. examiners State Nebr., 1988-98; cons. cleft palate team State of Nebr., 1986; asst. clin. prof. U. Nebr.; mem. Nebr. State Bd. Examiners. Contbr. articles to profl. jours. Capt. USNR, ret. Fellow ACS, Internat. Coll. Surgeons; mem. Am. Soc. Plastic and Reconstructive Surgery, Assn. Mil. Surgeons U.S., Assn. Mil. Plastic Surgeons, British Assn. for Surgery of the Hand, Royal Soc. Medicine, Am. Cleft Palate Assn., AMA, Am. Soc. Maxillo-Facial Surgery, Am. Assn. Hand Surgery, Lancaster County Med. Soc. Avocations: hunting, fishing, camping. Office: 1730 S 70th St Ste 210 Lincoln NE 68506-1668

METZEN, JAMES P. state legislator, banker; b. Oct. 1943; m. Sandie Metzen; two children. Student, U. Minn. Banker; mem. Minn. Ho. of Reps., St. Paul, 1975-86, Minn. Senate from 39th dist., St. Paul, 1986—. Chmn. govt. op. and vets. com.; mem. jobs, energy and cmty. devel., state govt. fin. divsn. commerce and consumer protection, rules and adminstrn. Minn. State Senate. Office: 312 Deerwood Ct South Saint Paul MN 55075-2102 also: State Senate State Capital Building Saint Paul MN 55155-0001

METZENBAUM, HOWARD MORTON, former senator, consumer organization official; b. Cleve., June 4, 1917; s. Charles I. and Anna (Klafter) M.; m. Shirley Turoff, Aug. 8, 1946; children: Barbara Jo, Susan Lynn Hyatt, Shelley Hope, Amy Beth. BA, Ohio State U., 1939, LLD, 1941. Chmn. bd. Airport Parking Co. Am., 1958-66, ITT Consumer Services Corp., 1966-68, ComCorp, 1969-74; U.S. senator State of Ohio, 1974, 1977-94; chmn. Consumer Fedn. Am., Washington. Mem. War Labor Panel, 1942-45, Ohio Bur. Code Rev., 1949-50, Cleve. Met. Housing Authority, 1968-70, Lake Erie Regional Transit Authority, 1972-73, Ohio Ho. of Reps., 1943-46, Ohio Senate, 1947-50; chmn. anti-trust sub-com., labor sub-com. U.S. Senate; mem. intell com., budget com., environ. and pub. works com., judiciary com., labor and human resources, energy and natural resources, dem. policy com. Trustee Mt. Sinai Hosp., Cleve., 1961—73, treas., 1966—73; nat. co-chmn. Nat. Citizen's Com. Conquest Cancer; former vice chmn. fellows Brandeis U.; chmn. Am. Friend Rabin Ctr., Tel Aviv; past bd. dirs. Coun. Human Rels., United Cerebral Palsy

Assn., Nat. Coun. Hunger and Malnutrition, Karamu House, St. Vincent Charity Hosp., Cleve., St. Jude Rsch. Hosp., Memphis. Mem. Order of Coif, Phi Eta Sigma, Tau Epsilon Rho. Home: 5610 Wisconsin Ave Bethesda MD 20815-4415

METZGER, KERRY R. state legislator; m. Karen Metzger; children: Robert, Ryan. BS, Juniata Coll.; DDS, Temple U. Dentist pvt. practice, New Phila., Ohio; councilman City of New Phila., 1988-94; pres. City Coun. of New Phila., 1992-94; rep. dist. 97 Ohio Ho. of Reps., Columbus, 1994—. Mem. Tuscarawas County Rep. Exec. Com. Named Internat. Senator Jaycees; recipient Presidential award of honor, Ohio Jaycees. Mem. Am. Dental Assn., Ohio Dental Assn., Tuscarawas County Dental Soc., Soc. Forensic Odontology, Tuscarawas C. of C., Tuscarawas Valley Civil War Roundtable. Address: 1203 3rd St NW New Philadelphia OH 44663-1303

MEULEMAN, ROBERT JOSEPH, banker; b. South Bend, Ind., May 1, 1939; s. Joseph and Louise (Dutrieux) M.; m. Judith Ann Mc Comb, July 1, 1961; children Joseph, Jennifer, Rachel. BA, U. Notre Dame, 1961; MBA, Mich. State U., 1962. Investment analyst Nat. Bank of Detroit, 1965-68, Heritage Investment Advisors, Milw., 1968-72; sr. investment officer St. Joseph Bank and Trust Co., South Bend, 1972-81; pres., CEO Amcore Financial, Inc., Rockford, Ill., 1981—. Bd. dirs. Amcore Fin. Bd. dirs. Swedish Am. Hosp. Found., Rockford, 1986—, Rockford Pro-Am., 1986—, Rockford YMCA, 1993. Served to 1st lt. U.S. Army, 1963-65. Mem. Chartered Fin. Analysts, Milw. Fin. Analysts, Rockford C. of C. (bd. dirs. 1985). Republican. Roman Catholic. Club: Rockford Country. Avocations: skiing, golf, tennis. Home: 5329 Gingeridge Ln Rockford IL 61114-5333 Office: Amcore Financial Inc 501 7th St Rockford IL 61104-1200

MEUSER, FREDRICK WILLIAM, retired seminary president, church historian; b. Payne, Ohio, Sept. 14, 1923; s. Henry William and Alvina Maria (Bouyack) M.; m. Jeanne Bond Griffiths, July 29, 1951; children: Jill Martha, Douglas Griffiths. AB, Capital U., 1945, BD, 1948, DD (hon.), 1989; STM, Yale U., 1949, MA, 1953, PhD, 1956; DD (hon.), Tex. Luth. Coll., 1980, Capital U., 1989; LHD (hon.), Augustana Coll., 1985. Ordained to ministry Am. Lutheran Ch., 1948; asst. pastor 1st Luth. Ch., Galveston, Tex., 1948, Christ Luth. Ch., North Miami, Fla., 1949-51; campus minister Yale U., 1951-53; prof. ch. history Luth. Theol. Sem., Columbus, Ohio, 1953-78, dean grad. studies, 1963-69, pres., 1971-78, Trinity Luth. Sem., Columbus, 1978-88; exec. sec. div. theol. studies Luth. Council in U.S.A., 1969-71; del. World Council Chs., 1968, Luth. World Fedn., 1970; v.p. Am. Luth. Ch., 1974-80; mem. Commn. for a New Luth. Ch., 1982-86; asst. pastor St. Paul Luth. Ch., Westerville, Ohio, 1995-97. Author: The Formation of the American Lutheran Church, 1958, Luther the Preacher, 1983; author: (with others) Church in Fellowship, 1963, Lutherans in North America, 1975; translator: (with others) What Did Luther Understand by Religion, 1977, The Reconstruction of Morality, 1979; editor and author: (with others) Interpreting Luther's Legacy, 1967. Recipient Disting. Churchman's award Tex. Luth. Coll., 1972, Joseph Sittler award Trinity Luth. Sem., 1990; named Outstanding Alumnus Capital U., 1977; Am. Assn. Theol. Schs. fellow, 1961-62 Home: 6392 Claypool Ct Columbus OH 43213-3435 Office: 2199 E Main St Columbus OH 43209-3913 E-mail: fredmeuser@aol.com.

MEYER, AUGUST CHRISTOPHER, JR. broadcasting company executive, lawyer; b. Champaign, Ill., Aug. 14, 1937; s. August C. and Clara (Rocke) M.; m. Karen Haugh Hassett, Dec. 28, 1960; children: August Christopher F., Elisabeth Hassett. BA cum laude, Harvard U., 1959, LLB, 1962. Bar: Ill. 1962. Ptr. Meyer-Capel, Champaign, Ill., 1962-77, of counsel, 1977—; owner, dir., officer Midwest TV, Inc., Sta. KFMB-TV-AM-FM, San Diego, Sta. WCIA-TV, Champaign, Ill. , Sta. WMBD-TV-AM, WMXP, Peoria, 1968—, pres., 1976—. Bd. dirs. BankIll., Main St. Trust Inc.; spl. asst. atty. gen. State of Ill., 1968-76. Chmn. bd. trustees Carle Found. Hosp., Urbana, Ill. Mem. Ill. Bar Assn., Champaign County Bar Assn. Club: Champaign Country. Home: 1408 S Prospect Ave Champaign IL 61820-6837 Office: Midwest TV Inc PO Box 197 100 W University Ave # 401 Champaign IL 61824-0197 also: Sta KFMB PO Box 85888 7677 Engineer Rd San Diego CA 92111-1515

MEYER, BRUD RICHARD, retired pharmaceutical company executive; b. Waukegan, Ill., Feb. 22, 1926; s. Charles Lewis and Mamie Olive (Broom) M.; m. Betty Louise Stine (dec. 1970); children: Linda (Mrs. Gary Stillabower), Louise (Mrs. Donald Knochel), Janet (Mrs. Gerald Cockrell), Jeff, Karen, Blake, Amy; m. Barbara Ann Hamilton, Nov. 26, 1970. B.S., Purdue U., 1949. With Eli Lilly & Co., Indpls., 1949-87, indsl. engr., 1949-56, supr. indsl. engr., 1956-59, sr. personnel rep., 1960-64, personnel mgr. Lafayette, Ind., 1964-67, asst. dir., 1967-69, dir. adminstrn., 1969-79, dir. personnel and public relations, 1980-87, ret., 1987. Bd. dirs. Lafayette Home Hosp., 1977— , Hanna Community Ctr., 1983—, Tippecanoe Hist. Corp., 1985—; bd. dirs. United Way Tippecanoe County, 1970-76, pres., 1974; bd. dirs. Legal Aid Soc. Tippecanoe County, 1973—, Jr. Achievement, pres., 1979; bd. dirs. Lilly Credit Union, 1969-75, pres., 1973-74; mem. Citizen's Com. on Alcoholism, 1966-72; bd. dirs. Greater Lafayette Cmty. Ctrs., 1975-79, pres., 1977-78; bd. dirs. Tippecanoe County Child Care, 1990—, pres., 1998-99; mem., mng. dir. Battle Tippecanoe Outdoor Drama Bd. With USAAF, 1943-45. Mem. Pi Tau Sigma, Lambda Chi Alpha, C. of C. Greater Lafayette (bd. dirs., v.p. 1969-73), Battleground Hist. Soc. Methodist. Home: 4217 Trees Hill Dr Lafayette IN 47909-3451 Office: Eli Lilly & Co PO Box 7685 Lafayette IN 47903-7685

MEYER, DANIEL JOSEPH, machinery company executive; b. Flint, Mich., May 31, 1936; s. John Michael and Margaret (Meehan) M.; m. Bonnie Harrison, June 22, 1963; children: Daniel P., Jennifer. BS, Purdue U., 1958; MBA, Ind. U., 1963. CPA, N.Y. Mgr. Touche, Ross & Co., Detroit, 1964-69; contr. Cin. Milacron, Inc., 1969-77, v.p. fin., treas., 1977-83, exec. v.p. fin. and adminstrn., 1983-86, pres., COO, 1987-90, pres., CEO, 1990-91, chmn., CEO, 1991-92, also bd. dirs. Bd. dirs. E.W. Scripps Inc., Hubbell Inc., Cin. Bell Inc., AK Steel. With U.S. Army, 1959. Mem. Am. Inst. CPAs, Kenwood Country Club (Cin.). Club: Kenwood Country (Cin.). Home: 8 Grandin Ln Cincinnati OH 45208-3304 Office: 2090 Florence Ave Cincinnati OH 45206-2425

MEYER, G. CHRISTOPHER, lawyer; b. Fremont, Nebr., Mar. 27, 1948; s. Gerald William and Mildred Ruth (Clausen) M.; m. Linda Haines, Dec. 27, 1969; children: Kate, Stacy, Jon, Robert. Student, Grinnell (Iowa) Coll., 1966-69; BA, U. Kans., 1970; JD, U. Pa., 1973. Bar: Ohio 1973, U.S. Dist. Ct. (no. dist.) Ohio 1975, U.S. Ct. Appeals (6th cir.) 1982. Assoc. Squire, Sanders & Dempsey, L.L.P., Cleve., 1973-82, ptnr., 1982—. Mem. ABA, Ohio State Bar Assn., Greater Cleve. Bar Assn. Office: Squire Sanders & Dempsey LLP 4900 Key Tower 127 Public Sq Cleveland OH 44114-1304 E-mail: cmeyer@ssd.com.

MEYER, HENRY LEWIS, III, banker; b. Cleve., Dec. 25, 1949; s. Henry Lewis and Anne (Taylor) M.; m. Jane Kreamer, July 15, 1978; children: Patrick Harrison, Andrew Taylor, Christopher Bicknell. BA, Colgate U., 1972; MBA, Harvard U., Boston, 1978. Asst. v.p. Soc. Nat. Bank, Cleve., 1972-76, v.p., 1978-81, sr. v.p., 1981-83; exec. v.p. Soc. Bank, Dayton, Ohio, 1983-85, pres., chief operating officer, 1985-87; sr. exec. v.p. Soc. Nat. Bank, Cleve., 1987-89, vice chmn. bd., 1989-90, pres., COO, 1990-93, pres., CEO, 1993-94, chmn. bd., CEO, 1994-95; exec. v.p. Soc. Corp., 1987-91, vice chmn. bd., 1991-94; exec. v.p. KeyCorp (formerly Soc. Corp.), 1994-95, sr. exec. v.p., COO, 1995-96, vice chmn. bd., COO, 1996-97, pres., COO, 1997—; pres., CEO KeyCorp, 2001—; exec. v.p. KeyCorp (formerly Soc. Corp.), 1994-95. Bd. dirs. Key Corp, The Lincoln Elec. Co. Trustee Am. Cancer Soc. (Cuyahoga County Unit), Cleve. Mus. Nat. History; vis. com. Case Western Res. U. Weatherhead Sch. Mgmt.; active The Holden Arboretum, Inroads, Northeast Ohio Coun. Higher Edn., Univ. Sch.; chmn. bd. trustees Sta. WVIZ-TV; mem. exec. com., bd. dirs. U. Hosps. Health Sys., Inc. Republican. Episcopalian. Clubs: Kirtland Country (Cleve.), The Union (Cleve.), Cleve. Skating, Pepper Pike (Cleve.), Club at Key Ctr. (Cleve.).

MEYER, JAMES B. retail executive; Dir. retail acctg. Spartan Stores, Grand Rapids, Mich., 1973-89, sr. v.p., CFO, 1989-96, COO, 1996-97, pres., CEO, 1997—, chmn., 2000—, also bd. dirs. Bd. dirs. Mich. Nat. Bank, Hope Network, Davenport Coll. Bd. dirs. Heart of West Mich. United Way, Employers Coalition Healing Racism, Mich. Econ. Devel. Coun.; corp. chair Year 2000 Juvenile Diabetes Found. Walk. Mem. Nat. Grocers Assn. (bd. mem.), Food Distbrs. Internat. (bd. mem.), Econ. Club Grand Rapids (bd. mem.). Office: Spartan Stores 850 76th St SW Grand Rapids MI 49518-8700

MEYER, MARK, state legislator; b. La Crosse, Wis., Sept. 3, 1963; Mem. Wis. Assembly from 95th dist., Madison, 1992-2000, Wis. Senate from 32nd dist., Madison, 2001—. Home: 9205 16th St La Crosse WI 54601-6132

MEYER, MAURICE WESLEY, physiologist, dentist, neurologist; b. Long Prairie, Minn., Feb. 13, 1925; s. Ernest William and Augusta (Warnke) M.; m. Martha Helen Davis, Sept. 3, 1946; children— James Irvin, Thomas Orville. B.S., U. Minn., 1953, D.D.S., 1957, M.S., 1959, Ph.D., 1961. Teaching asst. U. Minn. Sch. Dentistry, 1954-55, USPHS fellow, 1955-56, rsch. fellow, 1956-57, mem. faculty, 1960—; prof. physiology, dentistry and neurology U. Minn., 1976-88, prof. emeritus, 1988—; investigator Ctr. Rsch. and Cerebral Vascular Disease, 1969—; dir. lab. Center Research and Cerebral Vascular Disease, 1975—; postdoctoral research fellow Nat. Inst. Dental Research, 1957-60, research fellow, 1958-61, mem. faculty, 1961—, asso. prof. neurology, 1974-80, mem. grad. faculty, 1973—; trainee Inst. Advanced Edn. in Dental Research, 1964—. Vis. asso. prof., also vis. research fellow dept. physiology and Sch. Dentistry Cardiovascular Research Inst., U. Calif., San Francisco, 1971 Contbr. articles to profl. jours. Served to col. Dental Corps AUS, 1943-85. Decorated D.F.C., Air medal with 3 oak leaf clusters. Fellow AAAS; mem. ADA, Minn. Dental Soc., Internat. Assn. Dental Research (pres. Minn. sect. 1967-68), Soc. Exptl. Biology and Medicine, Am. Physiol. Soc., Microcirculatory Soc., Am. Assn. Dental Schs. (chmn. 1972-73), Can. Physiol. Soc., Sigma Xi, Omicron Kappa Upsilon. Club: Masons. Home: 560 Rice Creek Ter NE Minneapolis MN 55432-4472 Office: U Minn 6-255 Millard Minneapolis MN 55455 E-mail: meyer109@tc.umn.edu.

MEYER, MICHAEL LOUIS, lawyer; b. Buffalo, Dec. 17, 1940; s. Bernard H. and Florence (Nusbaum) M.; m. Jo Ann Ackerman, Sept. 21, 1990. AB, Princeton U., 1962; LLB, Harvard U., 1965. Bar: Ill. 1965, D.C., 1978. Assoc. Schiff Hardin & Waite, Chgo., 1965-72, ptnr., 1972—. Lt. USN, 1965-68. Mem. ABA (mem. fed. regulation of security com.), Chgo. Bar Assn., Chgo. Coun. Lawyers, Chgo. Yacht Club, Metropolitan Club Office: Schiff Hardin & Waite 7200 Sears Tower Ste 1200 Chicago IL 60606

MEYER, PAUL REIMS, JR. orthopedic surgeon; b. Port Arthur, Tex. s. Paul Reims and Evelyn (Miller) M.; m. Lesa W. Meyer; children: Kristin Lynn, Holly Dee, Paul Reims III, Stewart Blair. BA, Va. Mil. Inst., 1954; MD, Tulane U., 1958; MA of Mgmt., J.L. Kellogg Grad. Sch. of Mgmt. (Northwestern U.), 1992. Dir. Spine Injury Ctr. Northwestern U., Chgo., 1972—, prof. orthopaedic surgery, 1981—. Cons. Nat. Inst. Disability and Rehab. Rsch. VA, Washington, 1978-2000; clin. prof. surgery Dept. Surgery, USUHS; mem. adv. com. World Rehab. Fund, 1990—; mem. bd. councilors Am. Acad. Orthopaedic Surgeons, 1993-96. Author: Surgery of Spine Trauma, 1988; patentee cervical orthosis. Col. M.C., USAR. Fellow ACS, Am. Acad. Orthop. Surgeons; mem. Sociéé Internationale de Chirurgie Orthopédique et de Traumatologie, Internat. Med. Soc. Paraplegia, Am. Trauma Soc. (bd. dirs. 1988—), Am. Orthop. Assn., Am. Spinal Injury Assn. (past pres.), Soc. Med. Cons. to Armed Forces, Mid-Am. Orthop. Assn. Roman Catholic. Avocations: photography, fishing, ham radio, aviation, boating. Office: Northwestern Meml Hosp 250 E Superior St Ste 619 Chicago IL 60611-2950 also: Northwestern Meml Hosp Ste 11-245 201 E Huron Chicago IL 60611 E-mail: Interspace@nwu.edu.

MEYER, RAYMOND JOSEPH, former college basketball coach; b. Chgo., Dec. 18, 1913; s. Joseph E. and Barbara (Hummel) M.; m. Margaret Mary Delaney, May 27, 1939 (dec. 1985); children— Barbara (Mrs. Gerald Starzyk), Raymond Thomas, Patricia (Mrs. Thomas Butterfield), Merianne (Mrs. James McGowan; dec. 1997), Joseph, Robert. A.B., U. Notre Dame, 1938. Asst. coach U. Notre Dame, 1941-42; basketball coach DePaul U., Chgo., 1942—. Author: How To Play Winning Basketball, 1960, Basketball as Coached by Ray Meyer, 1967, Ray Meyer, 1 Coach, 1980, Coach, 1987. Named Coach of Yr. Chgo. Basketball Writers, 1943, 44, 48, 52, Coach of Yr. Nat. Assn. Basketball Coaches, 1978-79, Sportwriters Coach of Yr., 1978, Salvation Man of Yr., 1990; recipient Marine Corps Sportsman of Yr. award, 1979, Bunn award, 1981, Victor award, 1981, Lincoln Acad. award, 1988, Nat. Basketball Coach's Golden Jubilee award, Notre Dame Lifetime Achievement award 1998; inducted into Basketball Hall of Fame, 1979, Basketball Hall of Fame Chgo., 1981, Basketball Hall of Fame Ill., Golden Anniversay award Nat. Basketball Coaches, 1992, Naismith Found. Good Sportsman's award, 1998. Mem. Nat. Basketball Coaches Assn. Roman Catholic. Home: 2518 W Cedar Glen Dr Arlington Heights IL 60005-4336 Office: 100 Turner Ave Elk Grove Village IL 60007-3933

MEYER, RICHARD CHARLES, microbiologist, educator; b. Cleve., May 2, 1930; s. Frederick Albert and Tekla Charlotte (Schrade) M.; m. Carolyn Yvonne Patton, Apr. 6, 1963; children: Frederick Gustav, Carl Anselm. B.Sc., Baldwin-Wallace Coll., 1952; M.Sc., Ohio State U., 1957, Ph.D., 1961. Teaching and research asst. Ohio State U., 1956-61, research assoc., 1961-62; microbiologist Nat. Cancer Inst., NIH, Bethesda, Md., 1962-64; asst. prof. vet. pathology and hygiene and microbiology U. Ill., Urbana-Champaign, 1965-68, assoc. prof., 1968-73, prof., 1973-89, prof. emeritus, 1989—. Served with C.E. U.S. Army, 1952-54. Mem. Am. Acad. Microbiology, AAAS, Am. Inst. Biol. Sci., Am. Soc. Microbiology, Gamma Sigma Delta, Phi Zeta. Republican. Lutheran. Home: 1504 S Buckthorn Ln Mahomet IL 61853-3632 Office: Dept Vet Pathobiology U Ill at Urbana-Champaign Urbana IL 61801

MEYER, RUSSELL WILLIAM, JR. aircraft company executive; b. Davenport, Iowa, July 19, 1932; s. Russell William and Ellen Marie (Matthews) M.; m. Helen Scott Vaughn, Aug. 20, 1960; children: Russell William, III, Elizabeth Ellen, Jeffrey Vaughn, Christopher Matthews, Carolyn Louise. BA, Yale U., 1954; LLB, Harvard U., 1961. Bar: Ohio 1961. Mem. firm Arter & Hadden, Cleve., 1961-66; pres., chief exec. officer Grumman Am. Aviation Corp., 1966-74; exec. v.p. Cessna Aircraft Co., Wichita, Kans., 1974-75, chmn. bd., chief exec. officer, 1975-2000, chmn., 2000—. Bd. dirs. Nations Bank, Pub. Broadcasting Svc., Welfare to Work Partnership; presdl. appointee Aviation Safety Commn., 1987—; mem. Pres.' Airline Commn., 1993; dir. Pub. Broadcasting Sys. Chmn. bd. trustees 1st Bapt. Ch., Cleve., 1972-74; bd. dirs. United Way, Wichita and Sedgwick County; trustee Wesley Hosp. Endowment Assn., Wake Forest Univ.; bd. govs. United Way Am., 1993—. With USAF, 1955-58. Recipient Collier trophy Nat. Aeronautic Assn., 1986, George S. Dively award Harvard U., 1992, Wright Bros. Meml. trophy, 1995, Disting. Svc. Citation U. Kans., 2000; named Kansan of the Yr., 1998. Mem. ABA, Ohio Bar Assn., Kans. Bar Assn., Cleve. Bar Assn., Gen. Aviation Mfrs. Assn. (chmn. bd. dirs. 1973-74, 81-82, 93-94), Wichita C. of C. (chmn. 1988—, bd. dirs.), Wichita Club, Wichita Country Club, Pine Valley Club, Cypress Point Club, Double Eagle Country Club, Flint Hills Nat. Club, Latrobe Country Club. Home: 600 N Tara Ct Wichita KS 67206-1830 Office: Cessna Aircraft PO Box 7704 1 Cessna Blvd Wichita KS 67215-1424

MEYER, SUSAN M. lawyer, company executive; b. 1943; BA in Philosophy and Psychology, Marquette U.; JD, Fordham U. Officer, investigator Washington Met. Police Dept.; gen. counsel Beatrice Consumer Durables, Northbrook, Ill., G.D. Searle & Co., Skokie; sr. counsel Beatrice Cos., Inc., Chgo., 1986-91; v.p., sec., dep. counsel Gen. Instrument Corp., 1991-98; v.p., sec., gen. counsel United Stationers Inc., Des Plaines, Ill., 1998—. Office: 2200 E Golf Rd Des Plaines IL 60016-1246

MEYER, WILLIAM MICHAEL, mortgage banking executive; b. Fort Wayne, Ind., Oct. 21, 1940; s. Henry and Lola Mae (Leedy) M.; m. Phyllis Ann Ruetschilling, Aug. 12, 1961; children: Michael Dean, Blaine Aaron, Nathan Daniel, Andrea Rene. Degree in Bus., Ind. U., 1970. V.p. Waterfield Mortgage Corp., Fort Wayne, 1963-73, First Nat. Bank, Colorado Springs, Colo., 1973-78, Underwood Mortgage Co., Lawrenceville, N.J., 1978-79, Mortgage Serv, South Bend, Ind., 1979-82; sr. v.p. Irwin Mortgage Corp., Indpls., 1982—. Bd. dirs. Ctrl. Ind. Quality Leadership Forum, Indpls. Bd. dirs. Edyvean Repertory Theatre, 1996-99. Mem. Mortgage Bankers Assn. (mem. com. 1979—), Ind. Mortgage Bankers (bd. dirs. 1992—), Rotary (Zionsville bd. dirs. 1990-93). Republican. Roman Catholic. Avocations: skiing, gardening, swimming, golf. Home: 12071 Sail Place Dr Indianapolis IN 46256-9441

MEYERS, CHRISTINE LAINE, marketing and media executive, consultant; b. Detroit, Mar. 7, 1946; d. Ernest Robert and Eva Elizabeth (Laine) M.; 1 child, Kathryn Laine; m. Oliver S. Moore III, May 12, 1990. BA, U. Mich., 1968. Editor indsl. rels. diesel divsn. Gen. Motors Corp., Detroit, 1968; nat. advt. mgr. J.L. Hudson Co., 1969-76, mgr. internal sales promotion, 1972-73, dir. pub., 1973-76; nat. advt. mgr. Pontiac Motor divsn., Mich., 1976-78; pres., owner Laine Meyers Mktg. Cos., Inc., Troy, 1978—; founder, owner CORP! Mag., 1998—. Dir. Internat. Inst. Met. Detroit, Inc. Contbr. articles to profl. publs. Mem. bus. adv. coun. Ctrl. Mich. U., 1977-79; mem. pub. adv. com. on jud. candidates Oakland County Bar Assn.; mem. adv. bd. Birmingham Cmty. Hosp., Bank of Am., 1999-2001; bd. dirs. YMCA, Mich., 1992-98, Haven, 1997—, Automation Alley, Oakland County, 1999—. Named Mich. Ad Woman of Yr., 1976, one of Top 10 Working Women, Glamour mag., 1978, one of 100 Best and Brightest Advt. Age, 1987, one of Mich.'s top 25 female bus. owners Nat. Assn. Women Bus. Owners, One of Top 10 Women Owned Bus., Mich., 1994; recipient Vanguard award Women in Comm., 1986. Mem. Internat. Assn. Bus. Communicators, Adcraft Club, Women's Advt. Club (1st v.p. 1975), Women's Econ. Club (pres. 1976-77), Internat. Women's Forum Mich. (founding pres. 1986-97), Internat. Inst. Detroit (bd. dirs. 1986-89), Detroit C. of C., Troy C. of C., Mortar Bd., Quill and Scroll, Pub. Rels. Com. Women for Uunted Found., Founders Soc. Detroit Inst. Arts, Fashion Group, Pub. Rels. Soc. Am., First Soc. Detroit (exec. com. 1970-71), Kappa Tau Alpha. Home: 5165 Longmeadow Rd Bloomfield Hills MI 48304-3657 Office: Laine Meyers Mktg Cos Inc 3645 Crooks Rd Troy MI 48084-1642 E-mail: chrism@lainemeyers.com.

MEYERS, GERALD CARL, educator, author, expert witness, consultant; b. Buffalo, Dec. 5, 1928; s. Meyer and Berenice (Meyers) M.; m. Barbara Jacob, Nov. 2, 1958. BS, Carnegie Inst. Tech., 1950, MS with distinction, 1954. With Ford Motor Co., Detroit, 1950-51, Chrysler Corp., Detroit and Geneva, 1954-62; with Am. Motors Corp., Detroit, 1962-84, v.p., 1967-72, group v.p. product, 1972-75, exec. v.p., 1975-77, pres., 1977-84, COO, 1977, chmn., CEO, 1977-82, ret., 1984; Ford disting. prof. Grad. Sch. Indsl. Adminstrn. Carnegie Mellon U., Pitts., 1985-96; prof. U. Mich. Bus. Sch., Ann Arbor, 1995—. Pres. Gerald C. Meyers Assocs., Inc., West Bloomfield, Mich.; adj. prof. Sch. Bus. U. Mich., Ann Arbor. Author: When It Hits the Fan, Managing the Nine Crises of Business; co-author: Dealers, Healers, Brutes and Saliors; bus. commentator Nat. Pub. Radio, Fox News Cable TV, CNBC TN Network; contbr. articles to N.Y. Times, Wall St. Jour., L.A. Times. 1st lt. USAF, 1951-53. Decorated Legion of Honor (France). Mem. Econ. Club Detroit, Tau Beta Pi, Phi Kappa Phi, Omicron Delta Kappa. Address: U Mich Bus Sch D 3246 701 Tappan Ave Ann Arbor MI 48109-1217 Office: 5600 W Maple Rd Ste B216 West Bloomfield MI 48322-3787

MEYERS, JOHN E. prosecutor; b. Ann Arbor, Mich., July 24, 1944; s. Roy E. and Emaline (Pryor) M.; m. Suzanne Meyers, June 7, 1966; children: Ben, Elizabeth, Tom, Peter. BA, David Lipscomb Coll., Nashville, 1966; JD, U. Toledo, 1969. Bar: Ohio 1969, U.S. Dist. Ct. (so. dist.) Ohio 1973, U.S. Dist. Ct. (no. dist.) Ohio 1976. Spl. agt. FBI, Washington/Savannah, 1969-73; pros. Mcpl. Ct. Bellevue (Ohio), 1974-84, Sandusky County Ct., Fremont, Ohio, 1985—; ptnr. Meyers & Wallingford, Bellevue. Pres. bd. trustees Bellevue Libr. Bd., 1977; v.p. trustees Bellevue Hosp. Bd., 1984. Mem. Ohio Pros. Attys. Assn. (exec. com. 1988—), Huron County Bar Assn. (sec. 1975), Bellevue C. of C. (pres. 1978-79), Rotary (pres. 1982). Republican. Ch. of Christ. Home: 412 W Main St Bellevue OH 44811-1334 Office: Meyers & Wallingford 117 W Main St Bellevue OH 44811-1329

MEYERS, PAMELA SUE, lawyer; b. Lakewood, N.J., June 13, 1951; d. Morris Leon and Isabel (Leibowitz) M.; m. Gerald Stephen Greenberg, Aug. 24, 1975; children: David Stuart Greenberg, Allison Brooke Greenberg. AB with distinction, Cornell U., 1973; JD cum laude, Harvard U., 1976. Bar: N.Y. 1977, Ohio 1990. Assoc. Stroock & Stroock & Lavan, N.Y.C., 1976-80; staff v.p., asst. gen. counsel Am. Premier Underwriters, Inc., Cin., 1980-96; legal counsel Citizens Fed. Bank, Dayton, 1997-98; gen. counsel, sec. Mosler Inc., Hamilton, 1998—2001. Bd. dirs. Hamilton County Alcohol and Drug Addiction Svc. Bd., 1996-2000, Adath Israel Synagogue, 1999—. Mem. Cin. Bar Assn., Harvard Club of Cin. (pres. 1998-99, bd. dirs. 1993-2000), Phi Beta Kappa. Jewish. Avocations: piano, reading, golf. Home: 3633 Carpenters Creek Dr Cincinnati OH 45241-3824

MEYERS, RICHARD JAMES, landscape architect; b. Columbus, Ohio, Jan. 25, 1940; s. Ralph Joseph and Margaret Mary (Kruse) M.; m. Mary Igoe, Jan. 12, 1963; children: Gregory James, Helen Marie, Andrew James. B.Landscape Arch., Ohio State U., 1961. Registered landscape architect, Ohio, Mich., Fla., Ind.; cert. Council Landscape Archtl. Registration Bds. Jr. planner Columbus Planning Commn. (Ohio), 1960-62; landscape architect Behnke-Nes & Assocs., Cleve., 1962-65, Arthur Hills & Assocs., Toledo, 1965-67; ptnr. Mortensen-Meyers Assocs., 1967-69; prin. MMSS Inc., 1969-71, The Collaborative, Inc., Toledo, 1973-99; bd. dirs., past pres. Council Landscape Archtl. Registration Bd., Syracuse, N.Y., 1978-86, Ohio Bd. Landscape Architect Examiners, 1975-83. Adv. bd. Ohio State U. Land Architecture, 1999—, Toledo Mcpl. Cemetery Commn., 1999—; bd. dirs. Toledo Botanical Gardens, 2000—. Active St. Vincent Hosp. and Med. Ctr. Assocs., Toledo, 1978-83; bd. dirs. Family Svcs. Greater Toledo, 1977-82, Toledo Central City Neighborhood, 2001—; com. mem. Toledo Met. Area Coun. of Govt., 1972-79, 87-89, Toledo Bot. Gardens Design Rev. Bd., 1988-90, Downtown Toledo Vision, Inc., 1988-99; chmn. Toledo Lucas County Plan Commn., 1989-99; chmn. Toledo Adminstrv. Bd. Zoning Appeals, 1994-99, Met. Parks Com. of 25, 1991, 1997; chmn. campaign divsn. United Way, 1991; adv. bd. U. Toledo-Stranahan Arboretum, 1994—, Scenic Ohio, 1996—; trustees adv. coun. Schedel Arboretum

& Gardens, 2000—. Dumbarton Oaks Jr. summer scholar, 1960; recipient First Honor Design award Am. Assn. Nurserymen, 1974; named Disting. Alumnus, Ohio State Univ. Coll. Engring., 1996. Fellow Am. Soc. Landscape Architects (merit design award Ohio chpt. 1975, 81, 83, 85, Outstanding Svc. to Profession award 1983, Ohio Chpt. medal 1984); mem. AIA, Ohio Chpt. of Am. Soc. Landscape Architects (v.p. 1974-76), Urban Land Inst., Soc. for Coll. and Univ. Planning, Am. Forestry Assn., Am. Planning Assn., Rails to Trails Conservancy, Ohio Pks. and Recreation Assn., Heatherdowns Country Club (bd. dirs. 1983).

MEYSMAN, FRANK L. food and consumer products executive; b. Belgium; Grad., U. Brussels, U. Ghent (Belgium). Various mktg. positions Procter & Gamble, Brussels and Hamburg, Germany, 1977-86; v.p. mktg. Douwe Egberts Belgium, 1986-89, pres., 1989-90, sr. v.p. corp. strategy, bus. devel., 1990-91; mem. coffee and grocery bd. Sara Lee/DE, Utrecht, The Netherlands, 1991-92, corp. v.p., 1992-94, sr. v.p., 1992-94, also chmn. bd. mgmt., 1994—; exec. v.p. Sara Lee Corp., Chgo., 1997—. Office: Sara Lee Corp Three 1st National Plz Chicago IL 60602-4260

MICALLEF, JOSEPH STEPHEN, retired lawyer; b. Malta, Oct. 19, 1933; came to U.S., 1949; s. John E. and Josephine (Brownrigg) M.; m. Jane M. Yungers, Sept. 5, 1959; children: Lisa R., Maura J. Fisk, Sara M. Hulse, Amy A., Joseph S. Jr. BA cum laude, U. St. Thomas, 1958, LLB, JD, 1962. Pres., CEO Fiduciary Counselling, Inc., St. Paul, 1961-71, dir., cons., 1971-95. Trustee Gt. No. Iron Ore Properties Trust, St. Paul, The Charles A. Lindbergh Fund, Mpls.; mem. bd. visitors U. Minn. Law Sch., Mpls. Past pres., mem. exec. com. Minn. Hist. Soc., St. Paul; bd. dirs. Minn. Air NG Hist. Found., Inc., Plymouth Music Series, Ramsey County Hist. Soc.; bd. overseers Hill Monastic Manuscript Libr.; past regent St. John's U., Collegeville, Minn.; mem. investment adv. com. Archdiocese St. Paul/Mpls.; mem. fin. coun. Cathedral of St. Paul; dir. emeritus Sci. Mus. Minn., St. Paul; trustee James Jerome Hill Ref. Libr., St. Paul. Decorated Knight of the Sovereign Mil., Order of Malta, 1981, Knight of the Equestrian Order of Holy Sepulchre of Jerusalem, Hon. Consul Gen. of Malta, St. Paul/Mpls. Mem. ABA (com. on real property, probate and trust law), Minn. Bar Assn. (subcom. on the Minn. nonprofit corp. act trust law com.), Minn. Coun. on Founds. (govt. rels. com.), Minn. Club (bd. govs.), Town & Country Club, Casino Maltese Club, The Union Club (Malta). Office: Great Northern Iron Ore Properties W 1290 First National Bank 332 Minnesota St Saint Paul MN 55101-1361

MICEK, ERNEST S. former food products executive; b. Arcadia, Wis., Feb. 18, 1936; m. Sally; 4 children. BS in Chem. Engring., U. Wis., 1959. Mgr. Cargill, Inc., Mpls., 1959, Spain, asst. v.p., gen. mgr. corn milling dept., 1973, v.p. milling divsn., 1978, pres. corn milling divsn., 1981, pres. food sector, 1992, exec. v.p., 1993, pres., 1994-98, chmn., pres., CEO, 1995-99. Bd. dirs. Cargill, Inc., Schneider Nat.; chmn. ECAT; mem. bd. overseers, mem. internat. adv. bd. Carlson Sch. Mgmt.; mem. Pres.'s Export Coun., Pacific Basin Econ. Coun., U.S. Sect. Bd. dirs. United Way Exec. Com., Mpls.; trustee U. St. Thomas., U. Wis. Alumni Rsch. Found. Recipient Disting. Svc. citation U. Wis. Dept. Engring., 1991; named Man of Yr., Consumers for World Trade, 1999; recipient Coya Knudson Humanitarian award 1999. Mem. Nat. Assn. Mfrs. (bd. dirs., exec. com.). Office: Adminstrv office Cargill Inc PO Box 5724 Minneapolis MN 55440-5724

MICHAEL, ALFRED FREDERICK, JR. physician, medical educator; b. Phila. s. Alfred Frederick and Emma Maude (Peters) M.; m. Jeanne Jones; children: Mary, Susan, Carol. M.D., Temple U., 1953. Diplomate: Am. Bd. Pediatrics (founding mem. sub-bd. pediatric nephrology, pres. 1977-80). Diagnostic lab. immunology and pediatric nephrology intern Phila. Gen. Hosp., 1953-54; resident Children's Hosp. and U. Cin. Coll. Medicine, 1957-60; postdoctoral fellow dept. pediatrics Med. Sch., U. Minn., Mpls., 1960-63, assoc. prof., 1965-68, prof. pediatrics, lab. medicine and pathology, 1968-88, dir. pediatric nephrology, 1997, Regents' Prof., 1986—, head Dept. Pediatrics, 1986-97, interim dean, 1996-97, dean, 1997—. Established investigator Am. Heart Assn., 1963-68. Past mem. editl. bd. Internat. Yr. Book of Nephrology, Am. Jour. Nephrology, Kidney Internat., Clin. Nephrology, Am. Jour. Pathology; contbr. articles to profl. jours. Served with USAF, 1955-57. Recipient Alumni Achievement award in clin. scis. Temple U. Sch. Medicine, 1988; NIH fellow, 1960-63; Guggenheim fellow, 1966-67; AAAS fellow, 1995. Mem. AAAS, AMA, Am. Acad. Pediat., Am. Soc. Clin. Investigation, Assn. Am. Physicians, Am. Pediat. Soc., Soc. for Pediat. Rsch., Am. Assn. Investigative Pathology, Am. Soc. Cell Biology, Ctrl. Soc. for Clin. Rsch., Am. Soc. Nephrology (coun., pres.-elect 1992—, pres. 1993), Internat. Soc. Nephrology, Soc. for Exptl. Biology and Medicine, Am. Fedn. Clin. Rsch., Minn. Med. Assn. Congregationalist. Home: 1986 Lower Saint Dennis Rd Saint Paul MN 55116-2820

MICHAEL, JONATHAN EDWARD, insurance company executive; b. Columbus, Ohio, Mar. 19, 1954; BA, Ohio Dominican Coll., 1977. CPA, Ohio. Acct. Coopers & Lybrand, Columbus, Ohio, 1977-82; chief acct. RLI Ins. Co., Peoria, Ill., 1982-84, controller, 1984-85, v.p. fin., CFO, 1985—, exec. v.p., 1991-94, pres., COO, 1994-2000, pres., CEO, 2001—, chmn. bd., 2002—. Roman Catholic. Club: Mt. Hawley Country (Peoria). Avocation: golf. Office: RLI Ins Co 9025 N Lindbergh Dr Peoria IL 61615-1499

MICHAEL, R. KEITH, theatre and dance educator; BS in Fine Art, State U. Pa.; MFA in Directing, U. Iowa; PhD in Theatre, U. Bristol, Eng. Mem. faculty Western Wash. U.; mem. theatre St. Cloud (Minn.) State U., chmn. dept. theatre, 1965-71; chmn. dept. theatre and drama Ind. U., Bloomington, 1971—. Program or archtl. cons. to 14 maj. theatres and State of Miss.; mem. adv. com. Nat. Soc. Arts and Letters. Host IU Jour. weekly PBS TV program. Recipient Ind. Gov.'s award, 1997. Mem. Nat. Assn. Schs. and Theatre (past pres.), Univ. and Coll. Theatre Assn. (past pres.), Univ./Resident Theatre Assn. (officer), Nat. Theatre Conf., North Ctrl. Assn. Colls. and Schs. Office: Ind U Bloomington Bryan Hall 100 Bloomington IN 47405-2618

MICHAELIDES, CONSTANTINE EVANGELOS, architect, educator; b. Athens, Greece, Jan. 26, 1930; came to U.S., 1955, naturalized, 1964; s. Evangelos George and Kalliopi Constantine (Kefallonitis) M.; m. Maria S. Canellakis, Sept. 3, 1955; children: Evangelos Constantine, Dimitri Canellakis. Diploma in Architecture, Nat. Tech. U., Athens, 1952; M.Arch., Harvard U., 1957. Practice architecture, Athens, 1954-55, St. Louis, 1963—; asso. architect Carl Koch, Jose Luis Sert, Hideo Sasaki, Cambridge, Mass., 1957-59, Doxiadis Assos., Athens and Washington, 1959-60, Hellmuth, Obata & Kassabaum, St. Louis, 1962; instr. Grad. Sch. Design Harvard U., 1957-59, Athens Inst. Tech., 1959-60; asst. prof. architecture Washington U., St. Louis, 1960-64, assoc. prof., 1964-69, prof., 1969-94, assoc. dean Sch. Architecture, 1969-73; dean Washington U., Sch. Architecture, 1973-93, dean emeritus, 1993—; Ruth and Norman Moore vis. prof. Washington U., St. Louis, 1995. Vis. prof. (Sch. Architecture), Ahmedabad, India, 1970; counselor Landmarks Assn. St. Louis., 1975-79 Author: Hydra: A Greek Island Town: Its Growth and Form, 1967; contbr. articles to profl. jours. Mem. Municipal Commn. on Arts, Letters, University City, Mo., 1975-81. Served to lt. Greek Army Res., 1952-54. Fellow AIA (Rsch. award 1963-64, Presdl. Citation 1992); mem. Tech. Chamber of Greece, Soc. Archtl. Historians, Modern Greek Studies Assn., Hellenic Soc. St. Louis (pres. 1991, 95, 96). Home: 735 Radcliffe Ave Saint Louis MO 63130-3139 Office: Washington U Sch Architecture 1 Brookings Dr Saint Louis MO 63130-4899

MICHAELIS, ELIAS K. neurochemist; b. Wad-Medani, Sudan, Oct. 3, 1944; came to U.S., 1962; married, 1967; 1 child. BS, Fairleigh Dickinson U., 1966; MD, St. Louis U. Med. Sch., 1969; PhD in Physiology and Biophysics, U. Ky., 1973. Spl. fellow rsch. dept. physiology and biophysics U. Ky., 1972-73, from asst. prof. to prof. depts. human devel. and biochemistry, 1982-87; chair pharmacology and toxicology U. Kans., Lawrence, 1988—. Dir. ctr. biomed. rsch. and Higuchi bioscis. rsch. ctr. U. Kans., 1988—. Mem. AAAS, Am. Soc. Neurochemistry, Am. Soc. Biochemistry and Molecular Biology, Internat. Soc. Biomedical Rsch. on Alcoholism, Soc. Neuroscience, N.Y. Acad. Sci. Achievements include research in characterization of L-glutamate receptors in neuronal membranes, in membrane protein isolation and chemical analysis, in characterization of membrane transport systems for amino acids, sodium, potassium, and calcium, in neuronal membrane biophysics, in molecular neurobiology.

MICHAELS, DINAH, radio personality; m. Randy Michaels, Oct. 25, 1997. BA Mass Comm., Baker U. With KBNU Campus Sta.; radio host KUDL, Westwood, Kans. Author: The Bride's Guide to Reality (How to Have the Wedding You Want on the Budget You Have), 1999. Avocations: horseback riding, tennis, movies. Office: KULD 4935 Belinder Westwood KS 66205

MICHAELS, JACK D. office furniture manufacturing executive; BSME, U. Cin. Various postions Internat. Harvester Co., sr. v.p., gen. mgr., mng. dir. Germany, worldwide pres. agrl. and constrn. equipment ops., J. I. Case Co.; pres.-internat. Hussmann Corp., pres., CEO; pres. Hon Industries, Inc., Muscatine, Iowa, 1990—, CEO, 1991—, chmn., 1996—. Office: Hon Industries Inc 414 E 3rd St PO Box 1109 Muscatine IA 52761-7109

MICHAELS, JENNIFER TONKS, foreign language educator; b. Sedgley, England, May 19, 1945; d. Frank Gordon and Dorothy (Compston) Tonks; m. Eric Michaels, 1973; children: Joseph, David, Ellen. MA, U. Edinburgh, 1967, McGill U., 1971, PhD, 1974. Teaching asst. German dept. Wesleyan U., 1967-68; instr. German dept. Bucknell (Pa.) U., 1968-69; teaching asst. German dept. McGill U., Can., 1969-72; prodn. asst. Pub. TV News and Polit. program, Schenectady, N.Y., 1974-75; from asst. prof. to assoc. prof. Grinnell (Iowa) Coll., 1975-87, prof., 1987—. Vis. cons. German dept. Hamilton Coll., 1981; cons. Modern Lang. dept. Colby Coll.; panelist NEH, 1985; spkr. in field. Author: D.H. Lawrence, The Polarity of North and South, 1976, Anarchy and Eros: Otto Gross' Impact on German Expressionist Writers, 1983, Franz Jung: Expressionist, Dadaist, Revolutionary and Outsider, 1989, Franz Werfel and the Critics, 1994; contbr. numerous articles, revs. to profl. jours. Mem. MLA, Am. Assn. Tchrs. of German, Soc. Exile Studies, German Studies Assn. (sec. treas. 1991-92, v.p. 1992-94, pres. 1995-96, numerous coms.). Democrat. Avocations: music, travel, reading. Office: Grinnell Coll German Dept PO Box 805 Grinnell IA 50112-0805 E-mail: michaels@grinnell.edu.

MICHAELS, ROBERT A. real estate development company executive; BSBA, JD, U. S.D. With Gen. Growth, 1972—, gen. counsel, exec. v.p., dir. corp. leasing; pres., CEO Gen. Growth Mgmt., Inc.; pres., COO Gen. Growth Properties, Inc. Bd. dirs. Gen. Growth Properties, Inc., Gen. Growth Mgmt., Inc.; bd. dirs. Ctr. for Urban Land Econs. Rsch., Sch. of Bus. U. Wis.-Madison.; spkr. in field. Editor Law Rev., U. S.D.; contbr. articles to profl. jours. Mem. ABA, S.D. Bar Assn., Iowa Bar Assn., Minn. Bar Assn., Internat. Coun. of Shopping Ctrs. (exec. com., bd. trustees, govt. affairs chmn. states Iowa, Nebr., S.D., state dir. Minn., S.D., N.D.). Office: 110 N Wacker Dr Chicago IL 60606-1511

MICHALAK, EDWARD FRANCIS, lawyer; b. Evanston, Ill., Sept. 6, 1937; s. Leo Francis Michalak and Helen Sophie (Wolinski) Krakowski. BSBA, Northwestern U., 1959; LLB, Harvard U., 1962. Bar: Ill. 1962. Assoc. McDermott, Will & Emery, Chgo., 1963-69, ptnr., 1969—. Served to sgt. USAR, 1962-68. Mem. Ill. Bar Assn., Chgo. Bar Assn., Beta Gamma Sigma, Beta Alpha Psi. Roman Catholic. Avocations: golf, opera. Home: 3455 Harrison St Evanston IL 60201-4953 Office: McDermott Will & Emery 227 W Monroe St 47th Fl Chicago IL 60606-5096 E-mail: emichalak@mwe.com.

MICHEL, ANTHONY NIKOLAUS, electrical engineering educator, researcher; b. Rekasch, Romania, Nov. 17, 1935; came to U.S., 1952; s. Anton Michel and Katharina (Metz) Malsam; m. Leone Lucille Flasch, Aug. 17, 1957; children: Mary Leone, Katherine Jean, John Peter, Anthony Joseph, Patrick Thomas. B.S.E.E., Marquette U., 1958, M.S. in Math., 1964, Ph.D. in Elec. Engring., 1968; D.Sc. in Math., Tech. U. Graz (Austria), 1973. Registered profl. engr., Wis. Engr. in tng. U.S. Army C.E., Milw., 1958-59; project engr. AC Electronics div. Gen. Motors Corp., 1959-62, sr. research engr., 1962-65; asst. prof. elec. engring. Iowa State U., Ames, 1968-69, assoc. prof., 1969-74, prof., 1974-84; prof. elec. engring. U. Notre Dame, Ind., 1984-87, chmn. dept. elec. and computer engring., 1984-88, Frank M. Freimann prof. engring., 1987—, dean coll. engring., 1988-98. Cons. Houghton Mifflin Co., 1975, Acad. Press, 1983; cons. editor William C. Brown Co. Pubs., Dubuque, Iowa, 1982-83. Author: (with others) Qualitative Analysis of Large Scale Dynamical Systems, 1977, Mathematical Foundations in Engineering and Science, 1981, Ordinary Differential Equations, 1982, Applied Linear Algebra and Functional Analysis, 1993, (with Derong Liu) Dynamical Systems with Saturation Nonlinearities, 1993, (with Kaining Wang) Qualitative Theory of Dynamical Systems, 1994, (with Kaining Wang) Qualitative Theory of Dynamical Systems, 2d edit., revised and expanded, 2001, (with Panos J. Antsaklis) Linear Systems, 1997, (with Derong Liu) Qualitative Analysis and Synthesis of Recurrent Neural Networks, 2002; contbr. articles to profl. jours., chpts. to books. Research grantee NSF, 1972— ; research grantee Dept. Def., 1968-72; Fulbright fellow Tech. U. Vienna, Austria, 1992; recipient Alexander von Humboldt Rsch. award U.S. Sr. Scientists, 1998. Fellow IEEE (mng. editor Trans. on Cirs. and Sys. 1981-83, Best Trans. Paper award 1978, 83, 93, Centennial medal 1984, Millenium medal 2000); mem. IEEE Cirs. and Sys. Soc. (pres.s 1989, Myril B. Reed Outstanding Paper award 1993, Tech. Achievement award 1995, Golden Jubilee medal 1999), IEEE Control Sys. Soc. (Disting. Mem. award 1998), Russian Acad. Engring. (hon.), Sigma Xi, Eta Kappa Nu, Pi Mu Epsilon, Phi Kappa Phi. Home: 17001 Stonegate Ct Granger IN 46530-6948 Office: U Notre Dame Dept Elec Engring Coll Engring Notre Dame IN 46556 E-mail: anthony.n.michel.1@nd.edu.

MICHELI, FRANK JAMES, lawyer; b. Zanesville, Ohio, Mar. 23, 1930; s. John and Theresa (Carlini) M.; m. Doris Joan Clum, Jan. 9, 1954; children: Michael John, James Carl, Lisa Ann, Matthew Charles. Student, John Carroll U., Cleve., 1947-48, Xavier U., Cin., 1949-50; LL.D., Ohio No. U., Ada., 1953. Bar: Ohio 1953. Since practiced in, Zanesville; partner Leasure & Micheli, 1953-65, Kincaid, Micheli, Geyer & Ormond, 1965-75, Kincaid, Cultice, Micheli & Geyer (and predecessor), 1982-92; ptnr. Micheli, Baldwin, Bopeley & Northrup, 1992—. Instr. bus. law Meredith Bus. Coll., Zanesville, 1956; lectr. on med. malpractice, hosp. and nurse liability. Dir. Public Service for, City of Zanesville, 1954. Mem. Internat. Assn. Ins. Counsel, Def. Rsch. Inst., Ohio Def. Assn., Am. Ohio bar assns., Am. Judicature Soc., Am. Arbitration Assn. (mem. nat. panel), Am. Bd. Trial Advs. (bd. dirs. Ohio chpt. 1991-95, pres. 1997). Club: Elk. Home: 160 E Willow Dr Zanesville OH 43701-1249 Office: PO Box 788 3808 James Ct Ste 2 Zanesville OH 43702-0788 E-mail: micheli@cyberzane.net.

MICHELSEN, JOHN ERNEST, software and internet services company executive; b. New Brunswick, N.J., May 11, 1946; s. Ernest Arnold and Ursula (Hunter) M.; B.S., Northwestern U., 1969; M.S., Stevens Inst. Tech., 1972; M.B.A. in Fin. with honors, U. Chgo., 1978; m. Ruth Ann Flanders, June 15, 1969; children— Nancy Ellen, Rebecca Ruthann. Real-time programmer Lockheed Electronics Co., Plainfield, N.J., 1969-72; control system designer Fermi Nat. Accelerator Lab., Batavia, Ill., 1972-75; chief system designer Distributed Info. Systems Corp., Chgo., 1975-78, v.p., 1978-79; mgr. M.I.S. adminstrn. FMC Corp., Chgo., 1979-82; pres. Infopro, Inc., 1982— . Mem. Assn. Computing Machinery, Phi Eta Sigma, Tau Beta Pi, Beta Gamma Sigma. Office: 2625 Butterfield Rd Oak Brook IL 60523-1234

MICHENER, CHARLES DUNCAN, entomologist, researcher, entomologist, educator; b. Pasadena, Calif., Sept. 22, 1918; s. Harold and Josephine (Rigden) Michener; m. Mary Hastings, Jan. 1, 1941; children: David, Daniel, Barbara, Walter. BS, U. Calif., Berkeley, 1939, PhD, 1941. Tech. asst. U. Calif., Berkeley, 1939-42; asst. curator Am. Mus. Natural History, N.Y.C., 1942-46, assoc. curator, 1946-48, research assoc., 1949—; assoc. prof. U. Kans., 1948-49, prof., 1949-89, prof. emeritus, 1989—, chmn. dept. entomology, 1949-61, 72-75, Watkins Disting. prof. entomology, 1959-89, acting chmn. dept. systematics, ecology, 1968-69, Watkins Disting. prof. systematics and ecology, 1969-89; dir. Snow Entomol. Museum, 1974-83, state entomologist, 1949-61. Vis. rsch. prof. U. Paraná, Curitiba, Brazil, 1955—56. Author (with Mary H. Michener): (book) American Social Insects, 1951; author: (with S. F. Sakagami) Nest Architecture of the Sweat Bees, 1962, The Social Behavior of the Bees, 1974; author: (with M. D. Breed and H. E. Evans) The Biology of Social Insects, 1982; author: (with D. Fletcher) Kin Recognition in Animals, 1987; author: (with R. McGinley and B. Danforth) The Bee Genera of North and Central America, 1994, The Bees of the World, 2000; contbr. articles to profl. jours.; editor: (book) Evolution, 1962—64; Am. editor: Insectes Sociaux, 1954—55, Am. editor: , 1962—90, assoc. editor: Ann. Rev. Ecology and Systematics, 1970—90. Recipient Disting. Rsch. medal, Internat. Soc. Hymenopterists, 2002; fellow Guggenheim, U. Paraná, 1955—56, Africa, 1966—67, Fulbright, U. Queensland, 1958—59; scholar Rsch., U. Costa Rica, 1963. Fellow: AAAS, Royal Entomol. Soc. London, Am. Acad. Arts and Scis., Am. Entomol. Soc., Entomol. Soc. Am. (C. V. Riley award 1999); mem.: NAS, Kans. Entomol. Soc. (pres. 1950), Linnean Soc. London (corr.), Soc. Systematic Zoologists (hon.; 1969), Russian Entomol. Soc. (hon.), Brazilian Acad. Scis. (corr.), Internat. Union Study Social Insects 1977—82, Am. Soc. Naturalists 1978, Soc. Study Evolution 1967. Home: 1706 W 2nd St Lawrence KS 66044-1016 Office: U Kans Snow Hall 1460 Jayhawk Blvd Lawrence KS 66045-7523 E-mail: michener@ku.edu.

MICHENFELDER, JOHN DONAHUE, anesthesiology educator; b. St. Louis, Apr. 13, 1931; s. Albert A. and Ruth J. (Donahue) Michenfelder; m. Margaret Grey Nick, Oct. 22, 1955 (dec. Dec. 1971); children: Carol, David, Joseph, Paul, Matthew, Laura; m. Mary Monica Milroy, Aug. 11, 1972; 1 child Patrick. BS, St. Louis U., 1951, MD, 1955. Diplomate Am. Bd. Anesthesiology. Intern Presbyn. St. Luke's Hosp., Chgo., 1955—56, resident in internal medicine, 1956; resident in anesthesiology Mayo Clinic, Rochester, Minn., 1958—61, cons. in anesthesiology, 1961—93; prof. anesthesiology Mayo Med. Sch., 1976—93, emeritus prof., 1993—. Author: Anesthesia and the Brain, 1988, Clinical Neuroanesthesia, 1990. Fellow Faculty Anaesthetists, Royal Coll. Surgeons Ireland, 1982, Royal Coll. Surgeons Eng., 1988; grantee NIH, 1966—89, 1991—95. Mem.: Assn. Univ. Anesthetists (councilman 1975—78), Inst. Medicine, Am. Soc. Anesthesiologists (Excellence in Rsch. award 1990, Disting. Svc. award 1990). Avocations: upland game bird hunting, gardening, reading, writing. Home: 325 1st Ave NW Oronoco MN 55960-1410 Office: Mayo Clinic Emeritus Office 200 1st St SW Rochester MN 55905-0002 E-mail: am31@pitel.net.

MICKEL, EMANUEL JOHN, foreign language educator; b. Lemont, Ill., Oct. 11, 1937; s. Emanuel John and Mildred (Newton) M.; m. Kathleen Russell, May 31, 1959; children: Jennifer, Chiara, Heather. BA, La. State U., 1959; MA, U. N.C., 1961, PhD, 1965. Asst. prof. U. Nebr., Lincoln, 1965-67, assoc. prof., 1967-68, Ind. U., Bloomington, 1968-73, prof., 1973—, dir. Medieval Studies Inst., 1976-91, chmn. French and Italian, 1984-95. Cons. NEH; French advisor Soc. Rencesvals, 1995-98; adv. bd. mem. Nineteenth Century French Studies, 1995—. Author: Marie de France, 1974, Eugene Fromentin, 1982, Ganelon Treason and the Chanson de Roland, 1989, Jules Vernes Complete Twenty Thousand Leagues Under the Sea, 1992, Enfances Godefroi and Retour de Cornumarant, 1999. Capt. U.S. Army, 1963-65. Grantee NEH, Washington, 1978-84; Lilly Open fellow Lilly Found., Indpls., 1981-82; Chevalier dans l'Ordre des Palmes Academiques, 1997. Avocations: music, theater, sports, travel, ancient literature. Office: French & Italian Dept Indiana Univ 642 Ballantine Hall Bloomington IN 47401-5020 E-mail: mickel@indiana.edu.

MICKELSON, JAN, radio personality; Radio host morning show Sta. WHO-AM, Des Moines. Office: WHO Radio 1801 Grand Ave Des Moines IA 50309*

MICKELSON, STACEY, state legislator; BA, Minot State U., 1994. Govt. rels. dir. Artspace Projects, Inc.; rep. Dist. 38 N.D. Ho. of Reps., 1994-2000, mem. fin. and taxation com., vice-chmn. transp. com. Mem. interim taxation, adminstrv. rules coms. Bowhay Inst. for Legis. Leadership and Devel. fellow. Mem. Am. Coun. Young Polit. Leaders, Darden Program Emerging Polit. Leaders, Flemming Fellows. Home: 410 Groveland Ave #702 Minneapolis MN 55403

MIDDAUGH, JAMES (MIKE), former state legislator; b. Paw Paw, Mich., Sept. 4, 1946; s. Orson William and Phyllis Jean M.; m. Mary Ann. Student, Ferris State Coll., 1965-68; BS in Edn., Western Mich. U., 1969. Rep. Mich. Dist. 45, 1983-92, Mich. Dist. 80, 1993-98. Del. Van Buren County Mich. State Rep. Conv., 1965-73; adminstrv. asst. Mich. State Sen. Harry Gast, 1970—; chmn. issues com. Mich. Ho. Reps., 1974—, asst. minority whip, vice chmn. conservation, recreation & environ. com., mem. corps. and fin. com., pub. utilities & liquor control com. Mem. NRA, Farm Bur., N.Am. Hunting Club, Ferris State Coll. Alumni Assn. (pres. 1975), Southwestern Mich. Assn. Law Enforcement Officers. Home: 35361 51st Ave Paw Paw MI 49079-8852 Address: State Capitol PO Box 30014 Lansing MI 48909-7514

MIDDELKAMP, JOHN NEAL, pediatrician, educator; b. Kansas City, Mo., Sept. 29, 1925; s. George H. and Clara M. (Ordelheide) M.; m. Roberta Gill, Oct. 3, 1949 (div. 1970); children— Sharon Ann, Steven Neal, Susan Jean, Scott Alan; m. Lois Harper, Mar. 1, 1974 B.S., U. Mo., 1946; M.D., Washington U., St. Louis, 1948. Diplomate Am. Bd. Pediatrics. Intern D.C. Gen. Hosp., Washington, 1948-49; resident St. Louis Children's Hosp., 1949-50, 52-53; instr. pediatrics Washington U., 1953-57, asst. prof. pediatrics, 1957-64, assoc. prof., 1964-70, prof., 1970-98, prof. emeritus, 1998—; dir. ambulatory pediatrics St. Louis Children's Hosp., 1974-91. Author: Camp Health Manual, 1984; contbr. articles, chpts. to profl. publs. Served to comdr. M.C., USNR, 1943-66. NIH postdoctoral fellow, 1961-62 Mem. Am. Acad. Pediatrics, Am. Soc. Microbiology, Infectious Diseases Soc. Am., Am. Pediatric Soc., Ambulatory Pediatric Assn., Sigma Xi, Alpha Omega Alpha Home: 8845 Paragon Cir Saint Louis MO 63123-1114 Office: 1 Childrens Pl Saint Louis MO 63110-1002

MIDGLEY, A(LVIN) REES, JR. reproductive endocrinology educator, researcher; b. Burlington, Vt., Nov. 9, 1933; s. Alvin Rees and Maxine (Schmidt) M.; m. Carol Crossman, Sept. 4, 1955; children: Thomas, Debra, Christopher. B.S. cum laude, U. Vt., 1955, M.D. cum laude, 1958. Intern

U. Pitts., 1958-59, resident dept. pathology, 1959-61, U. Mich., Ann Arbor, 1961-63, instr. pathology, 1963-64, asst. prof., 1964-67, assoc. prof., 1967-70, prof., 1970—, dir. Reproductive Scis. Program, 1968—. Chmn. BioQuant of Ann Arbor, Inc., 1985-89. Contbr. articles to med. jours. Recipient Parke-Davis award, 1970; Ayerst award Endocrine Soc., 1977; Smith Kline Bio-Sci. Labs. award, 1985; NIH grantee, 1960—; Mellon Found. grantee, 1979-91. Mem. Soc. Study Reprodn. (pres. 1983-84), Endocrine Soc., Am. Assn. Pathology, Am. Physiol. Soc. Home: 101 W Liberty St Apt 340 Ann Arbor MI 48104-1359 Office: U Mich Rm 1101 Reproductive Scis Program 300 N Ingalls Bldg Fl 11 Ann Arbor MI 48109-2007

MIES, RICHARD W. career officer; b. Chgo. m. Sheila McCann; children: Rachel Anne, Sara Elizabeth. BS, U.S. Naval Acad., 1967; M, Harvard U., 1982. Commd. USN, 1967, advanced through grades to adm., 1998; comdr. in chief U.S. Strategic Command. Office: 901 SAC Blvd Offutt A F B NE 68113-6000

MIGLIN, MARILYN, cosmetic executive; Student, Northwestern U. Profl. ballerina; model Marshall Fields; founder, owner Marilyn Miglin Cosmetic Co., 1963—. Active Mayor Richard M. Daley's spl. com. tourism; officer Chgo. Conv. and Tourism Bur.; apptd. Gov. James Edgar Econ. Devel. Bd.; past pres. Oak St. Coun.; founder Women of Destiny (mentoring program). Named in her honor Marilyn Miglin Day, Chgo., 1998. Office: 120 E Oak St Chicago IL 60611-1204

MIHM, MICHAEL MARTIN, federal judge; b. Amboy, Ill., May 18, 1943; s. Martin Clarence and Frances Johannah (Morrissey) M.; m. Judith Ann Zosky, May 6, 1967; children— Molly Elizabeth, Sarah Ann, Jacob Michael, Jennifer Leah BA, Loras Coll., 1964; JD, St. Louis U., 1967. Asst. prosecuting atty. St. Louis County, Clayton, Mo., 1967-68; asst. state's atty. Peoria County, Peoria, Ill., 1968-69; asst. city atty. City of Peoria, 1969-72; state's atty. Peoria County, Peoria, 1972-80; sole practice, 1980-82; U.S. dist. judge U.S. Govt., 1982—; chief U.S. dist. judge U.S. Dist. Ct. (ctrl. dist.) Ill., 1991-98. Chmn. com. internat. jud. rels. U.S. Jud. Conf., 1994—96, mem. exec. com., 1995—97, mem. com. jud. br., 1987—93, mem. com. internat. jud. rels., 1998—; mem. Supreme Ct. Fellows Commn., 2000—; adj. prof. law John Marshall Law Sch., 1990—. Past mem. adv. bd. Big Brothers-Big Sisters, Crisis Nursery, Peoria; past bd. dirs. Salvation Army, Peoria, W.D. Boyce council Boy Scouts Am., State of Ill. Treatment Alternatives to Street Crime, Gov.'s Criminal Justice Info. Council; past vice-chmn. Ill. Dangerous Drugs Adv. Council; trustee Proctor Health Care Found., 1991—. Recipient Good Govt. award Peoria Jaycees, 1978 Mem. Peoria County Bar Assn. Roman Catholic. Office e-mail: michael. Office: US Dist Ct 204 Federal Bldg 100 NE Monroe St Peoria IL 61602-1003 E-mail: mihm@ilcd.uscourts.gov.

MIKA, JOSEPH JOHN, library school director, educator, consultant; b. McKees Rocks, Pa., Mar. 1, 1948; s. George Joseph and Sophie Ann (Stec) M.; m. Marianne Hartzell; children: Jason-Paul Joseph, Matthew Douglas, Meghan Leigh. BA in English, U. Pitts., 1969, MLS, 1971, PhD in Libr. Sci., 1980. Asst. libr., instr. Ohio State U., Mansfield, 1971-73; asst. libr., asst. prof. Johnson State Coll., Vt., 1973-75; grad. asst., tchg. fellow Sch. Libr. and Info. Sci., U. Pitts., 1975-77; asst. dean, assoc. prof. libr. svc. U. So. Miss., Hattiesburg, 1977-86; dir. libr. and info. sci. program Wayne State U., 1986—95, 2002—, prof., 1994—2001. Cons. to libraries; co-owner Libr. Jobs Network, Libr. Tng. Network. Editor Jour. of Edn. for Libr. and Info. Sci., 1995—. Col. USAR. Decorated DSM. Mem. ALA (councilor 1983-86, 98-2001, chmn. constrn. and bylaws com. 1985-86), Assn. Libr. and Info. Sci. Edn. (chmn. membership com. 1982-83, chmn. nominating com. 1982, exec. bd. 1986), Miss. Libr. Assn. (pres.-elect 1985), Mich. Libr. Assn. (chair libr. edn. com. 1989), Leadership Acad. (oversight com. 1989-95), Assn. Coll. and Rsch. Librs. (chmn. 1982-83, chmn. budget com. 1982-83), Soc. Miss. Archivists (treas., exec. bd. 1981-83), Mich. Ctr. for the Book (chair 1994-2001), Kiwanis (Hattiesburg), Beta Phi Mu (pres.-elect 1987-89, pres. 1989-91), Phi Delta Kappa. E-mal. Home: 222 Abbott Woods Dr East Lansing MI 48823-1995 Office: Wayne State U Libr and Info Sci Program 106 Kresge Library Detroit MI 48202 E-mail: aa2500@wayne.edu.

MIKELSONS, J. GEORGE, air aerospace transportation executive; Chmn., CEO Am. Trans Air, Inc., Indpls., 1980-98, chmn., 1998—. Office: Am Trans Inc Indpls Internat Airport PO Box 51609 Indianapolis IN 46251-0609

MIKESELL, MARVIN WRAY, geography educator; b. Kansas City, Mo., June 16, 1929; s. Loy George and Clara (Wade) M.; m. Reine-Marie de France, Apr. 1, 1957. B.A., UCLA, 1952, M.A., 1953; Ph.D., U. Calif.-Berkeley, 1959. Instr. to prof. geography U. Chgo., 1958—, chmn. dept. geography, 1969-74, 83-86. Del. U.S. Nat. Commn. for UNESCO Author: Northern Morocco, 1961; editor: Readings in Cultural Geography, 1962, Geographers Abroad, 1973, Perspectives on Environment, 1974. Fellow Am. Geog. Soc. (hon.); mem. Assn. Am. Geographers (pres. 1975-76, Disting. Career award 1995). Club: Quadrangle. Home: 1155 E 56th St Chicago IL 60637-1530 Office: Com Geog Studies 5828 S University Ave Chicago IL 60637-1583 E-mail: mmikesel@uchicago.edu.

MILBERT, ROBERT P. state legislator; b. June 1949; m. Vicky Milbert; three children. BA, Dartmouth Coll. Dist. 39B rep. Minn. Ho. of Reps., St. Paul, 1986—. Former vice chmn. gaming divsn. gen. legis., judiciary, vet. affairs and gaming coms., Minn. Ho. of Reps.; vice chmn. internat. trade, tech. and econ. devel. divsn. com. on commerce and econ. devel.; mem. taxes com. Office: 243 State Office Bldg Saint Paul MN 55155-0001

MILBRETT, TIFFENY CARLEEN, professional soccer player; b. Portland, Oreg., Oct. 23, 1972; Degree in comms. mgmt., U. Portland. Mem. U.S. Women's Nat. Soccer Team. Recipient Gold Medal Centennial Olympic Games, 1996, 3d pl. medal, 1995, Silver medal World Univ. Games, 1993; mem. championship team, Montricoux, France, 1993. Office: c/o US Soccer Fedn 1801 S Prairie Ave # 1811 Chicago IL 60616-1319

MILENTHAL, DAVID, advertising executive; B in Journalism, Ohio State U. Mgr. comms. Ohio Blue Shield; dir., organizer Pub. Interest Ctr., Ohio Environtl. Protection Agy.; pres., CEO Milenthal Advt. Agy.; exec. v.p. Hameroff/Milenthal, Inc.; pres., CEO HMS Ptnrs., chmn. Recipient Silver medal award Advt. Fedn. of Columbus; named Man of Yr. Temple Israel, Ten Outstanding Young Citizens Jaycees, People to Watch Columbus Monthly. Office: HMS Ptnrs Ste 5 250 Civic Center Dr S Columbus OH 43215-5086

MILES, WENDELL A. federal judge; b. Holland, Mich., Apr. 17, 1916; s. Fred T. and Dena Del (Alverson) M.; m. Mariette Bruckert, June 8, 1946; children: Lorraine Miles, Michelle Miles Kopinski, Thomas Paul. AB, Hope Coll., 1938, LLD (hon.), 1980; MA, U. Wyo., 1939; JD, U. Mich., 1942; LLD (hon.), Detroit Coll. Law, 1979. Bar: Mich. Ptnr. Miles & Miles, Holland, 1948-53, Miles, Mika, Meyers, Beckett & Jones, Grand Rapids, Mich., 1961-70; pros. atty. County of Ottawa, 1949-53; U.S. dist. atty. Western Dist. Mich., Grand Rapids, 1953-60, U.S. dist. judge, 1974—, chief judge, 1979-86, sr. judge, 1986—. Cir. judge 20th Jud. Cir. Ct. Mich., 1970-74; instr. Hope Coll., 1948-53, Am. Inst. Banking, 1953-60; adj. prof. Am. constl. history Hope Coll., Holland, Mich., 1979— ; mem. Mich. Higher Edn. Commn.; apptd. Fgn. Intelligence Surveillance Count, Washington, 1989—. Pres. Holland Bd. Edn., 1952-63. Served to capt. U.S. Army, 1942-47. Recipient Liberty Bell award, 1986. Fellow Am. Bar Found.; mem. ABA, Mich. Bar Assn., Fed. Bar Assn., Ottawa County Bar Assn., Grand Rapids Bar (Inns of Ct. 1995—), Am. Judicature Soc., Torch Club, Rotary Club, Masons. Office: US Dist Ct 236 Fed Bldg 110 Michigan St NW Ste 452 Grand Rapids MI 49503-2363 E-mail: miles@miwd.uscourts.gov.

MILEWSKI, BARBARA ANNE, pediatrics nurse, neonatal intensive care nurse; b. Chgo., Sept. 11, 1934; d. Anthony and LaVerne (Sepp) Witt; m. Leonard A. Milewski, Feb. 23, 1952; children: Pamela, Robert, Diane, Timothy. ADN, Harper Coll., Palatine, Ill, 1982; BS, Northern Ill. U., 1992; postgrad., North Park Coll. RN, Ill.; cert. CPR instr. Staff nurse Northwest Community Hosp., Arlington Heights, Ill., Resurrection Hosp., Chgo.; nurse neonatal ICU Children's Meml. Hosp.; day care cons. Cook County Dept. Pub. Health. CPR instr. Stewart Oxygen Svcs., Chgo.; instr., organizer parenting and well baby classes and clinics; vol. Children's Meml. Hosp.; health coord. CEDA Head Start; cons. day care Cook County Dept. Pub. Health; mem. adv. bd. Cook County Child Care Resource and Referral. Vol. first aid instr. Boy Scouts Am.; CPR instr. Harper Coll., Children's Meml. Hosp.; dir. Albany Park Cmty. Ctr. Head Start, Chgo.; day care cons. Cook County Dept. Pub. Health. Mem. Am. Mortar Bd., Sigma Theta Tau.

MILEY, GEORGE HUNTER, nuclear and electrical engineering educator; b. Shreveport, La., Aug. 6, 1933; s. George Hunter and Norma Angeline (Dowling) M.; m. Elizabeth Burroughs, Nov. 22, 1958; children: Susan Miley Hibbs, Hunter Robert. B.S. in Chem. Engring., Carnegie-Mellon U., 1955; M.S., U. Mich., 1956, Ph.D. in Chem.-Nuclear Engring., 1959. Nuclear engr. Knolls Atomic Power Lab., Gen. Electric Co., Schenectady, 1959-61; mem. faculty U. Ill., Urbana, 1961—, prof., 1967—, chmn. nuclear engring. program, 1975-86, dir. Fusion Studies Lab., 1976—, fellow Ctr. for Advanced Study, 1985-86; dir. rsch. Rockford Tech. Assocs. Inc., 1990-94; pres., dir. rsch. NPL Assocs., 1994—. Vis. prof. U. Colo., 1967, Cornell U., 1969-70, U. New South Wales, 1986, Imperial Coll. of London, 1987; mem. Ill. Radiation Protection Bd., 1988—; mem. Air Force Studies Bd., 1990-94; chmn. tech. adv. com. Ill. Low Level Radioactive Waste Site, 1990-96; chmn. com. on indsl. uses of radiation Ill. Dept. Nuclear Safety, 1989—. Author: Direct Conversion of Nuclear Radiation Energy, 1971, Fusion Energy Conversion, 1976; editor Jour. Fusion Tech., 1980-2001; U.S. assoc. editor Laser and Particle Beams, 1982-86, mng. editor, 1987-91, editor-in-chief, 1991-2002; U.S. editor Jour. Plasma Physics, 1995—. Served with C.E. AUS, 1960. Recipient Western Electric Tchg.-Rsch. award, 1977, Halliburton Engring. Edn. Leadership award, 1990, Edward Teller medal, 1995, Scientist of Yr. award Jour. New Energy, 1996; Inst. for New Energy 1996 Scientist of the Yr.; NATO sr. sci. fellow, 1975-76, Guggenheim fellow, 1985-86, Japanese Soc. Promotion of Sci. fellow, 1994. Fellow IEEE, Am. Nuclear Soc. (dir. 1980-83, Disting. Svc. award 1980, Outstanding Achievement award Fusion Energy divsn. 1992), Am. Phys. Soc.; mem. Am. Soc. Engring. Edn. (chmn. energy conversion com. 1967-70, pres. U. Ill. chpt. 1973-74, chmn. nuclear divsn. 1975-76, Outstanding Tchr. award 1973), Sigma Xi, Tau Beta Pi. Presbyterian. Achievements include research on fusion, energy conversion, reactor kinetics. Office: U Ill 214 Nuclear Engring Lab 103 S Goodwin Ave Urbana IL 61801-2901 E-mail: georgehm@aol.com.

MILKMAN, ROGER DAWSON, genetics educator, molecular evolution researcher; b. N.Y.C., Oct. 15, 1930; s. Louis Arthur and Margaret (Weinstein) M.; m. Marianne Friedenthal, Oct. 18, 1958; children: Ruth Margaret, Louise Friedenthal, Janet Dawson Milkman Lussenhop, Paul David. A.B., Harvard U., 1951, A.M., 1954, Ph.D., 1956. Student, asst., instr., investigator Marine Biol. Lab., Woods Hole, Mass., 1952-72, 88-96; instr., asst. prof. U. Mich., Ann Arbor, 1957-60; assoc. prof., prof. Syracuse U., N.Y., 1960-68; prof. biol. scis. U. Iowa, Iowa City, 1968-2001, prof. emeritus, 2001—, chmn. univ. genetics PhD program, 1992-93. Vis. prof. biology Grinnell (Iowa) Coll., 1990; mem. genetics study sect. NIH, 1986-87; NSF panelist, 1996-99. Translator: Developmental Physiology, 1970; editor: Perspectives on Evolution, 1982, Experimental Population Genetics, 1983, Evolution jour., 1984-86; mem. editl. bd. Jour. Bacteriology, 1998-2000; contbr. articles to profl. jours. Sec. Soc. Gen. Physiologists, 1963-65, Am. Soc. Naturalists, 1980-82; alumni rep. Phillips Acad., Andover, Mass., 1980-94. NSF grantee, 1959— ; USPHS grantee, 1984-87. Fellow AAAS; mem. Am. Soc. for Microbiology, Genetics Soc. Am., Corp. Marine Biol. Lab., Soc. for Gen. Microbiology (U.K.), Soc. Study Evolution, Soc. Molecular Biology and Evolution, Internat. Soc. for Molecular Evolution. Jewish. Avocation: mountain hiking. Home: 12 Fells Rd Falmouth MA 02540-1626 Office: Marine Biol Lab Lillie 503 Woods Hole MA 02543-1015

MILL, JETH, performing company executive; Exe. dir. Des Moines Symphony. Office: Des Moines Symph 221 Walnut St Des Moines IA 50309*

MILL, SETH, orchestra executive; BA in Edn., Ohio U. With Nat. Pub. Radio, Washington, 1975-83; asst. mgr. Pitts. Symphony, 1983-89; mgr. Northeastern Pa. Philharmonic, Scranton, 1990-95; exec. dir. Lincoln (Nebr.) Symphony Orch., 1995-99, Des Moines Symphony, 1999—. Office: Des Moines Symphony 221 Walnut St Des Moines IA 50309-2101

MILLAR, JAMES F. pharmaceutical executive; Exec. v.p. No. Group Cardinal Health Inc., Dublin, with distbn., pres. drug wholesaling opers. Office: Cardinal Health Inc 7000 Cardinal Pl Dublin OH 43017-1092

MILLARD, CHARLES PHILLIP, manufacturing company executive; b. Janesville, Wis., Apr. 21, 1948; s. Duane Francis and Mary Lou (Ganley) M.; m. Mary Franzen, Oct. 7, 1967 (div. June 13, 1990); children: Katherine, Laura. Student, U. Wis., Janesville, 1966-67. Spot welder Gen. Motors Corp., Janesville, 1966-67; plant mgr. Insta-Foam Products, Addison, Ill., 1967-72; warehouse mgr. Ram Golf Corp., Elk Grove, 1972-77; master scheduler Gandalf Data Inc., Wheeling, 1977-84, corp. mfg. coord., 1984-85; corp. mktg. coord. Gandalf Technologies Inc., 1985-87, corp. strategist, 1988-89; internat. rsch. analyst Gandalf Data Inc., 1989-90; asst. mgr. safety/security Fellowes Mfg. Co., Itasca, Ill., 1990-93; process specialist, cons. Janesville, Wis., 1993-94; asst. mgr. Janesville Travel Ctr., 1994-95; prodn. material coord. Alliant TechSystems, 1995-96; prodn. inventory control mgr. fabrication divsn. Freedom Plastics, 1997-99; armed security staff U.S. Attys. Office, Fed. Cthse. & FEMA Facilities, Madison, 2000. Patrol Officer Des Plaines (Ill.) Police Res., 1987-89; vol. with Alzheimer patients, 1999-2000. Mem. Am. Mgmt. Assn., Am. Mktg. Assn., Furniture Workers Union, Am. Fedn. Police, Nat. Rifle Assn. Avocations: physical fitness, motorcycling, home improvements, auto mechanics.

MILLEN, MATT, professional sports team executive; b. Hokendauqua, Pa., Mar. 12, 1958; m. Patricia Millen; children: Marianne, Michalyn, Marcus;1 child Matthew Jr. Student Pa. State U. Linebacker Oakland/L.A. Raiders, 1980—88, San Francisco 49ers, 1989—90, Washington Redskins, 1991; game analyst CBS, Fox TV; pres., CEO Detroit Lions, 2001—. Named to NFL Pro Bowl Team, 1988. Office: Detroit Lions 1200 Featherstone Rd Pontiac MI 48342

MILLER, ARNOLD, retired newspaper editor; b. Cleve., May 24, 1931; s. Ben and Fanny (Keller) M.; m. Loretta Cooney, June 29, 1957 (div. 1977); children: Adrienne, Evan, Bryn, Alyssa. BS in Journalism, Kent State U., 1956. Copy editor News-Sentinel, Fort Wayne, Ind., 1956; asst. city editor Beacon Jour., Akron, Ohio, 1957-65; mng. editor Morning Herald, Hagerstown, Md., 1965-69; reporter, columnist, asst. news editor Cleve. Press, 1969-72; mng. editor Chronicle-Telegram, Elyria, Ohio, 1972-97, ret., 1997. With U.S. Army, 1953-54. Mem. Assoc. Press Mng. Editors Assn., Md.-Del. Press Assn., Ohio UPI Editors Assn. (pres. 1978), Assoc. Press Soc. Ohio (adv. bd. 1992-93). Jewish. Home: 1550 Cedarwood Dr Apt D Cleveland OH 44145-1811

MILLER, ARTHUR HAWKS, JR. librarian, archivist, educator; b. Kalamazoo, Mar. 15, 1943; s. Arthur Hawks and Eleanor (Johnson) M.; m. Janet Carol Schroeder, June 11, 1967; children: Janelle Miller Moravek, Andrew Hawks. Student, U. Caenoo Coll., Calvados, France, 1963-64; AB, Kalamazoo Coll., 1965; AM in English, U. Chgo., 1966, AM in Librarianship, 1968; PhD, Northwestern U., 1973; postgrad., Lake Forest Grad. Sch. Mgmt., 1990—91. Reference libr. Newberry Libr., Chgo., 1966-69, asst. libr. pub. svcs., 1969-72; coll. libr. Lake Forest (Ill.) Coll., 1972-94, archivist and libr. for spl. collections, 1994—. Co-author: 30 Miles North: A History of Lake Forest College, Its Town, and Its City of Chicago, 2000, Lake Forest Estates, People, and Culture, 2000. Pres. Lake Forest/Lake Bluff Hist. Soc.,. 1982-85, Ill. Ctr. for Book Bd., 1992-93; with Ragdale Found., 1992-96, Lake Forest Found. for Hist. Preservation, 1997—, v.p., 2000—. Mem. Caxton Club. Presbyterian. Home: 169 Wildwood Rd Lake Forest IL 60045-2462 Office: Lake Forest Coll Donnelley Libr 555 N Sheridan Rd Lake Forest IL 60045-2399 Fax: 847-735-6296. E-mail: amiller@lakeforest.edu.

MILLER, ARTHUR J., JR. state legislator; b. Detroit, July 11, 1946; m. Marsha Ann; children: Holly A., Nicole M., Arthur J. III, Derek E. Student, Eastern Mich. U. Mem. Mich. Senate from 10th dist., Lansing, 1977—; Dem. Leader of the Senate, 1985—. City coun. Warren, Mich., v.p., pres. Address: PO Box 30036 Lansing MI 48909-7536 Also: State Senate 11139 Olive St Warren MI 48093-6557

MILLER, BENJAMIN K. retired state supreme court justice; b. Springfield, Ill., Nov. 5, 1936; s. Clifford and Mary (Luthyens) M. BA, So. Ill. U., 1958; JD, Vanderbilt U., 1961. Bar: Ill. 1961. Ptnr. Olsen, Cantrill & Miller, Springfield, 1964-70; prin. Ben Miller-Law Office, 1970-76; judge 7th jud. cir. Ill. Cir. Ct., 1976-82, presiding judge Criminal div., 1977-81, chief judge, 1981-82; justice Ill. Appellate Ct., 4th Jud. Dist., 1982-84, Ill. Supreme Ct., Springfield, 1984-2001, chief justice, 1991-93, ret., 2001. Adj. prof. So. Ill. U., Springfield, 1974—; chmn. Ill. Cts. Commn., 1988-90; mem. Ill. Gov.'s Adv. Coun. on Criminal Justice Legis., 1977-84, Ad Hoc Com. on Tech. in Cts., 1985—. Mem. editorial rev. bd. Illinois Civil Practice Before Trial, Illinois Civil Trial Practice Pres. Cen. Ill. Mental Health Assn., 1969-71; bd. govs. Aid to Retarded Citizens, 1977-80; mem. Lincoln Legals Adv. Bd., 1988—. Lt. USNR, 1964-67. Mem. ABA (bar admissions com. sect. of legal edn. and admissions to bar 1992—), Ill. State Bar Assn. (bd. govs. 1970-76, treas. 1975-76), Sangamon County Bar Assn., Ctrl. Ill. Women's Bar Assn., Am. Judicature Soc. (bd. dirs. 1990-95), Abraham Lincoln Assn. (bd. dirs. 1988-98). Address: 1918 Jeanette Ln Springfield IL 62702

MILLER, BERNARD J., III, advertising executive; b. 1949; BS in Mktg., Ind. U., 1971; M in Advt., Northwestern U., 1972. With brand mgmt. Alberto Culver, Chgo., 1972-74; pres. Columbian Advt. Del, 1974—. Office: Columbian Advt Del 201 E Ohio St Chicago IL 60611-3238

MILLER, BERNARD JOSEPH, JR. advertising executive; b. Louisville, July 31, 1925; s. Bernard J. Sr. and Myrtle (Herrington) M.; m. Jayne Hughes, Aug. 7, 1948 (div. Oct. 1970); children: Bernard J. III, Jeffrey, Janet Marie.; m. Brita Naujok, Nov. 24, 1970; 1 child, Brian. BS, Ind. U., 1949. Merchandising mgr. Brown-Forman Distillers, Inc., Louisville, 1949-54; v.p. Phelps Mfg. Co., Terre Haute, Ind., 1954-60; pres. Columbian Advt. Inc., Chgo., 1960-87, chmn., 1987—. 2d lt. USAF, 1943-46, PTO. Mem. Point of Purchase Advt. Inst. (dir. 1970-73), Saddle and Cycle Club (bd. dirs. 1987-90, 99—). Avocations: tennis, downhill skiing, collecting first edition autographed books. Office: Columbian Advt Inc 201 E Ohio St Chicago IL 60611-3238

MILLER, BEVERLY WHITE, past college president, education consultation; b. Willoughby, Ohio; d. Joseph Martin and Marguerite Sarah (Storer) White; m. Lynn Martin Miller, Oct. 11, 1945 (dec. 1986); children: Michaela Ann, Craig Martin, Todd Daniel, Cass Timothy, Simone Agnes. AB, Western Res. U., 1945; MA, Mich. State U., 1957; PhD, U. Toledo, 1967; LHD (hon.), Coll. St. Benedict, St. Joseph, Minn., 1979; LLD (hon.), U. Toledo, 1988. Chem. and biol. researcher, 1945-57; tchr. schs. in Mich., also Mercy Sch. Nursing, St. Lawrence Hosp., Lansing, Mich., 1957-58; mem. chemistry and biology faculty Mary Manse Coll., Toledo, 1958-71, dean grad. div., 1968-71, exec. v.p., 1968-71; acad. dean Salve Regina Coll., Newport, R.I., 1971-74; pres. Coll. St. Benedict, St. Joseph, Minn., 1974-79, Western New Eng. Coll., Springfield, Mass., 1980-96, pres. emerita, 1996—. Higher edn. cons., 1996—; cons. U.S. Office Edn., 1980; mem. Springfield Pvt. Industry Coun./Regional Employment Bd., exec. com., 1982-94; mem. Minn. Pvt. Coll. Coun., 1974-79, sec., 1974-75, vice chmn., 1975-76, chmn., 1976-77; cons. in field. Author papers and books in field. Corporator Mercy Hosp., Springfield, Mass. Recipient President's citation St. John's U., Minn., 1979; also various service awards; named disting. alumna of yr. U. Toledo, 1998. Mem. AAAS, Am. Assn. Higher Edn., Assn. Cath. Colls. and Univs. (exec. bd.), Internat. Assn. Sci. Edn., Nat. Assn. Ind. Colls. and Univs. (govt. rels. adv. com., bd. dirs. 1990-93, exec. com. 1991-93, treas. 1992-93), Nat. Assn. Biology Tchrs., Assn. Ind. Colls. and Univs. of Mass. (exec. com. 1981-96, vice chmn. 1985-86, chmn. 1986-87), Nat. Assn. Rsch. Sci. Tchg., Springfield C. of C. (bd. dirs.), Am. Assn. Univ. Adminstrs. (bd. dirs. 1989-92), Delta Kappa Gamma, Sigma Delta Epsilon. Office: 6713 County Road M Delta OH 43515-9778

MILLER, BRANT, meteorologist; m. Lisa Miller; 2 children. With Sta. WLS AM/FM, Sta. WTMX-FM; weather forecaster Fox 32, 1989; weekend weather forecaster NBC 5, Chgo., 1991—; weekday morning weather forecaster Sta. WUSN-FM, Sta. WJMK-FM. Recipient Chgo. Emmy awards, 1997, 1999, 2000, First pl. Silver Dome awards, Ill. Broadcasters Assn., 1999, 2000. Avocations: gardening, tinkerer, home repair aficionado. Office: NBC 5 454 N Columbus Dr Chicago IL 60611*

MILLER, CANDICE S. state official; b. May 7, 1954; m. Donald G. Miller; 1 child, Wendy Nicole. Student, Macomb County C.C., Northwood U. Sec., treas. D.B. Snider, Inc., 1972-79; trustee Harrison Twp., 1979-80, supr., 1980-92; treas. Macomb County, 1992-95; sec. of state State of Mich., Lansing, 1995—. Mem. Lake St. Clair Blue Ribbon Commn. Chair John Engler for Gov. campaign, Macomb County; del. Rep. Nat. Conv., 1996; co-chair Rep. Platform Com., 1996, Dole/Kemp Presdl. Campaign, Mich., 1996, Bush/Cheney Presdl. Campaign, Mich., 2000; mem. Carehouse-Macomb County Child Adv. Ctr., Selfridge Air Nat. Guard Base Cmty. Coun., Detroit Econ. Club; mem. adminstrv. bd. Mich. State, mem. safety commn. Avocations: boating, yacht racing. Office: Treasury Building 430 W Allegan Fl 1 Lansing MI 48918-0001 E-mail: candicem@sosmail.state.mi.us.

MILLER, CARL GEORGE, automotive parts manufacturing executive; b. Milw., Oct. 3, 1942; s. Carl Conrad and Agnes Frances (Patla) M.; m. Patricia Ann Smith, Apr. 27, 1968; children: Gregory, Brian. BS, St. Louis U., 1964. CPA, Mo. Audit mgr. Ahrens & McKeon, CPAs, St. Louis, 1967-73; supr. internal audit Gen. Dynamics Corp., 1973-75, mgr. fin. analysis, 1975-78, dir. fin. analysis, 1978-80; v.p., contr. Quincy (Mass.) Shipbldg. div. Gen. Dynamics Corp., 1980-86; v.p. fin. Cessna Aircraft Co., Wichita, Kans., 1986-88; v.p., contr. Ft. Worth div. Gen. Dynamics Corp.,

Ft. Worth, 1988-90; v.p., contr. TRW, Inc., Cleve., 1990-96, exec. v.p., CFO, 1996—. Mem. adv. coun. So. U. and A&M Bus. Sch., Case Western Reserve U. Acctg. Dept. Mem. AICPA, Fin. Execs. Inst. (com. on corp. reporting), Mfr. Alliance for Productivity and Innovation (fin. coun. II), Mo. Soc. CPA, Mayfield Country Club, Delta Sigma Pi (pres. 1963-64). Republican. Lutheran. Avocations; traveling, reading. Office: TRW Inc 1900 Richmond Rd Cleveland OH 44124-3760

MILLER, CHARLES S. clergy member, church administrator; Exec. dir. Division for Church in Society of the Evangelical Lutheran Church in America, Chicago, Ill. Office: Evangelical Lutheran Church Am 8765 W Higgins Rd Chicago IL 60631-4101

MILLER, CURTIS HERMAN, bishop; b. LeMars, Iowa, May 3, 1947; s. Herman Andrew and Verna Marion (Lund) M.; m. Sharyl Susan VanderTuig, June 2, 1969; children: Eric, Nathan, Paul. BA, Wartburg Coll., 1969; MDiv., Wartburg Sem., 1973; DD (hon.), Wartburg Coll., 1987. Assoc. pastor Holy Trinity Luth. Ch., Dubuque, Iowa, 1973-75; pastor St. Paul Luth. Ch., Tama, 1975-82; coord. for congl. life Am. Luth. Ch. Iowa dist., Storm Lake, 1982-87; bishop Western Iowa Synod Evang. Luth. Ch. in Am., 1987—. Bd. regents Waldorf Coll., Forest City, Iowa, 1987—; bd. dirs. Luth. Social Svcs. of Iowa, Des Moines, 1987. Office: Evang Luth Ch Am Western Iowa Synod PO Box 577 Storm Lake IA 50588-0577

MILLER, DALE KEITH, lawyer; b. St. Joseph, Mo., Nov. 2, 1946; s. Harold E. and Estella M. Miller; children: Nathan Keith, Cory Daniel. BSBA, U. Mo., 1968, JD, 1973. Ptnr. Sears & Miller Law Office, Savannah, Mo., 1973-77; pvt. practice, 1977—. Asst. city atty., Savannah, 1973-76; dep. juvenile officer 5th Judicial Cir. Mo., Savannah, 1975-76; prosecuting atty. Andrew County, Savannah, 1977-82, 91-94, Holt County, Oregon, Mo., 1996-98. With U.S. Army, 1969-71. Mem. Boy Scouts Am. (charter orgn. rep. Troop 60 1996-97), Am. Legion, Savannah Lions Club (pres. 1984), Savannah Lodge (master #71 AF&AM 1982). Office: PO Box 315 Savannah MO 64485-0315

MILLER, DANE ALAN, medical device manufacturing company executive; b. Belle Fountaine, Ohio, Feb. 7, 1946; s. Ersie E. and Ruth E. (Shumaker) M.; m. Mary Louise Schilke, Feb. 26, 1965; children: Kimberly Ruth, Stephany Marie. B.S. in Mech. Materials Science Engring., Gen. Motors Inst., 1969; M.S. in Materials Sci.-Biomed. Engring., U. Cin., 1971, Ph.D. in Materials Sci.-Biomed. Engring., 1974. Coop. engring. student Frigidaire div. GMC, Dayton, Ohio, 1964-68; dir. devel. engring. and custom Products Zimmer div. Bristol Meyers, Warsaw, Ind., 1972-75; dir. biomed. engring. Cutter Biomed. div. Cutter Labs., San Diego, 1975-78; pres. Biomet. Inc., Warsaw, 1978—. Elder, bldg. com. Warsaw Presbyn. Ch.; mem. community devel. com. City of Warsaw, Winona Lake Preservation Assn., Winona Community High Sch. Choir Boosters; mem. pres. com. Grace Coll. and Seminary; bd. dirs. First Source Bank of South Bend, Ind., Kosciusko Community Hosp. Named Outstanding Small Bus. Person in State of Ind., SBA, 1984. Mem. ASTM (surgical implant com.), Internat. Soc. Bio-materials, Orthopedic Research Soc., Soc. Plastic Engrs., NAE, Lodge: Rotary. Office: PO Box 587 Warsaw IN 46581-0587

MILLER, DAVID, state legislator, lawyer; b. Batavia, Iowa, Nov. 24, 1946; m. Pam Miller; 4 children. BA, Denver U., 1969; JD, U. Iowa, 1974. Pvt. practice, Batavia, Iowa, 1974-98; mem. Iowa Senate from 47th dist., Des Moines, 1998—; vice chair agr. com. Iowa Senate, mem. human resources com., mem. jud. com., mem. local govt. com., mem. natural resources and environment com. With U.S. Mil., 1970-72. Mem. Iowa State Bar Assn., Iowa Cattle Assn., Farm Bur., Lions. Republican. Office: State Capitol 9th And Grand Des Moines IA 50319-0001 E-mail: david_miller@legis.state.ia.us.

MILLER, DAVID GROFF, insurance agent; b. Kansas City, Kans., Aug. 17, 1949; s. Vincent G. and Ruth (Whitton) M.; m. Marjorie Zwiers, 1979. BA, U. Kans., 1972. CLU. Press aide to U.S. Senator James B. Pearson, 1974-75; fed. grant adminstr. Kans. Gov. Robert Bennett, 1975-78; brokerage rep. Paul Revere Co., Overland Park, Kans., 1979-85; prin. Miller Agy., Inc., Eudora, 1985—. Rep. dist. 43 Kans. State Reps., 1981-91; chmn. Kans. State Rep. Party, 1995-98. Mem.: Ind. Ins. Agts., Omicron Delta Kappa. Methodist. Office: Miller Agy Inc PO Box 460 Eudora KS 66025-0460

MILLER, DAVID HEWITT, environmental scientist, writer; b. 1918; m. Enid Woodson Brown; 1 child (dec.). AB cum laude, UCLA, 1939, MA, 1944; PhD, U. Calif., Berkeley, 1953; DLitt (hon.), U. Newcastle, 1979. Meteorologist U.S. Corps Engrs., 1941-43; forecaster TWA, 1943-44; climatologist Quartermaster Gen.'s Office, 1944-46; hydrometeorologist Corp. Engrs. Snow Investigations, San Francisco, 1946-53; geographer U.S. Natick (Mass.) Labs., 1953-59; hydrometeorologist U.S. Forest Svc., 1959-64; prof. geography U. Wis., Milw., 1964-75, prof. atmospheric scis., 1975—; sr. acad. meteorologist NOAA, 1981-82. Fulbright lectr., Australia, 1966, 71, 79; exchange scientist Acad. Scis., Moscow, 1969; adv. com. climatology Nat. Acad. Scis., 1958-64 Author: Snow Cover and Climate, 1955; (with others) Snow Hydrology, 1956, Heat and Water Budget of Earth's Surface, 1965, Energy at the Surface of the Earth, 1981, Water at the Surface of the Earth, 1977; translator: Climate and Life (M.I. Budyko), 1974. NSF fellow, 1952-53. Fellow AAAS (life); mem. Am. Geophys. Union (life, transl. bd. 1972-76), Am. Meteorol. Soc. (profl. life), Assn. Am. Geographers, Assn. Pacific Coast Geographers, Inst. Australian Geographers, We. Snow Conf., Phi Beta Kappa, Sigma Xi. Office: Univ Wis Dept Geoscis PO Box 413 Milwaukee WI 53201-0413

MILLER, DAVID W. lawyer; b. Indpls., July 1, 1950; s. Charles Warren Miller and Katherine Louise (Beckner) Dearing; m. Mindy Miller, May 20, 1972; children: Adam David, Ashley Kay, Amanda Katherine Kupfer. BA, Ind. U., Bloomington, 1971; JD summa cum laude, Ind. U., Indpls., 1976. Bar: Ind. 1977. Investigator NLRB, Indpls., 1971-76; assoc. Roberts & Ryder, 1977-80, ptnr., 1981-86, Baker & Daniels, Indpls., 1986—. Bd. dirs. Everybody's Oil Corp., Anderson, Ind. Bd. dirs. S. Madison Cmty. Found., Pendleton, Wis. Mem. Ind. Bar Assn. (chmn. labor law sect. 1981-82). Republican. Office: 300 N Meridian St Ste 2700 Indianapolis IN 46204-1750

MILLER, DON WILSON, nuclear engineering educator; b. Westerville, Ohio, Mar. 16, 1942; s. Don Paul and Rachel (Jones) M.; m. Mary Catherine Thompson, June 25, 1966; children: Amy Beth, Stacy Catherine, Paul Wilson Thompson. BS in Physics, Miami U., Oxford, Ohio, 1964, MS in Physics, 1966; MS in Nuclear Engring., Ohio State U., 1970, PhD in Nuclear Engring., 1971. Rsch. assoc. Ohio State U., Columbus, 1966-68, univ. fellow, 1968-69, tchg. assoc., 1969-71, asst. prof. nuclear engring., 1971-74, assoc. prof., 1974-80, chmn. nuclear engring. program, 1977-97, prof., 1980—, dir. nuclear reactor lab., 1977—. Sec., treas. Cellar Lumber Co., Westerville, Ohio, 1972-84, 85—; cons. Monsanto Rsch. Corp., Miamisburg, Ohio, 1979, NRC, Washington, 1982-84, 99—, Scantech. Corp., Santa Fe, 1984-95, Neoprobe Corp., Columbus, 1990, Electric Power Rsch. Inst., Palo Alto, Calif., 1992-94; mem. adv. com. on reactor safeguards Nuclear Regulator Commn., 1995-99. Patentee in field; contbr. articles to profl. jours. Mem. Westerville Bd. Edn., 1976-91, pres., 1977-78, 86-88; mem. Ohio Sch. Bd.'s Assn., Columbus, 1976-91; mem. fed. rels. com. Nat. Sch. Bd.'s Assn., Washington, 1984-86. With USAR, 1960-68. Named Tech. Person of Yr. Columbus Tech. Coun., 1979; named to All Region Bd. Ohio Sch. Bd's. Assn., 1981, 86, Westerville South H.S. Hall of Fame, 1996; recipient Coll. of Engring Rsch. award Ohio State U., 1984, Disting. Alumnus award, 1999; Achievement award Mid Ohio Chpt Multiple Sclerosis Soc., 1988. Fellow Am. Nuclear Soc. (chmn. edn. divsn. 1986-87, bd. dirs. 1989-91, chair human factors divsn. 1993-94, v.p./pres. elect 1995-96, pres. 1996-97, Cert. Appreciation 1991); mem. IEEE (sr. mem.), Am. Soc. Engring. Edn. (chmn. nuclear engring. divsn. 1978-79, Glenn Murphy award 1989), Instrument Soc. Am. (sr. mem.), Nuclear Dept. Heads Orgn. (chmn. 1985-86), Westerville Edn. Assn. (Friend of Edn. award 1992), Rotary (Courtright Cmty. Svc. award 1989), Kiwanis, Hoover Yacht Club, Alpha Nu Sigma (chmn. 1991-93). Avocations: sailing, Am. history, traveling, amateur radio (extra class license). Home: 172 Walnut Ridge Ln Westerville OH 43081-2464 Office: Ohio State U Dept Mech Engring Nuclear Engring Program 206 W 18th Ave Columbus OH 43210-1189 E-mail: miller.68@osu.edu.

MILLER, DONALD, food products executive; CFO Schwans Sales Enterprises, Marshall, Minn., v.p. fin., CEO. Office: Schwans Sales Enterprises 115 W College Dr Marshall MN 56258-1747

MILLER, DREW, financial management company executive; b. West Chester, Pa., Aug. 1, 1958; s. Raymond and Carol (Canfield) M.; m. Annabeth D.; 1 child, Anna Clarice. BS, USAF Acad., Colo., 1980; M in Pub. Policy, Harvard U., 1982, PhD, 1985. Cert. mgmt. acct., cert. fin. planner. Intelligence officer USAF, 1980-87; mgr. Con Agra, Inc., 1987-94; pres. Heartland Mgmt. Cons. Group, Papillion, Nebr., 1994—, Fin. Continuum, LLC, 1998-2000; mergers and acquisitions advisor, 2001—. V.p. Fin. Dynamics, Inc., Papillion, 1997-98. County commr. Sarpy County, Nebr., 1990-94; mem. Bd. Regents U. Nebr., 1994—. Republican. Home: 1904 Barrington Pkwy Papillion NE 68046-4152 E-mail: drmiller@drewmiller.com.

MILLER, DWIGHT WHITTEMORE, lawyer; b. Worcester, Mass., July 8, 1940; s. Fred Hamilton and Jeanette (Lewis) M.; m. Mary Francisco, June 22, 1963; children— Rebecca, David. A.B., Colgate U., 1962; J.D., Boston Coll., 1965. Bar: Vt. 1965, MO. 1969, Law clk. U.S. Dist. Ct. Vt., 1965-66; sole practice, Brattleboro, Vt., 1966-68; with Monsanto Co., St. Louis, 1968-72; gen. counsel Stromberg Carlson Communications, Inc., St. Louis, 1972-75, Pott Industries, Inc., St. Louis, 1975-85; gen. solicitor Mo. Pacific R.R., St. Louis, 1985-86, Union Pacific R.R., 1991—; ptnr. Thompson & Mitchell, St. Louis, 1987-91; Mem. ABA, Order of Coif. Unitarian. Office: 210 N 13th St Saint Louis MO 63103-2329

MILLER, EDWARD BOONE, lawyer; b. Milw., Mar. 26, 1922; s. Edward A. and Myra (Munsert) M.; m. Anne Harmon Chase Phillips, Feb. 14, 1969 (dec. Dec. 2001); children by previous marriage: Barbara Miller Anderson, Ellen Miller Gerkens, Elizabeth Miller Lawhun, Thomas; stepchildren: T. Christopher Phillips, Sarah Phillips Parkhill. B.A., U. Wis., 1942, LL.B., 1947; student, Harvard Bus. Sch., 1942-43. Bar: Wis. 1947, Ill. 1948. With firm Pope, Ballard, Shepard & Fowle, Chgo., 1947-51, 52-70, ptnr., 1953-70, 75-93, mng. partner, 1979-82, chmn. labor and employment law dept., 1975-76, 87-88, 90-91; of counsel Seyfarth Shaw, 1994—. Mem. adv. com. Ctr. for Labor Mgmt. Dispute Resolution, Stetson U., 1984—, Inst. Indsl. Rels., Loyola U., 1987-91, Kent Pub. Employee Labor Rels. Conf., 1988—, Ill. Ednl. Labor Rels. Bd., 1988—; exec. asst. to industry mems. Regional Wage Stblzn. Bd., Chgo., 1951-52, industry mem., 1952; chmn. NLRB, Washington, 1970-74; mem. panel of labor law experts Commerce Clearing House, 1987—; dir. Chgo. Wheel & Mfg. Co., 1965-70, 75-88, Andes Candies, Inc., 1965-68, 75-80 Mem. Gov. Ill. Commn. Labor-Mgmt. Policies for Pub. Employees, 1966-67; chmn. Midwest Pension Conf., 1960-61; mem. labor relations com. Ill. C. of C., 1953-70; bd. dirs. Am. Found. Continuing Edn., 1960-69. Served to lt. USNR, 1943-46. Mem. ABA (NLRB practice and procedures com., internat. labor law com.), Ill. Bar Assn., Wis. Bar Assn., Chgo. Assn. Commerce and Industry (chmn. labor relations com. 1980-86, bd. dirs. 1987-97), Am. Employment Law Coun. (mem. adv. bd. 1995—), Coll. Labor and Employment Lawyers (emeritus mem.), Order of Coif. Republican. Congregationalist. Clubs: Legal (Chgo.), Law (Chgo.), Cliff Dwellers (Chgo.). Home: 632 Chatham Rd Glenview IL 60025-4402 Office: 55 E Monroe St Chicago IL 60603-5713 E-mail: milleed@seyfarth.com.

MILLER, ELLEN, advertising executive; Pres. health care mktg. svcs. Draft Worldwide (formerly DraftDirect Worldwide), Chgo. Office: Draft Worldwide 633 N Saint Clair St Chicago IL 60611-3234

MILLER, EUGENE ALBERT, banker; married. B.B.A., Detroit Inst. Tech., 1964; grad., Sch. Bank Adminstrn., Wis., 1968. With Comerica Bank-Detroit (formerly The Detroit Bank, then Detroit Bank & Trust Co.), 1955—, v.p., 1970-74, contr., 1971-74, sr. v.p., 1974-78, exec. v.p., 1978-81, pres., 1981-89, CEO, 1989—, chmn., 1990—; with parent co. Comerica Inc. (formerly DETROITBANK Corp.), 1973—, treas., 1973-80, pres., 1981—, CEO, 1989-92, chmn. bd., 1990-92; pres., COO Comerica Inc. (merged with Manufacturers Nat. Corp.), Detroit, 1992-2000; chmn., CEO Comerica Bank (merged with Manufacturers Nat. Corp.), 1993—. Office: Comerica Inc Mail Code 3382 500 Woodward Ave Detroit MI 48226-5480

MILLER, FRANCES SUZANNE, historic site curator; b. Defiance, Ohio, Apr. 17, 1950; d. Francis Bernard Johnson and Nellie Frances (Holder) Culp; m. James A. Batdorf, Aug. 7, 1970 (div. Aug. 1979); 1 child, Jennifer Christine Batdorf; m. Rodney Lyle Miller, Aug. 8, 1982 (div. Apr. 1987). BS in History/Museology, The Defiance Coll., 1990; AS in Bus. Mgmt., N.W. Tech. Coll., 1986. With accts. receivable dept. Ohio Art Co., Bryan, Ohio, 1984-87; leasing agent Williams Met. Housing Authority, 1987-91; acting site mgr. James A. Garfield Nat. Historic Site, Mentor, Ohio, 1991—. Mem. AAUW (pres. 1993-95, treas. 1995-98), Nat. Trust Hist. Preservation, Ohio Mus. Assn., Ohio Assn. Host. Socs. and Mus., Cleve. Restoration Soc., Phi Alpha Theta. Avocations: needlework, reading. Office: Apt B14 8060 Deepwood Blvd Mentor OH 44060-7789

MILLER, FREDERICK WILLIAM, publisher, lawyer; b. Milw., Mar. 18, 1912; s. Roy W. and Kathryn (Oehlers) M.; m. Violet Jane Bagley, Mar. 31, 1939. B.A., U. Wis., 1934, LLB, 1936. Bar: Wis. 1936. Assoc. Tenney & Davis, Madison, 1935-36; atty. State of Wis., 1936-77; pub. The Capital Times Co., 1979—, also dir.; dir. Madison Newspaper, Inc., 1970—, chmn. bd., 1980—; dir. Evjue Found., Inc., Madison, 1957—. Trustee Evjue Charitable Trust, Madison, 1970— . Mem. Wis. Bar Assn. Clubs: Madison Club, Univ. Club. Office: Capital Times Co PO Box 8056 1901 Fish Hatchery Rd Madison WI 53713-1248

MILLER, GARY J. political economist; b. Urbana, Ill., Jan. 2, 1949; s. Gerald J. and Doris Elaine (Miner) M.; m. Anne Colberg, Jan. 29, 1971; children: Neil, Ethan. BA, U. Ill., 1971; PhD, U. Tex., 1976. Asst. prof. Calif. Inst. Tech., Pasadena, 1976-79; assoc. prof. Mich. State U., East Lansing, 1979-86; Taylor prof. polit. economy Washington U., St. Louis, 1986-97; assoc. dean for acad. affairs Olin Sch. Bus., 1995-96, prof. polit. sci. Author: Cities by Contract, 1981, Reforming Bureaucracy, 1987, Managerial Dilemmas, 1992. NSF grantee, 1981, 83, 92. Mem. Phi Beta Kappa, Phi Kappa Phi (Disting. Faculty award 1994). Democrat. Office: Washington U Dept Polit Sci 1 Brookings Dr Dept Polit Saint Louis MO 63130-4899 E-mail: gjmiller@artsci.wustl.edu.

MILLER, HAROLD EDWARD, retired manufacturing conglomerate executive, consultant; b. St. Louis, Nov. 23, 1926; s. George Edward and Georgenia Elizabeth (Franklin) M.; m. Lilian Ruth Gantner, Dec. 23, 1949; children— Ellen Susan, Jeffrey Arthur. B.S.B.A., Washington U., St. Louis, 1949. Vice pres. Fulton Iron Works Co., St. Louis, 1968-71, pres., 1971-79, chmn. bd., 1979-90; v.p. Katy Industries Inc., Elgin, Ill., 1976-77, exec. v.p., 1978-90, also dir., to 1990; pres. HM Consulting, Palatine, Ill., 1990—. Internat. cons. Vigel Spa, Italy; v.p. Vigel U.S.A. Inc., 1996—. Served with U.S. Army, 1945-46. Mem. Barrington Tennis Club, Inverness Golf Club. Presbyterian. E-mail: hmillercons84@cs.com.

MILLER, IRVING FRANKLIN, chemical engineering educator, biomedical engineering educator, academic administrator; b. N.Y.C., Sept. 27, 1934; s. Sol and Gertrude (Rochkind) M.; m. Baila Hannah Milner, Jan. 28, 1962; children: Eugenia Lynne, Jonathan Mark. BS in Chem. Engring., NYU, 1955; MS, Purdue U., 1956; PhD, U. Mich., 1960. Rsch. scientist United Aircraft Corp., Hartford, 1959-61; from asst. prof. to prof., head chem. engring. Poly. Inst. Bklyn., 1961-72; prof. bioengring., head bioengring. program U. Ill., Chgo., 1973-79, acting head sys. engring. dept., 1978-79, assoc. vice chancellor rsch., dean Grad. Coll., 1979-85, prof. chem. engring., head chem. engring., 1986-95, dir. Ctr. for Advanced Edn. and Rsch., 1989-90, dir. Office of Spl. Projects, 1990-92, dir. bioengring. program, 1992-95; dean Coll. Engring. U. Akron, Ohio, 1995-98, prof. biomed. engring., 1998-2000; dir. tech. con. svc. BioTech-Plex Corp., 2002—. Cons. to industry; cons. NAS, NIH; dir. distance learning programs Ohio Aerospace Inst., 1998—2000. Editor: Electrochemical Bioscience and Bioengineering, 1973; contbr. articles profl. jours. Mem. AIChE, AAAS, Am. Chem. Soc., Biomed. Engring. Soc., N.Y. Acad Scis. Home: 1746 N Larrabee St Chicago IL 60614-5634 E-mail: ifmiller@uic.edu.

MILLER, JAMES GEGAN, research scientist, physics educator; b. St. Louis, Nov. 11, 1942; s. Francis John and Elizabeth Ann (Caul) M.; m. Judith Anne Kelvin, Apr. 23, 1966; 1 child, Douglas Ryan. A.B., St. Louis U., 1964; M.A., Washington U., 1966, Ph.D., 1969. Asst. prof. physics Washington U., St. Louis, 1970-72, assoc. prof., 1972-77, prof. physics, 1977—, dir. lab. for ultrasonics, 1987—, rsch. asst. prof. medicine, 1976-81, rsch. assoc. prof. medicine, 1981-88, rsch. prof. medicine, 1988-2000, prof. biomed. engring., 1998—, Albert Gordon Hill prof. physics, 1999—, prof. medicine, 2000—. Contbr. articles to profl. jours.; patentee in field. Recipient I-R 100 award Indsl. Research Devel. Mag., 1974, 78; NIH, NASA grantee, NIH Merit Award, 1998. Fellow IEEE (sr., gov. com. Ultrasonics, Ferroelectrics and Frequency Control Soc. 1978-80,86-88, 92-94), Am. Inst. Ultrasound in Medicine, Acoustical Soc. Am., Am. Inst. Med. and Biol. Engring.; mem. Am. Phys. Soc., Sigma Xi (nat. lectr. 1981-82). Home: 444 Edgewood Dr Saint Louis MO 63105-2016 Office: PO Box 1105 Saint Louis MO 63188-1105

MILLER, JAY ALAN, retired civil rights association executive; b. Cleve., Feb. 8, 1928; s. Herbert Phillip Miller and Ruth Weisbach; m. Joyce Dannen, Feb. 1, 1952 (div. Oct. 1964); children: Joshua, Adam, Rebecca; m. Mary Lou Edelstein Kaplan, Dec. 2, 2000. BSc, U. Ill., 1950. Organizer Amalgamated Clothing Workers, Chgo., 1950-52, bus. agt., edn. dir. Wilkes-Barre, Pa., 1956-61; organizer United Packing House Workers, Chgo., 1952-53; reporter Cleve. Press, 1954-56; peace edn. dir. Am. Friends Svc. Com., Chgo., 1961-65; exec. dir. ACLU of Ill., 1965-71,78-2001, ACLU of No. Calif., San Francisco, 1971-74; assoc. dir. legis. office ACLU, Washington, 1975-78. Pres. AFL-CIO Labor Coun., Hazelton, Pa., 1959-61, mem. trade union delegation to USSR, 1960; chmn. Turn Toward Peace, Chgo., 1962-64; coord. Com. for a Test Ban Treaty, Ill. and Wis., 1962-63; dep. dir. Ill. Rally for Civil Rights, Chgo., 1964. With U.S. Army, 1946-48, PTO.

MILLER, JOHN, foundation administrator; BA in Psychology, U. Del., 1970. Exec. v.p. Am. Cancer Soc., Jefferson City, Mo., 1979-83, Am. Coll. Sports Medicine, Indpls., 1983-88, Am. Camping Assn., Martinsville, Ind., 1988-97, Nat. Muzzle Loading Rifle Assn., Friendship, 1997—. Cons. CUBE, Inc., 1988-90. Vol. leadership devel. Am. Cancer Soc.; active numerous civic orgns., including Kingsway Christian Ch., Indpls., Indpls. Conv. and Vis. Assn., 1985-86, XXIII FIMS World Congress on Sports Medicine, Brisbane, Australia/speaker, 1986, others. Mem. Am. Soc. Assn. Execs. Office: Nat Muzzle Loading Rifle Assn PO Box 67 Friendship IN 47021-0067

MILLER, JOHN ALBERT, university educator, consultant; b. St. Louis County, Mo., Mar. 22, 1939; s. John Adam and Emma D. (Doering) M.; m. Eunice Ann Timm, Aug. 25, 1968; children: Michael, Kristin. AA, St. Paul's Coll., 1958; BA with high honors, Concordia Sr. Coll., 1960; postgrad., Wash. U., St. Louis, 1960-64; MBA, Ind. U., 1971, DBA in Mktg., 1972. Proofreader, editor Concordia Pub. House, St. Louis, 1960-62, periodical sales mgr., 1964-68; asst. prof. Drake U., Des Moines, 1971-74; cons. FTC, Washington, 1974-75; vis. assoc. prof. Ind. U., Bloomington, 1975-77; assoc. prof. U. Colo., Colorado Springs, 1977-79, prof., 1977-86, prof. mktg., resident dean, 1980-84; v.p. market devel. Peak Health Care Inc., 1984-85; dean Valparaiso (Ind.) U., 1986-96, prof. mktg., 1986—. Cons. and rschr. govt. and industry; dir. health maintenance orgn.; bd. dirs. Ind. Acad. Social Scis., 1988-90; adv. bd. N.W. Ind. Small Bus. Devel. Ctr., 1989-91; consulting dean USIA project to form Polish Assn. of Bus. Schs., 1995. Author: Labeling Research The State of the Art, 1978; contbr. articles to profl. jours. Mem. Colorado Springs Symphony Orch. Coun., 1980-86; cons. Citizens Goals of Colorado Springs, 1985-86, Jr. League Colorado Springs, 1981-82; bd. dirs. Christmas in April-Valparaiso, 1991-96, Assn. Luth. Older Adults, 1998—. With U.S. Army, 1962-64. U.S. Steel fellow, 1970-71. Mem. Assn. Consumer Rsch. (chmn. membership 1978-79), Am. Mktg. Assn. (fed. govt. liaison com. 1975-76), Am. Acad. Advt., Ind. Acad. Social Scis. (bd. dirs. 1988-90), Greater Valparaiso C. of C. (accreditation com. 1991, planning com. 1989-92, chair 1992), Am. Assembly Collegiate Schs. Bus. (internat. affairs com. 1991-93, mem. peer rev. team 1994, 96, com. mem., seminar leader, faculty mem., program chair for New Deans seminar and other workshops 1992—), Beta Gamma Sigma, Alpha Iota Delta. Lutheran. Avocations: racquetball, jogging, walking. Home: 1504 Del Vista Dr Valparaiso IN 46385-3322 Office: Valparaiso U Dept Mktg Valparaiso IN 46383

MILLER, JOHN ROBERT, oil industry executive; b. Lima, Ohio, Dec. 28, 1937; s. John O. and Mary L. (Zickafoose) M.; m. Karen A. Eier, Dec. 30, 1961; children: Robert A., Lisa A., James E. BSChE with honors, U. Cin., 1960, D.Comml. Sc. hon., 1983. With Standard Oil Co., Cleve., 1960-86, dir. fin., 1974-75, v.p. fin., 1975-78, v.p. transp., 1978-79, sr. v.p. tech. and chems., 1979-80, pres., COO, 1980-86; bd. dirs.; pres., CEO TBN Holdings, 1986-2000; chmn., CEO Petroleum Ptnrs., 2000—. Bd. dirs. Cambrex Corp., Eaton Corp.; former chmn. Fed. Res. Bank, Cleve.; mem. adv. bd. SiTech. Mem. Pepper Pike Club, The Country Club, Chagrin Valley Hunt Club, Tau Beta Pi. Office: Petroleum Ptnrs Inc 29325 Chagrin Blvd Ste 301 Cleveland OH 44122 E-mail: office@johnrmiller.com.

MILLER, JOHN WILLIAM, JR. bassoonist; b. Balt., Mar. 11, 1942; s. John William and Alverta Evelyn M.; m. Sibylle Weigel, July 12, 1966 (div. 2000); children: Christian Desmond, Andrea Jocelyn, Claire Evelyn. BS, M.I.T., 1964; MusM with highest honors, New Eng. Conservatory, 1967, Artist's Diploma, 1969. Instr. bassoon Boston U., 1967-71, U. Minn., 1971—; prin. bassoonist, founding mem. Boston Philharmonia Chamber Orch., 1968-71; prin. bassoonist Minn. Orch., Mpls., 1971—. Dir. Boston Baroque Ensemble, 1963-71, John Miller Bassoon Symposium, 1984—; mem. Am. Reed Trio, 1977—; faculty Sarasota Music Festival, 1986—, Affinis Seminar, Japan, 1992; vis. faculty Banff Ctr. for Arts, 1987; faculty Nordic Bassoon Symposium, 1993—. Soloist on recs. for Cambridge, Mus. Heritage Soc., Pro Arte; featured guest artist 1st Internat. Bassoon Festival, Caracas, Venezuela, 1994. Recipient U.S. Govt. Fulbright award, 1964-65,

Irwin Bodky award Cambridge Soc. Early Music, 1968 Mem. Internat. Double Reed Soc., Minn. Bassoon Assn. (founder) Home: 706 Lincoln Ave Saint Paul MN 55105-3533 Office: 1111 Nicollet Mall Minneapolis MN 55403-2406

MILLER, JOHN WINSTON, academic administrator; m. Barbara Miller; children: Lauren, Elizabeth, Raymond. BS in Journalism, Ohio U., 1969; MS in Edn., No. Ill. U., 1972; PhD in Edn., Purdue U., 1975. Pub. sch. tchr., Chgo. and Ind.; from asst. prof. to prof., assoc dean edn. Wichita State U., 1974—86; prof., dean Coll. Edn. Ga. So. U., 1986—93, Fla. State U., 1993—99; chancellor U. Wis., Whitewater, Wis., 1999—. Office: U Wis-Whitewater 800 W Main St Whitewater WI 53190

MILLER, JOSEF M. otolaryngologist, educator; b. Phila., Nov. 29, 1937; married, 1960; 3 children. BA in Psychology, U. Calif., Berkeley, 1961; PhD in Physiology and Psychology, U. Wash., 1965; MD (hon.), U. Göteborg, Sweden, 1987; MD (h.c.), U. Turku, Finland, 1995. USPHS fellow U. Mich., 1965-67, rsch. assoc., asst. prof. dept. Psychology, 1967-68, prof., dir. rsch. dept. Otolaryngology, dir. Kresge Hearing Rsch. Inst., 1984—; asst. prof. depts. Otolaryngology, Physiology and Biophysics U. Wash., Seattle, 1968-72, rsch. affiliate Regional Primate Rsch. Ctr, 1968-84, assoc. prof., 1972-76, acting chmn. dept. Otolaryngology, 1975-76, prof., 1976-84; Lunn and Ruth Townsend prof. comm., 1996—. Mem. study sect. Nat. Inst. Neurol. and Communicative Disorders and Stroke, NIH, 1978-84, ad hoc bd. dirs. sci. counselors, 1988; sci. rev. com. Deafness Rsch. Found., 1978-83, chair, 1983—; mem. faculty Nat. Conf. Rsch. Goals and Methods in Otolaryngology, 1982; adv. com. hearing, bio-acoustics and biomechanics Commn. Behavioral and Social Scis. and Edn., Nat. Rsch. Coun., 1983—; hon. com. Orgn. Nobel Symposium 63, Cellular Mechanisms in Hearing, Karlskoga, Sweden, 1985; cons. Otitis Media Rsch. Ctr., 1985-89, Pfizer Corp., 1988; faculty opponent U. Göteborg, Sweden, 1987; rsch. adv. com. Gallaudet Coll., 1987; chair external sci. adv. com. House Ear Inst., 1988-91; author authorizing legis. Nat. Inst. Deafness and Other Comm. Disorders, NIH, 1988, co-chair adv. bd. rsch. priorities com., bd. dirs. Friends adv. coun., 1989—, chair rsch. subcom., 1990-93, treas., bd. dirs., 1996—; grant reviewer Mich. State Rsch. Fund, NSF, VA; reviewer numerous jours. including Acta Otolaryngologica, Jour. Otology, Physiology and Behavior, Science. Mem. editorial bd. Am. Jour. Otolaryngology, 1981—, AMA, Am. Physiology Soc., Annals of Otology, Rhinology and Laryngology, 1980—, Archives of Oto-Rhino-Laryngology, 1985-93, Hearing Rsch., Jour. Am. Acad. Otolaryngology-Head and Neck Surgery, 1990—. Bd. dirs. Internat. Hearing Found., 1985—. Fellow U. Wash., 1962-65, Kresge Hearing Rsch. Inst., U. Mich., 1965-67; recipient award Am. Acad. Otolaryngology; grantee Deafness Rsch. Found., U. Wash., 1969-71; rsch. grantee NIH, 1969-73. Mem. AAAS, Am. Acad. Otolaryngology and Head and Neck Surgery (com. rsch. in otolaryngology 1971-82, continuing edn. com. 1975-79, NIH liaison com. 1988—, program steering com. jour. 1990, Pres. Citation 1997), Am. Auditory Soc., Am. Otological Soc., Am. Neurotological Soc., Am. Otologic Honor Soc., Acoustical Soc. Am. (com. rsch. psychol., physiol. acoustics 1969-78), Fedn. Am. Physiol. Soc., Fedn. Am. Socs. Exptl. Biology, Soc. Neurosci., Assn. Rsch. Otolaryngology (sec.-treas. 1979-80, pres. elect 1981, pres. 1982. program dir. mtg. 1983, award of merit com. 1985, 95-96, chair 1988, program dir., pres. symposium homeostatic mech. of inner ear 1993), Finnish Acad. Otolaryngology (hon.), Sigma Xi. Office: U Mich Kresge Hearing Rsch Inst 1301 E Ann St Rm R5032 Ann Arbor MI 48109-0506

MILLER, JOSEPH IRWIN, automotive manufacturing company executive; b. Columbus, Ind., May 26, 1909; s. Hugh Thomas and Nettie Irwin (Sweeney) M.; m. Xenia Ruth Simons, Feb. 5, 1943; children: Margaret Irwin, Catherine Gibbs, Elizabeth Ann Garr, Hugh Thomas, II, William Irwin. Grad., Taft Sch., 1927; AB, Yale U., 1931, MA (hon.), 1959, LHD (hon.), 1979; MA, Oxford (Eng.) U., 1933; LLD, Bethany Coll., 1956, Tex. Christian U., Ind. U., 1958, Oberlin Coll., Princeton, 1962; LL.D., Hamilton Coll., 1964, Columbia, 1968, Mich. State U., 1968, Dartmouth, 1971, U. Notre Dame, 1972, Ball State U., 1972, Lynchburg Coll., 1985; L.H.D. (hon.), Case Inst. Tech., 1966, U. Dubuque, 1977; Hum.D., Manchester U., 1973, Moravian Coll., 1976. Assoc. Cummins Engine Co., Inc., Columbus, Ind., 1934—, v.p., gen. mgr., 1934-42, exec. v.p., 1944-47, pres., 1947-51, chmn. bd., 1951-77, chmn. exec. com., 1977-95; dir., 1995-97; hon. chmn. Cummins Engine, 1997—. Pres. Irwin-Union Bank & Trust Co., 1947-54, bd. dir., 1937—, chmn., 1954-75; chmn. exec. com. Irwin Union Corp., 1976-90, hon. chmn., 1997—; bd. dirs. Irwin Fin. Corp., 1990—; mem. Commn. Money and Credit, 1958-61, Pres.'s Com. Postal Reorgn., 1968, Pres.'s Com. Urban Housing, 1968; chmn. Pres.'s Com. on Trade Rels. with Soviet Union and Eastern European Nations, 1965, Nat. Adv. Commn. on Health Manpower, 1966; vice chmn. UN Commn. on Multinat. Corps., 1974; adv. council U.S. Dept. Commerce, 1976; mem. Study Commn. on U.S. Policy Toward So. Africa, 1979-81. Pres. nat. Coun. Chs. of Christ U.S.A., 1960-63; trustee Nat. Humanities Ctr., 1978-90, Carnegie Instn., Washington, 1988-91; mem. cen. and exec. coms. World Coun. Chs., 1961-68; trustee Ford Found., 1961-79, Yale Corp., 1959-77, Urban Inst., 1966-76, Mayo Found., 1977-82; fellow Branford Coll. Recipient Rosenberger award U. Chgo., 1977, 1st MacDowell Colony award, 1981; hon. fellow Balliol Coll., Oxford (Eng.) U.; Benjamin Franklin fellow Royal Soc. Arts. Fellow Am. Acad. Arts and Scis., Royal Inst. Brit. Architects (hon.); mem. AIA (hon.), Am. Philos. Soc., Ind. Acad., Bus. Coun., Conf. Bd. (sr.), Phi Beta Kappa, Beta Gamma Sigma. Mem. Christian Ch. Office: 301 Washington St Columbus IN 47201-6743

MILLER, KAREN L. dean, nursing educator; BSN, Case Western Res. U.; MSN, PhD in Nursing, U. Colo. V.p. The Children's Hosp., Denver; assoc. prof. Coll. Nursing U. Colo. Health Scis. Ctr.; dean, prof. Sch. Nursing U. Kans., 1996—, dean Sch. Allied Health, 1998—. Mem. editl. bd. IMAGE: Jour. Nursing Scholarship. Grantee NIH, 1992. Fellow Am. Acad. Nursing; mem. ANA, ANA Coun. Nurse Rschrs., Am. Orgn. Nurse Execs., Coun. on Grad. Edn. for Nursing Adminstrn., Midwest Alliance in Nursing, Midwest Nursing Rsch. Soc., Sigma Theta Tau (collateral reviewer rsch. com.). Office: U Kans Sch Nursing 390 Rainbow Blvd Kansas City KS 66160-0001

MILLER, KENNETH GREGORY, retired air force officer; b. Bryan, Tex., July 28, 1944; s. Max Richard and Catherine Mae (Sultzman) M.; m. Ann Marguerite Perpich, Nov. 25, 1966; children: Keith G., Deborah J., Craig S. BS in Aero. Engring., Purdue U., 1966; MS in Systems Mgmt., U. So. Calif., 1970; grad., Nat. War Coll., Washington, 1986; postgrad., U. Va., 1988. Commd. 2d lt. USAF, 1966, advanced through grades to brig. gen., 1995; with Office Sec. Def., Washington, 1980-81; various positions to dir. field ops. F-16 System Program Office, Wright-Patterson AFB, Ohio, 1981-86; chief engring. div. Sacramento Air Logistics Ctr., McClellan AFB, Calif., 1986-87; dir. materiel mgmt. Ogden Air Logistics Ctr., Hill AFB, Utah, 1987-89; vice comdr. Acquisition Logistics Div., Wright-Patterson AFB, 1989-90; comdr. Air Force Contract Mgmt. Divsn., Kirtland AFB, N.Mex., 1990; comdr. western dist. Def. Contract Mgmt. Command, L.A., 1990-91; dir. C-17 Program Office, Wright-Patterson AFB, 1991-93; dep. asst. sec. for acquistion USAF, Washington, 1993-94, dir. supply hdqrs., 1994-95; v.p. for gulf ops. BDM Fed., 1995-96; group v.p. for advanced tech. svcs. group RJO Enterprises, Inc., 1997; sr. v.p. Dayton ops. CACI, Inc., 1997-99; group v.p. Air Force programs Anteon Corp., 1999—. Mem. engring. bd. visitors Purdue U. Decorated Disting. Svc. medal, Legion of Merit (2), Def. Superior Svc. medal; recipient award of merit Freedom Found; named Outstanding Aerospace Engr., Purdue U., Disting. Engring. Alumnus, Purdue U., 2001; named to ROTC Hall of Fame, 2001. Mem. Nat. Contract Mgmt. Assn. (bd. advisors 1990-92), Soc. Logistics Engrs., Nat. Def. Indsl. Assn. Office: 1560 Wilson Blvd Ste 800 Arlington VA 22209 E-mail: kmiller@anteon.com.

MILLER, LLOYD DANIEL, real estate agent; b. Savannah, Mo., May 25, 1916; s. Daniel Edward and Minnie (Wiedmer) M.; m. Mabel Gertrude Kurz, June 9, 1939; children: Sharon Miller Schumacher, Donna Miller Bodinson, Rosemary Rae Miller, Jeffrey Lloyd. B.S. in Agrl. Journalism, U. Mo., 1941. Reporter, feature writer, photographer, market editor Corn Belt Farm Dailies, Chgo., Kansas City, Mo., 1941-43; asst. agrl. editor U. Mo., 1946; dir. pub. relations Am. Angus Assn., Chgo., 1946-67, St. Joseph, Mo., 1967, asst. sec., dir. pub. relations, 1968, exec. sec., 1968-78, sr. cons., 1978-81; realtor The Prudential Summers Realtors, 1978—. Mem. U.S. Agrl. Tech. Adv. Com. on Livestock and Livestock Products for Trade Negotiations, 1975-79. Bd. dirs. Mo. Western State Coll. Found., 1976-82, pres., 1978-79; deacon Wyatt Park Bapt. Ch.; chmn. Heartland Ctr., Heartland Hosp. West, 1987-89, bd. dirs. 1987-95. With AUS, 1943-45. Recipient Silver Anvil award Pub. Relations Soc. Am., 1962, Faculty-Alumni award U. Mo.-Columbia, 1975 Mem. Nat. Assn. Realtors, St. Joseph Area C. of C. (pres. 1969, dir., chmn. agri-bus. coun. 1971), St. Joseph Regional Bd. Realtors (pres. 1986), Realtors Land Inst. (v.p. Mo. chpt. 1987-90), Am. Angus Heritage Found., Masons (32 deg.), Shriners, Kiwanis, Sigma Delta Chi. Home: 3302 N Woodbine Rd Apt 10 Saint Joseph MO 64505-9323 Office: 1007 E Saint Maartens Dr Saint Joseph MO 64506-2993

MILLER, ORLANDO JACK, physician, educator; b. Oklahoma City, May 11, 1927; s. Arthur Leroy and Iduma Dorris (Berry) M.; m. Dorothy Anne Smith, July 10, 1954; children: Richard Lawrence, Cynthia Kathleen, Karen Ann. BS, Yale U., 1946, MD, 1950. Intern St. Anthony Hosp., Oklahoma City, 1950-51; asst. resident in obstetrics and gynecology Yale-New Haven Med. Center, 1954-57, resident, instr., 1957-58; vis. fellow dept. obstetrics and gynecology Tulane U. Service, Charity Hosp., New Orleans, 1958; hon. research asst. Galton Lab., Univ. Coll., London, 1958-60; instr. Coll. Physicians and Surgeons Columbia U., N.Y.C., 1960, asso. dept. obstetrics and gynecology, 1960-61, asst. prof., 1961-65, asso. prof., 1965-69, prof. dept. human genetics and devel., dept. obstetrics and gynecology, 1969-85; asst. attending obstetrician, gynecologist Presbyn. Hosp., 1964-65, assoc., 1965-70, attending obstetrician and gynecologist, 1970-85; prof. molecular biology, genetics and ob-gyn. Wayne State U. Sch. Medicine, Detroit, 1985-94, prof. Ctr. for Molecular Medicine and Genetics, 1994-96, prof. emeritus, 1996—, chmn. dept. molecular biology and genetics, 1985-93, dir. Ctr. for Molecular Biology, 1987-90. Bd. dirs.Am. Bd. Med. Genetics, 1983-85, v.p., 1983, pres., 1984, 85. Author: (with E. Therman) Human Chromosomes, 2000; editor Cytogenetics, 1970-72; assoc. editor: Birth Defects Compendium, 1971-74, Cytogenetics and Cell Genetics, 1972-97; mem. editl. bd. Cytogenetics, 1961-69, Am. Jour. Human Genetics, 1969-74, 79-83, Gynecologic Investigation, 1970-77, Teratology, 1972-74, Cancer Genetics and Cytogenetics, 1979-84, Jour. Exptl. Zoology, 1989-92, Chromosome Rsch., 1994-99; mem. editl. bd. com. Genomics, 1987-93, assoc. editor, 1993-96; mem. adv. bd. Human Genetics, 1978-98; cons. Jour. Med. Primatology, 1977-94; consulting editor McGraw-Hill Yearbook of Sci. and Tech., 1995—, Encyclopedia of Science and Technology, 1997—; contbr. chpts. to textbooks and articles to med. and sci. jours. Mem. sci. adv. com. on rsch. Nat. Found. March of Dimes, 1967-96, mem. sci. com., 1996—; mem. sci. rec. com. Basil O'Connor starter grants, 1973-77, 86-94; mem. human embryology and devel. study sect. NIH, 1970-74, chmn., 1972-74; mem. com. for study of inborn errors of metabolism NRC, 1972-74; mem. sci. adv. com. virology and cell biology Am. Cancer Soc., 1974-78, mem. sci. adv. com. cell and devel. biology, 1986-90; mem. human genome study sect. NIH, 1991-94; U.S. rep. permanent com. Internat. Congress of Human Genetics, 1986-91. With AUS, 1951-53. James Hudson Brown Jr. fellow Yale U., 1947-48; NRC fellow, 1953-54; Population Council fellow, 1958-59; Josiah Macy Jr. fellow, 1960-61; NSF sr. postdoctoral fellow U. Oxford, 1968-69; vis. scientist U. Edinburgh, 1983-84; Disting. vis. fellow, Fogarty Internat. fellow LaTrobe U., Melbourne, Australia, 1992; recipient Pres. Disting. Scientist award Soc. for Gynecol. Investigation, 1999. Fellow AAAS; mem. AAAS, Am. Genetic Assn., Am. Soc. Cell Biology, Am. Soc. Human Genetics (bd. dirs. 1970-73, 86-90), Genetics Soc. Am., Genetics Soc. Australia, Human Genome Orgn., Acad. Scholars, Wayne State U. (life, pres. 1996-97), Sigma Xi. Presbyterian. Home: 1915 Stonycroft Ln Bloomfield Hills MI 48304-2339 Office: 540 E Canfield St Detroit MI 48201-1928 E-mail: ojmiller@cmb.biosci.wayne.edu.

MILLER, PATRICIA LOUISE, state legislator, nurse; b. Bellefontaine, Ohio, July 4, 1936; d. Richard William and Rachel Orpha (Williams) M.; m. Kenniteh Orlan Miller, July 3, 1960; children: Tamara Sue, Matthew Ivan. RN, Meth. Hosp. Sch. Nursing, Indpls., 1957; BS, Ind. U., 1960. Staff nurse Cmty. Hosp., Indpls., 1958, Meth. Hosp., Indpls., 1959; office nurse A.D. Dennison, MD, 1960-61; rep. State of Ind. Dist. 50, Indpls., 1982-83; senator State of Ind. Dist. 32, 1983—; health welfare and aging com., 1983-90; mem. labor and pension com., 1983-94; mem. edn. com., 1984-90; legis. appt. and elections com., chmn. interim study com. pub. health and mental health Ind. Gen. Assembly, 1986; chair Senate Enfiron. Affairs, 1990-92; health and environ affairs, 1992—; mem. election com., 1992—; mem. budget subcom. Senate Fin. Com., 1995—. Mem. Bd. Edn. Met. Sch. Dist., Warren Twop., 1974-82, pres., 1979-80, 80-81; mem. Warren Twp. Citizens Screening Com. for Sch. Bd. Candidates, 1972-74, 84, Met. Zoning Bd. Appeals, Divsn. I, apptd. mem. City-County Coun. on Aging, Indpls. 1977-80; mem. State Bd. Vocat. and Tech. Edn., 1978-82, sec., 1980-82; mem. gov.'s Select Adv. Commn. for Primary and Secondary Edn., 1983; precinct committeeman Rep. Party, 1968-74, ward vice-chmn., 1975-78, ward chmn., 1978-85, twp. chmn., 1985-87; vice chmn. Marion County Rep., 1986—; del. Rep. State Copnv., 1968, 74, 76, 80, 84, 86, 88, 90, 92, 94, sgt. at arms, 1982, mem. platform com., 1984, 88, 90, 92, co-chmn. Ind. Rep. Platform Com., 1992; del. Rep. Nat. Conv., 1984, alternate del., 1988, Rep. Presdl. Elector Alternate, 1992; active various polit. campaigns; bd. dirs. PTA, 1967-81; pres. Grassy Creek PTA, 1971-72; state del. Ind. PTA, 1978; mem. child car adv. com. Walker Career Ctr., 1976-80, others; bd. dirs. Ch. Fedn. Greater Indpls., 1979-82, Christian Justice Ctr., Inc., 1983-85, Gideon Internat. Aux., 1977Y; mem. United Meth. Bd. Missions Aux. Indpls., 1974-80, v.p., 1974-76, mem. nominating com., 1977; bd. dirs. Lucille Raines Residence, Inc., 1977-80; exec. com. S. Ind. Conf. United Meth. Women, 1977-80, lay del. s. Ind. Conf. United Meth. Ch., 1977—, fin. and adminstrn. com., 1979-88, planning and rsch. com., 1980-88, co-chmn. law adv. com., chmn. health and welfare, conf. coun. ministries, also mem. task force, bd. ordained ministry, also panel, chmn. com. on dist. superintendency, dist. coun. on ministries; sec. Indpls. S.E. Dist. Council on Minstries, 1977-78, pres. 1982; chmn. council on ministries Cumberland United Meth. Ch., 1969-76; chmn. stewardship com. Old Bethal United Meth. Ch., 1982-85, fin. com., 1982-85, adminstrv. bd., mem. council on ministries, 1981-85; co-chair Evangelism Com., 1994—; jurisdictional del. United Meth. Ch., 1988, 92; alternate del. United Methodist Ch. Gen. Conf., 1988, del. 1992; mem. adv. com. Warren Fine Arts Found., 1991—; mem. adv. bd. St. Francis Hosp., 1992—; mem. health and human svcs. com. Midwest Legis. Conf., 1995. Recipient Lambda Theta Honor for Outstanding contbr. in fiedl of end., 1976; named Woman of Yr. Cumberland Bus. and Profl. Women, 1979; Ind. Vocat. Assn. citation award, 1984, others. Mem. Indpls. dist. Dental Soc. Women's Aux., Ind. Dental Assn. Women's Aux., Am. Dental Assn. Women's Aux., Coun. State Govt. (intergovtl. affairs com.), Nat. Conf. State Legis. (vice chmn. health com. 1994—), Warren Twp. Rep., Franklin Rep., Lawrence Rep., Center Twp. Rep., Fall Creek Valley Rep, Marion County Coun. Rep. Women (3rd v.p. 1986-89), Ind. Women's Rep. (legis. chair 1988-89), Nat. Fedn. rep. Women, Beech Grove Rep., Perry Twp. Rep., Indpls. Women's Rep. Club (3rd v.p. 1989—), Indpls. Press Club.

MILLER, PATRICK WILLIAM, research administrator, educator; b. Toledo, Sept. 1, 1947; s. Richard William and Mary Olivia (Rinna) M.; m. Jean Ellen Thomas, Apr. 5, 1974; children: Joy, Tatum, Alex. BS in Indstrl. Edn., Bowling Green State U., 1971, MEd in Career Edn. and Tech., 1973; PhD in Indstrl. Tech. Edn., Ohio State U., 1977; Master's cert. Govt. Contract Adminstrn., George Washington U., 1995. Tchr. Montgomery Hills Jr. High Sch., Silver Spring, Md., 1971-72, Rockville (Md.) High Sch., 1973-74; asst. prof. Wayne State U., Detroit, 1977-79; assoc. prof., grad. coord. indstrl. edn. and tech. Western Carolina U., Cullowhee, N.C., 1979-81; assoc prof. U. No. Iowa, Cedar Falls, 1981-86; dir. grad. studies practical arts and vocat.-tech. edn. U. Mo., Columbia, 1986-89; devel. editor Am. Tech. Pubs., Homewood, Ill., 1989-90; proposal mgr. Nat. Opinion Rsch. Ctr. U. Chgo., 1990-96; dir. grants & contracts City Colls. Chgo., 1996-99; assoc. v.p. acad. affairs Prairie State Coll., 1999—, also dean workforce devel. and career edn., 1999—. Pres. Patrick W. Miller and Assocs., Munster, Ind., 1981—; presenter, advisor and cons. in field. Author: Nonverbal Communication: Its Impact on Teaching and Learning, 1983, Teacher Written Tests: A Guide for Planning, Creating, Administering and Assessing, 1985, Nonverbal Communication: What Resarch Says to the Teacher, 1988, How To Write Tests for Students, 1990, Nonverbal Communication in the Classroom, 2000, Nonverbal Communication in the Workplace, 2000, Grant Writing: Strategies for Developing Winning Proposals, 2000, Test Development: Guidelines, Practical Suggestions and Examples, 2001; mem. editl. bd. Jour. Indsl. Tchr. Edn., 1981-88, Am. Vocat. Edn. Rsch. Jour., 1981-85, 94—, Tech. Tchr., 1982-84, Jour. Indsl. Tech., 1984—, Jour. Vocat. and Tech. Edn., 1987-90, Human Resource Devel. Quar., 1989—; also articles. Sec. U. No. Iowa United Faculty, Cedar Falls, 1983-84, pres., 1984-86. Lance cpl. USMC, 1966-68, Vietnam. Recipient editl. recognition award Jour. Indsl. Tchr. Edn., 1984, 86, 88; named One of Accomplished Grads. of Coll. Tech., Bowling Green State U., 1995. Mem. ASTD, Am. Ednl. Rsch. Assn., Assn. for Career and Tech. Edn., Am. Vocat. Edn. Rsch. Assn., Nat. Assn. Indsl. Tech. (chmn. rsch. grants 1982-87, pres. industry div. 1991-92, chmn. exec. bd. 1992-93, past pres. 1993-94, Leadership award 1992, 93), Nat. Assn. Indsl. and Tech. Tchr. Educators (pres. 1988-89, past pres. 1989-90, trustee 1990-93, Outstanding Svc. award 1988, 90), Internat. Tech. Edn. Assn., Coun. Tech. Tchr. Edn., Epsilon Pi Tau, Phi Delta Kappa. Office: Prairie State Coll 202 S Halsted St Chicago Heights IL 60411-8226 E-mail: miller9147@aol.com., pwmiller@online.com.

MILLER, PAUL DAVID, aerospace executive; BA, Fla. State U.; MBA, U. Ga. Commd. USN, advanced through grades to four star adm.; comdr.-in-chief U.S. Atlantic Command; supreme allied comdr.-Atlantic NATO; with Litton Marine Sys., 1995-99; pres. Sperry Marine Inc.; CEO Alliant Techsystems, Inc., Hopkins, Minn., 1999—, also chmn. bd. dirs. Office: Alliant Techsystems Inc 600 2d St NE Hopkins MN 55343

MILLER, PAUL DEAN, breeding consultant, geneticist, educator; b. Cedar Falls, Iowa, Apr. 4, 1941; s. Donald Hugh and Mary (Hansen) M.; m. Nancy Pearl Huser, Aug. 23, 1965; children: Michael, Steven. BS, Iowa State U., 1963; MS, Cornell U., 1965, PhD, 1967. Asst. prof. animal breeding cornell U., Ithaca, N.Y., 1967-72; v.p. Am. Breeders Svc., De Forest, Wis., 1972-95; exec. dir. Nat. Dairy Herd Improvement Assn., 1996—; pres. Windsor (Wis.) Park Inc., 1985—. Adj. prof. U. Wis., Madison, 1980—. Contbr. articles to profl. jours. Mem. Beef Improvement Fedn. (disting. svc. award 1980), Am. Soc. Animal Sci., Am. Dairy Sci. Assn., Nat. Assn. Animal Breeders (dir. 1983, v.p. 1986). Republican. Office: Nat Dairy Herd Improvement 3021 E Dublin Granville Rd Columbus OH 43231-4031 Home: 6301 Fox Run Sun Prairie WI 53590-9357 E-mail: pdmil@aol.com.

MILLER, PAUL J. lawyer; b. Boston, Mar. 27, 1929; s. Edward and Esther (Kalis) M.; children— Robin, Jonathan; m. Michal Davis, Sept. 1, 1965; children— Anthony, Douglas B.A., Yale U., 1950; LL.B., Harvard U., 1953. Bar: Mass. 1953, Ill. 1957. Assoc. Miller & Miller, Boston, 1953-54; assoc. Sonnenschein Nath & Rosenthal, Chgo., 1957-63, ptnr., 1963—. Bd. dirs. Oil-Dri Corp. Am., Chgo. Trustee Latin Sch. of Chgo., 1985-91. 1st lt. JAGC, U.S. Army, 1954-57. Fellow Am. Bar Found.; mem. Tavern Club, Saddle and Cycle Club, Law Club, Phi Beta Kappa. Avocation: sailing. Office: Sonnenschein Nath & Rosenthal 233 S Wacker Dr Ste 8000 Chicago IL 60606-6491 E-mail: pjm@sonnenschein.com.

MILLER, PEGGY GORDON ELLIOTT, university president; b. Matewan, W.Va., May 27, 1937; d. Herbert Hunt and Mary Ann (Renfro) Gordon; m. Robert Lawrence Miller, Nov. 23, 2001; children from previous marriage: Scott Vandling III, Anne Gordon. BA, Transylvania Coll., 1959; MA, Northwestern U., 1964; EdD, Ind. U., 1975. Tchr. Horace Mann H.S., Gary, Ind., 1959-64; instr. English Am. Inst. Banking, 1969-70, Ind. U. N.W., Gary, 1965-69, lectr. Edn., 1973-74, asst. prof. edn., 1975-78, assoc. prof., 1978-80, supr. secondary student tchg., 1973-74, dir. student tchg., 1975-77, dir. Office Field Experiences, 1977-78, dir. profl. devel., 1978-80, spl. asst. to chancellor, 1981-83, asst. to chancellor, 1983-84, acting chancellor, 1983-84, chancellor, 1984-92; pres. U. Akron, Ohio, 1992-96, S.D. State U., 1998—. Sr. fellow Nat. Ctr. for Higher Edn., 1996-97; vis. prof. U. Ark., 1979-80, U. Alaska, 1982; bd. dirs. Lubrizol Corp., A. Schulman Corp., First Nat. Bank Brookings, Commn. on Women in Higher Edn., Akron Tomorrow, Ohio Aerospace Consortium, Ohio Super Computer Com.; holder VA Harrington disting. chair in edn., 1994-96, Charles G. Herbrich chair in leadership mgmt., 1996— Author: (with C. Smith) Reading Activities for Middle and Secondary Schools: A Handbook for Teachers, 1979, Reading Instruction for Secondary Schools, 1986, How to Improve Your Scores on Reading Competency Tests, 1981, (with C. Smith and G. Ingersoll) Trends in Educational Materials: Traditionals and the New Technologies, 1983, The Urban Campus: Educating a New Majority for a New Century, 1994, also numerous articles. Bd. dirs. Meth. Hosp., N.W. Ind. Forum, N.W. Ind. Symphony, S.D. Art Mus., Boys Club N.W. Ind., Akron Symphony, NBD Bank, John S. Knight Conv. Ctr., Inventure Pl., Akron Roundtable, Cleve. Com. Higher Edn. Recipient Disting. Alumni award Northwestern U., VA Disting. Alumni award, 1994, numerous grants; Am. Council on Edn. fellow in acad. adminstrn. Ind. U., Bloomington, 1980-81. Mem. Assn. Tchr. Educators (nat. pres. 1984-85, Disting. Mem. 1990), Nat. Acad. Tchrs. Edn. (bd. dirs. 1983—), Ind. Assn. Tchr. Educators (past pres.), North Ctrl. Assn. (mem. commn. at large), Am. Assn. State Colls. and Univs. (sr. fellow 1996-98, acting v.p. divsn. acad. and internat. programs 1997, bd. dirs.), Am. Coun. Edn. (bd. dirs.), Leadership Devel. Coun. ACE, Ohio Inter Univ. Coun. (chairperson), Internat. Reading Assn., Akron Urban League (bd. dirs.), P.E.O., Cosmos Club, Phi Delta Kappa (Outstanding Young Educator award), Delta Kappa Gamma (Leadership/Mgmt. fellow 1980), Pi Lambda Theta, Pi Kappa Phi, Chi Omega. Episcopalian. Avocation: music. Home: 929 Harvey Dunn St Brookings SD 57006-1347 Office: South Dakota State Univ Office of the Pres Adminstrn Bldg 201 Brookings SD 57007-0001 Home: 3891 Spyglass Hill Rd Sarasota FL 34238 E-mail: Peggy_Miller@sdstate.edu.

MILLER, REGINALD WAYNE, professional basketball player; b. Riverside, Calif., Aug. 24, 1965; Student, UCLA. Profl. basketball player Indiana Pacers, 1987—. Named to NBA All-Star Team, 1990, 94, Dream Team I, 1994, Dream Team II, 1996. Achievements include being a holder of NBA Playoff record most three-point field goals in one quarter (5), 1994, co-holder NBA Playoff record most three-point field goals in one half (6), 1994, 95; first Pacers player to surpass 15,000 career points/5 time all star. Office: c/o Indiana Pacers Market St Arena 300 E Market St Fl 1 Indianapolis IN 46204-2603*

MILLER, RICHARD J. wholesale pharmaceutical distribution company executive; V.p. auditing Cardinal Health, Inc., 1994-95, v.p. contr., 1995-99, corp. v.p., 1999, exec. v.p., 1999, CFO, exec. v.p., 1999—. Office: Cardinal Health Inc 7000 Cardinal Pl Dublin OH 43017

MILLER, RICK FREY, emergency physician; b. Peoria, Ill., July 27, 1946; s. Richard Ross and Mildred (Frey) M.; m. Cheryl Kay Hasty, June 1, 1968; children: Richard Andrew, Jennifer Caroline, Heidi Sue. BS in Math., BS in Chemistry, Bradley U., 1969; MD, U. Ill., 1974. Bd. cert. emergency medicine and pediats. Program dir. emergency medicine St. Francis Med. Ctr., Peoria, Ill., 1980-88, med. dir. Life Flight, 1985-91, chmn. dept. emergency medicine, dir. emergency med. svcs., 1988—. Contbr. book chpt.: Emergency Medicine Clinics of North America, 1992. Bd. dirs. Prevent Child Abuse-Ill., Springfield, 1991-98, Mental Health Assn. of Illinois Valley, Peoria, 1996-98; co-lay dir. Teens Encounter Christ, Peoria, 1997. Recipient Ptnrs. in Peace award Ctr. for Prevention of Abuse, 1996. Fellow Am. Coll. Emergency Physicians, Am. Acad. Pediats.; mem. Soc. Acad. Emergency Medicine. Avocations: skiing, bicycling. Office: OSF St Francis Med Ctr 530 NE Glen Oak Ave Peoria IL 61637-0001

MILLER, ROBERT ARTHUR, former state supreme court chief justice; b. Aberdeen, S.D., Aug. 28, 1939; s. Edward Louis and Bertha Leone (Hitchcox) Miller; m. Shirlee Ann Schlim, Sept. 5, 1964; children: Catherine Sue, Scott Edward, David Alan, Gerri Elizabeth, Robert Charles. BSBA, U. S.D., 1961, JD, 1963. Asst. atty. gen. State of S.D., Pierre, 1963—65; pvt. practice law Philip, 1965—71; state atty. Haakon County, 1965—71; city atty. City of Philip, 1965—71; judge State of S.D. (6th cir.), Pierre, 1971—86, presiding judge, 1975—86; justice S.D. Supreme Ct., 1986—2001, chief justice, 1990—2001, ret., 2001—. Bd. dirs. Nat. Conf. of Chief Justices, 1996—97, State Justice Inst., 1998—, chair, 1998—; trustee S.D. Retirement Sys., Pierre, 1974—85, chmn., 1982—85; mem. faculty S.D. Law Enforcement Tng. Acad., 1975—85; bd. dirs. U. S.D. Law Sch. Found., 1990—. Mem. S.D. State Crime Commn., 1979—86; mem. adv. commn. S.D. Sch. for the Deaf, 1983—85, Comm. Svcs. to Deaf, 1990—92; cts. counselor S.D. Boy's State, 1986—, Nat. Awards Jury Freedoms Found., 1991. Mem.: S.D. Judge's Assn. (pres. 1974—75), State Bar of S.D., Elks. Roman Catholic. Avocations: golf, hunting. Office: SD Supreme Ct State Capitol Bldg 500 E Capitol Ave Pierre SD 57501-5070*

MILLER, ROBERT BRANSON, JR. retired newspaper publisher; b. Battle Creek, Mich., Aug. 10, 1935; s. Robert Branson and Jean (Leonard) M.; m. Pattricia E. Miller; children: Melissa Ann, Gregory Allen, Jennifer Lynn, Jeffrey William. Grad., Hotchkiss Sch., Lakeville, Conn., 1953; BA, Mich. State U., 1959. Advt. salesman State Jour., Lansing, Mich., 1959-61, circulation sales rep., 1961-62, reporter, 1962-65, nat. advt. mgr., 1965-66; asst. to pub. Idaho Statesman, Boise, 1966-69, pub., 1971-79, Daily Olympian, Olympia, Wash., 1969-71, Battle Creek Enquirer, 1979-90, chmn., 1990-91. Bd. dirs. Battle Creek chpt. ARC; advisor Big Bros./Big Sisters; sr. advisor United Way; trustee Miller Found., Battle Creek. With USNR, 1956-58.

MILLER, ROBERT EARL, engineer, educator; b. Rockford, Ill., Oct. 4, 1932; s. Leslie D. and Marcia V. (Jones) M. BS, U. Ill., 1954, MS, 1955, PhD, 1959. Asst. prof. theoretical and applied mechanics U. Ill., Urbana, 1959-61, assoc. prof., 1961-68, prof., 1968-94, prof. emeritus, 1994—. Cons. in field to industry U.S. Army; in various positions in industry, summers, 1963-68 Contbr. articles to profl. jours. Mem. AIAA, Am. Soc. Engrng. Edn. (Disting. Engrng. award 1991), ASCE. Office: U Ill 216 Talbot Lab 104 S Wright St Urbana IL 61801-2935 E-mail: rem@uiuc.edu.

MILLER, ROBERT G. retail executive; b. Cin., Sept. 7, 1936; s. Peter G. and Mildred (Behner) M.; m. Sharon T. Miller, Oct. 2, 1976 (div. July 1989); children: Lori A. Miller, Lynda S. Miller, Michael A. Miller. , U. Cin., Cin., 1964. Store mgr. Mc Alpins, Cin., 1975—. Bd. dirs. YMCA, Blue Ash, Ohio, 1990—. Mem. Lions Club. Republican. Avocations: sports fisherman, tennis, golf. Home: 1815 Williams Ave Cincinnati OH 45212-3557 Office: Mc Alpins Kenwood 7913 Montgomery Rd Cincinnati OH 45236-4303

MILLER, ROBERT JAMES, educational association administrator; b. Mansfield, Ohio, Jan. 27, 1926; s. Dennis Cornelius and Mabel (Snyder) M.; m. Jerri Ann Burran, June 5, 1952; children: Robert James Jr., Dennis Burran. Student, Heidelberg Coll., 1946-47; BS, U. N.Mex., 1950, MA, 1952; postgrad., Miami U., Oxford, Ohio, 1951-55; MBA, Fla. Atlantic U., 1978. Asst. exec. sec. Phi Delta Theta Hdqrs., Oxford, 1951-54, adminstrv. sec., 1954-55, exec. v.p., 1955-91; pres. Phi Delta Theta Found., 1984-96; bus. mgr. The Scroll, 1955-91; cons., 1997—. Dir. Interfrat. Found., 1995—. Editor: Phikeia—The Manual of Phi Delta Theta, 1951, 19 edits., 1989, Phis Sing, 1958, Constitution and General Statutes of Phi Delta Theta, Fraternity Education Foundations, 1962, Directory of Phi Delta Theta, 1973. Chmn. United Appeal, Oxford, 1960; bd. dirs. U. N.Mex. Alumni Assn., 1961-68, Work Devel. Assn., 1999—; pres. Fedn. of Clubs, Oxford, 1964, McGuffey PTA, 1971, Miami U. Art Mus., 1993-94, McCullough-Hyde Hosp., Oxford, 1966, chmn. endowment adv. com., 1988-89; vol. leader Boy Scouts Am., Oxford, 1966-79. Recipient citizen of yr. award City of Oxford, 1968, citation Theta Chi, 1967, Order of Interfrat. Svc. Lambda Chi Alpha, 1994, interfrat. leadership award Sigma Nu, 1994, accolate for intrafraternity svc. Kappa Alpha, meritorious svc. award Boy. Scouts Am., 1977, others; Interfrat. Inst. fellow Ind. U., 1988. Mem. Nat. Intrafraternity Conf. (various coms. 1954-96, gold medal 1992), Am. Soc. Assn. Execs. (cert.), Cin. Soc. Assn. Execs., Fraternity Execs. Assn. (pres. 1962-63, disting. svc. award 1991), Edgewater Conf. (pres. 1978-79), Summit Soc., Country Club Oxford (bd. dirs.), Order of Symposiarchs, Order of Omega, Rotary (founder Oxford club 1965, pres. 1966, merit award 1974, dist. gov. S.W. Ohio 1978-79, study group exch. leader South Africa 1992), Blue Key, Phi Delta Kappa, Omicron Delta Kappa. Home: 170 Hilltop Rd Oxford OH 45056-1572 Office: Phi Delta Theta Ednl Found 2 S Campus Ave Oxford OH 45056-1801

MILLER, ROBERT L., JR. federal judge; b. 1950; m. Jane Woodward. BA, Northwestern U., 1972; JD, Ind. U., 1975. Law clk. to presiding justice U.S. Dist. Ct. (no. dist.) Ind., 1975; judge St. Joseph Superior Ct., South Bend, Ind., 1975-86, chief judge, 1981-83; judge U.S. Dist. Ct. (no. dist.) Ind., 1985—. Office: US Dist Ct 325 Fed Bldg 204 S Main St South Bend IN 46601-2122

MILLER, ROBERT STEVENS, JR. finance professional; b. Portland, Oreg., Nov. 4, 1941; s. Robert Stevens and Barbara (Weston) M.; m. Margaret Rose Kyger, Nov. 9, 1966; children: Christopher John, Robert Stevens, Alexander Lamont. AB with distinction, Stanford U., 1963; LLB, Harvard U., 1966; MBA, Stanford U., 1968. Bar: Calif. bar 1966. Fin. analyst Ford Motor Co., Dearborn, Mich., 1968-71, spl. studies mgr. Mexico City, 1971-73; dir. fin. Ford Asia-Pacific, Inc., Melbourne, Australia, 1974-77, Ford Motor Co., Caracas, Venezuela, 1977-79; v.p., treas. Chrysler Corp., Detroit, 1980-81, exec. v.p. fin., 1981-90, vice chmn., 1990-92; sr. ptnr. James D. Wolfensohn, Inc., N.Y.C., 1992-93; chmn. Fed. Mogul corp., Smithfield, Mich. Chmn. bd. dirs. Morrison Knudsen Corp., 1995-96, Waste Mgmt., Inc., 1997—; bd. dirs. Fed.-Mogul, Pope & Talbot, Symantec, Morrison Knudsen; chmn. bd. Waste Mgmt. Inc., 1997—. Office: Fed Mogul Corp 26555 Northwestern Hwy Southfield MI 48034

MILLER, SAMUEL H. company executive; Co-chmn. Forest City Mgmt. Inc., Cleve., 1989—. Office: FOREST CITY ENTERPRISES, INC. 1100 TERMINAL TOWER 50 Public Sq.,Ste 1170 Cleveland OH 44113-2203

MILLER, STEPHEN RALPH, lawyer; b. Chgo., Nov. 28, 1950; s. Ralph and Karin Ann (Olson) M.; children: David Williams, Lindsay Christine. m. Sheila L. Krysiak, Feb. 2, 1998. BA cum laude, Yale U., 1972; JD, Cornell U., 1975. Bar: Ill. Assoc. McDermott, Will & Emery, Chgo., 1975-80, income ptnr., 1981-85, equity ptnr., 1986—, mgmt. com. mem., 1992-95. Mem. spl. task force on post-employment benefits Fin. Acctg. Standards Bd., Norwalk, Conn., 1987-91. Contbr. articles to profl. jours. Mem. Chgo. Coun. on Fgn. Rels., 1978—, mem. devel. com., 1997—, chair mem. devel. subcom., 1999—; trustee police pension bd., Wilmette, Ill., 1992-98; trustee Seabury We. Theol. Sem., Evanston, Ill., 1994—, chancellor, 1996-97, chair trusteeship com., 2000—. Mem.: ABA, Lawyers' Club of Chgo., Yale Club Chgo. Avocations: sailing, water skiing, cross-country skiing. Office: McDermott Will & Emery 227 W Monroe St Ste 4700 Chicago IL 60606-5096 E-mail: smiller@mwe.com.

MILLER, STEVEN, medical administrator; Grad., U. Mo., Kansas City. Nephrology fellow Wash. U., 1988, hosp. staff, faculty, 1990—, dir. hypertension clinic divsn. nephrology; med. dir. systemwide renal network Barnes-Jewish Hosp.; chief med. officer Wash. U. Sch. Medicine-Barnes Jewish Hosp. Assoc. prof. medicine Wash. U. Sch. of Medicine.

MILLER, SUSAN ANN, school system administrator; b. Cleve., Nov. 24, 1947; d. Earl Wilbur and Marie Coletta (Hendershot) M. BS in Edn., Kent State U., 1969; MEd, Cleve. State U., 1975; PhD, Kent State U., 1993. Cert. supt.; cert. elem. prin., cert. elem. supervisor; cert. Learning Disabled/Behavior Disabled tchr.; cert. tchr. grades 1-8; cert. sch. counselor; lic. counselor. Tchr., guidance counselor, interim prin. North Royalton City Schs., Ohio, 1969-84; dir. elem. and spl. edn., acting supt., asst. supt. Ednl. Svc. Ctr. of Cuyahoga County , Valley View, 1984—. Contbr. articles to profl. jours. Grantee Latchkey Program, State Dept. Edn., North Coast Leadership Forum, Peer Assistance and Rev., Entry Yr. Program, Alt. H.S. Mem. ASCD, Coun. Exceptional Children, Phi Delta Kappa. Office: ESC Cuyahoga County 5700 W Canal Rd Valley View OH 44125-3326 Home: 7236 Morning Star Trail Sagamore Hills OH 44067 E-mail: susan.a.miller@lnoca.org.

MILLER, TERRY ALAN, chemistry educator; b. Girard, Kans., Dec. 18, 1943; s. Dwight D. Miller and Rachel E. (Detjen) Beltram; m. Barbara Hoffmann, July 16, 1966; children: Brian, Stuart. BA, U. Kans., 1965; PhD, Cambridge (Eng.) U., 1968. Disting. tech. staff Bell Telephone Labs, 1968-84; vis. asst. prof. Princeton U., 1968-71; vis. lectr. Stanford U., 1972; vis. fgn. scholar Inst. Molecular Sci., Okazaki, Japan, summer 1983; Ohio eminent scholar, prof. chemistry Ohio State U., Columbus, 1984—. Chair Molecular Spectroscopy Symposium, Columbus, 1992—. Mem. editl. bd. Jour. Chem. Physics, 1978-81, Jour. Molecular Spectroscopy, 1982-87, Laser Chemistry, 1986—, Rev. of Sci. Instruments, 1986-89, Jour. Phys. Chemistry, 1989-95, Jour. Optical Soc. Am., 1989-95, Chemtracts, 1989-90, Ann. Revs. Phys. Chemistry, 1989-94, Jour. Molecular Structure, 1996—; contbr. more than 250 articles to profl. jours. Recipient Bourke medal Royal Soc. Chemistry, 1998; Marshall fellow Brit. Govt., 1965-67, NSF fellow, 1967-68. Fellow Optical Soc. Am. (Meggars award 1993), Am. Phys. Soc. (H.P. Broida award 1999); mem. Am. Chem. Soc. (councilor), Coblentz Soc. (Bomen-Michaelson award 1995). Office: Ohio State U 120 W 18th Ave Columbus OH 43210-1106

MILLER, TERRY MORROW, lawyer; b. Columbus, Ohio, Mar. 11, 1947; s. Robert E. and Elizabeth Jane (Morrow) M.; m. Martha Estella Johnson, Mar. 20, 1976; 1 child, Timothy. BS, Ohio State U., 1969, JD, 1975. Bar: Ohio 1975, U.S. Ct. Appeals (6th cir.) 1979, U.S. Supreme Ct. 1980. Asst. atty. gen. State of Ohio, Columbus, 1975-77; ptnr. Miller & Noga, 1977-81; assoc. Vorys, Sater, Seymour and Pease, 1981-85, ptnr., 1986—. Trustee Columbus Literacy Coun., 1997—. Sgt. U.S. Army, 1969-71, Okinawa. Mem. Ohio State Bar Assn., Columbus Bar Assn., Little Turtle Country Club (mems. coun. 1997-2000, pres. 1998-2000). Avocations: golf, Ohio history. Home: 288 E North Broadway Columbus OH 43214-4114 Office: Vorys Sater Seymour et al PO Box 1008 52 E Gay St Columbus OH 43215-3108

MILLER, THOMAS J. state attorney general; b. Dubuque, Iowa, Aug. 11, 1944; s. Elmer John and Betty Maude (Kross) Miller; m. Linda Cottington, Jan. 10, 1981; 1 child Matthew. BA, Loras Coll., Dubuque, 1966; JD, Harvard U., 1969. Bar: Iowa 1969. With VISTA, Balt., 1969—70; legis. asst. to U.S. rep. John C. Culver, 1970—71; legal edn. dir. Balt. Legal Aid Bur., part-time faculty U. Md. Sch. Law, 1971—73; pvt. practice McGregor, Iowa, 1973—78; city atty., 1973—79, Marquette; atty. gen. of Iowa, 1978—90, 1994—; ptnr. Faegre & Benson, Des Moines, 1991—95. Chmn. Microsoft case exec. com.; co-chmn. Airline Competition Working Group; pres. 2d Dist. New Dem. Club , Balt., 1972. Mem.: NAAG (pres. 1989—90, chmn. consumer protection, ins., budget, and antitrust coms., Wyman award 1990), ABA, Iowa Bar Assn., Common Cause. Roman Catholic. Office: Office of the Atty Gen Hoover State Office Bldg 1305 E Walnut St Des Moines IA 50319-0112*

MILLER, THOMAS WILLIAMS, former university dean; b. Pottstown, Pa., July 2, 1930; s. Franklin Sullivan and Margaret (Williams) M.; m. Edythe Edwards, Dec. 20, 1952; children: Theresa, Thomas, Christine, Stefanie. B.S. in Music Edn, West Chester (Pa.) State Coll., 1952; M.A., East Carolina U., Greenville, N.C., 1957; Mus.A.D. (Univ. fellow), Boston U., 1964. Dir. instrumental music Susquenita (Pa.) High Sch., 1955-56; instr. trumpet East Carolina U., 1957-61; asst. dean East Carolina U. (Sch. Music), 1962-68, dean, 1969-71; vis. prof. U. Hawaii, Honolulu, 1968; dean Sch. Music Northwestern U., Evanston, Ill., 1971-89; dean emeritus Northwestern U., 1989—. Contbr. articles to profl. jours. Assoc. Nat. Arts, 1989. Served with AUS, 1952-55. Named Distinguished Alumnus West Chester State Coll., 1975 Mem. Nat. Arts Assn., Music Educators Nat. Conf. (life), Nat. Assn. Schs. Music (hon. life, grad. commr. 1974-79, v.p. 1979-82, pres. 1982-85, chmn. grad. com. 1985-86, bd. dirs. 1986-89), Coll. Music Soc., Pi Kappa Lambda (hon. life regent, nat. pres. 1976-79), Phi Mu Alpha Sinfonia (hon. mem., Orpheus award 1989), Sigma Alpha Iota. Home: 3121 Walden Ln Wilmette IL 60091-1139 Office: Sch of Music Northwestern U Evanston IL 60208-0001

MILLER, TICE LEWIS, theatre educator; b. Lexington, Nebr., Aug. 11, 1938; s. Tice M. and Thyra V. (Lewis) M.; m. Carren J. Miller, Sept. 6, 1963; children: Dane, Graeme. BA, Kearney State Coll., 1960; MA, U. Nebr., 1961; PhD, U. Ill., 1968. Instr. Kansas City (Mo.) Jr. Coll., 1961-62; asst. prof. U. West Fla., Pensacola, 1968-72; from assoc prof. to prof. U. Nebr., Lincoln, 1972—, chair, 1989-96, pres. acad. senate, 2002—. Chair commn. on accreditation Nat. Assn. Schs. of Theatre, 1997-99. Author: Bohemians and Critics, 1981; co-editor: Shakespeare Around the Globe, 1986, Cambridge Guide World Theatre, 1988 (Hewitt award 1989), Cambridge Guide American Theatre, 1993, The American Stage, 1993; mem. editl. bd. Theatre History Studies, 1980--. Bd. dirs., ATHE, 1987-89, Lincoln Midwest Ballet Co., 1989-91, Theatre Arts for Youth, Lincoln, 1975-76, Pensacola Theatre, 1970-71. Lt. comdr. USNR 1962-65. Am. Theatre fellow, Mid-Am. Theatre Conf. fellow; inducted in Nebr. Repertory Theatre Hall of Fame. Fellow Great Plains Assn.; mem. Am. Soc. for Theatre Rsch. Democrat. Unitarian. Office: U Nebr Dept Theatre Arts Lincoln NE 68588 E-mail: tmiller1@unl.edu.

MILLER, VERNON DALLACE, retired minister; b. McClure, Ill., Sept. 27, 1932; s. Homer Lee and Marie Kathleen (White) M.; m. Alice Elizabeth Wright, July 25, 1954; children: Ronald, Philip, Elizabeth, Annette, Douglas. Student, Moody Bible Inst., 1950-53, S.E. Mo. State, 1954, So. Ill. U., 1956-57; BA, Cedarville Coll., 1963, LittD, 1988. Ordained to min. Bapt. Ch., McClure, 1953. Pastor Camp Creek Bapt. Ch., Murphysboro, Ill., 1953-54, Bible Fellowship Bapt. Ch., Carterville, 1954-57, Faith Bapt. Ch., Mattoon, 1957-60, Immanuel Bapt. Ch., Arcanum, Ohio, 1961-63; editor, bus. mgr. Regular Bapt. Press, Chgo., 1963-70; pres. Ch. Bldg. Cons., 1971-87; exec. editor, treas. Gen. Assn. of Regular Bapt. Chs., Schaumburg, Ill., 1987-97; ret., 1997. Mem. exec. bd. Awana Youth Assn., Streamwood, Ill., 1965-83, Grand Rapids (Mich.) Bapt. Coll. and Sem., 1981-91, Shepherds Bapt. Ministries, Union Grove, Wis., 1965-96. Editor: (mag.) The Baptist Bulletin, 1987-97. Del. Ill. Small Bus. Com., Springfield, Ill., 1984. Mem. Christian Ministries Mgmt. Assn. Republican.

MILLER, WILLARD, JR. mathematician, educator; b. Ft. Wayne, Ind., Sept. 17, 1937; s. Willard and Ruth (Kemerly) Miller; m. Jane Campbell Scott, June 5, 1965; children: Stephen, Andrea. S.B. in Math., U. Chgo., 1958; Ph.D. in Applied Math, U. Calif.-Berkeley, 1963. Vis. mem. Courant Inst. Math. Scis., NYU, 1963-65; mem. faculty U. Minn., 1965—, prof. math., 1972—, head Sch. Math., 1978-86; co-prin. investigator Inst. Math. and its Applications, 1980-94, assoc. dir., 1987-94, dir., 1997—2001; assoc. dean Inst. of Tech., 1994-97; acting dean Inst. of Tech., 1995. Author: Lie Theory and Special Functions, 1968, Symmetry Groups and Their Applications, 1972, Symmetry and Separation of Variables, 1977; assoc. editor Jour. Math. Physics, 1973-75, Applicable Analysis, 1978-90. Mem. AAAS, Soc. Indsl. and Applied Math. (mng. editor Jour. Math. Analysis 1975-81), Am. Math. Soc., Sigma Xi. Home: 4508 Edmund Blvd Minneapolis MN 55406-3629 Office: Univ Minn Sch Math Minneapolis MN 55455

MILLER, WILLIAM CHARLES, theological librarian, educator; b. Mpls., Oct. 26, 1947; s. Robert Charles and Cleithra Mae (Johnson) M.; m. Brenda Kathleen Barnes, July 24, 1969; children: Amy Renee, Jared Charles. BA, Ind. Wesleyan U., 1968; MLS, Kent State U., 1974, PhD, 1983; postgrad., U. Kans., 1984; MA in Religious Studies, Ctrl. Bapt. Theol. Sem., 1988; MBA, MidAm. Nazarene U., Olathe, KS, 1997; STM, Nashotah House, 2001. Ordained to ministry Ch. of Nazarene, 1986. Libr. technician Kent State U., 1972-74; catalog libr. Mt. Vernon Nazarene Coll., Ohio, 1974-76, catalog and acquisitions libr., 1976-78; dir. libr. svcs., prof. theol. bibliography Nazarene Theol. Sem., Kansas City, Mo., 1978—, dean for adminstrn., 1996-98, 99—. Adj. rsch. assoc. U. Kans., 1984-85; adj. prof. MidAm. Nazarene U., Olathe, Kans., 1994-2000; bd. dirs. Small Libr. Computing Inc.; pres. Mo. Libr. Network Corp., St. Louis, Mo., 1998-2001. Author: Holiness Works: A Bibliography, 1986; editor TUG Newsletter, 1984-87, bd. dirs., 1985-88; editor Jour. Religious and Theol. Info., 1990-98. With U.S. Army, 1968-72. Mem. ALA, Am. Assn. Higher Edn., Assn. Study Higher Edn., Bibliog. Soc. Am., Bibliog. Soc. London, Kansas City Met. Libr. Network (coun. mem. 1987-89), Am. Theol. Libr. Assn. (bd. dirs. 1985-88), Kansas City Theol. Libr. Assn. (pres. 1985-89), Wesleyan Theol. Soc., Ch. Eng. Record Soc., Beta Phi Mu. Home: 18290 W 155th Ter Olathe KS 66062-6718 Office: Nazarene Theol Sem 1700 E Meyer Blvd Kansas City MO 64131-1246 E-mail: wcmiller@nts.edu.

MILLER-LERMAN, LINDSEY, state supreme court justice; b. L.A., July 30, 1947; BA, Wellesley Coll., 1968; JD, Columbia U., 1973; LHD (hon.), Coll. of St. Mary, Omaha, 1993. Bar: N.Y. 1974, U.S. Dist. Ct. (so. dist.) N.Y. 1974, U.S. Ct. Appeals (2d cir.) 1974, Nebr. 1976, U.S. Dist. Ct. (ea. dist.) N.Y. 1975, U.S. Dist. Ct. Nebr. 1976, U.S. Ct. Appeals (8th cir.) 1979, U.S. Supreme Ct. 1982, U.S. Ct. Appeals (6th cir.) 1984, U.S. Ct. Appeals (10th cir.) 1987. Law clk. U.S. Dist. Ct., N.Y.C., 1973-75; from assoc. to ptnr. Kutak Rock, Omaha, 1975-92; judge Nebr. Ct. Appeals, Lincoln, 1992-98, chief judge, 1996-98; justice Nebr. Supreme Ct., 1998—. Contbr. articles to profl. jours. Bd. dirs. Tuesday Musical, Omaha, 1985—. Office: Nebr Supreme Ct State Capitol Rm 222 Lincoln NE 68509

MILLICHAP, JOSEPH GORDON, neurologist, educator; b. Wellington, Eng., Dec. 18, 1918; came to U.S., 1956, naturalized, 1965; s. Joseph P. and Alice (Flello) M.; m. Mary Irene Fortey, Feb. 25, 1946 (dec. Oct. 1969); children: Martin Gordon, Paul Anthony; m. Nancy Melanie Kluczynski, Nov. 7, 1970 (dec. Apr. 1995); children: Gordon Thomas, John Joseph. M.B. with honors in Surgery, St. Bartholomew's Med. Coll., U. London, Eng., 1946, M.D. in Internal Medicine, 1951, diploma child health, 1948. Diplomate: Am. Bd. Pediatrics, Am. Bd. Neurology and Child Neurology, Am. Bd. Electroencephalography. Intern, resident St. Bartholomew's Hosp., 1946-49, Hosp. Sick Children, London, 1951-53, Mass. Gen. Hosp., Boston, 1958-60; pediatric neurologist NIH, 1955-56; USPHS fellow neurology Mass. Gen. Hosp., Boston, 1958-60; cons. pediatric neurology Mayo Clinic, 1960-63; pediatric neurologist Children's Meml. Hosp., Northwestern Med. Center, Chgo., 1963—; prof. neurology and pediatrics Northwestern U. Med. Sch., 1963—. Cons. surgeon gen. USPHS; mem. med. adv. bds. Ill. Epilepsy League, Muscular Dystrophy Found., Cerebral Palsy Found., 1963—; vis. prof. Gt. Ormond St. Hosp., U. London, 1986-87. Author: Febrile Convulsions, 1967, Pediatric Neurology, 1967, Learning Disabilities, 1974, The Hyperactive Child with MBD, 1975, Nutrition, Diet and Behavior, 1985, Dyslexia, 1986, Progress in Pediatric Neurology, 1991, Vol. II, 1994, Vol. III, 1997, Environmental Poisons in Our Food, 1993, A Guide to Drinking Water, Hazards and Health Risks, 1995, Attention Deficit Hyperactivity and Learning Disorders, 1998, (with G.T. Millichap) The School in a Garden, 2000; editor Jour. Pediatric Neurology Briefs; contbr. articles to profl. jours., chpts. to books. Chmn. research com. med. adv. bd. Epilepsy Found., 1965— . Served with RAF, 1949-51. Named New Citizen of Year in Met. Chgo., 1965; recipient Americanism Medal D.A.R., 1972, Brennemann award Chgo. Pediat. Soc., 1998; USPHS research grantee, 1957 Fellow Royal Coll. Physicians; mem. Am. Neurol. Assn., Am. Pediatric Soc., Am. Soc. Pediatric Research, Am. Acad. Neurology, Am. Soc. Pharmacology and Exptl. Therapeautics, Soc. Exptl. Biology and Medicine, Am. Bd. Psychiatry and Neurology (asst. examiner 1961—), A.M.A. Episcopalian. Home: PO Box 11391 Chicago IL 60611-0391 Office: Children's Meml Hosp Box 51 2300 N Childrens Plz Chicago IL 60614-3394

MILLION, KENNETH RHEA, management consultant; b. Trenton, Ohio, July 3, 1939; s. Clara (Poff) Gardner; divorced; 1 child, Kimberley Rhea Stang. BSBA, U. Cin., 1963. With human resources mgmt. dept. Bendix Corp., Hamilton, Ohio, 1962-65, Cin., 1965-69; dir. pers. Lunkenheimer Co., 1969-73; v.p. human resources Clopay Corp., 1973-75; pres. Mgmt. Performance Inc., 1975-78; pres., owner Million & Assocs., Inc., 1978—. Internat. amb. People to People and Am. Soc. Pers. Adminstrn., 59 countries. Mem. Kiwanis (v.p. Cin. 1985-86). Republican. Home: 135 Garfield Pl Apt 619 Cincinnati OH 45202-5743 Office: 1831 Carew Tower Cincinnati OH 45202

MILLMAN, IRVING, microbiologist, educator, retired inventor; b. N.Y.C., May 23, 1923; BS, City Coll. N.Y., 1948; MS, U. Ky., 1951; PhD, Northwestern U., 1954. Asst. prof. Northwestern U., 1954; formerly with Armour & Co., Pub. Health RSch. Inst. of N.Y.C., Merck Inst. Therapeutic Rsch.; adj. prof. Hahnemann U., Phila. Inducted Nat. Inventors Hall of Fame, 1993. Fellow Am. Acad. Microbiology; mem. N.Y. Acad. Scis., AAAS, Am. Soc. Microbiology. Achievements include development of test to identify Hepatitis B in blood samples. Office: Nat Inventors Hall Fame

221 S Broadway St Akron OH 44308-1505 also: Sch of Med MCP Hahnemann U 2900 W Queen Ln Philadelphia PA 19129-1033

MILLNER, ROBERT B. lawyer; b. N.Y.C., Apr. 20, 1950; s. Nathan and Babette E. (Leventhal) M.; m. Susan Brent, June 5, 1983; children: Jacob, Daniel, Rebecca. BA, Wesleyan U., 1971; JD, U. Chgo., 1975. Bar: Ill. 1975. Law clk. to Hon. George C. Edwards U.S. Ct. Appeals for 6th Cir., Cin., 1975-76; with Sonnenschein Nath & Rosenthal, Chgo., 1976—, ptnr., 1982—. Mem. Panel of Bankruptcy Trustees, Chgo., 1992-97. Editorial bd. Jour. Corp. Disclosure and Confidentiality, 1989-92; contbr. articles to profl. jours. Trustee Anshe Emet Synagogue, Chgo., 1990-93; v.p. Am. Jewish Cong. midwest region, 1995—. Fellow: Am. Bar Found.; mem.: Comml. Bar Assn. (hon. overseas mem.), Chgo. Bar Assn., Am. Bankruptcy Inst., ABA (co-chair bankruptcy and insolvency com. litigation sect. 1992—95, 2001—), Wesleyan Alumni Club Chgo. (pres. 1988—90), Std. Club, Legal Club, Phi Beta Kappa. Office: Sonnenschein Nath & Rosenthal 8000 Sears Tower Chicago IL 60606

MILLOY, FRANK JOSEPH, JR. surgeon; b. Phoenix, June 26, 1924; s. Frank Joseph and Ola (McCabe) M. BS, Notre Dame U., 1946; MS, Northwestern U., 1949, MD, 1947. Diplomate Am. Bd. Surgery and Thoracic Surgery. Intern Cook County Hosp., Chgo., 1947-49, resident, 1953-57; practice medicine, specializing in surgery Lake Forest, Ill., 1958—. Hon. attending staff Presbyn.-St. Lukes Hosp.; former mem. attending staff Cook County Hosp.; mem. staff U. Ill. Rsch. Hosp.; clin. assoc. prof. surgery, U. Ill. Med. Sch.; assoc. prof. surgery Rush Med. Sch. Contbr. more than 35 articles to profl. jours., chpts. to books. Cons. West Side Vet. Hosp. Served as apprentice seaman USNR, 1943-45; lt. M.C., USNR, 1950-52; PTO. Mem.: ACS, Soc. Med. History Chgo. (pres.), Cook County Hosp. Surg. Alumni Assn., Karl Meyer Surg. Soc. (sec.), Warren Cole Surg. Soc. (past sec.), Ill. Thoracic Surg. Soc. (past pres.), Soc. Thoracic Surgeons, Am. Coll. Chest Physicians, Internat. Soc. Surgery, Chgo. Surg. Soc., Univ. Club (Chgo.), Met. Club, Phi Beta Po. Home: 574 Jackson Ave Glencoe IL 60022-2036

MILLS, CHARLIE, healthcare supplies and products company executive; b. Sept. 30, 1961; BS, MBA, Cornell U. With IBM; then joined Medline Industries, Mundelein, Ill., 1986, pres. textile divsn., now CEO, 1997—.

MILLS, JAMES STEPHEN, medical supply company executive; b. Chgo., Sept. 29, 1936; s. Irving I. and Beatrice (Shane) M.; m. Victoria L. Krisch, Mar. 23, 1973; children: Charles, Donald, Margaret. B.S. in Bus., Northwestern U. Vice pres. sales Mills Hosp. Supply Co., Chgo., 1961-66; pres. Medline Industries Inc., Northbrook, Ill., 1966-75, co-chair, 1975—. Served with AUS, 1958-64. Jewish. Home: 500 N Green Bay Rd Lake Forest IL 60045-2146 Office: Medline Industries Inc 1 Medline Pl Mundelein IL 60060

MILLS, MORRIS HADLEY, state senator, farmer; b. Indpls., Sept. 25, 1927; s. Howard S. and Bernice H. (Sellars) M.; m. Mary Ann Sellars, 1954; children: Douglas, Fred, Gordon. BA in Econs., Earlham Coll., 1950; MBA, Harvard U., 1952. Treas. Maplehurst Farms, Inc., Indpls., 1952-62; ptnr. Mills Bros. Farms, 1962—, treas., 1972—; also bd. dir.; mem. Ind. Ho. of Reps., 1970-72, Ind. Senate, 1972—, asst. pres. pro tem, chmn. budget subcom. fin., chmn. commerce and consumer affairs com. Chmn. bd. AMSCOR, Indpls., 1982— ; dir. Maplehurst Group; mem. Pres. Reagan's adv. council on continuing edn., Washington, 1982— . Mem. Greater Indpls. Progress Com., Conner Prairie Settlement Adv. Coun.; bd. dirs. Corp. Sci. and Tech. Marion County Farm Bur.; asst. treas. Valley Mills Friends Ch.; mem. Decatur Township Rep. Club. Served with U.S. Army, 1946-47. Recipient Spl. award Ind. Vocat. Assn., 1976, Spl. award Ind. State Tchrs. award Assn., 1978. Mem. Lions. Republican. Mem. Soc. of Friends. Office: Ind Senate Dist 35 200 W Washington St Indianapolis IN 46204-2728

MILLS, P. GERALD, retail executive; b. 1929; With L.S. Ayres & Co., buyer, stores mgr., pres., CEO; chmn., CEO Dayton Hudson's, Mpls., 1978-81, Detroit, 1981-82; exec. v.p. Dayton Hudson Corp., 1982-85; chmn. bd., pres., CEO Jacobson Stores, Inc., Jackson, Mich., 1996—. Bd. dirs. Comerica Inc., Detroit, Norwest Bank, Mpls. Chmn. bd. trustees Earlham Coll., Richmond, Ind.; bd. dirs. Detroit Renaissance Found., Indpls. Symphony Orch. Office: Jacobson Stores Inc 3333 Sargent Rd Jackson MI 49201-8847 Fax: (516) 764-1479.

MILLS, RICHARD HENRY, federal judge; b. Beardstown, Ill., July 19, 1929; s. Myron Epler and Helen Christine (Greve) M.; m. Rachel Ann Keagle, June 16, 1962; children: Jonathan K., Daniel Cass. BA, Ill. Coll., 1951; JD, Mercer U., 1957; LLM, U. Va., 1982. Bar: Ill. 1957, U.S. Dist. Ct. Ill. 1958, U.S. Ct. Appeals 1959, U.S. Ct. Mil. Appeals 1963, U.S. Supreme Ct. 1963. Legal advisor Ill. Youth Commn., 1958-60; state's atty. Cass County, Virginia, Ill., 1960-64; judge Ill. 8th Jud. Cir., 1966-76, Ill. 4th Dist. Appellate Ct., Springfield, Ill., 1976-85, U.S. Dist. Ct. (cen. dist.) Ill., Springfield, 1985—. Adj. prof. So. Ill. U. Sch. Medicine, 1985—; mem. adv. bd. Nat. Inst. Corrections, Washington, 1984-88, Ill. Supreme Ct. Rules Com., Chgo., 1963-85. Contbr. articles to profl. jours. Pres. Abraham Lincoln coun. Boy Scouts Am., 1978-80. With U.S. Army, 1952-54, Korea, col. res.; maj. gen. Ill. Militia. Recipient George Washington Honor medal Freedoms Found., 1969, 73, 75, 82, Disting. Eagle Scout Boy Scouts Am., 1985. Fellow Am. Bar Found.; mem. ABA, Nat. Conf. Fed. Trial Judges (chmn. 1999-00), Ill. Bar Assn., Chgo. Bar Assn., Cass County Bar Assn. (pres. 1962-64, 75-76), Sangamon County Bar Assn., 7th Cir. Bar Assn., Am. Law Inst., Fed. Judges Assn., Army and Navy Club (Washington), Sangamo Club, Masons (33 degree), Lincoln-Douglas Am. Inn of Ct. 150 (founding, pres. 1991-93). Republican. Office: US Dist Ct 600 E Monroe St Ste 117 Springfield IL 62701-1659

MILLSTONE, DAVID JEFFREY, lawyer; b. Morgantown, W.Va., 1946; AB, Johns Hopkins U., 1968; JD, U. W.Va., 1971. Bar: Ohio 1971. Ptnr. Squire, Sanders & Dempsey LLP, Cleve., intrnat. coord. labor and employment practice. Co-author: (book) Wage Hour Law—How to Comply, 2001; editor: (manual) Ohio and Fed. Employment Law Manual, 2001. Mem.: ABA. Office: Squire Sanders & Dempsey 4900 Key Tower 127 Public Sq Ste 4900 Cleveland OH 44114-1304 E-mail: dmillstone@ssd.com.

MILNIKEL, ROBERT SAXON, lawyer; b. Chgo., Aug. 17, 1926; s. Gustav and Emma Hazel (Saxon) M.; m. Virginia Lee Wylie, July 26, 1969; children: Robert Saxon Jr., Elizabeth Wylie. AB, U. Chgo., 1950, JD, 1953. Bar: Ill. 1953, U.S. Dist. Ct. 1954. Assoc. Traeger, Bolger & Traeger, Chgo., 1953-57, Heineke, Conklin & Schrader, Chgo., 1958-66; ptnr. Peterson & Ross, 1966—. With USN, 1944-46, PTO. Mem. Beta Theta Pi (pres. chpt. and alumni assn.), Cliffdwellers Club (bd. dirs. Arts Found.) Republican. Lutheran. Home: 601 Ridge Rd Kenilworth IL 60043-1042 Office: Peterson & Ross 200 E Randolph St Ste 7300 Chicago IL 60601-7012 E-mail: milnikel@enteract.com.

MILSTED, AMY, biomedical educator; BSEd, Ohio State U., 1967; PhD, CUNY, 1977. Lectr. Hunter Coll./CUNY, 1970-76; instr. Carnegie-Mellon U., Pitts., 1976-77; postdoctoral fellow Muscular Dystrophy Assn./Carnegie-Mellon U., 1978-79; rsch. assoc. Case Western Res. U., Cleve., 1979-82; rsch. chemist VA Med. Ctr., 1982-87; project staff The Cleve. Clin. Found., 1987-89; asst. staff dept. brain and vascular rsch. Cleve. Clinic Found., 1989-93; grad. faculty Sch. Biomed. Scis. Kent (Ohio) State U., 1995—; assoc. prof. dept. biology U. Akron, Ohio, 1993-2000, prof. biology, 2000—. Adj. faculty biology dept. Cleve. State U., 1991-97. Contbr. articles to profl. jours. Mem. Am. Heart Assn., Inter-Am. Soc. Hypertension, Am. Chem. Soc., Endocrine Soc., AAAS, Assn. Women in Sci. Office: University of Akron Dept of Biology Asec 279 Akron OH 44325-3908 E-mail: milsted@uakron.edu.

MILTON, CHAD EARL, lawyer; b. Brevard County, Fla., Jan. 29, 1947; s. Rex Dale and Mary Margaret (Peacock) M.; m. Ann Mitchell Bunting, Mar. 30, 1972; children: Samuel, Kathleen, Kelsey. BA, Colo. Coll., 1969; JD, U. Colo., 1974; postgrad., U. Mo., 1976-77. Bar: Colo. 1974, Mo. 1977, U.S. Dist. Ct. Colo. 1974, U.S. Dist. Ct. (we. dist.) Mo. 1977. Counsel Office of Colo. State Pub. Defender, Colo. Springs, 1974-76; pub. info. officer, counsel Mid-Am. Arts Alliance, Kansas City, Mo., 1977-78; claims counsel Employers Reinsurance Corp., 1978-80; sr. v.p. Media/Profl. Ins., 1981-2000; sr. v.p. nat. practice leader, intellectual property & media Marsh, 2000—. Reporter, photographer, editor Golden (Colo.) Daily Transcript, 1970; investigator, law clk. Office of Colo. State Pub. Defender, Denver, Golden, 1970-74; participant Annenberg Project on the Reform of Libel Laws, Washington, 1987-88; adj. prof., comm. and advt. law Webster U., 1989-93; lectr. in field. Pres. bd. dirs. Folly Theater, 1992-94. Mem. ABA (chair intellectual property law com. of the torts and ins. practice sect., forum com. on comm. law, ctrl. and Ea. European law initiative), Mo. Bar Assn., Kansas City Met. Bar Assn., Libel Def. Resource Ctr. (editorial bd., exec. com.). Avocations: tennis, golf, skiing, sailing, antique maps. Home: 8821 Alhambra St Shawnee Mission KS 66207-2357 Office: Marsh 2405 Grand Blvd Kansas City MO 64108-2510 E-mail: chad.e.milton@marsh.com.

MINER, THOMAS HAWLEY, international entrepreneur; b. Shelbyville, Ill., June 19, 1927; s. Lester Ward and Thirza (Hawley) M.; m. Lucyna T. Minciel, July 22, 1983; children: Robert Thomas, William John. Student, U.S. Mil. Acad., 1946-47; BA, Knox Coll., 1950; JD, U. Ill., 1953. Bar: Ill. 1954. Atty. Continental Ill. Nat. Bank & Trust Co., Chgo., 1953-55; pres. Harper-Wyman Internat. (S.A.), Venezuela and Mex., 1955-58, Hudson Internat. (S.A.), Can. and Switzerland, 1958-60, Thomas H. Miner & Assoc., Inc., Chgo., 1960—; chmn. Miner, Fraser & Gabriel Pub. Affairs, Inc., Washington, 1982-88, Miner Systems, Inc., 1981—. Bd. dirs. Lakeside Bank, Worldschool, Bright Oceans Internat. Corp.; chmn. Ill. dist. export coun. U.S. Dept. Commerce, 1971—; sec. Consular Corps. Chgo., 1986—88; chmn. Mid-Am. China Mgmt. Tng. Ctr., Global Software Source. Chmn. bd. dirs. Sch. Art Inst. Chgo., 1977-81; bd. govs., life mem., sustaining fellow Art Inst. Chgo.; former chmn. UN Assn., Chgo.; founder, chmn. Mid-Am. Com., 1968—; former mem. bd. dirs. UNICEF, NAM, Internat. Trade Policy Com. and Working Group on Commonwealth of Ind. States and Ea. Europe; trustee 4th Presbyn. Ch., Chgo., Roosevelt U., Chgo., 1996; bd. advisors Mercy Hosp.; vice chmn. Chgo. Sister Cities; mem. adv. bd. Internat. Inst. Edn.; bd. dirs. Internat. Sister Cities. With USNR, 1945-46; mem. Pres. Coun. U. Ill. Found. Capt. U.S. Army, 1946-47. Decorated commendatore Ordine al Merito della Repubblica Italiana; recipient Alumni Achievement award Knox Coll., 1974, Gold Medallion award Internat. Visitors Ctr. Chgo., 1989; named One of Chgo.'s 10 Outstanding Young Men, 1962, Chicagoan of Year Chgo. Assn. Commerce and Industry, 1968, Alumni of Month Coll. Law U. Ill., Nov. 1970, Aug. 1984; hon. consul Republic of Senegal, 1970-88. Mem. Am. Mgmt. Assn., Chgoland C. of C., Mid-Am. Arab C. of C. (founder, former pres.), Chgo. Bar Assn., Chgo. Com., Chgo. Coun. Fgn. Rels. (past dir.), Coun. of the Ams., Internat. Trade Club (past dir., pres.), Japan-Am. Soc., Nat. Coun. U.S.-China Trade, Nat. Acad. Scis. (pres. coun.), English Speaking Union (dir., past chmn.) Trade and Econs. Coun. USA-CIS (dir.), U.S.-Russia Bus. Coun., Mus. Contemporary Art, Newcomen Soc. N.Am., U.S.-China Bus. Coun., U.S.-Arab C. of C. (bd. dirs.), U.S.-Mex. C. of C. (bd. dirs.), Thomas Minor Soc., Chgo. Club, Econ. Club, Grant Park Concerts Soc., Chgo. Farmers Club, Mid-Am. Club, Univ. Club (Washington), Univ. Club (Milw.), Hillsboro Club (Fla.), Tryall Golf and Beach Club (Jamaica), Rotary, Phi Delta Phi, Phi Gamma Delta. Office: 150 N Michigan Ave Chicago IL 60601-7553 also: 2400 Virginia Ave NW Washington DC 20037-2612 also: Miner Farms Shelbyville IL 62565 E-mail: ltminer@aol.com.

MINGE, DAVID, former congressman, lawyer, law educator; b. Clarkfield, Minn., 1942; m. Karen Aaker; children: Erik, Olaf. BA in History, St. Olaf Coll., 1964; JD, U. Chgo., 1967. Atty. Faegre & Benson, Mpls., 1967-70; prof. law U. Wyo., 1970-77; atty. Nelson, Oyen, Torvik, Minge & Gilbertson, 1977-93; mem. 103d-106th Congresses from 2nd Minn. Dist., 1993-2001. Cons. Ho. Jud. Com., Subcom. Adminstrv. Law U.S. Congress, 1975; formerly atty. Minn. Valley Coop. Light and Power Assn., 1984-93; chair Agrl. Law Sect., Minn. State Bar Assn. 1990-92, adv. bd. Western Minn. Legal Svcs., 1978-84; bd. dirs. Legal Advice Clinics, Ltd., Hennepin County, Western Minn. Vol. Atty. Program Clk. Montevideo Sch. Bd., 1989-92; dir. Montevideo Community Devel. Corp.; steering com. Clean Up the River Environ., 1992 ; co-coord. Montevideo area CROP Walk for the Hungry, Multi-church Vietnamese Refugee Resettlement Com., Montevideo, 1978-90; bd. dirs. Montevideo United Way, Model Cities Program, Kinder Kare; chair AFS Montevideo chpt. Mem. Minn. Bar Assn., Chippewa County Bar Assn. (chair), Montevideo C. of C., Kiwanis (pres.) Address: Rte 4 Box 183 Montevideo MN 56265

MINICHELLO, DENNIS, lawyer; b. Cleve., June 9, 1952; s. Ernest Anthony and Mary Theresa (Rocci) M.; m. Janine Stevens, Feb. 14, 1987. BA in Econs., MA in Econs., Ohio U., 1974; JD, Northwestern U., 1978. Bar: U.S. Dist. Ct. (no. dist.) Ill., U.S. Ct. Appeals (7th cir.), Supreme Ct. Ill., U.S. Supreme Ct. Assoc. Haskell & Perrin, Chgo., 1978-84; ptnr. Tribler & Marwedel, 1984-89, Keck, Mahin & Cate, Chgo., 1989—. Contbr. articles to profl. jours. Bd. dirs. Great Lakes Naval and Maritime Mus. Fulbright scholar, 1974-75. Mem. ABA, Ill. State Bar Assn., Chgo. Bar Assn. (mem. transp. com.), Maritime Law Assn. (proctor), Casualty Adjusters Assn. Chgo., The Propeller Club U.S. (pres. 1983-84), Port Chgo., Met. Club. Roman Catholic. Avocations: sailing, reading, running. Office: Marwedel Minichello & Reeb PC 10 S Riverside Plz Ste 660 Chicago IL 60606-3709

MINISH, ROBERT ARTHUR, lawyer; b. Mpls., Dec. 25, 1938; s. William Arthur and Agnes Emilia (Olson) M.; m. Marveen Eleanor Allen, Sept. 16, 1961; 1 child, Roberta Ruth. BA, U. Minn., 1960, JD, 1963. Bar: Minn. 1963. Assoc. Popham, Haik, Schnobrich & Kaufman, Ltd., Mpls., 1963-67, 1967-97; ptnr. Hinshaw & Culbertson, 1997—. Bd. dirs. Braas Co., Mpls. Mem. ABA, Minn. Bar Assn. Avocations: fishing, traveling. Home: 331 Pearson Way NE Minneapolis MN 55432-2418 Office: Hinshaw & Culbertson 3100 Piper Jaffray Tower 222 S 9th St Minneapolis MN 55402-3389

MINKOWYCZ, W. J. mechanical engineering educator; b. Libokhora, Ukraine, Oct. 21, 1937; came to U.S., 1949; s. Alexander and Anna (Tokan) M.; m. Diana Eva Szandra, May 12, 1973; 1 child, Liliana Christine Anne B.S. in Mech. Engring., U. Minn., 1958, M.S. in Mech. Engring., 1961, Ph.D. in Mech. Engring, 1965. Asst. prof. U. Ill., Chgo., 1966-68, assoc. prof., 1968-78, prof., 1978—. Cons. Argonne Nat. Lab, Ill., 1970-82, U. Hawaii, Honolulu, 1974-94. Founding editor-in-chief (jour.) Jour. Numerical Heat Transfer, 1978—; editor: Internat. Jour. Heat and Mass Transfer, 1968-, Rheologically Complex Fluids, 1972, Internat. Comms. in Heat and Mass Transfer Jour., 1974-, Handbook of Numerical Heat Transfer, 1988—, Advances in Numerical Heat Transfer, Vol 1, 1997, Vol. 2, 1999, (book series) Computational and Physical Processes in Mechanics and Thermal Sciences, 1979-, Advances in Numerical Heat Transfer, 1996-, Vol. 1, 1997, Vol. 2, 1999—; contbr. articles to profl. jours. Recipient Silver Circle for Excellence in Teaching, U. Ill.-Chgo., 1975, 76, 81, 86, 90, 94, Harold A. Simon award Excellence in Teaching, 1986, Ralph Coats Roe Outstanding Tchr. award Am. Soc. Engring. Edn., 1988, U. Ill. Disting. Tchr. award, 1989. Fellow ASME (Heat Transfer Meml. award 1993); mem. Sigma Xi, Pi Tau Sigma. Republican. Ukrainian Catholic. Office: U Ill Dept Mech Engring Mail Code 251 842 W Taylor St Chicago IL 60607-7021 E-mail: wjm@uic.edu.

MINNESTE, VIKTOR, JR. retired electrical company executive; b. Haapsalu, Estonia, Jan. 15, 1932; s. Viktor and Alice (Lembra) M. BSEE, U. Ill., 1960. Elec. engr. Bell & Howell Co., 1960-69; microstatics divsn. A-M Co., 1969-71, multigraphics divsn., 1972-73; elec. engr. bus. products group Victor Comptometer Co. (merged with Walter Kidde Corp.), Chgo., 1973-74, svc. mgr. internat. group, 1974-75, supr. elecs. desing group, 1975-82; project engr. Warner Electric, 1982-84; systems engr. Barrett Elecs., 1984-85; phone engr. Williams Elecs., 1986-88; cons. engr., 1988-92; ind. contractor, 1993-95; ret., 1995. Pub. Motteid/Thoughts, 1962-68. Chmn. Estonian-Ams. Polit Action Com., 1968-72. With AUS, 1952-54. Home and Office: 3134 N Kimball Ave Chicago IL 60618-6856

MINOGUE, JOHN P. academic administrator, priest, educator; b. Chgo. B in Philosophy, St. Mary's Sem.; MDiv, Deandreis Inst. Theology, 1972; M in Theology, DePaul U., 1975; D in Ministry, St. Mary of the Lake Sem., 1987. Ordained Vincentian priest, 1972. Vincentian priest Congregation of the Mission; instr. theology, dir. clin. pastoral placement programs St. Thomas Sem., Denver, 1972-76; instr. grad. theology, asst. then acad. dean DeAndreis Inst., 1976-83; pres. DePaul U., Chgo., 1993—. Trustee DePaul U., 1991—; bd. dirs. DePaul U. Corp., 1981-91; adj. prof. Sch. New Learning DePaul U., 1984—, instr. law and med. ethics Coll. Law DePaul U., 1989—; asst. prof. clin. ob.-gyn. Northwestern U.; instr. health care ethics St. Joseph Coll. Nursing, Joliet, Ill., Northwestern Sch. Nursing, Chgo.; cons. nat. heatlh care ethics, patient decision-making. Office: De Paul U 1 E Jackson Blvd Chicago IL 60604-2287

MINOR, CHARLES DANIEL, lawyer, director; b. Columbus, Ohio, May 28, 1927; s. Walter Henry and Helen Margaret (Bergman) M.; m. Mary Jo Klinker, Dec. 27, 1950; children: Elizabeth, Daniel, Amy. B.S. in Bus. Adminstrn, Ohio State U., 1950, J.D. summa cum laude, 1952. Bar: Ohio 1952. Mem. firm Vorys, Sater, Seymour and Pease, Columbus, 1952—, ptnr., 1957-93, of counsel, 1993—. Bd. dirs. Inland Products, Inc., Worthington Industries, Inc. Served with USNR, 1945-46. Mem. Columbus, Ohio State bar assns., The Columbus Club, Double Eagle Club, Scioto Country Club. Republican. Office: Vorys Sater Seymour & Pease 52 E Gay St Columbus OH 43215-3161 E-mail: ldminor@vssp.com.

MINOR, MELVIN G. state legislator; b. Aug. 24, 1937; m. Carolyn Minor. Student, Emporia State U. Kans. state rep. Dist. 114; farmer. Mem. Masons, Shriners (Wichita Consistory).

MINOR, ROBERT ALLEN, lawyer; b. Washington, Oct. 20, 1948; s. Robert Walter and Joan (Allen) M.; m. Sue Ellyn Blose, June 13, 1981; children: Robert Barratt, Sarah Allen. AB in English, Duke U., 1970; JD, Ohio State U., 1975. Bar: Ohio 1975, U.S. Dist. Ct. (so. dist.) Ohio 1976, D.C. 1979. Assoc. Vorys, Sater, Seymour & Pease, LLP, Columbus, Ohio, 1975-82, ptnr., 1982—. Author seminar articles. With U.S. Army, 1970-72. Mem. Ohio Bar Assn., Columbus Bar Assn., Athletic Club Columbus, Scioto Country Club. Republican. Presbyterian. Office: Vorys Sater Seymour & Pease LLP PO Box 1008 52 E Gay St Columbus OH 43215-3161

MINOR, RONALD RAY, minister; b. Aliceville, Ala., Nov. 3, 1944; s. Hershel Ray and Minnie Ozell (Goodson) M.; m. Gwendolyn Otella Newsome, July 25, 1970; 1 child, Rhonda Rene. BA in Ministerial, Southeastern Bible Coll., 1971, BA in Secondary Edn., 1973; DDiv, Southern Bible Coll., 1984. Ordained to ministry Pentecostal Ch. of God, 1968. Gen. sec. Pentecostal Ch. of God, Joplin, Mo., 1979—, dist. supt. Philadelphia, Miss., 1975-79, pastor Bartow, LaBelle, Fla., Orient Park Tabernacle, Tampa. Pres. Pentecostal Young People's Assn., Fla. and Miss.; sec. Gen. Bd. Pentecostal Ch. of God, Joplin, 1979; bd. dirs. Nat. Assn. Evangs., Wheaton, Ill., 1981-96; adv. coun. Am. Bible Soc., N.Y.C., 1979—; sec. Commn. Chaplains, Washington, 1991-95. Home: 2625 Markwardt Joplin MO 64801-5353 Office: Pentecostal Ch of God 4901 Pennsylvania Ave Joplin MO 64804-4947

MINOW, JOSEPHINE BASKIN, civic volunteer; b. Chgo., Nov. 3, 1926; d. Salem N. and Bessie (Sampson) Baskin; m. Newton N. Minow, May 29, 1949; children: Nell, Martha, Mary. BS, Northwestern U., 1948. Asst. to advt. dir. Mandel Brothers Dept. Store, Chgo., 1948-49; tchr. Francis W. Parker Sch., 1949-50; vol. in civil and charitable activities, 1950—; bd. dirs. Juvenile Protective Assn., Chgo., 1958—, pres., 1973-75. Bd. dirs. Parnham Trust, Beaminster, Dorset, Eng. Author: Marty the Broken Hearted Artichoke, 1997. Founder, coord. Children's div. Hospitality and Info. Svc., Washington, 1961-63; mem. Caucus Com., Glencoe, Ill., 1965-69; co-chmn. spl. study on juvenile justice Chgo. Community Trust, 1978-80; chmn. Know Your Chgo., 1980-83; bd. dirs. Chgo. Coun. Fgn. Rels.; trustee Chgo. Hist. Soc., Ravinia Festival Assn.; mem. women's bd. Field Mus., U. Chgo.; founding mem., v.p. women's bd. Northwestern U., 1978; bd. govs. Chgo. Symphony, 1966-73, 76— ; mem. Citizens Com. Juvenile Ct. of Cook County, 1985-96; exec. com. Northwestern U. Libr. Coun., 1974-96; co-chair grandparents' adv. com. Chgo. Children's Mus., 1999; bd. dirs. Jane Addams Juvenile Ct. Found. Recipient spl. award Chgo. Sch. and Workshop for Retarded, 1975, Children's Guardian award Juvenile Protective Assn., 1993. Mem. Hebrew Immigrant Aid Soc. (bd. dirs. 1977-98, award 1988), Friday Club, Northmoor Country Club, The Arts Club. Democrat. Jewish. Office: Chgo Hist Soc Clark St at North Ave Chicago IL 60614

MINOW, NEWTON NORMAN, lawyer, educator; b. Milw., Jan. 17, 1926; s. Jay A. and Doris (Stein) M.; m. Josephine Baskin, May 29, 1949; children: Nell, Martha, Mary. BS, Northwestern U., 1949, JD, 1950, LLD (hon.), 1965, U. Wis., Brandeis U., 1963, Columbia Coll., 1972, Govs. State U., 1984, De Paul U., 1989, RAND Grad. Sch., 1993, U. Notre Dame, 1994, Roosevelt U., 1996, Barat Coll., 1996, Santa Clara U. Sch. Law, 1998. Bar: Wis. 1950, Ill. 1950. With firm Mayer, Brown & Platt, Chgo., 1950-51, 53-55; law clk. to chief justice Fred. M. Vinson, 1951-52; adminstrv. asst. to Ill. Gov. Stevenson, 1952-53; spl. asst. to Adlai E. Stevenson in presdl. campaign, 1952, 56; ptnr. firm Stevenson, Rifkind & Wirtz, Chgo., N.Y.C. and Washington, 1955-61; chmn. FCC, Wash., 1961-63; exec. v.p., gen. counsel, dir. Ency. Brit., Chgo., 1963-65; ptnr. Sidley Austin Brown & Wood, 1965-91, counsel, 1991—. Former trustee, past chmn. bd., adv. trustee Rand Corp.; past chmn. Chgo. Ednl. TV; chmn. pub. rev. bd. Arthur Andersen & Co., 1974-83; chmn. bd. trustees Carnegie Corp. of N.Y., 1993-97, trustee, 1987-97; Annenberg U. prof. com. policy and law Northwestern U., 1987—; dir. Annenberg Washington Program, 1987-96; bd. dirs. Moore Corp. Author: Equal Time: The Private Broadcasters and the Public Interest, 1964; co-author: Presidential Television, 1973, Electronics and the Future, 1977, For Great Debates, 1987, Abandoned in the Wasteland: Children, Television, and the First Amendment, 1995; contbr.: Aw We Knew Adlai. Trustee Notre Dame U., 1964-77, 83-96, life trustee, 1996, Mayo Found., 1973-81; trustee Northwestern U., 1975-87, life trustee, 1987—; co-chmn. presdl. debates LWV, 1976, 80, presdl. debate commn., 1993—; bd. govs. Pub. Broadcasting Svc., 1973-80, chmn. bd., 1978-80; chmn. bd. overseers Jewish Theol. Sem., 1974-77; trustee Chgo. Orchestral Assn., 1975-87, life trustee, 1987—. With AUS, 1944-46. Named 1 of Am.'s 10 Outstanding Young Men 1961; recipient George Foster Peabody Broadcasting award, 1961; Ralph Lowell award, 1982 Fellow Am. Bar Found., Am. Acad. Arts and Scis.; mem. Northwestern U. Alumni Assn. (medal 1978), Comml. Club (pres. 1987-88), Chgo. Club, Century Club (N.Y.C.). Democrat. Office: Sidley Austin Brown & Wood Ste 4800 10 S Dearborn St Chicago IL 60603 E-mail: nminow@sidley.com.

MINTZER, DAVID, physics educator; b. N.Y.C., May 4, 1926; s. Herman and Anna (Katz) M.; m. Justine Nancy Klein, June 26, 1949; children: Elizabeth Amy, Robert Andrew. B.S. in Physics, Mass. Inst. Tech., 1945, Ph.D., 1949. Asst. prof. physics Brown U., 1949-55; research asso. Yale U., 1955-56, assoc. prof., dir. lab. marine physics, 1956-62; prof. mech. engring. Northwestern U., Evanston, 1962-91, prof. physics and astronomy, 1968-91, prof. emeritus mech. engring., prof emeritus physics and astronomy, 1991—; assoc. dean McCormick Sch. Engring. and Applied Sci., 1970-73, acting dean, 1971-72, v.p. for rsch., dean sci., 1973-86, spl. asst. to pres., 1986-87, prof. emeritus mech. engring., physics and astronomy, 1991—. Mem. mine adv. com. Nat. Acad. Sci.-NRC, 1963-73; mem. Ill. Gov.'s Commn. on Sci. and Tech., 1987-88; mem. adv. bd. Applied Rsch. Lab. Pa. State U., 1976-82, chmn., 1980-81. Contbr. numerous chpts. to books, papers to profl. publs. Trustee EDUCOM interuniv. communications coun., 1975-83, vice chmn., 1977-78, chmn., 1978-81; trustee Adler Planetarium, 1976-92, life trustee, 1992—; bd. dirs. Rsch. Park, Inc., Evanston, 1986-92, treas., 1986-91; trustee Ill. Math. and Sci. Acad., 1986-97, mem. exec. com., 1989-95, chmn. alliance coun., 1991-93; chmn. bd. dirs. Heartland Venture Capital Network, Inc., 1987-90; bd. dirs. Tech. Innovation Ctr., Inc., 1990-92, treas., 1990-92. Fellow Am. Phys. Soc., Acoustical Soc. Am.; mem. ASME, Am. Astron. Soc., Sigma Xi, Tau Beta Pi, Pi Tau Sigma. Achievements include research on underwater acoustics and rarefied gas dynamics. Office: 332 Villena Way Palm Desert CA 92260-2172 E-mail: dmin@northwestern.edu.

MIRKIN, BERNARD LEO, clinical pharmacologist, pediatrician; b. Bronx, N.Y., Mar. 31, 1928; s. Max and Esther M.; m. Phyllis Korduner, Aug. 1954 (dec. 1982); children: Lisa Mia, Mara Rebecca; m. Sarah Solotaroff, 1986; stepchildren: Jennifer, Rachel, Jacob. AB, NYU, 1949; PhD, Yale U., 1953; MD, U. Minn., 1964. Asst. prof. pharmacology SUNY, Downstate Med. Center, 1954-60; Ford Found. postdoctoral fellow Karolinska Inst., Stockholm, 1960-61; USPHS post-doctoral fellow Yale U., 1961-62; resident in pediatrics U. Minn. Hosp., Mpls., 1964-66; asst. prof. U. Minn. Med. Sch., 1966-67, assoc. prof., 1967-72; prof. pediatrics, pharmacology and biol. chemistry, dir. div. clin. pharmacology U. Minn. Health Sci. Ctr., 1972-89; prof. pediatrics and molecular pharmacology Northwestern U. Med. Sch., Chgo., 1989—; head, dir. rsch. Inst. for Edn. and Rsch. Children's Meml. Hosp., 1989—99; assoc. dean rsch. Northwestern U. Med. Sch., 1994—96; dir. rsch. emeritus Inst. for Edn. and Rsch. Children's Meml. Hosp., Chgo., 2000—. Cons. Office of Technology Assessment, U.S. Congress, WHO, U.S. Pharmacopeia, PhARMA Found., Nat. Inst. Health; fellow Jesus Coll., Oxford U., 1974. Author: Perinatal Pharmacology and Therapeutics, 1976, Clinical Pharmacology: A Pediatric Perspective, 1978. postdoctoral fellow Karolinska Inst. Stockholm 1960-61 Served with M.C. U.S. Army, 1954-56. Mem. AAAS, Soc. Pediat. Rsch., Am. Assn. Cancer Rsch., Am. Pediat. Soc., Am. Soc. Pharm. Exptl. Therapeutics, Am. Soc. Clin. Pharm. and Therapeutics. Home: 427 Greenleaf St Evanston IL 60202-1328 Office: Childrens Meml Inst Edn and Rsch Mailcode # 117 2300 N Childrens Plz Chicago IL 60614-3363 E-mail: b-mirkin@northwestern.edu.

MIRKIN, CHAD A. chemistry educator; BS in Chemistry, Dickinson Coll., 1986; PhD, Pa. State U., 1989. Asst. prof. chemistry Northwestern U., Evanston, Ill., 1991-95, assoc. prof. chemistry, 1995-97, prof. chemistry, 1997-2000, George B. Rathmann prof. chemistry, 2000—. Contbr. articles to profl. jours. NSF postdoctoral fellow MIT, 1989-91; recipient Beckman Young Investigators award, 1992-94, Disting. New Faculty award Camille and Henry Dreyfus Found., 1991-96, Young Investigator Rsch. award NSF, Young Prof. award DuPont, Young Investigator award ONR, Inventors award B.F. Goodrich, Wilson prize, award in pure chemistry Am. Chem. Soc.; grantee USN. Mem. Am. Chem. Soc. Achievements include research nanotechnology biosensors and new ligand design in synthetic organometallic chemistry. Office: Northwestern U Dept Chemistry 2145 Sheridan Rd Evanston IL 60208-3113 E-mail: camirkin@chem.nwv.edu.

MIRMAN, JOEL HARVEY, lawyer; b. Toledo, Dec. 3, 1941; s. Benjamin and Minnie (Krapifko) M.; children: Lisa, Julie, Benjamin. BBA, Ohio U., 1963; JD, Ohio State U., 1966. Bar: Ohio 1966, U.S. Dist. Ct. (so. dist.) Ohio 1966, U.S. Supreme Ct. 1972. Ptnr. Topper, Alloway, Goodman, DeLeone & Duffey, Columbus, Ohio, 1966-85, Benesch, Friedlander, Coplan & Aronoff, 1986-93; shareholder Buckingham, Doolittle & Burroughs, Columbus, Ohio, 1994—. Lectr. Ohio CLE Inst., Columbus, 1972—. Author direct examination CLE materials; contbr. articles to profl. jours. Mem. Ohio Elections Commn., 1976-80, vice-chmn. 1980. Mem. Capital Club, Worthington Hills Country Club, Worthington Hills Civic Assn. (pres. 1992-93), Assn. Trial Lawyers Am. (chmn. family law sects. 1993-94). E-mail: jmirman@bdblaw.com.

MIRONOVICH, ALEX, publisher; b. Brooklyn, N.Y., Nov. 30, 1952; s. Peter Mironovich and Olga Sachrina; m. Cynthia Ann Wuss, July 23, 1983; children: Britany, Nicholas. BA in psychology, City U., N.Y.C., 1970-74. Sales rep. House Beautiful mag., N.Y.C., 1976-79, Sawyer Ferguson Walker, N.Y.C., 1979-82, Creative Ideas for Living, N.Y.C., 1982-83, Parents mag. G and J, N.Y.C.; assoc. pub. Y.M. Gruner and Jahr, N.Y., 1986-88, pub., 1988; former pub. Better Homes and Gardens, N.Y.C.; pres. pub. group, exec. v.p. Playboy Enterprises Inc., Chgo., 1999—. Office: Playboy Enterprises Inc 680 N Lake Shore Dr Chicago IL 60611-4402

MIRSKY, ARTHUR, geologist, educator; b. Phila., Feb. 8, 1927; s. Victor and Dorothy M.; m. Patricia Shorey, Dec. 22, 1961; 1 dau., Alexis Catherine. Student, Bklyn. Coll., 1944-45, 46-48; BA, U. Calif., 1950; MS, U. Ariz., 1955; PhD, Ohio State U., 1960. Cert. geologist, Ind. Field uranium geologist AEC, S.W. U.S., 1951-53; cons. uranium geologist Albuquerque, 1955-56; asst. dir. Inst. Polar Studies, Ohio State U., 1960-67; adj. asst. prof. geology Ohio State U., 1964-67; from asst. prof. geology to prof. Ind. U.-Purdue U., Indpls., 1967-94, prof. emeritus, 1994—, coord. geology, 1967-69, chmn. dept. geology, 1969-93. Contbr. articles to profl. jours. Served with USN, 1944-46. Mem. AAAS, AAUP, Am. Inst. Profl. Geologists, Geol. Soc. Am., Nat. Assn. Geosci. Tchrs., Am. Geol. Inst., Soc. Sedimentary Geology, Ind. Acad. Sci., Sigma Xi. Office: Indiana U-Purdue U Dept Geology 723 W Michigan St Indianapolis IN 46202-5132 E-mail: amirsky@iupui.edu.

MISCHKA, THOMAS, marketing professional; Degree in computer sci., U. Wis.-Oshkosh. Computer programmer Aid Assn for Lutherans, Appleton, Wis., 1982-98, v.p. nat. mktg., 1998—. Mem. Christus Luth. Ch., Greenville, Wis. Mem. Am. Mgmt. Assn. Office: Aid Assn for Lutherans 4321 N Ballard Rd Appleton WI 54919-0001

MISCHKE, CARL HERBERT, religious association executive, retired; b. Hazel, S.D., Oct. 27, 1922; s. Emil Gustav and Pauline Alvina (Polzin) M.; m. Gladys Lindloff, July 6, 1947; children: Joel, Susan Mischke Blahnik, Philip, Steven. B.A., Northwestern Coll., Watertown, Wis., 1944; M.Div., Wis. Luth. Sem., Mequon, 1947. Ordained to ministry Evang. Lutheran Ch. Parish pastor Wis. Synod, 1947-79; pres. Western Wis. Dist. Evang. Luth. Ch., Juneau, 1964-79; v.p. Wis. Luth. Synod, Milw., 1966-79, pres., 1979-93; retired, 1993.

MISCHKE, CHARLES RUSSELL, mechanical engineering educator; b. Glendale, N.Y., Mar. 2, 1927; s. Reinhart Charles and Dena Amelia (Scholl) M.; m. Margaret R. Bubeck, Aug. 4, 1951; children: Thomas, James. BSME, Cornell U., 1947, MME, 1950; PhD, U. Wis., 1953. Lic. mechanical engr. Iowa, Kans. Asst. prof. mech. engring. U. Kans., Lawrence, 1953-56, assoc. prof. mech. engring., 1956-57; prof., chmn. mech. engring. Pratt Inst., N.Y.C., 1957-64; prof. mech. engring. Iowa State U., Ames, 1964—, Alcoa Found. prof., 1974. Author: Elements of Mechanical Analysis, 1963, Introduction to Computer-Aided Design, 1968, Mathematical Model Building, 1972; editor: Standard Handbook of Machine Design, 1996, Mechanical Engineering Design, 6th edit., 2001, 8 Mechancal Designers Workbooks, 1990, Fundamentos de Diseno Mechanico, 4 vols., 1994. Scoutmaster Boy Scouts Am., Ames. With USNR, 1944-75, mem. Res. ret. Recipient Ralph Teetor award Soc. Automotive Engrs., 1977, best book award Am. Assn. Pubs., 1986, Legis. Teaching Excellence award Iowa Assembly, 1990, Ralph Coates Roe award Am. Soc. for Engring. Edn., 1991. Fellow ASME (life, Machine Design award 1990); mem. Am. Soc. Engring. Edn. (Centennial cert. 1993), Am. Gear Mfrs. Assn., Scabbard and Blade, Cardinal Key, Sigma Xi, Phi Kappa Phi, Pi Tau Sigma. Avocations: model building, railway history, diesel locomotive engineer, B&SV railroad. Office: Iowa State U Dept Mech Engring Ames IA 50011-0001

MISHLER, CLIFFORD LESLIE, publisher; b. Vandalia, Mich., Aug. 11, 1939; s. Nelson Howard and Lily Mae (Young) M.; m. Sandra Rae Knutson, Dec. 21, 1963 (dec. July 8, 1972); m. Sylvia M. Leer, Feb. 27, 1976; children: Sheila, Sharon, Susan. Student, Northwestern U., 1957-58. Author, pub. ann. edits. Ann. Studies U.S. and Can. Commemorative Medals and Tokens, 1958-63; assoc. editor Numismatic News, Krause Publs., Iola, Wis., 1963-64, editor, 1964-66, numismatic editor all publs., 1966-75, exec. v.p., pub. all numismatic publs., 1975-78, exec. v.p., pub. all products, 1978-88, sr. v.p., pub. all Numismatic products, 1988-89, sr. v.p. ops., 1989-90; pres. Krause Publs., Iola, Wis., 1991-99. Chmn. bd. dirs. Krause Publs., 2000—; bd. dirs. First State Bank Iola, 1972-83, Scandinavia Telephone Co., 1981-97, TDS Telecom cmty. bd., 1997-2000; ex-officio dir. Iola Old Car Show, Inc., 1985—; mem. coins and medals adv. panel Am. Revolution Bicentennial Commn., 1970-75; mem. ann. assay commn. U.S. Mint, 1973. Co-author: Standard Catalog of World Coins, ann. 1972—; contbr. articles New Book Knowledge, ann. 1969-81. Bd. dirs. William R. Higgins, Jr. Found., 1991—. Recipient The Internat. Vreneli Preistrager: The "Friendly Prize" for lifetime numismatic achievements, Munzen-Revue, Basel, Switzerland, 2001. Fellow Am. Numismatic Soc. (life mem., coun. mem. 1997—); mem. Am. Numismatic Assn. (life mem., medal of merit 1983, Farran Zerbe meml. disting svc. award 1984, Glen Smedley meml. dedicated svcs. award 1991, Lifetime Achievement award 1997), Token and Medal Soc. (life mem., pres. 1976-78, editor jour. 1964-68, disting. svc. award 1966, 80), Numismatists Wis. (life mem., pres. 1974-76, meritorious svc. award 1972), Soc. Internat. Numismatics (award of excellence 1981), Blue Ridge Numismatic Assn. (life mem., hall of fame 1994), Tex. Numismatic Assn. (life mem., hall of fame 1993), Ind. State Numismatic Assn. (life mem., founders award 1993), Ctrl. States Numismatic Soc. (life mem., medal of merit 1984), Wis. Commemorative Quarter Coun., Iola Lions (Melvin Jones fellow 1996). Home: 100 Island Dr Iola WI 54945-9485 Office: 700 E State St Iola WI 54990-0001

MISKOWSKI, LEE R. retired automobile executive; b. Stevens Point, Wis., Mar. 27, 1932; s. Paul P. and Marie Grace (Glazer) M.; m. Billie Poulson, 1963; children: Christine, Katherine. BBA, U. Wis., 1954, MBA, 1957. V.p. Ford of Europe Ford Motor Co., Cologne, Germany, 1977-80, gen. mktg. mgr. Ford div. Dearborn, Mich., 1980-83, v.p., gen. mgr. parts and svc. div., 1989-91, v.p., gen. mgr. Lincoln-Mercury div., 1991-94, ret., 1994. Bd. dirs. Wolverine Brass, Inc., U. Wis. MC Found., Bradford Equities. Chmn. Hospice of Mich., 1996-98; vice chmn. Hospice of Mich. Found.; chmn. bd. dirs. Mich. Parkinson Found., Detroit, 1992-94, bd. dirs. Bradford Equities, Wolverine Bradd, Autocaraft, 1994-2000. With U.S. Army, 1954-56. Mem. Oakland Hills Country Club. Roman Catholic. Avocations: tennis, golf, reading, travel.

MITCHELL, BERT BREON, literary translator; b. Salina, Kans., Aug. 9, 1942; s. John Charles and Bernita Maxine (Breon) M.; m. Lynda Diane Fink, July 21, 1965; children: Kieron Breon, Kerry Archer. BA, U. Kans., 1964; PhD, Oxford U., 1968. Asst. prof. German and comparative lit. Ind. U., Bloomington, 1968-71, assoc. prof., 1971-78, prof., 1978—, assoc. dean Coll. Arts and Scis., 1975-77, chmn. comparative lit., 1977-85, dir. Wells Scholars program, 1988-98, dir. The Lilly Libr., 2001—. Dir. The Lilly Libr., 2001—. Author: James Joyce and the German Novel, 1922-1933, 1976, Beyond Illustration: The Livre d'Artiste in the Twentieth Century, 1976, The Complete Lithographs of Delacroix's Faust and Manet's The Raven, 1981; editor: Literature and the Other Arts, 1978, Metamorphosis and the Arts, 1979, Paul Morand, Fancy Goods/Open All Night, 1984; translator: Heartstop (Martin Grzimek), 1984, Selected Stories (Siegfried Lenz), 1989, The Musk Deer and Other Stories (Vilas Sarang), 1990, Looking Back (Lou Andreas-Salomé), 1991, Shadowlife (Martin Grzimek), 1991, Laura's Skin (J.F. Federspiel), 1991, The Color of the Snow (Rüdiger Kremer), 1992, Knife Edge (Ralf Rothmann) 1992, In the Kingdom of Enki (Vilas Sarang), 1993, The Silent Angel (Heinrich Böll), 1994, On the Glacier (Jürgen Kross), 1996, The God of Impertinence (Sten Nadolny), 1997, The Mad Dog (Heinrich Böll), 1997, The Trial (Franz Kafka), 1998. Rhodes scholar, 1964-68; Danforth fellow, 1964-68, Woodrow Wilson fellow, 1964, Alexander-von-Humboldt fellow, 1971, Translation fellow Nat. Endowment for Arts, 1989, Mellon fellow U. Tex., 1999; recipient Frederic Bachman Lieber Meml. award for disting. teaching, 1974, hon. citation Columbia Translation Ctr., 1990, Theodore Christian Hoepfner award So. Humanities Rev., 1995, Katharine and Daniel Leab award, 2001. Mem. MLA (chair William Riley Parker prize selection com. 1994), P.E.N., Am. Comparative Lit. Assn., Am. Lit. Translators Assn. (pres. 1985-87, Alta prize for disting. translation 1992), Am. Translators Assn. (com. lit. transl. 1983-84, German Lit. prize for disting. translation 1987, chmn. honors and awards com. 1995. hon. citation for disting. transl. 1999), Nat. Coun. Tchrs. of English (chair com. on comparative and world lit. 1995-98), James Joyce Found., Franz Kafka Soc., Samuel Beckett Soc., So. Comparative Lit. Assn., Brit. Comparative Lit. Assn., Internat. Comparative Lit. Assn., Am. Antiquarian Soc. Office: BH657 Indiana U Bloomington IN 47405 E-mail: mitchell@indiana.edu.

MITCHELL, CAMERON M. restaurant executive; b. Columbus, Ohio, June 14, 1963; s. Earnest Edward and Joan (Kellough) M. Assoc. with honors, Culinary Inst. Am., Hyde Park, N.Y., 1986. Kitchen mgr. Max & Ermas Restaurants, Columbus, Ohio, 1981-84; chef Fifty Five at Crossroads Restaurant, 1986-87, gen. mgr., 1989-90; exec. chef Fifty Five on the Blvd., 1987, gen. mgr., 1987-89; ops. mgr. Fifty Five Restaurant Grove, 1990-2000; prin., owner Cameron Mitchell Restaurants, Ohio, 2000—. Dir. 55 Catering, Columbus; trustee Touchstone Cafe Inc., Columbus, 1988-90; alumni rep. Culinary Inst. Am.; chmn. Taste of Nation event, Columbus, 1990. Chmn., founder Core program, 1988—; mem. Downtown Columbus Planning Com., 1988; mem. Make Room Columbus Project. Named Citizen of Yr., Open Shelter, Columbus, 1990. Mem. Am. Culinary Fedn., Nat. Restaurant Assn., Ohio Restaurant Assn., Columbus Chefs Assn. Republican. Avocations; golf, reading, philanthropy, travel, food and wine. Office: Cameron Mitchell Restaurants 1245 Olentangy River Rd Columbus OH 43212-3118

MITCHELL, EARL WESLEY, clergyman; b. Excelsior Springs, Mo., Mar. 16, 1931; s. Earl Van and Ora Leah (Butterfield) M.; m. Mary Lou Bell, June 8, 1956; children: Susan Yvonne, Randall Bruce. Ordained to ministry Christian Union Ch., 1971. Min. Vibbard (Mo.) Christian Union Ch., 1962-69, Liberty (Mo.) Christian Ch., 1969-77, Barwick Christian Union Ch., Cameron, Mo., 1977-80, Independence (Mo.) Christian Union Ch., 1980-95; assoc. pastor Flack Meml. Christian Union Ch., Excelsior Springs, Mo., 1995—. Former mem. state exec. bd. Christian Union Mo., 1995-98; area rep. Mo. Christian Union USA; former mem. gen. exec. bd., former editor C.U. Witness. Sgt. USAF, 1951-55. Avocations: music, woodworking, painting, photography. Home and Office: 618 Henrie St Excelsior Springs MO 64024-2022

MITCHELL, EDWARD JOHN, economist, retired educator; b. Newark, Aug. 15, 1937; s. Edward Charles and Gladys (Werner) M.; m. Mary Josephine Osborne, June 14, 1958; children: Susan, Edward. B.A. summa cum laude, Bowling Green State U., 1960; postgrad. (Social Sci. Research Council fellow), Nuffield Coll., Oxford U., Eng., 1963-64, Ph.D. in Econs. (NDEA fellow 1960-63, NSF fellow 1964-65), 1966. Lectr. in econs. Wharton Sch., U. Pa., 1964-65; economist Rand Corp., 1965-68; mem. Inst. Advanced Study, Princeton, N.J., 1968-69; sr. economist Pres.'s Council Econ. Advs., Washington, 1969-72; vis. assoc. prof. econs. Cornell U., 1972-73; assoc. prof. bus. econs. U. Mich., 1973-75, prof., 1975-88, prof. emeritus bus. econs. and pub. policy, 1988—; pres. Edward J. Mitchell Inc., Ann Arbor, 1977—. Dir. nat. energy project Am. Enterprise Inst., 1974-76; pres. Fountainhead Investment Co., 1984— Author: U.S. Energy Policy: A Primer, 1974, Dialogue on World Oil, 1974, Financing the Energy Industry, 1975, Vertical Integration of the Oil Industry, 1976, The Deregulation of Natural Gas, 1983; contbr. articles to profl. jours. Home: 310 Penny Ln Santa Barbara CA 93108-2601 Office: Grad Sch Bus U Mich Ann Arbor MI 48109 E-mail: mitchell296@home.com.

MITCHELL, GARY R. former state official; b. Dickinson County, Kans. BS in Econs. and History, Kans. State U., 1978, postgrad. Chief of staff U.S. Ho. of Reps. Com. on Agr.; mem. staff Senator Pat Roberts U.S. Ho. of Reps.; sec. Kans. Dept. Health and Environment, Topeka, 1997-99. Office: Kans Dept Health and Environment 900 SW Jackson St Rm 620 Topeka KS 66612-1220

MITCHELL, GEORGE TRICE, physician; b. Marshall, Ill., Jan. 20, 1914; s. Roscoe Addison and Alma (Trice) M.; m. Mildred Aletha Miller, June 21, 1941; children: Linda Sue, Mary Kathryn. BS, Purdue U., 1935; MD, George Washington U., 1940. Intern Meth. Hosp., Indpls., 1940-41; gen. practice medicine, Marshall, 1946—. Mem. courtesy staff Union and Regional Hosps., Terre Haute, Ind.; clin. assoc. Sch. Basic Medicine, U. Ill.; mem. recruitment and retention com. U. Ill. Coll. Medicine, Rockford; chmn. bd. dirs. 1st Nat. Bank, Marshall. Author: Dr. George-An Account of the Life of a Country Doctor, 1993. Mem. adv. coun. premedicine Eastern Ill. U., 1965-69; alt. del. Rep. Conv., 1968, del., 1972; trustee Lakeland Jr. Coll., 1978-92. Lt. col. USAAF, 1941-45. Named Health Practitioner of Yr. Ill. Rural Health Assn., 1993; recipient Disting. Svc. award, Lake Land Coll., 1992, Purdue Alumni Assn. Citizenship award, 1996. Fellow Am. Acad. Family Physicians (Family Physician of Yr. 1993); mem. AMA, Ill. Med. Soc. (2d v.p. 1980-81), Clark County Med. Soc. (pres.), Aesculapian Soc. of Wabash Valley (pres. 1965), Nat. Rural Health Assn. (Practitioner of Yr. 19951999 Disting. Svc. award), Ill. Rural Health Assn. (bd. dirs.), Clark County Hist. Soc. (pres. 1968-70), Masons (32 degree), Shriners. Methodist. Home: 15923 N Oak Crest Rd Marshall IL 62441-4332 Office: 410 N 2d St Marshall IL 62441-1010

MITCHELL, GERALD LEE, state legislator; b. Jacksonville, Ill., June 18, 1942; m. Janet L. Conway; 3 children. BS, Eureka Coll., 1968; MS, Ill. State U., 1974; EdS, Western Ill. U., 1992. Tchr., coach Eureka Mid. Sch., 1968-70; prin. elem. K-8 schs. Mt. Sterling, Ill., 1975-81; prin. Rock Falls Jr. H.S., 1983; asst. prin. Dixon H.S., 1986; prin. elem., mid., and h.s., 1974-86; dir. evaluation and edn. svc. Dixon Dist., 1986-92; asst. supt., 1992-93; from ctrl. adminstrn. through supt. schs. Dixon Cmty. Unit Schs. Dist. # 170, 1994; supt., 1993-94; Ill. state rep. Dist. 73, 1995—. Mem. ASCD, Nat. Staff Devel., Coun., Am. Assn. Sch. Adminstrs., Ill. Assn. Sch. Bd. Office: 100 E 5th St Rock Falls IL 61071-1780

MITCHELL, JAMES AUSTIN, insurance company executive; b. Cin., Dec. 16, 1941; s. James Austin and Jeannette Louise (Stiles) M.; 1 child, J. David. A.B., Princeton U., 1963. CLU; chartered fin. cons.; FSA. Various positions Conn. Gen. Life Ins. Co., Hartford, 1963-73, v.p., controller, 1973-77; v.p., chief fin. officer Aetna Ins. Co., 1977-82; pres. Cigna RE Corp., 1982-84; chmn., pres., CEO IDS Life Ins. Co., Mpls., 1984—; exec. v.p. mktg. & products, chmn. subs. Am. Express. Dir. IDS Fin. Services and Affiliated Cos., Mpls. Mem. exec. com. Mpls. Inst. Arts, 1987—; bd. dirs. Mpls. YMCA. With U.S. Army, 1964-70. Fellow Soc. Actuaries; mem. Soc. C.L.U.s Republican. Presbyterian. Club: Minneapolis. Avocations: tennis; skiing; reading. Home: 142 Groveland Ter Minneapolis MN 55403-1148 Office: IDS Life Ins Co 2900 IDS Tower 10 Minneapolis MN 55440

MITCHELL, JAMES EDWARD, physician, educator; b. Chgo., June 19, 1947; s. James Edward and Elizabeth Latimer M.; m. Karen Antrim, June 14, 1969; children: James, Katherine. BA, Ind. U., 1968; MD, Northwestern U., 1972. Diplomate Am. Bd. Psychiatry Neurology. Intern Ind. U., Mpls., 1979-90; resident Northwestern U., 1990-96; from asst. prof. to prof. U. Minn., 1979-90, prof., 1990-96; prof., chmn. dept. neuroscience sch. medicine & health sci. U. N.D., Fargo, 1996—. Pres., scientific dir. Neuropsychiat. Rsch. Inst., Fargo, 1996—. Named Tchr. of Yr., N.D. Psychiat. Residents Assn., 1997-98, 98-99. Fellow Am. Psychiat. Assn., Am. Assn. Social Psychiatry; mem. Acad. Eating Disorders (pres.-elect 1999—), Eating Disorders Rsch. Soc. (sec.-treas. 1995—). Avocations: canoeing, art, traveling. Office: Neuropsychiat Rsch Inst PO Box 1415 700 1st Ave S Fargo ND 58107 Fax: 701-293-3226. E-mail: mitchell@medicine.nodak.edu.

MITCHELL, JAMES W. state official, former state legislator; b. Springfield, Mo., June 30, 1950; s. James Robert and Shirley (Sharp) M.; m. Terri Lea Starmer; 1 child, Mona. BA, Drury Coll., 1973, MA, 1081. Pres. Mitchell Bros. Farms, Richland, Mo., 1980-86; owner, mgr. Jim Mitchell Ins. Agy., 1984—; mem. Mo. Ho. of Reps., Jefferson City, 1983—; bd. dirs. State Bd. of Probation and Parole, Mo., 1997—. Alderman City of Richland, 1978-83; bd. dirs. Mo. Ozarks Econ. Opportunity Corp., 1983—; pres. Cmty. Assn., 1976-79. Recipient award of merit Mo. Tchrs. Assn., 1979, Meritorious Svc. award St. Louis Globe Dem., 1984-86; named Outstanding Rural Freshman Legislator, 1982-84. Mem. NRA, Pulaski County Landowners Assn., Phi Delta Kappa, Sigma Nu. Republican.

MITCHELL, JOHN LAURIN AMOS, biological science educator; b. Lincoln, Nebr., July 18, 1944; s. William A. and Ruth Chilla (Cobbey) M.; m. Gail Ann Kurtz, July 13, 1968; children: Jill, Todd. BA, Oberlin Coll., 1966; PhD, Princeton U., 1970. Postdoctoral fellow McArdle Inst. Cancer Rsch., Madison, Wis., 1970-73; asst. prof. No. Ill. U., DeKalb, 1973-78, assoc. prof., prof., 1983—. Inventor in field; contbr. articles to profl. jours.

MITCHELL, LEE MARK, communications executive, investment fund manager, lawyer; b. Albany , N.Y., Apr. 16, 1943; s. Maurice B. and Mildred (Roth) M.; m. Barbara Lee Anderson, Aug. 27, 1966; children: Mark, Matthew. AB, Wesleyan U., 1965; JD, U. Chgo., 1968. Bar: Ill. 1968, D.C. 1969, U.S. Supreme Ct. 1972. Assoc. Leibman, Williams, Bennett, Baird & Minow, Chgo. and Washington, 1968-72, Sidley & Austin, Washington, 1972-74, ptnr., 1974-84, 92-94; exec. v.p. and gen. counsel Field Enterprises, Inc., Chgo., 1981-83, pres., CEO, 1983-84, Field Corp., 1984-92; prin. Golder, Thoma, Cressey, Rauner, Inc., Chgo., 1994-98; ptnr. Thoma Cressey Equity Ptnrs., Inc., 1998—. Chmn. Chgo.

Stock Exch., Inc. Author: Openly Arrived At, 1974, With the Nation Watching, 1979; co-author: Presidential Television, 1973. Bd. visitors U. Chgo. Law Sch., 1984—86, Medill Sch. Journalism, Northwestern U., 1984—91; pres. bd. govs. Chgo. Met. Planning Coun., 1988—91; mem. midwest regional adv. bd. Inst. Internat. Edn., 1987—99; trustee Ravinia Festival Assn., 1989—97, Northwestern U., Northwestern Meml. Hosp.; U.S. del. Brit. Legis. Conf. on Govt. and Media, Ditchley Park, England, 1974; adv. com. LWV Presdl. Debates, Washington, 1979—80, 1982. Mem.: Econ. Mid-Am. Club, ABA, Comml. Club Chgo. Home: 135 Maple Hill Rd Glencoe IL 60022-1252 Office: Thoma Cressey Equity Ptnrs Sears Tower Ste 9200 233 S Wacker Dr Chicago IL 60606-6306 E-mail: LMitchell@thomacressey.com.

MITCHELL, NED, state legislator; Mayor City of Sesser (Ill.); auditor Ill. Comptroller, 1977—; mem. Ill. Senate, Springfield, 1999—. Democrat. Office: State Capitol Capitol Bldg M 103 F Springfield IL 62706-0001 also: 112 E Market St Christopher IL 62822-1742

MITCHELL, ORLAN E. clergyman, former college president; b. Eldora, Iowa, Mar. 13, 1933; s. Frank E. and Alice G. (Brown) M.; m. Verlene J. Huehn, June 10, 1952; children: Jolene R., Stephen M., Nadene A., Timothy M., Mark E. B.A., Grinnell Coll., 1955; B.D., Yale U., 1959, M.Div., 1965; D.Min., San Francisco Theol. Sem., 1976. Ordained to ministry United Ch. of Christ, 1959; pastor chs. Sheridan Twp., Iowa, 1954-55, New Preston, Conn., 1956-59, Clarion, Iowa, 1959-69, Yankton, S.D., 1969-77; pres. Yankton (S.D.) Coll., 1977-96; conf. minister Iowa Conf. United Ch. Christ; ret., 1996. Cons. in field. Mem. Sch. Bd., Clarion, Iowa, 1965-69, mem., Yankton, S.D., 1973-77, pres., 1976; bd. dirs. Lewis and Clark Mental Health Center. Mem. S.D. Found. Pvt. Colls., S.D. Assn. Pvt. Colls., Colls. of Mid-Am. Democrat. Lodges: Kiwanis; Masons. Office: 725 Park St Grinnell IA 50112-2235 E-mail: orlanm@pcpartner.net.

MITSCHER, LESTER ALLEN, chemist, educator; b. Detroit, Aug. 20, 1931; s. Lester and Mary Athelda (Pounder) M.; m. Betty Jane McRoberts, May 29, 1953; children: Katrina, Kurt, Mark. B.S., Wayne U., 1953, Ph.D., 1958. Research scientist, group leader Lederle Labs., Pearl River, N.Y., 1958-67; prof. Ohio State U., Columbus, 1967-75, U. Kans., Lawrence, 1975—, chmn. dept. medicinal chemistry, 1975-92; intersearch prof. Victorian Coll. of Pharmacy, Monash U., Melbourne, Australia, 1975—. Cons. NIH, Am. Cancer Soc., Abbott Labs., Pharmacia Labs. Author: (with D. Lednicer) The Organic Chemistry of Drug Synthesis, Vol. 1, 1976, Vol. 2, 1980, Vol. 3, 1984, Vol. 4, 1990, The Chemistry of the Tetracycline Antibiotics, 1978; co-author: The Green Tea Book, 1997; editor-in-chief Medicinal Research Reviews, 1995-99; contbr. over 235 articles to profl. jours. Recipient Disting. Alumnus award Sch. Pharmacy, Wayne State U., 1980, 97, Research Achievement award Acad. Pharm. Scis., 1980, 97, Volweiler research award Am. Assn. Colls. Pharmacy, 1985, Higuchi-Simmons award U. Kans., 1986. Fellow AAAS; mem. Am. Soc. Pharmacognosy (pres. 1992-93), Am. Chem. Soc. (former chmn. councilor medicinal chemistry divsn., Bristol-Myers Smissman rsch. award 1989, Med. Chemistry award 2000), Chem. Soc. London, Japanese Antibiotics Assn., Soc. Heterocyclic Chemistry, Internat. Union of Pure and Applied Chemistry (commr. medicinal chemistry divsn.), Internat. Orgn. for Chemistry in Developing Countries (steering com.). Presbyterian. Office: Dept Medicinal Chemistry U Kans Lawrence KS 66045 E-mail: lmitscher@ku.edu.

MITSEFF, CARL, lawyer; b. Detroit, Nov. 16, 1928; s. Frank H. and Katherine (Schaffer) M.; m. Phyllis Schlitters, June 28, 1952; children: C. Randall, Bradley Scott, Julie, Emily, Faye. B.S., Wayne State U., 1952, LL.B., 1955. Bar: Mich. 1956. Practiced in Detroit, 1956—; staff atty. Burroughs Corp., 1955-60; mem. firm LeVasseur, Mitseff, Egan & Capp, 1960-80, Mitseff & Baril, 1980-85, Fitzgerald, Hodgman, Cox, Cawthoren & McMahon, 1986-90, Cox & Hodgman, 1990—. Spl. asst. atty. gen. State of Mich.; lectr. in field. Named to Mich. Workers Compensation Hall of Fame, 2000. Mem. ABA, State Bar Mich., Internat. Assn. Ins. Counsel, Internat. Assn. Indsl. Accident Bds. and Commns., Detroit Athletic Club (bd. dirs.), Beavers (pres.), Lochmoor Club, Grosse Pointe Yacht Club, Pi Kappa Alpha, Delta Theta Phi. Home: 612 N Brys Dr Grosse Pointe Woods MI 48236-1247 Office: 1001 Woodward Ave Ste 1000 Detroit MI 48226-1904

MITSTIFER, DOROTHY IRWIN, honor society administrator; b. Gaines, Pa., Aug. 17, 1932; d. Leonard Robert and Laura Dorothy (Crane) Irwin; m. Robert Mitchell Mitsifer, June 17, 1956 (dec. Aug. 1984); children: Kurt Michael, Brett Robert. BS, Mansfield U., 1954; MEd, Pa. State U., 1972, PhD, 1976. Cert. home economist. Tchr. Tri-County High Sch., Canton, Pa., 1954-56, Loyalsock Twp. Sch. Dist., Williamsport, 1956-63; exec. dir. Kappa Omicron Phi, 1964-86, Kappa Omicron Phi, Omicron Nu, Haslett, Mich., 1986-90, Kappa Omicron Nu, East Lansing, 1990—. Prof. continuing edn. Pa. State U., University Park, 1976-80; prof. Mansfield (Pa.) U., 1980-86, pres.'s intern, 1984-86. Editor Kappa Omicron Nu Forum, 1986—; contbr. articles to profl. jours. Pres., bd. dirs. Profl. Devel. Ctr. Adv. Bd., Vocat. Edn., Pa. State U., 1980-86. Mem. ASCD, Am. Home Econs. Assn., Mich. Home Econs. Assn. (exec. dir. 1986-96), Am. Vocat. Assn., Am. Soc. Assn. Execs., Assn. Coll. Honor Socs. (sec.-treas. 1976—), Coll. Edn. Alumni Soc. Pa. State U. (pres. 1986-88, bd. dirs. 1980-90), Kappa Delta Pi. Avocations: sewing, camping, fishing. Home: 1425 Somerset Close St East Lansing MI 48823-2435 Office: Kappa Omicron Nu 4990 Northwind Dr Ste 140 East Lansing MI 48823-5031 E-mail: dmitstifer@kon.org.

MIXON, A. MALACHI, III, medical products executive; m. Barabara Mixon; 2 children. BA, MBA, Harvard U. CEO, chmn. Invacare Corp., Elyria, Ohio. Chmn. bd. trustees Cleve. Clinic Found. Office: Invacare Corp 1 Invacare Way PO Box 4028 Elyria OH 44036-2125 Fax: 440-366-9008.

MIYAMOTO, RICHARD TAKASHI, otolaryngologist; b. Zeeland, Mich., Feb. 2, 1944; s. Dave Norio and Haruko (Okano) M.; m. Cynthia VanderBurgh, June 17, 1967; children: Richard Christopher, Geoffrey Takashi. BS cum laude, Wheaton Coll., 1966; MD, U. Mich., 1970; MS in Otology, U.So. Calif., 1978; D in Engring. (hon.) Rose Hulman Inst. of Tech., 2001. Diplomate Am. Bd. Otolaryngology. Intern Butterworth Hosp., Grand Rapids, Mich., 1970-71, resident in surgery, 1971-72; resident in otolaryngology Ind. U. Sch. Medicine, 1972-75; fellow in otology and neurotology St. Vincent Hosp. and Otologic Med. Group, L.A., 1977-78; asst. prof. Ind. U. Sch. Medicine, Indpls., 1978-83, assoc. prof., 1983-88; prof. 1988—; chmn. 1987—, chief Otology and Neurotology dept. Otolaryngology, Head and Neck Surgery, Ind. U., 1982—, chmn. dept. Otolaryngology, 1987—, Arilla DeVault prof., 1991; chief Otolaryngology, Head and Neck Surgery Wishard Meml. Hosp., 1979—. Mem. editorial bd. Laryngoscope, Am. Jour. of Otology, Otolaryngology-Head and Neck Surgery, European archives of Oto-Rhino-Laryngology, Anales de Otorrinolaringologia Mexicana; contbr. articles to profl. jours. Mem. adv. coun. Nat. Inst. Deafness and other communication disorders, 1989-94; mem. med. adv. bd. Alexander Graham Bell Assn. for the Deaf, The Ear Found. Served to maj. USAF, 1975-77. Named Arilla DeVault Disting. investigator Ind. U., 1983. Fellow Am. Acad. Otolaryngology (gov. 1982—), ACS, Am. Otological, Rhinological, and Laryngological Soc. (Thesis Disting. for Excellence award), Am. Neurotology Soc. (pres. elect 1999-2000, pres. 2000-01), Am. Auditory Soc. (mem. exec. com. 1985—); mem. Am. Acad. Pediats., N.Y. Acad. Scis., Otosclerosis Study Group (coun. 1993—), Am. Otol. Soc. (coun. 1992—), Marines Meml. Assn., Assn. Rsch. Otol. (pres. elect 2000-2001, pres. 2001-), Wheaton Coll. Scholastic Honor Soc., Cosmos Club of Washington, Columbia Club of Ind., Royal Soc. Medicine London, Collegium Oto-Laryngologicum Amecitiae Sacrum; Alpha Omega Alpha, Psi Iote X. Office: Ind U Sch Med 702 Barnhill Dr Indianapolis IN 46202-5128

MLOCEK, SISTER FRANCES ANGELINE, financial executive; b. River Rouge, Mich., Aug. 4, 1934; d. Michael and Suzanna (Bloch) M. BBA, U. Detroit, 1958; MBA, U. Mich., 1971. CPA, Mich. Bookkeeper Allen Park (Mich.) Furniture, 1949-52, Gerson's Jewlery, Detroit, 1952-53; jr. acct. Meyer Dickman, CPA, Algaze, Staub & Bowman, CPAs, 1953-58; acct., internal auditor Sisters, Servants of Immaculate Heart of Mary Congregation, Monroe, Mich., 1959-66, asst. gen. treas., 1966-73, gen. treas., 1973-76; internal auditor for parishes Archdiocese of Detroit, 1976-78; asst. to exec. dir. Leadership Conf. of Women, Silver Spring, Md., 1978-83; dir. of fin. Nat. Conf. of Cath. Bishops/U.S. Cath. Conf., Washington, 1989-94; CFO Sisters Servants of the Immaculate Heart of Mary, Monroe, Mich., 1994—. Trustee SSIHM Charitable Trust, Monroe, 1988—. Author: (manual) Leadership Conference of Women Religious/Confernce of Major Superiors of Men, 1981. Treas. Zonta Club of Washington Found., Washington, 1983-88, pres., 1992-93; bd. dirs. Our Lady of Good Counsel High Sch., Wheaton, Md., 1983-89. Mem. AICPA, D.C. Inst. CPAs (mem. not-for-profit com. 1992-94, CFOs com. 1990-94. Democrat. Roman Catholic. Office: Sisters Servants Immaculate Heart Mary 610 W Elm Ave Monroe MI 48162-7909

MOAWAD, ATEF, obstetrician, gynecologist, educator; b. Beni Suef, Egypt, Dec. 2, 1935; came to U.S., 1959; s. Hanna and Baheya (Hunein) M.; m. Ferial Fouad Abdel Malek, Aug. 22, 1966; children: John, Joseph, James. Student, Cairo U. Sch. Sci., 1951-52; MB, BCh, Cairo U. Sch. Medicine, 1957; MS in in Pharmacology, Jefferson Med. Coll., 1963. Diplomate Am. Bd. Ob-Gyn; licentiate Med. Coun Can. Rotating intern Cairo U. Hosp., 1958-59, Elizabeth (N.J.) Gen. Hosp., 1959-60; resident in ob-gyn. Jefferson Med. Coll. Hosp., Phila., 1961-64; lect. dept. pharmacology U. Alta., Can., 1966; asst. prof. dept. ob-gyn. and pharmacology U. Alta., Can., 1967-70, assoc. prof. Can., 1970-72; assoc. prof. dept. ob-gyn. and pharmacology U. Chgo., 1972-75, prof. dept. ob-gyn. and pediatrics, 1975—, co-dir. perinatal ctr., 1974-80; obstetrician-gynecologist, chief obstetrics, co-dir. perinatal ctr. The Chgo. Lying-in Hosp. U. Chgo., 1980—, Blum Riese prof. ob-gyn., chief maternal fetal medicine, 2001—, interim chair dept. ob-gyn., 2002—. Vis. investigator dept. ob-gyn. U. Lund, Sweden, 1969. Co-author book chpts., jour. articles. Mem. perinatal adv. com. Chgo. March of Dimes, 1977—, health profl. adv. com., 1983—; mem. perinatal adv. bd. com. State of Ill., 1978—; mem. Chgo. Maternal Child Health Adv. Com., chmn., 1991—; mem. Mayor's Adv. Com. on Infant Mortality, 1991—. Fellow Jefferson Med. Coll., 1960-61, Case Western Reserve U., 1964-65; grantee Brush Found., 1966-67, Maternal Fetal Medicine Units Network NIH, 1994; recipient award Phila. Obstet. Soc., 1964, Disting. Teaching award Am. Profs. Gynecology and Obstetrics, 1993. Fellow Am. Coll. Ob-Gyn. (Purdue-Frederick award 1978), Royal Coll. Surgeons (Can.); mem. Soc. for Gynecol Investigation, Pharmacol. Soc. Can., Am. Gynecol. and Obstet. Soc., Soc. Perinatal Obstetricians, N.Y. Acad. Scis., Chgo. Gynecol. Soc., Can. Med. Assn., Christian Med. Soc., Edmonton Obstetrics Soc. Office: U Chgo Dept Ob-Gyn 5841 S Maryland Ave MC 2050 Chicago IL 60637-1463 E-mail: amoaroad@babies.bsd.uchicago.edu.

MOBBS, MICHAEL HALL, lawyer; b. Lawrenceburg, Tenn., Dec. 25, 1948; s. Hershel Leon and Doris (Davis) M.; children: Michael Hall Jr., Clifton Stevenson, Ellene Glenn. BA summa cum laude, honors with exceptional distinction in Russian studies, Yale U., 1971; JD, U. Chgo., 1974. Bar: Ala. 1974, D.C. 1978, U.S. Supreme Ct. 1980. Assoc. Bradley, Arant, Rose & White, Birmingham, Ala., 1974-77; assoc. Stroock & Stroock & Lavan, Washington, 1977-81, ptnr., 1990-93; ptnr. Squire, Sanders & Dempsey, LLP, 1994—, mng. ptnr. Moscow, 1995—; rep. of sec. def. to Strategic Arms Reduction Talks, Washington and Geneva, 1982-85; spl. counsel to head of del. and rep. of sec. def. to Negotiations on Nuclear and Space Arms, Washington and Geneva, 1985; asst. dir. of U.S. Arms Control and Disarmament Agy., Washington, 1985-87. Ford Fund scholar, 1967-71; Bates fellow, 1970; recipient Fellows' prize Jonathan Edwards Coll. Yale U., 1971. Mem. ABA (mem. com. on Ctrl. and Ea. European law initiatives), Am. Soc. Internat. Law, Ala. State Bar, D.C. Bar, Phi Beta Kappa. Democrat. Clubs: Yale of N.Y.C.; City Tavern (Washington). Author: (with George G. Lorinczi) An Importer's Roadmap to U.S. Import Restrictions, 1980, CBMs For Stabilizing the Strategic Nuclear Competition, 1986, Remarks on Verification of Arms Control Agreements, 1988, (with William J. Vanden Heuvel) Overview of the Laws Governing Foreign Investment in the USSR, 1990, On the Road in Eastern Europe, 1991, Environmental Protection in the CIS and Eastern Europe: Emerging Trends May Affect Your Business, 1993. Office: c/o McDermott Will & Emery 227 W Monroe St Ste 3200 Chicago IL 60606-5018 also: Ul Gasheka 7 Ste 610 123056 Moscow Russia

MOBERG, DAVID OSCAR, sociology educator; b. Montevideo, Minn., Feb. 13, 1922; s. Fred Ludwig and Anna E. (Sundberg) M.; m. Helen H. Heitzman, Mar. 16, 1946 (dec. Oct. 16, 1992); children: David Paul, Lynette, Jonathan, Philip; m. Marlys Taege, July 23, 1994. AA, Bethel Jr. Coll., 1942; AB, Seattle Pacific Coll., 1947; MA, U. Wash., 1949; PhD, U. Minn., 1952. Assoc. instr. U. Wash., Seattle, 1948-49; faculty Bethel Coll., St. Paul, 1949-68, prof. sociology, 1959-68, chmn. dept. social scis., 1952-68; prof. sociology Marquette U., Milw., 1968-91, prof. emeritus, 1991—, chmn. dept. sociology and anthropology, 1968-77. Cons. Nat. Liberty Found., 1970-71, Fetzer Inst., 1995-96; rsch. cons. Internat. Luth. Women's Missionary League, 1997-99, Bonnie Walker & Assocs., 1997-99; cons. Nat. Interfaith Coalition on Aging, 1973-75, mem. nat. adv. bd., 1980-89; guest rschr. Sociology of Religion Inst., Stockholm, summer 1978; adj. prof. San Francisco Theol. Sem., 1964-73, McCormick Theol. Sem., 1975-78, 81-82; vis. prof. U. So. Calif., 1979, Princeton Theol. Sem., 1979, So. Bapt. Theol. Sem., 1982, Soc. for Care of the Handicapped in the Gaza Strip of Palestine, 1995; mem. adv. bd. Ecumenical Ministry with Mature Adults, 1983-92; resource scholar Christianity Today Inst., 1985—; mem. bd. adv. editors Haworth Pastoral Press, 1998—. Author: The Church as A Social Institution, 1962, 2d edit. 1984, (with Robert M. Gray) The Church and the Older Person, 1962, 2d edit., 1977, Inasmuch: Christian Social Responsibility in the 20th Century, 1965, White House Conference on Aging: Spiritual Well-Being Background and Issues, 1971, The Great Reversal: Evangelism and Social Concern, 1972, 2d edit, 1977, Wholistic Christianity, 1985, Woman of God: An Assessment of the Spirituality of Women in the LCMS, 1999; also articles, chpts. in symposia.; editor: International Directory of Religious Information Systems, 1971, Spiritual Well-Being: Sociological Perspectives, 1979, Rev. Religious Research, 1968-72, Jour. Am. Sci. Affiliation, 1962-64, Adris Newsletter, 1971-76, Aging and Spirituality: Spiritual Dimensions of Aging Theory, Research, Practice, and Policy, 2001; co-editor Research in the Social Scientific Study of Religion, 1986—; assoc. editor: Social Compass, 1968—; mem. editl. bd. Christian Univ. Press, 1979-84, Perspectives on Sci. and Christian Faith, 1988—; consulting editor Calif. Sociologist, 1982-96. Fulbright lectr. U. Groningen, Netherlands, 1957-58, Fulbright lectr. Muenster U., West Germany, 1964-65. Fellow Am. Sci. Affiliation (editor jour. 1962-64, publs. com. 1984-91, social ethics com. 1985-88, program chair 1995-96), Gerontol. Soc. Am.; mem. Am. Sociol. Assn., Internat. Sociol. Assn. (sociology of religion rsch. com. 1972—), Wis. Sociol. Assn. (pres. 1969-71), Midwest Sociol. Assn. (Wis. bd. dirs. 1971-73), Assn. Devel. Religious Info. Sys. (coord. ADRIS 1971—, editor ADRIS newsletter 1971-76), Religious Rsch. Assn. (editor Rev. Religious Rsch. 1968-72, contbg. editor 1973-77, assoc. editor 1983—, bd. dirs. 1959-61, 68-72, pres. 1981-82, H. Paul Douglass lectr. 1986), Assn. for Sociology of Religion (exec. coun. 1971-73, pres. 1976-77), Soc. for Sci. Study Religion (exec. coun. 1971-74, sr. editl. cons. SSSR-RRA History Project 1995-99), Evangelicals for Social Action (planning com. 1973-75), Christian Sociol. Soc. (steering com. 1973-81, newsletter lit. reviewer 1981-93), Family Rsch. Coun. (assoc. 1985-88, rsch. network 1989-98), Psychologists Interested in Religious Issues (profl. affiliate 1984-99), Univ. Faculty for Life, Midwest Coun. for Social Rsch. on Aging (fellow 1961-64, 87—), Am. Soc. on Aging, Forum on Religion and Aging, Fairview Elder Enterprises (bd. dirs. 1989—). Home and Office: 7120 W Dove Ct Milwaukee WI 53223-2766 E-mail: david.moberg@marquette.edu.

MOBERLY, THOMAS, uniform company executive; b. 1948; With G & K Svcs., Inc., 1974—, exec. v.p., 1993-97, pres., CEO Minn., 2000—. Office: G & K Svcs Inc 5995 Opus Pky Ste 500 Minnetonka MN 55343 Fax: (612) 912-5500.

MOBLEY, EMILY RUTH, library dean, educator; b. Valdosta, Ga., Oct. 1, 1942; d. Emmett and Ruth (Johnson) M. AB in Edn., U. Mich., 1964, AM in Libr. Sci., 1967, postgrad., 1973-76. Tchr. Ecorse (Mich.) Pub. Schs., 1964-65; adminstrv. trainee Chrysler Corp., Highland Park, Mich., 1965-66, engring. libr., 1966-69; libr. II Wayne State U., Detroit, 1969-72, libr. III, 1972-75; staff asst. GM Rsch. Labs. Libr., Warren, Mich., 1976-78, supr. reader svcs., 1978-81; libr. dir. GMI Engring. & Mgmt. Inst., Flint, 1982-86; assoc. dir. for pub. svcs. & collection devel., assoc. prof. libr. sci. Purdue U. Librs., West Lafayette, Ind., 1986-89, acting dir. librs., assoc. prof. libr. sci., 1989, dean librs., prof. libr. sci., 1989—; Esther Ellis Norton Disting. Prof. Libr. Sci. Purdue U., 1997—. Adj. lectr. U. Mich. Sch. Libr. Sci., Ann Arbor, 1974-75, 83-86; grants reader Libr. of Mich., 1980-81; project dir. Mideastern Mich. Region Libr. Cooperation, 1984-86; cons. Libr. Coop. of Macomb, 1985-86, Clark-Atlanta U., 1990-91; search com. for new dir. of libr. Smithsonian Instn., 1988; mem. GM Pub. Affairs Subcom. on Introducing Minorities to Engring.; presenter in field. Author: Special Libraries at Work, 1984, numerous other publs.; mem. editl. bd. Reference Svcs. Rev., 1989—, Infomanage, 1993-97. Mem. corp. vis. com. for librs. MIT, 1990—, Carnegie-Mellon U., 1998—; mem. Ind. Statewide Libr. Automation Task Force, 1989-90; mem. state tech. strategy subcom. on info. tech. and telecomms. Ind. Corp. for Sci. & Tech., 1989; mem. nat. adv. com. Libr. of Congress, 1988; trustee Libr. of Mich., 1983-86, v.p., 1986, long range plan com., 1979-82, task force on document access and delivery, 1977-79; info. project mem. Rep. Nat. Conv., 1980; bd. dirs. Small Farms Assn., Southfield, Mich., Lafayette Symphony Orch., YWCA. Recipient Bausch & Lomb award for sci. achievement, 1960, Cert. for Outstanding Performance in Acad. Achievement State of Mich. Ho. of Reps., 1976, Spl. Tribute for Outstanding Contbns. Libr. of Mich. Bd. Trustees, 1986, Disting. Alumnus award U. Mich. Sch. Info. & Libr. Studies, 1989; U. Mich. Regents Alumni scholar, 1960-64; CIC doctoral fellow in libr. sci., 1973-76. Mem. ALA (com. on accreditation, subcom. to rev. 1972, standards for accreditation 1988-89, OLOS minority internship com. 1988-89, nominating com. 1992-93, mem. coun. resolutions com. 1993-97), Assn. Coll. & Rsch. Librs. (task force on libr. sch. curriculum 1988-89, com. on profl. edn. 1990-92), Libr. Adminstrn. & Mgmt. Assn., Assn. Rsch. Librs. (bd. dirs. 1990-93), Spl. Librs. Assn. (pres. 1987-88, fellow 1991, com. mem.), Alpha Kappa Alpha, Phi Kappa Phi, Sigma Xi, Iron Key. Office: Purdue U Librs Stewart Ctr Lafayette IN 47907

MOBLEY, TONY ALLEN, foundation executive, former university dean, recreation educator; b. Harrodsburg, Ky., May 19, 1938; s. Cecil and Beatrice (Bailey) M.; m. Betty Weaver, June 10, 1961; 1 child, Derek Lloyd. BS, Georgetown Coll., 1960; MS, Ind. U., 1962, D Recreation, 1965; MRE, So. Sem., Louisville, 1963. Chmn. dept. recreation and pks. Western Ill. U., Macomb, 1965-72, Pa. State U., University Park, 1972-76; prof., chmn. recreation and pks., dean Sch. Health, Phys. Edn. and Recreation Ind. U., Bloomington, 1976—; exec. dir. Ind. U. Found., 2002—. Chair health adv. coun. White River Park Commn., State of Ind., 1979—; v.p Ind. Sports Corp., Indpls., 1983-89; bd. dirs. Nat. Inst. for Fitness and Sport, Indpls., 1984-93; J.B. Nash scholar, lectr. Am. Assn. Leisure and Recreation, Reston, Va., 1985. Contbr. over 50 articles to profl. jours. Bd. dirs. Monroe County YMCA, Bloomington, 1984-88, United Way, Bloomington, 1994—; mem. Gov.'s Coun. for Phys. Fitness and Sport, 1991—. Am. Coun. Edn. adminstrv. internship fellow, N.C. State U., 1970-71. Fellow Am. Acad. Pk. and Recreation Adminstrn. (pres. 1985-86); mem. Nat. Recreation and Pk. Assn. (pres. 1978-79, Nat. Disting. Profl. award 1981), Assn. Rsch., Adminstrn., Profl. Couns. and Socs. (pres. 1986-87, award 1987), Am. Alliance Health, Phys. Edn., Recreation and Dance (Coll. and Univ. Adminstrs. Coun. Honor award 1986, R. Tait McKenzie award 1996), Soc. Pk. and Recreation Edn. (pres. 1974-75, award 1978), Ind. Pk. and Recreation Assn. (Outstanding Profl. award 1985). Avocations: golf, travel. Office: Ind U Found PO Box 500 Bloomington IN 47402

MOCK, DEAN R. state legislator; Owner, operator, Mock's TV Sales and Svc.; mem. from 48th dist., Ind. State Ho. of Reps., 1976—. mem. pub. policy com., ethics com., vets. affairs com., county and twp. com., labor and employment com., age and agine com., chmn. rds. and transp. com.; pres. Ind. Electric Svc. Assn. Del. Ind. Rep. State Conv., 1978-80. Mem. Elkhart C. of C., Am. Fedn. Musicians, Masons, Shriners, Scottish Rite, Moose. Home: 54135 County Road 7 Elkhart IN 46514-3076

MODIC, STANLEY JOHN, business editor, publisher; b. Fairport Harbor, Ohio, Dec. 29, 1936; s. Frank and Mary (Zakrajsek) M.; m. Albina DiMichele, May 27, 1961; children— Mark Francis, Laurel Marie. BS in Commerce, Ohio U., 1958. Musician, band leader, 1953-58; Reporter The Telegraph, Painesville, Ohio, 1960-63, city editor, 1964-65; asst. editor Steel Mag., Cleve., 1965-67, news editor, 1968-70; mng. editor Industry Week (formerly Steel Mag.), Cleve., 1970-72, exec. editor, 1972; editor Industry Week, 1972-86; sr. editor Industry Week (formerly Steel Mag.), 1986-89, editor-in-chief Purchasing World Mag., 1989-90, Tooling and Prodn. Mag., 1990—. Mcpl. clk. Fairport Harbor, 1960-61; mem. Fairport Harbor Village Council, 1962-63, pres., 1962-63. Recipient G.D. Crane award Am. Bus. Press, 1991; named Slovenian Man of Yr., Fedn. Slovenian Homes, Cleve., 1998. Mem.: Press Club (pres. Cleve. chpt. 1978—79), Hungarian Culture Club, Am. Slovenian Club (Fairport Harbor) (pres. 2002—), KC, Elks, Sigma Delta Chi (pres. Cleve. chpt. 1975—76). Home: 5842 Woodhill St Painesville OH 44077-5167 Office: 6001 Cochran Rd 1st Fl Cleveland OH 44139-3310 E-mail: smodic@nelsonpub.com.

MODISETT, JEFFREY A. lawyer, state attorney general, business executive; b. Windfall, Ind., Aug. 10, 1954; s. James Richard and Diana T. Modisett; m. Jennifer Ashworth, June 9, 1990; children: Matthew Hunter Ashworth, Haden Nicholas. BA, UCLA, 1976; MA, Oxford (Eng.) U., 1978; JD, Yale U., 1981. Bar: Ind., Calif., D.C. Clk. to Hon. R. Peckham U.S. Dist. Ct. (no. dist.) Calif., San Francisco, 1981—82; asst. U.S. atty. Office U.S. Atty. (ctrl. dist.) Calif., L.A., 1982—88; issues dir. Evan Bayh for Gov., Indpls., 1988; exec. asst. to gov. State of Ind., 1988—90; prosecutor Marion County, 1991—94; sr. counsel Ice Miller Donadio & Ryan, 1995—96; atty. gen. State of Ind., 1997—2000; dep. CEO, gen. counsel Dem. Nat. Conv., 2000; co-CEO TechNet, Palo Alto, Calif., 2000—; ptnr. Manatt Phelps & Phillips LLP. Chmn. Gov. Commn. for Drug Free Ind., Indpls., 1989—, Gov. Coun. on Impaired and Dangerous Driving, Indpls., 1989—; pres. Family Advocacy Ctr., Indpls., 1991—94, Hoosier Alliance Against Drugs, Indpls., 1993—96; dir. Cmty. Couns. of Indpls., 1991—93; chmn. Ind. Criminal Justice Inst., Indpls., 1989—90, dir., 1989—; vice chmn. Juvenile Justice and Youth Gang Study Com., Indpls., 1992—94; legal analyst Sta. WTHR-TV, Indpls., 1995—96. Author: Prosecutor's Perspective, 1991—94; editor-in-chief: Yale Jour. Internat. Law, 1980—81. Co-chair Ind. State Dem. Coordinated Campaign,

Indpls., 1996. Named Top Lawyer, Indpls. Monthly mag., 1993; named to Sagamore of Wabash, State of Ind., 1995; recipient Spl. Enforcement award, U.S. Customs, 1988, Child Safety Adv. award, Automotive Safety for Children, 1997, STAR Alliance Impact award, 1998, Spirit of Ind. award, Am. Lung Assn., 1999. Mem.: Indpls. Bar Assn., Ind. Bar Assn. Avocation: bicycling.

MOE, ROGER DEANE, state legislator, secondary education educator; b. Crookston, Minn., June 2, 1944; s. Melvin Truman and Matheldia (Njus) M.; m. Paulette Moe; four children. BS, Mayville State Coll., 1966; student, Moorhead State Coll., 1969, N.D. State U., 1970. Tchr. Ada (Minn.) H.S., 1966—; v.p. Coleman, Christison Advt. Agy.; mem. Minn. Senate from 2nd dist., St. Paul, 1970—. Chmn. rules and adminstrn. com., mem. ethics and campaign reform, edn., and higher edn. coms., Minn. State Senate. Ward del. Ada, Minn., 1970; state del. Minn. Dem.-Farmer-Labor Conv., 1970. Mem. NEA, Ada Edn. Assn., Jaycees. Office: RR 3 Box 86A Erskine MN 56535-9532 also: State Senate 208 Capitol 75 Constitution Ave Saint Paul MN 55155-1601

MOE, THOMAS O. lawyer; b. Des Moines, 1938; BA, U. Minn., 1960, LLB, 1963. Bar: Minn. 1963. Ptnr. Dorsey & Whitney LLP, Mpls., 1964-89, chmn., mng. ptnr., 1989-99, chmn., 1999—. Mem. Order of Coif. Office: Dorsey & Whitney 220 S 6th St Ste 2200 Minneapolis MN 55402-1498

MOEDDEL, CARL K. bishop; b. Cin., Dec. 28, 1937; Auxiliary bishop Archdiocese of Cin., 1993—. Office: 100 E 8th St Cincinnati OH 45202-2129

MOELLER, ROBERT JOHN, management consultant, consultant; b. Mpls., July 20, 1938; s. Ben G. and Catheryn D. M.; m. Sharon Lee Holmberg, Sept. 1, 1962; children: Mark Thomas (dec.), Maria Therese. BBA, U. Minn., 1962, MBA, 1965; grad. exec. mgmt. program, Columbia U., 1972; grad. exec. internat. mgmt., Mankato U., 1990. Asst. brand mgr. toiletries Procter & Gamble, Cin., 1965-68; group product mgr. No. div. Am. Can Co., Greenwich, Conn., 1968-71, dir. mktg. Dixie div., 1971-73; v.p. mktg. and sales Tonka Toy Co., Mpls., 1973-77, Toro Co., Mpls., 1977-79, v.p. gen. mgr. outdoor appliance div., 1979-80, v.p. gen. mgr. irrigation div., 1980-84, exec. v.p. internat. and irrigation div., 1984-88; pres., COO Mackay Envelope Corp., 1988-90; sr. v.p. mktg. meat sector Cargill, Inc., 1991-94; pres. Moeller Mgmt. Cons., 1992-98. Bd. dirs. Vista Info. Solutions. Chmn. 2002, Voyageur Outward Bound Sch., 1993-99; bd. dirs. State of Minn. Prison Industries, St. Paul, 1984—; commr. Chaska (Minn.) Planning Commn., 1988-98; pres. Dist. 112 Ednl. Found., Chaska, 1987-92; pres. Chaska Civic Theatre, 1978-80; chmn. S.W. Metro Transit Commn., 1998—, Jonathan Archtl. Rev. Commn., 1976-78, Mpls. United Way, 1997-98, bd. dirs., 1999-2002. With USN, 1955-61. Recipient Crystal Achievement award for human svcs. First Nat. Bank of Chaska, 1996. Avocations: skiing, sailing, tennis, music, golf.

MOEN, RODNEY CHARLES, state legislator, retired naval officer; b. Whitehall, Wis., July 26, 1937; s. Edwin O. and Tena A. (Gunderson) M.; m. Catherine Jean Wolfe, 1959; children: Scott A., Jon C. (dec.), Rodd M., Catherine J., Daniel M. Student, Syracuse U., 1964-65; BA, U. So. Calif., 1972; postgrad., Ball State U., 1975-76. Gen. mgr. We. Wis. Comm. Coop., Independence, 1976-83; mem. Wis. Senate from 31st dist., Madison, 1983—; chair health, utilities, vets. and mil. affairs com. Wis. Senate, 1983—, asst. majority leader. Contbg. editor Govt. Photography, 1970-74. Lt. USN, 1955-76, Vietnam. Home: 18775 Dewey St Whitehall WI 54773-0215 Office: State Capitol PO Box 7882 Madison WI 53707-7882

MOESER, ELLIOTT, principal; Prin. Nicolet High Sch., Glendale, Ill., 1990-97, dist. adminstr., 1990—. Recipient Blue Ribbon Sch. award, 1990-91. Office: Nicolet High Sch 6701 N Jean Nicolet Rd Glendale WI 53217-3799

MOESER, JAMES CHARLES, university chancellor, musician; b. Colorado City, Tex., Apr. 3, 1939; s. Charles Victor and Virginia (James) M.; m. Jesse Kaye Edwards, Jan. 26, 1963 (div. July 1984); children: James Christopher, Kathryn Carter; m. Susan Kay Smith Dickerson, June 21, 1987. B.Mus., U. Tex., 1961, M.M., 1964; postgrad. (Fulbright grantee), Hochschule fur Musik, Berlin, 1961-62; D.M.A. (Univ. fellow), U. Mich., 1966. Chmn. dept. organ, asst. prof. organ U. Kans., 1966-69, assoc. prof., 1969-74, prof., 1974-86, dean Sch. Fine Arts, 1975-86, Carl and Ruth Althaus disting. prof. organ, 1985-86; organist, choirmaster Plymouth Congl. Ch., Lawrence, Kans., 1967-86; organist nat. conf. Music Tchrs. Nat. Assn., Portland, Oreg., 1972, L.A., 1974; dean Coll. Arts and Architecture, Pa. State U., State College, 1986-96; chancellor U. Nebr., Lincoln, Nebr., 1996—2000, U.N.C. - Chapel Hill, Chapel Hill, NC, 2000—. Concert organist, on tour, W. Ger., 1977, Lisbon (Portugal) Festival, 1978, 81, recitals for, Musica Festiva da Costa Verde, Portugal, 1981; organist concerts, W. Ger., 1982, 86, 87; world premier Paul Creston's 3d Symphony for Organ and Orchestra, Kennedy Ctr., Washington, 1982. Bd. govs. Josephson Inst. Ethics; bd. trustees N.C. Symphony Soc., Inc., 2001—; mem. vis. com. Meml. Ch., Harvard U. Recipient Palmer Christian award U. Mich., 1981, Disting. Alumnus awrd Grad. Sch. U. Tex., 2001; Kent fellow Danforth Found.; Danforth Assoc. Mem. Am. Guild Organists (past dean chpt., nat. dir. student groups 1973-75, nat. chmn. com. on profl. edn. 1983— , chmn. 2d nat. conf. on organ pedagogy 1984, 3d nat. conf. 1986, v.p. 1986—). Episcopalian. Home: 1000 Raleigh Rd Chapel Hill NC 27517-4415 Office: UNC Office of the Chancellor PO Box 9100 Chapel Hill NC 27599-0001 E-mail: james_moeser@unc.edu.

MOFFATT, JOYCE ANNE, performing arts executive; b. Grand Rapids, Mich., Jan. 3, 1936; d. John Barnard and Ruth Lillian (Pellow) M. BA in Lit., U. Mich., 1957, MA in Theatre, 1960; HHD (hon.), Profl. Sch. Psychology, San Francisco, 1991. Stage mgr., lighting designer Off-Broadway plays; costume, lighting and set designer, stage mgr. stock cos., 1954-62; nat. subscription mgr. Theatre Guild/Am. Theatre Soc., N.Y.C., 1965-67; subscription mgr. Theatre, Inc.-Phoenix Theatre, 1963-67; cons. N.Y.C. Ballet and N.Y.C. Opera, 1967-70; asst. house mgr. N.Y. State Theater, 1970-72; dir. ticket sales City Ctr. of Music and Drama, Inc., N.Y.C., 1970-72; prodn. mgr. San Antonio's Symphony/Opera, 1973-75; gen. mgr. San Antonio Symphony/Opera, 1975-76, 55th St. Dance Theater Found., Inc., N.Y.C., 1976-77, Ballet Theatre Found., Inc./Am. Ballet Theatre, N.Y.C., 1977-81; v.p. prodn. Radio City Music Hall Prodns., Inc., 1981-83; artist-in-residence CCNY, 1981—; propr. mgmt. cons. firm for performing arts N.Y.C., 1983—; exec. dir. San Francisco Ballet Assn., 1987-93; mng. dir. Houston Ballet Assoc., 1993-95; gen. mgr. Chgo. Music and Dance Theater, Inc., 1995—. Cons. Ford Found., N.Y. State Coun. on Arts, Kennedy Ctr. for Performing Arts; mem. dance panels N.Y. State Coun. on Arts, 1979-81; mem. panels for Support to Prominent Orgns. and Dance, Calif. Arts Coun., 1988-92. Appointee San Francisco Cultural Affairs Task Force, 1991; chmn. bd. dirs. Tex. Inst. for Arts in Edn., 1994—; trustee Internat. Alliance of Theatrical Stage Employees Local 16 Pension and Welfare Fund, 1991-94; bd. dirs. Rudolf Nureyev Dance Found., Chgo., 1998—. Mem. Assn. Theatrical Press Agts. and Mgrs., Actors Equity Assn., United Scenic Artists Local 829, San Francisco Visitors and Conv. Bur. (bd. dirs.), Argyle Club (San Antonio). Office: Chicago Music & Dance Theater Mezz Level 203 N La Salle St Chicago IL 60601-1210

MOFFETT, DAVID MCKENZIE, bank executive; b. Daytona Beach, Fla., Feb. 22, 1952; s. James Denny Jr. and Dorothy McCall (McKenzie) M.; m. Cynthia Ann Daugherty, Aug. 25, 1973 (div. Oct. 1977); m. Katherine Ann Martin, May 26, 1979; children: Jeffrey Martin, Layne McCall, Hilary Marie. BA, Okla. U., 1974; MBA, So. Meth. U., 1975; grad. Stonier Sch. Banking, Rutgers U., 1981. Planning analyst First Nat. Bank & Trust Co., Tulsa, 1975-76, fin. analyst, 1978, v.p., 1978-80, sr. v.p., 1981-86, exec. v.p., 1987—; CFO Firstar Corp., Milw.; CFO, chmn. U.S. Bancorp (formerly Firstar Corp.), Minneapolis, 2001—. Faculty grad. sch. banking U. Wis., 1986; adj. prof. U. Tulsa. Bd. dirs. Leadership Tulsa, Inc., 1985-87, Arts & Humanities Council, Tulsa, 1986, Salvation Army, 1986, St. John's Episc. Ch., Tulsa, 1987. Recipient Chmn.'s award bd. dirs. First Nat. Bank, 1980. Mem. Nat. Asset/Liability Mgmt. Assn. (charter), Bank Adminstrn. Inst. (treasury mgmt. com. 1984, investment banking com. 1987). Republican. Episcopalian. Clubs: Tulsa, Cedar Ridge Country (Tulsa). Avocations: running, golf, skiing, scuba diving, bicycling. Office: US Bancorp US Bank Pl 601 2nd Ave S Minneapolis MN 55402

MOFFITT, DONALD L. state legislator; b. Knox County, Feb. 18, 1947; s. Russell Wellington and Gertrude (Johnson) M.; m. Carolyn J. Lock; children: Linda J., Justin L., Amanda H. BS, U. Ill., 1969. Tchr.; Dist. 94 rep. Ill. Ho. Reps., Springfield, 1993—; treas. West Ill. Police Tng. Orgn. Mem. Knox County bd., 1978-84, chmn. 1982-84, treas. 1984-93; mem. Agr. Housing and Edn. Com. Ill. Ho. Reps., 1993—; sec. Agr. and Edn. Twp. and County Com., 1995—. Mem. Carver Cmty. Action Agy. Recipient Friend of Agr. award Ill. Farm Bur., 1994—. Mem. Ill. Farm Bur., Lions Club, Masons, Alpha Zeta, Omicron Delta Kappa. Address: RR 1 Box 160 Gilson IL 61436-9707 Also: 5 Weinberg Arcade Galesburg IL 61401

MOGERMAN, SUSAN, state agency administrator; Dir. State of Ill. Historic Preservation Agy., Springfield. Office: State Ill-Hist Preservation Agy 500 E. Madison Springfield IL 62701-1028

MOGK, JOHN EDWARD, law educator, association executive, consultant; b. Detroit, Feb. 10, 1939; s. Clifford Anthony and Evelyn Lenore (Paselk) M.; m. Lylas Heidi Good, Aug. 23, 1964; children: Marja, Tenley, Matthew. BBA, U. Mich., 1961, JD with distinction, 1964; diploma in comparative law, U. Stockholm, 1965. Bar: N.Y. 1966, Mich. 1970. Assoc. atty. Shearman & Sterling, N.Y.C., 1964-68; mem. faculty Wayne State U. Sch. Law, 1968—, dir. grad. studies, 1990-95. Pres. MERRA Rsch. Corp., 1974-94; cons. econ. and urban devel., arbitrator; vis. prof. U. Utrecht, The Netherlands, 2000. Editor Michigan International Lawyer and Utilities Law Rev.; contbr. articles to profl. jours. Chmn. Mich. TOP Task Force, 1972; vice chmn. Mich. Constrn. Code Commn., 1973; mem. exec. com. Southeastern Mich. Coun. Govts., 1970; chmn. Detroit Sch. Boundary Commn., 1970, Downtown Detroit Vacant Bldg. Com., 1991-93; mem. Detroit Bd. Edn., 1970; mgr. Detroit Empowerment Zone Proposal, 1994; project exec. New Detroit Stadium, 1995; pres. Habitat for Humanity Detroit, 1999. Named Outstanding Contbr. Internat. Law Sect., State Bar of Mich., 2001, Outstanding Wayne State U. Assoc. Prof., 1971, Outstanding Wayne Law Sch. Prof., 1977, 83, 93, 97, Outstanding Young Man in Detroit, 1972, One of Ten Outstanding Young Men in U.S., 1973, One of Four Outstanding Vols. in U.S., 1974; recipient Presdl. citation Wayne State U., 1977, State of Mich., 1988, 94; Am.-Scandinavian fellow, 1965; vis. fellow U. Warwick, Eng., 1985-86. Mem. ABA, Mich. Bar Assn. (Outstanding Achievement award Internat. Law Sect. 2001), Assn. of Bar of City of N.Y. Home: 1000 Yorkshire Rd Grosse Pointe Park MI 48230-1432

MOHAN, JOHN J. lawyer; b. St. Louis, May 22, 1945; s. John Joseph and Virginia Loretta (Durkin) M.; m. Elaine Bronwyn Lipe, May 29, 1982; children: Bryn Elizabeth, John Burke. BS Indsl. Engring., St. Louis U., Sch. Engring. and Earth Scis., 1967; JD, St. Louis U., 1971. Bar: Mo. 1971, Ill. 1971, U.S. Dist. Ct. (we. dist.) Mo. 1971, U.S. Dist. Ct. (ea. dist.) Mo. 1980, U.S. Dist. Ct. (so. dist.) Ill. 1981, U.S. Ct. Appeals (8th cir.) 1987. Asst. prosecuting atty. St. Louis County, 1971-72; asst. cir. atty. St. Louis Cir. Atty's. Office, 1972-74; spl. asst. state's atty. St. Clair County Atty's. Office, Belleville, Ill., 1974—; assoc. Lashley, Caruthers, Theis, Rava & Hamel, St. Louis, 1979-80; ptnr. Schreiber, Tueth & Mohan, Clayton, Mo., 1981-83, Danis, Reid, Murphy, Tobben, Schreiber & Mohan, Ladue, 1983-87, Hinshaw & Culbertson, St. Louis, 1987-97, Blackwell, Sanders, Peper, Martin, St. Louis, 1998-2000, Mickes, Tueth, Keeney, Cooper, Mohan & Jackstadt, P.C., 2000—. Mem. U. Mo. Law Sch. Found. Scholarship. Mem. ABA, Am. Arbitration Assn. (cert. mediator, arbitrator 1988—), Ill. State Bar Assn., Mo. Bar, Bar Assn. Met. St. Louis, St. Clair County Bar, St. Louis County Bar, Def. Rsch. Inst., Mo. Orgn. Def. Lawyers, Pinnacle Arbitration and Mediation Svcs. (cert. mediator, arbitrator 1997—), Phi Delta Phi. Home: 529 Big Horn Basin Ct Wildwood MO 63011-4818 Office: Mickes Tueth Keeney Cooper Mohan Jackstadt PC 425 S Woods Mill Rd Ste 300 Saint Louis MO 63017

MOHAN, KSHITIJ, healthcare company executive; b. India, Jan. 26, 1945; came to U.S., 1965; B in Physics, Patna U., India; M in Physics, U. Colo.; D in Physics, Georgetown U. Various positions U.S. FDA; with White House Office of Mgmt. and Budget; v.p., corp. regulatory affairs Baxter Healthcare, Deerfield, Ill., 1988-90, v.p., scientific affairs for I.V. systems, 1990-95, corp. v.p. rsch. and tech. svcs., 1995—. Bd. dirs. KeraVision, Inc., others; chair Baxter Worldwide Tech. Coun. Mem. Health Industry Mfrs. Assn. (bd. dirs.). Office: Baxter Healthcare One Baxter Pkwy Deerfield IL 60015-4633

MOHIUDDIN, SYED MAQDOOM, cardiologist, educator; b. Hyderabad, India, Nov. 14, 1934; came to U.S., 1961, naturalized, 1976; s. Syed Nizamuddin and Amat-Ul-Butool Mahmoodi; m. Ayesha Sultana Mahmoodi, July 16, 1961; children: Sameena J., Syed R., Kulsoom S. MB, BS, Osmania U., 1960; MS, Creighton U., Omaha, 1967; DSc, Laval U., Que., Can., 1970. Diplomate Am. Bd. Internal Medcine (cardiovascular disease). Intern Altoona (Pa.) Gen. Hosp., 1961-62; resident in cardiology Creighton Meml. Hosp., also St. Joseph Hosp., Omaha, 1963-65, mem. staff, 1965—; prof. adjoint Laval U. Med. Sch., 1970; practice medicine specializing in cardiology Omaha, 1970—; prof. Creighton U. Med. Sch., 1977—, assoc. dir. div. cardiology, 1983-96; prof. pharmacy practice Creighton U. Sch. Pharmacy, 1986—; dir divsn. cardiology, 1996—; assoc. chair for acad. affairs dept. medicine, 1998—. Cons. Omaha VA Hosp. Rsch. fellow Med. Rsch. Coun. Can., 1968; grantee Med. Rsch. Coun. Can., 1970; grantee NIH, 1973. Fellow ACP, Am. Coll. Cardiology (gov. for Nebr. 1987-90), Am. Coll. Clin. Pharmacology, Am. Coll. Chest Physicians; mem. AAAS, Am. Heart Assn. (fellow coun. clin. cardiology, bd. dirs. 1973-75), Am. Fedn. Clin. Rsch., Nebr. Heart Assn. (chmn. rsch. com. 1974-76, dir. 1973—), Gt. Plains Heart Com. (Nebr. rep. 1976-84, pres. 1977-78), N.Y. Acad. Scis., Nebr. Cardiovascular Soc. (pres. 1980-81). Democrat. Islam. Home: 12531 Shamrock Rd Omaha NE 68154-3529 Office: Cardiac Ctr Creighton U 3006 Webster St Omaha NE 68131-2027

MOHLER, STANLEY ROSS, physician, educator; b. Amarillo, Tex., Sept. 30, 1927; s. Norton Harrison and Minnie Alice (Ross) M.; m. Ursula Luise Burkhardt, Jan. 24, 1953; children: Susan Luise, Stanley Ross, Mark Hallock. BA, MA, U. Tex., 1953, MD, 1956. Diplomate Am. Bd. Preventive Medicine. Intern USPHS Hosp., San Francisco, 1956-57; med. officer Center Aging Research, NIH, Bethesda, Md., 1957-61; dir. Civil Aeromed. Rsch. Inst., FAA, Oklahoma City, 1961-66, chief aeromed. applications divsn. Washington, 1966-78; prof., vice chmn. dept. community medicine, dir. aerospace medicine Wright State U. Sch. Medicine, Dayton, Ohio, 1978—. Rsch. assoc. prof. preventive medicine and pub. health U. Okla. Med. Sch., 1961—; vice-chmn. Am. Bd. Preventive Medicine, 1978—, sec.-treas., 1980—. Co-editor: Space Biology and Medicine (5 vols.), 1995 (Life Scis. Book award Internat. Acad. Astronautics); contbr. articles to profl. jours. Bd. dirs. Sr. Citizens Assn. Oklahoma City, 1962— , Flying Physicians Assn., 1961—. Served with AUS, 1946-48. Recipient Gail Borden Rsch. award, Boothby award Aerospace Med. Assn., 1966, FAA Meritorious Svc. award, 1974, Cecil A. Brownlow Publ. award Flight Safety Found., 1998; co-recipient Life Scis. Book award in space, biology and medicine Internat. Acad. Astronautics, 1995. Fellow Geriatrics Soc., Aerospace Med. Assn. (pres. 1983, Harry G. Moseley award 1974, Lyster award 1984, Louis H. Bauer Founders award 1998), Am. Coll. Preventive Medicine, Gerontol. Soc.; mem. AMA, Aircraft Owners and Pilots Assn. (Sharples award 1984, Hubertus Strughold award 1991), Alpha Omega Alpha. Home: 6539 Reigate Rd Dayton OH 45459-3214 Office: Wright State U Sch Medicine PO Box 927 Dayton OH 45401-0927

MOHN, MELVIN PAUL, anatomist, educator; b. Cleve., June 19, 1926; s. Paul Melvin and Julia (Jacobik) M.; m. Audrey Faye Lonergan, June 28, 1952; children— Shorey Faye, Andrew Paul A.B., Marietta Coll., 1950; Sc.M., Brown U., 1952, Ph.D. in Biology, 1955. Instr. SUNY Downstate Med. Ctr., Bklyn., 1955-59, asst. prof., 1959-63; asst. prof. anatomy U. Kans. Sch. Medicine, Kansas City, 1963-65, assoc. prof., 1965-72, prof., 1972-89, prof. emeritus, 1989—. Cons. Nat. Med. Audiovisual Ctr., Atlanta, 1972; vis. lectr. U. Miami Sch. Medicine, Fla., 1966. Bd. dirs. U. Kans. Med. Ctr. Credit Union, 1968-77, Kansas City Youth Symphony, 1972-77; mem. U.S. Pony Club, 1964-71, Med. Arts Symphony, 1965-71, 90—, Spring Hill Chorale, 1990—. Served with USN, 1944-46, PTO. McCoy fellow, 1950, Arnold biology fellow, 1954 Fellow AAAS; mem. Am. Soc. Zoologists, Am. Assn. Anatomists, Am. Inst. Biol. Sci., Phi Beta Kappa, Sigma Xi, Beta Beta Beta. Republican. Methodist. Club: Lions, Rotary, Lodge: Masons. Home: Yankee Bit Farm 23595 W 223rd St Spring Hill KS 66083-4029 Office: U Kans Med Ctr Dept Anatomy 39th and Rainbow St Kansas City KS 66103

MOHR, L. THOMAS, newspaper executive; b. Endicott, N.Y., Dec. 25, 1955; s. Lionel Charles and Anne (Tredwell) M.; m. Pageen Rogers, July 13, 1985; children: Mary Catherine, Jack. BA with honors, Queens U., Kingston, Ont., Can., 1979; MBA, U. Calif., Berkeley, 1987. Gen. mgr. Foster City (Calif.) Progress, 1981-82; classified advt. mgr. Peninsula Times Tribune, Palo Alto, Calif., 1982-85, mktg. mgr., 1985-86, advt. sales dir., 1986-87; dir. mktg. and advt. sales Bakersfield Californian, 1987-90; classified advt. dir. Star Tribune, Mpls., 1990-93, v.p., 1993-96, sr. v.p., gen. mgr., 1996-98, sr. v.p. mktg., 1998—. Chmn. bd. Cookie Cart; bd. dirs. Children's Theatre. Mem. Newspaper Assn. Am. (bd. dirs. mktg. com. 1997—, bd. dir. display fedn. 1997—). Republican. Roman Catholic. Avocations: running, tennis, golf, cross country skiing. Office: Star Tribune 425 Portland Ave Minneapolis MN 55488-0002 Home: 612 Post Oak Cir Brentwood TN 37027-5189

MOHR, TERRENCE B. food company executive; With Quaker Oats Co., Chgo., 1987—, sr. v.p. customer orgn., 1997—. Office: Quaker Oats Co 321 N Clark St Ste Ll2 Chicago IL 60610-4790

MOHS, FREDERIC EDWARD, lawyer; b. Madison, Wis., Mar. 16, 1937; s. Frederic E. and Mary Ellen Reynolds M.; m. Mary M. Mohs, June 14, 1959; children: Paula A., Nicole L. BS, U. Wis., 1959, JD, 1964. Bar: Wis. 1964. Assoc. Axley, Brynelson, Madison, Wis., 1964-67; ptnr. Mohs, MacDonald, Widder & Maradise, 1967—. Bd. dirs. U. Wis. Hosps. and Clinics, Madison, 1998—, Madison Gas and Electric Co., Madison, 1975—. Regent U. Wis., Madison, 1997—. Mem. Downtown Madison Rotary. Republican. Office: Mohs MacDonald Widder & Paradise 20 N Carroll St Madison WI 53703 E-mail: fred@mmwp-law.com.

MOLARO, ROBERT S, state legislator, lawyer; b. Chgo., June 29, 1950; BS, Loyola U.; JD, John Marshall Law Sch. Dist. 12 senator Ill. Senate, Springfield, 1993—. Del. Dem. Nat. Conv. 1988. Home: 2650 W 51st St Chicago IL 60632-1560

MOLDENHAUER, JUDITH A. graphic design educator; b. Oak Park, Ill., Feb. 28, 1951; d. Raymond L. and Jean Marie (Carqueville) M. BFA, U. Ill., 1973; MA, Stanford U., 1974; MFA, U. Wis., 1977. Design supr. N.E. Mo. State U., Kirksville, Mo., 1977-79; asst. prof. design, design dept. Kans. City Art Inst., 1979-83; asst. prof. art, graphic design Sch. Art U. Mich., Ann Arbor, 1983-92; vis. lectr. Wayne State U., 1990-92, asst. prof. graphic design, 1992-98, assoc. prof. graphic design, 1998—, area coord. graphic design, 1992—. Free-lance designer The Detroit Inst. Arts, Toledo (Ohio) Mus. Art, Burroughs Corp. (Unisys) Detroit, Detroit Focus Gallery; vis. designer N.S. Coll. Art and Design, 1986; juror Ohio Mus. Assn., 1986, Collaborator Presdl. Initiative "Healthy Start": prenatal and pre-conceptional booklets and ednl. modules designs, 1992—; presenter 8th Internat. Congress Women's Health Issues, U. Sask., 1997, 9th Internat. Congress on Women's Health Issues, Alexandria, Egypt, 1998, Internat. Inst. Info. Design, Schwarzenberg, Austria, 1998, Read Me exhbn., Bern, Switzerland, 1999, Expert Forum Manual Design, Malardalen U., Eskilstuna, Sweden, 2000; co-prin. investigator FIPSE grantee Dept. Edn., 2000; participant Read Me exhbn., Winterthur, Switzerland, 1999, 19th Biennale Graphic Design, Brno, Czech Rep., Nat. Inst. Design, Ahmenbad, India, 2000. Contbr. articles to profl. jours. Recipient award of distinction, merit award Am. Assn. Museums, 1985, 86, Excellence Design award Beckett Paper Co., 1991, gold award for softcover books Printing & Pub. Competition, 1994, Am. Graphic Design award, 1996, 98; Rackham grantee U. Mich., 1987, grantee Nat. Endowment for Arts, 1988. Mem. Am. Ctr. Design, Univ. and Coll. Designers Assn. (merit award 1979, gold award 1979), Coll. Art Assn. (chmn. panel 1991), Women's Caucus for Art (panel chmn. 1987), Amnesty Internat., Women in Design (excellence award Chgo. 1985, Sierra Club, Audubon Soc. Lutheran. Office: Wayne State U Dept Art and Art History 150 Art Bldg Detroit MI 48202 E-mail: FrogBoddg@aol.com.

MOLDENHAUER, WILLIAM CALVIN, soil scientist; b. New Underwood, S.D., Oct. 27, 1923; s. Calvin Fred and Ida (Killam) M.; m. Catherine Ann Maher, Nov. 26, 1947; children— Jean Ann, Patricia, Barbara, James, Thomas B.S., S.D. State U., 1949; M.S., U. Wis., 1951, Ph.D., 1956. Soil surveyor S.D. State U., Brookings, 1948-54; soil scientist U.S. Dept. Agr., Big Spring, Tex., 1954-57, soi. scientist Ames, Iowa, 1957-72, Morris, Minn., 1972-75; rsch. leader Nat. Soil Erosion Rsch. Lab., Agrl. Rsch. Svc. U.S. Dept. Agr., West Lafayette, Ind., 1975-85; prof. dept. agronomy Purdue U., 1975-85, prof. emeritus, 1985—. Contbr. articles to profl. jours. Served with U.S. Army, 1943-46 Fellow Am. Soc. Agronomy, Soil Sci. Soc., Soil Conservation Soc. Am. (pres. 1979), World Assn. Soil and Water Conservation (pres. 1983-85, exec. sec. 1985—). Home and Office: 317 Marvin Ave Volga SD 57071-2011

MOLER, DONALD LEWIS, educational psychology educator; b. Wilsey, Kans., Jan. 12, 1918; s. Ralph Lee and Bessie Myrtle (Berry) M.; B.S., Kans. State Tchrs. Coll., Emporia, 1939; M.S., U. Kans., Lawrence, 1949, Ph.D., 1951; m. Alta Margaret Ansdell, Nov. 6, 1942; 1 son, Donald Lewis Jr. Tchr., Centralia (Kans.) High Sch., 1939-42, Carthage (Mo.) High Sch., 1946-48; asst. dir. Reading Clinic, U. Kans., 1948-51; dir. reading program Ea. Ill. U., 1951-70, prof. dept. ednl. psychology and guidance, 1963— , chmn. dept., 1963-84, dean Sch. Edn., 1980; vis. scholar U. Fla., 1965. Served with Signal Corps, U.S. Army, 1942-46. Recipient C.A. Michelman award, 1974; Disting Svc. award Ill. Assn. Counselor Educators, 1985. Mem. Ill. Guidance and Pers. Assn. (pres. 1968-69), Ill. Counselor Educators and Suprs., Ill. Coll. Pers. Assn., Am. Pers. and Guidance Assn. (senator 1970-71), Assn. Counselor Edn. and Supervision, Assn. Humanistic Edn. and Devel., Phi Delta Kappa, Xi Phi, Pi Omega Pi, Pi Kappa

Delta, Sigma Tau Gamma. Methodist. Assoc. editor Ill. Guidance and Pers. Assn. Quar., 1970-84, mng. editor, 1984— . Home: 407 W Hayes Ave Charleston IL 61920-3303 Office: Ea Ill U Dept Ednl Psychology and Guidance Charleston IL 61920

MOLFENTER, DAVID P. former electronics executive; b. 1945; Former CEO Hughes Def. Comm., Fort Wayne, Ind.; now v.p. Raytheon Sys., 1995—. Office: Raytheon Sys 1010 Production Rd Fort Wayne IN 46808-4106

MOLIERE, JEFFREY MICHAEL, cardiopulmonary administrator; b. San Pedro, Calif., Nov. 22, 1948; s. Dwight Hedrick and Geraldine Stabile. AA, L.A. Harbor Coll., 1968; postgrad., Calif. State U., Long Beach, 1968-69; cert. in respiratory care, Calif. Coll. for Health Sci., 1982, Biosystems Inst., 1984; assoc. degree, Ind. U., Indpls., 1987, B in Gen. Studies, 1990; MS in Cmty. Health Adminstrn., Calif. Coll. for Health Sci., 1994; postgrad., So. Calif. U. for Profl. Study. Registered respiratory therapist, respiratory care practitioner; cert. pulmonary tech. Nat. Inst. Occupl. Safety and Health; cert. advanced cardiac and basic life support instr., neonatal advanced life support; cert. disability analyst, diplomate Am. Bd. Disability Analysts. Alt. supr. Good Samaritan Hosp., Vincennes, Ind., 1976-79; critical care technician Winona Meml. Hosp., Indpls., 1979-80; neonatal ICU-critical care technician Mercy Hosp., Urbana, Ill., 1980-82; cardio-pulmonary supr. Winona Meml. Hosp., Indpls., 1982-92; dir. pulmonary svcs. MidWest Med. Ctr., 1992-93; mgr., bronchoscopy, pulmonary function testing, respiratory care VA Med. Ctr., 1993-96, ednl. coord., EEO counselor, 1993-96; mgr. cardiopulmonary, neurology, Sleep/Wake Ctr. Cmty. Hosps., 1996—, dir. Respiratory Care Tutorial Ctr. Mem. adj. faculty Ind. Vocat.-Tech. Coll., 1993—, Calif. Coll. Health Scis., Southern Calif. U. for Profl. Studies, 2001; adv. bd. Allied Health Ind. U., 1995—. Mem. adv. bd. Allied Health Ind. Vocat. Tech. Coll., 1987—. Mem. Nat. Bd. Respiratory Care (panel of cons. to exam. com.), Am. Assn. for Respiratory Care (clin. practice guideline rev. bd.), Ind. Soc. for Respiratory Care, Nat. Bd. for Respiratory Care, Am. Bd. Disability Analysts (charter, diplomate, sr. disability analyst), Alpha Sigma Lambda (charter, Membership award 1990).

MOLINARI, MARCO, marketing executive; b. Stockholm, Sept. 15, 1969; m. Lisa Molinari; 2 children. Degree in mktg., St. Louis U.; M in Internat. Bus., Thunderbird U. Formerly with mktg. and sales, various mgmt. positions Goodyear Tire & Rubber Co., Stockholm, past mng. dir. England, past regional mktg. dir. Ohio, v.p. sales and mktg. N.Am. Tires, 1996—. Office: Goodyear Tire & Rubber Co 1144 E Market St Akron OH 44316-0002

MOLITOR, PAUL LEO, professional baseball coach; b. St. Paul, Aug. 22, 1956; m. Linda Kaplan; 1 child, Blaire. Student, U. Minn., 1975-77. Baseball player Milw. Brewers, 1978-92, Toronto Blue Jays, 1992-95, Minnesota Twins, Mpls., 1996-98, coach, 1999—. Mem. Am. League All-Star Team, 1980, 85, 88, 91-94. Named Am. League Rookie of Yr. Sporting News, 1978, Sporting News Coll. All-America Team, 1977; recipient Silver Slugger award, 1987, 88, 93, World Series MVP award, 1993, Midwest League MVP award. Office: Hubert H Humphrey Metrodome Minnesota Twins 34 Kirby Puckett Pl Minneapolis MN 55415-1523

MOLITORIS, BRUCE ALBERT, nephrologist, educator; b. Springfield, Ill., June 26, 1951; s. Edward and Joyce (Tomasko) M.; m. Karen Lynn Wichterman, June 16, 1973; children: Jason, Jared, Julie. BS, U. Ill., 1973, MS in Nutrition, 1975; MD, Wash. U., 1979. Resident Sch. Medicine U. Colo., Denver, 1979-81, nephrology fellow, 1981-84, asst. prof. medicine, 1984-88, assoc. prof. medicine, 1988-93, prof., 1993; dir. nephrology Ind. U. Med. Sch., Indpls., 1993—; vis. scientist U. Colo., MCDB, Boulder, 1989-90, Max Planck Inst., Federal Republic of Germany, 1984-85. NIH reviewer, 1991-94; dir. home dialysis Denver VA Ctr., 1984-93; vis. scientist dept. molecular biology Colo. State U., Ft. Collins, 1998. Mem. editl. bd. Am. Jour. Physiology, 1989—, Am. Jour. Kidney Diseases, 1991, Am. Jour. Kidney Disease, 1996; assoc. editor Jour. Investigative Medicine, 1994-99; contbr. articles to profl. jours. Pres. Cherry Creek Village South Homeowners Assn., 1989-90, Pickwick Commons Home Owners Assn., 1999; v.p. Our Father Luth. Ch., Denver, 1989-90; coun. mem. King of Glory Luth. Ch., Indpls., 1999-2002; coach Cherry Creek Soccer Assn., Greenwood Village, 1988-91, Centennial Little League Titans Basketball; bd. dirs. CSSA, 1993. Recipient Upjohn Achievement award, 1979, Liberty Hyde Bailey award, 1973. Mem. Am. Assn. Physicians, Am. Soc. Nephrology (program chmn. 2003), Internat. Soc. Nephrology, N.Y. Acad. Sci., Am. Soc. Clin. Investigation, Am. Fedn. for Clin. Rsch. (nat. counselor 1991-94), Western Assn. Physicians. Avocations: bridge, fishing, antiques, hiking. Office: Indiana Univ Med Ctr Fesler Hall 115 1120 South Dr Indianapolis IN 46202-5135 E-mail: bmolitor@iupui.edu.

MOLL, CURTIS E. manufacturing executive; b. 1933; Diploma, Wesleyan Coll., 1961, So. Meth. U., 1963. Chmn., CEO MTD Products Inc. Office: MTD Products Inc PO Box 368022 Cleveland OH 44136-9722

MOLL, JOSEPH EUGENE, chemical engineer, chemical company executive; b. Evansville, Ind., Sept. 3, 1950; s. Jacob Eugene and Mary Ann (Zenthoefer) M., m. Karen Jean Pennington, Aug. 20. 1977; children: Laura, Angela, Jared. BS in Chem. Engring., Purdue U., 1972. Cert. ofcl. USS Swimming. Mem. mfg. mgmt. staff GE, Selkirk, Danville, N.Y., Ill, 1972-74, product devel. engr. Pittsfield, Mass., 1974-75; tech. specialist Betz Labs., Kokomo, Ind., 1975-78, account mgr. Evansville, 1978-88; account exec. GE Betz, 1988-90; area mgr. Betz Dearborn divsn. Hercules Corp., 1990—. Mem. Mayor's Tech. Adv. Com., Mt. Vernon, Ind., 1983—Instr. ARC, Evansville, 1971-73; ofcl. Ill. High Sch. Assn., Danville, 1972-73; min. of the word St. Matthew's Ch., Mt. Vernon, Ind., 1980—; amb. Promise Keepers Men's Ministry, 1994—, Sunday sch. tchr., 1996—; asst. cubmaster Boy Scouts Am., 1993-96, asst. scoutmaster, 1997—. Mem. AICE (v.p. 1971-72), Tech. Assn. of Pulp and Paper Industry, Am. Water Works Assn., Purdue Alumni Assn. (life), John Purdue Coaches Club, Elks, Omega Chi Epsilon, Triangle Fraternity. Roman Catholic. Avocations: golf, weight tng., swimming, bible study group. Home and Office: 28 Parkridge Dr Mount Vernon IN 47620-9405 E-mail: joe.e.moll@betzdearborn.com.

MOLL, RUSSELL ADDISON, aquatic ecologist, science administrator; b. Bound Brook, N.J., Aug. 12, 1946; s. Addison and Celeste (Carrier) M. PhD, SUNY, Stony Brook, 1974; MS, U. Mich., 1983. Rsch. assoc. Brookhaven Nat. Lab., Upton, N.Y., 1972-74; rsch. investigator U. Mich., Ann Arbor, 1974-76, asst. rsch. scientist, 1976-81, assoc. rsch. scientist, 1981—; asst. dir. Mich. Sea Grant, 1988—; dir. Coop. Inst. Limnology and Ecosystems Rsch., U. Mich., 1989—. Univ. rep. Mich. Aquatic Scis. Consortium, 1989—; cons. Applied Scis. Assocs., Narragansett, R.I., 1988. Contbr. articles to profl. jours. Recipient numerous rsch. grants including NOAA, EPA, NSF, NASA, Agy. Internat. Devel. Mem. AAAS, Am. Soc. Limnology and Oceanography, Ecol. Soc. Am., Oceanographic Soc. Achievements include research in study of phytoplankton and bacteria dynamics in Great Lakes, effects of toxic materials on phytoplankton and bacteria, and ecological analysis of a large river and estuary in West Africa.

MOLL, WILLIAM GENE, broadcasting company executive; b. Sikeston, Mo., Dec. 25, 1937; s. John Alexander and Letha Ann (McDowell) M.; m. Marilyn Lewis, Aug. 2, 1957; children: David William, Craig Lewis. Student, So. Ill. U., 1955-57, Anderson Coll., 1957-58; B.S. in Edn., S.E. Mo. State Coll., 1960; M.A., U. Tex., 1963. Announcer, program dir. Sta. KSIM, Sikeston, Mo., 1954-57, 58-59; announcer Sta. WCBC, Anderson, Ind., 1957; announcer, writer, dir., news anchor KFVS-TV, Cape Girardeau, Mo., 1959-62; producer, dir., writer KLRN-TV, Austin, Tex., 1962-64, mgr. sta. ops. San Antonio, 1964-69; v.p., gen. mgr. WSMW-TV, Worcester, Mass., 1969-72; with KENS-TV, San Antonio, 1972-87, pres., gen. mgr., 1977-81, chmn., 1981-87; pres., chief exec. officer Harte-Hanks TV Group, 1979-81, Harte-Hanks Broadcasting & Entertainment, 1981-87, chmn. TV group, 1981—; sr. v.p. Harte-Hanks Communications, Inc., 1981-87. Pres. WNBC-TV, N.Y.C., 1989-92, WKRC-TV, Cin., 1992—. Bd. dirs. San Antonio Art Inst., 1974—, chmn., 1978-81; bd. dirs. Goodwill Industries, 1973-87, pres., 1987-88; bd. dirs. San Antonio Symphony Soc., 1979-85, United Way San Antonio, 1979-82, Friends of the McNay, 1979-81, Media-Advt. Partnership for Drug-Free Am., 1987—; pres., chmn. Dan Beard Coun. Boy Scouts of Am., Cin., 1996—. Mem. Tex. Assn. Broadcasters (dir. 1976—, sec.-treas. 1981—, pres. 1983), TV Bur. of Advt. (bd. dirs. 1980—, sec. 1981-83, chmn. 1983-85, pres./chief exec. officer 1987-89), CBS TV Affiliates Assn. (bd. dirs. 1980-83), Internat. Radio TV Found. (bd. dirs. 1985-88), Advt. Council (bd. dirs. 1987-89), Electronic Media Rating Council (bd. dirs. 1987-89). Clubs: Torch (San Antonio), Giraud (San Antonio); Oak Hills Country. Office: WKRC-TV 1906 Highland Ave Cincinnati OH 45219-3104

MOLLER, JAMES HERMAN, physician, pediatrician educator; b. Fresno, Calif., Aug. 12, 1933; s. Leonard Hansen and Eloise Jean (Hunter) M.; m. Carol Suzanne Eymann, Sept. 8, 1957; children: James, Elizabeth. AB, Stanford U., 1954, MD, 1958. Instr. pediatrics U. Minn., Mpls., 1965-66, asst. prof., 1966-70, assoc. prof., 1970-73, prof., 1973—, Dwan prof., 1975—, interim head pediatrics, 1976-78, 97-99, chief pediatrics, 1976-78; head pediatrics, 1999—; chief of staff U. Minn. Hosp., 1984-89. Vis. prof. Nat. Heart & Lung Inst., London, 1989-90, Inst. Child HEalth, London, 1989-90. Bd. dirs. U. Minn. Hosp., 1984-89, Mpls. Children's Health Ctr., Mpls., 1975-78, Children's Hosp., St. Paul, 1975-78, Minn. Assn. Pub. teaching Hosps., Mpls., 1984-89, Variety Club Heart Assn., Mpls., 1980-83. Capt. U.S. Army, 1961-63. Fellow Am. Acad. Pediatrics (exec. bd. 1991-92, dist. chmn. 1991-92, alternate dist. chmn. 1985-91, Ross Edn. award 1989), Am. Coll. Cardiology; mem. Am. Heart Assn. (pres. 1993-94, v.p. 1986-91, bd. dirs. 1986-95, award of Merit 1989), Am. Fedn. Clin. Rsch., Am. Pediatric Soc., Am. Bd. Pediatrics, Nat. Bd. Med. Examiners, Midwest Soc. Pediatric Cardiology Soc., Minn. Med. Assn. (interspeciality coun. 1979-82, resource group child health 1980-82), Minn. Acad. Medicine, Mpls. Met. Pediatric Soc, No. Pediatric Cardiology Soc. (pres. 1978-79), Midwest Soc. Pediatric Rsch.. Soc. Pediatric Rsch., Hennepin County Med. Soc. (bd. dirs. 1986—), Irish Am. Paediactric Soc., British Paediactric Cardiac Assn.; Coun. Med. Specialty Socs. (bd. dirs., 1991—), Sub-bd. Pediatric Cardiology (chmn. 1992—), Internam. Heart Found. (pres. 1997-98), World Heart Fedn. (bd. dirs. 1999). Independent. Congregationalist. Avocations: gardening, travel, oriental carpets, reading. Home: 4816 Sheridan Ave S Minneapolis MN 55410-1917 Office: U Minn 420 Delaware St SE Minneapolis MN 55455-0374

MOLNAR, DONALD JOSEPH, landscape architecture educator; b. Springfield, Ill., Dec. 24, 1938; s. Joseph and Mabel Irene (Woods) M.; m. Carol Jeanette Smith, Aug. 22, 1958; children: Elaina Deanne, Amy Lynn, Holly Suzanne. BFA in Landscape Architecture, U. Ill., 1960, MFA in Landscape Architecture, 1964. Landscape architect Simonds and Simonds, Pitts., 1961-63; landscape architect campus planning U. Ill., Urbana, 1963-72, asst. dir., planner capital programs Urbana and Chgo., 1971-81; assoc. prof. landscape architecture Purdue U., West Lafayette, Ind., 1981-85, dir. landscape architecture coop. program, 1983—, prof. landscape architecture, 1985—, chair landscape architecture program, 1987—, dir. internat. exch. landscape architecture, 1988—. Cons. to architect, engrs., park agys., 1964—, Mobile Homes Mfrs. Assn., Chgo., 966-76; prin. Profl. Searches for Landscape Archs., employment cons., 2000—. Author: Anatomy of a Park, 2d edit., 1986; illustrator: Anatomy of a Park, 1971, Visual Approach to Park Design, 1980; developer software CompuPave, 1992, PaveCAD, 1996. Mem., program coord. Champaign (Ill.) Devel. Coun., 1966-78. Named Hon. Parks Commr., Champaign Park Dist., 1981. Fellow Am. Soc. Landscape Architects (licensing com. Ill. chpt. 1968-70, registration com. Ind. chpt. 1982-85, pres. 1991-92, award 1982). Avocations: travel, computers. Office: Purdue U Landscape Architecture Prog 1165 Horticulture Bldg West Lafayette IN 47907-1165

MOLNAU, CAROL, state legislator; b. Sept. 17, 1949; m. Steven F. Molnau; 3 children. Attended, U. Minn. Mem. Minn. Ho. of Reps., 1992—. Active Our Saviors Luth. Ch., 4-H, Chaska City Coun. Mem. Agrl. Com., Econ. Devel., Infrastructure & Regulation Fin.-Transportation Fin. Divsn., Fin. Inst. & Ins.: Internat. Trade & Economic Devel. Republican. Office: State Capitol 443 State Office Bldg Saint Paul MN 55155-0001 Home: PO Box 24 Cologne MN 55322-0024

MOLONEY, THOMAS E. lawyer; b. Rockville Ctr., N.Y., Jan. 9, 1949; BS, U. Dayton, 1971; JD, U. Notre Dame, 1974. Bar: Ohio 1974. Prin. Am. Energy Svcs., Inc., Columbus, Ohio. Office: Am Energy Svcs Inc 1105 Schrock Rd Ste 602 Columbus OH 43229-1174

MOLYNEAUX, DAVID GLENN, newspaper travel editor; b. Marion, Ind., Oct. 16, 1945; s. Glenn Ingersol and Barbara Wingate (Draudt) M.; children: Miles David, Rebecca Susan; m. Judi Dash, May 15, 1994. BS in Econs., Miami U., Oxford, Ohio, 1967. Reporter The Plain Dealer, Cleve., 1967-75, city editor, 1976-78, assoc. editor, 1979-80, editorial page editor, 1980-82, travel editor, 1982—. Editor: 75 Years-An Informal History of Shaker Heights, 1987. Trustee Shaker Heights Pub. Libr., 1987—. With U.S. Army, 1968-70. Mem. Cleve. Press Club. Office: Plain Dealer 1801 Superior Ave E Cleveland OH 44114-2198

MONA, DAVID L. public relations executive; b. Mpls., May 4, 1943; BA in Journalism and Mass Communication, U. Minn, 1965. Reporter, editor Sta. WCCO-TV, 1962-65; reporter Mpls. Tribune, 1965-69; mgr. media rels. Luth. Brotherhood, 1969-70; dir. corp. communications Internat. Multifoods, 1970-78; v.p. communications The Toro Co., 1978-81; pres. David L. Mona Assocs., from 1981; chief exec. officer Mona, Meyer, McGrath & Gavin (now Shandwick USA); now mng. dir. Office: Shandwick USA Ste 500 8400 Normandale Lake Blvd Bloomington MN 55437-3889

MONA, STEPHEN FRANCIS, golf association executive; b. N.Y.C., June 9, 1957; s. Francis Joseph and Lucille (Croce) M.; m. Mary Jo Abate, May 21, 1983 (div. 1990); 1 child, Meredith Iris; m. Cynthia Kaye Davidson, Aug. 29, 1992; stepchildren: Kinyon Murphy Vinson, Stephen Brett Vinson. BA in Journalism, San Jose State U., 1980. Sports writer Tri-Valley News, Danville, Calif., 1977-78, Tri-Valley Herald, Livermore, 1978-80; tournament dir. Northern Calif. Golf Assn., Pebble Beach, 1980-81; asst. mgr., press relations U.S. Golf Assn., Far Hills, N.J., 1981-83; exec. dir. Ga. State Golf Assn., Atlanta, 1983-93; CEO Golf Course Supt.'s Assn. of Am., 1993—. Bd. dirs. Ga. Turf Grass Found., Norcross, Ga., 1988-93; treas. Ga. Jr. Golf Found., Atlanta, 1986-93. Named Golf Writer of the Yr., Northern Calif. PGA, Calif. 1980; Sports Story of the Yr., Contra Costa Press Club, Walnut Creek, Calif., 1977, 1978. Mem. Ga. Soc. Assn. Execs. (pres. 1993), Internat. Assn. Golf Adminstrs. (pres. 1990), Am. Soc. Assn. Execs., K.C. Soc. Assn. Execs. (pres. 2000), Aluamar Country Club. Republican. Roman Catholic. Avocations: golf, reading, yardwork. Office: GCSAA 1421 Research Park Dr Lawrence KS 66049-3858 E-mail: smona@gcsaa.org.

MONACO, JOHN J. molecular genetics research educator; Prof. U. Cin. Sch. of Medicine, Howard Hughes Med. Inst., 1994-2001. Recipient Eli Lilly and Co. Rsch. award in Microbiology and Immunology, Am. Soc. Microbiology, 1995, Investigator award Pharmingen/Am. Assn. Immunologists, 1997. Office: U Cin Sch Medicine Dept Molecular Genetics 231 Albert Sabin Way Cincinnati OH 45267-0524 E-mail: john.monaco@uc.edu.

MONAGHAN, DAVID A. corporate lawyer; b. St. Louis, Mar. 9, 1956; BS, William Jewell Coll., 1978; JD, U. Mo., Columbia, 1985. Bar: Mo. 1985. Asst. gen. coun. Am. Family Ins. Group, Madison, Wis. Office: American Family Ins Group 6000 American Pkwy Madison WI 53783-0002

MONAGHAN, THOMAS JUSTIN, former prosecutor; J.D., U. Nebr. Law School. Adjunct faculty College of St. Mary, Nebr., 1985—91; ptnr. Monaghan, Tiedman & Lynch, Omaha, 1978—93; U.S. atty. Dept. Justice, 1993—2001. Office: Monaghan Group 1321 Jones St Omaha NE 68102

MONAHAN, LEONARD FRANCIS, musician, singer, composer, publisher; b. Toledo, Aug. 19, 1948; s. Leonard Francis and Theresa Margaret (Geraldo) M.; m. Elaine Ann Welling, Oct. 14, 1978. BS in Psychology and Philosophy, U. Toledo, 1980. Musician, writer Len Monahan Prodns., Toledo, 1971-75; musician, composer, pub. World Airwave Music, 1975—. Founder Red Dog Records Label. Author: If You Were Big and I Were Small, 1971, The Land of Echoing Fountains, 1972, Sending You My Thoughts, 1987, Another Road, 1987, Tapping at Your Window, 1988, Voice of the Guitar, 2000; composer numerous songs. Recipient Internat. Recognition of Christmas Music. Mem. Broadcast Music Inc., Internat. Platform Assn., Nat. Assn. Independent Recording Distbrs. Home: Catania Regency 2151 Carlmont Dr Apt 102 Belmont CA 94002-3408 E-mail: lfmwriter@aol.com.

MONAHAN, MICHAEL T. bank executive; BBA, U. Notre Dame, 1960; MBA, U. Mich., 1967. Pres. Comercia Inc. Office: Comercia Tower at Detroit Ctr 500 Woodward Ave Detroit MI 48226-3416

MONAHAN, WILLIAM T. computer company executive; V.p. electro and communication sys. group 3M, Austin; pres., CEO Nat. Info. Infrastructure Testbed, Inc., 1995—; CEO Imation Corp., Oakdale, Minn., 1996—. Office: Imation Corp 1 Imation Pl Oakdale MN 55128-3414

MONDALE, JOAN ADAMS, wife of former Vice President of United States; b. Eugene, Oreg., Aug. 8, 1930; d. John Maxwell and Eleanor Jane (Hall) Adams; m. Walter F. Mondale, Dec. 27, 1955; children— Theodore, Eleanor Jane, William Hall. BA, Macalester Coll., 1952. Asst. slide librarian Boston Mus. Fine Arts, 1952-53; asst. in edn. Mpls. Inst. of Arts, 1953-57; weekly tour guide Nat. Gallery of Art, Washington, 1965-74; hostess Washington Whirl-A-Round, 1975-76; ambassador to Japan, 1993-96. Author: Politics in Art, 1972, Letters from Japan, 1998. Mem. bd. govs. Women's Nat. Dem. Club; hon. chmn. Fed. Coun. on Arts and Humanities, 1978-80; bd. dirs. Associated Coun. of Arts, 1973-75, Reading Is Fundamental, Am. Craft Coun., N.Y.C., 1981-88, J.F.K. Ctr. Performing Arts, 1981-90, Walker Art Ctr., Mpls., 1987-93, Minn. Orch., Mpls., 1988-93, 97—, St. Paul Chamber Orch., 1988-90, Northern Clay Ctr., 1988-93, St. Paul, 1988-93, Nancy Hauser Dance Co., Mpls., 1989-93, Minn. Landmarks, 1991-93, Walker Art Ctr., Mpls., 1997—; trustee Macalester Coll., 1986—; mem. commn. Nat. Portrait Gallery, 1997—; chair Hiawatha Light Rail Transit Pub. Art and Design com., 2000—. Mem. Phi Beta Kappa Epsilon. Presbyterian. Home: 2116 Irving Ave S Minneapolis MN 55405-2541 E-mail: diggerkpr@aol.com.

MONDALE, THEODORE ADAMS, former state senator; b. Mpls., Oct. 12, 1957; s. Walter Frederick and Joan (Adams) M.; m. Pamela Burris, June 12, 1988; children: Louis F., Amanda J., Berit C. BA in History, U. Minn., 1985; JD, William Mitchell Coll. Law, 1988. Assoc., law firm Larkin, Hoffman Daly & Lindgren, 1988-91; state senator Minn. State Senate, St. Paul, 1990—; v.p. pub. programs United HealthCare; atty. in pvt. practice Mpls. Legal counsel United HealthCare Corp., Mpls. Press aide Carter for Pres. Com., 1976; surrogate speaker Carter Reelection Com., 1979-80, Mondale for Pres. Com., 1983-84; midwest dir. Dukakis for Pres. Com., 1988. Home: 3800 France Ave S Saint Louis Park MN 55416-4912 Address: 220 6th St NW Saint Paul MN 55112-6817

MONDALE, WALTER FREDERICK, former Vice President of United States, diplomat, lawyer; b. Ceylon, Minn., Jan. 5, 1928; s. Theodore Sigvaard and Claribel Hope (Cowan) M.; m. Joan Adams, Dec. 27, 1955;children: Theodore, Eleanor, William. BA cum laude, U. Minn., 1951, LLB, 1956. Bar: Minn. 1956. Law clk. Minn. Supreme Ct.; pvt. practice law, 1956-60; atty. gen. State of Minn., 1960-64; U.S. senator from Minn., 1964-77; v.p. served under Pres. James Carter U.S., 1977-81; mem. Nat. Security Council, 1977-81; mem. firm Winston & Strawn, 1981-87; ptnr. Dorsey & Whitney, Mpls., 1987-93; U.S. amb. to Japan Tokyo, 1993-96. Author: The Accountability of Power*Toward a Responsible Presidency, 1975; mem. Minn. Law Rev. Dem. nominee for Pres. U.S., 1984. With U.S. Army, 1951-53. Presbyterian. Democrat.

MONDER, STEVEN I. orchestra executive; b. Newark, Mar. 12, 1945; B in Mus. Edn., Coll. Conservatory of Music, 1968, M in Mus. Edn., 1970. Tchr. orch., chorus, humanities McAuley H.S., Cin., 1970-71; prodn. mgr. Cin. Symphony Orch., 1971, asst. mgr., 1971-74, mgr., 1974-76, gen. mgr., 1976-89, exec. dir., 1989-98, pres., 1998—. Prodn. stage mgr. Cin. Opera Co., 1970, 71, adminstr., 1973. Office: Cin Symphony Orch Music Hall 1241 Elm St Cincinnati OH 45210-2231

MONE, ROBERT PAUL, lawyer; b. Columbus, Ohio, July 23, 1934; s. Henry P. and Ann E. (Freedlund) M.; m. Lucille L. Willman, May 3, 1960; children: Robert, Maria, Andrew, Richard. BA, U. Dayton, 1956; JD, U. Notre Dame, 1959. Bar: Ohio 1959. Law clk.to presiding judge U.S. Dist. Ct. (no. dist.) Ohio, Cleve., 1960-62; assoc. George, Greek, King, et al, Columbus, 1962-66, ptnr., 1966-79, McConnaughey, Stradley, et al, Columbus, 1979-81, Thompson Hine & Flory LLP, Columbus, 1981—. Cpl. U.S. Army, 1959-60. Mem. ABA, Ohio State Bar Assn., Fed. Energy Bar Assn., Columbus Bar Assn., Nat. Generation and Transmission Coop. Lawyers Assn. (1st pres.), Rotary. S Home: 2300 Tremont Rd Columbus OH 43221-3706 Office: Thompson Hine & Flory LLP 10 W Broad St Ste 700 Columbus OH 43215-3435

MONELLO, JOSEPH D. financial asset management company executive; b. 1945; V.p., contr. Kansas City (Mo.) Southern Industries, Inc., CFO, head fin. svcs. divsn., 1997—. Office: 114 W 11th St Kansas City MO 64105-1804 Fax: 816-983-1459.

MONGELLUZZO, JOHN ANDREW, lawyer; b. Lima, Ohio, Dec. 29, 1958; s. John Jr. and Virginia (Guagenti) M.; m. Kerry Jean Power, June 18, 1983. BA, U. Cin., 1981; JD, Capital U., 1984. Bar: Ohio 1984. Staff atty. savings and loan assns., securities Ohio Dept. Commerce, Columbus, 1985-86; counsel, sec. Structural Dynamics Rsch. Corp., Cin., 1986—. Vol. United Way, Clermont County, Ohio, 1987. Mem. ABA, Ohio State Bar Assn., Cin. Bar Assn., Am. Corp. Counsel Assn., Am. Soc. Corp. Secs. Republican. Roman Catholic. Office: Structural Dynamics Rsch 2000 Eastman Dr Milford OH 45150-2712 Home: 7875 Shawnee Run Rd Cincinnati OH 45243-3134

MONICAL, ROBERT DUANE, consulting structural engineer; b. Morgan County, Ind., Apr. 30, 1925; s. William Blaine and Mary Elizabeth (Lang) M.; m. Carol Arnetha Dean, Aug. 10, 1947 (dec. 1979); children: Mary Christine, Stuart Dean, Dwight Lee; m. Sharon Kelly Eastwood, July 13, 1980; 1 stepson, Jeffrey David Eastwood. B.S.C.E., Purdue U., 1948, M.S.C.E., 1949. Engr. N.Y.C. R.R., Cin., 1949-51, So. Rwy., Cin., 1951; design engr. Pierce & Gruber (Cons. Engrs.), Indpls., 1952-54; founder, partner Monical & Wolverton (Cons. Engrs.), 1954-63, Monical Assocs., Indpls., 1963—, pres., 1975—; v.p. Zurwelle-Whittaker, Inc. (Engrs. and Land Surveyors), Miami Beach, Fla., 1975-90. Mem. Ind. Adminstrv. Bldg. Council, 1969-75; chmn., 1973-75; mem. Meridian St. Preservation Commn., 1971-75, Ind. State Bd. of Registration for Profl. Engrs. and Land Surveyors, 1976-84, chmn., 1979, 83 Served with USNR, 1943-46, USAR, 1948-53. Mem. ASCE (Outstanding Civil Engr. award Ind. sect. 1987), Cons. Engrs. Ind. (pres. 1969, Cons. Recognition award 1986), Am. Cons. Engrs. Council (pres. 1978-79), Ind. Soc. Profl. Engrs. (Engr. of Yr. 1980), Nat. Soc. Profl. Engrs., Am. Concrete Inst., Am. Inst. Steel Constrn., Indpls. Sci. and Engring. Found. (pres. 1992-93), Am. Legion, Lions, Masons, Shriners. Mem. Christian Ch. Home and Office: 18831 Whitcomb Pl Noblesville IN 46060-8130 E-mail: rduane@juno.com.

MONK, SUSAN MARIE, physician, pediatrician; b. York, Pa., May 7, 1945; d. John Spotz and Mary Elizabeth (Shelly) M.; m. Jaime Pacheco, June 5, 1971; children: Benjamin Joaquin, Maria Cristina. AB, Colby Coll., 1967; MD, Jefferson Med. Coll., 1971. Diplomate Am. Bd. Pediatrics. Pediatrician Children's Med. Ctr., Dayton, Ohio, 1975—; asst. clin. prof. pediat. Wright State U., 1976—83, 1983—2000, asst. prof., 2000—. Mem. bd. dirs. Children's Med. Ctr., Dayton, 1991-96, chief-of-staff, 1992-94. Mem. Am. Acad. Pediatrics, We. Ohio Pediatric Soc., Pediatric Ambulatory Care Soc. Avocations: reading, gardening, travel, movies, theater. Office: Childrens Health Clinic 722 Valley St Dayton OH 45404-1845

MONROE, HASKELL MOORMAN, JR. university educator; b. Dallas, Mar. 18, 1931; s. Haskell M. and Myrtle Marie (Jackson) M.; m. Margaret Joan Phillips, June 15, 1957; children: Stephen, Melanie, Mark, John. BA, Austin (Tex.) Coll., 1952, MA, 1954; PhD, Rice U., Houston, 1961; doctorate (hon.) , Austin Coll., 1984. From instr. to prof. Tex. A&M U., 1959-80; asst. dean Tex. A&M U. (Grad. Sch.), 1965-68, asst. v.p. acad. affairs, 1972-74, dean faculties, 1974-80, assoc. v.p. acad. affairs, 1977-80; pres. U. Tex., El Paso, 1980-87; chancellor U. Mo., Columbia, 1987-91, prof. history, 1987-97, chancellor emeritus, prof. history, 1997—; dean faculties emeritus, dir. Heritage Preservation Program Tex. A&M U., College Station, 1998. Instr. Schreiner Inst., Kerrville, Tex., summer 1959; vis. lectr. Emory U., summers 1967, 72; faculty lectr. Tex. A&M U., 1972; alumni lectr. Austin Coll., 1980; bd. dirs. Southwestern Bell Corp., Boone County Nat. Bank, SBC Comms., Inc.; history adv. com. Sec. Air Force, 1987-87; orientation com. Dept. Def.-Joint Chiefs, 1986; adv. bd. Army Command and Gen. Staff Sch., 1986-88; trustee Schreiner U., 2000—. Contbr. articles, revs.; editor: Papers of Jefferson Davis, 1964-69; adv. editor: Texana, 1964-71; bd. editorial advisers: Booker T. Washington Papers, 1965-85 . Bd. dirs. Brazos Valley Rehab. Ctr., 1975-77, Salvation Army, El Paso, 1984-87, Columbia, Mo., 1988-97, Crime Stoppers of El Paso, United Way Columbia, 1988-94, Keep Brazos Beautiful, 1999-, Washington-on-the-Brazos State Park Assn., 2002-; trustee Bryan Hosp., 1976-79, chmn., 1979; bd. ch. visitors Austin Coll., 1977-78; deacon First Presbyn. Ch., Bryan, 1961-63, elder, 1965-67, 69-71, 73-74, clk. of session, 1973-74, chmn. pulpit nominating com., 1971-72; mem. presbytery's coun. Presbytery of Brazos, 1969-71, mem. resources for the 80s steering com., 1978-80; elder 1st Presbyn. Ch., El Paso, 1984-87, 1st Presbyn. Ch., Columbia, 1994-96; mem. exec. bd. Great Rivers coun. Boy Scouts Am., 1990-97; mem. Pres. Coun. NCAA, 1986-87; chmn. Jefferson Davis award com. Confederate Mus., 1996-97; bd. dirs. Salvation Army, 1989-97. Recipient Citation of Appreciation, LULAC, 1982, Honor award Salvation Army, 1997, also numerous achievement awards; grantee Social Sci. Rsch. Coun., Tex. A&M U., Huntington Libr., Intrafraternity and Sorority Outstanding Tchr. award, 1997; named Ky. Col., 1967; named to Legends of Aggieland, 1998. Mem. Am. Hist. Assn., Orgn. Am. Historians, So. Hist. Assn. Hist. Found. Presbyn. and Reformed Chs. (pres. 1970-72), Coll. Football Assn. (chmn. bd. 1989-90, bd. dirs.), Truman Scholarship Panel, Soc. Conf. Deans Faculties and Acad. V.P.s (pres. 1978), Rotary (El Paso, hon. Columbia, Mo., Bryan, Tex., Paul Harris fellow 1986, 2000). Home: 1005 Sonoma Cir College Station TX 77845-7907 Office: Tex A&M U 207 Evans Libr College Station TX 77843 E-mail: hmonroe@tamu.edu.

MONROE, JEFF, state legislator; Rep. S.D. State Dist. 24. Health and human svcs. com. S.D. Ho. Reps., local govt. com.; pvt. practice chiropractic neurology. Address: 362 S Pierre St Pierre SD 57501-3137

MONROE, MURRAY SHIPLEY, lawyer; b. Cin., Sept. 25, 1925; s. James and Martha (Shipley) M.; m. Sally Longstreth, May 11, 1963; children: Tracy, Murray, Courtney, David. BE, Yale U., 1946, BS, 1947; LLB, U. Pa., 1950. Bar: Ohio 1950, U.S. Dist. Ct. (so. dist.) Ohio 1954, U.S. Dist. Ct. (mid. dist.) Tenn. 1981, U.S. Dist. Ct. (mid. dist.) N.C. 1974, U.S. Dist. Ct. (mid. dist.) Pa. 1986, U.S. Dist. (ea. dist.) Pa. 1960, U.S. Dist. Ct. (we. dist.) Mo. 1974, U.S. Dist. Ct. Mass. 1978, U.S. Dist. Ct. (ea. dist.) La. 1979, U.S. Dist. Ct. (no. dist.) Ill. 1980, U.S. Ct. Appeals (4th cir.) 1984, U.S. Ct. Appeals (6th cir.) 1969, U.S. Supreme Ct. 1977, U.S. Ct. Appeals (3d cir.) 1990. Assoc. Taft, Stettinus & Hollister, Cin., 1950-58, ptnr., 1958-96; of counsel, 1997—. Mem. lawyers com. Nat. Ctr. for State Cts., 1985-96; faculty Ohio Legal Ctr. Inst., 1970-93. Contbr. articles to profl. jours. Trustee, treas. The Coll. Prep. Sch., 1972-76; trustee The Seven Hills Schs., 1982-88, chmn. bd., 1982-85. 2d lt. USNR, 1943-46. Recipient award Seven Hills Schs., 1985. Fellow Ohio Bar Found.; mem. ABA (speaker symposiums), Ohio Bar Assn. (coun. dels. 1977-82, bd. govs. antitrust sect. 1960-95, dir. emeritus 1995—, chmn. bd. govs. 1973-75, Merit award 1976, speaker symposiums), Bankers Club (Cin.), Cin. Country Club, Met. Club, Tau Beta Pi. Republican. Episcopalian. Avocations: sailing, tennis.

MONROE, THOMAS EDWARD, industrial corporation executive; b. Ironton, MO, Nov. 19, 1947; s. Donald Mansfield and Edwina Frances (Carr) M.; children: Thomas Edward II, Katherine Jenna. B.A., Drury Coll., 1969; postgrad., Washington U. Sch. Bus. Adminstrn., St. Louis, 1970. Acctg. mgr., asst. contr. Am. Transit Corp., St. Louis, 1970-74; mgr. corp. devel., asst. treas. Chromalloy Am. Corp., 1974-77, v.p. fin., 1977-78, exec. v.p., 1978-82; dir. Chromalloy Fin. Corp., 1976-82, Am. Universal Ins. Co., 1978-82; chmn. Capital Assocs. Corp., 1982—, Fed. Air Ambulance, The Safe Deposit Co., CompuVault, Inc., James Flying Svc., Inc., Lindbergh Leasing, Inc., Vault II, LLC. Trustee Kingsbury Place Assn. Mem. Algonquin Club. Presbyterian. Office: Capital Assocs Corp 515 S Lindbergh Blvd Saint Louis MO 63131-2731 E-mail: monroes@swbell.com.

MONSON, DAN, college basketball coach; b. Spokane, Wash., Oct. 6, 1961; BS in Math., U. Idaho, 1985; MS in Athletic Adminstrn., U. Ala., 1988. Asst. coach Oregon City H.S., 1985-86; grad. asst. U. Ala., Birmingham, 1986-88; asst. coach Gonzaga U. Bulldogs, Spokane, 1988-94, assoc. head coach, 1994-97, head coach, 1997-99; West Coast Conf. regular season champions, 1998; advanced to 2d round Nat. Invitation Championship, 1998; reached NCAA Sweet 16, 1998-99; ranked 13th in NCAA, 1998-99; head coach U. Minn. Gophers, 1999—. Named Coach of Yr., 1998, Nat. Rookie Coach of Yr., Basketball Times, 1998. Office: Univ of Minn Student Devel & Athletics 141 BFAB Minneapolis MN 55455-0100

MONSON, DAVID CARL, school superintendent, farmer, state legislator, insurance agent; b. Langdon, N.D., July 30, 1950; s. Carl Arthur and Shirley Jean (Klai) M.; m. Mary Kathryn Greutman, July 8, 1972; children: Cordell Carl, Cale David, Jared Arthur. Cert. tchr., adminstr., N.D. Sci. tchr. Hankinson (N.D.) Pub. Sch., 1972-75; tchr. Nekoma (N.D.) Pub. Sch., 1975-76; tchr., prin. NeKoma (N.D.) Pub. Sch., 1976-79; tchr., supt. Nekoma (N.D.) Pub. Sch., 1979-80; tchr., prin. Milton (N.D.)-Osnabrock High Sch., 1981-84; supt. Adams (N.D.) Pub. Schs., 1984-88; ins. agt. N.Y. Life, Fargo, N.D., 1988-95; self-employed ins. agt., Osnabrock, 1988—; farmer, 1975—; mem. N.D. Ho. of Reps., Bismarck, 1993—, asst. majority leader, 1998—; supt. Edinburg (N.D.) Pub. Schs., 1995—. Dir. N.Am. Indsl. Hemp Coun., 1999—. Leader Bobcats 4-H Club, 1988—2001; mem. sch. bd. dirs. Osnobrock Sch. Bd., 1989—2001. Mem. N.D. Farm Bur., N.D. Coun. Sch. Adminstrs., Eagles, KP (grand sec. N.D. and Sask. 1985-93, award 1990). Republican. Lutheran. Avocations: skiing, gardening, hunting, coin collecting. E-mail: dmonson@state.nd.us.

MONSON, DIANNE LYNN, literacy educator; b. Minot, N.D., Nov. 24, 1934; d. Albert Rachie and Iona Cordelia (Kirk) M. BS, U. Minn., 1956, MA, 1962, PhD, 1966. Tchr. Rochester (Minn.) Pub. Schs., 1956-59, U.S. Dept. Def., Schweinfurt, West Germany, 1959-61, St. Louis Park (Minn.) Schs., 1961-62; instr. U. Minn., Mpls., 1962-66; prof. U. Wash., Seattle, 1966-82; prof. literacy edn. U. Minn., Mpls., 1982-97, prof. emeritus, 1997—. Chmn. curriculum and instrn. U. Minn., 1986-89. Co-author: (with Scott Foresman) Reading, 2000, New Horizons in the Language Arts, 1972, Children and Books, 6th edit., 1981, Experiencing Children's Literature, 1984, (monograph) Research in Children's Literature, 1976, Language Arts: Teaching and Learning Effective Use of Language, 1988, Reading Together: Helping Children Get A Good Start With Reading, 1991; assoc. editor: Dictionary of Literacy, 1995. Recipient Outstanding Educator award U. Minn. Alumni Assn., 1983, Alumni Faculty award U. Minn. Alumni Assn., 1991. Fellow Nat. Conf. Rsch. in English (pres. 1990-91); mem. ALA, Nat. Coun. Tchrs. English (exec. com. 1979-81), Internat. Reading Assn. (dir. 1980-83, Arbuthnot award 1993, Reading Hall of Fame 1997), U.S. Bd. Books for Young People (pres. 1988-90). Lutheran. Home: 515 S Lexington Pkwy # 604 Saint Paul MN 55116 E-mail: monso001@tc.umn.edu.

MONTAG, JOHN JOSEPH, II, librarian; b. Omaha, Jan. 8, 1948; s. John Joseph and Ruth Helen (Johnston) M.; m. Linda Kay Lubanski, Apr. 8, 1971; children: Nicole Elizabeth, Megan Kristine. BA, Midland Luth. Coll., 1970; postgrad., Wash. State U., 1970-74; MA, U. Iowa, 1976; postgrad., U. Nebr., 1982-84. English tchr. pub. schs., Nebr., Iowa, 1972-75; reference librarian Concordia Coll., Moorhead, Minn., 1976-81; asst. prof. library sci. U. Nebr., Lincoln, 1981-84; dir. Office of Info. State Library Iowa, Des Moines, 1984-86, state librarian, 1986-87; dir. Thomas Library Wittenberg U., 1987-95, Cochrane-Woods Libr. Nebr. Wesleyan U., Lincoln, 1995-97, dir. libr. and computer svcs., 1997-99, univ. libr., 1999—. Trustee Bibliog. Ctr. for Research, Denver, 1986-87; adv. bd. No. Lights Library Network, Detroit Lakes, Minn., 1980-81; chair Southwest Ohio Consortium Higher Edn. Libr. Coun., 1991-94; mem. exec. com. Nebr. Inst., 1998—. Contbr. articles to profl. jours. Co-founder Nebr. Found. for Oral History, 2001—. Univ. Found. library improvement grantee, U. Nebr., 1983; Challenge grantee NEH, 1992. Mem. ALA, Assn. Coll. and Research Libraries, Nebr. Ind. Coll. Libr. Consortium (chmn. libr. dirs. 2000—). Office: Cochrane Woods Libr Nebr Wesleyan U 5000 Saint Paul Ave Lincoln NE 68504-2760

MONTAGUE, DROGO K. urologist; b. Alpena, Mich., Dec. 11, 1942; s. Frank Wright and Susan Alice (Kidder) M.; m. Margaret Mary Barrett; children: Mark Andrew, Lisa Joy. Student, U. Mich., 1963, MD cum laude, 1968. Diplomate Am. Bd. Urology. Intern Cleve. Clinic Hosp., 1968-69, resident in gen. surgery, 1969-70, resident in urology, 1970-73; assoc. staff urologist Cleve. Clinic Found., 1973-75, staff urologist, 1975—, head sect. prosthetic surgery, 1981—, urology residence program dir., 1985—, dir. Ctr. for Sexual Function, 1987—; prof. surgery Ohio State U. Coll. Medicine, 1992—. Trainee cardiovascular rsch. tng. program NIH, 1962-68; trustee Am. Bd. Urology, 1989-95, mem. examination com., 1975-80, examiner cert. exam., 1980-88, rep. to Am. Bd. Med. Specialties, 1989-95. Reviewer various publs. in field; contbr. numerous articles to profl. publs., chpts. to books; editor: Disorders of Male Sexual Function, 1988, Surgical Treatment of Erectile Dysfunction, 1993; author audiovisual tapes in field; mem. editl. bd. Jour. Urology. James B. Angell scholar, 1961, 62, Nat. Found. scholar, 1963-68; recipient Russell and Mary Hugh Scott Edn. award, 1989, Iowa Rsch. award, 1967. Fellow ACS; mem. Am. Urolog. Assn. (chmn. sci. exhibits com. North Cen. sect. 1977, mem. residency edn. com. 1979-83, vice chmn. audio visual com. 1989-95, mem. various coms., editor Am. Urolog. Assn. Video Libr. 1995—, chmn. audio visual com. 1996—), Am. Assn. Genitourinary Surgeons, Cleve. Urolog. Soc. (sec.-treas. 1978-80, v.p. 1980-81, pres. 1981-82, 94-95), Soc. for Study of Impotence (pres. 1995). Office: Cleve Clinic Found Urol Inst 9500 Euclid Ave Cleveland OH 44195-0001

MONTELEONE, PATRICIA, academic dean; Dean St. Louis U. Sch. Medicine. Office: St Louis U Sch Medicine 1402 S Grand Blvd Saint Louis MO 63104-1004

MONTGOMERY, ANN D. federal judge, educator; b. Litchfield, Minn., May 9, 1949; m. Theodore Smetak; 2 children; 1 stepchild. BS, U. Kans., 1971; JD, U. Minn., 1974. Bar: Minn. 1974, U.S. Dist. Ct. Minn., U.S. Ct. Appeals (8th cir.), U.S. Supreme Ct. Law clk. D.C. Ct. Appeals, Washington, 1974-75; asst. U.S. atty. Dist. Minn., Mpls., 1976-83; mcpl. judge Hennepin County, 1983-85; judge Hennepin County Dist. Ct., 1985-94, U.S. Magistrate Ct., 1994-96; federal judge U.S. Dist. Ct., Mpls., 1996—. Adj. prof. U. Minn. Law Sch., Mpls., 1988—; steering com. mem., dir. criminal divsn. Minn. Jud. Coll., 1990-94. Recipient Trial Judge of Yr. award Am. Bd. Trial Advocates, 1996. Mem. FBA, Minn. Dist. Judges Assn., Minn. Bar Assn., Minn. Women Lawyers (Myra Bradwell award 2000), Hennepin County Bar Assn. (Professionalism award 1993). Office: US Dist Ct 300 S 4th St Minneapolis MN 55415-1320 Fax: 612-664-5097. E-mail: admontgomery@mnd.uscourts.gov.

MONTGOMERY, BETTY DEE, state attorney general, former state legislator; BA, Bowling Green State U.; JD, U. Toledo, 1976. Former criminal clk. Lucas County Common Pleas Ct.; asst. pros. atty. Wood County, Ohio, 1977—78, pros. atty., 1981—88, City of Perrysburg, 1978—81; mem. Ohio Senate, 1989—94; atty. gen. State of Ohio, Columbus, 1995—. Mem.: Wood County Bar Assn. Office: Attorney Generals Office State Office Tower 30 E Broad St Columbus OH 43215-3414

MONTGOMERY, CHARLES BARRY, lawyer; b. Latrobe, Pa., Apr. 17, 1937; BA cum laude, Muskingum Coll., 1959; JD, U. Mich., 1962. Bar: Ill. 1962, U.S. Dist. Ct. (no. dist.) Ill. 1982, U.S. Supreme Ct. 1971. Atty. Jacobs & McKenna, 1962-67; founder, ptnr. Jacobs, Williams and Montgomery, Ltd., 1967-85; sr. ptnr. Williams Montgomery & John Ltd., Chgo., 1985—. Instr. advocacy inst. U. Mich., Ann Arbor, 1985, advanced program Nat. Inst. Trial Advocacy, 1986, trial acad. Internat. Assn. Def. Counsel, 1987, law inst. program Def. Rsch. Inst; pub. spkr. litigation. Contbr. articles to profl. jours. Fellow Internat. Acad. Trial Lawyers; mem. ABA (vice-chair medicine and law com. 1989-90), Am. Arbitration Assn., Chgo. Bar Assn., Def. Rsch. Inst., Ill. Assn. Def. Trial Counsel, Ill. Assn. Hosp. Attys., Ill. State Bar Assn., Internat. Assn. Def. Counsel, Soc. Trial Lawyers, Legal Club of Chgo., Trial Lawyers Club of Chgo. Office: Williams Montgomery & John Ltd Ste 2100 20 N Wacker Dr Chicago IL 60606-3094 E-mail: cbm@willmont.com.

MONTGOMERY, GARY B. manufacturing executive; CFO Amsted Industries Inc., Chgo. Office: Amsted Industries Inc 205 N Michigan Ave Chicago IL 60601

MONTGOMERY, JEFFREY THOMAS, baseball player; b. Wellston, Ohio, Jan. 7, 1962; BS Computer Sci., Marshall Coll., 1984. With Cin. Reds, 1983-88, Kansas City Royals, 1988-99. Mem. Am. League All-Star Team, 1992-93, 96. Names Am. League Fireman of Yr., Sporting News, 1993. Office: Kansas City Royals Kauffman Stadium PO Box 419969 Kansas City MO 64141-6969

MONTGOMERY, R. LAWRENCE, speciality department store chain executive; b. 1949; Pres., CEO Black's divsn. Allied Store Corp., 1985-87; sr. v.p., dir. stores, gen. mdse. mgr. Softlines L.S. Ayres divsn. May Dept. Stores, 1987-88; sr. v.p., dir. stores Kohl's Corp., Menomonee Falls, Wis., 1988-93, exec. v.p., 1993-96, vice chmn., 1996—, CEO, 1999—, also bd. dirs. Office: Kohn's Corp N56w17000 Ridgewood Dr Menomonee Falls WI 53051-5660

MONTGOMERY, REX, biochemist, educator; b. Halesowen, Eng., Sept. 4, 1923; came to U.S., 1948, naturalized, 1963; s. Fred and Jane (Holloway) M.; m. Barbara Winifred Price, Aug. 9, 1948 (dec.); children: Ian, David, Jennifer, Christopher. BSc, U. Birmingham, Eng., 1943, PhD, 1946, DSc, 1963. Rsch. assoc. U. Minn., 1951-55; mem. faculty U. Iowa, Iowa City, 1955—, prof. biochemistry, 1963—, assoc. dean U. Iowa Coll. Medicine, 1974-95, v.p. rsch., 1989-90. Vis. prof. Nat. Australian U., 1969-70; mem. physiol. chemistry study sect. NIH, 1968-72; mem. drug devel. contract rev. com., 1975-87; chmn. com. biol. chemistry NAS, 1961-64; pesticide and fertilizer adv. bd. Iowa Dept. Agr., 1990-91; bd. dirs. Wallace Tech. Transfer Found., 1989-93; chmn. bd. dirs. Neurotron Inc., 1990-95; mem. rsch. com. Iowa Corn Promotion Bd., 1995—; rsch. dir. Biotech. Byproducts Consortium, 1989—; cons. in field. Author: Chemical Production of Lactic Acid, 1949, Chemistry of Plant Gums and Mucilages, 1959, Quantitative Problems in Biochemical Sciences, 2d edit., 1976, Biochemistry: A Case-Orientated Approach, 6th edit., 1996; mem. editl. adv. bd. Carbohydrate Rsch., 1968-80; mem. editl. bd. Molecular Biotherapy, 1988-92; contbr. articles to profl. jours. Postdoctoral fellow Ohio State U., 1948-49; fellow Sugar Research Found., Dept. Agr., 1949-51 Home: 701 Oaknoll Dr Iowa City IA 52246-5168 Office: U Iowa Coll Medicine Dept Biochemistry Iowa City IA 52242 E-mail: rex-montgomery@uiowa.edu.

MONTGOMERY, ROBERT RENWICK, medical association administrator, educator; b. New Castle, Pa., June 3, 1943; BS in Chemistry, Grove City Coll., 1965; MD, U. Pitts., 1969. Diplomate Am. Bd. Pediatrics. Intern Childrens Hosp. Phila. U. Pa., 1969-70; resident Harriet Lane Svc. Johns Hopkins Hosp., 1972-73, fellow, 1972-73, U. Colo., 1973-76, Scripps Clinic and Rsch. Found., 1976-77; gen. med. officer USPHS, Chinle, Ariz., 1970-71, dep. chief pediatrics Tuba City, 1971-72; rsch. clin fellow in pediatric hematology U. Colo., 1973-76; rsch. fellow in molecular immunology Scripps Clinic and Rsch. Found., 1976-77; acting dir. Mountain States Regional Hemphilia Program U. Colo., 1977-78, asst. prof. dept. pediatrics, 1977-80, co-dir. coagulation rsch. labs., asst. dir. mountain sates regional hemophilia program, 1978-80; asst. prof. dept. pediatrics Med. Coll. Wis., 1980-81; dir. hemostasis program Milwaukee Children's Hosp., 1980-84; med. dir. Great Lakes Hemophilia Found., 1980-84; dir. regional homeostasis reference lab. The Blood Ctr. Southeastern Wis., 1981—; cons. hemostasis lab., dept. pathology The Children's Hosp. Wis., 1981—; assoc. prof. dept. pediatrics Med. Coll. Wis., 1981-84; sr. investigator The Blood Ctr. Southeastern Wis., 1982—, section head hemostasis rsch.; scientific dir. Great Lakes Hemophilia Found., 1984-96; assoc. dir. rsch. The Blood Ctr. Southeastern Wis., 1984-86; assoc. clin. prof. dept. pediatrics Med. Coll. Wis., clin. prof. dept. pediatrics, 1986-96, prof. pediatrics, 1996—, vice chmn. rsch. dept. pediatrics, 1998—; dir. rsch. The Blood Ctr. Southeastern Wis., 1986-98; acting sect. head coagulation lab., dept. pathology Med. Coll. Wis., 1986-87; faculty med. tech. Marquette U., Milw., 1986-92; clin. prof. dept. pathology Med. Coll. Wis., 1987—; v.p., dir. rsch. to exec. v.p. and dir. rsch. The Blood Ctr. Southeastern Wis., 1988-96, 96-98. Mem. med. adv. com. Great Lakes Hemophilia Found., 1980-96, exec. com. 1995—; mem. libr. com., human rsch. rev. com. The Blood Ctr. Southeastern Wis., 1981—, mem. rsch. mgmt. group, rsch. strategic planning com., 1983—; mem. subcom. FVIII and von Willebrand factor Internat. Congress Thrombosis and Haemostasis, 1984—; mem. radiation safety com. The Blood Ctr. Southeastern Wis., 1984—; ad hoc reviewer Heart Lung and Blood Inst., NIH, 1984—; mem. Inst. Biosafety com. The Blood Ctr. Southeastern Wis., 1985—; chmn. rsch. review com. Nat. Hemophilia Found., 1987-96, mem. rsch. rev. com., 1996—; ad hoc reviewer com. B Nat. Heart, Lung and Blood Inst., 1991—; chmn. von Willebrand subcom. Hemophilia Rsch. Soc., 1990-97; pres. Hemophilia Rsch. Soc., 1990-93; exec. sec. Hemphilia Rsch. Soc. of N.A., 1993—; mem. med. scientific adv. com. Nat. Hemophilia Found., 1992-95; mem. bd. dirs. Wis. Sickle Cell Disease Comprehensive Ctr., 1992-93; chair med. adv. coun. Great Lakes Hemophilia Found., Milw., 1992-96; mem. blood diseases and resources adv. com. Nat. Heart, Lung, and Blood Inst., 1992-95; prof. pediat. Med. Coll. Wis., 1996—. Sr. asst. surgeon USPHS, Indian Health Svc., 1971-72. Recipient Nat. Rsch. Svc. award Heart Lung and Blood Inst., NIH, 1975-77, Young Investigator award, 1978-81, Established Investigator award Am. Heart Assn., 1982-87, Jack Kennedy Alumni Achievement award Groce City Coll., 1985, Dr. Murray Thelin award Nat. Hemophilia Found., 1991. Mem. AAAS, Am. Soc. Clin. Investigators, Am. Soc. Pediatric Hematology/Oncology, Am. Soc. Hematology, Am. Fedn. Clin. Rsch., Am. Heart Assn., Internat. Soc. Thrombosis and Hemostasis, Soc. Pediatric Rsch., Hemophilia Rsch. Soc. Office: Blood Center of SouthEastern Wis Blood Research Institute 1701 W Wisconsin Ave Milwaukee WI 53233-2113

MONTGOMERY, WILLIAM ADAM, lawyer; b. Chgo., May 22, 1933; s. John Rogerson and Helen (Fyke) Montgomery; m. Jane Fauver, July 28, 1956 (div. Dec. 1967); children: Elizabeth, William, Virginia; m. Deborah Stephens, July 29, 1972; children: Alex, Katherine. AB, Williams Coll., 1955; LLB, Harvard U., 1958. Bar: D.C. 1958, Ill. 1959, U.S. Ct. Appeals (7th cir.) 1959, U.S. Supreme Ct. 1977. Atty. civil div., appellate sect. Dept. Justice, Washington, 1958—60; assoc. Schiff Hardin & Waite, Chgo., 1960—68, ptnr., 1968—93; v.p., gen. counsel State Farm Ins. Cos., Bloomington, 1994—97, sr. v.p., gen. counsel, 1997—99; ptnr. Schiff Hardin & Waite, Chgo., 1999—. Author: (39 corp. practice series) Tying Arrangements, 1984; contbr. articles to profl. jours. Fellow: Am. Coll. Trial Lawyers; mem.: ABA (coun. antitrust sect. 1989—92), Seventh Cir. Bar Assn. (pres. 1988—89), Chgo. Bar Assn., Econ. Club Chgo., Lawyers Club Chgo. Avocations: skiing, woodturning. Office: Schiff Hardin & Waite 6600 Sears Tower Chicago IL 60606 E-mail: wmontgomery@schiffhardin.com.

MONTGOMERY, WILLIAM A. lawyer; b. Chgo., Aug. 15, 1960; s. William A. and Jane (Fauver) M. BA, Furman U., 1982; JD, Washington U., St. Louis, 1986. Bar: Mo. 1986, Ill. 1987. Of counsel Walgreen Co., Deerfield, Ill., 1987—. Contbr. articles to profl. jours. Mem. ABA, Ill. State Bar Assn., Mo. Bar Assn. Office: Walgreen Co 200 Wilmot Rd Deerfield IL 60015-4616

MONTO, ARNOLD SIMON, epidemiology educator; b. Bklyn., Mar. 22, 1933; s. Jacob and Mildred (Kaplan) M.; m. Ellyne Gay Polsky, June 15, 1958; children: Sarah D. Monto Maniaci, Jane E., Richard L., Stephen A. BA in Zoology, Cornell U., Ithaca, N.Y., 1954; MD, Cornell U., N.Y.C., 1958. Diplomate Am. Coll. Epidemiology. Intern, asst. resident in medicine Vanderbilt U. Hosp., Nashville, 1958—60; USPHS postdoctoral fellow in infectious disease Stanford U. Med. Ctr., Palo Alto, Calif., 1960—62; mem. staff virus diseases sect. mid. Am. rsch. unit Nat. Inst. Allergy and Infectious Disease, Panama, 1962—65; asst. prof. U. Mich. Sch. Pub. Health, Ann Arbor, 1965—76, chmn. dept. population planning and internat. health, 1993—97, dir. Ctr. for Population Planning, 1993—97, prof. epidemiology, 1996—, dir. Mich. Bioterrism and Health Preparedness Ctr., 1976—; dir. Mich. Bioterrorism and Health Preparednedd Rsch. and Tng. Ctr. Vis. scientist Clin. Rsch. Ctr., Northwick Park Hosp., Harrow, Eng., 1976; scholar-in-residence bd. on sci. and tech. for internat. devel. NAS and Inst. Medicine, Washington, 1983-84; vis. scientist div. communicable diseases WHO, Geneva, 1986-87; mem. pulmonary diseases adv. com. Nat. Heart, Lung and Blood Inst., Bethesda, Md., 1979-83; mem. nat. adv. coun. Nat. Inst. Allergy and Infectious Diseases, Bethesda, 1989-93, Contbr. articles to med. jours. Recipient career devel. award NIH. Fellow Am. Coll. Epidemiology, Infectious Diseases Soc. Am.; mem. APHA (governing coun. 1978-80), Am. Epidemiol. Soc. Achievements include research on respiratory viral infections in the community; demonstration of effectiveness of influenza vaccine in severe disease in the elderly; prevention of spread of influenza virus and treatment of illness, occurrence, causes and treatment of common cold. Office: U Mich Sch Pub Health I 109 Observatory St Ann Arbor MI 48109-2029

MONTROSS, ERIC SCOTT, professional basketball player; b. Sept. 23, 1971; s. Scott and Janice M.; m. Laura, Aug. 27, 1994. Student in Speech Comm., U. N.C. Ctr. Boston Celtics, 1994-96, N.J. Nets, 1996-97, Phila. 76ers, 1997-98, Detroit Pistons, 1998—. Named All-Am. Second team AP, All-ACC First team, All-Tournament teams ACC, NCAA East Region, NCAA Final Four, All-Rookie Second team, Schick, 1994-95. Avocations: reading, bass fishing, skeet shooting, travel, country music. Office: Detroit Pistons The Palace of Auburn Hills Two Championship Dr Auburn Hills MI 48326

MONTY, MITCHELL, landscape company executive; Pres. Suburban Landscape Assocs., Inc., 1981—. Office: Suburban Landscape Associates Inc 20875 N Brady St Davenport IA 52804-9305

MOODY, JAMES T(YNE), federal judge; b. LaCenter, Ky., June 16, 1938; BA, Ind. U., 1960, JD, 1963. Bar: Ind. 1963, U.S. Dist. Ct. (no. and so. dists.) Ind. 1963, U.S. Supreme Ct. 1972. Atty. Cities of Hobart and Lake Station, Ind., 1963-73; sole practice Hobart, 1963-73; judge Lake County (Ind.) Superior Ct., 1973-79; magistrate U.S. Dist. Ct. (no. dist.) Ind., Hammond, 1979-82, judge, 1982—; mem. faculty bus. law Ind. U., 1977-80. Republican Office: US Dist Ct 128 Fed Bldg 507 State St Hammond IN 46320-1533

MOODY, SUSAN S. bank executive; Exec. v.p. corp. banking NBD Bancorp Inc., Detroit; exec. v.p. corp & instl. banking 1st Chgo. NBD Corp., exec. v.p. cmml. banking mgmt. Office: First Chgo NBD Corp Ste 0184 9th Fl One First National Plz Chicago IL 60670

MOON, HARLEY WILLIAM, veterinarian; b. Tracy, Minn., Mar. 1, 1936; s. Harley Andrew Moon and Catherine Mary (Engesser) Lien; m. Irene Jeannette Casper, June 9, 1996; children: Michael J., Joseph E., Anne E., Teresa J. BS, U. Minn., 1958, DVM, 1960, PhD, 1965. Diplomate Am. Bd. Veterinary Pathologists. Instr. Coll. Vet. Medicine U. Minn., St. Paul, 1960—62, NIH postdoctoral fellow, 1963—65; vis. scientist Brookhaven Nat. Lab., Upton, NY, 1965—66; assoc. prof. Coll. Vet. Medicine U. Sask., Saskatoon, Canada, 1966—68; rsch. vet. Nat. Animal Disease Ctr. Agrl. Rsch. Svc., USDA, Ames, Iowa, 1968—88, ctr. dir., 1988—95; Franklyn Ramnsey chair in veterinary medicine & prof., 1996—; dir. Plum Island Animal Disease Ctr. USDA, 1995—96; prof. in charge Vet. Med. Rsch. Inst., 1996—. Assoc. prof. Iowa State U., Ames, 1970—73, prof., 1972—74; cons. U. N.C., Chapel Hill, 1985—92, Pioneer Hy-Bred Internat., Johnson, Iowa, 1986—92. Contbr. Recipient Superior Svc. award, USDA. Mem.: NAS, AAAS, NAS, AVMA, Am. Soc. Microbiologists, Am. Coll. Vet. Pathologists, Phi Zeta, Sigma Xi. Avocation: farming. Office: Iowa State University Veterinary Medicine Research Institute 1802 Elmwood Dr Ames IA 50011-0001

MOON, HAROLD WARREN, JR. professional football player; b. L.A., Nov. 18, 1956; m. Felicia Hendricks; children: Joshua, Jeffrey, Chelsea, Blair. Degree in comm., U. Wash., 1978. With Edmonton Eskimos, 1978-84, Houston Oilers, 1984-94, Minn. Vikings, 1994-97, Seattle Seahawks, 1997-98, Kansas City Chiefs, 1998—. Named to Pro Bowl, 1988-93, Sporting News NFL All-Pro team, 1990. Achievements include AFC Passing Leader, 1992; holds NFL single-season records for most passes attempted-665, 1991; most passes completed-404, 1991, sheares NFL single game record for most times sacked-12, 1985; shares NFL single season records for most games with 300 or more yards passing-9, 1990, most fumbles-18, 1990; Played in Grey Cup CFL Champioship Game 1978-82. Address: Kansas City Chiefs 1 Arrowhead Stadium Kansas City MO 64129

MOON, HENRY, academic administrator; BA in Geography, Va. Poly. Inst. and State U., 1978; MS in Geography, U. Ala., 1984; PhD in Geography, U. Ky., 1986. Edn. advisor Toledo Indsl., Recreation and Employee Svcs. Coun., Inc., 1995—; acad. advisor The Buckeye Ctr., 1994—; prof. geography and planning U. Toledo, 1986—, dean Univ. Coll., 1995-98, provost, v.p. undergrad. and grad. edn., 1999—. Cons., presenter and rschr. in field. Author: Environmental Geography Lab Manual, 1986, Environment Geography Lab Manual, 2d edit., 1990, The Interstate Highway System, 1994; co-author: A Workbook in Human Geography, 1987; contbr. chpts. to books and articles to profl. jours.; jour. article reviewer; software reviewer; manuscript reviewer; book reviewer; grant program reviewer, others. Advisor Area Growth Com., 1986-90, Ashland Ave. Revitalization Com., 1986-90, Buckeye Basin Mgmt. Team, 1986-90, City of Toledo, 1986—, Toledo Met. Area Coun. Govts., 1986—, Viva! Toledo, 1986-90, Collingwood Springs Redevel. Corp., 1987—, Com. of 100, 1987-92, Heritage South Comml. Revitalization Assn., 1987—, Toledo-Lucas County Port Authority, 1987—, Archbold Area Schs., 1991—; mem. Toledo Met. Area Coun. of Govts. N.W. Ohio Strategic Planning Conf./Gen. Assembly, 1989; chair Toledo Met. Area Coun. Govts. Com. One, 1989-91, Toledo Met. Area Coun. Govts. Citizen Adv. Com., 1990-92, N.W. Ohio Passenger Rail Task Force, 1993; mem. Toledo Express Airport Master Planning Com., 1991-92, City of Toledo and Lucas County, Overall Econ. Devel. Planning Com., 1995—, City of Toledo Competitive Coun., 1995; trustee Arrowhead Park Assn., 1995-98, Greater Toledo Conv. and Visitors Bur., 1996-99, N.W. Ohio Distance Learning Consortium, 1997—. Recipient Most Outstanding Paper award 62nd Annual Meeting of the Ala. Acad. Sci., 1984, GM Vol. Spirit award, 1995; grantee U. Ala. Student Govt. Assn., 1984, Ala. Acad. Sci., 1984, Collingwood Springs Redevel. Corp., 1987, U. Toledo Office of Rsch., 1987, Toledo-Lucas County Port Authority, 1988, Toledo Met. Area Coun. Govts., 1988, U.S. Dept. Energy, 1991, 92, 94, Williams County Econ. Devel. Corp., 1994, Environ. Sys. Rsch. Inst., Inc., 1995, Nat. Aero. and Space Adminstrn., 1996, many others. Fellow Ohio Acad. Sci. (v.p. geography sect. 1990-92), Assn. Am. Geographers (chair East Lakes divsn., Disting. Svc. award East Lakes divsn. 1996), Am. Land Resource Assn. (charter mem. 1985-87), Toledo Area C. of C. (advisor 1986—). Office: Office of the Provost U Toledo Bancroft St Toledo OH 43606-3390

MOONE, ROBERT H. finance company executive; BA in Psychology, Ohio State U., 1966. With State Auto Fin. Corp., Columbus, Ohio, 1970, br. underwriting mgr., 1980, mgr. sales devel., dir. mktg., dir. sales and mktg., pres., 1996—, CEO, 1999—. Office: State Auto Fin Corp 518 E Broad St Columbus OH 43215-3901

MOONEY, JAMES P. chemicals executive; BA in History, Quincy U. Pres., CEO Mooney Chems., Inc., 1979-91; CEO OM Group Inc., Cleve., 1991—, also chmn. bd. dirs. Mem. Nat. Paint & Coatings Assn., Nat. Fed. Paint, Tech.'s Chems. Mgmt. Coun., Chem. Mfrs. Assn., Cobolt Devel. Inst. (bd. dirs.). Office: OM Group Inc 50 Public Sq,ste 3500 Cleveland OH 44113-2201

MOONEY, KEVIN W. telecommunications executive; BS in Fin., Seton Hall U.; MBA in Fin., Ga. State U. Various mgmt. positions New Jersey Bell, AT&T, BellSouth Cellular, BellSouth, Inc.; CFO Cin. Bell, Inc.; exec. v.p. Broadwing, Inc., Cin. Office: 401 E 4th St PO Box 2301 Cincinnati OH 45201-2301

MOOR, ROB, professional basketball team executive; b. Geneva, Switzerland; came to U.S., 1966; Degree, U. Calif., Irvine. Staff in distribution MGM Studios; staff in royalties, licensing and profits Twentieth Century Fox Studios; exec. v.p. Los Angeles Kings NHL; pres. Minn. Timberwolves, 1994—. Mem. Greater Minneapolis C. of C. (bd. dirs.). Office: Minn Timberwolves 600 1st Ave N Ste Sky Minneapolis MN 55403-1416

MOOR, ROY EDWARD, finance educator; b. Riverside, Calif., Oct. 11, 1924; s. Hugh Erin and Clara Viola Moor; m. Beverly A. Colbroth, Aug. 29, 1959; children— Cynthia Ann, Sheryl Lynn B.A., UCLA, 1949; Ph.D., Harvard U., 1958. Vice pres., chief economist Fidelity Bank, Phila., 1965-68; vice pres., chief economist Drexel Firestone, 1968-71, Warburg Paribas Becker, N.Y.C., 1971-81; sr. v.p., chief economist First Chgo. Corp., 1981-86; prof. fin. Ill. Inst. Tech., Chgo., 1986—. Dir. Nat. Bur. Econ. Research, Cambridge, Mass. Author: Federal Budget as an Economic Document, 1962 Fellow Nat. Assn. Bus. Economists (pres. 1973) Home: 1013 Woodrush Ct Westmont IL 60561-8823 Office: Ill Inst Tech 10 W 31st St Chicago IL 60616-3729 E-mail: rbmoor@kwom.com.

MOORADIAN, ARSHAG DERTAD, internist, educator; b. Aleppo, Syria, Aug. 20, 1953; arrived in U.S., 1981; s. Dertad and Araxi (Halajian) Mooradian; m. Deborah Lynn Miles, June 25, 1985; children: Arshag Dertad, Jr., Ariana Araxie. BS, Am. U., Beirut, 1976, MD, 1980. Diplomate Am. Bd. Internal Medicine. Asst. prof. medicine UCLA, 1985-88; assoc. prof. U. Ariz., Tucson, 1988-91; prof. St. Louis U., 1991. Contbr. articles to profl. jours. Grantee VA, 1985—97. Mem.: Am. Diabetes Assn. (chmn. task force micronutrients 1990—91, chmn. coun. nutrition and metabolism 2000—02), Endocrine Soc., Gerontol. Soc. Am., Am. Fedn. Clin. Rsch. Mem. Armenian Orthodox Ch. Achievements include identification of a potential biomarker of aging;research in on age-related changes in the blood-brain barrier;research in on age-related changes in thyroid hormone action;research in on diabetes related changes in the central nervous system. Office: Saint Louis U Med Sch 1402 S Grand Blvd Saint Louis MO 63104-1004

MOORE, ANDREA S. state legislator; b. Libertyville, Ill., Sept. 2, 1944; Attended, Drake U. m. William Moore; 3 children. Mem. Ill. Ho. of Reps., 1993—; mem. com. on elections and state govt.; mem. com. on aging; mem. cities and villages com.; mem. environ. and energy com.; mem. labor and commerce com.; mem. com. on healthcare; mem. revenue and commerce com. Republican. Home: 361 S Saint Marys Rd Libertyville IL 60048-9407 Office: Ill Ho of Reps State Capitol Springfield IL 62706-0001 also: 2014-h Stratton Bldg Springfield IL 62706-0001 also: 131 E Park Ave Libertyville IL 60048-2800

MOORE, C. BRADLEY, chemistry educator; b. Boston, Dec. 7, 1939; s. Charles Walden and Dorothy (Lutz) Moore; m. Penelope Williamson Percival, Aug. 27, 1960; children: Megan Bradley, Scott Woodward. BA magna cum laude, Harvard U., 1960; PhD, U. Calif., Berkeley, 1963. Predoctoral fellow NSF, 1960-63; asst. prof. chemistry U. Calif., Berkeley, 1963-68, assoc. prof., 1968-72, prof., 1972-2000, vice chmn. dept., 1971-75, chmn. dept. chemistry, 1982-86, dean Coll. Chemistry, 1988-94, prof. grad. sch., 2000—; v.p. rsch. Ohio State U., Columbus, Disting. prof. math. and phys. sci., prof. chemistry, 2000—. Assoc. prof. Faculty Scis., Paris, 1970, 75; Miller Rsch. Prof. U. Calif., Berkeley, 1972-73, 87-88; vis. prof. Inst. for Molecular Sci., Okazaki, Japan, 1979, Fudan U., Shanghai, 1979, adv. prof., 1988—; vis. fellow Joint Inst. for Lab. Astrophysics, U. Colo., Boulder, 1981-82; faculty sr. scientist (Chemical Sci. Div.) Lawrence Berkeley Nat. Lab., 1974-2000, divsn. dir., 1998-2000: mem. editl. bd. Jour. Chem. Physics, 1973-75, Chem. Physics Letters, 1980-85, Jour. Phys. Chemistry, 1981-87, Laser Chemistry, 1982—; mem. Basic Energy Scis. adv. com. Office Sci. U.S. Dept. Energy. Editor: Chemical and Biochemical Applications of Lasers; assoc. editor Annual Review of Physical Chemistry, 1985-90; contbr. articles to profl. jours. Trustee Sci. Svc., 1995—, Sci. and Tech. Campus; mem. bd. govs. Ohio Supercomputer Centing Chair; rsch. officer Coun. of Ohio Bd. of Regents; pres. Ohio State U. Rsch. Found., chmn. bd. Recipient Coblentz award, 1973, E.O. Lawrence Meml. award U.S. Dept. Energy, 1986, Lippincott award, 1987, 1st award Inter-Am. Photochem. Soc., 1988; nat. scholar Harvard U., 1958-60; fellow Alfred P. Sloan Found., 1968, Guggenheim Found., 1969, Humboldt Rsch. award for Sr. U.S. Scientists, 1994. Fellow AAAS, Am. Acad. Arts and Scis., Am. Phys. Soc. (Plyler award 1994); mem. NSF adv. com. for education and human resources directorate, chair subcom. policy and planning 1997-99, NAS (chmn. com. undergrad. sci. edn. 1993-97, class I membership com., 1998-2000, 2002, 2000 nominating com.), Am. Chem. Soc. (past chmn. divsn. phys. chemistry, Calif. sect. award 1977). Avocation: cycling. Office: Ohio State U 208 Bricker Hall 190 N Oval Mall Columbus OH 43210-1321 E-mail: moore.1@osu.edu.

MOORE, DENNIS, congressman; b. Anthony, Kans., 1945; m. Stephene; 7 children. BS, U. Kans., 1967; JD, Washburn U., 1970. Bar: Kans. 1970. Asst. atty. gen. State of Kans., 1971-73; pvt. practice, 1973-76; dist. atty. Johnson County, 1977-89; ptnr. Erker & Moore, LLC, 1991-98, Smith, Gill, Fisher & Butts, 1989-91; mem. U.S. Congress from 3d Kans. dist., 1999—. Mem. House Com. on Fin. Svcs. Sci. and the Budget. Elected to Johnson County C.C. bd. trustees, 1993; re-elected, 1997; bd. dirs. Johnson County Safehome, Coalition for Prevention of Child Abuse, Kans. Child Abuse Prevention Coun., CASA (Ct. Appointed Spl. Advocate), United Cmty. Svcs., Cmty. Corrections Adv. Bd.; unsuccessful Dem. candidate for state atty. gen., 1986. With U.S. Army, U.S. Army Res. Democrat. Achievements include personally prosecuting more than 25 felony jury trials; led Consumer Protection Divsn. in the investigation and successful prosecution of a nat. oil co. charged with rigging gas pumps to cheat consumers; established a victim assistance unit; was cited by an ind. cons. hired by the Johnson County Bd. Commrs. as running the most efficient office in Johnson County govt.; served as pres. Kans. County and Dist. Atty.'s Assn. Office: 431 Cannon Hob Washington DC 20515-0001*

MOORE, DENNIS J. electronics executive; b. 1938; Grad., U.S. Naval Acad., 1961. bd. dirs. Instron Corp., adv. bd. Allendale Mutual Ins. Co., trustee Naval Acad. Found. Exec. mgmt. mktg., research and devel. Rosemount, Inc.; pres. Beckman Indsl., 1984-87, Electronics & Space Corp., 1987-89; group v.p. Emerson, 1989-90; pres., COO ESCO Techs., Inc., 1990-92, chmn., CEO, 1992—. Office: Esco Techs Inc 8888 Ladue Rd Ste 200 Saint Louis MO 63124-2090

MOORE, DORSEY JEROME, dentistry educator, maxillofacial prosthetist; b. Boonville, Mo., Feb. 8, 1935; s. Lloyd Elliott Moore and Mary Elizabeth (Day) Katemann; m. Mary Louise Foote, May 2, 1959; children: Elizabeth L., David J. DDS, U. Mo., Kansas City, 1959. Diplomate Am. Bd. Prosthodontics. Commd. ensign USN, 1955, advanced through grades to capt., 1973; gen. practice dentistry various naval stas., 1959-63; practice in prosthodontics USS Proteus AS-19, 1963-66; resident in prosthodontics and maxillofacial prosthetics Naval Dental Sch., Bethesda, Md., 1966-69, chief maxillofacial prosthetics divsn., 1969-70; sr. dental advisor Naval Adv. Group, Comdr. Naval Forces, Saigon, Vietnam, 1970-71; chief maxillofacial prosthetics div. Nat. Naval Dental Ctr., 1971-76; chief maxillofacial prosthetics br. Naval Regional Med. Ctr., Great Lakes, Ill., 1976-79, ret., 1979; vis. lectr. U. Mo. Sch. Dentistry, Kansas City, 1976-79, H.G.B. Robinson prof., chmn. dept. removable prosthodontics, 1979-2000, Hamilton G.B. Robinson emeritus prof. dentistry, 2000, ret., 2000; chief maxillofacial prosthetics Truman Med. Ctr., Kansas City, Mo., 2000—. Assoc. prof. U. Saigon Sch. Dentistry, 1970-71; advisor to Min. of Health, Saigon, 1970-71; profl. lectr. George Washington U., Washington, 1971-76; clin. assoc. prof. surgery U. Kans. Sch. Medicine, 1987—; cons. maxillofacial prosthetics NIH Treatment Ctr., 1973—, Nat. Cancer Inst., 1973—, VA Hosp., North Chicago, Ill., 1976—, ADA Couns. Dental Edn., Hosp. Dental Svc. and Commn. on Accredition, 1978—; vice chancellor Devel. Adv. Com., 1983—; examiner Mo.

MOORE, EMILY ALLYN, pharmacologist; b. Evansville, Ind., Apr. 3, 1950; m. Robert Alan Yount, Nov. 25, 1972 (div. Feb. 1986); 1 child, Joseph Taylor; m. Robert E. Moore Jr., Aug. 11, 1990; 1 child, Alexander Allyn. AB in Chem. Biology, Ind. U., Bloomington, 1971; MS in Applied Computer Sci., Purdue U., Indpls., 1985; PhD in Pharmacology, Ind. U., Indpls., 1976. Vis. asst. prof. biology Ind. U., Bloomington, 1979, rsch. assoc. in biochemistry Indpls., 1979-81, rsch. assoc., 1982-83, computer programmer for med. genetics, 1983-85, asst. scientist. med. genetics, 1985-87; tech. assessment specialist Boehringer Mannheim Corp., 1987, mgr. sci. info., 1987-89; mgr. Tech. Assess, 1989-93, quality process analyst, 1993-94. Contbr. articles to profl. jours. Officer or bd. dirs. LWV, Hendricks County, Ind., 1977-84; elder St. Luke's United Ch. of Christ, Speedway, Ind., 1983-85; mem. adv. bd. Operation SMART, Indpls., 1989-90. Achievements include participation in creation of first DNA bank for storage of DNA samples for future use in diagnosis of genetic diseases.

MOORE, GARRY ALLEN, state legislator; b. Yankton, S.D., May 14, 1949; m. Connie Moore; 4 children. Student, S.D. State U., 1967-69. Mem. S.D. Ho. of Reps., 1991-98, mem. judiciary com., taxation com., local govt. com., health and human svcs. com.; mem. S.D. Senate from 18th dist., Pierre, 1999—; mem. judiciary com., govt. audit and ops. com. S.D. Senate, taxation com., transp. com., corrections commn. Sales mgr. Bob's Candy Svc., Yankton. Past mem. exec. bd. State Dem. Party; chmn. Yankton Sch. Bd., 1982-88. Mem. S.D. Wholesalers Assn. (past pres.). Home: 2310 Western Ave Yankton SD 57078-1419

MOORE, GWENDOLYNNE, state legislator; Mem. Wis. Senate from 4th dist., Madison, 1992—. Home: 4043 N 19th Pl Milwaukee WI 53209-6806 Office: Wis State Assembly State Capital Madison WI 53702-0001

MOORE, HERMAN JOSEPH, professional football player; b. Danville, Va., Oct. 20, 1969; BA in Rhetoric & Comm. Studies, U. Va., 1991. Wide receiver Detroit Lions, 1991—. Named to The Sporting News All-Am. 1st team, 1990; selected to Pro Bowl, 1994. Office: Detroit Lions 1200 Featherstone Rd Pontiac MI 48342-1938

MOORE, JOHN EDWARD, marketing professional, freelance writer; b. Watertown, Wisc., Sept. 18, 1920; s. John Martin and Grace Marie (Dent) M.; m. Barbara J. Gates, Sept. 21, 1947 (div. 1957); m. Sally Elizabeth Bond, Oct. 18, 1958; children: Gerald Ian, Helen Louise, Jeffrey Craig, Tracy Patricia. U. Wisc., 1946. Mktg. rsch. mgr. Procter & Gamble (Manila) Phillippines, 1949-57; staff assignment Overseas Div. Procter Gamble, Cin., 1958-62; mkt. rsch. mgr. Procter & Gamble Scandinavia, Newcastle, Tyne, U.K., 1962-64, Export & Spl. Ops., Procter & Gamble A.G., Geneva, Switzerland, 1964-75; assoc. mgr. mkt. rsch. Procter & Gamble, Cin., 1976-79, internat. mktg. rsch. mgr., 1980-84; cons. J.E. Moore, 1984-95; freelance writer, 1990—. Pres. Philippine (Manila) Radio Broadcasting Corp., 1952-54, mem. European Opinion and Mktg. Congress, 1964-75. Contbr. articles to profl. jours. Chmn. Boy Scouts of Am. Geneva, 1975, pres. Cin. Youth Symphony Orch. 1980-82, Men's com. Cin. Art Mus. 1984-90, Duveneck Assn., 1990-99, fund raiser Art Acad., Cin. 1987; chmn. Duveneck Assn., 1999. With U.S. Army, ETO. Recipient Market Rsch. Pioneer award, Philippines, 1987. Mem. Am. Assn. Individual Investors, Smithsonian Assocs., Am. Assn. Retired Persons, Internat. Visitors Ctr. Episcopalian. Avocations: golf, freelance writing, travel. Home and Office: 6235 Nuevelle Ln Cincinnati OH 45243-2355

MOORE, JOHN EDWIN, JR. college president; b. Aurora, Mo., Nov. 7, 1942; s. John Edwin and Emma Lou (Harback) M.; children: John E. III, Catherine Porter. BA cum laude, Yale U., 1964, MA in Teaching, 1965; EdD, Harvard U., 1971. Tchr. N.C. Advancement Sch., Winston-Salem, 1965-66; rsch. asst. Tech. Edn. Rsch. Ctr., Cambridge, Mass., 1969-70; adminstrv. asst., treas. Kirkwood Sch. Dist. R-VII, St. Louis, 1970-73, asst. supt., treas., 1973-74; adj. prof. U. Mo., 1973-74; v.p. Athens (Greece) Coll., 1974-75; asst. commr. edn. Dept. Elem. and Secondary Edn., Jefferson City, Mo., 1975-83; pres. Drury U., Springfield, 1983—. Part-time instr. Far-East div. U. Md., 1967-68. Bd. dirs. United Way Ozarks, campaign chmn., 1988; bd. dirs. Mo. Colls. Fund, chmn., 1988-89; bd. dirs. Make-A-Wish Found.; chmn. bd. dirs. Am. Nat. Fish & Wildlife Mus., 1998—. With U.S. Army, 1966-68. Recipient Vincent Conroy Meml. award Harvard Grad. Sch. Edn., 1971; named one of Outstanding Young Men Am., 1973. Mem. Springfield Area C. of C. (v.p. 1988, bd. dirs. Springfieldian of Yr. 1989), Nat. Assn. Intercollegiate Athletics (coun. pres.'s), Rotary (pres. Springfield chpt. 1988-89). Presbyterian (elder). Avocations: hunting, fishing, gardening, conservation. Home: 1234 N Benton Ave Springfield MO 65802-1902 Office: Drury U 900 N Benton Ave Springfield MO 65802-3712

MOORE, JOHN RONALD, manufacturing executive; b. Pueblo, Colo., July 12, 1935; s. John E. and Anna (Yesberger) M.; m. Judith Russelyn Bauman, Sept. 5, 1959; children: Leland, Roni, Timothy, Elaine. BS, U. Colo., 1959; grad. advanced mgmt. program, Harvard Grad. Sch. Bus., 1981. Mgmt. trainee Montgomery Ward & Co., Denver, 1960-65; distbn. mgr. Midas Internat. Corp., Chgo., 1965-71; v.p., gen. mgr. Midas, Can., Toronto, Ont., 1972-75; pres. Auto Group Midas Internat. Corp., Chgo., 1976-82, pres., chief exec. officer, 1982-98; ret., 1998. Bd. dirs. Goodwill Industries, Met. Chgo. Bd. dirs. Lake Forest Grad. Sch. Mgmt.; mem. bus. adv. coun. U. Colo. Sch. Bus. Mem. Harvard Bus. Sch. Alumni Assn., U. Colo. Alumni Assn., Chgo. Coun. Fgn. Rels., Econ. Club Chgo., Comml. Club Chgo. Republican.

MOORE, JOHN WILLIAM, former university president; b. Bayonne, N.J., Aug. 1, 1939; s. Frederick A. and Marian R. (Faser) M.; m. Nancy Baumann, Aug. 10, 1968; children: Matthew, Sarah, David. BS in Social Sci. and Edn., Rutgers U., 1961; MS in Counseling and Student Pers. Svcs., Ind. U., 1963; EdD, Pa. State U., 1970. Asst. to dean Coll. Edn. Pa. State U., University Park, 1968-70; asst. to dean students U. Vt., Burlington, 1970-71, asst. prof. edn. adminstrn., 1973-76, asst. v.p. acad. affairs, 1973-76, assoc. v.p. acad. affairs, 1976-77; v.p. policy and planning Old Dominion U., Norfolk, Va., 1977-78, exec. v.p., 1982-85; pres. Calif. State

U., Stanislaus, Turlock, 1985-92, Ind. State U., 1992-2000. Author: (with others) The Changing Composition of the Work Force: Implications for Future Research and Its Application, 1982, also articles, papers presented at profl. meetings Pres. United Way, Modesto Calif., 1989; campaign chair United Way Wabash Valley, Terre Haute, Ind.; bd. dirs. Pvt. Industry Coun., Modesto, 1989, Union Hosp., Swope Mus., Am. Assn. Colls. and Univs.; bd. dirs., exec. com. Alliance for Growth and Progress, Terre Haute, Ind., 1992—, Terre Haute C. of C., Wabash Valley United Way, Bus. and Modernization Tech. Corp., Ind. Econ. Devel. Commn., PSI Energy. Recipient Disting. Svc. award Old Dominion U. Alumni Assn., 1985, Hispanic C. of C., 1982; recipient Community Svc. award Norfolk Commn. Edn., 1985, Leadership award United Way,1 986, Svc. award Pvt. Industry Coun., 1989; Alumni fellow Pa. State U., 1990. Mem. Am. Assn. State Colls. and Univs. (rep. Calif. chpt. 1988-92, bd. dirs. 1994—), Gould Med. Found. (bd. dirs. 1988-92, trustee 1988-92), Modesto Symphony Orch. Assn. (bd. dirs. 1990-92), Am. Coun. Edn., Commn. on Women in Higher Edn., Turlock C. of C. (bd. dirs. 1988-92), Rotary. Methodist. Avocations: fitness training, skiing, coaching youth sports, golf. Office: Ind State U Condit House Terre Haute IN 47809-0001

MOORE, JOSEPH ARTHUR, alderman, lawyer; b. Chgo., July 22, 1958; s. Max Dale and Marilyn Ruth (Herzog) M.; m. Elaine Carol Weiss, Sept. 24, 1988; children: Nathan Alexander, Zachary Arthur. BA, Knox Coll., Galesburg, Ill., 1980; JD, DePaul U., Chgo., 1984. Bar: Ill. Atty. City of Chgo. Dept. of Law, 1984-91; alderman 49th Ward, Chgo., 1991—. Mem. adv. bd. Dev Corp. North, Chgo., 1993—. Pres. Network 49, Chgo., 1987-90; bd. dirs. Citizen Action, Washington, 1994-97, Ill. Pub. Action, Chgo., 1991-97, Ind. Voters Ill., Chgo., 1986-97, Citizen Action. Ill., 1998—; mem. energy, environment and natural resources steering com. Nat. League of Cities, 1998—, vice chair, 2001—. Dan Coman scholar DePaul U. Coll. Law, 1984. Democrat. Roman Catholic. Office: 7356 N Greenview Ave Chicago IL 60626-1924 E-mail: aldmoore@aol.com.

MOORE, KAREN NELSON, judge; b. Washington, Nov. 19, 1948; d. Roger S. and Myrtle Nelson; m. Kenneth Cameron Moore, June 22, 1974; children: Roger C., Kenneth N., Kristin K. AB magna cum laude, Radcliffe Coll., 1970; JD magna cum laude, Harvard U., 1973. Bar: DC 1973, Ohio 1976, U.S. Ct. Appeals (DC cir.) 1974, U.S. Supreme Ct. 1980, U.S. Ct. Appeals (6th cir.) 1984. Law clk. Assoc. Justice Harry A. Blackmun, U.S. Supreme Ct., Washington, 1974—75; assoc. Jones, Day, Reavis & Pogue, Cleve., 1975—77; asst. prof. Case Western Res. Law Sch., 1977—80, assoc. prof., 1980—82, prof., 1982—95; judge U.S. Ct. Appeals (6th cir.), 1995—. Vis. prof. Harvard Law Sch., 1990—91. Mem. Harvard Law Rev., 1971—73; contbr. articles. Trustee Lakewood Hosp., Ohio, 1978—85, Radcliffe Coll., Cambridge, 1980—84. Fellow: Am. Bar Found.; mem.: Harvard U. Alumni Assn. (bd. dirs. 1984—87), Am. Law Inst., Phi Beta Kappa. Office: US Ct Appeals 6th Cir 328 US Courthouse 201 Superior Ave E Cleveland OH 44114-1201

MOORE, KENNETH EDWIN, pharmacology educator; b. Edmonton, Alta., Can., Aug. 8, 1933; came to U.S., 1957, naturalized, 1966; s. Jack and Emily Elizabeth (Tarbox) M.; m. Barbara Anne Stafford, Sept. 19, 1953; children— Grant Kenneth, Sandra Anne, Lynn Susan. B.S., U. Alta., 1955, M.S., 1957; Ph.D., U. Mich., 1960. Instr. pharmacology Dartmouth Med. Sch., Hanover, N.H., 1960-61, asst. prof., 1962-66; assoc. prof. pharmacology Mich. State U., East Lansing, 1966-70, prof., 1970—, chmn. dept. pharmacology and toxicology, 1987—2001. Vis. scholar Cambridge (Eng.) U., 1974; instr. Lansing Community Coll., 1975-81; cons. NIH, also pharm. industry. Author 1 book; contbr. articles to profl. jours. Fellow Am. Coll. Neuropsychopharmacology; mem. Am. Soc. Pharmacology and Exptl. Therapeutics (chmn. bd. publs. trustees 1992-96, pres. 1998-2000), Soc. Exptl. Biology and Medicine, Soc. Neuroscis. Home: 4790 Arapaho Trl Okemos MI 48864-1402 Office: Dept Pharmacology Mich State U East Lansing MI 48824 E-mail: moorek@pilot.msu.edu.

MOORE, KENNETH CAMERON, lawyer; b. Chgo., Oct. 25, 1947; s. Kenneth Edwards and Margaret Elizabeth (Cameron) M.; m. Karen M. Nelson, June 22, 1974; children: Roger Cameron, Kenneth Nelson, Kristin Karen. BA summa cum laude, Hiram Coll., 1969; JD cum laude, Harvard U., 1973. Bar: Ohio 1973, U.S. Dist. Ct. Md. 1974, U.S. Ct. Appeals (4th cir.) 1974, D.C. 1975, U.S. Dist. Ct. (no. dist.) Ohio 1976, U.S. Ct. Appeals (6th cir.) 1977, U.S. Ct. Appeals (D.C. cir.) 1979, U.S. Supreme Ct. 1980. Law clk. to judge Harrison L. Winter U.S. Ct. Appeals (4th cir.), Balt., 1973-74; assoc. Squire, Sanders & Dempsey, Washington, 1974-75, Cleve., 1975-82, ptnr., 1982—, mem. fin. com., 1990—, profl. ethics ptnr., 1996—. Chmn. Ohio Fin. Com. for Jimmy Carter presdl. campaign, 1976; del. Dem. Nat. Conv., 1976; chief legal counsel Ohio Carter-Mondale Campaign, 1976; trustee Hiram Coll., 1997—, mem. exec. com., 1999, chair audit com., 1999, vice chair bd. trustees, 2000—, chair faculty affairs subcom. of ednl. policy com., 2000—. With AUS, 1970-76. Mem. ABA, Fed. Bar Assn., Ohio Bar Assn., Cleve. Bar Assn., Cleve. City Club. Home: 15602 Edgewater Dr Cleveland OH 44107-1212 Office: Squire Sanders & Dempsey 4900 Society Ctr 127 Public Sq Ste 4900 Cleveland OH 44114-1304

MOORE, KENNETH JAMES, agronomy educator; b. Phoenix, June 6, 1957; s. George Taylor and Barbara Joyce (Amy) M.; m. Gina Marie McCarthy Aug. 11, 1979; children: Ellyn Elizabeth, David Taylor, Mark Daniel. BS in Agr., Ariz. State U., 1979; MS in Agronomy, Purdue U., 1981, PhD in Agronomy, 1983. Asst. prof. agronomy U. Ill., Urbana, 1983-87; assoc. prof. N.Mex. State U., Las Cruces, 1988-89; rsch. agronomist Agrl. Rsch. Svc., USDA, Lincoln, Nebr., 1989-93; prof. Iowa State U., Ames, 1993—. Adj. assoc. prof. U. Nebr. Lincoln, 1989-93, prof., 1993-96; sr. rsch. fellow Ag Rsch. Grasslands, New Zealand, 1998. Author: Crop Science Laboratory Manual, 1988; editor Crop Mgmt., 2002--; assoc. editor Agronomy Jour., 1989-93, tech. editor, 1994-97; assoc. editor Crop Sci., 1994; contbr. chpts. to books. Bd. dirs. Lincoln Children's Mus., 1991-93, Children's Svcs. of Ctrl. Iowa, 1996-97; bd. dirs. Children's Mus. Ctrl. Iowa, 1997-2002, pres., 2000-01; mem. mgmt. com. N.E. YMCA, Lincoln, 1991-93; mem. youth policy forum Lincoln YMCA, 1991-92. Recipient Point of Light award USDA, 1991. Fellow Am. Soc. Agronomy, Crop Sci. Soc. Am. (divsn. chmn. 1990-92, Young Crop Scientist award 1993); mem. Am. Forage and Grassland Coun. (Outstanding Young Scientist award 1982, merit award 1991), Am. Soc. Animal Sci., Am. Dairy Sci. Assn. Republican. Presbyterian. Avocations: swimming, fishing, music. Office: Iowa State U Agronomy Dept 1567 Agronomy Hl Ames IA 50011-0001

MOORE, MITCHELL JAY, lawyer, law educator; b. Lincoln, Nebr., Aug. 29, 1954; s. Earl J. and Betty Marie (Zimmerlin) M.; m. Sharon Lea Campbell, Sept. 5, 1987. BS in Edn., U. Mo., Columbia, 1977, JD, 1981. Bar: Mo. 1981, U.S. Dist. Ct. (we. dist.) Mo. 1981, Tex. 1982, U.S. Ct. Appeals (8th cir.) 1998. Sole practice, Columbia, Mo., 1981—. Coordinating atty. student legal svcs. ctr. U. Mo., Columbia, 1983-89. Mem. Columbia Substance Abuse Adv. Commn., 1989—; bd. dirs. Planned Parenthood of Ctrl. Mo., Columbia, 1984-86, Opportunities Unltd., Columbia, 1984-86, ACLU of Mid-Mo., 1991-98; Libertarian candidate for Atty. Gen. of Mo., 1992, 2000, for 9th congl. dist. U.S. Ho. of Reps., 1994, 96, for Mo. State Rep. 23d dist., 1998, for Atty. Gen. Mo., 2000; mem. Probation and Parole Citizens Adv. Bd., 1997-99. Mem. Boone County Bar Assn., Assn. Trial Lawyers Am., Phi Delta Phi. Libertarian. Unitarian. Avocations: softball, camping, Tae Kwon Do. Office: 1210 W Broadway Columbia MO 65203-2126 E-mail: mmoore259@mchsi.com.

MOORE, OLIVER SEMON, III, publishing executive, consultant; b. Jersey City, July 26, 1942; s. Oliver S. and Ann Loy (Spies) M.; m. Dina Downing DuBois, Feb. 23, 1961 (div. 1974); 1 child, Deborah; m. Christine Laine Meyers, May 12, 1990; 1 child, Kathryn Laine. BA, U. Va., 1964. Chief bur. Richmond (Va.) Times-Dispatch, 1964-66; corr. Time mag., N.Y.C., 1966-67, contbg. editor, 1967-68; assoc. editor Newsweek, 1969-71; freelance writer, 1972-75; mng. editor Motor Boating and Sailing, N.Y.C., 1976-78, editor, 1980-82; exec. editor US Mag., N.Y. Times Co., 1978-80; dep. editor Town & Country Mag., N.Y.C., 1982-84; editor Sci. Digest Mag., 1984-86; pub. dir. Yachting Mag., 1986-95; editorial dir. Outdoor Life, 1993-95; v.p. The Outdoor Co., 1994-95; editor-at-large Motor Boating & Sailing, 1995—2001; pres. Alamo Pub. Svcs., Inc., Detroit, 1995—. Co-founder, chmn. bd. Corp! (Mag.), 1998. Author: (poems) Voices International, 1969; contbg. editor Sports Afield, 1996—; photographer (mags.) Motor Boating and Sailing, Yachting, Working Woman, (books) Lines to a Little Girl, Rancho Paradiso. Recipient Merit award Art Dirs. Club, 1981, award of merit Soc. Publ. Designers, 1981, Excellence in Media award Nat. Arbor Day Found., 1985. Mem. Am. Soc. Mag. Editors, Mag. Pubs. Assn. (nat. mag. award 1995), N.Y. Yacht Club, Grosse Pointe (Mich.) Club, Bayview (Mich.) Yacht Club, The Huntsman (Mich.), Wyndeme Club (Fla.). Republican. Episcopalian. Avocations: sailing, antique cars. Office: Corp! 3645 Crooks Rd Troy MI 48084-1642

MOORE, PATRICK J. paper company executive; Asst. treas. Jefferson Smurfit Corp., St. Louis, 1987-90, treas., 1990-93, v.p., treas., 1993-94; v.p., gen. mgr. Indsl. Packaging divsn., 1994-96; v.p., CFO Smurfit-Stone Container Corp., Chgo., 1996—. Office: Smurfit-Stone Container Corp 150 N Michigan Ave Chicago IL 60601-7568

MOORE, RAYMOND A. consultant, retired agriculture educator; b. Britton, S.D., Nov. 16, 1927; s. Arthur L. and Anna (Schuur) M.; m. Marlys Schiefelbein, Jun 17, 1951; children: Craig, Jay, Kent, Jeff. BA in Agrl. Edn. and Econs., S.D. State U., 1951, MS in Agronomy, 1958; PhD in Crop Physiology and Ecology, Purdue U., 1963. Instr. vocat. agriculture Bennett County H.S., Martin, S.D., 1951-56; instr., prof., adminstr. S.D. State U., Brookings, 1956-94, dir. emeritus agrl. expt. sta., 1994—. Cons. Coop. States Rsch. Svcs. USDA, Washington, Producers Renewable Products, St. Paul. Contbr. chpts. to books, articles to profl. jours. With USN, 1945-47. Nat. Sci. Faculty fellow forage & pasture mgmt. CSRS/U.S. Dept. Agriculture, 1965; Citizens Ambassador Program People to People Internat. travel grantee, U.S. Dept. Agriculture travel grantee. Mem. Am. Soc. Agronomy, Kiwanis Internat., Sigma Xi, Gamma Sigma Delta. Avocations: hunting, fishing, gardening, farming. Home: 207 17th Ave Brookings SD 57006-2609 Office: SD State U PO Box 2207 Brookings SD 57007-0001

MOORE, RICHARD KERR, electrical engineering educator; b. St. Louis, Nov. 13, 1923; s. Louis D. and Nina (Megown) M.; m. Wilma Lois Schallau, Dec. 10, 1944; children: John Richard, Daniel Charles. BS, Washington U. at St. Louis, 1943; PhD, Cornell U., 1951. Test equipment engr. RCA, Camden, N.J., 1943-44; instr. and rsch. engr. Washington U., St. Louis, 1947-49; rsch. assoc. Cornell U., 1949-51; rsch. engr., sect. supr. Sandia Corp., Albuquerque, 1951-55; prof., chmn. elec. engring. U. N.Mex., 1955-62; Black and Veatch prof. U. Kans., Lawrence, 1962-94; prof. emeritus, 1994—; dir. remote sensing lab. U. Kans., 1964-74, 84-93. Pres. Cadre Corp., Lawrence, 1968-87; cons. cos., govt. agys. Author: Traveling Wave Engineering, 1960; co-author: (with Ulaby and Fung) Microwave Remote Sensing, Vol. I, 1981, Vol. II, 1982, Vol. III, 1986; contbr. to profl. jours. and handbooks. Lt. (j.g.) USNR, 1944-46. Recipient Achievement award Washington U. Engring. Alumni Assn., 1978, Outstanding Tech. Achievement award IEEE Geosci. and Remote Sensing Soc., 1982, Louise E. Byrd Grad. Educator award U. Kans., 1984, Irving Youngberg Rsch. award U. Kans., 1989, Australia prize, 1995. Fellow AAAS, IEEE (sect. chmn. 1960-61, Outstanding Tech. Achievement award coun. oceanic engring. 1978); mem., NAE, AAUP, Am. Soc. Engring. Edn., Am. Geophys. Union, Internat. Sci. Radio Union (chmn. U.S. commn. F 1984-87, internat. vice chmn. commn. F 1990-93, chmn. 1993-96), Kiwanis, Sigma Xi, Tau Beta Pi. Presbyterian (past elder). Achievements include research in submarine communications, radar altimetry, radar as a remote sensor, radar oceanography; patent for polypanchromatic radar. Home: 1712 Carmel Dr Lawrence KS 66047-1840 Office: U Kans R S & Remote Sensing Lab 2335 Irving Hill Rd Lawrence KS 66045-7612 E-mail: rmoore@sunflower.com.

MOORE, ROBERT, protective services official; b. Pontotoc, Miss., Sept. 11, 1943; married; 2 children. Degree, Rock Valley C.C., Rockford, Ill., 1976; BA, U. Ill., Springfield, 1980, MA, 1985. Worker Chrysler Corp., Belvidere, Ill., 1966-70; dep. sheriff Winnebago County Sheriff's Dept., Rockford, 1970-72; dir. equal employment opportunity Ill. State Police, Springfield, 1976-84, dir. internal affairs, 1985; dep. chief of police Savannah (Ga.) Police Dept., 1985-87; dep. dir. children and family svcs. Springfield Police Dept., 1987, chief internal affairs, 1988-92, ret., 1993; U.S. marshal U.S. Ct., Ctrl. dist. Ill., 7th cir., Springfield, 1994—. Contbr. articles to profl. publs. Recipient NAACP Affirmative Action award, 1982, Human Rels. award Human Rels. Commn., 1993. Mem. Nat. Orgn. Black Law Enforcement Execs. (pres. local chpt. 1990-94), Internat. Police Chiefs Assn., Frontiers Internat. Baptist. Avocations: golf, writing, reading. Office: Office of US Marshal Fed Bldg US Ct 7th Cir 600 E Monroe St Springfield IL 62701-1626

MOORE, TERRY L. financial executive; CPA, Ohio. CFO, CEO Nationwise Automotive, Inc.; CFO, treas. Shoe Corp. Am.; contr. Drug Emporium, Inc., Powell, Ohio, CFO, 1999—. Office: Drug Emporium Inc 155 Ravines Dr Powell OH 43065

MOORE, THOMAS EDWIN, biology educator, museum director; b. Champaign, Ill. s. Gerald E. and Velma (Lewis) M.; m. E. Eleanor Sifferd, Feb. 4, 1951; children: Deborah S., Melinda S. BS, U. Ill., 1951, MS, 1952, PhD, 1956. Tech. asst. Ill. Natural History Survey, Urbana, 1950-56; instr. zoology U. Mich., Ann Arbor, 1956-59, asst. prof. zoology, 1959-63, assoc. prof. zoology, 1963-66, prof. biology, 1966—, curator insects, 1956—, dir. exhibit mus., 1988-93. Vis. prof. Orgn. for Tropical Studies, San Jose, Costa Rica, 1970, 72; bd. dirs. Orgn. Tropical Studies, San Jose, 1968-79; mem. steering com. tropical biome U.S. Internat. Biol. Program, 1969-72; mem. conf. planning com. Nat. Inst. for Environment, 1991-92; mem. steering com. Univ. Colloquium on Environ. Rsch. and Edn., 1991-93, grievance com. U. Mich., 1997-98, faculty handbook com., 1997-98. Co-editor: Lectures on Science Education, 1991-1992, 1993; Cricket Behavior and Neurobiology, 1989; author movie 17-Year Cicadas, 1975, tv, 1998. County rep. Huron River Watershed Coun., Ann Arbor, 1987-95; mem. Mich. H.S. Accreditation Adv. Com., Ann Arbor, 1988-92; mem. U. Mich. Senate Adv. Com. on Univ. Affairs, 1993-96, vice chair, 1995-96; bd. mem. U. Mich. Acad. Freedom Lecture Fund, 1995—, treas., 1995-98; cons. NSF Visual Tech. in Environ. Curricula, 1994-97. Rsch. grantee NSF, 1963-66, 66-69, 96-97, rsch. equipment grantee, 1984-86, rsch. grantee Def. Advanced Rsch. Project Agy./Office of Naval Rsch. 1998—. Fellow AAAS, AAUP (pres. U. Mich. chpt. 1996—, exec. bd. Mich. conf. 1996-98), Royal Entomol. Soc. London, Linnaen Soc. London; mem. Assn. Tropical Biology (pres. 1973-75), Sigma Xi (pres. U. Mich. chpt 1994-96, coun. 1993-98). Home: 4243 N Delhi Rd Ann Arbor MI 48103-9485 Office: Mus of Zoology U Mich Ann Arbor MI 48109-1079

MOORE, VERNON JOHN, JR. pediatrician, lawyer, medical consultant; b. Chgo., Mar. 18, 1942; s. Vernon John Moore; m. Rutheva deVera Dizon, Feb. 27, 1979; children: Christopher, Joseph. BS, Loyola U., Chgo., 1964, JD, 1986; MD, U. Ill.-Chgo., 1968. Bar: Ill. 1986, U.S. Dist. Ct. (no. dist.) Ill. 1986. Intern St. Joseph Health Care Ctrs. and Hosp., Chgo., 1968-69, resident in pediats., 1971-74, chief resident, 1972-74, mem. med. staff, 1974-76, 78-86; pvt. practice, 1974-76, 97—; mem. med. staff Naval Hosp. Great Lakes, 1976-78; med. officer Chgo. Mil. Entrance Processing Sta., 1996—, Midwest Ctr. for Youth and Families, Kouts, Ind., 1997—; mem. med. staff Ill. Masonic Med. Ctr., Chgo., 1997—, Swedish Covenant Hosp., Chgo., 1998—, Luth. Gen. Hosp., Park Ridge, Ill., 1998—, Alexian Bros. Med. Ctr., Elk Grove Village, 2000—. Asst. dir. pediat. edn. St. Joseph Health Care Ctrs. and Hosp., 1974-76, co-dir., 1978-86, acting chmn. dept. pediats., 1985-86; clin. assoc. prof. pediat. Loyola U., Maywood, Ill., 1981-87; med. cons. CNA Ins. Cos., Chgo., 1987-94; pediatric med. cons. Hartgrove Hosp., Chgo., 1996—, Alexian Bros. Behavioral Health Hosp., Hoffman Estates, Ill., 1999-2001. Part-time staff Chgo. office Sen. Everett M. Dirksen, 1961-64. With USN, 1969-71, 76-78; capt. USNR, 1983—. Fellow Am. Acad. Pediat.; mem. Ill. Bar Assn. (chmn. standing com. on interprofl. coop. 1991-92, mem. health law sect. coun. 1997-98), U. Ill. Alumni Assn. (bd. dirs. 1983-89), Alumni Assn. Coll. Medicine U. Ill. (alumni councillor 1989-99), U. Ill. Pres. Coun. Republican. Roman Catholic. Home: 146 Park Ave River Forest IL 60305-2040 Office: 5758 N California Ave Chicago IL 60659-4726

MOORE, WARD WILFRED, medical educator; b. Cowden, Ill., Feb. 12, 1924; s. Cecil Leverett and Velma Leona (Frye) M.; m. Frances Laura Campbell, Jan. 29, 1949; children— Scott Thomas, Ann Gail, Brian Dean, Kevin Lee. A.B., U. Ill., 1948, M.S., 1951, Ph.D., 1952; DSc (hon.), Mahidol U., Bangkok, 2001. Instr., rsch. assoc. U. Ill., 1952-54; asst. prof. Okla. State U., Stillwater, 1954-55, Ind. U., Bloomington, 1955-59, assoc. prof., 1959-66, prof. physiology, 1966-89, prof. physiology and biophysics emeritus, 1989—, acting chmn. dept. anatomy, 1971-73, assoc. dean basic med. scis., 1971-89, assoc. dean, dir. med. scis. program, 1976-89. Vis. prof. Postgrad. Med. Center, Karachi, Pakistan, 1963-64; staff mem. Rockefeller Found., 1968-71; vis. prof., chmn. dept. physiology, faculty sci. Mahidol U., Bangkok, Thailand, 1968-71 Served with U.S. Army, 1943-46. Mem. Am. Physiol. Soc., Endocrine Soc., Am. Soc. Nephrology, Soc. Study Reproduction, Am. Assn. Anatomists, Soc. Exptl. Biology and Medicine, Am. Assn. Med. Colls., AAAS, Am. Inst. Biol. Scis., AAUP, Ind. Acad. Sci., Ind. Hist. Soc., Soc. Sons of Am. Revolution, Sigma Xi, Phi Sigma. Office: Indiana U Jordan Hall # 105 Bloomington IN 47405 Home: 3500 E Bradley St Bloomington IN 47401-4201 E-mail: moorew@indiana.edu.

MOORHOUSE, LINDA VIRGINIA, symphony orchestra administrator; b. June 26, 1945; d. William James and Mary Virginia (Wild) M. BA, Pa. State U., 1967. Sec. San Antonio Symphony, Tex., 1970-71, adminstrv. asst., 1971-75, asst. mgr., 1975-76; exec. dir. Canton (Ohio) Symphony, 1977—. Mem. Ohio Arts Coun. Music Panel, 1980-82, 87-89, Mich. Arts Coun. Music Panel, 1986. Bd. dirs. Stark County unit Arthritis Fedn., 1986-92, treas., 1989-91; bd. dirs. Canton Palace Theatre Assn., treas., 1994-96, pres., 1998-99; active Cen. Stark County United Way Allocations Panel, 1991-96. Mem. Met. Orch. Mgrs. Assn. (pres. 1983-85), Orgn. Ohio Orchs. (pres. 1985-86), Am. Symphony Orch. League (bd. dirs. 1983-85, nat. 1st ladies' site com. 1997—), Stark County Women's Hall of Fame (charter inductee), Soroptomist (Canton, Ohio, Women of Distinction 1992), Nat. First Ladies Libr. Office: Canton Symphony Orch 1001 Market Ave N Canton OH 44702-1024

MOORING, F. PAUL, physics editor; b. Pitt County, N.C., Feb. 6, 1921; s. Benjamin Arthur and Amanda Elizabeth (Congleton) M.; m. Jean Louise Carpenter, Aug. 28, 1948; children: Cecily Hamm, Carol Larson, Margaret. BA, Duke U., 1944; PhD, U. Wis., 1951. Instr. Duke U., Durham, N.C., 1943-46; teaching asst. U. Wis., Madison, 1946-50, rsch. asst., 1950-51; physicist Argonne (Ill.) Nat. Lab., 1951-83; editor, cons. Am. Inst. Physics, Argonne, 1983—. Adj. prof. St. Louis U., 1966-83. Contbr. articles to profl. jours. Pres. The Ill. Prairie Path, Wheaton, Ill., 1971-93, Ill. Audubon Soc., Wayne, Ill., 1978-81. Fulbright Rsch. fellow U. Helsinki, 1962-63. Mem. AAAS, Am. Phys. Soc. Democrat. Home: 295 Abbotsford Ct Glen Ellyn IL 60137-4803 E-mail: fmooring@aol.com.

MOOTY, BRUCE WILSON, lawyer; b. Mpls., May 27, 1955; s. John William and Virginia Mae (Nelson) M.; m. Ann Tracy Grogan, May 1, 1982; children: Katharine Grogan, Allison Taylor, Megan Ann. Student, Amherst Coll., 1973-74; BA summa cum laude, U. Minn., 1977, JD cum laude, 1980. Bar: Minn. 1980, U.S. Dist. Ct. Minn. 1980, U.S. Ct. Appeals 1983. Assoc., shareholder, officer, dir. Briggs & Morgan, P.A., Mpls., 1980-93; mng. ptnr. Gray, Plant, Mooty, Mooty & Bennett, P.A., 1993—; also bd. dirs. Pres., chmn. bd. dirs. A Better Chance Found., Edina, Minn., 1988, Minn. Amateur Baseball Found., Mpls., 1992; mem. coun. Colonial Ch. Edina, 1992. Mem. ABA, Minn. Bar Assn. (community rels. com. 1992—), Hennepin County Bar Assn., Ramsey County Bar Assn., Minikahda Club (sec.), Phi Beta Kappa, Phi Kappa Phi. Office: Gray Plant Mooty Mooty & Bennett 3400 City Ctr 33 S 6th St Ste 3400 Minneapolis MN 55402-3796 Home: 7021 Antrim Rd Minneapolis MN 55439-1709

MOOTY, JOHN WILLIAM, lawyer; b. Adrian, Minn., Nov. 27, 1922; s. John Wilson and Genevieve (Brown) M.; m. Virginia Nelson, June 6, 1952 (dec. 1964); children: David N., Bruce W., Charles W.; m. Jane Nelson, Jan. 15, 1972. BSL, U. Minn., 1943, LLB, 1944. Bar: Minn. 1944. Ptnr. Gray, Plant, Mooty & Bennett, Mpls., 1945—. Bd. dirs. Internat. Dairy Queen, Inc., Bur. of Engraving, Inc., Riverway Co. and subs., Rio Verde Svcs., Inc., Ariz. Author: (with others) Minnesota Practice Methods, 1956. Chmn. Gov.'s Task Force on Edn., 1981; pres. Citizens League Mpls., 1970; acting chmn. Republican Party of Minn., 1958. Mem. ABA, Minn. Bar Assn., Hennepin County Bar Assn., U. Minn. Alumni Assn. (pres. 1982), Tonto Verde Country Club, Minikahda (Mpls.) Club, Mpls. Club. Home: 6601 Dovre Dr Minneapolis MN 55436-1711

MORA, ANTONIO GONZALEZ , III, broadcast journalist; b. Havana, Cuba, Dec. 14, 1957; came to U.S., 1960; s. Antonio Gonzalez Jr. and Natalia (Sandoval) M.; m. Julie Good, Aug. 27, 1994; children: Clara, Antonio Daniel. JD, U. Catolica Andres Bello, Caracas, Venezuela, 1980; LLM, Harvard U., Cambridge, Mass., 1981; DHL, Our Lady of Holy Cross, New Orleans, 2000. Assoc. Debevoise & Plimpton, N.Y.C., 1981-88; anchor Sta. WXTV, Secaucus, N.J., 1990-91, Sta. WNJU, Teterboro, 1991; anchor Nightside NBC, Charlotte, N.C., 1992; reporter, anchor Sta. WTVJ-TV, Miami, 1992-93; host Good Day LA Sta. KTTV-FOX, L.A., 1993-94; host Good Morning America Sunday ABC, N.Y.C., 1994-95, correspondent, 1995-99, news anchor Good Morning America, 1999—. Recipient Emmy award, 2000, Peabody award, 2000, Edward R. Murrow award, 2000. Mem. Coun. Fgn. Rels. Office: ABC News 147 Columbus Ave New York NY 10023*

MORA, JAMES ERNEST, professional football coach, professional sports team executive; b. Glendale, Calif., May 24, 1935; s. Mario Joseph and Helen Laverne (Thompson) M.; m. Connie Beatrice Saunders, Dec. 18, 1959; children— James L., Michael J., Stephen P. B.S., Occidental Coll., 1957; M.A., U. So. Calif., 1967. Asst. coach U. Washington, Seattle, 1975-78, Seattle Seahawks, Seattle, 1978-82, New England Patriots, Foxboro, MA, 1982-83; head coach Philadelphia Stars (name changed to Baltimore Stars), Baltimore, MD, 1983-86, New Orleans Saints, New Orleans, 1986-96, head coach, v.p. L.A., 1994-96; commentator NFC Football, 1997; head coach Indianapolis Colts, Ind., 1998—. Served to capt. USMCR, 1957-60 Mem. Am. Football Coaches Assn. Republican. Lutheran Avocations: working out; golf; skiing; reading; biking. Office: care Indpls Colts PO Box 535000 Indianapolis IN 46253-5000 also: care Indpls Colts 7001 W 56th St Indianapolis IN 46254-9725

MORACZEWSKI, ROBERT LEO, publisher; b. Saint Paul, Nebr., May 13, 1942; s. Leo and Florence (Wadas) M.; m. Virginia Kay Rohman, July 26, 1960; children— Mark, Matthew, Monika, Michael BS in Agrl. Journalism, U. Nebr., 1964. Assoc. editor Farmer Mag. Webb Co., St. Paul, 1964-72; mng. editor Farm Industry News Webb Co., 1972-74; editor Big Farmer Mag., Chgo., 1974-75; editorial dir. Webb Agrl. Services, St. Paul, 1976; editor The Farmer, The Dakota Farmer Webb Co., 1983-89; group pub. Webb Co., 1989-90, sr. v.p., 1990—. Chmn. Minn. Agri-Growth Coun. Contbr. articles to profl. jours. Mem. sponsors bd. Nat. FFA. Recipient numerous media awards. Mem. Am. Agrl. Editors Assn., Nat. Agrl. Mktg. Assn. Roman Catholic Home: 32993 Kale Ave Chisago City MN 55013-2644 Office: Primedia Bus Media 7900 Internat Dr Minneapolis MN 55425 E-mail: bmoraczewski@primediabusiness.com.

MORAN, DANIEL AUSTIN, mathematician, educator; b. Chgo., Feb. 17, 1936; s. Austin Thomas and Violet Lillian (Johnson) M.; m. Karen Krull, Sept. 14, 1963; children: Alexander, Claudia. B.S. summa cum laude, St. Mary's of Tex., 1957; M.S., U. Ill., 1958, Ph.D., 1962. Research instr. U. Chgo., 1962-64; asst. prof. Mich. State U., 1964-68, assoc. prof., 1968-76, prof. math., 1976—. Vis. scholar U. Cambridge, 1970-71, U. North Wales, 1978 Contbr. articles to profl. jours. Mem. Math. Assn. Am., Sigma Xi, Pi Mu Epsilon, Delta Epsilon Sigma, Kappa Mu Alpha. Roman Catholic. Home: 2633 Roseland Ave East Lansing MI 48823-3870 Office: Dept Math Michigan State Univ East Lansing MI 48824

MORAN, GLENN J. corporate lawyer; BA, Pa. State U., 1969; JD, Temple U., 1972. Bar: Pa. 1972. Lawyer-major appliance group Gen. Electric, 1973-77; sr. lawyer Frito Lay, Inc., Pepsico, 1977-79; v.p., gen. counsel, sec. LTV Corp., Cleve. Office: LTV Corp 200 Public Sq Cleveland OH 44114-2301

MORAN, JAMES BYRON, federal judge; b. Evanston, Ill., June 20, 1930; s. James Edward and Kathryn (Horton) M.; children: John, Jennifer, Sarah, Polly; stepchildren: Katie, Cynthia, Laura, Michael. AB, U. Mich., 1952; LLB magna cum laude, Harvard U., 1957. Bar: Ill. 1958. Law clk. to judge U.S. Ct. of Appeals (2d cir.), 1957-58; assoc. Bell, Boyd, Lloyd, Haddad & Burns, Chgo, 1958-66, ptnr., 1966-79; judge U.S. Dist. Ct. (no. dist.) Ill., Chgo., 1979—. Dir. Com. on Ill. Govt., 1960-78, chmn., 1968-70; vice chmn., sec. Ill. Dangerous Drug Adv. Coun., 1967-74; dir. Gateway Found., 1969— ; mem. Ill. Ho. of Reps., 1965-67; mem. Evanston City Council, 1971-75. Served with AUS, 1952-54. Mem. Chgo. Bar Assn., Chgo. Council Lawyers, Lawyers Club, Phi Beta Kappa. Home: 117 Kedzie St Evanston IL 60202-2509 Office: US Dist Ct 219 S Dearborn St Ste 2050 Chicago IL 60604-1800 E-mail: jbm117@aol.com.

MORAN, JERRY, congressman; m. Robba A. Moran. Senator dist. 37 State of Kans.; mem., asst. majority whip U.S. Congress from 1st Kans dist., 1997—, mem. agr., transp., infrastructure, vets. affairs coms., steering com. Republican. Home: 2758 Thunderbird Dr Hays KS 67601-1403 Office: US Ho of Reps 1519 Longworth Hob Washington DC 20515-0001*

MORAN, JOHN, religious organization administrator; b. Oct. 4, 1935; m. Retha Jean Patrick; children: John II, James, Helen. Missionary, Nigeria, 1963-68, 2001—; pastor, 1969-87; vice dist. supt. North Ctrl. Dist., Missionary Church, Ind., 1977-81; pres. Missionary Ch., Ft. Wayne, 1987-2001. Mem. exec. bd. World Relief Corp., 1998—. Author: Joy in a Roman Jail, 1984, Taking the High Ground, 1997. Mem. Nat. Assn. Evang. (mem. exec. bd. 1987-97). Office: Missionary Ch PO Box 9127 3811 Vanguard Dr Fort Wayne IN 46809-3304 E-mail: moranjprj@aol.com., johnpmoran@aol.com.

MORAN, MICHAEL ROBERT, corporate lawyer; BS, U. Ill., 1967; JD, DePaul U., 1972. Bar: Ill. 1972. V.p.-adminstrn. Spiegel, Inc., 1982-87, v.p., sec. gen. counsel Ill., 1988-96, sr. corp. v.p., sec., gen. counsel, 1996-97, pres., chief legal officer, 1997—, chmn. office of the pres., chief legal officer, 1998—. Mem. Ill. Retail Mchts. Assn. (chmn. bd. dirs., mem. credit com.), Nat. Retail Fedn. Office: Spiegel Inc 3500 Lacey Rd Downers Grove IL 60515-5421

MORAN, ROBERT FRANCIS, JR. library director; b. Cleve., May 3, 1938; s. Robert Francis Sr. and Jeanette (Mulholland) M.; m. Judith Mary Pacer, Dec. 28, 1968; children: Mary Jeanette, Catherine, Margaret. BA, Cath. U. Am., Washington, 1961, MLS, 1965; MBA, U. Chgo., 1976. Head librarian St. Patrick's Sem., Menlo Park, Calif., 1965-69; coordinator and reference librarian U. Chgo., 1969-72; serials librarian U. Ill., Chgo., 1972-78, acquisitions librarian, 1977-80; dir. library services Ind. U. Northwest, Gary, 1980—, asst. vice chancellor tech., 1991-99. V.p., sec., treas. Northwest Ind. Area Library Services Authority, Merrillville, 1982-91. Asst. editor Libr. Adminstrn. and Mgmt.; contbr. articles to profl jours. Mem. ALA, Libr. Adminstrn. and Mgmt. Assn. (com. chmn. 1981-86, sect. chmn. 1986-88, chmn. program com. 1988-91, chair nominating com. 1991-92, networked info. discussion group 1994-98, govtl. affairs com. 1998-2000). Democrat. Roman Catholic. Office: Ind Univ NW Library 3400 Broadway Gary IN 46408-1101

MORAVEC, CHRISTINE D. SCHOMIS, medical educator; b. L.A., Apr. 26, 1957; BA, John Carroll U., 1978, MS, 1984; PhD, Cleve. State U., 1988. Tchr. Trinity H.S., Garfield Heights, Ohio, 1978-80; grad. teaching asst. dept. biology John Carroll U., Cleve., 1982-84; rsch. assoc. dept. cardiovascular biology Cleve. Clinic Found., 1990-93, project scientist dept. cardiovascular biology, 1990-93, asst. staff dept. cardiovascular biology, 1993-94; asst. prof. dept. physiology & biophys. Case Western Res. U. Sch. Medicine, Cleve., 1993—. Adj. asst. prof. Cleve. State U., 1994—; asst. staff Ctr. Anesthesiology Rsch. Cleve. Clinic Found., 1994—. Contbr. articles to profl. jours. Grad. fellow Cleve. Clinic Found., 1984-88, Postdoctoral fellow, 1988-89, recipient Tarazi fellow, 1989. Mem. Am. Physiol. Soc., Am. Heart Assn. (basic sci. coun. 1990—; Established Investigatorship award 1995), Ohio Physiol. Soc., Electron Microscopy Soc. Northeastern Ohio, Cardiac Muscle Soc. Office: Cleve Clin Found Ctr Anesthesiology Found 9500 Euclid Ave # FF40 Cleveland OH 44195-0001

MORCOTT, SOUTHWOOD J. automotive parts manufacturing company executive; b. 1939; married Student, Davidson Coll.; MBA, U. Mich. Pres. Dana Corp., Toledo, 1963—, sales engineer, plant mgr. Tyston, Ind., 1963-75; pres. Dana World Trade Corp., 1969; v.p. ops. Hayes Dana Ltd. Dana Corp., 1975-77, exec. v.p., gen. mgr., 1977-78, pres. Hayes-Dana Ltd., 1978-80, group v.p. Dana svc. parts group, 1980-84, pres. N.Am. ops., 1984-86, pres., chief operating officer, 1986-89, chief exec. officer, 1989-99, also chmn., dir., 1990-2000; ret., 2000. Office: Dana Corp PO Box 1000 Toledo OH 43697-1000

MOREHOUSE, LAWRENCE GLEN, veterinarian, educator; b. Manchester, Kans., July 21, 1925; s. Edwy Owen and Ethel Merle (Glenn) M.; m. Georgia Ann Lewis, Oct. 6, 1956; children: Timothy Lawrence, Glenn Ellen. BS in Biol. Sci., DVM, Kans. State U., 1952; MS in Animal Pathology, Purdue U., 1956, PhD, 1960. Lic. vet. medicine. Veterinarian County Animal Hosp., Des Peres, Mo., 1952-53; supr. Brucellosis labs. Purdue U., West Lafayette, Ind., 1953-60; staff veterinarian lab. svcs. USDA, Washington, 1960-61; discipline leader in pathology and toxicology, animal health divsn. USDA Nat. Animal Disease Lab., Ames, Iowa, 1961-64; prof., chmn. dept. veterinary pathology U. Mo. Coll. Vet. Medicine, Columbia, 1964-69, 84-86, dir. Vet. Med. Diagnostic Labr., 1968-88, prof. emeritus, 1986—. Cons. USDA, to comdg. gen. U.S. Army R & D Command, Am. Inst. Biol. Scis., NAS, Miss. State U., St. Louis Zoo Residency Tng. Program, Miss. Vet. Med. Assn., Okla. State U., Pa. Dept. Agr., Ohio Dept. Agr. Co-editor: Mycotoxic Fungi, Mycotoxins, Mycotoxicoses: An Encyclopedic Handbook , 3 vols., 1977; contbr. numerous articles on diseases of animals to profl. jours. Active Trinity Presbyn. Ch., Columbia, 1989-92; bd. dirs. Mo. Symphony Soc., Columbia, 1989-92. Pharmacists mate second class USNR, 1943-46, PTO; 2d. lt. U.S. Army, 1952-56. Recipient Outstanding Svc. award USDA, 1959, merit cert., 1963, 64, Disting. Svc. award U. Mo. Coll. Vet. Medicine, 1987, Dean's Impact award, 1996. Fellow Royal Soc. Health London; mem. Am. Assn. Vet. Lab. Diagnosticians (E.P. Pope award 1976, chmn. lab. accreditation bd. 1972-79, 87-90, pres. 1979-80, sec.-treas. 1983-87), World Assn. Vet. Lab. Diagnosticians (bd. dirs. 1984-94, dir. emeritus 1994—), N.Y. Acad. Sci., U. S. Animal Health Assn., Am. Assn. Lab. Animal Sci., Mo. Soc. Microbiology, Am. Assn. Avian Pathologists, N.Am. Conf. Rsch. Workers in Animal Diseases, Mo. Univ. Retirees Assn. (v.p. 1996-98, pres. 1998-99). Presbyterian. Avocations: classic cars, boating, genealogy. Home: 916 Danforth Dr Columbia MO 65201-6164 Office: U Mo Vet Med Diagnostic Lab PO Box 6023 Columbia MO 65205-6023

MORELACK, MIKE, radio personality; b. Pensacola, Fla., Dec. 12; 1 child. Student, Marion Mil. Inst., U. Ala. Radio host WDAF, Westwood, Kans., 1980—. Avocations: horseback riding, collecting antique guns, classic cars. Office: WDAF 4935 Belinder Rd Westwood KS 66205*

MORENCY, PAULA J. lawyer; b. Oak Park, Ill., Mar. 13, 1955; AB magna cum laude, Princeton U., 1977; JD, U. Va., 1980. Bar: Ill. 1980, U.S. Dist. Ct. (no. dist.) Ill. 1980, U.S. Ct. Appeals (7th cir.) 1981, U.S. Ct. Appeals (5th cir.) 1990, U.S. Dist. Ct. (ctrl. dist.) Ill. 1999, U.S. Dist. Ct. (ea. dist.) Wis. 2000. Assoc. Mayer, Brown & Platt, Chgo., 1980-86, ptnr., 1987-94, Schiff Hardin & Waite, Chgo., 1994—. Adj. prof. trial advocacy Northwestern U. Sch. Law, Chgo., 1997--; faculty Midwest Regional, Nat. Inst. for Trial Advocacy, 1988—; mem. pres.'s council Dominican U., 1998—. Author: Cross-Examination of a Franchise Executive, 1995, Insurance Coverage Issues in Franchise and Intellectual Property Litigation, 1996, Re-Emergence of Franchise Class Actions, 1997, Judicial and Legislative Update: ABA Forum on Franchising, 1999, How to Find, Use and Defend Against the Expert Witness, 2000, Dealing With System Change in a High-Tech World, 2001. Mem. ABA (forum franchising, governing com., litigation sect., intellectual property sect.), Chgo. Coun. of Lawyers (bd. govs. 1989-93), Constnl. Rights Found. Chgo. (chair 2001). Office: Schiff Hardin & Waite 7300 Sears Tower Chicago IL 60606

MORFORD, JOANN (JOANN MORFORD-BURG), state senator, investment company executive; b. Miller, S.D., Nov. 26, 1956; d. Darrell Keith Morford and Eleanor May (Fawcett) Morford-Steptoe. BS in Agrl.-Bus., Comml. Econs., S.D. State U., 1979; cert. in personal fin. planning, Am. Coll., 1992. Chartered fin. cons. Agrl. loan officer 1st Bank System, Presho, S.D., 1980-82, Wessington Springs, 1982-86, Am. State Bank, Wessington Springs, 1986; registered investment rep. ARM Fin. Svcs. Inc., 1986-96; Miller, 1997—; mem. S.D. State Senate, Wessington Springs, 1990-96, majority whip, 1993-94, minority whip, 1995-96, mem., 1990-97, Miller, 1997-98; ins. agt. Western Fraternal Life Assn., 2001—. Mem. senate appropriations com. 1993-98; chair senate ops. and audit com. 1993, 94; mem. ops. and audit com., 1995-98; mem. Nat. Conf. State Legislators' Assembly of Fed. Issues Environ. Com., 1994-98, vice chair, 1996-97. Mem. Midwestern-Can. task force Midwest Conf., 1990-94; mem. transp. com., commerce com., taxation com. S.D. State Senate, Pierre, 1990-92; treas. twp. bd. Wessington Springs, 1990-92; mem. Wessington Springs Sch. Improvement Coun., 1992-95. Fleming fellow Ctr. Policy Alternatives, 1996. Mem.: S.D. Farmers Union, Bus. and Profl. Women, Alumni Coun. Young Polit. Leaders (China delegation 1996, host El Salvador delegation 1999), Future Farmers Am. (adv. bd. Wessington Springs chpt. 1984—96), S.D. State U. 4-H Alumni Assn., Order Ea. Star (various offices 1980—). Democrat. Methodist. Home and Office: PO Box 21 Miller SD 57362-0021

MORFORD, JOHN A. investment company executive; CFO V.T. Inc., Shawnee Mission, Kans. Office: VT Inc PO Box 795 Shawnee Mission KS 66201-0795

MORGAN, DENNIS RICHARD, lawyer; b. Jan. 3, 1942; s. Richard and Gladys Belle (Brown) Morgan. BA, Washington and Lee U., 1964; JD, U. Va., 1967; LLM in Labor Law, NYU, 1971. Bar: Ohio 1967, Va. 1967, U.S. Ct. Appeals (4th cir.) 1968, U.S. Ct. Appeals (6th cir.) 1971, U.S. Supreme Ct. 1972. Law clk. to chief judge U.S. dit. Ct. (ea. dist.) Va., 1967—68; mem. Marshman, Snyder & Seeley, Cleve., 1971—72; dir. labor rels. Ohio Dept. Adminstrv. Svcs., 1972—75; asst. city atty. Columbus, Ohio, 1975—77; dir. Ohio Legis. Reference Bur., 1979—81; assoc. Clemans, Nelson & Assocs., 1981; pvt. practice, 1978—92. Lectr. in field; guest lectr. Cen. Mich. U., 1975; judge moot ct. Ohio State U. Sch. Law, 1981, 83, grad. divsn., 73, 74, 76; guest lectr. Baldwin-Wallace Coll., 1973; legal counsel Dist. IV Comms. Workers Am., 1982—88; pers. dir. Pub. Utilities Commn., Ohio, 1989—91; asst. atty. gen. State of Ohio, 1991—. Negotiator Franklin County United Way, 1977—81; regional chmn. ann. alumni fund-raising program U. Va. Sch. Law; mem. Greater Hilltop Area Commn., 1989—; pres. Woodbrook Village Condominium Assn., 1985—; trustee Hilltop Civic Coun., Inc., 1997—99; vice-chmn. Franklin County Dem. Party, 1976—82; dem. com. person Ward 58, Columbus, 1973—95; chmn. rules com. Ohio State Dem. Conv., 1974; co-founder, trustee Greater West Side Dem. Club; bd. dir. Hilltop Civic Coun., Inc., 1997—99. Capt. U.S. Army, 1968—70. Recipient Am. Jurisprudence award, 1967; scholar Robert E. Lee Rsch., 1965. Mem.: ABA, Am. Judicature Soc., Fed. Bar Assn., Indsl. Rels. Rsch. Assn., Columbus Metropolitan club (charter), Pi Sigma Alpha. Roman Catholic. Home: 1261 Woodbrook Ln # G Columbus OH 43223-3243

MORGAN, E. A. church administrator; Chaplain Ch. of the Living God Exec. Bd., Cin., 1984—. Office: Ch of the Living God 400 S Franklin St Decatur IL 62523-1316

MORGAN, JANE HALE, retired library director; b. Dines, Wyo., May 11, 1926; d. Arthur Hale and Billie (Wood) Hale; m. Joseph Charles Morgan, Aug. 12, 1955; children: Joseph Hale, Jane Frances, Ann Michele. BA, Howard U., 1947; MA, U. Denver, 1954. Staff Detroit Pub. Libr., 1954-87, exec. asst. dir., 1973-75, dep. dir., 1975-78, dir., 1978-87; ret., 1987. Mem. Mich. Libr. Consortium Bd.; exec. bd. Southeastern Mich. Regional Film Libr.; vis. prof. Wayne State U., 1989—. Trustee New Detroit, Inc., Delta Dental Plan of Mich., v.p. Delta Dental Fund, Delta Dental Plan of Ohio; v.p. United Southwestern Mich.; pres. Univ.-Cultural Ctr. Assn.; bd. dirs. Rehab. Inst., YWCA, Met. Affairs Corp., Literacy Vols. Am., Detroit, Mich. Ctr. for the Book, Interfaith Coun.; bd. dirs., v.p. United Comty. Svcs. Met. Detroit; chmn. Detroiters for Adult Reading Excellence; chmn. adv. coun. libr. sci. U. Mich.; mem. adv. coun. libr. sci. U. Mich., mem. adv. coun. libr. sci. Wayne State U.; dir. Met. Detroit Youth Found.; chmn. Mich. LSCA adv. coun.; mem. UWA Literacy Com., Attys. Grievance Com., Women's Commn., Mich. Civil Svc. Rev. Com.; vice-chair Mich. Coun. for Humanities; v.p. Commn. for the Greening of Detroit; adv. com. Headstart; mem. Detroit Women's Com., Detroit Women's Forum, Detroit Exec. Svc. Corps.; sec., treas. Delta Dental Fund, pres., 1999. Recipient Anthony Wayne award Wayne State U., 1981, Summit award Greater Detroit C. of C.; named Detroit Howardite of Year, 1983 Mem. ALA, AAUW, Mich. Library Assn., Women's Nat. Book Assn., Assn. Mcpl. Profl. Women, NAACP, LWV, Women's Econ. Club, Sorosis Club (v.p.), Alpha Kappa Alpha. Democrat. Episcopalian.

MORGAN, JOHN BRUCE, hospital care consultant; b. Youngstown, Ohio, Oct. 25, 1919; s. John Benjamin and Ida May (Lane) M.; m. Marian Frampton, July 11, 1969; children: John B., Carolyn, Leonard, Suzanne (dec.). BS, Miami U., 1941; MBA, Harvard U., 1946. Field rep. Gen. Motors Acceptance Corp., Youngstown, 1941; pres. Asso. Hosp. Service, Inc., 1947-74, Hosp. Care Corp. (Blue Cross), Cin., 1974-83, cons., 1983—; pres. Health Maintenance Plan, 1974-83, Health Care Mutual, Cin., 1974-83. Chmn. bd. govs., chmn. exec. com. Blue Cross Assn., Chgo., 1981-82; chmn. bd. Community Life Ins. Co., Worthington, Ohio, 1979-83; mem. joint exec. com. Blue Cross-Blue Shield Assns., mem. joint bds., Chgo.; mem. bus. adv. com. Miami U., Oxford, Ohio. Gen. chmn. United Fund campaign, Youngstown, 1965; pres. Cancer Soc., 1965; chmn. bd. trustees Ch. of the Palms, 1996. Served with AUS, 1942-46. Mem. Am. Hosp. Assn. (Justin Ford Kimball award 1983), Ohio Hosp. Assn., Ohio C. of C. (bd. dirs.), Youngstown Area C. of C. (pres. 1966-67), Delray Beach, Fla. C. of C., Delray Dunes Golf and Country Club (bd. dirs., v.p.), Rotary (bd. dirs. Delray Beach club, pres. 1992, Paul Harris fellow), Masons, Elks, Sigma Alpha Epsilon, Delta Sigma Pi. Mem. United Ch. of Christ. Home: 9 Slash Pine Dr Boynton Beach FL 33436-5524 Office: 1351 William Howard Taft Rd Cincinnati OH 45206-1721

MORGAN, ROBERT ARTHUR, accountant; b. Decatur, Ill., Oct. 23, 1918; s. Robert Howard and Katherine (Massey) M.; m. Julia Ann Franklin, June 28, 1941; children: Robert A., Susan Ruth. BS, U. Ill., 1941. Acct. Pure Oil Co., 1941, Caterpillar Tractor Co., Peoria, Ill., 1945-56, controller, 1956-78; mem. Fin. Acct. Standards Bd., Stamford, Conn., 1978-82; cons. Morton, Ill., 1982—. Contbr. articles to acctg. periodicals. Past mem. fin. acctg. standards adv. coun. Fin. Acctg. Found.; pres. bd. edn. Morton Twp. High Sch., 1960-61. Civilian auditor AUS, 1942-44. Mem. Nat. Assn. Accts. (nat. dir., nat. v.p. 1965-66, chmn. mng. practices 1974-75), Machinery and Allied Products Inst. (fin. coun. II 1956-78), Fin. Execs. Inst. (mem. com. corp. reporting 1977-78), Internat. Fedn. Accts. (chmn. com. fin. and mgmt. acctg. 1983).

MORGAN, ROGER JOHN, research scientist, university official; b. Manchester, England, Nov. 2, 1942; came to U.S., 1968; s. Leslie Budworth and Hilda May (Bevins) M.; m. Anne Christine Cheetham, Sept. 23, 1967; children: Jacqueline, Nicholas, Melissa. BS in Chemistry with honors, U. of London, 1965; PhD in Polymer Phyics, U. of Manchester, 1968. Asst. rsch. prof. Washington U., St. Louis, 1968-72; scientist McDonnell Douglas Rsch. Labs., 1972-78; group leader Lawrence Livermore (Calif.) Nat. Lab., 1978-85; mem. tech. staff Rockwell Internat., Thousand Oaks, Calif., 1985-93; head of composites Mich. Molecular Inst., Midland, 1986-93; dir. Advanced Materials Engring. Expt. Sta., Mich. State U., 1993-2000; dir. Polymer Tech. Ctr., Tex. A&M U., College Station, 2000—. Dir. Advanced Materials Engring. Experiment Sta., Mich. State U., Midland, 1993—. Co-editor: Advanced Composites Bull., 1989-96; mem. editl. adv. bd. Jour. Composite Materials, 1985—, Jour. Advanced Materials, 1991-96; contbr. over 150 articles to profl. jours. Mem. Am. Chem. Soc., Soc. for Advancement of Materials and Process Engrs. Achievements include research in composites/polymer science. Office: Tex A&M U Dept Mech Engring College Station TX 77843-3123 E-mail: rmorgan@mengr.tamu.edu.

MORGAN, VICTORIA, performing company executive, choreographer; BFA, U. Utah, 1973, MFA magna cum laude, 1976. Prin. dancer Ballet West, 1969-78, San Francisco Ballet, 1978-87; resident choreographer San Francisco Opera; artistic dir. Cin. Ballet, 1997—. Lead dancer with roles in numerous classical, neoclassical and modern ballets including works by George Balanchine, Forsynthe, and Kudelka; dancer in lead roles for TV and film; choreographer, creating over 40 works for 20 ballet and opera cos. across U.S. including Utah Ballet, Pacific Northwest Ballet, Glimmerglass Opera and Cin. Opera; creator, prodr. ballet CD-ROM; choreography featured in documentary: The Creation of O.M.O. Office: Cincinnati Ballet 1555 Central Pkwy Cincinnati OH 45214-2863 E-mail: vmorga@cincinnatiballet.com.

MORGAN, VIRGINIA MATTISON, magistrate judge; b. 1946; BS, Univ. of Mich., 1968; JD, Univ. of Toledo, 1975. Bar: Mich. 1975, Federal 1975, U.S. Ct. Appeals (6th cir.) 1979. Tchr. Dept. of Interior, Bur. of Indian Affairs, 1968-70, San Diego Unified Schs., 1970-72, Oregon, Ohio, 1972-74; asst. prosecutor Washtenaw County Prosecutor's Office, 1976-79; asst. U.S. atty. Detroit, 1979-85; magistrate judge U.S. Dist. Ct. (Mich. ea. dist.), 6th circuit, 1985—. Mem. bd. Fed. Jud. Ctr., 1997—; mem. jud. conf. U.S. Com. on Long Range Planning, 1993-96. Recipient Spl. Achievement award Dept. of Justice, Disting. Alumni award U. Toledo, 1993. Fellow Mich. State Bar Found.; mem. FBA (chpt. pres. 1996-97), Fed. Magistrate Judges Assn. (pres. 1995-96). Office: US Courthouse 231 W Lafayette Blvd Detroit MI 48226-2700

MORGENSTERN-CLARREN, PAT, federal judge; b. 1952; AB in Polit. Sci., U. Mich., 1974; JD, Case Western Res. U., 1977; LLM, London Sch. Econs./Polit. Sci., 1979. Law clk. to Hon. Jack Grant Day Ohio Ct. Appeals (8th dist.), 1977-78; assoc. to ptnr. Hahn Loeser & Parks, Cleve., 1979-87, 87-95; bankruptcy judge U.S. Bankruptcy Ct., 1995—. Mem. bankruptcy appellate panel U.S. Ct. Appeals (6th cir.), 1999—. Assoc. editor Case Western Res. U. Law Rev. Mem. Order of Coif, Soc. of Benches. Office: US Bankruptcy Ct 3201 Key Tower 127 Public Sq Ste 3001 Cleveland OH 44114-1309

MORIARTY, DONALD WILLIAM, JR. bank executive; b. Amarillo, Tex., Sept. 15, 1939; s. Donald William and Lorraine Julia (Walck) Moriarty; m. Rita Ann Giller, Nov. 28, 1964; children: Mary Kathleen, Jennifer Ann, Anne Marie, Kerry Lee, Erin Teresa. Student, St. Benedict's Coll., 1957-59, 60-61; BSc, Washington U., 1962; MSc, St. Louis U., 1965, PhD, 1970. Cost acct. Emerson Electric, St. Louis, 1959-63; grad. fellow in econs. St. Louis U., 1963-65, instr., 1965-68; asst. prof. U. Mo., 1968-70; with Fed. Res. Bank of St. Louis, 1968-83, v.p., 1971-74, sr. v.p., controller, 1974-77, 1st v.p., 1977-83; sr. v.p. Gen. Bancshares Corp., 1983-86; exec. v.p. Commerce Bancshares, Inc., 1986-87; bank cons., 1987-89; pres., CEO, bd. dirs. Duchesne Bank, St. Peters, Mo., 1989-95; sr. cons. Universal Fin. Group, Inc., 1996—; assoc. prof. bus. Font Bonne U., St. Louis, 1998—. Vis. instr. Webster Coll., 1975—82; adviser City of Des Peres, Mo., chmn. fin. com., Mo., 1976—78, chmn. mgmt. com., Mo., 1978—81, mem. pers. commn., Mo., 1978—81, mem. planning and zoning com., Mo., 1981—83; bd. dirs. Mid-Am. Payments Exch., Duchesne Bank. Mem. parent's coun. Creighton U., Omaha, 1995—97; mem. adv. bd. St. Joseph Acad., 1982—86; mem. pres.'s coun. St. Louis U., 1983—; dist. chmn. Boy Scouts Am., 1991—93, vice chmn., 1994—2001; trustee, chmn. St. Joseph Hosp., 1982—93; bd. dirs. ea. Mo. region NCCJ, 1987—93. Recipient Alumni Merit award, St. Louis U., 1979. Mem.: Am. Mgmt. Assn., Am. Fin. Assn., Am. Econ. Assn., St. Peters C. of C., Alhpa Kappa Psi, Beta Gamma Sigma.

MORIARTY, JOHN TIMOTHY, writer, transportation consultant; b. Cleve., Jan. 23, 1939; s. James Joseph and Margaret (Healy) M.; m. Angela Marie Veneziano, June 29, 1968; children: Patrick J., Sean Gerald. Student, John Carroll U., 1957, Cleve. State U., 1964-67. Traffic analyst, Cleve., 1957-82; transp. cons. Norfolk So. R.R., 1982—. Author: One Square Mile of Mayhem, 1998, Honest John, 1998, The Phantom Employee, 1998, Sister Mommy, 1999, Thin Ice, 2001. With U.S. Army, 1961-63. Mem. Ill. Internat. Freight Coun. Roman Catholic. Avocations: basketball, billiards, reading. Home: Apt 2615 1111 Independence Ave Akron OH 44310-1896

MORISATO, SUSAN CAY, actuary; b. Chgo., Feb. 11, 1955; d. George and Jessie (Fujita) M.; m. Thomas Michael Remec, Mar. 6, 1981. BS, U. Ill., 1975, MS, 1977. Actuarial student Aetna Life & Casualty, Hartford, Conn., 1977-79; actuarial asst. Bankers Life & Casualty Co., Chgo., 1979-80, asst. actuary, 1980-83, assoc. actuary, 1983-85, health product actuary, 1985-86, v.p., 1986-95, sr. v.p., 1996—, also bd. dirs. Participant individual forum Health Ins. Assn. Am., 1983; spkr. in field. Adv. panel on long term care financing Brookings' Inst. Fellow Soc. Actuaries (workshop leader 1990, 93, news editor health sect. news 1988-90); mem. Am. Acad. Actuaries, Health Ins. Assn. Am. (long term care task force 1988—, chair 1993-95, tech. adv. com. 1991-93, legis. policy com. 1996-99, nominating com. 1996-98, other coms., policy coord. coun. 1999—, sr. mkt. task force chair 2000-01, Founders award 1996), Life Ins. Mgmt. Rsch. Assn. (strategic mktg. ins. com. 2001-, long-term care conf. Sharing the Burden 1994), Nat. Assn. Ins. Commrs. (ad hoc actuarial working group for long term care nonforfeiture benefits 1992), Am. Coun. Life Ins. (accelerated benefits/long term care com. 1997-2001), Chgo. Actuarial Assn. (sec. 1983-85, program com. 1987-89), Health Ins. Assn. Am. (Founders award 1996), Phi Beta Kappa, Kappa Delta Pi, Phi Kappa Phi. Office: Bankers Life & Casualty Co 222 Merchandise Mart Plz 19th Fl Chicago IL 60654 E-mail: s.morisato@banklife.com.

MORITZ, DONALD BROOKS, mechanical engineer, consultant; b. Mpls., June 17, 1927; s. Donald B. and Frances W. (Whalen) M.; m. Joan Claire Betzenderfer, June 17, 1950; children: Craig, Pamela, Brian. B.S. in Mech. Engring., U. Minn., 1950; postgrad., Western Res. U., 1956-58. Registered profl. engr., Ill. Minn., Ohio. V.p., gen. mgr. Waco Scaffold Shoring Co., Addison, Ill., 1950-72; group v.p. Bliss and Laughlin Industries, Oak Brook, 1972-83; sr. v.p. AXIA Inc. (formerly Bliss and Laughlin Industries, 1983-84, exec. v.p., chief operating officer, 1984-88; cons. Exec. Svc. Corps Chgo., 1988—; pres. Image-A-Nation, Unltd., 1988—. Bd. dirs. Am. Photographic Acad. Patentee in field. Served with USN, 1945-46. Mem. ASME, Scaffold and Shoring Inst. (founder, past pres.), Mensa, Meadow Club. Office: Moritz and Assocs PO Box 305 Clarendon Hills IL 60514-0305

MORK, GORDON ROBERT, historian, educator; b. St. Cloud, Minn., May 6, 1938; s. Gordon Matthew and Agnes (Gibb) M.; m. Dianne Jeannette Muetzel, Aug. 11, 1963; children: Robert, Kristiana, Elizabeth. Instr. history U. Minn., Mpls., 1966; lectr., asst. prof. U. Calif., Davis, 1966-70; mem. faculty Purdue U., West Lafayette, Ind., 1970—, assoc. prof., 1973-94, prof. history, 1994—, dir. honors program in the humanities, 1985-87, dir grad. studies in history, Am. studies, 1987-93, mem. Jewish studies com., 1980—, head dept. history, 1998—; resident dir. Purdue U.-Ind. U. Program, Hamburg, Fed. Republic Germany, 1975-76; rsch. fellow in humanities U. Wis., Madison, 1969-70. Mem. test devel. com., advanced placement European history Ednl. Testing Svc., 1993-99, chair, 1995-99. Author: Modern Western Civilization: A Concise History, 3d edit., 1994; editor: The Homes of Ober-Ammergau, 2000; mem. adv. bd. Teaching History, 1983—, History Tchr., 1986—. Mem. citizens task force Lafayette Sch. Corp., 1978-79; bd. dirs. Ind. Humanities Coun., 1986-89; bd. dirs., sec. Murdock-Sunnyside Bldg. Corp., 1980—; elder Cen. Presbyn. Ch., Lafayette, 1973-75, deacon, 1996-99, trustee, 2001—. Mem. Internat. Soc. History Didactics (v.p. 1991-95, 96-00), Am. Hist. Assn., German Studies Assn., Soc. History Edn., Com. for History in the Classroom (treas. 1990-93), Phi Beta Kappa. Home: 1521 Cason St Lafayette IN 47904-2642 Office: Purdue U Dept of History West Lafayette IN 47907-1358 E-mail: gmork@purdue.edu.

MORLEY, GEORGE WILLIAM, gynecologist; b. Toledo, June 6, 1923; s. Francis Wayland and Florence (Sneider) M.; m. Constance J. Morley, July 27, 1946 (dec. 1960); children: Beverly, Kathryn, George W. Jr.; m. Marcheta F. Morley, June 14, 1963. BS, U. Mich, 1944, MD, 1949, MS, 1955; cert. in Gynecologic Oncology, Am. Bd. Ob-Gyn., 1974. Diplomate Am. Bd. Ob-Gyn. Intern U. Mich. Hosp., 1949-50, asst. resident, 1950-51, resident, 1951-52, jr. clin. instr., 1952-53, sr. clin. instr., 1953-54; mem. faculty Sch. Medicine U. Mich., Ann Arbor, 1956—, prof. ob.-gyn., 1970-97, dir. gynecology svc., 1973-85, dir. gynecologic oncology svc., 1964-86, 94-95, Norman F. Miller prof. dept. ob.-gyn., 1987-98, assoc. chmn., 1987-91, prof. emeritus, 1997—. Chmn. Mich. Jud. Commn., Lansing, 1988-92. Contbr. to med. publs. George W. Morley professorship established U. Mich., 1995. Fellow, ACS (bd. govs. 1986-91), Am. Coll. Ob.-Gyn. (pres. 1987); mem. Rotary. Republican. Presbyterian. Avocations: golf, music. Home: 1120 Chestnut St Ann Arbor MI 48104-2826 Office: U Mich Med Ctr 1500 E Medical Center Dr Ann Arbor MI 48109-0005 E-mail: gwmorley@umich.edu.

MORLEY, HARRY THOMAS, JR. real estate executive; b. St. Louis, Aug. 13, 1930; s. Harry Thomas and Celeste Elizabeth (Davies) M.; m. Nelda Lee Mulholland, Sept. 3, 1960; children: Lisa, Mark, Marci. BA, U. Mo., 1955; MA, U. Denver, 1959. Dir. men's student activities Iowa State Tchrs. Coll., 1955-57; dir. student housing U. Denver, 1957-60; pvt. practice psychol. consulting St. Louis, 1960-63; dir. adminstrn. County of St. Louis, Mo., 1963-70; regional dir. HUD, Kansas City, 1970-71, asst. sec. adminstrn., 1971-73; pres. St. Louis Regional Commerce and Growth Assn., 1973-78, Taylor, Morley, Inc., St. Louis, 1978—. Teaching cons.-lectr. Washington U., St. Louis, 1962-70; bd. dirs. Mid-Am. Alliance Corp. and Life Ins. Co. Bd. dirs., mem. exec. com. St. Louis Coll. Pharmacy; past chmn. Better Bus. Bur.; chmn. Mo. Indsl. Devel. Bd., Mo. State Hwy. Commn.; bd. dirs. St. Luke's Hosps., St. Johns Hosp., Downtown St. Louis, Inc., Laclede's Landing Redevel. Corp. Served with USN, 1951-53. Mem. Am. Nat. Assn. Homebuilders, St. Louis Homebuilders Assn. (pres.), St. Louis Advt. Club, Mo. Athletic Club, St. Louis Club, Noonday Club, Castle Oak Country Club, Round Table Club, Sunset Country Club. Republican. Methodist. Home: 14238 Forest Crest Dr Chesterfield MO 63017-2818 Office: 17107 Chesterfield Airport Chesterfield MO 63005 E-mail: harrym@taylormorley.com.

MORLEY, JOHN EDWARD, physician; b. Eshowe, Zululand, South Africa, June 13, 1946; came to U.S., 1977; s. Peter and Vera Rose (Phipson) M.; m. Patricia Morley, Apr. 4, 1970; children: Robert, Susan, Jacqueline. MB, BCh, U. Witwatersrand, Johannesburg, South Africa, 1972. Diplomate Am. Bd. Internal Medicine, subspecialty cert. endocrinology and geriatrics. Asst. prof. Mpls. VA Med. Ctr. and U. Minn., 1979-81; assoc. prof. U. Minn., Mpls., 1981-84; prof. UCLA San Fernando Valley, 1985-89; dir. GRECC Sepulveda (Calif.) VA Med. Ctr., 1985-89; Dammert prof. gerontology, dir. div. geriatric medicine St. Louis U. Med. Ctr., 1989—; dir. geriatric rsch., edn. and clin. ctr. St. Louis VA Med. Ctr., 1989—. Mem. adv. panel of geriatrics and endocrinology U.S. Pharmacopeial Conv., Inc., Rockville, Md., 1990—. Author: (with others) Nutritional Modulation of Neuronal Function, 1988, Neuropeptides and Stress, 1988, Geriatric Nutrition, 1990, 2d edit., 1995, Medical Care in the Nursing Home, 1991, 2d edit., 1997, Endocrinology and Metabolism in the Elderly, 1992, Memory Function and Aging Related Disorders, 1992, Aging and Musculoskeletal Disorders, 1993, Aging, Immunity and Infection, 1994, Sleep Disorders and Insomnia in the Elderly, 1993, Quality Improvement in Geriatric Care, 1995, Focus on Nutrition, 1995, Applying Health Services Research to Long-Term Care, 1996, Cardiovascular Disease in Older People, 1997, Hydration and Aging, 1997, Advances in Care of Older People with Diabetes, 1999, Endocrinology of Aging, 1999, Science of Geriatrics, 2000, Subacute Care, 2000; mem. editl. bd. Peptides, 1983—, Internat. Jour. Obesity, 1986-89, Jour. Nutritional Medicine, 1990—, Clinics in Applied Nutrition, 1990-92; editor geriatrics sect. Yearbook of Endocrinology, 1987—, Nursing Home Medicine, 1992-97, Clin. Geriatrics, 1992-97, Sandwich Generation, 1997, others; editor Jour. Gerontology: Med. Scis., 2000—. Mem. adv. bd. Alzheimer's Assn., St. Louis, 1990-92; mem. adv. com. for physicians Mo. Divsn. Aging, Jefferson City, 1990—; bd. dirs. Mo. Assn. Long Term Care Physicians, 1991—, Long Term Care Ombudsman Program, St. Louis, 1992, Fund for Psychoneuroimmunology, 1990—, Hamilton Hts. Health Resource Ctr., 1992—. Recipient Mead Johnson award, Am. Inst. Nutrition, 1985, Cmty. Svc. award, BREM, 1997, Robert H. Bollinger Disting. Acad. award, U. Kans., 1997, Longevity prize, Ispen Found., 1999, Circle award, Am. Dietetics Assn., 2001, Nasher/Manning award, Am. Geriatric Soc., 2002. Mem. ACP (geriatrics subcom. 1991-92), Am. Soc. Clin. Investigation, Endocrine Soc., Am. Fedn. Clin. Rsch., Am. Acad. Behavioral Sci., Gerontology Soc. Am., Am. Diabetes Assn., Am. Soc. Pharmacy and Therapeutics, Soc. for Neurosci., La Asociacion de Gerontologica y Geriatrica, A.C. (hon.), Assn. Dirs. Geriatric Acad. Programs. Office: Saint Louis U Sch Medicine 1402 S Grand Blvd Rm M238 Saint Louis MO 63104-1004

MORLEY, MICHAEL B. public relations executive; b. Madras, India, Nov. 18, 1935; s. Gordon and Violet M.; m. Ingrid Hellman, Aug. 20, 1957; children: Andrew, Helen, Ann. Attended, Eastbourne Coll. Dir. Harris & Hunter Pub. Rels., 1960-67; mng. dir. Daniel J. Edelman, 1967; pres. Edelman Internat., 1970, Edelman N.Y., 1994—; dep. chmn., pres. Edelman Worldwide, 2000—. Comms. Advt. and Mktg. Edn. Found. fellow, 1981; decorated Knight of First Class, Order of Lion, Rep. Finland, 1978. Mem. Internat. Pub. Rels. Assn., Internat. Pub. Rels., Brit. C. of C., Japan Soc., Bus. Coun. Internat. Understanding, Inc., Korea Soc. Home: 1 Devon Pl Cresskill NJ 07626-1608 Office: Edelman Pub Rels Worldwide 200 E Randolph St Fl 62 Chicago IL 60601-6436

MORLOCK, CARL GRISMORE, physician, medical educator; b. Crediton, Ont., Can., Sept. 11, 1906; came to U.S., 1934, naturalized, 1939; s. Charles Edward and Emma (Grismore) M.; m. Katherine Ruth Mercer, Sept. 18, 1937; children: Anne Louise, William Edward. B.A., U. Western Ont., 1929, M.D., 1932; fellow internal medicine, Mayo Found., Grad. Sch. U. Minn., 1934-37; M.S. in Medicine, U. Minn., 1937. Intern Victoria Hosp., London, 1932-33, resident, 1933-34; practice medicine specializing in internal medicine and gastroenterology Rochester, Minn., 1934—; assoc.prof. internal medicine Mayo Found., 1949-62, prof. clin. medicine, 1962-72; prof. medicine Mayo Med. Sch., 1972—. Contbr. articles on gastrointestinal subjects to med. jours. Fellow ACP; mem. Am., Minn. med. assns., Osler Med. Soc., Am. Gastroent. Assn., Gideons Internat. Sigma Xi, Alpha Omega Alpha. Baptist. Home: 211 2nd St NW # 401 Rochester MN 55901-2807 Office: Mayo Clinic 200 1st St SW Rochester MN 55905-0002

MORNEAU, ROBERT FEALEY, bishop, writer; b. New London, Wis., Sept. 10, 1938; s. Leroy Frederick and Catherine (Fealey) M. M.A., Catholic U., 1962; D.Div.(hon.), 1979. Ordained priest Roman Catholic Ch., 1966, consecrated bishop, 1979. Instr. philosophy Silver Lake Coll., Manitowoc, Wis., 1966-78; dir. ministry to priests program Green Bay, 1979-85; aux. bishop Diocese of Green Bay, 1979—. Chmn. Commn. on Prison Reform, Wis. Cath. Conf.; lectr. in field. Author: Our Father Revisited, 1978, Trinity Sunday Revisited, 1980, Discovering God's Presence, 1980, Mantras for the Morning, 1981, Mantras for the Evening, 1982, Principles of Preaching, 1982, Seasonal Themes, 1984, Mantras for Midnight, 1985 and others; author tape series from Alba House; ; contbr. articles to profl. jours. Bd. trustees St. Norbert Coll. Mem. Nat. Conf. Catholic Bishops, Bishops Com. on Priestly Formation, Com. on Edn. U.S. Catholic Conf. Office: PO Box 23825 Green Bay WI 54305-3825

MORNHINWEG, MARTY, professional football coach; b. Edmond, Okla., Mar. 29, 1962; m. Lindsay Mornhinweg. Coach U. Mont., 1985; grad. asst., quarterback coach U. Tex., El Paso, 1986—87; coach running backs No. Ariz. U., 1988; offensive coord./quarterbacks S.E. Mo. State U., 1989—90; coach offensive line, tight ends U. Mo., 1991—93; offensive coord. No. Ariz. U., 1994; offensive asst., quality control, quarterback coach Green Bay Packers, Wis., 1995—96; offensive coord. San Francisco 49ers, 1997—2000; head coach Detroit Lions, 2001—. Office: Detroit Lions 1200 Featherstone Rd Pontiac MI 48342 also: Detroit Lions, Inc 222 Republican Drive Allen Park MI 48101*

MORRILL, R. LAYNE, real estate broker, executive, professional association administrator; m. Brenda Morrill; 1 child Rochelle Dawn. Cert. real estate broker. Pres. Shepherhd of the Hills, Realtors, Kimberling City, Branson, Mo., 1960—; mem. exec. com. Nat. Assn. Realtors, 1988—, pres., 1998—99, also bd. dirs. and mem. exec. com., 1988—. Regional v.p. Nat. Assn. Realtors, Ark., Kans., Mo., Okla., 1988; chair realtors polit. action com., 88; dir. Bank Kimberling city, Mo., Rural Mo. Cable TV, Inc. White River Valley Electric Coop., Branson, Mo., KAMO Electric Coop., Vinita, Okla., Nat. Rural utilities Coop. Fin. Corp., Herndon, Va. Mem.: Tri-Lakes Bd. Realtors (pres.), Mo. Assn. Realtors (pres., bd. dirs. 1962—, Realtor of the Yr. award 1979). Office: Nat Assn Realtors 430 N Michigan Ave Chicago IL 60611-4011

MORRIS, G. RONALD, industrial executive; b. East St. Louis, Ill., Aug. 30, 1936; s. George H. and Mildred C. M.; m. Margaret Heino, June 20, 1959; children: David, Michele, James. BS in Metall. Engring, U. Ill., 1959. Metall. engr. Delco-Remy div. Gen. Motors Corp., 1959-60; factory metallurgist Dubuque Tractor Works, John Deere Co., Iowa, 1960-66; with Fed.-Mogul Corp., 1966-79, v.p., group mgr. ball and roller bearing group, 1979; pres. Tenneco Automotive div. Tenneco, Inc., Deerfield, Ill., 1979-82; pres., chief exec. officer PT Components, Inc., Indpls., 1982-88; vice-chmn. Rexnord Corp., 1988-89; chmn., pres., chief exec. officer CTP Holdings Inc., 1986-88; chmn. Integrated Technologies, Inc., Indpls., 1990-92, also bd. dirs.; pres., chief exec. officer Western Industries, Inc., Milw., 1991-99. Chmn. bd. dirs. Milnot Holding Corp., St. Louis, NN, Inc., Erwin, Tenn.; bd. dirs. Dalco Metals, Inc., Walworth, Wis., Hines Hort., Inc., Irvine, Calif. Mem. Pres.'s Coun., U. Ill., mem. adv. bd. Coll. Engring., mem. sr. adv. bd. Sch. Materials Sci. and Engring; mem. U. Ill. Found. Mem. ASM, SAE, Exmoor Country Club (Highland Park, Ill.), The Landings Club (Savannah, Ga.), Masons, Scottish Rite Consistory, Kiwanis Internat. Republican. Presbyterian.

MORRIS, JOHN H. company executive; BS, U. W.Va.; MBA, Case Western Res. U. Mgmt. positions Gen. Tire & Rubber Co., Armstrong Cork Co.; dir. corp. mktg., corp. v.p. RPM, Inc., 1977-81, exec. v.p. Indsl. Group, 1981—. Dir. Fifth Third Bank, Northeastern Ohio. Office: 2628 Pearl Rd Medina OH 44256-7623

MORRIS, MATTHEW CHRISTIAN, baseball player; b. Middletown, N.Y., Aug. 9, 1974; Attended, Seton Hall Univ. Played Team USA, 1994; pitcher St. Louis Cardinals, 1997—. Named All-Am. Office: St Louis Cardinals 250 Stadium Plz Saint Louis MO 63102*

MORRIS, MICHAEL DAVID, chemistry educator; b. N.Y.C., Mar. 27, 1939; s. Melvin M. and Rose (Pollock) M.; m. Leslie Tuttle, June 5, 1961; children: Susannah, David, Rebecca, Ari. BA in Chemistry, Reed Coll., 1960; PhD in Chemistry, Harvard U., 1964. Asst. prof. Pa. State U., University Park, Pa., 1969; assoc. prof. U. Mich., Ann Arbor, 1969-82, prof., 1982—. Assoc. chmn. U. Mich., Ann Arbor, 1992-97. Editor: Spectroscopic and Microscopic Imaging of the Chemical State, 1993; mem. editorial bd. Applied Spectroscopy, 1994— (Gold medal N.Y. sect. 1993), Spectrochim Acta Rev., 1987-92, editor, 1993. Recipient Anachem award Assn. Analytical Chemists, 1997. Mem. Am. Chem. Soc. (award in Spectrochemical Analysis Divsn. Analytical Chemistry 1995), Soc. Applied Spectroscopy (Strock award 1995), Microbeam Analysis Soc. Office: Univ Mich Dept Chemistry Ann Arbor MI 48109 E-mail: mdmorris@umich.edu.

MORRIS, NAOMI CAROLYN MINNER, medical educator, administrator, researcher, consultant; b. Chgo., June 8, 1931; d. Morris George and Carrie Ruth (Auslender) Minner; m. Charles Elliot Morris, June 28, 1951; children: Jonathan Edward, David Carlton. BA magna cum laude, U. Colo., 1952, MD, 1955; MPH magna cum laude, Harvard U., 1959. Diplomate Am. Bd. Preventive Medicine. Rotating intern L.A. County Gen. Hosp., 1955-56; clin. fellow in pediats. Mass. Gen. Hosp., Boston, 1957; pub. health physician Mass. Dept. Health, 1957-58; clin. pediatrician Norfolk (Va.) King's Daus. Hosp., 1959-61; from rsch. assoc. to prof. dept. maternal/child health Sch. Pub. Health, U. N.C., Chapel Hill, 1962-70, 71-74, chair dept., 1975-77; prof., dir. cmty. pediats. U. Health Scis., Chgo. Med. Sch., 1977-80; prof. Sch. Pub. Health, U. Ill., Chgo., 1980—, dir. cmty. health scis. divsn., 1980-95. Advisor to chief pub.health officer, Guam, 1970-71; mem. liaison com. with Lake County Med. Soc. 1978-80; nursing divsn. adv. com. Lake County Health Dept., 1978-98; resource person Ill. 1980 White Ho. Conf. on Children, 1979-80; participant Enrich-A-Life series Chgo. Dept. Health, 1984-85, Ill. Health and Hazardous Substance Registry Pregnancy Outcome Task Force, 1984-86; mem. profl. adv. bd. Beethoven Project Ctr. Child Devel., 1986-96; mem. planning com. for action to reduce infant mortality Chgo. Inst. Medicine, 1986-89; founding mem. Westside Futures Infant Mortality Network, 1986; mem. Ill. vital stats. supplement Ill. Dept. Pub. Health, 1987; investigator and team leader Rev. Mo. Families Maternal and Child Health State Svcs., 1989; mem. children and youth 2000 task force MacArthur Found., 1992—; active Ill. Caucus on Teenage Pregnancies, 1978—, Chgo. Dept. Health Child Health Task Force, 1982-83, HSC Interprofessional Edn. Com., 1983-84, Med. Task Force Project Life, 1983-88, Women's Studies Curriculum Com., 1985-90, Com. Rsch. on Women, 1985-90, Mayor's Adv. Com. on Infant Mortality, 1986—, Gov. Adv. Coun. on Infant Mortality, 1988-96, Ctr. for Rsch. on Women Fellowship Com., 1993-98; cons. pediat. nursing resources group Ill. Dept. Pub. Health, 1983-84; cons. Cook County Hosp. Study of Preventive Childhood Obesity, 1983-84. Contbr. chapters to books, articles to profl. jours. Mem. Ill. MCH Coalition, 1994—, Voices for Ill. Children, 1993—, Children and Youth 2000, 1992—. Fellow APHA (task force on adolescence maternal and child health sect. 1977-85, sec. 1979-80, cons. manpower project 1982-83, publ. bd. 1985-87, coun. pediat. rsch. to Am. Acad. Pediats. 1985-92, Martha May Eliot award outstanding contbns. to field of maternal and child health 1999), Am. Coll. Preventive Medicine, Am. Acad. Pediats. (Ill. chpt. com. on sch. health, 1992-94, and com. adolescent health 1993—); mem. Ambulatory Pediat. Assn., Assn. Tchrs. Maternal and Child Health (exec. com. 1981-87, com. on tng. and continuing edn. needs of MCH/CCS dirs. 1982-83, liaison com. to fed. DCMH office 1983-87, pres. 1983-85), Chgo. Pediat. Soc., Phi Beta Kappa, Alpha Omega Alpha, Delta Omega, Sigma Xi. Avocations: photography, swimming, reading, classical music, travel. Office: U Ill Chgo Sch Pub Health 1603 W Taylor St Chicago IL 60612-4246 E-mail: numi@uic.edu.

MORRIS, NORVAL, criminologist, educator; b. Auckland, New Zealand, Oct. 1, 1923; s. Louis and Vera (Burke) M.; m. Elaine Richardson, Mar. 18, 1947; children: Gareth, Malcolm, Christoper. LLB, U. Melbourne, Australia, 1946, LLM, 1947; PhD in Criminology (Hutchinson Silver medal 1950), London Sch. Econs., 1949. Bar: called to Australian bar 1953. Asst. lectr. London Sch. Econs., 1949-50; sr. lectr. law U. Melbourne, 1950-58, prof. criminology, 1955-58; Ezra Ripley Thayer teaching fellow Harvard Law Sch., 1955-56, vis. prof., 1961-62; Boynthon prof., dean faculty law U. Adelaide, Australia, 1958-62; dir. UN Inst. Prevention Crime and Treatment of Offenders, Tokyo, Japan, 1962-64; Julius Kreeger prof. law and criminology U. Chgo., 1964—, dean Law Sch., 1975-79. Chmn. Commn. Inquiry Capital Punishment in Ceylon, 1958-59; mem. Social Sci. Rsch. Coun. Australia, 1958-59; Australian del. confs. div. human rights and sect. social def. UN, 1955-66; mem. standing adv. com. experts prevention crime and treatment offenders. Author: The Habitual Criminal, 1951, Report of the Commission of Inquiry on Capital Punishment, 1959, (with W. Morison and R. Sharwood) Cases in Torts, 1962, (with Colon Howard) Studies in Criminal Law, 1964, (with G. Hawkins) The Honest Politicians Guide to Crime Control, 1970, The Future of Imprisonment, 1974, Letter to the President on Crime Control, 1977, Madness and the Criminal Law, 1983, Between Prison and Probation, 1990, The Brothel Boy and Other Parables of the Law, 1992, The Oxford History of the Prison, 1995, Maconochie's Gentlemen, 2001. Served with Australian Army, World War II, PTO. Decorated Japanese Order Sacred Treasure 3d Class. Fellow Am. Acad. Arts and Scis. Home: 1207 E 50th St Chicago IL 60615-2908 Office: U Chgo Law Sch 1111 E 60th St Chicago IL 60637-2776 E-mail: norval_morris@law.uchicago.edu.

MORRIS, RALPH WILLIAM, chronopharmacologist; b. Cleveland Heights, Ohio, July 30, 1928; s. Earl Douglas and Viola Minnie (Mau) M.; m. Carmen R. Mueller; children: Christopher Lynn, Kirk Stephen, Timothy Allen and Todd Andrew (twins), Melissa Mary. BA, Ohio U., Athens, 1950, MS, 1953; PhD, U. Iowa, 1955; postgrad., Seabury-Western Theol. Sem., 1979-81, McHenry County Coll., 1986-88. Research fellow in pharmacology, then teaching fellow U. Iowa, 1952-55; instr. dept. pharmacology Coll. Medicine, 1955-56; asst. prof. dept. pharmacognosy and pharmacology Coll. Pharmacy, 1956-62, assoc. prof., 1962-69; prof. Med. Center, U. Ill., 1969-98, prof. emeritus, 1998, adj. prof. dept. pharmacodynamics, 1998-2000. Mem. adv. com. 1st aid and safety Midwest chpt. ARC, 1972-83; cons. in drug edn. to Dangerous Drug Commn., Ill. Dept. Pub. Aid, Chgo., Ill. Dept. Profl. Regulataions, Ill. Dept. Corrections and suburban sch. dists.; adj. prof. edn. Coll. Edn., U. Ill., Chgo., 1976-85; vis. scientist San Jose State U., Calif., 1982-83, St. George Med. Sch., Grenada, 1994. Referee and contbr. articles to profl. and sci. jours., lay mags., radio and TV appearances. Trustee Palatine (Ill.) Pub. Libr., 1967-72, pres., 1969-70; trustee North Suburban Libr. System, 1968-72, pres. 1970-72, mem. long-range planning com., 1975-81; chmn. Ill. Libr. Trustees, 1970-72, intellectual freedom com.; mem. Title XX Ill. Citizens Adv. Coun., 1981-83; trusteee McHenry (Ill.) Pub. Libr. Dist., 1987-89, pres., 1987-89; trustee St. Gregory's Abbey, Three Rivers, Mich., 1989-96; bd. dirs. North Suburban Libr. Found., Wheeling, Ill,. 1998-99; bd. dirs. United Campus Ministry U. Ill. at Chgo., 1983-87; pres. R.W. Morris & Assocs., 1988—; v.p. Lake Barrington Shores Condo X Assn., bd. dirs., 1999—; mem. archtl. commn. Lake Barrington Shores Master Bd., 1999—. Recipient Golden Apple Teaching award U. Ill. Coll. Pharmacy, 1966; cert. of merit Town of Palatine, 1972 Mem. AAAS, Am. Assn. Coll. Pharmacists, Internat. Soc. Chronobiology, European Soc. Chronbiology, Am. Soc. Pharmacology and Exptl. Therapeutics, Am. Library Trustee Assn., Ill. Library Trustee Assn. (v.p. 1970-72, dir. 1969-72), Sigma Xi, Rho Chi, Gamma Alpha. Episcopalian. Home and Office: 584 Shoreline Dr Lake Barrington IL 60010-3883 Fax: 847 304-5314. E-mail: raphaelmor@aol.com.

MORRIS, STEPHEN R. state legislator; b. Garden City, Kans., Jan. 4, 1946; m. Barbara Morris, 1968; children: Stephanie, Susan, Sara Beth. BS, Kans. State U., 1969. Farmer, Hugoton, Kans.; mem. from dist. 39 Kans. Senate, Topeka, 1992—; vice chmn. agr. com. Kans. State Senate, mem. energy and natural resources com., mem. emergency med. svc. bd., coord. coun. on early childhood devel. svc. With USAFR, 1974—. Mem. Kans. State U. Alumni Assn. Address: 600 S Trindle St Hugoton KS 67951-2734

MORRIS, THOMAS WILLIAM, symphony orchestra administrator; b. Rochester, N.Y., Feb. 7, 1944; s. William H. and Eleanor E. M.; m. Jane Allison, Aug. 7, 1965; children: Elisa L., Charles A., William H. A.B., Princeton U., 1965; M.B.A., Wharton Sch. U. Pa., 1969. Adminstrv. asst., Ford Found. fellow for adminstrv. interns in arts Cin. Symphony, 1965-67; payroll clk. bus. office Boston Symphony Orch., 1969-71, asst. mgr. bus. affairs, 1971-73, mgr., 1973-78, gen. mgr., 1978-86, v.p. spl. projects and planning, 1986; pres. Thomas W. Morris and Co., Inc., Boston, 1986-87; exec. dir. Cleve. Orch., 1987—. Chmn. policy com. Maj. Orch. Mgrs., 1977-79; chmn. orch. panel Nat. Endowment for Arts, 1979-80. Chmn. Cleve. Cultural Coalition, 1992-95; mem. Cleve. Bicentennial Commn., 1993-97; mem. bd. overseers Curtis Inst. Music, 1998—. Mem. Am. Symphony Orch. League (dir. 1977-79) Office: Cleve Orch Severance Hall 11001 Euclid Ave Cleveland OH 44106-1713

MORRISON, ANDREW J. marketing professional; b. Pitts., Mar. 7, 1949; s. James E. and Doris A. (Addicks) M.; m. Kathleen Ann Steiner, Dec. 27, 1969; children: Alanna Christine, James Jason. BA, U. Mich., 1971, PhD, 1980. Sr. v.p. Market Opinion Rsch., Detroit, 1980-89; prin., founder Market Strategies, Inc., Livonia, Mich., 1989-93, pres., CEO, 1994—. Contbr. chpts. to books, also articles to profl. publs., including Mktg. Rsch. Mag., Comm. Rsch., Am. Behavioral Scientist. Mem. Am. Mktg. Assn. (editor mag. 1996-98), Am. Assn. Pub. Opinion Rsch. Office: Market Strategies Inc 20255 Victor Pkwy Ste 400 Livonia MI 48152-7003

MORRISON, CLINTON, banker; b. Mpls., Mar. 26, 1915; s. Angus Washburn and Helen (Truesdale) M.; m. Mary K. Morrison. B.A., Yale U., 1937; M.B.A., Harvard U., 1939. With Shell Oil Co., N.Y.C., St. Louis, 1939-41; with Vassar Co., Chgo., 1946-48, Holding Co., Mpls., 1948, First Nat. Bank, Mpls., 1955-80, former vice chmn. bd., chmn. trust com. Former dir. Gt. No. Ins. Co., Minn. Title Fin. Corp., Munsingwear, Inc.; Dep. regional dir. Far East Fgn. Operations Adminstrn. for U.S. Govt., 1953- 55; mem. Internat. Pvt. Investment Adv. Council to AID, Dept. State, 1967-68, Nat. Adv. Council on Minority Bus. Enterprise, 1968-72 Life trustee Mpls. Art Inst., Mpls. Coll. Art and Design; former trustee Lakewood Cemetery Assn. Served to maj. Q.M.C. AUS, 1942-46. Mem. U.S. C. of C. (chmn. 1975-76), Bankers Assn. (exec. com. trust div. 1969-72), Twin Cities Soc. Security Analysts, Mpls. Econ. Roundtable. Home: 2400 Cedar Point Dr Wayzata MN 55391-2618 Office: 730 Second Ave South Ste 1350 Minneapolis MN 55402

MORRISON, DEBORAH JEAN, lawyer; b. Johnstown, Pa., Feb. 18, 1955; d. Ralph Wesley and Norma Jean (Kinsey) Morrison; m. Ricardo Daniel Kamenetzky, Sept. 6, 1978 (div. Nov. 1991); children: Elena Raquel, Julia Rebecca. BA in Polit. Sci., Chatham Coll., 1977; postgrad., U. Miami, Fla., 1977-78; JD, U. Pitts., 1981. Bar: Pa. 1981, Ill. 1985. Legal asst. Klein Y Mairal, Buenos Aires, Argentina, 1978-79; legal intern Neighborhood Legal Svcs., Aliquippa, Pa., 1980-81; law clk. Pa. Superior Ct., Pitts., 1981-84; atty. John Deere Credit Co., Moline, Ill., 1985-89; sr. atty. Deere & Co., 1989-96, sr. counsel, 1996—. Mem. ABA, Pa. Bar Assn., Phi Beta Kappa, Order of the Coif. Democrat. Mem. United Church of Christ. Office: Deere & Co 1 John Deere Pl Moline IL 61265-8098

MORRISON, DONALD WILLIAM, lawyer; b. Portland, Oreg., Mar. 31, 1926; s. Robert Angus and Laura Calista (Hodgson) M.; m. Elizabeth Margaret Perry, July 25, 1953; children: Elizabeth Laura, Carol Margaret. B.S.E.E., U. Wash., 1946; LL.B., Stanford U., 1950. Bar: Oreg. 1950, Calif. 1950, N.Y. 1967, Ill. 1968, Ohio 1974. Assoc. Pendergrass, Spackman, Bullivant & Wright, Portland, 1950-57, ptnr., 1957-60; gen. atty. Pacific N.W. Bell, Portland, 1960-66; atty. AT&T, N.Y.C., 1966-68; counsel Ill. Bell Telephone Co., Chgo., 1968-74; v.p., gen. counsel Ohio Bell Telephone Co., Cleve., 1974-91; of counsel Arter & Hadden, 1991—. Trustee Citizens League Rsch. Inst., Cleve. Chamber Music Soc.; trustee, mem. exec. com. Cleve. Coun. on World Affairs; mem. adv. com. Cleve. Play House; mem. adv. com., trustee Cleve. Bot. Garden; trustee Cleve. Archaeol. Soc. With USN, 1943—50. Recipient various bar and civic appreciation awards. Mem. ABA, Ohio State Bar Assn., Bar Assn. Greater Cleve., Oreg. State Bar Assn., Calif. Bar Assn., The Country Club, Rowfant Club. Office: Arter & Hadden 1100 Huntington Bldg Cleveland OH 44115

MORRISON, HARRY, chemistry educator, university dean; b. Bklyn., Apr. 25, 1937; s. Edward and Pauline (Sommers) M.; m. Harriet Thurman, Aug. 23, 1958; children: Howard, David, Daniel. BA, Brandeis U., 1957; PhD, Harvard U., 1961. NATO-NSF postdoctoral fellow Swiss Fed. Inst., Zurich, 1961-62; rsch. assoc. U. Wis., Madison, 1962-63; asst. prof. chemistry Purdue U., West Lafayette, Ind., 1963-69, assoc. prof., 1969-76, prof., 1976—, dept. head, 1987-92, dean Sch. Sci., 1992—2002. Acad. adv. com. Indsl. Rsch. Inst., 1993-96; mem. sci. adv. bd. Photogen, Inc. Contbr. numerous articles to profl. jours. Bd. fellows Brandeis U. Mem. Am. Chem. Soc., Am. Soc. Photobiology, Inter-Am. Photochem. Soc., Coun. for Chem. Rsch. (chmn. 1995), Phi Beta Kappa, Sigma Xi. Office: Purdue U Sci Adminstrn Math Bldg West Lafayette IN 47907-1390

MORRISON, JAMES FRANK, optometrist, state legislator; b. Colby, Kans., Apr. 11, 1942; s. Lloyd Wayne and Catherine Louise (Beckner) M.; m. Karen Jean Carr, Aug. 25, 1963; children: Mike, Jeff, Scott. Student, U. Kans., 1960-64; BS, OD, So. Coll. Optometry, 1967. Pvt. practice, 1969-75; founder, chief staff N.W. Kans. Ednl. Diagnostic and Referral Ctr. Children, Inc., Colby; asst. chief engr. Sta. KXXX-FM, 1977-80, chief engr., 1980-82; prof. vision dept. Colby Community Coll., 1979-84; mem. Kans. Ho. Reps., Topeka, 1992—. Cubmaster pack 140 Cub Scouts Am., 1970-80, dist. chmn., 1977-79. Fellow Am. Acad. Optometry, Coll. Optometrists in Vision Devel.; mem. Am. Optometric Assn., Am. Soc. Broadcast Engrs., Kans. Soc. Broadcast Engrs. (founder, pres. 1970-71), Kans. Optometric Assn., Kans. Assn. Children with Learning Disabilities, Mo. Optometric Assn., Thomas County Assn. Retarded Children, Rotary, Lions , Kiwanies (pres. 1971-72), Masons, Shriners. Rotary. Mem. Assemblies of God. Ch. Avocations: amateur radio, photography, astronomy. Home: 3 Cottonwood Dr Colby KS 67701-3902 Office: Morrison Optometric Assocs 180 W 6th St Colby KS 67701-2315

MORRISON, JOSEPH YOUNG, transportation consultant; b. Flushing, N.Y., Jan. 4, 1951; s. William Barrier and Barbara Helen (Lowe) M.; children: Susan Parker, Travis Barrier. AS, Montreat (N.C.)-Anderson Coll., 1971; BA, Oglethorpe U., 1989. Dept. head J.C. Penny & Co., Atlanta, 1971-74; uniform patrol officer City of Atlanta, 1974-80; spl. agt. U.S. Dept. Transp., Atlanta, 1980-82; group dir. safety and ins. Western Express, 1982-85; dir. safety Taylor Maid Transp., Albany, 1985-86; v.p. risk mgmt. Burlington Motor Carriers, Inc., Daleville, Ind., 1986-96; pres. Motor Carrier Safety Cons. Inc., Noblesville, 1996-97; v.p. safety & risk mgmt. LinkAmerica Corp., Tulsa, Okla., 1997—; pres. Nat. Transp. Cons., Inc., Noblesville, Ind., 1997—. Contbg. author: Guide to Handling Hazardous Material, 1986. Mem. Am. Trucking Assn. (hazardous materials com. 1982-86, chmn. injury control com. 1984-88, safety mgmt. coun. 1982—, interstate carrier conf. 1985—, nat. freight claims and security coun. 1985—, Safety Improvement awards, Accident Reduction awards, Injury Reduction awards), Kenilworth Civic Club (treas. Stone Mountain Ga. chpt. 1981-83, pres. 1983-84), Am. Soc. Safety Engrs., Sertoma Club, Sigma Alpha Epsilon. Methodist. Avocations: home remodeling, restoring old cars. Home: 7111 Oakview Cir Noblesville IN 46060-9419 Office: Nat Transp Cons 1109 S 10th St PO Box 2067 Noblesville IN 46061-2067 E-mail: jmorrison@ntconsult.com.

MORRISON, MICHAEL GORDON, university president, clergyman, history educator; b. Green Bay, Wis., Mar. 9, 1937; s. Gordon John and Gertrude (Crilly) M. A.B., St. Louis U., 1960, M.A., Ph.L., St. Louis U., 1965, S.T.L., 1969; Ph.D., U. Wis., 1971. Ordained priest Roman Catholic Ch., 1968. Joined S.J., 1955; asst. v.p. acad. affairs Marquette U., Milw., 1974-77; v.p. acad. affairs Creighton U., Omaha, 1977-81, acting pres., 1981, pres., 1981-2000, dir. Mem. governing bd. Creighton Prep. Sch., 1993-99. Bd. dirs. Health Future Found., 1983-2000, Xavier U., 1992-98; mem. cons. com. SAC, 1988-99; mem. adv. bd. Salvation Army, 1992-2000; trustee Duchesne Acad. of Sacred Heart, 1995-2000; bd. dirs. Red Cloud Indian Sch., 1997-2000; bd. trustees, Loyola U., Chgo., 1998-2000. Recipient Human Rights award Anti-Defamation League, 1982, Humanitarian award Nat. Conf. Christians and Jews, 1989. Mem. Assn. Jesuit Colls. and Univs. (bd. dirs.), Assn. Ind. Colls. and Univs. Nebr. (bd. dirs. 1981-2000), Nat. Assn. Ind. Colls. and Univs. (bd. dirs. 1993-2000), Greater Omaha C. of C. (bd. dirs. 1993-2000), Alpha Sigma Nu, Beta Alpha Psi. Office: Creighton U 2500 California Plz Omaha NE 68178-0001

MORRISON, PORTIA OWEN, lawyer; b. Charlotte, N.C., Apr. 1, 1944; d. Robert Hall Jr. and Josephine Currier (Hutchison) M.; m. Alan Peter Richmond, June 19, 1976; 1 child, Anne Morrison. BA in English, Agnes Scott Coll., 1966; MA, U. Wis., 1967; JD, U. Chgo., 1978. Bar: Ill. 1978. Ptnr., mem. exec. com. Piper Marbury Rudnick & Wolfe, Chgo., 1978—. Lectr. in field. Pres. Girl Scouts of Chgo. Mem.: ABA, Comml. Real Estate Women, Chgo. Fin. Exch., Pension Real Estate Assn., Chgo. Bar Assn. (real property com., subcom. real property fin., alliance for women), Am. Coll. Real Estate Lawyers (treas., bd. govs.). Office: Piper Rudnick 203 N La Salle St Ste 1800 Chicago IL 60601-1210 E-mail: portia.morrison@piperrudnick.com.

MORRISS, FRANK HOWARD, JR. pediatrics educator; b. Birmingham, Ala., Apr. 20, 1940; s. Frank Howard Sr. and Rochelle (Snow) M.; m. Mary J. Hagan, June 29, 1968; children: John Hagan, Matthew Snow. BA, U. Va., 1962; MD, Duke U., 1966. Diplomate Am. Bd. Pediatrics, Am. Bd. Perinatal and Neonatal Medicine. Intern Duke U. Med. Ctr., Durham, N.C., 1966-67, resident in pediatrics, 1967-68, fellow in neonatology, 1970-71, U. Colo., Denver, 1971-73; asst. prof. to prof. U. Tex. Med. Sch., Houston, 1973-86; prof. U. Iowa Coll. Medicine, Iowa City, 1987—, chmn. dept., 1987—. Editor: Role of Human Milk in Infant Nutrition and Health, 1986; contbr. numerous articles to profl. jours, chpts. to books. Lt. comdr. USN, 1968-70. NIH grantee, 77-87, 90—. Mem. Am. Pediatric Soc., Soc. Pediatric Rsch., Am. Acad. Pediatrics, Soc. Gynecol. Investigation, Midwest Soc. Pediatric Rsch., Assn. Med. Sch. Pediatric Dept. Chmn. Methodist. Avocation: tennis. Office: U Iowa Hosps & Clinics Dept Pediatrics Iowa City IA 52242

MORRISSEY, BILL, state agency administrator; Dir. Minn. Dept. Natural Resources, Office Ops. Pks. & Recreation, St. Paul, 1993—. Office: Minn Dept Natural Resources Office Ops Pks & Recreation 500 Lafayette Rd N Saint Paul MN 55155-4002 Fax: 651-296-4799.

MORRISSEY, MARY F. (FRAN), human resource consulting company executive; Cert. profl. employer specialist. Acctg., tax profl., small bus. cons., 10 yrs.; formre owner, mgr. profl. employer orgn.; co-founder, pres., CEO, Staff Mgmt., Inc., Rockford, Ill., 1983—. Part-owner John Morrissey, Accts., Rockford; presenter to state and fed. legislators, regulatory agys. and profl. orgns.; sec., mem. bd. Merc. Bank; bd. dirs. Inst. for Accreditation Profl. Employer Orgns. Bd. dirs. Swedish Am. Health Sys., Rockford; active numerous civic orgsn. Named One of Top 25 Women Bus. Owners, Crain's Chgo. Bus., 1993, 95, Connie Tremulis award for bus. owners YWCA, Rockford, 1998. Mem. Soc. for Human Resource Mgmt. (accredited sr. profl. in human resources), Nat. Assn. Profl. Employer Orgns. (past bd. dirs. and past pres.), former mem. profl. stds. com., also former chmn., past mem. comm. network, mgmt. performance, membership, govt. affairs, and edn. coms.), Midwest Assn. Profl. Employer Orgns. (past pres.), Nat. Assn. Women Bus. Owners (One of Top 25 Women Bus. Owners 1993, 95), Rockford Area C. of C. (coun. of 100, Woman Bus. Owner of Yr. 1998)), Rockford Women's Club, also others. Office: Staff Mgmt Inc 5919 Spring Creek Rd Rockford IL 61114-6447 Fax: 815-282-0515.

MORRIS-TATUM, JOHNNIE, state legislator; Mem. Wis. State Assembly. Address: 3711 W Douglas Ave Milwaukee WI 53209-3620

MORRONE, FRANK, electronic manufacturing executive; b. Marano Marchesato, Cosenza, Italy, May 13, 1949; s. Luigi and Emma (Molinaro) M.; m. Katherine Ann Kuehn, Feb. 1, 1975; children: Louis H., Cecilia E., Joseph V. BSEE, U. Wis., 1972; MBA, Northwestern U., 1993. Project engr. 3M Co., St. Paul, 1972—73; product engr., mgr. Eaton Corp., Kenosha, Wis., 1973—79; chief elec. engr. Tree Machine Tool, Racine, 1979—80; v.p. engring. MacPower divsn. Manu-Tronics, Inc., Kenosha, 1980—84, exec. v.p., 1984—99, bd. dirs., sec., 1988—99; v.p. ops. Sanmina Corp., 1999—2001, sr. v.p., 2001—. Mem. exec. bd. southeast coun. Boy Scouts Am., Racine, 1987—; bd. dirs. Kenosha Libr., 1987-98, U. Wis.-Parkside Benevolent Found., 2000—; mem. mgmt. coun. Lakeview Tech. Acad., 1997-99. Mem. IEEE, Kenosha County Club (bd. dirs.). Office: Sanmina Corp 8701 100th St Pleasant Prairie WI 53158-2202

MORROW, ANDREW NESBIT, interior designer, business owner; b. Fremont, Nebr., Feb. 22, 1929; s. Hamilton N. and May (Oberg) M.; m. Margaret M. Stoltenberg; children: Megan Beth, Molly Jean, Andrew C. BFA, U. Nebr., 1950. Interior designer Hardy Furniture, Lincoln, Nebr., 1950-61, Morrow Interiors, Lincoln, 1961—. Bd. visitors Found. for Interior Design Edn. and Rsch., 1976-84; mem. standards com. Found. for Interior Design Edn. and Research, N.Y.C. Exhibitor Fremont Art Gallery, 1986, Haymarket Art Gallery, 1984. Pres. First Luth. Ch., Lincoln, 1987-90; bd. dirs. Lincoln Symphony, 1988-91, Nebr. Republicans for Choice, 1992, Luth. Family Svcs. of Nebr., 1994, Luth. Family Svc. Nebr. Found., 1995—; treas. NCID, 1992—. Fellow Am. Soc. Interior Designers (bd. dirs. Nebr.-Iowa chpt. 1974-78, pres. 1986-88); mem. Interior Design Educators Council (hon.). Republican. Avocations: gardening, horseback riding, cross-country skiing. Home: 301 Park Vista Lincoln NE 68510 Office: Morrow Interiors Inc 1010 K St Lincoln NE 68508-2880

MORROW, ELIZABETH HOSTETTER, sculptress, museum administrator, farmer, educator; b. Sibley, Mo., Feb. 28, 1947; d. Elman A. and Lorine H. Morrow; married, 1970 (div. 1979); children: Jan Pawel, Lorentz Arthur. Student, William Jewell Coll., 1958-59, Colo. Coll., 1959-60, U. Okla., 1960-62; BFA, U. Kans., 1964, MFA, 1967; postgrad., U. Minn., 1965, U. Kans., 1968. Pres. E. Morrow Co., Kansas City, Mo., 1966-67; head dept. art U. Hawaii, Honolulu, 1968-69, Tarkio (Mo.) Coll., 1970-74; exec. dir. Pensacola (Fla.) Mus. Art, 1974-76; pres., owner Blair-Murrah Exhbns., Sibley, Mo., 1980—. Pres. bd. trustees, CEO Blair-Murrah, Inc., 1991—; sec.-treas. Coun. for Cultural Resources, 1995—. Del. White House Conf. on Small Bus., 1986. Lew Wentz scholar U. Okla., 1960-62. Mem. Internat. Coun. of Mus., Internat. Coun. Exhbn. Exch., Internat. Soc. Appraisers, Am. Assn. Mus., Internat. Trade Club of Greater Kansas City, Nat. Assn. Mus. Exhibitions, Ft. Osage Hist. Soc., Friends Art, Internat. Com. Fine Arts, Internat. Com. Conservation, Internat. Sculpture Ctr., DAR (regent Ft. Osage chpt.), Delta Phi Delta. Republican. Avocations: historical and cultural activities, antique cars, midwest farm auctions, genealogy. Home: RR # 1 Sibley MO 64088 Office: Blair-Murrah Vintage Hill Orch Sibley MO 64088 also: 7 rue Muzy PO Box Nr 554 1211 Geneva 6 Switzerland E-mail: elizabethmorrow@blair-murrah.org., exhibits@blair-murrah.org.

MORROW, GRANT, III, medical research director, physician; b. Pitts., Mar. 18, 1933; married, 1960; 2 children. BA, Haverford Coll., 1955; MD, U. Pa., 1959. Intern U. Colo., 1959-60; resident in pediat. U. Pa., 1960-62, fellow neonatology, asst. instr., 1962-63, instr., 1963-66, assoc., 1966-68, asst. prof., 1968-70, assoc. prof., 1970-72, U. Ariz., 1972-74, prof., 1974-78, assoc. chmn. dept., 1976-78; med. dir. Columbus (Ohio) Children's Hosp., 1978-94; prof. neonatology and metabolism, chmn. dept. Ohio State U., 1978-94; med. dir., dir. divsn. molecular and human genetics Children's Hosp. Rsch. Found., Columbus, 1994-98. Med. dir. Children's Rsch. Inst., Columbus, Ohio, 1978—. Mem. Am. Pediat. Soc., Am. Soc. Clin. Nutrition, Soc. Pediat. Rsch. Achievements include research on children suffering inborn errors of metabolism, mainly amino and organic acids. Office: Children's Rsch Inst 700 Childrens Dr Columbus OH 43205-2696 Fax: (614) 722-2716. E-mail: morrowg@pediatrics.ohio-state.edu.

MORROW, RICHARD MARTIN, retired oil company executive; b. Wheeling, W.Va., Feb. 27, 1926; married. B.M.E., Ohio State U., 1948. With Amoco Corp., 1948-91; v.p. Amoco Prodn. Co., 1964-66; exec. v.p. Amoco Internat. Oil Co., 1966-70, Amoco Chem. Corp., 1970-74, pres., 1974-78, Amoco Corp., 1978-83, chmn. chief exec. officer, 1983-91; ret., 1991. Trustee U. Chgo. and Rush-Presbyn. St. Luke's Med. Ctr. Office: 200 E Randolph Dr Ste 7909 Chicago IL 60601-7704

MORSCH, THOMAS HARVEY, lawyer; b. Oak Park, Ill., Sept. 5, 1931; s. Harvey William and Gwenodyne (Maun) M.; m. Jacquelyn Casey, Dec. 27, 1954; children: Thomas H. Jr., Margaret, Mary Susan, James, Kathryn, Julia. BA, Notre Dame U., 1953; B.S.L., Northwestern U., 1953, J.D., 1955. Bar: Ill. 1955, D.C. 1955. Assoc. Crowell & Leibman, Chgo., 1955-62; ptnr. Leibman, Williams, Bennett, Baird & Minow, 1962-72, Sidley & Austin, Chgo., 1972-97, counsel, 1998-2000. Bd. dirs. Chgo. Lawyers Com. for Civil Rights Under Law, chmn., 1982-83; bd. dirs. Pub. Interest Law Initiative, pres., 1993-95; No. Dist. Ill. Civil Justice Reform Com., 1991-95, Ill. Equal Justice Commn., 1999—; mem. vis. com. Law Sch. Northwestern U., 1989-90, dir. Small Bus. Opportunity Ctr., 1998—, assoc. clin. prof., 1998—. Pres. Republican Workshops of Ill., 1970; gen. counsel Ill. Com. to Re-elect the Pres., 1972; mem. LaGrange Plan Commn., Ill., 1972-80, LaGrange Fire and Police Commn., 1968-72; trustee LaGrange Meml. Hosp., 1983-89; adv. bd. Catholic Charities of Chgo., 1985— Fellow Am. Coll. Trial Lawyers; mem. ABA, Ill. State Bar Assn., Chgo. Bar Assn. (bd. mgrs. 1979-81), DC Bar Assn., Northwestern Law Sch. Alumni Assn. (pres . 1988-89), Chgo. Bar Found. (bd. dirs., pres. 1995-97), 7th Cir. Bar Assn. Roman Catholic. Clubs: Univ. (Chgo.),, LaGrange Country, Palisades Park Country (Mich.), Point O'Woods Country (Mich.) Home: 301 S Edgewood Ave La Grange IL 60525-2153 Office: Northwestern U Sch Law 357 E Chicago Ave Chicago IL 60611 E-mail: tmorsch@law.northwestern.edu.

MORSE, PETER HODGES, ophthalmologist, educator; b. Chgo., Mar. 1, 1935; s. Emerson Glover and Carol Elizabeth (Rolph) M. AB, Harvard U., 1957; MD, U. Chgo., 1963. Diplomate: Am. Bd. Ophthalmology. Intern U. Chgo. Hosp., 1963-64; resident Wilmer Inst. Johns Hopkins Hosp., Balt., 1966-69; fellow, retina service Mass. Eye and Ear Infirmary, Boston, 1969-70; asst. prof. ophthalmology, chief retina service U. Pa., 1971-75, assoc. prof., 1975, U. Chgo., 1975-77; prof. ophthalmology, 1979-93; sec. dept. ophthalmology, 1976-77; chief retina service, prof., 1979-93; clin. prof. ophthalmology U. S.D. Sch. Medicine, Sioux Falls, 1993—. Prof. La. State U., 1978; chmn. dept. ophthalmology, chief retina service Ochsner Clinic and Found. Hosp., New Orleans, 1977-78; clin. prof. Tulane U., 1978 Author: Vitreoretinal Disease: A Manual for Diagnosis and Treatment, 1979, 2d edit., 1989, Practical Management of Diabetic Retinopathy, 1985; co-editor: Disorders of the Vitreous, Retina, and Choroid; bd. editors Perspectives in Ophthalmology, 1976— , Retina, 1980— ; contbr. articles to profl. jours. Served with USNR, 1964-66. Fellow ACS, Coll. Ophthalmologists Eng., Am. Acad. Ophthalmology, Royal Soc. Health (Eng.), Royal Coll. Ophthalmologists (Eng.); mem. AMA, La. Med. Soc., Orleans Parrish Med. Soc., New Orleans Acad. Ophthalmology, La. Ophthalmol. and Otolaryngol. Soc., Miss. Ophthalmol. and Otolaryngol. Soc., Assn. Rsch. Vision and Ophthalmology, Retina Soc., Soc. Heed Fellows, Ophthalmol. Soc. U.K., Pan Am. Assn. Ophthalmology, Oxford Ophthalmol. Congress, All-India Ophthalmol. Soc., Soc. Eye Surgeons, Vitreoretinal Soc. (India), Sigma Xi. Republican. Episcopalian. Home: 1307 S Holly Dr Sioux Falls SD 57105-0221 Office: Sioux Valley Clin Dept Ophthalmology 1100 E 21st St Sioux Falls SD 57105-1002

MORSS, LESTER ROBERT, chemist; b. Boston, Apr. 6, 1940; s. Sumner M. and Sylvia F. (Woolf) M.; m. Helaine Sue Gubin, June 19, 1966; children: Sydney, Benjamin, Rebecca, Alisa. BA, Harvard U., 1961; PhD, U. Calif., Berkeley, 1969. Postdoctoral rsch. assoc. Purdue U., West Lafayette, Ind., 1969-71; from asst. prof. to assoc. prof. Rutgers U., New Brunswick, N.J., 1971-80; chemist, sr. chemist Argonne (Ill.) Nat. Lab., 1980—. Vis. prof. U. Liège, Belgium, 1978-79, U. Paris, Orsay, 1993. Author, co-editor: The Chemistry of the Actinide Elements, 1986, Syntheses of Lanthanide and Actinide Compounds, 1991; editor procs. Rare Earth Rsch. Conf., 1986—. Lt. USN, 1961-65. Recipient Sr. Scientist award Alexander von Humboldt Found., 1992. Fellow AAAS; mem. Am. Chem. Soc. (sec. div. nuclear chemistry and tech. 1990-92, chair divsn. nuclear chemistry and tech. 1999), Am. Nuclear Soc., Sigma Xi (pres. Argonne chpt. 1988-89). Jewish. Home: 1s680 Verdun Dr Winfield IL 60190-1716 Office: Argonne Nat Lab Chem Tech Divsn Bldg 205 Argonne IL 60439

MORTENSEN-SAY, MARLYS, school system administrator; b. Yankton, S.D., Mar. 11, 1924; d. Melvin A. and Edith L. (Fargo) Mortensen; m. John Theodore Say, June 21, 1951; children: Mary Louise, James Kenneth, John Melvin, Margaret Ann. BA, U. Colo., 1949, MEd, 1953; Adminstrv. Specialist, U. Nebr., 1973. Tchr. Huron (S.D.) Jr. H.S., 1944-48, Lamar (Colo.) Jr. H.S., 1950-52, Norfolk Pub. Sch., 1962-63; sch. supr. Madison County, Madison, Nebr., 1963-79. Mem. ASCD, NEA (life) AAUW, Am. Assn. Sch. Adminstrs., Dept. Rural Edn., Nebr. Assn. County Supts., N.E. Nebr. County Supts. Assn. Assn. Sch. Bus. Ofcls., Nat. Orgn. Legal Problems in Edn., Nebr. Edn. Assn., Nebr. Sch. Adminstrs. Assn. Republican. Methodist. Home: 1222 W S Airport Rd Norfolk NE 68701-1349

MORTENSON, M. A., JR. construction executive; Chmn., pres., ceo M. A. Mortenson Co., Mpls., 1960-98, chmn., CEO, 1998—. Office: M A Mortenson Co 700 Meadow Ln N Ste 710 Minneapolis MN 55422-4817

MOSELEY-BRAUN, CAROL, ambassador, former senator; b. Chgo., Aug. 16, 1947; d. Joseph J. and Edna A. (Davie) Moseley; m. Michael Braun, 1973 (div. 1986); 1 child, Matthew. BA, U. Ill., Chgo., 1969; JD, U. Chgo., 1972. Asst. U.S. atty. U.S. Dist. Ct. (no. dist.) Ill., 1973-77; mem. Ill. Ho. of Reps., 1979-88; recorder of deeds Cook County, Ill., 1988-92; U.S. senator from Ill. Washington, 1993-99; Am. ambassador to New Zealand and Samoa U.S. Dept. State, 1999—.

MOSER, DEBRA KAY, medical educator; BSN magna cum laude, Humboldt State U., Arcata, Calif., 1977; M in Nursing, UCLA, 1988, D in Nursing Sci., 1992. RN, Calif., Ohio; cert. pub. health nurse, Calif. Staff nurse, relief supr. med.-surg. fl. Mad River Cmty. Hosp., Arcata, 1977-78, staff/charge nurse intensive care/cardiac care unit, 1978-86; clin. nursing instr. Humboldt State U., 1985-86; staff/charge nurse surg. ICU Santa Monica (Calif.) Hosp., 1987-88; spl. reader UCLA Sch. Nursing, 1990-91, rsch. assoc., 1986-91, clin. rsch. nurse, 1988-92, project dir., 1991-92, asst. prof., 1992-94; asst. prof. dept. adult health and illness Ohio State U. Coll. Nursing, Columbus, 1994-98, assoc. prof. dept. adult health and illness,

1998—. Mem. working group on ednl. strategies to Prevent Prehosp. Delay in Patients at High Risk for Acute Myocardial Infraction, Nat. Heart Attack Alert Program, NIH, Nat. Heart, Lung and Blood Inst., 1993-95; abstract grader sci. sessions program Am. Heart Assn., 66th Sci. Sessions, 1993, 96; grad. advisor Sigma Theta Tau-Gamma Tau chpt., 1993-94; mem. med. adv. com. Westside YMCA Cardiac Rehab. Program, 1993-94; mem. Task Force on Women, Behavior and Cardiovasc. Disease NIH, Nat. Heart, Lung and Blood Inst., 1991; coord. cont. care CHF cmty. case mgmt. Mt. Carmel Health Sys., Columbus, Ohio, 1997—; presenter in field. Reviewer Am. Jour. Critical Care, 1992—, Heart and Lung, 1991—, Progress in Cardiovasc. Nursing, 1993—, Heart Failure: Evaluation and Care of Patients With Left-Ventricular Systolic Function, 1993, Intensive Coronary Care, 5th edit., 1994, Rsch. in Nursing & Health, 1995—, Jour. Am. Coll. Cardiology, 1995; co-editor Jour. Cardiovasc. Nursing, 1997—; mem. editl. bd. Am. Jour. Critical Care, 1994—, Jour. Cardiovasc. Nursing, 1995—; contbr. articles to profl. jours., chpts. to books. Recipient scholarship UCLA, 1988-90, scholarship Kaiser Permanente Affiliate Schs., 1990, Ednl. Achievement award LA-AACN, 1990, Alumni rsch. award UCLA, 1990, rsch. abstract award AACN-IVAC, 1993, Heart Failure Rsch. prize AHA Coun. Cardiovascular Nursing/Otsuka Am. Pharm., Inc., 1995; grantee Sigma Theta Tau-Gamma Tau chpt., 1989-90, AACN, 1989-90, 92-93, NIH, Nat. Ctr. Nursing Rsch., 1990-92, UCLA Program in Psychneuroimmunology, 1992-93, UCLA Sch. Nursing, 1993, UCLA Acad. Senate, 1993-94, AACN/Sigma Theta Tau Internat., 1994-95, NIH, Nat. Inst. Nursing Rsch., 1991-96, Sigma Theta Tau Epsilon chpt., 1995, Ohio State U., 1995, Nat. Am. Heart Assn., 1995—. Mem. AACN (Critical Care Rsch. Abstract award 1995, 98), Am. Heart Assn. Coun. Cardiovasc. Nursing (New Investigator award 1995, Heart Failure Rsch. prize 1995), Am. Psychol. Soc., Heart Failure Soc. Am., AHA (fellow Coun. Cardiovascular Nursing), Sigma Theta Tau (mem. rsch. com. 1990-94, Excellence in Rsch. award Gamma Tau chpt. 1993). Office: Ohio State U Coll Nursing Dept Adult Health & Illness 1585 Neil Ave Columbus OH 43210-1216 Home: Apt 1010 4390 Clearwater Way Lexington KY 40515-6375

MOSES, ABE JOSEPH, international financial consultant; b. Springfield, Mass., July 15, 1931; s. Mohammed Mustapha and Fatima (Merriam) M.; m. Donna C. Moses (dec. 1987); children: James Douglas, John C., Peter J.; m. Mary Jo Morris, Aug. 25, 2001. BA, Amherst Coll., 1955; MA in Internat. Affairs, Johns Hopkins U., 1957. Legis. aide Sen. J.F. Kennedy, 1955-57; fgn. service officer Dept. State, 1960-65; v.p., gen. mgr. Libyan Desert Oil Co., Texfel Petroleum Corp., Tripoli, Libya, 1965-67; v.p. adminstrn., fin. Occidental Petroleum Corp., Libya, 1967-70; v.p. fin., dir. Northrop Corp., 1970-74; chmn. Transworld Trade Ltd., Washington, 1971—; v.p., mng. dir. world adv. group Chase Manhattan Bank, 1974-80; pres. Berkshire Properties, 1976-95; pres., COO, Grolier Internat., Inc., Danbury, Conn., 1980-82; CEO, dir. Galadari Bros., Dubai, United Arab Emirates, 1982-86; internat. bus. and fin. cons. Traxol, 1986—; fin. cons. Govt. Costa Rica, 1986-89. Chmn. Aviation Sys. Corp., Northampton, Mass., 1974, Dillon Internat., Akron, Ohio, 1986—; mng. dir. Sheraton Suites Akron, Cuyahoga Falls, Ohio, 1990—; owner's rep. Monarch Sheraton Hotel, Springfield, Mass., 1993-95; bd. dirs., v.p. Morgan Freeport Co., Hudson, Ohio; bd. dirs. Seeds of Peace, Washington; gen. ptnr. BPM Ltd. Partnership, 1995—. Pres., bd. dirs. Riverside Cmty. Urban Redevel. Corp.; mem. exec. com., bd. dirs. Near East Found., N.Y.C., 1978—; pres. Riverfront Ctr. Assn., Cuyahoga Falls, 1992-95; bd. dirs. Gulfcoast Radio Ptnrs., 1997-99, Capitol City Radio Ptnrs., 1998-2000, Ind. Radio Ptnrs., Commonwealth Opera Co., Northampton, Mass. Capt. USAF, 1957-60. Ford Found. fellow Johns Hopkins U., 1955, Barr Found. fellow, 1955-57. Democrat. Home: 16 Highmeadow Rd Northampton MA 01062-2625 Office: Riverside CURC 1989 Front St Cuyahoga Falls OH 44221-3811 E-mail: abejmoses@aol.com.

MOSES, GREGORY H., JR. health services administrator; m. Johnella Moses. Lead engagement ptnr. Sister Mercy Health Corp.; ptnr.-in-charge Healthcare Consulting Group, N.Y., N.J.; ptnr. Coopers & Lybrand; pres., COO United Am. Healthcare Corp., Detroit, 1998—. Office: United Am Health Care Corp 1155 Brewery Park Blvd Ste 200 Detroit MI 48207-2640 Fax: 313-393-7944.

MOSES, WINFIELD CARROLL, JR. state legislator, construction company executive; b. Ft. Wayne, Ind., Feb. 20, 1943; s. Winfield C. and Helen A. (O'Neil) M.; children: Elizabeth, Christopher. AB in Econs, Ind. U., 1964, MBA in Fin, 1966. Apt. builder, Ft. Wayne, 1966—; mem. Ft. Wayne City Coun., 1972-79; mayor City of Ft. Wayne, 1980-87; mem. Ind. Ho. of Reps., Indpls., 1992—. Founding pres. Washington House, 1973-76, Citizen Energy Coalition, 1974-75; active Art Mus.; mem. Ind. Urban Enterprise Zone Bd., Ind. Bus. Modernization Bd. Mem. C. of C., Rotary. Democrat. Unitarian. Office: 6000 N Oak Blvd Fort Wayne IN 46818-2438

MOSKAL, ROBERT M. bishop; b. Carnegie, Pa., Oct. 24, 1937; s. William and Jean (Popivchak) M. BA, St. Basil Coll. Sem., Stamford, Conn., 1959; lic. sacred theology, Cath. U. Am., 1963; student, Phila. Mus. Acad. and Conservatory of Mus., 1963-66. Ordained priest Ukrainian Cath. Ch. 1963. Founder, pastor St. Anne's Ukrainian Cath. Ch., Warrington, Pa., 1963-72; sec. Archbishop's Chancery, Phila., 1963-67; apptd. vicechancellor Archeparchy of Phila., 1967-74; pastor Annunciation Ukrainian Cath. Ch., Melrose Park, Phila., 1972-74; named monsignor, 1974; chancellor archdiocese, pastor Ukrainian Cath. Cathedral of the Immaculate Conception, Phila., 1974-84; apptd. bishop, 1981; Ordained titular bishop of Agathopolis and aux. bishop Ukrainian-Rite Archeparcy of Phila., 1981-83; first bishop Diocese of St. Josaphat, Parma, Ohio, 1983—. Pro-synodal judge Archdiocean Tribunal, Phila., 1965-67; founder Ukrainian Cath. Hour: God is with Us, Sta. WIBF-FM, Phila, 1972-77, Christ Among Us, Sat. WTEL, 1975—; mem. Ukrainian Cath. Ch. Liturgical Subcommn., 1980; host to His Holiness Pope John Paul II. Bd. dirs. Ascension Manor, Inc., Phila., 1964-84, sec.-treas., 1964-78, exec. v.p., 1977-84. Office: PO Box 347180 5720 State Rd Parma OH 44134-2500

MOSKOS, CHARLES C. sociology educator; b. Chgo., May 20, 1934; s. Charles and Rita (Shukas) M.; m. Ilca Hohn, July 3, 1966; children—Andrew, Peter. BA cum laude, Princeton, 1956; MA, UCLA, 1961, PhD, 1963; LHD (hon.) , Norwich U., 1992, Towson U., 2002. Asst. prof. U. Mich., Ann Arbor, 1964-66; assoc. prof. sociology Northwestern U., Evanston, Ill., 1966-70, prof., 1970—. Fellow Progressive Policy Inst., 1992—; mem. Presdl. Commn. on Women in the Mil., 1992. Author: The Sociology of Political Independence, 1967, The American Enlisted Man, 1970, Public Opinion and the Military Establishment, 1971, Peace Soldiers, 1976, Fuerzas Armadas y Societdad, 1984, The Military--More Than Just A Job?, 1988, A Call to Civic Service, 1988, Greek Americans, 1989, Soldiers and Sociology, 1989, New Directions in Greek American Studies, 1991, The New Conscientious Objection, 1993, All That We Can Be, 1996, Reporting War When There Is No War, 1996, The Media and the Military, 2000, The Postmodern Military, 2000. Chmn. Theodore Saloutos Meml. Fund; mem. Archdiocesean Commn. Third Millenium, 1982-88; mem adv. bd. Vets. for Am., 1997—; mem. Congl. Commn. on Mil. Tng. and Gender-Related Issues, 1998-99, Nat. Security Study Group, 1998-2001. Served with AUS, 1956-58. Decorated D.S.M., Fondation pour les Etudes de Def. Nat. (France), S.M.K. (The Netherlands); named to Marshall rsch. chair ARI, 1987-88, 95-96; Ford. Found. faculty fellow, 1969-70; fellow Wilson Ctr., 1980-81, guest scholar, 1991; fellow Rockefeller Found. Humanities, 1983-84, Guggenheim fellow, 1992-93, fellow Annenberg Washington Program, 1995; grantee 20th Century Fund, 1983-87, 92-94, Ford Found., 1989-90; recipient Nat. Educator Leadership award Todd Found., 1997, Book award Washington Monthly, 1997, Honored Patriot award Selective Svc. Sys., 1998; Pub. Policy fellow Wilson Ctr., 2002; Eisenhower chair Royal Mil. Acad. Netherlands, 2002. Mem. Am. Sociol. Assn., Internat. Sociol. Assn. (pres. rsch. com. on armed forces and conflict resolution 1982-86), Am. Polit. Sci. Assn., Inter-Univ. Seminar on Armed Forces and Soc. (chmn. 1987-99), Am. Acad. Arts and Scis. Greek Orthodox. Home: 2440 Asbury Ave Evanston IL 60201-2307

MOSKOWITZ, HERBERT, management educator; b. Paterson, NJ, May 26, 1935; s. David and Ruth (Abrams) M.; m. Heather Mary Lesgnier, Feb. 25, 1968; children: Tobias, Rebecca, Jonas. BS in Mech. Engring., Newark Coll. Engring., 1956; MBA, U.S. Internat. U., 1964; PhD, UCLA, 1970. Rsch. engr. GE, 1956-60; systems design engr. Gen. Dynamics Convair, San Diego, 1960-65; asst. prof. Purdue U., West Lafayette, Ind., 1970-75, assoc. prof., 1975-79, prof., 1979-85, Disting. prof., 1985-87, James B. Henderson Disting. prof., 1987-91, Lewis B. Cullman Disting. prof. mfg. mgmt., 1991—, dir. Dauch Ctr. Mgmt. Mfg. Enterprises. Cons. AT&T, Inland Steel Co., Abbott Labs., others; adv. panelist NSF, 1990—. Author: Management Science and Statistics Texts, 1975-90; assoc. editor Decision Scis. Jour., 1984-90, Jour. Behavioral Decision Making, 1986-90; contbr. articles to jours. in field. Bd. dirs. Sons of Abraham Synagogue, Lafayette, Ind., 1970—; mem. Lafayette Klezmorem, 1973—. Capt. USAF, 1956-60. Recipient Disting. Doctoral Student award UCLA Alumni Assn., 1969-70; Fulbright Rsch. scholar, 1985-86. Fellow Decision Scis. Inst. (sec. 1985-87, v.p. 1978-80); mem. Ops. Rsch. Soc. Am./Inst. Mgmt. Sci. (liaison officer 1977—, panel mem., advisor NSF and Fulbright Scholar program 1993—), Tau Beta Pi, Pi Tau Sigma. Jewish. Avocations: Jewish music, tennis. Home: 1430 N Salisbury St West Lafayette IN 47906-2420 Office: Purdue U Krannert Grad Sch Mgmt Ctr Mgmt Mfg Enterprises West Lafayette IN 47907-1310

MOSKOWITZ, ROLAND WALLACE, internist; b. Shamokin, Pa., Nov. 3, 1929; MD, Temple U., 1953. Intern Temple U. Hosp., Phila., 1953-54; fellow in internal medicine Mayo Clinic, Rochester, Minn., 1954-55, 57-60; mem. staff U. Hosps. Cleve.; prof. medicine Case Western Res. U. Sch. Medicine, Cleve. Mem.: ACR, Alpha Omega Alpha. Office: U Hosps Cleve Divsn Rheum Diseases 11100 Euclid Ave Cleveland OH 44106-1736 E-mail: rolliemoskowitz@aol.com.

MOSS, GERALD S. dean, medical educator; b. Cleve., Mar. 4, 1935; s. Harry and Lillian (Alter) M.; m. Wilma Jabak, Sept. 1, 1957; children: William Alan, Robert Daniel, Sharon Lynn. BA, Ohio State U., 1956, MD cum laude, 1960. Diplomate Am. Bd. Surgery (apptd. assoc. examiner com. 1989); lic. Ill. Intern Mass. Gen. Hosp., Boston, 1960-61, resident, 1961-65; from asst. prof. to assoc. prof. dept. surgery Coll. Medicine U. Ill., Chgo., 1968-72, prof., 1973-77, 89—, head dept. surgery, 1989, dean, 1989—; prof. dept. surgery Pritzker Sch. Medicine U. Chgo., 1977-89. Tutor in surgery Manchester (Eng.) Royal Infirmary, 1964; asst. chief surgical svcs. VA West Side Hosp., Chgo., 1968-70; attending surgeon dept. surgery Cook County Hosp., Chgo. 1970-72, chmn. 1972-77; dir. surgical rsch. Hektoen Inst. for Med. Rsch., Cook County Hosp., 1972-77, Michael Reese Hosp. and Med. Ctr., Chgo., 1977-89, chmn. dept. surgery, 1977-89, chief svc. 1989, trustee, 1981, and numerou coms.; appointed to Nat. Rsch. Coun., NAS, 1966-68, Ad Hoc Subcom., NAE, 1970, Ad Hoc Study Sect., 1970, del. to Third Joint U.S-USSR Symposium, 1983, Blood Diseases and Resources Adv. Com., 1984-88, Planning Com. for discussing key blood problems, Nat. Heart and Lung Inst., 1987, chmn. Plasma and Plasma Products Com., 1979, bd. dirs., 1983, v.p., 1985, Ad Hoc Transition Com., Am. Blood Commn., 1989, Panel on Rsch. Opportunities, Office Naval Rsch. Program, 1987, exec. com., coord. com., Nat. Blood Edn. Program, 1988, Tech. Adv. Task Force Am. Hosp. Assn., 1988, chmn. review panel contract proposals, NIH, 1975, program project site visit, 1976, chmn. site-visit review group, 1977, adv. com. Blood Resources Work group, 1978, Planning Com. for Consensus, 1987, Small Bus. Innovation Rsch., 1988, Med. Rsch. Scv. Merit Review Bd. VA, 1978-81, Liaison Com. Graduate Med. Edn. AMA, 1979, and numerous other coms. for various med. organizations; cons. Nat. Heart and Lung Inst., Transfusion Medicine Acad. Awardees Program; vis. prof. Montefiore Med. Ctr. Bronx, N.Y., 1986, Ohio State U., 1988, U. N.Mex., Albuquerque, 1989, Seton Med. Ctr., Austin, Tex., 1990, U. Ill. Coll. Medicine, Peoria, 1991; guest lectr., participant numerous meetings, symposiums; cons. in field. Contbr. numerous articles to profl. jours., chpts. to books.. With USN, 1965—68, Vietnam. Teaching fellow Harvard Med. Sch., 1962; recipient Stitt Lectr. award Assn. Mil. Surgeons U.S.A., 1981; grantee U.S. Navy, 1969-84, U.S. Army, 1971-74, 75-78, NIH, 1969, 83-84, Dept. Pub. Health, 1973, HEW, 1974-77, UpJohn, 1974, Northfield Labs. 1985-89. Fellow ACS (pre and postoperative care com. 1975-83, rep. Am. blood commn. 1977—, mem. various coms., speaker various symposiums), Am. Soc. Surgery Trauma; mem. Am. Surgical Assn. (rep. Nat. Soc. Med. Rsch. 1984-88), Am. Trauma Soc., Am. Physicians Fellowship (rep. Israel Med. Assn.), Assn. Acad. Surgery (chmn. membership selection com. 1973-75, pres. elect 1974-75, pres. 1975-76, exec. coun. 1977-79), Soc. Univ. Surgeons (rep. Nat. Soc. Med. Rsch. 1973-77, com. Surgical Edn. 1979-81), Ctrl. Surgical Soc. (rep. Nat. Soc. Med. Rsch. 1973-77), Shock Soc. (chmn. planning com. 1986, chmn. program com. 1986, pres. elect 1986-87, pres. 1987-88), Soc. for Surgery Alimentary Tract (mem. com. west north ctrl. region 1978-82), Internat. Soc. Blood Transfusion, Surgical Biology Club II, Nat. Soc. for Med. Rsch., Collegium Internationale Chirugiae Digestivae, Societe Internationale de Chirugie, Sigma XI, Alpha Omega Alpha (faculty advisor 1972-73). Office: U Ill Coll Medicine Chgo 1853 W Polk St # M/C 784 Chicago IL 60612-4316

MOSS, JOEL CHARLES, radio production director; b. N.Y.C., Oct. 10, 1949; s. S. Herbert and Sylvia (Rosenberg) M.; m. Cynthia Louise Lamb, Nov. 27, 1983; children: Joshua David, Alyson Rachel. Student, N.Y. Tech., Old Westbury, 1968-70. Program dir. STa. WLIR-FM, Garden City, N.Y., 1975-77; air talent Sta. WNEW-FM, N.Y.C., 1979-81; program dir. Sta. WPFB, Middletown, Ohio, 1982-84; prodn. dir., soundtrack producer Sta WEBN, Cin., 1984—. Copywriter radio show VD Walk-In Clinic, 1974 (Clio awrd 1974); writer, producer radio commls. WEBN Tee-Shirts, 1987 (Addy award 1987), Omni-Netherland Plaza, 1987 (Addy award 1987); radio parody Without Radio, 1990 (Firsty award 1990), Fireworks Promos (Radio and Prodn. award 1991), 1991. Office: Sta WEBN 1111 Saint Gregory St Cincinnati OH 45202-1770

MOSS, RANDY, professional football player; b. Feb. 13, 1977; , Marshall U. Wide receiver Minn. Vikings, 1998—. First round draft pick NFL, 1998; named Rookie of Yr. NFL, 1998. Achievements include Marshall U. record holder for touchdowns in a career. Ranks second in total yards and third in total receptions. Office: MN Vikings 9520 Viking Dr Eden Prairie MN 55344-3898

MOSS, RICHARD L. physiology educator; b. Fond du Lac, Wis., Nov. 2, 1947; s. Robert C. and Lenore H. Moss; m. Susan L. Rusch, Aug. 17, 1968; 1 child, James P. BS in Biology, U. Wis., Oshkosh, 1969; PhD in Physiology and Biophysics, U. Vt., 1975. Rsch. assoc. Boston Biomed. Rsch. Inst., 1975-79; asst. prof. physiology U. Wis., Madison, 1979-83, assoc. prof., 1983-87, prof., 1987—, chair dept. physiology, 1988—. Dir. U. Wis. Cardiovascular Rsch. Ctr., 1995—; mem. cellular pharmacology and physiology rsch. study com. Am. Heart Assn., Dallas, 1990-93, Established Investigator, 1981-86; mem. physiology study sect. NIH, 1994—. Mem. editl. bd. Biophys. Jour., 1985-92, Jour. Gen. Physiology, 1987-91, Am. Jour. Physiology: Cellular, 1990-96, Physiol. Revs., 1985-91, Jour. Physiology (London), 1995—; contbr. articles to Biophys. Jour., Circulation Rsch., Nature, Jour. Physiology. NRSA fellow NIH, 1976-78. Achievements include research on regulation of heart and skeletal muscle contraction by selective extraction and/or exchange of regulatory protein from permeabilized muscle preparations, implicating role of thick filament proteins (i.e. light chain-2 and C-protein) in regulation of tension and kinetics of contraction. Office: U Wis Med Sch 1300 University Ave Madison WI 53706-1510

MOSSMAN, ROBERT GILLIS, IV, civil and environmental engineer; b. Youngstown, Ohio, Jan. 28, 1960; s. Robert Gillis III and Carol (Hoyt) M. B Engring., Youngstown State U., 1984. Engr. Lynn, Kittenger & Noble, Inc., Warren, Ohio, 1984-85, Thomas Fok & Assocs., Ltd., Youngstown, 1985-86, Daniel C. Baker Assocs., Inc., Beaver, Pa., 1986-87; cons. Youngstown, 1987—. Avocations: photography, poetry, dancing, art, nature study. Home and Office: 58 Norwick Dr Youngstown OH 44505-1626 E-mail: mossydork@prodigy.net.

MOSTER, MARY CLARE, public relations executive; b. Morristown, N.J., Apr. 7, 1950; d. Clarence R. and Ruth M. (Duffy) M.; m. Louis C. Williams, Jr., Oct. 4, 1987. BA in English with honors, Douglass Coll., 1972; MA in English Lit., Univ. Chgo., 1973. Accredited pub. rels. counselor. Editor No. Trust Bank, Chgo., 1973-75, advt. supr., 1975-77, communications officer, 1977-78; account exec. Hill & Knowlton, Inc., 1978-80, v.p., 1980-83, sr. v.p., 1983-87, sr. v.p., mng. dir., 1987-88; staff v.p. comms. Navistar Internat. Corp., 1988-93; v.p. corp. comms. Comdisco, Inc., Rosemont, Ill., 1993—. Bd. dirs. The Pegasus Players, 1993-2000. Author poetry, poetry translation. Bd. govs. Met. Planning Coun., Chgo., 1988-94; fellow Leadership Greater Chgo., 1989-90; bd. dirs. New City YMCA, Chgo., 1986-92; corp. devel. bd. Steppenwolf Theatre Co., Chgo., 1988-90; mem. The Chgo. Network, 1994—, bd. dirs., 1996-99. Mem. Nat. Investor Rels. Inst. (bd. dirs. 1988-89, 90-99, pres. Chgo. chpt. 1998-99), Arthur W. Page Soc., Pub. Rels. Soc. Am., Internat. Women's Forum. Avocations: sailing, cross-country skiing. Office: Comdisco Inc 6111 N River Rd Rosemont IL 60018-5158

MOTTLEY, JAMES DONALD, state legislator, lawyer; b. Alamogordo, N.Mex., Aug. 29, 1954; s. Harry Edward Mottley Jr. and Linnie Sue (Tate) Johnson; m. Patricia Chris Cooper, June 30, 1980 (div. May 1984). BA in Polit. Sci. magna cum laude, Wright State U., 1975, MS in Econs., 1976; JD, Salmon P. Chase Coll. of Law, 1991. Bar: Ohio, 1991, U.S. Dist. Ct. (so. dist.) Ohio 1992. Fin. mgr. NCR Corp., Dayton, Ohio, 1977-81, mgr. cash mgmt. and investment banking, 1982-84; asst. to county commr. Montgomery County, 1981-82; treas. NCR Credit Corp., 1984-87; chief dep. county auditor Montgomery County Auditors Office, 1987-91; assoc. Taft, Stettinius & Hollister, Cin., 1991-92; ptnr. Flanagan, Lieberman, Hoffman & Swaine, Dayton, 1993—; mem. Ohio Ho. of Reps., Columbus, 1993—. Mem. ctrl. and exec. coms. Orgn. Montgomery County Rep. Party, Dayton, 1985—. Mem. Optimists, Masons (master). Presbyterian. Avocation: flying. Home: 1641 Longbow Ln West Carrollton OH 45449-2344 Office: Ohio Ho of Reps 77 S High St Fl 13 Columbus OH 43215-6199

MOUL, MAXINE BURNETT, state official; b. Oakland, Nebr., Jan. 26, 1947; d. Einer and Eva (Jacobson) Burnett; m. Francis Moul, Apr. 20, 1972; 1 child, Jeff. BS in Journalism, U. Nebr., 1969; DHL (hon.), Peru State Coll., 1993. Sunday feature writer, photographer Sioux City Iowa Jour., 1969-71; reporter, photographer, editor Maverick Media, Inc., Syracuse, Nebr., 1971-73, editor, pub., 1974-83, pres., 1983-90; grant writer, asst. coord. Nebr. Regional Med. Program, Lincoln, 1973-74; lt. gov. State of Nebr., 1991-93; dir. Dept. Econ. Devel., 1993-99; pres. Nebr. Cmty. Found., 1999—. Mem. Dem. Nat. Com., Washington, 1988-92, Nebr. Dem. State Ctrl. Com., Lincoln, 1974-88; del. Dem. Nat. Conf., 1972, 88, 92; mem. exec. com. Nebr. Dem. Party, Lincoln, 1988-93. Recipient Margaret Sanger award Planned Parenthood, Lincoln, 1991, Champion of Small Bus. award Nebr. Bus. Devel. Ctr., Omaha, 1991, Toll fellowship Coun. State Govts., Lexington, Ky., 1992. Mem. Bus. and Profl. Womem, Nebr. Mgmt. Assn. (Silver Knight award 1992), Nat. Conf. Lt. Govs. (bd. dirs. 1991-93), Nebr. Press Women, Women Execs. in State Govt., Cmty. Devel. Soc., U. Nebr.-Lincoln Journalism Alumni. Democrat. Avocations: reading, gardening. Office: Nebr Cmty Found 317 S 12th St Lincoln NE 68508-2108

MOUL, WILLIAM CHARLES, lawyer; b. Columbus, Ohio, Jan. 12, 1940; s. Charles Emerson and Lillian Ann (Mackenbach) M.; m. Margine Ann Tessendorf, June 10, 1962; children: Gregory, Geoffrey. BA, Miami U., Oxford, Ohio, 1961; JD, Ohio State U., 1964. Bar: Ohio 1964, U.S. Dist. Ct. (so. dist.) Ohio 1965, U.S. Ct. Appeals (2d cir.) 1982, U.S. Ct. Appeals (6th cir.) 1984, U.S. Ct. Appeals (3d cir.) 1985. Assoc., ptnr. George, Greek, King, McMahon & McConnaughey, Columbus, 1964-79; ptnr. McConnaughey, Stradley, Mone & Moul, 1979-81; ptnr.-in-charge Thompson, Hine & Flory, 1981-89, exec. com., 1989-98. Chmn. Upper Arlington Civil Svc. Commn., Ohio, 1981-86. Mem. ABA, Ohio State Bar Assn. (labor sect. bd. dirs. 1983—), Columbus Bar Assn. (chmn. ethics com. 1980-82), Lawyers Club Columbus (pres. 1976-77), Athletic Club, Scioto Country Club, Wedgewood Country Club, Masons. Lutheran. Home: 2512 Danvers Ct Columbus OH 43220-2822 Office: Thompson Hine & Flory 10 W Broad St Ste 700 Columbus OH 43215-3435

MOULDER, WILLIAM H. chief of police; b. Kansas City, Mo., Feb. 19, 1938; s. Roscoe B. and Charleen M. (Flye) M.; m. Louise M. Pollaro, Aug. 2, 1957; children: Deborah, Ralph, Robert. BA, U. Mo., Kansas City, 1971, MA, 1976. Cert. police officer, Mo., Iowa. From police officer to maj. Kansas City (Mo.) Police Dept., 1959-84; chief of police City of Des Moines, 1984—. Mem. Internat. Assn. Chiefs of Police, Police Exec. Rsch. Forum, Iowa Police Exec. Forum. Avocations: racquetball, travel. Office: Office of Police Chief 25 E 1st St Des Moines IA 50309-4800

MOUNTS, NANCY, secondary education educator; Tchr. home econs. North High Sch., Sioux City, Iowa; tech. prep. specialist Cen. Campus, 1995—. Recipient State Tchr. of Yr. Home Econs. award Iowa, 1992. Office: Cen Campus 1121 Jackson St Sioux City IA 51105-1434

MOUROU, GERARD A. research administrator; BS in Physics, U. Grenoble, France, 1967; MS in Physics, U. Orsay, France, 1970; PhD in Physics, U. Paris, 1973. Sci. cooperant Université Laval, Quebec, Canada, 1970-73; postdoctoral fellow San Diego State U., 1973-74; scientist Lab. for Laser Energetics U. Rochester, N.Y., 1979-88, group leader Picosecond Rsch. Group, Lab. for Laser Energetics, 1979-88, sr. scientist Lab. for Laser Energetics, 1981-88, assoc. prof. Inst. Optics, 1983-87, divsn. dir. Ultrafast Science Divsn., Lab. for Laser Energetics, 1986-88, prof. Inst. Optics, 1987-89; prof. Dept. Elec. Engring. and Computer Scis., Coll. Engring. U. Mich., 1988—, dir. Ctr. for Ultrafast Optical Science NSF and Tech. Ctr., 1991—. Vis. prof. U. Tokyo, Japan, 1994; prof. physics, mcpl. chair Université Joseph Fourier, Grenoble, France, 1994; mem. editl. bd. Laser Focus. Contbr. numerous articles to scientific jours. Recipient R.W. Wood prize Optical Soc. of Am., 1995. Fellow Optical Soc. Am. Achievements include numerous patents in field including apparatus for switching high voltage pulses, light activated solid state switch, avalanche effect light activated solid state switching, microwave pulse generation with light activated semiconductor switch and control of transmission of microwaves using light activated semiconductors, laser system using organic dye laser and laser amplifier for generation of picosecond laser pulses, sweep drive circuit for streak camera image converter, photoelectron switching in semiconductors in the picosecond domain, measurement of electrical signal with Ps resolution, electro-optical wide band signal measurement system, CW pumped variable repetition rate regenerative laser amplifier, amplification of ultrashort pulses with Nd: glass amplifiers pumped by alexandrite free running laser. Office: University of Michigan Ctr for Ultrafast Optical Science 2200 Bonisteel Blvd Rm 6117 Ist Ann Arbor MI 48109-2099

MOUSER, LES, broadcasting executive; Pres., COO Campbell Mithun Esty, Minn. Office: care Campbell Mithun Esty 222 S 9th St Minneapolis MN 55402-3389

MOUSSEAU, DORIS NAOMI BARTON, retired elementary school principal; b. Alpena, Mich., May 6, 1934; d. Merritt Benjamin and Naomi Dora Josephine (Pieper) Barton; m. Bernard Joseph Mousseau, July 31, 1954. AA, Alpena Community Coll., 1954; BS, Wayne State U., 1959; MA, U. Mich., 1961, postgrad., 1972-75. Profl. cert. ednl. adminstr., tchr. Elem. tchr. Clarkston (Mich.) Community Schs., 1954-66; elem. sch. prin. Andersonville Sch., Clarkston, 1966-79, Bailey Lake Sch., Clarkston, 1979-94; ret., 1994. Oakland County rep. Mich. Elem. and Mid. Schs. Prins. Assn. Retirees Task Force, 1996. Cons., rsch. com. Youth Assistance Oakland County Ct. Svcs., 1968-88; leader Clarkston PTA, 1967-94; chair Clarkston Sch. Dist. campaign, United Way, 1985, 86; mem. allocations com. Oakland County United Way, 1987-88. Recipient Outstanding Svc. award Davisburg Jaycees, Springfield Twp., 1977, Vol. Recognition award Oakland County (Mich.) Cts., 1984, Heritage Chair for 40 yrs. svc. with Clarkston (Mich.) Cmty. Schs., 1994. Fellow ASCD, MACUL (State Assn. Ednl. Computer Users); mem. NEA (del. 1964), Mich. Elem. and Middle Sch. Prins. Assn. (treas., regional del. 1982—, pres.-elect Region 7 1988-89, program planner, pres. 1989-90, sr. advisor 1990-91, Honor award Region # 7 1991), Mich. Edn. Assn. (pres. 1960-66, del. 1966), Clarkston Edn. Assn. (author, editor 1st directory 1963), Women's Bowling Assn., Elks, Spring Meadows Golf Club (Sr. Ladies Net Champion 1999), Phi Delta Kappa, Delta Kappa Gamma (pres. 1972-74, past state and nat. chmn., Woman of Distinction 1982). Republican. Avocations: golf, gardening, reading, cross country skiing, clarinet. Home: 6825 Rattalee Lake Rd Clarkston MI 48348-1955

MOUSTAKIS, ALBERT D. prosecutor; b. Cairo, Feb. 5, 1956; came to U.S., 1959; s. David and Jeanette (Sayegh) M.; m. Anna Marie Marfredonia, 1982; m. Laura J. Moustakis, July 1, 1991; children: Matalyn Jean, Sydney Rae. BA, Loyola U., Chgo., 1978; JD, Nova Ctr. for Study Law, 1982. Pvt. practice, Downers Grove, Ill., Chgo.; atty. Nielsen & Nielsen, Eagle River, Wis.; pvt. practice; dist. atty. State of Wis. Pres. Walter E. Meml. Libr. Fund, Eagle River, 1993-94. Mem. Rotary (pres. 1995). Avocations: golf, hockey.

MOYER, KEITH J. publishing executive; Exec. editor Fresno (Calif.) Bee, pub., 1997—. Office: Star Tribune 425 Portland Avenue Minneapolis MN 55488

MOYER, THOMAS J. state supreme court chief justice; b. Sandusky, Ohio, Apr. 18, 1939; s. Clarence and Idamae (Hessler) M.; m. Mary Francis Moyer, Dec. 15, 1984; 1 child, Drew; stepchildren: Anne, Jack, Alaine, Elizabeth. BA, Ohio State U., 1961, JD, 1964. Asst. atty. gen. State of Ohio, Columbus, 1964-66; pvt. practice law, 1966-69; dep. asst. Office Gov. State of Ohio, 1969-71, exec. asst., 1975-79; assoc. Crabbe, Brown, Jones, Potts & Schmidt, 1972-75; judge U.S. Ct. Appeals (10th cir.), 1979-86; chief justice Ohio Supreme Ct., 1987—. Sec. bd. trustees Franklin U., Columbus, 1986-87; trustee Univ. Club, Columbus, 1986; mem. nat. council adv. com. Ohio State U. Coll. Law, Columbus. Recipient Award of Merit, Ohio Legal Ctr. Inst.; named Outstanding Young Man of Columbus, Columbus Jaycees, 1969. Mem. Ohio State Bar Assn. (exec. com., council dels.), Columbus Bar Assn. (pres. 1980-81), Critchon Club, Columbus Maennerchor Club. Republican. Avocations: sailing, tennis. Office: Ohio Supreme Ct 30 E Broad St Fl 3 Columbus OH 43215*

MOYNIHAN, WILLIAM J. museum executive; b. Little Falls, N.Y., Apr. 8, 1942; s. Bernard J. and Mary A. (Flynn) M.; m. Irene A. Sheilds, July 2, 1966; children: Patricia, Erin, Sean. BA, SUNY, Binghamton, 1964; MA, Colgate U., 1966; PhD, Syracuse U., 1973. From asst. to assoc. prof. Colgate U., Hamilton, NY, 1973—77, from asst. to assoc. dean faculty, 1977—80, dean students, 1980—83, dean coll., 1983—88; v.p.m. dir. Am. Mus. Natural History, NYC, 1988—95; pres., CEO Milw. Pub. Mus., 1995—2002; ret., 2002. Bd. dirs. N.Y. State Mus.; adv. com. arts and culture Congressman J. Nadler, N.Y.C., 1993-95. Adv. editor Curator jour., 1991-95. Mem. Am. Mus. Assn., Am. Assn. Museums (mem. ethics com., bd. dirs.), Wis. Acad. of Scis., Arts and Letters (councillor-at-large 1995—), Univ. Club. Home: RD 1 84 Eaton St Hamilton NY 13346 Address: 1626 N Prospect Ave Apt 1707 Milwaukee WI 53202-2422

MRAZEK, DAVID ALLEN, pediatric psychiatrist; b. Ft. Riley, Kans., Oct. 1, 1947; s. Rudolph George and Hazel Ruth (Schayes) M.; m. Patricia Jean, Sept. 2, 1978; children: Nicola, Matthew, Michael, Alissa. AB in Genetics, Cornell U., 1969; MD, Wake Forest U., 1973. Lic. psychiatrist, child psychiatrist, N.C., Ohio, Colo., D.C., Va., Md., Minn.; med. lic. N.C., Ohio, D.C., Va., Md., Minn. Lectr. child psychiatry Inst. of Psychiatry, London, 1977-79; dir. pediatric psychiatry Nat. Jewish Ctr. for Immunology and Respiratory Medicine, Denver, 1979-91; chmn. psychiatry Children's Nat. Med. Ctr., Washington, 1991-98; chair psychiatry and behavioral scis. George Washington U. Sch. Medicine, 1996-2000; dir. Children's Rsch. Inst. Neurosci., 1995-98; chair psychiatry and psychology Mayo Clinic, Rochester, Minn., 2000—; prof. psychiatry, psychology and pediat. Mayo Sch. Medicine, 2000—. Asst. prof. psychiatry U. Colo. Sch. Medicine, 1979-83, assoc. prof. psychiatry and pediatrics, 1984-89, prof., 1990-91; prof. psychiatry and pediatrics George Washington U. Sch. Medicine, 1991-2000, Leon Yochelson prof. psychiatry and behavioral scis. Contbr. articles and book chpts. on child devel. and asthma to profl. publs. Recipient Rsch. Scientist Devel. awards NIMH, 1983-88, 88-91, Irving Phillips Meml. award for outstanding rsch. in prevention Acad. Child and Adolescent Psychiatry, 2000. Fellow Am. Acad. Child Psychiatry, Royal Soc. Medicine, Am. Psychiat. Assn. (Blanche F. Ittleson award 1996, Agnes Purcell McGavin award 1999), Royal Coll. Psychiatrists; mem. Am. Coll. Psychiatrists, Group for the Advancement of Psychiatry, Colo. Child and Adolescent Psychiatry Soc. (pres. 1984), Benjamin Rush Soc. Office: Mayo Clinic Dept Psychiatry/Pschology 200 1st St SW Rochester MN 55905 Fax: (507) 266-3319. E-mail: mrazek.david@mayo.edu.

MRVAN, FRANK, JR. state legislator; b. East Chgo., Ind., Apr. 11, 1933; m. Jean Mrvan; three children, Judith, Frances, Frank. , Ind. U., Am. Inst. Banking. Asst. v.p. First Nat. Bank East Chgo.; mem. Ind. Senate from 1st. dist., 1978-94, 98—; asst. chmn. minority caucus, 1981-82. Mem. health and environ. affaris com., ins. and fin. instns. com., edn. comm., appt. and claims com., govt. and regulatory coms. Mem. Hammond Planning Commn.; mem. Ind. State Commn. for Handicapped; mem. Hammond City Coun. Mem. KC, PTA (past pres.), Hammond Young Dems., Lake County Fish and Game Protective Assn., Am. Legion. Office: Ind Senate Dist 1 200 W Washington St Indianapolis IN 46204-2728

MUCHIN, ALLAN B. lawyer; b. Manitowoc, Wis., Jan. 10, 1936; s. Jacob and Dorothy (Biberfeld) M.; m. Elaine Cort, Jan. 28, 1960; children: Andrea Muchin Leon, Karen, Margery Muchin Goldblatt. BBA, U. Wis., Manitowoc, 1958, JD, 1961. Gen. counsel IRS, Chgo., 1961-65; assoc. Altman, Kurlander & Weiss, 1965-68, ptnr., 1968-74; co-mng. ptnr. Katten Muchin & Zavis, 1974-95, chmn. bd., 1995—. Bd. dirs. Chgo. Bulls, Chgo. White Sox, Alberto-Culver Co., Acorn Investment Trust; bd. visitors U. Wis. Law Sch.; trustee Noble St. Charter Sch. Pres. Lyric Opera Chgo., 1993—; mem. adv. com. Am. Com. for Weizmann Inst. of Sci., Chgo., 1991—. Mem. Econ. Club Chgo., Comml. Club Chgo. Avocations: travel, tennis, reading. Office: Katten Muchin Zavis 525 W Monroe St Ste 1600 Chicago IL 60661-3693

MUCKERMAN, NORMAN JAMES, priest, writer; b. Webster Groves, Mo., Feb. 1, 1917; s. Oliver Christopher and Edna Gertrude (Hartman) M. B.A., Immaculate Conception Coll., 1940, M. in Religious Edn., 1942. Ordained priest Roman Catholic Ch., 1942. Missionary Redemptorist Missions, Amazonas, Para, Brazil, 1943-53, procurator missions St. Louis, 1953-58; pastor, adminstr. St. Alphonsus Ch., Chgo., 1958-67, St. Gerard, Kirkwood, Mo., 1967-71; mktg. mgr. circulation Liguori Pubs., Liguori, 1971-76; editor Liguorian Mag., 1977-89. Author: How to Face Death Without Fear, 1976, Redemptorists on the Amazon, 1992, Preparation for Death, 1998, Into Your Hands, 2001, From the Heart of St. Alphonsus, 2002; contbg. editor: Liguorian, 1989—95. Recipient Nota Dez award Caixa Fed. Do Para, Brazil, 1958 Mem. Cath. Press Assn. (cons. 1971-95, bd. dirs. 1976-85, pres. 1981-84, St. Francis De Sales award 1985). Avocations: golf; travel; reading. E-mail: nmuckerman@compuserve.com.

MUDGE, RANDAL J. investment company executive; Pres. Olde Fin. Corp., Detroit, until 1999. Office: H&R Block Fin Advisors 751 Griswold St Detroit MI 48226-3224

MUEHLBAUER, JAMES HERMAN, manufacturing executive; b. Evansville, Ind., Nov. 13, 1940; s. Herman Joseph and Anna Louise (Overfield) M.; m. Mary Kay Koch, June 26, 1965; children: Stacey, Brad, Glen, Beth, Katy. BSME, Purdue U., 1963, MS Indsl. Adminstrn., 1964. Registered profl. engr. Engr. George Koch Sons, Inc., Evansville, 1966-67, chief estimator, 1968-72, chief engr., 1973-74, v.p., 1975-81, dir., 1978—, exec. v.p., 1982-98, Koch Ent., Inc., 1999—; pres. George Koch Sons LLC, 1999—. V.p., bd. dirs. Brake Supply Co., Evansville, Gibbs Die Casting Corp., Henderson, Ky., Uniseal, Inc., Evansville; bd. dirs. Fifth Third Bank Indiana, George Koch Sons (Europe) Ltd., Lichfield, Eng., Red Spot Paint & Varnish Co., Inc., Evansville, Koch Air LLC, Evansville, George Koch Sons de Mex., Monterrey, George Koch Sons GmbH, Cologne. Co-author: Tool & Manufacturing Engineering Handbook, 1976; patentee in paint finishing equipment. Bd. dirs., past pres. Evansville Indsl. Found., 1980—; bd. dirs., past pres., past campaign chmn. United Way S.W. Ind., Evansville, 1983—; bd. dirs., past vice-chmn. Univ. So. Ind. Found., Evansville, 1988-2001; bd. dirs. Deaconess Hosp., Evansville, 1986—, treas., 1991-96, vice-chmn., 1999—; bd. dirs. Cath. Found. Southwestern Ind., 1998—; dir. bd. visitors U. So. Ind. Sch. Bus., 1997—, chmn., 2001-02; bd. dirs. Ind. Assn. United Ways, 2000—; mem. Brute Soc., Cath. Diocese Evansville, 1997, Equestrian Order of the Holy Sepulchre of Jerusalem, 1996—. Named Engr. of Yr. S.W. chpt. Ind. Soc. Profl. Engrs., 1983; recipient Tech. Achievement award Tri-State Coun. for Sci. and Engring., Evansville, 1984, Purdue U. Alumni Citizenship award, 1991. [e]m. Soc. Mfg. Engrs. (past nat. chmn. finishing and coating tech. divsn.), ASME, NSPE, Evansville Country Club, Evansville Petroleum Club, Evansville Kennel Club (bd. dirs. 1997-2001). Republican. Roman Catholic. Home: 2300 E Gum St Evansville IN 47714-2338 Office: Koch Enterprises 14 S 11th Ave Evansville IN 47744-0001 E-mail: jhm@kochllc.com.

MUELLER, CHARLES FREDERICK, radiologist, educator; b. Dayton, Ohio, May 26, 1936; s. Susan Elizabeth (Wine) W.; m. Kathe Louise Lutterbei, May 28, 1966; children: Charles Jeffrey, Theodore Martin, Kathryn Suzanne. BA in English, U. Cin., 1958, MD, 1962. Diplomate Am. Bd. Radiology, Am. Bd. Nuclear Medicine. Asst. prof. radiology U. N.Mex., Albuquerque, 1968-72, assoc. prof. radiology, 1972-74, Ohio State U., Columbus, 1974-79, acting chmn. dept. radiology, 1975, prof. radiology, 1979—, prof. radiology, dir. post grad. program radiology, 1980-2000, acting chmn. dept. radiology, 1990—93. Bd. dirs. Univ. Radiologists, Inc., Columbus, v.p., 1980-86; pres., founder Ambulatory Imaging, Inc., Columbus, 1985—. Author: Emergency Radiology, 1982; contbr. articles to profl. jours.; editl. bd. Emergency radiology, 1995—; editor Internat. Trauma, Am. Jour. Roentgenology, 1997—. Com. chmn. Boy Scouts of Am., Columbus, 1980-84. Served to capt. USAF, 1966-68. Research grantee Ohio State U. 1975, Gen. Electric Co., 1986-88; Gold medalist ASER, 2001. Fellow Am. Coll. Radiologists; mem. AMA, Assn. Univ. Radiologists, Am. Roentgen Ray Soc., Am. Soc. Emergency Radiology (founder 1988, pres. 1993-94, Gold medal 2001), Radiol. Soc. N.Am., N.Mex. Soc. Radiologists (pres. 1973-74), Ohio State Radiol. Soc. (pres. 1986-87). Republican. Presbyterian. Lodges: Commandery #6, Consistory. Avocations: flying, fly fishing, hiking. Office: Ohio State Univ Hosps Dept Radiology 410 W 10th Ave Columbus OH 43210-1240

MUELLER, CHARLES WILLIAM, electric utility executive; b. Belleville, Ill., Nov. 29, 1938; s. Charles A. and Clara R. (Jorn) M.; m. Janet Therese Vernier, July 9, 1960; children: Charles R., Michael G., Craig J. BSEE, St. Louis U., 1961, MBA, 1966. Registered profl. engr., Mo., Ill. Engr. Union Electric Co., St. Louis, 1961-75, supervisory engr., 1975-77, asst. dir. corp. planning, 1977-78, treas., 1978-83, v.p. fin., 1983-88, sr. v.p. adminstrv. svcs., 1988-93; pres., CEO Ameren Corp., 1994-98, pres., CEO, chmn., 1998—. Dep. chmn. The Fed. Res. Bank of St. Louis; chmn. bd. Webster U.; bd. dirs. Electric Energy Inc., Regional Commerce and Growth Assn., Edison Electric Inst., Angelica Corp., United Way of Greater St. Louis, BJC Health Sys., Kiel Ctr. Corp.; dir. Assn. of Edison Illuminating Cos., St. Louis Children's Hosp., St. Louis Sci. Ctr., Civic Progress, The Mcpl. Theatre Assn. Mem. IEEE, Mo. Athletic Club, St. Clair Country Club, The Bogey Club, Saint Louis Club. Avocations: tennis, boating, travel. Office: Ameren Corp 1901 Chouteau Ave Saint Louis MO 63103-3003

MUELLER, JOHN ERNEST, political science educator, dance critic and historian; b. St. Paul, June 21, 1937; s. Ernst A. and Elsie E. (Schleh) M.; m. Judy A. Reader, Sept. 6, 1960; children: Karl, Karen, Susan AB, U. Chgo., 1960; MA, UCLA, 1963, PhD, 1965. Asst. prof. polit. sci. U. Rochester, N.Y., 1965-69, assoc. prof., 1969-72, prof., 1972-2000, prof. film studies, 1983-2000, founder, dir. Dance Film Archive, 1973—; prof. polit. sci. Ohio State U., 2000—. Lectr. on dance in U.S., Europe, Australia, 1973—; OP-ED columnist Wall St. Jour., 1984—, L.A., Times, 1988—, N.Y. Times, 1990—; mem. dance panel NEA, 1983-85; columnist Dance Mag., 1974-82; dance critic Rochester Dem. and Chronicle, 1974-82; mem. adv. bd. Dance in Am., PBS, 1975; chmn. Nat. Security Studies Ohio State U. Author: War, Presidents and Public Opinion, 1973 (book selected as one of Fifty Books That Significantly Shaped Public Opinion Rsch. 1946-95 Am. Assn. Pub. Opinion Rsch. 1995), Dance Film Directory, 1979, Astaire Dancing: The Musical Films, 1985 (de la Torre Bueno prize 1983), Retreat From Doomsday: The Obsolescence of Major War, 1989, Policy and Opinion in the Gulf War, 1994, Quiet Cataclysm: Reflections on the Recent Transformation of World Politics, 1995, Capitalism, Democracy, and Ralph's Pretty Good Grocery, 1999; co-author: Trends in Public Opinion: A Compendium of Survey Data, 1989; editor: Approaches to Measurement, 1969, Peace, Prosperity, and Politics, 2000; co-editor Jour. Policy Analysis and Mgmt., 1985-89; mem. editl. bd. Pub. Opinion Quar., 1988-91, Jour. Cold War Studies, 1999—; prodr. 12 dance films/recorded commentator on 2nd soundtrack of laser disc edit. Swing Time, 1986; co-adapter (musical) A Foggy Day, 1998; prodr. Shaw Festival Niagara-on-the-Lake, Ont., 1998, 99. Grantee NSF, 1967-70, 74-75, NEH, 1972-73, 74-75, 77-78, 79-81; Guggenheim fellow, 1988. Mem. Am. Acad. Arts and Scis., Am. Polit. Sci. Assn., Dance Critics Assn. (bd. dirs. 1983-85). Home: 420 W 5th Ave Columbus OH 43201-3159 Office: Ohio State U Polit Sci Dept Columbus OH 43210-1373

MUELLER, KURT M. hotel executive; Pres. Motels Am., Des Plaines, Ill.; CFO MOA Hospitality Inc., 1997—, pres., CFO. Office: Hospitality Inc 701 Lee St Ste 1000 Des Plaines IL 60016-4555

MUELLER, MARYLIN, graphic supply company executive; Pres., CEO Mueller Graphic Supply Co. Office: 11475 W Theodore Trecker Way Milwaukee WI 53214-1138

MUELLER, WALT, state legislator; b. Springfield, Mo., Dec. 12, 1925; BS, U. Kans. Mem. Mo. State Ho. of Reps. Dist. 93, 1973-93, Mo. State Senate Dist. 15, 1993—. Address: 12325 Manchester Rd Saint Louis MO 63131-4316

MUELLER, WILLARD FRITZ, economics educator; b. Ortonville, Minn., Jan. 23, 1925; s. Fritz and Adele C. (Thormaehlen) M.; m. Shirley I. Liesch, June 26, 1948; children: Keith, Scott, Kay. B.S., U. Wis., 1950, M.S., 1951; Ph.D., Vanderbilt U., 1955. Asst. prof. U. Calif., Davis, 1954-57; prof. U. Wis., 1957-61; chief economist small bus. com. U.S. Ho. of Reps., 1961; chief economist, dir. bur. econs. FTC, 1961-68; exec. dir. President's Cabinet Com. on Price Stability, 1968-69; William F. Vilas rsch. prof. econs., agrl. and applied econs., Law Sch. emeritus U. Wis., Madison, 1969—. Past bd. editors Rev. Ind. Orgn., Antitrust Law and Econ. Rev., Antitrust Bull., Jour. Reprints for Antitrust Law and Econs. Served with USN, 1943-46. Recipient Distinguished Service award FTC, 1969 Fellow Am. Agrl. Econs. Assn.; mem. Am. Econ. Assn., Am. Agr. Econ. Assn. (profl. excellence awards in policy contbn. 1980, in communications 1985, in rsch. discovery 1988). Assn. Evolutionary Econs. (pres. 1974-75), Indsl. Orgn. Soc. (pres. 1989-90), Argus Econ. Svcs. (pres.). Unitarian. Home: 121 Bascom Pl Madison WI 53705-3975 Office: U Wis 427 Lorch St Madison WI 53706-1513 E-mail: wfritzmueller@aol.com.

MUFSON, STUART LEE, astronomer, educator; b. Phila., May 16, 1946; BA, MS, U. Pa., 1968; MS, U. Chgo., 1970, PhD in Astronomy and Astrophysics, 1974. Rsch. assoc. Nat. Radio Astron. Obs., 1973-75; NRC assoc. Marshall Space Flight Ctr., NASA, 1975-77; chmn. dept. astronomy Ind. U., Bloomington. Prin. investigator NASA, 1977—. Mem. Internat. Astron. Union, Am. Astron. Soc. Achievements include research on high energy astrophysics, neutrino astronomy, cosmic ray research, evolution of supernova remnants. Office: Dept Astronomy Ind Univ Bloomington IN 47405-4200

MUGNAINI, ENRICO, neuroscience educator; b. Colle Val d'Elsa, Italy, Dec. 10, 1937; came to U.S., 1969. children: Karin E., Emiliano N.G. MD summa cum laude, U. Pisa, Italy, 1962. Microscopy lab. rsch. fellow dept. anatomy U. Oslo Med. Sch., 1963, asst. prof., head of electron microscopy lab., 1964-66, assoc. prof., 1967-69; prof. biobehavioral scis. and psychology, head lab. of neuromorphology U. Conn., Storrs, 1969-95; E.C. Stuntz prof. cell biology, dir. Inst. for Neurosci., Northwestern U., Chgo., 1995—. Vis. prof. Dept. Anatomy Harvard U., Boston, 1969-70; traveling lectr. Grass Found., spring 1986, fall 1990. Mng. editor USA Anatomy and Embryology Jour., 1989—; contbr. more than 150 articles to books and jours. Recipient Decennial Camillo Golgi award Acad. Nat. dei Lincei, 1981, Sen. Javits Neurosci. Rsch. Investigator award NIH, 1985-92. Mem. AAAS, Am. Assn. Anatomists, Am. Soc. Cell Biology, Internat. Brain Rsch. Orgn., Internat. Soc. Developmental Neurosci., Norwegian Nat. Acad. Scis. and Letters, Soc. Neurosci., Cajal Club (pres. 1987-88). Office: U Northwestern Inst Neurosci 5-474 Searle Bldg 320 E Superior St Chicago IL 60611-3010

MUIR, WILLIAM LLOYD , III, academic administrator; b. Norton, Kans., Mar. 20, 1948; s. John Thomas and Rosalie June (Benton) M. BBA, Kans. State U., 1977. Asst. sec. of state State of Kans., Topeka, 1971-72, fin. adminstr. atty. gen. office, 1972-79, comptr. Office of Gov., 1979-87, sec. of cabinet, 1979-87, asst. sec. adminstrn., 1986-87; dir. econ. devel. Kans. State U., Manhattan, 1987-91, asst. to v.p., dir. cmty. rels., 1991—, faculty rep., senator Student Governing Assn., 1992—, mem. union governing bd., 1997—. Vice chmn. housing appeals bd. City of Manhattan, 1996—, mem., vice chmn. econ. devel. adv. bd., 1999—2002; trustee Kans. State U. Found., 1993—; mem. Leadership Kans., 1989; state officer Native Sons and Daus., 1997—2002, pres., 2001; bd. dirs. United Way Riley County, 1989—99, chmn., 1992. Mem. Friends of Cedar Crest Assn., Nat. Geog. Soc., Sierra Club, Masons (Scottish rite), Blue Key, Alpha Tau Omega (nat. officer), Alpha Kappa Psi. Episcopalian. Avocations: travel, volunteer work, advising. Home: 2040 Shirley Ln Manhattan KS 66502-2059 Office: Kansas State U 122 Anderson Hall Manhattan KS 66506-0100 E-mail: billmuir@ksu.edu.

MUIRHEAD, VINCENT URIEL, retired aerospace engineer; b. Dresden, Kans., Feb. 6, 1919; s. John Hadsell and Lily Irene (McKinney) M.; m. Bobby Jo Thompson, Nov. 5, 1943; children: Rosalind, Jean, Juleigh. B.S., U.S. Naval Acad., 1941; B.S. in Aero. Engring, U.S. Naval Postgrad. Sch., 1948; Aero. Engr., Calif. Inst. Tech., 1949; postgrad., U. Ariz., 1962, 64, Okla. State U., 1963. Midshipman U.S. Navy, 1937, commd. ensign, 1941, advanced through grades to comdr., 1951; nav. officer U.S.S. White Plains, 1945-46; comdr. Fleet Aircraft Service Squad, 1951-52; with Bur. Aeros., Ft. Worth, 1953-54; comdr. Helicopter Utility Squadron I, Pacific Fleet, 1955-56; chief staff officer Comdr. Fleet Air, Philippines, 1956-58; exec. officer Naval Air Tng. Center, Memphis, 1958-61; ret., 1961; asst. prof. U. Kans., Lawrence, 1961-63, assoc. prof. aerospace engring., 1964-76, prof., 1976-89, prof. emeritus, 1989—, chmn. dept., 1976-88. Cons. Black & Veatch (cons. engrs.), Kansas City, Mo., 1964— Author: Introduction to Aerospace, 1972, 5th edit., 1994, Thunderstorms, Tornadoes and Building Damage, 1975. Decorated Air medal. Fellow AIAA (assoc.); mem. Am. Acad. Mechanics, Am. Soc. Engring. Edn., Tau Beta Pi, Sigma Gamma Tau. Mem. Ch. of Christ (elder 1972-96). Achievements include research on aircraft, tornado vortices, shock tubes and waves. Home: 503 Park Hill Ter Lawrence KS 66046-4841 Office: Dept Aerospace Engring Univ Kans Lawrence KS 66045-0001 E-mail: vmuirhead@aol.com.

MUKERJEE, PASUPATI, chemistry educator; b. Calcutta, India, Feb. 13, 1932; s. Nani Gopal and Probhabati (Ghosal) M.; m. Lalita Sarkar, Feb. 29, 1964 (dec.); m. Mina Maitra, Nov. 14, 1998. B.Sc., Calcutta U., 1949, M.Sc., 1951; Ph.D., U. So. Calif., 1957. Lectr., vis. asst. prof. U. So. Calif., 1956-57; rsch. assoc. Brookhaven Nat. Lab., L.I., 1957-59; reader in phys. chemistry Indian Assn. Cultivation of Sci., Calcutta, 1959-64; guest scientist U. Utrecht, Holland, 1964; sr. scientist chemistry dept. U. So. Calif., 1964-66; vis. assoc. prof. U. Wis., Madison, 1966-67, prof. Sch. Pharmacy, 1967-94, emeritus prof., 1994—. Vis. prof. Indian Inst. Tech., Kharagpur, 1971-72; mem. commn. on colloid and surface chemistry Internat. Union Pure and Applied Chemistry Contbr. articles to profl. jours.; mem. editl. bd. Jour. Colloid and Interface Sci., 1978-80, Asian Jour. Pharm. Scis., 1978-85, Colloids and Surfaces, 1980-86. Grantee USPHS, NSF, Nat. Bur. Stds., Petroleum Rsch. Fund. Fellow AAAS, Acad. Pharm. Scis., Am. Inst. Chemistry; mem. Am. Chem. Soc. (editorial bd. Langmuir 1985-86), Am. Pharm. Assn., Acad. Pharm. Scis., Rho Chi. Home: 5526 Varsity Hl Madison WI 53705-4652 Office: 777 Highland Ave Madison WI 53705-2222

MULCAHY, MICHAEL J. light contruction and agricultural manfucturing; b. Detroit, Dec. 6, 1947; BS, U. Detroit, 1966, JD, 1969. Bar: Mich. 1969. Assoc. Raymond & Prokop, P.C., Southfield, Mich.; v.p., gen. counsel, sec. Gebl Co., West Bend, Wis. Office: Gebl Co PO Box 179 143 Water St West Bend WI 53095-3400 Fax: 262-334-6603.

MULCAHY, ROBERT WILLIAM, lawyer; b. Milw., Jan. 11, 1951; s. T. Larry and Mary Margaret (Chambers) M.; m. Mary M. Andrews, Aug. 3, 1974; children: Molly, Kathleen, Margaret, Michael. BS, Marquette U., 1973, JD, 1976. Staff atty. NLRB, Milw., 1976-79; ptnr. Mulcahy &

Wherry, S.C., 1979-90, Michael, Best & Friedrich, Milw., 1990—. Bd. dirs. WERC Coun. on Mcpl. Collective Bargaining, 1990-93. Co-author: Strike Prevention and Control Handbook, 1983, Comparable Worth: A Negotiator's Guide, 1985, Public Sector Labor Relations in Wisconsin, 1994. Bd. dirs. Milw. Repertory Theater, 1993-97; chmn. Charles Allis/Villa Terrace, 1991—; mem. St. Monica Parish Coun., 1988-96; chmn. Whitefish Bay Police Commn.; divsn. chmn. United Performing Arts Fund, 1993-94; co-chair Villa Terrace Garden Renaissance Project, 2000—. Mem. ABA, State Bar Wis. (chair labor sect. 1986-87), Milw. Bar Assn. (co-chair labor sect. 1988-95), Nat. Assn. Counties, Nat. Pub. Employers Labor Rels. Assn., Nat. Assn. Coll. & Univ. Attys., Wis. Counties Assn., Indsl. Rels. Rsch. Assn., Mgmt. Resources Assn., Wis. Sch. Attys. Assn., Milw. Area Mcpl. Employers Assn. Office: Michael Best & Friedrich 100 E Wisconsin Ave Ste 3300 Milwaukee WI 53202-4108 E-mail: rwmulcahy@mbf-law.com.

MULCH, ROBERT F., JR. physician; b. Quincy, Ill., June 21, 1951; s. Robert Franklin and Martha Jo (Nisi) M.; m. Barbara Ann Best, Apr. 5, 1975; children: Matthew, Luke. BS, U. Ill., 1973; MD, Rush Med. Coll., Chgo., 1977. Diplomate Am. Bd. Family Practice; cert. in geriatrics. Intern Riverside Meth. Hosp., Columbus, Ohio, 1977-78, resident in family practice, 1978-80; family physician Hillsboro (Ill.) Med. Ctr., Hillsboro, Ill., 1980—; ptnr., assoc. med. dir. Springfield Clin., 1998—. Asst. clin. prof. family medicine So. Ill. U., Springfield, 1981—; advisor Montgomery County Counseling Ctr.; reviewer Ctrl. Ill. Peer Rev. Orgn. Fellow Am. Acad. Family Practice; mem. AAFP, Am. Cancer Soc., Am. Coll. Physician Execs. Lutheran. Avocations: computers, boating, swimming. Office: Hillsboro Med Ctr SC 1250 E Tremont St Hillsboro IL 62049-1912 E-mail: rmulch@mcleodusa.net., rmulch@springfieldclinic.com.

MULDER, DONALD WILLIAM, physician, educator; b. Rehobath, N.Mex., June 30, 1917; s. Jacob D. and Gertrude (Hofstra) M.; m. Gertrude Ellens, Feb. 22, 1943. B.A., Calvin Coll., 1940; M.D., Marquette U., 1943; M.S., U. Mich., 1946. Intern Butterworth Hosp., Grand Rapids, Mich., 1943-44; resident U. Hosp., Ann Arbor, 1944-46, Denver, 1947-49; asst. prof. medicine in neurology U. Colo., 1949-50; prof. neurology Mayo Found. Faculty, 1964—, Mayo Med. Sch., 1973—; cons. neurology Mayo Clinic, Rochester, Minn., 1950—, gov., 1962-69, chmn. dept. neurology, 1966-71, pres. staff, 1971—, Andersen prof. neurology, 1977-83, prof. emeritus, 1983—; sci. advisor ALS. Contbr. articles on neuromuscular disease to sci. jours. Ret. capt. USNR. Recipient Disting. Alumni award Calvin Coll., 1992. Fellow A.C.P., Am. Acad. Neurology; mem. Am. Neurol. Assn. (hon.). Office: 200 1st St SW Rochester MN 55905-0001 Home: Apt 1307 211 2nd St NW Rochester MN 55901-2897

MULDER, GARY, religious publisher; Office: CRC Publ 2850 Kalamazoo Ave SE Grand Rapids MI 49508-1433

MULDER, RICHARD DEAN, state legislator; b. Rock Valley, Iowa, May 8, 1938; m. Ruth Maxine Van Buren; 4 children. BS, S.D. State U., 1960; MD, U. Iowa, 1968. Intern McKennan Hosp., Sioux Falls, S.D., 1969; family practice, 1982—; Minn. state rep., 1994—. Presenter in field. Bush Clin. fellowship; recipient Disting. Alumnus award U. S.D. Sch. Medicine Alumni Found., 1991. Mem. AMA, Minn. Med. Assn., Am. Acad. of Family Physicians, Minn. Acad. of Family Physicians (S.W. chpt., Merit award 1984, 1989), Lyon/Lincoln Med. Assn., Am. Assn. of Med. Examiners, Minn. Coroner's and Med. Examiners Assn., Phi Beta Phi. Home: PO Box A Ivanhoe MN 56142-2100

MULLAN, JOHN FRANCIS (SEAN MULLAN), neurosurgeon, educator; b. County Derry, Northern Ireland, May 17, 1925; came to U.S., 1955; naturalized, 1962; s. John and Mary Catharine Ann (Gilmartin) M.; m. Vivian C. Dunn, June 3, 1959; children: Joan Claire, John Charles, Brian Francis. MB, BCh, BAO, Queen's U., Belfast, Northern Ireland, 1947, DSc (hon.), 1976; postgrad., McGill U., 1953-55. Diplomate Am. Bd. Neurol. Surgery. Trainee gen. surgery Royal Victoria Hosp., Belfast, 1947-50, trainee in neurosurgery, 1951-53; trainee gen. surgery Guy's Hosp. and Middlesex Hosp., London, 1950-51, Montreal Neurosurg. Inst., Que., Can., 1955; asst. prof. neurol. surgery U. Chgo., 1955-61, assoc. prof., 1961-63, prof., 1963—, John Harper Seeley prof., chmn. dept., 1967-93, emeritus, 1993—, dir. Brain Rsch. Inst., 1970-84. Author: Neurosurgery for Students, 1961; contbr. over 150 articles to profl. jours.; mem. editorial bd. Jour. Neurosurgery, 1974-84, Archives of Neurology, 1976-87. Recipient Olivecrona medal Karolinska Inst., 1976, Wilder Penfield medal Can. Neurosurg. Soc., 1979, Jamieson medal Australian and New Zealand Neurosurg. Soc., 1980. Fellow ACS, Royal Coll. Surgeons; mem. Soc. Neurol. Surgeons (past pres.), Acad. Neurol. Surgery, Am. Assn. Neurol. Surgeons, Am. Neurol. Assn., Cen. Neurosurg. Soc., Chgo. Neurol. Soc., World Fedn. of Neurosurg. Socs. (sec. 1989-93, hon. pres. 1993—). Roman Catholic. Achievements include conducting research on vascular diseases of the brain, pain, head injury. Avocations: walnut tree farming, gardening. Office: U Chgo Med Ctr 5841 S Maryland Ave Chicago IL 60637-1463

MULLEN, EDWARD JOHN, JR. Spanish language educator; b. Hackensack, N.J., July 12, 1942; s. Edward J. and Elsie (Powell) M.; m. Helen Cloe Braley, Apr. 2, 1971; children: Kathleen, Julie Ann. BA, W.Va. Wesleyan Coll., 1964; MA, Northwestern U., 1965, PhD, 1968. Asst. prof. modern langs. Purdue U., West Lafayette, Ind., 1967-71; assoc. prof. Spanish U. Mo., Columbia, 1971-78, prof. Spanish, 1978—. Author: La Revista Contemporáneos, 1972, Carlos Pellicer, 1977, Langston Hughes in the Hispanic World and Haiti, 1977, The Life and Poems of a Cuban Slave: Juan Francisco Manzano 1797-1854, 1981, Critical Essays on Langston Hughes, 1986, Sendas Literarias: Hispanomerica, 1988, El cuento hispánico, 1994, 96, 99, Afro-Cuban Literature: Critical Junctures, 1998; co-editor Afro-Hispanic Rev., 1987—; editor: The Harlem Group of Negro Writers (Melvin B. Tolson), 2000. Recipient Diploma de Honor Instituto de Cultura Hispánica, 1964; Woodrow Wilson fellow, 1964-65; Northwestern U. fellow, 1965-67; summer research grantee U. Mo., 1972, 76; grantee Am. Council Learned Socs., 1979 Mem. MLA, Am. Assn. Tchrs. Spanish and Portuguese, Assn. of Depts. Fgn. Langs. (pres. 1989-91). Home: 207 Edgewood Ave Columbia MO 65203-3413 Office: U Mo Dept Romance Langs 143 Arts And Sci Bldg Columbia MO 65211-0001 E-mail: mullene@missouri.edu.

MULLEN, J. THOMAS, lawyer; b. Evanston, Ill., Aug. 27, 1940; BSE, Princeton U., 1963; JD cum laude, U. Mich., 1967. Bar: Ill. 1967. Ptnr. Mayer, Brown, Rowe & Maw, Chgo.; ptnr.-in-charge London office, 1974-78. Bd. dirs. Legal Assistance Found. Chgo., 1979-85. Mem. ABA, Chgo. Bar Assn., Chgo. Coun. Lawyers. Office: Mayer Brown & Platt 190 S La Salle St Ste 3100 Chicago IL 60603-3441 E-mail: tmullen@mayerbrownrowe.com.

MULLEN, RUSSELL EDWARD, agricultural studies educator; b. Atlantic, Iowa, Sept. 4, 1949; AA, Southwestern C.C., Creton, Iowa, 1969; BS in Agriculture, N.W. Mo. State U., 1971, MS in Edn., 1972; PhD in Crop Physiology and Mgmt., Purdue U., 1975. Grad. asst. N.W. Mo. State U., Maryville, 1971-72; grad. teaching asst. Purdue U., West Lafayette, Ind., 1972-74, grad. instr., 1974-75, temporary asst. prof., 1975-76; asst. prof. U. Fla., Gainesville, 1976-78; from asst. prof. to prof. Iowa State U., Ames, 1978—. Recipient Ensminger Interstate Disting. Tchr. award Nat. Assn. Colls. Tchrs. Agriculture, 1992, Am. Soc. Agronomy Resident Edn. award, 1999; Am. Soc. Agronomy fellow, 1998. Office: Iowa State U Dept Agronomy 1126 Agronomy Hl Ames IA 50011-0001

MULLENS, DELBERT W. automotive executive; CEO Wesley Ind., Inc., Bloomfield Hills, MI. Office: Wesley Ind Inc 41000 Woodward Ave #395E Bloomfield Hills MI 48304

MULLER, JOHN BARTLETT, university president; b. Port Jefferson, N.Y., Nov. 8, 1940; s. Frederick Henry and Estelle May (Reeve) M.; m. Barbara Ann Schmidt, May 30, 1964 (dec. 1972); m. Lynn Anne Spongberg, Oct. 10, 1987. AB in Polit. Sci., U. Rochester, 1962; postgrad. in apologetics, Westminster Sem., Phila., 1962-63; MS in Psychology, Purdue U., 1968, PhD in Psychology, 1975. Asst. prof. psychology Roberts Wesleyan Coll., Rochester, N.Y., 1964-66, acting chmn. div. behavioral sci., dir. instl. research, 1967-70; vis. asst. prof. psychology Wabash Coll., Crawfordsville, Ind., 1970-71; research assoc. Ind. U.-Purdue U., Indpls., 1971-72; prof. psychology, v.p. for acad. affairs Hillsdale (Mich.) Coll., 1972-85; pres. BMW Assocs., Osseo, Mich., 1984-85, Bellevue (Nebr.) U., 1985—. Bd. dirs. Nebr. Ind. Coll. Found., Omaha, Assn. Ind. Colls. Nebr., Lincoln; bd. advisors Wells Fargo Bank of Omaha, Applied Info. Mgmt. Inst., Am. Nat. Bank. Contbr. articles to profl. jours. and textbooks. Bd. govs. Boys Club of Omaha. Nat. Inst. Mental Health fellowship Purdue U., 1963, Nat. Tchg. fellowship Fed. Govt., 1967, Townsend fellowship U. Rochester, 1962. Mem. APA, Bellevue C. of C. (bd. dirs. 1989-95), Phi Beta Kappa, Phi Kappa Phi. Republican. Home: 13303 Lochmoor Cir Bellevue NE 68123-3770 Office: Bellevue U Office of the Pres 1000 Galvin Rd S Bellevue NE 68005-3098 E-mail: Jmuller@Bellevue.edu.

MULLER, MARCEL W(ETTSTEIN), electrical engineering educator; b. Vienna, Austria, Nov. 1, 1922; came to U.S., 1940; s. Georg and Josephine (David) M.; m. Esther Ruth Hagler, Feb. 2, 1947; children: Susan, George, Janet. BSEE, Columbia U., 1949, AM in Physics, 1952; PhD, Stanford U., 1957. Sr. scientist Varian Assocs., Palo Alto, Calif., 1952-66; prof. elec. engring. Washington U., St. Louis, 1966-91, prof. emeritus, rsch. prof., 1991—. Vis. lectr. U. Zurich, Switzerland, 1962-63; vis. prof. U. Colo., Boulder, summer 1969; vis. scientist Max Planck Inst., Stuttgart, Fed. Republic of Germany, 1976-77; cons. Hewlett-Packard Labs., Palo Alto, 1985-89, SRI Internat., Menlo Park, Calif., 1986—. Sgt. U.S. Army, 1943-46. Recipient Humboldt prize Alexander von Humboldt Soc., 1976; Fulbright grantee, 1977, grantee NSF, 1967—. Fellow IEEE, Am. Physical Soc. Achievements include development of Maser quantum noise theory; developments in micromagnetism; contributions to magnetic information storage; invention Magneprint security system. Home: 4954 Lindell Blvd Saint Louis MO 63108-1500 Office: Washington Univ Campus Box 1127 1 Brookings Dr Saint Louis MO 63130-4899 E-mail: mwm@ee.wustl.edu.

MULLER, MERVIN EDGAR, information systems educator, consultant; b. Hollywood, Calif., June 1, 1928; s. Emanuel and Bertha (Zimmerman) M.; m. Barbara McAdam, July 13, 1963; children: Jeffrey McAdam, Stephen McAdam, Todd McAdam. AB, UCLA, 1949, MA, 1951, PhD, 1954. Instr. in math. Cornell U., 1954-56; rsch. assoc. in math. Princeton U., 1956-59; sr. statistician, dept. mgr. IBM, N.Y.C., White Plains, 1956-64; sr. scientist statis. and elec. engring. Princeton U., 1968-69; prof. computer sci. and stats. U. Wis., 1964-71; prof. computer sci. George Mason U., 1985; dept. dir. World Bank, Washington, 1971-81, sr. advisor, 1981-85; Robert M. Critchfield prof. computer info. sci. Ohio State U., 1985-98, prof. emeritus, 1994-98, dept. chair, 1985-94. Chair sci. and tech. info. bd. NRC, NAS; bd. dirs. Advanced Info. Tech. Ctr., Columbus, Ohio. Mem. editl. bd. Computation and Stats., 1990, Jour. Computational and Graphical Stats., 1990; contbr. numerous articles to profl. jours. Bd. trustees First Unitarian Ch., Bethesda, Md., 1975-79. Rsch. grantee AT&T, Columbus, Ohio, 1987. Fellow Am. Statis. Assn., World Acad. Productivity Sci.; mem. Internat. Statis. Inst. (steering com. Internat. Rsch. Ctr., 1987-89), Internat. Assn. for Statis. Computing (sci. sec. 1979-83, pres. 1977-79). Avocations: reading, jogging, walking, bridge. Home: 4571 Clairmont Rd Upper Arlington OH 43220-4501 Office: Ohio State U Dept Computer Info Sci Rm 395 2015 Neil Ave Dept Computer Columbus OH 43210-1210 E-mail: mullee@columbus.rr.com.

MULLIGAN, MICHAEL DENNIS, lawyer; b. St. Louis, Mar. 9, 1947; s. Leo Virgil and Elizabeth (Leyse) M.; m. Theresa Baker, Aug. 7, 1971; children: Brennan, Colin. BA in Biology, Amherst Coll., 1968; JD, Columbia U., 1971. Bar: Mo. 1971, U.S. Dist. Ct. (ea. dist.) Mo. 1972, U.S. Ct. Appeals (8th cir.) 1982, U.S. Tax Ct. 1985. Law clk. to judge U.S. Dist. Ct. (ea. dist.) Mo., 1971-72; assoc. Lewis, Rice & Fingersh, L.C., St. Louis, 1972-80, ptnr., 1980—. Mem. editl. bd. Estate Planning Mag., 1985—. Served as cpl. USMC, 1968-70. Fellow Am. Coll. Trust and Estate Counsel; mem. ABA (mem. real property, probate and trust, and taxation sects.), Mo. Bar Assn. (mem. probate and trust, taxation sects.). Office: Lewis Rice & Fingersh LC 500 N Broadway Ste 2000 Saint Louis MO 63102-2147 E-mail: mmulligan@lewisrice.com.

MULLIGAN, ROSEMARY ELIZABETH, legislator; b. Chgo., July 8, 1941; d. Stephen Edward and Rose Anne (Sannasardo) Granzyk; children: Daniel R. Bonaguidi, Matthew S. Bonaguidi. AAS, Harper Coll., Palatine, Ill., 1982; student, Ill. State U., 1959-60. Paralegal Miller, Forest & Downing Ltd., Glenview, Ill., 1982-91; ind. contractor mcpl. law, 1991—. Paralegal seminar educator Harper Coll. Program chair White House Women's Econ. Leadership Summit, 1997. Pro-choice activist and mem. Ill. Ho. of Reps., 1993—, chmn. human svcs. appropriations com.; gov.'s workgroup on early childhood; gov.'s wokforce investment bd., 1999—. Recipient Disting. Alumnus award Ill. C.C. Trustee Assn., 1993, Legislator of Yr. award Ill. Assn. Cmty. Mental Health Agys., 1996, Heart Start award Nat. Ctr. Clin. Infant Programs, Legis. Leadership award Ill. Alcoholism and Drug dependence Assn., 1996, Cert. Appreciation Ill. Libr. Assn., Legis. cert. appreciation Delta Kappa Gamma Soc., 1997, Ida B. Wells-Barnett award, 1996; named Top 100 Women Making a Difference Today's Chgo. Woman, 1997; Flemming fellow Ctr. for Policy Alts., 1994. Mem. LWV, Nat. Women's Polit. Caucus, Ill. Fedn. Bus. and Profl. Women (Outstanding Working Woman of the Yr. 1997), Ill. Women in Govt., Chgo. Women in Govt. Rels., Ill. Fedn. Bus. and Profl. Women (nat. legis. platform rep. 1991-92, chair Outstanding Working Women of Ill. 1991-92, state membership chair 1989-90, state legis. co-chair, nat. platform rep. 1988-89, state legis. chair, nat. platform rep. 1987-88). Roman Catholic. Avocations: politics, tennis, reading. Home: 856 E Grant Dr Des Plaines IL 60016-6260 Office: Ill Ho of Reps State Capitol Springfield IL 62706-0001 also: 932 Lee St Ste 201 Des Plaines IL 60016-6594

MULLIKIN, THOMAS WILSON, mathematics educator; b. Flintville, Tenn., Jan. 9, 1928; s. Houston Yost and Daisy (Copeland) M.; m. Mildred Virginia Sugg, June 14, 1952; children— Sarah Virginia, Thomas Wilson, James Copeland. Student, U. South, 1946-47; A.B., U. Tenn., 1950; postgrad., Iowa State U., 1952-53; A.M., Harvard, 1954, Ph.D., 1958. Mathematician Rand Corp., Santa Monica, Calif., 1957-64; prof. math. Purdue U., 1964-93, interim v.p., dean grad. sch., 1991-93, dean grad. sch., prof. math emeritus, 1993—. Served with USNR, 1950-52. Mem. Am. Math. Soc., AAAS, Sigma Xi. Home: 104 Club Ct Cape Carteret NC 28584-9736

MULLIN, CHRIS(TOPHER) PAUL, professional basketball player; b. N.Y.C., July 30, 1963; Student, St. John's U., 1981-85. Basketball player Golden State Warriors, 1985-97, Ind. Pacers, 1997—. Mem. U.S. Olympic Team (received Gold medal), 1984, 92. Recipient Wooden award, 1985; named to Sporting News All-Am. First Team, 1985, NBA All-Star team, 1989-93, NBA First Team, 1992. Office: Ind Pacers 300 E Market St Indianapolis IN 46204-2603

MULROW, PATRICK JOSEPH, medical educator; s. Patrick J. and Delia (O'Keefe) M.; m. Jacquelyn Pinover, Aug. 8, 1953; children: Deborah, Nancy, Robert, Catherine. AB, Colgate U., 1947; MD, Cornell U., 1951; MSc (hon.), Yale U., 1969. Intern N.Y. Hosp., 1951-52, resident, 1952-54; instr. physiology Med. Coll. Cornell U., 1954-55; research fellow Stanford U., 1955-57; instr. medicine Yale U., 1957-60, asst. prof., 1960-66, assoc. prof., 1966-69, prof. medicine, 1969-75; chmn. dept. medicine Med. Coll. Ohio, Toledo, 1975-95, prof. medicine, 1975—. Chmn. ednl. com. Council for high blood pressure rsch. Am. Heart Assn., 1968-70, mem. exec. com., 1986-96, vice-chmn. of coun., 1990-92, chmn. 1992-94, past chmn., 1995-96; mem. study sect. NIH, 1970-74. Editorial bd. Jour. Clin. Endocrinology and Metabolism, 1966-70, 75-79, Endocrine Rsch., 1974—, Jour. Exptl. Biology and Medicine, Hypertension, 1994-98; contbr. articles to profl. jours. With USNR, 1944-46. Mem. ACP, Am. Soc. Clin. Investigation, Assn. Am. Physicians, Am. Physiol. Soc., Endocrine Soc., Am. Fedn. Clin. Rsch., Am. Clin. and Climatol. Assn., Am. Heart Assn. (nat. rsch. com., chmn. cardiovasc. regulation rsch. study com. 1986-91), Assn. Profs. Medicine, Assn. Program Dirs. in Internal Medicine, Cen. Soc. Clin. Rsch. (pres. 1988-89), Internat. Soc. Hypertension, World Hypertension League (sec.-gen. 1995—), Inter-Am. Soc. Hypertension, Sigma Xi (pres. Yale chpt. 1965-66), Alpha Omega Alpha. Home: 9526 Carnoustie Rd Perrysburg OH 43551-3501 Office: Med Coll of Ohio Dept of Medicine PO Box 10008 Toledo OH 43699-0008

MULROY, THOMAS ROBERT, JR. lawyer; b. Evanston, Ill., June 26, 1946; s. Thomas Robert and Dorothy (Reiner) M.; m. Elaine Mazzone, Aug. 16, 1969. Student, Loyola U., Rome, 1966; BA, U. Santa Clara, Calif., 1968; JD, Loyola U., Chgo., 1972. Bar: Ill. 1973, U.S. Dist. Ct. (no. dist.) Ill. 1973, U.S. Ct. Appeals (7th cir.) 1973. Asst. U.S. atty. No. Dist. Ill., Chgo., 1972-76; ptnr. Jenner & Block, Chgo. 1976—, chmn. products liability group; adj. prof. Northwestern U. Sch. Law, Chgo., 1978-85, Loyola U. Sch. Law, 1983—, DePaul U. Sch. Law, Chgo., Nova U. Ctr. for Study of Law. Editor: Annotated Guide to Illinois Rules of Professional Conduct; contbr. articles to profl. jours.; bd. dirs. Loyola U. Trial Advocacy Workshop, 1982—, Legal Assistance Found., Ill. Inst. for Continued Legal Edn.; chmn. inquiry panel Ill. Atty. Registration and Disciplinary Commn., spl. counsel, 1989—. Mem. Chgo. Crime Commn., 1978—. Mem. ABA, (torts and ins. pratcie, chmn. rules and evidence com.), Am. Judicature Soc., Fed. Trial Bar, Legal Club Chgo., Law Club, 7th Fed. Cir. Bar Assn., Chgo. Bar Assn., Ill. Assn. Def. Trial Counsel, Ill. Bar Assn. Clubs: Univ., Execs. of Chgo., Union League. Office: Jenner & Block 1 E Ibm Plz Fl 42 Chicago IL 60611-3586

MUMA, LESLIE M. data processing executive; Pres. Fiserv, Brookfield, Wis., 1984—, vice chmn., 1995-99, CEO, 1999—, chmn. bd. dirs., 2000—. Office: Fiserv 255 Fiserv Dr Brookfield WI 53045

MUMAW, JAMES WEBSTER, lawyer, director; b. Youngstown, Ohio, Apr. 11, 1920; s. Daniel W. and Helen (James) M.; m. Lois M. Baird, May 28, 1948; children: Thomas, Daniel, William. A.B., Coll. of Wooster, 1941; J.D., U. Cin., 1948. Bar: Ohio 1949. Since practiced in, Youngstown; partner Luckhart, Mumaw, Morrisroe & Zellers and predecessor firm, 1959-66; mem. firm Luckhart, Mumaw, Zellers & Robinson, 1966—. Dir. Ohio Bar Title Ins. Co., 1955-91, Western Res. Bank of Ohio, 1963-95. Mem. Youngstown City Bd. Edn., 1972-75; pres. Christ Mission Kindergarten Assn., Goodwill Industries, 1967-69; trustee Ohio Land Title Assn., 1975-78, v.p., 1981, pres., 1982-83, Penn Ohio Coll., 1989-96. Served with AUS, 1943-46. Mem. Ohio State Bar Found. (life), ABA, Ohio State Bar (exec. com. 1978-81), Mahoning County Bar Assn. (pres. 1963-64), Am. Judicature Soc., Phi Alpha Delta. Presbyterian (elder, trustee). Club: Kiwanian. Home: 845 Wildwood Dr Youngstown OH 44512-3244 Office: 3810 Starr Centre Dr Canfield OH 44406-8003

MUMFORD, MANLY WHITMAN, lawyer; b. Evanston, Ill., Feb. 25, 1925; s. Manly Stearns and Helen (Whitman) M.; m. Luigi Thorne Horne, July 1, 1961; children— Shaw, Dodge A.B., Harvard U., 1947; J.D., Northwestern U, Chgo., 1950. Bar: Ill. 1950, U.S. Supreme Ct. 1969. Assoc. Chapman and Cutler, Chgo., 1950-62, ptnr., 1963-90. Author: The Old Family Fire, 1997; contbr. articles to profl. jours. Served with USNR, 1942-46 Fellow Am. Coll. Bond Counsel (hon.); mem. Nat. Assn. Bond Lawyers (Bernard P. Friel medal 1987). Democrat. Clubs: Cliff Dwellers, University, Chgo. Literary. Avocation: computers. Home: 399 W Fullerton Pky Chicago IL 60614-2810 Office: 22 W Monroe St Ste 1503 Chicago IL 60603-2505 E-mail: manly@mumford.cx.

MUMPER, LARRY A. state legislator; b. Loudenville, Ohio, July 25, 1937; m. 3 children. B in Edn., Ohio Northern U.; MA, Mount St. Joseph Coll. Mem. Marion City Coun., 1992-95, Marion County Commn., 1995-97, Ohio Senate from 26th dist., Columbus, 1997—.

MUNDAY, DAVE, radio personality; children: Patrick, Chris. With KY 102, KEBQ; prodn. dir. KLSO, Fox & chiefs Radio Network; radio host Oldies 95 FM, Mission, Kans. Ack announcer State Fair Motor Speedway, Mo. State Fair Grounds, I-70 Speedway. Office: Oldies 95 5800 Ridgewood Dr 6th Fl Mission KS 66202*

MUNGER, CHARLES T. diversified company executive; b. 1924; married. Ptnr. Wheeler Munger & Co., 1961-76; chmn., CEO, Blue Chip Stamps, 1976-78; vice chmn. Berkshire Hathaway, Inc., Omaha, 1978—, also chmn., CEO Wesco Fin. subs. Office: Berkshire Hathaway Inc 1440 Kiewit Plz Omaha NE 68131-3302

MUNGER, PAUL R. civil engineering educator; b. Hannibal, Mo., Jan. 14, 1932; s. Paul Oettle and Anne Lucille (Williams) M.; m. Frieda Ann Mette, Nov. 26, 1954; children: Amelia Ann Munger Fortmeyer, Paul David, Mark James, Martha Jane Munger Cox. BSCE, Mo. Sch. Mines and Metallurgy, 1958, MSCE, 1961; PhD in Engring. Sci., U. Ark., 1972. Registered profl. engr., Mo., Ill., Ark., Minn. Instr. civil engring Mo. Sch. Mines and Metallurgy, Rolla, 1958-61, asst. prof., 1961-65; assoc. prof. U. Mo., 1965-73, prof., 1973-99, prof. emeritus, 2000—; dir. Inst. River Studies, U. Mo., 1976-93; exec. dir. Internat. Inst. River and Lake Systems, U. Mo., 1984-93, interim chmn. CE dept., 1998-99, prof. emeritus, 2000. Mem. NSPE, Mo. Soc. Profl. Engrs., Am. Soc. Engring. Edn., ASCE, Nat. Coun. Engring. Examiners (pres. 1983-84), Mo. Bd. Architects, Profl. Engrs. and Land Surveyors (chmn. 1978-84, 95-2002).

MUNKVOLD, GARY P. plant pathologist, educator; BS in Forestry, U. Ill., 1986, MS in Plant Pathology, 1988; PhD in Plant Pathology, U. Calif., Davis, 1992. Grad. rsch. asst. Ill. Natural History Survey, Champaign, 1986-88; grad. rsch. asst. dept. plant pathology U. Calif., Davis, 1988-92; asst. prof., ext. plant pathologists dept. plant pathology Iowa State U., Ames, 1993-98, assoc. prof., ext. plant pathologist dept. plant pathology, 1998—. Recipient Novartis award Am. Phytopathol. Soc., 2000. Office: Iowa State U Dept Plant Pathology 317 Bessey Hall Ames IA 50010 Fax: 515-294-9420. E-mail: munkvold@iastate.edu.

MUNOZ, ANTONIO, state legislator; b. Chgo., Feb. 18, 1964; m. Patricia; 3 children. Officer Chgo. Police Dept.; mem. Ill. Senate, Springfield, 1999—, mem. edn., lic. activities, pub. health & welfare coms. Mem. mayor's lic. commn., Local Liquor Control Sect., Chgo., 1990, Dept. Aviation, Mayor's Office Budget & Mgmt. With U.S. Army. Mem. FOP. Democrat. Office: State Capitol Capitol Bldg M103 E Springfield IL 62706-0001 also: 3720 W 26th St Chicago IL 60623-3824

MUNRO, DONALD JACQUES, philosopher, educator; b. New Brunswick, N.J., Mar. 5, 1931; s. Thomas B. and Lucile (Nadler) M.; m. Ann Maples Patterson, Mar. 3, 1956; 1 child, Sarah de la Roche. A.B., Harvard U., 1953; Ph.D. (Ford Found. fellow), Columbia U., 1964. Asst. prof. philosophy U. Mich., 1964-68, asso. prof., 1968-73, prof. philosophy, 1973-96, prof. philosophy and Asian langs., 1990-96; prof. emeritus philosophy and Chinese, 1996—; chmn. dept. Asian langs. and cultures U. Mich., 1993-95; vis. research philosopher Center for Chinese Studies, U. Calif., Berkeley, 1969-70; asso. Center for Chinese Studies, U. Mich., 1964—; chmn. com. on studies of Chinese civilization Am. Council Learned Socs., 1979-81. Mem. Com. on Scholarly Communication with People's Republic China, NAS, 1978-82, China Council of Asia Soc., 1977-80, Com. on Advanced Study in China, 1978-82, Nat. Com. on U.S.-China Rels., Nat. Faculty of Humanities, Arts and Scis., 1986—; Evans-Wentz lectr. Stanford U., 1970; Fritz lectr. U. Wash., 1980; Gilbert Ryle lectr. Trent U., Ont., 1983; John Dewey lectr. U. Vermont, 1989; vis. rsch.scholar Chinese Acad. Social Scis. Inst. Philosophy, Beijing, 1983, dept. philosophy Beijing U., 1990. Author: The Concept of Man in Early China, 1969, the Concept of Man in Contemporary China, 1977;, editor: Individualism and Holism, 1985, Images of Human Nature: A Sung Portrait, 1988, The Imperial Style of Inquiry in Twentieth Century China, 1996. Mem. exec. com. Coll. Literature, Sci. and The Arts U. Mich., 1986-89. Served to lt. (j.g.) USNR, 1953-57. Recipient letter of commendation Chief Naval Ops.; Disting. Svc. award U. Mich., 1968, Excellence in Edn. award, 1992; Rice Humanities award, 1993-94; Nat. Humanities faculty fellow, 1971-72; John Simon Guggenheim Found. fellow, 1978-79; grantee Social Sci. Rsch. Coun., 1965-66, Am. Coun. Learned Socs., 1982-83, China com. grantee NAS, 1990. Mem. Assn. for Asian Studies (China and Inner Asia Council 1970-72), Soc. for Asian and Comparative Philosophy. Club: Ann Arbor Racquet. Home: 14 Ridgeway St Ann Arbor MI 48104-1739 Office: Dept Philosophy U Mich Ann Arbor MI 48104

MUNSON, BRUCE N. state legislator; BS, Ball State U.; JD, Ind. U., Indpls. Bar: Ind. Atty. in pvt. practice; mem. from 35th dist. Ind. State Ho. of Reps., 1992—, mem. commerce and econ. devel. com., mem. family, children and human affairs coms. Bd. dirs. Century Legal Svc. Program; mem. lega. adv. com. Habitat for Humanity. Mem. Century City Bus. Assn., Dalaware County Rep. Men's Club, Kiwanis, Century Ind. Old Car Club. Address: 7009 W Santa Fe Dr Muncie IN 47304-9342 Also: 2710 Buryewood Dr Muncie IN 47304

MUNSON, DAVID ROY, state legislator; b. Sioux Falls, S.D., Apr. 16, 1942; s. Roy Elmer Munson and Theil Severson; m. Linda Marie Carlson, 1972; children: Steven David, Paul James, John Jeffrey. BA, Sioux Falls Coll.; postgrad., Augustana Coll. Mem. S.D. Ho. of Reps., 1979-96, asst. majority whip, 1983-84, 89-90, mem. commerce and health and human svc. coms.; vice chmn. state affairs com.; banker; mem. S.D. Senate from 10th dist., Pierre, 1996—. Mem. commerce, labor and regulation coms., state-fed. assembly Nat. Conf. State Legislators. Past mem. Sioux Vocat. Bd.; mem. Multiple Sclerosis Bd., Luth. Social Svc. Consumers Credit Adv. Bd. and Cmty. Disabilities Svc. Bd.; mem. S.D. Devel. Corp.; mem. Sioux Empire Fire Bd. Fellow Augustana Coll. Mem. NEA. Home: 1009 N Sycamore Ave Sioux Falls SD 57110-5748

MUNSON, DONALD E. state legislator; Mem. S.D. Ho. of Reps.; mem. govt., oper. and audit, taxation and transp. coms.; corp. mgr., acct. Address: PO Box 731 Yankton SD 57078-0731

MUNSON, RICHARD HOWARD, horticulturist; b. Toledo, Dec. 20, 1948; s. Stanley Warren and Margaret Rose (Winter) M.; m. Joy Ellen Smith, July 8, 1972; children: Sarah Joy, David Remington. BS, Ohio State U., 1971; MS, Cornell U., 1973, PhD, 1981. Plant propagator The Holden Arboretum, Mentor, Ohio, 1973-76; asst. prof. Agrl. Tech. Inst., Wooster, 1976-78, Tex. Tech U., Lubbock, 1981-84; dir. botanic garden Smith Coll., Northampton, Mass., 1984-95; exec. dir. The Holden Arboretum, Kirtland, Ohio, 1995-2000; dir. botanic garden U. Mo., Columbia, Mo., 2001—. V.p. Childs Park Found., Northampton, Mass., 1985-95. Ret. lt. col. USAR, 1971-99. Recipient Disting. Alumnus award Ohio State U. Coll. Agr., 1998. Mem. Internat. Plant Propagators Soc., Am. Soc. for Hort. Sci., Am. Assn. Bot. Gardens and Arboreta (com. chmn. 1987-92), Internat. Assn. Plant Taxonomy, Sigma Xi, Pi Alpha Xi, Gamma Sigma Delta. Methodist. Avocations: fishing, golf, woodworking, gardening. Office: University of Missouri General Svcs Bldg Columbia MO 65211-3200

MUNYER, EDWARD A. zoologist, museum administrator; b. Chgo., May 8, 1936; s. G. and M. Munyer; m. Marianna J. Munyer, Dec. 12, 1981; children: Robert, William, Richard, Laura, Cheryl. BS, Ill. State U., 1958, MS, 1962. Biology tchr. MDR High Sch., Minonk, Ill., 1961-63; instr. Ill. State U., Normal, 1963-64; curator zoology Ill. State Mus., Springfield, 1964-67, asst. dir., 1981-98, asst. dir. emeritus, 1998—; assoc. prof. Vincennes (Ind.) U., 1967-70; dir. Vincennes U. Mus., 1968-70; assoc. curator Fla. Mus. Natural History, Gainesville, 1970-81. Mem. Mus. Accreditation Vis. Com. Roster, 1976—. Contbr. articles to profl. jours. Mem. Am. Assn. Mus. (bd. dirs. 1990-95), Assn. Midwest Mus. (pres. 1990-92, lifetime achievement award for disting. svc. 1998), Ill. Assn. Mus. (bd. dirs. 1981-86, lifetime profl. achievement award 1998), Wilson Ornithol. Soc. (life). Office: Ill State Mus Spring & Edward Sts Springfield IL 62706-0001 E-mail: eammjm@springnet1.com.

MURAT, WILLIAM M. district director; b. Stevens Point, Wis., Dec. 4, 1957; s. James L. and Rose Murat. BS, U. Wis., Stevens Point, 1980; JD, U. Wis., Madison, 1983; MBA, Columbia U., 1992. Asst. dist. atty. to dist. atty. Portage County, Wis., 1983-88, dist. atty., 1988-91; assemblyman Wis. State Dist. 71, 1995-99. Vice chmn. Portage County Dem. Com., 1976-80, chmn., 1985-86; exec. dir. Wis. Young Dems., 1978-79, pres., 1982-83; mem. exec. com. Seventh Dist. Dems., Wis., 1978-80, 82-90; adminstrv. com. Wis. Dem. Com., 1982-99; mem. Dem. Nat. Com., 1997-99; 1st vice chair Dem. Wis., 1997-99. Mem. Phi Delta Phi, Pi Kappa Delta. Home: PO Box 111 10 Coronado Ct Apt 3 Madison WI 53705-4262

MURATA, TADAO, engineering and computer science educator; b. Takayama, Gifu, Japan, June 26, 1938; arrived in U.S., 1962; s. Yonosuke and Ryu (Aomame) M.; m. Nellie Kit-Ha Shin, 1964; children: Patricia Emi, Theresa Terumi B.S.E.E., Tokai U., 1962; M.S.E.E., U. Ill., 1964, Ph.D. in Elec. Engring., 1966. Research asst. U. Ill., Urbana, 1962-66; asst. prof. U. Ill. at Chgo., 1966-68, assoc. prof., 1970-76, prof., 1977—; assoc. prof. Tokai U., Tokyo, Japan, 1968-70. Vis. prof. U. Calif., Berkeley, 1976-77; cons. Nat. Bur. Stds., Gaithersburg, Md., 9184-85; panel mem. NAS, Washington, 1981-82, 83-85; vis. scientist Nat. Ctr. For Sci. Rsch., France, 1981; guest rschr. Gesellschaft für Mathematik und Datenverarbeitung, Germany, 1979; Hitachi-Endowed prof. Osaka (Japan) U., 1993-94. Editor IEEE Trans. on Software Engring., 1986-92; assoc. editor Jour. of Cirs., Sysems and Computers, 1990—; contbr. articles to sci. and engring. jours. Recipient C.A. Petri Disting. Tech. Achievement award Soc. Design and Process Scis., 2000; Sr. univ. scholar award U. Ill., 1990; NSF grantee, 1978— , U.S.-Spain coop. rsch. grantee, 1985-87. Fellow IEEE (golden core charter mem. IEEE Computer Soc., Donald G. Fink Prize award 1991); mem. Assn. Computing Machinery, Info. Processing Soc. Japan, European Assn. for Theoretical Computer Sci., Upsilon Pi Epsilon (hon.). Avocations: golf, travel. Office: U Ill Dept Computer Sci m/c 152 851 S Morgan St Chicago IL 60607-7042 E-mail: t.murata@ieee.org.

MURDOCK, CHARLES WILLIAM, lawyer, educator; b. Chgo., Feb. 10, 1935; s. Charles C. and Lucille Marie (Tracy) M.; m. Mary Margaret Hennessy, May 25, 1963; children: Kathleen, Michael, Kevin, Sean. BSChemE, Ill. Inst. Tech., 1956; JD cum laude, Loyola U., Chgo., 1963. Bar: Ill. 1963, Ind. 1971. Asst. prof. law DePaul U., 1968-69; assoc. prof. law U. Notre Dame, 1969-75; prof., dean Law Sch. Loyola U., Chgo., 1975-83, 86—; dep. atty. gen. State of Ill., 1983-86; of counsel Chadwell & Kayser, Ltd., 1986-89. Vis. prof. U. Calif., 1974; cons. Pay Bd., summer 1972, SEC, summer 1973; co-founder Loyola U. Family Bus. Program; arbitrator Chgo. Bd. Options Exch., Nat. Assn. Securities Dealers, N.Y. Stock Exch., Am. Arbitration Assn.; co-founder, mem. exec. com. Loyola Family Bus. Ctr., 1990—; bd. dirs. Plymouth Tube Co., 1993—. Author: Business Organizations, 2 vols., 1996; editor: Illinois Business Corporation Act Annotated, 2 vols., 1975; tech. editor The Business Lawyer, 1989-90. Chmn. St. Joseph County (Ind.) Air Pollution Control Bd., 1971; bd. dirs. Nat. Center for Law and the Handicapped, 1973-75, Minority Venture Capital Inc., 1973-75. Capt. USMCR. Mem. ABA, Ill. Bar Assn. (cert. of award for continuing legal edn.), Chgo. Bar Assn. (cert. of award for continuing legal edn., bd. mgrs. 1976-78), Ill. Inst. Continuing Legal Edn. (adv. com) Roman Catholic. Home: 2126 Thornwood Ave Wilmette IL 60091-1452 Office: Loyola U Sch Law 1 E Pearson St Chicago IL 60611-2055 E-mail: cmurdoc@luc.edu.

MURNANE, MARGARET MARY, engineering and physics educator; b. Limerick, Ireland, Jan. 23, 1959; d. Matthew and Helen (Bourke) M.; m. Henry Cornelius Kapteyn, Mar. 26, 1987. MSc, U. Coll. Cork, Ireland, 1983; PhD, U. Calif., Berkeley, 1989. Postdoctoral researcher U. Calif., Berkeley, 1990; asst. prof. Wash. State U., Pullman, 1990-95; assoc. prof. U. Mich., Ann Arbor, 1995—. Presdl. Young Investigator awardee NSF, 1991, Sloan Found. fellow, 1992, Presdl. faculty fellow NSF, 1993. Mem. Am. Phys. Soc. (Simon Ramo award 1990, Maria Goeppert-Mayer award 1997), Optical Soc. Am., Soc. Photo-Optical Instrumentation Engrs., Assn. for Women in Sci. Office: U Mich Ctr for Ultrafast Optics 2200 Bonisteel Blvd Ann Arbor MI 48109-2099

MURPHY, ANDREW J. managing news editor; Mng. editor news The Columbus (Ohio) Dispatch, mng. editor, 1990—. Office: The Columbus Dispatch 34 S 3rd St Columbus OH 43215-4241

MURPHY, DIANA E. federal judge; b. Faribault, Minn., Jan. 4, 1934; d. Albert W. and Adleyne (Heiker) Kuske; m. Joseph Murphy, July 24, 1958; children: Michael, John E. BA magna cum laude, U. Minn., 1954, JD magna cum laude, 1974; postgrad., Johannes Gutenberg U., Mainz, Germany, 1954—55, U. Minn., 1955—58; LLD, St Johns U., 2000. Bar: Minn. 1974, U.S. Supreme Ct. 1980. Assoc. Lindquist & Vennum, 1974—76; mcpl. judge Hennepin County, 1976—78, Minn. State dist. judge, 1978—80; judge U.S. Dist. Ct. for Minn., Mpls., 1980—94, chief judge, 1992—94; judge U.S. Ct. of Appeals (8th cir.), Minneapolis, 1994—. Chair U.S. Sentencing Commn., 1999—. Bd. editors: Minn. Law Rev., Bd. editors: Georgetown U. Jour. on Cts., Bd. editors: Health Scis. and the Law, 1989—92. Dir. Nat. Assn. Pub. Interest Law Fellowships for Equal Justice, 1992—95; Bd. dirs. Mpls. United Way, 1985—2001, treas., 1990—94, vice-chmn., 1996—97, chmn. bd. dirs., 1997—98; bd. dirs. Bush Found., 1982—, chmn. bd. dirs., 1986—91, also organizer, 1st chmn. adv. coun.; bd. dirs. Amicus, 1976—80; mem. Mpls. Charter Commn., 1973—76; bd. dirs. Ops. De Novo, 1971—76, chmn. bd. dirs., 1974—75; mem., chmn. bill of rights com. Minn. Constl. Study Commn., 1971—73; regent St. Johns U., 1978—87, 1988—98, vice-chmn., chmn. bd., 1985—98, bd. overseers sch. theology, 1998—2001; mem. Minn. Bicentennial Commn., 1987—88; trustee Twin Cities Pub. TV, 1985—94, chmn. bd., 1990—92; trustee, treas. U. Minn. Found., 1990—; bd. dirs. Sci. Mus. Minn., 1988—94, vice-chmn., 1991—94; trustee U. St. Thomas, 1991—; Bd. dirs. Spring Hill Conf. Ctr., 1978—84. Recipient Amicus Founders' award, 1980, Outstanding Achievement award, U. Minn., 1983, YWCA, 1981, Disting. Citizen award, Alpha Gamma Delta, 1985, Devitt Disting. Svc. to Justice award, 2001, Disting. Alumnus award, U. Minn. Law Sch., 2002; scholar Fulbright. Fellow: Am. Bar Found.; mem.: ABA (mem. ethics and profl. responsibility judges adv. com. 1981—88, standing com. on jud. selection, tenure and compensation 1991—94, mem. standing com. on fed. jud. improvements 1994—97, Appellate Judges conf. exec. com. 1996—99, chmn. ethics and profl. responsibility judges adv. com. 1997—2000), Fed. Jud. Ctr. (bd. dirs. 1990—94, 8th cir. jud. coun. 1992—94, convener task force 1993, mem. U.S. jud. conf. com. on ct. adminstrn. and case mgmt. 1994—99, chair gender fairness implementation com. 1997—98, 8th cir. jud. coun. 1997—), Hist. Soc. for 8th Cir. (bd. dirs. 1988—91), Fed. Judges Assn. 1982—, (v.p. 1984—89, pres. 1989—91), U. Minn. Alumni Assn. (bd. dirs. 1975—83, nat. pres. 1981—82), Minn. Women Lawyers (Myra Bradwell award 1996), Nat. Assn. Women Judges (Leadership Judges Jud. Adminstrn. award 1998), Nat. Assn. Governing Bds. Univs. Colls. (dir. 1998—), Am. Judicature Soc. (bd. dirs. 1982—93, v.p. 1985—88, treas. 1988—89, chmn. bd. 1989—91), Am. Law Inst., Hennepin County Bar Assn. (gov. coun. 1976—81), Minn. Bar Assn. (bd. govs. 1977—81), Order of Coif, Phi Beta Kappa. Office: 11 E US Courthouse 300 S 4th St Minneapolis MN 55415-1320

MURPHY, GORDON JOHN, electrical engineer, educator; b. Milw., Feb. 16, 1927; s. Gordon M. and Cecelia A. (Knerr) M.; m. Dorothy F. Brautigam, June 26, 1948; children— Lynne, Craig. BS, Milw. Sch. Engring., 1949; MS, U. Wis., 1952; PhD, U. Minn., 1956. Asst. prof. elec. engring. Milw. Sch. Engring., 1949-51; systems engr. A C Spark Plug divsn. GM, 1951-52, cons., 1959-62; instr. U. Minn., 1952-56, asst. prof. elec. engring., 1956-57; assoc. prof. elec. engring. Northwestern U., Evanston, Ill., 1957-60, prof.., 1960-97, head dept. elec. engring., 1960-69, dir. Lab. for Design of Electronic Systems, 1987-97, prof. emeritus, 1997—. Cons. numerous corps., 1959—; founder, 1st chmn. Mpls. chpt. Inst. Radio Engrs. Profl. Group on Automatic Control, 1956-57, Chgo. chpt., 1959-61; pres. IPC Systems, Inc., 1975—; expert witness in patent suits, 1997—. Author: Basic Automatic Control Theory, 1957, 2d edit., 1966, Control Engineering, 1959; contbr. articles, papers to profl. jours.; patentee TV, electronic timers, periodontal instruments and motion control systems. Mem. indsl. adv. com. Milw. Sch. Engring., 1971-2001. Served with USN, 1945-46. Recipient ECE Centennial medal U. Wis., 1991, Outstanding Alumnus award Milw. Sch. Engring. Alumni Assn., 1974; named One of Chgo.'s Ten Outstanding Young Men Chgo. Jaycees, 1961. Fellow IEEE (for edn. and rsch. in automatic control 1967); mem. feedback control systems com. 1960-68, discrete systems com. 1962-68, adminstrv. com. profl. group on automatic control 1966-69, chmn. membership and nominating coms. 1966-67); mem. Am. Automatic Control Coun. (edn. com. 1967-69), Engr.'s Coun. for Profl. Devel. (guidance com. 1967-69), Nat. Electronic Conf. (bd. dirs. 1983-85), Am. Electronics Assn. (exec. com. M.W. coun. 1990-93), Sigma Xi, Eta Kappa Nu, Tau Beta Pi. Home: 638 Garden Ct Glenview IL 60025-4105 Office: Northwestern U Elec Engring Dept Evanston IL 60201

MURPHY, HAROLD, state legislator; Student, Northeastern Ill. U. Owner, operator King's Lake Resort, Ind.; mem. Ill. Ho. of Reps. from 30th dist. Supervising mgr. Charles Chew Facility, Sec. of State of Ill.; alderman Markham, Ill. Democrat.

MURPHY, JANET GORMAN, college president; b. Holyoke, Mass., Jan. 10, 1937; d. Edwin Daniel and Catherine Gertrude (Hennessey) Gorman. BA, U. Mass., 1958, postgrad., 1960-61, EdD, 1974, LLD (hon.), 1984; MEd, Boston U., 1961. Tchr. English and history John J. Lynch Jr. H.S., Holyoke, 1958-60; tchr. English Chestnut Jr. H.S., Springfield, Mass., 1961-63; instr. English and journalism Our Lady of Elms Coll., Chicopee, 1963-64; mem. staff Mass. State Coll., Lyndonville, Vt., 1977-83; pres. Mo. Western State Coll., St. Joseph, 1983—. Mem. campaign staff Robert F. Kennedy Presdl. Campaign, 1967. Recipient John Gunther Tchr. award NEA, 1961, award Women's Opportunity Com., Boston Fed. Exec. Bd., 1963, Phi Delta Kappa Educator of Yr. award NAACP, 1992; named one of 10 Outstanding Young Leaders of Greater Boston Area, Boston Jr. C. of C., 1973. Office: Mo Western State Coll Office of the President 4525 Downs Dr Saint Joseph MO 64507-2246

MURPHY, JIM, state legislator; b. St. Louis, Feb. 4, 1925; s. William Francis and Jane Marie (Lavin) M.; m. Carol Pell Popovsky, 1961; children: Karen Ann, James William. BA, St. Louis U., 1948. Alderman, Crestwood, Mo., 1981-83; mem. Mo. State Ho. of Reps. Dist. 95, 1983—. Del. Mo. State Rep. Conv., 1984, 92. Recipient Globe-Dem. Meritorious Svc. award. Home: 9314 Cordoba Ln Saint Louis MO 63126-2708

MURPHY, JUDITH CHISHOLM, trust company executive; b. Chippewa Falls, Wis., Jan. 26, 1942; d. John David and Bernice A. (Hartman) Chisholm. BA, Manhattanville Coll., 1964; postgrad., New Sch. for Social Research, 1965-68, Nat. Grad. Trust Sch., 1975. Asst. portfolio mgr. Chase Manhattan Bank, N.A., N.Y.C., 1964-68; trust investment officer Marshall & Ilsley Bank, Milw., 1968-72, asst. v.p., 1972-74, v.p., 1974-75; v.p., treas. Marshall & Ilsley Invesmtent Mgmt. Corp., 1975-94; v.p. Marshall & Ilsley Trust Co., Phoenix, 1982—, Marshall & Ilsley Trust Co. Fla., Naples, 1985—; v.p., dir. instnl. sales Marshall & Ilsley Trust Co., Milw., 1994-97, sr. v.p., 1997-98, M&I Investment Mgmt. Corp., 1998—. Coun. mem. Am. Bankers Assn., Washington, 1984-86; govt. relations com. Wis. Bankers Assn., Madison, 1982-88. Contbr. articles to Trusts & Estates Mag., 1980, ABA Banking Jour., 1981, Maricopa Lawyer, 1983. Chmn. Milw. City Plan Commn., 1986—97; commr. Milw. County Commn. on Handicapped, 1988—90; bd. dirs. Cardinal Stritch Coll., Milw., 1980—89, Children's Hosp. Wis., Milw., 1989—98, Milw. Ballet Co., 1996—2001, Milw. Ctr. for Independence, 1999—, Girl Scouts Milw. Area, 2002—. Recipient Outstanding Achievement award YWCA Greater Milw., 1985, Sacajawea award Profl. Dimensions, Milw., 1988, Pro Urbe award Mt. Mary Coll., 1988, Vol. award Milw. Found., 1992; named Disting. Woman in Banking, Comml. West Mag., 1988. Mem. Milw. Analysts Soc. (sec. 1974-77, bd. dirs. 1977-80), Fin. Women Internat. (bd. dirs., v.p. 1976-80), Am. Inst. Banking (instr. 1975-78), TEMPO (charter), Profl. Dimensions (hon.), University Club, Woman's Club Wis., Rotary. Democrat. Roman Catholic. Home: 3622 N Lake Dr Milwaukee WI 53211-2644 Office: M&I Investment Mgmt Corp 1000 N Water St Milwaukee WI 53202-3197

MURPHY, MARTIN JOSEPH, JR. cancer research center executive; b. Colorado Springs, Dec. 29, 1942; s. Martin Joseph Sr. and Gertrude F. (Heffting) M.; m. Ann A. Flesher, May 29, 1965; children: Siobhan, Deirdre, Martin Joseph III, Sean, Brendan. BS, Regis Coll., 1964; MS, N.Y.U., 1967, PhD, 1969. Vis. fellow Inst. de Pathologie Cellulaire, Paris, 1969-71, Christie Hosp., Manchester, Eng., 1971-72; visiting fellow John Curtin Sch. of Med. Rsch., Canberra, Australia, 1972-74; asst. prof. Sch. Medicine Cornell U., N.Y.C.; dir. Bob Hipple Lab for Cancer Rsch., 1977-85; dir. hematology tng. program Sloan-Kettering Inst. for Cancer Rsch., 1978-79; prof. Sch. of Medicine Wright State U., Dayton, 1984—; pres., CEO Hipple Cancer Rsch. Ctr., 1985-99. Chmn. bd. dirs. AlphaMed Press, Inc., Dayton; bd. dirs. Dayton Clin. Oncology Program. Editor: In Vitro Aspects of Erythropoleis, 1978, Blood Cell Growth Factors: Their Biology and Clinical Applications, 1990, Blood Cell Growth Factors: Their Utility in Hematology and Oncology, 1991; editor-in-chief Internat. Jour. Cell Cloning, 1982-93, Stem Cells, 1993—; exec. editor The Oncologist; contbr. articles to profl. jours. NIH postdoctoral fellow, 1969-70, Damon Runyon fellow, 1970-71, Spl. fellow Leukemia Soc. Am., 1971, Pro Am. award Dayton Exec. Club. Mem. Assn. of Am. Cancer Inst., Am. Soc. Hematology, Am. Soc. Oncology, Am. Assn. for Cancer Rsch., Internat. Soc. for Exptl. Hematology, Dayton Area Cancer Assn. (trustee). Avocation: photography. Office: Wright State U Sch Medicine 3640 Col Glenn Hwy Dayton OH 45435

MURPHY, MARY C. state legislator; BA, Coll. St. Scholastica; postgrad., U. Wis., Superior, Am. U., Ind. U. H.s. tchr.; mem. Minn. Ho. of Reps., 1976—. Mem. judiciary fin. com., chair ethics com., mem. capital investments com., labor-mgmt. rels. com.; active del. Duluth Central Labor Body AFL-CIO; mem., lector St. Raphael's Parish; dir. State Democratic Farmer-Labor Party, 1972-74, chmn. 8th Dist. credentials com., 1974— , chmn. St. Louis County Legis. Delegation, 1985-86. Mem. Duluth Fedn. Tchrs. (1st v.p. 1976-77, various coms.), Minn. Fedn. Tchrs. (legis. com. 1972-75), Am. Fedn. Tchrs. (del. nat. convs.), Minn. Hist. Soc., Alpha Delta Kappa. Office: 100 Constitution Ave Saint Paul MN 55155-1232

MURPHY, MAX RAY, lawyer; b. July 18, 1934; s. Loren A. and Lois (Mink) M.; children: Michael Lee, Chad Woodrow. BA, DePauw U., 1956; JD, Yale U., 1959; postgrad., Mich. State U., 1960. Bar: Mich. 1960. Assoc. Glassen, Parr, Rhead & McLean, Lansing, Mich., 1960-67, Lokker, Boter & Dalman, Holland, 1967-69; ptnr. Dalman, Murphy, Bidol, & Bouwens, P.C., 1969-91, Cunningham Dalman, P.C., Holland, 1991—. Instr. Lansing Bus. U., 1963-67; asst. pros. atty. Ottawa County, Mich., 1967-69. Democratic candidate for Ingham County (Mich.) Pros. Atty., 1962, 1964. Mem. ABA, Ottawa County Bar Assn. (sec. 1970-71), Mich. Bar Assn. (mem. family law sect.). Home: 3169 E Crystal Waters 3 Holland MI 49424-8091 Office: 321 Settlers Rd Holland MI 49423-3778 E-mail: mmurphy@sirus.com.

MURPHY, MICHAEL B. state legislator; m. Suzanne Thompson. BA, U. Notre Dame, 1979. TV, polit. reporter, 1979-87; dir. comm. Lt. Gov. John Mutz, 1987-89; pub. rels. mgr. Melvin Simons Assocs., 1989-92; dir. spl. projects Anthem, Inc., 1992—; mem. Ind. State Ho. of Reps. Dist. 90, asst. Rep. floor leader, mem. labor and employment coms. Chmn. bd. Monarch Inc. Sec. Rep. 6th Dist. Com., 1993-2001, mem. edn. com., 2001—.

MURPHY, MICHAEL EMMETT, retired food company executive; b. Winchester, Mass., Oct. 16, 1936; s. Michael Cornelius and Bridie (Curran) M.; m. Adele Anne Kasupski, Sept. 12, 1959; children: Leslie Maura, Glenn Stephen, Christopher McNeil. B.S. in Bus. Adminstrn, Boston Coll., 1958; M.B.A., Harvard, 1962. Financial analyst Maxwell House div. Gen. Foods Corp., White Plains, N.Y., 1962-64, cost mgr. San Leandro, Calif., 1964-65, controller Jacksonville, Fla., 1965-67, Hoboken, N.J., 1967-68, mgr. fin. planning and analysis, 1968-69; mgr. planning Hanes Corp., Winston-Salem, N.C., 1969-70, corp. controller, 1970-72; v.p. adminstrn. Hanes Corp. (Hanes Knitwear), 1972-74; v.p. fin. Ryder System Inc., Miami, Fla., 1974-75, exec. v.p., 1975-79; exec. v.p., dir. Sara Lee Corp., Chgo., 1979-93, vice chmn., 1993-97. Bd. dirs. GATX Corp., Payless Shoe Source, Inc., Am. Gen. Corp., Coach Inc., Bassett Furniture Industries, Inc., No. Funds. Mgmt. adviser Jr. Achievement, 1965-66; mem. exec. com. Hudson County Tax Rsch. Coun., 1967-68; trustee Boston Coll., 1980-88; chmn. Civic Fedn. Chgo., 1984-86; bd. dirs. Jobs for Youth, Chgo., 1983-86, Lyric Opera, 1986—; bd. dirs. Northwestern Meml. Hosp., Chgo., 1989-2000, Big Shoulders Fund, Chgo. Ctrl. Area Com., 1995—, Chgo. Cultural Ctr. Found., 1995—; prin. Chgo. United, 1995-98. Mem. Nat. Assn. Mfrs. (bd. dirs. 1989-96, dir. Big Shoulders Fund 1995—), Fin. Execs. Inst., Hoboken C. of C., Winson-Salem C. of C., Miami C. of C., Internat. Platform Assn., UN Assn., Ouimet Scholar Alumni Group, Beta Gamma Sigma. Roman Catholic. Home: 1242 N Lake Shore Dr Chicago IL 60610-2361 Office: Sara Lee Corp 3 First National Plz Chicago IL 60602

MURPHY, PATRICK JOSEPH, state representative; b. Dubuque, Iowa, Aug. 24, 1959; s. Lawrence John and Eileen (Heitz) M.; m. Therese Ann Gulick, Dec. 27, 1980; children: Jacob, John, Joey, Natalie. BA, Loras Coll., 1980. Transporter, security and safety officer, mental health technician Mercy Health Ctr., Dubuque, Iowa, 1975-88; documentation specialist software systems Cycare Systems Inc., 1988-90; state representative State of Iowa, Des Moines, 1989—. Adv. com. Iowa Birth Defects, 1995. Recipient Robert Tyson award Cmty. Action Assn., 1993, Pub. Svc. award Coalition for Family and Children's Svcs., 1994; Henry Toll fellow, 1996. Mem. NAACP, YMCA, Dubuque Mental Health Assn. (bd. dirs., Legis. of Yr.), Loras Club, FDR Club. Democrat. Roman Catholic. Avocations: weightlifting, jogging. Home: 155 N Grandview Ave Dubuque IA 52001-6325 Office: Ho Of Reps Des Moines IA 50319-0001

MURPHY, RAYMOND, state legislator; b. St. Louis, Dec. 15, 1937; m. Lynette; eight children. Student, Detroit Inst. Tech. Mem. Mich. Ho. of Reps from dist. 17, Lansing, 1983-94, Mich. Ho. of Reps from dist. 7, Lansing, 1995-98, Mich. Senate from 3rd dist., Lansing, 1998—. Spkr. pro tem Mich. Ho. Reps., chair labor com., mem bus. & fin. com., house oversight com., tourism & recreation coms. Real estate broker. Mem. NAACP, Nat. Black Caucus State Legis., Elks, Masons, Lions, Optimist. Office: State Capitol PO Box 30036 Lansing MI 48909-7514

MURPHY, SANDRA ROBISON, lawyer; b. Detroit, July 28, 1949; m. Richard Robin. BA, Northwestern U., 1971; JD, Loyola U., Chgo., 1976. Bar: U.S. Dist. Ct. (no. dist.) Ill. 1976. Assoc. Notz, Craven, Mead, Maloney & Price, Chgo., 1976-78; ptnr. McDermott, Will & Emery, 1978—. Mem. ABA (family law sect.), Ill. Bar Assn. (chair sect. family law coun. 1987-88), Chgo. Bar Assn. (chair matrimonial law com. 1985-86), Am. Acad. Matrimonial Lawyers (sec. 1990-91, v.p. 1991-92, pres. Ill. chpt. 1992-93, pres.-elect 1994-95, pres. 1995-96), Legal Club Chgo.

MURPHY, SHARON MARGARET, educator; b. Milw., Aug. 2, 1940; d. Adolph Leonard and Margaret Ann (Hirtz) Feyen; m. James Emmett Murphy, June 28, 1969 (dec. May 1983); children: Shannon Lynn, Erin Ann; m. Bradley B. Niemcek, Aug. 7, 1999. BA, Marquette U., 1965; MA, U. Iowa, 1970, PhD, 1973. Cert. K-14 tchr., Iowa. Tchr. elem. and secondary schs., Wis., 1959-69; dir. publs. Kirkwood C.C., Cedar Rapids, Iowa, 1969-71; instr. journalism U. Iowa, Iowa City, 1971-73; asst. prof. U. Wis., Milw., 1973-79; assoc. prof. So. Ill. U., Carbondale, 1979-84; dean, prof. Marquette U., Milw., 1984-94; prof. Bradley U., Peoria, Ill., 1994—, provost, v.p. acad. affairs, 1994-97, pres. Cmty. Career and Tech. Ctr., 1997-98. Pub. rels. dir., editor Worldwide mag., Milw., 1965-68; reporter Milw. Sentinel, 1967; Fulbright sr. lectr. U. Nigeria, Nsukka, 1977-78. Author: Other Voices: Black, Chicano & American Indian Press, 1971; (with Wigal) Screen Experience: An Approach to Film, 1968; (with Murphy) Let My People Know: American Indian Journalism, 1981; (with Schilpp) Great Women of the Press, 1983; editor: (with others) International Perspectives on News, 1982. Bd. dirs. Dirksen Congl. Leadership Ctr., 1994-2000; Dow Jones Newspaper Fund, N.Y., 1986-95, Peoria Symphony; mem. Peoria Riverfront Commn., 1995-2000, co-chair Peoria Race Rels. Com. Recipient Medal of Merit, Journalism Edn. Assn., 1976, Amoco Award for Teaching Excellence, 1977, Outstanding Achievement award Greater Milw. YWCA, 1989; named Knight of Golden Quill, Milw. Press Club, 1977; Nat. headliner Women in Communication, Inc., 1985. Mem. Assn. Edn. in Journalism and Mass Comm. (pres. 1986-87), Soc. Profl. Journalists, Nat. Press Club. Democrat. Roman Catholic. Office: Bradley U Global Comm Ctr Peoria IL 61625-0001 E-mail: smm@bradley.edu.

MURPHY, STEVE, radio personality; Grad. History, Rutgers U. With Sta. WCCO Radio, Mpls., news anchor, mng. editor. Office: WCCO 625 2nd Ave S Minneapolis MN 55402*

MURPHY, STEVEN LESLIE, state legislator, utilities company official; b. San Francisco, Sept. 9, 1957; s. Russell Jr. and Helen Glendora (Black) M.; m. Robin Estelle Stelling, Feb. 9, 1979; children: Nikolaas Russell, Matthew Steven. AS in Bus. Mgmt., Red Wing (Minn.) Tech. Coll., 1992. Operator No. St, Red Wing, 1981—; mem. Minn. Senate from 29th dist., St. Paul, 1992—. Steward Unit 47 Local 949 Internat. Brotherhood Elec. Workers, Red Wing, 1987—. Bd.dirs. CSAP Open/Charity Golf Tournament, Frontenac, Minn.; co-chair Fireman Caucus, Minn. Legislature, 1992—; vice-chair Vets. Com., Minn. Senate, 1992—. Served with USMC, 1976-80. Mem. Am. Legion, Marine Corps League. Mem. Democratic-Farmer Labor Party. Methodist. Avocations: hunting, fishing, youth activities coach. Home: PO Box 40 Red Wing MN 55066-0040 Office: Minn State Senate State Capital Bldg 301 Saint Paul MN 55155-0001

MURPHY, TOM, radio personality; b. Lorain, Ohio; m. Tracey Murphy; 1 child Sean. Radio host WNWV, Elyria, Ohio. Avocation: auto racing. Office: WNWV 538 W Broad St PO Box 4006 Elyria OH 44036*

MURRAY, CONNIE WIBLE, state official, former state legislator; b. Tulsa, Oct. 13, 1943; d. Carl Prince Lattimore and Jimmie Bell Henry; m. Jarrett Holland Murray, May 4, 1995. Cert. of oral hygiene, Temple U., 1965; BA, Loyola Coll., 1975; JD, U. Md., 1980. Registered dental hygienist, Bethlehem, Pa., 1965-66, Joppa, Md., 1966-77; law clk. Hon. Albert P. Close, Belair, 1980-81; atty., 1981-85; realtor, 1985-90; mem. Mo. Ho. of Reps., Jefferson City, 1990-96; pub. svc. commr. State of Mo., 1997—. House mgr. Articles ot Impeachment of Judith Moriarty, Mo. Sec. of State, 1994; mem. budget com. Mo. Ho. of Reps., also mem. appropriations social svcs. and corrections com., judiciary and ethics com., civil and criminal law and accounts, opers. and fin. com., interim com. for fed. funds and block grants, commn. on intergovtl. affairs, commn. on mgmt. and productivity, legis. oversight com. for ct. automation, ho. automation com. Bd. dirs. North Springfield Betterment Assn., 1989; vocat. adv. bd., dir. house intern programs Nat. Conf. State Legislators. Named Outstanding Freshman Legis. on Health Care Issues, Mo. Rep. Caucus, 1992; recipient Jud. Conf. Legis. award Mo. Jud. Conf., 1994, Outstanding Woman Legis. award Assn. Probate and Assoc. Cir. Judges, 1995. Mem. LWV (bd. dirs. Springfield 1989, treas.), Nat. Order Women Legis., Nat. Conf. State Legis., Nat. Women's Polit. Caucus, Women Legis. Mo., Mo. Bar Assn. (Adminstr. for Justice award), Am. Legis. Exch. Counsel, Ctr. for Am. Women in Politics, Greene County Bar Assn., Forum-A Women's Network, Women in Govt. Avocations: golf, bicycling, jogging, travel. Home: 2118 S Catalina Ave Springfield MO 65804-2829 Office: Mo Gen Assembly State Capitol Office Bldg Jefferson City MO 65101-6806

MURRAY, DANIEL RICHARD, lawyer; b. Mar. 23, 1946; s. Alfred W. and Gloria D. Murray. AB, U. Notre Dame, 1967; JD, Harvard U., 1970. Bar: Ill. 1970, U.S. Dist. Ct. (no. dist.) Ill. 1970, U.S. Ct. Appeals (7th cir.) 1971, U.S. Supreme Ct. 1974. Ptnr. Jenner & Block, Chgo., 1970—. Trustee Chgo. Mo. and Western Rlwy. Co., 1988-97; adj. prof. U. Notre Dame, 1997—. Co-author: Secured Transactions, 1978, Illinois Practice: Uniform Commercial Code with Illinois Code Comments, 1997, Uniform Laws Annotated—Uniform Commercial Code Forms and Materials, 2001. Bd. regents Big Shoulders Fund, Archdiocese of Chgo., Bernadin Ctr., Cath. Theol. Union. Mem.: Assn. Transp. Practitioners, Transp. Lawyers Assn., Am. Coll. Comml. Fin. Lawyers, Am. Coll. Bankruptcy, Am. Law Inst., Am. Bankruptcy Inst., Cath. Lawyers Guild (bd. dirs.), Lawyers' Club Chgo. Roman Catholic. Home: 1307 N Sutton Pl Chicago IL 60610-2007 Office: Jenner & Block One IBM Plz Chicago IL 60611-3605 E-mail: dmurray@jenner.com.

MURRAY, DELBERT MILTON, manufacturing engineer; b. Fordland, Mo., Aug. 22, 1941; s. Chester Augustus and Iris Morene (Hamilton) M.; m. Orilla Maxine Stoaks, Sept. 15, 1962; children: Cynthia Ann, Norman Lee, Orilla Mae, Delbert Lynn. BS, S.W. Mo. State U., 1963. Prodn. planner McDonnell Douglas Corp., St. Louis, 1963-65; tool planning engr. The Boeing Corp., Wichita, Kans., 1965-70; indsl. engr. NCR Corp., 1972-77; sr. mfg. engr. Emerson Electric Co., Ava, Mo., 1977-96; mfg. engr. Copeland Corp., 1997—. Chmn. Mt. Zion Ch. of God., Mo., 1977-97; fire chief Ava Rural Fire Dept., 1998—. Mem. NRA, N.Am. Hunting Club, Gideons. Republican. Avocations: hunting, fishing, photography, woodworking. Home: RR 1 Box 305 Ava MO 65608-9720 Office: Copeland Corp 1400 NW 3D St Ava MO 65608 E-mail: dmmurray@fidnet.com.

MURRAY, DIANE ELIZABETH, librarian; b. Detroit, Oct. 15, 1942; d. Gordon Lisle and Dorothy Anne (Steketee) LaBoueff; m. Donald Edgar Murray, Apr. 22, 1968. AB, Hope Coll., 1964; MLS, Western Mich. U., 1968; MM, Aquinas Coll., 1982; postgrad., Mich. State U., East Lansing, 1964-66. Catalog libr., asst. head acquisitions sect. Mich. State U. Librs., East Lansing, 1968-77; libr. tech. and automated svcs. Hope Coll., Holland, Mich., 1977-88; dir. librs. DePauw U., Greencastle, Ind., 1988-91; acquisitions libr. Grand Valley State U., Allendale, Mich., 1991—. Sec., vice chair, chairperson bd. trustees Mich. Libr. Consortium, Lansing, 1981-85. Vice pres. Humane Soc. of Putnam County, Greencastle, 1990-91; bd. dirs., Loutit Dist. Libr., 1999—. Mem. ALA. Methodist. Avocations: dog breeding and showing, handbell ringing. Office: Grand Valley State U Zumberge Libr Allendale MI 49401 E-mail: murrayd@gvsu.edu.

MURRAY, JAMES A. bishop; b. July 5, 1932; Bishop of Kalamazoo Roman Cath. Ch., Mich., 1997—. Office: Kalamazoo Diocese 215 N Westnedge Ave Kalamazoo MI 49007-3718

MURRAY, JOHN PATRICK, psychologist, educator, researcher; b. Cleve., Sept. 14, 1943; s. John Augustine and Helen Marie (Lynch) M.; m. Ann Coke Dennison, Apr. 17, 1971; children: Jonathan Coke, Ian Patrick. PhD, Cath. U. Am., 1970. Rsch. dir. Office U.S. Surgeon Gen. NIMH, Bethesda, Md., 1969-72; asst. to assoc. prof. psychology Macquarie U., Sydney, Australia, 1973-79; vis. assoc. prof. U. Mich., Ann Arbor, 1979-80; dir. youth and family policy Boys Town Ctr., Boys Town, Nebr., 1980-85; prof., dir. Sch. Family Studies and Human Svcs. Kans. State U., Manhattan, 1985-98, interim assoc. vice provost rsch., 1998—. Scholar-in-residence Mind Sci. Found., San Antonio, 1996-97; mem. children's TV com. CBS, 1996-99. Author: Television and Youth: 25 Years of Research and Controversy, 1980, The Future of Children's TV, 1984, (with H.T. Rubin) Status Offenders: A Sourcebook, 1983, (with E.A. Rubenstein, G.A. Comstock) Television and Social Behavior, 3 vols., 1972, (with A. Huston and others) Big World, Small Screen: The Role of Television in American Society, 1992, (with C. Fisher and others) Applied Developmental Science, 1996; contbr. numerous articles to profl. jours. Mem. Nebr. Foster Care Rev. Bd., 1982-84; mem. Advocacy Office for Children and Youth, 1980-85; mem. Nat. Coun. Children and TV, 1982-87; trustee The Villages Children's Homes, 1986—, Menninger Found., 1996—; mem. children's TV adv. bd. CBS-TV, 1996—. Fellow Am. Psychol. Assn. (pres. div. child youth and family svcs. 1990); mem. Internat. Comm. Assn., Soc. Rsch. in Child Devel., Royal Commonwealth Soc. (London), Manhattan Country Club. Home: 1731 Humboldt St Manhattan KS 66502-4140 Office: Kans State U Office Vice Provost Rsch 101 Fairchild Hall Manhattan KS 66506-1100 E-mail: jpm@ksu.edu.

MURRAY, PATRICK ROBERT, microbiologist, educator; b. L.A., Jan. 15, 1948; married, 1970; 3 children. BS, St. Mary's Coll., Calif., 1969; MS, U. Calif., L.A., 1972, PhD in Microbiology, 1974. Rsch. fellow clinical microbiology Mayo Clinic & Mayo Found., 1974-76; asst. prof. medicine Wash. U. Sch. Med., 1976-82, assoc. dir., 1976; dir. clinical microbiology Barnes Hosp., St. Louis, 1977—, dir. postdoctoral training program, 1982—; assoc. prof. medicine Wash. U. Sch. Medicine, 1983—. Cons. St. Luke's Hosp., 1985—; mem. Nat. Com. Clinical Lab. Standards, 1980—; chmn. exam com. Am. Bd. Medical Microbiologist, 1982—, mem. joint standards and exam com., 1985—; bd. dirs. Southwestern Assn. Clinical Microbiologist; chmn. Clinical Microbiologist Divsn. Am. Soc. Microbiologist. Becton Dickinson Co. Clinical Microbiology award Am. Soc. Microbiology, 1993. Fellow Am. Acad. Med. Microbiologist, Infectious Disease Soc; mem. Am. Assn. Pathologist, Am. Soc. Microbiologist, Med. Mycol Soc. Am., Am. Federation Clinical Rsch., Sigma Xi. Achievements include research in new diagnostic and therapeutic tests for clinical microbiology. Office: Washington Univ Div of Lab Medicine 660 S Euclid Ave Saint Louis MO 63110-1093

MURRAY, RAYMOND HAROLD, physician; b. Cambridge, Mass., Aug. 17, 1925; s. Raymond Harold and Grace May (Dorr) M.; children—Maureen, Robert, Michael, Margaret, David, Elizabeth, Catherine, Anne. BS, U. Notre Dame, 1946; MD, Harvard U., 1948. Diplomate Am. Bd. Internal Medicine, also Sub-bd. Cardiovascular Disease. Practice medicine, Grand Rapids, Mich., 1955-62; asst. prof. to prof. medicine Ind. U. Sch. Medicine, 1962-77; prof. dept. medicine Coll. Human Medicine Mich. State U., Lansing, 1977-95, chmn. dept. medicine Coll. Human Medicine, 1977-89, emeritus, 1995—. Chmn. aeromed.-bioscis. panel Sci. Adv. Bd., USAF, 1977-81; mem. adv. coun. Office Alternative Medicine/NIH, 1997-99. Contbr. numerous articles to profl. publs. Served with USNR, 1942-45; Served with USPHS, 1950-53. Fellow ACP (gov. Mich. chpt. 1994-98); mem. Am. Heart Assn. (fellow coun. clin. cardiology), Am. Fedn. Clin. Rsch. E-mail: Raymondmur@aol.com.

MURRAY, ROBERT WALLACE, chemistry educator; b. Brockton, Mass., June 20, 1928; s. Wallace James and Rose Elizabeth (Harper) M.; m. Claire K. Murphy, June 10, 1951; children: Kathleen A., Lynn E., Robert Wallace, Elizabeth A., Daniel J., William M., Padraic O'D. AB, Brown U., 1951; MA, Wesleyan U., Middletown, Conn., 1956; PhD, Yale U., 1960. Mem. tech. staff Bell Labs., Murray Hill, N.J., 1959-68; prof. chemistry U. Mo., St. Louis, 1968-81, chmn. dept., 1975-80, Curators' prof., 1981-2000, Curators' prof. emeritus, 2001—. Vis. prof. Engler-Bunte Inst. U. Karlsruhe, Fed. Republic Germany, 1982, dept. chemistry Univ. Coll., Cork, Ireland, 1989; cons. to govt. and industry. Co-editor: Singlet Oxygen, 1979; contbr. articles to profl. jours. Mem. Warren (N.J.) Twp. Com., 1962-63, mayor, 1963; mem. Planning Com. and Bd. Health, 1962-64, Bd. Edn., 1966-68. Served with USN, 1951-54; Lt. comdr. USNR. Grantee EPA, NSF, NIH, Office of Naval Research. Fellow AAAS, Am. Inst. Chemists, N.Y. Acad. Scis.; mem. Am. Soc. Photobiology, Am. Chem. Soc., The Oxygen Soc., Sigma Xi. Home: 1810 Walnutway Dr Saint Louis MO 63146-3659 Office: Univ Mo Dept Chemistry Saint Louis MO 63121

MURREY, DANA L. state legislator; Mem. dist. 69 Mo. Ho. of Reps. Office: 2422 Mary Ave Rm 409 B Saint Louis MO 63136-3829

MURRY, CHARLES EMERSON, lawyer, official; b. Hope, N.D., June 23, 1924; s. Raymond Henry and Estelle Margarete (Skeim) M.; m. Donna Deane Kleve, June 20, 1948; children: Barbara, Karla, Susan, Bruce, Charles. B.S., U. N.D., 1948, J.D., 1950. Bar: N.D. 1950. Mem. firm Nelson and Heringer, Rugby, N.D., 1950-51; dir. N.D. Legis. Council, 1951-75; adj. gen. with rank of maj. gen. State of N.D., Bismarck, 1975-84; mgr. Garrison Diversion Conservancy Dist., 1985-93. Cons. Council State Govts.; mem. res. forces policy bd. Sec. of Def. Vice-pres. Mo. Slope Luth. Home of Bismarck, 1965-66. Served with AUS, 1942-45. Decorated D.S.M., Legion of Merit, Meritorious Service medal, Bronze Star, Army Commendation medal; Fourragere Belgium; Orange Lanyard Netherlands; recipient Sioux award U. N.D., 1970; Gov.'s award of excellence, 1971; Nat. Leadership award Bismarck C. of C., 1971 Mem. Adjs. Gen. Assn. (exec. com., sec. 1983-84), Nat. Legis. Conf. (past chmn.), N.G. Assn., Am. Bar Assn., N.D. Bar Assn., Commrs. Uniform State Laws. Lutheran. Lodges: Elks, Masons. Office: 5505 Ponderosa Ave Bismarck ND 58503-9159 E-mail: murryce@webtv.net.

MURTAUGH, CHRISTOPHER DAVID, lawyer; b. Darby, Pa., Oct. 25, 1945; s. John Michael and Rita (Sullivan) M.; m. Nancy R. Hanauer, Nov. 30, 1968; children: Jason C., Colin M., Alison M. AB, U. Ill., 1967, JD, 1970. Bar: Ill. 1970, Fla. 1973, U.S. Dist. Ct. (no. dist.) Ill. 1975. Ptnr. Winston & Strawn, Chgo., 1974—, capital ptnr., 1987—, real estate dept. chmn., 1994—. Mem. Glen Ellyn (Ill.) Capital Improvements Com., 1985-89, Glen Ellyn Plan Com., 1989-96, Met. Planning Coun., 1995—; bd. visitors U. Ill. Coll. of Law, 1998—. Lt. USNR, 1971-74. Mem. ABA, Am. Coll. Real Estate Lawyers, Fla. Bar Assn., Ill. State Bar Assn., Chgo. Bar Assn., Urban Land Inst., Internat. Coun. Shopping Ctrs., Order of Coif. Office: Winston & Strawn 35 W Wacker Dr Ste 4200 Chicago IL 60601-1695 E-mail: cmurtaug@winston.com.

MUSA, SAMUEL ALBERT, university executive; m. Judith Friedman; children: Gregory, Jeffrey. BA, BSEE, Rutgers U., 1961; MS in Applied Physics, Harvard U., 1962, PhD in Applied Physics, 1965. Rsch. scientist Gen. Precision Inc., Little Falls, N.J., 1965-66; asst. prof. elec. engring. U. Pa., Phila., 1966-71; project leader Inst. for Def. Analyses, Arlington, Va., 1971-78; dep. dir. Office of Under Sec. Def., Washington, 1978-83; dir. rsch. and advanced tech. E-Systems, Inc., Dallas, 1983-86, v.p. rsch. and advanced tech., 1986-95; exec. dir. Ctr. Display Tech. and Mfg. U. Mich., 1995-99; assoc. v.p. for strategic initiative Northwestern U., Evanston, Ill., 1999—. Mem. sci. adv. bd. USAF, 1987-91; mem. adv. bd. Def. Intelligence Agy., Army Sci. Bd. Contbr. articles to profl. jours. Recipient Exceptional Civilian Svc. award, Sec. of Air Force, cert. of appreciation, Sec. Def. Fellow IEEE; mem. AIA (tech. and ops. coun. 1986-95, vice chmn. 1993, chmn. 1994), Sigma Xi, Tau Beta Pi, Pi Mu Epsilon. Office: 1801 Maple Ave Evanston IL 60208-0001

MUSACCHIO, ROBERT A. medical association administrator; B of Econs., SUNY; D of Econs., U. Wis. Sr. v.p. membership & info., chief info. officer AMA, Chgo. Bus. dir., mng. editor AMA's Health Insight, AMA's Website; mem. bd. advisors Intel. Contbr. articles to profl. jours. Office: Jour Am Med Assn 515 N State St Chicago IL 60610-4325

MUSCHLER, AUDREY LORRAINE, insurance broker; b. New Britain, Conn., May 24, 1928; d. Leonard Marl and Carolyn Dorothy (Low) Jackson; m. Arthur F. Muschler, Aug. 28, 1954; children: George F., James A., John L. Grad., Edgewood Coll., 1948. Agt. Fidelity Mut. Life Ins. Co., Chgo., 1953-63; ins. broker Oak Brook, Ill., 1975—. Co-author: Oak Brook, a concise history of the Village, 1990. Co-founder, 1st pres. Oak Brook Hist. Soc., 1975—, Fullersburg Hist. Found., Oak Brook, 1986—; co-founder, v.p., treas. Salt Creek Greenway Assn., Oak Brook, 1988-97; co-founder, co-dir, Mayslake Landmark Conservancy, Oak Brook, 1993-2000; active Grace Episcopal Churchwomen, 1970—, pres., 1987-89. Mem. Nat. Assn. Life Underwriters, DuPage Life Underwriters, PEO Sisterhood (pres. 1985-87). Republican. Avocation: historic preservation. Home: 55 Yorkshire Woods Oak Brook IL 60523-1472 E-mail: artimusm@aol.com.

MUSCOPLAT, CHARLES, dean; b. St. Paul; B in Chemistry, D in Vet. Microbiology, U. Minn. Faculty mem. vet. medicine U. Minn., 1976-83, prof. dept. animal sci., dean Coll. Agrl., Food and Environ. Scis., v.p. for agrl. policy, dir. Minn. Agrl. Experiment Sta., 1999—. Bd. dirs. Minn. Acad. Sci.; mem. bd. on agr. NAS/NRC/ mem. bd. on sci. and tech. Internat. Devel.; mem. planning group Nat. Strategy for Biotech., U.S.-Indonesia Agrl. Biotechnology Workshop; sci. advisor State Dept. and the U.S. Agy. for Internat. Devel. Contbr. articles to profl. jours. Achievements include developed the nations first biotechnology animal health product (Genecol 99); played a key role in the development for the first U.S. biotechnology plant product herbicide-tolerant corn. Office: Coll Agrl Food & Environ Scis Rm 277 CofH 1420 Eckles Ave Saint Paul MN 55108

MUSER, TONY, manager professional athletics; b. L.A., Aug. 1, 1947; m. Nancy Muser; children: Tony Jr., Michael, Kristi. Student, San Diego Mesa Jr. Coll. Maj. league baseball player Boston, 1969, White Sox, 1971-75, Balt., 1975-77, Milw. Brewers, 1978; profl. baseball player Seibu Lions, Japanese Pacific League, 1979; mgr. Stockton A, Calif. League, 1980, El Paso AA then Vancouver AAA, 1983; 3rd base coach Milw. Big League Staff, 1985-88, hitting instr., 1987-89; amateur, maj. league crosschecker Milw. West Coast, 1991; mgr. Denver AAA, Am. Assn., 1991-92, Milw. Brewers; bullpen coach Chgo. Cubs, 1993, 3rd base coach then hitting coach, 1994-97; mgr. Kansas City Royals, 1997—. Named Calif. League Champions, 1980, Mgr. of Yr., Am. Assn., 1991. Office: Kansas City Royals Baseball Club PO Box 419969 Kansas City MO 64141-6969*

MUSHALA, MICHAEL C. career officer; BS in Materials Engring., Rensselaer Polytech. Inst., 1969, MS in Materials Engring., 1971, D in Materials Engring., 1973. Commd. 2d lt. USAF, 1969, advanced through grades to brig. gen., 1996; T-38 instr. pilot Vance AFB, Okla., 1975-76; chief T-38 pilot for operational test/evaluation Hdqrs. Air Tng. Command, Randolph AFB, Tex., 1976-78, ops. staff officer, dir. for ops. staff, 1978-79; instr. dept. of engring. mechanics USAF Acad., Colorado Springs, Colo., 1979-82; aide-de-camp to the chief of staff Hdqrs. Supreme Allied Powers Europe, Mons, Belgium, 1983-85; investment strategy mgr. Andrews AFB, Md., 1985-86; chief, plans divsn., sci. and tech. deputate, 1986-87; exec. officer to dep. chief of staff, tech. and plans, 1987-88; dep. program dir., space systems divsn. Nat. Aeronautics and Space Adminstrn. Advanced Launch Sys., L.A., 1988-90; sr. mil. asst. to undersec. of def. for acquisition Office of the Sec. of Def., The Pentagon, Washington, 1991-92; F22 sys. program dir. Air Force Material Command, Hanscom AFB, Mass., 1996—. Sr. rsch. fellow Indsl. Coll. of the Armed Forces, 1991. Office: ASC/YF 2130 5th St Bldg 50 Wright Patterson AFB OH 45433-7003

MUSIAL, STAN(LEY) (FRANK MUSIAL), hotel and restaurant executive, former baseball executive, former baseball player; b. Donora, Pa., Nov. 21, 1920; s. Lukasz M.; m. Lillian Labash, 1939; children: Richard, Geraldine, Janet, Jean. Ed. high sch., Donora. Baseball player St. Louis Cardinals Farm Team, 1938-41; 1st baseman, outfielder St. Louis Cardinals, Nat. League, 1941-63; sr. v.p. St. Louis Cardinals, 1963-91; pres. Stan Musial & Biggies, Inc., St. Louis. Author: Stan Musial: The Man's Own Story, 1964. Served with USNR, World War II. Voted Nat. League Rookie of Yr., 1943; named most valuable player Nat. League, 1943, 46, 48; mem. Nat. League All-Star Team, 1943-44, 46-63; voted most valuable player Baseball Writers Com., 1946; Maj. League Player of Year Sporting News, 1946, 51; Sid Mercer award N.Y. Baseball Writers, 1947; Kenesaw Mountain Landis Meml. plaque, 1948; Sports Illus. Sportsman of Yr., 1957; recipient Freedom Leadership medal, 1968; named to Baseball Hall of Fame, 1969; holder .331 lifetime batting average. Office: Stan the Man Inc 1650 Des Peres Rd Ste 125 Saint Louis MO 63131-1899

MUSSALLEM, MICHAEL A. healthcare company executive; BChemE, Rose-Hulman Inst. Tech., 1974. With Union Carbide, Baxter Healthcare, Deerfield, Ill., 1979—, various positions in mfg., engring. and product devel., gen. mgr. Access products, v.p. product devel. Parenterals, gen. mgr. Pharms. divsn., pres. Bentley divsn., group v.p. Baxter Surg. Group, chmn. Baxter Asia-Pacific Bd., group v.p. Baxter cardiovascular and biopharms. Bd. dirs. Calif. Health Care Inst., Med. Tech. Leadership Forum, Evanston Northwestern Healthcare.

MUSSER, TERRY M. state legislator; Mem. Wis. State Assembly. Home: W13550 Murray Rd Black River Falls WI 54615-5102

MUSTOE, THOMAS ANTHONY, physician, plastic surgeon; b. Columbia, Mo., June 29, 1951; s. Robert Moore and Carolyn (Swett) M.; m. Kathryn Claire Stallcup, Aug. 13, 1977; children: Anthony, Lisa. BA cum laude in biology, Harvard Coll., 1973, MD cum laude, 1978. Diplomate Am. Bd. Otolaryngology, Am. Bd. Plastic Surgery. Rsch. assoc. dept. microbiology Harvard Med. Sch., Cambridge, Mass., 1976-77; intern in medicine Mass. Gen. Hosp., Boston, 1978-79; resident in surgery Peter Bent Brigham Hosp., 1979-80; resident in otolaryngology Mass. Eye and Ear Infirmary, 1980-82, chief resident, 1982-83; resident in plastic surgery Brigham and Women;s Hosp., Children's Hosp., 1983-84, chief resident, 1984-85; asst. prof. in surgery Wash. U. Sch. Medicine, St. Louis, 1985-89, assoc. prof., 1989-91; prof., chief divsn. plastic surgery Northwestern U. Med. Sch., Chgo., 1991—; plastic surgeon Northwestern Meml. Hosp., 1991—, Evanston Hosp., 1991—, Children's Meml. Hosp., 1992—, Shriner's Hosp. Chgo., 1994—. Co-chmn. Gorden Rsch. Conf., 1995; spl. cons. FDA, 1994—98; mem. sci. adv. panel Biologies, 1997, NCI, 1998; lectr. seminars, 2001. Editl. bd. Archives of Surgery, 1992—, Plastic and Reconstructive Surgery, 1993-2001, Wound Repair and Regeneration, 1992—, Jour. Surg. Rsch., 1997—; contbr. articles to profl. jours., more than 200 publs., book chpts.; book reviewer. Harvard Nat. scholar, 1969-73; Rhodes scholar candidate, Harvard Coll., 1973. Fellow: ACS (adv. coun. plastic surgery 1999—2002, surg. forum com. 1999—2002, surg. biology club III); mem.: AMA, Coun. Plastic Surger Org., Double Boarded Soc. (pres. 1995—98), Chgo. Surg. Soc., Chgo. Plastic Surg. Soc. (sec. 1996—97), Wound Healing Soc. (program com. 1990, audit com. 1992, program com. 1992, bd. dir. 1993—96, program com. 1994, fin. com. 1994—96, program com. 1997, pres. 1997—99), Assn. Acad. Chmn. Plastic Surgery (matching program and ctrl. application svc. com. 1994), Soc. U. Surgeons, Soc. Head and Neck Surgeons (membership com. 1993—95), Plastic Surgery Rsch. Coun. (rep. coun. acad. surgeons 1991—94, com. indsl. rels. 1992, program com. 1992—94, 1995, Judge Snyder & Crikelair awards 1991), Midwest Assn. Plastic Surgeons, Lipoplasty Soc. N.Am. (lipoplasty ednl. rsch. found. 1998—2000), Am. Assn. Plastic Surgery (rsch. and edn. com. 1994—96, chmn. 1996, mem. com. 1998—, co-chmn.ASPRS-ASAPS task force on emerging trends 1999—2000, chmn. instl. coun. com. 1999—), Am. Soc. Plastic and Reconstructive Surgery (rsch. fund proposal com. 1987—92, plastic surgery device com. 1989—93, resource book for plastic surgery residents com. 1991—93, socioecon. 1992—94, sci. program com. 1993—95, chmn. device and tecyhnique assessment com. 1994—96, co-chmn. gen. reconstruction subcom. 1995, ultrasonic lipectomy task force 1995—96, task force for outcomes and guidelines 1995—98, devices and tech. com. 1995—98, chmn. instrnl. com. 1999—2002, chmn. edn. com. 1999—, chmn. resource book com.), Aesculapian Club, Sigma Xi. Avocations: reading, golf, gardening, sports. Home: 144 Greenwood St Evanston IL 60201-4712

MUTCH, DUANE, state legislator; b. Grand Forks, N.D., May 13, 1925; m. Dolores, 1949; children: Martha, John, Paul. Mem. N.D. Senate, 1959—, chmn. indsl., bus. and labor com., mem. transp. com. Distbr. bulk oil and propane. Mem. Am. Legion, Farm Bur. Office: 711 Terry Ave Larimore ND 58251-4526 Address: PO Box 416 Larimore ND 58251-0416

MUTTI, ALBERT FREDERICK, minister; b. Hopkins, Mo., Feb. 13, 1938; s. Albert Frederick and Phyllis Margaret (Turner) M.; m. Etta Mae McClurg, June 7, 1959; children: Timothy Allen, John Frederick, Martin Kent. AB, Cen. Meth. Coll., 1960; MDiv., Garrett-Evang. Theol. Sem., 1963; DMin., St. Paul Sch. Theology, 1975; DD, Baker U., 1993, Ctrl. Meth. Coll., 2000. Civ pastor Union Star Charge, Mo., 1963-65; sr. pastor Crossroads Parish, Savannah, 1965-74; assoc. coun. dir. Mo. West Conf. UMC, Kansas City, 1974-80, coun. dir., 1980-82; sr. pastor First United Meth. Ch., Blue Springs, Mo., 1982-87; dist. supt. Cen. Dist. UMC, 1987-89; dist. supr. Kansas City N. Dist., 1989-92; bishop Kans. Area United Meth. Ch., Topeka, 1992—. Chair Savannah Cmty. Betterment, 1971; bd. mem. St. Mary's Hosp., Blue Springs, 1986; dir. ARC, Savannah, 1968; bd. Discipleship, Nashville, bd. Global Ministries, N.Y.; pres. Mo. Coun. Chs., Jefferson City, Gen. Commn. on Christian Unity, Dean Mo. Area Ministers Sch., Curator, Ctrl. Meth. Coll.; trustee St. Paul Sch. Theology; organizer Rural, Religion and labor Coun. Kans. Named Disting. Alumni Ctrl. Meth. Coll.; recipient Grad. award St. Paul Sch. Theology. Home: 6841 SW Dunstan Ct Topeka KS 66610-1406 Office: 4201 SW 15th St Topeka KS 66604-2412 E-mail: ksbishumc@mindspring.com.

MUTZENBERGER, MARV, state legislator; m. Barbara; 3 children. Student, Wartburg Coll., Wartburg Sem. Mem. N.D. Ho. of Reps., 1991—, mem. human svcs. com., mem. vet. affairs com., mem. fed. govt. com., mem. judiciary com., mem. nat. resources com.; mem. N.D. Senate, Dist. 32. Prof.; minister. Mem. Social Svc. Bd. Bush fellow. Mem. AARP, Elks, Eagles. Home: 205 E Arbor Ave Apt 112 Bismarck ND 58504-5703

MYERS, ANNE M. developer; Sec., pub. rels. adminstr. Ch. of the Brethren, 1987-97; dir. devel. Timbercrest Retirement Cmty., North Manchester, Ind., 1990—. Office: Timbercrest Retirement Cmty 2201 East St North Manchester IN 46962-9654

MYERS, DANIEL N. lawyer, association executive; b. Independence, Kans., Sept. 17, 1942; s. James Kenneth and Evalyn Clair Petty (Feather) M.; m. Eileen Carruthers, Dec. 14, 1966; children: Yvette Christine, John Joseph. AA, Coffeyville Coll., 1961; BA, U. Okla., 1963; JD, Georgetown U., 1975. Bar: Va. 1976, U.S. Ct. Customs and Patent Appeals 1977, Ill. 1991. Asst. to pres. J.V. Hurson Assoc., Inc., Washington, 1968-74; mgr. fed. legis. affairs AICPA, 1974-77; dir. legis. svcs., assoc. counsel Nat. LP-Gas Assn., Arlington, Va., 1977-79; gen. counsel, v.p. govt. relations Nat. Propane Gas Assn., 1979-88, exec. v.p. Lisle, Ill., 1989—. Contbr. articles on good samaritan laws and genealogy to various publs. Bd. dirs. Washington Area State Rels. Group, 1980-82, mem. energy task force White House Conf. on Small Bus., 1980; chmn. good samaritan coaliton hazardous materials Adv. Coun., Washington, 1982-88; mem. motor carrier adv. com. Fed. Hwy. Adminstrn., Washington, 1982-88. Sgt. U.S. Army, 1964-68. Mem. Am. Soc. Assn. Execs. (legal sect. coun. 1980—, chmn. legal sect. 1991-92, bd. dirs. 1991-92), Spl. Indsl. Radio Svc. Assn. (bd. dirs. 1979-88), Indsl. Telecomm. Assn. (bd. dirs. 1995-97), Chgo. Soc. Assn. Execs., Nat. Vol. Firefighters Coun. Found. (bd. dirs. 1995-97). Avocations: golf, genealogy, racquetball, woodworking. Office: 1600 Eisenhower Ln Lisle IL 60532-2167 E-mail: dmyers@npga.org.

MYERS, DON V. state legislator; m. Mary Myers. Rep. dist. 82 State of Kans., 1993—. Republican. Home: 613 N Briarwood Rd Derby KS 67037-2112

MYERS, GARY, public relations executive; BS, U. Mo., 1971. Pres., CEO Morgan & Myers, Jefferson, Wis., 1997—. Recipient Founder award Agrl. Rels. Coun., 1984. Mem. Pub. Rels. Soc. Am., Coun. Pub. Rels. Firms, Nat. Agrl. Mktg. Assn. Office: Morgan & Myers 146 E Milwaukee St Jefferson WI 53549-1696

MYERS, HOWARD SAM, lawyer; b. Bremerhaven, Germany, Sept. 23, 1947; BA, U. N.D., 1969; JD, U. Va., 1972. Bar: Va. 1972, Minn. 1976. Ptnr. Myers Thompson P.A., Mpls., 1976—. Adj. prof. law William Mitchell Coll. Law, 1983-90. Mem. Am. Immigration Lawyers Assn. (pres. 1991-92). Office: Myers Thompson PA 123 3rd Ave S Ste 603 Minneapolis MN 55401-2522

MYERS, JOHN JOSEPH, bishop; b. Ottawa, Ill., July 26, 1941; s. M.W. and Margaret Louise (Donahue) M. BA maxima cum laude, Loras Coll., 1963; Licentiate in Sacred Theology, Gregorian U., Rome, 1967; Doctor of Canon Law, Cath. U. Am., 1977; DD (hon.), Apostolic See, Vatican City, 1987. Ordained priest Roman Cath. Ch., 1966, bishop, 1987. Asst. pastor Holy Family Parish, Peoria, Ill., 1967-70; asst. dept. internat. affairs U.S. Cath. Conf., Washington, 1970-71; asst. pastor St. Matthew Parish, Champaign, Ill., 1971-74; vice chancellor Cath. Diocese Peoria, 1977-78, vocation dir., 1977-87, chancellor, 1978-87, vicar gen., 1982-90, co-adjutor bishop, 1987-90; bishop of Peoria, 1990—. Bd. govs. Canon Law Soc. Am., Washington, 1985-87; bd. dirs. Nat. Cath. Bio Ethics Ctr., Boston, 1999—; mem. sem. com. Mt. St. Mary's Sem., Md., 1989-94; bd. trustees Cath. U. Am., Washington, 1999—. Author: (commentary) Book V of the Code of Canon Law, 1983; contbr. numerous articles to religious publs. Mem. Canon Law Soc. Am., Nat. Conf. Cath. Bishops. Roman Catholic. Office: Cath Diocese Peoria PO Box 1406 607 NE Madison Ave Peoria IL 61603-3832

MYERS, JON D. state legislator; m. Cheryl Myers; children: Shon, Jerrod, Ashley. BS, Urbana U. City councilman, Lancaster, Ohio; state rep. Dist. 78 Ohio State Congress, state rep. Dist. 6, 1993—. Employee Am. Electric Power, Lancaster. Named Freshman Legislator of Yr., 1992. Mem. Lancaster Law Commn. (chmn.), Friends of Lancaster Parks, Cameo and Cmty. Concerts, C. of C.

MYERS, JUDITH A. state legislator; b. Winamac, Ind., Oct. 29, 1939; m. Mel; 5 children. BS, Purdue U. Mem. Ill. Senate, Springfield, 1997—, mem. agrl. & conservation, exec. appts., local govt. coms. Recipient Athena Woman of Yr. award, 1992, Woman of Distinction award AAUW. Republican. Office: State Capitol Bldg M106 Springfield IL 62706-0001 also: 119 1/2 S Gilbert St Danville IL 61832-6229

MYERS, KENNETH ELLIS, hospital administrator; b. Battle Creek, Mich., Jan. 1, 1932; s. Orlow J. and Kathryn (Brown) M.; m. Nancy Lee Lindgren, June 9, 1956; children— Cynthia Lynn, Anne Lisa, Thomas Scot, Susan Elaine. BBA, U. Mich., 1956, MBA, 1957. Research analyst Bur. Bus. Research, U. Mich., 1956-57; in financial mgmt. Burroughs Corp., Detroit, 1957-66; controller William Beaumont Hosp., Royal Oak, Mich., 1966-68, asso. dir., 1968-69, hosp. dir., 1969-80, exec. v.p., 1976-80, pres., 1981-97; retired. Pres. Trinity Loss Prevention Systems, 1980-81. Elder Bloomfield Hills Christian Ch., 1979-82, Grace Chapel, 1988-92, 95-2000; bd. visitors Oakland Sch. Bus. Adminstrn., 1978-92; mem. adv. bd. Salvation Army, 1985-99; bd. dirs. William Tyndale Coll., 1992—, West Bloomfield Bldg. Authority, 1978—, William Beaumont Hosp., 1971—; trustee St. Mary's Hosp., 1992-97. Mem. Mich. Hosp. Assn. (past chmn.), Vol. Hosps. Am. Enterprises (bd. dirs. 1984-87), Full Gospel Businessmen's Fellowship, Bloomfield Hills Country Club, Belleair Country Club, Old Club, Phi Delta Theta, Beta Gamma Sigma. Home: 6085 Simsbury Ct West Bloomfield MI 48322-3567

MYERS, LONN WILLIAM, lawyer; b. Rockford, Ill., Nov. 14, 1946; s. William H. and Leona V. (Janvrin) M.; m. Janet L. Forbes, May 14, 1968; children: Andrew, Hillary, Corwin. BA, Mich. State U., 1968; MBA, Ind. U., 1973; JD, Harvard U., 1976. Bar: Ill. 1976, U.S. Ct. of Fed. Claims 1977, U.S. Tax Ct. 1977, U.S. Ct. Appeals (7th cir.) 1977. Ptnr. McDermott, Will & Emery, Chgo., 1976—. Served to maj. USAR, 1968-80. Mem. ABA (capital recovery and leasing com. tax sect., tax exempt fin. com. tax sect.). Episcopalian. Home: 1711 Highland Ter Glenview IL 60025-2284 Office: McDermott Will & Emery 227 W Monroe St Chicago IL 60606-5096

MYERS, MARY KATHLEEN, publishing executive; b. Cedar Rapids, Iowa, Aug. 19, 1945; d. Joseph Bernard and Marjorie Helen (Huntsman) Weaver; m. David F. Myers, Dec. 30, 1967; children: Mindy, James. BA in English and Psychology, U. Iowa, 1967. Tchr. Lincoln H.S., Des Moines, 1967-80; editor Perfection Learning Corp., 1980-87, v.p., editor-in-chief, 1987-93; pres., founding ptnr. orgn. to promote Edward de Bono Advanced Practical Thinking Tng., 1992—. Pres. Innova Tng. & Cons., Inc., 2000—. Editor: Six Thinking Hats, 1991, Lateral Thinking, 1993, Direct Attention Thinking Tools, 1997, Total Creativity, 1997. Adv. bd. Sch. Bus., Econs. and Acctg., Simpson Coll., 1998—. Mem. ASTD, Am. Creativity Assn. (bd. dirs. 1997—, pres. 1999), Instrnl. Systems Assn. (v.p. mem. svcs. 2002—). Home: 813 56th St West Des Moines IA 50266-6314 Office: APTT 2882 106th St # 200 Des Moines IA 50322-3771 E-mail: kymers@aptt.com.

MYERS, MINOR, JR. academic administrator, political science educator; b. Akron, Ohio, Aug. 13, 1942; s. Minor and Ruth (Libby) M.; m. Ellen Achin, Mar. 21, 1970; children: Minor III, Joffre V.A. B.A., Carleton Coll., Northfield, Minn., 1964; M.A., Princeton U., 1967, Ph.D., 1972. From instr. to assoc. prof. Conn. Coll., New London, 1968-81, prof. govt., 1981-84; provost, dean of faculty, prof. polit. sci. Hobart and William Smith Colls., Geneva, 1984-89; pres., prof. polit. sci. Ill. Wesleyan U., Bloomington, 1989—. Adv. Numismatic Collection Yale U., 1975-84; chmn. adv. coun. Lyman Allyn Mus., 1976-81, 82-84, pres., 1982-84. Author: Liberty Without Anarchy: A History of the Society of the Cincinnati, 1983, The Insignia of the Society of the Cincinnati, 1998; (with others) Arnold O. Beckman, One Hundred Years of Excellence, 2000, (with others) New London County Furniture, 1974, (with others) The Princeton Graduate School: A History, 1978, 2nd edit., 1997, (with others) American Interiors: A Documentary History from the Colonial Era to 1915, 1980. Asst. sec. gen. Soc. of the Cin., 1983-86, sec.-gen., 1986-89; trustee Inst. for Internat. Edn. Students, 1992-98, Found. for Ind. Higher Edn., 1999—, Nat. Merit Scholarship Corp., 1999-2002; pres. Associated Colls. Ill., 1999-2001. Mem. Grolier Club (N.Y.C.), Princeton Club (N.Y.C.), University Club (Chgo.), Caxton Club (Chgo.), Phi Beta Kappa, Sigma Xi. Office: Ill Wesleyan U PO Box 2900 Bloomington IL 61702-2900

MYERS, PHILLIP SAMUEL, mechanical engineering educator; b. Webber, Kans., May 8, 1916; s. Earl Rufus and Sarah Katharine (Breon) M.; m. Jean Frances Alford, May 26, 1943; children: Katharine Myers Muirhead, Elizabeth Myers Baird, Phyllis Myers Rathbone, John, Mark. BS in Math. and Commerce, McPherson Coll., 1940; BSME, Kans. State Coll., 1942; PhDME, U. Wis., 1947. Registered profl. engr., Wis. Instr. mech. engring. Ind. Tech. Coll., Ft. Wayne, summer 1942; instr. U. Wis., Madison, 1942-47, asst. prof., 1947-50, assoc. prof., 1950-55, prof., 1955-86, emeritus prof., 1986—, chmn. dept. mech. engring., 1979-83. Cons. Diesel Engine Mfrs. Assn., U.S. Army, various oil and ins. cos. Contbr. articles to profl. jours. Chmn. Pine Lake com. W. Wis. Conf. Meth. Ch., 1955-60; Mem. Village Bd., Shorewood Hills, 1962-67. Recipient B.S. Reynolds Teaching award, 1964, McPherson Coll. Alumni citation of merit, 1971; Dugald Clerk award, 1971 Fellow ASME (Diesel Gas Power award 1971, Soichiro Honda award 1993), Soc. Automotive Engrs. (Colwell award 1966, 79, Horning award 1968, nat. pres. 1969, hon. mem.), AAAS; mem. NAE, Am. Soc. for Engring. Edn., Blue Key, Sigma Xi, Phi Kappa Phi, Sigma Tau, Pi Tau Sigma (Gold medal 1949), Tau Beta Pi (Ragnar Onstad Svc. to Soc. award 1978). Mem. Brethren Ch. Achievements include patents in field.

MYERS, PHILLIP WARD, otolaryngologist; b. Evanston, Ill., Nov. 11, 1939; s. R. Maurice and Vivian (Ward) M.; m. Lynetta Sargent, Dec. 22, 1963; children: Andrea, Ward, Alycia, Amanda, Andrew. B.S., Western Ill. U., 1961; M.D., U. Ill., 1965. Diplomate: Am. Bd. Otolaryngology. Intern St. Paul-Ramsey Hosp., 1965-66; resident in otolaryngology U. Louisville, 1966-68; resident Northwestern U., 1968-70, fellow, 1970-71; practice medicine specializing in otolaryngology Springfield, Ill., 1973—; clin. prof. otolaryngology So. Ill. U., 1973—. Served to maj. M.C. AUS, 1971-73. Fellow Am. Soc. for Head and Neck Surgery, Am. Acad. Facial Plastic and Reconstructive Surgery; ACS, Am. Acad. Otolaryngology-Head and Neck Surgery. Achievements include research in perilymphatic fistulas. Home: 3423 N Oak Hill Rd Rochester IL 62563-9273 Office: 331 W Carpenter St Springfield IL 62702-4901

MYERS, RICHARD P. state legislator; Ill. state rep. Dist. 95, 1995—. Office: PO Box 170 331 N Lafayette St Macomb IL 61455-1505

MYERS, WILLIAM, food container manufacturing executive; CFO, treas. Dart Container, Mason, Mich., now treas. Office: Dart Container 500 Hogsback Rd Mason MI 48854-9547

MYERS, WOODROW AUGUSTUS, JR. physician, health care management director; b. Indpls., Feb. 14, 1954; s. Woodrow Augustus Sr. and Charlotte T. (Tyler) M.; m. Debra Jackson, June 23, 1973; children: Kimberly Leilani, Zachary Augustus. BS, Stanford (Calif.) U., 1973, MBA, 1982; MD, Harvard U., 1977. Intern in internal medicine Stanford U. Med. Ctr., 1977-78, resident in internal medicine, 1978-80, fellow, critical care medicine, 1980-81; asst. prof. critical care medicine San Francisco Gen. Hosp., 1982-84; physician health advisor com. on labor and human resources U.S. Senate, Washington, 1984; commr. Ind. Dept. of Health, Indpls., 1985-90; health commr. N.Y.C. Dept. of Health, 1990-91; corp. med. dir. Assoc. Group, Indpls., 1991-95; dir. health care mgmt. Ford Motor Co., Dearborn, Mich., 1996—. Asst. prof. medicine Cornell Med. Coll., N.Y.C., 1990-91; trustee Stanford U., 1987-92; assoc. prof. medicine Ind. U. Sch. Medicine, 1992-95; assoc. clin. prof. medicine Wayne State U., 1997—; adj. assoc. prof. internal medicine U. Mich., 1998—; bd. dirs. Somnus Med. Techs. Bd. dirs. Stanford Health Systems, 1994-97, U. Calif.-San Francisco/Stanford Health Care, 1997; bd. overseers Harvard U., 1996—; mem. Medicare Payment Adv. Commn., 1997—; vice-chmn. vis. com. Harvard Med. Sch., 1997—. Robert Wood Johnson clin. scholar, Stanford U., 1980-82. Fellow ACP; mem. AMA, Inst. Medicine of NAS, Nat. Med. Assn. Office: Ford Motor Co The American Rd WHQ-500 Dearborn MI 48121-1899

MYERSON, ROBERT J. radiation oncologist, educator; b. Boston, May 12, 1947; s. Richard Louis and Rosemarie M.; m. Carla Wheatley, Aug. 8, 1970; 1 child, Jacob Wheatley. BA, Princeton U., 1969; PhD, U. Calif., Berkeley, 1974; MD, U. Miami, 1980. Diplomate Am. Bd. Radiology. Asst. prof. dept. physics Pa. State U., State Coll., 1974-76; fellow Inst. Advanced Studies, Princeton, N.J., 1976-78; resident U. Pa. Hosp., Phila., 1981-84; assoc. prof. radiology Washington U. Sch. Medicine, St. Louis, 1984-97, prof. radiology, 1997—. Contbr. articles to profl. jours. Recipient Career Devel. award Am. Cancer Soc., 1985. Fellow Am. Coll. Radiology; mem. Am. Coll. Radiation, Am. Soc. Therapeutic Radiologists, Am. Phys. Soc. Democrat. Jewish. Avocation: bicycling. Office: Washington U Radiation Oncology Ctr Box 8224 4921 Parkview Pl Saint Louis MO 63110-1001 E-mail: myerson@radonc.wustl.edu.

MYERSON, ROGER BRUCE, economist, game theorist, educator; b. Boston, Mar. 29, 1951; s. Richard L. and Rosemarie (Farkas) M.; m. Regina M. Weber, Aug. 29, 1982; children: Daniel, Rebecca. AB summa cum laude, SM, Harvard U., 1973, PhD, 1976. Asst. prof. decision scis. Northwestern U., Evanston, Ill., 1976-78, assoc. prof., 1979-82, prof., 1982-2001, Harold Stuart prof. decision scis., 1986-2001, prof. econs., 1987-2001; W.C. Norby prof. econs. U. Chgo., 2001—. Guest researcher U. Bielefeld, Federal Republic of Germany, 1978-79; vis. prof. econs. U. Chgo., 1985-86, 2000-01. Author: Game Theory: Analysis of Conflict, 1991; mem. editorial bd. Internat. Jour. Game Theory, 1982-92, Games and Econ. Behavior, 1988-97; assoc. editor Jour. Econ. Theory, 1983-93; also articles. Guggenheim fellow, 1983-84; Sloan rsch. fellow, 1984-86. Fellow Econometric Soc., Am. Acad. Arts and Scis. (Midwest v.p. 1999-2002). Office: U Chgo Dept Econs 1126 E 59th St Chicago IL 60637

MYHAND, WANDA RESHEL, paralegal, legal assistant; b. Detroit, Aug. 15, 1963; d. Ralph and Geraldine (Leavell) M. Office mgr./adminstrv. asst. Gregory Terrell & Co., CPA, Detroit, 1987-90; legal sec. Ford Motor Co., 1990-91; office mgr. M.G. Christian Builders, Inc., 1991; paralegal, legal asst. Law Office of Karri Mitchell, 1991-98; legal sec., paralegal The KPM Group, Southfield, Mich., 1998—. Vol. UNCF Telethon Detroit, 1988. Mem. NAFE. Avocations: crossword puzzles, travel, theatre and concerts.

MYKLEBY, KATHY, newscaster, reporter; Degree, U. Iowa, 1976. With KRNA-FM Radio, Iowa City, 1976, WKY-Radio, Oklahoma City, 1976—80, WVTV-TV Channel 18, Milw., 1980; reporter, anchor WISN, 1980—. Active telethon Children's Miracle Network; co-chmn. Briggs and Stratton Run/Walk for Children's Hosp. of Wis. Recipient Regional award for best TV feature, UP Internat., 1984, Best Single Report Contbg. to Cmty. Welfare award, Milw. Press Club, 1987, Press Club award, 1992, Best Spot News award, Wis. Broadcasters Assn., 1997. Office: WISN PO Box 402 Milwaukee WI 53201-0402

MYRA, HAROLD LAWRENCE, publisher; b. Camden, N.J., July 19, 1939; s. John Samuel and Esther (Christensen) M.; m. Jeanette Austin, May 7, 1966; children: Michelle, Todd, Gregory, Rick, Joshua, Lindsey. B.S., East Stroudsburg State Coll., 1961; Litt.D., John Wesley Coll., 1976; D.Lit., Biola U., 1984; DLitt, Gordon Coll., 1992. Tchr. Pocono Mountain Jointure, Cresco, Pa., 1961; editorial asst. Youth for Christ Internat., Wheaton, Ill., 1961-62, asso. editor, 1962-64, mng. editor, 1964-65, dir. of lit., 1965-66; v.p. lit. div., pub. Campus Life, Wheaton, 1966-75; pres., chief exec. officer Christianity Today, Inc., Carol Stream, Ill., 1975—. Author: No Man in Eden, 1969, Michelle, You Scallawag, I Love You, 1972, The New You, 1972, The Carpenter, 1972, Elsbeth, 1975, Is There a Place I Can Scream?, 1976, Santa, Are You For Real?, 1979, Love Notes to Jeanette, 1979, The Choice, 1980, Halloween, 1982, Your Super-Terrific Birthday, 1985, Living By God's Surprises, 1988, Children in the Night, 1991, The Shining Face, 1993, Morning Child, 1994, Surprised by Children, 2001. Presbyterian. Home: 1737 Marion Ct Wheaton IL 60187-3319 Office: Christianity Today 465 Gundersen Dr Carol Stream IL 60188-2498

MYRDAL, ROSEMARIE CARYLE, state official, former state legislator; b. Minot, N.D., May 20, 1929; d. Harry Dirk and Olga Jean (Dragge) Lohse; m. B. John Myrdal, June 21, 1952; children: Jan, Mark, Harold, Paul, Amy. BS, N.D. State U., 1951. Registered profl. first grade tchr., N.D. Tchr., N.D., 1951-71; bus. mgr. Edinburg Sch. Dist., 1974-81; mem. N.D. Ho. of Reps., Bismarck, 1984-92, mem. appropriations com., 1991-92; lt. gov., State of N.D., Bismarck, 1992—. Sch. evaluator Walsh County Sch. Bds. Assn., Grafton, N.D., 1983-84; evaluator, work presenter N.D. Sch. Bds. Assn., Bismarck, 1983-84; mem. sch. bd. Edinburg Sch. Dist., 1981-90; adv. com. Red River Trade Corridor, Inc., 1989—. Co-editor: Heritage '76, 1976, Heritage '89, 1989. Precinct committeewoman Gardar Twp. Rep. Com., 1980-86; leader Hummingbirds 4-H Club, Edinburg, 1980-83; bd. dirs. Camp Sioux Diabetic Children, Grand Forks, N.D., 1980-90, N.D. affiliate Am. Diabetes Assn., Families First-Child Welfare Reform Initiative, Region IV, 1989-92; dir. N.D. Diabetes Assn., 1989-91; chmn. N.D. Ednl. TelecommunicationsCoun., 1989-90; vice chmn. N.D. Legis. Interim Jobs Devel. Commn., 1989-90. Mem. AAUW (pres. 1982-84 Pembina County area), Pembina County Hist. Soc. (historian 1976-84), Northeastern N.D. Heritage Assn. (pres. 1986-92), Red River Valley Heritage Soc. (bd. dirs. 1985-92). Lutheran. Club: Agassiz Garden

(Park River) (pres. 1968-69). Avocations: gardening, architectural history, ethnic foods, historic/cultural preservation. Office: 600 E Boulevard Ave Bismarck ND 58505-0660 Home: 12987 80th St NE Edinburg ND 58227-9635*

NAADEN, PETE, former state legislator; m. Mary Ellen; 12 children. farmer, rancher. City councilman; mem. N.D. Senate, 1973—, vice chm. appropriations com. Mem. Lions Club, Farm Bur., N.D. Pork Producers, N.D. Stockman's Assn. Home: PO Box 53 Braddock ND 58524-0053

NABEL, GARY J. internal medicine and biological chemistry educator; BA in Biochemistry magna cum laude, Harvard Coll., 1975; PhD in Cell and Devel. Biology, Harvard U., 1980, MD, 1982. Instr. biology Harvard U., Boston, 1980-81, resident tutor in biology, 1980-83, clin. fellow medicine, 1983-85; intern and resident in internal medicine Brigham and Women's Hosp., 1983-85; instr. Harvard med. Sch., 1984-87; assoc. Howard Hughes Med. Inst., Whitehead Inst., MIT, Lab. David Baltimore, 1985-87; assoc. physician Brigham and Women's Hosp., 1985-87; asst. prof. internal medicine and biol. chemistry U. Mich., Ann Arbor, 1987-90, asst. investigator Howard Hughes Med. Inst., 1987-91, assoc. prof. internal medicine and biol. chemistry, 1990-93, assoc. investigator Howard Hughes Med. Inst., 1991-94, prof. internal medicine and biol. chemistry, 1993—, investigator Howard Hughes Med. Inst., 1994—, Henry Sewall prof., 1995—. Mem. AIDS rsch. adv. com. Nat. Inst. Allergy and Infectious Diseases, NIH. Contbr. articles to profl. jours. Fellow Dana-Farber Cancer Inst., Harvard U., 1980-84; Harvard Nat. scholar, 1971-75, Harvard Grad. Nat. scholar, 1976-82; recipient Mallinkrodt Book prize, 1975, James Tolbert Shipley prize for rsch. Harvard Med. Sch., 1982, Ofcl. citation Conn. State Gen. Assembly for Contbns. to Human Gene Therapy, 1992, Young Investigator award Midwest Am. Fedn. for Clin. Rsch., 1992, Amgen award Am. Soc. Biochemistry and Molecular Biology, 1996. Mem. Am. Soc. Clin. Investigation, Assn. Am. Physicians. Office: Univ Mich 4520 MSRBI 1150 W Medical Center Dr Ann Arbor MI 48109-0726

NACLERIO, ROBERT MICHAEL, otolaryngologist, educator; b. N.Y.C., Mar. 30, 1950; s. Albert Paul and Lee Ann (Rabinowitz) N.; m. Sharon Ann Silhan, Mar. 30, 1983; children: Jessica, Daniel. BA, Cornell U., 1972; MD with honors, Baylor U., 1976. Diplomate Am. Bd. Otolaryngology. Intern in surgery Johns Hopkins Hosp., Balt., 1976-77, resident in surgery, 1977-78; resident in otolaryngology Baylor Coll. Medicine, Houston, 1978-80, chief resident in otolaryngology, 1982-83; fellow in clin. immunology divsn. Johns Hopkins U. Sch. Medicine, Balt., 1980-82, asst. prof. medicine and otolaryngology, 1983-87, asst. prof. pediat., 1986-87, dir. divsn. pediat. otolaryngology, 1986-94, assoc. prof. otolargyngology, medicine and pediat., 1987-92, prof. otolaryngology, medicine and pediat., 1992-94; chief of otolaryngology, head and neck surgery U. Chgo., Chgo., 1994—. Cons. Richardson-Vicks Inc., 1986-89, 90, NIH, 1987, Proctor & Gamble, 1987, 94, Sandoz Rsch. Inst., 1988, Schering Rsch., 1988, Wallace Labs., 1989, Joint Rhinologic Conf., 1989, Internat. Congress Rhinology, 1991, Norwich-Eaton Pharm. Inc., 1991-92, Ciba-Geigy Corp., 1991-92, Mktg. Corp. Am., 1993—, Astra, others; mem. med. bd. Children's Ctr., 1991-94, other local comms.; reviewer Am. Jour. Rhinology, others; lectr. in field. Editor: Rhinoconjuctivitis: New Perspectives in Topical Treatment, 1988; asst. editor: Am. Jour. Rhinology, 1986—, Rhinology, 1988—; mem. editl. bd. Otolaryngology-Head and Neck Surgery, 1990-97, Laryngoscope, 1990—, Jour. Allergy and Clin. Immunology, 1992-97; contbr. numerous chpts. to books, papers and abstracts to profl. jours. and procs. Fellow ACS, Am. Acad. Otolaryngology-Head and Neck Surgery (mem. com. 1985-90, 90-92, subcom. 1987-92), Am. Laryngol., Rhinol. and Otol. Soc., Inc.; mem. Am. Acad. Allergy and Immunology (mem. com. 1983-88, 88-89, 88-95, chmn. com. 1990-91, 91—, Jerome Glazer Meml. lectureship), Am. Fedn. Clin. Rsch., Am. Soc. Pediat. Otolaryngology (mem. rsch. com. 1990-94, chmn. subcom. 1990), Soc. Univ. Otolaryngologists-Head and Neck Surgeons, Pan-Am. Assn. Otorhinolaryngology, Internat. Symposium on Infection and Allergy of the Nose (v.p.). Office: U Chgo Section of O-HNS 5841 S Maryland Ave # 1035 Chicago IL 60637-1463 E-mail: rnacleri@surgery.bsd.uchicago.edu.

NADEAU, STEVEN C. lawyer; b. Schenectady, N.Y., July 6, 1954; AB magna cum laude, Boston Coll., 1974, JD cum laude, 1977. Bar: Mich. 1977. Mediator Wayne County Cir. Ct., 1983-88; mem. Honigman Miller Schwartz and Cohn, Detroit. Coord. dir. Sediment Mgmt. Work Group, 1998—. Mem. ABA (sect. natural resources), State Bar Mich. (sect. environ. law), Detroit Bar Assn. Office: Honigman Miller Schwartz and Cohn 660 Woodward Ave Ste 2290 Detroit MI 48226-3506 E-mail: snadeau@honigman.com.

NADER, ROBERT ALEXANDER, judge, lawyer; b. Warren, Ohio, Mar. 31, 1928; s. Nassef J. and Emily (Nader) N.; m. Nancy M. Veauthier. B.A., Western Res. U., 1950, LL.B., 1953. Bar: Ohio 1953. Ptnr. Paul G. Nader, Warren, 1953-83. Pres. Warren City Police and Fire Pension Bds., 1960-66; trustee Office Econ. Opportunity, 1970-72; mem. Warren City Coun., 1960-66, pres. pro tem, 1964-66; mem. Ohio Ho. of Reps., 1971-83, chmn. reference com., 1977-81, chmn. judiciary com., 1981-83; presiding judge Trumbull County Ct. Common Pleas, 1983-91; judge Ohio 11th Dist. Ct. Appeals, 1991—; trustee Family Svc. Assn., 1959-65. With AUS, 1946-48. Recipient Outstanding Young Man of Yr. award, 1964, award Am. Arbitration Assn., 1965, Community Action award Warren Area Bd. Realtors, 1967, Outstanding Svc. award Kent State U., Trumbull campus. 1978, Outstanding Svc. award Children's Rehab. Ctr., 1980; named to Warren High Sch. Disting. Alumni Hall of Fame, 1993. Mem. Ohio State Bar Assn., Trumbull County Bar Assn. (past pres.), Ct. Appeals Judges Assn. (chmn. legis. com. 1995-98), Trumbull County Law Libr. Assn. (trustee 1958-72), Trumbull New Theatre (past pres.), KC, Elks, Lambda Chi Alpha. Roman Catholic. Home: 798 Wildwood Dr NE Warren OH 44483-4458 Office: 11th Dist Ct # Appeals 111 High St NE Warren OH 44481

NADLER, MYRON JAY, lawyer, director; b. Youngstown, Ohio, July 22, 1923; s. Murray A. and Jean (Davis) N.; m. Alice Blue, Nov. 4, 1951; children: Jed M., Wendy D., John M.S. Student, N.Mex. State Coll., 1943-44; BS in Econs. Wharton Sch., U. Pa., 1947; JD with distinction, U. Mich., 1949. Bar: Ohio 1950. Pres., shareholder Nadler, Nadler & Burdman Co., L.P.A., Youngstown, 1950-95, pres., 1950-95; ret., 1996. Asst. editor Mich. Law Rev., 1949; instr. Youngstown U. Law Sch., 1952-59. Author: (with Saul Nadler) Nadler on Bankruptcy, 1965, April's Bankruptcy Forms and Practice, 1964; contbr. articles to profl. jours. Chmn. exec. budget com. United Appeal, Youngstown, 1964-66, v.p., 1967-70; co-chmn. Mayor's Commn. Human Rights, 1957; mem. Mahoning County Planning Commn., 1965-71, Nat. Budget and Consultation Com., 1967-70; trustee Cmty. Corp., Youngstown, v.p., 1977-82, chmn. pers. com., 1974-92; bd. dirs. Ctr. for Learning, Villa Maria, Pa., 1969-95, pres., 1981-89, chmn. bd., 1989-94. With AUS, 1943-45. Decorated Purple Heart with oak leaf cluster. Mem. Fellows of Ohio Bar Assn. Found., ABA, Ohio Bar Assn., Mahoning County Bar Assn., Scribes Assn. Legal Writers, Comml. Law League Am., Squaw Creek Country Club (pres. 1966-68), Hamlet Country Club. Clubs: Squaw Creek Country (pres. 1966-68); Hamlet Country Home: 601 Pine Lake Dr Delray Beach FL 33445-9042 also: 4326 Creekside Blvd Vienna OH 44473 Office: 20 Federal Plz W Ste 600 Youngstown OH 44503-1423

NAEGELE, JR. ROBERT O. professional sports team executive; m. Ellis Naegele; 4 children. BA in Sociology, Dartmouth Coll., 1961. Chmn. Naegele Comms., Inc.; ptnr. Rollerblade, Inc., 1985—95, chmn., 1995; chmn. Minn. Wild Minn. Hockey Ventures Group, St. Paul, 1997—. Mem.: Inline Skating Assn. (exec. com.), St. Paul Area C. of C. (chmn. bd. dirs.). Office: 317 Washington St Saint Paul MN 55102

NAEGER, PATRICK A. state legislator; Mem. dist. 155 Mo. Ho. of Reps. Office: 1083 Pcr 906 Perryville MO 63775-6141

NAFZIGER, ESTEL WAYNE, economics educator; b. Bloomington, Ill., Aug. 14, 1938; s. Orrin and Beatrice Mae (Slabaugh) N.; m. Elfrieda Nettie Toews, Aug. 20, 1966; children: Brian Wayne, Kevin Jon. B.A., Goshen Coll., 1960; M.A., U. Mich., 1962; Ph.D., U. Ill., 1967. Rsch. assoc. Econ. Devel. Inst., Enugu, Nigeria, 1964-65; asst. prof. Kans. State U., Manhattan, 1966-73, assoc. prof., 1973-78, prof., 1978-99, univ. disting. prof., 1999—; Fulbright prof. Andhra U., Waltair, India, 1970-71; fellow East West Ctr., Honolulu, 1972-73. Vis. scholar Cambridge U., 1976; vis. prof. Internat. U. Japan, Yamato-machi, 1983; external rsch. fellow World Acad. Devel. and Coop., College Park, Md., 1984-85; Indo-Am. Found. scholar Andura U., Waltair, India, 1993; World Inst. for Devel. Econ. Rsch., UN Univ., Helsinki, Finland, 1996-98. Author: African Capitalism, 1977, Class, Caste and Entrepreneurship, 1978, (with others) Development Theory, 1979, Economics of Political Instability, 1983, Economics of Developing Countries, 1984, 2d edit., 1990, 3d edit., 1997, Entrepreneurship Equity and Economic Development, 1986, Inequality in Africa, 1988 (named one of Outstanding Acad. Books, Choice 1989-90), The Debt Crisis in Africa, 1993, Poverty and Wealth, 1994, Learning From the Japanese, 1995, Fathers, Sons, and Daughters: Industrial Entrepreneurs under India's Liberalization, 1998; co-editor: War, Hunger, and Displacement, 2 vols., 2000, Prevention of Humanitarian Emergencies, 2002. Sec. bd. overseers Hesston Coll., Kans., 1980-85; chmn. Lou Douglas Lecture Series, 1984-91, 92-93; pres. faculty senate Kans. State U., 1990-92. Recipient Honor Lectr. award Mid Am. State U.'s Assn., 1984-85; grantee Social Sci. Found., 1969 Mem. Am. Econ. Assn., AAUP (pres. chpt. 1981-82), African Studies Assn., Assn. Comparative Econ. Studies, Omicron Delta Epsilon (hon.), Phi Kappa Phi (hon.) Democrat Avocations: reading; running. Home: 1919 Bluestem Ter # 785 Manhattan KS 66502-4508 Office: Kans State U Dept Econs Waters Hall Manhattan KS 66506-4001

NAGEL, SIDNEY ROBERT, physics educator; b. N.Y.C., Sept. 28, 1948; s. Ernest and Edith (Haggstrom) N. BA, Columbia U., 1969; MA, Princeton U., 1972, PhD, 1974. Rsch. assoc. Brown U., Providence, 1974-76; asst. prof. physics U. Chgo., 1976-81, assoc. prof., 1981-84, prof., 1984—, assoc. dean divsn. phy. scis., 1997-2000, Louis Block prof., 1998-2000, assoc. dean divsn. phy. scis., 1997-2000, Stein-Freiler disting. svc. prof., 2001—. Contbr. articles to profl. jours. Recipient Klopsteg Meml. Lecture award Am. Assn. Physics Tchrs., 1998; Alfred Sloan Found. fellow, 1978-82. Fellow AAAS, Am. Phys. Soc. (Oliver E. Buckley prize 1999), Am. Acad. Arts and Scis. Home: 4919 S Blackstone Ave Chicago IL 60615-3003 Office: U Chgo 5640 S Ellis Ave Chicago IL 60637-1433

NAGIN, LAWRENCE M. lawyer; b. 1941; married. BA, U. So. Calif., 1962; JD, U. Calif., Hastings, 1965. Dep. pub. defender Pub. Defender's Office, 1966-68; pvt. practice law Beverly Hills, Calif., 1968-74; spl. counsel aviation matters City Atty's. Officer, L.A., 1974-76; sr. asst. city atty. L.A. Dept. of Airports, 1976; formerly v.p. Flying Tiger Line, Inc., L.A., sr. v.p., gen. counsel adminstrn., from 1984; exec. v.p. corp. affairs, gen. counsel United Airlines, Inc. (UAL Corp.), Elk Grove Village, Ill., 1990-96, U.S. Airways Inc., Arlington, Va., 1996—. Office: US Airways Inc 2345 Crystal Dr Arlington VA 22227-0001

NAGLICK, ROBERT A. automotive suppliers holding company executive; BSBA, Wayne State U.; MS in Fin., Walsh Coll. CPA. Divsn. cost devel. and pricing mgr. United Techs. Automotive; divsn. contr. Lear Siegler Corp.; dir. ops. fin. ASC Inc.; CFO ASC Exterior Techs., Bingham Farms, Mich., 2000—. Office: Ste 401 30400 Telegraph Rd Bingham Farms MI 48025 Office Fax: 248-723-5536.

NAGORSKE, LYNN A. bank executive; Pres., CEO TCF Nat. Bank Minn., Mpls., 1997—. Office: TCF Nat Bank 801 Marquette Ave Minneapolis MN 55402-3475

NAGY, LOUIS LEONARD, engineering executive, researcher; b. Detroit, Jan. 15, 1942; s. Alex and Helen Nagy; m. Dianna M. Skarjune, Aug. 5, 1961; children: Tammy, Kimberly, Kristine, Amanda. BSEE, U. Mich., Dearborn, 1965; MSEE, U. Mich., Ann Arbor, 1969, PhDEE, 1974. Registered profl. engr. Rsch. engr. U. Mich., Ann Arbor, 1962-69; staff rsch. engr. GM R & D Ctr., Warren, Mich., 1969-98; sr. staff rsch. engr. Delphi Rsch. Labs., 1999—. Contbr. articles to profl. jours.; patentee in field. Bd. dirs. Convergence Ednl. Found., Birmingham, Mich., 1990-97, Convergence Transp. Electronics Assn., Birmingham, 1990-97. Recipient 1998 R&D 100 award R&D Mag. Fellow IEEE; mem. Convergence Fellowship (bd. dirs. 1988-96), Vehicular Tech. Soc. (Spl. Recognition award 1979, Avant Garde award 1986, Paper of Yr. 1975), Soc. Automotive Engrs., Tau Beta Pi, Eta Kappa Nu. Avocations: electronics, antennas, radar, automotive radar, microwaves. Office: Delphi Rsch Labs MC 483-478-105 51786 Shelby Pkwy Shelby Township MI 48315

NAHAT, DENNIS F. artistic director, choreographer; b. Detroit, Feb. 20, 1946; s. Fred H. and Linda M. (Haddad) N. Hon. degree, Juilliard Sch. Music, 1965. Prin. dancer Joffrey Ballet, N.Y.C., 1965-66; prin. dancer Am. Ballet Theatre, 1968-79; co-founder Cleve. Ballet, 1976, Sch. of Cleve. Ballet, 1972; founder, artistic dir. San Jose Cleve. Ballet, 1985, Sch. Cleve. San Jose Ballet, 1996; founder New Sch. of Cleve. San Jose Ballet, 1996—. Co-chair Artists Round Table Dance USA, 1991; trustee Cecchetti Coun. Am., 1991; mem. adv. bd. Ohio Dance Regional Dance Am. Prin. performer Broadway show Sweet Charity, 1966-67; choreographer Two Gentlemen of Verona (Tony award 1972), 1969-70; (ballet) Celebrations and Ode (resolution award 1985), 1985, Green Table, Three Virgins and a Devil (Isadora Duncan award 1985); conceived, directed, choreographed Blue Suede Shoes, PBS, 1997-98. Grantee Nat. Endowment Arts, 1978, Andrew Mellow Found., 1985; recipient Outstanding Achievement award Am. Dance Guild, 1995, 96, 2000—. Avocation: master chef. Office: Cleve San Jose Ballet 3615 Euclid Ave Ste 1A Cleveland OH 44115-2527 also: Cleve San Jose Ballet PO Box 1666 San Jose CA 95109-1666 also: San Jose Cleve Ballet 40 N 1st St San Jose CA 95113-1200

NAHRWOLD, DAVID LANGE, surgeon, educator; b. St. Louis, Dec. 21, 1935; s. Elmer William and Magdalen Louise (Lange) N.; m. Carolyn Louise Hoffman, June 14, 1958; children: Stephen Michael, Susan Alane, Thomas James, Anne Elizabeth. AB, Ind. U., 1957, MD, 1960. Diplomate Am. Bd. Surgery, Am. Bd. Thoracic Surgery. Intern, then resident in surgery Ind. U. Med. Ctr., Indpls., 1960-65; postdoctoral scholar in gastrointestinal physiology VA Ctr., UCLA, 1965; asst. prof. surgery Ind. U. Med. Sch., 1968-70; assoc. prof. Coll. Medicine Pa. State U., 1970-73; vice-chmn. dept. surgery Pa. State U., 1971-82, assoc. provost, dean health affairs, 1981-82, prof., chief divsn. gen. surgery, 1974-82; Loyal and Edith Davis prof., chmn. dept. surgery Northwestern U. Med. Sch., Chgo., 1982-97; surgeon-in-chief Northwestern Meml. Hosp., 1982-97; pres., CEO Northwestern Med. Faculty Found., Inc., 1996-99; prof. surgery, exec. assoc. dean clin. affairs Northwestern U. Med. Sch., 1997-99, prof. emeritus, 1999—. Mem. Nat. Digestive Disease Adv. Bd., 1985—89; bd. dirs. Am. Bd. Surgery, vice chmn., 1994—95, chmn., 1995—96; bd. dirs. Northwestern Healthcare Network; mem. exec. bd. Am. Bd. Med. Splty., 1997—, pres., 2002—; mem. exec. com. Accreditation Coun. for Grad. Med. Edn., 1999—2000. Editor emeritus Jour. Laparoendoscopic Surgery, 1997—; mem. editl. bd. Surgery, 1981-94, Archives of Surgery, 1983-93, Digestive Surgery, 1986-99, Am. Jour. Surgery, 1994-2000, Jour. Gastrointestinal Surgery, 1996-2000, Current Opinion in Gen. Surgery, Jour. Lithotripsy and Stone Disease, 1988-92; contbr. articles to profl. jours. With M.C., U.S. Army, 1966-68. Fellow: ACS (bd. govs. 1992—98, vice chmn. 1994—96, chmn. bd. govs. exec. com. 1996—98, interim dir. 1999—2000, bd. regents, Disting. Svc. award 2001), Philippine Coll. Surgeons (hon.); mem.: AMA, Chgo. Surg. Soc. (pres. 1993—94), Chgo. Med. Soc., We. Surg. Assn., Soc. Univ. Surgeons, Soc. Surgery Alimentary Tract 1989—90, (trustee), Soc. Clin. Surgery (sec. 1984—88), Internat. Biliary Assn., Ill. Surg. Soc., Ill. State Med. Soc., Internat. Fedn. Surg. Colls. (hon.; treas. 1999—2002), Gastroenterology Rsch. Group, Collegium Internat. Chirurgiae Digestive (pres. U.S. chpt. 1988—90), Ctrl. Surg. Assn. (sec. 1994—97, pres.-elect 1997—98, pres. 1998—99, pres. Found. 2002—), Assn. Surg. Edn., Assn. Acad. Surgery, Am. Surg. Assn. (2d v.p. 1993—94), Am. Phys. Soc., Alpha Omega Alpha, Sigma Xi. Office: Dept Surgery Galter 10-105 251 E Huron St Chicago IL 60611-2908 E-mail: dnahrwol@nmh.org.

NAIMARK, ARNOLD, medical educator, physiologist, educator; b. Winnipeg, Man., Can., Aug. 24, 1933; s. Harvey and Lisa N.; m. Barbara Jean Alder, Feb. 28, 1960; children: David, Mila. MD, BSc in Medicine, U. Man., 1957, MSc, 1960; postgrad., U. London, 1962-63, U. Calif., 1960-62; LLD (hon.), Mt. Allison U., 1986, U. Toronto, 1997. Registrar in medicine Hammersmith Hosp., London, 1962-63; asst. prof. physiology U. Man., 1963-64, assoc. prof., 1965-66, prof., 1967-71, acting head dept. physiology, 1966-67, head dept., 1967-71, dean Faculty Medicine, 1971-81, pres. and vice chancellor, 1981-96, prof. medicine and physiology, 1971—, dir. Ctr. for Advancement Medicine, 1996—. Dir. Health Scis. Ctr., 1971-99; cons. to govt. agys. and founds.; chmn. Can. Health Svcs. Rsch. Found., Can. Biotech. Adv. Com.; dir. Can. Imperial Bank of Commerce, Urban Idea Ctr., Inspiraplex Ltd.; mem. adv. coun. Order of Can., 1988-89; v.p., Can., Inter-Am. Orgn. for Higher Edn., 1993-95. Contbr. articles to profl. jours. Mem. nat. hon. bd. dirs. Juvenile Diabetes Fedn. Internat. Can. Lt. Royal Can. Arty., 1950-53. Decorated officer Order of Can.; recipient Queen Elizabeth Silver Jubilee medal; Symons medal Commonwealth Univs.; medal in physiology U. Man., 1955; Stefansson Meml. prize, 1957; Prowse prize in clin. rsch., 1959; Isbister scholar, 1950-53, 54-56 Fellow Royal Coll. Physicians, AAAS, Royal Soc. Can. (G. Malcolm Brown award 1987, com. univ. rsch. 1989-91); mem. Can. Med. Assn., Can. Physiol. Soc., Am. Physiol. Soc., Can. Soc. Clin. Investigation, Med. Rsch. Soc. Gt. BRit., Assn. Chairmen Depts. Physiology, Can. Tb and Respiratory Disease Assn., Assn. Commmonwealth Univs. (coun. 1985-91), Assn. Univs. and Colls. Can. (pres. 1986-88), Am. Heart Assn., Assn. Commonwealth Univs. (chmn. 1988), Can. Soc. for Acad. Medicine. Office: U Man Ctr for Adv Medicine 730 William Ave Ste 230 Winnipeg MB Canada R3E 3J7

NAIR, RAGHAVAN D. accountant, educator; b. Dehradun, United Provinces, India, Oct. 23, 1951; came to U.S., 1973; s. Keshavan R. and Parvati Nair; m. Ruth Marie Nair, 1976; 1 child, Andrea. BA, U. Madras, India, 1970, MA, 1972; MBA, U. Mich., 1974, PhD, 1977. CPA, Wis. Prof. U. Wis., Madison, 1978—, sr. assoc. dean acad. affairs Sch. Bus., 1994—, dir. internat. programs, 1996—; faculty fellow Fin. Acctg. Standards Bd., Norwalk, Conn., 1984-86; faculty resident Arthur Andersen & Co., Chgo., 1991—, dir. PhD Program, 1987-90, chmn. dept. acctg., 1991-94; dir. Arthur Andersen Ctr. Fin. Reporting, 1992-93; prof. acctg. and info. systems Price Waterhouse, 1993—; dir. Ctr. Internat. Bus. Edn. and Rsch., Madison, 1998—. Invited speaker various corps., pub. acctg. firms, mgmt. and exec. edn. groups, 1982—. Contbr. articles to profl. jours. Pres. John Muir PTO, Madison, Wis., 1988-89. Recipient Excellence in Teaching award Lawrence J. Larson Sch. Bus., 1992. Mem. AICPA, Parkwood Hills Community Assn. (treas. 1987-89), Am. Acctg. Assn., Wis. Inst. CPAs (Outstanding Educator award 1989), Bascom Hill Soc., Blackhawk Country Club (bd. dirs. 1994-96). Avocations: golf, marathon running.

NAIR, VASU, chemist, educator; BSc in Chemistry with high honors, U. Otago, Dunedin, New Zealand, 1963; PhD, U. Adelaide, Australia, 1966, DSc (hon.), 1991. Rsch. assoc. U. Ill., Urbana, 1967-68; rsch. fellow Harvard U., Cambridge, Mass., 1968-69; from asst. prof. chemistry to assoc. prof. U. Iowa, Iowa City, 1969-79, prof., 1980—, U. Iowa Found. Disting. prof. chemistry, 1993—. Cons. Miles Lab., West Haven, Conn., 1987, Burroughs Wellcome Co., Rsch. Triangle Park, N.C., 1984-96, Nucleotide Chemistry, Integrated DNA Techs., Inc., Iowa City, 1988-93, Nucleoside Chemistry, San Diego, 1988-94, NIH, 1989—, Lipitek Internat., San Antonio, Tex., Gensia Pharms.; dir. U. Iowa HIgh-Field NMR Facility, 1982-86; assoc. chair dept. chemistry U. Iowa, 1991-93, mem. U. Iowa Biosci. Com., 1995—, Faculty Senate, 1996—. Contbr. over 200 articles and abstracts to profl. jours.; speaker in field; patentee: 3 U.S. patents, 2 on antiviral chemicals, 1 on a potential anti-AIDS agent. Recipient Disting. Vis. Scholar award U. Adelaide, Australia, 1987, Sci. medal, Iowa Acad. Scis., numerous rsch. grants and awards. Fellow AAAS; mem. Internat. Soc. Antiviral Rsch., Internat. Soc. Nucleic Acid Chemistry, Am. Soc. Microbiology, Am. Chem. Soc. Office: Univ Iowa Chemistry Dept Iowa City IA 52242

NAIR, VELAYUDHAN, pharmacologist, medical educator; b. India, Dec. 29, 1928; arrived in U.S., 1956, naturalized, 1963; s. Parameswaran and Ammini Nair; m. Jo Ann Burke, Nov. 30, 1957; children: David, Larry, Sharon. Ph.D. in Medicine, U. London, 1956, D.Sc., 1976. Research assoc. U. Ill. Coll. Medicine, 1956-58; asst. prof. U. Chgo. Sch. Medicine, 1958-63; dir. lab. neuropharmacology and biochemistry Michael Reese Hosp. and Med. Center, Chgo., 1963-68, dir. therapeutic research, 1968-71. Vis. assoc. prof. pharmacology FUHS/Chgo. Med. Sch., 1963—68, vis. prof., 1968—71, prof. pharmacology, 1971—, vice chmn. dept. pharmacology and therapeutics, 1971—76, dean Sch. Grad. and Postdoctiral Studies, 1976—, v.p. for rsch., 1999—, disting. prof., 2001; vis. prof. Harvard U., 1994, Johns Hopkins Sch. Medicine, 1995. Contbr. articles to profl. jours. Recipient Morris Parker award, U. Health Scis./Chgo. Med. Sch., 1972. Fellow: AAAS, Am. Coll. Clin. Pharmacology, N.Y. Acad. Scis.; mem.: AAUP, Internat. Soc. Devel. Neurosci., Am. Coll. Toxicology, Internat. Soc. Chronobiology, Soc. Neurosci., Soc. Exptl. Biology & Medicine, Pan Am. Med. Assn. (coun. on toxicology), Royal Inst. Chemistry (London), Brit. Chem. Soc., Am. Chem. Soc., Soc. Toxicology, Radiation Rsch. Soc., Am. Soc. Clin. Pharmacology & Therapeutics, Am. Soc. Pharmacology & Exptl. Therapeutics, Internat. Soc. Biochem. Pharmacology, Internat. Brain Rsch. Orgn., Cosmos Club (Washington), Alpha Omega Alpha, Sigma Xi. Office: FUHS Chgo Med Sch 3333 Green Bay Rd North Chicago IL 60064-3037

NAIRN, RODERICK, immunologist, biochemist, educator; b. Dumbarton, Scotland, Mar. 25, 1951; came to U.S., 1976; s. James Bell and Muriel Elizabeth (Hyde) N.; m. Morag Gilhooly, Dec. 29, 1971; 1 child, Carolyn Mhairi. BS, U. Strathclyde, Glasgow, Scotland, 1973; PhD, U. London, 1976. Postdoctoral fellow Albert Einstein Sch. Medicine, N.Y.C., 1976-81; asst. prof. U. Mich. Med. Sch., Ann Arbor, 1981-87, assoc. prof., 1987-95, dir. student biomed. rsch. programs, 1989-92, dir. med. scientist tng. program, 1992-95; prof., chair dept. med. microbiology and immunology Sch. Medicine, Creighton U., Omaha, 1995—, interim dean, 1997-98, sr. assoc. dean academic affairs, 1998—. Contbr. chpts. to books, articles to profl. jours. Grantee NIH, Am. Cancer Soc. Mem. AAAS, Am. Che. Soc., Soc. for Microbiology, Am. Assn. Immunologists. Presbyterian. Office: Creighton U Sch Medicine Dept Med Microbiology & Immu Omaha NE 68178-0001 E-mail: rnairn@creighton.edu.

NAJARIAN, JOHN SARKIS, surgeon, educator; b. Oakland, Calif., Dec. 22, 1927; s. Garabed L. and Siranoush T. (Demirjian) N.; m. Arlys Viola Mignette Anderson, Apr. 27, 1952; children: Jon, David, Paul, Peter. AB with honors, U. Calif., Berkeley, 1948; MD, U. Calif., San Francisco, 1952; LHD (hon.), Univ. Athens, 1980; DSc (hon.), Gustavus Adolphus Coll., 1981; LHD (hon.), Calif. Luth. Coll., 1983. Diplomate Am. Bd. Surgery. Surg. intern U. Calif., San Francisco, 1952-53, surg. resident, 1955-60, asst. prof. surgery, dir. surg. research labs., chief transplant service dept. surgery, 1963-66, prof., vice chmn., 1966-67; spl. research fellow in immunopathology U. Pitts. Med. Sch., 1960-61; NIH sr. fellow and assoc. in tissue transplantation immunology Scripps Clinic and Research Found., La Jolla, Calif., 1961-63; Markle scholar Acad. Medicine, 1964-69; prof., chmn. dept. surgery U. Minn. Hosp., Mpls., 1967-93; med. dir. Transplant Ctr., clin. chief surgery Univ. Hosp., 1967-94; chief hosp. staff U. Minn. Hosp., Mpls., 1970-71, Regents' prof., 1985-95, Jay Phillips Disting. Chair in Surgery, 1986-95, prof. emeritus, prof. surgery, 1995—. Spl. cons. USPHS, NIH Clin. Rsch. Tng. Com., Inst. Gen. Med. Scis., 1965-69; cons. U.S. Bur. Budget, 1966-68; mem. sci. adv. bd. Nat. Kidney Found., 1968; mem. surg. study sect. A div. rsch. grants NIH, 1970; chmn. renal transplant adv. group VA Hosps., 1971; mem. bd. sci. cons. Sloan-Kettering Inst. Cancer Rsch., 1971-78; mem. screening com. Dernham Postdoctoral Fellowships in Oncology, Calif. div. Am. Cancer Soc. Editor: (with Richard L. Simmons) Transplantation, 1972; co-editor: Manual of Vascular Access, Organ Donation, and Transplantation, 1984; mem. editorial bd. Jour. Surg. Rsch., 1968—, Minn. Medicine, 1968—, Jour. Surg. Oncology, 1968—, Am. Jour. Surgery, 1967—, assoc. editor, 1982—; mem. editorial bd. Year Book of Surgery, 1970-85, Transplantation, 1970—, Transplantation Procs, 1970—, Bd. Clin. Editors, 1981-84, Annals of Surgery, 1972—, World Jour. Surgery, 1976—, Hippocrates, 1986—, Jour. Transplant Coordination, 1990—; assoc. editor: Surgery, 1971; editor-in-chief: Clin. Transplantation, 1986—. Bd. dirs., v.p. Variety Club Heart Hosp., U. Minn.; trustee, v.p. Minn. Med. Found. Served with USAF, 1953-55. Hon. fellow Royal Coll. Surgeons of Eng., 1987; hon. prof. U. Madrid, 1990; named Alumnus of Yr., U. Calif. Med. Sch., San Francisco, 1977; recipient award Calif. Trudeau Soc., 1962, Ann. Brotherhood award NCCJ, 1978, Disting. Achievement award Modern Medicine, 1978, Internat. Gt. Am. award B'nai B'rith Found., 1982, Uncommon Citizen award, 1985, Sir James Carreras award Variety Clubs Internat., 1987, Silver medal IXth Centenary, U. Bologna, 1988, Humanitarian of Yr. award, U. Minn., 1992, Najarian Festschrift award Am. Jour. Surgery, 1993, Jubilee medal Swedish Soc. Medicine, 1994. Fellow ACS; mem. Internat. Pediat. Transplantation Assn. (pres. 1998—), Soc. Univ. Surgeons, Soc. Exptl. Biology and Medicine, AAAS, Am. Soc. Exptl. Pathology, Am. Surg. Assn. (pres. 1988-89), Am. Assn. Immunologists, AMA, Transplantation Soc. (v.p. western hemisphere 1984-86, pres. 1994-96), Am. Soc. Nephrology, Internat. Soc. Nephrology, Am. Assn. Lab. Animal Sci., Assn. Acad. Surgery (pres. 1969), Internat Soc. Surgery, Soc. Surg. Chairmen, Soc. Clin. Surgery, Central Surg. Assn., Minn., Hennepin County med. socs., Mpls., St. Paul, Minn., Howard C. Naffziger, Portland, Halsted surg. socs., Am. Heart Assn., Am. Soc. Transplant Surgeons (pres. 1977-78), Council on Kidney in Cardiovascular Disease, Hagfish Soc., Italian Research Soc., Minn. Acad. Medicine, Minn. Med. Assn., Minn. Med. Found., Surg. Biology Club, Sigma Xi, Alpha Omega Alpha, others. Office: U Minn Surgery Dept Mayo Meml Bldg Box 195 516 Delaware St SE Minneapolis MN 55455-0374

NAJITA, TETSUO, history educator; b. Honokaa, Hawaii, Mar. 30, 1936; s. Niichi and Kikuno (Bamboku) N.; m. Elinor Moon, Aug. 2, 1958; children: Mie Kim, Kiyoshi Young. BA, Grinnell Coll., 1958; MA, Harvard U., 1960, PhD, 1965; LLD, Grinnell Coll., 1989. Asst. prof. Carleton Coll., Northfield, Minn., 1964-66, Wash. Univ., St. Louis, 1966-68; assoc. prof. U. Wis., Madison, 1968-69; Robert S. Ingersoll disting. prof. History/Japanese studies U. Chgo., 1969—, dir. Ctr. for East Asian Studies, 1974-80, assoc. dean, 1983-87, master collegiate div. social scis., 1983-87. John A. Burns disting. visiting chair U. Hawaii, Manoa, 1994; chair dept. history U. Chgo., 1994-97; Ena H. Thompson lectr. Pomona Coll., 1996; Catherine Gould Chism vis. prof. U. Puget Sound, Tacoma; Maruyame Masao lectr. U. Calif., Berkeley, 2000. Author: Hara Kei in the Politics of Compromise, 1969 (J.K. Fairbank prize Am. Hist. Assn.), Intellectual Foundations of Modern Japanese Politics, 1974, Visions of Virtue in Tokugawa Japan, 1987, Tokugawa Political Writings, 1998. Recipient Yamagata Banto prize Prefecture of Osaka, 1989; grantee NEH 1973-74, 1980-81; Fulbright fellow 1961-63, 68, Guggenheim fellow 1980-81. Fellow Am. Acad. Arts and Scis.; mem. Am. Hist. Assn., Assn. for Asian Studies (v.p., pres. 1991-93), Phi Beta Kappa. Office: U Chgo Dept History 1126 E 59th St Chicago IL 60637-1580

NAKAJIMA, YASUKO, medical educator; b. Osaka, Japan, Jan. 8, 1932; came to U.S., 1962, 69; m. Shigehiro Nakajima; children: Hikeko H., Gene A. MD, U. Tokyo, 1955, PhD, 1962. Intern U. Tokyo Sch. Medicine, 1955-56, resident, 1956-57, instr., 1962-67; assoc. prof. Purdue U., West Lafayette, Ind., 1969-76, prof., 1976-88; prof. anatomy and cell biology U. Ill. Coll. Medicine, Chgo., 1988—. Vis. rsch. fellow Coll. Physicians and Surgeons, Columbia U., N.Y.C., 1962-64; asst. rsch. anatomist UCLA Sch. Medicine, 1964-65; vis. rsch. fellow Cambridge U., 1967-69; mem. study sect. NIH, 1996-98. Contbr. articles to sci. jours. Fulbright travel grantee, 1962-65; Univ. scholar U. Ill., 1997—. Mem. AAAS, Am. Physiol. Soc., Soc. Neurosci., Am. Soc. Cell Biology, Am. Assn. Anatomists, Biophys. Soc., Marine Biol. Lab. Corp. Office: U Ill Coll Medicine Dept Anatomy m/c 512 808 S Wood St Chicago IL 60612-7300

NAKER, MARY LESLIE, legal firm executive; b. Elgin, Ill., July 6, 1954; d. Robert George and Marilyn Jane (Swain). BS in Edn., No. Ill. U., 1976, MS in Edn., 1978, postgrad., 1980, Coll. Fin. Planning, 1990. Cert. tchr., Ill., fin. paraplanner. Retail sales clk. Fin'n Feather Farm, Dundee, Ill., 1972-75; pvt. practice tchr. South Elgin, 1974-78; tchg. asst. Sch. Dist #13, Bloomingdale, 1976-78, substitute tchr.; office mgr. Tempo 21, Carol Stream, 1978-82, LaGrange, 1982-85; sales coord. K&R Delivery, Hinsdale, 1986-89; fin. planner coord. Elite Adv. Svcs., Inc., Schaumburg, 1989-90; adminstrv. coord. Export Transports, Inc., Elk Grove Village, 1990-98; adminstrn. mgr. SBS Worldwide Chgo. Inc., Bensenville, 1998-99; office adminstr. DiMonte & Lizak, Attys. at Law, Park Ridge, 2000—. Leader Girl Scouts U.S.A., 1972-77, camp counselor, 1972-79. Music Scholar PTA, U. Wis., 1967, PTA, U. Iowa, 1968-69. Mem. Nat. Geographic Soc., Smithsonian Assn. Lutheran. Avocations: ceramics, bowling, knitting, camping, sewing. Home: 2020 Clearwater Way Elgin IL 60123-2588 Office: DiMonte & Lizak 216 Higgins Rd Park Ridge IL 60068-5706

NAMBU, YOICHIRO, physics educator; b. Toyko, Jan. 18, 1921; arrived in U.S., 1952; m. Chieko Hida Nambu, Nov. 3, 1945; 1 child Jun-ichi. Research asst. U. Tokyo, 1945—49; prof. physics Osaka City U., Japan, 1950—56; mem. Inst. Advanced Study, 1952—54; research assoc. U. Chgo., 1954—56, mem. faculty, 1956—, prof. physics, 1958, Disting. prof., 1971—; emeritus, 1991—. Contbr. articles to profl. jours. Recipient J.J. Sakurai prize, Am. Phys. Soc., 1994, Wolf prize in Physics, 1994. Mem.: NAS, Am. Phys. Soc., Am. Acad. Arts and Scis. Office: Univ of Chicago Enrico Fermi Inst 5740 S Ellis Ave Chicago IL 60637-1434

NANAGAS, MARIA TERESITA CRUZ, pediatrician, educator; b. Manila, Jan. 21, 1946; came to U.S., 1970; d. Ambrosio and Maria (Pasamonte) Cruz; m. Victor N. Nanagas, Jr.; children: Victor III, Valerie, Vivian. BS, U. of the Philippines, 1965, MD, 1970. Diplomate Am. Bd. Pediat. Intern, resident St. Elizabeth's Hosp., Boston, 1971-74; fellow in ambulatory pediat. North Shore Children's Hosp., Salem, Mass., 1974-75; active staff medicine Children's Med. Ctr., Dayton, Ohio, 1976—, head divsn. gen. pediat., 1988-90, 95-97, co-interim head ambulatory pediat., 1989-90, med. dir. ambulatory pediat., 1990—. Clin. asst. prof. pediat. Wright State U., Dayton, 1977-83, clin. assoc. prof. pediat., 1983—, selective dir., 1989—, assoc. prof. pediat., 2000—; clin. asst. prof. family practice Wright State U., Dayton, 1999—; dir., preceptor Wright State U. residents continuing clinic Children's Med. Ctr., 1989—, attending physician family practice programs, 1978—. Active Miami Valley Lead Poisoning Prevention Coalition, 19926. Fellow Am. Acad. Pediat.; mem. Western Ohio Pediat. Soc., Ambulatory Pediat. Assn. Office: Children's Med Ctr Health Clinic 1 Childrens Plz Dayton OH 45404-1898

NANNE, LOUIS VINCENT, professional hockey team executive; b. Sault Ste. Marie, Ont., Can., June 2, 1941; s. Michael and Evelyn N.; m. Francine Yvette Potvin, Aug. 27, 1962; children: Michelle, Michael, Marc, Marty. B.S. in Mktg., U. Minn., 1963. Mem. Minn. North Stars hockey club, 1967-78, v.p., gen. mgr., 1978-88, pres., 1988-91; sr. v.p. Piper Capital Mgmt., Mpls., 1991-95; exec. v.p. Voyageur Asset Mgmt., 1995—. Bd. govs. Nat. Hockey League, 1981-91; mem. internat. com. USA Hockey. Bd. dirs. Mpls. C.C. Found., 1986-90, Children's Home Soc., 1998—. Recipient Lester Patrick award NHL, 1989; named among Top 50 Players in 50 Yrs.; inducted into U. Minn. Hall of Fame, U.S. Hockey Heritage Hall of Fame award, Sault St. Marie Hall of Fame, U.S. Hockey Hall of Fame. Mem. Interlachen Country Club (bd. dirs. 1992-95), Spring Hill Golf Club (bd. dirs. 1996—). Roman Catholic. Office: Voyageur Asset Mgmt 90 S 7th St Minneapolis MN 55402-3903

NANNEY, DAVID LEDBETTER, genetics educator; b. Abingdon, Va., Oct. 10, 1925; s. Thomas Grady and Pearl (Ledbetter) N.; m. Jean Kelly, June 15, 1951; children: Douglas Paul, Ruth Elizabeth Beshears. A.B., Okla. Bapt. U., 1946; Ph.D., Ind. U., 1951; Laurea honoris causa, U. Pisa, Italy, 1994. Asst. prof. zoology U. Mich., Ann Arbor, 1951-56, asso. prof., 1956-58; prof. zoology U. Ill., Urbana-Champaign, 1959-76, prof. genetics and devel., 1976-86, prof. ecology, ethology and evolution, 1987-91, prof. emeritus, 1991—. Sr. postdoctoral fellow Calif. Inst. Tech., 1958-59; predoctoral fellow NIH, Ind. U., 1949-51 Author: (with Herbert Stern) The Biology of Cells, 1965, Experimental Ciliatology, 1980. Recipient Disting. Alumnus award Okla. Bapt. U., 1972; named Disting. Lectr. Sch. Life Scis., U. Ill., 1981; Preisträger, Alexander von Humboldt Stiftung, Fed. Republic Germany, 1984. Fellow AAAS, Am. Acad. Arts and Scis.; mem. Genetics Soc. Am., Am. Genetic Assn. (pres. 1982), Soc. Protozoologists. Home: 703 W Indiana Ave Urbana IL 61801-4835 Office: U Ill Dept Animal Biology 505 S Gregory St Urbana IL 61801 E-mail: d-nanney@uiuc.edu.

NAPADENSKY, HYLA SARANE, engineering consultant; b. Chgo., Nov. 12, 1929; d. Morris and Minnie (Litz) Siegel; m. Arnaldo I. Napadensky; children: Lita, Yafa. BS in Math., MS in Math., U. Chgo. Design analysis engineer Internat. Harvester Co., Chgo., 1952-57; dir. rsch. Ill. Inst. Tech. Rsch. Inst., 1957-88; v.p. Napadensky Energetics Inc., Evanston, Ill., 1988-94; engring. cons., Lutsen, Minn., 1994-98. Contbr. numerous articles to profl. jours. Bd. overseers Armour Coll. Engring. Ill. Inst. Tech., 1988-93. Mem. NAE, Sigma Xi. Home and Office: 3284 W Highway 61 Lutsen MN 55612-9537

NAPOLI, WILLIAM BILL, state legislator; Rep. S.D. State Dist. 35. Taxation com. S.D. Ho. Reps., transp. com.; owner Car Mus. Address: 6180 S Highway 79 Rapid City SD 57702-8467

NARAHASHI, TOSHIO, pharmacology educator; b. Fukuoka, Japan, Jan. 30, 1927; arrived in U.S., 1961; s. Asahachi and Itoko (Yamasaki) Ishii; m. Kyoko Narahashi, Apr. 21, 1956; children: Keiko, Taro. BS, U. Tokyo, 1948, PhD, 1960. Instr. U. Tokyo, 1951-65; research assoc. U. Chgo., 1961, asst. prof., 1962, Duke U., Durham, N.C., 1962-63, 65-67, assoc. prof., 1967-69, prof., 1969-77, head pharmacology div., 1970-73, vice chmn. dept. physiology and pharmacology, 1973-75; prof., chmn. dept. pharmacology Northwestern U. Med. Sch., Chgo., 1977-94; Alfred Newton Richards prof. Med. Sch. Northwestern U., 1983—, John Evans prof. Evanston, 1986—. Mem. pharmacology study sect. NIH, 1976-80; mem. rsch. rev. com. Chgo. Heart Assn., 1977-82, vice chmn. rsch. coun., 1986-87, chmn., 1988-90; mem. Nat. Environ. Health Scis. Coun., 1982-86; rev. com. Nat. Inst. Environ. Health Scis., 1991-95. Editor: Cellular Pharmacology of Insecticides and Pheromones, 1979, Cellular and Molecular Neurotoxicology, 1984, Insecticide Action: From Molecule to Organism, 1989, Ion Channels, 1988—; specific field editor Jour. Pharmacology and Exptl. Therapeutics, 1972-97; assoc. editor Neurotoxicology, 1994—; contbr. articles to profl. jours. Recipient Javits Neurosci. Investigator award, NIH, 1986. Fellow AAAS; mem. Am. Soc. for Pharmacology and Exptl. Therapeutics (Otto Krayer award 2000), Am. Physiol. Soc., Soc. for Neurosci., Biophys. Soc. (Cole award 1981), Soc. Toxicology (DuBois award 1988, Merit award 1991, 1st Ann. Disting. Investigator Lifetime Achievement award 2001), Agrochem. Divsn. Am. Chem. Soc. (Burdick L. Jackson Internat. award 1989). Home: 175 E Delaware Pl Apt 7911 Chicago IL 60611-7745 Office: Northwestern U Med Sch Dept Mol Pharmaco Biol Chem 303 E Chicago Ave Chicago IL 60611-3008 E-mail: tna597@northwestern.edu.

NARBER, GREGG ROSS, lawyer; b. Iowa City, Sept. 4, 1946; s. James R. and Marguerite Maxine (Lasher) N.; m. Kathleen Joyce Andriano; children: Joshua Ross, Zachary Edward. BA, Grinnell Coll., 1968; MA, JD, Washington U., St. Louis, 1971. Bar: Iowa 1971, U.S. Ct. Mil. Appeals 1974, U.S. Supreme Ct. 1974. Atty. The Principal Fin. Group, Des Moines, 1975-76, asst. counsel, 1976-80, assoc. counsel, 1980-85, counsel, 1985-89, v.p., gen. counsel, 1989-92, sr. v.p., gen. counsel, 1993—. Bd. dirs. Sargasso Mut. Ins. Co., Bermuda, Ban Renta Co. Seguros de Vida, Chile; prin. Life Compania de Seguros, S.A., Argentina, Internat. Argentina S.A., Compania de Seguros de Retiro S.A., Argentina; lectr. Iowa Humanities Bd., 1981-82, Arts Midwest, 1987. Co-author: New Deal Mural Projects in Iowa, 1982; also articles; artist various works. Pres. intercultural program Am. Field Svc. Internat., West Des Moines, 1990-94; mem. acquisitions com., bd. trustees Edmundson Art Found./Des Moines Art Ctr., 1989—, pres. 1998-99; bd. dirs. Des Moines Symphony, 1989-94, Metro Arts Coun. Greater Des Moines, 1990-94, Edmundson Art Found., 1992—, pres. 1998—. Mem. ABA (ho. of dels. 1995-98), Iowa Bar Assn., Polk County Bar Assn., Prairie Club (sec. 1982-84, 86-87, pres. 1991-92), West Des Moines Soccer Club (coach 1982-89, referee 1984-89). Democrat. Mem. Congregational Ch. Avocations: art history and collecting, soccer. Home: 711 High St Des Moines IA 50392-0001 Office: The Prin Fin Group 711 High St Des Moines IA 50392-0002

NASH, DONALD GENE, commodity investigator; b. Paris, July 20, 1945; s. Lelan and Mildred (Washburn) N.; m. Jo Ann Bellew, Aug. 29, 1964; children— Stacey Alan, Ryan Christopher, Shaun Christian B.S., So. Ill. U., 1967, M.S., 1969; postgrad., DePaul U., 1970-71. Farm mgr., test farms So. Ill. U., Carbondale, 1968-69; economist Commodity Futures Trading Commn., Chgo., 1969-77; v.p.-ops. Mid. Am. Commodity Exch., 1977-86; sr. investigator divsn. enforcement Commodity Futures Trading Commn., 1986—. Bd. trustees Friends of Danada. With N.G. U.S. Army, 1968—74. Recipient Outstanding Mktg. award Wall St. Jour., 1966, award of merit Am. Farm Econ. Assn., 1967, cert. of merit Commodity Exch. Authority, merit award Naperville Art League, 1994, Honorable Mention award Danada Nature Show, 1995. Methodist. Avocations: photography; woodworking; sketching. Home: 923 Bainbridge Dr Naperville IL 60563-2002 Office: Commodity Futures Trading Commn 300 S Riverside Plz Ste 1600N Chicago IL 60606-6615 E-mail: dnash@cftc.gov.

NASH, GORDON BERNARD, JR. lawyer; b. Evergreen, Ill., Feb. 24, 1944; s. Gordon Bernard and Lilyan (Grafft) N.; m. Roseanne Joan Burke, Aug. 24, 1968; children: Caroline, Brian, Terry, Maureen. BA, Notre Dame U., 1966; JD, Loyola U., Chgo., 1969. Bar: Ill., U.S. Dist. Ct. (no. dist.) Ill. Atty. Office U.S. Atty. No. Dist. Ill., Chgo., 1971-78; ptnr. Gardner, Carton & Douglas, 1978—. Chmn. Ill. Bd. Ethics, Springfield, 1980-85. Served to capt. U.S. Army, 1969-71. Recipient John Marshall award U.S. Dept. Justice, 1978, Spl. Commendation award, 1975, Disting. Achievement award Internat. Acad. Trial Lawyers, 1969. Mem. ABA, Ill. Bar Assn., Chgo. Bar Found. Local Chpt. (bd. dirs. 1983-85, 87-89), Fed. Bar Assn. (bd. govs. 1986-91), Chgo. Bar Assn. (bd. mgrs. 1983-85, pres. 1990-91), Constl. Rights Found. Com. (bd. dirs. 1993—, chmn., 1998-2001), Am. Coll. Trial Lawyers, Ctr. for Conflict Resolution (bd. 1992-2000, v.p. 1995-2000), Chgo. Inn of Ct. (pres. 1996-97), Olympia Fields Country Club. Democrat. Roman Catholic. Home: 5101 Harvey Ave Western Springs IL 60558-2042 Office: Gardner Carton & Douglas Quaker Tower 321 N Clark St Ste 3400 Chicago IL 60610-4795 E-mail: gnash@gcd.com.

NASH, JOHN ARTHUR, bank executive; b. Indpls., Mar. 12, 1938; s. Basil and Harriet Nash; m. Susan Moss; children: John, Bill, Stacia. BS, Ind. U., 1960, MBA, 1961. Account officer Nat. City Bank, Cleve., 1961-66; v.p. Irwin Union Bank, Columbus, Ind., 1966-71, exec. v.p., 1971-75, pres., 1975-79, Irwin Fin. Corp., Columbus, 1975—, also bd. dirs. Ind., 1972—. Bd. dirs. Irwin Union Bank, Irwin Mortgage Corp., Irwin Ventures, Irwin Home Equity Corp., Irwin Cap. Holdings. Chmn. bd. trustees Columbus Regional Hosp., Columbus Econ. Devel. Bd.; past chmn. Heritage Fund Bartholomew County, Columbus; mem. adv. bd. Ind. U.-Purdue U., Indpls. 2d lt. U.S. Army, 1961-63. Recipient Sagamore of Wabash award Gov. of Ind., 1991. Mem. Am. Bankers Assn. (mem. bank leadership coun.), Ind. Bankers Assn. (bd. dirs., past chmn., chmn. govt. rels. com.), Ind. U. Alumni Assn. (pres. 1991-92). Office: Irwin Fin Corp 500 Washington St Columbus IN 47201-6230 E-mail: john.nash@irwinfinancial.com.

NASH, NICHOLAS DAVID, retailing executive; b. Mpls., June 11, 1939; s. Edgar Vanderhoef and Nancy (Van Slyke) N. AB, Harvard U., 1962; MEd, Bowling Green State U., 1970; PhD, U. Minn., 1975. Head lower sch. Maumee Valley (Ohio) Country Day Sch., 1965-71; assoc. dir. Univ. Council for Ednl. Adminstrn.; adj. asst. prof. Ohio State U., 1975-78; v.p. programming Minn. Public Radio, St. Paul, 1978-82, Am. Pub. Radio, St. Paul, 1982-85; pres. The Nash Co., 1985—. Bd. dirs. Artspace Projects, Inc. Author works in field. Bd. dirs. Nash Found., 1975—. Mem. University Club St. Paul. Episcopalian. Home: 1340 N Birch Lake Blvd Saint Paul MN 55110-6716 Office: 2179 4th St Ste 2H Saint Paul MN 55110-3041

NASS, CONNIE KAY, state auditor; m. Alan Nass; 3 children. V.p. Nass & Son, Inc., 1974—; auditor State of Ind., 1999—. Bd. Senator Richard Lugar's Excellence in Pub. Svc. Program. Bd. mem. Huntingburg Utility Bd., 1975—; city coun. mem., Huntingburg, 1979-88, mayor, 1988-96; mgr. municipally owned utility cos., Huntingburg, 1988-96; candidate for lt. gov. State of Ind., 1995-96; mem. GOP Platform Com., 1992; del. Rep. Nat. Conv., 1996; bd. dirs. Welborn Found. Evansville, S.W. Ind. Regional Health Care Ctr., Inc.; adv. bd. AAA, Evansville, 1990—; mem. fin. com. and emergency svcs. com. ARC Greater Indpls., 1999—; nat. gen. synod del. Ind.-Ky. Conf. United Ch. of Christ, 1981, com. on planning and evaluation, 1990—, bd. dirs., 1996—; Sunday sch. tchr., music dir. Salem United Ch. of Christ. Recipient Protect Our Woods Environtl. award, 1995; named Outstanding Rep. Woman Ind. Reps Mayor's Assn., 1995. Mem. Nat. Automated Clearing House Assn. (internet coun., electronic benefits coun., strategic expansion bd.), Nat. Assn. State Auditors, Comptrs. and Treas., Network Women in Bus., Women Execs. in State Govt., Ind. State Auditor Adv. Coun., Ind. Farm Bur., Ind. Assn. of Cities and Towns (bd. dirs.), Dubois County GOP Women's Club (pres. 1996-98), Marion County GOP Women's Club, Huntingburg C. of C. Office: State House Rm 240 200 W Washington St Indianapolis IN 46204-2728

NASS, STEPHEN L. state legislator; b. Whitewater, Wis., Oct. 7, 1952; BS, U. Wis., Whitewater, 1978, MSEd in Sch. Bus. Mgmt., 1990. Former payroll benefits analyst, info. analyst/negotiator; now mem. Wis. State Assembly. Mem. bd. visitors U. Wis., Whitewater. Served with Air N.G., Desert Shield and Desert Storm. Mem. Am. Legion, VFW, Nat. ASsn. Parliamentarians, Wis. Assn. Parliamentarians, Kiwanis. Home: W8948 Willis Ray Rd Whitewater WI 53190-3752

NASSER, JACQUES, former automotive company executive; b. Dec. 12, 1947; Australian citizen; Degree in Bus. Studies, Royal Melbourne Inst. Tech. With Ford of Australia, 1968-73; mem. fin. staff N.Am. Truck ops. Ford Motor Co., 1973, mgr. profit analysis, mgr. product programming Australia, 1973-75, various positions Internat. Automotive ops., from 1975, with Asia-Pacific and Latin-Am. ops., 1970s and 80s; dir., vp.. fin. and adminstrn. Autolatina joint venture Brazil and Argentina, 1987-90; pres., CEO Ford of Australia, 1990-93; chmn. Ford of Europe Fort Motor Co., 1993-96; v.p. Ford Motor Co., 1993-96, chmn. Ford of Europe, pres. Fort Automotive ops., exec. v.p., 1996—, pres., CEO, 1999—2001.

NATARUS, BURTON F. lawyer, municipal legislator; b. Wausau, Wis. BS in Polit. Sci., U. Wis., 1956, JD, 1960; postgrad., John F. Kennedy Sch. Govt., 1993. Pvt. practice law, Chgo.; elected alderman 42d Ward, 1971; chmn. Chgo. City Coun. Com. Traffic Control and Safety, 1997—; mem. Chgo. Plan Com. State St. Com., 1997—. Mem. Mayor's Zoning Reform Commn.; mem. Ctrl. Area Planning Task Force. Mem. 2000 Yr. Chgo. Trade Del. to China. Capt. USAR, ret. Mem. City Club, Greater North Mich. Ave Assn., Streeterville C. of C., River North Assn., North Dearborn Assn., North State, Astor, Lake Shore Dr. Assn., Streeterville Orgn. Active Residents, Washington Sq. Assn., State Street Coun., Ctrl. Mich. Ave. Assn. Address: 30 N La Salle St Ste 2900 Chicago IL 60602-2584 Office: City Hall Rm 306 121 N Lasalle St Chicago IL 60602-1202

NATHAN, PETER E. psychologist, educator; b. St. Louis, Apr. 18, 1935; s. Emil and Kathryn (Kline) N.; m. Florence I. Baker, Nov. 26, 1959; children: David Edward, Anne Miller, Laura Carol, Mark Andrew. AB, Harvard U., 1957; PhD, Washington U., 1962. Research fellow psychology Harvard U., 1962-64, research asso., 1964-68, asst. prof. psychology, 1968-69; research psychologist Boston City Hosp., 1964-68, dir. alcohol study unit, 1967-70; prof. Rutgers U., New Brunswick, N.J., 1969-89, dir. clin. psychology tng., 1969-87, dir. Alcohol Behavior Research Lab., 1970-87, chmn. dept. clin. psychology, 1976-87, dir. Ctr. Alcohol Studies, 1983-89, Henry and Anna Starr prof. psychology, 1983-89; sr. program officer, health program MacArthur Found., 1987-89; v.p. acad. affairs, found. disting. prof. psychology U. Iowa, 1990—, dean faculties, 1990-93, provost, 1993-95, acting pres., 1995. Mem. advisory council VA, 1972-76; chmn. alcoholism com. Nat. Inst. on Alcohol Abuse and Alcoholism, 1973-76, co-chmn. spl. rev. com., 1985, mem. nat. adv. coun., 1990-94; mem. psychol. scis. fellowship rev. com. NIMH, 1977-79; chmn. N.J. State Community Mental Health Bd., 1981-84; mem. working group substance use disorders, DSM-IV. Author: Cues, Decisions, and Diagnoses, 1967, Psychopathology and Society, 1975, 2d edit., 1980, Experimental and Behavioral Approaches to Alcoholism, 1978, Alcoholism: New Directions in Behavioral Treatment and Research, 1978, Clinical Case Studies in the Behavioral Treatment of Alcoholism, 1982, Professionals in Distress, 1987, Neuropsychological Deficits in Alcoholism, 1987, Introduction to Psychology, 1987, 2d edit., 1990, Abnormal Psychology, 1992, 2d edit., 1996, A Guide to Treatments that Work, 1998, 2d edit., 2002; exec. editor: Jour. Studies Alcohol, 1983—90; assoc. editor Am. Psychologist, 1977—85, Contemporary Psychology, 1991—97, Prevention and Treatment,

1998—2001, Psychol. Bull., 2002—, mem. editl. bd. Jour. Clin. Psychology, 1969—95, Jour. Cons. Clin. Psychology, 1973—95, Profl. Psychology, 1976—89. Fellow Am. Psychol. Assn. (chmn. sect. 3 div. 12 1976-77, rep. to council 1976-79, 82-85, pres. div. 12 1984-85; Disting. Contbns. to Knowledge award 1999). Democrat. Jewish. Home: 248 Black Springs Cir Iowa City IA 52246-3800 Office: Univ Iowa E119 Seashore Hall Iowa City IA 52242-1316 E-mail: pnathan@blue.weeg.uiowa.edu.

NATHANIEL, archbishop; b. Aurora, Ill., June 12, 1940; s. Joseph and Vera (Boytor) P. BA, St. Propcopius Coll., 1962; MDiv, Pontifical Gregorian U., Rome, 1966. Ordained priest Romanian Greek Cath. Ch., 1966; consecrated bishop Romanian Orthodox Episcopate of Am., 1980; elevated to archbishop, 1999. Asst. pastor St. Michael Byz Ch., Aurora, 1967; parish priest Holy Cross Romanian Orthodox Ch., Hermitage, Pa., 1975-80; aux. bishop Romanian Orthodox Episcopate of Am., Orthodox Ch. in Am., Jackson, Mich., 1980-84, ruling bishop Detroit, 1984—; mem. Holy Snyod Orthodox Ch. in Am., Syosset, N.Y., 1980—; Episcopal moderator Pastoral Life Ministries, O.C.A., 1991—. Bd. dirs. Moldovita Romanian Orthodox Ch., Hayward, Calif, 1982; tchr. summer youth programs Romanian Diocese; confessor to sisterhood Holy Transfiguration Monastery; rep. Conf. on Monasticism, Cairo, 1978; participant Monastic Consultation, Cairo, 1979, Seventh Assembly, Vancouver, Can., 1983; active mem. diocesan liturgical commn.; spkr., lectr. in field. Author: Holy Icons, 1969; editor newspaper Solia; contbr. numerous articles to profl. jours. Chmn. Romanian-Am. Heritage Ctr., Grass Lake, Mich.; organizer, chmn. Help for Romania Nat. Relief Fund and Help the Children of Romania Relief Fund; chmn. Congress of Romanian Ams., 1991—; mem. adv. bd. Orthodox Christian Laity, 1999—; pres. Ctr. for Orthodox Christian Studies, St. Andrew, Detroit, 2000. Home and Office: Romanian Orthodox Episcopate Am 2535 Grey Tower Rd Jackson MI 49201-9120 also: PO Box 185 Grass Lake MI 49240-0185 E-mail: hg.bnpopp@aol.com.

NATZ, JACQUES, news director; b. Paris, Dec. 3, 1955; BA in Journalism, U. Mo., 1977. News dir. WTHR-TV, Indpls., 1996—. Recipient Emmy award, 1985. Mem. Radio TV News Dir.'s Assn. Office: WTHR-TV 1000 N Meridian St Indianapolis IN 46204-1076

NAUERT, PETER WILLIAM, insurance company executive, lawyer; b. Rockford, Ill., May 3, 1943; s. Robert W. and Irene H. (Hippenbecker) N.; B.S., Marquette U., 1965; J.D., George Washington U., 1968. children: Heather, Justin, Jonathan. Bar: D.C. 1968, Ill. 1969, U.S. Ct. Appeals (7th cir.) 1969, U.S. Supreme Ct. 1971. Vice pres. Pioneer Life Ins. Co. of Ill., Rockford, 1968-75, pres., chmn., CEO, 1975—; chmn., CEO Pioneer Fin. Svcs., Inc., chmn. Ceres Group Inc., Strongsville, Ohio; Mem. ABA, Ill. Bar Assn., Winnebago County Bar Assn., Rockford C. of C., Young Pres. Orgn., World Pres. Assn., University Club, Rockford Country Club. Office: Ceres Group Inc PO Box 247007 Omaha NE 68124

NAUGLE, ROBERT PAUL, dentist; b. Cleve., May 3, 1951; s. Paul Franklin Albert and Olga (Bigadza) N.; m. Nancy Elaine Baker, June 14, 1975; 1 child, Jennifer Elaine. BS, Heidelberg Coll., Tiffin, Ohio, 1973; DDS, Case Western Res. U., 1977. Pvt. practice, Uniontown, Ohio, 1980—. Capt. USAF, 1977-80. Mem. ADA, Am. Soc. Dentistry for Children, Ohio Dental Assn., Acad. Gen. Dentistry, Acad. Sports Dentistry, Stark County Dental Soc., Akron Dental Soc., Air Force Assn., Rotary (past program chmn. Uniontown, Student of Month chmn., past pres., past v.p., past treas., Paul Harris fellow, past sgt.-at-arms, cmty. svc. chmn., cmty. svc. chmn.). Republican. Mem. United Church of Christ. Office: 13027 Cleveland Ave NW Uniontown OH 44685-8430

NAULT, WILLIAM HENRY, publishing executive; b. Ishpeming, Mich., June 9, 1926; s. Henry J. and Eva (Perrault) N.; m. Helen E. Matthews, Nov. 28, 1946; children: William Henry, Rebecca Nault Marks, Ronald, George, Peter, Julia Nault Doyle, Robert, David. AB, No. Mich. U., 1948, LittD (hon.), 1988; MA, U. Mich., 1949; EdD, Columbia U., 1953, LHD (hon.), 1980, LLD (hon.), 1986, LittD (hon.), 1988. Dir. adult edn., Battle Creek, Mich., 1948-49; guidance counselor, 1949-50; prin. W.K. Kellogg High Sch., Battle Creek, 1950-53; research assoc. Columbia U., 1953-54; asst. supt. Ridgewood, N.J., 1954-55; adj. prof. Patterson State Coll., 1954-55; dir. research World Book, Inc. (formerly Field Enterprises Edn. Corp.), Chgo., 1955-63, v.p., 1963-66, sr. v.p., editorial dir., 1966-68, exec. v.p. and editorial dir., 1968-83; pres., pub., chief operating officer World Book, Inc., 1983-84, gen. chmn. editorial adv. bds., 1968-99, pub., 1983-95, pub. emeritus, 1995—. Past vice chmn. Govt. Adv. Com. on Internat. Library and Book Programs, U.S. Dept. State; past mem. nat. adv. bd. Ctr. on Edn. Media and Materials for Handicapped; past mem. exec. bd. Commn. Instns. Higher Edn., North Central Assn. Colls. and Secondary Schs.; mem. dean's adv. council Coll. Bus. and Pub. Adminstrn., U. Mo., Columbia; mem. nat. council Inst. Internat. Edn. Author material on courses of study. Mem. alumni com. Columbia Tchrs. Coll. Capital Campaign; mem. White House Conf. on Youth, White House Conf. on Librs., White House Conf. on Edn.; pres. Oak Park (Ill.) Bd. Edn., 1960-63; v.p. LaGrange (Ill.) Libr. Bd.; bd. regents Lincoln Acad., Ill.; past trustee Adler Planetarium, De Paul U., Chgo. Geol. Soc.; bd. dirs. H.V. Phalin Found. Grad. Study, World Book, Inc., A.J. Nystrom Co., Field Edn. Co., Libr. Movens, Inc.; mem. adv. bd. Rosary Coll.; mem. liberal arts and scis. adv. council De Paul U. Served with F.A., AUS, 1944-45. Recipient Columbia U. Tchrs. Coll. medal for disting. svc. in edn.; named Disting. Alumnus No. Mich. U., U. Mich., Columbia U. Fellow AAAS; mem. ALA, Chgo. Planetarium Soc. (trustee), Chgo. Geog. Soc. (dir.), Am. Acad. Polit. and Social Sci., Am. Edn. Rsch. Assn., Am. Assn. Sch. Adminstrs., ASCD, Chgo. Pubs. Assn. (past pres.), Ill. Assn. Sch. Adminstrs., Ill. Acad. Sci., NSTA, Nat. Council Tchrs. English, Assn. Am. Geographers, Assn. Childhood Edn. Internat., NAESP, Nat. Assn. Secondary Sch. Prins., Council for Advancement Sci. Writing, Internat. Platform Assn., Nat. Council Social Studies, Nat. Soc. Study Edn. Roman Catholic. Clubs: Mid-Am, Mchts. and Mfrs. Office: World Book Inc 525 W Monroe St Chicago IL 60661-3629 E-mail: naultwh@aol.com.

NAUMANN, JOSEPH FRED, bishop; b. St. Louis, June 4, 1949; BA, Cardinal Glennon Coll., St. Louis, 1971; degree in theology, Kenrick Sem., St. Louis, 1975. Transitional deacon St. Christopher's Parish, Florissant, Mo., 1974-75; assoc. pastor St. Dominic Savio Parish, Affton, 1975-79, Our Lady of Sorrows Parish, St. Louis, 1979-84; part-time assoc. pastor Most Blessed Sacrament Parish, 1984-89; pastor Ascension Parish, Normandy, Mo., 1989-94; apptd. vicar gen., archdiocese of St. Louis Vicar for Fin., 1994—; aux. bishop of St. Louis/Titular Bishop of Caput Cilla, 1997—. Office: 4445 Lindell Blvd Saint Louis MO 63108-2403

NAVARRE, RICHARD A. mining executive; Dir. fin. planning Peabody Group, St. Louis, 1993, v.p., CFO, exec. v.p., CFO, 2001—. Pres., v.p. fin., controller Peabody COALSALES; bd. advisors Coll. Bus. and Adminstrn. and Sch. Acct. So. Ill. U., Carbondale Office: Peabody Group 701 Market St Saint Louis MO 63101 E-mail: publicrelations@peabodygroup.com.

NAVARRE, ROBERT WARD, manufacturing company executive; b. Monroe, Mich., May 21, 1933; s. Joseph Alexander N.; m. Barbara Anne Navarre, June 26, 1953; children— Veo Anne, Robert Ward, Jan Louise. B.S. in Commerce, U. Notre Dame, 1955; grad., exec. program Stanford U., 1979. Sales mgr. Marben Corp., Jackson, Mich., 1958-64; mktg. adminstr. Simpson Industries, Litchfield, 1964-67, pres., CEO, 1967-89, chmn., 1989-97, also bd. dirs. Bd. dirs. Webster Industries. Chmn. Jackson/Hillsdale Mental Health Service Bd., 1972-78; mem. Hillsdale Schs. Bd. Edn., 1972-76. Mem. NAM (regional vice chmn. 1978-79, chmn. membership com. 1979-80, bd. dirs.), Mich. Mfg. Assn. (bd. dirs., chmn. 1991—). Roman Catholic. Office: Simpson Industries Inc 47603 Halyard Dr Plymouth MI 48170-2429

NAVRATIL, ROBERT J. financial executive; Prin. in charge of property The RREEF Funds, Chgo., 1989—. Office: 41st Fl 875 N Michigan Ave Fl 41 Chicago IL 60611-1803

NAYLOR, JAMES CHARLES, psychologist, educator; b. Chgo., Feb. 8, 1932; s. Joseph Sewell and Berniece (Berg) N.; m. Georgia Lou Mason, Feb. 14, 1953; children— Mary Denise, Diana Darice, Shari Dalice. B.S., Purdue U., 1957, M.S., 1958, Ph.D., 1960. Asst. prof. Ohio State U., 1960-63, asso. prof., 1963-67, prof. vice chmn. dept. psychology, 1967-68; prof. Purdue U., Lafayette, Ind., 1968-86, head dept. psychol. scis., 1968-79; prof., chmn. dept. psychology Ohio State U., Columbus, 1986-98, prof. emeritus, 1999—. Fulbright rsch. scholar, Umea, Sweden, 1976; Disting. scholar, vis. scientist Flinders U., South Australia, 1982-83, UNESCO ednl. cons. to Hangzhou U., Peoples Republic of China, 1984; chmn. Coun. Grad. Depts. Psychology, 1993-94; lead reviewer Psychology Program Rev., State U. Sys. Fla., 1996. Author: Industrial Psychology, 1968, A Theory of Behavior in Organizations, 1980; founder, editor: Organizational Behavior and Human Decision Processes; mem. editorial bd.: Prof. Psychology; Contbr. articles to profl. jours. Served with USN, 1950-54. Fellow AAAS, Am. Psychol. Soc., Am. Psychol. Assn.; mem. Psychonomic Soc., Psychmetric Soc., Internat. Assn. Applied Psychology, Soc. Organizational Behavior (founder), Midwestern Psychol. Assn. (coun. 1994-97), Phi Beta Kappa, Sigma Xi. Home: 176 Tucker Dr Columbus OH 43085-3064 Office: Ohio State U Dept Psychology Columbus OH 43210 E-mail: naylor.2@osu.edu.

NAYLOR, JEFFREY GORDON, consumer products company executive; b. Montreal, Que., Can., Nov. 15, 1958; s. Gordon Charles and Patricia Grace (Pryde) N.; m. Shawn Elizabeth Baker, Oct. 6, 1984; 1 child, Madeleine Baker Naylor. BA in econs., Northwestern U., 1980, MBA, 1982. CPA, Ill. Pub. acct. Deloitte, Haskins & Sells, Chgo., 1982-86; assoc. N.Am. Venture Capital, 1986-88; mgr. mergers and acquisitions A.C. Nielsen, Northbrook, Ill., 1988-90, dir. fin. analysis, 1990-91; dir. finance Kraft Foods Sales, Northfield, Ill., 1991-93, Kraft Foods Corp., Northfield, 1993-95; v.p. credit divsn. Sears Roebuck & Co., Hoffman Estates, Ill., 1995—; v.p., contr The LimitedInc; CFO, sen. v.p. fin. Dade Behring, Dearfield, Ill, 2000—. Prof. acctg. Keller Grad. Sch. Mgmt., Chgo., 1987-91. Treas. Episcopal Ch. of Northwestern U., Evanston, 1996—; mem. Brookfield Zoo, 1995—, Northwestern U. "N" Club, 1980—. Mem. AICPA, Ill. CPA Soc. Episcopalian. Avocations: competitive swimming, Sunday Sch. tchr., gourmet cooking, reading, ice skating.

NAZETTE, RICHARD FOLLETT, lawyer; b. Eldora, Iowa, July 27, 1919; s. Hilmer H. and Genevieve A. (Follett) N.; m. Joan Chehak, June 20, 1942; children— Ronald D., Randall A. B.A., U. Iowa, 1942, J.D. with distinction, 1946. Bar: Iowa bar 1946. Practiced in, Cedar Rapids, 1946—; partner firm Nazette, Marner, Wendt, Knoll & Usher, 1968—; asst. atty. Linn County, Iowa, 1951-56; county atty., 1957-63. Dir. United States Bank, Cedar Rapids, 1968-91, State Surety Co., Des Moines, 1966-78 Bd. dirs. Linn County Health Center, 1968-73, chmn., 1968-69; mem. Iowa Bd. Parole, 1981-84. Served with AUS, 1942-44. Fellow Am. Bar Found., Iowa Bar Assn. (bd. govs. 1972-76), Iowa State Bar Found.; mem. Linn County Bar Assn. (pres. 1963), Iowa County Attys. Assn. (pres. 1959), Iowa Acad. Trial Lawyers (pres. 1964), Sigma Phi Epsilon. Republican. Presbyterian. Clubs: Masons, Shriners, Jesters, Elks, Optimists (internat. v.p. 1955). Home: 2224 Country Club Pkwy SE Cedar Rapids IA 52403-1639 Office: 100 1st St SW Cedar Rapids IA 52404-5701 E-mail: r.nazette@nazmar.com.

NEAGLE, DENNIS EDWARD (DENNY NEAGLE), professional baseball player; b. Gambrills, Md., Oct. 13, 1968; Grad. high sch., Gambrills, Md.; student, U. Minn. With Minn. Twins, 1991; pitcher Pitts. Pirates, 1992-96, Atlanta Braves, 1996-98, Cin. Reds, 1999—. Selected to N.L. All-Star Team, 1995. Achievements include being a mem. Pitts. Pirates N.L. East Champions, 1992. Office: Cin Reds Cinergy Field 100 Cinergy Fld Cincinnati OH 45202-3543

NEAL, HOMER ALFRED, physics educator, researcher, university administrator; b. Franklin, Ky., June 13, 1942; s. Homer and Margaret Elizabeth (Holl) Neal; m. Donna Jean Daniels, June 16, 1962; children: Sharon Denise, Homer Alfred. BS in Physics with honors, Ind. U., 1961; MS in Physics (John Hay Whitney fellow), U. Mich., 1963, PhD in Physics, 1966. Asst. prof. physics Ind. U., 1967—70, assoc. prof., 1970—72, prof., 1972—81, dean research and grad. devel., 1976—81; prof. physics SUNY, Stony Brook, 1981—87, provost, 1981—86; prof. physics, chmn. U. Mich., Ann Arbor, 1987—93, v.p. rsch., 1993—97, interim pres., 1996—97, prof. of physics, 1987—2000, Samuel A. Goudsmit disting. prof. physics, 2000—, dir. of atlas project, 1997—. Bd. dirs. Ford Motor Co., Covanta Corp.; mem. Nat. Sci. Bd., 1980—86; mem. adv. coun. Oak Ridge Nat. Lab., 1993—99; mem. external adv. coun. Nat. Computational Sci. Alliance, 1997—; mem. applications strategy coun. Univ. Corp. for Advanced Internet Devel., 2000—; chmn. Argonne Zero Gradient Synchrotron Users Group, 1970—72; trustee Argonne Univs. Assn., 1971—74, 1977—80; physics adv. panel NSF, 1976—79, chmn. physics adv. panel, 1987—89; high energy physics adv. panel U.S. Dept. Energy, 1977—81. Contbr. articles to profl. jours. Mem. bd. regents Smithsonian Instn., 1989—; trustee Ctr. for Strategic and Internat. Studies, 1990—2000; Oak Ridge (Tenn.) Nat. Lab., 1993—; mem. bd. overseers Superconducting Super Collider, 1989—93; trustee Environ. Rsch. Inst. of Mich., 1994—96; N.Y. Sea Grant Inst., 1982—86. Recipient Stony Brook medal, 1986, Ind. U. Disting. Alumni award, 1994; fellow NSF, 1966—67, Sloan, 1968, Guggenheim, 1980—81. Fellow: AAAS, Am. Acad. Arts and Scis., Am. Phys. Soc.; mem.: Univs. Rsch. Assn., Sigma Xi. Office: Dept of Physics Rm 2477 Randall Lab 500 East University Ann Arbor MI 48109-1120

NEAL, MO (P. MAUREEN NEAL), sculptor; b. Houston, Oct. 26, 1950; d. Gordon Taft and Mary Louise (O'Connor) N.; m. Thomas Alan Buttars, Jan. 2, 1984. BA cum laude, Wash. State U., 1988; MFA, Va. Commonwealth U., 1991. Assoc. prof. art and art history U. Nebr., Lincoln, 1994—. Adj. faculty dept. fine arts U. S.D., Vermillion, 1991-92. Grantee S.D. Arts Coun., 1992, 94, Nat. Endowment for Arts, 1994; fellow Nebr. Arts Coun., 1998. Mem. Mid Am. Coll. Art Assn. (bd. dirs. 1997, pres. 2000-02), Phi Beta Kappa. Democrat. Office: U Nebr Dept Art & Art History Rm 120 Richards Hall Lincoln NE 68588-0114 E-mail: moneal@unl.edu.

NEAL, STEVEN GEORGE, journalist; b. Coos Bay, Oreg., July 3, 1949; s. Ernest L. and Ellen Louise (Williams) N.; m. Susan Christine Simmons, May 8, 1971; children: Erin, Shannon. BS in Journalism, U. Oreg., 1971; MS in Journalism, Columbia U., 1972. Reporter Oreg. Jour., Portland, 1971, Phila. Inquirer, 1972-78; gen. assignment reporter, White House corr., polit. writer Chgo. Tribune, 1979-87; polit. editor Chgo. Sun-Times, 1987-92, polit. columnist, 1987—. Bd. govs. White House Corrs. Assn., Washington, 1981-83. Co-author: Tom McCall: Maverick, 1977; author: The Eisenhowers, 1978, Dark Horse: A Biography of Wendell Willkie, 1984, McNary of Oregon, 1985, Rolling on the River: The Best of Steve Neal, 1999; editor: They Never Go Back to Pocatello: The Essays of Richard Neuberger, 1988; contbr. to Am. Heritage, The Nation, The N.Y. Times Books Rev., Dictionary of Am. Biography. Recipient William H. Jones award Chgo. Tribune, 1984; Robert W. Ruhl lectr. U. Oreg., Eugene, 1984; Col. Robert R. McCormick fellow, McCormick Found., Chgo., 1989; Hoover Libr. Assn. scholar, West Branch, Iowa, 1989. Roman Catholic. Home: 411 N Elm St Hinsdale IL 60521-3709 Office: Chgo Sun-Times Inc 401 N Wabash Ave Rm 110 Chicago IL 60611-5642

NEALE, GARY LEE, utilities executive; b. Lead, S.D., Mar. 3, 1940; s. Vearl J. and Gladys M. (Trenkle) N.; m. Sandra C. Lovell, June 16, 1962; children: David G., Julie C. BA in Econs., U. Wash., 1962, MBA, 1965. Loan examiner Wells Fargo, 1966-69; sr. fin. analyst Kaiser Industries, 1969-70; chmn., pres., chief exec. officer Planmetrics, Chgo., 1970-89; pres., chief oper. officer No. Ind. Pub. Svc. Co., Hammond, 1989-93; chmn., pres., CEO Ni Source Inc. (formerly No. Ind. Pub. Svc. Co.), 1993—. Bd. dirs. Modine Mfg., Racine, Wis., Am. Gas Assn., Arlington, Va., Ind. Gas Assn./Ind. Electric Assn., Indpls., Nipsco Industries Inc., Hammond. Bd. dirs. N.W. Ind. Symphony, 1990; mem. Ind. Energy Policy Forum, 1991. Lt. (j.g.) USN, 1962-64. Mem. Econ. Club Chgo., Chgo. Univ. Club, NYU Club. Office: NiSource Inc 801 E 86th Ave Merrillville IN 46410-6272

NEALE, HENRY WHITEHEAD, plastic surgery educator; b. Richmond, Va., July 18, 1940; s. Richard C. and Eva W. Neale; m. Margaret C. Neale, June 20, 1964; children: Leigh, Jennifer, Henry Whitehead Neale Jr., William. BS, Davidson Coll., 1960; MD, Med. Coll. Va., 1964. Diplomate Am. Bd. Surgery, Am. Bd. Plastic Surgery . Intern Mercy Med. Ctr., Springfield, Ohio, 1964—65; resident in gen. surgery U. Cin. Med. Ctr., 1965—71, dir. divsn. plastic, reconstructive and hand surgery, 1974—; resident in plastic surgery Duke U. Med. Ctr., Durham, NC, 1971—74; fellow in hand surgery, Christine Kleinert hand fellow U. Louisville, 1973; asst. prof. surgery U. Cin. Coll. Medicine, 1974—77, assoc. prof., 1977—82, prof., 1982—; active staff, dir. hand surgery and plastic surgery clinics U. Cin. Med. Ctr. Hosp. Group, 1974—, prof., chmn. divsn. plastic surgery, 1974—. Guest examiner Am. Bd. Plastic Surgery , 1986—90, dir., 1990—96, com. on plans and qualifying exam. com., liaison to Am. Bd. Surgery , 1993—96, exec. com. , 1993—, chmn. certifying examing com. , 1993—95, ethics com. , 1993, chmn.-elect , 1995—96; dir. burn reconstructive and plastic surgery, co-dir. hand surgery svc. Shriners Burns Inst., Cin., 1983—; dir. divsn. plastic, reconstructive and hand surgery and plastic surgery clinic Childrens Hosp. Med. Ctr., Cin., 1983—; assoc. attending staff Good Samaritan Hosp.; courtesy staff Christ Hosp., Jewish Hosp.; presenter in field. Mem. editl. bd.: Jour. Plastic and Reconstructive Surgery, 1989—; contbr. articles to profl. jours. Grantee Rsch. grant, Eli Lilly Co., 1979—91. Fellow: ACS; mem.: AMA, Plastic Surgery Rsch. Coun., Ohio Valley Soc. Plaastic and Reconstructive Surgery (pres. 1985—86), Ohio Med. Assn., Greater Cin. Soc. Plastic and Reconstructive Surgeons 1988—89, Grad. Surg. Soc. Cin., Cin. Surg. Soc., Assn. Acad. Chairmen in Plastic Surgery, Acad. Medicine Cin., Am. Soc. for Surgery of Hand, Am. Soc. Plastic and Reconstructive Surgeons, Am. Soc. for Aesthetic Plastic Surgery, Am. Cleft Palate Assn., Am. Burn Assn., Am. Assn. Plastic Surgeons. Home: 2970 Alpine Ter Cincinnati OH 45208-3408 Office: U Cin Coll Medicine Plastic Reconst and Hand Su 231 Bethesda Ave Cincinnati OH 45267-0001

NEAMAN, MARK ROBERT, hospital administrator; b. Buffalo, Oct. 22, 1950; married. B, Ohio State U., 1972, MHA, 1974. Adminstrv. asst. Evanston (Ill.) Hosp., 1974-76, asst. to v.p., 1976-78, asst. v.p., 1978-80, v.p., 1980-84, sr. v.p., 1984-85, pres., exec. v.p., 1985-90, pres., 1990-92, pres., CEO, 1992—. Trustee Healthcare Leadership Coun. Fellow Am. Coll. Healthcare Execs. (regent northern Cook County, Ill. 1990—, RS Hudgens award 1988). Home: 263 W Onwentsia Rd Lake Forest IL 60045-2826 Office: Evanston Hosp 2650 Ridge Ave Evanston IL 60201-1781

NEASE, STEPHEN WESLEY, college president; b. Everett, Mass., Jan. 15, 1925; s. Floyd William and Madeline Anzelette (Nostrand) N.; m. Dorothy Christine Hardy, June 17, 1946; children: Linda Carol Nease Scott, Floyd William II, Stephen Wesley Jr., David Wayne, Melissa Jo Nease Wallace. A.B., Brown U., 1946; Th.B., Eastern Nazarene Coll., 1947, D.D., 1966; Ed.M., Boston U., 1956; postgrad., Harvard Div. Sch., 1946-48. Ordained to ministry Ch. of the Nazarene, 1951; pastor East Side Ch. of the Nazarene, Newark, 1948-50; dean men, instr. religion Ea. Nazarene Coll., Wollaston, Mass., 1950-53, dir. devel., 1953-66, pres. emeritus; founding pres. Mt. Vernon (Ohio) Nazarene Coll., 1966-72, pres. emeritus; pres. Bethany (Okla.) Nazarene Coll., 1973-76, Nazarene Theol. Sem., Kansas City, Mo., 1976-80, Eastern Nazarene Coll., Wollaston, Mass., 1981-89; edn. commr. Ch. of the Nazarene, 1989-94; exec. dir. Capital and Endowment Devel., Mt. Vernon, Ohio, 1994—. Served with USNR, 1943-46. Office: 51 Haverhill Rd Windham NH 03087-1515

NECHEMIAS, STEPHEN MURRAY, lawyer; b. St. Louis, July 27, 1944; s. Herbert Bernard and Toby Helen (Wax) N.; m. Marcia Rosenstein, June 19, 1966 (div. Dec. 1981); children: Daniel Jay, Scott Michael; m. Linda Adams, Aug. 20, 1983. BS, Ohio State U., 1966; JD, U. Cin., 1969. Bar: Ohio 1969. Ptnr. Taft, Stettinius & Hollister, Cin., 1969—. Adj. prof. law No. Ky. U., Chase Coll. Law. Tax comment author: Couse's Ohio Form Book, 6th edit., 1984. Mem. Ohio State Bar Assn. (chmn. taxation com.), Cin. Bar Assn. (chmn. taxation sect. 1985), Legal Aid Soc. Cin. (pres., trustee). Democrat. Jewish. Home: 3122 Walworth Ave Cincinnati OH 45226-1047 Office: 1800 Star Bank Ctr 425 Walnut St Cincinnati OH 45202-3923

NECHIN, HERBERT BENJAMIN, lawyer; b. Chgo., Oct. 25, 1935; s. Abraham and Zelda (Benjamin) N.; m. Susan Zimmerman (div.); 1 child, Jill Rebecca; m. Roberta Fishman, Oct. 24, 1976; 1 child, Stefan. BA with distinction, honors in History, Northwestern U., 1956; JD, Harvard U., 1959. Bar: Ill. 1960. From assoc. to ptnr. Brown Fox & Blumberg, Chgo., 1960-75; ptnr. Taussig Wexler & Shaw, 1975-79, Fink Coff Stern, Chgo., 1979-81, Holleb & Coff, Chgo., 1981-2000; prin. Levin & Schreder, 2000—. Contbr. articles to profl. jours. Pres. Emanuel Congregation, Chgo., 1994-97. Staff sgt. USAR, 1960-66. Mem. ABA, Ill. Bar Assn., Chgo. Bar Assn. (chmn. trust law com. 1990-91), Am. Coll. Trust and Estate Counsel, Standard Club, Cliff Dwellers Club, Phi Beta Kappa. Office: Levin & Schreder 120 N LaSalle St Ste 3800 Chicago IL 60602-2417 E-mail: Herb@LevinSchreder.com.

NEEDHAM, GEORGE MICHAEL, association executive; b. Buffalo, July 3, 1955; s. Paul James and Dolores Ann (Duffy) N.; m. Joyce Elaine Leahy, Nov. 28, 1992; 1 stepchild, Katherine Callison. BA in English, SUNY, Buffalo, 1976, MLS, 1977. Various profl. positions Charleston (S.C.) County Libr., 1977-84; dir. Fairfield County Dist. Libr., Lancaster, Ohio, 1984-89; mem. svcs. dir. Ohio Libr. Assn., Columbus, 1990-92; exec. dir. Pub. Libr. Assn., Chgo., 1993-96; state librarian State of Mich., Lansing, 1996-99; v.p. mem. svcs. OCLC Online Computer libr. Ctr., Dublin, 1999—. Mem. adv. bd. Libr. Video Project, 1996—. Co-author: A Director's Checklist for Connecting Public Libraries to the Internet, 1995; author (book revs.) Booklist, 1994—, (video revs.), Libr. Jours., 1979—. Bd. dirs. Fairfield County chpt. ARC, Lancaster, 1984-88, Mt. Prospect Theatre Soc., Mt. Prospect, Ill., 1993-96, Lib. Media Project, 1997—. Mem. ALA, Pub. Libr. Assn., Ohio Libr. Assn. Avocations: acting, traditional folk music, writing, 2-time Jeopardy champion. Office: OCLC Online Computer Libr Ctr 6565 Frantz Rd Dublin OH 43017-3395 E-mail: needhamg@oclc.org.

NEEDHAM, GLEN RAY, entomology and acarology educator, researcher; b. Lamar, Colo., Dec. 25, 1951; s. Robert Lee and Evor Elaine (Kern) N.; m. Karla Marie Lohr, May 28, 1983; children: Kathleen Marie,

John Harrison, Elizabeth Anne. BS, S.W. Okla. State U., 1973; MS, Okla. State U., 1975, PhD, 1978. Grad. rsch. asst. Okla. State U., Stillwater, 1974-78; asst. prof. Ohio State U., Columbus, 1978-84, assoc. prof., 1984—, co-organizer and coord. acarology summer program. Co-editor: Africanized Honey Bees and Bee Mites, 1988, Acarology IX: Proceedings and Symposia. Donor ARC, Columbus. Recipient Dist. Alumnus award Okla. State U., 1992. Mem. Acarology Soc. Am. (pres. 1994), Entomol. Soc. Am., Soc. Vector Ecology, Ohio Acad. Sci., Gamma Sigma Delta, Sigma Xi. Methodist. Achievements include research in tick and dust mite biology and control. Office: Ohio State U 484 W 12th Ave Columbus OH 43210-1214 E-mail: needham.1@osu.edu.

NEEDLEMAN, BARBARA, newspaper executive; BS in Eng., Northwestern Univ., 1994. V.p. Tribune Media Svcs., Chgo., 1993—. Office: Tribune Media Svcs 435 N Michigan Ave Ste 1500 Chicago IL 60611-4012

NEEL, HARRY BRYAN, III, surgeon, scientist, educator; b. Rochester, Minn., Oct. 28, 1939; s. Harry Bryan and May Birgitta (Bjornsson) N.; m. Ingrid Helene Vaga, Aug. 29, 1964; children: Carlton Bryan, Harry Bryan IV, Roger Clifton. BS, Cornell U., 1962; MD, SUNY-Bklyn., 1966; PhD, U. Minn., 1976. Diplomate Am. Bd. Otolaryngology. Intern Kings County Hosp., Bklyn., 1966-67; resident in gen. surgery U. Minn. Hosps., Mpls., 1967-68; resident in otolaryngology Mayo Grad. Sch. Medicine Mayo Clinic, Rochester, Minn., 1970-74, cons. in otorhinolaryngology, 1974—, cons. in cell biology, 1981—, assoc. prof. otolaryngology and microbiology Med. Sch., 1979-84, prof., 1984—, also chmn. dept. otolaryngology. Mem. adv. com. Pitts. Eye and Ear Found. Author: Cryosurgery for Cancer, 1976; contbr. chpts. to books, articles to profl. jours. V.p. bd. dirs. Minn. Orch. in Rochester, Inc., 1982, pres., chmn., 1983—84; mem. devel. com. Minn. Orchestral Assn., 1983, Mayo Found., 1983—86; bd. dirs. Mayo Health Plan, 1986—92, chmn., 1990—92; mem. bd. Mayo Mgmt. Svcs., Inc., 1992—94; mem. bd. regents U. Minn., 1991—, chair faculty staff, student affairs com., 1993—95, 1999, vice chmn. bd., 1995—97, chmn. fin. and ops. com., 1999—2001, mem. audit com., 1995—2000, chair litigation com., 2001—; bd. dirs. Greater Rochester Area Univ. Ctr., 1993—; trustee U. Minn. Found., 1996—, mem. fin. com., 1999—2001; chmn. U. Minn. Investment Adv. Com., 1999—2002; mem. State Commn. on U. Minn. Excellence, 2002, commn. on U. Minn. Excellence, 2002—. Recipient travel award Soc. Acad. Chmn. Otolaryngology, 1974, Ira J. Tresley rsch. award Am. Acad. Facial and Reconstructive Surgery, 1982, Master Tchr. award in surgery Alumni Assn. Coll. Medicine, SUNY, Health Sci. Ctr., Bklyn., 1991, Notable award Nat. Assn. Collegiate Women Athletic Admsintrs., 1992, The Best Doctors in Am. award Woodward/White, 1992-93, 94-99. Mem. AMA, ACS (bd. govs. 1985-90, devel. bd. 1988—, treas. 1990-98, sec.-treas. Minn. chpt. 1983-85, pres. 1988-89), Am. Acad. Otolaryngology-Head and Neck Surgery (prize for basic rsch. in otolaryngology 1972, bd. dirs. 1988-91, established Neel Disting. Rsch. Lectureship Endowment Fund 1994, audit com. 1998-2000, chair investment adv. com. 1995—, chmn. audit com. 1999-2000), Minn. Med. Assn., Zumbro Valley Med. Soc., Am. Broncho-Esophagological Assn. (pres.-elect 1988, pres. 1989-90), Am. Laryngological, Rhinological and Oto. Sco. (Mosher award 1980, pres.-elect 1995-96, centennial pres. 1996-97, investment com. 1994—), Am. Laryngological Assn. (Casselberry award 1985, sec. 1988-93, v.p. 1994, pres. 1994—, Newcomb award 1996, Baker lectr. 1998), Assn. for Rsch. in Otolaryngology, Assn. Acad. Depts. in Otolaryngology (sec.-treas. 1984-86, pres.-elect 1986, pres. 1988-9), Alumni Assn. Cornell U. (Outstanding Alumni award 1985), Collegium ORL Amicitiae Sacrum (bd. dirs. 2000—), Am. Bd. Otolaryngology (bd. dirs. 1986—, treas. 1998—), Am Laryngol. Voice Rsch. and Edn. Found. (charter bd. dirs. 1996—). Republican. Presbyterian. Club: Rochester Golf and Country. Home: 828 8th St SW Rochester MN 55902-6310 Office: Mayo Clinic 200 1st St SW Rochester MN 55905-0002

NEFF, ROBERT CLARK, SR. lawyer; b. St. Marys, Ohio, Feb. 11, 1921; s. Homer Armstrong and Irene (McCulloch) N.; m. Betty Baker, July 3, 1954 (dec.); children: Cynthia Lee Neff Schifer, Robert Clark Jr., Abigail Lynn (dec.); m. Helen Picking, July 24, 1975. BA, Coll. Wooster, 1943; postgrad., U. Mich., 1946-47; LLB, Ohio No. U., 1950. Bar: Ohio 1950, U.S. Dist. Ct. (no. dist.) Ohio, 1978. Pvt. practice, Bucyrus, Ohio, 1950—; ptnr. Neff Law Firm Ltd.; law dir. City of Bucyrus, 1962-95. Chmn. blood program Crawford County (Ohio) unit ARC, 1955-89; life mem. adv. bd. Salvation Army, 1962—; clk. of session 1st Presbyn. Ch., Bucyrus, 1958-96; bd. dirs. Bucyrus Area Cmty. Found., Crawford County Bd. Mental Retardation and Devel. Disabilities, 1977-82. With USNR, WWII; comdr. Res. ret. Recipient "Others" plaque for 30 yrs. adv. bd. svc. Salvation Army, Ohio No. U. Coll. Law Alumni award for cmty. svc., 1996; inducted Ohio Vets. Hall Fame, Columbus, 1996. Mem. Ohio Bar Assn., Crawford County Bar Assn., Naval Res. Assn., Ret. Officers Assn., Am. Legion, Bucyrus Area C. of C. (past bd. dirs., Outstanding Citizen award, 1973, Bucyrus Citizen of Yr. 1981), Kiwanis (life mem., past pres.), Masons. Republican. Home: 1085 Mary Ann Ln Bucyrus OH 44820-3145 Office: 840 S Sandusky Ave PO Box 406 Bucyrus OH 44820-0406 Fax: 419-562-1660. E-mail: nefflaw@cybrtown.com.

NEFF, ROBERT MATTHEW, lawyer, financial services executive; b. Huntington, Ind., Mar. 26, 1955; s. Robert Eugene and Ann (Bash) N.; m. Lee Ann Loving, Aug. 23, 1980; children: Alexandra, Graydon, Philip. BA in English, DePauw U., 1977; JD, Ind. U., Indpls., 1980. Bar: Ind. 1980, U.S. Dist. Ct. (so. dist.) Ind. 1980, U.S. Supreme Ct., 1993. Assoc. Krieg, DeVault, Alexander & Capehart, Indpls., 1980-85, ptnr., 1986-88, Baker & Daniels, Indpls., 1988-92; of counsel, 1993-96; dept. to chmn. Fed. Housing Fin. Bd., Washington, 1992-93; pres., CEO Circle Investors, Inc., Indpls., 1993-97, also bd. dirs.; chmn., CEO Senex Fin. Corp., 1998—. Mem. faculty Grad. Sch. of Banking of South, 1988—90; chmn. Liberty Bankers Life Ins. Co., 1995—98, Am. Founders Life Ins. Co., Laurel Life Ins. Co., Aztek Life Assurance Co., 1996—97. Exec. editor Ind. Law Rev., 1979-80. Participant Lacy Exec. Leadership Conf., Indpls., 1985-86; trustee DePauw U., 1977-80. Mem. ABA (chmn. bus. law com. young lawyers divsn. 1988-90, banking law com. 1990-92), Ind. Bar Assn. (chmn. corps. banking and bus. law sect. 1987-88), James Whitcomb Riley Meml. Assn. (bd. govs. 1999—), DePauw Alumni Assn. (bd. dirs. 1982-88), Phi Kappa Psi, Phi Beta Kappa. Avocations: tae kwon do, golf. Home: 7202 Merriam Rd Indianapolis IN 46240 Office: Senex Fin Corp 3500 DePauw Blvd # 3050 Indianapolis IN 46268 E-mail: neffrm@senexco.com.

NEGISHI, EI-ICHI, chemistry educator; arrived in U.S., 1960; BS in Organic Chemistry, U. Tokyo, 1958; PhD in Organic Chemistry, U. Pa., 1963. Rsch. chemist Teijin Ltd., 1958-65; postdoctoral assoc. Purdue U., 1966-68, asst. to H.C. Brown, 1968-72; asst. prof. Syracuse (N.Y.) U., 1972-76, assoc. prof., 1976-79; prof. Purdue U., West Lafayette, Ind., 1979-99, Herbert C. Brown disting. prof., 1999—. Lectr. in field. Recipient A. von Humboldt Rschr. award 1998—; Fulbright scholar, 1960-63. Mem.: Royal Soc. Chemistry (Sir E. Frankland Prize lectureship 2000), Japan Chem. Soc. (award 1998), Am. Chem. Soc. (Organometallic Chemistry award 1998), Sigma Xi, Phi Lambda Epsilon. Office: Purdue U Chem Dept 1393 Brown Labs West Lafayette IN 47907-1393 E-mail: negishi@purdue.edu.

NEHRA, GERALD PETER, lawyer; b. Detroit, Mar. 25, 1940; s. Joseph P. and Jeanette M. (Bauer) N.; m. children: Teresa, Patricia; m. Peggy Jensen, Sept. 12, 1987. B.I.E., Gen. Motors Inst., Flint, Mich., 1962; JD, Detroit Coll. Law, 1970. Bar: Mich. 1970, N.Y. 1972, Colo. 1992, U.S. Dist. Ct. (ea. dist.) Mich. 1970, U.S. Dist. Ct. (so. dist.) N.Y. 1972, U.S. Dist. Ct. (no. dist.) N.Y. 1976, U.S. Ct. Appeals (6th cir.) 1978. Successively engr., supr., gen. supr. Gen. Motors Corp., 1958-67; mktg. rep. to regional counsel IBM Corp., 1967-79; v.p. gen. counsel Church & Dwight Co., Inc., 1979-82; dep. chief atty. Amway Corp., 1982-83; dep. gen. counsel, 1983-92; dir. legal div., 1989-91; sec., dir. corp. law, 1991-92; v.p. gen. cousnel Fuller Brush, Boulder, Colo., 1991-92; pvt. practice, 1992—. Adj. instr. Dale Carnegie Courses, 1983-91. Recipient Outstanding Contbn. award Am. Cancer Soc., 1976. Mem. ABA, Mich. Bar Assn., Colo. Bar Assn., N.Y. State Bar Assn. Home and Office: 1710 Beach St Muskegon MI 49441-1008 E-mail: gnehra@mlmatty.com.

NEIDHARDT, FREDERICK CARL, microbiologist, educator; b. Phila., May 12, 1931; s. Adam Fred and Carrie (Fry) N.; m. Elizabeth Robinson, June 9, 1956 (div. Sept. 1977); children: Richard Frederick, Jane Elizabeth; m. Germaine Chipault, Dec. 3, 1977; 1 son, Marc Frederick. BA, Kenyon Coll., 1952, DSc (hon.), 1976; PhD, Harvard U., 1956; DSc (hon.), Purdue U., 1988, Umea U., 1994. Research fellow Pasteur Inst., Paris, 1956-57; H.C. Ernst research fellow Harvard Med. Sch., 1957-58, instr., then assoc., 1958-61; mem. faculty Purdue U., 1961-70, assoc. prof, then prof., assoc. head dept. biol. scis., 1965-70; mem. faculty U. Mich., Ann Arbor, 1970—, chmn. dept. microbiology and immunology, 1970-82, F.G. Novy disting. univ. prof., 1989-99, F.G. Novy disting. univ. prof. emeritus, 2000—, assoc. dean faculty affairs, 1990-93, assoc. v.p. for rsch., 1993-96, acting v.p. for rsch., 1996-97, interim v.p. for rsch., 1997, v.p. for rsch., 1998. Cons. Dept. Agr., 1964-65; mem. grant study panel NIH, 1965-69, 88-92; mem. commn. scholars Ill. Bd. Higher Edn., 1973-79; mem. test com. for microbiology Nat. Bd. Med. Examiners, 1975-79, chmn., 1979-83; mem. sci. adv. com. Neogen Corp., 1982-92; mem. basic energy scis. adv. com. U.S. Dept. Energy, 1994-98; Wellcome vis. prof. in microbiology U. Ky., 1986. Author books and papers in field; mem. editorial bd. profl. jours. Recipient award bacteriology and immunology Eli Lilly and Co., 1966; Alexander von Humboldt Found. award for U.S. sr. scientist, 1979; NSF sr. fellow U. Copenhagen, 1968-69 Mem. Am. Soc. Microbiology (pres. 1981-82), Am. Acad. Arts and Scis., Am. Soc. Biochemistry and Molecular Biology, Am. Inst. Biol. Scis., Genetics Soc. Am., Soc. Gen. Physiology, Waksman Found. for Microbiology (bd. dirs. 1996—, pres. 2001—), Phi Beta Kappa, Sigma Xi. Office: U Mich Med Sch Dept Microbiology and Immunology Ann Arbor MI 48109-0620 E-mail: fcneid@umich.edu.

NEIDIG, BRYCE P. farmer, farm association administrator; Pres. Nebr. Farm Bur.; owner, gen. farming operation Madison, Nebr. Office: 5225 S 16th St PO Box 80299 Lincoln NE 68512

NEIMAN, JOHN HAMMOND, lawyer; b. Des Moines, Jan. 8, 1917; s. Donald Edwin and Bessie A. (White) N.; m. Madeline Clare Flint, July 2, 1941; children— Richard F., Donald F., Nancy J. B.A., Drake U., 1939, J.D., 1941. Bar: Iowa 1941. Ptnr. Neiman, Neiman, Stone & Spellman, Des Moines, 1946-92, Neiman, Stone, McCormick, Attys., Des Moines, 1992—; exec. v.p., sec. Nat. Assn. Credit Mgmt., 1956-83. Mem. ethics com. Iowa Senate, 1969-73, probate rules com. Iowa Supreme Ct., 1977-81; mem., chmn. Client Security and Atty. Disciplinary Commn., Iowa, 1974-85. Pres. bd. councilors Drake U. Law Sch., 1968; pres. Northwest Community Hosp., Des Moines, 1974-77 Recipient Centennial award Drake U., 1981 Fellow Am. Bar Found., Comml. Law Found., Iowa State Bar Found. (50 Yr. award 1995); mem. ABA (bd. govs. 1984-85, ho. of dels. 1978-87, profl. discipline com. 1979-84, forum com. 1985-89, responsibility for clients protection 1989-90), Iowa Bar Assn. (bd. govs. 1963-67, pres. 1967-68, award of merit 1975), Polk County Bar Assn. (pres. 1960-61), Comml. Law League Am., Iowa State Bar Found. (sec. 1975-78, pres. 1988-92, 50 Yr. Svc. award 1995), Wakonda Club (pres. 1973), Met. Club (pres. 1981-82, 84-86). Republican. Methodist. Home: 3514 Wakonda Ct Des Moines IA 50321-2648 Office: Neiman Stone & McCormick 7405 University Ave Ste 10 Des Moines IA 50325-1343

NEIN, SCOTT R. state legislator; b. Hamilton, Ohio, Apr. 13, 1951; m. Janis Nein; children: Jason, Courtney, Beckett, Brody. BS, Bowling Green State U., 1974. Mem. Ohio Ho. of Reps from 58th dist., Columbus, 1991-95, Ohio Senate from 4th dist., Columbus, 1995—. Agt. Miller Ins.; mem. Butler County Rep. exec. com. Recipient Congl. appt. 8th Congl. Dist. Awards Coun., 1987. Mem. Prol. Ins. Agts. Assn., Ohio Ind. Ins. Agts. Assn., Middletown Ind. Ins. Agts. Assn. (past pres.), Rotary (past pres., Paul Harris Fellow), Middletown C. of C. (bd. dirs.), Farm Bur.

NELSEN, WILLIAM CAMERON, foundation executive, former college president; b. Omaha, Oct. 18, 1941; s. William Peter and Ellen Lucella (Cameron) N.; m. Margaret Leone Rossow, May 30, 1981; children by previous marriage: William Norris, Shawna Lynn; 1 adopted dau., Sarah Ruth. BA, Midland Luth. Coll., Fremont, Nebr., 1963; MA, Columbia U., 1966; PhD, U. Pa., 1971; Fulbright scholar, U. Erlangen, W. Ger., 1964; D (hon.), Midland Luth. Coll., 1995. Program exec. Danforth Found., St. Louis, 1970-73; asst. dean, then v.p., dean coll. St. Olaf Coll., Northfield, Minn., 1973-80; dir. Project on Faculty Devel. Assn. of Am. Colls., 1979; pres. Augustana Coll., Sioux Falls, S.D., 1980-86, Citizens' Scholarship Found. of Am., St. Peter, Minn., 1986—. Bd. dirs. 1st Nat. Bank and Bancommunity Svc. Corp., St. Peter, Minn. Author: Effective Approaches to Faculty Development, 1980, Renewal of the Teacher Scholar, 1981, also articles. Bd. dirs. S.D. Symphony, 1980-85, Sioux Falls YMCA, 1980-86, Luth. Edn1. Conf. N.Am., 1982-86, Sioux Falls United Way, 1983-86; nat. bd. advisors Coun. Aid to Edn.; mem. nat. coun. Connect Am., Points of Light Found; chmn. bd. U.S. Dream Acad.; mem. exec. bd. Nat. Assembly; charter bd. dirs. Nat. Scholarship Providers Assn.. Recipient McKee award for outstanding nat. leadership in edn. Nat. Assn. Ptnrs. in Edn., 1999; Danforth Grad. fellow, 1963, Woodrow Wilson fellow, 1963. Mem. Am. Assn. Higher Edn., Assn. Am. Colls. (bd. dirs. 1984-86), Shoreland Country Club (pres. 1996-99), Consortium for Advancement of Pvt. Higher Edn., Coun. of Ind. Colls., Nat. Dollars for Scholars, Rotary Club. Republican. Lutheran. Home: 804 Spruce Pl Saint Peter MN 56082-1598 Office: Citizens' Scholarship Fund Am PO Box 297 Saint Peter MN 56082-0297 E-mail: wcnelsen@csfa.org.

NELSON, BEN, senator; b. McCook, Nebraska, May 17, 1941; m. Diane Nelson; 4 children. Law degree, Univ. Nebr., 1970, M, 1965, BA in philosophy, 1963. Lawyer, bus. exe., govt. offical in insurance regulation & industry issues; CEO Ctrl Nat. Insurance Group; chief staff, exe. v.p. Nat. Assn. Insurance Commr.; dir. Nebr. Dept. Insurance; state senator U.S. Senate, 2000. Recipient Thomas Jefferson Freedom award, Eagle award, Nat. Eagle Scout Assn., Groundwater Achievement award, Spirit of Enterprise award, U.S. Chamber of Commerce, 2002. Mem.: Veterans Affairs Com., Agriculture Com., Senate Armed Svcs. Com. Democrat. Avocations: reading, hunting, fishing. Office: NE Senator 720 Hart Senate Office Bldg Washington DC 20510*

NELSON, CAROLYN, state legislator; b. Madison, Wis., Oct. 8, 1937; m. Gilbert W. Nelson; children: Paul, John, Karla. BS, N.D. State U., 1959, MS, 1960. Sr. instr. in math. N.D. State U., 1968—; mem. N.D. Ho. of Reps., 1986-88, 92-94, N.D. Senate from 21st dist., 1994—; mem. judiciary com., vet. affairs com. N.D. Senate, minority caucus leader, 2000—. Mem. N.D. State Investment Bd., 1989-92. Mem. Bd. Edn., Fargo, N.D., 1985-91, pres., 1989-90; trustee N.D. Tchrs. Fund for Retirement, 1985-92, pres., 1990-92; mem. N.D. PTA, pres., 1978-81, N.D. Women's and Children's Caucus. Recipient Merit Svc. award Gamma Phi Beta, 1978, 90, Legis. Voices award Children's Caucus, 1995; named Legislator of Yr., N.D. Bar Assn., 2000, N.D. Student Assn., 2001. Mem. LWV, Am. Guild English Handbell Ringers (area chmn. 1982-84, nat. bd. dirs. 1982-90), N.D. Fedn. Music Clubs (life; pres. 1997-2001, Rose Fay Thomas fellow 2001), Gamma Phi Beta, Phi Kappa Phi, Sigma Alpha Iota. Address: 1125 College St Fargo ND 58102-3433 Office: ND Senate State Capitol Bismarck ND 58505

NELSON, CHARLOTTE BOWERS, public administrator; b. Bristol, Va., June 28, 1931; d. Thaddeus Ray and Ruth Nelson (Moore) Bowers; m. Gustav Carl Nelson, June 1, 1957; children: Ruth Elizabeth, David Carl, Thomas Gustav. BA summa cum laude, Duke U., 1954; MA, Columbia U., 1961; MPA, Drake U., 1983. Instr. Beaver Coll., 1957-58, Drake U., Des Moines, 1975-82; office mgr. LWV of Iowa, 1975-82; exec. asst. Iowa Dept. Human Svcs., 1983-85; exec. dir. Iowa Commn. on Status of Women Dept. Human Rights, 1985—. Bd. dirs., pres. LWV, Beloit, Wis., 1960-74; bd. dirs. LWV, Des Moines, 1974-82, Westminster House, Des Moines, 1988-97, pres. 1996-97. Recipient Gov.'s Golden Dome award as Leader of the Yr., 2002; named Visionary Woman, Young Women's Resource Ctr., 1994. Mem. Am. Soc. Pub. Adminstrn. (mem. exec. coun. 1984-92, 98-99, past pres., Mem. of Yr. 1993), Phi Beta Kappa, Pi Alpha Alpha. Home: 1141 Cummins Cir Des Moines IA 50311-2113 Office: Human Rights Dept Lucas State Office Bldg Des Moines IA 50319-0001 E-mail: charlotte.nelson@dhr.state.ia.us., nelson514@aol.com.

NELSON, DARRELL WAYNE, university administrator, scientist; b. Aledo, Ill., Nov. 28, 1939; s. Wayne Edward and Olive Elvina (Peterson) N.; m. Nancyann Hyer, Aug. 27, 1961; children: Christina Lynne, Craig Douglas. BS in Agriculture, U. Ill., 1961, MS in Agronomy, 1963; PhD in Agronomy, Iowa State U., 1967. Cert. profl. soil scientist. Div. chief U.S. Army Chem. Corps., Denver, 1967-68; asst. prof. Purdue U., West Lafayette, Ind., 1968-73, assoc. prof., 1973-77, prof. agronomy, 1977-84; dept. head U. Nebr., Lincoln, 1984-88, dean for agr. rsch. and dir. Nebr. Agrl. Experiment Sta., 1988—. Cons. U.S. EPA, Washington, 1977-79, Ind. Bd. of Health, Indpls., 1977-83, Eli Lilly Co., Indpls., 1976. Editor: Chemical Mobility and Reactivity in Soils, 1983. Served to capt. U.S. Army, 1967-68. Fellow AAAS, Am. Soc. Agronomy (bd. dirs., pres.-elect, pres. 2001, CIBA-Geigy award 1975, Agronomic Achievement award 1983, Environ. Quality Rsch. award 1985), Soil Sci. Soc. Am. (bd. dirs., pres. elect 1992, pres. 1993, past. pres. 1994); mem. Internat. Soil Sci. Soc., Lions Lodge (treas. 1980-83, Lafayette, Ind. chpt.). Presbyterian. Avocations: fishing, skiing, jogging. Office: Univ of Nebr Agrl Rsch Divsn Lincoln NE 68583-0704 E-mail: dnelson1@unl.edu.

NELSON, DAVID ALDRICH, judge; b. Watertown, N.Y., Aug. 14, 1932; s. Carlton Low and Irene Demetria (Aldrich) Nelson; m. Mary Dickson, Aug. 25, 1956; 3 children. AB, Hamilton Coll., 1954; postgrad., Cambridge U., Eng., 1954—55; LLB, Harvard U., 1958. Bar: Ohio 1958, N.Y. 1982. Atty.-advisor Office of the Gen. Counsel, Dept. of the Air Force, 1959—62; assoc. Squire, Sanders & Dempsey, Cleve., 1958—67, ptnr., 1967—69, 1972—85; judge U.S. Ct. Appeals (6th cir.), Cin., 1985—99, sr. judge, 1999—. Gen. counsel U.S. Post Office Dept., Washington, 1969—71; sr. asst. postmaster gen., gen. counsel U.S. Postal Svc., Washington, 1971; nat. coun. Ohio State U. Coll. Law, 1988—98. Trustee Hamilton Coll., 1984—88. Recipient Benjamin Franklin award, U.S. Post Office Dept., 1969; scholar Fulbright, 1954—55. Fellow: Am. Coll. Trial Lawyers; mem.: Cin. Bar Assn., Ohio Bar Assn., Fed. Bar Assn., Emerson Lit. Soc., Ct. of Nisi Prius (sgt. emeritus), Phi Beta Kappa. Office: US Ct Appeals 6th Cir Potter Stewart US Ct House 5th and Walnut St Cincinnati OH 45202-3988

NELSON, DAVID LEONARD, process management systems company executive; b. Omaha, May 8, 1930; s. Leonard A. and Cecelia (Steinert) N.; m. Jacqueline J. Zerbe, Dec. 26, 1952; 1 child, Nancy Jo. BS, Iowa State U., 1952. Mktg. adminstr. Ingersoll Rand, Chgo., 1954-56; with Accuray Corp., Columbus, Ohio, 1956-87, exec. v.p., gen. mgr., 1967, pres., 1967-87, chief exec. officer, 1970-87; pres. process automation bus. unit Combustion Engring., Inc., 1987-90; pres. bus. area process automation Asea Brown Boveri, Stamford, Conn., 1990-91, v.p. customer satisfaction Ams. region, 1991-93, v.p. customer support Ams. region, 1994-95; chmn. bd. dirs. Herman Miller Inc., Zeeland, Mich., 1995-2000, counsel, 2000—. Patentee in field. Served to capt. USMCR, 1952-54. Mem. IEEE, Instrument Soc. Am., Newcomen Soc. N.Am., Tau Beta Pi, Phi Kappa Phi, Phi Eta Sigma, Delta Upsilon. Home: 1113 Roundhouse Ln Alexandria VA 22314-5935

NELSON, DENNIS LEE, finance educator; b. Randall, Minn., Nov. 4, 1929; s. George Otto and Emma Ida (Schwanke) N.; m. Joyce Marie Prozinski, Aug. 25, 1956; children: Constance, Kristin, Norma Joan. BS, St. Cloud State U., 1954; MA, U. Minn., 1964, PhD in Econs., 1970. Prof. econs. U. Minn., Duluth, 1964—, dir. ctr. for econ. edn., 1967-71, grad. faculty, 1970—, head dept. econs., 1971-77, assoc. chancellor, 1977-88, vice chancellor fin. ops., 1987-88. Mem. faculty Westhill Coll., U. Birmingham, Eng., 1996-97; instnl. rep. for adminstrs. on Nat. Collegiate Athletic Assn., 1978-87; adminstr., vis. faculty Oxford U., Eng., 1997, Yonsei U., Seoul, 1988, Moscow U., 1978, 84. Author econ. textbooks. Recipient Disting. Alumnus award U. Minn. Mem. Duluth Blueline Club, Duluth Quarterback Club, UMD Rasmussen Fund, UMD Hoop Club, Pres. Club U. Minn. Lutheran. Avocations: gardening, writing, reading, woodworking, bridge. Home: On the Lake 21190 Forest Rd Little Falls MN 56345-4065 Office: U Minn 10 University Dr Duluth MN 55812-2403

NELSON, DON JEROME, electrical engineering and computer science educator; b. Nebr., Aug. 17, 1930; s. Irvin Andrew and Agnes Emelia (Nissen) N. BSc, U. Nebr., 1953, MSc, 1958; PhD, Stanford U., 1962. Registered profl. engr., Nebr. Mem. tech. staff AT&T Bell Labs., Manhattan, N.Y., 1953, 55; instr. U. Nebr., Lincoln, 1955-58, from asst. to assoc. prof., 1960-63, dir. computer ctr., 1963-72, prof. electrical engring., 1967—, prof. computer sci., 1969—, co-dir. Ctr. Comm. & Info. Sci., 1988-91, dir. rsch. computing group, 1993-97; gen. mgr. Interactive Info. R&D, 1997—. Cons. Union Life Ins., Lincoln, 1973, Nebr. Pub. Power Dist., Columbus, 1972-83, Taiwan Power Co., Taipei, 1974. 1st lt. USAF, 1953-55. Mem. IEEE (sr., Outstanding Faculty award 1989), Assn. Computing Machinery. Republican. Home: 4911 Concord Rd Lincoln NE 68516-3330 Office: U Nebr Dept Elec Engring 209N WSEC Lincoln NE 68588-0511 E-mail: nelson@izrd.com., nelson@yoda.unl.edu.

NELSON, DUANE JUAN, minister; b. Urbana, Ill., Nov. 19, 1939; s. Elmer Andrew and Mabel Mae (Jones) N.; m. Marlys Mavis Klaustermeier-Hawkinson, Aug. 30, 1974; children: Matthew, Joshua, Joel. BA, Wartburg Coll., Waverly, Iowa, 1961; MDiv, Wartburg Theol. Sem., Dubuque, 1965. Ordained to ministry Luth. Ch., 1966. Pastor St. Paul's Luth. Ch., Massillon, Ohio, 1966-67, Hope Luth. Ch., Indpls., 1967-69, Grace Luth. Ch., Westchester, Ill., 1977-78; sr. chaplain Minn. Rec./Diag. Ctr., Lino Lakes, 1970-75; criminal justice chaplain Luth. Social Svc., Washington, 1975-77; staff chaplain Unity Med. Ctr., Fridley, Minn., 1978-81; sr. chaplain Anoka (Minn.) Metro-Reg. Treatment Ctr., 1981—. Sec. bd. Ch. in Soc., St. Paul Synod, 1986-90; mem. specialized pastoral com., bd. for ministry St. Paul Area Synod, 1991—; mem. chaplaincy adv. bd. HHS, 1990—; program chmn. Assn. of Mental health Chaplains, Midwest states, 1973-75. Writer, producer Multi-Media presentation, Celebrate Life, 1986, Your Part in God's World, 1988, Aging: Keenagers in Prime Time, 1996, others. Pres. Coalition for Criminal Justice Reform, Washington, 1976; co-founder Pastoral Care sect. Minn. Chem. Dependency Assn., St. Paul, 1983; lectr. health care workshops; v.p. Guardian Angel Corp., St. Paul; mem. State of Minn. AIDS Steering Com., 1985-86; co-prs. MVHS Boosters, 1994-95; actor Cmty. Theater. Mem. Assn. for Clin. Pastoral Edn., Minn. State Chaplains Assn. (chmn. 1990-96, treas. 1990—, vol. prison chaplain 1989-90), Anoka County Corrections Outpatient Treatment Program, Castle Singers (pres. 1960). Office: Anoka Metro-Reg Trtmt Ctr 3301 7th Ave Anoka MN 55303-4516 E-mail: duane.nelson@state.mn.us.

NELSON, E. BENJAMIN, senator, former governor, lawyer; b. McCook, Nebr., May 17, 1941; s. Benjamin Earl and Birdella Ruby (Henderson) N.; m. Diane C. Gleason, Feb. 22, 1980; children from a previous marriage: Sarah Jane, Patrick James; stepchildren: Kevin Michael Gleason, Christine Marie Gleason. BA, U. Nebr., 1963; MA, 1966, JD, 1970; LLD (hon.), Creighton U., 1992, Peru State Coll., 1993. Bar: Nebr. 1970. Instr. dept. philosophy U. Nebr., 1963-65; supr. Dept. Ins. State of Nebr., Lincoln, 1965-72; dir. ins., 1975-76; asst. gen. counsel, gen. counsel, sec., v.p. The Ctrl. Nat. Ins. Group Omaha, 1972-75; exec. v.p., 1976-77; pres., 1978-81; CEO, 1980-81; of counsel Kennedy, Holland, DeLacy & Svoboda, Omaha, 1985-90; gov. State of Nebr., Lincoln, 1991-98; of counsel Lumson, Dugan and Murray, Omaha, 1999—; U.S. Senator from Nebr., 2001—. Co-chmn. Carter/Mondale re-election campaign, Nebr., 1980; chair Nat. Edn. Goals Panel, 1992-94; co-founder Gov.'s Ethanol Coalition, chair, 1991, 94; pres. Coun. of State Govs., 1994. Recipient Disting. Eagle award Nat. Eagle Scout Assn., 1994; named Amb. Plenipotentiary, 1993. Mem. ABA, Nat. Assn. Ind. Insurers, Nat. Assn. Ins. Commrs. (exec. v.p. 1982-85), Nebr. Bar Assn., Consumer Credit Ins. Assn., Midwestern Govs. Assn. (chair 1994), Western Govs. Assn. (vice chair 1994, chair 1995), Happy Hollow Club, Omaha Club, Hillcrest Country Club. Democrat. Methodist. Office: US Senate 720 Hart Senate Office Bldg Washington DC 20510

NELSON, FRANKLIN W. commissioner, state; Commr. Kans. Bank Commr.'s Office, Topeka. Office: Kans Bank Commrs Office 700 SW Jackson St Ste 300 Topeka KS 66603-3757

NELSON, GARY J. state legislator; m. Linda; 3 children. Degree, Concordia Coll. Farmer; mem. N.D. Senate, 1977—; minority whip, 1991; majority whip. Past pres. Cent. Cass Sch. Bd.; farmer. Mem. Farm Bur., Crop Improvement Assn., Casselton Cmty. Club, Masons, N.D. Wildlife Fedn., Wildlife Club. Office: PO Box 945 Casselton ND 58012-0945 also: State Senate State Capital Bismarck ND 58505

NELSON, GARY MICHAEL, lawyer; b. Mpls., July 12, 1951; s. Emery Marshal and Henrietta Margaret (Flategraff) Nelson; m. Deb Snyder; 1 child Courtney Snyder ; children: Rachel Mary, Amy Margaret. BA, Gustavus Adolphus Coll., St. Peter, Minn., 1973; JD, Harvard U., 1976. Bar: Minn. 1976, U.S. Dist. Ct. Minn. 1976. Ptnr., CEO Oppenheimer Wolff & Donnelly, Mpls., 1976-97; exec. v.p., gen. counsel, corp. sec. Ceridian Corp., 1997—. Chair corp. practice inst. Minn. Inst. Legal Edn., Mpls., 1978-93. Sec., v.p. Mpls. Girls' Club, 1978-83. Recipient Significant Contbns. award Am. Girls' Clubs Am., 1982. Mem. ABA. Lutheran. Avocations: fishing, hunting, hiking, reading. Home: 2685 Maplewood Rd Wayzata MN 55391 Office: Ceridian Corp 3311 E Old Shakopee Rd Minneapolis MN 55425-1640

NELSON, GLEN DAVID, medical products executive, physician; b. Mpls., Mar. 28, 1937; s. Ralph and Edna S. Nelson; m. Marilyn Carlson, June 30, 1961; children: Diana, Curtis, Wendy. AB, Harvard U., 1959; MD, U. Minn., 1963. Diplomate Am. Bd. Surgery, also sub-bd. bariatric and peripheral vascular surgery. Intern Hennepin County Gen. Hosp., Mpls., 1963-64, resident in gen. surgery, 1964-69; staff surgeon Park Nicollet Med. Ctr. (formerly St. Louis Park Med. Ctr.), 1969-86, pres., chmn. bd. trustees, 1975-86; chmn., CEO Am. Med Ctrs., 1984-86; exec. v.p. Medtronic, Inc., 1986-88, vice chmn., 1988—2002, also bd. dirs.; prin., owner GDN Holdings, LLC, Minnetonka, 2002—. Clin. prof. dept. surgery U. Minn.; bd. dirs. Carlson Cos., Inc., Mpls., St. Paul Cos., Medtronic, Inc., Mpls., Advanced BioSurfaces, Inc., Itamar Med. Ltd. Bd. visitors Johns Hopkins U.; mem. deans coun. Harvard. Fellow ACS (del.); mem. AMA, Am. Acad. Med. Dirs., Am. Coll. Physician Execs., Hennepin County Med. Assn., Greater Mpls. C. of C. (chmn. 1987), Jackson Hole Group. Office: GDN Holdings LLC 301 Carlson Parkway Ste 315 Minnetonka MN 55305

NELSON, H. H. RED, insurance company executive; b. Herman, Nebr., June 2, 1912; m. Ruth Hansen; children: John, Steve. BA, U. Nebr., 1934, JD, 1937. Bar: Iowa, Nebr. 1938; CLU, 1948. Asst. mgr. life accident group depts. Travelers Inc. Co., Omaha, 1939-44; chmn. bd. Redlands Ins. Co., 1945—, Ins. Agts. Inc., Council Bluffs, Iowa, 1945—, Am. Agrisurance Co., Council Bluffs, 1969—, Am. Growers Ins., Council Bluffs, 1995—, Acceptance Ins., Tex., Council Bluffs, 1988—; chmn. Silverstone Group, 1997-2001, chmn. emeritus, 2001—. Chmn. Redland Group Cos. Pres. United Fund, Western Iowa council Boy Scouts Am.; bd. dirs. Nat. Scout Council; pres. Christian Home Orphanage, Council Bluffs Indsl. Found. Named to, Iowa Ins. Hall of Fame, 1997. Office: Silverstone Group 300 W Broadway Ste 200 Council Bluffs IA 51503-9099 E-mail: hhnelson@ssgi.com.

NELSON, HARRY DONALD, telecommunications executive; b. Chgo., Nov. 23, 1933; s. Harry E. and Elsie I. (Liljedahl) N.; m. Carol J. Stewart, Mar. 31, 1957; children: Donald S., David S., Sharon J. Arnold. BS, Northwestern U., Evanston, Ill., 1955, MBA, 1959. Sales rep., sales trainer Procter & Gamble, Chgo., 1955-58; sales adminstr. internat. products GE, N.Y., Ky., 1959-70, Md., Ohio, 1959-72, product mgr., 1978-81; mgr. mktg. Tex. Instruments, Dallas, 1972-74; v.p. mktg. Rockwell Internat., Anaheim, Calif., 1975, HMW-Pulsar, Lancaster, Pa., 1976-78, Genesco, Nashville, 1981-83; v.p. cellular ops. Tel. and Data Systems, Chgo., 1983-85; pres., CEO U.S. Cellular, 1985—. Mem. Dean's Adv. Bd. Kellogg Sch. Mgmt. Northwestern U., Evanston, 1994—, Alumni Adv. Bd., 1991—. With U.S. Army, 1956-57. Recipient Dean's Alumni award Kellogg Sch. Mgmt., 1996. Mem. Cellular Telecomm. Industry Assn. (treas., bd. dirs., exec. com. 1986—, Pres.'s award 1996). Republican. Baptist. Avocations: paperweight collecting, antique sales, stamp and coin collecting. Office: US Cellular 8410 W Bryn Mawr Ave Ste 700 Chicago IL 60631-3486

NELSON, HERBERT LEROY, psychiatrist; b. Eddyville, Iowa, June 15, 1922; s. Albert and Bessie Mae (Durham) Nelson; m. Carol Lorayne Hofert, Dec. 23, 1943; children: Richard Kent, Vicki Lurae, Thadeus Leroy, Cylda Vermae. B.A., U. Iowa, 1943, M.D., 1946. Diplomate Am Bd Psychiatry and Neurology. Intern Univ Hosps. of U. Iowa, Iowa City, 1946-47; resident Brooke Army Med. Ctr, Fort Sam Houston, Tex, 1947-49, U.S. VA Hosp., Knoxville, Iowa, 1949-51, Oreg. State Hosp., Salem, 1951-52, clin. dir., 1952-63; asst. prof. psychiatry U. Iowa, Iowa City, 1963-66, assoc. prof., 1966-73, prof., 1973-84, prof. emeritus, 1984—; dir. Iowa Mental Health Authority, Iowa City, 1968-82; med. dir. Mideast Iowa Community Mental Health Ctr., 1969-84. Adj prof Tulane Univ, New Orleans, 1974—77. Co-author: 4 monographs; contbr. articles to profl jours. Served as capt MC U.S. Army, 1947—49. Fellow: Am Psychiat Asn; mem.: AMA, Am Col Mental Health Adminrs, Am Asn Psychiat Adminrs, Johnson County Med Soc, Iowa Psychiat Soc (pres 1970—71, chmn subcom psychiat care 1973—77). Republican. Methodist. Avocations: gardening, fishing, woodworking, painting, travel. Home and Office: 1400 Laura Dr Iowa City IA 52245-1539 Personal E-mail: hlnelson@mehsi.com.

NELSON, KEITHE EUGENE, state court administrator, lawyer; b. Grand Forks, N.D. m. Shirley Jeanne Jordahl, June 10, 1955; children: Kirsti Lynn Nelson Hoerauf, Scott David, Kenen Edward, Karen Lee Nelson Strandquist. PhB, U. N.D., 1958, JD, 1959. Bar: N.D. 1959, U.S. Ct. Mil. Appeals 1967., U.S. Supreme Ct. 1967. With Armour & Co., Grand Forks, 1958-59; commd. 2d lt. USAF, 1958, advanced through grades to maj. gen., 1985, judge advocate N.D. and, Fed. Republic Germany and Eng., 1959-73, chief career mgmt., 1973-77; comdt. USAF JAG Sch., Montgomery, Ala., 1977-81; staff judge adv. Tactical Air Command USAF, Hampton, VA., 1981-82, SAC, Omaha, 1984-85; dir. USAF Judiciary, Washington, 1982-84; dep. JAG USAF, 1985, JAG, 1988-91, JAG, 1988, ret. JAG, 1991; dir. jud. planning Supreme Ct. N.D.; state ct. administr., 1992—. Chmn. editorial bd. USAF Law Rev., 1977-81. Decorated D.S.M., Legion of Merit with two oak leaf clusters. Mem. ABA. Lutheran. Avocations: skeet shooting, hunting, tennis, theater. Home: 800 Munich Dr Bismarck ND 58504-7050

NELSON, LAWRENCE EVAN, business consultant; b. Chgo., Dec. 3, 1932; s. Evan Thomas and Elizabeth Marie (Stettka) N.; m. Jean H. Clayton, July 11, 1953; children: Lori Jean, Lawrence Evan. BS with honors, So. Ill. U., 1959; MBA, U. Chgo., 1969. CPA, Ill. Sr. acct. Price Waterhouse & Co., CPA's, Chgo., 1959-65; sec.-treas. Bradner Cen. Co., 1965-73; pres. Protectoseal Co., Bensenville, Ill., 1973-84, Plan Ahead Inc., Palos Park, Ill, 1984—. Author: (book) Personal Financial Planning, 1985. Treas. City of Palos Heights, Ill., 1964-68, alderman, 1970-71; trustee Palos Heights FPD, 1977—. Served with USNR, 1952-56. Mem. Am. Inst. CPA's, Ill. Soc. CPA's. Office: Plan Ahead Inc PO Box 164 Palos Park IL 60464-0164

NELSON, MARILYN C. hotel executive, food service executive, travel services executive, marketing professional; b. Mpls. m. Glen Nelson; children: Diana, Curtis C., Wendy. Student, U. Sorbonne, Paris, Inst. Hautes Etudes Econ., Geneva; degree in internat. econs. with honors, Smith Coll., 1961; DBA (hon.), Johnson & Wales U.; DHL (hon.), Coll. St. Catherine, Gustavus Adolphus Coll. Securities analyst Paine Webber, Mpls.; co-owner Citizens State Bank, Waterville, Minn., 1971—; COO Carlson Cos., Inc., Mpls., 1997—, pres., CEO, chmn., 1998—, also bd. dirs. Co-chair Carlson Holdings, Inc., 1991—; dep. chair Thomas Cook Holdings; co-chair Carlson Wagonlit Travel, 1994—; disting. vis. prof. Johnson & Wales U.; bd. dirs. Exxonmobil Corp., Qwest, Inc. Pres. United Way Mpls., campaign chair, 1984; bd. dirs. United Way Am.; chair Super Bown Task Force, Mpls.; bd. dirs. U.S. Nat. Tourism Orgn., 1996—, Ctr. for Internat. Leadership, 1990—; mem. Internat. Adv. Coun., 1996—; mem. disting. adv. coun. Coll. of St. Catherine, 1989—; mem. Bretton Woods Com., 1986—; hon. bd. dris. Svenska Inst., Stockholm, 1993—; mem. adv. bd. Hubert H. Humphrey Inst. Pub. Affairs, 1992-96; co-founder Minn. Women's Econ. Roundtable, 1974—; chair Minn. Super Bowl Task Force, 1992; chair, founder Midsummer Internat. Festival of Music; co-chair New Sweden '88; past bd. dirs. Guthrie Theatre, Greater Mpls. coun. Girl Scouts U.S., Jr. Achievement, Jr. League Mpls., KTCA Pub. TV, Minn. Congl. Award, Minn. Opera Co., Women's' Assn. Minn. Symphony Orch.; trustee Smith Coll., Northampton, Mass., 1980-85, Macalester Coll., St. Paul, 1974-80. Named Woman of Yr., Minn. Exec. Women in Tourism, Sales Exec. of Yr., Sales and Mktg. Exec. of Mpls., Person of Yr. Travel Agt. mag., 1997, Woman of Yr. Roundtable for Women in Foodsvc., 1995, Outstanding Individual in Tourism, Minn. Office of Tourism, 1992, Woman of Yr., Minn. Exec. Women in Tourism, 1991-92, The Top 25 Execs. Yr. Bus. Week, 1999, Exec. Yr. Corp. Report Minn., 1999; recipient Minn. Congl. award for initiative and svc. to cmty., cert. of commendation State of Minn., Cmty. Svc. award YWCA, Independence award Vinland Nat. Ctr., Cmty. Svc. award Park-Nicollet Med. Ctr., Outstanding Mktg. Exec. of Yr. award, Minn. Distributive Edn. Club Am., Career Achievement award Sales and Mktg. Execs. Mpls., Outstanding Achievement award United Way Mpls., Extraordinary Leadership award Greater Mpls. C. of C., Disting. Svc. award United Way of Am., 1984-90, Nat. Caring award Caring Inst., 1995, Outstanding Bus. Leader award Northwood U., 1995, The 50 Most Powerful Women award in Am. Bus. Fortune, 1998, United Way Minn. Disting. Svc. award United Way's highest vol. honor, 1998, Good Neighbor award WCCO Radio, 1999, Caring Heart award charitable contbns. by Larry King Cardiac Found., 1999, Am.'s 100 Most Important Women award Ladies' Home Jr., 1999, The 50 Most Powerful Women in Bus. Fortune 1999, The Most Powerful Women in Travel #1 Travel Agent, 1999, Svc. Above Self award The Rotary Club Downtown, Minn., 1999, The Top 500 Women-Owned Bus.'s award Working Women, 2000, The 25 Most Influential Executives award Leisure Travel News, 2000, Northwest Airlines Disting. World Traveler award Hospitality Sales and Mktg. Assn. Internat., 2000. Mem. Hennepin County Med. Soc. Auxiliary, Jr. League Mpls., Minn. Meetings, Smith Coll. Alumni Assn., Smith Club Mpls., Woodhill Country Club, Mpls. Club, N.W. Tennis Club, Nat. Ctr. for Social Entrepreneurs, Com. of 200, Minn. Orchestral Assn., Orphei Dranger, Alpha Kappa Psi. Office: Carlson Cos Inc Carlson Parkway Minneapolis MN 55459-8215

NELSON, MARY ELLEN DICKSON, retired actuary; b. Mpls., Mar. 24, 1933; d. William Alexander and Laura Winona (Baxter) Dickson; m. David Aldrich Nelson, Aug. 25, 1956; children: Frederick Dickson, Claudia Baxter, Caleb Edward. BA, Vassar Coll., 1954; postgrad., Cambridge (Eng.) U., 1954-55. Rsch. assoc. N.Am. Life & Casualty Co., Mpls., 1955-56; actuarial asst. John Hancock Mut. Life Ins. Co., Boston, 1956-58; actuary David R. Kass & Assocs., Cleve., 1973-74; pres. Nelson & Co., 1975, Conrad, Nelson & Co., Cleve., 1975-81, Nelson & Co., Cleve./Cin., 1981-99. Bd. dirs. Blount Internat. Inc. and its subs. Blount, Inc., Montgomery, Ala., 1986—99, Broadwing, Inc., Union Ctrl. Life Ins. Co., Cin. Scholar Fulbright, 1954—55. Fellow: Soc. Actuaries, Phi Beta Kappa; mem.: Am. Acad. Actuaries, Midwest Benefits Conf. (chair 1991), Cin. Actuaries Club. Republican.

NELSON, PAMELA A. state legislator; m. Vic Nelson; 2 children. Mem. S.D. State Ho. of Reps., 1986-88, S.D. State Senate, 1988-96; commr. SD pub. utilities commn., Pierre, 1997—. Democrat. Roman Catholic. Mem. Kiwanis W, mem. LWV. Home: 2505 S Marion Rd Sioux Falls SD 57106-0842 Office: Pub Utilities Commn Capitol Bldg 1st Fl 500 E Capitol Ave Pierre SD 57501-5070

NELSON, PHILIP EDWIN, food scientist, educator; b. Shelbyville, Ind., Nov. 12, 1934; s. Brainard R. and Alta E. (Pitts) N.; m. Sue Bayless, Dec. 27, 1955; children: Jennifer, Andrew, Bradley. BS, Purdue U., 1956, PhD, 1976. Plant mgr. Blue River Packing Co., Morristown, Ind., 1956-60; instr. Purdue U., West Lafayette, 1961-76, head dept. food sci., 1984—. Cons. PEN Cons., West Lafayette, 1974; chair Food Processors Inst., Washington, 1990-93. Editor: Fruit Vegetable Juice Technology, 1980, Principles of Aseptic Processing and Packaging, 1992. Recipient Pers. Achievement award USDA, 1997. Fellow Inst. Food Techs. (Indsl. Achievement award 1976, Nicholas Appert award 1995, 49'er Svc. award 1995, Tanner Lectr. 1999, pres. 2001—); mem. AAAS, Sigma Xi, Phi Tau Sigma (pres. 1976-77). Achievements include 11 U.S. and foreign patents. Office: Purdue U Dept Food Sci 1160 Food Sci Bldg West Lafayette IN 47907-1160 E-mail: pen@purdue.edu.

NELSON, PRINCE ROGERS See PRINCE

NELSON, RALPH ALFRED, physician; b. Mpls., June 19, 1927; s. Alfred W. and Lydia (Johnson) N.; m. Rosemary Pokela, Aug. 7, 1954; children— Edward Ancher, Audrey Anne, Elizabeth Marie, Andrew William, Evan Robert. B.A., U. Minn., 1949, M.D., 1953, Ph.D., 1961. Diplomate Am. Bd. Internal Medicine. Intern Cook County (Ill.) Hosp., 1953-54; resident U. Minn. Hosps., Mpls., 1954-55, U. Minn., Mpls., 1955-56; fellow in physiology Mayo Grad. Sch., Rochester, Minn., 1957-60, resident in internal medicine, 1976-78; practice medicine specializing in internal medicine and clin. nutrition Sioux Falls, S.D., 1978-79, Urbana, Ill., 1979—. Bd. dirs. Scott Research Lab., Fairview Park Hosp., Cleve., 1962-67; assoc. in physiology Western Res. U., Cleve., 1962-67; asst. prof. physiology Mayo Grad. Sch., 1967-73, Mayo Med. Sch., 1973, assoc. prof. nutrition, 1974; cons. in nutrition Mayo Clinic, 1967-76; assoc. prof. medicine U. S.D. Sch. Medicine, Sioux Falls, 1978-79; prof. nutrition U. Ill. Coll. Medicine, Urbana-Champaign, 1979— , chmn. dept. medicine prof. nutritional sci., physiology, biophysics dept. food sci. Sch. Agr., 1979—, also prof. medicine, exec. head dept. internal medicine , 1989—, exec. head four sites of Coll. Medicine, 1989—; dir. research Carle Found. Hosp., Urbana, 1979— ; cons. nutritional support service Danville (Ill.) VA Hosp., 1980—. Co-author: The Mayo Clinic Renal Diet Cookbook, 1974; contbr. articles on nutrition, physiology, and hibernation to sci. jours.; editor: Geriatrics, 1980— , The Physician and Sportsmedicine, 1980-88, Am. Jour. Clin. Nutrition, 1980-83. Cons. in nutrition Nat. Cancer Inst., 1976; cons. in nutrition HEW, 1976, 79, 89, Nat. Heart and Lung Inst., 1976. Served with USAF, 1945-47. Fulbright scholar, Morocco, 1988. Fellow ACP; mem. Am. Physiol. Soc., Am. Inst. Nutrition, Am. Soc. Clin. Nutrition, Central Soc. Clin. Research, Am. Gastroent. Assn. Lutheran. Home: 2 Illini Cir Urbana IL 61801-5813 Office: Carle Foundation Hospital 611 W Park St Urbana IL 61801-2529 E-mail: r-nelson@staff.UIUC.edu.

NELSON, RALPH STANLEY, lawyer; b. Mpls., Mar. 15, 1943; s. Stanley L. and Louise M. Nelson; m. Judy E. Nelson, July 8, 1867; children: Sara C., Amy E., David A. BS in Bus. Adminstrn., U. Minn., 1966; JD with honors, Drake U., 1972. Bar: Minn. 1973, Wash. 1982, Tex. 1985. Assoc. Wiese and Cox, Ltd., Mpls., 1973-76; atty. Burlington No. R.R., St. Paul, 1976-81; sr. corp. counsel Burlington No. Inc., Seattle, 1981-85; v.p. law and adminstrn. Burlington Motor Carriers Inc., Ft. Worth, 1985-88, exec. v.p. and gen. counsel, 1988-93, sr. v.p., gen. counsel Daleville (Indpls.), Ind., 1993-96, Trism Inc., Kennesaw, Ga., 1996-2001, exec. v.p., gen. counsel, 2001—, pres., CEO, 2001—. Mem. law rev. Drake U. Capt. USMC, 1966-70. Mem. Order of the Coif. E-mail: rnelson@trism.com.

NELSON, RANDY J. psychology educator; b. Detroit, Jan. 13, 1954; s. Ralph Edward and Ada B. Nelson; m. Anne Courtney DeVries. AB in Psychology with honors, U. Calif., Berkeley, 1978, MA in Psychology, 1980, PhD in Psychology, 1983, PhD in Endocrinology, 1984. Rsch. asst. Dr. F.A. Beach U. Calif., Berkeley, 1978, Dr. I Zucker U. Calif., Berkeley, 1978-84; post doctoral fellow U. Tex., Austin, 1984-86; asst. prof. psychology The Johns Hopkins Univ., Balt., 1986-91, assoc. prof. psychology, 1991-96, assoc. prof. population dynamics, 1991-96, prof. psychology, neurosci., population dynamics, 1996-2000; disting. prof. social and behavioral scis. Ohio State U., 2000—, prof. psychology and neurosci., 2000—. Grant application reviewer NIH, 1986-87, 95—, NSF, 1986—, NSF program officer, 1995-96, 97-98; jour. reviewer Animal Behavior, Brain Rsch., Biology of Reproduction, Jour. Biol. Rhythms, Jour. Comparative Neurology, Jour. Comparative Psychology, Jour. Mammology, Jour. of Reproduction & Fertility, Jour. Exptl. Psychology, Jour. Reproduction, Fertility & Devel., Jour. Pineal Rsch., Neuroendocrine Letters, Nature, Neurobehavioral Toxicology and Teratology, Neuroendocrinology, Physiology and Behavior, Sci., Procs. of NAS. Author: An Introduction to Behavioral Endocrinology, 1995; contbr. numerous articles to profl. jours. including Nature, Jour. of Nervous and Mental Disease, Jour. Comparative Psychology, Jour. Exptl. Zoology, Biology of Reproduction, Jour. of Urology, Physiology and Behavior, Am. Jour. Physiology, Physiological Zoology, Behavioral and Brain Scis., Can. Jour. Zoology, others; mem. editorial bd. Behavioral Neuroscience, J. Pineal Rsch. Recipient postdoctoral fellowship NIH, 1984-86, James A. Shannon award Nat. Cancer Inst., 1992-94. Mem. Soc. for Neurosci., Am. Soc. Mammalogists, Animal Behavior Soc., Soc. for Study of Biolog. Rhythyms, Soc. for the Study of Reproduction (mem. edn. com. 1982-83, 85-86, chairperson edn. com. 1986-87, editor newsletter 1986-88, membership com. 1990-94), Phi Beta Kappa, Sigma Chi, Psi Chi. Office: Ohio State U Dept Psychology & Neuroscience 09 Townshend Hall Columbus OH 43201-2222 E-mail: rnelsont@osu.edu.

NELSON, RICHARD ARTHUR, lawyer; b. Fosston, Minn., Apr. 8, 1947; BS in Math., U. Minn., 1969, JD, 1974. Bar: Minn. 1974, U.S. Ct. Appeals (D.C. cir.) 1975, U.S. Dist. Ct. Minn. 1975. Law clk. U.S. Ct. Appeals (D.C. cir.), Washington, 1974-75; ptnr. Faegre and Benson, Mpls., 1975—. Seminar lectr. in employee benefits and labor laws, 1983—. Note and articles editor Minn. Law Rev., 1973-74. Active Dem.-Farmer-Labor State Cen. Com., Minn., 1976—, del. dist. and local coms. and convs., 1970—, state exec. com., 1990—; student rep. bd. regents U. Minn., Mpls., 1973-74; mem. adv. coun. IRS Mid-States Key Dist. EP/EO, 1996-2000, IRS Ctrl. Mountains Region TE/GE, 2001—; chair Mpls. Pension Coun., 1999-2000. Served with U.S. Army, 1970-72. Mem. ABA, Minn. Bar Assn. (chair employee benefits sect. 1997-98), Order of Coif, Tau Beta Pi. Lutheran. Office: Faegre and Benson 90 S 7th St Ste 2200 Minneapolis MN 55402-3901 E-mail: rnelson@faegre.com.

NELSON, RICHARD DAVID, lawyer; b. Chgo., Jan. 29, 1940; s. Irving E. and Dorothy (Apolsky) N.; m. Davida Distenfield, Dec. 17, 1960; children: Cheryl, Laurel. BS in Acctg., U. Ill., 1961, LLB, 1964. Bar: Ill. 1964. Ptnr. Defrees & Fiske Law Offices, Chgo., 1964-81; ptnr., counsel, chief adminstrv. officer Heidrick & Struggles, Inc., 1981—2001; pres. Galrk Sheridan, Inc., Highland Park, 2001—. Bd. dirs., exec. com. Heidrick & Struggles, Inc., Chgo., 1981-99. Pres. Jewish Cmty. Ctrs. of Chgo., 1987-89; chmn. Sign Graphics Task Force, Highland Park, Ill., 1986-88, Bus. and Econ. Devel. Commn., Highland Park; chmn. Econ. Devel. Commn. Highland Park, 1993-96, Ft. Sheridan Joint Plan Commn., 1997-2000, Bus. and Econ. Devel. Commn., Highland Park, 2000—. Mem. ABA, Ill. State Bar Assn., Chgo. Bar Assn., Standard Club, Northmoor Country Club. Office: Galrk Sheridan Inc 1896 Sheridan Rd Ste 200 Highland Park IL 60035-4635

NELSON, RICHARD L. physician; b. Evanston, Ill., Oct. 11, 1946; BA in Classics, Stanford U., 1968; MD, U. Chgo., 1972. Intern U. Ill., Chgo., 1972-73, resident, 1973-79; with U. Ill. Hosps., 1980—, prof. surgery, 1999—, asst. prof. epidemiology, 1986—. Mem. Am. Coll. Surgeons.

NELSON, ROBERT EDDINGER, management and development consultant; b. Mentone, Ind., Mar. 2, 1928; s. Arthur Irven and Tural Cecile (Eddinger) N.; m. Carol J., Nov. 24, 1951; children: Janet K., Eric P. BA, Northwestern U., 1949; LHD, Iowa Wesleyan Coll., 1969, North Ctrl. Coll., 1987. Asst. dir. alumni rels. Northwestern U., Evanston, Ill., 1950-51; v.p., dir. pub. rels. Iowa Wesleyan Coll., Mt. Pleasant, 1955-58; vice chancellor for devel. U. Kansas City, 1959-61; v.p. instl. devel. Ill. Inst. Tech., Chgo., 1961-68; pres. Robert Johnston Corp., Oak Brook, Ill., 1968-69, Robert E. Nelson Assocs., Inc., Oak Brook, 1969—. Bd. dirs. Chautauqua Workshop in Fund Raising and Instl. Relations, Continental Bank of Oak Brook Terr., The Sun Cos.; nat. conf. chmn. and program dir. Am. Coll. Pub. Relations Assn., 1961; trustee, Iowa Wesleyan Coll., 1962-68; faculty mem. Ind. U. Workshops on Coll. and Univ. Devel., 1963-65, Lorretto Heights Summer Inst. for Fund Raising and Pub. Relations, 1964-68; mem. Pub. Review Panel for Grants Programs, Lilly Endowment, Inc., 1975. Contbr. chpt. to Handbook of College and University Administration, 1970. With U.S. Army, 1951-54. Mem. Coun. on Fin. Aid to Edn. (bd. dirs. 1957-63), Pub. Rels. Soc. Am., Nat. Soc. Fund Raisers, Nat. Small Bus. Assn., Chgo. Soc. Fund Raising Execs., Blue Key, Execs. Club, Econ. Club, Union League, DuPage Club, Masons, Delta Tau Delta. Methodist. Home and Office: 5 Oakbrook Club Dr N101 Oak Brook IL 60523-1348

NELSON, STEVEN CRAIG, lawyer; b. Oakland, Calif., May 11, 1944; s. Eskil Manfred and Florence Lucille (Boatman) N.; m. Kathryn Cassel Stoltz, Nov. 30, 1974 (div. Apr. 1997); children: Carleton Philip, Whitney Cassel. BA in Econs. with exceptional distinction, Yale U., 1966, LLB, 1969. Bar: DC 1969, Minn. Supreme Ct. 1975, U.S. Supreme Ct. 1973. From atty. adviser to asst. legal adviser U.S. Dept. State, Washington,

1969-74; from assoc. to ptnr. Oppenheimer, Wolff, Foster, Shepard & Donnelly, St. Paul and Mpls., 1975-85; ptnr. Dorsey & Whitney, Mpls., 1985—. Mem. bd. appeals NATO, Brussels. 1977—; adj. prof. law U. Minn, 1980-86; speaker in field. Contbr. articles to profl. jours. Mem. ABA (chmn. internat. law and practice 1988-89), Minn. Bar Assn., Am. Fgn. Law Assn., Am. Soc. Internat. Law, Internat. Bar Assn. (mem. coun. 1996—), Union Internat. des Avocats (1st v.p. 1991-94), Minikahda Club. Presbyterian. Avocations: golf, tennis, skiing, sailing. Office: Dorsey & Whitney 220 S 6th St Ste 2200 Minneapolis MN 55402-1498

NELSON, THOMAS GEORGE, consulting actuary; b. Mason City, Iowa, Mar. 27, 1949; s. George Burton and Bonny Sue (Sharp) N.; m. Beverlee Joan Trindl, Sept. 28, 1974; children: Kristen Elizabeth, Joseph Charles. BA in Math., U. Iowa, 1971; MA in Math., U. Mich., 1972. Actuary CNA, Chgo., 1972-80; consulting actuary William M. Mercer, Inc., 1980-82, A.S. Hansen, Inc., Chgo., 1982-83; sr. consulting actuary, prin., nat. dir. health, bd. dirs. Milliman & Robertson, Inc., 1983—. Mem. task force on acctg. for non-pension retiree benefits Fin. Acctg. Standards Bd., Norwalk, Conn., 1986-90. Contbr. articles to profl. jours. Fellow, 1972, teaching fellow, 1972, U. Mich. Fellow Soc. Actuaries; mem. Am. Acad. Actuaries (bd. dirs. 1989-92, chmn. com. on health and welfare plans 1984-89, com. on rels. with accts. 1987-89, budget and fin. com. 1987-89, chmn. audit subcom. 1991-92, task force on taxation employee benefits 1986), Conf. of Consulting Actuaries (bd. dirs. 1989-95, v.p. 1991-92, exec. com. 1991-95, treas. 1992-95, chmn. com. on recognition of continuing profls. 1989-92, com. on health issues 1985-91), Chgo. Actuarial Soc. Roman Catholic. Avocations: tennis, golf, music. Home: 820 N Waiola Ave La Grange Park IL 60526-1452 Office: Milliman & Robertson Inc 55 W Monroe St Ste 4000 Chicago IL 60603-5001

NELSON, VIRGINIA SIMSON, pediatrician, physiatrist, educator; b. L.A. d. Jerome and Virginia (Kuppler) Simson; children: Eric, Paul. AB, Stanford U., 1963, MD, 1970; MPH, U. Mich., 1974. Diplomate Am. Bd. Pediatrics, Am. Bd. Phys. Medicine and Rehab. Pediatrician Inst. Study Mental Retardation and Related Disabilities, U. Mich., Ann Arbor, 1973-80; mem. faculty phys. medicine and rehab. dept. U. Mich. Med. Ctr., 1980-83, 85—, resident in phys. medicine and rehab., 1983-85, chief pediatric phys. medicine and rehab. physician, 1985—. Contbr. articles to profl. jours. Office: Univ Mich Med Ctr F7822 Mott Hospital Ann Arbor MI 48109-0230

NELSON, WILLIAM GEORGE, IV, software company executive; b. Phila., May 26, 1934; s. William George III and Eleanor (Boyle) N. BA in Chemistry, Swarthmore Coll., 1956; MBA in Finance, U. Pa., 1958; PhD in Econs., Rice U., 1965. Various positions Du Pont Co., 1957-62, Monsanto Co., St. Louis, 1965-76; vis. asst. prof. Washington U., 1966-75; sr. v.p. Chase Econs./Interactive Data, Waltham, Mass., 1976-83; pres. Pansophic Systems, Lisle, Ill., 1983-90; pres., CEO OnLine Software, Ft. Lee, N.J., 1990-91, bd. dirs.; pres., CEO Pilot Software, Boston, 1992-94; CEO Harris Data Corp., 1990—; pres., CEO Clarendon Capital Corp., Boston, 1995-96; chmn. GEAC Computer Corp. Ltd., North York, Ont., Can., 1996—, CEO Can., 1996-99. Bd. dirs. GEAC, Toronto, Manugistics, Rockville, Md., Harris Data, Waukesha, Wis., HealthGate Data, Boston. Bd. dirs. Swarthmore Coll. NFS fellow in econs., 1963-65. Office: HarrisData 611 N Barker Rd Brookfield WI 53045-5977

NEMCOVA, EVA, professional basketball player; b. Czech Republic, Dec. 3, 1972; came to U.S., 1997; Guard A.S. Montferrand, France, 1993-96, Bourges, France, 1996-97, Cleveland Rockers, (WNBA), 1997—. Named Best Player European Championship, 1995, 96. Avocations: volleyball, handball, football, mountain biking. Office: Cleve Rockers Gund Arena 1 Center Ct Cleveland OH 44115-4001

NEPPLE, JAMES ANTHONY, lawyer; b. Carroll, Iowa, Jan. 5, 1945; s. Herbert J. and Cecilia T. (Irlmeier) N.; m. Jeannine Ann Jennings, Sept. 9, 1967; children: Jeffrey B., Scott G., Carin J., Andrew J. BA, Creighton U., 1967; JD, U. Iowa, 1970; postgrad. in bus., Tex. Christian U., 1971; LLM in Taxation, NYU, 1982. Bar: Iowa 1970, Ill. 1973, U.S. Dist. Ct. (so. dist.) Iowa 1972, U.S. Dist. Ct. (cen. dist.) Ill. 1972, U.S. Dist. Ct.(no. dist.) Iowa 1975, U.S. Ct. Appeals (7th and 8th cirs.) 1975, U.S. Supreme Ct. 1975, U.S. Ct. Claims 1976, U.S. Tax Ct. 1976. Tax acct. Arthur Young & Co., Chgo., 1970; v.p., treas., bd. dirs. Stanley, Rehling, Lande & VanDerKamp, Muscatine, Iowa, 1972-92; pres. Nepple, VanDerKamp & Flynn, P.C., Rock Island, Ill., 1992-98; prin. Nepple Law Offices, P.L.C., 1999—. Scoutmaster Boy Scouts Am., Muscatine, 1982-85; trustee State Hist. Soc. Iowa, 1986-92, vice-chmn., 1991-92; bd. dirs. Iowa Hist. Found., 1988-95, pres., 1991-93. Capt. U.S. Army, 1971-72. Recipient Gov.'s Vol. award State of Iowa, 1988, 90, Jr. Achievement of the Quad Cities Bronze award, 1996, Silver award, 2000. Fellow Am. Coll. Trust and EstateCounsel, Am. Bar Found., Iowa Bar Found.; mem. ABA (tax sect. 1972—, chair agrl. tax com. 2001—); mem. Ia (tax com. 1979-91, chmn. 1988-91), Fed. Bar Assn., Ill. Bar Assn. (mem. fed. tax. sect. coun. 1993-99, chair 1997-98), Muscatine Bar Assn. (pres. 1982-83), Scott County Bar Assn., Rock Island County Bar Assn., Iowa Assn. Bus. and Industry (tax. com. 1978—, chmn. 1986-88, leadership Iowa award 1985), Quad City Estate Planning Coun. (pres. 1987), Muscatine C. of C. (pres. 1985), Geneva Golf and Country Club (pres. 1990-91), Kiwanis (pres. Muscatine chpt. 1978), Elks. Republican. Roman Catholic. Home: 2704 Mulberry Ave Muscatine IA 52761-2746 Fax: 563-264-6844. E-mail: jim@nepplelaw.com.

NESBITT, JOHN ARTHUR, recreation service educator, recreation therapy educator; b. Detroit, Mar. 29, 1933; s. John Jackson and Anna Maye (Hartley) N.; m. Dolores Antonia Gutierrez, Apr. 8, 1961; children: John Arthur, Victoria Bowen. Student, Howe Mil. Sch., 1945-51, Olivet Coll., 1952-53; BA, Mich. State U., 1955; MA, Columbia U., 1961, EdD, 1968. Registered hosp. recreation dir.; cert. therapeutic recreation specialist. Program dir. Jaycees Internat., Miami, Fla., 1957-60; therapeutic recreation specialist Rusk Inst. Rehab. Medicine, NYU-Bellevue Med. Ctr., 1960-61; dir. World Commn. on Vocat. Rehab., Rehab. Internat., N.Y.C., 1963—65; dep. dir. gen. World Leisure and Recreation Assn., 1964—68; asst. sec. gen. Rehab. Internat., 1966-68; asst. prof., coordinator rehab. svcs., leisure studies San Jose State U., 1968-69, assoc. prof., dir. Inst. interdisciplinary studies, 1969-72; assoc. prof., chmn. recreation edn. program U. Iowa, Iowa City, 1972-76, prof. therapeutic recreation svc. dept. leisure studies, 1976-91, prof. emeritus therapeutic recreation svc. dept. leisure studies, health and physical edn. studies, 1991—; prof., chmn. dept. leisure studies, 1986-87. Pres., CEO Spl. Recreation disABLED Internat., Inc., 1978—; dir. Com. for U.S. People to People Program, 1964—; chmn. com. recreation and leisure U.S. Pres.'s Com. on Employment of Handicapped, 1972-81; dir. Internat. Ctr. on Spl. Recreation, 1978—; vice chmn. People to People Com. Disability, 1996—. Author, editor books in field; editor Alert Mag., 1956, Jaycees Internat. World, 1957-60, Internat. Rehab. of Disabled Rev., 1965-68, Therapeutic Recreation Jour., 1968-70, Jour. Iowa Pks. and Recreation, 1974-76, Play, Recreation and Leisure for People Who Are Disabled, 1977, Fed. Funding for Spl. Recreation, 1978, New Concepts and New Processes in Spl. Recreation, 1978, New Horizons in Profl. Tng. in Recreation Service for Handicapped Children and Youth, 1983, Nisbet/Nesbitt Family Surname Assn. Newsletter, 1983-86, Spl. Recreation for disABLED Digest, 1983—, Spl. Recreation Compendium, 1986, USA Ban Fireworks and Fireworks Safety Campaign Bull., 1988—, UNAGRAM, 1997-99; sr. editor Recreation and Leisure Service for Disadvantaged, 1969; editor, compiler Spl. Recreation Compendium of 1,500 Resources for Disabled People, 3d edit., 1989, Special Recreation for disABLED Press, University Heights, Iowa, 1989. Bd. dirs., treas. United Cerebral Palsy Assn., San Mateo and Santa Clara County, 1970-72; bd. dirs. Harold Russell Found., 1971-73, Goodwill Industries Santa Clara County, 1969-72, rehab. counselor, master therapeutic recreation specialist; bd. dirs. Hawkeye Area Poverty Cmty. Action Program, Iowa, Iowa Pk. and Recreation Assn., Am. Leisure and Recreation Assn., Washington, others; bd. dirs., state v.p. Iowa Aging Coalition, Iowa; bd. dirs., founding pres. Santa Clara County Assn. on Recreation Handicapped, Iowa; bd. dirs., tech. adv. Disability Internat. Found., 1997—. With USAFR, 1955-57; maj. Ret. Recreation Svc. Ill and Handicapped fellow; recipient numerous awards and citations for work with handicapped, including Torch of Gold award Nat. Boy Scouts Am., Appreciation award Philippines Found. Mem. Nat. Therapeutic Recreation Soc. (pres. 1970-71, Disting. Svc. award), Nat. Rehab. Assn., Am. Assn. Leisure and Recreation (bd. dirs. 1977-80), Nat. Consortium on Phys. Edn. and Recreation for Handicapped (pres. 1976-77), Nat. Forum Comml. Recreation and Handicapped (chmn. 1979), AAHPER, Iowa Parks and Recreation Assn. (bd.dirs. 1973-75, 89-90), Nat. Rehab. Counseling Assn., Council Exceptional Children, Pi Sigma Epsilon. Presbyterian. Avocations: arts, gardening, travel, genealogy, community service. Office: Spl Recreation Disabled Internat 701 Oaknoll Dr Iowa City IA 52246 E-mail: john-nesbitt@uiowa.edu.

NESS, ROBERT, state legislator, education consultant; b. 1935; m. Marianne Ness; four children. BS, Bemidji State U.; MA, U. Minn. Edn. cons.; constrn. mgr.; Dist. 20A rep. Minn. Ho. of Reps., St. Paul, 1993—. Home: 24966 729th Ave Dassel MN 55325-3436

NESTER, WILLIAM RAYMOND, JR. retired academic administrator and educator; b. Cin., Feb. 19, 1928; s. William Raymond and Evelyn (Blettner) N.; m. Mary Jane Grossman; children: William Raymond, Mark Patrick, Brian Philip, Stephen Christopher. BS, U. Cin., 1950, EdM, 1953, EdD, 1965. Dir. student union U. Cin., 1952-53, asst. dean of men, 1953-60, dean of men, 1960-67, assoc. prof. edn., 1965-70, dean of students, 1967-69, vice provost student and univ. affairs, 1969-76, prof. edn., 1970-78, assoc. sr. v.p., assoc. provost, 1976-78; v.p. student svcs. Ohio State U., Columbus, 1978-83, prof. edn., 1978-83; pres. Kearney State Coll., Nebr., 1983-91, prof. edn., 1983-93; chancellor U. Nebr., Kearney, 1991-93, prof. emeritus, chancellor emeritus, 1993—; v.p. university relations devel. No. Ky. U., 1996-99. Pres. emeritus Mus. Nebr. Art, 1991—; cons. on higher edn., 1993—. Pres. Metro-Six Athletic Conf., 1975-76, Ctrl. States Intercollegiate Conf., 1986-89. Mem. Am. Assn. State Colls. and Univs. (bd. dirs.), Ctrl. States Intercollegiate Conf. (pres.), Nat. Assn. Student Pers. Adminstrs. (past regional v.p., mem. exec. com.), Am. Assn. Higher Edn., Ohio Assn. Student Pers. Adminstrs. (past pres.), Nat. Intrafrat. Conf. (pres. 1991-92), Frat. Scholarship Officers Assn. (past pres.), Mortar Bd., Pi Kappa Alpha Found. (nat. pres. 1978-80, past pres. ednl. found.), Omicron Delta Kappa, Phi Delta Kappa, Phi Alpha Theta, Phi Eta Sigma, Sigma Sigma. Episcopalian. Home: 7674 Coldstream Dr Cincinnati OH 45255-3932 E-mail: wrnchanem@cs.com.

NETHERLAND, JOSEPH H. manufacturing executive; BS in Indsl. Engring., Ga. Inst. Tech.; MBA, U. Pa. Bus. planner machinery group FMC Corp., 1973-78, ops. mgr. ordnance divsn., 1978-83, mgr. fluid control divsn., 1983-84, mgr. wellhead divsn., 1984-85, gen mgr. wellhead divsn., 1985-89, gen. mgr. specialized machinery group, 1989-99, pres., 1999—. Bd. dirs. Am. Petroleum Inst. Office: FMC Corp 200 E Randolph St Ste 5200 Chicago IL 60601-6662

NETHING, DAVID E. state legislator; m. Marjorie; 3 children. Degree, Jamestown Coll., U. N.D. Attorney; mem. N.D. Senate, 1966—; majority whip, 1974-86; mem. appropriations com. Past pres. Nat. Conf. State Legislators, Found. State Legislators, Coun. State Govt.; past mem. adv. commn. Intergovt. Rels.; past adm. Conf. of U.S. Mem. ABA, Am. Legion, Masonic Bodies, Rotary (past pres.), Elks (past bd. dirs, past exalted ruler), N.D. Affiliate Diabetic Assn. Office: PO Box 1059 Jamestown ND 58402-1059 also: State Senate State Capital Bismarck ND 58505

NETTELS, GEORGE EDWARD, JR. mining executive; b. Pittsburg, Kans., Oct. 20, 1927; s. George Edward and Mathilde A. (Wulke) N.; m. Mary Joanne Myers, July 19, 1952; children: Christopher Bryan, Margaret Anne, Katherine Anne, Rebecca Jane. BSCE, U. Kans., Lawrence, 1950. With Black & Veatch Engrs., Kansas City, Mo., 1950-51, Spencer Chem. Co., Kansas City, 1951-55, Freeto Constrn. Co., Pittsburg, 1955-57; pres. Midwest Minerals, Inc., 1957—; chmn. bd. McNally Pittsburg Mfg. Corp., 1970-76, pres., CEO, 1976-87, ret., 1987. Past chmn. bd. Nat. Limestone Inst.; bd. dirs. Pitts. Indsl. Devel. Com. Mem. bd. advisors U. Kans. Endowment Assn.; mem. Kans. U. Chancellor's Club, Kans., Inc.; past pres. Bd. Edn. 250, Pittsburg; past chmn. bd. trustees Mt. Carmel Hosp.; past mem. Kans. Commn. Civil Rights; chmn. Kans. Republican Com., 1966-68; Kans. del. Rep. Nat. Conv., 1968, Kans. Bus. and Industry Com. for Re-election of Pres., 1972. With AUS, 1946-47. Recipient Disting. Svc. citation U. Kans., 1980, Disting. Engring. citation U. Kans., 1985; named Kansan of Yr. Natives Sons and Daus. Kans., 1986. Mem. ASCE, NAM (past. dir.), Kans. C. of C. and Industry (dir., chmn. 1983-84), Kans. Right to Work (dir.), Pittsburg C. of C. (past dir.), Kans. U. Alumni Assn. (pres. 1977), Kans. Leadership Com., Crestwood Country Club, Wolf Creek Golf Club (Olathe), Tau Beta Pi, Omicron Delta Kappa, Beta Theta Pi. Office: Midwest Minerals Inc 509 W Quincy St Pittsburg KS 66762-5689 E-mail: george@midwestminerals.com.

NETTL, BRUNO, anthropology and musicology educator; b. Prague, Czechoslovakia, Mar. 14, 1930; s. Paul and Gertrud (Hutter) N.; m. Wanda Maria White, Sept. 15, 1952; children: Rebecca, Gloria. AB, Ind. U., 1950, PhD, 1953; MA in L.S, U. Mich., 1960; LHD (hon.) , U. Chgo., 1993; LHD (hon.) , U. Ill., 1996, Carleton Coll., 2000, Kenyon Coll., 2002. Mem. faculty Wayne State U., Detroit, 1953-64, asst. prof., 1954-64, music librarian, 1958-64; mem. faculty U. Ill., Urbana, 1964—, prof. music and anthropology, 1967—, chmn. div. musicology, 1967-72, 75-77, 82-85. Vis. lectr., Fulbright grantee U. Kiel, Fed. Republic of Germany, 1956-58; cons. Ency. Britannica, 1969—, also on ethnomusicology to various univs.; vis. prof. Williams Coll., 1971, Wash. U., 1978, U. Louisville, 1983, U. Wash., 1985, 88, 89, 93, 95, 98, 2000, Fla. State U., 1988, Harvard U., 1989, U. Alta., 1991, Colo. Coll., 1992, Northwestern U., 1993, U. Minn., 1994, U. Chgo., 1996, Carleton Coll., 1996, U. So. Calif., 2002. Author: Theory and Method in Ethnomusicology, 1964, Music in Primitive Culture, 1956, Folk and Traditional Music of the Western Continents, 1965, 2d edit., 1973, Eight Urban Musical Cultures, 1978, The Study of Ethnomusicology, 1983, The Western Impact on World Music, 1985, The Radif of Persian Music, 1987, rev. edit., 1992, Blackfoot Musical Thought, 1989, Comparative Musicology and Anthropology of Music, 1991, Heartland Excursions, 1995, In the course of Performance, 1998, Encounters in Ethnomusicology, a Memoir, 2002; co-author Excursions in World Music, 1992, 3rd edit., 2000; editor Ethnomusicology, 1961-65, 98-2002, Yearbook of the International Folk Music Council, 1975-77; sr. adv. editor Garland Ency. of World Music; contbr. articles to profl. jours. Recipient Koizumi prize in ethnomusicology, Tokyo, 1994. Fellow Am. Acad. of Arts and Scis.; mem. Soc. Ethnomusicology (pres. 1969-71), Am., Internat. musicol. socs., Internat. Coun. for Traditional Music, Coll. Music Soc. Home: 1423 Cambridge Dr Champaign IL 61821-4958 Office: U Ill Sch Music Urbana IL 61801

NETZLEY, ROBERT ELMER, state legislator; b. Laura, Ohio, Dec. 7, 1922; s. Elmer and Mary (Ingle) N.; m. Marjorie Lyons; children: Kathleen, Carol Anne, Robert. Grad. Midshipman Sch., Cornell U., 1944; BS, Miami U., 1947. State rep. 7th Dist. Ohio State Congress, 1961-82, state rep. Dist. 68, 1982—. Pres. Miami County Young Reps., Ohio, 1952-54; chmn. Miami County Rep. Ctrl. and Exec. com., 1958—; del. Rep. Nat. Conv., 1980, presdl. elector, 1980; sec.-treas., part owner Netzley Oil Co., 1947—; v.p. Romale Inc., 1961—. Recipient Purple Heart, Am. and Pacific Theaters. Mem. VFW, Miami County Heart Coun., Am. Legion, AmVets, Grange, Laura Lions; Phi Kappa Tau.

NETZLOFF, MICHAEL LAWRENCE, pediatric educator, endocrinologist, geneticist; b. Madison, Wis., Sept. 11, 1942; s. Harold Harvey Netzloff and Garnet Lucille (Wilson) MacFarlane; m. Cheryl Lynne Crandall, July 20, 1963; children: Michelle Lynne, Rochelle Anne, Cherie Lucille. BS with high honors, Eckert Coll., 1964; MS, U. Fla., 1968, MD, 1969. Diplomate Am. Bd. Pediatrics, Am. Bd. Pediatric Endocrinology, Am. Bd. Med. Genetics. Rsch. fellow, rsch. trainee dept. of anat. scis. U. Fla. Coll. Medicine, Gainesville, 1965-69, intern and resident in pediat., 1969-71, clin. and rsch. fellow divsn. genetics, endocrinology and metabolism, dept. pediat., 1971-73, instr. in pediat., 1973-74, asst. prof. of pediat., 1974-79; assoc. prof. of pediat. and human devel. Mich. State U. Coll. of Human Medicine, East Lansing, 1979-85, dir. of pediatric endocrinology, pediat. and human devel., 1981-89, dir. divsn. of human genetics, genetic toxicology, endocrinology and oncology, pediat. and human devel., 1982-89, prof. dept. pediat. and human devel., 1985—, chmn. dept., 1987-91; vis. prof. dept. pediat. U. Mich., 1992-93, dir. divsn. clin. genetics, 1993—, acting dir. pediat. endocrinology, diabetes & metabolism, 1999—. Cons. Juvenile Diabetes Found., Lansing, 1981-95; mem. diabetes adv. coun. Mich. State Dept. Pub. Health and Chronic Disease Control, Lansing, 1980-90. Recipient Carithers award for Child Health and Human Dev., U. Fla. Coll. Medicine, 1969, Edward Bogen fellowship U. Fla. Coll. Med., 1972, Basil O'Connor rsch. grant Nat. Found. March of Dimes, 1973, pediatric residency teaching award, Grad. Med. Edn., Inc., Mich. State U.. Affiliated Residency program, 1982, 86. Fellow Am. Acad. Pediatrics; mem. Assn. Clin. Scis. Inst. (sci. com. 1979-96), Am. Diabetes Assn. (coun. on diabetes in youth 1979-96), Am. Pediatric Soc., Lawson-Wilkins Pediatric Endocrine Soc., Mich State Med. Soc., Midwest Soc. for Pediat. Rsch., Ingham County Med. Soc., Soc. for Pediatric Rsch., Teratology Soc., Sigma Xi. Democrat. Lutheran. Home: 4432 Greenwood Dr Okemos MI 48864-3044 Office: Mich State U Dept Pediatrics B240 Life Scis East Lansing MI 48824-1317 E-mail: netzlofl@msu.edu.

NEUBAUER, CHARLES FREDERICK, investigative reporter; b. Berkeley, Ill., Feb. 13, 1950; s. Fred Charles and Dolores Jeanne (Pries) N.; m. Sandra Carol Bergo, Oct. 4, 1975; 1 child, Michael Frederick. B.S.J., Northwestern U., 1972, M.S.J., 1973. Investigator Better Govt. Assn., Chgo., 1971-73; investigative reporter Chgo. Today, 1973-74, Chgo. Tribune, 1974-83, Chgo. Sun Times, 1983—. Recipient Pulitzer prize local reporting, 1976; Edward Scott Beck award for domestic reporting Chgo. Tribune, 1980 Office: 401 N Wabash Ave Chicago IL 60611-5642

NEUDECK, GEROLD WALTER, electrical engineering educator; b. Beach, N.D., Sept. 25, 1936; s. Adolph John and Helen Annette (Kramer) N.; m. Mariellen Kristine MacDonald, Sept. 1, 1962; children: Philip Gerold, Alexander John. BSEE, U. N.D., 1959, MSEE, 1960; PhD in Elec. Engring., Purdue U., 1969. Asst. prof. U. N.D., Grand Forks, 1960-64; grad. instr. Purdue U., West Lafayette, Ind., 1964-68, asst. prof., 1968-71, assoc. prof., 1971-77, prof. elec. engring., 1977—, asst. dean engring., 1988-90, assoc. dir. NSF/ERC Engring., 1988-94, dir. Optoelectronics Rsch. Ctr., 1993-96. Cons. in field. Author: Electric Circuit Analysis and Design, 1976, 2d edit., 1987, Junction Diode/Bipolar Transisters, 1983, 2d edit., 1989; author, editor: Modular Series on Solid State Devices, 1983; contbr. over 230 articles to profl. jours.; inventor/13 U.S. patents in field. Bd. dirs. W. Lafayette Devel. Commn., 1990—, Greater Lafayette Pub. Transp., 1975-80; pres. Lafayette Tennis, 1976-78. Recipient Dow Outstanding Faculty award Am. Soc. Engring. Edn., 1972, Western Elec. Fund award, 1974-75, D.D. Ewing award Purdue U., 1973, A.A. Potter award, 1973, Honeywell Teaching award, 1995, Aristotle award Semicondr. Rsch., 2001. Fellow IEEE (Harry S. Nyquist award 1992, editor Transactions on Electron Devices 1994-97); mem. Am. Vacuum Soc., Sigma Xi, Eta Kappa Nu, Sigma Tau, Sigma Pi Sigma. Avocations: tennis, backpacking, fishing, woodworking, bread baking. Office: Purdue U 1285 Elec Engring Bldg West Lafayette IN 47907-1285

NEUEFEIND, WILHELM, economics educator, university administrator; b. Viersen, Germany, Mar. 6, 1939; came to U.S., 1977; m. Ingrid Leuchtenberg, Mar. 30, 1966; children: Nicole, Bettina. MBA, U. Cologne, Germany, 1962, MA in Math., 1969; PhD in Econs., U. Bonn, 1972. Lectr. econs. U. Bonn, 1973—77; prof. econ. Washington U., St. Louis, 1977; chmn. dept. econs. Wash. U., 1983—99. Contbr. articles to profl. jours. Mem. Econometric Soc., Am. Econ. Assn., Assn. for Advancement Econ. Theory. Office: Washington U Dept Econs 1 Brookings Dr # 1208 Saint Louis MO 63130-4899

NEUFELD, MELVIN J. state legislator; m. Maxine Neufeld. Student, Tabor Coll. Rep. dist. 115 State of Kans. Mem. NRA, Lions Club, Nat. Railroaders Club. Republican. Address: RR 1 Box 13 Ingalls KS 67853-9706

NEUHAUSER, DUNCAN VON BRIESEN, medical educator; b. Phila., June 20, 1939; s. Edward Blaine Duncan and Gernda (von Briesen) Neuhauser; m. Elinor Toaz, Mar. 6, 1965; children: Steven, Ann. BA, Harvard U., 1961; MHA, U. Mich., 1963; MBA, U. Chgo., 1966, PhD, 1971. Research assoc. U. Chgo., 1965—70; asst. prof. Sch. Pub. Health, Harvard U., Boston, 1970—74, assoc. prof., 1974—79; cons. in medicine Mass. Gen. Hosp., Boston, 1975—80; assoc. dir. Health Systems Mgmt. Ctr. Case Western Res. U., Cleve., 1979—85, prof. epidemiology, biostats., orgnl. behavior, 1979—, prof. medicine, 1981—, prof. family medicine, 1990—, Charles Elton Blanchard prof. health mgmt., 1995—, co-dir. Health Systems Mgmt. Ctr., 1985—. Mem. biomedical staff Metroheatlh Med. Ctr., 1981—; adj. mem. med. staff Cleve. Clinic Found., 1984—99; vis. prof. Vanderbilt U. Sch. Nursing, 1998—, Karolinska Med. Sch., Stockholm, 2002—. Author: numerous books, sci. papers; editor (jours.): Health Matrix, 1982—90, Med. Care, 1983—87. Vice chmn. bd. dirs. Vis. Nurse Assn. Greater Cleve., 1983—84, chmn., 1984—85; bd. dirs. New Eng. Grenfell Assn., Boston, 1972—, Braintree (Mass.) Hosp., 1975—86; trustee Internat. Grenfell Assn., St. Anthony, Canada, 1975—83, Blue Hill (Maine) Hosp., 1983—94, chmn., 1993—94; trustee Hough Norwood Health Ctr., 1983—94, chmn., 1993—94; mem. vis. com. Columbia U. Sch. Nursing, 2000—. Recipient E.F. Meyers Trustee award, Cleve. Hosp. Assn., 1987, Hope award, Nat. Multiple Sclerosis Soc., 1992, Neuhauser lectr., Soc. Pediatric Radiology, 1982, Freedlander lectr., Ohio Permanente Med. Group, 1986, Univ. medal, Tohoku Med. U., Sendi, Japan, 2001; fellow Kellogg, 1963—65; scholar Keck Found., 1982—. Mem.: Soc. for Clin. Decision Making, Inst. Medicine NAS, Cleve. Skating Club, Kollegewidgwok Yacht Club (Blue Hill) (commodore 1991—93), St. Botolph Club (Boston), Beta Gamma Sigma. Home: 2655 N Park Blvd Cleveland Heights OH 44106-3622 Office: Case Western Reserve U Med Sch 10900 Euclid Ave Cleveland OH 44106-4945 Fax: 216-368-3970. E-mail: dvn@po.cwru.edu.

NEUMAN, LINDA KINNEY, state supreme court justice; b. Chgo., June 18, 1948; d. Harold S. and Mary E. Kinney; m. Henry G. Neuman; children: Emily, Lindsey. BA, U. Colo., 1970, JD, 1973; LLM, U. Va., 1998. Ptnr. Betty, Neuman, McMahon, Hellstrom & Bittner, 1973-79; v.p., trust officer Bettendorf Bank & Trust Co., 1979-80; dist. ct. judge, 1982-86; supreme ct. justice State of Iowa, 1986—. Mem. adj. faculty U. Iowa Grad. Sch. of Social Work, 1981; part-time jud. magistrate Scott County, 1980-82; mem. Supreme Ct. continuing legal edn. commn.; chair Iowa Supreme Ct. commn. planning 21st Century; mem. bd. counselors Drake Law Sch., time on appeal adv. com. Nat. Ctr. State Cts. Trustee St. Ambrose U. Recipient Regents scholarship, U. Colo. award for disting. svc. Fellow

ABA (chair appellate judges conf., mem. appellate standards com., JAD exec. coun.); mem. Am. Judicature Soc., Iowa Bar Assn., Iowa Judges Assn., Scott County Bar Assn., Nat. Assn. Woman Judges (bd. dirs.), Dillon Am. Inn of Ct., U.S. Assn. Constl. Law. E-mail: linda.k.neuman@jb.state.ia.us.*

NEUMANN, FREDERICK LLOYD, plant breeder; b. Waterloo, Iowa, Apr. 9, 1949; s. Lloyd Frederick and Leita Evangeline (Otto) N.; m. Diane Marie Brown, Aug. 18, 1973 (div. 1995); children: Bradley, Brian; m. Jamie Lynn Cox, June 22, 1996. BS, Iowa State U., 1972, MS, 1974. Rsch. dir., plant breeder Ames (Iowa) Seed Farms, Inc., producers hybrid popcorn seed, 1973-85; plant breeder Crow's Hybrid Corn Co., Milford, Ill., 1985-93; sales rep. Tri-State Foods, Springfield, 1993-94; meat packer Swissland Packing, Ashkum, 1994—. Mem. research com. Popcorn Inst., Chgo., 1976-85, mem. prodn. and seed research subcom., 1982-85. Treas. Laurel Tree Nursery Sch., Inc., 1981-83; bishop's com. St. Paulinus Epsicopal Ch., 1986-87; stephen min. 1st Christian Ch., 1989—, deacon, 1989, elder, 1990-91, 93-94, 96-98, 2000—. Mem. Am. Soc. Agronomy, Iowa Crop Improvement Assn. (com. to recommend to bd. dirs. certification requirelemts for hybrid corn and hybrid sorghum 1979), Crop Sci. Soc. Am., Phi Kappa Phi, Gamma Sigma Delta. Republican. Mem. Disciples of Christ. Home and Office: 202 Wilson Dr Watseka IL 60970-7603

NEUMANN, MARK W. former congressman, real estate developer; b. Waukesha, Wis., Feb. 27, 1954; m. Sue; 3 children. BS, U. Wis., Whtiewater, 1975; MS, U. Wis., River Falls, 1977. Real estate developer Neumann Devels. (now named Numann Corp.), 1980—; mem. 104th and 105th Congresses from 1st Wis. dist., 1994-97. Mem. appropriations, nat. security, vets. affairs, HUD and ind. agys., budget coms. Address: W330 N6233 Hasslinger Dr Nashotah WI 53058-9432

NEUMANN, ROY COVERT, architect; b. Columbus, Nebr., Mar. 1, 1921; s. LeRoy Franklin and Clara Louise (Covert) N.; m. Hedy Charlotte Schultz, Aug. 28, 1948; children: Tali, Scott. Student, Midland Coll., 1939-40, U. Calif.-Berkeley Armed Forces Inst., overseas, 1942-43; AB, U. Nebr., 1948, BArch, 1949; MA, Harvard U., 1952; postgrad., U. Wis., Iowa State U. Registered profl. architect, Iowa, Nebr., Kans., Minn., S.D., N.Y., N.J., Mass., Ohio, Pa., Tenn., Ky., Va., W.Va., Ga., Mich., Mo., Ill., Wis., Tex., Colo. Ptnr., architect R. Neumann Assocs., Lincoln, Nebr., 1952-55; officer mgr. Sargent, Webster, Crenshaw & Folley, Schenectady, N.Y., 1955-59; dir. architecture, ptnr. A.M. Kinney Assocs., Cin., 1959-65; officer mgr. Hunter, Campbell & Rea, Johnstown, Pa., 1965-66; dir. architecture, ptnr. Stanley Cons., Muscatine, Iowa, 1966-76; pres., chmn. bd. Neumann Monson P.C., Iowa City, 1976—. Ptnr. Clinton St. Ptnrs., Iowa City, 1983—, Iris City Devel. Co. Mt. Pleasant, Iowa, 1986, Linn Mar Elem./Mid. Sch., Marion, Iowa. Prin. works include Harbour Facilities, Antigua, W.I., S.C. Johnson Office Bldg., Racine, Wis., Iowa City Transit Facility Bldg., addition to Davenport Ctrl. High Sch., V.A. Adminstrv. Office Bldg., Iowa City, Johnson County Office Bldg., Iowa City Mercer Park Aquatic Ctr., Iowa City, Coll. Bus. U. Iowa, Iowa City, renovation Lawrence County Courthouse, Deadwood, S.D., H.S. and Elem. Schs., Mt. Pleasant, Iowa. Mem. bd. edn. Muscatine Community Sch. Dist., 1974-76. Served with USN, 1942-46, PTO. Recipient Honor award Portland Cement Assn., 1949, Lorraine D. Wright award for outstanding constrn. Camanche (Iowa) H.S., 1998-99. Mem. AIA (Honor award 1975), Constrn. Specifications Inst. (pres. 1974-76, Honor award 1983, 84, 85, 86), Soc. Archtl. Historians, Archtl. Assn. London, U. Nebr. Alumni Assn., Harvard U. Alumni Assn., Iowa City C. of C., Phi Kappa Psi, Univ. Athletic Club (Iowa City), Masons, Ea. Star, Elks Republican. Presbyterian. Avocations: golf, fishing, medieval history, big band music. Home: 2014 Burnside Dr Muscatine IA 52761-3510 Office: Neumann Monson Architects 111 E College St Iowa City IA 52240-4012

NEUMANN, THOMAS ALAN, educational administrator; b. Green Bay, Wis., Apr. 7, 1949; s. William and Elena (Peabody) N.; m. Carla Simonson, Aug. 17, 1974; children: Nathaniel, Amanda. BSN, U. Wis., 1977; MSN, U. Minn., 1982; BS in Edn., U. Wis., 1972. RN, Wis. Instr. diploma nursing program Mounds-Midway Sch. Nursing, St. Paul, 1980-83; staff devel. instr. Hennepin County Med. Ctr., Mpls., 1983-84; instr. in AD nursing Western Wis. Tech. Coll., LaCrosse, 1984-86; chair nursing practice and edn. com. Nat. Coun. of State Bds. of Nursing, Chgo., 1989-92; adminstrv. officer Wis. Dept. Regulation and Licensing; assoc. dean health, human and protective svcs. Madison (Wis.) Area Tech. Coll., 2000—. Cons. Wis. Bd. Nursing, 1986-99; v.p. Nat. Coun. State Bds. Nursing, 1994-96, pres., 1996-98. Mem. Sigma Theta Tau. Home: 652 Birch Ct Verona WI 53593-1660 Office: Madison Area Tech Coll 3550 Anderson St Madison WI 53704-2520

NEUMANN, WILLIAM ALLEN, state supreme court justice; b. Minot, N.D., Feb. 11, 1944; s. Albert W. and Opal Olive (Whitlock) N.; m. Jaqueline Denise Buechler, Aug. 9, 1980; children: Andrew, Emily. BSBA, U. N.D., 1965; JD, Stanford U., 1968. Bar: N.D. 1969, U.S. Dist. Ct. N.D. 1969. Pvt. practice law, Williston, N.D., 1969-70, Bottineau, 1970-79; former judge N.D. Judicial Dist. Ct., N.E. Judicial Dist., Rugby and Bottineau, 1979-92; justice N.D. Supreme Ct., Bismarck, 1993—. Chmn. elect N.D. Jud. Conf., 1985-87, chmn. 1987-89. Mem. ABA, State Bar Assn. N.D., Am. Judicature Soc. (bd. dirs. 1998—). Lutheran. Office: ND Supreme Ct Jud Wing 1st Fl Dept 180 600 E Boulevard Ave Bismarck ND 58505-0530*

NEUMARK, MICHAEL HARRY, lawyer; b. Cin., Oct. 28, 1945; s. Jacob H. and Bertha (Zubor) N.; m. Sue Daly, June 5, 1971; children: Julie Rebecca, John Adam. BS in Bus., Ind. U., 1967; JD, U. Cin., 1970. Bar: Ohio 1970, D.C. 1972. Atty. chief counsel's office IRS, Washington, 1970-74, acting br. chief, 1974-75, sr. atty. regional counsel's office, 1975-77; assoc. Paxton & Seasongood Legal Profl. Assn., 1977-80; ptnr. Thompson, Hine & Flory, 1980—, mem. mgmt. com., 1993—. Chmn. So. Ohio Tax Inst., 1987; mem. IRS and Bar Liaison Com., 1991-93; spkr. at profl. confs. Contbr. articles to profl. jours. Bd. dirs. 1987 World Figure Skating Chamionship, Cin., 1986-89; precinct exec. Hamilton County Rep. Orgn., 1980-86; vol. referee Hamilton County Juvenile Ct., 1980-86; trustee Cin. Contemporary Arts Ctr., St. Rita Sch. for Deaf, 1991-97, Legal Aid Soc. Cin., 1997—. Recipient Commendation Resolution Sycamore Twp., 1987. Mem. ABA (del. 1999—), Ohio State Bar Assn., Cin. Bar Assn. (pres. 1996-97, recognition award 1985, treas., bd. trustees 1988-91, trustee 1992—, chair tax sect., 1990-91), Leadership Cin., Ohio Met. Bar Assn. (pres. 1996-97), Kenwood Country Club, Indian Hill Club, Ohio Met. Bar (pres. 1996-97), Cin. Acad. of Leadership for Lawyers (founder, chair). Republican. Avocations: golf, travel. Office: Thompson Hine & Flory 312 Walnut St Ste 1400 Cincinnati OH 45202-4089

NEUSCHEL, ROBERT PERCY, management consultant, educator; b. Hamburg, N.Y., Mar. 13, 1919; s. Percy J. and Anna (Becker) N.; m. Dorothy Virginia Maxwell, Oct. 20, 1944; children: Kerr Anne Ziprick, Carla Becker Neuschel Wyckoff, Robert Friedrich (Fritz). BA, Denison U., 1941; MBA, Harvard U., 1947. Indsl. engr. Sylvania Elec. Products Co., Inc., 1947-49; with McKinsey & Co., Inc., 1950-79, sr. partner, dir., 1967-79; prof. corp. governance, assoc. dean J. L. Kellogg Grad. Sch. Mgmt.; former dir. Northwestern U., assoc. dean J.L. Kellogg Sch. Mgmt. Mem. exec. bd. Internat. Air Cargo Forum, 1988—; mem. com. study air passenger svc. and safety NRC, 1989—; bd. dirs. Butler Mfg. Co., Combined Ins. Co. Am., Templeton, Kenley & Co., U.S. Freightways Co.; lectr. in field; mem. McKinsey Found. Mgmt. Rsch., Inc.; transp. task force Reagan transition team; chmn. bd. dirs. Internat. Intermodal Expn. Atlanta. Author: The Servant Leader: Unleashing the Power of Your People, 1998; co-author: Emerging Issues in Corporate Governance, 1983; contbr. over 125 articles to profl. jours. Pres. Bd. Edn., Lake Forest, Ill., 1965-70; rep. Nat. council Boy Scouts Am., 1970—, mem. N.E. exec. coun., 1969—; chmn. bd. Lake Forest Symphony, 1973; bd. dirs. Loyola U., Chgo., Chgo. Boys' Club, Nat. Ctr. Voluntary Action, Inst. Mgmt. Consultants; trustee N. Suburban Mass Transit, 1972-73, Loyola Med. Ctr.; mem. adv. coun. Kellogg Grad. Sch. Mgmt., Northwestern U., White House conferee Drug Free Am.; mem. Nat. Petroleum Coun. Transp. and Supply Com. Served to capt. USAAF, World War II. Named Transporation Man of Yr. Chitransp. Assoc., 1994; recipient Salzberg medallion Syracuse U., 1999. Fellow Acad. Advancement Corp. Governance; mem. Transp. Assn. Am., Nat. Def. Transp. Assn. (subcom. transp. tech. agenda 1990—), Intermodal Assn. N.Am. (chmn. bd. dirs.). Presbyterian (ruling elder). Clubs: Harvard Bus. Sch. (pres. 1964-65), Economic, Executive, Chicago, Mid America, Mid-Day (Chgo.); Onwentsia (Lake Forest). Home: 101 Sunset Pl Lake Forest IL 60045-1834 Office: 2001 Sheridan Rd Evanston IL 60208-0849 E-mail: cs-neuschel@nwu.edu.

NEUVILLE, THOMAS M. state legislator, lawyer; b. Marinette, Wis., Jan. 31, 1950; s. Morris and Dallas (Thompson) N.; m. Marilynn Hamilton, Jan. 31, 1976; children: Mark, John, Anne, Luke, Maggie. BSChemE, Mich. Tech. U., 1972; JD, William Mitchell Law Sch., St. Paul, 1976. Bar: Minn. 1976, U.S. Dist. Ct. Minn. 1977. Ptnr. Grundhoefer & Neuville, Northfield, Minn., 1976-82, pres., atty., 1982—; delegate State Republican Party, 1988, 90, 92, 94; mem. Minn. Senate, Saint Paul, 1990—. Arbitrator Am. Arbitration Assn., 1988—; civil and family arbitrator Hennepin County Dist. Ct., Mpls., 1986—. Treas. Rice County Rep. Com., 1982—. Mem. ABA, Minn. Bar Assn., Northfield C. of C. (pres. 1986-87), Tau Beta Pi. Roman Catholic. Avocations: golf, guitar, basketball. Home: PO Box 7 515 Water St S Northfield MN 55057-2033 Office: Grundhoefer & Neuville PO Box 7 Northfield MN 55057-0007 Address: Minn Senate 123 State Capitol 100 Constitution Ave Saint Paul MN 55155-1232

NEVILLE, DALLAS S. protective services official; married; 1 child. Student, Chippewa Valley Tech. Coll. Deputy sheriff Clark County Sheriff's Dept., Neillsville, Wis., 1980-94; U.S. marshal U.S. Marshal's Svc., Madison, 1994—. Office: US Marshals Svc US Courthouse 120 N Henry St Ste 440 Madison WI 53703-2559

NEVILLE, JAMES MORTON, retired lawyer, consumer products executive; b. Mpls., May 28, 1939; s. Philip and Maurene (Morton) N.; m. Judie Martha Proctor, Sept. 9, 1961; children: Stephen Warren, Martha Maurene Hereford. BA, U. Minn., JD magna cum laude, 1964. Bar: Minn. 1964, Mo. 1984. Assoc. Neville, Johnson & Thompson, Mpls., 1964-69, ptnr., 1969-70; assoc. counsel Gen. Mills, Inc., 1970-77, sr. assoc. counsel, 1977-83, corp. sec., 1976-83; v.p., sec., asst. gen. counsel Ralston Purina Co., St. Louis, 1983-84, v.p., gen. counsel, sec., 1984-96, v.p., gen. counsel, 1996-2000, v.p., sr. counsel, 2000-01; ret., 2001; chmn. The Thompson Ctr., 2002—. Lectr. bus. law. U. Minn., 1967-71. Named Man of Yr., Edina Jaycees, 1967. Mem. ABA, Mo. Bar Assn., U.S. Supreme Ct. Bar Assn., St. Louis Bar Assn., U. Minn. Law Sch. Alumni Assn., Old Warson Country Club, Ladue Racquet Club, Order of Coif, Phi Delta Phi, Psi Upsilon. Episcopalian. Home: 9810 Log Cabin Ct Saint Louis MO 63124-1133 E-mail: jnev57@aol.com.

NEVIN, JOHN ROBERT, business educator, consultant; b. Joliet, Ill., Jan. 27, 1943; s. Robert Charles and Rita Alice (Roder) N.; m. Jeanne M. Conroy, June 10, 1967; children: Erin, Michael. BS, So. Ill. U., 1965; MS, U. Ill., 1968, PhD, 1972. Asst. prof. bus. U. Wis., Madison, 1970—77, assoc. prof. bus., 1977—83, prof. bus., 1983—, Wis. disting. prof. bus., 1988—89, Grainger Wis. disting. prof. bus., 1989—, exec. dir. Grainger Ctr. for Supply Chain Mgmt., 1992—, assoc. dean masters program, 1999—2002. Mem. investment adv. com. Venture Investors of Wis., Inc., Madison, 1986-99. Author: International Marketing: An Annotated Bibliography, 1983; mem. editl. bd. Jour. of Mktg. Channels, The Haworth Press, Inc., 1991—; contbr. articles to profl. jours. Bd. dirs. Madison civic Ctr., 1983-99. Mem. Am. Mktg. Assn. (bd. dirs. PhD consortium 1979, editorial bd. Jour. of Mktg. Chgo. chpt. 1983-97), Assn. for Consumer Rsch. Avocations: golf, skiing, running. Home: 7514 Red Fox Trl Madison WI 53717-1860 Office: U Wis Grainger Ctr Supply Chain Mgmt 975 University Ave Madison WI 53706-1324 E-mail: jnevin@bus.wisc.edu.

NEVIN, ROBERT CHARLES, information systems executive; b. Dayton, Ohio, Nov. 4, 1940; s. Robert Steely and Virginia (Boehme) N.; m. Linda Sharon Fox, Apr. 16, 1966; children: Heather, Andrew. B.A., Williams Coll., 1962; M.B.A., U. Pa., 1970. Fin. planning mgr. Huffy Corp., Dayton, Ohio, 1971-72, asst. treas., 1972-73, treas., 1973-75, v.p. fin., 1975-79, exec. v.p., 1982-85; pres., gen. mgr. Frabill Sporting Good, Milw., 1979-82; exec. v.p. Reynolds & Reynolds, Dayton, Ohio, 1985-88, pres. bus. forms divsn., 1988-97; pres. automotive group, 1997—. Bd. dirs. Reynolds & Reynolds, Olympic Title Ins. Co. Bd. dirs., pres. Camp Fire Girls, Dayton, 1975; bd. dirs. ARC, 1977; participant, then trustee Leadership Dayton, 1986-95; vice chmn. Med. Am. Corp.; trustee, treas. Victory Theater Assn., 1985-91, Dayton Mus. Natural History, 1982-96; trustee, chmn. Alliance for Edn., Dayton Art Inst. 1st lt. USN, 1962-70. Mem. Beta Gamma Sigma, Racquet (Dayton), Dayton Country, Country Club of the North. Republican. Episcopalian. Office: Reynolds & Reynolds PO Box 1005 Dayton OH 45401-1005

NEVLING, LORIN IVES, JR. museum administrator; b. St. Louis, Sept. 23, 1930; s. Lorin I. and Rose Elizabeth (Meyer) N.; m. Janet Frances Sullivan, June 1, 1957; children— Lorin, Luara, Mark, James, John. B.S., St. Mary's Coll., 1952; postgrad., U. Notre Dame, 1952-53; A.M., Washington U., St. Louis, 1957, Ph.D., 1959. Research asst. flora of Panama Mo. Bot. Garden, St. Louis, 1957-58, 59; asst. curator Gray Herbarium, 1963-69, curator herbarium, 1969-73, mem. faculty arts and scis., 1966-73; curator Arnold Arboretum, 1969-73, lectr. biology, 1969-73, coordinator bot. systematic collections, 1972-73; curator Field Mus. Natural History, Chgo., 1973-80, chmn. dept. botany, 1973-77, asst. dir. sci. and edn., 1978-80, dir., 1980—. Cons. and lectr. in field. Contbr. articles to sci. jours.; assoc. editor Rhodora, 1964-70; mem. editorial bd. Anales del Instituto de Biologia, Mexico, 1970-74. Bd. dirs. Ill. Inst. Natural Resources, 1979— . Served with U.S. Army, 1953-55. Recipient Outstanding Vol. award United Way Met. Chgo., 1978; NSF grantee, 1970-81; Van Blarcom scholar, 1959. Fellow AAAS; mem. Am. Inst. Biol. Scis. (governing bd. 1974-77), Am. Assn. Museums, Bot. Soc. Am., Assn. for Tropical Biology (travel grantee 1966), Internat. Assn. Plant Taxonomy, Am. Soc. Plant Taxonomists (pres. 1977, council 1974-78, George R. Cooley award 1970), Linnean Soc. London, Sociedad Botanica de Mexico, Sigma Xi. Office: Ill Nat History Survey Nat Resources Bldg 607 E Peabody Dr Champaign IL 61820-6917

NEW, ROSETTA HOLBROCK, home economics educator, nutrition consultant; b. Hamilton, Ohio, Aug. 26, 1921; d. Edward F. and Mabel (Kohler) Holbrock; m. John Lorton New, Sept. 3, 1943; 1 child, John Lorton Jr. BS, Miami U., Oxford, Ohio, 1943; MA, U. No. Colo., 1971; PhD, The Ohio State U., 1974; student Kantcentrum, Brugge, Belgium, 1992, Lesage Sch. Embroidery, Paris, 1995, Kent State U., 1998. Cert. tchr., Colo. Tchr. English and sci. Monahans (Tex.) H.S., 1943-45; emergency war food asst. U.S. Dept. Agr., College Station, Tex., 1945-46; dept. chmn. home econs., adult edn. Hamilton (Ohio) Pub. Schs., 1946-47; tchr., dept. chmn. home econs. East H.S., Denver, 1948-59, Thomas Jefferson H.S., Denver, 1959-83; mem. exec. bd. Denver Pub. Schs.; also lectr.; exec. dir. Ctr. Nutrition Info. U.S. Office of Edn. grantee Ohio State U., 1971-73. Mem. Cin. Art Mus., Nat. Trust for Historic Preservation. Mem. Am. Home Econs. Assn., Am. Vocat. Assn., Embroiders Guild Am., Hamilton Hist. Soc., Internat. Old Lacers, Ohio State U. Assn., Ohio State Home Econs. Alumni Assn., Fairfield (Ohio) Hist. Soc., Republican Club of Denver, Internat. Platform Assn., Phi Upsilon Omicron. Presbyterian. Lodges: Masons, Daughters of the Nile, Order of Eastern Star, Order White Shrine of Jerusalem. Home and Office: 615 Crescent Rd Hamilton OH 45013-3432

NEWBLATT, STEWART ALBERT, federal judge; b. Detroit, Dec. 23, 1927; s. Robert Abraham and Fanny Ida (Grinberg) N.; m. Flora Irene Sandweiss, Mar. 5, 1965; children: David Jacob, Robert Abraham, Joshua Isaac. BA with distinction, U. Mich., 1950, JD with distinction, 1952. Bar: Mich. 1953. Ptnr. White & Newblatt, Flint, Mich., 1953-62; judge 7th Jud. Cir. Mich., 1962-70; ptnr. Newblatt & Grossman (and predecessor), Flint, 1970-79; judge U.S. Dist. Ct. (ea. dist.) Mich., 1979-93, sr. judge, 1993—. Adj. instr. U. Mich.-Flint, 1977-78, 86. Mem. Internat. Bridge Authority Mich., 1960-62. Served with AUS, 1946-47. Mem. Fed. Bar Assn., State Bar Mich., Dist. Judges Assn. 6th Circuit. Jewish. Office: PO Box 522 Glen Arbor MI 49636-0522

NEWBORG, GERALD GORDON, state archives administrator; b. Ada, Minn., Dec. 13, 1942; s. George Harold and Olea (Halstad) N.; m. Jean Annette Gruhl, Aug. 14, 1964; children: Erica, Annette. BA, Concordia Coll., Moorhead, Minn., 1964; MA, U. N.D., 1969; MBA, Ohio State U., 1978. Cert. archivist. Tutor, preceptor Parsons Coll., Fairfield, Iowa, 1964-67; state archivist Ohio Hist. Soc., Columbus, 1968-76; v.p. Archival Systems Inc., 1978-81; state archivist State Hist. Soc. of N.D., Bismarck, 1981—. Instr. Franklin U., Columbus, 1974; adj. prof. Bismarck State Coll., 1985-86. Co-author: North Dakota: A Pictorial History, 1988. Recipient Resolution of Commendation Ohio Ho. of Reps., Columbus, 1976. Mem. Soc. Am. Archivists, Nat. Assn. Govt. Archives & Records Adminstrs. (bd. dirs. 1984-86, sec. 1994-99), Midwest Archives Conf., N.D. Libr. Assn. (exec. bd. 1985-86). Home: 1327 N 18th St Bismarck ND 58501-2827 Office: State Hist Soc 612 E Boulevard Ave Bismarck ND 58505-0660

NEWBY, JOHN ROBERT, metallurgical engineer; b. Kansas City, Mo., Nov. 17, 1923; s. Merritt Owen and Gladys Mary (McCleery) N.; m. Audry Marie Loniker, Sept. 21, 1963 (div. 1980); children: Deborah A., Walter J., William F., Matthew O., Robert J. BA, U. Mo., Kansas City, 1947; BS in Metall. Engring., Colo. Sch. Mines, 1949; MS, U. Cin., 1963. Cert. profl. engr. Chemist Bar Rusto Plating Corp., Kansas City, 1949; supr. United Chromium, Ferndale, Mich., 1949-52; prin. rsch. metallurgist Armco Inc., Middletown, Ohio, 1952-85; prin. John Newby Cons., 1985—. Cons. Phoenix Cons., Inc., Cin., 1988—. Author, editor: Formability 2000, 1982, Metallic Materials, 1978, Sheet Metal Forming, 1976; editor: Mechanical Testing, Vol. 8, 9th edit., 1985. Scoutmaster Boy Scouts Am., Middletown, 1952-86, now asst. dist. commr.; chmn. Safety Coun., Middletown, 1978-80. Staff sgt. USAF, 1943-46, PTO. Fellow ASTM (chmn. 1963—, chmn. E-28 com. on mech. testing 1998-2002, Award of Merit 1984), ASM (sustaining mem., chpt. chmn. 1970, Award of Merit 1980); mem. SAE (sect. chmn. 1984). Democrat. Achievements include patent for high strength formable steel sheet; development of interstitial free steel, strain analysis process for metallic sheet formability. Home and Office: 100 Marymont Ct Middletown OH 45042-3735

NEWCOMB, MARTIN EUGENE, JR. chemistry educator; b. Mishauaha, Ind., Nov. 17, 1946; s. Martin Eugene and Yolanda Frances (Saliani) N.; 1 child, Jennifer Ruth. BA, Wabash Coll., 1969; PhD in Chemistry, U. Ill., 1973. Asst. prof. Tex. A&M U., College Station, 1973-81, assoc. prof., 1981-85, prof. chemistry, 1985-91, Wayne State U., Detroit, 1991-2001; prof. U. Ill., Chgo., 2001—. Contbr. articles to Accounts of Chem. Rsch., 1988, Jour. Am. Chem. Soc. 1989— Named Dreyfus Tchr.-Scholar, Camille and Henry Dreyfus Found., 1980-85. Mem. AAAS, Am. Chem. Soc.(Arthur C. Cope Scholar award, 1994, James Flack Norris award in Physical Organic Chemistry, 2000). Office: U Ill Chgo Dept Chemistry Chicago IL 60607

NEWELL, DANIEL K. utilities company executive; CFO, sr. v.p. fin. Northwestern Corp., Sioux Falls, S.D., mng. dir., CEO. Office: Northwestern Corp 125 S Dakota Ave Sioux Falls SD 57104

NEWLIN, CHARLES FREMONT, lawyer; b. Palestine, Ill., Nov. 18, 1953; s. Charles Norris and Regina Helen (Correll) N.; m. Jean Bolt, Jan. 6, 1975; children: Christian N., Charles W., Ethan A. BA in Polit. Sci. summa cum laude, Ill. Wesleyan U., 1975; JD cum laude, Harvard U., 1978. Bar: Ill. 1978, U.S. Dist. Ct. (no. dist.) Ill. 1978, U.S. Tax Ct. 1980. Law clk. Sugarman, Rogers, Barshak & Cohen, Boston, 1976-78; assoc. Mayer, Brown & Platt, Chgo., 1978-84, ptnr., 1985-94, Sonnenschein, Nath & Rosenthal, 1994—. Adj. prof. law DePaul U., Chgo., 1986-90; lectr. in field. Contbg. author: Am. Law of Property, 1975, Trust Adminstrn. Ill., 1983, 87, 92, 99, Bogert on Trusts, 1986-91, The Lawyer's Guide to Retirement, 1991, 94; contbr. articles to profl. jours. Scouting coord. DuPage area coun. Boy Scouts Am., Woodridge, Ill., 1984-86; bishop's counselor Mormon Ch., Woodridge, 1984-86; mem. planned giving com. Ill. divsn. Am. Cancer Soc., 1988—, chair, 1997—; active Boys and Girls Clubs of Chgo., 1993—; mem. bd. dirs. Suburban Chgo. Planned Giving Coun., 1996—, Ill. Inst. for Continuing Legal Edn., 1999—; vol. legal cons. The Tower Chorale, Western Springs, Ill., 1989-91. Fellow Am. Coll. Trust and Estate Counsel; mem. Chgo. Bar Assn., Chgo. Estate Planning Coun. Democrat. Mormon. Office: Sonnenschein Nath & Rosenthal 8000 Sears Tower Chicago IL 60606

NEWMAN, ANDREA FISCHER, air transportation executive; AB, U. Mich., 1979; JD, George Washington U., 1983. Sr. v.p. govt. affairs Northwest Airlines, Detroit. Bd. regents U. Mich., Ann Arbor, 1994—; vice chmn. George W. Bush for Pres. Campaign, co-chmn. fin. com. Mich., 2000; bd. dirs. Mich. Econ. Devel. Corp. Found., Mich. Thanskgiving Day Parade Found., Isiah Thomas Found. Mem.: Detroit Econ. Club (v.p.). Office: Northwest Airlines Detroit Met Airport North Terminal Mezzanine Level Detroit MI 48242

NEWMAN, ANDREW EDISON, restaurant executive; b. St. Louis, Aug. 14, 1944; s. Eric Pfeiffer and Evelyn Frances (Edison) N.; m. Peggy Gregory, Feb. 14, 1984; children: Daniel Mark, Anthony Edison. BA, Harvard U., 1966, MBA, 1968. With Office of Sec. Def., Washington, 1968-70; with Edison Bros. Stores, Inc., St. Louis, 1970-95, v.p. ops. and adminstrn., 1975-80, dir., 1978-96, exec. v.p., 1980-86, chmn., 1987-95; chmn., CEO Race Rock Internat., 1995—. Bd. dirs. Sigma-Aldrich Corp., St. Louis, Lee Enterprises, Davenport, Iowa. Trustee Washington U. Office: 8000 Maryland Ave Saint Louis MO 63105-3752

NEWMAN, BARBARA MILLER, psychologist, educator; b. Chgo., Sept. 6, 1944; d. Irving George and Florence (Levy) Miller; m. Philip r. Newman, June 12, 1966; children: Samuel Asher, Abraham Levy, Rachel Florence. Student, Bryn Mawr Coll.; AB with honors in Psychology, U. Mich., 1966, PhD in Devel. Psychology, 1971. Undergrad. research asst. in psychology U. Mich., 1963-64, research asst. in psychology, 1964-69, teaching fellow, 1965-71, asst. project dir. Inst. for Social Research, 1971-72, univ. lectr. in psychology and research assoc., 1971-72; asst. prof. psychology Russell Sage Coll., 1972-76, assoc. prof., 1977-78; assoc. prof. dept. family rels. and human devel. Ohio State U., 1978-83, prof., 1983-86, assoc. provost for faculty recruitment and devel., 1987-92, prof., 1992-2000; prof. dept. human devel. and family studies U. R.I., 2000—. Mem. Eastern Psychol. Assn., Soc. Research in Child Devel., AAAS, Am. Psychol. Assn., Am. Psychol. Soc., Nat. Council Family Relations, Groves Conf. on Marriage and Family, Midwestern Psychol. Assn., Soc. for

Research on Adolescence, Am. Assn. Family and Consumer Scis. Author books including: (with P. Newman) Living: The Process of Adjustment, 1981; Development Through Life, 1995, 7th edit., 1999; Understanding Adulthood, 1983; Adolescent Development, 1986; When Kids Go to College, 1997; contbr. articles to profl. publs. Office: U RI Human Devel and Family Studies 112 Transition Ctr Kingston RI 02881 E-mail: bnewman@uri.edu.

NEWMAN, CHARLES A. lawyer; b. L.A., Mar. 18, 1949; s. Arthur and Gladys Newman; children: Anne R., Elyse S. BA magna cum laude, U. Calif., 1970; JD, Washington U., 1973. Bar: Mo. 1973, U.S. Dist. Ct. (ea. dist.) Mo. 1973, U.S. Ct. Appeals (8th cir.) 1975, U.S. Supreme Ct. 1976, D.C. 1981, U.S. Tax Ct. 1981, U.S. Claims Ct. 1981, U.S. Ct. Appeals (11th cir.) 1994, U.S. Ct. Appeals (9th cir.) 1995, U.S. Dist. Ct. (ctrl. dist.) 1996, U.S. Ct. Appeals (3d, 5th, 7th and 10th cirs.) 1996, U.S. Ct. Appeals (6th cir.) 1997. From assoc. to ptnr. Thompson & Mitchell, St. Louis, 1973-96; ptnr. Thompson Coburn, 1996-97, Bryan Cave LLP, St. Louis, 1997—. Lectr. law Washington U., St. Louis, 1976-78. Bd. dirs. Hawthorn Found., 1997-2000; trustee Mo. Bar Found., 1990-96, mem. Mo. Bar Bd. Govs, 1980-84; bd. dirs. United Israel Appeal, N.Y.C., 1990-93, Coun. Jewish Fedns., N.Y.C., 1992-95, United Jewish Appeal Young Leadership Cabinet, N.Y.C., 1985-88, Ctr. for Study of Dispute Resolution, 1985-88, Legal Svcs. Ea. Mo., 1985-94, St. Louis Community Found., 1992-2001, vice-chmn. 1997-99, St. Louis chpt. Young Audiences 1993-95, Planned Parenthood St. Louis, 1986-89, Jewish Fedn., St. Louis, 1986-98, asst. treas., 1989-90, v.p. fin. planning, 1990-93, asst. sec., 1994-95; v.p. Repertory Theatre, St. Louis, 1986-89, sr. v.p., 1990-91; pres. St. Louis Opportunity Clearinghouse, 1974-78. Recipient Lon O. Hocker Meml. Trial award Mo. Bar Found., 1984. Mem. Bar Assn. Met. St. Louis (Merit award 1976). Democrat. Avocations: golf, reading, music, sailing. Office: Bryan Cave LLP One Metropolitan Square Saint Louis MO 63102-2750

NEWMAN, DIANA S. development consultant; b. Toledo, June 15, 1943; d. Fred Andrew and Thelma Elizabeth (Hewitt) Smith; m. Dennis Ryan Newman, Feb. 15, 1964; children: Barbara Lynn Newman LaBine, John Ryan, Elizabeth Anne. Student, Oberlin Coll., 1961-64. Asst. treas. Marble Cliff Quarries Co., 1964-68; community vol., 1968-83; dir. Ohio Hist. Found., Columbus, 1983-90; v.p. advancement The Columbus (Ohio) Found., 1990-95; pres. Philanthropic Resource Group, Columbus, 1995—. Bd. dirs. Nat. Com. on Planned Giving, 1999—. Chair governing com. First Community Ch., 1983-88; bd. dirs. LWV, 1968-72, Ohio Mus. Assn., 1985-90, Nat. Soc. Fundraising Execs. Cen. Ohio chpt., Columbus, 1983—, Crittenton Family Svcs., Columbus, 1992-95; founder Franklin County Com. on Criminal Justice, Columbus, 1972; past pres. Jr. League Columbus. Mem. Ctrl. Ohio Planned Giving Coun. (bd. dirs. 1990—, pres. 1998), Columbus Female Benevolent Soc. (bd. dirs. 1984—). Home: 1944 Chatfield Rd Columbus OH 43221-3702 Office: Philanthropic Resource Group 1944 Chatfield Rd Columbus OH 43221-3702

NEWMAN, JOAN MESKIEL, lawyer; b. Youngstown, Ohio, Dec. 12, 1947; d. John F. and Rosemary (Scarmuzzi) Meskiel; children: Anne R., Elyse S. BA in Polit. Sci., Case-Western Reserve U., 1969; JD, Washington U., St. Louis, 1972, LLM in Taxation, 1973. Bar: Mo. 1972. Assoc. Lewis & Rice, St. Louis, 1973-80, ptnr., 1981-90, Thompson Coburn, St. Louis, 1990—. Adj. prof. law Washington U. Sch. Law, St. Louis, 1975-92; past pres. St. Louis chpt., mem. Midwest Pension Conf. Mem. nat. coun. Washington U. Sch. Law, 1988—91; chmn. bd. dir. Great St. Louis coun. Girl Scouts USA, 1975—92, officer, 1978—92; mem. cmty. wide youth svcs. panel United Way Greater St. Louis, 1992—96; fin. futures task force Kiwanis Camp Wyman, 1992—93; chmn. staff blue ribbon fin. com. Sch. Dist. , Clayton, 1986—87; vol. Women's Self Help Ctr.; bd. dir., exec. com. Girl Scouts USA, 1993—99, nat. treas., 1996—99; bd. dirs. Met. Employment and Rehab. Svcs., 1980—2001, chmn. bd. dir., 1994—96; bd. dirs. Jewish Ctr. Aged, 1990—92, bd. dir., 1999—2001, Jewish Fedn. St. Louis, 1991—96, City Mus., 1998—2001, Parents as Tchrs., 2000—; chmn. bd. dir. Women of Achievement, 1993—96; bd. dir. United Way Greater St. Louis, 2000—, Oasis, 1999—2001; bd. dirs. MERS/Goodwill Industries, 2001—, Walker Scottish Rite Ctr., 2002—. Named Woman of Achievement St. Louis, 1991. Mem. Mo. Bar Assn. (staff pension and benefits com. 1991—), Bar Met. St. Louis (past chmn. taxation sect.), St. Louis Forum, Order of Coif (hon.). Office: Thompson Coburn LLP US Bank Plz Ste 3300 Saint Louis MO 63101-1643

NEWMAN, JOHN KEVIN, classics educator; b. Bradford, Yorkshire, Eng., Aug. 17, 1928; came to U.S., 1969, naturalized, 1984; s. Willie and Agnes (Shee) N.; m. Frances M. Stickney, Sept. 8, 1970; children: Alexandra, John, Victoria. B.A. in Lit.-Humaniores, Exeter Coll., Oxford U., 1950, B.A. in Russian, 1952, M.A., 1953; Ph.D., Bristol U., 1967. Classics master St. Francis Xavier Coll., Liverpool, Eng., 1952-54, Downside Sch., Somerset, Eng., 1955-69; mem. faculty U. Ill., Urbana, 1969—, prof. classics, 1980—, chmn. dept., 1981-85. Author: Augustus and the New Poetry, 1967, Latin Compositions, 1976, Pindar's Art, 1984, The Classical Epic Tradition, 1986, Roman Catullus, 1990, Lelio Guidiccioni, Latin Poems, 1992, Augustan Propertius, 1997; co-author: (with A.V. Carozzi) Horace-Benedict de Saussure, 1995; editor: Ill. Classical Studies, 1982-87; contbr. The New Princeton Encyclopedia of Poetry and Poetics, 1993. Mem. sr. common room Corpus Christi Coll., Oxford U., 1985-86 Recipient silver medals Vatican, Rome, 1960, 62, 65, 97. Roman Catholic. Home: 703 W Delaware Ave Urbana IL 61801-4806 Office: Dept Classics U Ill 4090 Fgn Lang Bldg 707 S Mathews Ave Urbana IL 61801-3625 E-mail: j-newman@uiuc.edu.

NEWMAN, JOHN M., JR. lawyer; b. Youngstown, Ohio, Aug. 15, 1944; BA, Georgetown U., 1966; JD, Harvard U., 1969. BAr: Ill. 1970, Calif. 1972, Ohio 1976. Law clerk ctrl. dist. U.S. Dist. Ct., Calif., 1969-70, asst. U.S. Atty. ctrl. dist., 1970-75; ptnr. Jones, Day, Reavis & Pogue, Cleve. Fellow Am. Coll. Trial Lawyers; mem. Phi Beta Kappa. Office: Jones Day Reavis & Pogue North Point 901 Lakeside Ave E Cleveland OH 44114-1190 E-mail: jmnewman@jonesday.com.

NEWMAN, JOSEPH HERZL, advertising consultant; b. N.Y.C., Dec. 1, 1928; s. Max A. and Tillie C. (Weitzman) N.; m. Ruth Zita Marcus, Dec. 19, 1954 (div. Feb. 1987); children: Deborah Lynn, David Alan, Mark Jonathan; m. Nancy Kramer Deutschman, Aug. 19, 1990; stepchildren: Pamela Sue Deutschman, Douglas Hayes Deutschman, Cindi Elaine Deutschman. AB, Bethany Coll., W.Va., 1949; MS Grad. Sch. Bus., Columbia U., 1956. With 20th Century Fox Film Corp., NYC, 1949—53; media supr. Fred Wittner Advt. Agy. (now Hammond Farrell Inc.), 1953—56; media dir. O.S. Tyson & Co. (now Poppe Tyson, Inc.), 1956—64; v.p., media dir. Marsteller Inc. (now Lord, Dentsu and Ptnrs.), 1965—85; v.p., assoc. media dir. HBM/Creamer, 1985—87, Della Femina, McNamee, Inc., NYC, 1987—89; pres. Newman And Assocs., Cleve., 1989—. Mem. faculty Advt. Age Media Workshop, 1972; past chmn. media mgrs. adv. com. Bus. Publs. Audit of Circulation Inc., N.Y.C.; condr. profl. media planning seminars, 1989-99. Contbr. articles to profl. jours. Past chmn. bus.-to-bus. media com. Am. Assn. Advt. Agys.; vice chmn. tax incentive rev. coun. City of Mayfield Heights, Ohio, 1994-97, chmn., 1997—. With U.S. Army, 1950-52. Mem. Bus. Mktg. Assn. (past mem. media comparability coun., media data form com. and rsch. resource com., Agy. Exec. of Yr., N.Y. chpt. 1960, 66, 71, 73, cert. bus. communicator). Home and Office: 6338 Woodhawk Dr Mayfield Heights OH 44124-4153 E-mail: nknewmansion@aol.com.

NEWMAN, LAWRENCE WILLIAM, financial executive; b. Chgo., Jan. 14, 1939; s. Eskil William and Adele Diane (Lawnicki) N.; m. Christine Harriet Jaronski, Sept. 22, 1962; children: Paul, Scott, Ron. BBS, U. Ill., 1965; MBA, Northwestern U., 1970. CPA, Ill. Auditor Price Waterhouse, Chgo., 1965-66; controller ECM Corp., Schaumburg, Ill., 1966-70, Nachman Corp., Des Plaines, 1970-76, v.p., treas., controller, 1976-79; v.p. fin. P & S Mgmt. Inc., Schiller Park, 1979-83; controller Underwriters Labs., Northbrook, 1983-86, asst. treas., 1986-89, v.p., 1990-98, treas., 1990-97; CFO, 1997—; sr. v.p. Underwriters Labs., Northbrook, 1998—. Mem. Fin. Execs. Inst., Am. Inst. CPA's. Club: Exec. of Chgo. Office: Underwriters Labs 333 Pfingsten Rd Northbrook IL 60062-2002

NEWSOM, GERALD HIGLEY, astronomy educator; b. Albuquerque, Feb. 11, 1939; s. Carroll Vincent and Frances Jeanne (Higley) N.; m. Ann Catherine Bricker, June 17, 1972; children: Christine Ann, Elizabeth Ann. BA, U. Mich., 1961; MA, Harvard U., 1963, PhD, 1968. Research asst. McMath-Hulbert Obs., Pontiac, Mich., summers 1959, 61; research asst. astronomy dept. U. Mich., Ann Arbor, 1959-61; research asst. Shock Tube Lab. Harvard U., Cambridge, Mass., 1962, 64-68; research asst. dept. physics Imperial Coll., London, 1968-69; asst. prof. astronomy Ohio State U., Columbus, 1969-73, assoc. prof., 1973-82, prof., 1982—, acting chmn. dept. astronomy, 1991-93, vice chmn. dept. astronomy, 1993—, acting asst. dean, 1985-86; sr. post-doctoral research asst. Physikalisches Institut, Bonn, Fed. Republic of Germany, 1978. Author: Astronomy, 1976, Exploring the Universe, 1979; contbr. articles to profl. and scholarly jours. Fellow Woodrow Wilson Found., 1961-62, NSF, 1961-63; grantee Noble Found., 1961-64. Mem. Internat. Astron. Union, Am. Astron. Soc. Home: 46 W Weisheimer Rd Columbus OH 43214-2545 Office: Ohio State U Dept Astronomy 140 W 18th Ave Columbus OH 43210-1173

NEWSOM, JAMES THOMAS, lawyer; b. Carrollton, Mo., Oct. 6, 1944; s. Thomas Edward and Hazel Love (Mitchell) N.; m. Sherry Elaine Retzloff, Aug. 9, 1986; stepchildren: Benjamin A. Bawden, Holly K. Bawden. AB, U. Mo., 1966, JD, 1968. Bar: Mo. 1968, U.S. Supreme Ct. 1971. Assoc. Shook, Hardy & Bacon, London and Kansas City, Mo., 1972, ptnr., 1976—. Mem. Mo. Law Rev., 1966-68. Lt. comdr. JAGC, USNR, 1968-72. Mem. ABA, Kansas City Met. Bar Assn., U. Mo. Law Sch. Law Soc., U. Mo. Jefferson Club, Order of Coif, Perry (Kans.) Yacht Club, Stone Horse Yacht Club (Harwich Port, Mass.). Avocations: skiing, sailing, car racing. Office: Shook Hardy & Bacon One Kansas City Pl 1200 Main St Ste 3100 Kansas City MO 64105-2139 E-mail: jnewsom@shb.com.

NEWTON, JOHN MILTON, academic administrator, psychology educator; b. Schenectady, Feb. 25, 1929; s. Harry Hazleton and Bertha A. (Lehmann) N.; m. Elizabeth Ann Slattery, Sept. 11, 1954; children: Patricia, Peter, Christopher. B.S., Union Coll., Schenectady, 1951; M.A., Ohio State U., 1952, Ph.D., 1955. Lic. psychologist, Nebr. Rsch. psychologist Electric Boat divsn. Gen. Dynamics Corp., Groton, Conn., 1957-60; mem. faculty U. Nebr., Omaha, 1960—, prof. psychology, 1966-99, chmn. dept., 1967-74, acting vice chancellor acad. affairs, 1994-95, prof. emeritus, 1999—, dean Coll. Arts and Scis., 1974-94, dean emeritus, 1999—. Cons. in field, 1960-72 Author research papers in field. Served to 1st lt. Med. Service Corps, AUS, 1955-57. Mem. Am. Psychol. Assn., Psychonomic Soc., Midwestern Psychol. Assn. Home: 5611 Jones St Omaha NE 68106-1232 Office: Univ of Nebr-Omaha Dept Psychology Omaha NE 68182-0001 E-mail: jnewton@mail.unomaha.edu.

NEWTON, WILLIAM ALLEN, JR. pediatric pathologist; b. Traverse City, Mich., May 19, 1923; s. William Allen and Florence Emma (Brown) N.; m. Helen Patricia Goodrich, Apr. 21, 1945; children: Katherine Germain, Elizabeth Gale, William Allen, Nancy Anne. B.Sc. cum laude, Alma (Mich.) Coll., 1943; M.D., U. Mich., 1946. Diplomate: Am. Bd. Pathology, Am. Bd. Pediatrics. Intern Wayne County Gen. Hosp., Detroit, 1947; resident in pediatric pathology/pathology/hematology Children's Hosp. Mich., 1948-50; res. in pediatrics Children's Hosp. Phila., 1950; dir. labs. Children's Hosp. Columbus, Ohio, 1952-88, rsch. pathologist, 1989—; mem. faculty Coll. Medicine, Ohio State U., 1952—, prof., 1965—, chief pediatric pathology, 1952-89, chief div. pediatric hematology, 1952-88, prof. emeritus, 1989—. Chmn. pathology com. Children's Cancer Study Group, 1965-91; chmn. Pathology Com. Intergroup Rhabdomyosarcoma Study Group; chmn. pathology com. Late Effects Study Group. Contbr. articles to med. jours. Trustee, mem. exec. com. Am. Cancer Soc., Ohio div., 1972-86; mem. adv. com. on childhood cancer Am. Cancer Soc.; chmn. exec. com. Consortium for Cancer Control of Ohio, 1982-86; mem. sci. adv. com. Armed Forces Inst. Pathology; pres. Internat. Conf. for Cure of Childhood Cancer in China, 2000—. Served to capt. M.C. U.S. Army, 1950-52, brig. gen. Res. ret. Mem. Ohio State Med. Assn. (com. on cancer), Midwest Soc. Pediatric Research (mem. council 1960-63, pres. 1964-65), Soc. Pediatric Research, Am. Pediatric Soc., Pediatric Pathology Club (pres. 1968-69), Am. Soc. Clin. Oncology, Internat. Soc. Pediatric Oncology, Sigma Xi, Phi Sigma Pi. Republican. Baptist. Home: 2500 Harrison Rd Johnstown OH 43031-9540 Office: 700 Childrens Dr Columbus OH 43205-2664 E-mail: wnewton@chi.osu.edu.

NEY, ROBERT W. congressman; b. Wheeling, W. Va., July 5, 1954; m. Candy (div.); children: Bobby, Kayla Marie. BS in Edn., Ohio State U., 1976. Am. Embassy tchr., supr. affiliate school of Shiraz (Iran), 1978; health and edn. program mgr. Ohio Office of Appalachia, 1979; safety dir. City of Bellaire, Ohio, until 1980; mem. Ohio Ho. of Reps., 1980-84, Ohio Senate, 1984-94, U.S. Congress from 18th Ohio dist., 1995—; mem. fin. svcs. com., transp. and infrastructure com., mem. adminstrn. com. Mem. Kiwanis, Elks, Lions, Sportsmen clubs, NRA. Office: US House of Reps 1024 Longworth Ho Office Bldg Washington DC 20515-3518 also: 3201 Belmont St Ste 604 Bellaire OH 43906-1547*

NEYER, JEROME CHARLES, consulting civil engineer; b. Cin., July 15, 1938; s. Urban Charles and Marie Helen (Hemsteger) N.; m. Judy Ann Drolet, June 17, 1961; children: Janet, Karen. BCE, U. Detroit, 1961; MCE, U. Wash., 1963. Registered profl. engr. 16 states. Facilities engr. Boeing Co., Seattle, 1961-62; found. engr. Metro Engrs., 1962-65; project engr. Hugo N. Helpert Assocs., Detroit, 1965-70; pres. NTH Cons. Ltd., Farmington Hills, Mich., 1970—. Adj. prof. U. Detroit, 1973-79. Contbr. articles to profl. jours. Mem. mineral well adv. bd., Lansing, Mich., 1975, mem. constrn. safety stds. bd., 1982; chmn. bldg. appeals bd. City of Farmington Hills, 1983. Mem. ASTM, ASCE (br. pres. 1973-74), Engring. Soc. Dtroit, Cons. Engrs. Mich. (pres. 1981), Mich. Soc. Profl. Engrs. (bd. dirs. 1980), Assn. Engring. Firms Practicing in the Geoscis. (pres. 1991). Roman Catholic. Avocations: golfing, tennis. Home: 26478 Ballantrae Ct Farmington Hills MI 48331-3528 Office: NTH Consultants Ltd 38955 Hills Tech Dr Farmington MI 48331-3434 E-mail: jneyer@nthconsultants.com.

NICHOL, NORMAN J. manufacturing executive; b. East Cleveland, Ohio, Feb. 12, 1944; s. Norman George and Irene Josephine (Peters) N.; m. Janice E. Nichol, Oct. 19, 1968; children: Gerard, Katherine. BBA, Kent State U. Mktg. trainee A.B. Dick Co., Chgo., 1968, sales rep., supr.-spl. markets mgr., 1971-75, br. mgr. Indpls. and Chgo., 1975-80, dir.-gen. mgr. internat., 1980-82, pres., 1982—, Rycoline Products Co., Chgo., 1985—, Sun Graphic Inc., Robersol Inc. With U.S. Army, 1968-70. Home: 1021 Dover Ct Libertyville IL 60048-3509 Office: Rycoline Products Inc 5540 N Northwest Hwy Chicago IL 60630-1134 E-mail: njnsplace@aol.com., norm.nichol@rycoline.com.

NICHOLAS, ARTHUR SOTERIOS, manufacturing company executive; b. Grand Rapids, Mich., Mar. 6, 1930; s. Samuel D. and Penelope A. (Kalapodes) N.; m. Bessie Zazanis, Aug. 25, 1957; children: Niki Stephanie, Arthur S., Thomas. B.S. in Chem. Engring, U. Mich., 1953; B.A. in Indsl. Mgmt, Wayne State U., 1957. Registered profl. engr., Mich. Project engr. B.F. Goodrich Co., 1953-54; plant mgr. Cadillac Plastics and Chem. Co., 1954-69; pres., chief exec. officer Leon Chem. and Plastics, Inc., Grand Rapids, 1960-69; with U.S. Industries, Inc., 1969-73, pres., chief operating officer, 1973; now pres. The Antech Group. Bd. dirs. ERO Industries, Inc. Patentee in field. Judge Jr. Achievement, Chgo. Served with USNR, 1948-49. Recipient Distinguished Alumni award Grand Rapids Jr. Coll., 1970 Mem. Young Pres. Orgn., Soc. Plastic Engrs., Mich. Acad. Sci., Arts and Letters, Chgo. Coun. on Fgn. Rels., Pres.' Assn. Mem. Greek Orthodox Ch. Clubs: Chgo. Athletic Assn. (Chgo.), Executives (Chgo.). Home: 655 Oak Rd Barrington IL 60010-3135 Office: 2300 Barrington Rd # 411 Hoffman Estates IL 60195-2082

NICHOLAS, RALPH W. cultural organization administrator; PhD, U. Chgo., 1962. William Rainey Herper prof. emeritus deptropology U. Chgo., 2000—; pres. elect Am. Inst. Indian Studies. Contbr. articles to profl. jours. Office: Am Inst Indian Studies 1130 E 59th St Chicago IL 60637 also: U Chgo Dept Anthropology 1126 E 59th St Chicago IL 60637

NICHOLAS, RALPH WALLACE, anthropologist, educator; b. Dallas, Nov. 28, 1934; s. Ralph Wendell and Ruth Elizabeth (Oury) N.; m. Marta Ruth Weinstock, June 13, 1963. BA, Wayne U., 1957; MA, U. Chgo., 1958, PhD, 1962. From asst. prof. to prof. Mich. State U., East Lansing, 1964-71; prof. anthropology U. Chgo., 1971—, chmn. dept., 1981-82, dep. provost, 1982-87, dean of coll., 1987-92, dir. Ctr. Internat. Studies, 1984-95, William Rainey Harper prof. anthropology and social scis., 1992-2000, William Rainey Harper prof. emeritus, 2000—; pres. Internat. House of Chgo., 1993-2000. Cons. Ford Found., Dhaka, Bangladesh, 1973 Author: (with others) Kinship Bengali Culture, 1977; editor: Jour. Asian Studies, 1975-78. V.p. Am. Inst. Indian Studies, 1974-76, treas., 1993-2001, pres.-elect 2001-2002, pres. 2002—; trustee Bangladesh Found. Ford Found. fgn. area tng. fellow, India, 1960-61; Sch. Oriental and African Studies research fellow, London, 1962-63; sr. Fulbright fellow, West Bengal, India, 1968-69 Fellow AAAS, Am. Anthrop. Assn., Royal Anthrop. Inst. (Eng.); mem. Assn. Asian Studies, India League of Am. Found. (trustee). Office: U Chgo Dept Anthropology 1126 E 59th St Chicago IL 60637-1580

NICHOLS, DAVID EARL, pharmacy educator, researcher, consultant; b. Covington, Ky., Dec. 23, 1944; s. Earl and Edythe Lee (Brooker) N.; m. Kathy J. Nichols; children: Charles D., Daniel P. BS, U. Cin., 1969; PhD, U. Iowa, 1973. Asst. prof. medicinal chemistry Purdue U., West Lafayette, Ind., 1974-79, assoc. prof., 1979-85, prof., 1985—. Founder, pres. Heffter Rsch. Inst.; co-founder Darpharma, Inc. Contbr. over 200 articles to sci. jours.; patentee in field. Grantee Nat. Inst. on Drug Abuse, 1978—, NIMH, 1978—. Fellow Am. Coll. Neuropsychopharmacology, Am. Pharm. Assn., Am. Assn. Pharm. Scientists. Office: Purdue U Sch Pharmacy West Lafayette IN 47907

NICHOLS, DONALD ARTHUR, economist, educator; b. Madison, Conn., Dec. 20, 1940; s. Edward Charles and Ruth (Nilson) Nichols; m. Linda Powley, Aug. 19, 1962 (dec. Oct. 1982); children: Charles Spencer, Elizabeth Clarke; m. Barbara Jakubowski Noel, May 22, 1983 (dec. Dec. 26, 2000); m. Jane Bartels, Sept. 26, 2001. B.A., Yale U., 1962, M.A., 1963, Ph.D., 1968. Mem. faculty dept. econs. U. Wis., Madison, 1966—, prof., 1977—, chmn. dept. econs., 1983-86, 88-90, mem. exec. com. faculty senate, 1987-90, chmn., 1989-90, dir. Robert M. LaFollette Sch. Pub. Affairs, 2002—; lectr. Yale U., 1970—71; sr. economist Senate Budget Com., Washington, 1975—76; dep. asst. sec. for econ. policy and rsch. Dept. Labor, 1977-79; dir. Ctr. for Rsch. on Wis. Economy. Econ. advisor to gov. State of Wis., 1983—86; exec. sec. Gov.'s Coun. Econ. Advisors, 1983—86; mem. Gov.'s Export Strategy Commn., 1994—95; bd. dirs. Thompson, Plumb Funds, Sustainable Woods Co-operative; cons. in field; dir. Ctr. for World Affairs and Global Economy, 1995—2000; affiliate Christensen Assocs., Madison, 1999—. Author: (with Clark Reynolds) Principles of Economics, 1970, Dollars and Sense, 1994; contbr. articles to profl. jours. Trustee U. Wis. Bookstore, 1990-95; bd. advisors Am. Players Theatre, Spring Green, Wis., 1993-2001. NSF fellow, 1963-66, 70-72; Nat. Commn. Employment Policy rsch. grantee, 1980-82; recipient William H. Kiekhofer Meml. Teaching prize U. Wis., 1973 Mem. Am. Econ. Assn., Econometric Soc., Royal Econ. Soc. Office: U Wis 1225 Observatory Dr Madison WI 53706

NICHOLS, ELIZABETH GRACE, nursing educator, dean; b. Feb. 1, 1943; d. Terence and Eleanor Denny (Payne) Quilliam; m. Gerald Ray Nichols, Nov. 20, 1965; children: Tina Lynn, Jeffrey David. BSN, San Francisco State U., 1969; MS, U. Calif., San Francisco, 1970, D of Nursing Sci., 1974; MA, Idaho State U., 1989. Staff nurse Peninsula Hosp., Burlingame, Calif., 1966-72; asst. prof. U. Calif.-San Francisco Sch. Nursing, 1974-82; chmn. dept. nursing Idaho State U., Pocatello, 1982-85; assoc. dean Coll. Health Scis. Sch. Nursing U. Wyo., Laramie, 1985-91, asst. to pres. for program revs., 1991-95; dean Coll. Nursing U. N.D., 1995—. Cons. U. Rochester, NY, 1979, Carroll Coll., Mont., 1980, divsn. Nursing Dept. HHS, Washington, U. Maine, Ft. Kent, 1992, Stanford Hosp. Nursing Svc., Calif., 1981—82, Ea. N.Mex. U., 1988, Met. State , Minn., 1998; cons. evaluator Higher Learning Commn., 1993—; site visitor CCNE, 1998—; mem. accreditation review com. The Higher Learning Commn., 2001—. Contbr. articles to profl. jours. Mem. adv. bd. dir. Ombudsman Svc. of Contra Costa Calif., 1979—82, U. Calif. Home Care Svc., San Francisco, 1975—82, Free Clin. of Pocatello, 1984; mem. bd. of rev. coun. baccalaureate & higher degree programs, 1990—92. Fellow ACE, U. Maine Sys., 1990—91. Fellow: Am. Acad. Nursing, Gerontol. Soc. Am. (chmn. clin. medicine sect. 1987, sec. 1990—93); mem.: ANA, Western Inst. Nursing (chmn. 1990—92, bd. govs. , bd. dir. mid-west alliance), Idaho Nurses Assn. (dist. 51 adv. bd. dir. 1982—84), ND Nurses Assn. (bd. dir.), Gerontol. Soc. Am., Oakland Ski Club. (1st v.p. 1981—82), Sigma Theta Tau. E-mail: elizabeth.nichols@mail.und.nodak.edu.

NICHOLS, JOHN DOANE, diversified manufacturing corporation executive; b. Shanghai, China, 1930; m. Alexandra M. Curran, Dec. 4, 1971; children: Kendra E., John D. III. BA, Harvard U., 1953, MBA, 1955. Various operating positions Ford Motor Corp., 1958-68; dir. fin. controls ITT Corp., 1968-69; exec. v.p., COO Aerojet-Gen. Corp., 1969-79, Ill. Tool Works Inc., Chgo., 1980-81, CEO, dir., 1982-95, chmn., 1986-96; pres., CEO Marmon Group Inc., Chgo. Bd. dirs. Household Internat., Philip Morris Cos., Inc., Rockwell Internat., Stone Container Corp.; overseer Harvard U., 1994-99, vis. com. Sch. Edn., com. athletics, com. univ. resources. Trustee U. Chgo., 1987-93, Lyric Opera Chgo., Mus. Sci. and Industry, Jr. Achievement Chgo., Chgo. Commerce Club Civic Com.; life trustee Chgo. Symphony Orch.; bd. dirs. Art Inst. Chgo., past chmn.; mem. bd. govs. Argonne (Ill.) Nat. Lab., 1988-93; mem. exec. com. Chgo. Cmty. Trust, 1997—. Mem. Harvard Club (N.Y., Chgo.), Indian Hill Club (Winnetka, Ill.), Chgo. Club, Comml. Club, Econ. Club Chgo. Office: Marmon Group Inc 225 W Washington St Chicago IL 60606

NICHOLS, RICHARD DALE, former congressman, banker; b. Ft. Scott, Kans., Apr. 29, 1926; s. Ralph Dale and Olive Marston (Kittell) N.; m. Constance Weinbrenner, Mar. 25, 1951 (dec. June 1994); children: Philip William, Ronald Dale, Anita Jane Nichols Bomberger; m. Linda Hupp, Apr. 21, 1996. BS in Agr. and BS in Journalism, Kans. State U., 1951. Info. counsel Kans. State Bd. Agr., Topeka, 1951-54; assoc. far, dir. Sta. WIBW, WIBW-TV, 1954-57; agr. rep. to v.p. Hutchinson (Kans.) Nat. Bank and Trust, 1957-69; pres., CEO Home State Bank, McPherson, Kans., 1969-79, chmn., pres., CEO, 1979-91; chmn. Home State Bank & Trust, 1985-91, 93—; mem. 102d Congress from 5th Kans. dist., 1991-92. Pres. Arts Coun., McPherson, 1979; 5th Dist. chmn. Kans. Rep. Party, 1986-89; bd. dirs. Camp Wood YMCA Camp, Elmdale, Kans., 1995; Meth. Ch. lay spkr., 1994—; bd. trustees Ctrl. Christian Coll., McPherson. Ensign USNR, 1944-47; ATO. Named Hon. Citizen N.Y.C., 1988. Mem. VFW, Kans. Bankers Assn. (pres. 1985-86), Am. Bankers Assn. (advisor 1986-88), Kans. Assn. Banking Ag. Reps. (pres. 1965), Am. Legion, McPherson C. of C. (pres. 1977), Kans. State U. Golden Key Alumni Assn. (pres.), Optimist (pres. Hutchinson club 1965), Rotary (pres. McPherson club 1978), Kans. Cavalry (cmdg. gen. 1986-89). Methodist. Home: 404 N Lakeside Dr Mcpherson KS 67460-3600 Office: Home State Bank and Trust PO Box 1266 Mcpherson KS 67460-1266

NICHOLS, ROBERT LEIGHTON, civil engineer; b. Amarillo, Tex., June 24, 1926; s. Marvin Curtis and Ethel Nichols; m. Frances Hardison, June 8, 1948; children: Eileen, William C., Michael L. B.S.C.E., Tex. A&M U., 1947, M.S.C.E., 1948. Grad. asst., instr. Tex. A&M U., 1947-48; assoc. Freese & Nichols (and predecessors), Ft. Worth, 1948-50, partner, 1950-77, v.p., 1977-88, pres., 1988-91, vice chmn., 1991-92, pres. emeritus, 1992—. Mem. Bldg. Stds. Commn., 1956—62. Chmn. Horn Frog dist. Boy Scouts Am., pres. Longhorn coun., 1990—93, Ozark Trails coun., 1998—99. Mem.: NSPE (pres. 1977—78), ASCE, Nat. Inst. Engring. Ethics 1995—97, Tex. Pub. Works Assn., Tex. Water Utilities Assn., Am. Pub. Works Assn., Water Environ. Assn. Tex. 1962—63, Water Environ. Fedn., Tex. Water Conservation Assn., Am. Water Works Assn., Tex. Soc. Profl. Engrs. 1965—66, C. of C. Webb City, Mo. (exec. dir. 1997—2001), Masons, Chi Epsilon, Tau Beta Pi. Methodist. Office: 1 S Main St Ste 102 Webb City MO 64870-2325 E-mail: rnl@freese.com.

NICHOLS, ROCKY, state representative, non-profit consultant; b. Topeka, Sept. 4, 1969; s. Kenneth Leroy and Rita Ann Nichols. BA in Polit. Sci., Washburn U., 1993. Lic. Nat. Soc. Fund Raising Execs. Legis. aide State of Kans., Topeka, 1991-92; state legislator 58th dist. State Ho. of Reps., 1992—; owner P.M. Consulting, 1993-97; dir. of devel. Family Svc. & Guidance Ctr., 1995-98; owner Fund Consulting, 1997—. Dir. Inst. for Comty. Partnerships, Washburn U., Topeka, 1995-97; mem. adv. bd. Pres.'s Com. on Mental Retardation, Washington, 1997-99; mem. adv. com. Capper Found., Topeka, 1995—; bd. dirs. Kans. Film Commn.; com. mem. Coun. of State Govt., Washington, 1997—. Plenary lectr. Pres.'s Com. on Mental Retardation, Washington, 1997; bd. dirs. Friends of Topeka Zoo, 1995—; Big Brother, Big Bros./Big Sisters Topeka, 1993-2000. Named Outstanding Pub. Ofcl. of Yr., Kans. Assn. of Mental Health Ctrs., 1996, Frank A. Hines Legislator of Yr., Kans. Chiropractic Assn., 1996, Legislator of Yr., Kans. Assn. Pub. Employees, 1994, 96, 97; BILLD fellow La Follette Inst. Pub. Affairs, Wis., 1997. Mem. ETAP (bd. dirs.), Highland Park Optimist Club (pres. 1997-98), Shawnee Heights Optimists Club, Highland Park Alumni Assn. (bd. dirs.). Democrat. Baptist. Avocations: exercise, computers. Home: 2329 SE Virginia Ave Topeka KS 66605-1358 Office: State Ho of Reps State Capitol Topeka KS 66612

NICHOLS, RONALD, state legislator; m. Sue; 4 children. BS, MS, N.D. State U. Mem. N.D. Ho. of Reps., 1991-2000, N.D. Senate from 4th dist., 2001—. Past. mem. fin. and taxation com. N.D. Ho. Reps., Agr. com., edn.; agr. loan officer; farmer, rancher. Mem. Stanley Cmty. Hosp.; past pres. coun. Holy Rosary Cath. Ch. Recipient Outstanding Agriculturist award N.D. State U. Mem. KC, Stanley Am. Legion (past comdr.), N.D. Stockman's Assn., Vietman Vet. Am. Home: 5837 73rd Ave NW Palermo ND 58769-9515

NICHOLSON, RALPH LESTER, botanist, educator; b. Lynn, Mass., Aug. 25, 1942; s. Nathan Aaron and Muriel Spinney (Buxton) N. BA, U. Vt., 1964; MS, U. Maine, 1967; PhD, Purdue U., 1972. Prof. dept. botany and plant pathology Purdue U., West Lafayette, Ind., 1972—. Contbr. chpts. to books, more than 100 articles to profl. jours. Active Big Bros./Big Sisters, Lafayette, Ind., 1974—. Fellow Am. Phytopathol. Soc. Office: Purdue U Botany and Plant Pathology Lafayette IN 47907 E-mail: nicholson@btny.purdue.edu.

NICHOLSON, WILLIAM NOEL, clinical neuropsychologist; b. Detroit, Dec. 24, 1936; s. James Eardly and Hazel A. (Wagner) N.; m. Nancy Ann Marshall, June 15, 1957; children: Anne Marie, Kristin, Scott. AB, Wittenberg U., 1959; MDiv, Luth. Theol. Sem., Phila., 1962; PhD, Mich. State U., 1972. Diplomate Am. Bd. Forensic Examiners, Am. Bd. Med. Psychotherapists; lic. clin. psychologist, Mich.; ordained to ministry Luth. Ch., 1962; cert. Nat. Register health Care Providers in Psychology. Parish pastor Our Saviour Luth. Ch., Saginaw, Mich., 1962-69; intern in psychology Ingham Mental Health Bd., 1971-72; resident in psychology Bay-Arenac Mental Health Bd., 1972-74; dir., psychologist Riverside Ctr., Bay City, Mich., 1974-75; pastor, psychologist Psych Studies & Clergy Consultation of Mich., 1989—. Pres. Bay Psychol. Assocs., P.C., Bay City, 1975— ; cons. Gov.'s Office of Drug Abuse, 1972-74. Author: A Guttman Facet Analysis of Attitude-Behaviors Toward Drug Users by Heroin Addicts and Mental Health Therapists, 1972, An Episcopalian Guide to the Augsburg Confession, 1997; contbr. articles to profl. jours. Mem. APA, Mich. Psychol. Assn., Mental Health Assn. (pres. Bay-ARenac chpt. 1981), Bay City Yacht Club. Office: Behavioral Med Ctr 3442 Wilder Rd Bay City MI 48706-2331 E-mail: fatherbill36@hotmail.com.

NICKEL, JANET MARLENE MILTON, geriatrics nurse; b. Manitowoc, Wis., June 9, 1940; d. Ashley and Pearl Milton; m. Curtis A. Nickel, July 29, 1961; children: Cassie, Debra, Susan. Diploma, Milw. Inst., 1961; ADN, N.D. State U., 1988. Nurse Milw. VA, Wood, Wis., 1961-62; supervising nurse Park Lawn Convalescent Hosp., Manitowoc, 1964-65; newsletter editor Fargo (N.D.) Model Cities Program, 1970-73; supervising night nurse Rosewood on Broadway, Luth. Hosps. and Homes, Fargo, 1973-92; assoc. dir. nursing Elim Care Ctr., 1992-94, night nurse, 1994—. Mem. Phi Eta Sigma. Home: 225 19th Ave N Fargo ND 58102-2352 Office: 3534 S University Dr Fargo ND 58104-6228

NICKELL, CECIL D. agronomy educator; BS, Purdue U., 1963; MS, Mich. State U., 1965, PhD, 1968. Asst. instr. crop sci. dept. Mich. State U., East Lansing, 1963-67; from asst. prof. to assoc. prof. soybean breeding Kans. State U., Manhattan, 1967-79; from assoc. prof. to prof. plant breeding U. Ill., Urbana, 1979-95, prof. plant breeding dept. crop scis., 1995—. Fellow Am. Soc. Agronomy (Achievement-Crops award for Crops 1995, Agron. Rsch. award 1998), Crop Sci. Soc. Am. Office: U Ill Dept Crop Scis 262 Nat Soybean Rsch Lab 1102 W Peabody Dr Urbana IL 61801

NICKELS, ELIZABETH ANNE, office furniture manufacturing executive; 2 children. BSBA in Acctg., Econs. and Bus. Admin., Aquinas Coll., 1983. CPA. CFO, mem. exec. and ops. coms. Universal Forest Products, Grand Rapids, Mich., 1993-2000; CFO Herman Miller, Inc., Zeeland, 2000—. Office: Herman Miller Inc 855 E Main Ave Zeeland MI 49464-0302

NICKELS, JOHN L. retired state supreme court justice; m. Merita Nickels; 7 children. Bachelor's degree, No. Ill. U.; law degree, DePaul U. Pvt. practice, 20 yrs; judge Appellate Ct.; cir. judge 16th Jud. Cir.; supreme ct. justice State of Ill., 1992-98; ret., 1998. Bd. dirs. Kane County Bank & Trust Co. Bd. trustees Waubonsee Coll.; mem. adv. coun. and found. Kaneland Sch. Dist.; mem. Kane County Planning Commn., Zoning Bd. Appeals; mem. St. Gall's Parish, Elburn. Home: 17901 Owens Rd. Maple Park IL 60151*

NICKERSON, DON C. lawyer, former prosecutor; U.S. atty. U.S. Dist. Ct. (So. Dist.), Iowa, 1993—2001; assoc. gen. counsel Wellmark Blue Cross & Blue Shield , 2001—. Office: Wellmark Blue Cross & Blue Shield of Iowa 636 Grand Ave Des Moines IA 50309-2565

NICKERSON, GREG, public relations executive; b. Iowa, Nov. 3, 1958; BS in Agrl. Journalism, Iowa State U., 981. Mkt. analyst, exec. editor Brock Assocs., Brookfield, Wis., 1981-85; with pub. rels. dept. Bader Rutter & Assocs., 1985-88, acctg. group supr., 1988-90, v.p., group supr., 1990-92, v.p., dir. pub. rels. group, 1992-98, exec. v.p., 1998—. Office: Bader Rutter & Assocs 13555 Bishops Ct Ste 300 Brookfield WI 53005-6231

NICKERSON, JAMES FINDLEY, retired educator; b. Gretna, Nebr., Dec. 16, 1910; s. Elmer Samuel and Lulu Perkins (Patterson) N.; m. Juanita M. Bolin, Mar. 3, 1934; children: Ann Rogers Nickerson Lueck, Maria De Miranda. BS, Nebr. Wesleyan U., 1932; MA, Columbia Tchrs. Coll., 1940; PhD, U. Minn., 1948; ScD (hon.), Yankton (S.D.) Coll., 1971. Tchr. pub. schs., Giltner, Nebr., 1932-35; sch. music supr. Gordon, 1936-38, Bayshore, L.I., 1939-41, Grand Island, Nebr., 1941-42; instr. Coll. Edn., music supr. high sch. U. Minn., 1942-46, vis. prof. Coll. Edn., summer 1948; asst. prof. music edn. U. Kans., 1946-48, assoc. prof., 1948-53. Rsch. assoc. dept. psychology U. So. Calif., assigned human factors div. U.S. Navy Electronics Lab., San Diego, 1953-54; dean edn., dir. summer quar., prof. psychology Mont. State U., 1954-64, head dept. psychology, 1954-56, rsch. assoc. Electronics Rsch. Lab, 1958-64; v.p. acad. affairs N.D. State U., Fargo, 1964-66; pres. Minn. State U ., Mankato, 1966-73, then pres. emeritus, disting. svc. prof., 1973-76; dir. Svc. Mems. Opportunity Colls., Am. Assn. State Colls. and Univs., Washington, 1973-81; dir. Northwestern Nat. Bank, Mankato, 1967-69; cons. publ. edn. Office Gov. Wash., 1964; exec. sec., study dir. interim com. edn. Wash. Legislature, 1959-60; chmn. regional conf. womanpower Nat. Manpower Coun. and Mont. State Coll., 1957; mem. steering com. Pacific N.W. Con. Higher Edn., 1962; mem. nat. adv. com. sci. edn. NSF, 1968-71, chmn., 1970-71; mem. vis. com. Harvard Grad. Sch. Edn., 1970-76, Schola Cantorum, N.Y.C., 1938-39, Choral Arts Soc., Washington, 1969-71. Stringbass Mont. State Coll. Symphonette, 1959-63, Mankato Symphony Orch., 1967-73, 83-93, bd. dirs., 1987-90. Recipient citation interim study Wash. Legislature and Gov., 1960, Outstanding Achievement award Bd. Regents U. Minn., 1968, Alumni award Nebr. Wesleyan U., 1968; Sec. Def. medal for outstanding pub. svc., 1981, citation Am. Coun. Edn., 1981; James F. Nickerson Medal of Merit for outstanding svc. to mil. edn. created by Am. Assn. Sr. Colls. and Univs., 1981; Danforth Found. adminstrn. grantee, 1969; named to Internat. Adult & Continuing Edn. Hall of Fame, 1999. Mem. Nat. Assn. State Univs. and Land Grant Colls. (senate, chmn. div. tchr. edn. 1962-65, sec. coun. acad. officers 1965), Am. Assn. State Colls. and State Univs. (bd. dirs. 1966-71), Am. Assn. Colls. Tchr. Edn. (bd. dirs. 1969-71), Am. Assn. Higher Edn. (chmn. resolutions com. 1974), Assn. Minn. Colls. (pres. 1972), Edn. Commn. States (commr. 1967-73, mem. task force on coordination, governance and structure postsecondary edn. 1973), Sigma Xi, Phi Mu Alpha Sinfonia. Home and Office: 301 S 5th St Apt 220 Mankato MN 56001-4580

NICOL, BRIAN, publishing executive; Publisher Home & Away, Inc., Omaha. Office: Home & Away Inc 10703 J St Omaha NE 68127-1023

NIEBYL, JENNIFER ROBINSON, obstetrician and gynecologist, educator; b. Montreal, Que., Can., Dec. 5, 1942; BSc, McGill U., Mont., 1963; MD, Yale U., 1967. Diplomate Am. Bd. Ob-Gyn., Am. Bd. Maternal and Fetal Medicine. Intern in Internal Medicine N.Y. Hosp.-Cornell Med. Ctr., 1967-68, resident in ob-gyn., 1968-70, Johns Hopkins Hosp., Balt., 1970-73, fellow in maternal and fetal medicine, 1976-78, mem. staff, 1973-88, U. Iowa Hosps. and Clinics, Iowa City, 1988—; prof., head ob-gyn. dept. U. Iowa Sch. Medicine, 1988—. Mem. ACOG, Am. Gynecol. and Obstetrical Soc., Soc. Gynecol. Investigation, Soc. Maternal Fetal Medicine, Inst. Medicine of NAS. Office: U Iowa Hosps & Clinics 200 Hawkins Dr Iowa City IA 52242

NIEDERHUBER, JOHN EDWARD, surgical oncologist and molecular immunologist, university educator and administrator; b. Steubenville, Ohio, June 21, 1938; s. William Henry and Helen (Smittle) N.; m. Tracey J. Williamson; children: Elizabeth Ann, Matthew John. BS, Bethany Coll., 1960; MD, Ohio State U., 1964. Diplomate Am. Bd. Surgery. Internship, surgery Ohio State U. Hosp., Columbus, 1964-65; resident, surgery U. Mich. Med. Ctr., Ann Arbor, 1967-69, NIH acad. trainee in surgery, 1969-71, resident, surgery, 1971-72, chief resident surgery, 1972-73, asst. prof. surgery and asst. prof. microbiology, 1973-77, dir. transplantation program, 1975-76, assoc. prof. surgery and assoc. prof. microbiology, 1977-80, chief divsn. surg. oncology and transplantation, sect. gen. surgery, 1979-82, sr. assoc. dean med. sch., 1983-86, assoc. dean rsch., 1982-86, chief divsn. surg. oncology sect. gen. surgery, 1982-86, prof. surgery, prof. microbiology and immunology, 1980-87; cons. Wayne County Gen. Hosp., Mich., 1973-84; cons. surgery Ann Arbor VA Hosp., 1973-87; prof. surgery, oncology, molecular biology and genetics The Johns Hopkins U. Sch. Med., Baltimore, 1987-91; Emile Holman prof. surgery, chair, dept. surgery, head sect. surgical scis. Stanford (Calif.) U. Sch. Medicine., 1991-95, prof. microbiology and immunology, 1991-97; chief of surgery Stanford (Calif.) U. Hosp., 1991-95; dir. planning Comp. Cancer Ctr. Stanford (Calif.) Med. Ctr., 1991-95; prof. surgery and oncology Sch. Medicine, asst. dean oncology, dir. Comprehensive Cancer Ctr. U. Wis., Madison, 1997—. Vis. prof. Howard Hughes Med. Inst. Dept. Molecular Biology and Genetics The Johns Hopkins U. Sch. Medicine, Baltimore, 1986-87; cons. in field. Authored books on cancer and surgery; mem. editl. bd. Jour. Immunology, 1981-85, Jour. Surg. Res., 1989-95, Current Opinion in Oncology, 1989—, Annals of Surgery, 1991—, Surg. Oncology, 1991—, Jour. Clin. Oncology, 1993, Annals of Surg. Oncology, 1993—, Jour. Am. Coll. Surgeons, 1994—, The Oncologist, 1995—, Surgery, 1999—; contbr. articles to profl. jours. Active NCI divsn. Cancer Treatment Bd. Scientific Councilors, 1986-91, chmn., 1987-91, Gen. Motors Cancer Rsch. Found. Awards Assembly, 1988-92, 98—. Served to capt. U.S. Army, 1965-67 Recipient USPHS Rsch. Career Devel. award Nat. Inst. Allergy and Infectious Disease, 1974-79, Disting. Faculty Svc. award U. Mich., 1978, Alumni Achievement award Ohio State U. Coll. Medicine, 1989, Alumni Achievement award in Medicine Bethany Coll., 1995; vis. rsch. fellow divsn. immunobiology Karolinska Inst., Stockholm, 1970-71, Am. Cancer Soc. Jr. Faculty Clin. fellow, 1977-79. Fellow ACS; mem. Am. Soc. Transplant Surgeons, Transplantation Soc., Am. Surg. Assn., Am. Assn. Immunologists, Am. Assn. Cancer Insts. (v.p. 1999—), Coller Surg. Soc., Soc. Univ. Surgeons, Assn. Acad. Surgeons, Soc. Surg. Oncology (v.p. 1999-2001, pres. 2001—), Ctrl. Surg. Soc., Am. Assn. Cancer Rsch., Am. Soc. Clin. Oncology, Soc. Clin. Surgery, Biology Club II, Robert M. Zollinger-Ohio State U. Surg. Soc., Pacific Coast Surg. Assn., Soc. Surgery of the Alimentary Tract, Soc. Surg. Oncology (v.p. 1999—). Avocations: golf, gardening. Office: U Wis Dir Comprehensive Cancer Ctr 600 Highland Ave Madison WI 53792-0001

NIEDERPRUEM, GARY J. metal company executive; Grad., Canisuis Coll.; MBA, U. Rochester. Sales/product mgmt. Ryerson Tull Inc., Buffalo, 1973-80, inside sales mgr. Mpls., 1980-85, gen. mgr. Buffalo, 1985-93, pres. Ryerson East, 1993-98, pres. Ryerson Ctrl., 1998-99, exec. v.p., 1998—. Office: Ryerson Tull Inc 2621 W 15th Pl Chicago IL 60608-1712

NIEFELD, JAYE SUTTER, advertising executive; b. Mpls., May 27, 1924; s. Julius and Sophia (Rosenfeld) N.; m. Piri Elizabeth Von Zabrana-Szilagy, July 5, 1947; 1 child, Peter Wendell. Cert., London U., 1945; BA, U. Minn., 1948; BS, Georgetown U., 1949; PhD, U. Vienna, 1951. Project dir. Bur. Social Sci. Research, Washington, 1952-54; research dir. McCann-Erickson, Inc., N.Y.C., 1954-57; v.p., dir. mktg. Keyes, Madden & Jones, Chgo., 1957-60; pres., dir. Niefeld, Paley & Kuhn, Inc., 1961-71; exec. v.p. Bozell, Inc., 1971-89; pres. The Georgetown Group, Inc., 1991—. Cons. U.S. Dept. State, Commerce, HEW, also others; lectr. Columbia U., Northwestern U., U. Chgo., 1989-94; chmn. Ctr. Advanced Comm. Rsch.; owner Glencoe Angus Farms, Glencoe Arabians; comm. adv. com. Arabian Horse Registry Am.; ptnr. Sunny Valley Farm, Talcott-Fromkin Freehold Assocs., Neptune Realty, J&J Enterprises; bd. dirs. Mktg. Decisions, Inc., E. Morris Comms., Inc. Author: The Making of an Advertising Campaign, 1989; (with others) Marketing's Role in Scientific Management, 1957, Advertising and Marketing to Young People, 1965, The Ultimate Overseas Business Guide for Growing Companies, 1990; contbr. articles to profl. jours. Mem. adv. bd. Glencoe Family Svc.; bd. dirs. Big Bros. Met. Chgo.; exec. v.p. City of Hope; mem. Theodore Thomas Soc. Chgo. Symphony Orch., Overture Soc. Lyric Opera Chgo. Capt. AUS, 1942-46. Decorated Bronze Star. Mem. Am. Assn. Pub. Opinion Rsch., Am. Film Inst., Am. Mktg. Assn., Am. Sociol. Assn., Smithsonian Instn., Internat. Arabian Horse Assn., Arabian Horse Registry (comm. com.), The Caxton Club, Chgo. Horticultural Soc. (governing bd.), Chgo. Coun. on Fgn. Rels. Home: 1011 Bluff St Glencoe IL 60022-1120 E-mail: Jaye8@msn.com.

NIEHM, BERNARD FRANK, mental health center administrator, retired; b. Sandusky, Ohio, Feb. 7, 1923; s. Bernard Frank and Hedwick (Panzer) N.; m. Eunice M. Patterson, Oct. 4, 1924; children— Julie, Patti, Bernie. BA, Ohio State U., 1951, MA, 1955, PhD in Ednl. Exceptional Children, Guidance and Couseling, Psychology, 1968. Tchr. pub. schs., Sandusky, 1951-57; chief ednl., vocat. and occupational therapy svcs. Vineland (N.J.) Tng. Sch., 1957-61; exec. dir. Franklin County Coun. Retarded Children, Columbus, Ohio, 1962-64; dir. Ohio Sheltered Workshop Planning Project Mental Retardation, 1964-66, coordinator mental retardation planning, 1966-68; project dir. Ohio Gov.'s Citizen Com. on Mental Retardation Planning, 1966-68; adminstr. Franklin County Program for Mentally Retarded, 1968-70; supt. Gallipolis (Ohio) State Inst., 1970-76; tchr. spl. edn. Ohio U., Columbus, 1975-77, dir. consultation and edn., 1977-79, dir., 1978-95; exec. dir. Woodland Ctrs. Inc., Gallipolis, 1995; ret. Woodland Farm, 1995. Pres. Gallco, 1989-90. Contbr. articles to profl. jours. Active Foster Grandparents Adv. Coun., Gallia County, 1974-76, Gallipolis State Inst. Parent Vol. Assn., 1970-76, Franklin County Bd. Mental Retardation, 1967-68; chmn. MGM dist. Tri-State Boy Scout Coun.; chmn. Meigs, Gallia, Mason Counties Boy Scout Dist., 1972-94; pres. Gallipolis Girls Athletic Assn. Booster Club, 1976—, Gallia County Arthritis Unit, 1986-96, Galleo Industries Bd. to Serve Handicapped Adults, 1987-94; pres. bd. dirs. Outreach Ctr. Gallia County, 1997-99; mem. Ch. Coun., St. Paul Luth. Ch., 1994-99, pres.; bd. dirs. United Cerebral Palsy, Columbus, 1968-70; mem. United Way Gallia County. With U.S. Army, 1943-46. Mem. Am. Assn. Mental Deficiency (past chmn. Ohio chpt., chmn. Great Lakes region), Am. Mental Health Adminstrs. (nat., Ohio chpts.), Nat. Rehab. Assn., Ohio Rehab. Assn., Ohio Assn. Retarded Children (2d v.p. 1974-76, dir.), Vocat. Rehab. Assn., Ohio Coun. Community Mental Health Ctrs., Gallia County Arthritis Assn. (pres. 1991—), Gallipolis Area C. of C., Gallipolis Rotary. Lutheran. Home: 1525 Mill Creek Rd Gallipolis OH 45631-8616 Office: Woodland Ctr Inc 3086 State Route 160 Gallipolis OH 45631-8418

NIELSEN, FORREST HAROLD, research nutritionist; b. Dancy, Wis., Oct. 26, 1941; s. George Adolph and Sylvia Viola (Blood) N.; m. Emily Joanne Currie, June 13, 1964; children: Forrest Erik, Kistin Emily. BS, U. Wis., 1963, MS, 1966, PhD, 1967. NIH grad. fellow, dept. biochemistry U. Wis., Madison, 1963-67; rsch. chemist, Human Nutrition Rsch. Inst. USDA, Beltsville, Md., 1969-70, rsch. chemist Human Nutrition Rsch. Ctr. Grand Forks, N.D., 1970-86, ctr. dir. and rsch. nutritionist, 1986-2001, rsch. nutritionist, 2001—. Adj. prof. dept. biochemistry and molecular biology, U. N.D., Grand Forks, 1971—, speaker in field. Assoc. editor Magnesium and Trace Elements Jour., 1990-93; mem. editl. bd. Jour. Trace Elements in Exptl. Medicine, 1988—, Biol. Trace Element Rsch. Jour., 1979—, Jour. Nutrition, 1984-88, Biofactors, 1997—; contbr. articles to profl. jours. Capt. U.S. Army, 1967-69. Recipient Klaus Schwarz Commemorative medal and award Internat. Assn. of Bioinorganic Scientists; named Scientist of Yr. U.S. Dept. Agrl., 1993. Mem. Internat. Soc. Trace Element Rsch. in Humans (gov. bd. 1989—, pres. 1992-95), Soc. for Exptl. Biology and Medicine, Am. Soc. for Nutritional Scis., N.D. Acad. Sci. (pres. 1988-89), Internat. Bone and Mineral Soc., Sigma Xi (pres. U. N.D. chpt. 1976-77). Lutheran. Achievements include patent for use of Boron Supplements to Increase in Vivo Production of Hydroxylated Steroids; discovery of the nutritional essentiality of the trace elements boron and nickel. Office: USDA ARS GFHNRC PO Box 9034 Grand Forks ND 58202-9034 E-mail: fnielsen@gfhnrc.ars.usda.gov.

NIELSEN, GEORGE LEE, architect; b. Ames, Iowa, Dec. 12, 1937; s. Verner Henry and Verba Lucile (Smith) N.; m. Karen Wall, Feb. 28, 1959; children: David Stuart, Kristina, Melissa. B.Arch., Iowa State U., 1961; M.Arch., M.I.T., 1962. Registered arch., Mass., Ohio, N.Y., Ill., Ind., Nat. Coun. Archtl. Registration Bds. Designer Perry, Shaw, Hepburn & Dean, Boston, 1961-64, F.A. Stahl & Assos., Cambridge, Mass., 1964-65; project architect Peirce & Pierce, Boston, 1965-70; project mgr. A.M. Kinney Assos., Cin., 1970—, partner, 1978—; sec. A.M. Kinney Assocs., Inc., Ill., 1993—, also dir.; v.p. A.M. Kinney Inc., 1992-94, pres., 1994-99, also dir.; sr. prin. A.M. Kinney Inc. Assocs., 1999—. Architect assoc. with major projects for Avco Rsch. Lab., Children's Hosp. Med. Ctr., Square D. Corp., Nalco Chem. Co., Olin Corp., Mead Johnson/Bristol Myers Squib, Cin. Gas and Elec. Co., Sandoz Pharm. Corp., Hoechst Celanese, Hoechst Marion Roussel, Witco Corp., Sotheby's, Shell Chem. Co., Bayer Corp., Univ. Ky. Served with U.S. Army, 1962-64. Mem. AIA (design awards 1970-71, 74, 78, 81, 91, 94, 95). Episcopalian. Home: 3419 Ault View Ave Cincinnati OH 45208-2518 Office: A M Kinney Inc 150 E 4th St Fl 6 Cincinnati OH 45202-4131 E-mail: nielsengl@amkinney.com.

NIELSEN, PAUL DOUGLAS, Air Force officer, engineering manager; b. New Orleans, Apr. 18, 1951; s. Jack Alton and Shirley Mae (Gillette) N.; m. Dorothy Webb Spragins, May 3, 1975; children: Eric Douglas, Kristin Echols, Steven Spragins. BS, USAF Acad., 1972; MS, U. Calif., Davis, 1973, PhD, 1981; MBA, U. N.Mex., 1977; postgrad., Nat. War Coll., 1988-89. Dir. engring., maj. Sec. of the Air Force Office of Spl. Projects, Los Angeles AFS, Calif., 1981-84; program dir., chief engr., lt. col. Electronic Systems Divsn., Hanscom AFB, Mass., 1984-88; mil. asst., col. Office of Asst. Sec. Def., Washington, 1989-92; comdr. Rome Lab., Griffiss AFB, N.Y., 1992-95; command dir. Cheyenne Mountain Ops. Ctr., Cheyenne Mountain Air Sta, Colo., 1995-96, chief ops., 1996-97; brig. gen., dir. plans N.Am. Aerospace Def. Command, Peterson AFB, Colo., 1997-99; vice comdr. Aero. Systems Ctr., Wright-Patterson AFB, Ohio, 1999-2000; maj. gen. Air Force Rsch. Lab., 2000—. Fellow Hertz Found., Livermore, Calif., 1972-73, 78-81. Mem. AIAA (sr.), Armed Forces Comm. and Electronics Assn., Air Force Assn. Home: 516 Metzger Dr Dayton OH 45433-1133 Office: AFRL/CC 1864 4th St 1 Wright Patterson AFB OH 45433-7130 E-mail: paul.nielsen@wpafb.af.mil.

NIEMEYER, GLENN ALAN, academic administrator, history educator; b. Muskegon, Mich., Jan. 14, 1934; s. John T. and Johanna F. (Walhout) N.; m. Betty Sikkenga, July 8, 1955; children: Kristin, Alexis, Sander BA in History, Calvin Coll., 1955; MA in History, Mich. State U., 1959, PhD in History, 1962. Tchr. soc. sci. Grand Haven Christian Sch., Mich., 1955-58; teaching asst., asst. instr. Mich. State U., East Lansing, 1958-63; asst. prof. history Grand Valley State U., Allendale, Mich., 1963-66, assoc. prof., 1966-70, prof., 1970—, dean Coll. Arts and Scis., 1970-73, v.p. of colls., 1973-76, v.p. acad. affairs, 1976—, provost, 1980—. Evaluator commn. on instns. of higher edn. North Ctrl. Assn., Chgo., 1974—, vice chair, 1994, chair, 1995, v.p., 1996, pres., 1997; mem. Acad. Officers, Pres.'s Coun. State Univs. of Mich. Author: The Automotive Career of Ransom E. Olds, 1963; contbr. articles and book revs. to profl. publs. Trustee Calvin Coll., Grand Rapids, Mich., 1974-80; trustee Unity Christian High Sch., Hudsonville, Mich., 1978-80, pres. bd., 1979-80 Mem. Am. Coun. on Edn., Am. Assn. Higher Edn. Mem. Christian Ref. Ch. Office: Grand Valley State U Allendale MI 49401

NIENKE, STEVEN A. construction company executive; b. 1950; Carpenter Halsey Tevis, Wichita, Kans., 1970-72; pres. Midwest Drywall Co. Inc., 1972—. Office: Midwest Drywall Co Inc 1351 S Reca Ct Wichita KS 67209-1848

NIENSTEDT, MONSIGNOR JOHN CLAYTON, educator, priest; b. Detroit, Mar. 18, 1947; s. John and Elizabeth S. (Kennedy) N. BA, Sacred Heart Sem., 1969; BST, Pontifical Gregorian U., 1972; Licentiate in Sacred Theology, Pontifical Inst. of St. Alphonsus, 1977, DST, 1985. Ordained deacon North Am. Coll., Rome, 1972, priest Sacred Heart Ch., Dearborn, Mich., 1974. Deacon intern Sacred Heart Parish, Dearborn, Mich., 1973-74; assoc. pastor Guardian Angels Ch., Clawson, 1974-76; priest/sec. Cardinal John Dearden, Archbishop, Detroit, 1977-80; apptd. minor official of 2nd grade Vatican Secretariate of State, 1980-85; temporary assoc. pastor St. Regis Parish, Birmingham, Mich., 1986; pastor St. Patrick's Parish, Union Lake, 1986-87; former rector Sacred Heart Major Sem., Detroit, former asst. prof. moral theology; auxiliary bishop Archdiocese of Detroit, 1996—. Part-time prof. Moral Theology St. John's Sem., Plymouth, Mich., 1977-78; weekend assoc. pastor St. Fabian's Parish, Farmington HIlls, Mich., 1977, Our Lady of Sorrow's Parish, Farmington, 1978-80; mem. med. moral com. Mich. Conf. for Cath. Health Facilities, 1977-80; served as Vicar Gen. of Archdiocese of Detroit, 1979-80; asst. chaplain Baby Jesus Hosp., Rome, Italy 1980-83; chaplain Bros. of Holy Cross assigned to Notre Dame High Sch. for Boys, Rome, 1981-84; instr. religion First Eucharist Program Marymont Internat. Sch., 1980-83; temp. assoc. pastor St. Regis Parish, Birminham, 1986; adj. prof. moral theology Orchard Lake Schs., 1986; bd. trustees Madonna Coll., 1989—, trustee com. acad. affairs, 1989—; mem. Midwest/Western Rector's Conf., 1987—, Wranglers, 1986-90, Archdiocesan Med. Moral Com., 1987—; presenter in field. Apptd. a Chaplain to His Holiness by Pope John Paul II bearing title Monsignor, 1985, a Prelate of Honor by Pope John Paul II, 1990. Mem. Cath. Theol. Soc. Am., Assn. Gov. Bds. of U. and Colls. (workshop theol. sch. trustees, chief execs. Cin. chpt. 1989), Midwest Assn. Theol. Schs. (ann. participation 1988, 89, 90), Assn. Am. Colls. (ann. participation 1990). Office: Diocese of New Ulm Catholic Pastoral Ctr 1400 6th St N New Ulm MN 56073

NIERSTE, JOSEPH PAUL, software engineer; b. Marion, Ind., Feb. 20, 1952; s. Louis Lemuel and Mary Catherine (Dragstrem) N.; m. Deborah Mae Goble, Sept. 20, 1986. BA Applied Piano, Bob Jones U., 1975; MM in Musical Performance, Ball State U., 1977, MS in Computer Sci., 1984. Instr. Marion Coll., 1983-84, Ball State U., Muncie, Ind., 1983-84; software engr. Tokheim Corp., Ft. Wayne, 1984, Delco Electronics, Kokomo, 1984-98, Delphi Delco Electronics Sys., Kokomo, 1998—. Mem. Pi Kappa Lambda. Republican. Baptist. Avocations: sports, music, computers. Home: 3508 Melody Ln W Kokomo IN 46902-7514 Office: Delphi Delco Electronics Systems CT-40-C PO Box 9005 Kokomo IN 46904-9005 E-mail: c2xjpn@eng.delcoelect.com.

NIGL, JEFFREY M. telecommunications company executive; b. 1958; CFO, v.p., treas. Electronic Telecomms. Inc., Waukesha, Wis. Office: Electronic Telecomms Inc 1915 MacArthur Rd Waukesha WI 53188

NIKOLAI, LOREN ALFRED, accounting educator, writer; b. Northfield, Minn., Dec. 14, 1943; s. Roman Peter and Loyola (Gertrude) N.; m. Anita Carol Baker, Jan. 15, 1966; children: Trishia, Jay. BA, St. Cloud State U., 1966, MBA, 1967; PhD, U. Minn., 1973. CPA, Mo. Asst. prof. U. N.C., Chapel Hill, 1973-76; assoc. prof. U. Mo., Columbia, 1976-80, prof., 1980-82, Ernst & Young Disting. prof. Sch. Accountancy, 1982—, dir. masters programs, 2002—. Author: Financial Accounting: Concepts and Uses, 1988, 3d edit., 1995, Intermediate Accounting, 1980, 8th edit., 2000, Accounting Information for Business Decisions, 1st edit., 2000. Recipient Faculty award of merit Fedn. Schs. of Accountancy, 1989, Disting. Alumni award St. Cloud U., 1990, Coll. of Bus. Faculty Mem. of Yr. award, 1991, Mo. Outstanding Acctg. Educators award, 1993; Kemper fellow U. Mo., 1992, Alumni award MU Faculty, 1996, UM Presdl. awd. for Outstanding Teaching, 1999; Coll. of Bus. Teacher of the Yr., 1999. Mem. AICPA, Am. Acctg. Assn., Mo. Soc. CPAs, Fedn. Schs. of Acctg. (pres. 1994). Office: U Mo Sch Accountancy 303 Cornell Hall Columbia MO 65211-0001

NIRO, CHERYL, lawyer; b. Feb. 19, 1950; d. Samuel James and Nancy (Canezaro) Ippolito; m. William Luciano Niro, July 1, 1979; children: Christopher William, Melissa Leigh. BS with highest honors, U. Ill., 1972; JD, No. Ill. U., 1980. Bar: Ill. 1981, U.S. Dist. Ct. (no. dist.) Ill. 1981, U.S. Ct. Appeals (7th cir.) 1990, U.S. Supreme Ct. 1999, cert.: negotiator, mediator, facilitator, bar: US Ct. Appeals (7th cir.), US Supreme Ct. 1999. Assoc. Pope Ballard Sheppard & Fowle, Chgo., 1980-81; ptnr. Partridge and Niro PC; now ptnr. Quinlan & Carroll, Chgo. Spec counsel to atty gen Office Ill Atty Gen; consult Ill Office Educ, 1975; conflict resolution program develop US Atty Gen; pres Assocs in Dispute Resolution Inc; exec dir Comt to Commerorate US Constituion in Ill, 1985—86; creator Bicentennial Law Sch Program; tchg asst program instrn lawyers mediation and negotiation worshops; guest lectr Harvard Univ; mem appt panel US Ct Appeals (7th cir). Chmn Task Force on Children; co-chair Ill Conclave on Legal Educ Ill State Scholar, 1968—72; bd dirs Univ Chicago Lying-In Hosp, 1982—. Named one of Ten Most Influential Women Lawyers in Ill, Am Lawyer Media, 2000. Mem.: ATLA, ABA (comn multijurisdictional practice, standing comt bar servs, dispute resolution sect coun, house delegs), Internat. Bar Assn., Ill Bar Asn (mem assembly 1993, bd govs 1994—97, treas 1995—96, 2d vpres 1997—98, pres 1999—2000, standing comt legal-related educ pub, pres. 1999—2000), Ill Trial Lawyers Asn. Home: 633 N East Ave Oak Park IL 60302-1715 Office: Quinlan & Carroll 30 N Lasalle St Ste 2900 Chicago IL 60602-2590 Business E-Mail: cniro@qclaw.com.

NISBET, THOMAS K. architect; b. Richland Center, Wis., Jan. 9, 1931; s. Thomas Kenneth and Eva Louise (Klein) N.; m. Lynnette Patricia MacIntyre, Aug. 27, 1954; children: Bruce W., Jay T., Christopher W. Student, Columbia Coll., 1949-51; BArch, Columbia U., 1955. Registered arch., N.Y., Wis. Apprentice arch. Albert M. Skinner AIA, Watertown, N.Y., 1946-49; asst. editl. Archtl. Record, N.Y.C., 1950-51; draftsman Weiler/Strang, Madison, Wis., 1952-55; arch. H.C. Montgomery AIA, Watertown, 1958-61; arch./assoc. Flad & Assocs., Madison, 1961-83; prin. Nisbet/Archs., 1983—. Mem. Wis. Examining Bd., 1982-83, Nat. Coun. Archs. Registration Bd., 1983. Works include co-designer Sentry Ins. home office, 1975 (honor award 1975), Wis. Telephone/ASC/WARF, 1970-75 (merit awards 1970-75), U. Wis. Libr./Vilas Hall (merit award 1974); awarded commission for Tri State Vets. Meml. with Severson/Schultz Sculptors. Deacon Westminster Presbyn. Ch., Madison, 1964; v.p., bd. dirs. Nakoma Golf Club, Madison, 1976-82. Recipient Columbia U. traveling fellowship Europe, 1957-58. Mem. AIA, Wis. Archs. Found. (pres. 1981-85). Avocations: art, photography. Office: Nisbet/Architects 4340 Hillcrest Cir Madison WI 53705-5017 E-mail: tknisbet@chorus.net.

NISBETT, RICHARD EUGENE, psychology educator; b. Littlefield, Tex., June 1, 1941; s. R. Wayne and Helen (King) N.; m. Susan Ellen Isaacs, June 29, 1969; children: Matthew, Sarah. AB summa cum laude, Tufts U., 1962; PhD, Columbia U., 1966. Asst. prof. psychology Yale U., New Haven, 1966-71; assoc. prof. psychology U. Mich., Ann Arbor, 1971-77, prof., 1977—, Theodore M. Newcomb prof. psychology, 1989-92, Theodore M. Newcomb disting. univ. prof. of psychology, 1992—. Author: (with others) Attribution: Perceiving the Causes of Behavior, 1972, Induction: Processes of Inference, Learning and Discovery, 1986, Rules for Reasoning, 1992, (with L. Ross) Human Inference: Strategies and Shortcomings of Social Judgment, 1980, The Person and the Situation, 1991, (with D. Cohen) Culture of Honor, 1996. Recipient Donald T. Campbell award for disting. rsch. in social psychology APA, 1982, Disting. Sci. Contbn. award APA, 1991, Am. Acad. Arts & Sci., 1992, Disting. Sr. Scientist award Soc. Exptl. Social Psychology, 1995, J. McKeen Cattell award, 1998; fellow Ctr. for Advanced Studies in Behavioral Scis., William James award Am. Psychol. Soc., 1995, John Simon Guggenheim fellow, 2001; Russell Sage Found. scholar, 2001, Nat. Acad. Sci., 2002. Office: U Mich 5261 ISR Rsch Ctr Group Dynamics Ann Arbor MI 48106

NISSEN, WILLIAM JOHN, lawyer; b. Chgo., July 28, 1947; s. William Gordon Jr. and Ruth Carolyn (Banas) N.; m. Patricia Jane Press, Jan. 16, 1971; children: Meredith Warner, Edward William. BA, Northwestern U., 1969; JD magna cum laude, Harvard U., 1976. Bar: Ill. 1976, U.S. Dist. Ct. (no. dist.) Ill. 1976, U.S. Ct. Appeals (7th cir.) 1981. Assoc. Sidley & Austin, Chgo., 1976-83, ptnr., 1983—. Gen. counsel Heinold Commodities, Inc., Chgo., 1982-84. Editor Harvard U. Internat. Law Jour., 1974-76. Served to lt. USN, 1969-73. Mem. ABA (co-chmn. futures regulation subcom. on pvt. litig. 1996-98), Chgo. Bar Assn. (chmn. futures regulation com. 1985-86), Am. Legion (comdr. union league post 758 1994-95), Union League Club Chgo. (dir. 1999—). Home: 348 Foss Ct Lake Bluff IL 60044-2753 Office: Sidley & Austin Bank One Plz 425 W Surf St Apt 605 Chicago IL 60657-6139

NITIKMAN, FRANKLIN W. lawyer; b. Davenport, Iowa, Oct. 26, 1940; s. David A. and Janette (Gordon) N.; m. Adrienne C. Drell, Nov. 28, 1972. BA, Northwestern U., 1963; LLB, Yale U., 1966. Bar: Ill. 1966, U.S. Dist. Ct. (no. dist.) Ill. 1967, U.S. Tax Ct. 1972, Fla. 1977, D.C. 1981. Assoc. McDermott, Will & Emery, Chgo., 1966-72, ptnr., 1973—. Co-author: Drafting Wills and Trust Agreements, 1990. Bd. dirs. Owen Coon Found., Glenview, Ill., 1985—, Jewish United Fund, Jewish Fedn. Met. Chgo., 1994—; bd. dirs. Spertus Inst. Jewish Studies, Chgo., 1991—, chmn. bd., 1999—. Fellow Am. Coll. Trust and Estate Coun., Am. Bar Found.; mem. Standard Club, Arts Club (Chgo.). Home: 365 Lakeside Pl Highland Park IL 60035-5371 Office: McDermott Will & Emery 227 W Monroe St Ste 4700 Chicago IL 60606-5096 E-mail: fnitikman@mwe.com.

NITSCHE, JOHANNES CARL CHRISTIAN, mathematics educator; b. Olbernhau, Germany, Jan. 22, 1925; came to U.S., 1956; s. Ludwig Johannes and Irma (Raecke) N.; m. Carmen Dolores Mercado Delgado, July 1, 1959; children: Carmen Irma, Johannes Marcos and Ludwig Carlos (twins). Diplom für Mathematik, U. Göttingen, 1950; PhD, U. Leipzig, 1951; Privatdozent, Tech. U. Berlin, 1955. Asst. U. Göttingen, 1948-50; rsch. mathematician Max Planck Institut für Strömungsforschung Göttingen, 1950-52; asst. Privatdozent Tech. U., Berlin, 1952-56; vis. assoc. prof. U. Cin., 1956-57; assoc. prof. U. Minn., Mpls., 1957-60, prof. math., 1960—, head Sch. Math., 1971-78. Vis. prof. U. P.R., 1960-61, U. Hamburg, 1965, Tech. Hochschule Vienna, 1968, U. Bonn, 1971, 75, 77, 80, 81, U. Heidelberg, 1979, 82, 83, U. Munich, 1983, U. Florence, 1983, Tech. Hochschule Aachen, 1997, 98; keynote speaker Festive Colloquium, U. Ulm, 1986; co-organizer workshop statis. thermodynamics and differential geometry U. Minn., 1991; keynote speaker Meml. Colloquium Tech. U. Berlin, 1991, speaker Internat. Workshop on Geometry and Interfaces, Aussois, France, 1990, others. Author: Vorlesungen uber Minimalflachen, Springer-Verlag, 1975, Lectures on Minimal Surfaces, 1989; mem. editorial bd. Archive of Rational Mechanics and Analysis, 1967-91; editor: Analysis, 1980—; assoc. editor: Contemporary Math., 1980-88, Zeitschrift für Analysis und ihre Anwendungen, 1993—; contbr. articles to profl. jours. Mem. Am. del. joint Soviet-Am. Symposium on Partial Differential Equations, Novosibirsk, 1963, U.S.-Japan Seminar on Differential Geometry, Tokyo, 1977; speaker 750th Berlin Anniversary Colloquium, Free U. Berlin, 1987. Recipient Lester R. Ford award for outstanding expository writing, 1975, George Taylor Disting. Svc. award U. Minn. Found., 1980, Humboldt prize for sr. U.S. scientists Alexander von Humboldt Found., 1981; Fulbright rsch. fellow Stanford, 1955-56. Fellow AAAS; mem. Am. Math. Soc., Circolo Matematico di Palermo, Deutsche Mathematiker-Vereinigung, Edinburgh Math. Soc., Gesellschaft für Angewandte Mathematik und Mechanik, Math. Assn. Am., N.Y. Acad. Scis., Österreichische Mathematische Gesellschaft, Soc. Natural Philosophy. Home: 2765 Dean Pky Minneapolis MN 55416-4382

NIX, EDMUND ALFRED, lawyer; b. Eau Claire, Wis., May 24, 1929; s. Sebastian and Kathryn (Keirnan) N.; m. Mary Kathryn Nagle Daley, Apr. 27, 1968; children: Kim, Mary Kay, Norbert, Edmund Alfred, Michael. B.S., Wis. State U., 1951; LL.B., U. Wis., 1954, postgrad. in speech, 1956-57. Bar: Wis. 1954. Practice in, Eau Claire, 1954-65; dist. atty. Eau Claire County, 1958-64; U.S. atty. Western Dist. Wis., Eau Claire, 1965-69, U.S. magistrate, 1969-70; dist. atty. La Crosse County, Wis., 1975-77; mcpl. judge City of La Crosse, 1992—. Co-chmn. United Fund, Eau Claire, 1958; Pres. Young Democrats Wis., 1951-53; mem. adminstrv. bd. Wis. Dem. party, 1953-54; chmn. 10th Congl. dist., 1965; sec. Kennedy for Pres. Club Wis., 1959-60. Served with AUS, 1954-56. Mem. Fed. Bar Assn., Wis. Bar Assn. (state chmn. crime prevention and control com.), La Crosse County Bar Assn. (pres.), Nat. Dist. Attys. Assn., KC. Roman Catholic. Office: 123 4th St N La Crosse WI 54601-3235 E-mail: nixe@ffax.net.

NIXON, CHARLES WILLIAM, acoustician; b. Wellsburg, W.Va., Aug. 15, 1929; s. William E. and Lenora S. (Treiber) Nixon; m. Barbara Irene Hunter, May 19, 1956; children: Timothy C., Tracy Scott. BS, Ohio State U., 1952, MS, 1953, PhD, 1960. Tchr. spl. edn. Ohio and W.Va. Pub. Schs., Wheeling, 1954—56; rsch. audiologist Aeromed Lab., Wright Patterson AFB, Ohio, 1956—67; supervisory rsch. audiologist Armstrong Lab., 1967—96, Veridian, Dayton, 1996—. Chair W4 Am. Nat. Stds. Inst., N.Y.C., 1968—96; U.S. rep. hearing protection Internat. Stds. Orgn., Geneva, 1968—96; USAF rep. NRC-NAS Hearing Com., Washington, 1976—94; chair robotics panel Joint Dirs. Labs., Washington, 1987—88. Author: reports and book chpts. Cpl. U.S. Army, 1953—55. Recipient Meritorious Svc. medal, U.S. Dept. Def., Dayton, Ohio, 1986, Outstanding Civilian Svc. award, 1996. Fellow: Acoustical Soc. Am.; mem.: Rsch. Soc. Am. Achievements include research in noise exposure, voice communications, hearing protection, sonic boom, active noise reduction, 3-D audio displays, others. Home: 4316 Sillman Pl Dayton OH 45440-1141 E-mail: cwnixon@aol.com.

NIXON, DAVID, dancer; b. Windsor, Ont., Can. Student, The Nat. Ballet Sch. With Nat. Ballet of Can., 1978-84, 1st soloist, 1982-84, prin. dancer, 1988-90; prin. dancer Berlin Opera Ballet, 1985-90, Bayerisches Staatsoper Ballet Munich, 1990-91; prin. dancer and 1st Ballet master Deutsche Opera Ballet Berlin, 1994-95; various guest appearances including Alexander Godunov and Stars, summer 1982, Milw. Ballet, 1984, Sydney Ballet Australia, 1984, World Ballet Festival Tokyo, 1985, 88, Hamburg Ballet, 1988, 89, Staatsoper Berlin, 1988-91, Bayerisches Staatsballet, 1988-90, Komische Opera Berlin, 1990-93; prodr. David Nixon's Dance Theatre, Hebbel Theatre, Berlin, 1990, 91; prodr., artistic dir. BalletMet, 1995-2001; choreographer Butterfly, 1983, La Follia, 1984, Dangerous Liaisons, 1990, 96, African Fantasy, 1990, Celebrate Mozart, 1991, Sudden Impulse, 1994, A Summer's Nights Reflections, 1995, Full-Length Nutcracker, 1995, Butterfly, 1996, Beauty and the Beast, 1997, Carmen, 1997, Romeo and Juliet, 1998, Swan Lake, 1998, Dracula, 1999, A Midsummer Nights Dream, 2000, A Celebration of Dance with Music by Gershwin, 2001; artistic dir. Northern Ballet Theatre, Eng., 2001—.

NIXON, JEREMIAH W. (JAY NIXON), state attorney general; b. DeSoto, Mo., Feb. 13, 1956; s. Jeremiah and Betty (Lea) Nixon; m. Georganne Nixon; children: Jeremiah, Will. BS in Polit. Sci., U. Mo., 1978, JD, 1981. Ptnr. Nixon, Nixon, Breeze & Roberts, Jefferson County, Mo., 1981—86; mem. Mo. State Senate from Dist 22, 1986—93; atty. gen. State of Mo., 1992—. Chmn. select com. ins. reform; creator video internat. devel. and edn. opportunity program. Named Outstanding Young Missourian, Jaycees, 1994, Outstanding Young Lawyer, Barrister's Mag., 1993; recipient Conservation Fedn. Mo award, 1992. Mem.: Mo. Assn. Trial Attys., Midwest Assn. Attys. Gen., Nat. Assn. Attys. Gen. Democrat. Methodist. Office: Atty Gen Office PO Box 899 Jefferson City MO 65102-0899*

NIXON, JUDITH MAY, librarian; b. Gary, Ind., June 14, 1945; d. Louis Robert Sr. and Mable Sophia (Reiner) Vician; m. Cleon Robert Nixon III, Aug. 20, 1967; 1 child, Elizabeth Marie. BS in Edn., Valparaiso U., 1967; MA in LS, U. Iowa, 1974. Tchr. U.S. Peace Corps, Kingdom of Tonga, 1968-69; popular books libr. Lincoln Libr., Springfield, Ill., 1971-73; reference libr. Cedar Rapids (Iowa) Pub. Libr., 1974-76; reference coord. U. Wis., Platteville, 1976-82; bus. libr. U. Ariz., Tucson, 1982-84; consumer and family sci. libr. Purdue U., West Lafayette, La., 1984-93, Krannert mgmt. and econs. libr., 1993—. Editor: Industry and Company Information, 1991, Organization Charts, 1992, 2d edit., 1996, Hotel and Restaurant Industries, 1993; editor quar. serial Lodging and Restaurant Index, 1985-93. Leader Girl Scouts U.S., Lafayette, 1985—. Recipient John H. Moriarty award Purdue U. Librs., 1989. Mem. ALA (chairperson bus. reference and svcs. sect. 1995-96, GALE Rsch. award for excellence in bus. librarianship 1994). Home: 2375 N 23rd St Lafayette IN 47904-1242 Office: Purdue U Mgmt and Econs Libr Krannert Grad Sch Mgmt West Lafayette IN 47907 E-mail: nixon@mgmt.purdue.edu.

NOALL, ROGER, bank executive; b. Brigham City, Utah, Apr. 1, 1935; s. Albert Edward Noall and Mabel Clayton; m. Judith Ann Stelter, Mar. 16, 1962 (div.); children: Brennan, Tyler; m. Colleen Henrietta Mannion. BS, U. Utah, 1955; LLB, Harvard U., 1958; LLM, NYU, 1959. Legal asst. Donavan, Leisure, Newton & Irvine, N.Y.C., 1959-61; assoc. Olwine, Connelly, Chase, O'Donnell & Weyher, 1961-65, ptnr., 1965-67; with Bunge Corp., 1967-85, exec. v.p., 1975-83; pres., chief fin. officer Centran Corp., Cleve., 1985-85; vice chmn., chief adminstrv. officer Soc. Corp., 1985—; sr. v.p., chief adminstrv. officer Key Corp., 1994—. Served in USNG, 1959. Office: Society Corp 127 Public Sq Cleveland OH 44114-1306

NOBACK, RICHARDSON KILBOURNE, medical educator; b. Richmond, Va., Nov. 7, 1923; s. Gustav Joseph and Hazel (Kilborn) N.; m. Nan Jean Gates, Apr. 5, 1947; children: Carl R., Robert K., Catherine E. MD, Cornell U., 1947; BA, Columbia U., 1993. Diplomate Am. Bd. Internal Medicine. Intern N.Y. Hosp., 1947-48; asst. resident Cornell Med. div. Bellevue Hosp., N.Y.C., 1958-50, chief resident, 1950-52; instr. medicine Cornell U., 1950-53; asst. prof. medicine SUNY Upstate Med. Ctr., Syracuse, 1955-56; assoc. prof. medicine U. Ky. Med. Ctr., Lexington, 1956-64; exec. dir. Kansas City (Mo.) Gen. Hosp. and Med. Ctr., 1964-69; assoc. dean, prof. medicine U. Mo. Sch. Medicine, Columbia, 1964-69, founding dean Kansas City, 1969-78, prof. medicine, 1969-90, prof. and dean emeritus, 1990—. Cons. U. Tenn., U. Mich., U. Del., Northeastern Ohio Group, U. Mo., Eastern Va. Med. Sch., Tex. Tech. U. Contbr. numerous articles to profl. jours. Bd. dirs. Kansas City Gen. Hosp., Truman Med. Ctr., Wayne Miner Health Ctr., Jackson County Med. Soc., The Shepherd's Ctr., Am. Fedn. Aging Rsch., Mo. Gerontol. Inst., The Shepherd's Ctrs. of Am.; dir. Mo. Geriatric Edn. Ctr., 1985-88. Capt. USAF Med. Svcs. 1953-55. Recipient medal of honor Avila Coll., Kansas City, 1968, merit award Met. Med. Soc., 1991, recognition award Mo. Soc. Internal Medicine, 1993. Mem. AMA, Mo. Med. Assn. (former mem. ho. of dels., v.p. 1992), Am. Geriatric Soc., Alpha Omega Alpha, Phi Kappa Phi. Avocations: photography, writing, travel. Home: 2912 Abercorn Dr Las Vegas NV 89134-7440 E-mail: Nanori@aol.com.

NOBLE, DOUGLAS ROSS, museum administrator; b. Sturgis, Ky., Jan. 19, 1945; s. Roscoe and Robbie Rae (Martin) N.; m. Catherine Ann Richardson, Nov. 3, 1973; children: Kate Faxon, Jennifer Martin. BS, Okla. State U., 1967; MSA, Ga. Coll., 1978; D Pub. Adminstrn., U. Ga., 1987. Asst. to dir. Savannah (Ga.) Sci. Mus., 1971-73; exec. dir. Mus. Arts and Scis., Macon, Ga., 1973-80; dir. museums Memphis Mus. Sys., 1980-2001; CEO Ind. State Mus., Indpls., 2001—. Mem. mus. assessment program Inst. of Mus. Services, Washington, 1982—, grant reviewer, 1983—; cons. Mus. Mgmt. Program, Sarasota, Fla., 1985. Contbr. articles to profl. jours. Grad., Leadership Memphis, 1984; bd. dirs. Memphis in May Internat. Festival. 1st lt. U.S. Army, 1968-70, Vietnam. Decorated Bronze Star. Mem. Natural Sci. for Youth Found. (trustee 1980-87, Naumburg award 1978), Am. Assn. Museums (S.E. rep. 1984-87, chmn. mus. assessment program adv. com. 1987-89, treas., v.p. fin. 1990-92, bd. dirs. 1997-2000, chmn. nature ctr. accreditation com. 1985), Southeastern Museums Conf. (pres. 1982-84, James R. Short Lifetime Achievement award 2000), Memphis Museums Roundtable (co-founder 1984, Thomas W. Briggs Cmty. Svc. award 2000). Episcopalian. Home: 310 E Ohio St Indianapolis IN 46204 Office: Ind State Mus 650 W Washington St Indianapolis IN 46204

NOBLE, ROBERT B. advertising executive; b. 1945; BFA, Southwest Mo. State U. With Batz, Hodgson & Nevwoehner Advt. Agy., St. Louis, 1965-69, Noble & Assocs., Springfield, Mo., 1969—, now pres., CEO. Address: Noble & Assoc 2155 W Chesterfield Blvd Springfield MO 65807-8650

NOBLITT, HARDING COOLIDGE, political scientist, educator; b. Marion, N.C., Oct. 31, 1920; s. Walter Tate and Nellie Mae (Horton) N.; m. Louise Hope Lester, July 3, 1943; 1 son, Walter Thomas. B.A., Berea Coll., 1942; M.A., U. Chgo., 1947, Ph.D., 1955. Mem. faculty Concordia Coll., Moorhead, Minn., 1950-90, prof. polit. sci., 1956-90, Wije Disting. prof., 1979-82, chmn. dept., 1964-72, prof. emeritus, 1990. Mem. editorial bd.: Discourse: A Review of the Liberal Arts, 1957-67, acting editor, 1959-60. Democratic candidate Congress, 1962; del. Dem. Nat. Conv., 1964; chmn. Profs. for Johnson-Humphrey, Minn., 1964; chmn. platform com. Dem. State Conv., 1968; mem. Gov.'s Citizens Council on Aging, 1963-68; mem. City Charter Commn., Moorhead, 1985— ; mem. Minn. Higher Edn. Coordinating Bd., 1971-81, sec., 1974-75, pres., 1979-80. Served with AUS, 1943-46, ETO. Recipient 1st ann. Great Tchr. award Concordia Coll., 1960; recipient Flaat Disting. Service award Concordia Coll., 1982 Mem. Am. Polit. Sci. Assn., Am. Legion, Phi Kappa Phi, Pi Gamma Mu, Tau Kappa Alpha, Pi Kappa Delta Presbyterian (elder). Home: 2014 4th St S Moorhead MN 56560-4131 Office: Concordia Coll Dept Polit Sci Moorhead MN 56560

NOCE, DAVID D. federal magistrate judge; b. 1944; AB, St. Louis U., 1966; JD, U. Mo., 1969. Bar: Mo. Law clk. to Hon. H. Kenneth Wangelin U.S. Dist. Ct. (ea. and we. dists.) Mo., 1972-73; law clk. to Hon. John F. Nangle U.S. Dist. Ct. (ea. dist.) Mo., 1973-75; asst. U.S. atty. Eastern Dist. Mo., St. Louis, 1975-76; magistrate judge U.S. Dist. Ct. (ea. dist.) Mo., 1976—. Adj. prof. law St. Louis U. Sch. Law, Washington U. Sch. Law, St.

Louis. Author: Jury Instructions Drafting Workbook West, 1999. Served with U.S. Army, 1970-72. Mem. ABA, Mo. Bar, Bar Assn. Met. St. Louis, Fed. Magistrate Judges Assn. Office: US Courthouse 17th Flr N 111 S 10th St Saint Louis MO 63102

NODDLE, HARLAN J. real estate developer; Chmn. bd. dirs. Noddle Devel. Co., 1979—. Office: Noddle Devel Co PO Box 542010 Omaha NE 68154-8010

NODDLE, JEFFREY, retail and food distribution executive; Various positions, including pres. 2 food divsns. Supervalu Inc., Eden Prairie, Minn., 1976-92, exec. v.p. mktg., 1992-95, exec. v.p. mktg.; pres., COO wholesale food cos., 1995-99, pres., COO, 2000-01, pres., CEO, 2001—. Office: Supervalu Inc 11840 Valley View Rd Eden Prairie MN 55344-3691*

NOE, JAMES KIRBY, computer consultant; b. Denver, June 21, 1951; s. George F. and Fern D. (Wilterdink) N. BSBA in Mgmt. Info., U. No. Colo., 1983. Cert. data processor, systems profl. Systems supr. USN Tactical Support Ctr., Sigonella, Sicily, Italy, 1978-79; tech. mgr. Empire Dispatch of No. Colo., Greeley, 1979-80; cons. Greeley C. of C., 1983; project mgr. software devel. Microhealth Systems Corp., Denver, 1983-84; database analyst Manville Corp., Littleton, 1984; leader project devel. Citicorp Diners Club, Englewood, 1985; cons. Mountain Bell Telephone, Denver, 1985-86; computer programmer Colo. Dept. Revenue, 1986-87; cons. DST Systems, Inc., Kansas City, Mo., 1987-91, Broadcast Data Systems, Kansas City, 1991-92, U.S. Sprint, Kansas City, 1992—2001. Pres. Pine Tree Players, Brunswick, Maine, 1976-77, Sigonella Theatre Co., 1978; bd. dirs. Theatre Assocs. Group, Inc., Denver, 1985-86, v.p., 1987. Recipient Eagle Scout award Boy Scouts Am., 1964, bronze palm, 1965, 5-Yr. Svc. award Am. Cancer Soc., Brunswick, 1977; named Outstanding Vol. Theatre Assocs. Group, Inc., 1987. Mem. Assn. for Computing Machinery (com. mem. 1984-98, chmn. Denver chpt. 1987), Data Processing Mgmt. Assn. (com. mem. 1984-98). Republican. Presbyterian. Avocations: gemology, theater. Home: 600 E 8th St Apt 813 Kansas City MO 64106-1621

NOEL, EDWIN LAWRENCE, lawyer; b. St. Louis, July 11, 1946; s. Thomas Currie and Christine (Jones) N.; m. Nancy Carter Simpson, Feb. 7, 1970; children: Caroline, Edwin C. BA, Brown U., 1968; JD cum laude, St. Louis U., 1974. Bar: Mo. 1974, U.S. Dist. Ct. (ea. dist.) Mo. 1974, U.S. Ct. Appeals (8th cir.) 1974, U.S. Ct. Appeals (6th cir.) 1978, U.S. Ct. Appeals (7th cir.) 1994, U.S. Supreme Ct. 1986. Ptnr. Armstrong, Teasdale, Schlafly & Davis, St. Louis, 1974—, mng. ptnr., 1993-97. Bd. dirs. Corley Printing Co., Elcom Industries, St. Louis, Home Fed. Savs. Bank of Mo., 1988-93. Bd. dirs. Edgewood Children's Ctr., St. Louis, 1982-92, St. Louis Assn. for Retarded Citizens, 1984-87, Churchill Sch., 1988-94, Whitfield Sch., 1991-95; chmn. Mo. Clean Water Comm., Jefferson City, 1982-86; chmn. environ. com. St. Louis Regional Commerce and Growth Assn., 1982-88. Mem. Mo. Bar Assn., Bar Assn. Met. St. Louis, Attys. Liability Assurance Soc. (bd. dirs. 1995—). Republican. Episcopalian. Home: 301 S Mcknight Rd Saint Louis MO 63124-1884 Office: Armstrong Teasdale LLP 1 Metropolitan Sq Ste 2600 Saint Louis MO 63102-2740 E-mail: enoel@armstrongteasdale.com.

NOEL, FRANKLIN LINWOOD, judge; b. N.Y.C., N.Y., Dec. 7, 1951; s. Charles Alexander and Mayme (Loth) N.; m. Ellen Barbara Perl, Sept. 15, 1979; children: Kate Alexandra, Charles David. BA, SUNY, Binghamton, 1974; JD, Georgetown U., 1977. Bar: D.C. 1977, U. S. Dist. Ct. D.C. 1978, U.S. Ct. Appeals (D.C. cir.) 1978, Pa. 1979, Minn. 1983, U.S. Ct. Appeals (8th cir.) 1983, U.S. Dist. Ct. Minn. 1984. Assoc. Arnold & Porter, Washington, 1977-79; asst. dist. atty. Phila. Dist. Attys. Office, 1979-83; asst. U.S. atty. U.S. Attys. Office, Mpls., 1983-89; U.S. magistrate judge U.S. Dist. Ct., 1989—. Legal writing instr. U. Minn., Mpls., 1989-92, adj. prof. Law Sch., 1996—. Mem. League of Am. Wheelman, Phi Beta Kappa. Episcopalian. Avocation: bicycling. Office: US Dist Ct 300 S 4th St Minneapolis MN 55415-1320

NOELKEN, MILTON EDWARD, biochemistry educator, researcher; b. St. Louis, Dec. 5, 1935; s. William Henry Noelken and Agnes (Westbrook) Burkemper; m. Carol Ann Agne, June 9, 1962. BA in Chemistry, Washington U., St. Louis, 1957, PhD in Chemistry, 1962. Rsch. chemist Ea. Regional Rsch., Dept. Agr., Phila., 1964-67; asst. prof. dept. biochemistry U. Kans. Med. Ctr., Kansas City, 1967-71, assoc. prof., 1971-81, acting chmn., 1973-74, prof., 1981—, interim chmn., 1993-94. Vis. prof. Fed. U. Minas Gerais, Brazil, 1978. Contbr. articles to profl. jours. Recipient Scholastic Achievement award Am. Inst. Chemists, Washington U., 1957; NSF fellow, Washington U., 1959. Mem. Am. Chem. Soc., Am. Soc. for Biochemistry and Molecular Biology, Biophysical Soc., Sigma Xi. Achievements include research in properties of antibody molecules related to antigen binding, stucture of collagen of basement membranes, and stability of proteins. Office: U Kans Med Ctr Dept Biochemistry 39th And Rainbow Blvd Kansas City KS 66160-7421 E-mail: mnoelken@kumc.edu.

NOER, RICHARD J. physics educator, researcher; b. Madison, Wis., July 3, 1937; s. Rudolf J. and Anita M. (Showerman) N.; m. Raymonde Tasset, Aug. 17, 1967; children— Geoffrey, Catherine B.A., Amherst Coll., 1958; Ph.D., U. Calif., Berkeley, 1963. Physicist Atomic Energy Research, Harwell, Eng., 1963-64; asst. prof. physics Amherst Coll., Mass., 1964-66, Carleton Coll., Northfield, Minn., 1966-68, assoc. prof. physics, 1968-72, prof. physics, 1972-98, dept. chair, 2001—02, Laurence McKinley Gould prof. natural scis., 1998—. Vis. physicist U. Paris, Orsay, France, 1972-73; physicist Ames Lab., Iowa, summers 1977-80, 82-84; rsch. physicist U. Geneva, 1980-81, 84-85; vis. scientist Cornell U., summers 1986, 88-91; vis. physicist Centre d'Etudes Nucléaires, Saclay, France, 1992-93; vis. scientist KEK High Energy Accelerator Rsch. Orgn., sokoba, Japan, 2000-01. Co-author: Revolutions in Physics, 1972; contbr. articles to profl. jours. Mem.: AAAS, Am. Assn. Physics Tchrs., Am. Phys. Soc., Sigma Xi, Phi Beta Kappa. Home: 101 Winona St Northfield MN 55057-2232 Office: Carleton Coll Dept Physics Northfield MN 55057

NOLAN, ALAN TUCKER, retired lawyer, labor arbitrator, writer; b. Evansville, Ind., Jan. 19, 1923; s. Val and Jeannette (Covert) N.; m. Elizabeth Clare Titsworth, Aug. 26, 1947 (dec. Nov. 1967); children: Patrick A., Thomas C., Mary F., Elizabeth T., John V.; m. Jane Ransel DeVoe, Feb. 7, 1970; adopted children: John C. DeVoe, Ellen R. DeVoe, Thomas R. DeVoe. AB in Govt., Ind. U., 1944, LHD (hon.), 1993; LLB, Harvard U., 1947. Bar: Ind. 1947. Law clk. U.S. Ct. Appeals (7th Cir.), Chgo., 1947-48; assoc. Ice, Miller, Donadio & Ryan, Indpls., 1948-58, ptnr., 1958-93, ret., 1993—. Chmn. Disciplinary Commn. Supreme Ct. Ind., Indpls., 1966-73. Author: The Iron Brigade, 1961, As Sounding Brass, 1964, Lee Considered, 1991; editor (with S. Vipond) Giants in Tall Black Hats, 1998, (with Gary Gallagher) The Myth of the Lost Cause and Civil War History, 2000, Rally Once Again, 2000; contbg. editor The Civil War, 1985-89; contbr. numerous articles to profl. jours. Life mem. NAACP Indpls., v.p., 1950-54; bd. dirs., founder Ind. Civil Liberties Union, Indpls., 1953-60; bd. dirs. Indpls. Art League, 1981-87; chmn., bd. trustees Ind. Hist. Soc., Indpls., 1986-93; trustee Eiteljorg Mus., Indpls., 1987-93. Fellow Co. Mil. Historians, Am. Bar Found., State Hist. Soc. Wis.; mem. ABA, Ind. Bar Assn., Indpls. Bar Assn. (bd. mgrs. 1958-60, chmn. Grievance Com. 1960-64), Indpls. Civil War Round Table, Ensemble Music Soc. (bd. dirs. 1999—). Democrat. Roman Catholic. Avocations: travel, gardening, reading. Home and Office: 4118 N Pennsylvania St Indianapolis IN 46205-2611 E-mail: indynolan@aol.com.

NOLAN, VAL, JR. biologist, lawyer; b. Evansville, Ind., Apr. 28, 1920; s. Val and Jeannette (Covert) N.; m. Susanne Howe, Dec. 23, 1946 (div. Aug. 29, 1980); children: Val, Ann Clare, William Alan; m. Ellen D. Ketterson, Oct. 17, 1980. A.B., Ind. U., 1941, J.D., 1949. Bar: Ind. 1949. Dep. U.S. marshal, 1941; agt. White House Detail, U.S. Secret Service, 1942; asst. prof. law Ind. U., 1949-52, assoc. prof., 1952-56, prof., 1956-85, prof. emeritus, 1985—, research scholar in zoology, 1957-68, prof. zoology, 1968-77, prof. biology, 1977-85; prof. emeritus, 1985—; acting dean Sch. Law, 1976, 80. Author: (with F.E. Horack, Jr.) Land Use Controls, 1955, Ecology and Behavior of the Prairie Warbler, 1978; editor Ind. Law Jour., 1945-46, Jour. Avian Biology, 1998—; co-editor Current Ornithology, 1994—. Served with USNR, 1942-46. Guggenheim fellow, 1957; recipient Ind. U. Disting. Alumni Svc. award, 1987; named to Acad. Law Alumni Fellows, Ind. U., 1988. Fellow AAAS, Am. Ornithologists Union (v.p. 1989-90, Brewster Meml. award 1986); mem. Brit. Ornithologists Union, Cooper Ornithol. Soc., Wilson Ornithol. Soc. (co-recipient Margaret M. Nice award 1998), Assn. Field Ornithologists, Ecol. Soc. Am., Am. Soc. Naturalists, Animal Behavior Soc., Deutsche Ornithologen-Gesellschaft, Nederlandse Ornithologische Unie, Soc. for Study of Reprodn., Phi Beta Kappa, Sigma Xi. Democrat. Home: 4675 E Heritage Woods Rd Bloomington IN 47401-9312

NOLAND, MARIAM CHARL, foundation executive; b. Parkersburg, W.Va., Mar. 29, 1947; d. Lloyd Henry and Ethel May (Beare) N.; m. James Arthur Kelly, June 13, 1981. BS, Case Western Res. U., 1969; M in Edn., Harvard U., 1975. Asst. dir admissions, fin. aid Baldwin-Wallace Coll., Berea, Ohio, 1969-72; asst. dir. admissions Davidson (N.C.) Coll., 1972-74; case writer Inst. Edn. Mgmt., Cambridge, Mass., 1975; sec., treas., program officer The Cleve. Found., 1975-81; v.p. The St. Paul Found., 1981-85; pres. Community Found. for S.E. Mich., 1985—. Bd. trustees Coun. Mich. Founds., 1988-98, Coun. on Founds., 1994-99, Henry Ford Health System, 1994—, Alma Coll., 1994—; commr. Detroit 300, 2000—01. Office: Community Found Southeastern Mich 333 W Fort St Ste 2010 Detroit MI 48226-3134 Business E-Mail: mnoland@voager.net.

NOLAND, N. DUANE, state legislator; b. Blue Mound, Ill., Sept. 12, 1956; m. Tina L. Beckett; children: Grant, Blake. BS with high honors, U. Ill., 1978. V.p. Noland Farms, 1982—; mem. Ill. Ho. of Reps. from 102d dist., 1990-98, Ill. Senate from 51st dist., 1998—. Minority vice spokesman Agr., Counties and Twps. Coms. Ill. Ho. of Reps., mem. Econ. and Urban Devel., Ins., Pub. Safety and Infrastructure Appropriations Coms. Recipient Award of Excellence Nat. Corn Growers Assn., Ill. Young Leader award Am. Soybean Assn.; named Outstanding Young Farmer, Decatur-Mason (Ill.) Jaycees. Mem. Ill. Corn Growers Assn. (bd. dirs., treas.), Macon County Farm Bur. (bd. dirs.), Corn-Soy Commodity Orgn. (chmn.), Masons, Aircraft Owners and Pilots Assn. Republican. Home: RR 2 Box 206 Blue Mound IL 62513-9557

NOLD, CARL RICHARD, state historic parks and museums administrator; b. Mineola, N.Y., Nov. 26, 1955; s. Carl Frederick and Joan Catherine (Heine) N.; m. Mary Beth Krivoruchka (div.). BA in History magna cum laude, St. John's U., Jamaica, N.Y., 1977; MA in History Mus. Studies, SUNY, Oneonta, 1982. Pres. Gregory Mus., Hicksville, N.Y., 1977; registrar N.Y. State Hist. Assn., Cooperstown, 1978-80; dir., curator Gadsby's Tavern Mus., Alexandria, Va., 1980-84; dir. State Mus. Pa., Harrisburg, 1984-91; exec. dir. Mackinac State Hist. Parks, Lansing, Mackinac Island, Mich., 1992—. Grant reviewer Inst. Mus. Svcs., Washington, 1982-90, 95—, mus. assessment prog. reviewer, 1985—, panelist, 1992-94; panelist mus. grant program Nat. Endowment for Humanities, 1990-93, panelist challenge grant program, 1997. Co-author: Gadsby's Tavern Mus. Interpretive Master Plan, 1984; contbr. articles to profl. jours. Mem. adv. bd. for Grad. History George Mason U., Fairfax, Va., 1982-84, Ctr. for Great Lakes Culture, Mich. State U., 2000—; adv. com. Susquehanna Mus. Art, Harrisburg, 1989-91; bd. dirs. Harrisburg-Hershey-Carlisle Tourism and Visitor Bur., 1987-91, bd. sec., 1990-91; mem. mayor's adv. bd. city of Mackinac Island, 1993—; mem. task force Mich. Cultural Tourism, 1998—. Mem. Assn. of Midwest Mus. (treas. 1998-2000, pres. 2000—), Mich. Mus. Assn. (bd. dirs. 1995-98, bd. sec. 1999-2001), Am. Assn. Mus. (vis. com. mus. accreditation 1989—, chmn. coun. of regions 2000-2001, MAP adv. com. 2002--), Am. Assn. for State and Local History (elections chmn. 1990), Cooperstown Grad. Assn. (bd. dirs. 1985-87).

NOLEN, WILFRED E. church administrator; Pres. Brethren Benefit Trust, 1983. Office: 1505 Dundee Ave Elgin IL 60120-1605

NOLTE, HENRY R., JR. lawyer, former automobile company executive; b. N.Y.C., Mar. 3, 1924; s. Henry R. and Emily A. (Eisele) Nolte; m. Frances Messner, May 19, 1951; children: Gwynne Conn, Henry Reed III, Jennifer Stevens, Suzanne Saunders. BA, Duke U., 1947; LLB, U. Pa., 1949. Bar: N.Y. 1950, Mich. 1967. Assoc. Cravath, Swaine & Moore, N.Y.C., 1951-61; assoc. counsel Ford Motor Co., Dearborn, Mich., 1961, asst. gen. counsel, 1964-71, assoc. gen. counsel, 1971-74, v.p., gen. counsel, 1974-89, Philco-Ford Corp., Phila., 1961-64; v.p., gen. counsel, sec. Ford of Europe Inc., Warley, Essex, Eng., 1967-69; gen. counsel fin. and ins. subs. Ford Motor Co., 1974-89; sr. ptnr. Miller, Canfield, Paddock & Stone, Detroit, 1989-93, of counsel, 1993—. Dir. emeritus Charter One Fin., Inc. Formerly vice chmn. and trustee Cranbrook Ednl. Cmty.; mem. Internat. and Comparative Law Ctr. of Southwestern Legal Found.; bd. dirs. Detroit Symphony Orch.; trustee Beaumont Hosp. Lt. USNR, 1943-46, PTO. Mem. ABA (past chmn. corp. law depts.), Mich. Bar Assn., Assn. Bar City N.Y., Assn. Gen. Counsel, Orchard Lake Country Club, Bloomfield Hills Country Club, Everglades Club (Fla.), Gulfstream Golf Club (Fla.), Ocean Club (Fla.). Episcopalian. Office: Miller Canfield Paddock & Stone 840 W Long Lake Rd Troy MI 48098-6356

NOONAN, SHEILA M. energy consulting company executive; BA in Bus. Adminstrn., U. St. Thomas; postgrad., Harvard U., Boston U. Numerous positions including dir. security & fire alarm bus. Honeywell; v.p. sales Cadence Networks, Cin. Office: Cadence Networks 105 E 4th St Ste 250 Cincinnati OH 45202-4006

NORBERG, ARTHUR LAWRENCE, JR. historian, physicist educator; b. Providence, Apr. 13, 1938; s. Arthur Lawrence Sr. and Margaret Helen (Riley) N. BS in Physics, Providence Coll., 1959; MS in Physics, U. Vt., 1962; PhD in History of Sci., U. Wis., 1974. Asst. prof. physics St. Michael's Coll., Winooski, Vt., 1961-63, 64-68; assoc. scientist Westinghouse Electric Co., Pitts., 1963-64; instr. in physics U. Wis., Whitewater, 1968-71; rsch. historian U. Calif., Berkeley, 1973-79; program mgr. NSF, Washington, 1979-81; dir. Charles Babbage Inst. for History of Info. Processing U. Minn., Mpls., 1981-93, 99—, prof. history of sci. and tech., 1995—, assoc. prof. computer sci., 1981-95, prof. computer sci., 1995—. Del. Am. Coun. Learned Socs., N.Y.C., 1981-87; mem. adv. coun. NASA, Washington, 1988-93; endowed ERA Land Grant chair U. Minn., 1989-93, 99—. Editor: Annals of the History of Computing, 1982-93; adv. editor Tech. and Culture, 1985-92, (book) Transforming Computer Technology: Information Processing for the Pentagon; contbr. articles to profl. jours. Founding pres. City Works-A Tech. Ctr., Mpls., 1987-90; exec. dir. Charles Babbage Found., 1984-94; trustee Charles Babbage Found., 1993-96. Fellow AAAS; mem. History of Sci. Soc. (treas. 1975-80), Brit. Soc. for History of Sci., Soc. for History of Tech., Sigma Xi. Office: U Minn Dept Computer Sci 4-192 EE/CS Bldg Minneapolis MN 55455-0290 E-mail: norberg@cs.umn.edu.

NORBERG, RICHARD EDWIN, physicist, educator; b. Newark, Dec. 28, 1922; s. Arthur Edwin and Melita (Roefer) N.; m. Patricia Ann Leach, Dec. 27, 1947 (dec. July 1977); children— Karen Elizabeth, Craig Alan, Peter Douglas; m. Jeanne C. O'Brien, Apr. 1, 1978. B.A., DePauw U., 1943; M.A., U. Ill., 1947, Ph.D., 1951. Research assoc., control sytems lab. U. Ill., 1951-53, asst. prof., 1953; vis. lectr. physics Washington U., St. Louis, 1954—, mem. faculty, 1955—, prof. physics, 1958—, chmn. dept., 1962-91. Mem. editl. bd. Magnetic Rsch. Rev. Served with USAAF, 1943-46. Fellow Am. Phys. Soc., Internat. Soc. Magnetic Research. Home: 7134 Princeton Ave Saint Louis MO 63130-2308 Office: Washington U Dept Physics PO Box 1105 Saint Louis MO 63188-1105

NORD, HENRY J. transportation executive; b. Berlin, May 1, 1917; came to U.S., 1937, naturalized, 1943; s. Walter and Herta (Riess) N.; children: Stephen, Philip. Student, U. Oxford, Eng., 1934, Northwestern U., 1938-40, Ill. Inst. Tech., 1942; JD, De Paul U., 1949. CPA, Ill. Apprentice in export, Hamburg, Germany, 1935- 37; with GATX Corp., Chgo., 1938-85, comptroller, 1961-67, v.p., 1967-71, exec. v.p., 1971-78, sr. v.p., 1978-80, v.p., 1980-82, cons., 1982-84, fin. cons., 1982—, dir., 1964-78. Dir. Planned Lighting, Inc. to 1988. Trustee DePaul U. Mem. Internat. Law Assn. Club: Tavern (Chgo.). Home: 1000 N Lake Shore Dr Chicago IL 60611-1308 Office: 55 W Monroe St Ste 500 Chicago IL 60603-5003

NORD, ROBERT EAMOR, lawyer; b. Ogden, Utah, Apr. 11, 1945; s. Eamor Carroll and Ella Carol (Winkler) N.; m. Sherryl Anne Smith, May 15, 1969; children: Kimberly, P. Ryan, Debra, Heather, Andrew, Elizabeth. BS, Brigham Young U., 1969; JD, U. Chgo., 1972. Bar: Ill. 1972, U.S. Dist. Ct. (no. dist.) Ill. 1972, U.S. Ct. Appeals (D.C. cir.) 1974, U.S. Dist. Ct. (mid. dist.) Fla. 1976, U.S. Ct. Appeals (7th cir.) 1977, U.S. Dist. Ct. (no. dist.) Ind. 1978, U.S. Dist. Ct. (no. dist.) Fla. 1979, U.S. Supreme Ct. 1981, U.S. Dist. Ct. (ea. dist.) Mich. 1984, U.S. Ct. Appeals (11th cir.) 1985, U.S. Ct. Appeals (3d cir.) 1996. Assoc. Chadwell & Kayser, Chgo., 1972-75; from assoc. to ptnr. Hinshaw & Culbertson, 1975—. Republican. Mormon. E-mail: rnord@hinshawculber+son.com. Home: 481 Woodlawn Ave Glencoe IL 60022-2175 Office: Hinshaw & Culbertson 222 N La Salle St Ste 300 Chicago IL 60601-1081 E-mail: rnord@hinshawlaw.com.

NORDBERG, JOHN ALBERT, federal judge; b. Evanston, Ill., June 18, 1926; s. Carl Albert and Judith Ranghild (Carlson) N.; m. Jane Spaulding, June 18, 1947; children: Carol, Mary, Janet, John Student, Carleton Coll., 1943-44, 46-47; J.D., U. Mich., 1950. Bar: Ill. 1950, U.S. Dist. Ct. (no. dist.) Ill. 1957, U.S. Ct. Appeals (7th cir.) 1961. Assoc. Pope & Ballard, Chgo., 1950-57; ptnr. Pope, Ballard, Shepard & Fowle, 1957-76; judge Cir. Ct. of Cook County, Ill., 1976-82, U.S. Dist. Ct. (no. dist.) Ill., Chgo., 1982-95, sr. judge, 1995—. Editor-in-chief, bd. editors Chgo. Bar Record, 1966-74 Magistrate of Cir. Ct. and justice of peace Ill., 1957-65. Served with USN, 1944-46; PTO Mem. ABA, Chgo. Bar Assn., Am. Judicature Soc., Law Club Chgo., Legal Club Chgo., Union League Club of Chgo., Order of Coif. Office: US Dist Ct #1886 219 S Dearborn St Chicago IL 60604-1706

NORDBY, EUGENE JORGEN, orthopedic surgeon; b. Abbotsford, Wis., Apr. 30, 1918; s. Herman Preus and Lucille Violet (Korsrud) N.; m. Olive Marie Jensen, June 21, 1941; 1 child, Jon Jorgen BA, Luther Coll., Decorah, Iowa, 1939; MD, U. Wis., 1943. Diplomate Am. Bd. Orthopaedic Surgery. Intern Madison Gen. Hosp., Wis., 1943-44, asst. in orthopedic surgery, 1944-48; practice medicine specializing in orthopedic surgery Madison, 1948—. Pres. Bone and Joint Surgery Assocs., S.C., 1969—91; chief staff Madison Gen. Hosp., 1957—63; assoc. clin. prof. U. Wis. Med. Sch., 1961—; bd. dirs. Wis. Physicians Svcs., 1958—, chmn., 1979—; dir. Wis. Regional Med. Program, Chgo. Madison and No. R.R.; bd. govs. Wils Health Care Liability Ins. Plan; chmn. trustees S.M.S. Realty Corp.; mem. bd. attys. Profl. Responsibility of Wis. Supreme Ct., 1992—. Assoc. editor Clin. Orthopaedics and Related Research, 1964—; mem. adv. edtl. bd. Spine, 1994-2000. Pres. Vesterheim Norwegian Am. Mus., Decorah, Iowa, 1968-97, pres. emeritus, 1997—. Served to capt. M.C., AUS, 1944-46 Decorated Knight 1st class Royal Norwegian Order St. Olav; named Notable Norwegian Dane County Norwegian-Am. Fest, 1995; recipient Disting. Svc. award Internat. Rotary,1 987, Den Hoyeste Aere award Vesterheim, 1993, Eugene J. Nordby Rsch. award established Internat. Intradiscal Therapy Soc., 1993, Lyman Smith, M.D. and Eugene J. Nordby, M.D. award for minimally invasive spine surgery established N.Am. Spine Soc., 1998, The Nordby Bldg. designated Wis. Phys. Svc. Health Ins. Co., 1998, Disting. Eagle Scout award, 2000. Fellow Wisdom Hall of Fame; mem. Acad. Orthopaedic Surgeons (bd. dirs. 1972-73), Clin. Orthopaedic Soc., Assn. Bone and Joint Surgeons (pres. 1973), Internat. Soc. Study Lumbar Spine, State Med. Soc. Wis. (chmn. 1968-76, treas. 1976-97, Coun. award 1976), Am. Orthopaedic Assn., N.Am. Spine Soc., Internat. Intradiscal Therapy Soc. (sec. 1987-99, exec. dir. 1996—), Wis. Orthopaedic Soc., Dane County Med. Soc. (pres. 1957), Nat. Exch. Club, Madison Torske Klubben (founder, pres. 1978-98, pres. emeritus 1998—), Norwegian-Am. Orthopaedic Soc., Am. Acad. Orthopedic Surgeons, Am. Orthopedic Assn., Phi Chi. Lutheran. Home: 7824 Courtyard Dr Madison WI 53719 Office: 2704 Marshall Ct Madison WI 53705-2256

NORDLAND, GERALD, art museum administrator, historian, consultant; b. Los Angeles; AB, JD, U. So. Calif. Dean of faculty Chouinard Art Sch., L.A., 1960-64; dir. Washington Gallery of Modern Art, 1964-66, San Francisco Mus. Art, 1966-72, Frederick S. Wight Art Galleries, UCLA, 1973-77, Milw. Art Mus., 1977-85; ind. curator, author, editor Chgo., 1985—. Author: Paul Jenkins, 1972, Gaston Lachaise/The Man and His Work, 1974, Richard Diebenkorn , 1987, rev. and expanded 2d edit. , 2001, Frank Lloyd Wright: In the Realm of Ideas, 1988, Zhou Brothers, 1994, Ynez Johnston, 1996, Lev Syrkin, 1998, Twentieth Century American Drawings, 1998. Gaston Lachaise Found. grantee, 1973-74; John Simon Guggenheim Found. fellow, 1985-86. Home and Office: 645 W Sheridan Rd Chicago IL 60613-3316

NORDLIE, ROBERT CONRAD, biochemistry educator; b. Willmar, Minn., June 11, 1930; s. Peder Conrad and Myrtle (Spindler) N.; m. Sally Ann Christianson, Aug. 23, 1959; children: Margaret, Melissa, John. B.S. St. Cloud State Coll., Minn., 1952; M.S., U. N.D., 1957, Ph.D., 1960. Tchg., rsch. asst. biochemistry U. N.D. Med. Sch., Grand Forks, 1955-60, rsch. prof. biochemistry, 1962-74, Chester Fritz disting. prof. biochemistry, 1974—, Cornatzer prof., chmn. dept. biochemistry and molecular biology, 1983-2000; Chesiter Fritz disting. emeritus prof., 2000—. Hon. prof. San Marcos U., Lima, Peru, 1981, 82—; emeritus prof., 2000-; NIH fellow Inst. Enzyme Rsch., U. Wis., 1960-61; mem. biochemistry study sect. NIH; merit rev. com. VA, 1994—; cons. enzymology Oak Ridge, 1961—; vis. prof. Tokyo Biomed. Inst., 1984; mem. predoctoral fellowship rev. group Howard Hughes Inst., 1990-93. Mem. editorial bd.: Jour. Biol. Chemistry, Biochimca et Biophysica Acta. Research publs. on enzymology relating to metabolism of various carbohydrates in mammalian livers, regulation blood sugar levels. Served with AUS, 1953-55. Recipient Disting. Alumnus award St. Cloud State U., 1983; recipient Sigma Xi Rsch. award, 1969, Golden Apple award U. N.D., 1968, Edgar Dale award U. N.D., 1983, Burlington No. Faculty Scholar award, 1987, Thomas J. Clifford Faculty Achievement award for excellence in rsch. U. N.D. Found., 1993. Mem. AAAS, Am. Soc. Biol. Chemistry and Molecular Biology, Am. Chem. Soc., Internat. Union Biochemists, Soc. Exptl. Biology and Medicine, Am. Inst. Nutrition, Sigma Xi, Alpha Omega Alpha. Home: 162 Columbia Ct Grand Forks ND 58203-2947 E-mail: rnordlie@medicine.nodak.edu .

NORDLUND, DONALD ELMER, manufacturing company executive; b. Stromsburg, Nebr., Mar. 1, 1922; s. E.C. and Edith O. (Peterson) N.; m. Mary Jane Houston, June 5, 1948; children: Donald Craig, William

Chalmers, Sarah, James. AB, Midland Coll., 1943; JD, U. Mich., 1948. Bar: Ill. 1949. With Stevenson, Conaghan, Hackbert, Rooks and Pitts, Chgo., 1948-55, A.E. Staley Mfg. Co., Decatur, Ill., 1956-85, v.p., dir., mem. exec. com., 1958-65, pres., chief operating officer, 1965-80, dir., mem. exec. com., 1965-85, also chmn., 1975-85; chief exec. officer Staley Continental, Inc., Rolling Meadows, Ill., 1985-88, chmn. and chief exec. officer, 1985-88. Past chmn. bd. trustees Millikin U., now hon. trustee; trustee Mus. Sci. and Industry, Chgo., Rush-Presbyn. St. Lukes Med. Ctr., Chgo.; bd. dirs. Lyric Opera Chgo.; mem. grad. dirs. coun. Decatur Meml. Hosp. Mem. ABA, Chgo. Bar Assn., Corn Refiners Assn. (bd. dirs., past chmn., now hon. dir.), Legal Club, Comml. Club, Chgo. Club, Tavern Club, Barrington Hills Club, Phi Alpha Delta.

NORDMAN, CHRISTER ERIC, chemistry educator; b. Helsinki, Finland, Jan. 23, 1925; came to U.S., 1948, naturalized, 1960; s. Eric Johan and Gertrud (Nordgren) N.; m. Barbara Lorraine Neal, Nov. 28, 1952 (div. 1993); children: Christina, Aleta, Eric, Carl; m. Outi Marttila, Dec. 28, 1994. Dipl. Ing., Finnish Inst. Tech., Helsinki, 1949; Ph.D., U. Minn., 1953. Research asso. Inst. Cancer Research, Phila., 1953-55; mem. faculty U. Mich., Ann Arbor, 1955—, prof. chemistry, 1964-95; prof. emeritus, 1995—. Mem. U.S. Nat. Com. Crystallography, 1970-72. Served with Finnish Army, 1943-44. NIH spl. fellow, 1971-72; recipient A.L. Patterson award, 1997. Fellow AAAS; mem. Am. Chem. Soc., Am. Phys. Soc., Am. Crystallographic Assn., Finnish Soc. Scis. and Letters. Home: 27 Haverhill Ct Ann Arbor MI 48105-1406 Office: Univ Mich Dept Chemistry Ann Arbor MI 48109

NORDWALD, CHARLES, state legislator; b. Aug. 25, 1955; m. Nina Hoelscher; 3 children. Mem. dist. 19 Mo. Ho. of Reps., 1992—; co-owner Allen & Nordwald Auction Svc., Warrenton, Mo. Mem. Warren County Fair Bd. Mem. NRA, Montgomery City C. of C., Elks Club. Office: 20 Hawthorne Warrenton MO 63383

NORGLE, CHARLES RONALD, SR. federal judge; b. Mar. 3, 1937; BBA, Northwestern U., Evanston, Ill., 1964; JD, John Marshall Law Sch., Chgo., 1969. Asst. state's atty. DuPage County, Ill., 1969-71, dep. pub. defender, 1971-73, assoc. judge, 1973-77, 78-81, cir. judge, 1977-78, 81-84; judge U.S. Dist. Ct. (no. dist.) Ill., Chgo., 1984—. Mem. exec. com. No. Dist. Ill.; mem. 7th Cir. Jud. Coun., 7th Cir. Jud. Conf. planning com., subcom. grant requests Fed. Defender Orgn., Fed. Defender Svcs. Com.; adj. faculty Northwestern U. Sch. Law, John Marshall Law Sch., Chgo.; pres. Atticus Finch Inn Ct. Mem. ABA, Fed. Bar Assn., Fed. Circuit Bar Assn., Ill. Bar Assn., DuPage County (Ill.) Bar Assn., Nat. Attys. Assn., DuPage Assn. Women Attys., Chgo. Legal Club, Northwestern Club. Office: US Dist Ct 219 S Dearborn St Ste 2346 Chicago IL 60604-1802

NORINS, ARTHUR LEONARD, physician, educator; b. Chgo., Dec. 2, 1928; s. Russell Joseph and Elsie (Lindemann) N.; m. Mona Lisa Wetzer, Sept. 12, 1954; children: Catherine, Nan, Jane, Arthur. B.S. in Chem. Engring, Northwestern U., 1951, M.S. in Physiology, 1953, M.D., 1955. Diplomate: Am. Bd. Dermatology; subcert. in dermatopathology. Intern U. Mich., Ann Arbor, 1955-56; resident in dermatology Northwestern U., Chgo., 1956-59; asst. prof. Stanford U., 1961-64; prof., chmn. dept. dermatology, prof. pathology Ind. U. Sch. Medicine, Indpls., 1964-93, prof. emeritus, 1993—. Mem. staff Riley Children's Hosp., Univ. Hosp., Wishard Hosp.; cons. VA Hosp. Contbr. articles to profl. jours. Capt. M.C. U.S. Army, 1959-61. Recipient Pres.' award Ind. U., 1979 Fellow ACP; mem. Am. Acad. Dermatology (bd. dirs.), Am. Dermatol. Assn., Soc. Pediatric Dermatology (founder, past pres.), Am. Soc. Dermatopathology, Am. Soc. Photobiology (founder), Soc. Investigative Dermatology. Home: 10100 Torre Ave Apt 211 Cupertino CA 95014-2168 Office: 550 University Blvd Ste 3240 Indianapolis IN 46202-5149

NORLING, RAYBURN, food service executive; b. 1934; Pres. Willmar (Minn) Poultry Co., Inc.; with Norling Farms, Inc., Svea, Minn., 1979—. Office: Willmar Poultry Co Inc 3735 County Road 5 SW Willmar MN 56201-9712

NORLING, RICHARD ARTHUR, health care executive; b. Waterbury, Conn., Dec. 9, 1945; s. Arthur and Alice Norling; m. Jeanne Marie Bone, Oct. 1, 1946; children: Jennifer, Stephanie. BS in Math., Tufts U., 1967; MS in Systems Engring., U. Ariz., 1969; MHA, U. Minn., 1975. Systems analyst Univ. Hosp., Tucson, 1969-70, mgr. systems engring., 1970-72, asst. to adminstr., 1972-73; adminstrv. resident Presbyn. Hosp. Ctr., Albuquerque, 1974-75; asst. dir. Calif. Med. Ctr., Los Angeles, 1975-77, assoc. dir., 1977-79, pres., exec. dir., 1979-86; exec. v.p. LHS Corp., from 1986; now pres., chief exec. officer Fairview Hosp. and Healthcare Svcs., Mpls. Mem. Joint Commn. on Accreditation of Healthcare Orgn.'s Adv. Group, 1993. Bd. mem. Am. Healthcare Systems, 1989, Augsburg Coll., 1992, Benefit Panel Svcs., 1991, Express Scripts, Inc., 1992, Hosp. Edn. and Rsch. Found., 1989, Minn. Bus. Partnerships, Inc., 1991. Kings Fund fellow, 1984-90; named Emerging Health Care Leader Assn. of Western Hosps. Mem. Am. Hosp. Assn. (chmn. various coms., coun. on fin. 1980-83), Am. Coll. Healthcare Execs., Edina Country Club, Mpls. Club. Congregationalist. Avocations: golfing, gardening, raquetball. Office: Fairview Hosp & Healthcare Svcs 2312 S 6th St Minneapolis MN 55454-1336

NORMAN, ART, newscaster; married. BS Math and Physics, Johnson C. Smith U. Tv engr. Sta. WCCB-TV, Charlotte, NC, 1969; reporter Sta. WPCQ-TV, Sta. WSOC-TV, Charlotte; reporter, weekend anchor Sta. WMAR-TV, Balt., 1979—82; gen. assignment reporter NBC 5, Chgo., 1982, co-anchors weekday editions 5 pm, 5:30 pm, 6 pm and 11 am. Spokesman, on air host of telethon United Negro Coll. Fund. Recipient award, N.C. Radio and TV News Dirs. Assn., 1975, Sch. Bell award, Nat. Assn. Educators, 1978, award, Internat. Radio and TV News Dirs. Assn., 1984, Emmy award, 1986, Wilbur award, Religious Pub. Rels. Coun., 1987, Chgo. Emmy award, 1989, award for Best Investigative Reporting, AP, 1992—93. Mem.: Omega Psi Phi. Office: NBC 454 N Columbus Dr Chicago IL 60611*

NORMAN, CHARLES HENRY, broadcasting executive; b. St. Louis, June 13, 1920; s. Charles Henry and Grace Vincent (Francis) N. BS, U. So. Calif., L.A., 1942. Announcer WIL, KSTL Radio Stas., St. Louis, 1948-55; owner Norman Broadcasting Co., 1961—. Lt. USN, 1943-45. Mem. St. Louis Ambassadros, Phi Kappa Phi. Episcopalian. Office: Portland Towers 265 Union Blvd Apt 1315 Saint Louis MO 63108-1240

NORMAN, JACK LEE, church administrator, consultant; b. Lancaster, Ohio, Aug. 5, 1938; s. Clearence Herbert and Jeanette Belle (Bennett) N.; m. Boneda Mae Coppock, June 30, 1957; children: Anthony Lee, Becky Lynn Norman Hux. Student, Circleville Bible Coll., Olivet U. Ordained min. Ch. of Christ, 1961. Pastor Chs. of Christ in Christian Union, Chillicothe, Ohio, 1959-62, 65-90, Winchester, 1962-65, dist. supt. Circleville, 1990—. Trustee Chs. of Christ in Christian Union, mem. dist. bd., mem. ch. ext. bd., mem. bd. exam. and ordination, mem. Evang. Christian Youth Bd. Trustee Circleville Bible Coll. Sgt. USNG, 1956-59. Avocations: fishing, boating, classic cars. Office: Ch of Christ in Christian Union PO Box 30 Circleville OH 43113-0030

NORMAN, LALANDER STADIG, insurance company executive; b. Binford, N.D., Apr. 10, 1912; s. John and Corinne (Stadig) N.; m. Garnet Johnston, Nov. 8, 1941; children: Eric John, Martha Mary Norman Neely, Carol Jean Norman Wellborn, Shirley Ann Norman Cook. A.B., U. Mich., 1935, M.B.A., 1937. Actuarial asst. Central Life Ins. Co. of Ill., Chgo., 1937-40, mgr. Eastern dept., 1940-41; actuary Mich. Life Ins. Co., Detroit, 1941-43; asst. actuary Guarantee Mut. Life Co., Omaha, 1946-49; asso. actuary Am. United Life Ins. Co., Indpls., 1949, actuary, 1950-77, dir., 1959-77, v.p., 1962-69, sr. v.p., 1969-77; ret., 1977. Bd. mgrs. AUL Fund B, 1969-84, chmn., 1973-84; actuary Ind. Dept. Ins., 1977-79 Bd. dirs. Cyprus Village Assn., 1981, 1983—85. Served with USNR, 1943—46. Recipient Navy Commendation award, 1946, Theta Xi Distinguished Service award, 1958. Fellow Soc. Actuaries; mem. Am. Acad. Actuaries, Indpls. Actuarial Club (past pres.), Woodland Country Club (Carmel), Sugarmill Woods Golf and Racquet Club, So. Woods Golf Club, Phi Beta Kappa, Theta Xi (regional dir. 1953-59), Phi Kappa Phi, Beta Gamma Sigma. Republican. Home: Sugarmill Woods 21 Graytwig Ct W Homosassa FL 34446-4727 Office: 1 American Sq Indianapolis IN 46282-0020

NORQUIST, JOHN OLAF, mayor; b. Princeton, N.J., Oct. 22, 1949; s. Ernest O. and Jeannette (Nelson) N.; m. Susan R. Mudd, Dec. 1986; children: Benjamin Edward, Katherine Elisabeth. Student, Augustana Coll., Rock Island, Ill., 1967-69; BS, U. Wis., 1971, MPA, 1988. Assemblyman Wis. State Assembly, Madison, 1974-82, co-chmn. state joint com. fin., 1980-81; mem. Wis. State Senate, 82-88, asst. majority leader, 1984-85, 87; mayor City of Milw., 1988—. Bd. dirs. Congress for the New Urbanism. Sgt. USAR, 1971-77. Mem. Wis. Alliance of Cities, Congress for New Urbanism (bd. dirs.). Democrat. Presbyterian. Avocation: map collecting. Office: Office of Mayor City Hall 200 E Wells St Rm 201 Milwaukee WI 53202-3515

NORRIS, ALAN EUGENE, federal judge; b. Columbus, Ohio, Aug. 15, 1935; s. J. Russell and Dorothy A. (Shrader) N.; m. Nancy Jean Myers, Apr. 15, 1962 (dec. Jan. 1986); children: Tom Edward Jackson, Tracy Elaine; m. Carol Lynn Spohn, Nov. 10, 1990. BA, Otterbein Coll., 1957, HLD (hon.), 1991; cert., U. Paris, 1956; LLB, NYU, 1960; LLM, U. Va., 1986; HLD, Capital U. Law Sch., 2001. Bar: Ohio 1960, U.S. Dist. Ct. (so. dist) Ohio 1962, U.S. Dist. Ct. (no. dist) Ohio 1964. Law clk. to judge Ohio Supreme Ct., Columbus, 1960-61; assoc. Vorys, Sater, Seymour & Pease, 1961-62; ptnr. Metz, Bailey, Norris & Spicer, Westerville, Ohio, 1962-80; judge Ohio Ct. Appeals (10th dist.), Columbus, 1981-86, U.S. Ct. Appeals (6th cir.), Columbus, 1986—. Contbr. articles to profl. jours. Mem. Ohio Ho. of Reps., Columbus, 1967-80. Named Outstanding Young Man, Westerville Jaycees, 1971; recipient Legislator of Yr. award Ohio Acad. Trial Lawyers, Columbus, 1972. Mem. Ohio Bar Assn., Columbus Bar Assn. Republican. Methodist. Lodge: Masons (master 1966-67). Office: US Ct Appeals 328 US Courthouse 85 Marconi Blvd Columbus OH 43215-2823

NORRIS, ALBERT STANLEY, psychiatrist, educator; b. Sudbury, Ont., Can., July 14, 1926; s. William and Mary (Zell) N.; m. Dorothy James, Sept. 2, 1950; children: Barbara Ellen, Robert Edward, Kimberly Ann. M.D., U. Western Ont., 1951. Intern Ottawa (Ont.) Civic Hosp., 1951-52; resident in psychiatry U. Iowa, Psychopathic Hosp., Iowa City, 1953-55, Boston City Hosp., 1955-56; practice medicine Kingston, Ont., Can., 1956-57; instr. Queen's U., 1956-57; asst. prof. psychiatry U. Iowa, 1957-62, asso. prof., 1962-64, 1965-66, prof., 1966-72; asso. prof. U. Oreg., 1964-65; prof. So. Ill. U. Sch. Medicine, Springfield, 1972-84, chmn. dept. psychiatry, 1972-82; prof. emeritus, 1984—; practice medicine specializing in psychiatry Cedar Rapids, Iowa, 1984—. Vis. prof. U. Auckland, N.Z., U. Otago, New Zealand, U. Liverpool. Contbr. chpts. to books, articles to med. jours. Fellow Am. Psychiat. Soc. (life); mem. AMA, Am. Psychopath. Assn., Soc. Biol. Psychiatry, Can. Psychiat. Soc., Am. Soc. Psychosomatic Ob-Gyn, Royal Soc. Medicine. Republican. Presbyterian. Home: 5 Penfro Dr Iowa City IA 52246-4927 Office: PO Box 1408 Cedar Rapids IA 52406-1408

NORRIS, ANDREA SPAULDING, art museum director; b. Apr. 2, 1945; d. Edwin Baker and Mary Gretchen (Brendle) Spaulding. BA, Wellesley Coll., 1967; MA, NYU, 1969, PhD, 1977. Intern dept. western European arts Met. Mus. Art, N.Y.C., 1970, 72; rsch. and editorial asst. Inst. Fine Arts NYU, 1971, lectr. Washington Sq. Coll., 1976-77; lectr. Queens Coll. CUNY, 1973-74; asst. to dir. Art Gallery Yale U., New Haven, 1977-80, lectr. art history, 1979-80; chief curator Archer M. Huntington Art Gallery, Austin, Tex., 1980-88; lectr. art history Dept. Art U. Tex., 1984-88; dir. Spencer Mus. Art U. Kans., Lawrence, 1988—. Co-author: (catalogue) Medals and Plaquettes from the Molinari Collection at Bowdoin College, 1976; author: (exhbn. catalogues) Jackson Pollock: New-Found Works, 1978; exhbn. The Sforza Court: Milan in the Renaissance 1450-1535, 1988-89. Mem.: Assn. Art Mus. Dir., Coll. Art Assn., Renaissance Soc. Am. (bd. dir. 2000—, v.p. for coms. 2002—), Phi Beta Kappa. Office: Spencer Mus Art U Kans 1301 Mississippi St Lawrence KS 66045-7500

NORRIS, JAMES RUFUS, JR. chemist, educator; b. Anderson, S.C., Dec. 29, 1941; s. James Rufus and Julia Lee (Walker) N.; m. Carol Anne Poetzsch, Dec. 28, 1963; children: Sharon Adele, David James. BS, U. N.C., 1963; PhD, Washington U., St. Louis, 1968. Postdoctoral appointee Argonne (Ill.) Nat. Lab., 1968-71, asst. chemist, 1971-74, chemist, 1974-79, photosynthesis group leader, 1979-95, sr. chemist, 1991-95; prof. dept. chemistry U. Chgo., 1995—. Prof. chemistry U. Chgo., 1984—; chmn. internat. organizing com. 7th Internat. Conf. on Photochemical Conversion and Storage of Solar Energy, Northwestern U., Evanston, Ill., 1988. Co-editor: Photochemical Energy Conversion, 1989; mem. editorial bd. Applied Magnetic Resonance Jour., 1989—. Recipient Disting. Performance award U. Chgo., 1977, 2 R&D 100 awards R&D mag., 1988, E.O. Lawrence Meml. award Dept. of Energy, 1990, Rumford Premium AAAS, 1992, Humboldt Rsch. award for Sr. Scientists, 1992, Zavoisky award Am. Acad. Arts and Scis., 1994. Mem. Am. Chem. Soc., Biophysical Soc. Achievements include discovery that the primary donor of photosynthesis is a dimeric special pair of chlorophyll molecules. Office: U Chgo Dept Chemistry 5735 S Ellis Ave Chicago IL 60637-1403

NORRIS, JOHN HART, lawyer, director; b. New Bedford, Mass., Aug. 4, 1942; s. Edwin Arter and Harriet Joan (Winter) N.; m. Anne Kiley Monaghan, June 10, 1967; children: Kiley Anne, Amy O'Shea. BA, Ind. U., 1964; JD, U. Mich., 1967. Bar: Mich. 1968, U.S. Ct. Claims 1975, U.S. Tax Ct. 1979, U.S. Ct. Mil. Appeals 1969, U.S. Supreme Ct. 1974. From assoc. to ptnr. Monaghan, Campbell, LoPrete, McDonald and Norris, 1970-83; of counsel Dickinson, Wright, Moon, Van Dusen & Freeman, 1983-84, ptnr., 1985—; dep. asst. atty. gen. State of Mich., 1997—. Natural gas law counsel to claims mediator Columbia Gas Transmission Corp.; chpt. 11 bankruptcy procs. in Wilmington, Del. Bankruptcy Ct., 1992—; dep. asst. atty. gen. State Mich., 1997—; bd. dirs. Prime Securities Corp., Ray M. Whyte Co., Ward-Williston Drilling Co., One Stop Cap. Shop. Contbr. articles to profl. jours. Mem. Rep. State Fin. Com.; founder, co-chmn. Rep. Majority Club; bd. trustees Boys and Girls Clubs of Southeastern Mich., 1979—, Mich. Wildlife Habitat Found., Mercy Coll., Detroit, Detroit Hist. Soc., 1984—; bd. trustees, bd. dirs. African Wildlife Found.; trustee, 1st vice chmn. Salk Inst., dir. One Stop Capital Shop, Detroit, 1999—. Recipient numerous civic and non-profit assn. awards. Fellow Mich. State Bar Found.; mem. ABA (litigation and natural resources sects.), Mich. Oil and Gas Assn. (legal and legis. com.), State Bar Mich. (chmn. environ. law sect. 1982-83, probate and trust law sect., energy conservation task force, oil and gas com.), Oakland County Bar Assn., Detroit Bar Assn. (pub. adv. com.), Am. Arbitration Assn., Fin. and Estate Planning Coun. of Detroit, Def. Orientation Conf. Assn., Detroit Zool. Soc., Blue Key Nat. Hon. Fraternity, Phi Delta Phi. Clubs: Bloomfield Hills Country, Thomas M. Cooley, Detroit Athletic, Econ. (Detroit), Hundred, Prismatic, Turtle Lake, Yondotega. Roman Catholic. Home: 1325 Buckingham Ave Birmingham MI 48009-5881 Office: Dickinson Wright 38525 N Woodward Ave Bloomfield Hills MI 48304-2971

NORRIS, RICHARD PATRICK, museum director, history educator; b. Galveston, Tex., May 21, 1944; s. William Gerard and Iris Elsa (Allington) N.; m. Therese Louise Aalid, July 27, 1974; children: William Gerard, John Patrick. BA, Ohio State U., 1966; MA, SUNY, Binghamton, 1968; PhD, U. Minn., 1976. Instr. U. Minn., Mpls., 1970-76; lectr. U. Md., Europe/Asia, 1976-78; dir. Chippewa Valley Mus., Eau Claire, Wis., 1978-80, Kalamazoo Valley Mus., 1985—; curator of history Mus. Sci. & Hist., Fort Worth, 1980-85. Lectr. Tex. Christian U., Fort Worth, Tex., 1981—85; cons. Am. Assn. Mus., Washington, 1979—, NEH, Washington, 1989; adj. prof. We. Mich. U., Kalamazoo, 1986—. Author: History by Design, 1984; book reviewer Mus. News, History News; contbr. articles to profl. jours. Mem.: Assn. Midwest Mus., Internat. Coun. Mus., Am. Assn. State and Local History, Am. Assn. Mus., Rotary (dir. Kalamazoo club 1991—93, pres. 1999—2000). Office: Kalamazoo Valley Museum PO Box 4070 Kalamazoo MI 49003-4070 E-mail: pnorris@kvcc.edu.

NORRIS, TRACY HOPKINS, retired public relations executive; b. Ainsworth, Iowa, Nov. 1, 1927; s. Lee E. and Ruth C. (Simpson) N.; m. Emilie Lathrop, Nov. 11, 1956; 1 child, Shawn Tracy. BA, Cornell Coll., Mt. Vernon, Iowa, 1952; MA, U. Iowa, 1957. Admissions counselor Cornell Coll., Mt. Vernon, 1952-54; dir. news bur. Wittenberg U., Springfield, Ohio, 1956-70; exec. dir. univ. relations and communications Ball State U., Muncie, Ind., 1970-88. Active United Way Springfield, Ohio, Muncie, 1965—. Served with USN, 1945-48. Recipient Silver Anvil award Pub. Relations Soc. Am., 1967. Mem. Council for Advancement and Support Edn., Exchange Club. Lutheran. Avocations: golf, travel, lawn and garden activities. Home: PO Box 2329 Muncie IN 47307 E-mail: tnorris629@aol.com.

NORRIS, WILLIAM C. retired computer systems executive; b. Inavale, Nebr., July 14, 1911; s. William H. and Mildred A. (McCall) N.; m. Jane Malley, Sept. 15, 1943; children: W. Charles, George, Daniel, Brian, Constance, Roger, Mary N., David. B.S., U. Nebr., 1932. Sales engr. Westinghouse Electric Mfg. Co., Chgo., 1935-41; v.p., gen. mgr. Engring. Research Assocs., 1946-55, Univac (div. Sperry Rand Corp.), 1955-57; pres. Control Data Corp., Mpls., 1957-77, past chmn., also bd. dirs.; chmn. William C. Norris Inst., Bloomington, Minn., 1988—. Bd. dirs. N.W. Bank Corp., N.W. Growth Fund, Tronchemics, Inc. Trustee Hill Reference Library; adv. com. White House Conf. on Balanced Nat. Growth and Econ. Devel., 1978— . Served to comdr. USNR, 1941-46. Recipient Nat. Medal Tech., 1986. Office: William C Norris Inst 2001 Killebrew Dr Ste 302 Bloomington MN 55425-1886

NORTH, DOUGLASS CECIL, economist, educator; b. Cambridge, Mass., Nov. 5, 1920; s. Henry Emerson and Edith (Saitta) North; m. Elisabeth Willard Case, Sept. 28, 1972; children from previous marriage: Douglass Alan, Christopher, Malcolm Peter. BA, U. Calif., Berkeley, 1942, PhD, 1952; D in Natural Scis. (hon.) , U. of Cologne, Federal Republic of Germany, 1988; D in Natural Scis. (hon.) , U. Zurich, Switzerland, 1993; D in Natural Scis. (hon.) , Stockholm Sch. of Econs., Sweden, 1994; D in Natural Scis. (hon.) , Prague Sch. Econs., 1995. Asst. prof. econs. U. Wash., 1950—56, assoc. prof., 1957—60, prof., 1960—83, prof. emeritus, 1983—, chmn. dept., 1967—79; dir. Inst. Econ. Research, 1960—66, Nat. Bur. Econ. Research, 1967—87; Spencer T. Olin prof. in arts and scis. Washington U., St. Louis, 1983—. Pitt prof. Am. history and instns. Cambridge U., 1981—82; fellow Ctr. for Advanced Study on Behavioral Scis., 1987—88. Author: The Economic Growth of the U.S. 1790-1860, 1961, Growth and Welfare in the American Past, 1966; author: (with L. Davis) Institutional Change and American Economic Growth, 1971; author: (with R. Miller) The Economics of Public Issues, 1971, 1974, 1976, 1978, 1980; author: (with R. Thomas) The Rise of the Western World, 1973; author: Structure and Change in Economic History, 1981, Institutions, Institutional Change and Economic Performance, 1990. Recipient Nobel Prize in Econ. Sci., Nobel Found., 1993; fellow, Guggenheim, 1972—73; grantee, Social Sci. Rsch. Coun., 1962, Rockefeller Found., 1960—63, Ford Found., 1961, 1966, NSF, 1967—73, Bradley Found., 1986—. Fellow: Am. Acad. Arts and Scis.; mem.: Econ. History Assn., The Brit. Acad. (corr.), Am. Econ. Assn. Office: PO Box 1208 Saint Louis MO 63188-1208

NORTH, JOHN E., JR. lawyer; b. Omaha, Feb. 26, 1952; s. John E. and Joyce (Zimmerman) N.; m. Pamela K. Black, Nov. 22, 1978; children: Stuart, Jeremy, Katherine, Jacqueline, Rebecca. BSBA, U. Nebr., 1974; JD, Creighton U., Nebr., 1977. Bar: Nebr. 1977, U.S. Dist Ct. Nebr. 1977, U.S. Ct. Appeals (8th cir.) Nebr. 1979, U.S. Tax Ct. Nebr. 1980, U.S. Dist Ct. (no. dist.) Texas, 1993. Assoc. McGrath, North, Dwyer, O'Leary & Martin, Omaha, 1977-78, Lathrop, Albright & Swenson, Omaha, 1978-80; ptnr. Fromkin, Herzog, Jabenis & North, 1980-84; prin. North & Black, PC, 1984-89, McGrath, North, Mullin & Kratz, PC, Omaha, 1989—. Mem. ABA, Nebraska State Bar Assn., Omaha Bar Assn., Nebraska Assn. Trial Attys. Office: McGrath North Mullin & Kratz Ste 1400 One Central Park Plz Omaha NE 68102-1680

NORTH, WALTER, state legislator; b. Jan. 31, 1933; Grad., Mich. State U. County commr.; mem. Mich. Senate from 37th dist., Lansing, 1995—. Chmn. agriculture & forestry com. Mich. State Senate, edn. com., transp. com., tourism com., joint com. on adminstrv. rules. Address: PO Box 30036 Lansing MI 48909-7536

NORTHRIP, ROBERT EARL, lawyer; b. Sleeper, Mo., May 8, 1939; s. Novel and Jessie (Burch) N.; m. Linda Kay Francis, June 15, 1968; children: Robert E. Jr., William F., Darryl F., David F. BA, Southwest Mo. State, 1960; MA, U. N.C., 1965; JD, U. Mo., 1968. Bar: Mo. 1968, U.S. Dist. Ct. (we. dist.) Mo. 1968, U.S. Ct. Appeals (10th cir.) 1976, U.S. Ct. Appeals (8th cir.) 1980, U.S. Ct. Appeals (9th cir.) 1983, U.S. Ct. Appeals (3d cir.) 1987, U.S. Supreme Ct. 1978. Ptnr. Shook, Hardy & Bacon, Kansas City, Mo., 1968—. Active Nelson Art Gallery, Soc. of Fellows, Kans. City, Mo. 1st lt. US Army, 1963-65. Mem. ABA, Mo. Bar Assn., Lawyers Assn. Kansas City, Mo. Orgn. Def. Lawyers, Kansas City Met. Bar Assn., U. Mo. Alumni Assn. (past pres. Kansas City chpt.), Nat. Soc. Arts and Letters. Republican. Avocations: baseball, football. Office: Shook Hardy & Bacon 25 Cannon St London EC4M 5SE England E-mail: rnorthrip@shb.com.

NORTON, LLOYD DARRELL, research soil scientist; b. Batesville, Ind., Oct. 20, 1953; s. Milton Walker and Enamay (Doan) N.; children: Benjamin D., Amber J., Jon A. BS, Purdue U., 1975, MS, 1976; PhD, Ohio State U., 1981. Soil scientist Ind. Dept. Natural Resources, Indpls., 1974; rsch. assoc. Purdue U., West Lafayette, Ind., 1975-77, Ohio State U., Columbus, 1977-82; soil scientist and dir. Nat. Soil Erosion Rsch. Lab. USDA, West Lafayette, 1982—; prof. agronomy and earth and atmospheric scis. Purdue U., 1982—. Cons. AID, Washington, 1986, 87, FAO, Rome, 1991; vis. scientist div. soils Commonwealth Sci. and Indsl. Rsch. Orgn., Canberra, Australia, 1990. Contbd. over 140 articles to profl. jours. Mem. Internat. Soc. Soil Sci. (cert. of appreciation 1988), Soil Sci. Soc. Am. (cert. of appreciation 1988), World Assn. Soil Water Cons. Office: Purdue U USDA Nat Soil Erosion Lab 1196 Soils West Lafayette IN 47907-1196

NORTON, PATRICK H. manufacturing company executive; b. Windsor, Ont., Can., May 23, 1930; s. H. Patrick and Alfreda (Haf) N.; m. Dorothy A. McAllen, Oct. 10, 1953; children: Patrick J., Mary Anne, Susan, Margaret, Michael, Thomas, John, Kathleen. BSME, U. Detroit, 1950. Pres. Ionic Internat., Inc., Detroit, 1965-75; chmn. Korest-Peterson Co., 1975-83; chmn. and chief exec. officer Chem. Handling Equipment Co., Toledo, 1980—, also bd. dirs. Bd. dirs. Korest-Peterson Co., ECO

Communications Co., JJ Bus. Products Co.. Patentee in field. Mem. Zoning Bd. Appeals, Beverly Hills, Mich., 1965-68. Served with U.S. Army, 1951-53. Recipient Edward Ignatius Rice award Christian Bros. Ireland, 1986. Mem. Am. Electroplaters Soc. (bd. dirs. 1954-86). Republican. Roman Catholic. Clubs: Plum Hollow Golf (Southfield, Mich.), Burning Tree Country (Mt. Clemens, Mich.). Avocations: golf, boating. Home: 17700 Northland Park Ct Southfield MI 48075-4302 Office: Chem Handling Equipment Co Inc 5656 Opportunity Dr Toledo OH 43612-2941

NORTON, PATRICK J. company executive; CPA. With Arthur Andersen, 1972-79; pres., CEO, dir. Barefoot, Inc.; CFO, bd. dirs. The Scotts Co., 1998—. Office: 41 S High St Ste 3500 Columbus OH 43215-6110

NORTON, ROBERT R., JR. former food products executive; b. 1946; BS, Mo. Western State Coll., 1966; MBA, N.W. Mo. State U., 1968. Sec., treas. Dugdale Packing Co., St. Joseph, Mo., 1966-86; with BeefAmerica Operating Co., Inc., Omaha, 1986-96, pres., 1988-96. Office: Beef America Ste 216 3610 Dodge St Omaha NE 68131-3218

NOSBUSCH, KEITH D. computer and electronics company executive; BS in Elec. and Computer Engring., U. Wis., Milw., 1974, MBA, 1976. Joined Allen-Bradley (subs. Rockwell Internat.), Milw., 1974; various mgmt. and exec.-level positions Rockwell Internat., pres. Automation Control Sys., 1998—. Office: Rockwell Internat Corp 1201 S 2d St Milwaukee WI 53204

NOSOFSKY, ROBERT M. psychology educator; Prof. psychology Ind. U., Bloomington. Recipient Troland Rsch. NAS, 1995. Office: Ind U Dept Psychology Bloomington IN 47405

NOTEBAERT, RICHARD C. retired telecommunications industry executive; b. 1947; married. With Wisconsin Bell, 1969-83; v.p. marketing and operations Ameritech, Chicago, 1983-86; pres. Ameritech Mobile Comm., 1986-89, Indiana Bell Telephone Co., 1989-92, Ameritech Services, 1992-93, pres., COO, 1993-94; chmn., pres., CEO Ameritech Corp., Chicago, 1994-2000, ret., 2000. Office: Aon Corp 4951 Indiana Ave Lisle IL 60532-3818

NOTTESTAD, DARRELL, state legislator; m. Ellen Nottestad; 2 children. Student, Mayville State Coll.; MEd, U. N.D.; postgrad., N.D. State U., Denver U., Ctrl. Mich. U. Sch. prin.; rep. Dist. 43 N.D. State U., mem. judiciary and natural resources com. Bd. dirs. Area Sch. Credit Union; mem. Grand Forks County Hist. Soc. Mem. Sons of Norway. Home: 2110 Westward Dr Grand Forks ND 58201-4167

NOTZ, JOHN KRANZ, JR. arbitrator and mediator, retired lawyer; b. Chgo., Jan. 5, 1932; s. John Kranz and Elinor (Trostel) N.; m. Janis Wellin, Apr. 23, 1966; children: Jane Elinor Notz (Mrs. Ian H. Watson), John Wellin. BA, Williams Coll., 1953; JD, Northwestern U., 1956. Bar: Ill. 1956, Fla. 1957, Wis. 1989, U.S. Supreme Ct. 1960. Assoc. 1st Nat. Bank Chgo., 1954, 1956; from assoc. to ptnr. Gardner, Carton & Douglas, Chgo., 1960-95, of counsel, 1990-95; ret., 1996. Arbitrator, mediator Am. Arbitration Assn., Chgo. Internat. Dispute Resolution Assn., NASD Dispute Resolution Inc., Nat. Futures Assn., N.Y. Stock Exch., Am. Stock Exch. Contbr. articles to profl. jours. Sec. State Corp. Acts Adv. Com., 1982-95, chmn., 1987-89; pres. Chgo. Lit. Club, 1996-97, Ill. Inst. Continuing Legal Edn., 1980-91, chmn., 1990-91; bd. dirs., pres. Black Point Historic Preserve, Inc.; trustee Graceland Cemetery; former trustee Beloit Coll. 1st lt. USAF, 1957-60. Recipient Svc. award Northwestern U., 1978 Fellow Am. Bar Found. (life), Ill. Bar Found. (life), Chgo. Bar Found. (life); mem. Am. Law Inst., Ill. State Bar Assn., Chgo. Bar Assn., Wis. State Bar, Lawyers Club City Chgo., Racquet Club Chgo., Lake Geneva (Wis.) Country Club, Mid-Day Club (Chgo.), Literary Club (Chgo.), Caxton Club (Chgo.), The Cliff Dwellers (Chgo.), Soc. of Archtl. Historians (treas.), Ill. State Hist. Soc. (advisor). Office: care Gardner Carton & Douglas 3100 Quaker Tower 321 N Clark St Chicago IL 60610-4795 E-mail: jnotz@gcd.com.

NOVAK, JOHN PHILIP, state legislator; b. Berwyn, Ill., Feb. 15, 1946; s. John Peter and Cordelia Ann (Moss) N.; (div.); 1 child, Todd Alexander. BS, Eastern Ill. U., Charleston, 1971, MA, 1973. Asst. pers. adminstr. Ill. Dept. Mental Health, 1973-76; pers. adminstr. Manville Corp., 1976-81; labor rels. adminstr. Am. Spring Wire, 1981-82; mem. Ill. Ho. of Reps. from 85th dist., 1987—. Mem. Agr., Edn. Appropriations, Environ. & Energy, Vet. Affairs Com. Ill. Ho. of Reps., vice chmn. Mcpl. and Conservation Laws Coms. Trustee Village of Bradley, Ill., 1975-82; treas. Kankakee County, Ill., 1982-86, 86-87, chmn., 1986-87, precinct committeeman, 1974-80, 86—; bd. dirs. Am. Cancer Soc., 1985-88. Decorated Unit Campaign Clusters; recipient Good Conduct medal, Agr. award, Ill. Farm Bur., 1987, 1988, Major Legislation Sponsorship award Northeastern Ill. Waterfowlers Assn., 1990, Friend of Edn. award Ill. Edn. Assn., 1990; named Outstanding Freshman Legislator, Ind. Cmty. Banks, 1987, Legislator of Yr., Ill. Assn. County Treas. Mem. Lions (treas. Bradley County chpt. 1982-83), Am. Legion (bd. dirs. Post No. 702 1981—), Vietnam Vets. Am. (bd. dirs. 1984—, Cert. of Recognition 1988), Moose, Pi Sigma Alpha. Democrat.

NOVAK, LESLIE HOWARD, lawyer; b. Chgo., May 10, 1944; s. Sidney and Sadie (Jensky) N.; m. Nancy Ruth Sherman, July 2, 1967; children: Heidi Ellen, Shani Beth. BS in Bus. with high distinction, U. Minn., 1966, JD cum laude, 1969. Bar: Minn. 1970, U.S. Dist. Ct. Minn. 1970, U.S. Ct. Appeals (8th cir.) 1974, U.S. Supreme Ct. 1995. Assoc. Robins, Kaplan, Miller & Ciresi, Mpls., 1969-77, ptnr., 1977-92, Mackall, Crounse & Moore, PLC., Mpls., 1992—, mng. ptnr., 1997-99. Bd. dirs. Am. Israel C. of C. and Industry of Minn., Mpls., 1981—, founding pres., 1981-91; founding sec., founding bd. dirs. Assn. N.Am.-Israel Chambers Commerce, Inc., 1993—; bd. dirs. United Jewish Fund and Coun., St. Paul, 1986—; founding dir. Illusion Theater and Sch.; past bd. dirs., past pres. Jewish Family Svc. of St. Paul; past bd. dirs. Mt. Zion Temple. Mem. Hillcrest Country Club, Gopher Golf Boosters Club (sec., bd. dirs.), Phi Delta Phi, Beta Gamma Sigma. Avocations: biking, golf, tennis, skiing. Office: Mackall Crounse & Moore PLC 1400 AT&T Tower 901 Marquette Ave Minneapolis MN 55402-2859 E-mail: lhn@mcmlaw.com.

NOVAK, RAYMOND FRANCIS, environmental health/toxicology research institute director, pharmacology educator; b. St. Louis, July 26, 1946; s. Joseph Raymond and Margaret A. (Cerutti) N.; m. Frances C. Holy, Apr. 12, 1969; children: Jennifer, Jessica, Janelle, Joanna. BS in Chemistry, U. Mo., St. Louis, 1968; PhD in Phys. Chemistry, Case Western Res. U., 1973. Assoc. in pharmacology Northwestern U. Med. Sch., Chgo., 1976-77, asst. prof. pharmacology, 1977-81, assoc. prof., 1981-86, prof., 1986-88; prof. pharmacology Wayne State U. Sch. Medicine, Detroit, 1988—; dir. Inst. Environ. Health Scis. Wayne State U., 1988—, dir. NIEHS Ctr. in Molecular and Cellular Toxicology with Human Application, 1994—. Mem. toxicology study sect. NIH, Bethesda, Md., 1984-88; adj. sci. Inhalation Toxicology Rsch. Inst., Lovelace Biomed. and Environ. Rsch. Inst., 1991-98; program leader Epidemiology and Environ. Carcinogenesis, Karmanos Cancer Inst. and Comprehensive Cancer Ctr., 1996-98. Assoc. editor Toxicol. Applied Pharmacology, 1992-96; editor Drug Metabolism and Disposition, 1994-2000; mem. editorial bd. Jour. Toxicology and Environ. Health, 19 87-92, In Vivo, 1986—, Toxic Substances Jour., 1993-98; mem. bd. pub. trustees Am. Soc. Pharmacology and Experimental Therapeutics, 1994-2000; contbr. articles to profl. jours. Recipient Disting. Alumni award U. Mo., St. Louis, 1988; grantee Nat. Inst. Environ. Health Sci., 1979—, Gen. Medicine sect. NIH, 1979-82, 89-94. Mem. Am. Soc. for Biochem. and Molecular Biology, Soc. Toxicology (councilor 1996-98, chmn. cont. edn. com. 1995-96), Am. Assn. for Cancer Rsch., Am. Soc. for Pharmacology and Exptl. Therapeutics (bd. publ. trustees 1994-99), Am. Soc. Hematology, Internat. Soc. for Study Xenobiotics. Office: Wayne State U Inst Environ Health Scis 2727 2nd Ave Rm 4000 Detroit MI 48201-2671 E-mail: R.Novak@wayne.edu.

NOVAK, STEVEN G. state legislator; b. May 26, 1949; m. Julie Novak; four children. BA, Hamline U.; postgrad., U. Minn., Duluth. Comm. coord. Minn. Mus. Art; v.p. devel. Ramsey Health Care, Inc., and Ramsey Found.; state rep. Minn. Ho. of Reps., St. Paul, 1975-82; Dist. 52 senator Minn. State Senate, 1982—. Chmn. jobs, energy and cmty. devel. com., mem. environ. and natural resources, jobs, energy and cmty. devel. (fin. divsn.), rules and adminstrn., taxes and tax laws, transp. and pub. transit, and fin. divsn. coms., Minn. State Senate. Office: 747 Redwood Ln Saint Paul MN 55112-6620 also: State Senate State Capital Building Saint Paul MN 55155-0001

NOVICH, NEIL S. metals distribution company executive; BA in Physics summa cum laude, Harvard U.; MS in Nuclear Engring., MS in Mgmt., MIT. Former dir. Bain & Co.; chmn., pres., CEO Ryerson Tull, Inc., Chgo., 1994—. Dir. W.W. Grainger, Inc. Trustee Field Mus. Natural History, Children's Home & Aid Soc. Ill.; mem. vis. com. Divsn. Phys. Scis., U. Chgo. Nat. Sci. Found. scholar, Ford scholar. Mem. Phi Beta Kappa. Office: Ryerson Tull Inc 2621 W 15th Pl Chicago IL 60608

NOVICK, ANDREW CARL, urologist; b. Montreal, Apr. 5, 1948; came to U.S., 1974; s. David and Rose (Ortenberg) N.; m. Thelma Silver, June 29, 1969 (div. Dec. 1983); 1 child, Lorne J.; m. Linda Friedman, May 24, 1992; children: Rachel H., Eric D. BSc, McGill U., Montreal, 1968, MD, CM, 1972. Diplomate Am. Bd. Urology. Resident in surgery Royal Victoria Hosp., Montreal, 1972-74; resident in urology Cleve. Clinic Found., 1974-77, staff dept. urology, 1977—, head sect. renal transplant, 1977—, chmn. dept. urology, 1985—, chmn. Organ Transplant Ctr., 1985—. Trustee Am. Bd. Urology, 1995—2001, Urology Residence Rev. Com., 1997—. Editor: Vascular Problems in Urology, 1982, Stewart's Operative Urology, 1989, Renal Vascular Disease, 1995, Innovations in Urologic Surgery, 1997; contbr. more than 500 articles to profl. jours. Fellow ACS, Med. Coun. Can.; mem. Am. Urol. Assn., Am. Assn. Genito-Urinary Surgeons, Clin. Soc. Genito-Urinary Surgeons. Home: 22325 Canterbury Ln Cleveland OH 44122-3901 Office: Cleve Clinic Found 9500 Euclid Ave A100 Cleveland OH 44195-0001

NOVICK, MARVIN, investment company executive, former automotive supplier executive, accountant; b. N.Y.C., July 16, 1931; s. Joseph and Anna Novick; m. Margaret A. Blau, Apr. 9, 1960; children: Jeffrey, Stuart, Barry. BBA, CCNY, 1952; MBA, NYU, 1955, postgrad., 1955-58. CPA, N.Y., Mich., La., N.C. Sr. v.p. Mich. Blue Cross/Blue Shield, Detroit, 1961-70; v.p., dir. fin. Meadowbrook Ins., Southfield, Mich., 1970-72; ptnr. Touche Ross and Co., Detroit, 1972-84; vice chmn. Dura Corp., Southfield, 1984-87, Wesnovtek Corp., Birmingham, Mich., 1987-91; pres. R&M Resources Inc., 1991—; advisor Meadowbrook Ins. Group, Southfield, Mich., 1995—. Chmn. Oak Park-Huntington Woods-Pleasant Ridge (Mich.) Dem. Orgn., 1970-72, 18th Dem. Congl. Dist., 1972-74; trustee Mich. Assn. for Emotional Children, 1965—, also past pres.; trustee Providence Hosp., Southfield, 1975-83, also past chmn., trustee bldg. bd., 1982-89; trustee Oak Park (Mich.) Bd. Edn., 1964-71, also past pres.; trustee Temple Beth El, Birmingham, Mich., 1968—, also past pres.; trustee, vice chmn. Union of Am. Hebrew Congregation, 1981—; chmn. fin. com., fin. sec. World for Prog. Judaism-Internat., 1985-99; chmn. pers. com. Jewish Welfare Found., 1987-91, assoc. chmn. cultural and edn. fedn. com., 1984-97, chmn. subcom. Israel and Overseas Com., 1988-99; mem. com. Jewish Agy. in Israel, 1987-99; vice chmn. fin. com., trustee Sinai Hosp., 1988-92, mem. audit com., 1995-97; trustee, treas. Mariners Inn, 1996-2000, Karmanos Cancer Inst.; bd. dirs. B'nai B'rith Centennial Lodge, 1970-79, past v.p.; trustee, mem. exec. com. Rose Hill Ctr., Inc., 1992—; mem. com. Hillel Ctr., U. Mich.; mem. various coms. Jewish Welfare Fedn. Recipient Honor and Service cert. Oak Park Bd. Edn., 1972, Past Pres. award Mich. Assn. Emotionally Disturbed Children, 1986; named one of Outstanding Young Men of Am., Outstanding Am. Found., 1968. Mem. Am. Inst. CPA's, Mich. Assn. CPA's, N.Y. State Assn. CPA's. Home: 12820 Burton St Oak Park MI 48237-1679

NOVIK, STEVE, finance company executive; BSBA, U. Mo., 1972; MBA, Washington U., 1974. Ptnr. KPMG Peat Marwick; from gen. prin. to CFO Steve Novik, St. Louis, 1983-95; CFO Edward Jones, 1995—. Office: Edward Jones 12555 Manchester Road Saint Louis MO 63131

NOVOTNEY, DONALD FRANCIS, superintendent of schools; b. Streator, Ill., July 10, 1947; s. Andrew Stephen and Irene Marie (Lux) Novotney; m. Jane Francis Loeffelholz, June 3, 1973; children: Nicole, Tara, Thomas, Michael, Theresa. BA, Loras Coll., 1969; MS in Tchg., U. Wis., Platteville, 1973; MS, U. Dayton, 1985. Cert. tchr., Wis.; cert. tchr. and adminstr., Ohio. Prin. Holy Ghost Sch., Dickeyville, Wis., 1969-75, St. John Sch., Green Bay, 1975-76, Beaver Dam (Wis.) Cath. Schs., 1976-83; coord. Jordan Cath. Schs., Rock Island, Wis., 1983-85; supt. schs. Diocese of Fargo, N.D., 1985-86, Diocese of La Crosse, Wis., 1987—. Mem. Nat. Cath. Edn. Assn. (del. to nat. congress for cath. schs.). Republican. Roman Catholic. Avocations: athletics, travel. Home: 3314 33rd St S La Crosse WI 54601-7706 Office: Diocese of La Crosse 3710 East Ave S La Crosse WI 54601-7215

NOVOTNY, DONALD WAYNE, electrical engineering educator; b. Chgo., Dec. 15, 1934; s. Adolph and Margaret Novotny; m. Louise J. Eenigenburg, June 26, 1954; children: Donna Jo Kopp, Cynthia Mason. BEE, Ill. Inst. Tech., 1956, MS, 1957; PhD, U. Wis., 1961. Registered profl. engr., Wis. Instr. Ill. Inst. Tech., 1957-58; mem. faculty U. Wis., Madison, 1958—, prof. elec. engring., 1969-96, chmn. dept. elec. and computer engring., 1976-80, Grainger prof. power electronics, 1990—, prof. emeritus, 1996—. Vis. prof. Mont. State U., 1966, Eindhoven (The Netherlands) Tech. U., 1974, Tech. U. Louvain, Belgium, 1986; Fulbright lectr. Tech. U. Ghent, Belgium, 1981; dir. Wis. Elec. Machines and Power Electronics Consortium, 1981—; assoc. dir. Univ.-Industry Rsch. Program, 1982-93; chmn. elec. engring. program Nat. Technol. U., 1989—; cons. to industry. Author: Introductory Electromechanics, 1965, Vector Control and Dynamics of AC Drives, 1996; also rsch. papers; assoc. editor: Electric Machines and Power Systems, 1976—. Recipient Kiekhofer tchg. award U. Wis., 1964, Benjamin Smith Reynolds tchg. award, 1984, Holdridge tchg. award, 1995, Nat. Technol. U. Outstanding Instr. award, 1996-2001, IEEE-IAS Outstanding Achievement award, 1998; Outstanding paper award Engring. Inst. Can., 1966; named IEEE-IAS Disting. Lectr., 1995; fellow GE, 1956, Ford Found., 1960; grantee numerous industries and govt. agys. Fellow IEEE (prize paper awards 1983, 84, 86, 87, 90, 91, 93, 94, 3d Millennium Medal 2000); mem. Am. Soc. Engring. Edn., Sigma Xi, Tau Beta Pi, Eta Kappa Nu. Congregationalist. Lodge: Rotary Home: 1421 E Skyline Dr Madison WI 53705-1132 Office: U Wis Dept Elec and Computer Engring 1415 Engineering Dr Madison WI 53706-1607 E-mail: novotny@engr.wisc.edu.

NOVOTNY, MILOS VLASTISLAV, chemistry educator; b. Brno, Czechoslovakia, Apr. 19, 1942; came to U.S., 1969; BS, U. Brno, Czechoslovakia, 1962, PhD, 1965. Rsch. assoc. Inst. Analytical Chemistry Czechoslovak Acad. Scis., Brno, 1965-68; rsch. assoc. Royal Karolinska Inst., Stockholm, 1968-69; rsch. assoc. dept. chemistry U. Houston, 1969-71; from instr. to Rudy prof. of chemistry Ind. U., Bloomington, 1971—. Office: Ind U Dept of Chemistry Bloomington IN 47405

NOWACKI, JAMES NELSON, lawyer; b. Columbus, Ohio, Sept. 12, 1947; s. Louis James and Betty Jane (Nelson) N.; m. Catherine Ann Holden, Aug. 1, 1970; children: Carrie, Anastasia, Emma. AB, Princeton U., 1969; JD, Yale U., 1973. Bar: Ill. 1973, N.Y. 1982, U.S. dist. Ct. (no. dist.) Ill. 1973, U.S. Ct. Appeals (7th cir.) 1978, U.S. Ct. Appeals (6th cir.) 1987, U.S. Supreme Ct. 1992. Assoc. Isham, Lincoln & Beale, Chgo., 1976-79; ptnr. Kirkland & Ellis, 1980—. Mem. Winnetka Sch. Bd. Dist. 36, Ill. 1983-91, bd. pres., 1989-91; mem. New Trier Sch. Bd., 1997-99, pres., 1997-98. Harlan Fiske Stone prize Yale U., 1972. Mem. ABA (forum com. on constrn. industry, litigation sect.), Mid-Am. Club, Skokie Country Club. Home: 708 Prospect Ave Winnetka IL 60093-2320 Office: Kirkland & Ellis 200 E Randolph St Fl 60 Chicago IL 60601-6636

NOWAK, JOHN MICHAEL, retired air force officer, company executive; b. Grand Rapids, Mich., Dec. 17, 1941; s. John F. and Dorothy F. (Smigiel) N.; m. Maureen K. Henry, Apr. 20, 1963; children: Kimberly, Susan, John, Michael, Lynn. BA in Sociology and Polit. Sci., Aquinas Coll., Mich., 1963; M in Mgmt., U. So.Calif., 1973. Commd. 2d lt. U.S. Air Force, 1963, advanced through grades to lt. gen., 1993; dir. maintenance Ogden Air Logistics Ctr., Hill AFB, Utah, 1984-86; dep. chief staff for maintenance Air Force Logistics Command, Wright-Patterson AFB, Ohio, 1986-89; dep. chief staff for logistics and engring. Hdqrs. Mil. Airlift Command, Scott AFB, Ill., 1989-92; dep. chief staff for logistics Hdqrs. Air Mobility Command, 1992; dir. of supply Hdqrs. U.S. Air Force, Washington, 1992-93, dep. chief for logistics, 1993-1995; pres., CEO Logtec, Fairborn, OH, 1995—. Decorated DSM, Legion of Merit, Bronze Star medal, Meritorious Svc. medal with 3 oak leaf clusters, Air Force Commendation medal. Avocations: golf, boating, fishing. Office: LOGTEC Inc 2900 Presidential Dr Ste 130 Fairborn OH 45324-6292 E-mail: nowakj@logtec.com.

NOWAK, PATRICIA ROSE, advertising executive; b. Toledo, Nov. 29, 1946; d. Robert Joseph and Hedwig Rose (Rutkowski) Stack; m. Casimir Robert Nowak Jr., June 3, 1967 (dec.); children: Martin Robert, Laura Kristen. Student, Bowling Green State U., 1964-67. Events dir. Sta. WTTO, Toledo, 1967-68; dir. spl. events Tiedtke's, 1968-72; dir. fashion and pub. rels. Lion Store, 1980-86; owner, mgr. Pat Nowak & Assocs., Sylvania, Ohio, 1986-90; dir. pub. rels., consumer affairs Seaway Foodtown Stores, Maamee, 1990—. Bd. dirs. State of Ohio Workforce Devel. Com. Contbr. articles to local newspaper. Auction chair Toledo Opera, 1978, 86-87, bd. dirs., 1998; bridge chair Toledo Symphony, 1987; gifts chair St. Johns H.S., Toledo, 1988-89; chair holiday parade Citifest, Toledo, 1988-89, Sapphire Ball, 1996; dir. opening ceremonies World Cup, Toledo, 1988-90; bd. dirs. Am. Heart Assn., Toledo Repertoire Theatre, Pvt. Industry Coun., Toledo Mus. Art, 1998; active Boy Scouts Am., Gov.'s Workforce Devel. Com. Recipient salute Old Newsboys, 1997. Mem. Toledo C. of C. (solicitation com., vol. award 1989), Jr. League Toledo (pub. rels. com. 1984-85). Roman Catholic. Home: 8130 Hidden Harbour Dr W Holland OH 43528-9398 Office: 1020 Ford St Maumee OH 43537-1820

NOWAK, ROBERT MICHAEL, chemist; b. South Milwaukee, Wis., Oct. 28, 1930; s. Casimer M. and Anita Marie (Anderson) N.; m. Susan Lora Boyd, Oct. 12, 1957; children: Karen Sue Nowak Sapsford, Janet Lynn Nowak McMorris. Student, U. Wis., Racine, 1949-51; BS, U. Wis., Madison, 1953; PhD, U. Ill., 1956. Rsch. chemist Phys. Rsch. Lab. , Dow Chem. Co., Midland, Mich., 1956-64, from group leader to asst. lab dir., 1964-72; dir. rsch. and devel. plastics dept. Dow Chem. Co., 1972-73, dir. rsch. and devel. Olefin and Styrene plastics depts., 1973-78, dir. rsch. and devel. plastics dept., 1978-83, dir. cen. rsch., 1983-90, chief scientist, dir. cen. rsch. and devel., 1990-94; pres., CEO Mich. Molecular Inst., 1994—. Contbr. articles to profl. jours.; patentee organic reaction mechanisms and reinforced plastics. Mem. NAE, AIChE, Am. Chem. Soc. Office: MI Molecular Inst 1910 W Saint Andrews Rd Midland MI 48640-2657 E-mail: nowak@mmi.org.

NOYES, RUSSELL, JR. psychiatrist; b. Indpls., Dec. 25, 1934; s. Russell and Margaret (Greenleaf) N.; m. Martha H. Carl, Nov. 13, 1960; children: Marjorie Noyes-Aamot, Nancy Heifner, James R. BS, DePauw U., 1956; MD, Ind. U., 1959. Diplomate Am. Bd. Psychiatry and Neurology. Intern Phila. Gen. Hosp., 1959-60; residency U. Iowa, Iowa City, 1961-63, asst. prof. psychiatry, 1966-71, assoc. prof., 1971-78, prof., 1978—. Co-author: The Anxiety Disorders, 1998; editor: Handbook of Anxiety, 1988-91; contbr. 250 articles to profl. jours. With USN, 1963-65. Fellow Am. Psychiat. Assn., Acad. Psychosomatic Medicine (pres. 1990-91); mem. Iowa Psychiat. Soc. (pres. 1986-87). Republican. Lutheran. Avocation: gardening. Home: 326 MacBride Rd Iowa City IA 52246-1716 Office: Psychiatry Rsch Med Edn Bldg Iowa City IA 52242-1009

NRIAGU, JEROME OKON, environmental geochemist; b. Ora-eri Town, Anambra, Nigeria, Oct. 24, 1942; came to U.S., 1993; s. Martin and Helena (Anaekwe) N.; children: Chinedu Delbert, Uzoma Vivian, Osita Jide. BSc with honors, U. Ibadan, Nigeria, 1965, DSc, 1987; MS, U. Wis., 1967; PhD, U. Toronto, Ont., 1970. Rsch. scientist Environment Can., Burlington, Ont., 1970-93; prof. environ. chem. sch. of pub. health U. Mich., Ann Arbor, 1993—; dir. environ. health scis. program, 1996-99; rsch. scientist Ctr. for Human Growth and Devel., U. Mich., 1997—. Adj. prof. U. Waterloo, Ont., 1985—96; vis. scientist NOAA, Ann Arbor, 1992; bd. dirs. Ecology Ctr. Mich., Alliance to End Childhood Lead Poisoning, Washington, 1998—. Author: Lead and Lead Poisoning in Antiquity, 1983; editor: (book series) Advances in Environmental Science and Technology, 1982—, Trace Metals in the Environment, 1996—, 29 books on various environ. topics, 1979—, Sci. of the Total Environment, 1983—; mem. editl. bds.: 9 jours.; contbr. articles to profl. jours. Recipient Rigler medal, Can. Soc. Limnologists, 1988; grantee Fulbright sr. fellowship, 2002. Fellow Royal Soc. Can. (Romanowski medal 1999); mem. Am. Pub. Health Assn., Geochem. Soc. Roman Catholic. Avocations: photography, reading (African authors), travel. Office: Univ of Michigan Environ/Indsl Health 109 Observatory St Ann Arbor MI 48109-2029 E-mail: jnriagu@sph.umich.edu.

NUGENT, DANIEL EUGENE, business executive; b. Chgo., Dec. 18, 1927; s. Daniel Edward and Pearl A. (Trieger) N.; m. Bonnie Lynn Weidman, July 1, 1950; children: Cynthia Lynn, Mark Alan, Dale Alan. BSME, Northwestern U., 1951. With U.S. Gypsum Co., Chgo., 1951-71, dir. corp. devel., to 1971; pres. Am. Louver Co., 1971-72; v.p. ops. ITT Corp., Cleve., 1972-74, exec. v.p. St. Paul, 1974-75; v.p., ops. Pentair, Inc., 1975, pres., COO, 1975-81, pres., CEO, 1981-86, chmn., CEO, 1986-92, chmn. exec. com., 1992-97, chmn. nominating com., dir., 1990-99; dir. exec. com. Fiberstar, Inc., St. Paul, 1999—. Bd. dirs., audit, exec., compensation and corp. governance coms. Apogee Enterprises, Inc.; dir. Wavecrest, Inc., 1997—. Vice-chmn. local planning commn., 1968-72; co-chmn. Wellspring, 1989-92; trustee Harper Coll., Palatine, 1970-73; mem. adv. commn. McCormick Engring. and Kelloggg Schs. at Northwestern U., MBA Sch. of St. Thomas U., St. Paul; mem. exec. com. Indian Head coun. Boy Scouts Am. With AUS, 1946-47. Mem. North Oaks Golf Club, Quail Creek Country Club (Naples). Republican. Presbyterian. E-mail: denugenta@aol.com.

NUGENT, DONALD CLARK, judge; b. Mpls., Mar. 7, 1948; s. Paul Donald and Kathleen June (Leasman) N. BA, Xavier U., 1970, Loyola U., Rome, 1969; JD, Cleve. State U., 1974. Bar: Ohio 1974. Prodn. supr. C.

Schmidt & Sons, Inc., Cleve., 1971-75; pros. atty. Cuyahoga County, Ohio, 1975-85, judge Common Pleas Ct., 1985—. Mem. Nat. Dist. Attys. Assn., Ohio Bar Assn., Greater Cleve. Bar Assn., Cuyahoga County Bar Assn. Roman Catholic. Avocations: marrathon running, classical guitar. Home: 328 Cornwall Rd Cleveland OH 44116-1629

NUGENT, JOHNNY WESLEY, state legislator, tractor company executive; b. Cleve., July 18, 1939; s. Carl Howard and Velma (Holland) N.; m. Nancy Carol Whiteford, Dec. 16, 1960; 1 child, Suzette. Grad. high sch., Aurora, Ind. Owner, mgr. Nugent Tractor Sales, Lawrenceburg, Ind., 1960—; mem. Ind. Senate from 43rd dist., Indpls., 1978—. Bd. dirs. 1st Nat. Bank Aurora. Commr. Dearborn County, Lawrenceburg, 1966-74. With USAR, 1957-64. Republican. Baptist. Office: Ind Senate Dist 43 200 W Washington St Indianapolis IN 46204-2728

NUGENT, SHANE VINCENT, lawyer; b. Bozeman, Mont., July 14, 1962; s. John Vincent Nugent and Marilyn Jean (Piotrowski) Cloven; m. Lori Sue Meyer, June 14, 1986; children: Justine Nicole, Cole Tyler. BA, Knox Coll., 1984; JD, Northwestern U., 1987. Bar: Ill. 1987. Assoc. Lord, Bissell & Brook, Chgo., 1987-93; pvt. practice Barrington, Ill., 1993-94; of counsel Blatt Hammestahr & Eaton, Chgo., 1994-96; pvt. practice Barrington, 1996-98; exec. v.p., COO Intelligent Learning Sys., Inc., Austin, Tex., 1998—. Contbr. articles to profl. jours. Recipient NASA Space Act award, 2000; named one of Outstanding Young Men Am., 1987. Mem. Chgo. Bar Assn., Beta Theta Pi (Ray M. Arnold prize Xi chpt. 1984, chpt. advisor 1987-92, asst. gen. sec. 1992-97), Xi Alumni (pres. 1992—).

NURNBERGER, JOHN I., JR. psychiatrist, educator; b. N.Y.C., July 18, 1946; married; 3 children. BS in Psychology magna cum laude, Fordham U., 1968; MD, Ind. U., 1975, PhD, 1983. Diplomate Am. Bd. Psychiatry and Neurology. Resident in psychiatry Columbia Presbyn. Med. Ctr., N.Y.C., 1975-78, med. officer sect. psychogenetics, 1977-78; sr. staff fellow, outpatient clinic adminstr. sect. psychogenetics NIH, Bethesda, Md., 1978-83, staff psychiatrist, chief NIMH Outpatients Clinic, 1983-86, acting chief sect. clin. genetics, 1986; prof. psychiatry, dir. Inst. Psychiatric Rsch., rsch. coord. dept. psychiatry Ind. U. Med. Ctr., Indpls., 1986—; prof. med. psychiatry, neurobiology and med. genetics Ind. U. Grad. Sch., 1987—; Joyce and Iver Small prof. psychiatry, dir. Inst. Psychiat. Rsch., Ind. U. Clin. cons. Cold Spring VA Hosp., 1986—; cons., lectr. in field. Editor-in-chief: Psychiatric Genetics; field editor: Neuropsychiatric Genetics; contbr. articles to profl. jours. NSF fellow, 1968; recipient NAMI Exemplary Psychiatrist award Nat. Alliance Mentally Ill, 1992, 94. Fellow Am. Psychiatric Assn., Am. Psychpathological Assn.; mem. AAAS, Am. Soc. Human Genetics, Internat. Soc. Psychiatric Genetics (bd. dirs.), Am. Coll. Neuropsychopharmacology, Soc. Light Treatment and Biol. Rhythms, Soc. Neursci., Assn. Rsch. in Nervous and Mental Disease, Soc. Biol. Psychiatry, Sigma Xi. Office: Ind U Sch Medicine Psychiatric Rsch Inst 791 Union Dr Indianapolis IN 46202-2873

NUSSBAUM, A(DOLF) EDWARD, mathematician, educator; b. Rheydt, Fed. Republic Germany, Germany, Jan. 10, 1925; came to U.S., 1947; s. Karl and Franziska (Scheye) N.; m. Anne Ebbin, Sept. 1, 1957; children: Karl, Franziska. MA, Columbia U., 1950, PhD, 1957. Mem. staff electronic computer project Inst. Advanced Study, Princeton, N.J., 1952-53, mem., 1962-63; instr. math U. Conn., Storrs, 1953-55; asst. prof. Rensselaer Poly. Inst., Troy, N.Y., 1956-58; vis. scholar Stanford U., Calif., 1967-68; asst. prof., then assoc. prof. Washington U., St. Louis, 1958-66, prof., 1966-95, prof. emeritus, 1995—. Contbr. articles to profl. jours. Grantee NSF, 1960-79 Mem. Am. Math. Soc. Home: 8050 Watkins Dr Saint Louis MO 63105-2517 Office: Washington U Dept Math Saint Louis MO 63130 E-mail: addi@math.wustl.edu.

NUSSBAUM, BERNARD J. lawyer; b. Berlin, Mar. 11, 1931; came to U.S., 1936; s. William and Lotte (Frankfurther) N.; m. Jean Beverly Enzer, Sept. 4, 1956; children— Charles, Peter, Andrew A.B., Knox Coll., 1948-52; J.D., U. Chgo., 1955. Assoc. Proskauer Rose Goetz & Mendelsohn, N.Y.C., 1955-56; assoc. Sonnenschein Nath & Rosenthal, Chgo., 1959-65, sr. ptnr., 1965—. Master bencher Am. Inns of Ct., 1986—; appointed to com. on civility 7th cir. U.S. Ct. Appeals, 1989-92. Editor U. Chgo. Law Rev., 1954-55; mem. nat. adv. bd. BNA Civil Trial Man., 1985—; contbr. articles to profl. jours. Mem. vis. com. U. Chgo. Law Sch., 1977-83. Served to capt. U.S. Army, 1956-59 Fellow Am. Bar Found., Ill. Bar Found. (charter); mem. ABA, Chgo. Bar Assn. (chmn. com. on fed. civil procedure 1968-69, mem. com. on judiciary 1970-76), Ill. Bar Assn. (council Antitrust sect. 1971-73, assembly del. 1972-80), U. Chgo. Law Sch. Nat. Alumni Assn. (pres. 1981-83), Law Club Chgo., Legal Club Chgo. Avocations: skiing; cycling. Office: Sonnenschein Nath & Rosenthal 8000 Sears Tower 233 S Wacker Dr Ste 8000 Chicago IL 60606-6491

NUSSBAUM, MARTHA CRAVEN, philosophy and classics educator; b. N.Y.C., May 6, 1947; d. George and Betty (Warren) Craven; m. Alan Jeffrey Nussbaum, Aug., 1969 (div. 1987); 1 child, Rachel Emily. BA, NYU, 1969; MA, Harvard U., 1971, PhD, 1975; LHD (hon.), Kalamazoo Coll., 1988, Grinnell Coll., 1993. Asst. prof. philosophy and classics Harvard U., Cambridge, 1975-80, assoc. prof., 1980-83; vis. prof. philosophy, Greek and Latin Wellesley (Mass.) Coll., 1983-84; assoc. prof. philosophy and classics Brown U., Providence, 1984-85, prof. philosophy, classics and comparative lit., 1985-87, David Benedict prof. philosophy, classics and comparative lit., 1987-89, prof., 1989-95; prof. law and ethics U. Chgo., 1995-96, prof. philosophy dept., 1995—, prof. Divinity Sch., 1995—, Ernst Freund prof. law and ethics Law Sch./Divinity Sch., 1996-99, assoc. mem. classics dept., 1996—. Rsch. advisor World Inst. Devel. Econs. Rsch., Helsinki, Finland, 1986-93; vis. prof. law U. Chgo., 1994. Author: Aristotle's De Motu Animalium, 1978, The Fragility of Goodness, 1986, Loe's Knowledge, 1990, The Therapy of Desire, 1994, Poetic Justice: The Literary Imagination and Public Life, 1996, For Love of Country, 1996; editor: Language and Logos, 1983; (with A. Rorty) Essays on Artistotle's De Anima, 1992, (with A. Sen) The Quality of Life, 1993, (with J. Brunschwig) Passions & Perceptions, 1993, (with J. Glover) Women, Culture and Development, 1995, Poetic Justice, 1996, Cultivating Humanity, 1997, Sex and Social Justice, 1998. Soc. Fellows Harvard U. jr. fellow, 1972-75, Humanities fellow Princeton U., 1977-78, Guggenheim Found. fellow, 1983, NIH fellow, vis. fellow All Souls Coll., Oxford, Eng., 1986-87; recipient Brandeis Creative Arts award, 1990, Spielvogel-Diamondstein award, 1991; Gifford lectr. U. Edinburgh, 1993. Fellow Am. Acad. Arts and Scis. (membership com. 1991-93, coun. 1992-96), Am. Philos. Soc.; mem. Am. Philos. Assn. (exec. com. Ea. divsn. 1985-87, chair com. internat. coop., ex-officio mem. nat. bd. 1989-92, chair com. on status of women 1994-97), Am. Philol. Assn., PEN. Office: U Chicago The Law Sch 1111 E 60th St Chicago IL 60637-2776

NUSSLE, JAMES ALLEN, congressman; b. Des Moines, June 27, 1960; s. Mark S. and Lorna Kay (Fisher) N.; m. Leslie J. Harbison, Aug. 23, 1986. BA, Luther Coll., Decorah, Iowa, 1983; JD, Drake U., 1985. Bar: Iowa 1985. Pvt. practice law, Manchester, Iowa, 1986; states atty. Delaware County Atty., 1986-90; mem. U.S. Congress from 2d Iowa dist., Washington, 1991—, mem. house ways and means com., chmn. house budget com. Lutheran. Avocation: guitar. Office: US Ho of Reps 303 Cannon Hob Washington DC 20515-0001*

NUTTER, FORREST, plant pathologist; BS in Botany, U. Md., 1976; MS in Plant Physiology, U. N.H., 1978; PhD, N.D. State U., 1983. Assoc. prof. plant pathology Iowa State U. Recipient CIBA-GEIGY award Am. Phytopathological Soc., 1995. Office: Iowa State University Plant Pathology Dept Ames IA 50011-0001

NYBERG, LARS, electronics company executive; b. Sweden; married; four children. BS in bus. adminstrn., U. Stockholm, 1974. With Philips Electronics NV, U.K., The Netherlands, Sweden, chmn., CEO comm. sys. divsn.; chmn., CEO AT&T Global Info. Solutions, mem. mgmt. exec. com., 1995-96; chmn., pres. and CEO NCR Corp., 1997—. Office: NCR Corp 1700 S Patterson Blvd Dayton OH 45479-0002

NYCKLEMOE, GLENN WINSTON, bishop; b. Fergus Falls, Minn., Dec. 8, 1936; s. Melvin and Bertha (Sumstad) N.; m. Ann Elizabeth Olson, May 28, 1960; children: Peter Glenn, John Winston, Daniel Thomas. BA, St. Olaf Coll., 1958; MDiv, Luther Theol. Sem., St. Paul, 1962; D of Ministry, Luth. Sch. Theology, Chgo., 1977. Ordained to ministry Am. Luth. Ch., 1962. Assoc. pastor Our Savior's Luth. Ch., Valley City, N.D., 1962-64, Milw., 1964-67, co-pastor, 1967-73, sr. pastor Beloit, Wis., 1973-82, St. Olaf Luth. Ch., Austin, Minn., 1982-88; bishop Southeastern Minn. Synod, Evang. Luth. Ch. in Am., Rochester, 1988—. Bd. dirs. Luth. Social Svcs. of Minn., Mpls., Bd. of Social Ministries, St. Paul, Minn. Coun. Chs., Mpls. Mem. bd. regents St. Olaf Coll., Northfield, Minn., 1988—. Avocations: skiing, trap shooting, golf.

NYE, MICHAEL EARL, former state legislator; b. Indpls., Aug. 3, 1946; s. Clair Zurmehly and Isabelle (Volk) N.; m. Marceline Leuzinger, 1974; children: Jessica E., Justin M. BS, Purdue U., 1968, JD, 1973. Rep. Mich. Dist. 58, Mich. Dist. 41, until 1998. Minority vice chmn. House Jud. Com. Mich. Ho. Reps., mem. conservation com., environ. com., recreation com., labor & tourism com., wildlife com., civil rights com., women's issues com. Farmer; pvt. practice law; adv. bd. State Bar Mich. Named environ. legis. of yr. Mich. Environ. Def. Assn., 1990, legis. of yr. Mich. Assn. Chiefs of Police. Mem. ABA, Am. Legion, Hillsdale County Bar Assn., Masons, Scottish Rite, Litchfield Exch. Clubs, Hillsdale Exch. Clubs, Mich. Farm Bur., Alpha Gamma Rho. Home: 7111 Anderson Rd Litchfield MI 49252-9772 Address: State Capitol PO Box 30014 Lansing MI 48909-7514

NYENHUIS, JACOB EUGENE, college official; b. Mille Lacs County, Minn., Mar. 25, 1935; s. Egbert Peter and Rosa (Walburg) N.; m. Leona Mae Van Duyn, June 6, 1956; children: Karen Joy, Kathy Jean, Lorna Jane, Sarah Van Duyn. AB in Greek, Calvin Coll., 1956; AM in Classics, Stanford U., 0961, PhD in Classics, 1963; LittD, Hope Coll., 2001. Asst. in classical langs. Calvin Coll., Grand Rapids, Mich., 1957-59; acting instr. Stanford (Calif.) U., 1962; from asst. prof. to prof. Wayne State U., Detroit, 1962-75, dir. honors program, 1964-75, chmn. Greek and Latin dept., 1965-75; prof. classics, dean for humanities Hope Coll., Holland, 1975-78, dean for arts and humanities, 1978-84, provost, 1984—2001, prof. and provost emeritus, 2001—; sr. rsch. fellow A.C. Van Raalte Inst., 2001—. Cons. Mich. Dept. Edn., Lansing, 1971-72, Gustavus Adolphus Coll., St. Peter, Minn., 1974, Northwestern Coll., Orange City, Iowa, 1983, Whitworth Coll., Spokane, Wash., 1987, The Daedalus Project, 1988; reviewer NEH, Washington, 1986-87, panelist, 1991; reviewer Lilly Endowment, Indpls., 1987-89, U.S. Dept. Edn., 1993, Mich. Humanities Coun., 1999-2001; vis. assoc. prof. U. Calif., Santa Barbara, 1967-68, Ohio State U., Columbus, 1972; vis. rsch. prof. Am. Sch. Classical Studies, Athens, Greece, 1973-74, also mem. mng. com.; vis. scholar Green Coll. Oxford U., 1989; mem. editl. adv. bd. Christianity and The Arts, 1998, chmn., 1999—. Co-author: Latin Via Ovid, 1977, rev. edit., 1982, A Dream Fulfilled: The Van Raalte Sculpture in Centennial Park, 1997; editor: Petronius: Cena Trimalchionis, 1970, Plautus: Amphitruo, 1970; authors articles in field. Elder Christian Ref. Ch., Palo Alto, Calif., 1960—62, elder, clk. Grosse Pointe, Mich., 1964—67, Holland, 1976—85, v.p., 1988—91, mem. exec. com., 1994—95; bd. trustees Calvin Theol. Sem., 2001—; chmn. human rels. coun. Open Housing Com., Grosse Pointe, 1971—73. Mem. Am. Philol. Assn., Danforth Assocs. (chmn. regional com. 1975-77), Mich. Coun. for Humanities (bd. dirs., 1976-84, 88-92, chmn. 1980-82, 96-99, Disting. Svc. award 1984), Nat. Fedn. State Humanities Couns. (bd. dirs. 1979-84, pres. 1981-83), Gt. Lakes Colls. Assn. (bd. dirs. 1991-93), Coun. on Undergrad. Rsch. (councilor-at-large 1993-99), Green Coll. Soc. (Oxford U.), Mortar Bd. (hon.), Eta Sigma Phi (hon.). Democrat. Avocations: photography, carpentry. Home: 51 E 8th St Ste 200 Holland MI 49423-3501 Office: Hope Coll Van Raalte Inst PO Box 9000 Holland MI 49422-9000

NYERGES, ALEXANDER LEE, museum director; b. Rochester, N.Y., Feb. 27, 1957; s. Sandor Elek and Lena (Angeline) N.; m. Kathryn Gray; 1 child, Robert Angeline. BA, George Washington U., 1979, MA, 1981. Intern The Octagon, Washington, 1976-79; archeol. asst. Smithsonian Instn., 1977; curatorial intern Nat. Mus. Am. History, 1978-79; adminstrv. asst. George Washington U., Washington, 1979-81; exec. dir. DeLand Mus. Art, Fla., 1981-85, Miss. Mus. Art, Jackson, 1985-92; dir. Dayton (Ohio) Art Inst., 1992—. Mem. grants panel Nat. Endowment for the Arts, 1988—; field surveyor Inst. Mus. Svcs., Washington, 1985-88, nat. review panel, 1990-92; treas., bd. dirs. Volusia County Arts Coun., Daytona Beach, Fla., 1983-85. Author: Selections from the Permanent Collection, 1999, In Praise of Nature: Ansel Adams and Photographers of the American West; contbr. articles to profl. jours. Bd. dirs. West Volusia Hist. Soc., 1984-85; pres. Miss. Inst. Arts and Letters, 1987-88; trustee Cultural Arts Ctr., DeLand, 1984-85, Miami Valley Cultural Alliance, 1993-95, Intermus. Conservation Lab., 1993-99, Montgomery County Arts and Culture Dist., 1994—; bd. trustees Montgomery Co. Convention and Vis. Bureau. U.S. Dept. Edn. scholar, 1973. Mem. DeLand Area C. of C. (bd. dirs., tourist adv. com. 1984-85), Assn. Art Mus. Dirs., Am. Assn. Mus. (S.E. regional rep. to non-print media com. 1983-85, nat. legis. com. 1986-93), Miss. Mus. Assn., Assn. Art Mus. Dirs., Southeastern Mus. Conf. (bd. dirs. 1991-92), Fla. Mus. Assn., Fla. Art Mus. Dirs. Assn., Cultural Roundtable (pres. 1993-95), Ohio Mus. Assn. (trustee 1993-98) Phi Beta Kappa. Avocations: photography, gardening, music, writing, sports, scuba diving. Home: 229 Volusia Ave Dayton OH 45409-2226 Office: Dayton Art Inst 456 Belmonte Park N Dayton OH 45405-4700 E-mail: anyerges@daytonartinstitute.org.

NYGAARD, LANCE COREY, nurse, data processing consultant; b. Casper, Wyo., June 21, 1952; s. Miles Adolph and Jenile Hansine (Mosman) N.; m. Susan Leigh Wilson, May 8, 1995; 1 child from previous marriage, Kari Melissa. AA in Nursing, U. S.D., 1980; BS in Chemistry, 1974; MLS, U. Ill., 1975. Libr. asst. Brookings Pub. Libr., S.D., 1971-75, asst. dir., 1975-77; emergency med. technician Brookings Hosp., 1976-78; sr. emergency med. technician Vermillion Ambulance, S.D., 1978-80; nurse McKennan Hosp., Sioux Falls, S.D., 1980-91, VA Hosp., 1991-96, Sioux Valley Hosp., 1996—, cardiovasc. data sys. coord., 1997—; owner operator Data Processing Svcs., Sioux Falls, 1983—; applications cons. Computer Dimensions, Sioux Falls, 1984-85. Fin. sec., mem. ch. coun. Holy Cross Luth. Ch., Sioux Falls, S.D., 1986-91, info. resources coord., 1991-92; troop leader Minn-Ia-Kota coun. Girl Scouts U.S., 1989—, region troop supr., 1991-95. Mem. Vermillion Chemistry Club (pres. 1973-74), Sioux Valley Rose Soc. (v.p. 1988-89, pres. 1989-90), Sons of Norway (guard 1976-77). Republican. Lutheran. Avocations: World War II military history, photography, amateur radio. Home: 3500 S Grace Cir Sioux Falls SD 57103-7226 Office: Sioux Valley Hosp 1100 S Euclid Ave Sioux Falls SD 57105-0496

NYHUS, LLOYD MILTON, surgeon, educator; b. Mt. Vernon, Wash., June 24, 1923; s. Lewis Guttorm and Mary (Shervem) N.; m. Margaret Goldie Sheldon, Nov. 25, 1949; children: Sheila Margaret, Leif Torger. BS, Pacific Luth. Coll., 1945; MD, Med. Coll. Ala., 1947; Doctor honoris causa, Aristotelian U., Thessalonika, Greece, 1968, Uppsala U., Sweden, 1974, U. Chihuahua, Mex., 1975, Jagallonian U., Cracow, Poland, 1980, U. Gama Filho, Rio de Janeiro, 1983, U. Louis Pasteur, Strasbourg, France, 1984, U. Athens, 1989. Diplomate Am. Bd. Surgery (chmn. 1974-76). Intern King County Hosp., Seattle, 1947-48, resident in surgery, 1948-55; practice medicine specializing in surgery Seattle, 1956-67, Chgo., 1967—; instr. surgery U. Wash., Seattle, 1954-56, asst. prof., 1956-59, assoc. prof., 1959-64, prof., 1964-67; Warren H. Cole prof., head dept. surgery U. Ill. Coll. Medicine, 1967-89, emeritus head, 1989—, prof. emeritus, 1993. Emeritus surgeon-in-chief U. Ill. Hosp.; sr. cons. surgeon Cook County, West Side VA, Hines (Ill.) VA hosps.; cons. to Surgeon Gen. NIH, 1965-69. Author: Surgery of the Stomach and Duodenum, 1962, 4th edit., 1986, named changed to Surgery of the Esophagus, Stomach and Small Intestine, 5th edit., 1995, Hernia, 1964, (book name change) Nyhus and Condon's Hernia, 5th edit., 2002, Abdominal Pain: A Guide to Rapid Diagnosis, 1969, 95, Spanish edit., 1996, Russian edit., 2001, Manual of Surgical Therapeutics, 1969, latest rev. edit., 1996, Mastery of Surgery, 1984, 3d edit., 1997, Spanish edit., 1999, Surgery Ann., 1970-95, Treatment of Shock, 1970, 2d rev. edit., 1986, Surgery of the Small Intestine, 1987; editor-in-chief Rev. of Surgery, 1967-77, Current Surgery, 1978-90, emeritus editor, 1991—; assoc. editor Quar. Rev. Surgery, 1958-61; editl. bd. Am. Jour. Digestive Diseases, 1961-67, Scandinavian Jour. Gastroenterology, 1966-97, Am. Surgeon, 1967-89, Jour. Surg. Oncology, 1969-99, Archives of Surgery, 1977-86, World Jour. Surgery, 1977-95; contbr. articles to profl. jours. Served to lt. M.C. USNR, 1943-46, 50-52. Decorated Order of Merit (Poland); postdoctoral fellow USPHS, 1952-53; recipient M. Shipley award So. Surg. Assn., 1967, Rovsing medal Danish Surg. Soc., 1973; Disting. Faculty award U. Ill Coll. Medicine, 1983, Disting. Alumnus award Med. Coll. Ala., 1984, Disting. Alumnus award U. Wash., 1993, 99; Guggenheim fellow, 1955-56. Fellow ACS (1st v.p. 1987-88), Assn. Surgeons Gt. Brit. and Ireland (hon.), Royal Coll. Surgeons Eng. (hon.), Royal Coll. Surgeons Ireland (hon.), Royal Coll. Surgeons Edinburgh (hon.), Royal Coll. Physicians and Surgeons Glasgow (hon.), Internat. Soc. Surgery Found. (hon., sec.-treas. 1992-2001); mem . Am. Gastroent. Assn., Am. Physiol. Soc., Pacific Coast Surg. Assn., Am. Surg. Assn. (recorder 1976-81, 1st v.p. 1989-90), Western Surg. Assn., Ctrl. Soc. Clin. Rsch., Chgo. Surg. Soc. (pres. 1974), Ctrl. Surg. Assn. (pres. 1984), Seattle Surg. Soc., St. Paul Surg. Soc. (hon.), Kansas City Surg. Soc. (hon.), Inst. Medicine Chgo., Internat. Soc. Surgery (hon. fellow 2001, pres. U.S. sect. 1986-88, pres. 34th World Congress 1991, internat. pres. 1991-93), Internat. Soc. for Digestive Surgery (pres. III world congress Chgo. 1974, internat. pres. 1978-84), Soc. for Surgery Alimentary Tract (sec. 1969-73, pres. 1974), Soc. Clin. Surgery, Soc. Surg. Chmn., Soc. U. Surgeons (pres. 1967), Duetschen Gesellschaft für Chirurgie (corr.), Polish Assn. Surgeons (hon.), L'Academie de Chirurgie (France) (corr.), Nat. Acad. of Medicine (France, Argentina and Brazil, hon.), Swiss Surg. Soc. (hon.), Brazilian Coll. Surgeons (hon.), Surg. Biology Club, Warren H. Cole Soc. (pres. 1981), Japan Surg. Soc. (hon.), Assn. Gen. Surgeons of Mex. (hon.), Columbian Surg. Soc. (hon.), Costa Rican Coll. Medicine & Surgery (hon.), Assn. Surgeons Costa Rica (hon.), Internat. Fedn. Surg. Colls. (hon. treas. 1992-99), Sigma Xi, Alpha Omega Alpha, Phi Beta Pi. Home: 310 Maple Row Winnetka IL 60093-1036 Office: U Ill Coll Medicine Dept Surgery MC 958 840 S Wood St Chicago IL 60612-7322

NYQUIST, KATHLEEN A. former publishing executive; b. Biloxi, Miss., May 14, 1955; d. Clarence and Marianne M. (Mahoney) Boehm; children: Lindsay, Eric. BS in Edn., Miami U., Oxford, Ohio, 1977. High sch. biology tchr., Ill., 1978-79; home tutor Fed. Homebound Program, 1980; from sci. editor to editorial v.p. Scott Foresman & Co., Glenview, 1981-89, creative dir., 1990, pub., 1992, pres., 1993-95; author, ednl. cons., 1996-2001. Parent rev. com. mem. Sch. Dist. 96, Buffalo Grove, Ill., 1991-92. Mem. ASCD, Nat. Coun. Tchrs. Math., Nat. Sci. Tchrs. Assn., Chgo. Book Clinic.

OAKAR, MARY ROSE, former congresswoman; b. Cleve., Mar. 5, 1940; d. Joseph M. and Margaret Mary (Ellison) O. BA in English, Speech and Drama, Ursuline Coll., Cleve., 1962, LHD (hon.); MA in Fine Arts, John Carroll U., Cleve., 1966; LLD (hon.), Ashland U., 1978, Ursuine Coll., 1984, St. Mary's Notre Dame, 1989, Baldwin Wallace Coll., 1988; LHD (hon.), Trinity Coll., 1987. Instr. English and drama Lourdes Acad., Cleve., 1963-70; asst. prof. English, speech and drama Cuyahoga Community Coll., 1968-75; mem. Cleve. City Council from 8th Ward, 1973-76, 95th-102nd Congresses from 20th Dist. Ohio, 1977-92; mem. Pepper Commn. on Long Term Health Care, chair subcom. internat. devel., fin., trade and monetary policy; chair task force on social security, elderly, women; chair subcom. on personnel and police; mem. banking, fin. and urban affairs com., select com. on aging, post office and civil service com., com. on house adminstrn., also numerous subcoms.; ptnr. Mary Rose Oakar and Assocs. Apptd. to Sec. Conf. to Establish Nat. Action Plan on Breast Cancer, 1994, by Pres. Clinton to bd. dirs. Bldrs., For Peace, 1994, to policy to White House Conf. on Aging. Founder, vol.-dir. Near West Side Civic Arts Center, Cleve., 1970; ward leader Cuyahoga County Democratic Party, 1972-76; mem. Ohio Dem. Central Com. from 20th Dist., 1974; trustee Fedn. Community Planning, Cleve., Health and Planning Commn. Cleve., Community Info. Service Cleve., Cleve. Soc. Crippled Children, Public Services Occupational Group Adv. Com., Cuyahoga Community Coll., Cleve. Ballet, Cleve. YWCA. Recipient Outstanding Service awards OEO, 1973-78, Community Service award Am. Indian Center, Cleve., 1973, Community Service award Nationalities Service Center, 1974, Community Service award Club San Lorenzo, Cleve., 1976, Cuyahoga County Dem. Woman of Yr., 1977, Ursuline Coll. Alumna of Yr. award, 1977, awards Irish Nat. Caucus, awards West Side Community Mental Health Center, awards Am. Lebanese League, awards Cleve. Fedn. Am.-Syrian Lebanese Clubs, Breast Cancer Awareness award Nat. Women's Health Resource Ctr., 1989, 1st lay recipient Barbara Bohen-Pfeiffer award Italian-Am. Found. Cancer Rsch., 1989, Disting. Svc. award Am. Cancer Soc., 1989, Myrl H. Shoemaker award Ohio Dem. Party, 1992, Philip Hart award Consumer Fedn. Am., 1987; cert. appreciation City of Cleve.; Woman of Yr. award Cuyahoga County Women's Polit. Caucus, 1983; decorated Knight of Order of St. Ladislaus of Hungary, Women in Aerospace Outstanding Ach. award, Black Focus Woman of the Decade award. Office: 1888 W 30th St Cleveland OH 44113-3447

OAKES, FRED D. editor; Editor Elks mag. The Elks of the USA, Chgo. Office: The Elks of the USA 425 W Diversey Pkwy Chicago IL 60614-6107

OAKES, LAURA, radio personality; Grad. Comms. and History, U. Minn.; postgrad., Brown Inst. With radio, Fergus Falls, Minn.; with radio and TV Duluth; news reporter, morning news anchor Sta. KDLH-TV; co-anchor 5 pm Sta. WCCO News Hour. Mem.: Minn. AP Broadcasters Assn. (bd. dirs.). Avocations: competitive figure skater, music, theater , sports. Office: WCCO 625 2nd Ave S Minneapolis MN 55402*

OAKES, ROBERT JAMES, physics educator; b. Mpls., Jan. 21, 1936; s. Sherman E. and Josephine J. (Olson) O.; children: Cindy L., Lisa A. B.S., U. Minn., 1957, M.S., 1959, Ph.D., 1962. NSF fellow Stanford U., 1962-64; asst. prof. physics, 1964-68; assoc. prof. physics Northwestern U., 1968-70, prof. physics, 1970-76, prof. physics and astronomy, 1976—. Vis. staff mem. Los Alamos Sci. Lab., 1971-92; vis. scientist Fermi Nat. Accelerator Lab., 1975—, CERN, 1966-67; mem. Inst. for Advanced Study, Princeton, 1967-68; vis. scientist DESY, 1971-72; faculty assoc. Argonne Nab. Lab., 1982— ; U.S. scientist NSF-Yugoslav joint program, 1982-92; panelist Nat. Rsch. Coun., 1990-98. A.P. Sloan fellow 1965-68; Air Force Office Sci. Rsch. grantee, 1969-71, NSF grantee 1971-87, Dept. Energy grantee, 1987—; named Fulbright-Hays Disting. prof. U. Sarajevo, Yugoslavia, 1979-80; recipient Natural Sci. prize China, 1993. Fellow Am.

Phys. Soc., AAAS; mem. N.Y. Acad. Sci., Ill. Acad. Sci., Physics Club (Chgo.), Sigma Xi, Tau Beta Pi. Club: Physics (Chgo.). Office: Northwestern U Dept Physics 2145 Sheridan Rd Evanston IL 60208-0834

OAKLEY, DEBORAH JANE, researcher, educator; b. Jan. 31, 1937; d. George F. and Kathryn (Willson) Hacker; m. Bruce Oakley, June 16, 1958; children: Ingrid Andrea, Brian Benjamin. BA, Swarthmore Coll., 1958; MA, Brown U., 1960; MPH, U. Mich., 1969, PhD, 1977. Dir. teenage and adult programs YWCA, Providence, 1959-63; editl. asst. Stockholm U., 1963-64; rsch. investigator, lectr. dept. population planning U. Mich., 1971-77, asst. prof. cmty. health programs, 1977-79, asst. prof. nursing rsch., 1979-81, assoc. prof., 1981-89, prof., 1989—, interim dir. Ctr. Nursing Rsch., 1988-90, acting dir. Ctr. Nursing Rsch., 1998. Vis. prof. Beijing Med. U., 1996—; prin. investigator NIH, CDC and pvt. found. funded rsch. grants and contracts on family planning, women's health and health care in China, mem. nat. adv. com. nursing rsch., 1993-97; mem. adv. workshop on Nat. Survey on Family Growth, 1994-97; co-chair Mich. Initiative for Women's Health, 1993-95. Author: (with Leslie Corsa) Population Planning, 1979; contbr. articles to profl. jours. Bd. dirs. Planned Parenthood Fedn. Am., 1975-80. Recipient Margaret Sanger award Washtenaw County Planned Parenthood, 1975, Outstanding Young Woman of Ann Arbor award Jaycees, 1970, Dist. Faculty award Mich. Assn. Gov. Bds., 1992, Blue Cross Blue Shield Found. of Mich. award for Excellence in Health Policy, 1996. Mem. APHA (chmn. population sect. coun.), Internat. Union Sci. Study Population, Midwest Nursing Rsch. Soc., Population Assn. Am., Delta Omega, Sigma Theta Tau (hon.). Democrat. Home: 5200 S Lake Dr Chelsea MI 48118-9481 Office: U Mich Sch Nursing Ann Arbor MI 48109-0482

OAKLEY, ROBERT ALAN, insurance executive; b. Columbus, Ohio, Nov. 1, 1946; s. Bernard Harmon and Mary Evelyn (Mosier) O.; m. Ann Lucille Liesenhoff, Aug. 3, 1968; children: Jeff, David. BS in Aero. Engring., Purdue U., 1968; MBA, Ohio State U., 1969, PhD in Fin., 1973. Mgr. fin. projects Nationwide Mut. Ins. Co., Columbus, 1976-79, regional controller, 1979-82, dir. ops. controls, 1982-83, v.p., corp. controller, 1983—, exec. v.p., CFO, 1993—. Author: Insurance Informations Systems, 1985. Capt. USAF, 1972-76. Mem. Fin. Mgmt. Assn., Fin. Execs. Inst., Am. Soc. CLU's. Avocations: golf, reading, teaching. Office: Nationwide One Nationwide Plz Columbus OH 43215-2220

OATES, JAMES G. advertising executive; b. Kenton, Ohio, Apr. 2, 1943; m. Sue Ann Minter; 2 children. BS, Ohio State U. Trainee Leo Burnett USA, Chgo., 1966-68, asst. acct. exec., 1968-69, acct. exec., 1969-73, acct. supv., 1973-74, v.p., 1974-77, acct. supv. GM Olds acct., 1977-80, mgmt. dir. Philip Morris account, 1980-84, sr. v.p., 1984-86, exec. v.p., 1986-90, vice chmn., dir. client svcs., 1990-92, bd. dirs., mem. exec. com., 1992—, group pres. Asia/Pacific, 1993-97; pres. Leo Burnett Co., 1997-2000, exec. cons., 2000—. Bd. dirs. The Advt. Coun. Mem. MBA adv. bd. Ohio State U.; Kellogg Adv. Bd.; active Chgo. Crime Commn. Mem. Am. Assn. Advt. Agys. (bd. govs. Chgo. chpt.). Office: Leo Burnett Co Inc 35 W Wacker Dr Chicago IL 60601-1648

OBAMA, BARACK A. state legislator; b. Hawaii, Aug. 4, 1961; m. Michelle. B, Columbia U., 1983; JD, Harvard U., 1991. Mem. Ill. Senate, Springfield, 1997—, mem. judiciary, pub. health & welfare coms. Chair Chto. Annebery Challenge; bd. dirs. Woods Fund Chgo. Recipient 40 Under 40 award Crains Chgo. Bus., 1993. Democrat. Office: State Capitol Capitol Bldg 105B Springfield IL 62706-0001 also: 1741 E 11th St Chicago IL 60649

O'BANNON, FRANK LEWIS, governor, lawyer; b. Louisville, Jan. 30, 1930; s. Robert Pressley and Rosella Faith (Dropsey) O'B.; m. Judith Mae Asmus, Aug. 18, 1957; children: Polly, Jennifer, Jonathan. AB, Ind. U., 1952, JD, 1957. Ind. 1957. Pvt. practice, Corydon; ptnr. Hays, O'Bannon & Funk, 1966-80, O'Bannon, Funk & Simpson, Corydon, 1980-88; mem. Ind. Senate, 1970-89, minority floor leader, 1979-89, asst. minority floor leader, 1972-76; lt. gov. State of Ind., 1989-97, gov., 1997—. Chmn., dir. O'Bannon Pub. Co., Inc.; chair Dem. Gov.'s Assn., 1999. Served with USAF, 1952-54. Mem. Ind. Dem. Editorial Assn. (pres. 1961), Am. Judicature Soc., Am. Bar Assn., Ind. Bar Assn. Democrat. Methodist. Office: Office of the Gov State Capitol Rm 206 Indianapolis IN 46204*

OBATA, GYO, architect; b. San Francisco, Feb. 28, 1923; s. Chiura and Haruko (Kohaski) O.; m. Majel Chance, 1947 (div. 1971); children: Kiku, Nori, Gen; m. Courtney Bean, Nov. 28, 1984; 1 child, Max. BArch, Washington U., St. Louis, 1945; MArch in Urban Design, Cranbrook Acad. Art, 1946. Registered architect 39 states, D.C. Sr. designer Skidmore, Owings, & Merrill, Chgo., 1947-51; designer Hellmuth, Yamasaki & Leinweber, Detroit, 1951-55; pres., chmn. bd. dirs. Hellmuth, Obata & Kassabaum, Inc., St. Louis, 1955-93. Affiliate prof. Washington U., 1971; frequent lectr. design and urban environment; serves on competition juries on design throughout country. Projects include Nat. Air and Space Mus., King Saud U., Riyadh, Saudi Arabia, Dalls and Houston Gallerias, King Khaled Airport, Riyadh, hdqrs. Kellogg Co., hdqrs. BP America, World Bank, Washington, St. Louis Union Sta., Met. Sq., Dallas-Ft. Worth Airport, Squibb Corp. Rsch. Ctr., Lawrenceville, N.J., Burger King Corp. Hdqrs., numerous others. Fellow AIA; mem. Log Cabin Club, Noonday Club, St. Louis Club. Avocations: skiing, tennis. Office: Hellmuth Obata & Kassabaum Inc 211 N Broadway # 600 Saint Louis MO 63102-2733

OBENBERGER, THOMAS E. lawyer; b. Milwaukee, Wis., Nov. 29, 1942; AB, Marquette U., 1965, JD, 1967. Bar: Wis. 1967. Law clk. to Hon. E. Harold Hallows Wis. Supreme Ct., 1967-68; ptnr. Michael, Best & Friedrich, Milw., 1968—. Mem. editorial bd. Marquette Law Rev., 1966-67. Mem. ABA. Office: Michael Best & Friedrich 100 E Wisconsin Ave #3300 Milwaukee WI 53202-4108

OBERHELMAN, DOUGLAS R. tractor company executive; CFO Caterpillar Inc., Peoria, Ill., v.p., dir. engine products divsn. Office: Caterpillar Inc 100 NE Adams St Peoria IL 61629-0002

OBERMAN, SHELDON ARNOLD, writer, educator; b. Winnipeg, Man., Can., May 20, 1949; s. Allan and Dorothy Oberman; m. Lee Anne Block, Sept. 8, 1973 (div. Mar. 9, 1990); children: Adam, Mira; m. Lisa Ann Dveris, Sept. 2, 1990; 1 child: Jesse. BA in English, U. Winnipeg, 1972; BA in English with honors, U. Jerusalem, Israel, 1973; teaching cert., U. Man., 1974. Tchr. W. C. Millar Collegiate, Altona, Man., Can., 1975-76, Joseph Wolinsky Collegiate, Winnipeg, Man., Can., 1976-95. Author: The Folk Festival Book, 1983, Lion in the Lake: A French English Alphabet Book, 1988, Julie Gerond and the Polka Dot Pony, 1988, TV Sal and the Game Show From Outer Space, 1993, This Business With Elijah, 1993, The Always Prayer Shawl, 1994, The White Stone in the Castle Wall, 1995, By the Hannukah Light, 1997, The Shaman's Nephew: A Life in the Far North, 1999, The Wisdom Bird: A Tale of Solomon and Sheba, 2000; co-editor: A Mirror of a People: The Canadian Jewish Experience in Poetry and Prose, 1985 (Sydney Taylor honor 2000, McNalley Robinson Book award 2001) Recipient Parents Choice Silver Honour, 1999, Norma Fleck award for children's non fiction, 1999, Parents Coun. Outstanding Book, 1999, Nat. Jewish Book award Jewish Book Coun., 1995, Sydney Taylor award, 1995, Best Book of the Yr. A Child's Mag., 1994, Pick of the List award Am. Bookseller, 1994, Can. Author Short Story award Canadian Author's Assn., 1987, Bliss Carmen Poetry prize Banff Sch. of Fine Arts, 1980; various writer and film maker grants. Avocations: public address, acting, collage sculptor, canoing. Home: 822 Dorchester Ave Winnipeg MB Canada R3M 0R7 E-mail: sobermon@mts.net.

O'BERRY, PHILLIP AARON, veterinarian; b. Tampa, Fla., Feb. 1, 1933; s. Luther Lee and Marjorie Mae (Mahlum) O'B.; m. Terri Martin, July 31, 1960; children: Kelly, Eric, Holly, Danny, Andy, Toby, Michael Asefa. BS in Agr., U. Fla., 1955; DVM, Auburn U., 1960; PhD, Iowa State U., 1967. With Agrl. Rsch. Svc. USDA, 1956—, asst. to dir. vet. scis. rsch. div. Md., 1967-72; asst. dir. Nat. Animal Disease Ctr., Ames, Iowa, 1972-73, dir., 1973-88, nat. tech. transfer coord., 1988—; prin. scientist Office Agr. Biotech., USDA, 1988-90. Adj. prof. Coll. Vet. Medicine, Iowa State U., 1973—; mem. expert panel livestock infertility FAO; sci. adv. com. Pan Am. Zoonosis Ctr., Buenos Aires; mem. Fed. Coun. Sci. and Tech.; mem. com. animal health, world food and nutrition study NRC; cons. Govt. of Italy, Govt. of Mex., USDA; mem. nat needs grad. fellowship rev. panel USDA, 1989-91, cons. agr. biotech. rsch. adv. com.; mem. sci. adv. bd. Biotech. R&D Corp., 1992-2001, sci. review bd. Am. Jour. Vet. Rsch., 1990-92; mem. USDA Patent Review Com., 1988—. Author 27 rsch. publs. Recipient Cert. of Merit, Agrl. Rsch. Svc., 1972, 84, Alumni Merit award Iowa State Club of Chgo., 1982, Cert. Appreciation, 1988, Tech. Transfer award 1989, USDA Disting. Alumnus award Auburn U., 1991; named Hon. Diplomate Am. Coll. of Vet. Microbiologists, 1995, Ames Citizen of the Yr., 2000, Iowa Gov.'s Vol. award, 2001. Mem. APHA, AVMA, AAAS, Nat. Assn. Fed. Vets., Iowa Vet. Med. Assn., N.Y. Acad. Scis., Conf. Rsch. Workers Animal Diseases, Am. Soc. Microbiology, Am. Assn. Lab. Animal Sci., U.S. Animal Health Assn., Am. Assn. Bovine Practitioners, Livestock Cons. Inst., Sigma Xi, Phi Zeta, Phi Kappa Phi, Gamma Sigma Delta (Alumni award Merit 1976), Alpha Zeta, Spades, Blue Key. Democrat. Home: 3319 Woodland St Ames IA 50014-3550 Office: Nat Soil Tilth Lab Rm 114 Ames IA 50011-0001 E-mail: usdaott@iastate.edu.

OBERSTAR, JAMES L. congressman; b. Chisholm, Minn., Sept. 10, 1934; s. Louis and Mary (Grillo) O.; m. Jo Garlick, Oct. 12, 1963 (dec. July 1991); children: Thomas Edward, Katherine Noelle, Anne-Therese, Monica Rose; m. Jean Kurth, Nov. 1993; stepchildren: Corinne Quinlan Kurth, Charles Burke Kurth, Jr. B.A. summa cum laude, St. Thomas Coll., 1956; postgrad. in French, Laval U., Que., Can.; M.S. in Govt. (scholar), Coll. Europe, Bruges, Belgium, 1957; postgrad. in govt, Georgetown U. Adminstrv. asst. Congressman John A. Blatnik, 1963-74; adminstr. Pub. Works Com. U.S. Ho. of Reps., 1971-74; mem. 94th-106th Congresses from 8th Minn. Dist., 1975—, ranking minority mem. transp. and infrastructure com. Mem. Am. Polit. Sci. Assn. Office: US Ho of Reps 2365 Rayburn Hob Washington DC 20515-2308*

OBERT, CHARLES FRANK, retired banker; b. Cleve., Apr. 28, 1937; s. Carl William and Irene Frances (Urban) O.; m. Linda Marie Thoss, June 3, 1961; children— Lisa Marie, Charles David. Student, Ohio State U., 1955-57. With Ameritrust Corp., Cleve., 1958-92, sr. v.p. affiliate bank div., 1975-80, sr. v.p. corp. service div., 1980-87, sr. v.p. br. adminstrn., 1987-92, mgmt. cons., 1993-2000; ret. Acoustical Cleaning Systems Inc., 2000, pres. Mem. Solon (Ohio) Recreation Commn., 1978-94, Solon Bd. Edn., 1986-94. Mem. Am. Inst. Banking, Am. Bankers Assn., Ohio Bankers Assn., Bank Adminstrn. Inst., Internat. Assn. Laryngectomees, Cleve. Hearing and Speech Ctr., Greater Cleve. Growth Assn., Solon C. of C. Home and Office: 8270 Pebble Creek Ct Chagrin Falls OH 44023-4866

OBERT, PAUL RICHARD, manufacturing executive; b. Pitts. s. Edgar F. and Elizabeth T. Obert. B.S., Georgetown U., 1950; J.D., U. Pitts., 1953. Bar: Pa. 1954, D.C. 1956, Ohio 1972, Ill. 1974, U.S. Supreme Ct. 1970. Sole practice, Pitts., 1954-60; asst. counsel H.K. Porter Co., Inc., 1960-62, sec., gen. counsel, 1962-71, Addressograph-Multigraph Corp., Cleve., 1972-74; v.p. law Marshall Field & Co., Chgo., 1974-82, sec., 1976-82; v.p., gen. counsel, sec. CF Industries, Inc., Long Grove, 1982—, also officer, dir. various subs. Served to lt. col. USAF. Mem. ABA (corp. gen. counsel com.), Pa. Bar Assn., Allegheny County Bar Assn., Ill. Bar Assn., Chgo. Bar Assn., Am. Soc. Corp. Secs., Am. Retail Fedn. (bd. dirs. 1977-80), Georgetown U. Alumni Assn. (bd. govs.), Pitts. Athletic Assn., Univ. Club (Chgo.), Delta Theta Phi. Office: CF Industries Inc 1 Salem Lake Dr Long Grove IL 60047-8401

OBEY, DAVID ROSS, congressman; b. Okmulgee, Okla., Oct. 3, 1938; s. Orville John and Mary Jane (Chellis) O.; m. Joan Therese Lepinski, June 9, 1962; children: Craig David, Douglas David. BS in Polit. Sci, U. Wis., 1960, MA, 1962. Mem. Wis. Gen. Assembly, 1963-69, asst. minority leader, 1967-69; mem. U.S. Congress from 7th Wis. dist., 1969—; ranking minority mem. appropriations com. Mem. adminstrv. com. Wis. Dem. Com., 1960-62 Named Edn. Legislator of Yr., Rural div. NEA, 1968; recipient Legislative Leadership award Eagelton Inst. Politics, 1964, award of merit Nat. Council Sr. Citizens, 1976, citation for legis. statesmanship Council Exceptional Children, 1976. Office: US Ho of Reps 2314 Rayburn HOB Washington DC 20515-4907*

O'BLOCK, ROBERT, entrepreneur, publishing executive; BS in Sociology, Pittsburg (Kans.) State U., 1972, MS in Sociology, 1973, EdS, 2001; PhD, Kans. State U., 1976; MA in Psychology, Newport U., 1998, PsyD in Psychology, 2000; MDiv, Trinity Coll., 2001, DMin, 2002. Ordained deacon So. Episcopal Ch., 1999; ordained priest Anglican Cath. Ch., 2002. Patrolman Frontenac (Kans.) Police Dept., 1971-73; probation officer Crawford County Juvenile Ct., 1973-74; spr. Children's Ct. Ctr., 1974; adminstrv. asst. to dean student affairs/cmty. svc. Labette Cmty. Jr. Coll., 1976; dir. night sch. Marymount Coll., 1976; asst. prof. dept. adminstrv. justice Wichita State U., 1977-79; assoc. prof. dept. criminal justice/polit. sci. Appalachian State U., Boone, N.C., 1979-89; prof., chair dept. adminstrn. of justice Coll. of Ozarks, Point Lookout, Mo., 1989-93; exec. dir. Am. Coll. Forensic Examiners, Springfield, 1994—. Founder Am. Bd. Forensic Medicine, Am. Bd. Forensic Examiners, Am. Bd. Forensic Psychol. Specializations, Am. Bd. Forensic Dentistry, Am. Bd. Forensic Engring. and Tech., Am. Bd. Forensic Nursing, Am. Bd. Law Enforcement Experts, Am. Bd. Forensic Acctg., Am. Bd. of Forensic Counselors, Am. Bd. Forensic Social Work; lectr., cons. in field. Author: Criminal Justice Research Sources, 1983, 3d edit., 1992, (with others) Security and Crime Prevention, 2d edit., 1990; founder, pub. The Forensic Examiner, Annals of the Am. Psychotherapy Assn., co-founder E Bus. Techs., contbr. articles to profl. jours., holder 14 U.S. fed. trademarks. Adv. bd. Larnard State Hosp. Grantee Gov.'s Com. on Criminal Adminstrn., 1976-77, 77, others. Mem.: APA, Am. Assn. Integrative Medicine (co-founder, CEO), Am. Coll. Forensic Examiners (founder), Am. Psychotherapy Assn. (founder, chmn., CEO). Home: 1646 S Cobblestone Ct Springfield MO 65809-2314 Office: 2750 E Sunshine St Springfield MO 65804-2047 E-mail: rloblock@aol.com.

O'BRIEN, DANIEL WILLIAM, lumber company executive; b. St. Paul, Jan. 6, 1926; s. Daniel W. and Kathryn (Zenk) O'B.; m. Sarah Ward Stoltze, June 20, 1952; children: Bridget Ann, Daniel William, Kevin Charles, Timothy John. Student, U. Dubuque, 1943, Ill. State U., 1944; BSL, U. Minn., 1948, JD, 1949. Bar: Minn. 1949. Practice in, St. Paul, 1950—; partner Randall, Smith & Blomquist, 1955-65; of counsel Doherty, Rumble & Butler, 1965-99; pres. F.H. Stoltze Land & Lumber Co., 1964—, Maple Island, Inc., 1968—. Served to ensign USNR, 1943-46. Mem. Minn., Ramsey County bar assns., World Pres's. Orgn., Chief Execs. Orgn. Office: 2497 7th Ave E Ste 105 North Saint Paul MN 55109-2902 Home: 3951 S Placita De La Moneda Green Valley AZ 85614-5063 E-mail: dwobrien@maple-island.com.

O'BRIEN, DONALD EUGENE, federal judge; b. Marcus, Iowa, Sept. 30, 1923; s. Michael John and Myrtle A. (Toomey) O'B.; m. Ruth Mahon, Apr. 15, 1950; children: Teresa, Brien, John, Shuivaun. LL.B., Creighton U., 1948. Bar: Iowa bar 1948, U.S. Supreme Ct. bar 1963. Asst. city atty., Sioux City, Iowa, 1949—54; county atty. Woodbury County, 1955—59; mcpl. judge Sioux City, 1959-60; U.S. atty. No. Iowa, 1961-67; pvt. practice law Sioux City, 1948—61; U.S. Dist. judge, 1978—; chief judge U.S. Dist. Ct. (no. dist.) Iowa, 1985-92, sr. judge, 1992—; pvt. practice law, 1967—78. Rep. 8th cir. dist. ct. judges to Jud. Conf. U.S., 1990-97. Served with USAAF, 1942-45. Decorated D.F.C., air medals. Mem. Woodbury County Bar Assn., Iowa State Bar Assn. Roman Catholic. E-mail: Dan_O'Brien@iand.uscourts.gov. Office: US Dist Ct PO Box 267 Sioux City IA 51102-0267 E-mail: Don_O'Brian@iand.uscourts.gov.

O'BRIEN, JAMES ALOYSIUS, foreign language educator; b. Cin., Apr. 7, 1936; s. James Aloysius and Frieda (Schirmer) O'B.; m. Rumi Matsumoto, Aug. 26,1961. B.A., St. Joseph's Coll., 1958; M.A., U. Cin., 1960; Ph.D., Ind. U., 1969. Instr. English, St. Joseph's Coll., Rensselaer, Ind., 1960-62; asst. prof. Japanese, U. Wis., Madison, 1968-74, assoc. prof., 1974-81, prof., 1981—, chmn. East Asian langs and lit., 1979-80, 82-85, 96—. Author: Dazai Osamu, 1975, Akutagawa and Dazai: Instances of Literary Adaptation, 1988; translator: Selected Stories and Sketches (Dazai Osamu), 1983, Three Works (Muro Saisei), 1985, Crackling Mountain and Other Stories (Dazal Osamu), 1989. Mem. MIddleton City Common Coun., 1996—. Ford Found fellow, 1965-66; Fulbright-Hays and NDEA fellow, 1966-68; Social Sci. Research Council fellow, 1973-74; Japan Found. fellow, 1977-78 Mem. Assn. Asian Studies, Assn. Tchrs. of Japanese (exec. com. 1981-84, dir. devel. 1981-83, pres. 1984-90) Home: 2533 Branch St Middleton WI 53562-2812 Office: U Wis Dept East Asian Langs-Lit 1220 Linden Dr Madison WI 53706-1525

O'BRIEN, JAMES PHILLIP, lawyer; b. Monmouth, Ill., Jan. 6, 1949; s. John Matthew and Roberta Helen (Cavanaugh) O'B.; m. Laurene Reason, Aug. 30, 1969 (div. 1980); m. Lynn Florsheim, Sept. 5, 1987. BA, Western Ill. U., 1971; JD, U. Ill., 1974. Bar: Ill. 1974. Asst. atty. gen. State Ill., Springfield, 1974-75; jud. clerk Ill. Appellate Ct., 1975-76; assoc. Graham & Graham, 1976-81; corp. counsel Am. Hosp. Assn., Chgo., 1981-84; ptnr., chmn. health care dept. Katten, Muchin & Zavis, 1984—. Task force med. malpractice reform legislation Am. Hosp. Assn., 1983-84, tax adv. com., 1987-91, tax reporting and compliance com., 1990-91; spkr. in field. Contbr. numerous articles to profl. jours. Recipient cert. recognition Ill. Dept. Children and Family Svcs., 1981; Edward Arthur Mellinger Found. scholar, Western Ill. U. 1971. Mem.: Am. Arbitration Assn. (Task Force Health Care Dispute Resolution 1982—84), Am. Health Lawyers Assn. Office: Katten Muchin & Zavis 525 W Monroe St Ste 1600 Chicago IL 60661-3693

O'BRIEN, JOHN FEIGHAN, investment banker; b. Cleve., Aug. 8, 1936; s. Francis John and Ann (Feighan) O'B.; m. Regina Quaid Harahan, June 27, 1959 (div. 1976); children: Regina, Victoria, Julie, John Jr.; m. Marilyn E. Schreiner. BS, Georgetown U., 1958. Salesman Appliance Mart, Cleve., 1958-59, ptnr., 1960-66; investment broker McDonald & Co. Investments, 1966-71, ptnr., 1971-83, exec. v.p., 1983-88, mng. dir., 1988-91, sr. mng. dir., 1993—. Bd. dirs. Hitchcock House, Cleve., 1978-89, Recovery Resources; chmn. Alcoholism Svcs. of Cleve., 1989-92, Alcohol and Drug-Addiction Svcs. Bd. of Cuyahoga County, 1992-98; trustee St. Edward H.S., Lakewood, Ohio, Alumnus of Yr., 1997,chmn. capital campaign, 1993-95; grand jury foreman Cuyahoga County, 2000. Named Good Fellow of Yr. Irish Good Fellows Club Cleve., 1996. Mem. Leadership Cleve., Greater Cleve. Growth Assn., Georgetown U. Alumni Assn. (alumni bd. senator, John Carrol award 1999), Westwood Country Club, Cleve. Yacht Club. Home: 8 Westhampton Dr Rocky River OH 44116-2300 also: 1800 S Ocean Dr Fort Lauderdale FL 33316-3704 Office: McDonald & Co Investments 18500 Lake Rd Ste 300 Rocky River OH 44116-1744 E-mail: jfeighanob@aol.com.

O'BRIEN, MARK J. real estate/residential construction executive; With Pulte Constrn., Bloomfield Hills, Mich., 1982—, pres. Pulte Homes West Fla. divsn., pres. Pulte Fla. region, pres. Pulte Home East, COO, 1997—. Office: Pulte Corp Ste 200 33 Bloomfield Hills Pkwy Bloomfield Hills MI 48304

O'BRIEN, NANCY LYNN, banker; b. Norfolk, Nebr., Sept. 6, 1951; d. Robert Sammie and Betty Ann (Petersen) Auten; m. Leo E. O'Brien, Aug. 3, 1984. B.S.E., U. Nebr.-Lincoln, 1972, M.A., U. Nebr.-Omaha, 1975, Ph.D., U. Nebr.-Lincoln, 1979. Tchr. spl. edn. Omaha Pub. Schs., 1973-79; devel. studies specialist Metro Tech. Community Coll., Omaha, 1979-80; coordinator personnel devel., 1980-81; mgr. tng. Omaha Nat. Bank, 1981-84, mgr. employment and tng., 1984— ; area rep/travel cons. Am. Leadership Study Groups, Worcester, Mass., 1977— ; grant mgr. Council for Exceptional Children, 1978; adj. faculty Coll. St. Mary's, Omaha, 1983— . Active United Way, Omaha; pres. Child Abuse Council, Omaha, 1982-83; pres. Council for Exceptional Children, 1981. Council for Exceptional Children, grantee, 1978. Mem. Am. Soc. Tng. and Devel. (dir.). Democrat. Lutheran. Home: 22627 Wilson Ave Waterloo NE 68069-9797

O'BRIEN, NANCY PATRICIA, librarian, educator; b. Galesburg, Ill., Mar. 17, 1955; d. Leo Frederick O'Brien and Yvonne Blanche (Uhlmann) O'Brien Tabb; 1 child, Nicole Pamela. AB in English, U. Ill., 1976, MS in LS, 1977. Vis. instr. U. Ill., Urbana, 1977-78, asst. prof. libr. adminstrn., 1978-84, assoc. prof., 1984-91, prof., 1991—, serials bibliographer, 1977-78, social sci. bibliographer collection devel. div., 1979-81, project dir. Title II-C grant, 1987-88, acting libr. and info. sci. libr., 1989-90, head Edn. and Social Sci. Libr., 1994—, coord. social scis. divsn., 1996—, edn. subject specialist, 1981—. Discussion leader Ill. White House Conf. on Libr. and Info. svcs., 1990; mem. nat. adv. bd. Office Ednl. Rsch. and Improvement, U.S. Dept. Edn., 1989-91; grant proposal reviewer NEH, 1991; mem. adv. bd. Ctr. for Children's Books, 1992-97; cons. Ark. Coll., 1989; chmn. rev. team Instrnl. Materials Ctr., U. Wis., Madison, 1989; chair exec. com. Nat. Edn. Network Nat. Libr. Edn. U.S. Dept. Edn., 1998—2001; presenter in field. Author: Test Construction: A Bibliography of Resources, 1988, (with Emily Fabiano) Core List of Books and Journals in Education, 1991; Education: A Guide to Reference and Information Sources, 2d edit., 2000; co-editor Media/Microforms column Series Rev., 1979-82; mem. editl. bd. Bull. Bibliography, 1982-90; asst. editor Libr. Hi Tech., 1983-85; editor EBSS Newsletter, 1990-91; contbr. articles to profl. jours., chpts. to books. Mem. ALA (Whitney-Carnegie grantee 1990-91), Am. Ednl. Rsch. Assn. (spl. interest group on libr. resources and info. tech.), Assn. Coll. and Rsch. Librs. (access policy guidelines task force 1990-95, vice chmn., chmn.-elect edn. and behavioral scis. sect. 1993-94, chmn. 1994-95, acad. status com. 1996—2000, Disting. Edn. and Behavioral Scis. Libr. 1997), Libr. Adminstrn. and Mgmt. Assn. (edn. and tng. com. pub. rels. sect. 1990-95), Resources and Tech. Svcs. Divsn.(micropub. com. 1982-85, chmn. 1983-85, cons. 1985-87). Office: U Ill Edn & Social Sci Libr 100 Main Libr 1408 W Gregory Dr Urbana IL 61801-3607 E-mail: n-obrien@uiuc.edu.

O'BRIEN, PATRICK WILLIAM, lawyer; b. Chgo., Dec. 5, 1927; s. Maurice Edward and Ellen (Fitzgerald) O'B.; m. Deborah Bissell, July 2, 1955; children: Kathleen, Mariellen, Patrick, James, Patricia. BS in Mech. Engring., Northwestern U., 1947, JD, 1950. Bar: Ill. 1951, U.S. Dist. Ct. (no. dist.) Ill. 1954, U.S. Dist. Ct. (so. dist.)Ill. 1956, U.S. Ct. Appeals (7th cir.) 1955, U.S. Ct. Appeals (8th cir.) 1972, U.S. Supreme Ct. 1970. Assoc. Bell, Boyd, Marshall & Lloyd, Chgo., 1950—51, Mayer, Brown, Rowe & Maw, Chgo., 1953—62, ptnr., 1962—94, sr. counsel, 1995—. Served to capt. USAF, 1951-53. Fellow Am. Coll. Trial Lawyers; mem. ABA, Ill. Bar Assn., Chgo. Bar Assn. Republican. Roman Catholic. Clubs: Chgo.,

Mid-Day, University, Westmoreland Country, Cliff Dwellers, Dairymen's Country. Office: Mayer Brown Rowe & Maw 190 S La Salle St Ste 3100 Chicago IL 60603-3441 Home: 2606 Park Pl Evanston IL 60201-1318

O'BRIEN, RICHARD L(EE), medical educator, academic administrator, physician, cell biologist; b. Shenandoah, Iowa, Aug. 30, 1934; s. Thomas Lee O'B. and Grace Ellen (Sims) Parish; m. Joan Frances Gurney, June 29, 1957; children: Sheila Marie, Kathleen Therese, Michael James, Patrick Kevin. MS in Physiology, Creighton U., 1958, MD, 1960. Diplomate: Nat. Bd. Med. Examiners. Intern and resident Columbia med. div. Bellevue Hosp., N.Y.C., 1960-62; postdoctoral fellow in biochemistry Inst. for Enzyme Research, U. Wis., 1962-64; asst. prof. to prof. pathology Sch. Medicine, U. So. Calif., L.A., 1966-82, dep. dir. Cancer Ctr., 1975-80, dir. rsch. and edn. Cancer Ctr., 1980-81, dir. Cancer Ctr., 1981-82; dean Sch. Medicine Creighton U., Omaha, 1982-92, acting v.p. health scis., 1984-85, v.p. health scis., 1985-99. Vis. prof. molecular biology U. Geneva, 1973-74; cons. in field; mem. cancer control research grants rev. com. NIH, Nat. Cancer Inst.; mem. Cancer Ctr. Support grant rev. com. Nat. Cancer Inst., 1984-88, chmn. 1987-88; co-chmn. United Way/CHAD Pacesetter campaign, 1988, 94. Contbr. articles; editor various profl. jours. Served to capt. U.S. Army, 1964-66. Spl. fellow Nat. Cancer Inst., 1967-69; Combined Health Agys. Drive—Health Citizen of Yr., 1986. Mem. ACP, Am. Assn. Pathologists, Am. Assn. Cancer Rsch., Am. Assn. Cancer Edn., AAAS, Am. Assn. Cancer Insts. (dir. 1982-83), Assn. Am. Med. Colls. (chmn. MCAT evaluation panel 1987-88, liaison com. on med. edn., 1988-93, co-chmn. 1989-93, adv. panel Strategic Planning Health Care Reform 1992-96), Assn. Acad. Health Ctrs. (long-range planning com. 1986, 2000, nominating com. 1987, 96, Task Force Health Care Delivery 1992, mem. task force on leadership and instl. values 1993-99, bd. dirs. 1998-99), Am. Cancer Soc. (adv. com. Inst. rsch. Grants 1977-80, Outstanding Leadership award, dir. Calif. div. 1980-82, dir. Nebr. divsn. 1992-96), Am. Hosp. Assn. (com. on med. edn. 1986-89), Alpha Omega Alpha. Home: 9927 Essex Dr Omaha NE 68114-3873 Office: Creighton Univ California At 24th Omaha NE 68178-0001 E-mail: rlo@creighton.edu.

O'BRIEN, RONALD JOSEPH, lawyer; b. Columbus, Ohio, Nov. 7, 1948; BA, Ohio Dominican Coll., 1970; JD, Ohio State U., 1974. Bar: Ohio 1974, U.S. Dist. Ct. (so. dist.) Ohio 1974, U.S. Supreme Ct. 1978, U.S. Ct. Appeals (6th cir.) 1982. Asst. prosecutor Franklin County, Columbus, 1974-77; chief prosecutor City of Columbus, 1978-85, city atty., 1986-96; pros. atty. Franklin County, Columbus, 1996—. Mem. Ohio Bar Assn., Columbus Bar Assn., Nat. Dist. Atty. Assn. Republican. Roman Catholic. Home: 543 Yaronia Dr N Columbus OH 43214-3137 Office: Hall of Justice 369 S High St Columbus OH 43215-4516

O'BRIEN, WILLIAM J., III, lawyer; BS, Holy Cross Coll., 1965; LLB, Yale U., 1969. Bar: N.Y. 1970, Mich. 1985. With Hughes Hubbard and Reed, N.Y.C. and Paris, 1969-75; asst. gen. counsel Chrysler Corp., Highland Park, 1983, assoc. gen. counsel, 1984, dep. gen. counsel, 1986, v.p., gen. counsel, sec., 1987; sr. v.p., gen. counsel DaimlerChrysler AG, 1998, 2001—. Office: DaimlerChrysler Corp CIMS 485-14-96 1000 Chrysler Dr Auburn Hills MI 48326-2766

O'BRIEN, WILLIAM JOHN, ecology researcher; b. Summit, N.J., Nov. 30, 1942; m. Mavion Meier, 1964; children: Connor, Shay, Lia BA, Gettysburg Coll., 1965; postgrad., Cornell U., 1965-69; PhD, Mich. State U., 1970. sch. rsch. assoc. Ctr. Northern Studies, 1977; disting. lectr. Kans. Acad. Sci., 1990. From asst. prof. to prof. aquatic ecology U. Kans., Lawrence, 1971—2000, full prof., 1982—, dir. exptl. and applied ecology program, 1994—99, chair dept. sys. and ecology, 1991—96. Rsch. scientist Ecosys. Ctr. Marine Biol. Lab., 1986—. Grantee NSF, 1975—. Mem.: Internat. Assn. Theoretical and Applied Limnology, Am. Fisheries Soc., Am. Soc. Limnology and Oceanography. Office: U NC Dept Biol 310 Eberhart Bldg Greensboro NC 27402

O'BRIEN, WILLIAM JOSEPH, materials engineer, educator, consultant; b. N.Y.C., July 25, 1940; s. William P. O'Brien; divorced; children: Anne Marie, Matthew. BS, CCNY, 1960; MS, NYU, 1962; PhD, U. Mich., 1967. Assoc. dir. rsch. J.F. Jelenko Inc., N.Y.C., 1956-61; from asst. to assoc. prof. Marquette U., Milw., 1961-67; mech. engr., dir. Biomaterials Rsch. Ctr., 1967-70; prof. biologic and materials scis. U. Mich., Ann Arbor, 1970—, dir. Biomaterials Rsch. Ctr., 1994—. Cons. WHO, N.Y.C., 1967-70, Johnson & Johnson, Inc., New Brunswick, N.J., 1970-83; chmn. rsch. com. Sch. Dentistry U. Mich., 1987-91. Editor: (book) Dental Materials, 1989; inventor Magnesia Ceramic, 1985. Recipient UN Cert., 1967, Disting. Contbn. award Mexican Prosthodontics Soc., 1991. Mem. Materials Rsch. Soc., Acad. Dental Materials, Adhesion Soc., Dental Materials Group (pres. 1985). Office: U Mich Biomaterials Rsch Ctr 1011 N University Ave Ann Arbor MI 48109-1078

O'CALLAGHAN, PATTI LOUISE, urban ministry administrator; b. Bklyn., Mar. 26, 1953; d. Cornelius Leo and Louise Patricia (Casey) O'C.; m. Mark A. Diekman, Dec. 17, 1977; children: Casey, Brian. BA in Biology, NYU, 1975; MS in Physiology, Colo. State U., 1983. Cert. in program adminstrn. Grad. asst. Colo. State U., Ft. Collins, 1975-78; rsch. technician Iowa State U., Ames, 1978-80; counselor trainer Tecumseh Planned Parenthood, Lafayette, Ind., 1985; program coord. Date-rape Awareness and Edn., 1986-89; dir. Tippecanoe Ct. Apptd. Spl. Advocates, 1989-2000; dir. social justice Lafayette (Ind.) Urban Ministry, 2001—. Mem. adv. commn. Ind. State Supreme Ct., Indpls., 1992-2000, chair, 1995-98; mem. Tippecanoe Child Abuse Prevention, 1992—, pres. 1996-98. Editor tng. manuals; contbr. articles to profl. jours. Mem. adv. com. Jour. and Courier, Lafayette, 1992-93; vol. adv. Urban Ministries Homeless Shelter, Lafayette, 1992-93; coach Tippecanoe Soccer Assn., West Lafayette, Ind., 1989—; coach girls soccer West Lafayette H.S., 1994—; sec., v.p., pres. West Lafayette Sch. Bd., 1988-96; mem. Tippecanoe County Child Protection Team, 1994-99; mentor Mothers Adv. Bd., 1994—. Recipient Salute to Women award in Govt. and Politics, 1997; named Ind. Child Adv. of Yr., 1992, Nat. CASA Dir. of Yr., 1995, Nat. Assoc. of Soc. Workers, Reg. 4 Citizen of the Year 1998, Sagamore of the Wabash, 2000. Mem. Ind. Chpt. for Prevention of Child Abuse, Ind. Advs. for Children (program com. 1991-92), Ind. Sch. Bd. Assn. (legis. com. 1991-92), Ctrl. Ind. Assn. Vol. Adminstrs., Assn. of Women in Sci., Nat. Ct. Apptd. Spl. Adv. Assn., West Lafayette Swim Club (v.p. 1989-92), West Lafayette City Coun. (pres. 2001). Democrat. Christian. Avocations: soccer, swimming, reading, camping, travel. Office: Lafayette Urban Ministry 525 N 4th St Lafayette IN 47901

OCHS, SIDNEY, neurophysiology educator; b. Fall River, Mass., June 30, 1924; s. Nathan and Rose (Kniaz) O.; m. Bess Ratner; children: Rachel F., Raymond S. Susan B. PhD, U. Chgo., 1952. Rsch. assoc. Ill. Neuropsychiat. Inst., Chgo., 1952-54; rsch. fellow Calif. Inst. Tech., Pasadena, 1954-56; asst. prof. dept. physiology U. Tex. Med. Br., Galveston, 1956-58; assoc. prof. dept. physiology Ind. U., Indpls., 1958-61, prof., 1961-94, prof. emeritus, 1994—. Author: Elements of Neurophysiology, 1965, Axoplasmic Transport and Its Relation to Other Nerve Functions, 1982; founding editor, editor-in-chief Jour. Neurobiology, 1969-76, assoc. editor, 1977-86. Served with U.S. Army, 1943-45 Mem. Internat. Brain Rsch. Orgn., Am. Physiol. Soc., Soc. Neurosci., Am. Soc. Neurochemistry, Peripheral Nerve Soc. Democrat. Jewish Office: Ind U Med Ctr Dept Cellular & Integ Physiology 635 Barnhill Dr Indianapolis IN 46202-5126

OCKERMAN, HERBERT W. agricultural studies educator; b. Chaplin, Ky., Jan. 16, 1932; m. Frances Ockerman (dec.). BS with Distinction, U. Ky., 1954, MS, 1958; PhD, N.C. State U., 1962; postgrad., Air U., 1964-70, Ohio State U., 1974, 83, 87 & 2001. Asst. prof. Ohio State U., Columbus, 1961-66, assoc. prof., 1966-71, prof., 1971—. Former mem. Inst. Nutrition and Food Tech.; judge regional and state h.s. sci. fairs, 1965—, Ham Contest, Ky. State Fair, Sausage and Ham Contest, Ohio Meat Processing Groups; cons. various food companies, 1975—, Am. Meat Inst., 1977-88, USDA, 1977-88, CRC Press., Inc., 1988—; bd. examiners U. Calcutta, 1987-88; examiner U. Mysore, India, 1990-97; expert witness, various firms, 1992—, UN expert 95; presenter in field. Contbr. over 1585 articles and abstracts to profl. jours. and conf. procs., 73 chpts. to books. Comdr, USAF, 1955-58. Fisher Packing scholar; named Highest Individual in Beef Grading, Kansas City Meat Judging Contest, 1952; recipient Cert. of Appreciation, Ohio Assn. Meat Processors, 1987-2000, Profl. Devel. award Cahill faculty, commendation for internat. work in agr. Ohio Ho. of Reps., badge of merit for svc. to agr. Polish Govt., plaque Argentina Nat. Meat Bd., animal sci. award Roussel UCALF, France, U. Assiuit, Egypt, silver platter Nat. Meat Bd., Sec. Agr., Livestock and Fishery, Argentina, Svc. award Coun. Grad. Students, Pomerance Tchg. award, Outstanding Alumni award U. Ky., also named to Hall of Disting. Alumni, 1995, award for outstanding ednl. achievements Argentine Soc. Agr., Coop. award vet. faculty U. Cordoba, Svc. award Panoma Legis. Br., Brazil; veterinary faculty U. Cordoba, Spain, 1982, 94, Nat. Chung-Hsing U., 1982, 95, Vet. Mus. Ciechanowcu, Poland, internat. award Inst. Food Tech., Assn. Nat. Tecnologis en Alimentos de Mexico, Can. Indst. Food Sci. and Tech., 1998, Appreciation plaque Republic of Argentina, 1999, Candle Stick of Knowledge, Ludhiana U., Punjab, India, 1999, internat. award Am. Meat Sci. Assn., 1999, 2000, Appreciation Plaque Am. Coll. Commerce, 1999, Plaque, Selcuk U., Turkey, 1999, Folklore and Cultural memento Sudanese Socs., Sudan U., 1999, Homage and Acknowledgment, Argentine Sec. Agr., 2000, Most Honored Guest, Weifang, China, 2001, World History award Jhadong U. Taiwan, China, 2001, plaque Congress of Hon., Cordoba, Spain, 2001, Light award Polish Acad. Sci. Mem. NAS, NCR, ASTM, Am. Meat Sci. Assn., Am. Soc. Animal Sci. (rsch. award 1987), Reciprocal Meat Conf., European Meeting of Meat Rsch. Workers, Polish Vet. Soc. (hon.), Inst. Food Technologists (nat. and OVS chpts.), Inst. Food Tech. (Internat. award 1998), Can. Meat Sci. Assn., Internat. Congress Meat Sci. and Tech., Rsch. in Basic Sci., Phi Beta Delta (treas. 1987, pres. 1991, internat. scholar award 1991, internat. faculty award 1991, Presdl. medallion award), Gamma Sigma Delta (rsch. award 1977, internat. award of merit 1988), Sigma Xi (outstanding advisor in coll. award 1995), Phi Beta Kappa (Outstanding Tchg. award 1997, Extension Diversity award 1997, Pomerene Tchg. Enhancement award 1997, Outstanding Internat. Faculty award 1997), Internat. Gamma Sigma Delta (Disting. Achievement Nat. award 1998), Phi Kappa Phi. Office: Ohio State U Meat Lab Animal Sci 2029 Fyffe Rd Columbus OH 43210-1007 E-mail: ockerman.2@osu.edu.

O'CONNELL, DANIEL CRAIG, psychology educator; b. Sand Springs, Okla., May 20, 1928; s. John Albert and Letitia Rutherford (McGinnis) O'C. B.A., St. Louis U., 1951, Ph.L., 1952, M.A., 1953, S.T.L., 1960; Ph.D., U. Ill., 1963. Joined Soc. of Jesus, 1945; asst. prof. psychology St. Louis U., 1964-66, asso. prof., 1966-72, prof., 1972-80, trustee, 1973-78, pres., 1974-78; prof. psychology Loyola U., Chgo., 1980-89, Georgetown U., Washington, 1990-98, emeritus, 1998—, chmn., 1991-96. Vis. prof. U. Melbourne, Australia, 1972, U. Kans., 1978-79, Georgetown U., 1986, Loyola U., Chgo., 1998—; Humboldt fellow Psychol. Inst. Free U. Berlin, 1968; sr. Fulbright lectr. Kassel U., W. Ger., 1979-80. Author: Critical Essays on Language Use and Psychology, 1988; contbr. articles to profl. jours. Recipient Nancy McNeir Ring award for outstanding teaching St. Louis U., 1969; NSF fellow, 1961, 63, 65, 68; Humboldt Found. grantee, 1973; Humboldt fellow Tech. U. of Berlin, 1987. Fellow Am., Mo. psychol. assns., Am. Psychol. Soc.; mem. Midwestern, Southwestern, Eastern psychol. assns., Psychologists Interested in Religious Issues, Psychonomic Soc., Soc. for Scientific Study of Religion, N.Y., Mo. acads. sci., AAUP, AAAS, Phi Beta Kappa. Home and Office: Loyola U Chgo Psychology Dept 6525 N Sheridan Rd Chicago IL 60626-5344 E-mail: doconn1@luc.edu.

O'CONNELL, DAVID PAUL, state legislator; b. Bottineau County, N.D., June 3, 1940; s. Basil and Dorothy (Zimny) O'C.; m. Anadine Picard, 1960; children: Russell, Patricia Hetland, Marlys. Student, N.D. U. Mem. N.D. Ho. of Reps., Bismark, 1983-88, N.D. Senate from 6th dist., Bismark, 1989—; chmn. joint constrn. revision com. N.D. Senate, vice chmn. edn., transp. coms. Farmer. Mem. Lansford Fire & Ambulance Squad. Named Legislator of Yr., N.D. Vocat. Edn., 1990. Mem. KC, Farmers Union, Farm Bur., C. of C. Home: 2531 Country Rd 30 Lansford ND 58750 Office: ND Senate State Capitol Bismarck ND 58501

O'CONNELL, JAMES JOSEPH, port official; b. Lockport, Ill., Feb. 7, 1933; m. Phyllis Ann Berard, Aug. 1, 1953; children: Lynn, Kathryn, Julia. BSBA, Lewis U., 1958. lic. pvt. pilot FAA. Recorder Will County, Joliet, Ill., 1976-88. Dir., treas., corp. sec., v.p. Joliet Regional Port Dist., 1972—; dir. Des Plaines Valley Enterprise Zone, Joliet; reg. lobbyist Ill. Assn. Pt. Dists., Ill. Real Estate Broker, 1959—; real estate cons. O'Connell Enterprises. Nat. dir., nat. U.S. pres. Internat. O'Connell Clan, Kerry County, Ireland, 1996—; precinct committeeman Will County, Joliet, 1962-72, exec. cen. committeeman, 1965-70, dir. Will County Young Reps., Joliet, 1984, sec. Will County Econ. Affairs Commn., Joliet; GOP candidate for Ill. dist. 11, U.S. Congress, 1994.; treas. U.S. Jaycee Found., 1999; treas. Joliet Housing Authority, 2000-2001. With U.S. Army, 1953-54, Korea. Mem. Ill. Assn. Port Dists. (sec., treas. 1982-86), Ill. Jaycees (senate pres. 1972-73, named to Hall of Fame 1993, Disting. Svc. award 1977), Joliet Flying Club (sec.), Joliet Navy League (pres. 1996—), KC (past Grand Knight 1972, 91), Joliet Exch. Club, Three Rivers Mfg. Assn. (pub. affairs com.), Joliet Columbian Club (pres.), Am. Legion (life, former post officer), VFW (life), U.S. Jr. C. of C. (found. trustee 1997-2001). Roman Catholic. Office: 1009 Western Ave Joliet IL 60435-6801

O'CONNELL, JOHN T. rental leasing company executive; CFO Enterprise Rent-A-Car Co., St. Louis. Office: Enterprise Rent A Car Co 600 Corporate Park Dr Saint Louis MO 63105

O'CONNELL, LAURENCE J. bioethics research administrator; b. Chgo., May 12, 1945; s. Joseph J. and Eleanor (Coleman) O'C.; m. Angela M. Schneider; 1 child, Coleman Brian. BA in Theology, U. Cath. de Louvain (Belgium), 1969, MA in Religious Studies, 1970, PhD, STD Religious Studies/Theology, 1976. Prof., dept. chair dept. theol. studies St. Louis U., 1979-82, 86-90; v.p. theology, mission and ethics Cath. Health Assn. U.S., St. Louis, 1985-89; pres., chief. Park Ridge Ctr. for the Study Health, Faith, Ethics, Chgo., 1989—. Adj. asst. prof. dept. medicine Stritch Sch. Medicine, Loyola U., Chgo., 1990—; bd. dirs. Am. Health Decisions, 1990—, SSM Health Care System, St. Louis, 1990—. Author: The Gospel Alive: The Care of Persons with AIDS and Other Diseases, 1988, Ethics Committees: A Practical Approach, 1986. Mem. Soc. for Bioethics Consultation (pres. 1989-91), Univ. Club Chgo. Home: 507 W Barry Ave Chicago IL 60657-5416 Office: Park Ridge Ctr 211 E Ontario St Ste 800 Chicago IL 60611-3279

O'CONNELL, MAURICE DANIEL, lawyer; b. Ticonderoga, N.Y., Nov. 9, 1929; s. Maurice Daniel and Leila (Geraghty) O'C.; m. Joan MacLure Landers, Aug. 2, 1952; children: Mark M., David L., Ann M., Leila K., Ellen A. Grad., Phillips Exeter Acad., 1946; AB, Williams Coll., 1950; LLB, Cornell U., 1956. Bar: Ohio 1956. Since practiced in, Toledo; assoc. Williams, Eversman & Black, 1956-60; ptnr. Robison, Curphey & O'Connell, 1961-95, of counsel, 1996—; spl. hearing officer in conscientious objector cases U.S. Dept. Justice, 1966-68. Mem. complaint rev. bd. Bd. Commrs. on Grievance and Discipline of Supreme Ct. Ohio, 1987. Mem. Ottawa Hills Bd. Edn., 1963-66, pres., 1967-69; former trustee Toledo Soc. for Handicapped; past trustee Woodlawn Cemetery; past trustee Toledo Hearing and Speech Center, Easter Seal Soc.; mem. alumni council Phillips Exeter Acad. Served to 1st lt. USMCR, 1950-53. Fellow Ohio State Bar Found.; mem. NW Ohio Alumni Assn. of Williams Coll. (past pres.), Ohio Bar Assn., Toledo Bar Assn. (chmn. grievance com. 1971-74), Kappa Alpha, Phi Delta Phi. Club: Toledo. Home: 3922 W Bancroft St Toledo OH 43606-2533 Office: 9th Flr Four SeaGate Toledo OH 43604

O'CONNOR, JAMES JOHN, retired utility company executive; b. Chgo., Mar. 15, 1937; s. Fred James and Helen Elizabeth O'Connor; m. Ellen Louise Lawlor, Nov. 24, 1960; children: Fred, John (dec.), James, Helen Elizabeth. BS, Holy Cross Coll., 1958; MBA, Harvard U., 1960; JD, Georgetown U., 1963. Bar: Ill. 1963. With Commonwealth Edison Co., Chgo., 1963-98, asst. to chmn. exec. com., 1964-65, comml. mgr., 1966, asst. v.p., 1967-70, v.p., 1970-73, exec. v.p., 1973-77, pres., 1977-87, chmn., 1980-98, CEO, also bd. dirs., 1998; chmn., CEO Unicom Corp., 1994-98, ret., 1998. Bd. dirs. Corning, Inc., Tribune Co., United Air Lines, Smurfit-Stone Container Corp. Mem. The Bus. Coun.; bd. dirs. Lyric Opera, Joffrey Ballet, Helen Brach Found.; bd. dirs., trustee Mus. Sci. and Industry, Chgo. Symphony; past chmn. Met. Savs. Bond Campaign; trustee Northwestern U.; bd. dirs., past chmn. Chgo. Urban League, Chicagoland C. of C.; past chmn. bd. trustees Field Mus. Natural History; life trustee Adler Planetarium, Mus. Sci. and Industry; mem. exec. bd. Chgo. Area coun. Boy Scouts Am.; chmn. Cardinal Bernardin's Big Shoulders Fund; exec. v.p. The Hundred Club Cook County; dir., past pres. Cath. Charities; past chmn., hon. dir. Am. Cancer Soc., Chgo. Conv. and Tourism Bur. With USAF, 1960-63. Mem. ABA, Ill. Bar Assn., Chgo. Bar Assn.

O'CONNOR, KAY F. state legislator; b. Everett, Wash., Nov. 28, 1941; d. Ernest S. and Dena (Lampers) Wells; m. Arthur J. O'Connor, Sept. 1, 1959; 6 children. Diploma, Lathrop H.S., Fairbanks, Alaska, 1959. Office mgr. Blaylock Chemicals, Bucyrus, Kans., 1981-84; store mgr. Copies Plus, Olathe, 1984-86; acct. Advance Concrete Inc., Spring Hill, 1986-92; mem. Kans. Ho. of Reps. from 14th dist., 1993-2000, Kans. Senate from 9th dist., 2001—. Exec. dir. Parents in Control, Inc.; bd. dirs. Hometel Ltd.; author sch. voucher legis. for State of Kans., 1994, 95, 96, 97, 98, 99; mem. corrections and juvenile justice oversight com., judiciary com., fed. and state affairs com., vice chair elections and local govt. com. Kans. Senate, 2001—. Republican. Roman Catholic. Avocations: choir directing, statue renovations, speaking on school vouchers. Home: 1101 N Curtis St Olathe KS 66061-2709 Office: PO Box 2232 Olathe KS 66051-2232 E-mail: kayoisok@comcast.net.

O'CONNOR, MAUREEN, state official, lawyer; b. Washington, Aug. 7, 1951; d. Patrick and Mary E. O'Connor; children: Alex, Ed. BA, Seton Hill Coll., 1973; postgrad., SUNY, 1975-76; JD, Cleve. State U., 1980. Pvt. practice, 1981-85; referee Probate Ct., 1985-93; judge Common Pleas, 1993-95; prosecutor Summit County, 1995-99; lt. gov., dir. Dept. Pub. Safety State of Ohio, 1999—. Dir. Summit County Child Support Enforcement Agy.; spkr. in field. Parishioner St. Vincent's Ch.; vol. Comty. Drug Bd., Am. Cancer Soc., bd. dirs.; bd. dirs. Victim Assistance, St. Edward Home, Fairlawn, Furnace St. Mission. Recipient MADD Law Enforcement award, 1997, Cleve. State Disting. Alumnae award for Civic Achievement, 1997. Mem. MADD, Nat. Dist. Attys. Assn., Nat. Child Support Enforcement Assn., Nat. Coll. Dist. Attys. Assn., Ohio Prosecuting Attys. Assn. (exec. com.), Ohio Family Support Assn., Atty. Gen.'s Prosecutor Liaison Com., Summit County Police Chiefs Assn., Summit Forum, Summit County Child Mortality. E-mail: ltgov.o'connor@das.state.oh.us. Office: Office of Lt Gov 77 S High St Fl 30 Columbus OH 43215-6108*

O'CONNOR, PATRICK J. state legislator; m. Susan Reckert; children: Patrick, Michael, Meghan. Student, U. Mo., St. Louis. Mem. Mo. State Ho. of Reps. Dist. 79, 1993—, mem. labor, higher edn., pub. health and safety coms., 1993—, mem. children, youth and family com., 1993—. Mem. Woodson Terrace Lion's Club, North County Labor Legis. Club, Pipefitters Local 562, N.W. Twp. Dem. Club (v.p.). Home: 1570 Ville Angela Ln Hazelwood MO 63042-1631

OCVIRK, OTTO GEORGE, artist; b. Detroit, Nov. 13, 1922; s. Joseph and Louise (Ekle) O.; m. Betty Josephine Lebie, June 11, 1949; children: Robert Joseph, Thomas Frederick, Carol Louise. B.F.A., State U. Iowa, 1949, M.F.A., 1950. Advt. artist apprentice Bass-Luckoff Advt. Agy., Detroit, 1941; engring. draftsman Curtiss-Wright Aircraft Corp., Buffalo, 1942; faculty Bowling Green (Ohio) State U., 1950—, assoc. prof., 1960-65, prof. art, 1965-85, prof. emeritus, 1985—. Exhibited in group shows at, Denver Mus. Art, 1949, 50, 53, Detroit Inst. Art, 71948, 49, 50, 53, 56, Dayton (Ohio) Art Inst., 1950, 51, 56, Ohio State U., 1953, Walker Art Center, Mpls., 1948, 49, Library of Congress, Washington, 1949, Bklyn. Mus., 1949, Joslyn Mus., Omaha, 1949, Colorado Springs Fine Arts Center, 1949; represented in permanent collections, Detroit Inst. Arts, Dayton Art Inst., Friends of Am. Art, Grand Rapids, Mich., State U. Iowa, Iowa City, Bowling Green State U.; (Recipient 24 nat., regional juried art exhbn. awards 1947-57, others.); Author: (with R. Stinson, P. Wigg, R. Bone and David Cayton) Art Fundamentals— Theory and Practice, 1960-97, 7th edit., 1994, 8th edit., 1997, 9th edit., 2001. Scoutmaster Toledo Area council Boy Scouts Am., 1960-63, asst. scoutmaster, 1963-74, dist. commr., 1978-80. Served with AUS, 1943-46. Recipient Silver Beaver award Boy Scouts Am., 1976, Magnifico award Medici Circle, Bowling Green State U., 1987. Mem. Delta Phi Delta (hon.) Methodist. Home and Office: 231 Haskins Rd Bowling Green OH 43402-2206

O'DANIEL, WILLIAM L. state legislator; b. Union County, Ky., Dec. 4, 1923; m. Norma Norris; 5 children. Student, Agr. Ext. Svc. Farmer, businessman; mem. Ill. Ho. of Reps., 1974-77; exec. dir. Agr. Stabilization and Conservation Svc. U.S. Dept. Agr., 1977-81; mem. Ill. State Senate from 54th dist. Vice chmn. Agr. Com. Ill. State Senate, mem. Revenue, Transp., Elec., Joint Com. on Adminstrv. Rules Coms. Decorated Purple Heart, Bronze Star. Home: RR 4 Mount Vernon IL 62864-9804

ODDEN, ALLAN ROBERT, education educator; b. Duluth, Minn., Sept. 16, 1943; s. Robert Norman and Mabel Eleanor (Bjornnes) Odden; m. Eleanor Ann Rubottom, May 28, 1966; children: Sarina, Robert. BS, Brown U., 1965; MDiv, Union Theol. Sem., 1969; MA, Columbia U., 1971, PhD, 1975. Tchr. N.Y.C. Pub. Schs., 1967-72; rsch. assoc. Teachers' Coll. Columbia U., 1972-75; dir. policy Edn. Commn. of the States, Denver, 1975-84; prof. U. So. Calif., L.A., 1984-93, U. Wis., Madison, 1993—. Rsch. dir. Sch. Fin. Commns., Conn., 1974—75, SD, 1975—76, Mo., 1975—76, Mo., 1993, Mo., 94, NY, 1978—81, NJ, 1991—92; co-dir. Consortium Policy Rsch. Edn.; cons. Nat. Govs. Assn., Nat. Conf. State Legislatures, U.S. Sec. Edn., U.S. Senate, U.S. Dept. Edn., many state legislatures and govs.; nat. rsch. coun. task force sch. fin. equity adequacy and productivity, 1996—99; ct. master Superior Ct. N.J. in Abbott V. Burke Sch. Fin. Case, 1997—98. Author: (book) Education Leadership for America's Schools, 1995; co-author: Financing Schools for High Performance, 1998, Paying Teachers for What They Know and Do, 1997, Paying Teachers for What They Know and Do, 2d edit., 2002, School Finance: A Policy Perspective, 1992, School Finance: A Policy Perspective, 2d edit., 2000, Reallocating Resources: How to Boost Student Achievement Without Spending More, 2001; editor: Education Policy Implementation, 1991, Rethinking School Finance, 1992, School-Based Financing, 1999; contbr.

articles to profl. jours., chapters to books. Mem. L.A. Chamber Edn. and Human Resources Commn., 1986, Gov.'s Sch. Fin. Commn., Calif., 1987, Calif. Assessment Policy Com., Gov.'s Edn. Task Force, Wis., 1996, Carnegie Corp. Task Force Edn. in the Early Yrs., 1994—96; mem. nat. rsch. coun. com. sch. fin. equity, adequcy and productivity, 1996—99; mem. Gov.'s Blue Ribbon Commn. State and Local Partnerships 21st Century, Wis., 2000. Grantee, Dept. Edn., Carnegie Corp., Spencer Found., Ford Found., Atlantic Philanthropic Svcs., Mellon Found., Carnegie Corp., Pew Charitable Trusts. Mem.: Nat. Soc. Study Edn., Politics Edn. Assn., Nat. Tax Assn., Am. Ednl. Fin. Assn. (pres. 1979—80), Am. Ednl. Rsch. Assn. Avocations: Lionel training collecting, youth soccer, baseball coach. Home: 3128 Oxford Rd Madison WI 53705-2224 Office: U Wis Sch Edn Wis Ctr Edn Rsch 1025 W Johnson St # 653E Madison WI 53706-1706 E-mail: arodden@facstaff.wisc.edu.

ODELBO, CATHERINE G. publishing executive; BA in Am. History with gen. honors, U. Chgo., 1985, MBA with honors, 2000. Mut. fund analyst Morningstar, Inc., Chgo., 1988-91, editor closed-end funds, 1991-95, pub. equities group, 1995-97, v.p. retail markets, 1997-98, sr. v.p. content devel., 1998-99; pres. Morningstar.com., 2000—. Mem. Phi Beta Kappa. Avocations: bridge, movies, reading. Office: Morningstar Inc 225 W Wacker Dr Chicago IL 60606-1224

O'DELL, JAMES E. newspaper publishing executive; V.p. ops. and techs. Chgo. Tribune, 1993-97, Chgo. Tribune Pub., 1997—. Office: Chgo Tribune Pub 435 N Michigan Ave Chicago IL 60611-4066

O'DELL, JANE, automotive company executive; Co-owner Westfall GMC Truck Inc., Kansas City, Mo. Office: Westfall GMC Truck Inc 3915 Randolph Rd Kansas City MO 64161-9383

O'DELL, MICHAEL RAY, accountant, banker; b. Camden, Ohio, Sept. 27, 1951; s. Donald Lee and Donna Louise (Buell) O'D. BS in Bus., Miami U., 1977; MBA, Xavier U., 1979. CPA, Ohio. Asst. trust officer First Nat. Bank Southwestern Ohio, Hamilton, Ohio, 1977-83, acctg. officer Middletown, 1983-86, comptroller, 1986-87, v.p., comptroller, 1987-96; CFO, sr. v.p. and sec. First Fin. Bancorp, Hamilton, OH, 1996—. Instr. microecons. Am. Inst. Banking, Cin., 1980-82; pres., bd. dirs. Cmty. First Fin., 1996—; bd. dirs. Sand Ridge Bank, Ohio City Ins. Agy.; bd. dirs., treas. First Fin. Bancorp Svc. Corp., 1999—. Bus. cons. applied econs. program Jr. Achievement, Springboro, Ohio, 1985. Served with USN, 1969-73. Mem. Am. Inst. CPA's, Ohio Soc. CPA's (com. chmn. 1985-88, pres. 1988-89, state dir. 1989-90). Club: Liberty (Ind.) Country. Avocation: golf. Home: 85B S Lafayette St Camden OH 45311-1019 Office: First Fin Banncorp 300 High St Hamilton OH 45011-6078

ODEN, ROBERT A., JR. college president; m. Teresa Oden; children: Robert, Katherine. BA in History and Lit., Harvard Coll.; MA in Religious Studies/Oriental Langs., Cambridge U.; MA in Theology, Harvard Divinity, 1972; D in Near Eastern Langs. and Lit., Harvard U., 1975; MA (hon.), Dartmouth Coll., 1987. Former mem. faculty Dartmouth Coll., 1975—, former prof., 1985—, chair dept. of religion, 1983-89; dir., founder Dartmouth's Humanities Inst.; headmaster Hotchkiss Sch., Lakeville, Conn.; pres. Kenyon Coll., Gambier, Ohio, 1995—. Chmn. com. on orgn. and policy Dartmouth Coll., com. on admissions and fin. aid; lectr. in field. Author: The Bible Without Theology, 1987. Mem. Conn. Assn. of Ind. Schs. (bd. dirs.). Avocations: fishing, running, religious studies, archaeology. Office: Kenyon Coll Office of Pres Gambier OH 43022-9623

ODLE, JOHN H. metal products executive; married; 2 children. BA in Pre-law, Miami U., Oxford, Ohio. Mgmt. trainee USX Corp., Cin., Pitts. and St. Paul, 1964-68; mktg. rep. RTI Internat. Metals, Inc., Niles, Ohio, 1968-73, gen. mgr. sales, 1978-81, v.p. sales, 1981-89, sr. v.p., 1989-96, exec. v.p. ops., mktg., purchasing, 1996—, also bd. dirs.; western regional mgr. Teledyne Allvac, 1973-78. Bd. dirs. Reamet S.A. Mem. Am. Soc. Metals, Internat. Titanium Assn. Office: RTI Internat Metals Inc 1000 Warren Ave Niles OH 44446-1168

O'DONNELL, F. SCOTT, banker; b. Brownsville, Pa., Sept. 20, 1940; s. Francis Horner and Rebecca (Warren) O'D.; m. Ann Bukmir, Dec. 30, 1976. BA, Grove City (Pa.) Coll., 1962; postgrad., U. Wis. Grad. Sch. Banking, 1970, Internat. Sch. Banking, U. Colo., 1972. Nat. bank examiner Comptroller of Currency, Cleve., 1965-71; supt. of banks State of Ohio, Columbus, 1975-77; sr. v.p. First Nat. Bank, Steubenville, Ohio, 1971-75; exec. v.p. Heritage Bancorp, 1977-80; from v.p. to exec. v.p. Soc. Corp., Cleve., 1980-95; dep. tax commr. State of Ohio, Columbus, 1996-99, supt. fin. instn., 1999—. Mem. state banking bd. Div. of Banks, Columbus, 1979-85, govt. affairs com. Ohio Bankers Assn., 1982-84. Served with USCG, 1963-69. Mem. Columbus Athletic Club, Pitts. Univ. Club, Belmont Hills Country Club, Lakewood Country Club. Avocations: travel, politics, antiques. Home: 31830 Lake Rd Avon Lake OH 44012-2022 Office: Ohio Divsn Fin Instns 77 S High St Fl 21 Columbus OH 43215-6199

O'DONNELL, GENE, retail executive; With Zayre, 1971-74; various Hills Dept. Stores, 1974-92; exec. v.p. True*Serve Corp. (formerly Hills Dept. Stores), 1992-99; exec. v.p. merchandising and mktg. Office Max, Inc., Shaker Heights, Ohio, 1999—. Office: Office Max Inc 3605 Warrensville Center Rd Shaker Heights OH 44122-5248

O'DONNELL, JAMES P. food service executive; B in Econs., U. Ky.; MBA in Fin., Xavier U. CMA. With fin. dept. Borden, Inc.; with ConAgra, 1978—, sr. v.p., CFO, exec. v.p., CFO, corp. sec., 1997—. Office: Conagra Inc One ConAgra Dr Omaha NE 68102-5001

O'DONNELL, KEVIN, retired metal products executive; b. Cleve., June 9, 1925; s. Charles Richard and Ella (Kilbane) O'Donnell; m. Ellen Blydenburgh, Aug. 16, 1965; children: Kevin, Susan, Michael, John, Maura, Neil, Megan, Hugh. AB, Kenyon Coll., Gambier, Ohio, 1947, PhD (hon.) in Law, 1980; MBA, Harvard U., 1947; PhD in Econs. (hon.) , Pusan (Korea) Nat. U., 1970, Ohio Wesleyan U., 1972. Gen. sales mgr. Steel Improvement & Forge Co., Cleve., 1947-60; mgmt. cons. Booz, Allen and Hamilton, 1960-62; gen. mgr., dir. Atlas Alloys-Rio Algom Corp., 1963-66; dir. Peace Corps, Seoul, Republic of Korea, 1966-70, dir. adminstrn. and fin., then dep. acting dir., 1970-71; assoc. dir. internat. ops. ACTION, 1971-72; exec. v.p. SIFCO Industries, Inc., Cleve., 1972-75, pres., chief oper. officer, 1976-83, pres., chief exec. officer, 1983-89, chief exec. officer, 1989-90, chmn., exec. comm., 1990-94; ret., 1994. Bd. dirs. Ctrl. Pk. Media Corp., Doyle Pacific Industries, Ltd.; chmn. Whole Health Mgmt., Inc., Cleve.; adv. dir. Plz. Group, Houston, Capital Strategies, Inc., Cleve. Mem. Washington Inst. Fgn. Affairs, Cleve. Com. Fgn. Rels., chmn., 1979—82, CCWA, 1982—89; pres. Guest Ho., Inc., 1990—92; trustee Alcohol Svcs., Cleve., 1993—, Cleve. Coun. World Affairs, Nat. Peace Corps. Assn. Decorated Order Civil Merit Republic of Korea. Mem.: Harvard Bus. Sch. Alumni Assn. (dir. Boston 1991—94), Army-Navy Club (Washington), Westwood Country Club, Pepper Pike Country Club, Union Club, 50 Club, First Friday Club, Harvard Bus. Sch. Club Cleve., Knights of Malta (master knight). Republican. Roman Catholic. Avocations: golf, reading. E-mail: kevodoncle@aol.com.

O'DONNELL, MARK JOSEPH, accountant; b. St. Louis, Mar. 28, 1954; s. William E. and Jeanne M. (Collins) O'D.; m. Jane E. Wismann, Sept. 29, 1973; children: Sean, Mark Jr., Kyle. BSBA magna cum laude, U. Mo., 1977. CPA, Mo. Cost acct. Hunter Engring., St. Louis, 1973-76; acct. Gen. Dynamics, 1976-77, Lester Witte & Co., St. Louis, 1977-80, mgr., 1980-82; ptnr. Bounds, Poger & O'Donnell, 1982-86, mng. ptnr., 1986-94; mng. prin. O'Donnell, Bonebrake & Co., P.C., 1994—. Named one of Outstanding Young Men Am., U.S. Jaycees, 1978. Mem. Am. Inst. CPA's, Mo. Soc. CPA's. Roman Catholic. Avocations: weight lifting, jogging, road cycling. Office: O'Donnell Bonebrake & Co PC 11457 Olde Cabin Rd Ste 310 Saint Louis MO 63141-7172

O'DONNELL, ROBERT PATRICK, priest; b. Gary, Ind., June 11, 1919; s. Liquori Alphonsus and Carolyn Emily (Senn) O'D. Student, Art Inst., Chgo.; BA, U. Chgo., 1943; MA, Cath. U., 1945; postgrad., Gregorian U., Rome, 1980-81. Ordained priest Roman Cath. Ch., 1949. Asst. Sacred Heart Ch., Russellville, Ky., 1950-52; adminstr. Our Lady of Lourdes Ch., Otway, Ohio, 1953-55; pub. rels. Glenmary Home Missioners, Glendale, 1956-60; chaplain Glenmary Sisters, Fayetteville, 1960-66; pastor Holy Redeemer Ch., Vancebury, Ky., 1987-94, St. Agnes Ch., Elkton, 1981-87, St. Mary & St. James Ch., Guthrie, St. Francis De Sales Ch., Idabel, Okla., 1987-94; with Glenmary Home Missioners, Cincinnati, 1994—. Editor, photographer, illustrator Glenmary's Challenge, Cin., 1952-80; designer/builder seven chs. in Ky., Ohio, N.C., 1952-64. Founder/designer: Appalachian Studios-resident artist, gen. mgr., 1966-80; composer music, producer: (musical) From Sheeba They Came, 1990; producer: (movie) Glenmary Story, 1958; other. With USN. With maritime svc. USN, 1943, ATO. Recipient Thomas Jefferson award, U.S. Office of Pres., 1979, Four Chaplains Nat. award Office of Four Chaplains Found., Phila., 1981; Art scholar U. chgo. Mem. Rotary (internat. exc. chmn. 1989-91), Phi Kappa Psi (pres. 1943). Home and Office: 100 Compton Rd 5C3 Cincinnati OH 45215-4141 E-mail: joedean@/starnet.com.

O'DONNELL, THOMAS MICHAEL, former brokerage firm executive; b. Cleve., Apr. 9, 1936; s. John Michael and Mary L. (Hayes) O'D.; m. Nancy A. Dugan, Feb. 4, 1961; children: Christopher, Colleen, Julie BBA, U. Notre Dame, 1959; MBA, U. Pa., 1960. Cert. Chartered Fin. Analyst. Fin. analyst Saunders Stiver & Co., Cleve., 1960-65; rsch. dir. McDonald & Co., 1965-66, exec. v.p. corp. fin., 1967-83, gen. ptnr., 1968-83; pres. McDonald & Co. Investments, Inc./McDonald & Co. Securities, 1984-88; chmn., chief exec. officer McDonald & Co. Securities, 1988-98. Bd. dirs. Seaway Food Town; mem. regional firms adv. com. N.Y. Stock Exch., 1986-92, chmn., 1991-92; dir. C.I.D. Venture Funds. Author: The Why and How of Mergers, 1968 Bd. dirs. Greater Cleve. Growth Assn., Inroads Northeast Ohio, PlayHouse Square Found.; bd. regents St. Ignatius High Sch., Cleve.; steering com. Leadership Cleve. Mem. Cleve. Soc. Security Analysts (cert.), Securities Industry Assn. (dir. 1988-94, chmn. 1993), Union Club, Westwood Country Club, 50 Club Cleve., Pepper Pike Club, Double Eagle Club. Roman Catholic. Avocation: golf. Home: 1790 Century Oaks Dr Cleveland OH 44145-3654

O'DONOHUE, WALTER JOHN, JR. medical educator; b. Washington, Sept. 23, 1934; s. Walter John and Mavis Leota (Terry) O'D.; m. Cynthia Ann Halminitoller, Aug. 10, 1957 (div. 1978); 1 child, Diane Louise; m. Maria Theresa Sauer, Nov. 27, 1978; children: Walter John III, Mary Theresa. BA, Va. Mil. Inst., 1957; MD, Med. Coll. Va., 1961. Diplomate Am. Bd. Internal Medicine, Am. Bd. Pulmonary Medicine. Resident internal medicine Med. Coll. Va., Richmond, 1961-63, 65-66, chief med. resident, 1966-67, cardio-pulmonary fellow, 1967-69, asst. prof. medicine, 1968-73, assoc. prof., 1973-77; prof. Creighton U., Omaha, 1977—, chief pulmonary medicine div., 1977—, chmn. dept. medicine, 1985-96, assoc. chair for edn., 1996—, dir. internal medicine residency program, 1985-98, assoc. dean grad. med. edn., 1998—. Editor: Current Advances in Respiratory Care, 1984, Long-term Oxygen Therapy: Scientific Basis and Clinical Application, 1995, Accurate Coding for Critical Care Services and Pulmonary Medicine, 1996-2002; contbr. more than 100 articles to med. jours., 30 chpts. to books. Served to capt. M.C., U.S. Army, 1963-65. Fellow ACP, Am. Coll. Chest PHysicians (regent 1986-88, gov. for Nebr. 1982-88); mem. AMA (CPT adv. com. 1992—, mem. ho. of dels., alt. del. for Am. Coll. Chest Physicians 1998—), Am. Lung Assn. (bd. dirs. 1981-87), Nebr. Lung Assn. (bd. dirs., pres. 1979-81), Am. Assn. Respiratory Care (chmn. bd. med. advisors 1986-87), Nat. Assn. Med. Dirs. for Respiratory Care (pres. 1995-97). Republican. Roman Catholic. Avocations: hunting, fishing. Home: 12773 Izard St Omaha NE 68154-1243 Office: Creighton U Sch Medicine 601 N 30th St Omaha NE 68131-2137 E-mail: wjo@creighton.edu.

O'DWYER, MARY ANN, automovitve executive; BS, DePaul U.; MS, Benedictine U. CPA. With Ernst and Young, McDonald's Corp.; various positions CC Industries (a Henry Crown Co.); sr. v.p. fin. ops., CFO Wheels, 1991—; sr. v.p fin & ops., CFO Frank Consol. Enterprises. Office: Frank Consol Enterprises 666 Garland Pl Des Plaines IL 60016

OEHME, FREDERICK WOLFGANG, medical researcher and educator; b. Leipzig, Germany, Oct. 14, 1933; arrived in came to U.S., 1934; s. Friedrich Oswald and Frieda Betha (Wohlgamuth) Oehme; m. Nancy Beth McAdam, Aug. 6, 1960 (div. June 1981); children: Stephen Frederick, Susan Lynn, Deborah Ann, Heidi Beth; m. Pamela Sheryl Ford, Oct. 2, 1981; 1 child April Virginia. BS in Biol. Sci., Cornell U., 1957, DVM, 1958; MS in Toxicology and Medicine, Kans. State U., 1962; DMV in Pathology, Justus Liebig U., Giessen, Germany, 1964; PhD in Toxicology, U. Mo., 1969. Diplomate Am. Bd. Toxicology, Am. Bd. Vet. Toxicology, Acad. Toxicol. Scis. Resident intern, Large Animal and Ambulatory Clinic Cornell U., 1957-58; gen. practice vet. medicine, 1958-59; from asst. to assoc. prof. medicine Coll. Vet. Medicine Kans. State U., 1959-66, 69-73, dir. comparative toxicology labs., 1969—, prof. toxicology, medicine and physiology Coll. Vet. Medicine, 1974-96, prof. toxicology, pathobiology, medicine and physiology, 1996—; postdoctoral research fellow in toxicology, NIH U. Mo., 1966-69. Cons. FDA, Washington, Ctr. for Vet. Medicine , Rockville, Md.; cons. animal care com. U. Kans., Lawrence, 1969—76, Syntex Corp., Palo Alto, Calif., 1976—77; mem. sci. adv. panel on PBB Gov.'s Office, State of MIch., 1976—77; mem. Coun. for Agrl. Sci. and Tech. Task Force on Toxicity, Toxicology and Environ. Hazard, 1976—83; cons., mem. adv. group on pesticides EPA, Cin., 1977—; expert state and fed. witness; advisor WHO, Geneva; presenter numerous papers to profl. meetings. Reviewer: Toxicology and Applied Pharmacology, reviewer: Spectroscopy, reviewer: numerous others. Mem. adv. coun. Cub Scouts Am., Eagle Scouts; mgr., coach Little League Baseball; active PTA; mem. Manhattan Civic Theatre; trustee Manhattan Marlin Swim Team; dir. meet Little Apple Invitational Swim Meet, 1984; mem. coun. Luth. Ch. Am., mem. sr. choir, numerous coms. Recipient Disting. Grad. Faculty award, Kans. State U., 1977—79, Dir.'s Letter of Commendation, FDA, 1983, Kenneth P. DuBois award, Midwest Soc. Toxicology, 1991, Kenneth F. Lampe award, Am. Acad. Toxicology, 1993, John Doull award, Ctrl. States Soc. Toxicology, 1994, medal, Azabu U., 1994, Silver award, Aristotelian U., 1995, others; fellow, Morris Animal Found., 1967—69. Fellow: Am. Acad. Vet. and Comparative Toxicology (past sec.-treas., numerous coms.), Am. Acad. Toxicology (past pres., numerous coms.); mem.: NRC (subcom. on organic contaminants in drinking water, safe drinking water com., adv. ctr. on toxicology assembly life scis. 1976—77, panel on toxicology marine bd., assembly of engring. 1976—79), AVMA (com. on environmentology 1971—73, adv. com. coun. on biol. and therapeuric agts. 1971—74, Samuel Shiedy award 1999), Nat. Ctr. Toxicol. Rsch. (vet. toxicology rep. sci. adv. bd., sci. adv. bd. 1974—77), N.Y. Acad. Scis., Soc. Toxicologic Pathologists, World Fedn. Clin. Toxicology Ctrs. and Poison Control Ctrs. (past pres.), Soc. Toxicology (numerous coms.), Cornell U. Athletic Assn., Manhattan Square Dance Club, Cornell U. Crew Club, Sigma Xi, Phi Zeta, Omega Tau Sigma. Republican. Avocations: historical readings, scientific writings, nature tours and walks, travel. Home: 148 S Dartmouth Dr Manhattan KS 66503-3079 Office: Kans State Univ Comparative Toxicology Labs 1800 Denison Ave Manhattan KS 66506-5660 E-mail: oehme@vet.ksu.edu.

OEHME, REINHARD, physicist, educator; b. Wiesbaden, Germany, Jan. 26, 1928; came to U.S., 1956; s. Reinhold and Katharina (Kraus) O.; m. Mafalda Pisani, Nov. 5, 1952. Dr. rer. nat., U. Goettingen, Germany, 1951; Diplom Physiker, U. Frankfurt am Main, Germany, 1948. Asst. Max Planck Inst. Physics, Goettingen, 1949-53; research asso. Fermi Inst. Nuclear Studies, U. Chgo., 1954-56; mem. faculty dept. physics and Fermi Inst., 1958—, prof. physics, 1964—; mem. Inst. Advanced Studies, Princeton, 1956-58. Vis. prof. Inst. de Física Teórica, São Paulo, Brazil, 1952-53, U. Md., 1957, U. Vienna, Austria, 1961, Imperial Coll., London, Eng., 1963-64, U. Karlsruhe, Fed. Republic Germany, 1974, 75, 77, U. Tokyo, 1976, 88; vis. scientist Internat. Centre Theoretical Physics, Miramare-Trieste, Italy, Brookhaven Nat. Lab., Lawrence Radiation Lab., U. Calif., Berkeley, CERN, Geneva, Switzerland, Max Planck Inst., Munich, Fed. Republic Germany, Rsch. Inst. for Fundamental Physics, Kyoto (Japan) U. Author articles in field, chpts. in books. Guggenheim fellow, 1963-64; recipient Humboldt award, 1974, Japan Soc. for Promotion of Sci. Fellowship awards, 1976, 88. Fellow Am. Phys. Soc. Office: Univ of Chicago Enrico Fermi Inst 5640 S Ellis Ave Chicago IL 60637-1433 E-mail: oehme@theory.uchicago.edu.

OELSLAGER, W. SCOTT, state legislator; b. Oct. 15, 1953; m. Elsie Price, 1994. BA, Mt. Union Coll., 1975; JD, Capitol U. Sch. Law, 2002. Aide to U.S. rep. Ralph Regula, 1973-78; asst. Sen. Thomas Walsh, 1981-84; mem. Ohio Senate from 29th dist., Columbus, 1985—. Mem. Hwy. & Transp. com.; chmn. com. on criminal justice Senate Judiciary, chmn. edn. com. , chmn. rules com. ; dir. pub. rels. Malone Coll., 1978—80; dir. svc. Ohio Auto Dealers Assn. Bd. dir. Akron & Canton Arthritis Found. Recipient Watchdog of Treas. award, 1986, 88, 90; Rep. Legis. of Yr. award Nat. Rep. Legis. Assn., 1986, Disting. Legis. award Assn. Ohio Health Commr., 1989, Lay Person of Yr. award Phi Delta Kappa, 1989, Pub. Officer of Yr. award Social Workers Assn., 1992, Legis. of Yr. award Common Cause of Ohio & Ohio Nurses Assn., 1993, Legis. of Yr. Ohio Acad. Trial Lawyers, Disting. Svc. award Ohio State Bar Assn. Home: 2853 Westmoreland Rd NW Canton OH 44718-3318 Office: State Senate State Capital Columbus OH 43215

OESTERLE, ERIC ADAM, lawyer; b. Lafayette, Ind., Dec. 2, 1948; s. Eric Clark and Germaine Dora (Seelye) O.; m. Carolyn Anne Scherer, Sept. 16, 1973; children: Adam Clark, Allison Margaret. BS, U. Mich., 1970, JD, 1973. Bar: Ill. 1973, U.S. Dist. Ct. (no. dist.) Ill. 1973, U.S. Ct. Appeals (7th cir.) 1987, U.S. Supreme Ct. 1986. Assoc. Sonnenschein, Carlin, Nath & Rosenthal, Chgo., 1973-80; ptnr. Sonnenschein Nath & Rosenthal, 1980—. Mem. ABA, Ill. Bar Assn., Chgo. Bar Assn. Home: 645 Lake Rd Glen Ellyn IL 60137-4249 Office: Sonnenschein Nath & Rosenthal 8000 Sears Tower 233 S Wacker Dr Ste 8000 Chicago IL 60606-6491 E-mail: eoesterle@sonnenschein.com.

OESTERLING, THOMAS OVID, retired pharmaceutical company executive; b. Butler, Pa., Mar. 6, 1938; s. Victor Kenneth and Marjorie Gertrude (Oswald) O.; m. Janet Westrick, Dec. 30, 1960 (div. 1983); children: Thomas, Jennifer, Daniel; m. Cynthia Adler, 1984 (div. 1987). B.S., Ohio State U., 1962, M.S., 1964, Ph.D., 1966. Rsch. assoc., rsch. head Upjohn Co., Kalamazoo, 1966-76; dir. R&D dermatol. divsn. Johnson & Johnson Corp., New Brunswick, N.J., 1976-78, dir. pharm. R&D, 1978-79; v.p. med. products R&D Mallinckrodt, Inc., St. Louis, 1979-83; sr. v.p. R&D Collaborative Rsch. Inc., Bedford, Mass., 1984-86, pres., 1986-89; chmn., pres., CEO Gliatech Inc., Cleve., 1989-2000; ret. Mem. faculty Arden House Conf. on Stability Evaluation Pharm. Dosage Forms, 1979 Contbr. numerous sci. articles to profl. jours.; patentee in field. Recipient Disting. Alumni award Ohio State U. Coll. Pharmacy, 1982; Parke Davis rsch. grantee, 1962-64; Am. Found. for Pharm. Edn. fellow, 1964-66 Mem. Am. Chem. Soc., Soc. Nuclear Medicine, Acad. Pharm. Scis., Soc. for Neurosci.

OETTINGER, JULIAN ALAN, lawyer, pharmacy company executive; BS, U. Ill., 1961; JD, Northwestern U., 1964. Bar: Ill. 1964. Atty. SEC, 1964-67, Walgreen Co., Deerfield, Ill., 1967-72, sr. atty., 1972-78, dir. law, 1978-89, v.p., gen. counsel, corp. sec., 1989-2000, sr. v.p., 2000—. Office: Walgreen Co 200 Wilmot Rd Deerfield IL 60015-4616

O'FLAHERTY, PAUL BENEDICT, lawyer; b. Chgo., Feb. 11, 1925; s. Benedict Joseph and Margaret Celestine (Harrington) O'F.; m. Catherine Margaret Bigley, Feb. 13, 1954; children: Paul, Michael, Kathleen, Ann, Neil. JD cum laude, Loyola U., Chgo., 1949. Bar: Ill. 1949, U.S. Dist. Ct. (no. dist.) Ill. 1949, U.S. Ct. Appeals (7th cir.) 1956, U.S. Supreme Ct. 1959. Ptnr. Madden, Meccia, O'Flaherty & Freeman, Chgo., 1949-56; ptnr. Groble, O'Flaherty & Hayes, 1956-63, Schiff Hardin & Waite, Chgo., 1963—. Mem. adj. faculty Loyola U., 1959-65 Author: (with others) Illinois Estate Administration, 1983; contbr. articles to profl. jours. Bd. advisors Cath. Charities, Chgo., 1979-92; trustee Clarke Coll., Dubuque, Iowa, 1982—. Served to 2d lt. U.S. Army, 1943-46. Fellow Am. Coll. Trust and Estate Counsel; mem. ABA, Ill. Bar Assn. (past chmn. fed. taxation sect. council), Chgo. Bar Assn. (past chmn. trust law com.), Chgo. Estate Planning Council Clubs: Union League, Metropolitan (Chgo.) Office: Schiff Hardin & Waite 6600 Sears Tower Chicago IL 60606

OGATA, KATSUHIKO, engineering educator; b. Tokyo, Jan. 6, 1925; came to U.S., 1952; s. Fukuhei and Teruko (Yasaki) O.; m. Asako Nakamura, Sept. 6, 1961; 1 son, Takahiko. B.S., U. Tokyo, 1947; M.S., U. Ill., 1953; Ph.D., U. Calif., Berkeley, 1956. Research asst. Sci. Research Inst., Tokyo, 1948-51; fuel engr. Nippon Steel Tube Co., 1951-52; mem. faculty U. Minn., 1956—, prof. mech. engring., 1961—; prof. elec. engring. Yokohama Nat. U., 1960-61, 64-65, 68-69. Author: State Space Analysis of Control Systems, 1967, Modern Control Engineering, 1970, 4th edit., 2001, Dynamic Programming, 1973, Ingenieria de Control Moderna, 1974, 3d edit., 1998, Metody Przestrzeni Stanow w Teorii Sterowania, 1974, System Dynamics, 1978, 3d edit., 1998, Engenharia de Controle Moderno, 1982, 2d edit., 1993, Teknik Kontrol Automatik, 1985, Discrete-Time Control Systems, 1986, 2d edit., 1995, Gendai Seigyo Riron, 1986, Dinamica de Sistemas, 1987, Solving Control Engineering Problems with MATLAB, 1994, Gendai Seigyo Kogaku, 1994, Designing Linear Control Systems with MATLAB, 1994, Kejuruteraan Kawalan Moden, 1996, Sistemas de Control en Tiempo Discreto, 1996, Projeto de Sistemas Lineares de Controle com MATLAB, 1996, Solucao de Problemas de Engenharia de Controle com MATLAB, 1997. Recipient Outstanding Adv. award Inst. of Tech., U. Minn., 1981, John R. Ragazzini Edn. award Am. Automatic Control Coun., 1999. Fellow ASME; mem. Sigma Xi, Pi Tau Sigma. Office: U Minn Dept Mech Engring Minneapolis MN 55455

OGG, WILLIAM L. state legislator; m. Janice Ogg; children: Julie Lynne, William Kenneta, Shana Jo. Student, Ohio U. Commr. Scioto County, Ohio; vice mayor, mem. city coun. City of Portsmouth, mayor; rep. dist. 92 Ohio Ho. Reps., Columbus. Chmn. Ohio Valley Regulation Devel. Commn., 1986-91. Named to Dem. Hall of Fame, Scioto County, 1990. Mem. Portsmouth C. of C.

O'HAGAN, JAMES JOSEPH, lawyer; b. Chgo., Dec. 29, 1936; s. Francis James and Florence Agnes (Dowgialo) O'H.; m. Suzanne Elizabeth Wiegand, June 28, 1958; children: Timothy, Karen, Peggy, Kevin. B in

Commerce, De Paul U., 1958, JD, 1962. Sr. ptnr. O'Hagan, Smith & Amundsen, Chgo., 1997—. Mem. Cook County Pres.'s Com. on the Cts. for the 21st Century, chmn. suburban subcom., 1998—2000; lawyer Chgo. Claim Mgrs. Assn., 1992—; chmn. USLaw Network, Inc., 2001—. Mem. ABA, Ill. Bar Assn. Chgo. Bar Assn., Internat. Assn. Def. Coun., Def. Rsch. Inst., Profl. Liability Underwriters Soc., Trial Lawyers Club. Roman Catholic. Avocations: golf, tennis, physical conditioning, painting, reading. Office: O'Hagan Smith & Amundsen 150 N Michigan Ave Chicago IL 60601-7553 E-mail: johagan@osalaw.com.

O'HAIR, JOHN D. lawyer; b. Detroit; m. Barbara Stanton. BA in Polit. Sci., DePauw U., 1951; JD, Detroit Coll. Law, 1954, LLD (hon.), 1992. Asst. corp. counsel City of Detroit; mem. Common Pleas Ct. Detroit, 1965-68; judge Wayne County Cir. Ct., 1968-83; corp. counsel Wayne County, 1983, prosecutor, 1983—. Assoc. prof., v.p., bd. trustees Detroit Coll. Law; chmn. Criminal Assessments Commn.; past vice-chmn., mem. adv. bd. Wayne County Comty. Corrections Bd.; mem. Housing and Pub. Safety Com., New Detroit, Inc., Prosecuting Attys. Coordinating Coun., Gun Violence Coalition; former instr. Mich. Jud. Inst.; former mem., vice-chmn. Mich. Jud. Tenure Commn. Mem. adv. bd. St. Ambrose Acad., Wayne County unit Am. Cancer Soc.; mem. Pres.'s Commn. on Model State Drug Laws; mem. adv. com. Drug Free Sch. Zones. With U.S. Army. Mem. Mich. State Bar (commn. on death and dying), Mich. Hospice Assn. (adv. bd.), Inc. Soc. Irish/Am. Lawyers (past pres.), Prosecuting Attys. of Mich. (past pres.), Prosecuting Attys. Assn. (chmn. legis. com.). Office: Office of Prosecuting Atty Frank Murphy Hall Justice 1441 Saint Antoine St Detroit MI 48226-2311

O'HALLERAN, MICHAEL D. insurance company executive; m. Kay; children: Meghan, Connor. Degree in acctg. and fin., U. Wis., Whitewater. Sr. exec. Wausau Ins. Cos., Gen. Reins., Alexander Re; sr. operating positions Aon Corp., Chgo., 1987, pres., COO; also bd. dirs. Bd. dirs. Cardinal Health, Inc., Optimark Techs., Inc.; COO Aon Group Inc. Dir. Spl. Children's Charities, Providence-St. Mel High Sch., Angus Robinson, Jr. Meml. Found.; mem. arts and letters adv. bd. U. Notre Dame; trustee Dublin City U., Ireland, dir. Coll. Ins. Mem. Econ. Club Chog., Young Pres.'s Orgn. Office: Aon Corp 123 N Wacker Dr Chicago IL 60606-1700

O'HARA, JOHN PAUL, III, orthopaedic surgeon; b. Detroit, June 10, 1946; m. Randy Baird, Mar. 11, 1987; children: Riley Anne, Nolan Baird, Evan John. BA, U. Mich., 1968, MD, 1972. Resident U. Va. Med. Ctr., Charlottesville, 1973-77; fellow Nuffield Orthopaedic Ctr., Oxford, Eng., 1977; practice medicine specializing in orthopaedic surgery Southfield, 1978—; staff Providence Hosp., Mich., 1978—, pres. elect med. staff, 1990, pres. med. staff, 1991; sect. chief orthopedics; pres. Porretta Orthopedic Ctr., 1996—, med. dir., 2001—. Pres. Providence Hosp. Med. Staff Research Found., 1984-85, bd. dirs., 1982—; bd. dirs. Mich. Master Health Plan, Southfield, 1982. Contbr. articles to profl. jours. Pres. Birmingham (Mich.) Little League Baseball. Recipient Disting. Alumni award Brother Rice High Sch., 1986. Fellow Am. Acad. Orthopaedic Surgery, Mid Am. Orthopaedic Soc.; mem. Detroit Orthopaedic Soc., Mich. Orthopaedic Soc., Detroit Acad. Orthopaedic Surgeons (past pres.), Oakland Hills Country Club (Birmingham, Mich.), Beverly Hills (Mich.) Club. Avocations: earthwatch vol., travel, sports. Home: 627 Waddington St Bloomfield Hills MI 48301-2346 Office: Porretta Orthopaedic Ctr 22250 Providence Dr Ste 401 Southfield MI 48075-6212

OHLDE, FREDERICK A. religious organization executive; BA, Concordia Tchr.'s Coll.; MA, Temple U. Adminstr. pvt. secondary sch., Phila.; joined Aid Assn. Lutherans, Appleton, Wis., 1975, sr. v.p. fraternal ops. Bd. visitors Sch. Human Ecology U. Wis., Madison. Office: Aid Assn Lutherans 4321 N Ballard Rd Appleton WI 54913-7729

OHM, HERBERT WILLIS, agronomy educator; b. Albert Lea, Minn., Jan. 28, 1945; s. Wilhelm Carl and Lena Ann (Finkbeiner) O.; m. Judy Ann Chrisinger, Aug. 8, 1964; children: Cari Lynn, David William. BS in Agrl. Edn., U. Minn., St. Paul, 1967; MS in Plant Breeding, N.D. State U., 1969; PhD in Plant Genetics and Breeding, Purdue U., 1972. Cert. agronomist. Asst. prof. Purdue U., West Lafayette, Ind., 1972-77, assoc. prof. agronomy, 1977-83, prof., 1983—. Team leader Interdisciplinary Wheat and Oat Genetics and Breeding Program, West Lafayette, 1980—, Interdisciplinary Purdue/AID Devel. Program, Burkina Faso, West Africa, 1983-85; mgr. hard red winter wheat rsch. Pioneer Hi-Bred Internat., Inc., Hutchinson, Kans., 1980. Contbr. book chpts. Recipient Soils and Crops Merit award Ind. Crop Improvement Assn., 1988, Merit award Orgn. of African Unity, 1989, Meritorious Svc. award Sci., Tech. and Rsch. Commn., 1989, Agronomic Acheivement award American Soc. of Agronomy, 1994, Sch. of Agr. Team award, 2000. Fellow: AAAS, Crop Sci. Soc. Am. (chmn. divsn. 1991), Am. Soc. Agronomy; mem.: Am. Registry Cert. Profls. in Agrl. Crops and Soils (cert.), Coun. Agrl. Sci. and Tech., Nat. Oat Improvement Coun. (chmn.), Am. Oat Workers Conf. Avocations: woodworking, music. Office: Purdue U Dept Agronomy Lilly Hall Life Scis West Lafayette IN 47907-1150

OKA, TAKESHI, physicist, chemist, astronomer, educator; b. Tokyo, June 10, 1932; arrived in Can., 1963, naturalized, 1973; s. Shumpei and Chiyoko O.; m. Keiko Nukui, Oct. 24, 1960; children: Ritsuko, Noriko, Kentaro, Yujiro. B.Sc., U. Tokyo, 1955, Ph.D., 1960; PhD (hon.), U. Waterloo, 2001. Rsch. assoc. U. Tokyo, 1960-63; fellow NRC Can., Ottawa, Ont., 1963-65, asst., 1965-68, assoc., 1968-71, sr. rsch. physicist, 1971-80; prof. U. Chgo., 1981—; Robert A. Millikan disting. prof., 1989—; prof. Enrico Fermi inst., 1993—. Mem. editorial bd. Chem. Physics, 1972-92, Jour. Molecular Spectroscopy, 1973—, Jour. Chem. Physics, 1975-77. Recipient Steacie prize, 1972; Earle K. Plyler prize, 1982. Fellow Royal Soc. Can., Royal Soc. London, Am. Phys. Soc., Optical Soc. Am. (William F. Meggers award 1997, Ellis R. Lippincott award 1998), Am. Acad. Scis. and Arts; mem. Am. Astron. Soc; Am. Chem. Soc. (E. Bright Wilson award, 2002). Office: U Chgo Dept Chemistry Astronomy & Astrophysics Chicago IL 60637 E-mail: t_oka@uchicago.edu.

O'KEEFE, MICHAEL DANIEL, lawyer; b. St. Louis, Jan. 3, 1938; s. Daniel Michael and Hanoria (Moriarty) O'K.; m. Bonnie Bowdern, July 11, 1964; children: Collen Coyne, Daniel Michael. AB, LLB, St. Louis U., 1961; postgrad., George Washington U., 1963. Bar: Mo. 1961, U.S. Ct. Appeals (8th cir.) 1961, U.S. Dist. Ct. (ea. dist.) Mo. 1961, Ill. 1975, U.S. Dist. Ct. (so. dist.) Ill. 1975, U.S. Ct. Appeals (5th and 7th cirs.) 1983, (10th cir.) 1995. Asst. atty. U.S. Ct. Appeals, St. Louis, 1962-63, 64-65; pvt. practice, 1964-67; ptnr. Lucas, Murphy & O'Keefe, 1967-74, Thompson & Mitchell, St. Louis, 1974-96. Adj. prof. trial practice Sch. of Law, St. Louis U., 1992—. Editor: American Maritime Cases, 1985—. Active Port Commn., St. Louis; trustee St. Louis U. Capt. USAF, 1962-64. Fellow Am. Coll. Trial Lawyers; mem. Internat. Assn. Def. Counsel, Fedn. Ins. and Corp. Counsel, Maritime Law Assn., USAZ, Nat. Assn. Railroad Trial Counsel, Am. Law Inst. Democrat. Roman Catholic. Avocations: reading, tennis, fencing, archaeology, microbiology. Home: 372 Walton Row Saint Louis MO 63108-1909 Office: Thompson Coburn One Firstar Plz Saint Louis MO 63101-1643

O'KEEFE, THOMAS JOSEPH, metallurgical engineer; b. St. Louis, Oct. 2, 1935; s. Thomas and Hazel (Howard) O'K.; m. Jane Gilmartin, Aug. 31, 1957; children— Thomas, Kathleen, Matthew, Daniel, Margaret, Robert. BS, Mo. Sch. Mines, 1958; PhD, U. Mo., Rolla, 1965. Process control engr. Dow Metal Products Co., Madison, Ill., 1959-61; mem. faculty U. Mo., Rolla, 1965—, prof. metall. engring., 1972—, Curators prof. metall. engring., 1985-86, Curators Disting. prof., 1986—. Rsch. technologist NASA, Houston, summer 1965; rsch. metall. engr. Ames (Iowa) Lab., 1966-67; rsch. metall. engr., cons. Cominco Ltd., Trail, B.C., Can., 1970-71; Disting. lectr. hydrometallurgy U. B.C., 1992, U. Mo.-Rolla Sch. Mining and Metallurgy Acad. Recipient Alumni Merit award U. Mo., Rolla, 1971, Outstanding Tchg. award, 1979, Silver medal paper award AESF, 1994; Jefferson-Smurfit fellow, 1984-85. Mem. AIME (dir. 1976-77, 79-81, EMD lectr. 1991), Testing Materials Soc., The Metall. Soc., Sigma Xi, Alpha Sigma Mu, Tau Beta Pi, Phi Kappa Theta (dir. 1965-77, cert. commendation 1970, pres. citation 1986). Home: 905 Southview Dr Rolla MO 65401-4720 Office: Material Research Center Univ Mo Rolla MO 65409

O'KEEFE, THOMAS MICHAEL, academic administrator; b. St. Cloud, Minn., Mar. 25, 1940; s. Thomas William and Genevieve B. (McCormick) O'K.; m. Kathleen Marie Gnifkowski, Aug. 20, 1966; children: Steven Michael, Ann Catherine. Student, Marquette U., 1961-65, BS, 1965; MS in Nuclear Physics, U. Pitts., 1968; DHL, Hamline U., 1989. Dir. edn. planning HEW, Washington, 1969-70, dep. asst. sec., 1977-80; v.p. Carnegie Found. for Advancement of Teaching, 1980-83; pres. Consortium for Advancement Pvt. Higher Edn., 1983-89; exec. v.p. McKnight Found., Mpls., 1989-99; commr. Dept. Human Svcs., State Minn., St. Paul, 1999—2002; pres. Mpls. Coll. Art and Design, 2002—. Dir. Washington internships in edn. George Washington U., 1970-73; dir. policy analysis and evaluation U. Ill., Chgo., 1973-74, assoc. v.p. acad. affairs, 1974-77; head U.S. del. to Orgn. Econ. Coop. and Devel., 1979, 80; mem. Carnegie Forum on Edn. and the Economy, 1985-88; mem. N.J. Commn. on Ind. Higher Edn., 1986-88; mem. task force on ind. higher edn. Edn. Commn. States, 1987-89; co-chair Program on Edn. in a Changing Soc., The Aspen Inst., 1987—. Contbr. articles to profl. jours.; contbg. editor: Change mag., 1985—2001; bd. dirs.: Editl. Project in Edn., 1984—93. Bd. dirs. The Edn. Resources Inst., Boston, 1987-94, Minn. Coun. on Founds., 1994-99, Minn. Pub. Radio, 1999—; trustee Buena Vista Coll., Storm Lake, Iowa, 1984-90; mem. Coun. on Fgn. Rels., 1995-99; bd. regents U. Minn., 1996—. Mem.: Mpls. Club. Democrat. Office: Mpls Coll Art and Design 2501 Stevens Ave S Minneapolis MN 55404

OKIISHI, THEODORE HISAO, mechanical engineering educator; b. Honolulu, Jan. 15, 1939; s. Clifford Muneo and Dorothy Asako (Tokushima) O.; m. Rae Wiemers, May 28, 1963; children: Christopher Gene, John Clifford, Mark William, Kenneth Edward Student, U. Hawaii, 1956-57; BS, Iowa State U., 1960, MS, 1963, PhD, 1965. Registered profl. engr., Iowa, Ohio. From asst. prof. to assoc. dean coll. engring. Iowa State U., Ames, 1967—. Cons. on fluid dynamics Contbr. articles to profl. jours. Served to capt. C.E., U.S. Army, 1965-67 Decorated Joint Services Commendation award; named Outstanding Prof., Iowa State U. student sect. ASME, 1983, Mech. Engring. Dept. Prof. of Yr., Iowa State U., 1977, 86, 90; recipient award for research NASA, 1975; Ralph R. Teetor award Soc. Automotive Engrs., 1976, Engring. Coll. Superior Teaching award Iowa State U., 1987, Cardinal Key Iowa State U., 1991. Fellow ASME (Melville medal 1989, 98); mem. AIAA, Sigma Xi. Republican. Mem. Ch. of Jesus Christ of Latter-day Saints. Club: Osborn Research Home: 2940 Monroe Dr Ames IA 50010-4362 Office: Iowa State U 104 Marston Hl Ames IA 50011-0001 E-mail: tedo@iastate.edu.

OKUN, MAURY, dance company executive; Exec. dir. Eisenhower Dance Ensemble, Troy, Mich. Office: Eisenhower Dance Ensemble Ste 214 755 W Big Beaver Troy MI 48084

OLDE, ERNEST J. investment company executive; Chmn. bd. dirs. Olde Fin. Corp., Detroit, until 1999. Office: H&R Block Fin Advisors 751 Griswold St Detroit MI 48226-3224

O'LEARY, DANIEL VINCENT, JR. lawyer; b. Bklyn., May 26, 1942; s. Daniel Vincent and Mary (Maxwell) O'L.; m. Marilyn Irene Gavigan, June 1, 1968; children: Daniel, Katherine, Molly, James. AB cum laude, Georgetown U., 1963; LLB, Yale U., 1966. Bar: Ill. 1967. Assoc. Wilson & Mc Ilvaine, Chgo., 1967—75, ptnr., 1975—87, Peterson & Ross, Chgo., 1987—94, Schwartz & Freeman, Chgo., 1994—95; of counsel Mandell, Menkes & Surdyk, LLC, 1995—. Pres., bd. dirs. Jim's Cayman Co., Ltd.; pres. TV and Radio Purchasing Group Inc.; asst. sec. L.M.C. Ins. Co. Bermuda, 1990—; pres. Wagering Ins. N.Am. Purchasing Group Inc., 1997—. Lt. comdr. USNR, ret. Mem. Kenilworth Sailing Club (commodore 1985-87). Roman Catholic. Avocations: fishing, scuba diving. Office: Mandel Menkes & Surdyk LLC Ste 300 333 W Wacker Dr Chicago IL 60606 E-mail: doleary@mms-law.net.

O'LEARY, DENNIS SOPHIAN, medical organization executive; b. Kansas City, Mo., Jan. 28, 1938; s. Theodore Morgan and Emily (Sophian) O'L.; m. Margaret Rose Wiedman, Mar. 29, 1980; children: Margaret Rose, Theodore Morgan. BA, Harvard U., 1960; MD, Cornell U., 1964. Diplomate Am. Bd. Internal Medicine, Am. Bd. Hematology. Intern U. Minn. Hosp., Mpls., 1964-65, resident, 1965-66, Strong Meml. Hosp., Rochester, N.Y., 1966-68; asst. prof. medicine and pathology George Washington U. Med. Ctr., Washington, 1971-73, assoc. prof., 1973-80, prof. medicine, 1980-86, assoc. dean grad. med. edn., 1973-77, dean clin. affairs, 1977-86; pres. Joint Commn. on Accreditation Healthcare Orgns., Oakbrook Terrace, Ill., 1986—. Med. dir. George Washington U. Hosp., 1974-85, v.p. Univ. Health Plan, 1977-85; pres. D.C. Med. Soc., 1983. Chmn. editl. bd. Med. Staff News, 1985-86; contbr. articles to profl. jours. Founding mem. Nat. Capital Area Health Care Coalition, Washington, 1982; trustee James S. Brady Found., Washington, 1982-87; bd. dirs. D.C. Polit. Action Com., 1982-84. Maj. U.S. Army, 1968-71. Recipient Community Service award D.C. Med. Soc., 1981, Key to the City, Mayor of Kansas City, Mo., 1982. Fellow Am. Coll. Physician Execs., ACP-Am. Soc. Internal Medicine; mem. AMA (resolution commendation 1981), Soc. Med. Adminstrs., Am. Hosp. Assn. (del. 1984-86, resolution commendation 1981), Internat. Club (Chgo.). Avocation: tennis.

O'LEARY, TIMOTHY MICHAEL, real estate corporation officer; b. Savanna, Ill., Mar. 24, 1946; s. John Patrick and Hazel O'Leary; m. Patricia Ann Woosnam; children: Kevin, Kathleen, Maureen, Mary Margaret, Michael, John. Student, Loras Coll., 1964-68; BS, No. Ill. U., 1970, MSBA, 1974. Systems programmer Newel Co., Freeport, Ill., 1970-71, acting mgr. accounts receivable, 1971-73; v.p., treas. HTO Real Estate Svcs., Chgo., Des Plaines, 1974-90, pres., treas. Northbrook, 1990-94; sr. v.p. Anderson Schroud Group, Schaumburg, 1994-96; pres. O'Leary Realty Corp., 1996—. Chmn. profl. stds. com. Chgo. Bd. Realtors, 1984-85; treas. The Real Estate Consortium, 1993, v.p., 1994-95. Mem. sch. bd. St. Luke Sch., River Forest, Ill., 1985-88, chmn. 1987-88; mem. troop com. Boy Scouts Am., 2000—. Mem. Soc. Indsl. and Office Realtors (vice chmn. regional seminar edn. 1984-87, exec. com. Chgo. chpt. 1987-91, nat. bd. dirs. 1987-90, treas. 1988, sec. 1989, v.p. 1990, pres. 1991), Oak Park Jaycees (past pres.), Realtors Nat. Mktg. Inst. (bd. dirs. Ill. chpt. cert. comml. investment 1988-89), Ill. Assn. Realtors (chmn. comml. indsl. subcom. 1990-91, chmn. CI com. 1991-92, Presdl. award 1991), Am. Soc. Real Estate Counselors, No. Ill. Comml. Assn. of Realtors (bd. dirs. 2001—), Realtors 40 Club (clk. 1985-86, cashier 1989-90, chmn. 1992), KC (dep. grand knight Queen of Peace coun. 2001—). Roman Catholic. E-mail: tim@olearyrealty.com.

OLEEN, LANA, state legislator; b. Kirksville, Mo., Apr. 26, 1949; d. Robert James and Frances (Primm) Scrimsher; m. Kent E. Oleen; children: Brooke, Bentson. BS in Edn., Ks. State Tchrs. Coll., 1972; MS in Curriculum, Emporia State U., 1977. Tchr., Council Grove, Kans., 1972-74, St. George, from 1978; communications coord. Woodward-Clyde Cons., San Francisco, 1974-75; dir. communication Kans. Dept. Human Resources; mem. Kans. State Senate, 1988—. Mem. Rep. Precinct Com., 1978—. Active Kans. Rep. Women, Riley County Rep. Women. Mem. NEA, Nat. Coun. Tchrs. of English. Lutheran. Office: Kansas Senate State Capitol Rm 136-N Topeka KS 66612 Address: 1619 Poyntz Ave Manhattan KS 66502-4148

OLEN, GARY, marketing company executive; b. Milw., Mar. 29, 1942; s. Norbert John and Irene (Rydlewicz) O.; m. Maryann Wozniak (div. May 1988); children: Wendy, Jeff. Grad. high sch., Milw. Rebuyer catalog div. J.C. Penney Co., Milw., 1960-67; buyer C&H Distbrs., 1967-70; mktg. dir. Fidelity Products, Mpls., 1970-77; owner, mgr. Sportsman's Guide, 1977-89, exec. v.p., prin., 1989—. Republican. Roman Catholic. Avocations: hunting, fishing, travel. Home: 4115 Havenhill Cir Saint Paul MN 55123-1661 Office: Sportsmans Guide 411 Farwell Ave South Saint Paul MN 55075-2464

OLESEN, DOUGLAS EUGENE, research institute executive; b. Tonasket, Wash., Jan. 12, 1939; s. Magnus and Esther Rae (Myers) Olesen; m. Michaele Ann Engdahl, Nov. 18, 1964; children: Douglas Eugene, Stephen Christian. BS, U. Wash., 1962, MS, 1963, postgrad., 1965—67, PhD, 1972. Rsch. engr. space research divsn. Boeing Aircraft Co., Seattle, 1963—64; with Battelle Meml. Inst., Pacific NW Labs., Richland, 1967—84, mgr. water resources systems sect., water and land resources dept., 1970—71, mgr. dept., 1971—75, dep. dir. rsch. labs., 1975, dir. rsch., 1975—79, v.p. inst., dir. NW divsn., 1979—84; exec. v.p., COO Battelle Meml. Inst., Columbus, Ohio, 1984—87, pres., CEO, 1987—2001; ret., 2001. Bd. dirs. Goodrich Co., BattellePharma, Inc., Battelle for Kids. Patentee process and sys. for treating wastewater. Mem. pres.'s coun. Columbus Mus. of Art; bd. dirs. Ohio State U. Found., Coun. on Competitiveness. Office: Battelle Meml Inst 505 King Ave Columbus OH 43201-2681

OLESZKIEWICZ, JAN ALOJZY, engineering educator; MS in Sanitary Engring. Design, Wroclaw (Poland) U., 1966; MS in Water Quality Mgmt., Vanderbilt U., 1972, PhD in Environ. Engring., 1974. Chartered engr. Chartered Inst. Water and Environ. Mgmt., 1998; diplomate Am. Acad. Environ. Engrs.; profl. engr., Can. Project mgr. indsl. wastes group DLA, Inc., Pitts., 1981-82; assoc. prof. civil engring. U. Man. (Can.), 1983-89, prof. civil engring., 1990—, adj. prof. dept. microbiology, 1988-96. Cons. US AID-RTI and LEMTECH Konsulting, Cracow, Poland, 1993—, evaln. hog manure processing techs. CETAC, Saskatoon, Sask., Can., 1998—, tng. operators of advanced WWTP in nutrient removal and biosolids, 1998—, rsch. to upgrade of 250 000/m3/d WWTP for Warsaw to biol. nutrient removal, 1999, numerous others; presenter in field. Author: Decision Maker's Manual of Sludge Management, 1998; co-author, editor, cons.: (handbook) Operation of Advanced Waste Treatment Plants, 1997, Decision Maker's Manual: Solid Waste Landfill, 1999; contbr. over 200 articles to profl. jours., chpts. to books. Recipient Premier of Man. award for excellence in r & d sustainable devel. 1995, 97, Dean of Engring. award, 1997, Gold Medal Polish Soc. Sanitary Engrs., 1997, Gold Medal Min. of Environ. Poland, 1998. Fellow Can. Soc. Civil Engring. (chair environ. engring. divsn. 1991-95, chair environ. splty. confs. 1994, co-chair 1996, Can. Soc. Civil Engring.-ASCE Internat. Conf. 1994, Can. Soc. Civil Engring.-Polish Soc. Sanitary Engrs.-ASCE Internat. Conf. 1996, 2000, Albert E. Berry medal 1998); mem. Water Environ. Fedn., Can. Water and Waste Assn., Internat. Water Assn., Tau Beta Pi. Achievements include research and development of anaerobic hybrid biological reactor technology for industrial wastes, sulphate reduction reactor and process technology for industrial waste water treatment, cold temperature SBR process for nitrogen removal in lagoon treating of slaughterhouse waste; pilot work of the first North American demonstration of the anaerobic co-composting of municipal sludge and solid waste; 3 patents on industrial waste and hog manure management. Office: U Manitoba Dept Civil Engr 15 Gillison St Winnipeg MB Canada R3T 5V6 Fax: (204) 474-7513. E-mail: oleszkie@cc.umanitoba.ca.

OLIAN, ROBERT MARTIN, lawyer; b. Cleve., June 14, 1953; s. Robert Meade and Doris Isa (Hessing) O.; m. Terri Ellen Ruther, Aug. 10, 1980; children: Andrew Zachary, Alix Michelle, Joshua Brett. AB, Harvard U., 1973, JD, M in Pub. Policy, 1977. Bar: Ill. 1977, U.S. Dist. Ct. (no. dist.) Ill. 1977, U.S. Ct. Appeals (7th cir.) 1983, U.S. Dist. Ct. (no dist. trial bar) Ill. 1992, U.S. Dist. Ct. (we. dist.) Mich. 1994. Assoc. Sidley & Austin, Chgo., 1977-84; ptnr. Sidley Austin Brown & Wood, 1985—. Editor: Illinois Environmental Law Handbook, 1988, 97. Panel atty. Chgo. Vol. Legal Svcs., Chgo., 1983—; mem. regional strategic planning/mktg. com. Alexian Bros. Ill., Inc., Elk Grove, 1985-88; trustee North Shore Congregation Israel, 1990—, sec., 1995-96, v.p., 1996—. Mem. ABA, Chgo. Bar Assn., Std. Club, Harvard Club (Chgo.). Jewish. Home: 85 Oakmont Rd Highland Park IL 60035-4111 Office: Sidley Austin Brown & Wood Bank One Plaza 10 S Dearborn St #5200 Chicago IL 60603-2003 E-mail: rolian@sidley.com.

OLIN, WILLIAM HAROLD, orthodontist, educator; b. Menominee, Mich., Mar. 7, 1924; s. Harold H. and Lillian (Hallgren) Olin; m. Bertha Spitters, May 6, 1950; children: William Harold, Paul Scott, Jon Edwards. DDS, Marquette U., 1947; MS, U. Iowa, 1948. Asst. prof. orthodontics Univ. Hosps., U. Iowa, Iowa City, 1948, assoc. prof., 1963-70, prof., 1970-93, prof. emeritus, 1995—. Chmn. bd. dirs. Hills Bank. Author: (book) Cleft Lip and Palate Rehabilitation, 1960; contbr. articles to profl. jours. Fund raiser, participant Ops. Smile. Served to capt. U.S. Army, 1952—54. Mem.: Am. Acad. Sports Dentistry (bd. dirs., sec./treas. 1989—95), Am. Cleft Palate Assn. (pres. 1970), Iowa Orthodontic Soc. 1959, Midwest Orthodontic Soc. 1968—69, Angle Orthodontic Soc. Midwest 1982, Univ. Athletic Club (bd. dirs.), Rotary (pres. Iowa City). Republican. Methodist. Avocations: coins, antique music boxes, sports, travel, political memorabilia. Home: 426 Mahaska Dr Iowa City IA 52246-1610

OLINGER, GORDON NORDELL, surgeon; b. Denver, 1942; MD, U. Rochester, 1968. Intern UCLA, 1968-69, resident, 1969-70, 72-74; resident in surgery NIH Clinic, Bethesda, Md., 1970-72; with Froedert Meml. Luth. Hosp.; prof., chmn. Med. Coll. Wis. Mem. ACS, Soc. Thoracic Surgery, Am. Assn. for Thoracic Surgery, Am. Surg. Assn. Office: Acad Faculty 9200 W Wisconsin Ave Milwaukee WI 53226-3522

OLINS, ROBERT ABBOT, communications research executive; b. Cambridge, Mass., Sept. 25, 1942; s. Harry and Janice Olins; m. Irma Westrich, June 16, 1967; 1 son, Matthew Abbot. Student, Hobart Coll., 1961-62, San Francisco Art Inst., 1962; BA, U. Mass., 1967; postgrad., U. Tampa, 1968; MA, U. Mo., 1969, PhD, 1972. With Marsteller, 1972, N.W. Ayer, 1972, Post, Keys & Gardner, Chgo., 1973, Young & Rubicam, Chgo., 1973-76, mng. dir. comm. rsch. divsn., 1976-77; pres., CEO, subs. Comm. Rsch. Inc., 1978—, owner, chmn., 1979—. Pres., chief exec. officer Insights, Chgo., 1976—. Contbr. articles to profl. jours. Recipient Chgo./4 award for creative excellence, 1974; overall winner Chgo. Mackinac race, 1981; Am. Assn. Advt. Agys. grantee, 1968-71 Mem.: Mid North Assn. (bd. dirs., chmn. planning), Am. Mktg. Assn., Chgo. Yacht Club, Lake Michigan Yachting Assn., U.S. Sailing Club, Skyline Club. Avocations: skiing, sailing, power boating. Office: Communications Rsch Inc 233 E Wacker Dr Apt 2105 Chicago IL 60601-5110 E-mail: cri77@aol.com.

OLIPHANT, PATRICK, cartoonist; b. Adelaide, Australia, July 24, 1935; came to U.S., 1964; s. Donald K. and Grace L. (Price) O.; children: Laura, Grant, Susan. L.H.D. (hon.), Dartmouth Coll., 1981. Copyboy, press artist Adelaide Advertiser, 1953-55, editorial cartoonist, 1955-64; world tour to study cartooning techniques, 1959; editorial cartoonist Denver Post, 1964-75, Washington Star, 1975-81, L.A. Times Syndicate, 1965-80, Universal Press Syndicate, 1980—; represented by Susan Conway Gallery, Washington. Author: The Oliphant Book, 1969, Four More Years, 1973, An Informal Gathering, 1978, Oliphant! A Cartoon Collection, 1980, The Jellybean Society, 1981, Ban this Book, 1982, But Seriously Folks, 1983, The Year of Living Perilously, 1984, Make My Day, 1985, Between a Rock and a Hard Place, 1986, Up to There in Alligators, 1987, Nothing Basically Wrong, 1988, What Those People Need Is a Puppy, 1989, Fashions for the New World Order, 1991, Just Say No, 1992, Why do I Feel Uneasy?, 1993, Waiting for the Other Shoe to Drop, 1994, Off to the Revolution, 1995, Maintain The Status Quo, 1996, So That Where They Come From, 1997, Oliphant's Anthem, 1998, Are We There Yet?, 1999, Now We'll Have to Spray for Politicians, 2000, When We Can't See the Forest for the Bushes, 2001. Recipient 2d Place award as funniest cartoonist Internat. Fedn. Free Journalists in Fleet St., London, 1958, Profl. Journalism award Sigma Delta Chi, 1966, Pulitzer prize for editl. cartooning, 1967, Cartoonist of Yr. award Nat. Cartoonist Soc., 1968, 72, Best in Bus. award Washington Journalism Rev., 1985, 87, Premio Satira Politica award Forte de Marmi, 1992, Thomas Nast award, 1992. Office: Universal Press Syndicate 4520 Main St Ste 700 Kansas City MO 64111-7701 also: care Susan Conway Gallery 1214 30th St NW Washington DC 20007-3401

OLIVER, EDWARD CARL, state legislator, retired investment executive; b. St. Paul, May 31, 1930; s. Charles Edmund and Esther Marie (Bjugstad) O.; m. Charlotte Severson, Sept. 15, 1956; children: Charles E., Andrew T., Peter A. BA, U. Minn., 1955. Sales rep. Armstrong Cork Co., N.Y.C., 1955; registered rep. Piper, Jaffray & Hopwood, Mpls., 1958; mgr. Mut. Funds Inc., subs. Dayton's, 1964, NWNL Mgmt. Corp. subs. Northwestern Nat. Life Ins. Co., Mpls., 1968-72, v.p., 1972-81, pres., dir., 1981-90; mem. Minn. State Senate, 1992—, asst. minority leader, 1998—. Arbitrator/mediator, Nat. Assn. Securities Dealers, 1988—; bd. dirs. 1st Minn. Bank, N.A. Commr. Gt. Lakes commn., 1993—; ch. elder, Presbyn. ch., Deephaven, Mpls. Mem. Internat. Assn. Fin. Planners (past pres. Twin City chpt., nat. governing com.), Psi Upsilon, Mpls. Club. Home: 20230 Cottagewood Rd Excelsior MN 55331-9300 Office: Washington Sq Securities Inc 100 Washington Ave S Ste 1600 Minneapolis MN 55401-2154 E-mail: sen.edward.oliver@senate.leg.state.mn.us.

OLIVER, G(EORGE) BENJAMIN, educational administrator, philosophy educator; b. Mpls., Sept. 17, 1938; s. Clarence P. and Cecile (Worley) O.; m. Paula Rae Foust, Sept. 15, 1963; children: Paul Benjamin, Rebecca Lee. BA with honors, U. Tex., 1960; MDiv, Union Theol. Sem., N.Y.C., 1963; MA, Northwestern U., 1966, PhD, 1967. Lectr. Northwestern U., Evanston, Ill., 1966-67; asst. prof. Hobart & William Smith Coll., Geneva, 1967-71, chmn. dept. philosophy, 1969-77, assoc. prof., 1971-77, prof., 1977; dean Southwestern U., Georgetown, Tex., 1977-89, provost, 1986-89; pres. Hiram (Ohio) Coll., 1989-2000, pres. emeritus, 2000—. Chmn. Coun. Acad. Deans and V.P.s of Tex., 1987-88. Contbr. articles to profl. jours. Trustee John Cabot U., Rome, 1989-2000, Grand River Acad., Austinburg, Ohio, 1991-2000, N.E. Ohio Coun. Higher Edn., 1991-2000, Ohio Found. Ind. Coll., 1989-2000, vice-chair, 1999-2000, exec. com., 1994-2000, co-chair strategic planning com., 1997-98; trustee Assn. Ind. Colls. and Univs. Ohio, 1993-2000, Nat. Assn. Ind. Colls. and Univs. Pol. Com. on Student Aid, 1999-2000, Am. Coun. Edn. Commn. Govtl. Rels., 1994-97, Cleve. Coun. on World Affairs, 1996-2000; chmn. bd. trustees East Ctrl. Coll. Consortium, 1993-95. Rockefeller Found. fellow, 1960-61, Internat. fellow Columbia U., 1962-63; rsch. grantee NEH, 1973-74. Mem. AAUP, Am. Coun. Edn. (commn. on govtl. rels.), Soc. for Values in Higher Edn., Assn. Ind. Coll. and Univs. Ohio (treas. 1993-94), East Ctrl. Colls. Consortium (chair, bd. trustees 1993-95), Ohio Found. Ind. Colls. (exec. com. 1994-2000, vice chair elect 1999-2000), Am. Assn. Higher Edn., Cleve. Coun. on Fgn. Rels. Episcopalian. Office: Hiram Coll Office of Pres Hiram OH 44234 E-mail: olivergben@msn.com.

OLIVER, GILDA MARIA, sculptor, painter, artist; b. Manhattan, N.Y., Nov. 16, 1961; d. Thomas Tobin and Francoise Marie (Bonamy) Krampf; m. Shawn James Francis McLean, Aug. 1, 1983 (div. Dec. 1986); 1 child, Cory Shawn McLean; m. Marc Scott Oliver (div. 1998). BFA cum laude, Wells Coll., Aurora, N.Y., 1984; BFA, N.Y.S. Coll. of Ceramics at Alfred U., 1994; MFA, Cranbrook Art Acad., 1997. Artist-in-residence Powabic Pottery, Detroit, 1997-98. Dir. corp. sales and rentals Cambridge (Mass.) Art Assn., 1988-92; tchrs. asst. art dept. Wells Coll., Aurora, 1980-84; prof. Ctr. for Creative Studies, Detroit, 1999—. Commissioned sculptures include Heather, 1984, Mark Phillips, 1987, Dr. Cutler-West, 1987, George Orwell, 1988, B.F. Skinner, 1988, Margaret Gibson, 1993 (nom. Pulitzer Prize award 1995), David McKain, 1992 (nom. Pulitzer Prize award 1995); one man show at A.R.C. Gallery, Chgo., 2001, Arianna Gallery, Royal Oak, Mich., 1998-2000; shows include U. Pitts., Bradford, Hanley Gallery, 1995; represented in collections Wells Coll., Aurora, 1984, Lillian Hellman, N.Y.C., 1984, Victoria and Richard MacKenzie-Childs, Ltd., Aurora, 1988, B.F. Skinner, Cambridge, 1989, Robert and Jane Saltonstall, Jr., Concord, Mass., 1989, David McKain and Margaret Gibson, Providence, R.I., 1995, Powabic Pottery, Detroit, 1999, 2000, 01, Sculpture, Objects and Functional Art Show, N.Y.C., 2000, 01, House and Garden Show, 2001; represented in galleries including Copley Soc., Boston, 1985-89, Cambridge Art Assn., 1988-90, Bella Luna Gallery, Boston, 1992-93, Brickbottom Gallery, Somerville, Mass., 1989-95, Loveed Gallery, 1995—, A.R.C. Gallery, Chgo., 2001; featured (cover) Am. Ceramics mag., Art in Am.; featured Artnews Mag., 2000, Ceramics Monthly, 1998, 99. Nominated Tiffany Comfort award, 1999; Fullbright finalist, 1997. Home: 19979 Spencer St Detroit MI 48234-3183 E-mail: Olvrgld@aol.com.

OLIVER, JERRY ALTON, protective services official; 4 children. BS in Criminal Justice, Ariz. State U., MS in Pub. Adminstrn., 1988; postgrad., Police Exec. Rsch. Forum, Washington. From patrolman to supr. Phoenix Police Dept., from supr. to asst. chief of police, 1971-90; dir. drug policy Memphis Police Dept.; chief of police Pasadena (Calif.) Police Dept., Richmond (Va.) Police Dept., 1995—. Founder Spl. Friends Project, Richmond, 1988—. Inductee Ariz. State U. Coll. Pub. Programs Hall of Fame, 1989; recipient Phoenix chpt. Image award NAACP, 1990, People of the Ur. award Law Enforcement News, 1999, Richmonder of the Ur. award Richmond Style Mag., 1999, U.S. Atty. Gen.'s award for outstanding contbns. to cmty. partnership for pub. safety, 2000, othrs. Office: Detroit Police Dept Chief of Police 1300 Beaubien Detroit MI 48226

OLIVER, JOHN PRESTON, chemistry educator, academic administrator; b. Klamath Falls, Oreg., Aug. 7, 1934; s. Robert Preston and Agnes May (McCornack) O.; m. Elizabeth Ann Shaw, Aug. 12, 1956; children: Karen Sue Oliver Vernon, Roy John, Gordon Preston. BA, U. Oreg., 1956; PhD, U. Wash., 1959. Asst. prof. chemistry Wayne State U., Detroit, 1959-64, assoc. prof., 1964-67, prof., 1967—, assoc. dean R&D, Coll. Liberal Arts, 1987-91, acting dean, 1991-92, interim dean Coll. Sci., 1992-93, dep. provost, 1996—. Chmn. organizing com. XIV Internat. Conf. on Organometallic Chemistry. Mem. Ferndale (Mich.) Bd. Edn., 1984-88. Mem. Am. Chem. Soc., Detroit sect. Am. Chem. Soc., Sigma Xi. Office: Wayne State Univ Rm 4101 FAB Detroit MI 48202-3489 E-mail: jpo@wayne.edu.

OLIVER, ROSEANN, lawyer; b. Chgo., Oct. 7, 1947; BA, Northwestern U., 1969; JD, Loyola U., 1972. Bar: Ill. 1972, U.S. Dist. Ct. (no. dist.) Ill. 1974, U.S. Ct. Appeals (7th cir.) 1974. Legal writing instr. I.I.T. Chicago-Kent Coll. Law, 1973-74, Loyola U., 1974-75; mem. Cook County Bd. Ethics. Articles editor Loyola Law Jour., 1971-72; contbr. articles to profl. jour. Mem. Ill. State Bar Assn., Chgo. Bar Assn. (spl. counsel 1981-82, chmn. standing com. on litigation 1985-88, amicus curiae com. 1989-95), 7th Cir. Bar Assn., Inns of Ct. Office: Cahill Christian & Kunkle 224 S Michigan Ave Ste 1300 Chicago IL 60604-2583

OLIVER, SOLOMON, JR. judge; b. Bessemer, Ala., July 20, 1947; s. Solomon Sr. and Willie Lee (Davis) O.; married; 2 children. BA, Coll. of Wooster, 1969; JD, NYU, 1972; MA, Case Western Res. U., 1974. Bar: Ohio 1973, U.S. Dist. Ct. (no. dist.) Ohio 1977, U.S. Ct. Appeals (6th cir.) 1977, U.S. Supreme Ct. 1980. Asst. prof. dept. polit. sci. Coll. of Wooster, Ohio, 1972-75; sr. law clk. to Hon. William H. Hastie U.S. Ct. Appeals (3d cir.), Phila., 1975-76; asst. U.S. atty. U.S. Atty.'s Office, Cleve., 1976-82, chief civil divsn., 1978-82; spl. asst. U.S. atty., chief appellate divsn. Dept. Justice, 1982, spl. asst. U.S. atty., 1982-85; prof. law Cleve. State U., 1982-94, assoc. dean faculty and adminstrn., 1991-94. Lectr. in law, trial practice Case Western Res. U., Cleve., 1979-82; vis. scholar Stanford U. Coll. Law, 1987; vis. prof. Comenius U., Bratislava, Czechoslovakia, 1991, Charles U., Prague, Czechoslovakia, 1991. Chair O.K. Hoover Scholarship com. Bapt. Ch., 1987-89; trustee Coll. of Wooster, Ohio, 1991-97, 2000—. Mem. ABA, Nat. Bar Assn. Office: US Dist Ct No Dist Ohio 300 US Courthouse 201 Superior Ave NE Cleveland OH 44114-1201 Fax: 216-522-7951.

OLIVER, THORNAL GOODLOE, health care executive; b. Memphis, Aug. 26, 1934; s. John Oliver and Evelyn Doris (Goodloe) Mitchell; m. Pauline Reid, Oct. 1, 1959. B.S., Tenn. State U., Nashville, 1956; M.H.A., Washington U., St. Louis, 1973. Cert. nursing home adminstr., Mo. Asst. dir., King Meml. Hosp., Kansas City, Mo., 1973-75; evening mgr. Truman Med. Ctr., Kansas City, Mo., 1975-77; asst. adminstr. Mid-Am. Radiation Ctr. U. Kans. Coll. Health Sci., Kansas City, Kans., 1977-81; dir. CHS, Inc., Leawood, Kans., 1981-82; adminstr. Poplar Bluff Hosp., Mo., 1982-83; adminstr. The Benjamin F. Lee Health Ctr., Wilberforce, Ohio, 1983-86; asst. clin. prof. Dept. Community Medicine, Wright State U., Dayton, 1986-89; asst. patent adminstr. Munson Army Hosp., Ft. Leavenworth, Kans., 1987—; cons. Urban Health Assocs., Nashville, 1986-87, others. Contbr. articles to profl. jours. Served with U.S. Army, 1957-59, USAR, 1959-63. Fellow Am. Coll. Hosp. Adminstrs.; mem. Am. Hosp. Assn., Nat. Assn. Health Services Execs., Am. Med. Record Assn., Mo. League of Nursing Home Adminstrs. Home: 10641 N Grand Ave Kansas City MO 64155-1655 Office: Munson Army Hosp Fort Leavenworth KS 66027

OLIVER, TIMOTHY ALLEN, lawyer; b. Lebanon, Ohio, July 13, 1950; s. George Wilbur and Ruthanna Mae (Ward) O.; m. Lois Anne Jacquemin, Oct. 28, 1972; children: Daniel, Matthew. BSBA, Ohio State U., 1971, JD, 1974. Bar: Ohio 1974, U.S. Dist. Ct. (so. dist.) Ohio 1975, U.S. Supreme Ct. 1978. Asst. pros. atty. County of Warren, Lebanon, 1974-76, 79-86, pros. atty., 1986—. Past ptnr. Oliver & Powell, Lebanon. Bd. dirs. Countryside YMCA, Lebanon, 1987-92, Warren/Clinton Drug and Alcohol Coun., Lebanon, 1987—; exec. com. Warren County Rep. Cen. Com., Lebanon, 1987—; trustee Coalition for Drug-Free Greater Cin., 1995—. Mem. ABA, Ohio Bar Assn., Warren County Bar Assn., Nat. Dist. Attys. Assn., Ohio Pros. Attys. Assn. (pres. 1998), Kiwanis (bd. dirs. Lebanon chpt. 1987-93, pres. 1991-92). Avocations: coaching, golf. Office: Warren County Prosecutor 500 Justice Dr Lebanon OH 45036-2379

OLIVIERI, JOSÉ ALBERTO, lawyer; b. San Juan, P.R., Aug. 28, 1957; s. José Juan Olivieri and Carmen Rivera; m. Jeanne Nikolai Olivieri, Aug. 12, 1978; children: Elisa, Lucas, Elena. BA in Polit. Sci. cum laude, Carroll Coll., 1978; JD, Marquette U., 1981. Bar: Wis. 1981. Lawyer Michael, Best & Friedrich, Milw., 1981. Asst. prof. law Marquette U., Milw., 1986-88, adj. prof., 1988—; bd. dirs. Firstar Bank, Milw. Articles editor Marquette Law Rev. Chmn. bd. dirs. Milw. Found., 1998; bd. dirs., pres. United Cmty. Ctr., Milw., 1987-92; mem. U. Wis. Bd. Regents, 1998—. Recipient Pro bono award Posner Found., Milw., 1985, Cmty. Svc. award Future Milw., 1987, Vol. Fundraiser award Nat. Assn. Fundraising Execs., 1993, Leadership award Milw. Civic Alliance, 1995; named Hispanic Man of Yr., United Migrant Opportunity Svcs., Milw., 1998. Mem. ABA, Wis. Hispanic Lawyers Assn. (pres. 1984), Wis. State Bar Assn. (chair labor and employment law sect. 1996), Milw. Bar Assn. Avocations: reading, sports. Office: Michael Best & Friedrich 100 E Wisconsin Ave Ste 3300 Milwaukee WI 53202-4108

OLLINGER, W. JAMES, lawyer, director; b. Kittanning, Pa., Apr. 5, 1943; s. William James and Margaret Elizabeth (Reid) Ollinger; m. Susan Louise Gerspacher, Oct. 20, 1979; children: Mary Rebecca, David James. BA, Capital U., Columbus, Ohio, 1966; JD, Case Western Res. U., 1968. Bar: Ohio 1968, US Dist Ct (no dist) Ohio 1971. Ptnr. Baker & Hostetler, Cleve., 1968—. Bd dirs Parts Assocs Inc, Cleveland, Ohio. Mem Bentleyville Village Coun, Ohio, 1990—93; mayor Bentleyville, 1997—99. Mem.: Order of Coif, Phi Delta Phi. Office: Baker & Hostetler 3200 Nat City Ctr 1900 E 9th St Ste 3200 Cleveland OH 44114-3475 E-mail: jollinger@bakerlaw.com.

OLMAN, GLORIA, secondary education educator; Tchr. Utica High Sch., Mich. Named Nat. H.S. Journalism Tchr. of Yr., 1992, Spl. Recognition advisor, 1981, Disting. Advisor Dow Jones Newspaper Fund Inc., 1987; named to Mich. Journalism Hall of Fame, 1997. Office: Utica High Sch 47255 Shelby Rd Utica MI 48317-3156

OLMAN, LYNN, state legislator; Rep. dist. 51 Ohio Ho. of Reps., Columbus, 1995—. Office: 604 Ford St Maumee OH 43537-1948

OLMSTEAD, WILLIAM EDWARD, mathematics educator; b. San Antonio, June 2, 1936; s. William Harold and Gwendolyn (Littlefield) Olmstead; m. Adele Cross, Aug. 14, 1957 (div. 1967); children: William Harold, Randell Edward. BS, Rice U., 1959; MS, Northwestern U., 1962, PhD, 1963. Mem. rsch. staff S.W. Rsch. Inst., San Antonio, 1959—60; Sloan Found. postdoctoral fellow Johns Hopkins, 1963—64; prof. applied math. Northwestern U., Evanston, Ill., 1964—, chmn. dept. engring. scis. and applied math., 1991—93. Vis. mem. Courant Inst. Math. Scis. NYU, 1967—68; faculty visitor U. Coll. London, England, 1973, Calif. Inst. Tech., 1987, 90. Contbr. articles to profl. jours. Named Technol. Inst. Tchr. of Yr., 1980, Charles Deering McCormick prof., 1994—97; recipient Award for Tchg. Excellence, Northwestern Alumni Assn., 1993. Mem.: Am. Contract Bridge League (silver life master), Soc. Indsl. and Applied Math. (editl. bd. jour. 1998—), Am. Phys. Soc., Am. Math. Soc., Am. Acad. Mechanics, Soc. Engring. Sci. (bd. dirs. 1998—2000), John Evans Club, Sigma Tau, Tau Beta Pi, Sigma Xi. Episcopalian. Home: 153 E Laurel Ave #203 Lake Forest IL 60045 Office: Northwestern U Dept Engring Scis And Applie Evanston IL 60208-0001

OLNESS, KAREN NORMA, pediatrics and international health educator; b. Rushford, Minn., Aug. 28, 1936; d. Norman Theodore and Karen Agnes (Gunderson) O.; m. Hakon Daniel Torjesen, 1962. BA, U. Minn., 1958, BS, MD, 1961. Diplomate Am. Bd. Pediatrics, Am. Bd. Med. Hypnosis. Intern Harbor Gen. Hosp., Torrance, Calif.; resident Nat. Children's Hosp. Med. Ctr., Washington; asst. prof. George Washington U., 1970-74; assoc. prof. U. Minn., Mpls., 1974-87; prof. pediat., family medicine and internat. health Case Western Res. U., Cleve., 1987—. Named Outstanding Woman Physician, Minn. Assn. Women Physicians, 1987; recipient Christopherson award Am. Acad. Pediat., 1998, Aldrich award, Am. Acad. Pediat., 1999; named to Cleve. Med. Hall of Fame, 2000. Fellow Am. Acad. Pediat. (chair internat. health sect. 2001), Am. Acad. Family Physicians, Am. Soc. Clin. Hypnosis (pres. 1984-86), Soc. Clin. and Exptl. Hypnosis (pres. 1991-93); mem. Soc. for Behavioral Pediatrics (pres. 1991-92), Northwestern Pediat. Soc. (pres. 1977), Internat. Hypnosis Soc. (pres.-elect 2000). Office: Case Western Res U 11100 Euclid Ave Cleveland OH 44106-1736 E-mail: kno@po.cwru.edu.

OLNEY, JOHN WILLIAM, psychiatry educator; b. Marathon, Iowa, Oct. 23, 1931; married, 1957; 3 children. BA, U. Iowa, 1957, MD, 1963. Diplomate Am. Bd. Psychiatry, Am. Bd. Neurology. Intern Kaiser Permanente Found., San Francisco, 1963-64; resident, 1964-68; from instr. to assoc. prof. psychiatry Washington U., St. Louis, 1968-77, prof. psychiatry and neuropathology Sch. Medicine, 1977—. NIMH biol. sci. trainee Washington U., 1966-68; asst. psychiatrist Barnes Hosp., 1968—; cons. psychiatrist Malcolm Bliss Mental Health Ctr., 1968—; elected to Inst. Medicine/NAS, 1996. Recipient Wakeman award Rsch. Neurosci., 1992; co-recipient Charles A. Dana award for Pioneering Achievements in Health, 1994. Mem. APA, Am. Assn Neuropathology, Soc. Neurosci. Assn. Rsch. Nervous & Mental Disorders, Psychiatric Rsch. Soc. Achievements include research in role of excitatory neurotoxins in disorders of the nervous system. Office: Washington U Dept Psychiatry Sch Med Saint Louis MO 63110

OLSEN, ARTHUR MARTIN, physician, educator; b. Chgo., Aug. 29, 1909; s. Martin I. and Aagot (Rovelstad) O.; m. Yelena Pavlinova, Sept. 16, 1936; children: Margaret Ann (Mrs. Frank A. Jost), David Martin, Karen Yelena (Mrs. Dori Kanellos), Mary Elizabeth. AB, Dartmouth Coll., 1930; MD, U. Chgo., 1935; MS, U. Minn., 1938. Diplomate Am. Bd. Internal Medicine. Intern Cook County Hosp., Chgo., 1935-36; fellow in medicine, resident Mayo Found., U. Minn., 1936-40, from instr. to prof. medicine, 1950-57, prof., 1957—. Cons. medicine Mayo Clinic, Rochester, Minn., 1940-76, chmn. divsn. thoracic diseases, 1968-71. Author numerous publs. on diseases of the lungs and esophagus. Mem. nat. heart and lung adv. coun. NIH, 1970-71; trustee Mayo Found., 1961-68, mem. subsplty. bd. pulmonary diseases, 1958—, chmn., 1961-63. Recipient Alexander B. Vishnevski medal Inst. Surgery, Moscow, 1966, Andres Bello medal Govt. of Venezuela, 1987, Disting. Alumnus award Rush Med. Coll., U. Chgo., 1989. Fellow ACP, Am. Coll. Chest Physicians (master, regent 1955—, chmn. 1959-66, pres. 1970, Disting. Fellow award 1978, dir. internat. activities 1976-83, cons. internat. activities 1983-85); mem. AMA (Billings gold meadl for exhibit on esophagitis 1955), Am. Soc. Gastrointestinal Endoscopy (pres. 1962-63), Minn. Respiratory Health Assn. (pres. 1964-68), Minn. Med. Assn., Am. Assn. Thoracic Surgery, Am. Thoracic Soc., Minn. Thoracic Soc. (pres. 1952), Am. Bronchoesophagol. Assn. (pres. 1969-70, Chevalier Jackson award 1973), Internat. Bronchoesophagol. Soc. (pres. 1979-81), Minn. Soc. Internal Medicine, Brit. Thoracic Soc. (hon.), Nat. Acad. Medicine of Buenos Aires (hon.), Portuguese Soc. Respiratory Pathology (corr.), Sigma Xi., Alpha Omega Alpha. Episcopalian. Home: 211 2nd St NW ALC #3-304 Rochester MN 55901

OLSEN, EDWARD JOHN, geologist, educator, curator; b. Chgo., Nov. 23, 1927; s. Edward John and Elizabeth (Bornemann) O.; children—Andrea, Ericka. A.B., U. Chgo., 1951, M.S., 1955, Ph.D., 1959. Geologist Geol. Survey Can., 1953, U.S. Geol. Survey, 1954—, Canadian Johns-Manville Co., Ltd., 1956, 57, 59; asst. prof. Case Inst. Tech., also Western Res. U., 1959-60; curator mineralogy Field Mus. Natural History, 1960-91, chmn. dept. geology, 1974-78; research assoc. prof. dept. geophys. scis. U. Chgo., 1977—. Adj. prof. U. Ill., Chgo. Circle, 1970-91. Assoc. editor Geochim. et Cosmochim. Acta., 1985-91. Fellow Mineral. Soc. Am.; mem. Mineral. Assn. Can., Geochem. Soc., Meteoritical Soc. Achievements include spl. research stability relations of minerals in earth's mantle and meteorites. Office: U Chgo Dept Geophys Sci Chicago IL 60637

OLSEN, GEORGE EDWARD, retired insurance executive; b. Antigo, Wis., Sept. 16, 1924; s. Hjalmar and Clara Marcella (Kramer) O.; m. Mary Susan Rice, Oct. 8, 1958 (div. Nov. 1969); children: Thomas George, Elizabeth Alice, James Phillip. BA, U. Wis., 1949. From underwriter to underwriting mgr. Employers Ins. Wausau, Milw., Phila., N.Y.C. and San Francisco, 1949-59; dir. casualty underwriting dept. Mut. Service Ins. Co., St. Paul, 1959-62; underwriting mgr. Celina Ins. Group, Cleve., 1962-71; mgr. nat. accounts Nationwide Ins. Co., Columbus, Ohio, 1971-74; v.p., regional mgr. Reinsurance Facilities Corp., 1974-78; pres., dir. Century Surety Co., 1978-89; treas., dir. Latitude Premium Fin. Co., 1987-90; dir. Proliance Ins. Co., Ohio, 1989-95. Prin. Ins. Mgmt. Advisors. With U.S. Army, 1943-45, ETO. Republican. Avocations: boating, travel.

OLSEN, LUTHER S. state legislator; b. Feb. 26, 1951; BA, U. Wis. Assemblyman Wis. State Dist. 41, 1994—. Owner (farm supply store) Omro. Mem. Berlin Area Bd. Edn., 1976-95. Home: 2021 Hwy 49 Berlin WI 54923 Office: PO Box 8952 Madison WI 53708-8952

OLSEN, REX NORMAN, trade association executive; b. Hazeltown, Idaho, Apr. 9, 1925; s. Adolph Lars and Pearl (Robbins) O. B.J., B.A. in English, U. Mo., 1950. Editor Clissold Pub. Co., Chgo., 1950-54; copy editor Am. Peoples Ency., 1955; asst. editor Am. Hosp. Assn., 1956-59, mng. editor, 1959-64, dir. jours. div., 1964-69, dir. publs. bur., 1969-75, exec. editor, asso. pub., 1975-79; v.p., treas. Am. Hosp. Pub., Inc., 1980-85; pres. Words Ltd., 1985—. Dir. publs. ETNA Comms., Chgo., 1997—. Served with USNR, 1943-46. Mem. Soc. Nat. Assn. Pubs. (sec. 1975-76, 2d v.p. 1976-77, 1st v.p. 1977-78, pres. 1978-79), Chgo. Bus. Publs. Assn. (dir. 1974-78, 4th v.p. 1978-79), Sigma Delta Chi. Home and Office: 3845 N Alta Vista Ter Chicago IL 60613-2907 E-mail: rexorudy@aol.com.

OLSEN, RICHARD GEORGE, microbiology educator; b. Independence, Mo., June 25, 1937; s. Benjamin Barth and Ruth Naomi (Myrtle) O.; m. Melinda J. Tarr; children: Cynthia Olsen-Noll, David G., Susan B. Dunham, John D. BA, U. Mo., Kansas City, 1959; MS, Atlanta U., 1963; PhD, SUNY, Buffalo, 1969. Tchr. Rustin High Sch., Kansas City, Mo., 1960-61; instr. Met. Jr. Coll., 1963-67; from asst. prof. to prof. microbiology Ohio State U., Columbus, 1969-89, prof. emeritus, 1989—; sci. dir. Cera Corp., Columbus, Ohio. Author: Immunology and Immunopathology, 1979, Feline Leukemia, 1981; contbr. articles to profl. jours.; 5 patents including method of recovering cell antigen and preparation of feline leukemia vaccine. NIH fellow SUNY-Buffalo, 1967-68; Nat. Cancer Inst. grantee, 1973—. Mem. Am. Soc. Microbiology, Internat. Assn. Research Leukemia, Am. Assn. Cancer Research, Internat. Soc. Immunopharmacology, Am. Soc. Virology Avocations: farming, wood working, Porsche club racing. Home: 63225 Jordan Ct Montrose CO 81401-9221 Office: Ohio State U 1925 Coffey Rd Columbus OH 43210-1005 E-mail: rgolsen@worldnet.att.net.

OLSON, DAVID WENDELL, bishop; b. St. Paul, Apr. 4, 1938; s. Wendell Edwin and Eva Victoria (Edstrom) O.; m. Nancy Grace Evans, July 9, 1961; children: Kathryn, Jonathan, Justin. BA, St. Olaf Coll., 1960; MDiv, Luther Sem., St. Paul, 1964. Ordained to ministry Am. Luth. Ch.,1964. Pastor St. Paul's Ch., Balt., 1964-69; co-pastor St. James Ch., Crystal, Minn., 1969-78; dir. North Mpls. Luth. Coalition, 1978-82; asst. prof. Luther N.W. Sem., St. Paul, 1982-84; asst. to bishop S.E. Minn. dist. Am. Luth. Ch., 1984-87; bishop Mpls. area synod Evang. Luth. Ch. in Am., Mpls., 1987—. Chair Robbinsdale (Minn.) Sch. Bd., 1976-82; trustee Fairview Hosp., Mpls. Bush Found. fellow, 1975; Regents scholar St. Olaf Coll. Office: Evang Luth Ch in Am 122 W Franklin Ave Ste 600 Minneapolis MN 55404-2455

OLSON, EDGAR, state legislator; b. Nov. 19, 1937; m. Phyllis Olson; 2 children. Degree, N.D. State U. Mem. Minn. Ho. of Reps., St. Paul, 1984-98. Mem. taxes, agr., local govt. and met. affairs coms., others; farmer. Democrat. Home: RR 3 Box 99 Fosston MN 56542-9546 Office: Minn Ho of Reps State Capitol Saint Paul MN 55155-0001

OLSON, GEN, state legislator; b. May 20, 1938; BS in Edn. with distinction, EdD, U. Minn. Mayor, Minnetrista, Minn., 1981-82; mem. Minn. Senate from 34th dist., St. Paul, 1983—. Former mem. Park and Recreation Commn., Planning and Zoning Commn., Police Commn., City Council. Republican. Office: Minn State Senate State Capitol Building Saint Paul MN 55155-0001

OLSON, GREGORY BRUCE, materials science and engineering educator, academic director; b. Bklyn., Apr. 10, 1947; s. Oscar Gustav Fritz and Elizabeth Rose (Dorner) Olson; m. Jane Ellen Black, May 10, 1980; 1 child Elise Marie. BS, MS in Materials Sci. and Engring., MIT, 1970, ScD in Materials Sci. and Engring., 1974. Rsch. assoc. dept. materials sci. and engring. MIT, Cambridge, 1974-79, prin. rsch. assoc., 1979-85, sr. rsch. assoc., 1985-88; prof. materials sci. and engring. Northwestern U., Evanston, Ill., 1988—, Wilson-Cook prof. engring. design, 1999—. Cons. Army Materials Tech. Lab., Watertown, Mass., 1975-88, Lawrence Livermore (Calif.) Nat. Lab., 1983-89; Jacob Kurtz Exchange Scientist Technion-Israel Inst. Tech., 1979; SERC vis. prof. U. Cambridge, 1992; assoc. chmn. dept. materials sci. and engring. Northwestern U., 1992-98, dir. materials tech. lab.-steel rsch.group, 1985—; founding mem. Questek Innovations LLC, 1997—. Editor: Innovative UHS Steel Technology, 1990, Martensite, 1992; contbr. numerous papers and articles to jours., encys., and symposia; inventor hydrogen-res. UHS steels, stainless bearing steel, ultrahard carburizing steels. Fellow AMAX Found., 1972-74; named N.Mex. Disting. lectr. in Materials, 1983; recipient Creativity Extension award NSF, 1983-85; Wallenberg grantee Jacob Wallenberg Found., Sweden, 1993, Technology Recognition award NASA, 1994, Tech. of Yr. award Industry Week mag. 1998. Fellow ASM (chmn. phase transformation com. 1987-90, Boston chpt. Saveur Meml. lectr. 1986, Phila. chpt. 1998, Alpha Sigma Mu lectr. 1996), ASM Internat., TMS-AIME (student affairs com.); mem. AAAS, Materials Rsch. Soc., Internat. Soc. Martensitic Transformation, ISS-AIME (M.R. Tenebaum award 1993), Assn. Univ. Related Rsch. Parks (Tech. Transfer award 1998). Lutheran. Avocations: sports cars, jazz trumpet. Office: Northwestern U Dept Materials Sci and Engring 2225 N Campus Dr Evanston IL 60208-3108

OLSON, JAMES CLIFTON, historian, university president; b. Bradgate, Iowa, Jan. 23, 1917; s. Arthur Edwin and Abbie (Anderson) O.; m. Vera Blanche Farrington, June 6, 1941; children: Elizabeth, Sarah Margaret. AB, Morningside Coll., 1938, LLD, 1968; MA, U. Nebr., 1939, PhD, 1942, LittD, 1980, Chonnam Nat. U., Korea, 1978. Instr. Northwest Mo. State Tchrs. Coll., summers 1940-42; dir. Nebr. State Hist. Soc., 1946-56; lectr. U. Omaha, 1947-50, U. Nebr., 1946-54, part-time assoc. prof., 1954-56, prof., chmn. dept. history, 1956-65, Bennett S. and Dorothy Martin prof. history, 1962-65; dean Grad. Coll., univ. research adminstr., 1966-68, vice chancellor, 1968; chancellor U. Mo.-Kansas City, 1968-76; interim pres. U. Mo. System, 1976-77, pres., 1977-84, pres. emeritus, 1984—; OAS prof. Am. history El Colegio de Mexico, Mexico City, 1962. Vis. prof. U. Colo., summer 1965. Author: J. Sterling Morton, 1942, The Nebraska Story, 1951, History of Nebraska, 1955, 3d edit. (with Ronald C. Naugle), 1997, (with Vera Farrington Olson) Nebraska is My Home, 1956, This is Nebraska, 1960, Red Cloud and the Sioux Problem, 1965, paper edit., 1975, 79, (with Vera Farrington Olson) The University of Missouri: An Illustrated History, 1988, Serving the University of Missouri: A Memoir of Campus and System Administration, 1993; contbg. author: The Army Air Forces in World War II, 1951, 53; editor: Nebraska History, 1946-56; contbr. articles to profl. jours., encys. Bd. dirs. Mid-Am. Arts Alliance; trustee Midwest Rsch. Inst., Kansas City. Mem. Am. Assn. State and Local History, Coun. Basic Edn., Am. Hist. Assn., Orgn. Am. Historians, State Hist. Soc. Mo. (1st v.p.), Nebr. State Hist. Soc., We. Hist. Assn., Cosmos Club, Phi Beta Kappa, Omicron Delta Kappa, Phi Kappa Phi, Pi Gamma Mu. E-mail: olsonja@umkc.edu.

OLSON, JOHN MICHAEL, lawyer; b. Grafton, N.D., Feb. 9, 1947; s. Clifford Inguold and Alice M. (Schwandt) O.; children: Dana Michel, Kirsten Lee. BA, Concordia Coll., Moorhead, Minn., 1969; JD, U. N.D., 1972. Bar: N.D. 1972. Asst. atty. gen. N.D. Atty. Gen.'s Office, Bismarck, 1972-74; state's atty. Burleigh County, 1974-82; pvt. practice, 1983-91; mem. 49th dist. N.D. Senate, 1983-91, minority leader, 1987-91; ptnr. Olson Cichy Bismarck, 1994—, Olson Cichy Attys., Bismarck, 1994—. Recipient Disting. Svc. award N.D. Peace Officers Assn., 1981, Outstanding Bismarcker award Bismarck Jaycees, 1981. Mem. N.D. Bar Assn. Republican. Lutheran. Office: 115 N 4th St Bismarck ND 58501-4002

OLSON, JUDITH MARY REEDY, public information officer, former state senator; b. Mitchell, S.D., June 24, 1939; d. John Marvin and Camille (Murphy) Reedy; m. Robert George Olson, Aug. 5, 1961; children: Jeffrey, Jennifer, Jon, Jaime, Jason, Jeremy. EdB, U. Tucson, 1961; MEd, S.D. State U., 1984; postgrad., U. S.D., 1985—. Cert. secondary tchr., edn. adminstrn. Tchr. jr. high sch. Mpls. Pub. Schs., 1961-63; mem. State Bd. Edn., S.D., 1972-83, pres., 1975-78; dir. S.D. Edn. Policy Seminar, 1975-79; substitute tchr. Rapid City (S.D.) Schs., 1979-81, tchr. adult basic edn., 1979-81, supr. community relations, 1981-88, supr. community edn., pub. info., 1988—; senator S.D. Legis. (dist. 33), Pierre, S.D., 1989—; edn. dir. Career Learning Center of the Black Hills. Speaker, cons. sch. bds., adminstrs., tchrs., sch. dists., pub. relations, various states, 1972—. Bd. dirs. Black Hills Symphony, 1987—; chair, S.D. State Democratic Party, 1998—. Mem. AAUW (Women of Worth award), Rotary, PEO, Delta Kappa Gamma. Democrat. Roman Catholic. Avocations: reading, spectator sports. Home: 4603 Ridgewood St Rapid City SD 57702-2063 Office: Rapid City Area Schs 300 6th St Rapid City SD 57701-2724

OLSON, KEVIN MEL, state legislator; Mem. S.D. State Senate, 1993—2001, mem. edn. and state affairs coms.; tchr.; mem. S.D. Ho. Reps., Pierre, 2002—. Ho. minority leader S.D. Ho. Reps., Pierre, 2002—, consumer and state affairs com. mem., 2002—. Home: 600 W 3rd Ave Mitchell SD 57301-2434 Office: SD State Senate State Capitol Pierre SD 57501

OLSON, MARK, state legislator; b. July 1955; Mem. from dist. 19A Minn. Ho. of Reps., St. Paul, 1993—; mem. civil law com., edn. policy com., family and early childhood edn. com., fin. com., health and human svcs. policy com. Carpenter, log home builder, qualified neutral mediator. Republican. Home: 17085 142nd St SE Big Lake MN 55309-8925 Office: 501 State Office Bldg Saint Paul MN 55155

OLSON, NORMAN FREDRICK, food science educator; b. Edmund, Wis., Feb. 8, 1931; s. Irving M. and Elva B. (Rhinerson) O.; m. Darlene Mary Thorson, Dec. 28, 1957; children: Kristin A., Eric R. BS, U. Wis., 1953, MS, 1957, PhD, 1959. Asst. prof. U. Wis.-Madison, 1959-63, assoc. prof., 1963-69, prof., 1969-93, dir. Walter V. Price Cheese Research Inst., 1976-93; dir. Ctr. Dairy Research, 1986-93; disting. prof. U. Wis.-Madison, 1993-97, prof. emeritus, 1997—. Cons. to cheese industry, 1997—. Author: Semi-soft Cheeses; inventor enzyme microencapsulation; sr. editor Jour. Dairy Sci., 1996-2000. Lt. U.S. Army, 1953-55. Recipient Laureate award Nat. Cheese Inst., 1998; named Highly Cited Rschr. ISI, 2002. Fellow Inst. Food Technologists (Macy award 1986), Am. Dairy Sci. Assn. (v.p. 1984-85, pres. 1985-86, Pfizer award 1971, Dairy Rsch. Inc. award 1978, Borden Found. award 1988, Hon. award 1997); mem. Inst. Food Technologists. Democrat. Lutheran Avocation: cross-country skiing. Home: 114 Green Lake Pass Madison WI 53705-4755 Office: U Wis Dept Food Sci Babcock Hall Madison WI 53706

OLSON, ROBERT GRANT, lawyer; b. Ft. Dodge, Iowa, Mar. 29, 1952; s. Grant L. and R. June (Pohlmann) O.; m. Cynthia Lynn Murray, Sept. 7, 1978; children: Brendon, Elisabeth, Jeffrey, Daniel. BS, Iowa State U., 1973; JD, U. Iowa, 1976. Bar: Mo., 1976, Ill. 1977. Ptnr. Thompson & Mitchell, St. Louis, 1976-92, Riezman & Blitz, P.C., St. Louis, 1992-2000, Stone, Leyton & Gershman, P.C., St. Louis, 2000—. Editor Jour. Corp. Law, 1975-76. Vol. Gephardt for Pres. Campaign, 1988, Carnahan for Lt. Gov. Campaign, 1988, Carnahan for Gov. Campaign, 1992., Habitat for Humanity; arbitrator Better Bus. Bur. Mem. ABA, Mo. Bar Assn., Ill. Bar Assn., Met. St. Louis Bar Assn., Downtown St. Louis Lions Club (pres. 1990-91). Home: 424 E Jackson Rd Saint Louis MO 63119-4128 Office: Stone Leyton & Gershman 7733 Forsyth Blvd Ste 500 Saint Louis MO 63105-1817

OLSON, ROBERT WYRICK, lawyer; b. Madison, Wis., Dec. 19, 1945; s. John Arthur and Mary Katherine (Wyrick) O.; m. Carol Jean Duane, June 12, 1971; children: John Hagan, Mary Catherine Duane. BA, Williams Coll., 1967; JD, U. Va., 1970. Assoc. Cravath, Swaine & Moore, N.Y.C., 1970-79; asst. gen. counsel Penn Cen. Corp., Cin., 1979-80, assoc. gen. counsel, 1980-82, v.p., dep. gen. counsel, 1982-87; sr. v.p., gen. counsel, sec. Am. Premier Underwriters, Inc. (formerly Penn Cen. Corp.), 1987-95, Chiquita Brands Internat., Inc., Cin., 1995—. Mem. ABA. Office: Chiquita Brands Internat 250 E 5th St Ste 25 Cincinnati OH 45202-4119 E-mail: bolson@chiquita.com.

OLSON, ROY ARTHUR, government official; b. Dec. 8, 1938; s. Elof Herman and Beatrice Lorraine (Dolezal) O.; m. Elisabeth Rigge Behrens, June 24, 1967; children: Heather Elisabeth, Peter Roy. BS, Northwestern U., 1960. Lic. real estate salesman, Ill. Writer, editor Chgo. Am., 1956-68; pres. Roy Olson Pub. Rels. Co., Oak Park, Ill., 1968-70; asst. regional adminstr. SBA, Chgo., 1970-95; Chgo. spokesman Ill. Dept. Transp., 1995—. Dir. Am. Food Industries, Chgo., Covenant Village Retirement Ctr., Northbrook, Ill., 1975-81, Brandel Care Ctr., Northbrook, 1975-81, Swedish Covenant Hosp., Chgo., 1995—. Chmn. Northbrook Covenant Ch., 1980-81, 97-2000. Mem. Soc. Profl. Journalists, Art Inst. Chgo., City Club (media com.), Execs. Club, Chgo. Press Club, Chgo. Headline Club (past dir. 1964-66), Northwestern Club. Home: 2015 Prairie St Glenview IL 60025-2824 Office: 310 S Michigan Ave Chicago IL 60604-4207 E-mail: olsonrb@aol.com.

OLSON-HELLERUD, LINDA KATHRYN, elementary school educator; b. Wisconsin Rapids, Wis., Aug. 26, 1947; d. Samuel Ellsworth and Lillian (Dvorak) Olson; m. H. A. Hellerud, 1979; 1 child Sarah Kathryn Hellerud. BS, U. Wis., Stevens Point, 1969, tchg. cert., 1970, MST, 1972; MS, U. Wis., Whitewater, 1975; EdS, U. Wis., Stout, 1978. Cert. K-12 reading tchr. and specialist. Clk. U. Counseling Ctr. U Wis., Stevens Point, 1965-69; elem. sch. tchr. Wisconsin Rapids, 1970-76; sch. counselor, 1976-79; dist. elem. guidance dir., 1979-82; elem. and reading tchr., K-1 early intervention team, 1982—; also cons. Adv. Moravian Ch. Sunday Sch. Mem.: NEA, Wood County Lit. Coun. (cons.), Wood County Hist. Soc., Wis. State Hist. Soc., Ctrl. Wis. Reading Assn. (family lit. com.), Wis. Reading Assn. (early intervention com.). United Ch. Christ. Avocations: literacy activities, piano, Spanish, technology, walking. Home: 1011 16th St S Wisconsin Rapids WI 54494-5371 Office: Howe Elem Sch Wisconsin Rapids WI 54494

OLSSON, BJÖRN ESKIL, railroad supply company executive; b. Kristianstad, Sweden, Oct. 7, 1945; came to U.S., 1990; m. Cecilia Lindblad, July 6, 1968; children: Fredrik, Karin, Eva. M Bus. and Adminstrn., U. Lund, Sweden, 1968. Internal auditor Kockums Mek. Verkstad, Malmö, Sweden, 1969-71, mgr. acctg. Sweden, 1971-74; v.p. fin. and adminstrn. Kockums Industri, Söderhamn, Sweden, 1974-76, Linden Alimak, Skellefteå, Sweden, 1976-81, Sonessons, Malmö, 1981-82; pres. Sab-Nife, 1982-87; v.p. corp. devel. Investment AB Cardo, 1987-90; pres., CEO Harmon Industries Inc., Blue Springs, Mo., 1990—. Bd. dirs. BJ Papperats, Malmo, Green & Co., Malmö; mem. adv. bd. Ctrl. Mo. State U. Bus. Sch., Warrensburg, 1991—. Staff sgt. Swedish Army, 1964-65. Avocations: golf, skiing. Office: Harmon Industries Inc 1600 NE Coronado Blue Springs MO 64014-6236

OLTMAN, C. DWIGHT, conductor, educator; b. Imperial, Nebr., May 27, 1936; s. George L. and Lois Beryl (Wine) O.; m. Shirley Jean Studebaker, May 30, 1966; children— Michelle Leigh, Nicole Alicia B.S., McPherson Coll., 1958; M.Mus., Wichita State U., 1963; postgrad., U. Cin., 1967-70; student, Nadia Boulanger, Paris, 1960, Pierre Monteux, 1963. Asst. prof. music Manchester Coll., North Manchester, Ind., 1963-67; prof. of conducting, music dir. symphony orch. and Bach Festival Baldwin-Wallace Coll., Berea, Ohio, 1970—; music dir. Ohio Chamber Orch., Cleve., 1972-92, laureate conductor, 1992—; music dir., prin. condr. Cleve. Ballet, 1976—; music dir. Cullowhee Music Festival, N.C., 1977-79; guest conductor Europe, Can., U.S.A. Mem. Am. Symphony Orch. League, Conductor's Guild. Democrat. Avocations: reading; walking; theater; spectator sports. Home and Office: 21631 Cedar Branch Trl Strongsville OH 44149-1287

O'MALLEY, JOHN DANIEL, law educator, banker; b. Chgo., Dec. 18, 1926; s. William D. and Paula A. (Skaugh) O'M.; m. Caroline Tyler Taylor, July 12, 1958; children: John Daniel, Taylor John. Grad., St. Thomas Mil. Acad., 1945; B.S., Loyola U., Chgo., 1950, M.A., 1952, J.D., 1953; grad., U.S. Army Intelligence Sch., 1962, Command & Gen. Staff Coll., 1965. Bar: Ill. 1953, Mich. 1954, U.S. Supreme Ct. 1962. Asst. prof. law Loyola U., 1953-59, asso. prof., 1959-65; formerly spl. counsel and bond claims mgr. Fed. Ins. Co.; prof. law Loyola U. Grad. Sch. Bus., 1965—, chmn. dept. law, 1968-86. Trust officer, v.p. First Nat. Bank Highland Park (Ill.), Marina City Bank, Chgo., Hyde Park Bank & Trust Co., 1970-75; exec. v.p. Harris Bank Winnetka, Ill., 1975-95. Author: Subrogation Against Banks on Forged Checks, 1967, Common Check Frauds and the Uniform Commercial Code, 1969; Contbr. articles to profl. jours. and law revs. Served to maj. AUS, 1945-47, 61-62. Decorated knight grand cross Papal Order of Holy Sepulchre, knight comdr. with star Constantinian Order of St. George (Italy), knight Order of St. Maurice and St. Lazarus (Italy), knight of Malta. Mem. ABA, Chgo., Ill., Mich. bar assns., Chgo. Crime Commn., French Nat. Hon. Soc., Am., Chgo. bus. law assns., Mil. Govt. Assn. Home: 1630 Sheridan Rd 6-L Wilmette IL 60091-1830 Office: Loyola U 820 N Michigan Ave Ste 1316 Chicago IL 60611-2147

O'MALLEY, KATHLEEN M. federal judge; b. 1956; AB magna cum laude, Kenyon Coll., 1979; JD, Case Western Reserve, 1982. Law clk. to Hon. Nathaniel R. Jones U.S. Ct. of Appeals, 6th circuit, 1982-83; with Jones, Day, Reavis & Pogue, Cleve., 1983-84, Porter, Wright, Morris & Arthur, Cleve., 1985-91; chief counsel, first asst. atty. gen., chief of staff Office of Atty. Gen., Columbus, 1991-94; district judge U.S. Dist. Ct. (Ohio no. dist.), 6th circuit, Cleve., 1994—. Mem. ABA, FBA, Anthony J. Celebrezze Inn of Ct., Order of Coif, Phi Beta Kappa. Office: US Courthouse 201 Superior Ave E Ste 135 Cleveland OH 44114-1201

O'MALLEY, KEVIN FRANCIS, lawyer, writer, educator; b. St. Louis, May 12, 1947; s. Peter Francis and Dorothy Margaret (Cradick) O'M.; m. Dena Hengen, Apr.2, 1971; children: Kevin Brendan, Ryan Michael. AB, St. Louis U., 1970, JD, 1973. Bar: Mo. 1973, U.S. Ct. Appeals D.C. 1974, U.S. Ct. Appeals (8th cir.) 1979, Ill. 1993. Trial lawyer U.S. Dept. Justice, Washington, 1973-74, Los Angeles, 1974-77, Phoenix, 1977-78, asst. U.S. atty. St. Louis, 1978-83. Adj. prof. law St. Louis U., 1979—; lectr. Ctrl. and Ea. European Law Initiative, Russian Fedn., 1996, Poland, 1999. Author: (with Devitt, Blackmar, O'Malley) Federal Jury Practice and Instruction, 1990, 92, (with O'Malley, Grenig & Lee), 1999, 2000, 01; contbr. articles to law books and jours. Community amb. Expt. in Internat. Living, Prague, Czechoslovakia, 1968; bd. dirs. St. Louis-Galway (Ireland) Sister Cities. Capt. U.S. Army, 1973. Recipient Atty. Gen.'s Disting. Service award U.S. Dept. Justice, 1977, John J. Dwyer Meml. Scholarship award, 1967-70. Fellow Am. Coll. Trial Lawyers; mem. ABA (chmn. govt. litigation counsel com. 1982-86, chmn. jud. com. 1986-87, chmn. com. on ind. and small firms, chmn. trial practice com. 1991-94, health care litigation 1994-98), Am. Law Inst., Met. Bar Assn. St. Louis (chmn. criminal law sect.), Nat. Inst. Trial Advocacy, Mo. Athletic Club. Roman Catholic. Office: 10 S Brentwood Blvd Ste 102 Saint Louis MO 63105-1694 E-mail: komalley@omalleylaw.com.

O'MALLEY, PATRICK J. state legislator; b. Evergreen Park, Ill., Oct. 22, 1950; BS, MS, Purdue U.; JD, John Marshall Law Sch. Mem. Ill. State Senate from 18th dist. Trustee Moraine Valley C.C.; pres. Palos Fire Protection Dist., Ill.; active Am. Cancer Soc., Vietnam Vets. Leadership Program, Coletta's of Ill. Found. Mem. Southwest Bar Assn., Chgo. Bar Assn. Republican. Home: 12744 S 87th Ave Palos Park IL 60464-1868

OMAN, RICHARD HEER, lawyer; b. Columbus, Ohio, Jan. 4, 1926; s. B. R. Oman and Marguerite H. (Oman) Andrews; m. Jane Ellen Wert, Oct. 5, 1963; children: Sarah M., David W. BA, Ohio State U., 1948, JD, 1951. Bar: Ohio 1951. Atty. Ohio Nat. Bank, Columbus, 1951-55; ptnr. Isaac, Postlewaite, O'Brien & Oman, 1955-71; dir. Columbus Found., 1955-77, counsel, 1955—; ptnr. Porter, Wright, Morris and Arthur (and predecessor firm), Columbus, 1972-89; of counsel Vorys, Sater, Seymour and Pease, 1990, ptnr., 1991-96, of counsel, 1997—. Mem. Columbus Airport Commn., 1960-64; trustee Reinberger Found., Cleve., 1980—, Columbus Acad., 1981-87, Grant Hosp., 1978-86, Harding Hosp., 1978-86; sr. warden Trinity Epsic. Ch., 1985-88. Fellow Ohio State Bar Found.; mem. ABA, Am. Coll. Trust and Estate Counsel, Ohio State Bar Assn. (past mem. bd. govs. probate and trust law sect.), Columbus Bar Assn., Columbus Club, Rocky Fork Hunt and Country Club, Nantucket (Mass.) Yacht Club, Kit Kat Club. Republican. Episcopalian. Office: Vorys Sater Seymour & Pease PO Box 1008 52 E Gay St Columbus OH 43215-3161 Fax: 614.714.4731. E-mail: rhoman@ussp.com.

O'MARA, JOHN ALOYSIUS, bishop; b. Buffalo, Nov. 17, 1924; s. John Aloysius and Anna Theresa (Schenck) O'M. Student, St. Augustine's Sem., Toronto, Ont., Can., 1944-51; J.C.L., St. Thomas U., Rome, 1953. Ordained priest Roman Catholic Ch., 1951; mem. chancery Archdiocese of Toronto, 1953-69; pres., rector St. Augustine's Sem., Toronto, 1969-75; pastor St. Lawrence Parish, Scarboro, Ont., 1975-76; bishop Diocese of Thunder Bay, 1976-94, Diocese of St. Catharines, 1994—. Pres. Ont. Conf. Cath. Bishops, 1986-92. Bd. dirs. Ont. Hosp. Assn., 1961-65; mem. Ont. Hosp. Services Commn., 1964-69. Named hon. prelate of Papal Household with title monsignor, 1954, hon. fellow U. St. Michael's Coll., Toronto, 1997. Mem. Cath. Ch. Ext. Soc. (bd. dirs. 1992-96), Cath. Health Assn. Ont. (bd. dirs. 1982-86, 88-92, 96—). Address: 122 Riverdale Rd Saint Catharines ON Canada L2R 4C2 E-mail: chancery@vaxxine.com.

O'MARA, THOMAS PATRICK, manufacturing company executive; b. St. Catharine's, Ont., Can., Jan. 17, 1937; s. Joseph Thomas and Rosanna Patricia (Riordan) O'M.; m. Nancy Irene Rosevear, Aug. 10, 1968; children: Patricia Catharine, Tracy Irene, Sara Megan. B.S., Allegheny Coll., 1958; M.S., Carnegie Inst. Tech., 1960. Mktg. analyst U.S. Steel Corp., Pitts., 1960-65; dir. info. systems AMPCO Pitts. (formerly Screw & Bolt Corp.), 1965-68; v.p., gen. mgr. Toy div. Samsonite Corp., Denver, 1968-73; regional mgr. Mountain Zone, Hertz Corp., 1973-75; asst. to chmn. Allen Group, Melville, N.Y., 1975-76; group exec. v.p. fin. and adminstrn. Bell & Howell Co., Chgo., 1976-77, corp. controller, 1977-78, corp. v.p., 1978-85, pres. visual communications, 1978-85; pres., chief operating officer, dir. Bridge Product Inc., Northbrook, Ill., 1985-87; chmn., chief exec. officer Micro Metl Corp., Indpls., 1987-91; chmn. Omara Ptnrs., 1992—. Bd. dirs. Loyola U. Press; trustee Barat Coll., 1994—. Mem. Lake Forest H.S. Bd., 1989-96, pres. 1993-96. With USAR, 1961-66. Mem. Econs. Club Chgo., Newcomen Soc. U.S., Sigma Alpha Epsilon, Knollwood Club. Home: 1350 Inverleith Rd Lake Forest IL 60045-1540

O'MEARA, JOHN CORBETT, federal judge; b. Hillsdale, Mich., Nov. 4, 1933; s. John Richard and Karolyn Louise (Corbett) O'M.; m. Penelope Reingier Appel, June 9, 1962 (div. Feb. 1975); children: Meghan Appel, John Richard, Corbett Edge, Patrick Fitzpatrick, Tighe Roberts; m. Julia Donovan Darlow, Sept. 20, 1975; 1 child, Gillian Darlow. AB, U. Notre Dame, 1955; LLB, Harvard U., 1962. Bar: Mich. 1962. Assoc. Dickinson, Wright, Moon, Van Dusen & Freeman, Detroit, 1962-70; mem. faculty U. Detroit, 1965-70; ptnr. Dickinson, Wright, Moon, Van Dusen & Freeman, Detroit, 1970-94, head of labor group, 1985-94; judge U.S. Dist. Ct., 1994—. Bd. dirs. Mich. Opera Theatre, Detroit. Contr. articles to profl. jours. Fin. chmn. Dem. Party Mich., 1968-70; chmn. U.S. Cts. Com. State Bar Mich., 1984-94. Lt. USN, 1955-59. Fellow Am. Coll. Trial Lawyers, Am. Bar Found.; mem. ABA, U.S. Supreme Court Bar, Am. Judicature Soc., Mich. State Bar Assn., 6th Cir. Court Appeals Bar (life mem., 6th Cir. Jud. Conf. 1986). E-mail: john_corbett_o'meara@ck6.uscourts.gov. Office: US Dist Ct 231 W Lafayette Blvd Detroit MI 48226-2700

O'MEARA, ONORATO TIMOTHY, academic administrator, mathematician; b. Cape Town, Republic of South Africa, Jan. 29, 1928; arrived in U.S., 1957; s. Daniel and Fiorina (Allorto) O'M.; m. Jean T. Fadden, Sept. 12, 1953; children: Maria, Timothy, Jean, Kathleen, Eileen. B.Sc., U. Cape Town, 1947, M.Sc., 1948; Ph.D., Princeton U., 1953; LLD (hon.), U. Notre Dame, 1987. Asst. lectr. U. Natal, Republic South Africa, 1949; lectr. U. Otago, New Zealand, 1954-56; mem. Inst. for Advanced Study, Princeton, N.J., 1957-58, 62; asst. prof., 1958-62; prof. math. U. Notre Dame, Ind., 1962-76, chmn. dept., 1965-66, 68-72, Kenna prof. math., 1976-98, provost, 1978-96, provost emeritus, 1996—, Kenna prof. emeritus, 1998—. Vis. prof. Calif. Inst. Tech., 1968; Gauss prof. Göttingen Acad. Sci., 1978; mem. adv. panel math. scis. NSF, 1974-77, cons., 1960—. Author: Introduction to Quadratic Forms, 1963, 71, 73, 2000, Lectures on Linear Groups, 1974, 2d edit., 1977, 3d edit., 1988, Russian translation, 1976, Symplectic Groups, 1978, 82, Russian translation, 1979, The Classical Groups and K-Theory (with A.J. Hahn), 1989; contbr. articles on arithmetic theory of quadratic forms and isomorphism theory of linear groups to Am. and European profl. jours. Mem. Cath. Commn. Intellectual and Cultural Affairs, 1962—, Commn. on Cath. Scholarship, 1997-99; life trustee U. of Notre Dame, 1996—. Recipient Marianist award U. Dayton, 1988; Alfred P. Sloan fellow, 1960-63. Mem. Am. Math. Soc., Am. Acad. Arts and Sci., Collegium (bd. dirs. 1992-96). Roman Catholic. Home: 1227 E Irvington Ave South Bend IN 46614-1417 Office: U Notre Dame Office of Provost Emeritus Notre Dame IN 46556

O'MEARA, THOMAS FRANKLIN, priest, educator; b. Des Moines, May 15, 1935; s. Joseph Matthew and Frances Claire (Rock) O'M. MA, Aquinas Inst, Dubuque, Iowa, 1963; PhD, U. Munich, Germany, 1967. Ordained priest Roman Cath. Ch., 1962. Assoc. prof. Aquinas Inst. of Theology, Dubuque, Iowa, 1967-79; prof. U. Notre Dame, South Bend, Ind., 1981-84, William K. Warren prof. of theology, 1985—. Author 14 books, including: Romantic Idealism and Roman Catholicism, 1983, Theology of Ministry, 1985, revised edit., 1999, Church and Culture, 1991,

Thomas Aquinas: Theologian, 1997, Erich Przywara, S.J., His Theology and His World, 2002. Mem. Catholic Theol. Soc. Am. (pres. 1980). Office: U Notre Dame Dept Of Theology Notre Dame IN 46556 E-mail: o'meara.1@nd.edu.

OMENN, GILBERT STANLEY, academic administrator, physician; b. Chester, Pa., Aug. 30, 1941; s. Leonard and Leah (Miller) O.; m. Martha Darling; children: Rachel Andrea, Jason Montgomery, David Matthew. AB, Princeton U., 1961; MD, Harvard U., 1965; PhD in Genetics, U. Wash., 1972. Intern Mass. Gen. Hosp., Boston, 1965-66, asst. resident in medicine, 1966-67; rsch. assoc. NIH, Bethesda, Md., 1967-69; fellow U. Wash., 1969-71, from asst. prof. medicine to assoc. prof., 1971-79, investigator Howard Hughes Med. Inst., 1976-77, prof. medicine, 1979-97, prof. environ. health, 1981—, chmn. dept., 1981-83; dean U. Wash. Sch. Pub. Health and Cmty. Medicine, 1982-97; exec. v.p. med. affairs, CEO health sys. U. Mich. Health Sys., Ann Arbor, 1997—; prof. internal medicine, human genetics and pub. health U. MIch., 1997—. Bd. dirs. Amgen, Rohm & Haas Co., Population Svcs. Internat.; White House fellow/spl. asst. to chmn. AEC, 1973-74; assoc. dir. Office Sci. and Tech. Policy, The White House, 1977-80; assoc. dir. human resources Office Mgmt. and Budget, 1980-81; vis. sr. fellow Wilson Sch. Pub. and Internat. Affairs, Princeton U., 1981; sci. and pub. policy fellow Brookings Instn., Washington, 1981-82; cons. govt. agys., Lifetime Cable Network; mem. Nat. Commn. on the Environment, Rene Dubos Ctr. for Human Environments, AFL-CIO Workplace Health Fund., Electric Power Rsch. Inst., Carnegie Commn. Task Force on Sci. and Tech. in Jud. and Regulatory Decision Making, adv. com. to dir., Ctrs. Disease Control, 1992-95, adv. com. Critical Technologies Inst., RAND; mem. Pres.'s Coun., U. Calif., 1992-97; chair, Pres. Congrl. Commn. on Risk Assessment and Risk Mgmt.; mem. Nat. Enterprise for the Environment. Co-author: Clearing the Air, Reforming the Clean Air Act, 1981. Editor: (with others) Genetics, Environment and Behavior: Implications for Educational Policy, 1972; Genetic Control of Environmental Pollutants, 1984; Genetic Variability in Responses to Chemical Exposure, 1984, Environmental Biotechnology: Reducing Risks from Environmental Chemicals through Biotechnology, 1988, Biotechnology in Biodegradation, 1990, Biotechnology and Human Genetic Predisposition to Disease, 1990, Annual Review of Public Health, 1991-97, Clinics in Geriatric Medicine, 1992; assoc. editor Cancer Rsch., Cancer Epidemiology, Biomarkers and Prevention, Environ. Rsch., Am. Jour. Med. Genetics, Am. Jour. Preventive Medicine; contbr. articles on cancer prevention, human biochem. genetics, prenatal diagnosis of inherited disorders, susceptibility to environ. agts., clin. medicine and health policy to profl. publs. Mem. Pres.'s Coun. on Spinal Cord Injury; mem. Nat. Cancer Adv. Bd., Nat. Heart, Lung and Blood Adv. Coun., Wash. State Gov.'s Commn. on Social and Health Svcs., Ctr. for Excellence in Govt.; chmn. awards panel Gen. Motors Cancer Rsch. Found., 1985-86; chmn. bd. Environ. Studies and Toxicology, Nat. Rsch. Coun., 1988-91; mem. Bd. Health Promotion and Disease Prevention, Inst. Medicine; mem. adv. com. Woodrow Wilson Sch., Princeton U., 1978-84; trustee Pacific Sci. Ctr., Fred Hutchinson Cancer Rsch. Ctr., Seattle Symphony Orch., Seattle Youth Symphony Orch., Seattle Chamber Music Festival, Santa Fe Chamber Music Festival, Univ. Mus. Soc., Ann Arbor; chmn. rules com. Dem. Conv., King County, Wash., 1972. Served with USPHS, 1967-69. Recipient Research Career Devel. award USPHS, 1972; White House fellow, 1973-74 Fellow ACP, AAAS, Nat. Acad. Social Ins., Western Assn. Physicians, Hastings Ctr., Collegium Ramazzini; mem. Inst. Medicine of NAS, White House Fellows Assn., Am. Soc. Human Genetics, Western Soc. Clin. Rsch., Assn. Am. Physicians, Am. Acad. Arts and Scis. Jewish. Home: 3340 E Dobson Ann Arbor MI 48105-2583 Office: Univ Mich M7324 Medical Sci I Bldg 1301 Catherine St Ann Arbor MI 48109-0626 Fax: 734-647-9739. E-mail: gomenn@umich.edu.

OMER, ROBERT WENDELL, hospital administrator; b. Salt Lake City, Feb. 10, 1948; s. Wayne Albert and Melva Bernice (Thunell) O.; m. Deborah Jackson, May 4, 1972;children: Melinda, Carmen, Creighton, Preston, Allison. BS in Biology, U. Utah, 1972; MHA, Washington U., St. Louis, 1975. V.p. St. Luke's Hosp., Cedar Rapids, Iowa, 1974-80; asst. adminstr. Franciscan Med. Ctr., Rock Island, Ill., 1980-82, Latter Day Saints Hosp., Salt Lake City, 1982-85, Clarkson Hosp., Omaha, 1985-93, v.p., COO, 1993-97; CEO Creighton St. Joseph's Clinics, 1998-99; pres., CEO MCH Health Sys., Blair, 1999—2001; CEO Cooper County Hosp., Boonville, Mo., 2002—. Bd. dirs. ARC, Heartland chpt. Omaha; bd. dirs. Nebr. Scanning Svcs. Lt. col. USAR, 1972. Fellow Am. Coll. Healthcare Execs. (regent); mem. Nebr. Hosp. Assn., Omaha C. of C. (Leadership Omaha award 1978), Omaha Healthcare Execs. Group (pres. 1989-90), Rotary (bd. dirs. 1990). Republican. Mem. Lds Ch. Avocations: jogging, history, cycling, backpacking, racquetball. Home: 513 Park Ave Boonville MO 65233

OMMODT, DONALD HENRY, retired dairy company executive; b. Flom, Minn., July 7, 1931; s. Henry and Mabel B. (Kvidt) Ommodt; m. Evelyn Mavis Billie, June 15, 1957; children: Linette, Kevin, Lee, Jodi. Student, Interstate Bus. Coll., Fargo, N.D. Acct. Farmers State Bank, Waubun, Minn., 1950-53; chief acct. Cass-Clay Creamery, Inc., Fargo, 1953-61, office mgr., 1961-65, gen. mgr., 1965-83, pres., 1983-96; ret. Pres. Messiah Luth. Ch., Fargo, 1976-78; mem. Minn. Dairy Task Force Com., 1988-90; bd. dirs. Communicating for Agr., Fergus Falls, Minn., 1977-80, Blue Cross of N.D., Fargo, 1971-88. Recipient Builder of the Valley award Minn. Red River Valley Devel. Assn., 1991, N.D. Milky Way award, 1993. Mem. Nat. Milk Prodrs. Fedn. (bd. dirs. 1996-97, hon. dir. for life 1998), N.D. Dairy Industries Assn. (bd. dirs., past pres.), Am. Dairy Assn. (bd. dirs. N.D. 1970-80), N.D. Dairy Product Promotion Commn. (bd. dirs. 1970-80), Messiah Found. Christian Communications (pres. 1987—), Moorhead C. of C.

O'MORCHOE, CHARLES CHRISTOPHER CREAGH, anatomical sciences educator, science administrator; b. Quetta, India, May 7, 1931; came to U.S., 1968; s. Nial Francis C. and Jessie Elizabeth (Joly) O'M.; m. Patricia Jean Richardson, Sept. 15, 1955; children: Charles Eric Creagh, David James Creagh. BA, Trinity Coll., Dublin (Ireland) U., 1953, MB, BCh, BAO, 1955, MA, 1959, MD, 1961, PhD, 1969, DSc, 1981. Resident Halifax Gen. Hosp., U.K., 1955-57; lectr. in anatomy Sch. Medicine Trinity Coll., Dublin (Ireland) U., 1957-61, 63-65, lectr. in physiology, 1966-67, assoc. prof. in physiology, 1967-68; instr. in anatomy Harvard Med. Sch., Boston, 1962-63; vis. prof. physiology U. Md. Sch. Medicine, Balt., 1961-62, assoc. prof. anatomy, 1968-71, prof. anatomy, 1971-74; chmn. anatomy bd. State of Md., 1971-73; prof., chmn. dept. anatomy Stritch Sch. Medicine Loyola U., Maywood, Ill., 1974-84; dean Coll. Medicine, U. Ill., Urbana-Champaign, 1984-98, prof. anat. scis. and surgery, 1984-98, emeritus dean and prof., 1998—. WHO cons., vis. prof. physiology Jaipur, India, 1967, S.M.S. Med. Coll., U. Rajasthan, vis. prof. anatomy, 1971. Assoc. editor: Anatomical Record, 1978-98, Am. Jour. Anatomy, 1987-91; contbr. articles to profl. jours. Elected fellow Trinity Coll., Dublin U., 1966; named faculty mem. of yr. Loyola U., Chgo., 1982. Mem. AMA, Am. Soc. Nephrology, N.Am. Soc. Lymphology (v.p. 1982-84, pres. 1984-86, sec. 1993-98, Cecil K. Drinker award 1992), Am. Assn. Anatomy Chairmen (emeritus), Am. Assn. Anatomists (dir. placement svc. 1981-91), Internat. Soc. Lymphology (exec. com. 1987-97, pres. 1993-95, Presdl. award 2001), Ill. State Med. Soc., Champaign County Med. Soc., Alpha Omega Alpha. Mem. Church of Ireland. Home: 5645 NE Lincoln Rd East Poulsbo WA 98370-7756 Office: U Ill Coll Medicine 190 Med Sci Bldg 506 S Mathews Ave Urbana IL 61801-3618 E-mail: cccom@uiuc.edu.

O'MORCHOE, PATRICIA JEAN, pathologist, educator; b. Halifax, Eng., Sept. 15, 1930; came to U.S., 1968; d. Alfred Eric and Florence Patricia (Pearson) Richardson; m. Charles Christopher Creagh O'Morchoe, Sept. 15, 1955; children: Charles E.C., David J.C. BA, Dublin U., Ireland, 1953, MB, Bch., BAO, 1955, MA, 1966, MD. Intern Halifax (Yorkshire) Gen. Hosp., Eng., 1955-57; instr., lectr. physiology Dublin U., 1957-61, 63-68; instr. pathology Johns Hopkins U., Balt., 1961-62, 68-72, asst. prof. pathology, 1972-74; rsch. assoc. surgery, pathology Harvard U., Boston, 1962-63; asst. prof. anatomy U. Md., 1970-74; assoc.prof., prof. pathology, anatomy Loyola U. Chgo., 1974-84; prof. pathology, cell and structural biology U. Ill., Urbana, 1984—, assoc. head dept. pathology, 1991-94, head dept. pathology coll. medicine, 1994-98; staff pathologist VA Hosp., Danville, Ill., 1989-98. Courtesy staff pathologist Covenant Hosp., Urbana, 1984-98, Carle Clinic, Urbana, 1990-98. Contbr. numerous articles to profl. jours. Recipient Excellence in Teaching award U. Ill., 1996, Spl. Recognition award U. Ill. Coll. Medicine at Urbana-Champaign, 1998. Mem. Internat. Acad. Cytology, Internat. Soc. Lymphology (auditor 1989-91, exec. com. 1991-93), N.Am. Soc. Lymphology (sec. 1988-90, treas. 1990-92, v.p. 1992-94, pres. 1994-98), Am. Soc. Cytology, Am. Assn. Anatomists, Ill. Soc. Cytology. Avocations: boating, needlework. Home: 5645 NE Lincoln Rd Poulsbo WA 98370-7756 Office: U Ill Coll Med 506 S Mathews Ave Urbana IL 61801-3618 E-mail: cccom@uiuc.edu.

OMTVEDT, CRAIG P. consumer products executive; m. Jane Omtvedt. Degree, U. Minn. Dir. of audit Fortune Brands, Inc., Lincolnshire, Ill., 1989-92, dep. contr., 1992-97, v.p., chief acctg. officer, 1997-99, sr. v.p., CFO, 1999—. Mem. Fin. Exec. Inst., Inst. of Mgmt. Accts., Tax Exec. Inst. Office: Fortune Brands Inc 300 Tower Pkwy Lincolnshire IL 60069

O'NEAL, MICHAEL RALPH, state legislator, lawyer; b. Kansas City, Mo., Jan. 16, 1951; s. Ralph D. and Margaret E. (McEuen) O'N.; children from a previous marriage: children: Haley Anne, Austin Michael; m. Cindy Wulfkuhle, Apr. 9, 1999. BA in English, U. Kans., 1973, JD, 1976. Bar: Kans. 1976, U.S. Dist. Ct. Kans. 1976, U.S. Ct. Appeals (10th cir.) 1979. Intern Legis. Counsel State of Kans., Topeka, 1975-76; assoc. Hodge, Reynolds, Smith, Peirce & Forker, Hutchinson, Kans., 1976-77; ptnr. Reynolds, Peirce, Forker, Suter, O'Neal & Myers, 1980-88; shareholder Gilliland & Hayes, P.A., 1988—, mng. ptnr., 2000—; mem. Kans. Ho. of Reps., 1984, chmn. jud. com., 1989-90, 93-94, 97—; pres. Gilliland & Hayes, P.C., 1999-2000; minority whip Kans. Ho. of Reps., 1991-92, majority whip, 1995-96, chmn. edn. com., 1995-96, mem. fiscal oversight com., 1997—, chair redistricting com., 2001—, mem. bus., commerce, labor com. Chmn. Ho. Reappointment Com., 2001, instr. Hutchinson C.C., 1977-88. Vice chmn. Rep. Ctrl. Com., Reno County, Kans., 1982-86; bd. dirs. Reno County Mental Health Assn., Hutchinson, 1984-89, YMCA, 1984-86, Crime Stoppers (ex-officio), Hutchinson; chmn. adv. bd. dirs. Wesley Towers Retirement Cmty., 1984-96; mem. Kans. Travel and Tourism Commn., 1990-94; mem. bd. govs. U. Kans. Law Sch., 1991—; mem. Kans. Sentencing Commn., 1997—. Recipient Leadership award Kans. C. of C. and Industry, 1985; named one of Outstanding Young Men Am., 1986. Mem. ABA, Nat. Conf. State Legislatures (criminal justice com.), Kans. Assn. Def. Counsel, Def. Rsch. Inst., Kans. Bar Assn. (prospective legis. com., Outstanding Svc. award), Hutchinson C. of C. (ex-officio bd. dirs., Leadership award 1984), Am. Coun. Young Polit. Leaders (del. to Atlantic conf. biennial assembly), Kans. Jud. Coun., Commn. on Uniform State Laws. Avocations: basketball, tennis, golf. Home: 8 Windemere Ct Hutchinson KS 67502-2020 Office: Gilliland & Hayes PA 2d Flr Box 2977 20 W 2nd Ave Hutchinson KS 67504-2977 E-mail: mroneal@southwind.net.

O'NEIL, J(AMES) PETER, computer software designer, educator; b. Rockville Center, N.Y., Apr. 2, 1946; s. Clement Lee and Frances Rita (Theis) O'N.; m. Carol Ann Sypniewski, June 8, 1968; children: Kelly Ann, Thomas Joseph. BA in Psychology, Loyola U., Chgo., 1968; MA in Sci. Edn., Webster Coll., St. Louis, 1972. Cert. elem. tchr. K-8, Mo., elem. tchr. K-8, Wis., dir. instruction, Wis. Tchr., student tchr. Sacred Heart Sch., Florissant, Mo., 1968-73; tchr. sci. Waunakee (Wis.) Mid. Sch., 1973-96, chmn. K-8 sci. dept., chmn. K-12 dept., 1984-92; learning coord. Deforest (Wis.) Area Sch. Dist., 1992—. Dir. Waunakee Summer Sci. Program, 1975-91; dir. instrn./tech. Brodhead Wis., 1996-99; designer sci. curriculum computer CD-ROM programs Sci. Curriculum Assistance Program and Elem. Sci. Curriculum Assistance Program, 1990—; dir. instrn. DeForest (Wis.) Area Sch. Dist., 2000--. Feature editor: Science Scope, 1989-96; contbr. over 30 activities and articles to profl. jours. Group worker settlement houses Chgo., St. Louis; mem. Parish Coun.; dir. Waunakee Area Edn. Found. Named Master Tchr. NSF, Waunakee, 1986-96; recipient Tchr. of Yr. award Waunakee, 1984, 90, 92, Kohl Found. award, 1992, Mid. Sch. Tchr. of Yr. award Wis., 1992-93. Mem. Nat. Sci. Tchrs. Assn., Wis. Soc. Sci. Tchrs., Wis. Elementary Sci. Tchrs., NEA, Wis. Ednl. Assn. Roman Catholic. Avocations: computers, sports, writing, jogging. Home: 119 Simon Crestway Waunakee WI 53597-1721 Office: Deforest Area Sch Dist 520 E Holum St De Forest WI 53532-1316 E-mail: jponeil@deforest.k12.wi.us.

O'NEIL, THOMAS J. mining company executive; BS in Mining Engring., Lehigh U.; MS, Pa. State U.; PhD, U. Ariz. Numerous sr. positions in minerals industry; head dept. mining and geol. engring. U. Ariz.; pres., COO Cleveland-Cliffs Inc., Cleve., 2000—. Mem. NAE, Am. Iron Ore Assn. (chmn.), Soc. Mining, Metallurgy and Exploration (dir., pres.-elect). Office: Cleveland-Cliffs Inc 1100 Superior Ave Cleveland OH 44114-2589

O'NEILL, BRIAN BORU, lawyer; b. Hancock, Mich., June 7, 1947; s. Brian Boru and Jean Anette (Rimpela) O'N.; m. Ruth Bohan, Sept. 18, 1991; children: Dru Groves, Brian Boru, Maggie Byrne, Phelan Boru, Ariel Margaret. BS, U.S. Mil. Acad., 1969; JD magna cum laude, U. Mich., 1974; D in Pub. Svc. (hon.), Northland Coll., 1999. Bar: Mich. 1974, U.S. Dist. Ct. Minn. 1977, U.S. Ct. Mil. Appeals 1975, U.S. Ct. Appeals (6th cir.) 1975, U.S. Ct. Appeals (8th cir.) 1977, U.S. Ct. Appeals (Fed. cir.) 1983, U.S. Ct. Appeals (7th cir.) 1985, U.S. Ct. Appeals (10th cir.) 1986, U.S. Ct. Appeals (9th cir.) 1990, U.S. Ct. Claims 1981, U.S. Supreme Ct. 1981. Asst. to gen. counsel Dept. Army, Washington, 1974-77; assoc., ptnr. Faegre & Benson, Mpls., 1977—. Mem. com. vis. Mich. Law Sch., 1994—; counsel Defenders of Wildlife, Washington, 1977—, also bd. dirs; counsel Sierra Club, Audubon Soc. Mng. editor: Mich. Law Rev., 1973—74. Served to capt. U.S. Army, 1969-77. Named Environmentalist of Yr. Sierra Club North Star, 1982, 96, 97, 98; recipient William Douglas award Sierra Club, 1985, Trial Lawyer of Yr. award Trial Lawyers for Pub. Justice, 1995. Fellow Am. Coll. Trial Lawyers, Order of the Coif; mem. Mpls. Golf, Mpls. Athletic. Office: Faegre & Benson 2200 Wells Fargo Tower 90 S 7th St Ste 2200 Minneapolis MN 55402-3901 E-mail: boneill@faegre.com.

O'NEILL, JOHN JOSEPH, speech educator; b. De Pere, Wis., Dec. 6, 1920; s. John Joseph and Elizabeth (Murray) O'N.; m. Dorothy Jane Arnold, Dec. 28, 1943; children— Katherine, Thomas, John, Philip. B.S., Ohio State U., 1947, Ph.D., 1951. From instr. to assoc. prof. speech Ohio State U., 1949-59; prof. speech U. Ill. at Champaign, 1959-91, prof. emeritus, 1991—; prof. audiology U. Ill. Coll. Medicine, Chgo., 1965-79, head speech and hearing sci. dept., 1973-79. Research assoc. U.S. Naval Sch. Aviation Medicine, summers 1953, 54; cons. in field. Co-author: Visual Communication, 1961, 81;, Hard of Hearing, 1964, Applied Audiometry, 1966. Pres. Columbus Hearing Soc., 1956-58; Bd. dirs. Champaign County Assn. Crippled-United Cerebral Palsy, 1961-63. Served with inf. AUS, 1942-46. Decorated Purple Heart, Bronze Star with oak leaf cluster, Jubilee of Liberty medal, France, 2000; recipient Disting. Alumnus award dept. speech Ohio State U., 1969, recipient honors, 1979. Fellow Am. Speech and Hearing Assn. (pres. 1969), Ohio Psychol. Assn.; mem. Am. Bd. Examiners Speech Pathology and Audiology (pres. 1967-68), Acad. Rehabilitative Audiology (pres. 1969) Home: 1203 W University Ave Champaign IL 61821-3224 E-mail: j-oneill@uiuc.edu.

O'NEILL, SHEILA, principal; Prin. Cor Jesu Acad., St. Louis. Recipient Blue Ribbon award U.S. Dept. Edn., 1990-91. Office: Cor Jesu Acad 10230 Gravois Rd Saint Louis MO 63123-4099

ONG, CHEE-MUN, engineering educator; b. Ipoh, Perak, Malaysia, Nov. 23, 1944; came to U.S., 1978; s. Chin-Kok Ong and Say-Choo Yeoh; m. Penelope Li-Lok, July 17, 1971; children: Yi-Ping, Yi-Ching, Chiew-Jen. BE with honors, U. Malaya, 1967; MS, Purdue U., 1968, PhD, 1974. Registered profl. engr. Ind., Eng. Plant engr. Guinness Brewery, Malaysia, 1967; asst. lectr. U. Malaysia, 1968-73, lectr., 1976-78; rsch. asst. Purdue U., West Lafayette, Ind., 1973-74, vis. asst. prof., 1975-76, asst. prof., 1978-81, assoc. prof., 1981-85, prof., 1985—. Cons. SIMTECH, West Lafayette, 1978-85, L.A. Water and Power Co., 1986-88, Caterpillar, 1993-94, Franklin Electric, 1997-98, P Plus Corp., 1999-, PPlus, 1999-, Unibus, 2002. Author: Dynamic Simulation of Electric Machinery, 1998; contbr. articles to jours. in field. Fulbright-Hayes scholar, 1967-68; UNESCO fellow, 1969-70. Fellow Inst. Elec. Engrs. (U.K.); mem. IEEE (sr.). Avocations: gardening, fishing, reading. Office: Purdue U Dept Elec/Computer Engring West Lafayette IN 47907-1285

ONG, JOHN DOYLE, ambassador, retired lawyer; b. Uhrichsville, Ohio, Sept. 29, 1933; s. Louis Brosee and Mary Ellen (Liggett) O.; m. Mary Lee Schupp, July 20, 1957; children: John Francis Harlan, Richard Penn Blackburn, Mary Katherine Caine. BA, MA, Ohio State U., 1954; LLB, Harvard, 1957; LHD, Kent State U., 1982; D Humanities (hon., Ohio State U., 1996; LHD (hon.), U. Akron, 1996. Bar: Ohio 1958. Asst. counsel B.F. Goodrich Co., Akron, 1961-66, group v.p., 1972-73, exec. v.p., 1973-74, vice chmn., 1974-75, pres., dir., 1975-77, pres., chief operating officer, dir., 1978-79, chmn. bd., pres., chief exec. officer, 1979-84, chmn. bd., chief exec. officer, 1984-96, chmn. bd., 1996-97, chmn. emeritus, 1997—; U.S. amb. to The Kingdom of Norway, 2002—. U.S. amb. Kingdom of Norway, 2002—. V.p. exploring Great Trail coun. Boy Scouts Am., 1974-77; bd. dirs. Nat. Alliance of Bus., 1981-84; trustee Mus. Arts Assn., Cleve., Bexley Hall Sem., 1974-81, Case Western Res. U., 1980-92, Kenyon Coll., 1983-85, Hudson (Ohio) Libr. and Hist. Soc., pres., 1971-72, Western Res. Acad., Hudson, 1975-95, pres. bd. trustees, 1977-95; nat. trustee Nat. Symphony Orch., 1975-83, John S. and James L. Knight Found., 1995-2002; mem. bus. adv. com. Transp. Ctr. Northwestern U., 1975-78, Carnegie-Mellon U. Grad. Sch. Indsl. Adminstrn., 1978-83; life trustee U. Chgo., 1991—; chmn. Ohio Bus. Roundtable, 1994-97; trustee Ohio Hist. Soc., 1998-2002; dir. New Amn. Schs., 1991, chmn., 1998-2002. Mem. Ohio Bar Assn. (bd. govs. corp. counsel sect. 1962-74, chmn. 1970), Rubber Mfrs. Assn. (bd. dirs. 1974-84), Chem. Mfrs. Assn. (bd. dirs. 1988-91, 94-97), Conf. Bd., Bus. Roundtable (chmn. 1992-94), Bus. Coun., Portage Country Club, Union Club, Links, Union League, Ottawa Shooting Club, Met. Club, Rolling Rock Club, Castalia Trout Club, Phi Beta Kappa, Phi Alpha Theta. Episcopalian. Home: 230 Aurora St Hudson OH 44236-2941 Office: United States Embassy Norway Drammensveien 18 0244 Oslo Norway

ONKEN, HENRY DRALLE, plastic surgeon; b. St.Louis, Feb. 22, 1932; s. John Werner and Clara Ruth (Dralle) O.; m. Deborah Dorsett Smith, June 3, 1961; children: John D., Michael D., Katherine Minna. AB, Princeton U., 1953; MD, Harvard U., 1957. Diplomate Am. Bd. Plastic Surgery. Resident in gen. and plastic surgery Barnes Hosp., St. Louis, 1957-66; practice medicine specializing in plastic surgery, 1966—. Pres. staff Deaconess Hosp., St. Louis, 1986-89. Bd. dirs. St. Louis Christmas Carolers, 1981—; co-chmn. Theater Factory of St. Louis, Webster Groves, Mo., 1984-88. Capt. USMC, 1962-64. Mem. AFTRA, Am. Soc. Plastic and Reconstructive Surgeons, Mo. State Med. Assn., Midwestern Assn. Plastic Surgeons (pres. 1996-97), St. Louis Area Soc. Plastic Surgeons, St. Louis Med. Soc. (councilor 1996-99), Univ. Club, Princeton Club, Aesculapian Club (Boston). Democrat. Avocations: acting, clarinet, singing, collecting old maps. Office: 141 N Meramec Ave Ste 2 Clayton MO 63105-3750 E-mail: donken@artsci.wustl.edu.

ONSAGER, DAVID RALPH, cardiothoracic surgeon, educator; b. Phoenix, Feb. 15, 1962; s. Ralph William and Margaret Carol (Engel) O. BA in Biochem., History & Sociology Sci., U. Pa., 1984; MD, Rush Med. Coll., 1988. Diplomate Nat. Bd. Med. Examiners, Am. Bd. Surgery, Am. Bd. Thoracic Surgery. Resident in gen. surgery Med. Coll. Wis. affiliated hosps., Milw., 1988-94; fellow in cardiopulmonary transplantation U. Wis. Hosp. and Clinics, Madison, 1994-95, fellow in cardiothoracic surgery, 1995-97, lectr. in cardiothoracic surgery, 1997-2000; attending surgeon Meth. Hosp., Omaha, 2000—. Contbr. articles to profl. jours. Recipient House Staff Excellence in Tchg. award Med. Coll. Wis., 1991, Cmty. Health Svc. award Rush Med. Coll., Chgo., 1988; Cancer Ctr. grantee Med. Coll. Wis., 1991. Fellow ACS (assoc.); mem. AMA, State Med. Soc. Nebr., Internat. Soc. Heart and Lung Transplantation, Soc. Thoracic Surgeons (candidate), Coun. Healthcare and Biomed. Advisors. Dem. Avocations: tennis, basketball, skiing, sailing, flying. Office: Cardiothoracic and Vascular Surgery 8111 Dodge St Ste 220 Omaha NE 68114-4117 Home: Apt 204 511 Aurora Ave Naperville IL 60540-6289 E-mail: donsager@earthlink.net.

OPAT, MATTHEW JOHN, lawyer; b. Riceville, Iowa, Nov. 5, 1952; s. Wesley John and Dolores Genevieve (Ludwig) O.; m. Therese Ann Dusheck, Aug. 13, 1977; children: Michael, Kristin, Steven. BA in History, U. Iowa, 1974; JD, Hamline U., 1977. Bar: Iowa 1977, Minn. 1977. Prin. Opat Law Office, Chatfield, Minn., 1977—. Atty. Fillmore County, 1997—. Mem. Fillmore County Bar Assn. (pres. 1984-85), Minn. State Bar Assn. (bd. dirs. 1985-87), Tenth Dist. Bar Assn. (chmn. ethics com. 1989-96). Office: 22 2nd St SE Chatfield MN 55923-1203

OPATZ, JOE, state legislator; BA, St. Cloud U.; MEd, Kent State U.; PhD in Edn., U. Minn. Mem. Minn. Ho. of Reps., St. Paul, 1993—. Univ. adminstr. Democrat. Home: 402 Riverside Dr SE Saint Cloud MN 56304-1032 Office: Minn Ho of Reps State Capitol Saint Paul MN 55155-0001

OPFER, DARRELL WILLIAMS, state representative, educator; b. Genoa, Ohio, June 17, 1941; s. Milton William and Iva Marie (Gleckler) O. BS in Edn., Bowling Green State U., 1963, MA, 1964. Cert. tchr., Ohio. Tchr. Peace Corps, Kenya, East Africa, 1965-68, Woodward High Sch., Toledo, 1969, Genoa High Sch., 1969-82; county commr. Ottawa County, Port Clinton, Ohio, 1983-92; state rep. State of Ohio, 1993-98. Sec. Dem. Party, Ottawa County, 1974-80; pres. Ottawa County Dem. Club, 1976-80. Named Outstanding Pub. Ofcl., Ohio Dirs.-Pvt. Industry Coun., 1992. Mem. Commodore Perry Fed. Credit Union (pres. 1982-92), Moose, Kiwanis. Mem. United Ch. of Christ. Home: 12342 W State Route 105 Oak Harbor OH 43449-9410

OPITZ, DAVID WILMER, corporate executive, state political party executi; b. Port Washington, Wis., Dec. 15, 1945; s. Wilmer Charles and Ella Lonsdale Opitz. BS, Carroll Coll., 1968. Pub. health biologist Waukesha County, Wis., 1968-70; with Aqua-Tech., Inc., Port Washington, 1971—; Chmn. Wisc. State Rep Party. Dir. environ. health Ozaukee County (Wis.), 1971-72; former Wis. State Rep.; former mem. Wis. State Senate, Dist. 20; chmn. Wis. State Rep. Party, 1992—; mem. Rep. Nat. Com., 1992—. Mem. Beta Pi Epsilon. Lutheran. Address: PO Box 31 Madison WI 53701-0031

OPPEGAARD, GRANT E. water transportation executive; b. 1943; M.B.A., U. of N.H., 1968. With Dayton Hudson Corp., Mpls., 1969-71, Minstar Inc., Mpls., 1971-82, Cuyuna Engine Co., Mpls., 1982-83, Allstate Lawn Products Inc., Mpls., 1983-84, C.V.N. Cos. Inc., Mpls., 1984-89, Fingerhut Cos. Inc., Hopkins, Minn., 1989-96; CEO Genmar Holdings Inc., Mpls., 1997—. Office: Genmar Holdings Inc Ste 2900 80 S 8th St Minneapolis MN 55402-2250

OPPERMAN, DWIGHT DARWIN, publishing company executive; b. Perry, Iowa, June 26, 1923; s. John H. and Zoa L. Opperman; m. Jeanice Wifvat, Apr. 22, 1942 (dec.); children: Vance K., Fane W. JD, Drake U., 1951, LLD (hon.), 1998. Bar: Iowa 1951, U.S. Supreme Ct. 1976, U.S Ct. Internat. Trade, 1988. Editor, asst. editorial counsel West Pub. Co., St. Paul, 1951-64, mgr. reporters and digest depts., 1964-65, v.p., 1965-68, pres., 1968-93, CEO, 1978-96, chmn., 1993-96; chmn. emeritus West Group, Eagan, 1996; chmn. Key Investment, Mpls., 1996—. Dir. Inst. Judicial Adminstrn. Chmn. Supreme Ct. Hist. Soc.; dir. Inst. Jud. Adminstrn.; bd. govs. Drake U., Des Moines; dir. Minn. D.A.R.E. Inc.; dir. Brennan Ctr. for Justice; trustee NYU Law Sch.; dir., Nat. Legal Ctr. for Pub. Interest, Nat. Ctr. for State Cts. Recipient Herbert Harley award Am. Judicature Soc., 1984, Justice award, 1992, 1st George Wickersham Founder's award Friends of Law Libr. of Congress, 1993, Lifetime Achievement award Minn. State Bar Assn., 1997. Fellow Am. Bar Found.; mem. ABA, Fed. Bar Assn., Am. Judicature Soc., Am. Law Inst., Drake U. Nat. Alumni Assn. (disting. svc. award 1974, Centennial award 1981, Outstanding Alumni award 1988), Minn. Club (pres. 1975-76), Mpls. Club. Office: Key Investment 601 2nd Ave S Ste 5200 Minneapolis MN 55402-4317

ORDONEZ, MAGGLIO, professional baseball player; b. Caracas, Venezuela, Jan. 28, 1974; Baseball player Chgo. White Sox, 1997—. Named to Am. League All Star Game, 1999. Office: Chgo White Sox 333 W 35th St Chicago IL 60616*

ORDWAY, ELLEN, biology educator, entomology researcher; b. N.Y.C., Nov. 8, 1927; d. Samuel Hanson and Anna (Wheatland) O. BA, Wheaton Coll., Mass., 1950; MS, Cornell U., 1955; PhD, U. Kans., 1965. Field asst. N.Y. Zool. Soc., N.Y.C., 1950-52; rsch. asst. Am. Mus. Natural History, 1955-57; tchg. asst. U. Kans., Lawrence, 1957-61, rsch. asst., 1959-65; asst. prof. U. Minn., Morris, 1965-70, assoc. prof. biology, 1970-85, prof., 1986-97, prof. emeritus, 1997, acad. advisor, 1997—. Cooperator and cons. USDA Bee Rsch. Lab., Tucson, 1971, 1983. Contbr. articles to profl. jours. Mgr. preserves Nature Conservancy, Mpls., 1975—; lectr. Morris area svc. clubs, 1972—; bd. dirs. County chpt. ARC, 1998—; bd. dirs. U. Minn. Morris Retirees Assn., 1997—, sec., treas. 1998—. Mem. AAAS, AAUP (v.p. 1975-76, sec.-treas. 1971-73 Morris chpt.), Kans. Entomol. Soc., Internat. Bee Rsch. Assn., Sigma Xi, Sigma Delta Epsilon. Episcopalian. Avocations: travel, photography, exploring natural environments, wilderness, areas. Office: U Minn Div Sci And Math Morris MN 56267 E-mail: ordwaye@mrs.umn.edu

O'REILLY, CHARLES TERRANCE, university dean; b. Chgo., May 30, 1921; s. William Patrick and Ann Elizabeth (Madden) O'R.; m. Rosella Catherine Neilland, June 4, 1955; children— Terrance, Gregory, Kevin, Joan Bridget, Kathleen Ann. B.A., Loyola U., Chgo., 1942, M.S.W., 1948; postgrad., U. Cattolica, Milan, Italy, 1949-50; Ph.D., U. Notre Dame, 1954. Instr. DePaul U., Chgo., 1948-49; asst. in psychology U. Cattolica, 1949-50; caseworker Cath. Charities, N.Y.C., 1953-54; exec. dir. Family Service, Long Branch, N.J., 1954-55; asst. prof. Loyola U., 1955-59; vis. lectr. Ensiss Sch. Social Work, Milan, 1959-60; asso. prof. U. Wis.-Milw., 1961-64; prof., asso. dir. U. Wis. Sch. Social Work, Madison, 1965-68; dean social welfare, v.p. acad. affairs SUNY-Albany, 1969-76; dean social work Loyola U., Chgo., 1976-92, dean emeritus, sr. prof., 1994—; vis. prof. sch. social work SS Maria Asunta, Rome, 1992-93. Author: OAA Profile, 1961, People of Inner Core North, 1965, Men in Jail, 1968, Italian Social Work Education 1946-1997, 1998, Italy's War of Liberation, 1998; contbr. articles to profl. jours. Pres. Community Action Commn. Dane County, Wis., 1967-68; bd. dirs. Council Community Services, Albany, Family and Children's Service, Albany; mem. adv. bd. Safer Found.; vice chmn. Ill. Pub. Aid Citizens Council. Served with AUS, 1942-46, 51-52. Fulbright scholar, 1949-50; fellow, 1959-60 Mem. AAUP, Nat. Assn. Social Workers. Roman Catholic. Home: 4073 Bunker Ln Wilmette IL 60091-1001 Office: Sch Social Work Loyola Univ Chicago IL 60611

O'REILLY, HUGH JOSEPH, restaurant executive; b. Emporia, Kans., July 20, 1936; s. Henry Charles and Mary Esther (Rettiger) O'R.; m. Eileen Ellen Browne, Feb. 11, 1961; 1 child, Hugh Jr. Student, St. Benedicts Coll., Atchison, Kans., 1954-57, Kansas City Conservatory of Music, 1957-58. Banquet mgr. Stouffer Corp., N.Y.C., 1958-61; gen. mgr. Howard Johnsons, L.I., N.Y., 1961-65; regional mgr. Malt Village Corp., St. Louis, 1965-68; ops. cons. McDonald's Corp., Chgo., 1968-78; pres., chief exec. officer O'Reilly Mgmt. Corp., Emporia, Kans., 1978—. Nat. advt. cons. McDonalds Operators Assn., Oak Brook, Ill., 1980-84. Republican. Roman Catholic. Lodge: Shriner. Avocations: golf, fishing. Office: 907 Commercial St Emporia KS 66801-2916

O'REILLY, JAMES THOMAS, lawyer, educator, author; b. N.Y.C., Nov. 15, 1947; s. Matthew Richard and Regina (Casey) O'R.; children: Jean, Ann. BA cum laude, Boston Coll., 1969; JD, U. Va., 1974. Bar: Va. 1974, Ohio 1974, U.S. Supreme Ct. 1979, U.S. Ct. Appeals (6th cir.) 1980. Atty. Procter & Gamble Co., Cin., 1974-76, counsel, 1976-79, sr. counsel for food, drug and product safety, 1979-85, corp. counsel, 1985-93, assoc. gen. counsel, 1993-98; adj. prof. in adminstrv. law U. Cin., 1980-97, vis. prof. law, 1998—. Cons. Adminstrv. Conf. U.S., 1981-82, 89-90, Congl. Office of Compliance, 1995-96; arbitrator State Employee Rels. Bd.; mem. Ohio Bishops Adv. Coun., Mayor's Infrastructure Commn., Cin. Environ. Adv. Coun. Author: Federal Information Disclosure, 1977, Food and Drug Administration Regulatory Manual, 1979, Unions' Rights to Company Information, 1980, Federal Regulation of the Chemical Industry, 1980, Administrative Rulemaking, 1983, Ohio Public Employee Collective Bargaining, 1984, Protecting Workplace Secrets, 1985, Emergency Response to Chemical Accidents, 1986, Product Defects and Hazards, 1987, Protecting Trade Secrets Under SARA, 1988, Toxic Torts Strategy Deskbook, 1989, Complying With Canada's New Labeling Law, 1989, Solid Waste Management, 1991, Ohio Products Liability Handbook, 1991, Toxic Torts Guide, 1991, ABA Product Liability Resource Manual, 1993, RCRA and Superfund Practice Guide, 1993, Clean Air Permits Manula, 1994, United States Environmental Liabilities, 1994, Elder Safety, 1995, Environmental and Workplace Safety for University and Hospital Managers, 1996, Indoor Environmental Health, 1997, Product Warnings, Defects & Hazards, 1999, Accident Prevention Manual, 2000; mem. editl. bd. Food and Drug Cosmetic Law Jour.; contbr. articles to profl. jours. Mem. Hamilton County Dem. Ctrl. Com. Served with U.S. Army, 1970-72. Mem. ABA (chmn. AD law sect.), FBA, Food and Drug Law Inst. (chair program com.), Leadership Cin. Democrat. Roman Catholic. Office: 24 Jewett Dr Cincinnati OH 45215-2648

OREL, HAROLD, literary critic, educator; b. Boston, Mar. 31, 1926; s. Saul and Sarah (Wicker) O.; m. Charlyn Hawkins, May 25, 1951; children: Sara Elinor, Timothy Ralston. BA cum laude, U. N.H., 1948; MA, U. Mich., 1949, PhD, 1952; postgrad., Harvard U., 1949. Teaching fellow U. Mich., 1948-52; instr. dept. English, U. Md., 1952-54, 55-56, overseas program Germany, Austria, Eng., 1954-55; tech. editor Applied Physics Lab., Johns Hopkins U., Balt., 1953-56; flight propulsion lab. dept. Gen. Electric Co., Cin., 1957; asso. prof. U. Kans., Lawrence, 1957-63, prof., 1963-74, Disting. prof. English, 1974-97, Disting. prof. emeritus, 1997—, asst. dean faculties and research adminstrn., 1964-67. Cons. to various univ. presses, scholarly jours., Can. Coun. Arts, Nat. Endowment Humanities, Midwest Rsch. Inst., 1958—93; lectr., Japan, 1974, Japan, 88, India, 85. Author: Thomas Hardy's Epic-Drama: A Study of The Dynasts, 1963, The Development of William Butler Yeats, 1885-1900, 1968, English Romantic Poets and the Enlightenment: Nine Essays on a Literary Relationship in Studies in Voltaire and the Eighteenth Century, vol. CIII, 1973, The Final Years of Thomas Hardy, 1912-1928, 1976, Victorian Literary Critics, 1984, The Literary Achievement of Rebecca West, 1985, The Victorian Short Story: Development and Triumph of a Literary Genre, 1986, The Unknown Thomas Hardy: Lesser-Known Aspects of Hardy's Life and Career, 1987, A Kipling Chronology, 1990, Popular Fiction in England, 1914-1918, 1992, The Historical Novel from Scott to Sabatini, 1995; contbg. author: Thomas Hardy and the Modern World, 1974, The Genius of Thomas Hardy, 1976, Budmouth Essays on Thomas Hardy, 1976, Twilight of Dawn: Studies in English Literature in Transition, 1987; contbr. numerous articles on English lit. history and criticism to various mags.; editor: The World of Victorian Humor, 1961, Six Essays in Nineteenth-Century English Literature and Thought, 1962, Thomas Hardy's Personal Writings: Prefaces, Literary Opinions, Reminiscences, 1966, British Poetry 1880-1920: Edwardian Voices, 1969, The Nineteenth-Century Writer and his Audience, 1969, Irish History and Culture, 1976, The Dynasts (Thomas Hardy), 1978, The Scottish World, 1981, Rudyard Kipling: Interviews and Recollections, 2 vols., 1983, Victorian Short Stories: An Anthology, 1987, Critical Essays on Rudyard Kipling, 1989, Victorian Short Stories 2: The Trials of Love, 1990, Sir Arthur Conan Doyle: Interviews and Recollections, 1991, Critical Essays on Sir Arthur Conan Doyle, 1992, Gilbert and Sullivan: Interviews and Recollections, 1994, Critical Essays on Thomas Hardy's Poetry, 1995, The Brontës: Interviews and Recollections, 1997, Charles Darwin: Interviews and Recollections, 2000; delivered orations Thomas Hardy ceremonies, Westminster Abbey, 1978, 90. With USN, 1944-46. Recipient Higuchi Endowment Rsch. Achievement award, 1990; grantee Am. Coun. Learned Socs., 1966, NEH, 1975, Am. Philos. Soc., 1964, 80. Fellow Royal Soc. Literature; mem. Thomas Hardy Soc. (v.p. 1968—), Am. Com. on Irish Studies (v.p. 1967-70, pres. 1970-72). Unitarian. Home: 713 Schwarz Rd Lawrence KS 66049-4507 Office: U Kans Dept English Lawrence KS 66045

OREN, DONALD G. transportation executive; Pres. Dart Transit Co., Eagan, Minn., 1979—. Office: Dart Transit Co 800 Lone Oak Rd Eagan MN 55121-2212

ORENTLICHER, DAVID, lawyer, physician; b. Washington, May 2, 1955; s. Herman Israel and Jeanette Adah (Levin) O. AB in Economics, Brandeis U., 1977; MD, Harvard U., 1981, JD, 1986. Bar: D.C. 1988, Ill. 1993, Ind. 1999. Med. intern U. Mich. Med. Ctr., Ann Arbor, 1981-82; pvt. practice Detroit, 1982-83; law clk. U.S. Ct. Appeals, Baton Rouge, 1986-87; assoc. Sidley & Austin, Washington, 1987-89; ethics and health policy counsel AMA, Chgo., 1989-95. Lectr. in law U. Chgo. Law Sch., 1993-95; adj. asst. prof. medicine Northwestern U. Med. Sch., Chgo., 1992-95; Samuel R. Rosen prof. of law, co-dir. Ctr. for Law and Health Ind. U. Sch. of Law, Indpls., 1995—. Contbr. articles to profl. jours. Mem. AMA, ABA, Am. Soc. Law, Medicine and Ethics. Avocations: cajun dancing, racquet sports. Address: Ind U Sch Law-Indianapolis 530 W New York St Indianapolis IN 46202-3225 E-mail: dorentli@iupui.edu.

ORFIELD, MYRON WILLARD, JR. state legislator, educator; b. Mpls., July 27, 1961; BA summa cum laude, U. Minn., 1983; grad., Princeton U., 1983-84; JD, U. Chgo., 1987. Bar: Minn. 1988. Law clk. Judge Gerald W. Heaney, U.S. Ct. Appeals, 8th Cir., 1987-88; rsch. assoc. Ctr. for Studies in Criminal Justice, U. Chgo., 1988-89; assoc. Faegre & Benson, 1989; asst. atty. gen. Minn. Atty. Gen.'s Office, 1989—; Bradley fellow Ctr. for Studies in Criminal Justice, U. Chgo., 1990-91; mem. Minn. Ho. of Reps. from dist. 60B, St. Paul, 1991-2000, Minn. Senate from 60th dist., St. Paul, 2001—. Adj. prof. law U. Minn., 1991—, Hamline U., 1991—; dir. Met. Area Protram, Mpls.' mem. com. on improving future of U.S. cities through improved met. governance Nat. Acad. Scis., 1996—. Author: Metropolitics, 1997; contbr. articles to profl. jours. Mem. Assn. Pub. Policy Analysis and Mgmt. (bd. dirs. 1997). Office: 521 State Office Bldg Saint Paul MN 55155-0001

ORIANI, RICHARD ANTHONY, metallurgical engineering educator; b. El Salvador, July 19, 1920; came to U.S., 1929, naturalized, 1943; s. Americo and Berta (Siguenza) O.; m. Constance Amelia Gordon, June 26, 1949; children— Margaret, Steven, Julia, Amelia. B. Chem.Engring, CCNY, 1943; M.S., Stevens Inst. Tech., 1946; M.A., Princeton U., 1948, Ph.D., 1949. Lab. asst. CCNY, 1943; chemist Bakelite Corp., Bloomfield, N.J., 1943-46; instr. physics Miss Fine's Finishing Sch., Princeton, 1946-47; research asso. Gen. Electric Corp. Research Lab., Schenectady, 1949-59; asst. dir. U.S. Steel Corp. Research Lab., Monroeville, Pa., 1959-80; prof. U. Minn., Mpls., 1980-89, dir. Corrosion Rsch. Ctr., 1980-87, prof. and dir. emeritus, 1989—. Cons. in field. Contbr. chpts. to books, articles to profl. jours. Founder, mem. Foxwood Civic Assn., Monroeville, 1959-80; founder, v.p. Monroeville Public Library, 1960-80. Recipient Alexander von Humboldt Sr. Scientist award, 1984, W.R. Whitney award, 1987. Fellow Am. Soc. for Metals, Am. Inst. Chemists, N.Y. Acad. Scis., Nat. Assn. Corrosion Engrs., Electrochem. Soc.; mem. AAAS, Am. Phys. Soc., Am. Inst. Metall. Engrs. Republican. Home: 4623 Humboldt Ave S Minneapolis MN 55409-2264 Office: U Minn 112 Amundson Hall 221 Church St SE Minneapolis MN 55455-0113 E-mail: orian001@tc.umn.edu.

ORIG, CARLENE, reporter; b. Oak Brook, Ill. Student, U. Ill., Chgo., Columbia Coll. Reporter WISN, Milw., 1999—, WICD-TV, Champaign, Ill. Avocations: reading, tennis, inline skating. Office: WISN PO Box 402 Milwaukee WI 53201-0402

ORIN, STUART I. lawyer; Exec. v.p. corp. affairs, gen. counsel UAL Corp., Elk Grove Village, Ill., 1996—. Office: UAL Corp PO Box 66100 Chicago IL 60666-0100

ORMESHER, DAVID T. advertising executive; married; 3 children. BA, Wheaton Coll.; MTS, Garrett-Evang. Theol. Sem. Disc kockey, N.J.; producer, journalist; CEO, founder Closer Look Group, Inc., Chgo., 1987—. Producer (documentary series) A Closer Look. Bd. dirs. Lyric Opera Guild, Shelter Now Internat. Mem. Assn. Multimedia Communicators, Chgo. Software Assn. Office: Closer Look Creative 212 W Superior St Ste 300 Chicago IL 60610-3557

ORMOND, PAUL A. health facility executive; b. Aurora, Ill. B in Econs. with honors, Stanford U., 1971; MBA, 1973. Mem. corp. staff, positions with Glass Container divsn. Owens-Ill., Inc. (O-I), 1973-77; nat. mktg. mgr. soft drinks Glass Container divsn., 1977-78; mgr. Atlanta sales dist., 1978-80; asst. gen. mgr. Gerresheimer Glas internat. affil. O-I, Germany, 1980-82; v.p. Glass Container group, 1982-84; v.p. packaging ops., dir. market strategy and devel. O-I, 1984-91; corp. v.p., 1986-91; pres., CEO Health Care and Retirement Corp. (HCR) subs. O-I, Toledo, 1986-91; chmn., pres., CEO HCR now independent co., 1991-96; pres., CEO Manor Care, 1996—. Bd. dirs. TRINOVA Corp., Nat. City Bank N.W. Office: Manor Care 333 N Summit St Toledo OH 43604

ORR, DANIEL, educator, economist; b. N.Y.C., May 13, 1933; s. Robert Connell and Lillian (Nagle) O.; m. Mary Lee Hayes, Oct. 12, 1957; children— Rebecca, Matthew, Sara. A.B., Oberlin Coll., 1954; Ph.D., Princeton, 1960. Ops. analyst Procter & Gamble Co., 1956-58; instr. econs. Princeton U., 1959-60; asst. prof. econs. Amherst Coll., 1960-61, Grad. Sch. Bus., U. Chgo., 1961-65; mem. faculty U. Calif. at San Diego, 1965-78, chmn. econs. dept., 1969-72; prof. econs., cons. in field; prof., head dept. econs. Va. Poly. Inst. and State U., 1978-89; prof. econs. U. Ill., Champaign-Urbana, 1989—, dept. head, 1989-00; prof. emeritus. Vis. prof. U. Nottingham, Eng., 1972, U. Calif., 1988, U. Warsaw, 1992. Author: Cash Management and the Demand for Money, 1970, Property, Markets and Government Intervention, 1976. Trustee Oberlin (Ohio) Coll., 1993—. Served with AUS, 1958. Mem. Am. Econ. Assn., Crystal Downs Country Club. Home: 1304 Taquaka Rd Frankfort MI 49635-9222 Office: U Ill 330 Commerce Bldg W 1206 S 6th St Champaign IL 61820-6978

ORR, J. RICHIE, physicist; b. Waukon, Iowa, Jan. 16, 1933; s. Lester Duncan and Carolyn (Dayton) O.; m. Suzanne Alice, June 20, 1961. BS in Physics with honors, U. Iowa, 1955; PhD, U. Wash., 1965. Rsch. engr. Boeing Aircraft Co., Seattle, 1956-60; rsch. asst. U. Wash., 1960-65; rsch. asst. prof. U. Ill., 1966-70; with Fermilab., Batavia, Ill., 1972—, formerly head accelerator div.; dir. spl. projects, 1986-89, assoc. dir. for adminstrn., 1989—. Contbr. articles to profl. jours. Recipient Nat. Medal of Tech. U.S. Dept. Commerce, 1989. Mem. Am. Phys. Soc., Phi Beta Kappa, Sigma Xi.

ORR, SAN WATTERSON, JR. lawyer; b. Madison, Wis., Sept. 22, 1941; s. San Watterson and Eleanor Augusta (Schalk) O.; m. Joanne Marie Ruby, June 26, 1965; children: San Watterson III, Nancy Chapman. BBA, U. Wis., 1963, JD, 1966. Bar: Wis. 1966; CPA, Wis. Sec., tres., bd. dirs. Yawkey Lumber Co., Wausau, Wis., 1971—; pres. Forewood, Inc., 1979—, also bd. dirs.; dir. M&I First Am. Bank, 1988—, vice chmn., 1997—; dir. Marshall & Ilsley Corp., 1994—; chmn. bd., chmn. exec. com. Wausau-Mosinee Paper Corp., 1997—. Dir. Wausau Ins. Cos., 1982-98, M&I Marshall & Ilsley Bank, Milw., MDU Resources Group, Inc., Bismarck, N.D., 1978-2000; chmn. Marathon Electric Mfg. Corp., Wausau, 1982-97, Mosinee (Wis.) Paper Corp., 1987-97; chmn. bd. Wausau Paper Mills Co., 1989-97. Editor: U. Wis. Law Rev., 1962-63. Bd. dirs. The Aytchmonde Woodson Found., Inc., Wausau, 1966—, The Leigh Yawkey Woodson Art Mus., Inc., Wausau, 1981—, Wis. Taxpayers Alliance, Madison, 1983—, Competitive Wis., Inc., Milw., 1989—, Wis. Mfrs. and Commerce, 2001—, U. Wis. Found., Madison, 1991—; dir. Wis. Policy Rsch. Inst., Milw., 1995—; mem. bd. regents U. Wis. Sys., Madison, 1993-2000, pres., 1998-2000; v.p., bd. dirs. Wausau YMCA Found., 1979—; dir. Wausau Health Found., Inc., 1981—, pres., 1998—. Mem. Wis. Bar Assn., Am. Law Inst., Wausau Club, Minocqua Country Club, Country Club of Fla. Office: Yawkey Lumber Co 500 3rd St Ste 602 Wausau WI 54403-4857

ORR, STEVEN R. health facility administrator; b. 1947; Undergrad. degree, Macalester Coll.; M in Hosp. Adminstrn., U. Minn., 1973. Tchr., coord. master's degree program in hosp. adminstrn. U. Minn., 1974-76; v.p. corp. planning, v.p. managed and affiliated hosp. divsn. Fairfield Community Hosps., Mpls., 1976-81; COO Mid-Atlantic Health Group, 1981-83, adminstr. Monmouth Med. Ctr. N.J., 1981-83; ptnr., cons. Peat, Marwick, Main & Co., Mpls., 1984-88; chmn., pres., CEO Lutheran Health Systems, Fargo, N.D., 1988—. Office: Luth Health System PO Box 6200 Fargo ND 58106-6200

ORTINO, HECTOR RUBEN, chemical company executive; b. Buenos Aires, July 23, 1942; came to U.S., 1983; s. Miguel and Maria Julia (Moauro) O.; m. Beatriz Monica Mayantz, Dec. 14, 1972; children: Nicolas Martin, Gabriela Andrea. B in Acctg. and Adminstrn., Buenos Aires U., 1971. Mng. dir. Ferro Argentina, Buenos Aires, 1976-81, also bd. dirs.; mng. dir. Ferro Mexicana, Mexico City, 1982-83, also bd. dirs.; asst. to v.p. fin. Ferro Corp., Cleve., 1983-84, v.p. fin., 1984—, chief fin. officer, 1987-93, exec. v.p., chief fin.-adminstrv. officer, 1993-96; pres. & COO Ferro Corp, 1996-99; chmn., CEO & pres. Ferro Corp., 1999—. Mem. Fin. Exec. Inst. Roman Catholic. Clubs: Cleve. Skating, Cleve. Athletic. Avocations: tennis, swimming, hunting. Home: 32100 Meadow Lark Way Pepper Pike OH 44124-5523 Office: Ferro Corp 1000 Lakeside Ave E Cleveland OH 44114-7000

ORTMAN, ELDON E. entomologist, educator; b. Marion, S.D., Aug. 11, 1934; s. Emil and Kathryn (Tieszen) O.; m. Margene Adrian, June 27, 1957; children— Karen, Connie, Nancy. AB, Tabor Coll., 1956; MS, Kansas State U., 1957, PhD, 1963. Rsch. entomologist USDA, No. Grain Insects Rsch. Lab., Brookings, S.D., 1961-68, dir., leader investigations, 1968-72; asst. prof. entomology S.D. State U., Brookings, 1961-63, assoc. prof., 1963-68, prof., 1968-72; asst. Entomology Rsch. Divsn. Office, Beltsville, Md., 1971; prof. entomology Purdue U., West Lafayette, Ind., 1972-89, head dept. entomology, 1972-89; assoc. dir. Ind. Agrl. Rsch. Programs, 1989—2001. Fellow AAAS; mem. Entomol. Soc. Am., Phi Kappa Phi, Gamma Sigma Delta, Sigma Xi. Achievements include research in plant resistance to insects and pest mgmt. Home: 3805 W Capilano Dr West Lafayette IN 47906-8881 E-mail: eeo@aes.purdue.edu.

ORTMAN, GEORGE EARL, artist; b. Oakland, Calif., Oct. 17, 1926; s. William Thomas and Anna Katherine (Noll) O.; m. Conni Whidden, Aug. 5, 1960 (dec.); 1 stepson, Roger Graham Whidden. Student, Calif. Coll. Arts and Crafts, 1947-49, Atelier Stanley William Hayter, 1949, Acad. Andre L'Hote, Paris, 1949-50, Hans Hoffman Sch. Art, 1949-50. Co-founder Tempo Playhouse, N.Y.C., 1954; Instr. painting and drawing NYU, 1962-65; co-chmn. fine arts Sch. Visual Arts N.Y.C., 1963-65; artist-in-residence Princeton U., 1966-69, Honolulu Acad. Art, 1969; head painting dept. Cranbrook Acad. Art, Bloomfield Hills, Mich., 1970-92. One-man exhbns. include Tanager Gallery, 1954, Wittenborn Gallery, 1955, Stable Gallery, 1957, 60, Howard Wise Gallery, 1962, 63, 64, 66, 69, Gimpel-Weitzenhoffer Gallery, 1972 (all N.Y.C.), Swetzoff Gallery, Boston, 1961-62, Fairleigh Dickinson U., 1962, Mirvish Gallery, Toronto, Can., 1964, Walker Art Center, Mpls., 1965, Milw. Art Center, 1966, Dallas Mus. Art, 1966, Portland Mus. Art, 1966, Akron Inst. Art, 1966, U. Chgo., 1967, Princeton U. Art Mus., 1967, Honolulu Acad. Art, 1969, Reed Coll., 1970, Cranbrook Acad. Art, 1970, 92, Indpls. Mus. Art, 1971, J.L. Hudson Gallery, Detroit, 1971, Gimpel-Weitzenhoffer, N.Y.C., 1972, 73, Gertrude Kasle Gallery, Detroit, 1976, Lee Hoffman Gallery, Detroit, 1977, Flint (Mich.) Mus. Art, 1977; other one-man exhbns. include Cranbrook Mus. Art, 1982; exhibited numerous group shows including Whitney Mus. Am. Art Annual, 1962, 63, 64, 65, 67, 73, Carnegie Internat., Pitts., 1964, 67, 70, Jewish Mus., N.Y.C., 1964, Corcoran Mus., Washington, 1964, others; represented permanent collections, Walker Art Center, Mpls., Mus. Modern Art, Whitney Mus. Am. Art, (both N.Y.C.), Guggenheim Mus., N.Y.C., Albright-Knox Mus., Buffalo, NYU, Christian Theol. Sem., Indpls., Indpls. Mus. Art, Cleve. Mus. Art, Mus. Am. Art, Washington, Honolulu Acad. Art, Newark Mus. Art, Container Corp. Am., Chgo. Ind. U. Music Bldg., Wausau (Wis.) Hosp. Center, Unitarian Ch., Princeton, Mfr. Hanover Trust Bldg., Albert Kahn & Assos., Detroit, Renaissance Center, Detroit, Mich. State Univ. Performing Arts Ctr., East Lansing, Detroit Inst. Arts. Guggenheim fellow, 1965-66; Ford Found. grantee, 1966; One of five Am. artists selected for 1965 Japanese Bi-ann.; recipient Gov. N.J.'s Purchase award 2d ann. exhbn. art, 1967; Best of Show Religion in Art Exhbn., Birmingham, Ala., 1966 Mem. Nat. Acad. of Design. also: Tim Hill Gallery 1527E 72d St Apt 12H New York NY 10021

ORTON, COLIN GEORGE, medical physicist; b. London, England, June 4, 1938; came to U.S., 1966; s. Frederick G. and Audrey V. (Sewell) O.; m. Barbara G. Scholes, July 25, 1964; children: Nigel, Susanne, Philip. BS in Physics with honors, Bristol U., 1959; MS in Radiation Physics, London U., 1961, PhD in Radiation Physics, 1965; MA (hon.), Brown U., 1976. ABR, ABMP. Instr. London U. St. Barts' Hosp., 1961-66; assoc. prof. NYU Med. Ctr., 1966-75, Brown U., R.I., 1975-81; prof., chief physicist Wayne State U., Harper Hosp., Detroit, 1981—. Dir., grad program, Wayne State U., 1981—. Author: Radiation Physics Review Books I, 1971, II, 1978; editor: Electron Treatment Planning, 1978, Progress in Medical Physics I, 1982, II, 1985, Radiation Dosimetry, 1986; editor Med. Physics, 1997—. Marie Curie Gold Medal, Health Physics Soc., 1987. Fellow Am. Assn. Physicists in Am. (pres. 1981, William D. Coolidge award 1993), Am. Coll. Med. Physics (chmn. 1985, Marvin M. D. Williams Award, 1997), Inst. Physics London, Am. Coll. Radiology; mem. Internat. Orgn. for Med. Physics (sec. gen. 1988-94, pres. 1997-2000), Am. Brechytherapy Soc. (pres. 2001—). Avocations: golf, badminton, tennis, running, squash. Home: 15810 Lakeview Ct Grosse Pointe Park MI 48230-1806 Office: Harper Hosp 3990 John R St Detroit MI 48201-2097 E-mail: ortonc@kci.wayne.edu.

ORVICK, GEORGE MYRON, church denomination executive, minister; b. Hanlontown, Iowa, Jan. 9, 1929; s. George and Mabel Olina (Mandsager) O.; m. Ruth Elaine Hoel, Aug. 25, 1951; children: Daniel, Emily, Mark, Kirsten. AA, Bethany Luth. Coll., Mankato, Minn., 1948, candidate of theology, 1953; BA, Northwestern Coll., Watertown, Wis., 1950. Ordained to ministry Evang. Luth. Synod, 1953. Pastor Our Saviour Luth. Ch., Amherst Junction, Wis., 1953-54, Holy Cross Luth. Ch., Madison, 1954-86; cir. visitor Evang. Luth. Synod, Mankato, 1964-69, pres., 1970—76, 1980—2002, dir. dept. archives and history, 2002—. Author: Our Great Heritage, 1966; columnist: The Luth. Sentinel, 1982-2002. Home: 1117 Lori Ln Mankato MN 56001-4728 Office: Evang Luth Synod 6 Browns Ct Mankato MN 56001-6121 E-mail: gorvick@blc.edu.

ORWOLL, GREGG S. K. lawyer; b. Austin, Minn., Mar. 23, 1926; s. Gilbert M. and Kleonora (Kleven) O.; m. Laverne M. Flentie, Sept. 15, 1951; children: Kimball G., Kent A., Vikki A., Tristen A., Erik G. BS, Northwestern U., 1950; JD, U. Minn., 1953. Bar: Minn. 1953, U.S. Supreme Ct. 1973. Assoc. Dorsey & Whitney, Mpls., 1953-59, ptnr., 1959-60; assoc. counsel Mayo Clinic, Rochester, Minn., 1960-63, gen. counsel, 1963-87, sr. legal counsel, 1987-91, sr. counsel, 1991-92. Gen. counsel, dir. Rochester Airport Co., 1962-84, v.p., 1981-84; gen. counsel Mayo Med. Svcs., Ltd., 1972-90; bd. dirs., sec. and gen. counsel Mayo Found. for Med. Edn. and Rsch., 1984-90; gen. counsel Mid-Am. Orthop. Assn., 1984—, Minn. Orthop. Soc., 1985-95; counsel Norwegian Am. Orthopaedic Soc., 1999—; asst. sec./sec. Mayo Found., Rochester, 1972-91; sec. Mayo Emeritus Staff, 1998-99, vice chair, 1999-2000, chair, 2000-2001; bd. dirs. Charter House, 1986-90; dir., officer Travelure Motel Corp., 1968-86; dir., v.p. Echo Too Ent., Inc.; dir., v.p. Oberhamer Inc., 1989-99; bd. dirs. Am. Decal and Mfg. Co., 1989-93, sec., 1992-93; adj. prof. William Mitchell Coll. Law, 1978-84. Contbr. articles and chpts. to legal and medico-legal publs.; mem. bd. editors HealthSpan, 1984-93; mem. editl. bd. Minn. Law Rev., 1952-53. Trustee Minn. Coun. on Founds., 1977-82, Mayo Found., 1982-86; trustee William Mitchell Coll. Law, 1982-88, 89-98, mem. exec. com. 1990-98; bd. visitors U. Minn. Law Sch., 1974-76, 85-91; mem. U. Minn. Regent Candidate Adv. Coun., 1988-99, Minn. State Compensation Coun., 1991-97. With USAF, 1944-45. Recipient Outstanding Svc. medal U.S. Govt., 1991. Mem. ABA, AMA (affiliate), Am. Corp. Counsel Assn., Minn. Soc. Hosp. Attys. (bd. dirs. 1981-86), Minn. State Bar Assn. (chmn. legal/med. com. 1977-81), Olmsted County Bar Assn. (v.p., pres. 1977-79), Rochester C. of C., U. Minn. Law Alumni Assn. (bd. dirs. 1973-76, 85-91), Rochester U. Club (pres. 1977), The Doctors Mayo Soc., Mid Am. Orthop. Assn. (hon.), Mayo Alumni Assn. (hon.), Phi Delta Phi, Phi Delta Theta. Republican. Home: 2233 5th Ave NE Rochester MN 55906-4017 Office: Mayo Clinic 200 1st St SW Rochester MN 55905-0002

OSBORN, KENNETH LOUIS, financial executive; b. Belleville, Ill., Jan. 9, 1946; s. William Arthur and Louise Mary (Brueggemann) O.; BBA, U. N.Mex., 1968; m. Roberta Marie Vodicka, Oct. 23, 1971; 1 son, David Anthony. Auditor, Ernst & Ernst, Albuquerque, 1968; budge mgr. Rockwell Internat., Chgo., 1970-74; mgr. internat. acctg. Allied Van Lines, Chgo., 1974-76; fin. mgr. Sealy, Inc., Chgo., 1976-79; sr. fin. analyst Newark Electronics, Chgo., 1979-80, internat. dir. credit, 1980-82; bus. mgr. Prime Computer, 1982-90; acctg. mgr., CFO Flexonics, Inc., Chgo., 1990-96; contr. and chief fin. ofcr. Jackson Industries, Chgo., 1996—; fin. cons. Am. European Expres. Mem. Rep. Nat. Com., presdl. task force. With AUS, 1968-70. Decorated Air medal. Mem. Mensa, Soc. Am. Baseball Rsch., Inst. Mgmt. Accts.

OSBORN, MARK ELIOT, dentist; b. Buffalo, Apr. 22, 1950; s. Thomas Earl and Ruth Frances (Martin) O. BA, U. Mo., Columbia, 1972; DDS, U. Mo., Kansas City, 1977. Dir. Westport Free Health Clinic, Kansas City, Mo., 1974-76; clinician St. Louis Dept. Health, 1977-82; gen. practice dentistry Troy, Mo., 1978-92; pvt. practice St. Louis, 1993-94; mem. gen. practice staff Gravois-Gustine Dental Group, 1994-96; pvt. practice gen. dentistry, 1996-97; pvt. practice Chestnut Park Dental, 1997—. Mem. ADA, Greater St. Louis Dental Soc. (bd. dirs. 1999—), Am. Soc. Dentistry for Children, St. Louis Dental Rsch. Group, Delta Sigma Delta, Troy C. of C., Rotary (Troy chpt., dir. dental program 1985—, sec. 1988, pres. 1989, bd. dirs. 1989-91). Home: 360 W Point Ct Saint Louis MO 63130-4028 Office: Chestnut Park Dental 4583 Chestnut Park Plz Ste 201 Saint Louis MO 63129-3163 E-mail: meosborn@swbell.net.

OSBORN, WILLIAM A. investment company executive; Chmn., CEO No. Trust Corp., Chgo. Office: No Trust Co 50 S Lasalle St Chicago IL 60675-0001

OSBORNE, QUINTON ALBERT, psychiatric social worker, inspector of institutional services; b. Hopkinsville, Ky., May 14, 1951; s. Willie Lee and Elizabeth (Talley) O.; m. Gwendolyn G. Flowers, Oct. 19, 1991; 1 adopted child, Quinton A. Jr.; children: Ashley Elain, Shelbie Elizabeth. BS in Sociology, Austin Peay State U., 1978; MS in Health Adminstrn., Calif. Coll. Health Sci., 1996. Lic. social worker, Ohio, Ky., D.C. Fin. specialist U.S. Army, Karlsruhe, Fed. Republic Germany, 1972-75; resident advisor Breckinridge Job Corps, Morganfield, Ky., 1978; clk., typist Govt. D.C., Washington, 1979; asst. worker's compensation Dept. Labor, Mt. Sterling, Ky., 1979-80; social svc. asst. U.S. Forest Svc., Mariba, 1980-85; mil. pay clk. Ky. N.G., Frankfort, 1985-86; social worker Cin. VA Med. Ctr., 1986-88; equal opportunity specialist US Dept. HUD, Columbus, Ohio, 1988-90; family tchr. Maryville Acad., 1991-93; inspector of instnl. svcs. Lebanon Correctional Instn., 1999; social worker Warren Correctional Instn., 1999—. Mem. Victorian Eva Vet. Group, Cin., 1975—, task force for homeless U.S. Dept. HUD, Columbus, 1988-89; chair ptnrs. in edn. VA Med. Ctr., Cin., 1986-88, Op. Feed, Columbus, 1988-89; social worker Vets. Homeless Program, Cin., 1988—; sect. and employees asst. coord., chairperson Adopt-A-Sch. Program, 1991—. Mem. Ptnrs. in Edn. (chairperson 1986-88), Alpha Phi Alpha (pres. Clarksville, Tenn. chpt. 1977-78), Alpha Phi Alpha (Clarksville chpt.). Republican. Baptist. Avocations: tennis, bowling, biking, reading, traveling. Home: 509 14th Ave Middletown OH 45044-5601 Office: Warren Correctional Instn Lebanon OH 45036

OSBORNE, TOM, congressman, former college football coach; b. Feb. 23, 1937; m. Nancy Tederman; children: Mike, Ann, Susie. B.A., Hastings Coll., 1959; M.A., U. Nebr., 1963, Ph.D. in Ednl. Psychology, 1965. Flankerback Washington Redskins, NFL, 1959-61, San Francisco 49ers, NFL, 1961-62; asst. football coach U. Nebr., 1962-73, head football coach, 1973-97; coach team U. Nebr. (Cotton Bowl), 1974, U. Nebr. (Sugar Bowl), 1971, U. Nebr. (Astro-Bluebonnet Bowl), 1976, U. Nebr. (Liberty Bowl), 1977, U. Nebr. (Sun Bowl), 1980, U. Nebr. (Orange Bowl), 1979, 83, 84, 89, 92-95; prof. emeritus U. Nebr., 1998-2000; mem. U.S. Congress from Nebr. 3rd Dist., 2001—; mem. agr. com., edn. and the workforce com., resources com. Served in U.S. Army. Named Big Eight Coach of Yr., 1975, 78, 80; named Bobby Dodds Nat. Coach of Yr., 1978 Coached team to NCAA Divsn. IA Nat. Championship, 1994-95. Office: US Ho of Reps 507 Cannon HOB Washington DC 20515-2703*

OSGOOD, CHRIS, professional hockey player; b. Peace River, Alta., Canada, Nov. 26, 1972; Goalie Detroit Red Wings, 1991—. Named to WHL East All-Star Second Team, 1990-91, Sporting News All Star Team, 1996; recipient Bill Jennings Trophy NHL, 1996; played in NHL All-Star Game, 1996. Office: New York Islanders Nassau Veterans Memorial Coliseum Uniondale NY 11553

OSGOOD, RUSSELL KING, academic administrator; b. Fairborn, Ohio, Oct. 25, 1947; s. Richard M. and Mary Russell Osgood; m. Paula Haley, June 6, 1970; children: Mary, Josiah, Micah, Iain. BA, Yale U., 1969, JD, 1974. Bar: Mass. 1974, U.S. Dist. Ct. Mass. (admitted to) 1976. Assoc. Hill & Barlow, Boston, 1974—78; assoc. prof. Boston U., 1978—80; prof. Cornell U., Ithaca, NY, 1980—88, dean law sch., 1988—98; pres. Grinnell (Iowa) Coll., 1998—. Lt. USNR, 1969—71. Mem.: Selden Soc., Stair Soc., Mass. Hist. Soc. Office: Grinnell Coll 1121 Park St Grinnell IA 50112-1640 E-mail: osgood@grinnell.com.

O'SHAUGHNESSY, JAMES PATRICK, lawyer; b. Rochester, N.Y., Mar. 3, 1947; s. John Andrew and Margaret May (Yaxley) O'S.; m. Terry Lee Wood. BS cum laude, Rensselaer Poly. Inst., 1972; JD, Georgetown U., 1977. Bar: Va. 1977, Ohio 1979, Wis. 1987. Assoc. Squire, Sanders & Dempsey, Cleve., 1978-81; ptnr. Hughes & Cassidy, Sumas, Wash., 1981-84; patent counsel Kimberly-Clark Corp., Neenah, Wis., 1984-85; ptnr. Foley & Lardner, Milw., 1986-96; v.p., chief intellectual property counsel Rockwell Internat. Corp., 1996—, corp. officer. Founder Innovatech Co., 1996—; mem. tech. adv. coun. Ideation Internat., Inc., 1999—; mem. adv. bd. Licensing Econs. Rev.; mem. bd. visitors Georgetown U. Sch. Nursing, 1996-2000; mem., bd. dir. Intellectual Property Owners; frequent lectr., chmn. seminars to legal and bus. groups. Contbg. author: Technology Licensing: Corporate Strategies for Maximizing Value, 1996, Profiting From Intellectual Capital: Extracting Value From Innovation, 1998; contbr. articles to profl. jours. Bd. dirs. Skylight Opera Theatre, 1991-92, Milw. Florentine Opera Co., 1999—. With USN, 1964-68. Mem. CPR Inst. for Dispute Resolution (mediation/arbitration panel), Lic. Execs. Soc., Am. Intellectual Property Law Assn., Assn. Chief Patent Coun.; Disabled Am. Vets., Tau Beta Pi, Alpha Sigma Mu. Home: 3207 W Donges Bay Rd Mequon WI 53092-5119 Office: Rockwell Automation Inc. 777 E Wisconsin Ave Ste 1400 Milwaukee WI 53202-5302

O'SHEA, LYNNE EDEEN, management consultant, educator; b. Chgo., Oct. 18, 1950; d. Edward Fisk and Mildred (Lessner) O'S. BA, BJ in Polit. Sci. and Advt., U. Mo., MA in Comms. and Mktg. Rsch., 1971; PhD in Consumer Cultures, Northwestern U., 1977; postgrad., Sch. Mgmt. and Strategic Studies, U. Calif., 1988. Congl. asst., Washington, 1969-70; brand mgr. Procter & Gamble Co., Cin., 1971-73; v.p. Foote, Cone & Belding, Inc., Chgo., 1973-79; v.p. corp. communications Internat. Harvester Co., 1979-82; dir. communications Arthur Andersen & Co., 1983-86; v.p. bus. devel. Gannett Co., Inc., 1987-94; pres., chief oper. officer Shalit Place L.L.C., 1995—; exec. v.p. Mus. Broadcast Comm., Chgo., 1996-97; cons. A.T. Kearney, Chgo., 1998—. Prof. mktg. U. Chgo. Grad. Sch. Bus., 1979—80, Kellogg Grad. Sch. mgmt., 1983—84, 1994—95, 2000—; exec.-in-residence DePaul U., 2000—; dir. AskRex.com, 1999—, Clark/Bardes Inc., 1999—. Bd. dirs. Off-the-Street Club, Chgo., 1977-86; mem. adv. bd. U. Ill. Coll. Commerce, 1980-95, Chgo. Crime Commn., 1987—; bus. adv. bd., DePaul U., 1989—, Roosevelt U., 1994—; dir., Merle Ruskin Theatre bd., 2001—. Recipient numerous Eagle Fin. Advt. awards, Silver medalist Am. Advt. Fedn., 1989; named Advt. Woman of Yr. Chgo. Advt. Club, 1989; named Glass Ceiling Commn., 1991-95, Com. 21st Century, 1992—. Fellow Internat. Leadership Forum; mem. Internat. Women's Forum (v.p. devel., v.p. communications, exec. com., bd. dir.), Chgo. Network, Women's Forum Chgo., Women's Forum Mich., Tarrytown Group, Social Venture Network, Execs. Club Chgo., Mid-Am. Club (bd. govs. 1990—), Women's Athletic Club Chgo., Cleve. Yachting Club. Office: AT Kearney Inc 222 W Adams St Fl 25 Chicago IL 60606-5227 E-mail: lynne.o'shea@atkearney.com., loshea@depaul.edu.

O'SHONEY, GLENN, church administrator; Exec. dir. Mission Svcs. of Luth. Ch. Mo. Synod Internat. Ctr., St. Louis. Office: Luth Ch Mo Synod Inter Ctr 1333 S Kirkwood Rd Saint Louis MO 63122-7226

OSIPOW, SAMUEL HERMAN, psychology educator; b. Allentown, Pa., Apr. 18, 1934; s. Louis Morris and Tillie Osipow; m. Sondra Beverly Feinstein, Aug. 26, 1956; children: Randall A., Jay I., Reva S., David S. B.A., Lafayette Coll., Easton, Pa., 1954; M.A., Columbia U., 1955; Ph.D., Syracuse U., 1959. Lectr. U. Wis., Madison, 1961; psychologist, asst. prof. Pa. State U., 1961-67; mem. faculty Ohio State U., Columbus, 1967-98, prof. psychology, 1969-98, chmn. dept., 1973-86, prof. emeritus, 1998—. Vis. prof. Tel Aviv U., 1972, U. Md., 1980—81; vis. rsch. assoc. Harvard U., 1965; cons. to govt. Author: Strategies in Counseling for Behavior Change, 1970, Theories of Career Development, 1968, 4th edit. 1996, Handbook of Vocational Psychology, 2 vols., 1983, 2d edit. 1995, A Survey of Counseling Methods, 1984; editor: Jour. Vocat. Behavior, 1970-75, Jour. Counseling Psychology, 1975-81, Applied and Preventive Psychology, 1993-99. Served to 1st lt. U.S. Army, 1959-61. Erskine fellow U. Canterbury, New Zealand, 1997. Mem. APA (bd. dirs. 1985-88), Nat. Register Health Svc. Providers in Psychology (bd. dirs. 1982-89, chmn. 1986-89). Home: 330 Eastmoor Blvd Columbus OH 43209-2022 E-mail: sosipow@aol.com.

OSMAN, STEPHEN EUGENE, historic site administrator; b. Berkeley, Calif., Aug. 8, 1949; s. Eugene Lee and June Elizabeth (Claus) O.; m. Wendy Kay Holmberg, June 21, 1975; children: Rachel Ann, Austin Thomas, Laurel Suzanne. BA in History and Edn. cum laude, St. Olaf Coll., 1971. Program mgr. Historic Ft. Snelling, St. Paul, 1971-85, dir., 1985—. Program mgr. Legis. Commn. on Minn. Resources, 1985; mem. Coun. on Am.'s Mil. Past, Midwest Open Air Mus. Coord. Coun.; lectr. in field. Author: The Soldiers Handbook, 1825, 1972; contbr. articles to profl. jours. Fellow Co. Mil. Historians; mem. Assn. Living History Farms and Agrl. Mus., Living History Soc. Minn. Republican. Lutheran. Avocations: 19th Century military uniforms and equipment, historic crafts. Office: Minn Hist Soc Ft Snelling History Ctr Saint Paul MN 55111 E-mail: stephen.osman@mnhs.org.

OSNES, LARRY G. academic administrator; b. Scottsbluff, Nebr., Oct. 30, 1941; s. Earl E. and Rose (DeRock) O.; m. Susan C.; 1 child, Justin. BA in History, Anderson Coll., 1963; MA in History, Wayne State Coll., 1965; PhD in History, U. Cin., 1970. Asst. prof. history and govt. U. Cin., 1967-69; dir. Am. studies Anderson (Ind.) Coll., 1970-75, chmn. dept. history, 1975-76, dean acadmeic devel., 1975-78, asst. corp. sec., dean academic devel. and pub. affairs, 1978-83; pres. Minn. Pvt. Coll. Coun., St. Paul, 1983-88, Hamline U., St. Paul, 1988—. Mem. Assoc. Colls. Twin Cities (chmn. 1988-90), Mpls. Club, St. Paul Athletic Club. Office: Hamline Univ 1536 Hewitt Ave Saint Paul MN 55104-1284

OSSKOPP, MIKE, state legislator; b. Oct. 3, 1951; m. Monica Osskopp; 2 children. BA, Inst. Broadcast Arts; MA, Moody Bible Inst. Minn. state rep. Dist. 29B, 1994—. Radio broadcast journalist. Home: PO Box 77 Lake City MN 55041-0077 Office: Minn Ho of Reps State Capitol Saint Paul MN 55155-0001

OSTER, LEWIS HENRY, manufacturing executive, engineering consultant; b. Mitchell, S.D., Jan. 18, 1923; s. Peter W. and Lucy (Goetsch) O.; m. Mary Mills, Aug. 17, 1948; children— David, Lewis, Nancy, Susan. B.S. in Engring., Iowa State U., 1948; M.B.A., Syracuse U., 1968. Registered profl. engr., Iowa. Mgr., Maytag Co., Newton, Iowa, 1953-59; sr. staff engr., mgr. Philco-Ford Corp., Phila., 1959-62; mgr. mech. and indsl. engring. Carrier Corp., Syracuse, N.Y., 1962-75; v.p. Superior Industries Internat., Van Nuys, Calif., 1981— ; v.p., gen. mgr. Superior/Ideal, Inc., Oskaloosa, Iowa, 1975— ; engring. cons., Louisville, 1951-53. Author: MTM Application Manual, 1957. Leader, Boy Scouts Am., Syracuse, 1965-73; fund chmn. United Fund, Syracuse, 1965-73. Served to lt. col. USAFR, 1942— ; ETO. Decorated Purple Heart, Disting. Flying Cross, air medal with four oak leaf clusters. Mem. Am. Inst. Indsl. Engrs. (pres. 1951-53), Oskaloosa Country Club, Retired Officers Assn., Elks, Am. Legion.

OSTERGREN, GREGORY VICTOR, insurance company executive; b. Mpls., May 27, 1955; s. Theodora Carl and Donna Marie Ostergren; m. Diane Jane Schaller, Oct. 12, 1985; children: Patrick, Cynthia. BS in Math., BA in Econs., U. Minn., 1977. Actuarial analyst Allstate Ins. Co., Northbrook, Ill., 1977-79; actuary MSI Ins. Co., Arden Hills, Minn., 1979-84, dir. actuarial dept., 1984-86, v.p. ops., 1986-90; chmn., pres., CEO Am. Nat. Property and Casualty Ins. Co., Springfield, Mo., 1990—, also bd. dirs. Chmn., Farm Family Ins. Cos., Albany, N.Y., 2001—; mem. governing bd. Minn., S.D. and N.D. Auto Assigned Risk, Mpls., 1984-90; bd. dirs. Guaranty Fed. Bank. Bd. dirs. United Way of Ozarks, Springfield, 1990-98, Springfield Pub. Sch. Found., 1994—; mem. cert. com. S.W. Mo. State U., Springfield, 1992-93; mem. steering com. Salvation Army, Springfield, 1992-93; chmn. adv. bd. Coll. Natural and Applied Scis. S.W. Mo. State U. Mem. Casualty Actuarial Soc., Am. Acad. Actuaries, Internat. Actuarial Assn., Midwest Actuarial Forum, Ins. Fraternity. Baptist. Avocations: golf, boating, scuba diving, reading, travel. Home: 1951 E Buena Vista St Springfield MO 65804-4326 Office: Am Nat Property Casualty 1949 E Sunshine St Springfield MO 65899-0001 E-mail: gostergren@anpac.com.

OSTHOFF, TOM, state legislator; b. 1936; m. Sandra Osthoff; 1 child. Student, U. Minn. Mem. Minn. Ho. of Reps., St. Paul, 1974—; asst. minority leader. Former chmn. transp. and transit com., mem. appropriations com., gaming com., others. Mgr. county records divsn. Ramsey County, Minn. Democrat. Office: 591 State Office Bldg Saint Paul MN 55155-0001

OSTMANN, CINDY, state legislator; BS, Lindenwood Coll. Tchr. Ft. Zumwalt Sch. Dist., 1958-62, 64-67, Fayetteville Sch. Sys., 1963-64; owner, mgr. residential property; mem. Mo. State Ho. of Reps. Dist. 14, 1992—, mem. children, youth and families com., mem. energy and environ. com., mem. local govt. and related matters com. Recipient Outstanding Contbr. to Edn. award Phi Delta Kappa, 1988. Mem. Coun. of Chambers Charter Govt. Com., St. Charles County Arts Coun., Grand Order of Pachyderm, Friends of St. Louis Symphony, Mo. Fedn. Rep. Women, First Capitol Rep. Club. Home: 445 Knaust Rd Saint Peters MO 63376-1713 Office: Mo Ho of Reps State Capitol Building Jefferson City MO 65101-1556

OSTRACH, SIMON, engineering educator; b. Providence, Dec. 26, 1923; s. Samuel and Bella (Sackman) O.; m. Gloria Selma Ostrov., Dec. 31, 1944 (div. Jan. 1973); children: Stefan Alan, Louis Hayman, Naomi Ruth, David Jonathan, Judith Cele; m. Margaret E. Stern, Oct. 29, 1975. BS in Mech. Engring, U. R.I., 1944, ME, 1949; MS, Brown U., 1949, PhD in Applied Math, 1950; DS (h.c.) Technion, Israel Inst. Tech., 1986; D of Eng. (hon.), Fla. State U., 1994; DS (hon.), U. R.I., 1995; ScD (hon.), Brown U., 1997. Rsch. scientist NACA, 1944-47; rsch. assoc. Brown U., 1947-50; chief fluid physics br. Lewis Rsch. Ctr. NASA, 1950-60; prof. engring., head div. fluid, thermal and aerospace scis. Case Western Res. U., Cleve., 1960-70, Wilbert J. Austin Distinguished prof. engring., 1970—; home sec. Nat. Acad. Engring., 1992—; dir. Nat. Ctr. for Microgravity Rsch. on Fluids and Combustion. Disting. vis. prof. City Coll. CUNY, 1966-67, Fla. A&M U., Fla. State U. Coll. Engring., 1990; Lady Davis fellow, vis. prof. Technion-Israel Inst. Tech., 1983-84; cons. to industry, 1960—; mem. rsch. adv. com. fluid mechanics NASA, 1963-68, mem. space applications adv. com., 1985—; hon. prof. Beijing U. Aeronautics and Astronautics, 1991; mem. space studies bd. Nat. Rsch. Coun., 1992, bd. govs., 1993—. Contbr. papers to profl. lit. Fellow Japan Soc. for the Promotion of Sci., 1987; recipient Conf. award for best paper Nat. Heat Transfer Conf., 1963, Richards Meml. award Pi Tau Sigma, 1964, Disting. Svc. award Cleve. Tech. Socs. Coun., 1987, Disting. pub. svc. medal NASA, 1993, Space Processing award Am. Inst. of Aeronautics and Astronautics, 1994 Fellow AIAA (Space Processing award 1993), ASME (hon., Heat Transfer Meml. award 1975, Freeman scholar 1982, Thurston lectr. 1987, Max Jacob meml. award 1983, Heat Transfer divsn. 50th Anniversary award 1988), Am. Acad. Mechanics; mem. NAE (chmn. com. on membership 1986, chmn. nominating com. 1989, chmn. awards com. 1990, sec., mem. space studies bd. 1992), Univs. Space Rsch. Assn. (trustee 1990), Soc. Natural Philosophy, Sigma Xi (nat. lectr. 1978-79), Tau Beta Pi. Home: 28176 Belcourt Rd Cleveland OH 44124-5618 Office: Case Western Res U Dept of Engineering Cleveland OH 44106

OSTROM, DON, political science educator; b. Chgo., Mar. 9, 1939; s. Irving and Margaret (Hedberg) O.; m. Florence Horan, Jan. 13, 1972; children: Erik, Rebecca, Katherine. BA, St. Olaf Coll., Northfield, Minn., 1960; MA, Washington U., 1970, PhD, 1972. Prof. polit. sci. Gustavus Adolphus Coll., St. Peter, Minn., 1972—; state rep. Minn. Ho. of Reps., St. Paul, 1988-96. Co-editor: Perspectives on Minnesota Government and Politics, 1998. Democrat. Home: 405 N 4th St Saint Peter MN 56082-1921 E-mail: dostrom@gac.edu.

OSTROM, VINCENT A(LFRED), political science educator; b. Nooksack, Wash., Sept. 25, 1919; s. Alfred and Alma (Knudson) O.; m. Isabell Bender, May 20, 1942 (div. 1963); m. Elinor Awan, Nov. 23, 1963. BA in Polit. Sci., UCLA, 1942, MA in Polit. Sci., 1945, PhD in Polit. Sci., 1950. Tchr. Chaffey Union H.S., Ontario, Calif., 1943-45; asst. prof. polit. sci. U. Wyo., Laramie, 1945-48, U. Oreg., Eugene, 1949-54, assoc. prof. polit. sci., 1954-58, UCLA, 1958-64; prof. polit. sci. Ind. U., Bloomington, 1964-90, Arthur F. Bentley prof emeritus polit. sci., 1990—. Hooker disting. vis. scholar McMaster U., 1984-85; rsch. assoc. Bur. Mcpl. Rsch., 1950, Resources for Future, Inc., 1962-64; assoc. dir. Pacific NW Coop. Program in Ednl. Adminstrn., 1951-58; co-dir. Workshop in Polit. Theory and Policy Analysis, Ind. U., Bloomington, 1973—; cons. and lectr. in field. Author: Water and Politics, 1953, The Political Theory of a Compound Republic, 1971, 2nd rev. edit., 1987, The Intellectual Crisis in American Public Administration, 1974, 2nd edit., 1989, The Meaning of American Federalism, 1991, The Meaning of Democracy and the Vulnerability of Democracies, 1997; co-author: Understanding Urban Government, 1973, Local Government in the United States, 1988; co-editor: Comparing Urban Service Delivery Systems, 1977, Guidance, Control and Evaluation in the Public Sector, 1986, Rethinking Institutional Analysis and Development, 1988, 2d. edit. 1993; mem. bd. editors Publius, 1972—; mem. editl. bd. Constnl. Polit. Economy, 1989—, Nigerian Jour. Fin. and Human Resources Mgmt., 1996—, Internat. Jour. Orgn. Theory and Behavior, 1997—; contbr. articles to profl. jours. Program coord. Wyo. Assessors' Sch., 1946-48, Budget Officer's Sch., 1947-48; exec. sec. Wyo. League of Municipalities, 1947-48; cons. Wyo. Legis. Interim Com., 1947-48, Nat. Resources, Alaska Constitutional Convention, 1955-56, Tenn. Water Policy Commn., 1956; mem. founding bd. Com. on Polit. Economy of the Good Soc., 1990—. Grantee and fellowships Social Sci.

Research Council, 1954-55, Ctr. Advanced Study in Behavioral Scis., 1955-56, Ctr. Interdisciplinary Rsch., 1981-82. Mem. AAAS, Am. Polit. Sci. Assn. (Spl. Achievement award for Significant Contbns. to Study of Federalism, 1991, Best Book on Federalism and Intergovtl. Rels. award 1999), Am. Econ. Assn., Am. Soc. Pub. Adminstrn., Pub. Choice Soc., Internat. Polit. Sci. Assn. Home: 5883 E Lampkins Ridge Rd Bloomington IN 47401-9726 Office: Ind U Workshop in Polit Theory 513 N Park Ave Bloomington IN 47408-3895 E-mail: workshop@indiana.edu., ghiggins@indiana.edu.

O'SULLIVAN, CHRISTINE, retired executive director social service agency, consultant; b. Washington, July 5, 1947; d. George Albert and Mary Ruth (Stalcup) Markward; m. Donald Phillip O'Sullivan, June 27, 1985; 1 child: Kimberly Molly. Sec. Gas Distributors Info. Svc., Washington, 1966-70; adminstr. asst. Nat. Airlines, 1970-71; office mgr. Tire Industry Safety Coun., 1971-75; pres. Type-Right Exec. Sec. Svc., Washington, Pitts., 1976-91; exec. dir. Eastside Cmty. Ministry, Zanesville, Ohio, 1991—2001. Chair FEMA Emergency Bd., Muskingum, Morgan and Perry Counties, Ohio, 1994-97, 99-2000; chair United Way Exec. Dirs. Coun., 1994-97; v.p. Muskingum County Hunger Network, Zanesville, 1993-99. Author: Write a Good Resume, 1976. Mem. task force Literacy Coun., 1993—2000; mem. steering com. Muskingum County Operation Feed, 1992—99; trustee Disability Network of Ohio-Solidarity, 2001; mem Zanesville City Sch. Bldg. Adv. Coun., Ohio, 2001—02; v.p. Muskingum County Women's Rep. Club, 1994, sec., 1995; mem. Downtown Clergy Assn., 1992—, pres., 1995—96; bd. dirs. Human Care Ministry, Ohio dist. Luth. Ch., Mo. Synod, PRO-Muskingum, 1995—2000; commr. Mo. Synod Luths. to Commn. on Religion in Appalachia, 1996—98; bd. dirs. Muskingum County Women's Coalition, 1994—97, Families and Children First Coun., 1995—2000, Interfaith Response to Ohio Disaster, 1988—91, Luth. Social Svcs. Emergency Assistance Com., 1998—99, Muskingum County Family Adv. Team, 2000—01. Recipient Cert. of Achievement for Mil. Family Support, U.S. Army, 1991, Excellence in Cmty. Svc. award Aid Assn. Luths., 1993, Excellence in Cmty. Svc. award Muskingum County DAR, 1994, Positive Action award, NOW, 1997, YWCA Woman of Achievement award, 1997, Americanism award VFW, 1992, Cmty. Involvement award Richvale Grange, 1997, Cmty. Citizen award State of Ohio Grange, 2000; named Outstanding Cmty. Vol. Zanesville Daybreak Rotary Club, 1997. Mem.: Bus. and Profl. Women's Club Zanesville, Nat. Multiple Sclerosis Soc. (program com. Buckeye chpt. 2001—02), Muskingum County Respiratory Assn. (bd. dirs. 2001—02), Disability Network Ohio Solidarity (trustee 2001—02), Richvale Grange, Kiwanis (Zanesville chpt. bd. dirs. 1997—99, spiritual aims com. chair Dist. 18 of Ohio 1998—99). Avocations: creative writing, music. Home: 509 Van Horn Ave Zanesville OH 43701-2562 Office: Eastside Cmty Ministry 221 Stillwell St PO Box 965 Zanesville OH 43702-0965 E-mail: eastsidecommunityministry@juno.com.

OTIS, JAMES, JR. architect; b. Chgo., July 8, 1931; s. James and Edwina (Love) O.; m. Diane Cleveland, Apr. 9, 1955; children: James III, Julie C., David C. BArch cum laude, Princeton U., 1953; postgrad., U. Chgo., 1955-57. Registered architect, Ill., Ariz., Colo., Ind., Iowa, Wis., N.Mex., Mo. Designer Irvin A. Blietz Co., Wilmette, Ill., 1955-57; pres. Homefinders Constrn. Corp., 1957-59, O & F Constrn. Co., Northbrook, Ill., 1959-61; chmn. bd., chief exec. officer Otis Assocs., Inc., 1960-89; pres. Otis Co., 1981—. Bd. dirs. Banco Popular, Chgo. Prin. works include GBC Corp. Hdqrs., Zurich Towers Office Complex, Schaumburg, Ill., AON Ins. Co. Corp. Hdqrs., Performing Arts Ctr., Northbrook, Ill., All State Regional Hdqrs., Skokie, Ill., Zurich Nat. Hdqrs.-Zurich Towers Schaumburg. Trustee Evanston (Ill.) Hosp., 1971-93, Better Govt. Assn., Chgo., Graham Found., 1984-86; chmn. bd. trustees North Suburban YMCA, Northbrook, 1990-97; governing mem. Shedd Aquarium; bd. govs. Chgo. Zool. Soc.; mem. adv. bd. Cook County Forest Preserve Dist.; mem. founder's coun. Field Mus., Chgo. Lt. USNR, 1953-55. Mem. AIA, Nat. Coun. Archtl. Registration Bds., Urban Land Inst., Northwestern U. Assocs., Chgo. Coun. Fgn. Rels. (assoc.), Internat. Wine and Food Soc., Princeton Club (pres. 1971-72), Econ. Club, Commonwealth Club, Chgo. Club, Comml. Club, Glen View Golf Club, Coleman Lake Club, Angler's Club. Republican. Episcopalian. Office: Otisco 1450 American Ln Ste 1250 Schaumburg IL 60173-6010 E-mail: jotisjr@otiscompany.com.

O'TOOLE, JAMES, state legislator; Mem. Mo. State Ho. of Reps. Dist. 68. Home: 5445 Finkman St Saint Louis MO 63109-3540

OTREMBA, KEN, state legislator; b. Oct. 29, 1948; m. Mary Ellen Otremba; 4 children. Minn. state rep. Dist. 11B, 1994—. Farmer. Home: RR 2 Box 17 Long Prairie MN 56347-9561 Office: Minn Ho of Reps State Capitol Saint Paul MN 55155-0001

OTT, ALVIN R. state legislator; Mem. Wis. Assembly from 3rd assembly dist. Home: PO Box 112 N8855 Church St Forest Junction WI 54123

OTT, BELVA JOLEEN, former state legislator; b. Wichita, Kans., June 5, 1940; d. Kenneth Theodore and Vera Esther (Harvey) Massey; m. Harold Arthur Ott, 1959; children: Teresa Dawn, Bruce Kenton. Mem. from dist. 92 Kans. State Ho. of Reps., 1977-82, 95-97, chmn. ho. election com., 1979-82. Mem. Women's Polit. Caucus; med. sec. Mid-Am. Heart Assn., Pa., 1977-81; mem. Kans. Fedn. Rep. Women; precinct committeewoman Sedgwick County Rep. Party, 1972—, ward chmn., 1973—; del. 4th Dist. Rep. Party Conv., 1976—; alt. del. Kans. State Rep. Conv., 1976. Mem. LWV, Am. Coun. Young Polit. Leaders, Sedgwick County Rep. Women's Club. Address: 821 Litchfield St Wichita KS 67203-3106

OTT, C(LARENCE) H(ENRY), citizen ambassador, accounting educator; b. Richmond, Mich., Jan. 20, 1918; s. Ferdinand and Wilhelmina (Radkte) O.; m. Helen Louis McKay, Oct. 29, 1942 (dec. Apr. 1994); children: James Richard, Dennis McKay, Richard Darrel, Delene Michelle. BA, Valparaiso U., 1940; MBA, Northwestern U., 1970; PhD, Southeastern U., 1980. CPA, N.Y.; cert. mgmt. acct., N.Y. Chief acct. G.E. X-Ray Corp., Chgo., 1940-41; pub. auditor Arthur Andersen & Co., 1941-43; renegotiator contracts U.S. Army Air Corps, 1943-45; internal auditor David Bradley Mfg. (Sears), Bradley, Ill., 1945-48; contr., treas. Manco Mfg. Co., 1948-59; owner, operator Yellow-Checker Cab Co., Kankakee, Ill., 1959-70; chmn. acctg., prof. Rochester (N.Y.) Inst. Tech., 1970-73, Southwestern Mich. Coll., Dowagiac, Mich., 1973—; citizen amb. People to People Internat., Kansas City, Mo., 1992—. Curriculum advisor Southwestern Mich. Coll., Dowagiac, 1992—. Del. to Russia to faciliate their transition to Dem. form of govt.; del. leader Wharton Sch. Fin., U. Pa., Phila., 1992, Citizen Ambassador to many countries including Tahita, Bora Bora, Moorea, Cuba, Quebec, Can., Ecuador, Galapagos Islands, Israel, Egypt, Hong Kong, Mainland China, Greece, Greek Islands, Turkey, Singapore, India, Japan, France, Morocco, Portugal, Spain, Russia, British Isles, Italy. Mem. Nat. Assn. Accts., Inst. Cert. Mgmt. Accts., Planning Execs. Inst. (spkr., chmn.), Alpha Kappa Psi, Pi Kappa Alpha, Pi Gamma Mu. Republican. Avocations: travel, golf, bowling, reading, exercise. Home: 30992 Middle Crossing Rd Dowagiac MI 49047-9268

OTT, KARL OTTO, nuclear engineering educator, consultant; b. Hanau, Germany, Dec. 24, 1925; came to U.S., 1967, naturalized, 1987; s. Johann Josef and Eva (Bergmann) O.; m. Gunhild G. Göring, Sept. 18, 1958 (div. 1986); children: Martina, Monika; m. Birgit Fehse, May 1, 1995. BS, J. W. von Goethe U., Frankfurt, Germany, 1948; MS, G. August U., Göttingen, Fed. Republic Germany, 1953, PhD, 1958. Physicist Nuclear Rsch. Ctr., Karlsruhe, Fed. Republic Germany, 1958-67, sect. head Fed. Republic Germany, 1962-67; prof. Sch. Nuclear Engring. Purdue U., West Lafayette, Ind., 1967-2001, prof. emeritus, 2001—. Cons. Argonne (Ill.) Nat. Lab., 1967—; prof. emeritus, 2001—. Author: Nuclear Reactor Statics, 1983, 2nd edit., 1989, Nuclear Reactor Dynamics, 1985, Chinese edit., 1991. Fellow Am. Nuclear Soc. (Arthur Holly Compton award 1993). Office: Sch Nuclear Engring Purdue U Lafayette IN 47907-1290 E-mail: ott@ecn.purdue.edu.

OTTE, FRANK J. federal judge; b. 1938; BS, Ind. U., 1960, JD, 1966. Pvt. practice law, Indpls., 1966-86; bankruptcy judge U.S. Dist. Ct. (so. dist.) Ind., 1986—. 1st lt. U.S. Army, 1960-63. Mem. Ind. Bar Assn., Indpls. Bar Assn., Nat. Conf. Bankruptcy Judges. Office: 335 US Courthouse 46 E Ohio St Indianapolis IN 46204-1903

OTTE, PAUL JOHN, academic administrator, consultant, trainer; b. Detroit, July 10, 1943; s. Melvin John Otte and Anne Marie (Meyers) Hirsch; children: Deanna Kropf, John. BS, Wayne State U., 1968, MBA, 1969; EdD, Western Mich. U., 1983. With Detroit Bank and Trust Co., 1965-68; teaching fellow Wayne State U., Detroit, 1968-69; auditor, mgr. Arthur Young & Co., 1969-75; contr., dir. Macomb Community Coll., Warren, Mich., 1975-79, v.p. bus., 1979-86; pres. Franklin U., Columbus, Ohio, 1986—, prof. undergrad. and grad. programs, 1986—. Author various tng. manuals, 1982. Cpl. USMC, 1961-65. Teaching fellow Wayne State U., 1968-69. Mem. AICPA, Mich. Assn. CPAs (chmn. continuing profl. edn. com. 1980-82, leadership com. 1981-83), Nat. Assn. Coll. and Univ. Bus. Officers (acctg. prins. com. 1986), Assn. Ind. Colls. and Univs. Ohio (bd. dirs.), Greater Detroit C. of C. (leadership award 1983), Columbus C. of C. (info. svc. com.). Roman Catholic. Avocations: travel, speaking engagements. Office: Franklin U 201 S Grant Ave Columbus OH 43215-5399

OTTINO, JULIO MARIO, chemical engineering educator, scientist; b. La Plata, Buenos Aires, Argentina, May 22, 1951; came to U.S., 1976; naturalized, 1990; s. Julio Francisco and Nydia Judit (Zufriategui) O.; m. Alicia I. Löffler, Aug. 20, 1976; children: Jules Alessandro, Bertrand Julien. Diploma in Chem. Engring., U. La Plata, 1974; PhD in Chem. Engring., U. Minn., 1979; exec. program Kellogg Sch. Mgmt., Northwestern U., 1995. Instr. in chem. engring. U. Minn., Mpls., 1978-79; asst. prof. U. Mass., Amherst, 1979-83, adj. prof. polymer sci., 1979-91, assoc. prof. chem. engring., 1983-86, prof., 1986-91; Chevron vis. prof. chem. engring. Calif. Inst. Tech., Pasadena, 1985-86; sr. rsch. fellow Ctr. for Turbulence Rsch. Stanford (Calif.) U., 1989-90; Walter P.Murphy prof. chem. engring. Northwestern U., Evanston, Ill., 1991-2000, chmn. dept. chem. engring., 1992-2000; McCormick Inst. prof., 2000—; George T. Piercy Disting. prof. U. Minn., 1998, prof. mech. engring., 2001—. Cons. to U.S. and European corps.; Allan P. Colburn Meml. lectr. U. Del., 1987; Merck Sharp & Dohme lectr. U. P.R., 1989, Stanley Corrsin lectr. Johns Hopkins U., 1991; Centennial lectr. U. Md., 1994, William N. Lacey lectr. Calif. Inst. Tech., 1994, P. V. Danckwerts Meml. lectr. Inst. Chem. Engring., Eng., 1999, Robb lectr. Pa. State U.; mem. tech. adv. bd. Dow Chem.; mem. bd. dirs. Coun. Chem. Rsch. Author: The Kinematics of Mixing: Stretching, Chaos and Transport, 1989; contbr. articles to profl. jours.; assoc. editor Physics Fluids A, 1991—; mem. editl. bd. Internat. Jour. Bifurc. Chaos, 1991—; assoc. editor Am. Inst. Chem. Engring. Jour., 1991-95, assoc. editor., 1995—; one man art exhibit, La Plata, 1974. Recipient Presdl. Young Investigator award NSF, 1984, Alpha Chi Sigma award AIChE, 1994, W.H. Walker award AIChE, 2001, E. Thiele award 2002; Univ. fellow U. Mass., 1988, J.S. Guggenheim fellow, 2001; Lacey lectureship, Calif. Inst. Tech., 1994, Danckwerts lectureship Royal Instn., 1999, Robb lectr. Pa. State U. Fellow Am. Phys. Soc., AAAS; mem. Am. Chem. Soc., Am. Phys. Soc., Soc. Rheology, Am. Soc. Engring. Edn., NAE, Sigma Xi (disting. lectr. 1997-99), Coun. for Chem. Rsch.(gov. bd. coun. 1999-2001). Achievements include research in fluid dynamics, chaos, complex systems, mixing and granular flows. Avocations: visual arts, painting. Home: 1092 Crescent Ln Winnetka IL 60093-1501 Office: Northwestern U Dept Chem Engring 2145 Sheridan Rd Evanston IL 60208-0834 E-mail: jm_ottino@northwestern.edu.

OTTO, CHARLOTTE R. consumer products company executive; b. Duluth, Minn., Aug. 15, 1953; BS, Purdue U., 1974, MS in Mgmt., 1976. With Procter & Gamble, 1976—, from asst. brand mgr. to brand mgr. various products, 1977-83, assoc. advt. mgr. paper products divsn., 1984-87, assoc. advt. mgr. toilet tissue/towels, paper products div., 1987-89, dir. issues mgmt., pub. affairs divsn., 1989-90, dir. pub. rels., pub. affairs divsn., 1990-91; v.p. pub. rels. Procter & Gamble USA, 1991-93; v.p. corp. comms. Procter & Gamble Worldwide, 1993-95, v.p. pub. affairs, 1995-96; sr. v.p. pub. affairs The Procter & Gamble Co., 1996-99, global pub. affairs officer, 1999—. Bd. dirs. The Brazelton Found., Inc.; bd. selectors The Jefferson Awards, Am. Inst. for Pub. Svc.; bd. dirs. Boys & Girls Clubs of Am., Cin. Playhouse in the Park, Joy Outdoor Edn. Ctr., Downtown Cin., Inc., Good Samaritan Hosp., Cin. chpt. ARC, Cin. Fire Mus., Great Cin. C. of C., Riverfront Advisors Commn.; trustee Arts & Cultural Coun. Greater Loveland. Recipient YWCA Career Woman of Achievement award, 1993, Woman of Distinction award Gt. Rivers coun. Girl Scouts Am., 1998. Mem. Commonwealth Club, Women's Capital Club, Queen City Club (bd. govs.), Club at Harper's Point. Office: Procter & Gamble Co 1 Procter And Gamble Plz Cincinnati OH 45202-3393

OUE, EIJI, conductor, music director; b. Hiroshima, Japan; Student, Toho Sch. Music, Tanglewood Music Ctr.; artist diploma in conducting, New England Conservatory Music. Assoc. condr. Buffalo (N.Y.) Philharmonic, 1987-91; music dir. Erie (Pa.) Philharmonic, 1991-95, Minn. Orch., 1995—. Co-creator, resident condr. Pacific Music Festival, Sopporo, Japan, 1990-92; music dir., condr. Grand Teton Music Festival, Wyo., 1997; guest condr. London Symphony Orch., Shinsei Symphony, N.Y. Philharmonic, Phila. Orch., Nat. Symphony, others. Recipient Koussevitzky prize Tanglewood, 1980, First prize Salzburg Mozarteum, 1981, Hans Haring Gold medal, 1981. Office: Minn Orch Orch Hall 1111 Nicollet Ave Minneapolis MN 55403-2406

OURADA, MARK, state legislator; b. Apr. 28, 1956; m. Christi Ourada. Student, St. John's U. Mem. Minn. Senate from 19th dist., St. Paul, 1994—. Former lab. technician. Address: 1110 Innsbrook Ln Buffalo MN 55313-1295 Office: Mem Senate State Capitol Saint Paul MN 55155-0001

OURADA, THOMAS D. state legislator; Home: 425 Dorr St Antigo WI 54409-1400

OUZTS, DALE KEITH, broadcast executive; b. Miami, Fla., Aug. 26, 1941; s. Jacob C. and Edna P. (Sloan) O.; m. Susan Ouzts; children: Dale Keith Jr., Karen, Ryan Keith. BJ, U. Ga., 1965, MA, 1966; postgrad. advanced mgmt. seminar, Harvard U., 1977. Mgr. Sta. WSJK-TV, Knoxville, Tenn., 1966-69; exec. v.p., gen. mgr. Sta. KPTS-TV, Wichita, Kans., 1969-72; gen. mgr. Sta. WSSR-FM, Springfield, Ill., 1972-77; sr. v.p. Nat. Pub. Radio, Washington, 1977-79; gen. mgr. Sta. WOSU-AM-FM and Sta. WOSU-TV, Ohio State U., Columbus, Ohio, 1979—; gen. mgr. Sta. WPBO-TV, Portsmouth, 1979—; Sta. WOSE-FM, Coshocton, 1996—; gen. mgr. Sta. WOSV-FM, Mansfield, Ohio, 1988—, Sta. WOSP-FM, Portsmouth, 1993—; assoc. prof. comm. Ohio State U., Columbus, Ohio, 1979—, assoc. prof. journalism, 1983—; pres. Sta. WOSU-AN-FM. Adminstrv. dir. Ohio State Awards, 1979-94; mem. Ohio Ednl. TV Stas., v.p., 1983-84, pres., 1988-90; pres. Ohio Pub. Radio, 1995—, Ohio Alliance for Pub. Telecom., 1996—; chmn. Nat. Pub. Radio, 1990-92; pres. Pub. Radio in Mid-Am., 1976-77, 85-87. Bd. dirs. Ctr. of Vocat. Alts. in Mental Health, 1985-93, 96—, sec.-treas., 1986-88, chmn., 1988-90, Pub. Radio Expansion Task Force, 1989-90; bd. dirs. Brule Conservation Trust, 1985-94, Columbus Zoo, 1984—, Mental Health Assn., Franklin County, 1987-93, Ohio China Coun., 1982-93, v.p., 1984-85, pres., 1987-89; advisor Chinese Student and Scholar Soc. at Ohio State U., 1987-91; program rev. panel Nat. Telecomms., 1988; mgmt. cons. Corp. for Pub. Broadcasting, 1975-95. Recipient Disting. Service award Nat. Pub. Radio, 1986, Disting. Service award Nat. Black Program Consortium, 1985, Disting. Service award PRIMA, 1977, 87, award for fundraising and promotion Corp. Pub. Broadcasting, 1971, Outstanding Broadcaster award Wichita (Kans.) Chpt. of Kappa Mu Psi, 1970, OEBIE award Ohio Ednl. Broadcasting Network Commn., 1987, Emmy award nomination Acad. TV Arts and Scis., 1987. Mem. Nat. Assn. Broadcasters, Ohio Alliance for Pub. Telecom. (pres. 1995-97), Ohio Assn. Broadcasters, Nat. Assn. State Univs. and Land Grant Colls. (mem. telecomms. com. 1980-93), Columbus Ducks Unltd. (bd. dirs. 1982-93), Scioto Valley Skeet Club (bd. dirs. 1982-92), Grand Hotel Hunt Club, Sawmill Athletic Club, Ohio-Rocky Mountain Elk Found., Rotary (Dublin-Worthington, v.p. 1988-89, pres. 1990-91). Avocations: racquetball, softball, golf, hunting, tennis. Home: 2038 Michelle Dr Grove City OH 43123-4019 Office: Sta WOSU 2400 Olentangy River Rd Columbus OH 43210-1027

OVAERT, TIMOTHY CHRISTOPHER, mechanical engineering educator; b. Chgo., Apr. 30, 1959; s. Walter Allen and Joyce Ann (Collins) O.; m. Valerie Mora, July 16, 1988; children: Teresa Noel, Christina Lynn. BSME, U. Ill., 1981; MEM, Northwestern U., 1985, PhD, 1989. Plant engr. Wells Mfg. Co.-Dura Bar Div., Woodstock, Ill., 1981-85; mech. engr. Nat. Inst. of Standards and Tech., Gaithersburg, Md., 1986; asst. prof. Penn State U., 1989-95; assoc. prof. Pa. State U., 1995-2000, prof., 2000, U. Notre Dame, Ind., 2000—. Assoc. editor ASME Trans., Jour. Tribology, 1998—; contbr. articles to profl. jours. Traffic safety com. Borough of State College, Pa., 1992. Named Nat. Young Investigator, NSF, 1992. Mem. ASME, Soc. Tribologists and Lubrications Engrs. Office: U Notre Dame 374 Fitzpatrick Hall Notre Dame IN 46556

OVERBECK, CARLA WERDEN, soccer player, coach; b. Pasadena, Calif., May 9, 1969; m. Greg Overbeck, Dec. 5, 1992; 1 child, Jackson. BS in Psychology, U. N.C., 1990. Asst. women's soccer coach Duke U., Durham, N.C. Mem. U.S. Nat. Women's Soccer Team, 1988—, including world championship FIFA Women's World Cup team, 1991, FIFA Women's World Cup team, 1995, gold medal U.S. Olympic Team, 1996. Named to Soccer Am. All-Freshman Team, 3-time NSCAA All-Am. Achievements: played 63 consecutive internat. games, a record for any U.S. nat. team player. Office: US Soccer Fedn 1801 S Prairie Ave Chicago IL 60616-1319

OVERBY, OSMUND RUDOLF, art historian, educator; b. Mpls., Nov. 8, 1931; s. Oscar Rudolph and Gertrude Christine (Boe) O.; m. Barbara Ruth Spande, Mar. 20, 1954; children: Paul, Katherine, Charlotte. B.A., St. Olaf Coll., 1953; B.Arch., U. Wash., 1958; M.A., Yale U., 1960, Ph.D., 1963. Asst. in instruction dept. of history of art Yale U., 1959-60, 61-62; architect Hist. Am. Bldgs. Survey, U.S. Nat. Park Service, 1960-61, summers 1959, 62, 63, 65, 68, 69, 70, 73, 85; lectr. dept. fine arts U. Toronto, Ont., Can., 1963-64; faculty dept. art history and archaeology U. Mo., Columbia, 1964—, dept. chmn., 1967-70, 75-77, prof. art history, 1979-98, prof. emeritus, 1998—, dir. Mus. of Art and Archaeology, 1977-83. Vis. prof. dept. architecture U. Calif., Berkeley, 1980; Morgan prof. U. Louisville, 1989; vis. prof. dept. art history and archaeology Washington U., St. Louis, 1996; bd. advisors Nat. Trust for Hist. Preservation, 1974-83; cons., panelist Nat. Endowment for Humanities, 1974— ; bd. Mo. Mansion Preservation Commn., 1974-87; advisor Heritage/St. Louis Survey, 1974-76; counsellor to St. Louis Landmarks Assn., 1977— ; chmn. Task Force on Hist. Preservation City of Columbia, 1977-78; cons. on hist. preservation; active Mo. Adv. Council on Hist. Preservation, 1967-82; lectr., exhibitor profl. confs. in field Author: Historic American Buildings Survey, Rhode Island Catalog, 1972, William Adair Bernoudy, Architect, Bringing the Legacy of Frank Lloyd Wright to St. Louis, 1999; co-author: Laclede's Landing, a History and Architectural Guide, 1977, The Saint Louis Old Post Office, A History and Architectural Guide to the Building and Its Neighborhood, 1979; co-author, editor: Illustrated Museum Handbook, A Guide to the Collections in the Museum of Art and Archaeology, University of Missouri-Columbia, 1982; editor in chief Buildings of the United States series, 1990-96; contbr. sects. to books, articles to profl. publs. in field. Served with U.S. Army, 1953-55. Recipient various fellowships and grants in field. Mem. Soc. Archtl. Historians (bd. dirs. 1968-73, 78-81, Jour. editor 1968-73, dir. Mo. Valley chpt., session chmn. ann. meeting 1976, v.p. 1982-86, pres. 1986-88, chmn. coms.), Mid-Continent Am. Studies Assn. (editorial bd. American Studies 1965-70), Midwest Art History Soc. (bd. 1975-78, gen. chmn. annual meeting 1977), Mid-Am. Coll. Art Assn. (session chmn. annual meeting 1975), Mo. Heritage Trust (pres. 1976-79, 81-83, bd. dirs. 1979—), Coll. Art Assn., Landmarks Assn. St. Louis. Lutheran. Home: 1118 W Rollins Rd Columbia MO 65203-2221 Office: U Mo Dept Art History & Archaeolo Columbia MO 65211-0001 E-mail: overbyo@missouri.edu.

OVERGAARD, MITCHELL JERSILD, lawyer; b. Chgo., Jan. 9, 1931; s. Kristen Mikkelsen and Rose Eunice (Jersild) O.; m. Joan Marquardt, Aug. 2, 1958; children: Wade, Kristin Bond, Neil. BA, U. Chgo., 1950, JD, 1953. Bar: Ill. 1957, U.S. Supreme Ct. 1975. Assoc. Dale, Haffner & Grow, Chgo., 1957-63; ptnr. Overgaard & Davis, 1963-2000, of counsel, 2001—. Dir. Cmty. Bank of Homewood-Flossmoor, Homewood, Ill., 1973—83. Trustee Village of Homewood, 1965-69, 85-95; commr. Homewood-Flossmoor Park Dist., 1969-77; past pres., bd. dirs. Family Svcs. and Mental Health Ctr. of South Cook County, Homewood Youth Coun.; bd. dirs. Ill. Philharm. Orch., 1992-95, South Star Svcs., 1998—. With U.S. Army, 1953-56. Mem.: Rotary. Mem. Reformed Ch. in America (elder) Home: 19137 Loomis Ave Homewood IL 60430-4431 Office: Overgaard & Davis 134 N La Salle St Chicago IL 60602-1086

OVERGAARD, ROBERT MILTON, retired religious organization administrator; b. Ashby, Minn., Nov. 6, 1929; s. Gust and Ella (Johnson) O.; m. Sally Lee Stephenson, Dec. 29, 1949; children: Catherine Jean Overgaard Thuleen, Robert Milton, Elizabeth Dianne Overgaard Almendinger, Barbara, Craig, David (dec.), Lori Overgaard Noack. Cert., Luth. Brethren Sem., 1954; BS, Mayville (N.D.) State U., 1959; MS, U. Oreg., 1970. Ordained to ministry Ch. Luth. Brethren Am., 1954. Pastor Elim Luth. Ch., Frontier, Sask., Can., 1954-57, Ebenezer Luth. Ch., Mayville, 1957-60, Immanuel Luth. Ch., Eugene, Oreg., 1960-63, 59th Street Luth. Ch., Bklyn., 1963-68, Immanuel Luth. Ch., Pasadena, Calif., 1969-73; exec. dir. world missions Ch. Luth. Brethren Am., Fergus Falls, Minn., 1973-86, pres., 1986—2001, ret., 2001. Editor Faith and Fellowship, 1967-75. Home: 806 W Channing Ave Fergus Falls MN 56537-3221 Office: Ch Luth Brethren Am PO Box 655 Fergus Falls MN 56538-0655 E-mail: rmo@clba.org.

OVERHAUSER, ALBERT WARNER, physicist; b. San Diego, Aug. 17, 1925; s. Clarence Albert and Gertrude Irene (Pehrson) Overhauser; m. Margaret Mary Casey, Aug. 25, 1951; children: Teresa, Catherine, Joan, Paul, John, David, Susan, Steven. AB, U. Calif., Berkeley, 1948, PhD, 1951; DSc (hon.) , U. Chgo., 1979; LLD (hon.) , Simon Fraser U., 1998. Research assoc. U. Ill., 1951—53; asst. prof. physics Cornell U., 1953—56, assoc. prof., 1956—58; supr. solid state physics Ford Motor Co., Dearborn, Mich., 1958—62, mgr. theoret. scis., 1962—69, asst. dir. phys. scis., 1969—72, dir. phys. scis., 1972—73; prof. physics Purdue U., West Lafayette, Ind., 1973—74, Stuart disting. prof. physics, 1974—. With USNR, 1944—46. Recipient Alexander von Humboldt sr. U.S. scientist award, 1979, Nat. medal of Sci., Pres. of U.S., 1994. Fellow: Am. Acad.

Arts and Scis., Am. Phys. Soc. (Oliver E. Buckley Solid State Physics prize 1975); mem.: NAS. Home: 236 Pawnee Dr West Lafayette IN 47906-2115 Office: Purdue U Dept Of Physics West Lafayette IN 47907 E-mail: awo@physics.purdue.edu.

OVERSCHMIDT, FRANCIS S. state legislator; Mem. Mo. State Ho. of Reps. Dist. 110. Home: 151 N Outer Rd Union MO 63084-4400

OVERTON, GEORGE WASHINGTON, lawyer; b. Hinsdale, Ill., Jan. 25, 1918; s. George Washington and Florence Mary (Darlington) O.; m. Jane Vincent Harper, Sept. 1, 1941; children— Samuel Harper, Peter Darlington, Ann Vincent A.B., Harvard U., 1940; J.D., U. Chgo., 1946. Bar: Ill. 1947, U.S. Dist. Ct. (no. dist.) Ill. 1947, U.S. Supreme Ct. 1951. Assoc. Pope & Ballard, Chgo., 1946-48; ptnr. Overton & Babcock, 1948-51, Taylor, Miller, Busch & Magner, Chgo., 1951-60; pvt. practice, 1960; sr. prin. Overton, Schwartz & Fritts and predecessor cos., 1961-81; of counsel Wildman Harrold Allen & Dixon, 1981—. Bd. dirs. Ill. Inst. Continuing Legal Edn., 1974-81, chmn. 1980-81; mem. com. on profl. responsibility of Ill. Supreme Ct., 1986-97, chmn., 1990-93. Contbr. articles to profl. jours. Ill. reporter Cornell U. Nat. Legal Ethics Project, 1981—; bd. dirs. Open Lands Project, 1961—, pres., 1978—81; bd. dirs. Canal Corridor Assn., 1981—, chmn., 1981—84. 1st lt. U.S. Army, 1942—45. Mem. ABA (mem. com. on counsel responsibility 1985—, com. on nonprofit corps., adv. coun. ethics 2000), Ill. Bar Assn., Chgo. Bar Assn. (bd. mgrs. 1981-83), Assn. of Bar of City of N.Y., Am. Law Inst., Univ. Club. Office: Wildman Harrold Allen & Dixon 225 W Wacker Dr Chicago IL 60606-1224 E-mail: overton@wildmanharold.com.

OVERTON-ADKINS, BETTY JEAN, foundation administrator; b. Jacksonville, Fla., Oct. 10, 1949; d. Henry and Miriam (Gordon) Crawford; children from previous marriage: Joseph Alonzo III, Jermaine Lamar; m. Eugene Adkins, Apr. 24, 1992. BA in English, Tenn. State U., 1970, MA in English, 1974; PhD in English, Vanderbilt U., 1980; student Inst. Ednl. Mgmt., Harvard U., 1990. Reporter Race Rels. Reporter Mag., Nashville, 1970-71; tchr. Met. Nashville Sch. System, 1971-72; instr., project dir. Tenn. State U., Nashville, 1972-76; asst. prof. Nashville State Tech. Inst., 1976-78, Fisk U., Nashville, 1978-83; assoc. dean. grad. sch. U. Ark., Little Rock, 1983-85, dean grad. sch., 1985-91; program dir. Kellogg Found., Battle Creek, Mich., 1991—; asst. dir. Kellogg Nat. Fellowship Program, 1991-94; coord. higher edn. programs Kellogg Found., 1994—. Instr. U. Tenn., Nashville, 1976-82; dir. rsch. sponsored programs U. Ark., 1986-88; bd. dirs. Ark. Sci. and Info. Liaison Office, 1984-91. Bd. dirs. Ark. Sci. and Tech. Authority, Little Rock, 1989—, Women's Project, 1986—, Ark. Pub. Policy Panel, 1988-91, No. Bank Women's Adv. Bd., 1988-91, Nashville Panel, 1974-83, Ctrl. Ark. Libr. Sys., 1990-91, Ark. coun. NCCJ, 1990-92, Bread for World, 1990-95; mem. Commn. on Edn. Credits and Credentials, Am. Coun. on Edn., 1989-95; chmn. bi-racial adv. com. Little Rock Sch. Dist., 1987— Fellow Am. Coun. Edn., 1981-82, W.K. Kellogg Found., 1988-93. Mem. Nat. Coun. Tchrs. of English, Coun. Grad. Schs., Coun. So. Grad. Schs., Women Color United Against Domestic Violence (pres.), An. Assn. High Edn., Rotary, Alpha Kappa Alpha. Democrat. Roman Catholic. Office: W K Kellogg Found One Michigan Ave E Battle Creek MI 49017

OVITSKY, STEVEN ALAN, musician, symphony orchestra executive; b. Chgo., Oct. 12, 1947; s. Martin N. and Ruth (Katz) O.; m. Camille Levy; 1 child, David Isaac. MusB, U. Mich., 1968; MusM, No. Ill. U., 1975. Fine arts dir. Sta. WNIU-FM Pub. Radio, Dekalb, Ill., 1972-76; program mgr. Sta. WMHT-FM Pub. Radio, Schenectady, N.Y., 1976-79; gen. mgr., artistic dir. Grant Park Concerts, Chgo., 1979-90; v.p., gen. mgr. Minn. Orch., Mpls., 1990-95; v.p., exec. dir. Milw. Symphony Orch., 1995-99, pres., exec. dir., 1999—. Panelist Ill. Arts Coun., 1986, 87, 88, Chgo. Artists Abroad, 1987-91, Nat. Endowment for the Arts, 1987-89, 98-99; bd. dirs. Ill. Arts Alliance, Chamber Music Chgo.; hon. dir. Chgo. Sinfonietta. With U.S. Army, 1968-71, Korea. Mem. NARAS, Am. Symphony Orch. League. Jewish. Avocations: audio, record collecting, softball. Office: Milw Symphony Orch 700 N Water St Ste 700 Milwaukee WI 53202-4278 Business E-Mail: ovitskys@milwaukeesymphonyorchestra.org.

OVSHINSKY, STANFORD ROBERT, physicist, inventor, energy executive, information company executive; b. Akron, Ohio, Nov. 24, 1922; s. Benjamin and Bertha T. (Munitz) O.; m. Iris L. Miroy, Nov. 24, 1959; children— Benjamin, Harvey, Dale, Robin Dibner, Steven Dibner. Student public schs., Akron; DSc (hon.), Lawrence Inst. Tech., 1980; DEng (hon.), Bowling Green State U., 1981; DSc (hon.), Jordan Coll., Cedar Springs, Mich., 1989. Pres. Stanford Roberts Mfg. Co., Akron, 1946-50; mgr. centre drive dept. New Britain Machine Co., Conn., 1950-52; dir. research Hupp Corp., Detroit, 1952-55; pres. Gen. Automation, Inc., 1955-58, Ovitron Corp., Detroit, 1958-2000; pres., CEO, chief scientist Energy Conversion Devices, Inc., Troy, Mich., 1978—. Adj. prof. engring. scis. Coll. Engring., Wayne State U.; hon. advisor for sci. and tech. Beijing (China) Inst. Aeronautics and Astronautics (name changed to Beijing U. Aeros. and Astronautics); chmn. Inst. for Amorphous Studies. Contbr. articles on physics of amorphous materials, neurophysiology and neuropsychiatry to profl. jours. Recipient Diesel Gold medal German Inventors Assn., 1968, Coors Am. Ingenuity award, 1988, Karl W. Böer solar energy medal of merit U. Del. and Interna. Solar Energy Soc., 1999; named to Mich. Chem. Engring. Hall of Fame, 1983, Mich. Scientist of Yr., Impression 5 Sci. Mus., 1987, Hero for the Planet, Time mag., 1999, Hero of Chemistry, Am. Chem. Soc., 2000, Sir William Grove award IAHE, 2000. Fellow AAAS, Am. Phys. Soc.; mem. IEEE (sr.), Soc. Automotive Engrs., N.Y. Acad. Scis., Electrochem. Soc., Engring. Soc. Detroit, Cranbrook Inst. Sci. (bd. govs. 1981). Office: Energy Conversion Devices Inc 2956 Waterview Dr Rochester MI 48309

OWEN, DAVE A. finance executive; B in Acctg., Ind. U. CPA. Sr. acct., auditor Price Waterhouse; with Essex Group, Inc., 1976, contr. magnet wire and insulation divsn., 1983-85, contr. wire and cable divsn., 1985-88, dir. treasury and fin. svcs., 1988-93, treas., 1992-94, v.p. fin., CFO, 1993-94, exec. v.p., CFO, 1994—. Bd. dirs. Cmty. Harvest Food Bank. Office: Essex Group 1601 Wall St Fort Wayne IN 46802-4352

OWEN, LYNN, state legislator; b. Lawrence County, Ala., Feb. 22, 1946; m. Diana; children: Amy, Andrew. Student, Washtenaw C.C., Cerritos Jr. Coll. Supervisor, assessor London Twp., Mich., 1978-84; rep. Mich. State 56, 1986-98; exec. asst. legal affairs Office of Atty. Gen., Lansing, Mich., 1998—. House appropriations com. Mich. Ho. Reps. Gov. bd. dirs. Monroe County Opportunity Program; pres. Milan Area Fire Dept.; chmn. London-Maybee-Raisinville Fire Dept. Named pub. servant of yr. Mich. chpt. Paralyzed Vet. Am., state legis. yr. Vientam Vets. Am.; recipient star award Dep. Sheriff's Assn.. Mem. Am. Legion, Disabled Am. Vets., Purple Heart Assn., West County Ambulance Assn. (former vice chair). Home: 2520 York Rd Lansing MI 48911-1237 Address: Olds Plz Bldg Rm 925 Lansing MI 48913-0001

OWEN, MICHEAL, agronomist, educator; Prof. dept. agronomy Iowa State U., Ames. Recipient CIBA-GEIGY/Weed Sci. Soc. Am. award CIBA-GEIGY Corp., 1992. Mem. Weed Sci. Soc. Am. (Outstanding Paper in Weed Tech. 1996), North Ctrl. Weed Soc. (Disting. Achievement award 1995). Office: Iowa State U Dept Agronomy 2104 Agronomy Hl Ames IA 50011-0001

OWEN, SUZANNE, retired savings and loan executive; b. Lincoln, Nebr., Oct. 6, 1926; d. Arthur C. and Hazel E. (Edwards) O. BSBA, U. Nebr., Lincoln, 1948. With G. F. Lessenhop & Sons, Inc., Lincoln, 1948-57, First Fed., Lincoln, 1963-91, v.p., dir. pers., 1975-81, 1st v.p., 1981-87, sr. v.p., 1987-91; ret., 1991. Mem. pers. bd. City of Lincoln, 1989-96. Mem. Lincoln Human Resources Mgmt. Assn., Wooden Spoon Club, Exec. Women's Breakfast Group, Thursday Morning Lecture Cir., Cmty. Women's Club, Lincoln Symphony Guild, Pi Beta Phi Alumnae, Order of Ea. Star, Phi Chi Theta. Republican. Christian Scientist.

OWENDOFF, STEPHEN PETER, lawyer; b. Morristown, N.J., Aug. 1, 1943; m.; 4 children. Student, Bowdoin Coll., 1966; BA, Kent State U., 1966; JD, Georgetown U., 1969. Bar: Ohio 1969. Assoc. Hahn Loeser & Parks and predecessor firms, Cleve., 1969-77; ptnr. Hahn Loeser & Parks (formerly Hahn, Loeser, Freedheim, Dean and Wellman), 1977—; mgmt. com. Hahn Loeser & Parks (formerly Hahn, Loeser, Freedheim Dean). Lectr. in field. Active Gesu Ch., University Heights, Ohio; mem. adv. bd. Learning About Bus., Inc.; past pres. Parmadale (Ohio) Adv. Bd.; bd. trustees, cmty. svcs. panel Fedn. Cath. Cmty. Svcs.; rep. United Way Assembly, Parmadale; bd. trustees LeBlond Housing Corp., Health Hill Hosp. Mem. Nat. Assn. Bond Lawyers, Nat. Assn. Coll. and Univ. Attys., Shaker Heights (Ohio) Country Club. Office: 3300 Bp Tower 200 Public Sq Cleveland OH 44114-2316

OWENS, CAROL, state legislator; Home: 144 County Road C Oshkosh WI 54904-9065 Office: Wis Assembly PO Box 8952 Madison WI 53708-8952

OWENS, JAMES W. manufacturing executive; With Caterpillar Inc., Peoria, Ill., 1972—, v.p. group svcs. divsn., 1993-94, group pres., 1994—; pres. Solar Turbines Inc. divsn., 1993. Office: Caterpillar Inc 100 NE Adams St Peoria IL 61629

OWENS, JOHN C. academic administrator; B.S., W. Texas State U.; M.S. , Texas Tech U; Ph.D., Iowa State U. Chief acad. officer N.Mex. State U., Las Cruces, 1999—2001; Vice Chancellor U. Nebr.- Lincoln , Nebr., 2001—. Office: U Nebr-Lincoln Varner Hall 3835 Holdrege Lincoln NE 68583

OWENS, JUDITH L(YNN), lawyer; b. Benkelman, Nebr., Oct. 17, 1942; d. Daniel E. and Estelle M. (Carlin) O. BA in History, MA in History, Creighton U., 1967, JD, 1978. Bar: Nebr. 1978. Adminstrv. asst. Creighton U., Omaha, 1968; grad. asst. Am. U., Washington, 1972; tchr. Omaha Pub. Schs., 1972-75; atty. Owens and Owens, Benkelman, 1979-82; legal counsel Nebr. Legislature, Lincoln, 1982-87; pvt. practice Benkelman, 1987—. Mem. delinquency prevention bd. City of Benkelman, 1995—; mem. juvenile delinquency prevention com. State of Nebr., Nebr. Crime Commn., Lincoln, 1994—; mem. cert. of need bd. State of Nebr. Health Dept., Lincoln, 1993—. Elected county atty. Dundy County, Benkelman, 1995—; del. Dem. Nat. Conv., San Francisci, 1984; bd. dirs., chair Cmty. Family Ctr., Benkelman, 1991-95. Mem. Internat. PEO (local pres. 1982—), Nebr. State Bar Assn. Avocations: reading, political and election work, theater, choral singing. Office: Box 316 508 Chief St Benkelman NE 69021

OWENS, SCOTT ANDREW, sales executive; b. Waconia, Minn., Jan. 6, 1958; s. John Herbert and Amy Lou (Anderson) O.; m. Cheri Lynn Anderson, Sept. 22, 1988 (div. Sept. 1995). BSBA magna cum laude, U. Nebr., Omaha, 1986. Adminstrv. asst. Hodne Stageberg Ptnrs., Mpls., 1978-80; pres. Orange Triangle Co., 1980; asst. mgr. Wendy's, 1980; pres. We Deliver, 1980-81; asst. mgr. Color Tile, Roseville, 1982-83; v.p. mktg. 20/20 Minn., St. Louis Pk., 1983; account rep. Unisys Corp., Minnetonka, 1986-88, sr. account rep. Eagan, 1988-89, third party sales mgr., 1990-91; v.p. mktg. TEP Systems, Bloomington, 1991-93; v.p. Benchmark Comms. Svc., Mpls., 1992—; strategic alliance regional mgr. Dataserv, a BellSouth Co., Eden Prairie, 1994-96; strategic alliance mgr. MAI Systems, Boston, 1996-97; mktg. dir. Triangle Fin. Svcs. & Internet Mktg. Group, Mpls., 1997—; area mgr. Sunrise Solutions, Inc., Edina, 1997-98; prof. ProCon Solutions, Inc., Plymouth, 1998—2000; area mgr. Internet Fin. Solutions, 2000—. Classroom cons. Jr. Achievement, Bloomington, Minn., 1990. Mem. Am. Mktg. Assn., Am. Prdn. Inventory Control Soc., Profl. Sales Assn., Sales and Mktg. Execs. Avocations: reading, writing, painting, architecture, photography, golf, travel. Home and Office: Benchmark Comm PO Box 582299 Minneapolis MN 55458-2299

OWENS, STEPHEN J. lawyer; b. Kansas City, Mo., June 4, 1955; BSPA, U. Mo., 1977; JD, Wake Forest U., 1980. Bar: Mo. 1980, U.S. Dist. Ct. (we. dist.) Mo. 1980, U.S. Ct. Appeals (8th cir.) 1981, U.S. Ct. Appeals (10th cir.) 1982, U.S. Ct. Appeals (5th cir.) 1988, U.S. Ct. Appeals (4th cir.) 1992. Law clerk to Hon. William R. Collinson U.S. Dist. Ct. (we. dist.) Mo., 1980-81; ptnr. Stinson, Mag & Fizzell, Kansas City, Mo., 1981—. Mem. ABA (litigation and natural resources divsns.), Mo. Bar, Kansas City Met. Bar Assn. Office: Stinson Mag & Fizzell PO Box 419251 Kansas City MO 64141-6251

OWENS, STEWART KYLE, food products executive; b. Dallas, Mar. 16, 1955; s. Jerry Paul and Jeanne (Garrett) O.; m. Lindy Gant; 1 child, Allison. BBA, So. Meth. U., 1977. Acctg. supr. Owens Country Sausage, Inc., Richardson, Tex., 1977-79, acctg. mgr., 1979-81, v.p. adminstrn., 1981-84, pres., chief oper. officer, 1984—. Bd. dirs. Bob Evans Farms Inc., Columbus, Ohio, Oklahoma Animal By-Products, Richardson. Mem. mgmt. Richardson YMCA, 1984-90; bd. dirs. Stonebridge Ranch Pres.'s Assn., McKinney, Tex., 1990. Mem. Young Pres.'s Assn., Stonebridge Country Club, Canyon Creek Country Club. Republican. Avocations: golf, water sports, R/C modeling. Home: 7304 Round Hill Rd Mc Kinney TX 75070-5713 Office: Bob Evan Farms Inc 3776 S High St Columbus OH 43207

OWENS, WILLIAM DON, anesthesiology educator; b. St. Louis, Dec. 12, 1939; s. Don and Caroline Wilhemena (Raaf) Owens; m. Patricia Gail Brown, Dec. 12, 1964; children: Pamela, David, Susan. AB, Westminster Coll., 1961; MD, U. Mich., 1965. Diplomate Am. Bd. Anesthesiology. Resident and fellow Mass. Gen. Hosp. and Harvard Med. Sch., Boston, 1969—72; instr. Harvard Med. Sch., 1972—73; asst. prof. anesthesiology Washington U. Sch. Medicine, St. Louis, 1973—76, assoc. prof., 1976—82, prof., 1982—, chmn. dept., 1982—92. Bd. trustees Barnes Hosp., St. Louis, 1987—89; bd. dir. Anesthesia Found., pres., 1999—; sec.-treas. An. Bd. Anesthesiology, 1991—94, pres., 1995—96. Contbr. Served to lt. comdr. USN, 1966—69. Fellow: Am. Coll. Anesthesiology (pres.-elect 1996—97); mem.: Assn. Univ. Anesthesiologists, Acad. Anesthesiology, Internat. Anesthesia Rsch. Soc., Am. Soc. Anesthesiologists (bd. dirs. 1989—99, 1st v.p. 1995—96, pres. 1997—98). Office: Washington U Sch Med Dept Anesthesiology 660 S Euclid Ave Saint Louis MO 63110-1010

OWNBY, JERRY STEVE, landscape architect, educator; b. Shawnee, Okla., Jan. 25, 1939; s. Hugh H. and N. Lorraine (Hopkins) O.; children by previous marriage: Gregory Steve, Mitchell Hugh; m. Arnola Colson, Dec. 19, 1971; 1 child, Steven Cory BS, Okla. State U., 1961; MS in Landscape Architecture, Kans. State U., 1964, M in Landscape Architecture, 1970. Coun. Landscape Archtl. Registration Bds. cert. and registered landscape architect, Ariz., Kans., Okla., Mo., Tex. Extension landscape architect Kans. State U., Manhattan, 1963-64, instr., 1969-70; landscape architect Beardsley & Talley, Seattle, 1964-65; extension specialist Okla. State U., Stillwater, 1965-69, from asst. prof. to prof. landscape architecture and coordinator landscape architecture, 1970-85; pvt. practice, 1985—. Chmn. Okla. Landscape Architect Registration Bd., 1980-85; mem. 1985 Expert Panel for Uniform Nat. Exam., 1984-85; gov.'s appointee Mo. Coun. Landscape Architects, 1991-97 Designs include Las Laderas residence, 1978 (Merit award 1981), Student Union courtyard Okla. State U., 1981 (Honor award 1983). Chmn. Oklahomans for Landscape Architecture, 1979-80; chmn., vice chmn. Stillwater Park and Recreation Adv. Bd., Okla., 1971-79. Recipient Outstanding Prof. award Okla. State U. chpt. Alpha Zeta, 1975, svc. award Stillwater City Commn., 1980, design awards Springfield Planning and Zoning Commn.., 1988, 89, 90, 99, design award Springfield Environ. Adv. Bd., 1990, Gov.'s landscape design award for Andy Williams' Moon River Theatre, Branson, Mo., 1992, for Charley Pride Theater, Branson, 1995, design award Watershed Com., 1993; alumni fellow Kans. State U., 1995. Fellow Am. Soc. Landscape Architects (v.p. 1983-85, Okla. chpt. Svc. award 1980); mem. Nat. Coun. State Garden Clubs (accredited instr. 1964—), Nat. Coun. of Educators in Landscape Architecture, Mo. Assn. of Landscape Architects, Coun. Landscape Archtl. Registration Bds. (cert.), Phi Kappa Phi, Sigma Lambda Alpha. Republican. Baptist Avocations: travel; photography; fishing. Home: 234 Sunset Cove # 109 Branson MO 65616-3604 Office: Ownby Assocs 654 S Hickory Ave Springfield MO 65809-1335 E-mail: jsownby@aol.com.

OWYANG, CHUNG, gastroenterologist, researcher; b. Chung King, China, Nov. 20, 1945; arrived in Can., 1965; s. Chi and Ching-Ying (Fung) O.; m. Jeannette Lim; children: Stephanie, Christopher. BS with honors, McGill U., Montreal, Can., 1968, MD, 1972. Diplomate Am. Bd. Internal Medicine, Gastroenterology; lic. Gen. Med. Coun., U.K., Que., Can., Min. Med. lic., Mich. med. lic. Intern in internal medicine Montreal Gen. Hosp./McGill U., 1972-73, resident in internal medicine, 1973-75; clin. teaching fellow in internal medicine McGill U., 1974-75; fellow in gastroenterology Mayo Clinic and Found., Rochester, Minn., 1975-78; instr. internal medicine Mayo Med. Sch., 1977-78; asst. prof. U. Mich., 1978-84, assoc. prof., 1984-88, assoc. chief divsn. gastroenterology, 1984-90, prof., 1988—, chief divsn. gastroenterology, 1991—, dir. med. procedures unit, 1992—. Assoc. dir. Gastrointestinal Peptide Rsch. Ctr., U. Mich., 1984-95, dir. 1996—; cons. Rsch. Coun. Janssen Pharmaceutica Inc., 1985—, Ann Arbor VA Med. Ctr., 1978—, NIH, Bethesda, Md., 1989-94, FDA, Bethesda, 1995—; H. Marvin Pollard chair in gastroenterology, U. Mich., 1996—; speaker, presenter in field. Co-author: Textbook of Gastroenterology, 1991, 2d edit. 1995, Atlas of Gastroenterology, 1992; mem. edit. bd. Pancreas, 1986—, Am. Jour. Physiology, 1988—, Regulatory Peptide Letter, 1988—, Gastroenterology, 1990—, guest editor, 1991—, Digestive Diseases, 1993—; contbr. numerous chpts. to books, articles to profl. jours., jours. refereed. Grantee in field. Fellow ACP; mem. Am. Assn. Physicians, Am. Soc. Clin. Investigation, Am. Gastroenterological Assn., Am. Pancreatic Assn., Am. Diabetes Assn., Am. Fedn. Clin. Rsch., Am. Motility Soc., Ctrl. Soc. Clin. Rsch., Internat. Assn. Pancreatology, Midwest Gut Club. Office: U Mich Med Ctr Divsn Gastroenterology PO Box 362 Ann Arbor MI 48106-0362

OXENDER, GLENN S. state legislator; b. Three Rivers, Mich.e, Aug. 8, 1943; s. Harry Bryan and Myrtle (Sherck) O.; m. F. Dianne Ellis, 1966; children: Xanne, Katrina, Robert, Kalynn, Melinda. BS, Manchester Coll., 1965; MA, Western Mich. U., 1969; postgrad., U. Mo., 1971. Math. tchr. Livonia (Mich.) Pub. Schs., 1965-66, Sturgis (Mich.) Pub. Schs., 1966-69, Sturgis H.S., 1969-82; rep. Mich. State Dist. 42, Mich. State Dist. 59, 1982-98. Farmer, 1974—; appropriations standing com. Mich. Ho. Reps., cmty. coll. subcom., mental health subcom., joint capital outlay subcom., state police subcom., mil. affairs subcom., ad hoc edn. com., chmn. K-12 Dept. Edn. subcom. Trustee Libr. Mich. Named outstanding legis. of yr., 1989, 94, Mich. Occupl. Edn. Assn.; recipient pres.'s award Mich. Assn. Sch. Bd., 1995. Mem. Sturgis Exch. Club, NEA, Mich. Edn. Assn., Sturgis Edn. Assn., Rotary, Nat. Rep. Legis. Assn., Am. Legis. Exch. Coun., Ctrl. Regional Edn. Lab. Home: 27221 Wait Rd Sturgis MI 49091-9154

OXLEY, DWIGHT K(AHALA), pathologist; b. Wichita, Kans., Dec. 2, 1936; s. Dwight K. Jr. and Ruth Erdene (Warner) O.; m. Patricia Warren, June 18, 1961; children: Alice DeBloois, Thomas Oxley. AB, Harvard U., 1958; MD, U. Kans., 1962. Diplomate Am. Bd. Pathology (trustee 1992—, pres. 1999), Am. Bd. Nuclear Medici ne. Pathologist Wesley Med. Ctr., Wichita, 1969-74, Eisenhower Med. Ctr., Rancho Mirage, Calif., 1974-78, St. Joseph Health Ctr., Kansas City, Mo., 1978-88; chmn. dept. pathology Wesley Med. Ctr., 1988—. Bd. editors Archives of Pathology and Lab. MEdicine, Chgo., 1984-95, Clinica Chimica Acta, Amsterdam, 1980-86, Am. Jour. Clin. Pathology, Chgo., 1974-80. Sr. warden St. Stephens Episcopal Ch., Wichita, 1994. Lt. commdr. USN, 1964-69. Fellow: Coll. Am. Pathologists (various offices), Am. Soc. Clin. Pathologists; mem.: Kans. Soc. Pathologists (pres. 1993—94), Am. Pathology Found. (bd. dirs. 1979—89). Republican. Avocations: music, athletics. Office: Wesley Med Ctr 550 N Hillside St Wichita KS 67214-4910

OXLEY, MARGARET CAROLYN STEWART, elementary education educator; b. Petaluma, Calif., Apr. 1, 1930; d. James Calhoun Stewart and Clara Thornton (Whiting) Bomboy; m. Joseph Hubbard Oxley, Aug. 25, 1951; children: Linda Margaret, Carolyn Blair Oxley Greiner, Joan Claire Oxley Willis, Joseph Stewart, James Harmon, Laura Marie Oxley Brechbill. Student, U. Calif., Berkeley, 1949-51; BS summa cum laude, Ohio State U., 1973, MA, 1984, postgrad., 1985, 88, 92. Cert. tchr., Ohio. 2d grade tchr. St. Paul Sch., Westerville, Ohio, 1973—. Presenter in field. Mem. editl. bd. Reading Tchr., vol. 47-48, 1993-94, Jour. Children's Lit., 1996—; co-author: Reading and Writing, Where it All Begins, 1991, Teaching with Children's Books: Path to Literature-Based Instruction, 1995, Adventuring With Books, 2000. Active Akita Child Conservation League, Columbus, Ohio, 1968-70. Named Columbus Diocesan Tchr. of Yr., 1988; Phoebe A. Hearst scholar, 1951, Rose Sterheim Meml. scholar, 1951; recipient Mary Karrer award Ohio State U., 1994. Mem. Nat. Coun. Tchrs. English (Notable Children's Books in the Lang. Arts com. 1993-94, chair 1995-96, treas. Children's Literature Assembly bd. dirs. 1996-99, co-chair fall breakfast children's lit. assembly, 2000—, excellence in poetry for children com. 2001-), Internat. Reading Ass (Exemplary Svc. in Promotion of Literacy award 1991), Literacy Connection (pres.), Children's Lit. Assembly, Ohio Coun. Tchrs. English Lang. Arts (Outstanding Educator 1990), Phi Kappa Phi, Pi Lambda Theta (hon.). Democrat. Roman Catholic. Avocations: reading, writing, travel, gardening, working with children. Home: 298 Brevoort Rd Columbus OH 43214-3826

OXLEY, MICHAEL GARVER, congressman; b. Findlay, Ohio, Feb. 11, 1944; s. George Garver and Marilyn Maxine (Wolfe) O.; m. Patricia Ann Pluguez, Nov. 27, 1971; 1 child, Michael Chadd. BA, Miami U., Oxford, Ohio, 1966; JD, Ohio State U., 1969. Bar: Ohio 1969, U.S. Supreme Ct. 1985. Agt. FBI, 1969-71; mem. Ohio Ho. of Reps., 1973-81, U.S. Congress from 4th Ohio dist., Washington, 1981—; chmn. fin. svcs. com. Mem. ABA, Ohio Bar Assn., Findlay Bar Assn., Soc. Former Spl. Agts. FBI, Ohio Farm Bur., Sigma Chi. Lodges: Rotary, Elks. Office: US Ho Reps 2233 Rayburn Ho Office Bldg Washington DC 20515-3504*

OXTOBY, DAVID WILLIAM, chemistry educator; b. Bryn Mawr, Pa., Oct. 17, 1951; s. John Corning and Jean (Shaffer) O., m. Claire Bennett, Dec. 17, 1977; children: Mary-Christina, John, Laura. BA, Harvard, 1972; PhD, U. Calif., Berkeley, 1975. Asst. prof. U. Chgo., 1977-82, assoc. prof., 1982-86, prof., 1986—, Mellon prof., 1987-92, dir. James Franck Inst., 1992-95, dean physical scis. divsn., 1995—, William Rainey Harper prof., 1996—. Co-author: Principles of Modern Chemistry, 1986, Chemistry: Science of Change, 1990. Trustee Bryn Mawr Coll., 1989—, Tchrs. Acad. Math. and Sci., 1999—; mem. bd. govs. Argonne Nat. Lab., 1996—, Astrophys. Rsch. Consortium, 1998—. Recipient Quantrell award U. Chgo., 1986; Alfred P. Sloan Found. fellow, 1979, John Simon Guggenheim Found. fellow, 1987; Camille and Henry Dreyfus Found. tchr.-

scholar, 1980. Fellow Am. Phys. Soc.; mem. Am. Chem. Soc., Royal Soc. Chemistry (Marlow medal 1983), Phi Beta Kappa. Office: James Franck Inst U Chgo 5640 S Ellis Ave Chicago IL 60637-1433

OZANNE, DOMINIC LAURANT, lawyer, construction company executive; b. Cleve., Apr. 10, 1953; s. Leroy and Betty Jean (Peyton) O. B.S./B.A., Boston U., 1975; J.D., Harvard U., 1978. Bar: Ohio 1979. Assoc. Thompson, Hine & Flory, Cleve., 1978-80; gen. counsel Ozanne Constrn. Co. Inc., Cleve. Trustee Ctr. for Venture Devel., Cleve., 1983— . Mem. Nat. Assn. Minority Contractors (sec. 1983). Roman Catholic. Office: Ozanne Constrn Co Inc 1635 E 25th St Cleveland OH 44114-4214

OZAWA, MARTHA NAOKO, social work educator; b. Ashikaga, Tochigi, Japan, Sept. 30, 1933; came to U.S., 1963; d. Tokuichi and Fumi (Kawashima) O.; m. May 1959 (div. May 1966). BA in Econs., Aoyama Gakuin U., 1956; MS in Social Work, U. Wis., 1966, PhD in Social Welfare, 1969. Asst. prof. social work Portland (Oreg.) State U., 1969-70, assoc. prof. social work, 1970-72; assoc. rsch. prof. social work NYU, 1972-75; assoc. prof. social work Portland State U., 1975-76; prof. social work Washington U., St. Louis, 1976-85, Bettie Bofinger Brown prof. social policy, 1985—. Author: Income Maintenance and Work Incentives, 1982; editor: Women's Life Cycle: Japan-U.S. Comparison in Income Maintenance, 1989, Women's Life Cycle and Economic Insecurity: Problems and Proposals, 1989; editl. bd. Social Work, Silver Spring, Md., 1972-75, 85-88, New Eng. Jour. Human Svcs., Boston, 1987—, Ency. of Social Work, Silver Spring, 1974-77, 91-95, 99—, Jour. Social Svc. Rsch., 1977-97, Children and Youth Svcs. Rev., 1991—, Social Work Rsch., 1994-97, Jour. Poverty, 1997—. Grantee Adminstrn. on Aging, Washington, 1979, 84, NIMH, 1990-93, Assn. for Pub. Policy Analysis and Mgmt. Mem. Nat. Assn. Social Workers (presdl. award 1999), Nat. Acad. Social Ins., Nat. Conf. on Social Welfare (bd. dirs. 1981-87), The Gerontol. Soc. Am., Coun. Social Work Edn., Soc. for Social Work and Rsch., Washington U. Faculty Club (bd. dirs. 1986-91). Avocations: photography, tennis, swimming, gardening. Home: 13018 Tiger Lily Ct Saint Louis MO 63146-4339 Office: PO Box 1196 Saint Louis MO 63188-1196 E-mail: awazo@gwbmail.wustl.edu.

OZMENT, DENNIS DEAN, state legislator; b. Farmington, Minn., May 2, 1945; s. Clyde Lee and Dolores (Bell) O.; m. Gayle Farrior, 1967; children: Wanda Kaye, Dennis Eugene. Student, U. Minn., Met. Cmty. Coll., Minn. Mem. Minn. Ho. of Reps., St. Paul, 1984—. Mem. edn. com., environ. and natural resources com., regulated industry com.; fire capt. Republican. Home: 3275 145th St E Rosemount MN 55068-5909 Office: Minn Ho of Reps State Capitol Saint Paul MN 55155-0001

PAANANEN, VICTOR NILES, English educator; b. Ashtabula, Ohio, Jan. 31, 1938; s. Niles Henry and Anni Margaret (Iloranta) P.; m. Donna Mae Jones, Aug. 15, 1964; children: Karl, Neil. AB magna cum laude, Harvard U., 1960; MA, U. Wis., 1964, PhD, 1967. Instr. English Wofford Coll., Spartanburg, S.C., 1962-63; asst. prof. Williams Coll., Williamstown, Mass., 1966-68, Mich. State U., East Lansing, 1968-73, assoc. prof., 1973-82, prof., 1982—, asst. dean Grad. Sch., 1977-82, chmn. dept. English, 1986-94. Vis. prof. Roehampton Inst., London, 1982, 96, hon. fellow, 1992. Author: William Blake, 1977, 2d edit., 1996, British Marxist Criticism, 2000; contbr. articles to profl. and scholarly jours. Univ. fellow U. Wis., 1962, 63-64, Roehampton Inst. hon. fellow, London, 1992—; Harvard Nat. scholar, 1956-60. Home: 350 Revere Beach Blvd 5-5W Revere MA 02151-4851 E-mail: paananen@msu.edu.

PAAVO, JARVI, conductor; b. Tallinn, Estonia; Studied under Leonard Bernstein; student in percussion and conducting, Tallinn Sch. Music, Curtis Inst. Music; student under Leonard Bernstein , L.A. Philharmonic Inst. Music dir. Cin. Symphony Orch., 2001—. Prin. guest conductor Royal Stockholm Philharmonic , City of Birmingham (Eng.) Symphony Orch., guest conductor N.Y. Philharmonic , Berlin Philharmonic, Munich Philharmonic, London Philharmonic , San Francisco Symphony , Phila. Orch. (Carnegie Hall debut) , NHK Symphony, Tokyo Symphony , Israel Philharmonic, St. Petersburg Philharmonic , Orch. Filarmonica della Scala, L.A. Philharmonic, Philharmonic orch. and many others, (works by Bernstein) City of Birmingham Symphony Orch., (recorded performances Stenhammar pieces) Royal Stockholm Philharmonic Orch., (recordings with Estonian composers Part, Tuur, and Tubin) Searching for Roots, Sibelius' Kullervo, Lemminkainen Suite , (concerts with cellist Turls Mork). Office: Cin Symphony Orch 1241 Elm St Cincinnati OH 45210*

PACE, ORLANDO LAMAR, football player; b. Sandusky, Ohio, Nov. 4, 1975; Attended , Ohio State Univ. Lineman St. Louis Rams, 1997—; winner Super Bowl 34, 2000; 1st overall pick NFL Draft, 1997; earned 2nd consecutive Pro Bowl Invitations; no sacks allowed St. Louis vs. Minn. , 1999. Donater Disadvantaged Kids; participant Spearheads Annual Offensive Line Thanksgiving Project, Chesterfield, Mo. Achievements include first to make history by becoming the first player to win two consecutive Lombardi awards in 1996. Office: 1 Rams Way St Louis MO 63045*

PACHECO, MANUEL TRINIDAD, academic administrator; b. Rocky Ford, Colo., May 30, 1941; s. Manuel J. and Elizabeth (Lopez) P.; m. Karen M. King, Aug. 27, 1966; children: Daniel Mark, Andrew Charles, Sylvia Lois Elizabeth. BA, N.Mex. Highlands U., 1962; MA, Ohio State U., 1966, PhD, 1969. Prof. edn., univ. dean Tex. A&I U., Laredo, 1972-77, exec. dir. Bilingual Edn. Ctr., Kingsville, 1980-82; prof. multicultural edn., chmn. dept. San Diego State U., 1977-78; prof. Spanish and edn. Laredo State U., 1978-80, pres., 1984-88; assoc. dean Coll. Edn. U. Tex., El Paso, 1982-84, exec. dir. for planning, 1984; chief policy aide for edn. to gov. N.Mex., 1984; pres. U. Houston-Downtown, 1988-91, U. Ariz., Tucson, 1991-97, U. Mo. Sys., Columbia, 1997—. Cons. lang. divsn. Ency. Britannica, 1965-72; bd. dirs. Valley Nat. Bank Corp., Nat. Security Edn. Program, ASARCO; mem. exec. com. Bus.-Higher Edn. Forum. Co-editor: Handbook for Planning and Managing Instruction in Basic Skills for Limited English Proficient Students, 1983; producer: (videotapes) Teacher Training, 1976. Treas. adv. com. U.S. Commn. on Civil Rights, L.A., 1987-91; trustee United Way of Houston, 1988-91; chmn. pub. rels. Buffalo Bayou Partnership, Houston, 1988-91; bd. dirs. Ctr. for Addiction and Substance Abuse, Greater Tucson Econ. Coun., Ariz. Econ. Coun., Ariz. Town Hall. Recipient Disting. Alumnus award Ohio State U., Columbus, 1984; named Most Prominent Am.-Hispancis Spanish Today mag., 1984, one of 100 Outstanding Hispanics Hispanic bus., 1988, Man of Yr. Hispanic Profl. Action Com., 1991; Fulbright fellow U. de Montepellier, France, 1962. Mem. Am. Assn. State Colls. and Univs., Nat. Acad. of Pub. Adminstrn., Hispanic Assn. Colls. and Univs., Tex. Assn. of Chicanos in Higher Edn., Rotary, Phi Delta Kappa. Office: U Mo Sys Office of Pres 321 University Hall Columbia MO 65211-3020 Business E-Mail: pachecom@umsystem.edu.

PACKARD, SANDRA PODOLIN, education educator, consultant; b. Buffalo, Sept. 13, 1942; d. Mathew and Ethel (Zolte) P.; m. Martin Packard, Aug. 2, 1964; children: Dawn Esther, Shana Fanny BFA, Syracuse U., 1964; MSEd, Ind. U., 1966, EdD, 1973. Cert. tchr. art K-12, N.Y. Asst. prof. art SUNY-Buffalo, 1972-74; assoc. prof. art Miami U., Oxford, Ohio, 1974-81, spl. asst. to provost, 1979-80, assoc. provost, spl. programs, 1980-81; dean Coll. Edn. Bowling Green State U., 1981-85; provost and vice chancellor for acad. affairs U. Tenn., Chattanooga, 1985-92; pres. Oakland U., Rochester, Mich., 1992-95, prof. edn., 1995—; sr. fellow, dir. tech. in edn. Am. Assn. State Colls. and Univs., 1995; coord. Nat. Coun. for Accreditation of Tchr. Edn., Washington, 1995—2001. Cons. Butler County Health Ctr., Hamilton, Ohio, 1976-78; vis. prof. art therapy Simmons Coll., 1979, Mary Mount Coll., Milw., 1981; bd. dirs. SE Ctr. for Arts in Edn., 1994-96; mem. corp. adv. com. Corp. Detroit Mag., 1994-95; cons. Univ. of the North, South Africa Project of the Am. Coun. on Edn., 1995; bd. mem. Fellows Coun. Am. Coun. on Edn., 1994-96. Sr. editor Studies in Art Edn. jour., 1979-81; editorial adv. bd. Jour. Aesthetic Edn., 1984-90; editor: The Leading Edge, 1986; contbr. articles to profl. jours., chpts. to conf. papers Chmn. com. Commn. on Edn. Excellence, Ohio, 1982-83, Tenn. State Peformance Funding Task Force, 1988, Tenn. State Task Force on Minority Tchrs., 1988; reviewer art curriculum N.Y. Bd. Edn., 1985; mem. supt. search com. Chattanooga Pub. Schs., 1987-88; mem. Chattanooga Met. Coun., 1987-88, Chattanooga Ballet Bd., 1986-88, Fund for Excellence in Pub. Edn., 1986-90, Tenn. Aquarium Bd. Advisors, 1989-92, Team Evaluation Ctr. Bd., 1988-90; mem. Strategic Planning Action Team, Chattanooga City Schs., 1987-88, Siskin Hosp. Bd., 1989-92, Blue Ribbon Task Force Pontiac 2010: A New Reality, City of Pontiac Planning Divsn., 1992—; steering com., cultural action bd. Chattanooga, planning com United Way, 1987; Jewish Fedn. Bd., 1986-91; mem. coun. for policy studies Art Edn. Adv. Bd., 1982-91; ex-officio mem. Meadow Brook Theatre Guild, 1992-95; bd. chair Meadow Brook Performing Arts Co., 1992-95; chair World Cup Soccer Edn. Com./Mich. Host Com. 1993-95; bd. dirs. Ptnrs. for Preferred Future, Rochester Cmty. Schs., 1992-95, Traffic Improvement Assn. Oakland County, 1992-95, Oakland County Bus. Roundtable, 1993-95; Rochester C. of C. host com. chair on edn. World Cup, 1992-95; mem. fin. adv. com. Jewish Fedn. Detroit, 1995-97; bd. dirs. United Way Southeastern Mich., 1992-95: bd. dirs. United Way Oakland County, 1992-95, Pontiac 2010: A New Reality, mayor's transition team city/sch. rels. task force: team evaluation leader Dept. of State Am. Univ. Bulgaria, 1995; bd. trustees Cohn's & Colitis Found., 1996-97. Am. Coun. on Edn. and Mellon fellow Miami U., 1978-79; recipient Cracking the Glass Ceiling award Pontiac Area Urban League, 1992. Fellow Nat. Art Edn. Assn. (disting.); mem. Am. Assn. Colls. for Tchr. Edn. (com. chair 1982-85), Am. Art Therapy Assn. (registered), Nat. Art Edn. Assn. Women's Caucus (founder, pres. 1976-78, McFee award 1986), Am. Assn. State Colls. and Univs. (com. profl. devel. 1993-95, state rep. 1994-95), Econ. Club Detroit (bd. dirs. 1992-95), Rotary Club, Great Lakes Yacht Club (social chmn. 1996-97, ground chmn., bd. dirs. 1997-98), Phi Delta Kappa (Leadership award 1985). Avocation: sailing. Home: Apt 204 6127 Orchard Lake Rd West Bloomfield MI 48322 Office: Oakland U 316 Odowd Hall Rochester MI 48309-4423 E-mail: packard@oakland.edu.

PADDOCK, STUART R., JR. publishing executive; Bd. chmn. Daily Herald/Sunday Herald, Arlington Heights, Ill.; pub. emeritus Daily Herald. Office: Daily Herald/Sunday Herald Paddock Publs PO Box 280 Arlington Heights IL 60006-0280

PAGAC, GERALD J. state agency administrator; Dir. Out Recreation, Ind.; divsn. dir. Ind. Dept. Natural Resources Divsn. State Pks., Indpls., 1993—. Office: Ind Dept Natural Resources Divsn State Pks 402 W Washington St Rm W298 Indianapolis IN 46204-2739 Fax: 317-232-4132.

PAGANO, JON ALLEN, data processing consultant; b. Kankakee, Ill., Dec. 26, 1958; s. Antoine and Agnes P. BA in Philosophy, U. Ill., 1979; BA in Computer Sci., North Cen. Coll., 1989. Computer ops. staff Roper Inc., Kankakee, 1979-81; programmer Harris Bankcorp, Chgo., 1981-84; cons. Circle Cons., Kankakee, 1984; sr. programmer/analyst First Nat. Bank, Chgo., 1984-86; programmer/analyst Internet Systems Corp., 1986-87; sr. systems analyst, mgr. Concord Computing Corp., Elk Grove, Ill., 1987-89; pres. Circle Cons., Naperville, 1989-2000, USBancorp, St. Paul, 2000—. Ednl. lobbying U. Ill., Urbana, 1986—, alumni networking North Cen. Coll., 1991—, bd. advocate, 1996—. Mem. ACM, IEEE, U. Ill. Alumni Assn. (Pres.'s Coun. 1988—, Bronze Circle 1988), Pres. Club North Ctrl. Coll., Univ. Ill. Alumni Bd. (adv. 1996—). Avocations: running, camping, hiking, bouldering. Home: 156 Dayton Ave Saint Paul MN 55104 Office: USBancorp 2751 Shepard Rd Saint Paul MN 55116-3061 E-mail: jon.pagano@usbank.com.

PAGE, ALAN CEDRIC, state supreme court justice; b. Canton, Ohio, Aug. 7, 1945; s. Howard F. and Georgianna (Umbles) P.; m. Diane Sims, June 5, 1973; children: Nina, Georgianna, Justin, Khamsin. BA, U. Notre Dame, 1967; JD, U. Minn., 1978; LLD, U. Notre Dame, 1993; LLD (hon.), St. John's U., 1994, Westfield State Coll., 1994, Luther Coll., 1995, U. New Haven, 1999. Bar: Minn. 1979, U.S. Dist. Ct. Minn. 1979, U.S. Supreme Ct. 1988. Profl. athlete Minn. Vikings, Mpls., 1967-78, Chgo. Bears, 1978-81; assoc. Lindquist & Vennum, Mpls., 1979-85; former atty. Minn. Atty. Gen.'s Office, 1985-92; assoc. justice Minn. Supreme Ct., St. Paul, 1993—. Cons. NFL Players Assn., Washington, 1979-84. Commentator Nat. Pub. Radio, 1982-83. Founder Page Edn. Found., 1988. Named NFL's Most Valuable Player, 1971, one of 10 Outstanding Young Men Am., U.S. Jaycees, 1981; named to NFL Hall of Fame, 1988, Coll. Football Hall of Fame, 1993. Mem. ABA, Minn. Bar Assn., Hennepin County Bar Assn., Minn. Minority Lawyers Assn., Minn. Assn. Black Lawyers. Avocations: running, biking. Office: 423 Minnesota Judicial Ctr 25 Constitution Ave Saint Paul MN 55155-1500

PAGE, ERNEST, medical educator; b. Cologne, Germany, May 30, 1927; came to U.S., 1936, naturalized, 1942; s. Max Ernest and Eleanor (Kohn) P.; m. Eva Veronica Gross, June 5, 1967; 1 son, Thomas J. A.B., Calif., Berkeley, 1949; M.D., Calif., San Francisco, 1952. Intern Peter Bent Brigham Hosp., Boston, 1952-53, resident, 1953-54, 57-58; research assoc. Harvard Med. Sch., 1957-65; assoc. prof. medicine and Physiology U. Chgo. Med. Sch., 1965-69, prof., 1969-98, prof. emeritus, 1998—. Editor: (jour.) Am, Jour. Physiology: Heart and Circulatory Physiology, 1981—86; editor: (sections) (handbook) Handbook of Physiology Vol. I The Heart, 2002. Served with AUS, 1945-46. Established investigator Am. Heart Assn., 1959-65 Mem. Am. Physiol. Soc., Biophys. Soc., Am. Soc. Cell Biology, Soc. Gen. Physiologists, Assn. Am. Physicians. Home: 5606 S Harper Ave Chicago IL 60637-1832 Office: U Chgo Med Sch 5841 S Maryland Ave Chicago IL 60637-1463 E-mail: epage@medicine.bscl.uchicago.edu.

PAGE, LINDA KAY, banking executive; b. Wadsworth, Ohio, Oct. 4, 1943; d. Frederick Meredith and Martha Irene (Vance P. Studnet, Ohio U., 1976-77; grad. banking program, U. Wis., 1982-84; BA, Capital U. cert. in pers. Am. Bankers Assn. Asst. v.p., gen. mgr. Bancohio Corp., Columbus, 1975-78, v.p., dist. mgr., 1979-80, v.p., mgr. employee rels., 1980-81, v.p., divsn. mgr., 1982-83; commr. of banks State of Ohio, 1983-87, dir. Dept. Commerce, 1988-90; pres., CEO Star Bank Ctrl. Ohio, 1990-92; state dir. Rural Devel/USDA, 1993-2000; pub. svc. dir. City of Columbus, 2000. Bd. dirs. Clark County Mental Health Bd., Springfield, Ohio, 1982-83, Springfield Met. Housing, 1982-83, Pvt. Industry Coun. Franklin County, 1990-2000—, Ohio Highe Edn. Facilities Commn., 1990-93, Ohio Devel. Corp., 1995—; bd. advisers Orgn. Indsl. Standards, Springfield, 1982-83; trustee League Against Child Abuse, 1986-90; treas. Ohio Housing Fin. Agy., 1980-90; vice chair Fed. Res. Bd. Consumer Adv. Coun., 1989-91; trustee, treas. Columbus State C.C. Found., 1990-2000, pres., 1997-99; bd. dirs. Columbus Urban league, 1992-98; mem. CompDrug Bd., 1998-2000. Recipient Leadership Columbus award Sta. WTVN and Columbus Leadership Program, 1975, 82, Outstanding Svc. award Clark County Mental Health Bd., 1983, Giles Mitchell Housing award, 1996. Mem.: LWV (treas. edn. fund 1992—2000), Women in Transp., Robert Morris Assocs., Women in Transp. (bd. trustees Ohio chpt. 2000, bd. dirs. 2002), Internat. Womens Forum, Am. Pub. Works Assn. (treas. Ohio chpt. 2000, treas. 2002), Ohio Mortgage Bankers Assn. (legis. commn. 1998), Ohio Devel. Assn., Ohio Bankers Assn. (bd. dirs. 1982—83, 1991—92), Conf. State Bank Suprs. (dist. chmn. 1984—85, sec.-treas. 1985—90, bd. dirs.), Women Execs. in State Govt., Am. Bankers Assn. (govt. rels. coun. 1990—92), Nat. Assn. Bank Women (pres. 1980—81). Democrat. Avocations: animal protection, reading, cultural arts, travel. Home: 641 Mirandy Pl Reynoldsburg OH 43068-1602 Office: 90 W Broad St Columbus OH 43215-9000 E-mail: lkpage@cmhmetro.net., lpage@ix.netcom.com.

PAGONIS, WILLIAM GUS, retired army general; b. Charleroi, Pa., Apr. 30, 1941; s. Constantinos V. and Jennie (Kontos) P.; m. Cheryl Elaine Miller, June 14, 1964; children: Gust, Robert. BS, Pa. State U., 1964, MBA in Bus. Logistics, 1970; D in Pub. Svc. (hon.), Washington Jefferson Coll., 1997. Commd. 2d lt. U.S. Army, 1964, advanced through grades to lt. gen., 1991; comdr. 1097th Transp. Co., Vietnam, 1968; div. transp. officer, then exec. officer 2d bn., 501st inf., 101st Airborne Div., Vietnam, 1970-71; pers. staff officer U.S. Army Mil. Pers. Ctr., Alexandria, Va., 1973-75; staff officer Office Chief of Legis. Liaison, Washington, 1975-76; comdr. 10th transp. bn. 7th Transp. Group, Ft. Eustis, Va., 1977-78; chief of staff 193d Inf. Brigade, Panama, 1980-81, comdr. Logistics Support Command Panama, 1981-82; comdr. Div. Support Command, 4th Inf. Div., Ft. Carson, Colo., 1982-85; dir. transp., energy and troop support Office Dep. Chief of Staff for Logistics, Washington, 1989-90; comdg. gen. 22d Support Command, Dhahran, Saudi Arabia, 1990-91, Saudi Arabia, 1990-92, 21st Support Command Europe, Germany, 1992-93; lt. gen., ret. U.S. Army, 1993; exec. v.p. logistics Sears & Roebuck Co., Hoffman Estates, Ill., 1993—. Author: Moving Mountains (Logistics Leadership and Management of the Gulf War), (one of top 30 best bus. books of 1992, top leadership book 1992 Soundview Exec. Book Summaries, 1992), 1992. Decorated D.S.M., Silver Star, Legion of Merit with oak leaf cluster, Bronze Star with 3 oak leaf clusters, Air medal with 2 oak leaf clusters, Meritorious Svc. medal with 4 oak leaf clusters, King Abdul Aziz 2d Class award Chief of Staff, Saudi Arabian Army, 1991, Kuwait Liberation medal Chief of Staff, Kuwait Army, 1992; recipient Merit and Honor award Govt. of Greece, 1991, Joseph C. Scheleen award Am. Soc. Transp. and Logistics, 1991, Man of Yr. award Modern Materials Handling, 1991, Grad. Man of Yr. award Alpha Chi Rho, 1991, AHEPA Man of Yr., 1992, Disting. Alumni award Pa. State U., 1994; named Hellenic Man of Yr., 1992; Pa. State U. fellow, 1992. Home: 25190 N Pawnee Rd Barrington IL 60010-1354 Office: Sears Roebuck & Co 3333 Beverly Rd Hoffman Estates IL 60192-3322

PAIGE, JEFFERY MAYLAND, sociologist, educator; b. Providence, June 15, 1942; s. Charles Warren and Dorothy Frances (Rice) P.; m. Karen Ericksen, Apr. 30, 1966 (div. 1980). AB summa cum laude, Harvard U., 1964; PhD, U. Mich., 1968. Asst. prof. U. Calif., Berkeley, 1968-76; assoc. prof. U. Mich., Ann Arbor, 1976-82, prof., 1982—, dir. ctr. for rsch. on social orgn., 1992-97; vis. scholar MIT, Cambridge, Mass., 1998. Vis. lectr. U. Ctrl. Am., San Salvador, El Salvador, 1990, Fla. Internat. U., Miami, 1992; internat. observer Nicaraguan Nat. Adv. Commn. on Atlantic Coast, Managua, 1986. Author: Agrarian Revolution, 1975 (Sorokin award 1976), Coffee and Power, 1997; co-author: The Politics of Reproductive Ritual, 1981. Fulbright fellow, 1990, Kellog fellow, 1991; rsch. grantee NSF, 1990-92. Mem. Am. Sociol. Assn. (coun. chair polit. econ. of world sys. sect. 1987-89), Latin Am. Studies Assn., Sociol. Rsch. Assn. Democrat. Avocations: hiking, Nordic and alpine skiing, sailing. Office: U Mich Dept Sociology Ann Arbor MI 48109

PAISLEY, KEITH WATKINS, former state senator, retired small business owner; b. Mpls., Dec. 29, 1928; s. Manley G. and Maxine Alice (Watkins) P.; m. Jean Clare Robson, Sept. 23, 1950; children: Mark, Susan, Julie, Jeanne. BA, Hamline U., 1950. Owner Robson Hardware, Sioux Falls, S.D., 1972-93; mem. S.D. Ho. of Reps., Pierre, 1981-84, S.D. Senate, Pierre, 1985-2000. Lutheran. Home: 2409 S Elmwood Ave Sioux Falls SD 57105-3315

PALAHNIUK, RICHARD JOHN, anesthesiology educator, researcher; b. Winnipeg, Man., Can., Dec. 5, 1944; s. George and Teenie (Lukinchuk) P.; m. Patricia June Smando, July 15, 1967; children: Christopher, Daniel, Andrew. BS in Medicine, MD, U. Man., 1968. Head obstetric anaesthesia Health Scis. Ctr., Winnipeg, 1973-79; prof. and chmn. of anaesthesia U. Man., 1979-89; prof. anesthesiology, head dept., dir. dept. anesthesiology U. Minn., Mpls., 1989—. Contbr. papers and book chpts. to profl. publs.; mem. editorial bd. Can. Jour. Anaesthesia, Toronto, 1985-89. Fellow Med. Rsch. Coun. Can., 1972, rsch. grantee, 1974-79. Fellow Royal Coll. Physicians of Can.; mem. Can. Anaesthetists' Soc., Am. Soc. Anesthesiology, Internat. Anesthesia Rsch. Soc. (editorial bd. Cleve. chpt. 1987—). Roman Catholic. Avocations: running, fishing, carpentry. Office: U Minn Med Sch Box 294 420 Delaware St SE Minneapolis MN 55455-0374

PALAMARA, JOSEPH, state legislator; b. s. Sam and Eleanor P.; m. Aline; children: Lauren Grace, Lance Joseph. BA, Mich. State U., 1975; JD, Detroit Coll. Law, 1985. Rep. Mich. State Dist. 30, 1985-94, Mich. State Dist. 24, 1995-98; county commr. Wayne County, Mich., 1998—. Majority whip Mich. Ho. Reps., chmn. election com., mem. corp. & fin. com., pub. health com., ins. com., jud. com.; pvt. practice law, Mich., 1986—. Home: 8963 Marquette Dr Grosse Ile MI 48138-1581

PALANS, LLOYD ALEX, lawyer; b. St. Louis, Aug. 6, 1946; s. Hyman Robert and Mae (Sherman) P.; m. Deborah Regn, Aug. 5, 1972; children: Emily Rebecca, Samantha Jane. BS, Tulane U., 1968; JD, U. Mo., 1972. Bar: Mo. 1972, U.S. Dist. Ct. (ea. and we. dists.) Mo. 1972, U.S. Ct. Appeals (8th cir.) 1972, U.S. Ct. Appeals (5th cir.) 1974, U.S. Supreme Ct. 1975, U.S. Ct. Appeals (9th cir.) 1992. Ptnr. Kramer, Chused, Kramer, Shostak & Kohn, St. Louis, 1972-77, Blumenfeld, Marx & Tureen, P.C., St. Louis, 1978-81, Gallop, Johnson & Neuman, St. Louis, 1981-90, Bryan Cave, LLP, St. Louis, 1990—. Adj. prof. Washington U. Sch. Law, St. Louis, 1989—. Bd. dirs. St. Louis Chpt. ARC, 1987—, St. Louis Chpt. Leukemia Soc., 1988—, Combined Health Appeal Greater St. Louis, 1988—, Combined Health Appeal of Am., 1990. Fellow Am. Coll. Bankruptcy; mem. ABA, Mo. Bar, St. Louis Met. Bar Assn. Office: Bryan Cave LLP 1 Metro Sq 211 N Broadway Saint Louis MO 63102-2733

PALERMO, GREGORY SEBASTIAN, architect; b. Westfield, N.Y., Oct. 28, 1946; s. Sebastian and Frances Joan (Ciminella) P.; divorced; children: Mark Sebastian, Christopher Anthony. BArch, Carnegie Mellon U., 1969; MArch in Urban Design, Wash. U., 1976. Registered architect, Mo., Calif., N.Y., Iowa. Architect PGAV Inc., St. Louis, 1976-79; sr. v.p. HOK, Inc., 1980-87; sr. assoc. Mackey Assocs., 1987-89; v.p., prin. Stone Marraccini Patterson, 1989-91. Affiliate asst. prof. Washington U. Sch. Arch., 1984-90; vis. assoc. prof. Iowa State U. Dept. Arch., 1992-95, assoc. prof., 1995-2001, prof., 2001—, undergrad. program coord., 1996-98, assoc. chair undergrad. program, 1999—; chair Des Moines Archtl. Adv. Com., 1996-97; mem. Des Moines Gateway Planning Com., 1996. Editorial bd. Iowa Architect mag., 1992—, assoc. ed., 1995—. Mem. Light Rail Transit Rev. Com., 1985, St. Louis Mayoral Task Force, 1986; exec/coun. Arts in Transit Com., St. Louis, 1987—; chmn. design rev. com.,St. Louis Metrolink Transit System, 1989-91; chair Nat. AIA Edn. Task Force, 1990; mem. Leadership St. Louis, 1990-91, Archtl. Adv. Commn. city of Des Moines, 1992-2000. Fellow AIA (bd. dirs., nat. v.p.); mem. Nat. Archtl. Accreditation Bd (pres. 1993-94). Office: Iowa State Univ Coll of Design Dept Architecture Rm 156 Ames IA 50011-0001

PALERMO, JAMES W. artistic director; b. Cleve. BMus, MMus, Ind. U. Gen. mgr. Evansville (Ind.) Philharmonic Orch., 1989-92; orch. mgr. Louisville Orch., 1992-95; artistic and gen. dir. Grant Park Orch., Chgo., 1995—. Musician Spoleo Festival Orch., Orquesta Sinfonica Del Valle, Cali, Columbia; intern Chgo. Office Fine Arts. Active Grant Park Cultural and Ednl. Cmty., program planning com. Sherwood Conservatory, search com. Chgo. Youth Symphony Orch., 25th anniversary com. Chgo. Opera Theater. Orch. Mgmt. fellow Am. Symphony Orch. League. Office: Grant Park Orch 425 E Mcfetridge Dr Chicago IL 60605-2791

PALIZZI, ANTHONY N. lawyer, retail corporation executive; b. Wyandotte, Mich., Oct. 27, 1942; s. Vincenzo and Nunziata (Dagostini) P.; children: A. Michael, Nicholas A. PhB, Wayne State U., 1964, JD, 1966; LLM, Yale U., 1967. Bar: Mich. 1967. Prof. law Fla. State U., Tallahassee, 1967-69; prof. law Tex. Tech U., Lubbock, 1969-71; atty. Kmart Corp., Troy, Mich., 1971-74, asst. sec., 1974-77, asst. gen. counsel, 1977-85, v.p., assoc. gen. counsel, 1985-91, sr. v.p., gen. counsel, 1991-92, exec. v.p., gen. counsel, 1992—. Editor law rev. Wayne State U., 1964-66 Chmn. Brandon Police and Fire Bd., Mich., 1982-87. Mem. ABA, Am. Corp. Counsel Assn., Mich. State Bar Assn. Roman Catholic.

PALLASCH, B. MICHAEL, lawyer, director; b. Chgo., Mar. 30, 1933; s. Bernhard Michael and Magdalena Helena (Fixari) P.; m. Josephine Catherine O'Leary, Aug. 15, 1981; children: Bernhard Michael III and Madeleine Josephine (twins). BSS, Georgetown U., 1954; JD, Harvard U., 1957; postgrad., John Marshall Law Sch., 1974. Bar: Ill. 1957, U.S. Dist. Ct. (no. dist.) Ill. 1958, U.S. Tax Ct. 1961, U.S. Ct. Claims 1961, U.S. Ct. Appeals (7th cir.) 1962. Assoc. Winston & Strawn, Chgo., 1958-66, resident mgr. br. office Paris, 1963-65, ptnr. Chgo., 1966-70, sr. capital ptnr., 1971-91; sr. ptnr. B. Michael Pallasch & Assocs., 1991—. Dir., corp. sec. Tanis, Inc., Calumet, Mich., 1972—, Greenbank Engring. Corp., Dover, Del., 1976-91, C.B.P. Engring. Corp., Chgo., 1976-91, Chgo. Cutting Svcs. Corp., 1977-88; corp. sec. Arthur Andersen Assocs., Inc., Chgo., 1976—, L'hotel de France of Ill., Inc., Chgo., 1980-85, Water & Effluent Screening Co., Chgo., 1988-91; dir. Bosch Devel. Co., Longview, Tex., 1977-87, Lor Inc., Houghton, Mich., 1977-87, Rana Inc., Madison, Wis., 1978-87, Woodlak Co., Houghton, 1977-87, Zipatone, Inc., Hillside, Ill., 1975-82, Keco Inc., Madison, 1977-81. Bd. dirs. Martin D'Arcy Mus. Medieval and Renaissance Art, Chgo., 1975— ; bd. dirs. Katherine M. Bosch Found., 1978— ; asst. sec. Hundred Club of Cook County, Chgo., 1966-73, bd. dirs., sec., 1974— . Served with USAFR, 1957-63. Knight of Merit Sacred Mil. Constantinian Order of St. George of Royal House of Bourbon of Two Sicilies, knight comdr. with star Sovereign Mil. Order of Temple of Jerusalem; named youth mayor City of Chgo., 1950; recipient Outstanding Woodland Mgmt. Forestry award Monroe County (Wis.) Soil and Water Conservation Dist., 1975. Mem. Ill. Bar Assn. (tax lectr. 1961), Advs. Soc., Field Mus. Natural History (life), Max McGraw Wildlife Found., English Speaking Union. Roman Catholic. Clubs: Travellers (Paris); Saddle and Cycle (Chgo.). Home: 737 W Hutchinson St Chicago IL 60613-1519 Office: 35 W Wacker Dr Ste 4700 Chicago IL 60601-1614

PALLMEYER, REBECCA RUTH, judge; b. Tokyo, Sept. 13, 1954; arrived in U.S., 1957; d. Paul Henry and Ruth (Schrieber) Pallmeyer; m. Dan P. McAdams, Aug. 20, 1977; children: Ruth McAdams, Amanda McAdams. BA, Valparaiso (Ind.) U., 1976; JD, U. Chgo., 1979. Bar: Ill. 1980, U.S. Ct. Appeals (7th cir.) 1980, U.S. Ct. Appeals (11th and 5th cirs.) 1982. Jud. clk. Minn. Supreme Ct., St. Paul, 1979-80; assoc. Hopkins & Sutter, Chgo., 1980-85; judge administrv. law Ill. Human Rights Commn., 1985-91; magistrate judge U.S. Dist. Ct. No. Dist. Ill., 1991-98, dist. judge, 1998—. Mem. jud. resources com. Jud. Conf. U.S., 1994—2000. Nat. adv. coun. Christ Coll., Valparaiso U., 2002—; bd. dirs. Augustana Ctr., 1990—91. Mem.: FBA (bd. mgrs. Chgo. chpt. 1995—99), Chgo. Bar Assn. (chair devel. law com. 1992—93, David C. Hilliard award 1990—91), Fed. Magistrate Judges Assn. (bd. dirs. 1994—97), Nat. Assn. Women Judges, Womens Bar Assn. Ill. (bd. mgrs. 1995—98), Valparaiso U. Alumni Assn. (bd. dirs. 1992—94). Lutheran. Avocations: choral music, sewing, running. Office: US Dist Ct 219 S Dearborn St Ste 2178 Chicago IL 60604-1877

PALM, GARY HOWARD, lawyer, educator; b. Toledo, Sept. 2, 1942; s. Clarence William Jr. and Emily Marie (Braunschweiger) P. AB, Wittenberg U., 1964; JD, U. Chgo., 1967. Bar: Ill. 1967, U.S. Dist. Ct. (no. dist.) Ill. 1967, U.S. Ct. Appeals (7th cir.) 1970, U.S. Supreme Ct. 1974. Assoc. Schiff Hardin & Waite, Chgo., 1967-70; dir. Edwin F. Mandel Legal Aid Clinic, 1970-91, atty., 1991-98; asst. prof. law U. Chgo., 1970-75, assoc. prof., 1975-83, prof., 1983-91, clin. prof., 1991—. Peer rev. reader, clin. edn. grants U.S. Dept. Edn., Washington, 1980, 81, 83, 84, 86, 87, Legal Svcs. Corp., 1986-87; chairperson-elect, chairperson sect. clin. legal edn. Assn. Am. Law Schs., 1985, 86. Vol. ACLU, Chgo., 1968-75. Mem. ATLA, ABA (clin. edn. com. 1974-80, membership com. 1984-85, skills tng. com. 1985-90, accreditation for Law Schs. 1987-94, mem. coun. sect. on legal edn. and admissions to the bar 1994—, liaison professionalism com. 1999—), Ill. State Bar Assn. (legal edn., admission and competence com. 1985-91, 93-99, com. on delivery legal svcs. 1999—), Chgo. Bar Assn., Chgo. Coun. Lawyers, Assn. Am. Law Sch. (clin. tchg. confs. 1985, 86, 87, 89, recipient Award for Outstanding Contbn. to Clin. Edn., sect. on legal edn. 1989, co-recipient of the award 1994), Clin. Legal Edn. Assn. (ad hoc com. on accreditation 1996, Clin. All Star 1996). Democrat. Home: 2800 N Lake Shore Dr Apt 3706 Chicago IL 60657-6254 Office: U Chgo Law Sch 1111 E 60th St Chicago IL 60637-2776

PALMBERG, PAUL W. retired electronics executive; Dir. R&D, gen. mgr. Phys. Electronics, Inc. (divsn. of Perkin-Elmer), Eden Prairie, Minn.; pres., CEO Phys. Electronics, Inc., 1994-97; ret., 1997. Mem. Am. Vacuum Soc. (Gaede-Langmuir award 1998). Office: Physical Electronics Inc US Corp Hqrs 6509 Flying Cloud Dr Eden Prairie MN 55344-3324 also: Am Vacuum Soc 120 Wall St Fl 32 New York NY 10005-4001

PALMER, BRADLEY BERAN, sportscaster; b. Madison, Wis., July 21, 1940; s. Robert and Cerise (Beran) P.; m. Patricia Carey, Oct. 19, 1974; two children. BS in Comms., U. Ill., 1963. Officer USN, U.S.S. Shangri-La, 1963-65; news anchor, reporter KGLO-AM/TV, Mason City, Iowa, 1965; news reporter WTVO-TV, Rockford, Ill., 1965-66; news writer, prodr. WGN-AM/TV, Chgo., 1966-68; sports dir. WBBM-AM, 1968-85; sports anchor, reporter WLS-TV, 1985—. Named Ill. Sportscaster of Yr., Nat. Sportscaster & Sportwriters Assn., 1980, 82, 86, 87, 88, 93, 95, 98.

PALMER, BRIAN EUGENE, lawyer; b. Mpls., May 16, 1948; s. Eugene Philip and Virginia Breeze (Rolfshus) P.; m. Julia Washburn Morrison, Dec. 29, 1972; 1 child, Julia Hunter. AB, Brown U., 1970; JD, William Mitchell Coll. of Law, 1974. Bar: Minn. 1974, U.S. Dist. Ct. Minn. 1975, U.S. Dist. Ct. (ea. dist.) Wis. 2001, U.S. Ct. Appeals (8th cir.) 1980, U.S. Ct. Fed. Claims 1984, U.S. Supreme Ct. 1980. Asst. pub. defender Hennepin County Pub. Defender, Mpls., 1974-78; assoc. Dorsey & Whitney LLP, 1978-82, ptnr., 1983—. Home: 1190 Lyman Ave Wayzata MN 55391-9671 Office: Dorsey & Whitney LLP 50 South Sixth St Ste 1500 Minneapolis MN 55402-1498 E-mail: palmer.brian@dorseylaw.com.

PALMER, CHARLES A. lawyer, educator; b. Jackson, Mich., Jan. 25, 1945; s. Robert E. and Gertrude (Caldwell) P.; m. Barbara Ann DiTiberio, May 10, 1975; children: Robert, Joseph, Christopher. BBA, U. Mich., 1967, JD, 1970. Bar: Mich. 1970, U.S. Dist. Ct. (we. and ea. dists.) Mich. 1970, U.S. Tax Ct. 1971, U.S. Ct. Appeals (6th cir.). Jud. clk. Ingham County Cir. Ct., Lansing, Mich., 1971; assoc. Cummins, Butter & Thorburn, 1971-72; prin. Charles A. Palmer, P.C., 1973-88; prof. law Thomas M. Cooley Law Sch., 1988—. Mayor, JAG, Mich. N.G., Jackson, 1978—; chmn. bd. dirs. Ind. Bank of South Mich., Leslie, 1989—. Pres. Legal Aid of Cen. Mich., Lansing. Mem. ABA, Mich. Bar Assn., Ingham County Bar Assn. Office: Independent Bank Corp 230 W Main St PO Box 491 Ionia MI 48846

PALMER, CHRIS, professional football coach; b. Brewster, N.Y., Sept. 23, 1949; m. Donna Palmer; children: Mark, Kristin. BS, MS, So. Conn. State U. Asst. coach U. Conn., 1972-75; wide receivers coach Lehigh U., 1975-76; offensive coord. Colgate U., 1976-82; offensive line coach Montreal Concords, 1983-84; coach receivers, quarterback coach, offensive coord. N.J. Generals, 1984-86; head coach U. New Haven, 1986-87, Boston U., 1988-89; coach wide receivers Houston Oilers, 1990-92; with New Eng. Patriots, 1994-97, quarterback coach, 1996-97; offensive coord. Jacksonville Jaguars, 1997-99; head coach Cleveland Browns, 1999—. Office: Cleveland Browns 1085 W 3rd St Cleveland OH 44114-1001

PALMER, CRUISE, newspaper editor; b. Kansas City, Kans., Apr. 9, 1917; s. Thomas Potter and Margaret Scroggs (McFadden) P.; m. Dorraine Humphreys, Sept. 7, 1946; children: Thomas Cruise, Martha D. Sprague. B.S. in Journalism, Kans. State U., 1938. With Kansas City (Mo.) Star, 1938—, news editor, 1963-64, mng. editor, 1965-66; exec. editor and bd. Star and Times, 1967—78, cons., 1978—. Dir. Purtec Systems, Inc. Mem. bd. govs. Am. Royal Live Stock and Horse Show Assn., 1967-91; bd. dirs. ARC, 1978-91, Kansas City Mayor's Corps Progress, 1978-91; found. trustee Kans. State U.; trustee Kansas City Sister Cities Commn., 1978-91. Served to lt. (j.g.) USNR, 1943-46. Recipient Distinguished Service award Kans. State U., 1967; First Place award Pro-Am. Southgate Open Golf Tournament, 1973; Second Place award Pro-Am. Hawaiian Open, 1973, 85; Third Place, 1981; First Place award Jim Colbert Celebrity Tournament, 1981, First Place Team award Kansas City area Am. Cancer Soc. Golf Tournament, 1986. Mem. Am. Soc. Newspaper Editors, Soc. Profl. Journalists, Kansas City Sr. Golf Assn., Kansas City Press Club (pres. 1953-54, 64-65, permanent trustee, pres. scholarship found. 1989), Kansas City Club, Chiefs Red Coat Club, Milburn Golf and Country Club, Beta Theta Pi (Greater Kansas City Beta of Yr. 1980). Episcopalian (former vestryman and lay reader). Home: Lakeview Retirement Village 14100 W 90th Ter Apt 504 Lenexa KS 66215-5430 Office: 1729 Grand Ave Kansas City MO 64108-1413

PALMER, DAVE RICHARD, retired military officer, academic administrator; b. Ada, Okla., May 31, 1934; s. David Furman and Lorena Marie (Clardy) P.; m. LuDelia Clemmer, Apr. 13, 1957; children: Allison, J. Kersten. BS, U.S. Military Acad., 1956; MA in History, Duke U., 1966; postgrad., Army War Coll., 1972-73; PhD (hon.), Duke U., 1990. Commd. U.S. Army, 1956, advanced through grades to lt. gen.; mem. faculty dept. history U.S. Mil. Acad., 1966-69; mem. staff (Pentagon), 1973-76, Joint Chiefs of Staff, 1979-81; comdr. Baumholder Mil. Community, W. Ger., 1981-83; dep. comdt. Command and Gen. Staff Coll., Ft. Leavenworth, Kans., 1983-85; comdg. gen. 1st Armored Div., W.Ger., 1985-86; supt. U.S. Mil. Acad., 1986-91, ret., 1991; pres. Walden U., 1995-99; CEO Walden Corp., 1999-2000. Author: The River and the Rock, 1969, The Way of the Fox, 1975, Summons of the Trumpet, 1978, 1794-America, Its Army, and The Birth of the Nation, 1994, First in War, 2000. Bd. dirs. Walden U., 1992-2001. Decorated Legion of Merit (3); Bronze Star (2), D.S.M.(2). Mem. Assn. U.S. Army, Armor Assn., Mil. History, Soc. Cin. E-mail: lucpalmer4@cs.com.

PALMER, DEBORAH JEAN, lawyer; b. Williston, N.D., Oct. 25, 1947; d. Everett Edwin and Doris Irene (Harberg) P.; m. Kenneth L. Rich, Mar. 29, 1980; children: Andrew, Stephanie. BA, Carleton Coll., 1969; JD cum laude, Northwestern U., 1973. Bar: Minn. 1973, U.S. Dist. Ct. Minn. 1973, U.S. Ct. Appeals (8th cir.) 1975, U.S. Supreme Ct. 1978, U.S. Ct. Appeals (11th cir.) 1999. Econ. analyst Harris Trust & Savs. Bank, Chgo., 1969-70; assoc. Robins, Kaplan, Miller & Ciresi LLP, Mpls., 1973-79, ptnr., 1979—. Trustee Carleton Coll., 1984-88; mem. bd. religious edn. Plymouth Congl. Ch., 1992-95; bd. dirs. Mpls. YWCA, 1996-99; mem. Dist. Minn. Civil Justice Reform Act Adv. Group, 1990-93; bd. dirs. RKM&C Found. Edn., Pub. Health & Social Justice, 1999—. Mem. ABA, Minn. Bar Assn., Minn. Women Lawyers Assn. (sec. 1976-78), Minn. Fed. Bar Assn. (chpt. bd. dirs. 1996-98), Hennepin County Bar Assn., Hennepin County Bar Found. (bd. dirs. 1978-81), Carleton Coll. Alumni Assn. (bd. dirs. 1978-82, sec. 1980-82), Women's Assn. of Minn. Orch. (bd. dirs. 1980-85, treas. 1981-83). Home: 1787 Colfax Ave S Minneapolis MN 55403-3008 Office: Robins Kaplan Miller & Ciresi LLP 800 Lasalle Ave Ste 2800 Minneapolis MN 55402-2015 E-mail: djpalmer@rkmc.com.

PALMER, DENNIS DALE, lawyer; b. Alliance, Nebr., Apr. 30, 1945; s. Vernon D. Palmer and Marie E. (Nelson) Fellers; m. Rebecca Ann Turner, Mar. 23, 1979; children: Lisa Marie, Jonathan Paul. BA, U. Mo., 1967, JD, 1970. Bar: Mo. 1970, U.S. Dist. Ct. (we. dist.) Mo. 1970, U.S. Ct. Appeals (8th and 10th cirs.) 1973, U.S. Supreme Ct. 1980. Staff atty. Legal Aid Soc. Western Mo., Kansas City, 1970-73; assoc. Shughart, Thomson & Kilroy, P.C., 1973-76, ptnr., bd. dirs., 1976—. Contbr. articles on franchise and employment law to legal jours. Bd. dirs., chmn. legal assts. adv. bd. Avila Coll., Kansas City, 1984-87. 2d lt. U.S. Army, 1970. Mem. ABA (litigation com. 1980, forum com. on franchising 1987), Mo. Bar Assn. (antitrust com. 1975—, civil practice com. 1975—), Kansas City Bar Assn. (chmn. franchise law com. 1987—), Univ. Club. Avocations: jogging, golf, tennis, outdoor activities, reading. Home: 13100 Canterbury Rd Leawood KS 66209-1700 Office: Shughart Thomson & Kilroy 12 Wyandotte Plz 120 W 12th St Fl 17 Kansas City MO 64105-1902

PALMER, JOHN BERNARD, III, lawyer; b. Ft. Wayne, Ind., May 18, 1952; s. John Bernard and Dorothy Alma (Lauer) P. BA, Mich. State U., 1974; JD, U. Mich., 1977. Bar: Ill. 1977, U.S. Dist. Ct. (no. dist.) Ill. 1977, U.S. Tax Ct. 1979. Assoc. Mayer Brown & Platt, Chgo., 1977-80, Hopkins & Sutter, Chgo., 1980-83, ptnr., 1983-2001, Foley & Lardner, Chgo., 2001—. Adj. prof. Ill. Inst. Tech.- Kent Coll. of Law, Chgo., 1984—. Mem. ABA. Office: Foley & Lardner Three First Nat Plaza Chicago IL 60602

PALMER, PATRICK EDWARD, radio astronomer, educator; b. St. Johns, Mich., Dec. 6, 1940; s. Don Edward and Nina Louise (Kyes) P.; m. Joan Claire Merlin, June 9, 1963; children: Laura Katherine, Aidan Edward, David Elijah. SB, U. Chgo., 1963; MA, Harvard U., 1965, PhD, 1968. Radio astronomer Harvard U., Cambridge, Mass., 1968; asst. prof. astronomy and astrophysics U. Chgo., 1968-70, assoc. prof., 1970-75, prof., 1975—. Vis. assoc. prof. astronomy Calif. Inst. Tech., Pasadena, 1972; vis. radio astronomer Cambridge (Eng.) U., 1973; vis. rsch. astronomer U. Calif., Berkeley, 1977, 86; vis. scientist Nat. Radio Astronomer Obs., 1980-2001. Contbr. articles on radio astron. investigations of comets and interstellar medium to tech. jours. Recipient Bart J. Bok prize for contbns. to galactic astronomy, 1969, Alfred P. Sloan Found. fellow, 1970-72, Helen B. Warner prize, 1975. Fellow AAAS (chmn. sect. D astronomy 1984); mem. AAUP, Am. Astron. Soc. (chmn. nominating com. 1981, mem. publs. bd. 1985-86, mem. Warner Prize selection com. 1977-78), Royal Astron. Soc., Internat. Astron. Union, U. Chgo. Track Club. Home: 5549 S Dorchester Ave Chicago IL 60637-1720 Office: Univ Chgo Astronomy & Astrophysics Ctr 5640 S Ellis Ave Chicago IL 60637-1433 E-mail: ppalmer@oskar.uchicago.edu.

PALMER, RAYMOND ALFRED, administrator, librarian, consultant; b. Louisville, May 8, 1939; BA in Biology, U. Louisville, 1961; MLS, U. Ky., 1966. Adminstrv. asst. Johns Hopkins Med. Libr., Balt., 1966-69; asst. librarian Harvard Med. Libr., Boston, 1969-74; health scis. librarian Wright State U., Dayton, Ohio, 1974-82, assoc. prof. library adminstrn., 1974-82; exec. dir. Med. Libr. Assn., Chgo., 1982-92, Am. Assn. Immunologists, Bethesda, Md., 1992-95; dir. info.-edn. svcs. Nat. Ctr. Edn. Maternal-Child Health Georgetown U., Arlington, Va., 1995-97—. Cons. Acad. Mil. Med. Scis. Libr., Beijing, 1990, Alzheimer's Assn., Chgo., 1991. Author: Management of Library Associations; mng. editor: Jour. Immunology, 1992-95; contbr. articles to profl. jours. Mem. ALA, Am. Soc. Assn. Execs., Greater Washington Soc. Assn. Execs., Spl. Librs. Assn., Biomed. Communication Network (chmn. 1980-82), Am. Mgmt. Assn. (strategic planning adv. coun. 1987-91), Coun. Biology Editors, Friends of Nat. Libr. Medicine (bd. dirs. 1989-92, 94-97), Internat. Fedn. Libr. Assns. and Instns. (exec. com. Round Table for Mgmt. of Libr. Orgns. 1989-92), Med. Libr. Assn. E-mail: rap539@aol.com.

PALMER, ROBERT ERWIN, association executive; b. Texarkana, Ark., Feb. 6, 1934; s. Burgess Prince and Ruth (Erwin) P. BJ, U. Tex., 1961. Reporter Texarkana Gazette, 1961; editor Southwestern Bell Telephone, Houston, 1961, info. specialist St. Louis, 1961-63; editor Shell Oil Co., Houston and Chgo., head office pub. relations N.Y.C.; dir. pub. relations Nat. PTA, Chgo., 1969-74; program dir. Nat. Assn. Realtors, 1974-76; corp. communications mgr. The Milw. Rd., 1976-78; staff v.p. Soc. Real Estate Appraisers, 1978-83, exec. v.p., 1983-90; sr. v.p. communications, 1991—; co. exec., v.p. Appraisal Inst., Chgo., 1992-93, v.p. mem. svcs., 1993-98. Bd. dirs. Tower Advt., Chgo., Costumes Unltd. ltd., Chgo. Founding mem. Chgo. Crime Commn., 1967. Served to staff sgt. USAF, 1953-57. Recipient Award of Merit, Chgo. Internat. Film Festival, 1970, 71, Spl. Corrs. Pring Feature award, 1971, 72, Golden Trumpet award Realtor Week promotion, 1975, Golden Trumpet award Pvt. Property Week promotion, 1977, Golden Trumpet award Realtor bicentennial program, 1977, Gold Circle award Chpt.-by-Chpt. program, 1982. Mem. Pub. Relations Soc. Am., Am. Soc. Assn. Execs., Sigma Delta Chi. Methodist. Club: Chgo. Headline.

PALMER, ROGER RAYMOND, accounting educator; b. N.Y.C., Dec. 31, 1926; s. Archibald and Sophie (Jarnow) P.; m. Martha West Hopkins, June 7, 1986; children by previous marriage: Kathryn Sue, Daniel Stephen, Susan Jo. BS, U. Wis., 1949; MBA, Cornell U., 1951; postgrad., NYU, 1951-54. Auditor, Ernst and Ernst, CPA's, N.Y.C., 1953-54; auditor Gen. Dynamics Corp., 1956-60; mgr. corp. audits Tex. Instruments, 1960-64; auditor 1st Nat. Bank, St. Paul, 1964-68, v.p. planning, 1968-69, v.p., comptr., 1969-75, sr. v.p., contr., 1975-82; chmn. dept. fin. Coll. of St. Thomas (now U. St. Thomas), 1996—. Dir. First Met. Travel, Inc.; guest lectr. U. Minn., 1966; conf. leader, speaker, 1959— Contbr. articles to publs. Bd. dirs. Waterford (Conn.) Civic Assn., 1959-60, Friends of St. Paul Pub. Library, 1967, Mpls. Citizens League; chmn. bd. dirs. Film in the Cities, 1983-85; mem. acctg. adv. council U. Minn.; trustee, chmn. fin. com. Hazelton Found. With U.S. Maritime Svc., 1945-47; with U.S. Army, 1954-56. Mem. Inst. Internal Auditors (pres. So. New Eng chpt. 1957-60, edn. chmn. Dallas 1961, Twin City chpt. 1965-66), Nat. Assn. Accts. (dir. Norwich, Conn. chpt. 1958-60), Nat. Assn. Accountants (St. Paul chpt. 1967), Assn. Bank Audit, Control and Operation, Am. Inst. Banking, Fin. Execs. Inst., Planning Forum (pres. Twin Cities chpt. 1984-85), Univ. Club (St. Paul). Club: St. Paul Athletic. Home: 415 Oak Ridge Dr San Marcos TX 78666 E-mail: rrpalmer@stthomas.edu.

PALMERI, SHARON ELIZABETH, freelance writer, community educator; b. Gary, Ind., July 23, 1948; d. Theodore and Alberta (Bias) Wozniak; m. John James Palmeri, Apr. 9, 1969: 1 child, Renee Suzanne. BS in Edn. English/Journalism with honor, Ind. U. NW, 1991. Health columnist Lake County Star, Crown Point, Ind., 1989-92; corr. Post Tribune, Gary, 1992-93; feature corr. The Munster (Ind.) Times, 1993—95; educator creative and news writing Merrillville (Ind.) Adult Edn., 1989—; educator writer's workshop Purdue U. Calumet, Hammond, Ind., 1990—95; educator creative writing Purdue U. N. Ctrl., Westville, 1995—. Bd. dirs. N.W. Ind. Arts and Humaniteis Consortium, Gary, 1994-2000; dir. Write-On Hoosiers, Inc., Crown Point, 1989—; educator news & creative writing Bethlehem Steel Career Devel. Ctr., 1996-98; educator news class Forest Ridge Acad., 1996—; book doctor, publicity agt., local book and mag. promoter The Creative Connection; educator New Class Forest Ridge Acad., 1996, No. Ind. Arts Assn., 1997—; educator, book dr., publicity agent, local book, mag. promoter. Exec. editor: Hoosier Horizon, 1991-96; co-editor: Hoosier Horizon Children's Mag., 1993—; contbr. short stories and essays to Spirits Mag., 1990, 91. Recipient Best of Show award Southlake Camera Club, Crown Point, 1975, Focal Point Camera Club, Portage, 1982. Mem. Nat. Coun. Tchrs. English, Soc. Profl. Journalists, N.W. Ind. Arts Assn. (educator 1997—), Communicators N.W. Ind., Ind. U. Alumni Assn., Kappa Delta Pi (newsletter editor 1991-94). Avocations: sailing, photography. Home and Office: 3605 Kingsway Dr Crown Point IN 46307-8934

PALMISANO, DONALD J. surgeon, educator; b. New Orleans, 1939; m. Robin Palmisano; 3 children. MD, Tulane U., 1963; JD, Loyola U., 1982. Diplomate Am. Bd. Surgery; bar: La. Intern Charity Hosp., New Orleans, 1963-64, resident in surgery, 1964-68, Lallie Kemp Charity Hosp., Independence, 1967-68; pvt. practice; clin. prof. surgery, clin. prof. med. jurisprudence Tulane U. Mem. Gov.'s Commn. on organ donations; chair La. Med. Disclosure Panel; founding mem. La. Med. Mutual Ins. Co.; lectr. in field. Contbr. articles to profl. publs. With USAF. Fellow ACS, AMSUS, SAFCS; mem. AMA (bd. trustees 1996—, chair devel. com., Physician Outreach Awards), La. State Med. Soc. (pres.). Avocation: photography. Office: AMA 515 N State St Chicago IL 60610-4325

PALMQUIST, MARK L. grain company executive; Grad., Gustavus Adolphus Coll., 1979; MBA, U. Minn. Grain buyer Cenex Harvest States, Inver Grove Heights, Minn., v.p., dir. grain mktg., 1990-93, sr. v.p., 1993—, exec. v.p., COO. Office: Cenex Harvest States 5500 Cenex Dr Inver Grove Heights MN 55077

PALO, NICHOLAS EDWIN, professional society administrator; b. Waukegan, Ill., Nov. 18, 1945; s. Edwin Arnold and Eevi Kustaava (Hukkala) P.; m. Lauren M. Reynolds, Aug. 18, 1990 (dec.). BA, U. Wis., Eau Claire, 1971; MS, U. Mo., 1975. Instr., coordinator U. Mo. Extension, Columbia, 1974-85; exec. officer Am. Bd. Profl. Psychology, 1984—. Pres. Columbia Community Band, 1987; chmn. Arts Resources Coun., Columbia, 1988; adv. bd. Columbia Art League. Mem. Am. Soc. Assn. Execs., Psychology Execs. Roundtable, Intertel, Mensa, Windjammers Unltd. Club, Am. Assn. Concert Bands Club, Internat. Trombone Assn., N.Am. Brass Band Assn., Phi Delta Kappa (hon.), Phi Mu Alpha (hon.). Democrat. Lutheran. Avocation: music. Home: 608 Spring Valley Rd Columbia MO 65203-2261 Office: Am Board of Profl Psychology 514 E Capitol Ave Jefferson City MO 65101-3008

PAMPUSCH, ANITA MARIE, foundation administrator; b. St. Paul, Aug. 28, 1938; d. Robert William and Lucille Elizabeth (Whaley) P. BA, Coll. of St. Catherine, St. Paul, 1962; MA, U. Notre Dame, 1970, PhD, 1972. Tchr. St. Joseph's Acad., St. Paul, 1962-66; instr. philosophy Coll. of St. Catherine, 1970-76, assoc. acad. dean, 1979, acad. dean, 1979-84, pres., 1984-97; Am. Council Edn. fellow Goucher Coll., Balt., 1976-77; pres. Bush Found., St. Paul, 1997—. Bd. dirs. St. Paul Cos.; head Women's Coll. Coalition, 1988-91. Author: (book rev.) Philological Quarterly, 1976; contbr. articles to profl. jours. Mem. adv. com. Instl. Leadership project, Columbia U., 1986—; dist. chmn. Rhodes Scholarship Selection com., Mo., Neb., Minn., Kans., N.D., S.D., 1987—; exec. com. Women's Coll. Coalition, Washington, 1985—. Mem. Coun. for Ind. Colls. (bd. dirs. 1987—, chair 1991—), Am. Philos. Assn., St. Paul C. of C. (bd. dirs. 1986—), St. Paul's Athletic Club, Mpls. Club, Phi Beta Kappa. Roman Catholic. Avocations: swimming, camping, reading, music. Home: 161 Stonebridge Rd Saint Paul MN 55118

PANCERO, JACK BLOCHER, restaurant executive; b. Cin., Dec. 27, 1923; s. Howard and Hazel Mae (Blocher) P.; m. Loraine Fielman, Aug. 4, 1944; children: Gregg Edward, Vicki Lee. Student, Ohio State U., 1941-44.

Ptnr. Howard Pancero & Co., Cin., 1948-66; stockbroker Gradison & Co., Cin., 1966-70; real estate assoc. Parchman & Oyler, Cin., 1972-87; v.p. Gregg Pancero, Inc., Kings Mills, Ohio, 1972—. Mem. Vineyards C. of C., Western Hills Country Club, Univ. Club (Cin.), Cin. Engrs. Table, Pelican Bay Club, Vineyard Country Club, Royal Poinciana Golf Club, Met. Club., Collier Athletic Club, Masons, Shriners. Methodist. Home and Office: 806 Rue De Vl Naples FL 34108-8531 Office: Kings Island Kenwood Ctr Bldg 7565 Kenwood Rd Cincinnati OH 45236-2800

PANG, JOSHUA KEUN-UK, trade company executive; b. Chinnampo, Korea, Sept. 17, 1924; came to U.S. 1951, naturalized, 1968; s. Ne-Too and Soon-Hei (Kim) P.; m. He-Young Yoon, May 30, 1963; children: Ruth, Pauline, Grace. BS, Roosevelt U., 1959. Chemist Realemon Co., Chgo., 1957-61; chief-chemist chem. divsn. Bell & Gossett Co., 1961-63, Fatty Acid Inc., divsn. Ziegler Chem. & Mineral Corp., Chgo., 1963-64; sr. chemist-supr. Gen. Mills Chems. Inc., Kankakee, Ill., 1964-70; pres., owner UJU Industries Inc., Broadview, 1971—, also dir. Bd. dirs. Dist. 92, Lindop Sch., Broadview, 1976-87; chmn. Proviso Area Sch. Bd. Assn., Proviso Twp., Cook County, Ill. 1976-77; bd. dirs. Korean Am. Cmty. Svcs., Chgo., 1979-80; mem. governing bd. Proviso Area Exceptional Children, Spl. Edn. Joint Agreement, 1981-84, 85-87; alumni bd. govs Roosevelt U., 1983-89; pres. Korean Am. Sr. Ctr., 1991-92; pres. Korean Am. Srs. Assn., Chicagoland, 1992—. Mem. Am. Chem. Soc., Am. Assn. Arts and Sci., Am. Inst. Parliamentarians (region 2 treas. 1979-81, region 2 gov. 1981-82), Internat. Platform Assn., Ill. Sch. Bd. Assn., Nat. Assn. Sch. Bds., Chgo. Area Parliamentarians, Parliamentary Leaders in Action (pres. 1980-81), Nat. Spkrs. Assn. (dir. Ill. chpt. 1981-82, nat. parliamentarian 1982-84, 2d v.p. chpt. 1983-84), Toastmasters (dist. gov. 1969-70), DADS Assn. U. Ill. (chmn. Cook County 1985-98, bd. dirs. 1987-95, treas. 1990-91, v.p. 1991-92), Korean Am. Assn. Chgo. (exec. dir. 1990), World Future Soc. (Chgo. area chpt. coord. 1988-99, pres. Greater Chicagoland Futurists 1991-95, 97-98, chmn. 1998 ann. conf. World Future Soc. Chgo.), Chicagoland C. of C. (ednl., environ. and Pacific-Rim coms., internat. divsn.). Home: 2532 S 9th Ave Broadview IL 60155-4804 Office: UJU Industries Inc PO Box 6351 Broadview IL 60155-6351 E-mail: jokupang@worldnet.att.net., j.pang@att.net.

PANICH, DANUTA BEMBENISTA, lawyer; b. East Chicago, Ind., Apr. 9, 1954; d. Fred and Ann Stephanie (Grabowski) B.; m. Nikola Panich, July 30, 1977; children: Jennifer Anne, Michael Alexei. AB, Ind. U., 1975, JD, 1978. Bar: Ill. 1978, U.S. Dist. Ct. (no. dist.) Ill. 1978, U.S. Dist. Ct. (ctrl. dist.) Ill. 1987, U.S. Ct. Appeals 1987, U.S. Dist. Ct. (no. dist.) Ind. 2001. Assoc. Mayer Brown & Platt, Chgo., 1978-86, ptnr., 1986—2001, Mayer Brown Rowe & Maw, Chgo., 2002—. Bd. dirs. Munster (Ind.) Med. Rsch. Found., 1990—. Mem. ABA, Ill. Bar Assn. Republican. Roman Catholic. Office: Mayer Brown Rowe & Maw 190 S La Salle St Ste 3100 Chicago IL 60603-3441 E-mail: dpanich@mayerbrownrowe.com.

PANKAU, CAROLE, state legislator; b. Aug. 13, 1947; m. Anthony John Pankau Jr., 1967; 4 children. BS, U. Ill., 1981. Mem. Ill. Ho. of Reps. from 49th dist., 1993—. Mem. DuPage County (Ill.) Bd., 1984-92; committeeman Bloomingdale Twp. Rep. Precinct 70; mem. Keeneyville (Ill.) Sch. Dist. 20; vice chair Bloomingdale Twp. Rep. Orgn. Mem. Bartlett, Roselle, Bloomingdale and Hanover C. of C. Home: 215 Heritage Dr Roselle IL 60172-2994 Office: Ill Ho of Reps Capitol Office 2122 Stratton Office Bldg Ofc Springfield IL 62706-0001 also: 1278B Lake St Roselle IL 60172-3364 E-mail: carole@punkan.org.

PANZER, MARY E. state legislator; b. Waupun, Wis., Sept. 19, 1951; d. Frank E. and Verna L. P.; 1 adopted child, Melissa. BA, U. Wis., 1974; mem., Wis. State Ho. Reps. from 53rd dist. Rep. State of Wis., Madison, 1980-93; mem. Wis. Senate from 20th dist., 1993—. Home: 635 W Tamarack Dr West Bend WI 53095-3653 Office: Wis State Senate State Capital Madison WI 53702-0001

PAPAI, BEVERLY DAFFERN, library director; b. Amarillo, Tex., Aug. 31, 1949; d. Clarence Wilbur and Dora Mae (Henderson) Daffern; m. Joseph Andrew Papai, Apr. 3, 1976. BS in Polit. Sci., West Tex. State U., Canyon, 1972; MSLS, Wayne State U., 1973. Head extension dept. and Oakland County Subregional Libr. The Farmington Cmty. Libr., Farmington Hills, Mich., 1973-79, coord. adult svcs., br. head, 1980-83, asst. dir., 1983-85, dir., 1985—. Cons. U.S. Office of Edn., 1978, Battelle Meml. Inst., Columbis, Ohio, 1980; presenter in field. Contbr. articles to profl. jours. Bd. dirs. Mich. Consortium, 1987-91, Oakland Literacy Coun., 1998—, vice chair, 2000-01, chair, 2001—; trustee Libr. of Mich., 1989-92, vice chair, 1991, 97-98, chair, 1992; del. White House Conf. on Librs. and Info. Svcs., 1991; founder, treas., fiscal agt. METRO NET Libr. Consortium, 1993—; mem. edn. com. Child Abuse and Neglect Coun. of Oakland County, 1998-2000; mem. Commn. on Children, Youth and Families, 1996—, Multiracial Cmty. Coun., 1995—; chair Edn. and Tng. Com., 2000—. Recipient Athena award Farmington/Farmington Hills C. of C. and Gen. Motors, 1994, Chairperson's Rainbow award, 2001; Amarillo Pub. Libr. Friends Group fellow, 1972, Wayne State U. Inst. of Gerontology fellow, 1972. Mem. ALA (officer), Mich. Libr. Assn. (chair specialized libr. svcs. roundtable 1975, chair conf. program 1982, chair pub. policy com. 1988-89, chair devel. com. 1994-95, chair ann. conf. and program coms. 1995-96, pres. 1996-97, Loleta D. Fyan award 1975), LWV of Mich., Farmington Exch. Club, Coun. on Resource Devel. Democrat. Roman Catholic. Home: 6805 Wing Lake Rd Bloomfield Hills MI 48301-2959 Office: The Farmington Cmty Libr 32737 W 12 Mile Rd Farmington Hills MI 48334-3302 E-mail: papaibev@farmlib.org.

PAPAZIAN, DENNIS RICHARD, history educator, political commentator; b. Augusta, Ga., Dec. 15, 1931; s. Nahabed Charles and Armanouhe Marie (Pehlevanian) P.; m. Mary Arshagouni. BA, Wayne State U., 1954; MA, U. Mich., 1958; NDG, Moscow State U., 1962; PhD, U. Mich., 1966. Head dept. social and behavioral scis. U. Mich., Dearborn, 1966-69, head div. lit., sci. and the arts, 1969-73, assoc. dean acad. affairs, 1973-74; dir. Armenian Assembly Am., Washington, 1975-79; dir. grad. studies U. Mich., Dearborn, 1979-85, prof. history, dir. Armenian Rsch. Ctr., 1985—. Fellow Ctr. for Russian and East-European Studies, U. Mich., Ann Arbor, 1982-92; chmn. bd. dirs. Mich. Ethnic Heritage Studies Ctr., U. Mich., 1987-92. Author: St. John's Armenian Church, 1974; editor: The Armenian Church, 1983, Out of Turkey, 1994; editor Jour. of Soc. Armenian Studies, 1994—. Bd. dirs. Armenian Apostolic Soc., Southfield, Mich., 1968-78; chmn. bd. dirs. Alex Manoogian Found., Taylor, Mich., 1969-77; mem. evaluation team Ind. Schs. Assn. Ctrl. States, Chgo., 1985; polit. commentator WXYZ-TV, ABC, Detroit, Southfield, 1984—, WWJ-Radio, Detroit, 1984—; bd. dirs. Southeastern Mich. chpt. ARC, 1988-98, chmn. internat. svcs. com., 1988-98, disaster and mil. family svcs. com., 1988-98. Scholar/diplomat U.S. Dept. State, Washington, 1976; grantee NEH, Washington, 1977, AID, Washington, 1978. Mem. AAUP (chpt. pres. 1962-65), Nat. Assn. Armenian Studies and Rsch. (bd. dirs. 1961-91), Nat. Ethnic Studies Assn. (bd. dirs. 1976-85), Am. Hist. Assn., Soc. Armenian Studies (pres. exec. com. 1988-91, 97—, sec./treas. exec. com. 1991-97), Am. Assn. Advancement of Slavic Studies, Am. Acad. Polit. Sci., Armenian Students Assn. (Arthur S. Dadian Armenian Heritage award 1993), Knights of Vartan. Armenian Orthodox. Avocations: reading; travel. Home: 1935 Bluff Ct Troy MI 48098-6616 Office: U Mich 4901 Evergreen Rd Southfield MI 48075 E-mail: papazian@umich.edu.

PAPPAGEORGE, JOHN, state official; b. Detroit, July 19, 1931; married; 3 children. BS, U.S. Mil. Acad., 1954; MA, U. Md., 1971; postgrad., U.S. Army War Coll., 1972-73. Active Oakland County Bd. Commrs., 1989-93; Rep. candidate U.S. House, 1992, 96. With U.S. Army, 1954-84. Greek Orthodox.

PAPPANO, ROBERT DANIEL, financial company executive; b. Chgo., Apr. 8, 1942; s. John Robert and Lucille Carmelita (Metallo) P.; m. Karen Marie Muellner, July 2, 1966; children: John, Kimberly, Robert, William. BS in Commerce, DePaul U., Chgo., 1964; MBA, Roosevelt U., Chgo., 1982. CPA, Ill. Audit supr. Alexander Grant & Co., Chgo., 1964-73; with W.W. Grainger, Inc., Lake Forest, Ill., 1973—, asst. to contr., 1973-75, contr., corp. acct., 1975-78, contr., asst. treas., 1978-84, v.p., contr., asst. treas., 1984-85, v.p., treas., asst sec., 1985-95; v.p. financial reporting and investor rels., 1995-99; v.p. fin. reporting W.W. Grainger, Inc., Lake Forest, 1999—. 1st lt. U.S. Army, 1965-67. Mem. AICPA, Ill. CPA Soc., Fin. Execs. Inst. Roman Catholic. Office: W W Grainger Inc 100 Grainger Pkwy Lake Forest IL 60045-5201

PAPPAS, EDWARD HARVEY, lawyer; b. Midland, Mich., Nov. 24, 1947; s. Charles and Sydell (Sheinberg) P.; m. Laurie Weston, Aug. 6, 1972; children: Gregory Alan, Steven Michael. BBA, U. Mich., 1969, JD, 1973. Bar: Mich. 1973, U.S. Dist. Ct. (ea. dist.) Mich. 1973, U.S. Dist. Ct. (we. dist.) Mich. 1980, U.S. Ct. Appeals (6th cir.) 1983, U.S. Supreme Ct. 1983. Ptnr. firm Dickinson & Wright, P.L.L.C., Detroit and Bloomfield Hi, Mich., 1973—. Mediator Oakland County Cir. Ct., Pontiac, Mich., 1983—; hearing panelist Mich. Atty. Discipline Bd., Detroit, 1983—, chmn., 1987—; mem. bus. tort subcom. Mich. Supreme Ct. Com. Standard Jury Instructions, 1992-94; bd. commrs. State Bar Mich., 1999—. Trustee Oakland Community Coll., Mich., 1982-90, Oakland-Livingston Legal Aid, 1982-90, v.p., 1982-85, pres., 1985-87; trustee, adv. bd. Mich. Regional Anti-Defamation League of B'nai B'rith, Detroit, 1983-90; planning commr. Village of Franklin, Mich., 1987-91, chmn. 1989-91, councilman, 1991-92, chmn. charter com., 1993-94; chmn. State Bar Mich. Long Range Planning com.; pres.-elect Oakland County Bar Assn., 1996-97, pres., 1997-98, chmn. Jud. Selection Task Force, 1997; bd. dirs. Franklin Found., 1989-92; trustee The Oakland Medication Ctr., 1992-96. Master Oakland County Bar Assn. Inn of Ct.; fellow Mich. State Bar Found., Oakland Bar-Adams Pratt Found., ABA Found.; mem. ABA, Fed. Bar Assn., State Bar Mich. (co-chmn. nat. moot ct. competition com. 1974, 76, com. on legal aid, chmn. standing com. on atty. grievances 1989-92, comml. litigation com., civil procedure com. 1992-94, bd. commrs. 1999—), Oakland County Bar Assn. (vice-chmn. continuing legal edn. com., chmn. continuing legal edn. com. 1985-86, mediation com. 1989-90, chmn. mediation com. 1990-91, bd. dirs. 1990-98, chmn. select com. Oakland County cir. ct. settlement week 1991, chmn. strategic planning com. 1992-93, editor Laches monthly mag. 1986-88, co-chair task force to improve justice systems in Oakland County 1993—, pres.-elect, bd. dirs. 1996-97, pres. 1997-98), Am. Judicature Soc., Mich. Def. Trial Lawyers, Def. Rsch. and Trial Lawyers Assn. (com. practice and procedure), B'nai B'rith Barristers. Home: 32223 Scenic Ln Franklin MI 48025-1702 Office: Dickinson Wright Moon Van Dusen & Freeman 525 N Woodward Ave Bloomfield Hills MI 48304-2971

PAPPAS, GEORGE DEMETRIOS, anatomy and cell biology educator, scientist; b. Portland, Maine, Nov. 26, 1926; James and Anna (Dracopoulos) Pappatheodoros; m. Bernice Levine, Jan. 14, 1952; children: Zoe Alexandra, Clio Nicollette. BA, Bowdoin Coll., 1947; MS, Ohio State U., 1948, PhD, 1952; DSc (hon.), U. Athens, Greece, 1988. Vis. investigator Rockefeller Inst., N.Y.C., 1952-54; assoc. in anatomy Coll. Physicians and Surgeons, Columbia U., 1956-57, asst. prof. anatomy, 1957-63, assoc. prof., 1963-66; prof. anatomy Albert Einstein Coll. Medicine, Yeshiva U., 1967-77, prof. neurosci., 1974-77, vis. prof. neurosci., 1977-97; prof., head dept. anatomy and cell biology U. Ill. Coll. Medicine, Chgo., 1977-96, prof. cell biology and psychiatry, 1996—. Trustee Marine Biol. Lab., Woods Hole, Mass., 1975-81 Author: (with others) The Structure of the Eye, 1961, Growth and Maturation of the Brain, vol. IV, 1964, Nerve as a Tissue, 1966, The Thalmus, 1966, Pathology of the Nervous System, vol. 1, 1968, Structure and Function of Synapses, 1972, Methodological Approaches to the Study of Brain Maturation and Its Abnormalities, 1974, Advances in Neurology, vol.12, 1975, The Nervous System, vol. 1 The Basic Neurosciences, 1975, Cellular and Molecular Basis of Synaptic Transmission, 1988, also author many conf. procs.; contbr. over 200 articles to profl. jours.; former mem. editorial bd. Anatomical Record, Biol. Bull., Brain Rsch., Jour. Neurocytology, Microstructure, Neurol. Rsch.; patentee method inducing analgesia by implantation of cells releasing neuroactive substances. Arthritis and Rheumatism Found. fellow, 1954-56; recipient career devel. award Columbia U., 1964-66; rsch. grantee NIH Fellow AAAS, N.Y. Acad. Scis., Inst. Medicine Chgo.; mem. Am. Soc. Cell Biology (pres. 1974-75), Am. Assn. Anatomists (chmn. pub. policy com. 1981-82), Assn. Anatomy Chmn. (exec. com. 1978-80, pres. 1981-82), Electron Microscopy Soc. Am. (program chmn. 1984-85), N.Y. Soc. Electron Microscopy (pres. 1967-68), Soc. for Neurosci. (pres. Chgo. chpt. 1985-86), Harvey Soc., Internat. Brain Rsch. Orgn., Cajal Club, Sigma Xi. Home: Apt 512 S 680 N Lake Shore Dr Chicago IL 60611 Office: U Ill Psychiat Inst MC 912 1601 W Taylor St Chicago IL 60612-4310 E-mail: gdpappas@uic.edu.

PAPPAS, SANDRA LEE, state legislator; b. Saint Paul, Minn., June 15, 1949; m. Neal Gosman, 1986; 3 children. BA, Met. State U., 1986; MPA, Harvard U., 1994. Mem. Minn. Ho. of Reps., St. Paul, 1984-90, Minn. Senate, St. Paul, 1990—. Part-time coll. instr. Mem. Dem. Farmer Labor Party. Home: 182 Prospect Blvd Saint Paul MN 55107-2136 Office: Minn State Senate 120 State Capitol 75 Constitution Ave Saint Paul MN 55155-1601

PAQUETTE, JACK KENNETH, management consultant, antiques dealer; b. Toledo, Aug. 14, 1925; s. Hector J. and Nellie (McCormick) P.; m. Jane Russell, Sept. 13, 1947; children: Jan Eriksen, Mark Russell, Mary Beth, John Eric. Student, Baldwin-Wallace Coll., 1943-44, Marquette U., 1944; BA, Ohio State U., 1949, MA, 1951; postgrad., Wayne State U., 1966. Editor monthly pub. Bur. Motor Vehicles, State of Ohio, 1947-49; asst. city editor, copy editor Ohio State Jour., 1949-51; copywriter Owens-Ill., Inc., Toledo, 1951-53, copy chief mktg. dept., 1953-55, asst. advt. mgr. mktg. dept., 1955-59; advt. mgr. Owens-Ill., Inc. (Libbey div.), 1959-61; mgr. advt. and sales promotion Owens-Ill., Inc. (Libbey products), 1961-64, mgr. customer mktg. services glass container div., 1964-67, dir. corporate orgn. planning, 1967-69, v.p. adminstrv. div., dir. corp. relations, 1969-70, corporate v.p., dir. corp. relations, 1970-80, corp. v.p., asst. to chmn. bd., 1980-84, cons., 1984-86; pres. Paquette Enterprises, 1984—; owner The Trumpeting Angel, antiques, 1985—. Mem. adv. bd. Cresset Chem. Co., 1987—. Author: A History of Owens-Illinois Inc., (1818-1984), 1985, The Glassmakers, Blowpipes, 2002. Bd. dirs. Toledo YMCA, 1970-74, Vis. Nurse Svc., 1970-73, Children's Svcs., 1973-80, Toledo coun. Boy Scouts Am., trustee, v.p. fin., 1978-84; trustee Owens Tech. Coll. Found, 1978-81; mem. Advt. Club Toledo, 1951-75, trustee, 1960-62; hon. bd. dirs. Greater Toledo area chpt. ARC, 1970—; mem. adv. bd. Mercy Hosp., Toledo, 1981-84, Mary's Adult Day Care Ctr., 1989-93, St. Anthony's Children's Ctr., 1993, Mid-Coast Hosp., Brunswick, Maine, 1998—; mem. pub. rels. com. Cath. U. Am., 1979-82; chmn. U.S. Savs. Bonds, Lucas County, 1977-79; trustee Bowling Green State U. Found., 1976-83, pres., 1980-82; mem. Nat. Commn. on a Free and Responsible Press, 1980-83; v.p. trustee, Toledo Repertoire Theatre, 1984-88; trustee Crosby Gardens, 1983-89, chmn. 1987-88; trustee Toledo Bot. Gardens, 1989-90, chmn. emeritus and hon. lifetime trustee, 1990—; mem. pres.'s coun. Toledo Mus. Art, Bowling Green State U.; trustee Riverside Hosp. Found., 1984-94, chmn. 1986-89; mem. Juvenile Justice Adv. Bd., 1986-87; advisor R.B. Hayes Presdl. Ctr., 1990-92. With USNR, 1943-46, PTO. Recipient Gold Key award Pub. Rel. News, 1970, Silver Anvil award Pub. Rel. Soc., 1971, 72; named to Toledo Clean Hall of Fame, 1983. Mem. Soc. Profl. Journalists (co-founder Columbus and Toledo chpts.), Ohio Mfrs. Assn. (v.p., trustee 1969-84), Keep Am. Beautiful, Inc. (nat. chmn., exec. com., 1978-84, chmn. emeritus, mem. nat. adv. coun. 1984—), Bus. Com. for the Arts (corp. liason 1980-84), U.S. C. of C. (cons. affairs com. 1980-84), Western Great Lakes Hist. Soc. (life, trustee 1998—), Lucas County/Maumee Valley Hist. Soc., Maine Maritime Mus., Toy Soldier Collectors of Am. Soc., Glass Club Toledo, USN Armed Guard Assn., Sampson WWII Navy Vets. Assn., OSU Alumni Assn. (life), Am. Legion (Toledo post), Pi Sigma Alpha. Clubs: Toledo Press (founding trustee), Toledo, Torch, Rotary (Paul Harris fellow). Home and Office: 2355 Parliament Sq Toledo OH 43617-1256

PARAGAS, ROLANDO G. physician; b. Philippines, Apr. 15, 1935; came to U.S., 1959; s. Epifanio Y. and Ester (Guiang) P.; m. Liwayway Galvey, May 5, 1963; children: Suzanne, Richard, Esther, Dawn. AA, U. Philippines, 1953; MD, Far Eastern U., 1958. Physician pvt. practice, Burlington, Iowa, 1968—. Fellow Am. Acad. Pediatrics; mem. AMA, Assn. Philippine Physicians in Am., Iowa Med. Soc. Office: 828 N 7th St Burlington IA 52601-4921

PARDUE, BILL, publishing executive; CEO U.S. Corp. and Fed. Markets divsn. Lexis-Nexis, Miamisburg, Ohio, 2000—. Office: Lexis-Nexis 9393 Springboro Pike Miamisburg OH 45342-4424

PARDUE, HARRY L. chemist, educator; b. Big Creek, W.Va., May 3, 1934; m. Mary Schultz; 1 child, Jonathan. BS, Marshall U., 1956, MS, 1957; PhD in Chemistry, U. Ill., 1961. From asst. to assoc. prof. Purdue U., West Lafayette, Ind., 1961-70, prof. chemistry, 1970—, head dept. chemistry, 1983-87. Recipient Am. Chem Soc. award in Analytical Chemistry, 1995. Mem. Am. Chem. Soc. (Chem. Instrumentation award Analytical Chem. divsn. 1982, Analytical Chemistry award 1995), Am. Assn. Clin. Chemists (award 1979, Samuel Natelson award 1982, Anachem award 1990). Achievements include research in instrumentation for chemical research, chemical kinetics. Office: Purdue U Dept Chem 1393 Brown Bldg Lafayette IN 47907-1393

PARETSKY, SARA N. writer; b. Ames, Iowa, June 8, 1947; d. David Paretsky and Mary E. Edwards; m. S. Courtenay Wright, June 19, 1976; children: Kimball Courtenay, Timothy Charles, Philip William. BA, U. Kans., 1967; MBA, PhD, U. Chgo., 1977. Mgr. Urban Rsch Ctr., Chgo., 1971-74, CNA Ins. Co., Chgo., 1977-85; writer, 1985—. Author: (novels) Indemnity Only, 1982, Deadlock, 1984 (Friends of Am. Writers award 1985), Killing Orders, 1985, Bitter Medicine, 1987, Blood Shot, 1988 (Silver Dagger award Crime Writers Assn., 1988), Burn Marks, 1990, Guardian Angel, 1992, Tunnel Vision, 1994, Hard Time: A V.I. Warshawski Novel, 1999, also numerous articles and short stories. Pres. Sisters in Crime, Chgo., 1986-88; dir. Nat. Abortion Rights Action League Ill., 1987—; mentor Chgo. inner-city schs. Named Woman of Yr. Ms mag., N.Y.C., 1987; recipient Mark Twain award for disting. contbns. to mid-western lit., 1996. Mem. Crime Writers Assn. (Silver Dagger award 1988), Mystery Writers Am. (v.p. 1989), Authors Guild, Chgo. Network Achievements include being the founder of two scholarships at U. Kans. Avocations: baseball, opera. Address: Sally McCartin Assoc PO Box 432 Millerton NY 12546-0432

PARHAM, ELLEN SPEIDEN, nutrition educator; b. Mitchells, Va., July 15, 1938; d. Marion Coote and Rebecca Virginia (McNiel) Speiden; m. Arthur Robert Parham, Jr., Dec. 16, 1961; children: Katharine Alma, Cordelia Alyx. BS in Nutrition, Va. Poly. Inst., 1960; PhD in Nutrition, U. Tenn., 1967; MSEd in Counseling, No. Ill. U., 1994. Registered dietitian; lic. clin. profl. counselor. Asst. prof. to prof. nutrition No. Ill. U., DeKalb, Ill., 1966—, coord. programs in dietetics, 1981-86, 90—, coord. grad. faculty sch. family, consumer, nutrition scis., 1985-87. Cons. on nutrition various hosps., clins. and bus., Ill., 1980—; founder, dir. Horizons Weight Control Program, DeKalb, 1983-91; founder, leader "Escaping the Tyranny of the Scale" Group, 1994—; co-chair Nutrition Coalition for Ill., 1989-90; ptnr., mgr. Design on Fabric, 1986—; adj. counselor Ctr. for Counsel, Family Svc. Agy. of DeKalb County. Bd. editors Jour. Nutrition Edn., 1985-90, 97—, Jour. Am. Dietetic Assn., 1991-97; contbr. articles to profl. jours. Recipient Fisher award excellence in svc., 2001. Mem. Am. Inst. Nutrition, Soc. Nutrition Edn., Am. Dietetic Assn (named Ill. Outstanding Dietetics Educator 2001, Excellence in Dietetics Edn. award 2001), Soc. Nutrition Edn. (treas. 1991-94, chair divsn. nutrition and weight realities 1995-96, Weight Realities Cert. of Achievement 1999), N.Am. Assn. Study Obesity. Avocations: painting in watercolor, gardening, reading.

PARINS, ROBERT JAMES, professional football team executive, judge; b. Green Bay, Wis., Aug. 23, 1918; s. Frank and Nettie (Denissen) P.; m. Elizabeth L. Carroll, Feb. 8, 1941; children: Claire, Andrée, Richard, Teresa, Lu Ann. B.A., U. Wis., 1940, LL.B., 1942. Bar: Wis. Supreme Ct. 1942. Pvt. practice, Green Bay, Wis., 1942-68; dist. atty. Brown County, 1949-50, cir. judge, 1968-82, res. judge, 1982—; pres. Green Bay Packers, Inc., 1982-90, chmn. bd., 1990-92; hon. chmn. bd., 1992-94. Mem.: Wis. State Bar Assn. Roman Catholic.

PARISEAU, PATRICIA, state legislator; b. St. Paul, Aug. 10, 1936; d. James Martin and Mary Margaret (May) Wright; m. Kenneth Edward Pariseau, July 9, 1960; children: Susan M., Douglas C., Penny A., Linda D., Barbara J., Jacqueline. RN, Ravenswood Hosp. Sch. Nursing, Chgo., 1957. Staff nurse Ravenswood Hosp., Chgo., 1957-58, St. Joseph's Hosp., St. Paul., 1958-59, Office of Drs. Roy & Hilker, St. Paul., 1959-60; aide to U.S. Senator Rudy Boschwitz, 1982-88; mem. Minn. Senate from 37th dist., 1989—. Mem. adv. bd. St. Paul chpt. ARC, 1986-88; vol., officer Minn. Ind. Rep. Com., 1972-83; bd. dirs. Ind. Sch. Dist. 192, Farmington, Minn., 1976-79. Mem. Minn. Waterfowl Assn., Farmington C. of C., Dakota Arts Coun., Ducks Unltd., Eagles Aux., Am. Legion Aux. (sec. Farmington chpt.), VFW Aux., So. Dakota County Sportsmen Club. Avocations: needlework, knitting, drawing, painting, traveling. Office: Minn Senate 109 State Ofc Bldg 100 Constitution Ave Saint Paul MN 55155-1232

PARISI, JOSEPH (ANTHONY), magazine editor, writer-consultant, educator; b. Duluth, Minn., Nov. 18, 1944; s. Joseph Carl Parisi and Phyllis Susan (Quaranta) Schlecht B.A. with honors, Coll. St. Thomas, 1966; M.A., U. Chgo., 1967, Ph.D. with honors, 1973. Asst. prof. Roosevelt U., Chgo., 1969-78; assoc. editor POETRY Mag., 1976-83, acting editor, 1983-85, editor, 1985—. Vis. prof. U. Ill., Chgo., 1978-87; cons., writer ALA, Chgo., 1980—; cons. NEH, 1983—. Author: The Poetry Anthology, 1912-1977, 1978, Voices and Visions Reader's Guide, 1987, Marianne Moore: The Art of a Modernist, 1990, (listener's guide) Poets in Person, 1992, 97, A History of Poetry in Letters, 2002, The Poetry Anthology, 1912-2002, 2002; contbr. articles and reviews to profl. jours.; producer, dir. (audio series on NPR) Poets in Person, 1991. Recipient Alvin Bentley award, Duns Scotus Coll., 1963; fellow, U. Chgo., 1966—69, Guggenheim, 2000, Churchill Coll., Cambridge. Mem. Arts Club of Chgo., Cliff Dwellers Club, Delta Epsilon Sigma Avocations: piano, photography, book and record collecting. Office: Poetry Mag 60 W Walton St Chicago IL 60610-7324

PARIZEK, ELDON JOSEPH, geologist, educator, dean; b. Iowa City, Apr. 30, 1920; s. William Joseph and Libbie S. P.; m. Mildred Marie Burger, Aug. 9, 1944; children— Richard, Marianne, Elizabeth, Amy. B.S., U. Iowa, 1942, M.S., 1946, Ph.D., 1949. Instr. U. Iowa, 1947-49; asst. prof. geology U. Ga., 1949-54, asso. prof., 1954-56, U. Kansas City, 1956-63; prof. U. Mo., Kansas City, 1963—, chmn. dept. geoscis., 1968-78; dean U. Mo. (Coll. Arts and Scis.), 1979-86. Served with USN, 1942-45. Fellow Geol. Soc. Am.; mem. AAUP, Assn. Mo. Geologists, AAAS, Sigma Xi.

Roman Catholic. Achievements include research, numerous publs. on mass wasting, slope failure, underground space, geology of West Mo. Home: 6913 W 100th Shawnee Mission KS 66212 Office: 5100 Rockhill Rd Kansas City MO 64110-2481

PARK, JOHN THORNTON, academic administrator; b. Phillipsburg, N.J., Jan. 3, 1935; s. Dawson J. and Margaret M. (Thornton) P.; m. Dorcas M Marshall; June 1, 1956; children: Janet Ernst, Karen Daily. BA in Physics with distinction, Nebr. Wesleyan U., 1956; PhD, U. Nebr., 1963. NSF postdoctoral fellow Univ. Coll., London, 1963-64; asst. prof. physics U. Mo., Rolla, 1964-68, assoc. prof. physics, 1968-71, prof., 1971-2000, prof. emeritus, 2000—, chmn. dept. physics, 1977-83, vice chancellor acad. affairs, 1983-85, 86-91, interim chancellor, 1985-86, 91-92, chancellor, 1992-2000, chancellor emeritus, 2000—. Vis. assoc. prof. NYU, 1970-71; pres. Talema Electronics, Inc., St. James, Mo., 1983-99, Tortran Corp., 1990—; prin. investigator NSF Rsch. Grants, 1966-92; bd. dirs. Mo. Tech. Corp., Jefferson City, Mo., 1994—, Mo. Enterprise, 1990—, Phelps County Bank, 1997—. Contbr. articles to profl. jours. Recipient Most Disting. Scientist award Mo. Acad. Sci., 1994. Fellow Am. Phys. Soc. (mem. divsn. elec. and atomic physics); mem. Am. Assn. Physics Tchrs., Rotary. Methodist.

PARKE, TERRY RICHARD, state legislator; b. Pittsfield, Ill., Feb. 21, 1944; m. Joanne Toombs; 2 children. BS, 1970. Ins. agt.; mem. Ill. Ho. of Reps. from 53d dist., 1985—. Rep. spokesman ins. com.; vice spokesman labor com.; mem. computer tech., conservation & land use, consumer protection, environment & energy coms.; co-chmn. Ill. Econ. & Fiscal Commn.; mem. Employee Suggestion Award bd.; past pres. Elgin Area Life Underwriters. Chmn. Bus. and Labor Am. Legis. Exch. Coun. Workers Compensation and Nat. Coun. of Ins. Legis., also pres.; past pres. N.W. Suburban Assn. Commerce and Industry; bd. dirs., Boy Scouts Northwest Suburban Coun., Girl Scouts Crossroads Coun. Mem. Rotary (past pres. Schaumburg club). Republican. Home: 1572 Rosedale Ln Hoffman Estates IL 60195-2653 Office: Ill Ho of Reps State Capitol Springfield IL 62706-0001

PARKER, ALAN JOHN, veterinary neurologist, educator, researcher; b. Portsmouth, Eng., Oct. 28, 1944; arrived in U.S., 1969, naturalized, 2002; s. William Barton and Emily (Begley) P.; m. Heather Margaret Nicholson, Oct. 30, 1971; children: Alyxander John, Robert William. B.Sc. with honors, Bristol U., 1966, B.V.Sc. with honors, 1968; M.S., U. Ill., 1973, Ph.D., 1976. Diplomate Am. Coll. Vet. Internal Medicine-Neurology, European Coll. Vet. Neurology. Intern Vet. Coll., U. Calif.-Davis, 1969-70; instr. vet. clin. medicine U. Ill., Urbana, 1970-71, 72-76, asst. prof., 1976-77, assoc. prof., 1977-82, prof., 1982-2000, prof. emeritus, 2001—. Cons. pharm. cos., seminar presenter; cons. in neurology Berwyn Vet. Hosp., Chgo., 1973— , Lake Shore Animal Hosp., Chgo., 1978— Contbr. numerous articles to sci. jours., chpts. to books. Active Boy Scouts Am., Champaign, Ill., 1982—; active Presbyn. Ch., Monticello, Ill., 1979—. Recipient Vigil Honor and Founder's award Order of the Arrow, Silver Beaver award Boy Scouts Am.; sci. grantee various orgns., 1972-2000. Mem. AVMA, Am. Animal Hosp. Assn., Brit. Vet. Assn., Ill. State Vet. Assn. Republican. Office: 2845 S Harlem Ave Berwyn IL 60402 E-mail: a-parker@staff.uiuc.edu.

PARKER, CHARLES WALTER, JR. consultant, retired equipment company executive; b. nr. Ahoskie, N.C., Nov. 22, 1922; s. Charles Walter and Minnie Louise (Williamson) P.; m. Sophie Nash Riddick, Nov. 26, 1949; children: Mary Parker Hutto, Caroline Parker Robertson, Charles Walter III, Thomas Williamson. B.S. in Elec. Engring, Va. Mil. Inst., 1947; Dr. Engring. (hon.), Milw. Sch. Engring., 1980. With Allis-Chalmers Corp., 1947-87, dist. mgr. Va., 1955-57, Phila., 1957-58, dir. sales promotion industries group Milw., 1958-61, gen. mktg. mgr. new products, 1961-62, mgr. mktg. services, 1962-66, v.p. mktg. and public relations services, 1966-70, v.p., dep. group exec., 1970-72, staff group exec. communications and public affairs, 1972-87, ret., 1987; prin. Charles Parker & Assocs., Ltd., Milw., 1987—. Founding mem. World Mktg. Contact Group, London; bd. dirs. Internat. Gen. Ins. Corp., Dinermite Corp. Gen. chmn. United Fund Greater Milw. Area, 1975; trustee Boy Scouts Am. Trust Fund, Milw.; bd. dirs., pres. Jr. Achievement; pres. bd. trustees Univ. Sch. Milw., 1978-80; trustee Carroll Coll., Waukesha, Wis.; bd. dirs. Milw. Children's Hosp.; bd. regents Milw. Sch. Engring.; mem. Greater Milw. Com.; chmn. bd. dirs. Milw. Found., 1987-89. Served to capt. AUS, 1943-46, ETO. Decorated Bronze Star. Mem. NAM (dir.), Wis. C. of C. (pres. 1974-76), Sales and Mktg. Execs. Internat. (pres., CEO 1974, 75, Eduardo Rihan Internat. Mktg. Exec. of Yr. award 1979), Wis. Mfrs. and Commerce Assn. (exec. com.), Pi Sigma Epsilon (pres. 1976-77, trustee and chmn. nat. edn. found. 1979-86), Kappa Alpha. Home: 4973 N Newhall St Milwaukee WI 53217-6049 Office: PO Box 92398 828 N Broadway Milwaukee WI 53202-3611

PARKER, GARY DEAN, manufacturing company executive; b. Omaha, Mar. 27, 1945; s. Norman and Dolores (Pierce) P.; m. Joanne Baker, Aug. 27, 1966; children: Jason E., Rodney R. B.S. in B.A., B.S. in Econs., Nebr. Wesleyan U. Dir. sales Lindsay Mfg. Co., Nebr., 1971-73, v.p. sales-mktg., 1973-76, sr. v.p., 1976-78, exec. v.p., 1978-83, pres., 1983—, dir., 1977—. Pres. Irrigation Assocs., Silver Springs, Md., 1981-82, dir., 1978-83; dir. Irrigation Found. & Research, Silver Springs, 1978— Mem. Nebr. Mfg. Assn. (pres. 1982-83), Delta Omicron Epsilon Lodge: Elks. Office: Lindsay Mfg Co PO Box 156 Lindsay NE 68644-0156

PARKER, GEORGE EDWARD, III, lawyer; b. Detroit, Sept. 26, 1934; s. George Edward and Lucia Helen (Muir) P.; m. Margaret G. Koehler; children— George, David, Benjamin AB, Princeton U., 1956; JD, U. Mich., 1959. Bar: Mich. 1959, D.C. 1981, Fla. 1982. Assoc. Miller, Canfield, Paddock & Stone, Detroit, 1959-68, ptnr., 1968-96, of counsel, 1996—; gen. counsel, sec. Republic Bancorp Inc., Ann Arbor, Mich. Bd. dirs. Univ. Liggett Sch.; trustee David Whitney Fund, Grayling Fund. Republican. Office: Miller Canfield Paddock et al 150 W Jefferson Ave Ste 2500 Detroit MI 48226-4416 E-mail: gparkerrbi@earthlink.net.

PARKER, KATHLEEN KAPPEL, state legislator; b. Pitts., Sept. 21, 1943; m. Keith Parker; 2 children. BA, U. Miami, 1968. Tax assessor Northfield Twp., 1979-83; mem. Regional Transp. Authority Bd., 1983-95; del. Ill. and Nat. Rep. Convs., 1988; Northfield Twp. coord. George Bush's Presdl. Campaign, 1988; mem. U.S. Archtl. and Transp. Barriers Compliance Bd., 1991-94; Ill. state sen., 1995—. Mem. Fin. Inst., vice chair Pub. Health and Welfare Coms., Transp. Com., 1995—, chair; co-owner Keith Parker and Assocs., 1985—; pres., bd. dirs. Chgo. divsn. Busch Jewelry Co., 1988-93. Chair Mental Health Task Force. Mem. Northeastern Ill. Planning Coun., Met. Planning Coun. Office: 191 Waukegan Rd Northfield IL 60093-2756

PARKER, LEE FISCHER, sales executive; b. Chgo., Nov. 28, 1932; d. Meyer Louis and Lena (Raphael) Fischer; m. Joseph Schwartz, Mar. 18, 1950 (div. Jan. 1986); 1 child, Steven Darryl; m. Robert K. Parker, Jan. 13, 1991. Student, Mallinkroudt Coll., Wilmette, Ill., 1976. Freelance fashion model, Chgo., 1958-78; sales assoc. Neiman-Marcus, Northbrook, Ill., 1978-79; owner Keystone Svcs., Woodale, 1969-82; sales assoc. Marshall Field's, Skokie, 1986-94, Jacobson's, Boca Raton, Fla., 1996-99. Fashion coord. Arnie's Restaurant, Chgo., 1964-68, Blackhawk Restaurant, Chgo., 1964-66, Jim Conway TV Show, Chgo., 1968-70. Appeared in movie, 2000. Mem. Brandeis Women's Aux., Holocaust Mus. Democrat. Jewish. Avocations: golf, dancing, reading.

PARKER, LEONARD S. architect, educator; b. Warsaw, Poland, Jan. 16, 1923; came to U.S. 1923; s. Rueben and Sarah (Kollica) Popuch; m. Betty Mae Buegen, Sept. 1, 1948 (dec. 1983); children— Bruce Aaron, Jonathan Arthur, Nancy Anne, Andrew David BArch., U. Minn., 1948; MArch., MIT, 1950. Sr. designer Eero Saarinen Assocs., Bloomfield Hills, Mich., 1950-56; CEO, chmn. bd., pres., dir. design The Leonard Parker Assocs., Mpls., 1957-97; pres., dir. design The Alliance Southwest, Phoenix, 1981-91; chmn. bd. dirs. The Leonard Parker Assn., Minn., 1997—. Prof. grad. program Sch. Architecture, U. Minn., Mpls., 1959—; pres. Minn. Archtl. Found., 1991. Author: Abandoning the Catalogs, 1979, Rivers of Modernism, 1986, Collaboration-Same Bed, Different Dream? Panel mem. Mpls. City Hall Restoration Com., Am. Arbitration Assn., USAF bd. visitors (chmn.). Served with U.S. Army, 1943-46; ETO Firm has received 84 nat. and regional awards for design excellence. Fellow AIA; mem. Minn. Soc. Architects (pres. 1981, Gold medal 1986, pres. Mpls. chpt. 1979), Tau Sigma Delta. Home: 3936 Willmatt Hl Hopkins MN 55305-5142 Office: The Leonard Parker Assocs 430 Oak Grove St Ste 300 Minneapolis MN 55403-3234

PARKER, LINDA BATES, professional development organization administrator; Grad., U. Dayton, U. Cin., Harvard U., 1991. Pres., founder Black Career Women, Cin. Dir. Career Devel. Ctr., mgmt. prof. U. Cin. Author: Career Portfolio; columnist for Nat. Black Collegian Mag.; presenter in field. Office: Black Career Women PO Box 19332 Cincinnati OH 45219-0332

PARKER, MICHAEL D. chemicals executive; BSChemE, U. Manchester (Eng.); MBA, Manchester Bus. Sch. With organics R & D Dow Internat., Freeport, Tex., 1968, prodn. engr., field sales position Birmingham, Eng., 1972-75, dist. sales mgr., 1975-77; product mktg. mgr. Epoxy resins Dow Europe, 1977, dir. mktg. inorganic chems., dir. mktg. organic chems., comml. dir. functional products dept., 1983-84; gen. mgr. splty. chems. dept. Dow U.S.A., Midland, Mich., 1984-87, group v.p. chems. and hydrocarbons, 1993-95; comml. v.p. Dow Pacific, Hong Kong, 1987-88, pres., 1988-93; pres., bus. v.p. chems. Dow N.Am., Midland, 1995—; exec. v.p. Dow Chem. Co., 1996—; also bd. dirs.; CEO Dow Chemical, Midland, Michigan, 2000. Bd. dirs. Dow Corning Corp. Bd. dirs. Nat. Legal Ctr. Pub. Interest. Mem. Nat. Assn. Mfrs. (bd. dirs.), Am. Plastics Coun. (bd. dirs.), Am. Chemistry Coun. Office: The Dow Chem Co 2030 Dow Ctr Midland MI 48674

PARKER, PATRICK STREETER, manufacturing executive; b. Cleve., 1929; BA, Williams Coll., 1951; MBA, Harvard U., 1953. With Parker-Hannifin Corp. and predecessor, Cleve., 1953— sales mgr. fittings div., 1957-63, mgr. aerospace products div., 1963-65, pres. Parker Seal Co. div., 1965-67, corp. v.p., 1967-69, pres., 1969-71, pres. and chief exec. officer, 1971-77, chmn. bd. and chief exec. officer, 1977-84, chmn. bd., 1984-99, pres., 1982-84, also bd. dirs., 1982-99, chmn. emeritus, 1999—. Bd. trustees Case Western Res. U.; With USN, 1954-57. Mem. Union Club, Country Club, Pepper Pike Club. Office: Parker Hannifin Corp 6035 Parkland Bvld Cleveland OH 44124-4141

PARKER, R. JOSEPH, lawyer; b. St. Louis, June 29, 1944; s. George Joseph and Ann Rosalie Parker; m. Theresa Gaynor, Aug. 26, 1967; children: Christa Michele, Kevin Blake. AB, Georgetown U., 1966; JD, Boston Coll., 1969. Bar: Ohio 1969. Law clk. to judge U.S. Ct. Appeals (6th Cir.), Akron, Ohio, 1969-70; assoc. Taft, Stettinius & Hollister, Cin., 1970-78, ptnr. 1978—. Arbitrator Am. Arbitration Assn., Cin., 1980—; faculty Nat. Inst. for Trial Advocacy, 1990—; faculty advanced trial advocacy program IRS, 1993. Editor Law Rev. Ann. Survey Mass. Law, 1967-69; contbg. author: Fed. Civil Procedure Before Trial-6th Circuit. Bd. dirs. West End Health Ctr., Inc., Cin., 1972-76, Legal Aid Soc. Cin., 1982-85; chmn. bd. dirs. Vol. Lawyers for Poor Found., Cin., 1986-88; master Am. Inn of Court, 1984—. Fellow Am. Coll. Trial Lawyers; mem. Ohio State Bar Assn., Cin. Bar Assn., Cin. Country Club, Order of Coif. Democrat. Roman Catholic. Office: 1800 Star Bank Bldg 425 Walnut St Cincinnati OH 45202-3923

PARKER, ROBERT FREDERIC, university dean emeritus; b. St. Louis, Oct. 29, 1907; s. Charles T. and Lydia (Gronemeyer) P.; m. Mary L. Warner, June 20, 1934; children: David Frederic, Jane Eleanor (Mrs. Howard H. Hush, Jr.). B.S., Washington U., St. Louis, 1925, M.D., 1929. Diplomate: Am. Bd. Microbiology. Asst. radiology Washington U. Med. Sch., 1929-30, instr. medicine, 1932-33; asst. Rockefeller Inst., 1933-36; mem. faculty Case Western Res. U., 1936—, prof. microbiology, 1954-77, prof. emeritus, 1977—, assoc. dean, 1965-73, dean, 1973-76, dean emeritus, 1976—. Mem. Cleve. Acad. Medicine (past bd. dirs.), Am. Soc. Clin. Investigation, Central Soc. Clin. Research, Am. Acad. Microbiology, Sigma Xi, Alpha Omega Alpha. Achievements include spl. research virus immunology, quantitative aspects virus infection, tissue culture, action of antibiotics. Home: 1890 E 107th St Apt 226 Cleveland OH 44106-2242

PARKER, SARA ANN, librarian, consultant; b. Cassville, Mo., Feb. 19, 1939; d. Howard Franklin and Vera Irene (Thomas) P. B.A., Okla. State U., 1961; M.L.S., Emporia State U., Kans., 1968. Adult svcs. librarian Springfield Pub. Libr., Mo., 1972-75, bookmobile dir., 1975-76; coord. S.W. Mo. Libr. Network, Springfield, 1976-78; libr. developer Colo. State Libr., Denver, 1978-82; state librarian Mont. State Libr., Helena, 1982-88, State Libr. Pa., Harrisburg, 1988-90; Pa. commr. librs., dep. sec. edn. State of Pa., 1990-95; state libr. State of Mo., Jefferson City, 1995—. Cons. and lectr. in field. Author, editor, compiler in field; contbr. articles to profl. jours. Sec., Western Coun. State Librs., Reno, 1984-88, mem. Mont. State Data Adv. Coun., 1983-88, Mont. Telecommunications Coun., 1985-88, WLN Network Coun., 1984-87, Kellogg ICLIS Project Mgmt. Bd., 1986-88; mem. adv. com. Gates Libr. Initiative, 1998—; mem. OCLC Strategic Directions and Governance Study Adv. Coun., 2000-01. Recipient Pres.'s award, Nature Conservancy, 1989, Friends award, Pa. Assn. Ednl. Comms. and Techs., 1989, Friend of Sch. Librs. award, Mo. Sch. Librs. Assn., 2000, Bohley Libr. Cooperation award, 2001; fellow Inst. Ednl. Leadership, 1982. Mem. ALA, Chief Officers State Libr. Agys. (pres. 1996-98), Mont. Libr. Assn. (bd. dirs. 1982-88), Mountain Plains Libr. Assn. (sec. chmn. 1980, pres. 1987-88). Home: PO Box 554 Jefferson City MO 65102-0554 Office: Mo State Libr PO Box 387 600 W Main St Jefferson City MO 65101-1532

PARKHURST, TODD SHELDON, lawyer; b. Evanston, Ill., Mar. 8, 1941; s. Don A. and Ruth Ellen (Sheldon) P.; m. Karen Judy Huckleberry, Sept. 2, 1968 (dec. Sept. 1969); m. Beverly Ann Susler, Aug. 15, 1976. BS in Gen. Engring., U. Ill., 1963; JD, U. Pa., 1966. Bar: Ill. 1968, U.S. Dist. Ct. (no. dist.) Ill. 1968, U.S. Dist. Ct. (ea. dist.) Wis. 1989, U.S. Ct. Appeals (7th cir.) 1977, U.S. Ct. Appeals Fed. Cir. 1978, U.S. Ct. Mil. Appeals, 1968, U.S. Patent and Trademark Office, 1973, U.S. Supreme Ct. 1973. Assoc. Wolfe, Hubbard, Voit & Osann, 1968-72; assoc. and ptnr. Trexler, Wolters, Bushnell & Fosse, Chgo., 1972-84; ptnr. Jenner & Block, 1984-87; ptnr., mgr. intellectual property practice Schiff Hardin & Waite, 1987-96; ptnr. Gardner, Carton & Douglas, 1996-98, Hill & Simpson, Chgo., 1998-2000; ptnr., mgr. intellectual property practice Holland & Knight, 2000—. Adj. prof. John Marshall Law Sch., Chgo., 1980-84, Ill. Inst. Tech.-Chgo. Kent Law Sch., 1989—. Contbr. articles to profl. jours. Mem. Lifeline Pilots, Inc., pres. 1994-96; hearing officer Ill. Pollution Control Bd., 1972-96. Mem. Am. Intellectual Property Law Assn., Licensing Execs. Soc., Chgo. Bar Assn., Patent Law Assn. Chgo., Chgo. Lit. Club (pres. 1989-90), Adventurers Club Chgo. (sec. 1988). Methodist. Avocations: flying, scuba diving, photography, theatrical acting. Home: 260 E Chestnut St Apt 4301 Chicago IL 60611-2474 Office: Holland & Knight 55 W Monroe St Ste 800 Chicago IL 60603-5004 E-mail: tparkhur@hklaw.com.

PARKINSON, MARK VINCENT, former state legislator, lawyer; b. Wichita, Kans., June 24, 1957; s. Henry Filson and Barbara Ann (Gilbert) Horton; m. Stacy Abbott, Mar. 7, 1983; children: Alex Atticus, Sam Filson, Kit Harlan. BA in Edn., Wichita State U., 1980; JD, Kans. U., 1984. Assoc. Payne and Jones Law Firm, Olathe, Kans., 1984-86; ptnr. Parkinson, Foth & Reynolds, Lenexa, 1986—; mem. Kans. Ho. Reps., 1990-92, Kans. Senate, 1993-97. Mem. ABA, Johnson County Bar Found. (pres. 1993—), Kans. Bar Assn. Republican. Avocations: travel, running, movies. Office: Parkinson Foth & Reynolds 13628 W 95th St Lenexa KS 66215-3304

PARKINSON, ROBERT L., JR. health facility administrator; BBA, MBA, Loyola U. With Abbott Labs., Abbott Park, Ill., 1977—, v.p. European ops., 1990-93, sr. v.p. chem. and agrl. products, 1993-95, sr. v.p. internat. ops., 1995-98, exec. v.p., dir., 1998-99, pres., COO, dir., 1999-2001, also bd. dirs.; chmn. Geneva (Switzerland) Proteomics, 2001—. Office: Geneva Proteomics Inc rue Pre-de-la-Fontaine 2 1242 Satigny Schweiz Switzerland

PARKINSON, WILLIAM CHARLES, physicist, educator; b. Jarvis, Ont., Can., Feb. 11, 1918; came to U.S., 1925, naturalized, 1941; s. Charles Franklin and Euphemia Alice (Johnston) P.; m. Martha Bennett Capron, Aug. 2, 1944; children: Martha Reed, William Reid. BSE, U. Mich., 1940, MS, 1941, PhD, 1948. Physicist Applied Physics Lab., Johns Hopkins U., 1942-46, OSRD, 1943-44; mem. faculty U. Mich., 1947—, prof. physics, 1958-88, prof. emeritus physics, 1988—, dir. cyclotron lab., 1962-77; mem. subcom. nuclear structure NRC, 1959-68; mem. nuclear physics sub panel mgmt. and costs nuclear program, 1969-70; adv. panel physics NSF, 1966-69. Cons. grad. sci. facilities, 1968, chmn. postdoctoral fellowship evaluation panel, 1969, cons. to govt. and industry, 1955— Quondam mem. Trinity Coll., Cambridge, Eng. Recipient Ordnance Devel. award Navy Dept., 1946; Fulbright research scholar Cavendish Lab., Cambridge U., 1952-53 Fellow Am. Phys. Soc.; mem. N.Y. Acad. Scis., Biophys. Soc., Grad. "M" Club (awarded hon. "M" 1991), Sigma Xi, Phi Kappa Phi, Kappa Kappa Psi. Achievements include invention of automatic judging and timing for swim meets, fast neutron spectroscopy using cyclotrons; development of high resolution nuclear spectroscopy with cyclotrons. Home: 1600 Sheridan Dr Ann Arbor MI 48104-4052 Office: Univ Mich Dept Physics Ann Arbor MI 48109 E-mail: wcpark@umich.edu.

PARKS, BLANCHE CECILE, public administrator; b. Leavenworth, Kans., Feb. 2, 1949; d. Nile Eugene Sr. and Fern (Dickinson) Williams; m. Sherman A. Parks Jr.; children: Michael A., Stacy M. BEd, Washburn U., 1971, MEd, 1976, postgrad., 1983-84. Tchr. Topeka Pub. Schs., 1971-76, reading specialist, 1979-84; ins. regulator Kans. Ins. Dept., Topeka, 1984-88; spl. asst. to sec. Kans. Dept. Human Resources, 1988-92; real estate lease adminstr. State of Kans., 1992—. Pres. Kans. Children's Svc. League, 1990-94, YWCA, Topeka, 1992-94; chmn. Topeka Human Rels. Commn., 1991-93; mem. Topeka Pub. Schs. Found., 1993-94; participant Leadership Topeka, 1994, Leadership Kans., 1994 Named The Outstanding Young Woman of Kans. Jaycee Women, 1984, 85, one of Outstanding Young Women Am., 1985. Mem. Jr. League of Topeka (Gold Rose award 1993), Jack and Jill Am., Kans. C. of C. (leadership award 1985), Links, Phi Kappa Phi, Phi Delta Kappa, Alpha Delta Kappa, Delta Kappa Gamma, (life) Delta Sigma Theta (v.p. 1980-82). Republican. Mem. A.M.E. Ch. Home: 3744 SE Fremont St Topeka KS 66609-1411

PARKS, PATRICK, English language educator, humanities educator; BA in Lit. and Mass Comms., Southwest State U., 1975; BS in English Edn. and Journalism, Bemidji State U., 1977; MFA in English, U. Iowa, 1982. Instr. English and journalism, newspaper advisor Harris-Lake Park H.S., Lake Park, Iowa, 1977-78, Ely (Minn.) H.S., 1978-79; tchg. asst. in rhetoric and lit. U. Iowa, Iowa City, 1981-82; instr. English and Journalism, pubs. advisor Muscatine (Ill.) C. C., 1982-86; prof. English and Humanities, dir. writers ctr. Elgin (Ill.) C. C., 1986-98, disting. prof. English and Humanities, 1998—. Instr. creative writing and composition evening program Southeastern C. C., Burlington, Iowa, 1979-80, creative writing Arts Outreach program U. Iowa, Iowa City, 1981, fiction writing The Writer's Workshop weekend program, 1982; facilitator No. Ill. Network Stff Devel., Lake Geneva, Wis., 1992, 1994; co-coord. ALA and Lila Wallace/Reader's Digest pilot program, Elgin, Ill., 1993; faculty adv. The Sarajevo Project, Elgin C. C., 1992—; presenter, lectr. in field. Editor, adv. (literary jour.) Farmer's Market; contbr. numerous stories, poems to literary jours., articles to profl. jours. Artist fellow Ill. Arts Coun. 1988; recipient Outstanding C. C. Professor of the Year award Carnegie Foun. Advancement of Tchg. and Coun. Advancement an Support of Edn. 1994, Outstanding Faculty award Ill. Cmty. Coll. Trustees Assn. 1994, Honorable Mention Fla. State U. World's Best Short Story Contest 1992, writing contest Rambunctious Review 1991, Excellence in Tchg. award Nat. Inst. Staf and Orgnl. Devel. 1991, First Place fiction writing contest Roselle Pub. Lib. 1988. Mem. Ill. Writers, Inc. (chair, bd. dirs.), Assoc. Writing Programs, C. C. Humanities Assn., Nat. Coun. Tchrs. English, Campus Compact Ctr. Cmty. Coll., Tchrs. and Writers Collaborative. Office: Elgin Comm Coll English Dept 1700 Spartan Dr Elgin IL 60123-7189

PARKS, ROBERT D. real estate company executive; Chmn. Inland Real Estate Investment Corp., Oak Brook, Ill., 1969—. Office: Inland Real Estate Investment Corp 2901 Butterfield Rd Ste 1 Oak Brook IL 60523-1190

PARKS, ROSA LOUISE, civil rights activist; b. Tuskegee, Ala., 1913; Stidemt, Ala. State Coll.; hon. degree, Shaw Coll. Former seamstress and housekeeper, Montgomery, Ala., Detroit, from 1957; office mgr. for Congressman John Conyers, Jr., from 1965; co-founder Rosa and Raymond Parks Inst. for Self-Devel., 1987—. Author: Quiet Strength, 1994 Formerly active Montgomery Voters League; mem. youth coun. NAACP, sec. Montgomery br., 1943; active SCLC. Recipient Spingarn medal NAACP, 1970, Martin Luther King Jr. award, 1980, Congl. Gold Medal of Honor, 1999, 31st NAACP Image award for outstanding supporting actress in a drama series for Touched by an Angel, 2000. Office: Rosa & Raymond Park Inst Ste 2200 Cadillac Sq Detroit MI 48226-1002

PARLOW, CYNTHIA MARIE, soccer player; b. Memphis, May 8, 1978; Student, U. N.C. Mem. U.S. Women's Nat. Soccer Team, 1996— (Gold medal 1996 Olympics).; mem. U.S. Under-20 Nat. Team, Nordic Cup championships, Denmark, 1997; mem. U-16 Nat. Team pool. Named Most Valuable Player 1995 Under-17 U.S. Youth Soccer nat. tournament; recipient Herman Trophy, Mo. Athletic Club Player of Yr. award, 1997; named Soccer Am. Freshman of Yr., 1995; voted All-ACC and ACC Rookie of Yr., 1995; named Most Valuable Player state and regional tournaments, 1994, Tenn. H.S. Player of Yr., 1994. Achievements: helped U. N.C. to NCAA Championship 1997; 1st-Team All-ACC Selection in 1997; named to 1997 NCAA All-Tournament Team. Office: US Soccer Fedn 1801-1811 S Prairie Ave Chicago IL 60616

PARMELEE, WALKER MICHAEL, psychologist; b. Grand Haven, Mich., Apr. 26, 1952; s. Walker Michael and Evelyn Mae (Essenberg) P.; m. Gayle Ann Klempel, Jan. 11, 1975; children: Morgan Christine, Kathryn Ann, Elizabeth Mae. BS, Ctrl. Mich. U., 1974, MA, cert. specialist in psychology, 1977; D in Counseling Psychology, Western Mich. U., 1986. Lic. psychologist, Mich. Sch. psychologist Oakridge Pub. Schs.,

Muskegon, Mich., 1977—82, Ravenna (Mich.) Schs., Muskegon Heights (Mich.) Schs., 1982—84; sr. staff therapist Steelcase Counseling Svcs., Grand Rapids, 1984—90; prin., psychologist Parmelee and Winebarger Psychol. Cons., Grand Haven, 1989—. Consulting psychologist Cross Rds. Family Ctr., Grand Haven, 1989—2000. Contbr. articles to profl. jours. Bd. dirs. Planned Parenthood, Muskegon, 1979-82, Harbinger Inc., Grand Rapids, 1986-90; elder 2d Ref. Ch., Grand Haven, 1989-92; mem. women and families adv. group Allegan, Muskegon, Ottawa Substance Abuse Agy., 1992-95. Mem. Am. Psychol. Assn., Am. Group Psychotherapy Assn., Nat. Assn. Child Alcoholics, Mich. Psychol. Assn., Mich. Sch. Psychologists. Avocations: woodworking, skiing, running, tennis, camping. Home: 215 Howard St Grand Haven MI 49417-1806 Office: Parmelee Psychology Ctr 321 Fulton Ave Grand Haven MI 49417-1231

PARMENTER, CHARLES STEDMAN, chemistry educator; b. Phila., Oct. 12, 1933; s. Charles Leroy and Hazeltene Lois (Stedman) P.; m. Patricia Jean Patton, Mar. 31, 1956; children: Tighe Stedman, Kyle Kirkland, Leigh Patton. BA, U. Pa., 1955; PhD in Phys. Chemistry, U. Rochester, 1963. Tech. rep. photo products E.I. du Pont de Nemours & Co., 1958; NSF fellow chemistry Harvard U., Boston, 1962-63, NIH rsch. fellow, 1963-64, from asst. prof. to prof., 1964-88; Disting. prof. chemistry Ind. U., Bloomington, 1988—. Simon H. Guggenheim fellow U. Cambridge, 1971-72; vis. fellow Joint Inst. Lab. Astrophysics, Nat. Bur. Standards and U. Colo., 1977-78, 92, Exeter Coll. Oxford U., 1999. Lt. USAF, 1956-58. Recipient Humboldt Sr. Scientist award Tech. U. Munchen, 1986; Fulbright Sr. Scholar Griffith U., Australia, 1980. Earle K. Plyler Prize, Am. Physical Soc., 1996. Fellow AAAS, Am. Phys. Soc. (Earle K. Plyler prize 1996); mem. NAS, Am. Acad. Arts and Scis., Am. Chem. Soc. (chmn. div. phys. chemistry 1986-87). Achievements include research in photochemistry, laser spectroscopy, energy transfer. Office: Ind U Dept of Chemistry Bloomington IN 47405

PARMER, JESS NORMAN, university official, educator; b. Elkhart, Ind., Nov. 23, 1925; s. Jess Noah and Zayda Irene (Tressler) P.; m. Bessie Norma Peterson, September 12, 1948; children: Thomas Norman, Sarah Irene. B.A., Ind. U., 1949; M.A., U. Conn., 1951; Ph.D., Cornell U., 1957. Resident in Malaya, Southeast Asia program, Cornell U., 1952-55; instr., then asst. prof. history U. Md., 1956-59; mem. faculty No. Ill. U., 1959-67, prof. history, 1960-67, chmn. dept., 1959-63; assoc. dean Coll. Arts and Scis. Ohio U., also dir. Center Internat. Studies, 1967-69, asst. dean faculties for internat. studies, 1969-75; v.p. acad. affairs Trinity U., San Antonio, 1975-82, prof. history, 1975-92; scholar in residence and dir. of special projects Ohio U., Athens, 1993-96; cons. business, govt., edn. Peace Corps rep. in Malaya, 1961-63, Tanzania, summer 1965, Malawi, summer, 1966, Korea, 1967; lectr. Fgn. Service Inst., 1958, 61, 65; vis. prof. history Nat. U. Malaysia, 1984; cons. social scis. com. Ill. Curriculum Program, 1961; cons. various corps.; vis. fellow Cornell U., 1987-88, vis. prof. 1989; luce scholar in res. Ohio U., 1990-91. Author: Governments and Politics of Southeast Asia, 2d edit., 1964, Colonial Labor Policy and Administration, 1960, Southeast Asia: Documents of Political Development and Change, 1974, People and Progress: A Global History, 1977; contbr. chpts. The World of Asia, 1995. Served with inf. AUS, 1944-46, ETO. Mem. AAUP, ACLU, Assn. Asian Studies (chmn. S.E. Asia regional coun. 1968-72, dir. 1969-72), Midwest Conf. Asian Affairs (chmn. library com. 1960-61), Southwest Conf. Asian Studies (pres. 1982-83), Am. Hist. Assn., Sons of the Am. Revolution, Torch Internat., Soc. of Ind. Pioneers, Tex. Soc. War of 1812. E-mail: bessnjess@cs.com.

PARRINO, CHERYL LYNN, federal agency administrator; b. Wisconsin Rapids, Wis., Jan. 21, 1954; m. Jack J. Parrino, Sept. 1, 1990; 1 child, George. BBA in Acctg., U. Wis., 1976. Auditor Pub. Svc. Commn. Wis., Madison, 1976-82, dir. utility audits, 1982-86, exec. asst. to chmn., 1986-91, commr., 1991-98, chmn., 1992-98; chmn., CEO Universal Svc. Adminstrv. Co., 1998—. Mem. adv. bd. Bellcore, 1991; vice chmn. bd. dirs. Wis. Ctr. Demand Side Rsch., Madison, 1991-92; chmn. bd. dirs. Wis. Pub. Utility Inst., Madison, 1992-95 Mem. Gov.'s Task Force Gross Receipts Tax, Madison, 1991-92, Gov.'s Task Force Alternative Fuels, Madison, 1992-98, Gov.'s Task Force Clean Air, Madison, 1992-98, Gov.'s Task Force Telecom., Madison, 1993-94. Mem. Nat. Assn. Pub. Utility Commrs. (exec. com. 1991, chmn. comm. com. 1992-98, pres. 1995-96, pres. Gt. Lakes conf. 1996). Republican. Lutheran. Avocations: snow skiing, tennis, traveling. Office: Universal Svc Adminstrv Co 583 Donofrio Dr Ste 201 Madison WI 53719-2096 Fax: (608) 827-8893.

PARRISH, MAURICE DRUE, museum executive; b. Chgo., Mar. 5, 1950; s. Maurice and Ione Yvonne (Columns) P.; m. Gail Marie Sims, Sept. 2, 1978; children: Theodore, Andrew, Brandon, Cara. BA in Arch., U. Pa., 1972; MArch, Yale U., 1975. City planner City of Chgo., 1975-81; architect John Hiltscher & Assocs., Chgo., 1981-83, Barnett, Jones & Smith, Chgo., 1983-84; zoning adminstr. City of Chgo., 1984-87, bldg. commr., 1987-89; dep. dir. Detroit Inst. of Arts, 1989-97, interim dir., 1997-99, exec. v.p., 1999—. Bd. dirs. Arts League of Mich., Detroit, 1994-97, Mosaic Youth Theatre Detroit, 2000—; co-chmn. Mayor's Affordable Housing Task Force, Chgo., 1984-89; chmn. Chgo. Elec. Commn., 1988-89; mem. Chgo. Econ. devel. Commn., 1987-89; pres. St. Philip Neri Sch. Bd., Chgo., 1981-85, South Shore Commn., Chgo., 1982-84. King Chavez Parks fellow U. Mich., 1991, H.I. Feldman fellow Yale U., 1972; Franklin W. Gregory scholar Yale U., 1974, Nat. Achievement scholar U. Pa., 1968. Mem. Am. Assn. Mus., Am. Assn. Mus. Adminstrs., Constrn. Specifications Inst., Lambda Alpha. Avocations: golf, chess, reading, astronomy. Office: Detroit Inst of Arts 5200 Woodward Ave Detroit MI 48202-4094 E-mail: mparrish@dia.org.

PARRISH, OVERTON BURGIN, JR. pharmaceutical corporation executive; b. Cin., May 26, 1933; s. Overton Burgin and Geneva Opal (Shinn) P. B.S., Lawrence U., 1955; M.B.A., U. Chgo., 1959. With Pfizer Inc., 1959-74; salesman Pfizer Labs., Chgo., 1959-62, asst. mktg. product mgr. N.Y.C., 1962-63, product mgr., 1964-66, group product mgr., 1966-67, mktg. mgr., 1967-68, v.p. mktg., 1969-70, v.p., dir. ops., 1970-71; exec. v.p. domestic pharm. div. Pfizer Pharms., 1971-72; exec. v.p., dir. Pfizer Internat. Divsn., 1972-74; pres., chief operating officer G.D. Searle Internat., Skokie, Ill., 1974-75, pres., chief exec. officer, 1975-77; pres. Worldwide Pharm./Consumer Products Group, 1977-86; pres., chief exec. officer Phoenix Health Care, Chgo., 1987—; chmn., CEO, bd. dirs. Wis. Pharmiacal Co., Inc., 1990-96; co-chmn. Inhalon Pharms., 1991-95, also bd. dirs.; chmn. ViatiCare Fin. Svcs. LLC, 1993—, also bd. dirs.; chmn., CEO, bd. dirs. The Female Health Co., 1996—. Chair Amreimmune Pharmaceuticals, Inc., 1999—; bd. dirs., chair Miicro Inc., 1999—; bd. dirs. Medic Group. Author: The Future Pharmaceutical Marketing; International Drug Pricing, 1971. Trustee Mktg. Sci. Inst.; trustee Food and Drug Law Inst., 1979-86 , Lawrence U., 1983-87, 98— . Served to 1st lt. USAF, 1955-57. Mem. Beta Gamma Sigma, Phi Kappa Tau. Home: 505 N Lake Shore Dr Chicago IL 60611-3427 Office: Phoenix Health Care 515 N State St Chicago IL 60610- E-mail: oparrish@aol.com.

PARRY, DALE D. newspaper editor; BS in Journalism cum laude, Ball State U., Muncie, Ind., 1981. Feature writer Richmond (Ind.) Palladium-Item, 1981-84, Cin. Enquirer, 1984-86; editor Today section The Dallas Morning News, 1987-90; assignment editor The Way We Live sect. Detroit Free Press, 1990-92, dep. features editor, 1992-94, features editor, 1993-96, asst. mng. editor, 1997-2000, dep. mng. editor, 2001—. Mem. Am. Assn. Sun. and Feature Editors. Office: Detroit Free Press 600 W Fort St Detroit MI 48226-2706

PARSONS, CHARLES ALLAN, JR. lawyer; b. Mpls., July 16, 1943; s. Charles Allan and Grace Adelaide (Covert) P.; m. JoAnne Ruth Russell, Oct. 16, 1965; children: Charles, Daniel, Nancy. BS, U. Minn., 1965, JD cum laude, 1972. Bar: Minn. 1972, U.S. Dist. Ct. Minn. 1972, U.S. Supreme Ct. 1995. Ptnr. Moss & Barnett, P.A., 1972—. Bd. dirs. Legal Advice Clinics Ltd., Mpls., 1975-93, Legal Aid Soc. Mpls., 1999—, first v.p., 2000—; bd. dirs. Mid-Minn. Legal Assistance, 2001—; chair steering com. S.E. Asian Legal Assistance Project, Mpls., 1988-93. Named Vol. Atty. of Yr., Legal Advice Clinics, Ltd., Mpls., 1990. Mem. ABA, Am. Coll. Real Estate Lawyers, Minn. State Bar Assn. (co-chair legis. com. real property sec. 1986—, coun. mem. 1986—, chair real property sect. 1993-94), Hennepin County Bar Assn. (chair real property sect. 1988-89). Roman Catholic. Avocations: reading, walking, biking, hiking. Office: Moss & Barnett PA 4800 Norwest Ctr 90 S 7th Minneapolis MN 55402-4119 E-mail: parsonsc@goldengate.net.

PARSONS, JEFFREY ROBINSON, anthropologist, educator; b. Washington, Oct. 9, 1939; s. Merton Stanley and Elisabeth (Oldenburg) P.; m. Mary Thomson Hrones, Apr. 27, 1968; 1 child, Apphia Hrones. B.S., Pa. State U., 1961; Ph.D., U. Mich., 1966. Asst. prof. anthropology U. Mich., Ann Arbor, 1966-71, assoc. prof., 1971-76, prof., 1976—, dir. mus. anthropology, 1983-86. Vis. prof. Universidad Nacional Autonoma de Mexico, 1987; vis. prof. Universidad Buenos Aires, 1994, Univ. Nac de Catamarca, Argentina, 1996, Univ. Nac de Tucuman, Argentina, 1996, Univ. Mayor de San Andres, Bolivia, 1999. Author: Prehistoric Settlement Patterns in the Texcoco Region, Mexico, 1971; (with William T. Sanders and Robert Stanley) The Basin of Mexico: The Cultural Ecology of a Civilization, 1979; (with E. Brumfiel) Prehispanic Settlement Patterns in the Southern Valley of Mexico, 1982; (with M. Parsons) Chinampa Agriculture and Aztec Urbanization in the Valley of Mexico, 1985; (with Mary H. Parsons) Maguey Utilization in Highland Central Mexico, 1990, The Production of Consumption of Salt During Postclassic Times in the Valley of Mexico, 1994; (with E. Brumfiel and M. Hodge) The Developmental Implications of Earlier Dates for Early Aztec in the Basin of Mexico, 1996; (with C. Hastings and R. Matos) Rebuilding the State in Highland Peru, 1997; A Regional Perspective on Inca Impact in the Sierra Central, Peru, 1998; (with C. hastings and R. Matos) Prehispanic Settlement Patterns in the Upper Mantaro-Tarma Drainage, Peru, 2000, The Last Saltmakers of Nexquipayac, Mexico, 2001. Rsch. grantee NSF, 1967, 70, 72-73, 75-76, 81, Nat. Geog. Soc., 1984, 86, 88. Mem. Am. Anthrop. Assn. (Alfred V. Kidder award 1998), Soc. Am. Archaeology, AAAS, Inst. Andean Rsch., Inst. Andean Studies, Sociedad Mexicana de Antropologia, Sociedad Argentina de Antropologia. Office: Museum of Anthropology U Mich Ann Arbor MI 48109

PARSONS, JOHN THOREN, corporate executive, inventor; b. Detroit, Oct. 11, 1913; s. Carl Berger and Edith Charlotte (Thorén) P.; m. Elizabeth Mae Shaw, Apr. 20, 1940; children: Carl A., John T. II, Robert S., Grant W., David C., Meredith W. Student, Wayne U., 1934; D of Engring. (hon.), U. Mich., 1988; LLD (hon.), Lake Superior State U., 1997. With Parsons Corp., Detroit & Traverse City, Mich., 1928-68, owner Traverse City, 1954-68, pres., 1956-68, Parsons Co., France, 1959-68; pres., owner The John T. Parsons Corp., Traverse City, Mich., 1968—. Invited lectr. Japan, Brazil, Germany. Inventor products and mfg. processes. Recipient Nat. Medal of Tech., U.S. Dept. Commerce, 1985, Jules Marie Jacquard award AIM Tech., 1968, Disting. Service award Nat. Tooling and Machining Assn., Citation Soc. Am. Value Engrs. Fellow Soc. Mfg. Engrs. (charter, internat. dir. 1992-93, citation 1975, inductee Inventors Hall of Fame 1993), Detroit Athletic Club. Republican. Lutheran. Avocations: music, reading, family. Home and Office: 1456 Brigadoon Ct # 3, # 6 Traverse City MI 49686-8013

PARTRIDGE, MARK VAN BUREN, lawyer, educator, writer; b. Rochester, Minn., Oct. 16, 1954; s. John V.B. and Constance (Brainerd) P.; m. Mary Roberta Moffitt, Apr. 30, 1983; children: Caitlin, Lindsay, Christopher. BA, U. Nebr., 1978; JD, Harvard U., 1981. Bar: Ill. 1981, U.S. Dist. Ct. (no. dist.) Ill. 1981, U.S. Dist. Ct. (ea. dist.) Mich. 1983, U.S. Ct. Appeals (fed. cir.) 1983, U.S. Ct. Appeals (4th cir.) 1986, U.S. Ct. Appeals (5th cir.) 1993, U.S. Ct. Appeals (3rd cir.) 1998. Assoc. Pattishall, McAuliffe, Newbury, Hilliard & Geraldson, Chgo., 1981-88, ptnr., 1988—. Adj. prof. John Marshall Law Sch., Chgo., 1987—; arbitrator Cook County Mandatory Arbitration Program, 1989—; v.p. Harvard Legal Aid Bur., 1980-81; mediator no. dist. Ill. Voluntary Mediation Program, 1997—; panelist World Intellectual Property Orgn., Domain Name Dispute Resolution Svc., 1999—. Contbr. articles to profl. jours.; mem. editl. bd. The Trademark Reporter, 1994-97; adv. bd. IP Litigator, 1995—. Vol. Chgo. Vol. Legal Svcs., 1983—. Mem. ABA (com. chmn. 1989-91, 94-99), Internat. Trademark Assn. (com. vice chmn. 1996), World Intellectual Property Orgn. (experts panel internet domain name process 1998-99), Am. Intellectual Property Law Assn. (com. chmn. 1989-91, 96-98, bd. dirs. 1998-2001), Intellectual Property Law Assn. Chgo. (com. chmn. 1993-96), Brand Names Ednl. Found. (moot ct. regional chmn. 1994-96, nat. vice-chmn. 1997-98, nat. chmn. 1998-99), Legal Club (v.p. 1998, pres. 1999), Lawyers Club Chgo. (pres. 2000, bd. dirs. 2000-01), Union League Club, Boy Scouts Am. Avocations: writing, music, genealogy, travel, internet. Office: Pattishall McAuliffe Newbury Hilliard & Geraldso 311 S Wacker Dr Ste 5000 Chicago IL 60606-6631 E-mail: mpartridge@pattishall.com.

PASCAL, ROGER, lawyer; b. Chgo., Mar. 16, 1941; s. Samuel A. and Harriet E. (Hartman) P.; m. Martha Hecht, June 16, 1963; children: Deborah, Diane, David AB with distinction, U. Mich, 1962; JD cum laude, Harvard U., 1965. Bar: Ill. 1965, U.S. Dist. Ct. (no. dist.) Ill. 1965, U.S. Ct. Appeals (7th cir.) 1969, U.S. Supreme Ct. 1976, Wis. 1985, U.S. Ct. Appeals (2d, 6th, 9th and 10th cirs.) 186. Assoc. Schiff Hardin & Waite, Chgo., 1965-71, ptnr., 1972—. Adj. prof. law Northwestern U. Law Sch., 1994—. Bd. dirs., mem. exec. com. Chgo. Law Enforcement Study Group, 1975-80, pres., 1978-80; pres. Harvard Law Soc. Ill., 1976-78; bd. dirs. ACLU of Ill., 1984—, gen. counsel, 1986—. Mem. ABA (antitrust, intellectual property, and litigation sects.), Pub. Interest Law Initiative (bd. dirs. 1989—, v.p. 1995-97, pres. 1997-98), Fund for Justice (v.p., bd. dirs. 1986-97), Chgo. Coun. Lawyers (bd. dirs. 1970-74, 80-84), Chgo. Legal Assistance Found. (bd. dirs. 1985-88), Univ. Club, Met. Club, Phi Beta Kappa. Office: Schiff Hardin & Waite 6600 Sears Tower Chicago IL 60606

PASULA, ANGELA MARIE, lawyer; b. Michigan City, Ind., Oct. 2, 1956; d. Edward Joseph Pasula and Theresa Jeanette (Stella) Hack; m. David Mark Prusa, June 19, 1982. BA in Polit. Sci. cum laude, Western Mich. U., 1977; JD, Valparaiso U., 1980. Bar: Mich. 1980. Asst. pros. atty. Kalamazoo (Mich.) Prosecutors Office, 1980-82, Berrien County Prosecutors Office, Niles, Mich., 1982—. Office: Berrien County Prosecutors Office 1205 Front St Niles MI 49120-1627

PATE, PAUL DANNY, mayor; b. Ottumwa, Iowa, May 1, 1958; s. Paul Devern and Velma Marie (McConnell) P.; m. Jane Ann Wacker, July 15, 1978; children: Jennifer Ann, Paul Daniel III, Amber Lynn. AA in Bus., Kirkwood Coll., 1978; cert. fin. mgmt. program, U. Pa., 1990. Exec. dir. Jr. Achievement, Cedar Rapids, Iowa, 1978-82; pres. PM Systems Corp., 1982—; senator Iowa State Senate, Des Moines, 1989-93; Sec. of State State of Iowa, 1994-98; mayor City of Cedar Rapids, 2002—. Chmn. Iowa Young Reps., Des Moines, 1989-93, Rep. Senate Campaign Com., 1990. Recipient Guardian Small Bus. award Nat. Fedn. Independent Bus., 1990; named Young Entrepreneur of Yr. U.S. Small Bus. Adminstrn., Iowa, 1988, Alumnus of Yr. Kirkwood Coll., Cedar Rapids, 1990. Methodist. Avocation: water skiing. Home: 6801 Bowman Ln NE Cedar Rapids IA 52402-1575 Office: PM Sys Corp 850 Robins Rd Hiawatha IA 52233-1320

PATEL, HOMI BURJOR, apparel company executive; b. Bombay, June 28, 1949; s. Burjor Ratan and Roshen Burjor (Marfatia) P.; married; children: Neville H., Cyrus H., Natasha E. BS in Stats., U. Bombay, 1973; MBA in Fin. and Mktg., Columbia U., 1975. Exec. asst. to pres. Corbin Ltd., N.Y.C., 1976, dir. mktg., 1978; with subs. Hartmarx Corp., Chgo., 1979—; v.p., gen. mgr. Fashionaire Apparel Inc., 1979-81; exec. v.p. Austin Reed of Regent St., 1981-82, M. Wile and Co., Buffalo, 1982-84; pres., chief exec. officer M. Wile & Co., Johnny Carson Apparel, Intercontinental Apparel, 1984—; group exec. v.p. Hartmarx Mens Apparel Group Corp., 1987-91, chmn., ceo Chgo., 1991-92; pres., COO Hartmarx Corp., 1992—, bd. dirs., 1994—2001, CEO, 2002—. Mem. Clothing Mfrs. Assn. Am. (bd. dirs. 1984—, chief labor negotiator for U.S. tailored clothing industry), Univ. Club N.Y., Chgo. Club. Office: Hartmarx Corp 101 N Wacker Dr Fl 23 Chicago IL 60606-1718

PATEL, VIRENDRA CHATURBHAI, mechanical engineer, educator; b. Mombasa, Kenya, Nov. 9, 1938; arrived in U.S., 1969, naturalized, 1975; s. Chaturbhai S. and Kantaben N. (Rai) Patel; m. Manjula Patel, May 29, 1966; children: Sanjay, Bindiya. BSc with honors, Imperial Coll., London, 1962; PhD, Cambridge (Eng.) U., 1965; Doctor honoris causa, Tech. U. Civil Engring., Bucharest, Romania, 1994. Sr. asst. in rsch. Cambridge U., 1965-69; vis. prof. Indian Inst. Tech., Kharagpur, 1966; cons. Lockheed Ga. Co., Marietta, 1969-70; mem. faculty U. Iowa, Iowa City, 1971—, prof. mech. engring., 1975—, chmn. div., 1976-82, chmn. mech. engring., 1978-82, U. Iowa Found. Disting. prof., 1990—, Edwin B. Green chair in hydraulics, 2000—, 2000—; research engr. Iowa Inst. Hydraulic Rsch., 1971—, dir., 1994—; hon. prof. Dharamsinh Desai Inst. Tech., 2002—. Mem. Iowa Gov. Sci. Adv. Coun., 1977—83; mem. resistance com. Internat. Towing Tank Conf., 1978—87; vis. prof. U. Karlsruhe, Germany, 1980—81, Ecole Nationale Superieure de Mechanique, Nantes, France, 1984, Nantes, 96; jubilee prof. Chalmers Inst. Tech., Goteborg, Sweden, 1988; cons. in field. Author: (book) Three Dimensional Turbulent Boundary Layers, 1972; contbr. articles to profl. jours.; assoc. editor: AIAA Jour., 1987—90. Recipient Sr. Scientist award, Alexander von Humboldt Found., 1980, 1993. Fellow: ASME (Fluids Engring. award 1997), AIAA (assoc.); mem.: Soc. Naval Archtl. Marine Engrs., Am. Soc. Engring. Edn., Pi Tau Sigma, Sigma Xi. Home: 60 Kennedy Pkwy Iowa City IA 52246-2780 Office: IIHR Hydroscience and Engring U Iowa 404 Hydraulics Laboratory Iowa City IA 52242-1585

PATRICK, JOHN JOSEPH, social sciences educator; b. East Chicago, Ind., Apr. 14, 1935; s. John W. and Elizabeth (Lazar) P.; m. Patricia Grant, Aug. 17, 1963; children— Rebecca, Barbara A.B., Dartmouth Coll., 1957; Ed.D., Ind. U., 1969. Social studies tchr. Roosevelt High Sch., East Chicago, 1957-62; social studies tchr. Lab. High Sch., U. Chgo., 1962-65; research assoc. Sch. Edn., Ind. U., Bloomington, 1965-69, asst. prof., 1969-74, assoc. prof., 1974-77, prof. edn., 1977—, dir. social studies devel. ctr., 1986—, dir. ERIC clearinghouse for social studies, social sci. edn., 1986—. Bd. dirs. Biol. Scis. Curriculum Study, 1980-83; ednl. cons. Author: Progress of the Afro-American, 1968, The Young Voter, 1974; (with L. Ehman, Howard Mehlinger) Toward Effective Instruction in Secondary Social Studies, 1974, Lessons on the Northwest Ordinance, 1987; (with R. Remy) Civics for Americans, 1980, rev. edit. 1986; (with Mehlinger) American Political Behavior, 1972, rev. edit. 1980, (with C. Keller) Lessons on the Federalist Papers, 1987; America Past and Present, 1983; (with Carol Berkin) History of the American Nation, 1984, rev. edit., 1987; Lessons on the Constitution, 1985, James Madison and the Federalist Papers, 1990, How to Teach the Bill of Rights, 1991, Ideas of the Founders on Constitutional Government: Resources for Teachers of History and Government, 1991, Young Oxford Companion to the Supreme Court of the United States, 1994, Founding the Republic: A Documentary History, 1995, (with Gerald Long) Constitutional Debates on Freedom of Religion: A Documentary History, 1999, (with Richard M. Pious and Donald A. Ritchie) The Oxford Essential Guide to the U.S. Government, 2000. Bd. dirs. Law in Am. Soc. Found., 1984-88, Social Sci. Edn. consortium, 1984—; mem. Gov.'s Task Force on Citizenship Edn., Ind., 1982-87; active Ind. Commn. on Bicentennial of U.S. Constn., 1986-92; bd. dirs. Coun. for the Advancement of Citizenship, Nat. History Edn. Network, 1994-96; mem. Natr. Coun. for History Standards, 1991-94. Mem. ASCD, Nat. Coun. Social Studies, Social Sci. Edn. Consortium (v.p. 1985-87), Coun. for Basic Edn., Am. Polit. Sci. Assn., Am. Hist. Assn., Orgn. Am. Historians, Phi Delta Kappa. Home: 1209 E University St Bloomington IN 47401-5045 Office: Ind U 2805 E 10th St Bloomington IN 47408-2601

PATRICK, THOMAS M. gas utility company executive; Pres., COO Peoples Energy Corp., Chgo., 1998—. Office: Peoples Energy Corp 130 E Randolph Dr 24th Fl Chicago IL 60601-6207

PATTEN, RONALD JAMES, retired university dean; b. Iron Mountain, Mich., July 17, 1935; s. Rudolph Joseph and Cecelia (Fuse) Pataconi; m. Shirley Ann Bierman, Sept. 5, 1959; children: Christine Marie, Cheryl Ann, Charlene Denise. BA, Mich. State U., 1957, MA, 1959; PhD, U. Ala., 1963. Acct. Price Waterhouse & Co., Detroit, 1958; instr. No. Ill. U., 1959-60; asst. prof. U. Colo., 1963-65; assoc. prof. Va. Poly. Inst. and State U., 1965-67, prof., 1967-73, head dept. accounting, 1966-73; dir. research Financial Accounting Standards Bd., Conn., 1973-74; dean Sch. Bus. Adminstrn., U. Conn., Storrs, 1974-88; chief of party-Eastern Caribbean Arthur D. Little Internat., 1988-89; dean Coll. Commerce and Kellstadt Grad. Sch. Bus. De Paul U., Chgo., 1989-99. Individual investors adv. com. N.Y. Stock Exch., 1993-98; cons. in field. Contbr. chapters to books, articles to profl. jours. Mem. West Towns Chorus; bd. dirs. U.S. com. UNICEF, Chgo., 1996—99. Recipient Nat. Quartermaster award Nat. Quartermaster, Assn., 1956; Earhart Found. fellow, 1962-63. Mem. AICPA, Am. Acctg. Assn., Inst. Mgmt. Accts., Acad. Internat. Bus. (Internat. Dean of Yr. award 1987), Internat. Assn. for Acctg. Edn. and Rsch., Chgo. Coun. Fgn. Rels., Ill. Coun. Econ. Edn. (Chgo., trustee 1989—, chmn. bd. trustees 1997-2000), Pacioli Soc., Heidelberg Club Internat., Scabbard and Blade, Golden Key, Beta Gamma Sigma (mem. bd. govs. 1975-90, nat. sec.-treas. 1980-82, nat. v.p. 1982-84, nat. pres. 1984-86), Beta Alpha Psi (bd. dirs. 1992-94), Delta Sigma Pi, Phi Kappa Phi, Delta Mu Delta. Avocations: hiking, skiing, golf, travel, softball. Home: 334 N Montclair Ave Glen Ellyn IL 60137-5253 E-mail: rpatten@depaul.edu.

PATTERSON, JAMES MILTON, marketing specialist, educator; b. DeQueen, Ark., Oct. 15, 1927; s. Charles Edward and Phoebe Allene (Steel) P.; m. Della Jeanne Hays, July 3, 1964; children— J. Marshall, Julia M.; children by previous marriage— Robert T., Donald A. BS, U.S. Mcht. Marine Acad., 1948; MBA (Teagle Found. fellow), Cornell U., 1954, PhD (Ford Found. dissertation fellow), 1961. Third mate Esso Shipping Co., 1948-52; instr. in bus. adminstrn. Northwestern U., 1957-60; lectr. Center for Programs in Govt. Adminstrn., U. Chgo., 1959; asst. prof. mktg. Ind. U., 1960-63, asso. prof., 1963-69, prof., 1969—, chmn. dept. mktg., 1972-78, asso. dir. Poynter Ctr., 1980, acting dir., 1981, co-sec. U. Faculty Coun., pres. Bloomington Faculty Coun.; dir. Ind. U. Inst. for Advanced Study, 1994-97. Bd. dirs. Inst. Advanced Study; cons. petroleum mktg.; expert witness on antitrust and mktg. Author: Marketing: The Firm's Viewpoint, 1964, Highway Robbery: An Analysis of the Gasoline Crisis, 1974, Competition Ltd.: The Marketing of Gasoline, 1972. With USNR, 1945-48. Mem. Assn. for Practical & Profl. Ethics. Democrat. Home: 1303 Dreams Landing Way Annapolis MD 21401-1035 Office: Ind U Inst Advanced Study Bloomington IN 47405 E-mail: tartan33@aol.com.

PATTERSON, JOHNNIE RAY, county convention and tourism executive; b. Monroe, Mich., Aug. 12, 1959; s. James Ray Patterson and Elgie (Drummonds) Grabitz; m. Shari Ann Ford, Dec. 1, 1989; children: Johnnie Ray Jr., Lauren Celine. Student, Monroe County C.C., Monroe; BEd, U.

Toledo, 1987, postgrad., 1987-88; grad., Agy. Mgmt. Tng. Coun., Detroit, 1993. Dist. mgr. Equitable Life N.Y., N.Y.C., 1988-95; fin. planner, pres. J.R. Patterson & Co. Tax & Mgmt. Svcs., Monroe, 1995—, owner, 1988—. Contbr. articles to profl. jours. Mem. exec. com. Monroe County Rep. Com., 1994—; bd. dirs. Monroe County Humane Soc., 1997—; trustee Soc. Mercy Meml. Hosp., 1995—. Named Small Bus. Person of Yr. Monroe County, 1997. Mem. Nat. Assn. Life Underwriters (Million dollar Roundtable 1996, 97, Nat. Quality award 1994, Nat. Sales Achievement award 1995), Monroe County C. of C. (bd. dirs. 1996—, chmn. Leadership Monroe program 1997—), Downtown Monroe Bus. Assn. (chmn. 1995—), Monroe County C.C. Alumni Assn. (bd. dirs. 1991—), Monroe Golf and Country Club. Roman Catholic. Avocations: weightlifting (nat. collegiate weightlifting champion NCAA 1985, 86), gardening, cigar and sports lover, father. Office: 101 W Front St Monroe MI 48161-2338

PATTERSON, MARIA JEVITZ, microbiology-pediatric infectious disease educator; b. Berwyn, Ill., Oct. 23, 1944; d. Frank Jacob and Edna Frances (Costabile) Jevitz; m. Ronald James Patterson, Aug. 22, 1970; children: Kristin Lara, Kier Nicole. BS in Med. Tech. summa cum laude, Coll. St. Francis, Joliet, Ill., 1966; PhD in Microbiology, Northwestern U., Chgo., 1970; MD, Mich. State U., 1984. Diplomate Am. Bd. Med. Examiners, Am. Bd. Pediatrics Gen. Pediatrics, Am. Bd. Pediatrics Infectious Diseases. Lab. asst., instr. med. microbiology for student nurses Med. Sch. Northwestern U., Chgo., 1966-70; postdoctoral fellow in clin. microbiology affiliated hosps. U. Wash., Seattle, 1971-72; asst. prof. microbiology and pub. health Mich. State U., East Lansing, 1972-77, assoc. prof., 1977-82, assoc. prof. pathology, 1979-82, lectr. dept. microbiology and pub. health, 1982-87, resident in pediatrics affiliated hosps., 1984-85, 86-87, clin. instr. dept. pediatrics and human devel., 1984-87, assoc. prof. microbiology-pub. health-pediatrics-human devel., 1987-90, prof., 1990—. Staff microbiologist dept. pathology Lansing Gen. Hosp., 1972-75; dir. clin. microbiology grad. program. Mich. State U., 1974-81, staff microbiologist, 1978-81; postdoctoral fellow in infectious diseases U. Mass. Med. Ctr., Worcester, 1985-86; asst. dir. pediatrics residency Grad. Med. Edn. Inc., Lansing, 1987-90; med. dir. Pediatrics Health Ctr. St. Lawrence Hosp., Lansing, Mich., 1987-90, Ingham Med. Ctr., 1990-94; cons. clin. microbiology Lansing Gen. Hosp., 1972-75, Mich. State U., 1976-82, Mich. Dept. Pub. Health, 1976—, Ingham County Health Dept., 1988—, Am. Health Cons., 1993, State of Mich. Atty. Gen. Office, 1994-98, Lansing Sch. Dist., 1998—, Mich. Antibiotic Residence Reduction, 1998—; cons. to editl. bd. Infection and Immunity, 1977, Mich. State U. AIDS Edn. Tng. Ctr, 2001—; presenter seminars. Contbg. author: Microbiology: Principles and Concepts, 1982, 4th edit., 1995, Pediatric Emergency Medicine, 1992, Principles and Practice of Emergency Medicine, 1997, Rudolph's Pediatrics, 2000; item writer certifying bd. examination Bd. Am. Acad. Pediats., 1990—, Am. Bd. Osteopathy, 1997—; contbr. articles to profl. jours. and publs. Mem. hon. com. Lansing AIDS Meml. Quilt, 1993. Recipient award for tchg. excellence Mich. State U. Coll. Osteo. Medicine, 1977, 78, 79, 80, 83, Disting. Faculty award Mich. State U., 1980, Woman Achiever award, 1985, excellence in pediatric residency tchg. award, 1988, Alumni Profl. Achievement award Coll. of St. Francis, 1991, excellence in diversity award Mich. State U., 2000, Weil Endowed Disting. Pediat. Faculty award, 2001; grantee renal disease divsn. Mich. Dept. Pub. Health 1976-82. Fellow Pediatric Infectious Diseases Soc., Infectious Diseases Soc. Am., Am. Acad. Pediatrics; mem. Am. Coll. Physician Execs., Am. Soc. Microbiology, Am. Soc. Clin. Pathologists (affiliate, bd. registrant), South Ctrl. Assn. Clin. Microbiology, Mich. Infectious Diseases Soc., N.Y. Acad. Scis., Kappa Gamma Pi, Lambda Iota Tau. Roman Catholic. Home: 1520 River Ter East Lansing MI 48823-5314 Office: Mich State Univ Microbiology/Pub Health East Lansing MI 48824-1101

PATTERSON, NEAL L. information systems company executive; BS in Fin., MBA, Okla. State U. Sys. cons., mgr. Arthur Andersen & Co., Kansas City, Mo.; co-founder, CEO, chmn. bd. dirs. Cerner Corp., 1979—. Trustee Midwest Rsch. Inst.; mem. steering com. Coun. Growing Cos. Named Entrepreneur of Yr., Ernst & Young, 1991. Mem. Health Execs. Network. Office: Cerner Corp 2800 Rockcreek Pkwy Ste 601 Kansas City MO 64117-2521

PATTERSON, SAMUEL CHARLES, political science educator; b. Omaha, Nov. 29, 1931; s. Robert Foster and Garnet Marie (Jorgensen) P.; m. Suzanne Louise Dean, June 21, 1956; children— Polly Ann, Dean Foster, Grier Edmund BA, U. S.D., 1953; MS, U. Wis., 1956, PhD, 1959. Asst. prof. polit. sci. Okla. State U., Stillwater, 1959-61; asst. prof. U. Iowa, Iowa City, 1961-64, assoc. prof., 1964-67, prof., 1967-85, Roy J. Carver prof., 1985-86; prof. Ohio State U., Columbus, 1986-98, prof. emeritus, 1998—. Vis. prof. U. Wis., 1962, U. Okla., 1968-78, U. Essex, Colchester, Eng., 1969-70, U. S.D., 2001. Author: (with others) Representatives and Represented, 1975, A More Perfect Union, 4th edit., 1989; co-author: The Legislative Process in the United States, 4th edit., 1986, Comparing Legislatures, 1979; editor: American Legislative Behavior, 1968; co-editor: Comparative Legislative Behavior: Frontiers of Research, 1972, Handbook of Legislative Research, 1985, Political Leadership in Democratic Societies, 1991, Parliaments in the Modern World, 1994, Great Theatre: The American Congress in the 1990s, 1998, Senates: Bicameralism in the Contemporary World, 1999; editor Am. Jour. Polit. Sci., 1970-73; co-editor Legis. Studies Quar., 1981-85; mng. editor Am. Polit. Sci. Rev., 1985-91. Served with U.S. Army, 1953-55 Recipient Disting. Scholar award Ohio State U., 1990; fellow social Sci. Rsch. Coun., 1961, 67, Guggenheim, 1984-85; vis. fellow Brookings Instn., 1984-85, Ctr. Advanced Study in Behavioral Scis., 1993-94; Fulbright Bologna chair, 1995. Mem. Internat. Polit. Sci. Assn., Am. Polit. Sci. Assn. (Frank J. Goodnow award, 2000), Midwest Polit. Sci. Assn. (pres. 1980-81), Phi Beta Kappa, Phi Kappa Phi, Pi Sigma Alpha. Office: Ohio State U Dept Polit Sci 2140 Derby Hall 154 N Oval Mall Columbus OH 43210-1330 E-mail: patpat851@aol.com.

PATTIS, MARK R. publishing company executive; b. Chgo., Mar. 15, 1953; BS in Econs. with hons., Swarthmore Coll.; postgrad. studies, U. Chgo., London Sch. Econs., Sorbonne, Paris. Banker Chase Manhattan Bank, Am. Nat. Bank, Chgo.; staff Marmon Group; exec. NTC/ Contemporary Publ. Co., Lincolnwood, Ill., 1977-, pres., CEO, 1996-2000, Next Chpt. Holdings, Highland Park, Ill., 2000—. Recipient Palmes Academiques award Govt. of France, 1993, Electronic Book award of excellence, Sony, 1994; nominated for Watson fellowship. Mem. Chgo. Book Clinic, U.S. Electronic Book Publ. Com. (co-chmn 1991-95), Multimedia and Electronic Book Internat. Com. (vice chmn.). Office: Next Chpt Holdings Ste 205 600 Center Ave Highland Park IL 60035

PATTIS, S. WILLIAM, publisher; b. Chgo., July 3, 1925; s. William Robert and Rose (Quint) P.; m. Bette Z. Levin, July 16, 1950; children: Mark Robert, Robin Quint Himovitz. BS, U. Ill., 1949; postgrad., Northwestern U., 1949-50. Exec. v.p., pub. United Bus. Publs., 1949-59; chmn., CEO 3M/Pattis, 1959-88; pres. NTC Pub. Group, Lincolnwood, Ill., 1961-96, Next Chapter Holdings, L.P., Highland Park, 1996—; dir. P-B Comm., Winnetka, 1978-98; vice-chmn. Profl. Media Group, Norwalk, Conn., 1999—. Bd. dirs. 1st Colonial/Highwood; mem. book and libr. com. USIA, Washington, 1986-89, chmn., 1989-93; mem. exec. com. Pub. Hall of Fame, 1987—; chmn. U.S.-USSR Bilateral Info. Talks, Moscow, 1990. Mem. Pres.'s Coun. Youth Opportunity, 1968-70; bd. dirs. Photography Youth Found., 1970-73, Expt. in Internat. Living, 1970, Inst. Human Creativity, 1983—, Fund for Am.'s Libraries, 1996-99; vice chmn. bd. dirs. Annenberg Ctr. for Health Scis., 1991—, vice chmn., 1996-99; trustee Eisenhower Med. Ctr., Rancho Mirage, Calif., 1989—, exec. com. mem., 1996—, chmn. investment com., 2000—; trustee Am. Coun. Tchrs. Russian, 1992-96; bd. dirs. Nat. Security Edn. Act, Washington, 1993-94; lord of manor, Kirkbride, Eng., 1989—. Recipient Human Rels. award Am. Jewish Com., 1971, Paul Simon award Ctrl. States Conf. on Tchg. Fgn. Langs., 1992. Mem. Standard Club (Chgo.), Club Internat. (Chgo.), Northmoor Country Club (Highland Park, Ill.), Tamarisk Country Club (Rancho Mirage). Home: 195 Elder Ln Highland Park IL 60035-5368 Office: Next Chpt Holdings Port Clinton Sq 600 Central Ave Highland Park IL 60035-3211 Home (Winter): 70843 Tamarisk La Rancho Mirage CA 92270 E-mail: bpattis@nextchapterholdings.com.

PATTON, RAY BAKER, financial consultant, real estate broker; b. Jan. 24, 1932; s. Dwight Lyman Moody and Opal (Hembre) P.; m. Gloria Ruth Chambers, June 6, 1954; children: David Baker, Dayna Erin. BA, U. Okla., 1955, MRCP, 1960, MAPA, 1969. Asst. dir. planning San Joaquin, Calif., 1959-61; dir. planning City of Norman, Okla., 1961-65, Oklahoma City, 1965-67, St. Louis County, Mo., 1967-71; pres. Creative Environs., Inc., Clayton, 1972-74; prin. Raymond B. Patton & Assocs., Ballwin, 1975-81; investment broker, ins. planner A.G. Edwards & Sons, Inc., Clayton, 1981-83; fin. planning coord., dir. seminars E.F. Hutton & Co., Inc., St. Louis, 1983-84; securities prin. Westport Fin. Group, Inc., 1984-86; securities products coord., agy. edn. coord., fin. planner Equitable Fin. Cos., 1986-91; bus. and fin. cons. Mo. Automative Svc. Assn., 1991-93; broker, sales assoc. Coldwell Banker Real Estate, Chesterfield, Mo., 1994-95. Pres. Patton Real Estate, Inc., 1975-81, Success Power, Inc., St. Louis, 1975-81, chmn. bd., CEO, 1989-93; dir. pub. works and planning, health commr., zoning enforcement officer City of Des Peres, Mo., 1977-79; zone mgr. Investors Diversified Svc.'s, Chesterfield, 1980-81; securities prin. The Patton Fin. Group, Inc., St. Louis, 1984-86; chmn. bd., CEO Body Works, St. Louis, 1989-93; faculty mem. Nat. Inst. Farm and land Brokers, 1971-76; motivational spkr.; cons. in field. Contbr. articles to profl. jours. Scoutmaster St. Louis Area coun. Boy Scouts Am., 1976-80, vice chmn. adult tng., 1977-83; mem. Christian Bus. Men's Com., Chesterfield; mem. adv. bd. Cleveland County (Okla.) Child Welfare, 1963-64; min. music Ballwin, 1978-83, choir cir. E. Free Ch., Ladue, Mo., 1986; vol. tutor OASIS, 1994-96; former choir dir. E. Free, Manchester, Md.; tutor O.A.S.I.S.. Parkway, S.D., 1993-96. Served with USMC, 1955-58. Named Outstanding Mcpl. Employee State of Okla., 1963, Woodbage staff Outstanding Adult Scout Leader Pioneer Dist. Boy Scouts Am., 1978, 79; recipient IDS Mercury award, 1980, A.G. Edwards & Sons Crest award, 1982, Outstanding Exec. award E.F. Hutton, 1983, Blue Chip award, 1983, designated fin. advisor award, 1984. Mem. Am. Inst. Cert. Planners, Am. Inst. Planners (pres.-elect Mo., Kans., Okla. chpt. 1957, co-founder St. Louis Metro sect. 1969), Inst. Cert. Fin. Planners, Internat. Platform Assn., Internat. Assn. Fin. Planners, Eagle Scout Assn. (life), Fellowship Christian Fin. Advisors, Lambda Chi Alpha (pres. 1953-54). also: 2612 87th Ter E Palmetto FL 34221-8374 Home: 2612 87th Ter E Palmetto FL 34221-8374

PAUL, ALLEN E. state legislator; b. Ind., Mar. 30, 1945; m. Terri Mann; 1 child, Allen H.L. BS in Polit. Sci. and History, Parsons Coll., 1967. Del. Rep. State Conv., 1972-88; mem. from dist. 27 Ind. Senate from 27th dist., 1986—; majority whip Senate Leadership, 1992—; mem. govt. and regulatory affairs, natural resources, rules and legislative procedures coms. Ind. Senate; pres. Innovative Industries, Inc., Richmond, Ind. Author: Vietnam Letters. Exec. bd. dirs. Richmond YMCA; past v.p. Civic Theatre, bd. dirs; past. pres. Wayne County Hist. Soc. and Mus.; past comdr. Sons of Vets. Hist. Group. Sgt. U.S. Army, 1967-70, Viet Nam. Decorated Bronze Star; recipient Sagamore of the Wabash Gov. Orr, 1988. Mem. VFW, AMVETS, Am. Legion, Marine Corps League (hon. life), Richmond and Wayne County C. of C. (free enterprise com., legis. com., small bus. com., Outstanding Svc. of Month award), Howe Mil. Acad. Alumni (bd. dirs.), Ind. Football Hall of Fame (past bd. mem.), Jaycees of Richmond, Rotary, Yorkfellow Luncheon Group, Tau Kappa Epsilon (past pres.). Republican. Methodist. Office: Ind Senate Dist 27 200 W Washington St Indianapolis IN 46204-2728

PAUL, ARA GARO, university dean; b. New Castle, Pa., Mar. 1, 1929; s. John Hagop and Mary (Injejikian) P.; m. Shirley Elaine Waterman, Dec. 21, 1962; children: John Bartlett, Richard Goyan. BS in Pharmacy, Idaho State U., 1950; MS, U. Conn., 1953, PhD in Pharmacognosy, 1956. Cons. plant physiology Argonne (Ill.) Nat. Lab., 1955; asst. prof. pharmacognosy Butler U., Indpls., 1956-57; faculty U. Mich., Ann Arbor, 1957—, prof. pharmacognosy, 1969—; dean U. Mich. Coll. Pharmacy, 1975-96; dean emeritus, prof. pharmacognosy. Vis. prof. microbiology Tokyo U., 1965-66; mem. vis. chemistry faculty U. Calif., Berkeley, 1972-73; del. U.S. Pharmacopeial Conv., 1980, 90; scholar-in-residence Am. Assn. Colls. Pharmacy, 1996, mem. exec. v.p. adv. com.; bd. grants Am. Found. Pharm. Edn., 1997—, chmn., 1999, co-chmn. endowment com., 2002--; mem. organizing com. Millennial World Congress Pharm. Scis., 1996-2000; mem. FIP Found., 2000—, chmn. bd. trustees, 2001--. Contbr. articles to profl. jours. Recipient Outstanding Tchr. award Coll. Pharmacy, U. Mich., 1969, Outstanding Alumnus award Idaho State U., 1976, Profl. Achievement award Coll. Pharmacy, Idaho State U., 1990; G. Pfeiffer Meml. fellow Am. Found. Pharm. Edn., 1965-66, Disting. Svc. Profile award Am. Found Pharm. Edn., 1992; fellow Eli Lily Found., 1951-53, Am. Found. Pharm. Edn., 1954-56, NIH, 1972-73. Fellow AAAS; mem. Am. Pharm. Assn., Am. Soc. Pharmacognosy, Acad. Pharm. Scis., Am. Assn. Colls. Pharmacy, Am. Assn. Pharm. Scientists, Phi Lambda Upsilon, Sigma Xi, Phi Delta Chi, Phi Sigma Kappa, Rho Chi. Home: 1415 Brooklyn Ave Ann Arbor MI 48104-4496 Office: U Mich Coll Pharmacy Ann Arbor MI 48109-1065 E-mail: arapaul@umich.edu.

PAUL, ELDOR ALVIN, agriculture, ecology educator; b. Lamont, Alta., Can., Nov. 23, 1931; s. Reinhold and Ida (Mohr) P.; m. Phyllis Ellen Furhop, Aug. 3, 1955; children: Lynette, Linda. BSc, U. Alta., 1954, MSc, 1956; PhD, U. Minn., 1958. Asst. prof. U. Saskatchewan, Saskatoon, Can., 1959-64, assoc. prof. Can., 1964-70, prof. Can., 1970-80; mem. faculty, chmn. dept. plant and soil biology U. Calif., Berkeley, 1980-85; mem. faculty, chairperson dept. of crop and soil sciences Mich. State U., East Lansing, 1985-94; prof. crop and soil sci., 1994—. Vis. prof. U. Ga., Athens, 1972-73, USDA, Ft. Collins, 1992-93. Author: Soil Microbiology and Biochemistry, 1988, 1996; editor: Soil Biochemistry, vols. 3-5, 1973-81; Soil Organic Matter in Temperate Agro Ecosystems, 1997; contbr. over 200 articles on microbial ecology and soil microbiology to sci. publs. Fellow AAAS, Soil Sci. Soc. Am., Can. Soc. Soil Sci., Am. Soc. Agronomy (Soil Sci. Rsch. award 1995); mem. Internat. Soc. Soil Sci. Soil Biology (chmn. 1978-82), Am. Soc. Microbiology, Am. Ecol. Soc. Home: 843 Rossum Dr Loveland CO 80537-7944 Office: Mich State U Dept Crop & Soil Scis East Lansing MI 48824

PAUL, JACK DAVIS, retired state official, addictions consultant; b. Bismarck, N.D., Mar. 16, 1927; s. Harry Ernest and Bernice Ambert (Davis) P.; m. Mary Ann Langness, Aug. 23, 1955; children: Steven, William. BSc in Law, U. N.D., 1956, LLB, 1957, JD, 1969. Bar: N.D. 1957; cert. master addiction counselor, addictions clin. supr., profl. educator; lic. social worker, N.D.; diplomate Internat. Orgn. for Treatment of Sex Offenders, 1986. Pvt. practice law, Bismarck, 1957-71; exec. sec., gen. counsel N.D. Trade Commn., 1965-69; master addiction counselor N.D. Corrections Dept., Bismarck, 1972-79, dir. programs, 1980-89; ret., 1989; acting warden, 1986, 88. Instr. alcohol and drug edn. St. Mary's Ctrl. High Sch., Bismarck, 1977-87; dir. penal family treatment N.D. State Penitentiary, 1976-89; lectr. psychology, sociology Bismarck State Coll., 1992-99; cons. additions, sex therapist and sex offender rehab. programs, prison treatment programs, Mandan, N.D., 1974—; lectr. on addictions, 1974—; mem. faculty N.D. Internat. Alcohol Studies, Grand Forks, 1980-83; cons. Internat. Orgn. for Treatment of Sex Offenders and Violence, 1979—, Johnson Inst., 1978-83. Mem. Mandan City Citizens Planning Com. for Law Enforcement, 1984; del. Nat. Conf. on Corrections Policy, Washington, 1986. With USN, 1945-46, PTO; capt. U.S. Army, 1949-53. Recipient citation for nat. flood relief Govt. of Netherlands, 1953. Mem. N.D. Social Workers Assn., N.D. Lic. Addiction Counselors (v.p. 1980). Democrat. Congregationalist. Avocations: volleyball, racquetball, golf, volunteering, reading. Home: 701 3rd Ave NW Mandan ND 58554-2810

PAUL, RICHARD R. military officer; BSEE, U. Mo., Rolla, 1966; MSEE, Air Force Inst. of Tech., 1971; disting. grad., Squadron Officer Sch., 1975, Air Command and Staff Coll., 1980, Naval War Coll., 1984. Commd. 2d lt. USAF, 1967, advanced through grades to maj. gen., 1995; nuclear safety engr. Air Force Weapons Lab., Kirtland AFB, N.Mex., 1967-69; missile trajectory engr. 544th Aerospace Reconnaissance Tech. Wing, Offutt AFB, Nebr., 1971-72; command and control project officer Hdqs. Strategic Air Command, 1972-76; command and control mgr. Hdqs. USAF, Washington, 1976-79; staff scientist Joint Strategic Target Planning Staff, Offutt AFB, 1980-83; dep. comdr. for advanced tech., electronic sys. divsn. Hanscom AFB, Mass., 1984-88; comdr. Wright Lab., Wright-Patterson AFB, Ohio, 1988-92; dir. sci. and tech. Hdqs. Air Force Materiel Command, 1992-97; comdr. Air Force Rsch. Lab., 1997—. Decorated Legion of Merit with oak leaf cluster. Office: AFRL/CC 1864 4th St Wright Patterson AFB OH 45433-7130

PAUL, RONALD NEALE, management consultant; b. Chgo., July 22, 1934; s. David Edward and Frances (Kusel) P.; m. Nona Maria Moore, Dec. 27, 1964 (div. Oct. 1981); children: Lisa, Karen, Brenda; m. Georgeann Elizabeth Lapkoff, Apr. 10, 1982. BS in Indsl. Engring., Northwestern U., 1957, MBA, 1958. Asst. to pres. Victor Comptometer Co., Chgo., 1958-64; cons. Corplan, 1964-66; pres. Technomic Inc., 1966—. Mng. ptnr. L/P Ptnrs., Chgo., 1978-84; bd. dirs. Summit Restaurants, Salt Lake City, 1990-96. Co-author: The 101 Best Performing Companies in America, 1986, Winning the Chain Restaurant Game, 1994. Mem. Am. Mktg. Assn., Am. Mgmt. Assn., Planners Forum, Pres.'s Assn., Product Devel. Mgmt. Assn., Beta Gamma Sigma. Avocations: reading, racquetball. Office: Technomic Inc 300 S Riverside Plz Ste 1940 Chicago IL 60606-6613 E-mail: rpaul@technomic.com.

PAUL, STEPHEN HOWARD, lawyer; b. Indpls., June 28, 1947; s. Alfred and Sophia (Nahmias) P.; m. Deborah Lynn Dorman, Jan. 22, 1969; children: Gabriel, Jonathan. AB, Ind. U., 1969, JD, 1972. Bar: Ind. 1972, U.S. Dist. Ct. (so. dist.) Ind. 1972. Assoc. Baker & Daniels, Indpls., 1972-78, ptnr., 1979—. Mem. bd. visitors Ind. U. Sch. Law, Bloomington. Editor in chief Ind. U. Law Jour., 1971. Pres. Belle Meade Neighborhood Assn., Indpls., 1974-78; v.p., counsel Brentwood Neighborhood Assn., Carmel, Ind., 1985-88, pres., 1988-91. Mem. ABA (state and local tax com. 1985—, sports and entertainment law com.), Am. Property Tax Counsel (founding mem.), Ind. State Bar Assn., Order of Coif. Office: Baker & Daniels 300 N Meridian St Ste 2700 Indianapolis IN 46204-1782

PAULS, JANICE LONG, state legislator; m. Ron Pauls. BS, Sterling (Kans.) Coll., 1973; JD, U. Kans., 1976. Rep. dist. 102 Kans. Ho. of Reps., mem. Judiciary, rules and regulations, transp., corrections and juvenile justice coms. Democrat. Home: 1634 N Baker St Hutchinson KS 67501-5621 Office: Kans Ho of Reps State Capitol Topeka KS 66612

PAULSEN, ERIK, state legislator; b. Bakersfield, Calif., May 14, 1965; s. Gerald and Janet (Lindfors) P.; m. Kelly Spowls, 1989; 1 child, Cassandra. BA, Olaf Coll., Norfield, Minn., 1987. Mktg. mgr. CVN Co., 1987-89; field dir. U.S. Sen. Rudy Baschwitz, 1989-90; legis. asst. U.S. Congressman Jim Ramstad, 1991-92, dist. dir., 1994; Minn. state rep. Dist. 42B, 1995—. Mem. C. of C. Address: 9158 E Staring Ln Eden Prairie MN 55347-2518

PAUP, THOMAS, retail department store executive; CFO Montgomery Ward & Co., Chgo. Office: Montgomery Ward & Co 1 Wards Plz 535 W Chicago Ave Chicago IL 60671

PAUPORE, JEFFREY GEORGE, lawyer; b. Iron Mountain, Mich., Feb. 22, 1949; s. John Cyril and Marion Maybelle (Plante) P.; m. Patricia Barbara Byzcek, Oct. 26, 1974; children: Kristin Leigh, Eric Jeffrey. BS, No. Mich. U., 1973; JD, Thomas M. Cooley Coll., 1982. Bar: Ariz. 1983, U.S. Dist. Ct. Ariz. 1985, Mich. 1990, Wis. 1994. Assoc. John Payant Attys., Iron Mountain, 1982, Sylvester & Assocs., Tucson, 1983-89; pvt. practice, 1989-90, Iron Mountain, Mich., 1990-96; elected prosecutor Dickinson County, 1997—. Bd. dirs. ARC, Iron Mountain, 1975-77; tribunal advocate Diocese Tucson, 1986, Ariz. Coll. Trial Advocacy. Mem. Mich. Bar Assn., Ariz. Bar Assn., ABA, Pima County Bar Assn. (vol. radio program 1985-89), Dickinson County Bar Assn., Iron Mountain Jaycees (v.p. 1974-76). Republican. Roman Catholic. Lodges: Elks (trustee Tucson club 1985-89). Avocations: jewelry making, hiking, swimming. Home: 429 Waverly St Kingsford MI 49802-6742 Office: Dickonson County Prosecutor Correctional Ctr Iron Mountain MI 49801

PAVALON, EUGENE IRVING, lawyer; b. Chgo., Jan. 5, 1933; m. Lois M. Frenzel, Jan. 15, 1961; children: Betsy, Bruce, Lynn. BSL, Northwestern U., 1954, JD, 1956. Bar: Ill. 1956. Sr. ptnr. Pavalon, Gifford, Laatsch & Marino, Chgo., 1970—. Adj. prof. Northwestern U. Sch. Law; mem. com. on discovery rules Ill. Supreme Ct., 1981—; lectr., mem. faculty various law schs.; bd. dirs. ATLA Mut. Ins. Co. Author: Human Rights and Health Care Law, 1980, Your Medical Rights, 1990; contbr. articles to profl. jours., chpts. in books. Former mem. state bd. dirs. Ind. Voters Ill. bd. overseers Inst. Civil Justice, Rand Corp., 1993-99; mem. vis. com. Northwestern U. Law Sch., 1990-96. Capt. USAF, 1956-59. Fellow Am. Coll. Trial Lawyers, Internat. Soc. Barristers, Internat. Acad. Trial Lawyers, Roscoe Pound Found. (life, pres. 1988-90); mem. ABA, Chgo. Bar Assn. (bd. mgrs. 1978-79), Ill. Bar Assn., Ill. Trial Lawyers Assn. (pres. 1980-81), Trial Lawyers for Pub. Justice (founding mem., v.p. 1991-92, pres.-elect 1992-93, pres. 1993-94), Assn. Trial Lawyers Am. (parliamentarian 1983-84, sec. 1984-85, v.p. 1985-86, pres.-elect 1986-87, pres. 1987-88), Am. Bd. Profl. Liability Attys. (diplomate), Am. Bd. Trial Advocates, Inner Circle of Advocates, Chgo. Athletic Assn., Std. Club. Home: 1540 N Lake Shore Dr Chicago IL 60610-6684 Office: Pavalon Gifford et al 2 N La Salle St Chicago IL 60602-3702 E-mail: pavalon@pglmlaw.com.

PAVELICH, DANIEL L. accounting, tax, management consulting executive; CEO BDO Seidman LLP, Chgo.; ret., 1999. Office: BDO Seidman LLP Two Prudential Plaza 130 E Randolph St Fl 2800 Chicago IL 60601-6300

PAVSEK, DANIEL ALLAN, banker, educator; b. Cleve., Jan. 18, 1945; s. Daniel L. and Helen A. (Femec) P. AB, Maryknoll Coll., Glen Ellyn, Ill., 1966; MA, Maryknoll Sch. Theology, Ossining, N.Y., 1971, Cleve. State U., 1972; PhD, Case Western Res. U., 1981; MS, George Washington U., 2000. Pres. Coun. Richmond Heights, Ohio, 1972-75; lectr. econs. Cleve. State U., 1972-75; asst. prof. Baldwin-Wallace Coll., Berea, Ohio, 1975-81; v.p., economist Ameritrust Co., Cleve., 1981-91; dean, prof. econs. Harry F. Byrd Jr. Sch. Bus. Shenandoah U., Winchester, Va., 1992-99, Durell prof. money and banking H.F. Byrd Jr. Sch. Bus., 1999—. Adj. prof. bus. adminstrn. Baldwin-Wallace Coll., Berea, Ohio, 1981-91 Mem. Am. Econ. Assn., Nat. Assn. Bus. Econs. Democrat. Home: 21343 Sawyer Sq Ashburn VA 20147-4728 E-mail: dpavsek@su.edu.

PAWLAK, ANDRZEJ M. electrical engineer; b. Poland; m. Ewa; 1 child, Patricia. MS in Electrical Engring., Posnan U. Tech., 1971; PhD, Silesian U. Tech., Gliwice, 1981. Staff rsch. engr. GM, 1981, sr. staff rsch. engr. electrical and electronics dept. Speaker in field. Recipient Achievement award Indsl. Rsch. Inst. Patentee in field. Office: GM R&D Ctr 30500 Mound Rd Warren MI 48092-2031

PAWLENTY, TIM, state legislator; b. Nov. 1960; m. Mary Pawlenty; 1 child. BA, JD, U. Minn. Chmn. Eagan Planning Commn., 1988-89; mem. Minn. Ho. of Reps. St. Paul, 1993—. Atty. Active Eagan city coun., 1990-92. Fannie Gilbertson Coll. scholar. Republican. Office: 4117 Countryview Dr Eagan MN 55123-3948

PAWLEY, RAY LYNN, zoological park consultant, real estate developer; b. Midland, Mich., Nov. 7, 1935; s. Lynn Richard and Alice Marie (Skelton) P.; m. Ethel Marie Condon, Feb. 19, 1955 (div. 1974); children: Ray Allyn, Shanna Sue, Cynthia Ann, Dawn Marie, Brandon Earl, Dareen Joy; m. Hedda P. Saltz, Mar. 16, 1997. Student, Mich. State U., 1954-57. Asst. curator, lectr. Black Hills Reptile Gardens, Rapid City, S.D., summers 1952-53; owner, adminstr. Reptile Exhibit, St. Ignace, Mich., 1957-59; animal coord. Marlin Perkin's Wild Kingdom (Don Meier Prodns.), Chgo., 1961-62; zoologist Lincoln Park Zool. Gardens, 1961-64; curator Brookfield (Ill.) Zoo, 1964-97; ret., 1997. Assoc. dept. zoology Field Mus. Natural History, Chgo.; internat. zoo and conservation cons., Russia, Latvia, Mex., Kenya, China, Ecuador, Czechoslovakia; past instr. herpetology Field Mus., Coll. of DuPage, Triton Coll.; assoc. zoologist Moscow Zool. Pk., Russia; info. resource for fed. and state wildlife agys.; lectr., cons. in field. Contbr. over 100 articles to profl. jours. and popular mags.; co-creator money bench Chgo. Children's Mus. Past v.p. Ill. Endangered Species Protection Bd., Springfield; liaison Endangered Species Tech. Adv. Com., Springfield. Mem. Am. Zoo Assn. (3d Outstanding Svc. awards), Chgo. Acad. Scis. (life), Chgo. Herpetological Soc. (life), Mensa. Avocations: hiking, archaeology, art, mechanics, paleontology. Home and Office: PO Box 218 Hinsdale IL 60522-0218 E-mail: raypawley@core.com.

PAYNE, PATRICIA A. marketing professional; V.p. mktg. Zaring Nat. Corp., 1987-97, sr. v.p. sales and mktg., 1997—. Office: Zaring Nat Corp 11300 Cornell Park Dr Ste 500 Cincinnati OH 45242-1885

PAYNE, THOMAS H. market research company executive; Pres., CEO Market Facts, Inc., Arlington Heights, Ill., 1996—. Office: Market Facts Inc 3040 W Salt Creek Ln Arlington Heights IL 60005-1085

PAYNE, THOMAS L. university official; b. Bakersfield, Calif., Oct. 17, 1941; s. Harry LeRoy and Opal Irene (Ansel) P.; m. Sharon Alice Lewis, Feb. 1, 1963; children: Jacob, Joanna. AA in Liberal Arts, Bakersfield (Calif.) Jr. Coll., 1962; BA in Zoology, U. Calif., Riverside, 1965, MS in Entomology, 1967, PhD in Entomology, 1969. Asst. prof. entomology and forest sci. Tex. A&M U., College Station, 1969-73, assoc. prof., 1973-78, prof., 1978-87, rsch. coord. USDA so. pine beetle program, 1974-78; prof. entomology, head dept. Va. Poly. and State U., Blacksburg, 1987-92; dir. Ohio Agrl. R & D Ctr., Wooster; assoc. dean rsch., assoc. v.p. agrl. adminstrn. Ohio State U. Coll. Agr., 1993—99; vice chancellor, dean agr., food and natural resources. U. Mo. Coll. Agr., Columbia, 1999—. Sec. protection sect. Nat. Planning Conf. for Rsch. in Forestry and assoc. Rangelands, 1977; bd. dirs. Urban Pest Control Rsch. Ctr. Endowment Fund, 1988—; dean's rep., ex officio mem. Va. Pesticide Control Bd., 1989—; vis. prof. Forest Zoology Inst., U. Freiburg, Germany, 1978. Editor: (with Birch and Kennedy) Mechanisms in Insect Olfaction, 1986; mem. editorial bd. Jour. Ga. Entomol. Soc., 1979-83; co-editor Jour. Insect Behavior, 1987—; contbr. chpts. to books. Pres., co-founder Brazos County Firefighters Assn., 1979-81; v.p., co-founder Precinct 2 Vol. Fire Dept., 1979-80, pres., 1982-86; author grant to build Edge Tex. Sr. Citizens Ctr., 1979; mem. Friends of Blacksburg Master Chorale. Recipient numerous awards, 1976—, including cert. of appreciation for svc. as rsch. coord. expanded so. pine beetle rsch. USDA, 1976, 78, 80, rsch. award Tex. Forestry Assn., 1977, awards Am. Registry Profl. Entomologists, 1979, Alexander von Humboldt Stiftung sr. U.S. scientist award, 1982, Faculty Disting. Achievement award in rsch. Assn. Former Students Tex. A&M U., 1985, A.D. Hopkins award for outstanding rsch.-adminstrn. in forest entomology, 1991; Volkswagenwerk fellow U. Freiburg, 1978. Mem. AAAS, Entomol. Soc. Am. (CIBA-GEIGY agrl. recognition award 1982), Internat. Soc. Chem. Ecology, Internat. Chemoreception Workshop on Insects, Internat. Union Forest Rsch. Orgns., Nat. Corn Growers Assn., So. Forest Insect Work Conf., Va. Agribus. Coun., Va. Agrl. Chem. and Soil Fertility Assn., Va. Hort. Soc. (exec. coun. 1989), Va. Corn Growers Assn., Va. Soybean Assn., Va. Pest Control Assn, Western Forest Insect Work Conf., Coll. Agr. and Life Scis. Agr. Faculty Assn., Sigma Xi, Gamma Sigma Delta. Office: Univ Missouri Coll Agr Food/Nat Resource 2-69 Agrl Bldg Columbia MO 65211-0001 E-mail: cafnr@missouri.edu.

PAZANDAK, CAROL HENDRICKSON, liberal arts educator; b. Mpls. d. Norman Everard and Ruth (Buckley) Hendrickson; m. Bruce B. Pazandak (dec. 1986); children: David, Bradford, Chris, Eric, Paul, Ann; m. Joseph P. O'Shaughnessy, May 1991 (dec. Feb. 2000). PhD, U. Minn., 1970. Asst. dir. admissions U. Minn., Mpls., 1970-72, asst. dean liberal arts, 1972-79, asst. to pres., 1979-85, office of internat. edn., acting dir., 1985-87, asst. prof. to assoc. to prof. liberal arts, 1970-96, prof. emerita, 1996—; ptnr. Hollrad-Pers. Consulting, Reykjavik, Iceland, 1999—. Vis. prof. U. Iceland, Reykjavik, 1984, periods in 1983, 86-99; vis. rsch. prof. U. Oulu, Finland, 1993; exec. sec. Minn.-Iceland Adv. Com., U. Minn., 1984—; cons. U. Iceland, 1983-98; co-chair Reunion of Sisters-Minn. and Finland Confs., 1986-98; sec. Icelandic Assn. of Minn., 1995-97. Editor: Improving Undergraduate Education in Large Universities, 1989. Past pres. Minn. Mrs. Jaycees, Mpls. Mrs. Jaycees; formerly bd. govs. St. John's Preparatory Sch., Collegeville, Minn.; former bd. trustees Coll. of St. Teresa, Winona, Minn.. Recipient Partnership award for contbn. to advancing shared interests of Iceland and Am., 1994; named to Order of the Falcon, Govt. of Iceland, 1990, Coll. Liberal Arts Alumna Notable Achievement, 1995, Pres.'s Club, U. Minn., 1996. Mem. APA, Waikoloa Village Outdoor Cir. Home: 4505 Harry's Ln Dallas TX 75229 Office: U Minn N 218 Elliott Hall 75 E River Rd Minneapolis MN 55455-0280 E-mail: carolpz@umn.edu.

PEACOCK, CHRISTOPHER A. investment company executive; b. 1946; Student, Wellington Coll., Berkshire, Eng. With Jones Lang Wooten (now Jones Lang LaSalle Inc.), Eng., 1972—, ptnr. Eng., 1974, mem. exec. bd. continent of Europe, 1985—, mng. ptnr. continent of Europe, chmn. leasing agy., 1992-96, European CEO, 1996-97, internat. CEO, 1997-99, pres., dep. CEO, COO, chmn. mgmt. exec. com., dir., 1999—. Fellow Royal Instn. Chartered Surveyors. Office: Jones Lang LaSalle Inc 200 E Randolph Dr Chicago IL 60601 Fax: 312-782-4339.

PEARCE, HARRY JONATHAN, lawyer; b. Bismarck, N.D., Aug. 20, 1942; s. William R. and Jean Katherine (Murray) P.; m. Katherine B. Bruk, June 19, 1967; children: Shannon Pearce Baker, Susan J., Harry M. BS, USAF Acad., Colorado Springs, Colo., 1964; JD, Northwestern U., 1967; Degree in Engring. (hon.), Rose-Hulman Inst. Tech., 1997; LLD (hon.), Northwestern U., 1998. Bar: N.D. 1967, Mich. 1986. Mcpl. judge City of Bismarck, 1970-76, U.S. magistrate, 1970-76, police commr., 1976-80; sr. ptnr. Pearce & Durick, Bismarck, 1970-85; assoc. gen. counsel GM, Detroit, 1985-87, v.p., gen. counsel, 1987-92, exec. v.p., gen. counsel, 1992-94, exec. v.p., 1994-95, vice chmn., 1996—. Bd. dirs. GM Corp., Hughes Electronics Corp., GM Acceptance Corp., Delphi Automotive Sys. Corp., Alliance of Automobile Mfrs. of Marriott Internat. Inc., Econ. Strategy Inst., Theodore Roosevelt Medora Found., MDU Resources Group, Inc., Nat. Def. U. Found., Detroit Investment Fund. Mem. law bd. Sch. Law, Northwestern U.; mem. bd. visitors U.S. Air Force Acad.; chmn. Product Liability Adv. Coun. Found.; founding mem. minority counsel demonstration program Commn. on Opportunities for Minorities in the Profession, ABA; chmn. The Sabre Soc., USAF Acad.; trustee Howard U., U.S. Coun. for Internat. Bus., New Detroit, Inc.; mem. The Mentor's Group Forum for U.S.-European Union Legal-Econ. Affairs, The Conf. Bd., Network of Employers for Traffic Safety's Leadership Coun., Pres.'s Coun. on Sustainable Devel., World Bus. Coun. for Sustainable Devel., World Economic Forum Coun. Innovative Leaders in Globalization. Capt. USAF, 1964-70. Named Michiganian of Yr., The Detroit News, 1997; Hardy scholar Northwestern U., Chgo., 1964-67, recipient Alumni Merit award, 1991. Fellow Am. Coll. Trial Lawyers, Internat. Soc. Barristers; mem. Am. Law Inst. Avocations: amateur radio, woodworking, sailing. Office: GM Corp 300 Renaissance Ctr PO Box 100 Detroit MI 48265-1000

PEARCE, ROBERT J. museum director; Exec. dir. London (Ont., Can.) Mus. Archaeology; prof. anthropology U. Western Ont. Office: London Mus Archaeology 1600 Attawandaron Rd London ON Canada N6G 3M6

PEARCE, ROBERT BRENT, agricultural studies educator; Prof. agr. Iowa State U., Ames, prof. agr. emeritus, 1999—. Fellow Nat. Assn. Colls. Tchrs. Agriculture, 1992. Office: Iowa State U Dept Agronomy 120 Agronomy Ames IA 50011-0001

PEARLMAN, JERRY KENT, electronics company executive; b. Des Moines, Mar. 27, 1939; s. Leo R. Pearlman; married; children: Gregory, Neal. BA cum laude, Princeton U., 1960; MBA, Harvard U., 1962. With Ford Motor Co., 1962-70; v.p. fin. dir. Behring Corp., 1970-71; from contr. to chmn. Zenith Electronics Corp., Glenview, Ill., 1971-95. Bd. dirs. Smurfit-Stone Container Corp, Ryerson-Tull Corp., Nanophase Techs., Evanston Northwestern Healthcare. Bd. dirs. Northwestern U. Office: 21 Linden Ave Wilmette IL 60091-2837 E-mail: jpearl@nwu.edu.

PEARLSTEIN, ROBERT M. physics educator; b. N.Y.C., Oct. 16, 1937; s. Joseph and Sylvia (Leibow) P.; m. Linda Ellen Schecter, June 19, 1960; children: Daniel A., Deborah N. AB in Physics, Harvard U., 1960; PhD in Physics, U. Md., 1966. Physicist Inst. Muscle Rsch. Marine Biol. Lab., Woods Hole, Mass., 1962-63; rsch. asst., pub. health svc. fellow U. Md., College Park, 1963-66; NSF postdoctoral fellow biology divsn. Oak Ridge (Tenn.) Nat. Lab., 1966-67, mem. rsch. staff biology divsn., 1967-76, leader photosynthesis group biology divsn., 1972-75, coord. solar energy rsch., 1975-77, mem. rsch. staff chemistry divsn., 1975-78; lectr. Oak Ridge Grad. Sch. Biomed. Scis. U. Tenn., 1969-78; sr. rsch. scientist Battelle Columbus (Ohio) Labs., 1978-82; prof., chmn. physics Ind. U.-Purdue U., Indpls., 1983-90, prof. physics, 1983—; Argonne fellow Argonne (Ill.) Nat. Lab., 1994—. Scholar Harvard Club Washington, 1955-56; jr. engr. Baird-Atomic, Inc., Cambridge, Mass., 1958-60; physicist Nat. Bureau Standards, Washington, 1960-61; teaching asst. U. Md., Colleg Park, 1962; predoctoral fellow Pub. Health Svc., 1965-66; postdoctoral fellow NSF, 1966-67; chmn. organizing com. Internat. Conf. on Photosynthetic Unit, Gatlinburg, Tenn., 1969-70; sec., treas. photochemistry and photobiology group Biophys. Soc., 1970-71; vis. scientist Swiss Fed. Inst. Tech., Zurich, summers, 1984, 85; lectr. Bat-Sheva summer sch. on photosynthesis Weizmann Inst., Rehovot, Israel, 1988; faculty rsch. participant Argonne Nat. Labs., summers, 1992, 93. Author: (with others) Excited States of Biological Molecules, 1976, Excitons, 1982, Photosynthesis: Energy Conversion by Plants and Bacteria, 1982, Advances in Photosynthesis Research, 1984, Antennas and Reaction Centers of Photosynthetic Bacteria—Structure, Interactions, and Dynamics, 1985, Photosynthesis, 1987, Photosynthetic Light-Harvesting Systems, 1988, The Photsynthetic Bacterial Reaction Center, 1988, Chlorophylls, 1991; assoc. editor Biophys. Jour., 1981-84; guest editor Photochemistry and Photobiology, 1971; mem. hon. editorial bd. Photochemistry and Photobiology, 1971-73; contbr. articles to profl. jours. Recipient Biological Physics prize Am. Physical Society, 1994 Fellow AAAS, Am. Phys. Soc. (chem. divsn., biol. physics divsn., biophys. lectr. Ohio State sect. Fall meeting 1969, publs. com. divsn. biol. physics 1975-78, program com. divsn. biol. physics 1975-76, exec. com. divsn. biol. physics 1982-85, fellowship com. divsn. biol. physics 1990—, Biol. Physics prize 1994); mem. Biophys. Soc., Am. Soc. Photobiology, Sigma Xi. Office: Ind U-Purdue U Dept Physics 402 N Blackford St Indianapolis IN 46202-3217

PEARSON, DONNA SUTHERLAND, retired lumber company executive; CEO Sutherland Lumber, Kansas City, Mo. Office: Sutherland Lumber Co 4000 Main St Kansas City MO 64111-2326

PEARSON, FORD G. automotive executive; CFO Frank Consolidated Enterprises Inc., Des Plaines, Ill., exec. v.p., COO. Office: Frank Consolidated Enterprises Inc 666 Garland Pl Des Plaines IL 60016-4725

PEARSON, GERALD LEON, food company executive; b. Mpls., June 24, 1925; s. Perry and Lillian (Peterson) P.; m. Beverly Mary Schultz, Nov. 10, 1946; children: Steven, Perry, Liecia. Grad., Trimont (Minn.) High Sch., 1943. Treas. Trimont Packing Co., 1946-52; v.p. Spencer Foods, Iowa, 1952-68, pres., chief exec. officer, 1969-80, chmn. bd., chief exec. officer, 1972-80; chmn. Beef Specialists of Iowa Inc., 1983-94. Bd. dirs. Graffaloy, Inc., El Cajon, Calif., dir. applied mem. tech., Minnetonka, Minn.; chmn., CEO World Champions of Golf Inc.; owner Brooks Golf Club, Okoboji, Iowa. Pres. Pearson Art Found.; bd. dirs. Bethany Coll., Lindsborg; commr. Nat. Mus. Am. Art-Smithsonian Instn., 1995-99; founder Internat. Ctr. for Jazz Found. With USN, 1943-46. Mem. Swedish Royal Roundtable, Swedish Council Am. (bd. dirs.). Home: Desert Highlands # 444 10040 E Happy Valley Rd Scottsdale AZ 85255-2395 Office: Brooks Golf Club PO Box 948 Okoboji IA 51355-0948 E-mail: brooksgolfclub@aol.com.

PEARSON, MARK, radio personality; Radio host midday weekday show Sta. WHO-AM, Des Moines. Office: WHO Radio 1801 Grand Ave Des Moines IA 50309*

PEARSON, NATHAN WILLIAMS, communications and investment executive; b. Sewickley, Pa., Aug. 1, 1951; s. Nathan Williams Sr. and Kathleen Patricia (McMurtry) P.; m. Jane Ruth Wallace, Oct. 12, 1985; children: Nathan McMurtry, Howe Quinn, Henry Wallace. BA and MA in Music, Conn. Wesleyan U., 1974; MBA, Columbia U., 1982. Pvt. practice cons., N.Y.C. and Washington, 1974-82; with McKinsey & Co., N.Y.C. and L.A., 1982-88; exec. v.p., chief fin. officer, mng. prin., sec., treas. Broadcasting Ptnrs., Inc., N.Y.C., 1988-95; chmn. Broadcasting Ptnrs., L.L.C., Rye, NY, 1995—; pres., CEO and chmn. RadioWave.com Inc., Chgo., 1999—2001; with Broadcasting Ptnrs., LLC. Vice chmn. No. Light Comms., Reykjavik, 1995-; mng. dir. Commonwealth Holdings, Inc., N.Y.C., 1996-99; operating affiliate McCown DeLeeuw & Co., N.Y.C., 1997-99. Author: "Goin' to Kansas City," 1987; producer LP records, TV and radio programs; contbr. articles to profl. jours. Sec., bd. dirs. CityLore, Inc., N.Y.C., 1986—, pres., 1990-92; pres. Young Audiences/N.Y.C., 1995-96; bd. dirs. Young Audiences, 1986—, Young Audiences, Inc., 1995—. Mem. Soc. for Ethnomusicology, Am. Folklore Soc., Wadawanuck Club, Nat. Assn. Broadcasting, Manursing Island Club, Hillsboro Club, Beta Gamma Sigma. Avocations: boardsailing, river running, hiking. Home: 3 Holly Ln Rye NY 10580-3953 Office: Broadcasting Ptnrs Rye NY 10580 E-mail: bili_pearson@prodigy.net.

PEARSON, PAUL HAMMOND, physician; b. Bolenge, Belgian Congo; s. Ernest B. and Evelyn (Utter) P. B.S., Northwestern, 1944, B.Medicine, 1946, M.D., 1947; M.P.H., UCLA, 1963. Diplomate: Am. Bd. Pediatrics. Intern Los Angeles County Gen. Hosp., 1946-47; resident Cin. Children's Hosp., 1949-51; fellow convulsive disorders and electroencephalography Johns Hopkins Hosp., Balt., 1951-53; resident in child psychiatry U. B.C., Can., Vancouver, 1976-77; practice medicine specializing in pediatrics L.A., 1953-62; chief mental retardation br. USPHS div. chronic disease, 1963-65; asst. dir. mental retardation program Nat. Inst. Child Health and Human Devel., NIH, 1965-66; spl. asst. to surgeon gen. USPHS, 1966-67; C.L. Meyer prof. child health, prof. pub. health and preventive medicine, dir. Meyer Children's Rehab. Inst., 1967-81, McGaw prof. adolescent medicine, dir. adolescent medicine, 1982-89, prof. emeritus dept. pediatrics, 1989—; mem. grad. faculty U. Nebr. Coll. Medicine, Omaha, 1967—, med. dir. Univ. Hosp. Eating Disorder Program, 1983-89, sr. cons. Univ. Hosp. Eating Disorder Program, 1989—. From instr. to asst. clin. prof. U. So. Calif. Med. Sch., 1953-62; from assoc. clin. prof. pediatrics to clin. prof. pediatrics Georgetown U. Sch. Medicine, Washington, 1963-67; Cons., mem. profl. services program com. United Cerebral Palsy Assn., 1969-72, mem. nat. awards com., 1971; Am. Acad. Pediatrics liaison rep. to Am. Acad. Orthopedic Surgery, 1969-73; apptd. to Nat. Adv. Council Services and Facilities for Developmentally Disabled Dept. Health. Edn. and Welfare, 1971-75; councilor Accreditation Council Facilities for Mentally Retarded, Joint Commn. on Accreditation Hosps., 1973-74; fellow adolescent medicine Boston Children's Hosp. Med. Center, 1981 Cons. editor: Am. Jour. Mental Deficiency, 1970-72; Contbr. articles to profl. jours. Mem. com. on accessible environments Nat. Acad. Scis., 1974-77. Served to capt. MC AUS, 1947-49. Mem. Am. Acad. Pediatrcs (com. on children with handicaps 1969-75, com. sect. on child devel. 1974—), Am. Assn. Mental Deficiency, Nat. Assn. for Retarded Children, Greater Omaha Assn. for Retarded Children (dir.), Am. Pub. Health Assn., Am. Acad. Cerebral Palsy and Developmental Medicine (exec. com. 1971-76, chmn. sci. program com. 1972-74, sec. 1974-77, mem. research and awards com. 1977-78, pres. 1981-82, bd. dirs. 1982-84), Assn. Univ.-Affiliated Facilities (exec. com. 1973— , v.p. 1974-75, pres. 1975-76, dir. 1971-78), Soc. Adolescent MedicineAlpha Omega Alpha. Home: 3247 N Boulder Cyn Mesa AZ 85207-1846 Office: U Nebr Med Ctr Dept Pediatrics Omaha NE 68198-0001

PEARSON, RONALD DALE, retail food stores corporation executive; b. Des Moines, 1940; married. B.S. in Bus. Adminstrn., Drake U., 1962. With Hy-Vee Food Stores, Inc. (name changed to Hy-Vee, Inc. in 1996), Chariton, Iowa, 1962—; pres. Hy-Vee, Inc., 1983—, chmn., pres., & CEO, 1989—. Dir. Beverage Mfrs., Inc., Civic Ctr. Cts., Inc. Office: Hy-Vee Inc 5820 Westown Pkwy West Des Moines IA 50266

PEARSON, WILBERT D. career officer; BS in Aerospace Engring., Tex. A&M U., 1969; postgrad., Ball State U., 1975. Commd. 2d lt. USAF, 1970, advanced through grades to brig. gen., 1997; F-4 combat pilot Korat Royal Thai AFB, Thailand, 1972-73; instr. pilot, standardization/evaluation pilot 22nd Tactical Fighter Squadron, Bitburg AB, West Germany, 1973-76; instr. pilot, wing weapons and tactics officer 53rd Tactical Fighter Squadron, West Germany, 1976-78; F-15 operational test pilot 422nd Fighter Weapons Squadron, Nellis AFB, Nev., 1978-81; F-4 and F-5 test pilot 6512 Test Squadron, Edward AFB, Calif., 1983-84, F-20 test pilot, 1984-85, dir. F-15 anti-satelite combined test force, 1985-87, comdr., 1987-89; dir. ops. mgmt. Hdqrs. AF Systems Command, Andrews AFB, Md., 1989-91; dep. for aeronautical systems Office of the Undersec. of Def. for Acquisition and Tech., Washington, 1992-96; vice comdr. Electronic Systems Ctr., Hanscom AFB, Mass., 1996-97; dir. ops., brig. gen. Hdqrs. Air Force Material Command, Wright-Patterson AFB, 1997—. Decorated DFC with two oak leaf clusters, Air medal with nine oak leaf clusters, Republic of Vietnam Gallantry Cross with palm, Republic of Vietnam campaign medal, Air Force Systems Command Primus award; Ira Eaker fellowship Air Force Assn., 1985. Office: HQ AFMC/DO 4375 Chidlaw Rd Ste 143 Wright Patterson AFB OH 45433-5066

PEAVY, HOMER LOUIS, JR. real estate executive, accountant; b. Okmulgee, Okla., Sept. 4, 1924; s. Homer Louis and Hattie Lee (Walker) P.; m. children: Homer Martin, Daryl Mark. Student, Kent State U., 1944-49; grad., Hammel-Actual Coll., Ohio, 1962. Sales supr. Kirby Sales, Akron, Ohio, 1948-49; sales mgr. Williams-Kirby Co., Detroit, 1949-50; area distributor Peavy-Kirby Co., Phila., 1953-54; salesman James L. Peaby Realty Co., Akron, 1964-65; owner Homer Louis Peavy Jr., Real Estate Broker, 1965—; pvt. practice acctg., 1962—. Fin. aid officer Buckeye Coll., Akron, 1982. Author: Watt Watts, 1969; poet: Magic of the Muse, 1978, P.S. I Love You, 1982; contbr. poetry to Am. Poetry Anthology, 1983, New Worlds Unlimited, 1984, Treasures of the Precioys Moments, 1985, Our World's Most Cherished Poems, 1985; songs: Sh...Sh, Sheree, Sheree, 1976, In Akron O, 1979; teleplay: Revenge, 1980. Bd. dirs. Internat. Elvis Gold Soc., 1978—; charter mem. Statue of Liberty-Ellis Island Found., 1984, Nat. Am. Indian, U.S. Holocaust Meml. Mus.; mem. Nat. Trust Hist. Preservation, Ohio Hist. Soc., Preservation/N.C., Japanese Am. Nat. Mus.; charter mem. USS Constn. Recipient Am. Film Inst. Cert. Recognition, 1982, Merit cert. World Poetry 10th ann. contest, 1985, Golden Poet award World of Poetry, 1985, 87-89. Mem. NAACP (mem.-at-large), Ohioana Libr. Assn., Internat. Black Writers Conf., Acad. Am. Poets, Poetry Soc. Am., Smithsonian Nat. Assocs., Manuscript Club Akron, Ohio Theatre Alliance, Kent State U. Alumni Assn. Democrat. Home and Office: 1160 Cadillac Blvd Akron OH 44320-2858

PECANO, DONALD CARL, automotive manufacturing executive; b. L.A., Dec. 2, 1948; s. Domenick Lawrence and Carlotta Noble (Martello) P.; m. Sandra Ann Tuminello, Apr. 26, 1969; children: Julia Ann, Melissa Ann, Donald Carl. BS in Acctg, Pa. State U., 1970; MBA in Mktg., Youngstown State U., 1981. CPA, Pa.; cert. mgmt. acct., cert. fin. mgr. Contr. Atlas Guard Svc. subs. SERVISCO, East Orange, N.J., 1974-76; asst. to pres. SERVISCO, Hillside, 1976-77; v.p. fin. Columbus Svcs., Inc. subs. SERVISCO, New Castle, Pa., 1977-82; dir. fin. East Mfg. Corp. and subs. cos., 1982-88, v.p. fin. and adminstrn., 1988-99, also mem. exec. com., exec. v.p., CFO, 1999—; v.p. fin. Intermodal Techs. Inc., 1991—. Bd. dirs. Intermodal Techs. Inc. Weatherhead fellow Case Western Res. U., 1995. Republican. Roman Catholic. Office: 1871 State Route 44 Randolph OH 44265

PECCARELLI, ANTHONY MARANDO, lawyer; b. Newark, Apr. 12, 1928; s. Adolph and Mary (Marano) P.; m. Mary Dearborn Hutchison, Dec. 23, 1953; children: Andrew Louis, David Anthony, Laura Elizabeth. BS, Beloit Coll., 1953; JD, John Marshall Law Sch., 1959; M in Jud. Studies, U. Nev., 1990. Bar: Ill. 1961, U.S. Dist. Ct. (no. dist.) Ill., U.S. Supreme Ct. Supr. real estate and claims Gulf Oil Corp., Chgo., 1956-61; asst. state's atty. DuPage County, Wheaton, Ill., 1961-65; first asst. state's atty. DuPage County State's Atty., 1965-69; mem.-del. Ill. Constnl. Conv., Springfield, 1969-70; exec. dir. Ill. State's Atty. Assn., Elgin, 1970-71; ptnr. Barclay, Damisch & Sinson, Chgo., 1971-79; assoc. cir. judge 18th Jud. Cir. Ct., Wheaton, 1979-82, cir. judge, 1982-93, chief judge, 1989-93, presiding judge domestic rels. divsn., 1982-83, presiding judge law divsn., 1987-89, chief judge, 1989-93; justice 2nd dist. Ill. Appellate Ct., 1993-94; state's atty. DuPage County, Ill., 1995-96; assoc., of counsel Ottosen Trevarthen Britz Kelly & Cooper, Ltd., 1996—. Exec. Conflict Resolution Ltd.; chair Ill. Jud. Conf. Ill. Supreme Ct., Springfield, 1987-89. Contbr. articles to profl. jours. Bd. dirs., treas. DuPage Coun. for Child Devel.; bd. dirs. Ctrl. DuPage Pastoral Counseling Ctr.; chair Wheaton Com. for Jud. Reform,

1962; trustee Midwestern U., 1993—, vice chmn., bd. trustees 1997-99. Cpl. USMC, 1946-48. Mem. DuPage County Bar Assn. (pres. 1972-73), DuPage County Legal Assistance Fedn. (pres. 1973-74), DuPage County Lawyer Referral Svc. (pres. 1972).

PECK, ABRAHAM, editor, writer, educator, magazine consultant; b. N.Y.C., Jan. 18, 1945; s. Jacob and Lottie (Bell) Peckolick; m. Suzanne Wexler, Mar. 19, 1977; children: Douglas Benjamin, Robert Wexler. BA, NYU, 1965; postgrad., CUNY, 1965-67; Cert. Advanced Exec. Program, Northwestern U., 1997. Engaged in community organizing and tutoring, 1962-64; with N.Y.C. Welfare Dept., 1965-67; free-lance writer, 1967—; writer, organizer Chgo. Action Youth Internat. Party, 1968; editor Chgo. Seed, 1968-70; treas. Seed Pub., Inc., 1968-70; mem. coordinating com. Underground Press Syndicate, 1969; assoc. editor Rolling Stone mag., San Francisco, 1975-76, contbg. editor, 1976-2001; cons. various mags., 1984—; ednl. cons. Asian Sources Media Group, Hong Kong, Manila, 1989-97; editl. co-auditor Advanstar Comm., 1999—; feature writer Chgo. Daily News, 1977-78; with features dept. Chgo. Sun-Times, 1978-81; from asst. prof. to prof. Medill Sch. Journalism, Northwestern U., 1981—2001, Theodore R. & Annie Laurie Sills prof. journalism, 2001—. Critic at large Sta. WBBM, 1979-82; editor, co-founder Sidetracks, alt. newspaper supplement, Chgo. Daily News, 1977-78; mem. exec. com. Assn. for Edn. in Journalism and Mass Communication, mag. divsn., 1987-89, 92-96, pres., 1994-95; mem. adv. bd. Academe mag., Am. Assn. Univ. Profs., 1990-2000, Heartland Jour., 1990—, Technos, 1992—, chair ethics sub-com., Am. Bus. Media, 2002; adv. bd. Asian Am. Journalists Assn., 2002; dir. mag. programs media mgmt. ctr. Northwestern U., 2002-. Editor: Dancing Madness, 1976; author: Uncovering the Sixties: The Life and Times of the Underground Press, 1985, 91; cons. editor, contbr.: The Sixties, 1977; contbr.: The Eighties: A Look Back, 1979, Voices From the Underground, 1993. Served with AUS, 1967. Office: Northwestern U Medill Sch Journalism 1845 Sheridan Rd Evanston IL 60208-0815 E-mail: a.peck@northwestern.edu.

PECK, GARNET EDWARD, pharmacist, educator; b. Windsor, Ont., Can., Feb. 4, 1930; s. William Crozier and Dorothy (Marentette) P.; m. Mary Ellen Hoffman, Aug. 24, 1957; children: Monique Elizabeth, Denise Anne, Philip Warren, John Edward. BS in Pharmacy with Distinction, Ohio No. U., 1957; MS in Indsl. Pharmacy, Purdue U., 1959, PhD, 1962. Sr. scientist Mead Johnson Research Center, 1962-65, group leader, 1965-67; assoc. prof. indsl. and phys. pharmacy Purdue U., West Lafayette, 1967-73, prof., 1973—, dir. indsl. pharmacy lab., 1975—, assoc. dept. head, 1989-96. Cons. in field. Contbr. articles to profl. jours. Mem. West Lafayette Mayor's Advisory Com. on Community Devel., 1973— ; mem. West Lafayette Citizen's Safety Com., 1974-81; mem. West Lafayette Park Bd., 1981— , pres., 1983-96. Served with U.S. Army, 1951-53. Recipient Lederle Faculty award Purdue U., 1976 Fellow APHA, AAAS, Am. Inst. Chem., Am. Assn. Pharmaceutical Scientists; mem. Am. Chem. Soc., Acad. of Rsch. and Sci. (Sidney Riegelman award 1994), Am. Assn. Colls. of Pharmacy, Cath. Acad. Sci. (founding mem.), KC, Rho Chi, Phi Lambda Upsilon, Phi Kappa Phi, Phi Sigma Lambda, Phi Lambda Sigma. Roman Catholic. Office: Purdue U Sch Pharmacy & Pharm Scis Dept Industrial & Physical Pharm West Lafayette IN 47907

PECK, WILLIAM ARNO, physician, educator, university official and dean; b. New Britain, Conn., Sept. 28, 1933; s. Bernard Carl and Molla (Nair) P.; m. Patricia Hearn, July 10, 1982; children by previous marriage: Catherine, Edward Pershall, David Nathaniel; stepchildren: Andrea, Elizabeth, Katherine. AB, Harvard U., 1955; MD, U. Rochester, N.Y., 1960; DSc (hon.), U. Rochester, 2000. Intern, then resident in internal medicine Barnes Hosp., St. Louis, 1960-62; fellow in metabolism Washington U. Sch. Medicine, 1963; mem. faculty U. Rochester Med. Sch., 1965-76, prof. medicine and biochemistry, 1973-76, head divsn. endocrinology and metabolism, 1969-76; John E. and Adaline Simon prof. medicine, co-chmn. dept. medicine Washington U. Sch. Medicine, St. Louis, 1976-89; physician in chief Jewish Hosp., 1976-89; prof. medicine and exec. vice chancellor med. affairs, dean sch. medicine, pres. univ. med. ctr. Washington U., 1989—. Chmn. endocrinology and metabolism adv. com. FDA, 1976-78; chmn. gen. medicine study sect. NIH, 1979-81; chmn. Gordon Conf. Chemistry, Physiology and Structure of Bones and Teeth, 1977; chmn. Consensus Devel. Conf. on Osteoporosis, NIH, 1984; co-chmn. Workshop on Future Directions in Osteoporosis, 1987; chmn. Spl. Topic Conf. on Osteoporosis, U.S. FDA, 1987; dir. Angelica Corp., Allied Healthcare Products, Hologic, Reinsurance Group of Am., TIAA-CREF Trust Co. Editor Bone and Mineral Rsch. Anns., 1982-88. Pres. Nat. Osteoporosis Found., 1985-90. Served as med. officer USPHS, 1963-65. Recipient Lederle Med. Faculty award, 1967, career program award NIH, 1970-75, commr.'s spl. citation FDA, 1988, Humanitarian award Arthritis Found. Ea. Mo., 1995, Founders award Nat. Osteoporosis Found., 1996, Humanitarian award Crohn's and Colitis Fedn. Am., 1999; Paul Harris fellow Rotary Found., 2001. Fellow AAAS, ACP; mem. Internat. Bone & Mineral Soc., Royal Soc. Medicine, Am. Assn. Clin. Endocrinologists, Am. Geriatrics Soc., Am. Soc. Biochemistry & Molecular Biophysics, Am. Soc. Bone and Mineral Rsch. (councilor 1978-81, pres.-elect 1982-83, pres. 1983-84), Am. Soc. Clin. Investigation, Am. Soc. Internal Medicine, Assn. Am. Med. Colls. (coun. deans adminstrv. bd. 1992—, chmn. 1996-97, chair elect 1997-98, chair 1998—, immediate past chair 1999), Assn. Am. Physicians, Endocrine Soc., Orthopaedic Rsch. Soc., Soc. Med. Adminstrs., St. Louis Metro. Med. Soc., St. Louis Soc. Internal Medicine (pres. 1986), Inst. Medicine Nat. Acad. Sci., Washington U. Health Adminstrn. Program Alumni Assn. (hon.), Research! Am. (vice chair 1999—), Pi Theta Epsilon (hon.), Sigma Xi, Alpha Omega Alpha (bd. dirs 1992-95). Home: 32 Huntleigh Downs Saint Louis MO 63131 Office: Washington U Sch Medicine 600 S Euclid Ave Saint Louis MO 63110-1010

PECK, WILLIAM HENRY, museum curator, art historian, archaeologist, author, lecturer; b. Savannah, Ga., Oct. 2, 1932; s. William Henry Peck and Mildred (Bass) Peck Tuten; m. Ann Amelia Keller, Feb. 2, 1957 (dec. 1965); children: Alice Ann, Sarah Louise; m. Elsie Holmes, July 8, 1967; 1 child, William Henry IV. Student, Ohio State U., 1950-53; BFA, Wayne State U., 1960, MA, 1961. Jr .curator Detroit Inst. Arts, 1960-62, asst. curator, 1962-64, assoc. curator, 1964-68, curator ancient art, 1968—, acting chief curator, 1984-88, sr. curator, 1988—. Lectr. art history Cranbrook Acad. Art, Bloomfield Hills, Mich., 1963-65; vis. lectr. U. Mich., Ann Arbor, 1970; adj. prof. art history Wayne State U., Detroit, 1966—; excavations in Egypt, Mendes, 1964-66, Precinct of Mut, Karnak, 1978—. Author: Drawings from Ancient Egypt, 1978, The Detroit Institute of Arts: A Brief History, 1991, Splendors of Ancient Egypt, 1978; co-author: Ancient Egypt: Discovering its Splendors, 1978, Mummies, Diseases and Ancient Cultures, 1980, also articles. With U.S. Army, 1953-55. Recipient award in the arts Wayne State U., 1985; Ford Motor Co. travel grantee, 1962; Am. Rsch. Ctr. Egypt fellow, 1971; Smithsonian Instn. travel grantee, 1975. Mem. Archaeol. Inst. Am., Am. Rsch. Ctr. Egypt, Internat. Assn. Egyptologists, Soc. Study Egyptian Antiquities, Am. Assn. Mus., Oriental Inst.-U. Chgo. Democrat. Episcopalian. Avocations: origami, performance of early music, collecting T.E. Lawrence material. Office: Inst Arts 5200 Woodward Ave Detroit MI 48202-4008 E-mail: wpeck@dia.org.

PEDDICORD, ROLAND DALE, lawyer; b. Van Meter, Iowa, Mar. 29, 1936; s. Clifford Elwood and Juanitas Irene (Brittain) P.; m. Teri Linn O'Dell; children: Erin Sue, Robert Sean. BSBA with honors, Drake U., 1961, JD with honors, 1962. Bar: Iowa 1962; cert. civil trial specialist Nat. Bd. Trial Advs. Asst. atty. gen. State of Iowa, 1962-63; assoc. Steward, Crouch & Hopkins, Des Moines, 1962-65; ptnr. Peddicord, Wharton, Spencer & Hook, 1965—. Lectr. in law Drake U., 1962-68; lectr. law Coll. Osteo. Medicine, Des Moines, 1965-72 Editor and chief Drake Law Rev., 1961-62 Past mem. nat. bd. dirs., nat. coun. YMCA of U.S.A., past vice chmn. nat. bd.; bd. dirs., past chmn. Greater Des Moines YMCA, 1968-89. With USMC, 1954-57. Mem. ABA, ATLA, Iowa Bar Assn., Polk County Bar Assn., Iowa Trial Lawyers Assn., Iowa Acad. Trial Lawyers, Am. Bd. Trial Advs. (mem. nat. bd., past pres. Iowa chpt.). Republican. Methodist. Office: 405 6th Ave Ste 700 Des Moines IA 50309-2415 also: Peddicord Wharton Spencer & Hook PO Box 9130 Des Moines IA 50306-9130 E-mail: Dale.Peddicord@Peddicord-Law.com.

PEDERSEN, DWITE A. state legislator; b. Chamberlain, S.D., Oct. 20, 1941; m. Priscilla Dougherty, Apr. 3, 1970; children: Andrew, Michaela, Megan. Undergrad., S.D. State U., S.D. So. State Tchrs. Coll.; B in human rels., Doane Coll., 1995. Cert. Gambling counselor Nebr. Nat. Assns. Alcoholism and Drug Abuse. Substance abuse counselor; acct., bus. adminstr. Internat. Harvester Co.; owner; counselor, adminstr. Boys Town; tchr.; mem. Nebr. Legislature from 39th dist., Lincoln, 1992—. Mem. Western Douglas Cty. C. of C., Elkhorn Eagles Club, Elkhorn Lions Club, St. Patrick's Cath. Ch. Men's Club. Mem. Nebr. and Nat. Assns. Alcoholism and Drug Abuse Counselors, Elkhorn Optimist Club (charter mem.), Nebr. Child Care Workers' Assn. (pres.). Roman Catholic. Office: State Capitol (Dist 39) Room 1018 PO Box 94604 Lincoln NE 68509-4604

PEDERSEN, KAREN SUE, electrical engineer; b. Indianola, Iowa, Apr. 27, 1942; d. Donald Cecil and Dorothy Darlene (Frazier) Kading; m. Wendell Dean Pedersen, May 6, 1961; children: Debra Ann Pedersen Schwickerath, Michael Dean. AA, Grand View Coll., Des Moines, 1975; BSEE, Iowa State U., 1977; MBA, Bentley Coll., Waltham, Mass., 1989. Registered profl. engr., Mass., Iowa, Ill. Engr. Iowa Power & Light Co., Des Moines, 1978-80, rate engr., 1980-84; sr. rsch. engr. Boston Edison Co., Boston, 1984-87, sr. engr., 1987-94, prin. rsch. analyst, 1994-98; sr. engr. Mid Am. Energy Co., Davenport, Iowa, 1998—. Ops. chmn. Old South Ch., Boston, 1989-98. Mem. IEEE (chmn. Iowa ctrl. sect. 1983-84, sec. Iowa-Ill. sect., exec. bd.), NSPE, Mass. Soc. Profl. Engrs. (pres. 1992-93, NSPE/PEI vice chair northeast region 1995-97, sec. 1997-98, chair elect 1998-99, v.p. NSPE/PEI, v.p NSPE 1999-2000, v.p. NSPE/North Ctrl. region 2001—), Eta Kappa Nu. Republican. Congregationalist. Office: Mid Am Energy Co 106 E 2nd St # D Davenport IA 52801-1502 E-mail: KSPedersen@midamerican.com.

PEDERSON, DONALD W. state legislature; b. Hasting, Nebr., Dec. 23, 1928; m. Virginia L. Cummings, Dec. 28, 1953; children: David, Steven, Scott, Jeff. Student, U. Nebr., Omaha, U. Nebr., Lincoln, Grinnell Coll. Lawyer; mem. Nebr. Legislature from 42nd dist., Lincoln, 1996—. Former mem., pres. N. Platte Bd. Edn., N. Platte Jr. Coll.; mem. Presbyn. Ch. N. Platte. Mem. Nebr. State Bar Assn., Lincoln County Bar Assn., Mid-Nebr. Cmty. Found. (former pres., bd. dirs.), Rotary. Home: 2011 Cedarberry Rd North Platte NE 69101-5943 Office: State Capitol Dist 42 PO Box 94604 Rm 1016 Lincoln NE 68509-4604

PEDERSON, GORDON ROY, state legislator, retired military officer; b. Gayville, S.D, Aug. 8, 1927; s. Roy E. and Gladys F. (Masker) P.; m. Betty L. Ballard, Mar. 8, 1955; children: James D., Carol A. Pederson Niemann, Nancy G. Pederson Holub, Gary W. Student, Yankton Coll., 1948-50, Fla. State U., 1963; advanced course, Infantry Sch., 1958-59. Drafted U.S. Army, 1945-47, commd. 2nd lt., 1952, advanced through grades to lt. col., 1967, served Korean War, 1950-54, served CONUS World War II, platoon leader 17th infantry regiment, 7th infantry divsn. Korea, 1953-54, rifle co. commdr. 10th mountain divsn. Germany, 1955-58, instr., dir. instrn. U.S. Army Jungle Warfare Tng. Ctr. Canal Zone, 1961-63, comdr. post Canal Zone, 1963-64, 1st brig., 1st infantry divsn. Vietnam, 1965-66, dir. tng. hdqs., 1966-68; advisor Ministry of Nat. Def., Rep. China on Taiwan, 1969-70; retired U.S. Army, 1970; rep. S.D. Ho. Reps., Pierre, 1977-99, 2001—; operator Dairy Queen, Wall, S.D., 1990-95. Chmn. transp. com. S.D. Ho. Reps., 1979-93, vice chair state affairs com., 1996-98, vice chair commerce com., 1998, chmn. budget audit com., 2001—, vice chmn. transp. com., 2001—. Del. S.D. Rep. Conv., 1974-78, 80, 82, 84, 86, 88, 90, 92, 94, 96, 98, 2000, 02, Nat. Rep. Conv., 1976, 80, 84, 88, 92, 96, 2000; bd. dirs. Legis. Rsch. Coun., 1988, 90, 92, 96, 98, 2001—. Decorated Bronze Star, Medal of Merit, U.S. Presdl. Unit Citation, Rep. Korea Presdl. Unit Citation, Rep. Vietnam Presdl. Unit Citation, Combat Infantry Badge with Star, Legion of Merit, Air Medal with 2 Oak Leaf Clusters, Army Accomodation medal with 2 oak leaf clusters, Cross of Gallantry with Palm, Republic Vietnam. Mem. VFW, DAV, Am. Legion, Retired Officers Assn., Wall C. of C., Internat. Lions Club, Sons of Norway. Lutheran. Home: PO Box 312 116 W 7th St Wall SD 57790 Office: SD Ho of Reps State Capitol Bldg Pierre SD 57501 E-mail: bpers@GWTC.net., gordonpederson@state.U.S.S.D.

PEDERSON, SALLY, lieutenant governor; b. Muscatine, Iowa, Jan. 13, 1951; d. Gerald and Wineva Pederson; m. James A. Autry, Feb. 6, 1982; children: Rick, Jim Jr., Ronald. Grad., Iowa State U., 1973. With Meredith Corp., 1973-84; sr. food editor Better Homes & Gardens mag.; lt. gov. State of Iowa, 1999—. Pres. Polk County Health Svcs.; bast bd. trustees Nat. Alliance for Autism Rsch.; pres. bd. trustees Autism Soc. Iowa; founding pres. The Homestead Living and Learning Ctr. for Adults with Autism; past cmty. bd. svcs. includes Des Moines Cmty. Playhouse, Very Spl. Arts Iowa, YWCA Aliber Child Care Ctr., YMCA Ctr. Br.; parent rep. Heartland AEA Autism Steering Com.; mem. Iowa State Spl. Edn. Adv. Bd; bd. dirs. Blank Children's Hosp., Mid-Iowa Health Found.; gov.'s appointee State Spl. Edn. Adv. Panel. Office: Office of Lt Governor State Capitol Bldg Des Moines IA 50319-0001*

PEDLEY, JOHN GRIFFITHS, archaeologist, educator; b. Burnley, Eng., July 19, 1931; arrived in U.S., 1959; s. George and Anne (Whitaker) Pedley; m. Mary Grace Sponberg, Aug. 30, 1969. BA, Cambridge (Eng.) U., 1953, MA, 1959; postgrad. (Norton fellow), Am. Sch. Classical Studies, Athens, Greece, 1963-64; PhD, Harvard U., 1965. Loeb rsch. fellow in classical archaeology Harvard U., Cambridge, Mass., 1969-70; asst. prof. classical archaeology and Greek U. Mich., Ann Arbor, 1965-68, assoc. prof., 1968-74, acting chmn. dept. classical studies, 1971-72, 75-76; dir. Kelsey Mus. Archaeology, 1973-86, prof., 1974—. Guest scholar J. Paul Getty Mus.; mem. staff excavations, Sardis, Turkey, 1962—64, Pylos, Greece, 1964; co-dir. excavations, Apollonia, Libya, 1966—68; field dir. Corpus Ancient Mosiacs, Tunisia, 1972—73; co-prin. investigator excavations, Carthage, North Africa, 1975—79; dir. excavations, Paestum, Italy, 1982—85, Paestum, 1993, Paestum, 95, Paestum, 1997—98; vis. scholar UCLA, 1989; resident in archaeology Am. Acad., Rome, 1990. Author: (book) Sardis in the Age of Croesus, 1968, Sardis in the Age of Croesus, reprint, 1999, Ancient Literary Sources on Sardis, 1972, Greek Sculpture of the Archaic Period: The Island Workshops, 1976, Paestum: Greeks and Romans in Southern Italy, 1990, Greek Art and Archaeology, 1992, Greek Art and Archaeology, 2d edit., 1998; co-author: Apollonia, the Port of Cyrene, 1977, The Sanctuary of Santa Venera at Paestum, Vol. 1, 1993, Corpus des Mosaiques de Tunisie, Vol. III, 1996; editor: New Light on Ancient Carthage, 1980; co-editor: Studies Presented to GMA Hanfmann, 1971. Fellow Am. Coun. Learned Socs., 1972—73, NEH, 1986; grantee, Am. Philol. Soc., 1979, Nat. Endowment Arts Mus., 1974, 1977, 1979, 1980, NEH, 1967, 1975, 1983, 1984. Home: 1720 Morton Ave Ann Arbor MI 48104-4522 Office: Dept Classical Studies Univ Mich Ann Arbor MI 48109 E-mail: jpedley@umich.edu.

PEDRAM, MARILYN BETH, reference librarian; b. Brewster, Kans., Apr. 3, 1937; d. Edgar Roy and Elizabeth Catherine (Doubt) Crist; m. Manouchehr Pedram, Jan. 27, 1962 (Oct. 28, 1984); children: Jaleh Denise, Cyrus Andre. BS in Edn., Kans. State U., 1958; MLS, U. Denver, 1961. Cert secondary educator, Mo. 7th grade tchr. Clay Ctr. (Kans.) Pub. Schs., 1958-59, Colby (Kans.) Pub. Sch. System, 1959-60; reference libr. Topeka (Kans.) Pub. Libr., 1961-62, extension dept. head, 1963-64, reference libr., 1964-65; br. libr. asst. Denver Pub. Libr., 1965-67; reference libr. Kansas City (Mo.) Pub. Libr., Plaza Br., 1974-79, Kansas City (Mo.) Main Libr., 1979—. Mem. AARP, ALA, Mo. Libr. Assn., Pub. Libr. Assn., Celiac Sprue Assn., Kans. State U. Alumni Assn., Nat. Parks and Conservation Assn. Avocations: flower gardening, gourmet cooking, travel, reading, walking. Office: Kansas City Pub Libr 311 E 12th St Kansas City MO 64106-2412

PEEBLES, CHRISTOPHER SPALDING, anthropologist, dean, academic administrator; b. Clearwater, Fla., May 26, 1939; s. Frederick Thomas and Corinne deGarmendia (Stephens) P.; m. Laura Ann Wisen, Oct. 6, 1993. AB, U. Chgo., 1963; PhD, U. Calif., Santa Barbara, 1974. Asst. prof. U. Windsor, Ont., Can., 1970-74; asst. curator U. Mich., Ann Arbor, 1974-81; prof. prehistory U. Amsterdam, The Netherlands, 1981-82; prof. Ind. U., Bloomington, 1983—, dean acad. computing, assoc. v.p., 1992—. Author: Excavations at Moundville, 1974, Representations in Archaeology, 1992. With USAF, 1956-60. Mem. Cosmos Club. Avocation: flying. Office: Ind U 116 Franklin Rd Bloomington IN 47405-1223 E-mail: peebles@indiana.edu.

PEEKEL, ARTHUR K. secondary school educator; Tchr. social scis. Rolling Meadows (Ill.) High Sch. Recipient State Tchr. of Yr. Social Scis. award Ill., 1992. Office: Rolling Meadows High Sch 2901 W Central Rd Rolling Meadows IL 60008-2536

PEERMAN, DEAN GORDON, magazine editor; b. Mattoon, Ill., Apr. 25, 1931; s. Staley Jacob and Irene (Monen) P. B.S. with highest distinction, Northwestern U., 1953; postgrad., Cornell U., 1953-54; B.D., Yale, 1959; D.D., Kalamazoo Coll., 1967. With Christian Century Found., 1959—; copy editor Christian Century mag., 1959-61, assoc. editor, 1961-64, mng. editor, 1964-81, exec. editor, 1981-85, sr. editor, 1985-98, contbg. editor, 1998—. Author: (with M.E. Marty) Pen-ultimates, 1963, (with Marty, L.M. Delloff, J.M. Wall) A Century of The Century, 1987; editor: Frontline Theology, 1967; co-editor: (with Marty) New Theology 1-10, 1964-73, A Handbook of Christian Theologians, 1965, enlarged edit., 1984, (with Alan Geyer) Theological Crossings, 1971. Contbr.: Chile: Under Military Rule, 1974; editor, contbr. Faithful Witness, 2002. Active Chgo. community theater groups. Recipient award for distinction in lay ministry within the church Yale Div. Sch., 1995. Mem. ACLU, Fellowship of Reconciliation, Amnesty Internat., Chgo. Religious Leadership Network on Latin Am., Phi Beta Kappa. Democrat. Baptist. Office: Christian Century Mag 104 S Michigan Ave Ste 700 Chicago IL 60603-5905

PEHLKE, ROBERT DONALD, materials and metallurgical engineering educator; b. Ferndale, Mich., Feb. 11, 1933; s. Robert William and Florence Jenny (McLaren) P.; m. Julie Anne Kehoe, June 2, 1956; children: Robert Donald, Elizabeth Anne, David Richard. B.S. in Engring, U. Mich., 1955; S.M., Mass. Inst. Tech., 1958, Sc.D., 1960; postgrad., Tech. Inst., Aachen, Ger., 1956-57. Registered profl. engr., Mich. Mem. faculty U. Mich., 1960—, prof. materials sci. and engring., 1968—, chmn. dept., 1973-84. Cons. to metall. industry; vis. prof. Tohoku U., Sendai, Japan, 1994; Campbell Meml. lectr., 2001. Author: Unit Processes of Extractive Metallurgy, 1973; Editor, contbr. numerous articles to profl. jours. Pres. Ann Arbor Amateur Hockey Assn., 1977-79. NSF fellow, 1955-56; Fulbright fellow, 1956-57 Fellow Am. Soc. Metals (tech. divsn. bd. 1982-84, sec. metals acad. com. 1977), Minerals, Metals and Materials Soc. of AIME (Gold Medal award extractive metallurgy divsn. 1976), Alpha Sigma Mu (disting. life, pres. 1977-78); mem. Iron and Steel Soc. of AIME (Disting. life mem., chmn. process tech. divsn. 1976-77, dir. 1976-79, Howe meml. lectr. 1980), Germany, London, Japan Socs. Iron and Steel, Am. Foundrymen's Soc., Am. Soc. Engring. Edn., Sigma Xi, Tau Beta Pi. Home: 9 Regent Dr Ann Arbor MI 48104-1738 Office: U Mich Materials Sci & Engring Dow Bldg 2300 Hayward St Rm 2146B Ann Arbor MI 48109-2136 E-mail: rdpehlke@engin.umich.edu.

PELHAM, JUDITH, health system administrator; b. Bristol, Conn., July 23, 1945; d. Marvin Curtis and Muriel (Chodos) P.; m. Jon N. Coffee, Dec. 30, 1992; children: Rachel, Molly, Edward. BA, Smith Coll., 1967; MPA, Harvard U., 1975. Various govt. postions, 1968-72; prin. analyst Urban Systems, Cambridge, Mass., 1972-73; dir. devel. and planning Roxbury Dental and Med. Group, Boston, 1975-76; asst. to dir. for gen. medicine and ambulatory care Peter B. Brigham Hosp., 1976-77, asst. dir. ambulatory care, 1977-79; asst. v.p. Brigham and Women's Hosp., 1980-81; dir. planning and mktg. Seton Med. Ctr., Austin, Tex., 1980-82, pres., 1982-92, CEO, 1987-92; pres., CEO Daughters of Charity Health Svcs., 1987-92, Mercy Health Svcs., Farmington Hills, Mich., 1993—2000, Trinity Health (merger of Mercy Health Svcs. and Holy Cross Health Sys.), Novi, 2000—. Bd. dirs. Amgen, Consol. Cath. Health Care; cons. Robert W. Johnson Found., 1979—80; mem. mgmt. bd. Inst. for Diversity in Health Mgmt., 1994—97; chair Coalition for Non-Profit Healthcare, 1997—2000, exec. com., 1997—. Contbr. articles to profl. jours. Trustee A. Shivers Radiation Therapy Ctr., Austin, 1982-92, Marywood Maternity and Adoption Agy., 1982-86; bd. dirs. Quality of Life Found., Austin, 1985, Austin Rape Crisis Ctr., adv. bd., 1986-88; bd. dirs., trustee League House, 1982-93, Seton Fund, 1982-93, Greater Detroit Area Health Coun., 1994—; mem. Gov's Job Tng. Coordinating Council, 1983-85; adv. council U. Tex. Social Work Found., 1983-85; charter mem. Leadership Tex., Austin, 1983-93. Recipient Leadership award YWCA, Austin, 1986. Fellow Am. Coll. Healthcare Execs., Am. Hosp. Assn., Tex. Hosp. Assn. (mem. various coms. 1982-87), Austin Area Rsch. Orgn., Tex. Conf. Health Facilities (bd. dirs. 1985-89, pres. 1988), Cath. Health Assn. (bd. dirs. 1987-95, com. on govt. rels. 1984-91, sec., treas. 1982-95, chair fin. com. 1992-95). Office: Trinity Health 27870 Cabot Dr Novi MI 48377

PELLEGRENE, THOMAS JAMES, JR. editor, researcher; b. Wilmington, Del., Dec. 26, 1959; s. Thomas J. and MaryBelle (McGowan) P.; m. Pamela Heinecke, Apr. 5, 1986. BS in Journalism, Northwestern U., 1981, MS in Journalism, 1982. Staff writer Ft. Wayne (Ind.) Journal-Gazette, 1982-87, bus. editor, 1987-95, asst. metro editor, 1995-98, mgr. news techs., 1998—. Mem. Soc. Profl. Journalists, Spl. Librs. Assn. Office: Fort Wayne Journal-Gazette 600 W Main St Fort Wayne IN 46802-1408 E-mail: tpellegrene@jg.net.

PELLOW, RICHARD MAURICE, former state legislator; b. Mpls., 1931; m. Jean Schwaab; 5 children. Grad. h.s. Mem. Minn. Ho. of Reps., 1988-92, 95-97. Former mem. commerce, econ. devel., edn., transp. coms.; currently self-employed. Address: 1354 Jackson St Saint Paul MN 55117-4614

PELOFSKY, JOEL, lawyer; b. June 23, 1937; s. Louis J. and Naomi (Hecht) Pelofsky; m. Brenda L. Greenblatt, June 19, 1960; children: Mark, Lisa, Carl. AB, Harvard U., 1959. Bar: Mo. 1962, U.S. Dist. Ct. (we. dist.) Mo. 62, U.S. Ct. Appeals (8th cir.) 68, U.S. Ct. Appeals (10th cir.) 70. Law clk. to judge U.S. Dist. Ct. (we. dist.) Mo., 1962—63; mem. Miniace & Pelofsky, Kansas City, Mo., 1962—63; asst. pros. atty. Jackson County, 1967—71; mem. Kansas City (Mo.) City Coun., 1971—79; judge U.S. Bankruptcy Ct. Western Dist. Mo., Kansas City, 1967—71; mem. Kansas City (Mo.) City Coun., 1971—79; ptnr. Shughart, Thomson & Kilroy P.C., 1986—95; appd. U.S. trustee Ark., Mo., Nebr., 1995—. Intermittent lectr. in law U. Mo.; mem. Region I Law Enforcement Assistance Adminstr. Mem. adv. bd. Urban League, Kansas City, Mo.; chmn. human resource devel. com. Mo. Mcpl. League; bd. dirs., mem. exec. com. Truman Med.

Ctr., Kansas City, Mo., pres. bd., 1988—90, chmn. bd., 1990—92; bd. dirs. Greater Kansas City Mental Health Found. Lt. U.S. Army, 1963—65. Mem.: ABA, Am. Coll. Bankruptcy, Comml. Law League, Kansas City Bar Assn., Mo. Bar. Office: US Trustee 400 E 9th St Ste 3440 Kansas City MO 64106-2625

PELOWSKI, GENE P., JR. state legislator; b. Feb. 1952; m. Deborah Pelowski; 2 children. BS, Winona State U. Mem. Minn. Ho. of Reps., St. Paul, 1986—. Mem. econ. devel. com., gen. legis. com., gaming com., edn. com., others, vicechmn. vet affairs and elec. coms.; educator; golf profl. Democrat. Home: 257 Wilson St Winona MN 55987-5238 Office: Minn Ho of Reps State Capitol Saint Paul MN 55155-0001

PELTON, RUSSELL MEREDITH, JR. lawyer; b. Chgo., May 14, 1938; BA, DePauw U., 1960; JD, U. Chgo., 1963. Bar: Ill. 1963, U.S. Supreme Ct. 1979. Assoc. Peterson, Ross, Schloerb & Seidel, Chgo., 1966-72, ptnr., 1972-90, Oppenheimer, Wolff & Donnelly, Chgo., 1990-2000, Chgo. mng. ptnr., 1992-95, 98-2000; ptnr. Ross & Hardies, 2000—. Co-founder, gen. counsel Chgo. Opportunities Industrialization Ctr., 1969—83; gen. counsel Delta Dental Plann Ill., 1979—96, Am. Assn. Neurol. Surgeons, 1983—. Pres. Wilmette Jaycees, 1970; chmn. Wilmette Sch. Bd. Caucus, 1970-71; Wilmette Dist. 39 Bd. Edn., 1972-80; bd. dirs. Wilmette United Way, 1980-86, campaign chmn., 1983-85, pres., 1985-86; Wilmette Zoning Bd. Appeals, 1989-2000, chmn., 1990-2000. Served to capt. USAF, 1963-66. Mem.: ABA, Soc. Trial Lawyers, Chgo. Bar Assn., Ill. Bar Assn., Ill. State Dental Soc. (hon.). Office: Ross & Hardies 150 N Michigan Ave Ste 2500 Chicago IL 60601-7567 E-mail: russell.pelton@rosshardies.com.

PELTZMAN, SAM, economics educator; b. Bklyn., Jan. 24, 1940; s. Benjamin Raphael and Ceil (Heller) P.; m. Nancy Virginia Bradney, Sept. 7, 1952; children: Shira Malka, Talya Rose. BBA, CCNY, 1960; PhD, U. Chgo., 1965. Prof. econs. UCLA, 1964-73; sr. staff economist Coun. Econ. Advisers, Washington, 1970-71; prof. econs. grad. sch. bus. U. Chgo., 1973-87, Sears, Roebuck prof., 1987-2001, dir. George J. Stigler Ctr. Study of Economy and the State, 1992—, Ralph and Dorothy Keller disting. svc. prof., 2001—. Vis. fellow Inst. for Advanced Study Hebrew U., Jerusalem, 1978; dir. CMP Industries LLC, 1995—; mem. coun. acad. advisers Am. Enterprise Inst., 1995—. Author: Political Participation and Government Regulation, 1998; co-author: Public Policy Toward Mergers, 1967; editor Jour. Law and Econs.; contbr. articles to profl. jours. Mem. Am. Econ. Assn., Mt. Pelerin Soc. Jewish. Office: U Chgo Grad Sch Bus 1101 E 58th St Chicago IL 60637-1511

PEMBERTON, BRADLEY POWELL, lawyer; b. Ft. Scott, Kans., June 15, 1952; s. Howard Duane and Juanita Lucille (Powell) P.; m. Kathleen Frances Querrey, May 22, 1976 (div. Feb. 1984); m. Lori Scott, June 18, 1994. BSBA, U. Mo., Columbia, 1974; JD, U. Mo., Kansas City, 1977. Bar: Mo. 1977, U.S. Dist. Ct. (we. dist.) Mo. 1981, U.S. Tax Ct. 1981; CPA, Mo. Tax acct. Alexander Grant & Co., Kansas City, Mo., 1977-79; shareholder Polsinelli, Shalton & Welte, 1979—; also bd. dirs. Polsinelli, White, Vardeman & Shalton. Active Vol. Atty. Project, Kansas City, 1984—; bd. dirs. Synergy House Inc., Kansas City, 1985-88, Youth Vol. Corps of Am., 1991—, March of Dimes, 1995—. Mem. ABA, Internat. Entrepreneurs Coun. (bd. dirs.), Mo. Bar Assn., Kansas City Bar Assn., AICPAs, Mo. Soc. CPAs, Kansas City C. of C., Entrepreneurs Club of Kansas City (bd. dirs.), KC. Avocations: tennis, golf, water skiing, snow skiing, private aviation. Home: 5806 W 131st St Shawnee Mission KS 66209-3639 Office: Polsinelli Shalton & Welte 700 W 47th St Ste 1000 Kansas City MO 64112-1805 E-mail: bpemberson@pswlaw.com.

PENA, ANTONIO FRANCISCO (TONY PENA), professional athletics coach; b. Monte Cristy, Dominican Republic, June 4, 1957; m. Amaris Pena; children: Tony, Jennifer Amaris. Profl. baseball player Pitts. Pirates, Nat. League, 1980-86, St. Louis Cardinals, 1986-89, Boston Red Sox, 1989—93, Cleveland Indians , 1994—97; mgr. Astros AAA farm club , New Orleans, 1997—2001; mgr. Kansas City Royals , 2002—. Player Major League All-Star Game, 1982, 84; winner Gold Glove. Office: Kansas City Royals One Royal Way Kansas City MO 64129*

PENCE, MIKE, congressman; b. Columbus, Ind. m. Karen; three children. Grad., Hanover Coll., 1981; JD, Ind. U. Sch. Law, 1986. Radio broadcaster The Mike Pence Show, 1992; host public affairs TV show, Indpls., 1995-99; mem. U.S. Congress from 2nd Ind. dist., 2001—. Named Asst. Majority Whip; mem. Congressional com. House Sci., House Agriculture; subcom. House Small Bus. on Reg. Reform and Oversight. Rep.; Christian. Office: 1605 Longworth House bldg Washington DC 20515*

PENDLEY, KEVIN, communication media executive; Bur. chief Bridge News, Chgo., 1996—. Office: Bridge News 30 S Wacker Dr Ste 1810 Chicago IL 60606-7404

PENISTEN, GARY DEAN, entrepreneur; b. Lincoln, Nebr., May 14, 1931; s. Martin C. and Jayne (O'Dell) P.; m. Nancy Margaret Golding, June 3, 1951; children: Kris D., Janet L., Carol E., Noel M. B.S. in Bus. Adminstrn., U. Nebr., Omaha, 1953; LLD (hon.), Concordia Coll., 1993. With Gen. Electric Co., 1953-74, mgr. group fin. ops. power generation group, 1973-74; asst. sec. navy fin. mgmt., 1974-77; sr. v.p. fin., chief fin. officer, dir. Sterling Drug Inc., N.Y.C., 1977-89; sr. v.p. fin., health group Eastman Kodak Co., 1989-90. Bd. dirs. Foster Ptnrs. Inc., chmn. bd. dirs. Acme United Corp. Mem. corp. adv. bd. U. Nebr. Coll. Bus., Omaha. Recipient Disting. Public Service award Navy Dept., 1977; Alumni Achievement citation U. Nebr., Omaha, 1975. Mem. Fin. Execs. Inst., Navy League of U.S., Army and Navy Club (Washington), Rotary, Union League (N.Y.), Ft. Lauderdale (Fla.) Country Club, White Eagle Golf Club (Naperville). Republican. Unitarian. Home and Office: 1409 Aberdeen Ct Naperville IL 60564-9787 E-mail: asnfm@aol.com.

PENKAVA, ROBERT RAY, radiologist, educator; b. Virginia, Nebr., Jan. 30, 1942; s. Joseph Evert and Velta Mae (Oviatt) P.; m. Kathy Bennett Secrest, Apr. 6, 1973; children: Ashley Secrest, J. Carson Bennett. AB BS, Peru State Coll., Nebr., 1963; MD, U. Nebr., Omaha, 1967. Intern Lincoln Gen. Hosp., Nebr., 1967-68; resident Menorah Med. Cen., Kansas City, 1968-71; chief resident Menorah Med. Ctr., 1970-71; adj. faculty U. Mo., 1970-71; staff radiologist Ireland Army Hosp., Ft. Knox, Ky., 1971-72, chief, dept. radiology & nuclear med., 1972-73; staff radiologist Deaconess Hosp., Evansville, Ind., 1973-99; mem. faculty U. So. Ind., 1973—; assoc. faculty Ind. U. Coll. Med., Bloomington, 1973—; med. dir. Sch. Radiol. Tech. U. So. Ind., Evansville, 1978—; dep coroner Vanderburgh County, 1991—; med. dir. Deaconess Breast Ctr., 1999—. Chmn. So. Ind. Health Sys., 1980-83; pres. Vanderburgh County Med. Soc. Svc. Bur., 1979—; mem. roentgen soc. liaison com. Ind. Bd. Health, 1968. Author numerous articles on med. ultrasound, nuclear med., angiography, and computed tomography. Chmn. profl. div. United Way of So. Ind., 1983; bd. dirs. S.W. Ind. Pub. Broadcasting, 1978-84, S.W. Ind. PSRO, 1982; v.p. Mesker Zoo Found., bd. dirs., 1991-95; mem. Evansville Pub. Safety Bd., 2000—. Maj. U.S. Army, 1971-73. Named Sci. Tchr. of Year, Lewis & Clark Jr. High Sch., 1963. Mem. AMA, Evansville Med. Radiol. Assn. (treas. 1987-98), Am. Soc. Breast Disease, Internat. Soc. Clin. Dosimetry, Tri-State Radiology Assn. (pres.), Vanderburgh County Med. Soc. (pres.), Physicians Svc. Bur. (treas.), Magnetic Resonance Imaging, Inc. (treas. 1995-98), Am. Coll. Radiology, Radiol. Soc. N.Am., Am. Roentgen Ray Soc., Am. Inst. Ultrasound in Medicine, Soc. Cardiovascular and Interventional Radiology. Avocations: golf, boating, flying. Office: 520 Mary St Ste #140 Evansville IN 47710

PENLAND, JAMES GRANVILLE, psychologist; b. Dallas, Mar. 1, 1951; s. James Marr and Katherine (Lindsley) P.; m. Michelle Elizabeth Stahl, Aug. 13, 1977; children: Abraham Christopher, Simon Peter, Zachary James. BA summa cum laude, Met. State Coll., 1977; MA, U. N.D., 1979, PhD, 1984. Instr. U. N.D., Grand Forks, 1978-83, statistician, 1981-84, psychologist, 1984-85; rsch. psychologist USDA, Agrl. Rsch. Svc., 1985—. Adj. prof. U. N.D., 1984—; mem. IOM FNB Panel on Micronutrients, Comm. Mil. Nutrition Rsch.; cons. in field. Mem. editl. bd. Nutritional Neurosci.; contbr. articles to profl. jours. Met. State Coll. scholar, 1977. Mem. APA, Am. Inst. Nutrition, Midwestern Psychol. Assn., N.D. Acad. Sci., Nat. Acad. Scis., Am. Statis Assn., Sigma Xi. Home: 1804 S 36th St Grand Forks ND 58201-5740 Office: USDA ARS GFHNRC Box 9034 2420 2nd Ave N Grand Forks ND 58202-9034 E-mail: jpenland@gfhnrc.ars.usda.gov.

PENNIMAN, NICHOLAS GRIFFITH, IV, retired newspaper publisher; b. Balt., Mar. 7, 1938; s. Nicholas Griffith Penniman III and Esther Cox Lony (Wight) Keeney; m. Linda Jane Simmons, Feb. 4, 1967; children: Rebecca Helmle, Nicholas G. V. AB, Princeton U., 1960; MA, Washington U., 1999. Asst. bus. mgr. Ill. State Jour. Register, Springfield, 1964-69, bus. mgr., 1969-75; asst. gen. mgr. St. Louis Post-Dispatch, 1975-84, gen. mgr., 1984-86, pub., 1986-99; sr. v.p. newspapers ops. Pulitzer Pub. Co., 1986-99; pres., CEO Pulitzer Comm. Newspapers Inc., 1997-99; chmn. bd. Penniman & Browne, Inc., Balt., 2001—. Chmn. Downtown St. Louis, Inc., 1988-90, Mo. Health and Ednl. Facilities Adminstrn., 1982-85, Ill. State Fair Bd., Springfield, 1973-75, Parks and Open Space Task Force St. Louis 2004, 1996-2000; pres. Caring Found. for Children, 1988-91, Forest Park Forever, 1991-93, St. Louis Sports Com., 1992-93, Gateway Parks and Trails 2004, 1999—; trustee St. Louis Country Day Sch., 1983-86; bd. dirs. Mo. Coalition for the Environment, 1997-2000, Randall Rsch. Ctr., Pineland, Fla., 2001--; 1st vice chair Am. Rivers, 1998. With U.S. Army, 1962—67. Mem.: St. Louis Country Club, Noonday Club (pres. 1994), Grey Oaks Country Club. Home: 611 Portside Dr Naples FL 34103-4118 E-mail: ngpiv@aol.com.

PENNINGTON, BEVERLY MELCHER, financial services company executive; b. Vermillion, SD, Feb. 8, 1931; d. Cecil Lloyd and Phyllis Cecelia (Walz) M.; m. Glen D., Sept. 1, 1965 (dec. Aug. 1986); 1 child, Terri Lynn. BS, U. S.D., Vermillion, 1952. Enrolled agt. cert. IRS 1989. Sec. budget dept. Bur. of Indian Affairs, Aberdeen, S.D., 1952-53, pvt. sec., 1953-54, U.S. P.H.S. Indian Health, Aberdeen, 1954-55; adminstr. asst. U.S. Pub. Health Svc., Anchorage, 1955-58, U.S. Pub. Health, Dental Pub. Health, Washington, 1958-61; grant adminstr. Dental Pub. Health, 1961-65; co-owner Penn Mel Marina, Platte, S.D, 1965-74, Pennington Tax Service, Platte, 1974-86, owner, 1986-93; pres., CEO, White Tiger Fin. Svc., Inc., 1994—. Contbr. articles to profl. jours. Mem. Platte Women's Club, sec., 1965-68, pres., 1968-70, 89-91; mem. Libr. Bd., Sec., 1982-85, treas., 1995—. Fellow Am. Soc. Tax Profls. (sec. 1989-91, 2d v.p. 1995, 1st v.p. 1996, pres. 1997); mem. NAFE, Platte C. of C. (v.p. 1989, pres. 1990), Lyric Theatre Mus. Soc. (pres. 1988-92), U.S. C. of C., Washington Dakota Cen. Com. Republican. Presbyterian. Avocations: collecting jewelry, reading, dress designing, gourmet cooking. Office: White Tiger Fin Svc Inc 420 Main St Platte SD 57369

PENSIS, HENRI BRAM, music educator, conductor; b. Luxembourg, Mar. 18, 1927; came to U.S., 1940; s. Henri Paul and Marielouise (Deltgen) P.; m. Patricia Adams Robinson, June 14, 1951; children: Henri Paul, Claude Norris. Student, Morningside Coll., 1944-45; MusB, Northwestern U., 1950, MusM, 1951, postgrad., 1952. Conductor Chamber Orch., Evanston, Ill., 1947-51; prof., chair music dept. Salem (W.Va.) Coll., 1952-55; asst. prof., conductor orch. Cen. Meth. Coll., Fayette, Mo., 1955-65; prof., conductor emeritus U. Wis., Oshkosh, 1965-95; music dir., conductor, mem. exec. com. Oshkosh Symphony Orch., 1967-96, music dir. laureate, 1998. Guest conductor Radio Luxembourg Symphony Orch., 1964, 72, 76, 78, 82, 84, 88; conducted Orchestre Philharmonique de Luxembourg Gala Concert in honor of father's death anniversary, October 1998. Recipient Key to City of Oshkosh, 1976, cert. of appreciation U.S. Amb. to Luxembourg, 1976, cert. of commendation Gov. of Wis., 1988: Henri B. Pensis Day declared in his honor, 1988, Maestro Pensis Week declared in his honor, 1996; selected as an influential citizen The Oshkosh Northwestern, 1993. Mem. Assn. Wis. Symphony Orchs. (exec. com. 1976—, past pres.; hon. life mem.), Am. Symphony Orch. League (hon.), Conductors Guild, Grand Ducal Inst. Arts and Letters Luxembourg, Phi Mu Alpha Sinfonia (life), Pi Kappa Lambda. Avocations: photography, collecting records, stereo equipment. E-mail: hbpensis@northnet.north.

PENSKE, ROGER S. manufacturing and transportation executive; b. 1937; married. Grad., Lehigh U., 1958. With Alcoa Aluminum, Pitts., 1958-63, George McKean Chevrolet, Phila., 1963-65; prin. Penske Corp., Red Bank, N.J., pres., chmn. bd.; chmn. bd. dirs., pres., CEO Penske Transp. Inc., Detroit; chmn. bd. dirs., pres. Pa. Internat. Raceway, Nazareth, 1986—; CEO Detroit Diesel Corp., chmn. bd. dirs.; pres. Competition Tire West, inc., Brooklyn, Mich.; chmn., CEO United Auto Grp. Chmn. bd. dirs. Penske Truck Leasing Corp., Penske Speedway, Inc., Detroit, Penske Automotive Group, Detroit, Outer Drive Holidays, Inc., Detroit, D Longo, Inc., El Monte, Calif.; sec. Ilmore Engring., Inc., Redford, Mich. Office: Penske Corp 8801 N Haggarty Rd Ann Arbor MI 48107

PEOPLES, JOHN, JR. physicist, researcher; b. S.I., N.Y., Jan. 22, 1933; s. John and Annie Alice (Wall) P.; m. Brooke Detweiler, Dec. 16, 1955; children— Jennet, Vanessa B.S. in Elec. Engring., Carnegie Inst. Tech., 1955; M.A. in Physics, Columbia U., 1961, Ph.D. in Physics, 1966. Engr. Martin Marietta Co., Middle River, Md., 1955-60; asst. prof. physics Columbia U., N.Y.C., 1966-69; asst. prof. Cornell U., Ithaca, N.Y., 1969-71, assoc. prof., 1972; scientist Fermilab, Batavia, Ill., 1972—, dir., 1989—; prof. physics Northwestern U., 1989—. Mem. high energy physics adv. panel Dept. Energy, Washington, 1976-80, 84-85 Contbr. articles to profl. jours. Alfred Sloan Found. fellow, 1970 Fellow AAAS, Am. Phys. Soc. (chmn. div. particles and fields 1984), Internat. Com. for Future Accelarators (chair). Home: 201 Ford St Geneva IL 60134-1449 Office: Fermi Nat Accelerator Lab MS 127 PO Box 500 Batavia IL 60510-0500 also: Fermilab Directors Office PO Box 500 Batavia IL 60510-0500

PEPE, STEVEN DOUGLAS, federal magistrate judge; b. Indpls., Jan. 29, 1943; s. Wilfrid Julius and Roselda (Gehring) P.; m. Janet L. Pepe. BA cum laude, U. Notre Dame, 1965; JD magna cum laude, U. Mich., 1968; postgrad., London Sch. Econs. and Polit. Sci., 1970-72; LLM, Harvard U., 1974. Bar: Ind. 1968, U.S. Dist. Ct. Ind. 1968, D.C. 1969, U.S. Dist. Ct. D.C. 1969, mass. 1973, Mich. 1974, U.S. Dist. Ct. (ea. dist.) Mich., 1983. Law clk. Hon. Harold Leventhal U.S. Cir. Ct. Appeals, Washington, 1968-69; staff atty. Neighborhood Legal Svcs. Program, 1969-70; cons. Office of Svcs. to Aging, Lansing, Mich., 1976-77, Adminstrn. Aging, Dept. Health and Human Svcs., 1976-78; U.S. magistrate judge Eastern Dist., Ann Arbor, Mich., 1983—. Mem. Biregional Older Am. Advocacy Assistance Resource and Support Ctr., 1979-81; cons., bd. dirs. Ctr. Social Gerontology (1988-93); clin. prof. law, dir. Mich. Clin. Law Program, U. Mich. Law Sch., 1974-83; adj. prof. law Detroit Mercy Sch. Law, 1985; lectr. U. Mich. Law Sch., 1985-97. Editor Mich. Law Rev.; contbr. articles to profl. jours. Recipient Reginald Heber Smith Cmty. Lawyer fellowship, 1969-70; Mich.-Ford Internat. Studies fellow, 1970-72, Harvard Law Sch. Clin. Teaching fellow, 1972-73. Mem. State Bar Mich., State Bar Ind., Fed. Bar Assn., Washtenaw County Bar Assn., Am. Inn Court XI, U. Detroit Mercy, Pi Sigma Alpha, Order of Coif. Office: US District Court PO Box 7150 Ann Arbor MI 48107-7150 E-mail: Steven_Pepe@mied.uscourts.gov.

PEPER, CHRISTIAN BAIRD, lawyer; b. St. Louis, Dec. 5, 1910; s. Clarence F. and Christine (Baird) P.; m. Ethel C. Kingsland, June 5, 1935 (dec. Sept. 1995); children: Catherine K. Peper Larson, Anne Peper Perkins, Christian B.; m. Barbara C. Pleiter, Jan. 25, 1996. AB cum laude, Harvard U., 1932; LLB, Washington U., 1935; LLM, Yale U., 1937. Bar: Mo. 1934. Pvt. practiced, St. Louis; of counsel Blackwell Sanders Peper Martin LLP. Lectr. various subjects Washington U. Law Sch., St. Louis, 1943-61; ptnr. A.G. Edwards & Sons, 1945-67; pres. St. Charles Gas Corp., 1953-72; bd. dirs. El Dorado Paper Bag Mfg. Co., Inc. Editor: An Historian's Conscience: The Correspondence of Arnold J. Toynbee and Columba Cary-Elwes, 1986. Mem. vis. com. Harvard Div. Sch., 1964-70; counsel St. Louis Art Mus. Sterling fellow Yale U., 1936. Mem. ABA, Mo. Bar Assn., St. Louis Bar Assn., Noonday Club, Univ. Club, Harvard Club, East India Club (London), Order of Coif, Phi Delta Phi. Roman Catholic. Home: 1454 S Mason Rd Saint Louis MO 63131-1211 Office: Blackwell Sanders Peper Martin LLP 720 Olive St Saint Louis MO 63101-2338 E-mail: cpeper@ospmlaw.com.

PEPPAS, NIKOLAOS ATHANASSIOU, chemical and biomedical engineering educator, consultant; b. Athens, Greece, Aug. 25, 1948; s. Athanassios Nikolaou Peppas and Alice Petrou Rousopoulou; m. Lisa Brannon, Aug. 10, 1988; 1 dau., Katherine. Diploma in Engring., Nat. Tech. U., Athens, 1971; ScD, MIT, 1973; D hon. causa, U. Parma, Italy, 1999, U. Ghent, Belgium, 1999, U. Ghent, U. Athens, 2000. Asst. prof. chem. engring. Purdue U., West Lafayette, Ind., 1976-78, assoc. prof., 1978-81, prof., 1981—, Showalter Disting. prof. of chem. and biomed. engring., 1993—. Vis. prof. U. Geneva, 1982-83, Calif. Inst. Tech., Pasadena, 1983, U. Paris, 1986, Hoshi U., Japan, 1994, Hebrew U., Jerusalem, 1994, U. Naples, 1995, U. Berlin, 2001, Complutense U. Madrid, 2001; adj. prof. U. Parma, Italy, 1987; cons. in field; mem. adv. bd. several cos. Author: Biomaterials, 1982, Hydrogels in Medicine and Pharmacy, 1987, One Hundred Years of Chemical Engineering, 1989, Pulsatile Drug Delivery, 1993, Biopolymers, 1993, Superabsorbent Polymers, 1994, Polymer/Inorganic Interfaces, 1995, Biomaterials for Drug and Cell Delivery, 1994; contbr. over 700 articles and over 300 abstracts to jours. Active Indpls. Symphony Orch., Indpls. Mus. Arts, Holy Trinity Orthodox Ch. Indpls. Recipient APV medal, Herbert McCoy award Purdue U. Fellow: AIChE (chmn. materials divsn. 1988—90, dir. bioengring. divsn. 1994—97, bd. dirs. 1999—, Materials Engring. Sci. award 1984, Bioengring. award 1994, Best Paper award 1994), Am. Phys. Soc., Italian Soc. Medicine and Scis., Am. Phys. Soc., Am. Assn. Pharm. Scientists (Rsch. Achievements Pharm. Tech. award 1999), Am. Inst. Med. Biol. Engrs., Soc. Biomaterials (pres.-elect 2002); mem.: numerous others, Polymer Pioneer, Am. Soc. Engring. Edn. (AT&T award 1982, Curtis McGraw award 1988, G. Westinghouse award 1992), Soc. Biomaterials (Clemson award 1992), Controlled Release Soc. (pres. 1987—88, Founders award 1991), N.Y. Acad. Scis., Am. Chem. Soc. Avocations: linguistics (conversant in 8 langs.), opera, rare maps, classical record collecting, wine collecting. Office: Purdue U Sch Chem Engring West Lafayette IN 47907

PEPPEL, MICHAEL E. computer company executive; BA, U. Notre Dame. Money desk mgr. Edward J. DeBartolo Corp., 1987-90; dir., CFO Diversified Data Products, Inc., 1990-96; v.p., CFO Miami Computer Supply Corp., Dayton, Ohio, 1996—. Office: Miami Computer Supply Corp 4750 Hempstead Station Dr Dayton OH 45429-5164 Fax: 937-291-8298.

PEPPER, J. STANLEY, construction company executive; BA, Monmouth Coll. Various positions Pepper Cos., Chgo., 1968-91, pres., COO, 1991-93, CEO, 1993—.

PEPPER, JOHN ENNIS, JR. consumer products company executive; b. Pottsville, Pa., Aug. 2, 1938; s. John Ennis Sr. and Irma Elizabeth (O'Connor) P.; m. Frances Graham Garber, Sept. 9, 1967; children: John, David, Douglas, Susan BA, Yale U., 1960; PhD (hon.), Mt. St. Joseph Coll., St. Petersburg (Russia) U., Xavier U. Staff asst. Procter & Gamble Co., Cin., 1963-64, asst. brand mgr., 1964-66, brand mgr., 1966-68, copy supr., 1968-69, brand promotion mgr., 1969-72, advt. mgr. bar soap and household cleaning products divsn., 1972-74, gen. mgr. Italy subs., 1974-77, divsn. mgr. internat., 1977-78, v.p. packaged soap and detergent divsn., 1978-80, group v.p. bar soap and household cleaning products divsn., 1980-81, group v.p. Europe, 1981-84, exec. v.p. U.S. bus., 1984-86, pres. U.S. Bus., 1986-90, pres. internat. bus., 1990-95, chmn. bd., chief exec., 1995-99; chmn. Proctor & Gamble Co., 1999—, exec. com. of bd., 2000—. Bd. dirs. Xerox Corp., Motorola, Inc., Boston Scientific Corp. Chmn. U.S. Advisory Com. for Trade Policy and Negotiations; co-chair Devel. campaign, mem., exec. com. Nat. Underground Railroad Freedom Ctr.; group chmn. Cin. United Appeal Campaign, 1980; bd. trustees Xavier U., 1985-89, mem. exec. com., 1989; trustee Cin. Coun. World Affairs, Cin. Art Mus., Ctr. Strategic & Internat. Studies, Christ Ch. Endowment Fund; fellow Yale Corp.; gen. chmn. United Way Campaign, 1994; mem. Gov.'s Edn. and Bus. Advisory Group, State of Ohio; mem. adv. coun. Yale Sch. Mgmt.; mem. schs. com. Cin. Bus. Com.; co-chmn., mem. exec. com. Cin. Youth Collaborative; mem. Total Quality Leadership steering com.; mem., bd. dirs. United Negro Coll. Fund; former v.p. Am. C. of C., Brussels, Belgium (1981-84); former mem. Cin. Symphony Bd. (1979-81), Cin. Art Mus. Served to lt. USN, 1960-63. Mem. Am. Soc. Corp. Execs., Grocery Mfrs. Am., Nat. Alliance Businessmen (chmn. communication com.), Partnership for a Drug-Free Am., Soap and Detergent Assn. (bd. dirs.), The Bus. Coun., Bus. Roundtable, Yale Club, Queen City Club, Commonwealth Club, Comml. Club (former pres.). Office: Procter & Gamble Co 1 Procter And Gamble Plz Cincinnati OH 45202-3393

PEPPER, JONATHON L. media executive; b. Dearborn, Mich., Aug. 23, 1955; s. Joseph Daniel and Norma (McIntyre) P.; m. Diane Sharon Garelis, May 12, 1984; children: Jonathon Jay, Lauren Claire, Scott Joseph. BA, Mich. State U., 1977. Copywriter Detroit Free Press, 1977-84, reporter, 1984-87; nat. corr. Detroit News, 1987-91, bus. columnist, 1991-2000; host talk show Sta. WXYT, 1995-96; assoc. bus. editor Detroit News, 1997-2000; pres. Small Times Media LLC, Ann Arbor, Mich., 2000—. Mem. Writers Guild Am., The Fairlane Club (vice chmn.). E-mail: jonpepper@ardesta.com.

PERELMAN, DAVID S. federal judge; b. 1934; Law clk. to Hon. Paul C. Weick U.S. Dist. Ct. No. Dist. Ohio and Sixth Cir. Ct. Appeals, 1958-60; law clk. to Hon. Ben C. Green U.S. Dist. Ct. (no. dist.) Ohio, 1962-79, magistrate judge, 1979—; pvt. practice, 1960. Office: US Dist Ct No Dist Ohio 424 US Courthouse 201 Superior Ave E Cleveland OH 44114-1201 Fax: (216) 522-2000.

PERES, JUDITH MAY, journalist; b. Chgo., June 30, 1946; d. Leonard H. and Eleanor (Seltzer) Zurakov; m. Michael Peres, June 27, 1972; children: Dana, Avital. BA, U. Ill., 1967; M Studies in Law, Yale U., 1997. Acct. exec. Daniel J. Edelman Inc., Chgo., 1967-68; copy editor Jerusalem (Israel) Post, 1968-71, news editor, 1971-75, chief night editor, 1975-80, editor, style book, 1978-80; copy editor Chgo. Tribune, 1980-82, rewriter, 1982-84, assoc. fgn. editor, 1984-90, nat. editor, 1990-95, nat./fgn. editor, 1995-96, specialist writer, 1997—; Yale Law fellow, 1996-97. Recipient Excellence in Coverage of Women and Gender, U. Mich., 2000, Media award for Excellence in Coverage of Women and Gender, 2000. Office: Chicago Tribune 435 N Michigan Ave Chicago IL 60611-4066 E-mail: jperes@tribune.com.

PEREZ, CARLOS A. radiation oncologist, educator; b. Colombia, Nov. 10, 1934; came to U.S., 1960, naturalized, 1969; children: Carlos S., Bernardo, Edward P. BS, U. de Antioquia, Medellin, 1952, MD, 1960. Diplomate: Am. Bd. Radiology (trustee 1985-97). Rotating intern Hosp. U. St. Vincente de Paul, Medellin and Caldas, 1958-59; resident Mallinckrodt Inst. Radiology Barnes Hosp., St. Louis, 1960-63, mem. faculty, 1964—; prof. radiation oncology Mallinckrodt Inst. Radiology Washington U., 1972—, dir. radiation oncology ctr., 1976—. Fellow radiotherapy M.D. Anderson Hosp. and Tumor Inst., U. Tex., Houston, 1963-64. Co-editor: Principles and Clinical Practice of Radiation Oncology, Principles and Practice of Gynecologic Oncology; mem. editl. bd. Internat. Jour. Radiation and Physics, 1975—, Cancer, 1993—; contbr. articles to med. jours. Recipient Am. Coll. of Radiology Gold Medal award, 1997. Fellow Am. Coll. Radiology; mem. AAAS, AMA, Am. Soc. Clin. Oncology, Am. Soc. Therapeutic Radiologists (pres. 1981-82, Gold medal 1992), Am. Radium Soc., Am. Assn. Cancer Rsch., Am. Assn. Cancer Edn., Radiol. Soc. N.Am., Mo. Radiol. Soc., Mo. Acad. Sci., Mo. Med. Soc., St. Louis Med. Soc., Greater St. Louis Soc. Radiologists, Radiation Rsch. Soc. Office: Washington U Radiation Oncology Ctr 4511 Forest Park Ave Ste 200 Saint Louis MO 63108-2190 Home: # 1204 8025 Bonhomme Ave Saint Louis MO 63105-3501 E-mail: perez@radonc.wustl.edu., caperez2@mehsi.com.

PEREZ, DIANNE M. medical researcher; b. Cleve., Dec. 13, 1959; BA in Chemistry and Biology with honors, Coll. of Wooster, 1982; PhD in Chemistry, Calif. Inst. Tech., 1988. Grad. rsch. asst. dept. chemistry Calif. Inst. Tech., Pasadena, 1982—87, grad. tchg. asst. introductory chemistry and biochemistry, 1982—87; sr. rsch. scientist Specialty Labs., Inc., Santa Monica, Calif., 1987—88; fellow dept. eye rsch. Doheny Eye Inst., L.A., 1988—89; fellow dept. heart and hypertension rsch. Cleve. Clinic Found., 1989—91, rsch. assoc. dept. cardiovasc. biology, 1992—93, project scientist dept. molecular cardiology, 1993—95, mem. asst. staff dept. molecular cardiology, 1996—. Coord. Molecular Cardiology's Protein Group Seminar Series Cleve. Clinic Found., 1994—95, supr. DNA Synthesis Core Facility Rsch. Inst., fellow's rep. Dept. Heart and Hypertension Rsch. to Divsn. Com.; adj. asst. prof. dept. pharmacology U. Ky., Lexington, 1994—; manuscript referee Molecular Pharmacology, Circulation Rsch., Cardiovasc. Rsch., Jour. Pharmacology and Exptl. Therapeutics, Gene, Biochemistry; lectr. in field. Contbr. articles to profl. jours.; patentee in field. Recipient Nat. Rsch. Svc. award, NIH, 1991; grantee Glaxo, 1994—; scholar Lubrizol, Coll. of Wooster, 1980. Mem.: AAAS, Am. Soc. Biochemistry and Molecular Biology, Am. Chem. Soc. (cert.), Am. Heart Assn. (Established Investigator award 1996), Am. Soc. Pharmacology and Therapeutics, Sigma Xi, Iota Sigma Pi, Phi Beta Kappa.

PEREZ, WILLIAM D. chemical company executive; Pres. SC Johson & Son, Inc., Racine, Wis., 1993-97, pres., CEO, 1997—. Office: SC Johnson & Son Inc 1525 Howe St Racine WI 53403-2236

PERKINS, MARK L. university chancellor; b. Richmond, Va., Oct. 13, 1948; m. Carolyn J. Snider; children: Patricia, Diana. BA in Psychology, St. Andrews Presbyn. Coll., 1972; MA, U. Ga., 1974, PhD in Psychometrics and Stats., 1976. With divsn. of pers. Gov.'s Office Commonwealth of Va., 1972-73; rsch. assoc., instr. U. Ga., Athens, 1973-76; various positions Old Dominion U., Norfolk, Va., 1976-86, exec. asst. to pres. for policy and planning, assoc. prof., 1981-82, assoc. exec. v.p., prof., 1982-86; v.p. for adminstrn., prof. Calif. State U., Stanislaus, Turlock, 1986-91, exec. v.p., prof., 1991-94; chancellor, prof. U. Wis., Green Bay, 1994—. Environ. mgmt. cons., 1990-95. Contbr. articles to profl. jours. Trustee Green Bay Symphony, 1995—; bd. dirs. Downtown Green Bay, Inc., 1996—, Weidner Ctr. Presents Inc., 1994—; trustee Calif. State U. Stanislaus Found., 1986-94, treas., 1986-94; mem. adv. coun. St. Vincent Hosp., 1994—. Named to Outstanding Young Men of Am., 1978. Mem. APA, Am. Ednl. Rsch. Assn., Am. Assn. for Higher Edn., Am. Assn. State Colls. and Univs., Soc. for Coll. and Univ. Planning, Green Bay Area C. of C./Ptnrs. in Edn. (exec. bd. 1996—), Green Bay Downtown Rotary Club, Phi Eta Sigma, Phi Kappa Phi, Kappa Delta Pi, Phi Delta Kappa. Avocations: running, racquetball, music. Office: U Wis Green Bay 2420 Nicolet Dr Green Bay WI 54311-7003

PERKINS, STEPHEN J. manufacturing executive; b. 1947; BS in Indsl. Engring., U. Pitts.; MBA, U. Chgo. Indsl. engr. U.S. Steel, 1968-71; with Copperweld Corp., 1971-79, Sr. Flexonics Inc., Bartlett, Ill., 1979-96, pres., CEO, 1983-96, Aftermarket Tech. Corp., Westmont, Ill., 1996-99; pres., COO, CEO-designate Comml. Intertech Corp., Youngstown, Ohio, 1999-2000; pres., CEO DT Industries, Inc., Springfield, Mo., 2000—. Office: DT Industries Inc 907 W 5th St Dayton OH 45407-3306

PERKINS, WILLIAM H., JR. finance company executive; b. Rushville, Ill., Aug. 4, 1921; s. William H. and Sarah Elizabeth (Logsdon) P.; m. Eileen Nelson, Jan. 14, 1949; 1 child, Gary Douglas. Ed., Ill. Coll. Pres. Howlett-Perkins Assos., Chgo. Mem. Ill. AEC, 1963-84, sec., 1970-84; mem. adv. bd. Nat. Armed Forces Mus., Smithsonian Instn., 1964-82 Sgt.-at-arms Democratic Nat. Conv., 1952, 56, del.-at-large, 1964, 68, 72; spl. asst. to chmn. Dem. Nat. Com., 1960; mem. Presdl. Inaugural Com., 1961, 65, 69, 73. Served with U.S. Army, 1944-46. Mem. Ill. Ins. Fedn. (pres. 1965-84), Ill. C. of C. (chmn. legis. com. 1971), Chgo. Assn. Commerce and Industry (legis. com., Raoul Wallenberg Humanitarian award 1993), Sangamo Club, Masons, Shriners. Methodist. Home: 52 N Cowley Rd Riverside IL 60546-2042 Office: 2501 South Des Plaines Ave North Riverside IL 60546-1521 Fax: (708) 795-1349.

PERKINSON, ROBERT RONALD, psychologist, consultant; b. Richmond, Va., Aug. 8, 1945; s. Gordon Archibald and Sarah (Haskins) P.; m. Elizabeth Godfrey Fly, July 27, 1968 (div. 1984); children: Robert Reps, Nyshie Page, Shane William; m. Angela Kaufman, Sept. 20, 1991. BS, Colo. State U., 1968; MS, Ea. Wash. State U., 1970; PhD, Utah State U., 1974. Lic. psychologist, S.D.; cert. chem. dependency counselor level III, S.D.; nat. cert. gambling counselor; nat. cert. alcohol and drug counselor; lic. marriage and family counselor, S.D. Juvenile ct. psychologist, Cedar City, Utah, 1971-72; psychologist in pvt. practice Jackson, Wyo., 1974-83; dir. psychol. svcs. Western Wyo. Mental Health Assn., 1977-78, psychologist, 1983—; psychologist, clin. dir. Keystone Treatment Ctr., 1988—. Cons. in field; chief psychologist Grand Teton Nat. Pk., Teton County Sheriff's Office and Police Dept. Copyrights: The Yellowstone Park Game, The Good Health Game, The Grizzly Control Team, Communication from God, Chemical Dependency Counseling, The Mystics, God Talks CD, Peace Will Come CD, The Treatment of Pathological Gambling: A Step By Step Approach. Author: Chemical Dependency Counseling: A Practical Guide, 1997, The Chemical Dependency Treatment Planner, 1998, God Talks to You, 2000, The Addiction Treatment Planner, 2001, Chemical Dependency Counseling: A Practical Guide, 2d edit., 2002; contbr. articles to profl. jours. Mem. APA, S.D. Psychol. Assn., S.D. Chem. Dependency Assn., Biofeedback Soc. Am. (bd. dirs. Wyo. br.), Wyo. Bd. Psychologist Examiners (pres. 1997, bd. dirs. S.D. coun. problem gambling), Nat. Registere of Health Svc. Providers in Psychology. Address: PO Box 159 Canton SD 57013-0159

PERKOFF, GERALD THOMAS, physician, educator; b. St. Louis, Sept. 22, 1926; s. Nat and Ann (Schwartz) Perkoff; m. Marion Helen Maizner, June 7, 1947; children: David Alan, Judith Ilene, Susan Gail. MD cum laude, Washington U., 1948. Intern Salt Lake City Gen. Hosp., 1948—49, resident, 1950—52; from instr. to asso. prof. medicine U. Utah, 1954—63; chief med. service Salt Lake VA Hosp., 1961—63; from assoc. prof. to prof. medicine Washington U. Sch. Medicine, St. Louis, 1963—79; chief Med. Svc., St. Louis City Hosp., 1963—68; prof. preventive medicine and pub. health, dir. divsn. health care rsch. Med. Svc. St. Louis City Hosp., 1968—79; Curators prof. and assoc. chmn. dept. family and cmty. medicine and prof. medicine U. Mo., Columbia, 1979—91, Curators prof. emeritus, 1991—, co-dir. program health care and human values, 1984—85. Chmn. nat. adv. com. Robert Wood Johnson Clin. Scholars Program, 1989—96; founder, dir. Med. Care Group Washington U., 1968—70. Contbr. articles to profl. jours. Career rsch. prof. neuromuscular diseases Nat. Found. Neuromuscular Diseases, 1961; dep. dir. Robert Wood Johnson Found. Generalist Physician Initiative, 1991—. Fellow Henry J. Kaiser Sr. fellow, Ctr. Advanced Studies in Behavioral Sci., 1976—77, 1985—86; scholar John and Mary R. Markle scholar med. sci., 1955—60. Mem.: Inst. Medicine (Nat. Acad. Scis.), Assn. Am. Physicians, Soc. Tchrs. Family Medicine, Am. Soc. Clin. Investigation. Home: 1300 Torrey Pines Dr Columbia MO 65203-4826 Office: U Mo Sch Medicine Dept Family & Community Medicine M228 Med Scis Columbia MO 65212-0001

PERKOVIC, ROBERT BRANKO, international management consultant; b. Belgrade, Yugoslavia, Aug. 27, 1925; came to U.S., 1958, naturalized, 1961; s. Slavoljub and Ruza (Pantelic) P.; m. Jacquelyn Lee Lipscomb, Dec. 14, 1957; children: Bonnie Kathryn, Jennifer Lee. M.S. in Econs, U. Belgrade, 1954; B.F.T., Am. Grad. Sch. Internat. Mgmt., 1960; grad. Stanford exec. program, Stanford U., 1970. Auditor Gen. Foods Corp., White Plains, N.Y., 1960-62, controller Mexico City, 1962-64; dir. planning Monsanto Co., Barcelona, Spain, 1964-67, dir. fin. Europe, Brussels, 1967-70, dir. fin. planning-internat., 1970-71, asst. treas., 1971-72, Brussels, 1972-74; corp. treas. Fiat-Allis Inc. & BV, Deerfield, Ill., 1974-78; v.p., treas. TRW Inc., Cleve., 1978-88; pres. RBP Internat. Cons., 1988—. Dir. U.S. Bus. Coun. for Southeastern Europe, Inc. Active Cleve. Commn. on Fgn. Relations. Inc. Served with Yugoslavian Army, 1944-47. Mem. Fin. Execs. Inst., Cleve. Treas. Club (bd. dirs., pres.), Assn. Corp. Growth (northeast Ohio chpt.), Latin Am. Bus. Assn. (co-founder), Mayfield Village (Ohio) Racquet Club. Office: RBP Internat Cons 26 Pepper Creek Dr Cleveland OH 44124-5248

PERLBERG, JULES MARTIN, lawyer; b. Chgo., Jan. 28, 1931; s. Maurice and Louise Mae (Schonberger) P.; m. Dora Ann Morris, Dec. 22, 1968; children: Julia, Michael. BBA with high distinction, U. Mich., 1952, JD with high distinction, 1957. Bar: Ill. 1958, D.C. 1964; C.P.A., Ill. Acct. Arthur Andersen & Co., Chgo., 1954-55; faculty U. Mich. Law Sch., Ann Arbor, 1957-58; assoc. Sidley & Austin and predecessor firm, Chgo., 1958-65, ptnr., 1966-98, sr. counsel, 1998—. Mem. Glencoe (Ill.) Bd. Edn., 1980-87, pres., 1985-86; bd. dirs. Juvenile Diabetes Found., Chgo., 1981-2001, v.p. 1983-85, treas., 1988-90, 96-98; exec. bd. Am. Jewish Com., Chgo., 1978-88, v.p., 1981-83; trustee New Trier Twp. Schs., 1987-91, pres., 1989-91; class co-chairperson parents com. Duke U., 1992-94. 1st lt. U.S. Army, 1952-54. Recipient Gold medal Ill. Soc. C.P.A.s, 1955 Mem. ABA, Chgo. Bar Assn., Lawyers Club, Mid-Day Club (Chgo.), Std. Club. Clubs: Legal, Law; Mid-Day (Chgo.); Standard. Home: 568 Westley Rd Glencoe IL 60022-1071 Office: Sidley Austin Brown & Wood Apt 605 425 W Surf St Chicago IL 60657-6139

PERLMAN, BURTON, judge; b. Dec. 17, 1924; s. Phillip and Minnie Perlman; m. Alice Weihl, May 20, 1956; children: Elizabeth, Sarah, Nancy, Daniel. BE, Yale U., 1945, ME, 1947; LLB, U. Mich., 1952. Bar: Ohio 1959, N.Y. 1953, Conn. 1952, U.S. Dist. Ct. (so. and ea. dists.) N.Y. 1954, U.S. Dist. Ct. (so. dist) Ohio 1959, U.S. Ct. Appeals (2d cir.) 1953, U.S. Ct. Appeals (6th cir.) 1959. Assoc. Armand Lackenbach, N.Y.C., NY, 1952—58; pvt. practice Cin., 1958—61; assoc. Paxton and Seasongood, 1961—67; ptnr. Schmidt, Effton, Josselson and Weber, 1968—71; U.S. magistrate U.S. Dist. Ct. (so. dist.) Ohio, 1971—76, U.S. bankruptcy judge, 1976—. Chief bankruptcy judge so. dist. Ohio, 1986—93; adj. prof. U. Cin. Law Sch., 1976—. Served with U.S. Army, 1944—46. Mem.: ABA, Cin. Bar Assn., Am. Judicature Soc., Fed. Bar Assn. Office: US Bankruptcy Ct Atrium 2 8th Fl 221 E 4th St Cincinnati OH 45202-4124

PERLMAN, HARVEY STUART, lawyer, educator; b. Lincoln, Nebr., Jan. 17, 1942; s. Floyd Ted and Rosalyn (Lashinsky) P.; m. Susan G. Unthank, Aug. 27, 1966; children: Anne, Amy. B.A., U. Nebr., 1963, J.D., 1966. Bar: Nebr. 1966, Va. 1980. Teaching fellow U. Chgo. Law Sch., 1966-67; mem. faculty U. Nebr. Sch. Law, 1967-74, prof., 1972-74; prof. law U. Va., Charlottesville, 1974-83; dean law U. Nebr., Lincoln, 1983—; exec. dir. Nebr. Commn. on Law Enforcement. Author: (with Edmund Kitch) Legal Regulation of the Competitive Process, 1972, 79, 86; asso. editor: Jour. Law and Human Behavior, 1974-86. Named Ida Beam Distinguished Vis. Prof. Law, U. Iowa, 1981-86. Mem. Am. Bar Assn., Nebr. Bar Assn., Law-Psychology Assn., Am. Law Inst. Office: U Nebr Coll Law Lincoln NE 68588

PERLMAN, LAWRENCE, retired business executive, corporate director, consultant; b. St. Paul, Apr. 8, 1938; m. Linda Peterson; children: David, Sara. BA, Carleton Coll., 1960; JD, Harvard U., 1963. Bar: Minn. 1963. Law. clk. for fed. judge, 1963; assoc., ptnr. Fredrikson & Byron, Mpls., 1964-75; gen. counsel, exec. v.p. U.S. pacing ops. Medtronic, Inc., 1975-78; sr. ptnr. Oppenheimer, Wolff & Donnelly, 1978-80; sec., gen. counsel, v.p. corp. svcs. Control Data Corp., 1980-82; pres. Comml. Credit Co., 1983-85; pres., CEO Imprimis Tech., 1985—88; pres., COO Control Data Corp., Mpls., 1989; pres., CEO Control Data Corp. (now Ceridian Corp.), 1990-92, chmn., CEO, 1992—2000; ret., 2000. Dir., chmn. Seagate Tech., 1989-2000; bd. dirs. Amdocs Ltd., Carlson Cos., Inc., The Valspar Corp.; chmn. Arbitron Inc.; trustee Carleton Coll. Bd. dirs. Walker Art Ctr.; regent Univ. of Minn., 1993-95; chmn. 21st Century Workforce Commn., 1999-2000. Address: 343 Union Plaza 333 Washington Ave N Minneapolis MN 55401

PERLMUTTER, DAVID H. physician, educator; b. Bklyn., May 11, 1952; s. Herman Arthur and Ruth (Jacobs) P.; m. Barbara Ann Cohlan, Feb. 7, 1981; children: Andrew, Lisa. BA, U. Rochester, 1974; MD, St. Louis U., 1978. Intern then resident in pediatrics U. Pa. Sch. Medicine, Phila., 1978-81; fellow in pediatric gastroenterology Harvard U. Sch. Medicine, Boston, 1981-84, instr. pediatrics, 1983-85, asst. prof. pediatrics, 1985-86; Donald Strominger prof. of pediatrics Washington U. Sch. Medicine, St. Louis, 1986-89, prof. cell biology, physiology, 1989—. Editor: Pediatric Rsch., 1990—; editl. bd. Gastroenterology, 1990—; dir. divsn. gastrology and nutrition and pediatrics; contbr. articles to profl. jours. Recipient Established Investigator award Am. Heart Assn., 1987, Rsch. Scholar award Am. Gastroent. Assn., 1985, RJR Nabisco Co., 1986. Mem. Soc. Pediatric Rsch. (coun. rep. 1990—), Am. Soc. Cell Biology, Am. Soc. Clin. Investigation. Office: Washington U Sch Medicine Dept Pediatrics 1 Childrens Pl Saint Louis MO 63110-1002

PERLMUTTER, NORMAN, finance company executive; b. 1934; BS, U. Ill., 1956. With Greenbawm Mortgage Co., Chgo., 1959-66, Heitman Fin. Svcs. Ltd., Chgo., 1966—, chmn., CEO. With USN, 1956-59. Office: Heitman Fin Ltd 180 N La Salle St Ste 3600 Chicago IL 60601-2805

PERLMUTTER, ROBERT, land company executive; Chmn., CEO David Street Land Co., Evanston, Ill., 1999—. Office: 630 David St Evanston IL 60602

PERLOW, GILBERT J(EROME), editor; b. N.Y.C., Feb. 10, 1916; s. David and Esther (German) P.; m. Mina Rea Jones. AB, Cornell U., 1936, MA, 1937; PhD, U. Chgo., 1940. Instr. physics U. Minn., Mpls., 1940-41; physicist Naval Ordnance Lab., Washington, 1941-42, Naval Rsch. Lab., Washington, 1942-52; rsch. assoc. physics dept. U. Minn., Mpls., 1952-53; assoc. physicist Argonne (Ill.) Nat. Lab., 1953-57, sr. physicist, 1957—; editor Jour. Applied Physics Am. Inst. Physics/Argonne Nat. Lab., 1970-73, editor Applied Physics Letters, 1970-90, consulting editor Applied Physics Letters, 1990-2000. Vis. assoc. prof. physics U. Wash., Seattle, 1957; vis. prof. German univs., Munich, Berlin; exch. physicist AERE Harwell, Berkshire, Eng., 1961. Contbr. over 70 articles to profl. jours., also chpts. to books; author numerous U.S. patents. Recipient Alexander von Humboldt award Alexander von Humboldt Found., Tech. U. Munich, 1972. Fellow Am. Phys. Soc.; mem. Chgo. Corinthian Yacht Club (life mem., commodore 1974). Avocations: sailing, woodworking, painting. Home: 4919 Northcott Ave Downers Grove IL 60515-3434 Office: Argonne Nat Lab Physics Divsn 9700 Cass Ave Argonne IL 60439-4803 E-mail: perlow@phy.anl.gov.

PERO, PERRY R. investment company executive; Sr. exec. v.p., CFO No. Trust Corp., Chgo., vice chmn., CFO. Office: No Trust Corp 50 S Lasalle St Chicago IL 60675-1006

PERRICONE, CHARLES, state legislator; b. Oct. 10, 1960; Student, Kalamazoo Coll., Western Mich. U. Rep. Mich. State Dist. 61, 1995—; spkr. of the house Lansing, 1999—. Vice chair tax policy com.; mem. corrections com., house oversight and ethics com., legis. coun.; asst. Rep. leader. Address: State Capitol PO Box 30014 100 Constitution Ave Lansing MI 48909-7536

PERRIN, KENNETH LYNN, university chancellor; b. L.A., July 29, 1937; s. Freeman Whitaker and Lois Eileen (Bowen) P.; m. Shirley Anne Cupp, Apr. 2, 1960; children: Steven, Lynne. BA, Occidental Coll., 1959; MA, Calif. State U., Long Beach, 1964; PhD, Stanford U., 1969. Lic. in speech pathology, Calif. Chmn. dept. communicative disorders U. Pacific, Stockton, Calif., 1969-77; dir. edn. and sci. programs Am. Speech-Lang.-Hearing Assn., Rockville, Md., 1977-80; dean faculty profl. studies West Chester U., Pa., 1980-82, acting acad. v.p., 1982, pres., 1983-91, Coun. on Postsecondary Edn., Washington, 1991-93; chancellor, system sr. v.p. U. Hawaii, Hilo and West Oahu, 1993-97; chancellor Ind. U., South Bend, 1997—. Bd. vis. C.C. Airforce, 1997—. Contbr. articles to profl. jours.; editor: Guide to Graduate Education Speech Pathology and Audiology, 1980. Bd. dirs. South Bend Meml. Hosp., 1997—, Pub. TV Sta., 1997—; trainee Vocat. Rehab. Adminstrn., 1965-69. Named Disting. Alumnus Sch. Humanities Calif. State U., Long Beach, 1988. Fellow Am. Speech-Lang.-Hearing Assn. Home: 52120 Sherford Ct Granger IN 46530-6287 Office: Indiana U South Bend PO Box 7111 South Bend IN 46634-7111

PERRIS, TERRENCE GEORGE, lawyer; b. L.A., Oct. 18, 1947; s. Theodore John Grivas and Penny (Sfakianos) Perris. BA magna cum laude, U. Toledo, 1969; JD summa cum laude, U. Mich., 1972. Bar: Ohio 1972, U.S. Tax Ct. 1982, U.S. Ct. Claims 1983, U.S. Supreme Ct. 1983. Law clk. to judge U.S. Ct. Appeals (2d cir.), N.Y.C., 1972-73; law clk. to Justice Potter Stewart U.S. Supreme Ct., Washington, 1973-74; assoc. Squire, Sanders & Dempsey LLP, Cleve., 1974-80; ptnr. Squire, Sanders & Dempsey, 1980—. V.p., trustee SS&D Found., Cleve., 1984—; nat. coord. Taxation Practice Area, 1987—, mgmt. com., 1996—2002; chmn. Cleve. Tax Inst., 1993; vis. prof. law U. Mich., 1996; adj. prof. Case Western Res. U., Cleve., 2001—02; lectr. in field. Vis. com. U. Mich. Law Sch., 1986—. Capt. U.S. Army, 1974. Mem.: ABA, Tax. Club Cleve., Supreme Ct. Hist. Soc., Cleve. Bar Assn., Ohio Bar Assn. (subchtp. C of internal revenue code task force), Pres.'s Club, Union Club Cleve., Club Cleve., U. Mich. Club Cleve., Order of Coif, Phi Kappa Phi. Republican. Eastern Orthodox. Avocation: landscape gardening. Office: Squire Sanders & Dempsey LLP 4900 Key Tower 127 Public Sq Cleveland OH 44114-1216 E-mail: tperris@ssd.com.

PERRUCCI, ROBERT, sociologist, educator; b. N.Y.C., Nov. 11, 1931; s. Dan and Inez (Mucci) P.; m. Carolyn Land Cummings, Aug. 4, 1965; children: Mark Robert, Celeste Ann, Christopher Robert, Alissa Cummings, Martin Cummings. B.S., SUNY, Cortland, 1958; M.S. (Social Sci. Research Council fellow), Purdue U., Ph.D., 1962. Asst. prof. sociology Purdue U., West Lafayette, Ind., 1962-65, asso. prof., 1965-67, prof., 1967—, head dept., 1978-87. Vis. Simon prof. U. Manchester (Eng.), 1968-69; Bd. dirs. Ind. Center on Law and Poverty, 1973-76 Author: Sociology, 1983, Circle of Madness, 1974, Divided Loyalties, 1980, The Triple Revolution, 1971, Profession Without Community, 1968, The Engineers and the Social System, 1968, Mental Patients and Social Networks, 1982, Plant Closings: International Context and Local Consequences, 1988, Networks of Power, 1989, Japanese Auto Transplants in the Heartland: Corporatism and Community, 1994, The New Class Society, 1999, Science Under Siege?, 2000; editor: The American Sociologist, 1982—, Social Problems, 1993-96, Contemporary Sociology, 2000-2003; contbr. articles to profl. jours. Served with USMC, 1951-53. Recipient grants, NSF, 1966—68, 1976—78, NIMH, 1969—72, Sloan Found., 2002—. Mem. Am. Sociol. Assn., Soc. Study Social Problems (dir. 1980-83, v.p. 1996-97, pres. 1999—), N. Central Sociol. Assn. (pres. 1973-74) Home: 305 Leslie Ave West Lafayette IN 47906-2411 Office: Dept Sociology Purdue U West Lafayette IN 47907

PERRY, BURTON LARS, retired pediatrician; b. Midland, Mich., Dec. 8, 1931; s. Willard Russell and Myrl Alice (Jacobsen) P.; m. Nancy Fawn Towsley, Aug. 24, 1956; children: Ellen, Willard. BS, U. Mich., 1953, MD, 1960. Diplomate Am. Bd. Pediats.; sub-bd. pediat. cardiology. Physician U. Mich., Ann Arbor, 1960-78, Childrens Hosp. Mich., Detroit, 1978-97. 1st lt. infantry, U.S. Army, 1954-56. Home: 1416 Dicken Dr Ann Arbor MI 48103-4417 Office: Childrens Hosp Mich 3901 Beaubien St Detroit MI 48201-2119

PERRY, CATHERINE D. judge; b. 1952; BA, Univ. of Okla., 1977; JS, Wash. Univ. Sch. of Law, 1980. Sec., law clk. Gillespie, Perry & Gentry, Sentinel, Okla., 1970, 77-78; with Armstrong, Teasdale, Kramer & Vaughn, St. Louis, 1980-90; magistrate judge U.S. Dist. Ct. (Mo. ea. dist.), 8th circuit, 1990-94; dist. judge U.S. Dist. Ct. (ea. dist.), 8th circuit, 1994—. Mem. Fed. Magistrate Judges Assn., Nat. Assn. of Women Judges, Am. Bar Assn., Mo. Bar Assn., Bar Assn. of Metropolitan St. Louis, Women Lawyers Assn. of Greater St. Louis. Office: US Courthouse 1114 Market St Rm 319 Saint Louis MO 63101-2038

PERRY, CHRIS NICHOLAS, retired advertising executive; b. Pitts., Dec. 25, 1945; s. Nicholas and Georgia (Demas) P.; Kathleen Clarke, June 19, 1971; children: Damien, Adam, Dana. BA, U. Pitts., 1968. With Youngstown (Ohio) Steel, 1968-70; creative supr. Ketchum Communications, Pitts., 1970-74; pres., creative dir. Hedding, Perry, Davis Inc., Charlotte, N.C., 1974-76; v.p., creative dir. Fahlgren & Swink Advt., Marion, Ohio, 1976-79, Meldrum and Fewsmith Communications, Inc., Cleve., 1979-82, sr. v.p. creative services, 1982-85, exec. v.p. creative services, 1985-86, pres., chief operating officer, 1986-87, chmn., chief exec. officer, creative dir., 1987-98, also bd. dirs. Mem. bd. disting. judges and advisors The N.Y. Festivals, 1988—. Recipient numerous awards for creative excellence. Mem. Am. Assn. Advt. Agys. (sec.-treas. cen. region 1990-91, chmn. 1992-93), Cleve. Advt. Club, Cleve. Soc. Communicating Arts (pres. 1985-87, Disting. Communicator award 1991), The Hermit Club, Columbia Hills Country Club, The Union Club, Firestone Country Club.

PERRY, EDWIN CHARLES, lawyer; b. Lincoln, Nebr., Sept. 29, 1931; s. Arthur Edwin and Charlotte C. (Peterson) P.; m. Joan Mary Hanson, June 5, 1954; children: Mary Mills, Judy Phipps, James Perry, Greg Perry, Jack Perry, Pricilla Hoffel Finger. BS, U. Nebr., 1953, JD, 1955. Bar: Nebr. 1955; U.S. Dist. Ct. Nebr., 1955; U.S. Ct. Appeals Nebr., 1968. Of counsel

Perry, Guthery, Haase & Gessford, P.C., Lincoln, 1957—. Chmn. Lincoln Lancaster County Planning Com., Madonna Rehab. Hosp. Fellow Am. Bar Found., Nebr. Bar Found.; mem. Nebr. State Bar Assn. (chair ho. dels. 1987-88, pres. 1991-92), Nebr. Coun. Sch. Attys. (pres. 1978-79), Lincoln Bar Assn. (pres. 1982-83). Republican. Roman Catholic. Office: Perry Guthery Haase & Gessford PC 223 S 13th St Ste 1400 Lincoln NE 68508-2005

PERRY, ESTON LEE, real estate and equipment leasing company executive; b. Wartburg, Tenn., Mar. 16, 1936; s. Eston Lee and Willimae (Heidle) P.; m. Alice Anne Schmidt, Oct. 21, 1961; children: Julie Anne, Jeffrey John, Jennifer Lee. BS, Ind. State U., 1961. With Oakley Corp., 1961—, dir., 1965—. Corp. officer Ind. State Bank, Terre Haute, 1975-80; pres. One Twenty Four Madison Corp., Terre Haute, 1979—, also bd. dirs., chmn. bd., 1981—; bd. dirs. Fifth Third Bank of Ind. Bd. dirs. Salvation Army, Terre Haute, 1975-91, mem. exec. adv. bd., 1979-87; bd. dirs. Vigo County Dept. Pub. Welfare, 1979-82, Jr. Achievement Wabash Valley, 1980-86; bd. dirs. United Way of Wabash Valley, 1984-89, chmn. fund campaign, 1984, bd. dirs. United Way of Ind., 1984-90, v.p., 1986, pres., 1988-89; trustee Oakley Found., 1970—; bd. dirs. Terre Haute Symphony Orch., 1984-87, Ind. State U. Found., 1988—, Goodwill Industries of Terre Haute, 1984-97, Leadership Terre Haute, 1984-88, Cen. Eastside Assocs., 1984-88, pres., 1984-85; mem. exec. com. Ind. State U. Found., 1990-94; bd. dirs. City of Terre Haute Hulman Links Commn., pres., 1986-91; mem. President's Assocs., Ind. State U., adv. bd.; bd. overseers Sheldon Swope Art Gallery of Terre Haute, 1984-87; bd. assocs. Rose Hulman Inst. Tech., 1986—. Served with U.S. Army, 1955-57. Mem. Jaycees Terre Haute (v.p. 1967-69), C. of C. Terre Haute (bd. dirs. 1984-93, vice chmn. 1986-88, chmn. 1990), Wabash Valley Pilots Assn., Aircarft Owners and Pilots Assn., Air Safety Found., Aviation Trades Assn., Country Club of Terre Haute (bd. dirs.), Aero Club of Terre Haute, Sycamore Athletic Scholarship Fund (Ind. State U.), Lions (pres. Terre Haute 1983-84), Elks, Lambda Chi Alpha. Home: 25 Bogart Dr Terre Haute IN 47803-2401 Office: 8 S 16th St Terre Haute IN 47807-4102 E-mail: bperry@oakleyusa.com.

PERRY, GEORGE, neuroscientist, educator; b. Lompoc, Calif., Apr. 12, 1953; s. George Richard and Mary Arlene (George) P.; m. Paloma Aguilar, May 21, 1983; children: Anne, Elizabeth. BA in Zoology with hons., U. Calif., Santa Barbara, 1974; PhD in Marine Biology, U. Calif., San Diego, 1979. Postdoctoral fellow Baylor Coll. Medicine, Houston, 1979-82; from asst. prof. to prof. pathology Case Western Res. U., Cleve., 1982-94, prof., 1994—, interim chmn. dept., 2001—. Tchg. asst. U. Calif., San Diego, 1977, Stanford U., 1978—79; mem. task force on Alzheimer's disease Ohio Gov., 1987, 90; mem. scientific adv. bd. Familial Alzheimer's Disease Rsch. Found., 1988—; mem., chair neurol. scis. study section NIH, Bethesda, Md., 1989—95; vis. scholar Sci.-by-Mail, 1991—94; cons. Nymox, Inc., Panacea Pharms., Inc., Prion Devel. Labs., Voyager; spkr. in field; mem. numerous rev. bds. nationally/internationally. Author: The Neuronal Cytoskeleton, 1992; co-author: (chpt.) Muscle and Cell Motility, 1982, Membranes in Growth and Development, 1982, Electron Microscopy and Alzheimer's Disease, 1986, Banbury Report 27, Molecular Neuropathology of Aging, 1987, Advances in Behavioral Biology, 1987, Fidia Research Series, 1988, Progress in Clinical and Biological Research: Alzheimer's Disease and Related Disorders, 1989, 93, International Congress Series: Molecular Biology and Genetics of Alzheimer's Disease, 1990, Neuroscience Year, 1992, Amyloid and Amyloidosis, 1993, Dementia in Parkinson's Disease, 1994, Non-Neural Cells in Alzheimer's Disease, 1995, Alzheimer's Disease: Aetiological Mechanism and Therapeutic Possibilities, 1996; editor-in-chief Jour. Alzheimer's Disease, 1998—; guest editor Clin. Neurosci., 1993; editor Biomed. Jour., 1994-95; assoc. editor Am. Jour. pathology, 1994-2000; mem. editl. bd. Am. Jour. Pathology, 1992—, Alzheimer Disease and Associated Disorders, 1994—, Alzheimer's Disease Rev., 1995—, Jour. Alzheimer's Disease,1997—, Jour. Exptl. Neurol., 1997-99, Molecular Chem. Neuropathology, 1997—, Jour. Neural Transmission, 1998—, Investigational Drugs Jour., 1998—, Brain Pathology, 1999—, Jour. Molecular Neurosci., 1999—, Antioxidant and Redox Signaling, 2000-2002, Research Signal Post, 2000—; reviewer Acta Neuropathol., Alan Liss Publ. Co., Am. Jour. Pathol., Ann Neurol, others; contbr. articles to Experimental Cell Rsch., Jour Cell Biology, Jour. Leukocyte Biology, Devel. Biology, Brain Rsch., Am. Jour. Pathology, Jour. Neurosci., European Jour. Cell Biology, Nature, Annals Neurology, Lancet, Acta Neuropathology, Jour. Neurochemistry, Neurosci. Letters, Hepatology, Jour. Hirnforsch, Cancer Letters, Neuroreport, Med. Hypotheses, Nature Medicine, Neurodegeneration, Brain Rsch. Protocols, others. Pres. Serra Club, 1995-97. Recipient Bausch and Lomb medal, 1971, Rsch. Career Devel. award, NIH, 1988—93, Temple award, Alzheimer's Assn., 1999, Career Devel. award, NIH, 1988, Disting. American of Portuguese Ancestry award, Portuguese-Am. Hist. Found., Inc., 2001; fellow Kennecott Copper fellow, 1974—75, Muscular Dystrophy Assn. fellow, 1980—82; grantee NIH, 1985—, grantee, Am. Health Assistance Found., 1988—90, 1997—99, Alzheimer's Assn., 1989—90, 1998—, Belgian Nat. Found. Sci. Rsch., 1994—, Neurogeriatrics Fund., 1995—96, 1997—, Britton Fund, 1996. Fellow AAAS; mem. AAUP (exec. com. 1996—, membership chair 1996-98, v.p. 1998-99, pres. 1999—), Am. Soc. Cell Biology (fellow 1992), Electron Microscopy Soc. N.E. Ohio (treas. 1986-88, trustee 1988-90, pres. 1990-91), Soc. Neurosci., Am. Assn. Neuropathologists (awards com. 1992-93, 95-2001, chmn. 2001, internat. congress neuropathology concilator 1995-2000), Am. Soc. Investigative Pathology (BioInfo Net 1996—, program com. 1998-2001), Oxygen Club, Soc. Neuroscientists Africa, Am. Soc. Neurochemistry, Am. Inst. Biol. Scis., Mitochondrion Rsch. Soc., U.S. and Can. Acad. of Pathology, Hispanic Med. Assn. (com. on status of Portuguese in medicine and sci.), Sigma Xi. Democrat. Roman Catholic. Home: 2500 Eaton Rd University Heights OH 44118-4339 Office: Case Western Res U Inst Path 2085 Adelbert Rd Cleveland OH 44106-2622 E-mail: GXP7@po.cwru.edu.

PERRY, HAROLD OTTO, dermatologist; b. Rochester, Minn., Nov. 18, 1921; s. Oliver and Hedwig Clara (Tornow) P.; m. Loraine Thelma Moehnke, Aug. 27, 1944; children— Preston, Oliver, Ann, John. AA, Rochester Jr. Coll., 1942; BS, U. Minn., 1944, MB, 1946, MD, 1947; MS, Mayo Grad. Sch. Medicine, 1953. Diplomate Am. Bd. Dermatology with spl. competence in dermatopathology. Intern Naval Hosp., Oakland, Calif., 1946-47; resident in dermatology Mayo Grad. Sch. Medicine, 1949-52; practice medicine specializing in dermatology Rochester, 1953-86; mem. staff Mayo Clinic, 1953-86, mem. emeritus staff, 1987—; instr., asst. prof., assoc. prof. Mayo Med. Sch., 1953-86, prof., 1978-83, Robert H. Kieckhefer prof. dermatology, 1978-83, head dept. dermatology, 1975-83, emeritus prof. dermatology, 1987—. Civilian cons. dermatology to surgeon gen. USAF, 1979-99. Contbr. articles to med. jours. and, chpts. to books. With USNR, 1943-45, 46-49. Inducted into Rochester (Minn.) C.C. Alumni Hall of Fame, 1993; recipient Disting. Alumnus award Mayo Found., 1995. Mem. AMA, Am. Acad. Dermatology (pres. 1981, Sulzberger internat. lectr. 1986, Gold Medal for visionary leadership 1998), Am. Dermatol. Assn. (bd. dirs. 1985-89, pres. 1989-90), Am. Bd. Dermatology (bd. dirs. 1979-90, v.p. 1989, pres. 1990), Noah Worcester Dermatol. Soc. (pres. 1969), Minn. Dermatol. Soc. (pres. 1967), Chgo. Dermatol. Soc., Internat. Soc. Tropical Dermatology, Minn. Med. Assn.; hon. mem. French Dermatol. Soc., Spanish Acad. Dermatology, Brazilian Dermatol. Soc., Ga. Dermatol. Soc., Iowa Dermatol. Soc., Korean Dermatol. Soc., Bolivar Soc. Dermatology, Jacksonville Dermatol. Soc., N.Am. Clin. Dermatol. Soc., Pacific Dermatol. Assn. Home: 3625 SW Bamber Valley Rd Rochester MN 55902 Office: Mayo Clinic Emeritus Staff Ctr 10th Fl Plummer Bldg Ctr Rochester MN 55905-0001

PERRY, JAMES ALFRED, b. Dallas, Sept. 27, 1945; BA in Fisheries, Colo. State U., 1968; MA, Western State Coll., 1973; PhD, Idaho State U., 1981. Sr. water quality specialist Idaho Div. Environ., Pocatello, 1974-82; area mgr. Centrac Assocs., Salt Lake City, 1982; H.T. Morse disting. prof. water quality U. Minn., St. Paul, 1982—, head dept. fisheries, wildlife, conservation biol., 2000—, dir. natural resources policy and mgmt., 1985—, dir. grad. studies in water resources, 1988—92; dep. dir. AID-funded Environ. Tng. Project for Ctrl. and Ea. Europe, 1992-96; spl. asst. to dean grad. sch. U. Minn., St. Paul, 1996-2000, dir. grad. studies in water resources, 1999—2001. Vis. scholar Oxford U., Green College, Eng., 1990-91; internat. cons. in water quality. Author: Water Quality Management of a Natural Resource, 1996, Ecosystem Management for Central and Eastern Europe, 2001; editor: Jour. Natural Resources and Life Scis. Edn. Charter mem. Leadership Devel. Acad., Lakewood, Minn., 1988; bd. dirs. Minn. Ctr. for Environ. Advocacy. Recipient Richard C. Newman Art of Tchg. award, 1998, Morse-Alumni award, 1999; ACOP/ESCOP nat. leadership fellow, 1995-96; CIC acad. leadership fellow, 2000-01. Mem.: The Soc. for Conservation Biology, The Wildlife Soc., Am. Fisheries Soc., N.Am. Benthol. Soc. (exec. bd. Albuquerque 1990—91), Internat. Soc. Theoretical and Applied Limnology, Internat. Water Resources Assn., Am. Water Resources Assn., Minn. Acad. Scis. (bd. dirs. 1987—90), Gamma Sigma Delta (merit award 2001), Xi Sigma Pi, Sigma Xi. Office: U Minn Dept Fisheries Wildlife amd Cpmservation Biology 204 Hodson Hall 1980 Folwell Ave Saint Paul MN 55108-1037 E-mail: jperry@umn.edu.

PERRY, JAMES BENN, casino and hotel executive; b. New Castle, Pa., Jan. 15, 1950; s. Samuel Wesley Jr. and Grace Elizabeth (Brumbaugh) P.; m. Cathy Ann Jackson, Dec. 27, 1982; children: James Benn Jr., Lauren Elizabeth, Julie Ann. BA in History, Ohio Wesleyan U., 1972; postgrad., Ariz. State U., 1975-76; student, Tulane U., 1968-70. CPA, N.J. Internal auditor Ramada Inns, Phoenix, 1976-78, regional controller, 1978-79; asst. controller Tropicana Hotel & Casino, Las Vegas, Nev., 1979-80, controller Atlantic City, 1980-82, v.p. fin., 1982-85; v.p., contr. Ramada Inns, Phoenix, 1985-87; sr. v.p., casino ops. Tropicana Hotel & Casino, Atlantic City, 1987-89; exec. v.p./asst., gen. mgr. ops. TropWorld Casino and Entertainment Resort, 1989-92, pres., gen. mgr., 1992—. Mem. AICPA, N.J. Soc. CPAs (chmn. gaming conf. com. 1985-86). Avocation: golf. Office: Argosy Gaming Co. 219 Piasa St. Alton IL 62002-6232

PERRY, JOSEPH N. bishop; b. Chgo., Apr. 18, 1948; Ordained priest Roman Cath. Ch., 1975. Pastor All Sts. Parish, Milw.; episcopal vicar Vicariate VI; consecrated aux. bishop, 1998; aux. bishop Archdiocese of Chgo., 1998—. Office: PO Box 733 South Holland IL 60473-0733

PERRY, KENNETH WILBUR, accounting educator; b. Lawrenceburg, Ky., May 21, 1919; s. Ollie Townsend and Minnie (Monroe) P.; m. Shirley Jane Kimball, Sept. 5, 1942; 1 dau., Constance June (Mrs. Linden Warfel). B.S., Eastern Ky. U., 1942; M.S., Ohio U., 1949; Ph.D., U. Ill., 1953; LL.D., Eastern Ky. U., 1983. C.P.A., Ill. Instr. Berea Coll., 1949-50, U. Ky., summer 1950; teaching asst. U. Ill. at Champaign, 1950-53, asst. prof. accounting, 1953-55, asso. prof., 1955-58, prof., 1958—, Alexander Grant prof., 1975—. Vis. prof. Northeastern U., summer 1966, Parsons Coll., 1966-67, Fla. A. and M. U., fall 1971; Carman G. Blough prof. U. Va., fall 1975; dir. Illini Pub. Co. Author: Accounting: An Introduction, 1971, Passing the C.P.A. Examination, 1964, (with N. Bedford and A. Wyatt) Advanced Accounting, 1960; contbg. author: Complete Guide to a Profitable Accounting Practice, 1965, C.P.A. Review Manual, 1971; Editor: The Ill. C.P.A, 1968-70; contbg. editor: Accountants' Cost Handbook, 1960. Served to maj. AUS, 1942-46; col. Res. ret. Named outstanding alumnus Eastern Ky. U., 1969 Mem. Am. Accounting Assn. (v.p. 1963, Outstanding Educator award 1974), Am. Inst. C.P.A.'s, Am. Statis. Assn., Nat. Assn. Accountants (dir. 1969-71), Ill. Soc. C.P.A.s (chair in accountancy), Beta Alpha Psi, Beta Gamma Sigma (Distinguished scholar 1977-78), Omicron Delta Kappa. Methodist. Home: 2314 Fields South Dr Champaign IL 61822-9302 Office: Commerce W U Ill Champaign IL 61822

PERRY, LEWIS CURTIS, historian, educator; b. Somerville, Mass., Nov. 21, 1938; s. Albert Quillen and Irene (Lewis) P.; m. Ruth Opler, June 5, 1962 (div. 1970); 1 child, Curtis Allen; m. Elisabeth Israels, Nov. 26, 1970; children: Susanna Irene, David Mordecai. A.B., Oberlin Coll., 1960; M.S., Cornell U., Ithaca, N.Y., 1964; Ph.D., Cornell U., 1967. Asst. prof. history SUNY, Buffalo, 1966-72, assoc. prof., 1972-78; prof. Ind. U. Bloomington, 1978-84; Andrew Jackson prof. history Vanderbilt U., 1984-99, dir. Am. Studies, 1992-95; John Francis Bannon prof. history St. Louis U., 1999—. Ampart lectr. U.S. Info. Service, India and Nepal, 1986, France, 1989; vis. prof. U. Leeds, 1988-89; vis. Raoul Wallenberg fellow Rutgers U., 1991-92. Author: Radical Abolitionism, 1973, reissue, 1995, Childhood, Marriage, and Reform, 1980, Intellectual Life in America, 1984, Boats Against the Current, 1993; co-author: Patterns of Anarchy, 1966, Antislavery Reconsidered, 1979; co-editor Moral Problems in American Life, 1998; editor: Jour. Am. History, 1978-84, American Thought and Culture Series, 1985—. Pres. Unitarian-Universalist Ch., Bloomington, Ind., 1983-84; mem. Ralph Waldo Emerson prize com. Phi Beta Kappa, 1997-99, chair, 1999. N.Y. State Regents fellow, 1965-66, Am. Coun. Learned Socs. fellow, 1972-73, Nat. Humanities Inst. fellow, 1975-76, John Simon Guggenheim Found. fellow, 1991, NEH fellow, 1987-88. Mem.: Soc. Historians Early Am. Republic, Am. Hist. Assn., Orgn. Am. Historians (editor 1978—84, exec. bd. 1996—99). Office: St Louis U Dept History 3800 Lindell Blvd Saint Louis MO 63108-3414 E-mail: perryl@slu.edu.

PERRY, MICHAEL CLINTON, physician, medical educator, academic administrator; b. Wyandotte, Mich., Jan. 27, 1945; s. Clarence Clinton and Hilda Grace (Wigginton) P.; m. Nancy Ann Kaluzny, June 22, 1968; children: Rebecca Carolyn, Katherine Grace. BA, Wayne State U., 1966, MD, 1970; MS in Medicine, U. Minn., 1975. Diplomate Am. Bd. Internal Medicine, Am. Bd. Hematology, Am. Bd. Oncology. Intern in internal medicine Mayo Grad. Sch. Medicine, Rochester, Minn., 1970-71, resident, 1971-72, fellow, 1972-75; instr. Mayo Med. Sch., 1974-75; asst. prof. U. Mo., Columbia, 1975-80, assoc. prof., 1980-85, prof., 1985—, chmn. dept. medicine, 1983-91, sr. assoc. dean, 1991-94, Nellie A Smith chair oncology, dir. div. hematology/oncology, 1994—. Prin. investigator Cancer and Leukemia Group B, Nat. Cancer Inst., Chgo., 1982—, exec. com., 1982-84, 1987-90. Author, co-author 30 book chpts.; editor: Toxicity of Chemotherapy, 1984, The Chemotherapy Source Book, 1992, 96, Comprehensive Textbook of Thoracic Oncology, 1996; contbr. articles to profl. jours. Recipient Faculty Alumni award U. Mo., Columbia, 1985, Disting. Alumnus award Wayne State U., 1995, Disting. Oncologist of Yr. award So. Assn. Oncology, 2000. Fellow ACP; mem. Am. Soc. Hematology, Am. Soc. Clin. Oncology, Cen. Soc. Clin. Research, Am. Soc. Internal Medicine (Young Internist of Yr. 1981), Sigma Xi, Alpha Omega Alpha. Home: 1112 Pheasant Run Columbia MO 65201-6254 Office: U Mo-Columbia 516 Ellis Fischel Cancer Ctr 115 Business Loop 70 W Columbia MO 65203-3244 E-mail: perrym@health.missouri.edu.

PERRY, NANCY, foundation administrator; m. Ken Perry; 1 child Brad. BS in Elem. Edn., U. Kans. Kindergarten tchr. Avondale East Elem. Sch.; host local Romper Room TV program; variety/talk show host; pres., CEO United Way of Greater Topeka. Mem. fin. and outreach coms., mem. altar guild Grace Episcopal Cathedral. Mem.: Rotary Club. Office: United Way of Greater Topeka 1315 SW Arrowhead Rd Topeka KS 66604

PERSAUD, TRIVEDI VIDHYA NANDAN, anatomy educator, researcher, consultant; b. Port Mourant, Berbice, Guyana, Feb. 19, 1940; arrived in Canada, 1972; s. Ram Nandan and Deen (Raggy) P.; m. Gisela Gerda Zehden, Jan. 29, 1965; children: Indrani Uta and Sunita Heidi (twins), Rainer Narendra. MD, Rostock U., Germany, 1965, DSc, 1974; PhD in Anatomy, U. West Indies, Kingston, Jamaica, 1970. Intern, Berlin, Germany, 1965-66; govtl. med. officer Guyana, 1966-67; lectr., sr. lectr. anatomy dept. U. West Indies, 1967-72; assoc. prof. anatomy dept. U. Man., Winnipeg, 1972-75, prof., 1975—, prof. ob-gyn., reproductive scis., 1979-99, prof. emeritus, 1999—, prof. pediatrics and child health, 1989—, prof., chmn./head dept. human anatomy & cell sci., 1977-93, dir. Teratology Rsch. Lab., 1972-97. Cons. in teratology, Children's Centre, Winnipeg, 1973—; mem. sci. staff Health Scis. Centre, Winnipeg, 1973—. Author, editor 22 med. textbooks, including: Early History of Human Anatomy: From Antiquity to the Beginning of the Modern Era, 1984, (with others) Basic Concepts in Teratology, 1985, Environmental Causes of Human Birth Defects, 1991, History of Human Anatomy: The Post-Vesalian Era, 1997, (with K.L. Moore) The Developing Human, 6th edit., 1998, Before We Are Born, 5th edit., 1998; contbr. numerous chpts. to books, over 200 articles to profl. jours. Recipient Carveth Jr. Scientist award Can. Assn. Pathologists, 1974, Albert Einstein Centennial medal German Acad. Scis., 1975, Dr. & Mrs. H.H. Saunderson award U. Manitoba, 1985, 12th Raymond Truex Disting. Lectureship award Hahnemann U., 1990. Fellow Royal Coll. Pathologists of London; mem. Can. Assn. Anatomists (pres. 1981-83, J.C.B. Grant award 1991), Am. Assn. Anatomists, Teratology Soc., European Teratology Soc. Office: U Man Dept Anatomy & Cell Sci 730 William Ave Winnipeg MB Canada R3E OW3 E-mail: persaud@ms.umanitoba.ca.

PERSHING, ROBERT GEORGE, telecommunications company executive; b. Battle Creek, Mich., Aug. 10, 1941; s. James Arthur and Beulah Francis P.; m. Diana Kay Prill, Sept. 16, 1961 (div. Jan. 1989); children: Carolyn, Robert; m. Charlene Jean Reed Wallis, Mar. 18, 1989 (div. Dec. 1995). BSEE, Tri-State Coll., 1961. Comm. engr. Am. Elec. Power, Ind., N.Y. and Ohio, 1961-69; design supr. Wescom, Inc., Ill., 1969-74; dir. engring. Tellabs, Inc., Lisle, 1974-78; pres., CEO Teltrend, Inc., St. Charles, 1979-89, chmn. bd., 1979-88; CEO DKP Prodns., Inc., 1986-89; exec. cons. Teltrend, 1979-93; asst. treas. Magnekopy, inc., Villa Park. Bd. dirs. TI Investors, Inc.; advisor entrepreneurial studies U. Ill.; engring. cons. Recipient Chgo. Area Small Bus. award, 1986., INC 500 awards, 1987, 88. Mem. IEEE. Office: 1519 Kirkwood Dr Geneva IL 60134-1659

PERSICO, VINCENT ANTHONY, state legislator; b. Oak Pk., Ill., Dec. 9, 1948; s. Vincent Michael and Lavergne (Gehrke) P.; (div.); 1 child, Derek. BA, U. Ill., 1971; MA, No. Ill. U., 1986. Tchr.; mem. Ill. Ho. of Reps. from 39th dist., 1991—. Mem. Edn. Appropriations, Elem. and Secondary Edn., Energy & Environ., Transp. & Motor Vehicles Coms. Ill. Ho. of Reps., vice spokesman Edn. Fin. Com. Trustee Milton Twp., Ill., 1988-91. Mem. Ill. Edn. Assn. Republican. Home: 711 Revere Rd Glen Ellyn IL 60137-5515 Office: Ill Ho of Reps State Capitol Springfield IL 62706-0001

PERSSON, ERLAND KARL, electrical engineer; b. Soderala, Sweden, Oct. 9, 1923; came to U.S., 1949, naturalized, 1953; m. Elaine Darm; children: Ann Monn, Eric. BSEE, U. Minn., 1955. Registered profl. engr., Minn. Prin. engr. Gen. Mills, Mpls., 1956-61; v.p. engring. Electro-Craft Corp., Hopkins, Minn., 1961-72; v.p. R & D, 1972-83; sr. v.p., chief tech. officer, 1983-86; pres. Erland Persson Co., Mpls., 1987—. Contbr. articles to profl. jours., chpts. to books. Patentee in field. Mem. mech. engring. adv. com. U. Minn.; bd. dirs. Minn. High Tech. Coun., 1984-86, mem., 1987. Fellow IEEE (life, mem. subcom. electric machines com., indsl. drives com.), Audio Engring Soc. (founder Midwest chpt. 1974); mem. Eta Kappa Nu. E-mail: persso002@tc.umn.edu.

PERSYN, MARY GERALDINE, law librarian, law educator; b. Elizabeth, N.J., Feb. 25, 1945; d. Henry Anthony and Geraldine (Sumption) P. AB, Creighton U., 1967; MLS, U. Oreg., 1969; JD, Notre Dame U., 1982. Bar: Ind. 1982, U.S. Dist. Ct. (no. and so. dists.) Ind. 1982, U.S. Supreme Ct. 1995. Social scis. libr. Miami U., Oxford, Ohio, 1969-78; staff law libr. Notre Dame (Ind.) Law Sch., 1982-84; dir. law libr. Valparaiso (Ind.) U., 1984-87, law libr., assoc. prof. law, 1987—. Editor Journal of Legislation, 1981-82; mng. editor Third World Legal Studies, 1986—. V.p. Ind. Coop. Libr. Svcs. Auth., 1997-98, pres., 1998-99. Mem. ABA, Ind. State Bar Assn., Am. Assn. Law Librs. Ohio Regional Assn. Law Librs. (pres. 1990-91), Ind. State Quilt Guild (pres. 1996-2000). Roman Catholic. Home: 1308 Tuckahoe Park Dr Valparaiso IN 46383-4032 Office: Valparaiso U Law Libr Sch Law Valparaiso IN 46383 E-mail: mary.persyn@valpo.edu.

PERTZ, DOUGLAS A. engineering executive; BS in Mech. Engring., Purdue U., 1975. Various exec. positions Caterpillar, Inc., Hong Kong, Malaysia, Singapore, Onan Corp.; group v.p. Danaher Corp.; pres., CEO Culligan Water Technologies, Inc., 1995-98; pres., COO IMC Global Inc., Northbrook, Ill., 1998-99, pres., CEO, officer, dir., 1999—. Office: IMC Global Inc 2100 Sanders Rd Northbrook IL 60062-6139

PERZ, SALLY, academic administrator, former state legislator; m. Joseph Perz; children: Allison, Julie, Melanie, Andrea, Brian. BA, Siena Heights. Ohio State rep. Dist. 52, 1993; mgmt. cons. Perz, Inc., 1996—; exec. dir. U. Toledo. Active Boy Scouts Am. Recipient Carlson Counyt Mktg. award, 1984-93, Women of Achievement award, 1993. Mem. Toledo Club, Toledo C. of C., Toledo Rotary, Toledo Sisters Cities (exec. bd.). Home: 3245 River Rd Toledo OH 43614-4218 Office: U Toledo 2801 W Bancroft St Toledo OH 43606-3328

PESHKIN, MURRAY, physicist; b. Bklyn., May 17, 1925; s. Jacob and Bella Ruth (Zuckerman) P.; m. Frances Julie Ehrlich, June 12, 1955; children— Michael, Sharon, Joel. B.A., Cornell U., 1947, Ph.D., 1951. Instr., then asst. prof. physics Northwestern U., 1951-59; physicist, then sr. scientist Argonne (Ill.) Nat. Lab., 1959—, assoc. dir. physics div., 1972-83. Fellow Weizmann Inst. Sci., Rehovoth, Israel, 1959-60, 68-69; sr. scientist SciTech Mus., Aurora, Ill., 1991—. Served with AUS, 1944-46. Home: 838 Parkside Ave Elmhurst IL 60126-4813 Office: Argonne Natl Lab Argonne IL 60439 E-mail: peshkin@anl.gov.

PESSIN, JEFFREY E. physiology educator; b. N.Y.C., Jan. 2, 1953; s. Al Pessin; m. Rene Debra Bronner, June 23, 1975; children: Jacob, Lauren, Melanie. BA in Chemistry, MA in Chemistry, CUNY, 1975; PhD in Biochemistry, U. Ill., 1980; postgrad., U. Mass., 1980. Grad. rsch. asst. U. Ill., Urbana, 1975-80; asst. prof. physiology U. Iowa, Iowa City, 1983-88, assoc. prof., 1988-91, prof., 1991—, assoc. dir. Diabetes and Endocrinology Rsch. Ctr., 1991—. Contbr. articles to Molecular and Cellular Biology, Endocrinology. Basil O'Connor rsch. scholar March of Dimes Birth Defects Found., 1987-90; grantee NIH, 1988-93. Mem. AAAS, NIH (mem. metabolism study sect. 1989-93), Am. Chem. Soc., Am. Diabetes Assn. (R & D award 1985-87, rsch. award 1995), Sigma Xi. Home: 924 Duck Creek Dr Iowa City IA 52246-8674 Office: U Iowa Dept Physiology and Biophysics Bowman Sci Bldg 5-530 Iowa City IA 52242

PESTILLO, PETER JOHN, lawyer, automotive executive; b. Bristol, Conn., Mar. 22, 1938; s. Peter and Ruth (Hayes) P.; m. BettyAnn Barraclough, Aug. 29, 1959; children: Kathleen, Karen, Kerry. BSS, Fairfield (Conn.) U., 1960; LLB, Georgetown U., 1963. Bar: D.C. 1964. Mgr. union relations planning Gen. Electric Co., N.Y.C., 1968-74; v.p. employee relations B.F. Goodrich Co., Akron, Ohio, 1974-80; v.p. labor relations Ford Motor Co., Dearborn, Mich., 1980-85, v.p. employee relations, 1985-86, v.p. employee and external affairs, 1986—; chmn., CEO Visteon Corp., Dearborn, Mich. Mem. adv. bd. United Found., Detroit. Mem. Am. Arbitration Assn. (dir.), U.S. C. of C. (labor relation com.), D.C.

Bar, Bus. Roundtable, Labor Policy Assn., Nat. Assn. Mfgs., UBA. Home: 338 Provencal Rd Grosse Pointe Farms MI 48236-2959 Office: Visteon Corp Fairlane Plaza North 290 Town Center Dr Fl 10 Dearborn MI 48126-2739

PETERLE, TONY JOHN, zoologist, educator; b. Cleve., July 7, 1925; s. Anton and Anna (Katic) P.; m. Thelma Josephine Coleman, July 30, 1949; children: Ann Faulkner, Tony Scott. BS, Utah State U., 1949; MS, U. Mich., 1950, PhD (univ. scholar), 1954; Fulbright scholar, U. Aberdeen, Scotland, 1954-55; postgrad., Oak Ridge Inst. Nuclear Studies, 1961. With Niederhauser Lumber Co., 1947—49, Macfarland Tree Svc., 1949—51; rsch. biologist Mich. Dept. Conservation, 1951—54; asst. dir. Rose Lake Expt. Sta., 1955—59; leader Ohio Coop. Wildlife Rsch. Unit U.S. Fish and Wildlife Svc., Dept. Interior, 1959—63; asso. prof., then prof. zoology Ohio State U., Columbus, 1959—89, prof. emeritus, 1989, chmn. faculty population and environmental biology, 1968—69, chmn. dept. zoology, 1969—81, dir. program in environ. biology, 1970—71; liaison officer Internat. Union Game Biologists, 1965—93; chmn. internat. affairs com., mem. com., ecotoxicology co-organizer XIII Internat. Congress Game Biology, 1979—80; proprietor The Iron Works, 1989—. Pvt. cons., 1989—; mem. com. rev. EPA pesticide decision making Nat. Acad. Scis.-NRC; mem. vis. scientists program Am. Inst. Biol. Scis.-ERDA, 1971-77; mem. com. pesticides Nat. Acad. Scis., com. on emerging trends in agr. and effects on fish and wildlife; mem. ecology com. of sci. adv. council EPA, 1979-87; mem. research units coordinating com. Ohio Coop. Wildlife and Fisheries, 1963-89; vis. scientist EPA, Corvallis, 1987. Author: Wildlife Toxicology, 1991; editor: Jour. of Wildlife Mgmt., 1969-70, 84-85, 2020 Vision Meeting the Fish and Wildlife Conservation Challenges of the 21st Century, 1992. Served with AUS, 1943-46. Fellow AAAS, Am. Inst. Biol. Scis., Ohio Acad. Sci.; mem. Wildlife Disease Assn., Wildlife Soc. (regional rep. 1962-67, v.p. 1968, pres. 1972, Leopold award 1990, hon. mem. 1990, Profl. award of merit North Ctrl. sect. 1993), Nat. Audubon Soc. (bd. dirs. 1985-87), Ecol. Soc., INTECOL-NSF panel U.S.-Japan Program, Xi Sigma Pi, Phi Kappa Phi. Home: 4072 Klondike Rd Delaware OH 43015-9513 Office: Ohio State U Dept Zoology 1735 Neil Ave Columbus OH 43210-1220

PETERS, DAVID ALLEN, mechanical engineering educator, consultant; b. East St. Louis, Ill., Jan. 31, 1947; s. Bernell Louis and Marian Louise (Blum) P.; children: Michael H., Laura A., Nathan C. BS in Applied Mechanics, Washington U., St. Louis, 1969, MS in Applied Mechanics, 1970; PhD in Aeros. and Astronautics, Stanford U., 1974. Assoc. engr. McDonnell Astronautics, 1969-70; rsch. scientist Army Aeronautics Lab., 1970-74; asst. prof. Washington U., 1975-77, assoc. prof., 1977-80, prof. mech. engring., 1980-85, chmn. dept., 1982-85; prof. aerospace engring. Ga. Inst Tech., Atlanta, 1985-91; dir. NASA Space Grant Consortium Ga. Inst. Tech., 1989-91; dir. Ctr. for Computational Mechanics Washington U., 1992—, prof. dept. mech. engring., 1991—, chmn. dept. mech. engring., 1997—, McDonnell Douglas prof. engring., 1999. Contbr. 65 articles to profl. jours. Recipient sci. contbn. award NASA, 1975, 76. Fellow AIAA, ASME; mem. Am. Helicopter Soc. (jour. editor 1987-90), Am. Soc. for Engring. Edn., Internat. Assn. for Computational Mechanics (charter), Am. Acad. Mechs., Pi Tau Sigma (gold medal 1978). Baptist. Home: 7629 Balson Ave Saint Louis MO 63130-2150 Office: PO Box 1185 Saint Louis MO 63188-1185

PETERS, DENNIS GAIL, chemist; b. L.A., Apr. 17, 1937; s. Samuel and Phyllis Dorothy (Pope) P. BS cum laude, Calif. Inst. Tech., 1958; PhD, Harvard U., 1962. Mem. faculty Ind. U., 1962—, prof. chemistry, 1974—, Herman T. Briscoe prof., 1975—. Co-author textbooks, contbr. articles profl. jours. Woodrow Wilson fellow, 1958-59; NIH predoctoral fellow, 1959-62; vis. fellow Japan Soc. for Promotion Sci., 1980; recipient Ulysses G. Weatherly award disting. teaching Ind. U., 1969, Disting. Teaching award Coll. Arts and Scis. Grad. Alumni Assn. Ind. U., 1984, Nat. Catalyst award for Disting. Teaching Chem. Mfrs. Assn., 1988, Henry B. Linford award The Electrochem. Soc., 2002; grantee NSF. Fellow Ind. Acad. Sci., Am. Inst. Chemists; mem. ACS (grantee, Div. of Analytical Chemistry award for excellence in teaching 1990, James Flack Norris award 2001). Home: 1401 S Nancy St Bloomington IN 47401-6051 Office: Dept Chemistry Ind U Bloomington IN 47405 Business E-Mail: peters@indiana.edu.

PETERS, GARY CHARLES, state legislator, lawyer, educator; b. Pontiac, Mich., Dec. 1, 1958; s. Herbert Garrett and Madeleine (Vignier) P.; m. Colleen Ochoa; children: Gary Jr., Madeleine, Alana. BA, Alma Coll., 1980; MBA, U. Detroit, 1984; JD, Wayne State U., 1989. Bar: Mich. 1990. Fin. cons., resident mgr., asst. v.p. Merrill Lynch, Pierce, Fenner & Smith, Inc., Rochester, Mich., 1980-89; br. mgr., v.p. Paine Webber, Inc., 1989—; mem. Mich. Snenate from dist. 14, Lansing, 1994—. Securities arbitrator, mediator Nat. Assn. Securities Dealers, N.Y. Stock Exchange, Am. Arbitration Assn., 1990—; adj. prof. Oakland U., Rochester, 1991-93, instr. Wayne State U., 1992-94; vice chair Mich. Senate Dem. Whip fin. com.; mem. edn. com., judiciary com., families, mental health and human svcs. com., econ. devel. & econ. trade com., law revision com. Mich. Sentencing Commn. Councilman City of Rochester Hills, 1992-94, mem. zoning bd. appeals and Paint Creek Trailways Commn., 1992-94; officer-at-large Mich. Dem. Party, 1996. Officer USNR, 1993—. Mem. Mich. State Bar Assn., Sierra Club, Phi Beta Kappa. Avocations: hiking, motorcycling, world travel, soaring, scuba diving. Home: 2645 Bloomfield Xing Bloomfield Hills MI 48304-1710 Office: PaineWebber Inc PO Box 80730 Rochester MI 48308-0730

PETERS, GORDON BENES, retired musician; b. Oak Park, Ill., Jan. 4, 1931; s. Arthur George and Julia Anne (Benes) P.; children: Rénee Kemper, Erica Kemper. Student, Northwestern U., 1949-50; Mus.B., Eastman Sch. Music, 1956, Mus.M., 1962. Percussionist Rochester (N.Y.) Philharmonic Orch., 1955-59; prin. percussionist Grant Park Symphony Orch., Chgo., 1955-58; mem. faculty Rochester Bd. Edn., 1956-57, Geneseo State Tchrs. Coll., 1957-58; acting prin. percussionist Rochester Philharm., N.Y., 1958-59; prin. percussionist and asst. prin. timpanist Chgo. Symphony Orch., 1959—2001; condr., adminstr. Civic Orch. Chgo., 1966-87; condr. Elmhurst Symphony Orch., 1968-73; ret., 2001. Instr. percussion instruments Northwestern U., 1963-68, lectr., 1991; guest conductor Bangor (Maine) Symphony, 1993. Author, pub. The Drummer: Man, 1975; arranger-pub. Marimba Ensemble arrangements; composer-pub.: Swords of Moda-Ling; editor: percussion column Instrumentalist mag, 1963-69; contbr. articles to profl. jours. Bd. dirs. Pierre Monteux Sch., Hancock, Maine, 1965-95. With U.S. Mil. Acad. Band, 1950-53. Recipient Pierre Monteux disciple award conducting, 1962, Prin. Timpani chair named GBP, Chgo. Youth Symphony Orch., 2000. Mem. Percussive Arts Soc. (pres. 1962-66), Am. Symphony Orch. League, Condrs. Guild (treas., exec. com. 1979-82, 86-90). Home (Winter): 824 Hinman Ave Apt 2N Evanston IL 60202-5906 Home (Summer): PO Box 403 Hancock ME 04640-0515

PETERS, HENRY AUGUSTUS, neuropsychiatrist; b. Oconomowoc, Wis., Dec. 21, 1920; s. Henry Augustus and Emma N. P.; m. Jean McWilliams, 1950; children— Henry, Kurt, Eric, Mark. BA, MD, U. Wis. Prof. dept. neurology and rehab. medicine U. Wis. Med. Sch., Madison, emeritus prof., 1996—. Mem. med. adv. bd. Muscular Dystrophy Assn. Served to lt. M.C. U.S. Navy. Fellow A.C.P.; mem. Wis. Med. Assn., Am. Acad. Neurology, Am. Psychiatric Assn. Club: Rotary. Office: 600 Highland Ave Madison WI 53792-0001

PETERS, HOWARD NEVIN, foreign language educator; b. Hazleton, Pa., June 29, 1938; s. Howard Eugene and Verna P.; m. Judith Anne Griessel, Aug. 24, 1963; children: Elisabeth Anne, Nevin Edward. BA, Gettysburg Coll., 1960; PhD, U. Colo., 1965. Asst. prof. fgn. langs. Valparaiso (Ind.) U., 1965-69, assoc. prof., 1969-75, dir. grad. divsn., 1967-70, acting dean Coll. Arts and Scis., 1970-71, assoc. dean Coll. Arts and Scis., 1971-74, dean Coll. Arts and Scis., 1974-81, prof. fgn. langs., 1975—, prof. fgn. langs. and lits., chair dept. fgn. langs. and lits., 1994—95, prof. emeritus fgn. langs. and lits., 1995—. Author (poetry) Espejo De Son, 1997. NDEA fellow, 1960-63 Mem. Midwest MLA, Phi Beta Kappa, Sigma Delta Pi, Phi Sigma Iota. Lutheran. Home: 860 N Cr 500 E Valparaiso IN 46383 Office: Meier Hall Rm 113 Valparaiso U Valparaiso IN 46383 E-mail: hpeters@exodus.valpo.edu.

PETERS, LEON, JR. electrical engineering educator, research administrator; b. Columbus, Ohio, May 28, 1923; s. Leon P. and Ethel (Howland) Pierce; m. Mabel Marie Johnson, June 6, 1953; children: Amy T. Peters Thomas, Melinda A. Peters Todaro, Maria C. Cohee, Patricia D., Lee A., Roberta J. Peters Cameruca, Karen E. Peters Ellingson. B.S.E.E., Ohio State U., 1950, M.S., 1954, Ph.D., 1959. Asst. prof. elec. engring. Ohio State U., Columbus, 1959-63, assoc. prof., 1963-67, prof., 1967-93, prof. emeritus, 1993—, assoc. dept. chmn. for rsch., 1990-92, dir. electro sci. lab., 1983-94. Contbr. articles to profl. jours. Served to 2d lt. U.S. Army, 1942-46, ETO. Fellow IEEE Home: 2087 Ellington Rd Columbus OH 43221-4138 Office: Ohio State U Electrosci Lab 1320 Kinnear Rd Columbus OH 43212-1156

PETERS, WILLIAM P. oncologist, science administrator, educator; b. Buffalo, Aug. 26, 1950; m. Elizabeth Zentai; children: Emily, Abigail, James. BS, BS, BA, Pa. State U., 1972; MPhil, PhD, Columbia U., 1976, MD, 1978; postgrad., Harvard U., 1984; MBA, Duke U., 1990. Diplomate Am. Bd. Internal Medicine, Am. Bd. Med. Oncology. Prof. medicine Duke U. Med. Ctr., Durham, N.C., 1993-95, assoc. dir. for clin. ops. Duke Comprehensive Cancer Ctr., 1994-95, dir. bone marrow transplant program, 1984-95; pres., CEO, Mich. Cancer Found., Detroit, 1995—; pres., dir., CEO Karmanos Cancer Inst., 1995—; prof. oncology, medicine, surgery and radiation oncology Wayne State U., 1995—, assoc. dean for cancer programs, 1995—. Sr. v.p. for cancer svcs. Detroit Med. Ctr.,, 1995—. Office: Karmanos Cancer Inst President's Office 110 E Warren Ave Detroit MI 48201-1312

PETERSEN, ANNE C.(CHERYL), foundation administrator, educator; b. Little Falls, Minn., Sept. 11, 1944; d. Franklin Hanks and Rhoda Pauline (Sandwick) Studley; m. Douglas Lee Petersen, Dec. 27, 1967; children: Christine Anne, Benjamin Bradfield. BA, U. Chgo., 1966, MS, 1972, PhD, 1973. Asst. prof., rsch. assoc. Dept. Psychiatry U. Chgo., 1972-80, assoc. prof., rsch. assoc., 1980-82; prof. human devel., head Dept. Individual and Family Studies Pa. State U., University Park, 1982-87, dean Coll. Health and Human Devel., 1987-92, prof. health and human devel., 1987-92; dean grad. sch., v.p. for rsch. throughout state U. Minn., Mpls., 1992-94, prof. adolescent devel. and pediatrics, 1992-96; dep. dir., COO NSF, Arlington, Va., 1994-96; sr. v.p. programs W.K. Kellogg Found., 1996—. Vis. prof., fellow Coll. Edn., R&D Psychology, Roosevelt U., Chgo., 1973-74; cons. Ctr. for Health Adminstrn. Studies U. Chgo., 1976-78, Ctr. for New Schs., Chgo., 1974-78, Robert Wood Johnson Found. Mathtech, Inc., 1987-89; coord. clin. rsch. tng. program Michael Reese Hosp. and Med. Ctr., Chgo., 1976-80, dir. Lab. for Study of Adolescence, 1975-82; mem. faculty Ill. Sch. for Profl. Psychology, 1978-79; statis. cons. Coll. Nursing U. Ill. Med. Ctr., 1975-83; assoc. dir. health program MacArthur Found., 1980-82, also cons. health program, 1982-88; chair sr. adv. bd. NIMH, 1987-88; mem. nat. adv. mental health coun. NIH, 1997—; trustee Nat. Inst. Statis. Scis., 1998—. Author: (books) Sex Related Differences in Cognition Functioning: Developmental Issues, 1979, Promoting Adolescent Health: A Diolog on Research and Practice, 1982, Firls at Puberty: Biological and psychosocial Perspectives, 1983, Brain Maturation and Cognitive Development: Comparative and Cross Cultural Perspectives, 1991, Narrowing the Margins: Adolescent Unemployment and the lack of a social role, 1991, Grofit: A Fortran Program for the Estimation of Parameters of a Human Growth Curve, 1972, Girls at Puberty: Biological and Psychosocial Perspectives, 1983, Adolescence and Youth: Psychological Development in a Changing World, 1984, Youth Unemployment and Society, 1994, Transitions Through Adolescence: Interpersonal Domains and Context, 1996; reviewer Jour. of Youth and Adolescence, 1975-80, Devel. Psychology, 1979—, Sci., 1979—, Jour. of Edn. Psychology, 1979—, Child Devel., 1980—, Jour. Edn. Measurement, 1980, Ednl. Researcher, 1980, Am. Ednl. Rsch. Jour., 1981—, Jour. of Mental Imagery, 1982-92, Sex Roles, 1984—; cons. editor Psychology of Women Quar., 1978-82, assoc. editor, 1983-86; adv. editor Contemporary Psychology, 1985-86; editorial bd. various profl. jours.; contbr. chpts. to books and articles to profl. jours. Bd. overseers Lewis Coll., Ill. Inst. Tech., 1980-82; mem. adv. bd. longitudinal data archive project Murray Ctr., Radcliffe Coll., 1985-91, mem. sci. adv. bd., 1983-91 Fellow: APA (chmn. task force on reproductive freedom 1979—81, program chmn. 1981—82, chmn. task force on long range planning 1986—89, pres. divsn. 7 1992—93), AAAS; mem.: NAS (nat. forum on future children and their families 1987—91, chmn. panel on child abuse and neglect 1991—93, mem. forum on adolescence Inst of Medicine 1997—2000, chair bd. on behavioral, cognitive and sensory scis. 1997—), Soc. for Rsch. on Adolescence (pres. 1990—92, past pres. 1992—94, chmn. nominations com. 1992—94), Acad. Europaea, Psychometric Soc., Behavior Genetics Assn., Assn. Women in Sci. (bd. dirs. 1996—2000), Am. Ednl. Rsch. Assn. (various offices), Internat. Soc. for the Study of Behavioral Devel. (coun. mem. 1995—2001, pres. elect 2002—04), Inst. for Medicine. Home: 3715 Blackberry Ln Kalamazoo MI 49008-3333

PETERSEN, DONALD SONDERGAARD, lawyer; b. Pontiac, Ill., May 14, 1929; s. Clarence Marius and Esther (Sondergaard) P.; m. Alice Thorup, June 5, 1954; children: Stephen, Susan Petersen Schuh, Sally Petersen Riordan. Student, Grand View Coll., 1946-48; B.A., Augustana Coll., Rock Island, Ill., 1951; J.D., Northwestern U., 1956. Bar: Ill. 1957. Assoc. Norman & Billick and predecessors, Chgo., 1956-64, ptnr., 1965-78; counsel Sidley & Austin, 1978-80, ptnr., 1980-93, ret., 1993. Pres. Chgo. Exhibitors Corp., Chgo., 1972-85. Bd. dirs. Mount Olive Cemetery Co. Inc., Chgo., 1972-90; bd. dirs. Augustana Hosp., 1983-87, Danish Old People's Home, 1976—; bd. dirs. Luth. Gen. Hosp., Park Ridge, Ill., 1968—, chmn., 1979-81, 89-91; bd. dirs. Luth. Gen. Health System and predecessors, Park Ridge, 1980-95, chmn., 1980-81, 83-85; bd. dirs., chmn. Parkside Health Mgmt. Corp., Parkside Home Health Svcs., 1985-88. With U.S. Army, 1951-53. Mem. Chgo. Bar Assn., Ill. State Bar Assn. Club: Union League (Chgo.). Home: 241 N Aldine Ave Park Ridge IL 60068-3009 Office: 55 W Monroe St Ste 2000 Chicago IL 60603-5008

PETERSEN, DOUGLAS ARNDT, financial development consultant; b. Albert Lea, Minn., Sept. 18, 1944; s. Arndt H. and Helen L. (Slater) P.; m. Winnifred K. Taylor, Aug. 14, 1964 (div. July 1970); children: Scott, Jennifer; m. Cynthia L. Schnabel, June 14, 1975; 1 child, Christopher. BS in Edn., Mankato State U., 1966, postgrad., 1966-68. Youth dir. Mankato (Minn.) YMCA, 1965-68; tchr. Mankato State U., 1965-68; exec. dir. YMCA Camp Christmas Tree, Mound, Minn., 1968-72; asst. exec. dir. West Suburban YMCA, Minnetonka, 1968-72; exec. dir. Eastside YMCA, Mpls., 1972-75; program/fin. devel. dir. Eastside Neighborhood Svc., 1975-79; asst. exec. dir. Mpls. Red Cross, 1979-89; dir. major/planned gifts ARC Nat. Staff, Mpls., 1989-91; pres./chief exec. officer/cons. D.A. Petersen Assocs., 1992—. Mem. St. Anthony/New Brighton Found. (chair 1988-92), YMCA Am. (pres. APD 1974), ARC (pres. MFDDC 1988-89). Lutheran. Avocations: travel, community service, scuba, canoeing, backpacking. Home: 3216 Skycroft Dr Minneapolis MN 55418-2552 Office: PO Box 18411 Minneapolis MN 55418-0411 E-mail: dapa@mindspring.com.

PETERSEN, JAMES L. lawyer; b. Bloomington, Ill., Feb. 3, 1947; s. Eugene and Cathryn Theresa (Hemmele) P.; m. Helen Louise Moser, Nov. 20, 1971; children: Christine Louise, Margaret Theresa. BA, Ill. State U., 1970; MA, U. Ill., Springfield, 1973; JD magna cum laude, Ind. U., 1976. Bar; Ind. 1976, Fla. 1980, U.S. Dist. Cts. (no. and so. Ind.), U.S. Ct. Appeals (7th cir.), U.S. Supreme Ct. Admissions officer U. Ill., Springfield, 1970-71, asst. to v.p., 1971-72, registrar, 1972-73; assoc. Ice Miller , Indpls., 1976-83, ptnr., 1983—. Pres. United Cerebral Palsy of Ctrl. Ind., 1981-83, pres. Found., 1988-90. Mem. ABA, Fla. Bar Assn., Ind. Bar Assn., Internat. Assn. Def. Counsel, Ill. State U. Alumni Assn. (pres. 1990-92), Ind. U. Law Alumni Assn. (bd. dirs. 1992—, pres. 1998-99), Order of Coif. Home: 11827 Sea Star Dr Indianapolis IN 46256-9400 Office: Ice Miller PO Box 82001 One American Sq Indianapolis IN 46282

PETERSEN, MAUREEN JEANETTE MILLER, management information consultant, former nurse; b. Evanston, Ill., Sept. 4, 1956; d. Maurice James and M. Joyce (Mielke) Miller; m. Gregory Eugene Petersen, July 7, 1984; children: Trevor James, Tatyana Brianne. BS in Nursing cum laude, Vanderbilt U., 1978; MS in Biometry and Health Info. Systems, U. Minn., 1984. Nurse U. Iowa Hosps. and Clinics, Iowa City, 1978-82; research asst. Sch. Nursing, U. Minn., Mpls., 1982-83; mgr. Accenture, 1984—. Mem. Mensa. Methodist. Avocation: travel. Home: 1050 County Rd C2 W Roseville MN 55113-1945 Office: Accenture 333 S 7th St Minneapolis MN 55402-2414 E-mail: peters10500@aol.com., maureen.j.m.petersen@accenture.com.

PETERSON, ANN SULLIVAN, physician, health care consultant; b. Rhinebeck, N.Y., Oct. 11, 1928; A.B., Cornell U., 1950, M.D., 1954; M.S. (Alfred P. Sloan fellow 1979-80), M.I.T., 1980. Diplomate Am. Bd. Internal Medicine. Intern, Cornell Med. Div.-Bellevue Hosp., N.Y.C., 1954-55, resident, 1955-57; fellow in medicine and physiology Meml.-Sloan Kettering Cancer Ctr., Cornell Med. Coll., N.Y.C., 1957-60; instr. medicine Georgetown U. Sch. Medicine, Washington, 1962-65, asst. prof., 1965-69, asst. dir. clin. research unit, 1962-69; assoc. prof. medicine U. Ill., Chgo., 1969-72, asst. dean, 1969-71, assoc. dean, 1971-72; assoc. prof. medicine, assoc. dean Coll. Physicians and Surgeons, Columbia U., N.Y.C., 1972-80; assoc. prof. medicine, assoc. dean Cornell U. Med. Coll., N.Y.C., 1980-83; assoc. dir. div. med. edn. AMA, Chgo., 1983-86, dir. div. grad. med. edn., 1986-89; v.p. Mgmt. Cons. Corp., 1989-93; ind. cons., Chgo., 1993—; mem. bd. regents Uniformed Svcs. U. of Health Scis., 1984-90. John and Mary R. Markle scholar, 1965-70. Fellow ACP; mem. Mortar Board, Alpha Omega Alpha, Alpha Epsilon Delta. Contbr. articles to med. jours.

PETERSON, BART, mayor; m. Amy Minick; 1 child, Meg. Grad., Purdue U., 1980; JD, U. Mich., 1983. Atty. Ice Miller Donadio & Ryan, Indpls.; from exec. asst. for environ. affairs to chief of staff Ind. Gov. Evan Bayh, 1989-95; pres. Precedent Cos., 1995; mayor City Indpsl., 2000—. Bd. mem. Ind. Nature Conservancy, Regenstrief Found. Office: 2501 City-County Bldg 200 E Washington St Indianapolis IN 46204-3307 E-mail: mayor@indygov.org.*

PETERSON, CARL V. professional football team executive; b. Mpls. 1 child, Dawn. BS in Kinesiology, UCLA, 1966, MS in Kinesiology, 1967, EdD in Adminstrn. in Higher Edn., 1970. Asst. coach Wilson High Sch., Calif., 1966, Loyola High Sch., 1967-68, Calif. State U., Somona, 1969-70, head coach, 1970-72; receivers coach UCLA, 1972-74, receivers coach, adminstrv. asst., 1974-76; coach recievers and tight ends Phila. Eagles, 1976, dir. player personnel, 1977-82; pres., gen. mgr. Phila. Stars, 1982-86; pres., gen. mgr., CEO, Kansas City Chiefs, Mo., 1988—. Pres., CEO, PhillySport Mag., Phila., 1987; mem. nat. bd. Maxwell Football Club and Pop Warner Little Scholar Orgn. Recipient USFL Exec. of Yr. award Sporting News, 1983, 84. Mem. Young Pres. Orgn. (Kansas City chpt.), World Press Orgn. Office: Kansas City Chiefs 1 Arrowhead Dr Kansas City MO 64129-1651

PETERSON, CLARK C. announcer, writer, poet, speaker; b. Pine City, Minn., Dec. 27, 1947; s. Carl A. and Bernice C. Peterson. AA, U. Minn., 1967, B Econs., 1969; A in Bible, Grace Bible Coll., 1993. Announcer Sta. KOLM/KWWK Radio, Rochester, Minn., 1974-84; pub. affairs specialist U.S. Army, Oklahoma City, 1985-97; announcer, writer Power Zone Wrestling Fedn., 1992-97; corr. Pro Wrestling Illustrated Mag., 1992-97; announcer, writer Mid-South Wrestling Fedn., Oklahoma City, 1998—; corr. The Wrestling Tribune, 1993—; host weekly pro wrestling radio talk show "The Three Count" aired throughout one-half of continental U.S., 2001—. Parade announcer Mora's (Minn.) Centennial, 1983; announcer Richards-Gebaur AFB Open House, Kansas City, Mo., 1973, Nat. Drum and Bugle Corps Contest, Stillwater, Minn., early 1980's; announcer, entertainment Rochester's (Minn.) 125th Anniversary, 1983; announcer, writer, entertainment Korn & Klover Karnival, Hinckley, Minn., 1973-87, 90-91; judge Miss Teen Minn. Pageant, St. Paul, 1984. Author: The Great Hinckley Fire, 1978, Blasted Unto a Pile of Rubble, 1995; co-author: In Their Name, 1995, We Will Never Forget, 1996, Forever Changed, 1998; contbg. author: Wrestling Title Histories, 2000. Mem., survivor Apr. 19, 1995 Oklahoma City Bombing, Family and Survivors United, 1995—; pub. rels. and advt. advisor Rep. campaign for Minn. Senate, 2000; bd. dirs. Grace Bible Coll., Morrisville, NC, 2002-. Served with USAF, 1970-74. Recipient Best Coverage of a Local Story in the U.S., AP, 1978, scholarship Fairfax U., 1988, Civil Svc. Achievement medal U.S. Army, 1997, 14 New Idea/Suggestion awards, One of the highest numbers in U.S. Civil Svc., 1997, 5th prize World-Wide Christmas Outdoor Lighting Display Contest, 1997; named among 25 winners Turner Broadcasting Wrestling Announcing Contest, 1992; inducted Profl. Wrestling's Wall of Fame, 1998. Avocations: outdoor Christmas lighting display, state and city flag collections, coin collecting.

PETERSON, COLLIN C. congressman; b. Fargo, N.D., June 29, 1944; children: Sean, Jason, Elliott. BA in Bus. Adminstrn. and Acctg., Moorhead State U., 1966. CPA, Minn. Senator State of Minn., 1976-86; mem. U.S. Congress from 7th Minn. dist., 1991—; mem. agrl. com., subcoms. gen. farm commodities, specialty crops and natural resources, livestock, environ. credit and rural devel.; mem. govt. ops. com., chmn. subcom. employment housing and aviation; mem. resource conservation com., rsch. and forestry subcom., livestock, dairy and poultry subcom., govt. reform and oversight com.; nat. econ. growth com., nat. resources and regulatory affairs com.-ranking minority mem., vet. affairs com. With U.S. Army N.G., 1963-69. Mem. Am. Legion, Ducks Unltd., Elks, Sportsmen's Club, Rural Caucus, Mainstream Forum, Cormorant Lakes Sportsmen Club, Congl. Sportsmen's Caucus, Mainstream Forum, Congl. Rural Caucus. Democrat. Office: US Ho of Reps 2159 Rayburn Hob Washington DC 20515-0001*

PETERSON, DAVID CHARLES, photojournalist; b. Kansas City, Mo., Oct. 22, 1949; s. John Edward and Florence Athene (Hobbs) P.; m. Adele Mae Johnson, Dec. 31, 1952; children: Brian David, Scott Ryun, Anna Victoria. BS in Edn., Kansas State U., 1971; BS in Journalism, U. Kans., 1973, BS in Journalism, 1974. Staff photographer Topeka Capital-Jour., 1975-77, Des Moines Register, 1977—. Photographer (photo essay) Shattered Dreams-Iowa's Rural Crisis, 1986 (Pulitzer prize 1987); exhibited at Creative Ctr. Photography, Tucson, 1989. Mem. Nat. Press Photographers Assn. (Nikon sabbatical 1986). Democrat. Home: 2024 35th St Des Moines IA 50310-4438 Office: Des Moines Register News Dept 715 Locust St Des Moines IA 50309-3767

PETERSON, DAVID MAURICE, plant physiologist, research leader; b. Woodward, Okla., July 3, 1940; s. Maurice Llewellyn and Katharine Anne (Jones) P.; m. Margaret Ingegerd Sundberg, June 18, 1965; children: Mark David, Elise Marie. BS, U. Calif., Davis, 1962; MS, U. Ill., 1964; PhD, Harvard U., 1968. Rsch. biologist Allied Chem. Corp., Morristown, N.J., 1970-71; plant physiologist U.S. Dept. Agr.-Agrl. Rsch. Svc., Madison, Wis., 1971—; from asst. to full prof. U. Wis., 1971—. Capt. U.S. Army, 1968-70. Fellow AAAS; mem. Am. Soc. Plant Biologists (editorial bd. 1984-86), Am. Assn. Cereal Chemists (assoc. editor 1988-91), Crop Sci. Soc. Am. (assoc. editor 1975-78). Office: USDA Cereal Crops Rsch Unit 501 Walnut St Madison WI 53726 E-mail: dmpeter4@wisc.edu.

PETERSON, DONALD MATTHEW, insurance company executive; b. Mt. Vernon, N.Y., Dec. 22, 1936; s. Cornelius J. and Catherine M. (Carney) P.; m. Patricia A. Frusciante, Sept. 10, 1960; children: Daniel, Linda, David, Debra, James. BA in Econs., LaSalle U., 1958. CLU; ChFC; FSA, MAAA, EA, RHU. Actuarial analyst Met. Life, N.Y.C., 1958-63; actuarial assoc. N.Am. Co. for Life and Health, Chgo., 1963-66; chmn. bd. dirs. Trustmark Ins. Co., Lake Forest, Ill., 1966—. Bd. dirs. Trustmark Ins. Co., Trustmark Life Ins. Co., Star Mktg. and Adminstrs., InfoTrust Coresource. Bd. dirs. Glenview (Ill.) Pub. Schs., 1973-76, Lake County (Ill.) United Way, 1989-96, Glenview Dist. 34 Found., 1990-93, Lake Forest Hosp., 1992-2001, Ill. Life Ins. Coun., 1990-94, Barat Coll., 1994-2001, Lake Forest Grad. Sch. Mgmt., 1995-2001. Mem. NALU, Nat. Assn. Health Underwriters, Am. Acad. Actuaries, Health Ins. Assn. Am. (bd. dirs. 1992-99), Am. Coun. Life Ins. (bd. dirs. 1995-98), Econ. Club Chgo., North Shore Country Club, Conway Farms Golf Club, Pelican Nest Golf Club, Exec. Club. Republican. Roman Catholic. Avocations: golf, curling, swimming, running. Office: Trustmark Ins Co 400 N Field Dr Lake Forest IL 60045-4809

PETERSON, DOUG, state legislator; b. 1948; m. Elly Peterson; 2 children. BS, Augustana Coll., Sioux Falls, S.D. Mem. Minn. Ho. of Reps., St Paul, 1990—. Mem. agrl. com., environ. and natural resources com., met. affairs com., others; tchr., farmer. Democrat. Home: RR 3 Box 90 Madison MN 56256-9452

PETERSON, FRANCIS, physicist, educator; Prof. physics dept. Iowa State U., Ames. Recipient Disting. Svc. Citation award, 1993. Mem. Am. Assn. of Physics Tchrs. Office: Iowa State U A 325 Physics Dept Ames IA 50011-0001

PETERSON, GALE EUGENE, historian; b. Sioux Rapids, Iowa, May 23, 1944; s. George Edmund and Vergene Elizabeth (Wilson) P. BS, Iowa State U., 1965; MA, U. Md., 1968, PhD, 1973. Instr. dept. history U. Md., College Park, 1971-72, Cath. U. Am., Washington, 1972-73; prin. investigator Gregory Directory project Orgn. Am. Historians, Bloomington, Ind., 1973-75; instr. dept. history Purdue U., West Lafayette, 1975-76; dir. U.S. Newspaper Project, Orgn. Am. Historians, Bloomington, 1976-78; exec. dir. Cin. Hist. Soc., 1978-96, exec. dir. emeritus, 1996—; exec. dir. Ohio Humanities Coun., 1998—. Author: (with John T. Schlebecker) Living Historical Farms Handbook, 1970, Harry S Truman and the Independent Regulatory Commissions 1945-52, 1985. Mem. Cin. Bicentennial Commn., 1983-88. Mem. Orgn. Am. Historians (treas. 1993—), Am. Assn. State and Local History, Am. Hist. Assn., Am. Assn. Mus., Assn. Midwest Museums (v.p.-at-large 1993-95, exec. v.p. 1995-96, pres. 1996-98), Nat. Coun. on Pub. History (bd. dirs. 1992-95). Office: Ohio Humanities Coun Ste 1620 471 E Broad St Columbus OH 43215-3857 E-mail: galep@one.net.

PETERSON, GARY, retail executive; With Wal-Mart Stores, 1984-88; sr. v.p. Carter Hawley Hale, L.A., 1988-91, Thrifty Drug Store, L.A., 1991-93; COO S.E. Frozen Foods LP, Miami, Fla., 1993-96, Blockbuster Video, 1996-2000; pres., COO OfficeMax, Inc., Shaker Heights, Ohio, 2000—. Office: Office Max Inc 3605 Warrensville Center Rd Shaker Heights OH 44122

PETERSON, JAMES LINCOLN, museum executive; b. Kewanee, Ill., Nov. 12, 1942; s. Reinold Gustav and Florence Josephine (Kjellgren) P.; m. M. Susan Pepin, Aug. 15, 1964; children: Hans C., Erika C. BA, Gustavus Adolphus Coll., 1964; PhD, U. Nebr., 1972. Sci. tchr. pub. schs., Ill. and Minn., 1964-68; research asst. U. Nebr., Lincoln, 1968-72; research assoc. U. Wis., Madison, 1972-74; staff ecologist Nat. Commn. Water Quality, Washington, 1974-75; v.p. research Acad. Nat. Scis., Phila., 1976-84, v.p. devel., 1982-84; pres. Sci. Mus. Minn., St. Paul, 1984—. Bd. dirs. Ea. Pa. chpt. Nature Conservancy, Phila., 1982-84, Downtown Coun., St. Paul, 1986-93, Keystone (Colo.) Ctr., 1989-93; mem. St. Paul Riverfront Commn., 1987-91; mem. adv. com. U. Minn. Coll. Biol. Scis., 1989-95. Mem. Assn. Sci. Mus. Dirs., Assn. Sci. and Tech. Ctrs. (pres. 1993-95), Sci. Mus. Exhibit Collaborative (pres. 1986-89), St. Paul C. of C. (bd. dirs. 1985-89), Informal Club. Office: Sci Mus Minn 30 10th St E Ste N Saint Paul MN 55101-2265

PETERSON, LARRY JAMES, medical educator, oral surgeon; b. Winfield, Kans., Apr. 23, 1942; m. Susan Bartlett; children: Brie, Tucker. BS, U. Kans., 1964; DDS cum laude, U. Mo., Kans. City, 1968; MS, Georgetown U., 1971. Diplomate Am. Bd. Oral and Maxillofacial Surgery. Oral surgery resident Georgetown U. Sch. Dentistry, Washington, 1968-71; active staff Eugene Talmadge Meml. Hosp., Augusta, Ga., 1971-75, John N. Dempsey Hosp., Farmington, Conn., 1975-82, Ohio State U. Hosp., Columbus, 1982—, Children's Hosp., Columbus, 1982—; asst. prof. oral surgery Med. Coll. Ga. Sch. Dentistry, Augusta, 1971-74, assoc. prof. oral surgery, 1974-75; assoc. prof. oral and maxillofacial surgery U. Conn. Sch. Dental Medicine, Farmington, 1975-81; program dir. oral and maxillofacial surgery residency U. Conn. Affiliated Program, 1980-82; prof. oral and maxillofacial surgery U. Conn. Sch. Dental Medicine, 1981-82; prof., chmn. oral and maxillofacial surgery and pathology Ohio State U. Coll. Dentistry, Columbus, 1982—. Adv. com. Am. Bd. Oral and Maxillofacial Surgeons 1980-86, assoc. subject leader 1982-84, subject leader 1984-86. Editor: (textbook) Contemporary Oral and Maxillofacial Surgery, (multi-vol. ref. book) Principles of Oral and Maxillofacial Surgery; contbr. over 40 articles to profl. jours., 25 chpts. to books; editor oral surgery sect. Clinical Dentistry, 1981-87, oral and maxillofacial surgery sect. Oral Surgery, Oral Medicine, Oral Pathology, 1992—, editor-in-chief 1993—; editl. bd. Jour. Oral and Maxillofacial Surgery 1991-92; presenter in field. Recipient awards Am. Coll. Dentists, 1984, Internat. Coll. Dentists, 1992; Mosby scholar 1968. Fellow Am. Dental Soc. of Anesthesiology; mem. ADA (cons., oral and maxillofacial surgery site visitor, commn. on dental accreditation 1985-91, nat. dental bd. test constrn. com. oral and maxillofacial surgery 1985-90, nat. dental bd. part II restructuring com. 1987-92, cons. coun. on dental therapeutics 1980-92), Am. Assn. of Oral and Maxillofacial Surgeons (rsch. adv. com. 1976-79, test constrn. com. 1978-91, com. on scientific sessions 1991-94, com. on residency edn. and tng. 1992—, del. Ho. Dels. 1991-94), Internat. Assn. for Dental Rsch., Am. Assn. Dental Schs., Acad. of Osteointegration, Assn. for Acad. Surgery, Surg. Infection Soc., Alliance for Prudent Use of Antibiotics, Ohio Dental Assn., Ohio Soc. Oral and Maxillofacial Surgeons, Great Lakes Soc. Oral and Maxillofacial Surgeons, Columbus Dental Soc., Sigma Xi, Omicron Kappa Upsilon. Office: Ohio State U Coll Dentistry Dept Oral and Max Surgery 305 W 12th Ave Columbus OH 43210-1267

PETERSON, MICHAEL K. political organization administrator; b. Ft. Dodge, Iowa, Feb. 13, 1960; s. Earl and LaVonne P. Peterson; m. Julie Kraft; children: Gabrielle, Keenan. BA, JD, U. Iowa. State rep. Dist. 95, Iowa, 1985-93, Dist. 80, 1993-94; chmn. Iowa State Dem. Party, 1995—; atty. Polking Law Office, Carroll. Mem. Iowa Bar Assn., Carroll County Optimists Club. Methodist. Home: 1713 NW Pine Rd Apt 8 Ankeny IA 50021-1241 Office: 5661 Fleur Dr Des Moines IA 50321-2841

PETERSON, NANCY, special education educator; AS, Webster State Coll., 1963; BS in Elem. Edn. magna cum laude, Brigham Young U., 1964, MS in Ednl. Psychology, 1966, PhD in Ednl. Psychology, 1969. Instr. in tchr. edn. Brigham Young U., Provo, Utah, 1966-69; asst. prof. edn. dept. spl. edn. U. Kans., Lawrence, 1969-74, dir. spl. edn. classes for handicapped children Clin. Tng. Ctr., 1969-89, project dir. head start tng., 1973-74, coord. edn. univ. affiliated facility Clin. Tng. Ctr., 1969-74, coord. pers. tng. programs in mental retardation, 1973-76, assoc. prof. edn., 1974-88, project dir. pers. tng. programs, 1986-93, prof. edn. dept. spl. edn., 1988—, dept. chair, 1994—. Rsch. sci. Bur. Child Rsch., U. Kans., 1969—; prin. investigator for Kans. U. Kans. Early Childhood Rsch. Inst., 1977-82 Recipient J.E. Wallace Wallin award Internat. Coun. Exceptional Children, 1993. Office: U Kans Dept Spl Edn 3001 Dole Bldg Lawrence KS 66045-0001

PETERSON, OSCAR EMMANUEL, pianist; b. Montreal, Que., Can., Aug. 15, 1925; s. Daniel and Olivia (John) P. Studied with Paul deMarky; LLD (hon.), Carleton U., 1973, Queen's U., 1976, Concordia U., 1979, McMaster U., 1981, U. of Victoria, 1981, U. Toronto, 1985, U. B.C., 1994; DMus (hon.), Mount Alison, N.B., 1980, U. Laval, 1985; LittD (hon.), York U., 1982; D.F.A. (hon.), Northwestern U., Evanston, Ill., 1983, Niagara U., 1996; MusD (hon.), U. Laval, 1985. Founder Advanced Sch. Contemporary Music, Toronto; former chancellor York U., 1991-94. Chancellor emeritus York U., 1994, leader seminars, 1994—; composer, writer. Began music career on weekly radio show, then with Johny Holmes Orchestra, Can., 1944-49; recorded with RCA Victor Records; appeared with Jazz at the Philharmonic, Carnegie Hall, 1949; toured the U.S. and Europe, 1950—; leader trio with Ray Brown, Irving Ashby, later Barney Kessel, Herb Ellis, Ed Thigpen, Sam Jones, Louie Hayes, concert appearances with Ella Fitzgerald, Eng., Scotland, 1955; appeared Stratford (Ont.) Shakespeare Festival, Newport Jazz Festival; recorded and performed solo piano works, 1972—; toured USSR, 1974, recordings with Billie Holiday, Fred Astaire, Benny Carter, Count Basie, Roy Eldridge, Lester Young, Ella Fitzgerald, Niels-Henning Orsted Pederson, Dizzy Gillespie, Harry Edison, Clark Terry; composer: Canadiana Suite, Hymn to Freedom, Fields of Endless Day, City Lights, Begone Dull Care, (with Norman McLaren) salute to Johann Sebastian Bach, music for films Big North and Silent Partner; author: Jazz Exercises and Pieces: Oscar Peterson New Piano Solos; numerous TV specials. Decorated officer Order of Canada, 1972, companion, 1984; recipient award for piano Down Beat mag. 13 times, Metronome mag. award, 1953-54, Edison award, 1962, Award of merit City of Toronto, (1st mention) 1973 (2d mention 1983), Diplome d'honneur Can. Conf. of the Arts, 1975, Grammy award 7 times, Olympic Key to Montreal, The Queen's medal, 1977, Genie Film award for film score The Silent Partner, 1978, Grand-Prix du Disques for Night Child album, 1981, Canadian Band Festival Award, 1982, Juno Hall of Fame award, 1982, George Peabody medal Peabody Conservatory of Music, Balt., 1987, Volunteer award Roy Thompson Hall, Toronto, 1987, Can. Club Arts and Letters award, N.Y.C., 1987, Officer in Order of Arts and Letters, France, 1989, Chevalier Order of Que., 1991, Lifetime Achievement Toronto Arts Award, 1991, appointed Order of Ontario, 1992, Lifetime Achievement Gov. Gens. award, 1992, Glenn Gould prize, 1993, Gemini Film award, 1993, Three-Key award Bern Internat. Jazz Festival, 1995, NARAS Grammy award for Lifetime Achievement, 1997, Loyola medal, 1997, Carnegie Hall Anniversary medal, Charlie Parker bronze medal, Ville de Salon de Provence medal, Award of Thanks, Mexico City; 12-time jazz poll winner Playboy mag.; named number one (piano) Jazz and Pop, Readers Poll 1968, 85; named to U. Calif. at Berkeley Hall of Fame, 1983, Contemporary Keyboard Hall of Fame, 1983; Oscar Peterson Day proclaimed by Baltimore, Oreg., 1981, 83; Oscar Peterson Scholarship founded in his honor Berklee Sch. of Music, Boston, 1982. Avocations: fly fishing, photography, astronomy. Office: Regal Recs Ltd 2421 Hammond Rd Mississauga ON Canada L5K 1T3

PETERSON, PATTY, radio personality; d. Willie and Jeanne Arland Peterson; m. Stuart Paster; 4 children. Radio show host Sta. WCCO Radio, Mpls., 1997—. Actor(actress): ; , musician commls., concerts, singer. Recipient 7 time Minn. Music award winner for Best Female Vocalist and Best Group. Office: WCCO 625 2nd Ave S Minneapolis MN 55402*

PETERSON, RICHARD WILLIAM, judge, lawyer; b. Council Bluffs, Iowa, Sept. 29, 1925; s. Henry K. and Laura May (Robinson) P.; m. Patricia Mae Fox, Aug. 14, 1949; children: Katherine Ilene Peterson Sherbondy, Jon Eric, Timothy Richard. BA, U. Iowa, 1949, JD with distinction, 1951; postgrad., U. Nebr.-Omaha, 1972-80, 86. Bar: Iowa 1951, U.S. Dist. Ct. (so. dist.) Iowa 1951, U.S. Supreme Ct. 1991, U.S. Ct. Appeals (8th cir.) 1997. Pvt. practice law, Council Bluffs, 1951—; U.S. commr. U.S. Dist. Ct. (so. dist.) Iowa, 1958-70. Part-time U.S. magistrate judge U.S. Dist. Ct. (so. dist.) Iowa, 1970-99; mem. nat. faculty Fed. Jud. Ctr., Washington, 1972-82; emeritus trustee Children's Square, U.S.A.; verifying ofcl. Internat. Prisoner Transfer Treaties, Mexico City, 1977, La Paz, Bolivia, 1980, 81, Lima, Peru, 1981. Author: The Court Moves West: A Study of the United States Supreme Court Decision of Appeals from the United States Circuit and District Court of Iowa, 1846-1882, 1988, West of the Nishnabotna: The Experiences of Forty Years of a Part-Time Judicial Officer as United States Commissioner, Magistrate and Magistrate Judge, 1958-1998, 1998; co-author: (with George Mills) No One is Above the Law: The Story of Southern Iowa's Federal Court, 1994; contbr. articles to legal publs. Bd. dirs. Pottawattamie County (Iowa) chpt. ARC, state fund chmn., 1957-58; state chmn. Radio Free Europe, 1960-61; dist. chmn. Trailblazer dist. Boy Scouts Am., 1952-55; mem. exec. coun. Mid-Am. Coun., 1976—. With inf. U.S. Army, 1943-46. Decorated Purple Heart, Bronze Star; named Outstanding Young Man Council Bluffs C. of C., 1959 Fellow Am. Bar Found. (life); mem. ABA, Am. Judicature Soc., Iowa Bar Assn. (chmn. com. fed. practice 1978-80, probate and trust coun. and sect. 1997—), Pottawattamie County Bar Assn. (pres. 1979-80), Fed. Bar Assn., Inter-Am. Bar Assn., Supreme Ct. Hist. Soc., Fed. Magistrate Judges Assn. (pres. 1978-79), Iowa Conf. Bar Assn. (pres. 1985-87), Hist. Soc. of U.S. Cts. Eighth Jud. Cir. (pres. 1989-99), Kiwanis (pres. Council Bluffs club 1957), Masons, Phi Delta Phi, Delta Sigma Rho, Omicron Delta Kappa. Republican. Lutheran. Home: 1007 Arbor Ridge Cir Council Bluffs IA 51503-5000 Office: PO Box 248 25 Main Pl Ste 200 Council Bluffs IA 51503-0790

PETERSON, ROBERT L. meat processing executive; b. Nebr., July 14, 1932; married; children: Mark R., Susan P. Student, U. Nebr., 1950. With Wilson & Co., Jim Boyle Order Buying Co.; cattle buyer R&C Packing Co., 1956-61; cattle buyer, plant mgr., v.p. carcass prodn. Iowa Beef Processors, 1961-69; exec. v.p. ops. Spencer Foods, 1969-71; founder, pres., chmn., chief exec. officer Madison (Nebr.) Foods, 1971-76; group v.p. carcass div. Iowa Beef Processors, Inc. (name now IBP, Inc.), Dakota City, Nebr., 1976-77, pres., COO, 1977-80, CEO, 1980-81, co-chmn. bd. dirs., 1981-82, CEO, CFO, 1980—, chmn., CEO. Served with Q.M.C. U.S. Army, 1952-54. Mem. Sioux City Country Club. Office: IBP Inc 800 Stevens Port Dr Dakota Dunes SD 57049-5005

PETERSON, RONALD ROGER, lawyer; b. Chgo., July 27, 1948; married; children: Elizabeth G., Ronald W. AB, Ripon, 1970; JD, U. Chgo., 1973. Bar: Ill. 1974, U.S. Dist. Ct. (no. dist.) Ill. 1974, U.S. Ct. Appeals (7th cir.) 1974, U.S. Dist. Ct. (ea. dist.) Wis. 1975, U.S. Dist. Ct. (no. dist.) Ind. 1978, U.S. Dist. Ct. (cen. dist.) Ill. 1980, U.S. Dist. Ct. (we. dist.) Mich. 1999, U.S. Ct. Appeals (8th cir.) 1984, U.S. Ct. Appeals (6th cir.) 1990, U.S. Ct. Appeals (9th cir.) 1996. Ptnr. Jenner & Block, Chgo., 1974—; commd. 2d lt. U.S. Army, 1968, advanced through grades to 1st lt., 1973, ret., 1978, with mil. intelligence, 1968-78. Mem. ABA, Chgo. Bar Assn., Internat. Soc. Insolvency Practitioners, Comml. Law League, Am. Bankruptcy Inst., Am. Coll. Bankruptcy Lawyers. Avocation: skiing. Office: Jenner & Block 1 E Ibm Plz Fl 4000 Chicago IL 60611-7603 E-mail: rpeterson@jenner.com.

PETERSON, WALLACE CARROLL, SR. economics educator; b. Omaha, Mar. 28, 1921; s. Fred Nels and Grace (Brown) P.; m. Eunice V. Peterson, Aug. 16, 1944 (dec. Nov. 1985); children: Wallace Carroll Jr., Shelley Lorraine; m. Bonnie B. Watson, Nov. 11, 1988 (dec. Oct. 1996). Student, U. Omaha, 1939-40, U. Mo., 1940-42; BA in Econs. and European History, U. Nebr., 1947, MA in Econs. and European History, 1948, PhD in Econs. and European History, 1953; postgrad., Handelshochschule, St. Gallen, Switzerland, 1948-49, U. Minn., 1951, London Sch. Econs. and Polit. Sci., 1952. Lic. pilot. Reporter Lincoln (Nebr.) Jour., 1946; instr. econs. U. Nebr., Lincoln, 1951-54, asst. prof., 1954-57, assoc. prof., 1957-61, prof., 1962—, chmn. dept. econs., 1965-75, George Holmes prof. econs., 1966-92; George Holmes prof. econs. emeritus, 1992—; v.p. faculty senate U. Nebr., Lincoln, 1972-73, pres. faculty senate, 1973-74; S.J. Hall disting. vis. prof. U. Nev., Las Vegas, 1983-84. Author: The Welfare State in France, 1960, Elements of Economics, 1973, Our Overloaded Economy: Inflation, Unemployment and the Crisis in American Capitalism, 1982, Market Power and the Economy, 1988, Transfer Spending, Taxes and the American Welfare State, 1991, Income, Employment and Economic Growth, 8th edit., 1996, Silent Depression: The Fate of the American Dream, 1994; co-author: (with F.R. Strobel) The Coming Class War: Power, Conflict and the Consequences of Middle Class Decline, 1998, The Social Security Primer: What Every Citizen Should Know, 1999, Pylon! The Omaha Air Races, 1931-1934, 2002. Mem. Nebr. Dem. Cen. Com., 1968-74, vice-chmn., chmn. Nebr. Polit. Accountability and Disclosure Commn., 1977-80; chmn. Nebr. Coun. Econ. Edn., 1976-77. Capt. USAAF, 1942-46. Recipient Champion Media award for Econ. Understanding, 1981; Fulbright fellow, 1957-58, 64-65; Mid-Am. State Univs. honor scholar, 1982-83. Mem. ACLU, AAUP (pres. Nebr. 1963-64, nat. coun.), Assn. for Evolutionary Econs. (pres. 1976, Veblen-Commons award 1991), Am. Econs. Assn., Midwest Econs. Assn. (pres. 1968-69), Mo. Valley Econ. Assn. (pres. 1989), Assn. Social Econs. (pres. 1992, Thomas F. Devine award 1995), Fedn. Am. Scientists, Antique Aircraft Assn., Aircraft Owners and Pilots Assn., Exptl. Aircraft Assn., Nat. Assn. R.R. Passengers. Office: U Nebr Dept Econs CBA Lincoln NE 68588-0489 E-mail: wcpeterson@mindspring.com.

PETERSON, WALTER FRITIOF, academic administrator; b. Idaho Falls, Idaho, July 15, 1920; s. Walter Fritiof and Florence (Danielson) P.; m. Barbara Mae Kempe, Jan. 13, 1946; children: Walter Fritiof III, Daniel John. BA, State U. Iowa, 1942, MA, 1948, PhD, 1951; HHD (hon.), Loras Coll., 1983; LHD (hon.), Clarke Coll., 1991; DHum (hon.), U. Dubuque, 1997. Asst. prof. history, chmn. dept. history Milw. Downer Coll., 1952-57, assoc. prof. history, chmn. social sci. div., 1957-64; assoc. prof. history Lawrence U., Appleton, Wis., 1964-67, prof. history, Alice G. Chapman libr., 1967-70; pres. U. Dubuque, 1970-90, chancellor, 1990—. Regional tng. officer Peace Corps, 1965-68; cons. history Allis-Chalmers Mfg. Co., 1959-75, Secura Ins. Group, 1968-92, Wm. C. Brown Pub. Co., 1981-92, bd. dirs. Editor: Transactions of Wis. Acad. Scis., Arts and Letters, 1965-72, The Allis-Chalmers Corporation: An Industrial History, 1977, A History of Wm. C. Brown Cos., 1994, A History of Hawkeye Bancorporation, 1996. Advisor Templeton Prize for Progress in Religion, 1986-91; bd. dirs. Finley Hosp., pres., 1983-84; chmn. Finley Health Found., 1986-95, Finley Health Found. Hall of Fame, 2000; bd. dirs. Dubuque Symphony Orch., Dubuque Art Assn., Jr. Achievement, Nat. River Hall of Fame, 1984; chmn. Iowa Assn. Coll. and Univ. Pres., 1975-76; chmn. Iowa Coll. Found., 1982-83; chair Grand Opera House Found., 1998—. With USAAF, 1942-45, PTO. Recipient Dubuque 1st Citizen award, 1990, Disting. Civic Svc. award, 1991, Benjamin Franklin award Nat. Soc. Fundraising Execs., 1994, Paul Harris fellowship, Duduque Rotary Club, 1993; named to Dubuque Bus. Hall of Fame, 1990 Mem. Iowa Assn. Ind. Colls. and Univs. (chmn. 1988-89), Dubuque County Hist. Soc. (bd. dirs.), Dubuque Golf and Country Club, Phi Alpha Theta, Kappa Delta Pi, Phi Delta Kappa. Office: U Dubuque Office of Chancellor 2000 University Ave Dubuque IA 52001-5050

PETERSON, WILLIAM E. state legislator; b. Chgo., Feb. 2, 1936; m. Patricia Guiffre; 3 children. BA, North Pk. Coll.; MS, No. Ill. U.; postgrad., Loyola U., Chgo. Tchr.; prin.; mem. Ill. Ho. of Reps. from 60th dist., 1983-93, Ill. State Senate from 26th dist., 1993—. Mem. Consumer Protection, Aging, Aeronauticsm, Counties and Twps. Coms. Ill. Ho. of Reps., Minority Spokesman, mem. Energy, Environ and Natural Resources, Ins. and Revenue Coms. Trustee, supr. Vernon Twp. (Ill.); active Lake County (Ill.) United Way. With U.S. Army Reserve. Mem. LWV, Lions. Republican. Home: 1480 Meadowlark Dr Long Grove IL 60047-9549 Office: Ill Senate State Capitol Springfield IL 62706-0001

PETKA, ED (EDWARD F.), state legislator; b. Chgo., Mar. 10, 1943; m. Phyllis Petka; children: Jennifer, Edward, Tanya, Melinda. AB, So. Ill. U., 1966; JD, John Marshall Law Sch., 1971. State's atty. Will County, Ill., 1976-86; mem. Ill. Ho. of Reps. from 82d dist., 1987-93, Ill. State Senate from 42d dist., 1993—, majority whip. Mem. Judiciary II, Exec. and Vet. Affairs, Cities and Villages, Election Law, Consumer Protection Coms, Ill. Ho. of Reps.; chair com. on exec. appts., vice chair exec. com., mem. ins. and pensions com., judiciary com. Ill. Senate Mem. Ill. State Attys. Assn. (past pres.). Republican. Home: 15210 Eyre Cir Plainfield IL 60544-1499 Office: 122 Capitol Bldg Springfield IL 62706

PETOSA, JASON JOSEPH, publisher; b. Des Moines, Apr. 26, 1939; s. Joseph John and Mildred Margaret (Cardamon) P.; m. Theodora Anne Doleski, Aug. 12, 1972; 1 son, Justin James. Student, Marquette U., 1957-59, St. Paul Sem., 1959-63, 65-67, Colegio Paolino Internationale, Rome, 1963-65. Asso. editor Cath. Home Mag., Canfield, Ohio, 1965-67, editor, 1968; dir. Alba House Communications, Canfield, 1968-71; with Office of Radio and TV, Diocese of Youngstown, Ohio, 1969-71; dir. pub. relations, instr. Alice Lloyd Coll., Pippa Passes, Ky., 1971-76; writer, cons. Bethesda, Ohio, 1976-79; pres., pub. Nat. Cath. Reporter, Kansas City, Mo., 1979-85; v.p., gen. mgr. Towsend-Kraft Pub. Co., Liberty, 1985-86; pres., pub. Steadfast Pub. Co., Kansas City, 1986—. Bd. dirs. David (Ky.) Sch., 1973-79; mem. Mayor's UN Day Com., Kansas City. Mem. Kansas City Direct Mktg. Assn., UN Assn. (bd. dirs. Met. Kansas City chpt., pres. 2000), Sigma Delta Chi. Roman Catholic. Office: 19 W Linwood Blvd PO Box 410265 Kansas City MO 64141-0265 E-mail: jasonpetosa@steadfastpublishing.com.

PETRAUSKAS, HELEN O. automobile manufacturing company executive; b. 1944; married. BS, Wayne State U., 1966, JD, 1971. Chemist, group supr. Sherwin-Williams Co., 1966-71; various positions Ford Motor Co., Dearborn, Mich., 1971-79, asst. dir. emissions and fuel economy cert., 1980-82, exec. dir. environ. and safety engring and rsch. staff, 1982-83, exec. dir. engring. and tech. staff, 1983, corp. v.p. environ. and safety engring., 1983—. Office: 1 American Rd Dearborn MI 48126-2701

PETRI, THOMAS EVERT, congressman; b. Marinette, Wis., May 28, 1940; s. Robert and Marian (Humleker) P.; m. Anne Neal, Mar. 26, 1983; 1 child, Alexandra. BA in Govt., Harvard U., 1962, JD, 1965. Bar: Wis. 1965. Law clk. to presiding justice U.S. Dist. (we. dist.) Wis., Madison, 1965-66; vol. Peace Corps, Somalia, 1966-67; aide White House, Washington, 1969-70; dir. crime and drug studies Pres.'s Nat. Adv. Coun. on

Exec. Orgn., 1969; pvt. practice Fond du Lac, Wis., 1970-79; mem. Wis. State Senate, Madison, 1973-79, U.S. Congress from 6th Wis. dist., Washington, 1979—; mem. edn. and workforce com., trans. and infrastructure com. Editor: National Industrial Policy: Solution or Illusion, 1984. Republican. Lutheran. Avocations: reading, swimming, hiking, biking, skiing. Office: US Ho of Reps 2462 Rayburn Bldg Washington DC 20515-0001*

PETRICK, ERNEST NICHOLAS, mechanical engineer, researcher; b. Pa., Apr. 9, 1922; s. Aurelius and Anna (Kaschak) P.; m. Magdalene Simcoe, June 13, 1946; children: Deborah Petrick Healey, Katherine, Denise, Victoria Petrick Kropp. B.S. in Mech. Engring, Carnegie Inst. Tech., 1943; M.S., Purdue U., 1948, Ph.D., 1955. Registered profl. engr., Mich. Faculty Purdue U., 1946-53; dir. heat transfer research Curtiss-Wright Corp., Woodridge, N.J., 1953-56; chief advanced propulson systems Curtiss-Wright Research divsn., Quehanna, Pa., 1957-60; chief research engr. Kelsey-Hayes Co., Detroit, 1960-65; chief scientist, tech. dir. U.S. Army Tank-Automotive Command, Warren, Mich., 1965-82; chief scientist, dir. engring. labs. Gen. Dynamics, 1982-87; engring. cons., 1987—; panel mem. combat vehicles NATO, 1973-82; mem. adv. bd. on basic combustion research NSF, 1973; chmn. advanced transp. systems com. White House Energy Project, 1973; mem. adv. com. NSF-RANN research program Drexel U. Coll. Engring., 1976-78; mem. Army Sci. Bd., 1983-89; cons. Air Force Studies Bd. NRC, 1991-93, cons. Def. Sci. Bd., 1994-95; cons. Nat. Acad. of Scis., 1997-99, 2001—. Adj. prof. engring. Wayne State U., Detroit, 1972-82, U. Mich., Ann Arbor, 1982-83. Contbr. articles on transp., ground vehicles, flight propulsion and project mgmt. to profl. jours. Lt. USNR, 1952—54. Recipient certificate of achievement U.S. Army, 1967, Outstanding Performance awards, 1970, 71, 76, 82, Outstanding Mech. Engring. award Purdue U., 1991; named Disting. Engring. Alumnus Purdue U., 1966 Mem. Soc. Automotive Engrs. (nat. dir. 1978-80), Am. Def. Preparedness Assn. (chmn. land warfare survivability divsn. 1990-95, Silver medal 1992, Recognition award 1992), Assn. U.S. Army, Sigma Xi, Pi Tau Sigma. Home: 1540 Stonehaven Rd Ann Arbor MI 48104-4150 Office: ENP Cons 1540 Stonehaven Rd Ann Arbor MI 48104

PETRICOFF, M. HOWARD, lawyer, educator; b. Cin., Dec. 22, 1949; s. Herman and Neoma P.; m. Hanna Sue, Aug. 11, 1974; children: Nicholas, Eve. BS, Am. U., 1967-71; JD, U. Cin., 1971-74; M in Pub. Adminstrn., Harvard U., 1980-81. Bar: Ohio, U.S. Ct. Appeals (D.C. cir.) 1977, U.S. Ct. Appeals (10th cir.) 1985, U.S. Ct. Appeals (6th cir.) 1989, U.S. Supreme Ct. 1989. Asst. city law dir. City of Toledo (Ohio), 1975-77; asst. atty. gen. Ohio Atty. Gen. Office, Columbus, 1977-82; ptnr. Vorys, Sater, Seymour & Pease, 1982—. Adj. prof. law Capital U. Law Sch., Columbus, 1991—. Contbr. articles to profl. jours. Reginald Heber Smith Found. fellow Washington, 1974-75. Mem. Ohio Bar Assn., Columbus Bar Assn., Ohio Oil and Gas Assn. Office: Vorys Sater Seymour & Pease PO Box 1008 52 E Gay St Columbus OH 43215-3161

PETRIDES, GEORGE ATHAN, ecologist, educator; b. N.Y.C., Aug. 1, 1916; s. George Athan and Grace Emeline (Ladd) P.; m. Miriam Clarissa Pasma, Nov. 30, 1940; children: George H., Olivia L., Lisa B. BS, George Washington U., 1938; MS, Cornell U., 1940; PhD, Ohio State U., 1948; postdoctoral fellow, U. Ga., 1963-64. Naturalist Nat. Park Service, Washington and Yosemite, Calif., 1938-43, Glacier Nat. Park, Mont., 1947, Mt. McKinley Nat. Park, Alaska, 1959; game technician W.Va. Conservation Commn., Charleston, 1941; instr. Am. U., 1942-43, Ohio State U., 1946-48; leader Tex. Coop. Wildlife Unit; assoc. prof. wildlife mgmt. Tex. A. and M. Coll., 1948-50; assoc. prof. wildlife mgmt., zool. and African studies Mich. State U., 1950-58, prof., 1958—; research prof. U. Pretoria, S. Africa, 1965; vis. prof. U. Kiel, Germany, 1967; vis. prof. wildlife mgmt. Kanha Nat. Park, India, 1983; del. sci. confs. Warsaw, 1960, Nairobi and Salisbury, 1963, Sao Paulo, Aberdeen, 1965, Lucerne, 1966, Varanasi, India, Nairobi, 1967, Oxford, Eng., Paris, 1968, Durban, 1971, Mexico City, 1971, 73, Banff, 1972, Nairobi, Moscow, The Hague, 1974, Johannesburg, 1977, Sydney, 1978, Kuala Lumpur, 1979, Cairns, Australia, Mogadishu, Somalia, Peshawar, Pakistan, 1980. Participant NSF Expdn., Antarctic, 1972, FAO mission to, Afghanistan, 1972, World Bank mission to, Malaysia, 1975 Author: Field Guide to Trees and Shrubs, 1958, 2d edit., 1972, Field Guide to Eastern Trees, 1988, 98, Field Guide to Western Trees, 1992, 98, First Guide to Trees, 1993, Trees of the California Sierra Nevada, 1996, Trees of the Pacific Northwest, 1998, Trees of the Rocky Mountains and Intermountain West, 2000, Trees of the American Southwest, 2000; editor wildlife mgmt. terrestrial sect. Biol. Abstracts, 1947-72; contbr. articles to biol. publs. Served to lt. USNR, 1943-46. Fulbright research awards in E. Africa Nat. Parks Kenya, 1953-54; Fulbright research awards in E. Africa Nat. Parks Kenya, Uganda, 1956-57; N.Y. Zool. Soc. grantee Ethiopia, Sudan, 1957; N.Y. Zool. Soc. grantee Thailand, 1977; Mich. State U. grantee Nigeria, 1962; Mich. State U. grantee Zambia, 1966; Mich. State U. grantee Kenya, 1969; Mich. State U. grantee Africa, 1970, 71, 73, 81; Mich. State U. grantee Greece, 1974, 83; Mich. State U. grantee Iran, 1974; Mich. State U. grantee Botswana, 1977; Mich. State U. grantee Papua New Guinea, Thailand, 1979; Iran Dept. Environment grantee, 1977; Smithsonian Instn. grantee India and Nepal, 1967, 68, 75, 77, 83, 85; World Wildlife Fund grantee W. Africa, 1968 Mem. Am. Ornithologists Union, Am. Soc. Mammalogists, Wildlife Soc. (exec. sec. 1953), Wilderness Soc., Am. Comm. Internat. Wildlife Protection, Ecol. Soc., Fauna Preservation Soc., E. African Wildlife Soc., Internat. Union Conservation Nature, Zool. Soc. So. Africa, Sigma Xi. Presbyterian. Home: 4895 Barton Rd Williamston MI 48895-9305 Office: Mich State U Dept Botany East Lansing MI 48824 E-mail: petrides@msu.edu.

PETRIE, BRUCE INGLIS, lawyer; b. Washington, Nov. 8, 1926; s. Robert Inglis and Marion (Douglas) P.; m. Beverly Ann Stevens, Nov. 3, 1950 (dec. Oct. 1993); children: Laurie Ann Roche, Bruce Inglis, Karen Elizabeth Medsger. BBA, U. Cin., 1948, JD, 1950. Bar: Ohio 1950, U.S. Dist. Ct. (so. dist.) Ohio 1951, U.S. Ct. Appeals (6th cir.) 1960, U.S. Supreme Ct. Assoc. Kunkel & Kunkel, Cin., 1950-51, Graydon, Head & Ritchey, 1951-57, ptnr., 1957—. Exec. prodr. (sch. video) Classical Quest, 2000; author: How To Get the Most Out of Your Lawyer, 2002; contbr. articles to legal jours. Mem. bd. Charter Com. Greater Cin., 1952—; pres. Charter Rsch. Inst., 2000; mem. bd. edn. Indian Hill Exempted Village Sch. Dist., 1965-67, pres., 1967; mem. adv. bd. William A. Mitchell Ctr., 1969-86; mem. Green Areas adv. com. Village of Indian Hill, Ohio, 1969-80, chmn., 1976-80; mem. Ohio Ethics Com., 1974-75; co-founder Sta. WGUC-FM; mem. WGUC-FM Cmty. Bd., 1974—, chmn., 1974-76; bd. dirs. Murray Seasongood Good Govt. Fund, 1975—, pres., 1989—; bd. dirs. Nat. Civic League, Cin. Vol. Lawyers for Poor Found., Linton Music Series, Amernet Chamber Music Soc.; founder Parents as Tchrs. Metro Housing Authority Commn., 1991—; elder, trustee, deacon Knox Presbyn. Ch.; a prin. advocate merit selection judges, Ohio; trustee, mem. bd., Seven Hills Neighborhood Houses, Inst. for Learning in Retirement; mem. bd. Hamilton County Good Govt. League; organizer Late Great Lakes Book Distbn. project. Recipient Pres.'s award U. Cin., 1976, Disting. Alumnus award, 1995. Fellow Am. Bar Found.; mem. ABA, Ohio Bar Assn., Cin. Bar Assn. (pres. 1981, Trustee's award 2000), Am. Judicature Soc. (Herbert Lincoln Harley award 1973, dir.), Nat. Civic League (Disting. Citizen award 1985, coun. 1984—), Am. Law Inst., Ohio State Bar Assn. Found. (Outstanding Rsch. in Law and Govt. award 1986, Charles P. Taft Civic Gumption award 1988, Ohio Bar medal 1988), Cincinnatus Assn., Order of Coif, Lit. Club, Univ. Club, Cin. Club. Avocations: tennis, squash, woodworking, writing, horticulture, music. Home: 2787 Walsh Rd Cincinnati OH 45208-3428 Office: Graydon Head & Ritchey 1900 Fifth 3d Ctr 511 Walnut St Ste 1900 Cincinnati OH 45202-3157

PETRILLO, NANCY, public relations executive; CFO, exec. v.p. Edelman Pub. Rels. Worldwide, Chgo. Office: Edelman Pub Rels Worldwide 200 E Randolph St Fl 63D Chicago IL 60601-6436

PETRO, JAMES MICHAEL, lawyer, politician; b. Cleve., Oct. 25, 1948; s. William John and Lila Helen (Janca) P.; m. Nancy Ellen Bero, Dec. 16, 1972; children: John Bero, Corbin Marie. BA, Denison U., 1970; JD, Case Western Res., 1973. Bar: Ohio 1973, U.S. Dist. Ct. (no. dist.) Ohio 1974, U.S. Ct. Appeals (6th cir.) 1981. Spl. asst. U.S. senator W.B. Saxbe, Cleve., 1972-73; asst. pros. atty. Franklin County, Ohio, 1973-74; asst. dir. law City of Cleve., 1974; ptnr. Petro & Troia, Cleve., 1974-84; dir. govt. affairs Standard Oil Co., 1984-86; ptnr. Petro, Rademaker, Matty & McClelland, 1986-93, Buckingham, Doolittle & Burroughs, Cleve., 1993-95. Mem. city coun. Rocky River, Ohio, 1977-79, dir. law, 1980; mem. Ohio Ho. of Reps., Columbus, 1981-84, 86-90; commr. Cuyahoga County, Ohio, 1991-95; Auditor of State of Ohio, 1995—. Mem. ABA, Ohio State Bar Assn., Cleve. Bar Assn. Republican. Methodist. Home: 1933 Lake Shore Dr Columbus OH 43204-4963 Office: 88 E Broad St Columbus OH 43215-3506 E-mail: petro@auditor.state.oh.us.

PETTEY, PATRICIA HUGGINS, county official; m. John M. Pettey. Rep. dist. 31 State of Kans., 1993-97; commr. Wyandotte County Unified Govt. Democrat. Home: 3500 Gibbs Rd Kansas City KS 66106-3810

PETTITT, JAY S. architect, consultant; b. Redford, Mich., Jan. 6, 1926; s. Jay S. and Florence Marian (Newman) P.; m. Ruth Elizabeth Voigt, June 21, 1947; children— J. Stuart, Laura Ellen, Patricia Lynn, Carol Ann B.Arch., U. Mich., 1951. Registered architect, Mich. Draftsman Frank J. Stepnoski and Son, Fond du Lac, Wis., 1951; project architect Albert Kahn Assocs., Inc., Detroit, 1951-62, chief archtl. devel., 1962-67, v.p., 1967-88, dir. architecture, 1975-88; archtl. cons. Beulah, Mich., 1988—. Active Jr. Athletic Assn., Redford, Mich., 1959-63; com. chmn. Boy Scouts Am., 1960-65; supr. Benzonia Twp. Served with U.S. Army. 1943-46, ETO. Fellow AIA; mem. Mich. Soc. Architects (pres. 1967), Am. Arbitration Assn., Am. Assn. Hosp. Planning, Engring. Soc. Detroit, U. Mich. Pres.' Club Avocations: sailing; skiing. E-mail: jaypettitt@bignetnorth.net.

PETTY, MARGE D. state senator; b. Ft. Wayne, Ind., Feb. 26, 1946; m. Tyrus C. Petty, 1968; children: Brandon, Megan. BS, Tex. Christian U., 1968; MEd, Kans. U., 1978; JD, Washburn U. Sch. Law, 1990. Tchr., 1968-69; mgmnt. consultant, 1981-; health educator, 1978-81; mem. City Council of Topeka, 1985-89; dep. mayor Topeka, 1986; mem. Kans. Senate, 1988-. Mem. Topeka Metro. Ballet, Chamber of Commerce, Mulvane Art Ctr. Episcopalian. Home: 106 SW Woodlawn Ave Topeka KS 66606-1241 Address: Kansas Senate State Capitol Rm 422-S Topeka KS 66612

PETYO, MICHAEL EDWARD, construction company owner; b. East Chicago, Ind., Mar. 29, 1949; m. Janet Lynn; 2 children. Candidate for Lake County Sheriff, 1994; Rep. candidate for U.S. House, 1st Dist., Ind., 1996.

PETZ, THOMAS JOSEPH, internist; b. Detroit, Feb. 10, 1930; s. Arthur J. and Marie (McCarthy) P.; m. Catherine Crowe, June 13, 1959; children: Thomas Jr., William, David, John, Catherine. BS, U. Detroit, 1951; MD, Wayne State U., 1955. Diplomate Am. Bd. Internal Medicine and Pulmonary Disease. Intern Harper Hosp., Detroit, 1955-56, resident, 1958-59, 60-62, U. Calif., San Francisco, 1959-60; clin. instr. Wayne State U., Detroit, 1962-72, assoc. prof., 1972-76, clin. assoc. prof., 1976-95, clin. prof., 1996-97, prof. emeritus, 1997—; pvt. practice pulmonary disease and internal medicine, 1962-72, St. Clair Shores, Mich., 1977-96; med.-legal cons. Grosse Pointe, 1996—. Chief pulmonary Wayne State U., Detroit, 1974-76, Harper Hosp., Detroit, 1972-79; dir. med. intensive care unit Harper Hosp., Detroit, 1977-83; chmn. dept. medicine Bon Secours Hosp., Grosse Pointe, Mich., 1984-86; chmn. Gen. Motors human rsch. com., 1995. Bd. govs. Wayne State Sch. of Medicine Alumni Assn., Detroit, 1981-85. Fellow Detroit Acad. Medicine (pres. 1982-83), Am. Coll. Chest Physicians; mem. Am. Coll. Physicians, Detroit Med. Club. Republican. Roman Catholic. Avocations: golf, skiing.

PETZOLD, JOHN PAUL, judge; b. 1938; BA, U. Maine, 1961; LLB, Washington & Lee U., 1962. Bar: Ohio 1962, Va. 1962. Pvt. practice law, Ohio, 1962-91; asst. atty. gen. State of Ohio, 1964-71; law dir. City of Miamisburg, Ohio, 1979-91; judge Montgomery County Common Pleas Ct., Dayton, 1991—. Bd. tax appeals City of Kettering, Ohio, 1971-91. Mem. ABA, Ohio State Bar Assn. (bd. govs., former chairperson young lawyers sect., chairperson pub. rels. com., vice chairperson lawyers assistance com., eminent domain com., banking, comml., and bankruptcy law com., pres. 1998-99), Dayton Bar Assn. (pres. 1989-90), Common Pleas Judge Assn. (mem. bd. commrs. on grievances and discipline 1995-97). Avocations: golf, swimming, writing, teaching, reading, genealogy. Office: Montgomery County Common Pleas Ct 41 N Perry St Dayton OH 45402-1431

PEVEC, ANTHONY EDWARD, bishop; b. Cleve., Apr. 16, 1925; s. Anton and Frances (Darovec) P. MA, John Carroll U., Cleve., 1956; PhD, Western Res. U., Cleve., 1964. Ordained priest Roman Catholic Ch., 1950. Assoc. pastor St. Mary Church, Elyria, Ohio, 1950-52, St. Lawrence Ch., Cleve., 1952-53; rector-prin. Borromeo Sem. High Sch., Wickliffe, Ohio, 1953-75; adminstrv. bd. Nat. Cath. Edn. Assn., 1972-75; pastor St. Vitus Ch., Cleve., 1975-79; rector-pres. Borromeo Coll., Wickliffe, 1979-82; aux. bishop Diocese of Cleve., 1982—. Mem. v.p. Slovenian-Am. Heritage Found., Cleve., 1975—. Honoree, Heritage Found., Cleve., 1982; named Man of Yr., Fedn. Slovenian Nat. Homes, Cleve., 1985, Cath. Man of Yr. KC, 1998, Man of Yr., Pioneer Assn., 2001; inducted into Hall of Fame, St. Vitus Alumni Assn., 1989, Wickliffe Hall of Fame, 2000. Mem. Nat. Conf. Cath. Bishops (com. on vocations 1984-86, com. on pro-life activities, 1990-92, com. on sci. and human values 1993-96, com. on priestly formation 1993—), U.S. Cath. Conf. (nat. adv. coun. 1996—). Democrat. Roman Catholic Avocations: reading; music. Home and Office: Diocese of Cleve 28700 Euclid Ave Wickliffe OH 44092-2527 E-mail: bpaepevec@dioceseofcleveland.org.

PEW, ROBERT CUNNINGHAM, II, office equipment manufacturing company executive; b. Syracuse, N.Y., June 4, 1923; s. Robert Carroll and Bernice (Evans) P.; m. Mary Bonnell Idema, Aug. 23, 1947; children: Robert Cunningham, John Evans, Kate Bonnell. B.A., Wesleyan U., Middletown Conn.; HHD (hon.), LLD (hon.), Aquinas Coll. Labor relations exec. Doehler-Jarvis Corp., Grand Rapids, Mich., 1948-51; with Steelcase Inc., 1952—, exec. v.p., 1964-66, pres., 1966-79, chmn. bd., pres., 1974-99. Dir. Old Kent Financial Corp., Foremost Corp. Am. Bd. control Grand Valley State Coll.; bd. dirs. Econ. Devel. Corp. Grand Rapids, Mich. Strategic Fund, Nat. Orgn. on Disability; mem. Gov.'s Commn. on Jobs and Econ. Devel. Served to 1st lt. USAAF, 1942-45; to capt. USAF, 1951-52. Decorated Purple Heart, Air medal with 2 oak leaf clusters. Mem. Grand Rapids C. of C. (dir.), Grand Rapids Employers Assn. (dir.), Chi Psi. Episcopalian. Clubs: Lost Tree (North Palm Beach Fla.); Peninsular; University, Kent Country (Grand Rapids). Home: 11307 Old Harbour Rd North Palm Beach FL 33408-3406 Office: PO Box 1967 Grand Rapids MI 49501-1967 also: Steelcase Inc 901 44th St SE Grand Rapids MI 49508-7575

PEYSER, JOSEPH LEONARD, educator, author, translator, historial researcher; b. N.Y.C., Oct. 19, 1925; s. Samuel and Sadye (Quinto) P.; m. Julia Boxer, May 30, 1948; children: Jay Randall, Jan Ellen. B.A., Duke U., 1947, M.A., 1949; profl. diploma, Columbia U., 1955; postgrad., U. Nancy, France, 1949-50; Ed.D., NYU, 1965. Prof., chmn. fgn. langs., adminstr. Nancy (France) École Normale, 1949-50; Tchr., chmn. fgn. langs. Monroe (N.Y.) Pub. Schs., 1951-54, Uniondale (N.Y.) Pub. Schs., 1954-61; asst. high sch. prin. Plainview, N.Y., 1961-63; mem. faculty Hofstra U., Hempstead, 1963-68, assoc. prof. edn., 1966-68; asst. dean, then asso. dean Hofstra U. (Sch. Edn.), 1964-66; interim dean Sch. Edn. Hofstra U., 1966-68; dean acad. affairs, prof. French and edn. Dowling Coll., Oakdale, N.Y., 1968-70, v.p. acad. affairs, dean faculty, 1970-73; prof. French and edn. Ind. U., South Bend, 1973-94, prof. emeritus French, 1994—, dean faculties, 1973-75, chmn. fgn. lang. dept., 1987-89. Vis. asst. prof. NYU, 1964-66; adj. asst. prof. L.I. U., 1961-63; prin. researcher, translator French Michilimackinac Rsch. Project, Mich., 1991—; rsch. reviewer NEH, 1994-98. Author: Letters from New France, 1981; rev. edit. Letters from New France: The Upper Country, 1686-1783, 1992; co-author, Fort St. Joseph, 1691-1781, 1991, The Fox Wars: The Mesquakie Challenge to New France, 1993, Jacques Legardeur de Saint-Pierre: Officer, Gentleman, Entrepreneur, 1996, On the Eve of the Conquest: Chevalier de Raymond's Critique of New France in 1754, 1997, Ambush and Revenge: George Washington's Adversaries in 1754, 1999; translator Fort St. Joseph Manuscripts, 1978, William Henry Harrison's French Correspondence, 1994; contbr. profl. publs. Bd. dirs. South Bend Symphony, 1979-86. Served with USNR, 1943-46. Recipient Founders Day award NYU, 1966, State Hist. Soc. of Wis. Hesseltine award, 1991, French Colonial Hist. Soc. Heggoy Book prize, 1994; tchg. fellow French Ministry Edn., 1949-50, Lilly Endowment faculty fellow, 1985-86, NEH fellow, 1988, 94-95, Lundquist faculty fellow, 1989-90; Newberry Libr. rsch. assoc., 1985-86. Mem. Ind. Hist. Soc. (Thornbrough award 1996), Hist. Soc. Mich., French Colonial Hist. Soc. (v.p. 1988-91, exec. com. 1988-94), Ctr. for French Colonial Studies.

PFAU, RICHARD ANTHONY, college president; b. N.Y.C., Feb. 19, 1942; s. Hugo and Irene Beatrice P.; m. Nancy Ann DiPace, Sept. 12, 1964; children: Bradley Madison, Aleksandra Nicole. AB, Hamilton Coll., 1964; MA, U. Va., 1973, PhD, 1975. Systems analyst Equitable Life Ins. Co., N.Y.C., 1964-66; asst. prof. history Dickinson Coll., Carlisle, Pa., 1975-80; assoc. prof., assoc. dean U. Miami, Coral Gables, Fla., 1980-85; dean of faculty, provost Emory (Va.) and Henry Coll., 1985-93; pres. Ill. Coll., Jacksonville, Ill., 1993—2002, Averett U., Danville, Va., 2002—. Author: No Sacrifice Too Great: The Life of Lewis L. Strauss, 1985. Contbr. articles, book revs. to profl. publs. Vestryman St. Thomas Episc. Ch., Abingdon, Va.; chmn., sec.-treas., exec. com., bd. dirs. Va. Found. for Humanities and Pub. Policy, Exec. Com. Fedn. Ind. Ill. Colls. and Univs.; mem. adv. bd. Salvation Army, Jacksonville. Capt. USAF, 1966-71. DuPont fellow, 1974-75; Hoover fellow, 1982. Mem. Omicron Delta Kappa, Alpha Psi Omega, Pi Delta Epsilon, Union League Club (Chgo.). Home: 500 Hawthorne Drive Danville VA 24541 Office: Averett Univ Pres Office 420 West Main Street Danville VA 24541

PFEIFER, PAUL E. state supreme court justice; b. Bucyrus, Ohio, Oct. 15, 1942; m. Julia Pfeifer; 3 children. BA, Ohio State U., 1963, JD, 1966. Asst. atty. gen. State of Ohio, 1967-70; mem. Ohio Ho. of Reps., 1971-72; asst. prosecuting atty. Crawford County, 1973-76; mem. Ohio Senate, 1976-92, minority floor leader, 1983-84, asst. pres. pro-tempore, 1985-86; ptnr. Cory, Brown & Pfeifer, 1973-92; justice Ohio Supreme Ct., 1992—. Chmn. jud. com. Ohio Senate, 10 yrs. Mem. Grace United Meth. Ch., Bucyrus. Mem. Bucyrus Rotary Club. Office: Supreme Court of Ohio 30 E Broad St Fl 3 Columbus OH 43215*

PFENDER, EMIL, mechanical engineering educator; b. Stuttgart, Germany, May 25, 1925; came to U.S., 1964, naturalized, 1969; s. Vinzenz and Anna Maria (Dreher) P.; m. Maria Katharina Staiger, Oct. 22, 1954; children: Roland, Norbert, Corinne. Student, U. Tuebingen, Germany, 1947-49; diploma in physics, U. Stuttgart, Germany, 1953, D Ing. in Elec. Engring., 1959. Assoc. prof. mech. engring. U. Minn., Mpls., 1964-67, prof., 1967—. Contbr. articles to profl. jours.; patentee in field. Fellow: ASME; mem.: NAE, IEEE (assoc.). Home: 1947 Bidwell St Saint Paul MN 55118-4417 Office: U Minn Dept of Mech Engrg 111 Church St SE Minneapolis MN 55455-0150 E-mail: pfender@tc.umn.edu.

PFENING, FREDERIC DENVER, III, manufacturing company executive; b. Columbus, Ohio, July 28, 1949; s. Frederic Denver Jr. and Lelia (Bucher) P.; m. Cynthia Gordon, July 1, 1978 (div. 1999); children: Lesley, Frederic Denver IV; m. Janet Evans, 1999. BA, Ohio Wesleyan U., 1971; MA, Ohio State U., Columbus, 1976. Various positions Fred. D. Pfening Co., Columbus, 1976-88, pres., 1988—. Bd. dirs. Friends of Ohio State U. Librs., 1988-94, 98—, Columbus State C.C. Devel. Found., 1991-99, Hist. Sites Found., Baraboo, Wis., 1984—, pres., 1987-91. Mem. Am. Soc. Bakery Engrs., Orgn. Am. Historians, Bakery Equipment Mfrs. Assn. (bd. dirs. 1985-91), Young Pres.'s Orgn., Circus Hist. Soc. (pres. 1986-89, mng. editor Bandwagon Jour.), Rotary. Office: 1075 W 5th Ave Columbus OH 43212-2629

PFISTER, KARL ANTON, industrial company executive; b. Ernetschwil St. Gallen, Switzerland, Oct. 17, 1941; came to U.S., 1966; s. Josef Anton and Paula Pfister; m. Karen Antonie Sievers; children: Kirsten, Marc, Theodore, Alexandra. Student trade sch., Rapperswil, Switzerland, 1957-61; student bus. sch., Zuerich, Switzerland, 1964-65. Tool and die maker H. Schmid, Rapperswil, Switzerland, 1957-61, Neher AG, Ebnat-Kappel, Switzerland, 1962-63; process engr. NCR, Buelach, Switzerland, 1964-66, Gretag, Regensdorf, Switzerland, 1966; tool and die maker Stoffel Fineflow Corp., White Plains, N.Y., 1966-67; mgr. mfg. Finetool Corp., Detroit, 1968; pres. Mich. Precision Ind., Inc., 1969—, MPI Internat. Inc., Rochester Hills, Mich., 1990—; chmn. bd., pres. Kautex N.Am., Inc., 1994; pres. Kloeckner Automotive, Inc., 1996, MPI Internat. Inc., Rochester Hills, 1998—. Dir. Kloeckner Capital Corp., Gordonsville, Va., MPI Internat., Inc. Consul, consulate Switzerland, Detroit, 1984—. Mem. Plum Hollow Club. Republican. Roman Catholic. Office: MPI Internat Inc 2129 Austin Ave Rochester Hills MI 48309-3668

PFLUM, BARBARA ANN, pediatric allergist; b. Cin., Jan. 10, 1943; d. James Frederick and Betty Mae (Doherty) P.; m. Makram I. Gobrail, Oct. 20, 1973; children: Christina, James. BS, Coll. Mt. St. Vincent, 1967; MD, Georgetown U., 1971; MS, Coll. Mt. St. Joseph, 1993. Cons. Children's Med. Ctr., Dayton, Ohio, 1975—, dir. allergy clinic, 1983-89; dir. allergy divsn. Hopeland Splty. Clinic, 1998-2000. Fellow Am. Acad. Pediatrics, Am. Acad. Allergy and Immunology, Am. Coll. Allergy and Immunology; mem. Ohio Soc. Allergy and Immunology, Western Ohio Pediatric Soc. (pres. 1985-86). Roman Catholic. Office: 207 E Stroop Rd Dayton OH 45429-2825 E-mail: bapflum@hotmail.com.

PHARES, E. JERRY, psychology educator; b. Glendale, Ohio, July 21, 1928; s. Bruce and Gladys (West) P.; m. Betty L. Knost, Aug. 6, 1955; 1 dau., Lisa M. B.A., U. Cin., 1951; M.A., Ohio State U., 1953, Ph.D., 1955. Faculty Kans. State U., Manhattan, 1955—, prof. psychology, 1964-91, prof. emeritus, 1991—, head dept., 1967-89. Vis. asso. prof. Ohio State U., Columbus, Ohio Wesleyan U., 1961-62 Author, co-author books.; Contbr. articles to profl. jours. Research grantee NIMH, 1960, 80; Research grantee NSF, 1964-76; Research grantee Population Council, 1971 Fellow Am. Psychol. Assn., Am. Psychol. Soc. Office: 2812 Nevada St Manhattan KS 66502-2330 E-mail: ephares@ksu.edu.

PHARES, LYNN LEVISAY, public relations communications executive; b. Brownwood, Tex., Aug. 6, 1947; m. C. Kirk Phares, Aug. 22, 1971; children: Laura, Margaret, Adele, Jessica. BA, La. State U., 1970; MA, U.

Nebr., 1987. Asst. to advt. mgr. La. Nat. Bank, 1970-71; writer, producer, asst. v.p., account exec. Smith, Kaplan, Allen & Reynolds, Inc., Omaha, 1971-80; assoc. dir. pub. affairs U. Nebr. Med. Ctr., 1980-83; dir. pub. rels. ConAgra Inc., Omaha, 1985-87, v.p. pub. rels., 1987-90, v.p. pub. rels. and cmty. affairs, 1990-97, v.p., corp. rels., 1997-2000. Pres. ConAgra Found., Feeding Children Better Found. Office: ConAgra Inc 1 ConAgra Dr Omaha NE 68102-5001

PHELPS, DAVID D. congressman; b. Eldorado, Ill., Oct. 26, 1947; m. Leslie Phelps; 4 children. BS, So. Ill. U. Mem. Ill. Ho. of Reps. from 118th dist., 1985-98; mem., chmn. healthcare com. 106th Congress from 19th Ill. dist., 1999—; mem. agr. com.; mem. small bus. Mem. Transp. and Motor Vehicles, Appropriations I, Energy, Environ. and Natural Resources, Edn. Appropriations, Human Svcs., Elem. and Secondary Edn., Counties and Twp., Econ. Devel. Coms. Ill. Ho. of Reps., vice chmn. Coal Devel. and Mktg., Econ. and Urban Devel. Coms., chmn. Health Care Com. Democrat. Home: RR 1 Box 114 Eldorado IL 62930-9727 Office: Ho. of Reps. 1523 Longworth Hob Washington DC 20515-0001*

PHENIS-BOURKE, NANCY SUE, educational administrator; b. Anderson, Ind., Oct. 29, 1943; d. Wilma (Anderson) Baker; m. Richard W. Phenis, June 11, 1966; 1 child, Heidi L. BA, Ind. State U., 1965; MA, Ball State U., 1974, postgrad., 1985. Elem. tchr. Highland Park (N.J.) Schs., 1966-68, Anderson City Schs., 1969-71; elem. tchr., tchr. gifted and talented South Madison Schs., Pendleton, Ind., 1974-85, elem. prin., 1985—. K-12 curriculum dir. South Madison Schs., 1984; mem. CAPE grant com. Eli Lilly Found., 2000. Bd. dirs. South Madison Community Found., Pendleton, 1991, First Am. Bank FirstGrant; devel. bd. St. John's Health Care Systems; mem. Prin.'s Leadership Summit, U.S. Dept. Edn., 2000. Recipient Outstanding Contbn. award Internat. Reading Assn., 1991; grantee Eli Lilly Found., 1993. Mem. NAESP (Ind. state rep. 1998—, membership adv. com. 1999), AAUW (pres. 1985-87), Ind. Assn. Sch. Prins. (bd. dirs. 1994—), First Am. (bd. dirs. 1992-95), Phi Delta Kappa (historian 1987, Leadership award 1994), Delta Kappa Gamma (sec. 1990-92, pres. 1992-94, Leadership/Adminstr. award 1993). Office: East Elem Sch 893 E Us Highway 36 Pendleton IN 46064-9580

PHIBBS, CLIFFORD MATTHEW, surgeon, educator; b. Bemidji, Minn., Feb. 20, 1930; s. Clifford Matthew and Dorothy Jean (Wright) P.; m. Patricia Jean Palmer, June 27, 1953; children— Wayne Robert, Marc Stuart, Nancy Louise B.S., Wash. State U., 1952; M.D., U. Wash., 1955; M.S., U. Minn., 1960. Diplomate Am. Bd. Surgery. Intern Ancker Hosp., St. Paul, 1955-56; resident in surgery U. Minn. Hosps., 1956-60; practice medicine specializing in surgery Oxboro Clinic, Mpls., 1962—, pres., 1985—; cons. to health risk mgmt. corps., 1994—. Mem. Children's Hosp. Ctr., Northwestern-Abbott Hosp., Fairview-Southdale Hosp., Fairview Ridges Hosp.; clin. asst. prof. U. Minn., Mpls., 1975-78, clin. assoc. prof. surgery, 1978—; med. dir. Minn. Protective Life Ins. Co. Contbr. articles to med. jours. Bd. dirs. Bloomington Bd. Edn., Minn., 1974— , treas., 1976, sec., 1977-78, chmn., 1981-83; mem. adv. com. jr. coll. study City of Bloomington, 1964-66, mem. community facilities com., 1966-67, advisor youth study commn., 1966-68; vice chmn. bd. Hillcrest Meth. Ch., 1970-71; mem. Bloomington Adv. and Rsch. Coun., 1969-71; bd. dirs. Bloomington Symphony Orch., 1976— , Wash. State U. Found., trustee, 1990—; dir. bd. mgmt. Minnesota Valley YMCA, 1970-75; bd. govs. Mpls. Met. YMCA, 1970—; bd. dirs. Bloomington Heart-Health Found., 1989—, Martin Luther Manor, 1989; pres. Oxboro Clinics, 1985—; bd. dirs. Bloomington History Clock Tower Assn., 1990—; bd. dirs. Fairview Hosp. Clinic, 1994—, Bloomington Sister city Orgn., 1999-, Bloomington Cmty. Found., 1997-, Bloomington Health Adv. Bd., 1999-, Com. on Cult. Competence Minnesota Med. Assn., 19986. Capt. M.C., U.S. Army, 1960-62. Mem. ACS, AMA (Physician Recognition awards 1969, 73, 76, 79, 82, 85, 88, 91, 94), Assn. Surg. Edn., Royal Soc. Medicine, Am. Coll. Sports Medicine, Minn. Med. Assn. (del. 1991-94), Minn. Surg. Soc., Mpls. Surg. Soc., Hennepin County Med. Soc., Pan-Pacific Surg. Assn., Jaycees, Bloomington C. of C. (chmn. bd. 1984, chmn. 1985-86). Home: 9613 Upton Rd Bloomington MN 55431-2454 Office: 600 W 98th St Minneapolis MN 55420-4773

PHILIP, JAMES (PATE PHILIP), state legislator; b. Elmhurst, Ill., May 26, 1930; married; 4 children. Student, Kansas City Jr. Coll., Kans. State Coll. Ret. dist. sales mgr. Pepperidge Farm, Inc.; rep. State of Ill., 1967-74, senator, 1975—. Asst. senate minority leader, 1979, senate minority leader, 1981-93, senate pres., 1993—; chmn. DuPage County Rep. Ctrl. Com.; committeeman Addison Twp. Precinct 52; past Jr. Nat. Rep. Committeeman. Past dir. Nat. Found. March of Dimes; past gen. chmn. Elmhurst March of Dimes; spl. events chmn. DuPage Heart Assn.; mem. DuPage Meml. Hosp. Century Club; dir. Ray Graham Assn. Handicapped Children; mem. bd. sponsors Easter Seal Treatment Ctr.; active Lombard YMCA; bd. dirs. Danada Sculpture Garden. With USMC, 1950-53. Recipient Ill. Coun. on Aging award, 1989, Leaders of 90's award Downers Grove Twp., 1989, Man of Yr. award United Hellenic Voters Am., 1989, Legis. of Yr. award Ill. County Treas.'s Assn., 1990, Tax$avers award Ill. Assn. County Auditors, 1990, Statesman of Yr. award Internat. Union of Operating Engrs. Local 150, 1991, Friend of Youth award Assn. Ill. Twp. Com. on Youth, 1991, Spl. Svc. award Serenity House, 1991, Recognition award DuPage Ctr. Independent Living, 1991. Mem. Am. Legion, Ill. Young Reps. (past pres.), DuPage County Young Rep. Fedn. (past chmn.), DuPage County Marine Corps League (life), DuPage Indsl. and Mfg. Assn. (past dir.), Suburban Bus. Mgmt. Coun. (past v.p.), Mil. Order Devil Dogs, Gocery Mgmt. and Sales Exec. Club Chgo., Exec. Club DuPage County, Shriners, Elks, Masons, Order of DeMolay (life), Moose. Office: Ill State Senate 327 Capitol Building Springfield IL 62706*

PHILIPSON, MORRIS, university press director; b. New Haven, June 23, 1926; s. Samuel and Edith (Alderman) P.; m. Susan Antonia Sacher, Apr. 26, 1961; children: Nicholas, Jenny, Alex. Diploma, U. Paris, 1947; B.A., U. Chgo., 1949, M.A., 1952; Ph.D. in Philosophy, Columbia U., 1959; L.H.D. (hon.), Coe Coll., 1985. Instr. English lit. Hofstra Coll., 1954—55; instr. philosophy Juilliard Sch. Music, 1955—58; lectr. Hunter Coll., 1957—60; editor Vintage Books, Alfred A. Knopf, Inc., N.Y.C., 1959—61, Modern Library, also trade books Random House, Inc., Pantheon Books, 1961—65; sr. editor Basic Books, N.Y.C., 1965—66; exec. editor U. Chgo. Press, 1966—67, dir., 1967—2000, dir. emeritus, 2000—. Author: Outline of Jungian Aesthetics, 1963, Bourgeois Anonymous, 1964, The Count Who Wished He Were a Peasant: A Life of Leo Tolstoy, 1967, Paradoxes, 1969, Everything Changes, 1972, The Wallpaper Fox, 1976, A Man in Charge, 1979, Secret Understandings, 1983, Somebody Else's Life, 1987; also short stories, articles; editor: Aldous Huxley on Arts and Artists, 1960, Aesthetics Today, 1961, Automation: Implications for the Future, 1962, (with Clapp, Rosenthal) Foundations of Western Thought, 1962. Served with AUS, 1944-46. Decorated comdr. Order Arts and Letters (France). Clubs: Arts (Chgo.), Caxton (Chgo.), Tavern (Chgo.), Quadrangle (Chgo.).

PHILLIPS, BARRY L. business executive; Pres., CEO Gradall Industries, Inc., New Philadelphia, Ohio. Office: Gradall Industries Inc 406 Mill Ave New Philadelphia OH 44663

PHILLIPS, CHARLES W. state agency administrator; BS in Indsl. Mgmt., U. Ky., 1950. Asst. examiner St. Louis dist. FDIC, 1950-54, examiner St. Louis dist., 1954-57; exec. v.p. Floyd County Bank, New Albany, Ind., 1958-62, pres., 1962-85; ret.; apptd. dir. Ind. Dept. Fin. Instns., 1989-97, 97—. Mem. Ind. Bank Law Study Commn., 1963-64; mem. state banking law steering com. Am. Bankers Assn., 1965-66, mem. leadership coun., 1980-82; chmn. mems. Ind. Dept. Fin. Instns., 1965-68; chmn. sr. mgmt. com. Ind. Bankers Assn., 1972, chmn. legis. com., 1973; bd. dirs. CSBS. Mem. bd. advisors Ind. U. S.E., 1973-78, chmn. bd. exec. 1976-82; charter dir. Leadership Louisville, 1978-81; dir. WKPC Ch. 15 PBS, Louisville, 1980-85, mem. bd. overseers, 1985-88; active Metro United Way. Recipient Chancellor's medallion for disting. svc. Ind. U. S.E., 1994. Office: Fin Instns Dept 402 W Washington St Rm W066 Indianapolis IN 46204-2763 E-mail: cphillips@dfi.state.in.us.

PHILLIPS, EDWARD JOHN, consulting firm executive; b. Phila., Sept. 8, 1940; s. Harold E. and Mary C. P.; m. Kathleen A. Everett, July 23, 1960; children: Elizabeth J., Edward J. B of Mech. Engring., Villanova U., 1973; MBA, Widener U., 1975. Registered profl. engr., Ill., Kans., Mo., Pa., Ohio; chartered engr., U.K. Tech. ops. mgr. Motorola, Inc., Franklin Park, Ill., 1976-81; v.p. engring. Rival Mfg. Co., Kansas City, Mo., 1981-82; prin., sr. cons. Richard Muther & Assocs., 1982-85; chmn. KANDE, Inc., Overland Park, Kans., 1983-86; pres., CEO Sims Cons. Group Inc., Lancaster, Ohio, 1986—; chmn. bd. dirs., pres. Sims Consulting Group. Bd. dirs. KANDE, Inc., Wilmington, Del. Author: Manufacturing Plant Layout, 1997; contbr. articles to profl. jours. Mem. NSPE, ASME (chmn. material handling divsn. 1989-91, mem. internat. mgmt. com. 1977), MIMechE, Soc. Mfg. Engrs., Tau Beta Pi, Pi Tau Sigma. Office: Sims Cons Group Inc PO Box 968 314 N Columbus St Lancaster OH 43130-3009

PHILLIPS, ELLIOTT HUNTER, lawyer; b. Birmingham, Mich., Feb. 14, 1919; s. Frank Elliott and Gertrude (Zacharias) P.; m. Gail Carolyn Isbey, Apr. 22, 1950; children— Elliott Hunter, Alexandra. A.B. cum laude, Harvard U., 1940, J.D., 1947. Bar: Mich. 1948. Since practiced in, Detroit; ptnr. Hill Lewis (formerly Hill, Lewis, Adams, Goodrich & Tait), 1953-89, of counsel, 1989-96, Clark Hill, 1996—. Chmn. bd. dirs. Detroit & Can. Tunnel Corp.; pres., dir. Detroit and Windsor Subway Co.; mem. Mich. Bd. Accountancy, 1965-73. Contbr. to legal and accounting jours. Chmn. bd. dirs. Southeastern Mich. chpt. ARC; pres., trustee McGregor Fund; trustee Boys Republic, Detroit Inst. for Children, United Way Southeastern Mich., Univ. Liggett Sch.; mem. nat. maj. gifts com. Harvard U., Harvard Pres.'s Assocs., 1974—99; Pres.'s Coun., 1990, mem. overseers com. to visit Law Sch., overseers com. univ. resouces, Mich. chmn. Harvard Coll. Fund; trustee, pres. Ch. Youth Svc.; mem. Detroit Area coun. Boy Scouts Am. Lt. comdr. USNR, 1946. Recipient Spitzley award Detroit Inst. for Children, 1986, Harvard Alumni Assn. Disting. Svc. award, 1991. Fellow Mich. State Bar Found. (life), Am. Bar Found. (life); mem. ABA, State Bar Mich., Detroit Bar Assn., Lincoln's Inn Soc., Soc. Colonial Wars in Mich. (gov. 1999—) and Fla., Country Club Detroit, Detroit Club (pres. 1988-89), Yondotega Club, Grosse Pointe Club, Harvard Ea. Mich. Club (pres. 1955-56, Disting. Alumnus award 1992), Harvard Club N.Y.C., John's Island Club. Episcopalian (vestryman, sr. warden). Home: 193 Ridge Rd Grosse Pointe Farms MI 48236-3554 E-mail: elliottphillips@earthlink.net.

PHILLIPS, FREDERICK FALLEY, architect; b. Evanston, Ill., June 18, 1946; s. David Cook and Katharine Edith (Falley) P.; m. Gay Fraker, 1983 (div. 1993). BA, Lake Forest Coll., 1969; MArch, U. Pa., 1973. Registered architect, Ill., Wis. Draftsman Harry Weese & Assocs., 1974, 75; architect pvt. practice, Chgo., 1976-81; pres. Frederick Phillips and Assocs., 1981—. Bd. dirs. Landmarks Preservation Coun., 1981-85, Chgo. Acad. Sci., 1988-97, Friends of Ceuros de Escazu, Costa Rica, 1992-95; mem. aux. bd. Chgo. Architecture Found., 1975-89. Recipient award Townhouse for Logan Sq. Competition, AIA and Econ. Redevel. Corp. Logan Sq., 1980, Gold medal award Willow St. Houses, Ill. Ind. Masonry Coun., 1981, Silver award for pvt. residence, 1989, Gold medal award pvt. residence, 1994, Three Record Houses awards Archtl. Record, 1990, 95, award 2d Compact House Design Competition, 1990, award of exellence for pvt. residence AIA/Nat. Concrete Masonry Assn., 1992, 98, award pvt. residence Am. Wood Coun., 1993, Honorable mention-Best in Am. Living award Profl. Builders Mag., 1995, Builder's Choice award pvt. residence, Builder Mag., 1996, Jury's Choice award pvt. residence Chgo. Athenaeum, 1996, Am. Architecture award Chgo. Athenaeum. Fellow AIA (Disting. Bldg. award for Willow St. Houses, Chgo. chpt. 1982, for Pinewood Farm 1983, for Pvt. Residences 1990, 92, 98, for Tower Ho., 2001, chmn. task group mfg. housing Nat. Com. Design 1994-96, mem. awards task group 1998—, chmn. 2000-2001); mem. Chgo. ARchtl. Club, Racquet Club (bd. govs. 1983-89), Arts Club, Cliff Dwellers Club (bd. govs. 1985-88). Office: Frederick F Phillips & Assocs 1456 N Dayton St Ste 200 Chicago IL 60622-2636

PHILLIPS, HARVEY, musician, soloist, music educator, arts consultant; b. Aurora, Mo., Dec. 2, 1929; s. Jesse E. and Lottie A. (Chapman) P.; m. Carol A. Dorvel, Feb. 22, 1954; children: Jesse E., Harvey G., Thomas A. Student, U. Mo., 1947-48, Juilliard Sch. Music, 1950-54, Manhattan Sch. Music, 1956-58; MusD (hon.), New England Conservatory of Mu, 1971; HHD (hon.), U. Mo., Columbia, 1987. Founder, v.p. Mentor Music, Inc., N.Y.C., 1958-79; v.p. Wilder Music, Inc., 1964-77, Magellan Music, Inc., N.Y.C., 1971—, Peaslee Music Inc., 1971—; mem. faculty Aspen Sch. Music, summer 1962, U. Wis., summer 1963, Hartt Sch. Music, Hartford, Conn., 1962-64, Mannes Sch. Music, N.Y.C., 1964-65; exec. v.p. Orch. USA, 1962-65; exec. v.p., pers. mgr., tubist Symphony of the Air N.Y.C., 1957-66; v.p. Brass Artists, Inc., N.Y.C., 1964—; adminstrv. asst. to Julius Bloom, Rutgers U., New Brunswick, N.J., 1966-67; v.p. fin. affairs New Englandonservatory of Music, Boston, 1967-71; mem. faculty Sch. Music, Ind. U., Bloomington, 1971-94, disting. prof. music, trustee, 1979, disting. prof. emeritus, 1994. Adv. bd. Am. Brass Chamber Music, Inc., 1971—; chmn. bd. Summit Brass/Keystone Brass Inst., 1985—92, Rafael Mendez Brass Inst., 1993—; cons. Margun Music, Inc., 1977—; bd. dirs. Summit Brass. Brass coach Festival at Sandpoint, Idaho, 1986-94; mem. faculty Joven Orch., Spain, 1987-94, Festival Casal Orch., San Juan, P.R., 1964-76; dir. 1st Internat. Tuba Symposium Workshop, 1973, Brass-Wind Music Studios, Carnegie Hall, N.Y.C., 1961-67; tubist, King Bros. Circus Band, 1947, Ringling Bros. & Barnum & Bailey Circus Band, 1948-50, N.Y.C. Ballet Orch., 1951-71, N.Y.C. Opera Orch., 1951-62, Voice of Firestone Orch., 1951-53, Sauter-Finegan Orch., 1952-53, Band of Am., 1952-54, NBC Opera Orch., 1956-65, Bell Tel. Hour Orch., 1956-66, Goldman Band, 1957-62; founding mem., tubist N.Y. Brass Quintet, 1954-67; condr., co-prodr. Burke-Phillips All Star Concert Band, 1960-62; co-founder, tubist Matteson-Phillips Tubajazz Consort, 1976—; founding mem. TubaShop Quartet, 1996—; rec. artist Crest Records, 1958-78—; originator Octubafest, TubaChristmas, Tubasantas, Tubajazz, TubaEaster, Tubacompany, Summertubafest; exec. editor Instrumentalist mag., 1986-96, bd. advisors, 1996—. Founder, pres. Harvey Phillips Found., Inc., N.Y.C., 1977—; bd. dirs. Mid-Am. Festival of the Arts, 1982-90, Bloomington Area Arts Coun., 1983-90; judge 1st Internt. tuba competition of CIEM Internat. Competition for Musical Performers, Geneva, 1991. Served with U.S. Army Field Band, 1955-56. Recipient Disting. Svc. to Music award Kappa Kappa Psi, 1978, Cmty. Svc. award City of Bloomington, 1978, Nat. Assn. Jazz Educators award, 1977, 78, Nat. Music Conf. award, 1977, T.U.B.A. award, 1978, MI Hummel The Tuba Player award, 1990, Disting. Achievement award Ednl. Press Assn. Am., 1991, Mentor Ideal award Assn. Concert Bands, 1994, Lifetime Achievement award United Music Instruments, 1995, Sudler award medal of the Order of Merit Sousa Found., 1995, Summit Brass Outstanding Svc. and Support Internat. Brassfest, 1995, Orpheus award Phi Mu Alpha Sinfonia, 1997; elected to Acad. Wind and Percussion Arts Nat. Band Assn., 1995; recipient Edwin Franko Goldman citation Am. Bandmasters Assn., 1996, Devel. of Mus. Artistry and Opportunities for Future Generations award Colonial Euphonium Tuba Inst., 1998, Lifetime Achievement award Rafael Mendez Brass Inst., 1998, Platinum Piston Lifetime Achievement award, U. Ga., 1999; Harvey Phillips Day proclaimed New England Conservatory Music, 1971, Harvey Phillips Day proclaimed Marionville, Mo. Bicentennial, 1976, Harvey Phillips Weekend Gov. of Mo., 1982; named hon. mem. U.S. Army Band, 1984. Mem. Am. Fedn. Musicians, Tubists Universal Brotherhood Assn. (bd. advs. 1973—, pres. 1984-87, hon.), Hoagy Carmichael Jazz Soc. (founder, acting pres. 1983—), Tau Beta Sigma, Phi Mu Alpha Sinfonia (Orpheus award 1997), Kappa Gamma Psi. Home and Office: Tubaranch 4769 S Harrell Rd Bloomington IN 47401-9028 Office: Sch of Music Ind U Bloomington IN 47405 E-mail: philliph@indiana.edu.

PHILLIPS, JAMES EDGAR, lawyer; b. N.Y.C., Aug. 30, 1947; s. Jack Louis Phillips and Jacqueline (Kasper) Ehrman; children: Zachary J., Mark H. BA, Boston U., 1971; JD, Case Western Reserve U., 1975. Bar: Ohio 1975, U.S. Supreme Ct. 1977, U.S. Dist. Ct. (so. dist.) 1978, U.S. Ct. Appeals (6th cir.) 1981, U.S. Dist. Ct. (no. dist.) 1982. Asst. prosecutor Franklin County Prosecutor Office, Columbus, Ohio, 1975-77, sr. asst. prosecutor, 1977-79; assoc. Vorys, Sater, Seymour & Pease, 1979-84, ptnr., 1984—; spl. prosecutor State of Ohio, 1993—. Gen. counsel Nat. Fraternal Order of Police, Washington, 1987—, Conrail Police #1, U.S. Postal Police #2; mem. Bd. Profl. Law Enforcement Certification; pres. Ohio Ctr. for Law-Related Edn., 1985-95; mem. Wong Sun Soc., 1997—. Author: Civil Recovery in Ohio, 1986, Collective Bargaining in the Pub. Sector, 1988; editor Bar Briefs; contbr. articles Jours., 1987-89. Fellow Ohio Bar Found., Columbus Bar Found., Ohio Bar Assn. (chmn. com. law-related edn. 1982-86), Columbus Bar Assn., Am. Judicature Soc., Sixth Cir. Jud. Conf. (life); bd. dirs. Ohio Assn. Criminal Defense Lawyers. Office: Vorys Sater Seymour & Pease PO Box 1008 52 E Gay St Columbus OH 43215-3161 E-mail: phillips@vssp.com.

PHILLIPS, JEANNE See VAN BUREN, ABIGAIL

PHILLIPS, JOHN, radio personality; b. Cin. Radio host, traffic reporter WEBN, Cin., 1983—. Office: WEBN 1111 St Gregory St Cincinnati OH 45202*

PHILLIPS, RONALD LEWIS, plant geneticist, educator; b. Huntington County, Ind., Jan. 1, 1940; s. Philemon Lewis and Louise Alpha (Walker) P.; m. Judith Lee Lind, Aug. 19, 1962; children: Brett, Angela. B.S. in Crop Sci., Purdue U., 1961, M.S. in Plant Breeding and Genetics, 1963, D (hon.), 2000; Ph.D. in Genetics, U. Minn., 1966; postgrad., Cornell U., 1966-67. Research and teaching asst. Purdue U., 1961-62; research and teaching asst. U. Minn., St. Paul, 1962-66, research assoc., 1967-68, asst. prof., 1968-72, assoc. prof., 1972-76, prof. genetics and plant breeding, 1976-93, Regents prof., 1993—, McKnight presdl. chair in Genomics, 2000—. Program dir. Competitive Rsch. Grants Office, USDA, Washington, 1979; mem. adv. grant panels NSF, USDA, AID; chmn. Gordon Conf. on Plant Cell and Tissue Culture, 1985; mem. sci. adv. coun. U. Calif. Plant Gene Expression Ctr., Berkeley, 1986-93, chair, 1992-93; vis. prof., Italy, 1981, Can., 1983, China, 1986, Japan, 1990, Morocco, 1996; dir. Plant Molecular Genetics Inst., 1991-94; chief scientist USDA, 1996-98; trustee Biol. Stain Commn.; mem. Nat. Plant Genetic Resources Bd.; mem. editl. bd. Proc. Nat. Acad. Sci., U.S., 1996-98; dir. Ctr. Microbial and Plant Genomics, 2000—. Co-editor: Cytogenetics, 1977, Molecular Genetic Modification of Eucaryotes, 1977, Molecular Biology of Plants, 1979, The Plant Seed: Development, Preservation and Germination, 1979, Genetic Improvement of Crops: Emergent Techniques, 1980, DNA-Based Markers in Plants, 1994, 2d edit., 2001; assoc. editor: Genetics, 1978-81, Can. Jour. Genetics and Cytology and Genome, 1985-90; mem. editl. bd. Maydica, 1978—, In Vitro Cellular and Devel. Biology, 1988-92, Cell Culture and Somatic Cell Genetics of Plants, 1983-91, Elaeis, 1994—, Proc. NAS; contbr. chpts. to Maize Breeding and Genetics, 1978, Staining Procedures, 1981, Chromosome Structure and Function, 1987, Corn and Corn Improvement, 1988, Plant Transposable Elements, 1988, Chromosome Engring. in Plants, 1991, Maize Handbook, 1994; contbr. sci. articles to profl. jours. Mem. chmn. coun. on ministries, lay leader United Meth. Ch., 1968, dir. Project AgGrad, 1983—; Cub Scout Pack co-chmn. Boy Scouts Am., 1976-77; judge Minn. Regional and State Sci. Fair, 1970-80. Recipient Purdue Agrl. Alumni Achievement award, 1961, Purdue Disting. Agrl. Alumni award, 1993; NSF fellow, 1961; NIH fellow, 1966-67; recipient Northrup King Oustanding Faculty Performance award, 1985, Crop Sci. Rsch. award, 1988, DeKalb Genetics Crop Sci. Disting. Career award, 1997. Fellow AAAS (chair-elect sect. D), Am. Soc. Agronomy, Crop Sci. Soc. Am. (awards com., divsn. chmn., bd. rep. 1988-91, pres.-elect 1998-99, pres. 1999-2000, past pres. 2000-01); mem. NAS (chair sect. 62), Genetics Soc. Am., Am. Soc. Agronomy (award student sect., Caleb-Dorr award), Sigma Xi, Gamma Alpha (nat. treas.), Gamma Sigma Delta (award of merit 1994), Alpha Zeta. Office: U Minn Dpt Agronomy-Plant Genetics Saint Paul MN 55108 E-mail: phill005@umn.edu.

PHILLIPS, SIDNEY FREDERICK, gastroenterologist, educator; b. Melbourne, Australia, Sept. 4, 1933; s. Clifford and Eileen Frances (Fitch) P.; m. Decima Honora Jones, Mar. 29, 1957; children: Penelope Jane, Nichola Margaret, David Sidney. M.B.B.S., U. Melbourne, 1956, M.D., 1961. Resident med. officer Royal Melbourne Hosp., 1957-61, asst. sub-dean clin. sch., 1961-62; research asso. Central Middlesex Hosp., London, 1962-63; rsch. assoc. Mayo Clinic, Rochester, Minn., 1963-66, cons. in gastroenterology, 1966-2000; prof. medicine Mayo Med. Sch., 1976-2000, prof. medicine emeritus, 2000—, dir. gastroenterology rsch. unit, 1977-94; program dir. Mayo Gen. Clin. Rsch. Ctr., 1974-87; dir. Mayo Digestive Diseases Core Ctr., 1984-90; Karl F. and Marjory Hasselman prof. rsch., 1994-2000. Editor: Digestive Diseases and Sciences, 1977-82, Gastroenterology International, 1990-95; sr. assoc. editor: Gastroenterology, 1991-96; contbr. chpts. to books, articles to profl. jours. Fellow ACP, Royal Coll. Physicians, Royal Australian Coll. Physicians; mem. Am. Motility Soc. (pres. 1994-96), Am. Soc. Clin. Investigation (emeritus), Gastroenterology Soc. Australia (hon.), Am. Gastroenterology Assn. Assn. Am. Physicians, Brit. Soc. Gastroenterology (hon.). Home: 1207 19th Ave NE Rochester MN 55906-4317 Office: St Mary's Hosp Gastroenterology Unit 200 1st St SW Rochester MN 55905-0001 E-mail: phillips.sidney@mayo.edu.

PHILLIPS, T. STEPHEN, lawyer; b. Tennyson, Ind., Oct. 1, 1941; AB, DePauw U., 1963; LLB, Duke U., 1966. Bar: Ohio 1966, Ind. 1967. Assoc. Frost & Jacobs, Cin., 1966-72, ptnr., 1972—. Adj. prof. North Ky. U. Chase Coll. Law, Highland Hights, 1983—. Contbg. editor: Ohio Probate Practice (Addams and Hosford), Page on Wills. Trustee Spring Grove Cemetery, Cin. Methodist. Office: Frost & Jacobs 2500 PNC Ctr 201 E 5th St Ste 2500 Cincinnati OH 45202-4182

PHILLIPS, TED, professional sports team executive; b. Oneida, NY, June 27, 1957; m. Katie Phillips; children: Matthew, Max, Frank. BBA in Acctg., U. Notre Dame, 1983; M Mtkg. and Mgmt., Northwestern U., 1989. Auditor, tax acct. Ernst & Whinney (now Ernst & Young), 1979—83; contr. Chgo. Bears , 1983—87, dir. fin., 1993, v.p. ops., 1993, CEO. Office: 100 Football Dr Lake Forest IL 60045

PHILLIPS, THOMAS JOHN, lawyer; b. Mpls., Nov. 24, 1948; BA, U. Minn., 1970; JD, U. Utah, 1973; LLM in Taxation, NYU, 1974. Bar: Wis. 1974. Ptnr. Quarles & Brady, Milw.; law clk. Utah Supreme Ct., Salt Lake City, 1972-73. Co-author: Wisconsin Limited Liability Company Forms and Practice Manual, 1999. Mem. ABA (corp. tax com. tax sect.), Wis. Bar Assn., Profl. Inst. Taxation, Mil. Tax Club, North Shore Country Club, Order of Coif. Avocations: gardening, golf, hockey, jogging, racquetball. Office: 411 E Wisconsin Ave Ste 2550 Milwaukee WI 53202-4409

PHILLIS, JOHN WHITFIELD, physiologist, educator; b. Port of Spain, Trinidad, Apr. 1, 1936; came to U.S., 1981; s. Ernest and Sarah Anne (Glover) P.; m. Pamela Julie Popple, 1958 (div. 1968); children: David,

Simon, Susan; m. Shane Beverly Wright, Jan. 24, 1969. B in Vet. Sci., Sydney (Australia) U., 1958, D in Vet. Sci., 1976; PhD, Australian Nat. U., Canberra, 1961; DSc, Monash U., Melbourne, Australia, 1970. Lectr./sr. Monash U., 1963-69; vis. prof. Ind. U., Indpls., 1969; prof. physiology, assoc. dean rsch. U. Man., Winnipeg, Can., 1970-73; prof., chmn. dept. physiology U. Sask., Saskatoon, Can., 1973-81, asst. dean rsch. Can., 1973-75; prof. physiology Wayne State U., Detroit, 1981—, chmn. dept. physiology, 1981-97. Mem. scholarship and grants com. Can. Med. Rsch. Coun., Ottawa, Ont., 1973-79; mem. sci. adv. bd. Dystonia Med. Rsch. Found., Beverly Hills, Calif., 1980-85, Curtis Rsch. Inst., Risingsun, Ohio, 1998-2000; mem. sci. adv. panel World Soc. for Protection of Animals, 1982-98; Wellcome vis. prof. Tulane U., 1986; mem. acad. scholars Wayne State U., 1995. Author: Pharmacology of Synapses, 1970; editor: Veterinary Physiology, 1976, Physiology and Pharmacology of Adenosine Derivatives, 1983, Adenosine and Adenine Nucleotides as Regulators of Cellular Function, 1991, The Regulation of Cerebral Blood Flow, 1993, Novel Therapies for CNS Injuries: Rationales and Results, 1996; editor Can. Jour. Physiology and Pharmacology, 1978-81, Progress in Neurobiology, 1973-97. Mem. grants com. Am. Heart Assn. of Mich., 1985-90, mem. rsch. coun., 1991-92, mem. rsch. forum com., 1991-96, chair, 1992-93; mem. Brain/Stroke Consortium Study Group, Am. Heart Assn., 1998. Wellcome fellow London, 1961-62; Can. Med. Rsch. Coun. grantee, 1970-81, rsch. prof., 1980; NIH grantee, 1983-2000. Mem. Brit. Pharmacol. Soc., Physiol. Soc., Am. Physiol. Soc., Soc. Neurosci., Internat. Brain Rsch. Orgn. Office: Wayne State U Dept Physiology 540 E Canfield St Detroit MI 48201-1928 E-mail: phillis@med.wayne.edu.

PHINNEY, WILLIAM CHARLES, retired geologist; b. South Portland, Maine, Nov. 16, 1930; s. Clement Woodbridge and Margaret Florence (Foster) P.; m. Colleen Dorothy Murphy, May 31, 1953; children— Glenn, Duane, John, Marla. B.S., MIT, 1953, M.S., 1956, Ph.D., 1959. Faculty geology U. Minn., 1959-70; chief geology br. NASA Lyndon B. Johnson Space Center, Houston, 1970-82, chief planetology br., 1982-89, ret., 1994. NASA prin. investigator lunar samples. Contbr. articles to profl. jours. Served with C.E. AUS, 1953-55. Recipient NASA Exceptional Sci. Achievement medal, 1972, NASA Cert. of Commendation, 1987; NASA rsch. grantee, 1972-94, NSF rsch. grantee, 1960-70. Mem. Am. Geophys. Union, AAAS, Mineral. Soc. Am., Geol. Soc. Am., Minn. Acad. Sci. (dir.), Sigma Xi. Home: 18063 Judicial Way S Lakeville MN 55044-8895

PHIPPS, JOHN RANDOLPH, retired army officer; b. Kansas, Ill, May 16, 1919; s. Charles Winslow and Kelsey Ethel (Torrence) P.; m. Pauline M. Prunty, Feb. 8, 1946; children: Charles W., Kelsey J. Phipps-Selander. B.S. in Econs. with honors, U. Ill., 1941; M.P.A., Sangamon State U., 1976; assoc. course, Command and Gen. Staff Coll., 1959, nuclear weapons employment course, 1962; course, U.S. Army War Coll., 1973, U.S. Nat. Def. U., 1978. Owner, operator chain shoe stores in, Eastern Ill., 1946-70; commd. 2d lt. F.A. U.S. Army, 1941, advanced through grades to capt., 1943; service in Philippines and Japan; discharged as maj., 1946; organizer, comdr. Co. E, 130th Inf., Ill.; N.G., Mattoon, 1947, comdg. officer 2d Bn., 130th Inf., 1951, lt. col. 2d Bn., 130th Inf., 1951; called to fed. service, 1952; adv. (29th Regt., 9th Republic of Korea Div.), 1952-53; comdr. officer 1st Bn., 130th Inf., Ill. N.G., 1954, col., 1959; comdg. officer 2d Brigade, 33d Div., 1963-67; asst. div. comdr. 33d Inf. Div., 1967, brig. gen., 1967; comdr. 33d Inf. Brigade, Chgo., 1967-70, Ill. Emergency Ops. Hdqrs., 1970, asst. adj. gen. Ill., 1970-77, acting adj. gen., 1977-78, adj. gen., 1978, promoted to maj. gen., 1978, now maj. gen. ret. Decorated Silver Star, Bronze Star, Disting. Service medal, Combat Infantry Badge, Army Disting. Service medal Ill., various Philippine and Korean decorations; State of Ill. Long and Honorable Service medal. Mem. VFW, Adj. Gens. Assn. U.S., N.G. Assn. U.S., N.G. Assn. Ill., Am. Legion, Amvets. Home: 100 Wabash Ave Mattoon IL 61938-4524 Office: Phipps 100 Wabash Ave Mattoon IL 61938-4524

PIASECKI, DAVID ALAN, social studies educator; b. Marquette, Mich., Sept. 14, 1956; s. Vincent Jerome and Irene Beatrice (Tousinant) P.; m. Linda Marie Anderson Piasecki, Aug. 2, 1985; children: Andrew Jacob, Zachary David. BA, No. Mich. U., 1978, MA, 1982, MA, 1984. Cert. 7-12 Social Studies, Sch. Adminstrn. and Prin. Supt., Alaska. Social studies tchr. Galena (Alaska) City Sch., 1978-80, Tanana (Alaska) H.S., 1980-85, activities dir., 1984-85; social studies tchr. Denali Borough Sch. Dist., Healy, Alaska, 1985-99; prin. Upsala (Minn.) H.S., 1999—. Student Taft Seminar For Tchrs., U. Alaska. Named Alaska Tchr. of Yr., Dept. Edn., Juneau and Anchorage, 1992, Railbelt Sch. Dist. Tchr. of Yr., NEA, Healy, 1992; recipient Secondary Econ. award Alaska Coun. on Econ. Edn., Fairbanks, Alaska, 1988, 91-92. Mem. NEA, Holy Mary of Guadalupe Cath. Ch., Nat. Alaska Coun. on Social Studies, Alaska Geographic Alliance, Nat. Coun. for Geographic Edn. Democrat. Roman catholic. Avocations: cross county skiing, basketball, tennis, hunting, travel. Home: PO Box 11 Upsala MN 56384-0011 Office: Upsala HS 415 S Main St PO Box 190 Upsala MN 56384-0190

PICHLER, JOSEPH ANTON, food products executive; b. St. Louis, Oct. 3, 1939; s. Anton Dominick and Anita Marie (Hughes) P.; m. Susan Ellen Eyerly, Dec. 27, 1962; children: Gretchen, Christopher, Rebecca, Josh. BBA, U. Notre Dame, 1961; MBA, U. Chgo., 1963, PhD, 1966. Asst. prof. bus. U. Kans., 1964-68, assoc. prof., 1968-73, prof., 1973-80; dean U. Kans. Sch. Bus., 1974-80; exec. v.p. Dillon Cos. Inc., 1980-82, pres., 1982-86; exec. v.p. Kroger Co., Cin., 1985-86, pres., COO, 1986-90, pres., CEO, 1990, chmn., CEO, 1990—, also bd. dirs. Spl. asst. to asst. sec. for manpower U.S. Dept. Labor, 1968-70; chmn. Kans. Manpower Svcs. Coun., 1974-78; bd. dirs. Cin. Milacron Inc., Federated Dept. Stores, Inc., Catalyst. Author: (with Joseph McGuire) Inequality: The Poor and the Rich in America, 1969; contbg. author: Creativity and Innovation in Manpower Research and Action Programs, 1970, Contemporary Management: Issues and Viewpoints, 1973, Institutional Issues in Public Accounting, 1974, Co-Creation and Capitalism: John Paul II's Laborem Exercens, 1983; co-editor, contbg. author: Ethics, Free Enterprise, and Public Policy, 1978; contbr. articles to profl. jours. Bd. dirs. Cin. Opera, 1987-96, adv. mem., 1996—; nat. bd. dirs. Boys Hope, 1983-96, Tougaloo Coll., 1986—; mem. Nat. Alliance of Bus. Bd., 1988-95, chmn., 1991-93; mem. fellow adv. com. Woodrow Wilson Found., 1990-93; mem. adv. bd. Salvation Army Sch. for Officers Tng., 1994-2000; mem. Cin. Bus. Com., 1991—, chmn., 1997-98. Recipient Disting. Svc. citation U. Kans., 1992, Disting. Svc. award Nat. Conf. Cmty. Justice, 2000; Woodrow Wilson fellow, Ford Found. fellow, Standard Oil Indsl. Rels. fellow, 1966; named Disting. Alumnus U. Chgo., 1994, William Booth award The Salvation Army, 1998, Horatio Alger award, 1999. Mem.: Greater Cin. C. of C. (trustee), Catalyst Bd., Bus. Roundtable, Comml. Club of Cin., Queen City Club. Office: Kroger Co 1014 Vine St Cincinnati OH 45202-1100

PICK, RUTH, research scientist, physician, educator; b. Carlsbad, Bohemia, Czechoslovakia, Nov. 13, 1913; came to U.S., 1949; d. Arthur and Paula (Lenk) Holub; m. Alfred Pick, May 28, 1938 (dec. Jan. 1982). M.D., German U., 1938. Resident in medicine Priessnitz Hosp., Graefenberg, Czechoslovakia, 1938; resident in psychiatry Hosp. Veleslavin, Prague, Czechoslovakia, 1945-47; extern in pathology State Hosp. Motol, 1948; research fellow cardiovascular dept. Michael Reese Hosp. & Med. Ctr., Chgo., 1949-50, research assoc., 1950-58, asst. dir., 1958-66, sr. investigator, 1966-71, chief exptl. atherosclerosis lab., 1971-83, attending physician div. cardiovascular diseases dept. medicine, 1964-98, chief cardiac morphology lab. Cardiovascular Inst., 1983-95; prof. emeritus medicine and pathology U. Chgo., 1973-98; part time rsch. assoc. Cardiovascular Inst., 1995-98, emeritus, 1998—. Mem. research council Chgo. Heart Assn., 1979-84, bd. govs., 1983, pres., 1985-86. Fellow Am. Heart Assn. (coun. on arteriosclerosis, coun. on circulation, established investigator), AAAS; mem. Am. Assn. Pathologists and Bacteriologists, Chgo. Heart Assn. (past pres. 1985-86), Am. Fedn. Clin. rsch., Am. Physiol. Soc., Ctrl. Soc. Clin. Rsch. Home: 400 E Randolph St Chicago IL 60601-7329 Office: Michael Reese Hosp and Med Ctr 2929 S Ellis Ave Chicago IL 60616-3395 E-mail: rpick2@compuserve.com.

PICKARD, WILLIAM FRANK, plastics company executive; b. LaGrange, Ga., Jan. 28, 1941; s. William H. and Victoria (Woodward) P. AS, Mott Community Coll., 1962; BS, Western Mich. U., 1964; MSW, U. Mich., 1965; PhD, Ohio State U., 1971; PhD in Bus. Adminstrn. (hon.), Cleary Coll., 1980. Dir. employment and edn. Urban League Cleve., 1965-67; exec. dir. NAACP, Cleve., 1967-69; assoc. dir. dept. urban studies Cleve. State U., 1971-72; assoc. prof. Wayne State U., Detroit, 1972-74; owner, operator McDonald's Restaurants, 1971—; chmn., chief exec. officer Regal Plastics, Roseville, Mich., 1985—. Vis. lectr. Cleve. State U., U. Chgo., Hiram Coll., U. Toledo, U. Mich., Case Western Res. U., Ohio State U., Wayne County Community Coll., McDonald's Hamburger U.; participant mgmt. seminar Case Western Res. U., Greater Cleve. Associated Found. and Rockefeller Found., 1968; chmn. Gov.'s adv. com. on minority bus., pres. 1976; bd. dirs. First Ind. Nat. Bank, Mich. Nat. Bank Corp., Farmington Hills. Mem. Pres.-elect Ronald Regan's transition team to SBA; chmn. econ. devel. com. Nat. Black Rep. Council, 1978, bd. dirs. com. to elect Gov. Ronald Reagan Pres., 1980, chmn. congl. liaison com., 1982; chmn. Mich. Reps. Urban Campaign to elect Gov. Reagan Pres., 1980; vice chmn. Mich. Rep. State Com., 1981; bd. control Grand Valley State Coll., Allendale, Mich.; bd. dirs. Oakwood Hosp., Kirkwood Gen. Hosp., Detroit, Detroit Black Causes, Detroit Econ. Devel. Corp., 1977, Nat. Minority Purchasing Council, Washington, Detroit Urban League, vice chmn.; appointed by Pres. Ronald Regan, and confirmed by U.S. Senate Chmn. of African Devel. Found., 1983. Named one of Ten Outstanding Young Men Cleve., Jaycees, 1969; Alice W. Gault schlor, 1962-63; Nat. Urban League fellow, 1964. Mem. Booker T. Washington Bus. Assn., NAACP, Jaycees, Alpha Phi Alpha. Home: 335 Pine Ridge Dr Bloomfield Hills MI 48304-2140 Office: 2990 W Grand Blvd Ste 15M Detroit MI 48202-3041

PICKERING, CHARLES W., JR. congressman; b. Laurel, Ms., Aug. 10, 1963; m. Leisha Jane Prather; children: Will, Ross, Jackson, Asher. BA in Bus. Adminstrn., U. Miss., 1986; MBA, Baylor U. Legis. asst. to U.S. Senator Trent Lott; apptd. to USDA; mem. U.S. Congress from 3d Mich. dist., 1996—. Mem. energy and commerce com., agriculture com., livestock, dairy and poultry subcom., forestry, resource conservation, rsch. subcom., Transp. and Infrastructure com., vice chair surface transp. subcom., aviation subcom., Sci. com., vice chair basic rsch. subcom., space subcom.; asst. minority whip; mem. House Rep. Policy com.; mem. exec. com. Nat. Rep. Congrl. com. Office: US House of Reps 427 Cannon House Office Bldg Washington DC 20515-0001

PICKLE, ROBERT DOUGLAS, lawyer, footwear industry executive; b. Knoxville, Tenn., May 22, 1937; s. Robert Lee and Beatrice Jewel (Douglas) P.; m. Rosemary Elaine Noser, May 9, 1964. AA summa cum laude, Schreiner Mil. Coll., Kerrville, Tex., 1957; BSBA magna cum laude, U. Tenn., 1959, JD, 1961; honor grad. seminar, Nat. Def. U., 1979; hon. grad., U.S. Army JAG Sch., U.S. Army Logistics Mgmt. Sch.; grad., U.S. Army Inf. Sch., Army Command-Gen. Staff Coll. Bar: Tenn. 1961, Mo. 1964, U.S. Ct. Mil. Appeals 1962, U.S. Supreme Ct. 1970. Atty. Brown Shoe Co., Inc., St. Louis, 1963-69, asst. sec., atty., 1969-74, sec., gen. counsel, 1974-85; v.p., gen. counsel, corp. sec. Brown Shoe Co., Inc. (formerly Brown Group, Inc.), 1985—. Indiv. mobilization augmentee, asst. army judge adv. gen. civil law The Pentagon, Washington, 1984-89. Provisional judge Municipal Ct., Clayton, Mo., summer 1972; chmn. Clayton Region attys. sect., profl. div. United Fund Greater St. Louis Campaign, 1972-73, team capt., 1974-78; chmn. City of Clayton Parks and Recreation Commn., 1985-87; liaison admissions officer, regional and state coordinator U.S. Mil. Acad., 1980—. Col. JAGC, U.S. Army, 1961-63. Decorated Meritorious Svc. medal; 1st U. Tenn. Law Coll. John W Green law scholar; recipient Cold War Recognition cert. Sec. Def. Fellow Harry S. Truman Meml. Library; mem. ABA, Tenn. Bar Assn., Mo. Bar Assn., St. Louis County Bar Assn., Bar Assn. Met. St. Louis, St. Louis Bar Found. (bd. dirs. 1979-81), Am. Corp. Counsel Assn., Am. Soc. Corp. Secs. (treas. St. Louis regional group 1976-77, sec. 1977-78, v.p. 1978-79, pres., mem. Quarter-Century Club 1979-80), U. Tenn. Gen. Alumni Assn. (pres., bd. dirs. St. Louis chpt. 1974-76, 80-84, bd. govs. 1982-89), U.S. Trademark Assn. (bd. dirs. 1978-82), Tenn. Soc. St. Louis (bd. dirs. 1980-88, treas., sec., v.p. 1984-87, pres. 1987-88), Smithsonian Nat. Assocs., World Affairs Coun. St. Louis, Inc., Am. Legion, University Club (v.p., sec. St. Louis chpt. 1976-81, bd. dirs. 1976-81), Stadium Club, West Point Soc. St. Louis (hon. mem., bd. dirs. 1992—), Conf. Bd. (coun. chief legal officers), Fontbonne Coll. Pres.'s Assocs. (O'Hara and Tower Socs), St. Louis U. Billiken Club, St. Louis U. DuBourg Soc. (hon. v.p.). Republican. Presbyterian. Avocations: reading, spectator sports. Home: 214 Topton Way Saint Louis MO 63105-3638 Office: Brown Shoe Co Inc 8300 Maryland Ave Saint Louis MO 63105-3645 E-mail: rpickle@brownshoe.com.

PICKLEMAN, JACK R. surgeon; MD, McGill U., Montreal, Que., Can., 1964. Intern Royal Victoria Hosp., Montreal, Que., Can., 1964-65; resident in surgery U. Chgo. Med. Ctr., 1967-73; asst. prof. surgery Loyola U., Chgo., 1973-77, assoc. prof. surgery, 1977-81, prof., chief gen. surgery, 1981—. Attending physician Loyola Med. Ctr., Maywood, Ill. Mem. ACS. Office: Loyola U Med Ctr 2160 S 1st Ave Maywood IL 60153-3304

PIDERIT, JOHN J. university educator; b. N.Y.C., Feb. 26, 1944; BA in Math. and Philosophy magna cum laude, Fordham U., 1967; Lic. in Sacred Theology cum laude, Philosophische und Theologische Hochschule Sankt Georgen, Frankfurt, West Germany, 1971; MPhil, Oxford U., 1974; MA, PhD in Econ., Princeton U., 1979. Ordained Jesuit priest Roman Cath. Ch., 1971. Tchr. math. Regis H.S., N.Y.C., 1967-68; asst. campus minister Fordham U., 1971-72, Princeton U., 1975-78, preceptor, 1976-77; asst. chairperson grad. studies Fordham U., 1984-88, dir. program internat. polit. econ. and devel., 1981-83, 87-88, asst. chairperson dept. econs., 1979-82, 88-89, asst. prof. econs., 1978-89, assoc. prof. econs., 1989-90; corp. v.p. Marquette U., 1990-93; pres. Loyola U. Chgo., 1993—. Vis. fellow Woodstock Theol. Ctr., Washington, summer 1982; sabbatical Santa Clara U., 1989-90; master Queen's Ct. Residential Coll., 1987-90; chmn. responsible investment com. N.Y. province SJ, 1986-88, mem. fin. com., 1986-88; mem. joint commn. govtl. rels. of Am. Coun. Edn., 1994—; mem. exec. com. Nat. Planning Com. Jesuit Assembly '89, 1988-90. Contbr. articles to profl. jours. Founder, moderator Friends of Loyola, 1987-90; pres. Univ. Neighborhood Housing Corp., 1986-90, Maroon Enterprises, Inc., 1986-90; trustee Canisius Coll., Buffalo, 1983-88, 89-94, Loyola Marymount U., L.A., 1996—, John Carroll U., University Heights, Ohio, 1996—; bd. dirs. Corp. Cmty. Schs. of Am., 1993—; promoter PIVOT H.S. and Middle Sch. with Milw. Pub. Schs., 1990-93; mem. Greater Milw. Edn. Trust, 1990-93; mem. steering com., chair edn. task force Milw. Cmty. Traffic Safety Com., 1991-93; mem. steering com. Libr. Literacy Soc. Milw., 1991-93; mem. scholarship com. Knitworkers Union Local 155, N.Y.C., 1982-90; mem. Princeton Schs. Com. N.Y. Region, 1985-88, chmn. Federation of Indp. Colls. and Univs., 1999—. Mellon grantee Fordham U., summer 1983, summer grantee Fordham U., 1979, Princeton U. fellow, 1974-78. Office: Loyola U Chgo 820 N Michigan Ave Chicago IL 60611-2147

PIECEWICZ, WALTER MICHAEL, lawyer; b. Concord, Mass., Jan. 27, 1948; s. Benjamin Michael and Cecelia (Makuc) P.; m. Anne T. Mikolajczyk, Oct. 28, 1978; children: Tiffany Anne, Stephanie Marie. AB magna cum laude, Colgate U., 1970; JD, Columbia U., 1973. Bar: Ill. 1973. Mem. firm Peterson & Ross, Chgo., 1987—. Bd. dirs. No. Data Systems, Inc., Steiner Co., Inc., Arrow Pattern & Foundry Co., Inc., Steiner Trust Co. Mem. ABA, Ill. Bar Assn., Chgo. Bar Assn., Chgo. Estate Planning Coun., Internat. Bus. Coun. Midwest, Phi Beta Kappa. Roman Catholic. Office: Peterson & Ross 200 E Randolph St Ste 7300 Chicago IL 60601-7012

PIEKARSKI, VICTOR J. lawyer; b. Lawrence, Mass., Feb. 20, 1950; BA cum laude, Boston Coll., 1971; MBA, U. Chgo., 1978; JD cum laude, Northwestern U., 1974. Bar: Ill. 1974, U.S. Ct. Appeals (7th cir.) 1977, U.S. Supreme Ct. 1978. Ptnr. Querrey & Harrow Ltd., Chgo., to 1997, O'Hagan, Smith and Amundsen, LLC, Chgo., 1997—. Mem. ABA, Def. Rsch. Inst. Office: O'Hagan Smith and Amundsen LLC 150 N Michigan Ave Ste 3300 Chicago IL 60601-7586 E-mail: vpiekarski@osalaw.com.

PIEPER, HEINZ PAUL, physiology educator; b. Wuppertal, Germany, Mar. 24, 1920; came to U.S., 1957, naturalized, 1963; s. Heinrich Ludwig and Agnes Marie (Koehler) P.; m. Rose Irmgard Hackl, Apr. 23, 1945. M.D., U. Munich, Germany, 1948. Resident 2d Med. Clinic, U. Munich, 1948-50, asst. prof. dept. physiology, 1950-57, Coll. Medicine, Ohio State U., Columbus, 1957-60, assoc. prof., 1960-68, prof., 1968—, chmn. dept. physiology, 1974-85, prof. emeritus, 1985—. Established investigator Am. Heart Assn., 1962-67 Mem. editorial bd.: Am. Jour. Physiology, 1973-82; contbr. articles on cardiovascular physiology to profl. jours. Mem. Am. Physiol. Soc., Ohio Acad. Scis., Sigma Xi. Home: 2206 SE 36th St Cape Coral FL 33904-4434 Office: Ohio State U Coll Medicine 333 W 10th Ave Columbus OH 43210-1239

PIEPHO, ROBERT WALTER, pharmacy educator, researcher; b. Chgo., July 31, 1942; s. Walter August and Irene Elizabeth (Huybrecht) Apfel; m. Mary Lee Wilson, Dec. 10, 1981. BS in Pharmacy, U. Ill.-Chgo., 1965; PhD in Pharmacology, Loyola U., Maywood, Ill., 1972. Registered pharmacist, Ill., Colo. Assoc. prof. U. Nebr. Med. Ctr., Omaha, 1970-78; prof. pharmacy, assoc. dean Sch. Pharmacy U. Colo., Denver, 1978-86; prof. pharmacol., dean U. Mo. Sch. Pharmacy, Kansas City, 1987—. Contbr. articles to profl. jours., chpts. to books. Pres. Club Monaco Homeowners Assn., Denver, 1980-82. Named Outstanding Tchr. U. Nebr. Coll. Pharmacy, 1975; recipient Arthur Hassan Colo. Pharmacal Assn., 1983, Excellence in Teaching U. Colo. Med. Sch., 1983 Fellow Am. Coll. Clin. Pharmacology (regent 1983-88, 91-96, pres. 1998-2000); mem. Am. Soc. Hosp. Pharmacists, Am. Soc. Pharmacology and Exptl. Therapeutics, Rho Chi Roman Catholic. Office: U Mo Sch Pharmacy 5005 Rockhill Rd Kansas City MO 64110-2239

PIERCE, HARVEY R. insurance company executive; Chmn., CEO Am. Family Ins. Group, Madison, Wis. Office: Am Family Ins Group 6000 American Pky Madison WI 53783-0001

PIERCE, ROY, political science educator; b. N.Y.C., June 24, 1923; s. Roy Alexander and Elizabeth (Scott) P.; m. Winnifred Poland, July 19, 1947 Ph.D., Cornell U., 1950. Instr. govt. Smith Coll., Northampton, Mass., 1950-51, asst. prof., 1951-56; asst. prof. polit. sci. U. Mich., Ann Arbor, 1956-59, assoc. prof., 1959-64, prof., 1964-94, prof. emeritus, 1993—. Vis. prof. Columbia U., 1959, Stanford U., 1966, U. Oslo, 1976, Ecole des Hautes Etudes en Sciences Sociales, Paris, 1978 Author: Contemporary French Political Thought, 1966, French Politics and Political Institutions, 1968, 2d edit., 1973, (with Philip E. Converse) Political Representation in France, 1986, Choosing the Chief: Presidential Elections in France and the United States, 1995. Served with USAF, 1943-46 Mem. Am. Polit. Sci. Assn. (co-winner Woodrow Wilson Found. award 1987, George H. Hallett Book award 1996). Office: Inst for Social Rsch U Mich Ann Arbor MI 48106 E-mail: tetons@umich.edu.

PIERRE, PERCY ANTHONY, university president; b. nr. Donaldsville, La., Jan. 3, 1939; s. Percy John and Rosa (Villavaso) P.; m. Olga A. Markham, Aug. 8, 1965; children: Kristin Clare, Allison Celeste. BSEE, U. Notre Dame, 1961, MSEE, 1963, D of Engring. (hon.), 1977; PhD in Elec. Engring, Johns Hopkins U., 1967; postgrad., U. Mich., 1968; DSc (hon.), Rensselear Poly. Inst. Asst. prof. elec. engring. So. U., 1963; instr. Johns Hopkins U., Balt., 1963-64; instr. physics Morgan State Coll., 1964-66; instr. info. and control engring. U. Mich., Ann Arbor, 1967-68; instr. systems engring. UCLA, 1968-69; research engr. in communications RAND Corp., 1968-71; White House fellow, spl. asst. Office of Pres., 1969-70; dean Sch. Engring., Howard U., Washington, 1971-77; program officer for engring. edn. Alfred P. Sloan Found., 1973-75; asst. sec. for research, devel. and acquisition U.S. Dept. Army, 1977-81; engring. mgmt. cons., 1981-83; pres. Prairie View (Tex.) Agrl. and Mech. U. System, 1983-89; Honeywell prof. elec. engring., 1989-90; v.p. rsch. and grad. studies Mich. State U., East Lansing, 1990-95, prof. elec. engring., 1995—. Dir. engring. coll. council Am. Soc. for Engring. Edn., 1973-75; mem. sci. adv. group Def. Communications Agy., 1974-75; mem. adv. panel Office Exptl. Research and Devel. Incentives, NSF, 1973-74; mem. Commn. Scholars To Rev. Grad. Programs, Ill. Bd. Higher Edn., 1972-74; mem. panel on role U.S. engring. sch. in fgn. tech. assistance, 1972, co-chmn. symposium on minorities in engring., 1973; mem. rev. panel for Inst. for Applied Tech., Nat. Bur. Standards, 1973-77; chmn. com. on minorities Nat. Acad. Engring., 1976-77; cons. to dir. Energy Rsch. and Devel. Adminstrn., 1976-77; mem. Army Sci. Bd., 1984; mem. adv. bd. Sch. Engring., Johns Hopkins U., 1981-84; cons. Office Sec. Def., 1981-84; mem. adv. bd. Lincoln Labs., MIT. Contbr. articles on communications theory to profl. publs. Trustee U. Notre Dame, 1974-77, 81—; trustee, mem. exec. com. Nat. Fund for Minority Engring. Students, 1976-77; bd. dirs. The Hitachi Found., 1987, Ctr. for Naval Analysis, 1986, Assn. Tex. Colls. and Univs.; pres. Southwest Athletic Conf., 1985-87, bd. dirs. CMS Corp., 1990—, Defense Sci., 1992-94, Old Kent Fin. Corp., 1993—, bd. trustee Aerospace Corp., 1991—. Recipient Disting. Civilian Service award Dept. Army, 1981; award of merit from Senator Proxmire, 1979. Mem. IEEE (sr. mem.; Edison award com. 1978-80), Sigma Xi, Tau Beta Pi. Home: 2445 Emerald Lake Dr East Lansing MI 48823-7256 Office: Mich State U 357 Engineering East Lansing MI 48824-1226

PIERSOL, LAWRENCE L. federal judge; b. Vermillion, S.D., Oct. 21, 1940; s. Ralph Nelson and Mildred Alice (Millette) P.; m. Catherine Anne Vogt, June 30, 1962; children: Leah C., William M., Elizabeth J. BA, U. S.D., 1962, JD summa cum laude, 1965. Bar: S.D. 1965, U.S. Ct. Mil. Appeals, 1965, U.S. Dist. Ct. S.D. 1968, U.S. Supreme Ct. 1972, U.S. Dist. Ct. Wyo. 1980, U.S. Dist. Ct. Nebr. 1986, U.S. Dist. Ct. Mont. 1988. Ptnr. Davenport, Evans, Hurwitz & Smith, Sioux Falls, S.D., 1968-93; judge U.S. Dist. Ct., 1993—; chief judge Dist. of S.D., 1999—. Mem. budget com. chair, economy sub com., Jud. Conf. U.S.; chmn. tribal ct. com., security com. 8th Cir. Jud. Coun.; editor-in-chief Law Review. Majority leader S.D. Ho. of Reps., Pierre, 1973-74, minority whip, 1971-72; del. Dem. Nat. Conv., 1972, 76, 80; S.D. mem. del. select commn. Dem. Nat. Com., 1971-75. Mem. ABA, State Bar S.D., Fed. Judges Assn. (bd. dirs., v.p.). Roman Catholic. Avocations: reading, running, painting, mountaineering. Office: US Dist Ct 400 S Phillips Ave Sioux Falls SD 57104-6824

PIERSON, EDWARD SAMUEL, engineering educator, consultant; b. Syracuse, N.Y., June 27, 1937; s. Theodore and Marjorie O. (Bronner) P.; m. Elaine M. Grauer, June 6, 1971; 1 child, Alan. BS in Elec. Engring., Syracuse U., 1958; SM, MIT, 1960, ScD, 1964. Asst. prof., fellow MIT, 1965-66; assoc. prof., assoc. dept. head U. Ill., Chgo., 1966-75; program mgr. Argonne Nat. Labs., Ill., 1975-82; head dept. engring. Purdue U. Calumet, Hammond, Ind., 1982-95, spl. asst. to chancellor for environ. programs, 1995—. Cons. Argonne Nat. Lab., 1972-75, 82-93, Solmecs

Corp., 1982-88, HMJ Corp., Washington, 1983-88, LM Mfg., 1994—. Contbr. articles to profl. jours. NSF fellow, 1958-60 Mem. IEEE, ASME, Am. Soc. Engring. Edn. Office: Purdue U Calumet Hammond IN 46323 E-mail: pierson@calumet.purdue.edu.

PIERSON, JOHN THEODORE, JR. manufacturer; b. Kansas City, Mo., Oct. 13, 1931; s. John Theodore and Helen Marguerite (Sherman) P.; m. Susan K. Chadwick, Apr. 16, 1977; children by previous marriage—Merrill Sherman, Karen Louise, Kimberly Ann. B.S.E., Princeton U., 1953; M.B.A., Harvard U., 1958. With Vendo Co., Kansas City, Mo., 1960—, gen. automatic products salesman, 1960-61, mgr. new products, 1961-63; v.p. sales equipment for Coca-Cola, 1963-66; pres. Vendo Internat., 1966-69, exec. v.p., chief operating officer, 1969-71, pres., chief exec. officer, 1971-74; pres. Preco Industries, Inc., 1976-97, chmn., 1997—. Chmn. Internat. Trade and Exhbn. Ctr. Co-author: Linear Polyethylene and Polypropylene: Problems and Opportunities, 1958. Trustee Midwest Rsch. Inst.; bd. dirs. and chmn. MidAm. Mfg. Tech. Ctr.; bd. dirs. Johnson County Bus. Tech. Ctr., Youth Symphony Kansas City, 1965-69; past trustee Pembroke-Country Day Sch., Barstow Sch.; past mem. adv. coun. U.S.-Japan Econ. Rels. Coun.; mem. coun. chmn. for exploring Boy Scouts Am., mem. Nat. coun. Lt. M.I. USNR, 1953-56. Mem. Kansas City C. of C., U.S. C. of C. (dir. 1970-74), River Club (pres. 1994-96), Kansas City Country Club. Home: 2801 W 63rd St Shawnee Mission KS 66208-1866 Office: 9705 Commerce Pkwy Lenexa KS 66219-2403

PIESHOSKI, MICHAEL J. construction executive; V.p., CFO Peter Kiewit Sons', Inc., Omaha, 2000—. Office: Peter Kiewit Sons Inc Kiewit Plz Omaha NE 68131

PIESTER, DAVID L(EE), magistrate judge; b. Lincoln City, Nebr., Nov. 18, 1947; s. George Piester; married; children. BS, U. Nebr., 1969, JD, 1972. Bar: Nebr. 1972, U.S. Dist. Ct. Nebr. 1972, U.S. Ct. Appeals (8th cir.) 1976, U.S. Supreme Ct. 1979. Staff atty. Legal Svcs. S.E. Nebr., Lincoln, 1972-73, exec. dir., 1973-79; asst. U.S. atty. Dept. Justice, 1979-81; magistrate judge U.S. Dist. Ct. Nebr., 1981—. Cons. Legal Services Corp., Nat. Legal Aid and Defender Assn., 1974-77. Mem. Lincoln Human rights commn., 1978-79. Mem. ABA (jud. adminstrn. divsn., Nat. Conf. Fed. Trial Judges), Nebr. State Bar Assn., Fed. Magistrate Judges Assn., Lincoln Bar Assn., Eighth Cir. Jud. Coun. (ex officio 1993-96). Office: US Dist Ct 100 Centennial Mall North 566 Fed Bldg Lincoln NE 68508

PIETROFESA, JOHN JOSEPH, education educator; b. N.Y.C., Sept. 12, 1940; s. Louis John and Margaret (Proietti) P.; m. Cathy Marks, June 22, 1985; children: John, Paul, Maria, Dolores. BE cum laude, U. Miami, 1961; MEd, 1963, Ed.D., 1967. Diplomate Am. Bd. Sexology; cert. cognitive behavior therapist, forensic counselor, sex therapist; lic. psychologist, social worker. Counselor Dade County (Fla.) pub. schs., 1965-67; prof. edn. Wayne State U., Detroit, 1967—; div. head theoret. and behavioral founds., 1977-83; dept. chair counselor edn., 1999—. Cons. to various schs., hosps. and univs. Author: The Authentic Counselor, 1971, 2nd edit., 1980, School Counselor as Professional, 1971, Counseling and Guidance in the Twentieth Century, 1971, Elementary School Guidance and Counseling, 1973, Career Development, 1975, Career Education, 1976, College Student Development, 1977, Counseling: Theory Research and Practice, 1978, Guidance: An Introduction, 1980, Counseling: An Introduction, 1984; mem. editl. bd. Counseling and Values, 1972-75. 1st lt. Mil. Police Corps, AUS, 1963-65. Mem. Am. Psychol. Assn., Am. Personnel and Guidance Assn., Mich. Personnel and Guidance Assn., Assn. Counselor Edn. and Supervision, Phi Delta Kappa. Home: PO Box 99 Bloomfield Hills MI 48303-0099 Office: Wayne State U 321 Education Detroit MI 48202

PIETROWSKI, ANTHONY, business executive; Founder, pres., CEO RDA Group, Inc., Bloomfield Hill, Mich., 1969—. Office: RDA Group Inc 450 Enterprise Ct Bloomfield Hills MI 48302-0386

PIGMAN, JACK RICHARD, lawyer; b. Fostoria, Ohio, June 5, 1944; s. Jack R. and A. Ada (McDevitt) P.; m. Judy Lynn Price, June 19, 1968 (div. 1983); m. Carolyn Ruth Parker, May 31, 1986; children: Shaeney E. Pigman Craig, J. Ryan Pigman, Adam Parker. BA, U. Notre Dame, 1966; JD cum laude, Ohio State U., 1969. Bar: Ohio 1969, U.S. Ct. Mil. Appeals 1970. Law clk. Ohio Supreme Ct., Columbus, 1969-70; assoc. Wright, Harlor, Morris & Arnold, 1970, 74-76; ptnr. Porter, Wright, Morris & Arthur and predecessor firms, 1977—. Speaker in field. Trustee Dublin Arts Coun., 2001—, Ctr. for New Directions, 1990-96, treas., 1996; trustee United Cerebral Palsy of Columbus and Franklin County, 1976-82, pres., 1980. Capt. JAG U.S. Army, 1970-74. Mem. Ohio State Bar Assn., Columbus Bar Assn. (chmn. bankruptcy com. 1982-84), Columbus Met. Club (trustee 1980-87, pres. 1985-86). Republican. Avocations: tennis, skiing, reading, cooking, photography. Office: Porter Wright Morris & Arthur 41 S High St Ste 2800 Columbus OH 43215-6194

PIIRMA, IRJA, chemist, educator; b. Tallinn, Estonia, Feb. 4, 1920; came to U.S., 1949; d. Voldemar Juri and Meta Wilhelmine (Lister) Tiits; m. Aleksander Piirma, Mar. 10, 1943; children: Margit Ene, Silvia Ann. Diploma in chemistry, Tech. U., Darmstadt, Fed. Republic of Germany, 1949; MS, U. Akron, 1957, PhD, 1960. Rsch. chemist U. Akron, Ohio, 1952-67, asst. prof., 1967-76, assoc. prof., 1976-81, prof., 1981-90, prof. emerita, 1990—, dept. head Ohio, 1982-85. Author: Polymeric Surfactants, 1992; editor: Emulsion Polymerization, 1982; contbr. articles to profl. jours. Recipient Extra Mural Rsch. award BP Am., Inc., 1989. Mem. Am. Chem. Soc. Avocations: swimming, skiing. Home: 3528 Adaline Dr Cuyahoga Falls OH 44224-3929 Office: U Akron Inst Polymer Sci Akron OH 44325-3909 E-mail: irja@uakron.edu.

PIKE, KERMIT JEROME, library director; b. East Cleveland, June 19, 1941; s. Frank James and Pauline Frances (Prijatel) P.; m. Joyce Rita Massillo, June 27, 1964; children: Christopher James, Laura Elizabeth. BA, Case Western Res. U., 1963, MA, 1965. Rsch. asst. Western Res. Hist. Soc., Cleve., 1965-66, curator manuscripts, 1966-72, chief libr., 1969-75, dir. libr., 1976—, COO, 1997—. Adj. prof. history, libr. sci. Case Western Res. U., 1975-84. Author: Guide to the Manuscripts and Archives, 1972, Guide to Shaker Manuscripts, 1974; editor: Guide to Jewish History Sources, 1983; Compiler: Guide to Major Manuscript Collections, 1987. Mem. Super Sesquicentennial Com., Cleve., 1971, Cleve. Bicentennial History Com., 1992—96, Ohio Preservation Coun., 1997—, Ohio Hist. Records Adv. Bd., 2002—; chmn. Family Heritage Adv. Bd., Numa Corp., 1995—99; chmn. vis. com. on humanities and arts Cleve. State U., 1980—82; trustee Nationalities Svc. Ctr., Cleve., 1978—86. Recipient Achievement award No. Ohio Live, Cleve., 1987; Spl. Recognition award Gov. Richard F. Celeste of Ohio, 1990. Mem. Soc. Ohio Archivists (co-founder 1968, pres. 1971-72), Black History Archives (founder 1970), Orgn. Am. Historians, Soc. Am. Archivists, Manuscripts Soc., Midwest Archives Conf., Ohio Geneal. Soc., Early Settlers Assn. of the Western Res., Rowfant Club, Lake County Farmers' Conservation Club, Lambda Chi Alpha. Roman Catholic. Home: 3985 Orchard Rd Cleveland OH 44121-2411 Office: Western Res Hist Soc 10825 East Blvd Cleveland OH 44106-1777 E-mail: kermit@wrhs.org.

PIKE, ROBERT WILLIAM, insurance company executive, lawyer; b. Lorain, Ohio, July 25, 1941; s. Edward and Catherine (Stack) P.; m. Linda L. Feitz, Dec. 26, 1964; children: Catherine, Robert, Richard. BA, Bowling Green State U., 1963; JD, U. Toledo, 1966. Bar: Ohio 1966, Ill. 1973. Ptnr. Cubbon & Rice Law Firm, Toledo, 1968-72; asst. counsel Allstate Ins. Co., Northbrook, Ill., 1972-74, assoc. counsel, 1974-76, asst. sec., asst. gen. counsel, 1976-77, asst. v.p., asst. gen. counsel, 1977-78, v.p., asst. gen. counsel, 1978-86, sr. v.p., sec., gen. counsel, bd. dirs., 1987-99, exec. v.p., 1999—. Bd. dirs. Allstate subs. Bd. dirs., exec. com. Assn. Calif. Ins. Cos., Nat. Assn. Ind. Insurers; mem. bd. overseers Inst. for Civil Justice. Served to capt. inf. U.S. Army, 1966-68. Mem. ABA, Ill. Bar Assn., Ohio Bar Assn., Ivanhoe (Ill.) Club. Roman Catholic. Home: 46 Fox Trl Lincolnshire IL 60069-4012 Office: Allstate Ins Co 2775 Sanders Rd Ste F8 Northbrook IL 60062-6127

PILAND, JOHN CHARLES, lawyer; b. Paxton, Ill., Dec. 6, 1961; s. Joseph C. and Jo Anne (Hortin) P.; m. Debra Ann Stewart, July 28, 1984; children: Jacqueline Prince, David Lincoln. BSBA, U. Ill., 1984, JD, 1987. Bar: Ill. 1987, U.S. Dist. Ct. (cen. dist.) 1988, U.S. Ct. Appeals (7th cir.) 1988, U.S. Supreme Ct. 1991. Atty. Heyl, Royster, Voelker & Allen, Urbana, Ill., 1987-95; spl. legal counsel to Ill. House Rep. Leader, 1993-94; state's atty. Champaign County, 1995—. Mem. nat. adv. coun. SBA, Washington, 1988-89; mem. gov.'s adv. bd., Springfield, Ill., 1988-90; mem. Ill. Truth-in-Sentencing Commn., 1995-98. Fl. page U.S. Ho. of Reps., Washington, 1979-80; legis. aide Ill. Ho. of Reps., Springfield, 1981-82. Harry S. Truman Found. scholar, 1982. Fellow Am. Bar Found.; mem. ABA, SAR, Ill. State Bar Assn. (bd. govs. 1995-2001), Champaign County Bar Assn., Nat. Dist. Attys. Assn., Ill. States Attys. Assn. (exec. com. 1995—), Lions, Masons, Rotary, Phi Alpha Delta. Republican. Office: Champaign County States Atty PO Box 785 Urbana IL 61803-0785

PILARCZYK, DANIEL EDWARD, archbishop; b. Dayton, Ohio, Aug. 12, 1934; s. Daniel Joseph and Frieda S. (Hilgefort) P. Student, St. Gregory Sem., Cin., 1948-53; PhB, Pontifical Urban U., Rome, 1955, PhL, 1956, STB, 1958, STL, 1960, STD, 1961; MA, Xavier U., 1965; PhD, U. Cin., 1969; LLD (hon.), Xavier U., 1975, Calumet Coll., 1982, U. Dayton, 1990, Marquette U., 1990, Thomas More Coll., 1991, Coll. Mount St. Joseph, 1994, Hebrew Union Coll.- Jewish Inst. Religion, 1997. Ordained priest Roman Catholic Ch. , 1959; asst. chancellor Archdiocese of Cin., 1961-63; synodal judge Archdiocesan Tribunal, 1971-82; mem. faculty Athenaeum of Ohio, St. Gregory Sem., 1963-74; v.p. Athenaeum of Ohio, 1968-74, trustee, 1974—; also rector St. Gregory Sem., 1968-74; archdiocesan dir. ednl. services, 1974-82; aux. bishop of Cin., 1974-82; vicar gen., 1974-82; archbishop of Cin., 1982—. Bd. dirs. Pope John Ctr., 1978-85; trustee Cath. Health Assn., 1982-85, Cath. U. Am., 1983-91, 97—, Pontifical Coll. Josephinum, 1983-92; v.p. Nat. Conf. Cath. Bishops, 1986-89, pres., 1989-92, chmn. Com. on Doctrine, 1996-2000; U.S. rep. Episc. Bd. Internat. Commn. on English in Liturgy 1987-97; chmn., 1991-97. Author: Praepositini Cancellarii de Sacramentis et de Novissimis, 1964—65, Twelve Tough Issues, 1988, We Believe, 1989, Living in the Lord, 1990, The Parish: Where God's People Live, 1991, Forgiveness, 1992, What Must I Do?, 1993, Our Priests: Who They Are and What They Do, 1994, Sacraments, 1994, Bringing Forth Justice, 1996, 1999, Thinking Catholic, 1998, Practicing Catholic, 1999, Believing Catholic, 2000, Live Letters, 2001. Ohio Classical Conf. scholar to Athens, 1966 Mem. Am. Philol. Assn. Home and Office: 100 E 8th St Cincinnati OH 45202-2129

PILCHEN, IRA A. editor; b. Chgo., Jan. 17, 1964; s. Bernard J. and Erna (Lee) P. BA in History, U. Ill., 1986. Assoc. editor Judicature jour., Chgo., 1991-98; dir. comms. Am. Judicature Soc., 1991-98; editor Student Lawyer mag. ABA Publishing, 1999—. Mem. adv. coun. Ill. State Justice Commn., 1995. Vol. interpretive guide Friends of the Chicago River, 1991—. Named Vol. of Yr., Friends of Chicago River, 1993. Avocations: swimming, bicycling, Chicago history. Office: ABA Publishing 750 N Lake Shore Dr Fl 8 Chicago IL 60611-4403

PILLSBURY, GEORGE STURGIS, investment adviser; b. Crystal Bay, Minn., July 17, 1921; s. John S. and Eleanor (Lawler) P.; m. Sally Whitney, Jan. 4, 1947; children: Charles Alfred, George Sturgis, Sarah Kimball, Katharine Whitney. BA, Yale U., 1943. Dir. emeritus Sargent Mgmt. Co. Mem. Seminole Golf Club (Juno Beach, Fla.), Lafayette Club, Woodhill Club, Minnetonka Yacht Club, Mpls. Club, River Club (N.Y.C.). Home: 1300 Bracketts Point Rd Wayzata MN 55391-9393 Office: 901 Marquette Ave Ste 2630 Minneapolis MN 55402-3230 E-mail: gspbury@smcinv.com.

PINCUS, THEODORE HENRY, public relations executive; b. Chgo., Sept. 15, 1933; s. Jacob T. and J. (Engel) P.; m. Sharon Barr, Jan. 16, 1988; children: Laura, Mark, Susan, Anne, Jennifer. BS in Journalism, Ind. U., 1955. Free-lance bus. writer, 1955-58; sr. exec. Harshe Rotman & Druck, Chgo., 1958-62; dir. comm. Theodore Pincus & Assocs., 1962-64; chmn., CEO, Fin. Rels. Bd., Inc. subs. BSMG Worldwide, 1995—98; vice chmn. BSMG Worldwide divsn. Interpub. Group, N.Y.C., 1998—2001; sr. cons. Interpub. Group, 2001—. Adj. prof. mktg. Northwestern U. Kellogg Grad. Sch., 2002—; pub. affairs advisor to Nelson Rockefeller, N.Y.C., 1960, 68; advisor U.S. Info. Agy., 1993—; former mem. adv. bd. NASDAQ. Author: Giveaway Day, 1977; contbr. articles to profl. publs. including Wall St. Jour., Fortune, and N.Y. Times. Active presdl. nomination campaigns; vice-chmn. Midwest region Am. Jewish Com.; mem. adv. bd. Ind. U. Bus. Sch.; bd. dirs. The Ill. Coalition. With USAF, 1955-57. Recipient numerous nat. awards for profl. excellence in investor rels. and corp.pub. rels. including Silver Anvil award Pub. Rels. Soc. Am., 1966, Civic Achievement award Am. Jewish Com., 1993; named Entrepreneur of Yr., Ernst & Young Merrill Lynch, 1998, Pub. Rels. Profl. of Yr., Pub. Rels. Soc. Am., 2002. Mem. Young Pres.'s Orgn., Nat. Investor Relations Inst. (founding), Std. Club. Club: Union League. Office: Theodore Pincus & Assocs 444 N Michigan Ave Ste 3530 Chicago IL 60611

PING, CHARLES JACKSON, philosophy educator, retired university president; b. Phila., June 15, 1930; s. Cloudy J. and Mary M. (Marion) P.; m. Claire Oates, June 5, 1951; children: Andrew, Ann Shelton. B.A., Rhodes Coll., 1951; B.D., Louisville Presbyn. Theol. Sem., 1954; Ph.D., Duke, 1961. Assoc. prof. philosophy Alma Coll., 1962-66; prof. philosophy Tusculum Coll., 1966-69, v.p., dean faculty, 1967-68, acting pres., 1968-69; provost Central Mich. U., Mt. Pleasant, 1969-75; pres. Ohio U., Athens, 1975-94, pres. emeritus, Trustee prof. philosophy and edn., 1994—, exec. dir. Manasseh Cutler Scholars Program, dir. Ping Inst. for Tchg. Humanities, 1994-99, dir. emeritus, 1999—. Bd. dirs. Wing Lung Bank Internat. Inst. for Bus. Devel., Hong Kong; trustee Louisville Presbyn. Theol. Sem., Muskingum Coll., Ohio; mem. adv. bd. Inst. Ednl. Mgmt. of Harvard U.; chair Commn. Planning for Future of Higher Edn., Kingdom of Swaziland; mem. Commn. on Higher Edn. Republic of Namibia. Author: Ohio University in Perspective, 1985, Meaningful Nonsense, 1966, also articles. Fulbright Sr. Rsch. scholar for So. Africa, 1995. Mem. Coun. on Internat. Ednl. Exch. (chair bd.), David C. Lam Inst. for East-West Studies (bd. dirs.), Coun. Internat. Exch. Scholars (bd. dirs., chair Africa com.). Office: Ohio U Office of Pres Emeritus Athens OH 45701 E-mail: ping@ohio.edu.

PINSKY, MICHAEL S. lawyer; b. Chgo., July 25, 1945; s. Joseph and Irene (Sodakoff) P.; m. Judy R. Rabin, Sept. 29, 1974; children: David, Susie, Jodie. BS, U. Ill., 1967; JD, DePaul U., 1971. Bar: Ill. 1971. Conferee, revenue agt. IRS, Chgo., 1967-72; ptnr. Levenfeld & Kanter, 1972-80, Levenfeld, Eisenberg Janger, Chgo., 1980-84, Vedder Price, Kaufman & Kammholz, Chgo., 1984-88, Gottlieb & Schwartz, Chgo., 1989-92; with Levin & Schreder, 1993-97, Altheimer & Gray, Chgo., 1997-2000, Schair, Burney, Ross & Citron, Ltd., 2000—. Bd. dirs. Better Boys Found., Chgo., 1989-94; mem. planned giving com. Am. Soc. for Technion, 1997—. Mem. Am. Bar Assn., Assn. of Bar of State of Ill., Assn. of Bar of City of Chgo. (com. chmn. 1984-86). Office: 222 N La Salle St Ste 1910 Chicago IL 60601-1102

PINSKY, STEVEN MICHAEL, radiologist, educator; b. Milw., Feb. 2, 1942; s. Leo Donald and Louise Miriam (Faldberg) P.; m. Sue Brona Rosenzweig, June 12, 1966; children: Mark Burton, Lisa Rachel. BS, U. Wis., 1964; MD, Loyola U., Chgo., 1967. Resident in radiology and nuclear medicine U. Chgo., 1968-70, chief resident in diagnostic radiology, 1970-71, asst. prof., 1973-77, assoc. prof. radiology and medicine, 1977-85, prof., 1985-89; prof., chmn. dept. radiology U. Ill., 1989-96, prof. radiology, 1996—. Dir. nuclear medicine Michael Reese Med. Ctr., Chgo., 1973-87, vice-chmn. radiology, 1984-87, chmn. radiology, 1987-93, v.p. med. staff, 1986-88, pres., 1988-90, trustee, 1984-86, 90-93; dir. nuclear medicine tech. program Triton Coll., River Grove, Ill., 1974-87. Contbr. chpts. to books, articles to med. jours. Maj., M.C., U.S. Army, 1971-73. Rsch. fellow Am. Cancer Soc., 1969-70. Fellow: Am. Coll. Nuclear Physicians (treas. 1982—84, Ill. del.), Am. Coll. Radiology; mem.: Ill. Radiologic Soc. (sec.-treas. 1992—94, pres.-elect 1994—95, pres. 1995—96, Chgo. chpt. Gold medal for disting. svc. 1999), Radiologic Soc. N.Am. (councilor 1994—99, chmn. tech. exhibits com. 1994—96, edn. coun. 1994—96), Soc. Nuclear Medicine (trustee 1979—87, pres. ctrl. chpt. 1980—81). Office: 1821 Lawrence Ln Highland Park IL 60035 E-mail: sspinsky1821@cs.com.

PIPER, ADDISON LEWIS, securities executive; b. Mpls., Oct. 10, 1946; s. Harry Cushing and Virginia (Lewis) P.; m. Louise Wakefield (div.); children: Gretchen, Tad, William; m. Cynthia Schuneman, Nov. 14, 1979; children: Elisabeth LaBelle, Richard LaBelle. BA in Econs., Williams Coll., 1968; MBA, Stanford U., 1972. Mktg. cons. Earl Savage and Co., Mpls., 1968-69; mem. capital market dept. Piper and Jaffray, 1969-70; asst. syndicate mgr. Piper, Jaffray and Hopwood, 1972-73, v.p., 1973-79, dir. trading, 1973-77, dir. sales, 1977-79, exec. v.p., dir. mktg., 1979-83, chief exec. officer, chmn. mgmt. com., 1983—, chmn. bd. dirs., 1988—. Adv. com. N.Y. Stock Exch., 1966-90; bd. dirs. Allina Health Systems, Greenspring Corp., Mpls., Minn. Bus. Partnership, Mpls., Abbott Northwestern Hosp., Mpls.; trustee CARE Found., Mpls. Fin. chmn. Senator Durenberger Fin. Com., Mpls., 1980-88; chmn. Minn. Pub. Radio, 1985-95. Mem. Securities Industry Assn. (bd. govs. 1986-90, tax policy com.), Country Club of the Rockies (Colo.), Mpls. Club, Ventana Canyon (Tucson), Woodhill Country Club (Wayzata). Republican. Episcopalian. Avocations: skiing, golfing, hunting, tennis, horses. Office: Piper Jaffray Cos J1012058 800 Nicollet Mall Ste 800 Minneapolis MN 55402-7020

PIPER, KATHLEEN, former political organization administrator; b. Ida County, Iowa; d. Pat and Rita Donahey McGuire; m. James Carl Piper, 1971; 2 children. Student, U. Iowa, Morningside Coll., Mt. Marty Coll. Co-owner Pied Piper Flower Shop, Yankton, S.D., 1986; vice chair Yankton County Dem. Com., 1980-95, state ctrl. committeewoman, 1995—; commr. Yankton County, 1986—, chair, 1996; state ctrl. com. S.D. Dem. Party, 1989-99, exec. bd., 1992-99, chairwoman, 1996-99. Mem. health care adv. com. Senator Tom Daschle, 1991—. Del. Nat. Dem. Conv., N.Y.C., 1992; mem. Gold adv. coun. appointed by Gov., 1993-95; participant Pres. Clinton and Hillary Rodham-Clinton's Health Care Inbitiative Rev., White House, 1993, Gt. Plains Rural Health Summit, 1994, Pres., Clinton and SBA Chief Roundtable Discussion Small Bus. and Health Care Reform, Washington, 1994; appointed del. White House Conf. Small Bus., 1994. Recipient Woman of Yr. award Ed Yankton Daily Press and Dakota, 1986, Emerging Leader for S.D. award Sioux Falls Argus Leader, 1990. Mem. S.D. County Commr. Assn. (exec. bd. 1992-94). Roman Catholic. Home: PO Box 737 Sioux Falls SD 57101-0737 Office: 405 James Pl Yankton SD 57078-1827

PIPER, ODESSA, chef; m. Terry Theise. Chef L'Etoile Restaurant, Madison, Wis., 1976—. Contbr. Wis. Pub. Radio, NPR; cons. Ctr. for Integrated Agrl. Sys., U. Wis., Madison. Contbr. Recipient award, James Beard Found., 2001. Mem.: Women Chefs and Restauranteurs (mem. scholarship com.), Chefs Collaborative 2000 (bd. dirs.). Office: L'Etoile Restaurant 25 N Pinckney Madison WI 53711

PIPER, PAT KATHRYN, state senator; b. Delavan, Minn., July 16, 1934; d. Claire I. and Geneva R. (Tibodeau) P. BA, Coll. St. Teresa, Winona, Minn., 1962; MA, Cath. U., 1972. Tchr. St. Augustine Sch., Austin, Minn., 1956-58, St. Francis Sch., Rochester, 1958-60, St. James (Minn.) Sch., 1960-61; catechist St. Catherine Sch. Ctr., Luverne, Minn., 1961-63, catechist, dir., 1964-67; catechist Area Ctr., Hayfield, 1963-64; dir. St. Ann's Ctr., Slayton, 1967-69, Christian Edn. Ctr., Austin, 1969-94; mem. Minn. Ho. of Reps., 1982-84, 84-86, Senate State of Minn., 1986-; chair Senate Family Svcs. Com. Contbr. articles to profl. jours. Active United Way, YMCA, Council for Handicapped, Salvation Army. Mem. LWV, Bus. and Profl. Women. Mem. Democrat Farmer Labor Party. Roman Catholic. Lodge: Zonta. Office: Minn State Senate 75 Constitution Ave Saint Paul MN 55155-1601

PIPPIN, M. LENNY, food products executive; CEO Lykes Bros. Inc., Tampa, Fla., 1997-99; pres. & CEO Schwan's Sales Enterprises, Marshall, MN. Office: Schwan's Sales Enterprises 115 W College Dr Marshall MN 56258

PIRAINO, THOMAS ANTHONY, lawyer; b. Cleve., July 12, 1949; s. Thomas Anthony and Margaret (Stephens) P.; m. Barbara McWilliams, Sept. 4, 1976; children: Margaret, Ann, Mary. BA in History, Allegheny Coll., 1971; JD, Cornell U., 1974. Bar: Ohio 1974. Assoc. counsel Parker-Hannifin Corp., Cleve., 1981-84, asst. gen. counsel, 1984-98, v.p., gen. counsel, sec., 1998—. Contbr. articles to legal jours. Mem. ABA, Ohio Bar Assn., Am. Corp. Counsel (sec. 1985—), Am. Soc. Corp. Secs. (pres. 1988—). Avocations: tennis, jogging. Office: Parker Hannifin Corp 6035 Parkland Blvd Cleveland OH 44124-4141

PIRKLE, WILLIAM H. chemistry educator; b. Shreveport, La., May 2, 1934; married, 1956; 4 children. BS, U. Calif., Berkeley, 1959; PhD in Chemistry, U. Rochester, 1963. NSF fellow Harvard U., 1963-64; asst. prof., 1964-69; assoc. prof. chemistry U. Ill., Urbana, 1969-80, prof. chemistry, 1980—. Vis. prof. U. Wis., Madison, 1971. Assoc. editor Enantiomer; mem. editl. bd. Jour. Liquid Chromatogrpahy, Chirality, HRC, Supramolecular Chemistry. Recipient A.J.P. Martin medal Chromatographic Soc. Gt. Britain, 1990, Merit award Chgo. Chromatography Discussion Group, 1991, Chirality medal Swedish Assn. Pharm. Scis., 1994, Robert Boyle Gold medal Royal Soc. of Chemistry, 1998, ISCO award U. Nebr., 1998, Ea. Analytical award in Separation Sci., 1998, Dal Nogare award Del. Valley Chromatography Forum, 2000; Alfred P. Sloan fellow, 1971-72. Mem. Am. Chem. Soc. (Chromatography award 1994), Am. Chem. Soc. Office: U Illinois 161 Roger Adam Lab 505 S Mathews Ave Urbana IL 61801-3617

PIRSCH, CAROL MCBRIDE, county official, former state senator, community relations manager; b. Omaha, Dec. 27, 1936; d. Lyle Erwin and Hilfrie Louise (Lebeck) McBride; m. Allen I. Pirsch, Mar. 28, 1954; children: Pennie Elizabeth, Pamela Elaine, Patrice Eileen, Phyllis Erika, Peter Allen, Perry Andrew. Student, U. Miami, Oxford, Ohio, U. Nebr., Omaha. Former mem. data processing staff Omaha Pub. Schs.; former mem. wage practices dept. Western Electric Co., Omaha; former legal sec.; former office mgr. Pirsch Food Brokerage Co., Inc.; former employment supr., mgr. pub. policy U.S. West Comm.; mem. Nebr. Senate, 1979-97; commr. Douglas County, 1997—, chair, 1999. Founder, 1st pres., bd. dirs. Nebr. Coalition for Victims of Crime; bd. dirs., treas. Centris Fed. Credit Union. Mem. Omaha Douglas County Bldg. Commn., 1997—, sec., 2000—. Recipient Golden Elephant award, Kuhle award Nebr. Coalition for Victims of Crime, 1986, Outstanding Legis. Efforts award YWCA,

1989, Breaking the Rule of Thumb award Nebr. Domestic Violence Sexual Assault Coalition, 1989, Cert. of Appreciation award U.S. Dept. Justice, 1988, Partnership award N.E. Credit Union League, 1995, Wings award LWV Greater Omaha, 1995, N.E. VFW Spl. Recognition award for Exceptional Svc., 1995, Cert. Appreciation, Nebr. Atty. Gen., 1995. Mem. VASA, Nat. Orgn. Victim Assistance (Outstanding Legis. Leadership award 1981), Freedom Found., Tangier Women's Aux., Footprinters Internat. (bd. dirs., sec.), Douglas County Hist. Soc., Nebr. Taxpayers Assn., Keystone Citizen Patrol (Keystoner of the Month award 1987), Audubon Soc., N.W. Cmty. Club, Benson Rep. Women's Club, Bus. and Profl. Rep. Women Club. Office: Legis Chambers 2 Douglas County Civic Ctr Omaha NE 68102 E-mail: cpirsch@aol.com.

PIRTLE, LAURIE LEE, women's university basketball coach; b. Columbus, Ohio, Jan. 1, 1958; BS in Phys. Edn., Ohio State U., 1980. Asst. coach girl's basketball William Fisher H.S., Lancaster, Ohio, 1981-82; coach women's basketball Capital U., Columbus, 1982-86, U. Cin., 1986—. Named Coach of Yr. Dist.III Ohio Athletic Commn. and Converse III, 1985-86, Ohio Intercoll. Coaches Assn., 1985, Metro Conf., 1989, Conf. USA, 1999, Leading Woman in Cin., 2000. Mem. Women's Basketball Coaches Assn., Greater Cin. and No. Ky., Women's Sports Assn. (mem. com.). Office: U Cin Athletics Dept PO Box 210021 Cincinnati OH 45221-0021

PISARCHICK, SALLY, special education educator; Tchr. spl. edn. Cuyahoga Spl. Edn. Svc. Ctr., Parma, Ohio, 1973-2000; dir. Ohio State Initiative Cuyahoga Spl. Edn. Regional Resource Ctr., 2000—. Recipient Sleznick award, Coun. of Admin. of Spec. Edn., 1994. Office: Cuyahoga Special Edn Regional Resource Ctr 15983 W 54th St Parma OH 44129

PITONIAK, GREGORY EDWARD, mayor; b. Detroit, Aug. 12, 1954; s. Anthony Edward and Constance Elizabeth (Matuszak) P.; m. Denise Ruth Kadi, Apr. 21, 1979; children: Gregory, Mallory. BA, U. Mich., 1976; Masters, U. N.C., 1980. Adminstrv. asst. Taylor (Mich.) Neighborhood Devel. Com., 1977-78; pers. analyst Downriver Community Conf., Southgate, Mich., 1978-79; dir. client svcs. Econ. Devel. Corp. Wayne County, Dearborn, 1979-84, exec. dir. Livonia, 1984-88; dir. econ. dev. Downriver Community Conf., Southgate, 1988; state rep. Mich. Ho. Reps., Lansing, 1989-97; mayor City of Taylor, 1997—. Councilman Taylor City Coun., 1981-88, chmn., 1983-85, 87-88; pres. Mich. Young Dems., 1982-84; treas. 15th Congl. Dist. Dem. Orgn., Taylor, 1988-90. Named Outstanding Young Person, Taylor Jaycees, 1987, State Legislator of Yr., Mich. Credit Union League, 1993. Mem. Am. Econ. Devel. Coun. (cert. econ. developer 1984), Am. Soc. Pub. Adminstrn., Polish Am. Congress, Dem. Club Taylor, KC. Roman Catholic. Home: 9686 Rose St Taylor MI 48180-3046 Office: City of Taylor 23555 Goddard Rd Taylor MI 48180-4116

PITOT, HENRY CLEMENT, III, pathologist, educator; b. N.Y.C., May 12, 1930; s. Henry Clement and Bertha (Lowe) Pitot; m. Julie S. Schutten, July 29, 1954; children: Bertha, Anita, Jeanne, Catherine, Henry, Michelle, Lisa, Patrice. BS in Chemistry, Va. Mil. Inst., 1951; MD, Tulane U., 1955, PhD in Biochemistry, 1959, DSc (hon.) , 1995. Instr. pathology Med. Sch. Tulane U., New Orleans, 1955-59; postdoctoral fellow McArdle Lab. U. Wis., Madison, 1959-60, mem. faculty Med. Sch., 1960—, prof. pathology and oncology, 1966-99, prof. emeritus, 1999—, chmn. dept. pathology, 1968-71, acting dean Med. Sch., 1971-73, dir. McArdle Lab., 1973-91. Recipient Borden Undergrad. Rsch. award, 1955, Leaderle Faculty award, 1962, Career Devel. award, Nat. Cancer Inst., NIH, 1965, Parke-Davis award, 1968, Noble Found. Rsch. award, 1984, Esther Langer award, U. Chgo., 1984, Hilldale award, U. Wis., 1991, Founders award, Chem. Industry Inst. Toxicology, 1993, Midwest Regional chpt. Soc. Toxicology award, 1996, Emeritus Faculty award, U. Wis. Med. Sch., 2001. Fellow: AAAS, N.Y. Acad. Scis.; mem.: Soc. Toxicologic Pathologists, Soc. Toxicology, Soc. Surg. Oncology (Lucy J. Wortham award 1981), Soc. Exptl. Biology and Medicine (pres. 1991—93), Am. Soc. Investigative Pathology 1976—77, Am. Cancer Soc. (life), Japanese Cancer Soc. (hon.), Am. Chem. Soc., Am. Soc. Biochemistry and Molecular Biology, Am. Assn. Cancer Rsch., Am. Soc. Cell Biology. Roman Catholic. Home: 314 Robin Pkwy Madison WI 53705-4931 Office: U Wis McArdle Lab Cancer Rsch 1400 University Ave Madison WI 53706-1599 E-mail: pitot@oncology.wise.edu.

PITT, BERTRAM, cardiologist, educator, consultant; b. Kew Gardens, N.Y., Apr. 27, 1932; s. David and Shirley (Blum) P., m. Elaine Liberstein, Aug. 10, 1962; children: Geoffrey, Jessica, Jillian BA, Cornell U., 1953; MD, U. Basel, Switzerland, 1959. Diplomate Am. Bd. Internal Medicine, Am. Bd. Cardiology. Intern Beth Israel Hosp., N.Y.C., 1959-60, resident Boston, 1960-63; fellow in cardiology Johns Hopkins U., Balt., 1966-67, from instr. to assoc. prof., 1967-77; prof. medicine, dir. div. cardiology U. Mich., Ann Arbor, 1977-91, prof. medicine Sch. Medicine, 1991—. Author: Atlas of Cardiovascular Nuclear Medicine, 1977; editor: Cardiovascular Nuclear Medicine, 1974; co-editor: Clinical Trials in Cardiology, 1997, Current Controlled Trials in Cardiovascular Medicine, 1999—. Served to capt. U.S. Army, 1963-65 Mem. ACP, Am. Coll. Cardiology, Am. Soc. Clin. Investigation, Assn. Am. Physicians, Am. Physiol. Soc., Am. Heart Assn., Assn. Univ. Cardiologists, Am. Coll. Chest Physicians, Royal Soc. Mich. Home: 24 Ridgeway St Ann Arbor MI 48104-1739 Office: U Mich Divsn Cardiology 1500 E Medical Center Dr Ann Arbor MI 48109-0005 E-mail: bpitt@umich.edu.

PITTELKO, ROGER DEAN, clergyman, religious educator; b. Elk Reno, Okla., Aug. 18, 1932; s. Elmer Henry and Lydia Caroline (Nieman) Pittelko. AA, Concordia Coll., 1952; BA, Concordia Sem., St. Louis, 1954, MDiv, 1957, STM, 1958; postgrad., Chgo. Luth. Theol. Sem., 1959-61; ThD, Am. Div. Sch., Pineland, Fla., 1968; DMin, Faith Evang. Luth. Sem., Tacoma, 1983. Ordained to ministry Luth. Ch., 1958. Vicar St. John Luth. Ch., S.I., NY, 1955—56, asst. pastor New Orleans, 1958-59; pastor Concordia Luth. Ch., Berwyn, Ill., 1959-63, Luth. Ch. of Holy Spirit, Elk Grove Village, 1963-67; chmn. Commn. on Worship, Luth. Ch.-Mo. Synod, 1982—92, chmn. Commn. on Worship, 1994—98, asst. bishop Midwest region English dist., 1983, pres. and bishop English dist., 1987-97, 3d v.p., 1997—; prof. pastoral theology Concordia Theol. Sem., Ft. Wayne, Ind., 1997—. Author: Guide to Introducing Lutheran Worship; contbr. articles. Mem.: Luth. Acad. for Scholarship, Concordia Hist. Inst., Itasca Country Club (Ill.), Maywood Sportsmans Club (Ill.). Republican. Office: Concordia Theol Seminary 6600 N Clinton St Fort Wayne IN 46825

PITTELKOW, MARK ROBERT, physician, dermatology educator, researcher; b. Milw., Dec. 16, 1952; s. Robert Bernard and Barbara Jean (Thomas) P.; m. Gail L. Gamble, Nov. 26, 1977; children: Thomas, Cameron, Robert. BA, Northwestern U., 1975; MD, Mayo Med. Sch., 1979. Intern then resident Mayo Grad. Sch., 1979-84, post-doctoral exptl. pathology, 1981-83; from asst. to assoc. prof. dermatology Mayo Med. Sch., Rochester, Minn., 1984-95, prof. dermatology, 1995—, assoc. prof. biochemistry and molecular biology, 1992—. Cons. Mayo Clinic/Found., Rochester, 1984— Fellow Am. Acad. Dermatology; mem. AAAS, Am. Dermatol. Assn., Soc. Investigative Dermatology, Am. Burn Assn., Am. Soc. Cell Biology, N.Y. Acad. Scis., Chi Psi. Home: 721 12th Ave SW Rochester MN 55902-2027 Office: Mayo Clinic 200 1st St SW Rochester MN 55905-0002

PITTMAN, PHILIP MCMILLAN, historian; b. Detroit, Apr. 6, 1941; s. Lansing Mizner and Sally Clotilde (Book) P.; m. Julie M. Ducharme, June 22, 1963 (div. 1975); children: Philip McMillan III, Mary Christine Steuart, Noel Ducharme; m. Adele Smith, June 26, 1976 (div. 1989); m. Margaret D. Schlueter, Aug. 26, 1990. AB, Kenyon Coll., 1963; MA, Vanderbilt U., 1964, PhD, 1967. Instr. Vanderbilt U., Nashville, 1966-67; asst. prof. U. Victoria, B.C., Can., 1967-68; assoc. prof. Marshall U., Huntington, W.Va., 1968-80; pres. W.Va. Assn. Coll. English Tchrs., 1978-79; author, historian Cedarville, Mich., 1980—; pub., salesman, v.p., sec., chmn. bd. Les Cheneaux Ventures Inc., 1985—. Adj. prof. W.Va. Coll. Grad. Studies, 1978-80. Author: The Les Cheneaux Chronicles: Anatomy of a Community, 1984, Ripples from the Breezes: A Les Cheneaux Anthology, 1988, North Shore Chinook: Lake Huron Salmon on Light Tackle, 1993, Don't Blame the Treaties: Native American Rights and the Michigan Indian Treaties, 1992; editor, compiler: The Portrayal of Life Stages in English Literature, 1500-1800, 1989, author various scholarly book reviews and articles. Active Les Cheaux Cmty. Action Com., 1985—, Mich. Nature Conservancy, 1994—; active Little Traverse Conservancy, 1990—, bd. dirs., 1994—; founding dir. Les Cheneaux Cmty. Found., 1997—; founding mem. Les Cheneaux Econ. Forum, 1997—. NEH fellow, 1971. Mem. Les Cheneaux Hist. Assn. (pres. 1987-89), Les Cheneaux Islands Assn. (pres. 1982-84, bd. dirs. 1996—), Les Cheneaux Club (sec. 1972-87, 97—), Delta Kappa Epsilon. Republican. Episcopalian. Avocations: sport fishing, boating, writing, walking in woods. Home: PO Box 187 Cedarville MI 49719-0187 Office: Les Cheneaux Ventures Inc RR 1 Box 15 Cedarville MI 49719-9706

PITTS, TERENCE RANDOLPH, museum director, consultant; b. St. Louis, Feb. 5, 1950; s. Benjamin Randolph and Barbara Avalon (Gilliam) P.; children: Jacob Richard, Rebecca Suzanne. BA, U. Ill., 1972, MLS, 1974; MA in Art History, U. Ariz., 1986. Registrar Ctr. for Creative Photography, Tucson, 1976-77, curator, 1978-88, dir., 1989-2000; exec. dir. Cedar Rapids (Iowa) Mus. Art, 2000—. Cons. Art and Architecture Thesaurus, Getty Mus., 1984—. Author: (with others) George Fiske: Yosemite Photographer, 1981, Edward Weston: Color Photography; author exhbn. catalogs Four Spanish Photographers, 100 Years of Photography in the American West, Photography in the American Grain, Reframing America. Fellow Nat. Endowment Arts, 1983; travel grantee Nat. Mus. Act, 1979, rsch. grantee U. Ariz., 1983. Office: Cedar Rapids Mus Art 410 3d Ave SE Cedar Rapids IA 52401 E-mail: pitts@crma.org.

PIVERONUS, PETER JOHN, JR. education educator; b. Boston, Nov. 29, 1941; s. Peter John Sr. and Rose Camella (Pasciuto) P.; m. Bonnie Jean Kennedy, June 7, 1969 (div. 1981); children: Elizabeth Schaeffler, William Schaeffler, Michelle Montesano; m. Eliabeth Doris Roth, Nov. 21, 1988; children: Shannon Roth, Sara Roth. BA, Boston U., 1964, MA, 1966; PhD, Mich. State U., 1972. Asst. prof. SUNY, Buffalo, 1967-69, Claflin Coll., Orangeburg, S.C., 1969-70; adj. prof. Lansing (Mich.) Community Coll., 1972—, Montcalm Community Coll., Sidney, Mich., 1973—, Jackson (Mich.) Community Coll., 1979—. Prof. humanities extended degree programs Cen. Mich. U., 1991—; vis. prof. Mich. State U., East Lansing, 1986, Alma (Mich.) Coll., 1987. Editor, contbr.: Conflict in Ireland, 1976; contbr. articles to profl. jours. Precinct del. Ingham County Dems., Lansing, 1980-81; trustee Southland Complex Condo Assn., Lansing, 1987-90; pres. Gaelic League of Lansing, 1981-82. HEW fellow Claflin Coll., 1969-70; postdoctoral rsch. grantee U. Mich. Ctr. for Russian and East European Studies, 1985. Mem. Am. Com. for Irish Studies, Nat. Ctr. for Employee Ownership, Irish-Am. Cultural Inst., Soc. for History of Discoveries, Mich. Assn. Higher Edn. (faculty senator 1978-79), Mich. Edn. Assn., Econ. and Bus. Hist. Soc. Unitarian. Avocations: reading, traveling, camping, boating. Home: PO Box 80452 Lansing MI 48908-0452 Office: Lansing Community Coll 419 N Capitol Ave Lansing MI 48933-1207

PIZER, HOWARD CHARLES, sports and entertainment executive; b. Chgo., Oct. 23, 1941; s. Edwin and Estyr (Seeder) P.; m. Sheila Graff, June 14, 1964; children: Jacqueline, Rachel. B.B.A., U. Wis., 1963; J.D. magna cum laude, Northwestern U., 1966. Assoc. McDermott, Will & Emery, Chgo., 1966-72; ptnr. Katten, Muchin, Zavis, 1972-74; exec. v.p., gen. counsel Balcor Co., Skokie, Ill., 1975-80; exec. v.p. Chgo. White Sox, Chgo., 1981—. Exec. v.p. United Ctr. Joint Venture. Past pres. Chgo. Spl. Olympics; bd. dirs. Chgo. Conv. and Tourism Bur., Inc., 1983—, Spl. Children's Charities, 1984—, Chgo. Baseball Cancer Charities, 1983—, Near West Side Cmty. Devel. Corp. Mem. Chgo. Bar Assn., Standard Club Chgo., Briarwood Country. Home: 300 Euclid Ave Winnetka IL 60093-3606 Office: Chgo White Sox 333 W 35th St Chicago IL 60616-3651

PLACHE, KIMBERLY MARIE, state legislator; b. Racine, Wis., Jan. 4, 1961; Student, U. Wis., Whitewater, 1978-81; BS, U. Wis., Parkside-Kenosha, 1984. Legis. asst. to state rep. Jeff Neubauer, 1984-88; mem. Wis. Assembly from 21st dist., madison, 1988-96, Wis. Senate from 21st dist., Madison, 1996—. Mem. NOW, AAUW, Wis. Action Coalition. Address: 2614 17th St Racine WI 53405-3522 Office: Wis State Assembly State Capital Madison WI 53702-0001

PLACHTA, LEONARD E. academic administrator; Pres. Ctrl. Mich. U., Mt. Pleasant, Mich., 1992—. Office: Ctrl Mich U 100 E Preston Rd Mount Pleasant MI 48859-0001

PLAGMAN, RALPH, principal; Prin. George Washington High Sch., Cedar Rapids, Iowa, 1981—. Recipient Blue Ribbon Sch. award Dept. Edn., 1983, 91, 2000. Office: George Washington High Sch 2205 Forest Dr SE Cedar Rapids IA 52403-1653

PLAKMEYER, STEVE, food service executive; CFO Gordon Food Svc. Inc., Grand Rapids, Mich. Office: Gordon Food Svc Inc 333 50th St SW Grand Rapids MI 49548

PLANK, BETSY (MRS. SHERMAN V. ROSENFIELD), public relations counsel; b. Tuscaloosa, Ala., Apr. 3, 1924; d. Richard Jeremiah and Bettye (Hood) P.; m. Sherman V. Rosenfield, Apr. 10, 1954. Student, Bethany (W.Va.) Coll., 1940-43; AB, U. Ala., 1944. Continuity dir. radio sta. KQV, Pitts., 1944-47; account exec. Mitchell McKeown Orgn., Chgo., 1947-54; pub. rels. counsel Chgo. chpt. A.R.C., 1954-57; dir. pub. rels. Chgo. Coun. on Fgn. Rels., 1957-58; v.p. Ronald Goodman Pub. Rels. Counsel, Chgo., 1958-61; exec. v.p., treas., dir. Daniel J. Edelman, Inc., 1961-73; dir. pub. rels. planning AT&T, N.Y.C., 1973-74; asst. v.p. corp. comm. Ill. Bell, Chgo., 1974-90; prin. Betsy Plank Pub. Rels., 1990—. Dep. chmn. VII World Congress on Pub. Rels., 1976; co-chmn. nat. commn. on Pub. Rels. Edn., 1984-86; mem. adv. bd. Ill. Issues, 1975—. Bd. dirs. United Way Chgo., 1986-90; chmn. Citizenship Coun. Met. Chgo., 1990-96, Betsy Plank chpt. Pub. Rels. Students Soc. Am., No. Ill. U.; trustee Found. for Pub. Rels. Rsch. and Edn., 1975-80; nat. bd. dirs. Girl Scouts U.S., 1975-85. Recipient Millennium award Coll. Journalism, U. Fla., 2000, Alexander Hamilton award, Inst. Pub. Rels., 2000; named one of World's 40 Leading Pub. Rels. Profls., Pub. Rels. News, 1984. Fellow Pub. Rels. Soc. Am. (accredited, nat. pres. 1973, Outstanding Profl. award 1977, Outstanding Cmty. Svc. award 1989, Disting. Svc. award 2001); mem. Publicity Club Chgo. (pres. 1963-64, Outstanding Profl. award 1961), Ill. Coun. on Econ. Edn. (past chmn. bd. trustees, Extraordinary Leadership award 2001), Internat. Pub. Rels. Assn., Chgo. Network (chmn. 1980-81), Arthur W. Page Soc. (lifetime achievement award 2000), Union League Club of Chgo., Econ. Club Chgo., Zeta Tau Alpha. Presbyterian. Home and Office: 421 W Melrose St Chicago IL 60657-3848

PLANT, THOMAS A. lawyer; b. 1948; Bar: Ohio, 1974. BA, Alfred U.; JD, Akron U. Sr. v.p., asst. gen. counsel Nat. City Corp., Cleve. Office: National City Corp 1900 E 9th St Fl 17 Cleveland OH 44114-3401

PLAPP, BRYCE VERNON, biochemistry educator; b. DeKalb, Ill., Sept. 11, 1939; s. Vernon Edgar and Eleanor Barbara (Kautz) P.; m. Rosemary Kuhn, June 13, 1962; children— Brendan Bryce, Laurel Andrea B.S., Mich. State U., East Lansing, 1961; Ph.D., U. Calif.-Berkeley, 1966. Research assoc. J.W. Goethe U., Frankfurt/Main, Germany, 1966-68; research assoc. Rockefeller U., N.Y.C., 1968-70; faculty U. Iowa, Iowa City, 1970—, prof. biochemistry, 1979—. Contbr. articles to profl. jours.; mem. editorial bd. Archives Biochemistry and Biophysics. Am. Cancer Soc. fellow, 1966-68 Mem. Am. Soc. for Biochemistry and Molecular Biology, Am. Chem. Soc., Sigma Xi Avocations: travel, sports. Office: U Iowa Dept Biochemistry 4-370 BSB Iowa City IA 52242 E-mail: bv-plapp@uiowa.edu.

PLASTER, GEORGE FRANCIS, Roman Catholic priest; b. Lafayette, Ind., Dec. 6, 1950; s. Robert Lee and Ann Elizabeth (Klinker) P. BS in Econs. and Fin., St. Joseph's Coll., Rensselaer, Ind., 1973; MDiv, Sacred Heart Sch. of Theology, Hales Corners, Wis., 1980. Ordained Roman Cath. Priest, 1980. Bank examiner dept. fin. instns. State of Ind., Indpls., 1973-76; deacon, assoc. pastor St. Patrick Ch., Kokomo, Ind., 1979-82; assoc. pastor Our Lady Mt. Carmel (Ind.), 1982-86, St. Charles Ch., Peru, Ind., 1986-88, St. Joan of Arc Ch., Kokomo, 1988-89; hosp. chaplain St. Vincent's Hosp., Indpls., 1989—. Spiritual counselor Jonah Ctr., Wabash, Ind., 1987-88; clin. pastoral educator Ctrl. State Hosp., Indpls., 1989-90, 91-92, 94-95. Mem. Nat. Right to Life, Washington, 1973—. Mem. Nat. Assn. Cath. Chaplains, KC (chaplain 1980-82, 84-85), Indpls. Cursillo (chaplain 1984, 89, 92, 96, 99). Avocation: playing organ and piano. Office: St Vincent Hosp 2001 W 86th St Indianapolis IN 46260-1991

PLATER, WILLIAM MARMADUKE, English language educator, academic administrator; b. East St. Louis, Ill., July 26, 1945; s. Everett Marmaduke and Marguerite (McBride) P.; m. Gail Maxwell, Oct. 16, 1971; children: Elizabeth Rachel, David Matthew. BA, U. Ill., 1967, MA in English, 1969, PhD in English, 1973. Asst. dir. Unit One, asst. to dean Coll. Liberal Arts and Scis. U. Ill., Urbana, 1971-72, acting dir. Unit One, 1972-73, asst. dean Coll. Arts and Scis., 1973-74, asst. dir. Sch. Humanities, 1974-77, assoc. dir., 1977-83, assoc. coordinator interdisciplinary programs, 1977-83; prof. English, dean Sch. Liberal Arts Ind. U., Indpls., 1983-87; dean of faculties Ind. U.-Purdue U., 1987—, exec. vice chancellor, 1988—. Bd. dirs. Met. Indpls. Pub. Broadcasting, Inc.; cons. in field. Author: The Grim Phoenix: Reconstructing Thomas Pynchon, 1978, also articles, revs., poetry. Trustee Coun. for Adult and Experiential Learning, 1995—; bd. dirs. Ind. Com. for Humanities, 1986—92, Ind. Repertory Theatre, 1987—93, Children's Mus., 1992—2001, U. Ill. YMCA, Urbana, 1982—83, Herron Gallery Contemporary Art, 1987—93; bd. govs. Ind. U. Ctr. on Philanthropy, 1997—; bd. dirs. Midwest Univs. Consortium for Internat. Activities, Inc., 1996—98. Recipient Program Innovation prize Am. Acad. Ednl. Devel., 1982. Home: 6477 Oxbow Way Indianapolis IN 46220- Office: IUPUI Adminstrn Bldg A0108 Indianapolis IN 46202 E-mail: wplater@iupui.edu.

PLATT, ANN, animal care company executive; Owner, pres. Pets Are Inn, Mpls. Office: Pets Are Inn 16526 W 78th St # 354 Eden Prairie MN 55346-4302

PLATT, JEFFREY LOUIS, surgeon, immunologist, educator, pediatric nephrologist; b. Mt. Vernon, N.Y., Mar. 21, 1949; s. Charles Alfred and Paula Platt; m. Agnes M. Schipper. BA in Politics with honors, NYU, 1971; postgrad., Columbia U., 1971-73; MD, U. So. Calif., 1977. Diplomate Am. Bd. Pediatrics, Nat. Bd. Med. Examiners. Intern in pediatrics Children's Hosp. L.A., 1977-78, resident, 1978-79, Della M. Mudd resident, 1979-80; med. fellow in pediatric nephrology U. Minn., Mpls., 1980-85, instr. dept. pediatrics, 1985-86, asst. prof., 1986-88, assoc. prof. pediatrics and cell biology and neuroanatomy, 1988-92; prof. surgery, pediatrics and immunology depts. Duke U., Durham, N.C., 1992—, Dorothy W. and Joseph W. Beard prof. exptl. surgery, 1994—; prof. surgery immunology and pediatrics Mayo Clinic, Rochester, Minn. Mem. editl. bd.: Transplantation, mem. editl. bd.: Transplant Immunology, mem. editl. bd.: Xenotransplantation, mem. editl. bd.: Jour. Heart Lung Transplant, mem. editl. bd.: Cellular Immunology; contbr. over 400 articles to med. jours.; author: 4 books. Recipient Clinician-Scientist award Am. Heart Assn., 1983-88, Established Investigator award Inst. Medicine of NAS. Mem. AAAS, Assn. Am. Physicians, Am. Heart Assn (coun. kidney in cardiovasc. disease, coun. basic sci.), Internat. Soc. Nephrology, Am. Assn. Immunologists, Am. Fedn. Clin. Rsch., Am. Soc. Nephrology, Am. Assn. Pathologists, Soc. for Devel. Biology, Clin. Immunology Soc., Soc. Pediatric Rsch., Soc. Glycobiology, Soc. Exptl. Biology and Medicine, Alpha Omega Alpha. Office: Mayo Found Medical Scis Bldg Rm 2 Rochester MN 55905-0001

PLATTHY, JENO, cultural association executive; b. Dunapataj, Hungary, Aug. 13, 1920; s. Joseph K. and Maria (Dobor) P.; m. Carol Louise Abell, Sept. 25, 1976 Diploma, Peter Pazmany U., Budapest, Hungary, 1942; PhD, Ferencz J. U., Kolozsvar, Hungary, 1944; MS, Cath. U., 1965; PhD (hon.), Yangmingshan U., Taiwan, 1975; DLitt (hon.), U. Libre Asie, Philippines, 1977. Lectr. various univs., 1956-59; sec. Internat. Inst. Boston, 1959-62; adminstrv. asst. Trustees of Harvard U., Washington, 1962-85; exec. dir. Fedn. Internat. Poetry Assns., 1976—. Pub. New Muses Quar., 1976— Author: Winter Tunes, 1974, Ch'u Yuan, His Life and Works, 1975, Springtide, 1976, Opera Bamboo, Collected Poems, 1981, The Poems of Jesus, 1982, Holiness in a Worldly Garment, 1984, Ut Pictures Poeta, 1984, European Odes, 1985, The Mythical Poets of Greece, 1985, Book of Dithyrambs, 1986, Asian Elegies, 1987, Space Ecologues, 1988, Cosmograms, 1988, Nova Comoedia, 1988, vols. II-III, 1992, Bartok: A Critical Biography, 1988, Plato: A Critical Biography, 1990, Near-Death Experiences in Antiquity, 1992, Celebration of Life, 1992, Idylls, 1992, Elegies Asiatiques, 1992, Paeans, 1993, Rhapsodies, 1994, Prosodia, 1994, Visions, 1994, Prophecies, 1994, Epyllia, 1994, Budapest-tol Tokyoig, 1994, 2d edit., 1995, Walking Two Feet Above the Earth, 1995, Dictionarium Cumanico Hungaricum, 1996, Emblems, 1996, Epodes, 1996, Aeolian Lilts, 1996, Transformations, 1996, Inexpressions, 1996, Songs of the Soul, 1996, Sacrifices, 1996, Gifts with Poetic Horizons, 1997, Imperceptions, Hermeneutics of Poetry, 1997, From Silence to Silence, New Perspectives in Poetry, 1997, Lincoln the Poet, an Epic Poem, 1997, Looking Away, 1998, Commitments, 1998, The Duino Elegies of Rilke, 1999, Symmetries with Poetic Discoveries, Part I, 1999, Cosmos Flowers with Poetic Discoveries, Part II, 1999, Dreamtide with Principia Spiritualia I (Discoveries III), 2000, Demonstrations with Principia Spiritualia II-III (Discoveries IV-V), 2000, Pictorial Bio-Bibliography, 2000, also numerous others, also translations; editor-in-chief Monumenta Classica Perennia, 1967-84. Named Poet Laureate 2d World Congress of Poets, 1973; recipient Confucius award Chinese Poetry Soc., 1974, Yunus Emre award 12th Internat. Congress of Poets, Istanbul, Turkey, 1991, Jacques Raphael-Leygues prize Société des Poètes Français, 1992, French Ordre des Arts et des Lettres (officer), 1992. Mem. PEN, ASCAP, Internat. Soc. Lit., Die Literarische Union, Internat. Poetry Soc., Acad. Am. Poets, Assn. Lit. Scholars and Critics, 3d Internat. Congress Poets (pres. 1976, poet laureate 1976), Nat. Assn. of Scholars. Office: Fedn Internat Poetry Assns 961 W Sled Cir Santa Claus IN 47579-6251

PLATZMAN, GEORGE WILLIAM, geophysicist, educator; b. Chgo., Apr. 19, 1920; s. Alfred and Rose I. K.; m. Harriet M. Herschberger, Feb. 19, 1945 (dec. 1985). BS, U. Chgo., 1940, PhD, 1948; MS, U. Ariz., 1941. Instr. U. Chgo., 1942-45, rsch. assoc., 1947-48, faculty, 1949—, head phys. scis. in coll., 1959-60, prof. geophys. scis., 1960-90, chmn. dept. geophys. scis., 1971-74, emeritus prof., 1990—. Cons. Inst. Advanced Study, Princeton, 1950-53 Author: A Catalogue of Early Printed Editions of the Works of Frédéric Chopin in the University of Chicago Library, 1997;

contbr. articles to profl. jours. Hydrologic engr. C.E., U.S. Army, 1945-46. Guggenheim fellow, 1967-68 Fellow AAAS, Am. Geophys. Union, Am. Meteorol. Soc. (editor jour. 1948-49, chmn. publs. com. 1966-70, Meisinger award 1966). Office: U Chgo Dept Geophys Scis 5734 S Ellis Ave Chicago IL 60637-1434

PLAUT, JONATHAN VICTOR, rabbi; b. Chgo., Oct. 7, 1942; s. W. Gunther and Elizabeth (Strauss) P.; m. Carol Ann Fainstein, July 5, 1965; children: Daniel Abraham, Deborah Maxine. BA, Macalester Coll., 1964; postgrad., Hebrew Union Coll., Jerusalem, 1967-68; BHL, Hebrew Union Coll., Cin., 1968, MA, 1970, DHL, 1977; DD (hon.), 1995. Ordained rabbi, 1970. Rabbi Congregation Beth-El, Windsor, Ont., Can., 1970-84; sr. rabbi Temple Emanu-El, San Jose, Calif., 1985-93; dir. comty. outreach and involvement Jewish Fed. of Met. Detroit, 1993-95; pres. JVP Fund Raising Cons., Inc., Farmington Hills, Mich., 1994—. Lectr. Assumption Coll. Sch., 1972-84, St. Clair Coll., 1982-84, U. Windsor, Ont., Can., 1984; adj. asst. prof. Santa Clara U., 1985-93; vis. Rabbinic scholar Temple Beth El, 1993—; pres. JVP Fund Raising Cons., 1994—; rabbi Congregation Beth El, Traverse City, Mich., 1999—, Temple Beth Israel, Jackson, Miss., 2000—. Contbg. author: Reform Judaism in America: A Biographical Dictionary and Sourcebook, 1993; editor: Through the Sound of Many Voices, 1982, Jour. Can. Jewish Hist. Soc., 1976-83; also articles; host weekly program Religious Scope, Sta. CBET-TV, Religion in News, Sta. CKWW, 1971-84. Pres. Jewish Nat. Fund Windsor, 1978-81, chmn. bd. dirs., 1981-84; chmn. United Jewish Appeal Windsor, 1981-83, State of Israel Bonds, Windsor, 1980; nat. bd. dirs. Jewish Nat. Fund Can., 1972-84; pres. Reform Rabbis of Can., 1982-84; bd. dirs. Can. Jewish Congress, 1978-84, Jewish Family Svc. Santa Clara County, 1987-90, Jewish Fedn. Greater San Jose, 1986-93; chaplain San Jose Fire Dept., 1987-93; mem. exec. cabinet United Jewish Appeal, Windsor, 1971-84, mem. nat. rabbinic cabinet, 1993-95; mem. exec. com. Windsor Jewish Community Coun., 1970-84, chmn. 1975-84; mem. adv. coun. Riverview unit Windsor Hosp. Ctr., 1972-81; pres. Credit Counselling Svc. Met. Windsor, 1977-79. Honoree Jewish Nat. Fund, 1985. Mem. NCCJ, Can. Jewish Congress (nat. exec. bd. 1978-84), Can. Jewish Hist. Soc. (nat. v.p. 1974-84), Calif. Bd. Rabbis, Rabbinic Assn. Greater San Jose (chmn. 1986-87), Ctrl. Conf. Am. Rabbis, Nat. Assn. Temple Educators. Home and Office: 30208 Kingsway Dr Farmington Hills MI 48331-1648 Fax: (248) 788-4144. E-mail: jvplaut@earthlink.net.

PLEAU, LAWRENCE WINSLOW, professional hockey coach, business executive; b. Boston, June 29, 1947; s. Ernest and Norma (Knowles) Pl.; m. Wendy Sargent MacDougall, May 3, 1969; children, Steven Lawrence, Shannon Lynn. Grad. high sch. Player Montreal (Que.) Canadiens, 1969-72, N.Eng. Whalers, Hartford, Conn., 1972-79; asst. coach Hartford Whalers, 1979-80, coach, gen. mgr., 1980-83, asst. gen. mgr., 1983-84, coach, 1988-89; coach, gen. mgr. Binghamton (N.Y.) Whalers, 1984-88. Player U.S. Olympic Hockey Team, Grenoble, France, 1968, U.S. Nat. Hockey Team, Stockholm, 1969, U.S.A. Hockey Team, Providence, 1976; radio, TV commentator, ESPN, Hartford, 1979-80; owner Bridge Marina Inc. With U.S. Army, 1967-69. Mem. All-Star Teams, 1973, 74, 75; named Coach of Yr. Am. Hockey League, 1986-87. Democrat. Avocations: deep sea fishing, golf, tennis. Office: care Hartford Whalers 1 Civic Center Plz Hartford CT 06103-1504

PLEHAL, JAMES BURTON, career officer; m. Sandra Plehal; 1 child, Andrew. BA in Polit. Sci. with hons, U. Utah, 1969; Diploma, U.S. Naval Submarine Sch. Ensign USN, 1969; advanced through ranks to rear adm. USNR; various assignments to Res. Cryptologic Area Coord., Ctrl., Naval Res. Security Group Program, 1995-99; comdr. Naval Res. Security Group Command, Ft. Worth, 1998—; asst. v.p. and fin. cons. Merrill Lynch, St. Paul; active duty dep. dir. Nat. Infrastructure Protection Ctr., Washington, 2001—. Mem., mental health provider Red Wing Charter Commn., Minn.; former city coun., Dist. Legal Ethics Com. Office: 1015 W 4th St Red Wing MN 55066-2421

PLESTED, WILLIAM G., III, surgeon; b. Wichita, Kans., 1936; BS, U. Colo.; MD, U. Kans., 1962. Diplomate Am. Bd. Surgery, Am. Bd. Thoracic Surgery. Intern UCLA, 1962-63, resident, 1963-68, asst. clin. prof. surgery; resident Mayo Clinic, Rochester, 1964; pvt. practice, 1970—. Bd. dirs. Santa Monica-UCLA Hosp., IPA, Blue Shield of Calif., Unihealth, Auto Digest Found. Mem. ACP, AMA (chair reference com. spl. com. to study AMA bd. trustees), Calif. Med. Assn. (pres.), L.A. County Med. Assn., Soc. of Thoracic Sugeons, Western Thoracic Surg. Assn.Soc. for Clin. Vascular Surgery, Pacific Coach Surg. Assn., Am. Soc. of Gen. Surgery. Office: AMA 515 N State St Chicago IL 60610-4325

PLETZ, THOMAS GREGORY, lawyer; b. Toledo, Oct. 3, 1943; s. Francis G. and Virginia (Connell) P.; m. Carol Elizabeth Connolly, June 27, 1969; children: Anne M., John F. BA, U. Notre Dame, 1965; JD, U. Toledo, 1971. Bar: Ohio 1971, U.S. Ct. Appeals (6th cir.) 1978, U.S. Supreme Ct. 1985. Ct. bailiff Lucas County Common Pleas Ct., Toledo, 1967-71; jud. clk. U.S. Dist. Ct. (no. dist.) Ohio, 1971-72; assoc. Shumaker, Loop & Kendrick, 1972-76, litigation ptnr., 1976—. Acting judge Sylvania (Ohio) Mcpl. Ct., 1990—; mem. Ohio Bar Bd. Examiners, 1993—, chmn., 1996-99. Active Toledo Parish Coun., 1987-2001; chmn., trustee Kiroff Trial Adv. Com., Toledo, 1982-91; mem. Nat. Conf. Bar Examiners Com., 1996-2001. With USNR, 1965-92; ret. CDR. Recipient Toledo Jr. Bar award, 1995. Mem. ABA, Ohio State Bar Assn., Toledo Bar Assn. (trustee 1981-93), Diocesan Attys. Bar Assn., 6th Cir. Jud. Conf. (life). Roman Catholic. Office: Shumaker Loop & Kendrick 1000 Jackson St Toledo OH 43624-1573 E-mail: tpletz@slk-law.com.

PLOTKIN, MANUEL D. management consultant, educator, former corporate executive and government official; s. Jacob and Bella (Katz) P.; m. Diane Fern Weiss, Dec. 17, 1967; 1 child, Lori Ann. BS with honors, Northwestern U., 1948; MBA, U. Chgo., 1949. Price economist, survey coordinator U.S. Bur. Labor Statistics, Washington, 1949-51, Chgo., 1951-53; sr. economist Sears Roebuck & Co., 1953-61, mgr. market research, 1961-66, chief economist, mgr. mktg. rsch., 1966-73, dir. corp. planning and research, 1973-77, exec. corp. planner, 1979-80; dir. U.S. Bur. Census, Washington, 1977-79; v.p., dir. group practice Divsn. Mgmt. Cons. Austin Co., Evanston, Ill., 1981-85; pres. M.D. Plotkin Research & Planning Co., Chgo., 1985—. Tchr. statistics Ind. U., 1953-54; tchr. econs. Wilson Jr. Coll., Chgo., 1954-55; tchr. quantitative methods and managerial econs. Northwestern U., 1955-63; tchr. mktg. rsch. and mktg. mgmt. DePaul U., Chgo., 1992-95; mem. Conf. Bd. Mktg. Rsch. Adv. Coun., 1968-77, chmn.-elect, 1977; chmn. adv. com. U.S. Census Bur., 1974-75; trustee Mktg. Sci. Inst., 1968-77; mem. Nat. Commn. Employment and Unemployment Stats., 1978-79, Adv. Coun. Edn. Stats., 1977-79, Interagy. Com. Population Rsch., 1977-79; mem. adv. coun. Kellstadt Ctr., DePaul U., 1987-92; trustee U.S. Travel Data Ctr., 1977-79. Contbr. articles to profl. jours. Served with AUS, 1943-46, ETO. Decorated Bronze Star medal with oak leaf cluster. Mem. Am. Mktg. Assn. (pres. Chgo. 1968-69, nat. dir. 1969-70, nat. v.p. mktg. rsch. 1970-72, nat. v.p. mktg. mgmt. 1981-83, pres., CEO 1985-86), Am. Statis. Assn. (pres. Chgo. 1966-67, Forecasting award 1963), Am. Econ. Assn., Nat. Assn. Bus. Economists, Planning Execs. Inst., World Future Soc., Midwest Planning Assn., U. Ill. Businessmen Rsch. Adv. Group, Chgo. Assn. Commerce and Industry, Beta Gamma Sigma, Alpha Sigma Lambda, Delta Mu Delta. Home and Office: 2650 N Lakeview Ste 3910 Chicago IL 60614-1831

PLOTNICK, HARVEY BARRY, publishing executive; b. Detroit, Aug. 5, 1941; s. Isadore and Esther (Sher) P.; m. Susan Regnery, Aug. 16, 1964 (div. Apr. 1977); children: Andrew, Alice; m. Elizabeth Allen, May 2, 1982; children: Teresa, Samuel. B.A., U. Chgo., 1963. Editor Contemporary Books, Inc., Chgo., 1964-66, pres., 1966-94; with Paradigm Holdings, Inc., Chgo., 1994—, CEO. CEO Molecular Electronics Corp., 2000—. Trustee U. Chgo., 1994—, Chgo. Acad. Scis., Argonne Nat. Lab. Office: Paradigm Holdings Inc 2 Prudential Plz Ste 3150 Chicago IL 60601-6790 E-mail: harvet1844@aol.com.

PLOTNIK, ARTHUR, author, columnist; b. White Plains, N.Y., Oct. 1, 1937; s. Michael and Annabelle (Taub) P.; m. Meta Von Borstel, Sept. 6, 1960 (div. 1979); children: Julia Nicole, Katya Michelle.; m. Mary Phelan, Dec. 2, 1983. B.A., State U. N.Y., Binghamton, 1960; M.A., U. Iowa, 1961; M.S. in L.S, Columbia U., 1966. Gen. reporter, reviewer Albany (N.Y.) Times Union, 1963-64; freelance writer, 1964-66; editor Librarians Office, Library of Congress, 1966-69; assoc. editor Wilson Library Bull., Bronx, N.Y., 1969-74; editor-in-chief Am. Libraries, Chgo., 1975-89; assoc. pub. ALA, 1989-97; editl. dir. ALA Editions, 1993-97; writer, 1997—. Adj. instr. journalism Columbia Coll., Chgo., 1988-89; speaker in field. Author: The Elements of Editing: A Modern Guide for Editors and Jouranlists, 1982, Jacob Shallus, Calligrapher of the Constitution, 1987, Honk If You're a Writer, 1992, The Elements of Expression, 1996, The Urban Tree Book, 2000; columnist: Editorial Eye, 1995—2001; contbg. editor: The Writer, 2000—; also fiction, articles, vide scripts, photographer: ; exec. prodr.: Libr. Video mag., 1986—91. Bd. dirs. Am. Book Awards, 1979-82; bd. advs. Univ. Press of Am., 1982— . Served with USAR, 1962-67. Fellow Iowa Writers Workshop Creative Writing, 1961; recipient award Ednl. Press Assn. Am., 1973 (3), 77, 82, 83; cert. of excellence Internat. Reading Assn., 1970, First Pl. award Verbatim essay competition, 1986, award Am. Soc. Bus. Press Editors, 1987. Mem. ALA, Am. Forests, Morton Arboretum, Treekeepers (Openlands Project). Home and Office: 2120 W Pensacola Ave Chicago IL 60618-1718 also: N E Pub Assocs Literary Agents PO Box 5 Chester CT 06412-0005 E-mail: baronplot@aol.com.

PLOWDEN, DAVID, photographer; b. Boston, Oct. 9, 1932; s. Roger and Mary Russell (Butler) P.; m. Pleasance Coggeshall, June 20, 1962 (div. 1976); children: John, Daniel; m. Sandra Oakes Schoellkopf, July 8th, 1977; children: Philip, Karen. BA Econs., Yale U., 1955; pvt. study with Minor White, Rochester, N.Y., 1959-60. Asst. O. Winston Link Studio, N.Y.C., 1958-59, George Meluso Studio, N.Y.C., 1960-62; photographer, writer, 1962—. Assoc. prof. Inst. Design, Ill. Inst. Tech., Chgo., 1978-86; lectr. U. Iowa Sch. Journalism, 1985-88; vis. prof. Grand Valley State Univ., 1988-90, 91—; artist-in-residence U. Balt., 1990-91. Author and photographer: Farewell to Steam, 1968, Lincoln and His America, 1970 (Benjamin Barondess award 1971), The Hand of Man on America, 1971, 2d edit, 1974, The Floor of the Sky: the Great Plains, 1972, Bridges: the Spans of North America, 1974, 2d edit. 1984, 3d edit., 2001, Commonplace, 1974, Tugboat, 1976 (notable Children's books ALA 1976, Children's Book Showcase 1976), Steel, 1981, An American Chronology, 1982 (Notable Books ALA 1982, Booklist's Best of the 80s 1989), Industrial Landscape, 1985, A Time of Trains, 1987, A Sense of Place, 1988, End of an Era: The Last of the Great Lakes Steamboats, 1992, Small Town America, 1994, Imprints: The Photographs of David Plowden, 1997; co-author, photographer, Nantucket, 1970, Cape May to Montauk, 1973, Desert and Plains, the Mountains and the River, 1975, The Iron Road, 1978 (notable children's books 1978, Honor list Horn Books 1979), Wayne County: the Aesthetic Heritage of a Rural Area, 1979; introduction The Gallery of World Photography/the Country, 1983; commd. illustrator Gems, 1967, The Freeway in the City, 1968, America the Vanishing, 1969, New Jersey, 1977, North Dakota, 1977, Vermont, 1979, New York, 1981, A Place of Sense, 1988; contbr. articles to numerous jours. including Time, Newsweek, Life, Audubon, Fortune, Smithsonian, Camera Arts; one-man shows include Columbia U., 1965, Smithsonian Instn., 1970, 71, 75, 76, 81, 89, Internat. Ctr. Photography, N.Y., 1976, Witkin Gallery, N.Y.C., 1979, Cin. Art Acad., 1979, The Gilbert Gallery, Chgo., 1980, 81, Chgo. Ctr. Contemporary Photography, 1982, Fed. Hall Mus., N.Y.C., 1982, Calif. Mus. Photography, Riverside, 1982-83, Chgo. Hist. Soc., 1985, Martin Gallery, Washington, 1987, Kunstmuseum, Luzern, Switzerland, 1987, Burchfield Ctr., Buffalo, 1987-88, Iowa State Mus., Des Moines, 1988-89, Catherine Edelman Gallery, Chgo., 1990, Grand Valley State U., 1993, Ewing Gallery, Washington, 1994, Beinecke Rare Book and Manuscript Lib. Yale U., 1997, Albright-Knox Art Gallery, 1997, Mus. Contemporary Photography, Chgo., 1998, Albin O. Kuhn Libr. & Gallery, U. Md., Balt., 1998, Tatar/Alexander Photogallery, Toronto, Ont., 1999, Lawrence Miller Gallery, N.Y.C., 2000; exhibited in group shows at Met. Mus. Art, N.Y.C., 1967, Kodak Gallery, N.Y.C., 1976, Currier Gallery Art, Manchester, N.H., 1978, Whitney Mus., 1979, Art Inst. Chgo., 1983-86, 87, Witkin Gallery, N.Y.C., 1988, Davenport (Iowa) Mus. Art, 1992, Mus. Contemporary Photography, Chgo., Ill., 1996, 98, 99, City, 2000, Peter Fetterman Gallery Photographic Works of Art, Santa Monica, Calif., 2001; represented in permanent collections Albright-Knox Gallery, Art Inst. Chgo., Calif. Mus. Photography, Ctr. Creative Photography, Chgo. Hist. Soc., Libr. Congress, Smithsonian Instn., U. Md., J.B. Speed Mus., Iowa Humanities Bd., Iowa State Hist. Dept., Burchfield Art Ctr., Buffalo and Erie County Hist. Soc., Internat. Mus. Photography George Eastman House, Internat. Ctr. Photography, Ekstrom Libr. U. Louisville, Beinecke Rare Book and Mauscript Library, Yale U., 1995—, Mus. Contemporary Photography, Chicy, Bayly Mus. U. Va., Charlottesville; PBS produced an hour long documentary film called David Plowden: Light, Shadow and Form. John Simon Guggenheim fellow, 1968; grantee N.Y. State Coun. Arts, 1966, 87, Smithsonian Inst., 1970-71, Dept. Transp. and Smithsonian Inst., 1975-76, H. E. Butt Found., 1977, United Bd. Homeland Ministries, 1976, Chgo. Hist. Soc., 1980-84, Seymour H. Knox Found., 1987, Baird Found., 1987, State Hist. Soc. Iowa, 1987-88, Iowa Humanities Bd., 1987-88; recipient Railroad History award, 1989; subjectof PBS documentary: David Plowden: Light, Shadow & Form. Mem. Am. Soc. Media Photographers. Home and Office: 609 Cherry St Winnetka IL 60093-2614 Fax: 847-446-2795. E-mail: dplowden@enteract.com.

PLUIMER, EDWARD J. lawyer; b. Rapid City, S.D., 1949; BA cum laude, U. S.D., 1971; JD cum laude, NYU, 1974. Bar: Minn. 1975. Law clk. to Hon. Robert A. Ainsworth, Jr. U.S. Ct. Appeals (5th cir.), 1974-75; ptnr. Dorsey & Whitney, Mpls., 1975—. Mem. Minn. Supreme Ct. ADR Task Force, 1988-92. Editor N.Y. U. Law Rev. Mem. Order of the Coif. Office: Dorsey & Whitney LLP Ste 1500 50 S 6th St Minneapolis MN 55402-1498 E-mail: pluimer.ed@dorseylaw.com.

PLUMLEY, S. PATRIC, retail executive; b. West Hamlin, W.Va., Jan. 2, 1949; s. Caudle and Nellie Brook (Honaker) P.; m. Rose M. McBee, Jan. 16, 1970. BA in Acctg. cum laude, U. South Fla., 1980, M Accountancy, 1986. CPA, Fla., Calif. Mem. acctg. staff Lucky Stores, Inc., Tampa, Fla., 1973-82, acctg. mgr., 1982-84, contr., 1984-86, v.p., contr. Buena Park, Calif., 1986-90, sr. v.p. adminstrn. Dublin, 1990-94; with Am. Stores, Inc., Salt Lake City, 1994—. Vice chmn. bd. dirs. Olive Crest, homes for abused children, Anaheim, Calif., 1988-90; bd. dirs. Jr. Achievement of Bay Area, 1992-94. With USN, 1967-71. Mem. AICPA, Inst. Mgmt. Accts. (cert.). Baptist. Avocations: golf, coin collecting. Office: Eagle Food Ctr 801 E First St Rte 67 & Knoxville Rd Milan IL 61264-6700

PLUMMER, ALFRED HARVEY, III, lawyer; b. Wabash, Ind., June 10, 1943; s. Alfred H. and Aileen (Kester) P.; m. Patricia Ann Hughes, June 5, 1966; children: Alfred H. IV, Ann H., Alexander J. BS, Ind. U., 1965, JD, 1968. Bar: Ind. 1968, U.S. Dist. Ct. (so. dist.) Ind. 1968, U.S. Dist. Ct. (no. dist.) Ind. 1980, U.S. Ct. Appeals (7th cir.) 1968. City atty. City of Wabash, Ind., 1968-72; atty. Town of LaFontaine, 1969--; pros. atty. Wabash County, Wabash, 1983--. Mem. Wabash (Ind.) C. of C. (pres. 1970), Rotary, Elks, Shriners (pres. 1988). Republican. Presbyterian. Office: Alfred H Plummer III 21-27 W Canal PO Box 421 Wabash IN 46992-0421

PLUMMER, PATRICIA LYNN MOORE, chemistry and physics educator; b. Tyler, Tex., Feb. 26, 2000; d. Robert Lee and Jewell Ovelia (Jones) Moore; m. Otho Raymond Plummer, Apr. 10, 1965; children: Patrick William Otho, Christina Elisa Lynne. BA, Tex. Christian U., Ft. Worth, Tex., 1960; postgrad., U. N.C., 1960-61; PhD, U. Tex., 1964; grad., Bryn Mawr Summer Inst., 1992. Instr., Welch postdoctoral fellow U. Tex., Austin, 1964-66; postdoctoral fellow Dept. Chemistry, U. Ark., Fayetteville, 1966-68; rsch. assoc. Grad. Ctr., Cloud Phys. Rsch., Rolla, Mo., 1968-73; asst. prof. physics U. Mo., 1973-77; assoc. dir. Grad. Ctr. Cloud Phys. Rsch., 1977-79, sr. investigator, 1980-85; assoc. prof. physics U. Mo., 1977-85, prof. dept. chemistry and physics, 1986—. Internat. sci. com. Symposium on Chemistry and Physics of Ice, 1982—, vice chair, 1996—, chair of Faculty Sen., 1995-96, pres. U. of Mo. Intercampo Fac. Sen., 1994-95. Assoc. editor Jour. of Colloid and Interface Sci., 1980-83; contbr. articles to profl. jours., chpts. to books. Rsch. grantee IBM, 1990-92, Air Force Office Rsch., 1989-91, NSF, 1976-86, NASA, 1973-78; Air Force Office Rsch. summer fellow, 1988, Bryn Mawr Summer Inst., 1992, Faculty fellow Cherry Emerson Ctr. for Sci. Computation, Emory U., 1998-99. Mem. Am. Chem. Soc., Am. Phys. Soc., Am. Geophys. Union, Sigma Xi (past pres.). Democrat. Baptist. Avocations: sailing, gardening, tennis, photography. Office: Univ of Missouri 314 Physics Bldg Columbia MO 65211-0001 Fax: (573) 882-4195. E-mail: plummerp@missouri,edu.

PLUNKETT, PAUL EDMUND, federal judge; b. Boston, July 9, 1935; s. Paul M. and Mary Cecilia (Erbacher) P.; m. Martha Milan, Sept. 30, 1958; children: Paul Scott, Steven, Andrew, Kevin BA, Harvard U., 1957, JD, 1960. Ptnr. Mayer Brown & Platt, Chgo., 1960-63, 78-83; asst. atty. U.S. Atty.'s Office, 1963-66; ptnr. Plunkett Nisin et al, 1966-78; sr. judge U.S. Dist. Ct. (no. dist.) Ill., 1983—. Adj. faculty John Marshall Law Sch., Chgo., 1964-76, 82—, Loyola U. Law Sch., Chgo., 1977-82. Mem. Fed. Bar Assn. Clubs: Legal, Law, Union League (Chgo.) Office: US Dist Ct Everett McKinley Dirksen Bldg 219 S Dearborn St Ste 1446 Chicago IL 60604-1705

PLUSH, MARK J. company executive; With Keithley Instruments, Inc., 1982, corp. officer, 1989, corp. contr., CFO, 1998—. Office: 28775 Aurora Rd Solon OH 44139-1837

PLUSQUELLIC, DONALD L. mayor; b. Akron, Ohio, July 3, 1949; m. Mary Plusquellic; children: Dave, Michelle. BS, Bowling Green State U., 1972; JD, U. Akron, 1981. Councilman Akron City Council, 1973-81, councilman-at-large, 1982-86, council pres., 1984-86; mayor City of Akron, 1987—. Trustee U.S. Conf. of Mayors. Home: 2785 Nesmith Lake Blvd Akron OH 44314-3427 Office: Office of the Mayor 200 Municipal Bldg 166 S High St Akron OH 44308-1626

POCHYLY, DONALD FREDERICK, physician, hospital administrator; b. Chgo., June 3, 1934; s. Frank J. and Vlasta (Bezdek) P.; m. Diane Dilelio, May 11, 1957; children: Christopher, Jonathan, David. M.D., Loyola U., 1959; M.Ed., U. Ill., 1971. Diplomate Am. Bd. Internal Medicine, Am. Bd. Geriatrics. Fellow ACP, 1966-67; asst. prof. med. edn. U. Ill., 1967-72, asso. prof., 1972-74; chmn. dept. health scis. edn. U. of Health Scis., Chgo. Med. Sch., 1975-77, provost, acting pres., 1977-79; prof. clin. medicine Loyola U., Chgo., 1980—; v.p. med. affairs N.W. Community Hosp., Arlington Heights, Ill. Chmn. com. rev. and recognition Am. Coun. Continuing Med. Edn., 1993; cons. Nat. Libr. Medicine, WHO. Contbr. articles to med. jours. Mem. AMA, Ill. Geriatrics Soc. (pres. Chgo. chpt. 1988-89), Ill. Med. Soc., Chgo. Med. Soc., Alpha Omega Alpha. Roman Catholic. Office: Northwest Community Hosp 800 W Central Rd Arlington Heights IL 60005-2392

PODANY, WILLIAM J. speciality discount retail company executive; b. 1948; Various sr. merchandising positions Allied Stores, 1978-87; various sr. mgmt. positions May Dept. Stores, 1987-92; exec. v.p. merchandising and logistics Carter Hawley Hale, 1992-94; exec. v.p. merchandising, mktg., logistics-store planning ShopKo Stores Inc., Green Bay, Wis., 1994-96, COO, 1996-97, pres., COO, 1997-99, pres., CEO, 1999—, chmn., 2000—. Named Retail Exec. of Yr., Discount Merchandiser, 2000. Office: ShopKo Stores Inc 700 Pilgrim Way Green Bay WI 54304-5276

POE, DONALD RAYMOND, state legislator; m. Carol Henrikson; children: Collette Schultz, Cherrilyn Mayfield, Lance. Grad., DeVry Inst. Tech., Chgo., 1963, Agriculture Leaders of Tomorrow, 1983. Farmer, Sherman, Ill., 1964—; mem. Ill. State Ho. of Reps. Dist. 99, 1995—. Mem. agriculture & conservation, appropriations-edn., elem. & secondary edn., higher edn., pers. & pensions coms. 99th Legis. Dist., Ill. Gen. Assembly; rep. Ill. Farm Bur., mem. state coun. bus.- edn. partnership Ill. State Bd. Edn., 1990—; mem., exec. bd. dirs. Ill. Farm Bur., past. pres., past mem. pub. rels. com. Bd. mem. Williamsvill Cmty. H.S., 1970-91, past pres.; fundraiser supr. Sherman United Meth. Ch., youth group leader, 1980-90, past chmn. bd., past chmn. bd. trustees com., pastor parish com.; active Sangamon County Sheriff's DUI Taskforce, 1995-96.

POEHLMANN, CARL JOHN, agronomist, researcher; b. Jamestown, Mo., Jan. 29, 1950; s. Edwin William and Lucille Albina (Neu) P.; m. Linda Kay Garner, Dec. 29, 1973; children: Anthony, Kimberly. BS, U. Mo., 1972, MS, 1978. Farmer, Jamestown, Mo., 1972-73; vocat. agrl. tchr. Linn (Mo.) Pub. Schs., 1973-75, Columbia (Mo.) Pub. Schs., 1975-78; dir., mgr. agronomy rsch. ctr. U. Mo., Columbia, 1978-2000; dir. MOAES Field Ops., 2000—. Mem. Am. Soc. Agronomy (div. A-7 chair 1985-86, bd. mem. 1991-94, cert. crop advisor 1993—), Crop Sci. Soc. Am., Soil Sci. Soc. Am., Internat. Assn. Mechanization Field Experiments. Mem. Christian Ch. (Disciples of Christ). Office: MU Field Ops 3600 New Haven Rd Columbia MO 65201

POEL, ROBERT WALTER, air force officer, physician; b. Muskegon, Mich., July 24, 1934; s. Abel John and Fannie M. (Vanderwall) P.; m. Carol Anne Noordeloos, June 24, 1960; children: Kathryn Anne Poel Engle, James Robert, Sharon Kay Poel Thompson. BS, Calvin Coll., 1957; MD, U. Mich., 1959. Diplomate Am. Bd. Surgery. Commd. capt. USAF, 1962, advanced through grades to brig. gen., 1988, ret., 1993; comdr. Hosp. Malmstrom AFB, Great Falls, Mont., 1971-73; dir. profl. svcs. Hdqrs. Tactical Air Command Command Surgeon's Office, Langley AFB, Va., 1973-74; div. chief, med. plans Office of Air Force Surgeon Gen., Wash., 1974-78; comdr. regional hosp. Sheppard AFB, Wichita Falls, Tex., 1978-83; dir. profl. svcs. Office of Air Force Logistics Command Surgeon, Wright-Patterson AFB, Ohio, 1983-85; vice-comdr. Wilford Hall USAF Med. Ctr., San Antonio, 1985-87; chief, quality assurance, dir. plans and resources Air Force Surgeon Gen., Bolling AFB, Washington, 1987-89; hosp. comdr. Malcolm Grow Med. Ctr., Andrews AFB, 1989-93; med. dir. near south office Meth. Occupational Healthctrs. Inc., Indpls., 1995—. Dir. Andrews Fed. Credit Union, 1991-95, vice chmn. bd. dirs., 1992-95. Advisor, bd. regents Uniformed Svcs. U. the Health Scis., Bethesda, Md., 1989-93; mem. pres. coun. Calvin Coll., 1990. Named Disting. alumnus, Calvin Coll., 1990; Paul Harris fellow Rotary Club of Wichita Falls, 1982. Mem. AMA, Am. Coll. Occupl. and Environ. Medicine, Assn. Mil. Surgeons of U.S. (life), Ret. Officers Assn. (life). Republican. Home: 12085 Waterford Ln Carmel IN 46033-5501 Office: 1101 Southeastern Ave Indianapolis IN 46202-3946 E-mail: poelrc@earthlink.net.

POELLOT, LUTHER, minister; b. Palatine, Ill., Oct. 23, 1913; s. Sigfried Daniel and Lisette (Brueggemann) P.; m. Esther Maaser, May 23, 1942; children: Sharon Ruth, Carolyn May Gluesenkamp, Marion Kay, Celia Louise (Mrs. Allen Thomas). Student, Concordia Coll., Milw., 1927-33, Concordia Sem., St. Louis, 1933-37, LittD, 1999. Ordained to ministry

Luth. Ch.-Mo. Synod, 1942. Head clk. Concordia Sem. Libr., St. Louis, 1937-39; missionary Ft. Myers, Fla., 1940; pastor Dallas, 1940-50, Mercedes, Tex., 1950-52, Pitcairn, Pa., 1952-62, Waterloo, Ont., Can., 1962-64. Indexer, editor Concordia Pub. House, St. Louis, 1964-78. Author: Revelation, 1962, 76, reprinted in Concordia Classic Commentary Series, 1987; translator chpts.: (J. Quenstedt's Theologia) The Nature and Character of Theology, 1986, The Holy Ministry, 1991, The Church, 1999; (M. Chemnitz's Enchiridion) Ministry, Word, and Sacraments, 1981; contbr. articles to profl. jours.; composer, poet. Home: 753 Buckley Rd Saint Louis MO 63125-5347

POGEMILLER, LAWRENCE J. state legislator; b. Sept. 18, 1951; 010 BS, U. Minn.; MPA, Harvard U. Mem. Minn. Ho. of Reps., St. Paul, 1981-82, Minn. Senate from 59th dist., St. Paul, 1983—. Chmn. edn. funding divsn. com., co-chmn. edn. com., mem. higher edn. divsn. com., tax laws com., others.; system project analyst. Democrat. Address: 201 University Ave NE Minneapolis MN 55413-2250 also: State Senate State Capital Building Saint Paul MN 55155-0001

POGUE, THOMAS FRANKLIN, economics educator, consultant; b. Roswell, NMex., Dec. 28, 1935; s. Talmadge Franklin and Lela (Cox) P.; m. Colette Marie LaFortune, June 10, 1961; children: Michael Frederick, Robert Franklin. BS, N.Mex. State U., 1957; MS, Okla. State U., 1962; PhD, Yale U., 1968. Asst. prof. econs U. Iowa, Iowa City, 1965-69, assoc. prof., 1970-75, prof., 1975—, chmn dept., 1983-84. Vis. prof. Tex. Tech. U., Lubbock, 1975-76, U. Adelaide, Australia, 1985, 89. Author: Government and Economic Choice, 1978; editor: State Taxation of Business, 1992; contbr. articles to profl. jours.; cons. on tax policy, welfare reform, pub. sch. fin., bus. taxation, and econ. devel. Tax Studies for Iowa, 1992, Minn, 1984, Ariz., 1989. Commd. officer with USAF, 1957-60. Grantee Nat. Inst. Justice, Washington, 1979, U.S. Dept. Transp., 1994. Mem. Am. Econ. Assn., Nat. Tax. Assn. Office: U Iowa Dept Econs 108 Pappajohn Bus Adminstrn Bldg Iowa City IA 52242 Home: 24 Colwyn Ct Iowa City IA 52245-1578 E-mail: thomas-pogue@uiowa.edu.

POHL, KATHLEEN SHARON, editor; b. Sandusky, Mich., Apr. 7, 1951; d. Gerald Arthur and Elizabeth Louise (Neukamm) P.; m. Bruce Mark Allen Reynolds, June 11, 1982. BA in Spanish, Valparaiso U., 1973; MA in English, No. Mich. U., 1975. Producer, dir. fine arts Sta. WNMU-FM, Marquette, Mich., 1981-82; instr. communications Waukesha County (Wis.) Tech. Inst., 1983; editor Ideals mag., Milw., 1983-85; editor, mng. editor Raintree Pubs., 1985-87; mng. editor, now exec. editor Country Woman mag., Greendale, Wis., 1987—; exec. editor Country Handcrafts mag., 1990-93, Taste of Home Mag., Greendale, Wis., 1993—; editor Talk About Pets, 1994-95. Author nature book series, 1985-87; sr. editor: Country Woman Christmas Book, 1996—; mng. editor: Irwin the Sock (Chgo. Book Clinic award 1988); exec. editor Taste of Home's Quick Cooking Mag., 1998—, Down the Aisle Countr Style, 2000, Taste of Home's Light & Tasty Mag., 2000—. Mem. Nat. Mus. of Women in Arts, Alpha Lambda Delta (hon.). Home: N54 W26326 Lisbon Rd Sussex WI 53089-4249 Office: Country Woman Mag 5400 S 60th St Greendale WI 53129-1404

POHLAD, CARL R. professional baseball team executive, bottling company executive; b. West Des Moines, Iowa; Ed., Gonzaga U. With MEI Diversified, Inc., Mpls., 1959—, chmn. bd., 1976-94; pres. Marquette Bank Mpls., N.A., pres., dir., Bank Shares, Inc.; owner Minn. Twins, 1985—. Dir. Meth. Hosp. Adminstrv. Group, T.G.I. Friday's, Tex. Air Corp., Ea. Airlines, Continental Air Lines, Inc., Carlson Cos. Inc. Address: Minnesota Twins Hubert H. Humphrey Metrodome 34 Kirby Puckett Pl Minneapolis MN 55415-1523

POINTER, PETER LEON, investment executive; b. Erie, Pa., Aug. 3, 1934; s. Leon Royce and Katherine (Hermen) P.; m. Linda Milla Jensen, Sept. 21, 1957; children: Philip Leon, David Andrew. BS in Econs., U. Pa., 1956; MBA, U. Mo., 1968. V.p. Roose-Wade & Co. Inc., Toledo, 1976-78; br. mgr. Wm. C. Roney & Co., Detroit, 1978-79; v.p. Lowe & Assocs., Columbus, Ohio, 1979-88; pres. Pointer Investment Co., 1988—. Arbitrator Nat. Assn. Security Dealers, Washington, 1987—; adv. com. mem. Dept. Commerce Div. of Securities, Columbus, 1988—. Trustee, sec.-treas. Univ. Urology Ednl. and Rsch. Found., 1993—. Lt. col. USAF, 1956-76. Mem. Brookside Golf and Country Club (treas., trustee 1991-94), Sigma Nu (treas. 1955-56). Republican. Methodist. Avocations: aviation, golf, gardening. Home: 2290 Haverford Rd Columbus OH 43220-4320 Office: Pointer Investment Co 1550 Old Henderson Rd Ste N 152 Columbus OH 43220-3626 E-mail: plpointer@ameritech.net.

POINTS, ROY WILSON, municipal official; b. Quincy, Ill., Oct. 21, 1940; s. Jess C. and Gladys (Wilson) P.; m. Karen Lee Olsen, July 23, 1966; children: Eric, Holly. BBA, Culver Stockton Coll., 1968. Tchr., coach Lewis County C-1, Ewing, Mo., 1968-69, Community Unit 3, Camp Point, Ill., 1969-78; real estate salesman Landmark, Quincy, 1978-80; supr. of assessment County of Adams, 1980-90; assessor City Twp. of Quincy, 1990—. Mem., chmn. Adams County Bd. Rev., 1977-80. Bd. dirs., 1st v.p., sec. Quincy Jaycees, 1970-76, Quincy Rotary East, 1980. Mem. Cert. Ill. Assessing Officers, Internat. Assn. Assessing Officers (cert. ednl. recognition 1988), Ill. Assessors Assn. (bd. dirs. 1992—), Twp. Ofcls. Ill. (bd. dirs. 1995-2001), North Ctrl. Regional Assn. Assessing Officers (bd. dirs. 1997—). Democrat. Avocations: fishing, hunting, jogging, raising cattle. Office: Quincy Twp Assessor City Hall Annex 706 Maine St Quincy IL 62301-4013

POLAKIEWICZ, LEONARD ANTHONY, foreign language and literature educator; b. Kiev, Ukraine, Mar. 30, 1938; came to the U.S., 1950; s. Wladyslaw and Aniela (Ossowska) P.; m. Marianne Helen Swanson, Sept. 7, 1963; children: Barbara, Kathryn, Janet. BS in Russian with distinction, BA in Internat. Rels., U. Minn., 1964; MA in Russian, U. Wis., 1968; cert. Russian area studies, 1969; PhD in Slavic Langs./Lit., U. Wis., 1978; diploma in Polish Curriculum and Instrn., Curie-Sklodowska U., Lublin, Poland, 1981. Instr. U. Minn., Mpls., 1970-78, asst. prof., 1978-90, assoc. prof., 1990—, Morse Alumni disting. teaching assoc. prof. Slavic langs. and literatures, dir. Inst. Langs., 1991-93, chair Slavic dept., 1993-97, 99-2000. Vis. asst. prof. U. London, Eng., fall 1984; dir. U. Minn. Polish Lang. Program, Curie-Sklodowska U., Lublin, Poland, summers 1984-89, dir. Russian Faculty Exch., Herzen Pedagogical U., St. Petersburg, Russia, 1993—; mem. selection com. Fulbright Tchr. Exch. Program, USIA, 1989, Title VI Dept. Edn., 1990, NEH Tchr.- Scholar Program, 1994; reviewer divn. ednl. programs NEH, 1990, translation program, 1993, 94; mem. rev. bd. Ctr. Applied Linguistics Polish Proficiency Test, 1990; mem. exec. com. Coun. on Internat. Edn., N.Y.C., 1991-94; mem. Russian Lang. Program Acad. Policy Com. CIEE, N.Y.C., 1994—; mem. nat. task force Polish Studies in Am., Ind. U., 1995-96; project dir. Nat. Coun. Orgns. of Less Commonly Taught Langs. Polish Lang. Learning Framework, 1995-2001; dir. U. Minn. Curie Sklodowska U. Faculty Exch., 1988—, U. Minn. Cath. U. of Lublin Faculty Exch., 1995-2001; coord. Def. Lang. Inst. Polish Proficiency Testing, 1998. Author: Supplemental Materials for First Year Polish, 1991, Supplemental Materials for Fifteen Modern Polish Short Stories, 1994, Directory of US Institutions of Higher Education and Faculty Offering Instruction in Polish Language, Literature and Culture, 1996-97, Intermediate Polish: A Cultural Reader with Exercises, 1999, (with Joanna Radwanska Williams and Waldemar Walczynski) Polish Language Learning Framework, 2001; assoc. editor Slavic and East European Jour., 1988-94; editl. bd. The Learning and Tchg. of Slavic Langs. and Cultures: Toward the 21st Century, 1996-2000; reviewer Choice Mag., Modern Lang. Jour., Canadian Slavonic Papers, Slavic and East European Jour. Bd. dirs. Immigration Hist. Rsch. Ctr., Mpls., 1984-89; co-founder Polish-Am. Cultural Inst., Mpls., 1986; vice-chair Polish Am. Congress' Commn. Edn., 1987; mem. gov.'s Commn. on Ea. Europe, St. Paul, 1991. With U.S. Army, 1961-63. Ford Found. fellow, 1964-65, Nat. Def. Edn. Act fellow, Title IV, 1966-68; grantee Kościuszko Found., 1981, Coun. for European Studies grantee Columbia U., 1981, 84, 86, Rsch. Assoc. grantee Russian and East European Ctr., U. Ill., 1982, 83, 84, Wasie Found. grantee, 1983, IREX Collaborative Activities and New Exchs. grantee, 1984, Ireland Travel grantee Trinity Coll., Dublin, 1984, Bush Found. Rsch. grantee, 1986-87, grantee U.S. Dept. Edn., 1988-91; Fulbright-Hays Group Projects Abroad grantee for Poland, 1989, USIA U. Linkage grantee for Poland, 1989-93, IREX Short Term Travel grantee, 1995, USIA Coll. & U. Affiliations grantee for Poland, 1995-2000; recipient Polanie Club of the Twin Cities Merit award, 1982, Curie-Sklodowska U. medal for acad. linkage devel., 1992, Cavalier's Cross of Order of Merit of Republic of Poland, 1999, Disting Svc. award Herzen Pedagogical U., St. Petersburg, Russia, 2002. Mem. AAUP, Am. Assn. for the Advancement Slavic Studies, Am. Assn. Tchrs. Slavic and East European Langs. and Lits. (com. on testing and profl. devel. 1997—, Excellence in Tchg. in U.S. award 1994), Internat. Czeslaw Milosz Soc. (pres. 1984-85), N.Am. Chekhov Soc., Am. Coun. Tchrs. of Russian, Polish Inst. Arts & Scis. Am. (N.Y.C., Waclaw Lednicki Humanities award com. 1996), Assn. Literary Scholars & Critics, Soc. of Lovers of the Russian Book, Irish Assn. of Russian and East European Studies, Polish Tchrs. Assn. of Am., Polish Studies Assn. (mem. biannual prize jury 1998), Bristol Group Internat. Assn. Tchrs. Polish, U. Minn. Acad. Disting. Tchrs. Roman Catholic. Avocations: reading, philatelics, genealogy, touring, gardening. Home: 466 Oak Creek Dr S Vadnais Heights MN 55127-7008 E-mail: polak001@tc.umn.edu.

POLARK, ROGER L. retail drug store executive; BS in Bus. Adminstrn., U. No. Iowa, 1970. With Arthur Andersen and Co.; asst. contr. Walgreen, 1977-78, contr., 1978-87, divsn. v.p. corp. acctg., 1987-88, v.p. adminstrn., 1988-95, sr. v.p., CFO Ill., 1995—. Office: Walgreen Co 200 Wilmot Rd Deerfield IL 60015-4616

POLASKI, ANNE SPENCER, lawyer; b. Pittsfield, Mass., Nov. 13, 1952; d. John Harold and Marjorie Ruth (Hackett) Spencer; m. James Joseph Polaski, Sept. 14, 1985. BA in Psychology, Allegheny Coll., 1974; MSW, U. Pa., 1976; JD, George Washington U., 1979. Bar: D.C. 1979, U.S. Dist. Ct. (D.C. dist.) 1980, U.S. Ct. Appeals (D.C. cir.) 1980, Ill. 1982, U.S. Dist. Ct. (no. dist.) Ill. 1982, U.S. Ct. Appeals (7th cir.) 1982. Law clk. to assoc. judge D.C. Ct., Washington, 1979-80; trial atty. Commodity Futures Trading Commn., Chgo., 1980-84, sr. trial atty., 1984, dep. regional counsel, 1984-88; assoc. Gottlieb and Schwartz, 1988-91; staff atty. Chgo. Bd. of Trade, 1991-92, sr. atty., 1992-94, asst. gen. counsel, 1994—. Mem. ABA, Chgo. Bar Assn. Office: Chgo Bd of Trade 141 W Jackson Blvd Chicago IL 60604-2992

POLIAN, BILL, professional football team executive; b. N.Y.C., Dec. 8, 1942; m. Eileen Polian; children: Lynn, Chris, Brian, Dennis. Grad., NYU. Asst. coach Manhattan Coll., 1965-67; asst. coach football U.S. Mcht. Marine Acad., 1968-70, head coach baseball, 1971-75; scout Kansas City Chiefs, 1978-82; dir. player personnel Winnipeg (Can.) Blue Bombers, 1983; dir. personnel Buffalo Bills, 1984-85, gen. mgr., v.p. adminstrn., 1985—. Mem. competition com. NFL, 1989—. Named NFL Exec. of Yr., 1991. Office: Indianapolis Colts 7001 West 56th St. Indianapolis IN 46254

POLICANO, ANDREW J. university dean; b. July 4, 1949; m. Susanne Policano; children: Emily, Keith. BS in Math., SUNY, Stony Brook, 1971; MA in Econs., Brown U., 1973, PhD in Econs., 1976. Asst. prof. U. Iowa, Iowa City, 1975-79, assoc. prof. dept. econs., 1979-81, prof., chair dept. econs., 1984-87, sr. assoc. dean academic affairs, 1987-88; prof. dept. econs. Fordham U., N.Y.C., 1981-84, asst. chair, dir. grad. studies, 1982-83; rsch. assoc. Ctr. for Study of Futures Markets Columbia U., 1982-86; dean divsn. social & behavioral sci. SUNY, 1988-91; dean Sch. Bus. U. Wis., Madison, 1991—. Guest prof. Inst. Advanced Studies, Vienna, Austria, 1985; dir. Nat. Guardian Life, Madison, 1991—; mem. Nat. Total Quality Forum Steering Com., Schaumburg, Ill., 1992—, Am. Assembly Collegiate Sch. Bus. Diversity Com., St. Louis, 1993—. Contbr. articles profl. jours. Recipient Disting. Alumnus award SUNY, Stony Brook, 1994. Mem. Rotary. Office: U Wis Sch Bus Grainger Hall 975 University Ave Rm 5110 Madison WI 53706-1324

POLICY, CARMEN A. professional sports team executive; b. Youngstown, Ohio, Jan. 26, 1943; s. Albert and Ruby (Tisone) P.; m. Aug. 8, 1964 (div. Mar. 1989); children: James, Daniel, Edward, Kerry, Kathy; m. Gail Marie Moretti, June 27, 1991. Grad., Youngstown State U., 1963; JD, Georgetown U., 1966. Bar: Ohio 1966, Va. 1966, D.C. 1966. Assoc. Nadler & Nadler, Youngstown, 1966-68; asst. prosecutor City of Youngstown, 1968-69; ptnr. Flask & Policy, Weimer & White, Youngstown, 1969-90; spl. counsel to atty. gen. State of Ohio, 1970-91; v.p., gen. counsel San Francisco 49ers, NFL, 1983-90, pres., 1990-99; pres., CEO Cleve. Browns, 1999—. Mem. various coms. NFL, 1990—; bd. dirs. World League Am. Football, N.Y.C., 1991—. Com. mem. various charities, Youngstown, 1969-90, San Francisco, 1990—. Mem. Va. Bar Assn., Ohio Bar Assn., D.C. Bar Assn. Roman Catholic. Avocations: scuba diving, hiking. Office: Cleve Browns Stadium 1085 W 3d St Cleveland OH 44114

POLIS, MICHAEL PHILIP, electrical and systems engineering educator; b. N.Y.C., Oct. 24, 1943; s. Max and Sylvia (Goldner) P.; m. Claudette Martin, May 28, 1966; children: Melanie Bobby, Martin Pascal, Karine Melissa. BSEE, U. Fla., 1966; MSEE, Purdue U., West Lafayette, Ind., 1968, PhD, 1972. Grad. instr. elec. engring. Purdue U., West Lafayette, 1966-71; postdoctoral fellow Ecole Polytechnique, Montreal, 1972-73, asst. prof. elec. engring., 1973-74, assoc. prof., 1974-82, prof., 1982-83; program dir. sys. theory NSF, Washington, 1983-87; chmn. dept. elec. and computer engring. Wayne State U., Detroit, 1987-93; dean Sch. Engring. and Computer Sci. Oakland U., Rochester, Mich., 1993-2001, prof. elec. and systems engring., 2001—. Expert witness various law firms, 1989—; cons. Mich. Bell-Ameritech, Detroit, 1989-95, ICAM Technologies, Inc., Montreal, 1981-83; vis. rsch. assoc. LAAS, Toulouse, France, 1978. Contbr. articles to profl. jours. Mem. IEEE (sr.), IEEE Control Sys. Soc. (bd. govs. 1993-95, 98-2000, Best Paper Trans. on Automatic Control 1974-75, Disting. Mem. 1993, v.p. mem. activities 1990-91, assoc. editor 1981-82). Office: Oakland Univ Sch Engring & Computer Sci Rochester MI 48309-4778

POLL, HEINZ, choreographer, artistic director; b. Oberhausen, Germany, Mar. 18, 1926; came to U.S., 1964, naturalized, 1975; s. Heinrich and Anna Margarete (Winkels) P. Co-founder, dir. The Dance Inst., U. Akron, 1967-77; founder, artistic dir., choreographer Ohio Ballet, Akron, 1968-99. Tchr. Chilean Instituto de Extension Musical, 1951-61, N.Y. Nat. Acad., 1965-66 Dancer Göttingen Mcpl. Theatre, 1947-49, Deutsches Theatre Konstanz, 1949-50, East Berlin State Opera, 1950-51, Nat. Ballet Chile, 1951-62, Ballet de la Jeunesse Musicales de France, 1963-64; guest appearances with Nat. Ballet Chile, 1964, Am. Dance Festival, 1965; choreographer works for Nat. Ballet Chile, Paris Festival Ballet, Ballet de la Jeunesses Musicales de France, Nat. Ballet Can., Pa. Ballet, Ohio Ballet, Limon Dance Co.; solo dancer Ellen Kogan. Recipient Ohio Dance award, 1983, 88-89, Achievement Dance award No. Ohio Live Mag., 1985-86, 88-89, 93-94, 94-95, 96-97, Cleve. Arts prize, 1995, Irma Lazarus Govs. award, 1999; Nat. Endowment for Arts grantee, 1974-75. Mem. NEA (dance panelist 1987-89, 92-93).

POLLACK, FLORENCE K.Z. management consultant; b. Washington; d. Charles and Ruth (Isaacson) Zaks; divorced; children: Melissa, Stephanie. BA, Flora Stone Mather Coll., Western Res. U., 1961. Chmn., CEO Exec. Arrangements, Inc., Cleve., 1978—. Lobbyist Ohio Citizens Com. for Arts, Columbus, 1975-83; mem. Leadership Cleve., 1978-79; trustee jr. com. Cleve. Orch., mem. pub. rels. adv. com.; trustee Great Lakes Theatre Festival, 1989-90; mem. pub. rels. adv. com., Cleve. Ballet, Dance Cleve., Jr. Com. of No. Ohio Opera Assn., Cleve. Opera, Shakers Lakes Regional Nature Ctr., Cleve. Music Sch. Settlement, Playhouse Sq. Cabinet, Cleve. Ctr. Econ. Edn., ARC, Cleve. Conv. and Visitors Bur., domed stadium adv. com.; bd. dirs. ARC, Great Lakes Theatre Festival, City Club of Cleve., Cleve. Ballet. Named Idea Woman of Yr., Cleve. Plain Dealer, 1975, to Au Courrant list Cleve. Mag., 1979, one of Cleve.'s 100 Most Influential Women, 1985, one of 1988 Trendsetters Cleve. Woman mag. Mem. Cleve. Area Meeting Planning, Skating Club, Univ. Club, Women's City Club, Playhouse Club, Shoreby Club. Avocations: arts, traveling, reading. Office: Exec Arrangements Inc 24800 Chargin Blvd Cleveland OH 44122 E-mail: executivearrange@ameritech.net.

POLLACK, GERALD LESLIE, physicist, educator; b. Bklyn., July 8, 1933; s. Herman and Jennie (Tenenbaum) P.; m. Antoinette Amparo Velasquez, Dec. 22, 1958; children: Harvey Anton, Samuela Juliet, Margolita Mia, Violet Amata. BS, Bklyn. Coll., 1954; Fulbright scholar, U. Gottingen, 1954-55; MS, Calif. Inst. Tech., 1957, PhD, 1962. Physics student trainee Nat. Bur. Standards, Washington, 1954-58, solid state physicist, 1961-65, cons. Boulder, Colo., 1965-70; assoc. prof. dept. physics Mich. State U., East Lansing, 1965-69, prof., 1969—; cons. NRC, Ill. Dept. Nuclear Safety; physicist Naval Med. Rsch. Inst., Bethesda, Md., summer 1979. Physicist USAF Sch. Aerospace Medicine, San Antonio, Tex., summer 1987. Co-author (with D.R. Stump): Electromagnetism, 2002; contbr. Fellow Am. Phys. Soc.; mem. AAAS, Am. Assn. Physics Tchrs. Office: Mich State U Dept Physics and Astronomy East Lansing MI 48824-1116

POLLACK, HENRY NATHAN, geophysics educator; b. Omaha, July 13, 1936; s. Harold Myron and Sylvia (Chait) P.; m. Lana Beth Schoenberger, Jan. 29, 1963; children: Sara Beth (dec.), John David. A.B., Cornell U., 1958; M.S., U. Nebr., 1960; Ph.D., U. Mich., 1963. Lectr. U. Mich., 1962, asst. prof., asso. prof., prof. geophysics, 1964—, assoc. dean for research, 1982-85, chmn. dept. geol. scis., 1988-91. Rsch. fellow Harvard U., 1963-64; sr. lectr. U. Zambia, 1970-71; vis. scientist U. Durham, U. Newcastle-on-Tyne, Eng., 1977-78, U. Western Ont., 1985-86; chmn. Internat. Heat Flow Commn., 1991-95. Fellow: AAAS, Geol. Soc. Am.; mem.: Am. Geophys. Union. Achievements include research on thermal evolution of the earth, recent climate change. Office: U Mich Dept Geol Scis Ann Arbor MI 48109

POLLACK, SEYMOUR VICTOR, computer science educator; b. Bklyn., Aug. 3, 1933; s. Max and Sylvia (Harrison) P.; m. Sydell Altman, Jan. 23, 1955; children: Mark, Sherie. BChemE, Pratt Inst., 1954; MChemE, Bklyn. Poly. Inst., 1960. Lic. chem. engr., Ohio. Engr. Schwarz Labs., Mt. Vernon, N.Y., 1954-55; design engr. Curtiss-Wright, Wood-Ridge, N.J., 1955-57, Fairchild Engines, Deer Park, N.Y., 1957-59, GE, Evendale, Ohio, 1959-62; rsch. assoc. U. Cin., 1962-66; prof. computer sci. Washington U., St. Louis, 1966-95, prof. emeritus, 1995—. Cons. Mo. Auto Club, St. Louis, 1969-82, United Van Lines, Fenton, Mo., 1984-86, Computer Sci. Accreditation Bd., N.Y.C., 1985-93. Author: Structured Fortran, 1982, UCSD Pascal, 1984, Studies in Computer Science, 1983, The DOS Book, 1985, Turbo Pascal Programming, 1991; cons. editor Holt Rinehart & Winston, N.Y.C., 1979-86. Bd. dirs. Hillel orgn., Washington U., 1983-84. Recipient Alumni Achievement award Pratt Inst., 1966, Outstanding Teaching award Burlington Northern Found., 1987. Mem. Assn. for Computing Machinery, Am. Assn. for Engring. Edn. Jewish. Avocations: classical and jazz piano, jogging. Office: Washington U PO Box 1045 Saint Louis MO 63188-1045

POLLAK, BARTH, mathematics educator; b. Chgo., Aug. 14, 1928; s. Samuel and Esther (Hirschberg) P.; m. Helen Charlotte Schiller, Aug. 22, 1954; children: Martin Russell, Eleanor Susan. BS, Ill. Inst. Tech., 1950, MS, 1951; PhD, Princeton U., 1957. Instr. math. Ill. Inst. Tech., Chgo., 1956-58; asst. prof. Syracuse (N.Y.) U., 1958-63; assoc. prof. U. Notre Dame, Ind., 1963-67, prof., 1967-2000, prof. emeritus, 2000—. Office: U Notre Dame Dept Math Notre Dame IN 46556

POLLAK, RAYMOND, general and transplant surgeon; b. Johannesburg, South Africa, Nov. 12, 1950; came to U.S., 1977; MB BCh, U. Witwatersrand, Johannesburg, 1973. Diplomate Am. Bd. Surgery. Rotating intern Gen. Hosp., Johannesburg, 1974; intern in surgery U. Ill. Hosps. and Clinics, Chgo., 1977-78, resident in surgery; immunology and transplant fellow U. Ill., 1982-84, assoc. prof. surgery, chief divsn. transplant dept. surgery, 1988-98, prof. surgery dept., surgeon, 1995—, chief divsn. transplant Peoria, 2000—. Fellow ACS, Royal Coll. Surgeons Edinburgh. Office: U Ill Dept Surgery 624 NE Glen Oak Ave North Bldg 2d Floor Peoria IL 61603-3135 Fax: 309-655-3630. E-mail: rpollak@uic.edu.

POLLARD, C(HARLES) WILLIAM, diversified services company executive; b. Chgo., June 8, 1938; s. Charles W. and Ruth Ann (Humphrey) P.; m. Judith Ann, June 8, 1959; children: Julie Ann, Charles W., Brian, Amy. A.B., Wheaton Coll., 1960; J.D., Northwestern U., 1963. Bar: Ill. 1963. Mem. firm Wilson and McIlvaine, 1963-67, Vescelus, Perry & Pollard, Wheaton, Ill., 1968-72; prof., v.p. fin. Wheaton Coll., 1972-77; sr. v.p. ServiceMaster Industries, Downers Grove, Ill., 1977-80, exec. v.p., 1980-81, pres., 1981-83, pres., COO, 1981-83; pres., CEO ServiceMaster Co., Downers Grove, Ill., 1983-93, chmn. bd. dirs., mem. exec. com., 1994—, now chmn., CEO. Bd. dirs. Wheaton Coll., Herman Miller, Inc., Provident Life and Accident Ins. Co. Office: The ServiceMaster 1 Servicemaster Way Downers Grove IL 60515-1700

POLLARD, MORRIS, microbiologist, educator; b. Hartford, Conn., May 24, 1916; s. Harry and Sarah (Hoffman) P.; m. Mildred Klein, Dec. 29, 1938; children: Harvey, Carol, Jonathan. D.V.M., Ohio State U., 1938; M.S., Va. Poly. Inst., 1939; Ph.D. (Nat. Found. Infantile Paralysis fellow), U. Calif.-Berkeley, 1950; D.Sc. (hon.) Miami U., Ohio, 1981. Mem. staff Animal Disease Sta., Nat. Agrl. Research Center, Beltsville, Md., 1939-42; asst. prof. preventive medicine Med. br. U. Tex., Galveston, 1946-48, assoc. prof., 1948-50, prof., 1950-61; prof. biology U. Notre Dame, Ind., 1961-66, prof., chmn. microbiology, 1966-81, prof. emeritus, 1981—, dir. Lobund Lab., 1961-85, Coleman dir. Lobund Lab., 1985—. Vis. prof. Fed. U. Rio de Janeiro, Brazil, 1977; vis. prof. Katholieke U., Leuven, Belgium, 1981; mem. tng. grant com. NIH, 1965-70; mem. adv. bd. Inst. Lab. Animal Resources NRC, 1965-68; mem. adv. com. microbiology Office Naval Research, 1966-68, chmn., 1968-70; mem. sci. adv. com. United Health Found., 1966-70; cons. U. Tex., M.D. Anderson Hosp. and Tumor Inst., 1958-66; mem. colon cancer com. Nat. Cancer Inst., 1972-76, chmn. tumor immunology com., 1976-79; mem. com. cancer cause and prevention NIH, 1979-81; program rev. com. Argonne Nat. Lab, 1979-85, chmn., 1983-85; lectr. Found. Microbiology, 1978 Editor: Perspectives in Virology Vol. I to XI, 1959-80; contbr. articles to profl. jours. Served from 1st lt. to lt. col. Vet. Corps, AUS, 1942-46. Recipient Disting. Alumnus award Ohio State U., 1979, Army Commendation medal, Presdl. citation, Hope award Am. Cancer Soc., 2000; named Hon. Alumnus U. Notre Dame, 1989; McLaughlin Faculty fellow Cambridge U., 1956; Raine Found. prof. U. Western Australia, 1975; vis. scientist Chinese Acad. Med. Scis., 1979, 81; hon. prof. Chinese Acad. Med. Scis., 1982. Mem. Am. Acad. Microbiology (charter), Brazilian Acad. Scis., Soc. Exptl. Biology and Medicine, Am. Soc. Microbiology (Acad. Sci. Achievement award 1990), Am. Soc.

Investigative Pathology, Am. Assn. Cancer Rsch., Am. Soc. Lab. Animal Sci., Assn. Gnotobiotics (pres.), Internat. Commn. Lab. Animal Sci., AAAS, Internat. Assn. Gnotobiology (pres.), Internat. Assn. Gnotobiotics (hon. pres. 1987), Sigma Xi, Phi Delta Epsilon (hon.), Phi Zeta (hon.). Home: 3540 Hanover Ct South Bend IN 46614-2331 Office: Lobund Lab Univ of Notre Dame Notre Dame IN 46556

POLLIHAN, THOMAS HENRY, lawyer; b. St. Louis, Nov. 15, 1949; s. C.H. and Patricia Ann (O'Brien) P.; m. Donna M. Bickhaus, Aug. 25, 1973; 1 child, Emily Christine. BA in Sociology, Quincy U., 1972; JD, U. Notre Dame, 1975; Exec. Masters in Internat. Bus., St. Louis U., 1992. Bar: Mo. 1975, Ill. 1976. Jud. law clk. to judge Mo. Ct. of Appeals, St. Louis, 1975-76; from assoc. to ptnr. Greenfield, Davidson, Mandelstamm & Voorhees, 1976-82; asst. gen. counsel Kellwood Co., 1982-89, gen. counsel, sec., 1989-93, v.p., sec., gen. counsel, 1993—2002, sr. v.p., 2002—. Trustee Quincy (Ill.) U., 1987-93, 97—, pres. alumni bd., 1986-87; pres. S.W. Neighborhood Improvement Assn., St. Louis, 1984, Quincy (Ill.) U. Found., 1993-94, 97—; dir., sec. New Piasa Chautauqua, Ill., 1996-97. Named Quincy U. Alumnus of Yr., 1997. Mem. Bar Assn. Met. St. Louis. Roman Catholic. Avocations: soccer, cycling. Home: 415 Spring Ave Saint Louis MO 63119-2634 Office: Kellwood Co 600 Kellwood Pkwy Ste 300 Chesterfield MO 63017-5897 E-mail: tom_pollihan@kellwood.com.

POLLNER, JULIA A. financial executive; BBA, Miami U., Oxford, Ohio. CPA, Ohio. With Red Roof Inns Inc., Columbus, Ohio, 1987; v.p., contr., asst. treas. Metatec Internat. Inc., v.p. fin., sec., treas., 1997—. Mem. AICPA, Ohio Soc. CPAs, Fin. Execs. Inst. Office: Metatec Internat Inc 7001 Metatec Blvd Dublin OH 43017-3219

POLLOCK, ALEXANDER JOHN, banker; b. Indpls., Jan. 28, 1943; s. Alex S. and Doris L. (VanHorn) P.; m. Anne M. Fryfogle, Jan. 27, 1968; children: Elizabeth, Alexander, Evelyn, James. B.A., Williams Coll., 1965; M.A., U. Chgo., 1966; M.P.A., Princeton U., 1969. Instr. philosophy Lake Forest Coll., (Ill.), 1967; with internat. banking dept. Continental Ill. Nat. Bank, Chgo., 1969-77, v.p., 1977-82, sr. v.p., 1982-85; prin. Nolan Norton & Co., 1985-86; chief fin. officer Marine Corp., Milw., 1986; pres. Marine Bank N.A., 1987; pres., CEO Cmty. Fed. Savs., St. Louis, 1988-90; vis. scholar Fed. Res. Bank of St. Louis, 1991; pres., CEO Fed. Home Loan Bank Chgo., 1991—. Life mem. Ctr. for Fin. Insts. and Mkts.; bd. dirs. Gt. Lakes Higher Edn. Corp.; past pres. Internat. Union for Housing Fin. Trustee Ill. Coun. on Econ. Edn.; Bd. dirs. Great Books Found. Mem.: Union League Club, Bankers Club of Chgo. (past pres.), Phi Beta Kappa. Office: Fed Home Loan Bank Chgo 8th Fl 111 E Wacker Dr Chicago IL 60601-4204 E-mail: alex_pollock@fhlbc.com.

POLLOCK, EARL EDWARD, lawyer; b. Decatur, Nebr., Feb. 24, 1928; s. Herman and Della (Rosenthal) P.; m. Betty Sokol, Sept. 8, 1951; children: Stephen, Della, Naomi. B.A., U. Minn., 1948; J.D., Northwestern U., 1953; LLD (hon.), Morningside Coll., 1995. Bar: D.C. 1955, Va. 1955, Ill. 1959, U.S. Supreme Ct. 1960. Law clk., chief justices Vinson and Warren, U.S. Supreme Ct. Washington, 1953-55; atty. antitrust div. Dept. Justice, Washington, 1955-56, asst. to solicitor gen., 1956-59; ptnr. Sonnenschein Nath & Rosenthal, Chgo., 1959—. Trustee Loyola U., Chgo., 1983-92; life trustee Northwestern Meml. Hosp.; dir. Fla. West Coast Symphony. Mem. Chgo. Bar Assn. (chmn. antitrust law com. 1967-68), ABA (chmn. antitrust law sect. 1979-80), Alumni Assn. Northwestern U. Sch. Law (pres. 1974-75, svc. award 1976). Office: Sonnenschein Nath 233 S Wacker Dr Ste 8000 Chicago IL 60606-6491

POLLOCK, GEORGE HOWARD, psychiatrist, psychoanalyst; b. Chgo., June 19, 1923; s. Harry J. and Belle (Lurie) P.; m. Beverly Yufit, July 3, 1946; children: Beth L. Pollock Ungar, Raphael E., Daniel A., Benjamin B., Naomi R. Pollock Sneider. BS, U. Ill., 1944, MD cum laude, 1945, MS, 1948, PhD, 1951. Diplomate Am. Bd. Psychiatry and Neurology. Intern Cook County Hosp., Chgo., 1945-46; resident Ill. Neuropsychiat. Inst., 1948-51; practice medicine, specializing in psychiatry, 1948-91. Clin. assoc. prof. dept. psychiatry Coll. Medicine, U. Ill., 1955-64, clin. prof., 1964-72; prof. psychiatry Northwestern U., 1972-93, Dunbar prof. psychiatry and behavioral scis. emeritus, 1993—, dir. rsch. dept. psychiatry/behavioral scis.m 1988-93, emeritus, 1993—; faculty Inst. for Psychoanalysis, Chgo., 1956-92, asst. dean edn., 1960-67, tng. analyst 1961-92, supervising analyst, 1962-92, dir. rsch., 1963-71, pres., 1971-89; exch. program participant Hampstead Child Therapy Clinic, 1962-63; pres. Ctr. Psychosocial Studies, 1972-90 Chmn. bd. editors Ann. of Psychoanalysis, 1971-89; mem. editorial bd. Jour. Am. Psychoanalytic Assn., 1971-74; mem. editorial bd. sect. psychoanalysis Psychiat. Jour. U. Ottawa Faculty Medicine, 1976—; corr. editor Jour. Geriatric Psychiatry, 1975—; Med. Problems of Performing Artists, Psychoanalytic Edn., Psychoanalytic Psychology, Internat. Forum for Psychoanalysis, Internat. Jour. Behavioral Scis. and the Law, Internat. Psychogeriatrics, Depression and Stress. Mem. med. adv. com. Planned Parenthood Assn., 1966-70; pres. governing bd. Parents Assn. Lab. Schs., U. Chgo., 1966-70; mem. med. adv. coun. Asthma and Allergy Found. for Greater Chgo. Capt. U.S. Army, 1946-48. Commonwealth fellow, 1951; research grantee Founds. Fund for Research in Psychiatry, 1960-65 Fellow Am. Coll. Psychiatrists, Am. Orthopsychiat. Assn., Am. Psychiat. Assn. (treas. 1980-86, pres. 1987-88), Am. Coll. Psychoanalysts (pres. 1985-86); mem. Internat. Psychogeriatrics (mem. editorial bds.), Am. Acad. Polit. and Social Sci., Am. Anthrop. Assn., Nat. Council on Family Relations, AAAS, AAUP, Profs., Am. Electroencephalographic Soc., Am. Heart Assn., Assn. for Research in Nervous and Mental Disease, Soc. for Exptl. Biology and Medicine, Ill., N.Y. acads. scis., Chgo. Psychoanalytic Soc. (pres. 1984-85), Soc. for Gen. Systems Research, AMA, World Med. Assn., Am. Name Soc., Am. Psychoanalytic Assn. (pres. 1974-75), Am. Psychol. Assn., Am. Psychosomatic Soc., Am. Pub. Health Assn., Am. Sociol. Assn., Assn. Am. Med. Colls., Ill. Psychiat. Soc. (pres. 1973-74), Sigma Xi, Alpha Omega Alpha, numerous others. Home: 5759 S Dorchester Ave Chicago IL 60637-1726 Office: 30 N Michigan Ave Chicago IL 60602-3402

POLLOCK, KAREN ANNE, computer analyst; b. Elmhurst, Ill., Sept. 6, 1961; d. Michael Paul and Dorothy Rosella (Foskett) P. BS, Elmhurst Coll., 1984; MS, North Cen. Coll., 1993. Formatter Nat. Data Corp., Lombard, Ill., 1985; computer specialist Dept. VA, Hines, 1985—. Lutheran. Avocations: cross-stitch, mystery books, bowling, bicycling, softball.

POLLOCK, ROBERT ELWOOD, nuclear scientist; b. Regina, Sask., Can., Mar. 2, 1936; s. Elwood Thomas and Harriet Lillian (Rooney) Pollock; m. Jean Elizabeth Virtue, Sept. 12, 1959; children: Bryan Thomas, Heather Lynn, Jeffrey Parker, Jennifer Lee. BSc with honors, U. Man., Can., 1957; MA, Princeton U., 1959, PhD, 1963. Instr. Princeton (N.J.) U., 1961-63, asst. prof., 1964-69, research physicist, 1969-70; Nat. Research Council Can. postdoctoral fellow Harwell, England, 1963-64; asso. prof. Ind. U., Bloomington, 1970-73, prof., 1973-84, disting. prof., 1984-2001, prof. emeritus, 2001—, dir. Cyclotron Facility, 1973-79, mem. nuc. sci. adv. com., 1977-80. Recipient Alexander von Humboldt Sr. U.S. Scientist award, 1985—88. Fellow: Am. Phys. Soc. (Bonner prize 1992). Home: 2811 Dale Ct Bloomington IN 47401-2414 Office: Ind U Swain Hall Dept Physics Bloomington IN 47405

POLLOCK, SHELDON IVAN, language professional, educator; b. Cleve., Feb. 16, 1948; s. Abraham and Elsie (Russ) P.; m. Estera Milman, Dec. 21, 1968 (div. May 1985); children: Nira, Mica; m. Ute Gregorius, 1991. AB, Harvard U., 1971, AM, 1973, PhD, 1975. Instr. Harvard U., Cambridge, Mass., 1974-75; asst. prof. U. Iowa, Iowa City, 1975-79, assoc. prof., 1979-85, prof., 1985-89; George V. Bobrinskoy prof. Sanskrit and Indic Studies U. Chgo., 1989—, chmn. Dept. S. Asian Langs. and Civilizations, 1991. Vis. prof. Collège de France, Paris, 1991; prin. investigator NEH collaborative rsch. project Literay Cultures in History, 1995-98. Author: Aspects of Versification in Sanskrit Lyric Poetry, 1977, Ramayana of Valmiki, Vol. II, 1986, Vol. III, 1991; regional editor: Harper Collins World Reader; contbr. articles to profl. jours. Am. Inst. Indian Studies sr. and short-term fellow, 1979, 84, 87, 94; Maharaja of Cochin Meml. lectr., Sanskrit Coll., Tripunithura, Kerala, 1989. Mem. Am. Oriental Soc., Assn. Asian Studies, Social Sci. Rsch. Coun. (Joint Com. on South Asia 1990-96). Office: U Chgo Dept South Asian Langs 1130 E 59th St Chicago IL 60637-1539

POLLOCK, STEPHEN MICHAEL, industrial engineering educator, consultant; b. N.Y.C., Feb. 15, 1936; s. Meyer and Frances R. Pollock; m. Bettina Dorn, Nov. 22, 1962; children: Joshua, Aaron, Ethan. B in Engring. Physics, Cornell U., 1958; SM, MIT, 1960, PhD in Physics and Ops. Research, 1964. Mem. tech. staff Arthur D. Little Inc., Cambridge, Mass., 1964-65; asst. prof. Naval Postgrad. Sch., Monterey, Calif., 1965-68, assoc. prof., 1968-69, U. Mich., Ann Arbor, 1969-73, prof., dept. indsl. and ops. engring., 1974—, chmn. dept., 1980-90. Cons. to over 40 orgns. Area editor Ops. Rsch. Jour., 1977-82; sr. editor Inst. Indsl. Engrs. Trans., 1985-89, Army Sci. Bd., 1994-99; contbr. more than 60 tech. papers to profl. jours. Fellow, Space Tech. Labs., 1960; sr. fellow NSF, 1975. Fellow: AAAS; mem.: Nat. Acad. Engring., Ops. Rsch. Soc. Am. (pres. 1986—87), Inst. Mgmt. Sci. Home: 2694 Wayside Dr Ann Arbor MI 48103-2251 Office: U of Mich Dept Indsl Ops Engring Ann Arbor MI 48109-2117

POLOVITZ, MICHAEL, state legislator; m. Barbara Polovitz; 4 children. MusM, U. Mich. Mem. N.D. Senate from 42d dist., Bismark, 2001—. With USN, 1944-46. Democrat. Office: 2529 9th Ave N Grand Forks ND 58203 E-mail: mpolovit@state.nd.us.

POLSKY, DONALD PERRY, architect; b. Milw., Sept. 30, 1928; s. Lew and Dorothy (Geisenfeld) P.; m. Corinne Shirley Neer, Aug. 25, 1957; children: Jeffrey David, Debra Lynn. BArch, U. Nebr., Lincoln, 1951; postgrad., U. So. Calif., 1956, U. Calif., Los Angeles, 1957, U. Nebr., Omaha, 1964, U. Ill., 1965. Project architect Richard Neutra, Architect, Los Angeles, 1953-56, Daniel Dworsky, Architect, Los Angeles, 1956; prin. Polsky, AIA & Assocs., 1956-62, Omaha, 1964—; dir. dept. architecture MCA, Inc., Universal City, Calif., 1962-64. Prin. works include Mills residence, 1958, apt. bldgs., 1960, Polsky residence, 1961, Milder residence, 1965. Chmn. Design Control I480 Study Mayor's Riverfront Devel., Omaha, 1969, 71; pres. Swanson Sch. Community Club, Omaha, 1972; mem. Mayor's Adv. Panel Design Services, Omaha, 1974; vice chmn. Omaha Zoning Bd. Appeals, 1976; dir. Siena/Francis House. Recipient archtl. awards Canyon Crier Newspaper, Los Angeles, 1960, House and Home Mag., Life Mag., AIA, Santa Barbara, Calif., 1962. Mem. AIA (pres. Omaha chpt. 1968), Nebr. Soc. Architects (pres. 1975, awards 1964, 68, 87, 91, 93, 94, 95, 97, Firm of Yr. 1997). Office: Donald P Polsky AIA & Assocs 8723 Oak St Omaha NE 68124-3051

POLSTER, DAN AARON, judge; b. Cleve., Dec. 6, 1951; s. Lewis H. and Elinor Ruth (Guren) P.; m. Deborah Ann Coleman, May 29, 1977; children: Joshua, Shira, Ilana. AB, Harvard U., 1972, JD, 1976; PhD (hon.), Cleve. Coll. Jewish Studies, 1988. Bar: Ohio 1976, U.S. Dist. Ct. (no. dist.) Ohio 1981, U.S. Ct. Appeals (6th cir.) 1982. Atty. Dept. Justice, Cleve., 1976-82, asst. U.S. atty., 1982-98; U.S. dist. judge U.S. Dist. Ct., Akron, Ohio, 1998—. Pres. bd. trustees Agnon Sch., Beachwood, Ohio, 1993-96; chmn. bd. govs. Cleve. Coll. Jewish Studies, Beachwood, 1984-88; bd. dirs. Jewish Comty. Fedn. Cleve., 1989-95, 96-2001. Recipient Special Achievement award U.S. Dept. Justice, 1980, 84, Special Commendation, 1988. Mem. Fed. Bar Assn., Cleve. Bar Assn. Jewish. Office: US Dist Ct 2 S Main St Akron OH 44308-1813 E-mail: dan_polster@ohnd.uscourts.gov.

POLSTON, MARK FRANKLIN, minister; b. Indpls., Feb. 9, 1960; s. Albert Franklin and Mildred (Wiggington) P.; m. Lisa Kaye Polston, July 21, 1984; children: Jordan Franklin, Jonathan Mark. AS, Somerset (Ky.) C. C., 1981; BS, Campbellsville Coll., 1984; JD, Ind. Sch. Law, 1995. Real estate agt. Homestead Real Estate, Somerset, 1978-89; pastor Trace Fork Separate Bapt. Ch., Liberty, Ky., 1979-81, Calvary Separate Bapt. Ch., Nancy, 1980-84, Harmony Separate Bapt. Ch., Jacksonville, Fla., 1984-85, Fairview Separate Bapt. Ch., Russell Springs, Ky., 1985-89, Calvary Separate Bapt. Ch., Nancy, 1989-91, Edinburgh (Ind.) Separate Bapt. Ch., 1991; sales rep. Sentry Ins., Somerset, 1989-91; dep. atty. gen. Ind. Atty. Gen., Indpls., 1992—. Clk. Gen. Assn. Separate Bapt., 1988-96; bd. dirs. Separate Bapt. Missions., Inc., 1988-92; adj. prof. Ind. Vocat. Tech. Coll., Indpls., 1993-95. Home: 787 Kitchen Rd Mooresville IN 46158-8057 Office: Ind Atty Gen 402 W Washington St Indianapolis IN 46204-2739 also: Edinburgh Separate Bapt Ch 905 S Main St Edinburgh IN 46124-1311

POLZIN, CHARLES HENRY, lawyer; b. Saginaw, Mich., June 9, 1954; s. James William and Dorothy Marie (Koski) P.; m. Roberta Anne Zaremba, May 26, 1984; children: Alexander James, Matthew Robert, Madelyn Marie. BA magna cum laude, Western Mich. U., 1975; JD cum laude, U. Mich., 1979. Bar: Mich. 1979. Assoc. Hill, Lewis, Adams, Goodrich & Tait, Detroit, 1979-81, Martin, Axe, Buhl & Schwartz, Bloomfield Hills, Mich., 1981-83, Hill, Lewis, Adams, Goodrich & Tait, Birmingham, 1983-86; ptnr. Hill Lewis, 1986-96; mem. Clark Hill P.L.C., 1996—. Mem. founders jr. coun. bd. Detroit Inst. Arts, 1986-92, treas., 1988-89, pres., 1989-91; bd. dirs. Coalition on Temporary Shelter, 1992—, pres., 1997—. Waldo Sangren scholar Western Mich. U., 1974. Mem. ABA, Oakland County Bar Assn. (chmn. continuing legal edn. com. 1986-88). Office: Clark Hill PLC 255 S Old Woodward Ave Fl 3D Birmingham MI 48009-6182

POMERANTZ, MARVIN ALVIN, business executive; b. Des Moines, Aug. 6, 1930; s. Alex and Minnie (Landy) P.; m. Rose Lee Lipsey, Nov. 12, 1950; children: Sandy Pomerantz, Marcie Morrison, Vickie Ginsberg, Lori Long. BS in Commerce, U. Iowa, 1952. Exec. v.p. Midwest Bag Co., Des Moines, 1952-60; founder, pres., gen. mgr. Gt. Plains Bag Corp., 1961-75; v.p. Continental Can Co. Inc., Greenwich, Conn., 1971-75; v.p., gen. mgr. Forest Products Brown Systems Operation (div. Continental Can Co. Inc.), 1975-77; pres. Diversified Group Internat. Harvester, Chgo., 1980-81, ex. v.p., 1981-82; pres., chmn., chief exec. officer The Mid-Am. Group, Des Moines, 1981—; chmn., chief exec. officer Gaylord Container Corp., Deerfield, Ill., 1986—2002. Mem. Greater Des Moines Commn.; trustee Drake U., 1978—; pres. Iowa State Bd. Regents, 1987-93, 95-96; mem. U.S. Olympic Budget and Audit Commn., Colorado Springs., Colo., 1989-92. Republican. Office: The Mid-Am Group 4700 Westown Pkwy Ste 303 West Des Moines IA 50266-6718

POMEROY, EARL R. congressman, former state insurance commissioner; b. Valley City, N.D., Sept. 2, 1952; s. Ralph and Myrtle Pomeroy; m. Laurie Kirby, Dec. 26, 1986. BA, U. N.D., 1974, JD, 1979. Atty. Sproul, Lenaburg, Fitzner and Walker, Valley City, 1979-84; commr. of ins. State of N.D., 1984-92; mem. U.S. Congress from N.D. (at large), Washington, 1993—; mem. ways and means com. State rep. N.D. Legis. Assembly, 1980-84. Recipient Found. award Rotary, 1975; named Outstanding Young North Dakotan N.D. Jaycees, 1982. Mem. Nat. Assn. of Ins. Commrs. (chmn. midwest zone 1987-88, exec. com. 1987-88), Phi Beta Kappa. Democrat. Presbyterian. Office: US Ho Rep 1110 Longworth Bldg Washington DC 20515-3401*

POND, PHYLLIS JOAN RUBLE, state legislator, educator; b. Warren, Ind., Oct. 25, 1930; d. Clifford E. and Rosa E. (Hunnicutt) Ruble; m. George W. Pond, June 10, 1951; children: William, Douglas, Jean Ann. BS, Ball State U., Muncie, Ind., 1951; MS, Ind. U., 1963. Tchr. home econs., 1951-54; kindergarten tchr., 1961-98; mem. Ind. Ho. of Reps., Inpdls., 1978—, majority asst. caucus chmn., vice chmn. ways and means com., 1995. Active Rep. Precinct Com., 1976—; del. Ind. Rep. Conv., 1976, 80, 84, 86, 88, 90, 92, 96, 2000; alt. del. Rep. Nat. Conv., 1980, del., 1996; alt. del. to Rep. Nat. conv., 2000. Mem. AAUW, Regional Red Cross Bio-Med. Bd., New Haven Am. Legion Aux., New Haven Woman's Club. Lutheran.

PONDER, DAN, public relations executive; MBA , BA, Mich. State U.; grad., Leadership Detroit X. Mem. pvt. co. adv. svc. Deloitte & Touche, Detroit; CFO Franco Pub. Rels. Group, 1985, CEO, 1985—93. Mem.: Henry Ford Estate Adv. Bd., Mich. Coun. Econ. Edn. (bd. trustees), Alliance for a Safer, Greater Detroit (mem. bd. dirs.), Mich. State Chamber, Detroit Regional Chamber (past chmn. small bus. exec. com., Svc. award 1996—97). Office: Franco Pub Rels Group 400 Renaissance Ctr Ste 1050 Detroit MI 48243 Office Fax: 313-567-4486. Business E-Mail: ponder@franco.com.*

PONDER, LESTER MCCONNICO, lawyer, educator; b. Walnut Ridge, Ark., Dec. 10, 1912; s. Harry Lee and Clyde (Gant) P.; m. Sallie Mowry Clover, Nov. 7, 1942; children— Melinda, Constance; m. Phyllis Gretchen Harting, Oct. 14, 1978 B.S. summa cum laude in Commerce, Northwestern U., 1934; J.D. with honors, George Washington U., 1938. Bar: Ark. 1937, Ind. 1948. Atty. Ark. Dept. Revenue, Little Rock, 1939-41; atty. IRS, Chgo. and Indpls., 1941-51; ptnr. Barnes & Thornburg and predecessor Barnes, Hickam, Pantzer & Boyd, Indpls., 1952—. Adj. prof. Sch. Law, Ind. U., Bloomington, 1951-54, Sch. Law, Ind. U., Indpls., 1954-63; lectr. polit. sci. Ind. U., Indpls., 1982-85. Author: United States Tax Court Practice & Procedure, 1976 Bd. dirs., vice chmn., chmn. Ind. chpt. The Nature Conservancy, 1981-89; mem. adv. coun. Ind. Dept. Natural Resources, 1986—; past bd. mem. Sigma Chi Found. Served with USN, 1942. Fellow Am. Bar Found., Ind. State Bar Found., Ind. Bar Found., Am. Coll. Tax Counsel; mem. ABA (coun., taxation sect. 1970-73, chair sr. lawyers div. 1993-94, adv. coun. Commr. Internal Revenue 1964—), Ind. State Bar Assn., Indpls. Bar Assn., Assn. of Seventh Fed. Cir. Republican. Presbyterian. Club: Meridian Hills Country (Indpls.). Lodge: Rotary (past bd. dirs.) Office: Barnes & Thornburg Merchants Bank Bldg Ste 1313 Indianapolis IN 46204-3506

PONDROM, LEE GIRARD, physicist, educator; b. Dallas, Dec. 26, 1933; s. Levi Girard and Guinevere (Miller) P.; m. Cyrena Jo Norman, Aug. 25, 1961. B.S., So. Meth. U., 1953; M.S., U. Chgo., 1956, Ph.D., 1958. Instr., dept. physics Columbia U., N.Y.C., 1960-63; assoc. prof. dept. physics U. Wis., Madison, 1963-69, prof. physics, 1969—, Robert Williams Wood prof., 1992—. Dept. chmn. U. Wis., 1997-2000; mem. high energy adv. com. Brookhaven Nat. Lab., 1973-75, chmn. Associated Universities, Inc., vis. com., 1987; mem. physics adv. com. Fermi Nat. Accelerator Lab., 1979-82, chmn., 1981-82; adv. com. for physics NSF, 1981-84; mem. high energy adv. panel (physics) U.S. Dept. Energy, 1981-84, 87-88, chmn. subcom. on detectors, 1987-88, mem. subpanel on future facilities, high energy physics, 1983, mem. subpanel on future modes of exptl. research in high energy physics, 1987; trustee Univs. Research Assn., 1973-76, 82-85; mem. sci. policy com. Stanford Linear Accelerator Ctr., 1984-88; mem. Internat. Com. Future Accelerators, 1984-90; chmn. Snowmass 1986 Summer Study on the SSC.; chmn. User's Orgn. for the SSC, 1987-89, mem. sci. policy com. SSC Lab., 1992; mem. CDRF awards com. to scientists in former Soviet Union, 1996. Contbr. articles to profl. jours. Served to 1st lt. USAF, 1958-60. J.S. Guggenheim Meml. fellow, 1971-72, Japan Soc. for Promotion of Sci. fellow; recipient Disting. Alumni award So. Meth. U., 1983, W.K.H. Panofsky award Am. Phys. Soc., 1994. Fellow Am. Phys. Soc. (chmn. div. particles and fields 1987, com. on status of women in physics 1989—, chmn. com. to award the Panofsky prize 1991); mem. AAAS, Phi Beta Kappa (pres. Wis. Alpha chpt. 1996-97). Episcopalian. Home: 210 Princeton Ave Madison WI 53705-4077 Office: U Wis Dept Physics Madison WI 53706 E-mail: pondrom@hep.wisc.edu.

PONITZ, DAVID H. former academic administrator; b. Royal Oak, Mich., Jan. 21, 1931; s. Henry John and Jeanette (Bouwman) P.; m. Doris Jean Humes, Aug. 5, 1956; children: Catherine Anne, David Robinson. BA, U. Mich., 1952, MA, 1954; EdD, Harvard U., 1964; degree (hon.), U. Dayton, 1996. Prin. Waldron (Mich.) Area Schs., 1956-58, supt., 1958-60; cons. Harvard U., Boston Sch. Survey, 1961-63; supt. Freeport (Ill.) Pub. Schs., 1962-65; pres. Freeport C.C., 1962-65, Washtenaw C.C., 1965-75, Sinclair C.C., 1975-97, pres. emeritus, 1997—. Cons. to community colls.; chmn., pres. Ohi Advanced Tech. Ctr. Mem. editorial adv. bd. Nations Schs, 1963-70; chmn. adv. bd. Community Coll. Rev, 1978-89. Past chmn. Dayton Mayor's Coun. on Econ. Devel., 1977-85; mem. Nat. Adv. Coun. on Nursing; former co-chair Performing Arts Edn. Task Force; bd. dirs. Alliance for Edn.; former campaign chmn. Ann Arbor and Dayton United Way; past vice chmn. Dayton Citizens Adv. Coun. for Desegregation Implementation; v.p. Miami Valley Rsch. Park; mem., past chmn. Area Progress Coun., Dayton; bd. dirs. Dayton Devel. Coun.; mem. F.S.B. bd. Citizens Fed. Banks, Universal Energy Systems Bd.; past chmn. Miami Valley Joint Labor/Mgmt. Profls., Area Progress Coun.; chmn. bd. dirs Ctr. Occupational R & D; bd. chair Wright Tech. Network; bd. dirs. Dean Family Funds; trustee Thomas B. Fordham Found.; mem. Midwestern Higher Edn. Commn.; vice chair Miami Valley Rsch. Found.; past chmn. bd. dirs. League Innovation C.C.; bd. dirs. Miami Valley Regional Planning Commn. Served with U.S. Army, 1954-56. Named Outstanding Alumnus, U. Mich., One of Top 100 Pres. in U.S. Coun. for Advancement and Support of Edn., Exec. of Yr., Bd. Realtors; named to Hall of Fame, Nat. Mgmt. Assn., 2001; recipient Presdl. medallion, Patron emeritus Horry-Georgetown Tech. Coll., Bogie Buster Red Jacket award, 1987, Thomas J. Peters award for Excellence, Assn. Cmty. and Jr. Colls., 1988, Marie N. Martin Chief Exec. Officer award, ACCT, 1989, The Living Legend award, Martin Luther King Jr. Holiday Celebration Com., 1991, Hon. Alumnus award, Sinclair, 1991, honor, India Found., 1992, Disting. Eagle Scout award, Nat. Eagle Scout Assn., 1993, Smitty award, Anti-Defamation award, Anti-Defamation League, 1996, Citizen Legion of Honor award, 1997, hon. award, Citizen Legion, 1997, Edn. award, Gov., 1999. Mem. Am. Assn. Community and Jr. Colls. (nat. future commn., bd. dirs., chmn. 1988-89, Nat. Leadership award 2002), Ohio Tech. and Community Coll. Assn. (pres. 1979-80), Nat. Mgmt. Assn. (Hall of Fame award 2001), Rotary. Methodist. Office: Sinclair Community Coll Office of Pres Emeritus 444 W 3rd St Dayton OH 45402-1421 Fax: 937-512-2865. E-mail: dponitz@sinclair.edu.

PONITZ, JOHN ALLAN, lawyer; b. Battle Creek, Mich., Sept. 7, 1949; m. Nancy J. Roberts, Aug. 14, 1971; children: Amy, Matthew, Julie. BA, Albion Coll., 1971; JD, Wayne State U., 1974. Bar: Mich. 1974, U.S. Dist. Ct. (ea. dist.) Mich. 1975, (we. dist.) Mich. 1986, U.S. Ct. Appeals (6th cir.) Mich. 1981, U.S. Supreme Ct. 1992. Assoc. McMachan & Kaichen, Birmingham, Mich., 1973-75; atty. Grand Trunk Western R.R., Detroit, 1975-80, sr. trial atty., 1980-89, gen. counsel, 1990-95; ptnr. Hopkins & Sutter, 1995-2000, Maxwell, Ponitz & Sclawy, Troy, 2000—01; of counsel Fabrizio & Brook, P.C., 2002—. V.p. Beverly Hills (Mich.) Jaycees, 1981. Served to capt. USAR, 1974-82. Mem. Mich. Bar Assn., Nat. Assn. R.R. Trial Counsel, Oakland County Bar Assn. Lutheran. Avocation: golf. Office: Fabrizio & Brook PC City Ctr Bldg 888 W Big Beaver Ste 1470 Troy MI 48084-4738 E-mail: japonitz@pbmaxwell.com.

PONKA, LAWRENCE JOHN, automotive executive; b. Detroit, Sept. 1, 1949; s. Maximillian John and Leona May (Knobloch) P.; m. Nancy Kathleen McNamara, Feb. 20, 1988. AA, Macomb County C. C., Mich., 1974; BS in Indsl. Mgmt., Lawrence Tech. U., 1978; MA in Indsl. Mgmt., Ctrl. Mich. U., 1983, postgrad. in Bus. Mgmt. Cert. internat. cons. Engr.'s asst. Army Tank Automotive Command, 1967-68; with Sperry and Hutchinson Co., Southfield, Mich., 1973, Chrysler Corp., Detroit, 1973, GM Corp., Warren, Mich., 1973-82, coord. engring. staff engring. systems, 1976-82; mfg. engr. Buick-Oldsmobile, Cadillac Group GM Assembly Divsn., Orion Pontiac, Mich, 1982-84; sr. anayst advanced vehicle engring. Chevrolet-Pontiac-Can. group Engring. Ctr., Warren, 1985-86; mfg. planning adminstr. Allanté Detroit Hamtramck Assembly Ctr. Cadillac Luxury Car Divsn., 1986-92, mgr. Cadillac Alante Assembly Ops., 1992—. Plant planning adminstr. Cadillac luxury car divsn. Detroit/Hamtramck Assembly Ctr., Cadillac El Dorado, Seville, Deville, Concours, 1993—, sr. mfg. project engr. N. Am. Ops., 1994, Flint, Mich., 96; advanced mfg. engr. N.Am. ops. mfg. process liaison Cadillac luxury car divsn., 1996—97; total mfg. integration engr. Advanced Product Devel. Ctr., 1997—2001, mfg. integration mgr., 2001; full size trucks Global Portfolio Devel. Ctr., 1997—; mem. people strategy team on environ. Cadillac Motor Car till 1992; mem. adj. faculty U. Phoenix Grad. Sch. Bus., Mich. campus. Elected del Dem. County Conv. With USAF, 1968—72. Decorated Air Force Commendation medal. Mem. DAV (life), Vietnam Vets Assn. (life), Am. Diabetes Assn. Roman Catholic. Home: 35537 Oakdale St Livonia MI 48154-2237 Office: U Phoenix Mich Campus 26999 Central Park Blvd Southfield MI 48076-4174 also: GM Corp Engring Ctr M/C 480-111-P04 30200 Mound Rd 111 Box 9010 Warren MI 48090-9010 E-mail: ljponka@prodigy.net.

PONKO, WILLIAM REUBEN, architect; b. Wausau, Wis., Apr. 4, 1948; s. Reuben Harrison and Ora Marie (Ranke) P.; m. Kathleen Ann Hilt, May 5, 1973; children: William Benjamin, Sarah Elizabeth. BArch magna cum laude, U. Notre Dame, 1971. Cert. Nat. Coun. Archtl. Registration Bds. V.p., arch., dir. ednl., instl. specialty Le Roy Troyer & Assocs. (now the Troyer Group), Mishawaka, Ind., 1971—; design instr. dept. arch. U. Notre Dame, 1976. Mem. Ind. State Bd. Registration for Architects, 1990—; mem. registration exam com. Nat. Coun. Archtl. Registration Bds., 1992—, vice chair 1996, chair 1997. Prin. archtl. works include: St. Peter Luth. Ch., Mishawaka, Ind., 1979, 4 brs. for South Bend Pub. Libr., 1983, Edward J. Funk & Sons office bldg. Taylor U., Upland, Ind., 1982, Taylor U. Lbir., carillon tower, 1985, Early Childhood Devel. Ctr. U. Notre Dame, 1994, Convents for Sisters of Holy Cross St. Mary's, Notre Dame, Ind., 1995. Mem. AIA (gold medal for exellence in archtl. edn. 1971), Ind. Soc. Archs. (Design Excellence award 1978, chpt. pres. 1985, Juliet Peddle award 2000). Office: The Troyer Group Inc 550 Union St Mishawaka IN 46544-2346

PONSETI, IGNACIO VIVES, orthopaedic surgery educator; b. Cuidadela, Balearic Islands, Spain, June 3, 1914; s. Miguel and Margarita (Vives) P.; 1 child, William Edward; m. Helena Percas, 1961. BS, U. Barcelona, 1930, MD, 1936, D honoris causa, 1984. Instr. dept. orthopaedic surgery State U. Iowa, 1944-57, prof., 1957—. Author papers and a book on cogenital and developmental skeletal deformities. Capt. M.C. Spanish Army, 1936-39. Recipient Kappa Delta award for orthopaedic rsch., 1955. Mem. Assn. Bone and Joint Surgeons, Am. Acad. Cerebral Palsy, Soc. Exptl. Biology and Medicine, Internat. Coll. Surgeons, N.Y. Acad. Sci., AMA (Ketoen gold medal 1960), Am. Acad. Orthopedic Surgeons, ACS, Am. Orthopedic Assn., Pediatric Orthopaedic Soc. (hon.), Iowa Med. Soc., Orthopedic Rsch. Soc. (Shands award 1975), Sigma Xi, Asociacion Argentina de Cirugia (hon.), Asociacion Balear de Cirugia (hon.), Sociedad de Cirujanos de Chile (hon.), Sociedad Espanola de Cirugia Ortopedica (hon.), Sociedad Brasilera de Ortopedia e Traumatologia (hon.). Home: 110 Oakridge Ave Iowa City IA 52246-2935 Office: Carver Pavilion U Iowa Hosps Iowa City IA 52242 E-mail: Ignacio-Ponseti@uiowa.edu.

PONTIKES, WILLIAM N. computer rental and leasing company executive; b. 1941; BA, So. Ill. U., 1968. With Ill. Police Dept., 1963-65, Comdisco, DesPlaines, Ill., 1973—, v.p. ops., 1975-76, sr. v.p. ops., 1976-77, dir., 1977—, exec. v.p. Des Plaines, I.L. With U.S. Army, 1963-65. Office: Comdisco Inc 6111 N River Rd Des Plaines IL 60018-5158

PONTIUS, STANLEY N. bank holding company executive; b. Auburn, Ind., Aug. 26, 1946; s. Clayton and Frances (Beuret) P.; m. Cheryl Ann Dawson, Aug. 3, 1968; children: Jarrod B., Dorian K. BS, Ind. U., 1968; grad., Stonier Grad. Sch. of Banking, 1979. Bank One, 1968-91; dir., pres., COO 1st Fin. Bancorp, Hamilton, Ohio, 1991, dir., pres., CEO, 1992—, 1st Nat. Bank of Southwestern Ohio, Hamilton, 1991-97, chmn., CEO, 1997-98, chmn., 1998—. Bd. dirs. Health Alliance Greater Cin., Ohio Casualty Corp., Fort Hamilton Health Network (chmn.), Hamilton Cmty. Found. With U.S. Army, 1968-70. Mem. Am. Bankers Coun., Hamilton-Fairfield Arts Assn. Leadership Hamilton, Metropolitan Growth Alliance, "The Community Banker" magazine (adv. bd.). Office: 1st Fin Bancorp 300 High St Hamilton OH 45011-6078

POOLE, WILLIAM, bank executive; b. Wilmington, Del., June 19, 1937; s. William and Louise (Hiller) P.; m. Mary Lynne Ahroon, June 26, 1960 (div. May 1997); children: William, Lester Allen, Jonathan Carl; m. Geraldine S. Stroud, July 12, 1997. AB, Swarthmore Coll., 1959, LLD (hon.), 1989; MBA, U. Chgo., 1963, PhD, 1966. Asst. prof. polit. economy Johns Hopkins U., Balt., 1963-69; professorial lectr. Am. U., Washington, 1970-71; assoc. professorial lectr. George Washington U., 1971-73; lectr. professorial lectr. Georgetown U., 1972, Harvard U., Cambridge, Mass., 1973; vis. lectr. MIT, 1974, 77; Bank Mees and Hope vis. prof. econs. Erasmus U. Rotterdam, 1991; prof. econs. Brown U., Providence, 1974-98, dir. ctr. for study fin. markets and insts., 1987-92, chmn. econs. dept., 1981-82, 85-86; economist Bd. Govs. of FRS, Washington, 1964, 69-70, sr. economist, 1970-74; pres., CEO Fed. Res. Bank, St. Louis, 1998—. Adviser Fed. Res. Bank, Boston, 1973-74, cons., 1974-81; vis. economist Res. Bank of Australia, 1980-81; mem. Coun. Econ. Advisers, 1982-85; adj. scholar Cato Inst., 1985-98. Mem. Am. Econ. Assn., Am. Fin. assn. (mem. nominating com. 1979), Western Econ. Assn. (mem. internat. exec. com. 1986-89, mem. nominating com. 1995). Office: Fed Res Bank St Louis 411 Locust St Saint Louis MO 63102-2005

POOLMAN, JIM, state legislator; b. Fargo, N.D., May 15, 1970; s. Robert Francis and Susan Faye (Brown) P. BBA, U. N.D., 1992, postgrad., 1994—. Sales cons. Straus Co., Grand Forks, N.D., 1987-95; state representative N.D. State Ho. of Reps., 1992—; trust officer First Am. Bank, 1995—. Task force State of N.D., Grand Forks, 1992; mem. United Hosp. Corp. United Health, Grand Forks, 1992—, Presdl. Search Com., U. N.D., 1992; bd. dirs. Red River Red Cross, 1995—. Mem. Toastmasters Internat. (sec.), Phi Delta Theta Alumni (varsity bachelors club scholarship ednl. found. 1992). Republican. Lutheran. Avocations: fishing, water sports, golf. Office: ND Ho of Reps State Capitol Bismarck ND 58505 Home: 505 Portage Dr Bismarck ND 58503-0266

POOR, JANET MEAKIN, III, landscape designer; b. Cin., Nov. 27, 1929; d. Cyrus Lee and Helen Keats (Meakin) Lee-Hofer; m. Edward King Poor III, June 23, 1951; children: Edward King IV, Thomas Meakin. Student, Stephens Coll., 1947-48, U. Cinn., 1949-51, Triton Coll., 1973-76. Pres. Janet Meakin Poor Landscape Design, Winnetka, Ill., 1975—. Chmn. bd. dirs. Cgho. Horticultural Soc., Chgo. Botanic Garden. Author, editor: Plants That Merit Attention Vol. I: Trees, 1984; contbr. articles to profl. jours. Participant in long range planning City of Winnetka, 1978-82, archtl. and environ. bd., 1980-84, beautification commn., 1978-84, garden coun., 1978-82; adv. coun., Sec. of Agr. Nat. Arboretum, Washington; nat. adv. bd. Filoli, San Francisco; trustee Ctr. Plant Conservation at Mo. Botanical Garden, St. Louis, also mem. exec. com.; mem. adv. coun. The Garden Conservancy, 1989—, chmn. Open Days Program; trustee Winnetka Congl. Ch., 1978-80; bd. dirs. Lady Bird Johnson Wildflower Ctr., Austin, Tex. Recipient merit award Hadley Sch. Blind, 1972; named Vol. of Yr. Hadley Sch. Blind. Mem. Chgo. Hort. Soc. (chmn. bd. dirs. 1987-93, medal 1984, gold medal garden design, exec. com., chmn. rsch. com., women's bd., designer herb garden Farwell Gardens at Chgo. Botanic Garden, Hutchinson medal 1994), Am. Hort. Soc. (bd. dirs., Catherine H. Sweeney award 1985), Garden Club Am. (chmn. nat. plant exchange 1980-81, chmn. hort. com. 1981-83, bd. dirs., 1983-85, corresponding sec. 1985-87, Horticulture award Zone XI 1981, Creative Leadership award 1986), Fortnightly Club, Garden Guild (bd. dirs.), Garden Club Am. (v.p. 1987-89, medal awards chmn. 1991-93, Medal of Honor 1994). Republican. Avocations: gardening, writing, music, hort. rsch., lecturing.

POORMAN, ROBERT LEWIS, education consultant, former college president; b. Germantown, Ohio, Dec. 9, 1926; s. Dale Lowell and Bernice Velma (Krick) P.; m. Lois May Romer, Dec. 26, 1949; children: Paula Beth, Janice Marie, Mark Leon, John Alex, Lisa Ann, Daniel Romer. Student, Ohio Wesleyan U., 1944-45, U. Va., 1945-46; B.S.Ed., Ohio State U., 1948, M.A., 1950; postgrad., U. So. Calif., 1951-53; Ed.D. (Kellogg fellow 1960-62, Disting. Scholar Tuition grantee 1960-62), UCLA, 1964. Tchr., counselor, adminstr., secondary schs., Colo., Mo., Ariz., 1948-57; registrar Phoenix Coll., 1957-60; intern Bakersfield Coll., 1960-63, asst. to pres., 1963-64, asso. dean instrn., 1964-65, dean students, 1965-67; founding pres. Lincoln Land Community Coll., 1967-88, pres. emeritus; edn. cons. MARA of Malaysia, 1983; higher edn. cons. Springfield, Ill., 1988—; interim pres. Parkland Coll., Champaign, 1989-90. Fulbright lectr., cons. to Lithuania, 1993, to Ukraine, 1996-97, to People's Rep. of China, 2000-01; vis. assoc. prof. Fla. Internat. U., 1994-95; cons. Citizens Dem. Corps., Ukraine, 1998, USIA, Lithuania, 1999, Hong Kong U., 2001. Contbr. articles to profl. jours. Bd. dirs. (past) United Way of Springfield, bd. dirs. Urban League of Springfield, Good Will Industries of Springfield, Springfield (Ill.) Symphony, Catholic Youth Orgn., Springfield, Gov.'s Prayer Breakfast, Springfield Mental Health, Griffin H.S. Bd., Diocesan Sem.; mem. adv. bd. Sacred Heart Acad., Springfield Commn. on Internat. Visitors, Sister Cities Assn. Served with USNR, 1944-46. Recipient Midwest region Chief Exec. Officer of Yr. Assn. Community Coll. Trustees, 1988, recognition Ill. Community Coll. Trustees Assn., 1988; named an Outstanding Chief Exec. Officer for Ill. Community Colls. U. Tex. Leadership Program, 1987; named a leader in shaping the century State Jour. Register, 1999; Phi Theta Kappa fellow, 1981. Mem. Am. Assn. Community and Jr. Colls., Ill. Council Public Community Coll. Pres. (sec. 1973-74, vice chmn. 1974-75, chmn. 1975-76), Council North Central Community and Jr. Colls. (exec. bd. 1979-81), North Central Assn. (cons., evaluator 1984-88) Republican. Roman Catholic. Home and Office: 2324 Willemoore Ave Springfield IL 62704-4362 Fax: 217-793-6939. E-mail: robert.poorman@llcc.edu.

POPE, DANIEL JAMES, lawyer; b. Chgo., Nov. 22, 1948; BA, Loyola U., Chgo., 1972; JD cum laude, John Marshall Law Sch., 1975; postgrad., U. Chgo., 1977-78. Bar: U.S. Merchant Marines 1966, Ill. 1975, U.S. Dist. Ct. (no. dist.) Ill. 1982, N.Y. 1983, U.S. Tax Ct. 1985, Tex. 1995, U.S. Supreme Ct. 1995. Corp. trust adminstr. Continental Bank, Chgo., 1972-74; assoc. Haskell & Perrin, 1975-77, Coffield, Ungaretti, Harris & Slavin, Chgo., 1977-81, ptnr., 1981-90, head litigation dept., 1988-90; ptnr. Seyfarth Shaw Fairweather & Geraldson, 1990-95, Bell, Boyd & Lloyd, 1996—. Adj. prof. John Marshall Law Sch., Chgo., 1978-79; appointed panel atty. Fed. Defender Program, Chgo., 1983. Mem. ABA, Pub. Interest Law Initiative (dir. 1989-91), Chgo. Athletic Club, Oak Park Country Club. Office: Bell Boyd & LLoyd 70 W Madison St Ste 3300 Chicago IL 60602-4284 Home: 3506 Cypress Creek Rd Champaign IL 61822-7948

POPE, KERIG RODGERS, magazine executive; b. Waukesha, Wis., Sept. 30, 1935; s. Kerig James Pope and Mildred (Offerman) Troemel; m. Claudia T. Koralewski, Nov. 1961 (div. 1975); children— Kerig William, Giles Thomas; m. Beth Leslie Kasik, May 24, 1980; children: Kolin Jared, Zoe Alissa. Grad., Art Inst. Chgo., 1958. Designer Jack Denst Wallpaper Designs, Chgo., 1958-60; designer Continental Casualty Ins. Co., 1960-62, Leo Burnett Adv. Agy., Chgo., 1962-63; art dir. Mercury Records Corp., 1963-66; mng. art dir. Playboy mag., 1966—. Exhibited in group shows Whitney Mus. Am. Art, N.Y.C., 1969, Mus. Contemporary Art, Chgo., 1972, Bienal de Sao Paulo, Brazil, 1973, Museo de Arte Moderno, Mexico City, 1974, Nat. Collection Fine Arts, Washington, 1979, Moderno, Mexico City, 1974, Mus. Contemporary Art, Chgo., 1996; represented in permanent collections Nat. Collection Fine Arts, Washington, Mus. Contemporary Art, Chgo., Smart Mus., U. Chgo. Recipient silver medal Communigraphics, N.Y.C., 1971, gold medal, 1971, 72; award of excellence Soc. Publ. Designers, 1979, 4 awards of excellence Design Ann., 1984, Silver medal Illustrators 29, 1986, Silver medal Soc. of Illustrators, 1988. Mem.: Soc. Publ. Arts (3 Silver awards 1987), Soc. Typog. Arts (Silver medal 1998, Gold medal 1999, 2001), Art Dirs. Club N.Y., Soc. Illustrators (Gold medal 1981, 1984, Silver medal 1988, Gold medal 1991, Silver medal 1998, Gold medal 1999), Arts Club (Chgo.). Club: Arts (Chgo.) Office: Playboy Enterprises Inc 680 N Lake Shore Dr Fl 15 Chicago IL 60611-4455 E-mail: kengp@playboy.com.

POPE, MARK ANDREW, lawyer, university administrator; b. Munster, Ind., May 22, 1952; s. Thomas A. and Eleanor E. (Miklos) P.; m. Julia Risk Pope, June 15, 1974; children: Brent Andrew, Bradley James. BA, Purdue U., 1974; JD cum laude, Ind. U., 1977. Bar: Ind. 1977, U.S. Dist. Ct. (so. dist.) Ind. 1977, U.S. Ct. Appeals (7th cir.) 1984. Assoc. Johnson & Weaver, Indpls., 1977-79, Rocap, Rocap, Reese & Young, Indpls., 1980-82, Dutton & Overman, Indpls., 1982-88, ptnr., 1988-89; asst. gen. counsel Lincoln Nat. Corp., Fort Wayne, Ind., 1989-91, sr. counsel, 1991-95, v.p. govt. rels., 1995-2001; dir. athletics Ind. U.-Purdue U., Ft. Wayne, 2001—. Bd. dirs. Ft. Wayne Bicentennial Coun.; pres., bd. dirs. ARCH, Inc., 1994-97. Bd. editors, devel. editor Ind. U. Law Rev., 1976-77 Mem. pres.'s coun. Purdue U., 1977—; applied eoncs. cons. Jr. Achievement, 1989-95; bd. dirs. Jr. Achievement of No. Ind., 1992-94; grad. Leadership, Fort Wayne, 1992; mem. parish coun. St. Elizabeth Ann Seton Ch., 1993-96, pres. 1993-95; bd. edn. mem. Bishop Luers H.S., 2000—; adv. coun. Ind. U. Bus. Sch., Purdue U., Fort Wayne, Ind., 2000-02; mem. bd. trustees Allen County War Meml. Coliseum, 2002--. Named Disting. Hoosier, Gov. of Ind., 1974. Fellow Ind. Bar Found., Indpls. Bar Found. (disting.); mem. ABA (dist. rep. young lawyers divsn. 1981-83, dir. 1983-84, liaison coord. 1985-86, 87-88, exec. coun. 1981-88, cabinet 1982-88, gen. practice sect. coun. mem. 1986—, membership chmn. 1987-89, chmn. career and family com. 1990-92, dir. 1991-93), Indpls. Bar Assn. (v.p. 1983, chmn. young lawyers divsn. 1981), 500 Festival Assocs. (vice-chmn. of 500 festival parade 1985-89), Orchard Ridge Country Club (bd. dirs. 1995—, sec. 1996-97, pres. 1999-2001). Avocations: tennis, golf, running. Office: Ind U-Purdue U at Fort Wayne Gates Sports Ctr 2101 E Coliseum Blvd Fort Wayne IN 46805-1499 E-mail: popem@ipfw.edu.

POPE, RICHARD M. rheumatologist; b. Chgo., Jan. 10, 1946; Student, Procopius Coll., 1963-65, U. Ill., 1965-66; MD, Loyola U., 1970. Diplomate Am. Bd. Internal Medicine. Intern in medicine Med. Ctr. Michael Reese Hosp., Chgo., 1970-71, resident in internal medicine, 1971-72; fellow in rheumatology U. Wash., Seattle, 1972-74; asst. clin. prof. medicine U. Hawaii, 1974-77; asst. prof. medicine U. Tex. Health Sci. Ctr., San Antonio, 1976-81, assoc. prof. medicine, 1981-85, Northwestern U. Med. Sch., 1985-88, prof. medicine, 1988—; attending physician Northwestern Meml. Hosp., Chgo., 1985—, VA Lakeside Med. Ctr., Chgo., 1985—, Rehab. Inst. Chgo., 1985—; divsn. chief rheumatology divsn. Northwestern U., Chgo., 1992—. Chief divsn. rheumatology VA Lakeside Med. Ctr., 1985-91, divsn. arthritis-connective tissue diseases Northwestern U. and Northwestern Meml. Hosp., 1989—, Northwestern Med. Faculty Found., 1989—; mem. program com. Cen. Soc. Clin. Rsch., 1987, cen. region Am. Rheumatism Assn., 1987; mem. sci. com. Ill. chpt. Arthritis Found., 1988-92, bd. dirs., 1990—, mem. chpt. rev. grants subcom., 1983-88, chmn. chpt. rsch. grant subcom., 1986-88, mem. rsch. com., 1986-88; mem. site visit teams NIH, 1986, 87, 89, 96, 97; cons. reviewer VA Merit Rev. Bd., 1984, 87, 91; cons. reviewer Arthritis Soc. Can., 1986, 87; mem. editl. adv. bd. Arthritis and Rheumatism Jour. Lab. and Clin. Medicine, 1992—. Author: (with others) The Science and Practice of Clinical Medicine, 1979, Proceedings of the University of South Florida International Symposium in the Biomedical Sciences, 1984, Concepts in Immunopathology, 1985, Biology Based Immunomodulators in the Therapy of Rheumatic Diseases, 1986, Primer on the Rheumatic Diseases, 1988; contbr. numerous articles to profl. jours. With U.S. Army, 1974-76. Anglo-Am. Rheumatology fellow, 1983. Mem. ACP, Am. Coll. Rheumatology (councillor cen. region coun. 1990-93, program com. 1983-86, 91), Am. Assn. Immunologists, Am. Fedn. Clin. Rsch., Am. Soc. Clin. Investigation, Lupus Found. Ill. (mem. adv. bd. 1990-93), Chgo. Rheumatism Assn. (pres. 1991-93), Cen. Soc. Clin. Investigation, Soc. Irish and Am. Rheumatologists (sec., treas. 1989-93), Univ. Rheumatology Coun. Chgo., Alpha Omega Alpha. Achievements include research in pathophysiology of rheumatoid arthritis, T cell activation, T cell receptor, macrophage gene expression. Office: Northwestern U Dept Divsn Rheumatology Ward 3-315 303 E Chicago Ave Chicago IL 60611-3093

POPE, ROBERT E(UGENE), fraternal organization administrator; b. Wellington, Kans., Sept. 10, 1931; s. Samuel E. and Opal Irene (Davis) P. BSChemE with honors, U. Kans., 1952, MS, 1958. Registered profl. engr., Kans. Asst. instr. U. Kans., Lawrence, 1952-56; lab. technician Monsanto Co., St. Louis, 1952; project engr. Mallinckrodt, Inc., 1953-59; traveling sec. Theta Tau, 1959-62, exec. sec., 1963-84, exec. dir., 1984-96, exec. dir. emeritus, 1996—. Carillonneur, Grace United Meth. Ch., St. Louis, 1985—, chmn. adminstrv. coun., 1991-95, trustee, 1997-99, comms. chmn. 2000—; trustee Theta Tau Ednl. Found., 1997—. Mem. Am. Soc. Assn. Execs. (life), Am. Soc. Engring. Edn., Profl. Fraternity Execs. Assn. (charter), Profl. Fraternity Assn. (exec. sec. 1977-86, Disting. Svc. award 1995), Creve Coeur Country Club, Theta Tau (Alumni Hall of Fame 1988, mem. bd. editors The Gear of Theta Tau 1993—, editor-in-chief 1996—), Tau Beta Pi, Phi Lambda Upsilon, Omicron Delta Kappa. Democrat. United Methodist. Avocations: physical fitness, sports, photography, stamp collecting, writing. Home: 13 Sona Ln Saint Louis MO 63141-7742 Office: Theta Tau 655 Craig Rd Ste 128 Saint Louis MO 63141-7168

POPLE, JOHN ANTHONY, chemistry educator; b. Burnham, Somerset, Eng., Oct. 31, 1925; s. Herbert Keith and Frances (Jones) Pople; m. Joy Cynthia Pople, Sept. 22, 1952; children: Hilary Jane, Adrian John, Mark Stephen, Andrew Keith. BA in Math., Cambridge U., Eng., 1946, MA in Math., 1950, PhD in Math., 1951. Rsch. fellow Trinity Coll., Cambridge U., England, 1951—54, lectr. in math. England, 1954—58; Ford vis. prof. chemistry Carnegie Inst. Tech., Pitts., 1961—62; Carnegie prof. chem. physics Carnegie-Mellon U., 1964—74, J.C. Warner prof., 1974—91; prof. Northwestern U., Evanston, Ill., 1986—. Recipient Chemistry prize, Wolf Found., 1992, Kirkwood medal, Am. Chem. Soc., 1994, J.O. Hirschfelder prize in theoretical chemistry, U. Wis., Theoretical Chemistry Inst., 1994, Nobel prize in chemistry, 1998. Fellow: AAAS, Royal Soc. London; mem.: NAS. Office: Northwestern U Dept Chemistry 2145 Sheridan Rd Evanston IL 60208-0834

POPOFF, FRANK PETER, chemical company executive; b. Sofia, Bulgaria, Oct. 27, 1935; came to U.S., 1940; s. Eftim and Stoyanka (Kossoroff) P.; m. Jean Urse; children: John V., Thomas F., Steven M. B.S. in Chemistry, Ind. U., 1957, M.B.A., 1959. With The Dow Chem. Co., Midland, Mich., 1959—, exec. v.p., 1985-87, dir., pres., chief executive officer, 1987-92; chmn., CEO, dir. Dow Chemical Corp., 1992-96, chmn., 1996—; exec. v.p., then pres. Dow Chem. Europe subs., Horgen, Switzerland, 1976-85. Bd. dirs. Dow Corning Corp., Am. Express, Chem. Bank & Trust Co., Chem. Fin. Corp., Midland. Mem. dean's adv. coun. Ind. U.; mem. vis. com. U. Mich. Sch. Bus.; mem. Pres.' Commn. Environ. Quality. Recipient Internat. Palladium medal, 1994, Société de Chimie Industrielle (Am. Section). Mem. Chem. Mfrs. Assn. (bd. dirs.), U.S. Coun. for Internat. Bus., Bus. Roundtable, Conf. Bd., Am. Chem. Soc. Office: Dow Chem Co 2030 Dow Ctr Midland MI 48674-0001

POPP, JOSEPH BRUCE, manufacturing executive; b. Chgo., July 9, 1919; s. Peter Leon and Anna (Chomyz) P.; m. Mabel Lydia Szymanski, Oct. 23, 1941 (dec. Mar. 1993); m. Elinor A. Maves, Jan. 27, 1996; children: Dianne, Lydia, Bruce, Anita, Gregory. Founder, owner Poultry Farm, Westville, Ind., 1941-48, Gary (Ind.) Undercoating Co., 1948-51; survey analyst George S. May Co., Chgo., 1952-54; gen. sales mgr. Maurey Instrument Corp., 1958-64; founder, owner Joe Popp Sales Co., North Riverside, Ill., 1964-89, Chart Pool USA Inc., Portage, Ind., 1966—. Inventor hand held berry picker, worldwide bloodhound property security (patents pending). Bd. dirs. YMCA Camp Tecumseh, Brookston, Ind., 1973—. Sgt. U.S. Army, 1942-46. Mem. Nat. Fedn. of Ind. Bus., Greater Portage C. of C., Ind. C. of C., Better Bus. Bur., The Gideons Internat. Republican. Home: 1133 Lincoln St Hobart IN 46342-6039 Office: Chart Pool USA Inc 5695 Old Porter Rd Portage IN 46368-1194

POPP, NATHANIEL, archbishop; b. Aurora, Ill., June 12, 1940; s. Joseph and Vera (Boytor) P. BA, Ill. Benedictine U., 1962; ThM, Pontifical Gregorian U., 1966. Ordained priest, 1966, bishop, 1980. Asst. priest St. Michael Byz Cath. Ch., Aurora, Ill., 1967; parish priest Holy Cross Romanian Orthodox Ch., Hermitage, Pa., 1975-80; aux. bishop Romanian Orthodox Episcopate of Am., Orthodox Ch. in Am., Jackson, Mich., 1980-84, ruling bishop, 1984—. Mem. Holy Synod, Orthodox Ch. in Am., Syosset, N.Y., 1980—, archbishop, 1999; participant Monastic Consultation World Coun. Chs., Cairo, 1979, 7th Assembly, Vancouver, Can., 1983; adv. bd. Orthodox Christian Laity, 1999—; pres. Ctr. for Orthodox Christian Studies, Detroit, 2000—. Author: Holy Icons, 1969; working editor: (monthly newspaper) Solia. Trustee Romanian-Am. Heritage Ctr., Grass Lake, Mich.; chmn. bd. dirs. Congress of Romanian Ams., 1990. Mem. Mineral and Rock Soc. Mich. Home: 2522 Grey Tower Rd Jackson MI 49201-9120 Address: PO Box 309 Grass Lake MI 49240-0309 E-mail: hgbnpopp@aol.com.

POPPEN, STEVE, professional sports team executive; m. Christy Poppen; children: Natalie, Andrew, Nathan, Avery. BA in Acctg., Evangel U., Springfield, Mo., 1991. CPA Mo. With bus. assurance grop PricewaterhouseCoopers LLP, Kansas City, Mo., 1991—99; dir. fin. Minn. Vikings Football Club Inc., Eden Prairie, 1999, v.p. fin. Office: 9520 Vikings Dr Eden Prairie MN 55344

POPPENHAGEN, RONALD WILLIAM, advertising agency executive; b. Chgo., Feb. 23, 1948; s. Andrew Charles and Elaine Edith (Larson) P.; m. Judy Diane Wagenblast, July 25, 1981. BA. in History and Lit., Augustana Coll., 1970. Reporter Sta. KBUR, Burlington, Iowa, 1970-71, Sta. KROS, Clinton, 1971-72, Sta. WDWS, Champaign, Ill., 1972-73, news dir., 1973-77; reporter The Morning Courier, Urbana, 1977-79; mng. editor The Daily Journal, Wheaton, 1979-80; met. editor The Southern Illinoisan, Carbondale, 1980-83; editor Green Bay (Wis.) News Chronicle, 1983-86, editor, gen. mgr., 1986-97; v.p., media dir. Wagenblast and Assocs., Green Bay, 1997—. Recipient Best Editls. award Wis. Newspaper

Assn., 1985, 86, 93, UPI, 1983-86, Best Local Column award, 1993. Avocation: railroads. Office: Wagenblast & Assocs 1524 University Green Bay WI 54302 E-mail: wagenblast@itol.com.

POPPER, ROBERT, law educator, former dean; b. N.Y.C., May 22, 1932; s. Walter G. and Dorothy B. (Kluger) P.; m. Mary Ann Schaefer, July 12, 1963; children: Julianne, Robert Gregory. BS, U. Wis., 1953; LLB, Harvard U., 1956; LLM, NYU, 1963. Bar: N.Y. 1957, U.S. Dist. Ct. (so. dist.) N.Y. 1962, U.S. Ct. Appeals (2d cir.) 1962, U.S. Supreme Ct. 1962, U.S. Dist. Ct. (ea. dist.) N.Y. 1969, U.S. Ct. Appeals (7th cir.) 1970, U.S. Ct. Appeals (8th cir.) 1971, Mo. 1971, U.S. Dist. Ct. (we. dist.) Mo. 1973. Trial atty. criminal br. N.Y.C. Legal Aid Soc., 1960-61; asst. dist. atty. N.Y. County, 1961-64; assoc. Seligson & Morris, N.Y.C., 1964-69; mem. faculty School of Law U. Mo, Kansas City, 1969-96, prof., 1973-96, acting dean, 1983-84, dean, 1984-93, dean and prof. emeritus, 1996—. Cons. and lectr. in field. Author: Post Conviction Remedies in a Nutshell, 1978, De-Nationalizing the Bill of Rights, 1979; contbr. articles to profl. jours. Bd. dirs. Midwestern Innocence Project. Fellow ABA; mem. Mo. Bar, Kansas City Met. Bar Assn., Mo. Inst. of Justice. Home: 6229 Summit St Kansas City MO 64113-1556 Office: U Mo Kansas City Sch Law 1500 Rockhill Rd Kansas City MO 64110-2467 Fax: (816) 235-5276. E-mail: popperr@umkc.edu.

PORCH, ROGER A. former state legislator; m. Lois Porch; 2 children. Grad., U. S.D. Mem. S.D. Ho. of Reps., 1985-90; mem. agr. and natural resources com., edn. com.; mem. S.D. State Senate, 1990-97, mem. agr. and natural resources coms., mem. edn., legis. procedure and state affairs coms.; rancher; loan officer. Address: PO Box 317 Philip SD 57567-0317

PORILE, NORBERT THOMAS, chemistry educator; b. Vienna, Austria, May 18, 1932; came to U.S., 1947, naturalized, 1952; s. Irving and Emma Porile; m. Miriam Eisen, June 16, 1957; 1 son, James. B.A., U. Chgo., 1952, M.S., 1954, Ph.D., 1957. Rsch. assoc. Brookhaven Nat. Lab., Upton, N.Y., 1957-59, assoc. chemist, 1959-63, chemist, 1963-64; vis. prof. chemistry McGill U., 1963-65; assoc. prof. chemistry Purdue U., West Lafayette, Ind., 1965-69, prof. chemistry, 1969—. Rsch. collaborator Brookhaven Nat. Lab., Argonne Nat. Lab., Los Alamos Sci. Lab., Lawrence Berkeley Lab.; vis. prof. Facultes des Scis., Orsay, France; fellow Soc. Promotion of Sci. in Japan, Inst. Nuclear Study, U. Kyoto, 1961. Editor: Radiochemistry of the Elements and Radiochemical Techniques, 1986-90. John Simon Guggenheim meml. fellow Institut de Physique Nucleaire Orsay, 1971-72; recipient F.D. Martin Undergrad. Teaching award, 1977; Von Humboldt Sr. U.S. Scientist award Philipps U., Marburg, W. Ger., 1982 Mem. Am. Chem. Soc., Am. Phys. Soc. Office: Purdue U Dept Chemistry Chemistry Bldg Lafayette IN 47907 E-mail: porile@purdue.edu.

PORTER, ANDREW CALVIN, educational administrator, psychology educator; b. Huntington, Pa., July 10, 1942; s. Rutherford and Grace (Johnson) P.; m. Susan Porter, June 5, 1967; children: Matthew, Anna, John, Joe, Kate. BS, Ind. State U., 1963; MS, U. Wis., 1965, PhD, 1967. Prof., co-dir. inst. rsch. on teaching Mich. State U., East Lansing, 1967-88; assoc. dir. basic skills group Nat. Inst. Edn., Washington, 1975-76; Anderson-Bascom prof. edn., prof. ednl. psychology, dir. Wis. Ctr. Edn. Rsch. U. Wis., Madison, 1988—. Vis. asst. prof. Ind. State U., Terre Haute, 1967; mem. adv. bd. Am. Jour. Edn., 1988—; chair bd. Internat. Studies, Nat. Acad. Scis., Nat. Rsch. Coun., 1993-2001; chmn. U.S. Dept. Edn., adv. coun. on edn. stats., 1994-2001. Author: Brookings Papers on Education Policy, 1998. Bd. dirs. Madison Urban League, 1992-96. Recipient Disting. Alumni award, Ind. U., 1994, award, U.S. Dept. Edn. Mem. Am. Ednl. Rsch. Assn. (pres. 2001), Nat. Coun. Edn. Measurement, Nat. Coun. Tchrs. Math., Psychometric Soc., Nat. Acad. Edn., Phi Delta Kappa (life). Office: U Wis Madison Wis Ctr Edn Rsch 1025 W Johnson St Madison WI 53706-1706 E-mail: andyp@education.wisc.edu.

PORTER, ARTHUR T. oncologist, educator, medical administrator; b. June 11, 1956; m. Pamela Porter; 4 children. Student, U. Sierra Leone, 1974-75; BA in Anatomy, Cambridge U., 1978, MB, BChir, MD, 1980, MA, 1984; DMRT, Royal Coll. Radiologists, Eng., 1985; postgrad., U. Alta., 1984-86; FRCPC, Royal Coll. Physicians and Surgeons, Can., 1986; cert. for physicians mgr. program, U. Toronto, 1990; MBA, U. Tenn., 1998. Lic., bd. cert., Mich., Can., Eng.; diplomate Health Care Adminstrn. House physician gen. medicine Norfolk and Norwich Hosp., Eng., 1981; house sugeon gen. surgery New Addenbrookes Hosp., Cambridge, Eng., 1981-82; sr. house officer clin. hematology No. Gen. Hosp., Sheffield, Eng., 1982; sr. house officer gen. medicine Huntington County Hosp., Hinchingbrooke Hosp., Eng., 1982-83; sr. house officer radiotherapy and oncology Norfolk and Norwich Hosp., Norwich, 1983-84; chief resident radiation oncology Cross Cancer Inst., Edmonton, Alta., Can., 1984-86, from radiation oncologist to sr. radiation oncologist Can., 1986-87, sr. radiation oncologist Can., 1987; asst. prof. medicine U. Alta., 1987, assoc. clin. prof. dept. surgery faculty medicine, 1988; head divsn. radiation oncology U. Western Ont., London, Can., 1988; cons. radiation oncologist, chief dept. radiation oncology London Regional Cancer Ctr., 1988, program dir. radiation oncology, 1989-91; chmn. dept. oncology Victoria Hosp. Corp., London, 1990; assoc. prof. dept. oncology U. Western Ont., 1990; program dir. radiation oncology Wayne State U., Detroit, 1991-92; prof., chmn. dept. radiation oncology Wayne State U. Sch. Medicine, 1991-99; chief Gershenson Radiation Oncology Ctr. Harper Hosp., 1991-99; radiation oncologist-in-chief Detroit Med. Ctr., 1991-99; pres., CEO Radiation Oncology R & D Ctr., Detroit, 1991-99; dir. multidisciplinary svcs. Meyer L. Prentice Comprehensive Cancer Ctr., 1992-99; chmn. radiation oncology Grace Hosp., 1993-99; assoc. dean Wayne State U. Sch. Medicine, 1998—. Pres., CEO Detroit Med. Ctr.; sr. v.p. Detroit Med. Ctr. Author: (with others) Fundamental Problems in Breast Cancer, 1985, Therapeutic Progress in Urological Cancers, 1988, Proceedings of the Consensus Meeting of the Treatment of Bladder Cancer-1987, 1988, Brachytherapy, 1989, High and Low Dose Rate Brachytherapy, 1989, Brachytherapy of Prostate Cancer, 1991; co-editor Treatment of Cancer, 1991—; assoc. editor Can. Jour. Oncology, 1990—, Antibody and Radiopharmaceuticals, 1992—; contbr. articles to profl. jours. Recipient Nat. award Sierra Leone, 1975-80, Commonwealth Found. scholarship, 1980, Best Doctor in Am. award, 1992, 93, 94, 95, 96, 97, 98, Testimonial Resolution, City of Detroit, 1993, Wayne County, 1993, Mich., 1997. Fellow Am. Coll. Angiology, Detroit Acad. Medicine, Royal Soc. Medicine, Royal Coll. Radiology, Am. Coll. Radiation Oncology (chancellor 1994-97); mem. AMA (Physicians Recognition award 1986), Am. Soc. Therapeutic Radiation Oncology, Am. Radium Soc., Am. Soc. Clin. Oncology, Am. Coll. Oncol. Adminstrs. (pres. 1994-96), Am. Acad. Med Adminstrs., Am. Endocurietherapy Soc. (pres. 1994-95), Mich. State Med. Soc., Mich. Soc. Therapeutic Radiation Oncology, Mich. Radiol. Soc. Detroit Med. Soc. (Ann. award for Excellence 1993), Wayne County Med. Soc., European Soc. Therapeutic Radiation Oncology, Brit. Inst. Radiology, Can. Oncology Soc., Can. Assn. Radiation Oncology, Royal Coll. Radiologists, Sierra Leone Med. and Dental Assn., Greater Detroit C. of C., Sigma Xi. Achievements include patent in a perineal applicator; research in novel methods in delivery dose, brachytherapy, intraoperative therapy, unsealed source therapy, verification and dosimetry, real time portal imaging, three-dimensional and planning, unsealed source dosimetry, the design of perineal applicators. Office: Detroit Med Ctr 3663 Woodward Ave Ste 200 Detroit MI 48201-2400 E-mail: ceo@dmc.org.

PORTER, CLOYD ALLEN, former state representative; b. Huntley, Ill., May 22, 1935; s. Cecil and Myrtle (Fisher) P.; m. Joan Hawkins, July 25, 1959; children: Ellen, LeeAnn, Jay, Joli. Grad. high sch., Burlington, Wis. Ptnr. Cecil W. Porter & Son Trucking, 1955-70; treas. Burlington Sand and Gravel, 1964-70; owner Cloyd A. Porter Trucking, Burlington, 1970-72; state rep. 43d dist. Wis. State Assembly, Madison, 1972-82, state rep. 66th dist., 1982-2001; ret., 2001. Mem. coun. on recycling, Wis., 1991-94, fire svc. legis. adv. com., 1987-94, legis. coun. com. on fire inspections and fire dues, 1991, legis. coun. spl. com. on emergency med. svcs., 1992-93, joint com. fins., 1995—, Am. Legislature Exch. Coun. Task Force on Fiscal Policy, 1995—, Nat. Coun. State Legislators com. sci., energy and environ. resources, v. chmn. joint fin. com., 1999-2000, budget conf. com., 1999-2000, nat. conf. state legis., 1999-2000, assembly on issues sci., energy, environ. resources com., 1999-2000, am. legis. exchange coun., 1999-2000, task force on tax and fiscal policy, 1999-2000, assembly com. on rules, 1999-2000. Contbr. articles to profl. jours. Chmn. Town of Burlington, 1971-75; state and met. affairs chmn. Jaycees, Wis., 1963, state v.p., 1969, adminstrv. asst., 1970, exec. v.p., 1971; mem. Wis. Conservation Congress for Natural Resources Leadership and Support in the State Assembly, 1994; hon. chair Walkathon for Healthier Babies, March of Dimes, Burlington, 1998. Recipient many awards and honors including being named hon. mem. State Fire Chiefs Assn., Wis., 1992, Guardian of Small Bus., NFIB, Wis., 1991, Friend of Agr., Farm Bur. of Wis., 1992, 94, Friend of Edn. Fair Aid Coalition, 1995, Cert. of Appreciation, Wis. Counties Assn., 1993, award Wis. State Fire Chiefs Assn., 1995, Inn Appreciation award Wis. Bed and Breakfast Assn., 1998, Bethel Baptist Ch. award Burlington, 1998, Svc. award Town of Salem, 1998, Mem. Appreciation award Tavern League of Wis., 1999; named Outstanding Legislator Wis. Counties Assn., 1996, 97-98; named to Vietnam Vets. Am. Legis. All-Star Team Wis. Coun. Vietnam Vets. Am., 1995-97. Mem. Wis. Alliance for Fire Safety. Republican. Roman Catholic. Home: 28322 Durand Ave Burlington WI 53105-9408

PORTER, DAVID LINDSEY, history and political science educator, author; b. Holyoke, Mass., Feb. 18, 1941; s. Willis Hubert and Lora Frances (Bowen) P.; m. Marilyn Esther Platt, Nov. 28, 1970; children: Kevin, Andrea. BA magna cum laude, Franklin Coll., 1963; MA, Ohio U., 1965; PhD, Pa. State U., 1970. Asst. prof. history Rensselaer Poly. Inst., Troy, N.Y., 1970-75, co-dir. Am. studies program, 1972-74; ednl. adminstrv. asst. Civil Svc. Office State of N.Y., 1975-76; asst. prof. history William Penn U., Oskaloosa, Iowa, 1976-77, assoc. prof. history, 1977-82, prof. history and polit. sci., 1982-86, Louis Tuttle Shangle prof. history and polit. sci., 1986—, chmn. Sperry & Hutchinson Found. lectureship series, 1980-82, acting chair social and behavioral scis. divsn., 2000—01. Supr. legis. internship program Iowa Gen. Assembly, 1978—, records inventory project Mahaska County, 1978-79, internship program Washington Ctr., 1985—; active Franklin D. Roosevelt Meml. Commn.; chpt. adviser Phi Alpha Theta, 1977—. Author: The Seventy-sixth Congress and World War II, 1939-40, 1979, Congress and the Waning of the New Deal, 1980; co-author: The San Diego Padres Encyclopedia, 2002; contbr. to Dictionary of American Biography, 1981, 88, 94, 95, Directory of Teaching Innovations in History, 1981, The Book of Lists #3, 1983, Biographical Dictionary of Internationalists, 1983, The Hero in Transition, 1983, Herbert Hoover and the Republican Era: A Reconsideration, 1984, The History of Mahaska County, Iowa, 1984, Franklin D. Roosevelt, His Life and Times: An Encyclopedic View, 1985, The Rating Game in American Politics: An Interdisciplinary Approach, 1987, Sport History, 1987, Book of Days, 1988, Sports Encyclopedia North America, 1988, The Harry S. Truman Encyclopedia, 1989, Encyclopedia of Major League Baseball Team Histories: The National League, 1991, Twentieth Century Sports Champions, 1992, Statesmen Who Changed the World, 1993, Ency. Modern Social Issues, 1996, Advanced Placement U.S. History 2, 1996, Encyclopedia of United States Popular Culture, 1997, Encyclopedia of Civil Rights, 1997, Encyclopedia of Propaganda, 1997, Total Padres, 1997, The Scribner Encyclopedia of American Lives, 1998, 99, 2001, 02, American National Biography, 1999, The Sixties in America, 1999, Racial and Ethnic Relations in America, 1999, History of Mahaska County, Iowa, 2000, Great Athletes, rev. edit., 2001, The Scribner Encyclopedia of American Lives, Sports Figures, 2002, Great Events: 1900-2001, rev. edit., 2002; editor, contbr.: Biographical Dictionary of American Sports: vols. Baseball, 1987, Football, 1987, Outdoor Sports, 1988, Basketball and Other Indoor Sports, 1989, 1989-92 Supplement for Baseball, Football, Basketball and Other Sports, 1992, 1992-95, Supplement for Baseball, Football, Basketball and Other Sports, 1995, African-American Sports Greats, 1995, Baseball, revised and expanded edit., 3 vols., 2000; compiler, A Cumulative Index to the Biographical Dictionary of American Sports, 1993; assoc. editor: (with others) American National Biography, 24 vols., 1999; contbr. weekly column to Oskaloosa Herald, 1994—, numerous articles to various dictionaries, directories, encys., jours., revs., newspapers, commentary to Nat. Pub. Radio. Mem. Franklin D. Roosevelt Meml. Commn.; participant Green Bay Packers Project, 1992; historian United Meth. Ch. Grantee NSF, 1967, NEH, 1974, Rensselaer Poly. Inst., 1974, Eleanor Roosevelt Inst., 1981, William Penn Univ., 1986, 89, 92; recipient Choice Outstanding Acad. Book awards, 1989. Mem. AAUP, Am. Hist. Assn., Orgn. Am. Historians, N.Am. Soc. for Sport History, Soc. History Am. Fgn. Rels., Ctr. for Study of the Presidency, Soc. Am. Baseball Rsch., Friends of the Nat. Baseball Hall of Fame, Popular Culture Assn., Profl. Football Rschrs. Assn., Coll. Football Rschrs. Assn., Coll. Football Hist. Soc., State Hist. Soc. Iowa, Mahaska County Hist. Soc. (v.p.), Iowa State UN Assn. (chmn. ann. assembly 1982, nat. soc. Disting. Svc. award 1981), Mahaska County UN Assn. (v.p.), Oskaloosa Babe Ruth League (bd. dirs.), Oskaloosa Cmty. Choir, Friends of Oskaloosa Pub. Libr. (mem. nominating com.), Friends of the Nat. Baseball Hall of Fame, Phi Alpha Theta, Kappa Delta Pi. Home: 2314 Ridgeway Ave Oskaloosa IA 52577-9109 Office: William Penn Univ Dept Social and Behavioral Scis Divsn Oskaloosa IA 52577-1757

PORTER, GREGORY W. state legislator; m. Yvette Brewster. BA, Earlham Coll. Property mgr. Cmty. Action of Greater Indpls.; mem. from 96th dist. Ind. State Ho. of Reps., 1992—. Mem. cts. and criminal code com., edn. com., pub. safety com., vice chmn. urban affairs com. Bd. dirs., pres. Near Eastside Fed. Credit Union, Friends of Urban League; bd. dirs. Indpls. Urban League; mem. Ch. Fedn. Greater Indpls.; mem. United N.W. Area Devel. Corp.; bd. dirs. Martin Ctr. Home: 3614 N Pennsylvania St Indianapolis IN 46205-3436 Office: Ind Ho of Reps State Capitol Indianapolis IN 46204

PORTER, JAMES MORRIS, retired judge; b. Cleve., Sept. 14, 1931; s. Emmett Thomas and Mary (Connell) P.; m. Helen Marie Adams, May 31, 1952; children: James E., Thomas W., William M., Daniel J. A.B., John Carroll U., 1953; J.D., U. Mich., 1957. Bar: Ohio 1957. Assoc. firm M.B. & H.H. Johnson, Cleve., 1957-62, McAfee, Hanning, Newcomer, Hazlett & Wheeler, Cleve., 1962-67; ptnr. firm Squire, Sanders & Dempsey, 1967-92; judge Ohio Ct. Appeals, 8th Dist., 1993-2000, Cuyahoga County Common Pleas Ct., Cleve., 2001. 1st lt. U.S. Army, 1953-55. Fellow Am. Coll. Trial Lawyers; mem. The Country Club (Cleve.). Republican. Roman Catholic.

PORTER, JOHN EDWARD, former congressman; b. Evanston, Ill., June 1, 1935; s. Harry H. and Beatrice V. P.; m. Kathryn Cameron; 5 children. Attended, MIT; BSBA, Northwestern U., 1958; JD with distinction, U. Mich., 1961; DHL, Barat Coll., 1988; LLD (hon.), Kendall Coll., 1992. Bar: Ill. 1961, U.S. Supreme Ct. 1968. Former honor law grad. atty., appellate div. Dept. Justice, Washington; mem. Ill. Ho. of Reps., 1973-79, 96-106th Congresses from 10th Ill. Dist., Ill., 1980-2001; mem. legis. select com. on aging, 1980-92; ptnr. Hogan & Hartson, Washington, 2001—. Founder, co-chmn. Congl. Human Rights Caucus; founder Congl. Coalition on Population and Devel. Past editor: Mich. Law Rev. Bd. dirs. PBS Recipient Best Legislator award League of Conservation Voters, 1973, Ind. Voters Ill., 1974, Chgo. Crime Commn., 1976, Lorax award Global Tomorrow Coalition, 1989, Spirit of Enterprise award U.S. C. of C., 1988, 89, 90, Golden Bulldog award Watchdogs of the Treasury, 12 times, Taxpayer's Friend award Nat. Taxpayers Union, Taxpayer Superhero award Grace Commn.'s Citizens Against Government Waste. Republican. Office: Hogan & Hartson 555 13th St NW Washington DC 20004*

PORTER, JOHN WILSON, education executive; b. Ft. Wayne, Ind., Aug. 13, 1931; BA, Albion Coll., 1953; MA, Mich. State U., 1957, PhD, 1962; D in Pub. Adminstrn. (hon.), Albion Coll., 1973; LLD (hon.), Mich. State U., 1977, Cleary Coll., 1987; LHD, Adrian Coll., 1970, U. Detroit, 1979; LLD, Western Mich. U., 1971, Eastern Mich. U., 1975; HHD, Kalamazoo Coll., 1973, Detroit Coll. Bus., 1975, Madonna Coll., Livonia, Mich., 1977; DEd, Detroit Inst. Tech., 1978; AA, Schoolcraft Coll., Livonia, Mich., 1979; DBA, Lawrence Inst. Tech., 1988; LLD, Cleary Coll., 1989. Counselor Lansing (Mich.) Pub. Schs., 1953-58; cons. Mich. Dept. Pub. Instrn., 1958-61; dir. Mich. Higher Edn. Assistance Authority, 1961-65; assoc. supt. for higher edn. Mich. Dept. Edn., 1966-69, state supt. schs., 1969-79; pres. Ea. Mich. U., Ypsilanti, 1979-89; v.p. Nat. Bd. for Profl. Teaching Standards, 1989; gen. supt. Detroit Pub. Schs., 1989-91; CEO Urban Edn. Alliance, Inc., Ypsilanti, Mich., 1991—. Mem. numerous profl. commns. and bds., 1959— , including Commn. on Financing Postsecondary Edn., 1972-74, Commn. for Reform Secondary Edn., Kettering Found., 1972-75, Edn. Commn. of States, 1973-79, Nat. Commn. on Performance-Based Edn., 1974-76, Nat. Commn. on Manpower Policy, 1974-79, Mich. Employment and Tng. Svcs. Coun., 1976-79, Nat. Adv. Coun. on Social Security, 1977-79, Commn. on Ednl. Credit, Am. Coun. on Edn., 1977-80; task panel on mental health of family Commn. on Mental Health, 1977-80; mem. Nat. Coun. for Career Edn. (HEW), 1974-76; pres. bd. dirs. Chief State Sch. Officers, 1974-79; pres. Coun. Chief State Sch. Officers, 1977-78; bd. dirs. Comerica Bank; former chmn. bd. Coll. Entrance Exam. Bd., 1984-86. Trustee Nat. Urban League, 1973-79, Charles Stewart Mott Found., 1981—, Albion Coll., 1989—; bd. dirs. Mich. Internat. Council, 1977—, Mich. Congress Parents and Tchrs.; mem. bd. overseers com. for Grad. Sch., Harvard U., 1980-88; mem. edn. com. NAACP; convener goal 6 Nat. Edn. Goals Panel, 1990—; mem. East Lansing Human Relations Commn.; chmn. Am. Assn. State Colls. and U.'s Task Force on Excellence in Edn.; mem. Mich. Martin Luther King, Jr. Holiday Commn., Gov.'s Blue Ribbon Commn. on Welfare Reform; trustee East Lansing Edgewood United Ch.; mem. Catherine McAuley Health Systems Bd., 1990—. Recipient numerous awards including Disting. Svc. award Mich. Congress Parents and Tchrs., 1963, Disting. Svc. award NAACP, Lansing, 1968; cert. of outstanding achievement Delta Kappa chpt. Phi Beta Sigma, 1970; award for disting. svc. Assn. Ind. Colls. and Univs. Mich., 1974; Disting. Alumni award Coll. Edn., Mich. State U., 1974; award for disting. svc. to edn Mich. State U., 1974; Disting. Alumni award, 1979; award for disting. svc. to edn. in Mich. Mich. Assn. Secondary Sch. Prins., 1974; President's award as disting. educator Nat. Alliance Black Sch. Educators, 1977; Marcus Foster Disting. Educator award, 1979; recognition award Mich. Ednl. Rsch. Assn., 1978; recognition award Mich. Assn. Secondary Sch. Prins., 1978; recognition award Mich. Assn. Intermediate Sch. Adminstrs., 1979; recognition award Mich. Assn. Sch. Adminstrs., 1979; Mich. Sch. Bus. Ofcls., 1979; resolution Mich. State Legislature, 1978; Anthony Wayne award Coll. Edn., Wayne State U., 1979; Educator of Decade award Mich. Assn. State and Fed. Program Specialists, 1979; Spirit of Detroit award Detroit City Coun., 1981; Disting. Svc. award Ypsilanti Area C. of C., 1988; Philip A. Hart award Mich. Women's Hall of Fame, 1988; Summit award Greater Detroit C. of C., 1991; Mich. State C. of C. award 1991; inducted Mich. Edn. Hall of Fame, 1992; John W. Porter Disting. Chair endowed at Eastern Mich. U., 1999; Coll. of Edn. bldg. at Eastern Mich. U. named for him, 1999; recipient Olivet Coll. award for Leadership and Social Responsibility, 2001. Mem. Am. Assn. Sch. Adminstrs., Am. Assn. State Colls. and Univs. (president's council, chmn. task force on excellence in edn.), Nat. Measurement Council, NAACP (life), Greater Detroit C. of C. (Summit award 1991), Mich. State C. of C. (Disting. Svc. and Leadership award 1991), Tuskegee Airmen (Disting. Svc. award 1991), Mich. PTA (hon. life), Ea. Mich. U. Alumni Assn. (Disting. Svc. award 1997), Econ. Club (dir. 1979), Sigma Pi Phi, Phi Delta Kappa. Office: Urban Edn Alliance Inc 1547 Fall Creek Ln Ann Arbor MI 48108-9579

PORTER, PHILIP WAYLAND, geography educator; b. Hanover, N.H., July 9, 1928; s. Wayland Robinson and Bertha Maria (LaPlante) P.; m. Patricia Elizabeth Garrigus, Sept. 5, 1950; children: Janet Elizabeth, Sara Louise, Alice Catherine. A.B., Middlebury Coll., 1950; M.A., Syracuse U., 1955; Ph.D., U. London, 1957. Instr. geography U. Minn., Mpls., 1957-58, asst. prof., 1958-64, assoc. prof., 1964-66, prof., 1966-2000, prof. emeritus, 2000—; assoc. to v.p. acad. affairs, also dir. Office Internat. Programs, 1979-83. Geography panel Com. on Space Programs for Earth Observations Nat. Acad. Scis., 1967-71; liaison officer Midwest Univs. Consortium for Internat. Activities, 1979-83 Author: (with Eric S. Sheppard) A World of Difference: Society, Nature, Development, 1998; contbr. articles to profl. jours. With AUS, 1952-54. Grantee Ctrl. Rsch. Fund, 1955-56, NSF, 1961-62, 78-80, 92-93, Social Sci. Rsch. Coun., 1966-67, Rockfeller Found., 1969, 71-73, Gen. Svc. Found., 1981-83, Exxon Edn. Found., 1983-84, Fulbright, 1992-93; Bush Sabbatical fellow, 1985-86. Mem. Assn. Am. Geographers. Home: 10 Burkehaven Terr Sunapee NH 03782-2402 Office: U Minn Dept Geography Minneapolis MN 55455 E-mail: pwporter@tds.net., porter@atlas.socsci.umn.edu.

PORTER, ROBERT HUGH, economics educator; b. London, Can., Jan. 25, 1955; came to U.S., 1976; s. Hugh Donald and Olive Marie (Anderson) P.; m. Therese Jane McGuire, June 20, 1981. BA with honors, U. Western Ont., London, 1976; PhD, Princeton U., 1981. Asst. prof. econs. U. Minn., Mpls., 1980-84; post doctoral fellow Bell Labs., Murray Hill, N.J., 1982-83; assoc. prof. SUNY, Stony Brook, 1984-87; mem. tech. staff Bell Communications Rsch., Morristown, N.J., 1986-88; prof. Northwestern U., Evanston, Ill., 1987—. Mem. bd. editors Am. Econ. Rev., 1987-88, 94-96; assoc. editor Internat. Jour. Indsl. Orgn., 1989-95; co-editor Econometrica, 1988-93, Rand Jour. Econs., 1995—; contbr. articles to profl. jours. NSF grantee, 1985, 88, 93, 97. Fellow Econometric Soc.; mem. Am. Econ. Assn., Can. Econs. Assn., Am. Acad. Arts and Scis. Home: 904 Michigan Ave Apt 1 Evanston IL 60202-5421 Office: Northwestern U Dept Econs 2003 Sheridan Rd Evanston IL 60208-0826

PORTMAN, ROB, congressman; b. Cin., Dec. 19, 1955; m. Jane Portman; children: Jed, Will. BA, Dartmouth Coll., 1979; JD, U. Mich., 1984. Ptnr. Head & Ritchey, Cin., 1986-89; assoc. counsel to President of U.S., then dep. asst. to President, dir. Office Legis. Affairs White House, Washington, 1989-92; mem. U.S. Del. to UN Subcom. on Human Rights, 1992, U.S. Congress from 2nd Ohio dist., 1993—; mem. ways and means com., budget com., ethics com.; chmn. Rep. leadership. Bd. trustees Springer Sch., The United Way, Hyde Park Community United Meth. Ch.; founding trustee Cin.-China Sister City Com.; former bd. dirs. United Home Care; vice chmn. Hamilton County George Bush for Pres. Campaign, 1988, 92; chmn. Rep. Early Bird Campaign com., 1992; del. Rep. Nat. Conv., 1988, 92; active Hamilton County Rep. Party Exec. com., Hamilton County Rep. Party Fin. Com. Mem. Cin. World Trade Assn. Office: US Ho of Reps 238 Cannon Hob Washington DC 20515-3502

PORTOGHESE, PHILIP SALVATORE, medicinal chemist, educator; b. N.Y.C., June 4, 1931; s. Philip A. and Constance (Antonelli) P.; m. Christine L. Phillips, June 11, 1960; children— Stephen, Stuart, Philip. B.S., Columbia U., 1953, M.S., 1958; Ph.D., U. Wis., 1961; Dr. honoris causa, U. Catania, Italy, 1986, Royal Danish Sch. Pharmacy, Copenhagen, 1992. Asst. prof. Coll. Pharmacy, U. Minn., Mpls., 1961-64, assoc. prof., 1964-69, prof. medicinal chemistry, 1969—, prof. pharmacology, 1987—, dir. grad. study in medicinal chemistry, 1974-86, head dept., 1974-83;

disting. prof. medicinal chemistry —, 2000. Cons. NIMH., 1971-72; mem. med. chemistry B sect. NIH, 1972-76; mem. pharmacology, substance abuse and environ. toxicology interdisciplinary cluster President's Biomed. Research Panel, 1975; mem. expert panel of Flavor and Extract Mfrs. Assn. of U.S., 1984—. Mem. editorial adv. bd. Jour. Med. Chemistry, 1969-71; editor-in-chief, 1972— ; mem. editorial adv. bd. Med. Chem. series, 1972-77. U.S. Army, 1954—56. Named Highly Cited Rschr., Inst. for Sci. Info., 2001; recipient Ernest H. Volwiler award (oustanding contbns. to pharm. scis., Am. Assn. Colls. Pharmacy, 1984, N.B. Eddy Meml. award, Coll. on Problems of Drug Dependency-NAS NRC, 1991, Merit award, NIH, 1997, Oak and the Tulip award, European Fedn. Medicinal Chemistry, 1999. Fellow AAAS, Acad. Pharm. Scis., Am. Assn. Pharm. Scientists (Rsch. Achievement award 1990); mem. Am. Chem. Soc. (Medicinal Chemistry award 1990, E.E. Smissman-Bristol-Meyers-Squibb award 1991, Alfred Burger award in medicinal chemistry 2000), Am. Soc. Pharm. Exptl. Therapeutics, Internat. Union Pure and Applied Chemistry (commn. on medicinal chemistry 1978-82, internat. com. med. chemistry 1982-85), Soc. Neurosci., Sigma Xi, Rho Chi (lecture award 1999), Phi Lambda Upsilon. Home: 17 Oriole Ln Saint Paul MN 55127-6334 Office: U Minn Coll of Pharmacy 308 Harvard St SE Minneapolis MN 55455-0353

POSCOVER, MAURY B. lawyer; b. St. Louis, Jan. 13, 1944; s. Edward and Ann (Chapnick) P.; m. Lorraine Wexler, Aug. 14, 1966; children: Michael, Daniel, Joanna. BA, Lehigh U., 1966; JD, Washington U., 1969. Bar: Mo. 1969. Assoc. Husch & Eppenberger LLC, St. Louis, 1969-75, ptnr., mem., 1975—. Lectr. Washington U., St. Louis, 1972—79. Editor-in-chief: The Business Lawyer, 1995-96; contbr. articles to profl. jours. Bd. dirs. Childhaven, St. Louis, 1978-92, pres. 1986; pres. Jewish Community Rels. Coun., 1990-92. Mem.: Am.-Israel C. of C. (pres. 1999—), Wash. U. Alumni Law Assn. 1980—81, Am. Judicature Soc. (dir. 1981—87), Mo. Bar Assn. (bd. govs. 1979—81), Bar Assn. Met. St. Louis (pres. 1983—84), ABA (bd. govs. 1999—, chmn. comml. fin. svcs. com. bus. law sect. coun., chair bus. law sect. 1997—98, editor-in-chief jour., mem. exec. com. bd. govs. 2001—, chair ops. and comms. com. 2001—), Mo. Athletic Club. Jewish. Office: Husch & Eppenberger LLC 190 Carondelet Plz Ste 600 Saint Louis MO 63105-3441 E-mail: maury.poscover@husch.com.

POSHARD, GLENN W. former congressman; b. Herald, Ill., Oct. 31, 1945; BA, So. Ill. U., 1970, MS, 1974, PhD, 1984. Tchr. high sch.; asst. dir. then dir. Ill. State Regional Edn. Svc. Ctr.; mem. Ill. State Senate, 1984-88, 101st-105th Congresses from 22nd (now 19th) Ill. Dist., 1989-98; tchr., adminstr. John A. Logan Coll., Carterville, Ill.; vice chancellor for adminstrn. So. Ill. U., Carbondale, 1999—. Founder The Poshard Found. for Abused Children. With U.S. Army. Democrat. Office: So Ill U Mail Code 4314 Carbondale IL 62901

POSLER, GERRY LYNN, agronomist, educator; b. Cainsville, Mo., July 24, 1942; s. Glen L. and Helen R. Posler; m. O. Shirley Weeda, June 23, 1963; children: Mark L., Steven C., Brian D. BS, U. Mo., 1964, MS, 1966; PhD, Iowa State U., 1969. Asst. prof. Western (Macomb) Ill. U., 1969-74; assoc. prof. Kans. State U., Manhattan, 1974-80, prof., 1980—, asst. dept. head, 1982-90, dept. head, 1990-98. Contbr. articles to profl. jours. and popular pubs., abstracts, book reviews. Fellow Am. Soc. Agronomy, Crop Sci. Soc. Am.; mem. Am. Forage Grassland Coun., Crop Science Soc. Am. (C-3 div. chmn. 1991), Coun. Agrl. Science Tech. (Cornerstone club), Nat. Assn. Colls. Tchrs. Agr. (tchr. fellow award 1978, ensminger interstate dist. teaching award, 1987, north cen. region dir. 1989, v.p. 1990, pres. 1991; life mem.), Kans. Assn. Colls. Tchrs. Agr. (pres. 1983-85), Kans. Forage Grassland Coun. (bd. dirs. 1989-92), Gamma Sigma Delta (Outstanding Faculty award 1991, pres. 1987). Home: 3001 Montana Ct Manhattan KS 66502-2300 Office: Kans State U Dept Agronomy Throckmorton Plant Sci Ctr Manhattan KS 66506 E-mail: gposler@oznet.ksu.edu.

POSNER, KATHY ROBIN, communications executive; b. Oceanside, N.Y., Nov. 3, 1952; d. Melvyn and Davonne Hope (Hansen) P. BA in Journalism, Econs., Manhattanville Coll., 1974. Fin. planner John Dreyfus Corp., Purchase, N.Y., 1974-80; corp. liaison Gulf States Mortgage, Atlanta, 1980-82; dir. promotion Gammon's of Chgo., 1982-83; coordinator trade show mktg. Destron, Chgo., 1983-84; pres. Postronics, 1984-87; v.p. Martin E. Janis & Co., Inc., 1987-90; pres., CEO Comm 2 Inc., 1990—. Editor: How to Maximize Your Profits, 1983; contbg. editor Internat. Backgammon Guide, 1974-84, Backgammon Times, 1981-84, Chgo. Advt. and Media; columnist Food Industry News. Bd. dirs. Chgo. Beautification Com., 1987, Concerned Citizens for Action, Chgo., 1987; mem. steering com. Better Boys Found.; campaign mgr. Brown for Alderman, Chgo., 1987; mem. bd. cons. Little City Found. Mem. NATAS, NOW, Women in Comm., Am. Soc. Profl. and Exec. Women, Women in Film-Chgo. (bd. dirs.), Mensa, Acad. Arts (v.p.), Ill. Restaurant Assn. (mem. adv. bd.), Chgo. Area Pub. Affairs Group, Baderbrau Beer Drinking Soc. (v.p. pub. rels.), Gammon's Chgo. (bd. dirs. 1980-83, editor newsletter 1982-83), Little City Found. (bd. dirs.), City Club Chgo. (bd. dirs.), Cavendish North Club (bd. dirs. 1984-87), Chgo. Legal Clinic (bd. dirs.), Met. Club, Plaza Club, Monroe Club, 410 Club Republican. Jewish. Avocations: backgammon, politics, reading. Home: 777 N Michigan Ave Apt 3208 Chicago IL 60611-2609 Office: Comm2 Inc 921 W Van Buren St Ste 240 Chicago IL 60607-3542 E-mail: kathyposner@aol.com.

POSNER, KENNETH ROBERT, former hotel corporation executive; b. Chgo., Sept. 2, 1947; m. Arlene Lynn Robinson, June 21, 1970; children: Zachary, Brennan B.S. in Acctg., So. Ill. U., 1970. C.P.A., Ill. Acctg. mgr. Jewel Cos., Inc., Melrose Park, Ill., 1970-72; audit ptnr. Laventhol & Horwath, Chgo., 1972-81; v.p. fin. Hyatt Corp., 1981-99; bd. dirs. Ill. CPA Soc., 2000—. also: Lodigan Inc 3445 Peachtree N E, Ste 700 Atlanta GA 30326

POSNER, RICHARD ALLEN, federal judge; b. N.Y.C., Jan. 11, 1939; s. Max and Blanche Posner; m. Charlene Ruth Horn, Aug. 13, 1962; children: Kenneth A., Eric A. AB, Yale U., 1959, LLD (hon.) , 1996; LLB, Harvard U., 1962; LLD (hon.) , Syracuse U., 1986; LLD (hon.) , Duquesne U., 1987, Georgetown U., 1992, U. Pa., 1997; PhD (hon.) , U. Ghent, 1995. Bar: N.Y. 1963, U.S. Supreme Ct. 1966. Law clk. to Hon. William J. Brennan Jr. U.S. Supreme Ct., Washington, 1962—63; asst. to commr. FTC, 1963—65; asst. to solicitor gen. U.S. Dept. Justice, 1965—67; gen. counsel Pres.'s Task Force on Commn. Policy, 1967—68; assoc. prof. Stanford U. Law Sch., Calif., 1968—69; prof. U. Chgo. Law Sch., 1969—78, Lee and Brena Freeman prof., 1978—81, sr. lectr., 1981—; circuit judge U.S. Ct. Appeals (7th cir.), Chgo., 1981—, chief judge, 1993—2000. Rsch. assoc. Nat. Bur. Econ. Rsch., cambridge, Mass., 1971—81; pres. Lexecon Inc., Chgo., 1977—81. Author: Antitrust Law: An Economic Perspective, 1976, Economic Analysis of Law, 5th edit., 1998, The Economics of Justice, 1981; author: (with William M. Landes) The Economic Structure of Tort Law, 1987; author: The Problems of Jurisprudence, 1990, Cardozo: A Study in Reputation, 1990, Sex and Reason, 1990, Sex and Reason, 1992; author: (with Tomas J. Philipson) Private Choices and Public Health: The AIDS Epidemic in an Economic Perspective, 1993; author: Overcoming Law, 1995, Aging and Old Age, 1995, The Federal Courts: Challenge and Reform, 1996, Law and Legal Theory in England and America, 1996, The Federal Courts: Challenge and Reform, 1997, Law and Literature, revised and enlarged edit., 1998, The Problematics of Moral and Legal Theory, 1999, An Affair of State: An Investigation, Impeachment, and Trial of President Clinton, 1999, Frontiers of Legal Theory, 2001, Breaking the Deadlock: The 2000 Election, The Constitution, and the Courts, 2001, Antitrust Law, 2d edit., 2001, Public Intellectuals, 2001; pres. Harvard Law Rev., 1961—62, editor Jour. Legal Studies, 1972—81, Am. Law and Econs. Rev., 1999—; author (with William M. Landes): The Essential Holmes, 1992. Fellow: AAAS, Brit. Acad., Am. Law Inst. (pres. 1995—96); mem.: Am. Law and Econ. Assn., Am. Econ. Assn., Century Assn. Office: US Ct Appeals 7th Cir 219 S Dearborn St Chicago IL 60604-1702

POSTHUMUS, RICHARD EARL, state offical, farmer; b. Hastings, Mich., July 19, 1950; s. Earl Martin and Lola Marie (Wieland) P.; m. Pamela Ann Bartz, June 23, 1972; children: Krista, Lisa, Heather, Bryan. BS in Agrl. Econs. and Pub. Affairs Mgmt., Mich. State U., 1972. Exec. v.p. Farmers and Mfrs. Beet Sugar Assn., Saginaw, Mich., 1972-74, Mich. Beef Commn., Lansing, 1974-78; dir. constituent relations Republican Caucus, Mich. Ho. of Reps., 1979-82, majority leader, 1991—; self-employed farmer, 1974—. Third vice-chmn. Mich. Republican Com., 1971-73; mem. Hope Ch. of the Brethren. Mem. Alpha Gamma Rho. Office: Office of Lt Gov PO Box 30013 State Capitol Bldg Lansing MI 48909*

POSTON, WALKER SEWARD, II, medical educator, researcher; BA in Biol. Scis., U. Calif., Davis, 1983; PhD in Psychology, U. Calif., Santa Barbara, 1990. Clin. psychology resident USAF Med. Ctr., Wright-PAtterson AFB, Ohio, 1989-90; dir. psychology svcs., asst. chief mental health svcs. 9th Med. Group, Beale AFB, 1990-92; fellow in behavioral medicine Wilford Hall Med. Ctr., 1992-93; chief health and rehab. psychology svc. Malcolm Grow Med. Ctr., 1993-95, faculty, 1993-95; clin. asst. prof. dept. med. and clin. psychology F. Edward Herbert Sch. Medicine, Bethesda, Md., 1993-95; asst. prof. medicine Baylor Coll. Medicine, Houston, 1995-99; asst. prof. U. Mo., Kansas City, 1999—. Rsch. exch. scientist Karolinska Inst., Stockholm, Sweden, 1997, 98. Contbr. articles to profl. jours. Recipient Minority Scientist Devel. award Am. Heart Assn., 1995; U. Calif. Doctoral scholars fellow, 1984-85, 85-86, 86-87, 88-89, Clin. fellow Wilford Hall Med. Ctr., Lackland AFB, 1992-93; Nat. Merit scholar, 1979-80. Office: Univ Mo 5319 Holmes St Kansas City MO 64110-2437

POTRIAS, STEVE, radio personality; Radio host Sta. KFGO-AM, Fargo, ND. Office: KFGO 1020 25th St S Fargo ND 58103*

POTTER, CALVIN J. state legislator; b. Sheboygan, Wis., Nov. 3, 1945; married. Student, U. Wis., Sheboygan; BA, Lakeland Coll., 1968; postgrad., U. Wis. Past Wis. state assemblyman dist. 26; with dist. 9 Wis. State Senate, 1990-98, chmn. edn. com.; asst. supt. Dept. Pub. Instrn., Madison, Wis., 1998—. Former tchr. Mem. Sheboygan County Hist. Soc. Mem. NEA, Wis. Edn. Assn., Izaak Walton League. Address: 808 Greentree Rd Kohler WI 53044-1414 Office: Dept Pub Instrn PO Box 7841 Madison WI 53707-7841

POTTER, JOHN WILLIAM, federal judge; b. Toledo, Oct. 25, 1918; s. Charles and Mary Elizabeth (Baker) P.; m. Phyllis May Bihn, Apr. 14, 1944; children: John William, Carolyn Diane, Kathryn Susan. PhB cum laude, U. Toledo, 1940; JD, U. Mich., 1946. Bar: Ohio 1947. Assoc. Zachman, Boxell, Schroeder & Torbet, Toledo, 1946-51; ptnr. Boxell, Bebout, Torbet & Potter, 1951-69; mayor City of Toledo, 1961-67; asst. atty. gen. State of Ohio, 1968-69; judge 6th Dist. Ct. Appeals, 1969-82, U.S. Dist. Ct., Toledo, 1982—, sr. judge, 1992—. Presenter in field. Sr. editor U. Mich. Law Rev., 1946. Pres. Ohio Mcpl. League, 1965; past assoc. pub. mem. Toledo Labor Mgmt. Commn.; past pres., bd. dirs. Commn. on Rels. with Toledo (Spain); past bd. dirs. Cummings Sch. Toledo Opera Assn., Conlon Ctr.; past trustee Epworth United Meth. Ch.; hon. chmn. Toledo Festival Arts, 1980. Capt. F.A., U.S. Army, 1942-46. Decorated Bronze Star; recipient Leadership award Toledo Bldg. Congress, 1965, Merit award Toledo Bd. Realtors, 1967, Resolution of Recognition award Ohio Ho. of Reps., 1982, Outstanding Alumnus award U. Toledo, 1966, conf. rm. named in his honor, U.S. Courthouse, Toledo, 1998; named to Field Arty. Officer Candidate Sch. Hall of Fame, 1999. Fellow Am. Bar Found., Am. Judicature Soc., 6th Jud. Cir. Dist. Judges Assn., Fed. Judges Assn.; mem. ABA, Ohio Bar Assn. (Found. Outstanding Rsch. award 1995), Toledo Bar Assn. (exec. com. 1962-64, award 1992), Lucas County Bar Assn., U. Toledo Alumni Assn. (past pres.), Toledo Zool. Soc. (past bd. dirs.), Old Newsboys Club, Toledo Club, Kiwanis (past pres.), Phi Kappa Phi. Home: 2418 Middlesex Dr Toledo OH 43606-3114 Office: US Dist Ct 307 US Courthouse 1716 Spielbusch Ave Toledo OH 43624-1363

POTTER, KEVIN, lawyer; Former dist. atty., Wood County, Wis.; former chmn. Wis. Tax Appeals Commn., Wis. Labor and Indsl. Review Commn.; U.S. Atty. We. Dist. Wis., Madison, 1991-93; mem. Brennan Steil Basting and MacDougall S.C., 1993—. Office: Brennan Steil Basting and MacDougall PO Box 990 22 E Mifflin St Ste 400 Madison WI 53701-0990

POTTER, MICHAEL J. retail stores executive; CFO, sr. v.p. Consolidated Stores Corp., Columbus, Ohio, pres., CEO OH. Office: Consolidated Stores Corp 300 Phillipi Rd Columbus OH 43228-5311

POTTER, ROSEMARY, state legislator; b. Apr. 15, 1952; m. Steve Nichols, 1994. BA, U. Wis., Milw., 1974, MA, 1983. Former dist. dir. Combined Health Appeal Wis. Ho. of Reps.; chairwoman Dem. Caucus; Wis. state assemblywoman Dist. 20, 1989-98; pub. polit. advocate Foley & Lardner, Milw., 1998—. Former tchr. Office: Doley & Lardner 1st Star Center 777 E Wisconsin Ave Ste 3800 Milwaukee WI 53202-5367 Home: W314n8709 Winchester Trl Hartland WI 53029-9525

POTTORFF, JO ANN, state legislator; b. Wichita, Kans., Mar. 7, 1936; d. John Edward McCluggage and Helen Elizabeth (Alexander) Ryan; m. Gary Nial Pottorff; children: Michael Lee, Gregory Nial. BA, Kansas State U., 1957; MA, St. Louis U., 1969. Elem. tchr. Pub. Sch., Keats and St. George, 1957-59; cons., elem. specialist Mid Continent Regional Edn. Lab., Kansas City, Mo., 1971-73; cons. Poindexter Assocs., Wichita, 1975; campaign mgr. Garner Shriver Congl. Camp, 1976; interim dir. Wichita Area Rape Ctr., 1977; conf. coord. Biomedical Synergistics Inst., Wichita, 1977-79; real estate sales asst. Chester Kappelman Group, 1979-98, J.P. Weigard & Sons, Wichita, 1998—; state rep. State of Kans., Topeka, 1985—. Mem. exec. com. Nat. Conf. State Legis. Com. Mem. sch. bd. Wichita Pub. Schs., 1977-85; bd. dirs. Edn. Consol. and Improvement Act Adv. com., Kans. Found. for the Handicapped; mem. Children and Youth Adv. com. (bd. dirs.); active Leadership Kans.; chairperson women's network Nat. Conf., State Legislators; mem. Wichita Children's Home Bd.; bd. dirs. Nat. Assessment Governing Bd.; chair edn. com. assembly on state issues Nat. Conf. State legislators. Recipient Disting. Svc. award Kans. Assn. Sch. Bds., 1983, Outstanding Svc. to Sch. Children of Nation award Coun. Urban Bds., 1984, awards Gov.'s Conf. for Prevention of Child Abuse and Neglect, Kans. Assn. Reading. Mem. Leadership Am. Alumnae (bd. dirs., sec) Found. for Agr. in Classroom (bd. dirs.), Jr. League, Vet. Aux. (pres.), Bd. Nat. State Art Agys., Rotary, Ky. Assn. Rehab. Facilities (Ann. award), Nat. Order Women in Legislature (past bd. dirs.), Nat. Conf. State Legislatures (chmn. edn. assembly state issues, exec. com.), Rotary, Chi Omega (pres.). Avocations: politics, traveling. Office: Weigard 6530 E 13th St N Wichita KS 67206-1247

POTTS, ANTHONY VINCENT, optometrist, orthokeratologist; b. Detroit, Aug. 10, 1945; m. Susan Claire, July 1, 1967; 1 child, Anthony Christian. Student, Henry Ford Community Coll., 1964-65, Eastern Mich. U., 1965-66; OD, So. Coll. Optometry, 1970; MS in Health Svcs. Mgmt., LaSalle U., 1995. Practice orthokeratology and contact lenses, Troy, Mich., 1975—. Adj. prof. optometry Ill. Coll. Optometry; lectr., author orthokeratology, contact lenses and astigmatism. Lt. comdr. USNR, MSC USNR, 1992—. Fellow Internat. Orthokeratology Soc. (membership chmn. 1976-83, bd. dirs. local chpt. 1976-83, chmn. Internat. Eye Rsch. Found. sect. 1981-83, bd. dirs. nat. chpt. 1985—, adminstrv. dir. nat. chpt. 1985—, chmn. nat. chpt. 1987—), Am. Acad. Optometry, Am. Optometric Assn.; mem. Am. Assn. Healthcare Execs., Armed Forces Optometric Soc., Nat. Eye Rsch. Found., Naval Order Am., Assn. of Mil. Surgeons of U.S., Naval Hosp. Am. Care Ctr., Am. Coll. Healthcare Execs. Roman Catholic. Office: Med Sq Troy 1575 W Big Beaver Rd Ste 11C Troy MI 48084-3525

POTUZNIK, CHARLES LADDY, lawyer; b. Chgo., Feb. 11, 1947; s. Charles William and Laverne Frances (Zdenek) P.; m. Mary Margaret Quady, Jan. 2, 1988; children: Kylie Brommell, Kathryn Mary. BA with high honors, U. Ill., 1969; JD cum laude, Harvard U., 1973. Bar: Minn. 1973. Assoc. Dorsey & Whitney LLP, Mpls., 1973-78, ptnr., 1979—. Co-head Broker-Dealer and Investment Markets Regulation Practice Group. Mem. Minn. State Bar Assn. (chmn. state securities law subcom. 1987-2000), Hennepin County Bar Assn., Minn. Securities Adv. Com., Phi Beta Kappa. Mem. Evang. Free Ch. Avocations: hunting, fishing, camping, canoeing, foreign travel. Office: Dorsey & Whitney LLP 50 South Sixth St Minneapolis MN 55402-1498 E-mail: potuznik.charles@dorseylaw.com.

POUCHE, FREDRICK, state legislator; b. Independence, Mo., Aug. 3, 1945; m. Martha M. Pouche; children: Sean R., Ash Thomas. BA in Bus. Adminstrn. summa cum laude, Park Coll., Parkville, Mo., 1980; MA in Bus. Adminstrn. and Mgmt. magna cum laude, Webster U., 1982. Prin. Pouche Corp.; adminstr. labor rels., sr. fin. analyst Trans World Airlines, 1965-84; fee agt. Mo. Dept. Revenue, 1985-89; auditor Platte County, 1989-91; state rep. 30th dist. Mo. Ho. of Reps., 1995-97. Candidate Mo. Ho. of Reps., 1982, 86, 88, 94; committeeman Platte County Rep. Com., 1983-84; staff rep. Ashcroft for Gov. Com., 1984; fin. chmn. Platte Rep. Com., 1984-85; dist. chmn. Dole for Pres. Com., 1987-88; Mo. del. Rep. Nat. Conv., 1988; Platte County coord. Roy Blunt for Gov. Com., 1994 Decorated Army Commendation medal with oak leaf cluster (2), others. Mem. KC (# 3430), Northland C. of C., South Platte Rotary Club (Paul Harris fellow), Platte Rep. Assn. Roman Catholic. Office: Mo Ho of Reps Rm 116-5 State Capitol Jefferson City MO 65101

POUR-EL, MARIAN BOYKAN, mathematician, educator; b. N.Y.C. d. Joseph and Mattie (Caspe) Boykan; m. Akiva Pour-El; 1 dau., Ina. A.B., Hunter Coll.; A.M., Harvard U., 1951, Ph.D., 1958. Assoc. prof. Pa. State U., 1962-64; mem. faculty U. Minn., Mpls., 1964—, prof. math., 1968—, U. of Minn. Mem. Inst. Advanced Study, Princeton, N.J., 1962-64; mem. coun. Conf. Bd. Math. Scis., 1977-82, trustee, 1978-81, mem. nominating com., 1980-82, chmn., 1981-82; lectr. internat. congresses in logic and computer sci., Eng., 1971, Hungary, 1967, Czechoslovakia, 1973,1998 Germany, 1983, 96, 97, Japan, 1985, 88, China, 1987; lectr. Polish Acad. Sci., 1974; lecture series throughout Fed. Republic of Germany, 1980, 1983 87, 89, 91,1996 Japan, 1985, 87, 90, 93, China, 1987, Sweden, 1983, 94, Finland, 1991, Estonia, 1991, Moscow, 1992, Amsterdam, 1992; mem. Fulbright Com. on Maths., 1986-89; invited spkr. Internat. Congress on Computability and Complexity Theory, Kazan U., Russia, 1997, Workshop on Computability and Complexity in Analysis, held in conjunction with 23rd Internat. Symposium on Math. Founds. of Computer Sci. and Computer Sci. Logic, Brno, Czech Republic, 1998, IEEE Workshop on Real Number Computation, 1998 Author: (with I. Richards) Computability in Analysis and Physics, 1989; author numerous articles on mathematical logic (theoretical computer sci.) and applications to mathematical and physical theory. Named to Hunter Coll. Hall of Fame, 1975; NAS grantee, 1966. Fellow AAAS, Japan Soc. for Promotion of Sci.; mem. Am. Math. Soc. (coun. 1980-88, numerous coms., spkr., orgn. spl. sessions on math. logic), Assn. Symbolic Logic, Math. Assn. Am. (nat. panel vis. lectrs.), Phi Beta Kappa, Sigma Xi, Pi Mu Epsilon, Sigma Pi Sigma. Achievements include research in mathematical logic (theoretical computer science) and in computability and noncomputability in physical theory—wave, heat, potential equations, eigenvalues, eigenvectors. Office: U Minn Sch Math Vincent Hall Minneapolis MN 55455-0488 E-mail: pourel@math.umn.edu.

POVINELLI, LOUIS A. aeronautical engineer; b. N.Y.C., June 10, 1931; With Bell Aircraft Corp., 1951-56; chief scientist turbomachinery and propulsion sys. NASA Glenn Rsch. Ctr., Cleve., 1960—. Program dir. Inst. for Computational Mechanics in Propulsion, 1987—. Contbr. over 110 articles to profl. jours. Recipient Aircraft Engine Tech. award IGTI, 1999. Fellow AIAA (Air Breathing Propulsion award 1997), ASME. Office: NASA Lewis Rsch Ctr Cleveland OH 44135-3191

POVISH, KENNETH JOSEPH, retired bishop; b. Alpena, Mich., Apr. 19, 1924; s. Joseph Francis and Elizabeth (Jachcik) P. A.B., Sacred Heart Sem., Detroit, 1946; M.A., Cath. U. Am., 1950; postgrad., No. Mich. U., 1961, 63. Ordained priest Roman Catholic Ch., 1950; asst. pastorships, 1950-56; pastor in Port Sanilac Mich., 1956-57, Munger, 1957-60, Bay City, 1966-70; dean St. Paul Sem., Saginaw, 1960-66, vice rector, 1962-66; bishop of Crookston Minn., 1970-75; bishop of Lansing Mich., 1975-95. Bd. consulators Diocese of Saginaw, 1966-70; instr. Latin and U.S. history St. Paul Sem., 1960-66 Weekly columnist Saginaw and Lansing diocesan newspapers. Bd. dirs. Cath. Charities Diocese Saginaw, 1969-70. Mem. Mich. Hist. Soc., Bay County Hist. Soc., Lions Club, KC (pres. Mich. Cath. Conf. 1985-95), Kiwanis.

POWELL, ANTHONY J. state legislator, lawyer; m. Betty Powell. Atty., Wichita, Kans.; mem. from dist. 85 Kans. State Ho. of Reps., Topeka. Home: 7313 Winterberry St Wichita KS 67226-2232 Office: Kans Ho of Reps State House Topeka KS 66612

POWELL, BARRY BRUCE, classicist, educator; b. Sacramento, Apr. 30, 1942; s. Barrett Robert and Anita Louise (Burns) P.; m. Patricia Ann Cox; children: Elena Melissa, Adam Vincent. BA in Classics, U. Calif., Berkeley, 1963, PhD, 1971; MA, Harvard U., 1965. Asst. prof. Northern Ariz. U., Flagstaff, 1970-73; from asst. prof. to prof. U. Wis., Madison, 1973—, chmn. dept. classics, 1985-92, chmn. program integrated liberal studies. Author: Composition by Theme in the Odyssey, 1973, Homer and the Origin of the Greek Alphabet, 1991, Classical Myth, 1995, 2d edit., 1997, 3d edit., 2000, New Companion to Homer, 1997, A Short Introduction to Classical Myth, 2001, Writing and the Origin of Greek Literature, 2002; writer screenplays; contbr. articles to profl. jours. Woodrow Wilson fellow, 1965. Mem. Am. Philol. Assn., Am. Sch. Classical Studies at Athens (mng. com), Archeol. Inst. of Am., Classical Assn. of Midwest and South, Am. Academy in Rome, Phi Beta Kappa (former pres. Madison chpt.). Home: 1210 Sweetbriar Rd Madison WI 53705-2228 Office: Univ Wis Dept Classics Madison WI 53707 E-mail: bbpowell@facstaff.wisc.edu.

POWELL, MICHAEL N. company executive; V.p., gen. mgr. Superior Valve divsn. Amcast Indsl. Corp., 1994-96, pres. Amcast Flow Control, 1996—. Office: PO Box 1008 Elkhart IN 46515-1008

POWER, JOSEPH EDWARD, lawyer; b. Peoria, Ill., Dec. 2, 1938; s. Joseph Edward and Margaret Elizabeth (Birkett) P.; m. Camille June Repass, Aug. 1, 1964; children— Joseph Edward, David William, James Repass Student, Knox Coll., Galesburg, Ill., 1956-58; B.A., U. Iowa, 1960, J.D., 1964. Bar: Iowa 1964. Law clk. to judge U.S. Dist. Ct., 1964-65; mem. Bradshaw, Fowler, Proctor & Fairgrave, P.C., Des Moines, 1965—. Bd. dirs. Moingona coun. Girl Scouts U.S.A., 1968-77, pres., 1971-74; bd. dirs. Des Moines United Way, 1976-82, v.p., 1979-81; trustee Am. Inst. Bus., 1987-2002, chmn., 1992-2002; bd. dirs. Iowa Law Sch. Found., 1992—. Plymouth Ch. Found., 1991-99; bd. dirs. Des Moines Found, 1996—, sec.-treas., 2001-; bd. dirs. Iowa Natural Heritage Found., 1995—, vice chmn., 2001-; mem. Des Moines Civil War Roundtable. Fellow Am.

Coll. Trust and Estate Counsel (state chair 1994-2000), Am. Coll. Real Estate Lawyers; mem. ABA, Iowa Bar Assn. (chmn. probate, property and trust law com. 1983-87), Polk County Bar Assn., Des Moines Estate Planners Forum (pres. 1982-83) Republican. Mem. United Ch. of Christ. Clubs: Des Moines, Rotary. Home: 4244 Foster Dr Des Moines IA 50312-2542 Office: Bradshaw Fowler Proctor & Fairgrave 801 Grand Ave Ste 3700 Des Moines IA 50309-2727 E-mail: www.power.edward@bradshawlaw.com.

POWERS, BRUCE THEODORE (TED POWERS), state legislator; b. Plymouth, Ind., June 24, 1934; s. Theodore Roosevelt and Mary (McKee) P.; m. Betty Mae Wehling; children: Cindy Jo (Mrs. John G.K. Kennedy), Shari Lynn (Mrs. Peter Bonneson), Charles Theodore. BMF, Phillips U., 1956; MME, Wichita State U., 1960; postgrad., Kans. U., 1963. Music tchr. Unified Sch. Dist. 263, 1956-92; band and vocal tchr. Mulvane, Kans., 1992—; mem. from dist. 81 Kans. State Ho. of Reps., 1993—. Mem. NRA, AARP, Numismatic Assn., Optimists, Lions, Phi Mu Alpha. Office: Capitol Bldg Rm 155E Topeka KS 67110

POWERS, DAVID RICHARD, educational administrator; b. Cambridge Springs, Pa., Apr. 5, 1939; s. William Herman and Elouise Fancheon (Fink) P.; m. Mary Julia Ferguson, June 11, 1960. Student, Pa. State U., 1957-60; BA, U. Pitts., 1963, MA, 1965, PhD, 1971. Dir. CAS advising ctr. U. Pitts., 1966-68, asst. dean faculty, 1968-70, asst. to chancellor, 1970-76, assoc. provost, 1976-78, vice provost, 1978-79; v.p. for acad. affairs George Mason U., Fairfax, Va., 1979-82; vice chancellor for acad. affairs W.Va. Bd. Regents, Charleston, 1982-88; exec. dir. Minn. Higher Edn. Coord. Bd., St. Paul, 1989-94, Nebr. Coord. Commn. Post-secondary Edn., Lincoln, 1994—. Prin. author: Making Participatory Management Work, 1983, Higher Education in Partnership with Industry, 1988; contbr. articles to Ednl. Record, Adult Learning, Forum for Applied Rsch. on Pub. Policy. Bd. trustees Western Govs. U. Grantee USOE Faculty Seminar, Taiwan, 1967, ARC Ctr. for Edn. & Rsch. with Industry Appalachian Regional Commn., 1983, Republic of China Sino-Am. Seminar, 1985; recipient Award for Acad. Quality W.Va. Coun. Faculty, 1986. Mem. Am. Assn. for Higher Edn., State Higher Edn. Exec. Officers, Nat. Postsecondary Edn. Coop., Western Coop. Ednl. Telecomm., Civil Air Patrol, Pi Sigma Alpha. Avocation: flying. Home: 16017 Middle Island Dr South Bend NE 68058-4311 Office: Nebr Coord Comm Post Secondary Edn PO Box 95005 Lincoln NE 68509-5005

POWERS, MARIAN, accounting educator; PhD in Acctg., U. Ill. Acctg. faculty Kellogg Grad. Sch. Mgmt. Northwestern U., Evanston, Ill., 1980-88; dept. acctg. U. Ill., Chgo., 1989-92; prof. acctg. Allen Ctr. Exec. Edn., 1987; vis. assoc. prof. acctg. Kellogg Grad. Sch. Mgmt. Northwestern U., 1993—. Rschr. in field. Contbr. articles to profl. jours.; co-author software. Mem. Am. Acctg. Assn., Ill. CPA Assn., European Acctg. Assn., Internat. Assn. Acctg., Edn. and Rsch., Am. Soc. Women Accts. (past pres. Chgo. chpt.), Edn. Found. Women in Acctg. (trustee 1999). Office: The Allen Ctr Northwestern U 633 Clark St Evanston IL 60208-0001

POWERS, MIKE, state legislator; b. Mar. 31, 1962; BA, U. Wis., Platteville. Assemblyman Wis. State Dist. 80, 1994—. Conservationist Green County Dept. Land Conservation. Address: PO Box 250 Albany WI 53502-0250

POWERS, PAUL J. manufacturing company executive; b. Boston, Feb. 5, 1935; s. Joseph W. and Mary T. Powers; m. Barbara Ross, June 3, 1961; children: Briana, Gregory, Jeffrey. BA in Econs., Merrimack Coll., 1956; MBA, George Washington U., 1962. Various mfg. and fin. positions with Chrysler Corp., Detroit and overseas, 1963-69; v.p., gen. mgr. Am. Standard, Dearborn, Mich., 1970-78; pres. Abex-Dennison, Columbus, Ohio, 1978-82; group v.p. Comml. Intertech Corp., Youngstown, 1982-84, pres., chief ops. officer, 1984-87, chmn., pres., CEO, 1987-00. Bd. dirs. 1st Energy Corp., Twin Disc, Inc., Global Marine Inc., CUNO, Inc., 19 96—. Bd. dirs. Youngstown Symphony, 1984-88. Lt. USNR, 1957-63. Mem. NAM (bd. dirs. 1986-93, 95—), Nat. Fluid Power Assn. (bd. dirs. 1984-87), Mfrs. Alliance (bd. dirs. 1995—), Youngstown Area C. of C. (bd. dirs. 1990—). Office: Commercial Intertech Corp PO Box 239 Youngstown OH 44501-0239

POWERS, RAMON SIDNEY, historical society administrator, historian; b. Gove County, Kans., Sept. 24, 1939; s. Sanford and Gladys Fern (Williams) P.; m. Eva Redin, Apr. 11, 1963; children: Elisabeth, Christina. AB, Ft. Hays (Kans.) State U., 1961, MA, 1963; PhD, U. Kans., 1971. Instr. western civilization U. Kans., Lawrence, 1963-67; asst. prof. history U. Mo., Kansas City, 1967-71; instr. Haskell Indian Jr. Coll., Lawrence, 1971-73; rsch. asst. Kans. Legis. Rsch. Dept., Topeka, 1973-77, rsch. analyst, 1977-78, prin. analyst, 1978-88; asst. exec. dir. Kansas State Hist. Soc., 1988, exec. dir., 1988—. Contbr. articles to various jours. Chair Eisenhower Centennial Adv. Com., Topeka, 1988-90, Kans. Antiquities Commn., 1988—, State Records Bd., 1988—, Sante Fe Natl. Hist. Trail Adv. Coun., 1988-96; mem. bd. review Kans. Hist. Sites, 1988—; mem. State Hist. Records Adv. Bd., 1988—, Gov.'s Commn. on Travel and Tourism, 1988—, mem. bd. dirs. Nat. Conf. of State Historic Preservation Officers, 1991-95. Recipient regional award Col. Dames Am., 1965, Disting. Alumni award Ft. Hays State U., 2000, Hays Rotary Club, 1978; travel grantee N.J. Hist. Commn., 1971, summer grantee NEH, 1973; elected to Kans. Bus. Hall of Fame (bd. dirs.), 1988. Mem. SAR (Thomas Jefferson chpt.), Am. Assn. State and Local History, Kans. Corral of the Westerns, Kans. History Tchrs. Assn., Western History Assn., Travel Industry Assn. (bd. dirs. 1988-92, 97—), Natural and Scientific Area Adv. Bd., 1998—, Santa Fe Trail Assn. Vice Pres., 1996-97; Greater Topeka C. of C., Topeka Heritage League, Sat. Night Literary Club. Office: Kans History Ctr 6425 SW 6th Ave Topeka KS 66615-1099 E-mail: ramonpowers@aol.com., rpowers@kshs.org.

POWLEN, DAVID MICHAEL, investment company executive; b. Logansport, Ind., May 28, 1953; s. Daniel Thomas and Bertha Frances (Cappa) P.; m. Karen Lamb Gentleman, Aug. 5, 1978 (div. Jan. 1984); 1 child, Brooks Ryan. AB, Harvard U., 1975, JD, 1978. Bar: Ind. 1978, U.S. Dist. Ct. (so. dist.) Ind. 1978, U.S. Ct. Appeals (7th cir.) 1985. Assoc. Barnes & Thornburg, Indpls., 1978-84, ptnr., 1985-01, chmn., adminstr. creditors rights dept.; mng. dir., co-mgr. restructuring group McDonald Investments Inc., Cleve., 2001—. Contbr. articles to profl. jours. Mem. ABA (bus. bankruptcy com., secured creditors and chpt. 11 subcom., comml. fin. svcs. com., creditors rights subcom.), Seventh Cir. Bar Assn., Ind. Bar Assn. (chmn. bankruptcy and creditors rights sect. 1990-91), Indpls. Bar Assn. (chmn. edn. com. 1984, chmn. ct. liaison com. 1985, bankruptcy and comml. law sect.), Am. Bankruptcy Inst., Turnaround Mgmt. Assn., Comml. Law League Am. (bankruptcy and insolvency sect.), Harvard Club, Phi Beta Kappa. Office: mail code OH-01-02-1645 McDonald Investments Inc 800 Superior Ave Ste 1600 Cleveland OH 44114 E-mail: dpowlen@mcdinvest.com.

POWSNER, EDWARD RAPHAEL, physician; b. N.Y.C., Mar. 17, 1926; m. Rhoda Lee Moscovitz , June 8, 1950; children: Seth, Rachel, Ethan, David. SB in Elec. Engring., MIT, 1948, SM in Biology, 1949; MD, Yale U., 1953; MS in Internal Medicine, Wayne State U., 1957; MHSA, U. Mich. Diplomate Am. Bd. Nuclear Medicine, Am. Bd. Pathology in clin. pathology and anatomic pathology, Am. Bd. Internal Medicine; lic. physician, Mich., Calif., N.Y. Intern Wayne County Gen. Hosp., Eloise, Mich., 1953-54, resident internal medicine, 1954-55, Detroit Receiving Hosp., 1955-56; fellow in hematology Wayne State U. and Detroit Receiving Hosp., 1957-58; clin. investigator VA Hosp., Allen Park, Mich., 1958-61, chief nuclear medicine svc., 1961-78; dir. clin. labs. Mich. State U., East Lansing, 1978-81; staff pathologist Ingham Med. Ctr., Lansing, Mich., 1978-81; dir. nuclear medicine St. John Hosp., Detroit, 1982-95. Rsch. asst. biology MIT, 1948-49, 50; asst. instr. medicine Wayne State U. Coll. Medicine, 1954-56, instr., 1959-61; assoc. prof. pathology Wayne State U. Sch. Medicine, 1961-68, assoc. medicine, 1961, prof. pathology, 1968-78; prof. pathology Mich. State U., 1978-81, assoc. chairperson, 1980-81, clin. prof., 1981-82; chief clin. labs. Detroit Gen. Hosp., 1969-73; chief lab. svcs. Health Care Inst., Wayne State U., 1976-78; mem. adv. coun. Nuclear Medicine Tech. Cert. Bd., 1990-91. Bd. editors Am. Jour. Clin. Pathology, 1963-76, 83-88; author 2 textbooks, 11 chpts., 50 peer reviewed papers, 17 abstracts and other publs. With U.S. Army, 1944-47. Mem. AMA (sect. coun. on pathology), Am. Soc. Clin. Pathologists (rep. 1987-89, 93-2000, govt. rels. com. 1993-95, mem. coun. nuclear medicine 1978-82, chmn. 1982-84), Am. Coll. Nuclear Physicians, Am. Soc. Nuclear Cardiology, Coll. Am. Pathologists, Detroit Acad. Medicine, Mich. Soc. Pathologists, Mich. State Med. Soc., Soc. Nuclear Medicine, Washtenaw County Med. Soc., Sigma Xi, Tau Beta Pi. Office: Eastside Nuclear Medicine 2363 E Stadium Blvd Ann Arbor MI 48104-4810 also: St John Hosp & Med Ctr 22101 Moross Rd Detroit MI 48236-2148

POZNANSKI, ANDREW KAROL, pediatric radiologist; b. Czestochowa, Poland, Oct. 11, 1931; came to U.S., 1957, naturalized, 1964; s. Edmund Maurycy and Hanna Maria (Ceranka) P.; children: Diana Jean, Suzanne Christine. BSc, McGill U., 1952, MD CM, 1956. Diplomate: Am. Bd. Radiology, Royal Coll. Physicians and Surgeons Can. Intern Montreal (Que., Can.) Hosp., 1956-57; resident Henry Ford Hosp., Detroit, 1957-60, staff radiologist, 1960-68, U. Mich. Med. Center, Ann Arbor, 1968-79; co.-dir. pediatric radiology C.S. Mott Children's Hosp., 1971-79; radiologist-in-chief Children's Meml. Hosp., Chgo., 1979-99; prof. radiology U. Mich., 1971-79, Northwestern U. Med. Sch., 1979—. Bd. dirs. Nat. Coun. on Radiation Protection, 1983-90; mem. Internat. Commn. on Radiologic Protection, 1981-89; mem. adv. panel on radiologic devices FDA, 1975-77, chmn., 1976-77; trustee Am. Bd. Radiology, 1993—. Author: The Hand in Radiologic Diagnosis, 1974, 2d edit., 1983, Practical Approaches to Pediatric Radiology, 1976; bd. editors: Skeletal Radiology, 1975-95, Radiographics, 1980-84, Pediatric Radiology, 1986-91. Fellow: Am. Coll. Radiology; mem.: AMA, Internat. Skeletal Soc. (founder, pres. 1992—94), John Caffey Soc., Radiol. Soc. N.Am., Can. Assn. Radiologists (hon.), European Soc. Radiology (hon.), Polish Radiol. Soc. (hon.), Soc. Pediatric Radiology 1980—81, Am. Roentgen Ray Soc. 1993—94, Alpha Omega Alpha. Home: 2400 N Lakeview Ave Chicago IL 60614-2747 Office: Childrens Meml Hosp 2300 N Childrens Plz Chicago IL 60614-3394 E-mail: apoznanski@ameritech.net.

PRABHUDESAI, MUKUND M. pathology educator, laboratory director, researcher, administrator; b. Lolyem, Goa, India, Mar. 17, 1942; came to U.S., 1967; s. Madhav R. and Kusum M. Prabhudesai; m. Sarita Mukund Usha, Feb. 1, 1972; 1 child, Nitin M. MB, BS (MD), G.S. Med., Bombay, 1967, postgrad., 1973-75. Diplomate Am. Bd. Pathology. Asst. pathologist Fordham Hosp., Bronx, N.Y., 1973-74, assoc. pathologist, 1974-76; assoc. dir. clin. pathology Lincoln Med., 1976, dep. dir. pathology, 1977-79; chief pathology and lab. medicine svc., coord. R&D VA Med. Ctr., Danville, Ill., 1979—, dir. electron microscopy lab., 1987—. Senator U. Ill. Chgo.; co-investigator U. Ill. Coll. Medicine, Urbana-Champaign, clin. prof. pathology and internal medicine, 1982—. Contbr. articles to Am. Jour. Clin. Nutrition, Jour. AMA, Am. Jour. Clin. Pathology. Member Gifted Student Adv. Bd., Danville, 1984-86; v.p. Am. Cancer Soc. Vermilion County chpt., 1982, pres., 1986-88. VA rsch. grantee, 1980-82, 82-85, 83. Fellow Coll. Am. Pathology (inspector 1981—, Ill. state del. to C.A.P. Ho. Dels. 1992—, mem. reference com. 1993); mem. AAAS, Am. Coll. Physician Execs., Ill. State Soc. Pathologists (bd. dirs. 1990—, chmn. membership com. 1990—). Achievements include development of cancer of bladder following portocarval shunting; research in adverse effects of alcohol on lung structure and metabolism; on effects of soy and bran on cholesterol, endocrine response to soy protein, in induction and reversibility of atherosclerosis in trout, effects of ethanol on Vitamin A, lymphatics in atherosclerosis, iron in atherosclerosis, development of dermofluorometer for detection of P.V.D. Office: VA Med Ctr Pathology and Lab Med Svcs 1900 E Main St Danville IL 61832-5100 E-mail: mukund.prabhudesai@med.va.gov.

PRAEGER, SANDY, state legislator; b. Oct. 21, 1944; m. Mark A. Praeger. Student, U. Kans., 1966. V.p. Douglas County Bank; mem. Kans. Senate from 2nd dist., Topeka, 1992—. Vice chmn. Douglas County Rep. Cent. Com.; chmn. Leadership Kans.; pres. bd. dirs. United Way. Home: 3601 Quail Creek Ct Lawrence KS 66047-2134 Office: Kans State Senate State Capitol Rm 128S Topeka KS 66612

PRAGER, STEPHEN, chemistry educator; b. Darmstadt, Germany, July 20, 1928; came to U.S., 1941, naturalized, 1950; s. William and Gertrude Ann (Heyer) P.; m. Julianne Heller, June 7, 1948. B.Sc., Brown, 1947; Ph.D., Cornell, 1951. Mem. faculty U. Minn., Mpls., 1952—, assoc. prof. chemistry, 1956-62, prof., 1962-90, prof. emeritus, 1990—. Cons. Union Carbide Corp., Oak Ridge, 1954-74 Asso. editor: Jour. Phys. Chemistry, 1970-79. Fulbright scholar and Guggenheim fellow, 1958, 59; Fulbright lectr. and Guggenheim fellow, 1966-67 Mem. Am. Chem. Soc., Am. Phys. Soc. Home: 3320 Dunlap St N Saint Paul MN 55112-3709 E-mail: psprager@cs.com.

PRANGE, ROY LEONARD, JR. lawyer; b. Chgo., Sept. 12, 1945; s. Roy Leonard and Marjorie Rose (Kauppi) P.; m. Carol Lynn Poels, June 5, 1971; children: David, Ellen, Susan. BA, U. Iowa, 1967; MA, Ohio State U., 1968; JD, U. Wis.-Madison, 1975. Bar: Wis. 1975, U.S. Dist. Ct. (we. and ea. dists.) Wis. 1975, U.S. Ct. Appeals (7th cir.) 1978, U.S. Supreme Ct. 1978. Assoc. Ross & Stevens, Svc. Corp., Madison, Wis., 1975-79, ptnr., 1979-90, Quarles & Brady, Madison, 1990—. Lectr. bankruptcy, debtor-creditor rights, U. Wis., Madison, 1982–. Contbr. Wis. Lawyer's Desk Reference Manual, 1987, Comml. Litigation in Wis. Practice Handbook, 1995, West's Bankruptcy Exemption Manual, 1997—. 1st lt. U.S. Army, 1969-72. Fellow Am. Coll. Bankruptcy; mem. ABA, Wis. State Bar (dir. bankruptcy, insolvency, creditors rights sect. 1985-91, chair 1990-92, mem. continuing legal edn. com. 1990-95), Am. Bankruptcy Inst., Dickens Fellowship (v.p. 1980-84). Avocations: swimming, bicycling, scuba diving. Office: Quarles & Brady PO Box 2113 1 S Pinckney St Madison WI 53703-2892

PRASAD, ANANDA SHIVA, medical educator; b. Buxar, Bihar, India, Jan. 1, 1928; came to U.S., 1952, naturalized, 1968; s. Radha Krishna and Mahesha (Kaur) Lall; m. Aryabala Ray, Jan. 6, 1952; children: Rita, Sheila, Ashok, Audrey. BSc, Patna (India) Sci. Coll., 1946, MB, BChir, 1951; PhD, U. Minn., 1957; doctorate honoris causa, U. Claude Bernard of Lyon, 1999. Intern Patna Med. Coll. Hosp., 1951-52; resident St. Paul's Hosp., Dallas, 1952-53, U. Minn., 1953-56, VA Hosp., Mpls., 1956; instr. dept. medicine Univ. Hosp., U. Minn., 1957-58; vis. assoc. prof. medicine Shiraz Med. Faculty, Nemazee Hosp., Shiraz, Iran, 1960; asst. prof. medicine and nutrition Vanderbilt U., 1961-63; mem. faculty, dir. div. hematology dept. medicine Wayne State U., Detroit, 1963-84, assoc. prof., 1964-68, prof., 1968-2000, dir. research dept. medicine, 1984-97, disting. prof., 2000—. Mem. staff Harper-Grace Hosp., VA Hosp., Allen Park, Mich.; mem. trace elements subcom. Food and Nutrition Bd., NRC-Nat. Acad. Scis., 1965-68, NIH Coun.; chmn. trace elements com. Internat. Union Nutritional Scis.; mem. Am. Bd. Nutrition; pres. Am. Coll. Nutrition, 1991-93. Author: Zinc Metabolism, 1966, Trace Elements in Human Health and Disease, 1976, Trace Elements and Iron in Human Metabolism, 1978, Zinc in Human Nutrition, 1979, Biochemistry of Zinc, 1993; editor: Clinical, Biochemical and Nutritional Aspects of Trace Elements, 1982, Am. Jour. Hematology, Jour. Trace Elements in Exptl. Medicine; editor: Zinc Metabolism, Current Aspects in Health and Disease, 1977; co-editor: Clinical Applications of Recent Advances in Zinc Metabolism, 1982, Zinc Deficiency in Human Subjects, 1983, Essential and Toxic Trace Elements in Human Health and Disease, 1988, Essential and Toxic Trace Elements in Human Health and Disease: An Update, 1993; Jour. Am. Coll. Nutrition; contbr. articles to profl. jours., also reviewer. Trustee Detroit Internat. Inst., Detroit Gen. Hosp. Research Corp., 1969-72. Recipient Rsch. Recognition award Wayne State U., 1964, award Am. Coll. Nutrition, 1976, Disting. Faculty Fellowship award Wayne State U., 1986, Medal of Honor, City of Lyon, France, 1989, Pioneer in Sickle Cell Disease Rsch. award Nat. Heart Lung Blood Inst./NIH, 1997; Pfizer scholar, 1955-56, WCMS Spl. Recognition award for Profl. Ach., 1998, Klaus Schwartz medal Internat. Assn. Bioinorganic Scientists, 2001, Spl. Recognition awrd Am. Assn. Physicists India, 2001. Master ACP (recipient Mich. Laureate award), Am. Coll. Nutrition; fellow AAAS, Am. Inst. Nutrition (trace elements panel), Internat. Soc. Hematology; mem. AMA (Goldberger award 1975), Internat. Soc. Trace Element Rsch. in Humans (pres. 1986-92, chmn. steering com. 1985-86, Raulin award 1989), Am. Soc. Clin. Nutrition (awards com. 1969-70), Am. Fedn. Clin. Rsch. (pres. Mich. 1969-70), Am. Physiol. Soc., Am. Soc. Clin. Investigation, Am. Soc. Hematology, Assn. Am. Physicians, European Acad. Scis., Arts and Humanities (corr.), Ctrl. Soc. Clin. Rsch., Soc. Exptl. Biology and Medicine (Councillor Mich. 1967-71), Wayne State U. Acad. Scholars (pres.-elect 1997-98, pres. 1998-99), Wayne County Med. Soc., Internat. Soc. Internal Medicine, Am. Soc. Clin. Nutrition (Robert H. Herman award 1984), Nutrition Soc. India (Gopalan oration award 1988), Nat. Heart, Lung, Blood Inst. NIH (mem. coun. 82-), Assn. of Am. Physicists of Indian Origin (Resch. award 2001), Cosmos Club (Washington), Sigma Xi. Home: 4710 Cove Rd Orchard Lake MI 48323-3604 Office: Univ Health Ctr 5-C 4201 Saint Antoine St Detroit MI 48201-2153

PRATHER, SUSAN LYNN, public relations executive; b. Melrose Park, Ill. d. Horace Charles and Ruth Anna Paula (Backus) P.; divorced. BS, Ind. U., 1973, MS, 1975. Arts adminstr. Lyric Opera Chgo., 1975; jr. account exec. Morton H. Kaplan Assocs., Chgo., 1976-78, sr. account exec., 1978-81; account supr. Ketchum Pub. Relations, 1981-83, v.p., 1983-87, v.p., group mgr., 1985-87; v.p., dir. pub. relations Cramer-Krasselt, 1987-95, sr. v.p., dir. pub. rels., 1996—. Cons. Velamints, Foster Wheeler, Kellogg Co., Battle Creek, Mich., 1985—, Village of Rosemont, Ill., PrincCo Personal Comm., Sr. Friendlys, Anti-Cruelty Soc. Chgo., Ill. State Toll Hwy. Authority. Singer various recitals; founder, dir. Chgo. Sports Hall of Fame, 1978-81. Mem. archives com. Chgo. Symphony Orch., 1986—, mem. long term planning com., 1987-89; mem. press advance team Papal Visit to Chgo., 1978; mem. White House Press Advance Team, Chgo., 1976-80. Mem. Pub. Rels. Soc. Am. (bd. dirs. Chgo. chpt. 1987—), Internat. Pub. Rels. Assn., Publicity Club (bd. dirs. 1986—, Merit award 1982, Golden Trumpet awards, Silver Trumpet awards), Bus. and Profl. Assn. Lutheran. Avocation: figure skating. Home: 155 N Harbor Dr Apt 2212 Chicago IL 60601-7321

PRATT, JOSEPH HYDE, JR. surgeon; b. Chapel Hill, N.C., Mar. 9, 1911; s. Joseph Hyde and Mary (Bayley) P.; m. Hazel Housman, Dec. 11, 1943; children: Judith Housman, Lisa Mary, Joseph Hyde. AB, U. N.C., 1933; MD, Harvrad U., 1937; MS, U. Minn., 1947. Diplomate Am. Bd. Surgery, Am. Bd. Ob-gyn. Intern Boston City Hosp., 1938-39; fellow surgery Mayo Found., Rochester, Minn., 1940-43; mem. staff Mayo Clinic, 1943—, head sect. in surgery, 1945-77, sr. gynecol. surgeon, 1958—. Prof. clin. surgery Mayo Grad. Sch. Medicine U. Minn., 1963—; prof. surgery Mayo Med. Sch., 1973—. Contbr. articles to med. jours. Mem. ACS (bd. govs. 1966-71, bd. regents 1971-80), AMA, ACOG, Ctrl. Assn. Ob-Gyn., Minn. Ob-Gyn. Soc., Western Surg. Assn., soc. Vaginal Surgeons (pres. 1979-80), Soc. Pelvic Surgeons (pres. 1968), So. Surg. Assn., Ob-Gyn. Travel Club (pres. 1993—), Sigma Xi, Nu Sigma Nu. Republican. Episcopalian. Home: 1159 Plummer Cir SW Rochester MN 55902-2035 Office: 200 1st St SW Rochester MN 55905-0001

PRATT, ROBERT WINDSOR, lawyer; b. Findlay, Ohio, Mar. 6, 1950; s. John Windsor and Isabelle (Vance) P.; m. Catherine Camak Baker, Sept. 3, 1977; children: Andrew Windsor, David Camak, James Robert. AB, Wittenberg U., Springfield, Ohio, 1972; JD, Yale U., 1975. Bar: Ill. 1975, U.S. Dist. Ct. (no. dist.) Ill. 1976, U.S. Dist. Ct. (we. dist.) Mich. 1995, U.S. Ct. Appeals (fed. cir.) 1984, U.S. Ct. Appeals (7th cir.) 1996. Assoc. Keck, Mahin & Cate, Chgo., 1975—81, ptnr., 1981—97; pvt. practice Wilmette, 1998—99; sr. asst. atty. gen. Office Ill. Atty. Gen., 1999—2001, chief antitrust bur., 2001—. Bd. dirs. Chgo. region ARC, 1985-96, vice chmn., 1988-92, chmn., 1992-96, bd. dirs. Mid-Am. chpt., 1992-96. Mem. ABA, Chgo. Bar Assn., Yale Club (Chgo.).

PRATTE, ROBERT JOHN, lawyer; b. Victoria, B.C., Can., Feb. 14, 1948; s. Arthur Louis Jr. and Marie Bertha (Latremouille) P.; children from previous marriage: Merie Elise, Jessica Louise, Allison Adele; m. Erica Catherine Street, Oct. 20, 1984; 1 child, Chelsea Nicole. BA, Northwestern U., 1970; JD, Tulane U., 1976. Bar: Minn. 1976, Ariz. 1997. Ptnr. Best & Flanagan, Mpls., 1976-84, Briggs & Morgan, Mpls., 1985—, head mortgage banking group. Editor: Mortgage Lending in Minnesota—A Desktop Reference Guide, 1990. Ex-officio mem. Wilderness Inquiry, Minn.; pres. Twin Cities Northwestern U. Alumni Assn., 1978; active Wayzata Cmty. Ch., Mpls. Fellow Am. Coll. Mortgage Attys. (regent) Home: 19900 Manor Rd Excelsior MN 55331-9256 Office: Briggs & Morgan 2400 IDS Ctr 80 S 8th St Ste 2400 Minneapolis MN 55402-2157 E-mail: rpratte@briggs.com.

PRAY, LLOYD CHARLES, geologist, educator; b. Chgo., June 25, 1919; s. Allan Theron and Helen (Palmer) P.; m. Carrel Myers, Sept. 14, 1946; children: Lawrence Myers, John Allan, Kenneth Palmer, Douglas Carrel. B.A. magna cum laude, Carleton Coll., 1941; M.S., Calif. Inst. Tech., 1943, Ph.D. (NRC fellow 1946-49), 1952. Geologist Magnolia Petroleum Co., summer 1942, U.S. Geol. Survey, 1943-44; hydrographic officer USN, 1944-46; Geologist U.S. Geol. Survey, 1946-56 part time; instr. to assoc. prof. geology Calif. Inst. Tech., 1949-56; sr. research geologist Denver Research Ctr., Marathon Oil Co., 1956-62, research assoc., 1962-68; prof. geology U. Wis., Madison, 1968-88; emeritus prof. geology, 1989—. Short course vis. prof. U. Tex., 1964, U. Colo., 1967, U. Miami, 1971, U. Alta., 1969, Colo. Sch. Mines, 1985; vis. scientist Imperial Coll. Sci. and Tech., London, 1977, U. Calif. Santa Cruz, 1987, Nat. Park Svc. Geology panel, 1993. Author articles sedimentary carbonates, the Permian Reef complex, stratigraphy and structural geology So. N.M. and W. Tex., porosity of carbonate facies, Calif. rare earth mineral deposits. Pres. Colo. Diabetes Assn., 1963-67, v.p., 1968; mem. adv. panel earth scis. NSF, 1973-76. Served as hydrographic officer USNR, 1944-46. Named Layman of Year Am. Diabetes Assn., 1968; recipient Disting. Teaching award U. Wis. Madison, 1988, Disting. Achievement citation Carleton Coll., 1991, Wallace Pratt Resources Stewardship award Guadalupe Mountains Nat. Pk., 1998. Fellow Geol. Soc. Am. (rsch. grants com. 1965-67, com. on nominations 1973, com.Penrose medal 1979-81); mem. Am. Assn. Petroleum Geologists (rsch. com. 1958-61, lectr. continuing edn. program 1966-69, continuing edn. com. 1978-80, Levorsen award 1966, Matson trophy 1967, Disting. lectr. 1986-87, 87-88, Disting. Educator award 1998), Soc. Sedimentary Geologists (hon. life mem. Permian Basin sect. 1977, hon. mem. internat. soc. 1982, sec.-treas. 1961-63, v.p. 1966-67, pres. 1969-70, Twenhofel award 1999), Am. Geol. Inst. (edn. com. 1966-68, ho. bd. dels. 1970-72), Phi Beta Kappa. Office: Univ Wis Dept Geology Madison WI 53706

PREBLE, ROBERT CURTIS, JR. insurance executive; b. Oak Park, Ill., Dec. 19, 1922; s. Robert Curtis and Dorothy (Seidel) P.; m. Lidia Blazik, May 29, 1963. BA, Amherst Coll., 1947; MBA, Harvard U., 1949, postgrad., 1971. CLU, Chartered Fin. Cons. Commd. 1st lt. U.S. Army, 1943—46, advanced through grades to capt., 1950—53; asst. to gen. supt., asst. buyer Carson Pirie Scott & Co., Chgo., 1949-52; with sales dept. Northwestern Mut. Life Ins. Co., 1952-53, Nat. Life Ins. Co., Chgo., 1953-59; prin. Preble Assocs., 1959—; pres., treas. Savs. Plans Inc., 1980—. Cons. Iowa Savs. & Loan League, 1959-82; consul of Colombia, 1981-86, Bolivia, 1965-70; bd. dirs., chmn. fin. com. Guardsman Life Ins. Co., 1962-74; chmn. exec. com. World Book Life Ins. Co., 1974-83; gov.'s adv. bd. Ill. Dept. Ins., 1965-70; dir. Scandia Savs. & Loan Assn., 1968-83, Chgo. Coun. on Fgn. Rels., 1971-77, Chgo. Estate Planning Coun., 1977-80. Dept. regional chmn. Dem. Nat. Fin. Com., 1952; bd. dirs. Sr. Ctrs. Met. Chgo., 1974—77, McCormick Theol. Sem., 1977—83; deacon 4th Presbyn. Ch. of Chgo., 1967—70. Recipient Svc. award Chgo. coun. Boy Scouts Am., 1962. Mem. Soc. Fin. Svc. Profls. (past pres. Chgo. chpt., Huebner scholar 1991, Grauer award 1998), Million Dollar Roundtable (life), Nat. Assn. Life Underwriters, Assn. Advanced Life Underwriting (founding pres. 1957), Harvard Bus. Sch. Assn. (alumni coun. 1977-82), Harvard Alumni Assn. (dir. 1980-82), Inst. Internat. Edn. (midwest adv. bd., 1979-99), Found. Study Cycles (internat. adv. bd.), Soc. Colonial Wars (coun.), Mil. Order World Wars, Univ. Club, Chgo. Club, Harvard Bus. Sch. Club (past pres.), Amherst Club (past pres.), Oak Park Country Club, Spanish Wells Country Club, Econ. Club Chgo., Chi Psi (past chmn. ednl. trust, pres. 1992-95, Svc. award 1986). Home: 300 N State St Apt 5406 Chicago IL 60610-4870 Office: Savs Plans Inc # 122-109 10 Trent Jones Ln Hilton Head Island SC 29928-7655

PREER, JOHN RANDOLPH, JR. biology educator; b. Ocala, Fla., Apr. 4, 1918; s. John Randolph Sr. and Ruth (Williams) P.; m. Louise Bertha Brandau; children: James Randolph, Robert William. BS with highest honors, U. Fla., 1939; PhD, Ind. U., 1947; D in Math. and Natural Scis., West Fäölische Wilhelms U., 1993. From asst. prof. to assoc. prof. to prof. depts. zoology and biology U. Pa., Phila., 1947-67, chmn. grad. group depts. zoology and biology, 1958-67, admissions officer grad. sch. arts and scis., 1960-61; prof. depts. zoology and biology Ind. U., Bloomington, 1968-77, chmn. dept. biology, 1977-79, disting. prof. depts. zoology and biology, 1977—, disting. prof. emeritus, 1988—. Contbr. 85 articles to profl. jours. and chpts. to books. Served to 1st lt. USAF, 1942-45, ETO. NSF sr. postdoctoral fellow, 1967-68, Guggenheim fellow 1976-77. Mem. AAAS, Nat. Acad. Scis. (elected 1976), Am. Inst. Biol. Scis., Am. Soc. Cell Biology, Am. Soc. Protozoology (pres. 1986-87), Phi Beta Kappa. Democrat. Methodist. Home: 1414 E Maxwell Ln Bloomington IN 47401-5143 Office: Ind Univ care Dept of Biology Bloomington IN 47405

PREISER, WOLFGANG FRIEDRICH ERNST, architect, educator, consultant, researcher; b. Freiburg, Germany, June 26, 1941; came to U.S., 1967; s. Gerhard Friedrich and Ursula Helene (von Huelsen) P.; m. Cecilia M. Fenoglio, Feb. 16, 1985; children: Johanna, Timothy, Andreas, Nicholas. Student, Vienna Tech. U., 1963; diploma in Engring., Architecture, U. Karlsruhe, 1967; M.Arch., Va. Poly. Inst. and State U., 1969; Ph.D. in Man-Environ. Relations, Pa. State U., 1973. Architect, Germany, Austria, Eng., 1960-66; prof. architecture Va. Poly. Inst. and State U., Pa. State U., U. Ill., U. N.Mex., U. Cin., 1970—; research architect constrn. engring. research lab. U.S. Army, 1973-76; co-dir. Inst. Environ. Edn., U. N.Mex., 1976-86; dir. Ctr. for R & D, U. N.Mex., Albuquerque, 1986-90; dir. research Archtl. Research Cons. Inc., 1976—. Lectr. ednl., profl. and civic groups worldwide; v.p. faculty club U. N.Mex., 1976-78; pres. Internat. Club, Va. Poly. Inst. and State U., 1968-69; rschr. in field. Editor, author 13 books on programming, post-occupancy evaluation, design review, pub. housing, universal design, and design rsch.; contbr. over 75 articles in field to books and profl. jours. Trustee Cin. Chamber Orch., 1992-98, v.p., 1995-98. Recipient Career award Environ. Design Rsch. Assn., 1999, Ann. Rieveschl award, U. Cin., 1999, MCB Univ. Press (U.K.) award for excellence, 1998, Faculty Devel. award for rsch. U. Cin., 1992, Faculty Achievement award, 1995, Pogue/Wheeler Traveling award, 1993, Dean's Spl. award, 1994, Finland's Inst. Tech. award, 1966, awards Am. Iron and Steel Inst., 1968, Progressive Arch. Ann., 1985, 89, undergrad. teaching award U. Ill., 1976, hon. mention 1st Kyoto award Internat. Coun. of Soc. for Indsl. Design, 1979; Fulbright fellow, 1967, 87, Ford Found. fellow, 1968, Nat. Endowment for Arts fellow, 1979, 82; grad. fellow U. Cin., 1996. Mem. Soc. Human Ecology (pres. 1980-86), Environ. Design Research Assn. (vice chmn. 1974-76, sec. 1973-74), Nat. Acad. Scis. (chmn. com. on programming and post-occupancy evaluation, bldg. research bd., 1985-86), U. Cin. Grad. Fellows (elected), Phi Kappa Phi. Office: U Cin Coll Daap Sch Architecture Cincinnati OH 45221-0001 E-mail: wolfgang.preiser@uc.edu.

PREISS, JACK, biochemistry educator; b. Bklyn., June 2, 1932; s. Erool and Gilda (Friedman) P.; m. Karen Sue; children: Jennifer Ellen, Jeremy Oscar, Jessica Michelle. BS in Chemistry, CCNY, 1953; PhD in Biochemistry, Duke U., 1957. Scientist NIH, Bethesda, 1960-62; asst. prof. dept. biochemistry, biophysics U. Calif., Davis, 1962-65, assoc. prof., 1965-68, prof., 1968-85, chair dept. biochemistry, 1971-74, 77-81; prof. dept. biochemistry Mich. State U., East Lansing, 1985-2000, univ. disting. prof., 2001—, chair dept., 1985-89, Univ. Disting. Prof., 2001—. Mem. editorial bd. Jour. Bacteriology, 1969-74, Arch. Biochem. Biophysics, 1969—, Plant Physiology, 1969-74, 77-80, assoc. editor, 1980-92, editor, 1993-95; editor Jour. Biol. Chemistry, 1971-76, 78-83, 94-99, 2000-04, Plant Physiol. Biochemistry, 1997—; 16th loomis lectr. Iowa State U., 1997-98. Recipient Camille and Henry Dreyfus Disting. scholar award Calif. State U., 1983, Alexander von Humboldt Stiftung Sr. U.S. Scientist award, 1984, Award of Merit, Japanese Soc. Starch Sci., 1992, Disting. Faculty Mem. award Mich. Assn. Governing Bds. of State Univs., 1997, Mich. Scientist of Yr. award Impressions 5 Mus., 1997, award lectr. Spanish Biochem. Soc., 2000; Alsberg-Schoch Meml. lectr. Am. Assn. Cereal Chemists, 1990, Nat. Sci. Coun. lectr. Republic of China, 1988; Guggenheim Meml. fellow, 1969-70, Japan Soc. for Promotion of Sci. fellow, 1992-93; grantee NIH, 1963-97, NSF, 1978-89, Dept. of Energy, 1993—, USDA, 1988—. Mem. AAAS, Am. Chem. Soc. (Charles Pfizer award in enzyme chemistry 1971), Biochem. Soc., Am. Soc. Biol. Chemists and Molecular Biology, Am. Soc. Microbiologists, Am. Soc. Plant Physiologists, Soc. for Complex Carbohydrates, Protein Soc., Pan Am. Soc. Biochemistry and Molecular Biology (sec. gen. 1994-96, vice chmn. 1997-99, chmn. 2000-2002). Office: Mich State Univ Dept Of Biochemistry East Lansing MI 48824 E-mail: preiss@msu.edu.

PREISTER, DONALD GEORGE, state legislator, greeting card manufacturer; b. Columbus, Nebr., Dec. 23, 1946; s. Maurice J. Preister and Leona T. (Dusel) Chereck. BS in Edn., U. Nebr., 1977. Unit dir. Boys' Clubs of Omaha, 1973-83; dep. city clk. City of Omaha, 1984-85; tchr. The Great Peace March, U.S., 1986; founder, owner Joy Creations, Co., Omaha, 1988—; mem. Nebr. Legislature from 5th dist., Lincoln, 1992—. Instr. Metro C.C., Omaha, 1979-80. Author: (sect.) Drug Abuse Prevention, 1977. Troop leader Boy Scouts Am., Omaha, 1973-83. Served with U.S. Army, 1966-68, Vietnam. Decorated Bronze Star. Mem. Vets. for Peace, Nebr. Sustainable Agr. Soc., Optimist. Democrat. Roman Catholic. Avocations: gardening, running, horses. Home: 3937 W St Omaha NE 68107-3152 Office: State Capitol Dist # 5 Lincoln NE 68509

PREKI, professional soccer player; b. Belgrade, Yugoslavia, June 24, 1963; Midfielder Red Star Belgrade, 1983, Kans. City Wizards, 1996—; mem. All-Star team, 1996-98. Named Maj. League Soccer MVP, 1997 Budweiser Scoring Champion. Office: Kans City Wizards 706 Broadway St Ste 100 Kansas City MO 64105-2306

PREM, KONALD ARTHUR, physician, educator; b. St. Cloud, Minn., Nov. 6, 1920; s. Joseph E. and Theresa M. (Willing) P.; m. Phyllis Edelbrock, June 14, 1947; children: Mary Kristen, Stephanie, Timothy. B.S., U. Minn., 1947; M.B., 1950, M.D., 1951. Diplomate: Am. Bd. Ob-Gyn (with spl. competence in gynecologic oncology). Intern Mpls. gen. Hosp., 1950-51; fellow dept. obstetrics and gynecology U. Minn., Mpls., 1951-54, instr., 1955-58, asst. prof., 1958-60, assoc. prof., 1960-69, prof., 1969-93; prof. emeritus, 1993—; dir. div. gynecologic oncology U. Minn., 1969-83, head dept. obstetrics and gynecology, 1976-84; prof. dept. surgery, 1993-96. Served to capt. USAR, 1941-46; brig. gen. M.C. USAR (Ret.). Decorated Legion of Merit. Mem. Am. Coll. Ob-Gyn, Am. Gynec. and Obstet. Soc., Central Assn. Ob-Gyn, Hennepin County Med. Soc., Soc. Pelvic Surgeons, Minn. Ob-Gyn Soc., Soc. Gynecologic Oncologists, Internat. Soc. Gynecologic Pathologists, Soc. Gynecologic Surgery, Minn. Acad. Medicine, Am. Radium Soc., Am. Assn. Pro-Life Ob-Gyn. Roman Catholic. Home: 15660-16 Place N Plymouth MN 55447-2497 Office: Mayo Mail Code 395 420 Delaware St SE Minneapolis MN 55455-0374 Fax: 612-626-0665.

PRENDERGAST, FRANKLYN G. health facility administrator, medical educator; MD, U. West Indies, 1968; PhD in Biochemistry, U. Minn., 1977; grad., Oxford U. With Mayo Clinic, Rochester, Minn., 1975—; prof. biochemistry, molecular biology, pharmacology Mayo Med. Sch.; interim dir. Mayo Cancer Ctr.; dir. Mayo Cancer Ctr, Rochester. Trustee Mayo Found.; bd. dirs. Eli Lilly and Co.; sci. adv. bd. BioDx Inc. Contbr. articles to profl. jours. Rhodes scholar. Office: Mayo Cancer Ctr 200 1st St SW Rochester MN 55905-0001

PRENSKY, ARTHUR LAWRENCE, pediatric neurologist, educator; b. N.Y.C., Aug. 31, 1930; s. Herman and Pearl (Newman) P.; m. Sheila Carr, Nov. 13, 1969. A.B., Cornell U., 1951; M.D., N.Y. U., 1955. Diplomate: Am. Bd. Psychiatry and Neurology. Intern Barnes Hosp., St. Louis, 1955-56; resident and research fellow in neurology Harvard U., Mass. Gen. Hosp., Boston, 1959-66; instr. neurology Harvard Med. Sch., 1966-67; mem. faculty Washington U. Sch. Medicine, St. Louis, 1967—, prof. pediatrics and neurology, to 1975, Allen P. and Josephine B. Green prof. pediatric neurology, 1975-2000, prof. emeritus of neurology, 2000—; pediatrician St. Louis Children's Hosp.; neurologist Barnes and Allied Hosps., Jewish Hosp., St. Louis. Author: (with others) Nutrition and the Developing Nervous System, 1975; editor: (with others) Neurological Pathophysiology, 2d edit, 1978, Advances in Neurology, 1976; mem. editorial bd. Pediatric Neurology, 1984-90, Jour. Child Neurology, 1985—. Served with USAF, 1957-59. Fellow Am. Acad. Neurology; mem. Am. Neurol. Assn., Am. Soc. Neurochemistry (mem. council 1973-77), Central Soc. Neurol. Research (pres. 1977-78), Child Neurology Soc. (pres. 1979-80, Hower award 2000), Am. Pediatric Soc., Internat. Child Neurology Assn., Japanese Soc. Child Neurology, Profs. Child Neurology (pres. 1984-86) Home: 15 Monarch Hill Ct Chesterfield MO 63005-4004 Office: 400 S Kingshighway Blvd Saint Louis MO 63110-1014

PRENTICE, MATTHEW, food service executive; b. Detroit, Dec. 1, 1958; married; four children. Student, Culinary Inst. Am. Pres. Unique Restaurant Corp., Franklin, Mich. Lectr. Wayne State U. Avocation: reading. Office: Unique Restaurant Corp 30100 Telegraph Rd Franklin MI 48025-4514

PRENTISS, C. J. state legislator; BA in Edn., Cleve. State U., 1969, MEd, 1975; cert., Kent State U., 1976; grad. Weatherhead Sch. Mgmt., Case Western Res. U., 1978. Mem. Ohio Ho. of Reps. from 8th dist., Columbus, 1990-98, Ohio Senate from 21st dist., Columbus, 1999—; mem. econ. devel., tech. and aerospace com., edn. com., fin. and financial instns. com., health, human svcs. and aging com. Chair edn. policy Ohio legislative Black Caucus and Black elected Democrats of Cleve., vice-chair edn. com. Nat. Conf. State Legislatures; past vice-chair HouseEdn. com., ways and means, ins.; mem. State Bd. Edn., 1984-90, chair lit. and youth-at-risk com., legis. stds. com., past chair joint select com. on infant health and family support. Past Vice-chair Black Leadership Cleve. Alumni; past mem. gov.'s com. Socially Disadvantaged Black Males. Office: Senate Bldg Rm 57 Columbus OH 43215

PRESCHLACK, JOHN EDWARD, management consultant; b. N.Y.C., May 30, 1933; s. William and Anna M. (Hrubesch) P.; m. Lynn A. Stanley, Dec. 29, 1962; children: John Edward Jr., James S., David C. BSEE, MIT, 1954; MBA, Harvard U., 1958. Ptnr. McKinsey & Co., Inc., N.Y.C., London, Düsseldorf, Germany, 1958-73; pres. ITEK Graphic Products Co., Lexington, Mass., 1973-77; pres., CEO Gen. Binding Corp., Northbrook, Ill., 1977-83; pres. Roberts & Porter, Inc., Des Plaines, 1984-86; sr. dir. Spencer Stuart, Chgo., 1987-96; chmn., pres. Jepcor, Inc., Lake Bluff, 1996—. Bd. dirs. Blyth Industries, Greenwich, Conn., 1989—. Trustee Chgo. Hort. Soc., 1979—; chmn. Lake Forest (Ill.) Planning Commn., 1982-88; alderman City of Lake Forest, 1990-96; mem. devel. com. MIT, 1986-92. Lt. USAF, 1954-56. Recipient Corp. Leadership award MIT, 1978. Mem. Onwentsia Club, Chgo. Club, John's Island Club. Republican. Roman Catholic. Avocations: tennis, golf, boating, travel. E-mail: jepcor@aol.com.

PRESKA, MARGARET LOUISE ROBINSON, education educator, administrator; b. Parma, N.Y., Jan. 23, 1938; d. Ralph Craven and Ellen Elvira (Niemi) Robinson; m. Daniel C. Preska, Jan. 24, 1959; children: Robert, William, Ellen Preska Steck. B.S. summa cum laude, SUNY, 1957; M.A., Pa. State U., 1961; Ph.D., Claremont Grad. Sch., 1969; postgrad., Manchester Coll., Oxford U., 1973. Instr. LaVerne (Calif.) Coll., 1968-75, asst. prof., asso. prof., acad. dean, 1972-75; instr. Starr King Sch. for Ministry, Berkeley, Calif., summer, 1975; v.p. acad. affairs, equal opportunity officer Minn. State U., Mankato, 1975-79, pres., 1979-92; project dir. Kaliningrad (Russia) Mil. Re-Tng., 1992-96; disting. svc. prof. Minn. State U., Winona, 1993—, pres. Inst. for Effective Tchg., 1993-96; owner BuildaBikeInc.com, 2000—. Bd. dirs. XCEL Energy Co., Norwest Corp., Exec. Sports Inc., 1996-98; pres. emerita Minn. State U., Mankato, 1992—; provost, CEO AbuDhabi Campus, Zayed U., United Arab Emirates, 1997-99. Pres. Pomona Valley chpt. UN Assn., 1968-69, Unitarian Soc. Pomona Valley, 1968-69, PTA Lincoln Elem. Sch., Pomona, 1973-74, Nat. Camp Fire Boys and Girls, 1986-88; mem. Pomona City Charter Revision Commn., 1972; chmn. The Fielding Inst., Santa Barbara, 1983-86; bd. dirs. Elderhostel Internat., 1983-87, Minn. Agrl. Interpretive Ctr. (Farmam.), 1983-92, Am. Assn. State Colls. and Univs., Moscow on the Mississippi - Minn. Meets the Soviet Union; nat. pres. Campfire, Inc., 1985-87; chmn. Gov.'s Coun. on Youth, Minn., 1983-86, Minn. Edn. Forum, 1984; mem. Gov.'s Commn. on Econ. Future of Minn., 1985—, NCAA Pres. Commn., 1986-92, NCAA Cost Cutting Commn., Minn. Brainpower Compact, 1985; commr. Great Lakes Govs.' Econ. Devel. Coun., 1986, Minn Gov.'s Commn. on Forestry. Carnegie Found. grantee Am. Coun. Edn. Deans Inst., 1974; recipient Outstanding Alumni award Pa. State, Outstanding Alumni award Claremont Grad. Sch., YWCA Leader award 1982, Exch. Club Book of Golden Deeds award, 1987; named One of top 100 alumni, SUNY, 1895-1985, 1985, Hall of Heritage award, 1988, Wohelo Camp Fire award, 1989. Mem. AAUW (pres. Mankato 1990-92), LWV, Women's Econ. Roundtable, St. Paul/Mpls. Com. on Fgn. Rels., Am. Coun. on Edn., Am. Assn. Univ. Adminstrs., Rotary, Benedicts Dance Club, Horizon 100. Unitarian. Home: 3573 Bailey Ridge Bay Woodbury MN 55125 Office: 4156 Pre Emption Rd Himrod NY 14842-9734 E-mail: mpreska@mediaone.net.

PRESS, CHARLES, retired political science educator; b. St. Louis, Sept. 12, 1922; s. Otto Ernst and Laura (Irion) P.; m. Nancy Miller, June 10, 1950; children: Edward Paul, William David, Thomas Leigh, Laura Mary. Student, Elmhurst (Ill.) Coll.; B of Journalism, U. Mo., 1948; M.A., U. Minn., 1951, Ph.D., 1953. Faculty N.D. Agrl. Coll., 1954-56; dir. Grand Rapids Area Study, 1956-57; with Bur. Govt., U. Wis., 1957-58; faculty Mich. State U., East Lansing, 1958-91, prof. polit. sci., 1964-91; emeritus, 1991—; chmn. dept. Mich. State U., 1966-73. Cons. Mich. Constl. Conv., 1962-63; supr. Ingham County, 1966-72; tchr. summers, London; tchr. U. N.S.W., Sydney, Mich. State U. Author: Main Street Politics, 1962, (with Charles Adrian) The American Government Process, 1965, Governing Urban America, 1968, 5th edit., 1977, American Politics Reappraised, 1974, (with Kenneth VerBurg) States and Community Governments in a Federal System, 1979, 3d edit., 1991, American Policy Studies, 1981, The Political Cartoon, 1982, (with others) Michigan Political Atlas 1984, (with Kenneth VerBurg) American Politicians and Journalists, 1988, (with Kenneth VerBurg) (weekly newspaper column) The Pros and Cons of Politics. Sec. Ingham County Bd. Health, 1983-93; chmn., mem. East Lansing Bd. Rev., 1966-86; bd. dirs. Urban League, 1971-73; mem. East Lansing Housing and Urban Devel. Commn., 1988-93. Served with AUS, 1943-45. Recipient Disting. Prof. award Mich. State U., 1980, Alumni Merit award Elmhurst (Ill.) Coll., 1995. Mem. Am. Polit. Sci. Assn., Midwest Polit. Sci. Assn. (pres. 1974-75), So. Polit. Sci. Assn., Mich. Conf. Polit. Scientists (pres. 1972-73), Nat. Municipal League, B.S.I. Home: 987 Lantern Hill Dr East Lansing MI 48823-2831 Office: Mich State U 315 S Kedzie Hall East Lansing MI 48824-1032 E-mail: pressc@pilot.msu.edu.

PRESSER, STEPHEN BRUCE, lawyer, educator; b. Chattanooga, Aug. 10, 1946; s. Sidney and Estelle (Shapiro) P.; m. Carole Smith, June 18, 1968 (div. 1987); children: David Carter, Elisabeth Catherine; m. ArLynn Leiber, Dec. 13, 1987; children: Joseph Leiber, Eastman Leiber. A.B., Harvard U., 1968, J.D., 1971. Bar: Mass. 1971, D.C. 1972. Law clk. to Judge Malcolm Richard Wilkey U.S. Ct. Appeals (D.C. cir.), 1971-72; assoc. Wilmer, Cutler & Pickering, Washington, 1972-74; asst. prof. law Rutgers U., Camden, N.J., 1974-76; vis. assoc. prof. U. Va., 1976-77; prof. Northwestern U., Chgo., 1977—, class 1940 rsch. prof., 1992-93, Raoul Berger prof. legal history, 1992—, assoc. dean acad. affairs Sch. Law, 1982-85. Prof. bus. law Kellogg Grad. Sch. Mgmt., Northwestern U., Chgo., 1992—. Author: (with Jamil S. Zainaldin) Law and Jurisprudence in American History, 1980, 4th edit., 2000, Studies in the History of the United States Courts of the Third Circuit, 1983, The Original Misunderstanding: The English, The Americans and the Dialectic of Federalist Jurisprudence, 1991, Piercing the Corporate Veil, 1991, revised ann., (with Ralph Ferrara and Meridith Brown) Takeovers: A Strategist's Manual, 2d edit., 1993, Recapturing the Constitution, 1994, (with Douglas W. Kmiec) The American Constitutional Order: History, Cases, and Philosophy, 1998; assoc. articles editor Guide to American Law, 1985. Trustee Village of Winnetka, Ill., 2000—; mem. acad. adv. bd. Washington Legal Found. Recipient summer stipend NEH, 1975; Fulbright Sr. scholar Univ. Coll., London Sch. Econs. and Polit. Sci., 1983-84, Inst. Advanced Legal Studies, 1996; Adams fellow Inst. U.S. Studies, London, 1996; assoc. rsch. fellow Inst. U.S. Studies, 1999—. Mem. Am. Soc. Legal History (bd. dirs. 1979-82), Am. Law Inst., Univ. Club Chgo. (bd. dirs. 1997-99, sec., 1999), Legal Club Chgo., Reform Club (London), Arts Club Chgo. Office: Northwestern U Law Sch 357 E Chicago Ave Chicago IL 60611-3069 E-mail: s-presser@law.northwestern.edu.

PRESSLEY, FRED G., JR. lawyer; b. N.Y.C., June 19, 1953; s. Fred G. Sr. and Frances (Sanders) P.; m. Cynthia Denise Hill, Sept. 5, 1981. BA cum laude, Union Coll., 1975; JD, Northwestern U., 1978. Bar: Ohio 1978, U.S. Dist. Ct. (so. dist.) Ohio 1979, U.S. Dist. Ct. (no. dist.) Ohio 1985, U.S. Dist. Ct. (ea. dist.) Wis. 1980, U.S. Ct. Appeals (6th cir.). Assoc. Porter, Wright, Morris & Arthur, Columbus, Ohio, 1978-85, ptnr., 1985—. Bd. dirs. Columbus Area Leadership Program, 1981-84, Franklin County Bd. Mental Retardation and Devel. Disabilities, Columbus, 1989-97, Union Coll., Schenectady, N.Y., 1992—. Recipient Civic Achievement award Ohio Ho. of Reps., 1988. Mem. ABA. Avocations: jogging, golf, basketball, military history. Office: Porter Wright Morris & Arthur 41 S High St Ste 2800 Columbus OH 43215-6194

PRESTON, ROBERT BRUCE, retired lawyer; b. Cleve., Feb. 24, 1926; s. Robert Bruce and Erma May (Hunter) P.; m. Agnes Ellen Stanley, Jan. 29, 1949; children— Robert B., Patricia Ellen Preston Kiefer, Judith Helen Preston Yanover. A.B., Western Res. U., 1950, J.D., 1952. Bar: U.S. Dist. Ct. (no. dist.) Ohio 1953, U.S. Ct. Appeals (6th cir.) 1959, U.S. Supreme Ct. 1964. Assoc. Arter & Hadden, Cleve., 1952-63, ptnr., 1964-93; ret., 1994. Dir. Service Stampings Inc., Willoughby, Ohio Vice pres. Citizens League Cleve., 1965; chmn. Charter Rev. Com., Cleveland Heights, Ohio, 1972; mem. Zoning Bd. Appeals, Cleveland Heights, 1974-76 Mem. Ohio Bar Assn., Greater Cleve. Bar Assn. Republican. Presbyterian. Avocations: tennis, fishing, travel. Home: 117 Manor Brook Dr Chagrin Falls OH 44022-4163 Office: Arter & Hadden 1100 Huntington Bldg Cleveland OH 44115

PRESZLER, GARY, commissioner, state; Commr. N.D. Banking and Fin. Instns. Dept., Bismarck. Office: ND Banking and Fin Instns Dept 2000 Schafer St Ste G Bismarck ND 58501-1204

PRETLOW, THOMAS GARRETT, physician, pathology educator, researcher; b. Warrenton, Va., Dec. 11, 1939; s. William Ribble and May (Tiffany) P.; m. Theresa Pace, June 29, 1963; children: James Michael, Joseph Peter, David Mark. AB, Oberlin Coll., 1960; MD, U. Rochester, 1965. Intern U. Hosps., Madison, Wis., 1965-66; fellow McArdle Lab., 1966-67; rsch. assoc. Nat. Cancer Inst., Bethesda, Md., 1967-69; asst. prof. pathology Rutgers Med. Sch., Piscataway, N.J., 1969-70; assoc. prof. pathology U. Ala., Birmingham, 1971-73, prof. pathology, 1974-83, prof. biochemistry, 1982-83; vis. prof. pathology Harvard Med. Sch., Boston, 1983-84; prof. pathology Case Western Res. U., Cleve., 1983—, prof. oncology, 1987—, prof. environ. health scis., 1991—, prof. urology, 1994—. Cons. NIH, Bethesda, 1976-2000, Am. Inst. Cancer Rsch., 1995-98; chmn. pathobiolog y 2 prostate cancer grant reviewer U.S. Army, 1998, 99. Mem. editl. bd. Cell Biophysics, Cambridge, Mass., 1978-82; editor: Cell Separation: Methods and Selected Applications, 5 vols., 1982, 83, 84, 87, Biochemical and Molecular Aspects of Selected Cancers, 2 vols., 1991, 94. Mem. exec. bd. Birmingham coun. Boy Scouts Am., 1979-83, Greater Cleve. coun. Boy Scouts Am., 1984-90. Served to lt. comdr. USPHS, 1967-69. Recipient Rsch. Career Devel. award Nat. Cancer Inst., 1973-78; grantee for cancer rsch. Mem. Am. Assn. Pathologists, Am. Assn. Immunologists, Internat. Acad. Pathology, Am. Soc. Clin. Oncology, Am. Assn. Cancer Rsch., Serra Club (pres. Birmingham chpt. 1982-83). Avocations: camping, fishing, Boy Scouts, classical music, biking. Home: 3061 Chadbourne Rd Cleveland OH 44120-2446 Office: Inst of Pathology Case Western Reserve U Cleveland OH 44106 E-mail: tgp3@po.cwru.edu.

PREUS, DAVID WALTER, bishop, minister; b. Madison, Wis., May 28, 1922; s. Ove Jacob Hjort and Magdalene (Forde) P.; m. Ann Madsen, June 26, 1951; children: Martha, David, Stephen, Louise, Laura. BA, Luther Coll., Decorah, Iowa, 1943, DD (hon.), 1969; postgrad., U. Minn., 1946-47; BTh, Luther Sem., St. Paul, 1950; postgrad., Union Sem., 1951, Edinburgh U., 1951-52; LLD (hon.), Wagner Coll., 1973, Gettysburg Coll., 1976; DD (hon.), Pacific Luth. Coll., 1974, St. Olaf Coll., 1974, Dana Coll., 1979, Tex. Luth. Coll., 1994; LHD (hon.), Macalester Coll., 1976. Ordained to ministry Luth. Ch., 1950; asst. pastor First Luth. Ch., Brookings, S.D., 1950-51; pastor Trinity Luth. Ch., Vermillion, 1952-57; campus pastor U. Minn., Mpls., 1957-58; pastor Univ. Luth. Ch. of Hope, 1958-73; v.p. Am. Luth. Ch., 1968-73, pres., presiding bishop, 1973-87; exec. dir. Global Mission Inst. Luther Northwestern Theol. Sem., St. Paul. Disting. vis. prof. Luther-Northwestern Sem., St. Paul, 1988-94; Luccock vis. pastor Yale Div. Sch., 1969; chmn. bd. youth activity Am. Luth. Ch., 1960-68; mem. exec. com. Luth. Council U.S.A.; v.p. Luth. World Fedn., 1977-90; mem. cen. com. World Council Chs., 1973-75, 80-90; Luth. del. White House Conf. on Equal Opportunity Chmn. Greater Mpls. Fair Housing Com., Mpls. Council Chs., 1960-64; Mem. Mpls. Planning Commn., 1965-67; mem. Mpls. Sch. Bd., 1965-74, chmn., 1967-69; mem. Mpls. Bd. Estimate and Taxation, 1968-73, Mpls. Urban Coalition; sr. public adv. U.S. del. Madrid Conf. of Conf. on Security and Cooperation in Europe, 1980-81; bd. dirs. Mpls. Inst. Art, Walker Art Center, Hennepin County United Fund, Ams. for Childrens Relief, Luth. Student Found., Research Council of Gt. City Schs., Urban League, NAACP; bd. regents Augsburg Coll., Mpls. Served with Signal Corps AUS, 1943-46, PTO. Decorated comdr.'s cross Royal Norwegian Order St. Olav, Order of St. George 1st deg. Orthodox Ch. of Georgia (USSR), 1989; recipient Regents medal Augustana Coll., Sioux Falls, S.D., 1973, Torch of Liberty award Anti-Defamation League, 1973, St. Thomas Aquinas award St. Thomas U., Pax Christi award St. John's Univ/. Collegeville, Minn., 1997.

PREUSS, ROGER E(MIL), artist; b. Waterville, Minn., Jan. 29, 1922; s. Emil W. and Edna (Rosenau) P.; m. MarDee Ann Germundson, Dec. 31, 1954 (dec. Mar. 1981). Student, Mankato Comml. Coll., Mpls. Sch. Art. Emeritus instr. seminar Mpls. Coll. Art and Design; emeritus Mpls. Inst. Arts Speakers Bur.; former judge ann. Goodyear Nat. Conservation Awards Program; founder U.S. Fed. Roger Preuss Waterfowl Prodn. Area, LeSueur County, Minn., 1997; former advisor Wildlife Forever Nat. Fish-Art Contest. Painter of nature art; one-man shows include: St. Paul Fine Art Galleries, 1959, Albert Lea Art Center, 1963, Hist. Soc. Mont., Helena, 1964, Brotherhood Fine Arts Ctr., 1965, Bicentennial exhbn., Le Sueur County Hist. Soc. Mus., Elysian, Minn., 1976, Merrill's Gallery of Fine Art, Taos, N.Mex., 1980; exhbns. include: Mpls. Inst. Art Msa exhibit, 1946, Midwest Wildlife Conf. Exhbn., Kerr's Beverly Hills, Calif., 1947, Laguna Art Mus., Calif., 1947, Joslyn Meml. Mus., Omaha, 1948, Hollywood Fine Arts Center, 1948, Minn. Centennial, 1949, Federated Chaparral Authors, 1951, Nat. Wildlife Art, 1951, 52, N.Am. Wildlife Art, dir. exposition, 1952, Ducks Unltd. Waterfowl exhibit, 1953, 54, St. Paul Winter Carnival, 1954, St. Paul Gallery Art Mart, 1954, Harris Fine Arts Center, Provo, Utah, 1969, Galerie Internationale, N.Y.C., 1972, Holy Land Conservation Fund, N.Y.C., 1976, Faribault Art Ctr., 1981, Wildlife Artists of the World Exhbn., Bend, Oreg., 1984, U. Art Mus., U. Minn., Mpls., 1990, Rochester Art Ctr., 1991, Minn. Hist. Soc.-Hill House, 1992, Bemidji Art Ctr., 1992, Jack London Ctr., Dawson City, Yukon Territory, Can., 1992, Weyerhaeuser Meml. Mus., Little Falls, Minn., 1995, Minn. Valley Nat. Wildlife Refuge Ctr., Bloomington, 1995, Sagebrush Artists Exhbn., Klamath Falls, Oreg., 1995; represented in permanent collections: Demarest Meml. Mus., Hackensack, N.J., Smithsonian Instn., N.Y. Jour. Commerce, Mont. Hist. Soc., Inland Bird Banding Assn., Minn. Capitol Bldg., Mont. State U., Wildlife Am. Collection, LeSueur Hist. Soc., Voyageurs Nat. Park Interpretive Ctr., Krause-Hartig VFW Post, Mpls., Nat. Wildlife Fedn. Collection, Minn. Ceremonial House, U.S. Wildlife Svc. Fed. Bldg., Fort Snelling, Minn., Crater Lake Nat. Park Visitors Ctr., VA Hosp., Mpls., Luxton Collection, Banff, Alta., Can., Internat. Inst. Arts, Geneva, Mont. Capitol Bldg., People of Century-Goldblatt Collection, Lyons, Ill., Harlem Savings Collection, N.Y.C., Weisman Art Mus., Mpls., Minn. Vets. Home, Mpls., Blauvelt Art Mus., Oradell, N.J., Roger Preuss Art Collection, Augustana Ctr. for Western Studies, Sioux Falls, S.D., Minn. Mus. Am. Art, St. Paul, U. Minn. Art Mus., C.M. Russell Mus., Great Falls, Mont., Le Sueur County Courthouse, Le Center, Minn., others, numerous galleries and pvt. collections; designer: Fed. Duck Stamp, U.S. Dept. Interior, 1949, Commemorative Centennial Pheasant Stamp, 1981, Gold Waterfowl medallion Franklin Mint, 1983, Gold Stamp medallion Wildlife Mint, 1983, 40th Anniversary Commemorative Fed. Duck Stamp etching, 1989; panelist: Sportsman's Roundtable, Sta. WTCN-TV, Mpls. (emeritus), from 1953; author: Is Wildlife Art Recognized Fine Art?, 1986; contbr.: Christmas Echos, 1955, Wing Shooting, Trap & Skeet, 1955, Along the Trout Stream, 1979; contbr. Art Impressions mag., Can., Wildlife Art, U.S.; also illustrations and articles in Nat. Wildlife and over 300 essays on North American animals, others.; assoc. editor emeritus: Out-of-Doors mag.; compiler and artist: Outdoor Horizons, 1957, Twilight over the Wilderness, 1972, 60 limited edition prints Wildlife of America, from 1970; contbr. paintings and text Minnesota Today; creator paintings and text Preuss Wildlife Calendar; inventor: paintings and text Wildlife Am. Calendar; featured artist Art West, 1980-84, Wildlife Art; featured in films Your BFA- Care and Maintenance, Black Ducks Along the Border. Del. Nat. Wildlife Conf.; bd. dirs. emeritus Voyageurs Nat. Park Assn., Deep-Portage Conservation Found.; bd. dirs. Wetlands for Wildlife U.S.A.; active Wildlife Am.; co-organizer, v.p., bd. dirs. Minn. Conservation Fedn., 1952-54; mem. U.S. Hospitalized Vets. Venison Program, 1957—; trustee Liberty Bell Edn. Found.; Waseca Arts Coun.; founder, dir. Roger Preuss Conservation Preserve for Study of Nature, 1990—. With USNR, World War II. Recipient Stamp Design award U.S. Fish and Wildlife Svc., 1994, Minn. Outdoor award, 1956, Patron of Conservation award, 1956, award for contbns. conservation Minn. Statehood Centennial Commn., 1958, 1st award Am. Indsl. Devel. Coun., citation of merit VFW, award of merit Mil. Order Cootie, 1963, merit award Minn. Waterfowl Assn., 1976, silver medal Nat. SAR, 1978, Svcs. to Arts and Environ. award Faribault Art Ctr., 1981, Ptnrs. for Wildlife award U.S. Fish and Wildlife Svc., 1994; named Wildlife Conservationist of the Yr., Sears Found.-Nat. Wildlife Fedn. program, 1966, Am. Bicentennial Wildlife Artist, Am. Heritage Assn., 1976; hon. mem. Ont. Chippewa Nation of Can., 1957; named Knight of Mark Twain for contbns. to Am. art Mark Twain Soc., 1978; named to Water, Woods and Wildlife Hall of Fame, named Dean of Wildfowl Artists, 1981, Hon. Ky. Col.; recipient hon. degree U.S. Vets. Venison program, 1980, Western Am. award significant contbns. to preservation arts and history No. Prairie Plains, Augustana Coll. Ctr. for Western Studies, Sioux Falls, S.D., 1992, Pub. Svc. award for outstanding contbns. to Am. conservation and environ. U.S. Dept. Interior, 1996; named creator first signed, numbered photolithographic print pub. in N.Am., 1959; documented Colorado Springs Fine Arts Ctr., 1993, colleague of Frederick R. Weisman Mus., Mpls., 1994; grantee NEH, 1995, Prairie Lakes Arts Coun., 1995. Fellow Internat. Inst. Arts (life), Soc. Animal Artists (emeritus), N.Am. Mycol. Assn., Nat. Wildlife Fedn. (nat. wildlife week chmn. Minn.), Minn. Ducks Unltd. (bd. dirs. emeritus), Minn. Artists Assn. (v.p., bd. dirs. 1953-59), Outdoor Writers Am. (emeritus), Soc. Artists and Art Dirs. (emeritus), Am. Artists Profl. League (emeritus), Mpls. Soc. Fine Arts, Wildlife Soc., Minn. Mycol. Soc. (pres. emeritus, hon. life mem.), Le Sueur County Hist. Soc. (hon. life mem.), Minn. Conservation Fedn. (hon. life), Wildlife Artists World (charter mem., emeritus internat. v.p., chmn. fine arts bd.), Internat. Platform Assn. (emeritus), Great Lakes Outdoor Writers (emeritus), The Prairie Chicken Soc. (patron), Mission Oceanic Arctic, 1992, Beaverbrook Club (hon. life), Minn. Press Club (emeritus), Explorers Club (N.Y.C., emeritus), Silver Lake Sports (hon.). Office: care Wildlife Am PO Box 580004-a Minneapolis MN 55458-0004

PREUSSER, JOSEPH WILLIAM, academic administrator; b. Petersburg, Nebr., June 18, 1941; s. Louis Henry and Elizabeth Sophia (Oberbrocking) P.; m. Therese Marie Mahoney, Aug. 12, 1967; children: Scott, Michelle, Denise. BA in Social Scis., Wayne State Coll., 1965; MA in Geography, U. Nebr., Omaha, 1971; PhD in Adminstrn., U. Nebr., 1978. Coord. social studies Lewis Ctrl. Cmty. Sch. Dist., Council Bluffs, Iowa, 1967-71; chmn. social sci. divsn., instr. Platte Jr. Coll., Columbus, Nebr., 1972-73; dean instrn./Platte campus Ctrl. C.C., 1973-82, v.p. ednl. planning cmty. edn., pres. Platte campus, 1982-84, pres. Grand Island, Nebr., 1984—. Mem. devel. com. Nebr. Tech. C.C., 1973-75, sec., dean instrn., 1974-76, chmn. pres.'s coun., 1990-91; mem. Archdiocese Omaha Bd. Edn., 1980-84; chmn. St. Bonaventure Bd. Edn., 1976-80; bd. dirs. Edgerton Edn. Found.; spkr. in field. Contbr. articles to profl. jours. Bd. dirs. Ctrl. Nebr. Goodwill Industries, Grand Island, 1987-95, treas., 1990-91, chmn. 1992; chmn. sustaining membership enrollment campaign Overland Trails Boy Scouts Am., 1990; mem. Columbus City Planning Commn., 1979-84, chmn., 1981, 82. With U.S. Army, 1959-61. Named one of Outstanding Young Mem of Am., 1976; recipient Nat. Leadership award U. Tex., 1988-89, Pres. of Yr. award Am. Assn. Women in Comm., 1996, award Nebr. Tech. C.C. Assn., Vision for Future award, 1999; named to Ctrl. Cath. H.S. Booster Club Hall of Fame, 1995. Mem. Am. Assn. Cmty. and Jr. Colls., Am. Voct. Assn., Nebr. Vocat. Assn. (Outstanding Svc. award 1986), Nebr. C.C. Assn. (coun. of pres. 1984—, pres. 1987, 93, 99), Rotary (Grand Island Noon Club bd. dirs. 1999-2000, pres. 1999, lt. gov. dist. 5630 1999—, Svc. award 1999), KC, Phi Delta Kappa. Democrat. Roman Catholic. Avocations: golfing, gardening, woodworking.

PRICE, CHARLES T. lawyer; b. Lansing, Mich., Feb. 11, 1944; BA, Ohio Wesleyan U., 1966; JD, Harvard U., 1969. Bar: Ohio 1969, U.S. Dist. Ct. (no. dist.) Ohio 1974, U.S. Ct. Appeals (6th cir) 1981, U.S. Supreme Ct. 1982, Ill. 1989. Former ptnr. Baker & Hostetler, Cleve.; pres., pub. Chgo. Sun-Times, 1987-88; exec. v.p. Sun-Times Co., 1989-92; ptnr. Foley & Lardner, Chgo., 2000—. Office: Foley & Lardner 330 N Wabash Ave Chicago IL 60611-3603

PRICE, CLARA SUE, state legislator; b. Sept. 10, 1953; m. Gary Price; 1 child. BA in Bus. Adminstrn., Minot State U., 1977. Mem. N.D. Ho. of Reps., 1991—, chmn. Rep. caucaus, 1993-94, vice chair human svcs. com., 1995, mem. transp. com., chmn. human svcs., 1997—. Employee benefit specialist BCBS of N.D., 1982-87; stockbroker INVEST, 1988-90; sec. Cal-Dak Cabinets, 1975—; owner, operator Dakota Gardens & Herbs, 1993—. Past mem. Minot Commn. Status of Women; bd. dirs. Trinity Health. Mem. Internat. Peace Garden, C. of C. Republican. Lutheran. Home: 3520 30th St NW Minot ND 58703-0312 Office: ND Ho of Reps State Capitol Bismarck ND 58505 E-mail: cprice@state.nd.us.

PRICE, DAVID CECIL LONG, physicist, researcher; b. London, Jan. 17, 1940; came to U.S., 1966; s. Cecil Long and Freda (Salusbury) P.; m. Marie-Louise Saboungi, Nov. 24, 1989; children: Morgan, Alkes. B.A., Cambridge U., 1961, M.A., 1962, Ph.D., 1966. Rsch. assoc. Brookhaven Nat. Lab., Upton, N.Y., 1966-68; mem. staff Argonne (Ill.) Nat. Lab., 1968—2002, dir. solid state sci. div., 1974-79, dir. intense pulsed neutron source program, 1979-81, sr. physicist, 1981—; dir. rsch. CRMHT, Orleans, France, 2001—. Vis. prof. Japanese Soc. Promotion Sci., 1977; disting. vis. prof.Grad. U. for Adv. Studies, Hayama, Japan, 2000; mem. panel research opportunities with low energy neutrons Nat. Acad. Scis., 1976-77; sr. sci. advisor physics panel Energy Research Adv. Bd., Dept. Energy, 1986-87. Editor: Neutron Scattering (Methods of Experimental Physics, vols. 23 A, B, C), 1986-87. Recipient U. Chgo. award for disting. performance at Argonne Nat. Lab., 1988, Warren prize Am. Cryst. Assn., 1997, Alexander von Humboldt Rsch. award, 1998. Fellow Am. Phys. Soc., Inst. Physics (U.K.). Home: 5492 S Everett Ave Chicago IL 60615-5918 Office: Argonne Nat Lab Argonne IL 60439

PRICE, HENRY ESCOE, broadcast executive; b. Jackson, Miss., Oct. 13, 1947; s. Henry E. Price Sr. and Alma Kate (Merrill) Noto; m. Maria Diane Harper, Apr. 8, 1972; children: Henry E. III, Norman Harper. BS in Radio, TV, Film, Journalism, U. So. Miss., 1972. Announcer, news dir. Sta. WROA Radio, Gulfport, Miss., 1967-69; comml. producer Sta. WJTV-TV, Jackson, 1969-73; prodn. mgr. Sta. WAAY-TV, Huntsville, Ala., 1973-77, Sta. WPEC-TV, West Palm Beach, Fla., 1977-79; dir. promotion Sta. WPTV-TV, Palm Beach, 1979-81; TV cons. Frank Magid Assoc., Marion, Iowa, 1981-83; dir. advt. and promotion Sta. WJLA-TV, Washington, 1983-84; v.p., dir. programming Sta. WUSA-TV, Gannett TV, 1984-88; pres., gen. mgr. Sta. WFMY-TV, Gannett TV, Greensboro, N.C., 1988-91, Sta. KARE-TV, Mpls., 1991-96; v.p., gen. mgr. Sta. WBBM-TV, CBS TV Stas., Chgo., 1996—. Pres. Carolina News Network, 1988-91; adj. faculty media mgmt. Ctr. Northwestern U., 2000—. Vice chair, bd. dirs. The Courage Ctr., Mpls.; regional dir. Nat. Conf.; mem. exec. com., bd. dirs. The Minn. Orch.; Pacesetter program chair Mpls. United Way Campaign; active Twin Cities Dunkers, Twin Cities Comm. Coun., 11 Who Care. Mem. Chgo. C. of C. (bd. dirs.), Ill. Broadcasters Assn. (bd. dirs.). Avocations: furniture design and constrn., reading, walking, bicycle riding. Home: PO Box 11847 Winston Salem NC 27116-1847 Office: Sta WBBM-TV CBS Television 630 N Mcclurg Ct Chicago IL 60611-4495

PRICE, HUBERT, state legislator; Rep. Mich. State Dist. 43, 1995—. Mem. Dem. Nat. Conv. 1983—. Address: PO Box 30014 Lansing MI 48909-7514

PRICE, JAMES TUCKER, lawyer; b. Springfield, Mo., June 22, 1955; s. Billy L. and Jeanne Adele Price; m. Francine Beth Warkow, June 8, 1980; children: Rachel Leah, Ashley Elizabeth. BJ, U. Mo., 1977; JD, Harvard U., 1980. Bar: Mo. 1980. Assoc. firm Spencer Fane Britt & Browne, Kansas City, 1980-86; ptnr. Spencer Fane Britt & Browne LLP, 1987—, chair environ. practice group, 1994—, mem. exec. com., 1997—. Mem. Brownfields Commn., Kansas City, 1999—; mem. steering com. Kansas City Bi-State Brownfields Initiative, 1997—. Contbr. to monographs, other legal publs. Mem. ABA (coun. sect. environ, energy and resources 1992-95, vice chmn. solid and hazardous waste com. 1985-90, chmn. 1990-92, chmn. brownfields task force 1995-97, vice chmn. environ. transactions and brownfield com. 1998-2000), Mo. Bar Assn., Kansas City Met. Bar Assn. (chmn. environ. law com. 1985-86), Greater Kansas City C. of C. (co-chair Brownfields Working Group, 1996-98, chmn. energy and environ. com. 1987-89). Office: Spencer Fane Britt & Browne LLP 1000 Walnut St Ste 1400 Kansas City MO 64106-2140 E-mail: jprice@spencerfane.com.

PRICE, JOSEPH MICHAEL, lawyer; b. St. Paul, Dec. 2, 1947; s. Leon and Rose (Kaufman) P.; m. Louise Rebecca Braunstein, Dec. 19, 1971; children: Lisa, Laurie, Julie. BA, U. Minn., 1969, JD, 1972. Bar: Minn. 1972, U.S. Dist. Ct. Minn. 1974. Ptnr. Faegre & Benson, Mpls., 1972—. Mem. Minn. Bar Assn., Hennepin County Bar Assn. Home: 4407 Country Club Rd Minneapolis MN 55424-1148 Office: Faegre & Benson 2200 Wells Fargo Ctr 90 S 7th St Ste 2200 Minneapolis MN 55402-3901 E-mail: jprice@faegre.com.

PRICE, LEONARD RUSSELL (LEN PRICE), state legislator; b. Sept. 21, 1942; m. Stephanie Wright; 3 children. BS, MS, U. Wis., River Falls. Mem. Minn. Ho. of Reps., St. Paul, 1982-90; vicechmn. gen. legis. com., vet. affairs com., gaming com.; mem. appropriations com., environ. and natural resource com.; mem. Minn. Senate from 57th dist., St. Paul, 1990—. Co-vice chmn. edn. com., mem. commerce and comsumer protection com., taxes com., others; tchr. Mem. NEA (life), Minn. Edn. Assn. Democrat. Home: 6264 Applewood Rd Woodbury MN 55125-1105 Office: Minn Senate State Capitol Saint Paul MN 55155-0001

PRICE, MARIAN L. state legislator; b. Page, Nebr., Aug. 6, 1938; children: Mark Reed Price, Penni Lou Price Godemann, Randall Joseph Price, Ronald Noble Price. Student, Wesleyan U., 1955-56; grad., Bryan Meml. Hosp. Sch., 1959. RN, Nebr. Formerly with Bryan Meml. Hosp.; former co-owner family restaurants, Lincoln, Nebr.; mem. Nebr. Legislature from 26th dist., 1998—. Bd. dirs. Home Health Svcs. for Independent Living, Inc., VITAL Inc. Mem. Lincoln Bd. Edn., 1985-98, pres., 1994-97, chair legis. subcom., 1997-98; chair Lancaster County Reorgn. Com., 1990-98; pres. Ednl. Svc. Unit No. 18, 1991-96; del. Nat. Sch. Bds. Assns. Fed. Rels. Network, 1989-98; mem. Bethany Christian Ch., Lincoln, past pres., mem. Christian women's fellowship, past ch. wedding coord.; past bd. dirs. Lincoln Cmty. Playhouse Guild. Mem. Bryan Meml. Sch. Nursing Alumnae Assn. (past bd. dirs.), Bethany Women's Club, Alpha Gamma Delta Alumnae Assn. (past bd. dirs.), Phi Sigma Alpha (past pres., bd. dirs.). Home: 6735 Lexington Cir Lincoln NE 68505-1338 Office: State Capitol Dist 26 PO Box 94604 Rm 1117 Lincoln NE 68509-4604

PRICE, PAUL L. lawyer; b. Chgo., Apr. 21, 1945; s. Walter S. and Lillian (Czerepkowski) L.; m. Dianne L. Olech, June 3, 1967; children: Kristen, Kathryn. BBA, Loyola U., Chgo., 1967; JD with honors, Ill. Inst. Tech., 1971. Bar: Ill. 1971, U.S. Dist. Ct. (no. dist.) Ill., U.S. Ct. Appeals (7th cir.). Tax acct. Arthur Anderson & Co., Chgo., 1970—71; assoc. Doyle & Tarpey, 1971—75, Gordon & Assocs., Chgo., 1975—76; from assoc. to ptnr. Pretzel & Stouffer, Chartered, 1976—96; ptnr. Price, Tunney, Reiter, 1996—. With USMC, 1969-70. Fellow: Am. Coll. Trial Lawyers; mem.: ABA, Ill. Inst. Tech.-Chgo. Kent Coll. Law Alumni Assn. (pres. 1989—90), Assn. Def. Trial Attys., Lawyers for Civil Justice (bd. dirs. 1999—2001), Def. Rsch. Inst. 1999—2001, Fedn. Def. and Corp. Counsel (pres. 1999—2000), Ill. Assn. Def. Trial Counsel 1990—91, Soc. Trial Lawyers, Ill. Bar Assn. Roman Catholic. Office: Price Tunney Reiter 200 N Lasalle St Ste 3050 Chicago IL 60601-1014

PRICE, ROBERT MCCOLLUM, computer company executive; b. New Bern, N.C., Sept. 26, 1930; B.S. in Math. magna cum laude, Duke U., 1952; M.S. in Applied Math., Ga. Inst. Tech., 1958. Research engr. Gen. Dynamics div. Convair, San Diego, 1954-56; research mathematician Ga. Inst. Tech., 1956-58; mathematician Standard Oil of Calif., San Francisco, 1958-61; with Control Data Corp., Mpls., from 1961, pres. systems and services, 1973-75, pres. systems, services and mktg., 1975-77; pres. Computer Co., Control Data Corp., 1977-80; pres., chief oper. officer Control Data Corp., 1980-86, pres., 1986-88, chmn., chief exec. officer, ret., from 1986, also dir. Office: DATALINK CORPORATION 8170 Upland Cir Chanhassen MN 55317-8589

PRICE, THEODORA HADZISTELIOU, individual and family therapist; b. Athens, Greece, Oct. 1, 1938; came to U.S. 1967; d. Ioannis and Evangelia (Emmanuel) Hadzisteliou; m. David C. Long Price, Dec. 26, 1966 (div. 1989); children: Morgan N., Alkes D.L. BA in History/Archaeology, U. Athens, 1961; DPhil, U. Oxford, Eng., 1966; MA in Clin. Social Work, U. Chgo., 1988; Diploma in Piano Teaching, Nat. Conservatory, Athens, 1958. Lic. clin. social worker; bd. cert. diplomate in clin. social work. Mus. asst. and resident tutor U. Sydney, Australia, 1966-67; instr. anthropology Adelphi U., N.Y.C., 1967-68; archaeologist Hebrew Union Coll., Gezer, Israel, 1968; asst. prof. classical archaeology/art U. Chgo., 1968-70; jr. rsch. fellow Harvard Ctr. Hellenic Studies, Washington, 1970-71; clin. social worker Harbor Light Ctr., Salvation Army, Chgo., 1988-89; therapist Inst. Motivational Devel., Lombard, Ill., 1989-90; caseworker Jewish Family & Community Svc., Chgo., 1989-90; staff therapist Family Svc. Ctrs. of South Cook County, Chicago Heights, 1990-91; pvt. practice child, adolescent, family therapy Bolingbrook, Ill., 1991—; dir. counseling svcs., clin. supr., psychotherapist The Family Link, Inc., Chgo., 1993; staff therapist Cen. Bapt. Family Svcs., Gracell Rehab., 1991, 91-92; casework supr., counselor Epilepsy Found. Greater Chgo., 1992-93; therapist children, adolescents and families dept. foster care Catholic Charities, 1993-94; individual and family therapist South Ctrl. Cmty. Svcs. Individual-Family Counseling Svcs., 1994-97. Lectr. in field; bd. mem., counselor Naperville Sch. for Gifted and Talented, 1982-84. Author: (monograph) Kourotrophos, Cults and Representations of the Greek Nursing Deities, 1978; contbr. articles to profl. jours. Meyerstein Traveling awardee, Oxford, Eng., 1963, 64; Eleutherios Venizelos scholar, 1962-65. Mem. NASW, Nat. Acad. Clin. Social Workers, Ill. Clin. Social Workers. Avocations: yoga, piano playing, dog training and therapy, hesychasm. Home and Office: 10 Pebble Ct Bolingbrook IL 60440-1557

PRICE, WILLIAM RAY, JR. state supreme court judge; b. Fairfield, Iowa, Jan. 30, 1952; s. William Ray and Evelyn Jean (Darnell) P.; m. Susan Marie Trainor, Jan. 4, 1975; children: Emily Margret, William Joseph Dodds. BA with distinction, U. Iowa, 1974; postgrad., Yale U., 1974-75; JD cum laude, Washington and Lee U., 1978. Bar: Mo. 1978, U.S. Dist. Ct. (we. dist.) Mo. 1978, U.S. Ct. Claims 1978, U.S. Ct. Appeals (8th cir.) 1985. Assoc. Lathrop & Norquist, Kansas City, Mo., 1978-84, ptnr., 1984-92, chmn. bus. litigation sect., 1987-88, 90-92, exec. com., 1989-92; judge Supreme Ct. Mo., Jefferson City, 1992—, chief justice, 1999—2001. G.L.V. Zumwalt monitoring com. U.S. Dist. Ct. (we. dist.) Mo., Kansas City. Pres. Kansas City Bd. Police Commrs.; mem. Together Ctr. & Family Devel. Ctr., Kansas City; chmn. merit selection com. U.S. marshal Western Dist. of Mo., Kansas City; bd. dirs. Truman Med. Ctr., Kansas City. Rockefeller fellow, 1974-75; Burks scholar Washington & Lee U., 1976. Mem. Christian Ch. Office: Supreme Ct Mo PO Box 150 207 W High St Jefferson City MO 65102-0150

PRICE, WILLIAM S. lawyer; b. Evanston, Ill., May 9, 1942; BSBA, Denver U., 1965; JD cum laude, Northwestern U., 1968. Bar: Ill. 1968. With Bell, Boyd & Lloyd, Chgo., 1968—. Mem. ABA, Nat. Assn. Bond Lawyers. Office: Bell Boyd & Lloyd Three First National Plz 70 W Madison St Ste 3300 Chicago IL 60602-4284

PRIDE, MIRIAM R. college president; b. Canton, China, June 6, 1948; d. Richard E. and Martha W. Pride; divorced. Grad., Berea College Found. Sch., 1966, College of Wooster, 1970; MBA, U. Ky., 1989. With sales room Boone Tavern Hotel Berea Coll., Berea, Ky., 1963-70; intern in administrn. in higher edn., head resident College of Wooster, Wooster, Ohio, 1970-72; accounts payable clerk, dir. Boone Tavern Hotel, head resident, dir. student activities Berea Coll., 1972-88; eligibility worker dept. human resources State of Ky., 1975-76; assistantship undergrad. advising coll. bus. U. Ky., 1987-89; asst. to pres. for campus life, v.p. for administrn., pres. Blackburn Coll., Carlinville, Ill., 1989—. Chmn. United Way Berea, Carlinville, 1989—92; fin. chmn. Carlinville Hosp., 1995—97; mem. Ill. Commn. on Status of Women; bd. dirs. Land of Lincoln Girl Scouts, 1993—2000, fin. chmn., 1995—2000, mem. nominating com., 2000—; bd. dirs. Carlinville Area Hosp., 1993—97, Assn. Presbyn. Colls. and Univs., Fedn. Ill. Colls. and Univs., 1993—, Federated Ch. Bd., 1998—2001. Mem. Carlinville C. of C. (bd. dirs.), Rotary (bd. dirs. 1996—). Mem. Federated Ch. Avocations: reading, walking, knitting. Office: Blackburn Coll Office of the President Carlinville IL 62626

PRIEVE, E. ARTHUR, arts administration educator; BBA in Adminstrn. and Art History, U. of Wis., 1959, MBA in Mgmt. and Orgn. Behavior, 1961; DBA in Mgmt. and Psych., George Washington U., Washington, 1965. Asst. dean adminstrv. affairs Sch. Bus. U. Wis., Madison, 1966-69, prof. mgmt. Grad. Sch. Bus., 1969—, dir. exec. MBA program, 1993—; dir. Ctr. For Arts Adminstrn., 1969—. Curriculum cons. for arts adminstrn.; cons. visual, performing and arts svc. orgns.; workshops and presentations on planning, bd. dirs. Mem. Assn. of Arts Adminstrn. Educators (chmn. U.S., Can.). Office: U Wis Ctr Arts Adminstrn 4171 Grainger Hall 975 University Ave Madison WI 53706-1324

PRIMM, EARL RUSSELL, III, publishing executive; b. Rhinelander, Wis., Oct. 24, 1958; s. Earl Russell and Betty Joan (Dennis) P. AB in Classics (hon.), Loyola U. Chgo., 1980; MA in Libr. Sci., U. Chgo., 1990. Asst. to edn. dir. J.G. Ferguson Pub. Co., Chgo., 1981-84; prodn. mgr. Joint Commn. on Accreditation of Hosps., 1984-85; sr. editor J.G. Ferguson Pub. Co., 1985-87; asst. editor U. Chgo. Press., 1987-88; editorial dir. J.G. Ferguson Pub. Co., Chgo., 1988-89; project mgr. Children's Press, 1989-92; exec. editor Franklin Watts, Inc., Chgo., N.Y.C., 1992-95; editl. dir.

Grolier Children's Pub., Danbury, Conn., 1995-97; pres. Editl. Directions, Inc., Chgo., 1997—. Mem. adv. bd. U. Chgo. Pub. Program, 1990-2000; judge Lambda Lit. awards, Washington, 1994-2000. Editorial chief: Career Discovery Encyclopedia, 1990; editor: Civil Rights Movement in America, 2nd edit., 1991, Extraordinary Hispanic Americans, 1991. Mem. crisis counselor Nat. Runaway Switchboard, Chgo., 1985-88; Horizon's hotline counselor, Chgo., 1987-88; bd. dirs. Gerber/Hart Libr. and Archives, Chgo., 1992-94. Named Honors Sr. of Yr., Loyola U. Chgo., 1980; recipient Mertz Latin Scholarship key Loyola U. Chgo., 1980. Mem. Pub. Triangle, Chgo. Book Clinic, Am. Libr. Assn. Democrat. Home and Office: 1000 W Washington Blvd #147 Chicago IL 60607-2148

PRINCE, ROBB LINCOLN, manufacturing company executive; b. Duluth, Minn., June 30, 1941; s. Milton H. and Katherine (Lincoln) P.; m. Jacqueline H. Marik, June 19, 1965; children: Daniel, Deborah. BA in Econs., Carleton Coll., 1963; MBA in Mktg., U. Pa., 1965. With mktg. planning United Airlines, Chgo., 1965-72; dir. planning Jostens Inc., Mpls., 1973-74, treas., 1975-79, v.p., treas., 1979-95, ret., 1995; dir. FORTIS Mut. Funds, Analysts Internat. Corp. Trustee Hamline U. With USN, 1966-69. Office: 5108 Duggan Plz Edina MN 55439-1453

PRINCE, THOMAS RICHARD, accountant, educator; b. New Albany, Miss., Dec. 7, 1934; s. James Thompson and Callie Florence (Howell) P.; m. Eleanor Carol Polkoff, July 14, 1962; children: Thomas Andrew, John Michael, Adrienne Carol. BS, Miss. State U., 1956, MS, 1957; PhD in Accountancy, U. Ill., 1962. CPA, Ill. Instr. U. Ill., 1960-62; mem. faculty Northwestern U. Kellogg Grad. Sch. Mgmt., 1962—, prof. acctg. info. and mgmt., 1969—, chmn. dept. acctg. info. and mgmt., 1968-75; prof. health industry mgmt. Northwestern U., 1980—; cons. in field. Dir. Applied Research Systems, Inc. Author: Extension of the Boundaries of Accounting Theory, 1962, Information Systems for Management Planning and Control, 3d edit, 1975, Financial Reporting and Cost Control for Health Care Entities, 1992, Product Life-Cycle Costing and Management of Large-Scale Medical Systems Investments, 1997, Strategic Management for Health Care Entities: Creative Frameworks for Financial and Operational Analysis, 1998. Served to 1st lt. AUS, 1957-60. Mem. Am. Accounting Assn., Am. Inst. C.P.A.s, Am. Econ. Assn., INFORMS, AHA, HFMA, HIMMS, AUPHA, Fin. Execs. Inst., AAAS, Ill. Soc. C.P.A.s, Inst. Mgmt. Acct., Alpha Tau Omega, Phi Kappa Phi, Omicron Delta Kappa, Delta Sigma Pi, Beta Alpha Psi. Congregationalist. Home: 303 Richmond Rd Kenilworth IL 60043-1138 Office: Northwestern U Leverone Hl Evanston IL 60208-0001 E-mail: t-prince@kellogg.northwestern.edu.

PRINCE, (PRINCE ROGERS NELSON), musician, actor; b. Mpls., June 7, 1958; s. John L. and Mattie D. (Shaw) Nelson; m. Mayte Garcia, 1996; 1 son (dec.). Singer, songwriter, actor. Albums include For You, 1978, Dirty Mind, 1979, Controversy, 1981, 1999, 1983, film star and soundtrack Purple Rain, 1984, Around the World in a Day, 1985 (Best Soul/Rhythm and Blues Album of the Yr., Downbeat readers poll, 1985), Parade, 1986, Chaos and Disorder, 1996, Sign O' the Times, 1987, Lovesexy, 1988, Batman: Motion Picture Soundtrack, 1989 (Soundtrack of Yr. award Playboy mag. readers' poll, Best Pop/Rock album Downbeat mag. readers' poll), (with the New Power Generation) Diamonds and Pearls, 1991, (symbol as title), 1992, Come, 1995; films include Purple Rain, 1984 (Acad. award for best original score 1985), film star and soundtrack Under the Cherry Moon, 1986, film star and soundtrack Sign O' the Times, 1987; film appearance and soundtrack Graffiti Bridge, 1990; formerly mem. group Prince and the Revolution (Best Soul/Rhythm and Blues Group of Yr. Downbeat mag. readers poll 1985); composer Show-girls, 1995, Girl 6, 1996, The Gold Experience, 1995, Crystal Ball, 1998, Rave Un2 the Joy Fantastic, 1999. Recipient 3 Grammy awards, 1985, Am. Music Achievement award for infuence on look and sound of the 80's, NAACP Spl. Achievement award, 1997; named Rhythm and Blues Musician of Yr. Down Beat mag. readers' poll, 1984, 1992. Office: Warner Bros Records 75 Rockefeller Plz New York NY 10019-6908

PRINGLE, BARBARA CARROLL, state legislator; b. N.Y.C., Apr. 4, 1939; d. Nicholas Robert and Anna Joan (Woloshinovich) Terlesky; m. Richard D. Pringle, Nov. 28, 1959; children: Christopher, Rhonda. Student, Cuyahoga C.C. With Dunn & Bradstreet, 1957-60; precinct committee-woman City of Cleve., 1976-77; elected mem. Cleve. City Coun., 1977-81; mem. Ohio Ho. of Reps., Columbus, 1982—. 20th dist. state ctrl. commetteewoman, 1982-92; asst. minority leader econ. devel. & small bus. com., pub. utilities com.; mem. Children & Family Svcs. com.; mem. Ohio Legis. Svc. Commn.; mem. Ohio Children's Trust Fund, Midwestern Legis. Conf. Coun. State Govts.' Com. Status Children. Vol. Cleve. Lupus Steering Com., various community orgns.; charter mem. Statue of Liberty Ellis Island Found. Recipient cert. of appreciation Cleve. Mcpl. Ct., 1977, Exch. Club Bklyn., 1978, Cmty. Recreation Appreciation award City of Cleve., 1978, Key to City of Cleve., 1979, Cleve. Area Soapbox Derby cert., 1976, 77, 81, cert. of appreciation Ward 9 Youth League, 1979-82, No. Ohio Patrolman's Benevolent Assn. award, 1983, Cuyahoga County Firefighters award, 1983, Outstanding Pub. Servant award for Outstanding Svc. to Hispanic Cmty., 1985, Nat. Sr. Citizen Hall of Fame award, 1987, cert. of appreciation Cleve. Coun. Unemployed Workers, 1987, Ohio Farmers Union award, 1990, award of appreciation United Labor Agy., 1993, Susan B. Anthony award, 1995. Mem. Nat. Order Women Legislators, Fedn. Dem. Women of Ohio, Nat. Alliance Czech Catholics, St. Michael Ch. Altar and Rosary Soc., Ward 15 Dem. Club, Polish Falcons. Democrat. Home: 708 Timothy Ln Cleveland OH 44109-3733

PRINGLE, LEWIS GORDON, marketing professional, educator; b. Lansing, Mich., Feb. 13, 1941; s. Gordon Henry and Lucile Roxana (Drake) P.; children: Lewis Gordon Jr., William Davis, Thomas Benjamin. B.A., Harvard U., 1963; M.S., M.I.T., 1965, Ph.D., 1969. Vice pres., dir. mktg. sci. BBDO, Inc., N.Y.C., 1968-73; asst. prof. mktg. Carnegie-Melon U., Pitts., 1973-74; exec. v.p., dir. rsch. svcs., corp. dir. BBDO, Inc., N.Y.C., 1978-91; exec. v.p. BBDO Worldwide, 1986-91; chmn., CEO BBDO Europe, 1986-91, LG Pringle and Assocs., 1992-95; Joseph C. Seibert prof. of mktg. Farmer Sch. Bus. Adminstrn., Miami U., Oxford, Ohio, 1995—. Bd. dirs. Yorktown U., prof. Author numerous articles in field. Active local Boy Scouts Am. Ford Found. fellow, 1967 Fellow Royal Statis. Soc.; mem. Market Rsch. Coun., Am. Psychol. Assn., European Soc. Mktg. and Opinion Rsch., Am. Mktg. Assn., Inst. Ops. Rsch. and Mgmt. Sci. Office: Silver Creek Farm 2858 N Stout Rd Liberty IN 47353

PRINGLE, ORAN ALLAN, mechanical and aerospace engineering educator; b. Lawrence, Kan., Sept. 14, 1923; s. Oran Allan and Mae (McClell) P.; m. Billie Hansen, June 25, 1947; children— Allan, Billie, James, Rebecca. B.S. in Mech. Engring. U. Kan., 1947; M.S., U. Wis., 1948, Ph.D., 1967. Registered profl. engr., Mo. Mech. engr. Black and Veatch (cons. engrs.), Kansas City, Mo., 1947-48; engr. Boeing Airplane Co., Wichita, 1952—; prof. U. Mo., Columbia, 1948—. Co-author: Engineering Metallurgy, 1957; contbr. articles to profl. lit. Bd. dirs. United Cerebral Palsy Boone County, Mo. Served with AUS, 1943-45. Ford Found. grantee. Mem. Am. Soc. M.E. (chmn. fastening and joining com., design engring. div.), Sigma Xi. Home: 1820 University Ave Columbia MO 65201-6004 Office: Dept Mech and Aerospace Engring U Mo Columbia MO 65201

PRINZ, RICHARD ALLEN, surgeon; MD, Loyola U., Chgo., 1972. Diplomate Am. Bd. Surgery, bd. dirs., 1994—. Intern Barnes Hosp., St. Louis, 1972-73, resident in surgery, 1973-74, Loyola U., Chgo., 1974-77, attending surgeon, 1980-93; staff Rush Presbyn.-St. Luke's Med. Ctr., 1993—; Helen Shedd Keith prof., chmn. dept. gen. surgery Rush U., 1993—. Mem. Am. Surg. Assn., Am. Assn. Endocrine Surgeons (pres. 1996), Midwest Surg. Assn. (pres. 1997), Western Surg. Assn. (treas. 1993-97). Office: Rush Presbyn/St Luke Med Ct 818 Professional Bldg 1725 W Harrison St Chicago IL 60612-3828 E-mail: rprinz@rush.edu.

PRIOR, DAVID JAMES, college dean; b. Anniston, Ala., Dec. 13, 1943; m. Merry Lucille; children: Andrea Suzanne, Christopher Sutton. AB, Olivet (Mich.) Coll., 1965; MS, Ctrl. Mich. U., 1968; PhD, U. Va., 1972. Postdoctoral fellow-neurobiology Princeton (N.J.) U., 1972-73; asst. prof. biolg. scis. U. Ky., Lexington, 1973-78, prof. biology, 1985-87, assoc. prof. physiology and biophysics, 1984-87, prof. physiology and biophysics Coll. Medicine, 1987; prof., chair biology No. Ariz. U., Flagstaff, 1987-92, dean Coll. Arts and Scis., 1992—. Office: U Wisconsin-Whitewater Office of Provost 800 W Main St. Whitewater WI 53190

PRIOR, GARY L. lawyer; b. Niagara Falls, N.Y., June 26, 1943; s. Harold D. and Adeline Thelma (Lee) P.; m. Nancy O'Shaughnessy, Aug. 23, 1975; children: Joseph Lee, Julia Elizabeth. BS, Tulane U., 1965; JD, U. Chgo., 1968. Bar: Ill. 1968, U.S. Dist. Ct. (no. dist.) Ill. 1968, U.S. Ct. Appeals (7th cir.) 1973, U.S. Ct. Appeals (3rd cir.) 1974, U.S. Trial Bar 1983, U.S. Supreme Ct. 1989, U.S. Dist. Ct. (we. dist.) Wis. 1992, U.S. Dist. Ct. (ea. dist.) Wis. 1993. Assoc. Rooks, Pitts & Poust, Chgo., 1968-71, McDermott, Will & Emery, Chgo., 1971-74, ptnr., 1974—, dir. trial dept. tng., 1980-85, mem. securities approval com., 1986—, mem. nominating com., chmn., 1988-89, partnership com., 1989-92, mem. mgmt. com., 1991-93. Mem. Phi Delta Phi. Avocations: farming, sports, family. Home: 2512 N Burling St Chicago IL 60614-2510 Office: McDermott Will & Emery 227 W Monroe St Ste 3100 Chicago IL 60606-5096

PRITCHETT, KELVIN, professional football player; b. Atlanta, Oct. 24, 1969; Student, U. Miss. Football player Detroit Lions, 1991-94, 99—. Jacksonville (Fla.) Jaguars, 1995-98. Office: Detroit Lions 1200 Featherstone Rd Pontiac MI 48342 also: Detroit Lions, Inc. 222 Republic Drive Allen Park MI 48101

PRITIKIN, DAVID T. lawyer; b. Freeport, Ill., May 2, 1949; BA summa cum laude, Cornell U., 1971; JD magna cum laude, Harvard U., 1974. Bar: Ill. 1974, U.S. Ct. Appeals (9th cir.) 1975, U.S. Ct. Appeals (7th cir.) 1976, U.S. Supreme Ct. 1977, U.S. Ct. Appeals (fed. cir.) 1993. Ptnr. Sidley & Austin, Chgo.

PRITZKER, ROBERT ALAN, manufacturing company executive; b. Chgo., June 30, 1926; s. Abram Nicholas and Fanny (Doppelt) P.; m. Mayari Sargent; children: James, Linda, Karen, Matthew , Liesel. B.S. in Indsl. Engring., Ill. Inst. Tech., Chgo., 1946; postgrad. in bus. adminstrn., U. Ill. Engaged in mfg., 1946—; chief exec. officer, pres., dir. Marmon Corp., Chgo., Marmon Indsl. Corp., Chgo.; pres., dir. The Colson Group, Inc.; pres., CEO Marmon Holdings, Inc., Marmon Industries, Inc., Chgo. Bd. dirs. Hyatt Corp., Chgo., Dalfort Corp., Union Tank Car Co.; vis. prof. Oxford U.; chmn. Nat. Assn. Mfrs. Chmn. bd. Pritzker Found., Chgo.; trustee, chmn. Ill. Inst. Tech., Chgo. Symphony Orch.; immediate past chmn. Field Mus. of Natural History; bd. dirs. Rush-Presbyn.-St. Luke's Med. Ctr. Mem. NAE, Nat. Assn. Mfrs. (former chmn.). Office: Marmon Group Inc 225 W Washington St Ste 1900 Chicago IL 60606

PRITZKER, THOMAS JAY, hotel business executive; b. Chgo., June 6, 1950; s. Jay Arthur and Marian (Friend) P.; m. Margot Lyn Barrow-Sicree, Sept. 4, 1977; children— Jason, Benjamin, David. BA, MBA, Claremont Men's Coll, 1976; JD, U. Chgo., 1976. Assoc. Katten, Muchin, Zavis, Pearl and Galler, Chgo., 1976-77; exec. v.p. Hyatt Corp., 1977-80, pres., 1980—; chmn. Hyatt Corp., Hyatt Internat. Corp., 1999—, Hyatt Hotels Corp., 1980—; ptnr. Pritzker & Pritzker, Chgo., 1980—. Pres., chmn. bd. dirs. The Pritzker Orgn., 1998; bd. dirs. First Health Group, Royal Caribbean Cruises Ltd. Trustee Art Inst. Chgo. 1988—, U. Chgo. Mem. ABA, Ill. Bar Assn., Chgo. Bar Assn., Standard Club, Lake Shore Country Club. Clubs: Standard (Chgo.); Lake Shore Country (Glencoe, Ill.). Office: Hyatt Corp 200 W Madison St38th Flr Chicago IL 60606

PROCHNOW, DOUGLAS LEE, lawyer; b. Omaha, Jan. 9, 1952; s. Albert Delmer and Betty Jean (Wood) P. BA with high distinction, U. Nebr., 1974; JD, Northwestern U., 1977. Bar: Ill. 1977, U.S. Dist. Ct. (no. dist.) Ill. 1977, U.S. Ct. Appeals (7th cir.) 1989, U.S. Supreme Ct. 2000. Assoc. Wildman, Harrold, Allen & Dixon, Chgo., 1977-84, ptnr., 1985—. Spl. asst. corp. counsel City of Chgo., 1986—87. Bd. dirs. Chgo. chpt. Prevent Child Abuse Am. Mem. ABA, ATLA (assoc.), Ill. Bar Assn., Chgo. Bar Assn., Soc. Trial Lawyers, Def. Rsch. Inst., Am. Health Lawyers Assn., Phi Beta Kappa, Phi Eta Sigma. Home: 1230 N State Pky Apt 6D Chicago IL 60610-2261 Office: Wildman Harrold Allen & Dixon 225 W Wacker Dr Chicago IL 60606-1224 E-mail: prochnow@wildmanharrold.com.

PROCTOR, BARBARA GARDNER, advertising agency executive, writer; b. Asheville, N.C. d. William and Bernice (Baxter) Gardner; m. Carl L. Proctor, July 20, 1961 (div. Nov. 1963); 1 son, Morgan Eugene. BA, Talladega Coll., 1954. Music critic, contbg. editor Down Beat Mag., Chgo., 1958—; internat. dir. Vee Jay Records, 1961-64; copy supr. Post-Keyes-Gardner Advt., Inc., 1965-68, Gene Taylor Assos., Chgo., 1968-69, North Advt. Agt., Chgo., 1969-70; contbr. to gen. periodicals, 1952—; founder Proctor & Gardner Advt., Chgo., 1970—, pres., CEO. Pres., CEO Proctor Comm. Network, Chgo. Mem. Chgo. Urban League, Chgo. Econ. Devel. Corp.; cons. pub. rels. and promotion, record industry. Author: (TV documentary) Blues for a Gardenia, 1963. Bd. dirs. People United to Save Humanity, Better Bus. Bur. Recipient Armstrong Creative Writing award, 1954; awards Chgo. Fedn. Advt., Frederick Douglas Humanitarian award, 1975; named Chgo. Advt. Woman of Yr., 1974. Mem. NARAS, Chgo. Media Women, Women's Advt. Club, N.Y. Art Dirs. Club, Woman's Day Club, Cosmopolitan C. of C. (dir.), Female Execs. Assn., Internat. Platform Assn., Smithsonian Instn. Assos.

PROFFER, ELLENDEA CATHERINE, publisher, author; b. Phila., Nov. 24, 1944; d. Joseph and Helen (Jardine) McEnness; m. Carl Ray Proffer, Oct. 1967. B.A., U. Md., 1966; M.A., Ind. U., 1968, Ph.D., 1971. Asst. prof. Slavic Wayne State U., Detroit, 1970-71; assoc. prof. humanities U. Mich., Dearborn, 1972-73; co-founder, 1971; since pres., owner Ardis Pubs., Ann Arbor. Author: The Early Plays of Mikhail Bulgakov, 1971, The Silver Age of Russian Culture, 1975; novel Double Wedding, 1982; Bulgakov, 1984; editor: Ardis Anthology of Recent Russian Literature, 1975, Ardis Anthology of New American Poetry, 1977, Tsvetaeva: A Photo Biography, 1980, Russian Literature Triquar, 1971— , Regency Miss (novel), 1978; co-editor: Ardis Anthology of Russian Futurism, 1980, Contemporary Russian Prose, 1982. NDEA fellow, 1968-69 Mem. Am. Assn. Advancement Slavic Studies, P.E.N.

PROFFITT, KEVIN, archivist; b. Hamilton, Ohio, Dec. 24, 1956; s. Henry C. and Marjorie O. (Elam) P.; m. Joan Moriarity, May 17, 1986. BA, Miami U., Oxford, Ohio, 1979; MA, Wright State U., 1980; MLS, U. Ky., 1998. Archivist Am. Jewish Archives, Cin., 1981—. Contbr. articles to profl. jours. Mem. Soc. Am. Archivists, Acad. Cert. Archivists (cert.), Midwest Archives Conf., Soc. Ohio Archivists (pres. 1987-89). Office: Am Jewish Archives 3101 Clifton Ave Cincinnati OH 45220-2404

PROFIT, KIRK A. former state legislator; b. Mt. Pleasant, Mich., Sept. 12, 1952; s. Lewis Edwin and Maxine (Merritt) P.; m. Sharon Grace Langen; children: Jennifer, Kristine, Kirk. BS, Ea. Mich. U.; JD, U. Detroit; DSc (hon.), Cleary Coll. Bar: Mich. Pvt. practice law, 1979-80; legal adv., undersheriff Washington County Sheriff's Dept., Mich., 1981-84; rep. Mich. Dist. 54, 1989-98; account exec. Govt. Cons. Svcs., Inc., Lansing, Mich., 1998—. Chmn. higher edn. com. Mich. Ho. Reps., ethics & oversight com., judiciary com., taxation com., bus. com., fin. com. Mem. Dem. Leadership Coun. Named legis. of yr. Police Officers Assn. Mich., 1991, Mich. Assn. Chiefs of Police, 1993; recipient disting. svc. award Ind. Colls. and Univs. Mich., 1994. Mem. Sierra Club, Optimists Internat. Home: 205 Valley Dr Ypsilanti MI 48197-4460 Office: Govt Cons Svcs Inc 530 W Ionia St Lansing MI 48933-1062

PROSSER, DAVID THOMAS, JR. judge, retired state legislator; b. Chgo., Dec. 24, 1942; s. David Thomas, Sr. and Elizabeth Averell (Patterson) Prosser. BA, DePauw U., 1965; JD, U. Wis., 1968. Bar: Wis. 1968. Lectr. Ind. U., Indpls., 1968-69; advisor U.S. Dept. Justice, Washington, 1969-72; adminstrv. asst. to U.S. Rep. Harold V. Froehlich, 1973-74; pvt. practice, 1975, Appleton, Wis., 1976; dist. atty. Outagamie County, 1977-78; state rep. State of Wis., Madison, 1979-96; commr. Tax Appeals Commn., 1997-98; justice Supreme Ct. Wis., 1998—. Commr. Nat. Conf. Commrs. Uniform State Laws, 1982—96; mem. Wis. Sesquecentennial Commn., Madison, 1993—99; minority leader Wis. Assembly, 1989—94, spkr., 1995—96. Mem.: Outagamie Bar Assn., Milw. Bar Assn., Dane Bar Assn., Wis. Bar Assn. Presbyterian. Avocation: art collector of American prints. Home: 2904 N Meade St Appleton WI 54911-1561 Office: Supreme Ct Wis PO Box 1688 Madison WI 53701-1688 E-mail: david.prosser@courts.state.wi.us.

PROSSER, FRANKLIN PIERCE, computer scientist; b. Atlanta, July 4, 1935; s. Edward Theron and Eunice (McDaniel) P.; m. Brenda Mary Lau, June 16, 1960; children: Edward, Andrea. B.S., Ga. Inst. Tech., 1956, M.S., 1958; Ph.D., Pa. State U., 1961. Prof. computer sci. Ind. U., Bloomington, 1969-99; asso. dir. Wrubel Computing Center, 1969-81, chmn. dept. computer sci., 1971-77, 87-93, spl. asst. for acad. computing, 1979-81; v.p. Logic Design, Inc., 1982-92. Cons. Lockheed Theoretical Physics Lab., Palo Alto, Calif., 1967 Home: 1200 S Longwood Dr Bloomington IN 47401-6072 Office: Ind U Dept Computer Sci Bloomington IN 47405

PROST, DONALD, former state legislator; Mem. Mo. State Ho. of Reps. Dist. 162, 1993-97; dir. joint com. on legis. rsch. State of Mo., 1997—. Office: Rm 117-A Mo State Capitol Jefferson City MO 65101

PROVUS, BARBARA LEE, executive search consultant; b. Washington, Nov. 20, 1949; d. Severn and Birdell (Eck) P.; m. Frederick W. Wackerle, Mar. 29, 1985. Student, NYU, 1969-70; BA in Sociology, Russell Sage Coll., 1971; MS in Indsl. Rels., Loyola U., Chgo., 1978; postgrad., Smith Coll., 1971. Sec. Booz, Allen & Hamilton, Chgo., 1973-74, mgr. tng., 1974-77, dir. rsch., 1977-79, cons. search, 1979-80; mgr. mgmt. devel. Federated Dept. Stores, Cin., 1980-82; v.p. Lamalie Assocs., Chgo., 1982-86; prin., founder Sweeney, Shepherd, Bueschel, Provus, Harbert & Mummert, Inc., 1986-91; founder Shepherd Bueschel & Provus Inc., 1992—. Bd. dirs. Anti-Cruelty Soc., Chgo., 1990—, pres., 1996-97; trustee Sage Colls., Troy, N.Y., 1999-2000. Mem. Assn. Exec. Search Cons. (dir. 1989-92), The Chgo. Network (bd. dirs. 1993—, chair 2000--), Econ. Club Chgo. Avocations: collecting rubber bands, modern art, baseball. Home: 3750 N Lake Shore Dr Chicago IL 60613-4238 Office: Shepherd Bueschel & Provus Inc 401 N Michigan Ave Ste 3020 Chicago IL 60611-4257

PRUGH, WILLIAM BYRON, lawyer; b. Kansas City, Mo., Jan. 3, 1945; s. Byron E. and Helen Prugh; m. Linda Stuart, Aug. 12, 1968; 1 child, K. Niccole. BA, U. Mo., Kansas City, 1966, JD, 1969, LLM in Taxation, 1971. Bar: Mo. 1969, U.S. Tax Ct. 1975, U.S. Supreme Ct. 1975, Kans. 1982. Assoc. Shughart Thomson & Kilroy, P.C., Kansas City, 1969—. Author, editor: Missouri Corporation Law and Practice, 1985, Missouri Taxation Law and Practice, 1987, 3d edit., 1996. Mem. ABA, Mo. Bar (chmn. taxation com. 1988-90, chmn. computer tech. com. 1989-91), Kansas City Met. Bar Assn. (chmn. tax com. 1989-90, chmn. computer law com. 1989-91, Pres. award 1988). Republican. Methodist. Office: Shughart Thomson & Kilroy 12 Wyandotte Plz 120 W 12th St Fl 18 Kansas City MO 64105-1902

PRUSI, MICHAEL, state legislator; Attended, No. Mich. U., Lansing. Rep. Mich. State Dist. 109, 1995—. Address: PO Box 30014 Lansing MI 48909-7514

PRUSSING, LAUREL LUNT, state official, economist; b. N.Y.C., Feb. 21, 1941; d. Richard Valentine and Maria (Rinaldi) Lunt; m. John Edward Prussing, May 29, 1965; children: Heidi Elizabeth, Erica Stephanie, Victoria Nicole Johanna. AB, Wellesley Coll., 1962; MA, Boston U., 1964; postgrad., U. Calif., San Diego, 1968-69, U. Ill., 1970-76. Economist Arthur D. Little, Cambridge, Mass., 1963-67, U. Ill., Urbana, 1971-72; mem. county bd. Champaign County, 1972-76, county auditor, 1976-92. Mem. local audit adv. bd. Office Ill. Compt., Chgo., 1984-92. Contbr. to Illinois Local Government: A Handbook, 1990. Founding mem. Citizens Forum on Gambling and Campaign Fin. Reform, 1999; downstate program dir. Citizen Action/Ill., 1999; lobbyist AAUW, Ill., Inc., 2001; state rep. 103d dist. Ill. Gen. Assembly, 1993—95; Dem. nominee Ill. 15th dist. U.S. Congress, 1996—98. Named Best Freshman Legislator Ind. Voters Ill., 1994; recipient Friend of Agriculture award Ill. Farm Bur., 1994; named to Legis. Honor Roll Ill. Environ. Coun., 1994. Mem. LWV, Govt. Fin. Officers Assn., U.S. and Can. (com. on acctg., auditing and fin. reporting 1980-88, Fin. Reporting award 1981-91, Disting. Budget award 1986), Nat. Assn. Local Govt. Auditors (charter), Ill. Assn. County Auditors (pres. 1984-85). Democrat. Home: 2106 Grange Dr Urbana IL 61801-6609

PRYCE, DEBORAH D. congresswoman; b. Warren, Ohio, July 29, 1951; BA cum laude, Ohio State U., 1973; JD with honors, Capital U., 1976. Bar: Ohio 1976. Former asst. city prosecutor, asst. city atty., first asst. city prosecutor, Columbus, Ohio; former judge Franklin County Mcpl. Ct.; mem. U.S. Congress from 15th Ohio dist., Washington, 1993—; mem. rules com. Republican. Presbyterian. Avocation: skiing.*

PRYOR, CHUCK, state legislator; m. Louella Pryor; children: Dustin, Ryan, Devon. Rep. dist. 116 State of Mo., Versailles, 1993—. Mem. agriculture com., commerce com., judiciary com., rules, joint rules, bills perfected and printed com., transp. com., tourism, recreation and cultural affairs com., iterim com. on agriculture, iterim joint com. on asset forfeitures, drug seizure and asset forfeiture com., joint com. on transp. oversight com. Chmn. bd. Versailles Christ. Ch.; bd. govs. Capitol Region Med. Ctr. Office: 410 Newton Rm 109-h Versailles MO 65084

PTAK, FRANK STANLEY, manufacturing executive; b. Chgo., Apr. 23, 1943; s. Frank J. and Stella R. (Los) P.; m. Karen M. Novoselsky, May 2, 1971; children: Jeffrey B., Jacquelyn F., Russell E. BSc, De Paul U., 1965. CPA, Ill. Sr. auditor Arthur Young & Co., Chgo., 1965-69; sr. rsch. cons. Kemper Fin. Svcs., 1969-71; asst. sec., mgr. acquisitions Sara Lee Corp., 1971-73, asst. treas., 1973-74, asst. to chmn., 1974, v.p. planning, 1974-75; bus. devel. mgr. ITW Conex, Des Plaines, Ill., 1975-77; mktg. mgr. ITW Shakeproof, Elgin, 1977-78, group pres., 1977-78, ITW Metal Components Cos., Glenview, 1978-91; exec. v.p. Global Automotive Components ITW Corp., 1991-95, vice-chmn., 1996—. Bd. dirs. Heller Fin., Kemper Ins., Snap-On Inc.; adv. coun. DePaul U. Coll. Commerce, Chgo., 1998. Patentee in field. Mem. AICPA, Assn. Corp. Growth, ITW Patent Soc. Jewish. Home: 849 Edgewood Ct Highland Park IL 60035-3714 Office: Illinois Tool Works 3600 W Lake Ave Glenview IL 60025-5811 E-mail: fptak@itw.com.

PUCKETT, C. LIN, plastic surgeon, educator; b. Burlington, N.C., Oct. 19, 1940; s. Harry W. and Lula C. Puckett; m. Florence Elizabeth Loy, June 18, 1961 (div. 1976); children: Loy C., Lisa A., Leslie A.; m. Patricia Louise Wells, June 17, 1984 (div. 1994); 1 child, Harry James; m. Teresa G. Teel, Nov. 24, 1995. MD, Bowman Gray Sch. Medicine, 1966. Assoc. in surgery Duke U. Med. Ctr., Durham, N.C., 1971-73; assoc. prof., head divsn. plastic surgery U. Mo. Med. Ctr., Columbia, 1976-81; prof., head attending plastic surgeon U. Mo. Med. Ctr., Truman VA Hosp., 1982—. Editl. bd. (jour.) Jour. Plastic & Reconstructive Surgery, 1994—2000; contbr. articles. Fellow: ACS (gov. 1992-98); mem.: Assn. Acad. Chmn. Plastic Surgery 9bd. dirs. 1985-, pres. 1987-88), So. Med. Assn., Plastic Surgery Rsch. Coun., Mo. Chpt. ACS, Internat. Microsurg. Soc., Am. Trauma Soc., Am. Soc. Surgery of the Hand, Am. Bd. Plastic Surgery (cert., bd. dirs. 1988-94, chmn. 1993-94), Am. Soc. Plastic Surgeons, Inc. (bd. dirs. 1985-, asst. sect. 1988, trustee 1990, chmn. 1992, parliamentarian 1993, various to pres. 1999), Am. Cleft Palate Assn., Am. Assn. Plastic Surgeons (trustee 1995), Am. Assn. hand Surgery 9bd. dirs. 1982-84, chmn. nominating com. 1985, v.p. 1987, pres.-elect 1988, pres. 1988-89), AMA, Alpha Omega Alpha, Sigma Xi. Republican. Avocation: breeding Quarter horses, Angus cattle. Office: U Mo Divsn Plastic Surgery 1 Hospital Dr Columbia MO 65212-0001 E-mail: puckettc@health.Missouri.edu.

PUCKETT, KIRBY, professional baseball team executive, former player; b. Chgo., Mar. 14, 1961; s. Catherine Puckett; m. Tonya Hudson; children: Catherine, Kirby, Jr. Student, Bradley U., Ill., Triton Coll. Baseball player Minnesota Twins, Mpls., 1982-96, exec. v.p., 1996—. Author: I Love This Game!, 1993, Be The Best You Can Be, 1993. Founder, benefactor Kirby Puckett Eight-Ball Invitational to benefit Children's Heart Fund, United Way. Recipient All-Star Most Valuable Player award, 1993, Gold Glove award, 1986-89, 1991-92, Silver Slugger award, 1986-89, 92, 94, All-Star team, 1986-94; named to Sporting News All-Star Team, 1986-89, 92, 94, Am. League All-Star Team, 1986-89, Am. League Batting Champion, 1989, Minn. Twins Most Valuable Player 1985, 86, 88, 89, 92; named Calif. League Player of the Yr., 1983, Most Valuable Player, Am. League Championship Series, 1991, Best Hitter and Most Exciting Player, Baseball America, 1992; inducted Triton Coll. Hall of Fame, 1993. Mem. Alexis de Tocqueville Soc. Achievements include: led Major League in hits 1988-92, highest batting average among active batters 1988-92, seasons with 200 or more hits: 1986-89, 92. Office: Minnesota Twins Hubert H Humphrey Metrodome 34 Kirby Puckett Pl Minneapolis MN 55415-1596

PUCKO, DIANE BOWLES, public relations executive; b. Wyndotte, Mich., Aug. 15, 1940; d. Mervin Arthur and Bernice Letitia (Shelly) Bowles; m. Raymond J. Pucko, May 22, 1965; children: Todd Anthony, Gregory Bowles. BA in Sociology, Bucknell U., Lewisburg, Pa., 1962. Accredited in pub. rels. Asst. to pub. rels. dir. Edward C. Michener Assocs., Inc., Harrisburg, Pa., 1962-65; advt./pub. rels. coord. Superior Switchboard & Devices, Canton, Ohio, 1965-66; editorial dir. women's svc. Hutchins Advt. Co., Inc., Rochester, N.Y., 1966-71; pres. Editorial Communications, Rochester and Elyria, Ohio, 1971-77; mgr. advt. and sales promotion Tappan Air Conditioning, Elyria, 1977-80; mgr. pub. affairs Kaiser Permanente Med. Care Program, Cleve., 1980-85; corp. dir. pub. affairs Keystone Health Plans, Inc., Camp Hill, Pa., 1985-86; v.p., dir. client planning Young-Liggett-Stashower, Cleve., 1986; v.p., dir. pub. rels. Marcus Pub. Rels., 1987-91; sr. v.p. Proconsul, 1991-95, also bd. dirs.; sr. ptnr. pub. rels. Poppe Tyson, 1995-96; managing dir. Bozell Pub. Rels., 1996-97; sr. counsel Pub. Rels. Ptnrs., Inc., 1997—. Mgr., role model Women in Mgmt. Field Placement program, Cleve. State U., 1983-92; pub. rels. adv. bd. profl. adviser, Pub. Rels. Student Soc. Am., Kent State U., 1988—. Bd. trustees, mem. exec. com., chmn. pub. rels. adv. com. Ronald MacDonald House of Cleve., 1993—; bd. dirs., chmn. pub. rels. com. Assn. Retarded Citizens, Cleve., 1987-91; mem. pub. rels.-mktg. com. Beech Brook, 1996—; mem. journalism comm. adv. bd. Elon Coll., 1998—. Recipient Woman Profl. Excellence award YMCA, 1984, MacEachern award Acad. Hosp. Pub. Rels., 1985, Bell Ringer award Cmty. Rels. Report, 1985, Bronze Quill Excellence award Internat. Assn. Bus. Communicators, 1992, 93, Cleve. Comms. award Women in Comms. Internat., 1993, 95, Tower award Bus./Profl. Advt. Assn., 1993, 95, Creativity in Pub. Rels. award, 1994, Silver Screen award U.S. Internat. Film & Video Festival, 1995, Silver Quill Excellence award Internat. Assn. Bus. Communicators, 1995, Internat. Assn. Bus. Communicators. Fellow Pub. Rels. Soc. Am. (bd. dirs. 1983-85, 86-94, officer 1991-95, mem. counselors acad. 1986—, Silver Anvil award 1985, Mktg./Consumer Rels. award East Ctrl. dist. 1992, 95, Lighthouse award 1995); mem. Press Club Cleve. (bd. dirs. 1989-96, v.p. 1990-96), Cleve. Advt. Club, Women's City Club Cleve., Nat. Agri-Mktg. Assn. (Nat. Merit award 2000). Republican. Methodist. Avocation: soccer. Home: 656 University Ave Elyria OH 44035-7278 Office: 6100 Rockside Woods Blvd Cleveland OH 44131-2366

PUFFER, RICHARD JUDSON, retired college chancellor; b. Chgo., Aug. 20, 1931; s. Noble Judson and Lillian Katherine (Olson) P.; m. Alison Foster Cope, June 28, 1952; children— Lynn, Mark, Andrew. Ph.B., Ill. Wesleyan U., 1953; M.S. in Edn, Ill. State U., 1962; PhD (Roy Clark Meml. scholar), Northwestern U., 1967. Asst. plant supt. J.A. Olson Co., Winona, Miss., 1957-59; tchr. Leroy Community Unit Dist. (Ill.), 1959-60; tchr., prin. Community Unit, Dist. 7, Lexington, Ill., 1960-62; asst. county supt. schs. Cook County, 1962-65; dean arts and scis. Kirkwood Community Coll., Cedar Rapids, Iowa, 1967-69; v.p. Black Hawk Coll., Moline, Ill., 1969-77, pres., 1977-82, chancellor, 1982-87; pres. The Ark Computer Ctr., 1989-92. Dir. W. Ctrl. Ill. Ednl. TV Corp., Springfield, Ill., 1977-87; cons. examiner North Central Assn., 1978-87. Editor: Cook County Ednl. Digest, 1962-65. Bd. dirs. Cedar Rapids Symphony, 1967-69, United Way of Rock Island and Scott Counties, Ill., 1978-80, Unitarian Universalist Dist. of Mich., 1995-98; bd. dirs., sec. West Shore Unitarian Universalist Congregation, 1996-99; sec., treas. Ill. Ednl. Retirement Cts., 1987-91; vice-chmn. Illini Hosp. Bd., 1988-93, chmn., 1993-95; bd. dirs. Illowa coun. Boy Scouts Am., 1979-83, v.p., 1981-83. With USNR, 1953-57. Mem. Rotary (pres. 1975-76, East Moline, Ill.), Green Medallion, Blue Key, Phi Delta Kappa, Pi Gamma Mu. Home and Office: 6191 Grace Ave Ludington MI 49431-8629

PUGH, COY, state legislator; b. Chgo., Feb. 27, 1952; s. Willie James and Martha (Nelson) P.; m. Laura L. Williams; children: Courtney, Leshawn. BA, Northeastern Ill. U., 1992. Adminstrv. asst. to State Rep. Ill. Ho. of Reps., 1984-86; owner Wescor Contracting, 1991-93; mem. Ill. Ho. of Reps., 1993—. Democrat. Home: 1748 N Mason Ave # 2 Chicago IL 60639-4011 Office: Mem Ho of Reps State Capitol Springfield IL 62706-0001

PUGH, DAVID L. manufacturing executive; b. Lynchburg, Va. m. Barbara Pugh; 2 children. BSEE, Duke U. Former chief mktg. officer, v.p. and gen. mgr. power equipment bus. unit Square D Co.; former plant mgr., v.p. constrn. sales Westinghouse Electric Corp.; former sr. v.p. Rockwell Automation, 1994-99; pres., COO Applied Indsl. Techs., Cleve., 1999-2000, pres., CEO, chmn. bd. dirs., 2000—. Office: Applied Indsl Techs 1 Applied Plz Cleveland OH 44115

PUGH, EDWARD W. state legislator; Atty.; mem. from dist. 61 Kans. State Ho. of Reps., Topeka, 1994-97; mem. Kans. Senate from 1st dist., 1998—. Address: 16705 Mil Trail Rd Wamego KS 66547

PUGH, RODERICK WELLINGTON, psychologist, educator; b. Richmond, Ky., June 1, 1919; s. George Wilmer and Lena Bernetta (White) P.; m. Harriet Elizabeth Rogers, Aug. 29, 1953 (div. 1955). BA, Fisk U., 1940; MA, Ohio State U., 1941; PhD, U. Chgo., 1949. Diplomate: Am. Bd. Profl. Psychology. Instr. Albany (Ga.) State Coll., 1941-43; psychology trainee VA, Chgo., 1947-49; lectr. Roosevelt U., 1951-54; staff clin. psychologist VA Hosp., Hines, Ill., 1950-54, asst. chief psychologist for psychotherapy, 1954-58, chief clin. psychology sect., 1958-60, supervising psychologist, coord. psychol. internship tng., 1960-66; pvt. practice clin. psychology Chgo., 1958—; assoc. prof. psychology Loyola U., 1966-73, prof., 1973-88, emeritus prof. psychology, 1989—. Cons. St. Mary of the Lake Sem., Niles, Ill., 1965-66, Ill. Div. Vocational Rehab., 1965-82, Center for Inner City Studies, Northeastern State U., Chgo., 1966-67, VA Psychology Tng. Program, 1966— , Am. Psychol. Assn. and Nat. Inst. Mental Health Vis. Psychologists Program, 1966-89; juvenile problems research rev. com. NIMH, 1970-74; cons. Center for Minority Group Mental Health Programs, 1975-77, cons. psychology edn. br., 1978-82; lectr. U. Ibadan, Nigeria, 1978; Mem. profl. adv. com. Div. Mental Health, City of Chgo., 1979-82; mem. adv. com. U.S. Army Command and Gen. Staff Coll., 1981-83 Author: Psychology and the Black Experience, 1972; Contbr.: chpt. in Black Psychology, 1972; Cons. editor: Contemporary Psychology, 1975-79; contbr. articles to profl. jours. Sec. bd. trustees Fisk U., 1968-78. Served to 2d lt. AUS, 1943-46, ETO. Vis. scholar Fisk U., 1966, vis. prof. in psychology, 1994. Fellow Am. Psychol. Soc., Am. Psychol. Assn. (nat. adv. panel to Civilian Health and Med. Program of Uniformed Services 1980-83, joint coun. on profl. edn. in psychology 1988-90); mem. Midwestern Psychol. Assn., Ill. Psychol. Assn. (chmn. legis. com. 1961, council mem. 1960-62, Disting. Psychologist award 1988, Outstanding Contbn. to Profession of Psychology award 2001), Soc. for Psychol. Study Social Issues, Assn. Behavior Analysis, AAUP, Sigma Xi, Alpha Phi Alpha, Psi Chi. Home: 5201 S Cornell Ave Chicago IL 60615-4207 Office: Loyola U 6525 N Sheridan Rd Chicago IL 60626-5344 E-mail: 72752.47@compuserve.com.

PUGH, THOMAS WILFRED, lawyer; b. St. Paul, Aug. 3, 1949; s. Thomas Leslie and Joann Marie (Tauer) P.; m. Susan Elizabeth Beattie, Sept. 12, 1971; children: Aimee Elizabeth, Douglas Thomas. AB cum laude, Dartmouth Coll., 1971; JD cum laude, U. Minn., 1976. Assoc. Thuet & Lynch, South St. Paul, 1976-79; ptnr. Thuet, Lynch & Pugh, 1980-85; atty., pres. Thuet, Pugh & Rogosheske, Ltd., 1986—; mem. Minn. Ho. of Reps., St. Paul, 1989—; Ho. dem. leader, 1999—. Mem. Supreme Ct. Task Force Conciliation Ct., St. Paul, 1992, Dakota County Tech. Coll. Adv. Bd., 1991—. Bd. dirs. Wakota Arena, South St. Paul, 1984-87; pres. Luther Meml. Ch., South St. Paul, 1983-84. Daniel Webster scholar Dartmouth Coll., 1970, Rufus Choate scholar, 1971. Mem. Minn. State Bar Assn., 1st Dist. Bar Assn., Ducks Unltd., Pheasants Forever, South St. Paul C. of C. (local issues chair 1982, Dedicated Svc. award 1983), South St. Paul Jaycees (pres. 1978-79, Key award 1979), Lions. Lutheran. Avocations: tennis, golf, hunting, fishing, reading. Office: Thuet Pugh & Rogosheske 222 Grand Ave South Saint Paul MN 55075-2237

PULIDO, JOSE S. physician; b. Apr. 29, 1956; BA with hons., U. Chgo., 1976, MS, 1977; MD, Tulane U., New Orleans, 1981; MBA, U. Iowa, 1993. Diplomate Am. Bd. Ophthalmology. Intern Tulane Affil. Hosps.-Charity Hosp., New Orleans, 1981-82; resident in ophthalmology U. Ill., Chgo., 1982-85, chief resident in ophthalmology, 1985-86; fellow vitreo-retinal surgery Bascome Palmer Eye Inst./U. Miami Sch. Medicine, 1986-87, fellow retina rsch., 1987; fellow ocular oncology Wills Eye Hosp./Thomas Jefferson U. Sch. Medicine, Phila., 1998; head and prof. dept. ophthalmology and visual scis. U. Ill., Chgo., 1998—. Instr. organic chemistry U. Chgo., 1976-77; asst. prof. ophthalmology Coll. of Medicine, U. Iowa, Iowa City, 1987-92, assoc. prof., 1992-97, prof. 1997-98, others. Reviewer numerous jours., including: Archives of Ophthalmology, 1985—, Ophthalmology, 1987—, Am. Jour. of Ophthalmology, 1992—, others; abstract editor: Diabetes 2000 Newsletter, 1992—, Ophthalmology World News, 1994-96, others; editor: Evidence-Based Eye Care, 1998—; contbr. articles to profl. jours. Mem. Am. Diabetes Assn. (del.), Am. Acad. Ophthalmology, Pan-Am. Acad. Ophthalmology, Retina Soc., Vitreous Soc., Fluorescein Reading and Macular Evaluation, Assn. for Rsch. in Vision and Ophthalmology, Am. Coll. Surgeons, Schepens Internat. Soc., Am. Ophthal. Soc., Macula Soc. Office: U Ill Chgo Eye Ctr 1855 W Taylor St Chicago IL 60612-7242

PULITZER, MICHAEL EDGAR, publishing executive; b. St. Louis, Feb. 23, 1930; s. Joseph and Elizabeth (Edgar) P.; m. Cecille Stell Eisenbeis, Apr. 28, 1970; children: Michael Edgar, Elizabeth E. Voges, Robert S., Frederick D., Catherine D. Culver, Christina H. Eisenbeis, Mark C. Eisenbeis, William H. Eisenbeis. Grad., St. Mark's Sch., Southborough, Mass., 1947; AB, Harvard U., 1951, LLB, 1954. Bar: Mass. 1954. Assoc. Warner, Stackpole, Stetson & Bradlee, Boston, 1954-56; reporter Louisville Courier Jour., 1956-60; reporter, news editor, asst. mng. editor St. Louis Post-Dispatch, 1960-71, assoc. editor, 1978-79; pub. Ariz. Daily Star, Tucson, 1971—; pres. chief operating officer Pulitzer Pub. Co. (and subs.), 1979-84, vice chmn., 1984-86, pres., 1986-99, also bd. dirs., CEO, 1988-99, chmn., 1993-99, Pulitzer Inc., 1999. Trustee St. Louis U., 1989—. Clubs: St. Louis Country; Mountain Oyster (Tucson). Office: Pulitzer Pub Co 900 N Tucker Blvd Saint Louis MO 63101-1069

PULLEN, PENNY LYNNE, non-profit administrator, former state legislator; b. Buffalo, Mar. 2, 1947; d. John William and Alice Nettie (McConkey) P. BA in Speech, U. Ill., 1969. Tv technician Office Instnl. Resources, U. Ill., 1966-68; cmty. newspaper reporter Des Plaines (Ill.) Pub. Co., 1967-72; legis. asst. to Ill. legislators, 1968-77; mem. Ill. Ho. of Reps., 1977-93, chmn. ho. exec. com., 1981-82, minority whip, 1983-87, asst. minority leader, 1987-93; pres., founder Life Advocacy Resource Project, Arlington Heights, Ill., 1992—. Exec. dir. Ill. Family Inst., 1993-94; dir. Legal Svcs. Corp., 1989-93; mem. Pres.'s Commn. on AIDS Epidemic, 1987-88; mem. Ill. Goodwill Del. to Republic of China, 1987. Summit conf. observer as mem. adhoc Women for SDI, Geneva, 1985; mem. Nat. Coun. Ednl. Rsch., 1983—88; dir. Eagle Forum of Ill., 1999—; Del. Rep. Nat. Conv., 1984; mem. Rep. Nat. Com., 1984—88; Del. Atlantic Alliance Young Polit. Leaders, Brussels, 1977; pres. Maine Twp. Rep. Women's Club, 1997—99, Rep. Women of Park Ridge, 2001—. Recipient George Washington Honor medal Freedoms Found., 1978, Dwight Eisenhower Freedom medal Chgo. Captive Nations Com., 1977, Outstanding Legislator awards Ill. Press Assn., Ill. Podiatry Soc., Ill. Coroners Assn., Ill. County Clks. Assn., Ill. Hosp. Assn., Ill. Health Care Assn.; named Ill. Young Republican, 1968, Outstanding Young Person, Park Ridge Jaycees, 1981, One of 10 Outstanding Young Persons, Ill. Jaycees, 1981. Mem. DAR, Am. Legis. Exch. Coun. (dir. 1977-91, exec. com. 1978-83, 2d vice chmn. 1980-83), Com. on the Status of Women (sec. 1997—).

PULTE, WILLIAM J. construction executive; Chmn. Pulte Homes Corp., 1950—. Office: Pulte Homes Corp 33 Bloomfield Hills Pkwy Bloomfield Hills MI 48304-2946

PUMPER, ROBERT WILLIAM, microbiologist, educator; b. Clinton, Iowa, Sept. 12, 1921; s. William R. and Kathrine M. (Anderson) P.; m. Ruth J. Larkin, June 24, 1951; 1 son. Mark. B.A., U. Iowa, 1951, M.S., 1953, Ph.D., 1955. Diplomate: Am. Soc. Microbiology. Asst. prof. Hahnemann Med. Coll., Phila., 1955-57; prof. microbiology U. Ill. Med. Sch., Chgo., 1957-92, prof. emeritus, 1992—, Raymond B. Allen Med. lectr., 1970, 74, 76, 87. Co-author: Essentials of Medical Virology; contbr. articles to profl. jours. Served with USAAF, 1942-46. Recipient Chancellors' award U. Ill., Bombeck award for excellence in med. edn., 1992. Mem. Tissue Culture Assn., Sigma Xi, Phi Rho Sigma. Lutheran. Home: 18417 Argyle Ave Homewood IL 60430-3007 Office: U Ill Med Sch Dept Microbiology 808 S Wood St Chicago IL 60612-7300

PUNDMANN, ED JOHN , JR. automotive company executive; b. St. Charles, Mo., Feb. 24, 1939; s. Ed J. Sr. and Ruth O. (Brehme) P.; m. Dolores Anne Lienau, June 15, 1963 (dec.); children: Mary Ann, Steven A., Susan K. BA, Westminster Coll., 1961. Jr. accountant Peat, Marwick & Mitchell, St. Louis, 1961-62; salesman Pundmann Ford, St. Charles, 1962-82, gen. mgr., 1982-92, pres., 1992—. Bd. dirs., chmn. First State Bank; bd. dirs. Mut. Fire Ins., St. Charles; mem. St. Charles City Tax Incremental Financing Commn., 1990-99; mem. Ford Motor Dispute Settlement Bd., 1993-94. Treas. St. Charles City Charter Commn., 1981; mem. St. Charles City Park Bd., 1981-82; chmn. St. Charles City Econ. Devel. Commn.; mem. St. Charles City Park Found. Bd., 1985—, also past pres.; St. Louis Regional Commerce and Growth Assn.; adv. bd. St. Charles County; mem. Handicapped Facilities Bd. St. Charles County, 1986-94, also past pres.; active St. Charles County Road Bd., 1996—; past pres. St. John United Ch. of Christ; bd. dirs. Emmaus Homes, 1981-91, Parkside Meadows Retirement Facility, 1982-2000, bd. dirs, 2001-; chmn. St. Charles City Charter Rev. Commn., 1991; bd. dirs. St. Charles Jaycee Village Retirement Home, 1980-90, Boone Ctr. Workshop, 1982-92, bd. dirs., 2001-; dist. chmn. Boy Scouts Am., 1979-82. Recipient Gov. of Mo. award, 1989, Mo. Time Quality Dealer award, 1995, United Ch. of Christ award, 1993, Jefferson award TV Sta. KSDK, St. Louis, 1996. Mem. Mo. Auto Dealers Assn. (bd. dirs. 1983—, treas. 1997-98, 2d v.p. 1998-99, 1st v.p. 1999-2000, pres. 2000-2001), Greater St. Louis Ford Dealers Assn. (past pres.), St. Charles C. of C. (past bd. dirs., pres., Citizen of Yr. award 1986, Small Bus. Person of Yr. 2002), Rotary (past pres.). Lodge: Rotary. Home: 3304 Lennox Dr Saint Charles MO 63301-0632 Office: Pundmann Ford 2727 W Clay St Saint Charles MO 63301-2566 E-mail: pundmann@nothnbut.net.

PUOTINEN, ARTHUR EDWIN, college president, clergyman; b. Crystal Falls, Mich., Sept. 7, 1941; s. Kaleva Weikko and Ines Pauline (Maki) P.; m. Judith Cathleen Kapoun, Aug. 8, 1964; children: Anne, Marjetta, Sara. AA, Suomi Coll., 1961; BA, Augustana Coll., Rock Island, Ill., 1963; MDiv, Luth. Sch. Theology, Chgo., 1967; MA, U. Chgo., 1969, PhD, 1973; MBA, Wake Forest U., 1984. Pastor Trinity Luth. Ch., Chgo., 1968-70; asst. prof. religion Cen. Mich. U., Mt. Pleasant, 1971-74; dean faculty Suomi Coll., Hancock, Mich., 1974-78; v.p. acad. affairs Lenoir-Rhyne Coll., Hickory, N.C., 1978-83; assoc. dean acad. affairs Roanoke Coll., Salem, Va., 1983-84; exec. dir. Luth. Ednl. Conf. of N.Am., Washington, 1984-88; pres. Grand View Coll., Des Moines, 1988-96; v.p., provost Finlandia U., Hancock, Mich., 1996—. Pastor ELCA No. Great Lakes Synod, Evang.-Luth. Ch. Am. Author: Finnish Radicals..., 1979; contbr. articles to books and jours. Grantee NEH, U.S. Dept. Edn. Democrat. Avocations: jogging, reading, travel. Home: 1404 Sugar Maple Ln Houghton MI 49931-2709 Office: Suomi Coll 600 Quincy St Hancock MI 49930-1806 E-mail: puotinin@mail.portup.com., apuotinen@accisd.k12.mi.us.

PURCELL, JAMES FRANCIS, former utility executive, consultant; b. Miles City, Mont., May 13, 1920; s. Robert E. and Mary A. (Hickey) P.; m. Dorothy Marie Abel, Nov. 4, 1944; children— Angela, Ann, Alicia, Anita, Alanna, James Francis, Andrea, Adria, Michael, Gregory, Amara. A.B. magna cum laude, U. Notre Dame, 1942; MBA, Harvard U., 1943. With McGraw-Hill Pub. Co., N.Y.C., 1946-48; dir. public relations Am. Maize Products Co., 1948-51; public relations cons. Selvage & Lee, Chgo., 1951-53; with No. Ind. Public Service Co., Hammond, 1953—, v.p. public relations, 1961-75, sr. v.p., 1975-84, bd. dirs., chmn. environ. and consumer affairs com.; owner, pres. James F. Purcell and Assocs., 1984—. Chmn. bd. govs. Our Lady of Mercy Hosp., Dyer, Ind., 1979-83; past chmn. Hammond Community Chest drive; past mem. nat. president's council St. Mary's (Ind.) Coll.; bd. dirs. Catholic Charities, 1965-85; chmn. bd. dirs. Bishop Noll Found., 1988-90. Served to lt. USNR, 1943-46. Named Man of Year Notre Dame U., 1967 Mem. Pub. Rels. Soc. Am. (past pres. Hoosier chpt.), N.W. Ind. Assn. Commerce and Industry (v.p., dir. 1979-83), Newcomen Soc. N. Am., Briar Ridge Country Club (Schererville), Serra Club (past pres. Calumet region), Notre Dame Club, Harvard U. Bus. Sch. Club of Chgo. Office: 2842 45th St Highland IN 46322-2905

PURDES, ALICE MARIE, retired adult education educator; b. St. Louis, Jan. 8, 1931; d. Joseph Louis and Angeline Cecilia (Mozier) P. AA, Belleville Area Coll., 1951; BS, Ill. State U., Normal, 1953, MS, 1954; cert., Sorbonne U., Paris, 1964; PhD, Fla. State U., Tallahassee, 1976. Cert. in music edn., elem. edn., secondary edn., adult edn. Tchg. and grad. asst. Ill. State U., 1953-54; music supr. Princeton (Ill.) Pub. Schs., 1954-55; music dir. Venice (Ill.) Pub. Schs., 1955-72, secondary vocal music dir., 1955-72; coord. literacy program Venice-Lincoln Tech. Ctr., 1983-86, chmn. lang. arts dept., 1983-96; ret., 1996. Tchr. in space candidate, 1985. Mem. St. Louis chpt. World Affairs Coun., UN Assn., Nat. Mus. of Women in the Arts, Humane Soc. of Am.; charter mem. St. Louis Sci. Ctr., Harry S. Truman Inst.; contbr. Old Six Mile Mus., 1981, Midland Repertory Players, Alton, Ill., 1991; chair Cystic Fibrosis Spring Bike-A-Thon, Madison, Ill., 1981, Granite City, Ill., 1985. Named to Ill. Sr. Hall of Fame, 2001; recipient gold medal, Nat. Senior Olympics, 1989, Senior World Games, 1992, Generations of Success Alumni award, Belleville Area Coll., 1998, gold medal, Nat. Sr. Olympics, 1989, Sr. World Games, 1992, several scholarships, Generations of Success Alumni award, Belleville Area Coll., 1998. Mem.: AAUW, Am. Fedn. Tchrs. (pres. 1957—58), Ill. Adult and Continuing Educators Assn., Am. Choral Dirs. Assn., Ill. Music Educators Assn. (Svc. award 2002), Music Educators Nat. Conf., Ill. State U. Alumni Assn., Slavic and East European Friends (life), Fla. State Alumni Assn., Lovejoy Libr. Friends, Nat. Space Soc., Western Cath. Union, Croation Fraternal Union, St. Louis Numis. Assn., Friends St. Louis Art Mus., Archaeol. Inst. Am., Travelers Abroad 1966—68, 1989—, Madison Rotary Club (internat. amb., Humanitarian award 1975). Roman Catholic. Avocations: bowling, travel. Home: PO Box 274 Madison IL 62060-0274

PURDOM, PAUL WALTON, JR. computer scientist; b. Atlanta, Apr. 5, 1940; s. Paul Walton and Bettie (Miller) P.; m. Donna Armstrong; children: Barbara, Linda, Paul B.S., Calif. Inst. Tech., 1961, M.S., 1962, Ph.D., 1966. Asst. prof. computer sci. U. Wis.-Madison, 1965-70, asst. prof., 1970-71; mem. tech. staff Bell Telephone Labs., Naperville, Ill., 1970-71; assoc. prof., chmn. computer sci. dept. Ind. U., Bloomington, 1977-82, prof. computer sci., 1982—. Grant researcher FAW, Ulm, Germany. Author: (with Cynthia Brown) The Analysis of Algorithms; assoc. editor: Computer Surveys; contbr. articles to profl. jours. NSF grantee, 1979, 81, 83, 92, 94. Mem. AAAS, Soc. for Indsl. and Applied Math., Assn. Computing Machinery, Sigma Xi. Democrat. Methodist Home: 2212 S Belhaven Ct Bloomington IN 47401-6803 Office: Ind U Dept Computer Science 215 Lindley Hall Bloomington IN 47405-4101 Business E-Mail: pwp@cs.indiana.edu.

PURDY, JAMES AARON, medical physics educator; b. Tyler, Tex., July 16, 1941; s. Walter Bethel and Florence (Hardy) P.; m. Marilyn Janette Coers, Jan. 29, 1965; children: Katherine, Laura. BS, Lamar U., 1967; MA, U. Tex., 1968, PhD, 1971. Asst. rsch. scientist U. Tex., Austin, 1969-71; rsch. asst. M.D. Anderson Hosp. and Tumor Inst., Houston, 1968-69, fellow in med. physics, 1972-73; instr. physics Sch. of Medicine, Washington U., St. Louis, 1973-76, asst. prof., 1976-79, assoc. prof., 1976-83, chief physics sect., 1976—, prof., 1983—, assoc. dir. Radiation Oncology Ctr., 1987—. Mem. NIH Radiaton Study sect. Divsn. Rsch. Grantes, 1991-95; Landauer lectr., Oakland, Calif., 1991. Editor: Three Dimensional Treatment Planning, 1991, Advances in Radiation Oncology, 1992, 3D Radiation Treatment Planning and Conformal Therapy, 1995, A Practical Guide to 3D Planning and Conformal Radiation Therapy, 1999, 3-D Conformal and Intensity Modulated Radiation Therapy: Physics and Clinical Applications, 2001; sr. physics editor: Jour. Radiation Oncology,

Biology, and Physics, 1996—. With USMC, 1961-64. Recipient William D. Coolidge award, 1997. Fellow Am. Assn. Physicists in Medicine (pres. 1985, Coolidge award 1997), Am. Coll. Radiology, Am. Coll. Med. Physics (chmn. bd. chancellors 1990, Marvin M.D. Williams award 1996); mem. Am. Inst. Physics, Am. Bd. Med. Physics (vice chmn. 1988-92), Am. Bd. Radiology, Am. Soc. Therapeutic Radiology and Oncology (ASTRO Gold medal 2000). Methodist. Avocation: travel. Home: 1452 Lost Hollow Ct Chesterfield MO 63005-4423 Office: Washington Univ Sch of Medicine 510 S Kingshighway Blvd Saint Louis MO 63110-1016

PURDY, JOHN EDGAR, manufacturing company executive; b. Detroit, June 17, 1919; s. William Everett and May Adeline (Fountain) P.; m. Elizabeth Anne Van Dyne; 1 child, Vannessa Anne. Grad. h.s., Mich. Founder, chmn. Dayton (Ohio) Showcase Co., 1947-87; pres. P-38 Nat. Assn., ret., 1987—. Capt. USAF, 1942-46. Decorated DFC with 2 oak leaf clusters, Purple Heart, Air medal with 6 oak leaf clusters. Mem. Am. Fighter Aces Assn. (pres. 1983-84), Am. Fighter Aces Mus. Found. (chmn. 1984-91), Nat. Aviation Hall of Fame (trustee 1978-86), Nat. Aviation Hall of Fame (bd. dirs. bd. of nominations), P-38 Nat. Assn. (pres. 1999-2001), Internat. Fighter Pilots Mus. Found. (trustee 1999—). Avocations: golf, aviation historian. Home: 6441 Far Hills Ave Dayton OH 45459-2725

PURI, MADAN LAL, mathematics educator; b. Sialkot, Feb. 20, 1929; came to U.S., 1957, naturalized, 1973; s. Ganesh Das and S. W. P.; m. Uma Kapur, Aug. 24, 1962; 3 children. B.A., Punjab U., India, 1948, M.A., 1950, D.Sc., 1975; Ph.D., U. Calif. at Berkeley, 1962. Head dept. math. D.A.V. Coll., Punjab U., 1955-57; instr. U. Colo., 1957-58; teaching asst., research asst., jr. research statistician U. Calif. at Berkeley, 1958-62; asst. prof., asso. prof. math. Courant Inst., N.Y. U., 1962-68; vis. asso. prof. U. N.C., summers 1966-67; prof. math. Ind. U., Bloomington, 1968—. Guest prof. stats. U. Gottingen, West Germany, 1972, Alexander von Humboldt guest prof., 1974-75; guest prof. U. Dortmund, West Germany, 1972, Technische Hochschule Aachen, West Germany, 1973, U. Goteborg, Chalmers U. Tech., both Sweden, 1974; vis. prof. U. Auckland, N.Z., 1977, U. Calif., Irvine, 1978, U. Wash., Seattle, 1978-79, U. Bern (Switzerland), 1982, Va. Poly. Inst., 1988; disting. visitor London Sch. Econs. and Polit. Sci., 1991; vis. prof. U. Göttingen, Germany, 1991, June-July 1992; rsch. fellow Katholieke U., Nijmegen, The Netherlands, 1992; vis. prof. U. Des Scis. et Tech. de Lille, France, 1994, U. Basel, Switzerland, 1995—, U. New South Wales, Australia, 1996; vis. univ. fellow Australian Nat. U., Canberra, Australia, 1999; guest prof. U. Konstanz, Germany, 2000, U. Gottingen, 2001. Co-author: Non Parametric Methods in Multivariate Analysis, 1971, Non Parametric Methods in General Linear Models, 1985. Editor Statochastic Process and Related Topics, 1975, Statistical Inference and Related Topics, 1975, Non Parametric Techniques in Statistical Inference, 1970; co-editor: Nonparametric Statistical Inference, Vols. I and II, 1982, New Perspectives in Theoretical and Applied Statistics, 1987, Mathematical Statistics and Probability Theory, Vol. A, 1987, Statistical Sciences and Data Analysis, 1993, Recent Advances in Statistics and Probability, 1994, Asymptotics in Statistics and Probability, 2000. Recipient Sr. U.S. Scientist award, Humboldt Preis, 1974-75, 83, 2001, Rsch. award Humboldt Found., U. Göttingen, 2001. Fellow Royal Statis. Soc., Inst. Math. Statistics, Am. Statis. Assn.; mem. Math. Assn. Am., Internat. Statis. Inst., Bernoulli Soc. Math. Stats. and Probability. Office: Ind U Dept Math Rawles Hall Bloomington IN 47405

PURKERSON, MABEL LOUISE, physician, physiologist, educator; b. Goldville, S.C., Apr. 3, 1931; d. James Clifton and Louise (Smith) P. AB, Erskine Coll., 1951; MD, U. S.C., Charleston, 1956. Diplomate Am. Bd. Pediat. Instr. pediat. Washington U. Sch. Medicine, St. Louis, 1961-67, instr. medicine, 1966-67, asst. prof. pediat., 1967-98, asst. prof. medicine, 1967-76, assoc. prof. medicine, 1976-89, prof., 1989-98, prof. emerita, 1998—, assoc. dean curriculum, 1976-94, assoc. dean acad. projects, 1994-98. Cons. in field. Editl. bd. Am. Jour. Kidney Diseases, 1981-87; contbr. articles to profl. jours. Trustee, mem. bd. counselors Erskine Coll., 1971—; trustee St. Louis Symphony Orch., Erskine Coll., 2000—. USPHS spl. fellow, 1971-72. Mem. Am. Heart Assn. (exec. com. 1973-81), Coun. on the Kidney, Am. Physiol. Soc., Am. Soc. Nephrology, Internat. Soc. Nephrology, Ctrl. Soc. Clin. Rsch., Am. Soc. Renal Biochemistry and Metabolism, Explorer's Club, Sigma Xi (chpt. sec. 1974-76). Home: 20 Haven View Dr Saint Louis MO 63141-7902 Office: Bernard Becker Med Libr Renal Div Dept PO Box 8132 Saint Louis MO 63156-8132 E-mail: purkerm@msnotes.wustl.edu.

PURNELL, JOHN H. beverage company executive; b. 1941; married. BSChemE, John Hopkins U., 1963; MBA, U. Pa., 1965. V.p. Anheuser-Busch, Inc., St. Louis, 1965-79; with Anheuser-Busch Cos., Inc., 1979—, sr. v.p., 1987-91; chmn., chief exec. officer Anheuser-Busch Internat., Inc., 1991—. Office: Anheuser-Busch Cos Inc 1 Busch Pl Saint Louis MO 63118-1852

PURSELL, CARROLL WIRTH, history educator; b. Visalia, Calif., Sept. 4, 1932; s. Carroll Wirth and Ruth Irene (Crowell) P.; m. Joan Young, Jan. 28, 1956 (dec. 1985); children: Rebecca Elizabeth, Matthew Carroll; m. Angela Woollacott, Dec. 20, 1986. B.A., U. Calif., Berkeley, 1956, Ph.D., 1962; M.A., U. Del., 1958. Asst. prof. history Case Inst. Tech., Cleve., 1963-65; asst. prof. U. Calif., Santa Barbara, 1965-69, asso. prof., 1969-76, prof., 1976-88; Adeline Barry Davee Disting. prof. history Case Western Res. U., Cleve., 1988—, chair history dept., 1998—. Mellon prof. Lehigh U., Bethlehem, Pa., 1974-76; vis. research scholar Smithsonian Instn., 1970 Author: Early Stationary Stem Engines in America, 1969, Military Industrial Complex, 1972, From Conservation to Ecology, 1973, White Heat, 1994, The Machine in America, 1995, American Technology, 2001. Fellow: AAAS; mem.: Am. Hist. Assn., Orgn. Am. Historians, Soc. History of Tech. (pres. 1990—92, pres. internat. com.for history of tech. 1998—2001, Leonardo da Vinci medal 1991), Phi Beta Kappa. Democrat. Office: Case Western Res U Dept History 11201 Euclid Ave Cleveland OH 44106-1717

PUSATERI, JAMES ANTHONY, judge; b. Kansas City, Mo., May 20, 1938; s. James A. and Madeline (LaSalle) P.; m. Jacqueline D. Ashburne, Sept. 1, 1962; children: James A., Mark C., Danielle L. BA, U. Kans., 1960, LLB, 1963. Bar: Kans. 1963, U.S. Dist. Ct. Kans. 1963, U.S. Ct. Appeals (10th cir.) 1964. Assoc. Payne, Jones, Chartered, Olathe, Kans., 1963-65, James Cashin, Prairie Village, 1965-69; asst. U.S. atty. Dept. Justice, Kansas City, 1969-76; judge U.S. Bankruptcy Ct. Dist. Kans., Topeka, 1976—. Active Prairie Village City Coun., 1967-69. Mem. Kans. Bar Assn., Topeka Bar Assn., Nat. Conf. Bankruptcy Judges, Am. Bankruptcy Inst., Sam A. Crow Am. Inn of Ct.

PUSATERI, LAWRENCE XAVIER, lawyer; b. Oak Park, Ill., May 25, 1931; s. Lawrence E. and Josephine (Romano) P.; m. Eve M. Graf, July 9, 1956; children: Joanne, Lawrence F., Paul L., Mary Ann, Eva. JD summa cum laude, DePaul U., 1953. Bar: Ill. 1953. Asst. state's atty. Cook County, 1957-59; ptnr. Newton, Wilhelm, Pusateri & Naborowski, Chgo., 1959-77; justice Ill. Appellate Ct., 1977-78; ptnr. Peterson, Ross, Scloerb & Seidel, 1978-95; of counsel Peterson & Ross, 1996—2000. Pres. Conf. Consumer Fin. Law, 1984-92, chmn. gov. com., 1993-99; mem. Ill. Supreme Ct. Com. on Pattern Jury Instrns., 1981-96; mem. adv. bd. Ctr. for Analysis of Alt. and Dispute Resolution, 1999—; mem. U.S. Senate Jud. Nominations Commn. State Ill., 1993, 95; exec. dir. State of Ill. Jud. Inquiry Bd., 1995-96; panel chmn. Cook County mandatory arbitration, 1990—, judicate Am. Arbitration; mem. Merit Selection Panel for U.S. Magistrate; lectr. law DePaul U., Chgo., 1962, Columbia U., N.Y.C., 1965, Marquette U., Milw., 1962-82, Northwestern U. Law Sch., Def. Counsel Inst., 1969-70; apptd. by U.S. Senator Paul Simon to Merit Screening Com. Fed. Judges, U.S. Atty. and U.S. Marshal, 1993, others; mem. task force indigent appellate def. Cook County Jud. Adv. Coun., 1992-95; mem. Ill. Gen. Assembly, 1964-68. Contbr. articles to profl. jours. Chmn. Ill. Crime Investigating Commn., 1967-68, chmn. Ill. Parole and Pardon Bd., 1969-70; bd. dirs. Ill. Law Enforcement Commn., 1970-72; chmn. Com. on Correctional Facilities and Services; exec. v.p. and gen. counsel Ill. Fin. Svcs. Assn., 1980-95; chmn. law forum Am. Fin. Svcs. Assn., 1975-76; mem. spl. commn. on adminstrn. of justice in Cook County, Ill. (Greylord Com.) 1984-90, bd. dirs. Chgo. Crime Commn., 1986-91; mem. Ill. Supreme Ct. Spl. Commn. on the Adminstrn. of Justice, Ill. Supreme Ct. Appointment, 1991. Served to capt. JAGC, AUS, 1955-58. Named One of Ten Outstanding Young Men in Chgo., Chgo. Jr. Assn. Commerce and Industry, 1960, 65; recipient Outstanding Legislator award Ill. Gen. Assembly, 1966. Mem. ABA (com. consumer fin. svcs. 1975-99, ho. dels. 1981-90, judicial adminstrn. divsn. 1980-95, mem. exec. com. lawyer's conf. 1994-95, mem. bench and bar rels. com. 1994-96, mem. adv. com. to Ill. State Del., Jud. Adminstrn. Divsn. in Recognition of Leadership in Improvement of Adminstrn. of Justice award 1993), Ill. State Bar Assn. (pres. 1975-76, com. on fed. jud. and related appointments; Abraham Lincoln Legal Writing award 1959, mem. adv. com., state del., 1994-99, bd. dirs., co-chmn. joint com. jud. compensation 2002-), Chgo. Bar Assn. (bd. mgrs. 1965-66), Fred B. Snite Found. (sec., counsel 1976-90), Gertrude and Walter Swanson Found. (sole trustee 1995—), Mid-Am. Club Chgo. Republican. Roman Catholic.

PUTATUNDA, SUSIL KUMAR, metallurgy educator; b. Santipur, W. Bengal, India, Jan. 31, 1948; came to U.S., 1983; s. Provat Chandra and Santi Kana Putatunda; m. Ivy M. George, June 7, 1984; children: Sujata, Shibani. BS, Instn. Engrs., Calcutta, 1975; MS, U. Mysore, India, 1979; PhD, Indian Inst. Tech., Bombay, 1983. Metallurgist Hindustan Copper Ltd., Khetri, Rajsthan, 1973-77; grad. rsch. asst. U. Mysore, Mangalore, India, 1977-79; R & D engr. Hindustan Electrographites, Bhopal, India, 1979-80; grad. rsch. asst. Indian Inst. Tech., Bombay, 1980-83; Fulbright scholar U. Ill., Urbana, 1983-84; assoc. prof. metallurgy Wayne State U., Detroit, 1985—. Govt. India scholar, New Delhi, 1977, 80; Fulbright fellow USIA, Washington, 1982. Mem. Am. Soc. Metals, The Metall. Soc., ASTM (editor spl. tech. pub. on fractography 1989), Iron and Steel Soc., Engring. Soc. Detroit. Home: 2732 Brady Dr Bloomfield Hills MI 48304-1725 Office: Wayne State U Coll Engring 5050 Anthony Wayne Dr Detroit MI 48202-3902 Fax: 313-577-3810. E-mail: sputa@chem1.eng.wayne.edu.

PUTH, JOHN WELLS, consulting company executive; b. Orange, N.J., Mar. 14, 1929; s. Leonard G. and Elizabeth R. (Wells) P.; m. Betsey Leeds Tait, Mar.1, 1952; children: David Wells, Jonathan Craig, Alison Leeds. BS cum laude, Lehigh U., 1952. Dir. mktg. Purolator Products, Rahway, N.J., 1955-61; pres., chief exec. officer Bridgeport (Conn.) Hardware Mfg. Co. subs. Purolator, 1962-65; group v.p. H.K. Porter Co., Pitts., 1965-72; pres., CEO Disston Inc., 1972-75, Vapor Corp., Niles, Ill., 1975-83; chmn., pres., CEO Clevite Industries Inc., Glenview, 1983-89; pres. JW Puth Assocs., Skokie, 1989—; gen. ptnr. BUCF III and BUCF IV venture capital funds, Chgo. Bd. dirs. L.B. Foster, Pitts., A.M. Castle & Co., Franklin Park, Ill., V.J. Growers Inc., Apopka, Fla., U.S. Freightways, Inc., Rosemont, Ill., George W. Schmidt Inc., Niles, Ill., Adams St. Ptnrs. LLC, Chgo., Guy & O'Neil, Fredonia, Wis.; advisor GTCR Funds, BWAY, Atlanta. Chmn. bd. trustees Hadley Sch. for Blind, Winnetka, Ill., 1982-84; trustee Lehigh U., Kenilworth Union Ch.; bd. dirs. Iaccoca Inst. With U.S. Army, 1946-47, PTO. Mem. Chgo. Club, Econ. Club, Comml. Club, Indian Hill Country Club, Old Elm Club, Loblolly Pines Club. Republican. Presbyterian. Home: 180 De Windt Rd Winnetka IL 60093-3744

PUTKA, ANDREW CHARLES, lawyer; b. Cleve., Nov. 14, 1926; s. Andrew George and Lillian M. (Koryta) P. Student, John Carroll U., 1944, U.S. Naval Acad., 1945-46; A.B., Adelbert Coll., Western Res. U., 1949, J.D., 1952. Bar: Ohio 1952. Practice law, Cleve.; instr. govt. Notre Dame Coll.; v.p. Koryta Bros. Coal Co., Cleve., 1952-56; supt. divsn. bldg. and loan assns. Ohio Dept. Commerce, 1959-63; pres., chmn. bd., CEO Am. Nat. Bank, Parma, Ohio, 1963-69; dir. fin. City of Cleve., 1971-74; dir. port control, 1974-78; dir. Cleve. Hopkins Internat. Airport, 1974-78. Mem. Ohio Ho. of Reps., 1953-56, Ohio Senate, 1957-58; dep. auditor, acting sec. Cuyahoga County Bd. Revision, 1970-71; mem. exec. com. Cuyahoga County Democratic Com., 1973-81, Assn. Ind. Colls. and Univs. Ohio, 1983-89; bd. govs. Sch. Law, Western Res. U., 1953-56; mem. exec. com. World Service Student Fund, 1950-52; U.S. rep. Internat. Pax Romana Congress, Amsterdam, 1950, Toronto, 1952; mem. lay advisory bd. Notre Dame Coll., 1968-90, trustee, 1990-93, hon. trustee, 1993—; mem. adv. bd. St. Andrew's Abbey, 1976-88 ; trustee Case-Western Res. U., Newman Found. No. Ohio, 1980-93, hon. trustee, 1993—; 1st v.p. First Cath. Slovak Union of U.S., 1977-80; pres. USO Council of Cuyahoga County, 1980-83. Voted an outstanding legislator Ohio Press Corrs., 1953; named to All-Star Legislative team Ohio Newspaper Corrs., 1955; named one of Fabulous Clevelanders Cleve. Plain Dealer, John Henry Newman honor Soc. Mem. Cuyahoga County, Cleve. Bar Assn., Nat. Assn. State Savs. and Loan Suprs. (past. nat. pres.), U.S. Savs. and Loan League (mem. legis com, 1960-63), Am. Legion, Ohio Mcpl. League (bd. trustees 1973), Parma C. of C. (bd. dirs., treas. 1965-67), Newman Fedn. (past nat. pres.), NCCJ, Catholic Lawyers Guild (treas.), Am. Ohio Bankers Assn., Am. Inst. Banking, Adelbert Alumni Assn. (exec. com.), Cathedral Latin Alumni Assn. (trustee 1952—), Internat. Order of Alhambra (internat. parliamentarian 1971—, past grand comdr., supreme advocate 1973), Amvets, KC, Pi Kappa Alpha, Delta Theta Phi (past. pres. Cleve. alumni senate, master inspector 1975). Office: 28 Pond Dr Cleveland OH 44116-1062

PUTNAM, J. E. (JIM), state legislator; b. Armour, S.D., Apr. 18, 1940; Grad. high sch., Armour, S.D. Mem. S.D. Ho. of Reps. from 19th dist., Pierre, 1993-2000; Ho. Asst. Majority Whip S.D. Ho. of Reps., 1993-2000; farmer; mem. S.D. Senate from 19th dist., Pierre, 2001—. Mem. appropriations com. (vice chair), legis. procedure com. Home: Rte 1 Box 98 Armour SD 57313-9749

PUTNEY, MARK WILLIAM, lawyer, utility executive; b. Marshalltown, Iowa, Jan. 25, 1929; s. Lawrence Charles and Geneva (Eldridge) P.; m. Ray Ann Bartnek, May 25, 1962 (dec. Feb. 2000); children: Andi Bartnek, William Bradford, Blake Reinhart. BA, U. Iowa, 1951, JD, 1957. Bar: Iowa 1957, U.S. Supreme Ct. 1960. Ptnr. Bradshaw, Fowler, Proctor & Fairgrave, Des Moines, 1961-72, of counsel, 1992-94; chmn., CEO. Bradford & Blake Ltd., Dakota Dunes, S.D., 1992—; pres., chmn., chief exec. officer Iowa Resources, Inc., 1984-90; chmn., chief exec. officer Iowa Power & Light Co., 1984-90, Iowa Gas Co., 1984-85, Midwest Resources Inc., 1990-92. Civilian aide to Sec. Army for Iowa, 1975-77; bd. dirs. Greater Des Moines YMCA, 1976-86, Boys' Home Iowa, 1982-86, Hoover Presdle. Libr. Assn., 1983—, U. Iowa Found., 1984—, Edison Electric Inst., 1986-89; bd. dirs. Greater Des Moines Com., 1984—, pres. 1988; bd. dirs. Assoc. Edison Illuminating Cos., 1988-93, pres., 1991-92; chmn. Iowa Com. Employer Support of Guard and Res., 1979-86; bd. dirs. Des Moines Devel. Corp., 1984-92, chmn., 1989-90. With USAF, 1951-53. Recipient Disting. Alumnus award U. Iowa, 1995. Mem. Iowa Utility Assn. (chmn. 1989, dir.), Des Moines Club (pres. 1977), Desert Forest Golf Club (Carefree, Ariz.), Masons, Shriners, Delta Chi, Phi Delta Phi. Republican. Episcopalian. Home: PO Box 19214 Reno NV 89511

PUTZELL, EDWIN JOSEPH, JR. lawyer, mayor; b. Birmingham, Ala., Sept. 29, 1913; s. Edwin Joseph and Celeste (Joseph) Putzell; m. Dorothy Corcoran Waters, Aug. 5, 1967; children from previous marriage: Cynthia Putzell Reidy, Edwin Joseph, III. AB, Tulane U., 1935; LLB, Harvard U., 1938. Bar: N.Y. 1939, U.S. Supreme Ct. 1945, Mo. 1947. Atty. Donovan, Leisure, Newton & Lumbard, N.Y.C. and Washington, 1937-42; asst. dir., exec. officer Office of Strategic Svcs., 1942-45; asst. treas. Monsanto Co., St. Louis, 1945-46, asst. sec., atty., 1946-51, sec., 1951-77, dir. law dept., 1953-68, v.p., gen. counsel, 1963-77; ptnr. Coburn, Croft, Shepherd, Herzog & Putzell, 1977-79; of counsel Coburn, Croft & Putzell, 1979-96; mayor City of Naples, Fla., 1986-90; of counsel Thompson & Coburn, St. Louis, 1996—. Dir. St. Louis Symphony Soc., 1955—69; pres. The Conservancy, Inc., 1981—85, chmn. bd. dirs., 1984—85; pres. Social Planning Coun., St. Louis, 1954—57; vice chmn. Westminster Coll., 1976—79; chmn. Sta. KETC-TV, St. Louis, 1977—79; trustee St. Luke's Hosp., 1973—79; pres. Hospice of Naples (Fla.) Cmty. Found., Collier County., 2002—; bd. dirs. The Moorings, Inc., Fla., Collier/Naplescape, Inc., Greater Naples Civic Assn., Naples Bot. Garden; vice chmn. St. Louis County Bd. Police Commrs., 1964—72; Big Cypress Basin bd. S. Fla. Water Mgmt. Dist., 1985—86; chmn. Naples Airport Authority, 1979—83, 1993—97. Mem.: ABA, Assn. Gen. Counsel, Am. Soc. Corp. Secs. (pres. 1968—69), St. Louis Bar Assn., Mo. Bar Assn., Naples Area C. of C., Naples Yacht Club, Noonday Club, Forum Club (v.p. 1998—2000, pres. 2002—), Bogey Club, Port Royal Golf Club, Hole in the Wall Golf Club, Delta Sigma Phi, Phi Beta Kappa. Episcopalian. Home: 1285 Gulf Shore Blvd N Naples FL 34102-4911 E-mail: depnaples@aol.com.

PYKE, JOHN SECREST, JR. lawyer, polymers company executive; b. Lakewood, Ohio, July 11, 1938; s. John S. and Elma B. Pyke; student Haverford Coll., 1956-58; BA, Columbia Coll., 1960, postgrad. Columbia Sch. Grad. Faculties, 1960-61; JD, Columbia Law Sch., 1964; m. Judith A., Dec. 26, 1970; 1 child, John Secrest, III. Bar: N.Y. 1965. Assoc. firm Townsend & Lewis (now Thacher, Proffit & Wood), N.Y.C., 1964-68; atty. M.A. Hanna Co., Cleve., 1968—, sec., 1973—, v.p., gen. counsel, 1979—. Trustee, Western Res. Acad., Hudson, Ohio, 1976—. Mem. ABA, Assn. Bar City N.Y., Am. Soc. Corp. Secs., Am. Corp. Counsel Assn., Union Club, Clifton Club, Cleve. Yachting Club. Author: Landmark Preservation, 1969, 2d edit., 1972. Office: MA Hanna Co 200 Public Sq Ste 36-5000 Cleveland OH 44114-2304

PYLE, DAVE, newspaper editor; Bur. chief AP, Mpls., 1980—. Office: 511 11th Ave S Ste 404 Minneapolis MN 55415-1568

PYLE, THOMAS F., JR. consumer products company executive; b. Phila., 1941; Diploma, La Salle U., 1962, U. Wis., 1963. Chmn., pres., CEO Rayovac Corp., Madison, Wis. Dir. Johnson Worldwide Assocs., Kewaunee Sci. Corp., Riverside Paper Corp. Office: Johnson Worldwide Associates PO Box 901 1326 Willow Rd Sturtevant WI 53177 also: Rayovac Corp 601 Ray O Vac Dr Madison WI 53711-2497

PYTELL, ROBERT HENRY, retired lawyer, former judge; b. Detroit, Sept. 27, 1926; s. Henry Carl and Helen (Zielinski) P.; m. Laurie Mazur, June 2, 1956; children: Mary Beth, Mark Henry, Robert Michael. JD, U. Detroit, 1951. Bar: Mich. 1952. Of counsel Pytell & Varchetti, P.C., Detroit, 1952-2001; asst. U.S. atty. Ea. Dist. Mich., 1962-65; judge Mcpl. Ct., Grosse Pointe Farms, Mich., 1967-85. With USNR, 1945-46. Mem. Am. Coll. Trust and Estate Coun., State Bar Mich. (mem. probate coun. probate sect. 1998-2000), Crescent Sail Yacht Club (Grosse Pointe), Delta Theta Phi. Roman Catholic. Office: 20100 Mack Ave Grosse Pointe Woods MI 48236

PYTTE, AGNAR, physicist, former university president; b. Kongsberg, Norway, Dec. 23, 1932; arrived in U.S., 1949, naturalized, 1965; s. Ole and Edith (Christiansen) Pytte; m. Anah Currie Loeb, June 18, 1955; children: Anders H., Anthony M., Alyson C. AB, Princeton U., 1953; AM, Harvard U., 1954, PhD, 1958. Faculty Dartmouth Coll., 1958—87, prof. physics, 1967—87, chmn. dept. physics and astronomy, 1971—75, assoc. dean faculty, 1975—78, dean grad. studies, 1975—78, provost, 1982—87; pres. Case Western Res. U., Cleve., 1987—99; adj. prof. physics Dartmouth Coll., 1999—. Rschr. in plasma physics; mem. Project Matterhorn Princeton U., 1959—60, U. Brussels, 1966—67, Princeton U., 1978—79; bd. dirs. Goodyear Tire & Rubber Co., A.O. Smith Corp. Bd. dirs. Accreditation Coun. for Grad. Med. Edn., 2000—, Sherman Fairchild Found., Inc., 1987—. Mem.: Am. Phys. Soc., Sigma Xi, Phi Beta Kappa. E-mail: agnar.x.pytte@dartmouth.edu.

QUADE, VICTORIA CATHERINE, editor, writer, playwright, producer; b. Chgo., Aug. 15, 1953; d. Victor and Virginia (Uryasz) Q.; m. Charles J. White III, Feb. 15, 1986 (div. Aug. 1996); children: Michael, David, Catherine. BS in Journalism, No. Ill. U., 1974. Staff reporter news divsn. The News-Tribune, LaSalle, Ill., 1975-77; staff writer news divsn. The News-Sun, Waukegan, 1977-81; staff writer ABA Jour., Chgo., 1981-85; mng. editor ABA Press, 1985-90, editor, 1990-2000, sr. editor, 1994-2000. Author: (poetry) Rain and Other Poems, 1976, Laughing Eyes, 1979, Two Under the Covers, 1981, (biography) I Remember Bob Collins, 2000; playwright Late Nite Catechism, 1993, (with Maripat Donovan) Room for Advancement, 1994, Mr. Nanny, 1997, (musical) Lost in Wonderland, 1998, (musical) Here Come the Famous Brothers, 2001; prodr. Late Nite Catechism, Mr. Nanny, Here Come the Famous Brothers, Christopher Carter Messes With Your Mind; contbr. to numerous anthologies and publs.; contbd. to: 20th Century Chicago: 100 Years, 100 Voices (contbd. the year 1953), owner/operator Crossroads Theater, Naperville, Ill. Recipient numerous awards from Soc. Nat. Assn. Publs., AP, UPI. Mem. Am. Soc. Bus. Press Editors (award), Chgo. Newspaper Guild (award), Am. Soc. Assn. Execs. (Gold Circle award 1989, 90). Avocations: traveling, photography.

QUALLS, ROXANNE, mayor; D (hon.), Cin. State Tech. and C.C., 1996. Former exec. dir. Women Helping Women; former dir. No. Ky. Rape Crisis Ctr.; former dir. Cin. office Ohio Citizen Action; councilwoman City of Cin., 1991-93, mayor, 1993-98, founder youth summer jobs program Artworks, Cin. Homeownership Partnership. Former chairperson Cin. City Council's Intergovtl. Affairs and Environment Com.; former vice chairperson Community Devel., Housing and Zoning Com.; mem. Gov.'s Commn. on Storage and Use of Toxic and Hazardous Materials, Solid Waste Adv. Com. of State of Ohio, Gov.'s Waste Minimization Task Force; former chair bd. commrs. Cin. Met. Housing Authority; bd. dirs. Shuttlesworth Housing Found. Hon. chair Friends of Women's Studies; mem. Jr. League Adv. Coun.; bd. dirs. Nat. Underground Railroad Freedom Ctr., Ctr. Voting and Democracy; past bd. didrs. No. Ky. Cath. Commn. Soc. Jusitice. Recipient Woman of Distinction award Girl Scouts U.S., 1992, Woman of Distinction award Soroptomists, 1993, Outstanding Achievement award Cin. Woman's Polit. Caucus, 1993, Women of Achievement award YWCA, 1994, Outstanding Svc. award Ohio Pub. Employees Lawyers Assn., 1996, Pub. Offcl. of Yr. award State of Cinn., 1996, Nat. Assn. Soc. Workers, 1996, Nat. Homebuilders Assn., 1997. Mem. Nat. Assn. Regional Couns. (former pres., 1st v.p., 2d v.p.), Ohio Ky. Ind. Regional Coun. Govts. (1st v.p., 2d v.p.). Fax: 513-352-5201.

QUAM, LOIS, healthcare company executive; MA in Philosophy, Politics, Econs., U. Oxford, 1985. Dir. rsch. and eval. United HealthCare, 1989-93, v.p. public sector svcs., 1993; sr. advisor White House Task Force Nat. Health Care Reform, 1993-96; CEO AARP/United divsn. United HealthCare, 1996-98; CEO Ovations (formerly Retiree and Sr. Svcs. Co. United HealthCare), Minnetonka, MN, 1998—. Office: Ovations United Health Group 500 Opus Ctr 9900 Bren Rd E Minnetonka MN 55343-9664

QUANDAHL, MARK C. state legislator, lawyer; b. Omaha, Oct. 10, 1961; m. Stacey Quandahl, May 24, 1986; children: Sarah, Scott, R.J. Grad., U. Nebr., 1984, grad., 1987. Bar: U.S. Dist. Ct. Nebr. 1987, U.S.

Dist. Ct. Iowa 1988. Atty. Brumbaugh & Quandahl, Omaha; mem. Nebr. Legislature from 31st dist., Lincoln, 1999—. Home: 16729 Leavenworth Cir Omaha NE 68118-2721 Office: State Capitol Dist 31 PO Box 94604 Rm 1010 Lincoln NE 68509-4604

QUARLES, BETH, civil rights administrator; Commr. Civil Rights Commn., Indpls. With presdl. task force, Mits task force, Muncie task force ADA; with Pecso CEO Learning Ctr.; active in youth leadership, employment opportunities and law enforcement ADA; hearing impaired cons.; condr. sign lang. classes. Bd. dirs. Open Door Comty., Muncie (Ind.) Pub. Libr., United Way, County Commty. Partnership on Disability, Muncie Civic Theater; vol. interpreter for deaf; mentor numerous minority bus. Recipient Frieda Dawkins award, Presdl. Points of Light award, also state, nat., and internat. awards for theatrical prodns. Office: Civil Rights Commn 100 N Senate Ave Rm W103 Indianapolis IN 46204-2273

QUARTON, WILLIAM BARLOW, broadcasting company executive; b. Algona, Iowa, Mar. 27, 1903; s. William B. and Ella B. (Reaser) Q.; m. Elnora Bierkamp, Aug. 24, 1935; 1 dau., Diane (Mrs. Waldo F. Geiger). Student, U. Iowa, 1921-22, George Washington U., 1923-25. Joined radio sta. KWCR, Cedar Rapids, Iowa, 1931; comml. mgr. radio sta. WMT, 1936, gen. mgr., 1943; exec. v.p. Am. Broadcasting Stas., Inc., 1959-68, chmn., 1968-70; chmn. bd. KWMT Inc., Ft. Dodge, Iowa, 1968-88, Cable Communications Iowa, Inc., 1971-83; pres. WMT-TV, Inc., 1959-68; chmn. adv. bd. CBS-TV Affiliates, 1960; Mem. bd. Iowa Ednl. Broadcasting Network, 1967-77; bd. govs. Pub. Broadcasting Service, 1973-78. Trustee Coe Coll., 1946-78; trustee, mem. exec. com. Herbert Hoover Presdl. Library; bd. regents State Iowa, 1965-71. Mem. Cedar Rapids C. of C. (pres. 1944), Nat. Assn. Broadcasters (chmn. TV bd. 1962-63, chmn. joint bd. 1963-64. Clubs: Ft. Lauderdale Country (Fla.), Coral Ridge Yacht (Ft. Lauderdale); Cedar Rapids Country. Lodge: Rotary. Home: 134 Kyrie SE Cedar Rapids IA 52403-1712 also: Plaza East 4300 N Ocean Blvd Fort Lauderdale FL 33308

QUAST, LARRY WAYNE, lawyer; b. Beulah, N.D., Aug. 13, 1945; s. Clarence and Lorraine (Meske) Q.; m. Linda Mae Borth, June 18, 1971; children: Tiffany, Phillip. BA cum laude, Dickinson Coll., 1968; JD, U. N.D., 1973. Bar: N.D. 1973, U.S. Dist. Ct. N.D. 1973. Small claims ct. referee, magistrate Grand Forks (N.D.) County, 1973-74; justice Mercer County, Stanton, N.D., 1974-78; assoc. Hagen, Quast & Alexander, Beulah, 1974—. Atty. City of Stanton, N.D., 1976—. Served to corpsman 4th class USN, 1968-70. Mem. ABA, N.D. Bar Assn. Lutheran. Avocations: raising and racing thoroughbred race horses. Home: 1050 Elbowoods Dr Hazen ND 58545-4912 Office: Hagen Quast Alexander PO Box 340 Beulah ND 58523-0340

QUAYLE, MARILYN TUCKER, lawyer, other: government, executive; b. 1949; d. Warren and Mary Alice Tucker; m. J. Danforth Quayle, Nov. 18, 1972; children: Tucker, Benjamin, Corinne. BA in Polit. Sci., Purdue U., 1971; JD, Ind. U., 1974. Pvt. practice atty., Huntington, Ind., 1974—77; ptnr. Krieg, DeVault, Alexander & Capehart, Indpls., 1993—2001; pres. BTC Inc., Phoenix, 2001—. Author (with Nancy T. Northcott): Embrace the Serpent, 1992; author: The Campaign, 1996.

QUEBE, JERRY LEE, retired architect; b. Indpls., Nov. 7, 1942; s. Charlie Christopher and Katheryn Rosella (Hankins) Q.; m. Mary Lee Darby (div.); children: Chad, Tara; m. Julie Ann Gordon (div.); 1 child, Dana Ann; m. Lisbeth Jane Gray, Mar. 16, 1986. BArch, Iowa State U., 1965. Registered Ill., Calif., Wis. Mem. staff Hansen Lind Meyer, Iowa City, 1965-70, assoc., 1970-74, prin., 1975-77, prin., v.p. Chgo., 1977-86; exec. v.p. VVKR, Inc., Alexandria, Va., 1986-93; prin., sr. v.p. Perkins & Will, Chgo., 1994-96, also bd. dirs.; sr. v.p. RTKL Assocs. Inc., 1996—2002, ret., 2002. Chmn. Cedar Rapids/Iowa City Architects Council, 1974. Author: Drafting Practices Manual, 1978; contbr. articles to profl. jours. Pres. bd. dirs. Mental Health Assn. of Greater Chgo., 1990-95. Fellow AIA, Am. Coll. Healthcare Archs.(founder); mem. Am. Hosp. Assn., Chgo. Health Exec. Forum, Forum for Health Care Planning (bd. dirs. 1992-99). Avocations: photography, sports car racing, woodworking. Home: 43495 Trout Creek Road Soldiers Grove WI 54655-7090 E-mail: jquebe@rtkl.com.

QUEEN, JOYCE ELLEN, elementary school educator; b. Cleve., Mar. 17, 1945; d. Wilbur Raynor and Mae (Reid) Closterhouse; m. Robert Graham Queen, Mar. 17, 1973. BA in Biology, Macalester Coll., 1966; MS in Conservation and Natural Resource Mgmt., U. Mich., 1968. Cert. tchr. biol. and earth scis., Ohio. Exhibitor, docent, coord. Grand Rapids (Mich.) Pub. Mus., 1967-68; tchr., naturalist Rose Tree-Media (Pa.) Outdoor Edn., 1967, Willoughby-East Lake (Ohio) Schs., 1969-70, Independence (Ohio) Schs., 1970-78; sci. tchr. grades 1-7, coord. sci. field trip Hathaway Brown Sch., Cleve., 1970—, primary sci. educator, 1970—, primary sci. dept. chair, 1999—. Designer Courtland Woods nature trail, 1986, designer sci. greenhouse, 1990-92; designer sci. classroom Van Dyke Architects/Hathaway Brown Sch., 1990-92; designer, coord. Dampeer Primary sci. courtyard, 1993, Oliva Herb Garden, 1998, Colini Landscape Design/Hathaway Brown Sch., Shaker Hts., Ohio; mem. ednl. adv. com. William G. Mather Vessel Mus., Cleve., 1992, Holden Arboretum, Kirtland, Ohio, 1992-97; workshop leader Lake Erie Islands Hist. Mus., South Bass Island, Ohio, 1992, H.B. Winter Sci. Symposium Workshop, 1994—; presenter Nat. Assn. Ind. Schs., Columbus, Ohio, 1993; workshop leader for schs. on garden design, sci. labs., and sci. discovery programs; children's garden design judge, 1999, 2000; youth divsn. judge Cleve. Botanic Garden Show, 2000. Contbr. articles to profl. jours. Design cons. Cleve. Bot. Garden and Floral Scape, 1998; active Belize (Ctrl. Am.) Tchrs. Workshop, 1994. Catalyst grantee Hathaway Brown Sch. Gt. Lks. Curriculum, 1991; recipient Environ. Edn. award Ohio Alliance for Environment, 1986, Presdl. Excellence in Elem. Sci. Tchg. award NSF, 1992, Sheldon Exemplary Equipment and Facilities award, 1992; Great Lakes Lighthouse Keepers Assn. scholar; Marine Ecology scholar Marine Resources, Inc., 1989. Mem. NSTA (recipient Exemplary Environ. and Facilities award with Sheldon Mfg. Co. 1992), Cleve. Regional Coun. Sci. Tchrs., Cleve. Coun. Ind. Schs., Cleve. Natural Hist. Mus., Cleve. Zool. Park, Ind. Sch. Assn. Ctrl. Sts., World Wise Sch. Peace Corp Pen Pal Exchange Progam. Presbyterian. Avocations: orchardist, naturalist, horticulturist. Office: Hathaway Brown Sch 19600 N Park Blvd Cleveland OH 44122-1899

QUENNEVILLE, JOEL, professional hockey coach; b. Windsor, Ont., Can., Sept. 15, 1958; m. Elizabeth Quenneville; children: Dylan, Lily, Anna. Hockey player, player coach St. John's Maple Leafs, 79-92; head coach Springfield Indians, Am. Hockey League, 1993-94; asst. coach Colo. Avalanche, 1995-96; head coach St. Louis Blues, NHL, 1997—. Named Most Valuable Defensemen, 1985, 86, Coach of Yr., NHL, 1999-2000. Office: Savvis Ctr 1401 Clark Ave Saint Louis MO 63103-2709

QUENON, ROBERT HAGERTY, retired mining consultant and holding company executive; b. Clarksburg, W.Va., Aug. 2, 1928; s. Ernest Leonard and Josephine (Hagerty) Q.; m. Jean Bowling, Aug. 8, 1953; children: Evan, Ann, Richard. B.S. in Mining Engring., W.Va. U., 1951; LL.B., George Washington U., 1964; PhD (hon.), U. Mo., 1979, Blackburn Coll., 1983, W.Va. U., 1988. Mine supt. Consol. Coal Co., Fairmont, W.Va., 1956-61; mgr. deep mines Pittston Co., Dante, Va., 1964-66; gen. mgr. Riverton Coal Co., Crown Hill, W.Va., 1966-67; mgr. ops. coal and shale oil dept. Exxon Co., Houston, 1967; pres. Monterey Coal Co., 1969-76; sr. v.p. Carter Oil Co., 1976-77; exec. v.p. Peabody Coal Co., St. Louis, 1977-78, pres., chief exec. officer, 1978-83, Peabody Holding Co., Inc., St. Louis, 1983-90, chmn., 1990-91. Bd. dirs. Newmont Mining Co., Denver, Ameren Corp., St. Louis, Laclede Steel Co., St. Louis, Miss. Lime Co., Alton, Ill.; bd. dirs., chmn. Fed. Res. Bank St. Louis, 1993-95, dep. chmn., 1990-92; mem. coal industry adv. bd. Internat. Energy Agy., 1980—, bd. chmn., 1984-90; chmn. Bituminous Coal Operator's Assn., 1980-83, 89-91. Trustee Blackburn Coll., Carlinville, Ill., 1975-83, St. Louis U., 1981-91; pres. St. Louis Art Mus., 1985-88. Served with AUS, 1946-47. Recipient Eavenson award Soc. Mining, Metallurgy, and Exploration, 1994, Erskine Ramsay award Am. Inst. Mining, Metallurgy. and Petroleum Engrs., 1985. Mem. Am. Mining Congress (vice-chmn. 1980-91), Nat. Coal Assn. (chmn. bd. 1978-80), U.S. C. of C. (dir. 1982-88). Office: PO Box 11328 Saint Louis MO 63105-0128

QURESHI, MOHAMMED YOUNUS, psychology educator, consultant; b. Haripur Hazara, Pakistan, Dec. 12, 1929; came to U.S., 1953; s. Mohammed Noor and Meryam Khatoon Q.; m. Nora Jane Knapp, May 27, 1958 (div. Nov. 1979); children: Ahmed, Amna, Shukria, Shawn; m. Farzana Kaukab, May 17, 1980; children: Ajmel, Sabeeha, Azem. PhD, U. Ill., 1958. Lic. psychologist, Wis.; diplomate Am. Bd. Psychol. Spltys. Asst. prof. psychology U. Minn., Duluth, 1960-62, U. N.D., Grand Forks, 1962-64; assoc. prof. psychology Marquette U., Milw., 1964-70, prof., 1970—, chmn. dept. psychology, 1971-77. Cons. psychologist. Author: Statistics and Behavior: An Introduction, 1980, 2d edit., 1991; contbr. articles to sci. and profl. jours. Pres. 81st St. Sch. PTA, 1968-70; merit badge counselor Milw. County coun. Boy Scouts Am., 1973-88; pres. Islamic Assn. Greater Milw., 1978-83. NIH grantee, 1962-69; Office of Edn. grantee, 1970-71; TOPS Club grantee, 1969-76. Mem. Am. Psychol. Assn., Psychometric Soc., Sigma Xi. Home: 2759 N 68th St Milwaukee WI 53210-1204 Office: Marquette U Schroeder Health Complex PO Box 1881 Milwaukee WI 53201-1881

QUICK, ALBERT THOMAS, law educator; b. Battle Creek, Mich., June 28, 1939; s. Robert and Vera Quick; m. Brenda Jones; children: Lori, Traci, Becki, Breton, Regan, Leigh. BA, U. Ariz., 1962; MA, Cen. Mich. U., 1964; JD, Wayne State U., 1967; LLM, Tulane U., 1974. Bar: Mich. 1968. Asst. prosecutor Calhoun County, Marshall, Mich., 1968-69; assoc. Hatch & Hatch, 1969-70; asst. prof. U. Maine, Augusta, 1970-73; prof. law U. Louisville, 1974-87, spl. asst. to univ. provost, 1983-87; dean, prof. law Ohio No. U., Ada, 1987-95; prof. law, dean U. Toledo, Ohio, 1995-99, dean and prof. emeritus, 1999—; of counsel Smith Haughey Rice & Roegge, Traverse City, Mich., 2002—. Co-author: Update Federal Rules of Criminal Procedure; contbr. articles to profl. jours. Trustee Traverse Dist. Libr. Recipient Medallion of Justice Nat. Bar Assn., 1995. Mem. ABA, ACLU, Mich. State Bar Assn., Willis Soc., Ohio State Bar Assn., Phi Kappa Phi, Coif. Episcopalian. Avocations: golf, art, reading. Office: 542 5th St Traverse City MI 49684-2408 E-mail: atquick@aol.com.

QUICK, EDWARD E. state legislator; b. Rich Hill, Mo., Feb. 16, 1935; City councilman, Kansas City, Mo., 1975-85; mem. Mo. Senate Dist. 17, 1985—. Office: 13004 County Road A Liberty MO 64068-8127 also: State Senate State Capitol Building Jefferson City MO 65101-1556 Address: 13004 County Rd A Liberty MO 64068-8127

QUIE, PAUL GERHARDT, pediatrician; b. Dennison, Minn., Feb. 3, 1925; s. Albert Knute and Nettie Marie (Jacobson) Quie; m. Elizabeth Holmes, Aug. 10, 1951; children: Katie, Bill, Paul, David. BA, St. Olaf Coll., 1949; MD, Yale U., 1953; PhD (hon.) , U. Lund, 1993. Diplomate Am. Bd. Pediat., Nat. Bd. Med. Examiners (mem.). Intern Hennepin County Hosp., 1953—54; pediatric resident U. Minn. Hosps., 1957—59; mem. faculty U. Minn. Med. Sch., 1959—, prof. pediatrics, 1968—99, prof. microbiology, 1974—99, assoc. dean of students, 1992—, Am. Legion meml. heart research prof., 1974—91, Regents prof., 1991; Regent's prof. emeritus, 1999—; interim dir. Ctr. for Biomed. Ethics U. Minn. Med. Sch., 1985—86; attending physician Hennepin County Hosp., 1959—91. Cons. U. Minn. Nursery Sch., 1959—91; chief of staff U. Minn. Hosp., 1979—84; vis. physician Radcliffe Infirmary, Oxford, England, 1971—72; mem. Adv. Allergy and Infectious Disease Coun., 1976—80; mem. pediat. com. NRC, 1978; mem. bd. sci. counselors Gamble Inst., 1985—90; vis. prof. U. Bergen, 1991; hon. prof. U. Hong Kong Med. Sch., 1995; vis. prof. pediat. Chubu Hosp., Nagasaki, Japan, 1996. Editl. bd. Pediat., 1970—76, Rev. Infectious Diseases, 1989—92. Pres. Fairview Found., 1998—99; bd. dirs. Ctr. for Victims of Torture. Med. officer USNR, 1954—57. Recipient E. Mead-Johnson award, Am. Acad. Pediat., 1971, Shotwell award, Hennipen Med. Soc., 2001; fellow Guggenheim, 1971—72, Alexander von Humboldt, 1986; scholar John and Mary R. Markle, 1960—65. Mem.: Eliz Glaser Pediat. AIDS Found., Minn. Acad. Medicine (pres. 1993—94), Assn. Am. Physicians, Am. Acad. Pediat., Minn. Acad. Pediat., Am. Soc. Clin. Investigation, Am. Pediatric Soc. (coun. 1976—83, pres. 1987—88), Soc. Pediatric Rsch., Infectious Diseases Soc. Am. (coun. 1977—82, pres. 1985, Bristol award 1994), Am. Soc. Microbiology, Am. Fedn. Clin. Rsch., Minn. Med. Found. 1986—88, N.W. Pediat. Soc., Inst. Medicine of NAS. Achievements include research in function of human leukocytes and international medical education and research. Home: 2154 Commonwealth Ave Saint Paul MN 55108-1717 Office: PO Box 293 Minneapolis MN 55440-0293 E-mail: quiex001@umn.edu.

QUIGLEY, HERBERT JOSEPH, JR. pathologist, educator; b. Phila., Mar. 6, 1937; s. Herbert Joseph and Mary Kathleen (Carney) G.; m. Jacqueline Jean Stocksdale, Nov. 28, 1965 (div. 1974); 1 child, Amelia Anne. BS in Chemistry, Franklin and Marshall Coll., 1958; MD, U. Pa., 1962. Diplomate Am. Bd. Pathology. Intern Presbyterias Hosp., NYC, 1962—66, resident, 1962—66; chief pathology Monroe County Hosp., Key West, Fla., 1966-68; from asst. prof. to assoc. prof. pathology Creighton U., Omaha, 1968-72, prof., 1972—; chief pathology svc. VA Med. Cr., 1968-88. Bd. dirs. Triton-Chito Inc., Omaha. Contbr. articles to profl. jours.; patentee in field. Bd. dirs., former pres., chmn. Nebr. Assn. Earth Sci. Clubs, Omaha, 1972—. Lt. comdr. USNR, 1966-68. Recipient career devel. award NIH, 1962-66, Borden prize for med. rsch. Borden Co., Inc., 1962; fellow NIH, Nat. Cancer Inst., 1958-62. Fellow Coll. Am. Pathologists, Am. Soc. Clin. Pathologists, Am. Inst. Chemists; mem. Nebr. Assn. Pathologists, N.Y. Acad. Scis. Republican. Roman Catholic. Avocations: paleontology, geology. Home: 9511 Mockingbird Dr Omaha NE 68127-2423 Office: VA Med Center 4101 Woolworth Ave Omaha NE 68105-1850

QUIGLEY, JOHN BERNARD, law educator; b. St. Louis, Oct. 1, 1940; s. John Bernard and Ruth Rosina (Schieber) Q. BA, Harvard U., 1962, MA, LLB, 1966. Bar: Ohio 1973, Mass. 1967, U.S. Dist. Ct. (so. dist.) Ohio 1976, U.S. Ct. Appeals (6th cir.) 1986, U.S. Supreme Ct. 1989. Research assoc. Harvard U. Law Sch., Cambridge, Mass., 1967-69; prof. law Ohio State U., Columbus, 1969—. Author: Basic Laws on the Structure of the Soviet State, 1969, The Soviet Foreign Trade Monopoly, 1974, Palestine and Israel: A Challenge to Justice, 1990, The Ruses for War: American Interventionism since World War II, 1992, Flight into the Maelstrom: Soviet Immigration to Israel and Middle East Peace, 1997, Genocide in Cambodia, 2000. Mem. Nat. Lawyers Guild (v.p. 1977-79), Am. Soc. Internat. Law, AAUP. Avocations: tennis, speed skating, violin. Office: Ohio State U Coll of Law Coll of Law 55 W 12th Ave Columbus OH 43210-1338

QUINLAN, MICHAEL ROBERT, fast food franchise company executive; b. Chgo., Dec. 9, 1944; s. Robert Joseph and Kathryn (Koerner) Q.; m. Marilyn DeLashmutt, Apr. 23, 1966; children: Kevin, Michael. BS, Loyola U., Chgo., 1967, MBA, 1970. With McDonald's Corp., Oak Brook, Ill., 1966—, v.p., 1974-76, sr. v.p., 1976-78, exec. v.p., 1978-79, chief ops. officer, 1979-80, pres. McDonald's U.S.A., 1980-82, pres., 1982-89, COO, 1982-87, CEO, 1987-97, chmn., 1989-97, also bd. dirs., 1992—. Republican. Roman Catholic. Clubs: Butterfield Country, Oakbrook Handball-Racquetball. Office: McDonald's Corp McDonalds Plaza Oak Brook IL 60523-2275

QUINN, ALEXANDER JAMES, bishop; b. Cleve., Apr. 8, 1932; Attended, St. Charles Coll., Catonsville, Md., St. Mary Sem., Cleve., Lateran Sem., Rome, Cleve. State U. Ordained priest Roman Cath. Ch., 1958. Titular, bishop, aux. bishop Cleve. Diocese, 1983, vicar western region. Office: 2500 Elyria Ave Lorain OH 44055-1367 E-mail: ajquinn@dioceseofcleveland.org.

QUINN, DENNIS B. English language and literature educator; b. Bklyn., Oct. 3, 1928; s. Herbert John and Thelma Leona (Warren) Q.; m. Eva M. Jensen, Aug. 13, 1952; children— Timothy, Monica, Alison. Student, Creighton U., 1948-50; B.A. in English, U. Wis., 1951, M.A. in English, 1952, Ph.D. in English, 1958. Instr. English U. Kans., Lawrence, 1956-60, asst. prof. English, 1960-64, assoc. prof. English, 1964-68, prof. English, 1968—, dir. Pearson Coll., 1968-75, dir. integrated humanities program, 1971-79. Author: Iris Exiled: A Synoptic History of Wonder, 2002; contbr. articles. Served with U.S. Army, 1946-48; Japan Recipient student Fulbright award, Leiden, The Netherlands, 1955-56, research Fulbright award, Salamanca, Spain, 1962-63; H. Bernard Fink Outstanding Tchr. award U. Kans., 1965, H.O.P.E. Teaching award, 1969; NEH grantee, 1971; Kemper Tchg. fellow, 1997. Roman Catholic Avocations: gardening, travel. Home: 1102 W 25th St Lawrence KS 66046-4441 Office: Univ Kansas Dept English Lawrence KS 66045-0001

QUINN, DONAL, diagnostic equipment company executive; BS in Econs., Cork U., Ireland. Exec. positions with Mallinckrodt Med., Abbott Labs.; group pres. Biology products divsn. Dade Behring, Deerfield, Ill., 1998-99, pres. Europe, Mid. East and Africa divsn., 1999—.

QUINN, PHILIP LAWRENCE, philosophy educator; b. Long Branch, N.J., June 22, 1940; s. Joseph Lawrence and Gertrude (Brown) Q. AB, Georgetown U., 1962; MS, U. Del., 1967; MA, U. Pitts., 1968, PhD, 1970; MA (hon.), Brown U., 1972. Asst. prof. philosophy Brown U., Providence, 1969-72, assoc. prof. philosophy, 1972-78, prof. philosophy, 1978-85, William Herbert Perry Faunce prof. philosophy, 1982-85; John A. O'Brien prof. philosophy U. Notre Dame, South Bend, Ind., 1985—. Author: (book) Divine Command and Moral Requirements, 1978; editor Faith and Philosophy, 1990-95; co-editor: A Companion to Philosophy of Religion, 1997, The Philosophical Challenge of Religious Diversity, 1999; contbr. articles to profl. jours. Fulbright fellow, 1962-63; Danforth fellow, 1967-69. Mem. Am Philos. Assn. (sec., treas. ea. divsn. 1982-85, chmn. career opportunities com. 1985-90, exec. com. ctrl. divsn. 1987-90, v.p. ctrl. divsn. 1993-94, pres. 1994-95, chair ctrl. divsn. nominating com. 1995-96, acting chair Nat. Bd. of Officers 1995-96, chair 1996-99), Philosophy of Sci. Assn. (nominating com. 1984-86), Soc. Christian Philosophers (exec. com. 1981-84), Am. Acad. Religion (steering com. philosophy of religion sect. 1999--). Roman Catholic. Avocations: reading, swimming, film, theater . Home: 1645 W Turtle Creek Dr South Bend IN 46637-5660 Office: Univ Notre Dame Dept Philosophy Notre Dame IN 46556

QUINN, R. JOSEPH, former judge; m. Carole Quinn. BA, St. John's U.; JD, Hamline U. Minn. State rep., 1983-90; judge Minn. Supreme Ct., 1991-99; ret., 1999. Office: Anoka County Court 325 E Main St Anoka MN 55303-2483

QUINNELL, BRUCE ANDREW, retail book chain executive; b. Washington, Jan. 6, 1949; s. Robert Kay and Marion Louise (Moseley) Q.; m. Aug. 31, 1972 (div. June 1986); children: Paul David, Andrea Carolyn; m. Marcia Melodie Mundie. BS in Acctg., Va. Poly. Inst. and State U., 1971, MA in Acctg., 1972. CPA, Ohio, Mo., Tex., Tenn. Sr. auditor Ernst & Whinney, Columbus, Ohio, 1972-75; treas., chief fin. officer Midway Ford Truck Ctr., Kansas City, Mo., 1975-82; sr. v.p., chief fin. officer Rsch. Health Svcs., 1982-85; sr. v.p. VHA Enterprises Inc., Irving, Tex., 1985-87; v.p., treas., chief fin. officer Dollar Gen. Corp., Nashville, 1987-92; exec. v.p. Pace Membership Warehouse, Englewood, Colo., 1992-93; exec. v.p., COO Walden Book Co., Stamford, Conn., 1993, pres., 1994-97, Borders Group, Inc., Ann Arbor, Mich., 1997-99; vice chmn. Borders Group Inc., 1999—. Bd. dirs. Advs. Tenn. State U. Coll. Bus., Nashville, 1991-92, Jr. Achievement Mid. Tenn., 1992, Hot Topic, Inc., 1998—; mem. adv. coun. Reading Is Fundamental, 1998—, chmn. adv. coun., 1999—. Mem. Fin. Execs. Inst., Am. Inst. CPA'S, Nat. Investor Rels. Inst. Republican. Lutheran. Avocations: racquetball, golf, scuba diving. Office: Borders Group Inc 100 Phoenix Dr Ann Arbor MI 48108-2202 E-mail: coobaq@bordersgroupinc.com.

QUINT, DOUGLAS JOSEPH, neuroradiology educator; b. N.Y.C., Apr. 25, 1956; s. George and Barbara (Gilder) Q.; m. Leslie Eisenbud, May 23, 1982; children: Mark Harry, Jason Meyer. BA, Wesleyan U., Middletown, Conn., 1978; MD, Cornell U., 1982. Diplomate Nat. Bd. Med. Examiners, Am. Bd. Radiology. Med. intern U. Mich. Hosps., Ann Arbor, 1982-83, resident in radiology, 1983-86; fellow in neuroradiology, mem. assoc. staff Henry Ford Hosp., Detroit, 1986-88; prof. neuroradiology and MRI U. Mich. Med. Sch., Ann Arbor, 1988—. Contbr. articles to med. jours. Mem. Am. Soc. Neuroradiology (sr.), Radiol. Soc. N.Am., Am. Roentgen Ray Soc., Am. Coll. Radiology, AMA. Avocations: softball, tennis, model trains, photography, profl. baseball. Office: U Mich Hosp Radiology Dept 1500 E Medical Ctr Dr Ann Arbor MI 48109-0030

QUINTANILLA, ANTONIO PAULET, retired physician, educator; b. Feb. 8, 1927; came to U.S., 1963, naturalized, 1974; s. Leandro Marino and Edel Paulet Quintanilla; m. Mary Parker Rodriguez, May 2, 1958; children: Antonio Paulet, Angela, Francis, Cecilia, John. PhD, San Marcos U., 1948, MD, 1957. Assoc. prof. physiology U. Arequipa, Peru, 1960-63; assoc. in physiology Cornell U., N.Y., 1963-64; prof. physiology U. Arequipa, 1964-68; assoc. prof. medicine Northwestern U., 1969-80, prof., 1980-2000; ret., 2000. Chief renal sect. VA Lakeside Hosp., 1976-90; cons. nephrologist Northwestern Meml. Hosp., Evanston Hosp., 1990-98, sr. attending emeritus; lectr. nat. Ctr. Advanced Med. Edn., Chgo.; mem. adv. bd. Am. Fedn. Clin. Rsch. Contbr. articles on renal disease to med. jours.; author books in English and Spanish, poetry, short stories. Fellow ACP; mem. Ctrl. Soc. Clin. Rsch., Internat. Soc. Nephrology, Am. Soc. Nephrology, Am. Physiol. Soc. Home: 650 S River Rd Unit 411 Des Plaines IL 60016-8428 E-mail: a.p.quintanilla@worldnet.att.net.

QUIRING, PATTI LEE, human resource consulting company executive; b. Indpls. d. Harold Woodrow and Flora Lee (Hoffman) Dulin; m. David Allen Niederhaus, June 1972; (div. May 1974); m. David Jonathon Quiring, Dec. 7, 1976; 1 child: Erin Ashley. AA, Ball State U., Muncie, 1972, BS, 1975; MBA, Ind. Wesleyan U., 1990. Profl. Sec. Summer employee P. R. Mallory and Co., Inc., Indpls., 1970, 1971; student asst. Ball State U., Muncie, Ind., 1970-72; adminstrv. asst. Ball Corp., 1972-74; student asst. Ball State U., 1975; adminstrv. asst. P. R. Mallory and Co., Inc., 1975-76; various mgmt. level positions Blue Cross and Blue Shield of Ind., Indpls., 1976-87; exec. recruiter Tech. Resource Group, 1988-91; pres. Quiring Assocs., Inc., 1991—. Co-facilitator Corp. Bd. Task Force, 1993—94; bd. dirs. Mega Sys, Inc. Co-chmn. venture com. United Way, 1991-93, mem. adv. com. women's divsn., 1991-94, bd. dirs., mem. exec. com., 1993-99, mem. goals and priorities com., 1993, vice chmn. agy. rels. cabinet 1993-94, chmn., 1995-98, co-chmn. campaign cluster, 1994-95, mem. campaign cabinet, 1995, N.E. area team leader, 1995; vol. Pan. Am. Games, Indpls., 1987; dir. alumni rels. Ball State U. Coll. Bus., Muncie,

1988-97, mem. alumni coun., 1994-97; bd. dirs. Heritage Place Sr. Citizens Ctr., Indpls., 1988-90, Indpls. YWCA, 1988-90, Feathercove Homeowners Assn., 1990-97, Geist Harbors Property Owner's Assn., 1994-97, Lawrence Twp. Found., 2000-01; corp. capt. Humane Soc., 1990-91; mem. mktg. com. Children's Mus., 1992-97, mem. bd. advisors, 1995—; mem. Equal Opportunity Adv. Bd., 1992-95, Indpls. BBB; bd. dirs. Lawrence Twp. Found., 2000—. Recipient Blue Cross award of Excellence, Indpls., 1985, City Ctr Vol. award, Indpls., 1985, Salute to Women of Achievement Individual award YWCA, 1993, Network of Women in Business Networker of Yr. award, 1993; named Blue Cross Bus. Women of Yr., Indpls. 1982, 86, Humane Soc. Outstanding Vol., Indpls., 1985. Mem. Ind. Assn. Pers. Svc. Bd., Network Women in Bus. (pres. 1993), Ind. C. of C. (small bus. coun. bd.), Nat. Assn. Pers. Svcs. (mem. bd.), Indpls. and Ind. C. of C. (bd. dirs.), Better Bus. Bur. Avocations: fishing, boating, arts, tennis. Office: Quiring Assocs Inc 7267 C Jessman Rd West Dr Indianapolis IN 46256

QUISENBERRY, NANCY LOU, university administrator, educator; b. Washington, Jan. 29, 1938; d. Joseph Franklin and Maud Helen (Fitch) Forbes; m. James D. Quisenberry, Feb. 6, 1960; 1 child, James Paul. BS in Home Econs., Ind. State Tchrs. Coll., 1960, MS in Home Econs., 1962; EdD, Ind. U., 1971. Cert. tchr., Ind. Home economics tchr. Honey Creek High Sch., Terre Haute, Ind., 1961-62; third grade tchr. Indpls. Pub. Sch., 1962-64; sustitute tchr. Dep. of Def., Baumholder, Fed. Republic Germany, 1964-65; first grade tchr. Wayne Twp. Schs., Indpls., 1966-67; assoc. faculty lang. arts Ind. U.-Purdue U., spring 1970; prof. curriculum and instruction So. Ill. U., Carbondale, 1971—, assoc. dean Coll. of Edn., 1976-96, interim dean, 1996-98. Cons. U. N.C., Durham, 1977, Ministry Edn., Bangkok, Thailand, 1980, 84, DePaul U., 1990, Ill. State U., 1997, Northeastern Ill. U., 1997; dir. tech. and tng. assistance grant Head Start-OCD, Carbondale, 1972-74, Cameroon project USAID, Carbondale, 1984-86; mem. Ill. State Tchr. Certification Bd., 1981-84, 84-87. Co-author: Early Childhood Education Programs: Developmental Objectives and Their Use, 1975, Play as Development, 1978, Educators Healing Racism, 1999. Chair candidacy com. Ctrl. So. Ill. Synod Evang. Luth. Ch. Am., Springfield, 1987-90, sec. multisynodical com., Chgo., 1987-90, synod coun., 1992-95; pres. Epiphany Luth. Ch. Coun., Carbondale, 1984-85, 89-92, 94-96; bd. dirs. Jackson County YMCA, 1988. Recipient Dare To Be Great award Ill. Women Adminstrs. and So. Ill. Region Ill. Women Adminstrs., 1989, Woman of Distinction award, So. Ill. U., 1992; grantee Bur. Educationally Handicapped, 1979-82, 90-95. Mem. Internat. Coun. on Edn. for Tchg. (bd. dirs., N.Am. v.p. 1992-94, pres.-elect 1997-2000, pres. 2000—), Assn. Childhood Edn. Internat. (chair tchr. edn. com. 1989-93, folio rev. coord. elem. edn. 1989-2001, sec.-treas. 1996—, Patty Hill Smith Lifetime Achievement award, pres.-elect 1998-2000, pres. 2001-03), Nat. Coun. for Accreditation Tchr. Edn. (bd. examiners 1987-98, new profl. tchr. project elem. edn. stds. drafting com. 1996-98, transition team elem. stds. 1998-2000, chair Rubics devel. com. 2001), Am. Assn. Colls. for Tchr. Edn. (chair adv. coun. state reps. 1987-88, bd. dirs. 1986-88, 91-94)), Ill. Assn. Colls. for Tchr. Edn. (pres. 1984-86), Assn. Tchr. Educators (chair com. racism from a healing perspective 1995-98), World Orgn. for Pre-sch. Edn. (U.S. nat. com., treas. 1997-99, chmn. strategic planning commn. 1999-2001, webmaster 2000—). Avocations: gardening, organ, flute, sewing, walking. Home: 3208 W Kent Dr Carbondale IL 62901-1917 Office: So Ill U Coll Edn Carbondale IL 62901-4624 E-mail: nancyq@siu.edu.

QUIST, GORDON JAY, federal judge; b. Grand Rapids, Mich., Nov. 12, 1937; s. George J. and Ida F. (Hoekstra) Q.; m. Jane Capito, Mar. 10, 1962; children: Scot D., George J., Susan E., Martha J., Peter K. BA, Mich. State U., 1959; JD with honors, George Washington U., 1962. Bar: D.C. 1962, Ill. 1964, U.S. Dist. Ct. (no. dist.) Ill. 1964, U.S. Supreme Ct. 1965, Mich. 1967, U.S. Dist. Ct. (we. dist.) Mich. 1967, U.S. Ct. Appeals (6th cir.) 1967. Assoc. Hollabaugh & Jacobs, Washington, 1962-64, Sonnenschein, Levinson, Carlin, Nath & Rosenthal, Chgo., 1964-66, Miller, Johnson, Snell & Cummiskey, Grand Rapids, 1967-72, ptnr., 1972-92, mng. ptnr., 1986-92; judge U.S. Dist. Ct. (we. dist.) Mich., 1992—. Bd. dirs. Wedgewood Acres-Ch. Youth Home, 1968-74, Mary Free Bed Hosp., 1979-88, Christian Ref. Publs., 1968-78, 82-88, Opera Grand Rapids, 1986-92, Mary Free Bed Brace Shop, 1988-92, Better Bus. Bur., 1972-80, Calvin Theol. Sem., 1992-93; bd. dirs. Indian Trails Camp, 1970-78, 82-88, pres., 1978, 88. Recipient Disting. Alumnus award George Washington U. Law Sch.. 1998 Mem. Am. Indicature Soc., Mich. State Bar Found., Univ. Club Grand Rapids, Order of Coif, Am. Inns Ct. Avocations: reading, travel. Office: 482 Ford Fed Courthouse 110 Michigan St NW Grand Rapids MI 49503-2313 E-mail: Gordon_J_Quist@miwd.uscourts.gov.

QUTUB, MUSA YACUB, hydrogeologist, educator, consultant; b. Jerusalem, June 2, 1940; came to U.S., 1960; s. Yacub and Sarah Qutub; married; children: Hanhia, Jennan, Sarmad, Muntaser, Aya, Saif, Tasneem. B.A. in Geology, Simpson Coll., Indianola, Iowa, 1964; M.S. in Hydrogeology, Colo. State U., 1966; Ph.D in Water Resources, Iowa State U. Sci. and Tech., 1969. Instr. earth sci. Iowa State U., Ames, 1966-69; from asst. prof. to prof. Northeastern Ill., Chgo., 1969-80, prof. geography and environ. studies, 1980—. Cons. hydrogeology, Des Plaines, Ill., 1970— ; sr. adviser Saudi Arabian Ministry Planning, Riyadh, 1977-78; leader U.S. environ. sci. del. to People's Republic of China, 1984; pres., founder Islamic Info. Ctr. Am. Author: Secondarty Environmental Science Methods, 1973; contbr. numerous articles to profl. jours.; editor Environ. Resource, Directory Environ. Educators and Cons. World. NSF grantee, 1970-71, 71-72, 72-73, 75, 76, Hew grantee, 1974, grantee Ill. Dept. Edn., 1970. Mem. AAAS, NSF (cons.), Am. Waterworks Assn., Am. Men and Women Sci., Nat. Assn. Geology Tchrs. (pres. central sect. 1974), Environ. Sci. Inst. (edn. com.), Internat. Assn. Advancement of Earth and Environ Sci. (pres. 1975—, founder), Ill. Earth Sci. Edn. (pres. 1971-73, founder), Phi Delta Kappa. Muslim. Avocations: tennis, track, cross country, soccer.

RAABE, WILLIAM ALAN, tax writer, business educator; b. Milw., Dec. 14, 1953; s. William Arthur and Shirley (Semmann) R.; m. Nancy Elizabeth Miller, Mar. 1989; children: Margaret Elisabeth, Martin William. BS, Carroll Coll., 1975; MAS, U. Ill., 1976, PhD, 1979. Wis. Disting. prof. U. Wis., Milw., 1979-96; tax edn. cons. Price Waterhouse Coopers, N.Y.C., 1990—; prof., dir. acctg. programs Samford U., Birmingham, Ala., 1997-2001; founding dean Sch. Mgmt., disting. prof. Capital U., Columbus, Ohio, 2001—. Vis. assoc. prof. Ariz. State U., Tempe, 1985; vis. faculty Ernst & Young, N.Y.C., 1990—, Deloitte & Touche, N.Y.C., 1998—, Calif. CPA Found., 1986, AICPA, 1984-94, Wis. Bar Assn., 1992; developer Estate Tax Planner, McGraw Hill Software, N.Y.C., 1980-88; expert witness, 1985—; cons. corp. income tax State Ala., 1997-01, State of Wis., 1995, 99. Author West's Federal Taxation, 1985—, West's Federal Tax Research, 1986—, Income Shifting After Tax Reform, 1987, Multistate Corporate Tax Guide, 1985-96; contbr. articles to profl. jours. Bd. dirs., pres. Luth. High Sch. Assn. Milw., 1991-96, Bethesda Luth. Home, Watertown, Wis., 1989-91, Concord Chamber Orch., Milw., 1983-88; mem. Econ. Devel. Com., Wauwatosa, Wis., 1986-89; faculty athletic rep. to NCAA from U. Wis. Milw., 1990-96; mem. Milw. Symphony Chorus, Master Singers of Milw., Samford Master Singers, Samford Die Kantorei; vice chair faculty senate Samford U., 2000-01. Fellow Am. Acctg. Assn., Nat. Ctr. for Tax Edn. and Rsch., Wis. Inst. CPAs (Educator of Yr. 1987), Ala. Acctg. Educators Assn. (pres. 1999-2000). E-mal. Office: Capital Univ Sch of Mgmt 2199 E Main St Bexley OH 43209

RABB, GEORGE BERNARD, zoologist, conservationist; b. Charleston, S.C., Jan. 2, 1930; s. Joseph and Teresa C. (Redmond) R.; m. Mary Sughrue, June 10, 1953. BS, Coll. Charleston, 1951, LHD (hon.), 1995; MA, U. Mich., 1952, PhD, 1957. Teaching fellow zoology U. Mich., 1954-56; curator, coord. rsch. Chgo. Zool. Park, Brookfield., Ill., 1956-64, assoc. dir. rsch. and edn., 1964-75, dep. dir., 1969-75, dir., 1976—. Rsch. assoc. Field Mus., 1965—; lectr. dept. biology U. Chgo., 1965-89; mem. Com. on Evolution Biology, 1969—; pres. Chgo. Zool. Soc., 1976—; steering com. Species Survival Commn., Internat. Union Conservation of Nature, 1983—, vice-chmn. for N.Am., 1986-88, dep. chmn., 1987-89, chmn., 1989-96, vice-chmn. comms., 1997—; chmn. policy adv. group Internat. Species Info. System, 1974-89, chmn. bd., 1989-92; pres. bd. dirs. Chgo. Wilderness Mag., 1999—; v.p. Fauna and Flora Internat., 1998—; chmn. bd. Ill. State Mus., 1999—. Fellow AAAS; mem. Am. Soc. Ichthyologists and Herpetologists (pres. 1978), Herpetologists League, Soc. Systematic Zoology, Soc. Mammalogists, Soc. Study Evolution, Ecol. Soc. Am., Soc. Conservation Biology (council mem. 1986), Soc. for Integrative and Comparative Zoology, Soc. Study Animal Behavior, Am. Assn. Museums, Am. Soc. Naturalists, Am. Assn. Zool. Parks and Aquariums (dir. 1979-80), World Assn. Zoos and Aquariums, Am. Com. Internat. Conservation (chmn. 1987—), World Conservation Union (hon. mem.), Chgo. Coun. Fgn. Relations (Chgo. com.), Economic Club Chgo., Tavern Club, Sigma Xi. Office: Brookfield Zoo 3300 Golf Rd Brookfield IL 60513-1095

RABIDEAU, PETER WAYNE, university dean, chemistry educator; b. Johnstown, Pa., Mar. 4, 1940; s. Peter Nelson and Monica (Smalley) R.; m. Therese Charlene Newquist, Sept. 1, 1962 (div.); children: Steven, Michael, Christine, Susan; m. Jennifer Lee Mooney, Nov. 15, 1986; children: Mark, Leah. BS, Loyola U., Chgo., 1964; MS, Case Inst. Tech., Cleve., 1967; PhD, Case Western Res U, Cleve., 1968. Postdoctoral asst. U. Chgo., 1968-69, instr., 1969-70; asst. prof. Ind. U.-Purdue U., Indpls., 1970-73, assoc. prof., 1973-76, prof., 1976-90, chmn. dept. chemistry, 1985-90; dean Coll. Basic Scis. La. State U., Baton Rouge, 1990-99; dean Coll. Liberal Arts and Scis. Iowa State U., Ames, 1999—. Program officer NSF, 1988-89. Contbr. numerous articles to profl. jours. Recipient rsch. award Purdue Sch. Sci. at Indpls., 1982, Outstanding Alumnus award chemistry dept. Case Western U., 2001. Fellow AAAS; mem. Am. Chem. Soc. (chmn. Ind. sect. 1974, councilor 1981-90). Home: 3509 Valley View Rd Ames IA 50014-4615 Office: Iowa State U Coll Liberal Arts and Scis 202 Catt Hall Ames IA 50011-1301 E-mail: rabideau@iastate.edu.

RABIN, JOSEPH HARRY, marketing research company executive; b. Chgo., Dec. 12, 1927; s. Morris and Libby (Broder) Rabinovitz; m. Barbara E. Leader, Oct. 31, 1954; children: Marc Jay, Michelle Ann, Deborah Susan. BSc, Roosevelt U., 1950; MBA, DePaul U., 1951. Account exec. Gould, Gleiss & Benn, 1951-56; asst. dir. mktg. rsch. Paper Mate Co., Chgo., 1956-63; pres. Rabin Rsch. Co., 1963—. Pres. Mather H.S. Coun., 1972-74; mem. adv. coun. U. Toledo, 1976-77, Kellstadt Ctr. DePaul U., 1986-93; mem. adv. com. Bur. of the Census, 1978-83; bd. dirs. Market Rsch. Inst., 1973-75, Ner Tamid Synagogue, 1976—, Jewish Vocat. Svc., 1977-80. With AUS, 1946-47. Mem. Am. Mktg. Assn. (pres. Chgo. chpt. 1961-62, nat. dir. 1973-75, nat. v.p. mktg. rsch. 1978-79, nat. pres. 1981-82), Assn. Consumer Rsch., Am. Statis. Assn. (pres. Chgo. chpt. 1962-63), Am. Assn. Pub. Opinion Rsch. Home: 7061 N Kedzie Ave Chicago IL 60645-2846 Office: Rabin Rsch Co 150 E Huron St Chicago IL 60611-2999

RABINOVICH, SERGIO, physician, educator; b. Lima, Peru, Apr. 8, 1928; m. Nelly; children— Gina, Sergio, Norca, Egla. M.D., San Fernando Med. Sch., U. San Marcos, Lima, Peru, 1953. Intern San Fernando Med. Sch., U. San Marcos, Lima, 1947-54; resident in medicine Grasslands Hosp., Valhalla, N.Y., 1954-57, Henry Ford Hosp., Detroit; prof., head dept. internal medicine U. Arequipa Med. Sch., 1960-61; asst. prof. dept. internal medicine U. Iowa, Iowa City, 1963-65, asst. prof., 1965-69; attending physician and cons. VA Hosp., Iowa City, 1965-73; assoc. prof. U. Iowa, 1969-73; prof., chief dept. medicine div. infectious disease So. Ill. U. Sch. Medicine, Springfield, 1973-96, prof., chmn. dept. medicine, 1974-88, pres. Faculty Coun., 1992-93, prof. emeritus, 1996. Author: (with I.M. Smith, S.T. Donta) Antibiotics and Infection, 1974. Fellow ACP, Infectious Disease Soc. Am.; mem. AMA, Am. Soc. Microbiology, N.Y. Acad. Sci., Am. Fedn. Clin. Research, AAAS, Am. Thoracic Soc., Ill. Thoracic Soc. (pres. 1978-79), Central Soc. Clin. Research, Sigma Xi. Office: So Ill U Sch Medicine 800 N Rutledge St Springfield IL 62794-9636

RABINOWITZ, PAUL H. mathematics educator; b. Newark, Nov. 15, 1939; BA, NYU, 1961, PhD, 1966. Prof. math. U. Wis., Madison. Mem. Am. Math. Soc., Soc. Indsl. & Applied Math. Office: U Wis Dept Math 450 Lincoln Dr Van Vleck Hall EB813 Madison WI 53706

RACCAH, DOMINIQUE MARCELLE, publisher; b. Paris, Aug. 24, 1956; arrived in U.S., 1964; d. Paul Mordechai and Colette Bracha (Madar) R.; m. Raymond W. Bennett, Aug. 20, 1980; children: Marie, Lyron, Doran. BA, U. Ill., Chgo., 1978; MS, U. Ill., Champaign-Urbana, 1981. Rsch. analyst Leo Burnett Advt., Chgo., 1980-81, rsch. supr., 1981-84, assoc. rsch. dir., 1984-87; pres., pub., owner Sourcebooks, Inc., Naperville, Ill., 1987—; co-CEO Login Pubs. Consortium, Chgo., 1990-99. Author Financial Sourcebooks' Sources, 1987. Recipient Blue Chip Enterprise award, 2000, Ernst & Young Entrepreneur of Yr. Ill. and N.W. Ind., 2000; named to Inc. 500 list; inducted into Univ. Ill. Entrepreneurship Hall of Fame, 2001. Mem. Pubs. Mktg. Assn., Am. Booksellers Assn., Am. Assn. Pubs. Avocations: photography, writing, history. Home: 26 N Webster St Naperville IL 60540-4527 Office: Sourcebooks Inc 1935 Brookdale Rd # 139 Naperville IL 60563-9245 E-mail: dominique@sourcebooks.com.

RADCLIFF, WILLIAM FRANKLIN, lawyer, director; b. Fredericksburg, Ind., May 21, 1922; s. Samuel Pearl and Hester Susan (Sherwood) R.; m. Elizabeth Louise Doeller Haines, May 15, 1982; children— Forrest Lee, Stephanie Anne; foster children— Cheryl Lynn, Sandra Lee, Richard Alan, Lezlie Laverne; stepchildren— Mark David, Laura Louise, Pamela Lynn, Veronica Leigh. B.A., Yale U., 1948; J.D., Ind. U., 1951. Bar: Ind. 1951. With DeFur, Voran, Hanley, Radcliff & Reed and predecessors, Muncie, Ind., 1951—, ptnr., 1954—. Dir., mem. exec. com. Am. Nat. Bank and Trust Co., Muncie . Author: Sherman Minton: Indiana's Supreme Court Justice, 1996, Sagamore of the Wabash. Pres. Delaware County Mental Health Assn., 1962-63; founding mem. Ind. Mental Health Meml. Found., 1962, sec., 1962-84; bd. dirs. Delaware County Cancer Soc.; trustee Acad. Community Leadership. Served with AUS, 1940-46, PTO Mem. ABA, Ind. Bar Assn., Muncie Bar Assn., Muncie-Delaware County C. of C. (pres. 1972-73) Clubs: Muncie Tennis and Country (bd. dirs., sec.), Muncie, Delaware Country (pres. 1972-73), Exchange (pres. 1962) (Muncie). Lodge: Masons Home: 1809 N Winthrop Rd Muncie IN 47304-2532 Office: 201 E Jackson St Muncie IN 47305-2832

RADER, RALPH TERRANCE, lawyer; b. Clarksburg, W.Va., Dec. 5, 1947; s. Ralph Coolidge and Jeanne (Cover) R.; m. Rebecca Jo Vorderman, Mar. 22, 1969; children: Melissa Michelle, Allison Suzanne. BSME, Va. Poly. Inst., 1970; JD, Am. U., 1974. Bar: Va. 1975, U.S. Ct. Customs and Patent Appeals, 1977, U.S. Dist. Ct. (ea. dist.) Mich. 1978, Mich. 1979, U.S. Ct. Appeals (6th cir.) 1979, U.S. Dist. Ct. (we. dist.) Mich. 1981, U.S. Ct. Appeals (fed. cir.) 1983. Supervisory patent examiner U.S. Patent Office, Washington, 1970-77; patent atty., ptnr. Cullen, Sloman, Cantor, Grauer, Scott & Rutherford, Detroit, 1977-88; ptnr. Dykema, Gossett, 1989-96, Rader, Fishman & Grauer, Bloomfield Hills, Mich., 1996—. Contbr. articles to profl. jours. Mem. adminstrv. bd. 1st United Meth. Ch., Birmingham, Mich., 1980—. With U.S. Army, 1970-76. Mem. ABA, Am. Patent Law Assn., Mich. Patent Law Assn., Mich. Bar (governing coun. patent, trademark and copyright law sect. 1981-84), Engring. Soc. Detroit, Masons, Tau Beta Pi, Pi Tau Sigma, Phi Kappa Phi. Methodist. Home: 4713 Riverchase Dr Troy MI 48098-4186 Office: Rader Fishman & Grauer 39533 Woodward Ave Ste 140 Bloomfield Hills MI 48304-5098 E-mail: rtr@raderfishman.com.

RADKE, RODNEY OWEN, agricultural research executive, consultant; b. Ripon, Wis., Feb. 5, 1942; s. Edward Ludwig and Vera Ione (Phillips) R.; m. Jean Marie Rutsch, Sept. 1, 1963; children: Cheryl Lynn, Lisa Diane, Daniel E. BS, U. Wis., 1963, MS, 1965, PhD, 1967. Rsch. scientist Monsanto Agrl. Co., St. Louis, 1969-75, sr. rsch. group leader, 1975-79, rsch. mgr., 1979-81, mgr. rsch., 1981-93; pvt. practice cons., 1993—2002; ret., 2002—. Contbr. articles to profl. jours.; patentee in field. Served to capt. U.S. Army, 1967-69. Mem. Weed Sci. Soc. Am., North Ctrl. Weed Sci. Soc. Lutheran. Avocations: power boating, soccer, gardening, woodshop. Home and Office: 1119 Grand Prix Dr Saint Charles MO 63303-6313

RADKOSKI, DONALD J. food products company executive; V.p., dir. fin., asst. tres. Bob Evans Farms, Columbus, Ohio, 1980-88, CFO, group v.p. fin., treas., 1988—. Office: Bob Evans Farms Inc 3776 S High St Columbus OH 43207-0863

RADLER, FRANKLIN DAVID, publishing holding company executive; b. Montreal, Que., Can., June 3, 1942; m. Rona Lassner, Mar. 26, 1972; children: Melanie, Melissa. MBA, Queen's U., Can., 1967. Pres., chief oper. officer, dir. Hollinger Inc., Toronto; exec. v.p. Argus Corp. Ltd.; co-chair, publ. Chgo. Sun-Times. Chmn. Am. Pub. Co., Jerusalem Post Ltd., Palestine Post Ltd. Office: Chgo Sun-Times 401 N Wabash Ave Chicago IL 60611-5642

RADMER, MICHAEL JOHN, lawyer, educator; b. Wisconsin Rapids, Wis., Apr. 28, 1945; s. Donald Richard and Thelma Loretta (Donahue) R.; children from previous marriage: Christina Nicole, Ryan Michael; m. Laurie J. Anshus, Dec. 22, 1983; 1 child, Michael John B.S., Northwestern U., Evanston, Ill., 1967; J.D., Harvard U., 1970. Bar: Minn. 1970. Assoc. Dorsey & Whitney, Mpls., 1970-75, ptnr., 1976—. Lectr. law Hamline U. Law Sch., St. Paul, 1981-84; gen. counsel, rep., sec. 163 federally registered investment cos., Mpls. and St. Paul, 1977—. Contbr. articles to legal jours. Active legal work Hennepin County Legal Advice Clinic, Mpls., 1971—. Mem. ABA, Minn. Bar Assn., Hennepin County Bar Assn. Club: Mpls. Athletic. Home: 4329 E Lake Harriet Pky Minneapolis MN 55409-1725 Office: Dorsey & Whitney 50 South 6th St Ste 1500 Minneapolis MN 55402

RADNOR, ALAN T. lawyer; b. Cleve., Mar. 10, 1946; s. Robert Clark and Rose (Chester) R.; m. Carol Sue Hirsch, June 22, 1969; children: Melanie, Joshua, Joanna. BA, Kenyon Coll., 1967; MS in Anatomy, Ohio State U., 1969, JD, 1972. Bar: Ohio 1972. Ptnr. Vorys, Sater, Seymour & Pease, Columbus, Ohio, 1972—. Adj. prof. law Ohio State U., Columbus, 1979-99. Contbr. articles to profl. jours. Bd. dirs., trustee Congregation Tifereth Israel, Columbus, 1975—, pres., 1985-87; trustee Columbus Mus. Art, 1995-98. Named Boss or Yr., Columbus Assn. Legal Secs., 1983. Fellow Am. Coll. Trial Lawyers; mem. ABA, Ohio State Bar Assn., Columbus Bar Assn., Def. Rsch. Inst., Internat. Assn. Def. Counsel. Avocations: reading, sculpture. Home: 400 S Columbia Ave Columbus OH 43209-1629 Office: Vorys Sater Seymour & Pease 52 E Gay St PO Box 1008 Columbus OH 43216-1008

RADOGNO, CHRISTINE, state legislator; b. Oak Park, Ill., Dec. 21, 1952; BA, MSW, Loyola U. Mem. Ill. Senate, Springfield, 1997—, mem. appropriations, commerce & industry & pub. health coms. Republican. Office: State Capitol Capitol Bldg M-121 Springfield IL 62706-0001 also: 521 S LaGrance Rd Ste 104 La Grange IL 60525

RAEBURN, JOHN HAY, English language educator; b. Indpls., July 18, 1941; s. Gordon Maurice and Katherine (Calwell) R.; m. Gillian Kimble, Aug. 18, 1963 (div. July 1979); children— Daniel Kennedy, Nicholas Kimble; m. Kathleen Kamerick, July 5, 1986. A.B. with honors, Ind. U., 1963; A.M., U. Pa., 1964, Ph.D., 1969. Asst. prof. U. Mich., Ann Arbor, 1967-74; vis. lectr. U. Iowa, Iowa City, 1974-75, assoc. prof., 1976-83, prof. English, 1983—; chmn. Am. Studies dept., 1983-85, 94-2000; chmn. English dept. U. Iowa, Iowa City, 1985-91; assoc. prof. U. Louisville, 1975-76. Author: Fame Became of Him: Hemingway as Public Writer, 1984; editor: (with others) Frank Capra: The Man and His Films, 1975 Mem. Am. Studies Assn., Orgn. Am. Historians. Democrat Home: 321 Hutchinson Ave Iowa City IA 52246-2407 Office: U Iowa Dept Am Studies Dept English 701 Jefferson Building Iowa City IA 52242-1418 E-mail: john-raeburn@iowa.edu.

RAGATZ, THOMAS GEORGE, lawyer; b. Madison, Wis., Feb. 18, 1934; s. Wilmer Leroy and Rosanna (Kindschi) Ragatz; m. Karen Christensen, Dec. 19, 1965; children: Thomas Rolf, William Leslie, Erik Douglas. BBA, U. Wis., 1957, LLB, 1961. CPA Wis.; bar: Wis. 1961, U.S. Dist. Ct. (ea. and we. dists.) Wis. 1961, U.S. Tax Ct. 1963, U.S. Ct. Appeals (7th cir.) 1965, U.S. Supreme Ct. 1968. Staff acct. Peat, Marwick, Mitchell & Co., Mpls., 1958; instr. Sch. Bus., U. Wis., Madison, 1958-60; formerly lectr. in acctg. and law Law Sch. U. Wis.; law clk. Wis. Supreme Ct., 1961-62; assoc. Boardman Suhr Curry & Field, Madison, 1962-64, ptnr., 1965-78, Foley & Lardner, Madison, 1978—, mng. ptnr., 1984-93, chmn. budget com., 1994-99. Dir. Sub-Zero Freezer Co., Inc., Mortenson, Matzell & Meldrem, Inc., Norman Bassett Found., Wis. Sports Found., United Way Found., Courtier Found.; dir., past pres. Wis. Sports Devel. Corp.; lectr. seminars on tax subjects. Author: The Ragatz History, 1989; contbr. Formerly dir. United Way, Meth. Hosp. Found; mem. U. Wis. Found., United Way of Dane County; former dir. United Way, Meth. Hosp.; mem. Wis. Found., United Way of Dane County; chmn. site selection com. U. Wis. Hosp.; bd. regents U. Wis., panel provision of legal svcs.; past pres. 1st Congl. Ch. Found.; bd. dirs. Met. YMCA, Madison, YMCA Found., Found. for Madison Pub. Schs.; pres. Bus. and Edn. Partnership, 1983—89, bd. dirs.; former moderator 1st Congl. Ch.; past pres. First Congl. Ch. Found.; former moderator 1st Congl. Ch.; chmn. site selection com. U. Wis. Hosp.; bd. regents U. Wis., panel provision of legal svcs.; bd. dirs. Met. YMCA, Madison, 1983—90, YMCA Found., Norman Bassett Found., Courtier Found.; pres. Bus. & Edn. Partnership, 1983—89, also bd. dirs. Fellow: Am. Bar Found.; mem.: ABA, Dane County Bar Assn. (pres. 1978—79, chmn. jud. qualification com., sec.), Wis. Inst. CPA, State Bar Wis. 1969—70, (bd. govs. 1971—75, chmn. fin. com. 1975—80, chmn. tax sect., chmn. spl. com. on econs., chmn. svcs. for lawyers com.), Wis. Bar Found., Seventh Cir. Bar Assn., Am. Judicature Soc., Order of Constantine, Bascom Hill Soc., Order of Coif, Madison Club (pres. 1980—81), Madison Club House Corp. 1999—, (bd. dirs.), Sigma Chi, Beta Gamma Sigma. Republican. Home: 3334 Lake Mendota Dr Madison WI 53705-1469 Office: Foley & Lardner PO Box 1497 Madison WI 53701-1497 also: Foley & Lardner 1st Wisconsin Ctr 777 E Wisconsin Ave Ste 3800 Milwaukee WI 53202-5302

RAGGIO, ROBERT FRANK, career officer; BEE, Mont. State U., 1966; MSc in Indsl. Engring., Purdue U., 1967. Commd. 2d. lt. USAF, 1966, advanced through grades to lt. gen., 1998; pilot McGuire AFB, N.J., 1968-70; rescue helicopter pilot Bergstrom AFB, Tex., 1970-71, Bien Hoa Air Base, South Vietnam, 1971, Udorn Royal Thai AFB, Thailand, 1971-72; instr. pilot Hill AFB, Utah, 1972-74; various assignments Aeronautical Sys. Ctr. Wright-Patterson AFB, Ohio, 1975-82, 88-96; comdr. Aeronautical Sys. Ctr. Wright-Patterson AFB, 1998—; various assignments The Pentagon, Washington, 1983-87, 96-98; exec. officer to comdr. Air Force Sys. Ctr. Andrews AFB, Md., 1987-88. Decorated D.S.M., Legion of Merit with oak leaf cluster, Air medal with oak leaf cluster, Meritorious Svc. medal with two oak leaf clusters, Vietnam Svc. medal with three svc. stars, Rep. of Vietnam Gallantry Cross with Palm. Home: 9401 David Andrew Way Dayton OH 45458-3644

RAGLAND, TERRY EUGENE, emergency physician; b. Greensboro, N.C., June 14, 1944; s. Terry Porter and Virginia Lucile (Stowe) R.; m. Marguerite Elizabeth Morton, May 15, 1976; children: Kenneth John McConnell, Ryan Lee Ragland. BS, Cen. Mich. U., 1966; MD, U. Mich., 1970. Diplomate Am. Bd. Internal Medicine, Am. Bd. Emergency Medicine. Intern St. Joseph Mercy Hosp., Ann Arbor, Mich., 1970-71, internal medicine resident, 1974-77, chief resident internal medicine, 1975-76, emergency physician, 1977-2001, med. dir. emergency ctr., 1985-97, chief of staff, 1996-97, assoc. dir. dept. emergency svcs., 1997-2000; CEO Secure Care, Inc., 1992—; pres. Huron Valley Phys. Assn., 1997-2000. Clin. asst. prof. U. Mich., Ann Arbor, 1981—; examiner Am. Bd. Emergency Medicine, 1983-2001; med. dir. Life Support Services, Ann Arbor, 1983-92; mem. Mercy Health Plans Bd., 1999-2000. Contbr. chpts. to book. Lt. USN, 1972-74. Fellow Am. Coll. Emergency Physicians; mem. Am. Coll. Physicians, Nat. Assn. Emergency Med. Technicians, Mich. State Med. Soc. (alt. del. 1982-84, 89-90, del. 1991-94, mem. jud. commn. 1999—), Mich. Emergency Med. Technicians Assn., Washtenaw County Med. Soc. (pres. 1993). Democrat. Avocations: trout fishing, gardening, skiing.

RAHMAN, YUEH-ERH, biologist; b. Kwangtung, China, June 10, 1928; came to U.S., 1960; d. Khon and Kwei-Phan (Chan) Li; m. Aneesur Rahman, Nov. 3, 1956; 1 dau., Aneesa. B.S., U. Paris, 1950; M.D. magna cum laude, U. Louvain, Belgium, 1956. Clin. and postdoctoral research fellow Louvain U., 1956-60; mem. staff Argonne (Ill.) Nat. Lab., 1960-72, biologist, 1972-81, sr. biologist, 1981-85; prof. pharmaceutics Coll. Pharmacy, U. Minn., Mpls., 1985—, dir. grad. studies, pharmaceutics, 1989-92, head dept. pharmaceutics, 1991-96, 97-98. Vis. scientist State U. Utrecht, Netherlands, 1968-69; adj. prof. No. Ill. U., DeKalb, 1971-85; cons. NIH.; Mem. com. of rev. group, div. research grants NIH, 1979-83 Author; patentee in field. Recipient IR-100 award, 1976; grantee Nat. Cancer Inst., Nat. Inst. Arthritis, Metabolic and Digestive Diseases. Fellow Am. Assn. Pharm. Scientists; mem. AAAS, Am. Soc. Cell Biology, N.Y. Acad. Scis., Radiation Rsch. Soc., Assn. for Women in Sci. (1st pres. Chgo. area chpt. 1978-79). Unitarian. Home: 939 Coast Blvd Unit 6G La Jolla CA 92037-4115 Office: Coll Pharmacy U Minn Minneapolis MN 55455

RAICHLE, MARCUS EDWARD, radiology, neurology educator; b. Hoquiam, Wash., Mar. 15, 1937; m. Mary Elizabeth Rupert, 1964; children: Marcus Edward, Timothy Stephen, Sarah Elizabeth, Katherine Ann. BS, U. Wash., 1960, MD, 1964. Diplomate Am. Bd. Psychiatry and Neurology. Intern Balt. City Hosps., 1964-65, resident, 1965-66; asst. neurologist N.Y. Hosp. Cornell Med. Ctr., N.Y.C., 1966-68, neurologist, chief resident, 1968-69; clin. instr. dept. medicine divsn. neurosci. U. Tex. Med. Sch., San Antonio, 1969-70; rsch. instr. Washington U. Sch. Med., St. Louis, 1971-72, from asst. prof. neurology to assoc. prof. neurology, 1972-78, from asst. prof. radiology (radiation scis.) to assoc. prof. radiology Edward Mallinckrodt Inst. Radiology, 1972-79, from asst. prof. to assoc. prof. biomedical engring., 1974-79, prof. neurology, 1978—, prof. radiology Edward Mallinckrodt Inst. Radiology, 1979—, prof. biomedical engring., 1979—. Instr. dept. neurology Cornell U. Med. Coll., N.Y.C., 1968-69; asst. neurologist Barnes Hosp., St. Louis, 1971-75, assoc. neurologist, 1975-78, neurologist, 1978—; cons. neurologist St. Louis Children's Hosp., 1975—; neurologist Jewish Hosp., St. Louis, 1984—, St. Louis Regional Hosp., 1985-97; mem. neurology study sect. A NIH, 1975-79; mem. com. cerebrovascular diseases Nat. Inst. Neurol. Diseases and Stroke, long range planning effort, 1978, basic sci. task force, 1978; mem ad hoc adv. panel, Nat. Inst. Neurol. Diseases and Stroke, 1983, chmn. PET grants spl. rev. com., 1983, chmn. brain imaging ctrs. spl. rev. com., 1985; mem. adv. bd. McDonnell-Pew Program cognitive neuroscience, 1989; other coms. Editorial bds. Stroke, 1974-82, Neurology, 1976-82, Annals of Neurology, 1979-86, Journal Cerebral Blood Flow and Metabolism, 1983-86, dep. chief editor, 1981-83, Brain, 1985-90, Human Neurobiology, 1985-87, Brain Research, 1985-90, Synapse, 1987-90, Jour. Neurosci., 1989-95, Jour. Cognitive Neurosci., 1989—, Cerebral Cortex, 1990—, Jour. Nuclear Medicine, 1990-96, Biol. Psychiatry, 1993—, Learning and Memory, 1993—; contbr. over 120 articles and revs. to sci. jours., over 75 chpts. to books. Major USAF, 1969-71. Recipient numerous awards, lectrs., fellows including Charles A. Dana award for pioneering achievements in health and edn. Dana Found., 1996. Mem. NAS, Inst. Medicine of NAS.

RAIKES, RONALD E. state legislator; b. Lincoln, Mar. 11, 1943; m. Helen Holz, Dec. 26, 1966; children: Heather, Abbie, Justin. BS in Farm Operation, Iowa State U.; MS in Agr. Bus., PhD in Agr. Econ., U. Calif. Former assoc. prof. dept. econs. Iowa State U.; farmer, cattle feeder, soil conservation contractor; mem. Nebr. Legislature from 25th dist., Lincoln, 1997, 98—. Mem. Nebr. Econ. Forecasting Adv. Bd., 1983-87. Mem. Nebr. Farm Bus. Assn., Nebr. Land Improvement Contractors Assn., Nebr. Agr. Rels. Coun., Agr. Builders Nebr. Home: 3221 S 76th St Lincoln NE 68506-4612 Office: State Capitol Dist 25 PO Box 94604 Rm 1008 Lincoln NE 68509-4604

RAILSBACK, MIKE, radio personality; b. St. Joseph, Mo., Mar. 16, 1958; m. Linda Railsback; children: Paul, Don. BS Agrl. Bus., Northwest Mo. State U. Radio host WDAF/61 Country, Westwood, Kans., 1989—. Office: WDAF/61 Country 4935 Belinder Rd Westwood KS 66205

RAINEY, WILLIAM JOEL, lawyer; b. Flint, Mich., Oct. 11, 1946; s. Ralph Jefferson and Elsie Matilda (Erickson) R.; m. Cynthia Hetsko, June 15, 1968; children: Joel Michael, Allison Elizabeth. AB, Harvard U., 1968; JD, U. Mich., 1971. Bar: N.Y. 1973, Wash. 1977, Ariz. 1987, Mass. 1992, Kans. 1997, U.S. Dist. Ct. (so. and ea. dists.) N.Y. 1973, U.S. Ct. Appeals (2nd cir.) N.Y. 1973, U.S. Dist. Ct. (we. dist.) Wash. 1977, U.S. Supreme Ct. 1976, U.S. Ct. Appeals (9th cir.) Wash. 1978, U.S. Dist. Ct. Ariz. 1987, U.S. Dist. Ct. Mass. 1992. Assoc. atty. Curtis, Mallet-Prevost, Colt & Mosle, N.Y.C., 1971-76; atty., asst. corp. sec. Weyerhaeuser Co., Tacoma, 1976-85; v.p., corp. sec., gen. counsel Southwest Forest Industries Inc., Phoenix, 1985-87; sr. v.p., corp. sec., gen. counsel Valley Nat. Corp. and Valley Nat. Bank, 1987-91; v.p., gen. counsel Cabot Corp., Boston, 1991-93; exec. v.p., gen. coun., corp. sec. Fourth Fin. Corp., Wichita, Kans., 1994-96; sr. v.p., gen. counsel, corp. sec. Payless ShoeSource, Inc., Topeka, 1996—. Editor U. Mich. Jour. Law Reform, 1970-71 Bd. dirs. Big Bros./Big Sisters, 1994-96. Maj. USAR, 1970-91. Mem. ABA (chmn. task force 1984-91), Wash. State Bar Assn., State Bar of Ariz., Assn. Bank Holding Cos. (steering com. 1989-91, chmn. lawyers com. 1990-91), Harvard Club of Phoenix (bd. dirs. 1989-91). Avocations: backpacking, running, fishing, bicycling. Home: 901 Deer Run Dr Lawrence KS 66049-4731 Office: Payless ShoeSource Inc PO Box 1189 Topeka KS 66601-1189

RAINS, JOANNE WARNER, nursing educator; b. Sioux Falls, S.D., June 27, 1950; d. Arnold D. and Arlene M. (Lawrence) W.; m. Daniel P. Rains, Dec. 13, 1975; children: David Warner, Isaac Daniel. BA, Augustana Coll., 1972; MA, U. Iowa, 1976; D of Nursing Sci., Ind. U., 1990. Vis. nurse Delaware County Vis. Nurse Assn., Muncie, Ind., 1976-77; cons. Ind. State Bd. Health, Indpls., 1977-78; instr. Briar Cliff Coll., Sioux Falls, 1981-82; adj. faculty Okla. Bapt. U., Shawnee, 1985; assoc. prof. Ind. U., Indpls., 1990—. Mem. exec. com. Friends Com. on Nat. Legis., Washington, 1992—; fellow Primary Health Care Policy, Washington, 1996; bd. trustees Earlham Coll. Campaign mgr. Doug Kinser for State Rep. Ind. House Dist. 54, 1988-94; exec. com., mem. New Castle (Ind.) Healthy City Com., 1989-99; chair residential drive Am. Cancer Soc., New Castle, 1989. Mem. ANA, Assn. Cmty. Health Nurse Educators (bd. dirs.), Ind. Polit. Sci. Assn. (v.p. 1993-94,. pres. 1994-95). Quaker. Office: Ind U 2325 Chester Blvd Richmond IN 47374-1220

RAINS, M. NEAL, lawyer; b. Burlington, Iowa, July 26, 1943; s. Merritt and Lucille (Lepper) R.; m. Jean Baldwin, July 26, 1980 (div. 1995); children: Robert Baldwin, Kathleen Kellogg. B.A. in Polit. Sci. with honors, U. Iowa, 1965; J.D., Northwestern U., 1968. Bar: Ohio 1968. Assoc. Arter & Hadden, Cleve., 1968-76, ptnr., 1976—2001, mem. exec. com., 1981-90, mem. mgmt. com., 1987-90, mng. ptnr., 1990-92; master bencher Inns of Ct., 1990—; ptnr. Frantz Ward LLP, Cleve., 2001—. Lectr. on profl. topics, including alternative dispute resolution, distbn. law, litigation practice and procedure, and antitrust. Contbr. articles to profl. jours. Former trustee Legal Aid Soc. Cleve.; trustee Cleve. Play House, mem. adv. coun., 1988—; trustee Citizens League Greater Cleve., Cleve. Art Assn. With U.S. Army, 1968-70 Fellow: Am. Bar Found.; mem.: ABA, Harold H. Burton Am. Inn Ct. (pres. 1999—2000), William K. Thomas Inn Ct. 1999—, Cleve. Bar Found. (trustee 1999—), Ohio Assn. Civil Trial Attys., Internat. Assn. Def. Counsel, Def. Rsch. Inst., Bar Assn. Greater Cleve. (chmn. young lawyers sect. 1975—76, cert. merit 1975), Ohio Bar Assn., Rowfant Club, City Club, Print Club (trustee 2001—), Cleve. Skating Club, Union Club, Phi Delta Phi, Omicron Delta Kappa, Phi Beta Kappa. Home: 18400 Shelburne Rd Shaker Heights OH 44118 Office: Frantz Ward LLP 55 Public Sq Cleveland OH 44113 E-mail: nrains@arterhadden.com.

RAJAN, FRED E. N. clergy member, church administrator; Exec. dir. Commn. for Multicultural Ministries of the Evangelical Lutheran Church in America, Chicago, Ill., 1992. Office: Evangelical Lutheran Church Am 8765 W Higgins Rd Chicago IL 60631-4101

RAJURKAR, KAMLAKAR PURUSHOTTAM, mechanical engineering educator; b. India, Jan. 6, 1942; came to U.S., 1975; s. Purushottam S. and Indira P. Rajurkar; m. Sanjivani K. Natu, Feb. 3, 1972; children: Piyush, Suneela. B.Sc., Vikram U., India, 1962, B.Engring. with honors, 1966; M.S., Mich. Tech. U., 1978, Ph.D., 1981. Lectr. mech. engring. Govt. Poly., Bhopal, India, 1966-75; grad. teaching and research asst. Mich. Tech. U., Houghton, 1975-81, asst. prof., 1981-83; assoc. prof. U. Nebr., Lincoln, 1983-88; Mohr prof. engring. and dir. Nontraditional Mfg. Rsch. Ctr., 1988—; Contbr. to profl. jours. Fellow ASME (Blackall Machine Tool and Gage award 1995), Soc. Mfg. Engrs.; mem. Internat. Inst. Prodn. Rsch., Tau Beta Pi. Home: 7308 Skyhawk Cir Lincoln NE 68506-4659 Office: University of Nebraska 175 Nebraska Hall Lincoln NE 68588-0158

RAKITA, LOUIS, cardiologist, educator; b. Montreal, Que., Can., July 2, 1922; came to U.S., 1951, naturalized, 1962; s. S. and Rose (Weinman) R.; m. G. Blanche Michlin, Dec. 4, 1945; 1 son, Robert M. B.A., Sir George Williams Coll., Montreal, 1942; M.D., C.M., McGill U., 1949. Diplomate: Am. Bd. Internal Medicine. Intern Montreal Gen. Hosp., 1949-50; resident in medicine Jewish Gen. Hosp., Montreal, 1950-51; fellow in medicine Alton Ochsner Med. Found., New Orleans, 1951-52; chief resident in medicine Cleve. City Hosp., 1952-53, Am. Heart Assn. fellow, 1954-55, Inst. for Med. Research, Cedars of Lebanon Hosp., Los Angeles, 1953-54; practice medicine specializing in internal medicine and cardiology Cleve., 1954—; instr. medicine Western Res. U., 1954-55, sr. instr., 1955-57, asst. prof., 1957-61, asso. prof., 1961-71; asst. vis. physician Cleve. City Hosp., 1954-57, vis. physician, 1957—; advanced fellow Cleve. Met. Gen. Hosp., 1959-61, dir. cardiology, 1966-87, immediate past dir., div. cardiology, 1987—; asso. div. of research in med. edn. Case Western Res. U., Cleve., 1969-75, prof. medicine, 1971-93, prof. emeritus medicine, 1993. Chmn. Phase IIA Cardiovascular com. Case Western Res. U., 1965-70, Faculty Senate Subcom. for Devel. and Evaluation of Ednl. Methods, 1969, chmn. Univ. Com. on Ednl. Planning, 1971-73, Faculty Coun. Sch. Medicine, 1979-80, Faculty Coun. Steering Com. Sch. Medicine, 1979-80, mem. bd. trustees Com. on Univ. Plans, 1971-73, Faculty Senate, Exec. Coun.; cons. in cardiology Luth. Med. Ctr., Cleve., 1970—, Crile VA Hosp., Cleve., 1969—; vis. cardiologist Sunny Acres Hosp., Cleve., 1973—; cardiologist rep. of del. to USSR, 1973. Author: (with M. Broder) Cardiac Arrhythmias, 1970, (with M. Kaplan) Immunological Diseases, 1972; Contbr. (with M. Kaplan) articles on cardiovascular diseases to profl. publs. Served with RCAF, 1942-45. Recipient Research Career Devel. award USPHS, 1962-69, Saltzman award Mt. Sinai Med. Health Found., 1997. Fellow ACP (Laureate award Ohio chpt. 1992), Am. Coll. Cardiology, Royal Coll. Physicians and Surgeons Can. (cert.), Am. Heart Assn. (mem. exec. com. N.E. Ohio chpt. 1972—, trustee 1969—, pres. N.E. Ohio chpt. 1972-74, coun. on clin. cardiology 1972—, chmn. various coms., v.p. North Ctrl. Region 1985-86, bd. dirs. 1985-86, hon. life trustee Northeast Ohio affiliate, vice chmn. task force on product licensing feasibility 1987—, Award of Merit 1987, Gold Heart award 1989); mem. AAUP, Am. Fedn. Clin. Rsch., Ctrl. Soc. Clin. Rsch., Soc. Exptl. Biology and Medicine, Cleve. Med. Libr. Assn. (trustee 1972—), Nat. Bd. Med. Examiners, The Press of Case Western Res. U. (adv. com. 1970), Nat. Heart and Lung Inst., Nat. Insts. Health (left ventricular assist device clin. trial program divsn. extramural affairs, data rev. bd. 1981—, adv. com. med. devices applications program 1971-75), Sigma Xi. Home: 24151 S Woodland Rd Cleveland OH 44122-3315 Office: 2500 Metrohealth Dr Cleveland OH 44109-1900

RAKOLTA, JOHN, JR. construction executive; b. Detroit, May 26, 1947; BSCE, Marquette U. Design engr. Bendix Machine Tool; mem. sr. staff aerospace sector engring. Allied Signal; chmn., CEO Walbridge Aldinger Co., Detroit. Mem. NAACP, Automotive Industry Action Group (bd. dirs.), Detroit Urban League, Engring. Soc. Detroit. Office: Walbridge Aldinger 613 Abbott St Ste 300 Detroit MI 48226-2521

RAKSAKULTHAI, VINAI, obstetrician, gynecologist; b. Rayong, Thailand, Mar. 20, 1942; came to U.S., 1968; s. Choosak and Ngo (Koo) R.; m. Vullapa Raksakulthai, Sept. 20, 1968; children: Vipavull, Vivian, Vipat. MD, ChiengMai Med. Sch., Thailand, 1966. Diplomate Am. Bd. Ob-Gyn. Intern New Britain (Conn.) Gen. Hosp., 1969; resident St. Joseph Mercy Hosp., Pontiac, Mich., 1970-72; practice medicine specializing in ob-gyn. Fredericktown, Mo., 1973—. Mem. Mo. Med. Assn., Mineral Area Med. Soc. Buddhist. Home: 201 Williams St Fredericktown MO 63645-1317 Office: 735 W Main Fredericktown MO 63645

RALPH, DAVID CLINTON, communications educator; b. Muskogee, Okla., Jan. 12, 1922; s. Earl Clinton and Rea Jane (Potter) R.; m. Kathryn Juanita Wicklund, Nov. 29, 1947; children: David Randall, Steven Wicklund. AA, Muskogee Jr. Coll., 1941; BS in Theatre, Northwestern U., 1947, MA in Theatre, 1948, PhD in Speech, 1953. Lectr. Ind. U., Hammond, 1947-48; instr. speech U. Mo., Columbia, 1948-53; tchr. debate-forensics summer program for high sch. students Northwestern U., Evanston, Ill., 1949-51; asst. prof. speech Mich. State U., East Lansing, 1953-57, assoc. prof., 1957-64, prof. speech and theatre, 1964-68, prof. communication, 1968-94, prof. emeritus, 1994—, dir. comm. undergrad. program, 1968-88. Cons. on pub. speaking, 1948—. Co-author: Group Discussion, 1954, 2d edit., 1956, Principles of Speaking, 1962, 3d edit., 1975; contbr. articles to profl. jours., chpts. to books. Coach Jr. League Boys' Baseball, Lansing, Mich., 1958-74; mem. civilian aux. to Lansing Fire Dept., 1987—. Lt. USNR, 1942-46, PTO, ETO. Named Hon. State Farmer, Future Farmers Am., 1965; recipient Community Svc. award Mich. State U. Sr. Class Coun., 1979, Outstanding Faculty award, 1987, 91; Teaching Excellence award State of Mich., 1990. Mem. AAUP, Nat. Communication Assn., Cen. States Communication Assn., Golden Key (hon., faculty advisor), Omicron Delta Kappa. Democrat. Methodist. Avocations: model trains and fire engines. Office: Mich State U Dept Communication East Lansing MI 48824

RALSTON, RICHARD H. lawyer; b. L.A., Sept. 28, 1942; BA, U. Kans., 1965; JD, U. Mo., Kansas City, 1969. Bar: Mo. 1969, U.S. Dist. Ct. (we. dist.) Mo., U.S. Ct. Appeals (8th cir.). Law clerk to Hon. Elmo B. Hunter U.S. Dist. Ct. (we. dist.) Mo., 1968-72, U.S. magistrate judge, 1976-88; prof. law Creighton U., 1972-76; mem. Polsinelli, White, Vardeman & Shalton, Kansas City, Mo., 1976—. Adj. prof. law U. Mo. Kansas City, 1977-79; chmn. subcom. on patterned civil jury instructions U.S. Ct. Appeals (8th cir.), 1986—. Editor-in-chief U. Mo. Kansas City Law Rev., 1968-69; contbr. articles to profl. jours. Mem. ABA (chmn. state membership com. 1988—), Mo. Bar (chmn. fed. practice com. 1988-92), Kansas City Met. Bar Assn. (exec. com. 1991-95), Ross T. Roberts Inn Ct. (master 1986-91), Phi Delta Phi. Office: Polsinelli White Vardeman & Shalton 700 W 47th St Ste 1000 Kansas City MO 64112-1805

RAMALINGAM, SUBBIAH, mechanical engineer, educator; MS in Mech. Engring., U. Ill., Urbana-Champaign, 1961, PhD, 1967. Prof. mech. engring. U. Minn., Mpls. Contbr. articles to profl. jours. Mem. NAE. Achievements include research in modeling thin films for tribological applications, intelligent sensors, real-time sensing for manufacturing automation, tribology, thin-film deposition processes and coating technology, machining theory, metal forming and manufacturing automation. Office: U Minn Engring Inst Tech 111 Church St SE Minneapolis MN 55455-0111

RAMDAS, ANANT KRISHNA, physicist, optics scientist; b. Poona, India, May 19, 1930; married, 1956. BSc, U. Poona, India, 1950, MSc, 1953, PhD in Physics, 1956. Rsch. assoc. physics, 1956-60; from asst. prof. to assoc. prof., 1960-67; prof. physics Purdue U., Lafayette, Ind., 1967—. Alexander von Humboldt U.S. sr. scientist, 1977-78. Fellow Am. Physical Soc. (Frank Isakson prize 1994), Indian Acad. Sci., Optical Soc. Am., Third World Acad. Scis. Achievements include research in spectroscopy; application of spectroscopic techniques to solid state physics; electronic and vibrational spectra of solids studied by absorption and emission spectra in the visible and the infrared and by Raman and Brillouin spectroscopy. Office: Purdue Univ Dept Of Physics West Lafayette IN 47907

RAMER, JAMES LEROY, civil engineer; b. Marshalltown, Iowa, Dec. 7, 1935; s. LeRoy Frederick and Irene (Wengert) Ramer; m. Jacqueline L. Orr, Dec. 15, 1957; children: Sarah T., Robert H., Eric A., Susan L. Student, U. Iowa, 1953-57; MCE, Washington U., St. Louis, 1976, MA in Polit. Sci., 1978; postgrad., U. Mo., 1984—. Registered profl. engr., land surveyor. Civil and constrn. engr. U.S. Army C.E., Tulsa, 1960-63; civil and relocations engr. U.S. State Dept., Del Rio, Tex., 1964; project engr. H.B. Zachary Co., San Antonio, 1965-66; civil and constrn. engr. U.S. Army C.E., St. Louis, 1967-76, tech. advisor for planning and nat. hydropower coord., 1976-78; project mgr. for EPA constrn. grants Milw., 1978-80; chief arch. and engring. HUD, Indpls., 1980-81; civil design and pavements engr. Whiteman AFB, Mo., 1982-86; project mgr. maintenance, 1993—; soil and pavements engr. Hdqrs. Mil. Airlift Command, Scott AFB, Ill., 1986-88. Project mgr. AF-1 maintenance hangar; cattle and grain farmer, 1982—; pvt. practice civil-mech. engr., constrn. mgmt., estimating, cost analysis, cash flow, project scheduling, expert witness, Fortuna, Mo., 1988—2001; chief constrn. inspector divsn. design and constrn. State of Mo., 1992—93; project engr. Mil. Housing, 2001—; adj. faculty civil engring. Washington U., 1968—78, U. Wis., Milw., 1978—80, Ga. Mil. Coll., Whiteman AFB, Longview Coll., Kansas City; adj. rsch. engr. U. Mo., Columbia, 1985—86; project engr., quality control officer Korte Constrn. Co. Author (tech. writing operation and maintenance manuals,): fin. reports and environ. control plans, designs & builds tech. and indsl. models. Mem.: AAUP, NSPE, ASCE, Soc. Am. Mil. Engrs., Optimists Internat. Lutheran. Achievements include patents for in diverse art, 9 copyrights;development of solar waterstill, deep shaft hydropower concept. Home: 11147 Angel Rd Fortuna MO 65034-2167

RAMEY, DENNY L. bar association executive director; b. Portsmouth, Ohio, Feb. 22, 1947; s. Howard Leroy and Norma Wylodine (Richards) R.; m. Jeannine Gayle Dunmyer, Sept. 24, 1971 (div. Nov. 1991); children: Elizabeth Michelle, Brian Michael. BBA, Ohio U., 1970; MBA, Capital U., 1976. Cert. assn. exec. Adminstrv. mgr. Transit Warehouse div. Elston Richards Storage Co., Columbus, Ohio, 1970-73; mgr. continuing profl. edn. Ohio Soc. CPA's, 1973-79; exec. dir. Engrs. Found. of Ohio, 1979-80; asst. exec. Ohio State Bar Assn., 1980-86, exec. dir., sec., treas., 1986—. Treas., exec. com., bd. dirs. Ohio Bar Liability Ins. Co., Columbus, 1986—; treas. Ohio State Bar Found., 1986—; treas. Ohio Legal Ctr. Ins., Columbus, 1988-91; sec. Ohio Printing Co., Ltd., 1991; v.p. Osbanet, Inc., 1993—; chmn. Lawriter LLC, 2000—; bd. dirs. OSBA.com, LLC. Mem.: Ohio Soc. Assn. Execs., Am. Soc. Assn. Execs., Nat. Assn. Bar Execs., Brookside Golf & Country Club, Scioto Country Club. Methodist. Avocations: tennis, golf, sports, music, wine appreciation. Office: Ohio State Bar Assn 1700 Lake Shore Dr PO Box 16562 Columbus OH 43216-6562 E-mail: dramey@ohiobar.org.

RAMIREZ, MANUEL ARISTIDES (MANNY RAMIREZ), professional baseball player; b. Santo Domingo, Dominican Republic, May 30, 1972; Grad. high sch., N.Y.C. Outfielder Cleve. Indians, 1993—. Named to The Sporting News Am. League Silver Slugger Team, 1995, mem. Am. League All-Star Team, 1995. Mem. Cleve. Indians Am. League Champions, 1995. Office: Boston Red Sox Feway Park 4 Yawkey Way Boston MA 02215*

RAMPERSAD, PEGGY A. SNELLINGS, sociologist; b. Fredericksburg, Va., Jan. 12, 1933; d. George Daniel and Virginia Riley (Bowler) Snellings; m. Oliver Ronald Rampersad, Mar. 19, 1955; 1 child, Gita. BA, Mary Washington Coll., Fredericksburg, 1953; student, Sch. of Art Inst. of Chgo., 1953-55; MA, U. Chgo., 1965, PhD, 1978. Grad. admissions counselor U. Chgo., 1954-57, adviser to fgn. students, 1958, dir. admissions Grad. Sch. Bus., 1959-63, rsch. project specialist Grad. Sch. Bus., 1970-78, pers. mgr. Grad. Sch. Bus., 1979-80, mgr. organizational devel. Grad. Sch. Bus., 1980-82, adminstr. dept. econs., 1983-95; cons. PSR Consulting, Chgo., 1995—. Cons. North Ctrl. Assn. Colls. and Secondary Schs., Chgo., 1964-70, Orchestral Assn. of Chgo. Symphony Orch., 1982, Chgo. Ctr. for Decision Rsch., 1982, Harvard U., 1993—. Exhibited paintings in juried shows at Va. Mus. Fine Arts, Art Inst. Chgo., others; editor North Cen. Assn. Quar., 1972; contbr. articles to profl. jours. U. Chgo. grad. fellow, 1963-67. Mem. AAUW, Am. Econ. Assn., Am. Acad. Polit. and Social Sci., Art Inst. Chgo. (museum assoc.), Pi Lambda Theta (past pres.). Episcopalian. Avocations: painting and drawing, music--especially opera, reading, walking. Home and Office: 28 Seneca Ter Fredericksburg VA 22401-1115

RAMSEY-GOLDMAN, ROSALIND, physician; b. N.Y.C., Mar. 22, 1954; d. Abraham L. and Miriam (Colen) Goldman; m. Glenn Ramsey, June 29,1 975; children: Ethan Ramsey, Caitlin Ramsey. BA, Case Western Res. U., 1975, MD, 1978; MPH, U. Pitts., 1988, DPH, 1992. Med. resident U. Rochester (N.Y.), 1978-81; chief resident Rochester Gen. Hosp., 1981-82; staff physician Univ. Health Svc., Rochester, 1982-83; rheumatology fellow U. Pitts., 1983-86, instr. medicine, 1986-87, asst. prof., 1987-91, co-dir. Lupus Treatment and Diagnostic Ctr., 1987-91; asst. prof. medicine Northwestern U., Chgo., 1991-96, assoc. prof. medicine, 1996—2001, prof. medicine, 2001—. Dir. Chgo. Lupus Registry, Northwestern U., Chgo., 1991—. Contbr. rsch. articles to profl. jours. Recipient

Finkelstein award Hershey (Pa.) Med. Ctr., 1986. Fellow ACP, Am. Coll. Rheumatology; mem. Soc. for Epidemiologic Rsch., Ctrl. Soc. Clin. Rsch. Office: Northwestern U Ward 3-315 303 E Chicago Ave Chicago IL 60611-3093 E-mail: rgramsey@northwestern.edu.

RAMSTAD, JIM, congressman, lawyer; b. Jamestown, N.D., May 6, 1946; s. Marvin Joseph and Della Mae (Fode) R. BA, U. Minn., 1968; JD with honors, George Washington U., 1973. Bar: N.D. 1973, D.C. 1973, U.S. Supreme Ct. 1976, Minn., 1979. Adminstrv. asst. to speaker Minn. Ho. Reps., 1969; spl. asst. to Congressman Tom Kleppe, 1970; pvt. practice law, Jamestown, 1973, Washington, 1974-1978, Mpls., 1978-90; mem. Minn. Senate, 1981-90, asst. minority leader, 1983-87; mem. U.S. Congress from 3rd Minn. dist., 1990—; adj. prof. Am. U., Washington, 1975-78. Bd. dirs. Children's Heart Fund, Lake Country Food Bank. Served as 1st lt. U.S. Army Res., 1968-74. Mem. Minn. Bar Assn., D.C. Bar Assn., N.D. Bar Assn., Hennepin County Bar Assn., U. Minn. Alumni Assn. (nat. dir.), Am. Legion, Wayzata C. of C., TwinWest C. of C., U. Minn. Alumni Club (past pres. Washington), Lions, Phi Beta Kappa, Phi Delta Theta. Republican. Office: 103 Cannon Ho Office Bldg Washington DC 20515-0001*

RAMUNNO, THOMAS PAUL, management consultant; b. Chgo., Sept. 13, 1952; s. Anthony Michael and Dorothy (Buriak) R.; m. Deborah G. Pauline Benton, Jan. 31, 1976 (div. 1991); 1 child, Michael Thomas. BBA, U. Ga., 1974, MBA, 1978. Treas. Concept Inc., Atlanta, 1974-77; product mgr. Johnson-Johnson, Inc., 1978-80; dir. Rollins Inc., 1979-80; cons. Chase Econometrics, 1980-83; v.p. comml. svcs., dir. corp. product mgmt./mktg. Union Trust Co. Md., 1983-84; prin., exec. v.p. Mktg. Scis. Group, Inc., Hunt Valley, Md., 1984-85; v.p., dir. Citicorp, Chgo., 1985-86; sr. mgr. fin. instns. consulting group Deloitte & Touche, 1987-90; dir. cons. svcs. FSA, Inc., 1990-92; CEO Adv. Scis. Group, 1991-98; pres. IASG, 1990-98; ptnr. Info. Scis., Inc., 1996-98; v.p., practice leader Metagroup Cons., 1998-2000; ptnr. KPMG Cons., 2000—01; mng. ptnr. Scient, Inc., 2001—; CEO, mng. ptnr. EVP/Chicago, 2001—. Home: 25 Commons Dr Palos Park IL 60464

RAN, SHULAMIT, composer; b. Tel Aviv, Oct. 21, 1949; came to U.S., 1963; m. Abraham Lotan, 1986. Studied composition with, Paul Ben-Haim, Norman Dello, Joio, Ralph Shapey; student, Mannes Coll. Music, N.Y.C., 1963-67. With dept. music U. Chgo., 1973—, William H. Colvin prof. music; composer-in-residence Chgo. Symphony Orch., 1990-97, Lyric Opera of Chgo., 1994-97. Compositions include 10 Children's Scenes, 1967, Structures, 1968, 7 Japanese Love Poems, 1968, Hatzvi Israel Eulogy, 1969, O the Chimneys, 1969, Concert Piece for piano and orch., 1970, 3 Fantasy Pieces for Cello and Piano, 1972, Ensembles for 17, 1975, Double Vision, 1976, Hyperbolae for Piano, 1976, For an Actor: Monologue for Clarinet, 1978, Apprehensions, 1979, Private Game, 1979, Fantasy-Variations for Cello, 1980, A Prayer, 1982, Verticals for piano, 1982, String Quartet No. 1, 1984, (for woodwind quintet) Concerto da Camera I, 1985, Amichai Songs, 1985, Concerto for Orchestra, 1986, (for clarinet, string quartet and piano) Concerto da Camera II, 1987, East Wind, 1987, String Quartet No. 2, 1988-89, Symphony, 1989-90, Mirage, 1990, Inscriptions for solo violin, 1991, Chicago Skyline for brass and percussion, 1991, Legends for Orch., 1992-93, Invocation, 1994, Yearning for violin and string orch., 1995, (opera) Between Two Worlds (The Dybbuk), 1995-97, Soliloquy, 1997, Vessels of Courage and Hope for orch., 1998, (flute concerto) Voices, 2000, Three Scenes for solo clarinet, 2000; commd. pieces include for Am. Composers Orch., Phila. Orch., Chgo. Symphony, Balt. Symphony, Chamber Soc. of Lincoln Ctr., Mendelssohn String quartet, Da Capo Chamber Players, Sta. WFMT, Lyric Opera Chgo.; composer and soloist for 1st performances Capriccio, 1963, Symphonic Poem, 1967, Concert Piece, 1971. Recipient Acad. Inst. Arts and Letters award, 1989, Pulitzer prize for music, 1991, Friedheim award for orchestral music Kennedy Ctr., 1992; Guggenheim fellow, 1977, 90. Office: U Chgo Dept Music 1010 E 59th St Chicago IL 60637-1512

RANCOURT, JAMES DANIEL, optical engineer; b. Maine; BA in Physics, Bowdoin Coll., 1963; MS in Physics, Carnegie Tech., 1965; PhD in Optical Scis., U. Ariz., 1974. Engr. Itek Corp., Lexington, Mass., 1965-69; rsch. assoc. U. Ariz., Tucson, 1969-74; engr. OCLI, Santa Rosa, Calif., 1974-95, chief scientist, 1996-97; dir. product devel. Guardian Industries Corp., Carleton, Mich., 1997—. Author: Optical Thin Films Users Handbook, 1987; patentee in field. Fellow Optical Soc. Am. Achievements include 13 patents. Office: Guardian Industries 14511 Romine Rd Carleton MI 48117-9706

RAND, KATHY SUE, public relations executive; b. Miami Beach, Fla., Feb. 24, 1945; d. William R. and Rose (Lasser) R.; m. Peter C. Ritsos, Feb. 19, 1982. BA, Mich. State U., 1965; MBA, Northwestern U., 1980. Asst. editor Lyons & Carnahan, Chgo., 1967-68; mng. editor Cahners Pub. Co., 1968-71; pub. rels. writer Super Market Inst., 1972-73; account supr. Pub. Communications Inc., 1973-77; divisional mgr. pub. rels. Quaker Oats Co., 1977-82; exec. v.p., dep. gen. mgr. Golin/Harris Communications, 1982-90; exec. v.p. Lesnik Pub. Rels., Northbrook, Ill., 1990-91; mng. dir. Manning, Selvage & Lee, Chgo., 1991—. Dir. midwest region NOW, 1972-74; mem. Kellogg Alumni Adv. Bd.; bd. dirs. Jr. Achievement of Chgo. Mem. Pub. Rels. Soc. Am. (Silver Anvil award 1986, 87), Pub. Club Chgo. (Golden Trumpet awards 1982-87, 90, 94, 95, 97, 98, 99, 2000), Northwestern Club Chgo., Kellogg Alumni Club, Beta Gamma Sigma. Home: 400 Riverwoods Rd Lake Forest IL 60045-2547 E-mail: ksrand@aol.com.

RAND, LEON, academic administrator; b. Boston, Oct. 8, 1930; s. Max B. and Ricka (Muscanto) Rakisky; m. Marian L. Newton, Aug. 29, 1959; children: Debra Ruth, Paul Martin, Marta Leah. B.S., Northeastern U., 1953; M.A., U. Tex., 1956, Ph.D., 1958. Postdoctoral fellow Purdue U., 1958-59; asst. prof. to prof. U. Detroit, 1959-68; prof., chmn. dept. chemistry Youngstown (Ohio) State U., 1968-74, dean grad. studies and research, 1974-81, acting acad. v.p., 1980; vice chancellor acad. affairs Pembroke (N.C.) State U., 1981-85; chancellor Ind. U.-S.E., New Albany, 1986-96; chancellor emeritus Ind. U., 1996—, prof. emeritus, 1999—; spl. asst. to chancellor IUPUI, 1996-98. Bd. dirs. INB Banking Co., Jeffersonville, Ind, Jewish Hosp., Louisville, Ky., 1991-96. Bd. dirs., mem. exec. com. Louisville (Ind.) Area chpt. ARC; bd. dirs. Floyd Meml. Hosp., New Albany, 1987-90. Mem. Am. Chem. Soc., Am. Inst. Chemists, Metroversity (bd. dirs.), Sigma Xi, Phi Kappa Phi. Home: 1785 Arrowwood Dr Carmel IN 46033-9019 E-mail: lrand@iupui.edu.

RAND, PETER ANDERS, architect; b. Hibbing, Minn., Jan. 8, 1944; s. Sidney Anders and Dorothy Alice (Holm) R.; m. Nancy Ann Straus, Oct. 21, 1967; children: Amy, Dorothy. BA, St. Olaf Coll., 1966; cert., Oslo Internat. Summer Sch., Norway, 1964, U. Minn. Sch. Architecture, 1969-72. Registered architect, Minn. Designer, architect, dir. pub. rels. Setter, Leach & Lindstrom, Inc., Mpls., 1972-78; dir. bus. devel, head Eden Prairie (Minn.) office Archtl. Design Group, Inc., 1979-80; dir. mktg. and publs. Minn. Soc. AIA, 1981-82, exec. dir., 1982-85, exec. v.p., CEO, 1986-98, v.p., 1999—. Pub. Architecture Minn. mag.; bd. dirs. MSAADA Architects & Engrs.; cons., archtl. designer. Bd. dirs. Project for Pride in Living, 1979-88, chmn., 1980-86; trustee Bethlehem Luth. Ch., 1980-86, chmn. bd. trustees, 1985, chmn. com. on worship, 1993-96, mem. ch. coun., 1993-96; mem. Minn. Ch. Ctr. Commn., 1981-89, chmn., 1985-88; sec. Coun. Archtl. Component Execs. of AIA, 1987, 92, pres., 1997-98; bd. dirs. Minn. Coun. Chs., 1985-89, sec., 1989; bd. dirs. Mpls. Coun. Chs., 1985-88; bd. dirs. Arts Midwest, 1987-96, treas., 1989, v.p., 1990-91, chmn., 1992-93; bd. dirs. Nordic Ctr., Preservation Alliance Minn., 1995—. Served with U.S. Army, 1966-69. Fellow AIA (jour. honor awrd 1981, Nat. Svc. award 1993); mem. Minn. Soc. AIA, Nat. Trust Hist. Preservation, Torske Klubben. Home: 1728 Humboldt Ave S Minneapolis MN 55403-2809

RANDA, RUDOLPH THOMAS, judge; b. Milw., July 25, 1940; s. Rudolph Frank and Clara Paula (Kojis) R.; m. Melinda Nancy Matera, Jan. 15, 1977; children: Rudolph Daniel, Daniel Anthony. BS, U. Wis.-Milw., 1963; JD, U. Wis.-Madison, 1966. Bar: Wis. 1966, U.S. Dist. Ct. (ea. and we. dists.) Wis. 1966, U.S. Ct. Appeals (7th cir.) 1973, U.S. Supreme Ct. 1973. Pvt. practice, Milw., 1966-67; prin. city atty. Office Milw. City Atty., 1970-75; judge Milw. Mcpl. Ct., 1975-79, Milw. County Cir. Ct., 1979-81, 82-92, Appellate Ct., Madison, 1981-82; fed. judge U.S. Dist. Ct. (ea. dist.) Wis., 1992—. Chmn. Wis. Impact, Milw., 1980—; lectr. Marquette U. Law Sch., Milw., 1980—. Capt. U.S. Army, 1967-69, Vietnam. Decorated Bronze Star. Mem. Milw. Bar Assn., Wis. Bar Assn., Trial Judges Wis., Am. Legion (adjutant Milw. 1980), Thomas More Lawyers Soc. (former pres. Milw. chpt.), Milw. Hist. Soc., Phi Alpha Theta. Roman Catholic. Office: US Courthouse 517 E Wisconsin Ave Rm 310 Milwaukee WI 53202-4504

RANDALL, GARY LEE, former state legislator; b. Ithaca, Mich., June 18, 1943; s. Clifton Peet and Elsie Mae (Martyn) R.; m. Brenda Faye Martin, 1973; children: Amy Kathryn, Clifton Lee. BA, Mich. State U., 1970; MA, Ctrl. Mich. U., 1972. Program dir. WFYC Radio, Alma, Mich., 1965-70; dir. pub. affairs WCMU TV/WCML TV, Mt. Pleasant, 1970-79; rep. Mich. Dist. 89, Mich. Dist. 93; clk. Mich. Ho. of Reps. Asst. Rep. leader Mich. Ho. Reps., former chair bus. & fin. com., mem. agriculture com., fin. com., edn. com., adminstrn. rules & capitol restoration coms. Trustee Libr. Mich. Mem. Assn. Edn. Broadcasters, Mich. Farm Bur., Lions, Jaycees, Elks, Sigma Delta Chi. Home: 1210 E Pickard Mount Pleasant MI 48858 Address: PO Box 30014 Lansing MI 48909-7514

RANDALL, GERARD, foundation administrator; Grad., Marquette U. Former social studies tchr. Dominican H.S., Milw.; former tchr. Milw. Pub. Schs.; pres., adminstr. Pvt. Industry Coun. Milwaukee County. V.p. bd. regents U. Wis., 1994—; bd. dirs. Milw. Pub. Mus., Milw. Symphony Orch., Marcus Ctr. for Performing Arts, Rosalie Manor. Recipient 2 bronze tchr. awards, Ameritech. Mem.: Phi Delta Kappa. Office: Pvt Industry Coun Milwaukee County 101 Pleasant St Ste 201 Milwaukee WI 53212

RANDALL, KARL W. aviation executive, lawyer; b. Mount Pleasant, Mich., Feb. 12, 1951; s. Herbert J. and Wilma E. (Worstell) R.; m. Natalie Kilmer Randall, Dec. 17, 1971; children: Adam B., Kara J. AA, Mich. Christian Coll., Rochester, 1971; BA, Oakland U., Rochester, 1977; JD, Wayne State U. Law Sch., Detroit, 1981. Bar: Mich., 1981, U.S. Dist. Ct., 1981, U.S. Ct. Appeals, 1983; cert. airport mgr., Mich., 1993. Quality contr. Staley SNO BOL Corp., Pontiac, Mich., 1971-72; engring. tech. Oakland Co. Drain Comm., 1972-83; sr. asst. corp. counsel Oakland County Corp. Counsel, 1983-93; mgr. aviation Oakland County Internat. Airport, Waterford, Mich., 1993—. Dir. Integrity Jour., Mt. Pleasant, 1980-98, Oakland County Coord. Child Care Coun., Waterford, 1992-97. Author, editor: (religious jour.) Integrity, 1982, 94-95. Mem. Rep. Com. Oakland County, 1988—, Exec. Club Oakland County, 1993—. Mem. Mich. Assn. Airport Execs. (exec.). Republican. Mem. Ch. of Christ. Avocations: physical fitness, motorcycling, jogging, golf, piano. Office: Oakland County Internat Airport 6500 Highland Rd Waterford MI 48327-1649 E-mail: randallk@co.oakland.mi.us.

RANDALL, LINDA LEA, biochemist, educator; b. Montclair, N.J., Aug. 7, 1946; d. Lowell Neal and Helen (Watts) R.; m. Gerald Lee Hazelbauer, Aug. 29, 1970. BS, Colo. State U., 1968; PhD, U. Wis., 1971. Postdoctoral fellow Inst. Pasteur, Paris, 1971-73; asst. prof. Uppsala (Sweden) U., 1975-81; assoc. prof. Washington State U., Pullman, 1981-83, prof. biochemistry, 1983-2000, U. Mo., Columbia, 2000. Guest scientist Wallenberg Lab., Uppsala U., 1973-75; study section NIH, 1984-88. Mem. edtl. bd. Jour. of Bacteriology, 1982-96; co-editor: Virus Receptors Part I, 1980; contbr. articles to profl. jours. Recipient Eli Lilly Award in Microbiology and Immunology, Am. Soc. Microbiology, Am. Assn. Immunologists, Am. Soc. Exptl. Pathology, 1984, Faculty Excellence Award in Rsch., Washington State U., 1988, Disting. Faculty Address, 1990, Parke-Davis award, 1995. Fellow AAAS, Am. Acad. Microbiology; mem. NAS, Am. Microbiol. Soc., Am. Soc. Biol. Chemists, Protein Soc. Avocation: dancing. Office: Univ Mo Dept Biochemistry 117 Schweitzer Hall Columbia MO 65211

RANDALL, WILLIAM SEYMOUR, leasing company executive; b. Champaign, Ill., July 5, 1933; s. Glenn S. and Audrey H. (Honnold) R.; m. Sharon Larsen; children: Steve, Cathy, Mike, Jennifer. B.S., Ind. State U., 1959. Controller Amana Refrigeration Co., Iowa, 1966-70; div. controller Trane Co., Clarksville, Tenn., 1970-74, corporate controller La Crosse, Wis., 1974-79; v.p., chief fin. officer Sta-Rite Industries, Milw., 1979-82; pres., owner Profl. Staff Resources, Inc., 1982—. Served with AUS, 1953-55. Mem. Financial Execs. Inst. Lodge: Rotary. Home: 13365 Tulane St Brookfield WI 53005-7141 Office: 14430 W Bluemound Rd Ste 103 Milwaukee WI 53226

RANDAZZO, RICHARD P. human resources professional; BSBA, Rochester Inst. Technology, 1965; MBA, Ind. U., 1967. Former various human resource mgmt. positions Xerox Corp.; former sr. v.p. human resources Asea Brown Boveri, Inc. Amerias Region, Conn.; sr. v.p. human resources Nextel Comms., Inc., 1994-97; v.p. human resources to sr. v.p. human resources Federal-Mogul Corp., Southfield, Mich., 1997-99, 99—. Office: Federal-Mogul Corp 26555 Northwestern Hwy Southfield MI 48034-2146

RANDEL, DON MICHAEL, academic administrator, musicologist; m. Carol Randel; children: Amy Elizabeth Keating, Julia, Emily Catherine Pershing, Sally Randel Eggert. AB, MFA, PhD in Music, Princeton U. With dept. music, dept. chair, vice provost Cornell U., 1968, assoc. dean Coll. Arts and Scis., dean Coll. Arts and Scis., 1991-95, provost, Given Found. prof. musicology, 1995-2000; pres. U. Chgo., 2000—. Editor: New Harvard Dictionary of Music, 1986, Harvard Biographical Dictionary of Music, 1996, Harvard Concise Dictionary of Music and Musicians, 1999; editor-in-chief Jour. Am. Musciological Soc., 1974-74. Recipient Hon. Woodrow Wilson fellow, Danforth Grad. fellow; Fulbright award. Office: U Chgo Adminstrn 502 5801 S Ellis Ave Chicago IL 60637-5418

RANDLE, JOHN, professional football player; b. Hearne, Tex., Jan. 12, 1967; Student, Trinity Valley C.C., Tex., Tex. A&I U. Defensive tackle Minn. Vikings, 1990—. Selected to Pro Bowl, 1993, 94; named to The Sporting News NFL All-Pro Team, 1994. Achievements tied AFC record for most sacks, 1994. Office: c/o Minn Vikings 9520 Viking Dr Eden Prairie MN 55344-3825

RANDOLPH, JACKSON HAROLD, utility company executive; b. Cin., Nov. 17, 1930; s. Dward Bradley and Cora Belle (Puckett) R.; m. Angelina Losito, June 20, 1958; children: Terri, Patti, Todd, Craig. B.B.A., U. Cin., 1958, M.B.A., 1968. C.P.A., Ohio. Acct. Arthur Andersen & Co., Cin., 1958-59; with Cin. Gas & Electric Co., 1959—, v.p. fin. and corp. affairs, 1981-85, exec. v.p., 1985-86, chmn., pres., CEO, from 1986, now chmn., also dir.; chmn. CINergy Corp., 1994—, now chmn.; former pres., now chmn. Union Light Heat and Power Co., Covington, Ky. Bd. dirs. Cen. Trust Bank, N.A., Cin. Fin. Corp., PNC Corp.; CEO CINergy Corp., 1994-95, chmn., 1995—. V.p., bd. dirs. Gen. Protestant Orphan Home, Cin., 1981-86; treas., bd. dirs. Cin. chpt. ARC, 1975— ; mem. adv. com. Catherine Booth Home, 1980— , Dan Beard council Boy Scouts Am., 1985. Served with USN, 1951-55. Mem. Cin. Country Club, Queen City Club, Met. Club, Bankers Club, Delta Sigma Pi, Phi Eta Sigma, Beta Gamma Sigma. Home: 414 Bishopsbridge Dr Cincinnati OH 45255-3900 Office: CINergy Corp 139 E 4th St Cincinnati OH 45202-4003 also: Union Light Heat & Power Co 107 Brent Spence Sq Covington KY 41011-1433

RANDOLPH, JOE WAYNE, machine manufacturing executive, stock broker; b. Madisonville, Ky., Aug. 5, 1938; s. Albert Clay and Helen (Brown) R.; m. Mary Ann Rabenau, July 20, 1963; children: Ann E., Charles J. BS, Murray State U., 1962, MS, 1964; MBA, Washington U./Lindenwood Coll., 1978. High sch. tchr. Benton (Ky.) Sch. System, 1962-64, St. Charles (Mo.) Sch. System, 1964-65; mfg. mgr. Sunnen Products Co., St. Louis, 1967-96; stock broker Linsco/Pvt. Ledger Securities, Washington, 1996-99. 1st lt. U.S. Army, 1965. Named Col., Hon. Order of Ky. Cols., 1990. Mem. AAIM Mgmt. Assn. (prodn. exec. round table, leader 1984—), Elks. Avocations: golf, fishing, travel, hunting. Home: 5700 Highway T Augusta MO 63332-1419 Office: 317 Elm St Washington MO 63090-2328

RANKIN, ALFRED MARSHALL, JR. business executive; b. Cleve., Oct. 8, 1941; s. Alfred Marshall and Clara Louise (Taplin) R.; m. Victoire Conley Griffin, June 3, 1967; children: Helen P., Clara T. BA in Econs. magna cum laude, Yale U., 1963, JD, 1966. Mgmt. cons. McKinsey & Co., Inc., Cleve., 1970-73; with Eaton Corp., 1974-81, pres. materials handling group, 1981-83, pres. indsl. group, 1984-86, exec. v.p., 1986, vice chmn., chief oper. officer, 1986-89; pres., COO NACCO Industries, Inc., 1989-91, pres., CEO, 1991-94, also bd. dirs., chmn., pres., CEO, 1994—; bd. dirs. The Goodrich Co., Vanguard Group. Bd. dirs. B.F. Goodrich Co., Vanguard Group. Former pres., trustee Hathaway Brown Sch.; trustee Univ. Hosps. Cleve., Mus. Arts Assn., Univ. Circle, Inc., Cleve. Mus. Art, John Huntington Art Trust, Cleve. Tomorrow; past chairperson The Cleve. Found. Mem. Ohio Bar Assn. Clubs: Chagrin Valley Hunt, Union, Tavern, Pepper Pike, Kirtland Country (Cleve.); Rolling Rock (Ligonier, Pa.); Met. (Washington). Office: NACCO Industries Inc 5875 Landerbrook Dr Ste 300 Mayfield Heights OH 44124

RANKIN, JAMES WINTON, lawyer; b. Norfolk, Va., Sept. 9, 1943; s. Winton Blair and Edith (Griffin) R.; m. Donna Lee Carpenter, June 25, 1966 (dec.); children— Thomas James, William Joseph, Elizabeth Jeanne; m. JoAnne Katherine Murray, Feb. 11, 1978. A.B. magna cum laude, Oberlin Coll., 1965; J.D. cum laude, U. Chgo., 1968. Bar: Ill. 1968, U.S. Dist. Ct. (no. dist.) Ill. 1969, U.S. Ct. Appeals (7th cir.) 1971, U.S. Ct. Appeals (5th cir.) 1979, U.S. Supreme Ct. 1975, Calif. 1986. Law clk. U.S. Dist. Ct. (no. dist.) Ill., 1968-69; assoc. Kirkland & Ellis, Chgo., 1969-73, ptnr., 1973—. Mem. ABA, Order of Coif, Mid-Am. Club, Univ. Club, Mich. Shores Club, Kenilworth Club, Ephriam Yacht Club. Presbyterian. Home: 633 Kenilworth Ave Kenilworth IL 60043-1070 Office: Kirkland & Ellis 200 E Randolph St Fl 54 Chicago IL 60601-6636

RANKIN, SCOTT DAVID, artist, educator; b. Newark, Mar. 21, 1954; s. Clymont J. and Jean L. (Lane) R.; m. Linda K. Piemonte, Sept. 3, 1989 (div. Apr. 2000). BFA, Tyler Sch. of Art, Phila., 1976; MFA, UCLA, 1980. Asst. prof. U. Iowa, Iowa City, 1985-86, U. Chgo., 1986-94; assoc. prof. Ill. State U., Normal, 1994—. Video cons. Math. Edn. Rsch. Project, L.A., 1991-93, 3d internat. math. and sci. study UCLA dept. psychology, 1994-95, 98-99. Prodr., dir.: (videotapes) Fugue, 1985, This and that (version 1), 1987, (version 2), 1990, The Pure, 1993, Wire, 1998, Flow, 2000, Central, 2001. Regional media arts fellow Nat. Endowment for Arts, 1984, visual artist's fellow Ill. Arts Coun., 1989, 90, visual artist's fellow Nat. Endowment for Arts, 1990, 93. E-mail: sdranki@ilstu.edu.

RANSEL, DAVID LORIMER, history educator; b. Gary, Ind., Feb. 20, 1939; s. Joseph A. and Patricia (Lorimer) R.; m. Therese Holma; children: Shairstin, Annaliisa. BA, Coe Coll., 1961; MA, Northwestern U., 1962; PhD, Yale U., 1969. Instr. Tollare Folkhogskola, Boo, Sweden, 1959-60; asst. instr. Yale U., New Haven, 1966-67; instr. U. Ill., Urbana, 1967-69, asst. prof., 1969-73, assoc. prof., 1973-81, prof., 1981-85, Ind. U., Bloomington, 1985—, Robert F. Byrnes prof. history, 2001—, dir. Russian and East European Inst., 1995—. Author: The Politics of Catherinian Russia, 1975, Mothers of Misery, 1988, Village Mothers: Three Generations of Change in Russia and Tataria, 2000; editor: The Family in Imperial Russia, 1978, Imperial Russia: New Histories for the Empire, 1998; editor/translator: Village Life in Late Tsarist Russia, 1993; editor Slavic Rev., Urbana, 1980-85, Am. Hist. Rev., Bloomington, 1985-95; bd. editors The History of the Family: An International Quarterly, Historisk Tidskrift, Kritika, Explorations in Russian and Eurasian History. Guggenheim fellow, 1989-90, Wilson fellow, 1989-90, NEH fellow, 1998-99; Fulbright-Hays grantee, 1979, 90, Irex grantee, 1990, 93. Mem. Am. Hist. Assn. (mem. gov. coun. 1985-95, mem. fin. com. 1989-95), Am. Assn. for Advancement of Slavic Studies (bd. dirs. 1979-85, mem. fin. com. 1980-85, chmn. com. on status of women 1991-93, mem. Irex program com. 1995-99). Avocations: classical guitar, sailing, running. Office: Ind Univ Russian/East European Inst 565 Ballantine Hall Bloomington IN 47401-5017 E-mail: ransel@indiana.edu.

RANTS, CAROLYN JEAN, college official; b. Hastings, Nebr., Oct. 3, 1936; d. John Leon and Christine (Helzer) Halloran; m. Marvin L. Rants, June 1, 1957 (div. July 1984); children: Christopher Charles, Douglas John. Student, Hastings Coll., 1954-56; BS, U. Omaha, 1960; MEd, U. Nebr., 1968; EdD, U. S.D., 1982. Tchr. elem. Ogallala (Nebr.) Community Sch., 1956-58, Omaha Pub. Schs., 1958-60, Hastings Pub. Schs., 1960-64, Grosse Pointe (Mich.) Community Schs., 1964-67; asst. prof., instr. Morningside Coll., Sioux City, Iowa, 1974-82, dean for student devel., 1982-84, v.p. for student affairs, 1984-94, interim v.p. for acad. affairs, 1992-94, v.p. enrollment and student svcs., 1994-96, v.p. adminstrn., 1996-99; exec. dir. enrollment svcs. Western Iowa Tech C.C., 1999—, dean of students, 2000—. Mem. new agy. com., chmn. fund distbn. and resource deployment com. United Way, Sioux City, 1987-94, co-chair, United Way Day of Caring, 1996; mem. Iowa Civil Rights Commn., 1989-97; bd. dirs. Leadership Sioux City, 1988-93, pres., 1992-93; bd. dirs. Siouxland Y, Sioux City, 1985-90, pres., 1988; bd. dirs. Girls, Inc., 1995—, New Perspectives, Inc., 1996—, pres. 1999, 2000; mem. Vision 2020 Cmty. Planning Task Force, 1990-92; pres. bd. dirs. Siouxland Youth Chorus, 2001—; bd. dirs. Sioux City Symphony, 2001—. Mem. Iowa Women in Edn. Leadership (pres. Sioux City chpt. 1986), Nat. Assn. Student Pers. Adminstrs.(region IV-E adv. bd.), Nat. Assn. for Women Deans, Adminstrs. and Counselors, Iowa Student Pers. Adminstr. (chmn. profl. devel. Iowa chpt. 1988-89, pres. 1991-92, Disting. Svc. award 1992), AAUW (corp. rep., coll./univ. rep. 1994-96), P.E.O. (pres. Sioux City chpt., Tri-State Women's Bus. Conf. (treas., planning com. Sioux City chpt. 1987-89), Quota Club (com. chmn. Sioux City 1987-89, v.p. 1992-94, pres. 1994-95, Siouxland Woman of Yr. award 1988), Sertoma (officer, bd. govs., regional dir.), Omicron Delta Kappa (faculty dir. province X 1996-99), Delta Kappa Gamma (state 1st v.p. 1993-95, state pres. 1995-97, internat. com. 1998-2000), Phi Delta Kappa (pres. 1988-89, Excellence in Leadership award 1998). Republican. Methodist. Avocations: handbells, cross-stitching. Home: 2904 S Cedar St # 4 Sioux City IA 51106-4246 Office: Western Iowa Tech Comm Coll PO Box 5199 4647 Stone Ave Sioux City IA 51102-5199 E-mail: rantsc@witcc.com.

RANUM, JANE BARNHARDT, state senator, lawyer; b. Charlotte, N.C., Aug. 21, 1947; d. John Robert and Gladys Rose (Swift) B.; m. James Harry Ranum, Mar. 29, 1972; 1 child, Elizabeth McBride. BS, East Carolina U., 1969; JD, Hamline U., 1979. Bar: Minn. 1979, U.S. Dist. Ct. Minn. 1979. Tchr. elem. sch. Durham County, Durham, N.C., 1960-70; tchr. Dept. Def., Baumholder, Germany, 1970-72, Dist. 196, Rosemount, Minn., 1972-76;

law cclk. Hennepin County Dist. Ct., Mpls., 1982; asst. county atty. Hennepin County, 1982—; mem. Minn. Senate, St. Paul, 1991—. Chmn. legislature commn. on children, youth and their families, 1993—, mem. rep. chem. abuse and prevention resource coun., 1993. Mem. exec. com., lobbying coord. Dem. Farmer Labor Feminist Caucus, St. Paul, 1980-84; bd. dirs. Project 13 for Reproductive Rights, Mpls., 1981-82; state del. Minn. Dem. Farmer Labor Party Conv., 1982, 84, precinct del., 1974—. Named Feminist of Yr., Minn. NOW, 1994, Legislator of Yr., Minn. Assn. for Retarded Citizens, 1994. Mem. Minn. Bar Assn., Minn. Women Lawyers, Minn. Family Support and Recovery Coun., Hennepin County Bar assn. Democrat. Home: 5045 Aldrich Ave S Minneapolis MN 55419-1207 Office: Minn Senate State Capitol Saint Paul MN 55155-0001

RAO, DABEERU C. epidemiologist, educator; b. Apr. 6, 1946; came to U.S., 1972; s. Ramarao Patnaik and Venkataratnam (Raghupatruni) R.; m. Sarada Patnaik, 1974; children: Ravi, Lakshmi. BS in Stats., Indian Statis. Inst., Calcutta, 1967, MS, 1968, PhD, 1971. Rsch. fellow U. Sheffield, Eng., 1971-72; asst. prof., geneticist U. Hawaii, Honolulu, 1972-78, assoc. prof., geneticist, 1978-80; assoc. prof., dir. divsn. biostats. Washington U. Med. Sch., St. Louis, 1980-82, prof. depts. biostats., psychiatry and genetics, 1982—. Adj. prof. math., 1982—, dir. div. biostats., 1980—. Author: A Source Book for Linkage in Man, 1979, Methods in Genetic Epidemiology, 1983, Genetic Epidemiology of Coronary Heart Disease, 1984; editor-in-chief Genetic Epidemiology jour., 1984-91; contbr. articles to profl. jours. Grantee NIH, 1978—. Mem. Am. Statis. Assn., Am. Soc. Human Genetics, Internat. Genetic Epidemiology Soc. (pres. 1996), Behavior Genetics Assn., Soc. Epidemiol. Rsch., Biomed. soc. Office: Washington U Sch Medicine Divsn Biostats Box 8067 660 S Euclid Ave Saint Louis MO 63110-1010 E-mail: rao@wubios.wustl.edu.

RAO, NANNAPANENI NARAYANA, electrical engineer; b. Kakumanu, Andhra Pradesh, India; m. Sarojini Jonnalagadda, June 10, 1955; children: Vanaja, Durgaprasad, Hariprasad. BSc in Physics, U. Madras, India, 1952; DMIT in Electronics, Madras Inst. Tech., 1955; MSEE, U. Wash., 1960, PhD in Elec. Engring, 1965. Acting instr. elec. engring. U. Wash., 1960-64, acting asst. prof., 1964-65; asst. prof. elec. engring. U. Ill., Urbana, 1965-69, assoc. prof., 1969-75, prof., 1975—, assoc. head elec. and computer engring., 1987—. Cons. Fakultas Teknik, Univ. Indonesia, Jakarta, 1985-86, 87. Author: Basic Electromagnetics with Applications, 1972, Elements of Engineering Electromagnetics, 5th edit., 2000; contbr. numerous articles to profl. jours. Recipient Engring. award Telugu Assn. N.Am., 1983, Excellence in Edn. award, 1999, Fakultas Teknik award Universitatas Indonesia, 1986. Fellow IEEE (Undergrad. Teaching award 1994); mem. Am. Soc. Engring. Edn. (AT&T Found. award for excellence in instrn. engring. students 1991), Internat. Union Radio Sci. (U.S. Commn. G). Achievements include contributions to engineering education in the United States and abroad. Home: 2509 S Lynn St Urbana IL 61801-6841 Office: U Ill Dept Elec & Computer Engring 1406 W Green St Urbana IL 61801-2918 E-mail: rao@ece.uiuc.edu.

RAO, PALAKURTHI S.C. soil science educator; b. Warangal, India, Feb. 15, 1947; came to U.S., 1967; s. Seshagiri and Arya (Kondapalli) R.; m. Keiko Yohena, June 7, 1970; 1 child, Masaru. BSc, A.P. Agrl. U., Hyderabad, India, 1967; MS, Colo. State U., 1970; PhD, U. Hawaii, 1974. Research assoc. U. Fla., Gainesville, 1975-77, assoc. research scientist, 1977-79, asst. prof. soil sci., 1979-82, assoc. prof., 1982-85, prof. of soil and water sci., 1985-99; Lee A. Reith disting. prof. Perdue U, W. Lafayette, IN, 1999—. Vis. prof. U. Hawaii, Honolulu, 1986—. Assoc. editor Jour. Environ. Quality, 1980-83; co-editor: Role of Unsaturated Zone in Hazardous Waste Disposal, 1983; co-editor Jour. Contaminant Hydrology, 1986. Mem. Internat. Soil Sci. Soc., Soil Sci. Soc. Am., Am. Geophys. Union, Am. Chem. Soc., Am. Soc. Agronomy. Avocations: outdoor sports, anthropology, history of sci. Office: Perdue U Civil Engineering 1284 Civil Engineering Bldg Lafayette IN 47907-1284

RAO, PRASAD, electronics executive; Pres., CEO, Cybertech Sys., Inc., Oak Brook, Ill. Office: Cybertech Systems Inc 1111 W 22d St Ste 800 Oak Brook IL 60523

RAO, VITTAL SRIRANGAM, electrical engineering educator; b. Inumpamula, India, June 8, 1944; came to U.S., 1981; s. Rangaiah Srirangam and Lakshmamma (Immadi) R.; m. Vijaya Morishetti, Feb. 28, 1965; children: Asha, Ajay. M of Tech., Indian Inst. Tech., 1972, PhD, 1975. Asst. prof. Indian Inst. of Tech., New Delhi, India, 1975-79; vis. prof. T.U., Halifax, N.S., Can., 1980-81; assoc. prof. U. Mo., Rolla, 1981-88, prof., 1988—; dir. Intelligent Systems Ctr., 1991—. Cons. Delco Remy, Anderson, Ind., 1985-87, Allison Gas Turbines, Indpls., 1986-87, U.S. Army Picatinny Arsenal, N.J., 1988-91. Contbr. articles to profl. jours. including Suboptimal/Near Optimal Control, Reduced Order Modeling Techniques, Robust Control, Large Space Structures, Smart Structures. Fellow AIAA (assoc.); mem. IEEE (sr., subsect. 1981-88, Centennial medal 1984). Achievements include devel. of reduced order modeling techniques for large space structures, interdisciplinary approach for control of smart structures and structural health monitoring. Home: 501 Oak Knoll Rd Rolla MO 65401-4727 Office: U Mo Intelligent Systems Ctr Rolla MO 65401

RAPOPORT, DAVID E. lawyer; b. Chgo., May 27, 1956; s. Morris H. and Ruth (Teckteil) R.; m. Andrea Gail Albun; children: Alyson Faith, Steven Andrew. BS in Fin., No. Ill. U., 1978; JD with high honors, Ill. Inst. Tech., 1981; cert. trial work, Lawyers Postgrad. Inst., Chgo., 1984; cert. civil trial specialist, Nat. Bd. Trial Adv., 1991. Bar: Ill. 1981, Wis. 1995, U.S. Dist. Ct. (no. dist.) Ill. 1981, U.S. Dist. Ct. (trial bar) Ill. 1993, U.S. Dist. Ct. (so. and ctrl. dists.), U.S. Ct. Appeals (7th cir.) 1981, U.S. Ct. Appeals (7th cir.) 1981, U.S. Ct. Appeals (4th cir.) 1996. Assoc. Katz, Friedman, Schur & Eagle, Chgo., 1981-90, of counsel, 1990—; ptnr. Baizer & Rapoport, of counsel Highland Park, Ill., 1990-95; founder, pres. Rapoport Law Offices, P.C. (formerly Rapoport & Kupets P.C.), 1995—. Instr. legal writing Ill. Inst. Tech.-Kent Coll. Law, Chgo., 1981, guest lectr., 1985—; instr. Ill. Inst. CLE, 1995—; arbitrator Cir. Ct. Cook County, Ill., Million Dollar Advs. Forum, 1995—; state coord., lead trial counsel, mem. plaintiff's steering com. In Air Disaster at Charlotte Douglas Airport, 1994; mem. lead counsel com. In Air Disaster at Morrisville, N.C., 1994; lead trial counsel, In The Air Disaster at Sioux Gateway Airport, 1989. Bd. dirs. Congregation Beth Judea, Long Grove, Ill. Fellow Roscoe Pound Found.; mem. ABA, ATLA (sustaining mem.), Ill. Bar Assn., Ill. Trial Lawyers Assn., Chgo. Bar Assn., Ill. Inst. for CLE, Trial Lawyers for Pub. Justice, Trial Lawyers for Pub. Justice, Trial Lawyers for Civil Justice, Lake County Bar Assn. Office: Rapoport & Kupets Law Offices 77 W Washington St Fl 20 Chicago IL 60602-2801 also: O'Hare Internat Ctr 20 N Clark Ste 3500 Chicago IL 60602

RAPOPORT, ROBERT MORTON, medical educator; b. Oakland, Calif., Nov. 20, 1952; married; 2 children. BA in Biological Scis., U. Calif., Santa Barbara, 1974; PhD in Pharmacology, U. Calif., L.A., 1980; postdoc. studies in Pharmacology, U. Va., 1980-81, Stanford U., 1981-83. Rsch. pharmacologist VA Med. Ctr., Palo Alto, Calif., 1983-84, Cin., 1984—. Asst. prof. dept. pharmacology and cell biophysics U. Cin., 1984-91, assoc. prof., 1991—; asst. dir. med. pharmacology, 1994; spkr. in field. Reviewer manuscripts. various jours., grants various assns.; contbr. over 100 articles to profl. publs. Grantee U. Calif., 1977, VA, 1983-86, 85-86, 87-90, NIH, 1985-87, 88-93, Am. Heart Assn. S.W. Ohio, 1985-86, 86-87, 88-89, 89-91, 91-92, U. Cin., 1985-86, Am. Heart Assn., 1987-90, 1995—, Veterans Affairs, 1994-95, 95—, Univ. Rsch. Coun., 1994-95, Parke-Davis, 1994, 95; recipient Rsch. Career Devel. award, 1986-91. Office: Dept Pharmacology Univ Cincinnati 231 Bethesda Ave Cincinnati OH 45267-0001

RAPP, GEORGE ROBERT (RIP RAPP), geology and archeology educator; b. Toledo, Sept. 19, 1930; s. George Robert and Gladys Mae (Warner) R.; m. Jeannette Messner, June 15, 1956; children: Kathryn, Karen. BA, U. Minn., 1952; PhD, Pa. State U., 1960. Asst. then assoc. prof. S.D. Sch. Mines, Rapid City, 1957-65; assoc. prof. U. Minn., Mpls., 1965-75, prof. geology and archeology Duluth, 1975-95, dean Coll. Letters and Sci., 1975-84, dean Coll. Sci. and Engring., 1984-89, dir. Archeometry Lab., 1975—; Regents' prof. geoarchaeology, 1995—. Prof. Ctr. for Ancient Studies, U. Minn., Mpls., 1970-93, prof. interdisciplinary archaeol. studies, 1993—; cons. USIA, Westinghouse Corp., Exxon Corp., Ford Found. Author, editor: Excavations at Nichoria, 1978, Troy: Archeological Geology, 1982, Archeological Geology, 1985, Excavations at Tel Michal, 1989, Encyclopedia of Minerals, 1989, Phytolith Systematics, 1992, Geoarchaeology, 1998, Artifact Copper Sources, 2000; mem. editl. bd. Jour. Field Archeology, 1976-85, Jour. Archeol. Sci., 1977-79, Geoarcheology Jour., 1984-92, Am. Jour. Archeology, 1985-92. NSF postdoctoral fellow, 1963-64, Fulbright-Hayes sr. rsch. fellow, 1972-73. Fellow AAAS (chmn. sect. E, 1987-88, nat. coun. 1992-95), Geol. Soc. Am. (Archeol. Geology award 1983), Mineral. Soc. Am.; mem. Nat. Assn. Geology Tchrs. (pres. 1986-89), Soc. for Archeol. Sci. (pres. 1983-84), Assn. Field Archeology (pres. 1979-81), Archaeol. Inst. Am. (Pomerance medal 1988), Sigma Xi (bd. dirs. 1990-98). Avocation: classical music, exercise, nutrition. Office: U Minn-Duluth Archaeometry Lab Duluth MN 55812

RAPP, GERALD DUANE, lawyer, manufacturing company executive; b. Berwyn, Nebr., July 19, 1933; s. Kenneth P. and Mildred (Price) R.; children: Gerald Duane Jr., Gregory T., Amy Frances Wanzek. B.S., U. Mo., 1955; J.D., U. Mich., 1958. Bar: Ohio bar 1959. Practice in, Dayton, 1960—; ptnr. Smith & Schnacke, 1963-70; asst. gen. counsel Mead Corp., Dayton, 1970, v.p. human resources and legal affairs, 1973, v.p., corp. sec., 1975, v.p., gen. counsel, corp. sec., 1976, v.p., gen. counsel, 1979, sr. v.p., gen. counsel, 1981-91, counsel to bd. dirs., 1991-92; of counsel Bieser, Greer & Landis, 1992—. Pres. R-J Holding Co., Weber Canyon Ranch, Inc. Sr. editor U. Mich. Law Rev., 1957-58. Past chmn. Oakwood Youth Commn.; past v.p., bd. dirs. Big Bros. Greater Dayton; mem. pres.'s visitors com. U. Mich. Law Sch.; past trustee Urbana Coll.; past pres., trustee Ohio Ctr. Leadership Studies, Robert K. Greenleaf Ctr., Indpls.; past pres. bd. trustees Dayton and Montgomery County Pub. Libr.; past. mem. bd. visitors Law Schs. of Dayton. 1st lt. U.S. Army, 1958-60. Mem. ABA, Ohio Bar Assn., Dayton Bar Assn., Moraine Country Club, Dayton Racquet Club, Dayton Lawyers Club, Met. Club Washington, Phi Kappa Psi, Phi Delta Phi, Beta Gamma Sigma. Presbyterian. Office: 108 Green St Dayton OH 45402-2835 Fax: 937-224-0403.

RAPP, ROBERT ANTHONY, metallurgical engineering educator, consultant; b. Lafayette, Ind., Feb. 21, 1934; s. Frank J. and Goldie M. (Royer) R.; m. Heidi B. Sartorius, June 3, 1960; children: Kathleen Rapp Raynaud, Thomas, Stephen, Stephanie Rapp Surface. BSMetE, Purdue U., 1956; MSMetE, Carnegie Inst. Tech., 1959, PhDMetE, 1960; D (hon.), Inst. Polytech., Toulouse, France, 1995. Asst. prof. metall. engring. Ohio State U., Columbus, 1963-66, assoc. prof., 1966-69, prof., 1969—, M.G. Fontana prof., 1988-95, Univ. prof., 1989-95, disting. univ. prof. emeritus, 1995—. Vis. prof. Ecole Nat. Superior d'Electrochimie, Grenoble, France, 1972-73, U. Paris-Sud, Orsay, 1985-86, Ecole Nat. Superior de Chimie, Toulouse, France, 1985-86, U. New South Wales, Australia, 1987; Acta/Scripta Metallurgica lectr., 1991; rsch. metallurgist WPAFB, Ohio, 1960-63. Editor: Techniques of Metals Research, vol. IV, 1982, High Temperature Corrosion, 1984; translator Metallic Corrosion (Kaesche), 1986; bd. rev. jour. Oxid. Metals; contbr. numerous articles to profl. jours. Decorated chevalier des Palmes Academiques; recipient Disting. Engring. Alumnus award Purdue U., 1988, B.F. Goodrich Collegiate Inventor's award, 1991, 92, Ulrick Evans award Brit. Inst. Corrosion, 1992; Guggenheim fellow, 1972; Fulbright scholar Max Planck Inst. Phys. Chemistry, 1959-60, Linford award for Disting. Tchg.,The Electrochem. Soc., 1998. Fellow: Nat. Assn. Corrosion Engrs. (W.R. Whitney award 1986), Electrochem. Soc. (HTM Divsn. Outstanding Achievement award 1992, Linford Tchr. award 1998), Mining Metals and Materials Soc. (R.F. Mehl medal 2000), Am. Soc. Metals Internat. (B. Stoughton award 1968, Howe gold medal 1974, gold medal 2000); mem.: Nat. Acad. Engring., French Soc. Metals and Materials (hon.). Lutheran. Home: 1379 Southport Dr Columbus OH 43235-7649 E-mail: bobheidirapp@msn.com., rapp.4@osu.edu.

RAPP, ROBERT NEIL, lawyer; b. Erie, Pa., Sept. 10, 1947; m. Sally K. Meder; 1 child: Jeffrey David. BA, Case Western Res. U., 1969, JD, 1972; MBA, Cleve. State U., 1989. Bar: Ohio 1972, U.S. dist. Ct. (no. dist.) Ohio 1973, U.S. Ct. Appeals (6th crct.) 1981, U.S. Supreme Ct. 1980. Assoc. Metzenbaum, Gaines & Stern, Co., L.P.A., Cleve., 1972-75; ptnr. Calfee, Halter & Griswold, 1975—. Adj. prof. law Case Western Res. U., 1975—78, 1994—98, Cleve. Marshall Coll. Law, Cleve. State U., 1976—82; practitioner-in-residence Cornell U. Law Sch., 1993; mem. legal adv. bd. Nat. Assn. Securities Dealers, 1992—96; mem. market ops. rev. com. Nasdaq Stock Market, 1996—; arbitrator, practitioner mediator Nat. Futures Assn. Contbr. numerous articles to law jours. Mem. ABA (sect. bus. law: mem. com. fed. regulation of securities, subcom. broker-dealer regulation, sect. litigation: mem. com. securities litigation), Am. Arbitration Assn. (securities arbitrator, mem. comml. adv. coun. Cleve. region), Ohio State Bar Assn. (elected mem. coun. dels. 1976-82, corp. law com. 1980—), Cleve. Bar Assn. (chmn. young lawyers sect. 1976-77), assoc. mem. cert. grievance com., sect. securities law: exec. coun. 1980-85, chmn. govt. liaison com. 1980-81). Office: Calfee Halter & Griswold LLP 1400 McDonald Investment Ct Cleveland OH 44114-2688 E-mail: rrapp@calfee.com.

RAPP, STEPHEN JOHN, international prosecutor; b. Waterloo, Iowa, Jan. 26, 1949; s. Spurgeon John and Beverly (Leckington) R.; m. Donna J.E. Maier, 1981; children: Alexander, Stephanie. AB cum laude, Harvard U., 1971; JD with honors, Drake U., 1973. Bar: Iowa 1974, U.S. Dist. Ct. (no. and so. dists.) Iowa 1978, U.S. Ct. Appeals (8th cir.) 1979, U.S. Supreme Ct. 1979. Rsch. asst. Office of U.S. Senator Birch Bayh, Ind., 1970; community program asst. HUD, Chgo., 1971; mem. Iowa Ho. Reps., 1972-74, 79-83, Coun. to Majority Caucus, Iowa Ho. Reps., 1975; staff dir., counsel subcom. on juvenile delinquency U.S. Senate, Washington, 1977-78; ptnr. Rapp & Gilliam, Waterloo, 1979-83; pvt. practice, 1983-93; U.S. atty. U.S. Dist. Ct. (no. dist.) Iowa, 1993—2001; sr. prosecuting atty. United Nations Internat. Crime Tribunal for Rwanda, 2001—. Del., mem. com. Dem. Nat. Conv., 1976, 80, 84, 88, 92; mem. Dem. Nat. Adv. Com. on Econ., 1982-84, chmn. Black Hawk Dem. Com., 1986-91; mem. Iowa Dem. Com., 1990-93, chair 2d C.D. Dem. Com., 1991-93. Mem. ABA, Iowa Bar Assn., Order of Coif. Methodist. Home: 219 Highland Blvd Waterloo IA 50703-4229 Office: K-708 UN-ICTR PO Box 6016 Arusha Tanzania E-mail: rapp@un.org.

RAPPAPORT, GARY BURTON, defense equipment executive; b. Mpls., Apr. 27, 1937; s. Max and Beatrice (Berkinsky) R.; m. Susan Heller, Nov. 26, 1961; children: Debra Lynn, Melissa Ellen. B.S., U. Pa., 1959. Asst. to pres. Napco Industries, Inc., Hopkins, Minn., 1959-61, v.p., 1961-65, exec. v.p., 1964-65, pres., 1965-74, CEO, 1974-84, Venturian Corp., Hopkins, 1984—, also chmn. bd. dirs. Dir. La Maur, Inc., Mpls., 1980-87. Chmn. bd. govs. Mt. Sinai Hosp., Mpls., 1979-81. Served with Air N.G., 1960-64. Jewish. Office: Venturian Corp 11111 Excelsior Blvd Hopkins MN 55343-3434

RAPPLEYE, RICHARD KENT, financial executive, consultant, educator; b. Oswego, N.Y., Aug. 10, 1940; s. Robert Edward and Evelyn Margaret (Hammond) R.; m. Karen Tobe Greenberg, Sept. 7, 1963; children: Matthew Walker, Elizabeth Marion. AB, Miami U., Oxford, Ohio, 1962; postgrad., Boston U., 1962-63; MBA, U. Pa., 1964; postgrad., DePaul U., 1965-66; MRA, U. Detroit-Mercy, 1997. CPA, Ill. Auditor DeLoitte Haskins & Sells, Chgo., 1962-67, mgmt. cons., 1967-71; controller United Dairy Industry Assn., Rosemont, Ill., 1971, dir. fin. and adminstrn., 1971-73, exec. v.p., 1973-74; asst. to exec. v.p. Florists' Transworld Delivery, Southfield, Mich., 1974-75, group dir. fin. and adminstrn., 1975-80; asst. treas. Erb Lumber Co., Birmingham, 1980, v.p. fin., chief fin. officer, 1981-83; v.p., sec.-treas. C.S. Mott Found., Flint, 1983-2000, v.p. field svcs., 2000—. Lectr. U. Mich., Flint, 1987-91, 98-99; cons. in field; instr. Oakland U., Rochester, Mich., 1981-83; bd. dirs. Treas. Council Mich. Founds, 1986-92, 96—. Trustee Mich. State Bar Fedn., 2001—. Mem. AICPAs, Mich. Assn. CPAs, Theosophical Soc., Masons, Rotary. Unitarian. Home: 503 Arlington St Birmingham MI 48009-1639 Office: CS Mott Found 2000 Town Center Ste 1900 Southfield MI 48075 E-mail: rrappleye@mott.org.

RASCHE, ROBERT HAROLD, banker, retired economics educator; b. New Haven, June 29, 1941; s. Harold A. and Elsa (Bloomquist) R.; m. Dorothy Anita Bensen, Dec. 28, 1963; children: Jeanette Dorothy, Karl Robert. B.A., Yale U., 1963; A.M., U. Mich., 1965, Ph.D., 1966. Asst. prof. U. Pa., Phila., 1966-72; assoc. prof. econs. Mich. State U., East Lansing, 1972-75, prof., 1975-98, prof. emeritus, 1999—; sr. v.p., dir. rsch. St. Louis Fed. Res. Bank, 1999—. Vis. scholar St. Louis Fed. Res., 1971-72, 76-77, 94-98, San Francisco Fed. Ses., 1985, Bank of Japan, Tokyo, 1990; disting. vis. prof. econs. Ariz. State U., Tempe, 1986; rsch. assoc. Nat. Bur. Econ. Rsch., Cambridge, Mass., 1982-91; mem. Mich. Gov. Coun. Econ. Advisers, 1992-96; mem. Shadow Open Market Com., 1973-98. Mem. Am. Econs. Assn. Lutheran. Home: 14531 Radcliffeborough Ct Chesterfield MO 63017-5626 Office: Fed Res Bank St Louis Rsch Divsn PO Box 442 Saint Louis MO 63166-0442 E-mail: rasche@msu.edu.

RASCO, KAY FRANCES, antique dealer; b. Rienzi, Miss., Nov. 13, 1925; d. Robert Franklin and Sophia Agnes (Kinningham) Dilworth; m. H. Manfred Ray, July 9, 1943 (div. 1950); 1 child, Manfred Ray; m. Lavon Rasco, Mar. 22, 1951; children: Francine, Karen. BA, U. Miss., 1948, MA, 1953; PhD, Northwestern U., 1966. Instr. English Western Ill. U., 1953-54, 56-60, Northwestern U., 1960-61; lectr. De Paul U., Chgo., 1969, 71-74; master tchr. English Yale U., New Haven, summers 1963,64, 66,67; tchr. English New Trier High Sch., Winnetka, Ill., 1961-69, 71-73; assoc. prof. English Am. U., Cairo, 1969-71; prof. drama Al Azhar U., 1976-77; sales assoc. Merrill Lynch Realty, Evanston, Ill., 1973-76, 78-83, mgr. area sales, 1983-89; owner Sarah Bustle Antiques, 1989—. Mem. Rotary Internat. (pres. Evanston Lighthouse Rotary 1999-2000). Home: 1211 Hinman Ave Evanston IL 60202-1312 Office: 821 Dempster St Evanston IL 60201-4303

RASHKIN, MITCHELL CARL, internist, pulmonary medicine specialist; b. N.Y.C., June 1, 1951; m. Karen B. Ohlbaum, Aug. 8, 1982. BS in Computer Sci., U. Mich., 1973, MD, 1977. Diplomate Am. Bd. Internal Medicine, subspecialty Pulmonary Disease, Nat. Bd. Med. Examiners; cert. in critical care medicine Am. Bd. Internal Medicine; insr. Advanced Cardiac Life Support. Intern U. Cin. Med. Ctr., 1977-78, resident, 1978-80, fellowship in pulmonary medicine, 1980-82, dir. med. intensive care unit, 1982—, program dir. critical care medicine, 1989-95, co-dir. pulmonary care unit, 1990-93, dir. respiratory therapy, 1993—, dir med. stepdown unit, 1993—, asst. prof. medicine, 1982-89, assoc. prof. medicine, 1989—. Asst. prof. clin. emergency medicine U. Cin. Hosps., 1988-90, assoc. prof. 1990—; fellowship dir. Pulmonary/Critical Care U. Cin. Med. Ctr., 1995—; mem. numerous hosp. coms. Fellow ACP, Am. Coll. Chest Physicians; mem. Am. Thoracic Soc., Ohio Thoracic Soc. Office: U Cin Med Ctr PO Box 670564 231 Bethesda Ave Rm 6004 Cincinnati OH 45229-2827 E-mail: mitchell.rashkin@uc.edu.

RASIN, RUDOLPH STEPHEN, corporate executive; b. Newark, July 5, 1930; s. Simon Walter and Anna Rasin; m. Joy Kennedy Peterkin, Apr. 11, 1959; children: Rudolph Stephen, James Stenning, Jennifer Shaw Denniston. BA, Rutgers Coll., 1953; postgrad., Columbia U., 1958-59. Mgr. Miles Labs., Inc., 1959-61; devel. mgr. Gen. Foods Corp., White Plains, N.Y., 1961-62; asst. to pres., chmn. Morton Internat. Inc., Chgo., 1962-72; pres. Rasin Corp., 1971—, Alliance Brands, LLC. Bd. dirs. Ctr. for Def. Info., 1972—, Geneva Lakes Conservancy, Gatherings Waters Land Trust. With USAF, 1954—56. Mem. Hinsdale Golf Club, Mid Am. Club (Chgo.), Lake Geneva Country Club, Williams Coll. Club (N.Y.C.), Chgo. Club. Mem. United Ch. of Christ. Home: 179 E Lake Shore Dr Chicago IL 60611 Office: Rasin Corp 21 S Clark St Chicago IL 60603

RASMUSSEN, EARL R, lumber company and home improvement retail executive; CFO Menards Inc, Eau Claire, Wis. Office: Menards Inc 4777 Menard Dr Eau Claire WI 54703-9625

RATAJ, EDWARD WILLIAM, lawyer; b. St. Louis, Oct. 14, 1947; m. Elizabeth Spalding, July 4, 1970; children: Edward, Suzanne, Anne, Thomas, Charles. BS in Acctg., St. Louis U., 1969, JD, 1972. Assoc. Bryan, Cave, McPheeters & McRoberts, St. Louis, 1972-82, ptnr., 1983—. Office: Bryan Cave McPheeters & McRoberts 211 N Broadway Saint Louis MO 63102-2733

RATHBUN, RANDALL KEITH, lawyer; b. Miami Beach, Fla., Aug. 24, 1953; s. Ronald K. and Betty L. (Stockstill) R.; m. Janet Sue Meyer, Oct. 8, 1983; children: Zachary Keith, Joshua George, Kelsea Rebecca. BS, Kans. State U., 1975; JD, Washburn U., 1978. Bar: Kans.. 1978, U.S. Dist. Ct. Kans. 1978, U.S. Ct. Appeals (10th cir.) 1985. Assoc. Curfman, Harris, Bell, Weigand & Depew, Wichita, Kans., 1978-80; ptnr. Depew, Gillen & Rathbun, 1980-93; U.S. atty. U.S. Dept. of Justice, Kans., 1993-96; ptnr. Depew & Gillen, 1996—. Bd. dirs. Washburn Law Jour., 1977-78. Chair 4th Congressional Dist. Democrats, Kans., 1986-88; exec. com. State Dem. Party, Topeka, 1986-88; del. Dem. Nat. Conv., Atlanta, 1988; treas. State Dem. Party, 1991—; officer, bd. dirs. Sedgwick County unit Am. Cancer Soc.-Wichita, 1984-90; bd. dirs. Kans. div. Am. Cancer Soc., Wichita, 1987-90. Mem. Wichita Bar Assn. (sec.-treas. 1991-92), Wichita Young Lawyers (pres. 1983-84), Kans. Bar Assn. Democrat. Methodist. Office: Depew & Gillen 151 N Main St Ste 800 Wichita KS 67202-1409

RATHI, MANOHAR LAL, pediatrician, neonatologist; b. Beawar, Rajasthan, India, Dec. 25, 1933; came to U.S. 1969; s. Bagtawarmal and Sitadevi (Laddha) R.; m. Kamla Jajoo, Feb. 21, 1960; children: Sanjeev A., Rajeev. MBBS, Rajasthan U., 1961. Diplomate Am. Bd. Pediats., sub-bd. Neonatal Perinatal Medicine; lic. physician, N.Y., Ill., Calif. Resident house physician internal medicine Meml. Hosp., Darlington, U.K., 1963-64; resident sr. house physician pediatrics Gen. Hosp., Oldham, U.K., 1964-65; dir. perinatal medicine Christ Hosp. Perinatal Ctr., Oak Lawn, Ill., 1974-98, attending physician Oakl Lawn, 1974—; assoc. prof. pediatrics Rush Med. Coll., Chgo., 1979—; cons. obstetrician Christ Hosp., Oak Lawn, 1976—; cons. neonatologist Little Co. of Mary Hosp., Evergreen Park, Ill., 1972—, Palos Cmty. Hosp., Palos Heights, 1978—; chmn. Midwest Neoped Assocs., Oak Brook, 1997—. Cons./lectr. in field. Contbr. articles to profl. jours.; editor: Clinical Aspects of Perinatal Medicine, 1984, Vol. I, 1985, Vol. II, 1986, Current Perinatology, 1989, Vol. II, 1990; editor with others: Perinatal Medicine Vol. I, 1978, Vol. I, 1980, Vol. II, 1982. Hummell Found. grantee, 1976-77, WyethLab grantee, 1977-78; recipient Physicians Recognition award AMA, 1971-74, 91-92, Outstanding New Citizen's award State of Ill., 1978, Asian Human Svcs. of Chgo., 1988, Nitric Oxide Study by Ohmeda, 1994-95. Fellow Am. Acad. Pediats. (perinatal sect., Ill. chpt. treas. 1994-96); mem. AMA, Chgo. Med. Soc., Ill.

Med. Soc., Chgo. Pediat. Soc., Med. Soc. County of Kings Bklyn., N.Y. Acad. Scis., Am. Thoracic Soc., Soc. Critical Care Medicine. Republican. Hindu. Office: Midwest Neoped Assocs Ltd 900 Jorie Blvd Ste 186 Oak Brook IL 60523-3808

RATHOD, MULCHAND, mechanical engineering educator; b. Pathri, India, Mar. 3, 1945; came to U.S., 1970, naturalized, 1981; s. Shamjibhai Laljibhai and Ramaben Rathod; m. Damayanti Thakor, Aug. 15, 1970; children: Prerana, Falgun, Sejal. BS in Mech. Engring., Sardar Patel U., India, 1970; MS, Miss. State U., 1972, PhD, 1975. Rsch. grad. asst. Miss. State U., 1970-75; cons. engr. Bowron & Butler, Jackson, Miss., 1975-76; asst. prof. Tuskegee Inst., Ala., 1976-78; mem. tech. staff Jet Propulsion Lab., Pasadena, Calif., summer 1980, 81; summer faculty IBM Corp., Endicott, N.Y., 1982-85; assoc. prof., coord. MET program SUNY, Binghamton, 1979-87; dir. engring. tech. divsn. Wayne State U., Detropit, 1987—. Cons. Interpine, Hattiesburg, Miss., 1977-79, Jet Propulsion Lab., 1980-83, IBM Corp., 1982-85; pres. Shiv-Parvati, Inc. 1982—. Contbr. articles to profl. jours.; patentee in field. Den leader Susquahanna coun. Boy Scouts Am., Vestal, N.Y., 1983-84. Recipient award NASA, 1981; grantee SUNY Found., 1984, Dept. Energy, 1978, GM, 1988-92, UAW Chrysler, 1990-91, Hudson-Webber Found., 1991-92, Ford, 1992-93, Kellogg Found., 1993-94, SME Found., 1994, Mich. Dept. Edn., 1994, NSF, 1995—. Fellow: ASME (cert. of appreciation 1991—2001, Dedicated Svc. award 1995, Ben C. Sparks medal 1998, cert. of appreciation 1982—89, BMW award 2001); mem.: ASHRAE, Profl. Order Engring. Tech., N.Y. State Engring. Tech. Assn., Am. Soc. Engring. Edn. (reviewer), India Assn. Miss. State U. (pres. 1972—73), Tau Beta Pi, Tau Alpha Phi (founder, faculty advisor 1989—), Pi Tau Sigma. Home: 1042 Woods Ln Grosse Pointe Woods MI 48236-1157 Office: Wayne State U Div Engring Tech Detroit MI 48202

RATNER, ALBERT B. building products company executive, land developer; b. Cleve., 1927; Grad., Mich. State U., 1951. With Forest City Enterprises, Inc., Cleve., 1964—, sec., 1960-68, exec. v.p., from 1968, now pres., chief exec. officer, dir., also co-chmn brd. Mem. exec. com., dir. Univ. Circle Devel. Corp.; dir. Am. Greetings Corp. Mem. Internat. Council Shopping Ctrs. Office: Forest City Enterprises Inc 1100 Terminal Tower 50 Public Sq # 1170 Cleveland OH 44113-2202

RATNER, CARL JOSEPH, theater director; b. Memphis, Sept. 17, 1957; MusB, Oberlin Conservatory of Music, 1980. Intern Juilliard Sch., N.Y.C., 1980-81, N.Y.C. Opera, 1981-82; asst. dir. Lyric Opera Chgo., 1982-84; prodn. asst. San Francisco Opera, 1985-86; asst. dir. Metropolitan Opera, N.Y.C., 1989-90; artistic dir. Chamber Opera Chgo., 1985-93, Chgo. Opera Theater, 1994-99. Home: 421 W Melrose St Apt 22A Chicago IL 60657-3881 Office: Chicago Opera Theater 70 E Lake St Ste 540 Chicago IL 60601-5990

RATNER, CHARLES A. real estate executive; Pres., CEO Forest City Enterprises, Inc., Cleve. Office: Forest City Enterprises Inc 50 Public Sq Ste 1100 Cleveland OH 44113-2267

RATNER, GERALD, lawyer; b. Chgo., Dec. 17, 1913; s. Peter I. and Sarah (Soreson) R.; m. Eunice Payton, June 18, 1948. PhB, U. Chgo., 1935, JD cum laude, 1937. Bar: Ill. 1937. Since practiced in, Chgo.; sr. ptnr. Gould & Ratner and predecessor firm, 1949—. Officer Henry Crown & Co., CC Industries, Inc., Material Svc. Corp., Freeman United Coal Mining Co., Mineral and Land Resources Corp.; lectr., writer on real estate law. Capt. AUS, 1942-46. Gerald Ratner Athletics Ctr. named in his honor, U. Chgo. Mem. ABA, Ill. Bar Assn., Chgo. Bar Assn., Order of Coif, Phi Beta Kappa. Home: 180 E Pearson St Apt 6205 Chicago IL 60611-2191 Office: 222 N La Salle St Ste 800 Chicago IL 60601-1086

RATNER, JAMES, real estate executive; m. Susan Ratner; 2 children. BA, Columbia U.; MBA, Harvard U. With Citibank, N.Y.C., Nasher Co., Dallas; pres. devel. divsn. Forest City Enterprises, Cleve., 1978—. Office: Forest City Mgmt Terminal Tower 50 Public Sq Ste 1100 Cleveland OH 44113-2267

RATNOFF, OSCAR DAVIS, physician, educator; b. N.Y.C., Aug. 23, 1916; s. Hyman L. and Ethel (Davis) Ratnoff; m. Marian Foreman, Mar. 31, 1945; children: William Davis, Martha. AB, Columbia U., 1936, MD, 1939; LLD (hon.) , U. Aberdeen, 1981; ScD (hon.) , Case Western Res. U., 1996. Intern Johns Hopkins Hosp., Balt., 1939—40; Austin fellow in physiology Harvard Med. Sch., Boston, 1940—41; asst. resident Montefiore Hosp., N.Y.C., 1942; resident Goldwater Meml. Hosp., 1942—43; asst. in medicine Columbia Coll. Physicians and Surgeons, 1942—46; fellow in medicine Johns Hopkins, 1946—48, instr. medicine, 1948—50, instr. bacteriology, 1949—50; asst. prof. medicine Western Res. U., Cleve., 1950—56; assoc. prof. Case Western Res. U., 1956—61, prof., 1961—; asst. physician Univ. Hosp., Cleve., 1952—67, physician, 1967—. Author: Bleeding Syndromes, 1960; mem. editl. bd.: Jour. Lab. Clin. Medicine, 1956—62, assoc. editor: , 1986—91, bd. rev. editors: , 1991—95, editl. adv. bd.: , 1995—; editor: Treatment of Hemorrhagic Disorders, 1968; editor: (with C.D. Forbes) Disorders of Hemostasis, 1984, Disorders of Hemostasis, 3rd edit., 1996; mem. editl. bd.: Circulation, 1961—65, mem. editl. bd.: Blood, 1963—69, mem. editl. bd.: , 1978—81, mem. editl. bd.: Am. Jour. Physiology, 1966—72, mem. editl. bd.: Jour. Applied Physiology, 1966—72, mem. editl. bd.: Jour. Lipid Rsch., 1967—69, mem. editl. bd.: Jour. Clin. Investigation, 1969—71, mem. editl. bd.: Circulation Rsch., 1970—75, mem. editl. bd.: Annals Internal Medicine, 1973—76, mem. editl. bd.: Perspectives in Biology and Medicine, 1974—, mem. editl. bd.: Thrombosis Rsch., 1981—84, mem. editl. bd.: Jour. Urology, 1981—88, mem. editl. bd.: Internat. Jour. Hematology, 1991—; contbr. articles to med. jours. Career investigator Am. Heart Assn., 1960—86. Maj. USMC, 1943—46. Named to Heart Hall of Fame, N.E. Ohio Heart Assn., 1989; recipient Henry Moses award, Montefiore Hosp., 1949, Disting. Achievement award, Modern Medicine, 1967, James F. Mitchell award, 1971, Murray Thelin award, Nat. Hemophilia Found., 1971, H.P. Smith award, Am. Soc. Clin. Pathology, 1975, Joseph Mather Smith prize, Columbia Coll. Physicians and Surgeons, 1976, Disting. Achievement in Med. Sci. award, U. Hosps. of Cleve., 1992, Saltzman award, Mt. Sinai Hosp. of Cleve., 1994. Master: ACP (John Phillips award 1974); fellow: AAAS; mem.: AMA, NAS (Kovalenko award 1985), Am. Soc. Biol. Chemists, Am. Physiol. Soc., Internat. Soc. Thrombosis (Grant award 1981, Spl. award 1993), Internat. Soc. Hematology, Am. Soc. Hematology (Dameshek award 1972), Assn. Am. Physicians (Kober lectr. 1985, Kober medal 1988), Ctrl. Soc. Clin. Rsch. (Disting. Svc. award 1992), Am. Soc. Clin. Investigation, Soc. Scholars Johns Hopkins U., Am. Fedn. Clin. Rsch. Home: 1801 Chestnut Hills Dr Cleveland OH 44106-4643 Office: Univ Hosps of Cleve Dept Medicine Cleveland OH 44106

RATTI, RONALD ANDREW, economics educator; b. Neath, West Glamorgan, Wales, Oct. 10, 1948; came to U.S., 1970; s. Ronald Rudolph and Janet (Marshall) R. BA, U. Lancaster, 1970; MA, Case Western Res. U., 1972; PhD, So. Meth. U., 1975. Asst. prof. to assoc. prof. U. Mo., Columbia, 1975-85, prof. econs., 1985—, chmn. dept., 1982-89. Vis. scholar Fed. Res. Bank Kansas City, Mo., 1978, Fed. Res. Bank St. Louis., 1984-85; acad. visitor London Sch. Econs., 1985; vis. Fulbright prof. Korea U., Seoul, 1996, Korea Inst. Fin., 1997. Contbr. articles to profl. jours. Office: U Mo Dept Econs 118 Profl Bldg Columbia MO 65211-0001

RAUENHORST, GERALD, architectural engineer, construction and development executive; b. Mpls., Dec. 8, 1927; s. Henry and Margaret (Keltgen) R.; m. Henrietta Schmoll, Sept. 2, 1950; children: Judith, Mark, Neil, Joseph, Michael, Susan, Amy. BA, U. St. Thomas, 1948, LLD, 1971; BSCE, Marquette U., 1951, LLD (hon.) , 2001. Instr. civil engring. Marquette U., Milw., 1950-51; engr. Peter Rasmussen & Son, Oshkosh, Wis., 1951-52, Viking Constrn., Mpls., 1952-53; pres., founder Rauenhorst Corp. (name changed to Opus Corp.), 1953—, chmn. bd., CEO, 1982—, founding chmn., 2000—. Chmn. and CEO Opus Nat., L.L.C., 1997—; dep. chmn. 1991-93, chmn. bd. dirs. Fed. Res. Bank, Mpls., 94-95, dir., chmn. human resources com. ConAgra, Omaha, 1982-98; bd. dirs. Cornerstone Properties, Inc., N.Y., 1993-98. Mem. devel. com. Papal Found.; trustee U. St. Thomas; chmn. bd. trustees Marquette U., 1985—87, trustee emeritus; dir. emeritus Cath. Cmty. Found.; treas. Papal Found. Recipient Disting. Engring. award Marquette U., 1974, Ernst & Young Lifetime Achievement award/Entrepreneur of Yr., 1997; named Alumnus of Yr., Marquette U., 1969, Coll. of St. Thomas, 1978, Minn. Exec. of Yr., Corp. Report mag., 1983, Developer of Yr., NAIOP, 1992, No. 1 Developer in Country, Nat. Real Estate Investor mag., 1995; named to Minn. Bus. Hall of Fame, 1980. Mem. ASCE, NSPE, World Pres. Orgn., Minn. Soc. Profl. Engrs., Mpls. Club, Interlachen Club, Naples Yacht Club, Port Royal Club, Royal Poinciana Golf Club, Serra Club (past gov. dist. 7, past pres. Mpls.), Knight of Holy Sepulchre, Knight of St. Gregory, Triangle. Roman Catholic. Avocations: fishing, golf, pottery. Office: Opus Corp PO Box 59110 Minneapolis MN 55459-0110

RAUGHTER, JOHN B. editor; Contbg. editor The Am. Legion, Indpls. Office: The Am Legion 5561 W 74th St Indianapolis IN 46268-4184

RAUSCHENBERGER, STEVEN J. state legislator; b. Elgin, Ill., Aug. 29, 1956; BBA, Coll. of William and Mary. Mem. Ill. State Senate, Dist. 33, Elgin Downtown Adv. Commn.; owner Rauschenberger Furniture Co.; gen. mgr. Ackerman Bros. Corp., Elgin, Ill. Active Boy Scouts Am. Home: 750 Jay St Elgin IL 60120-8240 Office: Ill Senate Mem State Capitol Springfield IL 62706-0001

RAVEN, FRANCIS HARVEY, mechanical engineering educator; b. Erie, Pa., July 29, 1928; s. Frederick James and Eleanor Elizabeth (Sopp) R.; m. Therese Mary Strobel, June 21, 1952; children: Betty, Ann, Paul, John, Mary, Cathy, Linda. BS in Math., Gannon Univ., 1948; BSME, Pa. State U., 1950, MSME, 1951; PhD, Cornell U., 1958. Design engr. Hamilton Standard div. United Techs., Hartford, Conn., 1951-54; instr. Cornell U., Ithaca, N.Y., 1954-58; asst. prof. mech. engring. U. Notre Dame, 1958-62, assoc. prof., 1962-66, prof., 1966—. Cons. microprocessor and computer control of robots and mech. systems; devel. Vector Loop Method (first analytical method for the design of mechanisms and cam systems.). Author: Automatic Control Engineering, 1961, 5th edit., 1995, Mathematics of Engineering Systems, 1966, Engineering Mechanics, 1973; pub. McGraw-Hill Book Co. Mem. ASME, Am. Soc. for Engring. Edn. (AT&T Teaching award 1968-69), Sigma Xi. Roman Catholic. Home: 52740 Brandel Ave South Bend IN 46635-1248 Office: U Notre Dame Dept Aerospace-Mech Engring Notre Dame IN 46556 E-mail: Francis.H.Raven.1@nd.edu.

RAVEN, PETER HAMILTON, botanical garden director, botany educator; b. Shanghai, China, June 13, 1936; s. Walter Francis and Isabelle Marion (Breen) R.; children— Alice Catherine, Elizabeth Marie, Francis Clark, Kathryn Amelia. AB with highest honors, U. Calif.-Berkeley, 1957; PhD, UCLA, 1960; DSc (hon.), St. Louis U., 1982, Knox Coll., 1983, So. Ill. U., 1983, Miami U., 1986, U. Goteborg, 1987, Rutgers U., 1988, U. Mass., 1988, Leiden U., The Netherlands, 1990; HHD (hon.), Webster U., 1989; D.Sc. (hon.), Universidad Nacional de La Plata, Argentina, 1991, Westminster Coll., 1992, U. Mo., 1992, Washington U., 1993, U. Conn., 1993; DSc (hon.), U. Cordoba, Argentina, 1993. Taxonomist, curator Rancho Santa Ana Botanic Garden, Claremont, Calif., 1961-62; asst. prof., then assoc. prof. biol. scis. Stanford U., 1962-71; dir. Mo. Bot. Garden, St. Louis, 1971—; adj. prof. biology St. Louis U., 1973—; Engelmann prof. botany Washington U., St. Louis, 1971—; adj. prof. biology U. Mo., 1976—. Sr. rsch. fellow New Zealand Dept. Sci. and Indsl. Rsch., 1969-70; v.p. XIII Internat. Bot. Congress, Sydney, 1981; Home Sec. Nat. Acad. Scis., 1987—; chmn. report rev. com. NRC, 1989—; mem. pres. com. Adv. on Sci. and Tech., 1994—; hon. vice-chair 27th Internat. Geographical Cong., 1992; hon. v.p. XV Internt. Bot. Cong., Tokyo, 1993; mem. Nat. Sci. Bd., 1990-94; mem. jury Internat. St. Francis Prize for Environment, 1990-93; mem. exec. com. Joint Appeal by Religion and Sci. for Environment, 1991—; mem. external adv. bd. Com. on Peabody Mus., Yale U., 1992-94; mem. coun. World Resources Inst., 1992—; mem. adv. com. Africa Ctr. for Resources and Environment, 1992—, Third World Found. N.Am., 1993; mem. adv. com. to biodiversity com. Chinese Acad. Scis., 1993—; mem. Exec. Com. Round Table, St. Louis, 1993—; mem. hon. fgn. adv. bd. Botanical Garden Orgn. Thailand, 1993—. Author: Native Shrubs of Southern California, 1966, (with P.R. Ehrlich, R.W. Holm) Papers on Evolution, 1969, (with H. Curtis) Biology of Plants, 1971, 4th edit., 1986, (with R.F. Evert and S.E. Eichhorn) 5th edit., 1992, (with B. Berlin and D. Breedlove) Principles of Tzeltal Plant Classification, 1974, (with G.B. Johnson) Biology, 1986, 3d edit., 1992, Understanding Biology, 1988, 3d edit., 1995; editor: (with L.E. Gilbert) Coevolution of Animals and Plants, 1981, (with F.J. Radovsky & S.H. Sohmer) Biogeography of the Tropical Pacific, 1984, (with others) Topics in Plant Population Biology, 1979, (with K. Iwatsuki and W.J. Bock) Modern Aspects of Species, 1986; editor-in-chief Brittonia, 1963-66; mme. editorial bd. Flora Neotropica, 1965-84; editor (with D.E. Osterbrock) Origins and Extinctions, 1988, paperback, 1992, (with R.M. Polhill) Advances in Legume Systematics, 1981 (with L. Berg and G.B. Johnson) Environment, 1995; mem. editorial bd. Evolution, 1963-65, 76-79, Memoirs of N.Y. Botanical Garden, 1966-84, N.Am. Flora, 1966-84, Am. Naturalist, 1967-70, Annual Rev. Ecology and Systematics, 1971-75, Flora of Ecuador, 1974—, Evolutionary Theory, 1975— , Adansonia, 1976—, Jour. Biogeography, 1978—, Science, 1979-82, Proceedings of U.S. Nat. Acad. Scis., 1980-87, World Book, Inc., 1982-86, Diversity, 1985-90, Bothalia, 1985—, Serie Botánica of the Anales del Instituto de Biología UNAM, 1989, Ecol. Applications, 1989-92, others; mem. adv. bd. Applied Botany Abstracts, 1981—, Tropical Plant Sci. Research, 1982—, Darwiniana, 1985—; mem. internat. editl. com. Acta Botánica Mexicana, 1987—; mem. internat. editl. adv. bd. Candollea, 1995—; mem. editl. bd. Botanical Bulletin Academia Sinica, 1988—, Botanical Mag., 1988-92, Chinese Jour. of Botany, 1991—, Edinburgh Jour. of Botany, 1994—; co-chmn. editl. com. Flora of China, 1988—; advisor Plants Today, 1988-89; contbr. over 400 articles to profl. jours. Bd. curators U. Mo., 1985-90; commr. Tower Grove Park, St. Louis, 1971—; mem. Arnold Arboretum Vis. Com., 1974-81, chmn. 1976-81; bd. overseers Morris Arboretum, 1977-81; mem. sci. adv. bd. Nat. Tropical Botanical Garden, 1975—; mem. Smithsonian Council, 1985-90; chmn. St. Louis Area Mus. Collaborative, 1985-91, Commn. for Flora Neotropica, 1985—; mem. Commn. on Mus. for New Century, 1981-84; mem. sci. and engring. panel Com. on Scholarly Communication with People's Republic China, 1981-85; chmn. com. to visit dept. organismic and evolutionary biology Harvard U., 1982-84, mem. 84-85; ednl. adv. bd. John Simon Guggenheim Meml. Found., 1986—; research assoc. botany Bernice P. Bishop Mus., 1985—; hon. trustee Acad. Sci. of St. Louis, 1986—; chmn. Internat. Union for the Conservation of Nature, World Wildlife Fund, 1984-87, hon. chmn. 1987-90; mem. adv. and tech. bd. Fundación de Parques Nacionales and Fundación Neotrópica, Costa Rica, 1988—; mem. Nat. Coun. World Wildlife Fund and Conservation Foun., 1989—, U.S. bd. dirs. 1983-88, bd. dirs. Conservation Found., 1985-88, sci. adv. com. Conservation Internat., 1988—, chmn's. coun., 1989, World Wildlife Fund, 1987-90, Conservation Found., 1989—, Found. Flora Malesianna, 1992—, Sci. Svc., 1993—; hon. scientific adv. com. XVII Pacific Sci. Congress, 1990-91; adv. bd. The Winslow Found., 1993—, The Internat. Sci. Camp The Earth We Share, 1993—; exec. bd. Internat. Sci. Found. for the Former Soviet Union, 1992—; internat. adv. bd. Fifth ICSEB Congress, Hungary, 1994—. Commn. mem. U.S. MAB, 1994-95. Recipient A.P. DeCandolle prize, Geneva, 1970; Disting. Service award Japan Am. Soc. So. Calif., 1977; award of Merit, Bot. Soc. Am., 1977; Achievement medal Garden Club Am., 1978; Willdenow medal Berlin Bot. Garden, 1979; Disting. Service award Am. Inst. Biol. Scis., 1981; Joseph Priestly medal, Dickinson Coll., 1982; Gold Seal medal Nat. Council of State Garden Clubs, 1982; Internat. Environ. Leadership medal UN Environ. Program, 1982; Spl. citiation Doña Doris Yankelewitz de Monge, 1985, Internat. Prize for Biology, Govt. Japan, 1986, Hutchinson medal Chgo. Hort. Soc., 1986, Archie F. Carr medal, 1987, Global 500 Honor Roll UN Environ. Program, 1987, Am. Fuchsia Soc. Achievement Medal, 1987, George Robert White Medal of Honor Mass. Horticultural Soc., 1987, Robert Allerton Medal Nat. Tropical Bot. Garden, 1988, Nat. Conservation Achievement award Nat. Wildlife Fedn., 1989, Delmer S. Fahrney medal Franklin Inst., Phila., 1989, (with E.O. Wilson) Environ. prize Institut de la Vie (Paris), 1990, Order of Golden Ark (officer), The Netherlands, 1990, award for Support of Sci. Coun. Sci. Soc. Pres., 1990, (with Norman Myers) Volvo Environ. prize, 1992, Pres.'s Conservation Achievement Awd., 1993, Nature Conservancyvement award TNC, 1993, Internat. award Internat. Inst. of St. Louis, 1994, Founder's Coun. Centennial Merit award The Field Mus. of Natural History, 1994, Sword of St. Ignatius Loyola award St. Louis U., 1994, Tyler Environ. Achievement prize, 1994, and numerous other botanical awards and honors; Guggenheim fellow, 1969-70; John D. and Catherine T. MacArthur Found. fellow, 1985-90, NSF postdoctoral fellow, Brit. Mus. London, 1960-61. Fellow Am. Acad. Arts and Scis. (com. on membership 1980-82), Linnean Soc. London (fgn. mem.), Calif. Acad. Scis. (CAS Fellow, Fellows' medal 1988), AAAS, Indian Nat. Sci. Acad., Third World Acad. Scis., World Acad. Art & Sci.; mem. NSF (systematic biology panel 1973-76, chmn. adv. com. for biol. behavioral and social scis. 1984-90), NAS (com. on human rights 1984-87, home sec. 1987—), Royal Danish Acad. Scis. and Letters (fgn. hon.), Royal Swedish Acad. Scis. (fgn.), Royal Soc. New Zealand (hon.), NRC (gov. bd. 1983-86, 87-88, chmn. com. on research priorities in tropical biology 1977-79, assembly life scis. 1979-81, com. on selected research problems in humid tropics 1980-82, commn. internat. relations 1981-82), Calif. Bot. Soc. (v.p. 1968-69), Am. Soc. Plant Taxonomists (pres. 1972), Assn. Systematics Collections (pres. 1980-82, Fed. Council Arts and Humanities, Nat. Geographic Soc. (com. on research and exploration 1982—), Internat. Orgn. Plant Biosystematists (v.p. 1989-92, pres. 92-95), Internat. Assn. for Plant Taxonomy (council 1981—), Orgn. Tropical Studies (treas. 1981-84, v.p. devel. 1984-85, pres. 1985-88, past pres. 1988-90, bd. dirs. 1981-91), Am. Soc. Naturalists (pres. 1983), Miller Inst. Basic Research in Sci. (adv. bd. 1983-89), Am. Inst. Biol. Scis. (pres. 1983-84), Mo. Acad. Scis., Geol. Soc. Am., Bot. Soc. Am. (pres. 1975, chmn. com. on sci. exchange with People's Republic China 1978-84), Assn. Tropical Biology (bd. dirs. 1981-85), Am. Assn. Mus. (exec. com. 1980-83), Assn. Sci. Mus. Dirs., Assn. Pacific Systematists, Sociedad Argentina de Botanica (socio honorario), Fundación Miguel Lillo (hon.), Soc. Systematic Zool., Sociedad Botánica de México (life), Assn. pour l'Etude Taxonomique de la Flore d'Afrique Tropicale, Orgn. for Phyto-Taxonomic Investigation of Mediterranean Area (council 1975-89), All-Union Botanical Soc. USSR (hon. fgn. mem.), Accademia Nazionale delle Scienze detta dei XL (fgn.), Am. Philosophical Soc, Russian Acad. Scis. (fgn. mem.), Nat. Acad. Scis. India (fgn. fellow 1990—), Academia de Ciencias Exactas, Físicas y Naturales, Austrian Acad. Scis., Academia Chilena de Ciencias, Academia Nacional de Ciencias, Academy Scis. Ukraine, Chinese Acad. Scis., Nature Conservancy (Pres. Conservation Achievement Awd., 1993), Phi Beta Kappa, Sigma Xi Office: Mo Bot Garden 4344 Shaw Blvd Saint Louis MO 63110-2226

RAVENCROFT, THOMAS A. food company executive; V.p. corp. planning Dean Foods Co., Franklin Park, Ill., 1979-88, group v.p., 1988-89, pres. dairy divsn., 1994-98, sr. v.p., 1989—, also bd. dirs. Office: 3600 River Rd Franklin Park IL 60131-2152

RAWDEN, DAVID, financial services company executive; CFO, Peregine, Southfield, Mich., until 1999; prin. Jay Alix & Assocs., 1999—. Office: Jay Alix & Assocs 4000 Town Center Ste 580 Southfield MI 48075

RAWLINS, RANDA, lawyer; Grad., Truman State U., 1979; JD, U. Mo., 1982. Bar: Mo., Kans., U.S. Dist. Ct. (ea. and we. dists.) Mo., U.S. Ct. Appeals (8th and 10th cirs.). Shareholder Niewald Waldeck & Brown, Kansas City, Kans. Bd. govs. Truman State U., 1997—; mem. Assn. of Governing Bds. of Univs. and Coll. Coun. of Bd. Chairs; vol. atty. CASA, Project Consent; mem. adv. bd. Inst. for Women in Pub. Life; lay leader St. John's United Meth. Ch., 1997—. Named one of 12 most disting. attys., Mo. Lawyers Weekly, 2001; recipient Pershing scholarship, Truman State U., Lon O. Hocke award, Mo. Bar Found., 1994. Mem.: Assn. Women Lawyers Greater Kansas City (2000 Woman of Yr.), Women Lawyers Greater Kansas City, Am. Bd. Trial Advocates, Kansas City Met. Bar Assn., Kans. Bar Assn. Office: 12 Wyandotte Plz 120 W 12th St Ste 1300 Kansas City MO 64105

RAY, DOUGLAS KENT, newspaper executive; Pres., CEO Daily Herald/Sunday Herald, Arlington Heights, Ill., 1970—. Office: Daily Herald/Sunday Herald Paddock Publs PO Box 280 Arlington Heights IL 60006-0280

RAY, EDWARD JOHN, economics educator, administrator; b. Jackson Heights, N.Y., Sept. 10, 1944; s. Thomas Paul and Cecelia Francis (Hiney) R.; m. Virginia Beth Phelps, June 14, 1969; children: Stephanie Elizabeth, Katherine Rebecca, Michael Edward. BA, CUNY, 1966; MA, Stanford U., 1969, PhD, 1971. Asst. prof. econs. Ohio State U., Columbus, 1970-74, assoc. prof., 1974-77, prof., 1977—, chmn. dept. econs., 1976-92, assoc. provost acad. affairs Office Acad. Affairs, 1992-93, sr. vice provost, chief info. officer Office Acad. Affairs, 1993-98, acting sr. v.p. and provost, 1997-98, exec. v.p., provost, 1998—. Cons. Dept. Labor, 1974-76, Dept. Commerce, 1977, AID, Office Tech. Assessment, winter 1982 Contbr. articles to profl. jours. Active Upper Arlington Civic Assn., Columbus, 1983—. Mem. Am. Econs. Assn., Phi Beta Kappa Home: 1977 Rosebery Dr Columbus OH 43220-3044 Office: Ohio State U Acad Affairs 203 Bricker Hall 190 N Oval Mall Columbus OH 43210-1321 E-mail: ray.1@osu.edu.

RAY, FRANK ALLEN, lawyer; b. Lafayette, Ind., Jan. 30, 1949; s. Dale Allen and Merry Ann (Fleming) R.; m. Carol Ann Olmutz, Oct. 1, 1982; children: Erica Fleming, Robert Allen. BA, Ohio State U., 1970, JD, 1973. Bar: Ohio 1973, U.S. Dist. Ct. (so. dist.) Ohio 1975, U.S. Supreme Ct. 1976, U.S. Tax Ct. 1977, U.S. Ct. Appeals (6th cir.) 1977, U.S. Dist. Ct. (no. dist.) Ohio 1980, Pa. 1983, U.S. Dist. Ct. (ea. dist.) Mich. 1983, U.S. Ct. Appeals (1st cir.) 1986; cert. civil trial adv. Nat. Bd. Trial Advocacy. Asst. pros. atty. Franklin County, Ohio, 1973-75, chief civil counsel, 1976-78; dir. econ. crime project Nat. Dist. Attys. Assn., Washington, 1975-76; assoc. Brownfield, Kosydar, Bowen, Bally & Sturtz, Columbus, Ohio, 1978, Michael F. Colley Co., L.P.A., Columbus, 1979-83; pres. Frank A. Ray Co., L.P.A., 1983-93, 2000—, Ray & Todaro Co., LPA, Columbus, 1993-94, Ray, Todaro & Alton Co., L.P.A., Columbus, 1994-96, Ray, Todaro, Alton & Kirstein Co., L.P.A., Columbus, 1996, Columbus, Ray, Alton & Kirstein Co., L.P.A., 1996-98; sr. ptnr. Ray & Alton, L.L.P., 1998-2000. Mem. seminar faculty Nat. Coll. Dist. Attys., Houston, 1975-77; mem. nat. conf. faculty Fed. Jud. Ctr., Washington, 1976-77; bd. editors Man. for Complex Litigation, Fed. Jud. Ctr., 1999—; bd. mem. bar examiners Ohio Supreme Ct., 1992-95, Rules Adv. Com., 1995-99. Editor: Economic Crime Digest, 1975-76; co-author: Personal Injury Litigation Practice in Ohio, 1988, 91. Mem. fin. com. Franklin County Rep. Orgn.,

Columbus, 1979-84; trustee Ohio State U. Coll. Humanities Alumni Soc., 1991-93, Nat. Coun. Ohio State U. Coll. Law Alumni Assn., 1998—; mem. Legal Aid Soc. of Columbus Capital Campaign Fund Cabinet, 1998. Capt. inf. U.S. Army, 1976. Named to Ten Outstanding Young Citizens of Columbus, Columbus Jaycees, 1976; recipient Nat. award of Distinctive Svc., Nat. Dist. Attys. Assn., 1977. Fellow: Ohio State Bar Found., Ohio Acad. Trial Lawyers (Pres.' award 1986), Roscoe Pound Found., Am. Coll. Trial Lawyers, Internat. Soc. Barristers, Columbus Bar Found.; mem.: ATLA (state del. 1990—92), ABA, Franklin County Trial Lawyers Assn. (pres. 1987—88, Pres.'s award 1990), Ohio Acad. Trial Lawyers 1989—90, Ohio State Bar Assn. (com. negligence law 1990—97), Million Dollar Advs. Forum, Columbus Bar Assn. (pres. 2001—02, Profl. award 1987), Am. Bd. Trial Advs. (sec. Ohio chpt. 2002—), Inns. of Ct. (pres. Judge Robert M. Duncan chpt. 1993—94). Presbyterian. Home: 2030 Tremont Rd Columbus OH 43221-4330 Office: 175 S 3rd St Ste 350 Columbus OH 43215-5188 E-mail: far@raylaw.com.

RAY, GARY J. food products executive; Chmn. bd. dirs. Rochelle (Ill.) Foods Inc.; exec. v.p. ops. Hormel Foods, Austin, Minn. Office: Hormel Foods 1 Hormel Pl Austin MN 55912-3680

RAY, JOHN WALKER, otolaryngologist, educator, broadcast commentator; b. Columbus, Ohio, Jan. 12, 1936; s. Kenneth Clark and Hope (Walker) R.; m. Susanne Gettings, July 15, 1961; children: Nancy Ann, Susan Christy. AB magna cum laude, Marietta Coll., 1956; MD cum laude, Ohio State U., 1960; postgrad., Temple U., 1964, Mt. Sinai Hosp., Columbia U., 1964, 66, Northwestern U., 1967, 71, U. Ill., 1968, U. Ind., 1969, Tulane U., 1969. Diplomate Am. Bd. Otolaryngology. Intern Ohio State U. Hosps., Columbus, 1960-61, clin. rsch. trainee NIH, 1963-65, resident dept. otolaryngology, 1963-65, 66-67, resident dept. surgery, 1965-66, instr. dept. otolaryngology, 1966-67, 70-75, clin. asst. prof., 1975-82, clin. assoc. prof., 1982-92, clin. prof., 1992-2000, clin. prof. emeritus, 2000—; hon. staff, past chief of staff Good Samaritan Hosp., also Bethesda Hosp., Zanesville, Ohio, 1967—. Hon. active staff Meml. Hosp., Marietta, Ohio, 1992—; radio-TV health commentator, 1982—. Contbr. articles to sci. and med. jours.; collaborator with surg. motion picture: Laryngectomy and Neck Dissection, 1964. Past pres. Muskingum chpt. Am. Cancer Soc.; bd. dirs. Zanesville Art Ctr. Capt. USAF, 1961-63. Recipient Barraquer Meml. award, 1965; named to Order of Ky. Col., 1966, Muskingum County Country Music Hall of Fame. Fellow ACS, Am. Soc. Otolaryn. Allergy, Am. Acad. Otolaryngology-Head and Neck Surgery (past gov.), Am. Acad. Facial Plastic and Reconstructive Surgery; mem. AMA, Nat. Assn. Physician Broadcasters, Muskingum County Acad. Medicine (past pres.), Ohio Med. Assn. (del.), Columbus Ophthalmol. and Otolaryn. Soc. (past pres.), Ohio Soc. Otolaryngology (past pres.), Pan-Am. Allergy Soc., Am. Acad. Invitro Allergy, Am. Soc. Contemporary Medicine and Surgery, Acad. Radio and TV Health Commentators, Fraternal Order of Police Assocs., Internat. Bluegrass Music Assn., Phi Beta Kappa, Alpha Omega Alpha, Beta Beta Beta. Presbyterian. Home: 1245 East Dr Zanesville OH 43701-1445

RAY, ROY LEE, state legislator, public finance consultant; b. Akron, Ohio, July 16, 1939; s. Charles Henry Ray and Geneva Lee (Edwards) Kendall; m. Frances Margaret Jordan, Aug. 24, 1968; children: Christopher Lee, Brian Edward. BS, Akron U., 1962. Sales rep. internat. div. Goodyear Tire & Rubber Co., Akron, 1962-68; stockbroker Francis I. DuPont & Co., 1968-69; rsch. analyst City of Akron, 1969-72, dep. dir. pub. svc., 1972-73, commr. pub. utilities, 1973-74, budget dir., 1974-79, fin. dir., 1977-79, mayor, mgr., safety dir., 1980-83; pres. Albrecht, Inc., Akron, 1983-85; cons. Ohio Co., 1988—; mem. Ohio Senate from 27th dist., Columbus, 1986—; fin. chmn. Ohio Senate, 1996—. State sen. Ohio Senate, 1986—. Pres. Ohio Mcpl. League, 1982-83; chmn. Conf. Ohio Big-City Mayors, 1981-83, N.E. Ohio Four-County Coord. Orgn., 1981-82; bd. trustees local United Way, Akron Gen. Med. Ctr., Am. Cancer Soc. Recipient Alumni Honor award U. Akron, 1987, Freshman of Yr. award Columbus Monthly mag., 1988. Mem. Kiwanis, Phi Kappa Tau (Ray C. Bliss award 1983), Omicron Delta Kappa. Office: 692 Sunnyside Ave Akron OH 44303-1756 also: Ohio Senate 1st Fl Rm 127 Senate Bldg Columbus OH 43215

RAY, WILLIS HARMON, chemical engineer; b. Washington, Apr. 4, 1940; BA, Rice Univ., 1962, BSChE, 1963; PhD, Univ. Minn., 1966. Asst. prof. chem. engring. Univ. Waterloo, 1966-69, assoc. prof., 1969-70; assoc. prof. to prof. State Univ. N.Y., Buffalo, 1970-76; prof. chem. engring. U. Wis., Madison, 1976-86, chmn. chem. engring., 1981-83, Steenbock prof. engring., 1986-96, Vilas prof., 1996—. Cons. 1967—; vis. prof. Rijksuniversiteit Gent & Univ. Leuven, 1973-74, Tech. Univ. Stuttgart, West Germany, 1974, dept. chem. engring. Univ. Minn., 1986, Cornell Univ., 1991; dist. vis. lectr. Univ. Alta, Can., 1982, McMaster Univ., Ont., 1985; lectr. Calif. Inst. Tech., 1988. Recipient Eckman award Am. Automatic Control Coun., 1969, A.K. Doolittle award Am. Chem. Soc., 1981, Prof. Progress award Am. Inst. Chem. Engring., 1982, Disn Reilly Lect. award Univ. Notre Dame, 1984, Edn. award Am. Automatic Control Coun., 1989; Guggenheim fellow 1973-74. Fellow Am. Inst. Chem. Engrs.; mem. IEEE, Nat. Acad. Engring., Am. Chem. Soc., Am. Soc. Engring. Edn., Soc. Industrial & Applied Math., Chem. Inst. Can., Sigma Xi. Office: Univ Wis Dept Chem Engring Madison WI 53706

RAYWARD, WARDEN BOYD, librarian, educator; b. Inverell, NSW, Australia, June 24, 1939; s. Warden and Ellie Rayward. B.A., U. Sydney, 1960; diploma in libr., U. NSW, 1964; M.S. in L.S., U. Ill., 1965; Ph.D., U. Chgo., 1973. Asst. state library, NSW, 1961-64; research librarian planning and devel., 1970; lectr. Sch. Librarianship U. NSW, Sydney, 1971-72, head sch. Info., Libr. and Archive Studies, 1986-92, prof., 1986-00, dean Faculty Profl. Studies, 1993-96, prof. emeritus, 2000—; asst. prof. U. Western Ont., 1973-74, Grad. Library Sch. U. Chgo., 1975-77, assoc. prof., 1978-80, prof., 1980-86; dean U. Chgo. Grad. Library Sch., 1980-86; rsch. prof. U. Ill., Champaign, 2000—. Cons. NEH, 1976-79, U.S. Dept. Edn., 1981; bd. govs. Charles Stuart U., 1994-96; bd. dirs. Internat. House-U. NSW, 1992-97; George A. Miller vis. prof. U. Ill., 1997-98; Leverhulme Trust vis. prof. Leed Met. U., 2002. Author: The Universe of Information: The Work of Paul Otlet for Documentation and International Organization, 1975 (also transl. Russian and Spanish); editor: The Variety of Librarianship: Essays in Honour of John Wallace Metcalfe, 1976, The Public Library: Circumstances and Prospects, 1978, Library Quar., 1975-79, Library History in Context, 1988, Libraries and Life in a Changing World: the Metcalfe Years 1920-1970, 1993; editor, translator: International Organization and the Dissemination of Knowledge: Selected Papers of Paul Otlet, 1990; editor Confronting the Future, University Libraries in the Next Decade, 1992, Developing a Profession in Librarianship in Australia: Travel Diaries and Other Papers of John Wallace Metcalfe, 1996; mem. internat. editorial adv. bd. World Book of Encyclopedia, 1990-97; contbr. articles to profl. jours. Coun. on Library Resources fellow, 1978, vis. fellow U. Coll. London, 1986, 90, Mortenson fellow U. Ill., 1992-93, Garfield fellow in hist. sci. lit., 2000. Mem. ALA, (hon.) Australian Library and Info. Assn., Bibliog. Soc. Australia and New Zealand, Am. Soc. for Info. Sci. Office: U Ill Grad Sch Libr and Info Scis 501 E Daniel St Champaign IL 61820-6211 E-mail: wrayward@alexia.lis.uiuc.edu.

RAZ, HILDA, editor-in-chief periodical, English educator; b. Rochester, N.Y., May 4, 1938; d. Franklyn Emmanuel and Dolly (Horwich) R.; m. Frederick M. Link, June 9, 1957 (div. 1969); children: John Franklin Link, Aaron Link; m. Dale Nordyke, Oct. 4, 1980. BA, Boston U., 1960. Asst. dir. Planned Parenthood League of Mass., Boston, 1960-62; edit. asst. Prairie Schooner, Lincoln, Nebr., 1970-74, contbg. editor, 1974-77, assoc. editor, 1977-87, acting editor, 1981-83, 85, poetry editor, 1980-87, editor-in-chief, 1987—; prof. dept Eng. U. Nebr., Lincoln, 1990—. Lectr., reader, panelist in field; participant many workshops, symposia, confs.; panelist creativity arts com. NEA, 2000; judge Kenyon Rev., 1990, Soc. Midland Authors Best Book of 1987 award, 198, Ill. Art Coun./NEA fellowships, 1987; bd. govs. Ctr. for Great Plains Studies, U. Nebr., 1989-95. Author: The Bone Dish, What Is Good, Divine Honors, 1988, Trans, 2001; editor: Best of Prairie Schooner: Fiction and Poetry, 2001, Best of Prairie Schooner: Essays, 2000, Living on the Margins, 1999, other books; editor Nebr. Humanist, 1990. Pres. Assoc. Writing Programs, bd. dirs., 1988-89, ex-officio pres., 1989-90, v.p., 1987-88; mem. program com. Friends of Librs. U. Nebr., 1989-90; bd. dirs. Nebr. Libr. Heritage Assn., 1988-91; mem. Mayor's Blue Ribbon Com. on Arts, 1985-88; bd. dirs. Planned Parenthood League Nebr., 1978-83, sec. bd. dirs., 1979-80, chairperson long-term planning com., 1980-81, 81-82. Recipient Literary Heritage award, Mayor's Art Awards, Lincoln, 1988; Bread Loaf scholar editors, 1974, poetry, 1985; Robert Frost fellow, 1988, 89, Mag. Panel fellow, 1993, 94. Avocations: gardening. Home: 960 S Cotner Blvd Lincoln NE 68510-4926 Office: Univ of Nebraska Lincoln Prairie Schooner 201 Andrews Hall Lincoln NE 68588-0334 E-mail: HRaz1@unl.edu.

RAZOV, ANTE, professional soccer player; b. L.A., Mar. 2, 1974; Student, UCLA, 1992-95. Forward L.A. Galaxy, 1996-97, Chgo. Fire, 1998-2000, team leading scorer, 1999; forward U.S. Nat. Team, 1999—. Avocations: reading mystery books, listening to reggae/hip hop music. Address: 12635 Heflin Dr La Mirada CA 90638

REA, DAVID K. geology and oceanography educator; b. Pitts., June 2, 1942; m. Donna M. Harshbarger, Feb. 11, 1967; children: Gregory, Margaret. AB, Princeton U., 1964; MS, U. Ariz., 1967; PhD, Oreg. State U., 1974. Prof. geology & oceanography U. Mich., Ann Arbor, 1975—. Assoc. dir. NSF Climate Dynamics Program, Washington, 1986-87; interim dir. Ctr. for Great Lakes and Aquatic Scis., 1988-89, chmn. dept. geol. scis., 1995-2000. Contbr. more than 300 articles, reports to profl. publs. Recipient numerous NSF rsch. grants, 1976—. Fellow Am. Geophys. Union, Geol. Soc. Am.

READ, SISTER JOEL, academic administrator; BS in Edn., Alverno Coll., 1948; MA in History, Fordham U., 1951; hon. degree, Lakeland Coll., 1972, Wittenburg U., 1976, Marymount Manhattan Coll., 1978, DePaul U., 1985, Northland Coll., 1986, SUNY, 1986, Lawrence U., 1997. Former prof., dept. chmn. history dept. Alverno Coll., Milw., pres., 1968—. Past pres. Am. Assn. for Higher Edn., 1976-77; mem. coun. NEH, 1977-84; bd. dirs. Ednl. Testing Svc., 1987-93, Neylan Commn., 1985-90; past pres. Wis. Assn. Ind. Colls. and Univs.; mem. Commn. on Status of Edn. for Women, 1971-76, Am. Assn. Colls., 1971-77. Bd. dirs. Jr. Achievement, State of Wis. Coll. Savs. Bd., Greater Milw. Com., YMCA, Profl. Dimensions, Wis. Found. Ind. Colls., 1990-99, Women's Philanthropy Inst., 1997-2000, Wis. Women Higher Edn. Leadership, 1997-2000. First recipient Anne Roe award Harvard U. Grad. Sch. Edn., 1980; recipient Morris T. Keaton award, Coun. for Adult and Experiential Learning, 1992; recipient Jean B. Harris award, Rotary; Paul Harris fellow, Rotary. Fellow Am. Acad. Arts and Scis., Wis. Acad. Arts and Scis. Office: Alverno Coll Office of Pres PO Box 343922 Milwaukee WI 53234-3922 E-mail: joel.read@alverno.edu.

READ, JOHN CONYERS, non-profit management consultant; b. N.Y.C., May 21, 1947; s. Edward Cameron Kirk and Louise (Geary) R.; m. Alexandra Gould, Mar. 30, 1968; children: Cameron Kirk, Trevor Conyers, Alexandra. AB, Harvard, 1969, MBA, 1971. Ops. rsch. analyst HEW, Washington, 1971-72; exec. asst. to dir. Cost of Living Council, 1973; chief econ. adviser to Gov. Mass., 1974; exec. asst., counselor to sec. labor Washington, 1975; asst. sec. labor for employment standards, 1976-77; dir. corp. employee rels., pers. Cummins Engine Co., Columbus, Ind., 1977-80, plant mgr., 1980-85; v.p. Midrange Engines, 1986-90; v.p., gen. mgr. engine group Donaldson Co., Inc., Mpls., 1990-92; exec. v.p., 1992-94; ptnr. Hidden Creek Industries, Mpls., 1996—; pres., CEO Heavy Duty Holdings, 1997-2000; pres. Read Ptnrs. Inc., 2001—02, Outward Bound U.S.A., Garrison, NY, 2002—. Cons. nat. productivity and energy policies; chmn. NAM Task Force on Wage and Price Policies, 1978-80; bd. dirs. MAC Equipment Co., Active Leasing Co. Author Ford Found. monograph on occupational disease and workers' compensation; contbr. articles to newspapers and mags. Trustee Nat. Ctr. Occupl. Readjustment, 1984-87; trustee N.C. Outward Bound Sch., dir., 1995—, chmn., 1997-2000; chmn. Charleston Pvt. Industry Coun., 1985; mem. plant closing task force U. S. Dept. Labor, 1986, mfg. task force NRC, 1989, critical industries task force Def. Dept., 1989. Mem. Nat. Assn. Mfrs. (bd. dirs., chair employee rels. com. 1993-95). Home: 2697 E Lake Of The Isles Pkwy Minneapolis MN 55408-1051

READ, SARAH J. lawyer; BA cum laude, Yale U., 1978; JD, U. Wis., 1981; postgrad., Ctr. for Conflict Resolution, Chgo., MIT-Harvard U. Bar: Wis. 1981, Ill. 1981, U.S. Dist. (we. dist.) Wis. 1981, U.S. Dist. Ct. (no. dist.) Ill. 1981. Ptnr. Sidley & Austin, Chgo., also mem. telecom., energy and petrochems. practice group, mem. alternative dispute resolution resource group. Mem. Ohio Telecom. Adv. Bd., 1984. Mem. ABA, Wis. Bar Assn., Chgo. Bar Assn., Order of Coif. Office: Sidley & Austin 1 S First National Plz Chicago IL 60603-2000 Fax: 312-853-7036.

READING, ANTHONY JOHN, business executive, accountant; b. London, Aug. 8, 1943; came to U.S., 1993; m. Myra Elizabeth Steer, Aug. 27, 1966; 1 child, Jason. Chartered acct. Mng. dir., dir. mfg., dir. fin. Donaldson Co. Inc., Brussels, 1970-80; group exec. Thomas Tilling Plc, London, 1980-83; divisional group chief exec. BTR Plc, 1983-87; group mng. dir. Polly Peck Internat., 1987-89, Pepe Group Plc, London, 1989-90; divisional dir. Tomkins Plc, 1990-92, also bd. dirs.; chmn., CEO Tomkins Corp., Dayton, Ohio, 1992—. Chmn. Orgn. Internat. Investment, Washington. Named Mem. of Most Excellent Order of Brit. Empire, Her Majesty Queen Elizabeth II, 1978. Fellow Inst. Chartered Accts. Eng. and Wales, Inst. Mgmt. Eng.; mem. Naval and Mil. Club London. Avocations: music, golf, water sports. Office: Tomkins Corp 4801 Springfield St Dayton OH 45431-1084 E-mail: areading@tomkins-industries.com.

REAMS, MICHAEL THOMAS, director, singer, actor; b. Peoria, Ill., Jan. 4, 1966; s. Thomas Clyde and Carol Ann (Wiltz) R. BA, Bradley U., 1988. Asst. mgr. Cabaret Music Theatre, Peoria, 1985-86; dir. park players Peoria Park Dist., 1987-88; mgr. Strawmill Playhouse, Peoria, 1989. Actor (mus.) Follies, 1985, Company, 1986, Do Black Patent Leather Shoes Really Reflect Up?, 1988, Sweeney Todd, 1989, Baby, 1989, A Funny Thing Happened on the Way to the Forum, 1990, Guys and Dolls, 1993, Damn Yankees, 1995, Into the Woods, 1995, Ruthless, 1996, It's A Bird, It's A Plane, It's Superman, 1996, The Fantasticks, 1997, (plays) Amadeus, 1987, The Nerd, 1988, 95, Noises Off, 1989, Bleacher Bums, 1992, Rumors, 1992, Lend Me A Tenor, 1993, (opera) Amahl and the Night Visitors, 1990; dir. (plays) The Dining Room, 1989, Social Security, 1990, Broadway Bound, 1991, A Day in Hollywood/A Night in the Ukraine, 1994, Nunsense, 1994, Nunsense II, 1995, Do Black Patent Leather Shoes Really Reflect Up?, 1996. Mem. Peoria Players Theatre, Cornstock Theatre. Avocations: cast recordings collector, writing.

REARDON, GEORGE M. human resources firm executive; BSBA, Ind. U.; JD, U. Fla. V.p., asst. gen. counsel Snelling & Snelling, Inc.; v.p., gen. counsel, corp. sec. The Talent Tree Corp., 1990-94; sole practice law Houston, 1994-98; sr. v.p., gen. counsel Kelly Svcs. Inc., Troy, Mich., 1998—. Served in U.S. Army, Vietnam. Office: Kelly Svcs Inc 999 W Big Beaver Rd Troy MI 48084-4716

REARDON, MARK, radio personality; b. Chgo. married; 2 children. B Journalism, U. Mo. News anchor, co-host morning show KPLA-FM, Columbia, Mo., news dir.; radio host KFRU-AM, 1992—96, KSD-AM, St. Louis, 1996, WTMJ, Milw., 1997—. Avocations: hunting, fishing, music, movies, thoroughbred racing, golf. Office: WTMJ 720 E Capital Dr Milwaukee WI 53212

REARDON, MICHAEL EDWARD, lawyer; b. Independence, Mo., Apr. 15, 1948; s. Neil Willison and Marjorie (Winters) R.; m. Gloria Kay Nelson, Jan. 31, 1970; children— Darin Thomas, Laura Michelle. B.A. magna cum laude, William Jewell Coll., 1970; J.D. with distinction, U. Mo.-Kansas City, 1973, LL.M. in Criminal Law, 1978. Bar: Mo. 1973, U.S. Dist. Ct. (we. dist.) Mo. 1974, U.S. Supreme Ct. 1978. Assoc. Morris, Larson, King, Stamper-Bold, Kansas City, Mo., 1973-74, M. Randall Vanet, North Kansas City, Mo., 1974-75; ptnr. Duncan, Russell & Reardon, Kansas City, 1975-82, Michael E. Reardon & Assocs., Kansas City, 1982-86; Clay County Pros. Atty., Liberty, Mo., 1987-98; pvt. practice, 1999—. Bd. dirs. Clay County Sheltered Facilities, 1982-84; chmn. Clay County Dem. Com., Kansas City, 1982-84; treas. Mo. 6th Congl. Dist. Dem. Com., 1982-86; bd. dirs. Clay County Investigative Squad, Liberty, 1987-98. Mem. Mo. Bar Assn., Mo. Assn. Trial Attys., Clay County Bar Assn., Kansas City Bar Assn., ATLA, Gladstone C. of C. Office: 5716 N Broadway St Kansas City MO 64118-3962

REARDON, NANCY ANNE, human resource executive; b. Little Falls, N.Y., Sept. 19, 1952; d. Warren Joseph and Elizabeth Owen (Tiel) Reardon; m. Steven Jonathan Sayer, Aug. 28, 1976; children: Scott Jason, Kathryn Anne. BS in Psychology, Union Coll., Schenectady, N.Y., 1974; MS in Social Psychology, Syracuse U., 1978. With GE Co., N.Y.C., 1979-85, Avon Products Inc., N.Y.C., 1985-89, Am. Express, N.Y.C., 1989-91; sr. v.p. human resources Duracell Internat., Inc., Bethel, Conn., 1991-97; sr. v.p. corp. affairs & human resources Borden Inc., Columbus, OH, 1997—. Adv. bd. mem. Catalyst, 1995. Mem. Human Resource Planning Soc. (bd. dirs. 1991-94, treas. 1992-93), N.Y. Human Resource Planners (bd. dirs., pres. 1989-91), Sr. Pers. Execs. Forum, Nat. Fgn. Trade Coun. (bd. dirs. 1995). Office: Borden Inc. 180 E Broad St Columbus OH 43215-3799

REARDON, THOMAS R. physician, medical association administrator; m. Elizabeth Reardon. MD, U. Colo., 1959. Intern Balt. City Hosp.; pvt. practice Portland, Oreg. Apptd. Congrl. Physician Payment Rev. Commn., 1986-94; mem. Pres. Commn. on Patient Rights and Quality Care. Chair of judges Portland Rose Festival Parade. With USAF, 1960-63. Mem. AMA (pres., chair bd. trustees 1997, mem. 1990—, exec. com. 1994—, sec. treas. 1994-95, vice chair bd. trustees 1995-97, hosp. med. staff sect. in ho. of dels. 1983-90, steering com.), Am. Rose Soc., Portland Rose Soc. (past pres.), Multnomah County Med. Soc. (pres. 1980-81, Disting. Svc. award 1982), Oreg. Med. Assn. (pres. 1983-84). Avocation: horticulture. Office: AMA 515 N State St Chicago IL 60610-4325

REASONER, WILLIS IRL, III, lawyer; b. Hamilton, Ohio, Dec. 24, 1951; s. W. Irl Jr. and Nancy Jane (Mitchell) R.; m. Lana Jean Mayes, Apr. 19, 1975 (div. Sept. 1985); 1 child, Erick; m. Joan Marie Mogil, Dec. 30, 1985; children: Scott, Sally. BA in History, Ind. U., 1974; JD cum laude, U. S.C., 1978. Bar: Ohio 1978, U.S. Dist. Ct. (so. dist.) Ohio 1978, U.S. Dist. Ct. (no. dist.) Ohio 1979, U.S. Ct. Appeals (6th cir.) 1988, U.S. Ct. Appeals (1st cir.) 1991, U.S. Ct. Appeals (7th cir.) 1999. Assoc. Porter, Wright, Morris & Arthur, Columbus, Ohio, 1978-83; ptnr. Baker & Hostetler, 1983-94, Habash, Reasoner & Frazier, 1994—. Mem. ABA, Ohio Bar Assn., Columbus Bar Assn. Home: 4005 Redford Ct New Albany OH 43054-9500 Office: Habash, Reasoner & Frazier 471 E Broad St Ste 800 Columbus OH 43215-3854

REBANE, JOHN T. lawyer; b. Bamberg, Germany, Oct. 29, 1946; s. Henn and Anna (Inna) R.; m. Linda Kay Morgan, Sept. 22, 1972; children: Alexis Morgan, Morgan James. BA, U. Minn., 1970, JD, 1973. Bar: Minn. 1973. Atty. Land O'Lakes, Inc., Arden Hills, Minn., 1973-80, assoc. gen. counsel, 1983, v.p., gen. counsel, 1984—. Sec. Land O' Lakes Farmland Feed LLC; sec., dir. Land O' Lakes Internat. Devel. Corp. Mem. ABA, Minn. Bar Assn., Hennepin County Bar Assn., Nat. Coun. Farm Coop. (gen.coun. com. chmn.). Office: Land O'Lakes Inc PO Box 64101 Saint Paul MN 55164-0101 E-mail: jreba@landolakes.com

REBEIZ, CONSTANTIN A. plant physiology educator, laboratory director; b. Beirut, July 11, 1936; came to U.S., 1969, naturalized, 1975; s. Anis C. and Valentine A. (Choueyri) R.; m. Carole Louise Conness, Aug. 18, 1962; children: Paul A., Natalie, Mark J. B.S., Am. U., Beirut, 1959; M.S., U. Calif. - Davis, 1960, Ph.D., 1965. Dir. dept. biol. scis. Agrl. Rsch. Inst., Beirut, 1965-69; research assoc. biology U. Calif. - Davis, 1969-71; assoc. prof. plant physiology U. Ill., Urbana-Champaign, 1972-76, prof., 1976—, dir. Lab. Plant Biochemistry and Photobiology, 1999—. Contbr. articles to sci. publs. plant physiology and biochemistry. Recipient Beckman Rsch. award, 1982, 1985, Funk award, 1985, Sr. Rsch. award, U. Ill., 1994, Presdl. Green Chemistry Challenge award, 1999, named One of 100 Outstanding Innovators, Sci. Digest, 1984—85; grantee John P. Trebellas Rsch. Endowment, 1986, C.A. and C.C. Rebeiz Endowment for basic rsch., 2000. Mem. Am. Soc. Plant Physiologists, Comite Internat. de Photobiologie, Am. Soc. Photobiology, AAAS, Lebanese Assn. Advancement Scis. (exec. com. 1967-69), Sigma Xi. Achievements include research on pathway of chlorophyll biosynthesis, chloroplast devel., bioengring. of photosynthetic reactors; pioneered biosynthesis of chlorophyll in vitro; duplication of greening process of plants in test tube, demonstration of operation of multibranched chlorophyll biosynthetic pathway in nature; formulation and design of laser herbicides, insecticides and cancer chemotherapeutic agents. Home: 301 W Pennsylvania Ave Urbana IL 61801-4918 Office: U Ill 240A Pabl Urbana IL 61801 E-mail: crebeiz@uiuc.edu.

RECHTZIGEL, SUE MARIE (SUZANNE RECHTZIGEL), child care center executive; b. St. Paul, May 27, 1947; d. Carl Stinson and Muriel Agnes (Oestrich) Miller; m. Gary Elmer Rechtzigel, Aug. 20, 1968 (div. Feb. 1982); children: Brian Carl, Lori Ann. BA in Psychology, Sociology, Mankato (Minn.) State U., 1969. Lic. in child care, Minn. Rep. ins. State Farm Ins. Co., Albert Lea, Minn., 1969-73; free-lance child caretaker, 1973-78; owner, dir. Lakeside Day Care, 1983—. Asst. Hawthorne Sch. Learning Ctr., Albert Lea, 1978-83. Mem. New Residents and Newcomers Orgn., Albert Lea, 1970—, past. pres.; asst. pre-sch. United Meth. Ch., Albert Lea, 1975-78, tchr. Sunday sch., 1976-80, tchr. Bible sch., 1980-85; active Ascension Luth. Ch., 1976-80. Mem. Freeborn Lic. Day Care Assn. (v.p. 1986, pres. 1987), AAUW (home tour 1977, treas. 1980-81), Bus. and Profl. Women, YMCA, Albert Lea Art Ctr. Republican. Club: 3M Families. Avocations: ceramics, calligraphy, painting, art, sewing. Home and Office: 1919 Brookside Dr Albert Lea MN 56007-2142

RECKER, THOMAS EDWARD, fraternal organization executive; b. Livonia, Mich., Feb. 28, 1960; s. Peter Edward and Patricia Ann (Heidenwolf) R. BA in Ednl. Psychology, U. Mich., 1982; MA in Coll. Student Personnel, Bowling Green State U., 1985. Asst. exec. dir. Grand Chpt. of Phi Sigma Kappa, Indpls., 1985-87, exec. dir., 1987-90; exec. v.p. Grand Chpt. of Phi Sigma Kappa and Phi Sigma Kappa Found., 1990—. Mem. Am. Soc. Assn. Execs., Assn. Frat. Advisers, Frat. Execs. Assn. Office: Phi Sigma Kappa Frat 2925 E 96th St Indianapolis IN 46240-1368

REDBURN, AMBER LYNNE, nurse; b. West Plains, Mo., Jan. 4, 1963; d. Norris Bert and Chlora Ivene (Brickey) Cozort; m. Timothy Mark Redburn, Apr. 26, 1997; 1 child, Corby Lee. BSN, Rockhurst Coll. and Rsch. Coll. of Nursing, Kansas City, Mo., 1985. RN, Mo. Psychiat. staff nurse Cox Med. Ctr. North, Springfield, Mo., 1985; psychiat. technician Park Cen. Hosp., 1985-86; orthop. staff nurse St. John's Regional Health Ctr., 1986-97; comprehensive care nurse Ozarks Med. Ctr., West Plains, 1997-98, nurse educator, 1998, also former instr. BLS, 1998; short term BLS instr. South Ctrl. Area Vocat.-Tech. Sch., 1998. Mem. com. St. John's Med. Explorer Post 339, 1989-90, pres., 1990-91; mem. Greene County Rep. Party-TARGET, 1993-97; mem. Rep. Nat. Com., 1995-98; mem. com. S.W. Mo. Nurses Recognition Dinner, 1992-97, chair, 1994-97; mem. West Plains Adult Day Svcs., 1997. Mem. Mo. Nurses Assn. (corr. sec., past bd. dirs., 4th dist., mem. nominating com., med.-surg. spl. interest group 1993-98, sec. 1996-98, regional dir. region F 1994-96, Mo. Nurses Assn.-PAC com. 1996—, comm. com. 1995-99, state bd. dirs. 1997-99, membership and mktg. com. 1997-99, nursing practice com. 1999), Nat. Assn. Orthopedic Nurses, Rsch. Coll. Alumni Assn., Rsch. Coll. Honor Soc.

REDDY, JANARDAN K. medical educator; b. Moolasaal, India, Oct. 7, 1938; MB, BS, Osmania U., Hyderabad, India, 1961; MD in Pathology, All India Inst. Med. Scis., 1965. Lic. physicain, Mo., Kans., Ill.; diplomate Am. Bd. Pathology. Rotating house officer Osmania Gen. Hosp., 1961-62; instr. pathology Kakatiya Med. Coll., Warangal, India, 1962-63, asst. prof. India, 1965-66; resident fellow pathology U. Kans. Med. Ctr., 1966-68, rsch. fellow pathology, 1968-70, asst. prof., 1970-73, assoc. prof., 1973-76, prof., 1976; prof. pathology Northwestern U. Med. Sch., Chgo., 1976—, dir. med. scientist tng. program, 1990-93, chmn. pathology, 1993—. Dir. anatomic pathology Northwestern Meml. Hosp., 1978-81, mem. med. staff, 1976—; mem. Northwestern U. Cancer Ctr., 1976—; mem. med. staff VA Lakeside Hosp., 1990—; group leader Chem.Carcinogenesis Rsch. Group, Northwestern U. Cancer Ctr., 1990—, assoc. dir. cancer edn., 1991—; mem. Task Force on an Environ. Sci./Policy Initiative, Northwestern U., 1991—; chmn. NIH clin. scis. study sect., 1990-91; mem. NIH spl. study sect., 1992; mem. com. on comparative toxicity of naturally occurring carcinogens, 1993—; mem. Nat. Toxicology Program Rev. Com., 1992—; mem. monograph com. WHO, Internat. Agy. on Cancer Rsch., Lyon, France, 1994. Mem. editl. bds. Jour. Histochemistry and Cytochemistry, 1973-76, Exptl. Pathology, 1982—, Toxicologic Pathology, 1983—, Internat. Jour. Pancreatology, 1986—, Lab. Investigation, 1988—, Carcinogenesis, 1989—, The Jour. Northwestern U. Cancer Ctr., 1990—, Gene Expression, 1990—, Internat. Jour. Toxicology, Occupational and Environ. Health, 1992—, Life Sci. Advanced, Oncology, 1991—; assoc. editor Jour. Toxicology and Environ. Health, 1984—, Cancer Rsch., 1985-90. Grantee Joseph Mayberry Endowment Fund, Cancer Rsch. Found., 1991-93, NIEHS, 1995—, NIGMS, 1992-2001, NIDDK, 1995—, NIGMS, 1992-97; merit scholar Osmania U., 1954-61, Govt. of Andhra Pradesh merit scholar, 1963-65; WHO Yamagiwa-Yoshida Internat. Cancer fellow in Japan, 1985; recipient NIH merit award, 1987, UN Devel. Programme-Tokten award, 1988, Fletscher scholar award, 1991; named George H. Joost Outstanding Basic Sci. Tchr., 1995, 97. Fellow AAAS, Assn. Scientists of Indian Origin in Am. (pres. 1983-84, sr. scientist award 1991), Soc. Toxicology (v.p. molecular toxicology speciality sect. 1990-91, pres. 1991-92, pres. carcinogenesis specialty sect. 1990-91, Kenneth P. Dubois award 1990), Am. Pancreatic Assn., Am. Assn. Pathologists (mem. program com. 1989-93), Am. Assn. Cancer Rsch. (mem. program com. 1990-91), Internat. Acad. Pathology, Am. Soc. Cell Biology, Histochem. Soc., Soc. Exptl. Biology and Medicine, Biochem. Soc. London, Soc. Toxicology Pathologists, Internat. Assn. Pancreatology, N.Y. Acad. Scis. Home: 1212 Asbury Ave Evanston IL 60202-1102 Office: Northwestern U Med Sch Dept Pathology Ward 6-204 303 E Chicago Ave Chicago IL 60611-3072

REDDY, VENKAT NARSIMHA, ophthalmologist, researcher; b. Hyderabad, India, Nov. 4, 1922; came to U.S., 1947; s. Malla and Manik (Devi) R.; m. Alvira M. DeMello, Dec. 10, 1955; children: Vinay Neville, Marlita Alvira. BSc, U. Madras, 1945; MS, PhD, Fordham U., 1952. Rsch. assoc. Coll. of Physicians and Surgeons Columbia U., N.Y.C., 1952-56, Banting and Best Inst., Toronto, Can., 1956; ass. and assoc. prof. ophthalmology Kresge Eye Inst. Wayne State U., Detroit, 1957-68; prof., biomed. scis., asst. dir. Eye Rsch. Inst. Oakland U., Rochester, Mich., 1968-75, prof., dir., 1975-98, Disting. prof. biomed. scis., dir., 1996-98; prof. ophthalmology Kellogg Eye Ctr. U. Mich., Ann Arbor, 1998—. Mem. study sect. NIH, Bethesda, 1966-70, nat. adv. eye coun., 1982-87, mem. bd. sci. counselors Nat. Eye Inst., 1977-81 Mem. editorial bd. Investigative Ophthalmology and Visual Scis., 1969-72, 78-88, Ophthalmic Research, 1978-90, Experimental Eye Research, 1985—; contbr. articles to profl. jours. Recipient Friendenwald award Assn. Rsch. in Ophthalmology, 1979, Rsch. award Cataract Rsch. Found., 1987, Merit award Nat. Eye Inst., 1989; named Scientist of Yr. State of Mich., 1991, Disting. Faculty Mem. Mich. Assn. Governing Bds. State Univs., 1994. Mem. AAAS, Internat. Soc. Eye Rsch., The Biochem. Soc., Assn. Rsch. in Vision and Ophthalmology (pres. 1985), Am. Soc. for Biochemistry and Molecular Biology, Soc. Free Radicals, Oxygen Soc. Sigma Xi. Achievements include research on cataract etiology, intraocular fluids dynamics relating to glaucoma, cell biology of lens, ciliary body and retinal pigment epithelium, cell differentiation. Office: U Mich Kellogg Eye Ctr 1000 Wall St Ann Arbor MI 48105-1912 E-mail: venreddy@umch.edu.

REDFERN, DONALD B. state legislator, lawyer; b. Nebraska City, Nebr., June 9, 1945; BA, Carleton Coll., 1967; JD, Columbia U., 1973. Ptnr. Redfern, Mason, Dieter, Larsen and Moore; mem. Iowa Senate from 12th dist., Des Moines, 1993—; mem. commerce com., mem. jud. com.; chair edn. com.; mem. rules and adminstrn. com. Adj. instr. U. No. Iowa. Bd. dirs. Cedar Valley Econ. Devel. Corp.; mem. Western Home, 1983-90, Friends of Sta. KHKE/KUNI Pub. Radio, 1985-87, Cedar Falls Pub. Libr., 1985-87; vol. Lawyers Project; mem. First United Meth. Ch.; mem. Cedar Valley Lakes Assn., 1987-90. Mem. Iowa Bar Assn., Hudson C. of C., Cedar Falls C. of C., Rotary (Cedar Falls), Waterloo C. of C. Republican. Office: State Capitol 9th And Grand Sts Des Moines IA 50319-0001 E-mail: don_redfern@legis.state.ia.us.

REDFIELD, JEAN M. electric power company executive; With McKinsey & Co., Inc.; mgr. corp. stratety Detroit Edison Co., 1994-97; pres. Detroit Edison Co. Am., 1997—. Office: Detroit Edison Co 2002 2d Ave Detroit MI 48226

REDFIELD, PAMELA A. state legislator; b. Chicago, Ill., Aug. 11, 1948; m. Jerry Redfield; 6 children. B in edn., U. Nebr., Omaha, 1969. Exec. dir. Omaha-Millard Rotary; libr. spcl.; election cons.; banker; mem. Nebr. Legislature from 12th dist., Lincoln, 1998—. Mem. Ralson Bd. Edn. 1992-1998. Coun. State Govt.; Nat. Conf. State Legislatures; Am. Legis. Exch. Conf.; Nat. Coun. Ins. Legislators.; chmn. Rotary Internat. Office: State Capitol (Dist 12) Room 1522 PO Box 94604 Lincoln NE 68509-4604

REDGRAVE, MARTYN R. hotel, food service executive; BA in Economics, Princeton U.; MBA in Finance, N.Y.U. V.p. finance, CFO Kentucky Fried chicken Corp.; CFO, exec. v.p Carlson Cos. Inc., Mpls., 1994—. Vol. United Way. Office: Carlson Cos Inc 1405 Xenium Lane N Plymouth MN 55441-8215 Business E-Mail: mredgrave@carlson.com.

REDLIN, ROLLAND W. state legislator; b. Lambert, Mont., Feb. 29, 1920; m. Christine Nesje; children: Ilene, Jeannette, Lisa, Daniel, Steven. Student, U. Wash., N.D. State Coll. Mem. N.D. Senate, 1958-64, mem. appropriations com.; mem. Congress, 1965-66; agr. cons. U.S. Dept. State, 1967; mem. N.D. Ho. of Reps. Cons. Bank of Agr. and Pub. Rels.; owner farm, past operator. Dem. candidate from N.D., Ho. of Reps., 1966, 68; pres. Minot Vocat. Workshop; trustee Nature Conservancy. Recipient Friend of Edn. award Minot Edn. Assn., 1988, Laura award for Dising. Svc. to Edn., 1991, Legis. award Libr. Assn. Mem. N.D. Bankers Assn., Farmers Union, Minot C. of C. Democrat. Office: 1005 21st St NW Minot ND 58703-1724 also: State Senate State Capitol Bismarck ND 58505

REDMAN, BARBARA KLUG, nursing educator; b. Mitchell, S.D. d. Harlan Lyle and Darlien Grace (Bock) Klug; m. Robert S. Redman, Sept. 14, 1958; 1 child, Melissa Darlien. BS, S.D. State U., 1958; MEd, U. Minn., 1959, PhD, 1964; LHD (hon.), Georgetown U., 1988; DSc (hon.), U. Colo., 1991. RN. Asst. prof. U. Wash., Seattle, 1964-69; assoc. dean U. Minn., Mpls., 1969-75; dean Sch. Nursing U. Colo., Denver, 1975-78; VA scholar VA Cen. Office, Washington, 1978-81; postdoctoral fellow Johns Hopkins U., Balt., 1982-83; exec. dir. Am. Assn. Colls. Nursing, Washington, 1983-89, ANA, Washington, 1989-93; prof. nursing Johns Hopkins U., Balt., 1993-95; dean, prof. Sch. Nursing U. Conn., Storrs, 1995-98; dean Coll. Nursing Wayne State U., Detroit. Vis. fellow Kennedy Inst. Ethics, Georgetown U., 1993-94; fellow in med. ethics Harvard Med. Sch., 1994-95. Author: Practice of Patient Education, 1968—; contbr. articles to profl. jours. Bd. dirs. Friends of Nat. Libr. of Medicine, Washington, 1987—. Recipient Disting. Alumnus award S.D. State U., 1975, Outstanding Achievement award U. Minn., 1989. Fellow Am. Acad. Nursing. Home: 12425 Bobbink Ct Potomac MD 20854-3005 Office: Wayne State U 5557 Cass Ave Detroit MI 48202-3615

REDMAN, CLARENCE OWEN, lawyer; b. Joliet, Ill., Nov. 23, 1942; s. Harold F. and Edith L. (Read) R.; m. Barbara Ann Pawlan, Jan. 26, 1964 (div.); children: Scott, Steven; m. 2d, Carla J. Rozycki, Sept. 24, 1983. BS, U. Ill., 1964, JD, 1966, MA, 1967. Bar: Ill. 1966, U.S. Dist. Ct. (ea. dist.) Ill. 1970, U.S. Ct. Appeals (7th cir.) 1973, U.S. Ct. Appeals (4th cir.) 1982, U.S. Supreme Ct. 1975. Assoc. Keck, Mahin & Cate, Chgo., 1969-73, ptnr., corp. ptnr., 1973—, CEO, 1986-97; of counsel Lord, Bissell & Brook, 1997—. Spl. asst. atty. gen. Ill., 1975-8; bd. dirs. AMCOL Internat. Corp. Mem. bd. visitors U. Ill. Coll. of Law, 1991-95. Capt. U.S. Army, 1967-69. Decorated Bronze Star. Mem. Ill. State Bar Assn. (chmn. young lawyers sect. 1977-78, del. assembly 1978-81, 84-87), Seventh Cir. Bar Assn. Office: Lord Bissell & Brook 115 S Lasalle St Ste 3200 Chicago IL 60603-3902

REDMOND, ROBERT FRANCIS, nuclear engineering educator; b. Indpls., July 15, 1927; s. John Felix and Marguerite Catherine (Breinig) R.; m. Mary Catherine Cangany, Oct. 18, 1952 (dec. May 1988); children: Catherine, Robert, Kevin, Thomas, John; m. Carole Moon Jacobs, Apr. 9, 1994. B.S. in Chem. Engring, Purdue U., 1950; M.S. in Math, U. Tenn., 1955; Ph.D. in Physics, Ohio State U., 1961. Engr. Oak Ridge Nat. Lab., 1950-53; scientist, adviser-cons. Battelle Meml. Inst., Columbus, Ohio, 1953-70; prof. nuclear engring. Ohio State U., 1970-92, assoc. dean. Coll. Engring., dir. Engring. Experiment Sta., 1977-92, acting dean, 1990-92, prof. emeritus mech. engring., assoc. dean emeritus, 1992—. Contbr. articles to profl. jours. V.p. Argonne Univs. Assn., 1976-77, trustee, 1972-80; mem. Ohio Power Siting Commn., 1978-82; trustee Edison Welding Inst., 1988-92. With AUS, 1945-46. Mem. Am. Nuclear Soc. (chmn. Southwestern Ohio sect.), AAAS, Nat. Regulatory Rsch. Inst. (bd. dirs. 1988-92), Trans. Rsch. Ctr., Am. Soc. Engring. Edn., Sigma Xi, Tau Beta Pi. Home: 4621 Nugent Dr Columbus OH 43220-3047 Office: Ohio State U Coll Engring Columbus OH 43220

REDWINE, JOHN NEWLAND, state legislator, physician; b. Pratt, Kans., Oct. 28, 1950; s. Albert Herold and Joyce Nadean (Durall R.; m. Barbara Ann Bomgaars, Dec. 27, 1975; children: John Newland II, William Merritt, Adam Boone. BA with honors, U. Kans., 1972; cert. med. technology, U. Tex. at Houston, 1974; DO, U. Health Scis., Kansas City, Mo., 1978. Diplomate Am. Bd. of Family Practice. Intern U. Hosp., Ctr. for Health Scis., Kansas City, Mo., 1978-79; family practice resident Siouxland Med. Edn. Found., Sioux City, Iowa, 1979-81; med. dir. Morningside Family Practice, 1981-95; v.p. St. Luke's Health Sys., Inc., 1995-2001; mem. Iowa Senate from 2nd dist., Des Moines, 1996—. Sr. aviation med. examiner FAA, 1979—95; clin. lectr. Iowa U. Coll. Medicine, Iowa City, 1983—95; past pres. Siouxland Med. Edn. Found., 1982—2001; past chmn. family practice St. Luke's Regional Med. Ctr., Sioux City, Iowa, pres.-elect, Iowa, 1993—95. Contbr. articles to profl. jours. Past v.p. Prairie Gold Area coun. Boy Scouts Am., Sioux City, bd. dirs. Mid.Am. coun., 1984—; bd. dirs. New Perspectives, Inc., 1996-2001, Sioux City Cmty. Sch. Dist., 1994-97, Crittenton Ctr., 2000—, Morningside Coll., 2000—; elected 2d dist. Iowa Senate, 1996—, asst. majority leader, 1998—. Recipient achievement award Upjohn Pharm. Co., Kansas City, 1978, Silver Beaver award Prairie Gold Area Coun., Boy Scouts Am., 1997, Pub. Ofcl. award Siouxland Dist. Health Dept., 1998, Leadership award Iowans for LIFE, 2000, Guardian of Small Bus. award Nat. Fedn. Ind. Bus., 2001, Iowa Friend of the Family award Christian Coalition Ia., 2001. Fellow Am. Acad. Family Physicians; mem. AMA, AOA, Iowa Med. Soc., Woodbury Med. Soc. (past pres.), Flying Physicians Assn. Republican. Avocation: politics. E-mail: jnredwine@hotmail.com.

REECE, MAYNARD FRED, artist, author; b. Arnolds Park, Iowa, Apr. 26, 1920; s. Waldo H. and Inez V. (Latson) R.; m. June Carman, Apr. 7, 1946; children: Mark A., Brad D. Privately educated. Artist Meredith Pub. Co., Des Moines, 1938-40; artist, asst., mus. dir. Iowa Dept. History and Archives, 1940-50. Artist: Fish and Fishing, 1963, Waterfowl of Iowa, 1943; watercolor Trout, Saturday Evening Post (award of Distinctive Merit 1962); watercolors 73 Fish, Life mag. (cert. of merit 1955); print of Water's Edge Canada Geese for Am. Artist Collection, Am. Artist Mag., 1985; author, artist: The Waterfowl Art of Maynard Reece, 1985, The Upland Bird Art of Maynard Reece, 1997. Chmn. Gov.'s Com. Conservation of Outdoor Resource, 1963-64; trustee Iowa Natural Heritage Found., Des Moines, 1979—; hon. trustee Ducks Unltd., Inc., 1983—; trustee J.N. "Ding" Darling Conservation Found., Inc., Des Moines, 1962—. Served with AUS, 1943-45. Recipient awards for duck stamps and others Dept. Interior, 1948, 51, 59, 69, 71; recipient award Govt. Bermuda, 1963, award Iowa Conservation Commn., 1972, 77, 80, 81, award Fish and Game Commn., Little Rock, 1982, 88, award Tex. Parks and Wild Life Dept., 1983, award Nat. Fish & Wildlife Found., 1988, award Wash. State Dept. Wildlife, 1989, award Idaho Dept. Fish & Game, 1998, 4 awards Ill. Dept. of Natural Resources, 1997-2000; named Artist of Yr. Ducks Unltd. Inc., 1973; chosen Master Artist 1989, Leigh Yawkey Woodson Art Mus., Wausau, Wis., 1989. Mem. Nat. Audubon Soc., Nat. Wildlife Fedn., Izaak Walton League Am. (hon. pres. 1974-75). Home and Office: 5315 Robertson Dr Des Moines IA 50312-2133

REECE, ROBERT WILLIAM, zoological park administrator; b. Saginaw, Mich., Jan. 21, 1942; s. William Andrews and Mary Barbara (Murphy) R.; m. Jill Whetstone, Aug. 21, 1965; children: William Clayton, Gregory Scott, Mark Andrews. B.S., Mich. State U., 1964; postgrad., U. West Fla., 1969-71, U. South Fla., 1974-76. Dir. Northwest Fla. Zool. Gardens, Pensacola, Fla., 1970-72; zool. dir. Lion Country Ga., Stockbridge, 1972-73; asst. dir. Salisbury Zoo, Md., 1976-77; dir. zoology Wild Animal Habitat, Kings Island, Ohio, 1977-92; exec. dir., then pres. The Wilds Internat. Ctr. for Preservation of Wild Animals, Cumberland, 1992—. Assoc. editor: Sci. Jour. Zoo Biology, 1982— . Lt. USN, 1964-69, Korea. Profl. fellow Am. Assn. Zool. Parks and Aqariums; mem. Cin. Wildlife Rsch. Fedn., Am. Soc. Mammalogists, Animal Behavior Soc., Captive Breeding Specialist Group, Species Survival Commn., Internat. Union for Conservation of Nature and Natural Resources. Republican. Episcopalian. Home: 11784 Canterbury Ave Pickerington OH 43147-8490 Office: The Wilds 14000 International Rd Cumberland OH 43732-9500

REED, JOHN SHEDD, former railway executive; b. Chgo., June 9, 1917; s. Kersey Coates and Helen May (Shedd) R.; m. Marjorie Lindsay, May 4, 1946; children: Ginevra, Keith, Helen, Peter, John Shedd Jr. Student, Chgo. Latin Sch., Hotchkiss Sch.; BS in Indsl. Adminstrn., Yale U., 1939; grad., Advanced Mgmt. Program, Harvard U., 1955. With A.T. & S.F. Ry., 1939-83; test dept. asst., successively spl. rep. to gen. supt. transp. Chgo.; transp. insp. Amarillo, Tex.; trainmaster Slaton, Pueblo, Colo.; supt. Mo. div., Marceline, Mo.; asst. to v.p. Chgo., 1957-59; exec. asst. to pres., 1957-59; v.p. finance, 1959-64; v.p. exec. dept., 1964-67; pres., 1967-78; chief exec. officer, 1968-82; chmn. bd., 1973-83. Pres. Santa Fe Industries, Inc., 1968-78, chmn. bd. dirs., CEO Santa Fe So. Pacific Corp., 1987, chmn., 1987-88. Dir. Nat. Merit Scholarship Corp., 1996, past chmn.; trustee Shedd Aquarium, Chgo., 1996, past pres.; v.p., dir. Alliance Francaise de Chicago. With USNR, 1940-45. Mem. Chgo. Club, Old Elm Club, Shoreacres Club, Onwentsia Club (Lake Forest). Home: 301 W Laurel Ave # 112 Lake Forest IL 60045-1180 Office: 224 S Michigan Ave Ste 200 Chicago IL 60604-2591

REED, JOHN WESLEY, lawyer, educator; b. Independence, Mo., Dec. 11, 1918; s. Novus H. and Lilian (Houchens) R.; m. Imogene Fay Vonada, Oct. 5, 1946 (div. 1958); m. Dorothy Elaine Floyd, Mar. 5, 1961; children: Alison A., John M. (dec.), Mary V., Randolph F., Suzanne M. AB, William Jewell Coll., 1939, LLD, 1995; LLB, Cornell U., 1942; LLM, Columbia U., 1949, JSD, 1957. Bar: Mo. 1942, Mich. 1953. Assoc. Stinson, Mag, Thomson, McEvers & Fizzell, Kansas City, Mo., 1942-46; assoc. prof. law U. Okla., 1946-49; assoc. prof. U. Mich., 1949-53, prof., 1953-64, 68-85, Thomas M. Cooley prof., 1985-87, Thomas M. Cooley prof. emeritus, 1987—; dean, prof. U. Colo., 1964-68, Wayne State U., Detroit, 1987-92, prof. emeritus, 1992—. Vis. prof. NYU, 1949, U. Chgo., 1960, Yale U., 1963-64, Harvard U., 1982, U. San Diego, 1993; dir. Inst. Continuing Legal Edn., 1968-73; reporter Mich. Rules of Evidence Com., 1975-78, 83-84; mem. faculty Salzburg Sem., 1962, chmn., 1964. Author: (with W.W. Blume) Pleading and Joinder, 1952; (with others) Introduction to Law and Equity, 1953, Advocacy Course Handbook series, 1963-81; editor in chief Cornell Law Quar., 1941-42; contbr. articles to profl. jours. Pres. bd. mgrs. of mins. and missionaries benefit bd. Am. Bapt. Chs. U.S.A., 1967-74, 82-85, 88-94; mem. com. visitors JAG Sch., 1971-76; trustee Kalamazoo Coll., 1954-64, 68-70. Recipient Harrison Tweed award Assn. Continuing Legal Edn. Adminstrs., 1983, Samuel E. Gates award Am. Coll. Trial Lawyers, 1985, Roberts P. Hudson award State Bar Mich., 1989. Fellow Internat. Soc. Barristers (editor jour. 1980—); mem. ABA (mem. coun. litigation sect.), Assn. Am. Law Schs. (mem. exec. com. 1965-67), Am. Acad. Jud. Edn. (v.p. 1978-80), Colo. Bar Assn. (mem. bd. govs. 1964-68), Mich. Supreme Ct. Hist. Soc. (bd. dirs. 1991—), Sci. Club Mich., Order of Coif. Office: U Mich Sch Law Ann Arbor MI 48109-1215 E-mail: reedj@umich.edu.

REED, KEITH ALLEN, lawyer; b. Anamosa, Iowa, Mar. 5, 1939; s. John Ivan and Florence Lorine (Larson) R.; m. Beth Illana Kesterson, June 22, 1963; children: Melissa Beth, Matthew Keith. BBA, U. Iowa, 1960, JD, 1963. Bar: Ill. 1963, Iowa 1963. Ptnr. Seyfarth Shaw, Chgo., 1963—. Co-author: Labor Arbitration in Healthcare, 1981; co-editor: Chicagoland Employment Law Manual, 1994, Employment and Discrimination, 1996, Federal Employment Law and Regulations, 1989-99, 2001-; co-contbr. articles to Am. Hosp. Assn. publs., 1986-89. Trustee Meth. Hosp. Chgo., 1985—; mem. ad hoc labor adv. com. Am. Hosp. Assn., Chgo., 1980—; bd. dirs. Lyric Opera Chgo. Ctr. for Am. Artists, pres., 1983-86. Mem. ABA (dir. health law forum 1979-82), Chgo. Bar Assn. (chair labor and employment law com. 1996-), Union League Club Chgo. (bd. dirs. 1985-88), Sunset Ridge Country Club (Northbrook, Ill.). Republican. Methodist. Avocations: music, community theater, tennis, golf. Office: Seyfarth Shaw 55 E Monroe St Ste 4200 Chicago IL 60603-5863

REED, M. SCOTT, accounting company executive; CFO Grant Thornton LLP, Chgo., 1997-99, CEO, 1999-2000. Office: Grant Thornton LLP One Prudential Plaza 130 E Randolph Dr Chicago IL 60601

REED, MICHAEL JOHN, dentist, college dean, oral biology educator; b. Wednesbury, Eng., Dec. 25, 1940; came to U.S., 1967, naturalized, 1972; s. Harry Ernest and Ida Veva (Heywood) R.; m. Pamela Twycross, July 4, 1965 (div. Feb. 1976); children: Justine Marianne, Helena Clare; m. Ingrid Liepins, Sept. 8, 1978; children: Kathryn Anne, Matthew Harrison. BS with honors, U. Durham, Eng., 1963; B in Dental Surgery, U. Newcastle-Upon-Tyne, Eng., 1967; PhD, SUNY, Buffalo, 1971. Lic. dentist U.K., N.Y., Miss. Instr. oral biology SUNY, Buffalo, 1971-72, asst. prof. oral biology, 1972-77, assoc. prof., 1977-79; asst. dean Sch. Dentistry, U. Miss., Jackson, 1980-85, assoc. dean, 1985; dean, prof. oral biology Sch. Dentistry, U. Mo., Kansas City, 1985—. Cons. Nat. Inst. Dental Rsch., Washington, 1975-85. Contbr. numerous articles to profl. jours. Recipient rsch. career devel. award NIH, 1975-80. Fellow Acad. Dentistry Internat., Internat. Coll. Dentists, Am. Coll. Dentists; mem. ADA (cons. 1982—, joint com. on nat. dental exam., 1988-93, chair 1992-93), Am. Assn. Dental Schs. (sect. chair 1985-86. chmn. schs. coun. of deans, 1992-93, pres. 1997-98), Am. Assn. Dental Rsch. (councillor 1974-76), Fedn. Dentaire Internat., Am. Assn. for Microbiology, Mid-Am. Masters Club, Omicron Kappa Upsilon. Episcopalian. Avocations: running, European current affairs. Home: 12812 Delmar St Leawood KS 66209-3319 Office: U Mo-Kansas City Sch Dentistry 650 E 25th St Kansas City MO 64108-2716

REED, SCOTT, automotive parts company executive; With Chrysler Corp., 1983-98; CFO Donnelly Corp., Holland, Mich., 1998, pres. Electronic Sys. Group, 2001—. Office: Electric Sys Group Donnelly Corp 49 W 3d St Holland MI 49423

REED, SUELLEN KINDER, state education administrator; BA in History, Polit. Sci.and Secondary Edn., Hanover Coll.; MA in Elem. Edn. and History, PhD in Adminstrn. and Supervision, Ball State U.; postgrad., Fla. Atlantic U., U. Scranton, Purdue U., Earlham Coll., Ind. U., Ind. State U. Cert. secondary tchr., elem. tchr., gifted and talented tchr., administr., supr., Fla., Ind., supt., Ind. Tchr. 5th and 6th grades Rushville (Ind.) Consol. Sch. Corp., 1967-70, asst. supt., 1987-91, supt., 1991-93; tchr. Shelbyville (Ind.) High Sch., 1970-71; tchr. 6th, 7th and 8th grade social studies, curriculum Broward County (Fla.) Sch. Corp., 1971-76; tchr. Rushville Jr. High Sch., 1976-77; asst. prin. Rushville Elem. Sch., 1977-79; prin. Frazee Elem. Sch., Connersville, Ind., 1979-87; asst. supt. Rushville Consolidated Schs., 1987-90, supt., 1991-93; supt. pub. instrn., chairperson bd. edn., CEO dept. edn. State of Indiana, Indpls., 1993—. Pres. N. Ctrl. Regional Edn. Lab., Oak Brook, Ill.; bd. trustees Hanover Coll., Commn. Drug-Free Ind. Commn. Cmty. Svc., Ind. Higher Edn. Telecom. Sys., Rush County Cmty. Found., Ctr. Agrl. Sci. Heritage; adv. council Ball State U., Sch. Continuing Studies Pub. Svc. (Outstanding Sch. Edn. Alumnus award 1994); bd. dirs. Nat. Children's Film Festival. Recipient Outstanding Svc. Pub. Interest award Ind. Optometric Assn., 1996, Ind. Crime Prevention Coalition award, 1996. Mem. ASCD (nat. and Ind. chpts.), Internat. Reading Assn., Nat. Assn. Elem. Sch. Prins. (assoc.), Ind. Assn. Pub. Sch. Supts., Ind. Assn. Elem. and Mid. Sch. Prins. (assoc.), Ind. Assn., Network Woman Adminstrs., Indpls. Zoo, Indpls. Art Mus., Bus. and Profl. Women of Rushville, Altrusa Club Connersville (chmn. internat. rels. 1979-87), Connersville Area Reading Coun., Smithsonian, Rushville County Players, Rotary (Rushville chpt.), Monday Cir., Delta Kappa Gamma (past pres., Phi Lambda Theta, Phi Delta Kappa (Conner Prairie), K-12 Compact Learning, Citizenship, Edn. Commn. States, Council Chief State Sch. Officers (pres.-elect.) Office: Superintendent Edn Dept 229 State House Indianapolis IN 46204-2798

REED, WILLIAM T. broadcasting executive; b. 1938; With Pub. TV, Reading, Calif., 1967-74, Pub. Broadcasting Sys., Washington, 1974-92; pres., gen. mgr. Sta. KCPT-TV, Kansas City, Mo., 1992—. Office: Sta KCPT-TV 125 E 31st St Kansas City MO 64108-3216

REEDER, ROBERT HARRY, retired lawyer; b. Topeka, Dec. 3, 1930; s. William Harry and Florence Mae (Cochran) R. AB Washburn U., 1952, JD, 1960. Bar: U.S. Dist. Ct. Kans. 1960, Kans. 1960, U.S. Supreme Ct. 1968. Rsch. asst. Kans. Legis. Council Rsch. Dept., Topeka, 1955-60; asst. counsel Traffic Inst., Northwestern U., Evanston, Ill., 1960-67, gen. counsel, 1967-92; exec. dir. Nat. Com. on Uniform Traffic Laws and Ordinances, Evanston, 1982-90. Co-author: Vehicle Traffic Law, 1974; The Evidence Handbook, 1980. Author: Interpretation of Implied Consent by the Courts, 1972. Served with U.S. Army, 1952-54. Mem. Com. Alcohol and Other Drugs (chmn. 1973-75). Republican. Methodist.

REEDY, JOHN J. (JOE), state legislator; b. Midland, S.D., Aug. 23, 1927; Grad. high sch., Vermillion, S.D. Mem. S.D. Ho. of Reps., Pierre, 1990-96, mem. agr. and natural resources and edn. coms.; owner Our Own Hardware, 1960-85; ins. salesman Mutual of Omaha, 1985—; mem. S.D. Senate from 17th dist., Pierre, 1996—. Home: 314 E Main St Vermillion SD 57069-2728 Office: SD Senate Members State Capitol Pierre SD 57501

REESE, POKEY, professional baseball player; b. Columbia, S.C., June 10, 1973; Baseball player Cin. Reds, 1997—. Recipient Gold Glove award Nat. League, 1999. Office: Cin Reds 100 Cinergy Field Cincinnati OH 45202*

REETZ, HAROLD FRANK, JR. industrial agronomist; b. Wat., Ill. s. Harold Frank and Evelyn Evedeen (Russell) R.; m. Christine Lee Kaiser, Aug. 25, 1973; children: Carrie, Wesley, Anthony. BS in Agrl. Sci., U. Ill., 1970; MS in Agronomy, Purdue U., 1972, PhD in Agronomy, 1976. Extension and rsch. specialist Purdue U., West Lafayette, Ind., 1974-82; regional dir. Potash & Phosphate Inst., Monticello, Ill, 1982—; v.p. Found. for Agronomic Rsch., 1996—. Cons. Control Data Corp., Mpls., 1978-82, Internat. Harvester Co., Chgo., 1979-82, Monsanto Agrl. Chem. Co., St. Louis, 1981-82; adj. prof. Crop Scis. U., Ill., 1999—. Author: Crop Simulation Model, CORNCROPS, 1976, several crops mgmt. computer programs; contbr. articles to profl. jours. Chmn. Ill. Com. for Agrl. Edn., 1987-89; mem. Ill. Groundwater Adv. Coun., 1988—2002; mem. Ill. Fertilizer Rsch. and Edn. Coun., Ill. Dept. Agr., 1989-98, Ill. Occupl. Skills Stds. Credentialing Coun., 2001—2002, Ill. Dept. Agr. Nutrient Mgmt. Com. Recipient Hon. mem. Hon. State Farmer Ill. Assn. FFA, Urbana, 1987; IFCA Spl. Recognition award Ill. Fertilizer and Chem. Assn., 1988, Site-Liner award Farm Chems., 1997, Alumni award of merit U. Ill., 2000. Fellow Crop Sci. Soc. Am., Am. Soc. Agronomy (Agronomic Industry award 2000); mem. Soil Sci. Soc. Am. (divsn. chmn. editl. bd., chmn. internat. cert. crop adviser exec. com. 1996-98), Ill. Assn. Vocat. Agrl. Tchrs. (hon. life 1989—), Gamma Sigma Delta (Merit award 2001). Methodist. Avocations: photography, travel, computers.

REEVE, JOHN NEWTON, molecular biology and microbiology educator; b. Wakefield, W. Yorkshire, Eng., June 21, 1947; came to U.S., 1979; s. Arthur Newton and Lilian Elsworth (Tallant) R.; m. Patricia Margaret Watson, Sept. 21, 1967; children: Simon Arthur, Daniel John. BS with 1st class honors, U. Birmingham, Eng., 1968; PhD, U. B.C., Vancouver, Can., 1971. Rsch. scientist U. Ariz., Tucson, 1971-73, Nat. Inst. Med. Rsch., Mill Hill, London, 1973-74; rsch. dir. Max-Planck Inst., Berlin, 1974-79; prof. microbiology Ohio State U., Columbus, 1979—, chmn. dept., 1985—, Rod Sharp prof. microbiology, 1999—. Cons. Battelle Rsch. Lab., Columbus, 1982-87, Govt. of Bulgaria, Sofia, 1987, Promega Corp., Madison, Wis., 1990, Procter and Gamble Co., Cin., 1990; mem. sci. adv. bd. BioTrol. Inc., Chaska, Minn., 1986-90; Disting. vis. prof. U. Adelaide, Australia, 1984, U. Wyo., Laramie, 1988, U. Calcutta, India, 1989, Frei U., Berlin, 1991, U. Karachi, Pakistan, 1995, U. Concepcion, Chile, 1995; mem. governing coun. So. Petrochems. Corp., Chennai, India, 1999—. Named Disting. Rsch. Scholar Ohio State U., 1989. Mem. Am. Soc. for Microbiology (lectr. Found. for Microbiology 1987-88, 94-96. chair Div. K, microbial physiol. 1998-99, coun. 2000—). Office: Ohio State U Dept of Microbiology 484 W 12th Ave Columbus OH 43210-1214 Fax: 614-292-8120. E-mail: reeve.2@osu.edu.

REEVE, LEE M. farmer; married; 3 children. BS in Agr. Econs., Kans. State U. Group mgr., owner Reeve Cattle Co., Garden City, Kans. Bd. dirs. Fidelity State Bank, Garden City, Garden City C. of C., Beef Empire Days, Garden City Fed. Land Bank. Mem. Agr. Value Added Processing Leadership Coun.; bd. dirs. Agrl. non-Food Use Task Force; mem. Kans. Coun. Vocat. Edn., Alt. Agr. Rsch. & Commercialization bd. Recipient Innovator of Yr. award State Bd. Agr., Environ. Achievement award Nat. Environ. Awards Coun., Wheeler McMillan award New Uses Coun., Disting. Agrl. Econs. Alumnus Kans. State U. Office: Reeve Cattle Co PO Box 1036 Garden City KS 67846-1036

REEVES, BRUCE, social worker; b. Centerville, Utah, Jan. 8, 1955; s. Leon W. and Maxine (Hodson) R. BA, U. Utah, 1979, MSW, 1983. Mental health caseworker Traveler's Aid Soc. Salt Lake, Salt Lake City, 1983-86; socialwork cons. Home Health of Utah, Bountiful, 1985-86; victim svcs. counselor Salt Lake County Atty's. Office, Salt Lake City, 1986-87; mgr., cons. AIDS and employee assistance program Aetna and Human Affairs Internat., 1987-96; dir. social work and therapies Paracelsus Home Care & Hospice, 1996-98; registrar, bus. mgr. Awakening Spirit Massage Sch., L.C., 1998-99; mgr. Christus St. Joseph Villa, 1999-2001; med. social worker Harmony Home Care and Hospice, 1999-2001; owner, operator Satori Pers. Coaching and Cons., 1999—; exec. dir. Violence Intervention Project, Thief River Falls, Minn., 2001—. Health educator Health Horizons, L.C., 1996-98; presenter in field. Bd. dirs. Walk-ons, Inc., Salt Lake City, 1989-98, Gay and Lesbian Cmty. Ctr. Utah, Salt Lake City, 1998-99, Utah chpt. Gay Lesbian Straight Edn. Network, 1996-99; mem. appropriations com. United Way Greater Salt Lake, Salt Lake City, 1990-99, bd. assocs. Ririe-Woodbury Dance Co., Salt Lake City, 1991-95, human svcs. com. Utah Stonewall Ctr., Salt Lake City, 1992-95. Mem.: NASW, Am. Soc. Aging, Gay Lesbian Straight Edn. Network. Democrat. Avocations: dance, theatre, music, literature. Office: Violence Intervention Project PO Box 96 Thief River Falls MN 56701

REGAN, GILBERT J. career officer, retired; BA in Econs., St. Michael's Coll., 1966; LLD, Harvard U., 1969. Commd. 2d lt. USAF, 1969, advanced through grades to brig. gen., 1996; asst. staff judge advocate 313th Combat Support Group, Forbes AFB, 1970-72; mil. judge Clark AB, Republic of the Philippines, 1972-74, 85-87, MacDill AFB, Fla., 1974-76; assoc. appellate govt. counsel Hdqrs. USAF, Washington, 1976-78, spl. counsel to judge advocate gen., 1978-81; staff judge advocate 836th Combat Support Group, Davis-Monthan AFB, Ariz., 1981-85, 13th Air Force, Clark AB, 1987-89; mil. asst. and spl. counsel to the gen. counsel of the AF Washington, 1989-91; staff judge advocate 22nd Air Force, Travis AFB, Calif., 1991-93, 15th Air Force, Travis AFB, 1993-94, Hdqrs. Pacific Air Forces, Hickam AFB, Hawaii, 1994-96; chief counsel Hdqrs. US Transp. Command, Scott AFB, Ill., 1996—; staff judge advocate Hdqrs. Air Mobility Command, 1996-2000. Ret., 2000. Contbr. articles to profl. publs. Decorated Legion of Merit with oak leaf cluster. Office: HQ AMC/JA 402 Scott Dr Unit 3l2 Scott Air Force Base IL 62225-5300

REGAN, TIMOTHY JAMES, grain company executive; b. Atchison, Kans., July 31, 1956; s. Vincent James and Phyllis (Brull) R.; m. Veronica Sue Kasten, June 25, 1977; children: Katrina Sue, Brian James. BS, Kans. State U., 1978. Corp. acct. Lincoln Grain Co., Atchison, 1978-80; acctg. supr. Pillsbury Co., St. Joseph, Mo., 1980, br. account mgr., 1980-82, Omaha, 1982, internal auditor Mpls., 1983, regional account mgr. Huron, Ohio, 1983-84, Scoular Grain Co., Omaha, 1984-87, controller, 1987-91, v.p., mem. exec. com., 1990-99, CFO, 1991—. Fin. advisor Grace Abbott Sch. PTO, Omaha, 1987, treas., 1990-91. Fin. adviser Grace Abbott Sch. PTO, Omaha, 1987, treas., 1990-91; bd. dirs. Cath. Charities, 1994-2000, treas., 1997-99; coach Little League Baseball and Soccer. Mem. KC, Elks. Republican. Roman Catholic. Avocations: jogging, basketball, coaching little league baseball and soccer. Office: Scoular Co 2027 Dodge St Omaha NE 68102 Home: PO Box 1331 Tulare CA 93275-1331

REGGIO, VITO ANTHONY, management consultant; b. Rochester, N.Y., Dec. 17, 1929; s. Salvatore and Carrie Angela (LoRe) R.; m. Mary Ann Dolores Pippie, Sept. 28, 1957; children: Salvatore, Angela. BS, Purdue U., 1952; postgrad. sch. modern langs., Middlebury Coll., 1948; postgrad. fellowship, U. Ky., U. Tenn. and U. Ala., 1952-53. Jr. engr. Rochester (N.Y.) Gas and Electric Co., 1950; designer/drafter Globe Constrn. Co., Rochester, 1951; rsch. analyst Commonwealth of Ky., Frankfort, 1952; orgn. & methods analyst, then wage adminstrn. specialist USN Dept. Indsl. Rels., Indpls., 1955-56; cons. mgmt. engr. to project mgr. to account exec. Bus. Rsch. Corp., Chgo., 1956-60; sr. cons. econ. feasibilities Ebasco Svcs., Inc., 1960-63, dir. pers. mgmt. cons. dept., 1970-77; regional mgr., orgn. and pers. mgmt. svcs. EBS Mgmt. Cons., 1963-65, nat. dir. orgn. and pers. mgmt. svcs., 1965-70; pres., bd. dirs. Reggio and Assocs., Inc., 1977—; mng. dir. Pay Data Svc., 1977—. Bd. dirs. Pay Data Svcs., Chgo. Contbr. papers to profl. publs. With U.S. Army, 1953-55. Named Solco Cultural Soc. fellow, Rochester, N.Y., 1948. Mem. Am. Compensation Assn., Am. Mgmt. Assn., Chgo. Compensation Assn., Soc. Human Resources Profls., Soc. Human Resources Mgmt., Human Resources Mgmt. Assn. Chgo., Western Soc. Engrs. E-mail: reggioassociates.com. Office: Reggio and Assocs Inc 4365 Lawn Ave Western Springs IL 60558-1465

REGNELL, BARBARA CARAMELLA, retired media educator; b. Paterson, N.J., May 5, 1935; d. William Joseph and Mafalda Erminia (Benedetto) Caramella; m. Joseph C. Tirre, July 12, 1958 (div. June 1977); children: Conrad J., William C.; m. John Albin Regnell, Apr. 2, 1983. BS, Syracuse U., 1957, MA, 1966; postgrad., Washington U., St. Louis, 1972. Editor, continuity dir. Sta. WWBZ-AM, Vineland, N.J., 1958; dir. publicity Conti Adv., Ridgewood, 1958; copywriter Sta. KCNY, San Marcos, Tex., 1959; tchr. Henninger High Sch., Syracuse, N.Y., 1966-67; instr. Belleville (Ill.) Area Jr. Coll., 1968; from instr. to assoc. prof. mass comm. So. Ill. U., Edwardsville, 1967-97, chmn. mass communications, 1985-95, prof. emerita, 1997—; comms. cons., 1997—. Trainer Nat. Iranian Radio, TV, Tehran, Iran, 1974-75; comms. cons., 1997—. Mem. NATAS (Silver Cir., mem. bd. govs. St. Louis chpt., 2d v.p., pres. 2002—), Mo. Osteoporosis Found. (pub. rels. com.), Delta Sigma Rho, Alpha Chi Omega. Republican. Home: 6 Hawthorne Ct Saint Louis MO 63122-4512

REGULA, RALPH, congressman, lawyer; b. Beach City, Ohio, Dec. 3, 1924; s. O.F. and Orpha (Walter) R.; m. Mary Rogusky, Aug. 5, 1950; children: Martha, David, Richard. BA, Mt. Union Coll., 1948, LLD, 1981; LLB, William McKinley Sch. Law, 1952; LLD, Malone Coll., 1976. Bar: Ohio 1952. Sch. adminstr. Stark County Bd. Edn., 1948-55; practiced law Navarre, 1952—; mem. Ohio Ho. of Reps., 1965-66, Ohio Senate, 1967-72, U.S. Congress from 16th Ohio dist., 1973—; vice chmn. appropriations com., chmn. subcom. depts. Labor, HHS, Edn.; ptnr. Regula Bros. Mem. Pres.'s Commn. on Fin. Structures and Regulation, 1970-71. Mem. Ohio Bd. Edn., 1960-64; hon. mem. adv. bd. Walsh Coll., Canton, Ohio; Trustee Mt. Union Coll., Alliance, Ohio, Stark County Hist. Soc., Stark County Wilderness Soc. With USNR, 1944-46. Recipient Community Service award Navarre Kiwanis Club, 1963; Meritorious Service in Conservation award Canton Audubon Soc., 1965; Ohio Conservation award Gov. James Rhodes, 1969; named Outstanding Young Man of Yr. Canton Jr. C. of C., 1957, Legis. Conservationist of Yr. Ohio League Sportsmen, 1969 Republican. Episcopalian. Office: US Ho of Reps 2306 Rayburn House Off Bldg Washington DC 20515-3516*

REH, THOMAS EDWARD, radiologist, educator; b. St. Louis, Sept. 12, 1943; s. Edward Paul and Ceil Anne (Golden) R.; m. Benedette Texada Gieselman, June 22, 1968; children: Matthew J., Benedette T., Elizabeth W. BA, St. Louis U., 1965, MD, 1969. Diplomate Am. Bd. Radiology, Nat. Bd. Med. Examiners. Intern St. John's Mercy Med. Ctr., St. Louis, 1969-70; resident St. Louis VA Hosp., 1970-73; fellow in vascular radiology Beth Israel Hosp., Boston, 1973-74; radiologist St. Mary's Health Ctr., St. Louis, 1974—, chmn. dept. radiology, 1986—; clin. asst. prof. radiology St. Louis U. Sch. Medicine, 1978-98, clin. prof. radiology, 1998—; clin. assoc. prof. radiology, 1989—. Fellow Am. Coll. Radiology; mem. AMA, Radiol. Soc. N.Am., St. Louis Met. Med. Soc., Alpha Omega Alpha, Alpha Sigma Nu, Delta Sigma Phi. Republican. Roman Catholic. Clubs: St. Louis, Confrerie des Chevaliers du Tastevin. Home: 9850 Waterbury Dr Saint Louis MO 63124-1046 Office: Bellevue Radiology Inc 4 Sunnen Bus Park Saint Louis MO 63143

REHBERG, KITTY, state legislator; b. Cedar Rapids, Iowa, Oct. 16, 1938; m. Franklin Rehberg; 3 children. Student, Rowly C.C. Mem. Iowa Senate from 14th dist., Des Moines, 1996—; mem. appropriations com., mem. rules and adminstrn. com.; vice chair edn. com. Des Moines; mem. natural resources and environment com. Republican. Office: State Capitol 9th And Grand Ave Des Moines IA 50319-0001 E-mail: kitty_rehberg@legis.state.ia.us.

REHERMAN, RONALD GILBERT, gas and electric company executive; b. Evansville, Ind., Aug. 14, 1935; s. Gilbert and Anna (Lawrence) R.; m. Rosalynn Reherman, Oct. 25, 1959; children: Robin, Chris, David. BS, U. Evansville, 1958; MBA, Ind. State U., 1971. Registered profl. engr., Ind. With So. Ind. Gas and Electric Co., Evansville, 1960—, v.p., dir. gas ops., 1982-84, exec. v.p., gen. mgr. ops., 1985-88; pres., COO So. Ind. Gas and Elec. Co., 1988-90, pres., CEO, 1990-92, pres., chmn., CEO, 1992—. Bd. dirs. Evansville Indsl. Found., Evansville Coun. Boy Scouts Am., Vision 2000, Deaconess Hosp., Evansville United Way, campaign chmn. 1986-87; bd. trustees Evansville Mus. With U.S. Army, 1958-60. Mem. Met. Evansville C. of C. (bd. dirs. 1987), Ind. C. of C. (exec. com.)/ Avocations: camping, reading, golf, skiing. Office: So Ind Gas & Electric Co 20 NW 4th St Evansville IN 47708-1724

REHM, JACK DANIEL, publishing executive; b. Yonkers, N.Y., Oct. 10, 1932; s. Jack and Ann (McCarthy) R.; m. Cynthia Fenning, Oct. 18, 1958; children: Lisabeth R., Ann M., Cynthia A., Jack D. Jr. BSBA, Coll. of the Holy Cross, 1954. Advt. sales trainee, asst. account exec. Batten, Barton, Durstine & Osborne, N.Y.C., 1954-59; mgr. Suburbia Today, 1959-62; with advt. sales dept. Better Homes and Gardens Meredith Corp., 1962-66, mgr. advt. sales Phila., 1966-67, N.Y.C., 1967-69, advt. sales dir. Better Homes and Garden mag., 1969-73, v.p., pub. dir. mag. divsn., 1973-75, v.p., pub. Better Homes and Gardens, pub. dir. mag. divsn., 1975-76, v.p. pub. group, gen. mgr., mag. pub., 1976-80, pres. pub. group Des Moines, 1980-86, exec. v.p. corp. svcs., 1986-88, pres., COO, 1988—, pres., CEO, 1989—, chmn., pres., CEO, 1992—, also bd. dirs. Bd. dirs. Norwest Bank Iowa, N.A., Vernon Co., Newton, Iowa, Internat. Multifoods, Mpls., Equitable of Iowa Cos., Am. Coun. for Capital Formation. Bd. govs. Drake U., 1988—; trustee Coll. Holy Cross, Worcester, Mass.; mem. bus. com. Mus. Modern Art, N.Y.C., Greater Des Moines Com., Inc.; chmn. Des Moines Devel. Corp., 1993-94; active Iowa Bus. Coun.; mem. mag. and print com. USIA. With U.S. Army, 1956-57. Mem. Mag. Pubs. Am. (bd. dirs. 1981—, chmn. 1983-85, Publisher of Yr. 1988), Pine Valley Golf Club, Scarsdale Golf Club, Wakonda Golf Club. Roman Catholic. Avocation: golf. Office: Meredith Corp 1716 Locust St Des Moines IA 50309-3023 Home: 7116 SE Greenview Pl Hobe Sound FL 33455-8041

REIBEL, KURT, physicist, educator; b. Vienna, Austria, May 23, 1926; came to U.S., 1938; s. Michael and Regina (Pak) R.; m. Eleanor Elvira Mannino, June 10, 1954; children— Leah, Michael, David B.A., Temple U., Phila., 1954; M.S., U. Pa., Phila., 1956, Ph.D., 1959. Jr. research assoc. in physics Brookhaven Nat. Lab., 1957-59; research assoc. U. Pa., Phila., 1959-61; asst. prof. Ohio State U., Columbus, 1961-64, assoc. prof., 1964-70, prof. physics, 1970-92, prof. emeritus, 1992—. Vis. scientist CERN, Geneva, Switzerland, 1968-69, 75-76 Author research papers on nuclear and elementary particle physics NSF fellow, 1954-56 Mem. Am. Phys. Soc., AAUP, Fedn. Am. Scientists, Union Concerned Scientists, Sigma Xi Jewish Office: Ohio State U Dept Physics 174 W 18th Ave Columbus OH 43210-1106

REICH, ALLAN J. lawyer; b. Chgo., July 9, 1948; s. H. Robert and Sonya (Minsky) R.; m. Lynne Susan Roth, May 23, 1971; children: Allison, Marissa, Scott. BA, Cornell U., 1970; JD cum laude, U. Mich., 1973. Bar: Ill. 1973, U.S. Dist. Ct. (no. dist.) Ill. 1973. Ptnr. McDermott, Will & Emery, Chgo., 1973-93; vice chmn. D'Ancona & Pflaum LLC, 1993—. Trustee Oakmark Family of Mutual Funds, 1994—. V.p., mem. exec. com. Coun. for Jewish Elderly, 1989—97; mem. men's coun. Mus. Contemporary Art, Chgo., 1988—89; mem. Chgo. exec. bd. Am. Jewish Com., 1989—, nat. bd. govs.; mem. met. Chgo. bd. Am. Heart Assn.; bd. dirs. Young Men's Jewish Coun., Chgo., 1974—84, Coun. for Jewish Elderly, 1986—97. Mem.: ABA, Chgo. Bar Assn., Execs. Club Chgo., Econ. Club Chgo., Northmoor Country Club (Highland Park, Ill.), Standard Club (Chgo.). Home: 936 Skokie Ridge Dr Glencoe IL 60022-1434 Office: D'Ancona & Pflaum LLC 111 E Wacker Dr Chicago IL 60601-3713 E-mail: areich@dancona.com.

REICH, VICTORIA J. consumer products company executive; b. Southborough, Mass., 1958; BS in Applied Math. and Econs., Brown U. With GE Co.; v.p., contr. Brunswick Corp., Lake Forest, Ill., 1996-2000, sr. v.p., CFO, 2000—. Office: Brunswick Corp 1 N Field Ct Lake Forest IL 60045-4811

REICHERT, DAVID, lawyer; b. Cin., Nov. 23, 1929; s. Victor E. and Louise F. Reichert; m. Marilyn Frankel, May 31, 1959; children— James G., Steven F., William M. BA, Bowling Green State U., 1951; JD, U. Cin., 1954. Bar: Ohio 1954, U.S. Supreme Ct. 1963. Ptnr. firm Porter, Wright, Morris & Arthur, formerly sr. ptnr. Reichert, Strauss & Reed and predecessors, Cin. Dir. numerous corps. Monthly columnist: Scrap Age mag, 1966-74; bd. editors: U. Cin. Law Rev, 1953-54. Pres. brotherhood Rockdale Temple, Cin., 1960-61, temple treas., 1973-75, v.p., 1975-79, pres., 1979-81; mem. Amberley Village Planning Commn. & Zoning Bd. Appeals, 1972-79, Ohio Solid Waste Adv. Group, 1974; treas. Contemporary Arts Ctr., Cin., 1973-75, pres., 1976-77, trustee, 1982-88; trustee Cin. Art Mus., 1978-93, v.p., 1992-93, chmn. vis. com. for contemporary art, 1990-92; trustee Jewish Publ. Soc., 1980-86, Cin. Sculpture Coun., 1984-87; mem. acquisitions com. Miami U. Art Mus., 1982-85. Mem. Cin. Print and Drawing Cir. (pres. 1974-76), The Literary Club (sec. 1988-91, v.p. 1991-92, pres. 1992-93), Losantiville Country Club (bd. govs. 1985-92, sec. 1986-90, pres. 1990-92), ISRI 20th Century Club (hon. 1998), Omicron Delta Kappa, Sigma Tau Delta, Phi Delta Phi, Zeta Beta Tau. Office: Porter Wright Morris & Arthur 250 E 5th St Ste 2200 Cincinnati OH 45202-5177

REICHERT, JACK FRANK, manufacturing company executive; b. West Allis, Wis., Sept. 27, 1930; s. Arthur Andrew and Emily Bertha (Wallinger) R.; m. Corrine Violet Helf, Apr. 5, 1952; children: Susan Marie, John Arthur. Cert. mktg., U. Wis., Milw., 1957; AMP, Harvard U., 1970; LLD (hon.), Marian Coll., 1994. Various mktg. positions GE, 1948-57; with Brunswick Corp., Lake Forest, Ill., 1957-95, pres. Mercury Marine div., 1972-77, corp. v.p., 1974-77, group v.p. Marine Power Group, 1974-77, pres., COO, 1977-93, CEO, 1982-95, chmn. bd. dirs., 1983-95, dir., 1977-82, chmn. emeritus, 1995—. Bd. dirs. Viad Corp., Phoenix, Strike Ten Entertainment, Inc. Trustee Carroll Coll., Waukesha, Wis., 1972; indsl. chmn. Fond du Lac United Fund, 1977; chmn. Internat. Bowling Mus. and Hall of Fame. With C.E. U.S. Army, 1951-53. Named Disting. Alumnus of the Yr., U. Wis., Milw. 1979, Top Chief Exec. Officer in Multi-Industry Group, Fin. World Mag., 1984; recipient Gold award in leisure industry Wall St. Transcript, 1983, 86, Bronze award in multi-industry category Wall St. Transcript, 1985, Leisure Industry Silver award, 1988. Mem. Am. Mgmt. Assn., U. Wis.-Milw. Alumni Assn., Knollwood Club, Harvard Club, Mid-Am. Club, Beta Gamma Sigma (hon.). Presbyterian. Avocations: golf, reading. Home: 580 Douglas Dr Lake Forest IL 60045-3342 Office: Brunswick Corp 1 N Field Ct Lake Forest IL 60045-4811

REICHGOTT JUNGE, EMBER D. former state legislator, web site design company executive, lawyer, writer, broadcast analyst; b. Detroit, Aug. 22, 1953; d. Norbert Arnold and Diane (Pincich) Reichgott; m. Michael Junge. BA summa cum laude, St. Olaf Coll., Minn., 1974; JD, Duke U., 1977; MBA, U. St. Thomas, 1991. Bar: Minn. 1977, D.C. 1978. Assoc. Larkin, Hoffman, Daly & Lindgren, Bloomington, Minn., 1977-84; counsel Control Data Corp., 1984-86; ptnr. The Gen. Counsel, Ltd., 1987—; mem. Minn. State Senate, 1983-2000, chmn. legis. com. on econ. status of women, 1984-86, vice chmn. senate edn. com., 1987-88, senate majority whip, 1990-94, chmn. property tax divsn. senate tax com., 1991-92, chmn. senate judiciary com., 1993-94, senate asst. majority leader, 1995-2000, chmn. spl. subcom. on ethical conduct; pres. Video on Wings, video to web co. Dem. endorsed candidate Minn. Atty. Gen., 1998; instr. polit. sci. St. Olaf Coll., Northfield, Minn., 1993; bd. dirs. Citizens Ind. Bank, St. Louis Park, Minn. Host cable TV monthly series Legis. Report, 1985-92. Trustee, bd. dirs. N.W. YMCA, New Hope, Minn., 1983-88; trustee, bd. dirs. United Way Mpls., 1989—; trustee, bd. dirs. Greater Mpls. Red Cross, 1988, chair, 2001; state co-chair Clinton/Gore Presdl. Campaign, Minn. Dem. Farmer-Labor Party, 1992, 96, del. Nat. Dem. Conv., 1984, 92, 96. Recipient Woman of Yr. award North Hennepin Bus. and Profl. Women, 1983, award for contbn. to human svcs. Minn. Social Svcs. Assn., 1983, Clean Air award Minn. Lung Assn., 1988, Disting. Svc. award Mpls. Jaycees, 1984, Minn. Dept. Human Rights award, 1989, Myra Bradwell award Minn. Women Lawyers, 1993, Disting. Alumnae award Lake Conf. Schs., 1993, Disting. Alumnae award St. Olaf Coll., 1998, awards for leadership Am. Lung Assn, 1999, Am. Heart Assn., 1997, Everyday Hero award Up with People, 1995, Unsung Hero award United Way of Mpls., 1999, 1st recipient of award named in her honor for prevention of sexual assault, 2000; charter inductee Robbinsdale H.S. Hall of Fame, 2000; author of Minn. charter sch. law, winner of "2000 Innovaions in Am. Govt. award. given by Harvard U. and Ford Found., others; named one of ten Outstanding Young Minnesotans, Minn. Jaycees, 1984, Policy Advocate of Yr., NAWBO, 1988, Woman of Achievement, Twin West C. of C., 1989, Marvelous Minn. Woman, 1993; youngest woman ever elected to Minn. Senate, 1983. Mem. Minn. Bar Assn. (bd. govs. 1992-96, Pro Bono Publico Atty. award 1990), Hennepin County Bar Assn., Corp. Counsel Assn. (v.p. 1989-96). Home: 7701 48th Ave N Minneapolis MN 55428-4515 Fax: 763-536-1447. E-mail: emberrj@msn.com.

REICIN, RONALD IAN, lawyer; b. Chgo., Dec. 11, 1942; s. Frank Edward and Abranita (Rome) R.; m. Alyta Friedland, May 23, 1965; children: Eric, Kael. BBA, U. Mich., 1964, MBA, JD cum laude, U. Mich., 1967. Bar: Ill. 1967, U.S. Tax Ct. 1967; CPA, Ill. Mem. staff Price Waterhouse & Co., Chgo., 1966; ptnr. Jenner & Block, 1967—. Bd. dirs. Nat. Kidney Found., Ill., 1978—, v.p., 1992-95, pres., 1995-98; bd. dirs. Ruth Page Found., 1985—, v.p., 1990—; bd. dirs. Scoliosis Assn. Chgo., 1981-90, Kohl Children's Mus., 1991-95, River North Chgo. Dance Co.,

1999—. Mem.: Chgo. Mortgage Attys. Assn., Chgo. Bar Assn., ABA, Lawyers (Chgo.), Exec., Beta Alpha Psi, Beta Gamma Sigma, Phi Kappa Phi. Office: Jenner & Block LLC 1 E Ibm Plz Fl 38 Chicago IL 60611-3586 E-mail: rreicin@jenner.com.

REID, DANIEL JAMES, public relations executive; b. Grand Rapids, Mich., Sept. 7, 1960; s. Robert Alexander and Janette Helen (Hickey) R.; m. Meredith Christine Ryan, Apr. 30, 1994; children: Ryan Paul, Katherine Baxter. BA, Mich. State U., 1983. Sr. account exec. Burson-Marsteller, Chgo., 1983-88; group dir. Ogilvy & Mather, 1988-90; sr. ptnr. FRB/BSMG Worldwide (subs. True North Comms.), 1990-98; sr. nat. mng. ptnr. BSMG Worldwide, 1998-2000, pres. fin. svcs., 2000—; exec. v.p. Weber Shandwick Worldwide, 2001—. Contbr. articles to profl. publs. and newspapers. Bd. dirs. Opportunity, Inc., Chgo., LEC Ltd. Mem. Union League Club Chgo. Republican. Roman Catholic. Office: Weber Shandwick 676 St Clair Chicago IL 60611

REID, IRVIN D. academic official; BS, MS in Exptl. Psychology, Howard U.; MA, PhD, U. Pa. Head dept. mktg. & bus. law U. Tenn., Chattanooga, 1979-83; assoc. prof. mktg. Howard U., Washington, 1978-79; cons. U.S. Consumer Product Safety Commn., 1977-78; sr. staff specialist in mktg. & econ. rsch. NASA, 1976-77, 78-79; asst. prof. mktg. coll. bus. Drexel U., 1970-78; pres. Montclair State Coll., Upper Montclair, N.J., 1989-97, Wayne State U., Detroit, 1997—. Bd. dirs. Detroit 300 Com., 1998—; exec. com. Detroit Med. Ctr., 1997—, Karmanos Cancer Inst., 1997—, New Detroit, 1998—, N.J./Israel Trade Commn., 1994-97, NCAA Pres.'s Commn., 1994-99, Nat. Conf. Christians and Jews, 1992-97, Mich. Econ. Devel. Corp., 1999—, Detroit Urban League, 1999—, Mich. Opera Theater, 1998—; steering com. Mich. Life Sci. Initiative, 2000—. Mem. Econ. Club Detroit, Univ. Cultural Ctr. Assn., Upper Montclair (N.J.) Country Club. Office: Wayne State U Office of the Pres Detroit MI 48201

REID, JAMES SIMS, JR. former automobile parts manufacturer; b. Cleve., Jan. 15, 1926; s. James Sims and Felice (Crowl) R.; m. Donna Smith, Sept. 2, 1950; children: Sally, Susan, Anne (dec.), Jeanne. AB cum laude, Harvard U., 1948, JD, 1951. Bar: Mich., Ohio 1951. Pvt. practice law, Detroit, 1951-52, Cleve., 1953-56; with Standard Products Co., 1956-99, dir., 1959, pres., 1962-89, chmn., chief exec. officer, 1989-99; ret., 1999. Trustee John Carroll U., 1967—, chmn., 1987-91, Musical Arts Assn. of Cleve. Orch., 1973—. Office: Hanna Bldg Ste 545 1422 Euclid Ave Cleveland OH 44115-1901

REID, MARILYN JOANNE, state legislator, lawyer; b. Chgo., Aug. 14, 1941; d. Kermit and Newell Azile (Hahn) N.; m. M. David Reid, Nov. 26, 1966 (div. Mar. 1983); children: David, Nelson. Student, Miami U., Oxford, Ohio, 1959-61; BA, U. Ill, 1963; JD, Ohio No. U., 1966. Bar: Ohio 1966, Ark. 1967, U.S. Dist. Ct. 1967. Trust adminstr. First Nat. Bank, Dayton, Ohio, 1966-67; assoc. Sloan & Ragsdale, Little Rock, 1967-69; ptnr. Reid and Reid, Dayton, 1969-76, Reid & Buckwalter, Dayton, 1975—; mem. Ohio Ho. of Reps., 1993-98. Mem. health ins. and HMO's com., chmn. ins. com., vets. com., pub. utilities com. Mem. Ohio adv. bd. U.S. Commn. Civil Rights; chmn., treas. various polit. campaigns, 1975—; trustee Friends Libr. Beavercreek (Ohio); bd. dirs. Beavercreek YMCA, 1985-88; active Mt. Zion United Ch. of Christ; chmn. Greene County Rep. Party. Mem. ABA, Ohio Bar Assn., Greene County Bar Assn., Beavercreek C. of C. (pres. 1986-87), Dayton Panhellenic Assn. (pres. 1982), Altrusa (v.p. Greene County 1978-79, pres. 1979-80), Lions (pres. Beavercreek 1975), Greene County Rep. Party (chmn.), Rotary, Kappa Beta Pi, Gamma Phi Beta (v.p. 1974-75). Mem. Ch. Christ. Avocations: tennis, skiing, boating, bridge. Office: Reid & Buckwalter 3866 Indian Ripple Rd Dayton OH 45440-3448

REID, ROBERT LELON, retired mechanical engineering educator, dean; b. Detroit, May 20, 1942; s. Lelon Reid and Verna Beulah (Custer) Menkes; m. Judy Elaine Nestell, July 21, 1962; children: Robert James, Bonnie Kay, Matthew Lelon. ASE, Mott C.C., Flint, Mich., 1961; BChemE, U. Mich., 1963; MME, So. Meth. U., 1966, PhDME, 1969. Registered profl. engr., Tenn., Tex., Wis. Asst. rsch. engr. Atlantic Richfield Co., Dallas, 1964-65; assoc. staff engr. Linde Div., Union Carbide Corp., Tonawanda, N.Y., 1966-68; from asst. to assoc. prof. U. Tenn., Knoxville, 1969-75; assoc. prof. Cleve. State U., 1975-77; from assoc. to full prof. U. Tenn., Knoxville, 1977-82; prof., chmn. U. Tex., El Paso, 1982-87; dean Coll. Engring., Marquette U., Milw., 1987-98, prof. mech. engring., 1998-2001; dean emeritus, 2001. Summer prof. NASA Marshall Space Ctr., Huntsville, Ala., 1970, EXXON Prodn. Rsch., Houston, 1972, 73, NASA Lewis Space Ctr., Cleve., 1986; cons. Oak Ridge Nat. Lab., 1974-75, TVA, 1978, 79, State of Calif., Sacramento, 1985, Tex. Higher Edn. Coordinating Bd., Austin, 1987. Contbr. articles 100 articles on heat transfer and solar energy. Grantee NSF, DOE, TVA, NASA, DOI, 1976-87; named Engr. of Yr. Engring. Socs. El Paso, 1986. Fellow ASME (Centennial medallion 1980, chmn. cryogenics com. 1977-81, chmn. solar energy divsn. 1983-84, chmn. Rio Grande sect. 1985-87, John Yellott award, 1997, Dedicated Svc. award 1998); mem. ASHRAE, Engrs. and Scientists Milw. (bd. dirs. 1988-93, v.p. 1989-90, pres. 1991-92), Wis. Assn. Rsch. Mgmt. (pres. 1996-97). Lutheran. Avocations: travel, classic car restoration.

REID, S.W. English educator; b. Neptune, N.J., Nov. 24, 1943; s. Sidney Webb and Mary Cook (Bennett) R.; m. Judith Wright, Aug. 22, 1969; 1 child, Laura. BA, Duke U., 1965; MA, U. Va., 1966, PhD, 1972. Grad. tchg. fellow U. Va., Charlottesville, 1968-70; asst. prof. English, Kent (Ohio) State U., 1970-75, assoc. prof., 1975-84, prof., 1984—, dir. Inst. Bibliography and Editing, 1985—. Vis. fellow Clare Hall, Cambridge (Eng.) U., 1992-93, life mem., 1993—. Textual editor Bicentennial Edition of Charles Brockden Brown, 6 vols., 1977-87; editor-in-chief: (Cambridge edits. of Joseph Conrad) The Secret Agent, 1990, Almayer's Folly, 1994. NDEA fellow U. Va., 1965-68; Rsch. grantee NEH, 1977-84. Office: Kent State University Inst Bibliography-Editing 1118 Library Kent OH 44242-0001

REID, WILLIAM HILL, mathematics educator; b. Oakland, Calif., Sept. 10, 1926; s. William Macdonald and Edna Caroline (Hill) R.; m. Elizabeth Mary Kidner, May 26, 1962; 1 child, Margaret Frances. BS, U. Calif., Berkeley, 1949, MS, 1951; PhD, Cambridge U., Eng., 1955, ScD (hon.), 1968; AM (hon.), Brown U., 1961. Lectr. Johns Hopkins U., Balt., 1955-56; NSF fellow Yerkes Observatory, Williams Bay, Wis., 1957-58; asst. prof. Brown U., Providence, 1958-61, assoc. prof., 1961-63, U. Chgo., 1963-65, prof., 1965-89, prof. emeritus, 1989—; prof. Ind. U.-Purdue U., Indianapolis, 1989—. Cons. research labs. Gen. Motors Corp., Warren, Mich., 1960-73. Author: (with P.G. Drazin) Hydrodynamic Stability, 1981; contbr. articles to profl. jours. Served with U.S. Mcht. Marine, 1945-47, with AUS, 1954-56. Fulbright research scholar Australian Nat. U., 1964-65. Fellow Am. Phys. Soc., Cambridge Philos. Soc.; mem. Am. Math. Soc., Am. Meteorol. Soc., Sigma Xi. Office: Ind U-Purdue U Dept Math Scis 402 N Blackford St Indianapolis IN 46202-3217 Home: 10900 Lightship Ct Fishers IN 46038-2651

REID-ANDERSON, JAMES, diagnostic equipment company executive; BS in Commerce with honors, U. Birmingham, Eng. Exec. level positions with Pepsico Inc., Grand Met. PLC, Mobil Oil Corp.; COO, chief adminstrv. officer Wilson Sporting Goods, Chgo., 1994-96; exec. v.p., CFO Dade Behring, Deerfield, Ill., 1996-97, exec. v.p., CFO, chief adminstrv. officer, 1997-99, pres., COO, 1999—. Fellow Chartered Assn. Cert. Accts.

REIDINGER, RUSSELL FREDERICK, JR. fish and wildlife scientist; b. Reading, Pa., June 19, 1945; BS, Albright Coll., 1967; PhD in Zoology, U. Ariz., 1972. Asst. prof. biology Augustana Coll., 1971-74; rsch. physiologist The Philippines, 1974-78; asst. mem., wildlife biologist Monell Chem. Senses Ctr., 1978-86; dir. Denver Wildlife Rsch. Ctr. U.S. Dept. Agr., Denver, 1987-93; dir. Ctr. Excellence Wildlife Mgmt. Lincoln U., Jefferson City, Mo., 1993—. Vis. prof. dept. zoology U. Philippines, 1975-78; cons. Bangladesh Agr. Rsch. Coun., USAID, 1977, Ministry Agrl. Devel. & Agrarian Reform, Nicaragua, 1981, CID, Uganda, 1996. Mem. Am. Soc. Mammalogists, Wildlife Soc., Nat. Animal Damage Control Assn. Office: Lincoln U Dept Ag Nat & Home Econ Jefferson City MO 65102-0029

REIDY, THOMAS ANTHONY, lawyer; b. Bronx, N.Y., Sept. 30, 1952; s. John Alexander and Elinor Ann (Tracey) R.; m. Victoria Mary Moxham, Mar. 12, 1977; children: J. Benjamin, Jacob T., Thomas A. II. BA with honors, Lehigh U., 1974; JD, U. Va., 1978. Bar: Ohio 1978, U.S. Dist. Ct. (so. dist.) Ohio 1980. Assoc. Moritz, McClure, Hughes, Kerscher & Price, Columbus, Ohio, 1978-80, Porter, Wright, Morris & Arthur, Columbus, 1980-87, ptnr., 1987-92; v.p. human resources and employment counsel The Longaberger Co., Dresden, Ohio, 1993-94, gen. counsel, 1994—. First v.p. Easter Seals Soc. Ctrl. Ohio, Columbus, 1990-92. Office: Longaberger Co PO Box 3400 Newark OH 43058-3400

REILLY, FRANK KELLY, business educator; b. Chgo., Dec. 30, 1935; s. Clarence Raymond and Mary Josephine (Ruckrigel) R.; m. Therese Adele Bourke, Aug. 2, 1958; children: Frank Kelly III, Clarence Raymond II, Therese B., Edgar B. BBA, U. Notre Dame, 1957; MBA, Northwestern U., 1961, U. Chgo., 1964, PhD, 1968; LLD (hon.), St. Michael's Coll., 1991. CFA. Trader Goldman Sachs & Co., Chgo., 1958-59; security analyst Tech. Fund, 1959-62; asst. prof. U. Kans., Lawrence, 1965-68, assoc. prof., 1968-72; prof. bus., assoc. dir. divsn. bus. and econ. rsch. U. Wyo., Laramie, 1972-75; prof. fin. U. Ill., Champaign-Urbana, 1975-81; Bernard J. Hank prof. U. Notre Dame, Ind., 1981—, dean Coll. Bus. Adminstrn., 1981-87. Bd. dirs., chmn. Brinson Funds, Assn. Investment Mgmt. and Rsch.; past chmn. Inst. Chartered Fin. Analysts; past chmn. bd. dirs. NIBCO Corp.; bd. dirs. Internat. Bd. CFPs, Discover Bank, Ft. Dearborn Income Securities, Battery Park High Yield Fund., Morgan Stanley Dean Witter Trust Fed. Savs. Bank (FSB). Author: Investment Analysis and Portfolio Management, 1979, 6th edit., 2000, Investments, 1982, 5th edit., 1999; co-editor: Ethics and the Investment Industry, 1989; editor: Readings and Issues in Investments, 1975, High Yield Bonds: Analysis and Risk Assessment, 1990; assoc. editor Fin. Mgmt., 1977-82, Quar. Rev. Econs. and Bus, 1979-87, Fin. Rev., 1979-87, 92—, Jour. Fin. Edn., 1981—, Jour. Applied Bus. Rsch., 1986—, Fin. Svcs. Rev., 1989-96, Internat. Rev. Econs. and Fin., 1992—, European Jour. Fin., 1994—. Arthur J. Schmidt Found. fellow, 1962-65; U. Chgo. fellow, 1963-65; recipient faculty award U. Notre Dame, 1999. Fellow Fin. Mgmt. Assn. (pres. 1983-84, chmn. 1985-91, bd. dirs.); mem. Midwest Bus. Adminstrn. Assn. (pres. 1974-75), Am. Fin. Assn., Western Fin. Assn. (exec. com. 1973-75), Ea. Fin. Assn. (exec. com. 1979-84, pres. 1982-83), Midwest Fin. Assn. (pres. 1993-94), Fin. Analysts Fedn., Acad. Fin. Svcs. (pres. 1990-91), Inst. Chartered Fin. Analysts (coun. of examiners, rsch. and edn. com., edn. steering com., C. Stewart Sheppard award 1991), Internat. Assoc. Fin. Planners (ednl. resource com., bd. dirs.), Assn. of Investment Mgmt. and Rsch. (Daniel J. Forrestal III Leadership award for profl. ethics 2001), Investments Analysts Soc. Chgo. (bd. dirs. 1988-89), Beta Gamma Sigma. Roman Catholic. Office: U Notre Dame Mendoza Coll Bus Notre Dame IN 46556-5646 E-mail: reilly.1@nd.edu.

REILLY, KEVIN P. academic administrator; BA, U. Notre Dame, 1971; MA, U. Minn., 1974, PhD in English, 1979. Teaching asst. dept. English U. Minn., Mpls., 1974-79, asst. to dir. undergrad. study dept. English, 1976-77; coord. project on ednl. advisement in the work setting N.Y. State Bd. Regents, 1979-80, dir. Teaching and Beyond project, 1983-84, dir. nat. program non-coll. sponsored instrn., 1979-84, dir. div. coll. and univ. evaluation, 1984-92; assoc. provost for acad. programs SUNY Sys., Albany, 1992—; also sr. fellow in univ./sch. rels. SUNY Systems, 1992—. Mem. vis. del. Am. educators to rev. sch. system in No. Ireland, 1990; lectr. and presenter in field. Editor: (with Carol Wolfe) A Guide to Educational Programs in Noncollegiate Organizations, 1983, (with Sheila Murdick) Teaching and Beyond: Nonacademic Career Programs for Ph.D.'s, 1984; contbr. numerous articles to profl. jours. Tutor, Literacy Vols. of Am., Schenectady, 1988-90. Recipient Mgmt. Performance awards N.Y. State, 1989, 90; recipient fellowships at U. Minn. Mem. MLA, Am. Assn. for Higher Edn., Am. Conf. for Irish Studies, Am. Ednl. Rsch. Assn., Assn. for Continuing Higher Edn., Irish Am. Cultural Inst. Home: 5325 Comanche Way Madison WI 53704-1021 Office: 432 N. Lake St. Madison WI 53706

REILLY, ROBERT FREDERICK, valuation consultant; b. N.Y.C., Oct. 3, 1953; s. James J. and Marie (Griebel) K.; m. Janet H. Steiner, Apr. 16, 1975; children: Ashley Lauren, Brandon Christopher, Cameron Courtney. BA in Econs., Columbia U., 1975, MBA in Fin., 1976. CPA, Ohio, Ill.; cert. mgmt. acct., CFA; cert. real estate appraiser; cert. review appraiser; cert. gen. appraiser Ill., Va., Utah, Oreg., N.Y.; cert. bus. appraiser; accredited bus. valuator. Sr. cons. Booz, Allen & Hamilton, Cin., 1975-76; dir. corp. planning Huffy Corp., Dayton, Ohio, 1976-81; v.p. Arthur D. Little Valuation, Inc., Chgo., 1981-85; ptnr., nat. dir. of valution svcs. Deloitte & Touche, 1985-91; mng. dir. Willamette Mgmt. Assocs., 1991—. Adj. prof. accounting U. Dayton Grad. Sch. Bus., 1977-81; adj. prof. fin. econs., Elmhurst (Ill.) Coll., 1982-87; adj. prof. fin. Ill. Inst. Tech. Grad. Sch. Bus., Chgo., 1985-91; adj. prof. taxation U. Chgo. Grad. Sch. Bus., 1985-87. Co-author: Valuing Small Businesses and Professional Practices, 1993, 4th edit., 2000, Business Valuation Video Course, 1993, Valuing a Business, 1995, 4th edit., 2000, Valuing Accounting Practices, 1997, Valuing Professional Practices--A Practitioner's Approach, 1997, Valuing Intangible Assets, 1998, Handbook of Advanced Business Valuation, 1999; editor, columnist Small Bus. Taxation, 1989-90, Bus. Valuation Rev., 1989-90, Jour. of Real Estate Acctg. and Taxation, 1991-93, Ohio CPA Jour., 1984-86, 91—, Jour. Property Taxation Mgmt., 1993—, Jour. Am. Bankruptcy Inst., 1993—; co-editor: Financial Valuation-Valuation of Business and Business Interests, 1997; contbr. more than 200 articles to profl. jours. Mem. AICPA, Am. Soc. Appraisers (mem. bd. examiners 1985-89), Nat. Assn. Real Estate Appraisers, Inst. Bus. Appraisers (life), Inst. Cert. Mgmt. Accts. (chpt. dir. 1976—), Inst. Property Taxation, Ill. Soc. CPAs, Ohio Soc. CPAs (chpt. dir. 1978-81), Accreditation Coun. Accountancy (accredited in fed. income taxation), Bus. Valuation Assn., Chgo. Soc. Investment Analysts, Inst. CFAs, Am. Bankruptcy Inst., Am. Econ. Assn., Nat. Assn. Bus. Economists, Appraisal Inst. Home: 310 Algonquin Rd Barrington IL 60010-6109 Office: 8600 W Bryn Mawr Ave Chicago IL 60631-3579

REIMAN, ROY J. publishing executive; Pub., founder Reiman Publs., Greendale, Wis., 1964—. Office: Reiman Publs 5400 S 60th St Greendale WI 53129-1404

REIMER, JUDY MILLS, pastor, religious executive; m. George G. Reimer, 1964; children: Todd, Troy. BA, Emory and Henry Coll., 1962; MDiv, Bethany Theol. Sem., 1994. Ordained into Set Apart Ministry, Ch. of the Brethren, 1994. Vol. Brethren Vol. Svc. NIH, Bethesda, Md., 1962-64, Hessish Lichtenau, Germany, 1964-65; elem. sch. tchr. Pub. and Private Schs., various cities, 1965-76; deacon Ch. of the Brethren, 1966—; mem Virlina Dist. Bd., 1978-90; chair of nurture com. Ch. of the Brethren Virlina Dist., 1979-82, chair of outdoor ministry, 1983-84, conf. speaker, 1992; founding pastor Ch. of the Brethren, Smith Mountain Lake, Va., 1996-98, gen. bd. exec. dir., 1998—; owner, sr. v.p. Harris Office Furniture Co., Roanoke, Va., 1976—. Co-chair and vice-chair of two Virlina Fin. Campaigns, Ch. of the Brethren, 1980s, mem. Gen. Bd., Ch. of Brethren, 1977-90; mem. PTA, United Way Allocation Com., Roanoke Valley Women Owners Assn. (charter mem.); adult advisor Nat. Youth Cabinet. 1991, 92; worship coord. Nat. Youth Conf. 1994 numerous other coms. for Ch. of Brethren; official observer for Nat. Coun. of Chs. at Nicaraguan Election, Feb., 1990; rep. of Ch. of the Brethren, 1989, Atlanta, The Torch of Conscience Campaign to sensitize congregation to the campaign to abolish death penalty; workshop leader across the denomination on leadership devel., pastor/spouse retreats, women's rallies, etc.; ann. conf. moderator elect, 1993-94. Mem. Inst. Indsl. Comml. Chaplains (chmn. bd. dirs. local unit, asst. treas. nat. bd.). Office: Church of the Brethren General Offices 1451 Dundee Ave Elgin IL 60120-1694

REIN, STANLEY MICHAEL, lawyer; b. St. Paul, Apr. 15, 1946; s. Clayton George Rein and Rose Gertrude (Mintz) Brown; m. Linda. R. Arnold; children: Gabriel Todd, Leah Suzanne. BA, U. Minn., 1968; JD cum laude, Harvard U., 1973. Bar: Minn. 1973, U.S. Tax Ct. 1973. Assoc. Dorsey & Whitney, LLP, Mpls., 1973-78; ptnr. Dorsey & Whitney LLP, 1979—. Mem. planned giving adv. coun. ARC Mpls. chpt., 1986, 88, planned giving adv. com. Minn. Pub. Radio, 1988-89; bd. dirs. South Metro Airport Action Council, Mpls., 1986, 87. With U.S. Army, 1968-70, Vietnam. Named in Best Lawyers in Am. Fellow Am. Coll. of Trust and Estate Counsel; mem. Minn. Bar Assn. (probate and trust law sect.), Hennepin County Bar Assn. (probate and trust law sect.), Phi Beta Kappa. Jewish. Avocations: reading, travel. Office: Dorsey & Whitney LLP 50 S 6th St Ste 1500 Minneapolis MN 55402-1498 E-mail: rein.stan@dorseylaw.com.

REINDL, JAMES, newspaper editor; Bur. chief AP, Chgo., 2000—. Office: 10 S Wacker Dr Ste 2500 Chicago IL 60606-7491

REINHARD, JOAO PEDRO, chemicals company executive; b. Sao Paulo, Brazil, Aug. 4, 1945; BA, MBA, Escola de Administracao de Empresas da Fundacao Vargas, Sao Paulo, Brazil, 1967. Fin. planning supr. Squibb do Brazil, Sao Paulo, 1968; credit mgr. Dow Quimica, 1970-72; fin. asst. Dow Latin Am., Miami, Fla., 1973; treas. Latin Am. Dow Lepetit Latin Am., 1974-76; corp. fin. planning mgr. The Dow Chem. Co., Midland, Mich., 1976-77; fin. dir. Dow Quimica S.Am., Sao Paulo, Brazil, 1978-80; treas. Dow Chem. Europe, Horgen, Switzerland, 1981-85; mng. dir. Dow Italy, Milan, 1985-87; v.p. Dow Europe, Horgen, Switzerland, 1985-87; treas. The Dow Chem. Co., Midland, Mich., 1988—, exec. v.p., CFO, 1995—. Bd. dirs. Liana Ltd., Midland, Mich., Dorinco Reinsurance Co., Midland, Dow Chem. Internat. BV, Midland, DCOMCO Inc., Midland, Dow Chm. Inter-Am. Ltd., Midland, Dow Chem. Internat. Inc. (Panama), Midland, , Dow Chem. Internat. Ltd., Midland, Midland Pipeline Corp., Dow Chem. Overseas Capital N.V., Midland, Bank Mendes Gans nv, Amsterdam, The Netherlands. Mem. Fin. Execs. Inst., Fin. Mgmt. Assn., Nat. Assn. Corp. Treasurers, Corp. Fin. Inst. Office: The Dow Chemical Co 2030 Dow Ctr Midland MI 48674-0001 E-mail: preinhard@dow.com.

REINHARD, SISTER MARY MARTHE, educational organization administrator; b. McKeesport, Pa., Aug. 29, 1929; d. Regis C. and Leona (Reese) R. AB, Notre Dame Coll.; MA, U. Notre Dame. Asst. prin. Regina H.S., Cleve., 1960-62, prin., 1963—65, Notre Dame Acad., Chardon, 1965-72; pres. Notre Dame Coll. of Ohio, Cleve., 1973-88; dir. devel. Sisters of Notre Dame Ednl. Ctr., Chardon, 1989—. Trustee, mem. exec. com. NCCJ, Cleve., 1987; mem. coun. Geagua United Way Svcs., 1990—97, vice chair fund raising, 1991—94, 1995—97; mem. adv. bd. Kent State U., Geauga campus, 1991—94; trustee Leadership Geauga, 1995—96; sec. Notre Dame Edn. Assn., 1990—98, pres., 1998—2001; mem. adv. bd. Regina H.S.; mem. distbn. com. McGinty Family Found., 1989—. Recipient Humanitarian award Cleve. chpt. NCCJ, 1990; named one of 100 most influential women in Cleve., Women's City Club, 1982, one of 79 most interesting people in Cleve., The Cleve. Mag., 1979; named Cleve. United Way Vol. of Yr., 1997, Woman of Yr., Notre Dame Coll. Ohio, 1989; elected to Hall of Excellence, Ohio Found. of Ind. Colls., 1996. Roman Catholic. Home and Office: 13000 Auburn Rd Chardon OH 44024-9331 E-mail: mreinhard@ndec.org.

REINHARD, PHILIP G. federal judge; b. LaSalle, Ill., Jan. 12, 1941; s. Godfrey and Ruth R.; married Virginia Reinhard; children: Bruce, Brian, David, Philip. BA, U. Ill., Champaign, 1962, JD, 1964. Asst. state atty. Winnebago County, 1964-67; atty. Hyer, Gill & Brown, 1967-68; state atty. Winnebago County, 1968-76; judge 17th Jud. Cir., 1976-80, Appellate Ct., 1980-92, U.S. Dist. Ct. (no. dist.) Ill., 1992—2001. Mem. security, space and facilities com. U.S. Jud. Conf. Mem. Am. Acad. Jud. Edn., Winnebago County Bar Assn. Office: US Courthouse 211 S Court St Rockford IL 61101-1219

REINHART, DIETRICH THOMAS, university president, history educator; b. Mpls., May 17, 1949; s. Donald Irving and Eleanor Therese (Noonan) R. BA in History, St. John's U., Collegeville, Minn., 1971; AM in History, Brown U., 1976, PhD in History, 1984. Benedictine monk St. John's Abbey, 1971—; prof. history St. John's U., 1981—, dean of the coll., 1988-91, pres., 1991—. Dir. liturgy St. John's Abbey, 1983-88. Bd. dirs. Minn. Pvt. Coll. Coun., 1991—, George A. MacPherson Fund, 1991—, Hill Monastic Manuscript Library, 1991—, Inst. for Ecumenical and Cultural Rsch., 1991—, First Am. Nat. Bank St. Cloud., 1992—; bd. overseers St. John's Prep. Sch., 1990—. Home: St Johns Abbey Collegeville MN 56321 Office: St John's U Office of Pres Collegeville MN 56321

REINHART, ROBERT ROUNTREE, JR. lawyer; b. Chgo., Oct. 21, 1947; s. Robert Rountree and Ruth (Duncan) R.; m. Elizabeth Aileen Plews, July 26, 1969; children: Andrea Jean, Jessica Elizabeth, Rebecca Jill. BA, Northwestern U., 1968; JD, U. Mich., 1971. Bar: Ill. 1971, Mich. 1972, Minn. 1973, U.S. Supreme Ct. 1976. Law clk. to judge U.S. Dist. Ct. (we. dist.) Mich., Grand Rapids, 1971-73; assoc. Oppenheimer Wolff & Donnelly, Mpls., 1973-77, ptnr., 1978-96, chair labor and employment bus. group, 1985-92; ptnr. Dorsey & Whitney, 1996—, chair labor and employment practice group, 2000—. Co-chmn. Upper Midwest Employment Law Inst., Mpls., 1984—; gen. counsel Minn. Empoyment Law Coun., 1990—. Mem. ABA (labor and employment, civil litigation sects.), Minn. Bar Assn. Office: Dorsey & Whitney Ste 1500 50 S 6th St Minneapolis MN 55402-1498 E-mail: reinhart.robert@dorseylaw.com.

REINKE, JOHN HENRY, educational administrator, clergyman; b. Covington, Ky., Sept. 14, 1915; s. Henry Tilden and Helena (Ungeheuer) R. B.A., Loyola U., 1937, M.A., 1942, postgrad., 1947-54, UCLA, 1948-49. Ordained priest Roman Cath. Ch., 1945; instr. psychology Loyola U., Chgo., 1947-54, vice chancellor, 1975-76, chancellor, 1976—; instr. psychology Xavier U., Cin., 1954-56, asst. prof., 1956-59; dir. guidance Loyola Acad., Wilmette, Ill., 1959-60, headmaster, 1960-65, pres., 1965-75; instr. music therapy Ind. U., Bloomington, summers 1958-60; trustee Regis Coll., Denver, 1973—, Xavier U., 1973—, Hadley Sch. for Blind, Winnetka, 1971—; chancellor emeritus Loyola U. of Chgo., Chgo., 1993—. Mem. Nat. Cath. Ednl. Assn., Nat. Sch. Public Relations Assn., Conf. Religious Dirs. Edn., Chgo. Art Inst., Field Mus., Nat. Assn. Ind. Schs., Jesuit Adminstrs. Assn., Nat. Cath. Guidance Conf. Clubs: Mid-Am, Internat, Plaza. Lodge: K.C. Achievements include 1st U.S. priest to appear as soloist with maj. symphony orch., Cin., 1956, 57, 60. Office: Loyola U 6525 N Sheridan Rd Chicago IL 60626-5385

REINKE, WILLIAM JOHN, lawyer; b. South Bend, Ind., Aug. 7, 1930; s. William August and Eva Marie (Hein) R.; m. Sue Carol Colvin, 1951 (div. 1988); children: Sally Sue Taelman, William A., Andrew J.; m. Elizabeth Beck Lockwood, 1991. AB cum laude, Wabash Coll., 1952; JD, U. Chgo., 1955. Bar: Ind. 1955. Assoc. Barnes & Thornburg and predecessors, South Bend, Ind., 1957-61, ptnr., 1961-96, of counsel, 1996—; former chmn. compensation com.; former mem. mgmt. com. Trustee Stanley Clark Sch., 1969-80, pres., 1977-80; mem. adv. bd. Salvation Army, 1973—, pres., 1990-92; bd. dirs. NABE Mich. chpt., 1990-94, pres. 1993-94, Isaac Walton League, 1970-81, United Way, 1979-81; pres. South Bend Round Table, 1963-65; trustee First Meth. Ch., 1976-70. Served with U.S. Army, 1955-57. Recipient Outstanding Local Pres. award Ind. Jaycees, 1960-61, Boss of Yr. award, 1979, South Bend Outstanding Young Man award, 1961. Mem. ABA, Ind. State Bar Assn., St. Joseph County Bar Assn., Ind. Bar Found. (patron fellow), Am. Judicature Soc., Ind. Soc. Chgo., Summit Club (past gov., founders com.), Rotary (bd. dirs. 1970-73, 94-97). Home: 51795 Waterton Square Cir Granger IN 46530-8317 Office: Barnes & Thornburg 1st Source Bank Ctr 100 N Michigan St Ste 600 South Bend IN 46601-1632

REINOEHL, RICHARD LOUIS, artist, scholar, martial artist; b. Omaha, Oct. 11, 1944; s. Louis Lawrence and Frances Margaret (Robinson) R.; 1 child, Joy Margaret Iroff-Reinoehl. BS in Sociology, Portland State U., 1970; MSW, U. Minn., Duluth, 1977; postgrad., Cornell U., 1984-88. Acting dir. Vanguard Group Homes, Virginia, Minn., 1976-77; dir. Minn. Chippewa Tribe Group Home, Duluth, 1978, Human Devel. Consortium, Minn., N.Y., Ohio, 1978—. Faculty Social Work Program U. Wis., Superior, 1981-84; adv. bd. Computers in Social Svcs. Network, 1982-85; mem. Com. on Internat. Social Welfare Edn., 1982-86, Am. Evaluation Assn., 1986-89; affiliate scholar Oberlin Coll., 1991—. Editor: Computer Literacy in Human Services Education, 1990, Computer Literacy in Human Services, 1990, Men of Achievement, 16th edit., 1993; mem. editorial bd. Computers in Human Svcs., 1983-96, 99, Jour. Technology in Human Scis., 1999—; assoc. editor book rev., 1996-99; contbr. numerous articles to profl. jours. Mem. Legis. Task Force Regional Alcoholism Bd., 1972-73, Assn. Drug Abuse, Prevention and Treatment, 1973-74, Minn. Pub. Health Assn., 1976-78, Minn. Social Svc. Assn., 1976-83, Wis. Coun. Social Work Edn., 1983-84, N.Y. State Coun. Family Rels., 1986-89, Nat. Coun. Family Rels., 1986-89; exec. bd. Duluth Community Action Program, 1982-83; Dem. precinct chair, Portland, Oreg., 1972-74; precinct vice-chair Dem. Farmer-Labor Party, Duluth, 1979-81, chair, 1981-83, 2d vice-chair exec. bd., 1981-83; mem. Zoning Appeals Bd., New Russia Twp., Ohio, 1996—; mem. art edn. com. Fireland Assn. Visual Arts, 1996-99; mem. land use planning com. New Russia Twp., Ohio, 1998—; chair Lorain County Comprehensive Plan Growth Mgmt. Com., 1999—; mem. Smart Devel. Coalition of Lorain County, 1998—, Lorain County Multi-Modal Transp. Planning Steering Com., 2000—, airport subcom., 2000—, roadways sub-com., 2000—, transit subcom., 2000—, info. tech. sub-com., 2000—. Mem. NASW (exec. com., chair program com. Arrowhead Region Minn. chpt., 1980-81, co-chair task force on computers in social work, 1981-82), Acad. Cert. Social Workers, Cornell U. Sailing Club (pres. 1990). Avocations: canoeing, antique Volkswagens, wilderness hiking. Office: Human Devel Consortium Inc 46180 Butternut Ridge Rd Oberlin OH 44074-9778 E-mail: richard.reinoehl@oberlin.edu.

REINSDORF, JERRY MICHAEL, professional sports teams executive, real estate executive, lawyer, accountant; b. Bklyn., Feb. 25, 1936; s. Max and Marion (Smith) Reinsdorf; m. Martyl F. Rifkin, Dec. 29, 1956; children: David Jason, Susan Janeen, Michael Andrew, Jonathan Milton. BA, George Washington U., 1957; JD, Northwestern U., 1960. Bar: D.C., Ill. 1960; CPA, Ill.; cert. specialist real estate securities, rev. appraiser; registered mortgage underwriter. Atty. staff regional counsel IRS, Chgo., 1960-64; assoc. law firm Chapman & Cutler, 1964-68; ptnr. Altman, Kurlander & Weiss, 1968-74; of counsel firm Katten, Muchin, Gitles, Zavis, Pearl & Galler, 1974-79; gen. ptnr. Carlyle Real Estate Ltd. Partnerships, 1971, 72; chmn. bd. Balcor Co., 1973-87; mng. ptnr. TBC Films, 1975-83; chmn. Chgo. White Sox, 1981—, Chgo. Bulls Basketball Team, 1985—; ptnr. Bojer Fin., 1987—. Lectr. John Marshall Law Sch., 1966-68; former bd. dirs. Shearson Lehman Bros., Inc., Project Academus of DePaul U., Chgo., Sports Immortals Mus., 1987-89, Com. Commemorate U.S. Constn., 1987; bd. dirs. La Salle Nat. Bank, La Salle Nat. Corp.; bd. overseers Inst. for Civil Justice, 1996-98; lectr. in real estate, sports and taxation. Author: (with L. Herbert Schneider) Uses of Life Insurance in Qualified Employee Benefit Plans, 1970. Co-chmn. Ill. Profls. for Senator Ralph Smith, 1970; mem. Chgo. region bd. Anti-Defamation League, 1986-2001; mem., trustee Ill. Inst. Tech., 1991-96; mem. Ill. Commn. on African-Am. Males, 1992—; bd. dirs. Chgo. Youth Success Found., 1992—, Corp. for Supportive Housing, 1995—; nat. trustee Northwestern U., 1993—; bd. govs. Hugh O'Brian Youth Found.; mem. internat. adv. bd. Barrow Neurol. Found., 1996-97; Chgo. Baseball Cancer Charities, 1994, 98; bd. trustees Equity Office Properties, 1997—. Recipient Hallmark award Chgo. Baseball Cancer Charities, 1986, Corp. Superstar award Ill. chpt. Cystic Fibrosis Found., 1988, Sportsman of Yr. award, 1994, Chicagoan of Yr. award Chgo. Park Dist., 1990, Kellogg Excellence award, 1991, Cmty. Hero award Interfaith Organizing Project, 1991, Operation Push Bridgebuilder award, 1992, Alumni Merit award Northwestern U., 1992, Ellis Island Medal of Honor award Nat. Ethnic Coalition of Orgns., 1993, Lifetime Achievement award March of Dimes, 1994, Hallmark Hall of Fame Civic award Ind. Sports Charities, 1994, Am. Spirit award USAF, 1995, Alpha Epsilon Pi Arthur and Simiteich Outstanding Alumnus award, 1995, Order of Lincoln, 1997, Mayor's medal Hon., 1997, Bklyn. Businessman of Yr., 1997; inductee B'nai B'rith Nat. Jewish Am. Sports Hall of Fame, 1994, Chgo. Sports Hall of Fame, 1997, Guardian of Children award Jewsih Coun. for Youth Svc., 1998. Mem.: FBA, ABA, Nat. Assn. Rev. Appraisers and Mortgage Underwriters, Nat. Sports Lawyers Assn., Chgo. Bar Assn., Ill. Bar Assn., Northwestern U. Law Sch. Alumni Assn. (bd. dirs.), Order of Coif, Comml. Club Chgo., Omega Tau Rho. Office: Chgo White Sox 333 W 35th St Chicago IL 60616-3651

REINSMA, HAROLD LAWRENCE, design consultant, engineer; b. Slayton, Minn., Sept. 6, 1928; s. Frank and Ida M. (Zabel) R.; m. Julia A. Tusek, Oct. 18, 1958; children: Frank, Michael, Diane. Student, Macalester Coll., 1948-50; BCE, U. Minn., 1953. Registered profl. engr., Ill. Cons. engr. GM Orr Engring. Co., Mpls., 1953-54; rsch. test engr. Caterpillar Tractor Co., Peoria, Ill., 1955-58, rsch. design engr., 1958-71, rsch. project engr., 1971-73, rsch. supervising engr., 1973-76, rsch. staff engr., 1976-91; design cons. Dunlap, 1991—. Achievements include 44 patents including 1st viable sealed and lubricated track, fundamental to success of a new generation of large high performance elevated sprocket tractors, also sealed maintenance-free linkage and large diameter high speed pressure balanced oil cooled brake wheel seals for mining trucks, all used in abrasive environments. Avocations: skiing, cycling, hiking, gardening. Home and Office: 13600 Lucerne Dr Dunlap IL 61525-9619

REISCH, MICHAEL STEWART, social work educator; b. N.Y.C., Mar. 4, 1948; s. Joseph and Charlotte (Rosenberg) R.; m. Amy Jane Lewis, May 21, 1972; children: Jennifer, Nikki. BA in History with highest honors, NYU, 1968; PhD in History with distinction, SUNY, Binghamton, 1975; MSW with honors, CUNY, 1979. Youth worker Washington-Heights-Inwood YM-YWHA, N.Y.C., 1965-66; editor, columnist Heights Daily News, Bronx, N.Y., 1966-68; rsch./teaching asst. SUNY, Binghamton, 1970-72; unit dir., program cons. Child Study Assn.-Wel Met, Inc., N.Y.C., 1970-72; asst. dir. youth div. Mosholu-Montefiore Community Ctr., Bronx, 1972-73; project dir. Silberman Found./N.Y. Assn. Deans, N.Y.C., 1973-74; asst. dean Sch. Social Welfare, asst. prof. SUNY, Stony Brook, 1974-79; asst. prof., then assoc. prof. Sch. Social Work U. Md., Balt., 1979-86; dir. Sch. Social Work, prof. social work/pub. adminstrn. San Francisco State U., 1986-95; prof. social work U. Pa., Phila., 1995-99, U. Mich., Ann Arbor, 1999—. Cons. and spkr. in field. Co-author: From Charity to Enterprise, 1989 (Social Sci. Book of Month), Social Work in the 21st Century, 1997, The Road Not Taken, 2001; editor, author various books in field; contbr. articles to profl. publs., chpts. in books. Cons. to numerous local, state, and fed. polit. campaigns, 1971—; mem. Gov.'s Adv. Coun. Human Resources, Md., 1983-86; pres. Welfare Advs., Md., 1983-86; campaign mgr. Rep. Barbara Mikulski, Balt., 1982; bd. dirs. Coleman Advs. for Children and Youth, 1987-95, San Francisco Internat. Program, 1987-95, Calif. Social Work Edn. Ctr., 1991-95, Ctr. for S.E. Asian Refugee Resettlement, 1992-95, Am. Jewish Congress, N. Calif., 1994-95, Coun. Internat. Programs, 1995, Phila. Citizens for Children and Youth, 1997-99; chair Children's Budget Task Force City of San Francisco, 1989-92; mem. Mayor's Adv. Coun. on Drug Abuse, San Francisco, 1988-91; mem. steering com. Poverty Action Alliance, 1993-95; mem. adv. com. Montreal Consortium for Human Rights Advocacy, 1995—. Woodrow Wilson Found. fellow, 1972-73. Mem. NASW (del. 1990-92, 94-96, chair peace and justice com. 1992-97), Coun. on Social Work Edn. (com. on status of women 1989-92, bd. dirs. 1993-97, chair commn. on ednl. policy 1994-97), Am. Hist. Assn., Social Welfare Action Alliance, Soc. for Social Work Rsch., Assn. for Advancement of Social Work with Groups, Assn. Cmty. Orgns. and Social Adminstrn. Avocations: travel, hiking, cooking, swimming, creative writing. E-mail: mreisch@umich.edu.

REISING, RICHARD P. lawyer; BA, Stanford U.; JD, U. Mo. Bar: Ill. 1970. Asst. gen. counsel, sec. Archer-Daniels-Midland Co., Decatur, Ill., v.p., sec., gen. counsel, 1991-97, sr. v.p., 1997—. Office: Archer-Daniels-Midland Co 4666 E Faries Pky Decatur IL 62526-5666

REITEMEIER, RICHARD JOSEPH, physician; b. Pueblo, Colo., Jan. 2, 1923; s. Paul John and Ethel Regina (McCarthy) Reitemeier; m. Patricia Claire Mulligan, July 21, 1951; children: Mary Louise, Paul, Joseph, Susan, Robert, Patrick, Daniel. AB, U. Denver, 1944; MD, U. Colo., 1946; MS in Internal Medicine, U. Minn., 1954. Diplomate Am. Bd. Internal Medicine . Intern Corwin Hosp., Pueblo, 1946—47; resident Henry Ford Hosp., Detroit, 1949—50, Mayo Found., Rochester, Minn., 1950—53; cons. internal medicine and gastroenterology Mayo Clinic, 1954—87; chmn. dept. internal medicine Mayo Clinic (Mayo Clinic and Mayo Med. Sch.), 1967—74, prof., 1971—; bd. govs. Mayo Clinic, 1970—74. Gov. Am. Bd. Internal Medicine , 1971—79, chmn., 1978—79, rep. to Federated Council Internal Medicine , 1977—80, 1983—84, accreditation council grad. med. edn. , 1979—85, chmn., 1982—83; governing bd. Am. Bd. Med. Specialties, 1983—86; sci. and med. dir. Ludwig Inst. Cancer Rsch., 1987—88; cons. Kaiser Family Med. Found., 1989—90; med. dir. Phoenix Alliance Inc., 1990—93. Author (with C.G. Moertel): Advanced Gastrointestinal Cancer, Clinical Management and Chemotherapy, 1969; contbr. articles to profl. jours. Trustee Mayo Found., 1970—74, St. Mary's Hosp., Rochester, 1976—82. With U.S. Army, 1947—49. Recipient Alumni award, U. Colo. Sch. Medicine, Irving Cutter award, Phi Rho Sigma, 1986, Disting. Alumnus award, Mayo Found., 1997. Master: ACP (regent 1979—82, gov. for Minn. 1975—79, pres. 1983—84, Alfred Stengel Meml. award 1990); fellow: AMA, Nat. Bd. Med. Examiners (treas. 1987—89), Am. Assn. Study Liver Disease, Am. Assn. Cancer Rsch., Inst. Medicine, Coun. Med. Splty. Socs., Am. Soc. Clin. Oncology, Am. Fedn. Clin. Rsch., Am. Clin. and Climatol. Assn., Am. Gastroenterol. Assn.; mem.: Alpha Omega Alpha. Republican. Roman Catholic. Home: 707 12th Ave SW Rochester MN 55902-2027 Office: 200 1st Ave SW Rochester MN 55902-3129

REITER, MICHAEL A. lawyer, educator; b. Pitts., Nov. 15, 1941; BS, U. Wis., 1963, MS, 1964, JD, 1967, PhD, 1969. Bar: Wis. 1967, Ill. 1975, U.S. Supreme Ct. 1975. Ptnr. Holleb & Coff, Chgo., 1987-99, Duane Morris LLC, Chgo., 1999—. Adj. prof. law Northwestern U., Chgo., 1977—99; mem. faculty Nat. Inst. Trial Advocacy, 1980—. Office: Duane Morris LLC 227 W Monroe St Ste 3400 Chicago IL 60606-5098

REITER, ROBERT EDWARD, banker; b. Kansas City, Mo., Dec. 27, 1943; s. Robert Vincent and Helen Margaret (Petrus) R.; m. Mary J. Darby, June 20, 1964; children: Mollie K., Jennifer M., Ellen R., Robert E. Jr. BA, Rockhurst Coll., 1964; JD, St. Louis U., 1967; LLM, U. Mo., Kansas City, 1969. Bar: Mo. 1967. Assoc. atty. Burke, Jackson & Millin, Kansas City, 1967-69; personal trust adminstr. City Nat. Bank and Trust Co., 1969-71; estate planning officer United Mo. Bank of Kansas City, 1971-73, v.p., 1973-80, sr. v.p., 1980-85; exec. v.p. UMB Bank, N.A., 1985—. Pres., corp. bd. Seton Ctr., Kansas City, 1992-95. Contbr. articles to profl. jours. Bd. of Counselors St. Joseph Health Ctr., Kansas City, 1977-85; pres. St. Joseph Health Ctr. Adv. Coun., Kansas City, 1985-86; treas., bd. trustees Endowment Trust Fund for Cath. Edn., 1989—; bd. regents Rockhurst U., 1999—, mem. planned giving coun., 1999—; mem. Diocesan Housing Cmty. Svcs. Commn. Grantee St. Louis U. Sch. of Law, 1964-67. Mem. Mo. Bar Assn., Kansas City Bar Assn. (chmn. employee benefits com. 1989-90), Employee Benefit Inst. (adv. bd. 1986—, chmn. 1989), Estate Planning Soc. Kansas City (pres. 1985-86), Serra Club of Kansas City (v.p. 1987-89). Home: 1024 W 70th St Kansas City MO 64113-2004 Office: UMB Bank NA 1010 Grand Blvd PO Box 419692 Kansas City MO 64141-6692

REITER, STANLEY, economist, educator; b. N.Y.C., Apr. 26, 1925; s. Frank and Fanny (Rosenberg) R.; m. Nina Sarah Breger, June 13, 1944; children: Carla Frances, Frank Joseph. AB, Queens Coll., 1947; MA, U. Chgo., 1950, PhD, 1955. Rsch. assoc. Cowles Commn., U. Chgo., 1948-50; mem. faculty Stanford U., 1950-54, Purdue U., 1954-67; prof. econs. and math. Northwestern U., 1967—, now Morrison prof. econs. and math. Coll. Arts and Scis., Morrison prof. managerial econs. and decision scis. Kellogg Grad. Sch. Mgmt. Dir. Ctr. for Math. Studies in Econs. and Mgmt. Sci.; cons. in field. Trustee Roycemore Sch., Evanston, Ill., 1969-71, treas., 1970-71. Served with inf. AUS, 1943-45. Decorated Purple Heart. Fellow Econometric Soc., AAAS; mem. Soc. Indsl. and Applied Math., Inst. Mgmt. Scis., Ops. Rsch. Soc. Am., Am. Math. Soc., Math. Assn. Am., Am. Acad. of Arts and Scis. Home: 2138 Orrington Ave Evanston IL 60201-2914 Office: Northwestern U Ctr for Math Studies 2001 Sheridan Rd Evanston IL 60208-0814 E-mail: s-reiter@northwestern.edu.

REITMAN, JERRY IRVING, advertising agency executive; b. Phila., Jan. 9, 1938; s. Benjamin and Ruth (Eisenberg) R.; m. Monica Birgitta Hall, Oct. 27, 1968; children: Jennifer Sharon, Sarah Beth. BS in Fin., Pa. State U., 1961. Exec. v.p., CEO Brit. Pubs., N.Y.C. and London, 1965-69; pres., pub. Acad. Media, Sherman Oaks, Calif., 1969-73; v.p. Pubs. Clearing House, Port Washington, N.Y., 1973-78; exec. v.p. Ogilvy & Mather, N.Y.C., 1978-81; with Scali, McCabe, Sloves, Inc., 1981-86; pres. Scali, McCabe, Sloves Direct; chmn. bd. dirs. The Reitman Group, 1986-87; exec. v.p The Leo Burnett Co., Chgo., 1986-96; pres., CEO, vice chair Internat. Data Response Corp., 1996—. Dir. Scandinavian Airlines Sys. Pub./Distbn. Svcs.; mem. adv. bd. Ill. Dept. Trade and Tourism, 1988—; internat. awards chmn., bd. dirs. John Caples Internat., 1989—; mem. Internat. Direct Mktg. Symposium, Zürich, Switzerland. Author: A Common Sense Approach to Small Business, 1968, Beyond 2000: The Future of Direct Marketing, 1994; contbr. articles to profl. jours. Trustee Locust Valley Libr. Assn., N.Y., 1982—; exec. com. mem. Pub. Hall of Fame, 1987—; bd. govs. Children's Miracle Network, 1992—, vice chmn., chmn. bd. govs., 1998—, 1999-2001; bd. dirs. Children's Meml. Found. Telethon, The Direct Mktg. Ednl. Found., exec, dir., 1996—. Anderson scholar, 1960; recipient Key to City, New Orleans, 1959, Silver Apple award N.Y. Direct Mktg. Club, 1989, Ed Mayer award Ednl. Found., 1996, Charles S. Downs award, 1997. Fellow Psychiat. Re-Edn. Assn.; mem. Am. Mktg. Assn. (at-large mem., 2000, bd. dirs.), Direct Mktg. Assn. (bd. mem. ethics com. 1984), Creative Guild (dir. 1984), Internat. Direct Mktg. Assn. (bd. dirs. 1981-82), Publ. Hall of Fame (exec. com. 1988—), Direct Mktg. Club N.Y. (pres. 1983-84), Beta Gamma Sigma, Delta Sigma Pi. Avocations: tennis; old car restoration; classical woodworking. Home and Office: Callahan Group LLC 2204 N Leavitt St Chicago IL 60647-3204 E-mail: jireitman@aol.com.

REITMAN, ROBERT STANLEY, business consultant, nonprofit agency advisor; b. Fairmont, W.Va., Nov. 18, 1933; s. Isadore and Freda A. (Layman) R.; m. Sylvia K. Golden, Dec. 24, 1955; children: Scott Alan, Alayne Louise. BS in Acctg., W.Va. U., 1955; JD, Case Western Res. U., 1958. Bar: Ohio 1958. Mem. firm Burke, Haber & Berick, Cleve., 1958-60, ptnr., 1960-68; exec. v.p., vice chmn. Tranzonic Cos. (formerly AAV Cos.), Pepper Pike, Ohio, 1968-70, pres., vice-chmn., 1970-73, chief exec. officer, pres., vice chmn., 1973-82, pres., chmn., CEO, 1982-98, chmn. emeritus, bd. dirs., 1998—; prin. Riverbend Advisors, 1998—. Mem. bus. adv. com. Mandel Ctr. for non-profit Orgn. Case We. Res. U., 1995-99, vis. com. Weatherhead Sch. of Bus., 1995—, vis. com. Sch. of Law, 1998—, chmn. Dean's Nat. Adv. Com., Sch. of Law, 1997-98; mem. pvt. banking adv. bd. Key Bank, N.A., 1997--. Mem. Rep. fin. com., Cuyahoga County, 1968-78; mem. Com. for Econ. Growth for Israel, Cleve., 1977-80, pres., 1978-80; mem. adv. coun. Cleve. Mus. Nat. History, 1982-85, Cleve. Opera, 1977—; del. Coun. of Jewish Fedns., N.Y.C., 1981-97; gen. co-chmn. Jewish Welfare Fund, Cleve., 1975-78, 81-85, gen. vice chmn., 1985-89, gen. chmn., 1989-91; sect. and div. chmn., team capt. United Way Svcs., 1974-97, mem. del. assembly, 1976-85, trustee, 1977-83, 84-90, 91—, v.p., 1985-88, chmn. nominating. com., 1988-90, campaign chmn., 1993, chair fund raising planning com., 1994-97, chair bd. trustees, 1997-2000, life trustee, 2000—; mem. employment com. Jewish Vocat. Svc., Cleve., 1974-83; bd. dirs. Capital for Israel, Inc., N.Y.C., 1986-87; nat. vice chmn. United Jewish Appeal, 1987-92, nat. allocations chmn., 1987-90, trustee, 1988-94, chair retirement fund com., 1994-97; trustee B'nai B'rith Hillel Found., 1975-81, Cleve. Jewish News, 1976-79, Ednl. TV Sta. WVIZ, Cleve., 1976-99, vice chmn. 1986-90, chmn. bd., 1990-97, immediate past chair, 1997-99, chair emeritus, 1999—; trustee, pres. Bus. Volunteerism Coun., 1994-96, chmn. 1996-97; trustee Jewish Cmty. Fedn. Cleve., 1983-98, 1999—, treas., 1991-94, v.p., 1995-97, Jewish Edn. Ctr. of Cleve., 1993-96, Cleve. Zool. Soc., 1972—, pres., 1979-87, chmn., 1987-92, chmn. emeritus, 1992—, chmn. JDC-Brookdale Inst. of Gerontology and Human Devel. (Israel), 1995; trustee Am. Jewish Joint Distbn. Com., 1988-96, 97—, United Israel Appeal, 1987-94, Mt. Sinai Med. Ctr., Cleve., 1976-96, chmn., 1982-85; trustee Cleve. State U. Devel. Found., 1988-89, Greater Cleve. Roundtable, 1991—; trustee The Wilds, 1995-99, adv. bd., 1999—, trustee, The Mt. Sinai Health Care Foundation, 1995—, vice chair 1998-2001, chair, 2001—. Mem. The 50 Club Cleve., Case We. Res. Univ. Sch. of Law Soc. Benchers, Am. Kennel Club (regional del. 1960-75), We. Res. Kennel Club (officer, trustee 1959-75), Beechmont Club (fin. com. 1972-80, house com. 1974), Pepper Pike Club, Union Club, Carambola Golf Club, Masons, Zeta Beta Tau, Tau Epsilon Rho. Avocations: golf, swimming, pure-bred dogs. Office: Riverbend Advisors 2087 Chagrin River Rd Gates Mills OH 44040-9740 E-mail: rsrform@megsinet.net.

REJAI, MOSTAFA, political science educator; b. Tehran, Iran, Mar. 11, 1931; came to U.S., 1954; s. Taghi and Forough (Lashgari) R. AA, Pasadena City Coll., 1957; BA, Calif. State U., L.A., 1959, MS, 1961; PhD, UCLA, 1964. Teaching fellow UCLA, 1963-64; asst. prof. polit. sci. Miami U., Oxford, Ohio, 1964-67, assoc. prof., 1967-70, prof., 1970-83, Disting. prof., 1983—. Vis. scholar Ctr. for Internat. Affairs, Harvard U., 1972, Hoover Instn. on War, Revolution and Peace, Stanford U., 1973, Inst. Internat. Studies, Iran, 1974-75; vis. prof. Western Coll., Oxford, 1971, 72. Author: World Military Leaders: A Collective and Comparative Analysis, 1996, The Strategy of Political Revolution, 1973, The Comparative Study of Revolutionary Strategy, 1977, Comparative Political Ideologies, 1984; (with Kay Phillips) Leaders of Revolution, 1979, World Revolutionary Leaders, 1983, Loyalists and Revolutionaries: Political Leaders Compared, 1988, Demythogizing an Elite: American Presidents in Empirical, Comparative, and Historical Perspectives, 1993, World Military Leaders: A Collective and Comparative Analysis, 1996, Leaders and Leadership: An Appraisal of Theory and Research, 1997, The Young George Washington in Psychobiographical Perspective, 2000, Political Ideologies: A Comparative Approach, 1991, 2d edit., 1995; editor, contbr.: Democracy: The Contemporary Theories, 1967, Decline of Ideology?, 1971; editor: Mao Tse-Tung on Revolution and War, 1969, rev. edit., 1970; assoc. editor Jour. Polit. and Mil. Sociology, 1973—; contbr. articles to profl. jours., book chpts. Recipient Outstanding Teaching award Miami U., 1970. Mem. Am. Polit. Sci. Assn. (polit. psychology sect.), Am. Sociol. Assn. (polit. soc. sect.), Internat. Polit. Sci. Assn., Internat. Soc. Polit. Psychology, Internat. Studies Assn., Inter-Univ. Seminar on Armed Forces and Soc., Conf. for Study Polit. Thought, Midwest Polit. Sci. Assn., So. Polit. Sci. Assn., Wesetern Polit. Sci. Assn., Pi Gamma Mu, Pi Sigma Alpha. Office: Miami U Dept of Political Science Oxford OH 45056

REKSTIS, WALTER J., III, lawyer; b. San Diego, 1945; BBA, U. Cin., 1968, JD, 1972. Bar: Ohio 1972. Ptnr. Squire, Sanders & Dempsey, Cleve. Office: Squire Sanders & Dempsey 4900 Key Tower 127 Public Sq Cleveland OH 44114-1304

RELIAS, JOHN ALEXIS, lawyer; b. Chgo., Apr. 2, 1946; s. Alexis John and Marie Helen (Metos) R.; m. Linda Ann Pontious, Nov. 27, 1971; children: Anne, Alexandra. BA, Northwestern U., Evanston, 1968; LLB, Northwestern U., Chgo., 1972. Bar: Ill., 1972, U.S. Dist. Ct. (no. dist.) Ill. 1972, U.S. Ct. Appeals (9th cir.) 1981, U.S. Ct. Appeals (7th cir.) 1983, U.S. Supreme Ct. 1997. Assoc. Vedder, Price, Kaufman & Kammholz, Chgo., 1972-78, ptnr., 1979-94, Franczek, Sullivan, Mann, Crement, Hein & Relias, Chgo., 1994—. Mem. bd. edn. Wilmette (Ill.) Sch. Dist. 39, 1989-97, 2001—, pres., 1992-93, 1995-96. Mem. Nat. Assn. Sch. Attys., Ill. Assn. Sch. Attys., Order of the Coif, Phi Beta Kappa. Greek Orthodox. Home: 2500 Kenilworth Ave Wilmette IL 60091-1337 Office: Franczek Sulian Mann Crement Hein & Relias 300 S Wacker Dr Chicago IL 60606-6680

RELLE, ATTILA TIBOR, dentist, geriodontist; b. Columbus, Ohio, Aug. 31, 1959; s. Ferenc Matyas and Trudi (Tubach) R.; m. Kim Ann McDonald, Apr. 26, 1986; 1 dau., Ilona. DDS, Case Western Reserve U., 1985; BS, Ohio State U., 1985, postgrad., 1985-88, 93, Wright State U. Sch. Medicine, 1988-93. Dentist Mobile Care Corp., Dublin, 1985; assoc. dentist Richard P. Deeds, DDS and Assocs., Columbus, 1985-86; dentist Family Dental and Denture Ctr. II, Dayton, Ohio, 1986-87; geriodontist Midwest Mobile Dental Care, Inc., Hamilton, 1988-91, Mobile Dental Care, Inc., Hamilton, 1991-92; dentist/owner Attila T. Relle, DDS and Assocs., Columbus, 1985—, Attila T. Relle, DDS & Assocs., Hilliard, 1995—; dentist Jerry Owens, D.D.S. and Assocs., Lancaster, Ohio, 1989-92; state dir. Ohio Residentcare dental geriatric program Meridian Svc. Care Corp. of Ohio, 1992-94, dentist/geriodontist, 1992-94. Co-chmn. Ohio Dental Careers Day, Columbus, 1980-81; regional dir. Midwest Mobile Dental Care, Inc., 1988-89; mem. adv. com. N.Am. Health Corp., 1989-92; sci. judge Ohio Acad. Sci., Delaware, 1985-92. Mem. Civitan Internat. (pres. Eastern Columbus Club 1986-87). Presbyterian. Avocations: tennis, snow skiing, soccer, string instruments, ice skating, aviation. Home: 5203 Carifa Ct Hilliard OH 43026-9589 Office: Attila T Relle DDS & Assocs 5203 Carifa Ct Hilliard OH 43026-9589 also: 4984 Scioto Darby Rd Ste 100 Hilliard OH 43026-1550 Business E-mail: relle.core@core.com.

RELLE, FERENC MATYAS, chemist; b. Gyor, Hungary, June 13, 1922; came to U.S., 1951, naturalized, 1956; s. Ferenc and Elizabeth (Netratics) R.; m. Gertrud B. Tubach, Oct. 9, 1946; children: Ferenc, Ava, Attila. BSChemE, MS, Jozsef Nador Poly. U., Budapest, Hungary, 1944. Lab. mgr. Karl Kohn Ltd. Co., Landshut, Germany, 1947-48; resettlement officer Internat. Refugee Orgn., Munich, 1948-51; chemist Farm Bur. Coop. Assn., Columbus, Ohio, 1951-56; indsl. engr. N.Am. Aviation, Inc., 1956-57; rsch. chemist Keever Starch Co., 1957-65, Ross Labs. divsn. Abbott Labs., Columbus, 1965-70, rsch. scientist, 1970-89; cons. in field. Chmn. Columbus and Ctrl. Ohio UNWeek, 1963; pres. Berwick Manor Civic Assn., 1968; trustee Stelios Stelson Found., 1968-69; deacon Brookwood Presbyn. Ch., 1963-65, 92-93, trustee, 1990-91. Decorated knight St. Stanislaus Order. Mem. Am. Chem. Soc. (alt. councilor 1973, chmn. long range planning com. Columbus sect. 1972-76, 78-80), Am. Assn. Cereal Chemists (chmn. Cin. sect. 1974-75), Ohio Acad. Sci., Arpad Acad. (gold medl mem.), Internat. Tech. Inst. (adv. dir. 1977-82), Nat. Intercollegiate Soccer Ofcls. Assn., Am. Hungarian Assn., Hungrian Cultural Assn. (pres. 1978-81), Ohio Soccer Ofcls. Assn., Columbus Mannerchor, Germania Singing and Sport Soc., Civitans (gov. Ohio dist. 1970-71, dist. treas. 1982-83, pres. Ea. Columbus 1963-64, 72-73, gen. sec. for Hungary 1991-92, Ea. European growth mgr. 1993-94, amb. at large 1994—, established 1st Civitan club in Hungary 1991, Ukrina 1992, Solvakia 1994, Internat. Gov. of Yr. awardd 1971, Internat. Honor Key 1992, master club builder award 1992, various other awards), World Fedn. Hungarian Engrs. Home and Office: 3487 Roswell Dr Columbus OH 43227-3560

RELWANI, NIRMAL MURLIDHAR (NICK RELWANI), mechanical engineer; b. Bombay, Aug. 9, 1954; came to the U.S., 1976; m. Prema Vasandani; children: Karuna, Daksh. BS in Mech. Engring., U. Baroda, 1976; student, U. Nebr., 1977-78; MS in Mech. Engring., U. Wis., Milw., 1980. Registered profl engr., Wis., Ill. Rsch. asst. dept. mech. engring. U. Nebr., Lincoln, 1978; design engr. Allis Chalmers Corp., Milw., 1978-80; engring. cons. Bombay, 1980-86; assoc. engr. IIT Rsch. Inst., Chgo., 1986; mech. engr. Gen. Energy Corp., Oak Park, Ill., 1987-89, Arrowhead Environ. Control, Chgo., 1989-90; environ. engr. Ill. Dept. Pub. Health, Bellwood, 1990-92; sr. environ. protection engr. field ops. sect. bur. air Ill. EPA, Maywood, 1992—. Recipient Cert. of appreciation Ill. EPA, 1993, 94. Mem. ASME, ASHRAE (energy conservation award 1991), Assn. Energy Engrs. (sr.). Home: 1806 Marne Rd (River Bend) Bolingbrook IL 60490-4589

RELYEA, CARL MILLER, hydrologist; b. Claverack, N.Y., Dec. 29, 1912; s. Charles Miller Croswell and Edna (Pulver) R.; m. Harriet Watson, Sept. 6, 1946 (dec. Nov. 1982); children: Richard, Deborah, Cornelia. AB, Columbia Coll., 1935; MA, Columbia U., 1938; postgrad., MIT, 1943. Organist, choirmaster Morrow Meml. Ch., Maplewood, N.J., 1937-41; meteorologist Air Corps, Pan Am., Weather Bur., Bermuda, 1946-48, Weather Bur., JFK Internat. Airport, N.Y., 1948-50; hydrologist Ohio River Forecast Ctr., Cin., 1950-65, hydrologist-in-charge, 1965-77; ret., 1977; dep. dir. Hamilton County Emergency Mgmt. Agy., Cin., 1979-2000. Contbr. articles to profl. jours. Organist Highland United Meth. Ch., Fort Thomas, Ky., 1962-99, now organist emeritus; clk. of vestry Grace Episcopal Ch., Cin. Capt. U.S. Army Air Corps, 1943-46. Recipient Pub. Svc. cert. Hamilton County Disaster Coun., Cin., 1990. Mem. Ret. Engrs. and Scientists Cin. (chmn. 1984-86), N.Y. Acad. Scis., Columbia U. Club N.Y., Downtown Kiwanis Club. Republican. Avocations: travel, music, organist, home maintenance. Home: 1346 Teakwood Ave Cincinnati OH 45224-2126 Office: Vol Hamilton County Emergency Mgmt Agy 2377 Civic Center Dr Cincinnati OH 45231-1305

REMINGER, RICHARD THOMAS, lawyer, artist; b. Cleve., Apr. 3, 1931; s. Edwin Carl and Theresa Henrietta (Bookmyer) Reminger; m. Billie Carmen Greer, June 26, 1954; children: Susan Greer, Patricia Allison, Richard Thomas. AB, Case-Western Res. U., 1953; JD, Cleve. State U., 1957. Bar: Ohio 1957, Pa. 1978, U.S. Supreme Ct. 1961. Pers. and safety dir. Motor Express, Inc., Cleve., 1954-58; mng. ptnr. Reminger & Reminger Co., L.P.A., 1958-90. Mem. nat. claims coun. adv. bd. Comml. Union Assurance Co., 1980—90; lectr. transp. law Fenn Coll., 1960—62; lectr. bus. law Case Western Res. U., 1962—64; lectr. products liability U. Wirtschaft at Schloss Gracht, Erfstadt-Liblar, Germany, 1990—91, Bar Assn. City of Hamburg, Germany, 1990; mem. faculty Nat. Inst. Trial Advocacy, 1992. Trustee Cerebral Palsy Assn., 1984—87, Cleve. Zool. Soc., Andrew Sch., 1984—96, Meridia Huron Hosp., Cleve., 1978—96, Cleve. Sch. Blind, 1987—88, Intracoastal Health Sys., Palm Beach, Fla., 1992—2000; mem. joint com. Cleve. Acad. Medicine-Greater Cleve. Bar Assn.; v.p. Cleve. Zool. Soc. With AC USNR, 1950—58. Mem.: ATLA, FBA, ABA (profl. responsiblity com. 1977—90, com. law and medicine), Palm Beach County Bar Assn., Internat. Ins. Law Soc., 8th Jud. Bar Assn. (life Ohio dist.), Am. Coll. Law and Medicine, Maritime Law Assn., Def. Rsch. Inst., Am. Judicature Soc., Ohio Assn. Civil Trial Attys., Soc. Ohio Hosp. Attys., Am. Soc. Hosp. Attys., Cleve. Assn. Civil Trial Attys., Transp. Lawyers Assn., Cleve. Bar Assn. (prof. liability com. 1977—90, chmn. med. legal com. 1978—79), Pa. Bar Assn., Ohio Bar Assn. (coun. dels. 1987—90, internat. law com. 1990—91), Internat. Bar Assn., Fedn. Ins. and Corp. Counsel, Internat. Soc. Marine Painters (profl. mem., v.p.), Oil Painters Am., Soc. Four Arts, Cleve.-Marshall Law Alumni Assn. (hon. trustee 1980—), Univ. Club (N.Y.C.), Salmagundi Club (N.Y.C.), Rolling Rock Club (Pa.), Kirtland Country Club, Everglades Club, Lost Tree Club (bd. govs. 1991—94), Hermit Club (pres. 1973—75), Union Club, Mayfield Country Club 1980—82, Case Res. Athletic Club (life). E-mail: monhegan1@aol.com.

RENARD, PAUL STEVEN, music educator; b. N.Y.C., May 5, 1934; s. Joseph Maurice and Elsie (Wolpow) R. Student, Miami (Fla.) Conservatory, 1947-48, Sch. of Am. Music, 1950-51; cert., Ida Elkan Sch. of Music, 1958. Staff concert organist Hammond Organ Co., N.Y.C., 1950-74; staff organist various TV stas., 1952-61, King Records and Riverside Records, N.Y.C., 1955-64; staff organist, ednl. dir. Lyon-Healy Music Co., Chgo., 1962-72; founder, dir. Paul Renard's Music Dynamics, 1972—. Cons. in field. Co-inventor first electric piano, Wurlitzer Mus. Instruments Co., 1953-54; author (software) Paul Renard's Music Dynamics, 1999; author numerous piano and organ texts; contbr. articles tor profl. jours. Office: 203 N Wabash Ave Ste 1510 Chicago IL 60601-2415

RENDER, LORNE, museum director; Dir. C.M. Russell Mus., Gt. Falls, Mont., Marianna Kistler Beach Art Mus., Manhattan, Kans., 1998—. Address: Marianna Kistler Beach Art Mus Kansas State U 701 Beach Ln Manhattan KS 66506

RENNER, ROBERT GEORGE, federal judge; b. Nevis, Minn., Apr. 2, 1923; s. Henry J. and Beatrice M. (Fuller) R.; m. Catherine L. Clark, Nov. 12, 1949; children: Robert, Anne, Richard, David. BA, St. John's U., Collegeville, Minn., 1947; JD, Georgetown U., 1949. Bar: Minn. 1949. Pvt. practice, Walker, 1949-69; U.S. atty. Dist. of Minn., 1969-77, U.S. magistrate, 1977-80, U.S. dist. judge, 1980-92, assumed sr. status, 1992—. Mem. Minn. Ho. of Reps., 1957-69. Served with AUS, 1943-46. Mem. FBA. Roman Catholic. Office: US Dist Ct 748 US Courthouse 316 Robert St N Saint Paul MN 55101-1495

RENNERFELDT, EARL RONALD, state legislator, farmer, rancher; b. Epping, N.D., July 10, 1938; s. Carl John and Margaret E. (Long) R.; m. Lois Ann Thune, Sept. 12, 1959; children: Charysse Renee, Carter Ryan. Student, NDSSS, Wahpeton, N.D., 1958. Farmer/rancher, Williston, N.D.; mem. N.D. Ho. of Reps., Bismarck, 1991—, chmn. nat. resources com. Bd. dirs. Am. State Bank. Mem. Lake Sacajawea Planning Bd., Williston, 1992; mem. Am. Legis. Exch. Coun., 1991-92; mem. adv. bd. N.D. State U. Exptl.. Sta.; bd. dirs. Mercy Med. Found., 1990-96. With U.S. Army, 1962-64. Recipient Harvest Bowl award N.D. State U., 1988; named Outstanding Young Farmer C. of C., 1972. Mem.: ND Durum Growers, Williston C. of C. (agrl. com., energy com.), Elks, Moose, Am. Legion. Republican. Mem. Evangelical Free Ch. Avocations: antiques, golf. Home and Office: 1704 Rose Ln Williston ND 58801-4362

RENO, ROGER, lawyer; b. Rockford, Ill., May 16, 1924; s. Guy B. and Hazel (Kinnear) R.; m. Janice Marie Odelius, May 17, 1952; children: Susan Marie, Sheri Jan Reno-Rudolph, Michael Guy. Student, Kenyon Coll., 1943-44, Yale U., 1944, U. Wis., 1946; A.B., Carleton Coll., 1947; LL.B., Yale U., 1950. Bar: Ill. 1950. Practiced in Rockford, 1950; assoc. firm Reno, Zahm, Folgate, Lindberg & Powell, 1950-56, partner, 1956-84, of counsel, 1984—. Chmn. Amcore Fin. Inc., 1982-95; atty. Rockford Bd. Edn., 1955-64. Past pres., bd. dirs. Childrens Home Rockford; trustee Swedish-Am. Hosp. Assn., 1967-77, Keith Country Day Sch. Served to 1st lt. USAAF, 1943-46. Mem. ABA, Ill. Bar Assn., Winnebago County Bar Assn. (pres. 1979-80) Republican. Methodist. Club: Forest Hills Country (Rockford). Home: 2515 Chickadee Trl Rockford IL 61107 Office: Reno Zahm Folgate Lindberg & Powell Amcore Fin Plaza Rockford IL 61104 Fax: 815-961-7723.

RENTER, LOIS IRENE HUTSON, librarian; b. Lowden, Iowa, Oct. 23, 1929; d. Thomas E. and Lulu Mae (Barlean) Hutson; m. Karl A. Renter, Jan. 3, 1948; children: Susan Elizabeth, Rebecca Jean, Karl Geoffrey. BA cum laude, Cornell Coll., 1965; MA, U. Iowa, 1968. Tchr. Spanish Mt. Vernon High Sch., 1965-67; head libr. Am. Coll. Testing Program, Iowa City, 1968-89, ret., 1989. Vis. instr. U. Iowa Sch. Library Sci., 1972-82. Mem. Phi Beta Kappa. Methodist. Home: 1308 Brendel Hill Dr NW Cedar Rapids IA 52405-1566 E-mail: KLRenter1308@home.com.

RENZAGLIA, KAREN A. biologist, educator; PhD, So. Ill. U. Vis. prof. dept. plant biology So. Ill. U., Carbondale. Recipient Edgar T. Wherry award Bot. Soc. Am., 1993, Michael Cichan award Bot. Soc. Am., 1999. Office: So Ill U Dept Plant Biology Mail Code 6509 Carbondale IL 62901-6509

REPLINGER, JOHN GORDON, architect, retired educator; b. Chgo., Nov. 9, 1923; s. Roy Lodawick and Dorothy Caroline (Thornstrom) R.; m. Dorothy Thiele, June 26, 1945; children: John Gordon Jr., Robert Louis, James Alan. B.S. in Architecture with highest honors, U. Ill., Urbana, 1949, M.S. in Architecture, 1952. Registered architect, Ill. Designer-draftsman L. Morgan Yost (Architect), Kenilworth, Ill., 1949-50; instr. U. Ill., 1951-53, asst. prof. architecture, 1953-57, assoc. prof. architecture, 1957-61, prof. architecture, 1961-85, prof. housing research and devel., 1972-85, prof. emeritus, 1985—, assoc. head dept. for acad. affairs, 1970-71; practice architecture Urbana, 1951—. Served as combat pilot USAAF, 1943-45. Decorated Air medal with oak leaf clusters; recipient Sch. medal AIA, 1949, List of Tchrs. Ranked as Excellent by Their Students award U. Ill., 1976, 77, 78, 82, 83; Allerton Am. travelling scholar, 1948 Mem. Nat. Trust Hist. Preservation. Home and Office: 403 Yankee Ridge Ln Urbana IL 61802-7113

REPPERT, RICHARD LEVI, lawyer; b. Phila., Nov. 6, 1948; s. William Downing and Angela R. (Schmid) R.; m. Faith Simpson, Dec. 30, 1972 (div. Aug. 1992); 1 child, Richard Jacob; m. Jeanette T. deHaven, Apr. 10, 1994. BA, Lehigh U., 1970; JD, Villanova U., 1974. Bar: Ohio 1974, U.S. Dist. Ct. (no. dist.) Ohio 1974, Pa. 1993. Assoc. Thompson, Hine and Flory, Cleve., 1974-82, ptnr., 1982-89, Jones, Day, Reavis & Pogue, Cleve., 1989—. Mem. ABA, Am. Coll. Real Estate Lawyers, Nat. Assn. Office and Indsl. Pks., Ohio State Bar Assn., Cleve. Bar Assn., Mortgage Bankers Assn. Greater Cleve. Office: Jones Day Reavis & Pogue North Point 901 Lakeside Ave Cleveland OH 44114-1190 E-mail: rreppert@jonesday.com.

REQUARTH, WILLIAM HENRY, surgeon; b. Charlotte, N.C., Jan. 23, 1913; s. Charles William and Amelia (George) R.; m. Nancy Charlton, 1948 (div. 1966); children— Kurt, Betsy, Jeff, Jan, Tim, Suzanna; m. Connie Harper, 1977. AB, Millikin U., 1934, LLD, 1996; MD, U. Ill., 1938, MS, 1939. Diplomate: Am. Bd. Surgery. Intern St. Luke's Hosp., Chgo., 1938-39; resident Cook County Hosp., 1940-42, 46-48; pvt. practice medicine, specializing in surgery Decatur, Ill., 1950—. Clin. prof. surgery U. Ill. Med. Sch., from 1962, now emeritus; Mem. Chgo. Bd. Trade. Author: Diagnosis of Abdominal Pain, 1953, The Acute Abdomen, 1958; also contbg. author chpts. books. Chmn. trustees Millikin U.; chmn. James Millikin Found.; bd. dirs. Decatur Meml. Hosp. Served to comdr. USNR, 1941-46. Mem. ACS, Cen. Surg. Assn., Western Surg. Assn., Chgo. Surg. Soc., Ill. Surg. Soc. (founder, pres. 1970-71), Am. Soc. Surgery Hand (founder), Am. Soc. Surgery Trauma, Soc. Surgery Alimentary Tract, Warren Cole Soc. (founder), Societe Internationale Chirurgie, Nat. Pilots Assn. (pres. 1960-61), Soaring Soc. Am., Sportsman Pilot Assn. (pres. 1966-67), Aerobatic Club Am., Internat. Aerobatic Club. Home: 1860 S Spitler Dr Decatur IL 62521-4417 Office: 158 W Prairie Ave Decatur IL 62523-1230 E-mail: bilreq@fginet.com.

RESCHKE, MICHAEL W. real estate executive; b. Chgo., Nov. 29, 1955; s. Don J. and Vera R. (Helmer) R.; m. Kim P. Shaw, July 17, 1977; children: Michael W. Jr., Tiffanie G., Taylor N. BS summa cum laude with univ. honors, No. Ill. U., 1977; JD summa cum laude, U. Ill., 1980. Bar: Ill. 1980; CPA, Ill. Assoc. Winston & Strawn, Chgo., 1980-82; also chmn. bd. dirs. The Prime Group, Inc., 1981—, pres., CEO, 1982—, also chmn. bd. dirs. Chmn. bd. dirs. Prime Retail, Inc., NASD: BLCI, Prime Groups Realty Trust (NYSE: PGE), Brookdale Living Cmtys. Inc. (NASD: BLCI), Horizon Group Properties, Inc. (NASD: HGPI). Mem. Chgo. Devel. Coun., 1987—. Mem. ABA, Ill. Bar Assn., Urban Land Inst., Chgo. Econ. Club, Real Estate Roundtable (dir.), Nat. Assn. Real Estate Investment Trusts, Order of Coif, Phi Delta Phi, Beta Alpha Psi. Office: The Prime Group 77 W Wacker Dr Ste 4200 Chicago IL 60601-1604

RESEK, ROBERT WILLIAM, economist; b. Berwyn, Ill., July 2, 1935; s. Ephraim Frederick and Ruth Elizabeth (Rummele) R.; m. Lois Doll, July 9, 1960; 1 child, Richard Alden. BA, U. Ill., 1957; AM, Harvard U., 1960, PhD, 1961. Vis. scholar MIT, Cambridge, 1967-68; asst. prof. econs. U. Ill., Urbana, 1961-65, assoc. prof., 1965-70, prof., 1970—; dir. Bur. Econ. and Bus. Rsch., 1977-89, acting v.p. for acad. affairs, 1987-89, v.p. for acad. affairs, 1989-94; prof. Inst. Govt. and Pub. Affairs, 1994—. Tchg. fellow Harvard U., 1959-61; vis. prof. U. Colo., 1967, 74, 75, 76, 82, Kyoto (Japan) U., 1976; cons. GM, 1964-66, U.S. Congress Joint Econ. Com., 1978-80, ABA, 1980-82; vis. scholar UCLA, 1994-95; co-dir. Midwest Economy: Issues and Policy, Midwest Govs. Conf., 1981; bd. dirs. Midwest U. Consortium Internat. Activities, v.p., 1991-94; mem. Ill. Gov.'s Econ. Policy Coun., 1999—. Co-author: Environmental Contamination by Lead and Other Heavy Metals— Synthesis and Modeling, 1978, Special Topics in Mathematics for Economists, 1976, A Comparative Cost Study of Staff Panel and Participating Attorney Panel Prepaid Legal Service Plans, 1981, Illinois Higher Education: Building the Economy, Shaping Society, 2000; editor: Illinois Economic Outlook, 1982-87, Illinois Economic Statistics, 1981, Economic Edge, 1996—; co-editor: The Midwest Economy: Issues and Policy, 1982, Frontiers of Business and Economic Research Management, 1983, Illinois Statistical Abstract, 1987. Mem. exec. com. Assn. Univ. bus. and Econ. Rsch., 1977-89, v.p., 1978-82, pres., 1982-83. Woodrow Wilson fellow, 1957; Social Sci. Rsch. Coun. grantee, 1964; NSF fellow, 1967-69, grantee, 1974-77; U.S. Dept. State scholar, Japan, 1976; grantee Ill. Bd. Higher Edn., 1998-99. Mem. Am. Statis. Assn., Econometric Soc., Beta Gamma Sigma, Phi Kappa Phi. Home: 201 E Holmes St Urbana IL 61801-6612 Office: Univ Ill 211 IGPA 1007 W Nevada St Urbana IL 61801-3812 E-mail: r-resek@uiuc.edu.

RESER, ELIZABETH MAY (BETTY RESER), bookkeeper; b. Le Roy, Kans., Sept. 4, 1939; d. William David II and Vera Hazel (Dreyer) Meats; m. William Joseph Reser, Sept. 26, 1958; children: Dee Anna Reser, Donna Sue Reser Larson. Diploma in computer programming, Control Data Inst., St. Louis, 1980; student, Washburn U., 1991. Cert. computer programmer, Mo. Computer programmer Regional Justice Info. Sys., St. Louis, 1980; sec. Shawnee Heights H.S., Tecumseh, Kans., 1973-78, bookkeeper, 1984-90. Treas. Secs. Assn. Shawnee Heights Unified Sch. Dist. 450, 1975-76, 86-87; vol. March of Dimes, Topeka, 1995-2001; mem. bd. trustees Susanna Wesley United Meth. Ch., Topeka, 1992-94, mem. prayer chain, 1993-94. Republican. Avocations: computers, quilting, shopping, crocheting, family activities. Home: 2849 SW Dukeries Rd Topeka KS 66614-4726

RESHOTKO, ELI, aerospace engineer, educator; b. N.Y.C., Nov. 18, 1930; s. Max and Sarah (Kalisky) R.; m. Adina Venit, June 7, 1953; children: Deborah, Naomi, Miriam Ruth. BS, Cooper Union, 1950; MS, Cornell U., 1951; PhD, Calif. Inst. Tech., 1960. Aero. research engr. NASA-Lewis Flight Propulsion Lab., Cleve., 1951-56, head fluid mechanics sect., 1956-57; head high temperature plasma sect. NASA-Lewis Research Center, 1960-61, chief plasma physics br., 1961-64; asso. prof. engring. Case Inst. Tech., Cleve., 1964-66, dean, 1986-87; prof. engring. Case Western Res. U., 1966-88, chmn. dept. fluid thermal and aerospace scis., 1970-76, chmn. dept. mech. and aerospace engring., 1976-79, Kent H. Smith prof. engring., 1989-98, Kent H. Smith prof. emeritus, 1999—. Susman vis. prof. dept. aero. engring. Technion-Israel Inst. Tech., Haifa, Israel, 1969-70; cons. United Technologies Research Ctr., Inst. Def. Analyses, Dynamics Tech. Inc., Micro Craft Tech., Martin-Marietta Corp., Rockwell Internat.; mem. adv. com. fluid dynamics NASA, 1961-64; mem. aero. adv. com. NASA, 1980-87, chmn. adv. subcom. on aerodynamics, 1983-85; chmn. U.S. Boundary Layer Transition Study Group, NASA/USAF, 1970—; U.S. mem. fluid dynamics panel AGARD-NATO, 1981-88; chmn. steering com. Symposium on Engring. Aspects Magneto-hydro-dynamics, 1966, Case-NASA Inst. for Computational Mechanics in Propulsion, 1985-92, USRA/NASA ICASE Sci. Coun., 1992; Joseph Wunsch lectr. Technion-Israel Inst. Tech., 1990. Contbr. articles to tech. jours. Chmn. bd. govs. Cleve. Coll. Jewish Studies, 1981-84; mem. bd. govs. Technion-Israel Inst. Tech., Haifa, Israel, 1999—; mem. NRC Air Force Sci. Tech. bd., 2000—. Guggenheim fellow Calif. Inst. Tech., 1957-59. Fellow ASME, AAAS, AIAA (Fluid and Plasma Dynamics award 1980, Dryden lectr. in rsch. 1994), Am. Phys. Soc. (vice-chmn. divsn. fluid dynamics 1998, chair-elect 1999, chair 2000, Otto Laporte award in fluid dynamics 1999), Am. Acad. Mechanics (pres. 1986-87); mem. NAE, AAUP, Ohio Sci. and Engring. Roundtable, Sigma Xi, Tau Beta Pi, Pi Tau Sigma. Office: Case Western Reserve Univ University Cir Cleveland OH 44106

RESNICK, ALICE ROBIE, state supreme court justice; b. Erie, Pa., Aug. 21, 1939; d. Adam Joseph and Alice Suzanne (Spizarny) Robie; m. Melvin L. Resnick, Mar. 20, 1970 PhB, Siena Heights Coll., 1961; JD, U. Detroit, 1964. Bar: Ohio 1964, Mich. 1965, U.S. Supreme Ct. 1970. Asst. county prosecutor Lucas County Prosecutor's Office, Toledo, 1964-75, trial atty., 1965-75; judge Toledo Mcpl. Ct., 1976-83, 6th Dist. Ct. Appeals, State of Ohio, Toledo, 1983-88; instr. U. Toledo, 1968-69; justice Ohio Supreme Ct., 1989—. Co-chairperson Ohio State Gender Fairness Task Force. Trustee Siena Heights Coll., Adrian, Mich., 1982— ; organizer Crime Stopper Inc., Toledo, 1981— ; mem. Mayor's Drug Coun.; bd. dirs. Guest House Inc. Mem. ABA, Toledo Bar Assn., Lucas County Bar Assn., Nat. Assn. Women Judges, Am. Judicature Soc., Toledo Women's Bar Assn., Ohio State Women's Bar Assn. (organizer), Toledo Mus. Art, Internat. Inst. Toledo. Roman Catholic Home: 2407 Edgehill Rd Toledo OH 43615-2321 Office: Supreme Ct Office 30 E Broad St Fl 3 Columbus OH 43215*

RESNICK, DONALD IRA, lawyer; b. Chgo., July 19, 1950; s. Roland S. and Marilyn B. (Weiss) R.; m. Jill Allison White, July 3, 1977; children: Daniel, Allison. BS with high honors, U. Ill., 1972; JD, Harvard U., 1975. Bar: Ill. 1975, U.S. Dist. Ct. (no. dist.) Ill. 1975. Assoc. Arvey, Hodes, Costello & Burman, Chgo., 1975-80, ptnr., 1981-83; sr. ptnr. Nagelberg & Resnick, 1983-89, Levenstein & Resnick, Chgo., 1989-91; chmn. real estate dept. Jenner & Block, 1992—. Bd. dirs. Ill. chpt. Real Estate/Investment Assn., Chgo., 1986—. Mem. ABA, Birchwood (Highland Park, Ill.) Club. Office: Jenner & Block 1 E Ibm Plz Fl 4000 Chicago IL 60611-7603 E-mail: dresnick@jenner.com.

RESS, CHARLES WILLIAM, management consultant; b. Columbus, Ohio, Aug. 6, 1933; s. George Leonard and Martha (Lake) R.; m. Virginia M. Beck, Aug. 28, 1954; children: Beverly Beck, Suzanne E., Charles W. Jr., Linda Perrins Foxworth, Jennifer Laurel Brulé. BS, Miami U., 1955; MA in Psychology, Rutgers U., 1969. Buyer The Higbee Co., Cleve., 1956-59; asst. to gen. mdse. mgr. The Halle Bros. Co., 1959-64; research dir. The Associated Mdse. Corp., N.Y.C., 1964-73; v.p. Mgmt. Horizons, Columbus, 1973-76; founder, chmn. bd. C.W. Ress & Assoc., Inc., 1976-90; gen. mgr. Levi Strauss & Co., 1990-94, mgmt. cons., 1994—. Lectr. in field. Author: Future Trends in Retailing, 1983, Trans National Retailing, 1988, Retailing 2000, 1991; contbr. articles to profl. jours. Republican. Avocations: cooking, wine tasting. Office: 3860 Lyon Dr Columbus OH 43220-4907 E-mail: Ressandress@Aol.com.

REST, ANN H. state legislator; b. Apr. 24, 1942; 1 child. BA, Northwestern U.; MA, U. Chgo.; MAT, MPA, Harvard U.; MBT, U. Minn. Mem. Minn. Ho. of Reps. dist. 46A, St. Paul, 1985-2000, Minn. Senate from 46th dist., St. Paul, 2001—. Chmn. taxes com., rules and legis. adminstrv. com., mem. ways and means com.; CPA. Recipient Women of Achievment award North Hennepin Bus. and Profl. Women, 1988; named Legislator of Yr., Politics in Minn., 1990. Mem. Resources for Adoptive Parents, Libr. Found. of Hennepin County, YMCA. Democrat. Home: 7611 36th Ave N Apt 322 Minneapolis MN 55427-2085 Office: Minn State Senate 439 State Office Bldg Saint Paul MN 55155-0001

REUBER, GRANT LOUIS, banking insurance company executive; b. Mildmay, Ont., Can., Nov. 23, 1927; s. Jacob Daniel and Gertrude Catherine (Wahl) R.; m. Margaret Louise Julia Summerhayes, Oct. 21, 1951 (dec. Feb. 1998); children: Rebecca, Barbara, Mary. BA, U. Western Ont., 1950; AM, Harvard U., 1954, PhD, 1957; LLD (hon.), Wilfred Laurier U., 1983, Simon Fraser U., 1985, U. Western Ont., 1985, McMaster U., 1994; postgrad., Cambridge U., 1954-55. Mem. research dept. Bank Can., Ottawa, 1950-52; mem. Can. Dept. Finance, 1955-57; asst. prof. econ. U. Western Ont., London, 1957-59, assoc. prof., 1959-62, prof., head dept., 1963-69, 1963-69; mem. bd. govs. U. Western Ont., London, 1974-78, acad. v.p., provost, 1975-78, chancellor, 1988-92; sr. v.p., chief economist Bank of Montreal, Que., Can., 1978-79, exec. v.p., 1980-81, dep. chmn., dep. chief exec. officer, 1981-83, dir., mem. exec. com., 1981-89, pres., chief operating officer, 1983-87, dep. chmn., 1987-89; dep. minister fin. Can., 1979-80; chmn. Can. Deposit Ins. Corp., 1993-99; sr. adv., dir. Sussex Circle, 1999—. Staff mem. Royal Commn. Banking and Fin., Toronto, 1962—63; chmn. Ont. Econ. Coun., 1973—78; cons. Can. Internat. Devel. Agy., 1968—69; hon. rsch. assoc. in econs. Harvard U., 1968—69; cons. devel. ctr. OECD, 1969—73; lectr. U. Chgo. Sch. Bus., 1992—93. Author: Private Foreign Investment in Development, 1973,

Canada's Political Economy, 1980; contbr. articles. Bd. dirs. Can. Merit Scholarship Found., 1994—2000; bd. govs. Royal Ont. Mus., 2000—02; pres. Can. Ditchley Found., 1981—. Decorated officer Order of Can. Fellow Royal Soc. Can.

REUM, JAMES MICHAEL, lawyer; b. Oak Park, Ill., Nov. 1, 1946; s. Walter John and Lucy (Bellegay) R. BA cum laude, Harvard U., 1968, JD cum laude, 1972. Bar: N.Y. 1973, D.C. 1974, U.S. Dist. Ct. (so. dist.) N.Y. 1974, Ill. 1979, U.S. Dist. Ct. (no. dist.) Ill. 1982. Assoc. Davis Polk & Wardwell, N.Y.C., 1973-78; assoc. Minority Counsel Com. on Judiciary U.S. Ho. of Reps., Washington, 1974; ptnr. Hopkins & Sutter, Chgo., 1979-93, Winston & Strawn, Chgo., 1994—. Midwest advance rep. Nat. Reagan Bush Com., 1980; nominee commr. Securities and Exchange Comm., Pres. Bush, 1992; mem. G.W. Bush fin. com, 2000. Served to SP4 USAR, 1969-75. Recipient Harvard U. Honorary Nat. Scholarship, 1964-72. Mem. Monte Carlo Country Club (Monaco), Univ. Club (N.Y.C.). Republican. Home: 12 E Scott St Chicago IL 60610-2320 Office: Winston & Strawn 35 W Wacker Dr Ste 4200 Chicago IL 60601-1695 E-mail: jreum@winston.com.

REUM, W. ROBERT, manufacturing executive; b. Oak Park, Ill., July 22, 1942; m. Sharon Milliken. BA, Yale U., 1964; JD, U. Mich., 1967; MBA, Harvard U., 1969. Dir. investment analysis City Investing Co., N.Y.C., 1969-72; v.p. corp fin. Mich. Nat. Corp., Bloomfield Hills, Mich., 1972-78; v.p., treas. White Motor Corp., Cleve., 1978-79; v.p. fin., CFO, Lamson & Sessions, 1980-82, The Interlake Corp., Oak Brook, Ill., 1982-88, exec. v.p., 1988-90, chmn., pres., CEO, 1991-99, Amsted Industries Inc., Chgo., 2001—, also bd. dirs. Bd. dirs. Lindberg Corp. Contbr. articles to Harvard Bus. Rev. Bd. dirs. Morton Arboretum, Lisle, Ill.; trustee Elgin (Ill.) Acad. Mem. Chgo. Golf Club, Chgo. Club, Rolling Rock Club (Ligonier, Pa.).

REUTER, HELEN HYDE, psychologist; b. McGehee, Ark. d. John Lloyd and Sallie Elizabeth (Holcomb) Hyde; m. George S. Reuter Jr.; children: Don N., M. Allan, K.L. BA, Westmar U., 1968; AM, U. S.D., 1969; PhD, Westgate U., 1976; LHD (hon.), Sioux Empire Coll.; LLD (hon.), St. John U., New Orleans; DD (hon.), Temple Bapt. Coll. Ordained So. Bapt. minister. Postmaster U.S. Post Office, College Heights, Ark.; sch. counselor various pub. sch. systems, Mo., Iowa; sch. psychologist Oak Park (Ill.) and River Forest High Sch.; v.p., sec. Internat. Assocs. for Christians, Holden, Mo. Cons. in field. Co-author: One Blood, 1964, 2d edit., 1988, Democracy and Quality Education, 1965, 2d edit., 1986. Named Mother of Yr., City of Monticello, 1960; cited as Psychologist of Yr., Internat. U., Lagos, Nigeria, 1992. Mem. P.E.O. (v.p.), Shakespeare Club (v.p.), Garden Club (v.p.). Democrat. Baptist. Avocations: travel, classical music. Home: 3100 Club Dr Apt 320 Lawrenceville GA 30044

REUTER, JAMES WILLIAM, lawyer; b. Bemidji, Minn., Sept. 30, 1948; s. John Renee and Monica (Dugas) R.; m. Patricia Carol Creelman, Mar. 30, 1968; children: Kristine, Suzanne, Natalee. BA, St. John's U., 1970; JD, William Mitchell Coll. Law, 1974. Bar: Minn. 1974, U.S. Dist. Minn. 1975, U.S. Ct. Appeals (8th cir.) 1985; cert. civil trial specialist. Editor West Pub. Co., St. Paul, 1970-73; assoc. Terpstra & Merrill, Mpls., 1974-77; ptnr. Barna, Guzy, Merrill, Hynes & Giancola, Ltd., 1977-89, Lindquist & Vennum, Mpls., 1989—. Recipient Cert. award Nat. Inst. Trial Advocacy, 1978. Mem. ABA (torts and ins. practice, and civil litigation sects.), ATLA, Minn. Bar Assn. (civil litigation and computer sects.), Hennepin County Bar Assn. (ins. com.), Anoka County Bar Assn. (pres. 1981-82). Avocations: skiing, golf, camping, reading. Office: Lindquist & Vennum 4200 IDS Ctr 80 S 8th St Ste 4200 Minneapolis MN 55402-2274

REVELLE, DONALD GENE, manufacturing and health care company executive, consultant; b. Cape Girardeau, Mo., July 16, 1930; s. Lewis W. and Dorothy R.; m. Jo M. Revelle, Aug. 1, 1954; children— Douglas, David, Daniel, Dianne BA, U. Mo., 1952; JD, U. Colo., 1957; grad., Harvard U. Bus. Sch., 1971. Dir. employee relations Westinghouse Corp., Pitts., 1957-65; asst. to v.p. Diebold Corp., 1966; v.p. human resources TRW Corp., Cleve., 1967-84; sr. v.p. human resources Black and Decker Co., Towson, Md., 1984-86; exec. v.p. corp. rels. Montefiore Acad. Med. Ctr., Bronx, 1987-98; pres., CEO Syzygy, Inc., 1998—. Univ. lectr.; cons. Duerba Ship, Blue Cross N.Y., Windsor Hosp., Salvation Army Contbr. articles to profl. jours. Mem. sch. bd. State of N.Y. Lt. USNR, 1952-54 Mem.: ABA (labor law com.), Human Resource Planning Soc., Fed. Bar Assn., Colo. Bar Assn., MBA Assn., Rotary. Methodist Home and Office: Syzygy Inc 29903 Baywood Ln Wesley Chapel FL 33543-9744

REVZEN, JOEL, conductor; BS, MS, The Juilliard Sch. Music; studies with Jorge Master, Jean Martinon,Margaret Hills, Abraham Kaplan. Mem. Fargo-Moorhead Symphony, Fargo, N.D., Berkshire Opera Co.; former dean St. Louis Conservatory Music. Recipient Grammy award for recording with Soprano Arleen Anger, 1993; named guest conductor of Kirov Opera, St. Petersburg, Russia, 1994, 95. Office: Fargo Moorhead Symphony 810 4th Ave S Moorhead MN 56560-2844

REXROTH, NANCY LOUISE, photographer; b. Washington, June 27, 1946; d. John Augustus and Florence Bertha (Young) R. B.F.A., Am. U., 1969; M.F.A. in Photography, Ohio U., Athens, 1971. Asst. prof. photography Antioch Coll., Yellow Springs, Ohio, 1977-79, Wright State U., Dayton, 1979-82; dealer Light Gallery, 1995—. Author: Iowa, 1976, The Platinotype, 1977, 1976. Nat. Endowment Arts grantee, 1973; Ohio Arts Council, 1981. Mem. Am. Massage Therapy Assn. Democrat. Home and Office: 2631 Cleinview Ave Cincinnati OH 45206-1810 E-mail: rexnex@cinci.com.

REYELTS, PAUL C. chemical company executive; MBA, Harvard U. V.p. corp. fin. dept. Piper, Jaffray & Hopwood; sr. v.p. fin., CFO Valspar Corp., Mpls. Office: Valspar Corp 1101 Third St South Minneapolis MN 55415

REYES, J. CHRISTOPHER, food products distribution executive; CEO Reyes Holdings, Lake Forest, Ill. Office: Reyes Holdings 225 E Deerpath Rd Lake Forest IL 60045 Office Fax: (847) 604-9972.

REYES, M. JUDY, food products distribution executive; CEO Reyes Holdings, Lake Forest, Ill. Office: Reyes Holdings 225 E Deerpath Rd Lake Forest IL 60045 Office Fax: (847) 604-9972.

REYNA, CLAUDIO, soccer player; b. Springfield, N.J., July 20, 1973; Student, U. Va. Midfielder Bayer Leverkusen (German Bundesliga), 1994-98, U.S. Nat. Soccer Team, Chgo., 1998—. Mem. 1994 World Cup Team. Named Freshman of Yr., Soccer Am., 1991, Player of Yr., 1992, 93, 3-time first-team All-Am., Nat. Soccer Coaches Assn. of Am.; recipient Player of Yr. award Mo. Athletic Club, 1992, 93. Office: US Soccer Fedn 1801 S Prairie Ave Chicago IL 60616-1319

REYNARD, CHARLES G. lawyer, educator; b. Indpls., Apr. 13, 1946; s. Granville G. R. and Helen (Rizzoli) Phoebus; m. Mary Anne Schierman; children: Rachel, Meghan. BA in English, St. Joseph's Coll., 1968; JD, Loyola U., 1974. Bar: Ill. 1974, U.S. Dist. Ct. (cen. dist.) Ill. 1985. Asst. state's atty. McLean County, Bloomington, Ill., 1975-78, state's atty., 1987—; pvt. practice, 1978-82; partner Reynard & Robb, 1982-87. Tchr., Chgo., 1968—; pres. McLean Child Protection Network, Bloomington, 1990-94; sec. McLean County Child Protection Network, 1994—. Author: Voir Dire in Child Sex Abuse Trials, 1996, The Violence Stops Here: Prosecuting Domestic Violence, 1999. Mem. Ill. Violence Prevention Authority, 1996—. Recipient Friend of Children award Youth Svcs. of Mid.-Ill., Bloomington, 1991-92, Human Dignity award Ill. Coalition Against Domestic Violence, 1998. Mem. Ill. State Bar Assn., Ill. State's Atty's. Assn. (bd. govs. 1991—), McLean County Bar Assn. Republican. Roman Catholic. Avocations: reading, writing, listening to music. Office: McLean County State's Attys Office 104 W Front St Ofc Bloomington IL 61701-5005 Business E-Mail: charles@mclean.gov.

REYNOLDS, A. WILLIAM, retired manufacturing company executive; b. Columbus, Ohio, June 21, 1933; s. William Morgan and Helen Hibbard (McCray) R.; m. Joanne D. McCormick, June 12, 1953; children: Timothy M., Morgan Reynolds Brigham, Mary Reynolds Miller. AB in Econs., Harvard U., 1955; MBA, Stanford U., 1957. Pres. Crawford Door Co., Detroit, 1959-66; staff asst. to treas TRW Inc., Cleve., 1957-59, asst. to exec. v.p. automotive group, 1966-67, v.p. automotive aftermarket group, 1967-70, exec. v.p. indsl. and replacement sector, 1971-81, exec. v.p. automotive worldwide sector, 1981-84; pres. GenCorp, Akron, Ohio, 1984-85, pres., chief exec. officer, 1985-87, chmn., CEO, 1987-94, chmn., 1994-95. Bd. dirs. Eaton Corp., Cleve., Boise (Idaho) Cascade Corp., Boise Cascade Office Products Corp., Itasca, Ill., Stant Corp., Richmond, Ind., Fed. Res. Bank Cleve., now chmn.; mem. dean's adv. coun. Stanford (Calif.) U. Grad. Sch. Bus., 1981-88. Chmn. United Way-Red Cross of Summit County, Ohio, 1987; trustee Univ. Hosps. of Cleve., 1984—, chmn., 1987-94. Mem. SAE, Bus. Roundtable (policy com.), Coun. on Fgn. Rels., Kirtland Country Club, Union Club, Rolling Rock Club, John's Island Club, Pepper Pike Club. Episcopalian. Avocations: hunting, fly fishing, skiing, golf. Office: Old Mill Investments Old Mill Group 1696 Georgetown Rd Ste E Hudson OH 44236-4094

REYNOLDS, DAVID L. state legislator; b. 1936; Grad., Nat. Tech. Sch., Cleve. Inst. Electronics. Rep. dist. 77 State of Mo., Florissant, 1994—. Mem. appropriations-health and mental health com., federal-state rels. and vet. affairs com. (vice chmn.), labor com., profl. registration and lic. com., local govt. and related matters (vice chmn.), workers comp. and employment security com. (vice chmn.), joint com. on wetlands com. (chmn.). Coun. mem. Florissant City (past pres.); pres. St. Louis County Mcpl. League; bd. mem. East-West Gateway Coord. Coun.; dir. North County, Inc.; vice chmn. North Star Boy Scouts of Am.; bd. mgrs. Emerson Family YMCA; dir. Father Dunne's Home for Boys. Mem. St. Sabina Men's Club, KC, St. Oliver Plunkett Ancient Order of Hiberians, Rotary, Florissant Valley C. of C., North County Athletic and Social Club. Democrat. Office: Mo Ho of Reps 201 W Capitol Ave Rm 411A Jefferson City MO 65101

REYNOLDS, ERNEST WEST, retired physician, educator; b. Bristow, Okla., May 11, 1920; s. Ernest West and Florence (Brown) R. B.S., U. Okla., 1942, M.D., 1946, M.S., 1952. Diplomate: Am. Bd. Internal Medicine. Intern Boston City Hosp., 1946-47; resident Grady Meml. Hosp., Atlanta, 1949-50; practice medicine Tulsa, Okla., 1953-54; prof. medicine U Mich., 1965-72; prof. medicine, dir. cardiology U. Wis., 1972-90, prof. emeritus, 1991—. Dir. Kellogg Found. Comprehensive Coronary Care Project, 1967-72; chmn. NIH Cardiovascular Study Sect. A, 1972-73 Mem. editorial bd.: Am. Heart Jour; Contbr. articles to profl. jours. Served to capt. AUS, 1947-49. Mem. Am. Heart Assn. (fellow coun. clin. cardiology), Ctrl. Soc. Clin. Rsch. Home: 17 Red Maple Trl Madison WI 53717-1515 Office: U Wis 600 Highland Ave Madison WI 53792-0001 E-mail: ewreynolds@prodigy.net.

REYNOLDS, FRANK EVERETT, religious studies educator; b. Hartford, Conn., Nov. 13, 1930; s. Howard Wesley and Caroline Mills Roys R.; m. Mani Bloch, Mar. 28, 1959 (dec. 1993); children: Roy Howard, Andrew Everett, Roger Frank; m. June Nash, Aug. 16, 1997. Student, Princeton U., 1948-51; B.A., Oberlin U., 1952; B.D., Yale Div. Sch., 1955; M.A., U. Chgo., 1963, Ph.D., 1971. Ordained to ministry Am. Baptist Ch., 1955. Program dir. Student Christian Ctr., Bangkok, Thailand, 1956-59; minister to fgn. students U. Chgo. Ecumenical Ministries, 1961-64; instr. U. Chgo., 1967-69, asst. prof. then assoc. prof., 1969-79, prof. history of religions and Buddhist studies, 1979-2001, prof. emeritus, 2001—; dir. Inst. for the Advanced Study of Religions/Martin Marty Ctr., 1991-2001. Tchr. Am. history and lit. Chulalongkorn U., Bangkok, 1956-59; co-dir. Liberal Arts and Study of Religions Project, 1985-90, NEH Sangitiyavasama Transl. Project, 1991-93. Author: (with others) Guide to Buddhist Religion, 1981, Two Wheels of Dhamma, 1971, Religions of the World, 3d edit., 1993; editor, co-translator: 3 Worlds According to King Ruang, 1981; co-editor: The Biographical Process: Studies in the History and Psychology of Religion, 1976, Religious Encounters with Death, 1977, Transitions and Transformations in the History of Religions, 1980, Anthropology and the Study of Religion, 1984, Cosmogony and Ethical Order, 1985, Myth and Philosophy, 1990, Beyond the Classics? Religious Studies and Liberal Education, 1990, Discourse and Practice, 1992, Religion and Practical Reason, 1994, Life of Buddhism, 2000, History of Religion Jour. 1977-2001, Towards a Comparative Philosophy of Religious Series, 1990-95, Religion in History, Society and Culture Series, 2001--; assoc. editor Jour. Religion, 1976—, Jour. Religious Ethics, 1981-2001; mem. editl. bd., History of Religion Jour., 2001—. Chair organizing com. Sawyer Seminar on Religious Law and Constrn. of Identities, 1996-97. Jacob Fox Found. fellow, 1952, Danforth Found. fellow, 1960, 64; sr. rsch. grantee Fulbright Commn., 1973-74, NEH, 1978-79. Mem. Am. Coun. Learned Socs. (com. on history of religions 1985-93), Am. Soc. Study Religion, Am. Acad. Religion (chmn. com. on history of religions 1993-96), Assn. Asian Studies (co-editor monograph series 1978-86, mem. Benda prize com. 1993-96), Internat. Assn. History of Religions, Internat. Assn. Buddhist Studies, Law and Soc. Home: 68 Prospect St Plainfield MA 01070 E-mail: freynold@midway.uchicago.edu.

REYNOLDS, JOHN FRANCIS, insurance company executive; b. Escanaba, Mich., Mar. 29, 1921; s. Edward Peter and Lillian (Harris) R.; m. Dorothy Gustafson, May 1, 1946; children— Lois, Margaret, Michael B.S., Mich. State U., 1942. Claims and assoc. surety mgr. Hartford Ins. Co., Escanaba, Mich. and Chgo., 1946-55; asst. v.p., bond mgr. Wolverine Ins. Co., Battle Creek, Mich., 1955-64, v.p. underwriting, 1964-69; Midwest zone underwriting mgr. Transamerica Ins. Co. (Wolverine Ins. Co.), 1969-74; pres., gen. mgr. Can. Surety Co. subs. Transamerica Ins. Co., Toronto, Ont., Canada, 1974-75; v.p. midwestern zone mgr. Transamerica Ins. Group, Battle Creek, Mich., 1975-83, pres., chief operating officer Los Angeles, 1983-84, chmn., chief exec. officer, 1984-85; apptd. spl. dep. ins. commr., dep. conservator Cadillac Inc. Co., 1989. Pres. Underwriting Exec. Council Midwest, 1967; dir. Underwriters Adjustment Bur., Toronto, 1974, Underwriters Labs. of Canada, Montreal, 1974; chmn. Mich. Assn. Ins. Cos., Lansing, 1976, Mich. Basic Property Ins. Assn., Detroit, 1973. Commr. City of Battle Creek, 1967-69; dir. Urban League, Battle Creek, 1969, 70, dir. Mich. Ins. Fedn., Lansing, 1975-83. Served to sgt. U.S. Army, 1942-45; New Guinea Roman Catholic Avocations: golf; fishing. E-mail: jackreynolds@prodigy.net.

REYNOLDS, JOHN W. federal judge; b. Green Bay, Wis., Apr. 4, 1921; s. John W. and Madge (Flatley) R.; m. Patricia Ann Brody, May 26, 1947 (dec. Dec. 1967); children: Kate M. Reynolds Lindquist, Molly A., James B.; m. Jane Conway, July 31, 1971; children: Jacob F., Thomas J., Frances P., John W. III. PhB, U. Wis., 1946, LLB, 1949. Bar: Wis. 1949. Since practiced in Green Bay; dist. dir. price stblzn., 1951-53; U.S. commr., 1953-58; atty. gen. of Wis., 1958-62; gov. State of Wis., 1963-65; U.S. dist. judge Ea. Dist. Wis., Milwa., 1965-71, chief judge, 1971-86, sr. judge, from 1986. Served with U.S. Army, 1942-46. Mem. State Bar Wis., Am. Law Inst., Fed. Judges Assn., Former Govs. Assn. Died Jan. 6, 2002.

REYNOLDS, MARTIN L. state legislator; b. Feb. 8, 1950; Mayor, Ladysmith, Wis., 1986-92; Wis. state assemblyman Dist. 87, 1990—. Plumbing and heating contractor. Mem. VFW, NRA, Am. Legion. Address: 101 Lake Ave E Ladysmith WI 54848-1304

REYNOLDS, R. JOHN, academic administrator, educator; b. Milw., Dec. 3, 1936; s. Edward R. and Elizabeth (Wickenhauser) R.; m. Carol G. Lucas, Dec. 15, 1956; children: John D., Katherine A. BEd, U. Wis., Whitewater, 1961; MA, No. Mich. U., 1967; PhD, So. Ill. U., 1971. Bus. instr. Green Bay (Wis.) Tech. Inst., 1964-65; dir. vocat. tng. No. Mich. U., Marquette, 1965-68; v.p. Tech. Edn. Corp., St. Louis, 1968-69, prof., 1969-71; acting dean, chmn dept. So. Ill. U., Carbondale, 1969-71, 74-80, 81-82; assoc. acad. dean N.H. Coll., Manchester, 1971-74; head. bus. and econs. dept. Lake Superior State U., Sault Ste. Marie, Mich., 1981-82; pres. Nat. Coll., Rapid City, S.D., 1982-84, Huron (S.D.) U., 1984-93, Tri-State U., Angola, Ind., 1993—. Cons. in field. Contbr. articles to profl. jours. Pres. Dakotaland Mus., Huron, 1986-91. Named Researcher of Yr. Ill. Bus. Edn. Assn., 1971. Office: Tri State Univ 1 University Ave Angola IN 46703-1764

REYNOLDS, RICHARD I. food products company executive; With Libbey Inc., Toledo, 1970—, v.p., CFO, now exec. v.p., COO, 1995—. Office: Libbey Inc 300 Madison Ave Fl 4 Toledo OH 43604-2634

REYNOLDS, ROBERT A., JR. electric distributor executive; Degree in bus., Stonehill Coll., 1972. Joined Graybar Electric Co., St. Louis, 1972, various mgmt. positions, v.p. commn./data divsn., 1991, pres., CEO. Office: Graybar Electric PO Box 7231 Saint Louis MO 63177

REYNOLDS, ROBERT HUGH, lawyer; b. St. Louis, Jan. 3, 1937; s. Leslie A. and Rebecca (McWaters) R.; m. Carol Jemison, Apr. 8, 1961; children: Stephen H., Cynthia C., Laura M. BA, Yale U., 1958; JD, Harvard U., 1964. Assoc. Barnes & Thornburg, Indpls., 1964-70, ptnr., 1970—, chmn. bus. dept., 1983-91; chmn. internat. practice group, 1992—. Co-chmn., editor Comml. Real Estate Financing for Ind. Attys., 1968; vice-chmn., co-editor Advising Ind. Businesses, 1974; chmn., editor Counseling Ind. Businesses, 1981, The Purchase and Sale of a Business, 1987. Bd. dirs. Crossroads Am. Coun. Boy Scouts Am., v.p., 1971-75, pres., 1987-89; v.p. Area 4 Ctrl. Region Boy Scouts Am., 1989-92, pres., 1992-93, pres. Ctrl. Region, 1993-96, Nat. Exec. Bd., 1993— (Silver Buffalo award); bd. dirs. Family Svc. Assn. Indpls., 1974-81, pres., 1978-80; bd. dirs. Family Svc. Am., 1979-88, Greater Indpls. Fgn. Trade Zone, 1987-2000, Indpls. Conv. and Visitors Assn., 1989-2000, Indpls. Econ. Devel. Corp., 1983-99, Greater Indpls. Progress Com., 1986-2000, exec. com., vice chmn. (Charles L. Whistler award); hon. trustee Children's Mus. Indpls., trustee, 1988-96, chmn., 1992-94; bd. dirs. Indpls. Downtown Inc., chmn., 1996-99; bd. gov. Legacy Fund, 1992—, v.chmn., 2000-; bd. dirs. Noyes Mem. Found., Japan-Am. Soc. Ind., pres., 1994—; vice chmn. TerraLex, 1996— Named Hon. Consul Gen. of Japan, 1999—. Fellow Ind. Bar Found., Indpls. Bar Found.; mem. ABA, Ind. Bar Assn. (chmn. corp., banking and bus. law sect. 1981-82, chmn. internat. sect. 1994-96), Internat. Bar Assn., Indpls. Bar Assn., Greater Indpls. C. of C. (bd. dirs., sec. 2000—), Econ. Club Indpls. (bd. dirs.). Republican. Clubs: Univ., Skyline (Indpls.). Lodge: Kiwanis. Office: Barnes & Thornburg 11 S Meridian St Indianapolis IN 46204-3535 E-mail: rreynolds@btlaw.com.

REYNOLDS, TOMMY, secondary school educator; b. Dec. 23, 1956; BSE ind. tech., CMSU, 1979, MS ind. voc. tech. edu., 1983. Secondary tchr. Lee's Summit (Mo.) North High Sch., 1979; tchr. PLJH, 1979-80, Lee's Summit High Sch., 1980—, Lee's Summit North High Sch., 1995-98; ind. tech. dept. coord., 1992-96. Recipient Tchr. Excellence award Internat. Tech. Edn. Assn., 1992. Office: Lee's Summit North High Sch 901 NE Douglas St Lees Summit MO 64086-4505

REYNOLDS, ZACKERY E. lawyer; b. Eureka, Kans., Dec. 19, 1957; BA, U. Kans., 1979; JD with honors, Washburn U., 1982. Bar: Kans. 1982, Mo. 1992. Pvt. practice, Fort Scott, Kans. Mem. ABA (exec. coun., young lawyers divsn. 1991-92), ATLA, Kans. Bar Assn. (pres.-elect 1998-99, v.p. 1997-98, sec.-treas. 1996-97, chair profl. ethics grievance com. 1993-95, pres. young lawyers sect. 1986-87, Oustanding Svc. award 1992), Mo. Bar Assn., Kans. Trial Lawyers Assn., Phi Delta Phi. Office: Reynolds Law Firm PA PO Box 32 102 S Jordan Fort Scott KS 66701

REYNOLDSON, WALTER WARD, retired state supreme court chief justice, lawyer; b. St. Edward, Nebr., May 17, 1920; s. Walter Scorer and Mabel Matilda (Sallach) R.; m. Janet Aline Mills, Dec. 24, 1942 (dec. 1986); children: Vicki, Robert; m. Patricia A. Frey, June 3, 1989. BA, State Tchrs. Coll., 1942; JD, U. Iowa, 1948; LLD (hon.), Simpson Coll., 1983, Drake U., 1987. Bar: Iowa 1948. Justice Iowa Supreme Ct., 1971-78, chief justice, 1978-87, sr. judge, 1989-93; of counsel Reynoldson Law Firm, Osceola, Iowa, 1993—. Adj. prof. law Drake U., 1989-93; county atty., Clarke County, Iowa, 1953-57. Contbg. author: Trial Handbook, 1969. Pres. Nat. Ctr. for State Cts., 1984-85; trustee Drake U., 1987-2000. Served with USNR, 1942-46. Recipient Osceola Community Svc. award, 1968 Fellow Am. Bar Found.; mem. Iowa Bar Assn. (chmn. com. on legal edn. and admission to bar 1964-71), Am. Judicature Soc. (bd. dirs. 1983-87, Herbert Harley award 1990), Iowa Acad. Trial Lawyers, Conf. Chief Justices (pres. 1984-85), Am. Coll. Trial Lawyers. Office: Reynoldson Law Firm 200 W Jefferson St Osceola IA 50213-1206

RHEIN, DAVE, newspaper editor; b. Chgo., Mar. 9, 1949; BE, Drake U., 1970. Deputy mng. editor Des Moines Register, 1995-99, asst. metro editor, 1999—. Office: Des Moines Register 715 Locust St Des Moines IA 50309-3767

RHIND, JAMES THOMAS, lawyer; b. Chgo., July 21, 1922; s. John Gray and Eleanor (Bradley) R.; m. Laura Haney Campbell, Apr. 19, 1958; children: Anne Constance, James Campbell, David Scott. Student, Hamilton Coll., 1940-42; A.B. cum laude, Ohio State U., 1944; LL.B. cum laude, Harvard U., 1950. Bar: Ill. bar 1950. Japanese translator U.S. War Dept., Tokyo, Japan, 1946-47; congl. liaison Fgn. Operations Adminstrn., Washington, 1954; atty. Bell, Boyd & Lloyd, Chgo., 1950-53, 55—, ptnr., 1958-92, of counsel, 1993—. Bd. dirs. Kewaunee Scientific Corp., Statesville, N.C. Commr. Gen. Assembly United Presbyn. Ch., 1963; life trustee Ravinia Festival Assn., Hamilton Coll., Clinton, N.Y., U. Chgo.; Northwestern Univ. Assocs.; chmn. Cook County Young Republican Orgn., 1957; Ill. Young Rep. nat. committeeman, 1957-58; v.p., mem. bd. govs. United Rep. Fund Ill., 1965-84; pres. Ill. Childrens Home and Aid Soc., 1971-73, life trustee; bd. dirs. E.J. Dalton Youth Center, 1966- 69; governing mem. Chgo. Symphony Orch., Chgo.; mem. Ill. Arts Council, 1971-75; mem. exec. com. div. Met. Mission and Ch. Extension Bd., Chgo. Presbytery, 1966-68; trustee Presbyn. Home, W. Clement and Jessie V. Stone Found., U. Chgo. Hosps. Served with M.I. AUS, 1943-46. Mem. ABA, Ill. Bar Assn., Chgo. Bar Assn. (bd. mgrs. 1967-69), Fed. Bar Assns., Chgo. Council on Fgn. Relations, Japan Am. Soc. Chgo., Lawyers Club Chgo., Phi Beta Kappa, Sigma Phi. Clubs: Chicago, Glen View (Ill.), Commercial (Chgo.), Mid-Day Club (Chgo.), Economic (Chgo.). Home: 830 Normandy Ln Glenview IL 60025-3210 Office: Bell Boyd & Lloyd 3 First National Pla 70 W Madison St Ste 3200 Chicago IL 60602-4244 E-mail: jrhind@bellboyd.com.

RHOADES, RODNEY ALLEN, physiologist, educator; b. Greenville, Ohio, Jan. 5, 1939; s. John H. and Floris L. Rhoades; m. Judith Ann Brown, Aug. 6, 1961; children: Annelisa, Kirsten. BS, Miami U., 1961; MS, 1963; PhD, Ohio State U., 1966. Asst. prof. Pa. State U., State Coll., 1966-72; assoc. prof., 1972-75; rsch. scientist NIH, Bethesda, Md., 1975-76; prof. Ind. U. Sch. Medicine, Indpls., 1976-81, 81—, chmn., 1981—. Dir. Indpls. Ctr. for Advanced Rsch. Author: Physiology, 1984; contbr. articles to profl.

jours. Fellow NASA, 1964-66; recipient Rsch. Career Devel. award NIH, 1975-80. Mem. Am. Physiol. Soc, AHA, Am. Thoracic Soc., Biophysics Soc., Sigma Xi. Home: 1768 Spruce Dr Carmel IN 46033-9025 Office: Ind U Sch Medicine 635 Barnhill Dr Indianapolis IN 46202-5126

RHOADS, PAUL KELLY, lawyer; b. La Grange, Ill., Sept. 4, 1940; s. Herbert Graves and Mary Margaret (Gurrie) R.; m. Katheryn Virginia Reissaus, Sept. 14, 1963; children: Elizabeth R. Saline, Katheryn R. Meek, Julia C. BA, Washington & Lee U., 1962; JD, Loyola U., Chgo., 1967. Bar: Ill. 1967, U.S. Dist. Ct. (no. dist.) Ill. 1967, U.S. Tax Ct. 1980. Trust officer 1st Nat. Bank Chgo., 1963-69; with Schiff Hardin & Waite, Chgo., 1969-98, ptnr., 1973-98; sole practitioner Western Springs, Ill., 1999—. Bd. dirs. McKay Enterprises, Chgo. Author: Starting a Private Foundation, 1993, Managing a Private Foundation, 1997; contbr. articles to profl. jours. and chpts. to books. Trustee Ill. Inst. Tech., 1985-95, Western Springs (Ill.) Hist. Soc., 1983-92, Philanthropy Roundtable, Washington, 1992-2000; bd. dirs. Cyrus Tang Scholarship Found., 1984-91; bd. overseers Ill. Inst. Tech. Chgo.-Kent Coll. Law, 1985-95; pres., bd. dirs. Grover Hermann Found., Chgo., 1984—; sec., bd. dirs. Western Springs Svc. Club, 1976-86; sec. Vandivort Properties, Inc., Cape Girardeau, Mo.; mem. adv. com. estate, tax and fin. planning Loyola U., 1986-92; adv. com. Thomas A. Roe Inst. for Econ. Policy Studies, Heritage Found., 1989—. Fellow Am. Coll. Trust and Estate Coun.; mem. Ill. State Bar Assn., Chgo. Bar Assn., Union League Club Chgo., Salt Creek Club (Hinsdale, Ill.) (pres. 1982, bd. dirs. 1981-83), Portage Lake Yacht Club (Onekama, Mich.) (commodore 1988, bd. dirs. 1985-89), Manistee (Mich.) Golf and Country Club. Republican. Avocations: sailing, golf, tennis. Office: 1000 Hillgrove Ave Western Springs IL 60558-1420 E-mail: paulkrhoads@aol.com.

RHODES, CHARLES HARKER, JR. lawyer; b. Chgo., May 24, 1930; s. Charles Harker and Claire (Hepner) R.; m. Mae Ellen Svoboda, Apr. 19, 1952; children: Charles Harker, James Albert, Edward Joseph. BA, U. Chgo., 1948, JD, 1951. Bar: Ill. 1951. Assoc. Schatz & Busch, Chgo., 1951-53; assoc. Sonnenschein Nath & Rosenthal, 1953-60, ptnr., 1961-92, ret. ptnr., 1992—. Dir. Ill. Inst. for Continuing Legal Edn., Springfield, 1977-84, 86-88; pres. Ill. Bar Automated Rsch., 1975-85. Trustee Nat. Ctr. for Automated Info. Rsch., N.Y.C., 1976-94; pres. B.R. Ryall YMCA, Glen Ellyn, Ill., 1967. Fellow Am. Bar Found., Chgo. Bar Found. (pres. 1977-80), Ill. Bar Found. (fellows chmn. 1990-91); mem. ABA (long range planning com. 1991-92, mem. pub. editorial bd. com. 1993-94), Ill. State Bar Assn. (bd. govs. 1975-79, chmn. liaison com. Atty. Registration and Disciplinary Commn. 1992-93), Chgo. Bar Assn. (libr., bd. mgrs. 1969-72), Am. Arbitration Assn. (arbitrator), Nat. Conf. Bar Founds. (trustee, pres. 1987-88), Met. Club Chgo. Republican. Presbyterian. Avocations: world travel, photography. Home: 267 N Montclair Ave Glen Ellyn IL 60137-5508 Office: Sonnenschein Nath & Rosenthal 233 S Wacker Dr Ste 8000 Chicago IL 60606-6491

RHODES, JIM, state legislator; b. Apr. 1942; m. Judy Rhodes. AA, U. Minn. Minn. state rep. Dist. 44B, 1993—, chair govt. ops. and vets. affairs com. Retail gen. mgr. Address: State Office Bldg Rm 409 Saint Paul MN 55155-0001

RHODES, STEVEN WILLIAM, judge; b. N.Y.C., Dec. 27, 1948; BS, Purdue U., 1970; JD, U. Mich., 1972. Bar: Mich. 1973, U.S. Dist. Ct. (ea. dist.) Mich. 1973. Law clk. U.S. Dist. Ct., Detroit, 1973; asst. U.S. atty. U.S. Atty.'s Office, 1974-77; U.S. magistrate U.S. Dist. Ct., 1981-85; pvt. practice Ann Arbor, Mich., 1977-81; judge U.S. Bankruptcy Ct., Detroit, 1985—, Bankruptcy Appellate Panel of the 6th cir. Ct., Detroit, 1997—. Adj. prof. Law Sch. U. Detroit, 1986, U. Mich., Ann Arbor, 1992, 94, 95. Author: Bankruptcy Cases for East Dist. Mich., 1987, 2d edit., 1990; co-author: Michigan Local Bankruptcy Court Rules Annotated, 1988; assoc. editor Am. Bankruptcy Law Jour., 1994-96, 97; contbr. articles to profl. jours. Office: US Bankruptcy Ct 211 W Fort St Ste 1800 Detroit MI 48226-3229

RHYNE, JAMES JENNINGS, condensed matter physicist; b. Oklahoma City, Nov. 14, 1938; s. Jennings Jefferson and Clyde Margaret (Russell) R.; m. Susan Margaret Watson, May 26, 1990; children: Nancy Marie, Edward Paxton. BS in Physics, U. Okla., 1959; MS in Physics, U. Ill., 1961; PhD in Physics, Iowa State U., 1965. Rsch. scientist Naval Ordnance Lab., White Oak, Md., 1965-75; rsch. physicist Nat. Inst. of Stds. and Tech., Gaithersburg, 1975-90; prof. physics U. Mo., Columbia, 1991—, dir. Rsch. Reactor Ctr., 1991-96. Adv. editor Jour. of Magnetism and Mag. Materials, 1990—; editl. bd. Jour. Applied Physics, 1986-89; co-editor procs. Fellow Am. Phys. Soc., Neutron Scattering Soc. Am. (pres. 1999—). Home: 2704 Westbrook Way Columbia MO 65203-5221 Office: U Mo Dept Physics And Astronomy Columbia MO 65211-0001 E-mail: rhynej@missouri.edu.

RIBBINS, MARK, radio personality; Radio host WNWV, Elyria, Ohio. Office: WNWV 538 W Broad St PO Box 4006 Elyria OH 44036

RIBEAU, SIDNEY A. academic administrator; M in Interpersonal Comm., U. Ill., 1973, D in Interpersonal Comm., 1979. Prof. comm. studies Calif. State U., L.A., 1976, chair Pan African studies dept., 1987; dean Coll. Liberal Arts Calif. Poly., San Luis Obispo, 1990, v.p. for acad. affairs Pomona, 1992; pres. Bowling Green (Ohio) U., 1995—. Bd. dirs. The Andersons Inc., Maumee, Ohio; lectr., spkr. and presenter in field. Co-author: African American Communication: Ethnic Identity and Cultural Interpretations, 1994 (Disting. Scholarship award Speech Comm. Assn.); contbr. papers to scholarly jours. Mem. Ohio Bd. Regent's Higher Edn. Funding Commn., Am. Coun. on Edn.'s Leadership and Instnl. Change Commn., Higher Edn. Bus. Coun., Urban League Toledo; bd. dirs. Toledo Symphony Orch. Mem. Bowling Green C. of C., Toledo C. of C. Office: Bowling Green State U Bowling Green OH 43403-0001

RICART, FRED, automotive company executive; Owner Ricart Automotive, Groveport, Ohio. Office: Ricart Automotive 4255 S Hamilton Rd Columbus OH 43227-1342

RICART, RHETT C. retail automotive executive; b. 1956; Grad., Ohio State U., 1977. Prin. Ricart Ford, Groveport, Ohio, 1977—, pres., CEO, 1988—; ceo Ricart Automotive, Columbus. Office: Ricart Automotive PO Box 27130 Columbus OH 43227-0130 also: Ricart Automotive 4255 S Hamilton Rd Groveport OH 43125-9332

RICE, DAVID LEE, university president emeritus; b. New Market, Ind., Apr. 1, 1929; s. Elmer J. and Katie (Tate) R.; m. Betty Jane Fordice, Sept. 10, 1950; children: Patricia Denise Rice Dawson, Michael Alan. B.S., Purdue U., 1951, M.S., 1956, Ph.D., 1958; degree (hon.), U. Evansville, 1994, U. So. Ind., 1995; LHD, U. Evansville, 1994; LLD, U. So. Ind., 1995. Dir. prof. research Ball State U., Muncie, Ind., 1958-66; v.p. Coop. Ednl. Research Lab., Inc., Indpls., 1965-67; research coordinator, bur. research HEW, Washington; dean campus Ind. State U., Evansville, 1967-71, pres. campus, 1971-85; pres. U. So. Ind., 1985-94, pres. emeritus, 1994—. Adminstrv. asst. Gov.'s Com. on Post High Sch. Orgn. Contbr. articles to profl. jours. Past mem. State Citizens Adv. Bd. Title XX Social Security Act; bd. dirs., past pres. bd. commrs. Evansville Housing Auth.; pres. Leadership Evansville, 1978-79; bd. dirs., past pres. S.W. Ind. Pub. TV, 1972—; chair Indian Pub. Broadcasting Sts., 1990-93; bd. dirs. Villages Inc.; mem. Buffalo Trace Coun. Boy Scouts Am., 1963_, New Harmony Commn., 1989-94; chair So. Ind. Rural Devel. Project., Inc.; bd. trustees Owen-Maclure Found. and Rapp Granary-Owen Found.; bd. dirs. So. Ind. Higher Edn. Inc., U. So. Ind. Found. With inf. U.S. Army, 1951-53. Decorated Bronze Star, Combat Infantryman's Badge; recipient Svc. to Others award Salvation Army, 1974, Citizen of Yr. award Westside Civitan Club, 1972, Boss of Yr. award Am. Bus. Women's Assn., 1976, Disting. Citizen of Yr. award Ivy Tech State Coll., 1994; David L. Rice Libr./U. So. Ind. named in his honor, 1994. Mem. DAR (medal of honor for cmty. svc. 1998), Am. Assn. Higher Edn., Am. Ednl. Rsch. Assn., Am. Assn. State Colls. and Univs., Nat. Soc. Study Edn., Met. Evansville C. of C. (dir.), Evansville Kennel Club, Petroleum Club, Rotary (civic award Evansville club 1985, life), Alpha Kappa Psi, Alpha Zeta, Phi Delta Kappa. Methodist. Home: 1223 S Main St New Harmony IN 47631 Office: Neef Lesueur House 404 Church St New Harmony IN 47631

RICE, JOHN RISCHARD, computer scientist, researcher, educator; b. Tulsa, June 6, 1934; s. John Coykendal Kirk and Margaret Lucille (Rischard) R.; m. Nancy Ann Bradfield, Dec. 19, 1954; children: Amy Lynn, Jenna Margaret. BS, Okla. State U., 1954, MS, 1956; PhD, Calif. Inst. Tech., 1959. Postdoctoral fellow Nat. Bur. Standards, Washington, 1959-60; rsch. mathematician GM Rsch. Labs., Warren, Mich., 1960-64; prof. Purdue U., West Lafayette, Ind., 1964-89, head dept. computer sci., 1983-96, disting. prof., 1989—. Editor-in-chief ACM Trans. Math. Software, N.Y.C., 1975-93; chmn. ACM-Signum, N.Y.C., 1977-79; dir. Computing Rsch. Bd., Washington, 1987-94; chair Computing Rsch. Assn., Washington, 1991-93. Author: The Approximation of Functions, 1964, Vol. 2, 1969, Numerical Methods, Software and Analysis, 1983; author and editor: Mathematical Software, 1971; editor: Intelligent Scientific Software Systems, 1991. Fellow AAAS, ACM (George Forsythe Meml. lectr. 1975); mem. IFIP (working group 2.5, vice chmn. 1977-91), Soc. Indsl. and Applied Math., Nat. Acad. Engring., Phi Kappa Phi. Home: 112 E Navajo St West Lafayette IN 47906-2153 Office: Purdue U Computer Sci Dept West Lafayette IN 47907

RICE, JON RICHARD, managed care administrator, physician; b. Grand Forks, N.D., July 10, 1946; s. Harry Frazer and Marian (Lund) R.; m. Roberta Jane Lindbergh, June 7, 1969; children: Kristen, Jennifer. BA, U. N.D., 1969, BS, 1970; MD, U. Tex., San Antonio, 1972; MS in Health Adminstrn., U. Colo., 1991. Intern U.S. Naval Hosp., San Diego, 1972-73; resident U. N.D. Sch. Medicine, Minot, 1975-77; physician Valley Med., Grand Forks, 1977-93; state health officer N.D. Dept. Health, Bismarck, 1993-97; dir. managed care Blue Cross Blue Shield of N.D., Fargo, 1997—. Contbg. author: Pilots, Personality and Performance. Lt. USN, 1972-75. Recipient Outstanding Vol. award Dakota Heart Assn., 1989, YMCA, 1992, Outstanding Health Care Provider Grand Forks C. of C., 1992, Award of Excellence N.D. Hosp. Assn., 1995. Mem. AMA, Am. Acad. Family Physicians, Am. Coll. Physician Execs., Alpha Omega Alpha. bus. Office: Blue Cross Blue Shield ND 4510 13th Ave S Fargo ND 58121-0002 E-mail: jon_rice_1999@yahoo.com., jon.rice@noridian.com.

RICE, JOY KATHARINE, psychologist, educational policy studies and women's studies educator; b. Oak Park, Ill., Mar. 26, 1939; d. Joseph Theodore and Margaret Sophia (Bednarik) Straka; m. David Gordon Rice, Sept. 1, 1962; children: Scott Alan, Andrew David. B.F.A. with high honors, U. Ill., Urbana, 1960; M.S., U. Wis., Madison, 1962, M.S., 1964, Ph.D., 1967. Lic. clin. psychologist. USPHS predoctoral fellow dept. psychiatry Med. Sch. U. Wis., Madison, 1964-65, asst. dir. Counseling Ctr., 1966-74, dir. Office Continuing Edn. Svcs., 1972-78, prof. ednl. policy studies and women's studies, 1974-95, clin. prof. psychiatry, 1995—; pvt. practice psychology Psychiat. Svcs., S.C., 1967—. Mem. State Wis. Ednl. Approval Bd., Madison, 1972-73; mem. Adult Edn. Commn., U.S. Office Career Edn., Washington, 1978 Author: Living Through Divorce, A Developmental Approach to Divorce Therapy, 1985, 2d edit., 1989; edit. bd. Lifelong Learning, 1979-86; cons. editor Psychology of Women Quar., 1986-88, assoc. editor, 1989-94; cons. editor Handbook of Adult and Continuing Education, 1989, Encyclopedia of Women and Gender, 2001; contbr. articles to profl. jours. Knapp fellow U. Wis.-Madison, 1960-62, teaching fellow, 1962-63; recipient Disting. Achievement award Ednl. Press Assn. Am., 1992. Fellow APA (exec. bd. psychology of women divsn. 1994—, internat. psychology divsn. 1998—, chair internat. com. for women 2000-02), Disting. Leadership award 2000-02; mem. Nat. Assn. Women in Edn. (editl. bd. jour. 1984-88, cons. editor Initiatives 1988-91), Internat. Coun. Psychologists, Am. Assn. Continuing and Adult Edn. (meritorious svc. award 1978-80, 82), TEMPO Internat. (bd. dirs., sec. 2000-02), Big Bros. Big Sisters of Dane County (pres. 2002, bd. dirs. 2001), Wis. Psychol. Assn., Phi Delta Kappa. Avocations: interior design, collecting art, gardening, travel. Home: 4230 Waban Hl Madison WI 53711-3711 Office: 2727 Marshall Ct Madison WI 53705-2255 E-mail: jkrice@facstaff.wisc.edu.

RICE, LINDA JOHNSON, publishing executive; b. Chgo., Mar. 22, 1958; d. John J. and Eunice Johnson; m. Andre Rice, 1984. BA Journalism, Univ. Southern California, Los angeles, 1980; MBA, Northwestern Univ., Evanston, 1988. With Johnson Pub. Co., 1980—, past v.p. and asst. to pub., pres., 1987—, also chief oper. officer; pres. Fashion Fair Cosmetics. Office: Johnson Pub Co Inc 820 S Michigan Ave Chicago IL 60605-2191

RICE, RICHARD CAMPBELL, retired state official, retired army officer; b. Atchison, Kans., Dec. 11, 1933; s. Olive Campbell and Ruby Thelma (Rose) R.; m. Donna Marie Lincoln, Aug. 4, 1956; children: Robert Alden, Holly Elizabeth. BS in History, Kans. State Univ., 1955; MA in Social Studies, Eastern Mich. Univ., 1965; grad., U.S. Army Command and Gen. Staff Coll., 1968, U.S. Army War Coll., 1977; attended, FBI Nat. Exec. Inst., 1990; grad. prog. for sr. execs., state and local govt., Harvard Univ., 1985. Commd. 2nd lt. U.S. Army, 1955; advanced through grades to col., 1976; with Joints Chief of Staff, Washington, 1975-76; fac. U.S. Army War Coll., Carlisle Barracks, PA, 1977-79; chief of staff Hdqrs. 3rd ROTC Region, Ft. Riley, KS, 1982-83; ret., 1983; dir. Mo. State Emerg. Mgmt. Agy., Jefferson City, 1983-85, Mo. Dept. Pub. Safety, Jefferson City, 1985-93. Trustee Mo. State Employees Retirement System, 1990-93; bd. visitors Nat. Emerg. Mgmt. Inst., 1991-92. Grad. Leadership, Mo., 1991; mem. Coordinating Coun. Health Edn., Mo.'s Chldrn. and Adolescents, Mo. Jail and Prison Overcrowding Task Force, Gov.'s Domestic Violence Task Force, Gov.'s Commn. on Crime, Gov.'s Adv. Coun. on Driving While Intoxicated, Mo. Children's Svcs. Commn., Blur Ribbon Commn. on Svcs. to Youth, Campaign to Protect Our Children; mem. policy com. Mo. Youth Initiative; chmn. Gov.'s Cabinet Coun. for Justice Adminstrn., Mo. Statistical Analysis Ctr. adv. bd., adv. bd. Mo. Criminal Hist. Records; bd. dirs. Mo. Law Enforcement Meml. Found., Gt. Rivers coun. Boy Scouts Am. (James E. West fellow), 1993—; bd. dirs. Mid-Mo. chpt. Alzheimer's Assn., 2002--; peer rev. cons. Nat. Inst. of Justice; chmn. Alliance for Uniform Hazmat Transp. Procedures, 1991-93. Decorated Legion of Merit, Bronze Star (3), Meritorious Svc. Medal (4), Air medal (2), Joint Svc. Commendation medal, Army Commendation medal (2); Republic of Vietnam Cross of Gallantry with Silver Star; recipient Conspicuous Svc. medal State of Mo., Silver Beaver award Boy Scouts Am.; James E. West fellow. Mem. Nat. Eagle Scout Assn., ASsn. U.S. Army, Soc. First Div., Am. Legion, VFW, Disabled Am. Vets., AMVETS, Mil. Order of World Wars, Nat. Soc., Sons Am. revolution, The Retired Ofcrs. Assn., Nat. Criminal Justice Assn. (bd. dirs. 1987-93), Rotary (Paul Harris fell.), St. Andrews Soc., Theta Xi. Republican. Avocation: sailing. E-mal. E-mail: rrice54864@aol.com.

RICE, WALTER HERBERT, federal judge; b. Pitts., May 27, 1937; s. Harry D. and Elizabeth L. (Braemer) R.; m. Bonnie Rice; children: Michael, Hilary, Harry, Courtney Elizabeth. BA, Northwestern U., 1958; JD, MBA, Columbia U., 1962; LLD (hon.), U. Dayton, 1991; DHL (hon.), Wright State U., 2000. Bar: Ohio 1963. Asst. county prosecutor, Montgomery County, Ohio, 1964-66; assoc. Gallon & Miller, Dayton, 1966-69; 1st asst. Montgomery County Prosecutor's Office, 1969; judge Dayton Mcpl. Ct., 1970-71, Montgomery County Ct. Common Pleas, 1971-80, U.S. Dist. Ct. (so. dist.) Ohio, 1980-95, chief judge, 1996—. Adj. prof. U. Dayton Law Sch., 1976—, bd. visitors, 1976— ; chmn. Montgomery County Supervisory Council on Crime and Deliquency, 1972-74; vice chmn. bd. dirs. Pretrial Release, Inc., 1975-79 Author papers in field. Pres. Dayton Area Coun. on Alcoholism and Drug Abuse, 1971-73; chmn. bd. trustees Stillwater Health Ctr., Dayton, 1976-79, Family Svc. Assn. Dayton, 1978-80; chmn. RTA in 2000 Com., 2003 Com. Designed To Bring Nat. Park to Dayton To Honor Wright Bros. and Birth of Aviation; chmn. Martin Luther King Jr. Meml. Com., Dayton Aviation Heritage Commn.; trustee Montgomery County Vol. Lawyers Project, Miami Valley Cultural Alliance, Barbara Jordan Com. Racial Justice; co-chmn., Dayton Dialogue on Race Rels.; former bd. mem. Sinclair C.C., U.S. Air & Trade Show. Recipient Excellent Jud. Service award Ohio Supreme Ct., 1976, 77, Outstanding Jud. Service award, 1973, 74, 76, Man of Yr. award Disting. Service Awards Council, Dayton, 1977, Outstanding Jurist in Ohio award Ohio Acad. Trial Lawyers, 1986, Pub. Ofcl. of Yr. award Ohio region of Nat. Assn. Social Workers, 1992, Humanitarian award NCCJ, 1993, City Mgr.'s Cmty. Svc. award City of Dayton, 1994, Paul Laurence Dunbar Humanitarian award, 1996, Pres.' award NAACP, 1996, greater Dayton Peace Bridge (civil rights) Hall of Fame, Mark of Excellence award, Nat. Forum Black Pub. Adminstrs., 2001. Mem. Dayton Bar Assn., Fed. Judges Assn., Carl D. Kessler Inn of Ct. (founder, former chmn.).

RICE, WILLIAM EDWARD, newspaper columnist; b. Albany, N.Y., July 26, 1938; s. Harry Edward, Jr. and Elizabeth (Lally) R.; m. Carol Timmon, June 3, 1978 (div.); m. Jill Van Cleave, Aug. 20, 1983. BA in History, U. Va., 1960; MS with honors, Columbia U., 1963. Reporter, editorial writer, critic Washington Post, 1963-69; student LeCordon Bleu, Paris, 1969-70; dir. L'Ecole de Cuisine, Bethesda, Md., 1971-72; freelance writer, restaurant critic Washingtonian Mag., 1971-72; exec. food editor Washington Post, 1972-80; editor-in-chief Food and Wine Mag., N.Y.C., 1980-85; food and wine columnist Chgo. Tribune, 1986—. Dining In columnist Gentlemen's Quarterly, 1987-89; chmn. restaurant awards com. James Beard Found., 1993-. Author: Feasts of Wine and Food, 1986, Steak Lovers Cookbook, 1997; editor: (with others) Where to Eat in America, 1978, 2d edit., 1980, 3d edit., 1987. Served with USN, 1960-62. Recipient Vesta award as outstanding newspaper food editor, 1979, Ordre du Merite Agricole (France), 1983 Home: 655 W Buena Ave Chicago IL 60613-2201 Office: Chgo Tribune Co Po Box 25340 435 N Michigan Ave Chicago IL 60611-4066 E-mail: wrice@tribune.com.

RICH, DANIEL HULBERT, chemistry educator; b. Fairmont, Minn., Dec. 12, 1942; married, 1964; 2 children. BS, U. Minn., 1964; PhD in Organic Chemistry, Cornell U., 1968. Rsch. assoc. organic chemist Cornell U., 1968; rsch. chemist Dow Chem. Co., 1968-69; rsch. assoc., organic chemist Stanford U., 1969-70; asst. prof. pharm. chemistry U. Wis., Madison, 1970-75, assoc. prof., 1975-81, prof. dept. medical chemistry, 1981—, prof. dept. organic chemistry, 1988—, Ralph F. Hirschmann prof. medicinal and organic chemistry, 1994—. Cons. biorganic natural product study sect., NIH, 1981-85, chmn., 1985. Recipient H.I. Romnes award, 1980, Vincent du Vigneaud award, 1990, Hitchings award for innovative methods in drug design, 1992, Alexander von Humboldt award, 1993, E. Volwiler award Am. Assn. Colls. Pharmacy, 1995; fellow NIH, 1968. Fellow AAAS, Am. Chem. Soc. (Ralph F. Hirschmann award in peptide chemistry 1993, divsn. medicinal chemistry award 1991, A.C. Cope scholar 1999), Am. Assn. Pharm. Sci. (rsch. achievement award 1992), Am. Assn. Coll. Pharmacy (Volwiler award 1995). Am. Peptide Soc. (R.B. Merrifield award 1999). Achievements include research in synthesis in peptides and hormones, inhibition of peptide receptors and proteases, characterization, synthesis and mechanisms of action of peptide natural products. Office: U Wis Dept Med Chemistry 7109 Rennebohm Hall 777 Highland Ave Madison WI 53705-2222

RICH, HARRY EARL, financial executive; b. Wichita, Kans., Mar. 5, 1940; s. Hubert E. and Lorene (Sadler) R.; m. Elfreda Elizabeth Babcock, Aug. 8, 1964; children: Lisa G., Carey E., Ashley H. BA, Harvard U., 1962, MBA, 1968. Pres. instrumentation divsn. Baxter Travenol, Deerfield, Ill., 1977-78; group v.p. Mallinckrodt, Inc., St. Louis, 1978-83; sr. v.p., chief fin. officer Brown Group, Inc., 1983-88, exec. v.p., chief fin. officer, 1988-00, also bd. dirs. Bd. dirs. Gen. Am. Capital Co. divsn. GenAm. Bd. dirs. Repertory Theatre, 1984-90, 1998—, pres. bd. dirs.,1988-90; treas., v.p. Fair Found., 1985-88; bd. trustees Mary Inst., 1986-90, Mary Inst./St. Louis Country Day Sch., 1990-97, chmn., 1995-97. Lt. USN, 1962-66. Avocations: tennis, jogging, sailing. Home: 101 Fair Oaks Saint Louis MO 63124-1579 Office: Brown Shoe Co Inc 8300 Maryland Ave Saint Louis MO 63105-3693

RICH, ROBERT EDWARD, lawyer; b. Corbin, Ky., Feb. 4, 1944; s. Edward Bluch and Marjorie Brooks (Wentworth) R.; m. Janet Sue Shearer, May 14, 1966; children: Susan M., Christopher R., David E., Sarah M. AB, U. Ky., 1966; JD, Harvard U., 1969. Bar: Ohio 1970. Jud. clk. U.S. Ct. Appeals for 6th Cir., Louisville, 1969-70; assoc. Taft, Stettinius & Hollister, Cin., 1970, ptnr., 1978—. Pres. Lighthouse Youth Svcs., Inc., Cin., 1985, YMCA, Frankfort, Ky., 2001, Ctr. for Hope, Inc., Mt. Health, Ohio, 1991, Cin. Bar Found., 1991. Mem. ABA, Cin. Bar Assn. Republican. Presbyterian. Home: 215 Hilltop Ln Wyoming OH 45215-4121 Office: 1800 Firstar Tower 425 Walnut St Cincinnati OH 45202-3923

RICH, S. JUDITH, public relations executive; b. Chgo., Apr. 14; d. Irwin M. and Sarah I. (Sandock) R. BA, U. Ill., 1960. Staff writer, reporter Economist Newspapers, Chgo., 1960-61; asst. dir. pub. rels. and communications Coun. Profit Sharing Industries, 1961-62; dir. advt. and pub. rels. Chgo. Indsl. Dist., 1962-63; account exec., account supr., v.p., sr. v.p., exec. v.p. and nat. creative dir. Edelman Pub. Rels. Worldwide, Chgo., 1963-85; exec. v.p., dir. Ketchum Pub. Rels. Worldwide, 1985-89, exec. v.p., exec. creative dir. USA, 1990-97, exec. v.p., chief creative officer worldwide, 1998—. Frequent spkr. on creativity and brainstorming; workshop facilitator. Contbr. articles to popular mags. Mem. pub. rels. adv. bd. U. Chgo. Grad Sch. Bus., Roosevelt U., Chgo., DePaul U., Chgo., Gov.'s State U. Recipient Pub. Rels. All-Star award for Creativity, Inside PR mag., 1999. Mem. Pub. Rels. Soc. Am. (Silver Anvil award, judge Silver Anvil awards), Counselors Acad. of Pub. Rels. Soc. Am. (exec. bd.), Chgo. Publicity Club (8 Golden Trumpet awards). Avocations: theatre, swimming, cycling, racquetball. Home: 2500 N Lakeview Ave Chicago IL 60614-1846 Office: Apt 2603G 2500 N Lakeview Ave Chicago IL 60614-1822

RICHARD, PATRICK, science research administrator, nuclear scientist; b. Crowley, La., Apr. 28, 1938; married; two children. BS, U. Southwestern La., 1961; PhD, Fla. State U., 1964. Rsch. assoc. prof. nuclear physics U. Wash., 1965-68; from asst. prof. to prof. physics U. Tex., Austin, 1968-72; dir. J.R. MacDonald Lab. physics dept., disting. prof. Kansas State U., 1972—. Cons. Columbia Sci. Rsch. Inst., 1969-71. Mem. Am. Phys. Soc. Office: Kans State U J R MacDonald Lab Physic Dept Cardwell Hall Manhattan KS 66506 also: Kans State U Physics Dept Cardwell Hall Manhattan KS 66506

RICHARDS, DANIEL WELLS, company executive; b. Taylor, Pa., Dec. 16, 1928; s. Daniel Wells and Bernice (Robling) R.; m. Helen Reilly, Feb. 10, 1979; children: Kenneth, Deborah, Thomas. BA, Dickinson Coll., 1950; postgrad., U. Pitts., 1953-54. Mgr. advt. prodn. Miller Machine Co., Pitts., 1954-55; mgr. sales promotion Gen. Paper Co., 1955-57; advt. and product mgr. Harris Seybold Co., Cleve., 1957-67; v.p. mktg. Colwell Systems Inc., Champaign, Ill., 1967-86, pres., 1986-91; Disting. lectr., exec. in residence Ill. State U., 1991-93; pres. D.W. Richards & Assocs., Champaign, 1994—. Mem. Urbana (Ill.) City Council, 1975-77; budget dir.

Ill. Humanities Council, 1980-84; bd. dirs. United Way Champaign County, 1987-92, Sinfonia da Camert, 1987-95. Served to lt. U.S. Army, 1950-53. Unitarian. Home and Office: 1704 Coventry Dr Champaign IL 61822-5242

RICHARDS, HUGH TAYLOR, physics educator; b. Baca County, Colo., Nov. 7, 1918; s. Dean Willard and Kate Bell (Taylor) R.; m. Mildred Elizabeth Paddock, Feb. 11, 1944; children: David Taylor, Thomas Martin, John Willard, Margaret Paddock, Elizabeth Nicholls, Robert Dean. BA, Park Coll., 1939; MA, Rice U., 1940, PhD, 1942. Research assoc. Rice U., Houston, 1942; scientist U. Minn., Mpls., 1942-43, U. Calif. Sci. Labs., Los Alamos, N.Mex., 1943-46; research assoc. U. Wis., Madison, 1946-47, mem. faculty, 1947-52, prof., 1952-88, prof. emeritus, 1988—, physics dept. chairperson, 1960-63, 66-69, 85-88. Assoc. dean Coll. Letters and Sci., U. Wis, 1963-66. Author: Through Los Alamos 1945: Memoirs of a Nuclear Physicist, 1993; contbr. articles to profl. jours. Fellow Am. Phys. Soc.; mem. Am. Assn. Physics Tchrs. Unitarian-Universalist. Achievements include neutron measurements first A-Bomb test; fission neutron (and other) spectra by new photo-emulsion techniques; mock fission neutron source; spherical electrostatic analyzer for precise reaction energy measurements; negative ion sources for accelerators (He ALPHATROSS, SNICS); accurate proton, deuteron, and alpha particle scattering and reaction cross sections; systematics mirror nuclei; isospin violations in nuclear reactions. Home: 1320 12th Ave E Apt # 115 Menomonie WI 54751

RICHARDS, JERRY LEE, academic administrator, religious educator; b. Lawrenceville, Ill., Nov. 4, 1939; s. Russell O. and Elvessa A. (Goodman) R.; m. Lee Ann, Apr. 25, 1986; children: Mark, Renee, Teresa, Angela. BA, Lycoming Coll., 1965; BD, Evang. Congregational Sch. Theology, 1967; MDiv, Garrett Theol. Sem., 1968; D in Ministry, St. Paul Sch. Theology, 1975. Ordained to ministry Meth. Ch., 1968. Pastor chs., Pa., 1960-65, Williamsport, Iowa, 1965-70; mem. faculty Iowa Wesleyan U., Mt Pleasant, 1970-85, prof. religion, dir. responsible social involvement Mt. Pleasant, 1975-85, v.p. for acad. affairs, 1975-82, pres., 1982-85; dir. gift planning U. Wis., Eau Claire, 1985—. Pres. Mental Health Inst. Aux., Mt. Pleasant, 1976. Mem. Phi Alpha Theta Office: U Wis Office of Devel 215 Schofield Hall Eau Claire WI 54702-4004

RICHARDSON, ALLISON, financial services company official; Grad. in acctg., Fordham U.; MBA in Fin., NYU, 1999. Mgr. assurance and adv. bus. svcs. Ernst & Young, Cleve. Former mentor Adlain Stevenson H.S., N.Y.C.; coord. co. vols. Coun. Fashion Designers Am.-Vogue Initiative/NYC AIDS Fund; counselor to young profls. Recipient Black Achiever in Industry award Harlem YMCA. Mem. Beta Alpha Psi. Office: Ernst & Young LLP 925 Euclid Ave Ste 1300 Cleveland OH 44115-1476

RICHARDSON, F. C. academic administrator; b. Memphis, Sept. 22, 1936; m. Bernice Tanner. AB in Biology, Rust Coll., 1960; MS in Biology, Atlanta U., 1964; PhD in Botany, U. Calif., Santa Barbara, 1967. Asst. prof. botany Ind. U. N.W., Gary, 1967-71, assoc. prof., 1971-82, prof., 1982-84, chair dept. biology, 1971-72, chair div. arts and scis., 1972-84; prof. Jackson (Miss.) State U., 1984-85, v.p. for acad. affairs, 1984-85, Moorhead (Minn.) State U., 1985-89; prof. SUNY Coll. at Buffalo, 1989, pres., 1989-96; chancellor Ind. U.-S.E., New Albany, 1996—. Cons., evaluator North Ctrl. Assn., 1987-89; mem. commn. on elem. schs. Mid. States Assn., 1990—; mem. Commn. on Minorities in Higher Edn., Am. Coun. on Edn.; mem. task force on outcomes and accountability Coun. on Postsecondary Edn., 1991—. Mem. editorial bd. Negro Ednl. Rev., 1977—, exec. editor, 1981—; contbr. numerous articles to profl. jours. Mem. fellowship selection com. for Martin Luther King, Jr. Fellowship Program, Woodrow Wilson Nat. Fellowship Found., Chgo., 1969-74; bd. dirs. Lake County Assn. for Retarded Citizens, 1969-75; chair Ind. U. N.W./Community Adv. Bd. for Spl. Svcs., 1970-74; mem. Gary Air Pollution Control Adv. Bd., 1970-84, chair; chair steering com. for creation of Gary Neighborhood Svcs., Inc., 1970-71, bd. dirs., 1971-84; mem. N.W. Ind. Clean Air Coordinating Com., N.W. Ind., 1970-73, Comprehensive Health Planning Coun., 1971-75, Com. on Sci. and Tech. R&D, State of Minn., 1987, Moorhead Chamber Edn. Task Force, 1987-88; mem. Gary Bd. Health, 1972-82, sec., 1976-79, pres., 1979-82; bd. dirs. Meth. Hosps., Gary, 1973-84, Med. Ctr. of Gary, Inc., 1975-81, Greater Buffalo Devel. Found., 1989—, Buffalo Soc. Natural Scis., 1989—, Western N.Y. Tech. Devel. Ctr., Inc., 1991—, Buffalo Fine Arts Acad., 1991—; mem. Lake area planning and allocation com. United Way, 1981-83, chair Lake area campaign exec. group, 1982-83, bd. dirs. United Way Buffalo and Erie County, 1990—; mem. local organizing com. World Univ. Games 1993, 1989—; mem. bd. govs. NCCJ of Western N.Y., 1989—. Univ. scholar Atlanta U., 1962-64; fellow NSF, 1966, U. Calif., 1967-68. Mem. Am. Inst. Biol. Scis., Bot. Soc. Am., Internat. Soc. Plant Morphologists, Am. Assn. State Colls. and Univs. (SCAN team 1986). Office: Ind U SE 4201 Grant Line Rd New Albany IN 47150-2158

RICHARDSON, KATHY KREAG, state legislator; Ed., Purdue U. Clk. Hamilton County Circuit Ct., 1984-91; mem. from 29th dist. Ind. State Ho. of Reps., 1992—. Mem. cts. and criminal code com., judiciary com., local govt., cityies and towns, county and twp. com., election and apportionment com., family and children com. Mem. Hamilton County Bd. Election Surps. Mem. Assn. Clks. Circuit Cts., Assn. Ind. Counties, Noblesville C. of C. (bd. dirs.), Noblesville H.S. Alumni Assn. (sec.), Kiwanis, Soroptimist, Republican Woman, Hamilton County Hist. Soc. Home: 1363 Grant St Noblesville IN 46060-1925 Office: Ind Ho of Reps State Capitol Indianapolis IN 46204

RICHARDSON, LAUREL WALUM, sociology educator; b. Chgo., July 15, 1938; d. Tyrrell Alexander and Rose (Foreman) R.; m. Herb Walum, Dec. 27, 1959 (div. 1972); children: Benjamin, Joshua; m. Ernest Lockridge, Dec. 12, 1981. AB, U. Chgo., 1955, BA, 1956; PhD, U. Colo., 1963. Asst. prof. Calif. State U., Los Angeles, 1962-64; postdoctoral fellow Sch. Medicine Ohio State U., Columbus, 1964-65, asst. prof. sociology, 1970-75, assoc. prof., 1975-79; prof. sociology Sch. Medicine Ohio State U., 1979—, prof. cultural studies, edn. policy and leadership; asst. prof. sociology Denison U., Granville, Ohio, 1965-69. Mem. editorial bd. Jour. Contemporary Ethnography, Symbolic Interaction, Gender & Soc., Qualitative Sociology, The Sociol. Quar. Author: Dynamics of Sex and Gender, 1977, 3d edit. 1988, The New Other Woman, 1985, Die Neve Andere, 1987, A Nova Outra Mulher, 1987, Writing Strategies: Reaching Diverse Audiences, 1990, Gender and University Teaching: A Negotiated Difference, 1995; editor: Feminist Frontiers, 1983, 5th edit., 2000, Fields of Play Constructing an Academic Life, 1997 (Charles H. Cooley award for best sociology book 1998); assoc. editor Symbolic Interaction; author more than 100 rsch. articles and papers. Ford Found. fellow, 1954-56; NSF dissertation fellow, 1960-62; post doctoral fellow Vocat. Rehab., Columbus, 1964; grantee Ohio Dept. Health, 1986-87, Nat. Inst. Edn., 1981-82, NIMH, 1972-74, NSF, 1963-64, NEH, 1992; recipient Disting. Affirmative Action award Ohio State U., 1983, Feminist Mentor award, 1998. Mem. Am. Sociol. Assn. (com. on coms. 1980-81, com. on pub. info. 1987—), North Ctrl. Sociol. Assn. (pres. 1986-87), Sociologists for Women in Soc. (coun. mem. 1978-80), Ctrl. Ohio Sociologists for Women in Soc. (past pres.), Women's Poetry Workshop, Soc. for Study of Symbolic Interaction (publs. com.). Avocations: hiking, poetry. Office: Ohio State Univ Dept of Sociology 190 N Oval Mall Columbus OH 43210-1328 E-mail: Richardson.9@osu.edu.

RICHARDSON, MARK, state legislator; b. Poplar Bluff, Mar. 19, 1952; married; children: Todd, Chris, Megan. BA in Polit. Sci. and History, MA in Psychology, S.E. Mo. State U.; JD, Memphis State U., 1980. City atty. City of Poplar Bluff, 1984-86; asst. prosecuting atty. City of Butler County, 1980-86; sr. ptnr. Richardson and Duncan; rep. Mo. Ho. of Reps., 1990—. Minority fl. leader Mo. Ho. of Reps., 1994; mem. follow ho. coms. accouts, ops. and fin., join com. on wetlands, judiciary and ethics, rules, join rules, bill perfected and printed, workers compensation; mem. govs. standing com. on job tng. and work force readiness, 1993—, mem. Rep. caucus com. for higher edn., policy devel. com. Rep. campaign com., mem. statewide bldg. code com., 1994—; bd. dirs. Mo. First Vote Program; del. Am. Coun. of Young Polit. Leaders to Austria and Hungary, 1992; ACYPL task force to the Pacific Mantle Countries of Sinapore, Thailand and South Korea. Scoutmaster Boy Scout Troop #166; elder, bd. dirs. First Christian Ch., Poplar Bluff; former pres. bd. Local Shelter Workshop, March of Dimes, Poplar Bluff H.S. task force on drug abuse. Recipient Award of Merit Boy Scouts Am., 1990; named Outstanding Young Men, 1981. Office: House of Reps Jefferson City MO 65101

RICHARDSON, RUDY JAMES, toxicology and neurosciences educator; b. May 13, 1945; B.S. magna cum laude, Wichita State U., 1967; Sc.M., Harvard U., 1973, Sc.D., 1974. Diplomate Am. Bd. Toxicology. Research geochemist Columbia U., N.Y.C., summer 1966; NASA trainee SUNY, Stony Brook, 1967-70; research biochemist Med. Research Council, Carshalton, Eng., 1974-75; asst. prof. U. Mich., Ann Arbor, 1975-79, assoc. prof., 1979-84, prof. toxicology, 1984—, assoc. prof. neurotoxicology neurology dept., 1987—, Dow prof. toxicology, 1998—, acting dir. dept. Toxicology, 1993, dir., 1994-99. Vis. scientist Warner-Lambert Co., Ann Arbor, 1982-83; vis. prof. U. Padua, Italy, 1991; cons. NAS, Washington, 1978-79, 84, Office Tech. Assessment U.S. Congress, 1988-90, Nat. Toxic Substance Disease Registry, 1990—; mem. sci. adv. panel on neurotoxicology EPA, 1987-89; chmn. work group on neurotoxicity guidelines Orgn. for Econ. Coop. and Devel., 1990, Nat. Inst. Orgnl. Safety and Health, 1990, 94; mem. acute cholinesterase risk assessement expert panel Internat. Life Scis. Inst., 1996; mem. steering com., working group Risk Sci. Inst., 1997; presenter sci. adv. panel U.S. EPA, 1998-99, WHO, Geneva, 1998; chair expert panel on dichlorvos neurotoxicity and cholinesterase inhibition SRA Internat., Washington, 1998-99; spkr. in field. Mem. editorial bd. Neurotoxicology, 1980—, Toxicology and Indsl. Health, 1986—, Toxicology and Applied Pharmacology, 1989-97, Jour. Toxicology and Environ. Health, 1997—; contbr. articles to profl. jours., chpts. to books. Mem. Mich. Lupus Found., Ann Arbor, 1979— Grantee NIH, 1977-86, 95—, EPA, 1977-86; invited speaker Gordon Conf., Meriden, N.H., 1984, Cholinesterase Congress, Bled, Yugoslavia, 1983. Mem. AAAS, Am. Coll. Toxicology, Soc. Toxicology (pres. neurotoxicology sect. 1987-88, councillor 1988-89), Soc. for Neurosci., Am. Diabetes Assn., Am. Chem. Soc., Internat. Soc. Neurochemistry, Internat. Brain Rsch. Orgn. Achievements include co-discoverer (with B.R. Dudek) of lymphocyte neurotoxic esterase (NTE); development of lymphocyte NTE as biomarker of exposure to neuropathic organophosphates; refinement of NTE assay for use in neurotoxicity testing. Office: U Mich Toxicology Program M 7525 Sph # 2 Ann Arbor MI 48109 E-mail: rjrich@umich.edu.

RICHARDSON, SHIRLEY MAXINE, genealogy editor; b. Rising Sun, Ind., May 3, 1931; d. William Fenton and Mary (Phillips) Keith; m. Arthur Lee Richardson, Feb. 11, 1950; children: Mary Jane Hunt, JoDee Mayfield, Steven Lee Richardson. Personnel mgr. Mayhill Pubs., Knightstown, Ind., 1967-87, prodn. mgr., 1975-87, editor, 1967-87; info. staff, assoc. editor Ind. Farm Bur., Inc., 1987-89, dir. info. and pub. rels., 1989-94; genealogy editor AntiqueWeek, 1996-2001; editor Knightstown Banner, 2001—. Avocations: travel, reading, boating, quilting. Home: 366 E Carey St Knightstown IN 46148-1208 Office: 24 N Washington St Knightstown IN 46148-1242 E-mail: srichardson@spitfire.net.

RICHARDSON, WILLIAM CHASE, foundation executive; b. Passaic, N.J., May 11, 1940; s. Henry Burtt and Frances (Chase) R.; m. Nancy Freeland, June 18, 1966; children: Elizabeth, Jennifer. BA, Trinity Coll., 1962; MBA, U. Chgo., 1964, PhD, 1971. Rsch. assoc., instr. U. Chgo., 1967-70; asst. prof. health services U. Wash., 1971-73, assoc. prof., 1973-76, prof., 1976-84, chmn. dept. health services, 1973-76, assoc. dean Sch. Pub. Health, 1976-81, acting dean, 1977, 78, dean Grad. Sch., vice provost, 1981-84; exec. v.p., provost, prof. dept. family and community medicine Pa. State U., 1984-90; pres. Johns Hopkins U., Balt., 1990-95, pres., prof. emeritus, 1995, prof. dept. health policy, mgmt., 1990-95, prof. emeritus, 1995—; pres., CEO W.K. Kellogg Found, Battle Creek, Mich., 1995—. Cons. in field; bd. dirs. Kellogg Co., CSX Corp., Mercantile Bankshares Corp., Mercantile-Safe Deposit & Trust Co., Coun. on Founds. Author: books, including Ambulatory Use of Physicians Services, 1971, Health Program Evaluation, 1978; contbr. articles to profl. jours. Mem. external adv. com. Fred Hutchinson Cancer Rsch. Ctr. Kellogg fellow, 1965-67 Fellow Am. Public Health Assn.; mem. Inst. Medicine, Nat. Acad. Scis. Office: WK Kellogg Found One Michigan Ave E Battle Creek MI 49017

RICHERSON, HAL BATES, physician, internist, allergist, immunologist, educator; b. Phoenix, Feb. 16, 1929; '; s. George Edward and Eva Louise (Steere) R.; m. Julia Suzanne Bradley (dec. 1996), Sept. 5, 1953; children: Anne, George, Miriam, Julia, Susan. BS with distinction, U. Ariz., 1950; MD, Northwestern U., 1954. Diplomate Am. Bd. Internal Medicine, Am. Bd. Allergy and Immunology, Bd. Diagnostic Lab. Immunology; lic. physician, Ariz., Iowa. Intern Kansas City (Mo.) Gen. Hosp., 1954-55; resident in pathology St. Luke's Hosp., Kansas City, 1955-56; trainee in neuropsychiatry Brooke Army Hosp., San Antonio, 1956; resident in medicine U. Iowa Hosps., Iowa City, 1961-64, fellow in allergy and immunology, 1964-66; fellow in immunology Mass. Gen. Hosp., Boston, 1968-69; instr. internal medicine U. Iowa Coll. Medicine, Iowa City, 1964-66, asst. prof., 1966-70, assoc. prof., 1970-74, prof., 1974-98, prof. emeritus, 1998—; acting dir. divsn. allergy/applied immunology U. Iowa Hosps. and Clinics, 1970-72, dir. allergy and clin. immunology sect., 1972-78, dir. divsn. allergy and immunology, 1978-91; gen. practice, asst. to Gen. Surgeon Ukiah, Calif., 1958; gen. practice medicine Holbrook, Ariz., 1958-61. Vis. lectr. medicine Harvard U. Sch. Medicine, Boston, 1968-69; vis. prof., rsch. scientist U. London and Brompton Hosp., 1984; prin. investigator Nat. Heart, Lung and Blood Inst., 1971-94, mem. pulmonary diseases adv. com., 1983-87; prin. investigator Nat. Inst. Allergy and Infectious Diseases, 1983-94; dir. Nat. Inst. Allergy and Infectious Diseases' Asthma and Allergic Diseases Ctr., U. Iowa, 1983-94; mem. VA Merit Rev. Bd. in Respiration, 1981-84; mem. com. NIH Gen. Clin. Rsch. Ctrs., 1989-93; mem. rev. reserve NIH, 1993-98; mem. bd. sci. advisors Merck Inst., 1990-94; presenter lectures, seminars, continuing edn. courses; mem. numerous univ., coll. and hosp. coms., 1970—; cons. Merck Manual, 1982, 87, 92, 96-97. Contbr. numerous articles and revs. to profl. jours., chpts. to books; reviewer Sci., Jour. Immunology, Jour. Allergy and Clin. Immunology, Am. Rev. Respiratory Disease, New Eng. Jour. Medicine, Ann. Internal Medicine. Served to capt. U.S. Army, 1956-58. NIH fellow 1968-69. Fellow ACP (Laureate award 1996), Am. Acad. Allergy Asthma & Immunology (Disting. Clinician award 1998); mem. AMA (mem. residency and rev. com. for allergy and immunology; mem. accreditation coun. for grad. med. edn. 1980-85, vice-chmn. 1984-85), AAAS, Iowa Med. Soc., Iowa Thoracic Soc. (chmn. program com. 1964-65, 69-71, pres. 1972-73, mem. exec. com. 1972-74), Am. Thoracic Soc. (bd. dirs. 1981-82, councilor assembly on allergy and immunology 1980-81, mem. nominating com. 1988-90), Iowa Clin. Med. Soc., Am. Fedn. Clin. Rsch., Am. Assn. Immunologists, Ctrl. Soc. Clin. Rsch. (chmn. sect. on allergy-immunology 1980-81, mem. coun. 1981-84), Alpha Omega Alpha. Avocations: reading, swimming, scuba diving. Home: 331 Lucon Dr Iowa City IA 52246-3300 Office: U Iowa Health Care Dept Internal Medicine 200 Hawkins Dr Iowa City IA 52242-1009 E-mail: richersonh@mchsi.com., hal-richerson@uiowa.edu.

RICHERT, PAUL, law educator; b. Elwood, Ind., Aug. 31, 1948; m. Catherine George Stanton, June 24, 1972; children: John, William. AB, U. Ill.-Urbana, 1970, MS, 1971; JD, Tulane U., 1977. Bar: Ohio 1977. Asst. law librarian U. Akron, 1977-78, law librarian, asst. prof. law, 1978-83, assoc. prof., 1983-87, prof. law, 1987—. Cons. to cts. Editor: Ohio Appellate Decision on Fiche, 1981; indexer Publs. Clearing House Bull., vols. 1-4. Mem. United Chs. of Christ. With U.S. Army, 1971-74. Mem. Am. Assn. Law Librs., Akron Bar Assn., ABA. Home: 2030 Ganyard Rd Akron OH 44313-6050 Office: U Akron Sch of Law Libr 150 University Ave Akron OH 44325-2902

RICHMAN, HAROLD ALAN, social welfare policy educator; b. Chgo., May 15, 1937; s. Leon H. and Rebecca (Klieman) R.; m. Marlene M. Forland, Apr. 25, 1965; children: Andrew, Robert. AB, Harvard U., 1959; MA, U. Chgo., 1961, PhD, 1969. Asst. prof., dir. Ctr. for Study Welfare Policy, Sch. Social Svc., U. Chgo., 1967-69, dean, prof. social welfare policy, 1969-78, Hermon Dunlap Smith prof., 1978—, dir. of ctr., 1978-81, dir. Children's Policy Rsch. Project, 1978-84, dir. Chapin Hall Ctr. for Children, 1985—2002, faculty assoc. Chapin Hall Ctr. for Children, 2002—, chmn. univ. com. on pub. policy studies, 1974-77. Chmn. Univ. Lab. Schs., 1985-88; cons. to gov. State of Ill., Edna McConnell Clark Found., 1984-95, Lilly Endowment, 1987-90, Ford Found., 1987-89; co-chair Aspen roundtable on comprehensive cmty. initiatives, 1993—. Chmn. editorial bd. Social Svcs. Rev., 1970-79; contbr. articles to profl. jours. Bd. dirs. Chgo. Com. Fgn. and Domestic Policy, 1969-78, S.E. Chgo. Commn., 1970—, Jewish Fedn. Met. Chgo., 1970-75, Ill. Facilities Fund, 1989-94, Welfare Coun. Met. Chgo., 1970-72, Erikson Inst. Early Childhood Edn., 1972-79, Nat. Urban Coalition, 1975-86, Family Focus, 1980-89, Jewish Coun. Urban Affairs, 1982-87, Ctr. for Study Social Policy, 1983-92, Nat. Family Resource Coalition, 1990-93, Pub./Pvt. Ventures, 1992-98, Benton Found., 1994—; bd. dirs. Israel Ctr. on Children, chmn., 1995—; bd. dirs. Jordan Children's Rsch. Ctr., 2001—, Michael Reese Health Trust, 2002-, U. Capttown Childen's Inst. Capt. USPHS, 1961-63. White House fellow, Washington, 1965-66; recipient Disting. Svc. citation U.S. Dept. Health, Edn. & Welfare, 1970, Quantrell award U. Chgo., 1990. Mem. White House Fellows Assn. (v.p. 1976-77), Am. Pub. Welfare Assn. (bd. dirs. 1989-92). Home: 5715 S Dorchester Ave Chicago IL 60637-1726 Office: U Chgo Chapin Hall Ctr for Children 1313 E 60th St Chicago IL 60637-2830

RICHMAN, JOHN MARSHALL, retired lawyer, business executive; b. N.Y.C., Nov. 9, 1927; s. Arthur and Madeleine (Marshall) R.; m. Priscilla Frary, Sept. 3, 1951; children: Catherine Richman Wallace, Diana H. BA, Yale U., 1949; LLB, Harvard U., 1952. Bar: N.Y. 1953, Ill. 1973. Assoc. Leve, Hecht, Hadfield & McAlpin, N.Y.C., 1952-54; mem. law dept. Kraft, Inc., Glenview, Ill., 1954-63, gen. counsel Sealtest Foods div., 1963-67, asst. gen. counsel, 1967-70, v.p., gen. counsel, 1970-73, sr. v.p., gen. counsel, 1973-75, sr. v.p. adminstrn., gen. counsel, 1975-79, chmn. bd., chief exec. officer, 1979, Dart & Kraft, Inc. (name changed to Kraft, Inc. 1986), Glenview, 1980; chmn. Kraft Gen. Foods, Ill., 1988-89; counsel Wachtell, Lipton, Rosen & Katz, Chgo., 1990-98. Bd. dirs. Archstone Cmtys.; life bd. dirs. Evanston Northwestern Healthcare. Life trustee Chgo. Symphony Orch.; trustee Northwestern U.; bd. dirs. Chgo. Coun. on Fgn. Rels., Lyric Opera Chgo., Norton Mus. Art, West Palm Beach. Fla. Mem. Comml. Club, Chgo. Club, Casino Club (Chgo.), Westmoreland Country Club (Wilmette, Ill.), Old Elm Club (Highland Park, Ill.), Lost Tree Club (N. Palm Beach, Fla.), Shoreacres, Lake Bluff, Ill., Racquet Club of Chgo. Congregationalist. Office: 179 E Lake Shore Dr Chicago IL 60611-1306

RICHMAN, STEPHEN ERIK, lawyer; b. Austin, Tex., Mar. 10, 1945; s. Allen A. and Erika (Zimmerman) R.; m. Frances Ellen Sharpe, Aug. 29, 1971; children: Joshua Eric, Wendy Michelle. BA magna cum laude, Amherst Coll., 1967; JD cum laude, Harvard U., 1970. Bar: Wis. 1972. Assoc. Webster Sheffield, N.Y.C., 1970-72, Quarles & Brady, Milw., 1972-78, ptnr., 1978—. Pres. Milw. Youth Symphony Orch., 1985-87, Milw. Jewish Fedn., 1996-98; chmn. Milw. Symphony Orch., 2000—; bd. dirs. Jewish Cmty. Found., Milw., 1992—. Mem. ABA, Nat. Assn. Bond Lawyers, State Bar Wis., Phi Beta Kappa. Home: 709 E Carlisle Ave Milwaukee WI 53217-4835 Office: Quarles & Brady 411 E Wisconsin Ave Ste 2550 Milwaukee WI 53202-4497

RICHMOND, JAMES GLIDDEN, lawyer; b. Sacramento, Feb. 20, 1944; s. James Gibbs and Martha Ellen (Glidden) R.; m. Lois Marie Bennett, Oct. 22, 1988; 1 child, Mark R. BS in Mgmt., Ind. U., 1966, postgrad., 1966-69, JD, 1969. Bar: Ind. 1969, Ill. 1991, U.S. Dist. Ct. (no. dist.) Ind. 1971, U.S. Dist. Ct. (so. dist.) Ind., 1969, U.S. Ct. Appeals (7th cir.) 1975, U.S. Tax Ct. 1980. Spl. agent FBI, 1970-74; spl. agent Criminal Investigation Divsn. IRS, 1974-76; asst. U.S. atty. no. dist. U.S. Atty. Office, Ind., 1976-80; assoc. Galvin, Stalmack & Kirschner, Hammond, 1980-81; pvt. practice Highland, 1981-83; ptnr. Goodman, Ball & Van Bokkelen, 1983-85; U.S. atty. no. dist. State of Ind., Hammond, 1985-91; spl. counsel to dep. atty. gen. of the U.S. U.S. Dept. Justice, Washington, 1990-91; mng. ptnr. Ungaretti and Harris, Chgo., 1991-92, ptnr., 1995—; exec. v.p., gen. counsel Nat. Health Labs., 1992-95. Practitioner in residence Ind. U. Sch. Law, Bloomington, 1989. Minority counsel senate republicans October Surprise Hearings, 1992. Fellow Am. Coll. Trial Lawyers. Republican. Avocation: fishing. Office: Ungaretti & Harris 3500 Three First National Plz Chicago IL 60602-4283

RICHMOND, RICHARD THOMAS, journalist; b. Parma, Ohio, May 16, 1933; s. Arthur James and Frances Marie (Visosky) R.; m. Charlotte Jean Schwoebel, Dec. 19, 1933; children: Kris Elaine, Leigh Alison, Paul Evan. AB, Washington U., St. Louis, 1961. Bur. mgr. UPI News Pictures, St. Louis, 1957-62; from asst. picture editor to editor color sect. Post-Dispatch, 1962-80, columnist Clayton, 1971—2001, editor calendar sect. St. Louis, 1983-94, asst. entertainment editor, 1995-96, prodn. coord. Get Out Mag., 1996-2000; v.p. Golden Royal Enterprises, 1976-78; pres. Oroquest Press, 1977-80; dir. U.S. Mortgage & Investment Corp., Hilton Head Island, N.C., 1977-81; pres. Magalar Mining, Texarkana, Ark., 1979-83. Co-author: Treasure Under Your Feet, 1974, In the Wake of the Golden Galleons, 1976, Diabetes: The Facts That Will Let You Regain Control of Your Life, 1986; editor: You Can Be Rich By Thursday, 1997, Male Homemaker's Handbook, 1997. Avocation: undersea treasure hunting. Home: 307 Lebanon Ave Belleville IL 62220-4126

RICHMOND, WILLIAM PATRICK, lawyer; b. Cicero, Ill., Apr. 5, 1932; s. Edwin and Mary (Allgier) R.; m. Elizabeth A., Jan. 9, 1954 (div.); children: Stephen, Janet, Timothy; m. Magda, June 8, 1992. AB, Albion Coll., 1954; JD, U. Chgo., 1959. Bar: Ill. 1959, N.Y. 1985. Assoc. Sidley & Austin, Chgo., 1960-67, ptnr., 1967-98, counsel, 1998—. Served with U.S. Army, 1954-56. Fellow Am. Coll. Trial Lawyers; mem. ABA, Soc. Trial Lawyers, Chgo. Bar Assn., Desert Forest Golf Club (Carefree, Ariz.), Ruth Lake Country Club (Hinsdale, Ill.). Republican. Methodist. . Home: 4 Tartan Ridge Rd Burr Ridge IL 60527-8904 Office: Sidley & Austin 425 W Surf St Apt 605 Chicago IL 60657-6139

RICHTER, GLENN, diagnostic equipment company executive; BBA, George Washington U.; MBA, Duke U. Various exec. level positions with Frito-Lay Co., McKinsey and Co.; sr. v.p., corp. contr. Dade Behring, Deerfield, Ill., 1997-99, CFO, 1999—.

RICHTER, JUDITH ANNE, pharmacology educator; b. Wilmington, Del., Mar. 4, 1942; d. Henry John and Dorothy Madelyn (Schroeder) R. BA, U. Colo., 1964; PhD, Stanford U., 1969. Postdoctoral fellow Cambridge (Eng.) U., 1969-70, U. London, 1970-71; asst. prof. pharmacology

Sch. Medicine Ind. U., Indpls., 1971-78, assoc. prof. pharmacology and neurobiology, 1978-84, prof., 1984—. Vis. assoc. prof. U. Ariz. Health Sci. Ctr., Tucson, 1983; mem. biomed. rsch. rev. com. Nat. Inst. on Drug Abuse, 1983-87. Mem. editorial bd. Jour. Neurochemistry, 1982-87; contbr. numerous articles to sci. jours. Scholar Boettcher Found., 1960-64; fellow Wellcome Trust, 1969-71. Mem. AAAS, Am. Soc. for Pharmacology and Exptl. Therapeutics (exec. com. neuropharmacology div. 1989-91), Am. Soc. for Neurochemistry, Internat. Soc. for Neurochemistry, Soc. for Neurosci., Women in Neurosci., Assn. Women in Sci., Phi Beta Kappa, Sigma Xi. Achievements include research in neuropharmacology, especially barbiturates, neurobiology of mutant mice and dopaminergic systems and painful neuropathies. Office: Ind U Sch Medicine 635 Barnhill Dr Indianapolis IN 46202-5126 E-mail: srichter@iupui.edu.

RICHTER, MITCH, state legislator; b. Suffrin, NY, Sept. 5, 1960; m. Julie Fee. B.A. Business, Black Hills State U., 1981. Rep. S.D. State Dist. 11, 1994—; Owner & operator Dairy Queen. Appropriations com. S.D. Ho. Reps. Address: 5801 W King Arthur Dr Sioux Falls SD 57106-0676 Office: SD Mem Ho of Reps State Captiol Pierre SD 57501

RICHTER, ROBERT C. automotive executive; CFO Dana Corp., Toledo. Office: Dana Corp PO Box 1000 4500 Dorr St Toledo OH 43697

RICKETTS, JOHN JOE, securities company executive; b. Nebraska City, Nebr., July 16, 1941; s. Donavon Platte and Florence Marie (Erhart) R.; m. Marlene Margaret Volkmer, June 15, 1963; children— J. Peter, Thomas, Laura, Todd. B.A., Creighton U., 1969. Counselor Father Flannagans Boys Home, Boys Town, Nebr., 1967-68; with sales dept. Dean Witter & Co., Omaha, 1968-74; investment counselor Ricketts & Co., Omaha, 1974-75; pres. Ameritrade, Inc., Omaha, from 1975, CEO 1982-99, co-CEO, 1999—. Republican. Roman Catholic. Office: Ameritrade Holding Corp 4211 S 102d St Omaha NE 68127

RIDEOUT, WALTER BATES, English educator; b. Lee, Maine, Oct. 21, 1917; s. Walter John and Helen Ruth (Brickett) R.; m. Jeanette Lee Drisko, Aug. 2, 1947; children: Linda Carolyn, Richard Bates, David John. A.B., Colby Coll., 1938; M.A., Harvard U., 1939, Ph.D., 1950. Teaching fellow English Harvard U., 1946-49, asst. prof., summer 1954, prof., summer 1969; from instr. to assoc. prof. English Northwestern U., Evanston, Ill., 1949-63, dir. program Bell System execs., 1957-58, 59-61; prof. English U. Wis., Madison, 1963—, Harry Hayden Clark prof. English, 1972—, chmn. dept., 1965-68, sr. vis. prof. Inst. Research in Humanities, 1968-69. Vis. prof. U. Hawaii, summer 1977; Disting. lectr. English Kyoto Am. Studies Summer Seminar, Kyoto, Japan, 1981 Author: The Radical Novel in the United States, 1900-1954, 1956; editor: (with Howard Mumford Jones) Letters of Sherwood Anderson, 1953, (with James K. Robinson) A College Book of Modern Verse, 1958, A College Book of Modern Fiction, 1961, The Experience of Prose, 1960, I. Donnelly-Caesar's Column, 1960, (with G.W. Allen and J.K. Robinson) American Poetry, 1965, Sherwood Anderson: Collection of Critical Essays, 1974. Recipient MidAm. award Soc. for Study of Midwestern Lit., Mich. State U., 1983, Outstanding Educator award, 1993; fellow Newberry Libr., 1951, Guggenheim fellow, 1957; Fulbright grantee to Kyoto, 1981. Mem. ACLU, MLA (mem. nat. exec. council 1970-73), Phi Beta Kappa. Home: Brookline Apts 7707 N Brookline Dr Apt 220 Madison WI 53719-3532 Office: Dept English U Wis 600 N Park St Madison WI 53706-1403

RIDGEWAY, LUANN, state legislator; m. Richard Ridgeway. Student, Am. U., 1977; BA in History and Polit. Sci., Westminster Coll., 1978; student, Oxford (Eng.) U., 1978; JD, U. Mo., 1981. Mem. Mo. State Ho. of Reps. Dist. 35, 1992—. Mem. criminal law com., judiciary com., urban affairs com., chldn., youth and families com., civil and administrv. law com., joint com. on administrv. rules. Mem. Mo. Bar Assn. Home: 19405 Platte County Line Rd Smithville MO 64089-8798 Office: Mo Ho of Reps State Capitol Building Jefferson City MO 65101-1556

RIDGLEY, THOMAS BRENNAN, lawyer; b. Columbus, Ohio, Apr. 29, 1940; s. Arthur G. and Elizabeth (Tracy) R.;); children: Elizabeth, Jennifer, Kathryn; m. Lisa Lester, Nov. 27, 1999 BA, Princeton (N.J.) U., 1962; JD with honors, U. Mich., 1965. Bar: Pa. 1965, Ohio 1968, U.S. Dist. Ct. (so. and no. dists.) Ohio, U.S. Dist. Ct. (ea. dist.) Pa., U.S. Ct. Appeals (6th, 3d and 10th cirs.), U.S. Supreme Ct. Assoc. Dechert, Price and Rhoades, Phila., 1965-67; ptnr. Vorys, Sater, Seymour and Pease, Columbus, 1967—. Author: Interstate Conflicts and Cooperation, 1986, (with others) Fending Off Corporate Raiders, 1987. Bd. dirs., mem. exec. com. United Way of Franklin County, Columbus, 1986-98; bd. dirs. Cmty. Shelter Bd., 1992-98, pres. 1997-98; bd. dirs. Columbus Bar Found., 1992-99, pres., 1998. Fellow Am. Coll. Trial Lawyers. Office: Vorys Sater Seymour & Pease 52 E Gay St Columbus OH 43215-3161

RIDGWAY, MARCELLA DAVIES, veterinarian; b. Sewickley, Pa., Dec. 24, 1957; d. Willis Eugene and Martha Ann (Davies) R. BS, Pa. State U., 1979; VMD, U. Pa., 1983; MS, U. Ill., 1997. Intern U. Ill., Urbana, 1983-84, resident in small animal internal medicine, 1984-87; small animal vet. Vet. Cons. Svcs., Savoy, Ill., 1987-97; clin. asst. prof. small animal vet. medicine U. Ill., Urbana, 1997—. Contbr. articles to profl. jours. Mem. Am. Vet. Med. Assn., Acad. Vet. Clinicians, Ea. Ill. Vet. Med. Assn. (pres. 2000-2001), Heartland Pathways (bd. dirs.), Savoy Prairie Soc. (pres. 1989—), Grand Prairie Friends (bd. dirs. 1993-96), Sangamon Valley Conservancy (bd. dirs. 1995—). Avocations: prairie conservation activities, hiking, sketching, canine collectibles. Home: 194 Paddock Dr E Savoy IL 61874-9663 Office: U Ill Vet Med Teaching Hosp 1008 W Hazelwood Dr Urbana IL 61802-4714

RIDLEN, SAMUEL FRANKLIN, agriculture educator; b. Marion, Ill., Apr. 24, 1916; s. Will and Leoma Josephine (Sneed) R.; m. Helen Louise Camp, Apr. 17, 1946; children: Judith Elaine, Barbara Jo, Mark Ellis. BS, U. Ill., 1940; MS, Mich. State U., 1957. Agr. instr. Westville (Ill.) Twp. High Sch., 1940-43; gen. mgr. Honegger Breeder Hatchery, Forrest, Ill., 1953-56; assoc. prof. poultry sci. U. Conn., Storrs, 1957-58; from asst. prof. to prof. poultry extension U. Ill., Urbana-Champaign, 1946-86, prof. emeritus poultry extension, 1986—, asst. head dept. animal scis., 1978-86. Author: An Idea and An Ideal-Nabor House Fraternity 1939-1989, 1989; poultry editorial cons. Successful Farming, Wonderful World Ency., 1960; poultry editor Am. Farm Youth, 1949-53, Ill. Feed Folks, 1949-53. Founding mem., charter mem. Nabor House Frat. Recipient Superior Svc. award U.S. Dept. Agr., 1982, Paul A. Funk Recognition award Coll. Agr., U. Ill., 1983, numerous others. Fellow Poultry Sci. Assn.; mem. World's Poultry Sci. Assn., Ill. State Turkey Growers Assn., Ill. Poultry Industry Coun., Ill Egg Market Devel. Coun. (adv. mem.), Ill. Animal Industry Coun., Coun. for Agr. Sci. and Tech., Ill. Alumni Assn. (life), DAV (life), Alpha Tau Alpha, Epsilon Sigma Phi, Gamma Sigma Delta (pres. 1982-83). Home: 1901 Lakeside Dr # C Champaign IL 61821-5997

RIEDL, JOHN ORTH, university dean; b. Milw., Dec. 9, 1937; s. John O. and Clare C. (Quirk) R.; m. Mary Lucille Priestap, Feb. 4, 1961; children: John T., Ann E., James W., Steven E., Daniel J. BS in Math. magna cum laude, Marquette U., Milw., 1958; MS in Math., U. Notre Dame, 1960, PhD in Math., 1963; postgrad., Northwestern U., 1963. Asst. prof. math. Ohio State U., Columbus, 1966-70, assoc. prof., 1970—, asst. dean Coll. Math. and Phys. Sci., 1969-74, assoc. dean, 1974-87, acting dean, 1984-86, spl. asst. to provost, 1987, dean, dir. Mansfield (Ohio) Campus, 1987—, exec. dean regional campus, 1988—. Panelist sci. edn. NSF, 1980-91; cons. Ohio Dept. Edn., 1989, Ohio bd. regents subsidy cons., 1991, 95, 97, 99, 2001. Pres., v.p. exec. com. Univ. Cmty. Assn., Columbus, 1970-78; mem. edn. commn. St. Peter's Schs., Mansfield, 1989-95; trustee Rehab. Svc. N. Ctrl. Ohio, Mansfield, 1990-99, v.p., 1993-94, pres., 1995-97; pres. Ohio Assn. Regional Campuses, 1993-94; co-chair capital campaign St. Peter's Schs., 1998. NSF grad. fellow, 1960, 61, 62; recipient Faculty Svc. award Nat. U. Continuing Edn. Assn., 1988, Creative Programming award, 1988. Mem. Math. Assn. Am. (chair com. on minicourse 1981-87), Downs Am. Chestnut Found. of Ohio (bd. dirs. 2001--), Rotary Internat. (bd. dirs., pres.-elect, pres.) C. of C. (bd. dirs.). Democrat. Roman Catholic. Avocations: fishing, woodworking, handball, gardening. Home: 745 Clifton Blvd Mansfield OH 44907-2284 Office: Ohio State U 1680 University Dr Mansfield OH 44906-1547 E-mail: riedl.1@osu.edu.

RIEDTHALER, WILLIAM ALLEN, risk management professional; b. Cleve., May 13, 1948; s. Robert Wilbert and Jean Margaret (Trojanowski) R.; m. Janet Louise Clark, Nov. 10, 1973; children: Jennifer Margaret, Valerie Gretchen. AS in Law Enforcement, Cuyahoga C.C., 1968; BA in Pub. Safety Adminstrn., BA in Criminal Justice Studies, Kent State, 1974; EMBA in Healthcare, Baldwin-Wallace Coll., 2000. Cert. instr. and peace officer; cert. tchr., Ohio, Fla., Tex., Mich. Police cadet Cleve. Police Dept., 1967-69, patrolman, 1969-74, detective, 1974-81, sgt. police, 1981-84; assoc. security advisor Cleve. Electric Illuminating Co., 1984-87, investigator, 1987-90; security advisor Centerior Energy Corp., Cleve., 1990-93, supr. claims Independence, 1993-96, mgr. risk mgmt., 1996-98; dir. spl. risk programs N.Am. Benefits Network, INc., Rocky River, Ohio, 1998—. Instr. gambling and vice Case Western Res. U., Cleve., 1979-90, Cleve. Police Acad., 1974—, Ohio Peace Officers Tng. Acad., 1976—, Cuyahoga County Sheriffs Officers Acad., Cleve., 1981—, Shaker Heights (Ohio) Police Acad., 1990—. Author: An Enforcement Guide to Carnival Games Gambling and Fraud, 1981, An Enforcement Guide to Monetary Operated Gambling Devices or Slot Machines, 2002; contbr. articles to profl. jours. Spl. dep. sheriff Cuyahoga County Sheriff's Office, Cleve., 1985—; trustee Cleve. Crime Clinic, 1999—; bd. govs. Nat. Healthcare Antifraud Assn., 1999—. Recipient Patrolman of Yr. award Cleve. Exchange Club, 1979. Mem. Am. Soc. Indsl. Security, Met. Crime Bur. (v.p. 1992-93, pres. 1994-95), German Am. Police Assn., Fraternal Order of Police, Cleve. Claims Assn. Republican. Achievements include participation in an expedition to recover shipwreck of 1857 gold-rush steamship off the Carolina coast;new species of golden coral (chrysogorgia herdendorfi) named in his honor. Home: 7992 Vesta Ave Northfield OH 44067-2048 Office: North Am Benefits Network Inc 19800 Detroit Rd Rocky River OH 44116-1816 E-mail: breidthaler@nabn.com., wreidthaler@enforcementguide.com.

RIEGER, MITCHELL SHERIDAN, lawyer; b. Chgo., Sept. 5, 1922; s. Louis and Evelyn (Sampson) R.; m. Rena White Abelmann, May 17, 1949 (div. 1957); 1 child, Karen Gross Cooper; m. Nancy Horner, May 30, 1961 (div. 1972); stepchildren: Jill Levi, Linda Hanan, Susan Perlstein, James Geoffrey Felsenthal; m. Pearl Handelsman, June 10, 1973; stepchildren: Steven Newman, Mary Ann Malarkey, Nancy Halbeck. AB, Northwestern U., 1944; JD, Harvard U., 1949. Bar: Ill. 1950, U.S. Dist. Ct. (no. dist.) Ill. 1950, U.S. Supreme Ct. 1953, U.S. Ct. Mil. Appeals 1953, U.S. Ct. Appeals (7th cir.) 1954. Legal asst. Rieger & Rieger, Chgo., 1949-50, assoc., 1950-54; asst. U.S. atty. No. Dist Ill., 1954-60, 1st asst., 1958-60; assoc. gen. counsel SEC, Washington, 1960-61; ptnr. Schiff Hardin & Waite, Chgo., 1961—, sr. counsel, 1998—. Instr. John Marshall Law Sch. Chgo., 1952-54. Contbr. articles to profl. jours. Active Chgo. Crime Commn., bd. dirs., 1998—; pres. Park View Home for Aged, 1969-71; Rep. precinct committeeman, Highland Park, Ill., 1964-68; bd. dirs. Spertus Mus. Judaica, 1987-91, vis. com., 1991—. Served to lt. (j.g.) USNR, 1943-46, PTO. Fellow Am. Coll. Trial Lawyers; mem. ABA, FBA (pres. Chgo. chpt. 1959-60, nat. v.p. 1960-61), Chgo. Bar Assn., Ill. Bar Assn., Am. Judicature Soc., 7th Circuit Bar Assn., Standard Club, Lawters Club Chgo., Vail Racquet Club, Phi Beta Kappa. Jewish. Avocations: photography, skiing, sailing. Home: 4950 S Chicago Beach Dr Chicago IL 60615-3207 Office: Schiff Hardin & Waite 6600 Sears Tower Chicago IL 60606 E-mail: mrieger@schiffhardin.com., msheridanr@aol.com.

RIEGSECKER, MARVIN DEAN, pharmacist, state senator; b. Goshen, Ind., July 5, 1937; s. Levi and Mayme (Kauffman) R.; m. Norma Jane Shrock, Aug. 3, 1958; children: Steven Scott, Michael Dean. BA in Pharmacy, U. Colo., 1967. Pharmacist Parkside Pharmacy, Goshen, Ind., 1967-73; pharmacist, mgr. Hooks Drugs, Inc., 1973-94; coroner Elkhart County, 1977-84; mem. Ind. Senate from 12th dist., Indpls., 1988—; pharmacist Walgreens, Goshen, 1994-96, Meijer, Goshen, 1998—. Bus. affairs cons. Goshen Health Sys., 1997-98. Rep. commr. Elkhart County, 1985-88; bd. commrs. pres., 1987-88; past adv. bd. dirs. Oaklawn Hosp.; past chmn. Michiana Area Coun. of Govts. Mem. Ind. Pharm. Assn. Republican. Mennonite. Avocation: jogging. Home: 1814 Kentfield Way Goshen IN 46526-5610 Office: Ind Senate Statehouse 200 W Washington St Indianapolis IN 46204-2728

RIELLY, JOHN EDWARD, educational association administrator; b. Rapid City, S.D., Dec. 28, 1932; s. Thomas J. and Mary A. (Dowd) R.; m. Elizabeth Downs, Dec. 28, 1957 (marriage annulled 1976); children: Mary Ellen, Catherine Ann, Thomas Patrick, John Downs; m. Irene Diedrich, Aug. 1, 1987. B.A., St. John's U., Collegeville, Minn., 1954; postgrad. (Fulbright scholar), London Sch. Econs. and Polit. Sci., 1955-56; Ph.D., Harvard U., 1961. Faculty dept. govt. Harvard U., 1958-61; with Alliance for Progress programs Dept. State, Washington, 1961-62; fgn. policy asst. to Sen. then Vice Pres. Hubert Humphrey, 1963-69; cons. office European and internat. affairs Ford Found., N.Y.C., 1969-70; sr. fellow Overseas Devel. Council, Washington, 1970-71; exec. dir. Chgo. Council on Fgn. Relations, 1971-74, pres., 1974—2001; vis. fellow Sidley & Austin, Chgo., 2001—. Adj. prof., Northwestern U., 2001—; cons. NSC; mem. adv. bd. Grad. Sch. Arts and Scis., Harvard U.; bd. dirs. Am. Coun. on Germany, Nat. Com. on U.S.-China Rels., China Coun. of Asia Soc., Am. Ditchley Found., Trilateral Comm., commn. on U.S.-Brazilian Rels.; past pres. Nat. Coun. Comty. World Affairs Orgns. Contbr. articles to profl. jours.; editor: American Public Opinion and U.S. Foreign Policy, 1975, 2d edit., 1979, 83, 87, 91, 95, 99; editl. bd. Fgn. Policy Quar., 1974—. Former trustee St. John's U. Recipient Legion d'Honneur, France, Distinguished Service Cross, Germany, Commendatore of the Italian Republic, Bernardo O'Higgins Award, Chile, The Golden Decoration, Austria, European Friendship Award, European Union, Order of Leopold (Belgium). Mem. Am. Polit. Sci. Assn., Council on Fgn. Relations, N.Y.C. Home: 2021 Kenilworth Ave Wilmette IL 60091-1519 Office: Sidley & Austin One First National Plz Chicago IL 60603

RIEMENSCHNEIDER, ALBERT LOUIS, retired engineering educator; b. Cody, Nebr., May 18, 1936; s. Albert L. and Agnes E. (Schilling) R.; m. Norma Mae Geisler, June 24, 1962 (dec.); children: Richard L., David F., Barbara J.; m. Sandra Ann Pryor, Feb. 14, 1998. BSEE, S.D. Sch. Mines and Tech., 1959, MSEE, 1962; PhD, U. Wyo., 1969. Registered profl. engr., S.D. Engr. Sperry Utah Corp., Salt Lake City, 1959-60; design engr. Dakota Steel & Supply Co., Rapid City, S.D., 1960-61; instr. U. Wyo., Laramie, 1961-67; chief engr. Dunham Assocs., Rapid City, 1974-80; grad. tchg. asst. S.D. Sch. Mines and Tech., 1961-62, asst. prof., 1967-73, assoc. prof., 1973-74, 80-84, prof., dept. head, 1983-95, prof., 1995-98, prof. emeritus, 1998—. Cons. ALR Engring., RE/SPEC, Inc., Rapid City, 1987—, HC Galloways, Black Hawk, S.D., 1999—. Mem. IEEE, NSPE, Am. Soc. Engring. Edn., Elks. Democrat. Episcopalian. Avocations: electronics, computers, hunting, fishing. Home and Office: ALR Engring 1204 Cheyenne Ave Alliance NE 69301-2529

RIENDEAU, DIANE, secondary school educator; Teacher Barrington (Ill.) H.S., Barrington, Ill., 1985—. Recipient Innovative Teaching Grants Program, Am. Assn. of Physics Teachers, 1992. Home: 310 James St Barrington IL 60010-3329 Office: Barrington HS 616 W Main St Barrington IL 60010-3015

RIES, THOMAS G. (TORCHY), former state legislator; m. Janet Ries; 7 children. Student, U. S.D. Cir. ct. judge; mem. S.D. Ho. Reps., 1984-88, 93-97, mem. judiciary com. and local govt. com.; mem. judiciary and transp. coms. Home: 420 S Lake Dr Watertown SD 57201-5433

RIESZ, PETER CHARLES, marketing educator, consultant; b. Orange, N.J., Apr. 30, 1937; s. Kolman and Ellen (Wachs) R.; m. Elizabeth Strider Dunkman, Dec. 28, 1968; children— Sarah Kathleen BS, Rutgers Coll., 1958; MBA, Columbia U., 1963, PhD, 1971. From asst. prof. to assoc. prof. U. Iowa, Iowa City, 1968-80, prof. mktg., 1980—, chmn. dept. mktg., 1981-87, Williams prof. tchg., 1994-97. Vis. prof. Boston U., 1974-75, Duke U., Durham, N.C., 1984-85; cons. in field. Contbr. articles to profl. jours. Recipient Teaching Excellence award HON Industries, 1989; named MBA Prof. of Yr., 1990; Old Gold fellow U. Iowa, 1972. Mem. Am. Chem. Soc., Am. Mktg. Assn. Democrat. Presbyterian Avocations: photography. Home: 2411 Tudor Dr Iowa City IA 52245-3638 Office: U Iowa Dept Mktg Coll Bus Adminstrn Iowa City IA 52242 E-mail: peter-riesz@uiowa.edu.

RIFE, JACK, state legislator; b. Muscatine, Iowa, Apr. 10, 1943; m. Sharon Cooper. AA, Muscatine (Iowa) C.C., 1963; BS, Iowa State U., 1966. Agrl. advisor Liberty Trust Bank, 1968-73; farmer, 1973—; mem. Iowa Senate, Des Moines, 1982—, minority leader 74th, 75th and 76th Gen. Assembly, senate minority leader, mem. legis. coun., chair health and human rights com., mem. appropriations com., mem. bus. and labor rels. com., mem. local govt. com., mem. natural resources and environment com. Mem. United Meth. Ch.; past pres. Ext. Coun.; mem. legis. contact Bi-Sttae Econ. Devel. Adv. Com. With U.S. Army, 1966-68. Mem. Cattlemen's Assn., Am. Legion (polit. liaison), Pork Prodrs. (past pres.), Wilton Farm Bur., Muscatine Farm Bur., Cedar County Farm Bur.,, Alpha Gamma Rho. Republican. Office: State Capitol 9th And Grand Ave Des Moines IA 50319-0001 E-mail: jack_rife@legis.state.ia.us.

RIFKIN, LEONARD, metals company executive; b. N.Y.C., Apr. 10, 1931; s. Irving W. and May (Goldin) R.; m. Norma Jean Smith, Aug. 22, 1954 (dec. Jan. 1983); children: Daniel Mark, Richard Sheldon, Martin Stuart; m. Ariel Kalisky, Jan. 14, 1984. B.S., Ind. U., Bloomington, 1952. Pres., CEO Omni Source Corp., Fort Wayne, Ind., 1960-98, chmn., CEO, 1998—. Bd. dirs. Steel Dynamics, Butler, Ind., Qualitech Steel, Indpls. Served with U.S. Army, 1956-58 Office: Omni Source Corp 1610 N Calhoun St Fort Wayne IN 46808-2762

RIGALI, JUSTIN F. archbishop; b. L.A., Apr. 19, 1935; s. Henry Alphonsus and Frances Irene (White) R. B in Sacred Theology, Cath. U. Am., 1961; Lic. in Canon Law, Gregorian U., Rome, 1963, D in Canon Law, 1964; LHD (hon.), St. Louis U., 1995. Ordained priest Apr. 25, 1961. Titular archbishop of Bolsena, 1985-94; sec. Congregation for Bishops Holy See, Vatican City, 1989-94, sec. Coll. of Cardinals, 1990-94; archbishop Archdiocese of St. Louis, 1994—. Pres. Pontifical Ecclesiastical Acad., 1985-89. Office: Archdiocese of St Louis 4445 Lindell Blvd Saint Louis MO 63108-2403

RIGGLEMAN, JAMES DAVID, former professional baseball team manager; b. Ft. Dix, N.J., Dec. 9, 1952; Degree in Physical Edn., Frostburg State U. Minor league baseball player, 1974-81; minor league baseball mgr., 1982-88, 91-92; dir. player devel., then coach St. Louis Cardinals, 1988-90; mgr. San Diego Padres, 1993-94, Chicago Cubs, 1995-99; bench coach Cleve. Indians, 1999—. Office: Cleve Indians 2401 Ontario St Cleveland OH 44115-4003

RIKLI, DONALD CARL, lawyer, deceased; b. Highland, Ill., June 16, 1927; s. Carl and Gertrude Louise (Stoecklin) R.; m. Joan Tate, Oct. 10, 1953; children: Kristine, David. AB, Ill. Coll., 1951; JD, U. Ill., 1953. Bar: Ill. 1953, U.S. Dist. Ct. (so. dist.) Ill. 1961, U.S. Ct. Appeals (7th cir.) 1968, U.S. Supreme Ct. 1974. Pvt. practice law, Highland, 1953-97. Atty. City of Highland, 1956-59; lectr. in field. Author: The Illinois Probate System, 1974, 75, 77, 78; bd. editors Illinois Real Property I, 1966, 71, Lawyers World, 1970-72, Law Notes, 1981-83, The Compleat Lawyer, 1985-87; contbr. over 60 articles to profl. jours. Mem. consistory United Ch. of Christ, 1960-62, 93-95. With U.S. Army, 1945-47. Fellow Am. Coll. Trust and Estate Counsel, Ill. Bar Found., Am. Bar Found.; mem. ABA (sec. chairperson gen. practice sect. 1990-91, Ho. of Dels. 1991-93, mem. coun. gen. practice sect. 1981-93, Sole Practitioner of Yr. 1990, posthumous Donald C. Rikli Solo Lifetime Achievement award gen. practice, solo practice and small firms sect.), Ill. Bar Assn. (chmn. Bill of Rights com. 1967-68, coun. estate planning probate and trust sect. 1976-81, sec. 1980-81), Madison County Bar Assn. (pres. 1966-67), Am. Acad. Estate Planning Attys. (bd. govs. 1994-95). Address: PO Box 366 Edwardsville IL 62025-0366

RIKOSKI, RICHARD ANTHONY, engineering executive, electrical engineer; b. Kingston, Pa., Aug. 13, 1941; s. Stanley George and Nellie (Gober) R.; m. Giannina Batchelor Petrullo, Dec. 18, 1971 (div. 1979); children: Richard James, Jennifer Anne; m. Carol Loestbron. BEE, U. Detroit, 1964; MSEE, Carnegie Inst. Tech., 1965; PhD, Carnegie-Mellon U., 1968; postdoctoral fellow, Case-Western Res. U./NASA, 1971. Registered profl. engr., Ill., Mass., Pa. Engr. 1st communication satellite systems Internat. Tel. & Tel., Nutley, N.J., 1961-64; engr. Titan II ICBM program Gen. Motors, Milw., 1964; trainee NASA, 1964-67; instr. Carnegie-Mellon U., Pitts., 1966-68; asst. prof. U. Pa., Phila., 1968-74; assoc. prof., dir. hybrid microelectronics lab., chmn. ednl. TV com. IIT, Chgo., 1974-80, chmn. ednl. TV com., 1974-80; rsch. engr. nuclear effects ITT Rsch. Inst., 1974-75; pres. Tech. Analysis Corp., 1980—. Engr. color TV colorimetry Hazeltine Rsch., Chgo., 1969; engr. Metroliner rail car/roadbed ride quality dynamics analysis U.S. Dept. Transp., ENSCO, Inc., Springfield, Va., 1970; pres. Tech. Analysis Corp., Chgo., 1978-91; contractor analysis of color TV receiver safety hazards U.S. Consumer Product Safety Commn., 1977, analysis heating effect in aluminum wire Beverly Hills Supper Club Fire, Covington, Ky., 1978; engr. GFCI patent infringement study 3M Corp., St. Paul, 1979-81; elec. systems analyst Coca-Cola Corp., Atlanta, 1983-91; fire investigator McDonald's Corp., Oak Brook, Ill., 1987-90; engring. analyst telephone switching ctrs. ATT, Chgo., 1990-91; expert witness numerous other govtl. and corp. procs.; evaluator Accreditation bd. Engring. and Tech., 2000—. Author: Hybrid Microelectronic Circuits, 1973; editor: Hybrid Microelectronic Technology, 1973; contbr. articles to profl. jours. Officer Planning Commn., Beverly Shores, Ind., 1987-93, trustee town coun., 1992—, police liason 1993-96, dir. emergency mgmt., 1998, coun. pres., 1999-2000; mem. Chgo. Coun. Fgn. Rels., USAF SAC Comdrs. Disting.is. Program; adv. coun. Nat. Park Svc. Ind. Dunes Nat. Lake Shore, 1993—. NASA fellow, 1964-67, 70. Mem. IEEE (sr. ednl. activities bd. N.Y.C. 1970-74, USAB career devel. com. 1972-74, editor Soundings 1973-75, Cassette Colloquia 1973-74, del. Popov Soc. Tech. Exch. USSR, mgr. Dial Access Tech. Edn. program 1972), Assn. for Media Based Continuing Engring. Edn. (bd. dirs.), Nat. Fire Protection Assn., Sigma Xi, Tau Beta Pi, Eta Kappa Nu. Republican. Avocations: sailing, travel. Home: One E Lakefront Dr Beverly Shores IN 46301-0444 Office: Tech Analysis Corp 1032 W Diversey Pkwy Chicago IL 60614-1317 E-mail: rikoski@technicalanalysiscorp.com.

RILEY, ANTONIO, state legislator; b. Aug. 22, 1963; BA, Carroll Coll. Former staff asst. to Milw. mayor City of Milw., 1990-92; Wis. state rep. Dist. 18, 1992—. Mem. Midtown Neighborhood Assn. Office: State Capitol PO Box 8953 Madison WI 53708-8953

RILEY, HUGH SANFORD, diversified financial services company executive; b. Montreal, Que., Can., Mar. 15, 1951; s. Robert Sanford Riley and Hope Meribeth Cameron (Stobie) Coyne; Deborah J. Doyle, Sept. 7, 1975. BA, Queen's U., Can., 1971; LLB, York U., Can., 1975. Assoc., then ptnr. Taylor McCaffrey Chapman & Sigurdson, 1976-85; v.p., then exec. v.p., COO Gt. Lakes Group Inc., 1985-89; exec. v.p., COO Trilon Fin. Corp., 1989; owner H.S. Riley Investors Group, Winnipen, Man., Can., 1989—. Bd. dirs. Trilon Fin. Corp., Gt. Lakes Group Inc., Northgate Explorations Ltd., Royal LePage Ltd., Comcheq Inc., Morgan Trust Co., 20/20 Group Fin. Ltd. Bd. dirs. Ont. Spl. Olympics. Mem. Law Soc. Man., Can. Hearing Soc. Found., Royal Can. Yacht Club. Office: HS Riley Investors Group Inc 1 Canada Ctr, 447 Portage Ave Winnipeg MB Canada R3C 3B6

RILEY, KEVIN M. principal; Prin. Gretna (Nebr.) Jr. Sr. High Sch., 1982-99, supt., 1999—. Recipient Blue Ribbon award U.S. Dept. Edn., 1990-91. Office: Gretna Sr High Sch 11705 S 216th St Gretna NE 68028-4729

RILEY, MICHAEL ROBERT, marketing and business development executive; b. Wisconsin Rapids, Wis., Apr. 17, 1938; s. Robert William and Anne Bates (Clark) R.; m. Judith Wood, Aug. 12, 1961; children: David T., Christopher W. BS, Hampton U., 1974; MS, Indsl. Coll. of Armed Forces, Washington, 1975; MPA, Golden Gate U., 1976, MBA, 1977. Commd. 2d lt. USAF, 1958, advanced through grades to lt. col., 1977, ret., 1979; mktg. exec. McDonnell Douglas Corp., St. Louis, 1979-90; pres. MRR Assocs., 1990—. Cons. Regional Commerce and Growth Assn., St. Louis, 1980-85, 90—. Pres. trustees Lake of the Woods Subdiv., St. Louis, 1980-85; pres. bd. dirs. St. Louis Chamber Chorus, 1986-88; mem. St. Louis Ambassadors, 1990—. Decorated D.F.C. with 2 oakleaf cluster, Bronze Star, Air medal with 23 oakleaf clusters; named Swimmer of the Yr., U.S. Amateur Athletic Union/NCAA, Portland, Oreg., 1956; recipient USAF Navigator Wings, Harlingen, Tex., 1959, USAF Pilot Wings, Chandler, Ariz., 1964, USN Wings, Beeville, Tex., 1971. Mem. Air Force Assn., Assn. Naval Aviation, Am. Mgmt. Assn., Internat. City Mgrs. Assn., Army Aviation Assn. Am., Am. Helicopter Soc., Navy League, River Rats. Avocations: sailing, golf, flying. Office: MRR Assocs 5846 Mango Dr Saint Louis MO 63129-2243

RILEY, NANCY MAE, retired vocational home economics educator; b. Grand Forks, N.D., May 1, 1939; d. Kenneth Wesley and Jeanne Margaret Olive (Hill) R. BS in Edn., Miami U., 1961; postgrad., Ohio U., 1964-69; MA, Marietta Coll., 1989. Cert. high sch. tchr. Tchr. home econs. Malta-McConnelsville (Ohio) High Sch., 1961-67; tchr. home econs. Waterford (Ohio) High Sch., 1968-92. Advisor Malta-McConnelsville Future Homemakers, 1961-66, Waterford Future Homemakers Am., 1968-92; advisor to state officer Ohio Future Homemakers Am., McConnelsville, 1963, Waterford, 1976. Leader Girl Scouts Am., McConnelsville, 1962-66, camp counselor, 1962-76; fair judge Waterford Cmty. Fair, Waterford, 1970-85. Mem.: DAR, NEA, Ohio Vocat. Assn. (life), Ohio Edn. Assn. (life; del. 1979), Am. Vocat. Assn. (life), Ohio Geneal. Soc., Daus. War of 1812 (pres. 1991—, state sec. 1995—97, state 2d v.p. 2001—), Daus. Union Vets. (del. 1992—, tent pres. 1993—98, dist. pres. 1996, Ohio Dept. pres. 1999), White Shrine of Jerusalem (worthy high priestess 1979—81, 1983), Order Eastern Star (worthy matron 1967—68, dep. grand matron 1978). Republican. Baptist. Avocations: ceramics, genealogy, camping, reading, handcrafts. Home: PO Box 137 Waterford OH 45786-0137 E-mail: rileyn@marietta.edu.

RILEY, PAUL E. retired judge; b. 1942; BS, St. Louis U., 1964, JD, 1967. Hearings examiner motor carrier divsn. Ill. Commerce Commn., 1967-69; from asst. pub. defender to chief pub. defender Office of Pub. Defender, 1969-82; prin. Law Office of Paul Riley, Edwardsville, Ill., 1969-72, Mudge Riley and Lucco, Edwardsville, 1972-85; assoc. judge State of Ill., 1985, cir. judge, 1986; judge U.S. Dist. Ct. (so. dist.) Ill., East St. Louis, 1994-99. Mem. ABA, Ill. State Bar Assn. (mem. assembly), Madison County Bar Assn. (pres. 1975). Office: US Dist Ct So Dist Ill Fed Courthouse 750 Missouri Ave East Saint Louis IL 62201-2954

RILEY, ROBERT BARTLETT, landscape architect; b. Chgo., Jan. 28, 1931; s. Robert James and Ruth (Collins) R.; m. Nancy Rebecca Mills, Oct. 5, 1956; children: Rebecca Hill, Kimber Bartlett. PhB, U. Chgo., 1949; BArch, MIT, 1954. Chief designer Kea, Shaw, Grimm & Crichton, Hyattsville, Md., 1959-64; prin. partner Robert B. Riley (A.I.A.), Albuquerque, 1964-70; campus planner, asso. prof. architecture, dir. Center Environ. Research and Devel., U. N.Mex., 1966-70; prof. landscape architecture and architecture U. Ill., Urbana-Champaign, 1970—, head dept. landscape architecture, 1970-85, dir. PhD program, 1999—; vis. prof. Harvard U., 1996-97; prof. emeritus, dir. joint PhD program U. Ill., 1997—. Sr. fellow landscape architecture studies Dumbarton Oaks/Harvard U., 1992—, chmn. fellows, 1996—; mem. rev. panel landscape architects Fed. Civil Service-Nat. Endowment Arts. Assoc. editor Landscape mag., 1967-70; editor Landscape Jour., 1987—. Served with USAF, 1954-58. Nell Norris fellow U. Melbourne, Australia, 1977; project fellow Nat. Endowment Arts, 1985 Fellow Am. Soc. Landscape Architects (Nat. Honor award 1979); mem. Coun. of Educators in Landscape Architecture, pres. 1984-85, chmn. bd. dirs. 1985-86, Outstanding Educator award 1992, Pres.'s award 1994, chmn. editl. adv. bd. Landscape Architecture 1996-99), AIA (Design award Md. 1962, N.Mex. 1968, Environ. Svc. award N.Mex. 1970), Environ. Design Rsch. Assn. (chmn. bd. 1990-91), Phi Beta Epsilon. Unitarian. Office: Univ Ill 101 Temple Buell Hall 611 E Lorado Taft Dr Champaign IL 61820-6921 Home: 407 E George Huff Dr Urbana IL 61801-6703

RINCK, JAMES RICHARD, lawyer; b. Grand Rapids, Mich., Mar. 6, 1958; s. Richard John and Ann Louise (Weening) R; m. Lorelei Landheer, Apr. 30, 1988. BA, Calvin Coll., 1975-79; JD, U. Ill., 1979-82. Bar: Mich. 1982, U.S. Dist. Ct. (we. dist.) Mich. 1982. Asst. prosecutor Muskegon County, Muskegon, Mich., 1983-84; sole practice Grand Rapids, 1984—. Deacon Westminster Presbyn. Ch., 1985-89, mem. pastoral search com., 1989-90; mem. exec bd. Kent County Dems., 1984—; mem. exec. bd. Mich. Young Dems., 1986-88, candidate Mich. State Senate, 1990; state asst. atty. gen., 1990-99; mem. Bd. Edn. of Grand Rapids, 1993—; bd. dirs. Grand Rapids Downtown Devel. Authority, 1995—. Mem. Mich. Bar Assn. (workers' compensation and negligence sects. 1987—, criminal law sect. 1983—), Grand Rapids Bar Assn., Nat. Orgn. Social Security Claimants Reps. (sustaining). Avocations: reading, sports, cooking. Home: 2353 Swensberg Ave NE Grand Rapids MI 49505-4066 Office: 1108 McKay Twr 146 Monroe Center St NW Grand Rapids MI 49503-2833

RINDEN, DAVID LEE, clergyman; b. Lake Mills, Iowa, Aug. 1, 1941; s. Oscar Henry and Iva (Stensrud) R.; m. Gracia Elizabeth Carlson, Sept. 11, 1966; children: Jonathan, Elizabeth, Amy. BA, Moorhead State U., 1964; diploma, Luth. Brethren Sem., 1966; postgrad., Seattle Pacific U., 1973. Ordained to ministry Luth. Ch., 1967. Pastor Bethesda Luth. Ch., Eau Claire, Wis., 1968-72, Maple Pk. Luth. Ch., Lynnwood, Wash., 1972-79; v.p. Ch. of the Luth. Brethren of Am., Fergus Falls, Minn., 1991—; editor Faith & Fellowship, 1979-2000; exec. dir. Faith and Fellowship Press Ch. of the Luth. Brethren of Am., 1979-2000; pastor Gethsemane Lutheran Ch., Rochester, Minn., 2000—. Chmn. com. on commitment Ch. of Luth. Brethren, Fergus Falls, 1981-82, com. on role of women in ch., 1984-86, chmn. com. on 90th anniversary, chmn. bd. publs., 1968-78. Editor: Explanation of Luther's Small Catechism, 1988; author: Biblical Foundations, 1981. Founding com. JAIL, Inc., Fergus Falls, 1991; pres. bd. dirs. Fergus Falls Fed. Community Credit Union, 1987-2000. Mem. Fergus Falls Ministerial Assn. (sec. 1989-90, v.p. 1991-92, pres. 1992-93), Kiwanis (pres. 1994-95, lt. gov. 1996-97). Home: 3610 4th Pl NW Rochester MN 55901-7502 Office: Gethsemane Lutheran Ch 2204 22d St NW Rochester MN 55901

RING, ALVIN MANUEL, pathologist, educator; b. Detroit, Mar. 17, 1933; s. Julius and Helen (Krolik) R.; m. Cynthia Joan Jacobson, Sept. 29, 1963; children— Jeffrey, Melinda, Heather. BS, Wayne State U., 1954; MD, U. Mich., 1958. Intern Mt. Carmel Hosp., Detroit, 1958-59; resident in pathology Michael Reese Hosp., Chgo., 1960-62; asst. pathologist Kings County Hosp., Bklyn., 1962-63; assoc. pathologist El Camino Hosp., Mountain View, Calif., 1963-65; chief pathologist, dir. labs. St. Elizabeth's Hosp., Chgo., 1965-72, Holy Cross Hosp., Chgo., 1972-87, Silver Cross Hosp., Joliet, Ill., 1990—. Instr. SUNY, 1962-63, Stanford U., 1963-65; asst. prof. pathology U. Ill., Chgo., 1966-69, assoc. prof., 1969-78, prof., 1978—; adj. clin. prof. No. Ill. U., 1981-87; adj. prof. med. edn. U. Ill. Coll. Medicine, 1988—; chmn. histotech. Nat. Accrediting Agy. for Clin. Lab Scis., 1977-81; mem. spl. adv. com. Health Manpower, 1966-71; pres. Spear Computer Users Group, 1981-82; mem. adv. com. Mid-Am. chpt. ARC, 1979-85; pres. Pathology and Lab Cons., Inc., 1985—; adj. prof., med. dir. Med. Tech., Moraine Valley C.C., 1994—; originator, coord. pathology, med. decision-making courses Nat. Ctr. for Advanced Med. Edn., 1981—, others; co-coord. computer courses Midwest Clin. Conf., 2000—. Author: Laboratory Correlation Manual, 1968, 82, 86, Laboratory Assistant Examination Review Book, 1971, Review Book in Pathology, Anatomic, 1986, Review Book in Pathology, Clinical, 1986; mem. editorial bd. Lab. Medicine, 1975-87; contbr. articles to med. jours. Fellow Coll. Am. Pathology (insp. 1973—, ins. com. 2002-), Am. Soc. Clin. Pathology; mem. AMA, Ill. Med. Soc., Chgo. Med. Soc. (alt. councilor 1980-85, mem. adv. com. on health care delivery), Ill. Pathol. Soc. (trustee 1997—), Chgo. Pathol. Soc. (censor 1980-88, exec. com. 1985-89, program. com. 1987—), Am. Assn. Blood Banks, Assn. Brain Tumor Rsch. (cons.), Exec. Svc. Corps (exec. cons. 1988—), Phi Lambda Kappa (chpt. pres.). Home: 100 Graymoor Ln Olympia Fields IL 60461-1213 Office: Silver Cross Hosp 1200 Maple Rd Joliet IL 60432-1497

RING, GERALD J. real estate developer, insurance executive; b. Madison, Wis., Oct. 6, 1928; s. John George and Mabel Sarah (Rau) R.; m. Armella Marie Dohm, Aug. 20, 1949; children: Michael J., James J., Joseph W. Student pub. schs., Madison. With Sub-Zero Freezer Co., Madison, 1948-70, mfr.'s rep., 1954-70; founder, pres. Parkwood Hills Corp., Madison, from 1965, Park Towne Devel. Corp., Madison, from 1969, Ring Devel. Co., 1992—. Bd. dirs.. CUNA Mut. Ins. Soc., CUNA Mut. Ins. Group, CUNA Mut. Investment Corp., CUDIS Ins. Soc., all Madison, 1968-98, exec. com., 1973-83, chmn. bd., 1979-81; bd. dirs. CUMIS Ins. Soc., mem. exec. com., 1973-83, chmn. bd., 1977-79; bd. dirs. CMCI Corp., mem. exec. com., 1974-83, chmn. bd., 1981-83; treas. CUNADATA Corp., 1974-81; bd. dirs. Wis. Credit Union League, 1958-79, pres., 1965-67; mem. Wis. Credit Union Rev. Bd., 1967-83, chmn., 1973-76, 82-83; bd. dirs. CUNA Credit Union Nat. Assn., Inc., 1964-81, League Life Ins. Co., League Gen. Ins. Co., Southfield, Mich., CUNA Mut. Fin. Svcs. Corp., Century Ins. Co. Am., Waverly., Iowa. Chmn. Greater Madison C. of C., 1980, bd. dirs., 1976-89, v.p. econ. devel., 1983-85, v.p. govtl. affairs, 1985-89, mem. capital fund raising com., 1983—, chmn. 1983-86; mem. Mayor's Emergency Housing Com., 1984-85; chmn. fin. com. St. Patrick's Congregation, 1983-89; bd. dirs. Cath. Charities of Madison, 1995—, pres., 1996-99; bd. dirs. Future Madison Housing Fund, 1997—. Served with USMC, 1951-53. Mem. Aircraft Owners and Pilots Assn. Roman Catholic. Lodge: Rotary. (bd. dirs. 1981-83). Home: 607 Farwell Dr Madison WI 53704-6029 Office: 402 S Gammon Rd Madison WI 53719-1002

RING, HERBERT EVERETT, management executive; b. Norwich, Conn., Dec. 19, 1925; s. Herbert Everett and Catherine (Riordan) R.; m. Marilyn Elizabeth Dursin, May 21, 1955 (dec. Jan. 1994); children: Nancy Marie, Herbert Everett. BA, Ind. No. U., 1971, MBA, 1973; AMP, Harvard U., 1981. V.p. ops. Ogden Foods, Inc., Toledo, 1963-74, sr. v.p. Boston, 1974-75; v.p. concessions SportSvc. Corp., Buffalo, 1976-78, sr. v.p., 1978-80, pres., 1980-83, bd. dir.; pres. Universal Mgmt. Concept Counseling, Sylvania, Ohio, 1983—; prin. Hysen Group II, Livonia, Mich., 1991-95. Counselor L.A. Olympic Concessions Food Svc., 1984, Phila. Meml. Stadium, 1985, Del. North Cos. Internat. London Eng., 1985-86, Chgo. Stadium Corp., 1989-92, Buffalo Sabres N.Y., 1992, Fine Host Inc. Greenwich Ct., 1993, Delaware North of Australia Ltd., 1994, Temp DNC Health Support Ltd., Wellington, New Zealand, 1995, Fanfare Enterprises, 1997, Geneva Lakes Kennel Club, Delavan, Wis., 1997, St. Francis Health Care Ctr., Greenspring, Ohio, 1998, Detroit Opera House, 2000; bd. dirs. Greenfield Restaurant Co., Inc., Letheby and Christopher Ltd., Reading, Berkshire, Eng., Air Terminal Svcs., Inc., The Aud Club, Inc., Bluegrass Turf Svc., Inc., Concession Suppliers, Inc., Cosel Drive-In Theatre, Inc., G&H Sports Concessions, Inc., Hazel Park Parking, Inc. Mem. Toledo Mus. Art., 1985-92. Sgt. Air Corps U.S. Army, 1944-46, ETO, USAF, 1950-51. Mem. Internat. Assn. of Auditorium Mgrs., N.W. Ohio Restaurant Assn. (bd. dirs. 1990-93), Am. Culinary Fedn. Inc., Harvard Bus. Club (Detroit). Roman Catholic. Home and Office: 5540 Radcliffe Rd Sylvania OH 43560-3740

RING, LEONARD M. lawyer, writer; b. Taurage, Lithuania, May 11, 1923; came to U.S., 1930, naturalized, 1930; s. Abe and Rose (Kahn) R.; m. Donna R. Cecrle, June 29, 1959; children: Robert Steven, Susan Ruth Student, N.Mex. Sch. Mines, 1943-44; LLB, DePaul U., 1949, JD; LLD (hon.), Suffolk U., 1990. Bar Ill. 1949. Spl. asst. atty. gen. State Ill., Chgo., 1967-72; spl. atty. Ill. Dept. Ins., 1967-73; spl. trial atty. Met. San. Dist. Greater Chgo., 1967-77; lectr. civil trial, appellate practice, tort law Nat. Coll. Advocacy, San Francisco, 1971, 72; chmn. and spl. atty. com. jury instrns. Ill. Supreme Ct., 1967—. Nat. chmn. Attys. Congl. Campaign Trust, Washington, 1975-79. Author: (with Harold A. Baker) Jury Instructions and Forms of Verdict, 1972. Editorial bd. Belli Law Jour., 1983— ; adv. bd. So. Ill. U. Law Jour., 1983— . Contbr. chpts. to books including Callaghan's Illinois Practice Guide, Personal Injury, 1988 and chpt. 6 (Jury Selection and Persuasion) for Masters of Trial Practice, also numerous articles to profl. jours. Trustee, Roscoe Pound-Am. Trial Lawyers Found., Washington, 1978-80; chmn. bd. trustees Avery Coonley Sch., Downers Grove, Ill., 1974-75. Served with U.S. Army, 1943-46 Decorated Purple Heart. Fellow Am. Coll. Trial Lawyers, Internat. Acad. Trial Lawyers, Internat. Soc. Barristers, Inner Circle Advs.; mem. Soc. Trial Lawyers, Am. Judicature Soc., Appellate Lawyers Assn. (pres. 1974-75), Assn. Trial Lawyers Assn. (nat. pres. 1973-74), Ill. Trial Lawyers Assn. (pres. 1966-68), Trial Lawyers for Pub. Justice (founder, pres. 1990-91), Chgo. Bar Assn. (bd. mgrs. 1971-73, 2d v.p. 1993), ABA (coun. 1983—, chair tort and ins. sect. 1989—, fed. jud. standing com. 7th cir. 1991—), Ill. Bar Assn., Kans. Bar Assn. (hon., life), Lex Legion Bar Assn. (pres. 1976-78), Met. Club, Plaza Club, Meadow Club, River Club, Monroe Club. Home: Ginger Creek 6 Royal Vale Dr Oak Brook IL 60523-1648 Office: Ill Supreme Ct PO Box 4987 Oak Brook IL 60522-4987

RING, TWYLA L. state legislator, newspaper editor; b. Sept. 15, 1937; m. Ardell Ring; 4 children. Student, Cambridge C.C. Mem. Minn. Senate from 18th dist., St. Paul, 1999—. Home: 8500 285th Ave NE North Branch MN 55056-6406 Office: Capitol 75 Constitution Ave Saint Paul MN 55155-1601

RINGEL, ROBERT LEWIS, university administrator; b. N.Y.C., Jan. 27, 1937; s. Benjamin Seymour and Beatrice (Salis) R.; m. Estelle Neuman, Jan. 18, 1959; children— Stuart Alan, Mark Joseph. B.A., Bklyn. Coll., 1959; M.S., Purdue U., 1960, Ph.D., 1962. cert. speech pathologist. Rsch. scientist, laryngeal rsch. lab. Ctr. Health Scis., UCLA, 1962-64; asst. prof. communication disorders U. Wis., 1964-66; from mem. faculty to provost Purdue U., 1966—91, provost, 1991—. Vis. prof. Inst. Neurology and Nat. Hosps. Coll. Speech Scis., U. London, 1985; cons. NIH, NEH, Bur. Edn. Handicapped of U.S. Office Edn.; bd. dirs. Indpls. Ctr. for Advanced Rsch., 1988-92; hon. prof. Coll. of Computer Scis. and Mgmt., Rzeszów, Poland, 2000—; bd. dir., faculty adv. Hillel Found. Purdue U., 2000-. Author sci. articles; contbr. to monographs and textbooks; cons. editor Chapman & Hall, London. Bd. dirs. Lafayette Home Hosp., 1978-87, Lafayette Symphony Orch., 1983-85. Recipient Research Career Devel. award Nat. Inst. Dental Research, 1967-70, Award for highest merit for sci. article Jour. Speech and Hearing Research, 1979, Disting. Alumnus award Bklyn. Coll., 1985; Para-Rabbi fellow Hebrew Union Coll., 2001—. Fellow Am. Speech and Hearing Assn. (v.p. Found. 1990—, honors 1998); mem. AAUP, Nat. Assn. State Univs. and Land Grant Colls. (exec. com. 1988-91, rsch. policy and grad. edn., exec. com. coun. on acad. affairs 1991—, com. on instnl. coop., exec. com. provosts instn. coop. com. 1991—), Sigma Xi (v.p. 1986—). Office: Purdue Univ Audiology & Speech Sci 1353 Heavilon Hall G-12B West Lafayette IN 47907-1353 Home: 208 Rosebank Ln West Lafayette IN 47906-8613

RINGEN, CATHERINE OLESON, linguistics educator; b. Bklyn., June 3, 1943; d. Prince Eric and Geneva Muriel (Leigh) Oleson; m. Jon David Ringen, Nov. 22, 1969; children: Kai Mathias, Whitney Leigh. Student, Cornell U., 1961-63; BA, Indiana U., 1970, MA, 1972, PhD, 1975. Vis. lectr. U. Minn., Mpls., 1973-74; asst. prof. U. Iowa, Iowa City, 1975-79, assoc. prof., 1980-87, prof., 1988—, chair linguistics, 1987-93. Author: Vowel Harmony: Theoretical Implications, 1988; co-editor Nordic Jour. Linguistics, 2001—; contbr. articles to profl. jours. Sr. Fulbright prof. Trondheim, Norway, 1980, Poznan, Poland, 1994-95. Mem. AAAS, Linguistic Soc. Am., Nordic Assn. Linguists, Phi Beta Kappa. Office: U Iowa Dept Linguistics Iowa City IA 52242 E-mail: catherine-ringen@uiowa.edu.

RINGLER, JAMES M. cookware company executive; b. 1945; BS, U. Buffalo, 1967, MBA, 1968. Mgr., cons. Arthur Andersen & Co., 1968-76; v.p. appliance group Tappan Co., Mansfield, Ohio, 1976-78, gen. v.p., mgr. appliance div., 1978-87, pres., COO, 1987-90, also bd. dirs., 1987-90; exec. v.p. Premark Internat., Inc., Deerfield, Ill., 1990-92, pres., COO, 1992-96, pres., CEO, 1996—, chmn., 1997—; vice chmn. Ill. Tool Works, Inc., Glenview, 1999—. Office: Premark Internat Inc 3600 W Lake Ave Glenview IL 60025-1215 also: Ill Tool Works Inc 3600 W Lake Ave Glenview IL 60025-1215

RINK, LAWRENCE DONALD, cardiologist; b. Indpls., Oct. 14, 1940; s. Joe Donald and Mary Ellen (Rand) R.; m. Eleanor Jane Zimmerly, Aug. 10, 1963; children: Scott, Virginia. BS, DePauw U., 1962; MD, Ind. U., 1966. Diplomate Am. Bd. Internal Medicine, Am. Bd. Cardiology, Critical Care Medicine. Clin. asst. prof. Ind. U. Med. Sch., Indpls., 1973-79, clin. assoc. prof., 1979-85, clin. prof. medicine, 1985—; cardiologist IMA, Inc., Bloomington, Ind., 1974-95; pres., CEO Internal Medicine Assocs., 1994—; dir. cardiac rehab. Bloomington Hosp., 1976—, dir. cardiology, 1983—; CEO, chmn. bd. dirs. IMA Inc., 1995—. Physician Ind. U. Basketball Team, 1979—; dir. med. edn. Bloomington Hosp., 1976—; med. dir. Track and Field Pan Am. Games, 1987; U.S. Olympic Physician Olympic Sports Festival, 1989, World Univ. Games, 1990, Olympic Games, Barcelona, 1992, World Univ. Games, Fukuoka, Japan, 1995, Korea, 1997, Majorca, Spain, 1999; N.Am. continent rep. Fed. Internat. Student Univ. Sports. Bd. dirs. J.O. Ritchie Soc., Ind. U. Med. Sch. Bd. dirs., dean's coun. Ind. U. Med. Sch., 1992—. Recipient Quality of Life award Major Bloomington, 1978; named Most Outstanding Flight Surgeon, USN, 1968, Most Outstanding Alumnus, Ind. U. Med. Sch., 1998. Fellow Am. Coll. Cardiology, Am. Heart Assn., Am. Soc. Critical Care, Am. Coll. Sports Medicine; mem. AMA, Ind. U. Med. Alumnae Assn. (pres. 1986-87, exec. alumna coun.). Avocations: reading, writing, golf, tennis. Office: IMA Inc 550 Landmark Ave Bloomington IN 47403

RINTAMAKI, JOHN M. automotive executive; BBA, U. Mich., 1964, JD, 1967. Bar: Mich. 1968, Pa. 1973. Sr. atty. internat. Ford Motor Co., 1978-84, assoc. counsel corp. and financings, 1984-86, asst. sec., assoc. counsel, 1986-92, sec., asst. gen. counsel, 1993-98, v.p., gen. counsel, sec., 1999-00, chief staff, 2000—. Office: Ford Motor Co One American Rd Dearborn MI 48126-1899

RIPLEY, JAMES W. food products executive; BA, Fairleigh Dickinson U. CPA. Acct. KPMG Peat Marwick; various positions Corn Product Internat., Bedford Park, Ill., 1968-97, v.p. fin. corn products, v.p. fin., CFO, 1997—. Office: Corn Products Internat 6500 S Archer Ave Bedford Park IL 60501

RIPPLE, KENNETH FRANCIS, federal judge; b. Pitts., May 19, 1943; s. Raymond John and Rita (Holden) Ripple; m. Mary Andrea DeWeese, July 27, 1968; children: Gregory, Raymond, Christopher. AB, Fordham U., 1965; JD, U. Va., 1968; LLM, George Washington U., 1972, LLD (hon.) , 1992. Bar: Va. 1968, N.Y. 1969, U.S. Supreme Ct. 1972, U.S. Supreme Ct. 1972, D.C. 1976, Ind. 1984, U.S. Ct. Appeals (7th cir.), U.S. Ct. Mil. Appeals, U.S. Dist. Ct. (no. dist.) Ind. Atty. IBM Corp., Armonk, NY, 1968; legal officer U.S. Supreme Ct., Washington, 1972—73, spl. asst. to chief justice Warren E. Burger, 1973—77; prof. law U. Notre Dame, 1977—; judge U.S. Ct. Appeals (7th cir.), South Bend, 1985—. Reporter Appellate Rules Com., Washington, 1978—85; commn. on mil. justice U.S. Dept. Def., Washington, 1984—85; cons. Supreme Ct. Ala., 1983, Calif. Bd. Bar Examiners, 1981, Anglo-Am. Jud. Exch., 1977; adv. com. Bill of Rights to Bicentennial Constn. Commn., 1989; adv. com. on appellate rules Jud. Conf. U.S., 1985—90, chmn., 1990—93; chmn. adv. com. on appellate judge edn. Fed. Jud. Ctr., 1996—. Author: Constitutional Litigation, 1984. With JAGC USN, 1968—72. Mem.: ABA, Am. Law Inst., Phi Beta Kappa. Office: US Ct of Appeals 208 US Courthouse 204 S Main St South Bend IN 46601-2122 also: Fed Bldg 219 S Dearborn St Ste 2660 Chicago IL 60604-1803

RIS, HANS, zoologist, educator; b. Bern, Switzerland, June 15, 1914; came to U.S., 1938, naturalized, 1945; s. August and Martha (Egger) R.; m. Hania Wislicka, Dec. 26, 1947 (div. 1971); children: Christopher Robert, Annette Margo; m. Theron Caldwell, July 14, 1980. Diploma high sch. teaching, U. Bern, 1936; Ph.D., Columbia, 1942. Lectr. zoology Columbia U., 1942; Seessel fellow in zoology Yale U., 1942; instr. biology Johns Hopkins U., 1942-44; asst. Rockefeller Inst., N.Y.C., 1944-46, assoc., 1946-49; assoc. prof. zoology U. Wis., Madison, 1949-53, prof., 1953-84, prof. emeritus, 1984—. Hon. prof. Peking U., Beijing, 1995—. Fellow AAAS, Am. Acad. Arts and Scis.; mem. Nat. Acad. Scis., Electron Microscopy Soc. Am. (Disting. Investigator award 1983), Am. Soc. for Cell Biology (E.B. Wilson award 1993). Achievements include research on mechanisms of nuclear division, chromosome structure, nuclear envelope, cell ultrastructure, electron microscopy. Office: U Wis Zoology Rsch 1117 W Johnson St Madison WI 53706-1705 E-mail: hris@facstaff.wisc.edu.

RISHEL, JAMES BURTON, manufacturing executive, director; b. Omaha, Apr. 27, 1920; s. James Blaine and Elizabeth Helen (Kerr) R.; m. Alice Jane Snyder, June 30, 1945; children: James Richard, Sara Jane Rishel Fields. BSME, U. Nebr., 1946. Profl. engr., Ohio. Pres. Corp.

Equipment Co., Cin., 1962-82; chmn. bd. Systecon Inc., 1982-2000; cons. Pumping Solutions LLC, 2000—. Author: The Water Management Manual, HVAC Pump Handbook, 1996; patentee hydraulic systems; contbr. numerous articles to profl. jours. Capt. USAF, 1942-46, 51-52. Fellow ASHRAE. Avocations: philanthropy, walking. Home: 7570 Thumbelina Ln Cincinnati OH 45242-4937 E-mail: jbrishel@fuse.net.

RISK, RICHARD ROBERT, health care executive; b. Chgo., Sept. 15, 1946; s. Clement Albert and Mary Catherine (Clarke) R.; m. Rebecca Ann Sandquist, Jan. 11, 1969 (div. Sept. 1984); children: Michael, Daniel, Laura; m. Louise L. Lawson, Dec. 1, 1984; stepchildren: Carrie Lawson, Valerie Lawson. BS in Econs., U. Ill., 1968; MBA in Health Adminstrn., U. Chgo., 1971. Asst. adminstr. U. Ill. Hosp., Chgo., 1969-72, Ctrl. DuPage Hosp., Winfield, Ill., 1972-74; mgmt. cons., v.p. Tribrook Group, Inc., Oak Brook, 1974-81; v.p. cons. svcs. Parkside Med. Svcs., Park Ridge, 1981-83; prin. health and med. divsn. Booz, Allen, & Hamilton, Inc., Chgo., 1983-84; exec. v.p. EHS Health Care, Oak Brook, 1984-92, pres., CEO, 1992-95, Advocate Health Care, Oak Brook, 1995—. Bd. dirs. Landauer Corp.; mem. faculty Healthcare Fin. Mgmt. Assn., 1978-86, Am. Assn. Hosps. Cons., 1978-84; bd. dirs., mem. ad hoc ins. com., fin. com. Premier; lectr. grad. program social scis. No. Ill. U., 1982-88; lectr., adv. bd. multi-hosp. system study Kellogg Sch. Health Mgmt. Program Northwestern U., 1985—; lectr. Grad. Program in Health Adminstrn. U. Chgo., 1982-94. Mem. access com. Gov.'s Task Force on Health Reform, 1992-94; mem. chancellor's adv. bd. U. Ill. at Chgo.; chair South Cook county region United Way. Fellow Am. Assn. Hosp. Cons. (bd. dirs., treas., chmn. govt. rels. com., chmn. membership task force, liaison Nat. Coun. Cmty. Hosps.); mem. Am. Hosp. Assn. (chair healthcare systems sect.), Ill. Hosp. Assn. (chmn. coun. on health fin., mem. strategic plan com., bd. dirs., treas.), U. Chgo. Hosp. Adminstrn. Alumni Assn. (pres. exec. com. alumni coun., chmn. 50th ann. com.), Chgo. Health Policy Rsch. Coun. Home: 801 Clinton Pl River Forest IL 60305-1501 Office: Advocate Health Care 2025 Windsor Dr Oak Brook IL 60523-1586

RISON, ANDRE, football player; b. Flint, Mich., Mar. 18, 1967; Student, Mich. State U. Wide receiver Indpls. Colts, 1989, Atlanta Falcons, 1990-95, Cleve. Browns, 1995-97, Kansas City Chiefs, 1997—. Named to Pro-Bowl, 1990, 91, Sporting News All-Pro team, 1990. Office: Kansas City Chiefs 1 Arrowhead Dr Kansas City MO 64129-1651

RISS, ROBERT BAILEY, real estate investor; b. Salida, Colo., May 27, 1927; s. Richard Roland and Louise (Roberts) R.; married; children: Edward Stayton, G. Leslie, Laura Bailey, Juliana Warren. BSBA, U. Kans., 1949. Pres. Riss Internat. Corp., Kansas City, Mo., 1950-80, chmn. bd., 1964-86; founder, chmn. bd., pres. Republic Industries, Inc., 1969-86; chmn. bd. Grandview Bank and Trust Co., 1969-86, Commonwealth Gen. Ins. Co., 1986-93. Chmn. bd. dirs., exec. com. Heart of Am. Fire and Casualty Co.; chmn. bd. dirs. Comml. Equipment Co. Vice chmn. bd. trustees Kansas U. Endowment Assn., 1980-89. Recipient Silver Beaver award Kansas City Area coun. Boy Scouts Am., 1972; Disting. Svc. citation U. Kans., 1976; Fred Ellsworth medal U. Kans., 1979; named Most Outstanding Young Man in Mo. U.S. Jr. C. of C., 1956 Mem. Kans. U. Alumni Assn. (nat. pres. 1969-70), Sigma Nu. Episcopalian.

RISSER, FRED A. state legislator; b. Madison, Wis., May 5, 1927; married; 3 children. BA, U. Oreg., LLB, 1952. Bar: Wis. Sole practice, Madison, 1952—; mem. Wis. Senate from 26th dist., 1962—; asst. minority leader Wis. State Senate, 1965-67, minority leader, 1967-75, pres. pro tem, 1975-79, pres., 1979-93, asst. minority leader, 1993-96, pres., 1996—. Mem. Wis. State Assembley, 1956-62; del. Democratic Conv., 1960, 64; presdl. elector-chmn. Wis. Electoral Coll., 1964; vice chmn. Bldg. Commn., Wis. also: 5008 Risser Rd Madison WI 53705-1365 Office: Madison Office, State Capitol Rm. 220 South, PO Box 7882 Madison WI 53707-7882 E-mail: sen.risser@legis.state.wi.us.*

RISSMAN, BURTON RICHARD, lawyer; b. Chgo., Nov. 13, 1927; s. Louis and Eva (Lyons) R.; m. Francine Greenberg, June 15, 1952; children: Lawrence E., Thomas W., Michael P. BS, U. Ill., 1947, JD, 1951; LLM, NYU, 1952. Bar: Ill. 1951, U.S. Dist. Ct. (no. dist.) Ill. 1954, U.S. Ct. Appeals (7th cir.) 1978, U.S. Supreme Ct. 1982. Assoc. Schiff, Hardin & Waite, Chgo., 1953-59, ptnr., 1959—, mem. mgmt. com., 1984-92, chmn. mgmt. com., 1986-90. Mem. faculty Practicing Law Inst. Bd. editor U. Ill. Law Forum, 1949-51; contbr. articles to profl. jours. 1st lt. JAGC USAF, 1952—53. Food Law fellow, 1951. Mem. ABA, Ill. Bar Assn., Chgo. Bar Assn., Chgo. Coun. Lawyers, Met. Club, Carlton Club. Office: Schiff Hardin & Waite 6600 Sears Tower Chicago IL 60606-6473

RISTOW, GEORGE EDWARD, neurologist, educator; b. Albion, Mich., Dec. 15, 1943; s. George Julius and Margaret (Beattie) R.; 1 child, George Andrew Martin. BA, Albion Coll., 1965; DO, Coll. Osteo. Medicine/Surgery, Des Moines, 1969. Diplomate Am. Bd. Psychiatry and Neurology. Intern Garden City Hosp., 1969-70; resident Wayne State U., 1970-74; fellow U. Newcastle Upon Tyne, 1974-75; asst. prof. dept. neurology Wayne State U., Detroit, 1975-77; assoc. prof. Mich. State U., East Lansing, 1977-83, prof., 1983-84, 95—, prof., chmn., 1984-95, prof. emeritus, 2001—. Fellow Am. Acad. Neurology, Royal Soc. Medicine; mem. AMA, Am. Osteo. Assn., Pan Am. Med. Assn., World Fedn. Neurology, Am. Coll. Neuropsychiatrists (sec.). Home: 2070 Riverwood Dr Okemos MI 48864-2814 E-mail: ristoowge@aol.com.

RITTER, FRANK NICHOLAS, otolaryngologist, educator; b. New Albany, Ind., July 30, 1928; s. Carl Joseph and Kathleen Mary (Wolfe) R.; m. Gertrude Erlacher; children: Raymond, Kathleen, Lawrence, Mary Elizabeth, Teresa, Joseph, Sharon, Michael. BS, Notre Dame U., 1949; MD, St. Louis U., 1953; MS, U. Mich., 1959. Diplomate Am. Bd. Otolaryngology (pres. 1990-93). Intern Mercy Hosp., Ohio, 1953-54; resident in otorhinolaryngology U. Mich. Hosp., 1954-60; asst. prof. otolaryngology U. Mich., Ann Arbor, 1960-65, assoc. prof., 1966-70, clin. prof., 1971—. Author: The Surgical Anatomy and Technique of Surgery on the Paranasal Sinuses, 1978, 3d edit. 1992; contbr. articles to profl. jours. Capt. USAF, 1955-57. Recipient Sr. award Med. Sch., U. Mich., 1965, Shovel award U. Mich. Med. Students, 1967. Mem. Am. Laryngol. Assn., Am. Otological Soc., Am. Acad. Otolaryngology, Head and Neck Surgery, Am. Bronchoesophagological Assn. (pres. 1985), Mich. Otolaryn. Soc. (pres. 1968), Soc. Univ. of Otolaryngologists, Triological Soc. (exec. sec. 1985-89, pres. 1993), Centurion (pres. 1984), Walter Work Soc. (pres. 1986). Roman Catholic. Avocations: golf, fishing. Office: Dept Otorhinolaryngology U Mich Ypsilanti MI 48197-1096

RITTER, ROBERT FORCIER, lawyer; b. St. Louis, Apr. 7, 1943; s. Tom Marshall and Jane Elizabeth (Forcier) R.; m. Karen Gray, Dec. 28, 1966; children: Allison Gray Campione, Laura Thompson Capstick, Elisabeth Forcier Schoenecker. BA, U. Kans., 1965; JD, St. Louis U., 1968. Bar: Mo. 1968, U.S. Dist. Ct. (ea. and we. dists.) Mo. 1968. U.S. Ct. Mil. Appeals 1972, U.S. Supreme Ct. 1972, U.S. Ct. Appeals (8th cir.) 1980, U.S. Dist. Ct. (so. dist.) Ill. 1982. Assoc. Gray & Sommers, St. Louis, 1968-71; ptnr. Gray Ritter & Graham, P.C., 1974—; chmn., pres. Gray & Ritter, 1983—. Bd. dirs. Marine Bank and Trust Co.; adv. com. 22d cir. Supreme Ct., 1985-92; mem. Supreme Ct. com. civil jury instrns., 1988—, U.S. Dist. Ct. adv. com., 1993-95; lectr. Contbr. articles to profl. jours. Bd. dirs. Cystic Fibrosis Found., Gateway chpt., pres., 1991. Capt. USAR, 1968-74. Recipient Law Week award Bur. Nat. Affairs, 1968, award of merit Nat. Conf. Met. Cts., 1995. Fellow Internat. Soc. Barristers (bd. govs. 1994—), Am. Coll. Trial Lawyers, Internat. Acad. Trial Lawyers; mem. ABA, Am. Judicature Soc., Assn. Trial Lawyers Am., Am. Bd. Trial Advocates (advocate), Bar Assn. Met. St. Louis (chmn. trial sect. 1978-79, exec. com. 1980-82, award merit 1976, award achievement 1982, chmn. bench bar conf. 1983), Mo. Bar Assn. (coun. practice and procedure com. 1972—, coun. tort law com. 1982—, bd. govs. 1984-91, fin. com. 1984-91), Mo. Bar Found. (outstanding trial lawyer award 1978), Lawyers Assn. St. Louis (exec. com. 1976-81, pres. 1977-78), Mo. Assn. Trial Attys. (bd. govs. 1984—), Noonday Club, Bellerive Country Club, John's Island Club (bd. dirs. 1998—), Racquet Club (bd. govs. 1988-93, pres. 1991-92), Red Stick Golf Club (founding mem.), Roaring Fork Club (founding mem.), Windsor Club. Presbyterian. Office: Gray Ritter & Graham PC 701 Market St Fl 8 Saint Louis MO 63101-1850 E-mail: rritter@grgpc.com.

RITTERSKAMP, DOUGLAS DOLVIN, lawyer; b. St. Louis, July 7, 1948; s. James Johnstone Jr. and Linn M. (Dolvin) R.; m. Linda S. Vansant, Mar. 23, 1974; 1 child, Tammy. AB, Washington U., 1970, JD, 1973; LLM in Taxation, NYU, 1978. Bar: N.Y. 1974, Mo. 1979. Assoc. Patterson, Belknap, Webb & Tyler, N.Y.C., 1974-78; jr. ptnr. Bryan Cave LLP (and predecessors), St. Louis, 1978-82; ptnr. Bryan Cave LLP, 1983—. Trustee Scottish Rite Clinic for Childhood Lang. Disorders of St. Louis, Inc., 1987-97, St. Louis Mission and Ch. Ext. Soc., United Meth. Ch., 1987-97, Mo. United Meth. Found., 1994—, The Coll. Sch., 1995—. Capt. USAR, 1970-79, active duty tng., 1973. Mem. ABA (employee benefits com. sect. taxation 1987-91, 96—), Bar Assn. Met. St. Louis (steering com. employee benefits 1989—), Masons (32d degree, knight comdr. ct. of honor), Shriners. Methodist. Home: 5223 Sutherland Ave Saint Louis MO 63109-2338

RITTINGER, CAROLYNE JUNE, retired newspaper editor; b. Swift Current, Sask., July 19, 1942; d. George Kelly Gaetz and Eva Evelyn (Hiebert) Olson; m. Robert Edward Rittinger, Aug. 16, 1958; children: Robert Wade, Angela Alison, Lisa Michelle. Women's editor Swift Current Sun, 1967-68; city editor Medicine Hat (Alta.) News, 1969-70; reporter Kitchener-Waterloo Record, Kitchener, Ont., 1972-75, copy editor, 1976, women's editor, then dist. editor, entertainment editor, wire editor, 1976-85, city editor, 1985-86, asst. mng. editor, 1986-89, mng. editor, 1989-92, editor, 1992—. Recipient News Story of Yr. award Calgary Women's Press Club, 1969, Best Feature Story on Fine Art award, 1970, Honorable Mention for A.R. McKenzie award for Info. Story, 1970; named Oktoberfest Woman of Yr., 1992. Avocations: downhill skiing, travel, live theatre. Office: Kitchener-Waterloo Record 225 Fairway Rd Kitchener ON Canada N2G 4E5

RITTMER, SHELDON, state senator, farmer; b. DeWitt, Iowa, Sept. 5, 1928; s. Elmer and Lois (Hass) R.; m. Elaine Heneke, June 11, 1950; children: Kenneth S., Lynnette Rittmer Jones, Robyn Jon (dec.), infant son (dec.). County supr. Clinton (Iowa) Conty Bd. Suprs., 1978-90; chmn. Clinton County Title III Com., 1987-90; v.p. Iowa Assn. County Suprs., Des Moines, 1989-90; mem. Iowa Senate from 19th dist., 1990—. Iowa Senate coms. Transportation, State Govt. (chair 1990-2000), Natural Resources, Ethics, Rules and Adminstrn., Health and Human Rights, mem. bd. Iowa Pub, Employees Retirement System. Chmn. 1st Luth. Ch., Maquoketa, Iowa, 1964-68; active Clinton County Hist. Soc., 1980—; mem. Elvira Luth. Ch. Recipient Spl. Recognition award Nat. Fedn. Ind. Bus., 1991-92, Spl. Recognition Iowa Soil Conservation award, 1994. Mem. Izaak Walton League Iowa, DeWitt Lions, Ducks Unlimited U.S.A, Clinton County Pork Prodr's. Assn., Clinton County Cattlemen's Assn., Pheasants Forever, City of Clinton C. of C., DeWitt C. of C., Bettendorf C. of C. Republican. Avocations: public speaking, com. rsch., reading, agriculture. Home: 3539 230th St De Witt IA 52742-9208 Office: State Senate of Iowa State Capital Des Moines IA 50319-0001 E-mail: sheldon.rittmer@legis.state.ia.us.

RIVARD, JEROME G. automotive engineer; b. Hudson, Wis., Nov. 21, 1932; BSME, U. Wis., 1955. Dir. engring. Bendix, 1962-76; chief engr. Ford Motor Co., 1976-86; vice pres., group exec. Bendix Electronics Group , 1986—88; pres. Global Tech. & Bus. Devel., Harrison Twp. , Mich., 1988—. Fellow IEEE, Soc. Automotive Engrs.; mem. NAE. Acheivements include research in the application of electronics to automotive systems. Office: 29401 S Seaway Ct Harrison Township MI 48045

RIVENESS, PHILLIP J. city official, former state legislator; b. Karlstad, Minn., Dec. 14, 1947; s. John Anders and Ruth (Olson) R.; m. Gail Elaine Coffin, 1968; 3 children. BA, U. Minn., 1969. Former mem. Minn. Ho. of Reps., St. Paul; senator Minn. Senate, 1991-97; mem. Mpls. St. Paul Met. Coun. Vicechmn. govt. ops. and reform com., mem. environ. and natural resources com., health care com., others.; exec dir. South Hennyson Svc. Coun., 1974-78; health care adminstr. Chmn. Bloomington Dem-Farmer-Labor Club, 1979-80. Democrat. Home: 5301 Northwood Rdg Minneapolis MN 55437-1717 Office: Met Coun Mears Park Ctr 230 E 5th St Saint Paul MN 55101

RIVERS, LYNN N. congresswoman; b. Augres, Mich., Dec. 19, 1956; 2 children. BA, U. Mich., 1987; JD, Wayne State U., 1992. Mem. sch. bd. City of Ann Arbor, Mich., 1984-92; mem. Mich. House of Reps., 1992-94, U.S. Congress from 13th Mich. dist., 1994—; mem. edn. and workforce com., sci. com., 1994. Office: US House Reps 1724 Longworth Bldg Washington DC 20515-2213*

RIVES, STANLEY GENE, university president emeritus; b. Decatur, Ill., Sept. 27, 1930; s. James A. and Frances (Bunker) R.; m. Sandra Lou Belt, Dec. 28, 1957; children: Jacqueline Ann, Joseph Alan. B.S., Ill. State U., 1952, M.S., 1955; Ph.D., Northwestern U., 1963; EdD (hon.), Lincoln Coll., 1998. Instr. W.Va. U., 1955-56, Northwestern U., 1956-58; prof. Ill. State U., Normal, 1958-80, Am. Council on Edn. Fellows Program, 1969-70, assoc. dean faculties, 1970-72, dean undergrad. instrn., 1972-80, assoc. provost, 1976-80, acting provost, 1979-80; provost, v.p. acad. affairs, prof. Eastern Ill. U., Charleston, 1981-83, pres., 1983-92, pres. emeritus, 1992—. Vis. prof. U. Hawaii, 1963-64 Author: (with Donald Klopf) Individual Speaking Contests: Preparation for Participation, 1967, (with Gene Budig) Academic Quicksand: Trends and Issues in Higher Education, 1973, (with others) Academic Innovation: Faculty and Instructional Development at Illinois State University, 1979, The Fundamentals of Oral Interpretation, 1981; contbr. articles to profl. jours. Bd. dirs. Ill. State Univs. Retirement System, 1992—, treas., 1995-2001, pres., 2001—; Ea. Ill. Univ. Found., 1993-98, also pres., 1996-98, East Ctrl. Ill. Devel. Corp., 1983-92, Charleston Area Econ. Devel. Found., 1986-92, Coles Together, 1988-92; mem. pres. commn. NCAA, 1986-91; trustee Nat. Debate Tournament, 1967-75. With U.S. Army, 1952-54. Recipient Alumni Achievement award Ill. State U., 1998, Co. of Edn. Hall of Fame. Mem. Am. Assn. State Colls. and Univs., Ill. State C. of C. (bd. dirs. 1990-92), Charleston C. of C. (bd. dirs. 1985-88), Theta Alpha Phi, Phi Kappa Delta, Pu Gamma Mu, Alpha Phi Omega, Alpha Zeta, Sigma Phi Epsilon (hon.). Home: 2231 Andover Pl Charleston IL 61920-3807 E-mail: srives@mcleodusa.net.

RIVET, JEANINE M. health plan administrator; BS in Nursing, Boston Coll.; MPH, Boston U. Sch. Public Health. From v.p. health svc. ops. to CEO United HealthCare, Minnetonka, Minn., 1990-98, CEO health plans, 1998—. Office: United HealthCare Group 300 United HealthCare Group Ctr 9900 Bren Rd E Minnetonka MN 55343-9664

RIZAI, MATTHEW M. marketing and finance professional; b. Istanbul, Turkey, Apr. 6, 1956; came to U.S. 1973; s. Andrew and Muriel (Wilson) Teneyck; m. Tonja M. Anstead, Mar. 14, 1987; 1 child, Aliyea Tiffany. BS, Mich. State U., 1978, MS, 1980, PhD, 1983; MBA Mktg. Fin., U. Chgo., 1990. Mgr. Modal Analysis Lab., Mich. State U., East Lansing, Mich., 1980-83; v.p. Computer Aided Design Software Inc., Oakdale, Iowa, 1983-84; cons. engr. NUTech Testing Corp., San Jose, Calif., 1984-85; sr. rsch. engr. GMC, Troy, Mich., 1985-90; assoc. Arch Devel. Corp., Chgo., 1989-90; pres., chief exec. officer Engring. Animation Inc., Ames, Iowa, 1990—. Office: Engring Animation Inc Isu Research Park 2625 Ames IA 50010

RIZER, FRANKLIN MORRIS, physician, otolaryngologist; b. Gallipolis, Ohio, Aug. 13, 1953; s. Franklin Morris and Wanda Mae (Potts) R.; m. Maria Nicolette Guglielmi, Feb. 8, 1986. BS cum laude, Ohio State U., 1975; MD, U. Cin., 1979; M in Med. Mgmt., Tulane U., 1997; MBA, Youngstown State U., 1998. Diplomate Am. Bd. Otolaryngology. Intern U. Calif., Davis, 1979-80; resident U. Wash., Seattle, 1980-81, Ea. Va. U. Coll. of Medicine, Norfolk, 1981-84; fellow House Ear Inst., 1984-87; chief otology St. Joseph's Riverside Hosp., Warren, Ohio, 1989—; assoc. prof. Ea. Va. Coll. of Medicine, Norfolk, 1987—, Northeastern Ohio U. Coll. of Medicine, Rootstown, 1987—, Ohio State U., Columbus, 1995—. Fellowship dir. Warren Otologic Group, Warren, 1991—. Contbr. articles to profl. jours. Trustee Makoning Valley Macintosh Users Group, Warren, 1989-92; active Leadership Warren, 1989; chmn., bd. dirs. Humility of Mary Integrated Delivery Network, 1995—. With USAF, 1971-73. Fellow Am. Acad. Otolaryngology; mem. Am. Acad. Facial Plastics, Am. Coll. Physician Execs., Am. Laryngological, rhinological and Otological Soc., Soc. of Wilderness Medicine, Undersea and Hyperbaric Med. Soc., Delta Mu Delta, Phi Kappa Phi. United Methodist. Avocations: scuba diving, bicycling, camping, gardening. Home: 469 Country Club Dr NE Warren OH 44484-4616 Office: Warren Otologic Group 3893 E Market St Ste 2 Warren OH 44484-4791

RIZZO, HENRY, state legislator; m. Silvia Rizzo; children: Tomy Mike, Johnny Joe. Mem. Mo. State Ho. of Reps. Dist. 40, 1985—. Mem. appropriations-gen. adminstrn. com., budget com., commerce com. (chmn.), local govt. and related matters com., urban affairs com., utilities regulation com. Home: 575 Harrison St Kansas City MO 64106-1265 Office: Mo Ho of Reps State Capitol Jefferson City MO 65101 Fax: 573-526-1947. E-mail: hrizzo@services.state.mo.us.

RIZZO, RONALD STEPHEN, lawyer; b. Kenosha, Wis., July 15, 1941; s. Frank Emmanuel and Rosalie (Lo Cicero); children: Ronald Stephen Jr., Michael Robert. BA, St. Norbert Coll., 1963; JD, Georgetown U., 1965, LLM in Taxation, 1966. Bar: Wis. 1965, Calif. 1967, Ill. 1999. Assoc. Kindel & Anderson, L.A., 1966-71, ptnr., 1971-86, Jones, Day, Reavis & Pogue, L.A., 1986-93, Chgo., 1993—. Bd. dirs. Guy LoCicero & Son Inc., Kenosha, Wis. Contbg. editor ERISA Litigation Reporter, 1994-99; mem. internat. adv. editl. bd. Jour. Pensions Mgmt. and Mktg. Schulte zur Hausen fellow Inst. Internat. and Fgn. Trade Law, Georgetown U., 1966. Fellow Am. Coll. Tax Counsel, Am. Coll. Employee Benefits Counsel (charter); mem. ABA (chmn. com. on employee benefits sect. on taxation 1988-89, vice chair com. on govt. submissions 1995-99), Los Angeles County Bar Assn. (chmn. com. on employee benefits sect. on taxation 1977-79, exec. com. 1977-78, 90-92), State Bar Calif. (co-chmn. com. on employee benefits sect. on taxation 1980), West Pension Conf. (steering com. L.A. chpt. 1980-83). Avocations: reading, golf, travel. Home: # 19C 1040 N Lake Shore Dr Chicago IL 60611-6164 Office: Jones Day Reavis & Pogue 77 W Wacker Ste 3500 Chicago IL 60601-1692 E-mail: rsrizzo@jonesday.com.

ROACH, JOHN ROBERT, retired archbishop; b. Prior Lake, Minn., July 31, 1921; s. Simon J. and Mary (Regan) R. B.A., St. Paul Sem., 1946; M.A., U. Minn., 1957; L.H.D. (hon.), Gustavus Adolphus Coll., St. Mary's Coll., St. Xavier U., Villanova U., U. St. Thomas, Coll. of St. Catherine. Ordained priest Roman Catholic Ch., 1946; instr. St. Thomas Acad., 1946-50, headmaster, 1951-68; named domestic prelate, 1966; rector St. John Vianney Sem., 1968-71; aux. bishop St. Paul and Mpls., 1971; consecrated bishop, 1971; pastor St. Charles Borromeo Ch., Mpls., 1971-73, St. Cecilia Ch., St. Paul, 1973-75; archbishop of, 1975-95. Appointed vicar for parishes, 1971, vicar for clergy, 1972— ; Episc. moderator Nat. Apostolate for Mentally Retarded, 1974; Mem. Priests Senate, 1968-72; pres. Priests Senate and Presbytery, 1970; chmn. Com. on Accreditation Pvt. Schs. in Minn., 1952-57; mem. adv. com. Coll. Entrance Exam. Bd., 1964; Episc. mem. Bishops and Pres.'s Com.; chmn. Bishops Com. to Oversee Implementation of the Call to Action Program, 1979-80; chmn. priestly formation com.; mem. Cath. Charity Bd. Trustee St. Paul Sem. Sch. Div., 1971-75, chmn., 1975-95; trustee Cath. U. Am., 1978-81, Coll. St. Catherine, 1975-95; chmn. bd. trustees St. Thomas Acad., U. St. Thomas, St. John Vianney Sem.; v.p. Nat. Conf. Cath. Bishops, 1977-80, pres., 1980-83, chmn. ad hoc com. on call to action, 1977; chair internat. policy com. U.S. Catholic Conf., 1990-93. Mem. Am. Coun. Edn. (del. 1963-65), Minn. Cath. Edn. Assn. (past pres.), Assn. Mil. Colls. and Schs. U.S. (past pres.), North Cen. Assn. Colls. and Secondary Schs., Nat. Conf. Cath. Bishops (adminstrv. com., priestly formation com., chmn. vocations com., priorities and plans com., com. on sexual abuse), U.S. Cath. Conf. (com. on social devel. and world peace 1990-93, priorities and plans com.), Nat. Cath. Edn. Assn. (chmn. bd. dirs.), Nat. Cath. Rural Life Conf. (past chmn. task force on food and agr. 1987-89). Address: Chancery Office 226 Summit Ave Saint Paul MN 55102-2121

ROACH, THOMAS ADAIR, lawyer, mediator, arbitrator; b. Akron, Ohio, May 1, 1929; s. Edward Thomas and Mayme Bernice (Turner) R.; m. Sally Jane Bennett, July 11, 1953; children: Thomas, David, James, Dorothy, Steven, Patrick. AB, U. Mich., 1951, JD with distinction, 1953. Bar: Mich. 1953. Assoc. McClintock, Fulton, Donovan & Waterman (and successor firms), Detroit, 1956-62, ptnr., 1962-87; counsel Bodman, Longley & Dahling, Detroit and Ann Arbor, Mich., 1988-90, ptnr. Detroit and Ann Arbor, Mich., 1990-2000, sr. lawyer, 2001—. Bd. dirs. Ferndale Labs, Inc., Canterbury Health Care, Inc. Contbr. articles to profl. jours. Vice chmn. 14th Congl. Dist. Democratic Orgn., 1971-75; chmn. platform and resolution com. Mich. Dem. Party, 1971-74, treas., 1975-87; permanent chmn. Dem. State Conv., 1976; mem. platform com. and drafting subcom. Dem. Nat. Conv., 1972, mem. rules com., 1980, alt. del., 1984; Bd. regents U. Mich., 1975-90; bd. dirs. Mich. Tech. Coun., 1983-92, vice chmn. 1984-86, south-ctrl. region 1992-95; pres. 9th Dist. Res. Policy Bd. 1976-77; nat. chmn. Ann Giving, U., Mich., 1987-97; mem. history and traditions com. U. Mich., 1998—; mem. Mich. Higher Edn. Assistance Authority, Mich. Higher Edn. Student Loan Authority, 1990-94, bd. dirs. Legal Counsel, 1999—, Great Sauk Trail Coun. Boy Scouts Am., 1993—; bd. dirs. Wolverine Coun. Boy Scouts Am., 1991-93; officer Compensation Commn. Pittsfield Twp., 1991-93. Served to capt. USCGR, 1953-56; res. group comdr., 1974-77. Mem. ABA, Fed. Bar Assn., Mich. Bar Assn. (chmn. constrn. law com. 1983-85), Detroit Bar Assn., Washtenaw County Bar Assn., Res. Officers Assn., Order of Coif (Disting. Alumni Achievement award, Spirit of Mich. award), Thomas M. Cooley Club, U. Mich. Club (gov. 1970-74), U. Mich. Alumni Assn. (bd. dirs. 1991-94, 95—, pres. 1995-97, pres. emeritus 2001-02), Rotary Club of Ann Arbor (bd. dirs. 1991-96, pres. 1994-95, chair Dist. Permanent Fund 1999-2001), Sigma Alpha Iota. Anglican. Home: 11825 Durston St Pinckney MI 48169-9502 Office: Bodman Longley & Dahling 110 Miller Ave Ste 300 Ann Arbor MI 48104-1339 E-mail: thomasa.roach@worldnet.att.net.

ROACH, WILLIAM RUSSELL, training and education executive; b. Bedford, Ind., 1940; s. George H. and Beatrice M. (Schoenlaub) R.; m. Margaret R. Balogh, 1961 (div. 1994); children: Kathleen L., Keith W. BS in Fin. and Acctg., UCLA, 1961. CPA, Calif. Internal auditor Hughes Aircraft Corp., L.A., 1962; sr. acct. Haskins & Sells, 1962-66; asst. to group v.p., asst. corp. contr. Lear Siegler, Inc., Santa Monica, Calif.,

1966-71; exec. v.p., corp. sec., dir. Optimum Sys. Inc., Santa Clara, 1972-79; pres., dir. Banking Sys. Inc. subs. Optimum Sys. Inc., Dallas, 1976-79, BancSystems, Inc., Santa Clara, 1976-79, DMA/Optimum Honolulu, 1978-79; v.p. URS Corp., San Mateo, Calif., 1979-81; pres. URS Internat., Inc., 1980-81; pres., CEO, dir. Advanced Sys., Inc., 1981-88. Pres., CEO, dir. Applied Learning Internat., Inc. (formed from merger of Advanced Systems, Inc. and Deltak Training Corp.), Naperville, Ill., 1981-88; sr. v.p., bd. dirs. Nat. Edn. Corp. (parent co. Applied Learning Internat.), Irvine, Calif., 1988-89; chmn. bd., CEO Plato Learning Inc. (former known as TRO Learning Inc. (acquisition and edn. group Control Data Corp.), Hoffman Estates, Ill., 1989-2000; guest speaker numerous industry related funtions including Rep. Platform Com., 1988. Mem. AICPA, Calif. Soc. CPAs, Biltmore Country Club, Marco Island Yacht and Sailing Club, Theta Delta Chi. E-mail: wrroach@plato.com.

ROBAK, JENNIE, state legislator; b. Suprise, Nebr., May 4, 1932; m. Cleo F. Robak; children: Karen, Kim, Frank, Kurt, Tony, Andrea. With Fed. Emergency Mgmt. Agy., Kansas City, Mo.; owner, operator RKR Foods, Inc.; mem. Nebr. Senate from 22d dist., Lincoln, 1988—. Trustee Jr. Achievement Columbus; bd. dirs. Platte County Red Cross; den mother Boy Scouts Am. Col. Nebr. Army N.G. Recipient Breaking Rule of Thumb award Nebr. Domestic Violence and Sexual Assault Coalition, 1989, Communicaiton and Leadership award Toastmasters Internat., 1992; named Woman of Distinction Soroptomist Internat. Colubmus, 1990. Mem. VFW Aux., Nat. Orgn. Vol. Leaders, Cath. Daus., Mrs. Jaycees, Kiwanis, Eagles Aux. Office: Rm 1118 State Capitol Lincoln NE 68509

ROBAK, KIM M. university official, lawyer; b. Columbus, Nebr., Oct. 4, 1955; m. William J. Mueller; children: Katherine, Claire. BA with distinction, U. Nebr., 1977, JD with highest distinction, 1985. Tchr. Lincoln (Nebr.) Pub. Schs., 1978-82; clerk Cline Williams Wright Johnson & Oldfather, Lincoln, 1983; summer assoc. Cooley Godward Castro Huddleson & Tatum, San Francisco, 1984, Steptoe & Johnson, Washington, 1985; ptnr. Rembolt Ludtke Parker & Berger, Lincoln, 1985-91; legal counsel Gov. E. Benjamin Nelson/State of Nebr., 1991-92, chief of staff, 1992-93; lt. gov. State of Nebr., 1993-98; v.p. external affairs, corp. sec. U. Nebr., 1999—. Chair Prairie Fire Internat. Symposium on Edn., 1986. Fellow Leadership Lincoln, 1986-87, program com., 1987-90; chair program com. Leadership Lincoln Alumni Assn., 1987, selection com., 1990; Dem. gen. counsel, Nebr., 1985-92; bd. dirs. women's ministries First Plymouth Congl. Ch., 1988-91, trustee, 1991-94, asst. moderator, 1999—; mem. Toll Fellowship Program, 1995; chair Nat. Conf. Lt. Govs., 1996; hon. chair Daffodil Day campaign Am. Cancer Soc.; hon. chair Walktoberfest, Am. Diabetes Assn.; hon. chair Nebr.'s campaign Prevent Blindness; hon. mem. Red Ribbon campaign Mothers Against Drunk Driving, 1994-95; active Groundwater Found., 1997, Medicaid Managed Care Commn., 1993—; bd. dirs. Nebr. Health Sys., 1997—, Nat. Found. Women Legislators Found., 1997-98; chair Nebr. Info. Tech. Commn., 1997-98; hon. Christmas chair Salvation Army, 1997; cert. program chair Nat. Order Women Legislators, 1997; bd. dirs. Doane Coll., 1997—, Lincoln Pub. Sch. Found., 1998—, Martin Luther Home Bd., 1999—; trustee Plymouth Congl. Ch., 1998—; mem. Lincoln Partnership for Econ. Devel. Bd., 1999—; bd. dirs. United Way, 2000—; mem. Wells Fargo Lincoln Adv. Bd., 2000—, Martin Luther Home Soc., 1999-2001. Named Notable Woman, First Plymouth Congl. Ch.'s Bd. Women's Ministries, 1996. Mem. ABA (steering com. 1997—), Nat. Inst. Trial Advocacy, Nebr. State Bar Assn. (ethics com. 1987-92, vice chair com. on pub. rels. 1988-92, chair com. on yellow pages advt. 1988, ho. of dels. 1988-95), Lincoln Bar Assn., U. Nebr. Coll. Alumni Assn. (bd. dirs. 1986-89), Updowntowners, Alzheimers Assn. (hon. chair Lincoln-Greater Nebr. chpt. 1996-98), Order of Coif. Office: 3835 Holdrege St PO Box 830745 Lincoln NE 68583-0745 E-mail: Krobak@uneb.edu.

ROBBINS, DARRYL ANDREW, pediatrician; b. Modesto, Calif., Sept. 16, 1945; s. Jerome and Grace (Bass) R.; m. Harriette Lee Eisenberg, June 12, 1971; children: Jennifer Lynn, Julie Ellen, Allison Beth. BS, Dickinson Coll., 1967; DO, Phila. Coll. Osteo. Medicine, 1971. Diplomate Am. Bd. Pediat. Intern Doctor's Hosp., Columbus, Ohio, 1971-72; resident in pediatrics Children's Hosp. Med. Ctr., Cin., 1972-75; practice medicine specializing in pediatrics Columbus, 1975—. Vice-chmn. Diocesan Child Guidance Ctr., Columbus, 1986; genetics svcs. adv. com. Ohio Dept. Health, 1978-86; pres. med. staff Columbus Children's Hosp., 1996. Trustee Columbus Children's Hosp., 2001, Children's Practicing Pediatricians, Columbus, 1991—94, bd. dirs., 1998—, pres., 2001—. Recipient Samuel Dalinsky Meml. award for Outstanding Graduating Resident Cin. Children's Hosp., 1975; named Pediatrician of Yr., Columbus Children's Hosp., 1982, 90. Fellow Am. Acad. Pediatrics; mem. Cen. Ohio Pediatric Soc. (pres. elect 1988, pres. 1989-90). Jewish. Home: 953 Old Farm Rd Columbus OH 43213-2674 Office: 453 Waterbury Ct Gahanna OH 43230-5309

ROBBINS, FREDERICK CHAPMAN, retired physician, medical school dean emeritus; b. Auburn, Ala., Aug. 25, 1916; s. William J. and Christine (Chapman) Robbins; m. Alice Havemeyer Northrop, June 19, 1948; children: Alice, Louise. AB, U. Mo., 1936, BS, 1938; MD, Harvard U., 1940; DSc (hon.) , John Carroll U., 1955, U. Mo., 1958, U. N.C., 1979, Tufts U., 1983, Med. Coll. Ohio, 1983; LLD, U. N.Mex., 1968. Diplomate Am. Bd. Pediatrics. Intern Children's Hosp., Boston, 1941—42, resident, 1940—41, resident in pediat., 1946—48; sr. fellow virus disease Nat. Rsch. Coun., 1948—50; staff rsch. divsn. infectious diseases Children's Hosp., Boston, 1948—50, assoc. physician, assoc. dir. isolation svc., assoc. rsch. divsn. infectious diseases, 1950—52; instr., assoc. in pediat. Harvard Med. Sch., 1950—52; dir. dept. pediatrics and contagious diseases Cleve. Met. Gen. Hosp., 1952—66; prof. pediatrics Case Western Res. U., 1950—80; dean Case Western Res. U. Sch. Medicine, 1966—80, dean emeritus, 2980—; prof. emeritus Case Western Res. U., 1987—, dir. Ctr. Adolescent Health Sch. Medicine; pres. Inst. Medicine, NAS, 1980—85. Vis. scientist Donner Lab. U. Calif., 1963—64. Pres. Soc. Pediatric Rsch. , 1961—62. Maj. U.S. Army, 1942—46. Decorated Bronze Star; co-recipient Nobel prize in physiology and medicine, 1954; recipient 1st Mead Johnson prize application tissue culture methods to study of viral infections, 1953, Med. Mut. Honor award, 1969, Ohio Gov.'s award, 1971. Mem.: Am. Philos. Soc., Am. Pediatric Soc, Am. Acad. Pediatrics, Am. Acad. Arts and Scis., Nat. Acad. Scis., Assn. Am. Med. Colls. (Abraham Flexner award 1987), Phi Gamma Delta, Sigma Xi, Phi Beta Kappa. Office: Case Western Res U Sch Med 10900 Euclid Ave Cleveland OH 44106-1712

ROBBINS, HENRY ZANE, public relations and marketing executive; b. Winston-Salem, N.C., Jan. 17, 1930; s. Romulus Mayfield and Vera Ethel (Daniel) R.; m. Barbara Anne Brown, Jan. 19, 1955; children: Zane Scott, Jill Stewart, Gail Ruth. AB, U. N.C., 1952; student, Emory U., 1952. Reporter Atlanta Constn., 1952; exhibit specialist Gen. Electric Co., Schenectady, 1952, employee relations specialist Cin., 1955, editor Schenectady, 1955, account supr. Winston-Salem, 1956-58, group supr. Schenectady, 1958-60; v.p., gen. mgr. Burson-Marsteller, Pitts. and Chgo., 1960-70, sr. v.p., 1970; pres., chief exec. officer SL&H-Robbins Inc., Chgo., 1970-72; also dir.; pres., chief exec. officer Beveridge Kraus Robbins & Manning, 1973-75; also dir.; pres., dir., chief exec. officer Beveridge and Robbins Inc., 1975-77; pres., chief exec. officer Financial Advt. of Ill., Inc.; mng. dir. Sports Mgmt. Group, 1975-77; dir. communications Arthur Andersen & Co., Chgo. and Geneva, Switzerland, 1977-81, dir. mktg. support services, 1981-89, dir. mktg. and comms., 1989-91; mem. Worldwide Alpha Group, 1991-96, exec. dir. global 1000 program, 1995—2000; prin. Arthur Andersen & Co., 1980—2000. Mem. journalism adv. com. Harper Coll., Palatine, Ill.; dir. Evanston Environ. Assn.; mem. Ladd Arboretum Commn., Evanston, Ill.; pub. rels. com. Chgo. Met. Crusade Mercy; mem. Nat. Task Force on Environment; cons. sec. Dept. Health, Edn. and Welfare, 1970; chmn. pub. rels. com. Honor Am. Day Com., 1970. Author: Vision of Grandeur, 1988, Globalizing the Enterprise, 2000; contbr. articles to profl. jours. Counselor Council of Mojave, 1972-74; gen. chmn. Chgo. Children's Classic Golf Tournament, 1974-77; chmn. Chgo. fin. com. Am.'s Freedom Train, 1976; chmn. fund devel. com. Presbytery of Chgo., 1977-83, maj. mission fund, 1977-79; dist. commr. Boy Scouts Am., 1976-79, chmn. Wildcat dist., 1980-83; mem. exec. bd. N.E. Ill. council, 1980-85; mem. Republican Citizens Com. Ill., 1960-61, Allegheny County (Pa.) Rep. Com., 1962-65; Trustee Roycemore Sch., Evanston, 1971-74; trustee, v.p. devel. Child and Family Services Chgo.; bd. dirs. Fellowship of Christian Athletes, U. N.C. Alumni Ill., Stockbrokers Assn. Chgo.; chmn. devel. com. Potawatamie Dist., 2000, chmn. fin. com., 2001. Served to 1st lt. AUS, 1952-54. Elected to N.C. Pub. Rels. Hall of Fame, 1994. Mem. Pub. Relations Soc. Am., Nat. Investor Relations Inst., Midwest Travel Writers Assn., Chgo. Ednl. TV Assn., Pub. Relations Counselors Roundtable, Am. Mgmt. Assn., Environ. Writers Assn. Am., Optimist Internat., Chgo. Assn. Commerce and Industry, Art Inst. Chgo., Univ. Club, Sunset Ridge Country Club, Optimist ClubChi Psi. Republican. Presbyterian. Home: 2759 Broadway Ave Evanston IL 60201-1556 Office: 33 W Monroe St Chicago IL 60603-5300

ROBBINS, JERRY HAL, educational administration educator; b. DeQueen, Ark., Feb. 28, 1939; s. James Hal and Barbara I. (Rogers) R. B.A. in Math, Hendrix Coll., 1960; M.Ed., U. Ark., 1963, Ed.D., 1966. Tchr. math. and music Clinton (Ark.) pub. schs., 1960-61; prin. Adrian (Mo.) High Sch., 1961-63; exec. sec. Ark. Sch. Study Council, Fayetteville, 1963-65; mem. faculty U. Miss., University, 1965-74, prof. ednl. adminstrn., 1970-74, chmn. dept. ednl. adminstrn., 1970-74; dean Coll. Edn., U. Ark., Little Rock, 1974-79; asso. v.p. for acad. affairs Ga. State U., Atlanta, 1979-84, dean Coll. Edn., 1984-90, prof. ednl. adminstrn., 1990-91; dean. Coll. Edn. Ea. Mich. U., Ypsilanti, 1991—. Co-author: (with S. B. Williams Jr.) Student Activities in the Innovative School, 1969, School Custodian's Handbook, 1970, Administrator's Manual of School Plant Administration, 1970. Mem. NEA, Am. Assn. Sch. Adminstrs., Am. Assn. Colls. Tchr. Edn. (dir. 1979-82, 2000—), Nat. Assn. Secondary Sch. Prins., So. Regional Council Ednl. Adminstrn. (pres. 1970-71), Tchr. Edn. Coun. State Colls. and Univs. (pres. 1998-99), Phi Delta Kappa, Kappa Delta Pi (v.p. chpt. devel. 1978-80, pres. elect 1980-82, pres. 1982-84, past pres. 1984-86) Mem. United Meth. Ch. Home and Office: 3384 Bent Trail Dr Ann Arbor MI 48108-9316 Office: Ea Mich U 310 Porter Bldg Ypsilanti MI 48197 E-mail: jerry.robbins@emich.edu.

ROBBINS, LAWRENCE HARRY, anthropologist, educator; b. Washington, Nov. 22, 1938; s. Maurice and Edith R.; m. Martha Ann Edwards, Dec. 16, 1967; children: Daniel, Brian, Michael, Mark. A.B., U. Mich., 1961, A.M., 1962; Ph.D., U. Calif., Berkeley, 1968. Asst. prof. U. Utah, 1967; mem. faculty Mich. State U., East Lansing, 1968—, prof. anthropology and African studies, 1977—, chairperson ANP dept., 1992-95. Vis. research asso. U. Nairobi, Kenya, 1969-70, Nat. Mus. Kenya, 1975-76; Fulbright vis. prof. U. Botswana, 1982-83; vis. archaeologist Nat. Mus. and Art Gallery, Botswana, 1982-83 Author: Stones, Bones and Ancient Cities, 1990; contbr. articles to profl. jours. Grantee NSF, 1965-66, 69-70, 75-77, 91-2000, Nat. Geographic Soc., 1987, 89. Mem. Am. Anthropol. Assn., Registry Profl. Archaeologists, Soc. Africanist Archeologists in Am., So. African Archeol. Soc., Botswana Soc. Office: Dept Anthropology Mich State U East Lansing MI 48824

ROBBINS, N. CLAY, foundation administrator; b. Indpls., May 30, 1957; m. Amy Robbins; 3 children. BA, Wabash Coll., Crawfordsville, Ind., 1979; JD, Vanderbilt U., 1982. Exch. assoc. European Econ. Cmty. law dept. Rycken Burlion Bolle & Houben, Brussels, 1985-86; assoc. Baker & Daniels, 1982-85, ptnr., 1985-92; v.p. cmty. devel. Lilly Endowment Inc., Indpls., 1993-94, pres., 1994—. Mem. bd. Nat. City Bank, Ind.; mem. drafting com. Ind. Nonprofit Corp. Act 1991. Past dir., pres. Indpls. Chamber Orch.; past dir. Damar Homes, Inc.; mem. bd. Ctrl. Ind. Corp. Partnership; vice chmn. policy planning exec. com. United Way Ctrl. Ind., chair strategic planning com. Mem. Ind. State Bar Assn., Indpls. C. of C. Methodist. Office: Lilly Endowment Inc 2801 N Meridian St PO Box 88068 Indianapolis IN 46208-0068

ROBBINS, OREM OLFORD, insurance company executive; b. Mpls., Feb. 5, 1915; s. Douglas Ford and Grace (Rorem) R.; m. Annette Strand Scherer, May 17, 1992; children: Ford M., Ross S., Gail R. Tomei, Cynthia R. Rothbard. BBA with distinction, U. Minn., 1936; BS in Law, William Mitchell Coll. Law, 1946, JD, 1948. Comml. rep. NW Bell Telephone Co., Mpls., 1936-48; dep. dir. U.S. Treas. Dept., 1948-49; sales rep. Conn. Gen. Life Ins. Co., 1949-56; founder, chmn. Security Life Ins. Co. Am., 1956—. Bd. dirs., past pres. Family and Children's Svcs., Mpls., 1968—; bd. govs., past chmn. Meth. Hosp., Mpls., 1960-90; past treas., bd. dirs. Goodwill/Easter Seals, St. Paul, 1958-68, 75-88; life trustee Hamline U., St. Paul, 1979—, chmn. bd. trustees, 1990-91. Col. U.S. Army, 1941-46. Decorated Legion of Merit; recipient Outstanding Achievement award U. Minn., 2001. Fellow Life Mgmt. Assn.; mem. Am. Soc. CLU (pres. Mpls. chpt. 1959), Health Underwriters Assn., Chartered Fin. Cons., Am. Legion, Skylight Club (Mpls.), Hole in the Wall Golf Club, Naples Yacht Club, Mpls. Club, Officer's Club, Masons. Republican. Methodist. Office: Security Life Ins Co Am 10901 Red Circle Dr Minnetonka MN 55343-9304 E-mail: oorobbins@securitylife.com.

ROBE, THURLOW RICHARD, engineering educator, university dean; b. Petersburg, Ohio, Jan. 25, 1934; s. Thrulow Scott and Mary Alice (McKibben) R.; m. Eleanora C. Komyati, Aug. 27, 1955; children: Julia, Kevin, Stephen, Edward. B.S.C.E., Ohio U., 1955, M.S. in Mech. Engring., 1962; Ph.D. in Applied Mechanics, Stanford U., 1966. Engr. Gen. Electric Co., Niles, Ohio, Cleve., Erie, Pa., Evendale,Ohio, 1954-60; instr. Ohio U., Athens, 1960-63; asst. prof to prof., assoc. dean U. Ky., Lexington, 1965-80; dean Ohio U., Athens, 1980-96, Cruse W. Moss prof. Engring. Edn., 1992-96, dir. Innovation Ctr. Authority, 1983-96; dean emeritus, Moss prof. emeritus Russ Coll. Engring. and Tech., Ohio U., Athens, 1996—; pres., chmn. bd. Q.E.D. Assocs., Inc., Lexington, 1975-83. Trustee Engring. Found. Ohio, 1988-94; bd. govs. Edison Materials Tech. Ctr., 1987-96; dir. T. Richard and Eleanora K. Robe Leadership Inst., Ohio U., 1997—. Contbr. articles to profl. jours.; patentee trailer hitch. Bd. dirs. Athens County Cmty. Redevel. Corp., 1980-86; treas. South Lexington Little League, 1976-80; vice chmn. Thoroughbred dist., Boy Scouts Am., 1975-77; pres. Tates Creek H.S. PTA, Lexington, 1975-76; bd. dirs. U. Ky. Athletics Ass.n, 1975-80; trustee Ohio U. Found. Bd. Trustees, 1998—. Maj. USAF Res., 1955-85. Recipient Alumni medal of merit Ohio U., 1993; named Am. Coun. on Edn. Adminstrn. fellow, 1970-71, Ohio U. Alumnus of Yr., 1996, inductee Acad. Disting. Grads., Russ Coll. Engring. & Tech., 2001. Mem. ASME, NSPE (Profl. Engring. in Edn. exec. bd., ctrl. region vice-chmn. 1987-89), Am. Soc. Engring. Edn. (Outstanding Contbn. in Rsch. award 1966), Athens Reading Club, Athens Symposiarchs, Rotary, Sigma Xi, Tau Beta Pi, Omicron Delta Kappa, Alpha Lambda Delta. Office: Russ Coll Engring & Tech Ohio U Athens OH 45701 E-mail: robe@ohio.edu.

ROBERSON, ROGER T. transportation executive; Chmn. Roberson Transp. Svcs., Mahomet, Ill., 1989—. Office: Roberson Transp Svcs 1100 S Roberson Dr Mahomet IL 61853-8532 also: PO Box 9800 Champaign IL 61826-8800

ROBERTS, A(RTHUR) WAYNE, organization administrator; b. Burlington, Vt., Feb. 25, 1944; s. Arthur William and Phyllis (Stockwell) R.; children: Arthur Weber, Morgan Wayne, Ethan Duvall. BS in Bus. Adminstrn., Babson Coll., 1964; MBA, U. Mass., 1967. IBM fin. analyst Space Guidance Ctr., 1965—; IBM fin. adviser Govt. Edn. Med. Region, Washington, 1965-66; advt. mktg. rep. IBM, Cin., 1966-72, account mgr. Albany, N.Y., 1972-75; pres., owner AWR Corp., 1973-80; asst. prof. econs. and mgmt. Johnson State Coll., 1974-80; sr. cons., regional polit. dir. Reagan-Bush Campaign Com. in Northeast, 1980; asst. dir. personnel for presdl. transition The White House, 1980-81, dep. dir. White House personnel, 1981; acting project mgr. U.S. Synthetic Fuel Corp., Washington, 1981; sec.'s regional rep. U.S. Dept. Edn., 1981-83, dep. under sec., 1983-86; pres. Lake Champlain Regional C. of C., Burlington, Vt., 1986—. Mem. Gov.'s Bd. on Small Bus., 1979; mem. Johnson State Small Bus. Adv. Bd. Vermont, 1982; del. Rep. Nat. Conv., 1980, 84, 88; mem. Chittenden County Rep. Com., South Burlington Rep. Com., Vt. Bush for Pres. Com., Bus. Roundtable, Vt. Bus. Forum; mem. bd. Vt./Can. Free Trade; mem. Small Bus. Adminstrn. Adv. Coun.; commr. Nat. Commn. Employment Policy, 1990-91. Recipient Commitment to Excellence in Edn. award Johnson State Coll. Found., 1985. Mem. Vt. State C. of C. (bd. dirs.). Home: 83 Laurel Hill Dr South Burlington VT 05403-7335 Office: Macalester College Saint Paul MN 55105

ROBERTS, CHARLES PATRICK (PAT ROBERTS), senator; b. Topeka, Apr. 20, 1936; m. Franki Fann, 1969; children: David, Ashleigh, Anne-Wesley. BS, Kans. State U., 1958. Pub. Litchfield Park, Ariz., 1962-67; adminstrv. asst. to U.S. Senator Frank Carlson, U.S. Senate, Washington, 1967-68; adminstrv. asst. to U.S. Congressman Keith Sebelius U.S. Ho. of Reps., 1968-80; mem. 97th to 104th Congresses from 1st Kans. Dist., 1980-96, U.S. Senate from Kans., Washington, 1997—; mem. agr., nutrition and forestry com.; mem. armed svcs. com.; chmn. ethics com.; mem. intelligence com. Served with USMC, 1958-62. Office: US Senate 302 Hart Senate Off Bldg Washington DC 20510-0001*

ROBERTS, DAVID, airport executive; Dir. Indpls. Internat. Airport. Office: Indpls Internat Airport Indpls Airport Authority 2500 S High School Rd Indianapolis IN 46241-4943

ROBERTS, DOUGLAS B. state official; Treas. State of Mich., Lansing, 1991-98, 2001—; v.p. best practices Lockhead Martin, 1998—2001. Office: Mich Dept Treasury Lansing MI 48922

ROBERTS, JAMES OWEN, financial planning executive, consultant; b. Madison, Wis., Aug. 19, 1930; s. John William and Sada (Buckmaster) R.; m. Georgianna Timmons, Jan. 30, 1954; children: Stephen, Susan, Ellen, Timmons. BS, Ohio State U., 1952; MBA, Case Western Res. U., 1970. With Owens-Ill., Inc., Toledo, 1952-71, food divsn. mgr. N.Y.C., 1963-66, br. mgr. Cleve., 1966-71; mgr. corp. fin. Stone & Webster Securities Corp., 1971-74; from regional dir. to pres. Mgmt. Planning, Inc., 1976-96, chmn., 1996—. Bd. dirs. Zaxis Internat., Inc.; lectr. valuation and bus. ownership succession. Contbr. articles to profl. jours. Trustee Applewood Ctrs. Found., 1996—, Soc. for the Blind, Cleve., 1983—86, Ohio Motorists Assn., 1985—94, chmn., 1990—92; pres. Childrens Svcs., Inc., 1986—88; trustee Great Lakes Theatre, co-chmn., 1998—2001; elder Fairmount Presbyn. Ch. 1st lt. USAF, 1952—54. Mem. Cleve. Skating Club, Nassau Club, Huron Yacht Club, Chgo. Athletic Assn. Republican. Avocations: sailing, skiing, hiking, photography. Home: 2323 Stillman Rd Cleveland OH 44118-3520 Office: Mgmt Planning Inc 545 Hanna Bldg Cleveland OH 44115 also: 101 Poor Farm Rd Princeton NJ 08540-1941 E-mail: jroberts@mpival.com.

ROBERTS, JOHN, radio personality; b. St. Louis; married; 2 children. Student, Meramec C.C., Lindenwood Coll. Music dir., announcer Classic 99, St. Louis. Office: Classic 99 85 Founders Ln Saint Louis MO 63105

ROBERTS, JOHN CHARLES, law educator; b. Aberdeen, S.D., Feb. 29, 1940; s. Jacob John Schmitt and Leona (Blethen) Blake; m. Kathleen Kelly (div. 1985); children: Katherine, John Charles Jr.; m. Lynn Dale Friedman, Dec. 22, 1985; 1 child, Emily Sara. B.S., Northwestern U., 1961; LL.B., Yale U., 1968. Bar: U.S. Dist. Ct. D.C. 1969, Mich. 1981. Assoc. Covington & Burling, Washington, 1968-71; assoc. dean, lectr. Yale U. Law Sch., New Haven, 1971-77; gen. counsel U.S. Senate Com. on Armed Services, 1977-80; adj. prof. law Washington Coll. Law, Am. U., 1978-80; dean, prof. law Wayne State U. Law Sch., Detroit, 1980-86; prof., dean Law Sch. DePaul U., Chgo., 1986-96, v.p. for univ. advancement, 1996-97, prof. law, 1997—. Mem. exec. com. Inst. for Continuing Legal Edn., Chgo., 1988-91. Mem. adv. com. Mich. Psychiat. Soc., 1980-86; bd. dirs. Constl. Rights Found., 1992-96. Lt. USN, 1961-65. Mem. ABA, Assn. Am. Law Schs. (mem. exec. com., chmn. sect. instn. advancement 1987-88, chmn., sec. adminstrn. law schs. 1993-94), Order of Coif. Democrat Avocations: collecting modern first editions. Office: DePaul U Coll Law 25 E Jackson Blvd Chicago IL 60604-2289

ROBERTS, PATRICK KENT, lawyer; b. Waynesville, Mo., Feb. 9, 1948; s. J. Kent and Winona (Clark) R.; m. Jeanne Billings, April 17, 1976; children: Christopher, Kimberly, Courtney. Student, U. Ill., Urbana, 1970; AB, U. Mo., 1970, JD, 1973. Bar: Mo. 1974, U.S. Dist. Ct. (we. dist.) Mo. 1974, U.S. Ct. Appeals (8th cir.) 1979. Lawyer U.S. Senator Stuart Symington, Columbia, Mo., 1973-76; ptnr. Daniel, Clampett, Powell & Cunningham, Springfield, 1976—2001; of counsel Cunningham, Harpool & Cordonnier, 2002—. Adj. faculty Webster U., 2000—. Mem. ctrl. com. Greene County Dems., Springfield, 1982-84, 88-90. Mem. ABA, Mo. Orgn. Def. Lawyers, Mo. Bar Assn., Springfield Met. Bar Assn. Democrat. Methodist. Lodge: Rotary. Office: Cunningham Harpool & Cordonnier PO Box 10306 3171 E Sunshine St Springfield MO 65804-2056

ROBERTS, THEODORE HARRIS, banker; b. Gillett, Ark., May 14, 1929; s. D. Edward and Gertrude (Harris) R.; m. Elisabeth Law, July 17, 1953; children: Susan, William (dec.), Julia, John. BA in Govt., Northwestern State U., 1949; MA in Polit. Sci., Okla. State U., 1950; postgrad., U. Chgo. Grad. Sch. Bus., 1956. With Harris Trust and Savs. Bank, Chgo., 1953-82; exec. v.p., sec., treas. Harris Bank and Harris Bankcorp Inc., 1971-82, dir., exec. com., 1975-82; pres. Fed. Res. Bank St. Louis, 1983-85; chmn. bd., chief exec. officer Talman Home Fed. Savs. & Loan, Chgo., 1985-92; pres. LaSalle Nat. Corp., 1992-95, retired. Sr. cons. ABN AMRO, 1995—. Mem. Chgo. Club, Comml. Club Chgo., Econ. Club Chgo., Exmoor Country Club (Highland Park, Ill.). Office: 135 S La Salle St Ste 1162 Chicago IL 60603-4500

ROBERTS, THOMAS MICHAEL, state legislator; b. Mar. 3, 1952; s. Harold Leonard and Susie (Williams) R.; m. Regina Michele Walker; children: Edward, Erienne. Student, Sinclair Cmty. Coll.; BA, Univ. Dayton, 1977. Clerk Montgomery County Clerk's Civil Divsn., 1972-77; supr. Montgomery County Auto Title Divsn., 1977; bailiff Montgomery County Common Pleas Ct., 1977-86; mem. Montgomery County Dem. Com., 1984; mem. congress adv. coun. U.S. Rep. Tony Hall, 1985; Ohio State rep. Dist. 37, 1986-92, Dist. 39, 1993—; mem. adv com. Dayton Job Corp., 1993—. Chmn. Aging & Housing Com., mem. agrl. & Natural resources, Children & Youth, Energy & Environ. com., Zone oversights & Policy adv. group Dept. Youth Svc., chmn. Select Com. Homeless & Affordable Housing, mem. Judiciary & Criminal Justice Com., Child Abuse and Juvenile Justice. Active Boy Scouts, 1986; co-chmn. pub. affairs com. Montgomery County Mental Health Assn., 1979-84, pres., 1986-87. Recipient Outstanding Young Man of Yr. award Montgomery Coun. Young Dem., 1982, Outstanding Achievement award, 1986, Ohio Homeless Coalition award, Spl. Contbr. award Ohio Housing Coalition, Pres.'s award

Ohio Youth Svc., Men & Women Courage award Cmty. Outreach. Mem. Dem. Voters League, Black Dem. of Ohio. Home: 1623 Kipling Dr Dayton OH 45406-4134 Office: Ohio Ho of Reps State House Columbus OH 43215

ROBERTS, WILLIAM EVERETT, lawyer; b. Pierre, S.D., May 12, 1926; s. Everett David and Bonnie (Martin) R.; m. Cynthia Cline, July 18, 1953; children: Catherine C. Roberts-Martin, Laura M., Nancy F., David H. BS, U. Minn., 1947; LLB, Yale U., 1950. Bar: Ind. 1950, U.S. Supreme Ct. 1964. Employee, ptnr. Duck and Neighbours, Indpls., 1950-58; ptnr. Cadick, Burns, Duck & Neighbours, 1958-60, Roberts, Ryder, Rogers & Scism, Indpls., 1960-85, Barnes & Thornburg, Indpls., 1986-93, of counsel, 1994—. Pres., bd. dirs. Park-Tudor Sch., Indpls., 1982-83; elder Second Presbyn. Ch., Indpls., 1962—; trustee Indpls. Mus. Art, 1978—; pres. New Hope of Ind., Indpls., 1986-87. Fellow Am. Bar Found.; mem. ABA, Ind. Bar Assn., Indpls. Bar Assn., Rotary, Meridian Hills Country Club (pres. 1983-84). Republican. Home: 10466 Spring Highland Dr Indianapolis IN 46290-1101 Office: Barnes & Thornburg 11 S Meridian St Ste 1313 Indianapolis IN 46204-3535

ROBERTSON, BIG O (OSCAR PALMER ROBERTSON), chemical company executive, former professional basketball player; b. Charlotte, Tenn., Nov. 24, 1938; BBBA, U. Cin., 1960. Player U.S. Olympic Basketball Team, 1960; basketball player Cin. Royals, 1960-70, Milw. Bucks, 1970-74; founder, pres., CEO, Orchem, Inc., Cin., 1981-1996, Orpack-Stone Corp., Herrin, Ill., 1990—, Orflex Ltd., Cin., 1995—, ORDMS, Marlton, N.J., 1997—. Player NBA Championship Team, 1971. Named Sporting News Coll. Player of Yr., 1958, 59, 60, Sporting News All-Star Fitrst Team, 1958, 59, 60, NBA Rookie of Yr., 1961, All NBA First Team, 1961-69; player NBA All Star Games, 1961-72; named MVP, NBA, 1964, M VP in NBA All-Star Games, 1961, 64, 69; named to NBA 35th Anniversary All-Star Team, 1980; elected to Naismith Meml. Basketball Hall of Fame, 1979 Office: Orchem Corp 4293 Mulhauser Rd Fairfield OH 45014-5450

ROBERTSON, CHARLES T., JR. air force Officer; BS in Engring., U.S. Air Force Acad., 1968; MS in Indsl. Mgmt., Cen. Mich. U., 1977; Grad., Squadron Officer Sch., Maxwell AFB, Ala., 1975, Nat. War Coll., Washington, 1985; postgrad., Harvard U., 1994. Commd. 2d. lt. USAF, 1968, advanced through grades to gen., 1998, various command assignments at squadron/wing levels; various to vice-dir. Joint Staff, Joint Chiefs of Staff, 1993-95; vice comdr. Air Mobility Command, Scott AFB, 1995-96; comdr. 15th Air Force, Travis AFB, Calif., 1996-98; comdr.-in-chief U.S. Transp. Command, Scott AFB, Ill., 1998—; comdr. Air Mobility Command, 1998—. Decorated Def. Disting. Svc. medal, Disting. Svc. medal, Legion of Merit with oak leaf cluster, Disting. Flying Cross with oak leaf cluster, Meritorious Svc. medal with two oak leaf clusters, Air medal with nine oak leaf clusters, Air Force Commendation medal with oak leaf clusters, Vietnam Svc. medal with four svc. stars, Republic of Vietnam Gallantry Cross with Palm, others. Office: USCINCTRANS/TCCC 508 Scott Dr Rm 339 Scott Air Force Base IL 62225-5313

ROBERTSON, DAVID WAYNE, pharmaceutical company executive; b. Dumas, Tex., July 30, 1955; s. R.L. and N.C. R. BS, Stephen F. Austin State U., 1977; MS, U. Ill., 1978, PhD, 1981. Sr. medicinal chemist Eli Lilly and Co., Indpls., 1981-84, rsch. scientist, 1985-87, sr. rsch. scientist, 1988-89, rsch. group leader, 1988-89, dir. cen. nervous system rsch., 1990-91; v.p. medicinal chemistry Ligand Pharms., Inc., San Diego, 1991-92, v.p. rsch., 1992-93, v.p. discovery rsch., 1993-96; exec. dir. R & D DuPont Pharm. Co., Wilmington, 1996-99; v.p. rsch. Pharmacia & Upjohn, Kalamazoo, 1999—2001; exec. dir. global rsch. and devel. Pfizer, Ann Arbor, 2002—. Contbr. articles to profl. jours. Mem. Soc. for Neurosci., Am. Soc. Pharmacology and Exptl. Therapeutics, Am. Chem. Soc. Office: Pfizer Global Rsch & Devel 2800 Plymouth Rd Ann Arbor MI 48105

ROBERTSON, EDWARD D., JR. retired state supreme court justice, lawyer; b. Durham, N.C., May 1, 1952; m. Renee Ann Beal; two children. BA, U. Mo., 1974, JD, 1977. Asst. atty. gen., Mo., 1978-79; assoc. mcpl. judge City of Belton, 1980-81, dep. atty. gen., 1981-85; justice Mo. Supreme Ct., Kansas City, 1985-98; counselor Bartimus Fickleton & Presley, Jefferson City, Mo. Office: Bartimus Fickleton & Presley 122 E High St Ste 3000 Jefferson City MO 65101-2960

ROBERTSON, JAMES MAGRUDER, geological research administrator; b. Port Clinton, Ohio, Sept. 24, 1943; married. BA, Carleton Coll., 1965; MS, U. Mich., 1968, PhD in Econ. Geology, 1972. Asst. prof. geology Mich. Technol. U., 1972-74; mining geologist N.Mex. Bur. Mines and Mineral Resources, 1974-86, sr. econ. geologist, 1986-88, assoc. dir., 1988-92; dir. and state geologist Wis. Geol. Survey, Madison, 1992—. Mem. Geochem. Soc., Geol. Soc. Am., Soc. Econ. Geology, Sigma Xi. Office: Univ Wisconsin Geol & Natural History Survey 3817 Mineral Point Rd Madison WI 53705-5121 also: Wis Geol Survey 3817 Mineral Point Rd Madison WI 53705-5121

ROBERTSON, JERRY EARL, retired manufacturing company executive; b. Detroit, Oct. 25, 1932; s. Earl Howard and Nellie (Wright) R.; m. Joanne Alice Wesner, Sept. 3, 1955; children: Scott Clark, Lisa Kay, Stuart Todd. B.S., Miami U., Oxford, Ohio, 1954; M.S., U. Mich., 1956, Ph.D., 1959. With Minn. Mining & Mfg. Co., St. Paul, 1963-94, tech. dir. med. products div., 1973-74, dept. mgr. surg. products dept., 1974-75, gen. mgr. surg. products div., 1975-79, div. v.p. surg. products div., 1979-80, group v.p. health care products and services, 1980-84, exec. v.p. life scis. sector, 1984-86, exec. v.p. life scis. sector and corp. svcs., 1986-94; ret., 1994. Bd. dirs. Coherent, Inc., Choice Hotels Internat., Steris Corp. Bd. reference MAP Internat., Brunswick, Ga., 1986-94; bd. dirs. Project HOPE, 1988-98, Manor Care Inc., 1989-98, Cardinal Health Distbn., Inc., 1991-99. Mem. Pharm. Mfrs. Assn. (bd. dirs. 1984-89), Health Industry Mfrs. Assn. (bd. dirs. 1982-91, chmn. 1990-91). Unitarian. Office: Minn World Trade Ctr 30 7th St E Ste 3050 Saint Paul MN 55101-4921

ROBERTSON, LEON H. management consultant, educator; b. Atlanta; s. Grady Jospeh and Pearline (Chandler) R. BS in Indsl. Mgmt., Ga. Inst. Tech., 1957, MS, 1959; postgrad., U. Okla.-Norman, 1958, U. Mich., 1961; PhD in Bus. Adminstrn., Ga. State U., 1968. Mgr. mgmt. cons. divsn. Arthur Andersen & Co., Atlanta, 1960-65; prof. bus. adminstrn. Ga. State U., 1965-75; corp. v.p. Tex. Gas Corp., Owensboro, Ky., 1975-78, sr. v.p., 1982-83; chmn., CEO Am. Carriers, Inc., Overland Park, Kans., 1978-88; chmn. bd. dirs. Midwest Coast Transport, 1988-89; prof. mgmt., dir. divsn. bus. adminstrn. U. Mo., Kansas City, 1990-96, prof. Internat. Acad. Programs, 1996-98, dir. Ctr. for Internat. Bus., 1999—. Office: Univ of Mo-Kansas City Henry W Bloch Sch Bus & Pub Admn 5110 Cherry St Kansas City MO 64110-2426

ROBERTSON, MARTHA RAPPAPORT, state legislator, consultant; b. Boston, Sept. 14, 1952; d. Jerome Lyle and Nancy (Vahey) Rappaport; divorced; 1 child, Colby. BA, Franklin & Marshall Coll., 1974; MBA, U. Pa., 1976. Mktg. and new bus. devel. exec. Gen. Mills, Inc., Mpls., 1976-91; mem. Minn. Senate from 45th dist., St. Paul, 1993—. Republican. Office: State of Minn 141 State Office Bldg Saint Paul MN 55155-0001

ROBERTSON, MICHAEL SWING, minister; b. Boston, July 20, 1935; s. Charles Stuart and Elizabeth (Swing) R.; m. Margaret Filoon, Sept. 17, 1960 (dec. Oct. 1996); children: Michael Swing, Ashlee Whipple, Christopher Filoon, Andrew Stuart; m. Emily Erickson, Feb. 22, 1998. A.B., Harvard U., 1957, grad. Advanced Mgmt. Program, 1979. With Robertson Factories, Inc., 1957-80, exec. v.p., 1968-73, pres., 1973-79, chmn. bd., 1979-80; dir. Robertson-Swing Co., 1980—; pres. The Berkley Co. Inc., 1981-90, Reactions Inc., 1985-90; treas. Falmouth Marine Inc., 1981-88; pres., treas. Orchard Computer Inc., 1984-91, chmn., treas., 1991-93; exec. sec. Nat. Assn. Congl. Christian Chs., Oak Creek, Wis., 1991-97; minister Pilgrim Congregational Ch., Taunton, Mass., 2000—; ch. coord. Cmty. Faith Alliance, Milw., 1997-2000; pres. Congl. Leadership Inst. Piedmont Coll., Ga., 1997—; exec. dir. Cmty. Village, Ltd., 1998-2000; pastor Pilgrim Congrl. Ch., Taunton, 2001—. V.p. adv. coun. Coll. of Bus. and Industry, Southeastern Mass. U., North Dartmouth, Mass., 1979-91; selectman, Town of Berkley, Mass., 1974-80, chmn. 1979-80; mem. Pres.'s Adv. Com. for Trade Negotiations, 1983-86; bd. dirs. Mass. Easter Seal Soc., 1977-91, pres. 1982-83; bd. dirs. Nat. Easter Seal Soc., 1985-91, Wis. Easter Seal Soc., 1994-95; chmn. Berkley Rep. Town com., 1977-91; mem. Pilgrim Congl. Ch., Taunton, Cmty. Bapt. Ch., Milw.; Rep. nominee U.S. Senate from Mass., 1976, nominee for Mass. state auditor, 1982; co-chmn. Mass Reagan for Pres. Com., 1980; Bristol County coord. Reagan/Bush campaign; co-chmn. Mass. Dole for Pres. Commn., 1987; chmn. Southeastern Mass. campaign Harvard Coll., 1981; chmn. Friends of Harvard Track, 1986-91; trustee Barnstable County Hosp., 1985-90, chmn., 1988. Mem. Harvard Varsity Club, Falmouth Yacht Club, Harvard Club of Boston. Home: 7 Swing Lane Falmouth MA 02540 Office: Pilgrim Congrl Ch 45 Broadway Taunton MA 02780-3120 Fax: 508-828-9147. E-mail: miker@cape.com.

ROBERTSON, PAUL JOSEPH, state legislator; b. Depauw, Ind., Apr. 25, 1946; s. William Edward and Mary Rita (Sieg) R.; m. Jill Ann Moss, 1971; children: Jennifer Lynn, Chad Alan, Heather Leigh, Jessica Moss. Student, Vincennes U., 1964-66; BS, Ind. State U., 1968, MS, 1970. Tchr., coach North Ctrl. H.S., 1968-69, Eng H.S., 1969-71, Vincennes H.S., 1971-73, Corydon H.S., 1973-85; mem. from 70th dist. Ind. State Ho. of Reps., 1978—. Del. Ind. State Dem. Conv., 1976-78; mem. Dem. Youth for Hamilton Campaign, 1974. Recipient Legis. award Ind. Alliance for Better Child Care, Legis. award UnitedWay. Mem. NEA, Ind. Tchrs. Assn., Lions, KC. Home: 8990 Bird Trail Rd NW Depauw IN 47115-8923 Office: Ind Ho of Reps State Capitol Indianapolis IN 46204

ROBERTSON, RICHARD EARL, physical chemist, educator; b. Long Beach, Calif., Nov. 12, 1933; s. Earl Austin and A. Isobel (Roberts) R.; m. Joyce W. Conger, Sept. 4, 1955 (div. 1972); children: Christopher, Jill; m. Patricia L. Richmond, Apr. 20, 1974. BA, Occidental Coll., L.A., 1955; student, UCLA, 1955-56; PhD, Calif. Inst. Tech., 1960. Phys. chemist rsch. lab. GE, Schenectady, N.Y., 1960-70; staff scientist Ford Motor Co., Dearborn, Mich., 1970-86; prof. materials sci. and engring. U. Mich., Ann Arbor, 1986—, dir. Macromolecular Sci. and Engring. Ctr., 1995-2000. Contbr. articles to profl. jours. Postdoctoral fellow Washington U., St. Louis, 1959-60. Fellow Am. Phys. Soc.; mem. Am. Chem. Soc., Sigma Xi. Office: U Mich Dept Materials Sci Eng Ann Arbor MI 48109-2136 E-mail: rer@umich.edu.

ROBERTSON, RICHARD STUART, insurance holding company executive; b. Spokane, Wash., June 14, 1942; s. Stuart A. and Marjory (Moch) R.; m. Trudy Ann Prendergast, July 31, 1976; children: Thomas Stuart, Richard Andrew. BS, Calif. Inst. Tech., 1963. Chief reinsurance actuary Lincoln Nat. Life Ins. Co., Ft. Wayne, Ind., 1963-74; sr. v.p., chief fin. officer Lincoln Nat. Corp., 1974-86, exec. v.p., CFO, 1986-92, exec. v.p., corp. risk officer, 1992-98; sr. v.p. Lincoln Nat. Reassurance Co., 1999—. Bd. dirs. Lincoln Re S.A., Lincoln China, Kyoei Lincoln Reins. Svc. Co., Linsco Reins. Co.; chmn. Actuarial Stds. Bd., 1996-97. Fellow Soc. Actuaries (pres. 1985-86); mem. Am. Acad. Actuaries (v.p. 1980-81, pres. elect 1998, pres. 1999). Episcopalian. Home: 12618 Aboite Center Rd Fort Wayne IN 46814-9725 Fax: 219-455-1036. E-mail: rrobertson@lnc.com.

ROBERTSON, TIMOTHY JOEL, statistician, educator; b. Denver, Oct. 4, 1937; s. Flavel P. and Helen C. (Oliver) Girdner; m. Joan K. Slater, Aug. 18, 1959; children— Kelly, Jana, Doug, Mike B.A. in Math., U. Mo., 1959, M.S. in Math., 1961, Ph.D. in Stats., 1966. Asst. prof. Cornell Coll., Mt. Vernon, Iowa, 1961-63; prof. stats. U. Iowa, Iowa City, 1965—. Vis. prof. U. N.C., Chapel Hill, 1974-75, U. Calif.-Davis, 1983-84; Eugene Lukacs Disting. vis. prof. Bowling Green State U., 1991-92; vis. lectr. Com. Pres. Statis. Soc., 1971-74. Author: (with F.T. Wright and R.L. Dykstra) Order Restricted Statistical Inference; assoc. editor Am. Math. Monthly, 1977-81; mem. editl. bd. Comms. in Stats., 1981-92; assoc. editor Jour. Am. Statis. Assn., 1990-96; contbr. numerous articles to profl. jours. Recipient Collegiate Teaching award U. Iowa, 1990. Fellow Am. Statis. Assn. (council 1974-75), Inst. Math. Stats., Internat. Statis. Inst.; mem. Math. Assn. Am., Sigma Xi, Sierra Club Democrat Avocations: canoeing, camping, bicycling, walking. Home: 673 Garfield Rd West Branch IA 52358-8574 Office: University of Iowa Dept Stats/Actuarial Sci Iowa City IA 52242

ROBERTSON, WILLIAM RICHARD, leverage buyout firm executive, former banker; b. Schenectady, N.Y., July 26, 1941; s. Bruce Manson and Mary Jo (Gillam) R.; m. Sarah Reed Parker, June 20, 1964; children: Deborah Graham, John William, Julie Elizabeth AB, Colgate U., 1964; MBA, Case Western Res. U., 1967. Nat. City Bank/Nat. City Corp., 1964-97; exec. v.p., chief fin. officer Nat. City Corp., Cleve., 1982-89, dep. chmn. bd. dirs., 1986-95; pres., 1995-97; mng. ptnr. Kirtland Capital Corp., 1997—. Bd. dirs. Kirtland Capital Corp. Trustee Coll. of Wooster, Ohio, 1982-91, Fairmount Presbyn. Ch., Cleve., 1983-86, St. Luke's Hosp., Cleve., 1984-97, Cleve. Ballet, 1985-89, United Way, 1986-97, Karamu House, 1988-95, Western Res. Hist. Soc., 1990—, Cleve. Mus. Art, 1991—, Salvation Army, 1985—, chmn. adv. bd., 1991-93; pres., trustee Big Bros. and Big Sisters, Cleve., 1973-80; chmn., bd. trustees United Way of Cleve., 1995-97, trustee Musical Arts Assn., 1994-97, chmn. vis. com. of Case Western Res. U. Weatherhead Sch. Mgmt., 1995-97. Mem. Fin. Execs. Inst., Cleve. Skating Club (pres. 1980-82), Union Club, Country Club, Pepper Pike Club, Ottawa Club, Desert Mountain Club. Republican. Avocations: travel, skiing, shooting, golf, history. Home: 13705 Shaker Blvd Cleveland OH 44120-5604 Office: Kirtland Capital Corp 2550 Som Center Rd Willoughby OH 44094-9655

ROBIE, JOAN, elementary school principal; Prin. Monteith Elem. Sch., Grosse Pointe, Mich., 1989—. Recipient Elem. Sch. Recognition award U.S. Dept. Edn., 1989-90 Office: Monteith Elem Sch 1275 Cook Rd Grosse Pointe Woods MI 48236-2511

ROBIN, RICHARD C. lawyer; b. Brownwood, Tex., July 12, 1945; s. Milton and Bernice F. (Fine) R.; children: Gregory, Max. B.A., Tulane U.; J.D., DePaul U. Bar: Ill. 1970, U.S. Dist. Ct. (no. dist.) Ill. 1971, U.S. Ct. Appeals (6th cir.), U.S. Ct. Appeals (7th cir.), Trial Bar (no. dist.) Ill. 1982. With civil trial div. Ill. Atty. Gen. Office, Chgo., 1970-74; assoc. firm Vedder Price Kaufman & Kammholz, Chgo., 1974-76, ptnr., 1976— . Mem. ABA, (com. on litigation), Chgo. Bar Assn. Office: Vedder Price Kaufman & Kammholz 222 N La Salle St Ste 2600 Chicago IL 60601-1100

ROBINER, DONALD MAXWELL, lawyer, former federal official; b. Detroit, Feb. 4, 1935; s. Max and Lucia (Chassman) Robiner; m. Phyllis F Goodman; children: Brian Roberts, Marc Roberts, Steven Ralph, Lawrence Alan. BA, U. Mich., 1957; postgrad., Wayne State U., 1957-58; JD, Case Western Res. U., 1961. Bar: Ohio 1961, US Supreme Ct 1964, US Ct Appeals (6th cir) 1965. Assoc. Metzenbaum, Gaines, Schwartz, Krupansky, Finley & Stern, Cleve., 1961-67; ptnr. Metzenbaum, Gaines, Krupansky, Finley & Stern, 1967-72; v.p. Metzenbaum, Gaines, Finley & Stern Co., L.P.A., 1972-77, Gaines, Stern, Schwarzwald & Robiner Co., Cleve., 1977-81; exec. v.p., sec. Schwarzwald, Robiner & Rock Co. LPA, 1981-90; prin. Buckingham, Doolittle & Burroughs Co, LPA, 1991-94; U.S. Trustee Ohio and Mich. region 9 U.S. Dept. of Justice, 1994—2001; of counsel Selkin, Billick & Harrold Co., LPA, Beachwood, Ohio, 2002—. V.p., sec. Richard L. Bowen & Assocs. Inc., Cleve., 1969—94; acting judge Shaker Heights Mcpl. Ct., 1973; mem. bd. bar examiners State of Ohio, Columbus, 1974—79; life mem. 6th Cir. Jud. Conf.; mediator alt ernate dispute resolution panel U.S. Dist. Ct. (no. dist.) Ohio, 1993—94. Sec. Friends of Beachwood Libr. Inc, Ohio, 1981—88; sec. Friends of Beachwood Libr. Inc., 1981—96, trustee, 1981—96. Recipient Cert Appreciation, Ohio Supreme Ct, 1974—79, Appreciation Award, Am Soc Appraisers, 1975. Mem.: Cleve. Bar Assn., Ohio Coun. Sch. Bd. Attys. (mem. exec. com. 1990—94), Am. Arbitration Assn. (Serv Award 1975), Comml. Law League Am., Am. Bankruptcy Inst., Jud. Conf. 8th Appellate Dist. Ohio (life), KP. Home: 3094 Richmond Rd Beachwood OH 44122-3247 Office: Commerce Park Four 23240 Chagrin Blvd Ste 450 Beachwood OH 44122 Fax: 216-831-1326. E-mail: DonRobiner@msn.com.

ROBINS, H(ENRY) IAN, medical oncologist; b. N.Y.C., Feb. 17, 1945; s. Edwin and Matilda (Morgenstern) R. AB in Biology, Boston U., 1966, AM in Biochemistry, 1968, PhD in Molecular Biology, 1971, MD, 1976. Diplomate Am. Bd. Internal Medicine, Am. Bd. Med. Oncology, Am. Bd. Forensic Medicine, Am. Bd. Forensic Examiners. Intern in internal medicine Univ. Hosps., Madison, Wis., 1976-77, resident in internal medicine, 1977-79; fellow in clin. oncology Wis. Clin. Cancer Ctr., 1979-81, fellow in rsch. oncology, 1981-82; instr. dept. human oncology, dept. medicine Dept. Human Oncology, Dept. Medicine U. Wis. Sch. Medicine, 1982-83, asst. prof., 1983-86, assoc. prof., 1986—; chief sect. med. oncology, dir. U. Wis. Sch. Medicine, 1990-95, prof. dept. human oncology, medicine and neurology, 1992—. Chmn. Systemic Hyperthermia Oncology Working Group. Contbr. numerous articles to profl. jours.; reviewer numerous sci. jours. including Biochem. Pharmacology, Internat. Jour. Radiation Biology, Jour. Clin. Oncology, New Eng. Jour. Medicine, others. Mem. N.Y. Acad. Scis., AAAS, ACP, Internat. Clin. Hyperthermia Soc. , Radiation Rsch. Soc., N.am. Hyperthermia Group, Oncology Group, Am. Fedn. clin. Rsch., Ea. Coop. Oncology Group, European Soc. Hyperthermic Oncology, Vet. Cancer Soc., Transplantation Soc., Collaborative Ocular Melanoma Study Group, N.Am. Brain Tumor Consortium, Am. Soc. Clin. Hypnosis, Minn. Soc. Clin. Hypnosis, Sigma Xi. Office: Clin Sci Ctr K4/662 U Wis Sch Med 600 Highland Ave Madison WI 53792-0001

ROBINS, JOEL, company executive; Pres. Robbins Trading Co., Chgo., 1983—. Office: Robbins Trading Co Ste 760 8700 W Bryn Mawr Ave # 7ths Chicago IL 60631-3512

ROBINS, LEE NELKEN, medical educator; b. New Orleans, Aug. 29, 1922; d. Abe and Leona (Reiman) Nelken; m. Eli Robins, Feb. 22, 1946 (dec. Dec. 1994); children: Paul, James, Thomas, Nicholas; m. Hugh Chaplin, Aug. 5, 1998. Student, Newcomb Coll., 1938-40; BA, Radcliffe Coll., 1942, MA, 1943; PhD, Harvard U., 1951. Mem. faculty Washington U., St. Louis, 1954—, prof. sociology in psychiatry, 1968-91, prof. sociology, 1969-91, prof. social sci., prof. social sci. in psychiatry, 1991-2000, prof. emeritus, 2001—. Past mem. Nat. Adv. Coun. on Drug Abuse; past mem. task panels Pres.'s Commn. on Mental Health; mem. expert adv. panel on mental health WHO; Salmon lectr. N.Y. Acad. Medicine, 1983; Cutter lectr. Harvard U., 1997. Author: Deviant Children Grown Up, 1966; editor 11 books; N.Am. Assoc. editor Internat. Jour. Methods in Psychiat. Rsch.; mem. editl. bd. Psychol. Medicine, Jour. Child Psychology and Psychiatry, Jour. Studies on Alcohol, Social Psychiatry and Psychiatric Epidemiology, Epidemiol. e Psichiat. Sociale; contbr. articles to profl. jours. Recipient Rsch. Scientist award USPHS, 1970-90, Pacesetter Rsch. award Nat. Inst. Drug Abuse, 1978, Radcliffe Coll. Grad. Soc. medal, 1979, Sutherland award Am. Soc. Criminology, 1991, Nathan B. Eddy award Com. on Problems of Drug Dependence, 1993, Spl. Presdl. Commendation Am. Psychiat. Assn., 1999, Am. Acad. Arts and Scis., 1999, Commendation and Appreciation award Harvard Inst. Psychiat. Epidemiology and Genetics, 2000; rsch. grantee NIMH, Nat. Inst. on Drug Abuse, Nat. Inst. on Alcohol Abuse and Alcoholism. Fellow Am. Coll. Epidemiology, Royal Coll. Psychiatrists (hon.), Am. Soc. Psychiatrists (hon.), Soc. Study of Addiction (hon.); mem. APHA (Rema Lapouse award 1979, Lifetime Achievement award sect. on alcohol and drug abuse 1994), Internat. Fedn. Psychiat. Epidemiology (com.1992-2002), World Psychiat. Assn. (sect. com. on epidemiology and cmty. psychiatry, 1985-2002, co-chmn. sect. on non-diagnostic instruments in psychiatry), Soc. Life History Rsch. in Psychopathology, Am. Coll. Neuropsychopharmacology, Internat. Sociol. Assn., Inst. Medicine, Am. Psychopath. Assn. (pres. 1987-88, Paul Hoch award 1978). Office: Washington U Med Sch Dept Psychiatry Saint Louis MO 63110 E-mail: lro6@aol.com.

ROBINS, MARJORIE MCCARTHY (MRS. GEORGE KENNETH ROBINS), civic worker; b. Oct. 4, 1914; d. Eugene Ross and Louise (Roblee) McCarthy; m. George Kenneth Robins, Nov. 9, 1940; children: Carol Robins Von Arx, G. Stephen, Barbara A. Robins Foorman. Mem. Mo. Libr. Commn., 1937-38; mem. bd. St. Louis Jr. League, 1945, 46; mem. bd. Occupational Therapy Workshop of St. Louis, 1941-46, pres., 1945, 46; mem. bd. Ladue Chapel Nursery Sch., 1957-60, 61-64, pres. bd., 1963, 64; past regional chmn. United Fund; past mem. St. Louis Met. Youth Commn., St. Louis Health and Welfare Coun.; bd. dirs. Internat. Inst. of St. Louis, 1966-72, 76-82, 83-92, sec., 1968, v.p., 1981; bd. dirs. Mental Health Assn. St. Louis, 1963-70, Washington U. Child Guidance and Evaluation Clinic, 1968-78; bd. dirs. Cen. Inst. for Deaf, 1970—, v.p., 1975-76, pres., 1976-78; bd. dirs. Met. St. Louis YWCA, 1954-63, 64-74, pres. bd., 1960-63, trustee, 1977—; mem. nat. bd. YWCA, 1967-79, nat. v.p., 1973-76; vol. tchr. remedial reading clinic St. Louis City Schs., 1968-71; trustee John Burroughs Sch., 1960-63, John Burroughs Found., 1965-80, Roblee Found., 1972—, Nat. YWCA Retirement Fund, 1979-88; bd. dirs. Gambrill Gardens United Meth. Retirement Home, 1979-85, Thompson Retreat and Conf. Center, 1981-87; bd. dirs. Springboard to Learning Inc., 1980-98, v.p., 1980-90; tutor I Have A Dream Found., 1995-98. Mem. Archaeol. Inst. Am. (bd. dirs. 1993-95, 97-00, treas. St. Louis chpt. 1985-87, 93-95), Vassar Club (sec. and pres. 1939-40), Wednesday Club (dir. 1968-70, 77-79, 80-81, 93-95), St. Louis. Home: 45 Loren Woods Saint Louis MO 63124-1903

ROBINSON, ALEXANDER JACOB, clinical psychologist; b. St. John, Kans., Nov. 7, 1920; s. Oscar Frank and Lydia May (Beitler) R.; m. Elsie Louise Riggs, July 29, 1942; children: Madelyn K., Alicia A., David J., Charles A., Paul S., Marietta J., Stephen N. BA in Psychology, MS in Clin. Psychology, Ft. Hays (Kans.) State U., 1942; postgrad., U. Ill., 1942-44. Cert. psychologist, sch. psychologist. Chief psychologist Larned (Kans.) State Hosp., 1948-53, with employee selection, outpatient services, 1953-55; sch. psychologist County Schs., Modesto, Calif., 1955-61, Pratt (Kans.) Jr. Coll., 1961-66; fed. grantee, writer assoc. dir. Exemplary Federally Funded Program for Spl. Edn., Pratt, 1966-70; dir. spl. edn., researcher Stafford County Schs., St. John, 1970-81, ret., 1981. Supr. testing and data Incidence of Exceptional Children in Kansas, Kans. State U., Ft. Hays, 1946; writer, asst. dir. Best Exemplary Federally Funded Program on Spl. Edn., Pratt, 1966-70; fed. grantee, researcher, writer, study dir. Edn. for the High-Performance Child, St. John, 1970—, Psychogenesis of the Sociopathic Personality, a longitudinal study. Minister, The Ch. of Jesus Christ. Served to 2d lt. U.S. Army, 1944-46, PTO. Mem. N.Y. Acad. Scis., Libr. of Congress. Lodge: Lions (program chmn. St. John 1974-76). Achievements include research on normal children with a learning disability and their specific developmental requirement. Avocations: history, ethnology, cultural anthropology, music, literature. Home and Office: 202 Grandview St Saint John KS 67576-2100

ROBINSON, BARRY R. lawyer; b. Dover, Ohio, Dec. 8, 1946; AB, Princeton U., 1969; JD cum laude, Ohio State U., 1972. Bar: Ohio 1972. Ptnr. Baker & Hostetler, Columbus, Ohio. Fellow Am. Coll. Trust and Estate Counsel; mem. ABA, Ohio State Bar Assn., Columbus Bar Assn. Office: Baker & Hostetler Capital Sq 65 E State St Ste 2100 Columbus OH 43215-4260

ROBINSON, DONALD PETER, musician, retired electrical engineer; b. Phila., Jan. 27, 1928; s. Warren Frederick and Marcella Theresa (Derry) R.; m. Beatrice Graves, Sept. 22, 1951 (dec.); children: Donald, Stephen, Sharon Robinson-Byrd, Michael; m. Mary Katherine Robertson, June 9, 1990. A.A., Temple U. Sch. Tech., 1956. Sr. engr./technician Gen. Electric Co., Utica, N.Y., 1956-89, ret., 1989; organist emeritus St. Joseph-St. Patrick's Ch., Utica, 1983— ; minister music/organist St. Paul's Baptist Ch., Utica, 1961-88; organist Utica Council K.C., 1969— ; organist/choir dir. 4th degree assembly Central N.Y. dist. K.C., 1985— ; producer, host Organ Loft radio program WLFH, Little Falls, N.Y., 1962-90; pipe organ cons. Served with AUS, 1948-54. Mem. Am. Guild Organists (past dean central N.Y. chpt.), Am. Theatre Organ Soc., Nat. Assn. R.R. Passengers (bd. dirs.), K.C. (past faithful navigator 4th degree assembly). Roman Catholic. Home: 715 Garfield Ave Rockford IL 61103-6023

ROBINSON, FARREL RICHARD, pathologist, toxicologist; b. Wellington, Kans., Mar. 23, 1927; s. Farrel Otis and Norine (Sloan) R.; m. Mimi Agatha Hathaway, June 5, 1949; children— Farrel Richard, Kelly S., E. Scott, Brian A. B.S., Kans. State U., 1950, D.V.M., M.S., 1958; Ph.D., Tex. A&M U., 1965. Diplomate: Am. Coll. Vet. Pathologists, Am. Bd. Vet. Toxicology (v.p. 1971-74, pres. 1976-79). Served with USN, 1945-46; commd. 2d lt. USAF, 1951, advanced through grades to lt. col., 1971; vet. pathologist Aerospace Med. Research Labs., Wright-Patterson AFB, Ohio, 1958-68; chief Vet. Pathology div. Armed Forces Inst. Pathology, Washington, 1968-74; ret., 1974; scientist assoc. Univs. Associated for Research and Edn. in Pathology, Inc., 1972-74; asst. clin. prof. pathology George Washington U. Sch. Medicine, 1972-74; instr. NIH Grad. Program, 1973-74; prof. toxicology-pathology Sch. Vet. Medicine, Purdue U., 1974-93; dir. Animal Disease Diagnostic Lab., 1978-85, head dept. vet. sci., 1978-85, head dept. vet. microbiology, pathology and pub. health, 1986-88, chief toxicology service, 1984-93; emeritus, 1993. Cons. vet. pathology USAF surg. gen. and asst. surg. gen. for vet. services, 1970-74 Mem. editorial bd. Human and Vet. Toxicology, 1976— . Contbr. sci. articles to profl. jours. Decorated USAF Commendation medal, Meritorious Service medal; recipient Aerospace Med. Research Labs. Scientist of Year award, 1967 Mem. AVMA, Am. Bd. Vet. Toxicology, Am. Coll. Vet. Pathology, Am. Assn. Vet. Lab. Diagnosticians (bd. govs.1980-85, v.p. 1986, pres. 1987), Wildlife Disease Assn., Conf. Rsch. Workers in Animal Disease, Soc. Toxicology, U.S. Animal Health Assn., Sigma Xi, Phi Kappa Phi, Alpha Zeta, Phi Zeta. Democrat. Methodist. Home and Office: 201 W 600 N West Lafayette IN 47906-9727 E-mail: frrob@wcis.cioe.com.

ROBINSON, JACK ALBERT, retail drug stores executive; b. Detroit, Feb. 26, 1930; s. Julius and Fannie (Aizkowitz) R.; m. Aviva Freedman, Dec. 21, 1952; children: Shelby, Beth, Abigail. B in Pharmacy, Wayne State U., 1952. Founder, chief exec. officer, chmn. bd. Perry Drug Stores, Inc., Pontiac, Mich., 1957-95; founder, chmn., pres. JAR Group LLC, Bloomfield, 1996. Former bd. dirs. Riser Foods, Inc.; former corp. dir. R & B Inc. Chmn. Wayne State U. Fund, Detroit, 1986, Concerned Citizens for the Arts in Mich., 1990, 91—; chmn. ann. fund Detroit Symphony Orch.; bd. dirs. United Way of Pontiac, Mich., 1986, United Found. of Detroit, 1986, Pontiac Area Urban League, Cmty. Found., S.E. Mich., Detroit Svc. Group, Save Orch. Hall, Inc., Cranbrook Inst. Sci., Jewish Fedn. Apts., Wetzman Inst. Sci., Holocaust Meml. Ctr., Harper-Grace Hosp., Detroit; past dir. Pontiac Symphony Boys Club, Detroit Osteo. Hosp.; pres. United Jewish Found. Met. Detroit, 1992, Greater Detroit Interfaith Round Table NCCJ, 1994-95, co-chmn., 1992; pres. Jewish Fedn. Met. Detroit, 1992-94. Recipient Disting. Alumni award Wayne State U. Coll. Pharmacy, 1975, Eleanor Roosevelt Humanities award from State of Israel, 1978, B'nai B'rith Youth Svcs. Am. Tradition award, 1982, Wayne State U. Disting. Alumni award, 1985, Tree of Life award Jewish Nat. Fund, 1985, Disting. Citizen award Pontiac Boy Scouts Am., 1985, Corp. Leadership award Wayne State U., 1985, Booker T. Washington Bus. Assn. Brotherhood award, 1986, Humanitarian award March of Dimes, 1987, award Weizmann Rsch. Inst., 1987, Humanitarian award Variety Club, 1988, Fred M. Butzel award Jewish Fedn. Met. Detroit, 1991, B'nai B'rith Great Am. Traditions award, 1991, Cmty. Svc. award Am. Arabic and Jewish Friends, 1995, Outstanding Philanthropic award Nat. Soc. Fundraising Execs., 1999, Mich. Hall of Fame award in Real Estate and Retailing, Internat. Coun. Shopping Ctrs., 2001; named Entrepreneur of Yr. Harvard U. Bus. Sch., Detroit, 1982. Mem.: Econ. Club (bd. dirs. Detroit chpt.), Am. Found. for Pharm. Edn. (bd. dirs.), Am. Pharm. Assn., Nat. Assn. Chain Drug Stores (chmn. 1987, Lifetime Achievement award 1995, Robert B. Begley award 1995). Avocations: skiing, jogging, photography, classical music, glass collecting. Office: JAR Group LLC Ste 330 38500 N Woodward Ave Bloomfield Hills MI 48304-2961

ROBINSON, JOHN HAMILTON, civil engineer; b. Kansas City, Mo., Feb. 14, 1927; s. David Beach and Aileen March (Weaver) R.; m. Patricia Ann Odell, June 17, 1949; children: John Hamilton, Patricia Ann, Donna Marie, Clinton Odell. B.S., U. Kans., 1949. Registered profl. engr., Kans. With Black & Veatch (cons. engrs.), Kansas City, Mo., 1949—, ptnr., 1956—, exec. ptnr., 1971-92, mng. ptnr., 1983-92, chmn. emeritus, 1993. Trustee Johnson County Community Coll.; deacon, elder 2d Presbyterian Ch., Kansas City, Mo. Served with USNR, 1945-46. Fellow ASCE (hon. mem.); mem. Am. Cons. Engrs. Coun. (chmn. com. of fellows), Cons. Engrs. Coun. Mo. (dir. 1972— , pres. 1976-77), Mo. Soc. Profl. Engrs., Kans. Engring. Soc. (Kans. Engr. of Yr. award 1983), Am. Water Works Assn. (v.p. 1985, pres. 1987, Fuller award 1983), U. Kans. Alumni Assn. (pres.), Water Pollution Control Fedn., Mission Hills Country Club, Vanguard Club, Mercury Club, Rotary, Tau Beta Pi, Sigma Tau, Omicron Delta Kappa, Beta Theta Pi. Home: 3223 W 67th St Shawnee Mission KS 66208-1846 Office: Black Veatch Engrs 8400 Ward Pky Kansas City MO 64114-2031

ROBINSON, JULIE ANN, federal judge; b. 1957; BS, U. Kans., 1978, JD, 1981. Bar: Kans. 1981. Asst. U.S. atty. for dist. Kans. U.S. Dept. Justice, Kansas City, Kans., 1983-94, sr. litigation counsel, 1991-94; law clk. to hon. Benjamin E. Franklin, U.S. Bankruptcy Ct. for Dist. Kans., 1981-83, bankruptcy judge, 1994—; judge bankruptcy appellate panel U.S. Ct. Appeals (10th cir.), 1996—. Instr. trial practice U. Kans. Sch. Law, 1989-90. Fellow Am. Bar Found.; mem. ABA, Nat. Conf. Bankruptcy Judges (fin. com., chmn. liaison com. to Nat. Bar Assn.), Kans. Bar Assn., Kan. Inn of Ct. Office: US Bankruptcy Ct 225 US Courthouse 444 SE Quincy Topeka KS 66683

ROBINSON, JUNE KERSWELL, dermatologist, educator; b. Phila., Jan. 26, 1950; d. George and Helen S. (Kerswell) R.; m. William T. Barker, Jan. 31, 1981. BA cum laude, U. Pa., 1970; MD, U. Md., 1974. Diplomate Am. Bd. Dermatology, Nat. Bd. Med. Examiners, Am. Bd. Mohs Micrographic Surgery and Cutaneous Oncology. Intern Greater Balt. Med. Ctr., Hanover, N.H., 1974, resident in medicine, 1974-75; resident in dermatology Dartmouth-Hitchcock Med. Ctr., Hanover, N.H., 1975-78, chief resident, clin. instr., 1977-78, instr. in dermatology, 1978; fellow Mohs; chemosurgery and dermatologic surgery NYU Skin and Cancer Clinic, N.Y.C., 1978-79; instr. in dermatology NYU, 1979; asst. prof. dermatology Northwestern U. Med. Sch., Chgo., 1979, asst. prof. surgery, 1980-85, assoc. prof. dermatology and surgery, 1985-91, prof. dermatology and surgery, 1991-98; prof. medicine and pathology, dir. divsn. dermatology Cardinal Bernardin Cancer Ctr., Loyola U. Med. Ctr., 1998—, program leader skin cancer clin. program, 1998—. Mem. consensus devel. conf. NIH, 1992; mem. panel on use of sunscreens Internat. Agy. for Rsch. on Cancer, WHO, 2000; lectr. in field. Author: Fundamentals of Skin Biopsy, 1985, also audiovisual materials; editor: (textbooks) Atlas of Cutaneous Surgery, 1996, Cutaneous Medicine and Surgery: An Integrated Program in Dermatology, 1996; mem. editl. bd. Archives of Dermatology, 1988-97; sect. editor The Cutting Edge: Challenges in Med. and Surg. Therapeutics, 1989-97; contbg. editor Jour. Dermatol. Surgery and Oncology, 1985-88; mem. editl. com. 18th World Congress of Dermatology, 1982; contbr. numerous articles, abstracts to profl. publs., chpts. to books. Bd. dirs. Northwestern Med. Faculty Found., 1982-84, chmn. com. on benefits and leaves, 1984, nominating com. 1988. Grantee Nat. Cancer Inst., 1985-91, Am. Cancer Soc., 1986-89, Skin Cancer Found., 1984-85, Dermatology Found., 1981-83, Northwestern U. Biomed. Rsch., 1981, Syntex, 1984. Fellow: Am. Coll. Chemosurgery (chmn. sci. program ann. meeting 1983, chmn. publs. com. 1986—87, chmn. task force on ednl. needs 1989—90, co-editor bull. 1984—87); mem.: Chgo. Dermatol. Soc., Women's Dermatol. Soc. (pres. 1990—92), Soc. Investigative Dermatology, Am. Soc. Dermatol. Surgery 1994—95, Dermatology Found. (trustee 1995—98), Am. Acad. Dermatology (asst. sec.-treas. 1995—98, sec.-treas. 1998—2001, bd. dirs. 1993—95, Stephen Rothman Lectr. award 1992, Presdl. citation 1992, 2000), Am. Dermatol. Assn., Am. Cancer Soc. (pres. Ill. divsn. 1996—98). Home: 132 E Delaware Pl Apt 5806 Chicago IL 60611-4951

ROBINSON, KAYNE, political organization officer; Donna Robinson. B, Drake U. With Des Moines Police Dept.; dep. Iowa chmn. Dole Presdl. campaign, 1988; Iowa chmn. Gramm Presdl. campaign, 1996; chmn. Iowa Reps., 1999—2001. With USMC. Named Police Officer of the Yr. Iowa Assn. Women Police. Mem. NRA (1st v.p.). Office: 521 E Locust St Des Moines IA 50309-1939*

ROBINSON, KEITH, newspaper editor; Bur. chief AP, Indpls., 2000—. Office: 251 N Illinois St Ste 1600 Indianapolis IN 46204-1943

ROBINSON, LARRY J. state legislator; m. Mary Lee; 2 children. BS, Valley City State U.; MS, N.D. State U. Mem. N.D. Senate from 24th dist., Bismark, 1989—; mem. appropriations com. N.D. Senate. Mem. Gov.'s Coun. on Human Resources, Com. on Status of Women; aux. svc. dir. Valley City State U. Bd. dirs., adv. com. Mercy Hosp.; mem. adv. com. Barnes County, Extension Adv. Coun., Hi Soaring Eagle Ranch. Mem. KC, Elks, Eagles, Kiwanis, C. of C. (past pres.), Masons, Phi Delta Kappa. Office: State Senate State Capitol Bismarck ND 58505 Home: 3584 Sheyenne Cir Valley City ND 58072-9545

ROBINSON, LARRY ROBERT, insurance company executive; b. Indpls., Feb. 7, 1936; s. Manuel H. Robinson and Barbara Dawson Robinson Trees; m. Sharon Moore, Aug. 3, 1957; children: Christopher, Lizbeth, Lara, Jeremy. BA, DePauw U., Greencastle, Ind., 1957. Actuarial trainee State Life Ins. Co., Indpls., 1957-63, asst. actuary, 1963-66, actuary, 1966-67, asst. v.p., actuary, 1967-70, v.p., actuary, 1970-80, sr. v.p., actuary, 1980-83, exec. v.p., 1983-99, pres., 1999—, also bd. dirs. Chmn. cost disclosure com. Am. Coun. Life Ins., Washington, 1985-87, chmn. actuarial com., 1990-91. Bd. dirs. Marion County Assn. Retarded Citizens, Indpls., 1980-86. With U.S. Army, 1961-62. Fellow Soc. Actuaries; mem. Am. Acad. Actuaries, Indpls. Actuarial Club (past pres.), Actuarial Club Ind., Ky. and Ohio (past pres.), Phi Beta Kappa. Office: State Life Ins Co Ste 368 1 American Sq Indianapolis IN 46282-0002 E-mail: Larry_Robinson@statelife.com.

ROBINSON, LESTER W. airport executive; B in Bus. Adminstrn., Mich. State U., 1973. CPA. With Coopers & Lybrand; CFO 1st Independence Corp., Detroit, 1980-83, pres., CEO, 1989-91; auditor gen. Wayne County, 1988-89, dept. dir. airports fin. & adminstrn. dept. airports, 1991-93, CFO dept. budget, 1993-95, dir. dept. airports, 2000—; corp. fin. rep. 1st Mich. Corp., 1995-2000. Office: Dept Aviation Detroit Met Airport Williams Rogell Dr Detroit MI 48242

ROBINSON, ROBERT GEORGE, psychiatry educator; b. Pitts., May 22, 1945; s. Robert Campbell and Rosetta M. (Martindale) R.; m. Gretchen Priscilla Smith, Jan. 5, 1974; children: Christopher, Jonathan. BS in Engring. Physics, Cornell U., 1967, MD, 1971. Intern Montefiore Hosp. and Albert Einstein Med. Ctr., 1971-72; resident Cornell U., White Plains, N.Y., 1972-73; rsch. assoc. NIMH, Washington, 1973-75; resident Johns Hopkins U., 1975-77, asst. prof. to assoc. prof., 1977-85, prof., 1985—; prof., head of dept. U. Iowa Coll. Medicine, Iowa City, 1990—, Paul W. Penningroth prof., 1996—. Mem. editorial bds. Jour. Neuropsychiatry & Clinical Neurosciences, Int. Jour. Psychiatry in Medicine, Psychiatry, J. Nervous and Mental Diseases. Author: The Clinical Neuropsychiatry of Stroke, 1998; editor: Depression and Coexisting Disease, 1989, Depression in Neurologic Disease, 1993; mem. editl. bd. Jour. Neuropsychiatry and Clin. Neuroscis., Internat. Jour. Psychiatry in Medicine, Psychiatry, Jour. Nervous and Mental Diseases; contbr. more than 300 articles and chpts. to publs. Rsch. Scientist award, NIMH, 1989; Mellon fellow Johns Hopkins U., 1977; recipient Rsch. prize Am. Psychiat. Assn., 1999, Acad. Pscyosomatic Medicine, 1999. Fellow APA, Am. Coll. Neuropsychopharmacology, Soc. for Neurosci.; mem. AAAS, Soc. Biol. Psychiatry, Johns Hopkins Soc. Scholars, Am. Neuropsychiat. Assn. (pres., 1998-99). Office: U Iowa Coll Med 200 Hawkins Dr Iowa City IA 52242-1009 E-mail: robert-robinson@uiowa.edu.

ROBINSON, SPENCER T. (HERK ROBINSON), professional baseball team executive; b. June 25, 1940; m. Kathy Robinson; children: Ashley, Amanda. Student, U. Miami, Washington U., St. Louis. With Cin. Reds., 1962-67; asst. Baltimore Orioles, 1968; asst. scouting dir. Kansas City Royals, 1969-72, dir. stadium ops., 1973-74, v.p., 1975-85, exec. v.p. adminstrn., 1985-90, v.p., 1975-85, exec. v.p., gen. mgr., 1990—, former mem. bd. dirs. Office: Kansas City Royals PO Box 419969 Kansas City MO 64141-6969

ROBINSON, STEPHEN MICHAEL, applied mathematician, educator; b. Columbus, Ohio, Apr. 12, 1942; s. Arthur Howard and Mary Elizabeth (Coffin) R.; m. Chong-Suk Han, May 10, 1968; children: Diana Marie, James Andrew. BA, U. Wis., 1962, PhD, 1971; MS, NYU, 1963; Doctor honoris causa, Univ. Zürich, 1996. Adminstr. U. Wis., Madison, 1969-72, asst. prof., 1972-75, assoc. prof., 1975-79, prof. indsl. engring. and computer scis., 1979—, chmn. dept. indsl. engring., 1981-84. Cons. to various agys. Dept. Def., 1971—. Editor: Math. of Ops. Rsch., 1981-86, assoc. editor, 1975-80, Jour. Ops. Rsch., 1974-86, Math. Programming, 1986-91; mem. bd. editors Annals Ops. Rsch., 1984-99, Set-Valued Analysis, 1992-99, Jour. Convex Analysis, 1994—; adv. editor Math. of Ops. Rsch., 1987—, Ops. Rsch. Letters, 2002-; mem. editl. bd. Springer Series in Ops. Rsch., 1996—; contbr. numerous articles to profl. jours. Trustee Village of Shorewood Hills, Wis., 1974-76, mem. fin. com. , 1973-87; bd. overseers Simon's Rock Coll., Great Barrington, Mass., 1991-2002. Capt. U.S. Army, 1963—69, Korea, Vietnam. Decorated Legion of Merit, Bronze star, Air medal, Army Commendation medal with 2 oak leaf clusters; recipient John K. Walker Jr. award, Mil. Ops. Rsch. Soc., 2001. Mem. Inst. for Ops. Rsch. and Mgmt. Scis. (mem. Ops. Rsch. Soc. Am. coun. 1991-94, sec. 2000—), Inst. Indsl. Engrs., Soc. Indsl. and Applied Math., Math. Programming Soc. (mem.-at-large of coun. 1991-94, George B. Dantzig prize 1997), Madison Club. Home: 1014 University Bay Dr Madison WI 53705-2251 Office: U Wis Dept Indsl Engring 1513 University Ave Madison WI 53706-1572 E-mail: smrobins@wisc.edu.

ROBIRDS, ESTEL, state legislator; Mem. Mo. State Ho. of Reps. Dist. 143, 1993—. Home: Rte 2 Box 2919 Theodosia MO 65761 Office: Mo Ho of Reps State Capitol Building Jefferson City MO 65101-1556

ROBITAILLE, LUC, professional hockey player; b. Montreal, P.Q., Can., Feb. 17, 1966; With Hull Olympiques Major Jr. Hockey League, Que., 1983-84, L.A. Kings, 1984-94, Pitts. Penguins, 1994-95, N.Y. Rangers, 1995-97, L.A. Kings, 1997—. Scored winning goal for nat. team of Can. at 1994 World Hockey Championship. Recipient Guy LaFleur trophy, 1985-86, Can. Hockey Player of Yr. award, 1985-86, Calder Meml. trophy, NHL Rookie of Yr., 1986-87; named to NHL All-Star team, 1987, 88, 90-91, 92-93. Office: Detroit Red Wings Joe Louis Arena 600 Civic Center Detroit MI 48226*

ROBLING, CLAIRE A. state legislator; b. Oct. 22, 1956; m. Tony Robling; 2 children. Student, Coll. St. Catherine. Mem. dist. 35 Minn. Senate, St. Paul, 1996—. Office: 100 Constitution Ave Saint Paul MN 55155-1232 Home: 1169 Butterfly Ln Jordan MN 55352-9476

ROBOL, RICHARD THOMAS, lawyer; b. Norfolk, Va., Feb. 8, 1952; s. Harry James and Lucy Henley (Johnson) R. BA, U. Va., 1974; JD, Harvard U., 1978. Bar: Va. 1979, Ohio 1996, U.S. Dist. Ct. (ea. dist.) Va. 1979, U.S. Ct. Appeals (4th cir.) 1979, U.S. Dist. Ct. (we. dist.) Va. 1981, U.S. Supreme Ct. 1982, D.C. 1991, U.S. Ct. Appeals (4th, 6th and 9th cirs.) 1995. Law clk. to presiding justice U.S. Dist. Ct. (ea. dist.) Va., 1978-79; ptnr. Seawell, Dalton, Hughes & Timms, Norfolk, 1979-87, Hunton and Williams, Norfolk, 1987-92; exec. v.p., gen. counsel Columbus Am. Discovery Group, Inc., 1992—. Adj. prof. U. Dayton Law Sch.; asst. prof. mil. sci. Capital U.; pro bono counsel Nat. Commn. for Prevention Child Abuse, Norfolk, 1983, Tidewater Profl. Assn. on Child Abuse, 1983, Parents United Va., 1981-82, Sexual Abuse Help Line, 1983-86; mem. Boyd-Graves Conf. on Civil Procedure in Va., 1981-87. Contbr. articles to law revs.; contbg. editor: International Law for General Practitioners, 1981. Bd. dirs. Va. Opera Assn. Guild, Norfolk, 1983-87, Tidewater br. NCCJ, 1991-92; deacon Ctrl. Bapt. Ch., Norfolk, 1980-83. Capt. USAR, 1992—. Fulbright scholar, 1974. Mem. Va. State Bar Assn. (bd. dirs. internat. law sect. 1984-87, chmn. 1982-83), Va. Young Lawyers Assn. (cir. rep. 1984-88), Va. Assn. Def. Attys., Maritime Law Assn., Norfolk-Portsmouth Bar assn. (chmn. speakers bur. 1987-88), Assn. Def. Trial Attys. (chmn. Va. 1987), Def. Rsch. Inst., 1982-88. Avocations: camping, rowing, scuba diving. Home: 60 Kenyon Brook Dr Worthington OH 43085-3629 Office: Columbus Am Discovery Group 433 W 6th Ave Columbus OH 43201-3136 E-mail: robol@ee.net.

ROBSON, JUDITH BIROS, state legislator; b. Cleve., Nov. 21, 1939; d. George John and Mary Grace (Millen) Biros; m. Arthur Robson, Sept. 2, 1961; children: Marybeth, Marc, Matthew. BSN, St. John Coll., Cleve., 1961; MS, U. Wis., 1976. RN. Staff nurse Beloit (Wis.) Hosp., 1967-73; nurse practitioner Dr. Ken Gold, Beloit, 1976-78; instr. Blackhawk Tech. Coll., Jonesville, Wis., 1978-87; mem. Wis. Assembly, 1987-98; mem Wis. Senate from 15th dist., Madison, 1998—. Mem. bd. Bedcore, Beloit, 1990, YWCA, Beloit, 1992; sec. Majority Party Caucus, 1990—. Recipient Clean 16 award Environ. Decade. Avocations: biking, skiing, gardening, photography. Office: State Legislature State Capital PO Box 7882 Madison WI 53707-7882

ROCCA, SUE, state legislator; b. May 12, 1949; AS, Ctrl. Mich. Coll. Commr. Macomb County, Mich.; rep. Mich. Dist. 30, 1995-2000. Vice chmn. health policy com. Mich. Ho. Reps., joint com. on adminstrv. rules & regulatory affairs. Office: Office Bd Commrs Macomb County Court Bldg 2nd Fl 40 Gratiot Ct Mount Clemens MI 48043-5719 Address: Mich State Capitol PO Box 30014 Lansing MI 48909-7514

ROCHA, CATHERINE TOMASA, municipal official; BA, U. Mo., 1977, MA, 1979. Cert. mcpl. clk. U. Mo., 1991. Student svc. coord., academic advisor U. Mo., Kansas City, 1979-84; dir. records records dept. Jackson County Courthouse, 1984-87; city clk. Office of the City Clk. City of Kansas City, 1988—. Mem. human rels. adv. commn., 1982-84; mem. bd. zoning commn., 1978-79. Author: (oral history) Black Baseball-The Kansas City Monarch Experience, 1978; editor: newsletter CCFOA, 1991-95. Bd. dirs. Trinity Luth. Hosp. Found., 1996, Women's Found. Gtr. Kansas City; chmn. Westside Fountain Com., 1995-97; former trustee, chmn. auction benefit Westport Alien Ctr.; bd. dirs. Trinity Hosp., 1998-99. Harvard U. fellow, 1990; named 25 Most Influential Hispanic Leaders in Kansas City Dos Mundos newspaper, 1994. Mem. Internat. Inst. Mcpl. Clks. (chmn. big cities com. 1991-94, Harvard grant allocation com. 1994-95, profl. status com. 1995-96), Mexican-Am. Women's Nat. Assn., Friends of Art Coun. (mem. exec. bd.), Southwest Blvd. Merchants Assn. (bd. dirs.), Westside Bus. Assn. (pres. 1996-97). Home: 4545 Wornall Rd Kansas City MO 64111-3270 Office: City of Kansas City Mo Office of the City Clk City Hall 25th Fl 414 E 12th St Kansas City MO 64106-2702

ROCHE, GEORGE CHARLES, III, college administrator; b. Denver, May 16, 1935; s. George Charles, Jr. and Margaret (Stewart) R.; children: George Charles, IV, Muriel Eileen, Margaret Clare, Jacob Stewart. B.S., Regis Coll., Denver, 1956; M.A., U. Colo., 1961, Ph.D., 1965. Tchr. jr. and sr. high schs., Salida, Colo., 1958-60; mem. faculty U. Colo., 1963-64, Colo. Sch. Mines, 1964-66; pres. Hillsdale (Mich.) Coll., 1971-99; ret., 1999. Dir. seminars Found. Econ. Edn., N.Y.C., 1966-71, trustee, 1971-90. Author: Power, 1967, American Federalism, 1967, Education in America, 1969, Legacy of Freedom, 1969, Frederic Bastiat: A Man Alone, 1971, The Bewildered Society, 1972, The Balancing Act: Quota Hiring in Higher Education, 1974, America by the Throat: The Stranglehold of Federal Bureaucracy, 1983, Going Home, 1986, A World Without Heroes, 1987, A Reason for Living, 1989, One By One, 1990, The Fall of the Ivory Tower: Government Funding, Corruption, and the Bankrupting of American Higher Education, 1994, The Book of Heroes: Great Men and Women in American History, 1998; also articles, newspaper column. Chmn. acad. adv. council Charles Edison Meml. Youth Bd., Nat. Council Ednl. Research, 1982-85. Served to 1st lt. USMCR, 1956-58. Recipient Freedom Leadership award Freedoms Found., 1972 Mem. Am. Hist. Assn., Am. Acad. Polit. and Social Sci., Am. Assn. Pres.'s Ind. Colls. and Univs., Mt. Pelerin Soc., Phila. Soc. Office: Hillsdale Coll 33 E College St Hillsdale MI 49242-1205

ROCHE, JAMES MCMILLAN, lawyer; b. Detroit, Apr. 16, 1934; s. James Michael and Louise Cullen (McMillan) R.; m. Laura Jane McMillion, Oct. 27, 1962; children: James, Laura, David, Elizabeth. AB, Holy Cross Coll., 1956; LLB, Harvard U., 1959; LLM, Georgetown U., 1962. Bar: Mich. 1959, Ill. 1962. Ptnr., mem. mgmt. com. McDermott, Will & Emery, Chgo., 1962-98, of counsel, 1998—. Bd. dirs. Time Med Labeling, Inc., Burr Ridge, Ill. Contbr. articles to profl. jours. Chmn. Chgo. Econ. Devel. Corp., 1979-81; pres. Village of Kenilworth, Ill., 1982-85; bd. dirs. St. Francis Hosp., Evanston, 1987-97. Served to capt. USAF, 1959-62. Mem. ABA, Ill. Bar Assn., Chgo. Bar Assn., Mich. Bar Assn., Glen View (Ill.) Golf Club, Monroe Club (Chgo.), The Boulders Club (Ariz.), Desert Forest Club. Roman Catholic. Avocations: golf, Indian art, wine. Office: McDermott Will & Emery 227 W Monroe St Ste 3100 Chicago IL 60606-5096

ROCHE, MARK A. consumer products company executive, lawyer; b. 1954; m. Barbara Roche. BA, U. Va.; JD, Cornell U. Bar: N.Y. 1980. From assoc. to counsel Chadbourne & Park LLP, N.Y.C., 1981-88; group gen. counsel Fortune Brands Inc., Deerfield, Ill., 1988-91, Lincolnshire, 1991-96, v.p., assoc. gen. counsel, 1996-98, v.p., gen. counsel, 1998-99, sr. v.p., gen. counsel, 1999—. Office: Fortune Brands Inc 300 Tower Pkwy Lincolnshire IL 60069-3640

ROCHKIND, LOUIS PHILIPP, lawyer; b. Miami, Fla., June 25, 1948; s. Reuben and Sarah R.; m. Rosalind H. Rochkind, July 4, 1971. BA in Psychology cum laude, U. Mich., 1970, JD cum laude, 1974. Bar: Mich. 1974, U.S. Dist. Ct. (ea. dist.) Mich. 1974. Ptnr. Jaffe, Raitt, Heuer & Weiss, Detroit, 1974—. Adj. prof. law Wayne St. U. Law Sch.; lectr. various profl. assns. and orgns. Assoc. editor U. Mich. Law Rev.; contbr. articles to profl. jours. publs. Mem. Am. Coll. Bankruptcy Lawyers, Detroit Bar Assn. (local rules in bankruptcy subcom. creditor-debtor law sect. 1980—), Phi Kappa Phi. Office: Jaffe Raitt Heuer & Weiss One Woodward Ave Ste 2400 Detroit MI 48226 E-mail: larrol@jafferaitt.com.

ROCK, HAROLD L. lawyer; b. Sioux City, Iowa, Mar. 13, 1932; s. Harold L. and Helen J. (Gormally) R.; m. Marilyn Beth Clark Rock, Dec. 28, 1954; children: Michael, Susan, John, Patrick, Michele, Thomas. BS, Creighton U., 1954, JD, 1959. Bar: Nebr., N.Y., Minn., Mont., Wyo. Law clk. to judge U.S. Ct. Appeals 8th Circuit, Omaha, 1959-60, Fitzgerald Hamer Brown & Leahy, Omaha, 1960-65; ptnr. Kutak Rock, 1965—. Chmn. Nebr. Bd. Bar Examiners, 1989-96; bd. dirs. Mid City Bank, Omaha. Bd. dirs. Douglas County Hist. Soc., 1992—, Nat. Equal Justice Libr., 1995—, Nebr. Nebr. Humanities Coun., 1996—. Served to 1st lt. U.S. Army, 1954-56. Recipient Alumni Achievement award Creighton U., 1995. Mem. ABA (ho. of dels. 1970-96, bd. govs. 1992-95), Nebr. Bar Assn. (ho. of dels., bd. dirs. 1985—, pres. 1988, Nebr. Bar found. bd. dirs., 1982—), Omaha Bar Assn. (pres. 1972-73), Omaha Legal Aid Soc. (pres. 1969-72), Nebr. State Bd. Pub. Accts. (bd. dirs. 1981-85). Roman Catholic. Office: Kutak Rock The Omaha Bldg 1650 Farnam St Ste A Omaha NE 68102-2186

ROCK, RICHARD RAND, lawyer, former state senator; b. Wichita Falls, Tex., Sept. 27, 1924; s. Parker Francis and Ruth Ann (Phillips) R.; m. Rosalee Deardorff, Aug. 23, 1947; children: Richard R. II, Darci Lee, Devon Ray, Robert Regan. BA, Washburn U., 1948, LLB, 1950, JD, 1970. Bar: Kans., U.S. Dist. Ct. Kans., U.S. Ct. Appeals (4th and 10th cirs.). Dir. indsl. rels. Maurer-Neuer Packers, Arkansas City, Kans., 1950-52, plant supt., 1952-54; atty. Rock, Smith & Mason, 1955-95; pres., owner Shreveport (La.) Packing Co., 1972-83, Amarillo (Tex.) Beef Processors, 1977-82, Lubbock (Tex.) Beef Processors, 1978-81, Montgomery (Ala.) Food Processors, 1978-91, Humboldt (Iowa) Sausage Co., 1985-92, Great Bend (Kans.) Packing Co., 1984-95; state senator, asst. minority leader State of Kans., 1988-96; chmn. Rockgate Mgmt. Co., Overland Park, Kans., 1997—. Chmn. bd. dirs. Rockgate Mgmt. Co., Overland Park, Kans. Judge Cowley County, Kans., 1952-56; state rep. State of Kans., 1957-61; authority mem. Kans. Turnpike Authority, 1980-83, chmn., 1993-97; commr. Children with Spl. Health Care Needs, Kans., 1993-95. Served USN Air Corps, 1943-45. Mem. Kans. Bar Assn., Nat. Counsel State Legislatures, Kans. C. of C., VFW. Democrat. Mem. Disciples of Christ. Avocations: golf, yard work. Address: US Marshal Kansas Federal Bldg 444 SE Quincy St Ste 456 Topeka KS 66683-3510

ROCK, RICHARD RAND, II, protective services official; b. 1949; BS, U. Kans, 1978; JD, Washburn U., 1988. Police officer U.S. Marshal's Svc., Lawrence, Kans., 1973-80; police lt. Largo Fla., 1980-85; atty. Mo., 1985-89, Kans., 1989-94; state rep. Kans. State Legislature 79th Dist., 1990-94; U.S. Marshall Dist. Kans., Topeka, 1994—. Office: US Marshals Svc Fed Bldg 444 SE Quincy St Ste 456 Topeka KS 66683-3576

ROCKENSTEIN, WALTER HARRISON, II, lawyer; s. Walter Harrison and Martha Lee (Morris) R.; m. Jodell Lynn Steinke, July 29, 1972; children: Martha Liv, Andrew Harrison. BA cum laude, Coll. of Wooster, 1965; LLB, Yale U., 1968. Bar: Minn. 1968, U.S. Dist. Ct. Minn. 1968, U.S. Ct. Appeals (8th crct.) 1977. Spl. asst. atty. gen., chief antitrust divsn. Office of Minn. Atty. Gen., 1970-72; assoc. Head & Truhn, 1972-73; alderman 11th ward Mpls. City Coun., 1974-83; assoc. Faegre & Benson, Mpls., 1984-85, ptnr., 1986—. Mem. Capital Long-Range Improvements Com., 1974-82, Gov.'s Econ. Roundtable, 1980-82, Hennepin County Waste Disposal & Energy Recovery Adv. Com., 1976-77; chmn. devel. strategies com. League of Minn. Cities, 1979-80, bd. dirs., 1980-83; Mpls. del. Metro. Aircraft Sound Abatement Coun., 1977-90, chmn., 1982-90; mem. aviation subcom. of transp. tech. adv. com. Metro. Coun., 1977-83; mem. airport noise adv. bd. Minn. Pollution Control Agy., bd. dirs. noise com., 1982-85, mem. tech. adv. com., 1990; adv. com. Nat. League of Cities, steering com. Environmental Quality, 1975-79, vice chmn., 1976, chmn., 1978, steering com. Energy, Environment and Natural Resources, 1980-83, Energy Task Force, 1977-79, Nat. Urban Policy Com., 1978; mem. Noise Task Force, Nat. League of Cities/Nat. Assn. of Counties, 1977-80; regional dir. Nat. Org. to Insure a Sound-Controlled Environment, 1976-90, v.p. legal affairs, 1983-90; cons. group nuclear waste mgt., U.S. Dept. Energy, 1978. Elder Westminster Presbyn. Ch., 1975-80, 95-2001, trustee, 1982-87, chair stewardship com., 1989, chair pastor nominating com., 1992-94, co-chair bldg. centennial com.; bd. dirs. Loring Nicollet-Bethlehem Cmty. Ctrs., Inc., 1984—, pres., 1988-92; bd. dirs. U. Minn. Underground Space Ctr. Adv. Bd., 1985-95, chair, 1988-95; bd. dirs. Minn. Ctr. for Book Arts, 1988-93; com. mem. Cub Scout pact 196, Diamond Lake Luth Ch., 1988-91, com. chair, 1990-91; alumni trustee, alumni bd. dirs. The Coll. of Wooster, 1990-96; com. mem. Boy Scout Troop 187, 1994-97; bd. dirs. Minn. Safety Coun., 1997—. Recipient Cert. of Appreciation, Upper Midwest chpt. Acoustical Soc. Am., 1977, Resolution of Appreciation, City of Mpls., 1983, Citation of Honor, Hennepin County, 1983, Cert. of Recognition, League of Minn. Cities, 1983, Hope of Rotary award City of Lakes Rotary Club, 1989, WCCO Good Neighbor award, 1992. Mem. Minn. State Bar Assn. (coun. mem. environ. and natural resources law sect. 1997-98, 99—), Hennepin County Bar Assn., Delta Sigma Rho-Tau Kappa Alpha, Phi Sigma Alpha. Republican. Presbyterian. Avocations: reading, backpacking, cross-country skiing, woodworking. Office: Faegre & Benson LLP 2200 Wells Fargo Ctr 90 S 7th St Minneapolis MN 55402-3901 E-mail: wrockenstein@faegre.com.

ROCKWELL, HAYS HAMILTON, bishop; b. Detroit, Aug. 17, 1936; s. Walter Francis and Kathryn (McElroy) R.; m. Linda Hullinger, Sept. 7, 1957; children: Keith, Stephen, Sarah, Martha. AB, Brown U., 1958; BD, Episcopal Theol. Sch., Cambridge, Mass., 1961; DD (hon.), Episcopal Theol. Seminary SW, Austin, Tex., 1984; BD, Kenyon Coll., 1974; HHD, St. Louis U., 1994. Ordained to ministry Episcopal Ch. as deacon, 1961, as priest, 1962; ordained bishop, 1991. Chaplain St. George's Sch., Newport, R.I., 1961-69, Univ. of Rochester, N.Y., 1969-71; dean Bexley Hall, Rochester, 1971-76; rector St. James' Ch., N.Y.C., 1976-91; bishop coadjutor Diocese of Mo., St. Louis, 1991-93, bishop, 1993—. Dir. Union Theol. Seminary, N.Y.C., 1976, 87, 91. Author: Steal Away, Steal Away Home, 1985. Mem. Coun. on Fgn. Rels., N.Y.C., 1988; former trustee U. Rochester, N.Y.C.; trustee Mo. Bot. Garden, St. Luke's Hosp., Mo. Mem. Century Assn. (N.Y.C.).

ROCKWELL, R(ONALD) JAMES, JR. laser and electro-optics consultant; b. Cin., May 7, 1937; s. Ronald James and Mary Cornelius (Thornton) R.; m. Diane Lundin, Feb. 3, 1968; children: James Gregory, Christopher Derrick. BS, U. Cin., 1960, MS, 1964. Directing physicist, assoc. prof. laser scis., laser research labs. Med. Center, U. Cin., 1963-76; dir. continuing edn. services Electro-Optical Systems Design Jour., Cin., 1976-77; v.p. laser/electro-optics Control Dynamics, Inc., 1977-79; pres. Rockwell Assocs., Inc. (cons. lasers, optics and electro-optics), 1979-89; pres., chief exec. officer Rockwell Laser Industries (cons. lasers, optics and electro-optics), 1989—. Exec. com. safe use lasers com. Am. Nat. Standards Inst., 1971-2000, chmn. control measures tech. com., 1971—; exec. sec. Laser Inst. Am., 1976-77, dir., 1972-92, pres., 1974; mem. adv. com. Laser History Project, 1983-89; dir. Laserworks, Inc., Rockwell Devel. Co.; cons. WHO, Internat. Electrotechnical Commn., founder Consortium of Laser and Tech. Cons., 1988; mem. tech. com. Laser Fire Protection of the Nat. Fire Protection Assn., 1991—. Co-author: Lasers in Medicine, 1971; author: Laser Safety Training Manual, 1982, Laser Safety in Surgery and Medicine, 1985, Laser Safety: Concepts, Analysis and Controls, 1992, Laser Safety: Modularized Training Package, 1994, Users Guide for Laser Safety, 1997, Multi-Lingual Laser Safety Training Program, 1998, Laser Accidents, a 30 Year Review, 2000, Medical User's Guide for Laser Safety, 2000; created software program: Laser Hazard Analysis, 1987, LAZAN for Windows, 1995, SKYZAN for Windows, 1996; co-developer: LASERNET page on the World-Wide Web (Internet), 1996; contbr. chpts. to books and articles to profl. jours.; editor jours. in field; mem. editl. bd. Jour. Laser Applications, 1994-99. Co-chmn. Internat. Laser Safety Conf., 1990, 92, mem. planning com., keynote spkr., 1997. Recipient Pres.' award Laser Inst. Am., 1985, Safety and Health award Am. Welding Soc., 2001. Fellow: Laser Inst. Am.; mem.: IEEE, Internat. Laser Display Assn., Midwest Bio-Laser Inst., Am. Soc. Laser Medicine and Surgery, N.Y. Acad. Scis., Newcomen Soc., Delta Tau Delta (dir. acad. affairs, nat. bd. dirs. 1975—83, D.S.C. award 1985), Sigma Xi (nat. lectr. 1971—75). Methodist. Achievements include designer, builder portable laser entertainment system in laser light artistic shows; patentee in field; co-developer laser safety awareness training program for world-wide web. Home: 6282 Coachlite Way Cincinnati OH 45243-2920 Office: PO Box 43010 7754 Camargo Rd Cincinnati OH 45243-2661 E-mail: BigJimR@aol.com.

ROCKWELL, WINTHROP ADAMS, lawyer; b. Pittsfield, Mass., May 7, 1948; s. Landon Gale Rockwell and Ruth (Adams) Lonsdale; m. Barbara Washburn Wood, June 20, 1970; children: Samuel Adams, Madeleine McCord. AB, Dartmouth Coll., 1970; JD, NYU, 1975. Bar: Minn. 1975, U.S. Dist. Ct. Minn. 1975. Asst. newsman fgn. desk N.Y. Times, N.Y.C., 1970-71; asst. to pres. Dartmouth Coll., Hanover, N.H., 1971-72; assoc. Faegre & Benson, Mpls., 1975-79; assoc. chief counsel Pres.'s Commn. on Accident at Three Mile Island, Washington, 1979; assoc. Faegre & Benson, Mpls., 1979-82, ptnr., 1983—, chmn. diversity com., 1990-95, head gen. litigation group, 1995—. Bd. dirs., v.p. Children's Theatre, Mpls., 1982-83; bd. dirs. Actors Theatre St. Paul, 1975-79, Trinity Films, Mpls., 1978-82, Minn. Ctr. for Book Arts, 1996—; mem. adv. bd. Univ. Minn. Joint Degree Program in Law, Health and the Life Scis. Brit.-Am. Project fellow, 1987. Mem. ABA, Minn. Bar Assn., Hennepin County Bar Assn., Am. Agrl. Law Assn., Adirondack 46ers, Adirondack Mountain Club. Avocations: writing, tennis, mountaineering, gardening. Home: 1901 Knox Ave S Minneapolis MN 55403-2840 Office: Faegre & Benson 2200 Wells Fargo Ctr 90 S 7th St Ste 2200 Minneapolis MN 55402-3901 E-mail: wrockwell@faegre.com.

RODEMAN, FREDERICK ERNEST, accountant; b. Chgo., Jan. 29, 1938; s. Ernest August and Elizabeth Mae (Penrod) R.; m. Marilyn Kay Paul, June 17, 1967. BBA, Ind. U., 1959; cert. bank controllership, U. Wis., 1975; MBA, De Paul U., 1976. CPA, Ind., Wis. Auditor Arthur Andersen & Co., Chgo., 1959-67; acct. mgr. A.B. Dick & Co., 1967-72; controller Beloit (Wis.) State Bank, 1972-77; pvt. practice acctg. Beloit, 1977—. Mem. Am. Inst. CPA's. Republican. Baptist. Home and Office: 2372 Tara Ct Beloit WI 53511-1938

RODENHUIS, DAVID ROY, meteorologist, educator; b. Michigan City, Ind., Oct. 5, 1936; married; 2 children. BS, U. Calif., Berkeley, 1959, Pa. State U., 1960; PhD in Atmospheric Sci., U. Wash., 1967. From asst. prof. to assoc. prof. dept. meteorology U. Md., College Park, 1968-75, assoc. prof. meteorology, 1976-84, dir. Climate Analysis Ctr., 1985-95, dir. Aviation Weather Ctr., 1996—. Exec. scientist U.S. com. global atmospheric rsch. program NAS, 1972; sci. officer World Meteorol. Orgn., 1975—; U.S.-U.S.S.R. exchange scientist, 1980. Mem. Am. Geophys. Union, Am. Meteorol. Soc. Achievements include research in tropical meteorology, convection models, dynamic climate models. Office: Aviation Weather Ctr 7220 NW 101st Terr Rm 101 Kansas City MO 64153-2371

RODGERS, CYNTHIA, anchor, correspondent; Anchor Sta. WIFR-TV, Rockford, Ill.; Chgo. bur. chief Knight-Ridder Fin. News; corr. CNN Fin. News, Chgo., Washington, anchor, corr. Chgo. Adj. prof. Northwestern U. Sch. Journalism, Evanston, Ill. Office: CNN 435 N Michigan Ave Chicago IL 60611-4066

RODGERS, JAMES FOSTER, association executive, economist; b. Columbus, Ga., Jan. 15, 1951; s. Laban Jackson and Martha (Jackson) R.; m. Cynthia Lynne Bathurst, Aug. 20, 1975. B.A., U. Ala., Tuscaloosa, 1973; Ph.D., U. Iowa, 1980. Fed. intern Office Rsch. and Stats., Social Security Adminstrn., Washington, 1976-77; rsch. assoc. Ctr. Health Policy Rsch., AMA, Chgo., 1979-80, rsch. dir., 1980-82, asst. to dep. exec. v.p. AMA, 1982-85; dir. AMA Ctr. Health Policy Rsch., 1985-96, v.p. health policy, 1996—. Contbr. articles on health econs. to profl. jours. Pharm. Mfrs. Assn. grantee, 1978; NSF grantee, 1978; Hohenberg fellow, 1969-70 Mem. Am. Econ. Assn., Am. Soc. Assn. Exec., Am. Statis. Assn., So. Econ. Assn., Western Econ. Assn. Home: 2233 N Orchard St Chicago IL 60614-3713 Office: AMA Ctr for Health Policy Rsch 515 N State St Chicago IL 60610-4325

RODGERS, LOUIS DEAN, retired surgeon; b. Centerville, Iowa, Nov. 24, 1930; s. John James and Anna Alice (Spraguer) R.; m. Gretchen Lynn Hendershot, Feb. 19, 1954; children: Cynthia Ann, Elizabeth Dee. MD, U. Iowa, 1960. Diplomate Am. Bd. Surgery. Intern Broadlawns Hosp., Des Moines, 1960-61; resident Meth. Hosp., 1961-65; pvt. practice, 1965-95. Chmn. dept. surgery Iowa Meth. Ctr., Des Moines, 1980-84, chief gen. surgery, 1982-95; clin. assoc. prof. surgery U. Iowa, Iowa City, 1983-95, ret., 1995 . Mem. steering com. gov.'s campaign Iowa Rep. Com., 1982; bd. dirs. Iowa Meth. Med. Found., Des Moines, 1983, Des Moines Synthony, 1984-90, Des Moines Children's Home, 1987-93. Staff sgt. U.S. Army, 1951-54. Recipient Disting. Alumni award Centerville Schs. Found., 1993; named Surg. Tchr. of Yr., Iowa Meth. Med. Ctr., 1978, 84. Fellow ACS (liaison to cancer com. 1973); mem. Western Surg. Assn. (Iowa trauma com. 1983), Iowa Acad. Surgery (pres. 1982-83), Throckmorton Surg. Soc. (pres. 1986), Des Moines Golf and Country. Republican. Home: 13138 Cedar Crest Ln Des Moines IA 50325

RODIBAUGH, ROBERT KURTZ, retired judge; b. Elkhart County, Ind., July 2, 1916; s. Ralph Leedy and Rose (Kurtz) R.; m. Doris Ann Siekemeyer, Jan. 1, 1942 (dec.); children: David L., Bob K.; m. Eunice Margaret Cline, Nov. 25, 1972. BSc, U. Notre Dame, 1940, JD, 1941. Bar: Ind. 1941, U.S. Dist. Ct. (no. dist.) Ind. 1946, U.S. Ct. Appeals (7th cir.) 1972, U.S. Supreme Ct. 1965. Dep. pros. atty. Ind. 60th Jud. Cir., St. Joseph County, 1948-50, 53-57; judge U.S. Bankruptcy Ct., No. Dist. Ind., South Bend, 1960-99, ret., 1999. Lectr. in law U. Notre Dame, 1973; atty. St. Joseph County Bd. Zoning Appeals, 1958-60. V.p. No. Ind. coun. Boy Scouts Am., 1967-77; bd. dirs. St. Joseph County chpt. ARC, 1970-77. Capt. U.S. Army, 1941-46, PTO. Recipient Silver Beaver award Boy Scouts Am., 1969. Mem. ABA, Seventh Fed. Cir. Bar Assn., Ind. Bar Assn., St. Joseph County Bar Assn. (gov. 1953-56), Comml. Law League, Nat. Conf. Bankruptcy Judges (dir. 1977-79), Exch. Club, Masons, DeMolay Club (Legion of Honor), Shriners, Rotary (South Bend, Ind. chpt.). Office: US Bankruptcy Ct PO Box 7003 401 S Michigan St South Bend IN 46601-2365

RODMAN, LEN C. civil and communication engineering executive; BS in Civil Engring., Iowa State U., 1971; MS in Environ. Engring., U. Mo., 1978. Civil engr. Black & Veatch, Kansas City, Mo., 1971—, group mng. ptnr., head N.Am. divsn. infrastructure bus., CEO, pres., 1998—. Office: Black & Veatch 8400 Ward Parkway Kansas City MO 64114 Fax: (913) 458-3511.

RODNEY, JOEL MORRIS, dean, campus executive officer; b. Bklyn., Nov. 9, 1937; s. Samuel Seymour and Jane (Loorya) R.; m. Judith DeStefano, July 22, 1994; children from previous marriage: Jonathan, Adam, Benjamin. BA cum laude, Brandeis U., 1959; PhD, Cornell U., 1965; attended, Inst. Ednl. Mgmt. Harvard U., 1976. From instr. to assoc. prof. Wash. State U., Pullman, 1963-70; chmn. div. social scis., assoc. prof. history Elmira (N.Y.) Coll., 1970-72, coordinator flood relief and community planning, 1973; dean arts and sci., prof. history Widener Coll., Chester, Pa., 1973-76, acting chief acad. officer, dean, 1976-77, chief acad. officer, dean, 1977-81, dir. univ. grad. programs, 1979-81; v.p. acad. affairs Salisbury (Md.) State Coll., 1981-86; provost Rockford (Ill.) Coll., 1986-90; CEO, dean U. Wis. -Washington County, West Bend, 1990—. Editor Albion, 1967-78; contbr. articles to profl. jours. Vice chmn. Md. Gov.'s Com. on Employment of Handicapped, 1985-86, chmn. and mem. Lower Shore divsn., 1983-86; chmn. adv. bd., mem. Crozer-Chester Med. Health Ctr., Chester, 1974-77; project evaluator NEH, 1986, RSA, 1993; mem., sec. Delaware County Mental Health/Mental Retardation Bd., 1975-81; adv. bd. Rehab. Inst. of Chgo., 1988-94; mem. coun. Ct. of Gov.'s Regents Coll., London, 1986-90, Rock Valley Coll. Indsl. Coun., Rockford, 1989-90; bd. dirs. Moraine Symphony Orch., 1990-93, Welcome Home, Inc., 1990—, pres., 1992—; citizens adv. bd. West Bend Bank One, 1991, Washington County Vol. Ctr., 1991-92; bd. dirs. The Threshold, 1992—, vice chair, 1990-2000, chair, 2000; apptd. to State Wis. Coun. Phys. Disabilities, 1994, vice chmn., 1995, chmn., 1996-2000; exec. com. Moraine area Tech. Prep. Coun., 1994—; mem. Wis. Gov.'s Com. on Persons with Disabilities, 1994-97, vice chmn., 1996; mem. adv. bd. S.E. Wis. Area Health Edn. Coun., 1995-96, West Bend Art Mus., 1996-2001, chair, 1999-2001; mem. West Bend C. of C. Ambs., 1995—; mem. Washington County Growth Mgmt. Task Force, 1996—, chair, 1999—; del. Washington County Reps., 1997—; bd. dirs. Kettle Moraine YMCA, 1999—. Recipient Disting. Service award Widener Meml. Sch., 1978, Award of merit Md. Gov.'s Com. on Employment of Handicapped, 1984; named to Legion of Honor, Chapel of Four Chaplains, 1978; honoree West Phila. Vets. and Handicapped Employment Com., 1977. Mem. Am. Assn. Acad. Deans, Conf. on Brit. Studies, Am. Assn. Univ. Adminstrs., Nat. Spinal Cord Injury Assn. (bd. dirs. Ill. chpt. 1988-90), Rotary, Phi Alpha Theta. Republican. Home: 229 Bittersweet Dr West Bend WI 53095-4907 Office: U Wis Washington County 400 S University Dr West Bend WI 53095-3619

RODOVICH, ANDREW PAUL, magistrate; b. Hammond, Ind., Feb. 24, 1948; s. Andrew H. and Julia (Makar) R.; m. Gail Linda Patrick, May 27, 1972; children: Caroline Anja, Mary Katherine, James Patrick. BA, Valparaiso (Ind.) U., 1970, JD, 1973. Bar: Ind. Ptnr. Hand, Muenich & Rodovich, Hammond, 1973-78; chief dep. prosecutor Lake County Prosecutor's Office, Crown Point, Ind., 1979-82; U.S. magistrate U.S. Dist. Ct., Hammond, 1982—. Referee Hammond City Ct., 1978; adj. prof. Valparaiso Law Sch., 1985—. Fellow Ind. Bar Found.; mem. Nat. Coun. U.S. Magistrates, Delta Theta Phi. Republican. Avocations: sports. Home: 7207 Baring Pky Hammond IN 46324-2218 Office: US Dist Ct 136 Federal Bldg Hammond IN 46320-1529

RODRIGUEZ, EDGAR, chef; b. Durango, Mex. Student, Cooking and Hospitality Inst. Chgo. Waiter, mgr., exec. chef Linda's Margaritas, Chgo.; exec. chef, co-owner Salbute, Hinsdale, 1997—. Active March of Dimes, Make A Wish Found., Share Our Strength, Meals on Wheels, Operation Frontline. Named One of Top 20 New Restaurants, Chgo. mag., 1998; recipient Four Forks rev., Chgo. Tribune. Office: Salbute 20 E 1st St Hinsdale IL 60521

RODRIGUEZ, MANUEL ALVAREZ, pathologist; b. Guantanamo, Cuba, Nov. 12, 1946; came to U.S., 1961, naturalized, 1970; s. Manuel and Maria Teresa (Alvarez) R.; children: Austin B., Matthew J. BSc in Biology, U. Nev., 1966; MT, St. Alexius Hosp., Bismarck, N.D., 1969; BSc in Medicine, U. N.D., 1971; MD, U. Tex., Galveston, 1973; flight surgeon training, Brooks AFB, San Antonio, 1992. Diplomate Am. Bd. Pathology. Rotating intern Meml. Med. Ctr., Corpus Christi, Tex., 1973-74; commd. USPHS, 1974, advanced through grades to comdr., 1993; gen. surgery resident USPHS Hosp., New Orleans, 1974-75, anatomic/clin. pathology resident, 1975-76, U. N.D. Sch. Medicine, Grand Forks, 1976-77, Touro Infirmary Hosp., New Orleans, 1977-79; pvt. practice Houston, 1979-89; sr. med. officer USPHS-USCG Med. Clinic, New Orleans, 1990-92; flight surgeon, sr. med. officer USPHS-Brooks AFB, San Antonio, 1992, USPHS-USCG Air Sta. Med. Clinic, Sitka, Alaska, 1992-96; clin. dir. USPHS, El Centro, Calif., 1997-98; sr. med. officer PHS Indian Health Ctr., White Earth, Minn., 1998—. Instr. pathology La. State U. Med. Sch., Baton Rouge, 1979-80; tchg. fellow pathology U. N.D. Med. Sch., Grand Forks, 1976-77. Contbr. articles to profl. jours. Dir. charitable donations mil. ann. drive USPHS-USCG, New Orleans, Sitka, 1990-96, Miami Lakes, Fla., 1996. Fellow Am. Acad. Family Practice, Coll. Am. Pathologists. Avocation: writing professional articles. Home: PO Box 354 Dakota City NE 68731

RODRIGUEZ, RAMIRO, chef; b. Guanajuato, Mex. Chef Carlos' Restaurant, Highland Park, Ill. Active James Beard Found., Share Our Strength, Meals on Wheels. Office: Carlos' Restaurant 429 Temple Ave Highland Park IL 60035

ROE, BYRON PAUL, physics educator; b. St. Louis, Apr. 4, 1934; s. Sam S. and Gertrude Harriet (Claris) R.; m. Alice Susan Krauss, Aug. 27, 1961; children: Kenneth David, Diana Carol. B.A., Washington U., St. Louis, 1954; Ph.D., Cornell U., 1959. Instr. physics U. Mich., Ann Arbor, 1959-61, asst. prof., 1961-64, assoc. prof., 1964-69, prof., 1969—. Guest physicist SSC Lab., 1991. Author: Probability and Statistics in Experimental Physics, 1992, 2d edit., 2001, Particle Physics at the New Millennium, 1996 (Libr. Sci. Book Club selection). CERN vis. scientist Geneva, 1967, 89; Brit. Sci. Rsch. Coun. fellow, Oxford, 1979; recipient inventor's prize CDC Worldtech, Edina, Minn., 1982, 83. Fellow Am. Phys. Soc. Home: 3610 Charter Pl Ann Arbor MI 48105-2825 Office: U Mich Physics Dept 500 E University Ave Ann Arbor MI 48109-1120 E-mail: byronroe@umich.edu.

ROE, JOHN H. manufacturing company executive; b. 1939; BA, Williams Coll., 1962; MBA, Harvard U., 1964. With Bemis Co. Inc., Mpls., 1964—, plant supt., 1964-67, sales rep., 1967-68, sales mgr., 1968-70, plant mgr., 1970-73, gen. mgr. film div., 1973-76, exec. v.p. ops., 1976-87, pres., chief oper. officer, from 1987, chief exec. officer, 1990—, also bd. dirs., chmn. Office: Bemis Co Inc 222 S 9th St Ste 2300 Minneapolis MN 55402-4099

ROE, ROBERT A. state legislator; b. Hayti, S.D., Mar. 3, 1954; BS, S.D. State U., 1976; postgrad., Northwestern U., 1979. Mem. S.D. Ho. of Reps., 1988—, Ho. Majority Whip, 1995—, mem. judiciary and state affairs coms.; stockbroker Piper, Jeffrey & Hopwood, 1984—. Home: 1820 Skyview Ln Brookings SD 57006-3535 Office: SD Ho of Reps State Capitol Pierre SD 57501

ROE, ROGER ROLLAND, JR. lawyer; b. Mpls., Dec. 31, 1947; s. Roger Rolland Roe Jr.; m. Paula Speltz, 1974; children: Elena, Madeline. BA, Grinnell Coll., 1970; JD, U. Minn., 1973. Bar: Minn. 1973, U.S. Dist. Ct. Minn. 1974, U.S. Ct. Appeals (8th cir.) 1977, U.S. Supreme Ct. 1978, Wis. 1988, U.S. Dist. Ct. Nebr. 1995, U.S. Dist. Ct. (ea. and we. dists.) Wis. Law clk. to Hon. Judge Amdahl Hennepin County Dist. Ct., Mpls., 1973-74; from assoc. to ptnr. Rider, Bennett, Egan & Arundel, 1974-91; mng. ptnr. Yaeger, Jungbauer, Barczak, Roe & Vucinovich, PLC, 1992-2000; ptnr. Best & Flanagan LLP, 2000—. Mem. nat. panel arbitrators Am. Arbitration Assn.; judge trial practice class and moot ct. competitions law sch. U. Minn.; guest lectr. Minn. Continuing Legal Edn. courses. Fellow Internat. Soc. Barristers; mem. ATLA (guest lectr.), Am. Bd. Trial Advs. (diplomat, Minn. chpt. pres. 1996-97), Minn. Trial Lawyers Assn., Million Dollar Round Table, Mich. Trial Lawyers Assn. Avocations: golfing, downhill skiing. Office: Best & Flanagan LLP 225 S 6th St # 4000 Minneapolis MN 55402

ROEHL, EVERETT, transportation executive; Owner Roehl Transport, Inc., Marshfield, Wis., 1963—. Office: Roehl Transport Inc PO Box 750 1916 E 29th St Marshfield WI 54449-0750

ROEHLING, CARL DAVID, architect; b. Detroit, June 25, 1951; m. Barbara K. Jeffries; children: Carl Robert, Kristin Virginia. BS in Architecture, U. Mich., 1973, MArch, 1975. Registered arch., Mich.; cert. Nat. Coun. Archtl. Registration Bd. Architect Minoru Yamasaki and Assocs., Inc., Troy, Mich., 1976-77; TMP Assocs., 1977-81; architect Harley Ellington Pierce Yee Assocs., Inc., Southfield, Mich., 1981-83, Giffels/Hoyem Basso Assocs., Troy, 1983-87, Smith, Hinchman & Grylls Assocs., Inc., Detroit, 1987—. With Chrysler World Hdqs., 1994. Prin. works include CBS/Fox Video Hdqrs., Livonia, Mich. (Honor award Mich. Masonry Inst., 1985), First Ctr. Office Bldg., Southfield, Mich. (Honor award FAIA Mich., 1988), Ind. U. Chemistry Bldg., Bloomington (Honor award AIA Detroit, 1990, AIA Mich., 1990), U. Mich. Aerospace Lab. Bldg., Ann Arbor, 1993, Los Alamos (N.Mex.) Materials Sci. Lab., 1993, others. Mem. AIA (Mich. chpg. pres. bd. dirs. 1989, mem. nat. com. on environ. 1991, Detroit chpt. pres. 1994, Young Arch. of Yr., AIA Detroit, 1986, AIA Mich., 1991, regional dir. 1996—, nat. bd. dirs.), Am. Archtl. Found. (bd. dirs. 1997—), Mich. Archtl. Found. (chmn. pres. scholarship program 1990). Office: Smith Group Inc 500 Griswold St Ste 200 Detroit MI 48226-3808

ROELL, STEPHEN A. manufacturing company executive; CFO Johnson Controls, Inc., Milw. Office: Johnson Controls Inc PO Box 591 Milwaukee WI 53201-0591

ROEMER, JAMES PAUL, data processing executive, writer; b. Cin., June 6, 1947; s. Charles William and Lillian (Vollman) R.; m. Patricia Pipenger: children: Kimberly, Michelle. Student, U. Cin., 1965-68; A.M.P., U. Va., 1978. Systems analyst Union Central Life Ins. Co., Cin., 1965-70; program and systems mgr. Computer Systems, Inc., Florence, Ky., 1970-72; mgr. data processing Mead Products, Dayton, Ohio, 1972-77; dir. ops. Mead Data Central, 1977-78, v.p. ops., 1978-80, acting pres., 1980-81, v.p. product devel., 1981-82, sr. v.p. legal, govt., acctg., sr. v.p. with responsibility for lexis, 1982-89; pres. Michie Group, Charlottesville, Va., 1989-91; pres., COO Bell and Howell Publs. Systems Co., 1991-93; pres., CEO Univ. Microfilms Internat., Ann Arbor, 1994-95; chmn., pres., CEO Bell & Howell, Skokie, Ill., 1995—. Active Harvard, 1989. Mem. Info. Industry Assn., Assn. for Info. and Image Mgmt. Republican. Roman Catholic. Home: 6271 Canterbury Dr Hudson OH 44236-3558 Office: Bell & Howell 5215 Old Orchard Rd Ste 1100 Skokie IL 60077-1076

ROEMER, TIMOTHY J. congressman; b. South Bend, Ind., Oct. 30, 1956; m. Sarah Lee Johnston, 1989. BA in pol. sci, U. Calif., San Diego, 1979; MA, PhD in internat. rels., U. Notre Dame, 1986. Staff asst. to congressman John Brademas U.S. Congress, def., trade and fgn. policy advisor to senator Dennis DeConcini; mem. U.S. Congress from 3rd Ind. dist., 1991—, mem. economic and ednl. opportunity com., mem. sci. com., mem. edn. and the workforce com. Adj. prof. Am. U. Office: US Ho of Reps 2352 Rayburn Hob Washington DC 20515-0001 also: 217 N Main St South Bend IN 46601-1216*

ROEMING, ROBERT FREDERICK, foreign language educator; b. Milw., Dec. 12, 1911; s. Ferdinand August and Wanda E. (Radtke) R.; m. Alice Mae Voss, Aug. 30, 1941; 1 child, Pamela Alice. BA in Econs./Acctg., U. Wis., 1934, MA in Italian, 1936, PhD in French, 1941. Mem. faculty U. Wis.-Milw., 1937—, prof. French and Italian, 1956—, assoc. dean Coll. Letters and Sci., asst. to provost for devel. of spl. programs, 1957-62, sole dir. dept. lang. labs., 1964-70, dir. English as 2d lang., 1967-70, founder and dir. Ctr. Twentieth Century Studies, 1970-74, prof. emeritus, 1980—; founder, chief investigator Camus Bibliography Research Collection, Golda Meir Library, 1985—. Rep. D.C. Heath Co., 1943-46; cons., 1946-50; cons. computer systems Harnischfeger Corp., Milw., 1953-57; chmn. tech. sect. Internat. Congress on Fgn. Lang. Tchg., Pädagogisches Zentrum, Berlin, summer 1964; guest InterAm. Congress of Linguists, Montevideo, Uruguay, 1966; ofcl. guest Romanian govt. 10th Internat. Congress Linguists, summer 1967; dir. Insts. in Adult Basic Edn., 1969, U.S. Office Edn.; pres., treas. Electronic Rsch. Instruments Co., Inc., Nashotah, Wis., 1969-93. Author: In the Land of the Immortals, 1934, (with C.E. Young) Introduction to French, 1951, Camus, A Bibliography, 1969, rev. and augmented computer-microfiche, 15th edit., 2000, Little Magazine Catalog, 1976, 77 (NEH grantee); editor: Modern Lang. Jour, 1963-70; contbr. numerous monographs and articles to profl. jours., 72 taped radio programs on French Black lit. Chmn. bldg. commn. Village of Chenequa, Wis., 1972-88; trustee, chmn. Midwest chpt. Jose Greco Found. for Hispanic Dance, Inc., 1970-76; mem. Wis. Bd. Nursing, 1977-79, chmn., 1979; mem. numerous nat. conservation orgns. and local civic groups. Decorated chevalier, officier, commandeur Ordre Palmes Académiques (France); recipient Travel award Italian Govt., summer, 1934. Mem. MLA (life, index com. 1970-79), Nat. Fedn. Modern Lang. Tchrs. Assn. (exec. com. 1963-70), Verband Deutscher Schriftsteller, Wis. News Photographers Assn. (hon. life, Pres.'s award 1972), Soc. des Etudes Camusiennes, Am. Assn. of French Acad. Palms, Wis. Assn. for the Blind and Physically Handicapped, Chenequa Country Club, Lake Country Racquet and Athletic Club, Phi Eta Sigma, Phi Kappa Phi, Tau Kappa Epsilon. Achievements include research in application of the computer to humanities, applied linguistics and contemporary French and Italian Literature. Home: 6078 N Oakland Hills Rd Chenequa WI 53058 Office: U Wis-Milw Golda Meir Libr W240 2311 E Hartford Ave Milwaukee WI 53211-3175 Fax: 414-229-6791.

ROEPER, RICHARD, columnist; b. Chgo., Oct. 17, 1959; s. Robert and Margaret R. BA, Ill. State U., 1982. Freelance writer, 1982-87; columnist Chgo.-Sun Times, 1987—. Talk show host Sta. WLS-FM, Chgo.; commentator Fox Thing in the Morning, Sta. WFLD-TV, Fox TV, Chgo. Recipient Outstanding Columnist Ill. Press Assn., 1992, Nat. Headliner award for top columnist Atlantic City Press Club, 1992, Emmy award, 1994. Mem. Am. Fedn. TV & Radio Artists, Chgo. Newspaper Guild. Office: Chgo Sun-Times 401 N Wabash Ave Chicago IL 60611-5642

ROESCH, ROBERT EUGENE, dentist; b. July 10, 1951; s. Wilber H. and Vivian (Reese) R.; m. Susan M. Tuttle, Aug. 25, 1973. BA, Midland Luth. Coll., 1973; DDS, U. Nebr., 1976. Pvt. practice, Fremont, Nebr., 1979—. Dental cons. Dodge County Am. Cancer Soc., Fremont, 1984-98; cons. Nebr. Dental Assn., Dodge County, 1979—, third party dental care com., 1984-88, del., 1991—, dental care com., 1993-95, legis. com., 1997—, chmn., 1998—, v.p. region 10 Acad. of Gen. Dentistry, 1990-91, dir., 1991-93, trustee, 1993-94, budget & fin. com., 1994-99, chmn. Acad. Gen. Dentistry, budget and fin. com., 1997, 98, 99, spkr. to house Acad. Gen. Dentistry, 1999—. Campaign chmn. Fremont United Way, 1987, v.p., 1988; pres. Sinai Luth. Ch. Coun., Fremont, 1983-84, bd. dirs., 1987-90; mem. endowment com. Sinai Luth. Ch., 1990-94; bd. dirs. Gannett Found., Ascertainments Com., Fremont, 1981-88, Dodge County Reps., Fremont, 1981-88; bd. dirs. Dodge County Hist. Soc., 1989-92, U. Nebr. Coll. Dentistry Alumni, 1996—, pres., 1998. Master Acad. Gen. Dentistry; fellow Internat. Acad. Dentistry, Internat. Coll. Dentistry; mem. ADA (alt. del. 2000), Acad. Operative Dentistry, Nebr. Acad. of Gen. Dentistry (pub. info. officer 1983-85, sec., treas. 1985-88, pres.-elect 1988-89, pres. 1990-92, exec. dir. 1992-94, continuing edn. chmn. 1994—, legis. chmn. 1997—), Nebr. Dental Assn. (v.p. 2000—), Am. Orthodontic Soc., Am. Assn. Functional Orthodontists, Am. Equilibration Soc., Omaha Dist. Dental Soc. (bd. dirs., pres.-elect 1996-97, pres. 1997-98), R.V. Tucker Nebr. study club) Salmon Soc., Dodge County Hist. Soc., Midland Coll. Alumni (bd. dirs. 1981-87, pres. 1983-84), Fremont Wellness Coun. (bd. dirs. 1996-98), Fremont C. of C. (diplomate 1985-94, bd. dirs. 1991-94, vice-chmn. memberships and membership svcs. 1989-90, vice-chmn. pub. affairs 1992-94), Optimists (bd. dirs. 1981-83, 84-88, pres. 1987, bd. dirs. Fremont club 1991-93), Fremont Indsl. Found., Main St. Fremont (orgn. com. 1995—, chmn. orgn. com. 1998—, bd. dirs. 1997—, 2d v.p. 1998, 1st v.p. 1999), Main St. Ambs. (co-chmn. 1997-98, chmn. 1998—), Fremont Tennis Assn., Am. Legion, Fremont Cmty. Players, Midland Luth. Coll. Boosters Club (bd. dirs. 1988-94), Tri Valley Dental Study Club (sec.-treas. 1983, v.p. 1984, pres. 1985, v.p. 1989). Avocations: tennis, traveling. Home: 2137 Nye Dr Fremont NE 68025-2210 Office: 553 N Broad St Fremont NE 68025-4930

ROESSLER, CAROL ANN, state legislator; b. Madison, Wis., Jan. 16, 1948; d. John J. and Lucile E. (Kraner) Murphy; m. Paul Roessler. BS, U. Wis., Oshkosh, 1972. Dir. nutrition program for older adults County of Winnebago, Wis., 1973-82; mem. Wis. Assembly, Madison, 1983-87, Wis. Senate from 18th dist., Madison, 1987—. Instr. pre-retirement planning Fox Valley Tech. Inst., 1978-81. Home: 1506 Jackson St Oshkosh WI 54901-2942 Office: PO Box 7882 Madison WI 53707-7882 E-mail: Sen.Roessler@legis.state.wi.us.

ROG, JOSEPH W. business executive; Chmn., pres., CEO Corrpro Cos., inc., Medina, Ohio. Office: Corrpro Cos Inc 1090 Enterprise Dr Medina OH 44256-1328

ROGALSKI, EDWARD J. university administrator; b. Manville, N.J., Feb. 16, 1942; s. Joseph Stanley and Wladyslawa (Kraszewski) R.; m. Barbara Ann Bogk, June 01, 1968; children: Edward, James, Daniel, David, Christopher. BA, Parsons Coll., 1965; MA, U. Iowa, 1968, PhD, 1985; LittD (hon.), Loras Coll., 1990. Dean of men, asst. dean of students Parsons Coll., Fairfield, Iowa, 1965-67; dean of students St. Ambrose Coll., Davenport, 1968-74, v.p. adminstrn., 1974-80, sr. v.p., 1980-86, exec. v.p., 1986-87; pres. St. Ambrose U., 1987—. Bd. dirs., past chmn. Genesis Med. Ctr.; bd. dirs. Genesis Health Sys., Genesis Health Svcs. Found., Firstar Bank Davenport N.A.; cons. ednl. divsn. Marriott Corp., 1988—. Past vice chairperson Civil Rights Commn., Davenport, 1975; bd. dirs. Handicapped Devel. Ctr., Davenport, 1987, Jr. Achievement, 1988, Big Brothers-Big Sisters, 1988, Iowa Coll. Found., 1992—. Grantee Kettering Found., 1968. Mem. Iowa Assn. Ind. Colls. and Univs. (exec. com. and past chmn., treas. 1992—), Nat. Assn. Ind. Colls. and Univs. (bd. dirs., past exec. sec.), Am. Assn. Higher Edn., Davenport One (bd. dirs. 1992, exec. com., past chair-elect), Rotary, Phi Delta Kappa. Roman Catholic. Home: 806 W Rusholme St Davenport IA 52804-1928 Office: St Ambrose U 518 W Locust St Davenport IA 52803-2898 E-mail: erogalsi@sau.edu.

ROGAN, ELEANOR GROENIGER, cancer researcher, educator; b. Nov. 25, 1942; d. Louis Martin and Esther (Levinson) G.; m. William John Robert Rogan, June 12, 1965 (div. 1970); 1 child, Elizabeth Rebecca. AB, Mt. Holyoke Coll., 1963; PhD, Johns Hopkins U., 1968. Lectr. Goucher Coll., Towson, Md., 1968-69; rsch. assoc. U. Tenn., Knoxville, 1969-73, U. Nebr. Med. Ctr., Omaha, 1973-76, asst. prof., 1976-80; assoc. prof. Eppley Inst., dept. pharm. scis. U. Nebr., 1980-90, prof. dept. pharm. scis. and dept. biochem. & molecular biol, 1990—. Contbr. articles to profl. jours. Predoctoral fellow USPHS, Johns Hopkins U., 1965-68. Mem. AAAS, Am. Assn. Cancer Rsch., Soc. Toxicology. Democrat. Roman Catholic. Home: 8210 Bowie Dr Omaha NE 68114-1526 Office: U Nebr Med Ctr Eppley Inst 986805 Nebr Med Ctr Omaha NE 68198-6805

ROGEN, MARK ENDRE, former state senator, farmer; b. Sioux Falls, S.D., Dec. 29, 1956; s. E. Ordell and Ruth Alice (Hess) R.; m. Kristen M. Halvorson, Aug. 30, 1985; children: Ariana, Melysa, Zachary. BS in Animal Sci., S.D. State U., 1979. Farmer, Sherman, S.D., 1979—; state senator State of S.D., Pierre, 1992-97. Bd. dirs. Hermanson (S.D.) Sch. Bd., S.D. Cattleman's Assn., 1985-88; pres. S.D. Corn Growers Assn., 1986-88; sec. Nat. Corn Growers Assn., St. Louis, 1987-89. Democrat. Lutheran. Home and Office: 48790 246th St Garretson SD 57030-5519

ROGERS, BRYAN LEIGH, artist, art educator; b. Amarillo, Tex., Jan. 7, 1941; s. Bryan Austin and Virginia Leigh (Bull) R.; m. Cynthia Louise Rice; 1 child, Kyle Austin Rogers. BE, Yale U., 1963; MS, U. Calif., Berkeley, 1966, MA, 1969, PhD, 1971. Design engr. Monsanto Co., Texas City, Tex., 1962; research engr. Rocketdyne, Canoga Park, Calif., 1963-64; research scientist Lawrence Livermore (Calif.) Lab., 1966; lectr. U. Calif., Berkeley, 1972-73; fellow Akademie der Bildenden Künste, Munich, 1974-75; prof. art San Francisco State U., 1975-88; head prof. sch. art Carnegie Mellon U., Pitts., 1988-99, dir. Studio for Creative Inquiry, 1989-99; dean, prof. Sch. of Art and Design U. Mich., Ann Arbor, 2000—. Fellow Ctr. Advanced Visual Studies MIT, Cambridge, Mass, 1981. Editor Leonardo Jour., San Francisco, 1982-85. One-man shows include: Laguna Beach (Calif.) Mus. Art, 1974, DeSaisset Art Gallery U. Santa Clara, Calif., 1974, San Francisco Mus. Modern Art, 1974, Baxter Art Gallery Calif. Inst. Tech., Pasadena, 1979, Contemporary Crafts gallery, Portland, Oreg., 1987; group exhbns. include: Berkeley (Calif.) Art Ctr., 1969, Hansen-Fuller Gallery, San Francisco, 1970, San Francisco Arts Commn. Gallery, 1984, Clocktower Gallery, N.Y.C., 1984, Otis-Parsons Gallery, L.A., 1985, P.P.O.W. Gallery, N.Y.C., 1985, 18th Internat. Bienal, São Paulo, Brazil, 1985, MIT, Cambridge, 1990, Objects Gallery, Chgo., 1992, ARTEC 93 Internat Biennale, Nagoya, Japan, 1993, Chgo. Cultural Ctr., 1993, Am. Iron and Steel Expo., Pitts., 1993, Pitts. Ctr. for Arts, 1994, Allegheny Coll. Gallery, Meadville, Pa., 1997, Aichi Art Ctr., Nagoya, Japan, 1997. Fellow NEA, Washington, 1981, 82, Deutscher Akademischer Austauschdienst, Fed. Republic of Germany, 1974, NSF, Washington, 1965-69; recipient SECA award San Francisco Mus. Modern Art, 1974. Office: Sch Art & Design Univ Michigan Ann Arbor MI 48109 E-mail: blrogers@umich.edu.

ROGERS, CHARLES EDWIN, physical chemistry educator; b. Rochester, N.Y., Dec. 29, 1929; s. Charles Harold and Maybelle (Johnson) R.; m. Barbara June Depuy, June 12, 1954; children: Gregory Newton, Linda Frances, Diana Suzanne. BS in Chemistry, Syracuse U., 1954; PhD in Phys. Chemistry, SUNY at Syracuse U., 1957. Rsch. assoc. dept. chemistry Princeton U., 1957-59, Goodyear fellow, 1957-59; mem. tech. staff Bell Telephone Labs., Murray Hill, N.J., 1959-65; assoc. prof. macromolecular sci. Case Western Res. U., Cleve., 1965-74, prof., 1974-98, prof. emeritus, 1998—. Sr. vis. fellow Imperial Coll., U. London, 1971; assoc. dir. Ctr. for Adhesives Sealants Coatings, Case Western Res. U., 1984-88, dir., 1988-91; co-dir. Edison Polymer Innovation Corp., Ctr. for Adhesives, Sealants and Coatings, 1991-97; cons. to polymer and chem. industries; devel. overseas ednl. instns. Editor: Permselective Membranes, 1971, Structure and Properties of Block Copolymers, 1977; contbr. numerous articles to profl. jours.; patentee in field. Served with U.S. Army, 1946-49. Mem. Am. Chem. Soc., Am. Phys. Soc., N.Am. Membrane Soc., Cleve. Coatings Soc., The Adhesion Soc. Home: 8400 Rockspring Dr Chagrin Falls OH 44023-4645 Office: Case Western Reserve U Dept Macromolecular Sc Cleveland OH 44106-7202 E-mail: cer@po.cwru.edu.

ROGERS, DARLA POLLMAN, lawyer; b. 1952; BA, Wheaton Coll.; JD, U. S.D. Bar: S.D. 1979. Ptnr. Meyer & Rogers, Pierre, S.D. Mem. ABA, S.D. Bar Assn. (pres.). Office: Meyer & Rogers PO Box 1117 Pierre SD 57501-1117

ROGERS, DAVID, apparel executive; With Pickwick Internat., Mpls.; pres. Wilson's The Leather Experts, Inc., Brooklyn Park, Minn., 1979—. Office: Wilsons The Leather Experts Inc 7401 Boone Ave N Brooklyn Park MN 55428-1080

ROGERS, DESIREE GLAPION, utilities executive; b. New Orleans, June 16, 1959; d. Roy and Joyce Glapion; 1 child, Victoria. B in Polit. Sci., Wellesley Coll., 1981; MBA, Harvard U., 1985. Customer svc. mktg. mgr. AT&T, N.J., 1985-87; dir. devel. Levy Orgn., Chgo., 1987-89; founder, pres. Mus. Ops. Consulting Assocs., 1989-91; dir. Ill. State Lottery, 1991-97; chief mktg. officer Peoples Energy, 1997—. Bd. dirs. Mus. Sci. and Industry, WTTW/Ch. 11, Ravinia; trustee Lincoln Park Zoo. Mem. The Econ. Club, Execs. Club. Office: Peoples Energy 130 E Randolph Dr Fl 18 Chicago IL 60601-6207

ROGERS, EARLINE S. state legislator; b. Gary, Ind., Dec. 20, 1934; d. Earl and Robbie (Hicks) Smith; m. Louis C. Rogers, Dec. 24, 1956; children: Keith, Dana. d. Earl and Robbie (Hicks) Smith; m. Louis C. Rogers, Dec.24, 1956; children: Keith, Dana. BS, Ind. U., 1957, MS, 1971. Mem. Ind. State Ho. Reps, 1982-90, Ind. State Senate from 14th dist., 1990—. Mem. appointment and claims com. (ranking minority mem.), edn. com., health and provider svcs. com., rules and legis. procedure com. Mem. NAACP, Nat. Coun. Negro Women, League Women Voters, Urban League, Black Prfl. Women, Am. Fedn. Tchrs., Ind. State Tchrs. Assn. Democrat. Avocations: reading, sewing. Office: Ind State Senate Dist 3 200 W Washington St Indianapolis IN 46204-2728

ROGERS, EUGENE JACK, medical educator; b. Vienna, Austria, June 13, 1921; came to U.S., 1937; s. Louis and Malvina (Haller) R.; m. Joyce M. Lighter, Feb. 9, 1952; children: Jay A., Robert J. B.S., CCNY; M.B., Chgo. Med. Sch., 1946, M.D., 1947. Diplomate Am. Bd. Phys. Medicine and Rehab. Intern Our Lady of Mercy Med. Ctr. and Cabrini Meml. Hosps., N.Y.C., 1946-48; resident Madigan Hosp., Tacoma, 1951, Mayo Clinic, Rochester, Minn., 1951, N.Y. Med. Coll. Met. Med. Ctr., 1953-55; USPHS fellow, 1955-56; ship's surgeon U.S. Lines, Grace Lines, N.Y.C., 1948-49; indsl. physician Abraham & Strauss Stores, Bklyn., 1949-51; practice medicine specializing in phys. medicine and rehab., 1956-73; dir. rehab. service, attending physician N.Y. City Hosp. Dept., 1955-73; prof. and chmn. dept. rehab. medicine Chgo. Med. Sch., North Chicago, Ill., 1973—. Cons. N.Y.C. Mayor's Adv. Com. for Aged, 1957; asst. prof. SUNY Downstate Med. Sch., Bklyn., 1958-73; med. dir. Schwab Rehab. Hosp., Chgo., 1973-75; acting chief rehab. service VA Center, North Chicgo, 1975-77; chmn. Ill. Phys. Therapy Exam. Com., 1977-78; examiner Am. Bd. Phys. Medicine and Rehab., 1983; sec., dir. Microtherapeutics, Inc., 1972 Editor: Total Cancer Care, 1975; contbr. articles to med. jours.; contbg. editor Ill. Med. Jour., 1983-89 Served to capt. U.S. Army, 1951-53. Recipient Bronze medal Am. Congress Rehab. Medicine, 1974 Fellow ACP, Am. Acad. Phys. Medicine and Rehab. (Cert. of Appreciation 1993); mem. Ill. Med. Soc. (chmn. workmen's compensation com. 1980-83), Ill. Soc. Phys. Medicine and Rehab. (pres. 1983-84), Chgo. Med. Sch. Faculty Assembly (spkr. 1978-80), Chgo. Med. Sch. Alumni Assn. (exec. com., asst. treas. 1983-93, treas. 1993—, sec. 1995-97, 1st v.p. 1999—, pres. 2001, Presdl. plaque Greater N.Y. chpt., Disting. Alumnus award 1980), Odd Fellows (pres. 1961-62), Alpha Omega Alpha, Phi Lambda Kappa (trustee 1980). Home: 1110 N Lake Shore Dr Chicago IL 60611-1054 Office: Finch U Health Scis Chgo Med Sch 3333 Green Bay Rd North Chicago IL 60064-3037 E-mail: eugenerogers@worldnet.att.net.

ROGERS, FRANK ANDREW, restaurant, hotel executive; b. Indpls., May 9, 1931; s. Andrew Jackson and Jane (Safford) R.; m. Beulah Frances White, Sept. 28, 1971; children: Jane, Debra, Anne, Gina, Andrea. BA in Bus., Ind. U., 1967. Chmn., pres., CEO Brown County Fed. Savs. and Loan, NAshville, Ind., 1963-80, Bloomington (Ind.) Nat. Bank, 1980-88; chmn., CEO Lake Shore Bank, Michigan City, Ind., 1984-88; pres. Nashville Hillside Corp., 1966—, Ordinary Corp., Nashville, 1974—, Brown County Inn, Inc., Nashville, 1992—; mgr. AbeMartin Lodge, 1962-66, 89—; pres. Nashville House, Inc., 1959—. Bd. dirs., chmn. First Bank Greenwood, Ind., Ind. Emergency Mgmt. Found. Mem., pres. Nashville Town Bd., 1959-62, Brown County Sch. Bd., Nashville, 1972-75, Monroe County Conv. and Visitors Bur., Bloomington, Ind.; bd. dirs. Bloomington Hosp., Citizens Bank of Cen. Ind., 1988-90, Brown Cmty. YMCA, 1999-; bd. dirs., pres. Brown County Conv. and Visitors Commn. Served with USN, 1950-54. Mem. VFW, Lions, Am. Legion, Ind. U. Alumni Assn. Home and Office: Nashville House PO Box 187 Nashville IN 47448-0187 E-mail: hhouse8007@aol.com.

ROGERS, JAMES DEVITT, judge; b. Mpls., May 5, 1929; s. Harold Neil and Dorothy (Devitt) R.; m. Leanna Morrison, Oct. 19, 1968. AB, Dartmouth Coll., 1951; JD, U. Minn., 1954. Bar: Minn. 1954, U.S. Supreme Ct. 1983. Assoc. Johnson & Sands, Mpls., 1956-60; sole practice, 1960-62; judge Mpls. Municipal and Dist. Ct., 1959-91. Mem. faculty Nat. Judicial Coll. Bd. dirs. Mpls. chpt. Am. Red Cross, chmn. service to mil. families and vets. com.; bd. dirs. Minn. Safety Council, St. Paul, 1988-91. Served to sgt. U.S. Army, 1954-56. Mem. ABA (chmn. nat. conf. spl. ct. judge, spl. com. housing and urban devel. law, traffic ct. program com., chmn. criminal justice sect., jud. adminstrn. div.), Nat. Jud. Coll. (bd. dirs.), Nat. Christmas Tree Grower's Assn. (pres. 1976-78), Mpls. Athletic Club. Congregational. Office: 14110 Prince Pl Minnetonka MN 55345-3027

ROGERS, JAMES EUGENE, electric and gas utility executive; b. Birmingham, Ala., Sept. 20, 1947; s. James E. and Margaret (Whatley) R.; m. Robyn McGill (div.); children: Chrissi, Kara, Ben; m. Mary Anne Boldrick, Oct. 28, 1977. BBA, U. Ky., 1970, JD, 1974. Asst. atty. gen. Commonwealth Ky., Louisville; asst. chief trial atty. Fed. Energy Regulation Commn., Washington, dep. gen. counsel litigation and enforcement; law clk. to presiding justice Supreme Ct Ky., Louisville; ptnr. Akin, Gump, Strauss, Hauer & Feld, Dallas, Akin Gump Strauss Hauer & Feld, Houston, 1985-86; formerly pres. Transwestern Pipeline; pres., CEO, chmn. CINergy Corp. (formerly PSI Resources, Inc.), Cin., 1994—. Bd. dirs. CINergy Corp., Fifth Third Bank, Edison Electric Inst., Duke Realty Investments, Inc. Trustee Nat. Symphony Orch.; bd. dirs. Cin. Mus. Assn., The Nature Conservancy-Ind. chpt., U. Ky. Bus. Partnership Found. Mem. Ky. Bar Assn., D.C. Bar Assn., Meridian Hills Country Club, Crooked Stick Golf Club, Queen City Club, Met. Club. Baptist. Avocations: tennis, biking, skiing, golf. Office: CINergy Corp 139 E Fourth St Cincinnati OH 45202-0960

ROGERS, JUSTIN TOWNER, JR. retired utility company executive; b. Sandusky, Ohio, Aug. 4, 1929; s. Justin Towner and Barbara Eloise (Larkin) R. AB cum laude, Princeton U., 1951; JD, U. Mich., 1954. Bar: Ohio 1954. Assoc. Wright, Harlor, Purpus, Morris & Arnold, Columbus, 1956-58; with Ohio Edison Co., Akron, 1958-93, v.p., then exec. v.p., 1970-79, pres., 1980-91, chmn. bd., 1991-93; ret., 1993. Past mem. coal adv. bd. Internat. Energy Agy. Past pres., trustee Akron Cmty. Trusts, Akron Child Guidance Ctr.; past chmn. Akron Assoc. Health Agys., U. Akron Assocs., Ohio Electric Utility Inst.; past chmn., trustee, mem. exec. com. trustees Akron Gen. Health Sys.; trustee Sisler McFawn Found., Cmty. Health Ventures, Inc., VNS-Hospice Found.; former trustee Stan Hywet Hall & Gardens; past dir. Edison Elec. Inst., Elec. Power Rsch. Inst., Assn. of Edison Illuminating Co.'s. Mem. Portage Country Club, Mayflower Club, Rockwell Springs Trout Club (Castalia, Ohio), Princeton Club (N.Y.C.), Phi Delta Phi, Beta Gamma Sigma.

ROGERS, MIKE, congressman; b. June 2, 1963; BA, Adrian Coll. Spl. agt. FBI; small bus. owner; mem. Mich. Senate from 26th dist., 1995-2000; vice chmn. judiciary com. Mich. Senate, mem. fin. svc., human resources, labor and vet affairs coms., mem. reappropriations com., mem. tech. and energy commn., mem. banking and fin. com.; mem. U.S. Congress from Mich. 8th dist., Washington, 2001—; mem. fin. svcs. and transp. coms. Office: District Office 1327 E. Michigan Ave. Lansing MI 48912*

ROGERS, MILLARD FOSTER, JR. art museum director emeritus; b. Texarkana, Tex., Aug. 27, 1932; s. Millard Foster and Jessie Bell (Hubbell) Rogers; m. Nina Olds, Aug. 3, 1963; 1 child Seth Olds. BA with honors, Mich. State U., 1954; MA, U. Mich., 1958; studied with, John Pope-Hennessy; LHD, Xavier U., 1987. Gosline fellow Victoria and Albert Mus., London, Eng., 1959; curator Am. art Toledo Mus. Art, 1959-67; coord. Ford Found. intern program; dir. Elvehjem Art Ctr., prof. art history U. Wis., Madison, 1967-74; dir. Cin. Art Mus., 1974-94, dir. emeritus, 1994—. Vis. scholar Principia Coll., Elsah, Ill., 1982, Elsah, 84; pres. Mariemont Preservation Found., Ohio, 1982—91, Ohio, 1995—2001; adj. prof. U. cin., 1987—91. Author: Randolph Rogers, American Sculptor in Rome, 1971, Spanish Paintings in the Cincinnati Art Museum, 1978, Favorite Paintings from the Cincinnati Art Museum, 1980, Sketches and Bozzetti by American Sculptors, 1800-1950, 1988, Rich in Good Works: Mary M. Emery of Cincinnati, 2000, John Nolen and Mariemont: Building a New Town in Ohio, 2001. Named Outstanding Citizen of Mariemont, 1991. Mem.: Am. Assn. Mus., Assn. Art Mus. Dirs. (hon.), Phi Beta Kappa. Office: 3610 Pleasant St Cincinnati OH 45227

ROGERS, PHIL, reporter; married; 1 child. BS Journalism, Okla. State U., 1977. News dir. Sta. KVRO-FM, Stillwater, Okla.; reporter Sta. KOMA-AM, Oklahoma City, 1977—79; news writer then afternoon news prodr. Sta. WBBM-AM, 1979—84, mng. editor, asst. news dir., on-air anchor, reporter; gen. assignment reporter Sta. WMAQ-TV, Chgo., 1993—. Recipient award, AP, awards for Best Radio Reporting, UPI, 3 Peter Lisagor awards, Chgo. Headline Club, Edward R. Murrow award, Radio and TV News Dirs. Assn. Avocation: lic. pilot. Office: NBC 454 N Columbus Dr Chicago IL 60611*

ROGERS, RICHARD DEAN, federal judge; b. Oberlin, Kans., Dec. 29, 1921; s. William Clark and Evelyn May (Christian) R.; m. Helen Elizabeth Stewart, June 6, 1947; children— Letitia Ann, Cappi Christian, Richard Kurt. B.S., Kans. State U., 1943; J.D., Kans. U., 1947. Bar: Kans. 1947. Ptnr. firm Springer and Rogers (Attys.), Manhattan, Kans., 1947-58; instr. bus. law Kans. State U., 1948-52; partner firm Rogers, Stites & Hill, Manhattan, 1959-75; gen. counsel Kans. Farm Bur. & Service Cos., 1960-75; judge U.S. Dist. Ct., Topeka, 1975—. City commr., Manhattan, 1950-52, 60-64, mayor, 1952, 64, county atty., Riley County, Kans., 1954-58, state rep., 1964-68, state senator, 1968-75; pres. Kans. Senate, 1975. Served with USAAF, 1943-45. Decorated Air medal, Dfc. Mem. Kans., Am. bar assns., Beta Theta Pi. Republican. Presbyterian. Club: Masons. Office: US Dist Ct 444 SE Quincy St Topeka KS 66683

ROGERS, RICHARD F. construction company executive, architect, engineer; b. Chgo., July 25, 1942; s. Frank S. and Emily H. (Novak) R.; m. Christina L. Rogers, June 30, 1963; children: Mitchell, Cynthia. B in Architectural Engineering, U. Ill., Chgo., 1964. Registered architect, Ill., Wis., Mich., profl. engr., Ill. Architect Einstein Assocs. Inc., Skokie, Ill., 1963-69; v.p. Land Am. Corp., Chgo., 1969-70; project architect M.A. Lombard Constrn. Co., Alsip, Ill., 1970-73; sr. project mgr. W.E. O'Neil Constrn. Co., Chgo., 1973-78; pres. A.C.M. Assocs. Inc., Mt. Prospect, Ill., 1978—. Mem.: AIA. Office: 1306 S Wolf Rd Wheeling IL 60090-6444

ROGERS, RICHARD HUNTER, lawyer, business executive; b. Flushing, N.Y., Sept. 11, 1939; s. Royden Harrison and Frances Wilma (Hunter) R.; children: Gregory P., Lynne A., Reade H. B.S. in Bus. Adminstrn, Miami U., 1961; J.D., Duke, 1964. Bar: Ill. 1964, Ohio 1973. Atty. Continental Ill. Nat. Bank, Chgo., 1964-65; sr. atty. Brunswick Corp., 1965-70; corporate counsel The A. Epstein Cos., Inc. (real estate developers), 1970-73; v.p., gen. counsel, sec. Price Bros. Co., Dayton, Ohio, 1973-82; v.p., divsn. mgr. Water Systems Tech. div. Price Bros. Co., 1982-85; pres. Internat. divsn. Price Bros. Co., 1986—88; pvt. practice law, 1988—; pres. Richard H. Rogers & Assocs. LPA. Pres. adv. coun. Miami U. Bus. Sch.; bd. dirs. Red and White Club, Miami U.; mem. Washington Twp. Task Force on Future Govt.; trustee Woodhaven, Inc.; mem. Washington Twp. Zoning Commn., 1990—, chmn., 1999—. Mem. ABA (forum com. on constrn.), Ill. Bar Assn., Ohio Bar Assn., Dayton Bar Assn. (chmn. corp. law dept. com. 1983-84, exec. com. 1986-87, editor Bar Briefs 1990-91), Miami U. Alumni Assn. (pres.), Miami U. Pres.'s Club. Office: 7333 Paragon Rd Ste 200 Dayton OH 45459-4157 Address: PO Box 751144 Dayton OH 45475-1144 E-mail: rhrlawoffice@aol.com.

ROGERS, RICHARD LEE, educator; b. N.Y.C., Sept. 17, 1949; s. Leonard J. and Beverly (Simon) R.; m. Susan Jane Thornton, Aug. 14, 1976; children: Caroline, Meredith. BA, Yale U., 1971, MA in Religion, 1973; postgrad., U. Chgo., 1977-80; MS in Edn., Bank St. Coll. Edn., N.Y.C., 1989. Tchr. Foote Sch., New Haven, 1974-77; devel. assoc. U. Chgo., 1980-81, spl. asst. to v.p. planning, 1981-82; spl. asst. to pres. New Sch. Social Rsch., N.Y.C., 1982-83, sec. of corp., then v.p., sec., 1983-94; pres. Coll. for Creative Studies, Detroit, 1994—. Office: Coll for Creative Studies 201 E Kirby St Detroit MI 48202-4048 E-mail: rrogers@ccscad.edu.

ROGERS, ROBERT ERNEST, medical educator; b. West Palm Beach, Fla., Nov. 16, 1928; s. Jessie H. and Willie L. (Bahr) Rogers; m. Barbara Ann Hill, May 16, 1950; children: Robert E., Jr., Stephanie Ann Thompson, Cheri Lee Heck. BS, John B. Stetson U., 1949; MD, U. Miami, 1957. Diplomate Am. Bd. Ob-gyn. Commd. 1st lt. M.C., U.S. Army, 1952, advanced through grades to col., 1971; intern Brooke Gen. Hosp., San Antonio, 1957-58, chief resident ob-gyn, 1960-61; resident in ob-gyn Jackson Meml. Hosp., Miami, Fla., 1958-60; fellow gynecology M.D. Anderson Hosp., Houston, 1965-66; asst. chief ob-gyn Tripler Army Med. Ctr., Honolulu, 1966-69; chmn. ob-gyn Walter Reed Med. Ctr., Washington, 1969-70, Madigan Army Med. Ctr., Tacoma, 1970-74; ret. U.S. Army, 1974; prof. Ind. U. Sch. Medicine, Indpls., 1974—, also chief gynecol. div., 1974—; chief ob-gyn svd. Wishard Meml. Hosp., 1983-87. Contbr. articles to profl. jours. Mem.: ACOG (chmn. gynecol. practice com., commr. practice), AMA, Internat. Soc. Advancement Humanistic Studies Medicine (pres. 1997—98), Soc. Gynecol. Oncologists, Soc. Gynecol. Surgeons 1983—84. Office: Ind U Sch Medicine 550 University Blvd Indianapolis IN 46202-5149 E-mail: Bobberogers@insightbb.com., reroger@iupui.edu.

ROGERS, RODDY JACK, civil, geotechnical and water engineer; b. Springfield, Mo. BSCE cum laude, U. Mo., 1981, MSCE, 1983, MS in Engring. Mgmt., 1990. Registered profl. engr., Mo. Asst. and staff engr. Dames and Moore Consulting Firm, Phoenix, 1983-85; project mgr. City Utilities, Springfield, 1985-90, sr. engr. civil engring. sect. system engring., 1990-97, dir. water engring., 1997—. Teaching asst. soil mechanics U. Mo., 1981-83, rsch. asst. soil mechanics lab., 1982-83; 5 time gov. appointee to Mo. Dam and Reservoir Safety Coun.; presented numerous papers. Contbr. articles to profl. jours. Trustee missions com. 1st Bapt. Ch., Springfield, 1989-94; judge sci. fair Springfield Pub. Schs., 1988-89; bd. dirs. Jr. Achievement, 1986-87; vol. Engring. Ministries Internat., 1988, 90-93. Needles scholar, Curators scholar; Recipient Young Engr. Awd., 1991, Nat. Soc. Profl. Engr. Mem. NSPE (chpt. treas. 1988-89, chpt. sec. mem. various coms., chpt. pres.-elect 1990-91, pres. 1991-92, Young Engr. of Yr. award Ozark chpt. 1990, Young Engr. of Yr. award 1991, Edmund Friedmund Young Engr. award for svc. to global cmty. 1991), ASCE, Am. Water Works Assn., Nat. Water Well Assn. (chair), Assn. State Dam Safety Ofcls. (award of excellence in dam safety), Mo. Soc. Profl. Engrs. (ethics task force chmn., Young Engr. of Yr. award 1990, Extra Mile Resolution award, nat. Ethics award), Mid-Mo. Soc. Civil Engrs. (3d v.p. 1989-90, 2d v.p. 1990-91, 1st v.p. 1991-92, pres. 1992-93), U. Mo.-Rolla Civil Engrs. Alumni Assn. (pres. Springfield chpt.), U. Mo.-Rolla Civil Engrs. Alumni Adv. Coun., Tau Beta Pi, Chi Epsilon. Home: 2241 E Powell St Springfield MO 65804-4692 Office: City Utilities Springfield PO Box 551 Springfield MO 65801-0551

ROGERS, ROY STEELE, III, dermatology educator, dean; b. Hillsboro, Ohio, Mar. 3, 1940; s. Roy S. Jr. and Anna Mary (Murray) R.; m. Susan Camille Hudson, Aug. 22, 1964; children: Roy Steele IV, Katherine Hudson. BA, Denison U., 1962; MD, Ohio State U., 1966; MS, U. Minn., 1974. Cert. dermatologist, dermatopathologist and immunodermatologist. Intern Strong meml. Hosp., Rochester, N.Y., 1966-67; resident Duke U. Med. Ctr., Durham, N.C., 1969-71, Mayo Clinic, Rochester, Minn., 1972-73, cons., 1973—, prof. dermatology, 1983—, dean Sch. Health Related Scis., 1991-99. Adv. coun. Rochester Community Coll., 1991-2000. Contbr. over 200 sci. articles to publs. Capt. USAF, 1967-69. Recipient Alumni Achievement award Ohio State U. Coll. of Medicine, 1991, Alumni citation Denison U., 1993, Faculty Svc. award Mayo Med. Sch., 1993. Mem. Am. Acad. Dermatology (bd. dirs. 1987-91, v.p.-elect 1998, v.p. 1999), Am. Soc. Dermatologic Allergy and Immunology (sec.-treas. 1988-2000), Am. Dermatologic Assn., Soc. Investigative Dermatology, Assn. Schs. Allied Health Professions, Dermatology Found. Avocations: travel, family, reading, walking. Home: 224 1st Ave SW Apt 27 Rochester MN 55902-3143 Office: Mayo Clinic 200 1st St SW Rochester MN 55905-0002

ROGERS, WILLIAM CECIL, political science educator, consultant; b. Manhattan, Kans., 1919; s. Charles Elkins and Sadie (Burns) R.; m. Mary Jane Anderson, Aug. 31, 1941; children: Shelley, Faith, Mary Sarah. B.A., U. Chgo., 1940, M.A., 1941, Ph.D., 1943. Asst. to dir. Pub. Adminstrn. Clearing House, Chgo., 1943-47; lectr. internat. relations U. Chgo., 1945-47; asst. prof. U. Va., 1947-48; asso. prof. polit. sci. Western Res. U., 1948-49; dir. World Affairs Center, U. Minn., Mpls., 1949-84; cons. Minn. Internat. Ctr., 1984—. Dir. Program Info. on World Affairs, Mpls. Star and Tribune, 1951-73. Author: Community Education in World Affairs, 1956, A Guide to Understanding World Affairs, 1966, Global Dimensions in U.S. Education: The Community, 1972; co-author: The Winter City Book, 1980. Pres. Minn. Jazz Sponsors, 1966-67; chmn. Mpls. Com. on Urban Environ., 1976-80. Mem. Nat. Univ. Extension Assn. (past sec.-treas.), Winter Cities Assn. (co-founder 1982). Home: 3510 Mckinley St NE Minneapolis MN 55418-1511 Office: 711 E River Rd Minneapolis MN 55455-0369

ROGNA, LAWRENCE G. packaging company executive; b. Detroit, Nov. 27, 1946; s. Guerino and Irvena (Goldsmith) R.; m. Cynthia Ruth Sharp, Feb. 21, 1981; children: Daniel, Angela. BA, U. Mich., 1968; MS in Adminstrn., George Washington U., 1972. Mgr. employee rels. McGraw-Edison Co., Elgin, Ill., 1976-78; mng. ptnr. People Mgmt., Inc., Palatine, 1978-81; v.p. human resources Rohr Industries, Inc., Chula Vista, Calif., 1981-88; sr. v.p. Gaylord Container Corp., Deerfield, Ill., 1988—. Sgt. U.S. Army, 1969-71. Avocations: golf, cycling, running. Office: Gaylord Container Corp 500 Lake Cook Rd Ste 400 Deerfield IL 60015-5269

ROGULA, JAMES LEROY, consumer products company executive; b. Rock Island, Ill., Nov. 8, 1933; s. Andrew and Nellie Pearl (Cook) R.; m. Adelaide F. Dittbrenner, May 29, 1960; children: James Lyle, Adelaide Ann, John Andrew. BA, Knox Coll., 1955; MBA, NYU, 1964. Group product mgr. Am. Chicle Co., Long Island City, N.Y., 1958-66; v.p. new product devel. Carter Wallace, Inc., N.Y.C., 1966-72; v.p. new products J.B. Williams Co., 1972-74; sr. v.p. E.J. Brach & Sons, Chgo., 1974-77; v.p., gen. mgr. A.E. Staley Mfg. Co., Oak Brook, 1977-80; exec. v.p. Booth Fisheries Corp., Chgo., 1980-82; v.p., gen. mgr. Arm & Hammer div. Church & Dwight, Inc., Princeton, NJ, 1982-90; pres. Am. Candy Co., Richmond, Va., 1990-94; group exec. v.p. N.Am. bus. groups Scotts Co., Marysville, Ohio, 1994—2001; pres., personal care domestic Church & Dwight Co. Inc., Princeton, 2001—. With U.S. Army, 1956-58. Mem. Sunset Ridge Country Club, Wedgewood Country Club. Home: 4 Grange Rd Pennington NJ 08534 Office: 469 N Harrison St Princeton NJ 08540-3510

ROHDE, BRUCE C. food company executive, lawyer; b. Sidney, Nebr., Dec. 17, 1948; BS, BA, Creighton U., 1971, JD cum laude, 1973. Bar: Nebr. 1974, U.S. Dist. Ct. Nebr. 1974, U.S. Tax Ct. 1975, U.S. Ct. Appeals (8th cir.) 1976, U.S. Ct. Appeals (5th cir.) 1979, U.S. Supreme Ct. 1980, U.S. Claims Ct. 1981, U.S. Ct. Appeals (D.C. cir.) 1982. Lawyer McGrath, North, Mullin & Kratz, Omaha, to 1996; pres., CEO Conagra Inc., 1996—. Mem. ABA (corp., banking and bus law sect., taxation sect., antitrust law sect., litigation sect.), Assn. Trial Lawyers Am., Nebr. Assn. Trial Lawyers, Nebr. State Bar Assn., Nebr. Soc. CPAs, Omaha Bar Assn., Beta Gamma Sigma, Beta Alpha Psi. Address: ConAgra Inc 1 ConAgra Dr Ste 302 Omaha NE 68102

ROHLIN, DIANE ELIZABETH, financial public relations executive; b. N.Y.C., June 18, 1958; d. Edward F. and Elaine (Wittenstein) R. BA, Mich. State U., 1979. Account exec. Prudential Bache, Chgo., 1980, A.G. Becker, Chgo., 1981-82; sr. ptnr., assoc. dir. market intelligence Fin. Rels. Bd., 1983-99, now assoc. mng. ptnr., 1999—. Republican. Avocations: reading, golfing, horseback riding. Office: Fin Rels Bd 875 N Michigan Ave Ste 2250 Chicago IL 60611-1879

ROHRBACH, LARRY, state legislator; b. California, Mo., Nov. 12, 1946; s. Emmet H. and Ruth (Bieri) R.; m. Beth Ann Connell, 1974; 1 child, Eva Beth. BS, Ctrl. Mo. State U., 1968. Mem. Mo. State Ho. of Reps. from 115th dist., Jefferson City, 1982-93; former asst. minority floor leader Mo. State Ho. of Reps., 1982-93; mem. Mo. Senate Dist. 6, Jefferson City, 1993—. Pres. Ctrl. Mo. State Rep. Club, 1968, Moniteau County Rep. Club, Mo., 1974-76; chmn. Moniteau County Rep. Com., 23rd Senate Dist. Rep. Com. Recipient Taxpayers Watchdog award, 1988. Mem. Mo. Farmers Assn., Moniteau County Farm Bur., Moniteau County Pork Prodrs. (pres. 1973). Home: 25420 Highway D California MO 65018-2707 Office: Rm 433 State Capitol Jefferson City MO 65101

ROITMAN, JUDITH, mathematician, educator; b. N.Y.C., Nov. 12, 1945; d. Leo and Ethel (Gottesman) R.; m. Stanley Lombardo, Sept. 26, 1978; 1 child, Ben Lombardo. BA in English, Sarah Lawrence Coll., 1966; MA in Math., U. Calif., Berkeley, 1971, PhD in Math., 1974. Asst. prof. math. Wellesley (Mass.) Coll., 1974-77; from asst. prof. to prof. math. U. Kans., Lawrence, 1977—. Author: Introduction to Modern Set Theory, 1990; contbr. articles to profl. jours. Grantee NSF, 1975-87, 92-95. Mem. Math. Assn. Am., Assn. Symbolic Logic, Am. Math. Soc., Assn. Women in Math. (pres. 1979-81, Louise Hay award 1996), Kans. Assn. Tchrs. Math., Nat. Assn. Tchrs. Math. Avocation: poetry. E-mail: roitman@math.ukans.edu.

ROIZEN, NANCY J. physician, educator; b. Hartford, Conn. m. Michael F. Roizen; children: Jeffrey, Jennifer. BS, Tufts U., 1968, MD, 1972. Diplomate Am. Bd. Pediats. Staff physician Oakland (Calif.) Children's Hosp., 1976-84; asst. prof. clin. pediats. Johns Hopkins Hosp., Balt., 1984-85; assoc. prof. pediat. and psychiatry U. Chgo., 1985—. Fellow Am. Acad. Pediats.; mem. Soc. for Devel. Pediats. (pres. 1996-98). Office: U Chgo Hosps MC 900 5841 S Maryland Ave Chicago IL 60637-1463

ROIZMAN, BERNARD, virologist, educator; b. Chisinau, Rumania, Apr. 17, 1929; arrived in U.S., 1947, naturalized, 1954; s. Abram and Liudmilla (Seinberg) Roizman; m. Betty Cohen, Aug. 26, 1950; children: Arthur, Niels. BA, Temple U., 1952, MS, 1954; ScD in Microbiology, Johns Hopkins, 1956; DHL (hon.), Gov.'s State U., 1984; MD (hon.), U. Ferrara (Italy), 1991; DSc (hon.), U. Paris, 1997, U. Valladolid, Spain, 2001. From instr. microbiology to asst. prof. Johns Hopkins Med. Sch., 1956—65; mem. faculty div. biol. scis. U. Chgo., 1965—, prof. microbiology, 1969-84, prof. biophysics, 1970—, chmn. com. virology, 1969-85, 88-01, Joseph Regenstein prof., 1981-83, Joseph Regenstein Disting. Svc. prof., 1984—, chmn. dept. molecular genetics and cell biology, 1985-88. Bd. dirs., co-founder Aviron, Inc., 1992—; convener herpes virus workshop, Cold Spring Harbor, NY, 1972; lectr. Am. Found. for Microbiology, 1974—75; mem. spl. virus cancer program devel. rsch. working group Nat. Cancer Inst., 1967—71, cons. inst., 1967—73; mem. steering com. human cell biology program NSF, 1971—74, cons. found., 1972—74; mem. adv. com. cell biology and virology Am. Cancer Soc., 1970—74; chmn. herpes virus study group Internat. Commn. Taxonomy of Viruses, 1971—73; mem. Internat. Microbiol. Genetics Commn. Internat. Assn. Microbiol. Scis., 1974—81; mem. sci. adv. coun. N.Y. Cancer Inst., 1971—88; mem. adv. bd. Leukemia Rsch. Found., 1972—77; mem. herpes-virus working team WHO/FDA, 1978—81; mem. bd. sci. cons. Sloan Kettering Inst., N.Y.C., 1975—81; mem. study sect. exptl. virology NIH, 1976—80; mem. task force on virology Nat. Inst. Allergy and Infectious Disease, 1976—77; mem. external adv. com. Emory U. Cancer Ctr., 1973—81, Northwestern U. Cancer Ctr., 1979—89; cons. Inst. Merieux, Lyon, France, 1979—91; mem. com. to establish vaccine priorities Nat. Inst. Medicine, 1983—85; chmn. sci. adv. bd. Tampa Bay Rsch. Inst., 1983—, chmn. bd. trustees, 1991—. Editor: (book) Herpes Viruses, Vol. 1, 1982, Herpes Viruses, Vol. 2, 1983, Herpes Viruses, Vols. 3 and 4, 1985, The Human Herpesviruses, 1993, Infectious Diseases in an Age of Change, 1995; adv. editor: Progress in Surface Membrane Science, 1972, editor-in-chief: Jour. Infectious Agts. and Disease, 1992—96, mem. editl. bd.: Jour. Hygiene, 1985—91, mem. editl. bd.: Infectious Diseases, 1965—69, mem. editl. bd.: Jour. Virology, 1970—, mem. editl. bd.: Jour. Intervirology, 1972—85, mem. editl. bd.: Archives of Virology, 1975—81, mem. editl. bd.: Virology, 1976—78, mem. editl. bd.: , 1983—, mem. editl. bd.: Microbiologica, 1978—, mem. editl. bd.: Cell, 1979—80, mem. editl. bd.: Gene Therapy, 1994; contbr. scientific papers, chapters to books. Trustee Goodwin Inst. Cancer Rsch., 1977—. Named hon. prof., Shandong Acad. Med. Scis., China, 1985; recipient Lederle Med. Faculty award, 1960—61, Career Devel. award, USPHS, 1963—65, Pasteur award, Ill. Soc. Microbiology, 1972, Esther Langer award for Achievement in Cancer Rsch., 1974, Outstanding Alumnus in Pub. Health award, Johns Hopkins U., 1984, ICN Internat. prize in Virology, 1988, J. Allyn Taylor Internat. prize in Medicine, 1997, Bristol-Myers Squibb award for Disting. Infectious Disease Rsch., 1998; fellow Travelling, Internat. Agy. Rsch. Against Cancer, Karolinska Inst., Stockholm, 1970; grantee Facutly Rsch. Assoc., Am. Cancer Soc., 1966—71, USPHS/NIH, 1958—, Am. Cancer Soc., 1962—90, NSF, 1962—79; scholar Am. Cancer Soc., Pasteur Inst. Paris, 1961—62. Fellow: Japanese Soc. for Promotion of Sci., Am. Acad. Arts and Scis.; mem.: NAS, Johns Hopkins U. Soc. Scholars, Chinese Acad. Engring. (fgn.), Hungarian Acad. Scis. (fgn.), Brit. Soc. Gen. Microbiology, Am. Soc. Molecular Biology and Biochemistry, Am. Soc. Virology, Am. Soc. Microbiology, Am. Assn. Immunologists, Am. Acad. Microbiology, Inst. Medicine, Quadrangle Club (Chgo.). Home: 5555 S Everett Ave Chicago IL 60637-1968 Office: U Chgo MB Kovler Viral Oncology Labs 910 E 58th St Chicago IL 60637-1432

ROJEK, KENNETH JOHN, health facility administrator, hospital; b. Chgo., Aug. 6, 1953; m. Carol Rojek; 2 children. BS with honors, U. Ill., 1975; MBA with honors, Roosevelt U., 1980. Diplomate Am. Coll. Healthcare Execs. Lab. mgr., tech. dir. Rush-Presbyn.-St. Lukes Med. Ctr., Chgo., 1977-80; adminstr. Wyler Children's Hosp., dept. pediatrics U. Chgo., 1980-86; v.p. Parkside Human Svcs., 1986-89, Luth. Gen. Med. Group, S.C., Chgo., 1989-92; sr. v.p. Luth. Gen. Hosp., Park Ridge, Ill., 1992-94, CEO, 1994-2000, Advocate North Side Health Network, 2000—. Adj. faculty U. Minn., St. Francis Coll., Joliet, Ill. Active numerous cmty. and civic orgns., cmty. devel. couns. Fellow Am. Coll. Med. Practice Execs. Med. Group Mgmt. Assn. Office: Ill Masonic Med Ctr 836 W Wellington Chicago IL 60657 E-mail: kenaojek@advocatehealth.com.

ROLEWICZ, ROBERT JOHN, estimating engineer; b. Chgo., Sept. 16, 1954; s. Frank Joseph and Margaret Mary (Ahlbach) R.; m. Vicki Lynn Heggeland, Sept. 1, 1985; children: Heather Margaret, Jeremy Robert. Diploma, Washburne Trade Sch., 1977. Level II inspector Kropp Forge Co., Chgo., 1974-77, chief cost estimator, 1978-88, mgr. estimating, chief estimating engr., 1989—. Pres. Kropp Employees Fed. Credit Union, 1986-88; founding mem. Metalworking Industry Adv. Coun., 1990. Committeeman Citizens to Reelect Jack Kubik, Cicero, Ill., 1984-96, Citizens to Reelect Judy Baar Topinka, Cicero, 1984-96; vol. instr. Boys Club, Cicero, 1975-84; bd. dirs. Cicero Family Svc. and Mental Health Ctr., 1979-87; supporter Cicero Police Benevolent Assn., 1990—, Misericordia Home for Developmentally Disabled, 1974—, Seguin Sch. for Retarded Citizens Assn., Inc., 1985—, Berwyn Libr. Bldg. Fund, Nat. Parks and Conservation Assn., 1990—; local area children's soccer coach; vol. cmty. based holiday baskets for needy families, 1979—, cmty. based drug awareness forum, 1985—; mem. Nat. Arbor Day Found., 2000— Recipient Hold My Hand award Children's Ctr. Cicero, 1982. Mem. VFW (life), Metalworking Industry Adv. Coun. (founding mem.), Vets. of Vietnam War Inc, Vietnam Vets. Am. Inc., Czechoslovak Soc. Am, Vietnow, Sacred Heart League, Cicero Hist. Soc., Brookfield Zoo, St. Jude League, Nat. Audubon Soc., St. Patrick H.S. Alumni Club, Kropp Key Club (pres. 1984—, Golden Anvil award 1989), Elks (mag. editor 1976—, exalted ruler 1981-82, 94-95, v.p. N.E. dist., P.E.R. plaque 1982, Elk of Yr. award Cicero-Berwyn 1989, 93, Govt. Rels. award 1989, Grand Lodge Order of Elks Disting. Citizenship award 1999, Grand Exalted Rulers Commendation award 1998-99, Grand Lodge Trail Blazer award 2000--01), Moose, Handyman Club Am., Nat. Home Gardening Club (charter mem. 2001—). Republican. Roman Catholic. Avocations: jogging, swimming, camping, canoeing, hiking. E-mail: rolewicz@webtv.net.

ROLLAND, IAN MCKENZIE, insurance executive, retired; b. Fort Wayne, Ind., June 3, 1933; s. David and Florence (Hunte) R.; m. Miriam V. Flickinger, July 3, 1955; children: Cheri L., Lawrence D., Robert A., Carol Ann, Sara K. B.A., DePauw U., 1955; M.A. in Actuarial Sci., U. Mich., 1956. With Lincoln Nat. Life Ins. Co., Ft. Wayne, 1956—, sr. v.p., 1973-75, pres., 1977-81, CEO, 1977-91, chmn., pres., 1981-92, chmn., CEO, 1992-98, ret., 1998. Pres. Lincoln Nat. Corp., 1975-91, CEO, 1977-91, chmn., CEO, 1992—; bd. dirs. Norwest Corp. Norwest Bank

(Ind.), No. Ind. Pub. Svc., Lincoln Fin. Corp., GTE North, Inc., Tokh Mem. adv. bd. Ind. U.-Purdue U., 1977, Fort Wayne Leadership, Fort Wayne Community Found., Corp. Innovation Devel. Ventures; bd. dirs. Associated Colls. Ind., Corp. Innovation Devel.; chmn. Ind. Fiscal Policy Com.; trustee Hudson Inst.; mem. Indiana Acad. Mem. Soc. Actuaries, Acad. Actuaries, Health Ins. Assn. Am., Am. Council Life Ins. (past chmn. bd. dirs.), Assoc. Ind. Life Ins. Cos. (exec. com.), Ind. Ins. Soc. (bd. dirs.), Internat. Ins. Soc. (bd. dirs.), Ind. C. of C. (mem. exec. com.). Office: Lincoln Nat Corp 200 E Berry St Fort Wayne IN 46802-2706

ROLLINS, ARLEN JEFFERY, osteopathic physician; b. Cleve., June 30, 1946; s. Lee Roy and Celia (Madorsky) R.; m. Deborah Joyce Gross, Dec. 18, 1971 (div.); children: Aaron Jason, Howard Philip, Lee Craig. AB, Miami U. of Ohio, 1968; DO, Chgo. Coll. Osteo. Medicine, 1973; MS in Occupl. Medicine Environ. Health, U. Cin., 1984. Diplomate Am. Bd. Preventive Medicine. Intern Phoenix Genl. Hosp., 1973-74; resident in environ. health/occupl. medicine Cin. Gen. Hosp.-U. Cin., 1974-77; plant physician Ford Motor Co., Cin., 1974-77, Walton Hills, Stamping Plant Divsn., Cleve., 1987—. Assoc. med. dir. East Side Occupl. Health Ctr., Cleve., 1977-79; med. dir. Ferro Corp., Cleve., 1979—, S.K. Wellman Corp., Cleve., 1979-87, Morgan Matroc, 1979—; pres. Occupl. Health Mgmt. Cons.; cons. occupl. health Ohio Bell Telephone Co., Cleve., 1981-87; cons. Occupl. Health Ctr., Univ. Hosps. of Cleve.; dir. occupl. health program Bedford Med. Ctr. Univ. Hosps. Cleve., 1990-99; corp. med. cons. Cleve.-Cliffs Inc., 1998—. Fellow Am. Acad. Occupl. Medicine, Am. Occupl. Med. Assn., Am. Coll. Preventive Medicine; mem. Ohio State Med. Assn., Cleve. Acad. Medicine (pub. health and immunization com., med.-legal com.), Western Res. Med. Dirs. Assn., Am. Osteo. Assn., Am. Osteo. Acad. Pub. Health and Preventive Medicine (past bd. dirs.). E-mail: arlenrollins@worldnet.att.net.

ROLLS, STEVEN GEORGE, chief financial officer; Joined BF Goodrich Co., Richfield, Ohio, 1981; asst. treas.; CFO Canadian and aerospace bus.; v.p., controller; CFO Convergys Corp. (subs. Cin. Bell Inc.), 1998—. Office: Convergys Corp PO Box 1638 Cincinnati OH 45201-1638

ROLOFF, MARVIN L. publishing executive; m. Shirley Sekas, June 27, 1959; children: Reed, Ross, Robyn. BA, Wartburg Coll., 1955; postgrad., U. Iowa, 1956; BD, Wartburg Theol. Sem., 1960, DD (hon.), 1997; ThM, Princeton Theol. Sem., 1961. Ordained to ministry Luth. Ch., 1961. Pastor youth and edn. Grace Luth. Ch., Green Bay, Wis., 1961-65; editor Augsburg Pub. Ho., Mpls., 1965-70, sr. editor children's curriculum divsn. parish edn., 1970-71, curriculum editl. dir. divsn. parish edn., 1971-74, dir. media resources divsn. life and mission in congregation, 1974-76, dir. edn. resources bd. of publ., 1976-87; dir. edn1. resources pub. Pub. Ho. of Evangelical Luth. Ch. Am., 1988-91; v.p. mktg. Augsburg Fortress, Pubs., 1991-93, v.p. customer resources and relationships, 1993-95, acting pres., CEO, 1995-96, pres., CEO, 1996—. Vis. prof. Christian edn. Luther Northwestern Theol. Sem., 1981, 83, 89, instr. Christian Edn. Inst., summers 1976-90; cons., chairperson youth/adult and children's coms. Curriculum Selection Conf. of Armed Forces, 1971-91; mem. resource planning groups Evangelical Luth. Ch. Am.; mem. publ. com. Augsburg Fortress, Pubs. Mem. Assn. Profs. and Rschrs. in Religious Edn., Protestant Ch.-Owned Pubs. Assn. (mem. edn. com., chair armed forces com. 1993—, mem. exec. com., bd. dirs. 1993—), Nat. Coun. Chs. (Augsburg Fortress, Pubs. rep. to ministries in Christian edn. com., mem. unit com. 1988—, mem. budget and fin. com. 1992—, mem. Bible translation and utilization com. 1994—). Protestant Ch.-Owned Pubs. Assn. (pres. 1998—). Office: Augsburg Fortress Pubs 100 S 5th St Ste 700 Minneapolis MN 55402-1219 Fax: 612-330-3583.

ROLSHOVEN, ROSS WILLIAM, legal investigator, artist; b. Mandan, N.D., Oct. 20, 1954; s. Raymond Paul and Bernice June (Mastel) R.; divorced; children: Ashley Anna, Carsen Ross. BA in Bus. Adminstrn., U. N.D., 1976. Lic. pvt. investigator, N.D., Minn. Claims adjuster, investigator Border Area Adjustments, Grand Forks, N.D., 1976-84; owner, mgr. Great Plains Claims, Inc., 1984—. Chmn. N.D. Claims Seminar, Grand Forks, 1988; guest lectr. U. N.D. Law Sch., 1993-96. Photographic exhibits include Artifacts, 1992 (1st pl. award 1992), Spirit of the Buffalo, 1992 (1st pl. award 1992), Grey Morn' on the Red, 1991 (Merit award 1991); featured artist Custer County Art Show, Miles City, Mont., 1995, Western Lines Art Exhibit at Empire Art Ctr., 2000; American Artists/ American Horses Exhibit, Ruidoso, N. Mex., 2000; sculpture How the West Was Won, 1992 (2d pl. award 1992). Mem. N.D. Mus. Art; patron Grand Forks Fire Hall Theater, 1988-92; mem. Fargo/Moorhead Art Assn., 1992; mem. bldg. restoration com. North Valley Arts Coun.; trustee, chmn. N.D. Cowboy Hall of Fame, 1998—; chmn. Ctrl. Bus. Dist. Authority, Grand Forks, 1998-2000. Recipient Svc. Recognition award United Way, 1984, Hist. Preservation award N.D. Hist. Soc., 1990, Buckskinner award Roughrider Internat. Art Show Com., 1994, 2d Pl. award Fargo Regional Art Show, 1994-95. Mem. Nat. Assn. Legal Investigators, Minn. Assn. Detectives, Red River Valley Claims Assn. (pres. 1986-87), Upper Red River Valley Claims Assn. (pres. 1988-89), Dakota Masters Club Swim Club. Avocations: photography, painting, horseback riding, swimming, archaeology. Office: Great Plains Claims Inc 220 S 3d St Grand Forks ND 58201-6345

ROMAN, TWYLA I. state legislator; m. John Roman; children: Lisa, Sheryl. Student, U. Akron, 1977-78. Trustee Springfield Twp., 1981-94; mem. Ohio State Ho. Reps., Columbus, 1994—. Mem. Summit County Emergency Mgmt. Planning and Exec. Commn. Mem. MADD, S.E. Bd. of Trade, Ohio Twp. Assn., Summit County Twp. Assn., Brimfield Meml. House Assn.

ROMANI, JOHN HENRY, health administration educator; b. Milan, Italy, Mar. 6, 1925; s. Henry Arthur and Hazel (Pettengill) R.; m. Barbara A. Anderson; children: David John, Paul Nichols, Theresa A. Anderson. BA, MA, U. N.H., 1949; PhD, U. Mich., 1955. Instr. U. N.H., 1950-51; instr. U. Mich., Ann Arbor, 1954-55, assoc. prof., asst. to assoc. dean Sch. Pub. Health, 1961-69, assoc. v.p., 1971-75, chmn. health planning and adminstrn., 1975-80, prof., 1971-93, prof. emeritus pub. health adminstrn., 1993—; interim chair Pub. Health Policy and Adminstrn., 1991-92. Asst. prof. We. Mich. U., 1956-57; assoc. dir. Cleve. Met. Svcs. Commn., 1957-59; assoc. prof. U. Pitts., 1959-61; vice chancellor, prof. U. Wis.-Milw., 1969-71; rsch. fellow Brookings Instn., 1955-56; mem. task force Nat. Commn. on Orgn. Cmty. Health Svcs., 1963-66; dir. staff Sec.'s Com. on Orgn. Health Activities, HEW, 1965-66; dir. Govtl. Affairs Inst., 1969-75, chmn., 1970-72; trustee Pub. Adminstrn. Svc., 1969-75, chmn., 1973-75; mem. Delta Dental Plan Mich., 1972-78, bd. dirs. 1972-78, chmn. consumers' adv. coun., 1975-77; bd. dirs. Ctr. for Population Activities, 1975-81, chmn., 1975-81; lifetime vis. prof. Capital U. Economics and Bus., Beijing, 1996—; rsch. assoc. Human Scis. Rsch. Coun., Pretoria, South Africa, 1999—. Author: The Philippine Presidency, 1956; editor: Changing Dimensions in Public Administration, 1962; contbr. articles to profl. jours. Mem. Citizens League, Cleve., 1957-59; mem. Ann Arbor Citizens Coun., 1965-69; bd. dirs. Southeastern Mich. Family Planning Project, 1975-77; trustee Congregational Summer Assembly, 1982-85; commr. Accrediting Commn. on Edn. for Health Svcs. Adminstrn., 1989-95. Served with AUS, 1943-46, ETO. Fellow Am. Pub. Health Assn. (chmn. program devel. bd. 1975-77, exec. bd. 1975-80, governing coun. 1975—, pres. 1979, chmn. publs. bd. 1984-88), Royal Soc. Health (hon.), Am. Polit. Sci. Assn. (life); mem. ASPA (past mem. coun.), Population Assn. Am., Phi Kappa Phi, Pi Sigma Alpha, Pi Gamma Mu, Delta Omega. Home: 2670 Bedford Rd Ann Arbor MI 48104-4010 Office: 2670 Bedford Rd Ann Arbor MI 48104-4010

ROMANOFF, MILFORD MARTIN, building contractor; b. Cleve., Aug. 21, 1921; s. Barney Sanford and Edythe Stolpher (Bort) R.; m. Marjorie Reinwald, Nov. 6, 1945; children: Bennett S., Lawrence M., Janet Beth (dec.). Student, U. Mich. Coll. Arch., 1939-42; BBA, U. Toledo, 1943. Pres. Glass City Constrn. Co., Toledo, 1951-55, Milford Romanoff, Inc., Toledo, 1956—. Co-founder Neighborhood Improvement Found. Toledo, 1960; active Lucas County Econ. Devel. Com., 1979—, Childrens Svcs. Bd. Lucas County, 1981—97, Arthritis Bd. Dirs., Crosby Gardens Bd. Advisors, 1983—96, Toledo Met. Area Govt. Exec. Com., 1996—; citizens adv. bd. Recreation Commn. Toledo, 1973—86; campus adv. com. Med. Coll. Ohio, 1980—; trustee Cummings Treatment Ctr. for Adolescents, 1981—; pres. Toledo Lodge, 1958—59, Cherry Hill Nursing Home, 1964—85; bd. dirs. Anti-Defamation League, 1955—60, Ohio Hillel Orgns., Lucas County Dept. Human Svcs., Arthritis Assn., 1995—, Comprehensive Addiction Svc. Sys., 1998, Kidney Found. Northwestern Ohio, 1986—, sec., 1989; vice chmn. Comprehensive Addiction Svc. Sys., 1999; chmn. Toledo Amateur Baseball and Softball Com., 1979—81; cons. U.S. Care Corp., 1985—; bd. govs. Toledo Housing for Elderly, 1982—84, sec., 1989, pres. bd. govs., 1990—, pres., 1991—; bd. adv. Ret. Sr. Vol. Program, 1987—89, chmn., 1988—90, 1993—, sec. adv. bd., 1990—; vice chmn. adv. bd. Salvation Army, 1986—87, chmn. adv. bd., 1988—90, ct. apptd. spl. advocate adv., bd. treas., 1988—; chmn. Mental Health Adv. Bd., 1983—84, sec., 1989; bd. dirs. Toledo Urban Forestry Commn., 1991—, pres., 1993, 1995, Lucas County Dept. Human Svcs. Bd.; adv. coun. Renaissance Sr. Apts., 1997, chmn. adv. coun., 1999; adv. bd. Lucas Co. Correctional Facility, 1999—; vice chmn. Compass Bd., 2000—; bd. dirs. Area Office on Aging of Northwest Ohio, 2001, Lucas County Mental Health, 2001; chair Compass Corp. for Recovery Svcs., 2002—; active Dem. Precinct Com., 1975—78; trustee Temple Brotherhood, 1956—58, bd. dirs., 1981—; pres. Ohio B'nai Brith, 1959—60. Mem.: Mental Health Bd. of Lucas County, Toledo Zool. Soc., Juvenile Justice (adv. bd.), U. Mich. Alumni Assn., Econ. Opportunity Planning Assn. Greater Toledo, Nat. Coun. on Alcoholism & Drug Dependence, Toledo Mus. Art (assoc.), U. Toledo Alumni Assn., Hadassah (assoc. Toledo chpt., juvenile correctoin bd. 2000—), Masons (Outstanding Cmty. Svc. award of Lucas County 2001), Zeta Beta Tau. Home and Office: Milford Romanoff Inc 2514 Bexford Pl Toledo OH 43606-2414

ROMERSA, ANTHONY JOSEPH, manufacturing executive; b. Washington, Feb. 23, 1945; s. Joseph Charles and Lucinda Antonio (Toffoli) R.; divorced; 1 child, Tanya. BS, U. Md., 1967, MBA, 1969. Asst. terminal mgr. Lehigh Cement Co., Richmond, Va., 1967-69; mgr. ops. and research mgmt. Mercury Marine Corp., Fond du Lac, Wis., 1970-74, dir. fin. planning, 1974-77; controller cons. div. Brunswick Corp., Skokie, Ill., 1977-78, dir. strategic planning, 1986—; controller, v.p. mktg. Vapor div. Brunswick Corp., Niles, 1979-84, v.p. G.M.R.R., 1985-86. Congl. rep. Ry Progress Inst., Alexandria, Va., 1984, 85, 86. Served to lt. USMC, 1966-67. Mem. Ry. Supply Agy., Ry. Progress Inst. (congl. rep. 1984, 85, 86), Am. Mgmt. Assn., Am. Pub. Transit. Assn. Republican. Roman Catholic. Club: Palatine Gymnastics (Ill.) Avocation: boating. Home: 179 Knobb Hill Ln Gurnee IL 60031-4427 Office: Brunswick Corp 1 N Field Ct Lake Forest IL 60045-4811

ROMPALA, RICHARD M. chemical company executive; B in Liberal Arts and Chem. Engring., Columbia U.; MBA, Harvard U. Bus. mgr. Olin Corp.; sr. v.p. ops. Mueller Brass Co.; joined PPG Industries, 1985, v.p. corp. devel., group v.p. chems., group v.p. coatings and resins; pres. Valspar Corp., Mpls., 1994, CEO, 1995—, chmn., 1998. Office: The Valspar Corp 1101 Third St S Minneapolis MN 55415

RONEN, CAROL, state legislator; b. Chgo., Mar. 28, 1945; BS, Bradley U.; MA, Roosevelt U. Dir. legis. and cmty. affairs Chgo. Dept. Human Svcs., 1985-89; exec. dir. Chgo. Commn. on Women, 1989-90; dir. planning and rsch. Chgo.-Cook County Criminal Justice Commn.; asst. commn. Chgo. Dept. Planning, 1991, Chgo. Dept. Housing; mem. Ill. Ho. of Reps., 1993-99, Ill. Senate from dist. 9, 2001—. Former pres. Ill. Task Force on Child Support; bd. dirs. Cook County Dem. Women, St. Martin De Porres Shelter for Women and Children, Alternatives Youth Orgn., Citizen Action Consumer Rights Orgn.; governing coun. Am. Jewish Congress Midwest Region; mem. Coun. Jewish Women. Democrat. Home: 6033 N Sheridan Rd Chicago IL 60660-3003 Office: Capitol Bldg Rm 413 Springfield IL 62706

ROOD, LEE, newspaper editor; b. Lincoln, Nebr., Dec. 22, 1966; BJ, U. Nebr., 1990. Gen. assignments reporter Des Moines Register, 1997—. Office: Des Moines Register Edit/715 Locust Des Moines IA 50309

ROOMANN, HUGO, architect; b. Tallinn, Estonia, Mar. 25, 1923; came to U.S., 1951, naturalized, 1957; s. Eduard August and Annette (Kask) R.; m. Raja R. Suursoho, Sept. 15, 1945; children— Katrin-Kaja, Linda-Anu. B.S., Inst. Tech. Carolo Wilhelmina, Braunschweig, W. Ger., 1950; M.F.A. in Arch. (scholar 1956-57), Princeton U., 1957. Archtl. engr. Austin Co., Roselle, N.J., 1951-54; archtl. designer Epple & Seaman, Newark, 1954-55, 57-61; propr. Hugo Roomann, Cranford and Elizabeth, N.J., 1961-66; partner A.M. Kinney Assocs. (Architects and Engrs.), Cin., N.Y.C. and Chgo., 1966-89. Dir. architecture, v.p. corp. ops. A.M. Kinney, Inc., Cin., 1967, 77, 89; dir. Walter Kidde Constructors, Inc., 1973, A.M. Kinney, Inc., A.M. Kinney Assocs. Inc., Chgo.; pres. Design Art Corp., 1986. Prin. works include Grad. Rsch. Ctr. for Biol. Scis., Ohio State U., 1970, Lloyd Libr., Cin., 1968, offices, labs. and mfg. facilities, Miles Labs., West Haven, Conn., 1969, Am. Mus. Atomic Energy, Oak Ridge, 1975, Renton K. Brodie Sci. Ctr., U. Cin., 1970, EPA Nat. Labs., Cin., 1975, NALCO Tech. Ctr., Naperville, Ill., 1979, Brown & Williamson Corp. Hdqrs., Louisville, 1983, U. Cin. Kettering Lab., 1989. Pres. Citizens League, Elizabeth, N.J., 1966, Estonian Heritage Assn. Cin., 1991-94; bd. dirs., pres. Inter-Ethnic Coun. of Greater Cin., 1992-95. Recipient Top Ten Plant award Factory mag., 1967, Top Ten Plant award Modern Mfg. mag., 1970 Mem. AIA (Ohio chpt. award for Renton K. Brodie Sci. Ctr. 1971, for NALCO Ctr. 1980), Cin. Preservation Assn., Princeton Club. Lutheran. Office: 2856 Observatory Ave Cincinnati OH 45208-2340

ROONEY, GEORGE WILLARD, lawyer; b. Appleton, Wis., Nov. 16, 1915; s. Francis John and Margaret Ellen (O'Connell) R.; m. Doris I. Maxon, Sept. 20, 1941; children: Catherine Ann, Thomas Dudley, George Willard. BS, U. Wis., 1938; JD, Ohio State U., 1948. Bar: Ohio 1949, U.S. Supreme Ct. 1956, U.S. Ct. Appeals 1956. Assoc. Wise, Roetzel, Maxon, Kelly & Andress, Akron, Ohio, 1949-54; ptnr. Roetzel & Andress, and predecessor, Akron, 1954—; dir. Duracote Corp. Nat. bd. govs. ARC, 1972-78; trustee, mem. exec. bd. Summit County chpt. ARC, 1968, 1975—; v.p. Akron coun. Boy Scouts Am., 1975—; pres. Akron Automobile Assn., 1980-83, trustee, 1983—; chmn. bd. Akron Gen. Med. Ctr., 1981-86, trustee, mem. exec. com., 1986—; trustee Mobile Meals Found., Bluecoats, Inc. Maj. USAAF, 1942-46. Decorated D.F.C. with 2 oak leaf clusters, Air medal with 3 oak leaf clusters; recipient Disting. Community Svc. award Akron Labor Coun.; Disting. Svc. award Summit County chpt. ARC, 1978. Mem. ABA, Ohio Bar Assn. Akron Bar Assn. Am. Judicature Soc., Rotary (past pres.), Portage Country Club (past pres.), Cascade Club (past chmn., bd. govs.), KC. Republican. Roman Catholic. Avocations: golf, travel, gardening. Home: 2863 Walnut Ridge Rd Akron OH 44333-2262 Office: Roetzel & Andress 222 S Main St Akron OH 44308-1533

ROONEY, MATTHEW A. lawyer; b. Jersey City, May 19, 1949; s. Charles John and Eileen (Dunphy) R.; m. Jean M. Alletag, June 20, 1973 (div. Dec. 1979); 1 child, Jessica Margaret; m. Diane S. Kaplan, July 6, 1981; children: Kathryn Olivia, S. Benjamin. AB magna cum laude, Georgetown U., 1971; JD with honors, U. Chgo., 1974. Bar: Ill. 1975, U.S. Dist. Ct. (no. dist.) Ill. 1975, U.S. Ct. Appeals (7th cir.). 1990. Law clk. to cir. judge U.S. Ct. Appeals (7th cir.), Chgo., 1974-75; assoc. Mayer, Brown, Rowe & Maw, 1975-80; ptnr. Mayer, Brown & Platt, 1981—. Assoc. editor U. Chgo. Law Rev., 1973. Fellow Am. Coll. Trial Lawyers; mem. ABA, 7th Cir. Bar Assn., Order of Coif, Phi Beta Kappa. Democrat. Roman Catholic. Avocations: jogging, golfing. Home: 2718 Sheridan Rd Evanston IL 60201-1754 Office: Mayer Brown Rowe & Maw 190 S La Salle St Ste 3100 Chicago IL 60603-3441 E-mail: mrooney@mayerbrownrowe.com.

ROONEY, PHILLIP B. service company executive; BA magna cum laude, St. Bernard Coll. Various positions, including pres. Waste Mgmt., 1969-97; various positions including pres. mgmt. svcs. Service Master Co., Downers Grove, Ill., 1997—. Trustee Notre Dame U.; mem. fin. coun. Archdiocese of Chgo.; chmn. sister Cities Internat.; mem. Civic Leadership Coun. of El Valor; dir. Ill. Tool Works, VanKampen Am. Capital. Recipient Semper Fidelis award Marine Corps Scholarship Found., Outstanding Svc. to Mil. award USO, El Valor's Corp. Visionary award, Man of Yr. award Ill. Viet Nam Vets. Mem. Econ. Club of Chgo. Office: ServiceMaster Co One Service Master Way Downers Grove IL 60515 E-mail: prooney@svm.com.

ROOP, JAMES JOHN, public relations executive; b. Parkersburg, W.Va., Oct. 29, 1949; s. J. Vaun and Mary Louise (McGinnis) R.; m. Margaret Mary Kuneck (div. 1982); m. Susan Lynn Hoell (div. 1989); m. Daisy P. Billue, 1990 (div. 1999). BS in Journalism, W. Va. U., 1971. Various account mgmt. postions Ketchum Pub. Rels., Pitts., 1972-77, v.p., 1977-79, Burson-Marsteller, Chgo., 1979-81; sr. v.p. Hesselbart & Mitten/Watt, Cleve., 1981-84, exec. v.p., 1984-86, pres., 1986-87, Watt, Roop & Co. (formerly Hesselbart & Mitten/Watt), Cleve., 1987-96; chmn., pres., CEO James J. Roop Co., 1996—. Contbr. articles to profl. jours. Mem. Leadership Clevel.; bd. dirs. Ctr. for Families and Children, Boys Hope, Kidney Found., Police Athletic League, Econs. Am. Fellow Pub. Rels. Soc. Am. (chmn. investor rels. sect. 1984-85, chmn. honors and awards com. 1995); mem. Nat. Investor Rels. Inst. (chpt. pres. Cleve./Akron chpt., sr. investor rels. roundtable), Cleve. Skating Club, Mayfield Country Club. Republican. Home: 2697 Scarborough Rd Cleveland Heights OH 44106-3241 Office: James J Roop Co 650 Huntington Bldg 925 Euclid Ave Cleveland OH 44115-1408

ROOT, WILLIAM LUCAS, electrical engineering educator; b. Des Moines, Oct. 6, 1919; s. Frank Stephenson and Helen (Lucas) R.; m. Harriett Jean Johnson, Dec. 10, 1918; children: William Lucas Jr., Wendy Elizabeth Root Cate. BEE, Iowa State U., 1940; MEE, MIT, 1943, PhD in Math., 1952. Staff mem. MIT Lincoln Lab., Lexington, Mass., 1952-61, group leader, 1959-61; lectr. Harvard U., Cambridge, 1958-59; visitor U. Wis., Madison, 1963-64; vis. prof. Mich. State U., East Lansing, 1966, 68, U. Calif., Berkeley, 1966-67; prof. aerospace engring. U. Mich., Ann Arbor, 1961-87, prof. emeritus, 1988—. Vis. fellow U. Cambridge (Eng.), 1970; mem. U.S. Army Sci. Bd., 1979-82. Co-author: Random Signals and Noise, 1958 (Russian and Japanese transls.); assoc. editor: (IEEE) Information Theory Transactions, 1977-79; Soc. Indsl. and Applied Math. Jour. Applied Mathematics, 1962-72; contbr. 65 articles to profl. jours., book chpts. and conf. procs. Served to lt. USMCR, 1943-45. NSF Sr. postdoctoral fellow, 1970, vis. fellow Cambridge Clare Hall, 1970; recipient Claude E. Shannon award IEEE Info. Theory Soc., 1986, Career Achievement award ComCon Conf. Bd., 1987. Life fellow IEEE (vice chmn. adminstrv. com. info. theory group 1965-66); mem. Am. Math. Soc. Home: PO Box 3785 Ann Arbor MI 48106-3785 Office: U Mich Dept Aerospace Engring Ann Arbor MI 48109

ROOT-BERNSTEIN, ROBERT SCOTT, biologist, educator; b. Washington, Aug. 7, 1953; s. Morton Ira and Maurine (Berkstresser) Bernstein; m. Michèle Marie Root-Bernstein, Sept. 2, 1978; children: Meredith Marie, Brian Robert. AB, Princeton U., 1975, PhD, 1980. Postdoctoral fellow Salk Inst. for Biol. Studies, La Jolla, Calif., 1981-82, rsch. assoc., 1983-84; from asst. to assoc. prof. Mich. State U., East Lansing, 1987-96, prof., 1996—. Cons. Parke-Davis Pharm. Rsch. Divsn., Ann Arbor, 1990-96, Chiron Corp., 1992-96; mem. adv. bd. Soc. for Advancement Gifted Edn., Chgo., 1987-92; Sigma Xi nat. lectr., 1994-96. Author: Discovering, 1989, Rethinking AIDS, 1993, Honey, Mud, Maggots and Other Medical Marvels, 1997, Sparks of Genius, 1999; columnist The Scis. mag., 1989-92; contbr. numerous articles to profl. jours. MacArthur Found. fellow, 1981-86; recipient D.J. Ingle Meml. Writing prize, 1988. Mem. Phi Beta Kappa (hon.), Sigma Xi. Avocations: drawing, painting, photography, cello. Office: Mich State U Dept Physiology Biomed & Phys Scis Bldg East Lansing MI 48824 E-mail: rootbern@msu.edu.

ROPER, DONNA C. archaeologist; Rsch. assoc. prof. dept. Sociology & anthrop. Kans. State U., Manhattan. Mem.: Kans. State Hist. Soc., Nebr. Assn. Profl. Archeologists (pres.). Home: 1924 Bluehills Rd Manhattan KS 66502-4503 Office: Kans State U Dept Sociology Anthrop & Social Work 204 Waters Hill Manhattan KS 66506*

ROPSKI, GARY MELCHIOR, lawyer; b. Erie, Pa., Apr. 19, 1952; s. Joseph Albert and Irene Stefania (Mszanowski) R.; m. Barbara Mary Schleck, May 15, 1982. BS in Physics, Carnegie-Mellon U., 1972; JD cum laude, Northwestern U. Sch. Law, 1976. Bar: Ill. 1976, U.S. Patent and Trademark Office 1976, U.S. Dist. Ct. (no. dist.) Ill. 1976, U.S. Ct. Appeals (7th cir.) 1977, U.S. Dist. Ct. (ea. dist.) Wis. 1977, U.S. Ct. Appeals (3d cir.) 1981, Pa. 1982, U.S. Ct. Claims 1982, U.S. Ct. Appeals (fed. cir.) 1982, U.S. Supreme Ct. 1982, U.S. Dist. Ct. (ea. dist.) Mich. 1984, U.S. Dist. Ct. (no. dist.) Calif. 1986. Assoc. Brinks Hofer Gilson & Lione, Chgo., 1976-81, shareholder, 1981—. Adj. prof. patents and copyrights Northwestern U. Sch. Law, Chgo., 1982-97. Contbr. numerous articles to profl. jours. Mem. ABA, Internat. Bar Assn., Internat. Trademark Assn., Am. Intellectual Property Law Assn., Ill. Bar Assn., Intellectual Property Law Assn. Chgo., Chgo. Bar Assn., Univ. Club, Chgo. Yacht Club. Roman Catholic. Office: Brinks Hofer Gilson & Lione Ste 3600 455 N Cityfront Plaza Dr Chicago IL 60611-5599 E-mail: gropski@brinkshofer.com.

RORIG, KURT JOACHIM, chemist, research director; b. Bremerhaven, Germany, Dec. 1, 1920; came to U.S., 1924, naturalized, 1929; s. Robert Herman and Martha (Grundke) R.; m. Helen Yonan, Mar. 20, 1949; children: James, Elizabeth, Miriam. BS, U. Chgo., 1942; MA, Carleton Coll., 1944; PhD, U. Wis., 1947. Lectr. Loyola U., Chgo., 1950-62; chemist to dir. Chem. Research G.D. Searle & Co., 1947-87; pres. Chemo-Delphic Cons. Ltd., 1987—. Adj. prof. chemistry U. Ill., Chgo., 1989—. Patentee in field. Mem. Sch. Bd., Wilmette, Ill., 1969-71. Mem. Am. Chem. Soc. (dir. Chgo. sect.), Am. Soc. Pharm. and Exptl. Therapeutics, N.Y. Acad. Scis., AAAS, Chgo. Chemists Club (past pres.) Presbyterian. Home and Office: 337 Hager Ln Glenview IL 60025-3329

ROSATI, ALLISON, newscaster; b. Dover, Del., 1963; married; 4 children. Grad. Speech and Comms. cum laude, Gustavus Adolphus Coll., 1985. Gen. assignment reporter Sta. KTTC-TV, Rochester, Minn., 1985, prodr., co-anchor of 6 pm and 10 pm newscasts, 1986—87; gen. assignment reporter Sta. WGRZ-TV, Buffalo, 1987, anchor 6 pm and 10 pm newscasts; anchor, reporter NBC 5, Chgo., 1990—97, co-anchor 10 pm newscast, 1997—, co-anchor weekday 6 pm newscast. Active Big Brothers/Big Sisters; bd. dirs., organizer Bowl for Kids and Celebrity Golf Outing; active Greater Chgo. Food Depository, March of Dimes, Salvation Army, Ronald McDonald House. Recipient 1st Decade award for Most Accomplished Alumna of the Decade, Gustavus Adolphus Coll., Nat.

Emmy award, Excellence in Comms. award, Justinian Soc. Chgo., David award for Achievement in Broadcasting, Joint Civic Com. Italian Ams., Dante award, 2001. Office: NBC 454 N Columbus Dr Chicago IL 60611*

ROSE, ALBERT SCHOENBURG, lawyer, educator; b. Nov. 9, 1945; s. Albert Schoenberg Sr. and Karleen (Klein) Rose; m. Nancy K. Rose; children: Claudia, Micah Daniel. BSBA, U. Ala., 1967; JD, Washington U., St. Louis, 1970; LLM in Taxation, George Washington U., 1974. Bar: Mo. 1970, U.S. Dist. Ct. (ea. dist.) Mo. 1970, U.S. Tax Ct. 1970, U.S. Ct. Mil. Appeals 1970, U.S. Supreme Ct. 1970. Ptnr. Lewis Rice & Fingersh, St. Louis, 2001—. Adj. prof. law Washington U., 1979-98, Fontbonne Coll., 1993-96. Co-author: Missouri Taxation Law and Practice, 1986, supplement, 1989. Capt. U.S. Army, 1970-74, Korea. Mem.: Civic Entrepreneurs Orgn. (Bd. dirs., sec.), Tax Lawyers Club (pres.), Mid.Am. Tax Conf. (chmn.). Office: Lewis Rice & Fingersh 500 North Broadway Ste 2000 Saint Louis MO 63102 E-mail: arose@lewisrice.com.

ROSE, DONALD MCGREGOR, retired lawyer; b. Cin., Feb. 6, 1933; s. John Kreimer and Helen (Morris) R.; m. Constance Ruth Lanner, Nov. 29, 1958; children: Barbara Rose Mead, Ann Rose Weston. AB in Econs., U. Cin., 1955; JD, Harvard U., 1958. Bar: Ohio 1958, U.S. Supreme Ct. 1962. Asst. legal officer USNR, Subic Bay, The Philippines, 1959-62, with Office of JAG The Pentagon, Va., 1962-63; assoc. Frost & Jacobs, LLP, Cin., 1963-70, ptnr., 1970-93, sr. ptnr., 1993-97, ret. ptnr., 1997. Co-chmn. 6th Cir. Appellate Practice Inst., Cin., 1983, 90, mem. 6th Cir. adv. com., 1990-98, chmn. subcom. on rules, 1990-94, chmn., 1994-96. Trustee Friends of Cin. Pks., Inc., 1980-89, 93-98, pres. 1980-86; trustee Am. Music Scholarship Assn., Cin., 1985-88; pres. Social Health Assn. Greater Cin. Area Inc., 1969-72; co-chmn. Harvard Law Sch. Fund for So. Ohio, Cin., 1985-87; pres. Meth. Union, Cin., 1983-85; chmn. trustees Hyde Pk. Cmty. United Meth. Ch., Cin., 1974-76, chmn. coun. on ministries, 1979-81, chmn. adminstrv. bd., 1982-84, chmn. mem. canvass, 1985, chmn. staff parish rels. com., 1988-90, chmn. commn. missions, 1993-95; trustee Meth. Theol. Sch. Ohio, vice chmn. devel. com., 1990-94, sec. 1992-94, chmn. devel. com., 1994-98, vice chmn., 1998, chmn., 1999—; loaned exec. United Way, Cin., 1999. Lt. USNR, 1959-63. Mem. Cin. Bar Assn., Cin. Citizens Police Assn., On Air Reader, Cin. Assn. for Blind, Univ. Club (Cin.), Cin. Country Club. Republican. Avocations: sailing, golf. Home: 8 Walsh Ln Cincinnati OH 45208-3435 also: 11 Blackstone Rd Boothbay Harbor ME 04538-1943 E-mail: dmrose@fbtlaw.com.

ROSE, JALEN, professional basketball player; b. Detroit, Jan. 30, 1973; s. Jeanne R. Student, U. Mich. Guard Denver Nuggets, 1994-96, Ind. Pacers, 1996—. Named Honorable Mention All-Am., AP, 1991; set Michigan freshman scoring record, 1991; selected as All-Am., Parade Magazine, Third-Team All-Am., USA Today; set Nuggets' rookie record for assists, 1994-95 season; named to All-Rookie Second Team, NBA, 1995 Office: Chicago Bulls United Center 1901 W. Madison St. Chicago IL 60612

ROSE, JOSEPH HUGH, clergyman; b. Jewett, Ohio, Nov. 21, 1934; s. Joseph Harper and Lottie Louella (VanAllen) R.; m. Nila Jayne Habig, Feb. 14, 1958; children: J. Hugh II, Stephanie Jayne, David William, Dawnella Jayne. ThB, Apostolic Bible Inst., St. Paul, 1955, DD, 1990. Ordained United Pentecostal Ch. Assoc. min. Calvary Tabernacle, Indpls., 1956-73; Ind. youth sec. United Pentecostal Ch., 1958-60, Ind. youth pres., 1960-72, bd. edn. Mo., 1974—, presbyter Ohio dist., 1975-97, hon. life presbyter Ohio, 1997; pastor Harrison Hills Ch., Jewett, Ohio, 1973—. Editor, Ind. Dist. News, 1959-70; narrator radio svc. Harvestime, 1961—. Republican. Avocations: travel. Office: United Pentecostal Ch 8855 Dunn Rd Hazelwood MO 63042-2212 E-mail: jhrhhupc@eohio.net., jhrose@upci.org.

ROSE, L. STEVEN See JASHEL, LARRY STEVEN

ROSE, MICHAEL DEAN, lawyer, educator; b. Johnstown, Pa., Oct. 22, 1937; BA, Ohio Wesleyan U., 1959; JD, Case Western Res. U., 1963; LLM, Columbia U., 1967. Bar: Ohio 1963. Assoc. firm Porter, Stanley, Treffinger & Platt, Columbus, Ohio, 1963-66; asst. prof. law Ohio State U., 1967-69, assoc. prof., 1969-72, prof., 1972-99, Lawrence D. Stanley prof. law, 1987-99, prof. emeritus, 1999—. Staff asst. to chief counsel IRS, Washington, 1970-71. Author: (with Leo J. Raskind) Advanced Federal Income Taxation: Corporate Transactions, 1978, (with Joseph S. Platt) A Federal Taxation Primer, 1973, Hornbook on Federal Income Taxation, 3d edit., 1988; editor Selected Federal Taxation Statutes and Regulations, 1973-99, Ohio Will Manual, 1986—. Fellow Am. Coll. Trust and Estate Counsel; mem. Am. Law Inst. Home: 1327 Friar Ln Columbus OH 43221-1527 Office: Ohio State U 55 W 12th Ave Columbus OH 43210-1338 E-mail: rose.4@osu.edu.

ROSE, ROBERT JOHN, bishop; b. Grand Rapids, Mich., Feb. 28, 1930; s. Urban H. and Maida A. (Glerum) R. Student, St. Joseph Sem., 1944-50; B.A., Seminaire de Philosophie, Montreal, Que., Can., 1952; S.T.L., Pontifical Urban U., Rome, 1956; M.A., U. Mich., 1962. Ordained priest Roman Catholic Ch., 1955; dean St. Joseph Sem., Grand Rapids, 1966-69; dir. Christopher House, 1969-71; rector St. John's Sem., Plymouth, Mich., 1971-77; pastor Sacred Heart Parish, Muskegon Heights, 1977-81; bishop Diocese of Gaylord, 1981-89, Diocese of Grand Rapids, 1989—. Mem. Nat. Conf. Cath. Bishops

ROSE, SHELDON, property manager; Pres., CEO Edward Rose Bldg. Enterprise, Farmington Hills, Mich., 1995—. Office: Edward Rose Bldg Enterprise PO Box 9070 30057 Orchard Lake Rd Farmington Hills MI 48333 Fax: 248-539-2125.

ROSE, STUART, retail executive; Chmn., CEO REX Stores Corp., Dayton, Ohio, 1981—. Office: REX Stores Corp 2875 Needmore Rd Dayton OH 45414-4301

ROSE, THOMAS ALBERT, artist, art educator; b. Washington, Oct. 15, 1942; s. Francis John and Ann Elizabeth (Voelkel) R.; m. Mary Melinda Moyer, Aug. 21, 1965; children: Sarah, Jessica. Student, U. Wis., 1960-62; BFA, U. Ill., 1965; MA, U. Calif., Berkeley, 1967; postgrad., Lund (Sweden) U., 1967-68. Instr. U. Calif., Berkeley, 1968-69, N.Mex. State U., Las Cruces, 1969-72; faculty mem. U. Minn., Mpls., 1972—, prof. art, 1983—, Fesler-Lampert chair in humanities, 2001—. Author: Winter Book, 1995; one-man shows include Clock Tower, N.Y.C., 1977, Truman Gallery, N.Y.C., 1977-78, Rosa Esman Gallery, N.Y.C., 1979, 81, 82, Marianne Deson Gallery, Chgo., 1984-86, Robert Thomson Gallery, Mpls., 1986, 91, 92, 95, Deson Saunders Gallery, Chgo., 1989, Mpls. Inst. Art, 1992, Weisman Art Mus., Mpls., 1994, Tweed Mus., Duluth, Minn., 1995, Steinbaum/Krauss Gallery, N.Y.C., 1996, 99, Brevard Mus. Art, Melbourne, Fla., 1997, Gensler Arch., Washington, 1999, Flanders Gallery, Mpls., 2000, Bernice Steinbaum Gallery, Miami, Fla., 2001; exhibited in group shows at Walker Art Ctr., Mpls., 1974, 76, 77, Whitney Mus. Downtown, N.Y.C., P.S. #1, N.Y.C., 1978, Wave Hill, Bronx, N.Y., 1981, Hirshhorne Mus., Washington, 1981, Am. Ctr. in Paris, 1982, Harvard U. Sch. Architecture, 1983, Cultural Ctr., Chgo., 1983, Hal Bromm Gallery, N.Y.C., Sheldon Mus., Lincoln, Nebr., 1989, Tampa (Fla.) Mus., 1988, MCAD, Mpls., 1996, Minn. Mus. Art, 1996, Socrates Sculpture Park, N.Y.C., Fla. Internat. U., Miami, 1997; represented in permanent collections Walker Art Ctr., Joslyn Mus., Omaha, Park St. Lofts, Springfield, Mass., U. Minn., Mpls., Am. Lung Assn. Target Ctr., Mpls., St. Lukes Episcopal Ch., Mpls.; set designer: Fool for Love, Cricket Theater, Mpls., 1985, Circus, Theater de Jeune Lune, 1986; project dir. Works of Art in Pub. Places for Humphrey Inst. Pub. Affairs, Mpls., 1988; prin. works include Minn. Zoo, Marine Edn. Ctr., Sacred Heart U., Fairfield, Conn., Berniece Steinbaum Gallery, Miami, 1999. Named Rockefeller resident, Bellagio, Italy, 1993; recipient McKnight Artist fellow, 1995, travel fellow, Dayton-Hudson/Jerome, 1990, 1995, Jerome Found. Arts, 1993—94, Mellon Found., 1993, Fesler-Lampert Chair in Humanities, 2002; fellow, Nat. Endowment for Arts, 1977, 1981, Bush Found., 1979, Minn. State Arts Bd., 1979, 1984, McKnight Found., 1981, McKnight Found. Rsch., 1993—96, McKnight Photography, 2002; grantee, Arts Bd. Opportunities, 1993. Home: 91 Nicollet St Minneapolis MN 55401-1513 Office: Univ Minn 208 Studio Arts 23D S Avenue Minneapolis MN 55425 E-mail: rosex001@umn.edu.

ROSE, WILLIAM, retired business executive; b. Waukegan, Ill., Nov. 7, 1919; s. Louis and Bertha Rose; m. Vivian May Gulledge, July 15, 1951; children: Whyland, Calvin, Marcia. LittD (hon.), Shimer Coll. Pres. Jobs Temporaries, Waukegan, 1951-86, ret., 1986. Fin. chmn. Boy Scouts Am., 1959-60, bd. dirs., 1966-71; mem. Lake County (Ill.) Mental Healt Adv. Com., 1971-80, bd. auditors Shields Twp., Ill., 1957-61; justice of peace Lake County, 1956-61, police magistrate, 1959-61; bd. dirs. Shimer Coll., Lake County Mental Health Clinic, 1957-68, United Community Services, 1964-71, Lake County Crime Commn., 1969-75; treas. Lake County Econ. Devel. Corp., 1982-83; bd. dirs., v.p. Lake County Welfare Council, 1963; bd. dirs. Pvt. Industry Council, 1977-83. Served with Signal Corps, AUS, 1944-46. Mem. Ind. Office Svcs. Inst. (pres. 1971-73), Nat. Assn. Temporary Svcs. (dir. 1975-78), Lake County Mental Health Soc. (pres. 1951), Waukegan-North Chgo. C. of C. (bd. dirs. 1968-74, pres. 1976), Am. Legion (comdr. 1951), VFW. Jewish (treas. congregation 1968-74, pres. 1976). Lodge: B'nai B'rith. Clubs: Waukegan Exchange (pres. 1963-64), North Shore Craftsman (pres. 1965). Home: 1075 E Victory Dr Ste 118 Lindenhurst IL 60046-7917

ROSEMARIN, CAREY STEPHEN, lawyer; b. Englewood, N.J., Aug. 19, 1950; s. Jack L. and Muriel Ruth (Gordon) R.; m. Joan Maxine Lafer, June 17, 1973; children: Benjamin Joseph, Meryl Ruth. BS, U. Mich., 1972; MS, Pa. State U., 1974; JD, U. Tenn., 1978. Bar: Tenn. 1978, Ill. 1982, U.S. Dist. Ct. (ea. dist.) Tenn. 1978, U.S. Dist. Ct. (no. dist.) Ill. 1982. Rsch. assoc. Union Carbide Corp., Oak Ridge Nat. Lab., 1974-80; asst. regional counsel U.S. EPA, Chgo., 1980-86; ptnr. Katten, Muchin, & Zavis, 1986-90, Jenner & Block, Chgo., 1990-99; prin. Law Offices of Carey S. Rosemarin, P.C., Northbrook, Ill., 1999—. Bd. dirs. Congregation Beth Judea, Long Grove, Ill. Mem. ABA, Tenn. Bar Assn., Chgo. Bar Assn. (chmn. environ. law com. 1985-86), Environ. Law Inst. (assoc.). Jewish. Avocations: licensed glider pilot, bicycling. Office: Law Offices of Carey S Rosemarin PC 707 Skokie Blvd Ste 505 Northbrook IL 60062-2893 Fax: 312-896-5786. E-mail: RosemarinLaw@141.com.

ROSEN, ELLEN FREDA, psychologist, educator; b. Chgo., Jan. 28, 1941; d. Samuel Aaron and Clara Laura (Pauker) R. BA, Carleton Coll., 1962; MA, U. Ill., 1965, PhD, 1968. Instr. psychology U. Ill., Urbana, 1966-67; prof. Coll. William and Mary, Williamsburg, Va., 1967-99; adean grad. studies and dir. Ctr. for Urban Mental Health Rsch. Chgo. State U., 1999—. Cons. Ctr. for Teaching Excellence Hampton (Va.) U., 1988-94; sr. rsch. scientist Behavioral Rsch. Ctr., Hampton U., 1997-99. Author: Ednl. Computer Software, (with E. Rae Harcum) The Gatekeepers of Psychology, 1993; contbr. articles to profl. jours. Mem. Soc. for Computers in Psychology, Psychonomic Soc., Ea. Psychol. Assn., Am. Psychol. Soc. Office: Office Grad Studies LIB 338 Chgo State Univ Chicago IL 60628 E-mail: EF-Rosen@csu.edu.

ROSEN, GEORGE, economist, educator; b. St. Petersburg, Russia, Feb. 7, 1920; s. Leon and Rebecca (Rosenoer) R.; m. Sylvia Vatuk; 1 son, Mark. BA, Bklyn. Coll., 1940; MA, Princeton U., 1942, PhD, 1949. Prof. econs. Bard Coll., Annandale-on-Hudson, N.Y., 1946-50; economist Dept. State, Washington, 1951-54, Council Econ. Indsl. Research, Washington, 1954-55, MIT, CENIS, Cambridge, 1955-59, UN, N.Y.C., 1959-60, Ford Found., N.Y.C., Nepal and India, 1960-62, Rand Corp., Santa Monica, Calif., 1962-67; chief economist Asian Devel. Bank, Manila, Philippines, 1967-71; prof. econs. U. Ill.-Chgo., 1972-85, prof. econs. emeritus, 1985—, head dept., 1972-77; fellow Woodrow Wilson Internat. Ctr., Washington, 1989-90. Adj. prof. Johns Hopkins U.-Nanjing U. Ctr. Chinese-Am. Studies, 1986-87; cons. USAID, Egypt, 1994; book rev. editor Econ. Devel. and Cultural Change, 1988-2001; treas. Am. Com. for Asian Econ. Studies, 1990-95; Golden Jubilee spkr. Dept. Commerce Osmania U., Hyderabad, India, 1999; disting. spkr. Ctr. for Advanced Study of Internat. Devel., Mich. State U., East Lansing, 1999. Author: Industrial Change in India, 1958, Some Aspects of Industrial Finance in India, 1962, Democracy and Economic Change in India, 1966, 67, Peasant Society in a Changing Economy, 1975, Decision-Making Chicago-Style, 1980, Western Economists and Eastern Societies, 1985, Industrial Change in India 1970-2000, 1988, Contrasting Styles of Industrial Reform: China and India in the 1980s, 1992, Economic Development in Asia, 1996; contbr. The India Handbook, 1997. Ford Found. fellow NYU, 1971-72; grantee U. Ill., 1977-78, Social Sci. Research Council and Am. Inst. Indian Studies, 1980-81, Am. Inst. Indian Studies, 1983-84, 87-88, Rockefeller Found. Bellagio Study Ctr., 1984. Office: U Ill Dept Econs M/C 144 601 S Morgan St Chicago IL 60607-7121

ROSEN, GERALD ELLIS, federal judge; b. Chandler, Ariz., Oct. 26, 1951; s. Stanley Rosen and Marjorie (Sherman) Cahn; m. Laurie DeMond; 1 child, Jacob DeMond. BA, Kalamazoo Coll., 1973; JD, George Washington U., 1979. Researchist Swedish Inst., Stockholm, 1973; legis. asst. U.S. Senator Robert P. Griffin, Washington, 1974-79; law clk. Seyfarth, Shaw, Fairweather & Gerardson, Wash., 1979; from assoc. to sr. ptnr. Miller, Canfield, Paddock and Stone, Detroit, 1979-90; judge U.S. Dist Ct. (ea. dist.) Mich., 1990—. Mem. Jud. Evaluation Com. (co-chmn. 1983-88), Detroit; adj. prof. law Wayne State U., 1992—, U. Detroit Law Sch., 1994—; mem. U.S. Jud. Conf. Com. on Criminal Law; lectr. CLE confs., others. Co-author: Federal Civil Trials and Evidence, 1999, Michigan Civil Trials and Evidence, 2001; contbr. articles to profl. jours. Rep. candidate for U.S. Congress, Mich., 1982; chmn. 17th Congl. Dist. Rep. Com., 1983-85; mem. Mich. Criminal Justice Commn., 1985-87; mem. Birmingham Athletic Club; bd. visitors George Washington U. Law Sch., 2000—; bd. dirs. Focus Hope, 2000—. Fellow Kalamazoo Coll. (sr. 1972); recipient Career Achievement award Rolex/Intercollegiate Tennis Assn. Mem. Fed. Judges Assn. (bd. dirs.). Jewish. Office: US Courthouse 231 W Lafayette Blvd Rm 802 Detroit MI 48226-2707

ROSEN, MATTHEW STEPHEN, botanist, consultant; b. N.Y.C., Oct. 7, 1943; s. Norman and Lucille (Cass) R.; m. Deborah Louise Mackay, June 16, 1974 (div. Feb. 1983); children: Gabriel Mackay, Rebecca Mackay; m. Kay Eloise Williams, July 11, 1987. MFSc, Yale U., 1972; BS, Cornell U., 1967. Instr. ornamental horticulture SUNY-Farmingdale, 1968-69; landscape designer Manhattan Gardener, N.Y.C., 1969-70; instr. ornamental horticulture McHenry County Coll., Crystal Lake, Ill., 1972-74; coord. agrl. studies, asst. prof. biology, chemistry Mercer County Community Coll., West Windsor, N.J., 1974-79; adminstr. Des Moines Botanical Ctr., 1979-96, horticulture divsn. mgr., 1996—. Consulting dir. West Mich. Horticultural Soc., 1993; judge Communities in Bloom, 2001, Am. in Bloom, 2002; cons. in field. Contbr. articles to profl. jours. Com. chmn. United Way Cen. Iowa, 1982, divsn. chmn. 1983-86, 88-89, 91, 2000, group chmn. 1987, chmn. arts adv. com. 1985-86, pres. 1986, bd. dirs. Arts and Recreation Council, 1985-86, com. chmn., 1992; mem. career vocat. com. Des Moines Indsl. Sch. Dist., 1986, co-chmn., 1987, mem. Ptnrs. for Progress com., 1988-90, mem. sci. monitoring program, 1991, 92; chmn. Two Rivers Festival, 1987-88; active Des Moines Sister City Program, Kofu, Japan, 1984, delegation, 1989, Naucalpan, Mexico, 1986, 87, Shijiazhuang, China, 1986, 90, 92, 95, 97; mem. edn. com. Am. Assn. Botanical Gardens & Arboretum, mem. membership com., mem. conservation com., bd. dirs., 1997—; judge Cmtys. in Bloom and Am. in Bloom, 2001. Mem. Am. Assn. Botanical Gardens and Arboreta (edn. com.), Greater Des Moines C. of C. (team leader 1984—, chmn. new mem. sales, chmn. 8 O'clock new, Pres. Cabinet award 1983, 84, 85, Achievement award C. of C. Fedn. 1986, mem. exec. com. 1995, 96, 97), East Des MoinesC. of C. (bd. dirs. 1992—, v.p., sec. 1993—, pres.-elect 1994, pres. 1995, 96, sister cities commn. 1994, china chair 1995, 96, 97—, treas. 1995, 96, 97—), Greater Des Moines Conv. and Visitors Bur. (chmn. new mem. sales com. 1988-89), Iowa Advt. Rev. Coun., Affiliate Pres.'s Coun. of Chambers (chair 1995, 97), bd. of dirs. DM Gen. Hosp., 1994-95, 96, 97, Bd. Coun. Internat. Trade, Latinos Unidos (bd. dirs. 1996, 97), Greater Des Moines C. of C. (bd. dirs. 1995—, mem. exec. com. 1995—), Rotary, Phi Kappa Phi, Pi Alpha Xi. Democrat. Jewish. Avocations: photography, reading, model trains, collecting old books, writing. Home: 1042 22nd St West Des Moines IA 50265-2219 Office: Des Moines Botanical Ctr 909 E River Dr Des Moines IA 50316-2854 E-mail: msrosen@ci.des-moines.ia.us.

ROSEN, STEVEN TERRY, oncologist, hematologist; b. Bklyn., Feb. 18, 1952; married, 1976; 4 children. MB, Northwestern U., 1972, MD, 1976. Genevieve Teuton prof., med. sch. Northwestern U., 1989—, dir. cancer ctr., 1989—. Dir. clin. programs Northwestern Meml. Hosp., 1989—. Editor-in-chief Jour. Northwestern U. Cancer Center, 1989—, Contemporary Oncology, 1990-95, Cancer Treatment and Rsch., 1995—, In Touch, 198—. Mem. AAAS, ACP, AMA, Am. Soc. Hematology, Am. Soc. Clin. Oncology, Ctrl. Soc. Clin. Rsch. Achievements include research in hematologic malignancies, lung cancer, breast cancer, biologic and hormonal therapies. Office: Northwestern U Olson Pavilion Rm 8250 303 E Chicago Ave Chicago IL 60611-3093

ROSEN, THOMAS J. food and agricultural products executive; 3 children. CEO Rosen's Diversified, Fairmont, Minn., 1986—. Bd. dirs. Morningside Coll., Danish Immigrants Coun. Minn. Mem. Minn. Agro-Growth Coun. Office: Rosen's Diversified 1120 Lake Ave Fairmont MN 56031-1939

ROSENAU, PETE, public relations executive; Owner, powersports franchises, import/export parts and accessories retail and wholesale operation; owner 6 new car franchises Honda, Hyundai, Mazda, Volkswagon, Toyota, Subaru, Mich.; chmn. Franco Pub. Rels. Group, 2002—. Bd. trustees YWCA Western Wayne County. Recipient Quality Dealer award, Time Mag., All-Star Dealer award (twice nominated), Sports Illustrated. Mem.: Henry Ford Cmty. Coll. (mem. found. bd.), BBB (serves exec. com.), Detroit Auto Dealers Assn. (past pres., exec. com., bd. dirs., co-chmn. 1997 and 1998 N.Am. Internat. Auto Shows, mem. bd. dirs. adv. ethics stds.). Office: Franco Pub Rels Group 400 Renaissance Ctr Ste 1050 Detroit MI 48243 Office Fax: 313-567-4486.*

ROSENBAUM, JACOB I. lawyer; b. Cleve., Oct. 4, 1927; s. Lionel C. and Dora (Heldman) R.; m. Marjorie Jean Arnold, Apr. 20, 1952; children: Laura Rosenbaum, Alexander, Judith Bartell JD, U. N.Mex., 1951. Bar: N.Mex. 1951, Ohio 1952. Pres. Ohio Savs. Assn., Cleve., 1955-60, sr. v.p., 1960-92, also dir.; ptnr. Burke, Haber & Berick, 1955-79, Arter & Hadden, Cleve., 1979-94, of counsel, 1994—. Pres. Kiwanis Found. of Cleve., 1994—; active Judson Retirement Cmty., Cleveland Heights, 1990—, trustee, 1994, pres., 1992; trustee Cleve. Zool. Soc., 1983—, Cleve. Nat. Air Show, 1981—, pres., 1987—90, 1994—, pres. Found., 1995—2000; trustee Golden Age Ctrs. of Cleve., 1996—; pres. Temple Emanu El, University Heights, 1965—67, 1995—; bd. dirs. U. N.Mex. Law Sch. Mem.: Cleve. Execs. Assn. (pres. 1989, chmn. 1990), Greater Cleve. Bar Assn., Ohio Bar Assn. (chmn. aviation law com. 1981—84), Lawyer-Pilots Bar Assn. (pres. 1981—82, editor jour. 1982—97), Kiwanis Club of Cleve. (pres. 1970—71). Democrat. Jewish. Home: 28050 N Woodland Rd Cleveland OH 44124-4521 Office: Arter & Hadden 1100 Huntington Bldg 925 Euclid Ave Cleveland OH 44115-1475

ROSENBAUM, JAMES MICHAEL, judge; b. Ft. Snelling, Minn., Oct. 12, 1944; s. Sam H. and Ilene D. (Bernstein) Rosenbaum; m. Marilyn Brown, July 30, 1972. BA, U. Minn., 1966. Bar: (Minn) 1969, (Ill.) 1970, (U.S. Supreme Ct.) 1979. VISTA staff atty. Leadership Coun. for Met. Open Cmtys., Chgo., 1969-72; assoc. Katz, Taube, Lange & Frommelt, Mpls., 1972-77; ptnr. Rosenbaum & Rosenbaum, 1977-79, Gainsley, Squier & Korsh, Mpls., 1979-81; U.S. dist. atty. U.S. Dept. Justice, 1981-85; judge U.S. Dist. Ct., Minn., 1985—, chief judge, 2001—. 8th cir. rep. Jud. Conf. U.S., 1997—, mem. Author: (booklet) Guide to Practice Civil Rights Housing, 1972; co-author: U.S. Courts Design Guide, 1991—96; contbr. Campaign chmn. People for Boschwitz, Minn., 1978; bd. vis. U. Minn. Law Sch. (pres. 1996-97). Mem.: FBA (bd. dirs., exec. com. 1999-2001). Republican. Jewish. Office: US Courthouse 300 S 4th St Minneapolis MN 55415-1320

ROSENBAUM, MICHAEL A. investor relations consultant; b. Chgo., May 13, 1953; s. Robert and Muriel (Caplan) R.; m. Jill Ann Rubenstein, Oct. 12, 1975; children: Susan Brooke, Stephanie Ilyse. BS in Communications, U. Ill., 1974; MBA, Roosevelt U., 1979. Reporter Peoria (Ill.) Jour. Star, 1974, Compass Newspaper, Hammond, Ind., 1974-75; corr. UPI, Chgo., 1975-78; mng. editor Purchasing World Mag., Barrington, Ill., 1978-79; chief Midwest bur. The Jour. of Commerce, Chgo., 1979-83; sr. assoc. The Fin. Rels. Bd., Inc., 1983-85, ptnr., 1985-88, sr. ptnr., 1988-90, dep. mng. ptnr., chief oper. officer, 1990—, pres., 1997; ptnr., dir. BSMG Worldwide, 1999—. Author: Selling Your Story to Wall Street: The Art and Science of Investor Relations, 1994; contbr. articles to profl. jours. Chmn. capital campaign Congregation Beth Judea, Long Grove, Ill., 1984-87, v.p. programming & membership, 1993-94; mem. capital campaign com. Infant Welfare Soc., Chgo., 1990-92, dir., 1993-97, v.p., 1994-97. Recipient Ann. Report Excellence award Fin. World Mag., 1988-95, Nat. Assn. of Investment Clubs, 1986, 88-95, Assn. of Publicly Traded Cos., 1988-95, Publicity Club of Chgo., 1989, 96, Equities Mag., 2000. Mem. Nat. Investor Rels. Inst., Nat. Assn. Corp. Dirs., Young Pres.'s Orgn. Jewish. Office: Financial Relations Bd John Hancock Ctr 875 N Michigan Ave Ste 2250 Chicago IL 60611-1805

ROSENBERG, CHARLES MICHAEL, art historian, educator; b. Chgo., Aug. 3, 1945; s. Sandor and Laura (Fried) R.; m. Carol Ann Weiss, June 25, 1967; children: Jessica Rachel, Jasper Matthew. BA, Swarthmore Coll., 1967; MA, U. Mich., 1969, PhD, 1974. Asst. prof. SUNY, Brockport, 1973-80; assoc. prof. U. Notre Dame, Ind., 1980-96, prof., 1996—. Author: 15th Century North Italian Painting and Drawing: Bibliography, 1986, Art and Politics in Late Medieval and Early Renaissance Italy, 1990, Este Monuments and Urban Development in Renaissance Ferrara, 1997; contbr. articles to Art Bull., Renaissance Quar., others. Kress Found. fellow Kunsthistorisches Inst., Florence, Italy, 1971-73, Am. Coun. Learned Socs. fellow, 1977-78, NEH fellow, Brown U., 1979-80, Villa i Tatti, Florence, 1985-86, Rome prize Am. Acad. Rome, 2000-01. Mem. Coll. Art Assn., Renaissance Soc. Am., Centro di Studi Europa Della Corti, Italian Art Soc. Office: Notre Dame U Dept Art Art History & Design Notre Dame IN 46556 E-mail: rosenberg.1@nd.edu.

ROSENBERG, GARY ARON, real estate development executive, lawyer; b. Green Bay, Wis., June 18, 1940; s. Ben J. and Joyce Sarah (Nemzin) R.; m. Gloria Davis, Nov. 1967 (div. 1975); children: Myra, Meredith; m. Bridgit A. Maile, Apr. 9, 1983. BS, Northwestern U., 1962, MBA, 1963; JD, U. Wis., 1966. Bar: Wis. 1966, Ill. 1967. Chmn., dir. The Rosenberg

Found., 1960—; atty. U.S. SEC, Washington, 1966-67; pvt. practice Chgo., 1967-74; founder, chmn. bd., CEO UDC Homes, Inc. (formerly UDC-Universal Devel., L.P.), 1968-1995; chmn., CEO, dir. Canterbury Devel. Corp., 1986—; dir. Olympic Cascade Fin. Corp., 1996-98, Nat. Securities, Chgo., 1996—; chair, pres., CEO, dir. OneStop Shop, Inc., 1998—; dir. hometouch Ctrs., Inc. Mem. adv. bd. Kellogg Grad. Sch. Mgmt. Northwestern U., Evanston, Ill., 1985—, founder, chmn. adv. bd. Kellogg Real Estate Rsch. Ctr., 1986—, adj. prof., 1982—; founder Shadow Hill Entertainment Corp., Beverly Hills, Calif., 1990. Recipient Arts Edn. Svc. award Ill. Alliance for Arts Edn., Chgo., 1988, Kellogg Schaffner Disting. Alumni award Kellogg Grad. Sch. Mgmt., 1993. Mem. Nat. Assn. Home Builders (coun. 1989-90), John Evans Club. Avocations: skiing, hiking, climbing, tennis, golf, reading. Office: hometouch Ctrs Inc Ste 3660 676 N Michigan Ave Chicago IL 60611-2866 E-mail: bamgar@interaccess.com.

ROSENBERG, RALPH, former state senator, lawyer, consultant, educator, foundation administrator; b. Chgo., Oct. 7, 1949; s. Nathan Benjamin and Rhea (Matlow) R.; m. Teresa Marie Sturm, July 11, 1989; children: Jacob Louis, Joel Patrick. BS in Commerce and Bus. Adminstrn., U. Ill., 1972; JD, Drake Law Sch., 1974. Bar: Iowa 1974. Sole practice Rosenberg Law Firm, Ames, Iowa, 1974—; mem. Iowa Ho. of Reps., Des Moines, 1981-90, Iowa Senate, Des Moines, 1990-94. Adj. faculty Des. Moines Area C.C., 1980—, Drake Law Sch., 1992, Upper Iowa U., 1993, Iowa State U., 1994—; dir. Environ. Planning Rsch. Group, Ames, 1976-77; exec. dir. Story County Legal Aid Soc., Nevada, Iowa, 1977-78; asst. Story County atty. County Attys. Office, Nevada, 1979-81; exec. dir., mng. atty. Youth Law Ctr., Des Moines, 1989-92; chair adv. bd. Inst. Pub. Leadership, 1994—; exec. dir. Coalition for Family and Childrens Svcs., 1995—; co-chair Iowans United for a Healthy Future. Author, editor: Public Interest Law, 1992; author: Family Theory, Law, Policy and Practice, 1994; editor: Descriptive Analysis of Iowa Environmental Agencies, 1977. Past chair Midwest Leadership Inst. of Coun. of State Govt.; bd. dirs. Jewish Cmty. Rels. Commn., Iowa Protection and Advocacy, regional adv. bd. Legal Svcs. Corp. Iowa, Child and Family Policy Ctr.; past bd. dirs. Co-op. Child Care Svcs., Cmty. Action Rsch. Group, Rural Iowa. Recipient Outstanding Contbn. to Well-being of Children award Youth and Shelter Svcs., 1992, Excellence in Svc. award Legal Svcs. Group, 1993, Iowa LWV Cornerstone award, 1994, Iowa Farmers' Union Friend of the Farmer award, 1994, Iowa Consumer Action Network Citizen Svc. award, 1994; named LEgislator of Yr., Sierra Club, 1988, Isaak Walton League, 1993, Common Ground award Inst. of Public Leadership, 1997; named Legis. Conservationist of Yr., Wildlife Soc., 1988, Elected Ofcl. of Yr., Iowa Corrections Assn., 1984. Mem.: Nat. Conf. State Legislators (criminal justice com. 1986—94), Iowa State Bar Assn. Home: 811 Ridgewood Ave Ames IA 50010-5823 Office: 1111 9th St Ste 200 Des Moines IA 50314-2527 E-mail: hn3957@earthlink.net.

ROSENBERG, ROBERT BRINKMANN, technology organization executive; b. Chgo., Mar. 19, 1937; s. Sidney and Gertrude (Brinkmann) R.; m. Patricia Margaret Kane, Aug. 1, 1959 (dec. Feb. 1988); children: John Richard Debra Ann; m. Maryann Bartoli Manrot, June 25, 1989. BSChemE with distinction, Ill. Inst. Tech., 1958, M.S. in Gas Tech, 1961, Ph.D. in Gas Tech, 1964. Registered profl. engr., Ill. Adj. asst. prof. Ill. Inst. Tech., 1965-69; mem. staff Inst. Gas Tech., Chgo., 1962-77, v.p. engrng. rsch., 1973-77; v.p. rsch. and devel. Gas Research Inst., Chgo., 1977-78, exec. v.p., sr. v.p., 1978-84, v.p., 1984-96; pres. RBR @ Vision, Burr Ridge, Ill., 1996—; also bd. dirs. IEA Internat. Ctr. for Gas Tech. Info. Tech. program dir. World Energy Congress, 1996—98. Author; patentee in field. Mem. Hinsdale (Ill.) Home Rule Ad Hoc Com., 1975-77; bd. dirs. Hinsdale Arts Coun., 1977-85, dir. emeritus, 1985-95; pres. Triangle Frat. Edn. Found., 1974-96, bd. dirs., 1996-2001, dir. emeritus; mem. vis. com. dept. chemistry U. Tex.; mem. adv. coun. U. Tex. Coll. Natural Scis. Found., 1990-95; pres. Lake Ridge Club Homeowners Assn., 2001—. Recipient Gas Industry Research award, 1985, Energy Exec. of Yr. award, 1987, Profl. Achievement award Ill. Inst. Tech. Alumni Assn., 1991. Mem. AIChE, Am. Gas Assn. (operating sect. award of merit 1989), Inst. Gas Engrs., Combustion Inst. (past treas. bd. cen. states sect.), Atlantic Gas Rsch. Exch. (chmn. mng. bd. 1980-96), Internat. Gas Union (U.S. rep. subcom. F-2 1974-83), Gas Appliance Engrs. Soc. (past trustee), Air Pollution Control Assn. (past sect. com. residential pollution sources), Triangle (svc. key and Outstanding Alumnus award 1987). Home: 28 Lake Ridge Club Dr Burr Ridge IL 60527-7937 Office: RBR @ Vision 28 Lake Ridge Club Dr Burr Ridge IL 60527-7937 E-mail: RBR@attbl.com.

ROSENBERG, ROBIN, executive chef; b. Sausalito, Calif., Mar. 25, 1958; div.; 1 child. AA, Columbia Coll. Banquet chef, exec. chef Hilton Hotels, 1985-95; chef de cuisine Levy Restaurant, Chgo. Caterer Fire and Ice Charity Ball, L.A., 1989, Golden Globe Awards, 1991. Avocations: exploring current food trends, taking road trips, skiing, going to horse races, photography. Office: Levy Restaurants 980 N Michigan Ave Chicago IL 60611-4501

ROSENBERG, SAMUEL NATHAN, French and Italian language educator; b. N.Y.C., Jan. 19, 1936; s. Israel and Etta (Friedland) R. AB, Columbia U., 1957; PhD, Johns Hopkins U., 1965. Instr. Columbia U., N.Y.C., 1960-61; lectr. Ind. U., Bloomington, Ind., 1962-65, asst. prof., 1965-69, assoc. prof. Ind., 1969-81, prof. dept. French and Italian, 1981-99, prof. emeritus, 2000—, chmn. dept., 1977-84. Author: Modern French CE, 1970, (with others) Harper's Grammar of French, 1983, (with W. Apel) French Secular Compositions of the 14th Century, 3 vols., 1970-72, (with H. Tischler) Chanter m'estuet: Songs of the Trouveres, 1981; translator: (with S. Danon) Ami and Amile, 1981, revised edit., 1996, Lyrics and Melodies of Gace Brulé, 1985, (with H. Tischler) The Monophonic Songs in the Roman de Fauvel, 1991, Lancelor-Grail Cycle, vol. 2, 1993, Chansons des trouvères, 1995, Songs of the Troubadours and Trouvères, 1997, (with others) Early French Tristan Poems, 2 vols., 1998. Pres. Mid-Am. Festival of the Arts, Inc., Bloomington, Ind., 1984-85. Woodrow Wilson Found. fellow, 1959-60; Fulbright fellow, 1960-61; Lilly Faculty fellow, 1986-87. Mem MLA, Am. Assn. Tchrs. French; mem. Medieval Acad. Am., Internat. Courtly Lit. Soc., Am. Literary Translators Assn., Phi Beta Kappa Home: PO Box 1164 Bloomington IN 47402-1164 E-mail: srosenbe@indiana.edu.

ROSENBERG, SHELI Z. investment company executive; Degree, Tufts U., Northwestern U. Atty. Cotton, Watt, Jones & King, 1966—70; mng. ptnr. Schiff Hardin & Waite, 1976—80; from gen. coun. to vice-chmn. Equity Group Investments, LLC, Chgo., 1980—2000, vice-chmn., 2000—. Bd. dirs. CVS Corp., Capital Trust, Cendant Corp., Dynegy, Inc., Manufactured Home Communities, Inc., Equity Residential Properties Trust, Equity Office Properties Trust, Ventas, Inc.; adv. bd. J.L. Kellogg Grad. Sch. Bus. N.W. Univ. Trustee Rush Presbyn. St. Luke's Med. Ctr., exec. com.; co-founder, pres. Ctr. for Exec. Women, J.L. Kellogg Grad. Sch. Bus., 2001—. Office: Equity Group Investments LLC 737 North Michigan Ave Ste 1405 Chicago IL 60611 E-mail: szr312@aol.com.

ROSENBLATT, KARIN ANN, cancer epidemiologist; b. Chgo., Apr. 22, 1954; d. Murray and Adylin Rosenblatt. BA, U. Calif., Santa Cruz, 1975; MPH, U. Mich., 1977; PhD, Johns Hopkins U., 1988. Postdoctoral fellow U. Wash., Seattle, 1987-89; staff scientist Fred Hutchinson Cancer Rsch. Ctr., 1989-91; asst. prof. U. Ill., Champaign, 1991-97, assoc. prof., 1997—. Vis. scientist Fred Hutchinson Cancer Rsch. Ctr., 1999-2000; vis. scholar U. Wash., 1999-2000. Fellow Am. Coll. Epidemiology; mem. APHA (governing councilor epidemiology sect. 1988-2000), Internat. Epidemiologic Assn., Internat. Genetic Epidemiology Soc., Soc. for Epidemiologic Rsch. Office: Dept Cmty Health 120 Huff Hall MC 588 1206 S 4th St Champaign IL 61820-6920

ROSENBLOOM, LEWIS STANLEY, lawyer; b. Fort Riley, Kans., Feb. 28, 1953; s. Donald and Sally Ann (Warsawsky) R.; m. Rochelle Leavitt, Dec. 16, 1973; children: Micah, Shaina. BA, Lake Forest Coll., 1974; JD with high honors, DePaul U., 1977. Bar: Ill. 1977, U.S. Dist. Ct. (no. dist.) Ill, 1977, U.S. Ct. Appeals (7th cir.) 1979, U.S. Supreme Ct. 1983, U.S. Ct. Appeals (9th cir.) 1987, U.S. Ct. Appeals (3rd cir.) 1993. Sr. acct. Gale, Takahasi & Channon, Chgo., 1973-74; law clk. to Hon. Robert L. Eisen U.S. Dist. Ct. (no. dist.) Ill., 1976; assoc. Nachman, Munitz & Sweig, Ltd., 1976-82, prin., 1982-87; ptnr., co-chmn. involvency, bankruptcy & bus. reorgn. dept. Winston & Strawn, 1987-93; ptnr., sr. corp. reorgn. counsel McDermott, Will & Emery, 1994—; chmn. distressed transactions SBU. Mem. bd. advisors to bankruptcy, comml. law advisor Bus. Laws, Inc., 1988—; lectr. in field. Contbr. articles to profl. jours. Mem. adv. com. and fin. subcom. Ill. Bd. Higher Edn., Springfield; mem. state edn. and legal aid subcom. Ill. Coun. on Children and Youth Welfare, Chgo. Coll. scholar Lake Forest Coll., 1973-74. Fellow Am. Coll. Bankruptcy; mem. ABA (bus. bankruptcy com. 1982—, chmn. new and pending bankruptcy legis. com. 1982-85, chmn. transp. reorganizations com. 1985-88), Chgo. Bar Assn. (bankrupcy reorganization com., co-chmn. subcom. on retention and fees 1987-88). Office: McDermott Will & Emery 227 W Monroe St Ste 3100 Chicago IL 60606-5096 E-mail: lrosenbloom@mwe.com.

ROSENBLUM, VICTOR GREGORY, political science and law educator; b. N.Y.C., June 2, 1925; s. George and Vera (Minster) R.; m. Louise Rann, Feb. 21, 1946; children: Susan, Ellen, Laura, Keith, Jonathan, Peter, Warren, Joshua. A.B., Columbia U., 1945, LL.B., 1948; Ph.D., U. Calif.-Berkeley, 1953; D.H.L., Hebrew Union Coll., 1970; D.L., Siena Heights Coll., 1982, Wabash Coll., 1998. Bar: Ill., N.Y., U.S. Supreme Ct. Lectr. polit. sci. U. Calif., Berkeley, 1949-52, asst. prof. polit. sci., 1953-57; assoc. prof. polit. sci. Northwestern U., 1958-63, prof. polit. sci. and law, 1963-68, 70-88, Nathaniel L. Nathanson prof., 1988—; pres. Reed Coll., Portland, Oreg., 1968-70. Sr. legal cons. project on bankruptcy govtl. studies div. Brookings Instn., 1964-69; vis. Fulbright lectr. Sch. Law U. Louvain, Belgium, 1966-67, vis. prof., 1978-79, 91-92; mem. Adminstrv. Conf. U.S., 1982-96. Editor in chief Adminstrv. Law Rev., 1958-62; author: Law As A Political Instrument, 1955, (with A.D. Castberg) Cases on Constitutional Law: Political Roles of the Supreme Court, 1973, (with Frances Zemans) The Making of a Public Profession, 1981; contbr. to law revs., also law and polit. sci. books. Staff assoc. Govtl. Affairs Inst., Washington, 1952-53; cons., assoc. counsel Subcom. on Exec. and Legis. Reorgn., Com. on Govt. Ops., U.S. Ho. of Reps., 1956-57; bd. dirs. Center for Adminstrv. Justice, 1972-78. Mem. ABA (council sect. adminstrv. law 1962-65, 72-75, chmn. 1977-78), Fed. Bar Assn., Am. Polit. Sci. Assn., Law and Soc. Assn. (pres. 1970-72), Am. Judicature Soc. (dir. 1982-90, chmn. bd. 1985-86), Assn. Am. Law Schs. (exec. com. 1984-88, pres. 1987), Consortium of Social Sci. Assns. (pres. 1987-88), Phi Beta Kappa, Pi Sigma Alpha. Democrat. Jewish. Home: 2025 Sherman Ave Evanston IL 60201-3268 Office: Northwestern U Sch Law 357 E Chicago Ave Chicago IL 60611-3059 E-mail: v-rosenblum@law.northwestern.edu.

ROSENFIELD, ROBERT LEE, pediatric endocrinologist, educator; b. Robinson, Ill., Dec. 16, 1934; s. Irving and Sadie (Ospide) R.; m. Sandra L. McVicker, Apr. 14, 1973. BS, Northwestern U., 1956; MD, 1960. Diplomate Am. Bd. Pediat. Endocrinology. Intern Phila. Gen. Hosp. and Children's Hosp., Phila., 1960-63, 65-68; practice specializing in pediat. endocrinology; prof. pediats., medicine U. Chgo., 1968—. Vis. prof. U. Dundee, 1986-87. Contbr. articles to profl. jours. Capt. USMC, 1963-65. Fogarty Sr. Internat. fellow, USPHS, Weizmann Inst., Israel, 1977-78. Mem. Am. Bd. Pediat. (sub.-bd. pediatric endocrinology 1983-86), Am. Pediat. Soc., Lawson Wilkins Pediatric Endocrinology Soc., Endocrine Soc., Soc. Gynecol. Invetigation, Soc. Dermatol. Investigation, Chgo. Pediat. Soc. (pres. 1981). Democrat. Jewish. Avocation: photography. Home: 1700 E 56th St Apt 3502 Chicago IL 60637-5099 Office: U Chgo Med Ctr 5841 S Maryland Ave Chicago IL 60637-1463

ROSENHEIM, EDWARD WEIL, English educator; b. Chgo., May 15, 1918; s. Edward Weil and Fannie (Kohn) R.; m. Margaret Morton Keeney, June 20, 1947; children: Daniel Edward, James Morton, Andrew Keeney. B.A., U. Chgo., 1939, M.A., 1946, Ph.D., 1953. Publicity writer Pub. Relations Service, Chgo., 1939-40; instr. Gary (Ind.) Coll., 1946; faculty U. Chgo., 1947—, prof. English, 1962—, David B. and Clara E. Stern prof., 1980-88, prof. emeritus, 1988—, assoc. chmn. dept. English, 1967-75, dir. broadcasting for univ., 1954-57; dir. Nat. Humanities Inst., 1977-80. Disting. vis. prof. Pa. State U., 1961; Disting. lectr. Nat. Coun. Tchrs. English, 1967; mem. Ill. Humanities Coun., 1982—, pres., 1985-87. Author: What Happens in Literature, 1960, Swift and the Satirist's Art, 1963; editor: Selected Prose and Poetry of Jonathan Swift, 1958, Jour. Gen. Edn., 1954-56; co-editor: Modern Philology, 1968-88. Served to capt. inf. AUS, 1941-46. Recipient Alumni Svc. medal U. Chgo., 1990; Willet Faculty fellow, 1962, Guggenheim Meml. fellow, 1967. Mem. Am. Soc. 18th Century Studies, Johnson Soc. (pres. Central region 1971) Clubs: Quadrangle, Wayfarers, Caxton Home: 5805 S Dorchester Ave Chicago IL 60637-1730 Office: 1050 E 59th St Chicago IL 60637-1559

ROSENHEIM, MARGARET KEENEY, social welfare policy educator; b. Grand Rapids, Mich., Sept. 5, 1926; d. Morton and Nancy (Billings) Keeney; m. Edward W. Rosenheim, June 20, 1947; children: Daniel, James, Andrew. Student, Wellesley Coll., 1943-45; J.D., U. Chgo., 1949. Bar: Ill. 1949. Mem. faculty Sch. Social Service Adminstrn., U. Chgo., 1950—, assoc. prof., 1961-66, prof., 1966—, Helen Ross prof. social welfare policy, 1975-96, dean, 1978-83; lectr. in law U. Chgo., 1980-97. Vis. prof. U. Wash., 1965, Duke U., 1984; Helen Ross prof. emerita U. Chgo., 1996—; acad. visitor London Sch. Econs., 1973; cons. Pres.'s Commn. Law Enforcement and Adminstrn. Justice, 1966-67, Nat. Adv. Commn. Criminal Justice Stds. and Goals, 1972; mem. Juvenile Justice Stds. Commn., 1973-78; trustee Carnegie Corp. N.Y., 1979-87; trustee Children's Home and Aid Soc. of Ill., 1981—, chair, 1996-98; chair CHASI Sys. Inc., 1998-2001; dir. Nat. Inst. Dispute Resolution, 1981-89, Nuveen Bond Funds, 1982-97; mem. Chgo. Network, 1983—. Editor: Justice for the Child, 1962; contbr. ; editor: Pursuing Justice for the Child, 1976; editor: (with F.E. Zimring, D.S. Tanenhaus, B. Dohrn) A Century of Juvenile Justice, 2002; editor: (with Mark Testa) Early Parenthood and Coming of Age in the 1990s, 1992; contbr. articles to profl. jours. Home: 5805 S Dorchester Ave Chicago IL 60637-1730 Office: 969 E 60th St Chicago IL 60637-2677 E-mail: mrosenhe@midway.uchicago.edu.

ROSENMAN, KENNETH D. medical educator; b. N.Y.C., Feb. 25, 1951; AB, Cornell U., 1972; MD, NY Med. Coll., 1975. Bd. cert. internal medicine; bd. cert. occupational and preventive medicine. Asst. prof. U. Mass., Amherst, 1979-81; dir. occupational and environ. health N.J. Dept. Health, Trenton, 1981-86; pvt. practice Plainsboro, N.J., 1986-88; assoc. prof. Mich. State U., East Lansing, 1988-93, prof., 1993—. Office: Mich State U 117 W Fee Hall East Lansing MI 48824-1316

ROSENOW, EDWARD CARL, III, medical educator; b. Columbus, Ohio, Nov. 2, 1934; s. Oscar Ferdinand and Mildred Irene (Eichelberger) R.; m. Constance Donna Grahame, Sept. 7, 1957; children: Sheryl Lynn, Scott Edward. BS, Ohio State U., 1955, MD, 1959; MS in Medicine, U. Minn., 1969. Diplomate Am. Bd. Internal Medicine, Am. Bd. Pulmonary Diseases. Intern Riverside Meth. Hosp., Columbus, Ohio, 1959-60; resident in internal medicine Mayo Grad. Sch. Medicine, Rochester, Minn., 1960-65, clin. fellow in thoracic diseases, 1965-66; cons. in internal medicine (pulmonary diseases) Mayo Clinic, 1966; instr. in medicine Mayo Grad. Sch. Medicine, 1969-73; asst. prof. medicine Mayo Med. Sch., 1973-77, assoc. prof. medicine, 1977-80, prof. medicine, 1980; chmn. divsn. pulmonary and critical care medicine, 1987-94; assoc. dir. internal medicine residency program Mayo Clinic, Rochester, 1977-79, program dir. internal medicine residency program, 1979-84, sec. Mayo staff, 1979; pres. Mayo staff, 1986; Arthur M. and Gladys D. Gray prof. medicine Mayo Clinic, Rochester, 1987-96, prof. emeritus, 1996—. Cons. NASA, Houston. Capt. M.C., U.S. Army, 1962-64. Recipient Alumni Achievement award Coll. Medicine Ohio State U., 1989, Disting. Mayo Clinician award, 1994, Henry S. Plummer Disting. Internist award, 1994, Karis award Mayo Clinic, 1996, Disting. Alumnus award Mayo Found., 1998; Edward W. and Betty Knight Scripps Professorship named in his honor Mayo Med. Sch., 1994, Edward C. Rosenow, III, Outstanding Subsplty. fellow award established in his honor. Fellow ACP (gov. Minn. chpt. 1987-91, Ralph S. Claypoole Sr. award for Lifetime Dedication to Patient Care 1995, Minn. chpt. Laureate award 1994, Disting. Lectr. award 1996), Am. Coll. Chest Physicians (master fellow, editl. bd. CHEST 1973-78, editor spl. case reports 1975-90, com. on postgrad. med. edn. 1978-84, sci. program com. 1982, com. on undergrad. med. edn. 1981-82, co-chmn. sci. program com. Internat. Coll. Chest Physicians meeting, Sydney, Australia, 1985, regent 1984-88, pres. elect 1988-89, pres. 1989-90, pres. Chest Found. 1998—, Dist. Lectr. award); mem. AMA, So. Minn. Med. Assn., Minn. Thoracic Soc., Am. Thoracic Soc., Sigma Xi. Office: Mayo Clinic Div Pulmonary Diseases 200 1st St SW Rochester MN 55905-0002

ROSENOW, JOHN EDWARD, foundation executive; b. Lincoln, Nebr., Sept. 15, 1949; s. Lester Edward and Lucille Louise (Koehler) R.; m. Nancy Kay Hadley; children: Matthew, Stacy. BS in Agrl. Engring., U. Nebr., 1971. Dir. of tourism Nebr. Dept. Econ. Devel., Lincoln, 1971-79, interim dept. dir., 1985; founder Nat. Arbor Day Found., 1972, exec. dir. million-mem., 1979-94, pres., 1994—. Co-author: (book) Tourism: the good, the bad, and the ugly, 1979. Democrat. Mem. United Ch. of Christ. E-mail: arborday.org. Office: Nat Arbor Day Found 211 N 12th St Lincoln NE 68508-1422

ROSENSHINE, ALLEN GILBERT, advertising agency executive; b. N.Y.C., Mar. 14, 1939; s. Aaron and Anna (Zuckerman) R.; m. Suzan Weston-Webb, Aug. 31, 1979; children: Andrew, Jonathan. A.B., Columbia Coll., 1960. Copywriter J.B. Rundle (advt.), N.Y.C., 1962-65; copywriter Batten, Barton, Durstine & Osborn, 1965, copy supr., 1967, v.p., 1968, asso. creative dir., 1970, sr. v.p., creative dir., 1975-77, exec. v.p., 1977-80, pres., 1980-82, chief exec. officer, 1981-86, chmn., 1983-86, also dir., mem. exec. com.; pres., chief exec. officer BBDO Internat., 1984-86, also bd. dirs.; pres., chief exec. officer Omnicom Group, 1986-88; chmn., chief exec. officer BBDO Worldwide, 1989—. Lectr. gen. studies Bklyn. Coll., 1961-65 Office: BBDO Worldwide Inc 1285 Avenue Of The Americas New York NY 10019-6028*

ROSENSTOCK, SUSAN LYNN, orchestra administrator; b. Bklyn., Nov. 2, 1947; BS, SUNY, Cortland, 1969; MBA, So. Meth. U., 1977, MFA, 1978. Asst. mgr. Columbus (Ohio) Symphony Orch., 1978-82; grants program dir., info. officer Greater Columbus Arts Coun., 1982-83, asst. dir. grants and adminstrn., 1983-84; dir. annual giving and spl. events Columbus Symphony Orch., 1984-86, dir. devel., 1986-90, orch. mgr., 1990-98, gen. mgr., 1998—. Panelist Ohio Arts Coun. Music Panel, 1986, 87, Challenge Grants Panel, 1991, J.C. Penney Gold Rule Award Judges Panel, 1993, 94. Mem. Am. Symphony Orch. League (devel. dirs. steering com. nat. conf. 1987, 88), Nat. Soc. Fund Raising Execs. (program com. Ctrl. Ohio chpt. 1988-94, chmn. program com. 1993, 94, bd. dirs. 1993-95, treas. 1995). Office: Columbus Symphony Orch 55 E State St Columbus OH 43215-4203 E-mail: susanr@columbussymphony.com.

ROSENTHAL, AMNON, pediatric cardiologist; b. Gedera, Israel, July 14, 1934; came to U.S., 1949, naturalized, 1959; s. Joseph and Rivka Rosenthal; m. Prudence Lloyd, July 22, 1962; children: Jonathan, Eben, Nathaniel. M.D., Albany Med. Coll., 1959. Intern Buffalo Children's Hosp., 1959-60; resident in pediatrics Children's Hosp. Med. Center, Boston, 1960-62, resident in pediatric cardiology, 1965-68; asso. prof. pediatrics Children's Hosp. Med. Center and Harvard U. Med. Sch., Boston, 1975-77; prof. pediatrics C.S. Mott Children's Hosp., U. Mich., Ann Arbor, 1977—, assoc. dir. dept. pediatrics, 1989-92, dir. pediatric cardiology, 1977-97. Served to capt. M.C. USAF, 1962-65. Amnon Rosenthal endowed professorship U. Mich., 1994. Mem. Am. Acad. Pediatrics, Soc. for Pediatric Rsch., Am. Pediatric Soc., Am. Heart Assn., Am. Coll. Cardiology, Am. Bd. Pediatrics, Am. Bd. Pediatric Cardiology (chmn. 1987-88). Office: CS Mott Childrens Hosp Ann Arbor MI 48109-0204 E-mail: amnonr@umich.edu.

ROSENTHAL, ARNOLD H. film director, producer, writer, graphic designer, calligrapher; b. Chgo., Jan. 31, 1933; s. Gus and Sara (Ariel) R.; children: Michel, Jason, Anthony. B.A., U. Ill., 1954. Graphic designer Whitaker-Guernsey Studios, Chgo., 1954-55; art dir. Edward H. Weiss Advt., 1956-60; owner Arnold H. Rosenthal & Assos., 1960-70; partner, creative dir., pres. Meyer & Rosenthal Inc. (mktg. communications), 1970-75; sr. v.p., creative dir. Garfield-Linn & Co. (Advt.), 1975-81; pres., exec. prodr./dir. Film Chgo., 1981—. TV comml. jury chmn. Chgo. Internat. Film Festival, 1977, 78, 79, 87, mem. governing bd., 1984—; represented at Moscow Film Fest, 1990; TV jury chmn. U.S. Festival, 1980; lectr. Columbia Coll., Purdue U., U. Ill., Ohio State U. Contbr. articles to profl. publs. Bd. dirs. Jewish United Fund. Served with AUS, 1955-56. Recipient creative awards Communication Clubs Chgo., N.Y.C., 1960—, Silver medal N.Y. Film Festival, 1986, Clio award, 1981. Mem. Soc. Typographic Arts (design awards 1958—, pres. 1971-72), Am. Inst. Graphic Arts (spl. award 1974), Dirs. Guild Am., Jazz Inst. Chgo. (charter, jazz drummer), Tau Epsilon Phi, Alpha Delta Sigma.

ROSENTHAL, IRA MAURICE, pediatrician, educator; b. N.Y.C., June 11, 1920; s. Abraham Leon and Jean (Kalotkin) R.; m. Ethel Ginsburg, Oct. 17, 1943 (dec.); children: Anne, Judith; m. Irene Farkis-Conn, Apr. 21, 2001. Student, CCNY, 1936-38; A.B., Ind. U., 1940, M.D., 1943. Intern Lincoln Hosp., N.Y.C., 1943-44; resident in pathology Albert Einstein Hosp., Phila., 1947-48; resident in pediatrics Fordham Hosp., N.Y.C., 1948-49; practice medicine specializing in pediatrics Bklyn., 1950-52; instr. U. Ill. Coll. Medicine, Chgo., 1953, asst. prof., 1953-55, assoc. prof., 1955-63, prof. pediatrics, 1963-90, prof. emeritus, 1990—, head dept., 1973-82; clin. prof. pediatrics Stritch Sch. Medicine Loyola U., Chgo., 1990-91, lectr., 1991-93; clin. assoc. in pediatrics U. Chgo., 1990-91, clin. prof. pediatrics, 1991—. Mem. med. service adv. com. Nat. Found. March of Dimes, 1975-80 Served to capt. U.S. Army, 1944-46. Mem. Am. Pediatric Soc., Soc. Pediatric Research, Acad. Pediatrics, Lawson Wilkins Pediatric Endocrine Soc., Endocrine Soc. Home: 5490 S South Shore Dr Chicago IL 60615-5984

ROSENTHAL, JOEL, manufacturing executive; b. Ft. Worth, Oct. 25, 1946; s. Melvin and Jane (Hertzman) R.; m. Susan Ellman, Nov. 15, 1970; children: Jackie Ilene, Harold Joseph. BBA, No. Tex. State U., 1969. V.p. First Street Corp., Ft. Worth, 1969-72; mgr. Edison Jewelers & Distbrs., 1972-73; v.p. Yankton Sioux Industries, Wagner, S.D., 1973-81, pres., 1981-85; cons., Canton, 1985—; pres. Ctrl. Plains Tractor Parts, Sioux Falls, 1986—. Cons. econ. devel. State of S.D., Pierre, 1985-86. Chmn. S.D. Rep. Com., 1995—; mem. Electoral Coll., 1996, 2000; pres. City Coun., Wagner, 1978-83; trustees, Carnegie Libr., Wagner, 1978-83; active Rep. Nat. Com., Washington, 1985—, S.D. Jud. Qualifications Commn., 1983-86, Pvt. Industry Coun., Pierre, 1985-86. Named S.D. Vol. of Yr. Office of Gov., 1983. Republican. Jewish. Home: PO Box 6 Canton SD 57013-0006 Office: PO Box 1818 Sioux Falls SD 57101-1818 Also: SD State Rep Party 401 E Sioux Ave Pierre SD 57501-3162

ROSENTHAL, LEIGHTON A. aviation company executive; b. Buffalo, Jan. 27, 1915; s. Samuel and Sadie (Dosberg) R.; m. Honey Rousuck, June 30, 1940; children: Cynthia, Jane. Student, Phila. Textile Sch.; grad. Wharton Sch., U. Pa.; hon. doctorate, Cleve. Coll. Jewish Studies, 1973. Pres. Cleve. Overall Co., 1956-61, Work Wear Corp., 1961-86, The Purity Uniform Service Inc., 1986-89, Lars Mgmt. div. Purity Uniform Service Inc., 1986-89, Lars Aviation Inc., 1990—. Chmn. Architecture Commn., City of Palm Beach, 1988-96. Trustee Jewish Cmty. Fedn. Cleve., Leighton A. Rosenthal Family Found.; bd. dirs. Ohio Motorists Assn. Fellow Am. Assn. Jewish Edn., Oakwood Club, Union Club, Poinciana Club, Marks Club, Annabels Club, Doubles Club, Harmonie Club. Office: Lars Aviation Inc The Halle Bldg 1228 Euclid Ave Ste 310 Cleveland OH 44115-1831

ROSENZWEIG, PEGGY A. state legislator; b. Detroit, Nov. 5, 1936; married; 5 children. BS, U. Wis., Milw., 1978; postgrad., Wayne State U. Wis. state assemblyman Dist. 98, 1982-92, Dist. 14, 1993; mem. Wis. Senate from 5th dist, Madison, 1993—. Former ranking minority mem. Health Com. Former dir. comty. rels. Milw. Regional Med. Ctr.; former pres. Med. Coll. Wis. Mem. LWV. Address: 6236 Upper Pkwy N Wauwatosa WI 53213-2430 Office: Wis State Senate State Capitol PO Box 7882 Madison WI 53707-7882

ROSENZWEIG, SAUL, psychologist, educator, administrator; b. Boston, Feb. 7, 1907; s. David and Etta (Tuttle) R.; m. Louise Ritterskamp, Mar. 21, 1941; children: Julia, Ann. A.B. summa cum laude, Harvard U., 1929, M.A., 1930, Ph.D., 1932. Research assoc. Harvard Psychol. Clinic, 1929-34, Worcester (Mass.) State Hosp., 1934-43; affiliate prof. Clark U., Worcester, 1938-43; chief psychologist Western State Psychiat. Ins. and Clinic, Pitts., 1943-48; lectr. psychology U. Pitts., 1943-48; assoc. prof. psychology and med. psychology Washington U., St. Louis, 1949-51, prof., 1951-75, prof. emeritus, 1975—; chief psychologist Child Guidance Clinic, 1949-59. Cons., mem. life scis. study sect. NIH, 1964-68; mng. dir. Found. for Idiodynamics and the Creative Process, 1972—; adj. prof. psychology St. Louis U., 1996—. Author: (with Kate L. Kogan) Psychodiagnosis, Grune and Stratton, 1949, Rosenzweig Picture-Frustration Study, 1948, Aggressive Behavior and the Rosenzweig Picture-Frustration Study, 1978, Freud and Experimental Psychology: The Emergence of Idiodynamics, 1986, Sally Beauchamp's Career, 1987, Freud, Jung, and Hall the King-Maker, 1992, 2d edit., 1994; assoc. editor: Jour. Abnormal and Social Psychology, 1950-56; cons. editor: Psychol. Monographs, 1948-57, Zeitschrift für Diagnostische Psychologie und Persönlichkeitsforschung, 1953-58, Diagnostica, 1959—; adv. editor: Jour. Cons. Psychology, 1959-64, Jour. Abnormal Psychology, 1965-67; mem. editorial bd. Aggressive Behavior, 1974—; contbr. articles to profl. jours. Fellow Am. Psychol. Assn. (rep. Internat. group for Coordination Psychiatry and Psychol. Methods 1955-61), Am. Psychopathol. Assn.; mem. Internat. Soc. for Research on Aggression (founding pres. 1972-73, archivist 1981-88), Soc. Prof. Emeriti Washington U. (founding pres. 1978), Sigma Xi, Phi Beta Kappa. Home: 8029 Washington Ave Saint Louis MO 63114-6333 Office: Washington U PO Box 1125 Saint Louis MO 63188-1125

ROSHOLT, ROBERT A. financial executive; b. Mar. 24, 1950; BA, St. Olaf Coll.; MBA, U. Rochester. Asst. v.p. Profit Planning Group First Chicago NBD Corp., Chgo., 1974-82, mem. Treasury Dept., 1982-87, head Treasury Dept., sr. v.p., 1987, CFO; exec. v.p. First Nat. Bank of Chgo., ADN Corp., Chgo. Office: ADN 123 N Wacker Dr Chicago IL 60606

ROSICA, GABRIEL ADAM, corporate executive, engineer; b. N.Y.C., Jan. 9, 1940; s. Gabriel J. and Elma (P.) R.; m. Bettina R. Nardozzi, Sept. 8, 1962; children: Gregory A., Julie Ann, Mark A. BA in Math. and Physics, Columbia U., 1962, BSEE, 1963; MSEE, Rensselaer Poly. Inst., 1966; MBA, Boston U., 1971. Registered profl. engr., Mass. Rsch. engr. United Aircraft Research Labs., East Hartford, Conn., 1963-67; mgr. electronic devel. The Foxboro (Mass.) Co., 1967-75, gen. mgr. U.S. div., 1975-77, v.p., 1977-80; pres., chief operating officer Modular Computer Systems, Inc., Ft. Lauderdale, Fla., 1980-82, pres., chmn., chief exec. officer, 1982-88; pvt. practice bus. cons. Boca Raton, 1988-91; sr. v.p. Elsag Bailey Corp., Pepper Pike, Ohio, 1991-92; exec. v.p. Bailey Controls Co., Wickliffe, 1993-94; COO Bailey Control Co., 1994-96; sr. v.p. Keithley Instruments, Solon, 1996-2001, exec. v.p., 2001—. Chmn. engring. adv. coun. U. Fla., Gainesville, 1987-90; chmn. hi tech adv. coun. Coll. Boca Raton, Fla., 1987-90. Mem. Pres.'s Coun. Fla. Atlantic U., Boca Raton, 1987-91; trustee Nova U., Ft. Lauderdale, Fla., 1987-94. Recipient Boston U. Chair, 1971, Outstanding Young Engr. of Year award Mass. Soc. Profl. Engrs., 1974. Mem. IEEE (sr. mem.), Am. Electronics Assn. (bd. dirs. 1987, chmn Fla. bd. dirs. 1987-88), Fla. High Tech. and Industry Coun. Home: 35640 Spicebush Ln Solon OH 44139-5063 Office: Keithley Instruments Inc 28775 Aurora Rd Solon OH 44139-1891 E-mail: gabe.rosica@att.net.

ROSIN, WALTER L. retired religious organization administrator; Sec. Luth. Ch.-Mo. Synod, St. Louis. Office: The Lutheran Ch-Missouri Synod 1333 S Kirkwood Rd Saint Louis MO 63122-7226

ROSKAM, JAN, aerospace engineer; b. The Hague, The Netherlands, Feb. 22, 1930; arrived in U.S., 1957; s. Kommer Jan and Agatha (Bosman) Roskam; m. Janice Louise Thomas-Barron, Dec. 21, 1994. MA in Aerospace Engring., Tech. U. Delft, 1954; PhD in Aeros. and Astronautics, U. Wash., 1965. Asst. chief designer Aviolanda Aircraft Co., Netherlands, 1954-57; sr. aerodynamics engr. Cessna Aircraft Co., Wichita, Kans., 1957-59; sr. group engr. Boeing Co., Wichita and Seattle, 1959-67; Ackers disting. prof. aerospace engring. U. Kans., Lawrence, 1967—; pres. Design, Analysis and Rsch. Corp., 1991—. Cons. to govt. and industry. Author: (book) Airplane Flight Dynamics and Automatic Flight Controls, 2 vols., 1979; co-author: Airplane Aerodynamics and Performance, 1981, Airplane Design, Part I-VIII, 1986. Fellow: AIAA, Soc. Automotive Engrs.; mem.: Exptl. Aircraft Assn., U.S. Chess Fedn., Koninklijk Instituut van Ingenieurs, Royal Aero. Soc., Am. Def. Preparedness Assn., Air Force Assn., Internat. Wildlife Assn., Aircraft Owners and Pilots Assn., Omicron Delta Kappa, Sigma Gamma Tau, Tau Beta Pi, Sigma Xi. Office: U Kans 2004 Lea Hl Lawrence KS 66045-0001 E-mail: roskam@ku.edn.

ROSKAM, PETER JAMES, state legislator, lawyer; b. Hinsdale, Ill., Sept. 13, 1961; s. Verlyn Ronald and Martha (Jacobsen) R.; m. Elizabeth Andrea Gracey, June 18, 1988; children: Gracey, James (dec.), Frances, Stephen, Alec. BA, U. Ill., 1983; JD, Ill. Inst. Tech., 1989. Bar: Ill. 1989. Tchr. All Saints Sch., St. Thomas, V.I., 1984-85; legis. asst. to Congressman Tom Delay U.S. Ho. of Reps., Washington, 1985-86, legal asst. to Congressman Henry Hyde, 1986-87; exec. dir. Ednl. Assistance Ltd., Glen Ellyn, Ill., 1987-93; ptnr. Salvi & Roskam, Wheaton, 1994—; mem. Ill. Gen. Assembly, Dist. 40, Springfield, 1993-98, Ill. Senate from dist. 20, 2001—. Legis. chmn. Ill. State Crime Commn. Republican. Mem. Evangelical Covenant Ch. Office: 213 W Wesley Ste 105 Wheaton IL 60187

ROSKENS, RONALD WILLIAM, international business consultant; b. Spencer, Iowa, Dec. 11, 1932; s. William E. and Delores A.L. (Beving) R.; m. Lois Grace Lister, Aug. 22, 1954; children: Elizabeth, Barbara, Brenda, William. BA, U. No. Iowa, 1953, MA, 1955, LHD (hon.), 1985; PhD, U. Iowa, 1958; LLD (hon.), Creighton U., 1978, Huston-Tillotson Coll., 1981, Midland Luth. Coll., 1984, Hastings Coll., 1981; LittD (hon.), Nebr. Wesleyan U., 1981; PhD (hon.), Ataturk U., Turkey, 1987; LHD (hon.), U. Akron, 1987; DSc (hon.), Jayewardenepura U., Sri Lanka, 1991; LHD (hon.), Am. Coll. of Greece, Athens, 1994. Lic. min. United Ch. of Christ (Congl. and E&R). Tchr. Minburn (Iowa) High Sch., 1954, Woodward (Iowa) State Hosp., summer 1954; asst. counselor to men State U. Iowa, 1956-59; dean of men, asst. prof. spl. edn. Kent (Ohio) State U., 1959-63, assoc. prof., then prof., 1963-72, asst. to pres., 1963-66, dean for adminstrn., 1968-71, exec. v.p., prof. ednl. adminstrn., 1971-72; chancellor, prof. ednl. adminstrn. U. Nebr., Omaha, 1972-76; pres. U. Nebr. System, 1977-89, pres. emeritus, 1989; hon. prof. East China Normal U., Shanghai, 1985; adminstr. USAID, Washington, 1990-92; pres. Action Internat., Inc., Omaha, 1993-96, Global Connections, Inc., Omaha, 1996—. Interim exec. officer Omaha Pub. Libr., 1996-98; mem. Bus.-Higher Edn. Forum, 1979-89, exec. com., 1984-87; mem. govtl. relations com. Am. Council Edn., 1979-83, bd. dirs., 1981-86, vice chair, 1983-84, chair, 1984-85; chmn. com. on financing higher edn. Nat. Assn. State Univs. and Land Grant Colls., 1978-83, vice chmn. com. on financing higher edn., 1983-84, chmn. com. on fed. student fin. assistance, 1981-87; mem. nat. adv. com. on accreditation and instl. eligibility U.S. Dept. Edn., 1983-86, chmn., bd. dirs., 1986; exec. bd. North Cen. Assn., 1979-84, chmn. exec. bd., 1982-84, pres., 1989-90; active Environ. Ams. Bd., 1991-92, Strategic Command Consultation Commn., 1993-96, Nat. Exec. Res. Corps, Fed. Office Emergency Preparedness, 1968-88; chmn. Omaha/Douglas Pub. Bldg. Commn., 1996—. Co-editor: Paradox, Process and Progress, 1968; contbr. articles profl. jours. Mem. Kent City Planning Commn., 1962-66; bd. dirs. United Ch. of Christ Bd. Homeland Ministries, 1968-74, Met. YMCA, Omaha, 1973-77, Mid-Am. council Boy Scouts Am., 1973-77, Midlands United Community Services, 1972-77, NCCJ, 1974-77, Omaha Rotary Club, 1974-77, Found. Study Presdl. and Congl. Terms, 1977-89, First Plymouth Congl. Ch., 1989-90, Midland Luth. Coll., 1993—, Coun. Aid to Edn., 1985-89, ConAgra, Inc., 1993—, Russian Farm Cmty. Project, Capitol Fed. Found., Topeka, Kans., 1999—; trustee Huston Tillotson Coll., Austin, Tex., 1968-81, chmn., 1976-78, Joslyn Art Mus., 1973-77, Nebr. Meth. Hosp., 1974-77, 1st Ctrl. Congregational Ch., Brownell-Talbott Sch., 1974-77, Harry S. Truman Inst., 1977-89, Willa Cather Pioneer Meml. and Ednl. Found., 1979-87; pres. Kent Area C. of C., 1966; mem. Met. Commn. Coll. Found., 1993-96. Decorated comdr.'s cross Order of Merit (Germany); recipient Disting. Svc. award for community svc., Kent, Ohio, 1967, Brotherhood award NCCJ, 1977, Americanism citation B'nai B'rith, 1978, Legion of Honor, Order of DeMolay, 1980, gold medal Nat. Interfrat. Coun., 1987, Agri award Triumph Agr. Expn., Omaha, 1989; named Nat. 4-H Alumnus, 1967, Outstanding Alumnus, U. No. Iowa, 1974, Midlander of Yr., Omaha World Herald, 1977, King Ak-Sar-Ben LXXXVI, 1980; named to DeMolay Hall of Fame, 1993; named Hon. Consul Gen. of Japan, 1999. Mem. AAAS, APA, AAUP, Am. Coll. Pers. Assn., Assn. Urban Univs. (pres. 1976-77), Am. Ednl. Rsch. Assn., Coun. on Fgn. Rels., Chief Execs. Orgn., Young Pres. Orgn., Scottish Rite (bd. dirs. Omaha coun. 1999—), Lincoln C. of C. (bd. dirs. 1989-90), Masons (33 deg.), Rotary (bd. dirs. Omaha 1974-77), Phi Delta Kappa, Phi Eta Sigma, Sigma Tau Gamma (pres. grand coun. 1968-70, Disting. Achievement award 1980, Disting. scholar 1981), Omicron Delta Kappa (nat. pres. 1986-90, Found. pres. 1986-96). Home: 10849 N 58th Plz Omaha NE 68152

ROSNER, JONATHAN LINCOLN, physicist, educator; b. N.Y.C., July 23, 1941; s. Albert Aaron and Elsie Augustine (Lincoln) R.; m. Joy Elaine Fox, June 13, 1965; children: Hannah, Benjamin. BA, Swarthmore Coll., 1962; MA, Princeton U., 1963, PhD, 1965. Research asst. prof. U. Wash., Seattle, 1965-67; vis. lectr. Tel Aviv U., Ramat Aviv, Israel, 1967-69; asst. prof. physics U. Minn., Mpls., 1969-71, assoc. prof., 1971-75, prof., 1975-82, U. Chgo., 1982—. Contbr. numerous articles to profl. and scholarly jours. Alfred P. Sloan fellow, 1971-73, Guggenheim fellow, 2002. Fellow Am. Phys. Soc. Democrat. Jewish. Avocations: fishing, hiking, skiing, amateur radio. Office: U Chgo Enrico Fermi Inst 5640 S Ellis Ave Chicago IL 60637-1433

ROSNER, ROBERT, astrophysicist, educator; b. Garmisch-Partenkirchen, Bavaria, Germany, June 26, 1947; came to U.S., 1959; s. Heinz and Faina (Brodsky) R.; m. Marsha Ellen Rich, Nov. 8, 1950; children: Daniela Karin, Nicole Elise. BA, Brandeis U., 1969; PhD, Harvard U., 1976. Asst. prof. Harvard U., Cambridge, Mass., 1978-83, assoc. prof., 1983-86; astrophysicist Smithsonian Astrophys. Observatory, 1986-87; prof. U. Chgo., 1987—, William E. Wrather prof., 1998—; chief scientist Argonne Nat. Lab., 2002—. Trustee Adler Planetarium, Chgo., 1989-98, chmn. dept. astronomy and astrophysics, 1991-97. Contbr. more than 150 articles to profl. jours. Woodrow Wilson fellow, 1969. Fellow Am. Phys. Soc.; mem. Am. Acad. Arts & Scis., Am. Astron. Soc., Soc. Indsl. and Applied Math., Am. Geophys. Union. Home: 4950 S Greenwood Ave Chicago IL 60615-2816 Office: U Chicago Astrophysics 5640 S Ellis Ave Chicago IL 60637-1433 E-mail: r-rosner@uchicago.edu.

ROSOWSKI, ROBERT BERNARD, manufacturing company executive; b. Detroit, July 23, 1940; s. Bernard and Anna (Maciag) R.; m. Kathleen Patricia Bates, Aug. 26, 1961; children: John, Paul, Mary, Judith. BS, U. Detroit, 1962; MBA, Mich. State U., 1974. CPA, Mich. Auditor, staff supr. Coopers and Lybrand, Detroit, 1962-71; fin. analyst Masco Corp., Taylor, Mich., 1971-73, controller, 1973-85, v.p., controller, 1985-96, v.p., controller and treas., 1996—. Bd. dirs. Acctg. Aid Soc. Met. Detroit, 1987—, Detroit Cath. Ctrl. H.S., 1999—; chmn. Oakwood Hosp. Found., 1990—; trustee Oakwood Healthcare System, 1997—. Mem. Am. Inst. CPA's, Mich. Assn. CPA's, Fin. Execs. Inst., Detroit Cath. Ctrl. Alumni Assn. (pres. 1999—). Avocations: golf, fishing, boating, photography. Office: Masco Corp 21001 Van Born Rd Taylor MI 48180-1300

ROSS, CARSON, state legislator; b. Warren, Ark., Dec. 15, 1946; m. Eloise E. Ross; children: Shelely, Carla, Diane. BS, BA, Rockhurst Coll., 1977. Mem. Mo. State Ho. of Reps. Dist. 55, 1988—, former minority whip, former mem. various coms. With Corp. Diversity, Hallmark Cards. Recipient Black Achievement in Industry award SCLC, 1985, Spirit of Enterprise award Chamber, 1991. Home: 3305 SW Park Ln Blue Springs MO 64015-7146 Office: Mo Ho of Reps State Capitol Jefferson City MO 65101

ROSS, DANIEL J.J. publishing executive; b. Albany, N.Y., June 2, 1943; AB, Hamilton Coll., 1966; MA, U. Fla., 1969. Prodn. mgr. U. Fla. Press, 1976-80; mktg. mgr. U. Ala. Press, 1980-85; asst. dir. Duke U. Press, 1985-89; editor-in-chief U. Nebr. Press, Lincoln, 1989-95, dir., 1995—. Office: 233 N 8th St Lincoln NE 68508-1305

ROSS, DEBRA BENITA, jewelry designer, marketing executive; b. Carbondale, Ill., May 1, 1956; d. Bernard Harris and Marian (Frager) R. BS, U. Ill., 1978; MS, U. Wis., 1979. Dir. mktg. Ambion Devel., Inc., Northbrook, Ill., 1983-89, Fitness Horizons, Inc., Northbrook, 1989-91, v.p. mktg., 1991-97; owner Benita Ross Designs, 1992—. Home: 1853 Mission Hills Ln Northbrook IL 60062-5760

ROSS, DONALD, JR. English language educator, university administrator; b. N.Y.C., Oct. 18, 1941; s. Donald and Lea (Meyer) R.; m. Sylvia Berger (div.); 1 child, Jessica; m. 2d, Diane Redfern, Aug. 27, 1971; children— Owen, Gillian BA, Lehigh U., 1963, MA, 1964; PhD, U. Mich., 1967. Asst. prof. English U. Pa., Phila., 1967—70; prof. English U. Minn., Mpls., 1970—, dir. composition program, 1982—86, dir. Univ. Coll., 1984—89. Author: American History and Culture from the Explorers to Cable TV, 2000; co-author: Word Processor and Writing Process, 1984, Revising Mythologies: The Composition of Thoreau's Major Works, 1988; co-editor, contbr.: American Travel Writers, 1776-1865, 1997, American Travel Writers, 1850-1915, 1998; contbr. articles to profl. jours. Grantee Am. Coun. Learned Socs., 1976, 90, NSF, 1974, Fund for Improvement of Postsecondary Edn., 1982-85; recipient Disting. Teaching award U. Minn., 1992. Mem. MLA, Assn. for Computers and Humanities (exec. sec. 1978-88). Office: U Minn Dept English 207 Lind Hall 207 Church St SE Minneapolis MN 55455-0152 E-mail: rossj001@umn.edu.

ROSS, DONALD ROE, federal judge; b. Orleans, Nebr., June 8, 1922; s. Roe M. and Leila H. (Reed) Ross; m. Janice S. Cook, Aug. 29, 1943; children: Susan Jane, Sharon Kay, Rebecca Lynn, Joan Christine, Donald Dean. JD, U. Nebr., 1948, LLD (hon.), 1990. Bar: Nebr. 1948. Practice law, Lexington, Nebr., 1948—53; mayor City of Lexington, 1953; assoc. Swarr, May, Royce, Smith, Andersen & Ross, 1956—70; U.S. atty. Dist. Nebr., 1953—56; gen. counsel Rep. party, Nebr., 1956—58; mem. Rep. Exec. Com. for Nebr., 1952—53; com. mem. Rep. Nat. Com., 1958—70, vice-chmn., 1965—70; sr. judge U.S. Ct. Appeals (8th cir.), 1971—.

ROSS, FRANK HOWARD, III, management consultant; b. Charlotte, N.C., Aug. 28, 1946; s. Frank Howard Jr. (dec.) and Alma (Richardson) R. (dec.); m. Beverly Hazel Ross, June 30, 1973 (dec.); children: Martha McCausland, Frank Howard IV. BS in Engring., N.C. State U., 1968. Cons. Fails & Assocs., Inc., Raleigh, N.C., 1968-73; ptnr. Ross-Payne & Assocs., Inc., Barrington, Ill., 1973—. Bd. dirs. Gilldorn Savs., Chgo., 1982-85, Brickman Industries, Inc., Chgo., 1980-90; CFO WRT, Inc., Chgo., 1993-95; pres., chmn. bd. dirs. Emerald Capital Investments, Inc., Barrington, 1993-97; adviser, spkr. on constrn. and fin.; bd. dirs. Sherman Plumbing, 1975-95. Author: More $ Through $ Management, 1975, MIS and You, 1978, Planning and Budgeting, 1979, Profit by Design, 1981, Pricing for Profit, 1983, Wealthbuilding, 1984, Equipment Cost Analysis, 1988, Survivial in a Tight Economy, 1988, Associated Landscape Contractors of America Operating Cost Survey, 1989, 91, Cash Flow, 1989, Dealing with the Competition of the 90's, 1990, Designing Your Accounting System, 1991, Bidding in a Tight Market, 1992, Industry's Wage and Benefit Study, 1992, Financing Your Business, 1993, Pricing, 1994, 2d edit., 1997, How Low Can You Go?, 1995, Valuing Your Business, 1998, Posturing for Growth and Prosperity, 1999. Mem. Presbyn. Ch. Barrington. Mem. Inst. Mgmt. Cons., Barrington Hills Country Club, Haig Point Country Club, Sigma Alpha Epsilon. Home and Office: Ross Payne Assocs Inc 536 Eton Dr Barrington IL 60010-2017

ROSS, LORI, radio personality; b. Delta, Ohio, May 14; Radio host Sta. WMBI-AM, Chgo. Avocations: photography, being outside, travel. Office: WMBI 820 LaSalle Blvd Chicago IL 60610*

ROSS, MONTE, electrical engineer, researcher; b. Chgo., May 26, 1932; s. Jacob Henry and Mildred Amelia (Feller) R.; m. Harriet Jean Katz, Feb. 10, 1957; children— Karyn, Dianne, Ethan B.S. in Elec. Engring., U. Ill., 1953; M.S., Northwestern U., 1962. Devel. engr. Chance Vought, Dallas, 1953-54; sr. electronics engr. Motorola, Chgo., 1955-56, project engr., 1957-59, assoc. dir. rsch., 1960-63; dir. rsch. Hallicrafters Co., Chgo., 1964-65; mgr. laser tech. McDonnell Douglas Astronautics Co., St. Louis, 1966-70, dir. laser comms.; program mgr. Laser Space Comms., 1971-87; pres. Ultradata Sys., Inc. (formerly Laser Data Tech.), St. Louis, 1987—. Mem. alumni bd. dept. elec. and computer engring. U. Ill., 1985-90; guest lectr. various univs.; cons. NSF. Author: Laser Receivers, 1966; tech. editor Laser Applications Series, vol. 1, 1971, vol. 2, 1974, vol. 3, 1977, vol. 4, 1980; patentee in field. Chmn. Laser Mus. and Space Signal Obs., 1997—. Recipient St. Louis High Tech. Entrepreneur of Yr. award, 1995; McDonnell Douglas Corp. fellow, 1985. Fellow IEEE; mem. Internat. Laser Comms. Soc. (pres. 1988-89), Sigma Xi. Home: 19 Beaver Dr Saint Louis MO 63141-7901 Office: Ultradata Sys Inc 1240 Dielman Ind Ct Saint Louis MO 63132-2212 E-mail: mross@ultradatasystems.com.

ROSS, RICHARD F. dean; DVM, Iowa State U., 1959, MS, 1960, PhD, 1965. Diplomate Am. Coll. Vet. Microbiologists. Postdoctoral fellow Pub. Health Svc., Rocky Mountain Lab., NIAID, Hamilton, Mont., 1965-66; prof. in charge Vet. Medicine Rsch. Inst. Iowa State U., 1985-92, assoc. dean for rsch. Coll. Vet. Medicine, 1990-92, interim dean Coll. Vet. Medicine, 1992-93, dean Coll. Vet. Medicine, 1993—; interim dean Coll. Agr. Iowa State U., Mont., 2000—; dean Coll. Agr., 2000—. Past pres. Internat. Orgn. for Mycoplasmology, Internat. Rsch. Program for Comparative Mycoplasmology, Conf. Rsch. Workers in Animal Disease; mem. panel bd. on agr. com. on CSRS animal health rsch. programs NRC; mem. edn. and econs. adv. bd. Sec. Agr. Nat. Agrl. Rsch. Ext.; mem. Sec. Agr. Strategic Planning Task Force on USDA Rsch. Facilities, 1996-99; mem. joint steering com. AVMA/AAHA/AAVMC, 1996-99; mem. Nat. Pork Prodrs. Rsch. Com.; reviewer CSRS Program Revs., Cooperative State Rsch. Svc. Spl. Grants Rev. Panel. Contbr. articles to profl. jours. Recipient Beecham award for rsch. excellence, 1985, Howard Dunne Meml. award Am. Assn. Swine Practitioners, 1988, Am. Vet. Medicine Assn. award for rsch. Am. Feed Mfrs. Assn., 1995, U.S. Sec. Agrl. award for personal and profl. excellence, 1996, Pres. award Iowa Vet. Med. Assn., Faculty citation Iowa State U. Alumni Assn.; named hon. master pork prodr. Iowa Pork Prodrs. Assn., Sr. U.S. scientist Alexander von Humboldt Found., Germany. Fellow Am. Acad. Microbiology; mem. Assn. Am. Vet. Med. Colls. (sec., pres.-elect, pres. 1997-98, past pres.). Achievements include research on mycoplasmal pneumonia of swine, including efforts to develop better serodiagnostic tests, to develop vaccines, and to evaluate chemotherapeutic agents for control of the disease. Office: Iowa State U Coll Vet Medicine 2508 Vet Med Ames IA 50011-1050 Fax: 515-294-6800. E-mail: rfross@iastate.edu.

ROSS, RICHARD FRANCIS, veterinarian, microbiologist, educator, dean; b. Washington, Apr. 30, 1935; s. Milton Edward and Olive Marie (Berggren) R.; m. Karen Mae Paulsen, Sept. 1, 1957; children: Scott, Susan D.V.M., Iowa State U., 1959, M.S., 1961, Ph.D., 1965. Oper. mgr. Vet. Lab. Inc., Remsen, Iowa, 1961—62; rsch. assoc. Iowa State U., Ames, 1959—61, asst. prof., 1962—65, assoc. prof., 1966—72, prof., 1972—, assoc. dir., assoc. dean Coll. Vet. Medicine, 1990—92, interim dean, 1992—93, dean Coll. Vet. Medicine, 1993—2000; interim dean, dean Coll. Agr., dir. Agrl. Expt. Sta. Rocky Mountain Lab., NIAID, Hamilton, 2000—02, postdoctoral fellow Mont., 1965—66. Sr. U.S. scientist Alexander von Humboldt Found., Bonn, Fed. Republic Germany, 1975-76; chmn. Internat. Research Program on Comparative Mycoplasmology, 1982-86; pres. Iowa State U. Research Found., Ames, 1984-86; Howard Dunne meml. lectr. Am. Assn. Swine Practitioners, 1984; mem. adv. bd. Sec. Agr., 1996—, mem. strategic planning task force USDA, 1997-99, mem. safegarding task force, 2001-2002. Contbr. numerous articles to profl. publs., 1963— Named Disting. Prof., Iowa State U., 1982, Hon. Master Pork Producer, Iowa Pork Producers Assn., 1985; recipient faculty citation Iowa State U. Alumni Assn., 1984, Beecham award for rsch. excellence, 1985, Howard Dunne Meml. award Am. Assn. Swine Practitioners, 1988, Am. Feed Mfg. award for rsch., 1995, Sec. of Agr. award for personal and profl. accomplishment, 1996, Gamma Sigma Delta Merit award for disting. achievement in agr. 2002. Mem. Am. Coll. Vet. Microbiologists (diplomate, vice chmn. 1974-75, sec.-treas. 1977-83), Am. Soc. Microbiology (chmn. div. 1985-86), Internat. Orgn. Mycoplasmology (chair 1990-92, Bd. Dirs. award 2002), AVMA, AAAS, Osborn Research Club, Conf. Rsch. Workers in Animal Diseases (coun. mem., pres. 1992), Assn. Am. Vet. Med. Colls. (pres. 1997-98). Republican. Lutheran Avocations: fishing, gardening, walking, reading. Home: 4022 Stone Brooke Rd Ames IA 50010-2900 Office: Iowa State U Coll Vet Medicine Ames IA 50011-0001

ROSS, RICHARD LEE, lawyer; b. Columbus, Ohio, Sept. 23, 1951; s. Richard Earl and Dorothy Mae (Fitch) R.; m. Diana E. Gifford, Aug. 17, 1974; children: Rebecca, Jeremiah. B.S., Centre Coll., 1973; J.D., Capital U., 1976. Bar: Ohio, U.S. Tax Ct., U.S. Supreme Ct., U.S. Dist. Ct. (so. dist.) Ohio. Law librarian Morgan County, McConnelsville, Ohio, 1977-80;

solicitor Stockport, Ohio, 1977-80; pros. atty. Morgan County, 1981—. Chmn. various Rep. coms. Mem. Ohio Pros. Attys. Assn., Morgan County Bar Assn., Nat. Dist. Attys. Assn., Nat. Sch. Attys. Assn., Rotary, Kiwanis (sec. 1977-79). Mem. Ch. of Christ. Avocations: golf, reading. Home: 1800 N Pleasant Valley Rd NW Malta OH 43758-9646 Office: 109 E Main St Mc Connelsville OH 43756-1125

ROSS, ROBERT EVAN, bank executive; b. Alliance, Ohio, Sept. 22, 1947; s. James Jacob Ross and Eva Mae (Forsha) Bodo; m. Susan Margaret Burd, June 20, 1970; children: Margaret Mae, James William. BBA, Kent State U., 1970; MBA, U. Chgo., 1977. Advisor to fraternities, dean of men's office Kent (Ohio) State U., 1970-71; trainee, supr. of trainees Northern Trust Co., Chgo., 1971-73, jr. analyst, 1973-74, trust rep., 1974-77, trust officer, 1977-81, v.p., div. head for personal fin. planning, 1981-85; portfolio mgr., investment rep. Morgan Stanley, 1985-89; pres. Northern Trust Bank in Winnetka, 1989-92; exec. v.p. Northern Trust Bank/Lake Forest, 1992-95, vice chmn., 1995-97, pres., CEO, 1997—; pres., CEO Northern Trust Bank-Ohio , 2001—. Bd. dirs. No. Trust Bank, Lake Forest, O'Hare, Ill., DuPage, Ill. Bd. dirs. The Camerata Singers of Lake Forest, Lake Forest Symphony, 1992—, Ragdale Found., 1999-2000; bd. govs. Ill. St. Andrew Soc., 1998—; suburban chair United Way North Region, 1993—; mem. centennial commn. on identity, values and comm. Kent State U., 1998; trustee DePaul U., Chgo., Barat Coll. Edn. Found. Avocations: sports, reading, stock market, painting. Office: No Trust Bank Lake Forest Deerpath And Bank Ln Lake Forest IL 60045

ROSS, ROBERT JOSEPH, retired professional football coach; b. Richmond, Va., Dec. 23, 1935; s. Leonard Aloysius and Martha Isabelle (MMiller) R.; m. Alice Louise Bucker, June 13, 1959; children: Chris, Mary Catherine, Teresa, Kevin, Robbie. BA, Va. Mil. Inst., 1959. Tchr., head football coach Benedictine High Sch., Richmond, 1959-60; tchr., coach Colonial Heights (Va.) High Sch., 1962-65; asst. football coach Va. Mil. Inst., Lexington, 1965-67, Coll. William and Mary, Williamsburg, Va., 1967-71, Rice U., Houston, 1971-72, U. Md., College Park, 1972-73; head football coach The Citadel, Charleston, S.C., 1973-77; head coach U. Md., College Park, 1982-87; head football coach Ga. Inst. Tech., Atlanta, 1987-91; asst. coach Kansas City (Mo.) Chiefs, 1978-82; head coach San Diego Chargers, 1992-96, Detroit Lions, 1997-2001. 1st lt. U.S. Army, 1960-62. Named Coach of Yr., Washington Touchdown Club, 1982, Kodak Coach of Yr., 1990, Bobby Dodd Coach of Yr., 1990, Bear Bryant Coach of Yr., 1990, Scripps-Howard Coach of Yr., 1990, Nat. Coach of Yr., CBS Sports, 1990, Coach of Yr., Walter Camp Football Found., 1990, NFL Coach of Yr. UPI, 1992, Pro Football Weekly, 1992, Pro Football Writers' Assn., 1992, Football News, 1992, Football Digest, 1992, Maxwell Football Club, 1992, AFC Coach of Yr. Kansas City 101 Banquet. Mem. Am. Football Coaches Assn., Coll. Football Assn. (coaching com. 1988-92). Roman Catholic.

ROSS, ROBERT THOMAS, neurologist, educator; b. Winnipeg, Man., Can., June 25, 1924; s. John L. and Alberta I. (Gray) R.; m. Margot Joan Ellacott, May 27, 1950; children: Gray T., John L., Mary E.; m. Angela Morrow Brady, Aug. 14, 1970; children: Diana Gray Salter, Drew Garland Salter. MD, U. Manitoba, 1948. Intern Winnipeg Gen. Hosp., 1947-50; resident Nat. Hosp. Queen Sq., London, 1950-52; lectr. dept anatomy U. Manitoba, Winnipeg, 1953-55, asst. prof. dept. medicine, 1955-59, assoc. prof., 1959-77, prof. medicine, 1977-2000, head sect. neurology, 1971-84, emeritus prof. medicine, 2000—. Editor., pub., founder: Can. Jour. Neurol. Scis., 1972-81; author: How to Examine the Nervous System, 3d edit., 1998; Syringobulbia-A Contribution to the Pathophysiology of the Brain Stem, 1986, Syncope, 1988. Trustee Man. Med. Svc., 1958-64; pres. United Health Found., Winnipeg, 1969-71; bd. dirs. Man. Med. Coll. Found., 1983-85, Winnipeg Libr. Found.; mem. senate U. Manitoba, 1988-99; bd. trustees Nat. Gallery of Can.; bd. govs. The Winnipeg Art Gallery, Manitoba Chamber Orch. Recipient E.L. Drewry prize E.L. Drewry Found., 1948; recipient Can. Centennial Medal, 1967, Queen Elizabeth Jubilee Medal, 1977. Fellow Royal Coll. Physicians (Can. and London), Am. Acad. Neurology; mem. Can. Neurol. Soc. (pres. 1971), Coll. Physicians and Surgeons of Man (pres. 1971), Am. Neurol. Assn., Order of Can. Baptist. Home: 312 Park Blvd Winnipeg MB Canada R3P OG7

ROSSER, RICHARD FRANKLIN, higher education consultant; b. Arcanum, Ohio, July 16, 1929; s. Harold Arm and Margaret (Whitacre) R.; m. Donna Eyssen., Mar. 21, 1951; children— Eric, Carl, Edward. B.A., Ohio Wesleyan U., 1951; M.P.A., Syracuse U., 1952, Ph.D., 1961. Joined U.S. Air Force, 1952, advanced through grades to col., 1968; prof. polit. sci. U.S. Air Force Acad., Colorado Springs, Colo., 1959-73, head dept., 1967-73, ret., 1973; prof. polit. sci., dean Albion (Mich.) Coll., 1973-77; pres. DePauw U., Greencastle, Ind., 1977-86, chancellor, 1986; pres. Nat. Assn. Ind. Colls. and Univs., Washington, 1986-93; cons. in higher edn. pvt. practice, Racine, Wis., 1993—. Author: An Introduction to Soviet Foreign Policy, 1969; Contbr. articles to profl. jours. Mem. univ. senate United Meth. Ch., 1980-84; mem. spl. commn. of Chief of Staff on Honor Code U.S. Mil. Acad., 1989; bd. visitors Air U., 1991-94; bd. trustees Ohio Wesleyan U., 1991—; mem. nat. adv. com. Instnl. Quality and Integrity, 1994—; co-chair Citizens for Librs., Grand Traverse County, 1995-96. Decorated Legion of Merit with oak leaf cluster. Mem. Phi Beta Kappa, Omicron Delta Kappa. Presbyterian. Home and Office: 31 Sumac Dr Brunswick ME 04011

ROSSI, ANTHONY GERALD, lawyer; b. Warren, Ohio, July 20, 1935; s. Anthony Gerald and Lena (Guarnieri) R.; m. Marilyn J. Fuller, June 22, 1957; children: Diana L., Maribeth, Anthony Gerald III. BS, John Carroll U., 1957; JD, Cath. U. Am., 1961. Bar: Ohio 1961. Ptnr. Guarnieri & Secrest, Warren, 1961—; former acting judge Warren Municipal Ct. Mem. Mahoning-Shenango Estate Planning Coun., 1968—, past sec.; past pres. Warren Olympic Club; past bd. govs. Cath. U. Am. Law Sch. Coun.; past trustee Trumbull Art Guild, Warren Civic Music Assn. Capt. Transp. Corps, AUS, 1957-65. Mem. ABA, Ohio Bar Assn., Trumbull County Bar Assn. (exec. com. 1975—, pres. 1976-77), Am. Arbitration Assn., Ohio State Bar Found., Ohio Motorist Assn. (corp. mem., trustee 1980-86, 92-98), Wolf's Club, KC, Elks, Ohio Acad. of Trial Lawyers. Home: 2500 Hidden Lakes Dr NE Warren OH 44484-4159 Office: 151 E Market St Warren OH 44481-1102

ROSSING, THOMAS D. physics educator; b. Madison, S.D., Mar. 27, 1929; s. Torstein H. and Luella E. Rossing; children: Karen, Barbara, Erik, Jane, Mary. BA, Luther Coll., 1950; MS, Iowa State U., 1952, PhD, 1954. Rsch. physicist Univac div. Sperry Rand, 1954-57; prof. physics St. Olaf Coll., 1957-71, chmn. physics dept., 1963-69; prof. physics No. Ill. U., DeKalb, 1971—, disting. rsch. prof., chmn. dept., 1971-73. Rschr. Microwave Lab., Stanford (Calif.) U., 1961-62, Lincoln Lab., MIT, Cambridge, Mass., summer 1963, Clarendon Lab., Oxford (Eng.) U., 1966-67, physics dept. MIT, 1976-77; rsch. assoc. Argonne (Ill.) Nat Lab., 1974-76, scientist-in-residence, 1990—; vis. lectr. U. New Eng., Armidale, Australia, 1980-81; vis. exch. scholar to China, 1988; guest rschr. Royal Inst. Tech., Stockholm, 1983, 84, 85, Inst. Perception Rsch., Eindhoven, The Netherlands, 1984, 85, Physikalisch-Technische Bundesanstalt, Braunschweig, Germany, 1988-89; guest rschr. Ecole Nat. Superiéure des Telecomm., Paris, 1996, Luleå U. Tech., Sweden, 1996, U. Calif., San Diego, 1998, Fraunhofer Inst., Stuttgart, Germany, 1998. Author 12 books in field; contbr. more than 300 articles to profl. publs. Recipient Robert Millikan medal, 2000. Fellow AAAS, Am. Phys. Soc., Acoustical Soc. Am. (Silver medal in mus. acoustics 1992), Acoustical Soc. India (hon.); mem. IEEE, Am. Assn. Physics Tchrs. (pres. 1991, Robert A. Milliken medal 2000), Catgut Acoustical Soc., Sigma Xi (nat. lectr. 1984-87), Sigma Pi Sigma. Achievements include research in musical acoustics, psychoacoustics, speech and singing, vibration analysis, magnetic levitation, environmental noise conrol, surface effects in fusion reactors, spin waves in metals, physics education; 9 U.S. and 11 foreign patents in field. Office: No Ill U Physics Dept Dekalb IL 60115

ROSSITER, ROBERT E. interior auto parts manufacturing executive; b. 1946; With Lear Siegler Inc., 1971-87, former pres. seating div.; pres., chief oper. officer Lear Seating Corp., Southfield, Mich., 1987-2000, also bd. dirs.; CEO, pres. Lear Corp., MI, 2000—. Office: Lear Seating Corp 21557 Telegraph Rd Southfield MI 48034

ROSSMANN, JACK EUGENE, psychology educator; b. Walnut, Iowa, Dec. 4, 1936; s. Wilbert C. Rossmann and Claire L. (Mickel) Walter; m. Marilyn Martin, June 14, 1958; children: Ann, Charles, Sarah. BS, Iowa State U., 1958, MS, 1960; PhD, U. Minn., 1963. Lic. psychologist, Minn. Asst. prof. Macalester Coll., St. Paul, 1964-68, assoc. prof., 1968-73, prof., 1973—, v.p. acad. affairs, 1978-86, chair dept. psychology, 1990-2000. Cons. Pers. Decisions Internat., Mpls., 1989—2000, Bush Found., 1993—; cons.-evaluator North Ctrl. Assn., 1975—. Author: (with others) Open Admissions at CUNY, 1975; contbr. articles to profl. jours. Bd. dirs. Twin City Inst. for Talented Youth, St. Paul, 1978-91; trustee United Theol. Sem., New Brighton, Minn., 1984-96. 2d lt. U.S. Army, 1959. Mem.: AAUP (pres. Minn. conf. 1993—95), APA, Minn. Psychol. Assn. (treas. 2001, pres.-elect 2002), Am. Assn. Higher Edn., Assn. Instl. Rsch., Am. Psychol. Soc. Home: 99 Cambridge St Saint Paul MN 55105-1947 Office: Macalester Coll 1600 Grand Ave Saint Paul MN 55105-1801 E-mail: rossmann@macalester.edu.

ROSSMANN, MICHAEL GEORGE, biochemist, educator; b. Frankfurt, Germany, July 30, 1930; s. Alexander and Nelly (Schwabacher) R.; m. Audrey Pearson, July 24, 1954; children— Martin, Alice, Heather. BSC with honors, Polytechnic, London, 1951, MSc in Physics, 1953; PhD in Chemistry, U. Glasgow, 1956; PhD (hon.) , U. Uppsala (Sweden), 1983, U. Strasbourg (France), 1984, Vrije U. Brussel, 1990, U. Glasgow (Scotland), 1993, U. York (England), 1994, U. Quebec (Can.), 1998. Fulbright scholar U. Minn., 1956-58; research scientist MRC Lab. Molecular Biology, Cambridge, Eng., 1958-64; asso. prof. biol. scis. Purdue U., West Lafayette, Ind., 1964-67, prof., 1967-78, Hanley Disting. prof. biol. scis., 1978—, prof. biochemistry, 1975—. Editor: The Molecular Replacement Method, 1972; contbr. more than 390 articles to profl. jours. Grantee NIH, NSF; recipient Fankuchen award Am. Crystallographc Assn., 1986, Horwitz prize Columbia U., 1990, Gregori Arminoff prize Royal Swedish Acad. Sci., 1994, Stein & Moore award Protein Soc., 1994, Ewald prize Internat. Union Crystallography, 1996, Cole award Biophysical Soc., 1998, Elion award Internat. Soc. for Antiviral Rsch., 2000, Ehrlich and Darmstaedter prize Paul Erhlich-Fedn., 2001. Mem. Am. Soc. Biol. Chemists, Am. Chem. Soc., Biophys. Soc. (Cole award 1998), Am. Crystallographic Assn. (Fankuchen award 1986), Brit. Biophys. Soc., Inst. Physics., Chem. Soc. (U.K.), AAAS, NAS, Indian Nat. Sci. Acad., Royal Soc., Nat. Sci. Bd., Lafayette Sailing Club. Democrat. Home: 1208 Wiley Dr West Lafayette IN 47906-2434 Office: Dept Biol Scis Purdue Univ West Lafayette IN 47907-1392 E-mail: mgr@indiana.bio.purdue.edu.

ROSSO, JEAN-PIERRE, electronics executive; b. Aix-les Bains, Savoie, France, July 11, 1940; Diploma in Civil Engring., Ecole Polytechnique, Lausanne, Switzerland, 1964; MBA, U. Pa., 1967. With Honeywell, 1989—, mgr. fin. and adminstrn., 1969-70, dir. African div., 1970-71, sales dir., 1971-75; v.p. bus. devel. Honeywell Europe SA, Brussels, 1981-83, pres., 1987—; v.p., gen. mgr. Honeywell Med. Electronics, N.Y.C., 1983-85; group v.p. Honeywell Info. Systems, Mpls., 1985-87; pres., chief exec. officer Rossignol Ski, Burlington, Vt., 1975-80; dir. gen. Rossignol SA, Voiron, France, 1980-81; chmn., cheif exec. officer Case Corp., Racine, Wis., 1991—. Avocations: golfing, skiing. Office: Case Corp 700 State St Racine WI 53404-3392

ROST, WILLIAM JOSEPH, chemist; b. Fargo, N.D., Dec. 8, 1926; s. William Melvin and Christine Ruth (Hamerlik) R.; m. Rita Cincoski, Sept. 15, 1951; children— Kathryn, Patricia, Carol. B.S., U. Minn., 1948, Ph.D., 1952. From asst. prof. to prof. pharm. chemistry Sch. Pharmacy U. Kansas City, Mo., 1952-63; prof. pharm. chemistry Sch. Pharmacy U. Mo., Kansas City, 1963—. Co-author: Principles of Medicinal Chemistry, 1974, 3d rev. edit., 1988; contbr. articles profl. jours. Mem. Am. Pharm. Assn., Am. Chem. Soc., Sigma Xi, Kappa Psi, Rho Chi, Phi Lambda Upsilon. Home: 709 W 115th Ter Kansas City MO 64114-5597 Office: U Mo Sch of Pharmacy Kansas City MO 64110

ROSTBERT, JIM, state legislator; b. May 28, 1956; m. Kathy Rostbert; 2 children. AA, Cambridge C.C.; postgrad., Met. State U. Minn. state rep. Dist. 18A, 1994—. Former vet. svc. officer. Address: 26450 Terrace Rd NE Isanti MN 55040-6143 Office: Minn Ho of Reps State Capitol Saint Paul MN 55155-0001

ROSTON, DAVID CHARLES, lawyer; b. Evanston, Ill., Oct. 15, 1943; BA cum laude, Brandeis U., 1964; JD cum laude, Harvard U., 1967. Bar: Ill. 1967. Ptnr. Altheimer & Gray, Chgo. Mem. pres. coun. Brandeis U. Mem. ABA, Ill. State Bar Assn., Chgo. Bar Assn. (chmn. com,. on profl. responsibility 1997-98). Office: Altheimer & Gray 10 S Wacker Dr Ste 4000 Chicago IL 60606-7407

ROTH, DANIEL BENJAMIN, lawyer, business executive; b. Youngstown, Ohio, Sept. 17, 1929; s. Benjamin F. and Marion (Benjamin) R.; m. Joann M. Roth; children: William M., Jennifer A., Rochelle. BS in Fin., Miami U., Oxford, Ohio, 1951; JD, Case-Western Res. U., 1956. Bar: Ohio 1956, U.S. Supreme Ct. 1960, D.C. 1983. Pres. Roth, Blair, Roberts, Strasfeld & Lodge, LPA, Youngstown, 1969—; co-founder, vice chmn. Nat. Data Processing Corp., Cin., 1961-69; chmn., pres., CEO Torent, Inc., Youngstown, 1971—, Morrison Metalweld Process Corp., 1979—; vice chmn. McDonald Steel Corp., 1980—, Torent Oil & Gas Co., 1979—, Vaughn Indsl. Car & Equipment Co., 1988—; bd. dirs. Morrison Metalweld Process Corp., $D. Bd. dirs. Gasser Chair Co., Hamlin Steel Products, Inc. Profl. singer: appearances including Steve Allen Show, 1952. Bd. dirs. Youngstown Symphony, Stambaugh Auditorium; bd. dirs. Youngstown Playhouse, v.p., 1991-93; pres. Rodef Sholom Temple, Youngstown, 1982-84. 1st lt. USAF, 1951-53, lt. col. Res., ret. Recipient Mgr. of Yr. award Mahoning Valley Mgmt. Assn., 1989, Man of Yr. award Youngstown YWCA, 1995. Mem. ABA, D.C. Bar Assn., Ohio Bar Assn., Mahoning County Bar Assn., Lawyer-Pilots Bar Assn., Soc. Benchers of Case Western Res. U. Law Sch., Youngstown Club, Pelican Marsh Club (Naples, Fla.), Pelican Isle Yacht Club (Naples), Zeta Beta Tau (nat. v.p. 1964-66), Omicron Delta Kappa, Phi Eta Sigma, Tau Epsilon Rho. Jewish. Home: PO Box 959 Canfield OH 44406-0959 Office: 600 City Centre One Youngstown OH 44503-1514

ROTH, DON, orchestra executive; m. Mary Ellen Roth; children: Florence, Daniel. Gen. mgr. Austin (Tex.) Symphony, 1977-80; mng. dir. Hartford (Conn.) Symphony, 1980-83; exec. dir. Syracuse (N.Y.), 1986; gen. mgr. San Francisco Symphony, 1987-90; exec. dir. Oreg. Symphony, Portland, 1990-98, pres., 1992-98; exec. dir. St. Louis Symphony Orch., 1998—. Office: St Louis Symphony Orch 718 N Grand Blvd Saint Louis MO 63103-1011

ROTH, JACK JOSEPH, historian, educator; b. Dec. 17, 1920; s. Max and Dinah (Kraus) R.; m. Sheilagh Goldstone. B.A., U. Chgo., 1942, Ph.D., 1955; postgrad., Inst. d'Études Politiques, Paris, 1949-50. Mem. faculty Roosevelt U., 1951-68, prof. history, chmn. dept., 1960-68; prof. history Case Western Res. U., Cleve., 1968—, chmn. dept., 1968-73; vis. asso. prof. history U. Chgo., 1962, professorial lectr. history, 1968; vis. prof. history U. Wis., 1964-65. Project dir.: The Persistence of Surrealism, Nat. Endowment for Humanities, festival, 1979, film, 1982; Translator: (Georges Sorel): Reflections on Violence, 1951, Sorel und die Totalitären Systeme, 1958, Revolution and Morale in Modern French Thought: Sorel and the Sorelians, 1963, The First World War: A Turning Point in Modern History, 1967, The Roots of Italian Fascism, 1967, Georges Sorel: on Lenin and Mussolini, 1977, The Revolution of the Mind: The Politics of Surrealism Reconsidered, 1977, The Cult of Violence: Sorel and the Sorelians, 1980; Contbr. articles to profl. jours., chpts. to books. Served with AUS, 1942-46. Recipient Penrose Fund award Am. Philos. Soc., 1964 Home: 24301 Bryden Rd Beachwood OH 44122-4038 Office: Dept History Case Western Res U Cleveland OH 44106

ROTH, JAMES R. lawyer; Degree in bus., Emporia State U.; JD, Washburn U. Ptnr. Woodard, Blaylock, Hernandez, Roth and Day, Wichita, Kans., 1979—. Mem. bd. govs. Washburn U., 1992—, chmn. bd., 1996—97. Office: Woodard Hernandez Roty & Day Emprise Bank Bldg 257 N Broadway Wichita KS 67202

ROTH, LAWRENCE MAX, pathologist, educator; b. McAlester, Okla., June 25, 1936; s. Herman Moe and Blanche (Brown) R.; m. Anna Berit Katarina Sundstrom, Apr. 3, 1965; children— Karen Esther, David Josef B.A., Vanderbilt U., 1957; M.D., Harvard U., 1960. Diplomate Am. Bd. Pathology. Rotating intern U. Ill. Research and Ednl. Hosps., Chgo., 1960-61; resident in anat. pathology Washington U. Sch. Medicine, St. Louis, 1961-64; resident in clin. pathology U. Calif. Med. Ctr., San Francisco, 1967-68; asst. prof. pathology Tulane U. Sch. Medicine, New Orleans, 1968-71; assoc. prof. pathology Ind. U. Sch. Medicine, Indpls., 1971-75, prof., 1975—, dir. div. surg. pathology. Series editor: Contemporary Issues in Surgical Pathology; mem. editl. bd. Am. Jour. Surg. Pathology, Human Pathology, Seminars in Diagnostic Pathology, Internat. Jour. Gynecol. Pathology, Endocrine Pathology; contbr. articles to med. jours. Served to capt. U.S. Army, 1965-67 Mem. Am. Assn. Investigative Pathologists, U.S. and Can. Acad. Pathology, Am. Soc. Clin. Pathologists, Coll. Am. Pathologists, Internat. Soc. Gynecol. Pathologists, Arthur Purdy Stout Soc. Surg. Pathologists, Assn. Dirs. Anatomic and Surg. Pathology. Home: 7898 Ridge Rd Indianapolis IN 46240-2538 Office: 550 University Blvd Indianapolis IN 46202-5149 E-mail: lroth@iupui.edu.

ROTH, PHILIP R. manufacturing executive; BS in Bus. Adminstrn., U. Mo.; MBA, Washington U. CPA. With Price Waterhouse Co., Valley Industries, Inc.; v.p. fin., CFO Wiegand Indsl. divsn. Emerson Electric Co.; v.p. fin., CFO Gardner Denver, Inc., Quincy, Ill., 1995—. Office: 1800 Gardner Expy Quincy IL 62305-9364

ROTH, ROBERT EARL, environmental educator; b. Wauseon, Ohio, Mar. 30, 1937; s. Earl Jonas and Florence Lena (Mahler) R.; m. Carol Sue Yackee, Aug. 8, 1959; children; Robin Earl, Bruce Robert. BS, Ohio State U., 1959, BS in Secondary Sci. Edn., MS in Conservation Edn., Ohio State U., 1960; PhD in Environ. Edn., U. Wis., 1969. Supr. conservation edn. Ethical Culture Schs., N.Y.C., 1961-63; naturalist, sci. tchr. Lakeside Sch., Spring Valley, N.Y., 1963-65; instr. No. Ill. U., Oregon, 1965-67; asst. prof. Ohio State U., Columbus, 1969-73, assoc. prof., 1973-78, prof. environ. edn. and sci. edn., 1978-2001, prof. emeritus, 2001—, chmn. divsn., 1973-84, coord. office internat. affairs, 1985-89, asst. dir., sch. sec. Sch. Natural Resources, 1989-93, acting dir. Sch. Natural Resources, 1993-94, assoc. dir., 1994-2001, state extension specialist Environ. Edn., 1993-2001. Rsch. & devel. assoc. Mosely & Assocs., Columbus, 1986-89; project cons. NARMA project, U.S. Agy. internat. Devel., Santo Domingo, Dominican Rep., 1982-87; cons. Richard Trott & Assocs., 1988-90, Kinzelman & Kline, 1990-2001, Midwest consortium Internat. Activity, 1995; evaluator Montclair State U., N.J. Sch. Conservation, 1999; workshop leader Carribean Conservation Assn., Bridgetown, Barbados, 1981-83; vis. scholar Indonesian Second U. Devel. project, Jakarta, 1988; AID lectr., Thesolonika, Greece, 1992. Exec. editor Jour. Environ. Edn., 1974-91 (Pub.'s prize 1970); contbr. articles to profl. jours. Committeeman Boy Scouts Am., 1983-86; adv. coun. McKeever Environ. Learning Ctr., Pa., 1977-83. Named vis. scholar, Uganda Makerere, 1989, Pacific Cultural Found., Taipei, Taiwan, 1989, 1999, 2001; recipient Pomerene Tchg. Enhancement award, Ohio State U., 1986, 1995, Environ. Edn. award, Ohio Alliance for the Enrivon., 1992, Outstanding Advising award, Coll. Food Agrl. and Environ. Scis., 1996. Mem.: Sch. Nat. Resource Alumni Assn. (inducted hon. 100), Nat. Sci. Tchrs. Assn. (life), N.Am. Assn. Environ. Edn. (life; bd. dirs. 1972—82, pres. 1977—78, Walt Jeske award 1988, Outstanding Contbns. to Rsch. award 2000). Avocations: swimming, canoeing, camping, fishing, travel. Home: 570 Morning St Columbus OH 43085-3775 E-mail: roth.3@osu.edu.

ROTH, SANFORD IRWIN, pathologist, educator; b. McAlester, Okla., Oct. 14, 1932; s. Herman Moe and Blanche (Brown) R.; m. Kathryn Ann Corliss, Sept. 3, 1961; children: Jeffrey Franklin, Elisabeth Francyne, Gregory James, Suzannah Joan. Student, Vanderbilt U., 1949-52; MD, Harvard U., 1956. Intern Mass. Gen. Hosp., Boston, 1956-57, resident in pathology, 1957-60, pathologist, 1962-75, Armed Forces Inst. Pathology, 1960-62; asst. prof. Med. Sch. Harvard U., 1962-69, assoc. prof. Med. Sch., 1969-75; pathologist, prof., chmn. dept. Coll. Medicine U. Ark., Little Rock, 1975-81; prof. Med. Sch. Northwestern U., Chgo., 1981-99, asst. dean admissions, 1998-2000, prof. emeritus, 2000—; chief lab. svc. VA Lakeside Med. Ctr., 1981-86. Attending pathologist Northwestern U. Hosp., 1981-99; vis. prof. pathology Harvard Med. Sch., 2001—; cons. in pathology Mass. Gen. Hosp., 2001—. With M.C. U.S. Army, 1960-62. Mem. AMA, AAAS, Am. Soc. Cell Biology, Coll. Am. Pathology, U.S.-Can. Acad. Pathology, Soc. for Investigative Dermatology, Ill. Med. Soc., Mass. Med. Soc. Home: 169 Tisquantum Rd Chatham MA 02633-2578 Office: Fruit St Boston MA 02114 E-mail: siroth@northwestern.edu.

ROTH, THOMAS, marketing executive; Grad., Western Mich. U. With Tarkenton and Co., Atlanta; founder HR Skills divsn. Nat. Edn. Tng. Group, 1988-92; dir. product devel. Wilson Learning Corp., Eden Prairie, Minn., 1981-88, v.p. product mgmt. in global R & D, 1992-94, v.p. product mgmt. and tng. group, 1994-99, v.p. global cons., 1999—. Cons. IBM, AT&T, Ford Motor Co., Pfizer, E.I. DuPont, Gen. Electric, Oracle, Dow Chem., Lucent, Tex. Instruments, Colgate-Palmolive, Honeywell, others; spkr. in field. Co-author: Creating the High Performance Team, 1987. Office: Wilson Learning Corp 7500 Flying Cloud Dr Eden Prairie MN 55344-3795

ROTHAL, MAX, director law department, lawyer; b. Norwalk, Ohio, Jan. 2, 1932; Student, Kent State U., 1951-53; LLB, U. Akron, 1957. Bar: Ohio, 1958, U.S. Dist. Ct. Ohio. Chief prosecutor Law Dept. City of Akron, Ohio, 1959-60, dir., 1987—. Mem. ABA, Ohio Defense Inst. Office: City of Akron Law Dept 161 S High St Akron OH 44308-1602 E-mail: rothama@ci.akron.oh.us.

ROTHENBERGER, DAVID ALBERT, surgeon; b. Sioux Falls, S.D., 1947; MD, Tufts U., 1973. Cert. colon and rectal surgery. Intern St Paul-Ramsey Med. Ctr., 1973-74, resident gen. surgery, 1974-78; fellow colon rectal surgery U. Minn., Mpls., 1978-79; mem. staff United Hosp., St. Paul; cln. prof. surgery U. Minn., Mpls., chief divsn. colon and rectal surgery; dir. U. Minn. Cancer Ctr.; pres. Am. Bd. Colon & Rectal Surgery, Taylor, Mich. Fellow ACS, Am. Soc. Colon and Rectal Surgeons (exec. coun., immediate past pres. 1997—), Am. Surg. Assn., Soc. for Surgery of the Alimentary Tract, Western Surg. Assn. Address: 2550 University Ave W Ste 313N Saint Paul MN 55114-1903 also: Box 450 Mayo Meml Bldg 420 Delaware St SE Minneapolis MN 55455-0374

ROTHERHAM, THOMAS G. diversified financial services company executive; BA, U. Iowa. From mem. staff to exec. ptnr. McGladrey & Pullen LLP, Davenport, Iowa, 1971-88, exec. ptnr., 1988—. Mem. AICPA (SEC regulations com., SEC practice section exec. com.), Minn. Soc. CPAs. Office: McGladrey & Pullen LLP 102 W 2nd St Fl 2 Davenport IA 52801-1803

ROTHERT, MARILYN L. dean, nursing educator; b. June 4, 1939; married; 3 children. BSN cum laude, Ohio State U., 1961; MA in Ednl. Psychol., Mich. State U., 1979, PhD in Ednl. Psychol., 1980. RN, Mich. Staff nurse Univ. Hosp., Columbus, Ohio, 1961; instr. sch. nursing Hurley Hosp., Flint, Mich., 1961-66; asst. instr. sch. nursing Mich. State U., East Lansing, 1967-77, grad. asst. dept. community health sci., 1977-80, asst. prof. Coll. Human Medicine, 1980-82, asst. prof., dir. lifelong edn. Coll. Nursing, 1982-84, asst. prof. Coll. Human Medicine, 1982-84, assoc. prof., dir. lifelong edn. Coll. Nursing, 1984-88, assoc. prof. Coll. Human Medicine, 1984-86, prof., dir. lifelong edn. Coll. Nursing, 1988-92, prof., assoc. dean outreach and profl. devel., 1992-96, prof., dean Coll. Nursing, 1996—. Cons. No. Ill. U., Ohio State U., Mich. State Dept. Natural Resources, Can. Nurses Assn., Mich. Judicial Inst., Med. Coll. Va., U. Wash., Kirtland Coll., Anderson Coll. Contbr. articles to profl. jours. Co-chmn. Capitol Health Event, 1987-88; mem. worksite health subcom. Mich. Dept. Pub. Health; mem. State 4-H Health Com. Coop. Extension Svc., 1972-75, 82—; mem. med. adv. com. Mich. Civil Svc. Health Screening Unit, 1984. Mem. ANA (mem. coun. continuing edn., nurse researchers), Mich. Nurses Assn. (chmn. continuing edn. adv. com. 1989), Soc. for Med. Decision Making, The Brunswik Soc., Soc. for Judgment and Decision Making, Soc. for Rsch. in Nursing Edn., Midwest Nursing Rsch. Soc., Am. Pub. Health Assn., Nat. Ctr. for Health Edn., Nat. League for Nursing, Mich. State U. Faculty/Profl. Women's Assn. (bd. dirs. 1989—), Capitol Area Dist. Nurses Assn. (mem. nom. com. 1984-86, continuing edn. com. 1984), Phi Kappa Phi. Office: Mich State U Coll Nursing A-230 Life Sci Bldg East Lansing MI 48824

ROTHMAN-DENES, LUCIA BEATRIZ, biology educator; b. Buenos Aires, Feb. 17, 1943; came to U.S., 1967; d. Boris and Carmen (Couto) Rothman; m. Pablo Denes, May 24, 1968; children: Christian Andrew, Anne Elizabeth. Lic. in Chemistry, Sch. Scis., U. Buenos Aires, 1964, PhD in Biochemistry, 1967. Vis. fellow NIH, Bethesda, Md., 1967-70; postdoctoral fellow biophysics U. Chgo., 1970-73, rsch. assoc., 1973-74, from asst. prof. to assoc. prof., 1974-83, prof. molecular genetics and cell biology, 1983—. Mem. microbial genetics study sect. NIH, 1980-83, 93-96, chair, 1994-96, mem. genetic basis of disease study sect., 1985-89, mem. coun. Ctr. for Sci. Rev., 2000—; mem. Damon Runyon and Walter Winchell Sci. Adv. Com., N.Y.C., 1989-93; mem. biochemistry panel NSF, 1990-92. Contbr. articles to profl. jours. Fellow AAAS, Am. Acad. Microbiology; mem. Am. Acad. Arts & Scis., Am. Soc. Microbiology (divsn. chair 1985, divsn. group II rep. 1990-92, vice chair GMPC 1995-99, chair GMPC 1999-2001), Am. Soc. Virology (councilor 1987-90), Am. Soc. Biochemistry and Molecular Biology. Office: Univ Chgo 920 E 58th St Chicago IL 60637-5415 E-mail: lbrd@midway.uchicago.edu

ROTHMANN, BRUCE FRANKLIN, pediatric surgeon; b. Akron, Ohio, July 11, 1924; s. Edwin Franklin Rothmann and Mary Madoline Policy; m. Lola May Secor, June 14, 1947; children: Susan Ann, Pamela Jane, Elizabeth Rothmann Rusnak. Student, Case Western Reserve U., 1942-43, Wesleyan U., 1943-44; MD, NYU, 1948. Diplomate Am. Bd. Surgery. Intern Akron City Hosp., 1948-49, from resident in surgery to chief resident surgeon, 1949-55; from resident pediatric surgeon to chief staff Children's Hosp., Akron, 1953-74; pvt. practice in surgery, 1955; pvt. practice in pediatric surgery, 1968—. Clin. instr. Case Western Reserve U., Cleve. 1962-64, asst. clin prof, 1967-83, assoc. clin. prof. pediatric surgery, 1968-99, assoc. clin. prof. emeritus, 1998—; asst. surgeon Univ. Hosp. Cleve. 1962-98; cons. in pediatric surgery Akron City Hosp.; v.p. Nat. Invention Ctr., Inc., 1990-92. Contbr. med. articles to profl. jours. Dir. Med. Outreach Children Hosp. Med. Ctr. of Akron, 1986—; bd. mgmt. Cuyahoga Falls Comty. YMCA, 1957-63; trustee Akron Symphony Orch., 1959-85, Akron Jr. Achievement, 1980-88, 1st Congl. Ch. Akron, 1960-64; mem. adv. bd. Children's Concert Soc., Akron, 1970—; bd. trustees Children's Family Care, 1984-86, Cuyahoga Falls H.S. Found., 1988—; pres., mem. exec. bd. Gt. Trail coun. Boy Scouts Am., coun. pres., 1997-99; mem. Nat. Inventors Hall of Fame, Cleve. Inst. Music, Nat. Inventors Hall of Fame Found. With USN, 1942-45, 50-52. Home: 3020 Kent Rd Cuyahoga Falls OH 44224-3044 Office: 330 Locust St Akron OH 44302-1801

ROTHMEIER, STEVEN GEORGE, merchant banker, investment manager; b. Mankato, Minn., Oct. 4, 1946; s. Edwin George and Alice Joan (Johnson) R. BBA, U. Notre Dame, 1968; MBA, U. Chgo., 1972. Corp. fin. analyst Northwest Airlines, Inc., St. Paul, 1973, mgr. econ. analysis, 1973-78, dir. econ. planning, 1978, v.p. fin., treas., 1978-82, exec. v.p., treas., dir., 1982-83, exec. v.p. fin. and adminstrn., treas., dir., 1983, pres., chief operating officer, 1984, pres., chief exec. officer, 1985-86, chmn., chief exec. officer, 1986-89, also bd. dirs.; pres. IAI Capital Group, Mpls., 1989-93; chmn., CEO Great No. Capital, St. Paul, 1993—. Bd. dirs. Gencorp, Precision Castparts, Dept. 56 Inc., Waste Mgmt., Inc., Am. Coun. on Germany, German Marshal Fund. Chmn. St. Agnes Found. Decorated Bronze Star. Mem. Mpls. Club, Chgo. Club. Republican. Roman Catholic. Office: Great Northern Capital 332 Minnesota St Ste W2900 Saint Paul MN 55101-1377

ROTHSTEIN, RUTH M. county health official; Dir. Cook County Hosp., Chgo., to 1999; chief Cook County Bur. of Health Svcs., 1999—. Office: Cook County Bur Hlth Svcs 1900 W Polk St Ste 220 Chicago IL 60612-3736

ROTUNDA, RONALD DANIEL, law educator, consultant; b. Blue Island, Ill., Feb. 14, 1945; s. Nicholas and Frances (Manna) R.; children: Nora, Mark. A.B. magna cum laude, Harvard U., 1967, J.D. magna cum laude, 1970. Bar: N.Y. 1971, U.S. Ct. Appeals (2d cir.) 1971, U.S. Ct. Appeals (D.C. cir.) 1971, U.S. Ct. Appeals (7th cir.) 1990, U.S. Supreme Ct. 1974, Ill. 1975. Law clk. U.S. Ct. Appeals (2d cir.), 1970-71; assoc. Wilmer, Cutler & Pickering, Washington, 1971-73; asst. majority counsel Watergate Com., U.S. Senate, 1973-74; spl. cons. Office of Ind. Counsel, 1997-99; asst. prof. U. Ill. Coll. Law, Champaign, 1974-77, assoc. prof., 1977-80, prof., 1980-93, Albert E. Jenner, Jr. prof. of law, 1993—2002; prof. law George Mason U., Arlington, Va., 2002—. Vis. prof. law European U. Inst., Florence, Italy, 1981, U. Ala., 1999; mem. profl. responsibility exam. com. Nat. Conf. Bar Examiners, 1980-87; constl. advisor Supreme Nat. Coun. Cambodia, 1993; cons. Supreme Ct. Moldova, 1996; vis. sr. fellow in constnl. studies Cato Inst., 2000. Author: (with Morgan) Problems and Materials of Professional Responsibility, 1976, 7th edit., 2000; (with Nowak and Young) Constitutional Law, 1978, (with Nowak) 2d edit., 1983, 3d edit., 1986, 4th edit., 1991, 5th edit., 1995, 6th edit., 2000, Modern Constitutional Law: Cases and Materials, 1981, 6th edit., 2000, (with Nowak) Treatise on Constitutional Law, 4 vols., 2d edit., 1992, 5 vols., 3d edit., 1999. Fulbright research scholar, Italy, 1981, Venezuela, 1986. Fellow Am. Bar Found. (life), Ill. Bar Found. (life); mem. Am. Law Inst. Roman Catholic Office: George Mason Univ Law School 3301 N Fairfax Drive Arlington VA 22201 E-mail: rrotunda@GMU.edu.

ROTZOLL, KIM BREWER, advertising and communications educator; b. Altoona, Pa., Aug. 21, 1935; s. Fredrick Charles and Anna (Brewer) R.; m. Nancy Benson, Aug. 26, 1961; children: Keith, Kristine, Amanda, Jason. BA in Advt., Pa. State U., 1957, MA in Journalism, 1965, PhD in Sociology, 1971. Account exec. Ketchum, Macleod and Grove, Pitts., 1957-61; instr. advt. Pa. State U., University Park, 1961-71; asst. prof. advt. U. Ill, Urbana, 1971-72, assoc. prof., 1972-78, prof., 1978—, rsch. prof., head advt. dept., 1983-92; dean Coll. Comms., 1992—. Lectr. in People's Republic of China, Bahrain. Author, co-author, editor: Is There Any Hope for Advertising, 1986, Advertising in Contemporary Society, 1990, 96, Media Ethics, 1995, 97, 2000, The Book of Gossage, 1995, Last Rights: Revisiting Four Theories of the Press, 1995. Named Disting. Advt. Educator of Yr. by Am. Advt. Fedn., 1992. Fellow Am. Acad. Advt. (pres. 1991); mem. Am. Advt. Found., Nat. Advt. Rev. Bd., Ill. Press Assn. Bd., Alpha Kappa Delta, Phi Kappa Phi. Democrat. Presbyterian. Avocations: reading, films, cycling. Office: U Ill 119 Gregory Hall 810 S Wright St Urbana IL 61801-3644 E-mail: krotzoll@uiuc.edu.

ROUGIER-CHAPMAN, ALWYN SPENCER DOUGLAS, furniture manufacturing company executive; b. Ostende, Belgium, Feb. 19, 1939; came to U.S., 1970; s. Douglas Alwyn and Simone (Stiernet) Rougier-C.; m. Christine Hayes, Mar. 14, 1964; children: Andrew Douglas, Duncan Peter Chartered Acct., City of London Coll., 1963. Chartered acct., Eng. and Wales; C.P.A., Mich. Articled clk. Spain Bros., London, 1958-64; mgr. Deloitte & Co., Brussels, 1964-70; ptnr. Seidman & Seidman, Grand Rapids, Mich., 1970-81; v.p. planning Steelcase Inc., 1981-83, sr. v.p., CFO, 1983—. Dir. Meijer, Inc. Pres. French Soc., Grand Rapids, Mich., 1974-75; treas., vice chmn. Opera Grand Rapids, 1981-86, pres., 1987-89; treas. Grand Rapids Symphony, 1991-96; bd. trustees Blodgett Meml. Hosp., 1989-98; bd. dirs. Fin. Execs. Inst., Western Mich., 1988-94, pres., 1991-92; mem. fin. com. Spectrum Health, 1998—. Fellow Inst. Chartered Accts. Eng. and Wales; mem. Am. Inst. C.P.A.s (computer exec. com. 1977-81), Mich. Assn. C.P.A.s (auditing standards com. 1973-78) Roman Catholic. Clubs: Cascade Country, Peninsular (Grand Rapids) Avocations: golf; tennis; squash; travel; music (symphony and opera). Office: 901 44th St SE Grand Rapids MI 49508-7575

ROULEAU, REYNALD, bishop; b. St.-Jean-de-Dieu, Que., Can., Nov. 30, 1935; Ordained priest, 1963, bishop, 1987. Bishop Churchill-Hudson Bay, 1987—. Home and Office: Diocese Churchill-Hudson Bay PO Box 10 Churchill MB Canada R0B 0E0

ROUNDS, M. MICHAEL, state legislator; b. Huron, S.D., Oct. 24, 1954; m. Jean Rounds; 4 children. B.S., S.D. State U., 1977. Mem. for dist. 24 S.D. State Senate, 1990—; minority whip, 1993-94; majority leader, 1994—; vice-chmn. legis. procedure com.; chmn. retirement laws com.; vice-chmn. state affairs com.; ins. & real estate exec. Office: SD Senate Mem State Capitol Pierre SD 54501 Home: 912 Woodridge Dr Pierre SD 57501-2366

ROUSH, SUE, newspaper editor; b. Mason City, Iowa., Dec. 26, 1957; BS in Journalism, Northwestern U., 1980. Mng. editor Universal Press Syndicate, Kansas City, Mo., 1995—. Office: Universal Press Syndicate 4520 Main St Ste 700 Kansas City MO 64111-7701

ROUSH, WILLIAM R. chemistry educator; BS in Chemistry, UCLA, 1974; PhD in Chemistry, Harvard U., 1977. Disting. prof. chemistry dept. Ind. U., Bloomington; Warner Lambert Park Davis prof. chemistry, chair chemistry U. Mich., Ann Arbor, 1997—. Recipient Arthur C. Cope Scholar award Am. Chem. Soc., 1994, Alan R. Day award Phila. Organic Chemist's Club, 1992. Office: U Mich Dept Chemistry Ann Arbor MI 48109

ROUSSEAU, EUGENE ELLSWORTH, musician, music educator, consultant; b. Blue Island, Ill., Aug. 23, 1932; s. Joseph E. and Laura M. (Schindler) R.; m. Norma J. Rigel, Aug. 15, 1959; children— Lisa-Marie, Joseph. B of Mus Edn., Chgo. Mus. Coll., 1953; MusM, Northwestern U., 1954; student, Paris Conservatory of Music, 1960-61; PhD, U. Iowa, 1962. Instr. Luther Coll., 1956-59; asst. prof. Cen. Mo. State Coll., 1962-64; prof. music Ind. U., Bloomington, 1964-88, disting. prof. music, 1988—; prof. U. Minn., 2000—. Guest prof. U. Iowa, 1964, Hochschule fur Musik, Vienna, Austria, 1981-82, Ariz. State U., 1984, Prague Conservatory Music, 1985, Showa Coll. Music, 1996, 98, Tokyo Coll. Music, 1997, Paris Conservatory, 1997; tchr. U. Wis.-Ext., 1969—; R&D of saxophone mouthpieces; music arranger; svc. on numerous acad. coms.; tchr. 1st course in saxophone Mozarteum in Salzburg, Austria, 1991—; mem. jury Munich Internat. competitions, 1987, 90, 2001, pres. of juries, 1991-92; first solo saxophonist to perform on Prague Spring Festival, 1993; mem. jury Can. Nat. Music competition, 1994; juror Japan Wind and Percussion Competition, 1997; v.p. jury Adolphe Sax Internat. Competition, Belgium, 1998. Worldwide concert saxophonist; Carnegie Hall debut, 1965; author: Marcel Mule: His Life and the Saxophone, 1982, Saxophone High Tones, 1978, Method for Saxophone (2 vols.), 1975; performer 1st solo saxophone recitals, several European cities, 1st Am. solo saxophone performance in Japan, 1984; 1st to record concert saxophone on compact disc (Delos); radio broadcasts in Berlin, Bremen, London, Montreal, Ostrava, Paris, Prague, Toronto, Vienna; saxophone recs. for Deutsche Gramophon, Golden Crest, Coronet, Delos, Liscio, ALM, McGill and RIAX. Instr., asst. band leader 25th Infantry Div. U.S. Army, 1954-56. Named Hon. Prof. Music, Prague Conservatory, 1993, Braga Inst., Italy; recipient Edwin Franko Goldman award, ABA, 1995, Disting. Alumni award, U. Iowa, 1996; grantee, Fulbright Found., 1960—61, Rsch. and Exchange Bd., 1985, NEA, 1986. Mem. N.Am. Saxophone Alliance (pres. 1978-80), Comite Internat. de Saxophone (pres. 1982-85), Coll. Music Soc., Clarinet and Saxophone Soc. (U.K.), Music Tchrs. Nat. Assn. (Tchr. of Yr. award for Ind. 1993), Fulbright Assn. (life), World Saxophone Congress (co-founder 1969, pres. organizing com. 2000--). Office: U Minn Sch Music Minneapolis MN 55455 E-mail: rouss007@tc.umn.edu.

ROVNER, ILANA KARA DIAMOND, federal judge; b. Riga, Latvia, 1938; arrived in U.S., 1939; d. Stanley and Ronny (Medalje) Diamond. AB, Bryn Mawr Coll., 1960; postgrad., U. London King's Coll., 1961, Georgetown U., 1961—63; JD, Ill. Inst. Tech., 1966; LittD (hon.) (hon.) , Rosary Coll., 1989, Mundelein Coll., 1989; DHL (hon.) (hon.) , Spertus Coll. of Judaica, 1992. Bar: Ill. 1972, U.S. Dist. . (no. dist.) Ill. 1972, U.S. Ct. Appeals (7th cir.) 1977, U.S. Supreme Ct. 1981, Fed. Trial Bar (no. dist.) Ill. 1982. Jud. clk. U.S. Dist. Ct. (no. dist.) Ill., Chgo., 1972—73; asst. U.S. atty. U.S. Atty.'s Office, 1973—77; dep. chief of pub. protection, 1975—76; chief pub. protection, 1976—77; dep. gov., legal counsel Gov. James R. Thompson, Chgo., 1977—84; dist. judge U.S. Dist. Ct. (no. dist) Ill., 1984—92; cir. judge U.S. Ct. Appeals (7th cir.), 1992—. Mem. Gannon-Proctor Commn. on the Status of Women in Ill., 1982—84; mem. civil justice reform act adv. com. 7th Cir. Ct., Chgo., 1991—95, mem. race and gender fairness com., 1993—; mem. fairness com. U.S. Ct. Appeals (7th cir.), 1996—, mem. gender study task force, 1995—96; mem. jud. conf. U.S. Com. Ct. Adminstrn. Case Mgmt., 2000—; ctrl. and east European law initiative vol. ABA, 1997—. Ctrl. and East European law initiative vol. ABA, 1997—; trustee Bryn Mawr Coll, Pa., 1983—89; mem. bd. overseers Ill. Inst. Tech./Kent Coll. Law, 1983—; trustee Ill. Inst. Tech., 1989—; mem. adv. coun. Rush Ctr. for Sports Medicine, Chgo., 1991—96; bd. dirs. Rehab. Inst. Chgo., 1998—; bd. visitors No. Ill. U. Coll. Law, 1992—94; vis. com. Northwestern U. Sch. Law, 1993—98, U. Chgo. Law Sch., 1993—96, 2000—; chair Ill. state selection com. Rhodes Scholarship Trust, 1998—2000. Named Today's Chgo. Woman of the Yr., 1985, Woman of Achievement, Chgo. Women's Club, 1986; named one of 15 Chgo. Women of the Century, Chgo. Sun Times, 1999; recipient Spl. Commendation award, U.S. Dept. Justice, 1975, Spl. Achievement award, 1976, Ann. Nat. Law and Social Justice Leadership award, League to Improve the Cmty., 1975, Ann. Guardian Police award, 1977, Profl. Achievement award, Ill. Inst. Tech., 1986, Louis Dembitz Brandeis medal for Disting. Legal Svc., Brandeis U., 1993, 1st Woman award, Valparaiso U. Sch. Law, 1993, ORT Women's Am. Cmty. Svc. award, 1987—88, Svc. award, Spertus Coll. of Judaica, 1987, Ann. award, Chgo. Found. for Women, 1990, Arabella Babb Mansfield award, Nat. Assn. Women Lawyers, 1998, award, Chgo. Attys. Coun. of Hadassah, 1999, 1st Woman award, Georgetown U. Law Ctr., 2001, others, Hebrew Immigrant Aid Soc. Chgo. 85th Anniversary honoree, 1996. Mem.: Decalogue Soc. of Lawyers (citation of honor 1991, Merit award 1997), Chgo. Coun. Lawyers, Chgo. Bar Assn. (commendation def. of prisoners com. 1987), Women's Bar Assn. Ill. (ann. award 1989, 1st Myra Bradwell Woman of Achievement award 1994), Fed. Judges Assn., Fed. Bar Assn. (mem. selection com. Chgo. chpt. 1977—80, treas. 1978—79, sec. 1979—80, 2d v.p. 1980—81, 1st v.p. 1981—82, pres. 1982—83, 2d v.p. 7th cir. 1983—84, v.p. 7th cir. 1984—85), Kappa Beta Pi, Phi Alpha Delta (hon.). Office: 219 S Dearborn St Ste 2774 Chicago IL 60604-1803

ROWARK, MAUREEN, fine arts photographer; b. Edinburgh, Midlothian, Scotland, Feb. 28, 1933; came to U.S., 1960, naturalized, 1970; d. Alexander Pennycook and Margaret (Gorman) Prezdpelski; m. Robert Rowark, May 3, 1952 (div. July 1965). 1 child, Mark Steven. Student, Warmington Bus. Coll., Royal Leamington Spa, Eng., 1950-51, Royal Leamington Spa Art Sch.; diploma, Speedwriting Inst., N.Y.C., 1961; AS in Edn., St. Clair County Community Coll., Port Huron, Mich., 1977, AA, 1978. Supr. proof reading Nevin D. Hirst Advt., Ltd., Leeds, Eng., 1952-55; publicity asst. Alvis Aero Engines, Ltd., Coventry, Eng., 1955-57; adminstrv. asst. Port Huron Motor Inn, 1964-66; adminstrv. asst. pub. rels. dept. Geophysics and Computer Svcs., Inc., New Orleans, 1966-68; sales mgr. Holiday Inn, Port Huron, 1968-70; adminstrv. asst. Howard Corp., 1971-73; sales and systems coord. Am. Wood Products, Ann Arbor, Mich., 1973-74; systems coord. Daniels & Zermack Architects, 1974; systems coord., cataloger fine arts dept. St. Clair County Community Coll., Port Huron, 1976-79; freelance fine arts photographer, 1978—. Photographer Patterns mag. front cover, 1978, Erie Sq. Gazette, 1979, Bluewater Area Tourism Bur. brochure, 1989, 92, 95, 97, 2000, 2001, Corits Castle, Lexington, 2002, Port Huron, Can. Legion, Wyo., Ont. Br., 1987, 88—, Grace Episcopal Ch. Mariner's Day, Port Huron, 1987, 92-2001, Homes mag., 1989. Photographer (one-woman shows) Grace Episcopal Ch., 1995, Port Huron Mus., 1995, St. Clair River Remedial Action Plan, 1995 (Best in Landscape Category), Mich. Waterways Coun. Girl Scouts Exhibit, 1996, exhibited in internat. shows Ann. Ea. Mich. Internat. Juried Exhbn., yearly , 1981—98 (Award of Excellence, 1982, Award of Excellence, 1983, Best Photography award, 1995, Best Photography award, 1996, Best Photography award, 1997), exhibited in group shows Ann. Ea. Mich. Internat. Juried Exhbn. , 2000, exhibited in internat. shows Our Town Juried Exhbn., 1997, St. Clair County C.C., 1983, 1986 (Award of Excellence, 1986), Gallery Lambton Juried Exhbn., Sarnia, Ont., Can., 1983—92 (Best Photography, 1988), 1994, 1996, 1997, 2000, Bluewater Bridge Juried Exhibit, 1988, Kaskilaaksontie Exhibit, Finland, 1991 (Par Excellence award), Swann Gallery, Detroit, 1996, St. Clair (Mich.) Art Gallery, Genesis Gallery, Lexington, Mich., others, represented in permanent exhibit Royal Can. Legion, Wyo. Br. Centaph, Capac State Bank, 1996, Grace Episcopal Ch., 1995, Thomas Edison Inn, Port Huron Hosp., 1996, Front Cover "Good Health News", 1997, costume modelling Bluewater Art Assn., 2000, 01, contbr. short stories to mags., photographer Bluewater Percussion Brochure , 2001. Cons., buyer interior decor Grace Episcopal Ch., 1994; active Port Huron Mus., 1978l; founder Red Hat Soc. Bluewater Les Chapeaux Rouge chpt., 2002. Recipient hon. mention Gallery Lambton, Sarnia, 1981, 2d pl. memoir writing women's history month St. Clair County C.C., 1999; winner 2d and 3d place awards Times Herald Newspaper, 1988, 1st place juried photography award Port Huron Art Festival, 1997. Mem. St. Clair County C.C. Alumni Assn., Phi Theta Kappa, Lambda Mu. Democrat. Episcopalian. Avocations: costumes and interior design, travel, theater, memoir writing. Home and Office: 3512 Walnut St Port Huron MI 48060 E-mail: ha-penerth-of-tar@prodigy.net.

ROWE, JOHN W. utility company executive; b. Wis. married; 1 son. Grad., U. Wis. Assoc. Isham, Lincoln & Beale, Chgo., 1970-78; ptnr., 1978-80; sr. v.p. law Conrail, 1980-84; pres., CEO Ctrl. Maine Power Co., 1984-89, New Eng. Electric Sys., 1989-98; chmn., pres., CEO Unicom and ComEd, 1998—. Bd. dirs. UnumProvident Corp., Fleet Boston Fin., Wis. Ctrl. Tranp. Co.; of counsel to trustees Chgo., Milw., St. Paul, Pacific Railroad Co. Bd. trustees Art Inst. Chgo., Chgo. Hist. Soc., Field Mus., Wis. Alumni rsch. Found., Am. Enterprise Inst., Ill. chpt. Nature Conservancy; vice-chmn. Edison Electric Inst.; nat. trustee Northwestern U.; past pres. USS Constitution Mus.; past chmn. Mass. Bus. Roundtable. Mem. Econ. Club. Chgo., Comml. Club Chgo. (civic com.), Order of the Coif, Phi Beta Kappa. Office: Unicom Corp 10 S Dearborn St Chicago IL 60603-2397

ROWE, JOHN WILLIAM, utility executive; b. Dodgeville, Wis., May 18, 1945; s. William J. and Lola (Rule) R.; m. Jeanne M.; 1 son, William John. BS, U. Wis., 1967, JD, 1970. Bar: Wis. 1970, Ill. 1970, U.S. Supreme Ct. 1979, Pa. 1982. Assoc. Isham, Lincoln & Beale, Chgo., 1970-77, ptnr., 1978-80; counsel to trustee Chgo. Milw. St. Paul & Pacific R.R., 1979-80; v.p. law Consol. Rail Corp., Phila., 1980-82, sr. v.p. law, 1982-84; pres., chief exec. officer Cen. Maine Power Co., Augusta, 1984-89; pres., CEO New Eng. Elec. System, Westboro, Mass., 1989-98, former bd. dirs.; chmn., pres., CEO Unicom Corp. & Commonwealth Edison Co., 1998-2000; pres., co-CEO Exelon Corp. Bd. dirs. UNUM Corp., UNUM Provident, Fleet Boston, Bank of Boston Corp. Pres. USS Constitution Mus., 1993-95, Edison Electric Inst., Field Mus. of Natural History; trustee Mechanics Hall, Pioneer Inst. Mem. Chgo. Club, Phi Beta Kappa. Home and Office: Unicom Corp Ten S Dearborn St # 37 Chicago IL 60603

ROWE, LISA DAWN, computer programmer/analyst, computer consultant; b. Kenton, Ohio, Feb. 2, 1966; d. Daniel Lee and Frances Elaine (Johnson) Edelblute; m. Jeffrey Mark Rowe, Feb. 13, 1982; children: Anthony David, Samantha Paige Elizabeth, Zane Thomas, Zachary Tyler. Student, Inst. of Lit., 1988-90, Acad. Ct. Reporting, 1988, Marion Tech. Coll., 1991-92; postgrad., Ohio State U., 1993—. Writer, model Newslife, Marion, Ohio, 1982-83; bookkeeper Nat. Ch. Residences, Columbus, 1985, Insty-Prints, Columbus, 1985; asst. editor Columbus Entertainment, 1984-85; book reviewer, writer Columbus Dispatch, 1989-91; writer Consumer News, Delaware, Ohio, 1989-90; computer programmer, supr. Dyserv, Inc., Columbus, 1986-92; bookkeeper, acct., office mgr. Marion Music Ctr., Inc., 1990; computer programmer EBCO Mfg., Columbus, 1992-93; sr. programmer/analyst Borden, Inc., 1993-94; computer cons. System X, 1994-95, LDA Systems, Dublin, 1995-96; pres. Rowe Techs. Inc. (formerly Jones, Mitchell Rowe & Assocs.), Marion, 1996—. Editor newsletter Assn. System Users, 1989-90; contbr. articles and revs. to profl. jours. Mem. NAFE, MADD, DAV (chaplain 1990). Republican. Mormon. Avocations: horseback riding, swimming, camping, fishing, reading. Home: 1150 Toulon Ave Marion OH 43302-6610 Office: Rowe Techs Inc 1150 Toulon Ave Marion OH 43302-6610 E-mail: Lisarowe@rowetech.com.

ROWE, MAX L. lawyer, corporate executive, management and political consultant, writer, judge; b. Dallas City, Ill., Aug. 14, 1921; s. Samuel Guy and Nellie (Moyes) R.; m. Maxine Marilyn Gladson, May 23, 1944; children: Melody Ann (Mrs. Gunn), Susan Elaine, Joyce Lynn, Andrew Blair. Student, Knox Coll., Galesburg, Ill., 1939-40; A.B., U. Ill., 1943, J.D., 1946; M.B.A., U. Chgo., 1952. Bar: Ill. 1947, Ind. 1954, also U.S. Supreme Ct. 1964. Pvt. practice in Aurora and Urbana, 1947; asst. to sec., asst. treas. Elgin Nat. Watch Co., 1948-50; gen. atty., asst. to pres.-treas.

Rival Packing Co., 1950- 51; gen. counsel, asst. sec.-treas. Victor Mfg. & Gasket Co., Chgo., 1951-54; sec. Mead Johnson & Co., Evansville, Ind., 1954-55; assoc. counsel Caterpillar Tractor Co., 1955-62; assoc. gen. counsel, sec., asst. treas. Thomas J. Lipton, Inc. and subs., 1962-68; v.p., treas. Seeburg Corp., Chgo., 1968-69; v.p. fin., law and adminstrn. Nightingale Conant Corp., 1970-71; pvt. legal practice, also mgmt. and polit. cons., 1968—; v.p. law, sec. Ward Foods, Inc., Wilmette, Ill., 1972-76; mem. firm Kirkland & Ellis, Chgo., 1978-87; pres., CEO Rowe Enterprises, 1987—; atty. Ill. Dept. Profl. Regulation, Chgo. and Springfield, 1987-92; adminstrv. law judge State of Ill., 1993—. Dir. Ward-Johnston, Inc., Ward Internat., Inc., Superior Potato Chips, Inc., Quinlan Pretzel Co., Honiron-Philippines, Inc.; instr. extension div. U. Ill., 1960-61, eve. div. Fairleigh Dickinson U., 1966-68; leader Am. Mgmt. Assn., other corp. seminars, 1966-87. Actor various TV, radio and print commercials, 1992—. Treas. Peoria County (Ill.) Republican Central Com., 1958-62, Rep. precinct committeeman, Peoria County, 1958-62, Bergen County, N.J., 1966-68, del., Rep. Nat. Conv., 1980; elder Presbyterian Ch., 1975—; mem. nat. adv. council SBA, 1976-78; chmn., mem. adv. bd. Ill. Dept. Personnel, 1979-82; mem. Ill. Compensation Rev. Bd., 1984-87; mem. Pres. Reagan's Nat. Commn. for Employment Policy, 1984-88; mem. U. Ill. Found. and Pres.'s Council, 1979—, bd. visitors Coll. of Law, 1993—; dir., mem. exec. com., chmn. Outreach and Devel., World Heritage Mus., 1992-98; dir., Spurlock Mus. of World Culture, 1998—; mem. bd. dirs. Oak Ridge Cemetary, 1994—. Served to 2d lt. AUS, 1943-45, newspaper columnist, 1994—, producer, writer, host of closed circuit TV programs, 1994—. Named Alumni of Month, U. Ill. Coll. Law, 1982; inductee Sr. Illinoisans Hall of Fame, 1995. Mem. Am. Mgmt. Assn., Conf. Bd., Am., Ill, Chgo., Sangamon County bar assns., Am. Soc. Corp. Secs., Phi Gamma Delta. Republican. Clubs: Union League (Chgo.), Execs. (Chgo.). Office: 49 Inverness Rd Springfield IL 62704-3110

ROWLAND, DOYLE ALFRED, federal judge; b. Northville, Mich., May 22, 1938; s. Doyle Vernal and Georgiana (Britcher) R.; m. Carol Ann Fritz, July 26, 1964; children: Doyle Andrew, Matthew Mark. BS, Ea. Mich. U., 1965; JD, Detroit Coll., 1967. Bar: Mich. 1968, U.S. Dist. Ct. (ea. dist.) Mich. 1968, U.S. Dist. Ct. (we. dist.) Mich. 1984. Asst. city atty. City of Midland, Mich., 1967-69; friend of the ct. Midland County, 1969-72; ptnr. Whittaker & Rowland, Midland, 1969-77; pros. atty. Midland County, 1977-81; pvt. practice Midland, 1981-84; U.S. magistrate judge Western Dist. Mich., Kalamazoo, 1984—. Mem. Midland County Bar Assn. (pres. 1978-79), Kalamazoo County Bar Assn. Office: US Dist Ct We Dist Mich 410 W Michigan Ave Kalamazoo MI 49007-3757

ROWLAND, HOWARD RAY, mass communications educator; b. Eddy County, N.Mex., Sept. 9, 1929; s. Lewis Marion and Ursula Lorene (Hunt) R.; m. Meredith June Lee, Apr. 19, 1951; children: Runay Ilene Olson, Rhonda Lee Fisher. B in Journalism, U. Mo., 1950; MS in Journalism, So. Ill. U., 1959; PhD, Mich. State U., 1969. Feature writer Springfield (Mo.) Newspapers, Inc., 1954; newspaper editor Monett (Mo.) Times, 1954-55; editl. writer So. Ill. U., Carbondale, 1955-59; pub. rels. dir. St. Cloud (Minn.) State U., 1959-86, asst. dean, 1986-87, 88-90; dir. Ctr. for British Studies, Alnwick, Eng., 1987-88, 90-91. Emeritus prof. St. Cloud State U., 1991—; cons. Conf. of Campus Ombudsmen, Berkeley, 1971; recorder Seminar on Fund Raising, Washington, 1985; bibliographer Higher Edn. Bibliography Yearbook, 1987. Author: American Students in Alnwick Castle, 1990, St. Cloud State University--125 Years, 1994; editor: Effective Community Relations, 1980; sect. editor: Handbook of Institutional Advancement, 1986; author book revs. Chair All-Am. City Com., St. Cloud, 1973-74. With U.S. Army, 1951-53. NDEA doctoral fellowship Mich. State U., 1967-69; recipient Appreciation award Mayor of St. Cloud, 1974, Disting Svc. award Coun. for Advancement and Support of Edn., 1985. Mem. Soc. of Profl. Journalists (Minn. chpt. pres. 1963-64, dep. dir. 1965-67), Coun. for Advancement and Support of Edn. (dist. 5 chair 1977-79, Leadership award 1979), Rotary Internat., Phi Delta Kappa (Mich. State U. chpt. pres. 1968-69, St. Cloud State Univ. chpt. pres. 1978-79). Presbyterian. Avocations: writing, fishing, travel, photography, antiques. Home: 29467 Kraemer Lake Rd Saint Joseph MN 56374-9646 E-mail: rjrowland@mymailstation.com.

ROWLAND, JAMES RICHARD, electrical engineering educator; b. Muldrow, Okla., Jan. 24, 1940; s. Richard Cleveland and Imogene Beatrice (Angel) R.; m. Jonell Condren, Aug. 24, 1963 (dec. May 1991); children: Jennifer Lynn, Angela Janel; m. Mary Anderson, Jan. 2, 1995. BSEE, Okla. State U., 1962; MSEE, Purdue U., 1964, PhD in Elec. Engring., 1966. Registered profl. engr., Okla. Instr. Purdue U., West Lafayette, Ind., 1964-65; from asst. to assoc. prof. Ga. Inst. Tech., Atlanta, 1966-71; from assoc. to full prof. Okla. State U., Stillwater, 1971-85; prof., chmn. dept. elec. and computer engring. U. Kans., Lawrence, 1985-89, prof., 1985—. Cons. Lockheed-Ga. Co., Marietta, 1966-71, U.S. Army Missile Command, Huntsville, Ala., 1969-79, Sandia Nat. Labs., Albuquerque, 1979, Puritan-Bennett, Lenexa, Kans., 1992. Author: Linear Control Systems, 1986; mem. editorial adv. bd. Computer and Elec. Engring., 1971-98; co-contbr. 50 articles to profl. jours. Fellow IEEE (edn. soc. pres. 1982-83, Centennial medal 1984, edn. soc. Achievement award 1986, edn. conf. award 1988, Region 5 Oustanding Educator award 1995), Am. Soc. Engring. Edn. (dir. grad. div. 1987-89), Eta Kappa Nu (dir. 1989-91), Kiwanis. Republican. Baptist. Avocations: golf, gardening. Home: 2424 Free State Ct Lawrence KS 66047-2831 Office: U Kans Dept Elec Engring & Computer Sci 415 Snow Hall Lawrence KS 66045-7504 E-mail: jrowland@ku.edu.

ROWLAND, PLEASANT, publisher, toy company executive; m. Jerry Frautschi. Grad., Wells Coll., 1962. Elem. tchr. Mass., Calif., Ga. and N.J.; TV news reporter, anchor KGO-TV, San Francisco; v.p. Boston Ednl. Rsch. Co., 1971-78; pub. Children's Mag. Guide, 1981-89; founder, pres. Pleasant Co., 1986—; vice chmn. Mattell, 1998—. Named one of 12 Outstanding Entrepreneurs, Inst. Am. Entrepreneurs, 1990, one of Am.'s Top 50 Women Bus. Owners, Working Women mag., 1993-98; recipient Best and Brightest in Mktg. award Advt. Age, 1993, Mem. Intenrat. Women's Forum, Com. of 200. Office: Pleasant Co/Am Girl 8400 Fairway Place PO Box 998 Middleton WI 53562-0998

ROWLAND, THEODORE JUSTIN, physicist, educator; b. Cleve., May 15, 1927; s. Thurston Justin and Lillian (Nesser) R.; m. Janet Claire Millar, June 28, 1952 (div. 1967); children: Theodore Justin, Dawson Ann, Claire Millar; m. Patsy Marie Beard, Aug. 21, 1968. BS, Western Res. U., 1948; MA, Harvard U., 1949, PhD, 1954. Rsch. physicist Union Carbide Metals Co., Niagara Falls, N.Y., 1954-61; prof. phys. metallurgy U. Ill., 1961-92, asst. dean Coll. Engring., acting assoc. dean Grad. Coll., 1990-91, prof. emeritus, 1992—; pres., dir. Materials Cons., Inc. Cons. physicist, 1961—; cons. metallurgist, 1976—. Editor 2 books; author monograph; contbr. articles to profl. jours. Fellow Am. Phys. Soc.; mem. AIME, AAAS, AAUP, Phi Beta Kappa, Sigma Xi. Achievements include initial verification of charge density waves in dilute alloys; original contributions to theory and experiment in nuclear magnetic resonance in metals. Home: 805 Park Lane Dr Champaign IL 61820-7613 Office: U Ill Dept Materials Sci and Engring 1304 W Green St Urbana IL 61801-2920 E-mail: trowland@staff.uiuc.edu.

ROWLETT, RALPH MORGAN, archaeologist, educator; b. Richmond, Ky., Sept. 11, 1934; s. Robert Kenny and Daisy (Mullikin) R.; m. Elsebet Sander-Jorgensen, Aug. 25, 1963 (div. Jan. 1986); children: Rolf Arvid, Erik Kenneth; m. Elizabeth Helen Dinan, Apr. 21, 1989 (div. Oct. 1995); 1 child, Helen Holly. Student, U. Ky., 1952-53; BA summa cum laude, Marshall U., 1956; postgrad., U. London, 1962-63; PhD, Harvard U., 1968. Instr. anthropology U. Mo., Columbia, 1965-67, asst. prof., 1967-69, assoc. prof., 1969-75, prof., 1975—. Postdoctoral fellow Ghent U., 1969 Co-author: Neolithic Levels on the Titelberg, Luxembourg, 1981, Meeting Anthropology Phase to Phase, 2000; anthropology editor Random House Unabridged Dictionary of English, 1980—; editor: Horizons and Styles, 1993, Horizons and Styles in West Eurasiatic Archaeology; developer thermoluminescence dating of flint, 1972; co-developer electron spin resonance dating of flint, 1981. 1st lt. arty., U.S. Army, 1956-58. Decorated officer Legion de Merit (Luxembourg); named Ky. col., 1976; grantee NSF, 1973-75, 76-79, 82-83, Svc. Archeologique de Neuchatel, 1989, British Coun., 1993, Acad. of Romania, 1996, Internat. Rsch. and Exch. Bd., 1997. Fellow Am. Anthrop. Assn.; mem. AAAS, Archaeol. Inst. Am., Soc. Am. Archaeology, Prehistory Soc., Societe Prehistorique de Luxembourg, Societe Archeologique Champenoise, English Heritage, Palomino Horse Breeders Assn. Democrat. Mem. Christian Ch. (Disciples of Christ) Home: Hollywell Hill 1197 State Road Ww Fulton MO 65251-5106 Office: Univ Mo Dept Anthropology Columbia MO 65211-0001

ROWLEY, JANET DAVISON, physician; b. N.Y.C., Apr. 5, 1925; d. Hurford Henry and Ethel Mary (Ballantyne) Davison; m. Donald A. Rowley, Dec. 18, 1948; children: Donald, David, Robert, Roger. PhB, U. Chgo., 1944, BS, 1946, MD, 1948; DSc (hon.) , U. Ariz., 1989, U. Pa., 1989, Knox Coll., 1991, U. So. Calif., 1992, St. Louis U., 1997, St. Xavier U., 1999, Oxford (Eng.) U., 2000. Diplomate Am. Bd. Med. Genetics. Rsch. asst. U. Chgo., 1949—50; intern Marine Hosp., USPHS, Chgo., 1950—51; attending physician Infant Welfare and Prenatal Clinics Dept. Pub. Health, Montgomery County, Md., 1953—54; rsch. fellow Levinson Found., Cook County Hosp., Chgo., 1955—61; clin. instr. neurology U. Ill., 1957—61; USPHS spl. trainee Radiobiology Lab. The Churchill Hosp., Oxford, England, 1961—62; rsch. assoc. dept. medicine and Argonne Cancer Rsch. Hosp. U. Chgo., 1962—69, assoc. prof. dept. medicine and Argonne Cancer Rsch. Hosp., 1969—77, prof. dept. medicine and Franklin McLean Meml. Rsch. Inst., 1977—84, Blum-Riese Disting. Svc. prof., dept. medicine and dept. molecular genetics and cell biology, 1984—, Blum-Riese Disting. Svc. prof. dept. human genetics, 1997—, interim dep. dean for sci. biol. scis. divsn., 2001—. Bd. sci. counsellors Nat. Inst. Dental Rsch., NIH, 1972—76, chmn., 1974—76; mem. Nat. Cancer Adv. Bd., Nat. Cancer Inst., 1979—84, Nat. Adv. Coun. for Human Genome Rsch. Inst., 1999—; adv. com. Frederick Cancer Rsch. Facility, 1983—84; bd. sci. counsellors Nat. Human Genome Rsch. Inst., NIH, 1994—99, chmn., 1994—97; adv. bd. Howard Hughes Med. Inst., 1989—94, MD Anderson Cancer Ctr., 1998—; vis. com. dept. applied biol. scis. MIT Corp. , 1983—86; bd. sci. cons. Meml. Sloan-Kettering Cancer Ctr., 1988—90; adv. com. Ency. Britannica U. Chgo., 1988—96; Bernard Cohen Meml. lectr. U. Pa., 1993; Katherine D. McCormick Disting. lectr. Stanford U., 1994; Donald D. Van Slyke lectr. Brookhaven Nat. Lab., 1994; Hilary Koprowski lectr. Thomas Jefferson U., 1994; W. Jack Stuckey Jr. lectr. Tulane Career Ctr., 1996; Presdl. Symposium Am. Soc. Pediatric Hematology/Oncology, 1995; Brit. Jour. of Haematology Plenary lectr. Brit. Soc. Haematology, 1997; Peacock Meml. lectr. in pathology U. Tex. Southwestern Med. Sch., 1997; Cosbie lectr. Royal Coll. Physicians and Surgeons Can., 1997; Richard Brunning lectr. U. Minn., 1999; Muriel Verder Millenium lectr. Evanston Hosp., 1999; Disting. Women in Medicine and Sci. lectr. Northwestern Med. Sch., 2000; Edward C. Hill lectr. U. Calif., San Francisco, 2000; Margaret Pitman lectr. NIH, 2000; plenary spkr. Spanish Soc. Hematology, 2000. Co-founder, co-editor: Genes, Chromosomes and Cancer, mem. editl. bd.: Oncology Rsch., mem. editl. bd.: Cancer Genetics and Cytogenetics, mem. editl. bd.: Internat. Jour. Hematology, mem. editl. bd.: Genomics, mem. editl. bd.: Internat. Jour. Cancer, mem. editl. bd.: Leukemia, past. mem. editl. bd.: Blood, past. mem. editl. bd.: Cancer Rsch., past. mem. editl. bd.: Hematol. Oncology, past. mem. editl. bd.: Leukemia Rsch.; contbr. chapters to books, articles to profl. jours. Adv. com. for career awards in biomed. scis. Burroughs Wellcome Fund, 1994—98; selection panel for Clin. Sci. award Doris Duke Charitable Found., 2000—; mem. Pres.'s Adv. Coun. on Bioethics, 2001—; nat. adv. com. McDonnell Found. Program for Molecular Medicine in Cancer Rsch., 1988—98; adv. bd. Leukemia Soc. Am., 1979—84; selection com. scholar award in biomed. sci. Lucille P. Markey Charitable Trust, 1984—87; trustee Adler Planetarium, Chgo., 1978—; med. adv. bd. G&P Charitable Found., 1999—. Co-recipient Charles Mott prize, GM Cancer Rsch. Found., 1989; named Chicagoan of Yr., Chgo. mag., 1998; recipient First Kuwait Cancer prize, 1984, Esther Langer award, Ann Langer Cancer Rsch. Found., 1983, A. Cressy Morrison award in natural scis., N.Y. Acad. Scis., 1985, Past State Pres. award, Tex. Fedn. Bus. and Profl. Women's Clubs, 1986, Karnofsky award and lecture, Am. Soc. Clin. Oncology, 1987, Antoine Lacassagne Lique prize, Nat. Francaise Contre le Cancer, 1987, King Faisal Internat. prize in medicine (co-recipient), 1988, Katherine Berkan Judd award, Meml. Sloan-Kettering Cancer Ctr., 1989, Steven C. Beering award, U. Ind. Med. Sch, 1992, Robert de Villiers award, Leukemia Soc. Am., 1993, Kaplan Family prize for cancer rsch. excellence, Oncology Soc. Dayton, 1995, Cotlove award and lecture, Acad. Clin. Lab. Physicians and Scientists, 1995, Nilsson-Ehle lecture, Mendelian Soc. and Royal Physiographic Soc., 1995, The Gairdner Found. award, 1996, medal of honor, Basic Sci. Am. Cancer Soc., 1996, Nat. Medal of Sci., 1998, Lasker award for clin. scis., 1998, Woman Extraordinaire award, Internat. Women's Assocs., 1999, Golden Plate award, Am. Acad. Achievement, 1999, Women Achieving Excellence award, YWCA of Met. Chgo., 2000, Philip Levine award, Am. Soc. Clin. Pathology, 2001, Emile M Chamot award, State Microsurg. Soc. Ill., 2001. Fellow: AAAS (nominating com. 1998); mem.: NAS (chmn. sect. 41 1995—99), Inst. Medicine (coun. 1988—90), Am. Assn. Cancer Rsch. (G.H.A. Clowes Meml. award 1989), Am. Soc. Hematology (lectr. Millenium Symposium 1999, Presdl. Symposium 1982, Dameshek prize 1982, Ham-Wasserman award 1995), Genetical Soc., Am. Soc. Human Genetics (pres.-elect 1992, pres. 1993, Allen award and lectr. 1991), Am. Philos. Soc., Am. Acad. Arts and Scis. (nominating com. 1998), Alpha Omega Alpha, Sigma Xi (William Proctor prize for sci. achievement 1989). Episcopalian. Home: 5310 S University Ave Chicago IL 60615-5106 Office: U Chgo 5841 S Maryland Ave Rm 2115 Chicago IL 60637-1463

ROY, DAVID TOD, Chinese literature educator; b. Nanking, China, Apr. 5, 1933; s. Andrew Tod and Margaret (Crutchfield) R.; m. Barbara Jean Chew, Feb. 4, 1967. AB, Harvard U., 1958, AM, 1960, PhD, 1965. Asst. prof. Princeton U., 1963-67; assoc. prof. U. Chgo., 1967-73, prof., 1973—99, prof. emeritus, 1999—, chmn. com. on Far Eastern Studies, 1968-70, chmn. dept. Far Eastern Langs. and Civilizations, 1972-75. Author: Kuo Mo-jo: The Early Years, 1971; contbr.: How to Read the Chinese Novel, 1990, Minds and Mentalities in Traditional Chinese Literature, 1999; co-editor: Ancient China: Studies in Early Civilization, 1978; translator: The Plum in the Golden Vase or Chin P'ing Mei, vol. 1, 1993, vol. 2, 2001. Served with U.S. Army, 1954-56. Ford Found. fellow, 1958-60, Jr. fellow Harvard Soc. Fellows, 1960-63, fellow Fulbright-Hays Commn., 1967, Chgo. Humanities Inst. fellow, 1994-95; grantee Am. Coun. Learned Socs., 1976-77, NEH, 1983-86, 95-96. Mem. Am. Oriental Soc., Assn. for Asian Studies. Democrat. Club: Quadrangle (Chgo.). Home: 5443 S Cornell Ave Chicago IL 60615-5603 Office: U Chgo 1050 E 59th St Chicago IL 60637-1559 E-mail: davidroy@midway.uchicago.edu.

ROY, ROBERT RUSSELL, toxicologist; b. Mpls., Sept. 14, 1957; s. Rudolph Russell and Arlene Charlotte (Miller) R.; m. Barbara Jane Richie, Oct. 10, 1987; children: Andrew, Katherine. BA cum laude, Augsburg Coll., 1980; MS, U. Minn., 1986, PhD, 1989. Bd. cert. in toxicology. Toxicologist, project mgr. Pace Labs., Inc., Mpls., 1989-90; toxicologist Minn. Dept. Health, 1990-93, Minn. Regional Poison Ctr., St. Paul, 1990-97; team leader, toxicology specialist 3M, 1997—, sr. toxicology specialist, 2000—. Lectr. U. Minn., Mpls., 1986-90, Midwest Ctr. Occupl. Health and Safety, St. Paul, 1990—, instr., 1989; adj. assoc. prof. U. Minn., 1993—; mem. grad. faculty in toxicology and pub. health U. Minn.; adj. asst. prof. emergency medicine Oreg. Health Sci. U., Portland. Mem. Mt. Carmel Luth. Ch. Coun., Mpls., 1983-85. Mem. Soc. Toxicology, Am. Indsl. Hygiene Assn., Delta Omega. Home: 6201 Near Mountain Blvd Chanhassen MN 55317-9117 Office: Corp Toxicology 3 M Ctr Bldg 220-2E-02 Saint Paul MN 55144-1000 E-mail: rroy@mmm.com.

ROYAL, HENRY DUVAL, nuclear medicine physician; b. Norwich, Conn., May 14, 1948; MD, St. Louis U., 1974. Diplomate Am. Bd. Internal Medicine; Am. Bd. Nuclear Medicine. Intern R.I. Hosp., Providence, 1974, resident in internal medicine, 1975-76; resident in nuclear medicine Harvard Med. Sch., Boston, 1977-79; from assoc. to staff physician Barnes Hosp., St. Louis, 1987—; from assoc. to cons. staff physician Children's Hosp., 1987—; prof. Washington U., 1993—. Co-team leader health effects sect. Internat. Atomic Energy Agy. Internat. Chernobyl Project, 1990; mem. Am. Bd. Nuclear Medicine, 1993-99; mem. com. on assessment of CDC radiation studies NRC/NAS, 1993-98; mem. sci. com. 1 and 4 Nat. Coun. on Radiation Protection and Measurements, 1993—; mem. coun. Nat. Coun. on Radiation Protection, 1996—, bd. dirs., 2000—; Vets. Adv. Com. on Environ. Hazards, 1997—. Contbr. articles to profl. jours. Mem. Soc. Nuc. Medicine (v.p. elect 2001), Alpha Omega Alpha. Office: Acad Faculty Mallinckrodt Inst Radiology 510 S Kingshighway Blvd Saint Louis MO 63110-1016

ROYHAB, RONALD, journalist, newspaper editor; b. Lorain, Ohio, Oct. 6, 1942; s. Halim Farah and Elizabeth Della (Naiser) R.; m. Roberta Lee Libb, Apr. 20, 1969; children: David Libb, Aaron Nicholas. Student, Lorain County (Ohio) Coll., Kent State U.; student grad. program, Am. U., Washington. Reporter Lorain Jour., 1966-69; reporter spl. assignment Scripps Howard Cin. Post, 1971-72; investigative reporter Scripps Howard Cleve. Press, 1972-75; chief bur. Scripps Howard Ohio Bur., Columbus, 1975-78; asst. mng. editor Scripps Howard News Svc., Washington, 1978-81; mng. editor Scripps Howard El Paso (Tex.) Herald Post, 1981-83; asst. mng. editor Scripps Howard Pitts. Press, 1983-92; assoc. editor Pitts. Post Gazette, 1992-93; mng. editor Toledo Blade, 1993-97, exec. editor, 1997—. Bd. dirs. Am. Lebanese Congress; mem. Knight in Order of St. Ignatius of Antioch, 1997. With USAR, 1964-70. Recipient 7 awards for Excellence Cleve. Newspaper Guild, 1972-75, Spl. Sect. awards Pa. Newspaper Pubs. Assn., 1985, 86, 88; named to DeMolay Legion of Honor, 1997; fellow Am. Polit. Sci. Assn., 1970-71. Mem. Am. Soc. Newspaper Editors, AP Soc. Ohio (past pres.), Ohio Newspaper Assn., Toledo Press Club (pres.). Eastern Orthodox. Home: 27262 Fort Meigs Rd Perrysburg OH 43551-1230 Office: Toledo Blade 541 N Superior St Toledo OH 43660-0002 E-mail: royhab@theblade.com.

ROZEBOOM, JOHN A. religious organization administrator; Dir. Christian Ref. Home Missions, 1983. Office: Christian Ref Ch in N Am 2850 Kalamazoo Ave SE Grand Rapids MI 49560-0001

ROZELL, JOSEPH GERARD, accountant; b. Kansas City, Kans., Mar. 20, 1959; s. Joseph Frank and Frances Elizabeth (Gojmeric) R. BSBA, Rockhurst Coll., 1981; MBA, U. Mo., Kansas City, 1992. Staff acct. Donnelly, Meiners & Jordan, Kansas City, Mo., 1981-82, Francis A. Wright & Co., Kansas City, 1982-88, Libby Corp., Kansas City, 1988-90, Sprint Corp., Overland Park, Kans., 1990—. Mem. Greater Kansas City Young Reps., pres. 1988-89; treas. Jackson County Rep. Com., 1989-97. Mem. AICPAs, Mo. Soc. CPAs (legis. com., liaison com.), Greater Kans. Jaycees (treas. 1988-89). Republican. Roman Catholic. Avocations: basketball, soccer, volleyball. Home: 12112 Madison Ct Kansas City MO 64145-1023

ROZELLE, LEE THEODORE, physical chemist, researcher; b. Rhinelander, Wis., Mar. 9, 1933; s. Theodore and Alice (Omholt) R.; m. Barbara J. Ingli, June 21, 1955; children— David, Steven, Carolyn, Ann, Kenneth B.S., U. Wis., 1955, Ph.D., 1960. Rsch. chemist DuPont Corp., Circleville, Ohio, 1960-63; prin. scientist-tech. coord. Honeywell Corp., Mpls., 1963-67; dir. chemistry div. North Star Rsch. Inst., 1967-74; v.p. R&D USCI div. C.R. Bard, Billerica, Mass., 1974-77; dir. engring. tech. div. Mellon Inst., Pitts., 1977-78; dir. rsch. and devel. Permutit Co., Monmouth Junction, N.J., 1978-80; v.p. rsch. and devel. Gelman Scis., Inc., Ann Arbor, Mich., 1980-82; v.p. sci. and tech. Culligan Internat. Co., Northbrook, Ill., 1982-87; assoc. dir. rsch. Olin Chems. Rsch. div. Olin Corp., Cheshire, Conn., 1987-92; cons. in water treatment tech., mktg. and mgmt., 1992—; pres., cons. Water Solutions, Inc., 1995—; exec. v.p. Puraq Water Systems, Inc., 1996—. Cons. in field; mem. Nat. Drinking Water Adv. Council EPA, 1987-90; mem. small bus. inovative rsch. com. U.S. EPA, 1999—. Contbr. chpts. to books, numerous articles to profl. jours. Bd. dirs. Unitarian Ch., Andover, Mass., 1974-77 NIH fellow, 1958-60; recipient Spl. Hominum award Nat. Sanitation Found., 1988. Fellow Am. Inst. Chemists; mem. AAAS, Am. Chem. Soc., Am. Soc. Artificial Internal Organs, Health Industry Mfrs. Assn. (chmn. spl. activities com.), Water Pollution Control Fedn., Water Quality Assn. (chmn. sci. adv. com., Award of Merit 1989), Am. Water Works Assn., Assn. Met. Water Agencies, Filtration Soc., Pacific Water Quality Assn. (bd. dirs. 1987-90, Robert Gans award 1988), Am. Soc. Agrl. Engring., Internat. Water Supply Assn., European Membrane Soc., N.Am. Membrane Soc., Asociacion Interamericano De Ingenieria Sanaitaria y Ambiental, Sigma Xi, Eta Phi Alpha, Phi Lambda Upsilon. Home and Office: 626 23rd St N La Crosse WI 54601-3825

ROZOF, PHYLLIS CLAIRE, lawyer; b. Flint, Mich., Aug. 3, 1948; d. Eugene Robert and Loveta Lucille Greenwood; m. Robert James Rozof, July 17, 1970 (dec. Oct. 1995); children: Nathan, Zachary. AB with high distinction, U. Mich., 1970, JD magna cum laude, 1977. Bar: Mich. 1977, Fla. 1978. Assoc. Honigman Miller Schwartz and Cohn, Detroit, 1977-81, ptnr., 1982—. Mem. Comml. Real Estate Women Detroit (pres. 1992-93). Office: Honigman Miller Schwartz & Cohn 2290 1st National Bldg Detroit MI 48226

RUB, TIMOTHY F. museum director; BA in Art History, Middlebury Coll., 1974; MA in Art History, NYU, 1979; MBA, Yale U., 1987; postgrad., Harvard U., 1998. Curatorial intern Met. Mus. Art, 1983; lectr. art and archtl. history Cooper-Hewitt Mus./Parsons Sch. Design, Stevens Inst. Tech., 1979-84; guest curator Bronx Mus. Arts, N.Y., 1985-86; curator Cooper-Hewitt Mus., N.Y.C., 1983-87; assoc. dir. Hood Mus. Dartmouth Coll., Hanover, N.H., 1987-91, dir., COO, 1991-2000; dir. Cin. Art Mus., 2000—. Office: Cin Art Mus 953 Eden Park Dr Cincinnati OH 45202-1596

RUBEN, ALAN MILES, law educator; b. Phila., May 13, 1931; s. Maurice Robert and Ruth (Blatt) R.; m. Betty Jane Willis, May 23, 1965. AB, U. Pa., 1953, MA, JD, U. Pa., 1956. Bar: Pa. 1957, Ohio 1972. Law clk. Supreme Ct. Pa., 1956-58; pvt. practice Phila., 1958-65; assoc. counsel Aetna Life & Casualty Co., Hartford, Conn., 1965-69; corp. counsel Lubrizol Corp., Cleve., 1969-70; prof. Cleve.-Marshall Coll. Law, Cleve. State U., 1970—; adj. prof. law Fudan U., Shanghai, People's Republic of China, 1993—; dep. to city solicitor Phila., 1958-61; dep. atty. gen. State of Pa., 1961-65; spl. counsel to U.S. Senate Subcom. on Nat. Stockpile, 1962; commentator Higher Edn. Issues Sta. WCLV-FM, Cleve., 1975-87. Mem. nat. panel labor arbitrators Nat. Acad. Arbitrators, Fed. Mediation and Conciliation Svc. and Am. Arbitration Assn., Ohio State Employment Rels. Bd.; lectr. law U. Conn. Law Sch., 1968; vis. prof. law FuDan U., Shanghai, Peoples Republic of China, 1988-89; cons. Shanghai Law Office for Fgn. Economy and Trade, Peoples Republic of China, 1991-94. Author: The Constitutionality of Basic Protection for the Automobile Accident Victim, 1968, Unauthorized Insurance: The Regulation of the Unregulated, 1968, Arbitration in Public Employee Labor Disputes: Myth, Shibboleth and Reality, 1971, Illicit Sex of Campus: Federal Remedies for Employment Discrimination, 1971, Model Public Employees Labor Relations Act,

1972, Sentencing the Corporate Criminal, 1972, Modern Corporation Law, supp. edit., 1978, An American Lawyer's Observations on the Inauguration of the Shanghai Stock Exchange, 1989, Ohio Limited Partnership Law, 1992—, Practice Guides, Ohio Limited Liability Company, Law, 1995—; co-editor: How Arbitration Works, 1997; contbr.: With an Eye to Tomorrow: The Future Outlook of the Life Insurance Industry, 1968, The Urban Transportation Crisis: The Philadelphia Plan, 1961, Philadelphia's Union Shop Contract, 1961, The Administrative Agency Law: Reform of Adjudicative Procedure and the Revised Model Act, 1963, The Computer in Court: Computer Simulation and the robinson Patman Act, 1964. Bd. dirs. U.S. Olympic Com., 1968-73; chmn. U.S. Olympic Fencing Sport Com., 1969-73; pres. U.S. Fencing Assn., 1968-73; capt. U.S. Pan-Am. Fencing Team, 1971, U.S. Olympic Fencing Team, 1972; bd. dirs. Legal Aid Soc. Cleve., 1973-77; trustee Cleve.-San Jose Ballet, 1999-2001. Winner Internat. Inst. Edn. Internat. Debate Championship, 1953; recipient Harrison Tweed Bowl and Am. Law Inst. prizes Nat. Moot Ct. Competition, 1955; named Guggenheim scholar, 1949-53, Fulbright scholar FuDan U., Shanghai, 1993-94. Mem. ABA, Ohio Bar Assn. (corp. law and profl. responsibility com.), Cleve. Bar Assn. (Securities Law Inst.), Assn. Am. Law Schs. (chmn. sect. law and edn. 1976-78), Internat. Indsl. Rels. Rsch. Assn., Internat. Soc. Labor Law, Internat. Bar Assn., Union Internat. Des Avocats, Internat. Law Assn., AAUP (pres. Ohio conf. 1974-75), Rowfant Club, Phi Beta Kappa, Pi Gamma Mu. Home: 9925 Lake Shore Blvd Bratenahl OH 44108-1052 Office: Cleve State U 18th St And Euclid Ave Cleveland OH 44115

RUBEN, GARY A. marketing and communications consultant; b. Cochem, Germany, Jan. 1, 1924; came to U.S., 1939, naturalized, 1943; s. Jules and Erna (Hirsch) R.; m. Irene Jehle, Aug. 12, 1962; 1 child, Monique L. Student, Acad. Comml. Art, Indpls., 1940-41. With advt. dept. Indpls. News, 1940-41; advt. mgr. Greater Indpls. Amusement Corp., 1941-42; pres. Ruben Advt. Agy., Indpls., 1948-68; chmn. bd. Ruben, Montgomery & Assos., 1968-76; pres. Prestige Program Sales Inc., 1973-76, Gary A. Ruben Inc. (advt. and mktg. cons.), Indpls., 1976—. Past lectr. advt. and bd. fellows Northwood Inst.; past pres. Nat. Fedn. Advt. Agys., 1971. Hon. trustee Indpls. Children's Mus. With Combat Engrs. AUS, 1943-46. Paul Harris fellow Rotary Internat. Home: 7370 Lions Head Dr Indianapolis IN 46260-3460 Office: 931 E 86th St Ste 206 Indianapolis IN 46240-1852

RUBENS, SIDNEY MICHEL, physicist, technical advisor; b. Spokane, Wash., Mar. 21, 1910; s. Max Zvoln and Jennie Golda (Rubinovich) R.; m. Julienne Rose Fridner, May 11, 1944; 1 child, Deborah Janet. BS, U. Wash., 1934, PhD, 1939. Instr. U. So. Calif., L.A., 1939—40; rsch. assoc. UCLA, 1940—41; physicist Naval Ordnance Lab., Washington, 1941—46, Engring. Rsch. Assocs., St. Paul, 1946—52; mgr. physics Univac divsn. Sperry Rand, 1958—61, dir. rsch., 1961-66, staff scientist, 1969—71, dir. spl. projects, 1971—75, cons., 1975—81; tech. advisor Vertimag Sys. Corp., 1981—, Advanced Rsch. Corp., Mpls., 1986—. Lectr. U. Pa., 1960-61; mem. adv. subcom. on instrumentation and data processing NASA, 1967-69; mem. panel on computer tech. NAS, 1969. Author: Amplifier and Memory Devices, 1965; contbg. author: Magnetic Recording—The First Hundred Years, 1999. Hon. fellow U. Minn., 1977—. Fellow IEEE (Magnetic Soc. info. storage award 1987, Millennium medal 2000); mem. AAAS, N.Y. Acad. Scis., Am. Phys. Soc., Am. Geophys. Union, Acad. Applied Sci., Minn. Acad. Sci., Am. Optical Soc., Phi Beta Kappa, Sigma Xi, Pi Mu Esilon. Achievements include patents in magnetic material and devices. Home: 1077 Sibley Hwy Apt 506 Saint Paul MN 55118-3616 Office: Advanced Rsch Corp 815 14th Ave SE Minneapolis MN 55414-1515

RUBENSTEIN, ALBERT HAROLD, industrial engineering and management sciences educator; b. Phila., Nov. 11, 1923; s. Leo and Jean (Kaplan) R.; m. Hildette Grossman, Sept. 11, 1949; children: Michael Stephen, Lisa Joan. BS in Indsl. Engring. magna cum laude (Sr. prize econs.), Lehigh U., 1949; MS in Indsl. Engring, Columbia, 1950, PhD in Indsl. Engring. and Mgmt, 1954; DEng (hon.), Lehigh U., 1993. Asst. to pres. Perry Equipment Corp., 1940-43; rsch. assoc. Columbia U., 1950-53; asst. prof. indsl. mgmt. MIT, 1954-59; prof. indsl. engring. and mgmt. scis. Northwestern U., 1959-97; emeritus prof., 1997—; Walter P. Murphy prof. Northwestern U., 1986—, dir. Ctr. for Info. Tech., 1986-97; pres. Internat. Applied Sci. and Tech. Assos., 1977—; vis. prof. U. Calif., Berkeley; pres. Sr. Strategy Group, 1995—. Adj. prof. U. Calif., San Diego, 1997—; cons. to govt. and industry. Dir. Narragansett Capital Corp. Author books and articles in field. Served with inf. AUS, World War II. Decorated Purple Heart, Combat Inf. badge.; Recipient Lincoln Arc Welding Found. prize paper, 1948, Pioneer in Innovation Mgmt. award Com. Innovation Mgmt., 1992; Omicron Delta Kappa annual fellow, 1949-50; Fulbright research fellow, 1955 Fellow IEEE (editor trans. 1959—, Engring. Mgr. of Yr. award 1992), Soc. Applied Anthropology; mem. AAAS (chmn. indsl. sci. and tech. sect. 1997—), Inst. Mgmt. Scis. (sr. mem., dir. studies for coll. on R & D 1960—, v.p. rsch. and edn. 1966-68) Home and Office: 1630 Chicago Ave Apt 2010 Evanston IL 60201-6025

RUBENSTEIN, JEROME MAX, lawyer; b. St. Louis, Feb. 16, 1927; s. Jacob J. and Anne (Frankel) R.; m. Judith Hope Grand, July 31, 1954; children— Edward J., Emily Rubenstein Muslin, Daniel H. AB, Harvard U., 1950, LLB, 1955. Bar: Mo. 1956, U.S. Dist. Ct. (ea. dist.) Mo. 1956, U.S. Ct. Appeals (8th cir.) 1956. Mem. English lit. faculty U. So. Philippines, Cebu, 1950-51; law clk U.S. Dist. Ct., St. Louis, 1955-56; assoc. Lewis, Rice, Tucker, Allen & Chubb, 1956-64, Grand, Peper & Martin, St. Louis, 1964-65, ptnr., 1965-66; jr. ptnr. Bryan Cave, 1966-67, ptnr., 1968-97, of counsel, 1998—. Dir. Commerce Bank, N.A. Bd. dirs. Independence Ctr., St. Louis, 1985-88, The Arts and Edn. Coun. Greater St. Louis, 1991-99. Served with USN, 1945-46. Bd. dirs. Independence Ctr., St. Louis, 1985. Served with USN, 1945-46 Mem. ABA, Mo. Bar Assn., St. Louis Bar Assn., Mo. Athletic Club, Harvard Club of St. Louis (pres. 1982-83, bd. dirs. 1983-90). Jewish. Avocations: jogging; tennis. Home: 7394 Westmoreland Dr Saint Louis MO 63130-4240 Office: Bryan Cave 1 Metropolitan Sq Ste 3600 Saint Louis MO 63102-2750

RUBENSTEIN, PAMELA SILVER, precision machinery executive; b. Lansing, Mich., May 12, 1953; d. Neil M. and Leah Rebecca (Coffman) Silver; m. Alec Robert Rubenstein. BA in Linguistics, U. Mich., 1974; MA in teaching English to spkrs. of other langs., Columbia U. Tchrs. Coll., 1976; MA in Linguistics, U. Ill., 1978, doctoral studies in linguistics, 1978-80. Instr. Columbia U. Tchrs. Coll., N.Y.C., 1976, U. Ill., Urbana, 1978, libr. Linguistic Dept., 1978-79; asst. libr. Ill. State Geol. Survey, 1979-80; tchr. Congregation Temple Israel, Springfield, Ill., 1980-81; adminstr., tchr. Springfield Bd. Jewish Edn., 1981-82; instr. Comm. Divsn. Lincoln Land C.C., Springfield, 1981-82; tchr. Cmty. Hebrew Sch., Charleston, S.C., 1982-83; instr. The Citadel and Coll. of Charleston, 1983; legal sec. Gibbs & Holmes, Charleston, 1984, May, Oberfell & Lorber, South Bend, Ind., 1984-88; instr. U. Notre Dame, 1987; tchr. Triton Sch. Corp., Bourbon, 1988-89; v.p. Allied Screw Products, Inc., Mishawaka, 1989—. Contbr. articles to profl. jours. Mem. Temple Beth-El Sisterhood, South Bend, 1987—, Hadassah (life mem.). Mem. Michiana Gem and Mineral Soc. (treas. 1995-98). Office: Allied Screw Products Inc 815 E Lowell Ave Mishawaka IN 46545-6480

RUBERG, ROBERT LIONEL, surgery educator; b. Phila., July 22, 1941; s. Norman and Yetta (Wolfman) R.; m. Cynthia Lief, June 26, 1966; children: Frederick, Mark, Joshua. BA, Haverford (Pa.) Coll., 1963; MD, Harvard U., 1967. Diplomate Am. Bd. Surgery, Am. Bd. Plastic Surgery. Instr. surgery U. Pa., Phila., 1972-75; asst. prof. Ohio State U., Columbus, 1975-81, assoc. prof., 1981-88, prof., 1988—. Bd. dirs. Am. Bd. Plastic Surgery, 1991-97, vice-chair, 1996-97; chmn. curriculum com. Coll. Medicine, Ohio State U., 1984-97; chief plastic surgery Ohio State U. Hosps., 1985—. Plastic Surgery Ednl. Found. research grantee, 1976, 78. Fellow ACS; mem. Am. Assn. Plastic Surgeons, Assn. Acad. Chairmen of Plastic Surgery (pres. 1994-95), Plastic Surgery Edn. Found. (pres. 2000-01, chair residency rev. com. for plastic surgery 2000—). Avocation: bicycling. Home: 100 Walnut Woods Ct Gahanna OH 43230-6200 Office: N325-B Means Hall 1654 Upham Dr Columbus OH 43210

RUBIN, ALAN J. environmental engineer, chemist, photgrapher; b. Yonkers, N.Y., Mar. 20, 1934; s. Jerome and Lydia R.; m. Ann Kopyt, June 17, 1962; 1 dau., Sara. B.S. in Civil Engring, U. Miami (Fla.), 1959; M.S. in San. Engring, U. N.C., Chapel Hill, 1962, Ph.D. in Environ. Chemistry, 1966. Civil engr. FAA, Ft. Worth, 1959-60; asst. prof. U. Cin., 1965-68; prof. civil engring. Ohio State U., Columbus, 1968-91, prof. emeritus, 1991—; with U.S. Geol. Survey, 1991-93. Vis. prof. Technion, Haifa, 1984. Editor 4 books on environ. chemistry; contbr. articles profl. jours. Served with AUS, 1953-55. Mem. Am. Water Works Assn., Water Pollution Control Fedn., Internat. Assn. Water Pollution Research. Achievements include research on giardia cysts, metal ion chemistry, flotation techniques, disinfection, flocculation, coagulation, adsorption, and other physical-chemical treatment processes. Home: 1438 Sherbrooke Pl Columbus OH 43209-3113 Office: Ohio State Univ Dept Civil and Environtl Engring Columbus OH 43210-1058 E-mail: arubin@columbus.rr.com.

RUBIN, JEAN ESTELLE, mathematics educator; b. Bklyn., Oct. 29, 1926; d. Leonard Lewis and Phyllis Irma (Mann) Hirsh; m. Herman Rubin, Mar. 23, 1952; children: Arthur Leonard, Leonore Anne Rubin Findsen. B.S., Queens Coll., 1948; M.A., Columbia U., 1949; Ph.D., Stanford U., 1955. Instr. Queens Coll., 1949-51, Stanford U., 1953-55; lectr. U. Oreg., 1955-59; asst. prof. Mich. State U., 1960-67; asso. prof. math. Purdue U., West Lafayette, Ind., 1968-75, prof., 1975—. Author: Set Theory for the Mathematician, 1967, Mathematical Logic: Applications and Theory, 1990; co-author: (with H. Rubin) Equivalents of the Axiom of Choice, 1963, Equivalents of the Axiom of Choice II, 1985, (with P. Howard) Consequences of the Axiom of Choice, 1998. Vol. West Lafayette Libr., 1981—; bd. dirs. Lafayette Symphony Orch., Inc., 1987-93, Friends of West Lafayette Libr., 1993—. Mem. Am. Math. Soc., Assn. Symbolic Logic, Math. Assn. Am. (vis. lectr. 1976-86), Purdue Staff Aero Club Inc. (bd. dirs. 1975-90). Home: 1214 W Sunset Ln West Lafayette IN 47906-2429 Office: Purdue U Math Dept West Lafayette IN 47907-1395

RUBIN, PATRICIA, internist; b. Apr. 27, 1962; MD, Wright State U., 1988. Cert. internal medicine. Resident in internal medicine U. Cin., 1988-91; fellow in cardiology U. Hosp., Cleve., 1991; rsch. fellow in cardiology U. Wash. Sch. Medicine, Seattle, 1993—; pvt. practice Cardiology One, Kent, Ohio. Recipient Clinician Scientist award Am. Heart Assn., 1995-96. Mem. ACP, AMA, ACC. Office: Cardiology One Box 8086 1330 Mercy Dr NW Ste 200 Canton OH 44708-2624

RUBIN, STANLEY GERALD, aerospace engineering educator; b. Bklyn., May 11, 1938; s. Harry Jack and Cele (Sake) R.; m. Carol Ruth Kalvin, Sept. 29, 1963; children— Stephany, Elizabeth, Barbara B.A.E., Poly Inst. Bklyn., 1959; Ph.D., Cornell U., 1963. Asst. prof. to prof. dept. aerospace engring. Poly. Inst. N.Y., Farmingdale, 1964-79, Assoc. dir. aerodynamic labs., 1977-79; prof. aerospace engring. and engring. mechanics U. Cin., 1979—2000, head dept., 1979-89, dir. NASA Univ. Space Engring. Ctr. on Health Monitoring Space Propulsion Systems, U. Cin., 1988-91, prof. emeritus, 2000—; sci. coun. Inst. for Computer Application in Sci./Engring. NASA Langley Rsch. Ctr., Hampton, Va., 1998—. Cons. Aerospace Corp., NASA AAC/ARTS, Allison (GM), others; mem. adv. com. Inst. for Computational Methods in Propulsion, NASA; keynote spkr. 9th Internat. Conf. Numerical Methods in Fluid Mechanics, Saclay, France Editor-in-chief Internat. Jour. Computers and Fluids, 1978—; contbr. articles to profl. jours. and Ann. Rev. Fluid Mechanics, 1992. NSF fellow, 1963-64; grantee Office Naval Research, 1978-88, AFOSR 1968-92, NASA, 1973— , others Fellow AIAA (assoc.), ASME; mem. Am. Soc. Engring. Edn., Sigma Xi, Sigma Gamma Tau, Tau Beta Pi Home: 10695 Deershadow Ln Cincinnati OH 45242 Office: U Cin ML 070 509 Old Chem Hall Cincinnati OH 45221-0070 E-mail: srubin@uceng.uc.edu.

RUBNITZ, MYRON ETHAN, pathologist, educator; b. Omaha, Mar. 2, 1924; s. Abraham Srol and Esther Molly (Jonich) R.; m. Susan Belle Block, Feb. 9, 1952; children: Mary Lu Rubnitz Roffe, Peter, Thomas (dec.), Robert. BSc, U. Nebr., l945; MD, U. Nebr., Omaha, 1947. Diplomate Am. Bd. Pathology. Intern Mt. Sinai Hosp., Cleve., 1947-48, fellow N.Y.C., l948-49; resident in pathology Michael Reese Hosp., Chgo., 1949-5l; pathologist VA Hosp., Hines, Ill., 1953-56, chief labs., 1956-93, cons., 1993—; assoc. prof. pathology Loyola U. Med. Sch., Maywood, 1963-70, prof., 1970-99, prof. emeritus, 1999—. Adj. prof. Ill. State U., Normal, 1979-96, U. St. Francis, Joliet, Ill., 1989—, Ea. Ill. U. Charleston, 1991—, Western Ill. U., Macomb, 1991—; clin. instr. Augustana Coll., Rock Island, Ill., 1991—. Chmn. candidates com. Village Caucus, Winnteka, Ill., l969-70; bd. dirs. Chgo. Commons Assn., 1968—, North Shore Sr. Ctr., 1998—; mem. New Trier High Sch. Caucus, Winnetka, l972-74. With AUS, 1943-46, PTO; lst lt. M.C., U.S. Army, l95l-53. Fellow Am. Soc. Clin. Pathologists, Coll. Am. Pathologists; mem. Internat. Acad. Pathology, Assn. VA Pathologists (pres. 1982-84), Chgo. Pathology Soc., Lake Shore Country Club (Glencoe, Ill.), North Shore Racquet Club, Mich. Shores Club (Wilmette, Ill.). Republican. Jewish. Avocations: electronics, tennis, travel. Home: 979 Sheridan Rd Winnetka IL 60093

RUCH, RICHARD HURLEY, manufacturing company executive; b. Plymouth, Ind., Apr. 15, 1930; s. Dallas Claude and Mabel (Hurley) R.; m. Patricia Lou Overbeek, June 27, 1931; children: Richard, Michael, Christine, Douglas. BA, Mich. State U., 1952. Stores acctg. supr. Kroger Inc., Grand Rapids, Mich., 1954-55; chief acct. Herman Miller Inc., Zeeland, 1955-58, controller, 1958-63, dir. mfg., 1963-67, v.p. mfg., 1967-77, v.p. adminstrn., 1978, v.p. corp. resources, 1979-85, chief fin. officer, sr. v.p., 1985-87, chief exec. officer, 1988-92, pres, chief exec. officer, 1990-92, also vice chair bd. dirs., 1992-95; chmn. of bd., 1995—. Active Hope Coll., Twentieth Century Club, Holland, Mich.; formerly active Holland C. of C., Zeeland Planning Com.; bd. dirs. Words of Hope, 1997. Mem. Scanlon Plan Assocs. (bd. dirs., past pres.). Avocations: tennis, running. Office: Herman Miller Inc 855 E Main Ave Zeeland MI 49464-1372

RUCKER, RICHARD S. information systems executive; b. Dayton, Ohio, Sept. 4, 1947; s. Wilbert Hunter and Estelle Janet Rucker. BBA, Wright State U., Dayton, 1976; MBA, Cen. Mich. U., 1987; PhD in Mgmt. Info. Systems, Kennedy-Western U., 1990. Asst. program mgr. Synergy, Inc., Dayton, 1968-78; mgr. data processing Ledex, Inc., Vandalia, Ohio, 1978-83; cons. analyst NCR Corp., Dayton, 1983-85; mgr. info. systems SelectTech Corp., 1985; dir. computing and tech. svcs. Dayton Bd. Edn., 1985-91, asst. supt. bus. and tech. svcs., 1991-92; v.p. Midwest region Metters Industries, Inc., 1992-97; CEO, pres. The Rucker Group, Dayton, 1997—. Pres. Richard S. Rucker & Assocs., Dayton, 1982-97. Bd. dirs. Dakota Youth Ctr., Dayton, 1983, Dayton Urban League, 1986—; mem. exec. council Congl. Adv. Council to U.S. Congressman Tony Hall, 1986. Named one of Outstanding Young Men Am., 1984, Man of Achievement, 1988. Mem. Kappa Alpha Psi. Democrat. Avocations: painting, reading, swimming, astro-physics, basketball. Home: 2914 Forest Grove Ave Dayton OH 45406-4039

RUCKER, ROBERT D. judge; b. Canton, Ga. married; 3 children. BA, Ind. U.; JD, Valparaiso Sch. of Law; LLM, U. Va. Dep. prosecuting atty., Lake County, Ind.; city atty. City of Gary; pvt. practice East Chicago; justice Ind. State Supreme Ct., Indpls., 1999—. Former vice chmn. Ind. Commn. for Continuing Legal Edn. Bd. dirs. Legal Svcs. of N.W. Ind. Decorated Vietnam Vet. Office: State House Rm 312 200 W Washington St Indianapolis IN 46204-2798*

RUDE, BRIAN DAVID, utilities company executive; b. Viroqua, Wis., Aug. 25, 1955; s. Raymond and Conelee (Johnson) R.; m. Karen Thulin; children: Erik, Nels. BA magna cum laude, Luther Coll., 1977; MA, U. Wis., Madison, 1994. Mem. Wis. Assembly, Madison, 1982-84, Wis. Senate, Madison, 1984-2000; pres. Wis. State Sen., 1993-96, 98. With corp. communications The Trane Co., La Crosse, Wis., 1981-85; dir. external rels. Dairyland Power Cooperative; chmn. Midwestern Higher Edn. Commn. Mem. Evang. Luth. Ch. Am. Coun. Mem. Lions, Sons of Norway, Norwegian-Am. Hist. Assn. (bd. dirs.), Rotary. Republican. Lutheran. Avocations: reading, gardening, traveling, fishing. Home: 307 Babcock St PO Box 367 Coon Valley WI 54623-0367 Office: 3400 East Ave S PO Box 817 La Crosse WI 54602 E-mail: bdr@dairynet.com.

RUDELIUS, WILLIAM, marketing educator; b. Rockford, Ill., Sept. 2, 1931; s. Carl William and Clarissa Euclid (Davis) R.; m. Jacqueline Urch Dunham, July 3, 1954; children: Robert, Jeanne, Katherine, Kristi. B.S. in Mech. Engring., U. Wis., 1953; M.B.A., U. Pa., 1959, Ph.D. in Econs., 1964. Program engr., missile and space vehicle dept. Gen. Electric Co., Phila., 1956-57, 59-61; sr. research economist North Star Research Inst., Mpls., 1964-66; lectr. U. Minn., 1961-64, asst. prof. mktg. Coll. Bus. Adminstrn., 1964, assoc. prof., 1966-72, prof., 1972—. Co-author: (with W. Bruce Erickson) An Introduction to Contemporary Business, 1973, rev. 4th edit., 1985, (with Eric N. Berkowitz, Roger A. Kerin and Steven W. Hartley) Marketing, 1986, rev. 7th edit., 20030, (with Krzysztof Przybytowski, Roger A. Kerin and Steven W. Hartley) Marketing na Przykładach, 1998, (with others) Mapketkht, 1st Russian edit., 2001; contbr. articles to profl. jours. Served with USAF, 1954-55. Home: 1425 Alpine Pass Minneapolis MN 55416-3560 Office: U St Thomas Grad Sch Bus MPL 331 1000 LaSalle Ave Minneapolis MN 55403-2005 E-mail: wrudelius@stthomas.edu.

RUDELL, MILTON WESLEY, aerospace engineer; b. Rice Lake, Wis., July 9, 1920; s. George C. and Edna (Bjoraa) R.; m. Doris Lorraine Shella, Nov. 30, 1941; children: Helen, Geoffrey, Lynn, Deborah, Leah, Andrea, Kessea, Eric, Erin. B in Aerospace Engring., U. Minn., 1946. Registered profl. engr. Chief tool engr. Boeing Aircraft Corp., Wichita, Kans. and Seattle, 1941-43, stateside and overseas field engr., 1943-45; chief fueling systems engr. N.W. Airlines, Mpls., 1946-50; pres. Rumoco Co., Frederic, Wis., 1950-68; registrar ECPI-Nat. IBM computer sch., Mpls., 1968-69; pres. Life Engring. Co., Milw. and Frederic, Wis., 1969—. Designer original med. surg. suture tape, 1951; designer 1st match-book cover with strike plate on rear side for safety, 1942; pioneered high-speed underwing fueling sys. for comml. aircraft and 1st hydrant ground fueling sys. for comml. aircraft; co-author Ops. & Maintenance Manual for B-29 aircraft, 1943. Founder Frederic Found. for Advanced Edn.; bd. dirs. Frederic Area Hist. Soc. Recipient WWII Aeronautical Engring. Citation from Pres. Eisenhower, 1944. Mem. Exptl. Aircraft Assn., Wis. Aviation Hall of Fame, Northwestern Wis. Mycol. Soc. (charter). Lutheran. Home and Office: PO Box 400 501 Wisconsin Ave N Frederic WI 54837-0400

RUDNICK, ELLEN AVA, health care executive; b. New Haven; d. Harold and C. Vivian (Soybel) R.; children from previous marriage: Sarah, Noah; m. Paul W. Earle. BA, Vassar Coll., 1972; MBA, U. Chgo., 1973. Sr. fin. analyst Quaker Oats, Chgo., 1973-75; various positions Baxter Internat., Deerfield, Ill., 1975-80, dir. planning, 1980-83, corp. v.p., 1985-1990; pres. Baxter Mgmt. Svcs., 1983-1990, HCIA, Balt., 1990-92, CEO Advs., Northbrook, Ill., 1992—; prin., chmn. Pacific Biometrics, Lake Forest, Calif., 1993-99; exec. dir., clin. prof. Entrepreneurship Program Sch. Bus. U. Chgo., 1999—. Bd. dirs. Liberty Mut. Ins., Oxford Health Plans, 2001—. Chief crusader Met. Chgo. United Way, 1982—85; mem. cir. friends Chgo. YMCA, 1985—89; bd. dirs. Evanston Northwestern-Highland Park Hosp., 1990—99, Health Mgmt. Sys., Oxford Health Plans, 2001—, Liberty Mut. Ins., 2001—, Evanston-Northwestern Hosp., 2000—; pres. coun. Nat. Coll. Edn., Evanston, Ill., 1983—93. Office: Univ Chgo Grad Sch Bus 1101 E 58th St Chicago IL 60637-1511

RUDNICK, PAUL DAVID, lawyer; b. Chgo., May 15, 1940; s. Harry Louis and Cele (Gordon) R.; m. Hope Korshak, June 13, 1963; children: William A., Carolyn. BS, Tulane U., 1962; JD cum laude, Northwestern U., 1965. Bar: Ill. 1965, Colo. 1994, U.S. Dist. Ct. (no. dist.) Ill. Assoc. Schiff, Hardin & Waite, Chgo., 1965-66; ptnr. Piper, Marbury, Rudnick & Wolfe, 1966-99, sr. counsel, 2000—. Editor Northwestern U. Law Rev., 1964-65; co-editor, author: Illinois Real Estate Forms, 1989. Mem. Pitkin County Colo. Planning and Zoning Commn. Mem. Am. Coll. Real Estate Lawyers, Internat. Found. Employee Benefits, Order of Coif. Office: Piper Marbury Rudnick & Wolfe 203 N La Salle St Ste 1800 Chicago IL 60601-1210 E-mail: paul.rudnick@piperrudnick.com.

RUDOLPH, CARL J. insurance company executive; Chartered life underwriter; cert. mgmt. acct.; CPA; cert. cash mgr. Dir. fin. planning & control sys. Aid Assn. Lutherans, Appleton, Wis., 1971-86, v.p., controller, 1986-97, v.p., controller, treas. corp. fin. svcs., 1997-99, sr. v.p., CFO, 1999—. Mem. Fin. Execs. Inst., Treasury Mgmt. Assn., AICPAs. Office: Aid Assn Lutherans 4321 N Ballard Rd Appleton WI 54919-0001

RUDOLPH, LAVERE CHRISTIAN, library director; b. Jasper, Ind., Dec. 24, 1921; s. Joseph Frank and Rose (Stradtner) R. A.B., DePauw U., 1948; B.D., Louisville Presbyn. Sem., 1951; Ph.D., Yale, 1958; student, U. Zurich, Switzerland, 1960; M.L.S., Ind. U., 1968. Ordained to Ministry Presbyn. Ch., 1950; pastor in Ind. and Conn., 1950-54; mem. faculty Louisville Presbyn. Sem., 1954-69, prof. ch. history, 1960-69; lectr. history U. Louisville, 1965-69; rare books bibliographer Van Pelt Library U. Pa.; head tech. services Lilly Library, Ind. U., 1970-78, curator of books, 1978-86, librarian emeritus, 1987—. Author: Hoosier Zion, 1963 (Thomas Kuch award Ind. U. Writers Conf. 1964), Story of the Church, 1966, Francis Asbury, 1966, Indiana Letters, 1979, Religion in Indiana, 1986, Hoosier Faiths, 1995. Served to capt. USAAF, 1940-46. Mem.: Presbyn. Hist. Soc., Am. Soc. Ch. History, Phi Beta Kappa. Democrat. Home: 1021 Sassafras Cir Bloomington IN 47408-1280 Office: Ind U Library Bloomington IN 47405

RUDSTEIN, DAVID STEWART, law educator; b. Leeds, Eng., Sept. 27, 1946; B.S., U. Ill., 1968, LL.M., 1975; J.D., Northwestern U., 1971. Bar: Ill. 1971, U.S. Supreme Ct. 1977. Teaching asst. U. Ill. Coll. Law, 1971-72; law clk. to Justice Walter V. Schaefer Supreme Ct. Ill., Chgo., 1972-73; asst. prof. law Ill. Inst. Tech.-Chgo. Kent Coll., 1973-76, assoc. prof., 1976-79, prof., 1979—, assoc. dean, 1983-87. Author: (with C.P. Erlinder and D. Thomas) Criminal Constitutional Law, 1990. Mem. ABA, Chgo. Council Lawyers, Order of Coif Office: Ill Inst Tech-Chgo 565 W Adams St Chicago IL 60661-3613

RUDY, LESTER HOWARD, psychiatrist, educator; b. Chgo., Mar. 6, 1918; s. Sol and Mildred (Weinzimmer) R.; m. Ruth Jean Schmidt, Nov. 25, 1950; 1 dau., Sharon Ruth. B.S., U. Ill., 1939, M.D., 1941; M.S. in Hosp. Adminstrn, Northwestern U., 1957. Diplomate: Am. Bd. Psychiatry and Neurology (exec. dir. 1972-86). Intern Cedars of Lebanon Hosp., Los Angeles, 1941-42; resident in psychiatry VA Hosp., Downey, Ill., 1946-48, staff psychiatrist, 1948-52, chief service, 1952-54; supt. Galesburg (Ill.) State Research Hosp., 1954-58; practice medicine specializing in psychiatry Chgo.; supt. Ill. State Psychiat. Inst., 1958-61, dir., 1961—, Ill. Mental

Health Insts., Chgo., 1967-75; prof. psychiatry U. Ill. Coll. Medicine, 1971-88, emeritus, 1988—, head dept. psychiatry, 1975-88, pres. hosp. staff, 1979-80; dir. U. Ill. Hosp., 1981-82; sr. med. dir. Health Care Compare, 1988—. Chmn. research rev. com. mental health services NIMH, 1972-73; AMA commr. Joint Commn. on Accreditation of Hosps., 1967-75; sr. cons. VA; cons. adv. bd. Chgo., Police Dept.; lectr. dept. psychiatry and neurology Loyola U., 1968-75; mem. Ill. Gov.'s Com. Competency to Stand Trial, 1968; cons. psychiatry Blue Cross/Blue Shield of Ill., 1996—, Cir. Ct. of Winnebago County (Ill.), 1995—. Contbr. articles to profl. jours. Served to col. AUS, 1942-46. Decorated Bronze Star with two oak leaf clusters Fellow Am. Psychiat. Assn. (chmn. ethics com. 1963, Simon Bolivar award 1985), Am. Coll. Psychiatrists (charter, Bowis award 1979); mem. Am. Acad. Psychoanalysis (sci. asso.), Ill. Psychiat. Soc. (pres. 1962-63), U. Ill. Med. Alumni Assn. (ann. outstanding achievement award 1980) Home: 6343 Collingswood Ct Rockford IL 61103-8961 Office: 912 S Wood St Chicago IL 60612-7325 E-mail: rjandlhr@aol.com.

RUEBEL, MARION A. university president; b. Manson, Iowa; B in Biol. Scis., U. No. Iowa, 1958, M in Sch. Adminstrn., 1962; PhD in Ednl. Adminstrn., Iowa State U., 1969. Asst. prof. secondary edn. U. Akron, 1970-73, dept. chmn., assoc. prof., 1973, asst. dean Coll. Edn., dean Univ. Coll., exec. asst. to pres., interim sr. v.p., dir. alumni affairs and govtl. rels., prof. edn.; pres. St. Vincent-St. Mary H.S., Akron, 1994-96, U. Akron, 1996-99, trustee prof., 1999—. Bd. dirs. Ohio Aerospace Inst., Northeastern Ohio Univs. Coll. of Medicine; mem. Ohio Scis. and Tech. Coun. Contbr. numerous papers, reports, and articles to profl. publs. Office: Univ of Akron Stitzleis Alumni Ctr Buchtel Common Akron OH 44325-2602

RUECK, JON MICHAEL, manufacturing executive; b. Riley, Kans., Oct. 23, 1940; s. G.M. Karl and Esther Margaret (Jones) R.; m. Connie Lee Dick Rueck, Apr. 14, 1962; children: Michael Jon, Robin Renee. BS in Nuclear Engring., Kans. State U., 1964, MS in Mech. Engring., 1971. Registered profl. engr., KS, Ohio. Radiation safety trainee Argonne Nat. Lab., Lemont, Ill., 1962; tech. sales trainee Owens-Corning Fiberglas Corp., Granville, Ohio, 1964-65, tech. sales Mpls., 1965-66, customer svc. engr. Granville, Ohio, 1966-67, environ. engr. Toledo, 1971-75; dir. plant ops. Leila Y. Post Montgomery Hosp., Battle Creek, Mich., 1975; environ. engr. Thompson Dehydrating Co., Topeka, 1976, Kans. Dept. Health Environ., Topeka, 1976-77; v.p. Hosp. Instrument Svc. Co., Silver Lake, Kans., 1977-80; supr. air pollution source monitoring Kans. Dept. of Health and Environ., 1979-85; chmn. Rueck Assocs., Silver Lake, Kans., 1985—; pres. Computers Et Cetera, 1995—. Cons. to Nat. Coun. Examiners for Engring. and Surveying, 1993—; fin. cons. Telecomms. Rsch. Assocs., 1999—. Co-author: Environmental Engineering Examination Guide & Handbook, 1996. Res. police officer St. Mary's (Kans.) Police Dept., 1981-86; lay spkr. Kans. East Conf., United Meth. Ch., 1979—, vol. coord. Topeka dist. disaster response, 1993, coord. Kans. East Conf. United Meth. Disaster Relief, 1994-2000; merit badge counselor Boy Scouts Am., Silver Lake, 1988—; del. candidate for Robertson for Pres., Shawnee County, Kans., 1988; coord. Kans. Interfaith Disaster Recovery, 1993; rural mail carrier, 1999-2000. Mem. Am. Acad. Environ. Engrs. (diplomate, chmn. admissions com. Annapolis, Md. 1986-90, state rep. Kans. 1990-99, chmn. air pollution exam sub-com. 1999—), Midwest Air and Waste Mgmt. Assn. (officer 1987-90), Kaw Valley Bicycle Touring Club (Topeka), Lions. Republican. United Methodist. Avocations: bicycling, vocalist, amateur radio, computers. Office: Rueck Assocs 617 Walnut St Silver Lake KS 66539-9467 E-mail: jrueck@ejmark.org.

RUEDEN, HENRY ANTHONY, accountant; b. Green Bay, Wis., Dec. 25, 1949; s. Bernard M. and Audrey Virgin R. BS, U. Wis., Green Bay, 1971; MBA, U. Wis., Oshkosh, 1973; postgrad., Internat. Grad. Sch., St. Louis, 1984—. CPA, Ill., Wis.; cert. mgmt. acct.; cert. internal auditor; cert. info. systems auditor; cert. cost analyst. Auditor U.S. Customs Svc., Chgo., 1974-86; systems acct. U.S. R.R. Retirement Bd., 1986—. With USAR, 1972-2000 (ret.), Desert Storm, 1991, Operation Joint Endeavor, Bosnia, 1996. Mem. CPAs For The Pub. Interest, Nat. Wildlife Fedn., Nat. Audubon Soc., Wis. Farm Bur., Wis. State Hist. Soc., Wis. Farm Bur. Fedn., Future Farmers Am., Am. Inst. CPAs, Wis. Inst. CPAs, Nat. Assn. Accts., Assn. Govt. Accts. Roman Catholic. Achievements include completed marathons in all 50 states and D.C. twice. Home: 2661 S Pine Tree Rd De Pere WI 54115-9028

RUEDENBERG, KLAUS, theoretical chemist, educator; b. Bielefeld, Germany, Aug. 25, 1920; came to U.S., 1948, naturalized, 1955; s. Otto and Meta (Wertheimer) R.; m. Veronika Kutter, Apr. 8, 1948; children: Lucia Meta, Ursula Hedwig, Annette Veronika, Emanuel Klaus. Student, Montana Coll., Zugerberg, Switzerland, 1938-39; licence es Scis., U. Fribourg, Switzerland, 1944; postgrad., U. Chgo., 1948-50; PhD, U. Zurich, Switzerland, 1950; PhD (hon.), U. Basel, Switzerland, 1975, U. Bielefeld, Germany, 1991, U. Siegen, 1994. Research assoc. physics U. Chgo., 1950-55; asst. prof. chemistry, physics Iowa State U., Ames, 1955-60, assoc. prof., 1960-62, prof., 1964-78, disting. prof. in sci. and humanities, 1978-91, disting. prof. emeritus, 1991—, sr. chemist Ames Lab., U.S. Dept. Energy, 1964-91, assoc., 1991—. Prof. chemistry Johns Hopkins, Balt., 1962-64; vis. prof. U. Naples, Italy, 1961, Fed. Inst. Tech., Zurich, 1966-67, Wash State U. at Pullman, 1970, U. Calif. at Santa Cruz, 1973, U. Bonn (Germany), 1974, Monash U. and CSIRO, Clayton, Victoria, Australia, 1982, U. Kaiserlautern, Germany, 1987; lectr. univs., rsch. instns. and sci. symposia, 1953—. Author articles in field; assoc. editor: Jour. Chem. Physics, 1964-67, Internat. Jour. Quantum Chemistry; Chem. Physics Letters, 1967-81, Lecture Notes in Chemistry, 1976—, Advances in Quantum Chemistry, 1987—; editor-in-chief Theoretica Chimica Acta, 1985-97; hon. editor Theoretical Chemistry Accounts, 1997—. Co-founder Octagon Center for the Arts, Ames, 1966, treas., 1966-71, also bd. dirs. Guggenheim fellow, 1966-67; Fulbright sr. scholar, 1982 Fellow: AAAS, Internat. Acad. Quantum Molecular Scis., Am. Inst. Chemists, Am. Phys. Soc.; mem.: AAUP, Am. Chem. Soc. (Midwest award 1982, nat. award in theoretical chemistry 2002), Phi Lambda Upsilon, Sigma Xi. Office: Dept Chemistry Iowa State Univ Ames IA 50011-0001

RUEGSEGGER, DONALD RAY, JR. radiological physicist, educator; b. Detroit, May 29, 1942; s. Donald Ray and Margaret Arlene (Elliot) R.; m. Judith Ann Merrill, Aug. 20, 1965 (div.); children: Steven, Susan, Mark, Ann; m. Patricia Ann Mitchell, Oct. 16, 1999. BS, Wheaton Coll., 1964; MS, Ariz. State U., 1966, PhD (NDEA fellow), 1969. Diplomate Am. Bd. Radiology. Radiol. physicist Miami Valley Hosp., Dayton, Ohio, 1969—, chief med. physics sect., 1983—. Physics cons. X-ray dept. VA Hosp., Dayton, 1970—; adj. asst. prof. physics Wright State U., Fairborn, Ohio, 1973—, clin. asst. prof. radiology, 1976-81, clin. assoc. prof. radiology, 1981—, group leader in med. physics, dept. radiol. scis. Med. Sch., 1978—. Mem. AAAS, Am. Assn. Physicists in Medicine (pres. Ohio River Valley chpt. 1982-83, co-chmn. local summer sch. arrangements com. 1986), Am. Coll. Radiology, Am. Coll. Med. Physics (founding chancellor), Am. Phys. Soc., Ohio Radiol. Soc., Health Physics Soc. Baptist. Home: 6252 Donnybrook Dr Centerville OH 45459-1837 Office: Radiation Therapy Miami Valley Hosp 1 Wyoming St Dayton OH 45409-2722

RUESINK, ALBERT WILLIAM, biologist, plant sciences educator; b. Adrian, Mich., Apr. 16, 1940; s. Lloyd William and Alberta May (Foltz) R.; m. Kathleen Joy Cramer, June 8, 1963; children: Jennifer Li, Adriana Eleanor. B.A., U. Mich., 1962; M.A., Harvard U., 1965, Ph.D., 1966. Postdoctoral fellow Swiss Fed. Inst. Tech., Zurich, 1966-67; prof. biology Ind. U., Bloomington, 1967—, spl. asst. to Pres. for Faculty Rels., 1999—. Recipient Amoco Teaching award Ind. U., 1980 Mem. AAUP (pres. chpt. 1978-79, 90-91), Am. Soc. Plant Physiologists, Bot. Soc. Am. Democrat. Mem. United Ch. of Christ. Home: 2605 E 5th St Bloomington IN 47408-4286 Office: Ind U Dept Biology 1001 E 3d St Bloomington IN 47405 E-mail: ruesink@indiana.edu.

RUFF, L. CANDY, state legislator; m. Gregory W. Ruff. Student, U. Kans. Rep. dist. 40 State of Kans., 1993—. Democrat. Home: 321 Arch St Leavenworth KS 66048-3421 Office: Kans Ho of Reps State Capitol Topeka KS 66612

RUFFER, DAVID GRAY, retired museum director, former college president; b. Archbold, Ohio, Aug. 25, 1937; s. Lawrence A. and Florence A. (Newcomer) R.; m. Marilyn Elaine Taylor, Aug. 23, 1958; children: Rochelle Lynne, Robyn Lynne, David Geoffrey. B.S., Defiance Coll., 1959; M.A., Bowling Green State U., 1960; Ph.D., U. Okla., 1964. Spl. instr. U. Okla., 1963-64; asst. prof. biology Defiance Coll., 1964-68, asso. prof., 1968-73, faculty dean, 1969-73; provost Elmira (N.Y.) Coll., 1973-78; pres. Albright Coll., Reading, Pa., 1978-91, U. Tampa, Fla., 1991-94; exec. dir. Dayton (Ohio) Soc. Natural History, 1995-99, ret., 2000—. Author: Exploring and Understanding Mammals, 1971; contbr. articles to profl. jours. NSF grantee, 1965, 67; Ohio Biol. Survey grantee, 1968-69 Fellow AAAS; mem. Am. Assn. Higher Edn., Animal Behavior Soc., Am. Soc. Mammalogists, Sigma Xi. Methodist. Club: Rotary. Home: 167 Mill Creek Rd Youngstown OH 44512-1402 E-mail: mdruffer@aol.com.

RUGLAND, WALTER S. fraternal benefit society executive; b. Appleton, Wis. BA, Luther Coll., 1959; MBA, U. Mich., 1961. With Conn. Gen. Life Ins. Co., until 1975; cons. actuary, equity prin. Milliman & Robertson, Inc., Hartford, Conn., 1975-98; exec. v.p., chief operating officer Aid Assn. Lutherans, Appleton, 1998—. Fellow Conf. Cons. Actuaries, Soc. Actuaries; mem. Am. Acad. Actuaries. Office: Aid Assn Lutherans 4321 N Ballard Rd Appleton WI 54919-0001 E-mail: walt_rugland@aal.org.

RUIZ, ANSELMO, chef; With Ambria, Chgo., 1983—, now exec. chef de cuisine. Office: Ambria 2300 N Lincoln Park W Chicago IL 60614

RUKAVINA, TOM, state legislator; b. Aug. 1950; m. Lenore Rukavina; 2 children. BA, U. Minn. Mem. Minn. Ho. of Reps., St. Paul. Mem. govt. ops. com., econ. devel. com., taxes com., environ. and natural resources com., vice chair labor mgmt. rels. com.; legal asst. Democrat. Home: 6930 Highway 169 Virginia MN 55792-8040 Office: Minn Ho of Reps House Standing Com State Capitol Cmn Saint Paul MN 55155-0001

RULAND, RICHARD EUGENE, English and American literature educator, critic, literary historian; b. Detroit, May 1, 1932; s. Eugene John and Irene (Janette) R.; m. Mary Ann Monaghan; children: Joseph, Michael, Paul, Susan; m. Birgit Noll. BA, Assumption Coll. U. Western Ont., Can., 1953; MA, U. Detroit, 1955; PhD, U. Mich., 1960. Instr., then asst. prof. English and Am. studies Yale U., New Haven, 1960-67, Morse rsch. fellow, 1966-67; prof. English and Am. lit. Washington U., St. Louis, 1967—, chmn. dept. English, 1969-74; chmn. comparative lit. program, 1993-94. Vis. Bruern prof. Am. lit. Leeds (Eng.) U., 1964-65; vis. Fulbright prof. U. Groningen, The Netherlands, 1975, Sch. of English and Am. Studies U. East Anglia, Eng., 1978-79; vis. disting. prof. Am. lit. Coll. of William and Mary, 1980-81. Author: The Rediscovery of American Literature: Premises of Critical Taste, 1900-1940, 1967, America in Modern European Literature: From Image to Metaphor, 1976, (with Malcolm Bradbury) From Puritanism to Postmodernism: A History of American Literature, 1991 (paperback 1992), translation into Czech and Hungarian, 1997; editor: Walden: A Collection of Critical Essays, 1967, The Native Muse: Theories of American Literature, Vol. I, 1972, 76, A Storied Land: Theories of American Literature, Vol. II, 1976; contbr. articles to profl. jours. Guggenheim Rsch. fellow, 1982-83. Mem. Assn. Depts. English (pres. 1974). Avocation: jazz musician. Office: Washington U Dept English Saint Louis MO 63130 E-mail: rruland@artsi.wustl.edu.

RULAU, RUSSELL, numismatist, author, consultant; b. Chgo., Sept. 21, 1926; s. Alphonse and Ruth (Thorsen) R.; m. Hazel Darlene Grizzell, Feb. 1, 1968; children by a previous marriage: Lance Eric, Carla Rae, Russell A.W., Marsha June, Scott Quentin, Roberta Ann, Kyle Christopher. Student, U. Wis., 1946-48. Enlisted U.S. Army, 1944-50; transferred to USAF, 1950-62; master sgt. USAFR, 1963-73; asst. editor Coin World newspaper, Sidney, Ohio, 1962-74; editor World Coins mag., 1964-74, Numis. Scrapbook mag., 1968-74; editl. coord. How to Order Fgn. Coins guidebook, 1966-74; editor-in-chief World Coin News newspaper, 1974-84, Bank Note Reporter, 1983-84; fgn. editor Numis News newspaper, 1974-77; cons. editor Std. Catalog of World Paper Money, 1975-83; contbg. editor Std. Catalog of World Coins, 1974-81; pres. House of Rulau, 1984—, Alpha Enterprises Inc., 1989—. V.p. Keogh-Rulau Galleries, Dallas, 1984-85, Pobjoy Mint, Ltd., Iola, Wis., 1985-97, cons., 1997-98; U.S. agent Christie's Pty. Ltd., 1992-95; chmn. bd. dirs. Thorsen Estates, Inc., 1998—; apptd. mem. U.S. Assay Commn., 1973. Author: (with George Fuld) Spiel Marken, 1962-65, American Game Counters, 1972, World Mint Marks, 1966, Modern World Mint Marks, 1970, (with J.U. Rixen and Frovin Sieg) Seddelkatalog Slesvig Plebiscit Zone Iog II, 1970, Numismatics of Old Alabama, 1971-73, Hard Times Tokens, 1980, 96, 2001, Early American Tokens, 1981, U.S. Merchant Tokens 1845-1860, 1982, U.S. Trade Tokens 1866-1889, 1983, Tokens of the Gay Nineties, 1987, Discovering America: The Coin Collecting Connection, 1989, Latin American Tokens, 1992, 2000, (with George Fuld) Medallic Portraits of Washington, 1985, 99, Standard Catalog of U.S. Tokens 1700-1900, 1994, 97, 99, Tokens of Spain since 1800, 2002; contbr. articles to profl. jours. Sec. Numismatic Terms Standardization Com., 1966-74; vice-chmn. Waupaca County Rep. Party, 1977-79, 88-89, chmn., 1979-82; chmn. county chairmen, 3d vice chmn. Wis. Rep. Party, 1981-83; del. Rep. Nat. Conv., 1980; exec. com. 6th Wis. Dist. Rep. Com., 1984-87. Recipient Clemy Literary award, 1993, Smedley Lifetime Achievement award, 1994, Numismatic Ambassador award, 1995; elector Numismatic Hall of Fame, 1995—; inductee Numismatic Hall of Fame, 2000. Fellow Royal Numis Soc., Am. Numis Soc.; mem. Token and Medal Soc. (editor 1962-63, gold cataloging medals 1982, 83, 92), Am. Numis Assn. (merit medal 1995, Lifetime Achievement award 2000), Canadian Numis Assn., Am.-Israel Numis. Assn., Md. Token & Medal Soc., Numis Lit. Guild (dir. 1974-78, editor 1984-86. Best Specialized Book awards 1985, 89, 92, 94, 97, 99), VFW (post commdr. 1985-89. 96-2001), Am. Legion (11th Airborne Divsn. Assn.). Lutheran. Home: N7747 County J Iola WI 54945-9710 Office: Thorsen Estates Inc PO Box 153 Iola WI 54945-0153 E-mail: rviking@athenet.net.

RULE, JOHN CORWIN, history educator; b. Evanston, Ill., Mar. 2, 1929; s. Corwin V. and Elaine (Simons) R. A.B., Stanford U., 1951, M.A., 1952, Harvard U., 1955, Ph.D., 1958. Tutor and fellow Harvard U., Cambridge, Mass., 1956-58; instr. Northeastern U., Boston, 1955-56; from instr. to prof. history Ohio State U., Columbus, 1958—; vis. asst. prof. Western Res. U., Cleve., 1961; vis. prof. Johns Hopkins U., Balt., 1968. Editor and contbg. author: Louis XIV and the Craft of Kingship, 1970; editor: Louis XIV, 1974, Letters from the Hague and Utrecht, 1711-1712, 1979, The Reign of Louis XIV, 1990. Folger Shakespeare Library fellow, 1968,, 1970; Huntington Library fellow, 1978; Am. Council Learned Socs. fellow, 1981 Fellow Royal Hist. Soc. (London); mem. Soc. for French Hist. Studies (sec. 1963-70, assoc. editor jour. 1975-86, co-pres. 1989-91), Signet Soc., Crichton Club. Democrat. Home: 118 E Beck St Columbus OH 43206-1110 Office: Dept History Ohio State U 230 W 17th Ave Rm 106 Columbus OH 43210-1367

RUMMAN, WADI (SALIBA RUMMAN), civil engineer, consultant; b. Beit-Jala, Palestine, Sept. 7, 1926; came to U.S., 1948, naturalized, 1959; s. Saliba Y. and Miladeh (Nasrallah) R.; m. Doris E. Reed, Sept. 6, 1955; children— Mary Elaine, Linda Jean. BSE, U. Mich., 1949, MSE, 1953, PhD, 1959. Field engr. Finkbeiner Pettis and Strout, Toledo, 1949; structural engr. Vogt, Ivers, Seaman and Assos., Cin., 1950-51, Giffels and Vallet, Inc., Detroit, 1951-52; instr. U. Mich., 1952-59, asst. prof. civil engring., 1959-64, assoc. prof., 1964-75, prof., 1975-88, prof. emeritus, 1988—. Cons. on design of reinforced concrete chimneys and other tower structures to industry and other agys. Author: Engineering, 1974, 3d edit., 1991. Fellow Am. Concrete Inst.; mem. ASCE (life), Am. Soc. Engring. Edn. (life), Internat. Assn. Bridge and Structural Engring., Sigma Xi, Chi Epsilon, Phi Kappa Phi. Home: 4648 Bayberry Cir Ann Arbor MI 48105-9762 Office: U Mich Dept Civil Engring Ann Arbor MI 48109 E-mail: wsrumman@umich.edu.

RUMSFELD, DONALD HENRY, federal official, former corporate executive; b. Chgo., July 9, 1932; s. George Donald and Jeannette (Husted) R.; m. Joyce Pierson, Dec. 27, 1954; 3 children. A.B., Princeton U., 1954; hon. degree, De Paul U. Coll. Commerce, Ill. Coll., Lake Forest Coll., Park Coll., Tuskegee Inst., Nat. Coll. Edn., Bryant Coll., Claremont (Calif.) Grad. Sch., Ill. Wesleyan U., RAND Grad. Sch., Hampden-Sydney Coll. Adminstrv. asst. U.S. Ho. of Reps., 1957-59; with A.G. Becker & Co., Chgo., 1960-62; mem. 88th-91st Congresses from 13th Ill. dist., Pres. Richard Nixon's Cabinet, 1969-73; dir. OEO, asst. to pres., 1969-70; counsellor to Pres., dir. econ. stabilization program, 1971-72; U.S. ambassador and permanent rep. to NATO, 1973-74; chief of staff for Pres. Gerald Ford, mem. Cabinet, 1974-75; sec. Dept. Def., 1975-77; pres., chief exec. officer, then chmn. G.D. Searle & Co., Skokie, Ill., 1977-85; spl. envoy of Pres. Ronald Reagan to Mid. East, 1983-84; sr. advisor William Blair & Co., Chgo., 1985-90; chmn., chief exec. officer General Instrument Corp., 1990-93; chmn. bd. dirs. Gilead Scis., Inc., Foster City, Calif., 1997—2001; sec. of def., 2001—. Bd. dirs. Amylin Pharms., Inc., Asea Brown Boveri, Ltd., Tribune Co.; bd. trustees RAND Corp., 1977—; chmn. U.S. Commn. to Assess the Ballistic Missile Threat to the U.S., 1998; commr. U.S. Fed. Trade Deficit Rev. Commn., 1999, U.S. Commn. to Assess Nat. Security Space Mgmt. and Orgn., 2000—. Naval Aviator USN, 1954-57. Recipient Presdl. Medal of Freedom, 1977, George Catlett Marshall award, Woodrow Wilson award, Dwight David Eisenhower medal. Office: Department of Defense 1000 Defense Pentagon Washington DC 20301-1000

RUNBECK, LINDA C. state legislator; b. June 11, 1946; m. Richard Runbeck; 1 child. BA, Bethel Coll., 1968. Former mem. Minn. Ho. of Reps., St. Paul; mem. various coms.; U.S. senator from Minn., 1993—. Mem. govt. ops. and reform com., mem. jobs, energy and cmty. devel com., others; advt. exec. Mem. League Women's Voters. Home: 48 E Golden Lake Rd Circle Pines MN 55014-1725 Office: Minn State Senate State Capitol Building Saint Paul MN 55155-0001

RUND, DOUGLAS ANDREW, emergency physician; b. Columbus, Ohio, July 20, 1945; s. Carl Andrew and Caroline Amelia (Row) Rund; m. Sue E. Padavana, 1980; children: Carie, Emily, Ashley. BA, Yale U., 1967; MD, Stanford U., 1971. Lic. physician Ohio, diplomate Nat. Bd. Med. Examiners, Am. Bd. Family Practice, Am. Bd. Emergency Medicine . Intern U. Calif. San Francisco-Moffett Hosp., 1971—72; resident in gen. surgery Stanford U., 1972—74, Robert Wood Johnson Found. clin. scholar in medicine, 1974—76; med. dir. Mid-Peninsula Health Svc., Palo Alto, Calif., 1975—76; clin. instr. dept. medicine and preventive medicine Stanford U. Med. Sch., 1975—76; assoc. prof., dir. divsn. emergency medicine Ohio State Coll. Medicine, 1982—87, dir. emergency medicine residency program, assoc. prof. dept. 1976—87, prof., chmn. dept. preventive medicine, 1988—90, prof., chmn. dept. emergency medicine, 1990—, prof., interim chmn. dept. family medicine, 1994—95, assoc. dean, 2001—. Attending staff Ohio State U. Hosps., 1976—; med. dir. CSCC, Emergency Med. Svcs. Dept.; pres. Internat. Rsch. Inst. Emergency Medicine; sr. rsch. fellow NATO: Health and Med. Aspects of Disaster Preparedness, 1985—87; mem. Residency Rev. Com. for Emergency Medicine, 1997—; vis. epidemiology and injury control U. Edinburgh, Scotland, 1987; working group, emergency and critical care in space NASA, 2001—; bd. dirs. Am. Bd. Emergency Medicine , 1988—97, sr. editor in tng. exam. , 1989—, pres., 1995—. Author: Triage, 1981, Essentials of Emergency Medicine, 1982, 2d edit., 1986, Emergency Radiology, 1982, Emergency Psychiatry, 1983, Environmental Emergencies, 1985; editor: Emergency Medicine Ann., 1983—84, Emergency Medicine Survey, Annals of Emergency Medicine, Annals of Emergency Medicine Symposium, 1986; editor: (in chief) Ohio State Series on Emergency Medicine, Emergency Medicine Observer, 1986—87; mem. editl. bd. : Physician, Sports Medicine, Emergency Med. Svcs.; co-author: Family Medicine Priciples and Practice, 1978, 2d edit., 1983; contbr. articles to profl. jours. Recipient Faculty Tchg. award, Ohio State U. Coll. Medicine Alumni Assn., 1999. Fellow: Am. Coll. Emergency Physicians (task force on substance abuse and injury control); mem.: IAAA, Internat. Soc. for Emergency Med. Svcs. (med. dir.), Columbus Med. Forum (pres. 1993—), Soc. Acad. Emergency Medicine (chmn. internat. com. 1991—), Assn. Acad. Chairs Emergency Medicine (pres. 1992—93), Nat. Inst. on Alcohol Abuse and Alcoholism, Alpha Omega Alpha. Office: Ohio State U HSL 016 376 W 10th Ave Columbus OH 43210-1240

RUNDIO, LOUIS MICHAEL, JR. lawyer; b. Chgo., Sept. 13, 1943; s. Louis Michael Sr. and Germaine Matilda (Pasternack) R.; m. Ann Marie Bartlett, July 10, 1971; children: Matthew, Melissa. BS in Physics, Loyola U., Chgo., 1965, JD, 1972. Bar: Ill. 1972, U.S. Dist. Ct. (no. dist.) Ill. 1972, U.S. Ct. Appeals (7th cir.) 1974, U.S. Dist. Ct. (ea. dist.) Mich. 1983. Assoc. McDermott, Will & Emery, Chgo., 1972-77, ptnr., 1978—. Served to 1st lt. U.S. Army, 1965-68, Vietnam. Mem. ABA, Chgo. Bar Assn. Home: 676 Skye Ln Barrington IL 60010-5506 Office: McDermott Will & Emery 227 W Monroe St Ste 3100 Chicago IL 60606-5096

RUNGE, KAY KRETSCHMAR, library director; b. Davenport, Iowa, Dec. 9, 1946; d. Alfred Edwin and Ina (Paul) Kretschmar; children: Peter Jr., Katherine. BS in History Edn., Iowa State U., 1969; MLS, U. Iowa, 1970. Pub. svc. libr. Anoka County Libr., Blaine, Minn., 1971-72; cataloger Augustana Coll., Rock Island, Ill., 1972-74; dir. Scott County Libr. Sys., Eldridge, Iowa, 1974-85, Davenport (Iowa) Pub. Libr., 1985—2001, Pub. Libr. Des Moines, 2001—. V.p. Quad-Cities Conv. and Visitors Bur., 1992—97, Quad-Cities Grad. Study Ctr., 1992—2001, Downtown Davenport Devel. Corp., 1992—2000, Hall of Honor Bd., Davenport Ctrl. H.S., 1992—95, Brenton Bank Bd., 1995—2001, Wells Fargo Bank Bd., 2001; steering com. Quad-Cities Visions for the Future, 1987—91, Humanities Iowa, 1993—2000, chair, 1998—99; bd. govs. Iowa State U. Found., 1991—; citizens adv. coun. Iowa State U., 1998—2000, Leadership Iowa, 1998—99; adv. bd. mem. U. Iowa Sch. Libr. Sci., 1999—, adj. prof., 2000—01; mem. Iowa State U. Found. Devel. Bd., 2000—; bd. dirs. Wells Fargo Bank, 2000—, River Ctr. for Performing Arts, Davenport, 1983—97, Iowa State U. Rsch. Pk., 1998—2000; chmn. bd. dirs. Am. Inst. Commerce, 1989—98; bd. dirs. Quest Ednl. Corp., 1999—, Davenport One, Downtown Devel., 2000—01. Recipient Svc. Key award Iowa State U. Alumni Assn., 1979, ALA/ALTA Nat. Advocacy Honor Roll award, 2000; named Quad City Panhellenic Woman of Yr., 1998. Mem. ALA (chmn. library adminstrs. and mgrs. div., fundraising section 1988), Iowa Library Assn. (pres. 1983, Mem. of Yr. award 2000), Pub. Library Assn. (bd. dirs. 1990-99, pres. 2000-2001), Iowa Edn. Media Assn. (Intellectual Freedom award 1984), Alpha Delta Pi (alumni state pres. 1978). Lutheran. Office: Pub Libr of Des Moines 100 Locust St Des Moines IA 50309-1791

RUNK, FRED J. insurance company executive; CFO Am. Fin. Group, Inc., Cin. Office: American Financial Group Inc 1 E 4th St Cincinnati OH 45202 Office Fax: (513) 579-2113.

RUNKLE, MARTIN DAVEY, library director; b. Cin., Oct. 18, 1937; s. Newton and Ilo (Neal) R.; m. Nancy Force, Aug. 7, 1965; children: Seth, Elizabeth. BA, Muskingum Coll., 1959; MA, U. Pitts., 1964, U. Chgo., 1973. Library systems analyst U. Chgo., 1970-75, head cataloging librarian, 1975-79, asst. dir. tech. services, 1979-80, dir. library, 1980—. Sr. lectr. grad. library sch. U. Chgo., 1977-90. Fulbright grantee, 1965. Mem. ALA, Univ. Club Chgo. Office: U Chgo 1100 E 57th St Chicago IL 60637-1596 E-mail: maru@midway.uchicago.edu.

RUOHO, ARNOLD EINO, pharmacology educator; b. Thunder Bay, Ont., Can., Nov. 26, 1941; s. Eino Armas and Toini Helen (Kuusisto) R.; m. Marjorie Denise Anderson, Aug. 21, 1965; children— David, Daniel, Jonathon B.S. in Pharmacy, U. Toronto, Ont., Can., 1964; Ph.D. in Physiol. Chemistry, U. Wis.-Madison, 1970. Helen Hay Whitney postdoctoral fellow U. Calif.-San Diego, 1971-74; asst. prof. pharmacology U Wis.-Madison, 1974-80, assoc. prof., 1980-84, prof., 1984—, acting chair dept. pharmacology Med. Sch., 1994-95, chair, 1995—, S. Jonathan Singer prof. and chair pharmacology, 1997—. Cons. NIH, Bethesda, Md., 1984— Contbr. articles to profl. jours., chpts. to books Den leader local council Boy Scouts Am., Madison, 1975-77, mem. at large, 1979— ; hockey coach, 1983— . Grantee March of Dimes, 1975-78, Pharm. Mfrs., 1975-76, NIH, 1975— Mem. AAAS. Lutheran

RUPERT, TIMOTHY G. metal products executive; BS in Math., Indiana U. of Pa. Mgmt. trainee in acctg. USX Corp., 1968, various analytical positions, 1968-79, asst. dist. mgr. Saddlebrook, N.J., 1979-81, sr. investment analyst N.Y., 1981-83, mgr. N.Y. treasury ops., 1983-84, gen. mgr. treasury coord., 1984-86, dir. corp. treasury adminstrn., 1986-88, dir. corp. fin., 1988-90, dir. corp. staff, 1990-91; exec. v.p., CFO RTI Internat. Metals, Inc., Niles, Ohio, 1991-99, pres., CEO, 1999—. Active United Way of Allegheny County, Boy Scouts Am.; grad. Leadership Pitts. Mem. Am. Inst. Mgmt. Accts., Fin. Execs. Inst., Youngstown/Warren Regional C. of C. (exec. mem.). Office: RTI Internat Metals Inc 1000 Warren Ave Niles OH 44446-1168

RUPNOR, JENNIFER, journalist; BA in Broadcast Journalism, U. Wis., Eau Claire, 2000. Mem. radio news staff WAXX-WAYY , 1997—2000; reporter, prodr. WEAU-TV, Eau Claire, Wis., 2000, anchor NewsCenter 13 sunrise and noon, 2000—. Avocations: baseball, mysteries. Office: WEAU-TV P oBox 47 Eau Claire WI 54702

RUPORT, SCOTT HENDRICKS, lawyer; b. Nov. 22, 1949; s. Fred Hendricks and Juyne (Kennedy) R.; m. Linda Darlene Smith, Sept. 12, 1970; children: Brittany Lyle, Courtney Kennedy. BSBA, Bowling Green U., 1971; JD, U. Akron, 1974. Bar: Ohio 1974, Pa. 1984, U.S. Dist. Ct. (no. dist.) Ohio 1974, U.S. Ct. Appeals (6th cir.) 1975, U.S. Supreme Ct. 1978; cert. civil trial specialist Nat. Bd. Trial Advocacy. Assoc. Schwab, Sager, Growenburgh, Rothal, Fort, Skidmore & Nukes, Akron, Ohio, 1974-76, Skidmore & George Co. LPA, Akron, 1976-79, Skidmore, Ruport & Haskings, Akron, 1979-83; ptnr. Roderick, Myers & Linton, 1983-85, Ruport Co. LPA, Akron, 1985—. Instr. real estate law U. Akron, 1976-77, adj. asst. prof. constrn. tech. Coll. Engring., 1983—. Capt. Fin. Corps. USAR, 1971-79. Mem. ABA, ATLA, Ohio Bar Assn., Ohio Acad. Trial Lawyers (chmn. civil and bus. litigation sect. 1989), Akron Bar Assn., Beta Gamma Sigma, Sigma Chi. Republican. Presbyterian. Office: Ruport Co LPA 3700 Embassy Pkwy Ste 440 Akron OH 44333-8367

RUPPEL, WILLIAM J. state legislator; m. Miriam ruppel. BS, Butler U.; MS, Manchester Coll. Tchr., coach Tippecanoe Valley Sch. Corp.; mem. from 22d dist. Ind. State Ho. of Reps., 1992—. Mem. aged and acing com., fin. instns. com., local govt., county and twp. coms., human affairs com., vice chmn. pub. safety com. Mem. North Manchester (Ind.) Vol. Fire Dept.; mem. North Manchester Police Res.; mem. Butler U. Alumni Bd. Mem. Ind. Vol. Fireman Assn., Farm Bur., Rotary. Home: 909 State Road 13 W North Manchester IN 46962-9127 Office: Ind Ho of Reps State Capitol Indianapolis IN 46204

RUSCH, THOMAS WILLIAM, manufacturing executive; b. Alliance, Nebr., Oct. 3, 1946; s. Oscar William and Gwen Falerne (Middleswart) R.; m. Gloria Ann Sutton, June 20, 1968 (div. Oct. 1979); children: Alicia Catherine, Colin William; m. Lynn Biebighauser, Jan. 17, 1981. BEE, U. of Minn., 1968, MSEE, 1970, PhD, 1973; MS in Mgmt. of Tech., U. Minn., 1993. Sr. physicist cen. rsch. 3M Co., St. Paul, 1973-77, rsch. specialist cen. rsch., 1977-79; project scientist phys. electronics div. Perkin Elmer Corp., Eden Prairie, Minn., 1979-83, sr. project scientist phys. electronics div., 1983-85, lab mgr. phys. electronics div., 1985-87, product mgr. phys. electronics div., 1987-88, sr. product mgr. phys. electronics div., 1988-93; v.p. product devel. Chorus Corp., St. Paul, 1993-94; pres. Creekside Techs. Corp., Plymouth, Minn., 1994—; v.p. Xoft microTube, Inc., 1998—; chief tech. officer Xoft MicroTube, INc., Fremont, Calif., 2001—. Editor: X-rays in Materials Analysis, 1986; co-author: Oscillatory Ion Yields, 1977; patentee in field. Recipient IR100 award for transfer vessel Rsch. and Devel. mag., 1981, IR100 award for energy analyser, 1985. Office: 49000 Milmont Dr Fremont CA 94538

RUSH, ANDRA M. transportation executive; MBA, U. Mich. CEO, pres. Rush Trucking, Wayne, Mich., 1984—. Office: Rush Trucking PO Box 1011 Wayne MI 48184-4011

RUSH, BOBBY L. congressman; b. Ga., Nov. 23, 1946; m. Carolyn Rush; 5 children. BA in Polit. Sci., Roosevelt U., 1974; MA in Polit. Sci., U. Ill., 1992. Fin. planner Sanmar Fin. Planning Corp.; assoc. dean Daniel Hale Williams U.; ins. agent Prudential Ins. Co.; city alderman Chgo., 1984-93; democratic committeeman Chgo. 2nd ward, 1984, 88, Central Ill., 1990; dep. chmn. Ill. Democratic Party, 1990; mem. U.S. Congresses from 1st Ill. Dist., 1993—. Chmn. Environ. Protection, Energy and Pub. Utilities com., Budget and Govt. Operations com., Capitol Devel. com., Hist. Landmark Preservation Com.; mem. Commerce com. Former mem. Student Non-Violent Coordinating com.; founder Ill. Black Panther Party; past coord. Free Breakfast for Children, Free Med. Clinic. With US Army, 1963-68. Recipient Ill. Enterprise Zone award Dept. Commerce and Community, Operation PUSH Outstanding Young Man award, Henry Booth House Outstanding Community Svc. award, Outstanding Bus. and Profl. Achievement award South End Jaycees, Chgo. Black United Communities Disting. Polit. Leadership award. Office: US Ho of Reps 2416 Rayburn House Office Bldg Washington DC 20515-0001*

RUSH, RICHARD R. academic administrator; Pres. Calif. State U. Channel Islands, Camarillo. Office: Calif State U Channel Islands 1 University Dr Camarillo CA 93012 Fax: 805-437-8414. E-mail: richard.rush@csuci.edu.

RUSHFELT, GERALD LLOYD, magistrate judge; b. Kansas City, Kans., Aug. 4, 1929; s. Henry Lawrence and Marie Ernestine (Heinrich) R.; m. Joy Marie Jungferman, May 28, 1960. AA, Graceland Coll., 1949; BA, U. Kans., 1953, LLB, 1958. Bar: Kans. 1958, U.S. Dist. Ct. Kans. 1958, U.S. Ct. Appeals (10th cir.) 1969. From assoc. to ptnr. Sullivant and Smith and successor firms, Kans. City, Overland Park, Kans., 1958-75; sr. ptnr. Rushfelt, Mueller, Lamar and Druten and successors, Overland Park, 1975-85; U.S. magistrate judge U.S. Dist. Ct. Kans., Kansas City, 1985—. Mcpl. judge pro tem City of Leawood (Kans.) 1977-85; critique instr. U. Kans. Law Sch., Lawrence, 1981-92. Active Roeland Park (Kans.) City Council, 1964-69. With U.S. Army, 1953-55. Fellow Am. Coll. Trial Lawyers, Internat. Soc. Barristers; mem. ABA, Kans. Bar Assn., Johnson County Bar Assn. (pres. 1986-87), Am. Bd. Trial Advocates, Earl E. O'Connor Am. Inn of Ct. Democrat. Mem. Cmty. Of Christ. Avocations: swimming, baseball, philately. Office: 208 US Courthouse 500 State Ave Rm 208 Kansas City KS 66101-2400

RUSNACK, WILLIAM C. petroleum company executive; Pres. ARCO Transp. Co., 1990-93, ARCO Products Co., 1993-97; pres., CEO, Clark USA Inc. (now Primcor), Glen Ellyn, Ill., 1998—, also bd. dirs. Bd. dirs. Flowserve. Office: Premcor 8182 Maryland Ave Saint Louis MO 63105

RUSSELL, FRANK ELI, retired newspaper publishing executive; b. Kokomo, Ind., Dec. 6, 1920; s. Frank E. and Maude (Wiggins) R.; children: Linda Carole Russell Atkins, Richard Lee, Frank E. III, Rita Jane Russell Eagle, Julie Beth Russell; m. Nancy M. Shover, Oct. 5, 1991. AB, Evansville Coll., 1942; JD, Ind. U., 1951; LLD (hon.), U. Evansville, 1985; HHD (hon.), Franklin Coll., 1989. Bar: Ind. 1951; CPA, Ind. Ptnr. George S. Olive & Co., Indpls., 1947-53; exec. v.p. Spickelmier Industries, Inc., 1953-59; bus. mgr. Indpls. Star & News, 1959-77; v.p., gen. mgr. Ctrl. Newspapers, Inc., Indpls., 1977-79, pres., 1979-95, chmn., bd. dirs., 1996-98; ret., 1998; also bd. dirs. Ctrl. Newsprint; pres. Bradley Paper Co., also bd. dirs. Past chmn. adv. bd. Met. Indpls. TV Assn., Inc.; trustee retirement trust Ctrl. Newspapers, Inc.; chmn. retirement com. Hoosier State Press. Bd. dirs. Ariz. Cmty. Found., 1992-96, Eiteljorg Mus., 1994—; trustee, chmn. bd. Nina Mason Pulliam Charitable Trust, 1997—. Recipient Life Salvation award Salvation Army, 1989, Disting. Alumni award Ind. U. Sch. Law, 1989, Life Trustee award U. Evansville, 1991, Ralph D. Casey award, 1997. Mem. ABA, AICPA, Ind. Bar. Assn., Indpls. Bar Assn. (past bd. dirs., past treas.), Ind. Assn. CPAs (past dir.), Tax Execs. Inst. (past pres.), Ind. Assn. Credit Mgmt. (dir., v.p.), Inst. Newspaper Controllers and Fin. Officers (dir., past pres.), Ind. Acad. Ind. Assn. Colls., Midwest Pension Conf. (Ind. chpt.), Newspaper Advt. Bur. (bd. dirs.), Salvation Army (life mem. award), Columbia Club, Meridian Hills Country Club, Masons, Shriners, Order of Coif, Phi Delta Phi, Sigma Alpha Epsilon. Methodist. Office: Nina Mason Pulliam Charitable Trust 135 N Pennsylvania St Ste 1200 Indianapolis IN 46204-1956

RUSSELL, GEORGE ALBERT, retired university president; b. Bertrand, Mo., July 12, 1921; s. George Albert and Martha (Cramer) R.; m. Ruth Ann Ashby, Nov. 11, 1944; children: George Albert, Frank Ashby, Ruth Ann, Cramer Anderson. B.S. in Elec. Engring, Mass. Inst. Tech., 1947; M.S., U. Ill., 1952, Ph.D. in Physics, 1955. Assoc. prof. So. Ill. U., 1960-62; faculty U. Ill., Urbana, 1962-72, prof. physics, 1963-72, assoc. dir. Materials Research Lab., 1963-68, assoc. head physics dept., 1968-70, assoc. dean Grad. Coll., 1970-72, vice chancellor research, dean Grad. Coll., 1972-77; chancellor U. Mo.-Kansas City, 1977-91; pres. U Mo. system admin., Columbia, Mo., 1991-96. Cons. Office Naval Research, 1961-76; dir. Microthermal Applications Inc.; dir. Kansas City Power and Light Co.; mem. adv. bd. dirs. Boatman's First Nat. Bank Kansas City; mem. acad. adv. panel Com. on Exchanges Vice chmn. Illini Union Bd., 1970; pres. Levis Faculty Center, 1972; chmn. bd. trustees AUA, 1977; mem. Mo. Sci. and Tech. Corp.; trustee Midwest Research Inst.; bd. dirs. Edgar Snow Meml. Fund, Inc. Served with USN, World War II. Mem. Am. Assn. Physics Tchrs., Am. Phys. Soc. Clubs: Champaign Country (pres. 1972), Mission Hills Country, Rockhill Tennis. Home and Office: 3601 Augusta Dr Columbia MO 65203-4820

RUSSELL, JEFFREY SCOTT, civil engineering educator; b. Alliance, Ohio, June 14, 1962; s. Ronald Francis Russell and Georgia Ann (Charleston) Holmes; m. Vicki Carolina Radford, Aug. 17, 1985; children: Nicole Lynne, Jacob Thomas, Matthew David, Rachel Marie. BS, U. Cin., 1985; MS, Purdue U., 1986, PhD, 1988. Grad. tchg. asst. Purdue U., West Lafayette, Ind., 1985-87, grad. rsch. asst., 1987-88, postdoctoral rsch. assoc., 1988-89; from asst. to assoc. prof. civil engring. U. Wis., Madison, 1989—. Lectr. Tex. A&M U., College Station, 1988—, U. Tex., Austin, 1992—, U. Wis., Madison Ext., 1990—. Editor Jour. Mgmt. in Engring., 1996—. Mem. Wis. Right to Life, Madison, 1989-94; project coord. U. Wis. Coll. Testament Distbn., Gideon's Internat., Madison West Camp, 1990—; dir. evangelistic ministries First Ch. of Nazarene, Madison, 1992-93. Recipient Presdl. Young Investigator award NSF, 1990, Edmund Friedman Young Engr. award for profl. achievement, 1993. Mem. ASCE (assoc., sec. constrn. div. 1989-92, Collingwood Prize 1991, Outstanding Profl. Civil and Environ. Engring. 1991, Walter L. Huber Civil Engring. Rsch. prize 1996, bd. dirs. 1998—), Am. Assn. Cost Engrs. (assoc.), Am. Soc. Engring. Edn., Constrn. Mgmt. Assn. Am., Sigma Xi, Tau Beta Pi. Achievements include identification of causes of constrn. contractor failure; devel. of analytical models to assist in predicting contractor failure prior to contract award. Office: U Wis-Madison 2304 Engring Hall 1415 Johnson Dr Madison WI 53706-1607

RUSSELL, JOHN THOMAS, state legislator; b. Lebanon, Mo., Sept. 22, 1931; s. Aubrey F. and Velma F. (Johnson) R.; m. Margaret Ann Carr, 1951; children: John Douglas, Georgia Jeanette, Sarah Melissa. Student, Drury Coll. Mem. Mo. Ho. of Reps., Laclede County, 1963-66, Mo. Ho. of Reps. Dist. 125, 1967-72, Mo. Ho. of Reps. Dist. 150, 1973-76, Mo. Senate from 33rd dist., Jefferson City, 1976—. Dir., officer Laclede Metal Product Co. and Detroit Tool & Engring. Co., Lebanon, 1957-89, now cons.; Gen. Alumni Supply Co., Kansas City, 1959—; with Mo. Transp. Co., Lebanon, 1960; ptnr. Faith Leasing Co., Lebanon, 1969—. Del. Rep. Nat. Conv., 1972. Mem. Kiwanis, Am. Legion, Mason (32 degree), Scottish Rite, Lebanon C. of C. Republican. Home: PO Box 93 Lebanon MO 65536-0093 Office: State Senate State Capitol Building Jefferson City MO 65101-1556 Fax: 573-751-2745. E-mail: jrusse01@services.state.mo.us.

RUSSELL, PAUL FREDERICK, lawyer; b. Kansas City, Mo., Feb. 3, 1948; s. Walter Edward and Dorothy Marie (Sickels) R.; m. Kerry Diann Anderson, June 2, 1973; children: Philip, Erin, Shannon, Kelsey, Scott. BA, Northwestern, 1970; JD, U. Mich., 1973. Bar: Ill. 1973, U.S. Dist. Ct. (no. dist.) Ill. 1973. Assoc. Vedder, Price, Kaufman & Kammholz, Chgo., 1973-79, ptnr., 1980—. Mem. ABA, Chgo. Bar Assn., Ill. State Bar Assn., Univ. Club (Chgo.), Mich. Shores Club. Office: Vedder Price 222 N La Salle St Chicago IL 60601-1003 E-mail: prussell@vedderprice.com.

RUSSELL, THOMAS R. medical association administrator; Exec. dir. ACS. Office: ACS 633 N Saint Clair St Chicago IL 60611-3234

RUSSELL, TIM, radio personality; m. Judy Russell. Radio host Sta. WCCO Radio, Mpls., 1973—93, now radio host; radio host Sta. KLBB-AM. (voice over): (films) Little Big League; voice over (nat. broadcast, regional radio, and TV commls.); writer, prodr., performer: play on CD and audiotape Tim Russell's Comedy Christmas Carol; and numerous others. Recipient Outstanding Broadcast Personality of Yr. award, Minn. Broadcasters Assn., 1996, Best Radio Host award, Mpls./St. Paul Mag., 1996. Avocations: travel, antiques. Office: WCCO 625 2nd Ave S Minneapolis MN 55402*

RUSSELL, WILLIAM STEVEN, finance executive; b. Evanston, Ill., Aug. 5, 1948; s. John W. and Lillian H. Russell; m. Susan M. Hanson, Aug. 20, 1972. BS, So. Ill. U., 1970. CPA, Ill. Sr. staff auditor Arthur Andersen & Co., Chgo., 1972-76; acctg. mgr., controller, asst. sec. and treas. Lawter Internat., Inc., Northbrook, Ill., 1976-86, treas., sec., 1986-87, v.p. fin., treas. and sec., 1987-96, pvt. investor, 1996—. Served with U.S. Army, 1970-72. Mem. Am. Inst. CPA's, Beta Alpha Psi, Beta Gamma Sigma. Roman Catholic. Home and Office: 51 Park Lane Park Ridge IL 60068-2834

RUSSI, GARY D. academic administrator; Pres. Oakland U., Rochester, Mich. Office: Oakland U Rochester MI 48309

RUST, EDWARD BARRY, JR. insurance company executive, lawyer; b. Chgo., Aug. 3, 1950; s. Edward Barry Sr. and Harriett B. (Fuller) R.; m. Sally Buckler, Feb. 28, 1976; 1 child, Edward Barry III. Student, Lawrence U., 1968-69; BS, Ill. Wesleyan U., 1972; JD, MBA, So. Meth. U., 1975. Bar: Tex. 1975, Ill. 1976. Mgmt. trainee State Farm Ins. Cos., Dallas, 1975-76, atty. Bloomington, 1976, sr. atty., 1976-78, asst. v.p., 1978-81, v.p., 1981-83, exec. v.p., 1983-85; pres., CEO State Farm Life Ins. Cos., 1985—87; CEO, chmn. State Farm Mutual Auto Ins. Co., 1987—. Pres. and bd. dirs. State Farm Investment Mgmt. Corp., State Farm Internat. Services, Inc., State Farm Cos. Found.; bd. dirs. exec. and investment coms. State Farm Annuity and Life Ins. Co., State Farm Mut. Automobile Ins. Co., State Farm Life Ins. Co., State Farm Fire and Casualty, State Farm Gen. Trustee Ill. Wesleyan U., 1985—; mem. adv. coun. Grad. Sch. Bus. Stanford U., 1987-94; mem. bus. adv. coun. Coll. Commerce and Bus. Adminstrn. U. Ill. Mem. Am. Enterprise Inst., Bus. Roundtable (chmn. edn. task force), Tex. State Bar Assn., Ill. Bar Assn., Am. Inst. Property and Liability Underwriters (trustee 1986-96), Ins. Inst. Am. (trustee 1986-96), Ins. Inst. for Highway Safety (vice chmn.), Nat. Alliance of Bus. (chmn. 1998—), Ill. Bus. Roundtable (chmn. 1998—). Office: State Farm Ins Cos 1 State Farm Plz E-12 Bloomington IL 61710-0001

RUST, LOIS, food company executive; Pres. Rose Acre Farms, Seymour, Ind., 1989—. Office: Rose Acre Farms PO Box 1250 Seymour IN 47274-3850

RUSTHOVEN, PETER JAMES, lawyer; b. Indpls., Aug. 12, 1951; s. Richard and Henrietta (Iwema) R.; children from previous marriage: Julia Faith, David James; m. Linda C. Bennett, Dec. 28, 1987; children: Mark Bennett, Matthew Boyd. A.B. magna cum laude, Harvard U., 1973, J.D. magna cum laude, 1976. Bar: Ind., 1976. Assoc. Barnes, Hickam, Pantzer & Boyd, Indpls., 1976-81; assoc. counsel to Pres. of U.S. White House, Washington, 1981-85; of counsel Barnes & Thornburg, Indpls., 1985-86, ptnr., 1987—. Counsel Presdl. Commn. on Space Shuttle Challenger Accident, 1986; spl. cons. U.S. Atty. Gen.'s Adv. Bd. on Missing Children, 1988; adj. fellow Hudson Inst., 1989-91, adj. sr. fellow, 1991—; sr. fellow Ind. Policy Rev. Found., 1991—; bd. advisors Indpls. Lawyers Chpt. Federalist Soc., 1993—, mem. nat. practitioners coun., 1995—. Contbr. monthly column The Am. Spectator mag., 1973-79; mem. bd. editors Harvard Law Rev., 1974-76, case editor, 1975-76; contbr. articles to nat. mags. Bd. dirs. Ednl. Choice Charitable Trust, 1994—, Legal Svcs. Orgn. Indpls., 1977-79; precinct committeeman Marion County Rep. Ctrl. Com., Indpls., 1978-81; state media dir. Ind. Reagan for Pres. Com., 1979-80, Ind. Reagan-Bush Com., 1980; speechwriter nat. Reagan for Pres. Campaign, 1980; mem. legal policy adv. bd. Washington Legal Found., 1989—; candidate for Rep nomination for U.S. Sen., Ind., 1998. Grantee Inst. Politics, Harvard U., 1972 Mem. Ind. Bar Assn., Indpls. Bar Assn., Phi Beta Kappa Roman Catholic Avocations: golf; contract bridge; baseball memorabilia. Office: Barnes & Thornburg 1313 Merchants Bank Bldg 11 S Meridian St Ste 1313 Indianapolis IN 46204-3535

RUTENBERG-ROSENBERG, SHARON LESLIE, retired journalist; b. Chgo., May 23, 1951; d. Arthur and Bernice (Berman) Rutenberg; m. Michael J. Rosenberg, Feb. 3, 1980; children: David Kaifel and Jonathan Reuben (twins), Emily Mara. Student, Harvard U., 1972; B.A., Northwestern U., 1973, M.S.J., 1975; cert. student pilot. Reporter-photographer Lerner Home Newspapers, Chgo., 1973-74; corr. Medill News Service, Washington, 1975; reporter-newsperson, sci. writer UPI, Chgo., 1975-84; ret., 1984. Interviewer: exclusives White House chief of staff, nation's only mother and son on death row; others. Vol. Chgo.-Read Mental Health Ctr. Recipient Peter Lisagor award for exemplary journalism in features category, 1980, 81; Golden Key Nat. Adv. Bd. of Children's Oncology Service Inc., 1981; Media awards for wire service feature stories, 1983, 84, wire service news stories, 1983, 84, all from Chgo. Hosp. Pub. Relations Soc. Mem. Profl. Assn. Diving Instrs., Nat. Assn. Underwater Instrs., Hon. Order Ky. Cols., Hadassah, Sigma Delta Chi, Sigma Delta Tau Home: 745 Marion Ave Highland Park IL 60035-5123

RUTHERFORD, DAN, state legislator; Degree, Ill. State U., 1978. Legis. asst. for State Rep. Tom Ewing, Ill., 1978-80; exec. dir. Ill. Reagan/Bush Com., 1980; asst. dir. Gov.'s Office of Pers., Ill., 1981; mem. adv. com. on internat. trade U.S. Govt. and Adv. Com. on Sports Medicine; mem. Livingston County Coun. for Econ. Devel., Ill.; Ill. State rep. Named One of the People to Watch in 1986 Chgo. Tribune. Mem. Livingston County Farm Bur., Ill. Corn Growers Assn., Pontiac C. of C., Pheasants Forever, Japan-Am. Soc. Republican. Home: 13266 E 950 North Rd Chenoa IL 61726-9049 Office: Ill Ho of Reps State Capitol Springfield IL 62706-0001

RUTKOFF, ALAN STUART, lawyer; b. Chgo., May 31, 1952; s. Roy and Harriet (Ruskin) R.; m. Mally Zoberman, Dec. 22, 1974; children: Aaron Samuel, Jordana Michal, Robert Nathaniel. BA with high distinction, U. Mich., 1973; JD magna cum laude, Northwestern U., 1976. Bar: Ill. 1976, U.S. Dist. Ct. (no. dist.) Ill. 1976, U.S. Ct. Appeals (7th cir.) 1977, U.S. Ct. Appeals (3d cir.) 1978, U.S. Supreme Ct. 1981, U.S. Ct. Appeals (5th cir.) 1983, U.S. Ct. Appeals (8th cir.) 1990, U.S. Dist. Ct. (we. dist.) Wis. 1996. Assoc. Altheimer & Gray, Chgo., 1976-80; ptnr. Kastel & Rutkoff, 1980-83, Holleb & Coff Ltd., Chgo., 1983-84, McDermott, Will & Emery, Chgo., 1984—. Pres. N. Suburban Synagogue Beth El, Highland Pk., Ill., 1999-2001.. Mem. ABA, Chgo. Bar Assn., Order of Coif. Home: 801 Timberhill Rd Highland Park IL 60035-5148 Office: McDermott Will & Emery 227 W Monroe St Ste 4400 Chicago IL 60606-5096 E-mail: arutkoff@mwe.com.

RUTKOWSKI, JAMES ANTHONY, former state legislator; b. Milw., Apr. 6, 1942; BS in Bus., Marquette U., 1964, JD, 1966. Former instr. Marquette U., Milw.; asst. instr. U. Wis.; state legis. State of Wis., Madison, 1970-98. With USAR, 1966-72. Recipient Clean 16 award, 1982, 88, 90, 94, Wis. Man of Achievement award, 1976. Mem. KC, Greendale Jaycee Roosters. Home: 4550 S 117th St Greenfield WI 53228-2451

RUTLEDGE, CHARLES OZWIN, pharmacologist, educator; b. Topeka, Oct. 1, 1937; s. Charles Ozwin and Alta (Seaman) R.; m. Jane Ellen Crow, Aug. 13, 1961; children: David Ozwin, Susan Harriett, Elizabeth Jane, Karen Ann. BS in Pharmacy, U. Kans., 1959, MS in Pharmacology, 1961; PhD in Pharmacology, Harvard U., 1966. NATO postdoctoral fellow Gothenburg (Sweden) U., 1966-67; asst. prof. U. Colo. Med. Ctr., Denver, 1967-74, assoc. prof., 1974-75; prof., chmn. dept. pharmacology U. Kans., Lawrence, 1975-87; dean, prof. pharmacology Purdue U., West Lafayette, Ind., 1987—, program dir. Discovery Park, 2001—. Contbr. articles on neuropharmacology to profl. jours. Grantee NIH, 1970-87. Mem. AAAS, Am. Soc. Pharmacology and Exptl. Therapeutics (councillor 1982 84, sec.-treas. 1990-93, pres. 1996-97), Am. Assn. Coll. Pharmacy (chmn. biol. scis. sect. 1983-84, chmn. coun. faculties 1986-87, chmn. coun. deans 1993-94, commn. implement change pharm. edn. 1989-92, pres. 1996-97), Soc. for Neurosci., Am. Pharm. Assn. Avocations: gardening, skiing. Home: 40 Brynteg Est West Lafayette IN 47906-5643 Office: Purdue U Office of Dean Sch Pharmacy 1330 R Heine Pharm Bldg West Lafayette IN 47907-1330 E-mail: chipr@pharmacy.purdue.edu.

RUTTAN, VERNON WESLEY, agricultural economist; b. Alden, Mich., Aug. 16, 1924; s. Ward W. and Marjorie Ann (Chaney) R.; m. Marilyn M. Barone, July 30, 1945; children: Lia Marie, Christopher, Alison Elaine, Lore Megan. BA, Yale U., 1948; MA, U. Chgo., 1950, PhD, 1952; LLD (hon.), Rutgers U., 1978; D Agrl. Sci. ((hon.), U. Kiel, Germany, 1986, Purdue U., 1991. Economist TVA, 1951-54; prof. agrl. econs. Purdue U., 1954-63; staff economist President's Council Econ. Advisers, 1961-63; economist Rockefeller Found., 1963-65; head dept. agrl. econs. U. Minn., St. Paul, 1965-70, Regent's prof., 1986-99, Regent's prof. emeritus, 2000—. Pres. Agrl. Devel. Council, N.Y.C., 1973-77 Author: (with Y. Hayami) Agricultural Development: An International Perspective, 1971, 85, Agricultural Research Policy, 1982, Aid and Development, 1989, U.S. Development Assistance Policy, 1996, Technology, Growth and Development, 2001. Recipient Alexander von Humboldt award, 1985. Fellow AAAS, Am. Acad. Arts and Scis., Am. Agrl. Econs. Assn. (pres. 1971-72, Publ. award 1956, 57, 62, 66, 67, 71, 79, 85, 97); mem. NAS. Home: 1666 Coffman St Apt 112 Saint Paul MN 55108-1326 Office: Dept Applied Econs U Minn Saint Paul MN 55108

RUWWE, WILLIAM OTTO, retired automotive engineer; b. Cuba, Mo., July 25, 1930; s. Otto Albert and Maude May (Hines) R.; m. Helen Leona Haynes, Jan. 1, 1958; children: Teresa Lynn, Nancy Jean. BS, Cen. Mo. State U., 1959. Engring. clk. Wagner Brake div. Cooper Industries, St. Louis, 1959-64, engr., 1964-67, quality control chemist, 1967-68, mfg. mgr., 1968-82, plant mgr., 1982-93; ret., 1993. Inventor electroless nickle plating process for cast iron, 1964, dissolution of crystal formation in brake fluid, 1971. With U.S. Army, 1951-53. Mem. Soc. Automotive Engrs. (cert., product bus. com.1985-90), St. Louis Geneal. Soc. Avocations: genealogy, history. Home: 540 Innsbrook Estates Dr Innsbrook MO 63390-5325

RUXIN, PAUL THEODORE, lawyer; b. Cleve., Apr. 14, 1943; s. Charles and Olyn Judith (Koller) R.; m. Joanne Camy, May 25, 1965; children; Marc J., Sarah. BA, Amherst Coll., 1965; LLB, U. Va., 1968. Bar: Ill. 1968, U.S. Dist. Ct. (no. dist.) Ill. 1968, U.S. Ct. Appeals D.C. 1972. Assoc. Isham, Lincoln & Beale, Chgo., 1968-73, ptnr., 1974-77; ptnr., chmn. energy utilities sect. Jones, Day, Reavis & Pogue, Cleve., 1977—. Mem. Hudson Archtl. and Hist. Bd. Rev., 1981-81; mem. Folger Shakespeare Libr. Com., 1999—; exec. bd. Greater Cleve. Boy Scouts Am., 1978-90; bd. dirs. Cleve. chpt. ARC, 1991-97. Mem. ABA, Ohio State Bar Assn. (pub. utilities sect.), Bar Assn. Greater Cleve., Fed. Energy Bar Assn. (com. chmn. 1981), Chgo. Bar Assn., Club at Soc. Ctr., Rowfant Club, Chgo. Club, Caxton Club, Grolier Club. Office: Jones Day Reavis & Pogue 77 W Wacker Dr Fl 35 Chicago IL 60601-1662 also: 901 Lakeside Ave Cleveland OH 44114-1116 E-mail: paultruxin@jonesday.com.

RYALL, JO-ELLYN M. psychiatrist; b. Newark, May 25, 1949; d. Joseph P. and Tekla (Paraszczuk) R. BA in Chemistry with gen. honors, Rutgers U., 1971; MD, Washington U., St. Louis, 1975. Diplomate Am. Bd. Psychiatry and Neurology. Resident in psychiatry Washington U., 1975-78, psychiatrist Student Health, 1978-83, clin. asst. prof. psychiatry, 1983—. Inpatient supr. Malcolm Bliss Mental Health Ctr., St. Louis, 1978-80, pvt. practtice medicine specializing in psychiatry, St. Louis, 1980—. Bd. dirs. Women's Self Help Ctr., St. Louis, 1980. Fellow: APA (pres. ea. Mo. dist. br. 1983—85, sect. coun. AMA 1986—99, dep. rep. to assembly 1994—97, rep. 1997—2001, dep. rep. area 4 2001—, chair bylaws com. 2000—); mem.: AMA (alt. del. Mo. 1988—90, 1993—94, del. 1995—, mem. coun. on constn. bylaws 1998—), Manic Depressive Assn. St. Louis (chmn. bd. dirs. 1985—89), Mo. State Med. Assn. (vice spkr. ho. of dels. 1986—89, spkr. 1989—92), St. Louis Met. Med. Soc. (del. to state conv. 1981—86, 1993—, councilor 1985—87, v.p. 1989), Am. Med. Women's Assn. (pres. St. Louis dist. br. 1981—82, 1992, regional gov. VIII 1986—89, spkr. ho. of dels. 1993—96), Washington U. Faculty Club. Office: 9216 Clayton Rd Ste 105 Saint Louis MO 63124-1515

RYAN, CARL RAY, electrical engineer, educator; b. Gateway, Ark., Mar. 3, 1938; s. Clarence and Stella (Schnitzer) R.; m. Arline Walker; children: Carline, Julie. BSEE, U. Ark., 1962; MSEE, Iowa State U., 1963; PhD in Elec. Engring., U. Mo.-Rolla, 1969, profl. degree Elec. Engring., 1994. Instr. U. Mo.-Rolla, 1968-69; sr. engr. Govt. Electronics Group, Motorola Inc., Scottsdale, Ariz., 1969-72, mem. tech. staff, 1972-76, sr. mem. tech. staff, chief engr., 1979-89, v.p. tech. staff, 1989-90, dir. communication systems tech., 1990-98; pres. CRF, LLC, Cassvile, Mo., 1998—. Prof. Mich. Tech. U., 1976-79; adj. prof. Ariz. State U., Tempe, 1980-89; panel mem. Internat. Solid States Circuits Conf., Phila., 1977; session chmn. Future Space Communications Tech. Workshop, Pasadena, Calif., 1980; external advisor Mich. Technol. U. Contbr. articles to profl. jours.; patentee in field Assoc. Motorola Sci. Adv. Bd. Served with USAF, 1956-60 Fellow IEEE (communications tech., solid state circuits, accreditation com., Dan Nobel fellow, chmn. Phoenix chpt. 1981-82, program chmn. 1989, gen. chmn. Phoenix Conf. on computers and communication 1988)

RYAN, DANIEL LEO, bishop; b. Mankato, Minn., Sept. 28, 1930; s. Leonard Bennett and Irene Ruth (Larson) R. BA, Ill. Benedictine Coll., 1952; JCL, Pontificia Università Lateranense, Rome, 1960. Ordained priest Roman Cath. Ch., 1956, consecrated bishop, 1981. Parish priest Roman Cath. Diocese, Joliet, Ill, 1956-82, chancellor, 1965-78, vicar gen., 1977-79, aux. bishop, 1981-84, bishop Springfield, Ill., 1984-99. Office: Diocese of Springfield PO Box 3187 1615 W Washington St Springfield IL 62702-4757 E-mail: dlryan@dio.org.

RYAN, GEORGE H. governor, pharmacist; b. Maquoketa, Iowa, Feb. 24, 1934; s. Thomas J. and Jeanette (Bowman) R.; m. Lura Lynn Lowe, June 10, 1956; children: Nancy, Lynda, Julie, Joanne, Jeanette, George. BS in Pharmacy, Ferris State Coll., Big Rapids, Mich. Mem. Ill. Ho. of Reps., 1973-82, minority leader, 1977-80, speaker, 1981-82; lt. gov. State of Ill., 1983-91, sec. of state, 1991-98, gov., 1999—. Mem. Kankakee County Bd., 1966-72, chmn., 1971-72; chmn. Ill. Literacy Coun., 1991—. With U.S. Army, Korea. Recipient Humphrey award Am. Pharm. Assn., 1980, Top award Ill. chpt. DARE, 1989, Govt. Leadership award Nat. Commn. Against Drunk Driving and MADD Govt. Leader Against Drunk Driving award, 1994-95, City Club of Chgo. Man of Yr. award, 1995. Mem. Am. Pharm. Assn., Ill. Pharm. Assn., One Hundred Club, Masons (33d degree). Republican. Methodist. Lodges: Elks, Moose, Shriners. E-mail: governor@state.il.us.*

RYAN, JACK, physician, retired hospital corporation executive; b. Benton Harbor, Mich., Aug. 26, 1925; s. Leonard Joseph and Beulah (Southworth) R.; m. Lois Patricia Patterson; children: Michele, Kevin, Timothy, Sarah, Daniel. AB, Western Mich. U., 1948; postgrad., U. Mich. Law Sch., 1949-50, Emory U., 1950-51; MD, Wayne State U., 1955. Intern St. Luke's Hosp., Saginaw, Mich., 1955-56; pres. Meml. Med. Ctr., Warren, 1956-77; v.p. med. affairs Detroit-Macomb Hosps. Corp., 1976-77, pres. and chief exec. officer, 1977-96; ret., 1996. Assoc. prof. medicine Wayne State U., Detroit, 1974—; bd. chmn. Mich. Hosp. Ins. Co., 1990—. Recipient Disting. Alumnus award Wayne State U. Med. Sch., 1974, Wayne State U., 1979, Western Mich. U., 1989, Disting. Key award Mich. Hosp. Assn., 1986, Tree of Life award Jewish Nat. Fund, 1996. Fellow Am. Coll. Family Physicians, Am. Coll. Physician Execs., Detroit Acad. Medicine; mem. Internat. Health Econs. and Mgmt. Inst. (charter), Econ. Club Detroit, Detroit Athletic Club, Renaissance Club, Red Run Club. Avocations: Civil War, history, golf, tennis. Home: 175 Hendrie Blvd Royal Oak MI 48067-2412

RYAN, JAMES LEO, federal judge; b. Detroit, Nov. 19, 1932; s. Leo Francis and Irene Agnes Ryan; m. Mary Elizabeth Rogers, Oct. 12, 1957; children: James R., Daniel P., Colleen M. Hansen, Kathleen A. LLB, U. Detroit, 1956; LLD (hon.) , U. Detroit , 1986; BA, U. Detroit, 1992; LLD (hon.) , Madonna Coll., 1976, Detroit Coll., 1978, Thomas M. Cooley Law Sch., Lansing, Mich., 1986. Justice of peace, Redford Twp., Mich., 1963—66; judge 3d Cir. Ct. of Mich., 1966—75; justice Mich. Supreme Ct., 1975—86; judge U.S. Ct. Appeals (6th cir.), 1986—. Faculty Nat. Jud. Coll., Reno; adj. faculty U. Detroit Sch. Law, Thomas M. Colley Law Sch.; adj. faculty, bd. dirs. Ave Maria Sch. Law. Contbr. articles to profl. jours. Capt. JAGC USNR, 1957—92, ret. mil. judge USNR. Mem.: Fed. Bar Assn., State Bar Mich., Fed. Judges Assn., KM, KC. Office: US Ct Appeals US Courthouse 231 W Lafayette Blvd Detroit MI 48226-2700

RYAN, JAMES E. state attorney general; b. Chgo., Feb. 21, 1946; m. Marie Ryan; children: John, Jim, Matt, Amy, Patrick, Anne Marie(dec.). BA in Polit. Sci., Ill. Benedictine Coll., 1968; JD, Ill. Inst. Tech., 1971. Bar: Ill. 1971. Asst. state's atty. criminal divsn. DuPage County State's Atty.'s Office, 1971—74, 1st. asst. state's atty., 1974—76; founder Ryan & Darrah; state's atty. DuPage County State's Atty.'s Office, 1984—94; atty. gen. State of Ill., 1994—. Named Lawyer of Yr., DuPage County Bar Assn., 1997; recipient numerous awards from various orgns. including, Nat. Assn. Counties, Alliance Against Intoxicated Motorists. Mem.: Ill. State's Attys. Assn. (past pres., Ezzard Charles award). Republican. Roman Catholic. Office: James R Thompson Ctr 100 W Randolph St Chicago IL 60601*

RYAN, JOAN, food company executive; BS in Acctg., U. Ill. CPA, Ill. Divsn. contr., CFO NutraSweet Co.; v.p. fin., CFO Ameritech Small Bus. Svcs., 1995-98; v.p., corp. contr. Alliant Foodservice, Inc., Deerfield, Ill., 1998-2000; CFO, Tellabs, Inc., Lisle, 2000—. Office: Tellabs Inc 4951 Indiana Ave Lisle IL 60532-1698

RYAN, JOHN MICHAEL, landscape architect; b. Chgo., Sept. 27, 1946; s. Terrance Joseph and Norma (Morris) R.; m. Victoria Jean Wheetley, June 26, 1986; children: Micheline Giannasi-Mennecke, Tony Giannasi, Nick Giannasi, Andrew Morris Jennings, Melissa Contance Victoria, Cameron Michael Montgomery. B in Landscape Architecture, U. Ill., 1969. Registered landscape architect, Ill., cert. Mich., registered Ariz., Ind., Wis., Tenn., cert. CLARB. Assoc. landscape architect Carl Garnder & Assocs., Inc., Chgo., 1969-71; sr. landscape architect Collaborative Rsch. & Planning, 1971-73; v.p. Michael L. Ives & Assocs., Inc., Downers Grove, Ill., 1973-84; pres. Ives/Ryan Group, Inc., Naperville, 1984—. Prin. works include renovation of Old Orchard Shopping Ctr., Skokie, Ill., Lake Katherine Nature Preserve, Palos Heights, Ill., Crystal Tree Residential Golf Course Cmty., Orland Park, Ill., Corporetum Office Campus, Lisle, Ill., Maravilla Rainforest Atrium, Vernon Hills, Ill. Trustee Wheaton Evangelical Free Ch., 2000—. Recipient Nat. Landscape award Am. Assn. Nurserymen, 1988, 92, Key award in landscape arch. Home Bldrs. Assn. Greater Chgo., 1981, 84, 90, Best Project Grand award Interiorscape mag., 2001. Mem. Am. Soc. Landscape Archs. (Merit award 1991, 94, 96), Assoc. Landscape Contractors Am. (Environ. Improvement Grand award 1997, 2000, Environ. Improvement honor award 2000), Ill. Landscape Contractors Assn. (Gold award 1991, 96, 2001, Silver award 1986, 90, 93, 2001, Merit award 1988, 91), Chgo. Hort. Soc., Perennial Plant Assn. (Nat. Honor award 1993), Morton Arboretum. Avocations: gardening, travel.

RYAN, JOHN WILLIAM, academic administrator; b. Chgo., Aug. 12, 1929; s. Leonard John and Maxine (Mitchell) R.; m. D. Patricia Goodday, June 20, 1949; children: Kathleen Elynne Ryan Acker, Kevin Dennis Mitchell, Kerrick Charles Casey. BA, U. Utah, 1951; MA, Ind. U., 1958, PhD, 1959, LLD (hon.), 1988, U. Notre Dame, 1978, Oakland City Coll., 1981, St. Joseph Coll., 1981, Hanover Coll., 1982, DePauw U., 1983, U. Ma., 1983, Manchester Coll., 1983, U. Evansville, 1985, Wabash Coll., 1986, Ind. U., 1988; DLitt (hon.), U. St. Thomas, 1977; D Pub. Adminstrn., Nat. Inst. Devel. Adminstrn., Thailand, 1991; LLD (hon.), U. Md., 1994. Rsch. analyst Ky. Dept. Revenue, Frankfort, 1954-55; vis. rsch. prof. U. Thammasat, Bangkok, Thailand, 1955-57; asst. dir. Inst. Tng. for Pub. Svc. Ind. U., 1957-58; successively asst. prof., assoc. prof. polit. sci., assoc. dir., Bur. Govt. U. Wis., 1958-62; exec. asst. to pres., sec. of univ. U. Mass., Amherst, 1962-63, chancellor Boston, 1965-68; v.p. acad. affairs Ariz. State U., 1963-65; v.p., chancellor regional campuses Ind. U., Bloomington, 1968-71, pres., 1971-87, pres. emeritus, 1987—, prof. polit. sci., 1968-95, prof. pub. and environ. affairs, 1981-95, prof. emeritus, 1995—; cons. AID, 1991-92; chancellor SUNY, Albany, 1997-99, chancellor emeritus, 2000—; hon. prof. Moscow State U., 1999. Interim pres. Fla. Atlantic U., 1989, U. Md., Balt., 1994; bd. dirs. Ind. U. Found., chmn. 1972-87; chmn. Nat. Adv. Bd. on Internat. Edn. Programs, 1985-89; chancellor SUNY System, 1996-2000. Contbr. articles to profl. jours. Bd. govs. Pub. Broadcasting Svc., 1973-82; bd. visitors Air U., 1974-81; chmn. Air Force Inst. Tech Subcom., 1976-81; mem. univ. adv. com. Am. Coun. Life Ins.; bd. dirs. Corp. Community Coun., 1976; mem. nat. adv. coun. Pan Am. Games, 1985; mem. adv. bd. Assocs. for Religious and Intellectual Life, 1984—; active United Way Ind. Centennial Commn. Mem. Am. Soc. Pub. Adminstrn. (pres. Ind. chpt. 1969-70, nat. chpt. 1972-73, nat. coun. from 1970, Ind. Soc. Chgo. (non-resident v.p. from 1976, Am. Polit. Sci. Assn., Assn. Asian Studies, Am. Coun. Edn., Assn. Am. Univs. (chmn. 1981-82), Nat. Acad. Public Adminstrn., Ind. Acad., Explorers Club, Adelphia (hon.), Columbia Club (Indpls.), Skyline Club, Cosmos Club (Washington), Athenaeum (London), KC, Equestrian Order of Holy Sepulchre, Elks, Phi Kappa Phi, Phi Alpha Theta, Pi Sigma Alpha, Beta Gamma Sigma, Kappa Sigma (worthy grand master 1985-87). Office: Ind U SPEA 415 1315 E 10th St Bloomington IN 47405-1701 E-mail: chancem123@aol.com., ryan@indiana.edu.

RYAN, JOSEPH W., JR. lawyer; b. Phila., June 24, 1948; s. Joseph W. Sr. and Marie R. (Hillgrube) R.; m. Mary Pat Law, Sept. 11, 1971; children: Caitlin, Joseph W. III. BA, St. Joseph's U., Phila., 1970; MA, Villanova U., 1971; JD, U. Va., 1978. Bar: Ohio 1978, U.S. Supreme Ct. 1982. Ptnr. Porter, Wright, Morris & Arthur, Columbus, Ohio, 1978—. Lectr. Sch. Dentistry Ohio State U., Columbus, 1982-89, Continuing Legal Edn. Inst., 1984—; mem. trial acad. faculty Internat. Assn. Def. Counsel, Boulder, Colo., 1994. Author: Use of Demonstrative Evidence, 1985; assoc. editor Litigation News, 1986—, editor in chief, 2000—. Trustee Columbus Zool. Assn., 1980-90; bd. dirs. Columbus Speech and Hearing Ctr., 1988-99, pres., 1995-96. Mem. ABA, Ohio State Bar Assn., Columbus Bar Assn., Internat. Assn. Def. Counsel, Am. Arbitration Assn. (panel of arbitrators). Republican. Roman Catholic. Office: Porter Wright Morris & Arthur 41 S High St 30 Columbus OH 43215-6101 E-mail: jryan@porterwright.com.

RYAN, MARK ANTHONY, architect; b. Council Bluffs, Iowa, Sept. 6, 1964; s. Paul Elmer and Darreline Kay (Wyland) R.; m. Shelli Ann Hagerbaumer, Sept. 26, 1992. BA in Architecture with distinction, Iowa State U., 1987; postgrad. Sch. of Law, Creighton U., 2000—. Registered profl. architect, Wis. Project architect U.S. Army C.E., Omaha, 1987-90, architect, security engr., 1990-91, environ. project mgr., 1991-96; owner, architect Ryan Designs, 1987—; project mgr. Bovis Constrn. Corp., 1997-2000; CEO, Ad Hoc Comm. Resources, LLC, 1999—. Owner The Ryan Co., Omaha, 1994-96; bd. adv. Fitness Plus, Council Bluffs, Iowa, 1990-92; expert witness for pvt. attys., Iowa and Nebr., 1991—. Chmn. City Devel. Commn., Council Bluffs, 1992; trustee San. and Improvement Dist. No. 142, Douglas County, Nebr., 1995-96. Scholar, State of Iowa, 1982, Valentino scholar, 2001. Mem. AIA (sec. S.W. Iowa sect. 1991, treas. 1992, v.p. 1993, pres. 1994-96), Am. Mil. Engrs., Nat. Trust for Hist. Preservation, Downtown Omaha Inc., Golden Key, Phi Kappa Phi, Tau Sigma Delta, Phi Delta Phi. Avocations: archl. restoration, biking, freshwater aquatics. Home and Office: Ad Hoc Communication Resources 9030 Raven Oaks Dr Omaha NE 68152-1759 E-mail: ryandesigns@nfinity.com.

RYAN, PATRICK G. diversified financial services company executive, director; b. Milw., May 15, 1937; m. Shirley Welsh, Apr. 16, 1966; children: Patrick Jr., Robert J., Corbett M. BS, Northwestern U., 1959. Sales agt. Penn Mut., 1959-64, Pat Ryan & Assocs., 1964-71; chmn., pres. Ryan Ins. Group Inc., 1971-82; pres., chief exec. officer Combined Internat. Corp. (now Aon Corp.), Northbrook, Ill., 1982—, bd. dirs., 1982—; chmn., pres., CEO Aon Corp., Chgo., 1990—. Bd. dirs. Sears Roebuck and Co., Chgo., Tribune Co., Chgo. Trustee Rush-Presbyterian-St. Luke's Med. Ctr., Chgo., chmn. bd. trustees; trustee Northwestern U., Field Mus. Natural History, Chgo. Office: Aon Corp 123 N Wacker Dr Chicago IL 60606-1700

RYAN, PATRICK MICHAEL, lawyer; b. Chgo., May 26, 1944; s. Edward Michael and Kathleen Teresa (Crimmins) R.; m. Holly Ann Daleske, Aug. 31, 1968; children: Rebecca Eileen, Brendan Patrick, Abigail Christine, Lucas Christopher. BA, St. Mary's Coll., Winona, Minn., 1966; JD, Marquette U., 1969. Bar: Wis. 1969. Law clk. Wis. Supreme Ct., Madison, 1969-70; ptnr. Quarles & Brady, Milw., 1970—. Dir. and officer several pvt. bus. corps. Mem. ABA, Wis. Bar Assn., Milw. Bar Assn., University Club. Avocations: reading, sports. Home: 363 Huntington Dr Cedarburg WI 53012-9507 Office: Quarles & Brady LLP 411 E Wisconsin Ave Ste 2550 Milwaukee WI 53202-4497 E-mail: pmr@quarles.com.

RYAN, PAUL, congressman; b. Janesville, Wis., 1970; son. Paul and Betty R. BS in Econs. and Polit. Sci., Miami (Ohio) U., 1992. Aide to Sen. Bob Kasten (R-Wis.), Washington; legis. dir. U.S. Senate; economic advisor, speechwriter Empower Am., Jack Kemp, Bill Bennett; mktg. cons. Ryan Inc., Central, Janesville; mem. U.S. Congress from 1st Wis. dist., 1999—; mem. ways and means com. Defeated former Kenosha City Coun. Pres. Lydia Spottswood in 1998 to succeed two-term Rep. Mark Neumann, who ran unsuccessfully for the Senate. Mem. Janesville YMCA, Janesville Bowmen Inc. and Ducks Unlimited. Republican. Roman Catholic. Office: 1217 Longworth Ho Office Bldg Washington DC 20515-4901*

RYAN, PRISCILLA E. lawyer; AB, Marquette U., 1969; JD, Loyola U., Chgo., 1982. Bar: Ill. 1982. With IRS, 1986-87; atty.-advisor Office Tax Policy, U.S. Treasury Dept., Washington, 1988-89; ptnr. Sidley & Austin, Chgo. Frequent spkr. on employee benefits. Contbr. articles to profl. jours. Mem. ABA. Office: Sidley & Austin 1 S First National Plz Chicago IL 60603-2000 Fax: 312-853-7036.

RYAN, TERRY, professional sports team executive; m. Karilyn Ryan; children: Tim, Kathleen. Diploma in Phys. Edn., U. Wis., 1979. Scouting dir. Minn. Twins, 1986-91; profl. scout N.Y. Mets, 1980-86; profl. baseball player Minn. Twins, 1972-76, v.p. player personnel, 1991-94, v.p., gen. mgr., 1994—. Office: Minnesota Twins 34 Kirby Puckett Pl Minneapolis MN 55415-1596

RYAN, THOMAS, food service executive; b. Grand Rapids, Mich., Jan. 15, 1957; m. Jody Ryan; three children. B in Food Sci., M in Lipid Toxicology, D in Flavor Sci., Mich. State U. Consumer product rschr. Procter & Gamble, Pillsbury; sr. dir. new product devel. Pizza Hut, 1988-96; v.p. bus. devel. Long John Silvers, Lexington, Ky., 1996-97; v.p. meal mgmt. McDonalds Corp., Oak Brook, Ill. Recipient Silver and Gold awards Am. Mktg. Assn. Avocations: dining, golfing, wine collecting. Office: 1 Mcdonalds Dr Oak Brook IL 60523-1911

RYAN, THOMAS F. lawyer; b. Detroit, Nov. 4, 1943; BS, Ferris State U., 1965; JD magna cum laude, Wayne State U., 1971. Bar: Ill. 1972, U.S. Supreme Ct. 1978. Ptnr. Sidley & Austin, Chgo., 1972—. Mem. adv. com. cir. rules 7th Fed Ct. Appeals. 1st lt. U.S. Army, 1966-68. Fellow Am. Coll. Trial Lawyers; mem. Chgo. Bar Assn. (mem. jud. evaluation com.), 7th Cir. Bar Assn. (bd. govs. 1986-89, 2nd v.p. 1990-91, pres. 1991-92). Office: Sidley & Austin Bank One Plz 425 W Surf St Apt 605 Chicago IL 60657-6139

RYAN, TIMOTHY, state legislator; BA in Polit. Sci., Bowling Green State U.; JD, Franklin Pierce Law Ctr. Mem. Ohio Senate from 32d dist., Columbus, 2001—. Trustee Found. Extended. Mem. KC, Sons Italy, Internat. Narcotics Enforcements Offices Assn., Ancient Order Hibernians, Elks. Democrat. Office: Rm # 056 Senate Bldg Columbus OH 43215

RYBA, JOHN J. state legislator; b. Aug. 10, 1929; m. Gertrude Ryba, 1954; children: Sue, Sandy, Steve. Former city councilman, Green Bay; former mem. Green Bay Planning Commn. Met. Sewerage Commn. and Transit Authority; Wis. state assemblyman Dist. 90, 1992—. Co-author: Informent Bill, Legalizing Pepper Protection Spray; author: Responsible Beverage Survey. Recipient Spl. Olympics Achievement award, 1991-92. Mem. VFW (life), Elks (life mem. lodge 259, Elk of Yr. 1988-91), Am. Legion (life mem.). Address: 714 Wilson Ave Green Bay WI 54303-4106 Office: Wis Assembly PO Box 8952 Madison WI 53708-8952

RYBAK, R.T. mayor; m. Megan O'Hara; 2 children. Mayor City of Minneapolis, Minn.; cons. various orgn.; gen. mgr. WCCO TV & WCCO Radio; v.p. Internet Broadcast Sys.; pub., mgr., bus. ops. Twin Cities Reader. Founder, mem. bd. Save the Water in Mpls.; served Minn. Soc. Architects, Night of the Penguin, Hennepin Ave. Adv. Com., Adv. Fedn. Minn., Eiji Oue Inaugural Com.; coach Little League Baseball, Youth Soccer; vol. reader Minn. Pub. Sch.; co-coord. Bill Bradley for Pres. , 2000; co-chair Tony Bouza for Gov., 1994. Office: 350 S Fifth St 331 City Hall Minneapolis MN 55415*

RYBERG, WILLIAM A. orchestra executive; BMus, Western Wash. State U.; MMus, Ind. U. Teller, loan officer, br. mgr., regional mgr. Ranier Nat. Bank; v.p., area mgr. West One Bank, Tacoma; v.p., dist. mgr. Key Bank, Wash., 1993-96; exec. dir. Bellingham (Wash.) Festival of Music, 1996-98; pres. Grand Rapids (Mich.) Symphony, 1998—. Office: Grand Rapids Symphony Ste 1 169 Louis Campau Promenade NW 1 Grand Rapids MI 49503-2629

RYCHLAK, JOSEPH FRANK, psychology educator, theoretician; b. Cudahy, Wis., Dec. 17, 1928; s. Joseph Walter and Helen Mary (Bieniek) R.; m. Lenora Pearl Smith, June 16, 1956; children: Ronald, Stephanie. B.S., U. Wis., 1953; M.A., Ohio State U., 1954, Ph.D., 1957. Diplomate Am. Bd. Examiners in Profl. Psychology. Asst. prof. psychology Fla. State U., Tallahassee, 1957-58, Washington State U., Pullman, 1958-61; assoc. prof., then prof. psychology St. Louis U., 1961-69; prof. psychology Purdue U., West Lafayette, Ind., 1969-83, interim dept. head, 1979-80; prof. Loyola U. Chgo., 1983-99, Maude C. Clarke prof. humanistic psychology, 1983—, prof. emeritus, 1999—. Dir. Human Relations Ctr., Pullman, Wash., 1958-61; research cons. AT&T, 1957-82. Author: The Psychology of Rigorous Humanism, 1977, 2d edit., 1988, Discovering Free Will and Personal Responsibility, 1979, A Philosophy of Science for Personality Theory, 2d edit., 1981, Personality and Life Style of Young Male Managers, 1982, (with N. Cameron) Personality Development and Psychopathology, 2d edit., 1985, Artificial Intelligence and Human Reason: A Teleological Critique, 1991; assoc. editor Psychotherapy: Theory, Research and Practice, 1965-76, Jour. Mind and Behavior, 1985-94, Logical Learning Theory: A Human Teleology and Its Empirical Support, 1994, In Defense of Human Consciousness, 1997. With USAF, 1946-49. Named Outstanding Contbr. to Human Understanding, Internat. Assn.

Social Psychiatry, 1971. Fellow Am. Psychol. Assn. (div. 24 pres. 1977-78, 86-87), Am. Psychol. Soc.; mem. Soc. Personality Assessment, Phi Beta Kappa Roman Catholic. Home: 916 Michigan Ave Apt 2 Evanston IL 60202-5416

RYCUS, MITCHELL JULIAN, urban planning educator, urban security and energy planning consultant; b. Detroit, June 20, 1932; s. Samuel Israel and Esther (Mitnick) R.; m. Carole Ann Lepofsky, Aug. 31, 1958; children: Lisa Karen Rycus Mikalonis, Peter Todd. BS in Math., U. Mich., 1958, MS in Math., 1961, MS in Physics, 1965, PhD in Urban and Regional Planning, 1976. Asst. rsch. scientist radiation lab. U. Mich., Ann Arbor, 1958-61, pvt. cons. extension gaming svc., 1972-77, rsch. assoc. Mental Health Rsch. Inst., 1977-80; asst. prof. Coll. Architecture and Urban Planning, 1980-83; assoc. prof. U. Mich., 1983-86; chmn. Coll. Architecture and Urban Planning, 1986-92, prof., 1989—; co-dir. Studies in Urban Security Group U. Mich., Ann Arbor, 1985—; mathematician Bendix Corp. & Rocketdyne, 1961-62; group scientist Conductron Corp., 1962-70; project assoc. Mich. State C. of C., Lansing, 1970-72. Cons. Community Systems Found., Ann Arbor, 1985— Contbr. rsch. reports, articles. Advisor assessment com. United Way of Washtenaw County, Ann Arbor, 1988-89. With USN, 1950-54. Recipient Faculty Recognition award U. Mich., 1982-83. Mem. AAAS, Am. Planning Assn. Democrat. Jewish. Avocation: computer applications to planning. Office: U Mich Coll Architecture & Urban Planning Ann Arbor MI 48109-2069

RYDELL, CATHERINE M. former state legislator; b. Grand Forks, N.D., May 8, 1950; d. Hilary Harold and Catherine F. (Ireland) Wilson; m. Charles D. Rydell, 1971; children: Kimberly, Jennifer, Michael. BS, U. N.D., 1971. Mem. N.D. Ho. of Reps., 1985—, mem. supreme ct. judicial planning, govt., vet. affairs com., past rep. caucus leader; exec. dir. Am. Acad. Neurology, St. Paul. Coord. cmty. svc. Bismarck Jr. Coll.; bus. mgr. surg. svc. St. Alexius Med. Ctr. Bd. dirs. Mission Valley Family, YMCA, N.D. Early Childhood Tng. Ctr., Ronald McDonald Found., CHAND; mem. state adv. bd. Casey Family Program, Juvenile Justice; mem. lay adv. bd. St. Alexius; mem. regional adv. bd. Luth. Social Svcs.; mem. N.D. State Centennial Com., N.D. State Mus. Art. Recipient Outstanding Svc. award Tobacco Free N.D., Legislator of Yr. award Children's Caucus, Guardian of Bus. award Nat. Fedn. Ind. Bus. Mem. Philanthropic and Edn. Orgn. Sisterhood, N.D. Med. Assn. (v.p.), Gamma Phi Beta. Office: Am Acad Neurology 1080 Montreal Ave Saint Paul MN 55116-2386

RYDER, HENRY C(LAY), lawyer; b. Lafayette, Ind., Feb. 18, 1928; s. Raymond Robert and Mina Elizabeth (Arnold) R.; m. Ann Sater Clay, Nov. 29, 1952 (dec.); children: David C., Sarah Paige Hugon, Anne M.; m. Velma Iris Dean, Aug. 27, 1976 BS, Purdue U., 1948; LLB, U. Mich., 1951; LLD, Hanover Coll., 1998. Bar: Mich. 1951, Ind. 1952, U.S. Dist. Ct. (so. dist.) Ind. 1953, U.S. Ct. Appeals (7th cir.) 1957, U.S. Supreme Ct. 1981. Assoc. Buschmann, Krieg, DeVault & Alexander, Indpls., 1953-57, ptnr., 1957-60, Roberts & Ryder and successor firms, Indpls., 1960-86, Barnes & Thornburg (merger), Indpls., 1987-95, of counsel, 1996—. Pres. Ind. State Symphony Soc. Inc., 1979-82, bd. dirs., 1972-91, trustee, 1991—; chmn. United Way of Greater Indpls., 1984; vice chmn. Greater Indpls. Progress Com., 1979-86, chmn., 1987-89, mem. exec. com., 1979-2000; trustee Purdue U., 1983-89, Hanover Coll., 1979—, chmn., 1988-98; bd. dirs. Hist. Landmark Found. of Ind., 1985-96, chmn., 1992-95; bd. dirs. Purdue Rsch. Found., 1992—; hon. v.p. Ind. Soc. Chgo.; bd. govs. Heartland Film Festival, 2000—. Lt. U.S. Army, 1951-53. Recipient Jefferson award Indpls. Star, 1983, Whistler award Greater Indpls. Progress Com., 1989; Sagamore of the Wabash, 1984; named Man of Yr., B'nai B'rith Soc., 1984, Ind. Acad., 1992, Lifetime Achievement award Nat. Soc. Fund Raising Execs., 1999. Fellow: Ind. Bar Found., Am. Bar Found.; mem.: ABA, Indpls. Bar Assn., Ind. Bar Assn., Ind. C. of C. (bd. dirs. 1991—94), Purdue U. Alumni Assn. (pres. 1975—77, Alumni Svc. award 1982, Citizenship award 1989), Indpls. Lit. Club, Kiwanis (pres. Indpls. 1983, Civic award 1981), Columbia Club (bd. dirs. 1987—90, sec. 1988, trustee 1990—, pres. Found. 1990—95, Benjamin Harrison award 1983, Columbian Student of Yr. award 2002), USAC Benevolent Found. (bd. dirs., pres. 1999—), USAC Properties (sec., bd. dirs.), U.S. Auto Club (Pres.'s award 1989, Eddie Edenburn award 2000), Lawyers Club (pres. Indpls. 1966). Republican. Presbyterian. Office: Barnes & Thornburg 11 S Meridian St Ste 1313 Indianapolis IN 46204-3535

RYDER, TOM, state legislator; b. Medora, Ill., May 17, 1949; m. Peggy Ryder; 2 children. BA, No. Ill. U.; JD, Washington and Lee U. Ill. state rep. Dist. 97, 1983—; mem. appropriations II, human svcs. Ill. Ho. Reps., state govt. adminstrn. transp. and motor vehicles coms., chmn. house rep. policy com., mem. health care, labor and commerce com., pub. safety, infrastructure appropriations coms., joint com. adminstrn. rules, minority dep. leader; minority dept. leader; atty. Mem. Ill. Nat. Guard. Mem. Lions, Elks, Moose, Am. Legion. Republican. Home: 309 N Liberty St Jerseyville IL 62052-1516 Office: Ill Ho of Reps Rm 314 State Capitol Springfield IL 62706-0001

RYDHOLM, RALPH WILLIAMS, advertising agency executive; b. Chgo., June 1, 1937; s. Thor Gabriel and Vivian Constance (Williams) R.; m. Jo Anne Beechler, Oct. 5, 1963; children: Kristin, Erik, Julia. BA, Northwestern U., 1958, postgrad. in bus. adminstrn, 1958-59; postgrad. Advanced Mgmt. Program, Harvard U., 1982. Acct. trainee, copywriter Young & Rubicam Advt., Chgo., 1960-63; copywriter Post-Keyes-Gardner Advt., 1963, E. H. Weiss Advt., Chgo., 1963-65; copy group head BBDO Advt., 1965-66; with J. Walter Thompson Advt., 1966-86, creative dir., v.p., 1969-76, exec. creative dir., 1976-86, sr. v.p., 1972-80, exec. v.p., dir., 1980-86; exec. v.p., chief creative officer, dir. Ted Bates Worldwide, N.Y.C., 1986-87; mng. ptnr., chmn. mgmt. com., chief creative officer, chmn., CEO EURO RSCG Tatham Advt., Chgo., 1987-98; pres. R2 Cons., 1999—; spl. counsel J. Walter Thompson, 1999-2000. Bd. dirs., ops. com., chmn. creative com., vice chmn., 1996, chmn., 1997-98; Am. Assn. Advt. Agys. guest spkr. Ad Age Workshop, 1969, 77, 86, Adweek Seminar, 1993, CLIO awards, 1995; keynote spkr. Stephen B. Kelly Awards, 1993, CEBA Awards, 1997; dir. Euro RSCG, USA.; chmn. CEBA Awards, 1997. Mem. assoc. bd. Newberry Libr. Assn., Friends com. Northwetern U.; adv. coun. Chgo. Pub. Edn. Fund; Prin. for a Day Chgo. Pub. Schs., 1998, 1999, 2000, 2001; chmn. bd. dirs. Am. Scandinavian Coun.; dir. Am. Assn. Advt. Agys. Found., 1997—99. Staff sgt. USAF, 1959—65. Recipient Clio awards, Internat. Broadcast award, Lion awards, Cannes Film Festival, Addy awards; named one of Top 100 Creative Ad People Ad Daily, 1972, Advt. Exec. of Yr. Adweek, 1991, Best Man in Advt. McCalls and Adweek, 1992; named to Creative Leader Hall of Fame, Wall St. Jour., 1994. Mem. ASCAP, Am. Advt. Fedn. (Silver medal Lifetime Svc. 1997), Chgo. Advt. Fedn., Chgo. Coun. on Fgn. Rels., Saddle and Cycle Club, Econ. Club Chgo. (bd. dirs. 1996-98), Northwestern Club Chgo., Harvard Club Chgo., Harvard Club Boston, Execs. Club Chgo., Tavern Club, Carlton Club, Chikaming Country Club (Mich.), Dunes Club (Mich.), Lost Dunes Club (Mich.), Internat. Club, Hon. Order Ky. Cols., Openlands, Friends of the Parks, Friends of Chgo. River, Fernwood, Art Inst. Chgo., Phi Delta Theta. E-mail: rydholm@aol.com.

RYDZEL, JAMES A. lawyer; b. Worcester, Mass., Nov. 13, 1946; s. Joseph S. and Shirley F. Rydzel; m. Mary C. Chandler; 1 child, Molly. BA, St. Louis U., 1968; JD, Duke U., 1971. Bar: Ohio, 1972, Fla. 1975, U.S. Dist. Ct. (no. dist.) Ohio, U.S. Dist. Ct. (ea. dist.) Mich., U.S. Ct. Appeals (2d, 3d, 4th and 6th cirs.). Ptnr. Jones, Day, Reavis & Pogue, Cleve., 1972—. Adj. prof. law Case Western Res. U. Bd. dirs. New Orgn. Visual Arts, 1990, Greater Cleve. Growth Assn., Citizens League. Mem. ABA (litigation labor and employment law com.), Ohio State Bar Assn., Fla. Bar Assn., Def. Rsch. Inst. Office: Jones Day Reavis & Pogue North Point 901 Lakeside Ave E Cleveland OH 44114-1190

RYERSON, DENNIS, editor; b. Ames, Iowa, Apr. 20, 1948; children: Carey, Kirsten. Student, Iowa State U., U. No. Iowa. Announcer, news dir. Sta. KWBG, Boone, Iowa; reporter, then city editor Cedar Falls Record; news editor Scottsbluff (Nebr.) Star-Herald; editl. page editor Vancouver (Wash.) Columbian; chief editl. writer, then editl. dir. Cleve. Plain Dealer; mng. editor news Denver Post; editor editl. pages Des Moines Register, 1989-94; exec. editor Great Falls (Mont.) Tribune, 1994-95; v.p., editor Des Moines Register, 1995—. Appeared on TV shows including Good Morning America, MacNeil/Lehrer News Hour, CBS Morning News, NPR's All Things Considered. Mem. Nat. Conf. Editl. Writers (past pres.), Am. Soc. Newspaper Editors. Office: Des Moines Register 715 Locust St Des Moines IA 50309-3767

RYMER, WILLIAM ZEV, research scientist, administrator; b. Melbourne, Victoria, Australia, June 3, 1939; came to U.S., 1971; s. Jacob and Luba Rymer; m. Helena Bardas, Apr. 10, 1961 (div. 1975); children: Michael Morris, Melissa Anne; m. Linda Marie Faller, Sept. 5, 1977; 1 child, Daniel Jacob. MBBS, Melbourne U., 1962; PhD, Monash U., Victoria, 1971. Resident med. officer dept. medicine Monash U., Victoria, 1964-66; Fogarty internat. fellow NIH, Bethesda, Md., 1971-74; rsch. assoc. Johns Hopkins U. Med. Sch., Balt., 1975-76; asst. prof. SUNY, Syracuse, 1976-78, Northwestern U., Chgo., 1978-81, assoc. prof., 1981-87, prof., 1987—; rsch. dir. Rehab. Inst. Chgo., 1989—. Contbr. articles to profl. jours. Grantee NIH, VA, Dept. of Def., Nat. Inst. Disability Rehab. Rsch., pvt. founds. Fellow Royal Australian Coll. Physicians; mem. Soc. Neurosci., Am. Soc. Biomechanics. Democrat. Avocations: tennis, racquetball. Office: Rehab Inst Chgo 345 E Superior St Chicago IL 60611-4805

RYNKIEWICZ, STEPHEN MICHAEL, journalist; b. Sheboygan, Wis., Oct. 20, 1955; s. Walter Paul and Ruth Catherine (Van Hercke) R.; m. Brenda Gail Russell, Sept. 27, 1986. BA, U. Wis., 1976. Various staff assignments Chgo. Sun-Times, 1979-97, real estate editor, 1990-97; Internet prodr. Chgo. Tribune, 1997-2000. Pres. Ill. Freedom of Info. Coun., 1991-93; mem. profl. faculty Columbia Coll., Chgo., 1998; dir. Nat. Assn. Real Estate Editors, 1999—. Pres. Chgo. Headline Club, 1991-92, treas., 2001—. Mem. Soc. Profl. Journalists (regional dir. 1992-95, sec. treas. 1995-96, membership chair 1997-98, diversity chair 1996-97), Nat. Soc. Real Estate Editors (bd. dirs. 1999—), Sigma Delta Chi Found. (bd. dirs. 1995-96). Office: 435 N Michigan Ave Ste 1115 Chicago IL 60611-4001

RYPSTRA, ANN, zoology educator; PhD, Pa. State U., 1982. Prof. zoology Miami U., Oxford, Ohio; also dir. Ecology Rsch. Ctr. Reviewer NSF. Contbr. articles to sci. jours., including Animal Behaviour, Jour. Arachnology, Oikos. Rsch. grantee NSF. Office: Miami U Dept Zoology Oxford OH 45056

RYSKAMP, BRUCE E. publishing executive; b. Grand Rapids, Mich., 1941; AB, Calvin Coll., 1962; MBA, Mich. State U., 1964. With R. H. Donnelly Corp., 1964-82; with Zondervan Pub. House Zondervan Corp., Grand Rapids, 1983—, v.p. book and bible pub. Zondervan Pub. House, 1986-93, pres., CEO, 1993—. Office: Zondervan Pub House 5300 Patterson Ave SE Grand Rapids MI 49512-9512

RYUN, JIM, congressman; b. Wichita, Kans. m. Anne Ryun; children: Ned, Drew, Catharine, Heather. Founder, pres. Jim Ryun Sports, Inc.; mem. Congress from 2d Kans. dist., 1996—. Participant Olympic Games, 1964, 68, 72. Recipient Silver medal 1500 meter run Olympic Games, 1968; held world record in the mile, 1500 meters, 800 yards. Office: 330 Cannon Ho Office Bldg Washington DC 20515-0001*

SAADA, ADEL SELIM, civil engineer, educator; b. Heliopolis, Egypt, Oct. 24, 1934; came to U.S., 1959, naturalized, 1965; s. Selim N. and Marie (Chahyne) S.; m. Nancy Helen Hernan, June 5, 1960; children: Christiane Mona, Richard Adel. Ingénieur des Arts et Manufactures, École Centrale, Paris, 1958; M.S., U. Grenoble, France, 1959; Ph.D. in Civil Engring, Princeton U., 1961. Registered profl. engr., Ohio. Engr. Société Dumez, Paris, 1959; research assoc. dept. civil engring. Princeton (N.J.) U., 1961-62; asst. prof. civil engring. Case Western Reserve U., Cleve., 1962-67, assoc. prof., 1967-72, prof., 1973—, chmn. dept. civil engring., 1978-98, Frank H. Neff prof. civil engring., 1987. R.J. Carroll Meml. lectr. Johns Hopkins U., 1990; cons., lectr. soil testing and properties Waterways Expt. Sta. (C.E.), Vicksburg, Miss., 1974-79; cons. to various firms, 1962— . Author: Elasticity Theory and Applications, 1974, 2d edit., 1993; contbr. numerous articles on soil mechanics and foundation engring. to profl. jours. Recipient Telford Prize Instn. of Civil Engrs., U.K., 1995, Disting. Leadership award Cleve. Tech. Socs., 2001. Fellow ASCE (named Outstanding Civil Engr. of Yr. Cleve. sect. 1992); mem. Internat. Soc. Soil Mechanics, ASTM, One Two One Athletic Club. Achievements include invention of pneumatic analog computer and loading frame. Home: 3342 Braemar Rd Shaker Heights OH 44120-3332 Office: Case Western Res U Dept Civil Engring Case Sch Engring Cleveland OH 44106 E-mail: axs31@po.cwru.edu.

SAAL, HOWARD MAX, clinical geneticist, pediatrician, educator; b. N.Y.C., Aug. 20, 1951; s. Josef and Ester (Morgenstern) S.; m. Cara Tina Schweitzer, May 3, 1987; 1 child, Rebecca. BS, U. Mass., Amherst, 1973, MS, 1975; MD, Wayne State U., 1979. Intern pediatrics U. Conn. Med. Ctr., 1979-80; resident pediatrics U. Conn. Health Ctr., 1980-82; fellow med. genetics U. Wash. Sch. Medicine, 1982-84; dir. cytogenetics U. Conn. Health Ctr., Farmington, 1984-87; vice chmn. med. genetics Children's Nat. Med. Ctr., Washington, 1987-93, head clin. genetics Cin., 1993—. Asst. prof. pediats. George Washington U., Washington, 1987-93, assoc. prof. pediats., 1993; assoc. prof. clin. pediats. U. Cin. Sch. Medicine, 1993—, prof. pediats., 2000—. Contbr. articles to profl. jours. Mem. med. adv. com. Nat. Neurofibromatosis Found., N.Y.C., 1987—; mem. health profl. adv. com. March of Dimes, Arlington, Va., 1991-93; bd. dirs. Capital Area March of Dimes, 1993. Tng. grantee NIH, 1979-82. Fellow Am. Acad. Pediats. (chmn. exec. com. for sect. on genetics and birth defects 1999—), Am. Coll. Med. Genetics; mem. Am. Soc. Human Genetics, Soc. Craniofacial Genetics (sec.-treas. 1990-96). Avocation: photography. Home: 3715 Monets Ln Cincinnati OH 45241-3847 Office: Childrens Hosp Med Ctr 3333 Burnet Ave Cincinnati OH 45229-3026

SABATINI, FRANK CARMINE, lawyer; b. Chgo., May 24, 1932; s. Carmine and Lisetta (Arguilla) S.; m. Alice C. Chandler, Dec. 28, 1955; children: Marcus, Matthew, Michael, Daniel. BS, Kan. U., 1954, LLB, 1957. Bar: Wis. 1958, Kans. 1957. Atty. Allis Chalmers Mfg. Co., Milw., 1958-59; mem. Lillard, Eideson, Lewis & Porter, Topeka, 1959-61; partner firm Colmerry, Davis, Bennett & McCue, 1968-69, Sabatini, Waggener, Vincent, Afterborn, & Hannah, 1969-94, Sabatini & Assocs., 1984—. Mem. Kans. Ho. of Reps., 1969-70; chmn. bd. Capital City State Bank.; Workmen's compensation examiner, 1967; chmn. Legal Aid Soc., 1966-68; instr. Kans. Bankers Assn., 1959-61. Chmn. Topeka chpt. March of Dimes, 1961; pres. Hayden Father and Friends, 1974; mem. sch. bd. St. Matthews Grade Sch., Topeka; bd. dirs. St. Francis Hosp.; mem. exec. bd. Boy Scouts Am. 1st lt. U.S. Army, 1957-58. Named Boss of Year Legal Sec. Assn. Kans., 1972; recipient Silver Beaver award Boy Scouts of Am., 1990, St. Lawrence Student Ctr. award, 1990. Mem. Topeka Bar Assn. (exec. com., chmn. ethics com.), Kans. Bd. Regents, Phi Kappa Theta. Club: Topeka Country. Home and Office: Sabatini & Assoc 3710 SW Topeka Blvd Topeka KS 66609-1230

SABATINO, THOMAS JOSEPH, JR. lawyer; b. Norwich, Conn., Dec. 3, 1958; s. Thomas J. and Germaine (Clement) S.; m. Joan Kathryn Turnbull, June 4, 1983. BA, Wesleyan U., Middletown, Conn., 1980; JD, U. Pa., 1983. Bar: Mass. 1983, Ill. 1985, Calif. 1989. Assoc. Testa, Hurwitz & Thibeault, Boston, 1983-85, Coffield Ungaretti Harris & Slavin, Chgo., 1985-86; corp. counsel Baxter Healthcare Corp., Deerfield, Ill., 1986-90; pres., CEO Secure Med. Inc., Mundelein, 1990-92; assoc. gen. counsel Am. Med. Internat., Dallas, 1992-93, v.p., gen. counsel, 1993-95; v.p., assoc. gen. counsel Tenet Healthcare Corp., 1995; v.p., assoc. gen. counsel, asst. sec. Baxter Healthcare Corp., Deerfield, Ill., 1995-97, corp. v.p., gen. counsel, 1997—. Office: Baxter Healthcare Corp One Baxter Pkwy Deerfield IL 60015

SABBAGHA, RUDY E. obstetrician, gynecologist, educator; b. Oct. 29, 1931; arrived in U.S., 1965, naturalized; s. Elias C. and Sonia B.S.; m. Asma E. Sahyouny, Oct. 5, 1957; children: Elias, Randa. BA, Am. U., Beirut, 1952, MD, 1958. Diplomate Am. Bd. Ob-Gyn. Sr. physician Tapline, Saudi Arabia, 1958-64; resident Northwestern Meml. Hosp./Prentice Women's Pavilion, Chgo., U. Pitts./Magee Women's Hosp., 1965—68; ob-gyn specialist Tapline, Saudi Arabia, 1969-70; tchg. fellow U. Pitts, 1965-68, asst. prof. ob-gyn, 1970-75; prof. Northwestern U., Chgo., 1975-94; med. dir. Obstet. and Gynecol. Ultrasound S.C., 1994—; clin. prof. U. Chgo. Pritzker Sch. Medicine, 1995-2000, prof., 1995—. Obstetrician, gynecologist Prentice Women's Hosp., Chgo., 1995—. Editor: Ultrasound Applied to Obstetrics and Gynecology, 1980, 3d edit., 1994; co-editor: Fetal Anomalies: Ultrasound Diagnosis and Postnatal Management, 2001; contbr. Fellow Am. Coll. Obstetricians and Gynecologists, Am. Inst. Ultrasound in Medicine; mem. Soc. Gynecol. Investigation, Am. Gynecol. and Obstet. Soc., Ctrl. Assn. Obstetricians and Gynecologists. Research on diagnostic ultrasound, obstetrics and gynecology. Office: 680 N Lake Shore Dr Ste 1430 Chicago IL 60611-8702 Fax: 312-656-9202.

SABERS, RICHARD WAYNE, state supreme court justice; b. Salem, S.D., Feb. 12, 1938; s. Emil William and Elrena Veronica (Godfrey) S.; m. Colleen D. Kelley, Aug. 28, 1965 (dec. Feb., 1998); children: Steven Richard, Susan Michelle, Michael Kelley; m. Ellie Schmitz, June 9, 2000. BA in English, St. John's U., Collegeville, Minn., 1960; JD, U. S.D., 1966. Bar: S.D. 1966, U.S. Dist. Ct. S.D. 1966, U.S. Ct. Appeals (8th cir.) 1983. From assoc. to ptnr. Moore, Rasmussen, Sabers & Kading, Sioux Falls, S.D., 1966-86; justice Supreme Ct. S.D., Pierre and Sioux Falls, 1986—. Mem. editorial bd. U. S.D. Law Rev., 1965-66. State rep. March of Dimes, Bismarck, N.D., 1963; bd. dirs. St. Joseph Cathedral, Sioux Falls, 1971-86; trustee, bd. dirs. O'Gorman Found., Sioux Falls, 1978-86; active sch. bd. O'Gorman High Sch., Sioux Falls, 1985-86. Lt. U.S. Army, 1960-63. Named Outstanding Young Religious Leader, Jaycees, Sioux Falls, 1971. Mem. ABA, S.D. Bar Assn., Inst. Jud. Adminstrn., St. John's Alumni Assn. (pres. Sioux Falls chpt. 1975-91). Republican. Roman Catholic. Avocations: tennis, skiing, sailing, sports, wood carving. Office: SD Supreme Ct 500 E Capitol Ave Pierre SD 57501-5070 Home: 5218 S Sweetbriar Ct Sioux Falls SD 57108-2855

SABIN, NEAL F. broadcast executive; b. Chgo., Sept. 27, 1956; BA, Northwestern U., 1978. Exec. v.p. Weigel broadcasting/WCIU TV, Chgo., 1994—; corp. program mgr. WPWR-TV, 1983-94. Office: 2154 W Windsor Ave Chicago IL 60625-1612 Fax: (312) 705-2656. E-mail: nsabin@wciu.com.

SABL, JOHN J. lawyer; b. L.A., June 16, 1951; AB with distinction, Stanford U., 1973, JD, 1976. Bar: Calif. 1976, Ill. 1977. Assoc. Sidley & Austin, Chgo., 1977-83; ptnr. Sidley Austin Brown & Wood, 1983-97, 2000—; exec. v.p., gen. counsel, sec. Conseco, Inc., Carmel, Ind., 1997-2000. Editorial bd. Stanford U. Law Review, 1974-75, assoc. mng. editor, 1975-76. Mem. ABA, Calif. Bar Assn., Ill. Bar Assn., Chgo. Bar Assn. (chmn. securities law commn. 1985-86), Phi Beta Kappa. Office: Sidley & Austin Bank One Plz 10 S Dearborn St Chicago IL 60603 E-mail: jsabl@sidley.com.

SABO, JULIE ANN, state legislator; b. Mar. 18, 1966; m. Peter Baatrup. BA, Augsburg Coll. Pub. sch. tchr.; vice chair jobs, housing and cmty. devel. com.; mem. edn. com.; mem. E-12 edn. budget divsn. com.; mem. fin. com., mem. transp. com.; mem. transp. and pub. safety budget divsn. com. Mem. Legis. Coordinating Commn. Home: 3319 E 26th St Minneapolis MN 55406 Office: 317 Capitol 75 Constitution Ave Saint Paul MN 55155-1206 E-mail: sen.julie.sabo@senate.leg.state.mn.us.

SABO, MARTIN OLAV, congressman; b. Crosby, N.D., Feb. 28, 1938; s. Bjorn O. and Klara (Haga) S.; m. Sylvia Ann Lee, June 30, 1963; children: Karin, Julie. BA cum laude, Augsburg Coll., Mpls., 1959; postgrad., U. Minn., 1961-62. Mem. Minn. Ho. of Reps. from 57B Dist., 1960-78, minority leader Dem.-Farmer-Labor party, 1969-72, speaker, 1973-78; mem. U.S. Congress from 5th Minn. Dist., 1979—; chmn. Dem. Study Group; dep. majority whip 96th to 103rd Congresses; mem. permanent select com. on intelligence 102d Congress; chmn. Ho. Budget Com. 103d Congress; ranking minority mem. house budget com. 104th-106th Congress, mem. standards of official conduct com., appropriations com., ranking minority mem. transp. subcom. Former mem. Nat. Adv. Commn. on Intergovtl. Rels.; past pres. Nat. Legis. Conf.; bd. regents Augsburg Coll. Mgr., player Dem. Congl. Baseball Team, 1987—. Recipient Disting. Alumni citation Augsburg Coll., Arms Control Leadership award Employees Union, Local 113, SEIU, AFL-CIO; named One of 200 Rising Young Leaders in Am. Time mag., 1974; Man of Yr. Mpls. Jr. C. of C., 1973-74, One of Ten Outstanding Young Men of Yr. Minn. Jr. C. of C., 1974; inducted Scandinavian Am. Hall of Fame, 1994. Mem. Nat. Conf. State Legis. Leaders (past pres.) Office: 2336 Rayburn Bldg Washington DC 20515-2305*

SABO, RICHARD STEVEN, electrical company executive; b. Walkertown, Pa., Jan. 1, 1934; s. Alex S. and Elizabeth (Haluska) S.; m. Gail P. Digon, Feb. 15, 1954; children: Gailyn J., Richard A., Kerry S., Dale A. BS in Edn., California (Pa.) U., 1955; MS in Edn., Edinboro (Pa.) U., 1965. Tchr. Northwestern Sch. Dist., Albion, Pa., 1955-65; prodn. technician The Lincoln Electric Co., Cleve., 1965-66, staff asst. mktg., 1966-70, mgr. pub. rels., 1971-86, asst. to chmn., 1986-96, dir. cop. comms. and investor rels.; also exec. dir. James F. Lincoln Arc Welding Found.; ret., 1999. Editor: The Procedure Handbook of Arc Welding, 1994, 10 other books on arc welding; contbr. numerous articles to profl. jours. Chmn. Area Recreation Bd., Chesterland, Ohio, 1970, West Geauga Boosters, Chesterland, 1973-77; mem., bd. dirs. Profit Sharing Coun. Am., 1991-99. Recipient Svc. award Future Farmers Am., 1970—, Svc. award U.S. Skill Olympics, 1980, Lakeland Community Coll. award, 1990, Ohio State U. Hon. Welding Engring. Alumni award, 1990, Calif. U. (Pa.) medallion of Distinction, 1990, Internat. Bus. Exec. of Yr. Internat. Acad. of Bus. Disciplines, 1997. Mem. Am. Welding Soc. (vice chmn. edn. and fin. com., mem. fin. com. 1988-94, speaker, various awards, Plummer lectr. 1992), Am. Soc. for Engring. Edn., Am. Inst. Steel Cons. (mem. edn. com. 1986—), Steel Plate Fabricators Assn. (past chmn. promotions com., mem. bd. dirs. profit sharing coun. 1991-99—), California U. Alumni Assn. (trustee 1983-99—). Republican. Presbyterian. Lodge: Masons. Avocations: golf, hunting, fishing, classical music.

SACHA, ROBERT FRANK, osteopathic physician; b. Each Chicago, Ind., Dec. 29, 1946; s. S. Frank John and Ann Theresa S.; m. Linda T. LePage, 1988; children: Joshua Jude, Josiah Gerard, Anastasia Levon, Jonah Bradley. BS, Purdue U., 1969; DO, Chgo. Coll. Osteo. Medicine, 1975. Diplomate Am. Bd. Pediatrics, Am. Bd. Allery and Immunology. Pharmacist, asst. mgr. Walgreens Drug Store, East Chicago, Ind., 1969-75; intern David Grant Med. Ctr., San Francisco, 1975-76, resident in pediatrics, 1976-78; fellow in allergy and immunology Wilford Hall Med. Ctr., 1978-80; staff pediatrician, allergist Scott AFB (Ill.), 1980-83; practice medicine specializing in allergy and immunology Cape Girardeau, Mo., 1983—. Assoc. clin. instr. St. Louis U., 1980—; clin. instr. Purdue U., 1971-72, Pepperdine U., 1975-76, U. Tex.-San Antonio, 1978-80, assoc. clin. instr. So. Ill. U. Pres., Parent Tchrs. League; bd. gov. Chgo. Coll. Osteopathic Medicine. Maj. M.C. USAF, 1975-83, comdr. USNR. Named one of Top Pediatricians 2002-2003, Pediatric Allergy, Immunology. Fellow Am. Coll. Allergy, Am. Coll. Chest Physicians, Am. Acad. Pediatrics, Am. Acad. Allergy-Immunology, Am. Assn. Cert. Allergists; mem. ACP, AMA, Am. Acad. Allergy, Assn. Mil. Allergists, Am. Coll. Emergency Physicians, Mil. Surgeons and Physicians. Republican. Lutheran. E-mail: lsacha@ldd.net.

SACHS, ALAN ARTHUR, lawyer, corporate executive; b. Bklyn., Feb. 7, 1947; s. Herman and Clara Ethel (Treinkman) S.; m. Marilyn Neda Mushlin, May 19, 1974; children: David Henry, Stephen Edward. B.A., Columbia U., 1967; J.D., Harvard U., 1970. Bar: N.Y. 1971, U.S. Dist. Ct. (ea. and so. dists.) N.Y. 1972, U.S. Ct. Appeals (2d cir.) 1973, U.S. Dist. Ct. (no. dist.) N.Y. 1977, Wis. 1983, Mo. 1989. Law clk. to judge U.S. Dist. Ct. (ea. dist.) N.Y., 1970-71; assoc. Cleary, Gottlieb, Steen & Hamilton, N.Y.C., 1971-79, Paskus, Gordon & Hyman, N.Y.C., 1979-81; sec., gen. counsel The Trane Co., LaCrosse, Wis., 1981-85; sr. v.p., gen. counsel, sec. Edison Bros. Stores Inc., St. Louis, 1985—. Mem. ABA, Am. Soc. Corp. Secs. Office: Edison Bros Stores Inc 501 N Broadway Saint Louis MO 63102-2102

SACHS, HOWARD F(REDERIC), federal judge; b. Kansas City, Mo., Sept. 13, 1925; s. Alex F. and Rose (Lyon) S.; m. Susanne Wilson, 1960; children: Alex Wilson, Adam Phinney. B.A. summa cum laude, Williams Coll., 1947; J.D., Harvard U., 1950. Bar: Mo. 1950. Law clk. U.S. Dist. Ct., Kansas City, Mo., 1950-51; pvt. practice law Phineas Rosenberg, 1951-56; with Spencer, Fane, Britt & Browne, 1956-79; U.S. dist. judge Western Dist. Mo., Kansas City, 1979—, chief dist. judge, 1990-92, now sr. judge. Contbr. articles to various publs.; contbr. chpt. to Mid-America's Promise, 1982. Mem. Kansas City Commn. Human Rels., 1967-73; chmn. Jewish Community Rels. Bur., 1968-71, Kansas City chpt. Am. Jewish Com., 1963-65; mem. exec. com. Nat. Jewish Community Rels. Adv. Coun., 1968-71; pres. Urban League Kansas City, 1957-58, Kansas City chpt. Am. Jewish Congress, 1974-77; co-chmn. Kansas City chpt. NCCJ, 1958-60; mem. Kansas City Sch. Dist. Desegregation Task Force, 1976-77; pres. Jackson County Young Democrats, 1959-60; treas. Kennedy-Johnson Club, Jackson County, 1960. Served with USNR, 1944-46. Mem. ABA, Mo. Bar, Kansas City Bar Assn., Am. Judicature Soc., Lawyers Assn. Kansas City, Dist. Judges Assn. (8th cir., pres. 1992-94), Phi Beta Kappa. Office: US Dist Ct US Courthouse 400 E 9th St Kansas City MO 64106-2607

SACHTLER, WOLFGANG MAX HUGO, chemistry educator; b. Delitzsch, Germany, Nov. 8, 1924; came to U.S., 1983; s. Gottfried Hugo and Johanna Elisabeth (Bollmann) S.; m. Anne-Lore Luise Adrian, Dec. 9, 1953; children: Johann Wolfgang Adriaan, Heike Kathleen Julia, Yvonne Rhea Valeska. Diplomchemiker, Tech. U., Braunschweig, Ger., 1949; Dr.rer.nat. (Ph.D), 1952. Research chemist Kon-Shell Lab., Amsterdam, Netherlands, 1952-71, dept. head Netherlands, 1972-83; extraordinary prof. chemistry U. Leiden, Netherlands, 1963-83; V.N. Ipatieff prof. Northwestern U., Evanston, Ill., 1983-96; chmn. Gordon Research Conf. Catalysis, N.H., 1985. Rideal lectr. Faraday div. Royal Soc. Chemistry, 1981; F. Gault lectr., 1991. Mem. editl. bd. Jour. Catalysis, 1976-88, Applied Catalysis, 1983-87, Catalysis Letters, 1987—, Advances in Catalysis, 1987—, Catalysis Today, 1996—, Catalysis Reviews, 1997—; contbr. numerous articles to sci. jours. Recipient Deutsche Gesellschaft Mineraloel und Kohle Kolleg, 1991. Fellow AAAS; mem. Royal Netherlands Acad. Scis., Internat. Congress Catalysis (pres. coun. 1992-96), Royal Dutch Chem. Soc. (hon. mem. catalysis divsn.), Am. Chem. Soc. (E.V. Murphee award 1987, Petroleum Chemistry award 1992), Catalysis Soc. N.Am. (Robert L. Burwell award 1985, E. Houdry award 1993). Home: 2141 Ridge Ave Apt 2D Evanston IL 60201-2788 Office: Northwestern U 2137 Sheridan Rd Evanston IL 60208-0001 E-mail: wmhs@northwestern.edu.

SACK, JAMES MCDONALD, JR. radio and television producer, marketing executive; b. London, Oct. 11, 1948; s. James McDonald and Ruth Elmore (Bryant) S.; m. Cheryl S. Gremaux, July 13, 1969 (div. June 1974); 1 child, Graehm McDonald; m. Svetlana Antsoulevich, Oct. 14, 1999. BA in History, Ind. U., 1975, MS in Telecomm., 1976. Coord. Latin Am. Ednl. Ctr., Ft. Wayne, Ind., 1979-81, Mayor's Office, Ft. Wayne, 1981-83; producer WMEE-WQHK Radio, 1983-85; owner, operator Festival Mgmt. and Devel., 1984—; owner Lily Co., 1991—2001; region sales mgr. Plan Mgmt., 1995-96; v.p. comm., mktg. United Way of Allen County, 1989-96; owner The Sack Co., 1996—. Pub. affairs prodr. WBYR/WFWA, Ft. Wayne; co-founder, treas. Vurpar Project (aid to Romania), 1999—. Producer radio documentary, 1985 (First Pl. award Ind. Broadcasters Assn., 1985), producer WFWA-PBS Eye on the Arts, 1987-89. Founder, pres. Germanfest of Ft. Wayne, 1981-92; pres. cable TV program adv. coun. City of Ft. Wayne; founder Ft. Wayne-Gera (Germany) Sister City Affiliation; commr. Ind. Hoosier Celebration, 1988; dir. Ind. Highland Games, 1992, cons., 1993-99; mktg. dir. Germanfest of Ft. Wayne, 1996-98; cmn. adv. bd. Ft. Wayne Cable Fund, 2000--; bd. dirs. Ft. Wayne Sister Cities Com., 2000—. Named Ky. Col., 1991. Mem. German Heritage Soc. (founder, bd. dirs. 1986-99), Ind. German Heritage Soc. (founder, bd. dirs. 1986-92, Gov.'s Commendation award 1983), N.Am. Sängerbund (sec. 1985-86), Männerchor Club (Ft. Wayne), Ft. Wayne Sport Club (sec. 1985-86, trustee 1987-89). Lutheran. Avocations: flying, politics, linguistics, travel. Home and Office: 902 West Rudisill Fort Wayne IN 46807 E-mail: jimsack@yahoo.com.

SADLER, DAVID GARY, management executive; b. Iowa City, Mar. 14, 1939; s. Edward Anthony and Elsie June (Sherman) S.; m. Karen Sadler. Student, St. Ambrose Coll., 1957-59; BS in Indsl. Adminstrn. and Prodn., Kent State U., 1961. Various mgmt. positions Ford Motor Co., Lorain, Ohio, 1962-67, Sperry-New Holland, Lebanon, 1967-71; mgr. mfg. Allis Chalmer, Springfield, Ill., 1971-72; dir. mfg. Purolator, Inc., Fayetteville, N.C., 1972-73; v.p. mfg. farm equipment and ops. truck div. White Motor Co., Eastlake, Ohio and Chgo., 1973-78; corp. v.p. mfg. Massey Ferguson Ltd., Toronto, Ont., Can., 1978-80, Internat. Harvester, Chgo., 1980-81, sr. v.p. ops. staff, 1981-82, v.p. bus. devel., 1982, pres. diversified group, 1982-83, pres. internat. group, 1983-85; pres. AMI, Inc., 1985-86; vice chmn., chief exec. officer Savin Corp., Stamford, Conn., 1986, chmn., chief exec. officer, 1986-89, also bd. dirs.; pres. Asset Mgmt. Internat., Westport, 1989-95; chmn., CEO, Rowe Internat., Grand Rapids, Mich., 1995-2000, also bd. dirs., 2000—01; CEO Merisel, Inc., El Segundo, Calif., also bd. dirs. Bd. dirs. greater Chgo. Safety Coun., 1981-84; mem. adb. bd. Hellmond Assocs. Opportunity Fund II. Roman Catholic. Home: 751 Bradford Farms Ln NE Grand Rapids MI 49525-3348 E-mail: davidgsadler@aol.com.

SADOWSKI, JAMES R. company executive; BS in Engring./Sci., MS, Case Inst. Tech. Various mgmt. positions Parker Hannifin Corp. and TRW Inc.; group v.p. Bertea Aerospace Group Parker Hannifin Corp., 1991-93; pres., COO Chart Industries, Cleve., 1993—. Office: Chart Industries 5885 Landerbrook Dr Ste 150 Cleveland OH 44124-4031 Fax: 440-753-1491.

SADOWSKI, RICHARD J. publishing executive; b. Mar. 26, 1947; Publ. Press-Telegram, Long Beach, Calif.; now pres., publ. St. Paul Pioneer Press. Office: St Paul Pioneer Press 345 Cedar St Saint Paul MN 55101-1057

SAEKS, ALLEN IRVING, lawyer; b. Bemidji, Minn., July 14, 1932; m. Linda J. Levin; 1 child, Adam Charles. BS in Law, U. Minn., 1954, JD, 1956. Bar: Minn. 1956, U.S. Dist. Ct. Minn. 1956, U.S. Ct. Appeals (8th cir.) 1957, U.S. Ct. Appeals (fed. cir.) 1959, U.S. Supreme Ct. 1959, U.S. Ct. Appeals (11th cir.) 1997; cert. civil trial specialist. Asst. U.S. atty. Dept. Justice, St. Paul, 1956-57; assoc. Leonard Street and Deinard, Mpls., 1960-63, ptnr., 1964—. Adj. prof. law U. Minn. Law Sch., 1960-65; chmn. Lawyer Trust Account Bd., Interest on Lawyers Trust Accounts, 1984-87. Chmn. Property Tax Com., 1986-87; bd. dirs. Citizens League, Mpls., 1984-87; pres. Jewish Cmty. Rels. Coun. of Minn. and the Dakotas, 1994-96. 1st lt. JAGC, U.S. Army, 1957-60. Recipient City of Mpls. award, 1996, Lifetime Commitment award Cardozo Soc., 2001. Fellow Am. Bar Found. (life); mem. ABA (commn. on interest on lawyers trust accts. 1990-93), Minn. State Bar Assn., Fund for the Legal Aid Soc. (chmn. 1997-98, Law Day Testimonial award 1996), Hennepin County Bar Assn. (pres. 1983-84), Order of Coif, Phi Delta Phi. Office: Leonard Street and Deinard 150 S 5th St Ste 2300 Minneapolis MN 55402-4238

SAFFELS, DALE EMERSON, federal judge; b. Moline, Kans., Aug. 13, 1921; s. Edwin Clayton and Lillian May (Cook) S.; m. Margaret Elaine Nieman, Apr. 2, 1976; children by previous marriage: Suzanne Saffels Gravitt, Deborah Saffels Godowns, James B.; stepchildren: Lynda Cowger Harris, Christopher Cowger. AB, Emporia State U., 1947; JD cum laude, LLB cum laude, Washburn U., 1949. Bar: Kans. 1949. Pvt. practice law, Garden City, Kans., 1949-71, Topeka, 1971-75, Wichita, Kans., 1975-79; U.S. dist. judge Dist. of Kans., Topeka, 1979—. County atty. Finney County, Kans., 1951-55; chmn. bd. Fed. Home Loan Bank Topeka, 1978-79; mem. Jud. Conf. Com. on Fin. Disclosure, 1993-99. Mem. bd. govs. Sch. Law Washburn U., 1973-85; pres. Kans. Dem. Club, 1957; Dem. nominee Gov. of Kans., 1962; mem. Kans. Ho. of Reps., 1955-63, minority leader, 1961-63; mem. Kans. Corp. Commn., 1967-75, chmn., 1968-75; mem. Kans. Legis. Coun., 1957-63; Kans. rep. Interstate Oil Compact Commn., 1967-75, 1st vice chmn., 1971-72; pres. Midwest Assn. Regulatory Commn., 1972-73, Midwest Assn. R.R. and Utilities Commrs., 1972-73; trustee Emporia State U. Endowment Assn.; bd. dirs. Nat. Assn. Regulatory Utility Commrs., 1972-75. Maj. Signal Corps U.S. Army, 1942-46. Fellow Am. Bar Found., Kans. Bar Found.; mem. ABA, Kans. Bar Assn., Wichita Bar assn., Am. Judicture Soc., Delta Theta Phi. Lutheran. Office: US Dist Ct 420 Federal Bldg 444 SE Quincy St Topeka KS 66683 Fax: (785) 295-2809.

SAFFERMAN, ROBERT SAMUEL, microbiologist, researcher; b. Bronx, N.Y., Dec. 19, 1932; s. Irving and Rose (Schuler) S.; m. Jewel S. Reisman, June 7, 1958; children— Karen M., Sharon L., Steven I. B.S., Bklyn. Coll., 1955; Ph.D., Rutgers U., 1960. With USPHS, Cin., 1959-64; with Dept. Interior, 1964-70, U.S. EPA, Cin., 1970—; chief virology sect. Environ. Monitoring and Support Lab. EPA, 1974-88, chief virology br. Environ. Monitoring Systems Lab., 1988-94; chief virology and parasitology br. Environ. Monitoring Sys. Lab., 1994-95; chief biohazard assessment rsch. br. Nat. Exposure Rsch. Lab., 1995—. Mem. Internat. Com. on Taxonomy of Viruses. Recipient Spl. Service award San. Engring. Ctr., USPHS, 1963; Gans medal Soc. Water Treatment and Examination, Eng., 1970; named Fed. Employee of Yr., Cin., 1974 Fellow Am. Acad. Microbiology; mem. Am. Soc. Microbiology, Sigma Xi. Home: 1669 Locksley St Cincinnati OH 45230-2220 Office: 26 Martin Luther King Dr W Cincinnati OH 45268-0001

SAFLEY, JAMES ROBERT, lawyer; b. Cedar Rapids, Iowa, Sept. 19, 1943; s. Robert Starr and Jean (Engelman) S.; m. Dianne Lee McInnis; children: Anne Michele, Jamie Leigh. BA, U. Iowa, 1965; JD, Duke U., 1968. Bar: Minn. 1968, U.S. Ct. Appeals (4th, 5th, 6th, 8th, 9th and 11th cirs.), U.S. Supreme Ct. Law clk. U.S. Dist. Ct. Minn., Mpls., 1968-69; assoc. Robins, Kaplan, Miller & Ciresi, 1969-74, ptnr., 1974—. Mem. adv. coun. Women's Intercollegiate Athletics, U. Minn., 1988-94; mem. Minn. Fed. Bar Assn. Commn. on ADR, 1995—. Mem. ABA, Minn. State Bar Assn. (antitrust sect. chmn. 1985-87), Hennepin County Bar Assn., Duke Law Alumni Assn. (bd. dirs. 2001--), Phi Beta Kappa. Office: Robins Kaplan Miller & Ciresi 2800 LaSalle Pla 800 Lasalle Ave Ste 2800 Minneapolis MN 55402-2015

SAGER, DONALD JACK, librarian, consultant, former publisher; b. Milw., Mar. 3, 1938; s. Alfred Herman and Sophia (Sagan) Sager; m. Sarah Ann Long, May 23, 1987; children: Geoffrey, Andrew. BS, U. Wis., Milw., 1963; MSLS, U. Wis., 1964. Sr. documentalist AC Electronics divsn. GM, Milw., 1958-63; teaching asst. U. Wis., Madison, 1963-64; dir. Kingston (N.Y.) Pub. Libr., 1964-66, Elyria (Ohio) Pub. Libr., 1966-71, Mobile Pub. Libr., 1971-75, Pub. Libr. Columbus and Franklin County, Ohio, 1975-78; commr. Chgo. Pub. Libr., 1978-81; dir. Elmhurst Pub. Libr., Ill., 1982-83, Milw. Pub. Libr., 1983-91; pub. Highsmith Press, Ft. Atkinson, Wis., 1991-2000; pres., CEO Gossage Sager Assocs. LLC, N.Y.C., 2000—. Secy Online Computer Library Ctr, 1977—78, disting vis scholar, 1982; chmn investment comt PLA Pub Library, 1985—89, chmn mus comt, 1989—91, mem hist comt, 1993—95, chmn PLA nat conf comt, 1986—88; bd dirs Coun Wis Libraries, 1982—91, Urban Libraries Coun, 1985—93, secy, 1991—93; adj faculty Univ Wis, Milwaukee, 1984—91; consult in field. Author: (book) Reference: A Programmed Instruction, 1970, Binders, Books and Budgets, 1971, Participatory Management, 1981, The American Public Library, 1982, Public Library Administrators Planning Guide to Automation, 1983, Managing the Public Library, 1984, Small Libraries, 1992, Small Libraries, 3d rev ed, 2000; co-editor: Urban Library Management Trends, 1989; contbg. editor: Public Libraries, 1990—; contbr. articles to profl jours. Pres Milwaukee Civic Alliance, 1990—91; chmn Milwaukee United Way Campaign, 1984; pres Milwaukee Westown Asn, 1987—90; bd dirs Goethe House, 1985—91. Mem.: ALA (coun mem 1995—, policy monitoring comt, awards comt, chmn core values task force), Library Admin Asn Wis (chmn 1987—88), Wis Library Asn Found 1986—88, Wis Library Asn, Chicago Book Clin, Ill Library Asn, Pub Library Asn (bd dirs, vpres, pres-elect, pres 1982—83), Exchange Club Milwaukee 1988—89. Home: 590 Wilmot Rd Deerfield IL 60015-3955 Office: Gossage Sager Assocs LLC 25 W 43d St Ste 812 New York NY 10036 E-mail: dsager@gossagesager.com.

SAGER, WILLIAM FREDERICK, retired chemistry educator; b. Glencoe, Ill., Jan. 22, 1918; s. Fred Anson and Alta (Stansbury) S.; m. Marilyn Olga Williams, Dec. 26, 1941; children: Karen Louise Sager Dickinson, Judith Lynn SagerPeyton), Kathryn Gwen Sager Potts. B.S. in Chemistry, George Washington U., 1939, M.A. in Organic Chemistry, 1941; Ph.D. in Organic Chemistry, Harvard U., 1948. Research chemist The Texas Co., 1941-45; prof. chemistry George Washington U., 1948-65, U. Ill.-Chgo., 1965-86, prof. emeritus, 1986—, chmn., 1965-80. Cons. to govt. and industry, 1952—. Founder, pres. Sager Innovations, Inc. Patentee (U.S. patents on evergy saving devices.). Recipient Disting. Service award U. Ill. Alumni Assn., 1985; Guggenheim fellow, 1954-55. Mem. Am. Chem. Soc., Sigma Xi, Alpha Chi Sigma. Home: 1552 John Anderson Dr Ormond Beach FL 32176-3567 Office: Dept Chemistry U Ill-Chicago Chicago IL 60680

SAHR, BOB, state agency administrator; s. Bob and Carla Sahr; m. Christine Sahr. Grad. with honors, U. Colo., 1989, JD. Sales and mktg. exec. Michelin Tire Corp.; gen. counsel Bur. of Pers., State of SD, SD; pub. utilities commr. State of SD, Pierre. Past pres. Oahe Habitat for Humanity; vol. Easter Seals; bd. dirs. Countryside Hospice, Pierre Mcpl. Libr. Mem.: State Bar SD (mem. commn.). Avocations: reading, movies, music, sports. Office: Pub Utilities Commn Capitol Bldg 1st Fl 500 E Capitol Ave Pierre SD 57501-5070

SAIN, MICHAEL KENT, electrical engineering educator; b. St. Louis, Mar. 22, 1937; s. Charles George and Marie Estelle (Ritch) S.; m. Frances Elizabeth Bettin, Aug. 24, 1963; children: Patrick, Mary, John, Barbara, Elizabeth. BSEE, St. Louis U., 1959, MSEE, 1962; PhD, U. Ill., 1965. Engr. Sandia Corp., Albuquerque, 1958-61, Vickers Electric Corp., St. Louis, 1962; instr. U. Ill., Urbana, 1962-63; asst. prof. U. Notre Dame (Ind.), 1965-68, assoc. prof., 1968-72, prof., 1972-82, Frank M. Freimann prof. elec. engring., 1982—. Vis. scientist U. Toronto, Ont., Can., 1972-73; disting. vis. prof. Ohio State U., Columbus, 1987; cons. Allied-Bendix Aerospace, South Bend, Ind., 1976—, Deere & Co., Moline, Ill., 1981, 82, Garrett Corp., Phoenix, 1984, GM, Warren, Mich., 1984-94; plenary spkr. IEEE Conf. on Decision and Control, 1990. Author: Introduction to Algebraic System Theory, 1981; editor: Alternatives for Linear Multivariable Control, 1978; hon. editor: Ency. of Systems and Control, 1987; editor jour. IEEE Trans. on Automatic Control, 1979-83; contbr. 350 articles to profl. jours., books and refereed proc; founding editor-in-cheif, IEEE Circuits and Systems Mag., 2001—. Grantee Army Rsch. Office, NSF, Ames Rsch. Ctr., Lewis Rsch. Ctr. NASA, Office Naval Rsch., Air Force Office Sci. Rsch., Law Enforcement Assistance Adminstrn., Clark-Hurth Components, Visteon. Fellow IEEE (prize papers com. 1992-96, chair 1994-96, awards bd. 1994-96, Alfred Noble prize com. 1995—); mem. Control Sys. Soc. IEEE (bd. govs. 1978-84, Disting. Mem. award 1983, Centennial medal 1984, Axelby prize chair 1991-97, awards com. chair 1993-97), Circuits and Sys. Soc. IEEE (co-chair internat. symposium on circuits and sys. 1990, newsletter editor 1990-2000, v.p. adminstrn. 1992-93, v.p. tech. activities 1994-95, Golden Jubilee medal 1999), Soc. Indsl. and Applied Math. Republican. Roman Catholic. Avocations: photography, swimming, jogging. Office: U Notre Dame Dept Elec Engring 275 Fitzpatrick Hall Notre Dame IN 46556-5637 E-mail: sain.1@nd.edu.

ST. ANTOINE, THEODORE JOSEPH, b. St. Albans, Vt., May 29, 1929; s. Arthur Joseph and Mary Beatrice (Callery) S.; m. Elizabeth Lloyd Frier, Jan. 2, 1960; children: Arthur, Claire, Paul, Sara. AB, Fordham Coll., 1951; JD, U. Mich., 1954; postgrad., U. London, 1957-58. Bar: Mich. 1954, Ohio 1954, D.C. 1959. Assoc. Squire, Sanders & Dempsey, Cleve., 1954; assoc., ptnr. Woll, Mayer & St. Antoine, Washington, 1958-65; assoc. prof. law U. Mich. Law Sch., Ann Arbor, 1965-69, prof., 1969—, Degan prof., 1981-98, Degan prof. emeritus, 1998—, dean, 1971-78. Pres. Nat. Resource Ctr. for Consumers of Legal Svcs., 1974—78; mem. pub. rev. bd. UAW, 1973—, chmn. pub. rev. bd., 2000—, chmn., 2000—; mem. Mich. Atty. Discipline Bd., 1999—, vice-chmn., 2000—; chmn. UAW-GM Legal Svcs. Plan, 1983—95; Mich. Gov.'s spl. counselor on workers' compensation, 1983—85; reporter Uniform Law Commrs., 1987—92; life mem. Clare Hall, Cambridge (Eng.) U. Co-author: (with R. Smith, L. Merrifield and C. Craver) Labor Relations Law: Cases and Materials, 4th edit., 1968, 10th edit., 1999; editor: The Common Law of the Workplace: The Views of Arbitrators, 1998; contbr. articles to profl. jours. 1st lt. JACG, U.S. Army, 1955-57. Fulbright grantee, London, 1957-58. Mem. ABA (past sec. labor law sect., coun. 1984-92), Am. Bar Found., State Bar Mich. (chmn. labor rels. law sect. 1979-80), Nat. Acad. Arbitrators (bd. govs. 1985-88, v.p. 1994-96, pres. 1999-2000), Internat. Soc. Labor Law and Social Security (U.S. br. exec. bd. 1983—, vice chmn. 1989-95), Am. Arbitration Assn. (bd. dirs. 2000—), Indsl. Rels. Rsch. Assn., Coll. Labor and Employment Lawyers, Order of Coif (life). Democrat. Roman Catholic. Home: 1421 Roxbury Rd Ann Arbor MI 48104-4047 Office: U Mich Law Sch 625 S State St Ann Arbor MI 48109-1215 E-mail: tstanton@umich.edu.

ST. CLAIR, DONALD DAVID, lawyer; b. Hammond, Ind., Dec. 30, 1932; s. Victor Peter and Wanda (Rubinska) Small; m. Sergine Anne Oliver, June 6, 1970 (dec. June 1974); m. Beverly Joyce Tipton, Dec. 28, 1987. BS, Ind. U., 1955, MS, 1963, EdD, 1967; JD, U. Toledo, 1992. Bar: Ohio 1992, U.S. Dist. Ct. (no. dist.) Ohio 1993, U.S. Supreme Ct., 1996. Assoc. prof. Western Ky. U. Coll. Edn., Bowling Green, 1967-68, U. Toledo, 1968-77, prof., 1977-92; atty., ptnr. Garand, Bollinger, & St. Clair, Oregon, Ohio, 1992-97; pvt. practice Law Offices Donald D. St. Clair, Toledo, 1997—. Mem. Ohio Coun. Mental Health Ctrs., Columbus, 1978-79; dir. honors programs U. Toledo. Author: (poetry) Daymarks and Beacons, 1983, Impressions from an Afternoon in a Paris Courtroom, 1998; contbr. articles to profl. jours. Organizer Students Toledo Organized for Peace, 1970-71; mem. Lucas County Dem. Party, 1990—. With U.S. Army, 1955-57. Mem. ABA, AAU (nat. bd. dirs. 1973-74), Am. Inns of Ct., Ohio Bar Assn., Toledo Bar Assn., Ohio Acad. Trial Lawyers, Toledo Power Squadron (comdg. officer 1981), Bay View Yacht Club, Ohio Criminal Def. Lawyers Assn., Lucas County Bar Assn., Maumee Valley Criminal Def. Lawyers Assn., Ottawa County Bar Assn., Masons (32 degree), Shriners, Ancient Order Friars, Phi Alpha Delta. Home: 3353 Christie Blvd Toledo OH 43606-2862 Office: 5415 Monroe St Toledo OH 43623-2800 E-mail: stclairlaw@attglobal.net.

ST. CYR, JOHN ALBERT, II, cardiovascular and thoracic surgeon; b. Mpls., Nov. 26, 1949; s. John Albert and Myrtle Lavira (Jensen) St. C.; m. Mary Helen Malinoski, Oct. 29, 1977. BA summa cum laude, U. Minn., 1973, BS, 1975, MS, 1977, MD, 1980, PhD, 1988. Teaching asst. dept. biochemistry U. Minn., Mpls., 1973, rsch. asst. dept. surgery, 1977-78, intern surgery dept. surgery, 1980-81, resident surgery, 1981-88, cardiovascular rsch. fellow dept. surgery, 1983-86, with dept. surgery, 1991-92; rsch. assoc. fellow Cardiovasular Pathology, United Hosp., St. Paul, 1987-88; cardiovascular surg. resident U. Colo., Dept. Cardiovascular Surgery, Denver, 1988-91; med. advisor Organetics, Ltd., Mpls., 1992, med. dir., 1992. Med. advisor Aor Tech., Inc., St. Paul, 1992; bd. dirs. Minn. Acad. Sci.; pres. Virotech, Inc., 1993-94; med./surg. cons. Medtronic, Inc., 1993—; ind. rsch., 1992—; dir. R&D Medcorp Internat., 1996, Jacqmar, Inc., 1996—; med. dir. IHI, 1996, First Circle Med., Inc., 1997-99; med. dir. Bioenergy Inc., 1998—. Contbr. Recipient NIH Rsch./Fellowship award, 1983-86, Grant in Aid Rsch. award Minn. Heart Assn., 1983-85, Med. Student Rsch. award Minn. Med. Found., 1980, Acad. Excellence award Merck Found., 1980. Mem. AAAS, AMA, Assn. Acad. Surgeons, Minn. Acad. for Scis., Am. Physiol. Soc., Am. Fedn. and Clin. Rsch., N.Y. Acad. Scis., Am. Heart Assn., Am. Med. Writers Assn., Internat. Soc. Heart Rsch., So. Med. Assn., Phi Kappa Phi. Republican. Achievements include patents for Achievements include patents in field with subsequent clinical studies.

ST. PIERRE, GEORGE ROLAND, JR. materials science and engineering administrator, educator; b. Cambridge, Mass., June 2, 1930; s. George Rol and Rose Ann (Levesque) St. P.; m. Roberta Ann Hansen, July 20, 1956; children: Anne Renee, Jeanne Louise, John David, Thomas George; m. Mary Elizabeth Adams, Dec. 11, 1976; m. Gretchen Ann Butrick, June 29, 2001. BS, MIT, 1951, ScD, 1954; DSc (hon.), Ohio State U., 1998. Rsch. metallurgist Inland Steel Co., 1954-56; faculty Ohio State U., 1956—, prof. metall. engring., 1957-88, assoc. dean Grad. Sch., 1964-66, chmn. metall. engring., 1983-88, chmn. mining engring., 1985-92; dir.

Ohio Mineral Rsch. Inst., 1984-92, prof., chmn. material sci. and engring., 1988-92, Presdl. prof., 1988-92, chmn., disting. u. prof. emeritus, 1992—; chief scientist Materials Directorate, Wright-Patterson AFB, 1995-96. Cons. in field; vis. prof. U. Newcastle, NSW, Australia, 1975; adv. com. materials sci. MIT, 1990-97; adv. bd. Argonne Nat. Lab., 1994—. Editor: Physical Chemistry of Process Metallurgy, Vols. 7 and 8, 1961, Advances in Transport Processes in Metallurgical Systems, 1992, Transactions Iron and Steel Soc., 1994—; contbr. articles to profl. jours. Bd. dirs. Edward Orton Jr. Ceramic Found., 1989-92. With USAF, 1956-57. Recipient Milton (Mass.) Clarence Boylston Sci. prize, 1947; MacQuigg award, 1971; Alumni Disting. Tchr. award, 1978; named Disting. scholar Ohio State U., 1988, Presdl. prof. Ohio State U., 1988. Fellow Minerals, Metals & Materials Soc., AIME (bd. dirs. 1988-91, 93-96, Educator award 1996), Am. Soc. Materials Internat. (Bradley Stoughton Outstanding Tchr. award 1961, Gold medal 1987, Albert E. White award 1997); mem. Am. Inst. Mining Metall. and Petroleum Engrs. (Mineral Industry Edn. award 1987), Iron and Steel Soc. (Elliott lectr. 1994), Am. Contract Bridge League (gold life master), Faculty Club (pres. 1990-92), Sigma Xi. Home: 4495 Carriage Hill Ln Columbus OH 43220-3801 Office: Ohio State U Dept Materials Sci/Engring 2041 N College Rd Columbus OH 43210-1124 E-mail: st-pierre.2@osu.edu.

ST. PIERRE, RONALD LESLIE, medical and public health educator, university administrator; b. Dayton, Ohio, Feb. 2, 1938; s. Leslie Frank and Ruth Eleanor (Rhoten) St.P.; m. Joyce A. Guilford, Apr. 1, 1961; children: Michele Christine, David Bryan. B.S., Ohio U., 1961; M.Sc., Ohio State U., 1962, Ph.D., 1965. Instr. anatomy Ohio State U., Columbus, 1965-67, asst. prof., 1967-69, assoc. prof., 1969-72, prof., 1972—, chmn. dept. anatomy, 1972-81, assoc. v.p. health scis., 1981-83, sr. assoc. v.p. health scis. and acad. affairs, 1983-2000, 2000—, assoc. dean Coll. Medicine and Pub. Health, 1987-96, vice dean Coll. of Medicine and Pub. Health, 1996-2000, exec. vice dean, 2000—, interim dean pub. health, 1999—; assoc. dir. Cancer Rsch. Ctr., 1974-78. Vis. research asso. Duke U., 1966-67; cons. Battelle Meml. Inst., Columbus. Contbr. articles to profl. jours. Chmn. Ohio Gov.'s Com. on Employment of Handicapped, 1970-78; mem. state exec. com. Presdl. Commn. Employment of Handicapped, 1970-78, chmn., 1971-72; mem. planning and adv. council White House Conf. on Handicapped Individuals, 1975-78; mem. Columbus Mayor's Com. on Internat. Yr. of Disabled. Recipient Lederle Med. Faculty award, 1968-71; prize for basic research South Atlantic Assn. Obstetricians and Gynecologists, 1968; Outstanding Individual award Ohio Rehab. Assn., 1969; Gov.'s award for community service, 1973 Mem. Am. Assn. Anatomists, Am. Assn. Immunologists, Soc. Exptl. Biology and Medicine, Sigma Xi (pres. Ohio State chpt. 1979-80) Republican. Presbyterian. Home: 8586 Button Bush Ln Westerville OH 43082-8675 Office: Ohio State U 218 Meiling Hall 370 W 9th Ave Columbus OH 43210-1238

SALAMME, MATT, reporter; married; 2 children. Airborne reporter WBBM-AM 780, Chgo.; weekend news anchor WLS-AM 890; fill-in airborne reporter Fox 32; reporter News Chopper 12 WISN 12, Milw., 1998—. Office: WISN PO Box 402 Milwaukee WI 53201-0402

SALAMON, MYRON BEN, physicist, educator, dean; b. Pitts., June 4, 1939; s. Victor William and Helen (Sanders) S.; m. Sonya Maxine Blank, June 12, 1960; children— David, Aaron. B.S., Carnegie-Mellon U., 1961; Ph.D., U. Calif., Berkeley, 1966. Asst. prof. physics U. Ill., Urbana, 1966-72, assoc. prof., 1972-74, prof., 1974—, program dir. Materials Research Lab., 1984-91, assoc. dean. Coll. Engring., 2000—. Vis. scientist U. Tokyo, 1966, 71, Tech. U. Munich, Fed. Republic Germany, 1974-75; cons. NSF; Disting. Vis. Prof. Tsukuba (Japan) U., 1995-96. Editor: Physics of Superionic Conductors, 1979; co-editor: Modulated Structures, 1979; divisional assoc. editor: Phys. Rev. Letters, 1992-96; contbr. sci. papers to profl. jours. Recipient Alexander von Humboldt Sr. U.S. Scientist award, 1974-75; NSF coop. fellow, 1964-66; postdoctoral fellow, 1966; A.P. Sloan fellow, 1972-73; Berndt Matthias scholar Los Alamos Nat. Lab., 1995-96; visiting scientist CNRS and Inst. Laue-Langevin Grenoble, France, 1981-82. Fellow Am. Phys. Soc. Office: U Ill Dept Physics 1110 W Green St Urbana IL 61801-9013

SALE, LLEWELLYN, III, lawyer; b. St. Louis, May 19, 1942; s. Llewellyn Jr. and Kathleen (Rice) S.; m. Cynthia Jean Bricker, Aug. 17, 1968 (div. Apr. 1995); children: Allyson J., Eryn E. AB cum laude, Yale U., 1964; LLB cum laude, Harvard U., 1967. Bar: Mo. 1967, U.S. Dist. Ct. (ea. dist.) Mo. 1967, U.S. Tax Ct. 1982, U.S. Ct. Claims 1985. From assoc. to ptnr. to mng. ptnr. Husch & Eppenberger, St. Louis, 1967-88; ptnr. Bryan Cave LLP, 1988—. Bd. dirs. Washington U. Child Guidance Clinic, St. Louis, 1978-80, Mental Health Assn. St. Louis, 1988-89. Mem. ABA, Bar Assn. Met. St. Louis (chmn. law econs. subcom. 1982), Media Club, Noonday Club. Avocations: spectator sports, jogging. Office: Bryan Cave 211 N Broadway Ste 3600 Saint Louis MO 63102-2733 E-mail: lsale@bryancavellp.com.

SALENTINE, THOMAS JAMES, pharmaceutical company executive; b. Milw., Aug. 8, 1939; s. James Edward and Loretta Marie (Burg) S.; m. Susan Anne Sisk, Apr. 16, 1966; children: Anne Elizabeth, Thomas James Jr. BS in Acctg., Marquette U., Milw., 1961. CPA, Ind., Wis. Sr. audit mgr. Price Waterhouse, Milw., 1961-74; dir. corp. acctg. Ward Foods Inc., Wilmette, Ill., 1974-78; corp. contr. Johnson Controls Inc., Milw., 1984-85; v.p., contr. Stokely Van Camp Inc., Indpls., 1978-87; exec. v.p., chief fin. officer Bindley Western Industries Inc., 1987—, also bd. dirs. Bd. dirs. Priority Healthcare Corp., Nat. Refrigeration Svcs. Inc. Chmn. com. United Way, Indpls., 1989-90. Lt. USN, 1962-65. Mem. AICPA, Fin. Execs. Inst. Republican. Roman Catholic. Home: 13540 Brentwood Ln Carmel IN 46033-9488 Office: Bindley Western Industries 8909 Purdue Rd Indianapolis IN 46268-3146

SALERNO, AMY, state legislator; m. Joe Armeni. BA, Youngstown State U., 1979; JD, Ohio State U., 1982. Bar: Ohio. Lawyer, small bus. owner, Columbus, Ohio; mem. Ohio Ho. of Reps. Past chmn. Italian Village Commn; former mem. bd. dirs. St. Mark's Comty. HealthCtr.; former mem. Victorian Village Commn., Downtown Housing Task Force, Columbus. Recipient Appreciation cert. Italian Village Commn, Victorian Village Commn., Columbus City Coun., Outstanding Orgn. award Short North Bus. Assn.

SALES, ANGEL RODOLFO, financial executive; b. Holguin, Oriente, Cuba, Sept. 20, 1948; came to U.S., 1961; s. Angel Alberto and Adeina Rosa (Paneque) S.; m. Barbara Cornell Felix, Aug. 26, 1972; children: Ashley Lynden, Alison Lane. BS, Ind. U., 1972, MBA, 1977. Mgmt. trainee Lincoln Nat. Bank, Ft. Wayne, Ind., 1972-73; asst. v.p. Am. Fletcher Nat. Bank, Indpls., 1973-77; treasury mgr. The Upjohn Co., Kalamazoo, 1977-82, v.p., treas., 1985-90; asst. treas. Midland-Ross Corp., Cleve., 1982-85; treas. Arvin Industries, Inc., Columbus, Ind., 1990-98, v.p. fin. planning and rels., 1998—; exec. v.p., CFO Arvin Roll Coater subs. Arvin Industries, Inc., Indpls., 1999-2000; pres. Roll Coater Subs. Arvin Meritor, Inc., 2000—01; v.p., CFO Best Access Sys., Indpls., 2001—. Bd. dirs. C. Brown Speech and Hearing Ctr., Kalamazoo, 1987-90, treas., 1989; bd. dirs. Columbus Econ. Devel. Bd., Columbus Regional Hosp. Found., Bartholomew Co. United Way, chmn. 1997—; adv. bd. Ind. U.-Purdue U., Columbus. Mem. Fin. Execs. Inst., Nat. Assn. Corp. Treas., Beta Gamma Sigma. United Methodist. Avocations: tennis, golf, art. Office: Best Access Sys 8900 Keystone Crossing Ste 1100 Indianapolis IN 46250 E-mail: Arsales@bestaccess.com.

SALIGMAN, HARVEY, retired consumer products and services company executive; b. Phila., July 18, 1938; s. Martin and Lillian (Zitin) S.; m. Linda Powell, Nov. 25, 1979; children: Martin, Lilli Ann, Todd Michael, Adam Andrew, Brian Matthew BS, Phila. Coll. Textiles and Sci., 1960. With Queen Casuals, Inc., Phila., 1960-88, v.p., 1966-68, pres., chief exec. officer, 1968-81, chmn., 1981-88; pres., chief operating officer Interco Inc., St. Louis, 1981-83, chief exec. officer, 1983-85, 1985-89, chmn., 1989-90; ret. Bd. dirs. Ameren Corp. (formerly Union Electric). Trustee Washington U., St. Louis, John Burroughs Sch., St. Louis Mem. St. Louis Club, Masons.

SALISBURY, ALICIA LAING, state senator; b. N.Y.C., Sept. 20, 1939; d. Herbert Farnsworth and Augusta Belle (Marshall) Laing; m. John Eagan Salisbury, June 23, 1962; children: John Eagan Jr., Margaret Salisbury La Rue. Student, Sweet Briar Coll., 1957-60; BA, Kans. U., 1961. Mem. Kans. Senate, 1985—, v.p., chmn. commerce com., telecomm. stragegic planning, 1995, vice chmn. ways and means com., mem. utilities com., jt. com. on econ. devel., mem. orgn. and calendar rules com., mem. jt. com. corrections and juvenile justice, mem. confirmations oversight com. Elected mem. State Bd. Edn., Topeka, 1981-85, Kans.; past pres. Jr. League of Topeka; trustee Leadership Kans., 1982-89; bd. dirs. Topeka Cmty. Found., 1983—, Topeka Pub. Sch. Found., 1985-89, Capitol Area Pla. Authority, 1989—, Kans. Inc., 1996—, Mid-Am. Mfg. Tech. Ctr., 1994-96, mem. workers' compensation fund oversight com., 1993— Stormont-Vail Hosp. Aux.; mem. adv. commn. Juvenile Offenders Program, Kans., 1985-95; mem. adv. bd. Topeka State Hosp., Kans. Action for Children, 1982—, Kans. Ins. Edn. Found., 1984-95, Youth Ctr. at Topeka, 1987—; steering com. One Stop Career Ctr., 1996, Interstate Cooperation Com. Coun. State Govts.; mem. Nat. Fedn. Rep. Women; past bd. mem. United Way Greater Topeka, ARC, Family Svc. and Guidance, Topeka, Shawnee County Mental Health Assn., Florence Crittenton Svcs., Topeka, Topeka City Commn. Govtl. Adv. Com.; chmn. Topeka State Hosp. Grounds Adv. Com.; mem. Kans. Workforce Investment Partnership Coun. Recipient Woman of Yr. award Topeka Panhellenic Coun., 1997. Mem. Nat. Conf. State Legislators (exec. com.), Nat. Rep. Legislators' Assn. (Nat. Rep. Legislator of Yr. 1993, Gold Rose award 1992, Bus. Guardian award 1990, 99, Outstanding Individual Legis. Achievement award 1989), Shawnee County Rep. Women, Kans. State Hist. Soc. (exec. com.), Kappa Kappa Gamma. Episcopalian. Avocations: tennis, downhill skiing, water sports, horseback ridng, gardening. Office: Kans State Senate State Capital Topeka KS 66612

SALISBURY, ROBERT HOLT, political science educator; b. Elmhurst, Ill., Apr. 29, 1930; s. Robert Holt and Beulah (Hammer) S.; m. Rose Marie Cipriani, June 19, 1953; children: Susan Marie, Robert Holt, Matthew Gary. AB, Washington and Lee U., 1951; MA, U. Ill., 1952, PhD, 1955. Mem. faculty Washington U., St. Louis, 1955-65, prof., 1965-97, prof. emeritus, 1997—, chmn. dept. polit. sci., 1966-73, 86-92, dir. Center for Study Pub. Affairs, 1974-77, Sidney W. Souers prof. govt., 1982-97. Vis. prof. SUNY, Buffalo, 1965, So. Ill. U., Edwardsville, 1975; affiliated scholar Am. Bar Found., 1981-95; cons. U.S. Conf. Mayors, 1965, Hartford (Conn.) C. of C., 1964, NSF, 1973. Author: Interest Groups Politics in America, 1970, Governing America, 1973, Citizen Participation in the Public Schools, 1980, Interests and Institutions, 1992, The Hollow Core, 1993; contbr. articles to profl. jours. Mem. St. Louis County Charter Commn., 1967, Gov.'s Commn. on Local Govt., 1968-69. Guggenheim fellow, 1990; Rockefeller Ctr. scholar, 1990. Mem. Mo. Polit. Sci. Assn. (pres. 1964-65), Am. Polit. Sci. Assn. (exec. council 1969-71, v.p. 1980-81), Midwest Polit. Sci. Assn. (pres. 1977-78), Pi Sigma Alpha. Democrat. Methodist. Home: 709 S Skinker Blvd Saint Louis MO 63105-3225 Office: Washington U Dept Polit Sci Saint Louis MO 63130 E-mail: rhsalisb@artsci.wustl.edu.

SALIT, GARY, lawyer; Corp. counsel Bell Howell Co., Skokie, Ill. Office: Bell & Howell Company 5215 Old Orchard Rd Ste 1100 Skokie IL 60077-1076

SALITERMAN, RICHARD ARLEN, lawyer; b. Aug. 3, 1946; s. Leonard Slitz and Dorothy (Sloan) S.; m. Laura Shrager, June 15, 1975; 1 child, Robert Warren. BA summa cum laude, U. Minn., 1968; JD, Columbia U., 1971; LLM, NYU, 1974. Bar: Minn. 1972, D.C. 1974. Mem. legal staff subcom. on antitrust and monopoly U.S. Senate, Washington, 1971-72; acting dir., dep. dir. compliance and enforcement divsn. Fed. Energy Office, N.Y.C., 1974; mil. atty. Presdl. Clemency Bd., White House, Washington, 1975; sr. ptnr. Saliterman & Saliterman, Mpls., 1975—. Adj. prof. law Hamline U., 1976-81. Author: Advising Minnesota Corporations and Other Business Organizations, 4 vols., 1975; chmn. Hennepin County Bar Jour., 1985-87. Trustee, sec. Hopkins Edn. Found.; trustee W. Harry Davis Found., 1990-96; pres. Twin Cities Coun.; mem. nat. bd. dirs. Navy League U.S., Washington, 1997—, nat. judge adv., 2001—.

SALIZZONI, FRANK L. finance company executive; b. 1938; m. Sarah Salizzoni; 3 children. BS, Pa. State U.; MBA, George Washington U. V.p., CFO TWA, 1984-87; exec. v.p., CFO USAir, Inc., 1990-94, pres., COO, 1994-96; pres. H&R Block, Kansas City, Mo., 1996-99, CEO, 1999—. Office: H&R Block 4400 Main St Kansas City MO 64111-1812

SALKIND, MICHAEL JAY, technology administrator; b. N.Y.C, Oct. 1, 1938; s. Milton and Esther (Jaffe) S.; m. Miriam E. Schwartz, Aug. 16, 1959 (div. 1979); children: Michael Jay, Elizabeth Jane, Jonathan Hillson, Joshua Isaac; m. Carol T. Gill, Dec. 23, 1990. B in Metall. Engring., Rensselaer Polytech. Inst., 1959, PhD, 1962. Chief advanced metallurgy United Techs. Rsch. Labs., East Hartford, 1964-68; chief structures and materials Sikorsky Aircraft div. United Techs. Corp., 1968-75; dir. product devel. Avco Systems div., 1975-76; mgr. structures NASA, 1976-80; dir. aerospace scis. Air Force Office of Sci. Rsch., 1980-89; pres. Ohio Aerospace Inst., 1990—. Adj. faculty metallurgy Trinity Coll., Hartford; adj. faculty aerospace U. Md., 1982-85; adj. faculty materials Johns Hopkins U., 1985-89; chair Ohio Math. and Sci. Coalition. Cons. editor Internat. Jour. Fibre Sci. and Tech.; editor Applications Composite Materials, 1973; contbr. to profl. jours. and textbooks. Evaluator Accreditation Bd. Engring. and Tech., 1989—; mem. Daniel Guggenheim Medal Bd. Awards, 1984-90; mem. Spirit of St. Louis Medal Bd., 1984-89; mem. bd. Citizens' Acad. Charter Sch.; mem. bd. NCCJ. Capt. U.S. Army, 1962-64. Fellow AAAS, AIAA (assoc.), ASM Internat.; mem. ASME (Disting. lectr. 1989-93), ASTM (chmn. com. D-30 on high modulous fibers and their composites 1968-74), Am. Helicopter Soc., AIME, Brit. Inst. Metals, Rsch. Soc. Am., Plansee Soc., Cosmos Club, Union Club, 50 Club, Leadership Cleve., Sigma Xi, Alpha Sigma Mu. E-mail: michaelsalkind@oai.org.

SALLEE, MARY LOU, state legislator; Mem. Mo. State Ho. of Reps. Dist. 144. Home: PO Box 128 Ava MO 65608-0128 Office: Mo Ho of Reps State Capitol Building Jefferson City MO 65101-1556

SALLEN, MARVIN SEYMOUR, investment company executive; b. Detroit, Oct. 15, 1930; s. Jack Samuel and Sara S.; m. Nancy Susan Berke; 1 child, Jack Samuel II. AB in Econs., U. Mich., 1952. V.p. Sonnenblick-Goldman Corp., Detroit, 1967-83; sr. v.p. Comerica Bank, 1983-87; pres. Comerica Mortgage Corp., 1983-87; mng. ptnr. Brick Ltd., Birmingham, Mich., 1988-90; mng. dir. Redcliffe Corp., 1990—.

SALLER, RICHARD PAUL, classics educator; b. Ft. Bragg, N.C., Oct. 18, 1952; s. George E. and Arthea E. (North) S.; m. Carol Joann Fisher, Jan. 12, 1974; children: John E., Benjamin T. BA in Greek and History, U. Ill., 1974; PHD in Classics, U. Cambridge, Eng., 1978. Asst. prof. Swarthmore (Pa.) Coll., 1979-84; assoc. prof. U. Chgo., 1984-89, prof., 1990—, dean of social scis., 1994—2001, provost, 2002—. Author: Personal Patronage, 1982, Patriarchy, Property and Death in the Roman Family, 1994; co-editor: Economy and Society in Ancient Greece, 1981; co-author: Roman Empire, 1987; editor Classical Philology, 1991-93. Rsch. fellow Jesus Coll., U. Cambridge, 1978-79; Ctr. for Adv. Study fellow, Stanford U., 1986-87; Trinity Coll., U. Cambridge fellow commoner, 1991. Mem. Am. Philol. Assn., Am. Hist. Assn. Office: U Chgo Dept History 1126 E 59th St Chicago IL 60637-1580

SALMANS, LARRY D. state legislator; b. Shamrock, Tex., Nov. 17, 1937; m. Marilyn Salmans. A in Bus. Law, U. Colo; BS in Psychology and Biology, Baylor U.; MD in Guidance Counseling, Phillips U. Cert. alcohol drug counselor. Enlisted USAF, 1960, command pilot, 1960-69, ret., 1969; psychologist Larned State Hosp., 1986-96; farmer, rancher Rock Creek Ranch, 1969-86; ret. dir. drug and alcohol svcs. Kans. State Hosp., Topeka; mem. Kans. Senate, 1996—, vice chmn. pub. health and welfare com., mem. transp. and tourism com., mem. ways and means com. Mem. VFW, Kans. Assn. Masters Psychologists, Kans. Alcohol and Drug Assn., Kans. Livestock Assn., Res. Officers Assn., Irrigation Assn. Republican. Office: 300 SW 10th Ave Topeka KS 66612-1504

SALMELA, DAVID DANIEL, architect; b. Wadena, Minn., Mar. 28, 1945; s. Laurie Fredrich and Lempi Christin (Matti) S.; m. Gladys Elaine Hanka, June 23, 1967; children: Cory, Chad, Tia, Kai, Brit. Grad. high sch., Sebeka, Minn. Registered profl. architect, Minn., Wis. Draftsman McKenzie Hague & Gilles, Mpls., 1965-66, A.G. McKee, Hibbing, Minn., 1966, ABI Contracting, Virginia, 1966-69, Archtl. Resources, Hibbing, 1969-70; designer, arch. Damberg Scott Peck & Booker, Virginia, 1970-89; arch. Mulfinger Susanka, Duluth, Minn., 1989-90; prin. Salmela Fospick Ltd., 1990-94, Salmela, Arch., Duluth, 1994—. Recipient Minn. Masonry Inst. award, 1987, citation Am. Wood Coun., 1994. Fellow: AIA (Honor award 1985, 1987, 1990, 1992—2000, Wood Design award 1998, Record House award 1998). Office: Architect 852 Grandview Ave Duluth MN 55812-1170 E-mail: ddsalmela@aol.com.

SALMON, STUART CLIVE, manufacturing engineer; b. London, 1952; BTech in Prodn. Engring. and Engring. Mgmt. with honors, Loughborough U., 1975; PhD, Bristol U., 1979. Apprentice Rolls-Royce Ltd., Derby, Eng., 1969-79; with Gen. Electric Aircraft Engine Group, Cin., 1979-83, engr. Evendale, Ohio, 1980-83; prin. Advanced Mfg. Sci. and Tech., Cin., 1983—. Adj. prof. mfg. engring. U. Cin., 1996—; presenter seminars. Author: Abrasive Machining Handbook, 1983, Modern Grinding Process Technology, 1992; contbr. articles to profl. jours., to McGraw-Hill Ency., 1982-83; patentee in field. Recipient Jim Bottorf award Abrasive Engring. Soc., 1986, Sir Walter Puckey prize, Inst. Prodn. Engrs., U.K., 1975; Rolls-Royce/Brit. Sci. Rsch. Coun. grantee, 1976. Fellow Soc. Mfg. Engrs. Office: Advanced Mfg Sci and Tech PO Box 60227 Rossford OH 43460-0227 Fax: 419-662-9553. E-mail: drsalmon@buckeye-express.com.

SALOMON, ROGER BLAINE, English language educator; b. Providence, Feb. 26, 1928; s. Henry and Lucia Angell (Capewell) S.; m. Elizabeth Helen Lowenstein, June 14, 1950; children— Pamela, Wendy. B.A., Harvard, 1950; M.A., U. Calif. at Berkeley, 1951, Ph.D., 1957. Instr. Mills Coll., Oakland, Calif., 1955-57; instr., then asst. prof. Yale U., New Haven, 1957-66; mem. faculty Case Western Res. U., Cleve., 1966—, prof. English, 1969—, Oviatt prof. English, 1990, chmn. dept., 1974-80, part-time prof. English, 1994-99; Oviatt prof. English emeritus, 1999—. Mem. adv. screening com. Am. lit. Sr. Fulbright-Hayes Program, 1973-76, chmn., 1975; mem. grants-in-aid selection com. Am. Council Learned Socs., 1976-78 Author: Twain and the Image of History, 1961, Desperate Storytelling: Post-Romantic Elaborations of the Mock-Heroic Mode, 1987. Served to 1st lt. USAF, 1952-53. Morse fellow, 1960-61; Guggenheim fellow, 1972-73 Mem. AAUP, MLA. Home: 2830 Coventry Rd Cleveland OH 44120-2231 Office: Case Western Reserve U Dept English Cleveland OH 44106

SALOMONE, JOSEPH ANTHONY, III, emergency medicine physician; b. Reno, June 5, 1958; s. Joseph Anthony and Peggy Ruth (Crompton) S.; m. Cynthia Amelia Douglas, Aug. 10, 1980; children: Joseph Kenneth, Christopher Anthony. BS, U. Nev., 1979, MD, 1983. Diplomate Am. Bd. Emergency Medicine. Intern in gen. surgery Truman Med. Ctr., Kansas City, 1983-84, resident in emergency medicine, 1984-86, fellow in emergency medicine, 1986-87, rsch. dir. emergency medicine, 1987-88, assoc. residency dir., 1990-97, residency dir., 1997—, assoc. prof. emergency medicine, 1994—; med. dir. Met. Ambulance Svcs., 1988-89; staff physician St. Joseph's Med. Ctr., Asheville, N.C., 1989-90. Chmn. Emergency Physicians Adv. Bd., Kansas City, 1992-94; mem. edn. com. SAEM, 1997—. Author: Toxicology Guide for Emergency Medicine, 1988, Emergency Medicine, 1995; editor: Critical Decision in Emergency Medicine, 1995. Cubmaster Pack 397 Boy Scouts Am., Kearney, Mo., 1994-96, webelos leader, 1993-95, den leader, asst. adminstr., 1991-93. Fellow Am. Coll. Emergency Medicine, Am. Acad. Emergency Medicine; mem. Am. Coll. Emergency Physicians (mem. emergency med. svcs. com. Mo. chpt. 1990-94), Soc. for Acad. Emergency Medicine, Coun. Residency Dirs., Nat. Assn. Emergency Med. Svc. Physicians (state liaison 1988-90). Baptist. Avocations: computers, sailing. Office: Truman Med Ctr Dept Emergency Medicine 2301 Holmes St Kansas City MO 64108-2640

SALTER, CHRISTOPHER LORD, geography educator; BA, Oberlin Coll., 1961; MA, U. Calif. Berkeley, 1968, PhD, 1970. Prof. geography U. Mo., Columbia. Recipient George J. Miller award Nat. Coun. for Geog. Edn., 1992, Disting. Geography Educator award Nat. Geog. Soc., 1990, Disting. Tchg. Achievement award Nat. Coun. for Geog. Edn., 1999, Disting. Faculty award U. Mo. Alumni Assn., 1999. Office: Univ Mo Dept Geography Dept Geography 3 Stewart Hall Columbia MO 65211-6170

SALTZMAN, BARRY, actor; b. Chgo., Nov. 1, 1961; s. Bernard William and Cynthia Iris (Gordon) S. BA in Theatre and Drama, Ind. U., 1983. Appeared in theatrical prodns. Rosencrantz and Guilderstern Are Dead, Stage Left Theatre, Chgo., 1984, On the Verge, Body Politic Theatre, Chgo., 1986, The Skin of Our Teeth, Baliwick Repertory, 1987, The Magic Barrel and Other Stories, Nat. Jewish Theatre, Skokie, Ill., 1988, Vampire Lesbians of Sodom, Royal George Theatre, Chgo., 1990, The Little Prince, Children's Classical Theatre Co., Chgo., 1990, Broadway Bound, Briar Street Theatre, Chgo., 1991, The Merry Widow, DuPage Opera Theatre, Glen Ellyn, Ill., 1991, The Miser, The Liar, Green Stockings, Festival Theatre, Wis., 1992, Julius Caesar, Next Theatre, Evanston, Ill., 1992, The Real Live Brady Bunch (nat. tour), 1993, Beachwood Palace Jubilee, L.A., 1994-95, Theft, Hudson Theatre, L.A., 1994, The Smell of Ennui, Theater/Theatre, L.A., 1995, The Big Time Jubilee, Acme Theatre, L.A., 1995-96, numerous others; on camera performances include Bradymania, ABC, 1993, others. Adminstr., fundraiser The Hunger Project, 1986-88; fundraiser Youth at Risk, 1988, AIDS Walk Chgo., 1990; group discussion leader, fundraiser Stop AIDS Chgo., 1987-90; various adminstrv. and enrollment roles Werner Erhard and Assocs., Chgo., 1986-90; mem. Human Rights Campaign Fund, 1990-94; adminstrv. vol. Gore-Lieberman, 2000; entertainment legal MGM Studios, 2001—. Recipient Medallion for Acting Excellence, Amoco Cos./Am. Coll. Theatre Festival, Kennedy Ctr., Washington, 1982. Mem. AFTRA. Home: 319 S Cloverdale Ave Los Angeles CA 90036-3433 E-mail: bjsaltzman@yahoo.com.

SALVENDY, GAVRIEL, industrial engineer, educator; b. Budapest, Hungary, Sept. 30, 1938; came to U.S., 1968; s. Paul and Katarina (Brown) S.; m. Catherine Vivien Dees, Apr. 1, 1966; children: Laura Dorit, Kevin

David. MSc in Engring. Prodn, U. Birmingham, Eng., 1966, PhD, 1968; Doctorate (hon.), Academia Sinica, 1995, Chinese Acad. Scis., 1995. Asst. prof. indsl. engring. SUNY, Buffalo, 1968-71; mem. faculty Purdue U., 1971—, prof. indsl. engring., chmn. human factors program, 1977, Fulbright distinguished prof., 1979-80, 81-82, NEC prof. indsl. engring., 1984-99; chmn. prof., head dept. indsl. engring. Tsinghua U., China, 2001—. Chmn. Internat. Commn. on Human Aspects in Computing, Switzerland, 1986-91. Co-author: Prediction and Development of Industrial Work Performance, 1973, Human Aspects of Computer Aided Design, 1987; sr. editor: Machine-Pacing and Occupational Stress, 1981, Social, Ergonomic and Stress Aspects of Work with Computers, 1987, Designing and Using Human-Computer Interfaces and Knowledge Based Systems, 1989; editor: Handbook of Industrial Engineering, 1982, 2d edit., 1992, Human Computer Interaction, 1984, Handbook of Human Factors, 1987, Cognitive Engineering in the Design of Human Computer Interaction and Expert Systems, 1987; founding editor: Internat. Jour. on Human-Computer Interaction, Internat. Jour. Human Factors in Mfg., Internat. Jour. of Cognitive Ergonomics; co-editor: Work with Computers: Organizational Management, Stress and Health Aspects, 1989, Human Computer Interaction: Software and Hardware Interfaces, 1993, Human-Computer Interaction: Applications and Case Studies, 1993, Design of Work and Development of Personnel in Advanced Manufacturing, 1994, Organization and Management of Advanced Manufacturing, 1994, Advanceds in Applied Ergonomics, 1996, Handbook of Human Factors and Ergonomics, 2d edit., 1997, Design of Computing Systems (2 vols.), 1997, Ergonomics in Manufacturing, 1998; contbr. articles to profl. jours., chpts. to books. Pres. Lafayette Jewish Sunday Sch., 1980-81. Recipient Mikhail Vasilievich Lomonosov medal USSR Acad. Sci., 1991. Fellow APA, Inst. Indsl. Engrs. (sr., Phil Carroll award 1973), Human Factors and Ergonomics Soc. (past officer), Ergonomics Soc. (hon., life mem.); mem. NAE. Office: Purdue U Sch Indsl Engring West Lafayette IN 47907

SALVESEN, B BEHAN-FORBES, artist; b. Elgin, Ill., Nov. 6, 1944; d. Donald Behan and Helen Elaine (Krajacik) Forbes; m. Bruce Michael Salvesen, Sept. 3, 1966. Studied with Elvira Spivey, Barrington, Ill., 1972-74; studied with Peter Schoelch, Cary, Ill., 1975-82; student, Am. Acad. Art, 1976, Sch. Art Inst. Chgo., 1980-82, Kulick-Startk Byzantine Jewelry Sch., 1983. Asst. to purchasing agt. Harnischfeger, Crystal Lake, Ill., 1962-64; rec. sec. Electric Mfrs. Credit Bur., Cary, 1964-66; student and practicing artist, 1968—. Illustrator: (book) There were Reasons, 1983. Recipient Award of Excellence, Ill.-Arlington Heights Fine Arts Festival, 1995, Best of Show award 20th Ann. Cambridge Art Fair, 1995, 19th Ann. Fine Arts Festival, Downers Grove, Ill., 1995. Democratic. Roman Catholic. Avocations: writing, poetry, jewelry crafting, cross-country skiing, hiking. Home: 1312 Whippoorwill Dr Crystal Lake IL 60014-2614

SALZMAN, ARTHUR GEORGE, architect; b. Chgo., June 20, 1929; s. Russell Harvey Salzman and Mildred Olive (Olsen) Erickson; m. Joan Marie Larson, Aug. 16, 1952; children: Lisa Jo Salzman Braucher, David Ralph. BS in Archtl. Engring., U. Ill., 1952; MArch, Ill. Inst. Tech., 1960. Registered architect, Ill., Mich., Nat. Coun. Archtl. Registration Bds. Architect Skidmore, Owings & Merrill, Chgo., 1960, Mies van der Rohe, Arch., Chgo., 1960-69; assoc. The Office of Mies Van Der Rohe, 1969-81; v.p. FCL Assocs., 1981-86; exec. v.p. Lohan Assocs., 1986-91; pvt. practice Evanston, Ill., 1992—. Bldg. code restructuring com. City of Chgo., 1994-96, bldg. code electronic version com., 1997, bldg. code rev. com., 1998—. Active Chgo. Com. on High Rise Bldgs.; bd. dirs. Savoy Aires, Evanston, 1985-88, 90-93, pres. 1992-93; v.p. Chgo. area Unitarian-Universalist Coun., Chgo., 1974-76. Cpl. U.S. Army, 1952-54. Mem. AIA (bd. dirs. Chgo. chpt. 1992-96, sec. 1994-96), Constrn. Specifications Inst., Bldg. Ofcls. and Code Adminstrs. Internat. (profl.), Coun. on Tall Bldgs. and Urban Habitat, Am. Assn. for Wind Engring., Precast-Prestressed Concrete Inst., Cliff Dwellers Club, North Shore Musicians Club. Avocations: community theater, choral singing, sailing. Home: 1018 Greenwood St Evanston IL 60201-4212 Office: 1603 Orrington Ave Ste 1060 Evanston IL 60201-5041 E-mail: salzmanagev@att.net.

SAMEROFF, ARNOLD JOSHUA, developmental psychologist, educator, research scientist; b. N.Y.C., Apr. 20, 1937; s. Stanley and Zeena (Shapiro) S.; m. Susan C. McDonough, Jan. 2, 1982; children: Shira, Rebecca, Crista, Andrew. BS, U. Mich., 1961; PhD, Yale U., 1965; MA (hon.), Brown U., 1987. Asst. prof. psychology, pediatrics and psychiatry U. Rochester, 1967-70, assoc. prof., 1970-73, prof., 1973-78, dir. developmental psychology tng. program, 1975-78; prof. psychology U. Ill., Chgo., 1978-86, assoc. dir. Inst. for Study Developmental Disabilities, 1978-86; assoc. dir., dir. rsch. Ill. Inst. for Developmental Disabilities, Ill. Dept. Mental Health and Developmental Disabilities, 1978-86; prof. psychiatry and human behavior Brown U., Providence, 1986-92; dir. Developmental Psychopathology Rsch. Ctr., Bradley Hosp., East Providence, 1986-92; prof. psychology, sr. rsch. scientist Ctr. for Human Growth and Devel. U. Mich., Ann Arbor, 1992—, dir. devel. and mental health Rsch. Ctr., 2000-01. Vis. prof. psychology Birkbeck Coll., U. London, 1974-75; vis. scientist Ctr. for Interdisciplinary Rsch., U. Bielefeld, Fed. Republic Germany, 1977-78; W.T. Grant Found. lectr. Soc. for Behavioral Pediatrics, 1984; dir. Summer Inst. on Human Devel. and Psychopathology, Ctr. for Advanced Study in Behavioral Scis., Stanford, Calif., 1989; mem. small grants adv. com. NIH, 1977-81, behavioral scis. assessment panel, 1987-88; mem. organizational planning com. Internat. Conf. for Infant Studies, 1980-84. Editor: (with R.N. Emde) Relationship Disturbances in Early Childhood: A Developmental Approach, 1989, (with F. Kessel and M. Bornstein) Contemporary Constructions of the Child: Essays in Honor of William Kessen, 1991, (with M. Haith) The Five to Seven Year Shift, 1996 (with F.F. Furstenberg et. al.) Managing to Make It: Urban Families and Adolescent Success, 1999, (with S. Miller) Handbook of Developmental Psychopathology, 2000; also monographs; mem. editl. bds. Devel. and Psychopathology, 1988-94, Jour. Devel. and Behavioral Pediatrics, 1989-93, Jour. Family Psychology, 1990-91, others. Mem. social and behavioral scis. rsch. adv. com. March of Dimes Birth Defects Found., 1977-94, rsch. adv. com. Little City Found., 1986-88; bd. dirs. Zero to Three: Nat. Ctr. for Infants Toddlers and Families, 1986—, exec. com., 1998—; mem. program on successful adolescent devel. among youth in high-risk settings John D. and Catherine T. MacArthur Found., 1986-95, network on early childhood transitions, 1989-92; mem. gov. coun. Soc. Rsch. in Child Devel., 1998—. Recipient rsch. scientist award NIMH, 1994-99; GE fellow Yale U., 1961; NIMH predoctoral rsch. fellow Yale U., 1962, NIMH postdoctoral rsch. fellow, 1965-67, Ctr. for Advanced Study in Behavioral Scis. fellow Stanford U., 1984-85. Fellow AAAS, Am. Acad. Mental Retardation, Am. Psychol. Soc., APA (mem. program com. devel. psychology divsn. 1978-90, chair 1979, mem. coun. 1980-83, mem.-at-large exec. com. 1985-88, pres. devel. psychology divsn. 1995-96, G. Stanley Hall rsch. award); mem. AAUP, Soc. for Rsch. in Child Devel. (governing coun. 1999—), World Assn. Infant Mental Health, Internat. Soc. for Infant Studies (pres. 2002—), Soc. for Rsch. on Adolescence, Zero-to-Three (bd. dirs. 1986—, exec. com. 1999—). E-mail: sameroff@umich.edu.

SAMIC, DENNIS R. career officer, retired; BSBA, Ohio State U., 1970; M in Systems Mgmt, U. Southern Calif., L.A., 1973. Commd. 2d lt. USAF, 1970, advanced through grades to brig. gen., 1994; base cost analysis officer, later base budget officer 306th Combat Support Group, McCoy AFB, Fla., 1970-73; budget analyst to exec. officer to dep. chief staff, comptr. Hdqs. USAF Europe, Ramstein AB, West Germany, 1973-77; comdr.'s aide, to asst. to comptr., asst. chief of staff Hdqs. Army and AF Exch. Svc., Dallas, 1977-80; fin. analyst, to chief Comptr. Plans divsn. Air Force Acctg. and Fin. Ctr., Lowry AFB, Colo., 1981-85, chief Ret. Pay Entitlements divsn., 1981-85; chief, comptr. info. architecture, exec. officer to comptr. Hdqs. USAF, the Pentagon, Washington, 1985-88; dep. chief of staff, contr., comptr. Hdqs. Alaskan Air Command, Elmendorf AFB, Alaska, 1989-90; asst. dep. chief of staff, fin. mgmt., comptr. Hdqs. Mil. Airlift Command, Scott AFB, Ill., 1990-92; comptr. Hdqs. Air Edn. and Tng. Command, Randolph AFB, 1992-95, Hdqs. Air Force Material Command, Wright-Patterson AFB, Ohio, 1995-99; ret., 1999. Decorated Legion of Merit. Office: HQ AFMC/FM 4375 Chidlaw Rd Ste 6 Wright Patterson AFB OH 45433-5066

SAMPANTHAVIVAT, ARUN, chef; b. Thailand; Student, U. Chgo. Owner, chef Arun's, Chgo. Named to Fine Dining Hall of Fame, Nation's Restaurant News; recipient Ivy award, Restaurants & Instns. mag., 1994, DiRoNA award, 1998, 1999. Office: Arun's 4156 N Kedzie Ave Chicago IL 60618

SAMPSON, EARLDINE ROBISON, education educator; b. Russell, Iowa, June 18, 1923; d. Lawrence Earl and Mildred Mona (Judy) Robison; m. Wesley Claude Sampson, Nov. 25, 1953; children: Ann Elizabeth, Lisa Ellen. Diploma, Iowa State Tchrs. Coll., 1943, BA, 1950; MS in Edn., Drake U., 1954; postgrad., No. Ill. U., Iowa State U., 1965-66, 74. Cert. tchr., guidance counselor, Iowa. Tchr. elem. sch. various pub. sch. sys., 1943-48; cons. speech and hearing Iowa Dept. Pub. Instrn., Des Moines, 1950-52; speech therapist Des Moines Pub. Schs., 1952-54, 55; lectr. spl. edn. No. Ill. U., DeKalb, 1964-65; tchr. of homebound Cedar Falls (Iowa) Pub. Schs., 1967-68; asst. prof. edn. U. No. Iowa, Cedar Falls, 1968; asst. prof., counselor Wartburg Coll., Waverly, Iowa, 1968-70; instr. elem. edn., then head of advising elem. edn. Iowa State U., Ames, 1972-82; field supr. elem. edn. U. Toledo, 1988, 89; ind. cons. Sylvania, Ohio, 1989—. Cons. Des Moines Speech and Hearing Ctr., 1958-59, bd. dirs., 1962, 63; cons. Sartori Hosp., Cedar Falls, 1967-69; bd. dirs. Story County Mental Health Ctr., Ames, 1972-74. NDEA fellow, 1965. Methodist. Avocations: public speaking on preservation of prose and poetry, reading, music, photography. Home: 4047 Newcastle Dr Sylvania OH 43560-3450

SAMPSON, JOHN EUGENE, consulting company executive; b. Feb. 25, 1941; s. Delbert John and Mary Etta (Dodrill) S.; m. Mary Margaret Treanor, Aug. 14, 1965; children: J. Mark, Sharon. AB with distinction, Nebr. Wesleyan U., 1963; MBA, Ind. U., 1964. Mgmt. asst., exec. trainee Office Sec. Def., Washington, 1963—64; mem. staff Com. Econ. Devel., 1964—69; coord. environ. planning Gen. Mills Inc., Mpls., 1969—72, mgr. devel. planning, 1972—74; dir. corp. planning Cen. Soya Co. Inc., Ft. Wayne, Ind., 1974—76, v.p. corp. planning, 1976—80, v.p. corp. planning and devel., 1980—82, v.p. corp. devel., corp. sec., 1982—84; v.p. corp. planning and devel. Internat. Multifoods, Inc., 1984—96; pres. Sampson Assocs., Edina, Minn., 1996—. Mem. bd. govs. Nebr. Wesleyan U., 1974-80; chmn. bd. trustees St. Joseph United Meth. Ch., Ft. Wayne, 1984; bd. dirs., treas. North Ind. United Meth. Found., 1981-84; lay mem. North Ind. Ann. Conf. United Meth. Ch., 1980-84; bd. dirs. Anthony Wayne coun. Boy Scouts Am., 1984; lay mem. Minn. Ann. Conf. United Meth. Ch., 1985-91, 97-00; chmn. conf. bd. devel. Minn. United Meth. Conf., 1986-91; chmn. bd. trustees Hennepin Ave. United Meth. Ch., Mpls., 1990-92, chair adminstrv. coun., 1993-95, lay leader, 1995-98; chair exec. com. North Naples (Fla.) United Meth. Ch., 2002—. Mem. Ind. U. Sch. Bus. Alumni Assn. (pres. 1984-85), Interlachen Country Club, Country Club of Naples. Home: 6612 Gleason Ter Edina MN 55439-1131 also: Unit 1701 4451 Gulf Shore Blvd N Naples FL 34103 Office: Sampson Assocs 5200 Willson Rd Ste 404 Edina MN 55424-1345

SAMPSON, RONALD ALVIN, advertising executive; b. Charlottesville, Va., Nov. 13, 1933; s. Percy Thomas Sampson and Lucile (Mills) Martin; m. Norvelle Ann Johnson, Aug. 8, 1959; children: David Alan, Cheryl Ann. BS in Commerce, DePaul U., 1956. Advt. sales rep. Ebony Mag., Chgo., 1959-63; merchandising rep. Foote, Cone & Belding Advt., 1963-66; account mgr. Tatham, Laird & Kudner Advt., 1966-78; account mgr., exec. v.p. Burrell, Advt., 1978-81; advt. agy. account mgr., sr. v.p. Darcy McManus Masius, 1981-88; advt. agy. account mgr., exec. v.p., dir. corp. devel. Burrell Comm. Group, 1990—. Mem. diversity com. Am. Advt. Fedn., 1996—. Bd. dirs. Cmty. Renewal Soc., Chgo., 1969-94; deacon Chgo. United, 1992-94; co-chair Protestants for Common Good, 1996—. With U.S. Army, 1956-58. Office: Burrell Comm Group 20 N Michigan Ave Chicago IL 60602-4811

SAMPSON, WILLIAM ROTH, lawyer; b. Teaneck, N.J., Dec. 11, 1946; s. James and Amelia (Roth) S.; 1 child, Lara; m. Drucilla Jean Mort, Apr. 23, 1988; stepchildren: Andy, Seth. BA in History with honors, U. Kans., 1968, JD, 1971. Bar: Kans. 1971, U.S. Dist. Ct. Kans. 1971, U.S. Ct. Appeals (10th cir.) 1982, U.S. Ct. Claims 1985, U.S. Ct. Appeals (8th cir.) 1992. Assoc. Turner & Balloun, Gt. Bend, Kans., 1971; ptnr. Foulston & Siefkin, Wichita, 1975-86, Shook, Hardy & Bacon, Overland Park, 1987—. Adj. prof. advanced litig. U. Kans., 1994; mem. faculty trial tactics inst. Emory U. Sch. Law, 1994-97; mem. merit selection panel U.S. Dist. Ct. Kans., 1999; lectr., presenter in field. Author: Kansas Trial Handbook, 1997; mem. Kans. Law Rev., 1969-71, editor, 1970-71; contbr. articles to profl. jours. Chmn. stewardship com. Univ. Friends Ch., Wichita, 1984-86; bd. dirs. Friends U. Retirement Corp., Wichita, 1985-87; chmn. capital fund drives Trinity Luth. Ch., Lawrence, Kans., 1990-93, mem. ch. coun., 1990-92; bd. dirs. Lied Ctr. of Kans., 1994-97. Lt. USNR, 1971-75. Named among Best Lawyers in Am. Fellow Am. Bar Found., Kans. Bar Found.; mem. ABA, Assn. Def. Trial Attys., Kans. Bar Assn. (chmn. Kasn. coll. advocacy 1986, long-range planning, CLE com. 1987-88), Douglas County Bar Assn., Johnson County Bar Assn. (bench-bar com. 1989-99, Boss of Yr. award 1990), Wichita Bar Assn. (bd. dirs. 1985-86), Am. Bd. Trial Advs. (pres. Kans. chpt. 1990-91, nat. bd. dirs. 1990-91), Internat. Assn. Def. Coun. (faculty mem. trial acad. 1994), Def. Rsch. Inst. (v.p. 2000—, nat. bd. dirs. 1998-2000, Kans. state rep. 1990-98, Exceptional Performance citation 1990, Outstanding State Rep. 1991-92, 94), Kans. Assn. Def. Counsel (pres. 1989-90, legis. coun. 1991, 93, William H. Kahrs Disting. Achievement award 1994), Kans. U. Law Soc. (bd. govs. 1993-96), Am. Inn Ct. (Judge Hugh Means chpt., Master of Bench), Lawrence Country Club, Order of Coif, Delta Sigma Rho, Phi Alpha Theta, Omicron Delta Kappa. Republican. Episcopalian. Avocations: jogging, golf, snow skiing, travel, reading. Office: Shook Hardy & Bacon 10801 Mastin Ste 1000 Overland Park KS 66210-1669 E-mail: wsampson@shb.com.

SAMRA, NICHOLAS JAMES, bishop; b. Paterson, N.J., Aug. 15, 1944; s. George H. and Elizabeth L. (Balady) S. BA, St. Anselm Coll., 1966; BD, St. John Sem., Brighton, Mass., 1970. Ordained priest Melkite-Greek Cath. Ch., 1970, bishop, 1989. Assoc. pastor St. Anne Ch., North Hollywood, Calif., 1970-78; pastor Holy Cross Ch., Anaheim, 1973-78, St. John The Bapt. Ch., Northlake, Ill., 1978-81, St. Michael Ch., Hammond, Ind., 1978-81, St. Anne Ch., West Paterson, N.J., 1981-89; aux. bishop Diocese of Newton, Mass., 1989—. Chaplain Police Athletic League Supporters, North Hollywood, 1970's; vicar gen., corp. v.p., and regional bishop of Midwest region, Diocese of Newton; translator articles on Melkite subjects; mem. Ecumenical Commn., L.A., 1974-78. Mem. Cath. Archives Assn. Home and Office: 8525 Cole Ave Warren MI 48093-5239

SAMS, DALLAS C. state legislator; b. Aug. 30, 1952; m. Elaine Sams; 4 children. Student, Brainerd (Minn.) Cmty. Coll.; BS, U. Minn., 1974. Mem. Minn. Senate from 11th dist., St. Paul, 1991—. Vice-chmn. health care com., mem. agrl. and rural devel. com., mem. govt. ops. and reform com., mem. health care com., family svc. fin. divsn. com., tax com., tax laws com.; farmer; farm bus. mgmt. instr. Home: RR 1 Box 258 Staples MN 56479-9801 Office: Minn Senate Mems State Capitol Saint Paul MN 55155-0001

SAMSON, ALLEN LAWRENCE, bank executive; b. Milw., Nov. 16, 1939; s. Harry E. and Rose (Landau) S.; m. Vicki Faye Boxer, July 3, 1977; children: Daniel, Rachel; children from previous marriage: Nancy, David. BS, U. Wis., 1962, LLB, 1965. Bar: Wis. 1965. Asst. dist. atty. Milw. County Dist. Attys. Office, 1965-67, dep. dist. atty., 1968-70; assoc. Samson & Nash, Milw., 1967-68; ptnr. Samson, Friebert, Sutton and Finerty, 1970-73; v.p., sec. Am. Med. Svcs., Inc., 1973-83, exec. v.p., chief exec. officer, 1983-86, chmn., chief exec. officer, 1986-90; cons. nursing homes Samson Med. Mgmt. Co., 1990-93; pres. Liberty Bank, 1994—2001; vice chmn. State Fin. Bank, 2001—. Pub. mem. nursing home study Wis. Legis. Bur., 1988-89; mem. bd. visitors U. Wis. Law Sch., 1992—; mem. health policy adv. coun. Med. Coll. Wis., 1992-96. Bd. dirs. Nat. Found. Jewish Culture, 1996—98; trustee Milw. Ballet, 1982—89, Milw. Art Mus., 2001—, pres. bd. trustees, 1992—95; bd. dirs. Milw. Symphony Orch., 1995—2002, treas., 1996—2000; bd. dirs. Wis. Womens Bus. Initiative, War Meml. Corp., 1993—95, Jewish Fedn., 1985—, pres., 2000—02; bd. dirs. Milw. Jewish Home, 1992—96, Jewish Cmty. Ctr., 1985—96; pres. Milw. Parks Found., 1998—; gen. chmn. Wis. Israel Bond Campaign, 1993—94, chmn., 1996—98, bd. dirs., exec. com., 1986—; gen. chmn. ann. camp Milw. Jewish Fedn., 1990—91; pres. Jewish Vocat. Svc., 1976—78; Alexis de Tocqueville's leadership chmn. United Way campaign, 1995. Recipient Kaplan prize for econ. devel. Govt. of Israel, 1986, United Way Fleur de Lys award, 1996, Israel Bonds Star of David award, 1999. Avocations: tennis, skiing, golf. Office: State Fin Bank 815 N Water St Milwaukee WI 53202-3529

SAMSON, FREDERICK EUGENE, JR. neuroscientist, educator; b. Medford, Mass., Aug. 16, 1918; s. Frederick Eugene and Annie Bell (Pratt) S.; m. Camila Albert; children Cecile Samson Folkerts, Julie Samson Thompson, Renée. DO, Mass. Coll. Osteopathy, 1940; PhD, U. Chgo., 1952. Asst. prof. U. Kans., Lawrence, 1952-57, prof. physiology, 1962-73, chmn., prof. dept. physiology and cell biology, 1968-73; prof. physiology U. Kans. Med. Ctr., Kansas City, 1973-89, prof. emeritus, 1989—; dir. Ralph L. Smith Rsch. Ctr. U. Kans., 1973-89. Staff scientist neurosci. rsch. program MIT, Cambridge, Mass., 1968-82, cons., 1982-91; vis. prof. neurobiology U. Catolica de Chile, Santiago, 1972; prof. Inst. de Investigaciones Citologicas, Valencia, Spain, 1981-89; hon. lectr. Mid-Am. State Univs. Assn., 1987. Editor: (with George Adelman) The Neurosciences: Paths of Discovery, II, 1992, (with Merrill Tarr) Oxygen Free Radicals in Tissue Damage, 1993; contbr. articles to profl. publs. Scientist, U.S.A., Spain Friendship Treaty, Madrid and Valencia, 1981. Staff sgt. U.S. Army, 1941-45, PTO. Recipient Rsch. Recognition award U. Kans. Med. Ctr., Kansas City, 1984; Van Liere fellow U. Chgo., 1948; Rawson fellow U. Chgo., 1949-51; USPHS fellow MIT, 1965 Fellow AAAS; mem. Am. Soc. Neurochemistry (chmn. program com. 1980), Am. Soc. Cell Biology (local host com. 1984), Am. Physiol. Soc. (emeritus 1990), Soc. Neurosci. (program com. 1972-73), The Oxygen Soc., N.Y. Acad. Sci., U. Chgo. Kansas City Club (chmn. alumni fund bd. 1975-82, pres. 1979-81), Sigma Xi (regional lectr. 1974-75, pres. Kansas City chpt. 1977-78, pres. neurosci. chpt. 1978). Avocations: writing, hand balancing. Home: 171 Lakeshore Dr S Lake Quivira KS 66217-8516 Office: U Kans Med Ctr Ralph L Smith Rsch Ctr Bldg 37 Kansas City KS 66160-0001

SAMSON, RICHARD MAX, theatre director, investment/real estate executive; b. Milw., June 13, 1946; s. Harry E. and Rose (Landau) S.; m. Nancy K. Pinter; children: Gina Shoshana, Alayna Tamar; (stepson) Christopher P. BA, U. Wis., 1968. Dir., owner The Puppet Co., Jerusalem, 1972-73; pres. Century Hall, Inc., Milw., 1974-75; dir. purchasing Am. Med. Svcs., Inc., 1973-74, v.p., 1974-82, exec. v.p., 1982-86, pres., 1986-90, Samson Investments, Milw., 1990—. Bd. dirs. Liberty Bank, Milw.; sec. Super Sitters, Mequon, Wis., 1987—. Co-prodr./dir. Loss of Breath: The Unfinished Life and Death of Edgar Allan Poe, 1999; co-creator/dir. Einstein: Hero of the Mind, 2002. Pres. bd. Theatre X, Milw., 1982, Holton Youth Ctr., Milw., 1994, Children's Outing Assn., 1996, Jewish Found. for Econ. Opportunity, 1996—; v.p. bd. ArtReach, Milw., 1987; bd. dirs. Bnai Or Religious Fellowship, 1988-93, Milw. Jewish Coun., 1992-94; mem. funding bd. Wis. Cmty. Fund, 1989-93; dir. Mask and Puppet Co. Milw., 1992—; treas. nat. bd. Am. for Peace Now, 2002. Recipient Humanitarian Peace award Ecumenical Refugee Coun., 1989, Social Justice award Wis. Cmty. Fund, 1997, Human Rels. award Wis. region NCCJ, 1998, Cmty. Svc. Human Rels. award, Wis. chpt. Am. Jewish Com., 2000. Mem. Ams. for Peace Now (bd. dirs. 1990—). Avocations: chess, comic collecting, puppetry. Office: Samson Investments 100A E Pleasant St Milwaukee WI 53212-3975

SAMUEL, ROGER D. newspaper publishing executive; Dir. advt. The Flint (Mich.) Jour., 1991-96, pub., 1996—. Office: The Flint Jour 200 E 1st St Flint MI 48502-1911

SAMUELSON, DONALD B. state legislator; b. Brainerd, Minn., Aug. 23, 1932; s. Walter H. and Ellen (Gallagher) S.; m. Nancy O'Brien, 1952; children: Stephen, Laura, Paula, Christine. Chmn. 6th Dist. Com. on Polit. Edn. State of Minn., 1960-66; mem. Minn. Ho. of Reps., St. Paul, 1969-76, 1981-82, Minn. Senate from 12th dist., St. Paul, 1982—; pres. Minn. Senate, 2001—. Chmn. Health & Human Svc. Fin. Div. Com., mem. Commerce and Consumer Protection, mem. Family Svc. Com., mem. Fin. and Health Care Com.; former foreman Bor-Son Construct Co.; union bus. mgr. Chmn. 6th Dist. Com. on Polit. Edn., Minn., 1960-66; mem. State Ctrl. Com. Dem-Farmer-Labor Party, 1964-66, former chmn. Crow Wing County. Mem. Housing and Redevel. Authority, Minn. AFL-CIO, Bricklayers Union, Elks, Eagles, Moose. Democrat. Home: 1018 Portland Ave Brainerd MN 56401-4133 also: 121 Capitol 75 Constitution Ave Saint Paul MN 55155-1606

SAND, HARVEY, state legislator; m. Eleanor; 5 children. Mem. N.D. Senate, 1993—, vice chmn. govt. affairs com., mem. bus., labor coms. Mem. Masonic Orders, Am. Legion. Home: HC 2 Box 28 Langdon ND 58249-9501 Office: ND Senate Mems State Capitol Bismarck ND 58505

SANDALOW, TERRANCE, law educator; b. Chgo., Sept. 8, 1934; s. Nathan and Evelyn (Hoffing) Sandalow; m. Ina Davis, Sept. 4, 1955; children: David Blake, Marc Alan, Judith Ann. AB, U. Chgo., 1954, JD, 1957. Bar: Ill. 1958, Mich. 1978. Law clk. to judge Sterry R. Waterman U.S. Ct. Appeals (2d cir.), 1957-58; law clk. to justice Potter Stewart U.S. Supreme Ct., Washington, 1958-59; assoc. Ross, McGowan & O'Keefe, Chgo., 1959-61; assoc. prof. law U. Minn., Mpls., 1961-64, prof., 1964-66; prof. law U. Mich., Ann Arbor, 1966-2000, dean Law Sch., 1978-87, Edson R. Sunderland prof. law, 1987-2000, dean emeritus and Edson R. Sunderland prof. law emeritus, 2000—. Author (with F. I. Michelman): (book) Government in Urban Areas, 1970; author: (with E. Stein) Courts and Free Markets, 1982; contbr. articles to legal jours. and periodicals. Mem. Mpls. Commn. Human Rels., 1965—66. Recipient Profl. Achievement award, U. Chgo. Alumni; fellow, Ctr. Advanced Study in Behavioral Scis., 1972—73. Fellow: Am. Acad. Arts Scis.; mem.: Order of Coif (nat. pres. 2001—), Phi Beta Kappa (hon.). Office: U Mich Law Sch Hutchins Hall Ann Arbor MI 48109-1215 E-mail: sandalow@umich.edu.

SANDBERG, JOHN STEVEN, lawyer; b. Mpls., Sept. 1, 1948; s. Donald and Margery Susan (Knudsen) S.; m. Cynthia A. Tucker, July 17, 1982; children: Jennifer, Adam, Luke, Abigail. AB with honors, U. Mo., Columbia, 1970, JD cum laude, 1972. Bar: Mo., Ill., U.S. Ct. Appeals (7th and 8th cirs.), U.S. Dist. Ct. (ea. and we. dists.) Mo., U.S. Dist. Ct. (so. and ctrl. dists.) Ill., U.S. Dist. Ct. (we. dist.) Ky. Ptnr. Coburn, Croft & Putzell, St. Louis, 1972-79, Sandberg, Phoenix & von Gontard, St. Louis, 1979—.

Author (books) Damages Deskbook, 1988, Missouri Product Liability Law, 1988. Pres. SAFE KIDS, St. Louis, 1989-96. Mem. Am. Bd. Trial Advocates. Office: Sandberg Phoenix & von Gontard One City Ctr Fl 15 Saint Louis MO 63101-1883

SANDER, DONALD HENRY, soil scientist, researcher; b. Creston, Nebr., Apr. 21, 1933; s. Paul L. and Mable O. (Wendt) S.; m. Harriet Ora Palmateer, Dec. 27, 1953; children: Ben, Joan. BS, U. Nebr., 1954, MS in Agronomy, 1958, PhD in Agronomy, 1967. Soil scientist, researcher USDA Forest Svc., Lincoln, Nebr., 1958-64; asst. prof. agronomy, soil fertility specialist Kans. State U., Manhattan, 1964-67; prof. agronomy U. Nebr., Lincoln, 1967-98; ret., 1998. Contbr. numerous rsch. articles to jours. including Soil Sci. Soc. Am. Jour. 1st lt. U.S. Army, 1954-56, Korea. Recipient Agronomic Achievement award, 1985, USDA Superior Svc. award, 1987, Soil Sci. Applied Rsch. award, 1989, Great Plains Leadership award, Denver, 1990. Fellow Am. Soc. Agronomy, Soil Sci. Soc. Am.; mem. Gama Sigma Delta, Sigma Xi. Republican. Presbyterian. Avocation: woodworking. Home: 6548 Darlington Ct Lincoln NE 68510-2362 Office: Univ Nebr Dept Agronomy Lincoln NE 68583

SANDERFORD, PAUL L. coach; b. Durham, N.C. m. Yvette Sanderford; 1 child Aaron. B Sociology, So. Meth. U., 1972; M Guidance Counseling, N.C. State U., 1974. Head coach women's basketball U. Nebr., Lincoln. Office: U Nebr 125 Bob DeVaney Sports Ctr Lincoln NE 68588*

SANDERMAN, MAURICE, construction company executive; b. 1940; Acct. Shepard, Schwartz & Harris, Chgo., 1961-68; with Kaufmann Broad Homes, Oak Brook, Ill., 1968-74, B.A. Storms Cons., Chgo., 1974-76; pres. Northbrook (Ill.) Devel. Corp., 1976-86; chmn. bd. dirs., CEO, pres. Sundance Homes Inc., Schaumburg, Ill., 1981—. Office: Sundance Homes Inc 70 E Lake St Ste 1600 Chicago IL 60601-5917

SANDERS, BARRY, retired football player; b. Wichita, July 16, 1968; s. William and Shirley Sanders. Student, Okla. State U., 1986-89. With Detroit Lions, 1989-99; retired, 1999. Led NFL in rushing, 1990, 94. Recipient Heisman Trophy award, 1988; named Sporting News Coll. Football Player of Yr., 1988, NFL Rookie of Yr., 1990; named to Sporting News Coll. All-Am. team, 1987, 88, All-Pro team, 1989-91, 93, Pro Bowl, 1989-96. Achievements include leading the NFL in rushing, 1990, 94. Office: Detroit Lions 1200 Featherstone Rd Pontiac MI 48342-1938

SANDERS, DAVID, university press administrator; BFA in Creative Writing, Bowling Green State U., 1977; MFA, U. Ark., 1983, postgrad., 1986-88. Owner, propr. Hays & Sanders Bookshop, Fayetteville, Ark., 1983-86; vis. asst. prof. dept. English U. Ark., 1984-88; asst. dir. U. Ark. Press, 1988-89, assoc. dir., 1989-90, assoc. dir., editor-in-chief, 1991-92; dir. Purdue U. Press, West Lafayette, Ind., 1992-95, Ohio U. Press/Swallow Press, Athens, 1996—. Author: Time in Transit, 1995, Nearer to Town, 1998; contbr. translations: Poetry Miscellany; Sparrow. Literature of the Western World, Vol. One, 1988; contbr. poetry to New Orleans Rev., Poetry East, Christian Sci. Monitor, S.I. Rev., Mankato Rev., Kans. Quar., Stand Mag., Yarrow, Caesura, Epigrammatist, Zone 3, Hiram Poetry Rev., others. Recipient Christopher McKean award for poetry, 1982, Kenneth Patchen Poetry award, 1982, Dudley Fitts Translation award, 1986, 87, Lily Peter Found. award, 1987. Office: Ohio Univ Press Scott Quadrangle Athens OH 45701

SANDERS, DAVID P. lawyer; b. Chgo., Sept. 24, 1949; BA with distinction, U. Wis., 1971; JD, Georgetown U., 1974. Bar: Ill. 1974, U.S. Ct. Appeals (7th and 4th cirs.) 1974, U.S. Dist. Ct. (no. dist. trial bar) Ill. 1974. Ptnr. Jenner & Block, Chgo. Adj. prof. trial advocacy Northwestern U., Chgo., 1981-91. Editor Am. Criminal Law Rev., 1974. Mem. ABA, Chgo. Coun. Lawyers (chmn. fed. jud. evaluation com. 1989—, mem. def. counsel sect. libel def. resource ctr.). Office: Jenner & Block One IBM Plz Chicago IL 60611

SANDERS, JACK FORD, physician; b. St. Louis, July 16, 1918; s. Ford and Viva (Marvin) S.; m. Gretchen A. Jellema, Feb. 2, 1945; children: Karen Jean, Vicki Leigh, Mary Beth, Donald Curtis, Wendy Lynn B.S. summa cum laude, Alma Coll., Mich., 1939; M.D., U. Mich., 1945; LL.D., Northwood U. Diplomate Am. Bd. Internal Medicine; cert. flight instr. aircraft and instruments, airplane single and multi-engine land and sea; flight safety counselor FAA; CAP check pilot; sr. aviation med. examiner. Intern Henry Ford Hosp., 1945-46, resident in internal medicine, 1947-50; practice medicine specializing in internal medicine Alma, Mich.; sr. attending physician internal medicine Butterworth Hosp., Blodgett Hosp., Grand Rapids; cons. St. Mary's Hosp., Ferguson-Droste-Ferguson Hosp.; med. dir. Mich. Masonic Hosp., Alma, 1960-77; med. dir. rehab. div., chmn. dept. medicine, chief staff Gratiot Community Hosp.; chmn. dept. medicine Tri-County Hosp., Edmore, Mich.; clin. assoc. prof. medicine Coll. Human Medicine, Mich. State U. Mem. Com. on Aging, Gov's Adv. Coun. on Heart Disease, Cancer and Stroke; del White Ho. Conf. on Aging; bd. dirs. Mich. Masonic Home and Hosp.; chmn. bd. Cen. Mich. Wendy's, Inc.; sec., treas. Gratiot Aviation, Inc. Contbr. articles to profl. jours. Chmn. bd. govs. Mich.; bd. dirs. Northwood U., Gratiot Cmty. Airport Bd. Instr. ACTS, U.S. Air Corps and lt. (j.g.) M.C., USNR, WWII. Fellow ACP, Am. Geriatrics Soc.; mem. AMA, Mich. State Med. Soc., Gratiot Med. Soc., Kent Med. Soc., Gratiot-Isabella-Clare County Med. Soc. (pres. 1965), Am. Diabetes Assn., Am. Heart Assn., Am. Multiple Sclerosis Soc., Mich. Crippled Children and Adults Soc., East Ctrl. Mich. Health Svc. Assn., Mason (33d degree), Rotary, Phi Sigma Pi (hon.). Home: 250 Purdy Dr Alma MI 48801-2174 Office: Mich Masonic Pathways Alma MI 48801-2174

SANDERS, JACQUELYN SEEVAK, psychologist, educator; b. Boston, Apr. 26, 1931; d. Edward Ezral and Dora (Zoken) Seevak; 1 son, Seth. BA, Radcliffe Coll., 1952; MA, U. Chgo., 1964; PhD, UCLA, 1972. Counselor, asst. prin. Orthogenic Sch., Chgo., 1952-65; research assoc. UCLA, 1965-68; cons. Osawatomie State Hosp. (Kans.), 1965-68; asst. prof. Ctr. for Early Edn., L.A., 1969-72; assoc. dir. Sonia Shankman Orthogenic Sch., U. Chgo., 1972-73, dir., 1973-93, dir. emeritus, 1993—; curriculum cons. day care ctrs. L.A. Dept. Social Welfare, 1970-72; instr. Calif. State Coll., L.A., 1972; lectr. dept. edn. U. Chgo., 1972-80, sr. lectr., 1980-93, clin. assoc. prof. dept. psychiatry, 1990-93, emeritus, 1993—; instr. edn. program Inst. Psychoanalysis, Chgo., 1979-82; reading cons. Foreman High Sch., Chgo. Author: Greenhouse for the Mind, 1989; editor: (with Barry L. Childress) Psychoanalytic Approaches to the Very Troubled Child: Therapeutic Practice Innovations in Residential & Educational Settings, 1989, Severly Disturbed Children and the Parental Alliance, 1992, (with Jerome M. Goldsmith) Milieu Therapy: Significant Issues and Innovative Applications, 1993, The Seevak Family, The Zoken Family; contbr. articles to profl. jours. Mem. vis. com. univ. sch. rels. U. Chgo.; bd. dirs. KAM Isaiah Israel Congregation, 1997-2001. UCLA Univ. fellow, 1966-68; Radcliffe Coll. Scholar, 1948-52; recipient Alumna award Girls' Latin Sch., Boston, Bettelheim award Am. Assn. Children's Residential Ctrs., Dist. Svc. award Radcliffe Assn. Mem. Assn. Children's Residential Ctrs. (past pres.), Quadrangle Club, Radcliffe Club (Chgo., sec/treas. 1986-87, pres. 1987-89), Harvard Club (Chgo., bd. dirs. 1986-2001). Home: 5842 S Stony Island Ave Apt 2G Chicago IL 60637-2033

SANDERS, JOE MAXWELL, JR. pediatrician, association administrator; b. Hartsville, S.C., July 5, 1940; m. Dorothy Garvin, June 6, 1963; children Joe M. III, Eric T. BS, The Citadel, 1962; MD, Med. U. S.C., 1967. Diplomate Am. Bd. Pediatrics. Rotating intern, resident in pediatrics Letterman Army Med. Ctr., San Francisco, 1967-70; fellow in adolescent medicine San Francisco Children's Hosp., 1970-71; chief adolescent medicine svc. Fitzsimmons Army Med. Ctr., 1971-86; dir. adolescent medicine svc. Med. Coll. Ga., 1986-88; assoc. exec. dir. Am. Acad. Pediatrics, Elk Grove Village, Ill., 1988-93, exec. dir., 1993—. Asst. clin. prof. pediatrics U. Colo. Health Scis. Ctr., 1971-76, assoc. clin. prof., 1976-83, clin. prof. 1983-86; assoc. prof. pediatrics Med. Coll. Ga., 1986-88; clin. prof. pediatrics, U. Chgo., 1991—; cons. for adolescent medicine Surgeon Gen. Army, 1976-86; mem. med. com. Rocky Mt. Planned Parenthood, 1981-86; vis. prof. dept. pediatrics U. Kansas (Wichita), 1984, 87, dept. pediatrics and family practice, E. Tenn. State U., Johnson City, 1985, U. Fla., Gainesville, 1987, Fitzsimmons Army Med. Ctr., Denver, 1989, U. Chgo., 1991, Baylor Coll., Houston, 1994, others. Contbr. numerous articles and abstracts to profl. jours., chpts. to books; mem. editl. bd. Jour. Current Adolescent Medicine, 1979-81, Substance Abuse: A Guide for Profls., 1985-88; reviewer Pediatrics, 1984—, Jour. Pediatrics, 1986—, Jour. Adolescent Health, 1986—, Am. Jour. Diseases of Children, 1987—, Jour. Am. Med. Assn., 1987—; guest lectr., speaker at many sci. confs. and med. soc. meetings. Mem. teenage coord. coun. Richmond County Health Dept., 1986-88, head start health adv. com. CSRA Econ. Opportunity Authority, Inc., 1986-88; med. cons. Alexian Bros. Med. Rels. Com. Decorated Legion of Merit, U.S. Army, 1987; recipient Adele Hoffman award, Sect. on Adolescent Health, 1988. Fellow Am. Acad. Pediatrics (com. on adolescence 1980-87, chmn. 1983-87, chmn. uniformed svcs chpt. 1981, 84, mem. exec. com. mil. pediatrics sect. 1976-79, sec.-treas. 1976-77, chmn. 1977-79, mem. steering com. to establish non-geographic mil. dist. chpt., mem sect. on adolescent health 1979—, program com. 1981-83, task force on substance abuse, chmn. 1984-85, cons. 85-87, task force on sch. based clinics, 1987—), Soc. Adolescent Medicine (edn. com., ambulatory care com., 1975-80, chmn. nominating com. 1978, exec. coun. 1980-83, chmn. awards com. 1990-93, pres. 1987-88, past pres's. coun. 1988—, Outstanding Achievement award 1994); mem. AMA (mem. planning com. nat. coalition on adolescent health, rep. Am. Acad. Pediatrics, Soc. Adolescent Medicine to Coalition 1987—, chmn. working group on rsch. agenda 1987-88, adv. com. on unintentional injuries 1987), Ambulatory Pediatric Assn., So. Soc. for Pediatric Rsch., Soc. Med. Cons. to Armed Forces, Order Mil. Med. Merit, Sigma Xi. Home: 449 W Rosiland Rd Palatine IL 60074-1098 Office: Am Acad Pediatrics 141 Nortwest Point Blvd Elk Grove Village IL 60007

SANDERS, KEITH PAGE, journalism educator; b. Ashland, Ohio, Sept. 25, 1938; s. Merwin Morse and Phyllis Pearl (Snyder) S.; m. Jane Carmel Adams, June 11, 1966; children: Paige Ann, Kevin Scott. BS in Journalism, Bowling Green State U., 1960; MS in Journalism, Ohio U., 1964; PhD in Mass. Comm., U. Iowa, 1967. Sports editor Ashland (Ohio) Times Gazette, 1960-61, Dover (Ohio) Daily Reporter, 1961-62; instr. journalism Bowling Green (Ohio) State U., 1963-64, U. Iowa, Iowa City, 1965-67; prof. journalism U. Mo., Columbia, 1967—2001, assoc. dean grad. studies Sch. Journalism, 1986-87, 90-91, O.O. McIntyre disting. prof., 1993, prof. emeritus, 2002—. Cons. in field. Contbr. articles to profl. jours. including Journalism Quar., Mass Media Rev., Jour. Broadcasting, Electronic Jour. of Comm.; assoc. editor Mass Comm. Rev., 1981-92, mem. editl. bd., 1972-98; mem. editl. bd. Journalism Monographs, 1973-80, Mass Comm. and Soc., 1998—. Recipient Award for Outstanding Achievement U. Mo. Alumni Assn., 1986; Joyce Swan Disting. Faculty award U. Mo., 1973; inducted into Columbia Bowling Hall of Fame, 1999. Mem. Internat. Soc. for Sci. Study of Subjectivity (treas. 1990-95), Assn. for Edn. in Journalism/Mass. Comm. (Trayes Prof. of Yr. 1987), Soc. Profl. Journalists, Mo, State Bowling Assn. (bd. dirs. 2000—), Kappa Tau Alpha, Omicron Delta Kappa. Avocations: bowling, golf, fishing. Home: 6551 N Creasy Springs Rd Columbia MO 65202-8093 Office: Univ of Missouri Sch Journalism Columbia MO 65211-0001 E-mail: sandersk@missouri.edu.

SANDERS, RICHARD HENRY, lawyer; b. Chgo., Apr. 10, 1944; s. Walter J. and Marian (Snyder) Sikorski; m. Sharon A. Marciniak, July 8, 1967 (div. Oct. 1979); 1 child, Douglas Bennett. BS, Loyola U., Chgo., 1967; JD, Northwestern U., 1969. Bar: Ill. 1969, Ind. 1990, D.C. 1990, U.S. Dist. Ct. (no. dist.) Ill. 1970, U.S. Dist. Ct. (no. and so. dists.) Ind. 1990, U.S. Ct. Appeals (7th cir.) 1990, U.S. Supreme Ct. 1990. Assoc. Vedder, Price, Kaufman & Kammholz, Chgo., 1969-76, ptnr., 1976—, mem. exec. com., 1991-93, health law area leader, 1989-91, 93-95, 2001—. Adj. prof. Sch. of Law Northwestern U., 1994—; mem. svc. dispute resolver panel Am. Health Lawyers Assn. Alt. Dispute Resolution, 2000—. Mem. ABA, Ill. Bar Assn. (chmn. health sect. 1989-90), Chgo. Bar Assn., Ind. Bar Assn., D.C. Bar Assn., Am. Health Lawyers Assn., Ill. Assn. Health Attys., Univ. Club, Evanston Golf Club (Skokie). Avocations: skiing, diving, photography, golf. Office: Vedder Price Kaufman & Kammholz 222 N La Salle St Ste 2600 Chicago IL 60601-1100 E-mail: rsanders@vedderprice.com.

SANDERS, WALLACE WOLFRED, JR. civil engineer; b. Louisville, June 24, 1933; s. Wallace Wolfred and Mary Jane (Brownfield) S.; m. Julia B. Howard, June 9, 1956; children— Linda, David. B.C.E., U. Louisville, 1955; M.S., U. Ill., Urbana, 1957, Ph.D., 1960; M.Engring., U. Louisville, 1973. Research asst., then research assoc. U. Ill., 1955-60, asst. prof., 1960-64; mem. faculty Iowa State U., Ames, 1964-98, prof. civil engring., 1970-98, assoc. dir. engring. research, 1980-91, assoc. dean research, 1988-91, interim asst. vice provost for research and advanced studies, 1991-92. Cons. to govt. and industry. Contbr. numerous papers to profl. jours. Bd. dirs. Northcrest Retirement Cmty., Ames, 1976-82, 92-98, pres., 1987-91, 96—; bd. dirs. Am. Bapt. Homes of the Midwest, Mpls., 1998—. Mem. ASCE (R.C. Reese research prize 1978), Am. Welding Soc. (Adams Meml. membership award 1971), Am. Ry. Engring. Assn., Am. Soc. Engring. Edn. Baptist. Home and Office: Iowa State U 1924 Northcrest Cir Ames IA 50010-5113 E-mail: wsanders@iastate.edu.

SANDERS, W(ILLIAM) EUGENE, JR. physician, educator; b. Frederick, Md., June 25, 1934; s. W(illiam) Eugene and E. Gertrude (Wilburn) S.; m. Christine Culp, Feb. 22, 1974. A.B., Cornell U., 1956, M.D., 1960. Diplomate: Am. Bd. Internal Medicine. Intern Johns Hopkins Hosp., Balt., 1960-61, resident, 1961-62; instr. medicine Emory U. Sch. Medicine, Atlanta, 1962-64; chief med. resident, instr. U. Fla. Coll. Medicine, Gainesville, 1964-65, asst. prof. medicine and microbiology, 1965-69, asso. prof., 1969-72; prof., chmn. dept. med. microbiology, prof. medicine Creighton U. Sch. Medicine, Omaha, 1972-95, prof. emeritus, 1995—. Cons.-in-research Fla. Dept. Health and Rehab. Services, 1966— Editor: Am. Jour. Epidemiology, 1974-95; contbr. sci. articles to profl. jours. Served as med. officer USPHS, 1962-64. Recipient NIH Research Career Devel. award, 1968-72; John and Mary R. Markle scholar in acad. medicine, 1968-73 Mem. Am. Soc. for Microbiology, Infectious Diseases Soc. Am., Soc. for Epidemiol. Research, Am. Lung Assn., Thoracic Soc., N.Y. Acad. Scis., Phi Beta Kappa, Sigma Xi, Phi Kappa Phi. Achievements include patent on enocin antibiotic and RBE limonene and perrilyl alcohol. Home: 1901 Pennsylvania Ave Englewood FL 34224 E-mail: ecsanders@gls3c.com.

SANDERSON, GEOFF, professional hockey player; b. Hay River, N.W.T., Can., Feb. 1, 1972; Hockey player Hartford, 1990-97, Carolina Hurricanes, 1997-98, Vancouver Canucks, 1998, Buffalo Sabres, 1998-2000, Columbus Blue Jackets, 2000—. Office: Columbus Blue Jackets 150 E Wilson Bridge Rd Columbus OH 43085-2328*

SANDERSON, GLEN CHARLES, science director; b. Wayne County, Mo., Jan. 21, 1923; married; 2 children. BS, U. Mo., 1947, MA, 1949; PhD, U. Ill., 1961. Game biologist Iowa State Conservation Commn., 1949-55, Ill. Dept. Conservation, 1955-60; from game biologist to prin. scientist emeritus, dir. Ill. Nat. History Survey, Champaign, 1955—90, prin. scientist emeritus, dir., 1990—; prof. U. Ill., 1965—92. Adj. rsch. prof. So. Ill. U., 1964, adj. prof. 1964-84. Editor Jour. Wildlife Mgmt., 1971-72. Recipient Oak Leaf award Nature Conservancy, 1975. Mem. AAAS, Am. Soc. Mammal, Am. Inst. Biol. Sci., Wildlife Soc. (Aldo Leopold Meml. award 1992). Achievements include research in population dynamics of wild animals, especially furbearers, physiological factors of reproductive and survival rates, and lead poisoning in waterfowl. Office: Ill Natural History Survey Ctr Wildlife Ecology 711 S State St Champaign IL 61820-5114

SANDESON, WILLIAM SEYMOUR, cartoonist; b. Mound City, Ill., Dec. 16, 1913; s. William Stephen and Jessie Mae (Mertz) S.; m. Ione Wear, June 4, 1938 (dec. 1975); 1 son, William Scott; m. Ruth Cress, Dec. 31, 1978. Student, Chgo. Acad. Fine Arts, 1931-32. Free-lance cartoonist for nat. mags., 1932-37; editorial cartoonist New Orleans Item-Tribune, 1937-41; cartoonist, picture editor and art dir. St. Louis Star-Times, 1941-51; editorial cartoonist Ft. Wayne (Ind.) News-Sentinel, 1951-82; ret., 1982. Drew daily cartoon feature for, Star-Times, Sketching Up With the News. Recipient Honor medal Freedoms Found., 1952, 53, 56, George Washington Honor medal, 1954, 55, 57, 58, 59, 60, Disting. Service award, 1961-72, cartoon award, 1982;, Ind. Sch. Bell award, 1967, Disting. Service awards, 1971-76, prin. cartoon award, 1977, cartoon award, 1978; co-recipient Pulitzer prize for gen. local reporting, 1982 Mem. Nat. Cartoonist Soc., Assn. Am. Editorial Cartoonists. Congregationalist. Club: Fort Wayne Press (pres. 1965). Home: 119 W Sherwood Ter Fort Wayne IN 46807-2846

SANDLER, NORMAN, business executive; Formerly dir. pub. rels. Motorola, Inc., Schaumburg, Ill., now dir. global strategic issues. Office: Motorola Inc 1303 E Algonquin Rd Schaumburg IL 60196-1079

SANDLOW, LESLIE JORDAN, physician, educator; b. Chgo., Jan. 7, 1934; s. Harry H. and Rose (Ehrlich) S.; m. Joanne J. Fleischer, June 16, 1957; children: Jay, Bruce, Lisa. BS, U. Ill., 1956; MD, Chgo. Med. Sch., 1960. Intern Michael Reese Hosp. and Med. Ctr., Chgo., 1961, med. resident, rsch. fellow gastrointestinal rsch., 1961-64, physician-in-charge clin. gastroenterology lab., 1963-74, asst. attending physician, 1964-67, assoc. attending physician, 1967-72, vice chmn. divsn. gastroenterology, dir. ambulatory medicine, 1968, dir. ambulatory care, 1969-76, attending physician, 1972—, assoc. med. dir., 1972-73; clin. asst. Chgo. Med. Sch., 1963-68, clin. instr., 1966; asst. prof. dept. medicine Pritzker Sch. Medicine, U. Chgo., 1973-76, assoc. prof., 1976-85, prof., 1985-90; prof. clin. medicine and med. edn. U. Ill. Coll. Medicine, Chgo., 1990-91, prof. medicine and med. edn., 1992—, sr. assoc. dean for grad. and continuing med. edn., 1993—, head dept. med. edn., 1993—, sr. assoc. dean for med. edn. affairs, 1994—. Dep. v.p. profl. affairs Michael Reese Hosp. and Med. Ctr., 1973-78, dir. Office Ednl. Affairs, 1976-81, assoc. v.p. acad. affairs, 1978-82, dir. quality assurance program, 1981-91, v.p. planning, 1982-83, v.p. profl. affairs and planning, 1983-88, dir. divsn. internal medicine, 1986-93, v.p. profl. and acad. affairs, 1988-91, med. dirs. acad. and med. affairs, 1992-94; med. dir. Michael Reese Health Plan, Inc., 1972-74, interim exec. dir., 1976-77; cons. gastroenterologist Ill. Ctrl. Hosp., 1978-80; vis. prof. Pontifica U. Catolica Rio Grande do Sul, Brazil, 1978, U. Fed. Espirito Santo, Brazil, 1978, Nordic Fedn. for Med. Understanding, Akureyri, Iceland, 1978, Seoul Nat. U. Sch. Medicine, 1981, Coll. Physicians and Surgsons, Kharachi, Pakistan, 1994, U. Tex., Ft. Worth, 1977, U. Ariz., Tucson, 1977, Loyola U. Med. Sch., Maywood, Ill., 1979; cons. in field; coord. Health Scis. Librs. in Ill.; mem. Midwest Med. Libr. Network; mem. subcom. on delivery of ambulatory med. care Inst. Medicine Chgo.; mem. cmty. resources task force Interinstnl. Cardiovascular Ctr.; chmn. steering group Ill. Regional Med. Program; past co-chmn. curriculum com. U. Chgo. Reviewer Rsch. in Med. Edn./Assn. Am. Med. Colls., 1985—, Acad. Medicine/Assn. Am. Med. Colls., 1989; contbr. numerous articles to profl. publs. Mem. Skokie (Ill.) Bd. Health, 1973-85, chmn., 1976-85; bd. dirs. Group Health Assn. Am., 1976-78, Portes Ctr., 1980—; bd. dirs. Good Health Program Skokie Valley Hosp., 1978-80; bd. dirs., exec. com. Rsch. and Edn. Found. of Michael Reese Hosp. Med. Staff, 1992—. Recipient numerous grants, including NIH, 1988, Michael Reese Hosp. Found., 1994-95, Chgo. Cmty. Trust, 1994-95. Fellow Am. Coll. Gastroenterology; mem. N.Y. Acad. Scis., Inst. Medicine, Assn. Am. Med. Colls., Am. Coll. Physician Execs. (co-chair resource mgmt. com. of quality assurance forum), Soc. Dirs. Med. Coll. Continuing Med. Edn., Soc. Dir. Rsch. in Med. Edn. Home: 2314 N Lincoln Park W Chicago IL 60614-3455 Office: U Ill Coll Medicine Med Edn MC 784 1819 W Polk St Chicago IL 60612-7331

SANDOR, RICHARD LAURENCE, financial company executive; b. N.Y.C., Sept. 7, 1941; s. Randolph Henry and Luba (Mirner) S.; m. Ellen Ruth Simon, June 27, 1963; children: Julie, Penya. B.A., CCNY, 1962; Ph.D., U. Minn., 1967. Asst. prof. applied econs. U. Calif, Berkeley, 1966-72; v.p., chief economist Chgo. Bd. Trade, 1972-75; v.p. ContiCommodity Services, Chgo., 1975-82; dir. ContiFin div. ContiCommodity Services, 1975-82; sr. v.p. instl. fin. futures Drexel Burnham Lambert, Inc., 1982-90; pres., CEO Indosuez Internat. Capital Markets, 1990-93; chmn. Indosuez Carr Futures, 1990-91, Hedge Fin. subs. CNA, 1997—; chmn., CEO Environ., Fin. Products, 1998—. Mem. Chgo. Bd. Trade, 1975—, bd. dirs., vice chmn., 2d vice chmn., 1996-98; exec. mng. dir. Kidder, Peabody Inc., N.Y.C., 1991-94, Non-resident Dir., CBOT; pres., CEO Centre Fin. Products Ltd., 1993-98; chmn., CEO, Environ. Fin. Products LLC, 1998—, mem. Index and Option Market, 1983—; sr. advisor PriceWaterhouseCoopers LLP, 1999—; bd. dirs. Chgo. Mercantile Exch., chmn., Hedge Fin. Products, Inc., 1997-99; dir., Sustainable Asset Mgmt./Sustainable Performance grp.; Internatl. Adv. Bd. of Maché à Terme Internatl. de France (MATIF); bd. dirs., Fin. Products Adv. Com. of The Commodity Futures Trading Commn., Benfield and Rea Investment Trust, Bear Stearns Fin. Products, Inc., Ben Stearns Trading Risk Mgmt., Inc., Altra Energy Bd., Altra Electronic Adv. Bd., Ctr. for Sustainable Devel. in Ams., Nextera Enterprises, Inc.; vis. scholar, Northwestern U., 1999—, bd. visitors of Internatl. Prog. Ctr., U. Oklahoma, Internat. Ctr. Photography, N.Y.C., First Fed. Savs. & Loan Assn. of Chgo., Sch. Art Inst. Chgo., Patsyss. plc, 2000—; vis. scholar Northwestern U., 1972-74; Martin C. Remer vis. Disting. prof. fin. Grad. Sch. Mgmt., 1974-75; cons. agribus. orgns., securities firms, banks, fgn. exchs., govts., 1969— ; mem. faculty NYU, 1964; mem. faculty U. Minn., 1963-67; mem. faculty Stanford U., 1969; disting. adj. prof. Grad. Sch. Bus. Columbia U., 1993; expert advisor UNCTAD; guest lectr. various univs., coms. and bds., Banking and Rsch. Ctr., Northwestern U., Columbia U. Futures Ctr.; bd. dirs. Ctrl. and S.W. Corp.. Dow Jones Sustainability Group Index GmbH.; life mem. London Internat. Fin. Future and Options Exch., London Clearing House. Contbr. articles to profl. journs., chpts. of books and handbooks. Vice chmn. bd. govs. Sch. of Art Inst. of Chgo.; bd. dirs. Lincoln Park Zool. Soc., 1985—. Summer faculty fellow U. Calif.; NSF grantee Mem. Am. Econ. Assn., Econometric Soc., Am. Fin. Assn., Am. Agrl. Econs. Assn. Club: Union League of Chgo. Home: 1301 N Astor St Chicago IL 60610-2186 Office: Environ 111 W Jackson Blvd Fl 14 Chicago IL 60604-3589

SANDROK, RICHARD WILLIAM, lawyer; b. Evergreen Park, Ill., July 8, 1943; s. Edward George and Gertrude Jeanette (Van Stright) Sandrok; m. Rebecca Fitzz, June 19, 1973; children: Richard William, Jr., Alexander Edward, Philip Robert, Erika Joy. BA, Wheaton (Ill.) Coll., 1965; JD, U. Ill., 1968. Bar: Ill. 1968, U.S. Dist. Ct. (no. dist.) Ill. 1971. Assoc. Hinshaw Culbertson Moelmann Hoban & Fuller, Chgo. and Wheaton, 1971-75, ptnr. Wheaton, 1976-89, Lisle, 1989—. Reviewer: Legal Checklists. Capt. U.S. Army, 1969—71. Mem.: ABA, Def. Rsch. Inst., Assn. Def. Trial Attys.,

DuPage County Bar Assn. (chmn. med./legal com. 1978—79), Am. Arbitration Assn. (arbitrator), Chgo. Bar Assn., Ill. Bar Assn. Home: 818 Revere Rd Glen Ellyn IL 60137-5537 E-mail: RWS283@aol.com.

SANDS, DEANNA, editor; Mng. editor Omaha World Herald, 95—. Office: Omaha World-Herald World-Herald Sq Omaha NE 68102-1138

SANDSTROM, DALE VERNON, state supreme court judge; b. Grand Forks, N.D., Mar. 9, 1950; s. Ellis Vernon and Hilde Geneva (Williams) S.; m. Gail Hagerty, Mar. 27, 1993; children: Jack, Carrie, Anne. BA, N.D. State U., 1972; JD, U. N.D., 1975. Bar: N.D. 1975, U.S. Dist. Ct. N.D. 1975, U.S. Ct. Appeals (8th cir.) 1976. Asst. atty. gen., chief consumer fraud and antitrust div. State of N.D., Bismarck, 1975-81, securities commr., 1981-83, pub. svc. commr., 1983-92, pres. commn., 1987-91, justice Supreme Ct., 1992—. Chair N.D. Commn. on Cameras in the Courtroom, 1993—, Joint Procedure Com., 1996—; mem. exec. com. N.D. Jud. Conf., 1995—, chair-elect, 1997-99, chair, 1999-2001; mem. Gov.'s Com. on Security and Privacy, Bismarck, 1975-76, Gov.'s Com. on Refugees, Bismarck, 1976; chmn. Gov's Com. on Comml. Air Transp., Bismarck, 1983-84. Mem. platform com. N.D. Reps., 1972, 76, exec. com., 1972-73, 85-88, dist. chmn., 1981-82; former chmn. bd. deacons Luth. Ch.; mem. ch. coun., exec. com., chmn. legal and constl. rev. com. Evang. Luth Ch. Am., 1993—; mem. exec. bd. dirs., No. Lights Coun., dist. chair Boy Scouts Am., 1998-2000. Named Disting. Eagle Scout, Boy Scouts Am., 1997. Mem. ABA, N.D. Bar Assn., Big Muddy Bar Assn., Nat. Assn. Regulatory Utility Commrs. (electricity com.), N.A. Assn. Securities Adminstrs., Order of De Molay (grand master 1994-95, mem. Internat. Supreme coun., Legion of Honor award), Nat. Eagle Scouts Assn. (regent for life), Shriners, Elks, Eagles, Masons (33d degree, chmn. grand youth com. 1979-87, Youth Leadership award 1986), Bruce M. VanSickle Am. Inn of Court (pres. 1999-2001). Office: State ND Supreme Court Bismarck ND 58505*

SANDVIG, SALLY, state legislator; m. Henry David Sandvig; 3 children. Student, N.D. State U. Sales rep. Avon; rep. Dist. 21 N.D. Ho. of Reps., mem. human svc. and govt. and vet. affairs coms. Precinct chmn., dist. sec. Dist. 21, Cass, N.D.; 4-H leader; client coun. mem. LAND; mem. Dem. Women. Soroptimist Internat. Tng. Awards scholar, 1988. Mem. Avon Pres.'s Club. Office: ND Ho of Reps State Capitol Bismarck ND 58505 Address: 201 11th St N Fargo ND 58102-4652

SANFILIPPO, JON WALTER, lawyer; b. Milw., Nov. 10, 1950; s. Joseph Salvator and Jeanne Catherine (Lisinski) S.; m. Pamela Joy Jaeger, July 8, 1972; children: Kerri, Jessica, Jennifer. AS, U. Wis., West Bend, 1972; BS, U. Wis., Milw., 1974, MS, 1978; JD, Marquette U., 1988; postgrad., Nat. Jud. Coll., 1996. Bar: Wis. 1988, U.S. Dist. Ct. (ea. dist.) Wis. 1988, U.S. Ct. Appeals (7th cir.) 1988, U.S. Dist. Ct. (we. dist.) Wis 1989. U.S. Supreme Ct. 1994; cert. elem. tchr., ednl. adminstr., Wis. Collection agt. West Bend Co., 1970-72; educator, athletic dir., coach St. Francis Cabrini, West Bend, 1974-77; clk. of cir. ct. Washington County, 1976-89; ptnr. Schowalter, Edwards & Sanfilippo, S.C., 1989-94; sch. prin.K-8 Campbellsport (Wis.) Sch. Dist., 1994-95; chief dep. clk. Cir. Ct. Milw. County, Milw., 1995—, acting clk., 1997-98; jud. ct. commr. Milw. County, 1997—. Judo tchr. City of West Bend, 1967—; phys. edn. instr., judo coach U. Wis., West Bend, 1992—; fellow ct. exec. devel. program Inst. Ct. Mgmt. Nat. Ctr. State Cts., 1999. Author: Judo for the Physical Educator, 1981, Proper Falling for Education Classes, 1981. Mem. sch. bd. West Bend Sch. Dist., 1979-80; dist. chmn. Wis. Clk. of Cts. Assn., 1976-79, mem. exec. com., 1976-82, 97-98, mem. legis. com., 1982-84, 97-98. Recipient cert. study internat. and Chinese law East Chinese Inst. Politics and Law, Willamette U. Law Sch., Shanghai, People's Republic China, 1988. Mem. ABA, Nat. Jud. Coll., Nat. Assn. for Ct. Adminstrn., Wis. Bar Assn. (bench/bar com. 1986-88, 97—), Milw. Bar Assn. (cts. com. 1995—, criminal bench/bar com. 1997—, family bench/bar coun. 1997—), Washington County Bar Assn., U. Wis.-Washington County Found. Inc. (bd. dirs. 1993-94), Assn. Wis. Sch. Adminstrs., Justinian Soc., Universal Tae Kwon Do Assn. (3d degree Black Belt 1988), U.S. Judo Assn. (6th degree Black Belt 1995), U.S. Martial Arts Assn. (7th degree Black Belt Judo 2000), Rotary (bd. dirs. West Bend Sunrise Club 1990-91, Paul Harris fellow). Roman Catholic. Avocations: Tae Kwon Do, Tai Chi, Judo, photography, model railroading. Office: Milw County Ct House Rm 104 901 N 9th St Milwaukee WI 53233-1425 E-mail: jon.sanfilippo@milwaukee.courts.state.wi.us.

SANFORD, BILL R. medical products executive; BS, Kans. State U. Pres., CEO Steris Corp., Mentor, Ohio, 1987—, also chmn. bd. dirs. Bd. dirs. Key Corp., Cleve. Clinic Found., Edison Biotechnology Ctr., Primus Ventur Ptnrs., neuroControl Corp., BIOMEC, Inc., Cleve. Tomorrow, Case Western Res. U., Health Industries Mfrs. Assn. Office: 5960 Heisley Rd Mentor OH 44060-1834 Fax: 440-639-4457.

SANGER, STEPHEN W. consumer products company executive; b. 1945; With Gen. Mills, Inc., Mpls., 1974—, v.p., gen. mgr. Northstar Divsn., 1983, v.p., gen. mgr. new bus. devel., 1986, pres. Yoplait USA, 1986, pres. Big G Divsn., 1988, sr. v.p., 1989, vice chmn. bd., 1992-96, pres., 1993-95, CEO, chmn. bd., 1995—. Bd. dirs. Donaldson Co., Inc., Mpls. Treas. Guthrie Theatre Found., Mpls. Office: Gen Mills Inc One General Mills Blvd Minneapolis MN 55426

SANGMEISTER, GEORGE EDWARD, lawyer, consultant, former congressman; b. Joliet, Ill., Feb. 16, 1931; s. George Conrad and Rose Engaborg (Johnson) S.; m. Doris Marie Hinspeter, Dec. 1, 1951; children: George Kurt, Kimberley Ann. BA, Elmhurst Coll., 1957; LLB, John Marshall Law Sch., 1960, JD, 1970. Bar: Ill. 1960. Ptnr. McKeown, Fitzgerald, Zollner, Buck, Sangmeister & Hutchison, 1969-89; justice of peace, 1961-63; states atty. Will County, 1964-68; mem. Ill. Ho. of Reps., 1972-76, Ill. Senate, 1977-87, 101st-103rd Congresses from 4th (now 11th) Dist. Ill., 1989-95; ret., 1995; cons. McKeown, Fitzgerald, Zollner, Buck, Hutchison, Ruttle and Assocs., 1990—. Chmn. Frankfort Twp. unit Am. Cancer Soc., Will County Emergency Housing Devel. Corp.; past trustee Will County Family Svc. Agy.; past bd. dirs. Joliet Jr. Coll. Found., Joliet Will County Ctr. for Econ. Devel., Silver Cross Found., Silver Cross Hosp. With inf. AUS, 1951-53. Mem. ABA, Ill. Bar Assn., Assn. Trial Lawyers Am., Am. Legion, Frankfort (past pres.), Mokena C. of C., Old Timers Baseball Assn., Lions. Home: 20735 Wolf Rd Mokena IL 60448-8927

SANNER, JOHN HARPER, retired pharmacologist; b. Anamosa, Iowa, Apr. 29, 1931; s. Lee Michael and Helen (Grace) S.; m. Marilyn Joan Eichorst, Dec. 28, 1958; children: Linda Leigh, Steven Bradley. BS, U. Iowa, 1954, MS, 1961, PhD, 1964. Rsch. investigator G.D. Searle & Co., Skokie, Ill., 1963-69, sr. rsch. investigator, 1969-75, rsch. fellow, 1975-86, ret., 1986—. Conducted pioneering rsch. in prostaglandin antagonists; contbr. articles to profl. jours. Mem. Deerfield (Ill.) Cable and Telecomm. Commn. 1st lt. USAFR, 1955-57. Mem. Am. Soc. for Pharmacology and Exptl. Therapeutics (ret.), Ill. Videomakers Assn., Wedding and Event Videographers Assn. Internat., Deerfield C. of C. Republican. Avocations: video photography and production. Office: Sanner Video Svc PO Box 199 Deerfield IL 60015-0199 E-mail: johnsanner@aol.com.

SANNER, ROYCE NORMAN, lawyer; b. Lancaster, Minn., Mar. 9, 1931; s. Oscar N. and Clara Sanner; m. Janice L. Sterne, Dec. 27, 1972; children— Michelle Joy, Craig Allen. BS, Minn. State U., Moorhead, 1953; LLB cum laude, U. Minn., 1961. Bar: Minn. 1961, U.S. Dist. Ct. Minn. 1961, U.S. Supreme Ct. 1981. Tchr. English Karlstad (Minn.) High Sch., 1955-57; counsel IDS Life Ins. Co., Mpls., 1961-68, v.p., gen. counsel, 1969-72, exec. v.p., gen. counsel, 1972-77; dir. corp. devel. Am. Express Fin. Advisors, Mpls., 1968-69, v.p., gen. counsel, 1975-78, v.p., 1978-80, v.p., gen. counsel, 1980-82; v.p. law Northwestern Nat. Life Ins. Co., 1982-83, sr. v.p., gen. counsel, sec., 1983-96, ReliaStar Fin. Corp. (formerly known as NWNL Cos., Inc.), Mpls., 1988-96; of counsel Maslon Edelman Borman & Brand, 1996—. Bd. dirs. Fairview Univ. Med. Ctr., Friendship Fund., Inc., Fraser Cmty. Svcs., Fairview Health Svcs. Served with U.S. Army, 1953-55. Mem. ABA, Minn. Bar Assn., Hennepin County Bar Assn., Fed. Bar Assn., Assn. of Life Ins. Counsel, Minn. Corp. Counsel Assn., Rotary. Home: 734 Widsten Cir Wayzata MN 55391-1784 Office: Maslon Edelman Borman & Brand 3300 Wells Fargo Ctr 90 S 7th St Ste 3300 Minneapolis MN 55402-4140 E-mail: rsampls@aol.com.

SANSTEAD, WAYNE GODFREY, state superintendent, former lieutenant governor; b. Hot Springs, Ark., Apr. 16, 1935; s. Godfrey A. and Clara (Buen) S.; m. Mary Jane Bober, June 16, 1957; children: Timothy, Jonathan. B.A. in Speech and Polit. Sci, St. Olaf Coll., 1957; M.A. in Pub. Address, Northwestern U., 1966; Ed.D., U. N.D., 1974. Tchr., Luverne, Minn., 1959-60; dir. forensics Minot (N.D.) High Sch., 1960-71, tchr. social sci., 1960-78; mem. N.D. Ho. of Reps., 1965-70, 83-85, N.D. Senate, 1971-73; lt. gov. N.D. Bismarck, 1973-81; supt. pub. instrn. N.D., 1985—. Served with AUS, 1957-59. Recipient Disting. Alumnus award St. Olaf Coll., 1991; named Outstanding Freshman Senator A.P., 1971, Outstanding Young Educator, N.D. Jr. C. of C., 1967, Outstanding Young Man, Minot Jr. C. of C., 1964; Coe Family Found. scholar, 1963, Eagleton scholar Rutgers U., 1969. Mem. N.D. Edn. Assn., NEA (legis. com. 1969—), Central States Speech Assn., Am. Forensic Assn., Jr. C. of C., Sons of Norway. Democrat. Lutheran (chmn. Western N.D. research and social action com. 1962-68). Clubs: Elk, Toastmaster. Home: 1120 Columbia Dr Bismarck ND 58504-6514 Office: Dept Pub Instrn 600 E Boulevard Ave Bismarck ND 58505-0660

SANT, JOHN TALBOT, lawyer; b. Oct. 7, 1932; s. John Francis and Josephine (Williams) S.; m. Almira Steedman Baldwin, Jan. 31, 1959; children: John Talbot Jr., Richard Baldwin, Frank Williams. AB, Princeton U., 1954; LLB, Harvard U., 1957. Bar: Mo. 1957. Assoc. Thompson, Mitchell, Douglas & Neill, St. Louis, 1958-60; atty. McDonnell Aircraft Co., 1960-61; asst. sec., 1961-62; sec., 1962-67, McDonnell Douglas Corp., St. Louis, 1967-76; asst. gen. counsel, 1969-74; corp. v.p. legal, 1974-75; corp. v.p., gen. counsel, 1975-88; bd. dirs., 1978-82; sr. v.p., gen. counsel, 1988-91; ptnr. Bryan Cave, 1991-96; of counsel, 1997. Vestry of St. Michael and St. George, St. Louis, 1979-82, 87-90, 93-95; bd. dirs. Grace Hill Neighborhood Svcs., Inc., St. Louis, 1987-93; pres. Grace Hill Settlement House, 1996-97; mem. transition task force Supt. Elect. of St. Louis Pub. Schs., 1996, found. dir. St. Louis Pub. Schs. Found., chair Partnership For Youth, Inc., 2001—. Mem. ABA (pub. contracts sec., coun. 1987-91), Mo. Bar Assn., St. Louis Bar Assn. Home: 9 Ridgewood St Saint Louis MO 63124-1849 Office: Bryan Cave 1 Metropolitan Sq Ste 3600 Saint Louis MO 63102-2750

SANTANGELO, MARIO VINCENT, dentist; b. Youngstown, Ohio, Oct. 5, 1931; s. Anthony and Maria (Zarlenga) S. Student, U. Pitts., 1949-51; DDS, Loyola U., Chgo., 1955, MS, 1960. Instr. Loyola U., 1957-60, asst. prof., 1960-66, assoc. prof., 1966-70, chmn. dept. radiology, 1962-70, dir. dental aux. utilization program, 1963-70, chmn. dept. oral diagnosis, 1967-70, asst. dean, 1969-70; pvt. practice, Chgo., 1960-70. Cons. Cert. Bd. Am. Dental Assts. Assn., 1967-75, VA Rsch. Hosp., 1969-75, Chgo. CSC, 1967-75; counselor Chgo. Dental Assts. Assn., 1966-69; mem. dental student tng. adv. com. divsn. dental health USPHS, HEW, 1969-71; cons. dental edn. rev. com. NIH, 1971-72; cons. region IV, USPHS, HEW, Atlanta, 1973-76, region V, Chgo., 1973-77; mem. Commn. on Dental Edn. and Practice, Fedn.Dentaire Internat., 1984-92; mem. bd. visitors Washington U. Sch. Dental Medicine, St. Louis, 1974-76 Contbr. articles to dental jours. Capt. USAF, 1955-57. Recipient Dr. Harry Strusser Meml. award NYU Coll. Dentistry, 1985. Fellow Am. Coll. Dentists (life); mem. ADA (life, asst. sec. coun. dental edn. 1971-81, acting sec. 1981-82, sec. 1982-90, dir. 1990-92, asst. sec. commn. on dental accreditation 1975-81, acting sec. commn. on continuing dental edn. 1981-82, sec. 1982-85), Ill. State Dental Assn. (life), Chgo. Dental Assn. (life), AMA (edn. work group 1982-86), Assembly Specialized Accrediting Bodies (coun. on postsecondary accreditation 1981-92, award of merit 1992), Am. Assn. Dental Schs., Odontographic Soc. Chgo. (life), Am. Acad. Oral Pathology, Am. Acad. Dental Radiology, Can. Dental Assn. (commn. on dental accrediation award of merit 1992), Am. Acad. Oral Medicine, Am. Assn. Dental Examiners (hon.), Blue Key, Omicron Kappa Upsilon, Xi Psi Phi. Home: 1440 N Lake Shore Dr Chicago IL 60610-1626

SANTE, WILLIAM ARTHUR, II, electronics manufacturing executive; b. N.Y.C., July 16, 1943; s. William Arthur and Grace Elizabeth (Burnat) S.; m. Kathleen Margaret Rourke, July 2, 1966; children: Jennifer, William, Timothy. BS, U. Detroit, 1965; MBA, U. Pitts., 1981. CPA, Mich. Mgr. Deloitte & Touche, Detroit, 1965-78; gen. auditor Rockwell Internat., Pitts., 1978—. Mem. AICPA, Mich. Assn. CPA's, Inst. Internal Auditors, Shannopin Club (Pitts.), Ozaukee Club. Republican. Roman Catholic. Office: Rockwell Internat Corp 1201 S 2nd St Milwaukee WI 53204-2410 E-mail: wasante@ra.rockwell.com.

SANTIAGO, BENITO RIVERA, professional baseball player; b. Ponce, P.R., Mar. 9, 1965; m. Bianca Santiago; 1 child, Benny Beth. Baseball player San Diego Padres, 1986-92, Florida Marlins, 1993-94, Cin. Reds, 1995, 2000—, Philadelphia Phillies, 1996, Toronto Blue Jays, 1997-98; catcher Chgo. Cubs, 1999. Named Nat. League Rookie of Yr. Baseball Writers' Assn. Am., 1987, Sporting News All-Star Team, 1987, 89, 91, 92; recipient Gold Glove award, 1988-90, Silver Slugger award, 1987-88, 90-91; holder maj. league rookie record for most consecutive games batted safely. Office: Cin Reds 100 Cinergy Fld Cincinnati OH 45202-3543

SANTIAGO, MIGUEL A. state legislator; b. P.R., May 24, 1953; 2 children. BA, Northwestern Ill. U.; MA, Gov.'s State U. Ill. state rep. Dist. 3, 1989—; mem. exec. fin. inst., vice chmn. human svcs. appropriations Ill. Ho. Reps., mem. reapportionment, regist and regulation, transp. and motor vehicles coms.; tchr. Democrat. Home: 7414 N Octavia Ave Chicago IL 60631-4435 Office: Ill Ho of Reps Rm 618 State Capitol Springfield IL 62706-0001

SANTONA, GLORIA, lawyer; b. Gary, Ind., June 10, 1950; d. Ray and Elvira (Cambeses) S.; m. Douglas Lee Frazier, Apr. 12, 1980. BS in Biochemistry, Mich. State U., 1971; JD, U. Mich., 1977. Bar: Ill. 1977. Atty. McDonald's Corp., Oak Brook, Ill., 1977-82, dir., 1982-86, assoc. gen. counsel, 1986-92, asst. v.p., 1989-93, v.p., sec., dep. gen. counsel, 1996-99, v.p., U.S. gen. counsel, sec., 1999-2001, sr. v.p., gen. counsel, sec., 2001—. Mem. ABA, Chgo. Assn., Am. Corp. Counsel Assn., Am. Soc. Corp. Secs. Office: McDonalds Corp 1 Mcdonalds Plz Oak Brook IL 60523-1911

SANTULLI, RICHARD T. executive; Chmn. Exec. Jet Aviation, Inc., Columbus, Ohio. Office: Exec Jet Aviation Inc 625 N Hamilton Rd Columbus OH 43219-1825 also: PO Box 369099 Columbus OH 43236-9099

SAPERSTEIN, LEE WALDO, mining engineering educator; b. N.Y.C., July 14, 1943; s. Charles Levy and Freda Phyllis (Dornbush) S.; m. Priscilla Frances Hickson, Sept. 16, 1967; children: Adam Geoffrey, Clare Freda. BS in Mining Engring., Mont. Sch. Mines, 1964; DPhil in Engring. Sci., Oxford U., 1967. Registered profl. engr., Ky., Mo., Pa. Laborer, miner, engr. The Anaconda Co., Butte, Mont., and N.Y.C., 1963-64; asst. prof. mining engring. Pa. State U., University Park, 1967-71, assoc. prof., 1971-78, prof., 1978-87, sect. chmn., 1974-87; prof., chmn. dept. mine engring. U. Ky., Lexington, 1987-93; dean, prof. mining engring. Sch. Mines and Metallurgy U. Mo., Rolla, 1993—. Chmn. engring. accreditation commn., 1989-90, bd. dirs. Accreditation Bd. for Engring. and Tech., 1992-2001, sec. of bd., 1995-98, pres.-elect, 1998-99, pres. 1999-2000, ABET fellow. Contbr. articles to refereed jours. Rhodes scholar Oxford U., 1964-67. Mem. NSPE, ASEE, Soc. Mining, metallurgy and Exploration, Inc. (disting. mem. AIME-Soc. Mining Engrs.), Am. Assn. Rhodes Scholars. Home: 801 Laurel Dr Rolla MO 65401-3841 Office: U Mo 305 V H Mc Nutt Hl Rolla MO 65409-0001 E-mail: saperste@umr.edu., saperste@rollanet.org.

SAPP, JOHN RAYMOND, lawyer; b. Lawrence, Kans., June 18, 1944; s. Raymond Olen and Amy (Kerr) S.; m. Linda Lee Tebbe, July 3, 1965; children: Jeffrey, Jennifer, John. BA, U. Kans., 1966; JD, Duke U., 1969. Bar: Wis. 1969, U.S. Dist. Ct. (ea. dist.) Wis. 1969, U.S. Ct. Appeals (7th cir.) 1974, U.S. Ct. Appeals (4th cir.) 1984, U.S. Supreme Ct. 1974. Assoc. Michael, Best & Friedrich, Milw., 1969-76, ptnr., 1976-90, mng. ptnr., 1990—. Dir. Roadrunner Freight Systems, Milw., 1992—. Bd. dirs. Milw. Symphony, 1981-95, mem. exec. com., 1993-95; bd. dirs. Boy Scouts Am., Milw., 1986—, pres. 1990-92; mem. Milw. Arts Bd., 1990, Greater Milw. Com.; bd. dirs. Zool. Soc., 1995—, v.p., 2000—; bd. dirs. Lex Mundi, 1997-2000, mem. exec. com., 1997-2001; bd. dirs. Jr. Achievement Greater Milw., 2001—. Avocations: golf, curling, print collecting. E-mail: jrsapp@mbf-law.com.

SARANOW, MITCHELL HARRIS, investment banker, business executive; b. Chgo., Oct. 14, 1945; B.S.B.A. with high distinction, Northwestern U., 1967; J.D. cum laude, Harvard U., 1971; M.B.A. with distinction (George F. Baker scholar), Harvard U. Bus. Sch., 1971; m. Linda Lee Billig, Sept. 8, 1973; children: Jennifer Wynne, Julie Ann, William L., David M. Bar: Ill. 1971, Mo. 1976, D.C. 1984; Assoc. firm Mayer, Brown & Platt, Chgo., 1971-73; investment banker Becker and Warburg, Paribas, Bicker Group, Inc., Chgo., 1973-75; v.p. fin. and law Sunmark Cos., St. Louis, 1975-79; v.p. fin., chief fin. officer CFS Continental, Inc., Chgo., 1979-83; pres., The Saranow Co., Chgo., 1983—; chmn. Fluid Mgmt. L.P., Wheeling, Ill. 1987; cons., dir. MidAtlantic Cable TV, Inc., Washington, 1983— . C.P.A., Ill. Mem. Am. Bar Assn., Beta Gamma Sigma, Phi Epsilon Pi. Clubs: Econs., Standard; Harvard Bus. Sch. Century. Office: Navigant Consulting Inc 615 N Wabash Ave Chicago IL 60611

SARETT, LEWIS HASTINGS, chemist, retired inventor, retired health/medical products executive; b. Champaign, Ill., Dec. 22, 1917; BS, Northwestern U., 1939; PhD, Princeton U., 1942. With Merck Rsch. Labs., Rahway, N.J., 1942, sr. v.p. science and tech.; ret., 1982. Inducted to Nat. Inventors Hall of Fame, 1980. Achievements include development of synthetic cortisone. Office: Nat Inventors Hall of Fame 221 S Broadway St Akron OH 44308-1505

SARGENT, JOHN, psychiatrist; MD, U. Rochester, 1973. Cert. psychiatry, child and adolescent psychiatry, pediatrics; approved clin. supr. Am. Assn. Marriage and Family Therapy. Intern and resident pediat. U. Wis., Madison, 1973-77; resident child and adolescent psychiatry Phila. Child Guidance Ctr., 1978-80; resident gen. psychiatry Hosp. U. Pa., Phila., 1984-87; dir. child and adolescent psychiatry U. Pa. Med. Sch., 1989-97, dir. adult residency program, 1989-97; mem. staff Children's Hosp. Phila., Phila. Child Guidance Ctr., 1980-97; dir. edn. and rsch., dean Karl Menninger Sch. Psychiatry & Mental Health Svcs., Topeka, 1997—. Assoc. prof. psychiatry and pediat. U. Pa. Med. Sch., 1987-97; Pfeitter/Adams prof. psychiatry Karl Menninger Sch. Psychiatry. Mem. editl. bd. Jour. Am. Acad. Child and Adolescent Psychiatry; co-author: Madness, Chaos and Violence: Therapy with Families at the Brink; co-editor: Primary Care Pediatrics; contbr. over 60 articles to profl. jours. Faculty mem., organizer Eastern European Child Abuse and Child Mental Health Program, Soros Found. and Children's Mental Health Alliance. Office: Menninger Rsch & Edn PO Box 829 Topeka KS 66601-0829 E-mail: sargenj@menninger.edu.

SARGUS, EDMUND A., JR. judge; b. Wheeling, W.Va., July 2, 1953; s. Edmund A. Sr. and Ann Elizabeth (Kearney) S.; m. Jennifer L. Smart, Jan. 7, 1978; 2 children. AB with honors, Brown U., 1975; JD, Case Western Res. U., 1978. Bar: Ohio 1978, U.S. Dist. Ct. (so. dist.) Ohio 1979, U.S. Dist. Ct. (no. dist.) Ohio 1981, U.S. Ct. Appeals (6th cir.) 1985, U.S. Dist. Ct. (no. dist.) W.Va. 1988, U.S. Ct. Appeals (4th cir.) 1988. Assoc. Cinque, Banker, Linch & White, Bellaire, Ohio, 1978-79, Stanley C. Burech, St. Clairsville, 1980-82; ptnr. Burech & Sargus, 1983-93; U.S. Atty. Dept. of Justice, Columbus, Ohio, 1993-96; dist. judge U.S. Dist. Ct. (so. dist.) Ohio, 1996—. Spl. counsel Ohio Atty. Gen., Columbus, 1979-93; treas. Coalition for Dem. Values, Washington, 1990-93. Solicitor Village of Powhattan Point, Ohio, 1979-93; councilman City of St. Clairsville, 1987-91. Mem. ABA, Ohio Bar Assn. Office: US Dist Ct 85 Marconi Blvd Columbus OH 43215-2823

SARICKS, JOYCE GOERING, librarian; b. Nov. 8, 1948; d. Joe W. and Lovella Goering; m. Christopher L. Saricks, Aug. 21, 1971; children: Brendan James, Margaret Katherine. BA with highest distinction in Eng.& Ger, U. Kans., 1970; MA in Comparative Lit., U. Wis., 1971; MA/MAT in Library Sci., U. Chgo., 1977. Reference librarian Downers Grove (Ill.) Pub. Library, 1977-80, head tech. svcs., 1980-83, coord. lit. and audio svcs., 1983—. Presenter workshops in field. Author: (with Nancy Brown) Readers' Advisory Service in the Public Library, 1989, revised edit., 1997, The Readers' Advisory Guide to Genre Fiction, 2001. Mem. Read Ill. adv. com., 1990-91. Woodrow Wilson fellow, 1970; recipient Allie Beth Martin award Pub. Library Assn., 1989, No. Ill. Libr. of Yr. award Windy City Romance Writers, 1995, Libr. of the Yr. award Romance Writers of Am., 2000. Mem. ALA, Ill. Library Assn., Adult Reading Round Table (founder), Phi Beta Kappa, Delta Phi Alpha, Pi Lambda Theta, Beta Phi Mu. Home: 1116 61st St Downers Grove IL 60516-1819 Office: Downers Grove Pub Library 1050 Curtiss St Downers Grove IL 60515-4606 E-mail: saricksj@juno.com.

SARWER-FONER, GERALD JACOB, physician, educator; b. Volkovsk, Grodno, Poland, Dec. 6, 1924; arrived in Can., 1932, naturalized, 1935; s. Michael and Ronia (Caplan) Sarwer-F.; m. Ethel Sheinfeld, May 28, 1950; children: Michael, Gladys, Janice, Henry, Brian. BA, Loyola Coll. U., Montreal, 1945, MD magna cum laude, 1951; DPsychiatry, McGill U., 1955. Diplomate: Am. Bd. Psychiatry and Neurology. Intern. Univ. Hosps. U. Montreal Sch. Medicine, 1950-51; resident Butler Hosp., Providence, 1951-52, Hosps. Western Res. U., Cleve., 1952-53, Queen Mary Vets. Hosp., Montreal, 1953-55; cons. psychiatry, dir. psychiatric rsch., 1955-61; lectr. psychiatry U. Montreal, 1953-55; lectr., assoc. prof. McGill U., 1955-70; dir. dept psychiatry Queen Elizabeth's Hosp, Montreal, 1964-71; prof. psychiatry U. Ottawa, Ont., 1971-89, prof., chmn. psychiatry, 1974-86, prof., 1989—; dir. dept. psychiatry Ottawa Gen. Hosp., 1971-87; dir. Lafayette Clinic, Detroit, 1989-92; prof. psychiatry and behavioral Neurosciences Wayne State U., 1989—. Cons. in psychiatry Ottawa Gen. Hosp., Royal Ottawa Hosp., Children's Hosp. of Eastern Ont., Ottawa, Windsor (Ont.) Western Hosp. Ctr., Ottawa Sch. Bd.; Z. Lebensohn lectr. Silbey Meml. Hosp. Cosmos Club, Washington, 1991; disting. lectr. XI World Congress Psychiatry, Hamburg, 1999. Editor: Dynamics of Psychiatric Drug Therapy, 1960, Research Conference on the Depressive Group of Illnesses, 1966, Psychiatric Crossroads-the Seventies, Research Aspects, 1972, Social Psychiatry in the Late 20th Century, 1993; editor in chief Psychiat. Jour. U. Ottawa, 1976-90, emeritus editor in chief, 1990—;

mem. editorial bds. of numerous internat. and nat. profl. jours.; editor numerous audio-video tapes; contbr. to more than 200 articles to profl. jours. Bd. govs. Queen Elizabeth Hosp., Montreal, 1966-71; life gov. Queen Elizabeth Hosp. Found.; cons. Protestant Sch. Bd., Westmount, Que., 1966-71; advisor Com. on Health, City of Westmount, 1969-71. Served to lt. col. Royal Can. A Med. Corps, 1949-62. Fulbright fellow, 1951-53; recipient Sigmund Freud award Am. assn. Psychoanalytic Physicians, 1982, William V. Silverberg Meml. award Am. Acad. Psychoanalysis, 1990, Poca award Assn. Psychiat. Out Patient Ctrs. Am., 1990; Simon Bolivar lectr. Am. Psychiat. Assn., New Orleans, 1981; Can. Decoration, Knight of Malta. Fellow: Am. Acad. Psychiatry and the Law (sr., pres. 1977, Silver Apple Award), World Psychiat. Assn. (chair Sci. program VI World Congress 1974—77, v.p. sect on edn. 1989—, mem. internat. adv. com. 9th World Congress Rio de Janeiro 1993, org. com. sci. program com. X World Congress in Madrid, dist. lectro. 1996, XI World Congress, Hamburg 1999, mem. nom. com.,), Benjamin Rush Soc. (founding menm., councillor), Am. Psychopathol. Assn., Am. Coll. Psychoanalysts (pres. elect. 1983, pres. 1984—85, Henry Laughlin Award 1986), Collegium Internat. Neuropsychopharmacology, Am. Coll. Psychiatrists (bd. regents 1978—80, pres. 1982—86, emeritus), Internat. Coll. Psychosomatic Medicine (sec.-gen. 1979—83), Royal Coll. Physicians and Surgeons (exec. sec. test psychiat. com. 1987—89), Am. Coll. Neuropsychopharmacology (life; charter fellow), Can. Coll. Neuropsychopharmacology (life; hon. found. 1958—64), Am. Psychiat Assn. (life; chair com., psychiarty, law 1975—77, chair sci. program com. 1997), Am. Coll. Psychoanalysts (life; 6th world congress of psychiatry), Am. Coll. Mental Health Adminstrn. (life), Can. Psychiat. Assn. (life; bd. dirs. 1958—62, founder, chair com., sect. psychotherapy 1962—64), AAAS, Royal Coll. Psychiatry (Found. fellow), Internat. Psychoanalytical Assn. (mem. program com. 31st cngress N.Y. 1979); mem.: Mich. Psychoanalytic Soc., Am. Psychoanalytic Assn., Cosmos Club, Royal Can. Mil. Inst. Club., Am. Assn. for Social Psychiatry (v.p. 1987—89, pres. elect 1990, pres. 1992—94), Can. Assn. Profs. of paychiatry 1976—77, Can. Psychoanalytic Soc. 1977—81, Bio. Psychiatry (sr., H. Azina Meml. lectr. 1963, pres. 1983—84, George M. Thompson Award 1997). Home and Office: 3220 Bloomfield Shr West Bloomfield MI 48323-3300 Fax: 248 855-8321. E-mail: sarwfon@aol.com.

SATERFIEL, THOMAS HORNE, education researcher, administrator; b. Hattiesburg, Miss., Dec. 14, 1950; s. Thomas Walton and Maybell (Horne) S.; m. Susan McKinley, June 1, 1974; children: Wayne Thomas, John Michael. BS, Miss. State U., 1972, MEd, 1973; PhD, Fla. State U., 1977; postgrad., Harvard U., 1985. Asst. prin. Tupelo (Miss.) Pub. Schs., 1972-73; tchr. math. Amory (Miss.) Pub. Schs., 1973-74; dir. devel. Blue Mountain (Miss.) Coll., 1974-75; asst. prof. ednl. psychology Miss. State U., Mississippi State, 1976-81, assoc. prof., 1981-85, dir. program. rsch. and evaluation for pub. schs., 1976-85; dep. state supt. Miss. Dept. Edn., Jackson, 1985-90; v.p. for rsch. Am. Coll. Testing (now ACT, Inc.), Iowa City, 1990-98, sr. v.p., 1998—. Mem. outcomes accreditation panel Office Gov. of Miss., Jackson, 1981-83, study commn. Coun. of Chief State Sch. Officers, Washington, 1985-90; chair planning and evaluation Southeastern Ednl. Rsch. Lab., Raleigh, N.C., 1987-90; exec. com. Nat. Forum on Ednl. Stats., Washington, 1989-90. Contbr. articles to profl. jours. Sec.-treas. Optimist Club, Starkville, Miss., 1977-85, bd. dirs., Jackson, 1985-90; deacon 1st Bapt. Ch., Starkville, 1982-85. Recipient Outstanding Young Adminstr. award Phil Hardin Found., 1975; named one of Outstanding Young Men in Am., U.S. Jaycees, 1977; Kellogg Nat. fellow W.K. Kellogg Found., 1983-86. Mem. Nat. Coun. on Measurement in Edn., Am. Ednl. Rsch. Assn., Am. Mgmt. Assn., Phi Kappa Phi, Phi Delta Kappa (pres. Mississippi State chpt. 1983-84, Peer award, 1982, Outstanding Educator award 1984). Avocations: music, running. Home: 49 Samuel Dr Iowa City IA 52245-5652 Office: ACT Inc 2201 N Dodge St Iowa City IA 52243-0001

SATHE, SHARAD SOMNATH, chemical company executive; b. Bombay, Oct. 10, 1940; came to U.S., 1967; s. Somnath Waman and Kamala S. (Bhave) S. m. Usha Moreshwar Tamhankar, Feb. 6, 1966; children: Vandana, Swapna. BS, U. Bombay, 1960; B in Pharmacy, Banaras Hindu U., 1963; PhD, Ind. U., 1971. Rsch. asst. CIBA Rsch. Ctr., Bombay, 1964-67; postdoctoral fellow Rsch. Triangle Inst., Raleigh, N.C., 1971-73; rsch. chemist Mallinckrodt, Inc., St. Louis, 1973-79, tech. supr., 1979-81, group leader, 1981-87, mgr. R & D, 1989-94; assoc. dir. rsch., 1995-98; dir. process rsch. Mallinckrodt Inc., St. Louis, 1998—. Patentee in field; contbr. articles to profl. jours. Pres. India Student Assn., Bloomington, Ind., 1969-70; mem. bd. of trustees India Assn. of St. Louis, 1980-85; pres. Sangeetha, St. Louis, 1986-87. Fellow Am. Inst. Chemistry, N.Y. Acad. Scis.; mem. Am. Chem. Soc. Avocations: music, tennis, reading. Office: Mallinckrodt Inc 2nd & Mallinckrodt St Saint Louis MO 63147

SATO, PAUL HISASHI, pharmacologist; b. Mt. Vernon, N.Y., Mar. 22, 1949; s. Yoshio and Lury (Shiogi) S.; m. Jeanne Ellen Courville, June 29, 1996. BS, Jamestown Coll., 1971; MS, NYU, 1972, PhD, 1975. Rsch. assoc. Roche Inst. Molecular Biology, Nutley, N.J., 1975-77; assoc. prof. Mich. State U., East Lansing, 1977—. Office: Mich State U Dept Pharmacology/Toxicol East Lansing MI 48824 E-mail: sato@msu.edu.

SATOVSKY, ABRAHAM, lawyer; b. Detroit, Oct. 15, 1907; s. Samuel and Stella (Benenson) S.; m. Toby Nayer, Sept. 4, 1938 (dec.); children: Sheldon Baer, James Bennett. B.A., U. Mich., 1928, J.D., 1930. Bar: Mich. 1930, U.S. Supreme Ct. 1930. Assoc. William Henry Gallagher, Detroit, 1930-65. Bldg. chmn. lawyers com. United Found. and Torch Dr. Co-chmn. profl. divsn. Allied Jewish Campaign; adv. coun. United Synagogue Am.; del. Jewish Cmty. Coun. Detroit; v.p. Mosies Chetim Orgn. Detroit; bd. dirs. Detroit Svc. Group, past chmn. fgn. mission; active fund raiser Greater Miami United Jewish Appeal; mem. fund dr. com. U. Mich. Law Sch.; trustee Clover Hill Park Cemetery, 1978-81, trustee emeritus, 1982—; bd. dirs. Congregation Shaarey Zedek, Southfield, Mich., past pres., 1959-62. Recipient Sem. award Jewish Theol. Sem. Am., 1952; citation of merit Jewish Welfare Fedn., Detroit; Jerusalem award State of Israel Bond Orgn.; numerous other awards. Mem. ABA, Mich. Bar Assn., Detroit Bar Assn., Oakland County Bar, Nat. Fedn. Jewish Men's Clubs (founder, past pres., hon. life pres., Gt. Lakes regional award 1977, Ma'Asim Tovim (Good Deeds) award 1989), Am. Arbitration Assn., Jewish Hist. Soc. Mich. (mem. adv. bd.), Am. Jewish Hist. Soc., Am. Judicature Soc., Men's Club Congregation Shaarey Zedek (past pres., hon. life pres.), Standard Club, B'nai B'rith (past pres. Detroit), Hadassah (life), Phi Beta Delta (merged with Pi Lambda Phi). Home and Office: 28455 Northwestern Hwy Southfield MI 48034-1823

SATTER, LARRY DEAN, nutritionist; b. Madelia, Minn., July 30, 1937; m. 1966; 3 children. BS, S.D. State U., 1960; MS, U. Wis., 1962, PhD in Biochemistry and Dairy Sci., 1964. Asst. prof. to assoc. prof. dairy sci. U. Wis., Madison, 1964-73, prof., 1973-81; mem. staff U.S. Dairy Forage Rsch. Ctr., U. Wis., USDA, 1981-87, dir., 1987-98, rsch. dairy scientist, 1998—. Recipient Am. Feed Mfrs. award, 1977. Mem. Am. Dairy Sci. Assn., Am. Soc. Animal Sci., Am. Inst. Nutrition. Office: U Wis USDA Dairy Forage Rsch Ctr 1925 Linden Dr W Madison WI 53706-1108 E-mail: ldsatter@facstaff.wisc.edu., lsatter@dfrc.wisc.edu.

SATTERLEE, TERRY JEAN, lawyer; b. Kansas City, Mo., Aug. 28, 1948; d. Charles Woodbury and Francis Jean (Shriver) S.; m. William W. Rice, Jan. 9, 1982; children: Cassandra Jean Rice, Mary Shannon Rice. BA, Kans. U., 1970; JD, U. Mo., 1974. Bar: Mo. 1974. Lawyer Arthur Benson Assocs., Kansas City, Mo., 1974-77, Freilich & Leitner, Kansas City, 1977-78, U.S. Environ. Protection Agy., Kansas City, 1978-83; of counsel Lathrop & Norquist, 1985-87, ptnr., 1987—, mem. exec. com., 1997-2001. Contbr. articles to profl. jours. Chmn. Bd. Zoning Adjustment, Kansas City, 1983-87, Mo. State Parks Adv. Bd., 1997-2002; Kansas City Hazardous Materials com; steering com. COMPASS Met. Planning, Kansas City, 1990-93. Mem. Mo. Bar Assn. (chair environ. com. 1990-93), Kansas City Bar Assn. (environ. com. chmn. 1986-90, chair 2001), Mo. C. of C. (natural resource coun. 1990-2002, bd. dirs. 1999-2002, chair 1998-2002), Kansas City C. of C. (environ. com. chmn. 1992), Women's Pub. Svc. Network (named Top 25 US Women in Bus. 2000). Democrat. Episcopalian. Office: Lathrop & Gage 2345 Grand Blvd Kansas City MO 64108-2612

SAUBERT, WALTER E. (WALLY SAUBERT), trucking and transportation company executive; b. Seattle; m. Alicejo Saubert. BS in Econs., U. Wash. Joined Am. Red Ball Internat., 1972, various mgmt. and exec.-level positions, v.p., gen. mgr., 1983; co-founder Red Ball Corp., 1985, CEO, 1989; chmn., CEO Atlas World Group, 1996—. With USMC, 1965-68, Vietnam.

SAUDER, MAYNARD, manufacturing company executive; b. Feb. 15, 1932; CEO Sauder Woodworking, Archibald, Ohio.

SAUER, GORDON CHENOWETH, dermatologist, educator; b. Rutland, Ill., Aug. 14, 1921; s. Fred William and Gweneth (Chenoweth) S.; m. Mary Louise Steinhilber, Dec. 28, 1944; children: Elisabeth Ruth, Gordon Chenoweth, Margaret Louise, Amy Kieffer.; m. Marion Green, Oct. 23, 1982. Student, Northwestern U., 1939-42; BS, U. Ill., 1943, MD, 1945. Diplomate Am. Bd. Dermatology and Syphilology. Intern Cook County Hosp., Chgo., 1945-46; resident dermatology and syphilology N.Y.U.-Bellevue Med. Center, 1948-51; dermatologist Thompson-Brumm-Knepper Clinic, St. Joseph, Mo., 1951-54; pvt. practice Kansas City, 1954—; mem. staff St. Luke's, Research, Kansas City Gen. hosps.; assoc. instr. U. Kans., 1951-56, vice-chmn. sect. dermatology, 1956-58, assoc. clin. prof., 1960-64, clin. prof., 1964-93; clin. prof. emeritus, 1993—; head sect. dermatology U. Kans., 1958-70. Clin. assoc., acting head dermatology sect. U. Mo., 1955-59, cons. dermatology, 1959-67, clin. prof., 1967—; cons. Munson Army Hosp., Ft. Leavenworth, Kans., 1959-68; dermatology panel, drug efficacy panel Nat. Acad. Sci.-FDA, 1967-69. Author: Manual of Skin Diseases, 1959, 7th edit., 1995, Teen Skin, 1965, John Gould Bird Print Reproductions, 1977, John Gould's Prospectuses and Lists of Subscribers to His Work on Natural History: With an 1866 Facsimile, 1980, John Gould The Bird Man, 1982, John Gould The Bird Man: Associates and Subscribers, 1995, John Gould The Bird Man: Bibliography 2, 1996, John Gould The Bird Man: Correspondence, Vol. 1 through 1838, 1998, vol. 2 through 1841, 1998, vol. 3, 1842-45, 1999; editor Kansas City Med. Bull., 1967-69; contbr. articles to profl. jours. Bd. dirs. Kansas City Area coun. Camp Fire Girls Am., 1956-59, Kansas City Lyric Theatre, 1969-74, Kansas City Chamber Choir, 1969-74, Chouteau Soc., 1985-97, U. Mo.-Kansas City Friends of Libr., 1988-92; bd. dirs. Mo. br. The Nature Conservancy, 1984-91. Sr. asst. surgeon USPHS, 1946-48. Named Dermatology Found. Practitioner of Yr., 1992; recipient Soc. for History of Natural History Founders' award, London, 2001. Fellow Am. Acad. Dermatology and Syphilology (dir. 1975-79, v.p. 1980); mem. Mo., Jackson County med. socs., Mo. Dermatol. Soc. (pres. 1974-75), Dermatology Found. (trustee 1978-83), Am. Ornithol. Union, Wilson Ornithol. Soc., Royal Australasian Ornithologists Union, Soc. Bibliography Natural History, Am. Dermatol. Assn., Alpha Delta Phi, Nu Sigma Nu. Presbyterian. Office: 6400 Prospect Ave Kansas City MO 64132-1180

SAUER, HARRY JOHN , JR. mechanical engineering educator, university administrator; b. St. Joseph, Mo., Jan. 27, 1935; s. Harry John and Marie Margaret (Witt) S.; m. Patricia Ann Zbierski, June 9, 1956; children: Harry John, Elizabeth Ann, Carl Andrew, Robert Mark, Katherine Anne, Deborah Elaine, Victoria Lynn, Valerie Joan, Joseph Gerard. BS, U. Mo., Rolla, 1956, MS, 1958; PhD, Kans. State U., 1963. Instr. mech. engring. Kans. State U., Manhattan, 1960-62; sr. engr., cons. Midwest Rsch. Inst., Kansas City, Mo., 1963-70; mem. faculty dept. mech. and aerospace engring. U. Mo., Rolla, 1957—, prof., 1966—, assoc. chmn., 1980-84, dean grad. study, 1984-92. Cons. in field; mem. Gov.'s Commn. on Energy Conservation, 1977; mem. Mo. Solar Energy Resource Panel, 1979-83; mem. Accreditation Bd. for Engring. and Tech. Co-author: Environmental Control Principles, 1975, 4th edit., 1985, Thermodynamics, 1981, Heat Pump Systems, 1983, Engineering Thermodynamics, 1985, Principles of Heating, Ventilating and Air Conditioning, 1991, 4th edit., 2001; contbr. articles to profl. jours. Pres. St. Patrick's Sch. Bd., 1970-72, St. Patrick's Parish Council, 1975-76. Recipient Ralph R. Teetor award Soc. Automotive Engrs., 1968; Hermann F. Spoehrer Meml. award St. Louis chpt. ASHRAE, 1979; also E. K. Campbell award of merit, 1983; Louise and Bill Holladay disting. fellow, 1999. Mem. ASME, ASHRAE (disting. svc. award 1981, exceptional svc. award 2001), NSPE, Soc. Automotive Engrs., Am. Soc. Engring. Edn., Mo. Soc. Profl. Engrs., Mo. Acad. Sci., Sigma Xi. Roman Catholic. Home: 10355 College Hills Dr Rolla MO 65401-7726 Office: Dept of Mech Engring U Mo Rolla MO 65401 E-mail: sauer@umr.edu.

SAUER, JEFF, university hockey coach; b. St. Paul; m. Jamie Sauer; children: Chip, Beth. BA in Sociology, Colo. Coll., 1965. Asst. hockey, baseball coach Colo. Coll., Colo. Springs, 1966-68, head coach hockey, 1971-82; asst.coach hockey U. Wis., Madison, 1968-71, head coach hockey, 1982—. Mem. U.S. Olympic Hockey Com., 1984; coach Olympic Festival, 1987, USA Select Team, Pravda Cup, Leningrad, Russia, 1989, Team USA, Goodwill Games, 1990, U.S. Nat. Team World Championships, 1995, U.S. Select Team, Tampere Cup, Finland, 1997, coach, organizer youth hockey camps in summer. Counselor Stan Mikita's Hockey Camp for Hearing Impaired, Chgo. Named We. Coll. Hockey Assn. Coach of Yr. 1972-73, 74-75 (Colo. Coll.); NCAA championship (Wis.) 1983, 90, WCHA championship 1987-88, 97-98, WCHA Playoff Championship, 1982-83, 87-88, 94-95. Office: U Wis/Kohl Ctr 601 W Dayton St Madison WI 53715-1206 E-mail: jbs@athletics.wisc.edu.

SAUER, MARK, professional sports team executive; b. Brooklyn, Nov. 17, 1946; m. Georgia Sauer; children: Peter, Alex. Bachelor's degree, U. Ill., 1968; MBA, Columbia U., 1971. V.p. Seven-Up Internat., 1976-80, Busch Entertainment Corp. subs. Anheuser-Busch, 1980-84; pres., CEO Civic Ctr. Corp. subs. Anheuser-Busch; dep. COO St. Louis Cardinals, exec. v.p., COO, 1989-91; pres. Kiel Ctr. Arena Project, St. Louis; pres., CEO Pitts. Pirates subs. Pitts. Assocs., 1991—, St. Louis Blues, 1996-. Vice chmn. St. Louis Blues Hockey Club, bd. dirs. Co-chmn. Pitts. Minority Bus. Opportunity Com. Mem. Greater Pitts. C. of C. (bd. dirs.). Office: Pitts Pirates 600 Stadium Cir Pittsburgh PA 15212-5731

SAUL, NORMAN EUGENE, history educator; b. LaFontaine, Ind., Nov. 26, 1932; s. Ralph Odis and Jessie (Neff) S.; m. Mary Ann Culwell, June 27, 1959; children: Alyssa, Kevin, Julia. B.A., Ind. U.- Bloomington, 1954; M.A., Columbia U., 1959, Ph.D., 1965; postgrad., Leningrad State U. (USSR), 1960-61. Asst. prof. Brown U., 1965-68; vis. assoc. prof. Northwestern U., 1969-70; assoc. prof. U. Kans., Lawrence, 1970-75, prof. history, 1975—, chmn. dept. history, 1981-89. Inst. Advanced Study, Princeton U., 2000. Author: Russia and the Mediterranean 1797-1807, 1970, Sailors in Revolt, 1978, Distant Friends: The United States and Russia, 1763-1867, 1991, Concord and Conflict: The United States and Russia, 1867-1914, 1996, War and Revolution: The United States and Russia, 1914-1921, 2001; editor: Russian-American Dialogue on Cultural Relations, 1776-1914, 1997. Fulbright scholar, London, 1954-55, Helsinki, 1968-69, Soviet Am. Exch. scholar Internat. Rsch. and Exch. Bd., Moscow, 1973-74, 91-92; fellow Ford Found., 1957-59, Hall Ctr. for Humanities, 1989, 95; recipient Byron Caldwell Smith Book award for Distant Friends Hall Ctr. for Humanities, 1993, Robert H. Ferrell book award for concert and conflict Soc. Historians Am. Fgn. Rels., 1997, Pub. Scholar award Kans. Humanities Coun., 1997, Higuchi Rsch. award U. Kans., 1997, Steeples award for Svc. to Kans., 2000, Herbert Hoover Libr. Assn. award, 2001. Mem. Am. Assn. Advancement of Slavic Studies, Kans. State Hist. Soc. Home: 1002 Crestline Dr Lawrence KS 66049-2607 E-mail: nsaul@ku.edu.

SAUL, WILLIAM EDWARD, civil engineering educator; b. N.Y.C., May 15, 1934; s. George James and Fanny Ruth (Murokh) S.; m. J. Muriel Held Eagleburger, May 11, 1976. BSCE, Mich. Tech. U., 1955, MSCE, 1961; PhD in Civil Engring., Northwestern U., 1964. Registerd profl. engr., Wis., Idaho, Mich., profl. structural engr., Idaho. Mech. engr. Shell Oil Co., New Orleans, 1955-59; instr. engring. mechanics Mich. Tech. U., Houghton, 1960-62; asst. prof. civil engring. U. Wis., Madison, 1964-67, assoc. prof., 1967-72, prof., 1972-84; dean, prof. civil engring. U. Idaho Coll. Engring., Moscow, 1984-90; prof. civil engring. Mich. State U., East Lansing, 1990—2000, chmn. dept. civil and environ. engring., 1990-95, chmn. emeritus, prof. emeritus, 2000. Cons. engr., 1961—; vis. prof. U. Stuttgart, Germany, 1970-71. Co-editor Conf. of Methods of Structural Analysis, 1976. Bd. dirs. Idaho Rsch. Found., 1984-90. Fulbright fellow 1970-71; von Humboldt scholar, 1970-71. Fellow ASCE (pres. Wis. sect. 1983-84), Mich. Soc. Profl. Engrs.; mem. NSPE, Internat. Assn. Bridge and Structural Engrs., Am. Concrete Inst., Am. Soc. Engring. Edn., Sigma Xi, Phi Kappa Phi, Tau Beta Pi, Chi Epsilon. Avocations: hiking, reading, travel, gadgets. Home: 1971 Cimarron Dr Okemos MI 48864-3905 Office: Mich State U 3546 Engring Bldg E East Lansing MI 48824

SAUNDERS, GEORGE LAWTON, JR. lawyer; b. Mulga, Ala., Nov. 8, 1931; s. George Lawton and Ethel Estell (York) S.; children: Kenneth, Ralph, Victoria; m. Terry M. Rose. B.A., U. Ala., 1956; J.D., U. Chgo., 1959. Bar: Ill. 1960. Law clk. to chief judge U.S. Ct. Appeals (5th cir.), Montgomery, Ala., 1959-60; law clk to Justice Hugo L. Black U.S. Supreme Ct., Washington, 1960-62; assoc. Sidley & Austin, Chgo., 1962-67, ptnr., 1967-90; founding ptnr. Saunders & Monroe, 1990—. With USAF, 1951-54. Fellow: ACLA; mem.: Chgo. Bar Assn., Ill. State Bar Assn., ABA, Law Club, Chgo. Club, Point-O-Woods Club, Quadrangle Club, Order of the Coif, Phi Beta Kappa. Democrat. Baptist. Home: 179 E Lake Shore Dr Chicago IL 60611-1306 Office: Saunders & Monroe 3160 NBC Tower 455 N Cityfront Plaza Dr Chicago IL 60611-5503

SAUNDERS, JOHN L. state agency administrator; Dir. Agr. Dept., Jefferson City, Mo. Office: Agr Dept PO Box 630 Jefferson City MO 65102-0630

SAUNDERS, KENNETH D. insurance company executive, consultant, arbitrator; b. Chgo., Jan. 4, 1927; s. Maurice and Mildred (Cochrane) S.; m. Jean S. Davies, Dec. 17, 1949; children: Karen Saunders Waugh, William Thomas. A.B., Dartmouth Coll., 1949. With Continental Casualty Co., Chgo., 1949-59, asst. v.p., 1957-59; exec. asst. Standard Accident Ins. Co., Detroit, 1959-62; with Combined Ins. Co. Am., Chgo., 1962-86, v.p., 1969-74, sr. v.p., 1974-86; with Rollins, Burdick, Hunter, 1986-87. With USMC, 1945-46. Mem. Tavern Club (Chgo.), Exmoor Country (Ill.) Club, John's Island (Fla.) Club. Office: 1418 Woodhill Dr Northbrook IL 60062-4661

SAUNDERS, LONNA JEANNE, lawyer, newscaster, talk show host; b. Cleve. d. Jack Glenn and Lillian Frances (Newman) Slaby. Student, Dartmouth Coll.; AB in Polit. Sci. with hons., Vassar Coll.; JD, Northwestern U., 1981; cert. advanced study in Mass Media, Stanford U., 1992. Bar: Ill. 1981. News dir., morning news anchor Sta. WKBK-AM, Keene, N.H., 1974-75; reporter Sta. KDKA-AM, Pitts., 1975; pub. affairs dir., news anchor Sta. WJW-AM, Cleve., 1975-76; helicopter traffic reporter WERE-AM Radio, 1976-77; morning news anchor Sta. WBBG-AM, 1978; talk host, news anchor Sta. WIND-AM, Chgo., 1978-82; atty. Arvey, Hodes, Costello & Burman, 1981-82; host, "The Stock Market Observer", news anchor WCIU-TV, 1982-85; staff atty. Better Govt. Assn., 1983-84; news anchor, reporter Sta. WBMX-FM, 1984-86; pvt. practice, 1985—; news anchor Sta. WKQX-FM, 1987. Instr. Columbia Coll., Chgo., 1987-90; guest talk host Sta. WMCA, N.Y.C., 1983, Sta. WMAQ, Chgo., 1988, Sta. WLS, Chgo., 1989, Sta. WWWE, Cleve., 1989, Sta. KVI, Seattle, 1994, WCBM-AM, Balt., 1996, WRC-AM, Wash., D.C., 1997; host, prodr. The Lively Arts, Cablevision Chgo., 1986; talk show host The Lonna Saunders Show, Sta. KIRO-AM, Seattle, 1995-96; news anchor, WTOP-AM Radio, Washington, D.C., 1996-97; talk host, "Today and Tomorrow show", WMAL-AM radio, Washington, D.C., 1997, freelance reporter, CBS Radio Network, N.Y.C., 1995—; writer, General Media, N.Y.C., 1996—; atty. Lawyers for Creative Arts, Chgo., 1985-91; guest columnist Gainesville (Fla.) Sun Newspaper, 1998-99; freelance writer Indians Ink mag., 1998—. Columnist Chgo. Life mag., 1986—; editl. bd. Jour. Criminal Law and Criminology, 1979-81; contbr. articles to profl. jours.; creator pub. affairs program WBBM-AM, Chgo., 1985. Recipient Akron Press Club award for best pub. affairs presentation, 1978; grantee Scripps Howard Found., 1978-81; AFTRA George Heller Meml. scholar, 1980-81. Fellow Am. Bar Found.; mem. ABA (mem. exec. coms. Lawyers and the Arts, Law and Media 1986-92, chmn. exec. com. Law and Media 1990-91, 91-92, Young Lawyers divsn. liaison to Forum Com. on Communications Law 1991-93, Commn. for Partnership Programs 1993-94, regional divsn. chair Forum on Communications Law 1995-96). Roman Catholic. Avocations: theater, piano, baseball.

SAUNDERS, MARY L. career officer; BS in Social Work, Tex. Woman's U., 1970; grad., Squadron Officer Sch., 1973; MA in Guidance and Counseling, Rider Coll., 1978; grad., Air War Coll., 1993; nat. security leadership course, Johns Hopkins U., 1997. Commd. 2d lt. USAF, 1971, advanced through grades to brigadier gen., 1997; air terminal ops. officer 610th Mil. Airlift Support Squadron, Yokota Air Base, Japan, 1973-75; dep. comdr., comdr. Mil. Air Traffic Coordinating Office Mil. Traffic Mgmt. Command, McGuire AFB, N.J., 1976-79; chief of transp. 6168th Combat Support Squadron, Taegu Air Base, South Korea, 1982-83; comdr. 475th Transp. Squadron, Yokota Air Base, Japan, 1983-84; transp. staff officer Joint Deployment Agy., MacDill AFB, Fla., 1986-88, J-5, U.S. Transp. Command, Scott AFB, Ill., 1988-90; chief contingency plans divsn. J-5, U.S. So. Command, Quarry Heights, Panam, 1990-92; chief logistic plans Hdqs. Air Force Res., Robins AFB, Ga., 1993-96; dir. transp. Office Dep. Chief Staff Installations/Logistics Hdqs. USAF, The Pentagon, Washington, 1996-98; comdr. Def. Supply Ctr. Columbus Def. Logistics Agy., Columbus, Ohio, 1998—. Decorated Legion of Merit, Def. Meritorious Svc. medal with oak leaf cluster, Meritorious Svc. medal with 2 oak leaf clusters. Mem. AAUS, NAFE, Air Force Assn., Nat. Def. Transp. Assn. Office: Def Supply Ctr Columbus PO Box 3990 Columbus OH 43216-5000

SAUNDERS, PHILIP D. professional basketball coach; b. Cleve., Feb. 23, 1955; m. Debbie Saunders; children: Ryan, Mindy, Rachel and Kimberly (twins). Student, U. Minn. Asst. coach U. Minn Golden Gophers, 1982-86, U. Tulsa, 1986-88; head coach Continental Basketball Assn. Rapid City (S.D.) Thrillers, 1988-89, La Crosse (Wis.) Catbirds, 1989-94, gen. mgr., 1991-93, team pres., 1991-94; head coach Continental Basketball Assn. Sioux Falls (S.D.) Skyforce; gen. mgr., head coach Minn. Timberwolves, 1995—. Named CBA Coach of the Yr., 1989, 92. Office: Minn Timberwolves 600 1st Ave N Minneapolis MN 55403-1400

SAUNDERS, TERRY ROSE, lawyer; b. Phila., July 13, 1942; d. Morton M. and Esther (Hauptman) Rose; m. George Lawton Saunders Jr., Sept. 21, 1975. BA, Barnard Coll., 1964; JD, NYU, 1973. Bar: D.C. 1973, Ill. 1976, U.S. Dist. Ct. (no. dist.) Ill. 1976, U.S. Ct. Appeals (7th cir.) 1976, U.S.

Supreme Ct. 1983. Assoc. Williams & Connolly, Washington, 1973-75, Jenner & Block, Chgo., 1975-80, ptnr., 1981-86, Susman, Saunders & Buehler, Chgo., 1987-94; pvt. practice Law Offices of Terry Rose Saunders, 1995—. Author: (with others) Securities Fraud: Litigating Under Rule 10b-5, 1989. Recipient Robert B. McKay award NYU Sch. Law. Mem. ABA (co-chair class actions and derivative suits com. sect. litig. 1992-95, task force on merit selection of judges, co-chair consumer and personal righs itig. com. sect. litig.), Ill. State Bar Assn., Chgo. Bar Assn., Order of Coif, Union League Club. Office: 30 N La Salle St Chicago IL 60602-2590 E-mail: trslawfirm@aol.com.

SAUNDERS, WARNER, newscaster; b. Chgo. m. Sadako Saunders. BA, Xavier U.; MA, Northwestern U. Instr. sociology Nat. Coll. Edn. Ind. U. Northwest, Gary, Ind., Northeastern Ill. U.; dir. cmty. affairs, host Common Ground Sta. WBBM-TV; with Sta. WMAQ-TV, Chgo., 1980—, sports anchor, reporter, 1982—89, host Warner pub. affairs talk show, 1983—90, co-anchor 6 pm and 10 pm newscasts. Recipient 16 Chgo. Emmy awards in news and programming. Mem.: Chgo. Assn. Black Journalists (past pres., Hull House Jane Addams award 1999). Office: NBC 454 N Columbus Dr Chicago IL 60611*

SAUNDERS, W(ARREN) PHILLIP, JR. economics educator, consultant, author; b. Morgantown, W.Va., Sept. 3, 1934; s. Warren Phillip and Thelma Marie (Dotson) S.; m. Nancy Lee Trainor, June 16, 1956; children: Kathleen M., Kevin W., Keith A., Kent T., Kristine A. BA, Pa. State U., 1956; MA, U. Ill., 1957; PhD, MIT, 1964. Instr. econs. Bowdoin Coll., Brunswick, Maine, 1961-62; rsch. assoc., from asst. to assoc. prof. econs. Carnegie-Mellon U., Pitts., 1962-70; prof. econs. Ind. U., Bloomington, 1970—; assoc. dean Coll. of Arts and Scis. Ind. U., 1974-78, chmn. dept. econs., 1988-92. Cons. Agy. for Instructional Tech., Bloomington, 1976-78, 81-84, 92-93. Author: (books) Political Dimension of Labor-Management Relations, 1986; author, editor: Framework for Teaching Basic Economic Concepts, 1995; (Workbooks) Introduction to Macroeconomics (18th edit.), 1998, Introduction to Microeconomics (18th edit.), 1998; contbr. articles to Am. Econ. Rev., 1964—. Chmn. staff-parish rels. com. First United Meth. Ch., Bloomington, 1982-94. Recipient Vilard award for disting. rsch., Nat. Assn. Econ. Educators, N.Y.C., 1986, Leavey award for edn. Freedoms Found., Valley Forge, Pa., 1986, Disting. Svc. award. Nat. Coun. Econ. Edn., 1995. Mem. Am. Econ. Assn., Midwest Econ. Assn. (1st v.p. 1988-89), Soc. Econs. Educators (pres. 1992-93). Home: 3725 E Brownridge Rd Bloomington IN 47401-4209 Office: Ind Univ Dept Econs Bloomington IN 47405 E-mail: saunders@indiana.edu.

SAVAGE, BLAIR DEWILLIS, astronomer, educator; b. Mt. Vernon, N.Y., June 7, 1941; s. Rufus Llewellyn and Christine (Burney) S.; m. Linda Jean Wilber, June 25, 1966; children: Reid Hamilton, Keith Wesley. B.Engring. Physics, Cornell U., 1964; M.S., Princeton U., 1966, Ph.D., 1967. Research assoc. Princeton U., 1967-68; asst. prof. U. Wis., Madison, 1968-73, assoc. prof., 1973-78, prof. astronomy, 1978—, chmn. dept., 1982-85, Karl Kansky prof. astronomy, 1999—. Vis. fellow Joint Inst. Lab. Astrophysics, Boulder, Colo., 1974-75; investigator space astronomy projects NASA, 1968—; bd. pres. Wis., Ind., Yale Nat. Optical Astronomy Obs. Telescope Consortium, 1990-96. Contbr. articles to profl. jours. Peyton fellow Princeton U., 1964-66; NASA fellow Princeton U., 1966-67; research grantee NASA, NSF, 1968— Mem. Am. Astron. Soc. (councilor 1994-97), Internat. Astron. Union, Nat. Rsch. Coun. (space sci. bd. mem. 1985-88, chmn. com. for space astronomy and astrophysics 1985-88, astronomy and astrophysics survey com. 1989-90, com. for astronomy and astrophysics 1998—), Assn. for Univ. Rsch. in Astronomy (bd. dirs. 1989-92), Tau Beta Pi. Home: 4015 Hiawatha Dr Madison WI 53711-3037 Office: Dept Astronomy U Wis 475 N Charter St Madison WI 53706-1507

SAVAGE, TERRY, television personality, columnist; Grad., U. Mich. Registered investment advisor stocks and commodity futures. Columnist Chgo. Sun Times, Chgo.; personal fin. columnist Barron's Online. Bd. dirs. McDonald's Corp.; spkr. in field. Host Money Talks; author: Terry Savage's New Money Strategies for the 90s, Terry Savage Talks Money: The Common-Sense Guide to Money Matters; columnist Chgo. Sun-Times. Dir. Chgo. Mus. Sci. and Industry, Northwestern Meml. Hosp. Corp., Econ. Club Chgo., Execs. Club Chgo., Jr. Achievement Ill., Ill. Coun. on Econ. Edn., Women's Bus. Devel. Ctr. Recipient Outstanding Consumer Journalism award Nat. Press Club, 1987, Dir.'s Choice award, 1993, Emmy award; Woodrow Wilson fellow in Am. history and econs. Mem. Phi Beta Kappa. Office: Chgo Sun-Times Hollinger Inc 401 N Wabash Ave Chicago IL 60611-5642 E-mail: savage@suntimes.com.

SAVAGEAU, MICHAEL ANTONIO, microbiology and immunology educator; b. Fargo, N.D., Dec. 3, 1940; s. Antonio Daniel and Jennie Ethelwin (Kaushagen) S.; m. Ann Elisa Birky, July 22, 1967; children— Mark Edward, Patrick Daniel, Elisa Marie B.S., U. Minn., 1962; M.S., U. Iowa, 1963; Ph.D., Stanford U., 1967, postgrad., 1968-70, UCLA, 1967-68. Research fellow UCLA, Los Angeles, 1967-68; lectr. Stanford U., Calif., 1968-69; from asst. to full prof. U. Mich., Ann Arbor, 1970—; sr. research fellow Max Planck Inst., Göttingen, Fed. Republic of Germany, 1976-77; fellow Australian Nat. U., Canberra, 1983-84; prof. microbiology and immunology U. Mich., Ann Arbor, 1978—, chmn. dept., 1982-85, 92—, prof. chem. engring., dir. cellular biotech. labs., 1988-91, dir. NIH tng. program in cellular biotechnology, 1991-92, dir. bioinformatics program, 1998-2001, Nicolas Rashevsky disting. univ. prof., 2002—. Cons. Upjohn Co., Kalamazoo, 1979—81, NIH, Bethesda, Md., 1981—82, Bethesda, 1994—95, Bethesda, 1997—2000, Synergen, Boulder, Colo., 1985—87, NRC/Howard Hughes Med. Inst., 1997—, NSF, 1999—, Swedish Found. for Strategic Rsch., 2001—02; assoc. mem. Ctr. for Integrative Genetics, Agrl. U. Norway, 2001—; mem. com. on progress and promise of sys. biology NAS, 2001—; vis. prof. dept. biochemistry U. Ariz., Tucson, 1994; mem. com. on progress and promise of sys. biology, NAS, 2002; cons. Swedish Found. for Strategic Rsch., Stockholm, 2001—02, Cigene Ctr. for Integrated Genetics, Agrl. U. Norway, Aas, 2001—. Author: Biochemical Systems Analysis, 1976; mem. editl. bd. Math. Scis., 1976-95, editor, 1995—; mem. editl. bd. Jour. Theoretical Biology, 1989-96, mem. adv. bd., 1996—; mem. editl. bd. Nonlinear World, 1992—, Nonlinear Digest, 1992—, inScight, 1998—, BioComplexity, 2000—; co-editor Math. Ecology, 1986—. Australian Nat. U. fellow, 1983-84; Guggenheim Found., fellow N.Y.C., 1976-77; Fulbright Found., sr. research fellow, Washington, Fed. Republic of Germany, 1976-77; sr. fellow Mich. Soc. Fellows, 1990-94; grantee NIH, NSF, ONR, 1964—. Fellow AAAS; mem. Am. Chem. Soc., Am. Soc. Microbiology, IEEE (sr.), Soc. Indsl. and Applied Math., Biophys. Soc., Soc. Gen. Physiologists, Soc. Math. Biology (bd. dirs. 1987-90), Internat. Fedn. Nonlinear Analysts (bd. dirs. 1997—). Office: U Mich Dept Microbiology and Immunology 5641 Med Sci II Ann Arbor MI 48109-0620

SAVARD, DENIS JOSEPH, former professional hockey player, coach; b. Pointe Gatineau, Que., Can., Feb. 4, 1961; With Chgo. Black Hawks, 1980-90, 96-97; ret., 1997; asst. coach devel. Chgo. Black Hawks, 1997—; with Montreal Canadiens, 1990-93, Tampa Bay Lightning, 1993-96. Mem. Stanley Cup championship team 1983; player NHL All-Star games, 1982-84, 86, 88, 91. Recipient Michel Briere trophy, 1979-80. Office: Chgo Blackhawks 1901 W Madison St Chicago IL 60612-2459

SAVELKOUL, DONALD CHARLES, retired lawyer; b. Mpls., July 29, 1917; s. Theodore Charles and Edith (Lindgren) S.; m. Mary Joan Holland, May 17, 1941; children: Jeffrey Charles, Jean Marie, Edward Joseph. BA magna cum laude, U. Minn., 1939; JD cum laude, William Mitchell Coll. Law, 1951. Bar: Minn. 1951, U.S. Dist. Ct. Minn. 1952, U.S. Ct. Appeals (8th cir.) 1960, U.S. Supreme Ct. 1971. Adminstrv. work various U.S. govt. depts., including Commerce, War, Labor, Wage Stblzn. Bd., 1940-51; mcpl. judge Fridley, Minn., 1952-53; pvt. practice law Mpls., St. Paul, Fridley, 1951-96; ret., 1997. Chmn. bd. Fridley State Bank, 1962-95; pres. Banrein, Inc., 1962-95, Babbscha Co., 1962-95; mem. faculty William Mitchell Coll. Law, 1952-59, corp. mem., 1956-99; sec. Fridley Recreation and Svc. Co., 1955-97; mem. Minn. Legislature, 1967-69. Mem. Gov.'s Com. Workers Compensation, 1965-67, Gov.'s Adv. Coun. on Employment Security, 1957-60, 62-63; gen. counsel Minn. AFL-CIO Fedn. Labor, 1952-71. 1st lt. AUS, 1943-46. Decorated Bronze Star; recipient Disting. Alumni award Coll. Liberal Arts U. Minn., 1995, Outstanding Alumnus award William Mitchell Coll. Law Alumni/ae Assn., 1997. Mem. ABA, Minn. Bar Assn. (chmn. 1957-58, bd. dirs. 1958-62, 68-69, labor law sect.), Justice William Mitchell Soc., Am. Legion, U. Minn. Pres.'s Club, Phi Beta Kappa. Roman Catholic. Office: 916 Moore Lake Dr W Fridley MN 55432-5148

SAVIA, ALFRED, conductor; b. Livingston, NJ; Asst. condr. Omaha Symphony, 1976-78, Fla. Symphony Orch., 1978-78, assoc. condr., 1979-86, prin. guest condr., 1986-87; asst. condr. Colo. Philharm., 1979-81; resident condr. New Orleans Symphony, 1986-88, assoc. condr., 1988-89; resident condr. Philharm. Orch. Fla. (now Fla. Philharm. Orch.), 1987-89; music dir. Evansville (Ind.) Philharm., 1989—; assoc. condr. Indpls. Symphony Orch., 1990-96, artistic dir., prin. condr. summer season, 1991-96. Guest condr. Indpls. Symphony, New Orleans Symphony, Kitchener-Waterloo Symphony, Can., Presdl. Symphony Ankara, Turkey, Aalborg Symphony, Denmark, Korea Philharm., San Antonio Symphony, Alabama Symphony, Hudson Valley Philharm., Fla. Symphony Orch., Colo. Philharm., Denver Chamber Orch., Lubbock Symphony, Nebr. Chamber Orch., Miami Ballet, Orlando Opera Co., St. Louis Symphony, R.I. Philharm., Nat. Repertory Orch., Ill. Symphony, Grant Park Symphony, Osnabruck Symphony Orch., others. Recipient High Fidelity Musical Am. Young Artist award, 1985. Office: Evansville Philharm Orch PO Box 84 Evansville IN 47701-0084 also: Parker Artists 382 Central Park W Apt 9G New York NY 10025-6032

SAVIANO, ANGELO, state legislator; b. May 20, 1958; m. Julia Thalji, 1987; 1 child, Bianca. BA, DePaul U., 1980. Supr. Leyden Twp., Franklin Park, Ill., 1989-93; Ill. state rep. Dist. 77, 1993—. Office: Ill Ho of Reps State Capitol 2112 N Stratton Bldg Springfield IL 62706-0001

SAVILLE, PAT, state senate official; b. Marysville, Kans., Sept. 10, 1943; Sec. Kans. Senate, Topeka, 1991—. Mem.: Am. Soc. Legis. Clks. and Secs. (past pres.). Office: Kans Senate State House 360 East Topeka KS 66612 E-mail: pats@senate.state.ks.us.

SAVINELL, ROBERT FRANCIS, engineering educator; b. Cleve., May 26, 1950; s. Robert D. and Lotte R. Savinell; m. Coletta A. Savinell, Aug. 23, 1974; children: Teresa, Robert, Mark. BSChemE, Cleve. State U., 1973; MS, U. Pitts., 1974, PhD, 1977. Registered profl. engr., Ohio. Rsch. engr. Diamond Shamrock Corp., Painesville, Ohio, 1977-79; assoc. prof. U. Akron, 1979-86; prof. Case Western Reserve U., Cleve., 1986—, dir. Ernest B. Yeager Ctr. for Electrochem. Scis., 1991—, assoc. dean engring., 1998—, interim dean of engring., 2000, dean engring., 2001. Divsn. editor Jour. Electrochem. Soc., 1988-91; N.Am. editor Jour. Applied Electrochemistry, 1991-97; contbr. articles to profl. jours. Named Presdl. Young Investigator, NSF, Washington, 1984-89, Outstanding Engring. Alumnus, Cleve. State U., 1984. Fellow Electrochem. Soc.; mem. AIChE (program chmn. 1986-92), Electrochem. Soc. (divsn. officer 1992—), Internat. Soc. Electrochemistry (v.p. 1995-98). Avocations: sailing, skiing. Office: Case Western Reserve U AW Smith Bldg Dept Chem Eng 10900 Euclid Ave Cleveland OH 44106-4901 E-mail: Rfs2@PO.cwru.edu.

SAVINI, DAVE, reporter; BA Broadcast Journalism, U. Dayton, 1989. Intern in investigative journalism NBC 5, Chgo., 1988—90; Raleigh bur. chief, investigative reporter Sta. WNCT-TV, Greenville, NC, 1990—92; investigative reporter, weekend anchor Sta. WROC-TV, Rochester, NY; investigative reporter NBC 5, Chgo., 1993—. Named Best Reporter, AP, 1995; recipient 2 Chgo. Emmy awards, 1998, Emmy for Outstanding Achievement award, 1999, 2 Peter Lisagor awards, 2000, award, Chgo. City Coun., Chgo. Emmy award, 1997, RTNDA award, Peter Lisagor award, 15 awards, AP, 5 Regional Radio & TV News Dirs. Assn. awards, 1999. Office: NBC 454 N Columbus Dr Chicago IL 60611*

SAWATSKY, BEN, church administrator; Exec. dir. Evangelical Free Church Mission, Bloomington, Minn., 1992. Office: The Evang Free Ch Am 901 E 78th St Bloomington MN 55420-1334

SAWYER, HOWARD JEROME, physician; b. Detroit, Nov. 17, 1929; s. Howard C. and Dorothy M. (Risley) S.; m. Janet Carol Hausen, July 24, 1954; children: Daniel William, Teresa Louise BA in Philosophy, Wayne State U., 1952, MD, 1962, postdoctoral, 1969-72. Diplomate Am. Bd. Preventive Medicine in Occupational and Environ. Medicine. Intern William Beaumont Hosp., Royal Oak, Mich., 1962-63, resident in surgery, 1963-64; chief physician gen. parts div. Ford Motor Co., 1964-66; med. dir. metall. products dept. Gen. Electric Co., Detroit, 1966-73, chem. and metal div., 1972-73; staff physician Detroit Indsl. Clinic, Inc., 1973-74; pres., med. dir. OccuMed Assocs., Inc., Farmington Hills, Mich., 1974-84; dir. OccuMed div. Med. Service Corp. Am., Southfield, 1984-86; dir. occupational, environ. and preventive medicine Henry Ford Hosp., 1987-91; pres. Sawyer Med. Cons., P.C., 1991—. Adj. asst. prof. occupational and environ. health scis. Wayne State U., 1974— , lectr. occpl. and environ. medicine Sch. of Medicine, 1998—; lectr. Sch. Pub. Health, U. Mich., Ann Arbor, 1977-88 ; cons. med. dir. St. Joe Minerals Corp., 1976-87, Chesbrough Pond's Inc., 1979-83; cons. Anaconda, Bendix, Borg Warner Chems., Fed. Mogul, Gen. Electric, Gt. Lakes Chems., other corps. Contbr. articles to profl. jours., chpts. to textbooks. Fellow Am. Coll. Preventive Medicine, Am. Occupational and Environ. Med. Assn., Mich. Occupational and Environ. Med. Assn. (pres. 1986), Am. Acad. Occupational Medicine; mem. AMA, Detroit Occupational Physicians Assn. (pres. 1984), Mich. State Med. Soc., Oakland County Med. Soc., Am. Indsl. Hygiene Assn., Mich. Indsl. Hygiene Soc. E-mail: buzsaw@mediaone.net.

SAWYER, JOHN, professional football team executive; s. Charles S.; m. Ruth Sawyer; children: Anne, Elizabeth, Catherine, Mary. Pres., part owner Cin. Bengals, Nat. Football League; pres. J. Sawyer Co., Ohio, Miss., Mont., Wyo.; vice pres Cin. Bengals. Office: J Sawyer Co Provident Towers Cincinnati OH 45202-3717 also: Cin Bengals One Bengals Dr Cincinnati OH 45204

SAWYER, RAYMOND TERRY, lawyer; b. Cleve., Oct. 1, 1943; s. R. Terry and Fanny Katherine (Young) S.; m. Katherine Margaret Schneider, Aug. 5, 1972; children: Margaret Young, John Terry. BA, Yale U., 1965; LLB, Harvard U., 1968. Bar: Ohio 1969, U.S. Dist. Ct. (no. dist.) Ohio 1970. Assoc. Thompson Hine LLP, Cleve., 1968-76, ptnr., 1976—83, 1986—2001, chmn. bus. transactions and org. dept., 1998—2001, of counsel, 2002—; exec. dir. Ohio Housing Fin. Agy., Columbus, 1983-84; counsel to gov. State of Ohio, 1984, chief of staff, 1985-86, chmn. Gov.'s commn. on housing, 1989-90. Bd. dirs. Premix, Inc., North Kingsville, Ohio. Vol. VISTA, East Palo Alto, Calif., 1968—69; mem. Tech. Leadership Coun., 1987—95, Leadership Cleve., 1986—87, Cleve. Found. Study Commn. on Med. Rsch. Edn., 1991—92; chmn. George W. Codrington Charitable Found.; mem. Ohio Bd. Regents, Columbus, 1987—96, chmn., 1992—93; trustee Cleve. Ballet, 1987—2000; trustee Cleve. Orch., 1993—; mem. exec. com. MetroHealth Sys., 1998—; mem. Julliard Coun. Julliard Sch.; mem. pres.'s adv. coun. Case Western Res. U. Named Man of Yr. Womanspace, 1982. Mem. ABA, Ohio State Bar Assn. (chair corp. law com. 1993-95), Clevel. Bar Assn., Yale U. Alumni Assn. (pres. Cleve. chpt. 1980-81), Assn. Yale Alumni (del. 1996-99). Democrat. Presbyterian. Office: Thompson Hine LLP 3900 Key Ctr Cleveland OH 44114-1216

SAWYER, ROBERT MCLARAN, history educator; b. St. Louis, Nov. 12, 1929; s. Lee McLaran and Harrie (Alcock) S.; m. Patricia Ann Covert, Nov. 23, 1955; children— Ann Marie, Lee McLaran, Gail Louise. B.S., S.E. Mo. State Coll., 1952; M.A., U. Ill., 1953; Ph.D., U. Mo., 1966. Tchr. Rolla (Mo.) Public Schs., 1955; asst. prof., then asso. prof. history U. Mo., Rolla., 1956-67; mem. faculty U. Nebr., Lincoln, 1967—, prof. history of edn., 1969—, chmn. dept. history and philosophy of edn., 1975-81; mem. council U. Nebr. (Coll. Arts and Scis.), 1979—. Vis. prof. Ark. State U., Jonesboro, summer 1966; proposal reviewer Nat. Endowment Humanities, 1979 Author: The History of the University of Nebraska, 1929-1969, 1973, The Many Faces of Teaching, 1987, The Art and Politics of College Teaching, 1992, The Black Student's Guide to College Success, 1993, The Handbook of College Teaching, 1994; also articles, revs. Served with AUS, 1953-55. Mem. Orgn. Am. Historians, History Edn. Soc., Am. Ednl. Studies Assn., Soc. Profs. Edn., Phi Alpha Theta, Phi Delta Kappa. Home: 2640 S 35th St Lincoln NE 68506-6623 Office: Univ Nebr 29 Henzlik Hall Lincoln NE 68588

SAWYER, THOMAS C. congressman; b. Akron, Ohio, Aug. 15, 1945; m. Joyce Handler, 1968; 1 child, Amanda. BA, U. Akron, 1968, MA, 1970. Pub. sch. tchr., Ohio; adminstr. state sch. for delinquent boys; legis. agt. Ohio Pub. Utilities Commn.; mem. Ohio House Reps., Columbus, 1977-83; mayor City of Akron, 1984-86; mem. U.S. Congress from 14th Ohio dist., Washington, 1987—; mem. energy and commerce com. Democrat. Office: US Ho of Reps 1414 Longworth Hob Washington DC 20515-3514 also: District Office 411 Wolf Ledges Parkway, Suite 105 Akron OH 44311*

SAWYERS, ELIZABETH JOAN, librarian, administrator; b. San Diego, Dec. 2, 1936; d. William Henry and Elizabeth Georgiana (Price) S. A.A., Glendale Jr. Coll., 1957; B.A. in Bacteriology, UCLA, 1959, M.L.S., 1961. Asst. head acquisition sect. Nat. Library Medicine, Bethesda, Md., 1962-63, head acquisition sect., 1963-66, spl. asst. to chief tech. services div., 1966-69, spl. asst. to assoc. dir. for library ops., 1969-73; asst. dir. libraries for tech. services SUNY-Stony Brook, 1973-75; dir. Health Scis. Library Ohio State U., Columbus, 1975-90, spl. asst. to dir. Univ. librs., 1990—. Mem. Assn. Acad. Health Scis. Library Dirs. (sec./treas. 1981-83, pres. 1983-84), Med. Library Assn., Am. Soc. for Info. Sci., Spl. Libraries Assn., ALA Office: Ohio State Univ Librs 1858 Neil Ave Columbus OH 43210-1225

SAWYIER, DAVID R. lawyer; b. Chgo., Feb. 2, 1951; BA, Harvard U., 1972, JD, 1977; MA, Oxford U., 1974; diploma law, Cambridge U., 1979. Bar: Ill. 1977, D.C. 1978. Law clerk U.S. Ct. Appeals D.C. cir., 1977-78; ptnr. Sidley & Austin, Chgo. Mem. ABA (bus. law sect.), Chgo. Bar Assn. (futures sect.). Office: Sidley & Austin Bank One Plz 425 W Surf St Apt 605 Chicago IL 60657-6139

SAXENMEYER, MARK HAROLD, television news reporter; b. Neptune, N.J., June 19, 1966; BA in Broadcast Journalism, U. Wis., Madison, 1989. Reporter KOVR-TV (formerly ABC, now CBS), Sacramento, 1989-93; spl. projects reporter WFLD-TV (Fox), Chgo., 1993—. Recipient Emmy awards, 1993-94, 96, Associated Press award, 1991, 93, 94, 95, 97, United Press Internat. award, 1995, 96, 97, alumni achievement award Minn. Pub. Schs., 1997. Home: 474 N Lake Shore Dr Chicago IL 60611-3400 Office: WFLD-TV 205 N Michigan Ave Chicago IL 60601-5927*

SAXTON, WILLIAM MARVIN, lawyer; b. Joplin, Mo., Feb. 14, 1927; s. Clyde Marvin and Lea Ann (Farnan) S.; m. Helen Grace Klinefelter, June 1, 1974; children: Sherry Lynn, Patricia Ann Painter, William Daniel, Michael Lawrence. A.B., U. Mich., 1949, J.D., 1952. Bar: Mich. Mem. firm Love, Snyder & Lewis, Detroit, 1952-53, Butzel, Long, Detroit, 1953—, dir., chmn., CEO, 1989-96, dir. emeritus, 1997—. Lectr. Inst. Continuing Legal Edn.; sec., bd. dirs. Fritz Broadcasting, Inc., 1983-97; mem. mediation tribunal hearing panel for 3d Jud. Dist. Mich., 1989—, 6th Jud. Dist., 1994—. Trustee Detroit Music Hall Ctr. Soc. for the Performing Arts, 1984-99; trustee Hist. Soc. U.S. Dist. Ct. (ea. dist.) Mich., 1992-95, pres., 1993-95. Recipient Distinguished award Mich. Road Builders Assn., 1987. Master of Bench Emeritus Am. Inn of Court; fellow Am. Coll. Trial Lawyers, Am. Bar Found., Am. Coll. Labor and Employment Lawyers, Mich. Bar Found.; mem. ABA, FBA, Detroit Bar Assn. (dir. 1974-79, Goodnow Pres.'s award 1996), Mich. Bar Assn. (atty. discipline panel, Disting. Svc. award 1998), Detroit Indsl. Rels. Rsch. Assn. (treas. 1980—, v.p. 1982, pres. 1984-85), Mich. Young Lawyers (pres. 1954-55), Am. Law Inst., Indsl. Rels. Rsch. Assn. Am. Arbitration Assn., U.S. 6th Cir. Ct. Appeals (life, mem. jud. conf., mem. bicentennial com.), Am. Inn Ct., Cooley Club, Renaissance Club, Detroit Golf Club (dir. 1983-89), Detroit Athletic Club. Office: Butzel Long 150 W Jefferson Ave Ste 900 Detroit MI 48226-4416

SAYATOVIC, WAYNE PETER, manufacturing company executive; b. Cleve., Feb. 8, 1946; m. Janice Elaine Zajac; children: Jason Scott, Jamie Elizabeth. BA in Econs., Syracuse U., 1967, MBA in Fin., 1969, fin. mgmt. program, 1969—72. Fin. and cost acctg. mgr. Lubriquip divsn. Houdaille Industries Inc., Solon, Ohio, 1972—88, contr. Hydraulics divsn. Buffalo, 1975-77, contr. Strippit divsn. Akron, 1977-79, treas. Ft. Lauderdale, Fla., 1979-86, v.p., treas., sec. Northbrook, Ill., 1986-88, IDEX Corp., Northbrook, 1988—, v.p. fin., CFO, sec., 1992-94, sr. v.p. fin., CFO, sec., 1994-98, sr. v.p. fin., CFO, 1998—. Mem. Mfrs.' Alliance for Productivity & Innovation (fin. coun.). Office: IDEX Corp 630 Dundee Rd Ste 400 Northbrook IL 60062-2745

SAYERS, GALE, computer company executive, retired professional football player; b. Wichita, Kans., May 30, 1943; s. Roger Earl and Bernice (Ross) S.; m. Ardythe Elaine Bullard, Dec. 1, 1973; children: Gale Lynne, Scott Aaron, Timothy Gale, Gaylon, Guy, Gary. Student phys. edn., Kans. U., N.Y. Inst. Finance. Running back Chgo. Bears Profl. Football Team, 1965-72; then asst. to athletic dir. Kans. U.; athletic dir. So. Ill. U., to 1981; v.p. mktg. Computer Suppy by Sayers, Northfield, Ill., 1984-86; pres. Crest Computer Supply Co., Skokie, 1986—; now pres., ceo Sayers Computer Source, Mt. Prospect. Columnist Chgo. Daily News. Author: (with Al Silverman) I Am Third, 1970. Co-chmn. legal def. fund sports com. NAACP; co-ordinator Reach-Out program, Chgo.; hon. chmn. Am. Cancer Soc.; commr. Chgo. Park Dist. Recipient numerous awards for playing, also holder numerous Nat. Football League records; named to Pro Football Hall of Fame, 1977 Mem. Kappa Alpha Psi. Office: Sayers Computer Source 1150 Feehanville Dr Mount Prospect IL 60056-6007

SAYERS, MARTIN PETER, pediatric neurosurgeon; b. Big Stone Gap, Va., Jan. 2, 1922; s. Delbert Bancroft and Loula (Thompson) S.; m. Marjorie W. Garvin, May 8, 1943; children: Daniel Garvin Sayers, Stephen Putnam Sayers, Julia Hathaway Sayers Bolton, Elaine King Sayers Buck. B.A., Ohio State U., 1943, M.D., 1945; postgrad., U. Pa., 1948-51. Intern Phila. Gen. Hosp., 1945-46; resident in neurosurgery U. Pa. Hosps., Phila., 1948-51; practice medicine specializing in neurosurgery Columbus, Ohio, 1951—; mem. faculty Ohio State U., 1951-87, clin. prof. neurosurgery, 1968-87, emeritus, chief dept. pediatric neurosurgery, 1960-87. Cons. Bur. Crippled Children Services Ohio.; Neurosurgeon Project Hope, Ecuador, 1964, Ceylon, 1968, Cracow, Poland, 1979 Served as lt. jr. grade M.C.,

USN, 1946-48. Mem. Am. Assn. Neurol. Surgeons (chmn. pediatric sect.), Congress Neurol. Surgeons (pres.), Neurosurg. Soc. Am. (pres.), Am. Soc. Pediatric Neurosurgery, Soc. Neurol. Surgeons. Office: 931 Chatham Ln Columbus OH 43221-2417

SAYRE, ROBERT FREEMAN, English language educator; b. Columbus, Ohio, Nov. 6, 1933; s. Harrison M. and Mary (White) S.; (divorced); children— Gordon, Nathan, Laura; m. Hutha Refle, May 7, 1988. BA, Wesleyan U., Middletown, Conn., 1955; PhD, Yale U., 1962. Instr. English U. Ill., Urbana, 1961-63; Fulbright lectr. Lund (Sweden) U., 1963-65; faculty U. Iowa, 1965-72, prof. English, 1972-98, prof. emeritus, 1998—. Dir. inter-profl. seminars NEH, 1978, 79; Fulbright lectr. Montpellier, France, 1984; exch. prof. U. Copenhagen, 1988-89; mem. adv. bd. Leopold Ctr. for Sustainable Agr., 1994—, chair, 1996—. Author: The Examined Self: Benjamin Franklin, Henry Adams and Henry James, 1964, Adventures, Rhymes and Designs of Vachel Lindsay, 1968; Thoreau and the American Indians, 1977; editor: A Week on the Concord and Merrimac Rivers, Walden, The Maine Woods, Cape Cod (H.D. Thoreau), 1985, Take This Exit: Rediscovering the Iowa Landscape, 1989, New Essays on Walden, 1992, American Lives: An Anthology of Autobiographical Writing, 1994, Recovering the Prairie, 1999, Take the Next Exit, 2000; contbr. articles to profl. jours. Guggenheim fellow, 1973-74. Mem. Am. Studies Assn., MLA.

SCALES, FREDA S. dean, nursing educator; BSN, Okla. Bapt. U., 1965; MSN, Ind. U., 1970; PhD, Purdue U., 1977. Mem. staff faculty Sch. Nursing Ind. U., Inpls., 1970-82; dean Coll. Nursing Valparaiso (Ind.) U., 1982—. Mem. ANA, Am. Assn. Coll. Nursing, Nat. League Nursing. Office: Valparaiso U Coll Nursing Valparaiso IN 46383 Fax: 219-464-5425.

SCALETTA, PHILLIP RALPH, III, lawyer; b. Iowa City, Dec. 18, 1949; s. Phillip Jasper and Helen M. (Beedle) S.; m. Karen Lynn Scaletta, May 13, 1973; children: Phillip, Anthony, Alexander. BSIM, MS, Purdue U., 1972; JD, Ind. U., 1975. Bar: Ind. 1975, U.S. Dist. Ct. Ind. 1975, Ill. 1993. Assoc. Ice Miller Donadio & Ryan, Indpls., 1975-81, ptnr., 1981—. Contbr. articles to profl. jours. Chmn. Ind. Continuing Legal Edn. Found., Indpls., 1989; mem. Environ. Quality Control Water Com., 1988-98. Mem. Ind. Bar Assn., Indpls. Bar Assn., Def. Rsch. Inst., Internat. Assn. Def. Counsel, Gyro Club Indpls. (v.p. 1992-93, pres. 1993-94, bd. dirs. 1990—). Avocations: golf, skiing, tennis. Home: 7256 Tuliptree Trl Indianapolis IN 46256-2136 Office: Ice Miller 1 American Sq Indianapolis IN 46282-0020

SCALLEN, THOMAS KAINE, broadcasting executive; b. Mpls., Aug. 14, 1925; s. Raymond A. and Lenore (Kaine) S.; m. Bille Jo Brice; children by previous marriage: Thomas, Sheila, Patrick, Eileen, Timothy and Maureen (twins). BA, St. Thomas Coll., 1949; JD, U. Denver, 1950. Bar: Minn. Asst. atty. gen. State of Minn., Mpls., 1950-55; sole practice, 1955-57; pres. Med. Investment Corp., 1957—, Internat. Broadcasting Corp., Mpls., 1977—; owner Harlem Globetrotters. Pres., exec. producer Ice Capades; chmn. bd. dirs. Century Park Pictures Corp., Los Angeles, chmn. bd. dirs. Blaine-Thompson Co., Inc., N.Y.C; chmn. Apache Plastics, Inc., Stockton, Calif. Served with AUS. Mem. World Pres. Orgn., Minn. Club, Calhoun Beach Club, L.A. Athletic Club. Clubs: University (St. Paul, Mpls.), Rochester (Minn.) Golf and Country, Edina (Minn.) Country, Athletic (Mpls.). Home: Heron Cove Windham NH 03087 Office: Internat Broadcasting Corp 80 S 8th St Ste 4701 Minneapolis MN 55402-2207

SCALLY, MARK, diversified financial services company executive; b. Jan. 11, 1947; BBA, U of Iowa. CPA, Calif. From mem. staff to chmn. bd., mng. ptnr. McGladrey & Pullen, LLP, Bloomington, Minn., 1971-84, chmn. bd., mng. ptnr., 1984—. Office: McGladrey & Pullen LLP 3600 W 80 St Ste 500 Davenport IA 52801-1803

SCAMINACE, JOSEPH M. paint store executive; Grad., U. Dayton; MBA, Case Western Res. U. Dir. mfg. Sherwin-Williams Co., Morrow, Ga., 1983, pres., gen. mgr. consumer group/predecessor coatings divsn. Cleve., 1997-99, pres., COO, 1999—. Office: Sherwin-Williams Co 101 Prospect Ave NW Cleveland OH 44115-1075

SCANLAN, JAMES PATRICK, philosophy and Slavic studies educator; b. Chgo., Feb. 22, 1927; s. Gilbert Francis and Helen (Meyers) S.; m. Marilyn A. Morrison, June 12, 1948. BA, U. Chgo., 1948, MA, 1950, PhD, 1956. Research fellow Inst. Philos. Research, San Francisco, 1953-55; instr. Case Inst. Tech., Cleve., 1955-56; from instr. to assoc. prof. Goucher Coll., Balt., 1956-68; prof., dir. Slavic Ctr. U. Kans., Lawrence, 1968-70; prof. Ohio State U., Columbus, 1971-91, dir. Slavic Ctr., 1988-91, prof. emeritus, 1992—. Vis. rsch. scholar Moscow State U., 1964-65, 69, 98, Acad. Scis. USSR, Moscow, 1978, 93, Russian State U. for the Humanities, 1995; fgn. vis. fellow Slavic Rsch. Ctr., Hokkaido U., Sapporo, Japan, 1987-88. Author: Marxism in the USSR, 1985, Dostoevsky the Thinker, 2002; editor: Historical Letters by Peter Lavrov, 1967, Soviet Studies in Philosophy, 1987—92, Russian Studies in Philosophy, 1992—97, Technology, Culture and Development: The Experience of the Soviet Model, 1992, Russian Thought After Communism, 1994; co-editor: Russian Philosophy, 1965, Marxism and Religion in Eastern Europe, 1976. Served with USMC, 1945-46. Woodrow Wilson Internat. Ctr. fellow, 1982; recipient Translation award Nat. Translation Ctr., 1967, Faculty Rsch. award Fulbright-Hays, 1982-83. Mem. Am. Philos. Assn., Am. Assn. Advancement Slavic Studies, Phi Beta Kappa. Home: 1000 Urlin Ave Apt 206 Columbus OH 43212-3324 E-mail: scanlan.1@osu.edu.

SCANLAN, MICHAEL, priest, academic administrator; b. Far Rockaway, N.Y., Dec. 1, 1931; s. Vincent Michael and Marjorie (O'Keefe) S. BA, Williams Coll., 1953; JD, Harvard U., 1956; MDiv, St. Francis Sem., Loretto, Pa., 1975; LittD (hon.), Coll. Steubenville, 1972; LLD (hon.), Williams Coll., Williamstown, Mass., 1978; PdD (hon.), St. Francis Coll., Loretto, Pa., 1987; STM, 3d Order Regular of St Francis, 1996. Ordained priest Roman Catholic Ch., 1964; Cross Pro Ecclesia et Pontifice, 1990. Acting dean Coll. Steubenville, Ohio, 1964-66, dean, 1966-69; rector pres. St. Francis Major Sem., Loretto, Pa., 1969-74; pres. Franciscan U. Steubenville, 1974-2000, chancellor, 2000—. Pres.(FIRE) Cath. Alliance for Faith, Intercession, Repentence and Evangelism, 1984—. Author: The Power in Penance, 1972, Inner Healing, 1974, A Portion of My Spirit, 1979, The San Damiano Cross, 1983, Turn to the Lord-A Call to Repentance, 1989, The Truth About Trouble, 1989, What Does God Want: A Practical Guide to Making Decisions, 1996, (with James Manney) Let the Fire Fall, 1997, The Holy Spirit: Holy Desire, 1998; chmn. editl. bd. New Covenant mag., 1985-92. Mem. Diocese of Steubenville Ecumenical Commn., 1964-69; bd. dirs. Rumor Control Ctr., Steubenville, 1968-69, C. of C., Steubenville, 1976-79; bd. trustees St. Francis Prep. Sch., Spring Grove, Pa., 1969-74; vice-chmn., bd. trustees St. Francis Coll., Loretto, Pa., 1969-74; trustee United Way, Steubenville, 1975-80; chmn. nat. svc. com. Cath. Charismatic Renewal, 1975-78. Staff judge adv. USAF, 1956-57. Named Sacrae Theologiae Magister Third Order Regular St Francis, 1996. Roman Catholic. Avocations: tennis, golf, skiing. Office: Franciscan U Office of Chancellor 1235 University Blvd Steubenville OH 43952-1796

SCANLAN, RICHARD THOMAS, classics educator; b. St. Paul, May 30, 1928; s. Robert Lawrence and Catherine (Rockstroh) S.; m. Donna Mary Campion, Dec. 29, 1951; children: John, Susan, Catherine, Anne, Margaret. B.S., U. Minn., 1951, M.A., 1952. Tchr. Hastings High Sch., Minn., 1953-55, Edina High Sch., 1955-67; prof. classics U. Ill., Urbana, 1967—. Ednl. cons., 1960-75 Author: Power in Words, 1983; computer courses, 1975, 77; Myths of Greece and Rome, 1986 Pres. bd. trustees Champaign Libr., 1980-92. With U.S. Army, 1946-48, Italy. Named Excellent Tchr. Am. Classical League, 1966; recipient Silver medal Nat. Coun. for Advancement of Edn., 1985. Mem. Am. Philol. Assn., Am. Classical League, Archaeol. Assn., Classical Assn. (Excellent Tchr.award 1974) Roman Catholic. Home: 2103 Noel Dr Champaign IL 61821-6552 Office: Univ of Ill Dept of Classics Urbana IL 61801

SCANLAN, THOMAS CLEARY, publishing executive, editor; b. Birmingham, Mich., May 18, 1957; s. Thomas Matthew and Emily (Cleary) S.; m. Sally Sachs, June 20, 1981; children: Bridget C., Thomas M., Patrick J. BS, St. Louis U., 1979. Salesman Walter Heller Co., Chgo., 1979-82; pub., editor Surplus Record, Inc., 1982—. Office: Surplus Record Inc 20 N Wacker Dr Chicago IL 60606-2806

SCARPA, ANTONIO, medicine educator, biomedical scientist; b. Padua, Italy, July 3, 1942; s. Angelo and Elena (DeRossi) S. MD cum laude, U. Padua, 1966, PhD in Pathology, 1970; MA (hon.), U. Pa., 1978. Asst. prof. biochemistry, biophysics U. Pa., Phila., 1973-76, assoc. prof., 1976-80, prof., 1980-86, dir. biomed. instrumentation group, 1983-86; prof. dept. pathology Jefferson U., 1986—; prof., chmn. dept. physiology and biophysics Case Western Res. U., Cleve., 1986—, dir. tng. ctr., program project, 1983—, prof. medicine, 1989—. Cons. study sect. NIH, Bethesda, 1984—, Am. Heart Assn., Dallas, 1986-91; pres., assoc. chair dept. physiology, 1993-94; vice chair Nat. Caucus Basic Sci. Presidents, Washington. Editor (books): Frontiers of Biological Energetics, Calcium Transport and Cell Function, Transport ATPases, Membrane Pathology, Membrane and Cancer Cells; editor (jours.) Archives Biochemistry and Biophysics, Cell Calcium, Biochemistry Internat., The Scientific Jour.; mem. editl. bd. Circulation Rsch., 1978-81, Biophys. Jour., 1979-82, Jour. Muscle Rsch., 1979—, Magnesium, 1982—, Physiol. Revs., 1982-90, FASEB Jour., 1987-92, Molecular Cellular Biochemistry, 1988—; contbr. numerous articles to profl. jours. Mem. Am. Soc. Physiologists, Am. Soc. Biol. Chemistry, Biophys. Soc. (exec. coun. 1980-83, 85-89, 94-97), U.S. Bioenergetics Group (program chmn. 1974-75, 82, 83, exec. officer 1985-90, assoc. chmn. dept. physiology, pres. 1993-95), Biophys. Soc. (treas. 1998—), Assn. Am. Med. Colls. (adminstrv. bd.). Avocations: farming, sailing, painting. Office: Case Western Reserve Univ Dept Of Physiology Cleveland OH 44106

SCARSE, OLIVIA MARIE, cardiologist, consultant; b. Chgo., Nov. 10, 1950; d. Oliver Marcus and Marjorie Ardis (Olsen) S. BS, North Park Coll., 1970; MD, Loyola U., Maywood, Ill., 1973. Diplomate Am. Bd. Internal Medicine, Am. Bd. Cardiovascular Diseases. Surg. intern Resurrection Hosp., Chgo., 1974; resident in internal medicine Northwestern U., 1974-77; cardiovascular disease fellow U. Ill., 1977-80; dir. cardiac catherization lab. Cook County Hosp., 1981; dir. heart sta. MacNeal Hosp., Berwyn, Ill., 1983; dir. electrophysiology Hines VA Hosp., Maywood, 1984-85; dir. progressive care Columbus Hosp., Chgo., 1985-88, pvt. practice, 1984—, Ill. Masonic Hosp., Chgo., 1989-96. Founder Physician Cons. for Evaluation of Clin. Pathways, Practice Parameters and Patient Care Outcomes, 1991—. Dir. continuous quality improvement Improvement Columbus, 1990-95; mem. presdl. ad hoc com. on prevention and treatment of domestic violence Chgo. Med. Soc., 1997—. Pillsbury fellow Pillsbury Fund, 1980. Fellow Am. Coll. Cardiology; mem. AMA, ACP, Chgo. Med. Assn., Ill. State Med. Assn., Am. Heart Assn. (coun. on clin. cardiology), Crescent Countries Found. for Med. Care, Physicians Health Network, Cen. Ill. Med. Rev. Orgn. Avocations: musician, ballet and tap dancer, actress, model, singer. Home and Office: 2650 N Lakeview Ave Apt 4109 Chicago IL 60614-1833 Fax: (773) 935-1039.

SCHAAL, BARBARA ANNA, evolutionary biologist, educator; BS in Biology with honors, U. Ill., Chgo., 1969; MPhil in Population Biology, Yale U., 1971, PhD in Population Biology, 1974. spkr. in field. Assoc. prof. biology Washington U., St. Louis, 1980-86, prof., 1986—; prof. genetics Wash. U. Sch. Medicine, Spencer T. Olin prof. biology in arts and scis., chair dept. biology, 1993-97, mem. various coms. Assoc. editor Molecular Biology and Evolution, Am. Jour. Botany, Molecular Ecology, Conservation Genetics. Trustee St. Louis Acad. Scis. Fellow AAAS; mem. NAS, Bot. Soc. Am. (pres. 1995-96, Merit award 1999), Nature Conservancy (trustee Mo. chpt.). Achievements include research on the evolutionary process within plant populations. Office: PO Box 1137 Saint Louis MO 63188-1137

SCHACHT, JOCHEN HEINRICH, biochemistry educator; b. Königsberg, Fed. Republic Germany, July 2, 1939; came to U.S., 1969; s. Heinz and Else (Sprenger) S.; m. Helga Hildegard Seidel, Jan..27, 1967; children: Miriam Helga, Daniel Jochen. BS, U. Bonn, Fed. Republic Germany, 1962; MS in Chemistry, U. Heidelberg, Fed. Republic Germany, 1965, PhD in Biochemistry, 1968. Asst. research chemist, Mental Health Research Inst. U. Mich., Ann Arbor, 1969-72, from asst. prof. to assoc. prof. biochemistry, Dept. Biol. Chemistry & Otolaryngology, 1973-84, prof., 1984—, chmn. grad. program in physiol. acoustics, 1981—; hon. prof. Med. Acad. of the Chinese PLA, Beijing, 1998. Vis. prof. Karolinska Inst., Stockholm, 1979-80; acting dir. Kresge Hearing Rsch. Inst., U. Mich., 1983-84, assoc. dir., 1989-99, dir., 2000—; mem. hearing rsch. study sect. USPHS, NIH, Nat. Inst. Neurol. and Communicative Disorders and Stroke, 1986-89, Task Force Nat. Strategic Rsch. Plan, Nat. Insts. Deafness and Communication Disorders, USPHS, NIH; hon. prof. Hunan Med. U., Changsha, China, 1999—, Tonghi Med. U., Wuhan, China, 1999—; guest prof. Fourth Mil. Med. U., Xian, China, 1999—. Mem. editl. bd. Hearing Rsch., 1990—; assoc. editor Audiology & Neuro-Otol., 1995—; contbr. more than 200 articles to profl. jours., book chpts., revs.; co-editor Neurochemistry of Cholinergic Receptors, 1974. Fogarty Sr. Internat. fellow NIH, 1979, Sen. J. Javitz Neurosci. investigator, 1984; recipient Chercheur Etranger rsch. award INSERM, Paris, 1986, 94, Animal Welfare award Erna-Graff Found., Berlin, 1987, Disting. Faculty Achievement award U. Mich., 1989, Employer of Yr. award Nat. Capital Assoc. Coop. Edn. and Gallaudet U., Washington. Mem. Deutsche Gesellschaft für Biologische Chemie, Am. Soc. Neurochemistry, Internat. Soc. Neurochemistry, Soc. for Neurosci., Assn. for Research in Otolaryngology, Am. Soc. Biol. Chemists, Assn. Espanola de Audiologia Exptl. Avocations: photography, travel, birding. Office: U Mich Kresge Hearing Rsch Inst Ann Arbor MI 48109-0506

SCHACTER, BRENT ALLAN, oncologist, health facility administrator; b. Winnipeg, Man., Can., June 1, 1942; s. Irvin C. and Claire (Easton) S.; m. Sora Ludwig, Dec. 20, 1981; children: Isanne, Jennifer, Miriam. BSc, MD with honors, U. Man., 1965. Intern Winnipeg Gen. Hosp., 1965-66, jr. asst. resident, 1967-68; asst. resident in internal medicine Barnes Hosp., St. Louis, 1968-69; clin. fellow hematology Barnes Hosp. and Washington U., 1969-70; rsch. fellow, asst. in medicine U. Tex. Southwestern Med. Sch., Dallas, 1970-72; asst. prof. internal medicine U. Man., Winnipeg, 1972-77, assoc. prof. medicine, 1977-87, prof., 1987—; pres., CEO CancerCare Manitoba, 1993—. Lectr. in field; sci. officer grant panel C, Nat. Cancer Inst. Can., 1978, mem., 1979-82; mem. Man. Health Rsch. Coun. grant panel, 1982-84, 89-91, Coun. for Canadian Strategy for Cancer Contro, 2002-; adv. bd. Can. Porphyria Found., 1988—; mem. steering com. Can. Strategy For Cancer Control, 1999—2002, co-chair steering com., 2000—; mem. steering com. Can. Cancer Stats., 2000—. Contbr. numerous articles and abstracts to profl. jours. Bd. dirs. Nat. Cancer Inst. Can., 2000—. Recipient Med. Rsch. Coun. Can. Vis. Scientist award, 1986; fellow Muscular Dystrophy Assn., 1964, John S. McEachern Meml. fellow Can. Cancer Soc., 1969-70, Med. Rsch. Coun. Can. fellow, 1970-72, Nat. Cancer Inst. of Can. rsch. fellow, 1966-67; Isbister scholar, 1962, 63, Med. Rsch. Coun. Can. scholar, 1975-80. Fellow Royal Coll. Physicians; mem. AAAS, Royal Coll. Physicians and Surgeons of Can. (specialty com. in med. oncology 1985-94, bd. med. examiners in med. oncology 1987-90, specialty com. in hematology 1989-93, core com. mem. 1990-96, chmn. bd. examiners med. oncology 1990-93, mem. regional adv. com. Sask./Man. dist. 1992-97), Am. Fedn. for Clin. Rsch., Can. Soc. for Clin. Investigation (awards com. 1980-82, chmn. 1981-82), Am. Soc. Hematology, Can. Soc. Hematology, Am. Soc. Clin. Oncology, Can. Bone Marrow Transplant Group, Can. Assn. Provincial Cancer Agys., Can. Hemophilia Soc. (mem. clinic dirs. group 1990-93, sec-treas. 1991-93) Avocations: cross-country skiing, scuba diving, model railroading. Home: 224 Lamont Blvd Winnipeg MB Canada R3P 0E9 Office: CancerCare Manitoba 675 McDermot Ave Winnipeg MB Canada R3E 0V9 E-mail: brent.schacter@cancercare.mb.ca.

SCHADE, STANLEY GREINERT, JR. hematologist, educator; b. Pitts., Dec. 21, 1933; s. Stanley G. and Charlotte (Marks) S.; m. Sylvia Zottu, Mar. 24, 1966; children: David Stanley, Robert Edward. BA in English, Hamilton Coll., 1955; MD, Yale U., 1961. Diplomate Am. Bd. Internal Medicine, Am. Bd. Hematology, Am. Bd. Oncology. Intern, resident, hematology fellow U. Wis., Madison, 1962-66; chief hematology Westside VA Hosp., Chgo., 1971-77; prof. medicine, chief hematology U. Ill., 1978—. Contbr. articles to profl. jours. Served to maj. U.S. Army, 1967-69. Fulbright fellow Tubingen, Fed. Republic of Germany, 1956. Fellow Am. Coll. Physicians; mem. Am. Soc. Hematology. Presbyterian. Avocation: medical ethics. Home: 189 N Delaplaine Rd Riverside IL 60546-2060 Office: Westside VA Med Ctr Dept Medicine MP111 820 S Damen Ave Chicago IL 60612-3728

SCHAEFER, DAVID ARNOLD, lawyer; b. Cleve., May 3, 1948; s. Leonard and Maxine V. (Bassett) S.; m. Riki C. Freeman, Aug. 8, 1971; children: Kevin, Lindsey, Traci. BS, Miami U., Oxford, Ohio, 1970; MA, Northwestern U., 1971; JD, Case Western Res. U., 1974. Bar: Ohio 1974, U.S. Dist. Ct. (no. dist.) Ohio 1974, U.S. Ct. Appeals (6th cir.) 1978, U.S. Supreme Ct. 1978. Ptnr. Guren, Merritt et al, 1980-84, Menexch. Friedlander et al, Cleve., 1984-93, McCarthy, Lebit, Crystal & Haiman, Cleve., 1993—. Author: Deposition Strategy, 1981, 2d edit., 1984; contbr. articles to profl. publs. Mem. ABA, Internat. Assn. Def. Counsel, Fed. Bar Assn. (pres. 1992-93), Nat. Inst. Trail Advocacy (faculty), 8th Cir. Jud. Conf. (life). Office: McCarthy Lebit Crystal & Haiman 1800 Midland Bldg 101 W Prospect Ave Ste 1800 Cleveland OH 44115-1027

SCHAEFER, FRANK WILLIAM, III, microbiologist, researcher; b. Dayton, Ohio, Sept. 1, 1942; s. Frank William Jr. and Irene Josephine (Krouse) S. BA, Miami U., Oxford, Ohio, 1964; MS, U. Cin., 1970, PhD, 1973. Rsch. assoc. parasitologist U. Notre Dame, South Bend, Ind., 1973-78; U.S. EPA EPA, Cin., 1978—. Mem. ASTM, AAAS, Am. Soc. Parasitology, Am. Soc. Microbiology, Am. Water Works Assn., Soc. Protozoologists, Sigma Xi. Home: 9948 McCauley Woods Dr Sharonville OH 45241-1489 Office: US EPA 26 Martin Luther King Dr Cincinnati OH 45268 E-mail: schaefer.frank@epa.gov.

SCHAEFER, GEORGE A., JR. bank executive; Pres., CEO Fifth Third Bancorp, Cin. Office: Fifth Third Bancorp Fifth Third Center 38 Fountain Square Plz Cincinnati OH 45263-0001

SCHAEFER, PATRICIA, librarian; b. Ft. Wayne, Ind., Apr. 23, 1930; d. Edward John and Hildegarde Hartman (Hormel) S. MusB, Northwestern U., 1951; MusM, U. Ill., 1958; AMLS, U. Mich., 1963. With U.S. Rubber co., Ft. Wayne, 1951-52; sec. to promotion mgr. Sta. WOWO, Ind., 1952, sec. to program mgr., 1953-55; coord. publicity and promotion Home Telephone Co., 1955-56; sec. Fine Arts Found., 1956-57; libr. asst. Columbus (Ohio) Pub. Libr., 1958-59; audio-visual libr. Muncie (Ind.) Pub. Libr., 1959-86, asst. libr. dir., 1981-86, libr. dir., 1986-95. Chmn. Ind. Libr. Film Cir., 1962-63; treas. Ind. Libr. Film Svc., 1969-70, 83-85; mem. trustee adv. coun. Milton S. Eisenhower Libr., Johns Hopkins U.; mem. presdl. counsellors Johns Hopkins U., 1994—; bd. dirs. Franklin Elec. Co., Inc. Weekly columnist Libr. Lines, Muncie Evening Press, 1981-83; program annotator Muncie Symphony Orch. and Masterworks Chorale; contbr. articles to profl. jours. Bd. dirs. Muncie Symphony Assn., 1964-74, 85-91, Ctrl. City Bus. Assn., 1986-92, Ind. Inst. Tech., Ptnrs. for the Enhancement of Cmty. Coop., Ind. Humanities Coun., 1996—, Sta. WIPB-TV; mem. adv. coun. Coll. Fine Arts, Ball State U.; mem. adv. com., bookshop dir. Midwest Writers Workshop, 1976-77; sec. Del. County Coun. for the ARts, 1978-79, pres., 1979-81, bd. dirs., 1985-86; mem. pres.'s coun. Berea Coll.; bd. dirs. Muncie YWCA, 1977-82, 85-89, 95-2001, treas. 1981-82, 88-89; bd. dirs. ARC, Hoosier Heartland chpt.; bd. govs. Minnetrista Cultural Ctr.; gen. chmn. Ind. Renaissance Fair, 1978-79; pres. Muncie Matinee Musicale, 1965-67; past pres. Ind. Film and Video Coun.; mem. adv. bd. Cmty. Found. Muncie and Delaware County; bd. dirs. Wapehani coun. Girl Scouts U.S., 1989-96; bd. dirs. Muncie Ctr. for Arts, 1999—. Named Woman Achievement Pub. Svc., 1986; recipient Sagamore of the Wabash award Gov. State of Ind., Outstanding Libr. award Ind. Libr. Fedn., 1995, Cert. of Congrl. Recognition, 1995, Cert. of Achievement, Women's Coalition, 1996, Cert. of Appreciation, Masterworks Chorale, 1998. Mem. ALA, Ind. Libr. Assn. (pres. 1987-88), Nat. League Am. Pen Women (pres. Muncie br. 1974-78), Altrusa (pres. 1986-87, cmty. svc. award 2000), Art Students League, Riley-Jones Club, Del. Country Club, Delta Zeta, Mu Phi Epsilon. Republican. Roman Catholic. Home: 5400 W Deer Run Ct Muncie IN 47304-5775 E-mail: patschaefer@mindspring.com.

SCHAFER, EDWARD T. governor; b. Bismarck, N.D., Aug. 8, 1946; s. Harold and Marian Schafer; m. Nancy Jones; children: Edward Thomas Jr., Ellie Sue, Eric Jones, Kari Jones. BSBA, U. N.D., 1969; MBA, Denver U., 1970. Quality control inspector Gold Seal, 1971-73, v.p., 1974, chmn. mgmt. com., 1975-78; owner/dir. H&S Distbn., 1976—; pres. Gold Seal, 1978-85, Dakota Classics, 1986—, TRIESCO Properties, 1986—, Fish 'N Dakota, 1990-94; gov. State of N.D., 1992-2000. Chmn. N.D. Micro Bus. Mktg. Alliance; pres. N.D. Heritage Group; adv. coun. Distributive Edn. Clubs of Am.; lectr. Hugh O'Brien Leadership Found.; counselor Junior Achievement; dir. Bismarck Recreation Coun.; trustee Missouri Valley Family YMCA; plankowner USS Theodore Roosevelt; ann. support com. Medcenter One Found.; mem. Bismarck State Coll. Found. Mem. NRA, Theodore Roosevelt Assn. (Theodore Roosevelt Medora Found., United Sportsman of N.D., U. N.D. Pres. Club, U. Mary Pres. Club, Bismarck-Mandan Rotary. Republican.

SCHAFER, JOHN FRANCIS, retired plant pathologist; b. Pullman, Wash., Feb. 17, 1921; s. Edwin George and Ella Frances (Miles) S.; m. Joyce A. Marcks, Aug. 16, 1947; children— Patricia, Janice, James BS, Wash. State U., 1942; PhD, U. Wis., 1950. Asst. prof. to prof. plant pathology Purdue U., 1949-68; head dept. plant pathology Kans. State U., 1968-72; chmn. dept. plant pathology Wash. State U., Pullman, 1972-80; integrated pest mgmt. coordinator sci. and edn. USDA, 1980-81, acting nat. research program leader plant pathology Agrl. Research Service, 1981-82, dir. cereal rust lab., 1982-87, biol. sci. collaborator, 1987-95; ret., 1995. Vis. rsch. prof. Duquesne U., 1965-66; adj. prof. plant pathology U. Minn., 1982-92. Contbr. articles to profl. jours., chpts. to books. With AUS, 1942-46. Phi Sigma scholar, 1942. Fellow AAAS, Ind. Acad. Sci., Am. Phytopathol. Soc. (past pres.); mem. Am. Soc. Agronomy, Crop Sci. Soc. Am., Coun. for Agrl. Sci. and Tech. Achievements include identification of increased resistance to wheat leaf rust by genetic recombination; demonstration of probabilities of virulence to genetic resistance combinations, of tolerance as a mechanism of disease control, and of use of cultivaral diversity for disease protection; bred (with others) over 30 disease resistant cultivars of cereal crops, including Arthur wheat. Home: 4949 Snyder Ln Apt 108 Rohnert Park CA 94928-4834 E-mail: joyjac@msn.com.

SCHAFER, MICHAEL FREDERICK, orthopedic surgeon; b. Peoria, Ill., Aug. 17, 1942; s. Harold Martin and Frances May (Ward) S.; m. Eileen M. Briggs, Jan. 8, 1966; children: Steven, Brian, Kathy, David, Daniel. BA, U. Iowa, 1964, MD, 1967. Diplomate Am. Bd. Orthopedic Surgery. Intern Chgo. Wesley Meml. Hosp., 1967-68; resident in orthop. surgery Cook County Program, Northwestern U., Chgo., 1968-72; asst. prof. orthop. surgery Northwestern U., 1977—; Reyerson prof. and chmn. dept. orthopedic surgery; asso. attending orthopedic surgeon Northwestern Meml. Hosp., 1974—. Adj. staff Children's Meml. Hosp., Chgo., 1974—; cons. VA Lakeside Hosp., 1974—; panelist Bur. Health Manpower, HEW, 1976; sec.-treas. Orthop. Rsch. and Edn. Found.; attending orthop. surgeon Northwestern Meml. Hosp., 1980—, exec. dir. Back and Neck Inst. Contbr. articles to profl. jours. Maj. U.S. Army, 1973-74. Fellow Am. Orthopaedic Assn., Am. Acad. Orthopaedic Surgeons; mem. AMA, Am. Orthopedic Soc. Sports Medicine, Ill. Med. Soc., Chgo. Med. Soc., Scoliosis Rsch. Soc. Roman Catholic. Home: 1815 Ridgewood Ln W Glenview IL 60025-2205 Office: Northwestern U Med School Ste 910 645 N Michigan Ave Chicago IL 60611-2876 E-mail: m-schafer@nwu.edu.

SCHAFER, SHARON MARIE, anesthesiologist; b. Detroit, Mar. 23, 1948; d. Charles Anthony and Dorothy Emma (Schweitzer) Pokriefka; m. Timothy John Schafer, Nov. 12, 1977; children: Patrick Christopher, Steven Michael. BS in Biology, Wayne State U., 1971, MD, 1975; MBA in Practice Mgmt., Madonna U., 2000. Diplomate Am. Bd. Anesthesiology. Intern, resident Sinai Hosp. Detroit, 1975-78; pvt. practice anesthesiology Troy, Mich., 1988—. Mem. AMA, Am. Soc. Anesthesiologists. Roman Catholic. Home and Office: 5741 Folkstone Dr Troy MI 48085-3154

SCHAFFER, JACK, former state senator; b. Chgo., Oct. 12, 1942; s. Raymond and Francis (Barter) S.; divorced; children: Neal, Todd, Ryan. BS, No. Ill. U., 1965. Plant mgr. Oak Mfg. Co., Crystal Lake, Ill., 1967-68; auditor McHenry County, 1968-72. Sgt. U.S. Army, 1965-67. Mem. Rotary. Office: Cmty Bankers Assn Ill 901 Community Dr Springfield IL 62703-5184

SCHAKOWSKY, JANICE, congresswoman; b. Chgo., May 26, 1944; d. Irwin and Tillie (Cosnow) Danoff; m. Harvey E. Schakowsky, Feb. 17, 1965 (div. 1980); children: Ian, Mary; m. Robert B. Creamer, Dec. 6, 1980; 1 stepchild, Lauren. BS, U. Ill., 1965. Cert. elem. tchr., Ill. Tchr. Chgo. Bd. Edn., 1965-67; organizer Ill. Pub. Action Coun., Chgo., 1976-85; exec. dir. Ill. State Coun. Sr. Citizens, 1985-90; mem. Ill. Ho. Reps., 1990-98, U.S. Congress from 9th Ill. dist., 1999—; mem. banking and fin. svcs. com., 1999—; mem. govt. reform com., 1999—. Bd. dirs. Ill. Pub. Action, 4 C's Day Care Coun., Evanston, Ill.; steering com. mem. Cook County Dem. Women, 1986-90; del. Nat. Dem. Conv., 1988; governing coun. Am. Jewish Congress, 1990—. Named Outstanding Legislator Interfaith Coun. for Homeless, 1993, Legislator of Yr. Ill. Nurses Assn., 1992, Ill. Assn. Cmty. Mental Health Agys., 1994, Coalition of Citizens with Disabilities and Ill. Coun. Sr. Citizens, 1993, Cmty. Action Assn., 1991, Champaign County Health Care Assn., 1992, Rookie of Yr. Ill. Environ. Coun., 1991. Mem. ACLU, NOW, Nat. Coun. Jewish Women, Ill. Pro-Choice Alliance, Evanston Mental Health Assn., Evanston Hist. Soc., Evanston Friends of Libr., Rogers Park Hist. Soc. Democrat. Jewish. Avocations: travelling, horsebackriding, reading. Home: 1101 Ridge Ave Evanston IL 60202-1231 Office: Ho of Reps 515 Cannon Hob Washington DC 20515-0001*

SCHALLENKAMP, KAY, academic administrator; b. Salem, S.D., Dec. 9, 1949; d. Arnold B. and Jennie M. (Koch) Krier; m. Ken Schallenkamp, Sept. 7, 1970; children: Heather, Jenni. BS, No. State Coll., 1972; MA, U. S.D., 1973; PhD, U. Colo., 1982. Prof. No. State Coll., Aberdeen, S.D., 1973-88, dept. chair, 1982-84, dean, 1984-88; provost Chadron (Nebr.) State Coll., 1988-92, U. Wis., Whitewater, 1992-97; pres. Emporia (Kans.) State U., 1997—. Cons. North Ctrl. Assn., nursing homes, hosps. and ednl. instns. Contbr. articles to profl. jours. Commr. North Ctrl. Assn., 1995-99. Bush fellow, 1980; named Outstanding Young Career Woman, Bus. and Profl. Women's Club, 1976. Mem. NCAA (pres.'s coun. 2000—), Kans. C. of C. (bd. dirs. 2000—), Am. Speech and Hearing Assn. (cert.), Rotary. Avocation: martial arts. Office: Emporia State U 1200 Commercial St Emporia KS 66801-5087 E-mail: schallka@emporia.edu.

SCHANFARBER, RICHARD CARL, real estate broker; b. Cleve., June 11, 1937; s. Edwin David and Helen (Newman) S.; m. Barbara A. Berger, Dec. 21, 1958 (div. Sept. 1981); children: Edwin Jeffrey, Lori Jo, Tammy Joy. Grad., NYU, 1959. Lic. FCC broadcast engr. Pres. Erieview Realty, Gates Mills, 1961—, Miller Warehouse, Gates Mills, 1968—2001, ERI Travel Co., Gates Mills, 1974—2001, ERI Sales Co., Gates Mills, 1979—, Eastgate Travel Svcs., Gates Mills, Ohio, 1987—2001. Pres. Shaker Hts. (Ohio) Alumni Assn., 1986-97, Cleve. Area Bd. Realtors, 1981, Cleve. Warehouseman Assn., 1977-79; chmn. City of Cleve. Landmarks Commn., 1984—. Mem. NRA (life), Nat. Assn. Realtors, Ohio Assn. Realtors, Cleve. Growth Assn., Cleve. Area Bd. Realtors. Avocation: real estate. Home: 6719 Sandalwood Dr Gates Mills OH 44040-9619 E-mail: richard@eri-group.com.

SCHAR, STEPHEN L. lawyer; b. Chgo., Oct. 19, 1945; s. Sidney and Lillian (Lieberman) Schar; m. Jessica S. Feit, Aug. 17, 1980; children: Scott Andrew, Elizabeth Loren. BA, U. Chgo., 1967; JD, DePaul U., 1970. Bar: Ill. 1970, U.S. Dist. Ct. (no. dist.) Ill. 1970. Assoc. Aaron, Aaron, Schimberg & Hess, Chgo., 1970-77, ptnr., 1977-80, Aaron, Schimberg, Hess, Rusnak, Deutsch & Gilbert, Chgo., 1980-84, Aaron, Schimberg, Hess & Gilbert, Chgo., 1984, Aaron, Schimberg & Hess, Chgo., 1984, D'Ancona & Pflaum, Chgo., 1985-98; mem. D'Ancona & Pflaum LLC, 1999—. Instr. estate planning Loyola U., Chgo., 1978—79. Bd. dirs. Jewish Children's Bur. Chgo., 1982—2001, pres., 1996—98, hon. dir., 2001—; pres. Faulkner Condominium Assn., Chgo., 1980—82, Carl Sandburg Village Homeowners Assn., Chgo., 1981—82. Mem.: Chgo. Estate Planning Coun., Chgo. Bar Assn. (pres. probate practice divsn. III 1979), Ill. Bar Assn. Home: 2155 Tanglewood Ct Highland Park IL 60035-4231 Office: D'Ancona & Pflaum LLC 111 E Wacker Dr Ste 2800 Chicago IL 60601-4209 E-mail: sschar@dancona.com.

SCHARF, CHARLES W. banking executive; married; two children. B, Johns Hopkins U., 1987; MBA, N.Y. U. With Comml. Credit Corp., 1987-95; various sr. positions to CFO Smith Barney, 1995-98; CFO global corp. & investment bank Citibank, 1998-2000; exec. v.p., CFO Bank One Corp., Chgo., 2000—. Office: Bank One Corp 1 Bank One Plaza Chicago IL 60670

SCHARFFE, WILLIAM GRANVILLE, academic administrator, educator; b. Saginaw, Mich., Mar. 12, 1942; s. William Edward and Marion Kittie (Granville) S.; m. Mary Jo Whitfield, Sept. 4, 1965; children: Sue L., William W. BA, Mich. State U., 1965, MA, 1969, PhD, 1977. Tchr. English Webber Jr. High Sch., Saginaw, 1965-66; tchr. speech Arthur Hill High Sch., 1966-68; staff asst. for pers. Saginaw City Schs., 1968-73, dir. pers., 1977-94, dir. employee devel. and media ops., 1994-99; prin. Zilwaukee Jr. High Sch., Saginaw, 1973-74; asst. prin. North Intermediate Sch., 1974-75, 1975-77; dir. policy svcs. Mich. Assn. Sch. Bds., Lansing, 1999—. Adj. asst. prof. Mich. State U., East Lansing, 1977; pvt. practice pers. cons., Saginaw, 1978—; adj. lectr. Ctrl. Mich. U., Mt. Pleasant, 1987, Mich. State U., 1977, Saginaw Valley State U., 1991. Author: (children's book) Elfred Alanzo & Santa's Surprise, 1987. Bd. dirs. Japanese Cultural Ctr. and Tea House, Saginaw, 1986-97, pres., 1993-95. Recipient Key Man award United Way Saginaw County, 1978, Outstanding Svc. award, 1978. Mem. Mich. Assn. Sch. Pers. Assn. (sec., bd. dirs. 1988-90, pres., bd. dirs. 1992-93), Mich. Mid. Cities Pers. and Labor Rels. Task Force (pres. 1980-82), Soc. For Human Resource Mgmt., Exch. Club (Saginaw chpt. pres. 1981), Saginaw Club (pres. 1996-97), Phi Delta Kappa. Republican. Episcopalian. Avocations: writing, golf, photography, public speaking. Home: 2812 Adams Blvd Saginaw MI 48602-3103

SCHARP-RADOVIC, CAROL ANN, choreographer, classical ballet educator, artistic director; b. Ypsilanti, Mich., Aug. 9, 1940; d. John Lewis and Mary Vivien (Alther) Keeney; m. Jack Laurel Scharp, July 28, 1958 (div. July 1970); children: Kathryn E., Mark A.; m. Srecko Radovic, Nov. 15, 1989. Studied with Pereslavic, Danilova; student, Harkness Ballet, N.Y.C., Joffrey Ballet, Eglevsky Ballet, Briansky Ballet, Darvesh Ballet, N.Y.C.; studied with Jurgen Schneider, Am. Ballet Theatre, 1983-93; studied with Janina Cunova, Luba Gulyeava, Australian & Kirov ballet cos., 1983-93; studied with Ninel Kurgapkina, Ludmila Synelnikova, Genhrich Mayorov, Kirov Ballet, 1987-89; studied with Ludmila Sakharova, Perm Ballet, 1993; studied with Ludmila Synelnikova, Bolshoi Ballet Sch., Moscow, 1989; studied with Inna Zubkhovskaya, Alex. Stiopin, Lydia Goncharova, Valentina Chistova and Mararita Zagurskaya, studied with Mdm. Trafimova, Nina Sakhrouskaya and Valentina Rumyantsema, Vaganova Ballet Acad., 1993. Ballet mistress Adrian (Mich.) Coll., 1982-84; founder, artistic dir. Ann Arbor (Mich.) Ballet Theatre, 1980—. Former regional field judge Nat. Ballet Achievement Fund; dir. seminars Marygrove Coll., Detroit. Choreographer Cinderella, 1980, Nightingale, 1980, Nutcracker, 1984, Carnival of the Animals, 1981, Carmen, 1983, Midsummer Nights Dream, 1982, Vivaldi's Spring, 1990, Opulence, 1984, La Boutique Fantasque, 1995, Handel's Alcina, 1985, Gymnopedie, 1985, Gershwin's Preludes, 1996, Ravel's Bolero, 1997, Dracula, 1997, others. Ruth Mott grantee for choreography, 1982. Mem. Mich. Dance Assn. Avocations: gardening, reading, writing. Home: 6476 Huron River Dr Dexter MI 48130-9796 Office: CAS Ballet Theatre Sch Ann Arbor Ballet Theatre 548 Church St Ann Arbor MI 48104-2563

SCHAUB, PAUL B. lawyer; b. Waseca, Minn., Jan. 11, 1965; s. Frank Joseph and Marjory Ann (Kean) S. BA, Creighton U., Omaha, 1987, JD, 1991. Bar: Nebr. 1992, U.S. Dist. Ct. Nebr. 1992. Assoc. Peetz, Sonntag & Goodwin, P.C., Sidney, Nebr., 1992-95; county atty. Cheyenne County, 1995—. Mem. Cheyenne County Lawyers Assn., Nebr. State Bar Assn. Republican. Avocations: racquetball, camping. Office: Office Cheyenne County Atty PO Box 217 Sidney NE 69162-0217 Home: 1932 Maple St Sidney NE 69162-1836

SCHEETZ, SISTER MARY JOELLEN, English language educator; b. Lafayette, Ind., May 20, 1926; d. Joseph Albert and Ellen Isabelle (Fitzgerald) S. AB, St. Francis Coll., 1956; MA, U. Notre Dame, 1964; PhD, U. Mich., 1970. Tchr. English, Bishop Luers High Sch., Fort Wayne, Ind., 1965-67; acad. dean St. Francis Coll. (now U. St. Francis), 1967-68, pres. Ft. Wayne, Ind., 1970-93, pres. emeritus, English lang. prof. Ind., 1993—. Mem. Delta Epsilon Sigma. Office: U St Francis 2701 Spring St Fort Wayne IN 46808-3939 E-mail: jscheetz@sf.edu.

SCHEEVEL, KENRIC JAMES, state legislator; b. July 7, 1956; m. Karen Dornink. BA, Northwestern Coll., 1978; BSME, S.D. State U., 1981. Mem. Minn. Senate from 31st dist., St. Paul, 1994—. Address: RR 2 Box 227 Preston MN 55965-9570

SCHEIBER, STEPHEN CARL, psychiatrist; b. N.Y.C., May 2, 1938; s. Irving Martin and Frieda Olga (Schor) S.; m. Mary Ann McDonnell, Sept. 14, 1965; children: Lisa Susan, Martin Irving, Laura Ann. BA, Columbia Coll., 1960; MD, SUNY, Buffalo, 1964. Diplomate Am. Bd. Psychiatry and Neurology. Intern Mary Fletcher Hosp., Burlington, Vt., 1964-65; resident in psychiatry Strong Meml. Hosp., Rochester, N.Y., 1967-70; asst. prof. U. Ariz., Tucson, 1970-76, assoc. prof., 1976-81, prof., 1981-86; exec. sec. Am. Bd. Psychiatry and Neurology, Inc., Deerfield, Ill., 1986-89, exec. v.p., 1989—. Adj. prof. psychiatry Northwestern U., Chgo. and Evanston, 1986—, Med. Coll. Wis., Milw., 1986—. Co-editor: The Impaired Physician, 1983, Certification, Recertification and Lifetime Learning in Psychiatry, 1994; contbr. articles to profl. jours. Mem. med. adv. com. Casas de los Ninos, Tucson, 1974-86; mem. mental health adv. com. Tucson Health Planning Coun., 1974-75; med. student interviewer Office of Med. Edn., 1975; mem. Glenbrook (Ill.) North H.S. Boosters Club, 1988-91; treas. Robert E. Jones Found., 1988-96. Surgeon USPHS, 1965-67. Recipient Outstanding Tchr. award, U. Ariz., 1986, Lifetime Achievement award, SUNY, Buffalo, 1998; grantee Group Therapy Outcome Studies on Inpatient Svc., 1980, Dialysis and Schizophrenia Pilot Project, NIH, 1978. Fellow: Group for Advancement of Psychiatry (invited mem., chmn. mem. edn. com. 1987—91, bd. dirs., sec. 1993—97, pres.-elect 1997—99, pres. 1999—2001), Assn. Acad. Psychiatry (parliamentary sec. 1979—84, treas. 1984—88, pres.-elect 1988—89, pres. 1989—90), Am. Assn. Dirs. Psychiat. Residency Tng. (pres. 1981—82), Am. Coll. Psychiatrists (bd. regents 1992—2001, treas. 1995—2001), Am. Psychiat. Assn. (chmn. impaired physician com. 1985—88, cons. 1988—92); mem.: Oracle Heights Club (pres. 1983—84). Democrat. Jewish. Office: Am Bd Psychiatry & Neurology 500 Lake Cook Rd Ste 335 Deerfield IL 60015-5635

SCHEID, LINDA J. state legislator; b. June 16, 1942; 2 children. BA, Coe Coll.; JD, William Mitchell Coll. Law. Bar: Minn. Mem. Minn. Ho. of Reps., 1976, 82-90; mem. 47th dist. Minn. Senate, St. Paul, 1996—. Home: 6625 81st Ave N Brooklyn Park MN 55445-2513 Office: 317 Capitol 75 Constitution Ave Saint Paul MN 55155-1601

SCHEIDT, W. ROBERT, chemistry educator, researcher; b. Richmond Heights, Mo., Nov. 13, 1942; s. Walter Martin and Martha (Videtich) S.; m. Kathryn Sue Barnes, Aug. 9, 1964; children: Karl Andrew, David Martin. BS, U. Mo., 1964; MS, U. Mich., 1965, PhD, 1968; postdoctoral studies, Cornell U., 1970. Asst. prof. U. Notre Dame, Ind., 1970-76, assoc. prof., 1976-80, prof., 1980—, William K. Warren prof., 1999—. Vis. prof. U. Wash., Seattle, 1980, U. Paris (Orsay), France, 1991, U. Strasbourg, France, 1998; mem. review sect. Metallobiochemistry NIH, Bethesda, 1991-96. Contbr. articles to profl. jours. Fellow AAAS; mem. Am. Chem. Soc. (assoc. editor Chem. Revs. jour. 1980-85), Am. Crystallographic Assn., Biophys. Soc., Sigma X. Democrat. Office: U Notre Dame Dept Chemistry Notre Dame IN 46556 E-mail: scheidt.1@nd.edu.

SCHEINFELD, JAMES DAVID, travel agency executive; b. Milw., Nov. 11, 1926; s. Aaron and Sylvia (Rosenberg) S.; children from previous marriage: John Stephen, Shaina, Robert Alan; m. Elna Magnusson, 1994. BA in Econs. magna cum laude, U. Wis., 1949. With Manpower, Inc., 1948-78, salesman, Chgo., 1949-51, br. mgr., 1951-53, nat. sales mgr., Milw., 1953-56, dir. sales, corp. sec., 1956-59, v.p. sales, 1959-62, exec. v.p. mktg., 1962-65, exec. v.p. (sr.), chief ops. officer, 1965-76, v.p. spl. projects, 1976-78, mem. exec. com., bd. dirs., 1959-76, cons., 1978-84; exec. v.p., chief exec. officer, bd. dirs. Transpersonal, Inc., Any Task Inc., Manpower Argentina, Manpower Europe, Manpower Ltd. (U.K.), Manpower Australia, Manpower Japan, Manpower Germany GmbH, Manpower Norway, Manpower Denmark, Manpower Venezuela, 1966-76; pres. Travway Internat. Inc. - Funway Holidays, Funjet, 1976-81, Aide Svcs., Inc., Tampa, Fla., 1976-81; pres., chief exec. officer Travelpower Inc., 1976-84; sr. v.p. Carlson Travel Network, 1984—. Mem. Hickory Travel Systems Inc., 1977-85, bd. dirs., 1978-85, pres., 1980-82, pres. emeritus, 1982—. Contbr. articles to profl. jours. Chmn. Cancer Crusade Milwaukee County, 1970; bd. dirs. Sinai-Samaritan Med. Ctr., Better Bus. Bur. Milw., 1979-90, Found. for Santa Barbara City Coll., 1989—, pres., 1996-2000; trustee U. Wis. Milw. Found., 1981-91, emeritus trustee, 1991—; mem. bus. adv. bd. U. Wis.-Milw., 1987—; chmn. bus. adv. bd. Santa Barbara City Coll., 1988-92; dir. Santa Barbara Trust for Hist. Preservation, 1995—, v.p., 1998—; mem. Greater Milw. Com., 1984-97. With USNR, 1944-46. Mem. Nat. Assn. Temporary Svcs. (pres. 1975-76, bd. dirs. 1969-77), Univ. Club Milw., La Cumbre Country Club (Santa Barbara), Rotary Club of Montecito Calif. Home and Office: 129 Rametto Rd Santa Barbara CA 93108-2317 E-mail: jimscheinfeld1@cox.net.

SCHELBLE, DANIEL TIMOTHY, emergency medicine physician; b. LaCrosse, Wis., July 9, 1946; s. Robert Martin and Pearl Elizabeth (Newman) S.; m. Susan Jean Sadler, Oct. 27, 1973; children: Anita Marie, Dana Marie. BS in Biology, Loras Coll., Dubuque, Iowa, 1968; MD in Medicine, U. Wis., 1972. Diplomate Am. Bd. Emergency Medicine, recert. Surgery intern Meth. Hosp., Dallas, 1972-73; emergency medicine resident Akron (Ohio) Gen. Med. Ctr., 1975-77, emergency medicine residency dir., 1978-80, emergency medicine dept. chmn., 1980—, emergency medicine svcs. staff, 1977—. Prof. clin. emergency medicine Northeastern Ohio Univ. Coll. Medicine, 1994—. Contbr. numerous articles and chpts. to med. publs. Mem. mayor's adv. com. on emergency med. svcs. City of Akron, 1980—; med. advisor Mogadore (Ohio) Fire Dept., 1991—. Lt. USN M.C., 1973-75. Fellow Am. Coll. Emergency Physicians (mem. Ohio chpt., bd. dirs., mem. reimbursement com. 1977—), Soc. Tchrs. of Emergency Medicine (bd. dirs., pres.-elect, pres., chmn. pub. rels. 1980—), Summit County Med. Soc. Republican. Avocations: physical fitness, 20th century American history. Office: Akron Gen Med Ctr 400 Wabash Ave Akron OH 44307-2463 E-mail: Lvanscoy@agmc.org.

SCHELLEN, NANDO, opera director; b. The Hague, The Netherlands, Oct. 11, 1934; came to U.S., 1993; m. Deborah Raymond, June 19, 1991; 4 children. Mng. dir. Netherlands Opera, 1969-79, assoc. gen. dir., 1979-87; gen. artistic dir. Sweelinck Conservatory of Music, Amsterdam, 1990-93; gen. dir. Indpls. Opera, 1993-96; dir. opera theatre No. Ariz. U., Flagstaff, 2000—. Freelance stage dir., 1982—. Home: 3841 Woodride E Way Flagstaff AZ 86004

SCHENDEL, DAN ELDON, management consultant, business educator; b. Norwalk, Wis., Mar. 29, 1934; s. Leonard A. and Marian T. (Koch) S.; m. Mary Lou Sigler, Sept. 1, 1956; children: Suzanne, Pamela, Sharon. BS in Metall. Engring., U. Wis., 1956; MBA, Ohio State U., 1959; PhD (Ford Found. fellow), Stanford U., 1963. With ALCOA, 1956, U.S. Civil Svc., 1959-60, SRI, 1963-65; prof. mgmt., dir. exec. edn. programs Purdue U., Lafayette, Ind., 1965-85; vis. prof. U. Mich., 1988-89, U. Chgo., 1990-91. Dean German Grad. Internat. Sch. Mgmt. and Adminstrn., Hannover, Germany; pres. Strat egic Mgmt. Assocs., Inc. Author: (with others) Strategy Formulation: Analytical Concepts, 1978, Divided Loyalties, 1980, Fundamental Issues in Strategy, 1994; editor: (with others) Strategic Management: A New View of Business Policy and Planning, 1979; founding editor Strategic Mgmt. Jour., 1980—. Served with USAF, 1956-59. Fellow Acad. Mgmt.; mem. Strategic Mgmt. Soc. (founding pres., exec. dir.), Lafayette Country Club, Univ. Club Chgo. Home: 1327 N Grant St West Lafayette IN 47906-2463 Office: Krannert Grad Sch Mgmt Purdue U West Lafayette IN 47907 E-mail: schendel@mgmt.purdue.edu.

SCHENKENBERG, MARY MARTIN, principal; b. Oakland, Calif., Nov. 29, 1944; d. Leo Patrick and Florence Kathryn (Brinkoetter) Martin; m. Philip Rawson Schenkenberg III, Aug. 20, 1966; children: Philip Rawson IV, Amy Lynn, Stephen Patrick. BA in English, Fontbonne Coll., 1966; MA Teaching in English, St. Louis U., 1975, PhD in English, 1991. Cert. tchr., Mo. Asst. prof. Fontbonne Coll., St. Louis, 1978-85; English dept. chair Nerinx Hall High Sch., 1979-89; asst. prof. Webster U., 1986-89; co-prin. Nerinx Hall High Sch., 1989-92, prin., 1992—. Adj. prof. St. Louis U., 1985-89; advanced placement reader Ednl. Testing Svc., Princeton, N.J., 1986-89. Author: (with others) The English Classroom in the Computer Age, 1991. Bd. mem. pres. Mary, Queen of Peace Sch., St. Louis, 1977. Mem. ASCD, Nat. Coun. Tchrs. English, Greater St. Louis Tchrs. English (bd. dirs. 1989—). Roman Catholic. Avocations: tennis, theater, travel. Office: Nerinx Hall High Sch 530 E Lockwood Ave Webster Groves MO 63119-3278

SCHERB, JEFF R. newspaper company executive; BA in Bus. Adminstrn., Computer Sci., Rutgers U. Mgmt. positions Commodore Internat. Ltd, Cullinet Software Inc.; v.p. systems devel. Turner Broadcasting; chief tech. officer, sr. v.p. R & D Dun & Bradstreet Software; sr. v.p., chief tech. officer Tribune Co., Chgo., 1999—. Office: Tribune Co 435 N Michigan Ave Chicago IL 60611-4066

SCHERER, ANITA (ANITA STOCK), gerontologist, marketing consultant; b. Sept. 20, 1938; d. William John Stock and Gertrud Clara (Kaufmann) Bacher; m. Richard Phillip Scherer, Nov. 25, 1961; children: William Richard, Christopher Howard. Student, U. Cin., 1956-57; AB, Jones Bus. Coll., 1958; BA, Coll. Mount St. Joseph, 1999. Acct. sec. Northlich, Stolley Inc., Cin., 1978-79, acct. asst., 1979-80, asst. acct. mgr., 1980-81, acct. mgr., 1981-84, mktg. svc. assoc., 1984-89, mgr., 1989-97. Lectr. local schs., univs., Cin. 1980-93; adv. bd. mem. performing arts Coll. Mount St. Joseph, Ohio, 1974-80; mktg. cons. for the over 50 market; trustee Arts and Humanities Resource Ctr. for Older Adults, 1990—, chmn. bd., 1991-93. Co-editor: monthly newsletter Badge, 1967-72; designer assorted notepads, 1986. Corr. sec. Delhi Police Assn. Inc., Ohio, 1967—72; pres. Delhi Hills Cmty. Coun., 1974—75; v.p. adminstr. Stagecrafters, Cin., 1983—85, publicity chmn., 1984—89; mktg. bd. mem. Contemp. Arts Ctr., 1985—97; chmn. Advt./Graphic Arts div. Fine Arts Fund Campaign, 1988; docent Cin. Art Mus., 2002; Lector Our Lady of Victory Roman Cath. Ch., Cin., 1972—. Winner nat. competition Am. Assn. Advt. Agys., 1980; recipient Outstanding Performance award Assn. Cmty. Theatres, Cin., 1983, Excellence in Acting award Ohio Cmty. Theatres Assn., 1984, Outstanding Achievement Gerontological Studies, Coll. Mount St. Joseph, 1999; first American to participate in Kalkriese dig, Germany, 1993, 95. Mem. Am. Mktg. Assn., Acad. Health Svcs. Mktg. (adv. bd. dirs. 1989-91), Cin. C. of C. (lectr. 1984-86). Avocations: travel, reading, medieval/renaissance history, community theater, archaeology. Home: 5511 Palomino Dr Cincinnati OH 45238-4143

SCHERER, GEORGE F. construction executive; Exec. v.p., treas., CFO, McCarthy Bldg. Cos., St. Louis. Office: McCarthy Bldg Cos 1341 N Rock Hill Rd Saint Louis MO 63124-1441

SCHERER, NORBERT FRANZ, chemistry educator; b. Milw., July 9, 1960; s. Franz and Ilse Scherer; m. Seung-Eun Choi, June 2, 1990; children: Matthew S., Amanda, Andrew. BS, U. Chgo., 1982; PhD, Caltech., 1989. NSF postdoctoral fellow U. Chgo., 1989-91, postdoctoral assoc., 1991-92; asst. prof. chemistry U. Pa., Phila., 1992-97; prof. chemistry U. Chgo., 1997—. Contbr. articles to sci. publs. Recipient Nat. Young Investigator award NSF, 1993-98; David and Lucile Packard fellow, 1993-98, Arnold and Mabel Beckman fellow, 1994-96, Alfred P. Sloan fellow, 1997; Camille Dreyfus tchr.-scholar, 1996. Mem. Am. Chem. Soc., Am. Phys. Soc., Optical Soc. Am.

SCHERER, RONALD CALLAWAY, voice scientist, educator; b. Akron, Ohio, Sept. 11, 1945; s. Belden Davis and Lois Ramona (Callaway) S.; children: Christopher, Maria. BS, Kent State U., 1968; MA, Ind. U., 1972; PhD, U. Iowa, 1981. Research asst. U. Iowa, Iowa City, 1979-81, asst. research scientist, 1981-83, adj. asst. prof., 1983-88, adj. assoc. prof., 1988—; adj. asst. prof. U. Denver, 1984-86; asst. adj. prof. U. Colo., Boulder, 1984-93, adj. assoc. prof., 1993-96; research scientist The Denver Ctr. for the Performing Arts, 1983-88, sr. scientist, 1988-96; lectr. voice and speech sci. Nat. Theatre Conservatory, Denver, 1990-94; asst. clin. prof. Sch. Medicine U. Colo., 1988-96; assoc. prof. Bowling Green State U.,

Ohio, 1996—2001, prof., 2001—. Adj. assoc. prof. U. Okla., 1992-96; affiliate clin. prof. U. No. Colo., 1993-96; Oberlin Coll. affiliate scholar, 1996—; mem. exec. and legis. bd. Nat. Ctr. for Voice and Speech, 1990-96. Author: (with Dr. I. Titze) Vocal Fold Physiology: Biomechanics, Acoustics and Phonatory Control, 1983; contbr. articles to profl. jours. Nat. Inst. Dental Research fellow, 1972-76. Fellow Internat. Soc. Phonetic Scis. (auditor 1988-91); mem. Internat. Arts Medicine Assn., Am. Speech-Lang.-Hearing Assn., Acoustical Soc. Am., Internat. Assn. Logopedics and Phoniatrics, Am. Assn. Phonetic Scis. (nominating com. 1985-87), Collegium Medicorum Theatri, Sigma Xi, Pi Mu Epsilon. Office: Bowling Green State U Dept Comm Disorders Bowling Green OH 43403-0001

SCHERER, VICTOR RICHARD, physicist, computer specialist, consultant, musician; b. Poland, Feb. 7, 1940; came to U.S., 1941; s. Emanuel and Florence B. Scherer; m. Gail R. Dobrofsky, Aug. 11, 1963; children: Helena Cecile, Markus David. BS magna cum laude, CCNY, 1960; MA, Columbia U., 1962; PhD, U. Wis., 1974. Health physics asst. Columbia U., N.Y.C., 1961-63; rsch asst. physics. dep. U. Wis., Madison, 1967-74; project assoc., project mgr. Inst. for Environ. Studies, World Climate-Food Rsch. Group, 1974-78; specialist computer systems U. Wis. Acad. Computing Ctr., 1978—; coord., sr. cons. Divsn. Info. Tech. U. Wis., Madison; concert pianist; tchr.; promoter contemporary composers. Researcher in particle physics, agroclimatology, soil-yield relationships and computer graphics; cons. on computer sys., electronic mail, geographic analysis, help desk and supercomputing applications. Fellow AEC, 1960-61. Mem. AAAS, Am. Phys. Soc., Am. Meteorol. Soc., Am. Soc. Agronomy, Assn. Computing Machinery, Nat. Computer Graphics Assn., Phi Beta Kappa, Sigma Xi. Office: U Wis-Madison Divsn Info Tech 1210 W Dayton St Madison WI 53706-1613

SCHERMER, LLOYD G. publishing and broadcasting company executive; b. St. Louis, 1927; married. Student Amherst U., 1950, Harvard U. Grad. Sch. Bus. Adminstrn., 1952. With Lee Enterprises, Inc., Davenport, Iowa, 1955— , pres., chief exec. officer, from 1974, now pres., also dir.; chmn. Newspaper Advt. Bur.; dir. Davenport Bank & Trust Co., NAPP Systems (USA), Inc. Bd. dirs. U. Mont. Found. Mem. Am. Soc. Newspaper Editors, Am. Newspaper Pubs. Assn. (dir.; dir. Found.). Office: Lee Enterprises Inc 400 PUTNAM BLDG. 215 N. MAIN ST ., STE 400 Davenport IA 52801-1924

SCHEUMANN, JOHN B. construction executive; BS, Ball State U. Chair, CEO Crossman Cmtys., Indpls., 1996—. Office: 92 N Meridian St Ste 300 Indianapolis IN 46204-3003

SCHEVE, MAY E. state legislator; b. St. Louis, June 27, 1964; d. Robert Anthony and May Ellen (Braun) S. BA, St. Louis U., 1987; postgrad., Webster U. Rep. Mo. State Ho. Reps. Dist. 98, 1991—. Committeewoman Gravois Twp. Dem. Club. Mem. Women Legislators, Third Congl. Women's Club (sec.), Women's Dem. Forum, Alpha Gamma Delta, Kappa Beta Phi. Office: Mo Ho of Reps State Capitol Bldg 201 W Capitol Ave Rm 401A Jefferson City MO 65101-1556

SCHIESER, HANS ALOIS, education educator; b. Ulm, Germany, July 15, 1931; came to U.S., 1965; s. Alois and Anna (Stegmann) S.; m. Margret H. Schröer, June 6, 1962; children: Peter, Elisabeth. BA, Kepler Gymnasium, Ulm, 1952; MA in Philosophy, Passau, Fed. Republic Germany, 1959; EdM, Pedagogic Acad., Weingarten, Fed. Republic Germany, 1962; PhD, Loyola U., 1970. Head tchr. Pestalozzischule, Ulm, 1964-65; learning disabilities tchr. Jeanine Schultz Meml. Sch., Skokie, Ill., 1966-67; co-dir. Oak Therapeutic Sch., Evanston, 1967-70; from assoc. prof. to prof. edn. DePaul U., Chgo., 1969-91, prof. emeritus, 1991—. Cons. in field; program cons. Delphian Soc., L.A., 1977-90; rschr., tchr. in Germany, 1991—; active in tchrs. edn. Midwest Montessori Tchr. Tng. Ctr., Evanston, Ill.; adv. bd. Verein Psychol.; vis. prof. State U. Chelyabinsk, State Linguistic U., Irkutsk, Russia 1998; ord. prof. Gustav-Siewerth-Akademie, Germany; prof. G. Siewerth Akademie (Germany). Author chpts. in books; contbr. articles to profl. jours.; adv. bd. Ann. Edits. Sociology, Dushkin Pub. Group, 1985-91. Pres. N.Am. Family Svc. Found., Oak Lawn, Ill., 1974-91; bd. dirs. S.O.S. Children's Villages USA, Washington, 1986-94; pres. emeritus S.O.S. Children's Village Ill., Inc., Chgo.; bd. govs. Invest-in-Am. Nat. Found., Phila., 1988-90. Rsch. grant DePaul U., 1985-86, Rsch. sabbatical, 1989. Mem. Am. Ednl. Studies Assn., Nat. Soc. for Study of Edn., Philosophy of Edn. Soc. U.S.A., Soc. Educators and Scholars (bd. dirs. 1984-90), Am. Montessori Soc., Thomas More Gesellschaft/Amici Mori Europe, Phi Delta Kappa (pres. Zeta chpt., Chgo. 1973-75). Home: Veilchenweg 9 D-89134 Bermaringen Germany also: 400 E Main/6B/DJURI Evanston IL 60202 Office: DePaul U 2320 N Kenmore Ave Chicago IL 60614-3210 E-mail: prof_schieser@hotmail.com.

SCHIFF, GILBERT MARTIN, virologist, microbiologist, medical educator; b. Cin., Oct. 21, 1931; married, 1955; 2 children. BS, U. Cin., 1953, MD, 1957. Intern U. Hosp., Iowa City, 1957-58, resident internal medicine, 1958-59; med. officer lab br. Communicable Diseases Ctr., Ga., 1959-61; head tissue culture investigation unit, perinatal rsch. br. Nat. Inst. Neurol. Diseases and Blindness, 1961-64; dir. clin. virology lab. U. Cin., 1964-78, asst. prof. medicine and microbiology, 1964-67, asst. prof. microbiology, 1967-71, prof. medicine Coll. Medicine, 1971—; pres. James N. Gamble Inst. Medical Rsch., 1984—. Attending physician dept. medicine Emory U., Atlanta, 1959-61; cons. com. maternal health Ohio State Med. Assn., 1964-70, Hamilton County Neuromuscular Diagnostic Clinic, 1966, 75, Contract Immunization Status in U.S., 1975-77; mem. com. viral hepatitis among dental pers. VA; mem. immunization practice adv. com. Surgeon Gen., 1971-75; dir. Christ Hosp Inst. Med. Rsch., Cin., 1974-83, chairperson libr. com., 1974—, mem. com. cancer programs, 1979—, mem. com. human rsch., 1980—, chairperson search com., dir. radiotherapy, 1980-82; mem. com. infection control, 1981—, mem. com. univ. liaisons, 1982—; mem. subcom. antimicrobial agents U.S. Pharmacopeia, 1977-80; mem. study sect., adv. com., review com. NIH; mem. com. Rubella immunization Ohio Dept. Health; com. Rubella control Cin. Dept. Health. Trustee Children's Hosp. Med. Ctr., rsch. com., 1985—; community adv. com. Hoxworth Blood Ctr., 1991—. Recipient career rsch. devel. award Nat. Inst. Child Health and Human Devel., 1970-74; grantee USPHS, 1964-67, Nat. found., 1965-67. Fellow ACP; mem. AAAS, Am. Soc. Microbiology, Am. Fedn. Clin. Rsch. (sec.-treas. 1967-70), Am. Pub. Health Assn., Sci. Rsch. Soc. Am., Ctrl. Soc. Clin. Rsch. (sec.-treas. 1977-81, v.p. 1983, pres. 1984), Infectious Disease Soc. Am. Am. Soc. Clin. Investigation, Sigma Xi. Office: Dept Pediatrics U Cincinnati Coll Med 3333 Burnet Ave Cincinnati OH 45229-3026

SCHIFF, JOHN JEFFERSON, JR. finance company executive; BA, Ohio State U. Chmn., CEO John J. & Thomas R. Schiff & Co., Inc., 1983-96; pres., CEO Cin. Fin. Corp., 1986—, also chmn. bd. dirs. Trustee Am. Inst. Charatered Property Casualty Underwriters; dir. 5th 3d Bancorp, Cinergy Corp., Std. Register Co., Cin. Bengals, Inc. Office: Cin Fin Group PO Box 145496 Cincinnati OH 45250-5496

SCHIFFER, JOHN PAUL, physicist, educator; b. Budapest, Hungary, Nov. 22, 1930; came to U.S., 1947, naturalized, 1953; s. Ernest and Elisabeth (Tornai) S.; m. Marianne Tsuk, June 28, 1960; children: Celia Anne, Peter Ernest. AB, Oberlin Coll., 1951; MS, Yale U., 1952, PhD, 1954; DSc (hon.), Notre Dame U., 1999. Research asso. Rice Inst., Houston, 1954-56; asst. physicist Argonne (Ill.) Nat. Lab., 1956-59, asso. physicist, 1960-63, sr. physicist, 1964—, assoc. dir. physics div., 1964-79, 83-99, dir. physics div., 1979-82, 99. Prof. physics U. Chgo., 1968-99, prof. emeritus, 1999; vis. asso. prof. Princeton, 1964; vis. prof. U. Rochester, N.Y., 1967-68; mem. adv. coms. nuclear physics Nat. Acad. Scis.; mem. program adv. or rev. coms. Los Alamos Meson Physics Facility, 1971-73, Ind. U. Cylotron Facility, 1974-77, Lab. for Nuclear Sci., M.I.T., 1975-79, Lawrence Berkeley Lab, Bevalac, 1978-80, Swiss Inst. Nuclear Research, 1981-85, Max Planck Inst. Nuclear Physics, 1982-85; mem. physics adv. panel NSF, 1971-73; mem. Nuclear Sci. Adv. Com. Dept. Energy/NSF, 1981-85, chmn., 1983-85; chmn. program adv. com. CEBAF, 1986-91; chmn. subcom. Implementation of 1989 Long Range Plan for Nuclear Sci.; chair Com. on Nuclear Physics, NRC, 1996—; Riken (Japan) Adv. Coun., 1996—. Editor: Comments on Nuclear and Particle Physics, 1971-75; assoc. editor Revs. Modern Physics, 1972-77; mem. editorial bd. Phys. Rev. C, 1983-85; editor: Physics Letters, 1978— ; mem. editorial com. ann. revs. of nuclear and particle sci., 1987-91; contbr. articles on nuclear structure physics and nuclear reactions to phys. jours. and books. Mem. cold fusion panel Dept. Energy, 1989. Recipient Alexander V. Humboldt Found. sr. U.S. scientist award, 1973-74; Wilbur Cross medal Yale U., 1985; Guggenheim fellow, 1959-60 Fellow AAAS (mem. coun., chair physics sect. 1992-93), Am. Acad. Arts and Scis., Am. Phys. Soc. (chmn. div. nuclear physics 1975-76, Tom W. Bonner prize 1976); mem. NAS, Royal Danish Acad. Scis. and Letters. Achievements include research on nuclear structure, Mössbauer effect, heavy-ion reactions, pion interactions in nuclei, quark searches, crystalline order in confined cold plasmas. Office: Physics Division Argonne Nat Lab Argonne IL 60439

SCHILLER, DONALD CHARLES, lawyer; b. Chgo., Dec. 8, 1942; s. Sidney S. and Edith (Lastick) S.; m. Eileen Fagin, June 14, 1964; children— Eric, Jonathan Student, Lake Forest Coll., 1960-63; J.D., DePaul U., 1966. Bar: Ill. 1966, U.S. Dist. Ct. (no. dist.) Ill. 1966, U.S. Supreme Ct. 1972. Ptnr. Schiller, DuCanto & Fleck (formerly Schiller & Schiller and Schiller & DuCanto), Chgo., 1966—; lectr. in law U. Chgo. Law Sch. Chair domestic rels. adv. com. Cir. Ct. Cook County, 1993—2001, exec. com., 1986—93; lectr. in law U. Chgo. Law Sch., 2001—; spkr. profl. confs. Contbr. chpts. and articles to profl. publs. Mem. steering com. on juvenile ct. watching, LWV, 1980-81. Recipient Maurice Weigle award Chgo. Bar Found., 1978, Disting. Alumni award, DePaul U., 1988, various certs. of appreciation profl. groups: named One of Am.'s Best Divorce Lawyers, Town and Country, 1985, 98, The Nat. Law Jour., 1987, The Best Lawyers in Am., 1987—, One of Chgo's. Best Div. Lawyers, Crain's Chgo. Bus., 1981, Today Chgo. Woman, 1985, Inside Chgo. mag., 1988, Chgo. Sun Times, 2000. Fellow Am. Bar Found., Am. Acad. Matrimonial Lawyers (nat. chair continuing legal edn. 1993-94); mem. ABA (bd. govs. 1994-97, chmn. family law sect. 1985-86, Ill. State del. 1980-84, mem. Ho. of Dels. 1984—, editor-in-chief Family Law Newsletter 1977-79; mem. editorial bd., assoc. editor Family Adv. Mag. 1979-84, speaker at confs. and meetings), Ill. Bar Assn. (pres. 1987-88, chmn. family law sect. 1976-77, editor Family Law Bull. 1976-77, bd. govs. 1977-83, treas. 1981-84, v.p. 1984-86, chmn. various coms., lectr., incorporator and pres. Ill. State Bar Assn. Mutual Ins. Co., Inc. 1988-89), Chgo. Bar Assn., Am. Coll. Family Law Trial Lawyers (diplomate). Office: Schiller DuCanto & Fleck 200 N La Salle St Ste 2700 Chicago IL 60601-1098 E-mail: dschiller@sdflaw.com.

SCHILLER, JAMES JOSEPH, lawyer; b. Cleve., July 1, 1933; s. Jacob Peter and Helen Elizabeth (Tosh) S.; m. Sara Brooke Wilson, Oct. 24, 1964; children: Charles A., Brooke V.G., Kristan W. BS, Case Inst. Tech., 1955; JD, U. Mich., 1961. Bar: Ohio 1962. Assoc. Marshman, Hornbeck & Hollington, Cleve., 1961-68; ptnr. Marshman, Snyder & Seeley, 1968-73, Zellmer & Gruber, Cleve., 1973-80, Weston, Hurd, Fallon, Paisley & Howley, Cleve., 1980-88, Porter, Wright, Morris & Arthur, Cleve., 1989-95, James J. Schiller & Assocs., Cleve., 1995—. Campaign mgr. John J. Gilligan for Gov. of Ohio, Cuyahoga County, 1970; campaign dir. U.S. Senator Howard M. Metzenbaum, Cleve., 1973; mem. Ohio Dem. Com., 1970-73; dep. registrar motor vehicles Dept. Hwy. Safety, Cuyahoga County, 1971-74; trustee Greater Cleve. Regional Transit Authority, 1985-87; vestryman Christ Episcopal Ch., Shaker Heights, Ohio, 1974-76, 90-93, clk., 1974-76, sr. warden, 1992-93; chmn. bd. suprs. ChristCh. Found., 1995—; trustee Recovery Resources, 1988—, chmn. bd. dirs., exec. com., 1994-96; trustee Ohio Ch. Orch., exec. com., 1996—; trustee Cleve. Ballet, 1997—. Lt. j.g. USNR, 1955-58. Recipient Cert. Commendation Bd. County Commrs., 1987. Mem. ABA, Ohio State Bar Assn. (ethics com. 1986-88), Cleve. Bar Assn., Rowfant Club (fin. com. 1988, coun. Fellowes 1990-91, 95—, advocate 1992-95, v.p. 1998-99, pres. 1999-2000), Union Club, Cleve. Skating Club. Avocations: sailing, skiing, restoring furniture. Home: 13415 Shaker Blvd Cleveland OH 44120-1586 Office: James J Schiller & Assocs 13224 Shaker Sq Ste 210 Cleveland OH 44120-2349

SCHILLER, WILLIAM RICHARD, surgeon; b. Bennett, Colo., Jan. 14, 1937; s. Francis T. and Frances M. (Finks) S.; m. Beverlee Schiller; children from previous marriage: Julie, Lisa. B.S., Drury Coll., Springfield, Mo., 1958; M.D., Northwestern U., 1962. Diplomate Am. Bd. Surgery; cert. of added qualifications in surg. critical care, 1987, recertified in surg. critical care, 1994. Intern Passavant Meml. Hosp., Chgo., 1962-63; resident Northwestern U. Clin. Tng. Program, 1963-68; assoc. prof. surgery Med. Coll Ohio, Toledo, 1970-78; prof. surgery U. N.Mex, Albuquerque, 1978-83; dir. Trauma Ctr. St. Joseph's Hosp., Phoenix, 1983-89; dir. burn and trauma ctr. Maricopa Med. Ctr., 1989-98; prof. surgery So. Ill. U., Springfield, 1998—. Clin. prof. surgery U. Ariz. Health Sci. Ctr.; prof. surgery Mayo Grad. Sch. Medicine, Rochester, Minn. Contbr. chpts. to books, articles to profl. jours. Served as maj. M.C. U.S. Army, 1968-70, Vietnam. Fellow ACS; mem. Am. Assn. Surgery of Trauma, Cen. Surg. Assn., Western Surg. Assn., Soc. Surgery of Alimentary Tract, Am. Burn Assn., Internat. Soc. of Surgery. Republican. Home: 4505 Innis Brk Springfield IL 62707-6713 Office: So Ill Univ Med Sch Trauma Ctr Dept Surgery Box 19638 Springfield IL 62794-9638 E-mail: wschiller@siumed.edu.

SCHILLING, DON RUSSELL, electric utility executive; b. Greenburg, Ind., June 11, 1951; s. Cloyd H. and Ruth V. (Knarr) S.; m. Teri L. Edwards, July 14, 1973; children: Jaclyn, Christopher. BS in Elec. Engring., Purdue U., 1973; MS in Bus. Adminstrn., Ind. U., Fort Wayne, 1977. Registered profl. engr., Ind. Elec. engr. Ind. and Mich. Electric Co., Fort Wayne, 1973-79; asst. gen. mgr. Decatur County REMC, Greensburg, Ind., 1979-86, pres., gen. mgr., 1986—; sec.-treas. Hometown Energy LLC, 2001—. Pres. Ind. Rural TV, Inc., 1988-89. Mem. IEEE, Greensburg Area C. of C. (pres. 1994), Lions, Masons. Baptist. Avocations: woodworking. Office: Decatur County REMC PO Box 46 Greensburg IN 47240-0046 E-mail: dschilling@dcremc.com.

SCHILLING, EMILY BORN, editor, association executive; b. Lawton, Okla., Oct. 2, 1959; d. George Arthur and Sumiko (Nagamine) Born; m. Mark David Schilling, June 26, 1995. BS, Ball State U., 1981. Cert. coop. communicator Nat. Rural Electric Coop. Assn. Feature writer The News-Sentinel, Fort Wayne, Ind., 1981-83; wire editor The Noblesville (Ind.) Daily Ledger, 1983; staff writer Ind. Statewide Assn. Rural Electric Coops., Indpls., 1983-84, mng. editor, 1984-85, editor, 1985—. Author: Power to the People, 1985. Mem. Coop. Communicators Assn. (Michael Graznak award 1990), Internat. Assn. Bus. Communicators (award of excellence dist. 7 1985), Women's Internat. Network of Utility Profls. (pres. 1999, Mem. of Yr. 1999, Power award 1994), Nat. Electric Coops. Statewide Editors Assn. Office: Ind Statewide Assn RECs 720 N High School Rd Indianapolis IN 46214-3756

SCHILLING, MIKE, state legislator; Rep. Mo. State Ho. Reps. Dist. 136. Home: 1027 S New Ave Springfield MO 65807-1346 Office: Mo Ho of Reps State Capitol Jefferson City MO 65101

SCHILLINGS, DENNY LYNN, history educator, grants manager; b. Mt. Carmel, Ill., June 28, 1947; s. Grady Lynn and Mary Lucille (Walters) S.; m. Karen Krek; children: Denise, Corinne. AA, Wabash Valley Coll., 1967; BEd, Ea. Ill. U., 1969, MA in History, 1972; MA in Adminstrn., Govs. State U., 1996; postgrad., Ill. State U., No. Ill. U. Grad. asst. dept. history Ea. Ill. U., Charleston, 1969; tchr. Edwards County High Sch., Albion, Ill., 1969-70, Sheldon (Ill.) High Sch., 1971-73, Homewood-Flossmoor (Ill.) High Sch., 1973—, grants and devel. mgr., 1994—. Participant, con. Atlantic Coun. U.S. and NATO, Washington, 1986, Internat. Soviet-U.S. Textbook Project Conf., Racine, Wis., 1987; moderator Soviet-U.S. Textbook Study: Final Report, Dallas, 1987; chair history content adv. com. Ill. Tchr. Certification Requirements Com. 1986; mem. Ill. State Bd. Edn., Com. to Establish Learner Outcomes, 1984, Joint Task Force on Admission Requirements Ill. State Bd. on Higher Edn., 1986—; mem. adv. com. for Jefferson Found. Sch. Programs, 1987-90, Ill. State Bd. Edn.'s Goals Assessment Adv. Com., 1987-90; chair Ill. Learning Standards Project, 1996-97. Author: (with others) Economics, 1986, The Examination in Social Studies, 1989, Links Across Time and Place: A World History, 1990, Illinois Government Text, 1990, Challenge of Freedom, 1990; author: The Living Constitution, 1991, 2d edit., 2002; co-editor: Teaching the Constitution, 1987; reviewer, cons. for ednl. instns. and organizations; chair editorial bd. Social Edn., 1983; contbg. editor Social Studies Tchr., 1987-88. Mem. steering com. Homewood-Floosmoor High Sch. Found., 1983-84; elected bd. edn. Homewood Elem. Dist. 153, 1999—. Mem. NEA, Am. Hist. Assn. (James Harvey Robinson prize com. 1990-91), Ill. Coun. Social Studies (v.p. 1981, editor newsletter 1979-84, pres. 1983), Ill. Edn. Assn. (Gt. Lakes coord. com. 1982-83), Nat. Coun. Social Studies (publs. bd. 1983-86, bd. dirs. 1987-90, 94-96, exec. com. 1989-90, chair conf. com. 1989-90, pres. 1993-94, program planning com. 1989, 91), Phi Alpha Theta. Avocations: computers, reading. Home: 18447 Aberdeen St Homewood IL 60430-3525 Office: Homewood-Flossmoor High Sch 999 Kedzie Ave Flossmoor IL 60422-2248 E-mail: dschillings@hfhighschool.org.

SCHILSKY, RICHARD LEWIS, oncologist, researcher; b. N.Y.C., June 6, 1950; s. Murray and Shirley (Cohen) S.; m. Cynthia Schum, Sept. 24, 1977; children: Allison, Meredith. BA cum laude, U. Pa., Phila., 1971; MD with honors, U. Chgo., 1975. Diplomate Nat. Bd. Med. Examiners, Am. Bd. Internal Medicine (subspecialty med. oncology); lic. physician, Mo., Ill. Intern, resident medicine Parkland Meml. Hosp., Southwestern Med. Sch., Dallas, 1975-77; clin. assoc. medicine br. and clin. pharmacology br. Divsn. Cancer Treatment, Nat. Cancer Inst., Bethesda, Md., 1977-80, cancer expert clin. pharmacology br., 1980-81; asst. prof. dept. internal medicine U. Mo. Sch. Medicine, Columbia, 1981-84; asst. prof. dept. medicine U. Chgo. Pritzker Sch. Medicine and Michael Reese Med. Ctrs., 1984-86, assoc. prof. dept. medicine, 1986-89; assoc. dir. joint sect. hematology and med. oncology U. Chgo. and Michael Reese Med. Ctrs., 1986-89; assoc. prof. dept. medicine, assoc. dir. sect. U. Chgo. Pritzker Sch. Medicine, 1989-91, prof. dept. medicine sect. hematology-oncology, 1991—; dir. U. Chgo. Cancer Rsch. Ctr., 1991-99; chmn. Cancer and Leukemia Group B, Chgo., 1995—; assoc. dean clin. rsch. biol. scis. divsn. U. Chgo., 1999—. Vivian Saykaly vis. prof. oncology McGill U., 1992; sci. com. Internat. Congress on Anti-Cancer Chemotherapy, 2002; adv. panel on hematologic and neoplastic disease U.S. Pharmacopeial Conv., 1991-95; bd. dirs. Assn. Am. Cancer Insts., 1995-99; cancer ctr. support grant rev. com. Nat. Cancer Inst., NIH, 1992-95; expert panel on advances in cancer treatment, 1992-93; mem. Cancer Ctrs. Working Group, 1996-97; oncologic drugs adv. com. FDA, 1996-2000, chmn., 1999-2000; mem. NCI Clin. Trials Implementation com., 1997-98; bd. scientific advisors Nat. Cancer Inst., 1999—. Mem. editl. bd. Investigational New Drugs, 1988-95, Jour. Clin. Oncology, 1990-93, Contemporary Oncology, 1991-95, Jour. Cancer Rsch. and Clin. Oncology, 1991—, Seminars in Oncology, 1997—; assoc. editor Clin. Cancer Rsch., 1994—, Cancer Therapeutics, 1997-99, Cancer, 2000—; contbr. articles to profl. jours., chpts. to books. With USPHS, 1977-80. Recipient Spl. Advancement for Performance award VA, 1983, Fletcher Scholar award Cancer Rsch. Found., 1989; grantee VA, 1981-87, Am. Cancer Soc., 1983-86, 92-95, Ill. Cancer Coun., 1985-86, Michael Reese Inst. Coun., 1985-86, Nat. Cancer Inst., 1987, 88-90, Burroughs-Wellcome Co., 1987-88, NIH/Nat. Cancer Inst., 1988— Fellow ACP; mem. AAAS, Am. Soc. Clin. Oncology (chmn. pub. rels. com. 1994-96, bd. dirs. 2002-), Am. Assn. Cancer Rsch. (chmn. Ill. state legis. com. 1992—), Am. Fedn. Clin. Rsch. (senator Midwest sect. 1983-84, councilor 1983-86, chmn.-elect 1987-88, chmn. 1988-89), Am. Cancer Soc. (bd. dirs. Ill. divsn. 1997—), Am. Assn. Cancer Edn., Am. Soc. Clin. Pharmacology and Therapeutics, Ctrl. Soc. Clin. Rsch., N.Y. Acad. Scis., Assn. Am. Cancer Insts. (bd. dirs. 1995-99), Chgo. Soc. Internal Medicine, Sigma Xi, Alpha Epsilon Delta, Alpha Omega Alpha. Office: U Chgo Biol Scis Divsn 5841 S Maryland Ave Chicago IL 60637-1463 E-mail: rs27@midway.uchicago.edu.

SCHIMBERG, A(RMAND) BRUCE, retired lawyer; b. Chgo., Aug. 26, 1927; s. Archie and Helen (Isay) S.; m. Barbara Zisook; children: Geoffrey, Kate. PhB, U. Chgo., 1949, JD, 1952. Bar: Ohio 1952, Ill. 1955, U.S. Supreme Ct. 1987. Assoc. Paxton & Seasongood, Cin., 1952-55; ptnr. Schimberg, Greenberger, Kraus & Jacobs, Chgo., 1955-65, Leibman, Williams, Bennett, Baird & Minow, Chgo., 1965-72, Sidley & Austin, Chgo., 1972-92, counsel, 1993-94; ret., 1994. Lectr. U. Chgo., 1953-54; gen. counsel Comml. Fin. Assn., 1978-94; past mem. editl. bd. Lender Liability News. Mng. and assoc. editor U. Chgo. Law Rev., 1951-52; contbr. articles to legal jours. Bd. dirs. U. Chgo. Law Sch. Alumni Assn., 1969-72; dir. vis. com. U. Chgo. Law Sch., 1980-83. Recipient Homer Kripke Lifetime Achievement award for contbns. to comml. fin. law, 1998. Mem. ABA (chmn. subcom. and charter mem. comml. fin. svcs. com.), Am. Coll. Comml. Fin. Lawyers (pres. 1994-95, bd. regents), Ill. Bar Assn. (chair comml. banking, bankruptcy sect. 1972-73), Chgo. Bar Assn. (chair ucc com., 1966, bd. mgrs. 1968-70, chair judiciary com. 1971-72), Law Club Chgo., Mid-Day Club, Lake Shore Country Club. Home: 132 E Delaware Pl Apt 5002 Chicago IL 60611-4944 Office: Sidley & Austin 55 W Monroe St Ste 2000 Chicago IL 60603-5008

SCHIMEK, DIANNA RUTH REBMAN, state legislator; b. Holdrege, Nebr., Mar. 21, 1940; d. Ralph William and Elizabeth Julia (Wilmot) Rebman; m. Herbert Henry Schimek, 1963; children: Samuel Wolfgang, Saul William. AA, Colo. Women's Coll., 1960; student, U. Nebr., Lincoln, 1960-61; BA magna cum laude, U. Nebr., Kearney, 1963. Former tchr. and realtor; mem. Nebr. Legislature from 27th dist., Lincoln, 1989—; chmn. govt., mil. and vets. affairs com. Nebr. Legislature, 1993-94, 99—, vice chair urban affairs com., 1995-98. Dem. Nat. committeewoman, 1984-88; chmn. Nebr. Dem. Com., 1980-84, mem. exec. com., 1987-88; past pres., sec. bd. dirs. Downtown Sr. Ctr. Found., 1990-96; mem. exec. bd. Midwestern Legis. Conf., 1995-96, co-chair health and human svcs. com., 1995-96; exec. dir. Nebr. Civil Liberties Union, 1985; former bd. dirs. Nebr. Repertory Theater, Exon Found., 1997—; mem. adv. bd. Martin Luther Home, 1997—; chair Midwestern legis. conf. Coun. of State Govts., 2000—. Toll fellow, 1999; recipient Outstanding Alumni award U. Nebr., 1989, Tribute award YWCA, 1992, Friend of Psychology award N.E. Psychol. Assn., 1998, Woman of Yr. award Nova Chpt. Bus. & Profl. Women, 1999, Disting. Svc. award Nat. Guard Assn., 2000, Legis. of Yr. award N.E. Dental Hygienists Assn., 2001, Disting. Svc. award N.E. League of Municipalities, 2002. Mem. Nat. Conf. State Legislators Women's Network (bd. dirs. 1993-96, 1st vice chmn.), PEO, Soroptimists, Delta Kappa Gamma (hon.), Mortar Bd. (cmty. advisor 1998, hon.). Democrat. Unitarian. Home: 2321 Camelot Ct Lincoln NE 68512-1457 Office: Dist # 27 State Capital Lincoln NE 68509

SCHIMKE, DENNIS J. former state legislator; m. Olive Young, Dec. 1964 (dec. 1998); 3 children. BS, U. N.D., 1968, MS, 1972. Bison rancher, Coteau Hills, ND, 1987—; tchr. h.s. math. and physics LaMoure, N.D., 1975-2000; lectr. math. N.D. State U., 2001—; rep. Dist. 28 N.D. Ho. of Reps., 1991-93, rep. dist. 26, 1995-97, mem. edn. and agr. com., 1991—93, 1995—97. Founding bd. dirs. N.D. Buffalo Assn., 1991—95. Home: PO Box 525 Edgeley ND 58433-0525

SCHINDEL, DONALD MARVIN, retired lawyer; b. Chgo., Jan. 5, 1932; s. Harry L. and Ann (Schiff) S.; m. Alice Martha Andrews, Apr. 24, 1960; children: Susan Yost, Judith Harris, Andrea Glickman. BS in Acctg., U. Ill., 1953; JD, U. Chgo., 1956. Ptnr. Sonnenschein, Nath & Rosenthal, Chgo., 1956-2000, ret., 2000. Author: Estate Administration and Tax Planning for Survivors, 1987, supplements, 1988-1996. Pres. United Way Highland Park-Highwood, Ill., 2000—02, Congregation Beth Or, Deefield, 1983—85. Fellow Am. Coll. Trust and Estate Counsel; mem. Chgo. Estate Planning Coun. (Austin Fleming Disting. Svc. award 1999), ABA, Ill. Bar Assn., Chgo. Bar Assn. (chmn. probate practice com. 1981-82). Club: East Bank (Chgo.) Avocations: tennis, travel, photography, carpentry, running, juggling. Home: 636 Rice St Highland Park IL 60035-5012 E-mail: dms@sonnenschein.com., dmschindel@aol.com.

SCHINDLER, JUDI(TH KAY), public relations executive, marketing consultant; b. Chgo., Nov. 23, 1941; d. Gilbert G. and Rosalie (Karlin) Cone; m. Jack Joel Schindler, Nov. 1, 1964; 1 child, Adam Jason. BS in Journalism, U. Ill., 1964. Assoc. editor Irving Cloud Publs., Lincolnwood, Ill., 1963-64; asst. dir. publicity Israel Bond Campaign, Chgo., 1965-69; v.p. pub. relations Realty Co. of Am., 1969-70; dir. pub. relations Pvt. Telecomm., 1970-78; pres. Schindler Comm., 1978—. Del. White House Conf. on Small Bus., Washington, 1980, 86; mem. adv. bd. Entrepreneurship Inst., Chgo., 1988-92. Bd. dirs. Family Matters Comty. Ctr.; mem. Chgo. bd. Roosevelt U.; leader luncheon coun. YWCA, Chgo., 1987, 89-90, 92; appointee small bus. com. Ill. Devel. Bd., 1988-89. Named Nat. Women in Bus. Adv. SBA, 1986, Chgo. Woman Bus. Owner of Yr., Continential Bank and Nat. Assn. Women Bus. Owners, 1989, Ill. Finalist Entrepreneur of Yr. award, 1991-92. Mem. Nat. Assn. Women Bus. Owners (pres. Chgo. chpt. 1980-81, nat. v.p. membership 1988-89), Small Bus. United of Ill., Publicity Club Chgo., Alpha Epsilon Phi. Office: Schindler Comm 500 N Clark St Chicago IL 60610-4288

SCHINK, JAMES HARVEY, lawyer; b. Oak Park, Ill., Oct. 2, 1943; s. Norbert F. and Gwendolyn H. (Hummel) S.; m. Lisa Wilder Haskell, Jan. 1, 1972 (div. 1980); children— David, Caroline, Elizabeth; m. April Townley, Aug. 14, 1982 BA, Yale U., 1965, JD, 1968. Bar: Ill. 1968, Colo. 1982. Assoc. Sidley & Austin, Chgo., 1968; law clk. to judge U.S. Ct. Appeals, 1968-69; assoc. Kirkland & Ellis, 1969-72, ptnr., 1972—. Sustaining fellow Art Inst. Chgo. Mem. ABA, Ill. Bar Assn., Chgo. Bar Assn., Chgo. Club, Saddle and Cycle Club, Mid-Am. Club, Econ. Club of Chgo., Chgo. Yacht Club, Vail Racquet Club, Yale Club of Chgo., Racquet Club Chgo., Game Creek Club. Republican. Presbyterian. Home: 1530 N State Pkwy Chicago IL 60610-1614 Office: Kirkland & Ellis 200 E Randolph St Ste 6100 Chicago IL 60601-6436

SCHIRN, JANET SUGERMAN, interior designer; b. Jersey City; d. Oscar H. and Mary (Lustig) S.; 1 child, Martha. BFA, Pratt Inst.; MFA, Columbia U.; postgrad. in Architecture, U. Ill. Tchr. N.Y.C. Bd. Edn.; dir. N.Y.C. Bd. Adult Edn.; pres. Janet Schirn Design Group, Chgo., N.Y.C., 1950—; prin. The J S Collection, N.Y.C., 1978—. Adj. prof. So. Ill. U., 1991-92; mem. adv. bd. Du Pont Co., Monsanto, 1981-89, So. Ill. U., 1990-95; mem. adv. bd. interior arch. dept. Columbia Coll., Iowa State u. Contbr. articles to interior design mag. Bd. dirs. Washington Archtl. Forum, 1992-96, Chgo. Archtl. Assistance Ctr., 1975, pres., 1982; adv. bd. mem. Mundelein Coll. dept. interior architecture, 1978; mem. Met. Planning Coun., Chgo., 1980—, Art Resources Tchg., 1984-95—; mem. aux. bd. Sch. of Art Ins., Ill. Arts Alliance, 1992—. Recipient award Chgo. Lighting Inst., 1989, 92, 93, 95, 97, 98, Villeroy and Boch gold award, 1990, Designer mag. residential award, 1990, Edward Fields 1st prize Rug Design, 1981, 91, 1st prize project awards ASID, 1993, 95, 96, 98, 99, 2000, 01. Mem. UNESCO (steering com. tall bldgs. and urban habitat coun.), Am. Soc. Interior Designers (nat. pres. 1986, nat. treas. 1984, regional v.p. 1981, pres. Ill. chpt. 1977-78, nat. dir. 1979-83, chmn. pub. affairs 1989, Designer of Distinction 1998), Illuminating Engring. Soc., Am. Inst. Architects (nat. urban planning and design com. 1981-85), Chgo. Network, Internat. Fedn. Interior Designers (exec. bd. dirs. 1992-96). Home: 220 E Walton St Chicago IL 60611-1507 Office: Janet Schirn Design Group 401 N Franklin St Chicago IL 60610-4400 also: 521 5th Ave New York NY 10175-0003

SCHIZAS, JENNIFER ANNE, law association administrator; b. Grand Island, Nebr., Aug. 18, 1959; d. John Delano and Jacqueline May (Pieper) S. BJ, U. Nebr., 1982. Rschr. U.S. Senator Carl T. Curtis, Washington, 1978; pub. rels. dir. Nebr. Solar Office, Lincoln, 1979; reporter Sta. WOWT-TV, Omaha, 1980-83; bur. chief Sta. KHAS-TV, Hastings, Nebr., 1983-84; divsn. dir. March of Dimes, Lincoln, 1986-90; exec. dir. Lincoln Arts Coun., 1990-92, Nebr. Food Industry Assn., Lincoln, 1992-93; dir. comm. Nebr. Bar Assn., 1993—. Mem. editor's exch. adv. bd. West Pub. CO., Eagan, Minn., 1995. Mem. Am. Soc. Assn. Execs., Nat. Assn. Bar Execs. (pub. rels. cons. 1995), Nebr. Soc. Assn. Execs. Sertoma Club (v.p.). Democrat. Greek Orthodox. Avocations: running, painting, antique collecting and refinishing. Office: Nebr Bar Assn 635 S 14th St Lincoln NE 68508-2700 Home: 4 Lake Hill Dr Durham NC 27713-8954 E-mail: jschizas@nebar.com.

SCHLAFLY, PHYLLIS STEWART, author; b. St. Louis, Aug. 15, 1924; d. John Bruce and Odile (Dodge) Stewart; m. Fred Schlafly, Oct. 20, 1949; children: John F., Bruce S., Roger S., Phyllis Liza Forshaw, Andrew L., Anne V. BA, Washington U., St. Louis, 1944, JD, 1978; MA, Harvard U., 1945; LLD, Niagara U., 1976. Bar: Ill. 1979, D.C. 1984, Mo. 1985, U.S. Supreme Ct. 1987. Syndicated columnist Copley News Svc., 1976—. Pres. Eagle Forum, 1975—; broadcaster Spectrum, CBS Radio Network, 1973-78; commentator Cable TV News Network, 1980-83, Matters of Opinion sta. WBBM-AM, Chgo., 1973-75. Author, pub.: Phyllis Schlafly Report, 1967—; author: A Choice Not an Echo, 1964, The Gravediggers, 1964, Strike From Space, 1965, Safe Not Sorry, 1967, The Betrayers, 1968, Mindszenty The Man, 1972, Kissinger on the Couch, 1975, Ambush at Vladivostok, 1976, The Power of the Positive Woman, 1977, First Reader, 1994, Turbo Reader, 2001; editor: Child Abuse in the Classroom, 1984, Pornography's Victims, 1987, Equal Pay for Unequal Work, 1984, Who Will Rock the Cradle, 1989, Stronger Families or Bigger Government, 1990, Meddlesome Mandate: Rethinking Family Leav, 1991. Del. Rep. Nat. Conv., 1964, 1968, 1984, 1988, 1992, 1996, alt., 1960, 1980, 2000; 1st v.p. Nat. Fedn. Rep. Women, 1964—67; nat. chmn. Stop ERA, 1972—; mem. Ronald Reagan's Def. Policy Adv. Group, 1980, Commn. on Bicentennial of U.S. Constn., 1985—91, Adminstrv. Conf. U.S., 1983—86; pres. Ill. Fedn. Rep. Women, 1960—64; mem. Ill. Commn. on Status of Women, 1975—85. Recipient 10 Honor awards Freedoms Found., Brotherhood award NCCJ, 1975; named Woman of Achievement in Pub. Affairs St. Louis Globe-Democrat, 1963, one of 10 most admired women in world Good Housekeeping poll, 1977-90. Mem. ABA, DAR (nat. chmn. Am. history 1965-68, nat. chmn. bicentennial com. 1967-70, nat. chmn. nat. def. 1977-80, 83-95), Ill. Bar Assn., Phi Beta Kappa, Pi Sigma Alpha. Office: Eagle Forum 7800 Bonhomme Ave Saint Louis MO 63105-1906 E-mail: phyllis@eagleforum.org.

SCHLEGEL, FRED EUGENE, lawyer; b. Indpls., July 24, 1941; s. Fred George and Dorothy (Bruce) S.; m. Jane Wessels, Aug. 14, 1965; children: Julia, Charles, Alexandra. BA, Northwestern U., 1963; JD with distinction, U. Mich., 1966. Bar: Ind. 1966. Assoc. lawyer Baker & Daniels, Indpls., 1966-72, ptnr., 1972—; vice chmn. Meridian St. Preservation Commn., 1975-90. Contbr. articles to profl. jours. Chmn. Indpls. Pub. Schs. Edn. Found., 1988-90; pres. Festival Music Soc., 1974-75, 79, 86-87; bd. dirs. Indpls. Symphony Orch., 1991—, Arts Coun. Indpls. Mem. ABA, Ind. Bar Assn., Energy Bar Assn., Northwestern U. Alumni Club Indpls. (pres. 1992-94). Republican. Presbyterian. Office: Baker and Daniels 300 N Meridian St Ste 2700 Indianapolis IN 46204-1782 E-mail: feschleg@bakerd.com.

SCHLEGEL, JOHN P. academic administrator; b. Dubuque, Iowa, July 31, 1943; s. Aaron Joseph and Irma Joan (Hingtgen) S. BA, St. Louis U., 1969, MA, 1970; BDiv, U. London, 1973; DPhil, Oxford U., 1977. Joined Soc. of Jesus, 1963, ordained priest Roman Cath. Ch., 1973. From asst. prof. to assoc. prof. Creighton U., Omaha, 1976-79, asst. acad. v.p., 1978-82; dean Coll. Arts and Scis. Rockhurst Coll., Kansas City, Mo., 1982-84, Marquette U., Milw., 1984-88; exec. and acad. v.p. John Carroll U., Cleve., 1988-91; pres. U. San Francisco, 1991-2000, Creighton U., Omaha, 2000—. Cons. Orgn. for Econ. Devel. and Cooperation, Paris, 1975-76. Author: Bilingualism and Canadian Policy in Africa, 1979; editor: Towards a Redefinition of Development, 1976; contbr. articles to profl. jours. Mem. Milwaukee County Arts Coun., 1986—88, Mo. Coun. on Humanities, Kansas City, 1984; trustee St. Louis U., 1985—91, Loyola U., Chgo., 1988—95, Loyola U. New Orleans, 1995—98, St. Ignatius H.S., Cleve., 1990—91, Loyola Coll. in Md., 1992—98, Xavier U., 1998—; bd. dirs. Commonwealth Club Calif., Calif. Coun. on World Affairs, 1997—99. Oxford U. grantee, 1974-76; Govt. of Can. grantee, 1977-78. Mem. Am. Coun. on Edn., Bohemian Club, Univ. Club. Avocations: racquet sports, classical music, cooking, hiking. Office: Creighton U Office Pres 2500 Calif Plz Omaha NE 68178 E-mail: jpschlegel@creighton.edu.

SCHLEICHER, DONALD, music director; Degree, U. Wis., Northwestern U.; studied with Gustav Meier, Simon Rattle, Seiji Ozawa, Maurice Abravanel, Roger Norrington, Joel Smirnoff, Leon Fleisher. Band dir. Williamsville (N.Y.) South High Sch., 1977-84; past mem. music faculty U. Wis., Stevens Point; past mem. conducting faculty U. Mich.; dir. orch. studies, condr. Univ. Symphony Orch., head grad. program in orch. conducting U. Ill.; music dir. Quad City Symphony Orch. Assn., Davenport, Iowa. Conducting fellow Tanglewood Music Ctr., 1993; music dir., prin. condr. Pine Mountain Music Festival, Mich., 1994—; condr. orchs. N.Y., Ala., Wis., Hawaii, R.I., Ill.; guest condr., resident Fla. State U., Ark. State U., U. Minn., U. Akron, Ohio U., U. Buffalo, Ithaca Coll., Ohio State U.; guest condr. orchs. Bridgeport, Conn., Tallahassee, Fla., Lansing, Mich., Ann Arbor, Mich., Southfield, Mich.past dir. Detroit Chamber Winds; guest condr. Chautauqua Festival, 1996, Taiwan Symphony Orch. Wind Ensemble; presenter conducting clinic at nat. convention Music Educators Nat. Conf., Kansas City, 1996. Condr. operas including La Boheme, Suor Angelica, Il Pagliacci, Susannah, The Barber of Seville, La Traviata, The Marriage of Figaro, Madama Butterfly, Carmen. Office: Quad City Symphony Orch PO Box 1144 Davenport IA 52805-1144

SCHLENDER, WILLIAM ELMER, management sciences educator; b. Sawyer, Mich., Oct. 28, 1920; s. Gustav A. and Marie (Zindler) S.; m. Lela R. Pullen, June 9, 1956 (dec. June 1983); m. Margaret C. Krahn, Mar. 3, 1987. A.B., Valparaiso U., 1941; M.B.A., U. Denver, 1947; Ph.D., Ohio State U., 1955. With U.S. Rubber Co., 1941-43, 46; asst. prof., assoc. prof. bus. adminstrn. Bowling Green State U., 1947-53; asst. prof. bus. orgn., prof. Ohio State U., 1954-65, asst. dean, 1959-62; assoc. dean Ohio State U. (Coll. Commerce and Adminstrn.), 1962-63; prof. mgmt. U. Tex., 1965-68, chmn. dept., 1966-68; dean Cleve. State U. Coll. Bus. Adminstrn., 1968-75, prof. mgmt., 1975-76; Internat. Luth. Laymen's League prof. bus. ethics Valparaiso (Ind.) U., 1976-79, Richard E. Meier prof. mgmt., 1983-86, Richard E. Meier prof. emeritus, 1986—. Vis. assoc. prof. mgmt. Columbia U., 1957-58; vis. prof. mgmt. U. Tex., Arlington, 1981-82; cons. in field; bd. govs. Internat. Ins. Soc., 1972-90. Author: (with M.J. Jucius) Elements of Managerial Action, 3d edit, 1973, (with others) Management in Perspective: Selected Readings, 1965; Editor: (with others) Management in a Dynamic Society, 1965; Contbr. (with others) articles to profl. jours. Served with AUS, 1943-45. Decorated Bronze Star. Recipient Exec. Order Ohio Comodr. for outstanding contbn. to growth and devel. of state. Fellow Acad. Mgmt.; mem. Indsl. Rels. Rsch. Assn. (pres. N.E. Ohio chpt. 1971-72), Am. Legion, Tau Kappa Epsilon, Soc. for Case Rsch., Rotary, Beta Gamma Sigma, Sigma Iota Epsilon, Pi Sigma Epsilon, Alpha Kappa Psi, Phi Kappa Phi. Home: PO Box 446 Sawyer MI 49125-0446 Office: Coll Bus Adminstrn Valparaiso U Valparaiso IN 46383 E-mail: bschlend@aol.com.

SCHLENSKER, GARY CHRIS, landscaping company executive; b. Indpls., Nov. 12, 1950; s. Christian Frederick and Doris Jean (Shannon) S.; m. Ann Marie Tobin, Oct. 27, 1979; children: Laura Patricia, Christian Frederick II. Student, Purdue U., 1969-71, 73; A Bus. Adminstrn., Clark Coll., 1979; cert. emergency med. technician, Ind. Vocat. Tech. Inst., Lafayette, 1974. Salesman Modern Reference, Indpls., 1971; orthopaedic technician St. Elizabeth Hosp., Lafayette, 1973-75, asst. mgr. ambulance service, 1975; sales asst. Merck, Sharpe & Dohme, Oakbrook, Ill., 1975-77; v.p. Turfco, Inc., Zionsville, Ind., 1977-84; pres. Turfscape, Inc., 1984—. Speaker Midwest Turf Conf., 1991; del. erosion and sediment control econ. summit Internat. Erosion Control Assn., New Orleans, 2000. With U.S. Army, 1971-73. Mem. ASTM (erosion control subcom.), BBB, Nat. Fedn. Ind. Bus., Midwest Turf Found., Ohio Turf Found., Internat. Erosion Control Assn. (bd. dirs. Gt. Lakes chpt. 1998—), U.S. C. of C., Ind. C. of C., Zionsville C. of C., Phi Kappa Psi. Presbyterian. Avocations: woodworking, golf.

SCHLESINGER, JOSEPH ABRAHAM, political scientist; b. Boston, Jan. 4, 1922; s. Monroe Jacob and Millie (Romansky) S.; m. Mildred Saks, Sept. 9, 1951; children: Elizabeth Hannah, Jacob Monroe. Student, Hobart Coll., 1938-40; A.B., U. Chgo., 1942; A.M., Harvard U., 1947; Ph.D., Yale U., 1955. Instr. Boston U., 1947-49; teaching fellow Wesleyan U., Middletown, Conn., 1952-53; mem. faculty Mich. State U., East Lansing, 1953—, prof. polit. sci., 1963—. Vis. prof. U. Calif., Berkeley, 1964-65 Author: How They Became Governor, 1957, Ambition and Politics: Political Careers in the United States, 1966, Political Parties and the Winning of Office, 1991, also articles. Del. Ingham County (Mich.) Democratic Conv., 1966-68. Served with AUS, 1943-45. Cowles fellow, 1950-51; Block fellow, 1951-52; grantee Social Sci. Research Council, 1955-57, 68-69; recipient Distinguished Faculty award Mich. State U., 1976, Sr. Fulbright award for Rsch. Western Europe, 1990—. Mem. Am. Polit. Sci. Assn. (coun. 1981-83, 1st ann. award for outstanding pub. paper 1986, Samuel Eldersveld award for lifetime achievement 1993), Midwest Polit. Sci. Assn. (v.p. 1969-70), So. Polit. Sci. Assn., Mich. Conf. Polit. Scientists, Acad. Polit. Sci. Democrat. Jewish. Home: 930 Roxburgh Ave East Lansing MI 48823-3131 Office: Dept Polit Sci Mich State Univ East Lansing MI 48824

SCHLESINGER, LEONARD ARTHUR, apparel company executive; b. N.Y.C., July 31, 1952; s. Joe and Edith (Smukler) S.; m. Phyllis Barbara Fineman, Dec. 23, 1972; children: Rebecca, Emily, Katharine. BA, Brown U., 1972; MBA, Columbia U., 1973; DBA, Harvard U., 1979. Mgr. Procter & Gamble, Green Bay, Wis., 1973-75; asst. prof., assoc. prof. bus. sch. Harvard U., Boston, 1978-85, prof. bus. adminstrn., 1988-98; exec. v.p., COO Au Bon Pain, Inc., 1985-88; sr. v.p. Brown U., 1998-99; exec. v.p., COO Limited Brands, 1999—. Bd. dirs. GC Companies, Chestnut Hill, Mass., 1997-00, Borders Group, Inc., Ann Arbor, Mich., 1995-00, Limited Brands, Columbus, Ohio, 1996—, Pegasystems, Inc., Cambridge, Mass., 1996-00. Editor: Human Resources Mgmt. Jour., Jour. Mgmt. Inquiry; contbr. 40 articles to profl. jours. Jewish. Avocation: travel, music, bicycling. Home: 12 Edge of Woods New Albany OH 43054 Office: Limited Brands 3 Limited Pkwy Columbus OH 43230-1467 E-mail: lschlesinger@limitedbrands.com.

SCHLESINGER, MILTON J. virology educator, researcher; b. Wheeling, W.Va., Nov. 26, 1927; s. Milton J. and Caroline (Oppenheimer) S.; m. Sondra Orenstein, Jan. 30, 1955. BS, Yale U., 1951; MS, U. Rochester, 1953; PhD, U. Mich., 1959. Rsch. assoc. U. Mich., Ann Arbor, 1953-56, 59-60; guest rsch. investigator Inst. Superiore di Sanita, Rome, 1960-61; rsch. assoc. MIT, Cambridge, 1961-64; asst. prof. virology Washington U. Sch. Medicine, St. Louis, 1964-67, assoc. prof., 1967-72, prof., 1972-99, chmn. exec. coun. divsn. biol. and biomed. scis., 1992-94, emeritus prof., 1999—. Vis. scientist Imperial Cancer Rsch. Fund, London, 1974-75; vis. scholar Harvard U., Cambridge, 1989-90, 95, 95-96; mem. adv. panels Am. Heart Assn., Dallas, 1975-78, NSF, Washington, 1978-82; mem. sci. adv. bd. Friedrich Miescher Inst., Basel, Switzerland, 1988—, chmn., 1992-98; nat. lectr. Sigma Xi, 1991-93. Editor: Heat Shock, 1982, Togaviridae and Flaviviridae, 1986, Lipid Modification of Proteins, 1992, (monographs) The Ubiquitin System, 1988, Stress Proteins, 1990; mem. editl. bd. virology, 1975-92, Jour. Biol. Chemistry, 1982-87, Molecular and Cellular Biology, 1983-92. Bd. dirs. ACLU, St. Louis, 1966-72, Coalition for Environ., St. Louis, 1989-92. Fellow AAAS; mem. Am. Biol. Chemistry and Molecular Biology, Am. Soc. Microbiology, Am. Soc. Virologists, Am. Chem. Soc. Office: Dept Molecular Micro 8230 Washington U Med Sch 660 S Euclid Ave Saint Louis MO 63110-1010

SCHLICHTING, CATHERINE FLETCHER NICHOLSON, librarian, educator; b. Huntsville, Ala., Nov. 18, 1923; d. William Parsons and Ethel Loise (Breitling) Nicholson; m. Harry Fredrick Schlichting, July 1, 1950 (dec. Aug. 1964); children: James Dean, Richard Dale, Barbara Lynn. BS, U. Ala., 1944; MLS, U. Chgo., 1950. Asst. libr. U. Ala. Edn. Libr., Tuscaloosa, summers 1944-45; libr. Sylacauga (Ala.) H.S., 1944-45, Hinsdale (Ill.) H.S., 1945-49; asst. libr. Centre for Children's Books, U. Chgo., 1950-52; instr. reference dept. libr. Ohio Wesleyan U., Delaware, 1965-69, asst. prof., 1969-79, assoc. prof., 1979-85, prof., 1985—, curator Ohio Wesleyan Hist. Collection, 1986—, student pers. libr., 1966-72. Author: Introduction to Bibliographic Research: Basic Sources, 4th edit., 1983, Checklist of Biographical Reference Sources, 1977, Audio-Visual Aids in Bibliographic Instruction, 1976, Introduction to Bibliographic Research: Slide Catalog and Script, 1980; info. cons. (documentary) Noble Achievements: The History of Ohio Wesleyan 1942-1992, 1992, 150 Years of Excellence: A Pictorial View of Ohio Wesleyan University, 1992. Mem. adminstrv. bd. Meth. Ch., 1973-81, chmn. adminstrv. bd., 1985—, mem. coun. on ministries, 1975-81, chmn., 1975-77, trustee, 1999—. Recipient Algernon Sidney Sullivan award U. Ala., 1944, Hon. Alumna award Ohio Wesleyan U., 1997; Ohio Wesleyan U.-Mellon Found. grantee, 1972-73, 84-85; GLCA Tchg. fellow, 1976-77. Mem. ALA, Ohio Libr. Assn., Midwest Acad. Libr. Conf., Acad. Librs. Assn. Ohio (dir. 1984-86), AAUP (chpt. sec. 1967-68), United Meth. Women (pres. Mt. Vernon dist. 1994-97, newsletter editor 1998—), Ohio Wesleyan Woman's Club (exec. bd. 1969-72, 77-79, 81-84, pres. 1969-70, sec. 1977-78), History Club (pres. 1971-72, v.p. 1978-79) Fortnightly Club (pres. 1975-76, 87-88), Am. Field Svc. (pres. Delaware chpt. 1975-76), Kappa Delta Pi, Alpha Lambda Delta. Democrat. Home: 57 Willow Brook Way S Delaware OH 43015 Office: Ohio Wesleyan U La Beeghly Library Delaware OH 43015

SCHLICKMAN, J. ANDREW, lawyer; b. Washington, Mar. 28, 1952; AB, Georgetown U., 1974; JD, U. Chgo., 1978. Bar: Ill. 1978, U.S. Supreme Ct. 1987. Ptnr. Sidley & Austin, Chgo. Coord. author: International Environmental Law and Regulation, 1991, 2d edit., 1994. Mem. ABA, Ill State Bar Assn.. Chgo. Bar Assn. Office: Sidley & Austin Bank One Plz 425 W Surf St Apt 605 Chicago IL 60657-6139

SCHLIEVE, HY C. J. school administrator; b. Mandan, N.D., Apr. 4, 1952; s. Calvin L. and Loretta L. (Johnson) S.; m. Terri Ann Hansen, Dec. 30, 1977; children: Derek, Aaron, Jessica. BA, N.D. State U., 1974, MS, 1984; EdD, Calif. Coast U., 1994. Tchr., coach Halliday (N.D.) Pub. Sch., 1974-75, Drake (N.D.) Pub. Sch., 1975-76, Montpelier (N.D.) Pub. Sch., 1976-81; prin. Unity Pub. Sch., Petersburg, N.D., 1981-83, Page (N.D.) Pub. Sch., 1983-85; supt. Wolford (N.D.) Pub. Sch., 1985-87, Garrison (N.D.) Pub. Schs., 1987-93; prin. Buhl Joint Sch. Dist. 412, Idaho, 1993-95, Oconto Falls Area Sch. Dist., Wis., 1995-99; supt. Ellendale (N.D.) Pub. Schs. #40, 1999—. Com. mem. NDASA Rsch. and Evaluation, Garrison, 1988-93; fiscal agt. Mo. Hills Consortium, McLean County, N.D., 1989-93; cons. asbestos Garrison Pub. Sch. Dist., 1987-93. Sec. Govtl. Affairs Com., Garrison, 1987-93; mem. Tourism Com., Garrison, 1988-92, Econ. Devel. Com., 1988-89. Recipient Nat. Superintendent of the Yr. awd., North Dakota, Am. Assn. of School Administrators, 1992. Mem. Nat. Assn. Secondary Sch. Prins. (prin. assessor tng. 1990), NSBA Fed. Policy Coords. Network. Avocations: golf, hunting, fishing, bowling, outdoor activities. Office: Ellendale Pub Schs PO Box 400 321 N 1st St Ellendale ND 58436 Home: 91 Prairieview Ellendale ND 58436-7401

SCHLITTER, STANLEY ALLEN, lawyer; b. Decorah, Iowa, Jan. 27, 1950; s. Joseph Everett and Lillian Helena (Helgerson) S.; m. Sheila Lynn Edwards, Sept. 24, 1977; children: Stephanie Anne, Joseph Allen, John Edward. BS, Iowa State U., 1972; JD, U. Iowa, 1977. Bar: Ill. 1977, U.S. Dist. Ct. (no. dist.) Ill. 1977, U.S. Ct. Appeals (7th cir.) 1981, U.S. Ct. Appeals (Fed. cir.) 1982, D.C. 1989. Assoc. Kirkland & Ellis, Chgo., 1977-84, ptnr., 1984-88, Washington, 1988-91, Jenner & Block, Chgo., 1991—. Mem. ABA, IEEE, Am. Intellectual Property Law Assn. Office: Jenner & Block One IBM Plaza Chicago IL 60611-3608

SCHLODER, JOHN E. museum director; BS, Duquesne U., 1969; diplôme d'Ancien Elève, L'Ecole du Louvre, Paris, 1973; licence L'Institut d'Art et d'Archéologie, U. Paris-Sorbonne, 1973, doctorat L'Institut d'Art et d'Archéologie, 1988; MPhil, Columbia U., 1980. Chargé de Mission Musée du Louvre, Paris, France, 1979-82; asst. curator Cleve. Mus. Art Edn Dept., 1982-85, assoc. curator, 1985-86, adminstr. pub. programs, 1986-88, asst. dir. edn. and pub. programs, 1988-92; dir. Birmingham (Ala.) Mus. Art, 1992-96, Jocelyn Mus. Art, 1997—. Vis. prof. Colégio Andrews, Rio de Janeiro, Brazil, 1980-81, Vaculdade Candido Mendes, Rio de Janeiro, 1981-82; adj. prof. dept. art history Case Western Res. U., Cleve., 1984-92; lectr. in field. Mus. rep. Northeastern Ohio Inter-Mus. Coun., 1984-92; trustee Cleve. Sch. Arts, 1991-92; active Southeast Mus. Conf., 1992—; mem. Leadership Birmingham, 1994-95; bd. dirs. Op. New Birmingham, 1993—; mem. Birmingham Olympic programming com., mem. outreach com., 1994—. Lurcy Trust fellowship, 1975, Columbia U. Traveling fellowship, 1975, 76, U. Cambridge, Eng. Leverhulme fellowship, 1977, Kellogg Project fellowship Smithsonian Instn., 1987; scholarship J. Paul Getty Trust, 1989; vis. Scholar grantee The Japan Found., 1995; recipient French Govt. award, 1975, award of achievement for best cmty. event Northern Ohio Live Mag., 1991. Mem. Am. Assn. Mus., Assn. Art Mus. Dirs., Internat. Lab. for Visitor Studies, Visitor Studies Assn., Ala. Mus. Assn., Birmingham Area Mus. Assn., Soc. de l'Historie de l'Art Français, Rotary Club Birmingham.

SCHLOERB, PAUL RICHARD, surgeon, educator; b. Buffalo, Oct. 22, 1919; s. Herman George and Vera (Gross) S.; m. Louise M. Grimmer, Feb. 25, 1950; children: Ronald G., Patricia Johnson, Marilyn A. Hock, Dorothy E. Schloerb Hoban, Paul Richard. AB, Harvard U., 1941; MD, U. Rochester, 1944. Intern U. Rochester Med. Sch., 1944-45, asst. resident, 1947-48, instr. surgery, 1952; rsch. fellow, resident Peter Bent Brigham Hosp., Boston, 1948-52; faculty U. Kans. Med. Ctr., Kansas City, 1952-79, prof. surgery, 1964-79, 88—, dean for rsch., 1972-79, dir. nutritional support svc., 1993—; prof. surgery U. Rochester (N.Y.) Med Ctr., 1979-88, adj. prof. surgery, 1988-90; surgeon Strong Meml. Hosp., 1979-88, dir. Surg. ICU, 1979-85, dir. surg. nutritional support service. Contbr. over 100 articles to profl. jours. Lt. (j.g.), M.C. USNR, 1944-45; to lt. 1953-55. Mem. AMA, ACS, AAAS, Am. Surg. Assn., Soc. U. Surgeons, Am. Physiol. Soc., Internat. Soc. Surgery, Ctrl. Surg. Assn., Am. Assn. for Surgery of Trauma, Am. Assn. Cancer Rsch., Biomed. Engring. Soc., Am. Inst. Nutrition, Am. Soc. Clin. Nutrition, Sigma Xi. Office: Dept Surgery U Kansas Med Ctr Kansas City KS 66160-0001

SCHLOSSMAN, JOHN ISAAC, architect; b. Chgo., Aug. 21, 1931; s. Norman Joseph and Carol (Rosenfeld) S.; m. Shirley Goulding Rhodes, Feb. 8, 1959; children: Marc N., Gail S. Mewhort, Peter C. Student, Grinnell Coll., 1949-50; BA, U. Minn., 1953, BArch, 1955; MArch, MIT, 1956. Registered architect, Ill. Archtl. designer The Architects Collaborative, Cambridge, Mass., 1956-57; architect Loebl Schlossman & Hackl and predecessors, Chgo., 1959-65, assoc., 1965-70, prin., 1970-98, cons. prin., 1998—. Bd. overseers Coll. Arch. Illinois Inst. Tech., Chgo.; founding bd. dirs. Chgo. Archtl. Assistance Ctr., 1974-79 Chmn. Glencoe Plan Commn., Ill., 1977-82; trustee Com. for Green Bay Trail, Glencoe, 1970-77, Chgo. Arch. Found., 1971-75, Graham Found. for Advanced Studies in Fine Arts, 1995-99, pres. 1999-2001; bd. dirs. Merit Music Program, Chgo., 1983-93, pres., 1988-90, hon. trustee 1996; governing mem. Chgo. Symphony Orch.; mem. founders coun. Field Mus., Chgo.; mem. zoning & planning com. Greater North Mich. Ave. Assn., Chgo., 2000-01; mem. Nat. Trust Coun., Nat. Trust for Hist. Preservation, Washington. Named dir. for life Young Men's Jewish Council, Chgo., 1971; Rotch travelling scholar, 1957; sustaining fellow Art Inst. Chgo. Fellow AIA (trustee ins. trust 1971-76, chmn. ins. com. 1974-75, v.p. Chgo. chpt. 1975, chmn. architects liability com. 1976, 80-82, hon. found. trustee 1995—), Archtl. Soc. of Art Inst. Chgo., Tavern Club (gov. 1986-88, v.p. 1990), The Club at Symphony Ctr., The Arts Club, Alpha Rho Chi, Office: Loebl Schlossman & Hackl 232 Mary St Winnetka IL 60093-1522

SCHLOTMAN, MICHAEL, food products executive; CFO Kroger, Cin. Office: Kroger 1014 Vine St Cincinnati OH 45202

SCHMALZ, DOUGLAS J. agricultural company executive; CFO Archer Daniels Midland Co., Decatur, Ill. Office: Archer Daniels Midland Co 4666 E Faries Pkwy Decatur IL 62526

SCHMELZER, WILHELM A. manufacturing executive; Degree in Acctg. and Fin., Fachhochschule, Cologne, Germany; student, Albion Coll. Various positions Federal-Mogul Corp., Southfield, Mich., 1969-95, v.p., group exec., 1995-98, exec. v.p. sealing systems, 1998, exec. v.p. Europe, 1998—. Bd. dirs. Federal-Mogul Corp. Fellow Carl Duisberg Found. Office: Federal-Mogul Corp 26555 Northwestern Hwy Southfield MI 48034-2146

SCHMETTERER, JACK BAER, federal judge; b. Chgo., Apr. 11, 1931; s. Samuel and Gertrude (Schiff) Schmetterer; m. Joan L. Ruther, Mar. 18, 1956 (dec.); children: Laura, Mark, Kenneth; m. Barbara Friedman, Sept. 2, 2001. BA, Yale U., 1952, JD, 1955. Bar: Ill. 1956. Instr. polit. sci. Yale U., New Haven, 1954-55, U. Ga., 1957-58; ptnr. Schmetterer & Schmetterer, Chgo., 1958-63; asst. U.S. atty. U.S. Dist. Ct. (no. dist.) Ill., 1963-68, 1st asst. U.S. atty., 1968-70; ptnr. Freeman, Schmetterer, Freeman & Salzman, 1970-71; 1st asst. states atty. State's Atty. of Cook County, 1971-73; assoc., ptnr., head of litigation Gottlieb & Schwartz, 1973—85; U.S. bankruptcy judge U.S. Bankruptcy Ct. (no. dist.) Ill., 1985—. Vis. prof. dept. criminal justice U. Ill., Chgo., 1974-76. Bd. dirs. Cook County Ct. Watchers, Inc., until 1985, Better Govt. Assn., until 1985; former mem. Northbrook Village Bd., North Shore Mass Transit Dist. Bd. With U.S. Army, 1956-58. Mem.: John Howard Assn. (chairperson 1997—99, bd. mem.), Fed. Bar Assn. (pres. Chgo. chpt. 1993—94), Fed. Trial Judges Conf., ABA, Just the Beginning Found. (v.p.), Decalogue Soc., Mackey-Wigmore Inn of Ct., Lawyers Club of Chgo. Office: US Bankruptcy Ct # 600 219 S Dearborn St Apt 600 Chicago IL 60604-1702

SCHMID, HARALD HEINRICH OTTO, biochemistry educator, academic director; b. Graz, Styria, Austria, Dec. 10, 1935; Came to U.S., 1962; s. Engelbert and Annemarie (Kletetschka) S.; m. Patricia Caroline Igou, May 21, 1977. MS, U. Graz, 1957, LLD, 1962, PhD, 1964. Rsch. fellow Hormel inst. U. Minn., Austin, 1962-65, rsch. assoc., 1965-66, asst. prof., 1966-70, assoc. prof., 1970-74, prof., 1974—. Cons. NIH, Bethesda, Md., 1977—; acting dir. Hormel inst. U. Minn., 1985-87, exec. dir., 1987-01; faculty mem. Mayo Med. Sch., Rochester, Minn., 1990—. Mng. editor Chemistry and Physics of Lipids, Elsevier Sci. Publs., Amsterdam, The Netherlands, 1984-01; contbr. numerous articles to profl. jours. Rsch. grantee NIH, 1967—. Mem. AAAS, Am. Soc. Biochemistry and Molecular Biology, Am. Chem. Soc., The Oxygen Soc. Avocations: yacht racing, downhill skiing, classical music. Home: 2701 2nd Ave NW Austin MN 55912-1195 Office: U Minn Hormel Inst 801 16th Ave NE Austin MN 55912-3679

SCHMIDT, ARLO E. state legislator; m. Marion Schmidt; 6 children. Grad., Am. Sch. Auctioneering. Auctioneer; rep. Dist. 12 N.D. Ho. of Reps., mem. indsl. bus. and labor and govt. and vet. affairs coms. Named to N.D. Auctioneers Hall of Fame. Mem. N.D. Auctioneers Assn. (past pres.), Legionnaires. Home: PO Box E Maddock ND 58348-0107 Office: ND Ho of Reps State Capitol Bismarck ND 58505

SCHMIDT, ARTHUR IRWIN, steel fabricating company executive; b. Sept. 9, 1927; s. Louis and Mary (Fliegel) S.; m. Mae Rosman, July 25, 1950; children: Jerrold, Cynthia, Elizabeth, Richard. Student, Colo. A&M Coll., 1946-47; BS in Aero. Engring., U. Ill., 1950. Sec. Rosman Iron Works, Inc., Franklin Park, Ill., 1950-86; pres. Rosman-Schmidt Steel Corp., 1986-00. With USNR, 1944-46, 51-52. Mem. B'nai Brith (trustee, past pres. Lincolnwood chpt.). Home: 1901 Somerset Ln Northbrook IL 60062-6067

SCHMIDT, CHUCK, professional football team executive; b. Detroit, Jan. 22, 1947; m. Sharon Schmidt; children: Scott, Krista, Matthew. Degree in bus., U. Mich.; grad. degree in fin., Wayne State U. Formerly with Ernst and Whinney; CPA Detroit Lions, from 1976, also contr., then v.p. fin., until 1987, exec. v.p., chief oper. officer, 1989—. Bd. dirs., sec., treas. Detroit Lions Charities; bd. dirs. CATCH, Pontiac (Mich.) Devel. Found. Office: Detroit Lions Pontiac Silver Dome 1200 Featherstone Rd Pontiac MI 48342-1938

SCHMIDT, GORDON PEIRCE, artistic director; Former dancer; resident choreographer Ballet Chgo., 1990-95; artistic dir. Grand Rapids (Mich.) Ballet, 1999—. Office: Grand Rapids Ballet Co 341 Ellsworth Ave Grand Rapids MI 49503-4045

SCHMIDT, JOHN RICHARD, agricultural economics educator; b. Madison, Wis., July 3, 1929; s. Oscar John and Alma Theodora (Ula) S.; m. Rosemary Pigorsch, Oct. 7, 1951; children: Janet, Deborah, Allen. B.S., U. Wis., 1951, M.S., 1953; Ph.D., U. Minn., 1960. Asst. prof. agr. econs. U. Wis., Madison, 1956-61, assoc. prof., 1961-65, prof., 1965-95, prof. emeritus, 1995—, chmn. dept., 1966-70; owner, mgr. JRS Computing Svcs., 1995—. Farm mgmt. cons. Am. Farm Bur. Fedn., Chgo., 1962; cons. Banco de Mexico, 1972-84, IBRD (World Bank), 1973-94; Agrl. Devel. Bank Iran, 1974-76; mem. adv. bd. Internat. Devel. Inst., 1983; faculty Salzburg Seminar, 1983, 85. Contbr. articles to tech. jours., also monographs, bulls. Bd. dirs. U. Wis. Credit Union, 1968-77, pres., 1969-75; mem. com. Wis.-Upper Mich. Synod Sem., 1972-75, mem. ch. coun. 1967-69, 72-75, pres. 1974-75. Mem. Am. Agrl. Econs. Assn., Rotary (pres. Madison West 1994-95), Delta Theta Sigma (nat. sec. 1962-64), Gamma Sigma Delta (pres. Wis. chpt. 1975). Lutheran. Home: 106 Frigate Dr Madison WI 53705-4426 Office: JRS Computing Svcs 6601 Grand Teton Plz Ste 4 Madison WI 53719-1049 E-mail: jrschmi1@facstaff.wisc.edu.

SCHMIDT, KATHLEEN MARIE, lawyer; b. Des Moines, June 17, 1953; d. Raymond Driscoll and Hazel Isabelle (Rogers) Poage; m. Dean Everett Johnson, Dec. 21, 1974 (div. Nov. 1983); children: Aaron Dean, Gina Marie; m. Ronald Robert Schmidt, Feb. 7, 1987. BS in Home Econs., U. Nebr., 1974; JD, Creighton U., 1987. Bar: Nebr. 1987, U.S. Dist. Ct. Nebr. 1987, U.S. Ct. Appeals (8th cir.) 1989, U.S. Supreme Ct. 1991. Apprentice printer, journeyman Rochester (Minn.) Post Bull., 1978-82; dir. customer info. Cornhusker Pub. Power Dist., Columbus, Nebr., 1982-83; artist Pamida, Omaha, 1983; offset artist Cornhusker Motor Club, 1983-84; assoc. Lindahl O. Johnson Law Office, 1987-88; pvt. practice, 1988-90; ptnr. Emery, Penke, Blazek & Schmidt, 1990-91; pvt. practice, 1992—. Atty. in condemnation procs. Douglas County Bd. Appraisers, Omaha, 1988-99, Sarpy County Bd. Appraisers, Omaha, 1999—; presenter Nebr. Sch. Bd. Assn., 1991, 92. Mem. Millard Sch. Bd., Omaha, 1989-96, treas. 1991, 92; mem. strategic planning com. Millard Sch. Dist., 1990; mem. Omaha Mayor's Master Plan Com., 1991-94. Named hon. mem. Anderson Mid. Sch., Omaha, 1991; recipient Award of Achievement, Nebr. Sch. Bd. Assn., 1991, 94. Mem. Nebr. Bar Assn., Omaha Bar Assn. (spkrs. bur. 1992—), Nat. Sch. Bd. Assn. (del. federal rels. network 1991-96, cert. recognition 1991). Republican. Lutheran.

SCHMIDT, MARK JAMES, state public health official; b. Milw., July 16, 1955; s. Warren J. and Carolyn Juel (Gissing) S.; m. Janet M. Schmidt, Oct. 5, 1991; children: Andrew T., Rachel M., Malia D.; stepchildren: Nathan A. and Aaron M. Stotts. BA, U. Wis., Eau Claire, 1977; MSc., Ill. State U., 1978. Dir. debate U. No. Iowa, Cedar Falls, 1978-79; dir. comm. Ill. Rep. Party, Springfield, 1979-83; asst. adminstr. driver svc. dept. Office of the Sec. State, Ill., 1983-87, asst. to dir., driver svc. dept., 1987-91; dir. pub. affairs Ill. Dept. Ctrl. Mgmt. Svcs., 1991-95; asst. dir. Ill. Dept. Pub. Health, Springfield, 1995-2000, acting dep. dir. Office of Health and Wellness, 1999-2000, dep. dir. Office of Health Promotion, 2000—. Guest lectr. cert. program in health policy Am. Osteo. Assn., 1997; guest lectr. Ill. Pub. Health Leadership Inst., 1999—2000, Leadership Springfield Conf., 1999, 2000; guest lectr. polit. comm. Ill. State U., Normal, 1980; guest lectr. social mktg. U. Ill., Springfield, 2001—02; cons. 6th Congl. Dist. Rep. Com., Lombard, Ill., 1985—90; rep. Ill. Drivers Lic. Compact Com., Falls Church, Va., 1987—91; mem. Ill. Rural Health Assn.; bd. dirs. Ill. Rural Ptnrs., Inc., 1995—2000, co-chmn. pub. sector, 1997—99; chair Rural Transp. Task Force, 1997—; mem. Ill. Rural Ptnrs. Telecomm. Commn., 1999—; keynote spkr. conf. on managed care Coop. Extension Svc., 1996; keynote spkr. Ill. Rural Poverty Conf., 1998, SIV Cancer Prevention and Control Conf., 2002; leader, mentor Mid-Am. Regional Pub. Health Leadership Inst., 1999—; chair Springfield Pub. Health and Safety Strategy Group, 1999—; mem. panel advisors Mayor Karen Hasarn, Springfield; chair Ill. Adoption Registry Adv. Coun., 1999—2001; staff Gov.'s Domestic Preparedness Conf., 2001; lectr. tobacco prevention and control Ill. Sch. Health Days, 2001; spkr. in field. Editor: Driver's Handbook (annual) Rules of the Road, 1984-91; editor Driver Svcs. Dept. newsletter, 1988-91, Rural Health News, 1999-2000; contbg. editor: Lyme Disease Handbook for Physicians, 1997, Management and Treatment of Lyme Disease, 1998; co-editor tng. manual for local bds. of health; contbr. articles to profl. jours. Debate strategist Fahner for Atty. Gen. Ill., 1982, Bertini for Congress, Chgo., 1982; advisor Richard Austin for Congress, Springfield, 1984; designer local advt. Al Salvi for Sec. of State of Ill., 1998; health care developer George Ryan for Gov. of Ill., 1998; coord. Citizens for Jim Edgar, Springfield, 1985-91; sr. staff, Ill. gubernatorial transition team, 1990-91; stage mgr. 1999 Ill. Gubernatorial Inauguration; chmn. pub. info. subcom. Ill. Comml. Drivers License Program, 1989-91; media coord. Lincoln Land C.C. Trustee Campaign, 1997; mem. local advance staff George W. Bush for Pres., 1999-2000; mem. long range planning com. 1st United Meth. Ch., Springfield; mem. Food and Nutrition Work Group, Ill. Farm Bill Task Force, 2001. Recipient Gov. Adminstrs. Recognition award Ill. Primary Health Care Assn., 1997, Presdl. award for Outstanding Contbn. Ill. Rural Health Assn., 1999. Fellow: Ill. Pub. Health Leadership Inst.; mem.: Ill. Pub. Health Assn., Order Ea. Star (chmn. Grand chpt. info. com. 2001—02), Masons. Republican. Methodist. Home: 37 Meander Pike Chatham IL 62629-1569 Office: Ill Dept Pub Health 535 W Jefferson St Springfield IL 62702-5058 E-mail: mschmidt@idph.state.il.us.

SCHMIDT, PATRICIA JEAN, special education educator; b. Cleve., June 15, 1941; Cert. applied lab. tech., Cuyahoga C.C., Cleve., 1967; student, IIT Tech. Coll., 2000—. Lic. student driver instr. Lab. sect. supr. Meridia Euclid (Ohio) Hosp., 1968-74; gen. lab. technician, 1974-94; student driving instr. Cleve., 1994-2000. Tutor deaf students in coll. math.; designer including vet.'s memls. Author: A Manual of Disciplines for Interpreters of the Deaf; composer, vocal and stage presentation coach; sculptor and designer. Active voter registration Rep. Party. Recipient Acad. award Math. Assn. Am., Washington, 1959. Mem. Nat. Assn. of the Deaf, Nat. Head Injury Found., Sweet Adeline Internat. Avocations: writing, stamp collecting, reading. Home: PO Box 43123 Cleveland OH 44143-0123

SCHMIDT, ROBERT CHARLES, JR. finance executive; b. Oklahoma City, Apr. 2, 1942; s. Robert Charles and Francis Laura (Schiele) S.; m. Susan G. Dietz-Felbinger, Nov. 8, 1974; children: Laura Stewart, Elizabeth Berry Saldebar. B.A., Westminster Coll., Fulton, Mo., 1964; postgrad., U. Okla., 1972, London Grad. Sch. Bus. Studies, 1974-76. Exec. trainee First Nat. Bank in St. Louis, 1967-68, comml. banker, 1968-74, v.p., mgr. client services div., 1974-76; v.p. treasury ops. Am. Express Co., N.Y.C., 1976-81, dep. treas., 1981-86; chmn. bd. Am. Express Export Credit Corp., 1982-86; group v.p., gen. mgr. Nat. Data Corp., Atlanta, 1986-88, exec. v.p., 1988-89, Capital Guaranty Corp., San Francisco, 1989-91; pres. Tampsco Enterprises, Inc., St. Louis, 1993; ptnr. The Whitelaw Group, 1994-96; pres. SCM Group, Inc., 1996—. Cons. City of N.Y., 1977 Loaned exec. United Fund, St. Louis, 1973; trustee Congl. Summer Assembly Edn. Fund, 1993—; Served with U.S. Army, 1965—67; dir. Crystal Lake Assn., The Endowment for Experimental Arch., Ltd. Decorated Army Commendation medal; recipient cert. of merit USO, 1966, Alumni Achievement award Westminster Coll., 1977 Mem. Treas. Group (chmn. 1982-83), Noonday Club (St. Louis), Crystal Downs Country Club (Frankfort, Mich.), Beta Theta Pi Republican. Episcopalian. Office: 230 S Bemiston Ave Ste 300 Saint Louis MO 63105-1907

SCHMIDT, STEPHEN CHRISTOPHER, agricultural economist, educator; b. Isztimer, Hungary, Dec. 20, 1920; came to U.S., 1949, naturalized, 1965; s. Francis Michael and Anne Marie (Angeli) S.; m. Susan M. Varszegi, Dec. 20, 1945; children— Stephen Peter, David William. Dr.Sc., U. Budapest, Hungary, 1945; Ph.D., McGill U., Montreal, Que., Can., 1958. Asst. head dept. Hungary Ministry Commerce, Budapest, 1947-48; asst. prof. U. Ky., Lexington, 1955-57, Mont. State U., Bozeman, 1957-59, U. Ill., Urbana-Champaign, 1959-63, assoc. prof., 1963-70, prof. agrl. mktg. and policy, 1970-91, prof. emeritus, 1991—. Fulbright grantee Bulgaria, 1992-93; Ford Found. fellow, 1959; Agrl. Devel. Coun. grantee, 1966, U. Man. Rsch. fellow, 1968-69, Ford Found. rsch. grantee, 1973, 74, Whitehall found. grantee, 1979, Internat. Inst. Applied Systems Analyses (Laxenburg, Austria) rsch. scholar, 1976-77, USDA Intergovtl. Personnel Act grantee, 1983-84. Mem. Am. Agrl. Econs. Assn. (award 1979), Internat. Assn. Agrl. Economists, Am. Assn. Advancement Slavic Studies, Ea. Econ. Assn., Sigma Xi, Gamma Sigma Delta. Office: 1301 W Gregory Dr Urbana IL 61801-9015 E-mail: scschmid@uiuc.edu.

SCHMIDT, THOMAS JOSEPH, JR. lawyer; b. New Haven, Jan. 16, 1945; s. Thomas Joseph and Rosemary (O'Shaughnessy) S.; m. Linda Diane Crider, Nov. 16, 1974; children: Elizabeth Anne, Thomas Joseph III, Karen Diana. AB, Xavier U., 1967; JD, U. Cin., 1970. Bar: Ohio 1970, U.S. Ct. Mil. Appeals 1970. Commd. 2d lt. U.S. Army, 1967, advanced through grades to capt., 1969-75; legal officer U.S. Army Corps Engrs., Ft. Hayes, Ohio, 1967-68, Ft. Knox, Ky., 1969-70; atty. U.S. Army JAGC, Ft. Benning, Ga., 1971-75; asst. counsel Midland Enterprises Inc., Cin., 1975-77, assoc. gen. counsel, 1977-83, gen. counsel, 1983-87, gen. counsel, sec., 1987-95, v.p., gen. counsel and sec., 1995—. Republican. Roman Catholic. Office: Midland Enterprises Inc 300 Pike St Cincinnati OH 45202-4222

SCHMIDT, THOMAS WALTER, airport executive; b. St. Paul, Nov. 16, 1938; s. Elmer John and Margaret Elizabeth (Cunnien) S.; m. Roxanne B. Therrien, Mar. 1, 1980; children: Susan, Johnette, Holly. BA, U. Minn., 1961. Accredited airport exec. Dir. aviation Burlington (Vt.) Internat. Airport, 1970-83; asst. dir. aviation McCarran Internat. Airport, Las Vegas, Nev., 1983-89; exec. dir. Capital Region Airport Authority, Lansing, Mich., 1989—. Dir., mem. exec. com. Greater Lansing Conv. and Visitors Bur., Lansing, 1993—; dir. Capital Choice program C. of C., Lansing, 1995—. Mem. Mich. Athletic Club. Office: Capital Region Airport Authority 4100 Capitol City Blvd Lansing MI 48906-2170

SCHMIDT, WAYNE WILLIAM, museum director, curator; b. Chicago, Ill., Mar. 31, 1945; s. Walter William and Gloria Louise (Schoenfeldt) S.; m. Kathleen Keating Anderson, Mar. 31, 1979 (div. May 1991); 1 child, Robert Joseph; m. Margaret Ann Brooks, Dec. 20, 1998; children: Jessica, Samantha. BA cum laude, Northeastern Ill. U., Chgo., 1971, attended, 1972-75. Sta. mgr. Inflight Svcs., N.Y.C., 1968-79; pres., CEO Great Lakes Naval and Maritime Mus., Chgo., 1979-86; exec. dir., COO Intrepid Sea-Air-Space Mus., N.Y.C., 1986-90; cons. Chgo., 1990-92; dir. Nat. Mus. Transp., St. Louis, 1992-98; pres., CEO, exec. dir. Strategic Air Command Mus., Omaha, 1998-2000; pres., CEO Mus. Assocs., St. Louis, 2000-01; dir. Mus. of Aviation Flight Tech. Ctr., Robins AFB, Ga., 2001—. Adv. Nat. Park Svc., Washington, 1993; v.p. Historic Naval Ships N.Am., Phila., 1976-80; adv. Assn. Railroad Mus., Phila., 1996-98. Cons. Webster's Illus. Dictionary, 1994-95, Arm. Accreditation Standards, 1996-97. V.p. Nationalities Coun. Ill., Chgo., 1970-80; mem. Internat. Naval Review, N.Y.C., 1986, Commissioning Com. U.S.S. Chgo., 1986; sec/-treas. Zachary and Elizabeth Fisher Armed Svcs. Found., N.Y.C., 1988-90. Served with USNR, 1963-65. Recipient Raymond Tucker award ASME, 1996. Mem. Am. Assn. Mus., Navy League. Republican. Roman Catholic. Avocations: sailing, golf, scale modeling, photography. Home: 119 Autumn Woods Dr Warner Robins GA 31088 Office: Mus Aviation Flight Tech Ctr 78ABW/MU 1942 Heritage Blvd Robins AFB GA 31098-1662 E-mail: wayne.schmidt@robins.af.mil.

SCHMIT, DAVID E. lawyer; b. Charleston, W.Va., Feb. 18, 1947; BSEE, U. Cin., 1969, MSEE, 1976; JD, No. Ky. U., 1975. Bar: Ohio 1975, U.S. Patent and Trademark Office. Mem. Frost & Jacobs, Cin. Office: Frost & Jacobs 2500 PNC Ctr 201 E 5th St Ste 2500 Cincinnati OH 45202-4182

SCHMITT, ANDREW B. business executive; Pres. NL Acme Tool, 1985-88; v.p., gen. mgr. Tri-State Oil Tools, Inc., Bossier City, La., 1988-90, pres., 1990; pres., CEO Layne Christensen Co., Mission Woods. Office: Layne Christensen Co Ste 100 1900 Shawnee Mission Pkwy Mission KS 66205-3600

SCHMITT, GEORGE FREDERICK, JR. materials engineer; b. Louisville, Nov. 3, 1939; s. George Frederick and Jane Limbird (Hurst) S.; m. Ann Cheatham, July 31, 1965; 2 children. BS, U. Louisville, 1962, MS, 1963; MBA, Ohio State U., 1966. Chief integration and ops. divsn. Air Force Rsch. Lab. USAF Materials Directorate, Wright Patterson AFB, Ohio, 1966—; advanced engring devel. mgr. USAF Materials Lab., 1986-90, chief plans and programs br. Wright AFB, 1989-90, asst. chief nonmetallic materials divsn., 1990-96. Guest lectr. U. Dayton, 1970, 95, Cath. U., 1973, U. Mich., 1975. Contbr. articles to profl. jours. Mem. Kettering (Ohio) Civic Band, 1965— , Affiliate Socs. Coun. Dayton, 1972-81; mem. Dayton Philharm Chorus, 1999—, Dayton Letter Carriers Band, 2000—. 1st lt. USAF, 1963-66. Named Fed. Profl. Employee of Yr., Dayton, 1972, One of Ten Outstanding Engrs., Engrs. Week, 1975; recipient Air Force Meritorious Civilian Svc. award, 1994, Burton award for svc., Playhouse South Cmty. Theater, 1998, Tech. Transfer award, Fed. Lab. Consortium, 2001. Fellow Soc. for Advancement Materials and Process Engrs. (Best Paper award 1973, nat. sec. 1975-76, nat. membership chmn. 1977-79, nat. v.p. 1979-81, nat pres. 1981-82, chmn. long-range planning com. 1983-87, trustee 1991—, chmn. Internat. SAMPE Symposium 1996, chmn. SAMPE Trophy com. 1998—), AIAA (assoc., materials tech. com.); mem. ASTM (rec. sec. 72-75, chmn. com. on erosion and wear 1976-79, chmn. liaison subcom. 1979-83, award of merit 1981), Am. Chem. Soc., Affiliate Socs. Coun. Dayton (chmn. 1978-79). Republican. Lutheran. Home: 1500 Wardmier Dr Dayton OH 45459-3354 Office: AFRL Materials and Mfg Directorate MLO Wright-Patterson AFB 2977 P St Bldg 653 Dayton OH 45433-7733 E-mail: george.schmitt@wpafb.af.mil.

SCHMITT, HOWARD STANLEY, minister; b. Waterloo, Ont., Can., Oct. 19, 1933; came to U.S., 1971; s. Delton Howard and Beulah (Weber) S.; m. Dorothy Jean West, May 20, 1960; children: Valerie Jean Schmitt Jones, Jeffrey Howard. B Theology, Toronto Bible Coll., Ont., Can., 1963. Ordained to ministry Mennonite Ch., 1963. Pastor Wanner Mennonite Ch., Cambridge, Ont., 1960-71, Calvary Mennonite Ch., Ayr, 1964-69, S. Union Mennonite Ch., West Liberty, Ohio, 1971-83; hosp. chaplain Mary Rutan Hosp., Bellefontaine, 1983-85; dir. devel. Adriel Sch., West Liberty, 1985-86; pastor Bay Shore Mennonite Ch., Sarasota, Fla., 1986-95, Sharon Mennonite Ch., Plain City, Ohio, 1995—. Sec. Mennonite Conf. Ont., Cambridge, 1970-71; overseer Ohio Conf. Mennonites, West Liberty, 1972-78, 84-86; moderator Southeast Mennonite Conf., Sarasota, 1989-92; mem. Mennonite Ch. Gen. Bd., 1991-95. Vice chair Mary Rutan Hosp. Bd., 1978-83; sec. Plain City Ch. Fellowship, 1997—. Recipient 13 Yrs. Svc. award Vol. Chaplains Group, Mary Rutan Hosp., 1985. Mem. Sarasota Mennonite Mins. Fellowship (past sec., chmn.), Plain City Pastors' Fellowship, Ctrl. Ohio Mennonite Pastor Peer Group, Ohio Conf. Mennonites Coun. E-mail: howjean@prodigy.net.

SCHMITT, JERRY, state legislator; b. Oak, Nebr., Aug. 28, 1938; m. Lavonne R. Holmes; children: Dennis, Bruce. Constrn. worker; mem. Nebr. State Patrol, 1962-92; mem. from dist. 41 Nebr. State Senate, Lincoln, 1992—, mem. govt., mil. and vet. affairs com., mem. banking, commerce and ins. com. Mem. Ord City Park Bd. Mem. NRA, Nebr. Hist. Soc., VFW, State Troopers Assn. Nebr. Office: Nebr State Senate State Capitol Rm 1202 Lincoln NE 68509

SCHMITT, MARK F. bishop; b. Algoma, Wis., Feb. 14, 1923; Ed., Salvatorian Sem., St. Nazianz, Wis., St. John's Sem., Collegeville, Minn. Ordained priest Roman Cath. Ch., 1948; titular bishop of Ceanannus Mor and aux. bishop of Green Bay, 1970-78; bishop of Marquette (Mich.), 1978-92; retired, 1992—. Office: Chancery Office 444 S 4th St PO Box 550 Marquette MI 49855-0550

SCHMITT, WOLF RUDOLF, consumer products executive; b. Koblenz, Germany, Mar. 12, 1944; s. Josef H. and M.H. (Baldus) S.; m. Toni A. Yoder, June 30, 1974. BA, Otterbein Coll., 1966; AMP, Harvard U. Bus. Sch., 1986. With Rubbermaid Inc., Wooster, Ohio, 1966—, pres., gen. mgr. housewares products div., 1984-91, exec. v.p., bd. dirs., 1987-91, pres., chief operating officer, 1991-92; chmn., CEO, 1993-99; ret., 1999. Bd. dirs. Parker Hannifin Corp., Kimberly-Clark Corp.; chmn. Value Am. Bd. dirs. Otterbein Coll., 1992—. Avocations: horticulture, tennis, sailing. Office: Trends 2 Innovation 105 E Liberty St Wooster OH 44691-4345

SCHMITZ, JOHN, grain company executive; BS in Acctg., St. Cloud State U. CPA, Minn. With Harvest States (merged with Cenex, now Cenex Harvest States), Inver Grove Heights, Minn., 1974—, v.p., contr., 1986, sr. v.p., CFO, 1999, exec. v.p., CFO. Mem. AICPA, Nat. Soc. Accts. for Cooperatives, Minn. Soc. CPAs. Office: Cenex Harvest States 550 Cenex Dr Inver Grove Heights MN 55077

SCHMITZ, ROGER ANTHONY, chemical engineering educator, academic administrator; b. Carlyle, Ill., Oct. 22, 1934; s. Alfred Bernard and Wilma Afra (Aarns) S.; m. Ruth Mary Kuhl, Aug. 31, 1957; children: Jan, Joy, Joni B.S. in Chem. Engring., U. Ill., 1959; Ph.D. in Chem. Engring., U. Minn., 1962. Prof. chem. engring. U. Ill., Urbana, 1962-79; Keating-Crawford prof. chem. engring. U. Notre Dame, Ind., 1979—, chmn. dept. chem. engring., 1979-81, dean engring., 1981-87, v.p., assoc. provost, 1987-95. Cons. Amoco Chems., Naperville, Ill., 1966-77; vis. prof. Calif. Inst. Tech., Los Angeles, 1968-69, U. So. Calif., Los Angeles, 1968-69 Contbr. articles to profl. jours. U.S. Army, 1953—55. Fellow, Guggenheim Found., 1968. Mem. Nat. Acad. Engring., Am. Inst. Chem. Engrs. (A.P. Colburn award 1970, R.H. Wilhelm award 1981), Am. Chem. Soc., Am. Soc. for Engring. Edn. (George Westinghouse award 1977) Roman Catholic. Roman Catholic. Home: 16865 Londonberry Ln South Bend IN 46635-1444 Office: U Notre Dame 301 Cushing Hall Notre Dame IN 46556 E-mail: schmitz.1@nd.edu.

SCHMUTZ, CHARLES REID, university foundation executive; b. Youngstown, Ohio, Jan. 26, 1942; s. Charles Edward and Alice Mae (Bliss) S.; m. Judith Rhodes Seiple, June 19, 1965; children: Charles Reid Jr., Andrew Edward, Jill Caroline. AB in Econs., Brown U., 1964. Lab. technician The Standard Slag Co., Youngstown, 1964-65, direct salesman Cleve., 1965-69, mktg. and prodn. scheduler Youngstown, 1969-73, mktg. and indsl. engr., 1973-85, gen. mgr., v.p. ops., 1985-89; pres. Youngstown State U. Found., 1989—. Bd. dirs. StanCorp., Youngstown. Bd. dirs. Youngstown Playhouse, Jr. Achievement Mahoning Valley. Named to Hall of Fame, Ohio Aggregates Assn., 1990. Mem. Rotary. Methodist. Avocations: golf, tennis.

SCHNABEL, ROBERT VICTOR, retired academic administrator; b. Scarsdale, N.Y., Sept. 28, 1922; s. Frederick Victor and Louise Elizabeth (Frick) S.; m. Ellen Edyth Foelber, June 7, 1946; children: Mark F., Philip P. Student, Concordia Sem., St. Louis, 1943-45; AB, Bowdoin Coll., 1944; MS, Fordham U., 1951, PhD, 1955; LLD (hon.), Concordia Coll., 1988. Tchr. St. Paul's Sch., Ft. Wayne, Ind., 1945-49; prin. St. Matthew's Sch., N.Y.C., 1949-52; assoc. supt. edn. Central Dist., Luth. Ch.-Mo. Synod, 1952-56; asst. prof. philosophy Concordia Sr. Coll., Ft. Wayne, 1956-60, assoc. prof., 1960-65, prof., acad. dean, 1966-71; pres. Concordia Coll., Bronxville, N.Y., 1971-76; acad. v.p., dean Wartburg Coll., Waverly, Iowa, 1976-78; pres. Valparaiso (Ind.) U., 1978-88. Cons. Luth. Edn. Conf. N.Am., 1977-88. Contbr. articles to profl. jours. Mem. AAUP, Luth. Acad. Scholarship, Assoc. Colls. Ind., Nat. Assn. Ind. Colls. and Univs., Rotary, Phi Delta Kappa. Office: Valparaiso Univ 23 Huegli Hall Valparaiso IN 46383

SCHNEIDER, ARTHUR SANFORD, physician, educator; b. Los Angeles, Mar. 24, 1929; s. Max and Fannie (Ragin) S.; m. Edith Kadison, Aug. 20, 1950; children: Jo Ann Schneider Farris, William Scott, Lynnellen. B.S., UCLA, 1951; M.D., Chgo. Med. Sch., 1955. Diplomate Am. Bd. Internal Medicine, Am. Bd. Pathology. Intern, Wadsworth VA Hosp., Los Angeles, 1955-56, resident, 1956-59, chief clin. pathology sect., 1962-68; mem. faculty UCLA, 1961-75, clin. assoc. prof., 1971-75; chair dept. clin. pathology City of Hope Med. Ctr., Duarte, Calif., 1968-75; prof., chair dept. clin. pathology Whittier Coll., 1974-75; prof., chair dept. pathology Chgo. Med. Sch., 1975—; chief lab. service VA Med. Ctr., North Chicago, Ill., 1975-86, chief lab. hematology, 1986-94. Contbr. numerous chpts. to books and articles to med. jours. Served to capt. M.C., USAF, 1959-61. Fellow ACP, Coll. Am. Pathologists, Am. Soc. Clin. Pathologists; mem. AAUP, AMA, Internat. Acad. Pathology, Am. Assn. for Investigative Pathology, Assn. Pathology Chairs, Acad. Clin. Lab. Physicians and Scientists, Am. Soc. Hematology, Am. Assn. Blood Banks, Am. Soc. Clin. Rsch., Ill. Med. Soc., Lake County Med. Soc., Sigma Xi, Alpha Omega Alpha, Phi Delta Epsilon. Office: Chgo Med Sch 3333 Green Bay Rd North Chicago IL 60064-3037 Fax: 847-578-5002. E-mail: arthur.schneider@finchcms.edu.

SCHNEIDER, CARL EDWARD, law educator; b. Exeter, N.H., Feb. 23, 1948; s. Carl Jacob and Dorothy (Jones) S.; m. Joan L. Wagner, Jan. 6, 1976. BA, Harvard Coll., 1972; JD, U. Mich., 1979. Curriculum specialist Mass. Tchrs. Assn., Boston, 1972-75; law clk. to judge U.S. Ct. Appeals (D.C. cir.), Washington, 1979-80; law clk. Potter Stewart U.S. Supreme Ct., 1980-81; asst. prof. law U. Mich., Ann Arbor, 1981-84, assoc. prof. law, 1984-86, prof. law, 1986—, prof. internal medicine, 1998—, Chauncey Stillman prof. ethics, morality and practice of law; vis. prof. U. Tokyo, 1998. Author: The Practice of Autonomy: Patients, Doctors and Medical Decisions, 1998, (with Margaret F. Brinig) An Invitation to Family Law, 1996; editor: (book) The Law and Politics of Abortion, 1980, Family Law in Action: A Reader, 1999 (with Margaret F. Brinig & Lee E. Teitelbaum), Law at the End of Life: The Supreme Court and Assisted Suicide, 2000; contbr. articles to profl. jours. Fellow Am. Council of Learned Socs., Ford Found., 1985, Hastings Ctr.; life fellow Clare Coll., Cambridge. Mem. Order of Coif. Office: U Mich Law Sch 801 Monroe St Ann Arbor MI 48109-1210

SCHNEIDER, CAROL ANN, staffing services company executive; d. Glenn William and Beatrice Helen Kluth; m. Leon A. Schneider, Feb. 4, 1961; children: Paul, Joel, Neil. BS in Bus. Edn., U. Wis., Whitewater, 1958; postgrad., U. Wis., 1971-74. Lic. secondary bus. educator, Wis., vocat. bus. educator, Wis.; cert. pers. cons.; sr. prof. in human resources. Bus. divsn. chair Milw. Area Tech. Coll.-North, Mequon, Wis., 1969-80, Port Washington (Wis.) Vocat., Tech. and Adult Sch., 1969-80; founder, CEO, chair of the bd. SEEK, Inc., Grafton, Wis., 1971—. Founder, mgr. The Schneider Co., LLC, Grafton, 1996—, ITech Profls., LLC, Grafton, 1998—; past pres. Wis. Assn. Staffing Svcs.; presenter in field. Fund raising chair St. Joseph's Ch.; founder, past co-chair Workforce 2010; founder, co-chair Ozaukee County Transp. Mgmt. Assn.; former bd. mem. Ozaukee County Econ. Devel. Corp.; bd. mem., capitol campaign mem. B.A.B.E.S. Recipient Celebrate Success award Wis. Women Entrepreneurs, 1993, named Outstanding Citizen, Grafton C. of C., Nat. Employer of Yr., Coun. for Exceptional Children Divsn. on Career Devel. and Transition, 1998, Outstanding Bus. of Yr., Grafton Area C. of C., 1998, Wis. Welfare-to-Work Small Bus. Person of Yr., U.S. Small Bus. Adminstrn., 1999; named Woman of Yr. Wis. Women Entrepreneurs, 2000. Mem. FOCUS (founder, past pres., past v.p.), Am. Staffing Assn. (nat. temporary help week regional chair), Wis. Assn. Pers. Svcs. (past pres.), Washington/Ozaukee County Pers. Mgmt. Assn. (past pres.), Ind. Bus. Assn. Wis. (past bd. mem., past pres., past v.p. state programs, current welfare reform chair, mem. of yr. award 1999). Republican. Roman Catholic. Avocations: community service, playing piano, reading, politics. Office: SEEK Inc 1160 Opportunity Dr Grafton WI 53024-0148

SCHNEIDER, DAN W. lawyer, consultant; b. Salem, Oreg., Apr. 28, 1947; s. Harold Otto and Frances Louise (Warner) S.; m. Nancy Merle Schmalzbauer, Mar. 29, 1945; children: Mark Warner, Edward Michael. BA cum laude, St. Olaf Coll., 1969; JD, Willamette U., 1974; LLM, Columbia U., 1975. Bar: Oreg. 1974, D.C. 1978, Ill. 1987. Trial atty. U.S. Dept. Justice Antitrust, Washington, 1975-79; dep. assoc. dir. U.S. SEC, 1979-86; gen. ptnr. Schiff Hardin & Waite, Chgo., 1986-95; name ptnr. Smith Lodge & Schneider, 1995-98; ptnr. Hopkins & Sutter, 1998-2000; internat. ptnr. Baker & McKenzie, 2000—. Bd. dirs. NygaarArt, Northfield, Minn. Contbr. articles to profl. jours. Trustee, sec. Ill. Acad. Fine Arts, Chgo., 1990-98; mem. adv. bd. Steensland Art Mus., Northfield, 1990—; mem. adv. bd. Hallie Ford Mus. Art, Salem, Oreg., 1999—. Recipient 1st prize Nathan Burkan Law Essay Competition ASCAP, N.Y., 1974, Christie award Securities Transfer Assn., 1987. Mem. Met. Club. Chgo., Monroe Club, Plaza Club. Avocations: art collecting, art writing, music composition. Office: Baker & McKenzie 1 Prudential Plz 130 E Randolph St Ste 3700 Chicago IL 60601-6342 E-mail: dan.w.schneider@bakernet.com.

SCHNEIDER, DAVID MILLER, lawyer; b. Cleve., July 27, 1937; s. Earl Philip and Margaret (Miller) S.; children: Philip M., Elizabeth Dale. B.A., Yale U., 1959; LL.B., Harvard U., 1962. Assoc. Baker & Hostetler, Cleve., 1962-72, ptnr., 1972-89; cons. Progressive Casualty Ins. Co., 1989-99; sec. The Progressive Corp., 1989-99. Trustee Alcoholism Svcs. of Cleve., 1977—, pres., 1980-82, chmn., 1982-84; v.p. Ctr. for Human Svcs., Cleve., 1980-83; trustee Cleve. chpt. NCCJ, 1986—. Mem. Ohio Bar Assn., Bar Assn. Cleve., Union Club, Tavern Club, Hunt Club, Town Club (Jamestown, N.Y.), Ojibway Club (Pointe au Baril, Ont., Can.). Republican. Episcopalian. Office: The Progressive Corp 300 N Commons Blvd Magfield Heights OH 44143 Home: 7100 South Ln Willoughby OH 44094-9389

SCHNEIDER, DONALD J. trucking company executive; b. 1935; BA, St. Norbert Coll., 1957; MBA, U. Pa. Pres. Schneider Transport Inc., Green Bay, Wis., 1957—, Schneider National, Inc. Office: Schneider National Inc PO Box 2545 Green Bay WI 54306

SCHNEIDER, JAMES JOSEPH, military theory educator, consultant; b. Oshkosh, Wis., June 18, 1947; s. Joseph Edward and Virginia Gertrude Schneider; m. Peggy L. Spees, July 28, 1973 (dec. May 1976); m. Claretta Virginia Burton, Nov. 11, 1984; children: Kevin, Jason, Jenifer, Julie. BA, U. Wis., Oshkosh, 1973, MA, 1974; PhD, U. Kans., 1992. Planning evaluator Winnegago County, Oshkosh, 1978-80; ops. rsch. analyst Tng. and Doctrine Command Analysis Ctr., Ft. Leavenworth, Kans., 1980-84; prof. mil. theory Sch. Advanced Mil. Studies U.S. Army Command and Gen. Staff Coll., 1984—. Adj. assoc. prof. history Russian and East European Studies Ctr., U. Kans., 1994—; vis. assoc. prof. philosophy St. Mary Coll., Leavenworth, Kans., 2000. Author: (monograph) Exponential Decay of Armies in Battle, 1985, The Structure of Strategic Revolution, 1994; also numerous articles. With U.S. Army, 1965-68, Vietnam. Recipient medal for civilian achievement Dept. Army, 1989, superior civilian svc. award, 2001, Bronze Order of St. George, U.S. Cav. Assn., 1990 Mem. Am. Hist. Assn., Mil. Ops. Rsch. Soc., Alpha Pi chpt. Phi Beta Delta. Office: U S Army Command/Gen Staff Coll Sch Advanced Mil Studies Fort Leavenworth KS 66027

SCHNEIDER, JOHN DURBIN, state legislator; b. St. Louis, Mar. 1, 1937; s. F. John and Kathleen (Durbin) S.; m. Mary Jo Steppan; children: Anne Marie, John Steppan, Robert Durbin. BS, JD, St. Louis U., 1960. Atty. Transit Casualty Co., 1960-65, chief trial atty., 1965-70; rep. Mo. Ho. Reps. Dist. 26, Jefferson City, 1969-70; mem. Mo. Senate Dist. 14, 1970—. Mem. St. Louis Bar Assn., Phi Delta Phi. Address: 3520 Tremont Dr Florissant MO 63033-3057 also: State Senate State Capitol Bldg Rm 422 Jefferson City MO 65101-1556

SCHNEIDER, MAHLON C. lawyer; b. 1939; BA, U. Minn., 1962, LLB, 1964. Bar: Minn. 1965. Atty. Green Giant Co., 1980, Pillsbury, 1980-84, v.p., gen. counsel foods divsn., 1984-89; corp. atty. Geo. A. Hormel & Co., Austin, Minn., 1989-90, v.p., gen. counsel, 1990-99, sr. v.p. external affairs, gen. counsel, 1999—. Office: Hormel Foods Corp 1 Hormel Pl Austin MN 55912-3680

SCHNEIDER, MARLIN DALE, state legislator; b. La Crosse, Wis., Nov. 16, 1942; s. Donald M. and Elva M. (Peterson) S.; m. Georgia Jean Johansen, 1973; children: Jeanine Marie, Molly Anne. BS, U. Wis., La Crosse, 1965; MST, U. Wis., Stevens Point, 1976; MS, U. Wis., 1979; cert. Police Acad., Madison Area Tech. Coll., 1982. Wis. state rep. Dist. 72, 1970—; Wis. state assemblyman Dist. 59, 1971-72. Asst. majority leader, 1989-90; asst. minority leader, 1995—; tchr. Lomira H.S., Wis., 1965-66, Lincoln H.S., Wisconsin Rapids, 1966-71. Mem. Nat. Conf. State Legis. NSF grantee in sociology La. State U., 1970; named one of Outstanding Young Men of Am., 1973, Wis. Men of Achievement, 1976. Mem. Moose (local 819), Sigma Tau Gamma. Address: 3820 Southbrook Ln Wisconsin Rapids WI 54494-7548

SCHNEIDER, MARY LEA, college administrator; Student, Cardinal Stritch Univ., 1960-63; BA in Theology and Philosophy, Marquette U., 1966, MA in Theology, 1969, PhD in Religious Studies, 1971. Asst. prof. dept. religious studies Mich. State U., 1971-79, assoc. prof., 1979-84, prof., 1984-90, acting chair dept. religious studies, 1988-90; pres. Cardinal Stritch Coll., Milw., 1990—. Vis. instr. theology dept. U. San Francisco, summer 1969, Creighton U., summers 1974-77; spkr., presenter papers, mem. seminars in field; cons. Lilly Endowment, 1988; various TV and radio interviews, 1985— Contbr. articles, revs. to profl. publs. Trustee Pub. Policy Forum, Mt. St. Clare Coll., Clinton, Iowa, 1995—; mem. program Peter Favre Forum; mem. Greater Milw. Com. NEH travel grantee, 1986-87, 1990, rsch. grantee Coll. Arts and Letters Mich. State U., 1987-88. Mem. Am. Acad. Religion (chair Thomas Merton consultation 1979-81), Coll. Theology Soc. (chair Detroit-Cleve. region 1975-77, mem. com. on membership and objectives 1977-79, program dir., chair ann. conv. 1981-84, 88, convenor ecclesiology sect. ann. conv. 1984-87, pres. 1988-90, bd. dirs. 1990-92), Cath. Theol. Soc. Am., Am. Cath. Hist. Soc., History of Women in Religious Network, Tempo (Greater Milw. com.), Wis. Assn. Ind. Colls. and Univs. (exec. com. 1995—, chair, 1997—). Home: 225 W Bradley Rd Milwaukee WI 53217-3154 Office: Cardinal Stritch Univ 6801 N Yates Rd Milwaukee WI 53217-3945

SCHNEIDER, MICHAEL JOSEPH, biologist; b. Saginaw, Mich., Apr. 21, 1938; s. Michael Elias and Jane (Moffitt) S.; m. Janet Marie Potter, Nov. 24, 1967. B.S., U. Mich., 1960; M.S., U. Tenn., 1962; Ph.D. (Hutchinson Meml. fellow 1963-64, John M. Coulter research fellow 1964-65), U. Chgo., 1965. Resident research asso. Nat. Acad. Scis., Beltsville, Md., 1965-67; USPHS fellow U. Wis., Madison, 1967-68; asst. prof. biology Columbia U., 1968-73; mem. faculty U. Mich., Dearborn, 1973—, prof. biology, 1975—, chmn. dept. natural scis., 1975-80, 83-89, assoc. provost for acad. affairs, 1990, interim provost, vice chancellor for acad. affairs, 1991. Vis. prof. Plant Research Lab., Mich. State U., East Lansing, 1980-81 Contbr. articles profl. jours. Mem. AAAS, Am. Soc. Plant Physiologists, Am. Soc. Photobiology, Sigma Xi. Home: 4654 Mulberry Woods Cir Ann Arbor MI 48105-9767 Office: U Mich-Dearborn Dept Nat Scis Dearborn MI 48128-1491

SCHNEIDER, ROBERT F. treasurer; b. 1961; With Kimball Internat., Inc., Jasper, Ind., corp. contr., 1990—, v.p., dir. acctg., 1992—, exec. v.p., CFO, asst. treas., 1997—. Office: Kimball Internat Inc 1600 Royal St Jasper IN 47549-1001

SCHNEIDER, ROBERT JEROME, lawyer; b. Cin., June 22, 1947; s. Jerome William and Agnes (Moehringer) S.; m. Janice Loraine Eckhoff, Dec. 13, 1968; children: Aaron Haisley, Jared Alan, Margot Laraine. BSME, U. Cin., 1970, JD, 1973. Bar: Ill. 1973, U.S. Dist. Ct. (no. dist.) Ill. 1973, U.S. Ct. Appeals (7th cir.) 1973, U.S. Ct. Appeals (fed. cir.) 1973. Ptnr. Mason, Kolehmainen, Rathburn & Wyss, Chgo., 1973-82; ptnr., asst. chmn. patents, chmn. intellect. property dept. McDermott, Will & Emery, 1982-94; chmn. intellectual property dept. Chapman & Cutler, 1995—. Mem. ABA, ASME, Ill. Bar Assn., Chgo. Bar Assn., Licensing Execs. Soc., Intellectual Property Law Assn. Chgo. (sec. 1981-83), Fedn. Internat. des Conseils en Proriete Industrielle, Assn. Internationale pour la Protection de la Propertiètè Industrielle, Internat. Trademark Assn., Internat. Trade Commn. Trial Lawyers Assn., Am. Intellectual Property Law Assn., Tower Club (bd. govs. 1988—, v.p. 1994-95, pres. 1995—), Univ. Club Chgo. Republican. Roman Catholic. Home: 1609 Asbury Ave Winnetka IL 60093-1303 Office: Chapman & Cutler Chicago IL 60601 Fax: 530-464-2529. E-mail: iplaw@chapman.com.

SCHNEIDER, STEVEN PHILIP, aerodynamics educator; b. Chgo., Aug. 4, 1960; s. Philip Walter and Barbara Jean (Brilla) S.; m. Lynette Diane Brown, Aug. 24, 1985; children: Ariel, Kaitlyn. BS with honor, Calif. Inst. Tech., 1981, MS in Aeronautics, 1984, PhD in Aeronautics, 1989. Engr., scientist Naval Ocean Systems Ctr., San Diego, 1981-83; rsch. fellow Calif. Inst. Tech., Pasadena, 1989; asst. prof. Sch. Aero. and Astronautical Engring., West Lafayette, Ind., 1989-95, assoc. prof., 1995—. Presenter in field. Contbr. articles and abstracts to profl. jours. Achievement Rewards for Coll. Scientists scholar, 1986-87. Fellow AIAA (assoc.); mem. Am. Phys. Soc. (fluid dynamics div. 1983—). Avocations: backpacking, bicycling. Office: Purdue U Airport Aerospace Scis Lab West Lafayette IN 47906

SCHNEIDER, THOMAS PAUL, non-profit agency administrator; b. June 5, 1947; s. Milton and Gloria (Bocaner) S.; m. Susan G. Stein, May 31, 1987; children: Rachel Jenny, Daniel Joshua. BA with honors, JD, U. Wis., 1972. U.S. atty. U.S. Dist. Dist. Ct. (ea. dist.) Wis., Milw., 1993-2001; exec. dir. youth svcs. COA Youth & Family Ctrs., 2001—. Mem. Wis. Bar Assn. Democrat. Jewish. Office: COA Youth & Family Ctrs 909 E North Ave Milwaukee WI 53212 E-mail: tomcoa@execpc.com.

SCHNEIDER-CRIEZIS, SUSAN MARIE, architect; b. St. Louis, Aug. 1, 1953; d. William Alfred and Rosemary Elizabeth (Fischer) Schneider; m. Demetrios Anthony Criezis, Nov. 24, 1978; children: Anthony, John and Andrew. BArch, U. Notre Dame, 1976; MArch, MIT, 1978. Registered architect, Wis. Project designer Eichstaedt Architects, Roselle, Ill., 1978-80, Solomon, Cordwell, Buenz & Assocs., Chgo., 1980-82; project architect Gelick, Foran Assocs., 1982-83; asst. prof. Sch. Architecture U. Ill., 1980-86; exec. v.p. Criezis Architects, Inc., Northfield, Ill., 1986—. Graham Found. grantee MIT, 1977, MIT scholar, 1976-78; Prestressed Concrete Inst. rsch. grantee, 1981. Mem. AIA, Chgo. Archtl. Club, Chgo. Women in Architecture, Am. Solar Energy Soc., NAFE, Jr. League Evanston, Evanston C. of C. Roman Catholic. Avocations: tennis, swimming. Office: 1775 Winnetka Ave Ste 100 Northfield IL 60093-3386

SCHNELL, CARLTON BRYCE, lawyer; b. Youngstown, Ohio, Jan. 1, 1932; s. Carlton Wilhelm and Helen Jean (Alexander) S.; m. Dorothy Stewart Apple, Aug. 15, 1953; children— Laura, Margaret, Heidi B.A., Yale U., 1953, LL.B., 1956. Bar: Ohio 1956. Assoc. Arter & Hadden, Cleve., 1956-65, ptnr., 1966-96, mng. ptnr., 1977-82, Washington, 1982-84. Exec. comm. mem. Greater Cleve. Growth Assn., Cleve., 1983-97; chmn. Build Up Cleve., 1981-89; profl. chmn. United Way, Cleve., 1983; co-chmn. Charter Rev. Commn., Cleve., 1983-84; pres. Citizen's League Rsch. Inst., 1992-95. Named Vol. of Yr., Leadership Cleve., 1985. Mem. Tex. Club Cleve. (pres. 1972-73), Cleve. Tax Inst. (chmn. 1978), Ohio C. of C. (trustee 1977-80) Republican. Presbyterian. Clubs: Tavern, Pepper Pike. Avocations: golf; tennis. Home: 31450 Shaker Blvd Pepper Pike OH 44124-5153

SCHNELL, ROBERT LEE, JR. lawyer; b. Mpls., Sept. 20, 1948; s. Robert Lee and Dorothy Mae (Buran) S.; m. Jacqueline Irene Husak, Dec. 19, 1969 (div. Aug. 1988); children: Robert Lee III, Elizabeth Anne, Jennifer Irene; m. Julie Ann Bemlott, Sept. 29, 1989; children: Helen Bridget, Michael Henry. BA cum laude, Princeton U., 1970; JD magna cum laude, Harvard U., 1974. Bar: Minn. 1974, U.S. Dist. Ct. Minn. 1974, U.S. Ct. Appeals (8th cir.) 1975, U.S. Supreme Ct. 1990. Assoc. Faegre & Benson, Mpls., 1974-81, ptnr., 1982—. Bd. dirs. United Way of Mpls., 1992-93. Office: Faegre & Benson 2200 Wells Fargo Ctr 90 S St Ste 2200 Minneapolis MN 55402-1109

SCHNOBRICH, ROGER WILLIAM, lawyer; b. New Ulm, Minn., Dec. 21, 1929; s. Arthur George and Amanda (Reinhart) S.; m. Angeline Ann Schmitz, Jan. 21, 1961; children: Julie A. Johnson, Jennifer L. Holmers, Kathryn M. Kubinski, Karen L. Holetz. BBA, U. Minn., 1952, JD, 1954. Bar: Minn. 1954. Assoc. Fredrikson and Byron, Mpls., 1956-58; pvt. practice, 1958-60; ptnr. Popham Haik, Schnobrich & Kaufman, 1960-97, Hinshaw & Culbertson, Mpls., 1997—. Bd. dirs. numerous corps., Mpls. With U.S. Army, 1954-56. Mem. ABA, Minn. Bar Assn., Hennepin County Bar Assn., Order of Coif, Law Rev. Roman Catholic. Avocations: family, jogging, reading, golf. Home: 530 Waycliff Dr N Wayzata MN 55391-1385 Office: Hinshaw & Culbertson 3100 Piper Jaffray Tower 222 S 9th St Minneapolis MN 55402-3389 E-mail: rschnobrich@hinshawlaw.com.

SCHNOLL, HOWARD MANUEL, investment banking and managed asset consultant; b. Milw., June 6, 1935; s. Nathan P. and Della (Fisher) S.; m. Barbara Ostach, Dec. 3, 1988; children: Jordan, Terry, Jeffrey, Robert, Tammy, Daniel. BBA, U. Wis., 1958. CPA, Wis.; cert. mgmt. cons.; registered investment advisor. Mng. ptnr. Nankin, Schnoll & Co., S.C., Milw., 1966-86; mng. ptnr., bd. dirs. BDO Seidman, 1986-90; pres., chief oper. officer Universal Med. Bldgs., L.P., Milw., 1990, also bd. dirs.; pres. Howard Schnoll & Assocs., 1991; mng. dir. Grande, Schnoll & Assocs., 1992-93; exec. mng. dir., COO Glaisner, Schilffarth, Grande & Schnoll, Ltd., 1993-98; exec. v.p., treas., bd. dirs. GS2 Securities, Inc., 1998-99; sr. v.p. B.C. Ziegler and Co., 1999—. Bd. dirs. Milw. World Festival, Inc., 1968—, City of Festivals Parade, Milw., 1983-89, Aurora Health Care Ventures, Milw. Heart Rsch. Found., Milw. Heart Inst., Arthritis Found.; pres. Milw. Coun. on Alcoholism and Drug Dependance, 1993—, bd. dirs.; pres., treas. Am. Heart Assn., Milw., 1978-82; capt. United Way, Milw., 1985; mem. Greater Milw. Com. Nat. Found. Ileitis and Colitis, Milw. chpt. Served to sgt. U.S. Army, 1956-63. Mem.: AICPA, Brynwood Country Club (bd. dirs., treas., pres. 1988—2000), Acct. Computer Users Tech. Exchange, Wis. Inst. CPAs, B'nai Brith 1960—62. Jewish. Avocations: golf, tennis. Office: BC Ziegler & Co 250 E Wisconsin Ave Ste 2000 Milwaukee WI 53202-4298 E-mail: hschnoll@ziegler.com.

SCHNOOR, JEFFREY ARNOLD, lawyer; b. Winnipeg, Man., Can., June 22, 1953; s. Toby and Ray (Kass) S. BA, U. Man., 1974, LLB, 1977. Bar: Man. 1978. Assoc. McJannet Weinberg Rich, Winnipeg, 1977-84, ptnr., 1984-86; exec. dir. Man. Law Reform Commn., 1986-97; dir. criminal justice policy Man. Dept. Justice, 1998—2002, exec. dir. policy devel. & analysis, 2002—. Pres. Fedn. Law Reform Agys. Can., 1995-98; del. Uniform Law Conf. Can., 1986—, exec. com. 1995-2001, chair civil sect., 1996-97, v.p., 1998-99, pres., 1999-2000. Trustee United Way of Winnipeg, 1990-97, 99—, exec. com., 1990-97, 2001— treas., 1991-92, pres., 1994-95, cmty. rels. com. 1995-98, chmn. 1996-97, chair United Way 2005 com., 1997-98, hon. solicitor, 2001—, chmn. 211 implementation com., 2001-; mem. R&D 2000 steering com., United Way of Can., 1995-98; bd. dirs. Winnipeg Libr. Found., 1997-2001; Man. Voluntary Sector Coun., 2001-. Named Queen's Counsel Govt. of Man., 1992; recipient Chair's award of distinction United Way of Can., 1997. Mem. Law Soc. Man. (lectr. bar admission course 1981-96), Man. Bar Assn. (governing coun. 1988-96, life mem.), Can. Bar Assn. (legis. and law reform com. 1994-2000, 2001— vice-chair 1997-2000, chair 2001—). Avocations: travel, languages, performing arts, fitness. Home: 2245 West Taylor Blvd Winnipeg MB Canada R3P 2J5 Office: Policy Development & Analysis 1210-405 Broadway Winnipeg MB Canada R3C 3L6 E-mail: jschnoor@gov.mb.ca.

SCHNUCK, CRAIG D. grocery stores executive; b. Apr. 20, 1948; BS, Cornell U., 1967, MBA, 1971. With Schnuck Markets, Inc., Hazelwood, Mo., 1971—, v.p., 1975-76, exec. v.p., sec., 1976-83, pres., chief exec. officer, 1983-91, also bd. dirs., 1991, chmn., CEO, 1991—. Office: Schnuck Markets Inc 11420 Lackland Rd Saint Louis MO 63146-3559

SCHNUCK, SCOTT C. grocery store executive; b. 1950; Pres., COO Schnuck Markets, Inc., St. Louis, 1992—. Office: Schnuck Markets Inc 11420 Lackland Rd Saint Louis MO 63146-3559

SCHNUCK, TERRY EDWARD, lawyer; b. St. Louis, Oct. 10, 1952; s. Donald Otto and Doris Irene (Letson) S.; m. Sally Barrows Braxton, May 24, 1980; children: Hadley Braxton, Terry Edward Jr. BA in Econs., Tulane U., 1975; MBA, Washington U., St. Louis, 1980; JD, St. Louis U., 1980. Bar: Mo. 1980. Assoc. Greensfelder, Hemker, Wiese, Gale & Chappelow, St. Louis, 1980-84; with Schnuck Markets Inc., Bridgeton, Mo., 1980—, chief legal counsel, sec. Bd. dirs. Arts and Edn. Coun. of Greater St. Louis, 1991—. Bd. dirs. Urban League of Met. St. Louis, 1987—. Mem. ABA, Mo. Bar Assn., Bar Assn. of Met. St. Louis, Better Bus. Bur. (bd. dirs. 1990—), Mo. Retailers Assn. (exec. bd. 1984—), Beta Theta Pi. Republican. Presbyterian. Club: Bellerive Country (St. Louis). Office: Schnuck Markets Inc 11420 Lackland Rd Saint Louis MO 63146-3559

SCHNUCK, TODD ROBERT, grocery store company executive; CFO Schnuck Markets, Inc., St. Louis. Office: Schnuck Markets Inc 11420 Lackland Rd Saint Louis MO 63146-3559

SCHNUR, ROBERT ARNOLD, lawyer; b. White Plains, N.Y., Oct. 25, 1938; s. Conrad Edward and Ruth (Mehr) S.; children: Daniel, Jonathan. BA, Cornell U., 1960; JD, Harvard U., 1963. Bar: Wis. 1965, Ill. 1966. Assoc. Michael, Best & Friedrich, Milw., 1966-73, ptnr., 1973—. Chmn. Wis. Tax News, 1983-90; adj. prof. tax law U. Wis. Law Sch., 1988—. Capt. U.S. Army, 1963-65. Fellow Am. Coll. Tax Counsel; mem. ABA, Wis. Bar Assn. (chmn. tax sect. 1986-88), Milw. Bar Assn. Home: 3093 Timber Ln Verona WI 53593 Office: Michael Best Friedrich 100 E Wisconsin Ave Ste 3300 Milwaukee WI 53202-4108 E-mail: raschnur@mbf-law.com.

SCHOBINGER, RANDY ARTHUR, state legislator; b. Minot, N.D., Dec. 15, 1969; Student, Minot State U., 1991-96. Warehouseman, Minot; mem. N.D. Senate from 3rd dist., Bismarck, 1994—; with Movers, Inc. Vice chmn. transp. com. State Senate of N.D., mem. edn. com.; endorsed candidate of the N.D. Repub. Party for State Treasurer, 1996. Office: ND State Capitol 600 Easy St Bismarck ND 58504-6239

SCHODORF, JEAN, state legislator; b. Cherry Point, N.C., June 11, 1950; m. Richard Schodorf; children: Brian, Kelly, Kristin. BA, U. N.Mex., 1972, MS, 1973; PhD, Wichita State U., 1981. Mem. Kans. State Senate, 2000—. Active USD 259 Bd. Edn., 1989—. Republican. Methodist. Home: 3039 Benjamin Ct Wichita KS 67204 Office: State Capitol Rm 143-N Topeka KS 66612 E-mail: jschodor@swbell.net.

SCHOELLER, DALE ALAN, nutrition research educator; b. Milw., June 8, 1948; s. Arthur B. and Anne Clare S.; m. Madeline Mary Juresh, Aug. 22, 1970; children: Nicholas Paul, Gregory Scott, Erica Lee. BS with honors, U. Wis., Milw., 1970; PhD, Ind. U., 1974. Postdoctoral fellow Argonne (Ill.) Nat. Lab., 1974-76; from asst. prof. to prof., also rsch. assoc. U. Chgo., 1976-91, assoc. prof., 1991—, prof., 1996; assoc. prof. U. Wis., Madison, 1997-98, prof., 1998—. Chmn. com. on human nutrition and nutritional biology U. Chgo., 1991-97. Author: (book chpt.) Obesity, 1992; co-author: (book chpt.) Annual Review of Nutrition, 1991. Mem. Am. Soc. Nutritional Scis. (v.p. elect 2001, Mead Johnson award 1987), Am. Soc. for Clin. Nutrition (Herman award 2000), Am. Soc. for Mass Spectrometry, N.Am. Soc. for Study of Obesity. Achievements include development of stable isotope methods for the study of human energy metabolism including first human use of doubly labeled water for measurement of free-living total energy expenditure. Office: U Wis Dept Nutrition 1415 Linden Dr Madison WI 53706-1527 E-mail: dschoell@nutrisci.wisc.edu.

SCHOENBERG, JEFFREY M. state legislator; b. Chgo., July 28, 1959; BA, Columbia U., 1983, Rugers U. Ill. state rep. Dist. 58, 1991—; mem. aging com. appropriations, edn. fin. Ill. Ho. Reps., environ. and energy, health care, human svcs. com.; dir. Roosevelt Ctr. for Am. Policy Studies. Democrat. Home: 3114 Hartzell St Evanston IL 60201-1126 Office: Ill Ho of Reps Rm M-2 State Capitol Springfield IL 62706-0001

SCHOENDIENST, ALBERT FRED (RED SCHOENDIENST), professional baseball coach, former baseball player; b. Germantown, Ill., Feb. 2, 1923; m. Mary Eileen O'Reilly; children: Colleen, Cathleen, Eileen, Kevin. Infielder St. Louis Cardinals, 1945-56, 61-63, N.Y. Giants, 1956-57, Milw. Braves, 1957-61; coach St. Louis Cardinals, 1961-64, 1979-95, Hitting Coach, mgr., 1964-77; coach Oakland Athletics, Calif., 1977-78. Mem. Nat. League All-Star team, 10 times, player in 9 games; mem. World Series Championship team, 1946, 57, 64; managed team to World Series Championship, 1967; inducted into Major League Baseball Hall of Fame, 1989. Office: Saint Louis Cardinals 250 Stadium Plz Saint Louis MO 63102-1722

SCHOENFELD, HANNS-MARTIN WALTER, accounting educator; b. Leipzig, Germany, July 12, 1928; came to U.S., 1962, naturalized, 1968; s. Alwin and Lisbeth (Kirbach) S.; m. Margit Frese, Aug. 10, 1956; 1 child, Gabriele. MBA, U. Hamburg, Fed. Republic Germany, 1952, DBA, 1954; PhD, U. Braunschweig, Fed. Republic Germany, 1966. Pvt. practice acctg., Hamburg, 1948-54; bus. cons. Europe, 1958-62; faculty accountancy U. Ill., Champaign/Urbana, 1962—, prof. acctg., bus. adminstrn. Urbana, 1967—, Weldon Powell prof. acctg., 1976, 80-81, H. T. Scovill prof. acctg., 1985-94; prof. emeritus, 1994—; dir. Office of West European Studies, 1982-84. Lectr., cons. in bus. and acctg., Eng., Belgium, Austria, Denmark, Brazil, Mex., Germany, Poland, Indonesia, Japan, Switzerland, Hungary, Czechoslovakia, 1962—; vis. prof. Econ. U. Vienna, Austria, 1984—, Handelshochschule, Leipzig, Germany, 1996—. Author: numerous books including Management Dictionary 2 vols., 4th edit, 1971, Cost Accounting, 8th edit, 1974-95, Management Development, 1967, Cost Terminology and Cost Theory, 1974, (with J. Sheth) Export Marketing: Lessons from Europe, 1981, (with H.P. Holzer) Managerial Accounting and Analysis in Multinational Enterprises, 1986, (with L. Noerreklit) Resources of the Firm, 1996. With German Army, 1944-45. Recipient Dr. Kausch prize for internat. integration of acctg. U. St. Gall, Switzerland, 1996. Mem. Am. Acctg. Assn. (chmn. internat. sect. 1976-77), Acad. Acctg. Historians (v.p. 1976-77, pres. 1978-79, Hour Glass award for best book publs. 1975), Acad. Internat. Bus., German Profs. Bus. Adminstrn., German Assn. Indsl. Engring., European Acctg. Assn., Coun. of European Studies, Internat. Assn. for Acctg. Edn. and Rsch., Beta Gamma Sigma, Beta Alpha Psi. Home: 1014 Devonshire Dr Champaign IL 61821-6620 Office: U Ill Dept Acctg 360 Commerce Bldg W 1206 S 6th St Champaign IL 61820-6915

SCHOENFELDER, LASKA, state commissioner, farmer; m. Mike Schoenfelder; 5 children. Student, Dakota Wesleyan U. Formerly with Dept. Commerce, Bur. Pers., Office Hwy. Safety; registrar of deeds Davison County, S.D., 1973-82; mem. S.D. Pub. Utilities Commn., Pierre, 1982—. Farmer, nr. Mt. Vernon, S.D.; mem. FCC Fed-State Joint Bd. Mem. Nat. Assn. Regulatory Utility Commrs. (com. oncomm. 1991—). Republican. Office: SD Pub Utilities Commn Capitol Bldg 1st Fl 500 E Capitol Ave Pierre SD 57501-5070 Fax: 605-773-3809.

SCHOENHARD, WILLIAM CHARLES, JR. health care executive; b. Kansas City, Mo., Sept. 26, 1949; s. William Charles S. and Joyce Evans (Thornsberry) Bell; m. Kathleen Ann Klosterman, June 3, 1972; children: Sarah Elizabeth, Thomas William. BS in Pub. Adminstrn., U. Mo., 1971; M of Health Adminstrn. with honors, Washington U., St. Louis, 1975. V.p., dir. gen. svcs. Deaconess Hosp., St. Louis, 1975-78; assoc. exec. dir. St. Mary's Health Ctr., 1978-81; exec. dir. Arcadia Valley Hosp., Pilot Knob, 1981-82, St. Joseph Health Ctr., St. Charles, 1982-86, St. Joseph Hosp. W., Lake St. Louis, 1982—86; exec. v.p., COO SSM Health Care, St. Louis, 1986—. Adv. bd. dirs. Firstar Bank, 1998-2001; regent Mo.-Gateway area Am. Coll. Healthcare Execs., 1997-2001. Contbr. articles to profl. jours. Mem. fin. com. Cath. Health Assn. U.S., 1999—; mem. adv. bd. St. Louis chpt. Lifeseekers, St. Louis, 1985—94; mem. bd. mgrs. Kirkwood-Webster (Mo.) YMCA, 1990—96, sec., 1996; mem. healthcare adv. bd. Sanford Brown Colls., 1992—94; del. Am. Hosp. Assn. Regional Policy Bd., 1999—; bd. trustees Mo. Hosp. Assn., 1999—, chmn., 2002—; mem. Greater St. Louis divsn. bd. dirs. Am. Heart Assn., 2001—; bd. dirs. St. Andrews Mgmt. Svcs., Inc., 1994—, Mid Am. Transplant Svcs., 1995—, Lindenwood U., 1997—, Civic Entrepreneurs Orgn., 1997—2000, Greater St. Louis Boy Scouts Am., 1997—; pres. Shaw Neighborhood Improvement Assn., St. Louis, 1979—80. With USN, 1971—72, Vietnam. Fellow Am. Coll. Health Care Execs. (bd. govs. 2002—); mem. VFW, Am. Legion, U.S. Navy League, Phi Eta Sigma, Pi Omicron Sigma, Delta Upsilon, Delta Sigma Pi. Roman Catholic. Avocations: reading, walking. Home: 420 Fairwood Ln Saint Louis MO 63122-4429 Office: SSM Health Care 477 N Lindbergh Blvd Saint Louis MO 63141-7832

SCHOENHOLZ, DAVID A. diversified financial services company executive; CFO Household Internat. Inc., Prospect Heights, Ill. Office: Household Internat Inc 2700 Sanders Rd Prospect Heights IL 60070-2701

SCHOENROCK, TRACY ALLEN, airline pilot, aviation consultant; b. Oshkosh, Wis., Jan. 11, 1960; s. Elder Roy and Shirley Mae (Rutz) S.; m. Kathleen Mary Neumann, Oct. 8, 1983; children: Amanda Beth, Veronica Grace, Shannon Traci. BS in Geography summa cum laude, U. Wis., Oshkosh, 1982. Charter pilot Basler Airlines, Oshkosh, 1977-82; pilot Simmons Airlines, Marquette, Mich., 1982-84, Northwest Airlines, St. Paul, 1984—; owner charter operation. Lutheran. Avocations: golf, travel, flying, electronics. Home and Office: 1345 Maricopa Dr Oshkosh WI 54904-8150

SCHOLER, SUE WYANT, state legislator; b. Topeka, Oct. 20, 1936; d. Zint Elwin and Virginia Louise (Achenbach) Wyant; m. Charles Frey Scholer, Jan. 27, 1957; children: Elizabeth Scholer Truelove, Charles W., Virginia M. Scholer McCal. Student, Kans. State U., 1954-56. Draftsman The Farm Clinic, West Lafayette, Ind., 1978-79; assessor Wabash Twp., 1979-84; commr. Tippecanoe County, Lafayette, Ind., 1984-90; state rep. Dist. 26 Ind. Statehouse, Indpls., 1990—. Asst. minority whip, 1992-94, Rep. whip, 1994-2000, asst. Rep. leader, 2001—; mem. Tippecanoe County Area Plan Commn., 1984-90; chmn. Midwestern legis. conf. CSG, 1998. Bd. dirs. Crisis Ctr., Lafayette, 1984-89, Tippecanoe Arts Fedn., 1990-99, United Way, Lafayette, 1990-93; mem. Lafayette Conv. and Visitors Bur., 1988-90. Recipient Salute to Women Govt. and Politics award, 1986, United Sr. Action award, Outstanding Legislator award, 1993, Small Bus. Champion award, 1995, Ind. Libr. Fedn. Legislator award, 1995, Disting. Legislator award Nat. Alliance for Mentally Ill, 1997, Friend of Cmty. Action award, 1999. Mem. Ind. Assn. County Commrs. (treas. 1990), Assn. Ind. Counties (legis. com. 1988-90), Greater Lafayette C. of C. (ex-officio bd. 1984-90), LWV, P.E.O., Purdue Women's Club (past treas.), Kappa Kappa Kappa (past pres. Epsilon chpt.)., Delta Delta Delta (past pres. alumnae, house corp. treas.). Republican. Presbyterian. Avocations: golf, needlework, reading. Home: 807 Essex St West Lafayette IN 47906-1534 Office: Indiana Statehouse 200 W Washington Indianapolis IN 46204

SCHOMMER, CAROL MARIE, principal; Prin. Madonna High Sch., 1985—. Recipient Blue Ribbon, 1990-91. Office: Madonna High Sch 4055 W Belmont Ave Chicago IL 60641-4731

SCHONBERG, ALAN ROBERT, management recruiting executive; b. N.Y.C., Oct. 23, 1928; s. Julius and Evelyn (Guzik) S.; m. Carole May Kreisman, Dec. 27, 1975; children: William, Evelyn, David, Jeffrey. Nat. sales mgr. Majestic Specialties, Inc., Cleve., 1953-63; pres. Internat. Personnel, Inc., 1963-65; chmn. Mgmt. Recruiters Internat., Inc., 1965-98, 1998—2000, chmn. emeritus, 2001—. Pres., bd. dirs. Jewish Vocat. Service, Cleve., 1983—; trustees Mt. Sinai Hosp. (now Mt. Sinai Found.), Cleve., bd. dirs. Cleve. Jewish News; gen. chmn. Welfare Fund Campaign; trustee Am. Jewish Commn., Mt. Sinai Med. Ctr., Hebrew Immigrant Aid Soc. Named one of Cleve.'s 86 Most Interesting People, Cleve. Mag., 1986, Man of Yr. local chpt. Orgn. through Rehab. and Tng., 1996, Entrepreneur of Yr. Inc. Mag., Merrill Lynch Ernst & Young, 1995; recipient Human Rels. award Cleve. chpt. Am. Jewish Com., 1998. Mem. Internat. Franchise Assn., Internat. Confederation Pvt. Employment Agys. Assns., Am. Mgmt. Assn., Assn. Human Resource Cons. (chmn. 1980—), Org. for Rehab. and Training (ORT), Assn. Am.-Israel C. of C. (pres.), Ohio Israel C. of C. (co-chmn.), Jewish Family Svcs. Assn. (v.p., pres. 1998-2002). Avocation: world travel. E-mail: aschonberg@adelphia.net.

SCHONBERG, WILLIAM PETER, aerospace, mechanical, civil engineering educator; b. N.Y.C., Mar. 25, 1960; s. Christian and Tamara (Kalnev) S.; m. Jane Heminover, Sept. 7, 1986; children: Christina Carol, Richard William, Peter James. BSCE cum laude, Princeton U., 1981; MS in Engring., Northwestern U., 1983, PhD, 1986. Asst. prof. civil engring. U. Ala., Huntsville, 1986-91, assoc. prof., 1991-94, prof., 1994-99, chair civil and environ. engring. dept., 1995-99; prof., chair U. Mo., Rolla, 1999—. Mem. working group NASA Boeing Space Sta., 1987-90. Contbr. articles to profl. publs. Recipient rsch. and creative works award U. Ala.-Huntsville Found., 1992; Walter P. Murphy fellow, 1981-82, summer faculty fellow NASA, 1987, 88, 94, 95, Air Force Office Sci. Rsch., 1992, 93; grantee U. Ala.-Huntsville Rsch. Inst., 1987-92. Fellow AIAA (assoc., Young Engr. of Yr. award 1990, Lawrence Sperry award 1995); mem. ASME, ASCE, Am. Acad. Mechanics, Tau Beta Pi. Avocations: astronomy, stamps, mystery novels, rock and roll music, travel. Office: U Mo Civil Engring Dept Rolla MO 65401 E-mail: wschon@umr.edu.

SCHÖNEMANN, PETER HANS, psychology educator; b. Pethau, Fed. Republic Germany, July 15, 1929; came to U.S., 1960, naturalized, 1965; s. Max Paul Franz and Hertha Anna (Kahle) S.; m. Roberta Dianne Federbush, Jan. 29, 1962; children: Raoul Dieter, Nicole Deborah. Vordiplom in Psychologie, U. Munich, 1956; Hauptdiplom in Psychologie, U. Goettingen, 1959; Ph.D., U. Ill., 1964. Thurstone postdoctoral fellow U. N.C., 1965-66; asst. prof., then assoc. prof. Ohio State U., 1966-69; postdoctoral fellow Ednl. Testing Service, Princeton, N.J., 1967-68; vis. prof. Technische Hochschule, Aachen, Fed. Republic Germany, 1981; mem. faculty Purdue U., 1969—, prof. psychology, 1971-2001, emeritus, 2001—. Vis. prof. Univs. Munich, Bielefeld and Braunschweig, 1984-85, Nat. Taiwan U., 1992, 96, 97. Author papers in field. Recipient Found. for the Advancement of Outstanding Scholarship award, Taiwan, 1996. Mem. Soc. Multivariate Exptl. Psychology. Office: Dept Psychol Scis Purdue U Lafayette IN 47907 E-mail: phs@psych.purdue.edu.

SCHONFELD, GUSTAV, medical educator, researcher, administrator; b. Mukacevo, Ukraine, May 8, 1934; came to U.S., 1946; s. Alexander Schonfeld and Helena Gottesmann; m. Miriam Steinberg, May 28, 1961; children: Joshua Lawrence, Julia Elizabeth, Jeremy David. BA, Washington U., St. Louis, 1956, MD, 1960. Diplomate Am. Bd. Internal Medicine. Intern. Bellevue Med. Ctr. NYU, 1960-61, resident in internal medicine, 1961-63; chief resident in internal medicine Jewish Hosp., St. Louis, 1963-64; from NIH trainee in endocrinology & metabolism to prof. Washington U., 1964—2002, Samuel B. Schechter prof. medicine, 2002—; rsch. assoc. Cochran VA Hosp., 1965-66, clin. investigator, 1968-70, cons. in internal medicine, 1972—; rsch. flight med. officer USAF Sch. Aerospace Medicine, Brooks AFB, Tex., 1966-68; from asst. physician to asst. physician Barnes Hosp., St. Louis, 1972—99; physician Barnes Jewish Hosp., 1999—; clin. instr. medicine Harvard U. Med. Sch., Boston, 1970-72; assoc. prof. metabolism and human nutrition, asst. dir. Clin. Rsch. Ctr. MIT, Cambridge, 1970-72. Mem. rsch. com. Mo. Heart Assn., 1978-80; expert witness working group on atherosclerosis Nat. Heart, Lung and Blood Inst., 1979, Nat. Diabetes Adv. Bd., 1979; mem. endocrinologic and metabolic drugs adv. com. USPHS, FDA, 1982-86; mem. nutrition study sect. NIH, 1984-88, spl. reviewer metabolism study sect.; mem. adult treatment guidelines panel Nat. Cholesterol Edn. Program, 1986; mem. Consensus Devel. Conf. on Triglyceride, High Density Lipoprotein and Coronary Heart Disease, 1992; cons. Am. Egg Bd., Am. Dairy Bd., Inst. Shortening and Edible Oils, Ciba-Geigy, Sandoz, Fournier, Parke-Davis, Bristol-Meyers Squibb, Monsanto/Searle. Past editor: Atherosclerosis, past mem. editl. bd.: Jour. Clin. Endocrinology and Metabolism, past mem. editl. bd.: Jour. Clin. Investigation, past mem. editl. bd.: Jour. Lipid Rsch., past assoc. editor: Circulation. Recipient Berg Prize in Microbiology, 1957, 58, Faculty/Alumni award Washington U., 1995; named Physician honoree Am. Heart Assn. Mo. Affiliate, 1995; grantee MERIT status NIH. Fellow ACP, AAAS; mem. Assn. Am. Physicians, Am. Soc. for Clin. Investigation, Am. Physiol. Soc., Am. Soc. Biol. Chemists, Am. Inst. Nutrition, Am. Diabetes Assn., Am. Heart Assn. (program com. coun. on atherosclerosis 1977-80, 86-88, nat. com. 1980-84, pathology rsch. com. 1980-83, budget com. 1991, awards com. 1992), Endocrine Soc., Alpha Omega Alpha. Office: Washington U Sch Medicine Box 8046 660 S Euclid Ave Saint Louis MO 63110-1010 E-mail: gschonfe@im.wustl.edu.

SCHOONHOVEN, RAY JAMES, retired lawyer; b. Elgin, Ill., May 24, 1921; s. Ray Covey and Rosina Madeline (Schram) (White) S.; m. Marie Theresa Dunn, Dec. 11, 1943; children: Marie Kathleen "Kamie", Ray James, Jr., Pamela Suzanne, John Philip, Rose Lynn. B.S.C., U. Notre Dame, 1943; J.D., Northwestern U., 1948. Bar: Ill. 1949, U.S. Supreme Ct. 1954, D.C. 1973, U.S. Ct. Mil. Appeals 1954. Assoc. Seyfarth, Shaw Fairweather & Geraldson, Chgo., 1949-57; ptnr. Seyfarth, Shaw Fairweather & Geraldson now Seyfarth Shaw, 1957-92; ret. Chief rulings and ops. br. Wage Stabilization Bd. Region VII, Chgo., 1951-52 Book rev. editor: Ill. Law Rev., 1948. Served to lt.comdr. USNR, 1942-62. Mem. ABA, Ill. State Bar Assn., Chgo. Bar Assn., D.C. Bar Assn., Chgo. Athletic Assn., Univ. Club. Chgo., Fed. Bar Assn., Order of Coif. Republican. Roman Catholic. Home: 1182 Lynette Dr Lake Forest IL 60045-4601 Office: Seyfarth Shaw 55 E Monroe St Ste 4200 Chicago IL 60603-5863

SCHORNACK, JOHN JAMES, accountant; b. Chgo., Nov. 22, 1930; s. John Joseph and Helen Patricia (Patrickus) S.; m. Barbara Anne Lelli, June 5, 1965; children: Mark Boyd, Anne Marguerite Schornack Trueman, Erin Keeley Schornack Dickes, Tracy Bevan Schornack Power. BS, Loyola U., 1951; MBA, Northwestern U., 1956; grad., Advanced Mgmt. Program, Harvard Bus. Sch., 1969. With Ernst & Young (formerly Arthur Young & Co.), 1955-91, partner, 1964-91; firm dir. personnel Ernst & Young LLP (formerly Arthur Young & Co.), N.Y.C., 1966-71, asst. mng. ptnr. N.Y.C. office, 1971-72, mng. ptnr., 1972-74, mng. ptnr. Chgo. office, 1976-85, mng. ptnr. Midwest region, vice chmn., 1985-91; mem. mgmt. com. Arthur Young & Co. Mgmt. com. Arthur Young & Co.; vice chmn., mng. ptnr. Midwest region Ernst & Young, 1989-91; bd. dirs., chmn. Ernst & Young Found., 1981-91; chmn., bd. dirs. North Shore Bancorp, Inc., 1992-, Wintrust Fin. Corp., 1996-. Pres. Chgo. Youth Ctrs., 1979-95; bd. govs. Chgo. Symphony, 1979-85, trustee, 1985—, life trustee; vol. United Way, 1975-92, dir., 1989-92; vis. adv. com. sch. accountancy DePaul U., 1980-83; mem. Loyola U. Citizens Bd., 1977-94, chmn., 1993-94; mem. adv. com. Northwestern U. Grad. Sch. Mgmt., 1967-91; coun. U. Chgo. Grad. Sch. Bus., 1982-91; bd. dirs. Met. Planning Coun., 1992-95; trustee Kohl Children's Mus., 1994—, Lyric Opera, 1984-92, Cath. Theol. Union, 1992-97, Graham Found., 1992-98; trustee Barat Coll., 1983-98, life trustee, 1999-2001, vice chmn., 1985-90, chmn., 1990-97; trustee St. Francis Hosp., 1986-97, vice chmn., 1991-94; trustee Night Ministry, 1998—. Mem. AICPA, Am. Acctg. Assn., Ill. Soc. CPA's, Midwest-Japan Assn. (chmn. 1983-99), Japan Am. Soc., 410 Club, Tavern Club, Chgo. Club, Glen View Club, Ocean Club, The Little Club. Home: 314 Regent Wood Rd Northfield IL 60093-2762 Office: Ernst & Young LLP Great Lakes Reg Office 233 S Wacker Dr Chicago IL 60606-6306 E-mail: northdel@aol.com.

SCHORR, ROGER J. business executive; Gen. mgr. Convergys Corp., Cin., 1993—. Office: Convergys Corp 4600 Montgomery Rd Cincinnati OH 45212-2697

SCHOTT, MARGE, former professional baseball team executive; b. 1928; d. Edward and Charlotte Unnewehr; m. Charles J. Schott, 1952 (dec. 1968). Owner Schottco, Cin.; ltd. ptnr. Cin. Reds, 1981-84, gen. ptnr., 1984—, owner, pres., 1985—, chief exec. officer. Office: Cin Reds 100 Cinergy Field Cincinnati OH 45202-3543

SCHOTTENFELD, DAVID, epidemiologist, educator; b. N.Y.C., Mar. 25, 1931; m. Rosalie C. Schaeffer; children: Jacqueline, Stephen. AB, Hamilton Coll., 1952; MD, Cornell U., 1956; MS in Pub. Health, Harvard U., 1963. Diplomate Am. Bd. Internal Medicine, Am. Bd. Preventive Medicine. Intern in internal medicine Duke U., Durham, N.C., 1956-57; resident in internal medicine Meml. Sloan-Kettering Cancer Ctr., Cornell U. Med. Coll., N.Y.C., 1957-59; Craver fellow med. oncology Meml. Sloan-Kettering Cancer Ctr., 1961-62; clin. instr. dept. pub. health Cornell U., N.Y.C., 1963-67, asst. prof. dept. pub. health, 1965-70, assoc. prof. dept. pub. health, 1970-73, prof. dept. pub. health, 1973-86; John G. Searle prof., chmn. epidemiology sch. pub. health U. Mich., Ann Arbor, 1986—, prof. internal medicine, 1986—. Vis. prof. epidemiology U. Minn., Mpls., 1968, 71, 74, 82, 86; W.G. Cosbie lectr. Can. Oncology Soc., 1987. Editor: Cancer Epidemiology and Prevention, 1982, 2d edit., 1996; author 9 books; contbr. more than 200 articles to profl. jours. Served with USPHS, 1959-61. Recipient Acad. Career award in Preventive Oncology, Nat. Cancer Inst., 1980-85. Fellow AAAS, ACP, Am. Coll. Preventive Medicine, Am. Coll. Epidemiology, Armed Forces Epidemiology Bd.; mem. soc. Epidemiologic Rsch. (pres. 1998—), Phi Beta Kappa. Office: U of Mich Sch Pub Health Dept Epidemiology 109 Observatory St Ann Arbor MI 48109-2029 E-mail: daschott@umich.edu.

SCHOTTENSTEIN, IRVING E. construction company executive; b. 1920; Apt. bldg. developer, 1966-73; pres., CEO M/I Schottenstein Homes Inc., Columbus, Ohio, 1973—; chmn. bd. dirs. M/I Real Estate Co., Inc.; ptnr. Brothers Realty Co. Address: MI Schottenstein Homes 3 Easton Oval Ste 500 Columbus OH 43219-6011

SCHOTTENSTEIN, JAY L. retail executive; b. 1954; Grad., Ind. U. With Schottenstein Stores, Columbus, Ohio, vice chmn., exec. v.p., CEO, 1992—; chmn., CEO Value City Department Stores, American Eagle Outfitters, Warrendale, Pa. Office: Schottenstein Stores 1800 Moler Rd Columbus OH 43207-1680 Address: Value City Department Stores Inc 3241 Westerville Rd Columbus OH 43224 also: American Eagle Outfitters 150 Thorn Hill Dr Warrendale PA 15086-7528

SCHOTTENSTEIN, ROBERT H. construction executive; Pres., vice chair M/I Schottenstein Homes, Columbus, Ohio, 1997—. Office: M/I Schottenstein Homes 3 Eastern Columbus OH 43219

SCHOTTENSTEIN, STEVEN, real estate development executive; COO, vice chair M/I Schottenstein Homes, Columbus, Ohio, 1990—. Office: M/I Schottenstein Homes 3 East St Ste 500 Columbus OH 43228-1107

SCHOUMACHER, BRUCE HERBERT, lawyer; b. Chgo., May 23, 1940; s. Herbert Edward and Mildred Helen (Wagner) S.; m. Alicia Wesley Sanchez, Nov. 4, 1967; children: Liana Cristina, Janina Maria. BS, Northwestern U., 1961; MBA, U. Chgo., 1963, JD, 1966. Bar: Nebr. 1966, U.S. Dist. Ct. Nebr. 1966, Ill. 1971, U.S. Dist. Ct. (no. dist.) Ill. 1971, U.S. Ct. Appeals (7th cir.) 1979, U.S. Supreme Ct. 1982, U.S. Ct. Fed. Claims 1986. Assoc. Luebs, Tracy & Huebner, Grand Island, Nebr., 1966-67, McDermott, Will & Emery, Chgo., 1971-76, ptnr., 1976-89, Querrey & Harrow, Ltd., Chgo., 1989—. Instr. bus. adminstrn. Bellevue Coll., Nebr., 1967-70; lectr. U. Md., Overseas Program, 1970. Author: Engineers and the Law: An Overview, 1986; contbg. author: Construction Law, 1986, Construction Law Handbook, 1999; co-author: Successful Business Plans for Architects, 1992; contbr. articles to profl. jours. Served to capt. USAF, 1967-71, Vietnam. Decorated Bronze Star, 1971. Fellow Am. Coll. Constrn. Lawyers; mem. ABA, AIA (profl. affiliate), Nebr. Bar Assn., Ill. State Bar Assn. (ad hoc com. large law firms 1992-98, chmn. membership and bar activities com. 1988-89, coun. ins. law sect. 1986-91, mem. spl. com. on computerized legal rsch. 1986-87), Chgo. Bar Assn. (chmn. fed. civil procedure com. 1982-83), Def. Rsch. Inst., Ill. Assn. Def. Trial Counsel, Chgo. Bldg. Congress (bd. dirs. 1985—, sec. 1987-89, 95—, v.p. 1989-91), Western Soc. Engrs. (assoc.), The Lawyers Club of Chgo., Tower Club (Chgo.), Univ. Club Chgo., Pi Kappa Alpha, Phi Delta Phi. Republican. Methodist. Office: Querrey & Harrow Ltd 175 W Jackson Blvd Ste 1600 Chicago IL 60604-2827

SCHOWALTER, WILLIAM RAYMOND, college dean, educator; b. Milw., Dec. 15, 1929; s. Raymond Philip and Martha (Kowalke) S.; m. Jane Ruth Gregg, Aug. 22, 1953; children: Katherine Ruth, Mary Patricia, David Gregg. BS, U. Wis., 1951; postgrad., Inst. Paper Chemistry, 1951-52; MS, U. Ill., 1953, PhD, 1957; PhD (hon.), Inst. Nat. Poly. Lorraine, France, 1996. Asst. prof. dept. chem. engring. Princeton U., 1957-63, assoc. prof., 1963-66, prof., 1966-86, Class of 1950 prof. engring. and applied sci., 1986-89, acting chmn. dept. chem. engring., 1971, chmn. dept. chem. engring., 1978-87, assoc. dean Sch. Engring. and Applied Sci., 1971-77, class of 1950 prof. engring. and applied sci. emeritus, 2000—; dean Coll. Engring. U. Ill., Urbana, 1989-2001, dean, prof. emeritus, 2001—; Mobil prof. chem. engring. Nat. U. Singapore, 1998, sr. advisor to vice-chancellor, 2001—. Sherman Fairchild disting. scholar Calif. Inst. Tech., 1977-78; vis. fellow U. Cambridge, Eng., 1974; vis. sr. fellow Sci. Rsch. Coun., U. Cambridge, Eng., 1970; cons. to chem. and petroleum cos.; editl. adv. bd. McGraw-Hill Pub. Co., 1964-92; co-chmn. Internat. Seminar for Heat and Mass Transfer, 1970; vis. com. for chem. engring. MIT, 1979-87, Lehigh U., 1980-87; mem. vis. com. Sch. Engring., Stanford U., 1990-2001; evaluation panelist Ctr. Chem. Engring. Nat. Bur. Standards, 1982-88, chmn., 1986-88; mem. commn. engring. and tech. sys. NRC, 1983-88; engring. rsch. bd., 1984-86, com. on chem. engring. frontiers; adv. coun. chem. engring. Cornell U., 1983-91; adv. coun. Sch. Engring., Rice U., 1986-92; adv. com. Ill. Inst. Tech., 1992-97; adv. coun. Coll. Engring., U. Calif., Berkeley, 1997-2001, Coll. Engring. U. Mich., 1997-2001, Carnegie Inst. Tech., 1999-2001; acad. adv. bd. Sematech Corp., 1992-2001; internat. adv. panel Nat. U. Singapore, 1996; Reilly lectr. in chem. engring. U. Notre Dame, 1985, Van Winkle lectr. in chem. engring. U. Tex., Austin, 1986, David M. Mason lectr. chem. engring. Stanford U., 1987; bd. dirs. Champaign (Ill.) Nat. Bank, 1991-95, BankIll. Trust Co., 1996-98; mem. fellowship program Packard Found. Sci. Adv. Panel, 1998—; adv. coun. Sch. Engring., Princeton U., 1999—. Author: Mechanics of Non-Newtonian Fluids, 1978; co-author: Colloidal Dispersions, 1989; mem. editl. com. Ann. Rev. Fluid Mechanics, 1974-80, Internat. Jour. Chem. Engring., 1974-94, Indsl. and Engring. Chemistry Fundamentals, 1975-78, Jour. Non-Newtonian Fluid Mechanics, 1976-2001, AIChE Jour., 1979-83; contbr. articles to profl. jours. Mem. Ill. Gov.'s Sci. Adv. Com., 1989-96. Served with U.S. Army, 1953-55. Decorated officier des Palmes Académiques (France), 1995; recipient Disting. Svc. citation Coll. Engring., U. Wis., Madison, 1983; Guggenheim fellow, 1987-88. Fellow AIChE (William H. Walker award 1982, bd. dirs. 1992-94), NAS (class membership com. 2000, 2002), Am. Acad. Arts and Scis.; mem. Am. Soc. Engring. Edn. (Lectr. award chem. engring. divsn. 1971, exec. com. engr. deans coun. 1992-95, vice-chair, engring. deans coun. pub. policy com. 1998, chair engring. deans coun. pub. policy com. 1999-2001), NAE (awards com. 1986-88, chmn. 1987, acad. adv. bd. 1991-94, chmn. 1992-94, coun. 1994-2000, Draper Award com. 2001-2002), Am. Chem. Soc., Soc. Rheology (exec. com. 1977-79, v.p. 1981-83, pres. 1983-85, Bingham medal 1988), Sigma Xi, Tau Beta Pi, Phi Lambda Upsilon, Phi Eta Sigma. Home: 1846 Maynard Dr Champaign IL 61822-5268

SCHRADER, DAVID FLOYD, state legislator; b. Oct. 23, 1952; s. Hubert F. and Violet L. (Marshall) S.; m. Roberta J. Sterling, July 15, 1974; children: Todd, JoAnna, Heather, Melissa. Grad. high sch., Monroe, Iowa, 1970. Owner, operator automotive fabrication bus., Monroe, 1970-93; owner, operator amusement and vending bus., 1980-88; mem. Iowa Ho. of Reps., Des Moines, 1987-90, asst. majority leader, 1991-92, asst. minority leader, 1993—, minority leader. Named Legis. Conservationist of 1993, Iowa Wildlife Fedn. Mem. Internat. Motor Contest Assn., NASCAR, Kiwanis. Democrat. Methodist. Office: Iowa Ho of Reps State Capitol Des Moines IA 50319-0001

SCHRADER, KEITH WILLIAM, mathematician; b. Neligh, Nebr., Apr. 22, 1938; s. William Charles and Gail (Hughes) S.; m. Carol Jean Taylor, Dec. 26, 1960; children: Jeffrey, Melinda. B.S., U. Nebr., 1959, M.S., 1961, Ph.D., 1966; postgrad., Stanford U., 1961-63. Engr. Sylvania Co., Mountain View, Calif., 1962-63; asst. prof. dept. math U. Mo.-Columbia, 1966-69, assoc. prof., 1969-78, prof., 1978-79, chmn. dept. math. prof., 1979-82, 85-88, prof. dept. math., 1988—. Bd. dirs. Schrader Inst. Early Learning, Columbia, 1970-83; mem. Planning And Zoning Commn., 1980-90. NASA grantee, 1967-68; NSF grantee, 1969-70 Mem. Am. Math. Soc., Sigma Xi, Sigma Phi Epsilon Office: Dept Math U Mo Columbia MO 65211-0001 E-mail: keiths99k@netscape.net.

SCHRADER, THOMAS F. utilities executive; b. Indpls., 1950; Grad., Princeton U., 1972, 78. Pres., COO WICOR, Inc., Milw., 1997-2000; sr. v.p. strategic process integration Wis. Electric, 2000—. Office: Wis Electric 626 E Wisconsin Ave Milwaukee WI 53202-4608

SCHRAG, EDWARD A., JR. lawyer; b. Milw., Mar. 27, 1932; s. Edward A. and Mabel Lena (Baumbach) S.; m. Leslie Jean Israel, June 19, 1954; children: Amelia Marie Schrag Prack, Katherine Allison Schrag Roberts, Edward A. III (dec.). B.S. in Econs, U. Pa., 1954; J.D., Harvard, 1960. Bar: Ohio 1961. Assoc., then firm partner, now of counsel Vorys, Sater, Seymour and Pease, Columbus, 1960—. Sec. Ranco Inc., 1972-87; trustee Lake of Woods Water Co., 1972-91; mem. Ohio div. Securities Adv. Com. Mem. Downtown Area Com., 1970-74. Served to lt. (j.g.) USNR, 1954-57. Mem. ABA, Ohio Bar Assn. (chmn. corp. law com. 1986-88, chmn. securities regulation subcom., spl. com. bus. cts., bd. govs., corp. counsel sect., chmn. 1991-93), Columbus Bar Assn., Columbus Area C. of C., Navy League, Alpha Tau Omega, Beta Gamma Sigma, Phi Sigma Alpha, Pi Gamma Mu. Episcopalian. Clubs: Capital, Crichton, Ohio State U. Pres.'s. Home: 9400 White Oak Ln Westerville OH 43082-9606 Office: Vorys Sater Seymour & Pease PO Box 1008 52 E Gay St Columbus OH 43216-1008

SCHRECK, ROBERT, commodities trader; b. 1944; With Pillsbury Co., Mpls., 1968-93, v.p.; exec. v.p. Commodity Specialists Co., 1993—. Office: Commodity Specialists Co 301 4th Ave S Minneapolis MN 55415-1015

SCHRECK, ROBERT A., JR. lawyer; b. Buffalo; BS in Bus. Adminstrn., Georgetown U., 1974; MBA, Northwestern U., 1975, JD, 1978. Bar: Ill. 1978. Ptnr. McDermott, Will & Emery, Chgo., 1978—. Mem. ABA. Office: McDermott Will & Emery 227 W Monroe St Ste 3100 Chicago IL 60606-5096 E-mail: rschreck@mwe.com.

SCHREIBER, BERTRAM MANUEL, mathematics educator; b. Seattle, Nov. 4, 1940; s. Isador and Amy (Hurwitz) S.; m. Rita Ruth Stusser, June 30, 1963; children: Susannah M. Schreiber Bechhofer, Deborah H. Schreiber Shapiro, Abraham D., Elisabeth T. Schreiber Seigel. BA, Yeshiva U., 1962; MS, U. Wash., 1966, PhD, 1968. Asst. prof. Wayne State U., Detroit, 1968-71, assoc. prof., 1971-78, prof., 1978—, chair dept. math., 1987-90. Vis. prof. Hebrew U., Jerusalem, 1975, 2000, Mich. State U., East Lansing, 1982-83, Nat. U. Singapore, 1992, U. New South Wales, Australia, 1992, Indian Statis. Inst., 1993, Tata Inst. Fund Res., Bombay, 1993, Bar Ilan U., 1993, Tel Aviv U., 1993, U. Utrecht, The Netherlands, 1993, U. Wroclaw, Poland, 1993, U. Paris VII, 1999, U. Granada, Spain, 1999-2000, U. Wash., Seattle, 2000. Contbr. articles to profl. jours. NSF grantee, 1968-87; Sci. and Engring. Rsch. Coun. Gt. Britain fellow U. Edinburgh, Scotland, 1976. Mem. Am. Math. Soc., Math. Assn. Am., Israel Math. Union, Edinburgh Math. Soc. Achievements include research in the fields of harmonic analysis, topological groups, and probability theory. Office: Wayne State U Dept Math Detroit MI 48202

SCHREIBER, JAMES RALPH, obstetrician, researcher; b. Rosebud, Tex., May 29, 1946; s. Lester B. and Jane Elinore (Hodges) Schreiber; m. Mary Celia Schmitt, Aug. 16, 1968; children: Lisa, Joseph, Laura, Cynthia. BA, Rice U., 1968; MD, Johns Hopkins U., 1972. Diplomate Am. Coll. Ob-gyn., Am. Bd. Reproductive Endocrinology. Intern. ob-gyn. U. So. Calif. Los Angeles County Hosp., 1972-73, resident ob-gyn., 1973-74, 76-78; fellow reproductive endocrinology NIH, Bethesda, Md., 1974-76; asst. prof. ob-gyn U. Calif., San Diego, 1978-82; assoc. prof. U. Chgo., 1982-87, prof., 1988-91; prof., chmn. dept. Washington U., St. Louis, 1991—. Contbr. articles to profl. jours. Grantee, NIH, 1978—. Mem.: Soc. Gynecologic Investigation. Home: 22 Frontenac Estates Saint Louis MO 63131-2600 Office: Washington U Sch Medicine Dept Ob-Gyn 4911 Barnes Hospital Plz Saint Louis MO 63110-1003 E-mail: schreiberj@msnotes.wustl.edu.

SCHREIBER, LOLA F. former state legislator; m. Marion Schreiber; 2 children. Student, S.D. State U. Mem. S. D. Ho. Reps., to 1997, vice-chmn. edn. com., mem. state affairs com. Chmn. edn. com., mem. judiciary com., mem. tax com., chmn. legislators exec. bd., 1995, 96, chmn. edn. com. Nat. Conf. State Legislators; commr. Edn. Commn. States; mem. policy and priorities com.; mem. adv. bd. Policymakers Inst., Danforth Found.; mem. Fin. Project. Home: 30045 173rd St Gettysburg SD 57442-5301

SCHREIBER, MARVIN MANDEL, agronomist, educator; b. Springfield, Mass., Oct. 17, 1925; s. William and Florence Schreiber; m. Phyllis E. Altman, Dec. 18, 1949; 1 child, Michelle. BS, U. Mass., 1950; MS, U. Ariz., 1951; PhD, Cornell U., 1954. Asst. prof. dept. agronomy Cornell U., Ithaca, N.Y., 1954-59; assoc. prof. dept. botany and plant pathology Purdue U., West Lafayette, Ind., 1959-73—, prof., 1973—; rsch. agronomist Agrl. Rsch. Svc. USDA, 1959—. Fellow AAAS, Am. Soc. Agronomy, Weed Sci. Soc. Am.; mem. Internat. Weed Sci. Soc. (pres. 1979-81), Controlled Release Soc., Coun. Agrl. Sci. and Tech., Sigma Xi. Avocations: golf, gardening. Office: Dept Botany & Plant Pathology Purdue U Lilly Hall Life Scis West Lafayette IN 47907

SCHREIER, KAREN ELIZABETH, judge; U.S. atty. U.S. Dept. Justice, Sioux Falls, S.D., 1993-99; judge U.S. Dist. Ct., Rapid City, SD, 1999—. Office: US Dist Ct 515 9th St Rapid City SD 57701-2626

SCHREINER, ALBERT WILLIAM, physician, educator; b. Cin., Feb. 15, 1926; s. Albert William and Ruth Mary (Neuer) S.; m. Jean Tellstrom, Dec. 12, 1953; 1 child, David William. BS, U. Cin., 1947, MD, 1949. Diplomate Am. Bd. Internal Medicine. Clin. investigator VA Hosp., Cin., 1957-59, chief med. service, 1959-68, dir. dept. internal medicine, 1968-93; dir. resident program internal medicine Christ Hosp., 1978-87; mem. faculty U. Cin. Coll. Medicine, 1955—, assoc. prof. medicine, 1962-67, prof. internal medicine, 1967-98, emeritus prof. internal medicine, 1998—; attending physician Cin. Gen. Hosp., 1957—. Cons. to med. dir. Gen. Electric, 1987-96; med. dirs. United Home Care Hospice, 1993-99, United Home Care Agy. Contbr. articles to profl. jours. Bd. dirs., chmn. health com. Cmty. Action Commn., 1968-71; trustee Drake Meml. Hosp., 1975-78, Leukemia Found. Southwest Ohio, Cancer Control, Am. Cancer Soc., bd. dirs. Hamilton County unit, 1990; bd. dirs., chair profl. affairs com. United Home Care Agy., 1998; bd. dirs. Gamble Inst. Med. Rsch., Cin., 1991-96. Fellow: ACP; mem.: Am. Soc. Clin. Rsch. Program Dirs. Internal Medicine, Assn. Program Dirs. Internal Medicine, Clin. Soc. Internal Medicine (pres. 1979—80), Ohio Soc. Internal Medicine (trustee 1978, sec.-treas. 1981—85, v.p. 1982—83, pres. 1984—85), Ohio Med. Assn., Am. Fedn. Clin. Rsch., N.Y. Acad. Scis., Am. Cancer Soc. (bd. dirs. Hamilton County unit 1990—92), Am. Leukemia Soc. (med. adv. exec. bd.), Phi Beta Kappa, Sigma Xi. Roman Catholic. Home: 8040 S Clippinger Dr Cincinnati OH 45243-3248 Office: 2139 Auburn Ave Cincinnati OH 45219-2906

SCHREINER, JOHN CHRISTIAN, economics consultant, software publisher; b. Los Angeles, Nov. 2, 1933; s. Alexander and Margaret S.; m. Marie Nielsen, June 19, 1967; children: Christian Alexander, Carl Arthur, Elizabeth, Nathan Alexander. B.S.M.E., U. Utah, 1958; M.B.A., Harvard U., 1960; Ph.D., UCLA, 1970. Chartered fin. analyst. Design engr. Eimco Corp., Salt Lake City and N.Y.C., 1957-59; credit exec. James Talcott, Inc., N.Y.C. and Boston, 1960-65; lectr. mgmt. U. Utah, 1965-66; mem. faculty Grad. Sch. Mgmt., U. Minn., Mpls., 1969-84, chmn. dept. fin. and ins., 1973-74, 76-81; pres. The Sebastian Group, Inc., 1984—. Dir. Deluxe Corp.; cons. to corps. and govt. agys. Co-author: Executive Recruiting: How Companies Obtain Management Talent, 1960; contbr. articles to profl. jours. Mem. Fin. Execs. Inst., Fin. Analysts Fedn., Tau Beta Pi, Phi Kappa Phi. Republican. Mem. Ch. Jesus Christ of Latter-day Saints (missionary, Ger. 1953-56). Club: Harvard Bus. Sch. Minn. Office: The Sebastian Group Inc 5730 Duluth St Minneapolis MN 55422-4000

SCHRIER, ARNOLD, historian, educator; b. N.Y.C., May 30, 1925; s. Samuel and Yetta (Levine) S.; m. Sondra Weinshelbaum, June 12, 1949; children— Susan Lynn, Jay Alan, Linda Lee, Paula Kay. Student, Bethany Coll., W.Va., 1943-44, Ohio Wesleyan U., 1944-45; B.S., Northwestern U., 1949, M.A., 1950, Ph.D. (Social Sci. Research Council fellow, Univ. fellow), 1956. Asst. prof. history U. Cin., 1956-61, assoc. prof., 1961-66, prof., 1966-95, dir. grad. studies history, 1969-78, Walter C. Langsam prof. modern European history, 1972-95; Walter C. Langsam prof. history emeritus, 1995—. Vis. asst. prof. history Northwestern U., Evanston, Ill., 1960; vis. assoc. prof. history Ind. U., Bloomington, 1965-66; vis. lectr. Russian history Duke U., 1966; disting. vis. prof. U.S. Air Force Acad., 1983-84; dir. NDEA Inst. World History for Secondary Sch. Tchrs., U. Cin., 1965; Am. del. Joint U.S.-USSR Textbook Study Commn., 1989. Author: Ireland and the American Emigration, 1958, reissued, 1970, paperback edit., 1997, The Development of Civilization, 1961-62, Modern European Civilization, 1963, Living World History, 1964, rev., 1993, Twentieth Century World, 1974, History and Life: the World and Its People, 1977, rev., 1993, A Russian Looks at America, 1979. Pres. Ohio Acad. History, 1973-74, Midwest Slavic Conf., 1980. Served with USNR, 1943-46, 52-54. Recipient Disting. Svc. award Ohio Acad. History, 1992; Am. Council Learned Socs. fgn. area fellow, 1963-64 Mem. World History Assn. (v.p. 1986-88, pres. 1988-90). Home: 10 Diplomat Dr Cincinnati OH 45215-2073 Office: Univ Cincinnati Dept History Mail Location 373 Cincinnati OH 45221-0001 E-mail: arnsond@aol.com.

SCHRIESHEIM, ALAN, research administrator; b. N.Y.C., Mar. 8, 1930; s. Morton and Frances (Greenberg) Schriesheim; m. Beatrice D. Brand, June 28, 1953; children: Laura Lynn, Robert Alan. BS in Chemistry, Poly. Inst. Bklyn., 1951; PhD in Phys. Organic Chemistry, Pa. State U., 1954; DSc (hon.) , No. Ill. U., 1991; PhD (hon.) , Ill. Inst. Tech., Chgo., 1992; Laureate, Lincoln Acad., 1996. Chemist Nat. Bur. Standards, 1954—56; with Exxon Rsch. & Engring. Co., 1956—83, dir. corp. rsch., 1975—79; gen. mgr. Exxon Engring., 1979—83; sr. dep. lab. dir., COO Argonne Nat. Lab., 1983—84, lab. dir., CEO, 1984—96, dir. emeritus, 1996—; prof. chemistry dept. U. Chgo., 1984—96, lectr. Bus. Sch., 1996—; prin. Washington Adv. Group, 1996—. Karcher lectr. U. Okla., 1977; Hurd lectr. Northwestern U., 1980; Rosensteil lectr. Brandeis U., 1982; Welsh Found. lectr., 87; com. svc. NRC, 1980—; vis. com. chemistry dept. MIT, 1977—82; mem. vis. com. mech. engring. and aerospace dept. Princeton (N.J.) U., 1983—87, mem. vis. com. chemistry dept., 1983—87; mem. Pure and Applied Chemistry Com.; del. to People's Republic of China, 1978; mem. Presdl. Nat. Commn. on Superconductivity, 1989—91, U.S.-USSR Joint Commn. on Basic Sci. Rsch., 1990—93; mem. U.S. nat. com. Internat. Union Pure and Applied Chemistry, 1982—85; mem. magnetic fusion adv. com. Divsn. Phys. Scis. U. Chgo. Magnetic Fusion adv. com. to U.S. DOE, 1983—86; mem. Dept. Energy Rsch. Adv. Bd., 1983—85, Congl. Adv. Com. on Sci. and Tech., 1985—96; mem. vis. com. Stanford (Calif.) U., U. Utah, Tex. A&M U., Lehigh U.; bd. govs. Argonne Nat. Lab., 1984—96; mem. adv. com. on space sys. and tech. NASA, 1987—93; mem. nuc. engring. and engring. physics vis. com. U. Wis., Madison; mem. Coun. Gt. Lakes Govs. Regional Econ. Devel. Commn., 1987—, rev. bd. Compact Ignition Tomamak Princeton U., 1988—91; advisor Sears Investment Mgmt. Co., 1988—89; bd. dirs. Petroleum Rsch. Fund, ARCH Devel. Corp., HEICO, Rohm and Haas Co., Smart Signal Corp.; adv. bd. Batterson Venture Ptnrs., Influx, UHV Aluminum, Valley Indsl. Assn., Coun. on Superconductivity for Am. Competitiveness; mem. State of Ill. Commn. on the Future of Pub. Svc., 1990—92; co-chair Indsl. Rsch. Inst. Nat. Labs./Industry Panel, 1984—87; mem. Nat. Acad. Engring. Adv. Commn. on Tech. and Soc., 1991—92, Sun Electric Corp. Bd., 1991—92, U.S. House of Reps. subcom. on Sci.-Adv. Group on Renewing U.S. Sci. Policy, 1992—96, Chgo. Acad. Scis. acad. coun., 1994—; mem. adv. bd. Chemtech; mem. sr. action group on R&D investment strategies Ctr. for strategic and Internat. Studies, 1995; bd. vis. Astronomy and Astrophysics Pa. State U., 1995—. Adv. bd.: Chemtech, 1970—85, editl. bd.: Rsch. & Devel., 1988—92, editl. bd.: Superconductor Industry, 1988—95; patentee in field. Mem. spl. vis. com. Field Mus. of Natural History, Chgo., 1987—88; trustee The Latin Sch. of Chgo., 1990—92; adv. bd. WBEZ Chicagoland Pub. Radio Cmty., 1990—96; mem. Conservation Found. DuPage County, 1983—96, Econ. Devel. Adv. Commn. of DuPage County, 1984—88, Ill. Gov.'s Commn. on Sci. and Tech., 1986—90, Inst. for Ill. Coun. Advisors, 1988—, Ill. Coalition Bd. Dirs., 1989—, Inst. for Ill. Adv. Rev. Panel, 1986—88, NASA Sci. Tech. Adv. Com. Manpower Requirements Ad Hoc Rev. Team, 1988—91, Ill. Sci. and Tech. Adv. Com., 1989—, chmn., 1997; mem. U. Ill. Engring. Vis. com., Urbana-Champaign, 1986—95; trustee Tchrs. Acad. for Math. and Sci. Tchrs. in Chgo., 1990—96; bd. visitors astronomy and astrophysics Pa. State U., 1995—; bd. dirs. LaRabida Children's Hosp. and Rsch. Ctr., 1987—95, Children's Meml. Hosp., Children's Meml. Inst. for Edn. and Rsch. Recipient Outstanding Alumni Fellow award, Pa. State U., 1985, laureate, Lincoln Acad. Ill., 1996, Disting. fellow, Poly. U., 1989. Fellow: AAAS (coun. del. chem. sect. 1986—92, sci. engring. and pub. policy com. 1992, standing com. audit 1992, bd. dirs. 1992—96, selection com. to bring FSU scientists to ann. mtg. 1995—), N.Y. Acad. Scis.; mem.: AIChE (award com. 1992—), NAE (adv. com. tech. and soc. 1991—92, mem. program adv. com. 1992—94, chair study fgn. participation in U.S. R&D 1993—96, NRC com. on dual use tech. 1996—97, com. to assess policies and practices of Dept. of Energy to design, ma 1998—99), Ctr. Strategic and Internat. Studies (sr. action group 1995—96), Indsl. Rsch. Inst. (fed. adv. com. to Fed. Sci. and Tech. Com. 1992—96, co-chmn. Nat. Labs. Indsl. Panel 1984—87, sr. action group on R&D Investment Strategies), Am. Nuc. Soc., Am. Petroleum Inst. (rsch. coord. coun.), Nat. Conf. Advancement Rsch. (conf. com. 1985—, site selection com. 1994, conf. com. 50th ann. 1996), Am. Mgmt. Assn. (R&D coun. 1988—), Am. Chem. Soc. (joint bd. coun. on sci. 1983—87, chmn. petroleum divsn. 1983—91, councilor, com. on chemistry and pub. affairs 1983—91, petroleum chemistry award 1969, 1995—96), Econ. Club, Comml. Club, Cosmos Club, Carleton Club (bd. govs. 1992—), Phi Lambda Upsilon, Sigma Xi. Home: 1440 N Lake Shore Dr Apt 31ac Chicago IL 60610-5927 Office: Argonne Nat Lab 9700 S Cass Ave Argonne IL 60439-4803

SCHRIVER, JOHN T., III, lawyer; b. Evanston, Ill., May 18, 1945; AB, Coll. of Holy Cross, 1967; JD, Georgetown U., 1971. Bar: Ill. 1971, Fla. 1972. Ptnr. McDermott, Will & Emery, Chgo. Mem. ABA, Chgo. Bar Assn., Fla. Bar. Office: McDermott Will & Emery 227 W Monroe St Ste 3100 Chicago IL 60606-5096

SCHROCK, EDWARD J. state legislator; b. Holdrege, Nebr., Aug. 20, 1943; m. Judith M. Grove, 1965; children: Ted, Tom. BA, Nebr. Wesleyan U., 1965. Farmer, Phelps County, Nebr.; mem. Nebraska Legislature, Lincoln, 1991, 92, 95—. Mem. Phelps County Sch. Bd. Dist. R-4. Mem. Holdrege Area C. of C., Natural Resources Commn., Nebr. Corn Growers Assn., Nebr. Corn Developers (utilization and mkt. coms. bds.), Ctrl. Irrigators Assn., Nebr. Cattlemens Assn.

SCHROCK, HAROLD ARTHUR, manufacturing company executive; b. Goshen, Ind., Apr. 10, 1915; s. Arthur E. and Anna (Shaner) S.; m. Thelma A. Hostetler, Sept. 3, 1938; children— Sara (Mrs. William Barrett), Susan (Mrs. John Graff), Cinda (Mrs. Stephen McKinney), Douglas. B.A, Goshen Coll., 1937. Chmn. bd. dirs. Starcraft Co., Goshen, 1967-71. Pres. Goshen Sash & Door Co., Smoker-Craft, Inc., New Paris, Earthway Products, Bristol, Inc., Goshen Iron & Metal Co.; chmn. 1st Nat. Bank of Goshen; v.p. Ind. Capital Co., Ft. Wayne; pres. Ivy Terrace, Inc., Goshen, Marque, Inc., Goshen. Past pres. Greater Goshen Assn., Jr. Achievement, Goshen Gen. Hosp., Goshen Pub. Library; pres. Goshen Hosp. Found. Mem. Goshen C. of C. (pres. 1952) Republican. Lutheran (v.p. vestry). Clubs: Elcona Country (Goshen), Maplecrest Country (Goshen); Vineyards Country, Naples, Fla.; Rotary (past pres.). Home: 506 N Front St Syracuse IN 46567-1257 Office: US 33 E Goshen IN 46526 Also: Goshen Sash & Door Co Inc 603 E Purl St Goshen IN 46526-4044

SCHROEDER, CHARLES EDGAR, investment management executive; b. Chgo., Nov. 17, 1935; s. William Edward and Lelia Lorraine (Anderson) S.; m. Martha Elizabeth Runnette, Dec. 30, 1958; children: Charles Edgar, Timothy Creighton, Elizabeth Linton. BA in Econs., Dartmouth Coll., 1957; MBA, Amos Tuck Sch., 1958. Treas. Miami Corp., Chgo., 1969-78, pres., 1978-2001, pres. emeritus, 2001—; chmn., bd. dirs Blvd. Bank of Chgo., 1981-91; chmn. Blvd. Bancorp., Inc., 1991-94. Bd. dirs. Nat.-Standard Co., Niles, Mich. Trustee Northwestern Meml. Hosp., 1985-2000, Northwestern U., 1989—. Lt. (j.g.) USN, 1958-60. Mem. Chgo. Club, Glen View Club, Comml. Club. Office: Miami Corp 410 N Michigan Ave Ste 590 Chicago IL 60611-4252

SCHROEDER, DAVID HAROLD, healthcare facility executive; b. Chgo., Oct. 22, 1940; s. Harry T. and Clara D. (Dexter) Schroeder; m. Clara Doorn, Dec. 27, 1964; children: Gregory D., Elizabeth M. BBA, Kans. State Coll., 1965; MBA, Wichita State U., 1968; postgrad., U. Ill., 1968-69. CPA Ill. Supt. cost acctg. Boeing Co., Wichita, Kans., 1965-68; sr. v.p., treas. Riverside Med. Ctr., Kankakee, Ill., 1971—; v.p., bd. dirs. Service Med., Inc., 1999—. Treas. Riverside Health Sys., 1982—, Kankakee Valley Health Inc., 1985—, Health Info. Sys. Coop., 1991—; v.p., treas. Oakside Corp., Kankakee, 1982—; bd. dirs. Harmony Home Health Svc., Inc., Naperville, Ill.; treas. Oak Surg. Inst., 2001—; mem. faculty various profl. orgns.; preceptor Gov.'s State U., University Park, Ill., 1987—, adj. prof. econs. divsn. health adminstrn., 1990—95; trustee Riverside Found. Trust, 1989—, RMC Found., 1989—, Sr. Living Ctr., 1989—, Alzehimer's Assn., 1997; pres. Kankakee County Mental Health Ctr., 1982—84. Contbg. author: book Cost Containment in Hospitals, 1980; contbr. articles to profl. jours. Active Make A Wish Found., 1994—; founder Kankakee Trinity Acad., 1980, Riverview Hist. Dist., 1982; dir. Kankakee County Hist. Soc., 1995, pres., 2001; mem. adv. bd. Students in Free Enterprise, Olivet Nazarene U., Kankakee, 1989—; pres. United Way Kankadee County, 1984—85; trustee, treas. Am. Luth. Ch.; pres. Riverside Employees Credit Union, 1976—79; chmn. Ill. Provider Trust, Naperville, 1983—85; dir. IPT Physician's Ins. Co. Ltd., 2001—; chmn. Ill. Provider Trust, Naperville, 2002—. Capt. U.S. Army, 1969—71. Fellow: Fin. Analysts Fedn. (bd. cert. in healthcare mgmt.), Healthcare Fin. Mgmt. Assn. (pres. 1975—76), Am. Coll. Healthcare Execs.; mem.: AICPA, Investment Analysts Soc. Chgo., Inc., Healthcare Fin. Mgmt. Assn. (William G. Follimer award 1977, Robert H. Reeves award 1981, Muncie Gold award 1987, Founders medal of honor 1990), Ill. CPA Soc., Fin. Exec. Inst., Nat. Assn. Accts., Inst. Chartered Fin. Analysts, Ill. Hosp. Assn. (chmn. coun. health fin. 1982—85), Packard Club, Classic Car Club Am., Masons, Kiwanis (pres.), Sigma Chi, Alpha Kappa Psi. Avocations: classical automobile restoration, architectural preservation, computers. Home: 901 S Chicago Ave Kankakee IL 60901-5236 Office: Riverside Med Ctr 350 N Wall St Kankakee IL 60901-2901 E-mail: David_Schroeder@rsh.net.

SCHROEDER, HORST WILHELM, food products executive; b. Schwerin, Germany, May 5, 1941; m. Gisela I. Kammin; 1 child, Bernd; stepchildren: Ralph, Isabel Lange. MBA, U. Gottingen, Hamburg, Fed. Republic Germany, 1965. Sr. auditor Price Waterhouse, Hamburg, 1966-70; fin. contr. Kellogg Co. of West Germany, Bremen, 1970-71, dir. fin., 1971-76, mng. dir., 1976-81; pres., chief exec. officer Kellogg Salada Can., Toronto, 1981-83; pres. Kellogg Internat., Battle Creek, Mich., 1983-86, Kellogg N.A., Battle Creek, 1986-88; exec. v.p. Kellogg Co., 1988, pres., chief oper. officer, 1988—. Mem. adv. bd. J.L. Kellog Grad. Sch.; Bd. of govs. St. Joseph Acad. of Food Mktg., Phila., 1986-88; mem. com. external affairs U. Ill., Chgo., 1987-88. Mem. Am. Health Found. (bd. dirs. 1987—), KC (pres. 1988—, bd. dirs. 1989—). Avocations: golf, tennis. Office: Am Italian Pasta Co 1000 Italian Way Excelsior Springs MO 64024

SCHROEDER, JOHN H. university chancellor; b. Twin Falls, Idaho, Sept. 13, 1943; s. Herman John and Azalia (Kimes) S.; m. Sandra Barrow; children: John Kimes, Andrew Barrow. BA, Lewis and Clark Coll., Portland, Oreg., 1965; MA, U. Va., 1967, PhD, 1971. Instr. history U. Wis., Milw., 1970-71, asst. prof., 1971-76, assoc. prof., 1976-86, prof., 1986—, Am. Coun. on Edn. fellow, 1982-83, assoc. dean, 1976-82, asst. to vice chancellor, 1982-85, acting vice chancellor, 1985-87, vice chancellor, 1987-90, chancellor, 1990-98, U. Wis. sys. prof., 1998—. Louis M. Sears Meml. lectr. Purdue U., 1978. Author: Mr. Polk's War: American Opposition and Dissent, 1973, The Commercial and Diplomatic Role of the American Navy 1829-1861, 1985, Matthew C. Perry: Antebellum Sailor and Diplomat, 2001. V.p. bd. dir. John Michael Kohlers Arts Ctr.; bd. dir. Wis. Hist. Soc. Recipient Edward and Rosa Uhrig award U. Wis.-Milw., 1974, Disting. Teaching award AMOCO/U. Wis.-Milw., 1975. Mem. Orgn. Am. Historians, Soc. for History of Early Republic, Soc. for History Am. Fgn. Rels., Rotary. Office: U Wis Dept History PO Box 413 2310 E Hartford Ave Milwaukee WI 53211-3165 E-mail: jhs@uwm.edu.

SCHROEDER, KENT A. lawyer; b. Genoa, Nebr., Apr. 7, 1943; m. Linda J. Sotherspoon, June 24, 1972; 1 child 3. BS, Iowa State U., 1965; JD, U. Nebr., 1968. Bar: Nebr. 68. Ptnr. Ross, Schroeder & Romatzke, Kearney, Nebr. Bd. dirs. Ctrl. C.C.; bd. regents U. Nebr., 1998—; trustee Good Samaritan Hosp., 1988—. Mem.: ABA, Nebr. Assn. Trial Attys. (bd. dirs.), Nebr. Bar Assn., Kearney C. of C., Kearney Cosmo. Club, Kearney Country Club, Phi Delta Phi, Phi Kappa Alpha. Mailing: 3003 Country Club Ln Kearney NE 68845-4047 Office: Ross Schroeder & Romatzke 220 W 5th St PO Box 1685 Kearney NE 68848-1685

SCHROEDER, STEPHEN ROBERT, psychology researcher; b. Leipsic, Ohio, Oct. 28, 1936; BA, Josephinum Coll., 1958; MA, U. Toledo, 1964; PhD, U. Pitts., 1967. Lic. psychologist, Ohio, N.C. Postdoctoral rsch. assoc. Learning Rsch. and Devel. Ctr., U. Pitts., 1967-68; clin. asst. prof. dept. psychology U. N.C., Chapel Hill, 1968-73, clin. assoc. prof. depts. psychology and psychiatry, 1973-77, rsch. assoc. prof. dept. psychology, 1977-87, rsch. sci. Biol. Scis. Rsch. Ctr., 1973-87, assoc. prof. dept. psychiatry, 1977-86, prof. dept. psychiatry, 1986-87; dir. psychology Murdoch Ctr., Butner, N.C., 1973-75, dir. rsch. and devel., 1975-77; prof. dept. psychology and psychiatry Ohio State U., Columbus, 1987-90, dir. The Nisonger Ctr., 1987-90; prof. dept. human devel. and family life U. Kans., Lawrence, 1990—, prof. dept. pharmacology and toxicology, 1990—, dir. Bur. Child Rsch., 1990—, dir. Schiefelbusch Inst. for Life Span Studies, 1990—. Mem. program com. Gatlinburg Conf. on Mental Retardation and Devel. Disabilities, 1977-92, program chmn., 1992—; mem. N.C. divsn. Mental Health and Mental Retardation Rsch. Grants Rev. Bd., 1977-86; mem. statewide lead screening com. N.C. Dept. Meternal and Child Health, 1979-86; founding chmn. Annie Sullivan Enterprises, Inc., 1982-89, active, 1989-92, chmn., 1992—; mem. rsch. grant rev. bd. Ont. Mental Health Found., 1984—; mem. internat. rsch. exch. subcom. for Rsch. in Ednl. Rehab. in U.S. and German Dem. Republic, 1984-90; gen. ad hoc mem. grant rev. bd. NIMH, 1984; mem. mental retardation study com. NICHD, 1989-90; rsch. cons. Am. Occupational Therapy Found., Inc.; cons. pediats. ward N.C. Meml. Hosp., 1977-86; cons. civil rights divsn. U.S. Dept. Justice, 1987—; cons. No. Va. Tng. Ctr., 1983-85, 91, Murdoch Ctr., Western Carolina Ctr., Caswell Ctr., 1977-89; bd. dirs. Corp. of Guardianship; active Ohio Devel. Disabilities Planning Coun., 1987-90, Kans. Planning Coun. on Devel. Disabilities Svcs., 1990—, Kans. Prevention Task Force, 1991—, Gov. Task Force on Respite Care, 1991—. Author, editor chpts. to books; editor Am. Jour. Mental Retardation, 1987—; co-editor Jour. Applied Rsch. in Mental Retardation, 1980-86, Rsch. in Devel. Disabilities, 1987—; mem. editl. bd. Jour. Applied Behaviour Analysis, 1973-74, Mental Retardation, 1977-93, Analysis and Intervention in Devel. Disabilities, 1981-82; guest reviewer Jour. Applied Behaviour Analysis, Pediat. Psychology, Am. Jour. Psychiatry, Jour. Autism and Childhood Scizophrenia, Child Devel., Sci., Perceptual and Motor Skills, Pediatrics, Neurotoxicology; contbr. articles, papers to profl. jours. Mem. adv. bd. Ohio United Cerebral Palsy, 1988-90; active Ohio Prevention Coalition, 1987-90. Recipient Karl Heinz Renker medallion for interdisciplinary sci. collaboration German Dem. Republic, 1989. Fellow APA (pres. divsn. 33 mental retardation 1986-87, Nicholas Hobbs award 1989); mem. AAAS, Am. Assn. Mental Retardation, Am. Acad. Mental Retardation, Assn. Advancement Behavior Therapy (task force on self-injurious behavior 1981-82), Assn. Behavior Analysis, N.Y. Acad. Scis., Sertoma Club. Office: U Kansas KS Ctr Rsch Mental Retardation 1052 Dole Human Devel Ctr Lawrence KS 66045-0001

SCHROER, EDMUND ARMIN, retired utility company executive; b. Hammond, Ind., Feb. 14, 1928; s. Edmund Henry and Florence Evelyn (Schmidt) S.; m. Lisa V. Strope; children: James, Fredrik, Amy, Lisa, Timothy, Suzanne. BA, Valparaiso U., 1949; JD, Northwestern U., 1952. Bar: Ind. 1952. Pvt. practice law, Hammond, 1952—; assoc. Crumpacker & Friedrich, 1952; ptnr. Crumpacker & Schroer, 1954-56; assoc., then ptnr. Lawyer, Friedrich, Petrie & Tweedle, 1957-62; ptnr. Lawyer, Schroer & Eichhorn, 1963-66; sr. ptnr. Schroer, Eichhorn & Morrow, Hammond, 1967-77; pres., CEO No. Ind. Pub. Svc. Co., Inc., 1977-93; chmn. No. Ind. Pub. Svc. Co., 1978-93, chmn., CEO, 1989-93, also bd. dirs.; chmn., pres., CEO NIPSCO Industries, Inc., 1987-93; cons. NIPSCO Industries Inc., Hammond, 1993-96; also bd. dirs.; ret. Asst. dist. atty., No. Ind., 1954-56; trustee Ill. Ins. Exch., 1993-95. Trustee Sch. Bd., Munster, Ind., 1969-71, pres., 1971; fin. chmn. Rep. Party, Hammond, 1958-62; del. Ind. Rep. Conv., 1958, 60, 64, 66, 68. Mem. Fed. Bar Assn., Am. Gas Assn. (chmn. 1986), Rotary (pres. Hammond club 1968). Lutheran. Home and Office: No Ind Pub Svc Co 5265 Hohman Ave Hammond IN 46320-1722

SCHROPP, TOBIN, lawyer; b. 1962; BS in Fgn. Svc., Georgetown U., 1984, JD, 1987, LLM in Taxation, 1991. Bar: 1987. V.p., gen. counsel Peter Kiewit Sons' Inc., Omaha. Office: Peter Kiewit Sons Inc 1000 Kiewit Plaza Omaha NE 68131

SCHUBERT, HELEN CELIA, public relations executive; b. Washington City, Wis. d. Paul H. and Edna (Schmidt) S. BS, U. Wis., Madison. Dir. pub. rels. United Cerebral Palsy, Chgo., 1961; adminstrv. dir. Nat. Design Ctr., 1962-67; owner Schubert Pub. Rels., 1967—. Bd. dirs. Fashion Group, Chgo., 1988-95. Mem. women's bd. Am. Cancer Soc., Chgo., 1988-96, Art Resources in Tchg., Chgo., 1988-92. Recipient Comm. award Am. Soc. Interior Designers, Chgo., 1979, 83, 88, 94; named to Chgo. Women's Hall of Fame City of Chgo., 1990. Fellow Nat. Home Fashion League; mem. Women's Ad Club Chgo. (pres. 1981-83, Woman of Yr. award 1987), Women in Comm. (pres. 1969-70, Matrix award Lifetime Achievement 1996), Am. Advt. Fedn. (lt. gov. 1983-85). Lutheran.

SCHUBERT, WILLIAM HENRY, curriculum studies educator; b. Garrett, Ind., July 6, 1944; s. Walter William and Mary Madeline (Grube) S.; children by previous marriage: Ellen Elaine, Karen Margaret; m. Ann Lynn Lopez, Dec. 3, 1977; children: Heidi Ann, Henry William. BS, Manchester Coll., 1966; MS, Ind. U., 1967; PhD, U. Ill., 1975. Tchr. Fairmount, El Sierra and Herrick Schs., Downers Grove, Ill., 1967-75; clin. instr. U. Wis., Madison, 1969-73; tchg. asst., univ. fellow U. Ill., Urbana, 1973-75, asst. prof. Chgo., 1975-80, assoc. prof., 1981-85, prof., 1985—, coord. secondary edn., 1979-82, coord. instrnl. leadership, 1979-85, dir. grad. studies Coll. Edn., 1983-85, coord. grad. curriculum studies, 1985—, coord. edn. studies, 1990-94, 96—, chair area curriculum and instrn., 1990-94. Vis. assoc. prof. U. Victoria (B.C., Can.), 1981; disting. vis. prof. U. S.C., 1986; presenter in field. Author: (with Ann Lopez) Curriculum Books: The First Eighty Years, 1980; Curriculum: Perspective, Paradigm and Possibility, 1986; (with Edmund C. Short and George Willis) Toward Excellence in Curriculum Inquiry, 1985, (with J. Dan Marshall and James T. Sears) Turning Points in Curriculum: A Contemporary American Memoir, 2000; editor: (with Ann Lopez) Conceptions of Curriculum Knowledge: Focus on Students and Teachers, 1982, (with George Willis) Reflections from the Heart of Educational Inquiry: Understanding Curriculum and Teaching Through the Arts, 1991, repub., 2001, (with William Ayers) Teacher Lore: Learning From Our Own Experience, 1992, repub., 1999, (with George Willis, R. Bullough, C. Kridel, J. Holton) The American Curriculum: A Documentary History, 1993; assoc. editor, editl. bd. Ednl. Theory; former mem. editl. bd. Ednl. Studies; former cons. editor Phenomenology and Pedagogy; adv. bd. Teaching Edn., Pi Lamda Theta Pubs., 1995—, Jour. Curriculum and Supervision; editl. bd. Curriculum and Teaching, emeritus editl. bd., Jour. Curriculum Theorizing, 1999—; editor: book series Student Lore, 1990—; cons. editor Jour. Curriculum Discourse and Dialogue; mem. adv. bd. Jour. Critical Issues in Curriculum and Instrn., 2000—; contbr. over 200 articles and chpts. to profl. pubs.; presenter in field. Mem. Internat. Acad. Edn. (elected 1997), Profs. of Curriculum (factotum 1984-85), Soc. for Study of Curriculum History (founding mem., sec.-treas. 1981-82, pres. 1982-83), Am. Ednl. Rsch. Assn. (chmn. creation and utilization of curriculum knowledge 1980-82, program chmn. curriculum studies divsn. 1982-83, sec. Divsn. B 1989-91, v.p. 2000-01), Am. Assn. Colls. for Tchr. Edn., John Dewey Soc. (bd. dirs. 1986-95, chair awards com. 1988-90, co-chair lectures commn. 1989-91, pres.-elect 1990-91, pres. 1992-93), ASCD (steering com. of curriculum com. 1980-83, publs. com. 1987-90, internat. polling panel 1990—), Am. Ednl. Studies Assn., World Coun. for Curriculum and Instrn., Soc. for Profs. of Edn. (exec. bd. 1997-88, pres.-elect 2000-01, pres. 2001—), Nat. Soc. for Study of Edn., Inst. Dem. in Edn., Masons, Scottish Rite, Phi Delta Kappa, Phi Kappa Phi (pres. U. Ill.-Chgo. chpt. 1981-82). Office: U Ill Coll Edn M/C 147 1040 W Harrison St Chicago IL 60607-7129 E-mail: schubert@uic.edu.

SCHUBERT, WILLIAM KUENNETH, hospital medical center executive; b. Cin., July 12, 1926; s. Wilfred Schubert and Amanda Kuenneth; m. Mary Jane Pamperin, June 5, 1948; children: Carol, Joanne, Barbara, Nancy. BS, U. Cin., 1949, MD, 1952; HHD (hon.), Coll. Mt. St. Joseph, Cin., 1997. Diplomate Am. Bd. Pediatrics. Pvt. practice specializing in pediatrics, Cin., 1956-63; dir. clin. research ctr. Children's Hosp. Med. Ctr., 1963-76; dir. div. gastroenterology Children's Hosp., 1968-79; prof. pediatrics U. Cin., 1969-96, prof. emeritus, 1997—, assoc. sr. v.p. for children's hosp. affairs Coll. Medicine, 1993-96; chief of staff Children's Hosp. Med. Ctr., Cin., 1972-88; chmn. dept. pediatrics U. Cin., 1979-93; dir. Children's Hosp. Rsch. Found., Cin., 1979-93; pres., CEO Children's Hosp. Med. Ctr., 1983-96, trustee, 1983—. V.p. Ohio Solid Organ Transplant Consortium, Columbus, 1986-87, pres., 1987-88, alt. trustee, 1988-96; trustee med. rsch. James N. Gamble Inst., Cin., 1989-95; bd. dirs. Choice Care Found., Health Found. of Greater Cin. Contbr. over 100 articles to profl. jours. Trustee Greater Cin. Hosp. Coun., 1986-96, Assn. of Ohio Children's Hosp., Columbus, 1986-96, Springer Sch., Cin., 1994—, Children's Convalescent Hosp., 1997—; chmn. Greater Cin. Hosp. Coun., 1989; co-chmn. Citizen's Com. for Med. Ctr., Cin., 1980-81; chmn. Hosp. Divsn. 1988 Fine Arts Fund, Cin., 1987; hon. trustee Babies' Milk Fund, Children's and Prenatal Clinics, Cin., 1994—. Recipient Disting. Alumni award u. Cin., 1992. Fellow Am. Acad. Pediatrics; mem. Am. Pediatric Soc. (councillor 1986-93), Soc. Pediatric Research, Assn. Med. Sch. Pediatric Dept. Chmn., Cin. Acad. Medicine, AMA, Midwestern Soc. for Pediatric Research, Am. Assn. for Study of Liver Diseases, Central Soc. Clin. Research, Am. Gastroenterological Assn., N.Am. Soc. Pediatric Gastroenterology, Nat. Reye's Syndrome Found. (med. dir. 1976-87), Internat. Assn. Study Liver Diseases. Club: Queen City (Cin.). Office: Children's Hosp Med Ctr 3333 Burnet Ave Cincinnati OH 45229-3026

SCHUCK, THOMAS ROBERT, lawyer, farmer; b. Findlay, Ohio, Feb. 7, 1950; s. Robert Damon and Katherine Margaretta (Beynon) S. BA, DePauw U., 1972; MA, U. Kent, U.K., 1974; JD, Harvard U., 1976. Bar: Ohio 1976, U.S. Dist. Ct. (no. dist.) Ohio 1977, U.S. Dist. Ct. (so. dist.) Ohio 1979, Ariz. 1990, U.S. Ct. Appeals (6th cir.) 1978, U.S. Ct. Appeals (9th cir.) 1991, U.S. Ct. Appeals Armed Forces, 2000. Law clk. U.S. Dist. Ct., Cleve., 1976-79; assoc. Taft, Stettinius & Hollister, Cin., 1979-87, ptnr., 1987—; owner, operator Rural Hill Farm. Participant Ohio Bench Bar Conf., Columbus, 1990, 91, Glenmoor Justice Inst., 2000; barrister Am. Inn of Ct., 1986-87, LEAD Clermont, 1997-98; mem. bar exam com. U.S. Dist. Ct. (so. dist.) Ohio; mem. merit panel for bankruptcy judge selection U.S. Ct. Appeals Sixth Cir., 1998. Contbg. author: Aids and the Law, 2d edit. 1992; contbr. articles to profl. jours. Trustee Mental Health Svcs. East, Inc., Cin., 1985-91; sec. bd. trustees Joy Outdoor Edn. Ctr., Inc., 1999—; mem. Clermont County Mental Health Bd., Batavia, Ohio, 1992-2000, vice chair, 1997-2000; mem. Clermont County Mental Retardation Developmental Disabilities Levy Steering Com., 1996, bd. trustees, 2000—, vice chmn., 2002-; mem. May Festival Assocs., Cin., 1984-86; spl. gifts com. Cin. Art Acad., 1987; mem. WGUC Radio Cmty. Bd., 1984-86. Rotary Internat. Found. grad. fellow, 1972, 73. Mem. FBA (pres. Cin. chpt. 1994-95, v.p. 6th cir. 1996-99, nat. sec. 2001—, nat. treas. 2001-02, nat. membership chair 1997-99, govt. rels. com.), Potter Stewart Am. Inn of Ct. (barrister 1986-87), U.S. Rowing Assn. (asst. referee), Harvard Club Cin. (pres. 1995-96), Camargo Hunt Club, Ohio Soc. (sec.), Soc. Bacchus Am., Masons, Phi Beta Kappa, Delta Chi, Phi Eta Sigma, Sigma Delta Chi. Republican. Methodist. Avocations: reading, photography. Home: PO Box 615 189 State Route 133 Felicity OH 45120 Office: 1800 Firstar Tower 425 Walnut St Cincinnati OH 45202-3923

SCHUCK, WILLIAM, state legislator; b. Findlay, Ohio, Dec. 12, 1951; s. Robert and Margaretta (Beynon) S. BA, Harvard Univ., 1974; MBA, JD, Cornell Univ., 1982. Mem. Columbus Devel. Com., Ohio, 1985-86; State Rep. Ohio Dist. 29, 1987—; lawyer Porter, Wright, Morris & Arthur, 1984—. Named Outstanding Citizen of Columbus, Jaycees, 1986. Mem. Columbus Athletic Club, Aladdin Shrine, Delta Epsilon. Address: Ohio Ho of Reps 13th Fl State House Columbus OH 43215

SCHUELE, DONALD EDWARD, physics educator; b. Cleve., June 16, 1934; s. Edward and Mildred (Matousek) S.; m. Clare Ann Kirchner, Sept. 5, 1956; children: Donna, Karen, Melanie, Judy, Rachel, Ruth. BS, John Carroll U., Cleve., 1956, MS, 1957; PhD, Case Inst. Tech., 1962. Instr. physics and math. John Carroll U., 1956-59; part-time instr. physics Case Inst. Tech., 1959-62, instr., asst. prof., assoc. prof., 1962-70; mem. tech. staff Bell Telephone Labs., 1970-72; assoc. prof. physics Case Western Res. U., 1972-74, prof., 1974—, dean undergrad. coll., 1973-76, chmn. dept. physics, 1976-78; vice dean Case Inst. Tech., 1978-83, v.p. for undergrad. and grad. studies, 1983-84, dean, 1984-86, prof. physics, 1986-88, dean math. and natural sci., 1988-89, Albert A. Michaelson prof. physics, 1989—, acting chmn. elec. engring. and applied physics, 1992-93. Cons. in field. Co-editor: Critical Revs. in Solid State Scis, 1969-84; contbr. articles to profl. jours.; patentee in field. Mem. adv. bd. St. Charles Borromeo Sch., 1970-72; pres. Seed Found., 1986-89; trustee St. Mary's Sem., 1980-93; mem. Olympic Sports Equipment and Tech. Com., 1982-93; trustee Newman Found., 1983—, Northeastern Ohio Sci. Fair, 1983—; mem. Diocesan Pastoral Coun., 1992-94; active Rep. Presdl. task force. Recipient Disting. Physics Alumnus award John Carroll U., 1983; NSF Faculty fellow, 1961-63; Sam Givelber fellow Case Alumni Assn., 2001. Mem.: North Coast Thermal Analysis Soc., Am. Assn. Physics Tchrs., Am. Phys. Soc. (vice chair Ohio sect. 1995—96, chair 1996—97), Newman Apostolate, Case Alumni Coun. (life; treas. 1992, 3d v.p. 2001—02), Tau Beta Pi, Sigma Xi, Alpha Sigma Nu. Republican. Roman Catholic. Achievements include patents fluid pressure device, impact wrench torque calibrator, detection of wear particles and other impurities in industrial fluids, electrical oil analysis instrument. Home: 4892 Countryside Rd Cleveland OH 44124-2513 Office: Case Western Res U 10900 Euclid Ave Cleveland OH 44106-1712 E-mail: des3@po.cwru.edu.

SCHUELER, JOHN R. newspaper executive; b. Grosse Point, MI; B.A., W. Mich. U. With Miami Herald, Miami, Fla.; pres. New England Newspapers; v.p. consumer mktg. & circulation The Orange County Register, Santa Ana, Calif., 1991, exec. v.p. & gen. mgr. 1992-95, pres., COO, 1995-98; publisher Star Tribune, Mpls., 1998—.

SCHUEPPERT, GEORGE LOUIS, financial executive; b. Merrill, Wis., July 1, 1938; s. George Henry and Eleanor Natalie (Pautz) S.; m. Kathleen Kay Carpenter, May 6, 1967; children— Steven Andrew, Stephanie Roanne, Stenning Karl BBA, U. Wis., Madison, 1961; MBA, U. Chgo., 1969. Treas., controller Steiger-Rathke Devel. Co., Phoenix, 1964-65; various positions Continental Ill. Nat., Chgo., 1965-76, 1981-86; mng. dir. Continental Ill. Ltd., London, 1977-81; sr. v.p. Continental Ill. Nat. Bank, Chgo., 1982-86; ptnr. Coopers & Lybrand, 1986-87; exec. v.p. fin. CBI Industries Inc, Oak Brook, Ill., 1987-95, also bd. dirs., 1987-95; exec. v.p., CFO Outboard Marine Corp., Waukegan, Ill., 1996-97. Bd. dirs. Wells Mfg. Co., Barrington Bank & Trust Co. Pres. Gt. Books Found.; chmn., bd. dirs. De Paul U. Gov. Asst. Program. Lt. (j.g.) USN, 1961-64. Recipient Herfurth award U. Wis., 1960 Mem. Econ. Club Chgo. (bd. dirs., chmn. membership com.). Republican. Avocations: history; civic affairs; architecture; travel; golf. Home: 97 Otis Rd Barrington IL 60010-5129 Office: Great Books Found 35 E Wacker Dr Ste 2300 Chicago IL 60601-2298

SCHUERER, NEAL, state legislator; b. Cedar Rapids, Iowa, Nov. 6, 1954; BA, Ctrl. Coll. Restauranteur, Amana, Iowa; mem. Iowa Senate from 30th dist., Des Moines, 1996—; mem. appropriations com., mem. bus. and labor rels. com.; mem. commerce com., mem. human resources com.; mem. state govt. com. Bd. dirs. Amana Ch. Soc., Sunday sch. supt.; mem. Amana Heritage Soc., Amana Colonies Land Use Dist., Amana Colonies Challenge 2000. Mem. Nat. Restaurant Assn., Iowa Hospitality Assn. Republican. Office: State Capitol 9th And Grand Ave Des Moines IA 50319-0001 E-mail: neal_schuerer@legis.state.ia.us.

SCHUESSLER, JOHN T. food service executive; BS, Spring Hill Coll. Mgr. trainee Wendy's franchise, Atlanta, 1974-76; joined Wendy's Internat., 1976; dist. mgr., dir. area ops., regional dir. various zones U.S., 1976-83; regional v.p. ea. divsn., 1983-84; zone pres., 1984-86; divsn. v.p., 1986-87; sr. v.p. N.E. region, 1987-95; exec. v.p. U.S. ops., 1995-97; pres., COO U.S. ops., 1997-2000; pres., COO Can., 1999-2000; pres., CEO, 2000—. Trustee Wendy's Nat. Advtsg. Program. Office: Wendy's Internat 4288 W Dublin-Granville Rd Dublin OH 43017

SCHUETTE, BILL, state legislator; b. Midland, Mich., Oct. 13, 1953; m. Cynthia; children: Heidi, Billy. Student, U. Aberdeen, 1974-75; B.S. in Fgn. Svc., Georgetown U., 1976; J.D., U. San Francisco, 1979. Bar: U.S. Supreme Ct. 1985. Atty., Midland, Mich., 1981—; Mich. field coordinator George Bush for Pres., 1979; Mich. polit. dir. Reagan/Bush for Pres., 1980; mem. 99th-101st Congresses from 10th Mich. dist., Washington, 1985-91, Mich. Senate from 35th dist., Lansing, 1994—. Dir. Mich. Dept. Agr., 1991-93; chair State Econ. Devel., Internat. Trade and Regulatory Affairs Com., 1995—. Office: PO Box 30036 Lansing MI 48909-7536

SCHUG, KENNETH ROBERT, chemistry educator; b. Easton, Pa., Aug. 27, 1924; s. Howard Lester and Marion Henry (Hulbert) S.; m. Miyoko Ishiyama, June 13, 1948; children: Carey Tyler, Carson Blake, Reed Porter. Student, Johns Hopkins U., 1942-43; B.A., Stanford U., 1945; Ph.D., U. So. Calif., 1955. Instr. Seton Hall Coll., South Orange, N.J., 1948-50; research assoc. U. Wis.-Madison, 1954-56; instr. Ill. Inst. Tech., Chgo.,

1956-59, asst. prof., 1959-65, assoc. prof., 1965-75, prof. chemistry, 1975—, chmn. dept. chemistry, 1976-82, 85-87, 89-90, assoc. chair dept. biol. chem. phys. sci., 1999-01. Project dir. Chgo. Area Health and Med. Careers Program, 1979—; project co-dir. Sci. and Math. Initiative for Learning Enhancement, 1985—; project dir. Howard Hughes Med. Inst. Undergrad. Biol. Scis. Program, 1992-97; cons. Argonne (Ill.) Nat. Lab., 1960-62. Co-author: Eigo Kagoku Ronbun no Kakikata, 1979; contbr. articles to profl. jours. Trustee Michael Reese Health Plan, Chgo., 1976-91, Michael Reese Trust, 1991—; bd. dirs. Hyde Park Consumers Coop. Soc., 1982-94. Fulbright scholar, 1964-65; grantee in field Mem. Am. Chem. Soc. (dir., officer Chgo. sect. 1978-84). Home: 1466 E Park Pl Chicago IL 60637-1836 Office: Ill Inst Tech Div Chemistry IIT Ctr Chicago IL 60616 E-mail: schug@lit.edu.

SCHUH, DALE R. insurance company executive; Joined Sentry Ins., A Mutal Co., Stevens Point, Wis., 1972, v.p. planning, 1988, pres., COO, 1996, CEO, pres., chmn., 1997—. Office: Sentry Ins A Mutual Co 1800 North Point Dr Stevens Point WI 54481

SCHUH, G(EORGE) EDWARD, university dean, agricultural economist; b. Indpls., Sept. 13, 1930; s. George Edward and Viola (Lentz) S.; m. Maria Ignez, May 23, 1965; children: Audrey, Susan, Tanya. BS in Agrl. Edn, Purdue U., 1952, DAgr (hon.), 1992; MS in Agrl. Econs., Mich. State U., 1954; MA in Econs, U. Chgo., 1958, PhD, 1961; prof. (hon.), Fed. U. Vicosa, Brazil, 1965; hon. doctorate, Purdue U., 1992. From instr. to prof. agrl. econs. Purdue U., 1959-79; dir. Center for Public Policy and Public Affairs, 1977-78; dep. undersec. for internat. affairs and commodity programs Dept. Agr., Washington, 1978-79, chair bd. for internat. food and agrl. devel., 1995—; prof. agrl. and applied econs., head dept. U. Minn., Mpls., 1979-84; dir. agr. and rural devel. World Bank, Washington, 1984-87; dean Humphrey Inst. for Pub. Affairs U. Minn., 1987—96; Orville and Jane Freeman Endowed chair Humphrey Inst. for Pub. Affairs, U. Minn., 1996—; regents prof. U. Minn., 1998—. Program advisor Ford Found., 1966-72; sr. staff economist Pres.'s Coun. Econ. Advisors, 1974-75; bd. on agr. NRC, 1998—; trustee Internat. Food Policy Rsch. Inst., 1997—. Author, editor profl. books; contbr. numerous articles to profl. publs. Served with U.S. Army, 1954-56. Fellow AAAS, Am. Acad. Arts and Scis., Am. Agrl. Econs. Assn. (Thesis award 1962, Pub. Rsch. award 1971, Article award 1975, Policy award 1979, Publ. of Lasting Value award 1988, bd. dirs. 1977-80, pres.-elect 1980-81, pres. 1981-82); mem. Internat. Assn. Agrl. Econs., Am. Econ. Assn., Brazilian Soc. Agrl. Economists. Office: Humphrey Ctr U Minn 301 19th Ave S Minneapolis MN 55455-0429 E-mail: geschuh@hhh.umn.edu.

SCHUL, BILL DEAN, psychological administrator, author; b. Winfield, Kans., Mar. 16, 1928; s. Fred M. and Martha Mildred (Miles) S.; m. Virginia Louise Duboise, Aug. 3, 1952; children: Robert Dean, Deva Elizabeth. BA, Southwestern Coll., 1952; MA, U. Denver, 1954; PhD, Am. Internat. U., 1977. Reporter, columnist Augusta (Kans.) Daily Gazette, 1954-58, Wichita (Kans.) Eagle-Beacon, 1958-61; youth dir. under auspices Kans. Atty. Gen., 1961-65; state dir. 7th Step Found., Topeka, 1965-66; mem. staff Dept. Preventive Psychiatry, Menninger Found., 1966-71; dir. cons. Ctr. Improvement Human Functining, Wichita, 1975—. Psychologist Ctr. Human Devel., Wichita. Mng. editor The Register, Oxford, Kans., 1988—; author: (with Edward Greenwood) Mental Health in Kansas Schools, 1965, Let Me Do This Thing, 1969, (with Bill Larson) Hear Me, Barabbas, 1969, How to Be An Effective Group Leader, 1975, The Secret Power of Pyramids, 1975, (with Ed Pettit) The Psychic Powre of Pyramids, 1976, Pyramids: The Second Reality, 1979, The Psychic Power of Animals, 1977, Psychic Frontiers of Medicine, 1977, Animal Immortality, 1990, Life Song, 1995, Synchronize Your Brain, 1997, Wayward Angel, 1988. Bd. dirs. Recreation Commn., Topeka, United Funds, Topeka, Acadic Inst., Trees for Life; v.p. Pegasus Way; pres. Intraface Corp., 1989—; mem. adv. bd. Clayton U. With USN, 1945-46. Recipient John H. McGinnis Meml. award Nonfiction, 1972, Am. Freedom Found. award, 1966, Spl. Appreciation award Kans. State Penitentiary, 1967. Mem. Acad. Parapsychology and Medicine, Kans. Coun. Children and Youth (pres. 1965-66), Assn. Strenghtening higher Realities and Aspirations of Man (pres. 1970-71), Smithsonian Instn., Lions (pores. 1957). Address: 7233 192d Rd Winfield KS 67156-9803 E-mail: schul@kcisp.net.

SCHULER, JAMES JOSEPH, vascular surgeon; b. Aurora, Ill., Feb. 12, 1946; s. Ella Schuler; m. Catherine Weller, 1969; children: James Jr., Matthew. BS, St. John's U., 1968; MD with hons., U. Ill., 1972, MS in Biochemistry, 1975. Diplomate Am. Bd. Surgery, Am. Bd. Vascular Surgery. Intern U. Ill., Chgo., 1972-73, resident, 1973-78, chief resident, 1978-79, instr., 1975-79, asst. prof., 1980-85, assoc. prof., 1985-92, prof. surgery, 1992—, chief divsn. vascular surgery, 1988—. Lectr. Cook County Grad. Sch., Chgo., 1991—; attending surgeon Cook County Hosp., Chgo., 1992—, West Side Vets. Hosp., Chgo., 1979—. Assoc. editor: Civilian Vascular Trauma, 1992; co-author numerous book chpts.; contbr. articles to profl. jours. Vascular Surgery fellow U. Ill., 1979-80; rsch. grantee numerous granting bodies, 1980—. Fellow ACS; mem. Am. Venous Forum, Soc. for Vascular Surgery, Western Surg. Assn., Internat. Soc. for Cardiovascular Surgery, Midwestern Vascular Surg. Soc., Alpha Omega Alpha. Republican. Roman Catholic. Avocations: hunting, fishing. Office: U Ill Hosp 1740 W Taylor St Ste 2200 Chicago IL 60612-7232

SCHULER, ROBERT HUGO, chemist, educator; b. Buffalo, Jan. 4, 1926; s. Robert H. and Mary J. (Mayer) S.; m. Florence J. Forrest, June 18, 1952; children: Mary A., Margaret A., Carol A., Robert E., Thomas C. BS, Canisius Coll., Buffalo, 1946; PhD, U. Notre Dame, 1949. Asst. prof. chemistry Canisius Coll., 1949-53; asso. chemist, then chemist Brookhaven Nat. Lab., 1953-56; staff fellow, dir. radiation research lab. Mellon Inst., 1956-76, mem. adv. bd., 1962-76; prof. chemistry, dir. radiation research lab. Carnegie-Mellon U., 1967-76; prof. chemistry U. Notre Dame, Ind., 1976—, dir. radiation lab., 1976-95, dir. emeritus, 1995—, John A. Zahm prof. radiation chemistry, 1986—; Raman prof. U. Madras, India, 1985-86. Vis. prof. Hebrew U., Israel, 1980. Author articles in field. Recipient Curie medal Poland, 1992. Fellow AAAS; mem. Am. Chem. Soc., Am. Phys. Soc., Chem. Soc., Radiation Research Soc. (pres. 1975-76), Sigma Xi. Club: Cosmos. Office: U Notre Dame Radiation Lab Notre Dame IN 46556 E-mail: schuler.1@nd.edu.

SCHULER, ROBERT LEO, appraiser, consultant; b. Cin., June 15, 1943; s. Del D. and Virginia D. (Heyl) S.; m. Shelagh J. Moritz, Aug. 11, 1962; children: Robert C., Sherry L. V.p. Comprehensive Appraisal Service, Cin., 1977—. Bd. dirs. Hamilton County Regional Planning Commn., Cin., 1987-88; mem. exec. com., past pres. OKI Regional Coun. Govts., Cin., 1981-92. Councilman City of Deer Park, Ohio, 1979-86; trustee Sycamore Twp., 1988-92; Ohio state rep. 36th dist., 1993—2000; active Scarlet Oaks Bus. Adv. Coun. Mem. Cin. Bd. Realtors, Ohio Assn. Realtors, Jaycees (v.p.), Nat. Assn. Independent Fee Appraisers, Appraisal Inst. Republican. Roman Catholic. Home: 3648 Jeffrey Ct Cincinnati OH 45236-1544 Office: 3648 Jeffrey Ct Cincinnati OH 45236-1544

SCHULFER, ROCHE EDWARD, theater executive director; b. Chgo., Sept. 26, 1951; s. Thomas Florian and Tess (Ronk) S.; m. Arlene Lencioni, June 2, 1973 (div. 1979); m. Linda Kimbrough, Aug. 2, 1986. BA in Econs., U. Notre Dame. Box office asst. Goodman Theatre, Chgo., 1973-74, asst. to mng. dir., 1974-77, gen. mgr., 1977-80, mng. dir., prodr., producing dir., exec. dir., 1980—. Mem. exec. com. League of Resident Theatres, Chgo., 1981, 83; pres. League of Chgo. Theatres, 1983-85, pres. Chgo. Theatre Found., 1985-87 ; bd. dirs. Chgo. Theatre Group, Lifeline Theatre, Theatre Comm. Group, Lawyers for Creative Arts. Mem. Am. Arts Alliance (chair), Ill. Art Alliance (pres.), Ill. Arts Coun. Office: Goodman Theatre 170 N Dearborn St Chicago IL 60601-3205

SCHULHOFER, STEPHEN JOSEPH, law educator, consultant; b. N.Y.C., Aug. 20, 1942; s. Joseph and Myrelle S.; m. Laurie Wohl, May 28, 1975; children: Samuel, Jonah. AB, Princeton U., 1964; LLB, Harvard U., 1967. Bar: D.C. 1968, U.S. Dist. Ct. (ea. dist.) Pa. 1973, U.S. Supreme Ct. 1973. Law clk. U.S. Supreme Ct., Washington, 1967-69; assoc. Coudert Freres, Paris, 1969-72; prof. law U. Pa., Phila., 1972-86; prof. U. Chgo., 1986—. speedy trial reporter U.S. Dist. Ct., Wilmington, Del., 1975-80; cons. U.S. EPA, Washington, 1977-78, U.S. Sentencing Commn., Washington, 1987-94. Author: Unwanted Sex: The Culture of Intimidation and the Failure of Law, 1998; Prosecutorial Discretion and Federal Sentencing Reform, 1979. Editor: Criminal Law and its Processes, 1983, 89, 95; contbr. articles to profl. jours. Trustee, Community Legal Services, Inc., Phila., 1981-86. Walter Meyer grantee Am. Bar Found., 1984. Mem. ACLU (Ill. bd. dirs. 1993-97), Law and Soc. Assn. Office: NYU Law Sch 40 Washington Sq S New York NY 10012

SCHULLER, DAVID EDWARD, cancer center administrator, otolaryngologist; b. Cleve., Oct. 20, 1944; m. Carole Ann Hauss, June 24, 1967; children: Rebecca, Michael. BA, Rutgers U., 1966; MD cum laude, Ohio State U., 1970. Diplomate Am. Bd. Otolaryngology 1975. Intern dept. surgery U. Hosps. Cleve., 1970-71; resident dept. otolaryngology Ohio State U., Columbus, 1971-72; resident dept. surgery U. Hosps. Cleve., 1972-73; fellow head and neck surgery Pack Med. Found. with John Conley, N.Y.C., 1973; resident dept. otolaryngology Ohio State U. Hosps., Columbus, 1973-75; fellow head and neck oncology and facial plastic and reconstructive surgery U. Iowa, Iowa City, 1975-76; from clin. instr. to prof. and chmn. dept. otolaryngology The Ohio State U., Columbus, 1971—, prof. sect. oral biology, Coll. Dentistry, 1990—; dir. Comprehensive Cancer Ctr., Columbus, 1997—, Arthur G. James Cancer Hosp. & Richard J. Solove Rsch. Inst., Columbus, 1988—; chair dept. otolaryngology Ohio State U., 1990—. Mem., chmn. various coms. Ohio State U. Hosps. and Coll. Medicine, 1976—; dir. CCC head and neck oncology program Ohio State U., 1977—, hosps. physician flr. coord. 10th flr., 1977-82, dir. laser-microsurgery teaching and rsch. lab., 1987-88; mem. various coms. Grant Hosp., 1980-84; mem. Accreditation Coun. for the Grad. Med. Edn. Residency Review Com. for Otolaryngology, 1985—, chmn., 1988—; vis. prof., lectr., ACS prof. clin. Oncology, 1989-94. numerous instns. Author: (books) (with others) Otolaryngology-Head and Neck Surgery-4 Vols., 1986, Textbook of Otolaryngology-7th Edit., 1988, Otolaryngology-Head and Neck Surgery-Update I, 1988, Musculocutaneous Flaps in Head and Neck Reconstructive Surgery, 1989, Otolaryngology-Head and Neck Surgery Update II, 1990, Otorinolaringologia-Cirugia de Cabeza y Culleo, 1991, Otolaryngology-Head and Neck Surgery-4 Vols., 1992; contbr. chpts. to books and articles to profl. jours.; mem. editorial bd. New Horizons in Otolaryngology/Head and Neck Surgery, 1982-87, The Laryngoscope, 1986—, Am. Jour. Otolaryngology, 1988—, Facial Plastic Surgery Internat. Quar. Monographs, 1992—; mem. rev. bd. Jour. Head and Neck Surgery, 1985—; mem. editorial rev. bd. Otolaryngology-Head and Neck Surgery, 1990—; reviewer New Eng. Jour Medicine, 1992—. Trustee Ohio Cancer Found., 1988—; dir. Am. Bd. Otolaryngology, 1988— Recipient Cert. of Appreciation, Scioto Meml. Hosp., 1982, Edmund Prince Fowler award Triological Soc., 1984; Henry Rutgers scholar Rutgers U., 1965-66; grantee Nat. Cancer Inst., 1980-88, 90-97, Bremer Found., 1982-83, 87-88, Photomedica Inc., 1986-89, Upjohn Co., 1986-90, others. Mem. AMA (mem. rev. panel Archives of Otolaryngology-Head and Neck Surgery 1984—), Am. Cancer Soc. (mem. instl. grant rev. com. 1980—, chmn. rehab. com. Franklin County unit 1981-82, mem. profl. edn. com. 1981—, chmn. 1982-85, v.p. 1982-83, pres. 1986, 87, trustee Ohio divsn. 1988—), Am. Assn. Cosmetic Surgeons, Am. Acad. Facial Plastic and Reconstructive Surgery (mem. rsch. com. 1977-82, chmn. residency rels. com. 1982-85, mem. program com. 1982-85, v.p. mid. sect. 1983-87, chmn. by-laws com. 1988-90, treas. 1988-90, Honor award 1989), Am. Coll. Surgeons, Am. Cleft Palate Assn., Assn. Am. Cancer Insts., Am. Soc. Head and Neck Injury, Am. Acad. Otolaryngology Head and Neck Surgery (mem. editorial bd. self-instructional package program 1982—, del. bd. govs. 1982-87, Honor award 1983), Am. Soc. Laser Medicine and Surgery, Am. Laryngological, Rhinological, Otological Soc., Inc., Am. Laryngological Assn., Am. Soc. Clin. Oncology (mem. program com. 1989—), Am. Assn. Cancer Researchers, Am. Soc. Head and Neck Surgery (mem. coun. 1983-86, chmn. scholastic and fellowship award com. 1984-86, mem. profl. rels. and pub. edn. com. 1989—), Southwest Oncology Group (chmn. head and neck com. 1983—), Collegium ORLAS, Ohio State Med. Assn. (pres. sect. otolaryngology 1987—), Ohio Soc. Otolaryngology (pres. 1985, 86, 87), Acad. Medicine of Columbus and Franklin County, Columbus E.E.N.T. Soc., Franklin County Acad. Medicine (mem. profl. rels. com. 1982—), Head and Neck Intergroup (vice-chmn. 1984-86, chmn. 1986-89), Assn. Rsch. Otolaryngology, Ohio State U. Med. Alumni Soc. (class rep. 1980—, v.p. 1987-88, pres. 1989-90), Med. Forum, Med. Review Club, Order of Hippocrates (charter), Alpha Omega Alpha. Office: 456 W 10th Ave Columbus OH 43210-1240 also: Ohio State Univ Comp Cancer Ctr 300 W 10th Ave Columbus OH 43210-1240

SCHULMAN, SIDNEY, neurologist, educator; b. Chgo., Mar. 1, 1923; s. Samuel E. and Ethel (Miller) S.; m. Mary Jean Diamond, June 17, 1945; children— Samuel E., Patricia, Daniel. B.S., U. Chgo., 1944, M.D., 1946. Asst. prof. neurology U. Chgo., 1952-57, asso. prof., 1957-65, prof., 1965-75, Ellen C. Manning prof., div. biol. scis., 1975-93, Ellen C. Manning prof. emeritus, 1993—. Served with M.C. AUS, 1947-49. Mem. Am. Neurol. Assn., U. Chgo. Med. Alumni Assn. (pres. 1968-69), Chgo. Neurol. Soc. (pres. 1964-65) Home: 5000 S East End Ave Chicago IL 60615-3140 Office: U Chgo Divsn Biol Scis CLI L633 (MC 7080) 5841 S Maryland Ave Chicago IL 60637

SCHULT, THOMAS P. lawyer; b. Great Falls, Mont., Sept. 12, 1954; s. Peter Henry and Louise (de Russy) S.; m. Margo C. Soulé, Sept. 18, 1982. BS in Russian History, U. Va., 1976, JD, 1979. Bar: U.S. Dist. Ct. (we. dist.) Mo. 1979, U.S. Ct. Appeals (10th cir.) 1983, U.S. Ct. Appeals (7th, 8th and llth cirs.) 1984, U.S. Ct. Appeals (5th cir.) 1985, U.S. Supreme Ct. 1987, U.S. Ct. Appeals (9th cir.) 1988. Ptnr. Lathrop Koontz & Norquist, Kansas City, Mo., 1979-89, Bryan Cave, Kansas City, 1989-94; Stinson, Mag & Fizzell, 1994-2001; ptnr. Berkowitz Feldmiller, 2001—. Committeeman Jackson County Reps., Kansas City, 1984—. Mem. ABA (products liability com.), Products Liability Adv. Coun., Mo. Bar Assn. (lectr. continuing legal edn.), Fedn. of Ins. and Corporate Counsel, Def. Rsch. Inst. Episcopalian. Office: Stinson Mag & Fizzell 1201 Walnut St Ste 2800 Kansas City MO 64106-2117

SCHULTE, DAVID MICHAEL, investment banker; b. N.Y.C., Nov. 12, 1946; s. Irving and Ruth (Stein) S.; m. Patricia Gordon, Sept. 5, 1999; children: Michael B., Katherine F. BA, Williams Coll., 1968; postgrad., Exeter Coll., Oxford (Eng.) U., 1968-69; JD, Yale U., 1972. Bar: D.C. 1973. Law clk. to Mr. Justice Stewart, U.S. Supreme Ct., 1972-73; spl. asst. to pres. N.W. Industries, Inc., Chgo., 1973-75, v.p. corp. devel., 1975-79, exec. v.p., 1979-80; sr. v.p. Salomon Bros., Chgo., 1980-84; mng. ptnr. Chilmark Ptnrs., 1984—. Editor-in-chief: Yale Law Jour, 1971-72. John E. Moody scholar Exeter Coll., Oxford U., 1968-69. Mem. Washington Bar Assn., Chgo. Club, Racquet Club, Bryn Mawr Country Club, Vineyard Golf Club. Office: Chilmark Ptnrs 875 N Michigan Ave Ste 3460 Chicago IL 60611-1957

SCHULTE, STEPHEN CHARLES, lawyer; b. Evanston, Ill., June 26, 1952; s. George John and Mary Ruth (Lamping) S.; m. Kathleen Ann O'Donnell, Sept. 4, 1982; children: Kate, Maureen, John. BA magna cum laude, St. Louis U., 1973, JD, 1976. Bar: Ill. 1976, U.S. Dist. Ct. (no. dist.) Ill. 1976, U.S. Ct. Appeals (7th cir.) 1991. Atty. Perz & McGuire, Chgo., 1976-83; ptnr. Winston & Strawn, 1983—. Founder, bd. dirs. Greater Orgn. for Less Fortunate (GOLF), Chgo., 1982—; fundraiser for Maryville Acad.; mem. Glenview Park Dist. Commn., 1989—, v.p., 1991-92, 98-99, pres., 1992-93, 99-2000. Mem. ABA, Ill. State Bar Assn., Chgo. Bar Assn., Ill. Trial Lawyers Assn., Ill. Assn. Def. Trial Counsel, Chgo. Vol. Legal Svcs., Nat. Legal Aid Defender Assn., Phi Beta Kappa. Avocations: basketball, baseball, golf, music, travel. Home: 941 Club Cir Glenview IL 60025-3101 Office: Winston & Strawn 35 W Wacker Dr Ste 4200 Chicago IL 60601-1695 E-mail: sschulte@winston.com.

SCHULTZ, CARL HERBERT, real estate management and development company executive; b. Chgo., Jan. 9, 1925; s. Herbert V. and Olga (Swanson) S.; m. Helen Ann Stevesson, June 6, 1948; children: Mark Carl, Julia Ann. B.S. in Gen. Engring., Iowa State U., 1948. With Schultz Bros. Co., 1948—, mdse. mgr. and store planner, 1962-70, v.p. Lake Zurich, Ill., 1968-72, pres., 1972-2000; chmn., 2000—; pres. Ill. Schultz Bros. Co., Ind. Schultz Bros. Co., Iowa Schultz Bros. Co., Wis. Schultz Bros. Co.; chmn. Schultz Bros. Co., 2000—. Mem. Lake Bluff (Ill.) Zoning Bd. Appeals, 1976-85, chmn., 1978-85. Served with U.S. Army, 1944-46. Mem. Lake Zurich Indsl. Coun. (sec. 1976), Assn. Gen. Mdse. Chains (dir. 1975-86, exec. com. 1983-86, chmn. nat. conv. 1982), Ill. Retail Mchts. Assn. (dir. 1984-89), Wis. Retail Fedn. (dir. 1981-89) Presbyterian. Club: Bath and Tennis (Lake Bluff). Home: 701 E Center Ave Lake Bluff IL 60044-2607 Office: 785 Oakwood Rd Ste 102S Lake Zurich IL 60047-1549

SCHULTZ, CLARENCE JOHN, minister; b. Morris Twp., Wis., Aug. 4, 1937; s. Clarence John Sr. and Ella Mae (Feavel) S.; m. Doroland Kay King, Aug. 24, 1957 (dec. Jan. 1974); children: Sharon Kay Braun, Susan May Schultz Rogers; m. Martha Ann Aylor, Apr. 5, 1975. BS, Bryan Coll., 1960. Ordained to ministry Conservative Congl. Ch., 1961. Min. 1st Congl. Ch., Herreid, S.D., 1961-66, Immanuel Evang. Congl. Ch., Sheboygan, Wis., 1966-77, Hope Congl. Ch., Superior, 1977-83, Zion Evang. Ch., Scottsbluff, Nebr., 1983-89, 1st Congl. Ch., Buffalo Center, Iowa, 1989-92, Kenosha, Wis., 1992-98, St. Lucas Cmty. Ch., Lake Elmo, Minn., 1998—. Mem. Conservative Congl. Christian Conf. (rec. sec. 1973-82, v.p. 1994-96, pres. 1996-99, Rocky Mountain area rep. 1987-89, endorser of chaplains 1988-2000, mem. credentials com. 1988—), Rotary (ch. chaplain com. 1993-95). Avocations: amateur radio, golf. Home and Office: 1195 Manning Ave N Lake Elmo MN 55042-9607 E-mail: stlucas@attbi.com., stlucas2000@netzero.net.

SCHULTZ, DALE WALTER, state legislator; b. Madison, Wis., June 12, 1953; s. Walter Albert and Lillian (Fortman) S.; m. Rachel Weiss, June 20, 1981; children: Katherine Ann, Amanda. BBA, U. Wis., 1975. Farm mgr., Hillpoint, Wis., 1975—; adminstrv. and legis. asst. Wis. State Senate, Madison, 1976-79; planning analyst State of Wis., 1979-82; mem. Wis. Assembly, 1982-91, Wis. Senate from 17th dist., Madison, 1991—; chair ins. com. Wis. Senate, 1995—, mem. audit com. joint com. rev. adminstrv. rules. Mem. citizens adv. bd. Sauk County (Wis.) Health Care Ctr.; mem. Sauk County Farm Bur. Recipient Disting. Svc. award FFA, 1994; named Legislator of Yr., Wis. Tech. Coll. Assn., 1994-95, Guardian of Small Bus., Nat. Fedn. Ind. Bus., 1994, Legislator of Yr., Vietnam Vets. Assn., 1994. Republican. Club: Rod & Gun (Hillpoint, Wis.). Lodges: Lions, Masons. Home: 515 N Central Ave Richland Center WI 53581-1702 Office: PO Box 7882 Madison WI 53707-7882

SCHULTZ, DENNIS BERNARD, lawyer; b. Detroit, Oct. 15, 1946; s. Bernard George and Madeline Laverne (Riffenberg) Schultz; m. Andi Lynn Leslie, Apr. 18, 1967; 1 child Karanne Anne. BS, Wayne State U., 1970; JD, Mich. State U., 1977. Bar: Mich. 1977, U.S. dist. Ct. (ea. and we. dists.) Mich., U.S. Ct. Appeals (6th cir.), U.S. Dist. Ct. (we. dist.) Pa. V.p. Barkay Bldg. Co., Ferndale, Mich., to 1976; law clk. Hon. George N. Bashara, Mich. Ct. Appeals, Detroit, 1977; shareholder Butzel Long, 1978—. Editor: Detroit Coll. Law Rev., 1977. Scholar Detroit Coll. Law Alumni Assn., 1976, Mich. Consol. Gas Co., 1977. Mem.: Mich. Bar Assn., Detroit Bar Assn. Republican. Roman Catholic. Avocations: boating, bicycling, golf.

SCHULTZ, ED, radio personality; Radio host News and Views weekdays Sta. KFGO-AM, Fargo, ND. Office: KFGO 1020 25th St S Fargo ND 58103*

SCHULTZ, HARRY, health science organization administrator; Dir. St. Boniface Gen. Hosp. Rsch. Ctr., Winnipeg, MB, Canada. Office: U Manitoba St Boniface Gen Hosp 351 Tache Ave Winnipeg MB Canada R2H 2A6

SCHULTZ, LOUIS EDWIN, management consultant; b. Foster, Nebr., Aug. 8, 1931; s. Louis Albert and Lula Pusey (Cox) S.; m. Mary Kathleen Peck, Mar. 3, 1962; children: Kurt Michael, Kristen Leigh. BSEE, U. Nebr., 1959; MBA, Pepperdine U., 1974. Mktg. mgr. Bell & Howell, Pasadena, Calif., 1962-70; dir. mktg. Cogar Corp., Utica, N.Y., 1970-71; product mgr. Pertec Corp., L.A., 1971-73; gen. mgr. Control Data Corp., Mpls., 1973-84; founder Process Mgmt. Internat., Inc., 1984, pres., 1984-99; ptnr., mng. dir. Bluefire Ptnrs., 1999—. Bd. dirs. CorCom Cos., Inc., Mpls., PMI Ltd, 1995-98; adv. bd. Inst. for Productivity Through Quality, U. Tenn., Knoxville, 1982-84; ptnr. CorCom Cos., Inc., 1997-99, ptnr.-mng. dir., Bulefire Ptrns. Author: Managing in the Worldwide Competitive Society, 1984, Quality Management Philosophies, 1985, Profiles in Quality, 1994; co-author: Quality Handbook for Small Business, 1994, Deming, The Way We Knew Him, 1995. Mem. Gov.'s Commn. on Productivity, St. Paul, 1986; chmn. Wirth Park Tree Restoration Com., Mpls., 1983; mem. Productivity Planning Com., St. Paul, 1985—. Staff sgt. USMC, 1952-54; advisor to Deming Forum, 1985—; judge Minn. Quality award, 1992. Recipient Profl. Partnership award U. Minn., 1987. Mem. Am. Soc. Performance Improvement (bd. dirs. 1984-89, outstanding svc. award), Minn. Coun. for Quality (bd. dirs. 1987-97), Human Sys. Mgmt. (editl. bd.), Asia-Pacific Orgn. Quality Control (life), Toastmasters Internat. Republican. Methodist. Office: Bluefire Ptnrs 150 S 5th St Ste 1300 Minneapolis MN 55402-4213 E-mail: lschultz@bluefirepartners.com.

SCHULTZ, LOUIS MICHAEL, advertising agency executive; b. Detroit, Aug. 24, 1944; s. Henry Richard and Genevieve (Jankowski) S.; children: Christian David, Kimberly Ann; m. Diane Lee; stepchildren: Vince, Andrea, Frank. B.A., Mich. State U., 1967; M.B.A., Wayne State U., 1970. Staff Campbell-Ewald, Warren, Mich., 1967-74, v.p. group dir., 1975-77, sr. v.p., assoc. dir., 1977-82, group sr. v.p., 1982-83, exec. v.p., 1984-87, Lintas: USA, 1987-94; chmn. Lintas: WW Media Coun., 1991; mem. devel. council IPG, N.Y.C., 1984—; pres., CEO CE Comm., 1994—; vice chmn. Campbell-Ewald, 1998-99; chmn., CEO Initiative Media N.Am., L.A., 2000—; chmn. Initiative Media WW, 2000. Advisor, Detroit Renaissance Com., 1981-84. With USAR, 1967-73. Mem. NATAS, Am. Women in Radio and TV, Am. Mktg. Assn., Detroit Advt. Assn., Promotion Mktg. Assn. (bd. dirs. 1999), Ad Club N.Y. (bd. dirs.), Adcraft Club, Old Club, Hidden Valley Club, Longboat Key Club, Detroit Athletic Club, Am. Advt. Fedn. (bd. dirs.), Forest Lake Country Club, Renaissance Club, Detroit Athletic Club. Episcopalian. Avocations: golf; tennis; travel. Home: 5011 Elmgate Dr Orchard Lake MI 48324-3014 Office: Initiative Media 5700 Wilshire Blvd Ste 400 Los Angeles CA 90036-3639

SCHULTZ, LOUIS WILLIAM, retired judge; b. Deep River, Iowa, Mar. 24, 1927; s. M. Louis and Esther Louise (Behrens) S.; m. D. Jean Stephen, Nov. 6, 1949; children: Marcia, Mark, Paul. Student, Central Coll., Pella, Iowa, 1944-45, 46-47; LLB, Drake U., Des Moines, 1949. Bar: Iowa. Claims supr. Iowa Farm Mut. Ins. Co., Des Moines, 1949-55; partner firm Harned, Schultz & McMeen, Marengo, Iowa, 1955-71; judge Iowa Dist. Ct. (6th dist.), 1971-80; justice Iowa Supreme Ct., 1980-93; county atty. Iowa County, 1960-68; ret., 1993. Served with USNR, 1945-46. Mem. Am. Bar Assn., Iowa Bar Assn. (bd. govs.), Iowa Judges Assn. (pres.)

SCHULTZ, RICHARD CARLTON, plastic surgeon; b. Grosse Pointe, Mich., Nov. 19, 1927; s. Herbert H. and Carmen (Huebner) S.; m. Pauline Zimmermann, Oct. 8, 1955; children: Richard, Lisa, Alexandra, Jennifer. McGregor scholar, U. Mich., 1946-49; M.D., Wayne State U., 1953. Diplomate Am. Bd. Plastic Surgery. Intern Harper Hosp., Detroit, 1953-54, resident in gen. surgery, 1954-55, U.S. Army Hosp., Fort Carson, Colo., 1955-57; resident in plastic surgery St. Luke's Hosp., Chgo., 1957-58, U. Ill. Hosp., Chgo., 1958-59, VA Hosp., Hines, Ill., 1959-60; practice medicine specializing in plastic surgery Park Ridge, 1961-96; retired, 1996; clin. asst. prof. surgery U. Ill. Coll. Medicine, 1966-70, assoc. prof. surgery, 1970-76, prof., 1976-96, head div. plastic surgery, 1970-87; pres. med. staff Luth. Gen. Hosp., Park Ridge, 1977-79. Vis. prof. U. Pitts., 1972, U. Miss., 1973, U. Pisa, Italy, 1974, Jikei U. Coll. Medicine, Tokyo, 1976, Ind. U., 1977, U. Helsinki, 1977, U. N.Mex., 1978, U. Milan, 1981, So. Ill. Sch. Medicine, 1982, Tulane U. Med. Sch., 1983, Shanghai 2d Med. Coll., 1984, U. Guadalajara (Mex.), 1986, Gazi U., Turkey, 1988, U. Coll. Medicine Tsuksba, Japan, 1996, Taegu (Korea) U., 1996; participant, guest surgeon Physicians for Peace, Turkey and Greece, 1988, Israel and Occupied Ters., 1990, Egypt, 1991, Lithuania, Estonia, 1993 (team leader); leader citizen amb. People to People Internat. Del. Plastic Surgeons to Albania & Russia, 1994, del. leader, Tibet and China, 1998. Author: Facial Injuries, 1970, 3d edit., 1988, Maxillo-Facial Injuries from Vehicle Accidents, 1975, Outpatient Surgery, 1979. Mem. sch. bd., Lake Zurich, Ill., 1966-72, pres., 1968-72; pres. Chgo. Found. for Plastic Surgery, 1966— . Served to capt. M.C., AUS, 1955-57. Recipient research award Ednl. Found. Am. Soc. Plastic and Reconstructive Surgery, 1964-65, Med. Tribune Auto Safety award, 1967, Robert H. Ivy award, 1969, Disting. Sci. Achievement award Wayne U. Coll. Medicine Alumni, 1975; Sanvenero-Rosselli award, 1981; Fulbright scholar U. Uppsala, Sweden, 1960-61 Fellow ACS (pres. local commn. on trauma 1985-87); mem. Am. Assn. Plastic Surgeons (trustee 1990-91), Am. Soc. Plastic and Reconstructive Surgeons, Midwestern Assn. Plastic Surgeons (pres. 1978-79), Chgo. Soc. Plastic Surgeons (pres. 1970-72), Midwestern Assn. Plastic Surgeons (pres. 1978-79), Am. Soc. Maxillofacial Surgeons (pres. 1988-89, award of honor 1986), Am. Assn. Automotive Medicine (pres. 1970-71, A. Merkin award 1982), Am. Cleft Palate Assn., Am. Soc. Aesthetic Plastic Surgery, Tord Skoog Soc. Plastic Surgeons (pres. 1971-75), Can. Soc. Plastic Surgery, Chilean Soc. Plastic Surgery (corr.), Japanese Soc. Plastic Surgery (corr.), Cuban Soc. Maxillofacial Surgery (corr.), Korean Soc. Plastic Surgery. Office: PO Box 357 Northport MI 49670-0357 Home: PO Box 357 Northport MI 49670-0357

SCHULTZ, RICHARD DALE, national athletic organization executive; b. Grinnell, Iowa, Sept. 5, 1929; s. August Henry and Marjorie Ruth (Turner) S.; m. Jacquilyn Lu Duistermars, June 26, 1949; children: Robert Dale, William Joel, Kim Marie. BS, Ctrl. Coll., Pella, Iowa, 1950; EdD (hon.), Ctrl. Coll., 1987; LLD (hon.), Wartburg Coll., 1988, Alma Coll., 1989, Luther Coll., 1991; PhD (hon.), U.S. Sports Acad., 1993; LLD (hon.), Daniel Webster Coll., 1997, Gettysburg Coll., 1998. Head basketball coach, athletic dir. Humboldt (Iowa) High Sch., 1950-60; freshman basketball coach U. Iowa, Iowa City, 1960-62, head baseball coach, assoc. basketball coach, 1962-70, head basketball coach, 1970-74, asst. v.p., 1974-76; dir. athletics and phys. edn. Cornell U., Ithaca, N.Y., 1976-81; dir. athletics U. Va., Charlottesville, 1981-87; exec. dir. NCAA, Mission, Kans., 1987-94; pres. Global Sports Enterprises, 1994-95; exec. dir. U.S. Olympic Com., Colorado Springs, Colo., 1995-2000; chmn. Mktg. Assocs. Internat., 2000—. Mem. honors ct. Nat. Football Found. and Hall of Fame, Nat. Basketball Hall of Fame, 1992; chmn. bd. NCAA Found., 1989; organizer Iowa Steel Mill, Inc.; bd. trustees Gettysburg Coll., 1996—. Author: A Course of Study for the Coaching of Baseball, 1964, The Theory and Techniques of Coaching Basketball, 1970; Contbr. articles to mags. Bd. dirs. Fellowship of Christian Athletes, 1986, chmn., 1990; chmn. Multiple Sclerosis, 1974-75; mem. Knight Found. Commn. on Intercollegiate Athletics, 1990—; mem. adv. com. on svc. acad. athletic programs Def. Dept. Recipient Disting. Alumni award Ctrl. Coll., Pella, 1970, 98, Lifetime Svc. award U. Iowa, 1994, Corbett award Nat. Assn. Collegiate Dirs. Athletics, 1994, medal of honor Ellis Island, 1997, Disting. Alumni award Ctrl. Coll., 1998, Casey award, 1999, Pres. and Mrs. Bush Cmty. Impact award 1999; mem. Basketball Hall of Fame Honor Ct., 1992, Sportsman of Yr. award Marine Corp., 1997; inducted into Iowa Baseball Hall of Fame, 1993. Mem. Nat. Assn. Coll. Basketball Coaches, Ea. Coll. Athletic Assn. (mem. exec. com. 1980-81), Am. Basketball Coaches Assn. (Award of Honor 1994), Am. Football Coaches Assn. (lifetime membership award 1995). Home: 3670 Twisted Oak Cir Colorado Springs CO 80904-4720 Office: 10975 Benson 12 Corporate Woods Ste 55 Overland Park KS 66210 E-mail: dschultz@maisponts.com.

SCHULTZ, RICHARD MICHAEL, biochemistry educator, researcher; b. Phila., Oct. 28, 1942; s. William and Beatrice (Levine) S.; m. Rima M. Lunin, Mar. 7, 1965; children: Carl M., Eli J. BA, SUNY, Binghamton, 1964; PhD, Brandeis U., 1969. Rsch. fellow Harvard U. Med. Sch., Boston, 1969-71; asst. prof. Loyola U. Stritch Sch. of Medicine, Maywood, Ill., 1971-78, assoc. prof., 1978-84, prof., 1984—, chmn. dept. molecular and cellular biochemistry, 1984-2000. Mem. adv. med. bd. Leukemia Rsch. Found., Chgo., 1987-91. Contbr. articles to profl. jours. and chpts. to books. Recipient Rsch. grants NIH. Achievements include in vivo evidence for the role of protease enzymes and their inhibitors in regulating tumor cell metastasis, oncogene pathways in metastasis, obtaining evidence on the nature of the transition-state in enzyme catalysis.. Office: Divsn Molecular & Cellular Biochemistry Loyola U Sch Medicine Maywood IL 60153 E-mail: rschult@lumc.edu.

SCHULTZ, RICHARD OTTO, ophthalmologist, educator; b. Racine, Wis., Mar. 19, 1930; s. Henry Arthur and Josephine (Wagoner) S.; m. Diane Haldane, Sept. 29, 1990; children: Henry Reid, Richard Paul, Karen Jo. BA, U. Wis., 1950, MS, 1954; MD, Albany Med. Coll., 1956; MSc, U. Iowa, 1960. Diplomate Am. Bd. Ophthalmology. Intern, Univ. Hosps., Iowa City, 1956-57, resident in opthalmology, 1957-60; chief ophthalmology sect. div. Indian health USPHS, Phoenix, 1960-63; practice medicine specializing in ophthalmology, 1963; NIH spl. fellow in ophthalmic microbiology U. Calif., San Francisco, 1963-64, clin. assoc., 1963-64, research assoc., 1963-64; assoc. prof., chmn. dept. ophthalmology Marquette U. Sch. Medicine (now Med. Coll. Wis.), Milw., 1964-68, prof., chmn., 1968-97, prof. ophthalmology, 1997—2000, prof. emeritus, 2000—. Mem. nat. adv. eye coun. NIH, 1984-88; cons. VA regional ctr. Milw. Children's, Columbia, Froedert and hosps., Milw. Contbr. articles to profl. jours. Served with USPHS, 1960-63. Fellow: ACS, Am. Ophthalmol. Soc., Am. Acad. Ophthalmology; mem.: Milw. Acad. Medicine, Med. Soc. Milwaukee County, Oxford Ophthalmol. Congress (Eng.), Rsch. to Prevent Blindness, N.Y. Acad. Scis., Assn. Rsch. Vision and Ophthalmology, Milw. Ophthal. Soc., Assn. Univ. Profs. Ophthalmology. Home: 13070 W Bluemound Rd 107 Elm Grove WI 53122-1973 Office: MCW Eye Inst 925 N 87th St Milwaukee WI 53226-4812 E-mail: roschulz@mcw.edu.

SCHULTZ, ROBERT J. retired automobile company executive; b. 1930; BSME, Mich. State U., 1953, MBA, 1969. With GM Corp., 1955-92, chief engr., 1977-81, gen. mgr. Delco Elecs. div., 1981-84, group dir. engr. Chevrolet, Pontiac Can. Group, 1984-85, group v.p. Chevrolet, Pontiac Can. Group, 1985-90, vice chmn., 1990-92; also chmn., pres., chief exec. officer GM Hughes Electronics Corp. Bd. dirs. MCT Corp.; bd. dirs. Delco Remy Internat. Bd. trustees Calif. Inst. Tech. With USAAF, 1953-55. Mem. NAE.

SCHULZ, KEITH DONALD, corporate lawyer; b. Burlington, Iowa, Dec. 20, 1938; s. Henry Carl and Laura Iral (Bowlin) S.; m. Emily Brook Roane, Apr. 19, 1985; children: Keith Jr., Sarah, Christine, Stefan. BA, U. Iowa, 1960, JD, 1963. Bar: Iowa 1963, Ill. 1966, Wis., 1990. Dep. Sec. of State, State of Iowa, Des Moines, 1965-66; atty. AT&T, Chgo., 1966-67; sec., gen. counsel Borg-Warner Acceptance Corp., 1967-74; asst. gen. counsel Borg-Warner Corp., 1974-84, v.p., gen. counsel, 1984-88; of counsel Bell, Boyd & Lloyd, 1988—. Chmn., CEO Downtown Ptnrs., Inc., 1995-96. Contbr. articles to Harvard Bus. Rev., Jour. for Corp. Growth. Chmn. bd. dirs. Vol. Legal Svcs. Found., Chgo., 1984-91; bd. dirs. Southeast Iowa Symphony Orch., pres., 1998-2000, Heritage Trust Found. Mem. Iowa Bar Assn., Chgo. Bar Assn. (chmn. corp. law depts. com. 1983-84), Wis. Bar Assn., Assn. of Gen. Counsel, Am. Soc. Corp. Secs., Law Club of Chgo. Clubs: University, Economic (Chgo.). Avocations: tennis, bicycling, skiing. Office: Bell Boyd & Lloyd 70 W Madison St Ste 3300 Chicago IL 60602-4284 E-mail: KDons@aol.com.

SCHULZ, MICHAEL JOHN, fire and explosion analyst, consultant; b. Milw., Oct. 7, 1958; s. John F. and JoAnn E. (Carlson) S.; children: Kari L., Brian M. BS in Fire and Safety Engring. Tech., U. Cin., 1996; grad., U.S. Fire Adminstrn. Acad. Cert. fire and explosion investigator; cert. fire protection specialist; cert. fire investigation instr.; cert. fire svc. instr. II; cert. Can. fire investigator. Fire investigator Cedarburg (Wis.) Police Dept., 1979-90; capt., fire investigator Cedarburg (Wis.) Fire Dept., 1981-90; sr. staff expert John A. Kennedy & Assoc., Hoffman Estates, Ill., 1990-2000; pres. M.J. Schulz Assocs., Inc., 2000—. Cons. U.S. Fire Adminstrn.; instr. fire tech. and police sci. depts. Milw. (Wis.) Area Tech. Coll.; instr. fire sci. tech. dept. William Rainey Harper C.C.; lectr. in field. Author: Manual for the Determination of Electrical Fire Causes, 1988, Guide for Fire and Explosion Investigations, 1992, 95, 98. Recipient Common Coun. Commendation, City of Cedarburg, Wis., 1986; named Firefighter of Yr., Ozaukee County Assn. Fire Depts., 1985. Mem. ASTM, Nat. Assn. Fire Investigators (bd. dirs. 1987—, nat. cert. bd. 1987—, chmn. edn. com., editor The Nat. Fire Investigator, Man of Yr. 1991), Nat. Fire Protection Assn. (tech. com. on fire investigations 1985—, fire svc. sect., sect. rep. tech. com. on fire investigations 1985-92, sec. rep. nat. conf. on fire investigation instrn., mem. bd. dirs. fire sci. and tech. educators sect.), Fire Marshal's Assn. N.Am. (assoc.), Nat. Inst. Bldg. Scis. (reviewing mem. fire rsch. sub-com.), Bldg. Ofcls. and Code Adminstrs. Internat., Soc. Automotive Enmgrs., Human Factors and Ergonomics Soc., So. Bldg. Code Congress Internat., Internat. Bldg. Code Ofcls., Internat. Assn. Arson Investigators (John Charles Wilson scholarship award 1982), Ill. Chpt. Internat. Assn. Arson Investigators, Internat. Soc. Fire Svc. Instrs., Am. Soc. Safety Engrs., Nat. Conf. Fire Investigation Instrn. (bd. dirs.), Wis. Soc. Fire Svc. Instrs., Ky. Cols. Republican. Lutheran. Avocations: amateur radio, flying. E-mail: mjschulz@mjschulz.com.

SCHULZE, FRANZ, JR. art critic, educator; b. Uniontown, Pa., Jan. 30, 1927; s. Franz and Anna E. (Krimmel) S.; m. Marianne Gaw, June 24, 1961 (div. 1975); children: F. C. Matthew, Lukas; m. Stephanie Mora, 1992. (div. 1996). Student, Northwestern U., 1943; PhB, U. Chgo., 1945; BFA, Sch. Art Inst. Chgo., 1949, MFA, 1950; postgrad., Acad. Fine Arts, Munich, Germany, 1956-57. Instr. art Purdue U., 1950-52; chmn. dept. art Lake Forest (Ill.) Coll., 1952-58, artist-in-residence, 1958-61, prof. art, 1961—, Hollender prof. art, 1974-91; art critic Chgo. Daily News, 1962-78, Chgo. Sun-Times, 1978-85. Adj. prof. U. Ill., Chgo., 1996; Chgo. corr. in art Christian Sci. Monitor, 1958-62; art and arch. critic The Chicagoan, 1973-74; mem. vis. com. dept. art U. Chgo., 1974—. Author: Art, Architecture and Civilization, 1969, Fantastic Images: Chicago Art Since 1945, 1972, 100 Years of Chicago Architecture, 1976, Stealing Is My Game, 1976, Mies van der Rohe: A Critical Biography, 1985, The University Club of Chicago: A Heritage, 1987, Mariotti, 1988; editor: Mies van der Rohe: Critical Essays, 1989, Mies van der Rohe Archive, 1993; co-editor Chicago's Famous Buildings, 1993, Philip Johnson: Life and Work, 1994, A. James Speyer, Architect, Curator, Exhibition Designer, 1997, The Farnsworth House, 1997, (with Rosemary Cowler and Arthur Miller) Thirty Miles North, 2000; contbg. editor Art News, 1973—, Inland Architect, 1975-94; corr. editor Art in Am., 1975—. Trustee Ragdale Found., Lake Forest, 1981— . Recipient Harbison award for tchg. Danforth Found. of St. Louis, 1971, Excellence in Architecture award Ill. Inst. Tech., 1999; Adenauer fellow, 1956-57; Ford Found. fellow, 1964-65; Graham Found. for Advanced Studies in the Fine Arts fellow, 1971, 81, 93; NEH fellow, 1982, 88; Skidmore Owings & Merrill Found. fellow, 1983; recipient Disting. Svc. award Chgo. Phi Beta Kappa Soc., 1972; Hon. Mention Hitchcock Book award Soc. Archtl. Historians, 1987. Mem. AAUP, Coll. Art Assn. (bd. dirs. 1983-86), Archives Am. Art (adv. com.), Soc. Archtl. Historians. Office: Lake Forest Coll Dept Art Lake Forest IL 60045 E-mail: schulze@lfc.edu.

SCHULZE, JOHN B. manufacturing executive; BBA, So. Meth. U., 1959; Advanced Mgmt. Program, Harvard U., 1984. Group v.p., sr. group v.p., sr. exec. v.p., CEO indsl. products group White Consol. Industries, 1962-87; pres., chief oper. officer Lamson & Sessions Co., Cleve., 1988, pres., chief exec. officer, 1989, chmn., pres., chief exec. officer, 1990—, also bd. dirs. Capt. USMC, 1959-62. Office: Lamson & Sessions 25701 Science Park Dr Cleveland OH 44122-7393

SCHULZE, RICHARD M. retail electronics company executive; b. 1941; With No. States Sales Co., 1962-66; founder, chmn., CEO Besy Buy Co., Inc., Eden Prairie, Minn., 1967—. Office: Best Buy Co 7075 Flying Cloud Dr Eden Prairie MN 55344-3538

SCHUMACHER, LESLIE, state legislator, artist; b. Oct. 4, 1955; m. Byron Schumacher; 2 children. Freelance artist, Princeton, Minn.; mem. Minn. Ho. of Reps., St. Paul, 1994—. Mem. Dem.-Farmer-Labor Party. Office: Minn Ho of Reps State Capitol Saint Paul MN 55155-0001

SCHUMAN, ALLAN L. chemical company executive; b. 1937; BS, NYU, 1955. With Ecolab Inc., St. Paul, 1957—, v.p. mktg. and nat. acctg., 1972-78, v.p. mktg. devel., 1978-79, now pres., CEO. Office: Ecolab Inc Ecolab Ctr Saint Paul MN 55102

SCHUMAN, LEONARD M. medical educator, academic administrator; b. Cleve., Mar. 4, 1913; AB, Oberlin Coll., 1934; MSc, Western Reserve U., 1939, MD, 1940. Diplomate Am. Bd. Preventive Medicine. Teaching and rsch. fellow in hygiene and bacteriology Sch. Medicine Western Reserve U., 1937-39; intern U.S. Marine Hosp., Chgo., 1940-41; asst. epidemiologist Ill. Dept. Pub. Health, 1941-42, dist. health supt. dist. # 2, 1943, asst. chief divsn. local health adminstrn., 1943-45, chief divsn. venereal disease control, 1947-50, acting chief divsn. communicable disease, 1949-50, dep. dir. divsn. preventive medicine, 1950-51, 53-54; assoc. prof. Sch. of Pub. Health U. Minn., 1954-58, prof. epidemiology, 1958-83, Mayo prof. emeritus, dir. epidemiology emeritus Sch. Pub. Health, 1983—. Epidemiologist U.S. Dept. of Def., 1951-53; vis. lectr. U. Ill. Sch. of Medicine, Chgo., 1947-54; lectr. communicable diseases Springfield Meml. Hosp., Sch. of Nursing, 1947-54; cons. Communicable Disease Ctr., USPHS, 1955-83, Air Pollution Med. Program, 1958—, Nat. Cancer Inst., 1958-79, Divsn. Radiol. Health, 1961-69, Chronic Disease Divsn., 1964-72, mem. Adv. Com. Bio-Effects of Radiation, 1966-69, Grant Rev. Com. for Prevention Ctrs., Ctrs. for Disease Control, 1986-93; cons. Minn. State Health Dept., 1955-90, mem. adv. com. cancer surveillance, 1981—, tech. adv. com. non-smoking and health, 1983—; cons. Hennepin County (Minn.) Gen. Hosp., 1955—. Contbr. articles to profl. jours. With USPHS, 1941-47. Rockefeller Found. fellow, 1946; recipient Samuel Harvey award Am. Assn. Cancer Edn., 1983, Wyeth award Pacific Coast Fertility Soc., 1983, Pioneer award Minn. Dept. of Health, 1991, Recognition award Hennepin County (Minn.) Cmty. Prevention Coalition, 1994, citation from Surgeon Gen. Jocelyn Elders, 1994, Recognition award Assn. Schs. Pub. Health, 1995; named Disting. Alumnus 2000, Case Western Reserve Sch. Medicine. Fellow APHA (chmn. infectious disease monograph subcom. 1961-68, mem. com. evaluations and standards 1962-66, governing coun. 1964-70, resolutions com. 1964-65, chmn. subcom. on drugs 1964-65, vice chmn. epidemiology sect. 1966, chmn. epidemiology sect. 1967, program area com. communicable diseases 1966-70, mem. tech. devel. bd. 1966-70, v.p. 1993-94, John Snow award 1983, Sedgwick Meml. medal 1996), Am. Coll. Epidemiology (bd. dirs. 1979-89, chmn. edn. com. 1985-92, Abraham H. Lilienfeld award 1989, cert. Appreciation 1991), Am. Heart Assn. (coun. epidemiology 1965, hon.); mem. AAAS, AAUP, Am. Assn. Pub. Health Physicians, Am. Coll. Preventive Medicine (sec. coun. rsch. 1956-59, chmn. 1959-64), Am. Epidemiol. Soc. (v.p. 1978), Am. Thoracic Soc. Am. Venereal Disease Assn., Am. Cancer Soc. (Minn. divsn.), Assn. Mil. Surgeons U.S., Assn. Tchrs. Preventive Medicine, Internat. Epidemiol. Soc., Internat. Soc. Cardiology, Internat. Soc. Thrombosis and Hemostasis, Mid. States Pub. Health Assn., Minn. Pub. Health Assn. (Pub. Health Achievement award 1987), N.Y. Acad. Scis., Pub. Health Cancer Assn., Soc. Epidemiol. Rsch. (exec. bd. 1980, award for Outstanding Contbns. to Field of Epidemiology 1992), Phi Beta Kappa, Alpha Omega Alpha, Phi Zeta, Sigma Xi, Phi Kappa Phi, Delta Omega (award selection com. 1985, pres. Pi chpt. 1985—, nat. pres.-elect 1990-92, pres. 1993-95). Office: U Minn Mayo Meml Bldg Box 197 420 Delaware St SE Minneapolis MN 55455-0374 Fax: 612-626-6931. E-mail: schum009@maroon.tc.umn.edu.

SCHUNK, MAE, state official; b. Greenwood, Wis., May 21, 1934; m. William Schunk; 1 child. BS in Elem. Edn., U. Wis., Eau Claire; MS in Gifted/Talented Edn., U. St. Thomas. Curriculum specialist, asst. prin., elem. tchr. various pub. schs.; enrichment specialist Phalen Lake Elem. Sch., St. Paul; lt. gov. State of Minn., 1999—. Mem. Minn. Exec. Coun.; chair Capitol Area Archtl. Planning Bd.; co-chair The Minn. Alliance with Youth, the NetDay Minn. Program, Minn. Office of Citizenship and Vol. Svcs. Avocations: flower and vegetable gardening, creative cooking and baking, stained glass, watercolor painting, fishing. Office: Office of Lt Governor 130 State Capitol Saint Paul MN 55155-0001*

SCHUPP, RONALD IRVING, clergyman, missionary; b. Syracuse, N.Y., Dec. 10, 1951; s. George August and Shirley Louise (Mitchell) S. Ordained ministry, The Old Country Ch., 1972; ordained Bapt. Ministry, 1976. Cert. Moody Bible Inst., 1986, 1988, Emmaus Bible Coll., 1996, 1997, Ctr. Biblical Counseling, 2001, Henry George Sch. of Soc. Sci.. Chgo., 2002; Advanced Cert. Evang. Tng. Assn., 1992. Missionary, asst. pastor The Old Country Ch. Inc., Chgo., 1972-76; missionary Solid Rock Bapt. Ch., 1976-89, Marble Rock Missionary Bapt. Ch. (Ch.-Lic. Pastoral Coun.) , Chgo., 1990—; field organizer and staff person Nite Pastor, 1972—78; Southern Culture Exchange, 1973—76; Alt. Christian Training Sch. Chgo., 1974—78; The Great Am. Coffeehouse, 1976—78; Chgo. Area Conf. on Hunger and Malnutrition, 1974—78. Asst. dir. Uptown Community Orgn, Chgo, 1974—76; dir. Chgo. Action Ctr, 1978—80; mem. Chgo. Clergy and Laity Concerned, 1981—87; Rep. Chgo. Welfare Rights Organ., 1986—88. Mem. Chgo. Coalition for the Homeless, 1988—99, vol. organizer, 1988—94, mem. empowerment adv. com., 1991—94; mem. steering com. 1st Congl. Dist. Ministerial Assn., 1993—95, chair housing com., 1993—95; Mem. Am. Assn. Christian Counselors , 2001—. Named Wa-Kin-Ya-Wicha-Ho Thunder Voice by trad. Lakota Elders, 1993, Kiyuyakki Northern Lights by Inuit Elder Etok, 1994; recipient Letter of Commendation, Chgo. Fire Dept., 1983, appreciation award, West Englewood United Orgn. / Clara's House Shelter, Chgo., 1992. Mem.: North Am. Shortwave Assn., AARP (life). Democrat. Avocation: radio. Home and Office: 6412 N Hoyne Ave Apt 3A Chicago IL 60645-5655

SCHURZ, FRANKLIN DUNN, JR. media executive; b. South Bend, Ind., May 22, 1931; s. Franklin Dunn and Martha (Montgomery) S.; m. Robin Rowan Tullis, Nov. 22, 1975 (div. 1985). AB, Harvard U., 1952, MBA, 1956, A.M.P., 1984. Exec. asst. South Bend Tribune, 1956-60, dir., 1971-76, sec., 1970-75, assoc. pub., 1971-72, editor, pub., 1972-82, exec. v.p., 1975-76, pres., 1976-82; asst. pub. Morning Herald and Daily Mail, Hagerstown, Md., 1960-62, pub., 1962-70, editor, 1966-70; pres. Schurz Communications, Inc., 1982—, treas., 1983-89. Bd. dirs. Atlantic Salmon Fedn., MSTV. Chmn. Ind. Arts Commn., 1979-81; bd. regents St. Marys Coll., Notre Dame, Ind., 1977-83; chmn. adv. coun. Coll. Arts and Letters Notre Dame U., 1980-82; bd. dirs. Ind. Endowment Ednl. Excellence Inc., Indpls., 1987-90; mem. pres.'s coun. Ind. U., Bloomington, 1988-94; bd. dirs. C-Span, 1997—, MSTV, 2001—. 2d lt. U.S. Army, 1952-54. Recipient Presdl. Award of Merit Nat. Newspaper Assn., 1965, Frank Rogers award Rotary, South Bend, 1980 Mem. Am. Press Inst. (bd. dirs. 1985-94), AP (chmn. audit com. 1979-84), Chesapeake AP Assn. (past pres.), Md.-Del.-D.C. Press Assn. (past pres.), Hoosier State Press Assn. (past pres.), Newspaper Advt. Bur. (past bd. dirs.), South Bend Mishawaka Area C. of C. (pres. 1980-82), Am. Soc. Newspaper Editors, Am. women in Radio and TV (Found. hon. trustee 1996—), Inland Press Assn., Inst. Newspaper Fin. Execs. (past pres.), South Bend Country Club, Nat. Press Club, Soc. Profl. Journalists. Presbyterian. Home: 1329 Erskine Manor Hl South Bend IN 46614-2186 Office: Schurz Communications Inc 225 W Colfax Ave South Bend IN 46626-1000

SCHURZ, SCOTT CLARK, journalist, publisher; b. South Bend, Ind., Feb. 23, 1936; s. Franklin Dunn and Martha (Montgomery) S.; m. Kathryn Joan Foley, Aug. 5, 1967; children: Scott Clark, Alexandra Carol, John Danforth. BA, Denison U., 1957; LHD (hon.), Ind. U., 2000. Asst. instr. U. Md., 1957-58; adminstrv. asst. South Bend Tribune, 1960-66; circulation cons. Imperial Valley Press, El Centro, Calif., 1966; pres. Hoosier Times, Inc.; dir., v.p. Schurz Comms., Inc.; pub., editor-in-chief Martinsville (Ind.) Reporter-Times, Ind., Bloomington Herald-Times, Bedford Times-Mail, Mooresville The Times, Beech Grove Southside Times; pres. Kiva Telecomm., Inc. Pres., Bloomington Boys' Club, 1970-71, Jr. Achievement Monroe County, 1971-73; bd. dirs. United Way Monroe County, 1979-81, Cmty. Found. Area Arts Coun. Served with U.S. Army, 1958-60. Mem. World Assn. Newspapers (bd. dirs.), Internat. Newspaper Mktg. Assn. (pres. 1986, treas. 1997—), Inland Daily Press Assn. (pres. 1989), Newspaper Assn. Am. (bd. dirs. 1992-95), Inter-Am. Press Assn. (bd. dirs. 1995—), Hoosier State Press Assn. (pres. 1989, 97), World Press Freedom Com. (exec. com.), Internat. Press Inst., Newspaper Advt. Bur. (bd. dirs. 1987-92), Newspaper Assn. Am. Found. (pres.). Republican. Presbyterian. Office: Hoosier Times Inc 1900 S Walnut St Bloomington IN 47401-7720

SCHUSTER, ELAINE, civil rights professional; b. Detroit, Sept. 26, 1947; d. William Alfred and Aimee Isabelle (Cote) LeBlanc; m. James William Schuster, Sept. 6, 1969; 1 child, Cambrian James. BA, Wayne State U., 1972, postgrad., 1974-75, paralegal cert., 1991. Asst. payments Mich. Dept. Social Svcs., Detroit, 1972-73; rights rep. Mich. Dept. Civil Rights, 1973-80, 82-87, 90, asst. dir. div., 1987-90, supr., 1993-97, dir. Svc. Ctr., 1997-99, contract coord., 1999—; ct. adminstr. Chippewa-Ottawa Conservation Ct., Bay Mills, Mich., 1980-82; quality assurance coord. State Mental Health Facility, Southgate, 1991-93; acting interim dir. Mich. Indian Commn., Detroit, 1995. Author: Critique, An Indian Tours Michilimackinac, 1981; contbr. articles and poems to mags. and profl. jours. Bd.

dirs. Tri-County Native Ams., Warren, Mich., 1982-89, sec. Native Am. Sesquicentennial subcom., Mich., 1987; mem. Linking Lifetimes, mentor program for Native Am. youth, 1992-93; sec., newsletter editor various civic orgns.; also other polit. and civic activities. Native Am. fellow Mich. State U., 1989. Mem. NAACP (housing com. S. Oakland br. 2000), ACLU (bd. dirs. Union-Oakland county 1987-88). Democrat. Avocations: exploring local historical and natural places of interest, historical re-enactment, research, fitness. Office: Mich Dept Civil Rights Cadillac Pl Ste 3-600 3054 W Grand Blvd Detroit MI 48202

SCHUTTA, HENRY SZCZESNY, neurologist, educator; b. Gdansk, Poland, Sept. 15, 1928; came to U.S., 1962, naturalized, 1967; s. Jakub and Janina (Zerbst) S.; m. Henryka Kosmal, Apr. 29, 1950; children—Katharine, Mark, Caroline. M.B., B.S., U. Sydney, Australia, 1955, M.D., 1968. Jr. resident, then sr. resident St. Vincent's Hosp., Sydney, 1956-58; acad. registrar, house physician Nat. Hosp. Nervous Diseases, London, 1958-62; neurologist Pa. Hosp., Phila., 1962-73; asso. prof. neurology U. Pa. Med. Sch., 1963-73; prof. neurology, chmn. dept. SUNY Downstate Med. Center, Bklyn., 1973-80; prof. U. Wis. Med. Sch., 1980-98, chmn. dept. neurology, 1980-95, prof. emeritus, 1999; prof. neurology U. Ariz., Tucson, 2001—. Achievements include research on bilirubin encephalopathy, cerebral edema, degeneration and regeneration of muscle, history of medicine. Home: 35 Mountain View Ln PO Box 4692 Tubac AZ 85646 Office: U Hosp 600 Highland Ave Madison WI 53792-0001 E-mail: hsschutta@aol.com.

SCHUTTER, DAVID JOHN, banker; b. Erie, Pa., Apr. 21, 1945; s. Donald John and Ruth Margaret (Hilbert) S. m. Ellen Carol Hoffman, June 18, 1967; children: David, Erica. BS with honors and distinction, Pa. State U., 1967; postgrad., Mich. State U., 1967-68, Ohio State U., 1973-75; cert., Stonier Grad. Sch. Banking, 1981. Asst. v.p. Huntington Nat. Bank, Columbus, Ohio, 1973-80; v.p. Ameritrust Co., Cleve., 1980-81, v.p., mgr. asset based lending dept., 1981-86, sr. v.p. secured lending div., 1986-89, dep. sr. loan adminstr., 1989-90, sr. cred. pol. off., 1990-92; sr. v.p., regional credit exec. Soc. Nat. Bank, 1992-94; exec. v.p., chief credit officer, 1994-97; exec. v.p., sr. lending officer Key Bank NA, Cleve., 1997—; exec. v.p., chief credit officer Key Corp., 2000—. Pres. AT Comml. Corp., 1986-96; panelist Robert Morris Assocs., Cleve., 1981, 93, mem., 1986—, Cleve. Bar Assn., 1986. Served to capt. U.S. Army, 1968-72. Mem. Nat. Comml. Fin. Assn. (bd. dirs. 1986—), Key Bank (dir., mem. exec. com., 2000—), Beta Gamma Sigma, Omicron Delta Epsilon. Office: Key Bank NA 127 Public Sq Cleveland OH 44114-1216 E-mail: david_schutter@keybank.com.

SCHUTZIUS, LUCY JEAN, retired librarian; b. Cin., Dec. 27, 1938; d. Gregory Girard and Harriet Elsa (Wiggers) Wright; m. Paul Robert Wilson, Aug. 25, 1962 (div. 1968); 1 child Ellen Field ; m. William Carl Schutzius, Dec. 12, 1976; stepchildren: Christopher Matthew, Catharine Alexander, John Benedict, Margaret Elizabeth. BA in French, Middlebury Coll., 1960; MLS, U. Ill., 1963. Tech. libr. Chanute AFB, Rantoul, Ill., 1963-65; libr. Coll. Prep. Sch., Cin., 1969-74; pub. svcs. libr. Raymond Walters Coll., 1974-79, dir. libr., 1979-92, sr. libr., 1988—2001, sr. libr. emerita, 2001—. Access svcs. libr. U. Cin. Coll. Engring., 1992—2001. Mem.: Friends of Univ. Librarians. Home: 3444 Stettinius Ave Cincinnati OH 45208-1204 E-mail: lucy.wilson@uc.edu.

SCHWAB, DAVID, state legislator; b. 1944; m. Phyllis Schwab, 1966; three children. Owner Schwab's Pines; farmer and businessman; rep. Mo. State Ho. Reps. Dist. 157. Former chmn. Farmers for Emerson Com.; former mem. Farmers for Ashcroft Com., Farmers to Elect Sen. Bon State Com.; mem. Mo. State Agr. Stabilization Conservation Com., Gov. Ashcroft's Adv. Coun. on Agr.; former committeeman Ward 6, Byrd; former pres. congregation St. Paul Luth. Ch., Jackson, Mo., Sunday sch. tchr., chmn. bd. elders, chmn. men's club; former mem. St. Paul Sch. Bd. Edn. Mem. Nat. Fedn. Ind. Businessmen, Am. Tree Farm Sys., Mo. State Christmas Tree Growers Assn., Cape County Far Bur. (past pres.), Jackson C. of C., NRA. Office: Mo Ho of Reps State Capitol 201 W Capitol Ave Rm 203B Jefferson City MO 65101-1556

SCHWAB, GLENN ORVILLE, retired agricultural engineering educator, consultant; b. Gridley, Kans., Dec. 30, 1919; s. Edward and Lizzie (Sauder) S.; married; children: Richard, Lawrence,Mary Kay. BS, Kans. State. U., 1942; MS, Iowa State U., 1947, PhD, 1951; postdoctoral, Utah State U., 1966. Registered profl. engr., Ohio. Instr. to prof. agrl. engring. Iowa State U., Ames, 1947-56; prof. agrl. engring. Ohio State U., Columbus, 1956-85, ret., 1985, prof. emeritus Ohio, 1985—. Co-author: Soil and Water Conservation Engineering, 4th edit., 1993, Agricultural and Forest Hydrology, 1986, Soil and Water Management Systems, 4th edit., 1996; contbr. articles to profl. jours. Served to capt. U.S. Army, 1942-46. Fellow Am. Soc. Agrl. Engrs. (bd. dirs. soil and water div. 1976-78, Hancock Brick and Tile Drainage Engr. 1968, John Deere medal 1987), ASTM, Soil and Water Conservation Soc. Am., Am. Geophys. Union, Internat. Commn. Irrigation and Drainage. Avocations: rock polishing, wood working, photography, traveling. Home: 2637 Summit View Rd Powell OH 43065-8446

SCHWAB, GRACE S. state legislator; m. Steven Schwab; 3 children. BS, postgrad., Mankato State U. Mem. Minn. State Senate, 2000—, mem. crime prevention com., edn. com., transp. com., E-12 edn. budget divsn. com., taxes com., income and sales tax budget divsn. com. Home: 1858 Greenwood Dr Albert Lea MN 56007 Office: 151 State Office Bldg Saint Paul MN 55155-1206 E-mail: sen.grace.schwab@senate.leg.state.mn.us.

SCHWAB, JAMES CHARLES, urban planner; b. Oceanside, N.Y., Dec. 20, 1949; s. Charles Francis and Hazel Dorothy (Waters) S.; m. Jean Catlett, June 8, 1985; children: Jessica, Anna. BA in Polit. Sci., Cleve. State U., 1973; MA in Urban & Regional Planning, MA in Journalism, U. Iowa, 1985. Purchasing agt. Kaufman Container Co., Cleve., 1973-75; rsch. assoc. No. Ohio Project on Nat. Priorities, 1975-76; sales rep. Met. Life Ins. Co., Willoughby Hills, Ohio, 1976-78; exec. dir. Iowa Pub. Interest Rsch. Group, Iowa City, 1979-81; rsch. asst. Legis. Extended Assistance Group, 1982-85; asst. editor Am. Planning Assn., Chgo., 1985-90, sr. rsch. assoc., 1990—. Author: Raising Less Corn and More Hell, 1988, Industrial Performance Standards for a New Century, 1993, Deeper Shades of Green, 1994; author, prin. investigator: Planning for Post-Disaster Recovery and Reconstruction, 1998, Planning and Zoning for Concentrated Animal Feeding Operations, 1998; editor Zoning News, 1990—, Environment and Devel., 1992-96; contbr. articles to profl. publs. Chmn. Environ. Concerns Working Group, Met. Chgo. synod Evang. Luth. Ch. Am., 1989—; chmn. Task Force on Care of Creation, Region 5, Dubuque, Iowa, 1992-93; mem. ch. coun. Augustana Luth. Ch., Chgo., 1990-93; co-leader Luth. Environ. Network of the Synods, 1997—. Mem. Soc. Midland Authors (bd. dirs., newsletter editor 1990-95, membership sec. 1995-97, chmn. non-fiction awards 1995-96, chmn. biography awards 2000-02, pres. 1997-99, treas. 1999-2001), Soc. Environ. Journalists, Soc. Profl. Journalists, Investigative Reporters and Editors, Am. Planning Assn., Am. Inst. Cert. Planners. Lutheran. Avocations: travel, reading history, health club workouts, ethnic restaurants. Home: 1755 N Campbell Ave Chicago IL 60647-5205 Office: Am Planning Assn 122 S Michigan Ave Ste 1600 Chicago IL 60603-6190 E-mail: jschwab@planning.org.

SCHWAN, ALFRED, food products executive; CEO, chmn. Schwan Sales Enterprises, Inc., Marshall, Minn., 1965-2000; chmn., 1965—. Office: Schwan Sales Enterprises 115 W College Dr Marshall MN 56258-1747

SCHWANDA, TOM, religious studies educator; b. E. Stroudsburg, Pa., Oct. 23, 1950; s. Theodore Frank and Madlyn Betty (Backensto) S.; m. Grace Elaine Dunning, July 30, 1977; children: Rebecca Joy, Stephen Andrew. Student, Worcester Polytechnic Inst., 1968-69; BA in Econ., Moravian Coll., 1969-72; student, Gordon-Conwell Sem., 1972-74; MDiv, New Brunswick Sem., 1975; DMin, Fuller Theol. Sem., 1992. Ordained to ministry Reformed Ch. in Am., 1975. Pastor Wanaque (N.J.) Reformed Ch., 1975-87; pastor congl. care Immanuel Reformed Ch., Grand Rapids, Mich., 1987-92; interim sr. pastor Remembrance Reformed Ch., 1992-93; rsch. fellow H. Henry Meeter Ctr. for Calvin Studies Calvin Coll., 1993-95; instr. spirituality and worship Bethlehem Ctr. for Spirituality, 1993—; dir. Reformed Spirituality Network, 1992—; assoc. for spiritual formation Reformed Ch. in Am., 1995-99; prof. spiritual formation Reformed Bible Coll., Grand Rapids, Mich., 1999—. Organizer, convener Gathering Reformed Spirituality, 1993, 94, 95, 97, 99, 2001; chair spirituality com. Synod of Great Lakes, 1989-2000, mem. Christian discipleship com., 1988-94; mem. ch. life, evangelism, missions com. South Grand Rapids Classics, chair, 1992; mem. commn. on worship Reformed Ch. in Am., 1978-94; mem. care of students com. Passaic Classis, 1975, 87, chair, 1978, 83-86, pres., 1979; adj. prof. spirituality and spiritual direction and worship Fuller Theol. Sem., San Francisco Theol. Sem., No. Bapt. Theol. Sem., Western Theol. Sem., Columbia Theol. Sem., Charlotte, Orlando, Reformed Theol. Sem., Charlotte. Author: Celebrating God's Presence: The Transforming Power of Public Worship, 1995; contbr. articles to religious jours.; author poetry; manuscript reader, evaluator religious pub. co. Established, managed Wanaque Cmty. Food Pantry, 1977-87; vol. Domestic Crisis Ctr., Grand Rapids, 1988—; bd. dirs. Nat. Inst. Rehabilitation Engring., Hewitt, N.J., 1984—, pres. bd. dirs., 1986—. Recipient Barnabas award Iglesia Cristiana Ebenezer, 1987. Mem. Czechoslovak Soc. Arts and Sci., Czechoslovak Hist. Conf., Soc. for Study of Christian Spirituality. Avocations: running, landscaping, genealogy/family history. Home: 6125 Capitan Dr SE Grand Rapids MI 49546-6721 Office: Reformed Bible Coll 3333 E Beltline Ave NE Grand Rapids MI 49525-9781 E-mail: tschwanda@reformed.edu.

SCHWANK, JOHANNES WALTER, chemical engineering educator; b. Zams, Tyrol, Austria, July 6, 1950; came to U.S., 1978; s. Friedrich Karl and Johanna (Ruepp) S.; m. Lynne Violet Duguay; children: Alexander Johann, Leonard Friedrich, Hanna Violet, Rosa Joy. Diploma in chemistry, U. Innsbruck, Austria, 1975, PhD, 1978. Mem. faculty U. Mich., Ann Arbor, 1978—, assoc. prof. chem. engring., 1984-90, acting dir. Ctr. for Catalysis and Surface Sci., 1985-90, prof., interim chmn. dept. chem. engring., 1990-91, assoc. dir. Electron Microbeam Analysis Lab., 1990—; chmn. dept. chem. engring., 1991-95; prof. chem. engring. U. Mich., Ann Arbor, 1995—. Vis. prof. U. Innsbruck, 1987-88, Tech. U. Vienna, 1988; cons. in field. Patentee bimetallic cluster catalysts, hydrodesulfurization catalysts and microelectronic gas sensors; contbr. over 100 articles to sci. jours. Fulbright-Hays scholar, 1978. Mem. AAAS, Am. Chem. Soc., Am. Inst. Chem. Engrs., Mich. Catalysis Soc. (sec.-treas. 1982-83, v.p. 1983-84, pres. 1984-85), Am. Soc. Engring. Edn. Home: 2335 Placid Way Ann Arbor MI 48105-1295 Office: U Mich Dept Chem Engring 2300 Hayward St Ann Arbor MI 48109-2136 E-mail: schwank@engin.umich.edu.

SCHWARTZ, ALAN E. lawyer, director; b. Detroit, Dec. 21, 1925; s. Maurice H. and Sophia (Welkowitz) S.; m. Marianne Shapero, Aug. 24, 1950; children: Marc Alan, Kurt Nathan, Ruth Anne. Student, Western Mich. Coll., 1944-45; BA with distinction, U. Mich., 1947; LLB magna cum laude, Harvard U., 1950; LLD, Wayne State U., 1983, U. Detroit, 1985. Bar: N.Y. 1951, Mich. 1952. Assoc. Kelley, Drye & Warren, N.Y.C., 1950-52; mem. Honigman, Miller, Schwartz & Cohn, Detroit, 1952—. Spl. asst. counsel N.Y. State Crime Commn., 1951; bd. dirs. Pulte Corp. Editor: Harvard Law Rev., 1950. Dir. Detroit Symphony Orch.; v.p., bd. dirs. United Found.; bd. dirs. Detroit Renaissance, New Detroit, Jewish Welfare Fedn. Detroit, Wayne State Univ. Found.; trustee Cmty. Found. for Southeastern Mich., Interlochen Arts Acad.; adv. mem. Arts Commn., City of Detroit; mem. investment com. Krespe Found. Served as ensign Supply Corps, USNR, 1945-46. Recipient Mich. Heritage Hall of Fame award, 1984, George W. Romney award for lifetime achievement in volunteerism, 1994, Max M. Fisher Cmty. Svc. award, 1997. Mem. Mich. Bar Assns. Clubs: Franklin Hills Country; Detroit, Economic (dir.). Office: Honigman Miller Schwartz & Cohn 2290 1st National Bldg Detroit MI 48226

SCHWARTZ, ALAN GIFFORD, sport company executive; b. N.Y.C., Nov. 7, 1931; s. Kevie Waldemar and Vera (Isaacs) S.; m. Roslyn Smulian, Sept. 6, 1958; children: Steven, Andrew, Sally, Elizabeth. BS, Yale U., 1952; MBA, Harvard U., 1954. Ptnr. Gifford Investment Co., Chgo., 1954—; CEO Tennis Corp. of Am., 1969—, chmn. bd., 1974—. Dir. Firstar Bank Ill., Comtrex Systems, Inc., Mt. Laurel, N.J.; trustee Roosevelt U., 1994—, Inst. European & Asian Studies, 1993—; v.p. U.S. Tennis Assn., 1994—. Contbr. articles to profl. jours.; editorial cons. Club Industry mag., 1985—. Bd. dirs. Grad. Sch. of Bus., Duke U., Durham, N.C., 1977—, McCormick Boys and Girls Club, 1989—. Elected to Club Industry Hall of Fame, 1987. Mem. Standard Club of Chgo., Exec. Club. Chgo. Jewish. Avocations: travel, tennis. Office: Tennis Corp of Am 3611 N Kedzie Ave Chicago IL 60618-4513

SCHWARTZ, ALAN LEIGH, pediatrician, educator; b. N.Y.C., Apr. 25, 1948; s. Robert and Joyce (Goldner) S.; m. Judith Child, June 22, 1974; 1 child, Timothy Child. BA, PHD in Pharmacology, Case Western Res. U., 1974, MD, 1976. Diplomate Am. Bd. Pediatrics. Intern Children's Hosp., Boston, 1976-77, resident, 1976-78, fellow Dana Farber Cancer Inst., 1978-80; instr. Harvard Med. Sch., 1980-81, asst. prof., 1981-83, assoc. prof., 1983-86; prof. pediatrics, molecular biology and pharmacology Washington U. Sch. Medicine, St. Louis, 1986—, chmn. dept. pediatrics, 1995—; chmn. faculty practice plan Washington U., 1999—2001. Vis. scientist MIT, Boston, 1979-82; mem. sci. adv. bd. Nat. Inst. Child Health and Human Devel., NIH, Bethesda, Md., 1988-94; investigator Am. Heart Assn. Alumni Endowed Prof. Pediats. Wash. U. Sch. Medicine, 1987-97, Harriet B. Spoehrer Prof. Pediats., 1997—. Mem. Inst. Medicine of NAS. Office: Washington U Sch Medicine Dept Pediatrics Box 8116 One Children's Pl Saint Louis MO 63110-1093

SCHWARTZ, DONALD LEE, lawyer; b. Milw., Dec. 8, 1948; s. Bernard L. and Ruth M. (Marshall) S.; m. Susan J. Dunst, June 5, 1971; children: Stephanie Jane, Cheryl Ruth. BA, Macalester Coll., 1971; JD, U. Chgo., 1974. Bar: Ill. 1974. Assoc. Sidley & Austin, Chgo., 1974-80, ptnr., 1980-88, Latham & Watkins, Chgo., 1988—. Chmn. Ill. Conservative Union, 1979-81, bd. dirs. 1977-85. Served with U.S. Army, 1971-77. Mem. ABA (uniform comml. code com., comml. fin. svcs. commn.), Ill. Bar Assn. (sec. coun. banking and bankuprtcy sect. 1982-83), Chgo. Bar Assn. (chmn. comml. law com. 1980-81, fin. insts. com. 1982-83), Ivanhoe Country Club, Sea Pines Country Club, Met. Club. Republican. Episcopalian. Avocation: golf. Home: 191 Park Ave Glencoe IL 60022-1351 Office: Latham & Watkins Ste 5800 Sears Tower Chicago IL 60606 E-mail: Donald.schwartz@lw.com.

SCHWARTZ, ELEANOR BRANTLEY, academic administrator; b. Kite, Ga., Jan. 1, 1937; d. Jesse Melvin and Hazel (Hill) Brantley; children: John, Cynthia. Student, U. Va., 1955, Ga. Southern Coll., 1956-57; BBA, Ga. State U., 1962, MBA, 11963, DBA, 1969. Adminstrv. asst. Fin. Agy., 1954, Fed. Govt., Va., Pa., Ga., 1956-59; asst. dean admissions Ga. State U., Atlanta, 1961-66, asst. prof., 1966-70; assoc. prof. Cleve. State U., 1970-75, prof. and assoc. dean, 1975-80; dean, Harzfeld prof. U. Mo., Kansas City, 1980-87, vice chancellor acad. affairs, 1987-91, interim chancellor, 1991-92, chancellor, 1992-99; prof. mgmt. U. Mo. Block Sch., 1999—. Disting. vis. prof. Berry Coll., Rome, N.Y. State U. Coll., Fredonia, Mons U., Belgium; cons. pvt. industry U.S., Europe, Can.; bd. dirs. Rsch. Med. Ctr., Waddell & Reed Funds, Inc., Toy and Miniature Mus., Menorah Med. Ctr. Found., NCAA, NCCJ, Econ. Devel. Corp. of Kansas City, Silicon Prairie Tech. Assn. Author: Sex Barriers in Business, 1971, Contemporary Readings in Marketing, 1974; (with Muczyk and Smith) Principles of Supervision, 1984. Chmn., Mayor's Task Force in Govt. Efficiency, Kansas City, Mo., 1984; mem. comm. unity planning and rsch. coun. United Way Kansas City, 1983-85; bd. dirs. Jr. Achievement, 1982-86. Named Career Woman of Yr., Kansas City, Mo., 1989; named one of 60 Women of Achievement, Girl Scouts Coun. Mid Continent, 1983; recipient Disting. Faculty award, Cleve. State U., 1974, Disting. Svc. award, Kans. State U., 1992, YWCA Hearts of Gold award, 2002. Mem.: Alpha Iota Delta, Golden Key, Phi Kappa Phi.

SCHWARTZ, GARRY ALBERT, advertising executive; b. Toledo, Jan. 4, 1949; s. Albert Theodore Otto and Ethel Anna (Weiler) S. BA in Speech, Adrian Coll., 1971; MA in Communication, Bowling Green State U., 1972; postgrad., Ind. U., 1974. Creative dir. S & L Advt. & P.R., Toledo, 1976-78; instr. U.S. Savings League Inst., 1977; conf. leader Aeroquip Corp., Jackson, Mich., 1978-79, sales promotion supr., 1979-87, advt. display mgr., 1987-88, sr. writer, producer, video, pub. rels., 1988-89, advt. prodn. supr., 1989-91; sr. copywriter Donald L. Arends, Inc., Oak Brook, Ill., 1992-96, Alexander Mktg. Svcs., Inc., Grand Rapids, Mich., 1996—. Mem. Lambda Iota Tau, Iota Beta Sigma, Pi Kappa Delta. Avocations: painting, stamp collecting. Home: 2045 Wyndham Hill Dr NE Grand Rapids MI 49505-6353 Office: Alexander Mktg Svcs Inc PO Box 601 Grand Rapids MI 49516-0601

SCHWARTZ, HOWARD WYN, business/marketing educator, consultant; b. Mpls., June 12, 1951; s. Jerry Schwartz and Geraldine (Berg) Brooks; m. Jeannie Marie Holtzmann, Aug. 2, 1975; children: Abigail Jorene, Rachel Elizabeth. BA cum laude, U. Minn., 1973, MBA, 1982, MEd, 1999. Acct. Med. Sch., U. Minn., 1973-77, bus. mgr. dept. neurology, 1977-79, adminstr. found. edn. dept., 1979-82, assoc. to chmn. dept. radiology, 1982-99; chmn. bus./mktg. edn. dept. Robbindale-Cooper H.S., New Hope, Minn., 1999—. Adj. instr. dept. radiology U. Minn., 1982—; pres. Bus. Mgmt. Svcs., Golden Valley, Miss., 1979—; lectr., author topics in bus./mktg. edn., 2000—. Editor-in-chief: RADWORKS Workload Measurement Manual, 1985-87; editor: Radiology Management, 1985-87, Purchasing the Radiology Information System, 1991, Current Concepts in Radiology Management, 1991; contbr. articles to profl. jours. Mem. Cystic Fibrosis Found., Minn., 1980—; chmn. Human Rights Commn., Robbinsdale, 1982-84; sec. Coord. Coun. Minority Concerns, 1984-85; chmn. imaging tech. adv. com. Univ. Hosp. Consortium, 1989-92; dir. Univ. Hosp. Consortium Svcs. Corp., 1990-92, Nat. Summit on Manpower, 1989-92; treas. Tech. Learning Campus Site Coun., Dist. 281, 1990-91, chmn. Bond Referendum campaign, 1995; pres. Armstrong H.S. Parent Assn., Dist. 281, 1991-92. Fellow Am. Healthcare Radiology Adminstrn. (regional pres. 1986-87, nat. pres. 1988-89, sec. edn. found. 1990-91, bd. dirs. edn. found. 1993-95, 97-98, Outstanding Author award 1990, 93, 96, Midwest Region Disting. Mem. award 1991, Gold award 1991); mem. Radiologists Bus. Mgrs. Assn., Delta Kappa Epsilon. Home: 7400 Winnetka Heights Dr Golden Valley MN 55427-3549 Office: PO Box 27405 Minneapolis MN 55427-0405 E-mail: Schwa006@ix.netcom.com., howard_schwartz@rdale.k12.mn.us.

SCHWARTZ, JOHN NORMAN, health care executive; b. Watertown, Minn., Dec. 13, 1945; s. Norman O. and Marion G. (Tesch) S. BA, Augsburg Coll., Mpls., 1967; MHA, U. Minn., 1969. Adminstrv. resident Luth. Hosp. and Med. Ctr., Wheat Ridge, Colo., 1968-69; asst. adminstr. St. Luke's Hosp., Milw., 1969-73, med. adminstr., 1973-75, v.p., 1975-84; sr. v.p. and chief oper. officer Good Samaritan Med. Ctr., 1984-85, pres. and chief exec. officer, 1985-88; exec. v.p. Aurora Health Care Inc., 1988-89; gen. mgr. SmithKline Beecham Clin. Labs., Schaumburg, Ill., 1989-90; chief exec. Trinity Hosp. of Advocate Health Care, Chgo., 1991—. Bd. dirs. Samaritan Health Plan, Milw., 1984-89. Bd. dirs. Gt. Lakes Hemophilia Found., Milw., 1975-89, S.E. Chgo. Devel. Commn., 1996—, East Side Bank, 1998—; Gov.'s appointee to Coun. on Hemophilia and Related Blood Disorders, Madison, 1978; mem. Sullivan Chamber Ensemble, Milw., 1975-84, South Chgo. YMCA, 1993—. Recipient Bd. Mem. of Yr. award Great Lake's Hemophilia Found., 1986, Outstanding Cmty. Leadership award Stony Island C. of C., 1996, Am. Hosp. Assn. Cir. of Distinction award, 1999; named Exec. of Yr. Coun. on Health and Human Svcs. Ministry, 1999. Fellow Am. Coll. Healthcare Execs. (regent 1993-99, Regent's award for sr. exec. leadership 1999). Lutheran. Avocations: jogging, photography, music, choral singing. Office: Trinity Hosp 2320 E 93rd St Chicago IL 60617-3983 E-mail: john.schwartz@advocatehealth.com.

SCHWARTZ, JOSEPH, English language educator; b. Milw., Apr. 9, 1925; s. Alfred George and Mary (Brandt) S.; m. Joan Jackson, Aug. 28, 1954; 1 son, Adam. B.A., Marquette U., 1946, M.A., 1947; Ph.D., U. Wis., 1952. Teaching asst. Marquette U., Milw., 1946-47, instr., 1947-48, 50-54, asst. prof., 1954-59, assoc. prof., 1959-64, prof., 1964-90, chmn. dept. English, 1963-75, prof. emeritus, 1990—. Teaching fellow U. Wis., 1948-50; Chmn. region X Woodrow Wilson Nat. Fellowship Found., 1967-73; pres. bd. edn. Archdiocese of Milw., 1977-79 Author: A Reader for Writers, 3d edit., 1971, Perspectives on Language, 1963, Province of Rhetoric, 1965, Poetry: Meaning and Form, 1969, Hart Crane: A Critical Bibliography, 1970, Hart Crane: A Descriptive Bibliography, 1972, Exposition, 2d edit., 1971, Hart Crane: A Reference Guide, 1983; sr. editor: Renascence Mag., 1978—. Recipient Distinguished Alumni award Marquette U. Sch. Speech, 1967, Outstanding Tchr. award Marquette U., 1974; Ford Found. grantee, 1956; Am. Council Learned Socs. grantee, 1972, 89; HEW grantee, 1966, 67 Mem. Nat. Coun. Tchrs. English (nat. dir. 1965-68), Modern Lang. Assn., Midwest Modern Lang Assn. (exec. com. 1973-76), Fellowship of Cath. Scholars (bd. dirs. 1987-90), Conf. on Christianity and Lit. (bd. dirs. 1987-90), Phi Beta Kappa, Alpha Sigma Nu (hon.). Republican. Roman Catholic. Home: 8516 W Mequon Rd # 112 Thiensville WI 53097-3100 Office: Marquette U PO Box 1888 Renascence Helfaer Bldg Milwaukee WI 53201-1888

SCHWARTZ, JUDY ELLEN, cardiothoracic surgeon; b. Mason City, Iowa, Oct. 5, 1946; d. Walter Carl and Alice Nevada (Moore) S. BS, U. Iowa, 1968, MD, 1971; M.P.H., Johns Hopkins U., 1996. Diplomate Am. Bd. Surgery, Am. Bd. Thoracic Surgery, Am. Bd. Med. Mgmt.; cert. physician exec. Cert. Commn. Med. Mgmt. Intern Nat. Naval Med. Ctr., Bethesda, Md., 1971-72, gen. surgery resident, 1972-76, thoracic surgery resident, 1976-78, staff cardiothoracic surgeon, 1979-82, chief cardiothoracic surgeon, 1982-83; chmn. cardiothoracic surg. dept. Naval Hosp., San Diego, 1983-85, quality assurance program dir., 1985-88. Exec. office Rapidly Deployable Med. Facility Four, 1986-88; asst. prof. surgery Uniformed Svcs. Univ. Health Sci., Bethesda, 1983-99; sr. policy analyst quality assurance Profl. Affairs and Quality Assurance, 1988-90, dep. dir. quality assurance, 1990; dir. clin. policy Health Svcs. Ops., Washington, 1990-94; head performance evaluation and improvement Nat. Naval Med. Ctr., 1994-99; cardiothoracic speciality cons. to naval med. command U.S. Navy, Washington, 1983-84; Dept. Def. rep. to Joint Commn. Accreditation Health Care Orgn. task force on info. mgmt., 1990-93, chmn. 1991-93, task force on IMS Tech., 1993-94; chmn. info mgmt. workshop Fed. Health Care Study Commn.'s Corrd. Fed. Health Care, 1993; corp. med. dir. Medctr. One Health Systems, 1999—, N.Dak. Dept. Corrections & Rehab., 1999-, VPMA Medcenter One, 2000; mem. bd. dir. SCCI; bd. trustees Medcenter One Health Sys., 1999-; mem. adv. com. BCBS Care Mgmt., 1999-. Contbr. articles to profl. pubs. Mem. nat. physician's leadership coun. VHA, 2000; bd. trustees St. Vincent's Nursing Home, 2001—.

Fellow Am. Coll. Cardiology, Am. Coll. Surgeons (com. allied health pers. 1985-91, exec. com. 1987-91, accreditation review com. edn. physician asst. 1988-94, treas. accreditation review com. 1991-93, sr. mem. com. allied health pers. 1991-94); mem. AMA, Am. Thoracic Soc., Am. Med. Women's Assn., Am. Mgmt. Assn., Am. Coll. Physician Execs. Office: Medcenter One Health Systems PO Box 5525 300 N 7th St Bismarck ND 58506-5525 E-mail: medicaldirector@mohs.org.

SCHWARTZ, MARK, retail executive; CEO Hechinger Investment, Largo, Md.; pres., COO KMart Corp., Troy, Mich., 2000—. Office: KMart Corp 3100 W Big Beaver Rd Troy MI 48084

SCHWARTZ, MICHAEL, university president, sociology educator; b. Chgo., July 29, 1937; s. Norman and Lillian (Ruthenberg) S.; m. Ettabelle Slutsky, Aug. 23, 1959 (div. Jan. 1998); children: Monica, Kenneth, Rachel; m. Joanne Rand Whitmore, Nov. 10, 1998. BS in Psychology, U. Ill., 1958, MA in Indsl. Rels., 1959, PhD in Sociology, 1962; LLD (hon.), Youngstown State U., 1990. Asst. prof. sociology and psychology Wayne State U., Detroit, 1962-64; asst. prof. sociology Ind. U., Bloomington, 1964, assoc. prof. sociology, 1966-70; prof., chmn. dept. sociology Fla. Atlantic U., Boca Raton, 1970-72, dean Coll. Social Sci., 1972-76; v.p. grad. studies and rsch. Kent (Ohio) State U., 1976-78, interim pres., 1977, acting v.p. acad. affairs, 1977-78, v.p. acad. and student affairs, 1978-80, provost, v.p. acad. and student affairs, 1980-82, pres., 1982-91; pres. emeritus and trustee's prof. Kent State U., 1991; interim pres. Cleve. State U., 2001—. Trustee Ctrl. State U., 1996-97; acting dir. Inst. for Social Rsch., Ind. U., 1966-67; tng. cons. Operation Head Start in Ind., 1964-70; cons. Office of Manpower, Automation and Tng., U.S. Dept. Labor, 1964-65. Cons. editor, Sociometry, 1966-70, assoc. editor, 1970; reader Am. Sociol. Rev. papers; author: (with Elton F. Jackson) Study Guide to the Study of Sociology, 1968; contbr. articles to profl. jours., chpts. to books. Chmn. Mid-Am. Conf. Coun. Pres.; rep. Nat. Coll. Athletic Assn. Pres.'s Commn.; chmn. divsn. I, 1988; corps evaluators North Ctrl. Assn. Colls. and Schs.; mem. bd. visitors Air U., USAF; mem. Akron (Ohio) Regional Devel. Bd., N.E. Ednl. TV of Ohio, Inc., N.E. Ohio Univs. Coll. Medicine; trustee Akron Symphony Orch. Assn.; mem. State of Ohio Post-Secondary Rev. Entity, 1995; mem. Assn. of Governing Bds. Commn. on Strengthening the Presidency. Recipient Disting. Tchr. award Fla. Atlantic U., 1970-71, Meritorious Svc. award Am. Assn. State Colls. and Univs., 1990; Michael Schwartz Ctr., Kent State U., named in his honor, 1991. Mem. Ohio Tchr. Edn. and Cert. Adv. Commn., Pine Lake Trout Club. Office: Kent State U 405 White Hl Kent OH 44242-0001 E-mail: mschwartz@educ.kent.edu.

SCHWARTZ, MICHAEL ROBINSON, health facility administrator; b. St. Louis, Mar. 18, 1940; s. Henry G. and Edith C. (Robinson) Schwartz; m. Kathleen Nowicki, Dec. 9, 1989; children from previous marriage: Christine, Richard. AB, Dartmouth Coll., 1962; MHA, U. Minn., 1964. Asst. in adminstrn. Shands Tchg. Hosp., Gainesville, Fla., 1966-67, asst. dir., 1967-68, assoc. dir., 1968-73; assoc. adminstr. St. Joseph Mercy Hosp., Pontiac, Mich., 1973-76, pres., 1976-85; exec. v.p. Mercy Health Svcs., Farmington Hills, 1985-96, COO, 1988-96; exec. v.p. Ea. Mich. region Sisters of Mercy Health Corp., 1991-92; pvt. practice Birmingham, Mich., 1996—. Non-resident lectr. U. Mich., 1982—93; cons. prof. Oakland U., 1980—88; asst. prof. hosp. adminstrn. U. Fla., 1967—73; pres. Eastern Mich. Regional Bd. Sisters of Mercy Health Corp., 1976—79; bd. dirs. Lourdes Nursing Home, 1973—83, v.p., 1981—84; bd. dirs. United Way-Pontiac/North Oakland, 1976—85, v.p., 1982—84; bd. dirs. Oakland Health Edn. Program, 1977—85, treas., 1978—79; bd. dirs. Blue Cross/Blue Shield of Mich., 1982—86, coms., 1978—86, chair hosp. contingent to participating hosp. agreement adv. com., 1989—96; bd. dirs. Greater Detroit Area Health Coun., 1983—88, 1993—96, Vis. Nurse Assn., Inc., 1997—, treas., 1998—99, vice chair, 1999—2000, chair, 2000—02; chmn. bd. dirs., pres. Accord Ins. Co. Ltd., 1983—88; chmn. bd. dirs. Mercy Health Plans, 1986—96, Venzke Svc. Co., 1983—88, pres., 1983—84; chmn. bd. dirs., pres. Venzke Ins. Co. Ltd., 1988—96; bd. dirs. Mercy Info. Sys., 1986—92, Pontiac Devel. Found., 1984—86; mem. audit and fin. com. Am. Healthcare Sys., 1988—92; mem. S.E. Mich. Hosp. Coun., chmn. pub. rels. com., 1983—85; bd. dirs. Hosp. Found., 1986—96; mem. Commonfund Healthcare Coun., 1999—; trustee Sisters of Mercy Health Corp., 1991—93, sec. bd. trustees, 1993. Mem. charitable trust Sisters of Mercy, Regional Cmty. Detroit, 1999—. With U.S. Army, 1964—66. Fellow: Am. Coll. Healthcare Execs. (mem. exec. com. higher edn. 1990—93, Mich. Regent's award 1992); mem.: Comprehensive Health Planning Coun. (com. mem. 1976—81), Am. Healthcare Sys. Risk Retention Group (bd. dirs. 1990—91), Mich. Hosp. Assn. (at-large rep. corp. bd. 1990—96, exec. com. 1992—96), Pontiac Urban League (pers. com. 1979). E-mail: swrtzmk@aol.com.

SCHWARTZ, RICHARD BRENTON, English language educator, university dean, writer; b. Cin., Oct. 5, 1941; s. Jack Jay and Marie Mildred (Schnelle) S.; m. Judith Mary Alexis Lang, Sept. 7, 1963; 1 son, Jonathan Francis. AB cum laude, U. Notre Dame, 1963; AM, U. Ill., 1964, PhD, 1967. Instr. English U.S. Mil. Acad., 1967-69; asst. prof. U. Wis.-Madison, 1969-72, assoc. prof., 1972-78, prof., 1978-81; assoc. dean U. Wis.-Madison (Grad. Sch.), 1977, 79-81; prof. English, dean Grad. Sch., Georgetown U., Washington, 1981-98, interim exec. v.p. for main campus academic affairs, 1991-92; interim exec. v.p. for the main campus Georgetown U., 1995-96; prof. English, dean Coll. Arts and Sci. U. Mo., Columbia, 1998—. Mem. exec. bd. Ctr. Strategic and Internat. Studies, 1981-87. Author: Samuel Johnson and the New Science, 1971 (runner-up Gustave O. Arlt prize), Samuel Johnson and the Problem of Evil, 1975, Boswell's Johnson: A Preface to the Life, 1978, Daily Life in Johnson's London, 1983, Japanese edit., 1990, After the Death of Literature, 1997, Nice and Noir: Contemporary American Crime Fiction, 2002, (novels) Frozen Stare, 1989, The Last Voice You Hear, 2001, After the Fall, 2002, Into the Dark, 2002, (short stories) The Biggest City In America, 1999 (Choice Mag. citation); editor: The Plays of Arthur Murphy, 4 vols., 1979, Theory and Tradition in Eighteenth-Century Studies, 1990; contbr. articles to profl. jours. Served to capt. U.S. Army, 1967-69. Decorated Army Commendation medal; recipient Presdl. medal Georgetown U., 1998; Nat. Endowment Humanities grantee, 1970, 87; Inst. for Research in Humanities fellow, 1976; Am. Council Learned Socs. fellow, 1978-79; H.I. Romnes fellow, 1978-81. Mem. Mystery Writers Am., Johnson Soc. So. Calif., Johnson Soc. of London, Am. Soc. Eighteenth-Century Studies, Coun. Grad. Schs., N.E. Assn. Grad. Schs. (exec. com. 1986-88), Assn. Grad. Schs. in Cath. Univs. (exec. com. 1984-87), Assn. Literary Scholars and Critics, Nat. Assn. Scholars, N.Am. Conf. Brit. Studies, Jefferson Club, Mosaic Soc., Alpha Sigma Nu, Alpha Sigma Lambda. Roman Catholic. Home: 5800 Highlands Pkwy Columbia MO 65203-5125 Office: U Mo Coll of Arts and Sci 317 Lowry Hall Columbia MO 65211-6080 E-mail: SchwartzRB@missouri.edu.

SCHWARTZ, RICHARD JOHN, electrical engineering educator, researcher; b. Waukesha, Wis., Aug. 12, 1935; s. Sylvester John and LaVerne Mary (Lepien) S.; m. Mary Jo Collins, June 29, 1957; children: Richard, Stephen, Susan, Elizabeth, Barbara, Peter, Christopher, Margaret. BSEE, U. Wis., 1957; SM, MIT, 1959, ScD, 1962. Mem. tech. staff Sarnoff Rsch. Labs. RCA, Princeton, N.J., 1957-58; instr. MIT, Cambridge, 1961-62; v.p. Energy Conversions, Inc., 1962-64; assoc. prof. Purdue U., West Lafayette, Ind., 1964-71, prof., 1972—, head dept., 1985-95, dean engring., 1995—2001, dir. Optoelectronic Ctr., 1986-89. Co-dir. Nano Tech. Ctr. Purdue U., W. Lafayette, Ind.; cons. solar cells, 1965—. Contbr. chpts. to books, articles to profl. jours. Served to 2nd lt. U.S. Army, 1957-58. Recipient Disting. Svc. medal U. Wis., 1989, Centennial medal, 1991. Fellow: IEEE (William R. Cherry award 1998); mem.: Nat. Elec. Engring. Dept. Heads Assn. (bd. dirs.). Achievements include development of high intensity solar cells, of surface charge transfer device, and of numerical models for solar cells. Office: Purdue U 1280 Engring Adminstrn West Lafayette IN 47907

SCHWARTZHOFF, JAMES PAUL, foundation executive; b. Waukon, Iowa, June 24, 1937; s. Harold J. and Mary (Regan) Schwartzhoff; m. Mary Lou Hess, Apr. 23, 1960; children: Tammara, Eric, Stephanie, Mark, Laurie, Michelle, Steven. B. U. Iowa, 1962. Asst. chief auditor Wis. Dept. Tax, Madison, 1962-67; mgr. treas. dept. Mead Johnson and Co., Evansville, Ind., 1967-69; v.p., treas., investment officer Kettering Found., Dayton, Ohio, 1969—. Chmn., treas. bd. Pastoral Counseling Ctr., Dayton, 1975-81; treas. Ohio River Rd. Runners, Dayton, 1986-87; spkr. nat. investment confs. Past treas. Nat. Issues Forums Inst., Coun. Pub. Policy Edn., Ctr. for Community and Ednl. Devel.; mem. Donor's Forum Ohio Fin. Com., 1990-92; mem. investment com. U. Dayton; adv. com. JMB Endowment and Found. Realty Funds, 1991-94. Cpl. U.S. Army, 1957-59. Mem. AICPA, Found. Fin. Officers Group, Southern Ohio Pension Fund Group. Avocations: bicycling, running, photography, woodworking, skiing. Office: Kettering Found 200 Commons Rd Dayton OH 45459-2799

SCHWARZ, EGON, humanities and German language educator, writer, literary critic; b. Vienna, Austria, Aug. 8, 1922; arrived in U.S., 1949, naturalized, 1956; s. Oscar and Erna S.; m. Dorothea K. Klockenbusch, June 8, 1950; children— Rudolf Joachim, Caroline Elisabeth, Gabriela Barbara. PhD, U. Wash., 1954; Hon. Doctorate, U. Vienna, 1997. Mem. faculty Harvard U., 1954-61; mem. faculty dept. Germanic langs. and lit. Washington U., St. Louis, 1961—, prof. German, 1963—, Rosa May Disting. Univ. prof. in the Humanities, 1975-93, prof. emeritus, 1993—. Vis. prof. U. Hamburg, Fed. Republic Germany, 1962-63, U. Calif., Berkeley, 1963-65, Middlebury Coll., 1969, U. Calif.-Irvine, 1977, U. Tübingen, 1986; William Evans prof. U. Otago, Dunedin, N.Z., 1984; Disting. scholar Ohio State U., Columbus, 1987, U. Graz, Austria, 1989, 93, U. Siegen, 1993-94. Author: Hofmannsthal und Calderon, 1962, Joseph von Eichendorff, 1972, Das verschluckte Schluchzen- Poesie und Politik bei Rainer Maria Rilke, 1972, Keine Zeit für Eichendorff: Chronik unfreiwilliger Wanderjahre; an autobiography, 1979, revised and expanded, 1992, Dichtung, Kritik, Geschichte: Essays zur Literatur 1900-1930, 1983, Literatur aus vier Kulturen: Essays und Besprechungen, 1987, Ich bin Kein Freund allgemeiner Urteile uber ganze Volker: Essays uber osterreischische, deutsche und judische literatur, 2000, Die japanische Mauer: Uhgewohnliche Reisegeschichten, 2002, also numerous other books. Recipient Joseph von Eichendorff medal, 1986, Austrian Medal of Honor for Arts and Scis., 1991, Alexander von Humboldt prize for fgn. scholars, 1995; Guggenheim fellow, 1957-58, Fulbright fellow, 1962-63, sr. fellow NEH, 1970-71, fellow Ctr. for Interdisciplinary Studies, Bielefeld, Germany, 1980-81; grantee Am. Coun. Learned Socs., 1962-63. Mem. MLA, Am. Assn. Tchrs. German, German Acad. Lang. and Lit. (hon.). Home: 1036 Oakland Ave Saint Louis MO 63122-6565 Office: Washington U German Dept Saint Louis MO 63130 E-mail: gabrielas@aol.com.

SCHWARZ, JOHN J.H. state legislator, surgeon; b. Chgo., Nov. 15, 1937; s. Frank William and Helen Veronica (Brennan) S.; m. Anne Louise Ennis, Jan. 16, 1971 (dec. Feb. 1990); 1 child, Brennan Louise. BA, U. Mich., 1959; MD, Wayne State U., 1964. Physician, surgeon, Battle Creek, Mich., 1974—; mayor City of Battle Creek, 1985-87; mem. Mich. Senate from 24th dist., Lansing, 1987—; pres. pro tempore of the Senate, 1993—. Trustee Olivet Coll., 1991—, Wayland Acad., 1992-96; trustee, treas. Am. Legacy Found. Lt. USN, 1965-67. Mem. AMA, ACS, Am. Soc. for Head and Neck Surgery. Republican. Roman Catholic. Office: State Senate State Capital Lansing MI 48909

SCHWARZ, STEVEN R. stationary company executive; Exec. v.p. supply divsn. United Stationers, Inc., Des Plaines, Ill., 1997—. Office: United Stationers Inc 2200 E Golf Rd Des Plaines IL 60016-1257

SCHWARZROCK, SHIRLEY PRATT, writer, lecturer, educator; b. Mpls., Feb. 27, 1914; d. Theodore Ray and Myrtle Pearl (Westphal) Pratt; m. Loren H. Schwarzrock, Oct. 19, 1945 (dec. 1966); children: Kay Linda, Ted Kenneth, Lorraine V. BS, U. Minn., 1935, MA, 1942, PhD, 1974. Sec. to chmn. speech dept. U. Minn., Mpls., 1935, instr. in speech, 1946, team tchr. in creative arts workshops for tchrs., 1955-56, guest lectr. Dental Sch., 1967-72, asst. prof. (part-time) practice adminstrn. Sch. Dentistry, 1972-80; tchr. speech, drama and English Preston (Minn.) H.S., 1935-37; tchr. speech, drama and English, dir. dramatics Owatonna (Minn.) H.S., 1937-39; tchr. creative dramatics and English, tchr.-counselor Webster Groves (Mo.) Jr. H.S., 1939-40; dir. dramatics and tchr.-counselor Webster Groves Sr. H.S., 1940-43; exec. sec. bus. and profl. dept. YWCA, Mpls., 1943-45; tchr. speech and drama Covent of the Visitation, St. Paul, 1958; editor pro-tem Am. Acad. Dental Practice Adminstrn., 1966-68. Guest tchr. Coll. St. Catherine, St. Paul, 1969; vol. mgr. Gift Shop, Eitel Hosp., Mpls., 1981-83, Edina Cmty. Resource Pool, 1992-95; cmty. citizen mem. planning, evaluating, reporting com. Edina Pub. Sch. Sys., 1993-96; tutor for reading, writing, and speaking, 1993-96; cons. for dental med. programs Normandale C.C., Bloomington, Minn., 1968; cons. on pub. rels. to dentists, 1954-96; guest lectr. to various dental groups, 1966-95; lectr. Internat. Congress on Arts and Comm., 1980, Am. Inst. Banking, 1981; condr. tutorials in speaking and profl. office mgmt., 1985-96; owner Shirley Schwawrzrock's Exec. Support Svc., 1989-99; cons. to mktg. comm. mgr. Ergodyne Corp., St. Paul, 1991-92; freelance editor med. support bus., 1992. Author: (books) (series) Coping With Personal Identity, Coping With Human Relationships, Coping With Facts and Fantasies, Coping With Teenage Problems, 1984; individual book titles include: Do I Know the "Me" Others See?, My Life-What Shall I Do With It?, Living With Loneliness, Learning to Make Better Decisions, Grades, What's So Important About Them, Anyway?, Facts and Fantasies About Alcohol, Facts and Fantasies About Smoking, Food as a Crutch, Facts and Fantasies About the Roles of Men and Women, You Always Communicate Something, Appreciating People-Their Likenesses and Differences, Fitting In, To Like and Be Liked, Can You Talk With Someone Else?, Coping With Emotional Pain, Some Common Crutches, Parents Can Be a Problem, Coping With Cliques, Crises Youth Face Today, Effective Dental Assisting, (with L.H. Schwarzrock) 1954, 59, 67, (with J.R. Jensen) 1973, 78, 82, (with J.R. Jensen, Kay Schwarzrock, Lorraine Schwarzrock) 1990, Workbook for Effective Dental Assisting, 1968, 73, 78, 82, 90; (with Donovan F. Ward) Effective Medical Assisting, 1969, 76, Manual for Effective Assisting, 1969, 76; (with C.G. Wrenn) The Coping With Series of Books for High School Students, 1970, The Coping With Manual, 1973, Contemporary Concerns of Youth, 1980; contbr. articles to profl. jours. Pres. Univ. Elem. Sch. PTA, 1955-56; vol. judge Minn. State Hist. Day Program, 1994-98. Fellow Internat. Biog. Assn.; mem. Minn. Acad. Dental Practice Adminstrn. (hon.), Authors Guild, Minn. Hist Soc., Minn. Geneal. Soc., Zeta Phi Eta (pres. 1948-49), Eta Sigma Upsilon. Home: 7448 W Shore Dr Edina MN 55435-4022

SCHWEICKART, JIM, advertising executive, broadcast consultant; b. Toledo, June 25, 1950; s. Norman Marvin and Anne Belle (Cress) S.; m. Deborah J., Aug. 14, 1971; children: Jennifer, Kimberly, Stephen. BA in Polit. Sci, Taylor U., Upland, Ind., 1972. News anchor, announcer Sta. WCMR, Elkhart, Ind., 1967-71; news anchor, disc jockey Sta. WWHC, Hartford City, 1971-72; gen. mgr. Sta. WTUC, Taylor U., 1971; news dir. Sta. WCMR, Elkhart, 1972-74; news anchor Sta. WOWO, Fort Wayne, Ind., 1974-78, Sta. KDKA, Pitts., 1978-79; gen. mgr. Sta. WBCL-FM, Fort Wayne, 1979-85; owner advt. agy., broadcast cons., 1984—. Bd. dirs. Christians for Polit. Alternatives; adv. bd. Taylor U., Fort Wayne campus. Republican. Baptist. Office: 3452 Stellhorn Rd Fort Wayne IN 46815-4630

SCHWEITZER, PETER, advertising agency executive; b. Chgo., Aug. 31, 1939; children: Mark, Cynthia, Jenifer, Samantha; m. Elaine Elkin, 1986; children: Dana, Taylor. B.A., U. of Mich., 1961; MBA, W. Mich. U., 1967. With Post div. Gen. Foods, 1961-69; v.p. Grey Advt., 1969-76; sr. v.p. J. Walter Thompson, 1976-79; sr. v.p. mktg. Burger King Corp., 1990; sr. v.p., gen. mgr., then exec. v.p., gen. mgr. J. Walter Thompson USA, Inc.-Detroit, 1995; v. chmn. of agency ops. J. Walter Thompson Co., Detroit, 1988-95, pres., 1995—. Office: J Walter Thompson Co 500 Woodward Ave 14th Fl Detroit MI 48226-3416 also: 466 Lexington Ave New York NY 10017-3140

SCHWEIZER, KENNETH STEVEN, physics educator; b. Phila., Jan. 20, 1953; s. Kenneth Paul and Grace Norma (Fischer) S.; m. Janis Eve Pelletier, Oct. 18, 1986; children: Gregory Michael, Daniel Patrick. BS, Drexel U., 1975; MS, U. Ill., 1976, PhD, 1981. Postdoctoral rsch. assoc. AT&T Bell Labs., Murray Hill, N.J., 1981-83; sr. mem. tech. staff Sandia Nat. Labs., Albuquerque, 1983-91; prof. materials sci. engring. and chemistry U. Ill., Urbana, 1991—, prof. chem. engring., 1998—, G. Ronald and Margeret H. Morris prof. materials sci., 2001—. Contbr. articles to profl. jours. Recipient Sandia award for Excellence, 1990, R&D 100 award, 1992, Award for Scientific Achievement in Materials Chemistry DOE, 1996, Burnett Tchg. award, 1997, Everitt Tchg. award, 2002. Fellow Am. Phys. Soc. (John H. Dillon medal 1991); mem. Am. Chem. Soc., Soc. Rheology, Sigma Xi, Pi Mu Epsilon. Office: U Ill Dept Materials Sci Engring 1304 W Green St Urbana IL 61801-2920 E-mail: kschweiz@uiuc.edu.

SCHWEMM, JOHN BUTLER, printing company executive, lawyer; b. Barrington, Ill., May 18, 1934; s. Earl M. and Eunice (Butler) S.; m. Nancy Lea Prickett, Sept. 7, 1956; children: Catherine Ann, Karen Elizabeth. AB, Amherst Coll., 1956; JD, U. Mich., 1959. Bar: Ill. 1959. With Sidley & Austin, Chgo., 1959-65; with legal dept. R.R. Donnelley & Sons Co., 1965-69, gen. counsel, 1969-75, v.p., 1971-75, pres., 1981-87, chmn., 1983-89, dir., 1980-92. Bd. dirs. William Blair Mut. Funds, Inc., Walgreen Co., USG Corp. Life trustee Northwestern U., Chgo. Mem. Law Club Chgo., Order of Coif, Phi Beta Kappa. Clubs: Chgo., Univ., Mid-Am., Comml., Hinsdale (Ill.) Golf, Old Elm. Home and Office: 2 Turvey Ct Downers Grove IL 60515-4530

SCHWEND, MICHAEL T. hospital administrator; m. Mary Jo Fitzpatrick. BS in Psychology, Truman State U., 1983, MA in Counseling and Guidance, 1990; MBA, William Woods U., 1997. Pres., CEO Preferred Family Healthcare, Kirksville, Mo. Mem. White House Commn. on Alcohol and Drug Abuse; sec. bd. govs. Truman State U., Kirksville, 2001—; former mem. Mo. Adv. Coun. on Alcohol and Drug Abuse; peer rev. specialist Tex. Commn. on Alcohol and Drug Abuse; active Kirksville R-III Athletic Booster Club; pres. bd. dirs. K-Life outreach program; active Immaculate Cath. Ch. Office: Preferred Family Healthcare 900 E LaHarpe Kirksville MO 63501

SCHWOY, LAURIE ANNETTE, soccer player; b. Balt., Feb. 14, 1978; Mem. U.S. Nat. Women's Soccer Team, 1997—, including U.S. Women's Cup, 1997; mem. Under-20 Women's Nat. Team, 1996—, including bronze medal team at Nordic Cup, Sweden, 1996, championship team, Nordic Cup, Denmark, 1997. Named Soccer Am. Freshman of Yr., 1996, voted ACC Rookie of Yr., 1996. Avocation: dancing. Office: US Soccer Fedn 1801-1811 S Prairie Ave Chicago IL 60616

SCIARRA, JOHN J. physician, educator; b. West Haven, Conn., Mar. 4, 1932; s. John and Mary Grace (Sanzone) S.; m. Barbara Crafts Patton, Jan. 9, 1960; chidren: Vanessa Patton, John Crafts, Leonard Chapman. BS, Yale U., 1953; MD, Columbia U., N.Y.C., 1957, PhD, 1963. Asst. prof. Columbia U., N.Y.C., 1964-68; prof., dept. head U. Minn. Med. Sch., Mpls., 1968-74; prof. Northwestern U. Med. Sch., Chgo., 1974—; chmn. ob-gyn Northwestern Meml. Hosp., 1974—. Editor Gyn-Ob Reference Series, 1973—, Internat. Jour. Gyn-Ob, 1985—. V.p. med. affairs Chgo. Maternity Ctr., Chgo., 1974—. Fellow ACS, Am. Coll. Ob-Gyn. (chmn. internal affairs com. 1985-89); Internat. Fedn. Gyn-Ob. (pres. 1991-94, pres. supporters assn. 1994-2000); mem. Assn. Profs. Gyn-Ob. (sec. 1976-79, pres. 1980-81), Am. Assn. Maternal and Neonatal Health (pres. 1980-89, coun. resident edn. in ob-gyn. 1988-92), Am. Fertility Soc. (Hartman award 1965, bd. dirs. 1971-73), Gyn-Ob. Med. Edn. Found. (sec.-treas. 1987-91, pres. 1991-93), Ctrl. Assn. Ob-Gyn. (trustees 1986-90, pres. 1990-91), Chgo. Gynecol. Soc. (pres. 1990-91), Internat. Soc. Gynecol. Endoscopy (v.p. 1997-99, pres. 1999-2001), Internat. Fedn. Ob-Gyn., Yale Club N.Y.C., Carleton Club (Chgo.). Club: Yale (N.Y.C.); Carleton (Chgo.). Avocation: photography, food, wine. Office: Northwestern U Med Sch 333 E Superior St Chicago IL 60611-3015 E-mail: jsciarra@nmh.org.

SCISM, DANIEL REED, lawyer; b. Evansville, Ind., Aug. 27, 1936; s. Daniel William and Ardath Josephine (Gibbs) S.; m. Paula Anne Sedgwick, June 21, 1958; children: Darby Claire, Joshua Reed. BA, DePauw U., 1958; JD, Ind. U., 1965. Bar: Ind. 1965, U.S. Dist. Ct. (so. dist.) Ind. 1965, U.S. Ct. Appeals (7th cir.) 1967, U.S. Supreme Ct. 1976. Reporter Dayton (Ohio) Jour.-Herald, 1958-59; editor Mead Johnson & Co., Evansville, 1961; first assoc., then ptnr. Roberts, Ryder, Rogers & Scism and predecessor firms, Indpls., 1965—86; ptnr. Barnes & Thornburg, 1987—. Cons. Ind. Personnel Assn., 1984—. Treas. Marion County chpt. Myasthenia Gravis Found., Indpls., 1970; v.p. Marion County Mental Health Assn., Indpls., 1970-71; pres. The Suemma Coleman Agy., Indpls., 1973-74; bd. dirs. Ind. Humanities Coun., 1995-2000, chmn. bd., 1997-98; trustee Indpls. Mus. Art, 2001—; pres. Persimmon Woods Homeowners Assn., 2001-02. With U.S. Army, 1959—62. Edwards fellow Ind. U., 1964. Mem. ABA, Ind. Bar Assn., Indpls. Bar Assn., Ind. State C. of C. (social legis. com. 1970-80). Methodist. Clubs: Indpls. Athletic; Woodland Country (bd. dirs. 1984-88, sec. 1998-99) (Carmel, Ind.). Home: 10909 300 Yard Dr Fishers IN 46038-9306 Office: Barnes & Thornburg 11 S Meridian St Indianapolis IN 46204-3535

SCOBIE, TIMOTHY FRANKLIN, lawyer; b. Chippewa Falls, Wis., July 8, 1964; s. William Mason and Nancy Anne (Clark) S.; m. Michelle Mae Michael, Aug. 10, 1991; 1 child, Lauren Michael. BA, Boston U., 1987; JD, Hamline U., 1990. Bar: Wis. 1991, Minn. 1991, U.S. Ct. Appeals (7th cir.) 1991. Staff atty. Wiley, Wahl et al, Chippewa Falls, 1990-92; dist. atty. County of Chippewa, 1992—. Mem. bd. alumni Breck Sch., Mpls., 1992—; mem bd. advisors U. Wis., Eau Claire, 1992—. Mem. Jaycees (v.p. 1994). Office: 711 N Bridge St Chippewa Falls WI 54729-1845

SCOGLAND, WILLIAM LEE, lawyer; b. Moline, Ill., Apr. 2, 1949; s. Maurice William and Harriet Rebecca S.; m. Victoria Lynn Whitham, Oct. 9, 1976; 1 child, Thomas. BA magna cum laude, Augustana Coll., 1971; JD cum laude, Harvard U., 1975. Bar: Ill. 1975, U.S. Dist. Ct. (no. dist.) Ill. 1975. Assoc. Wildman, Harrold, Allen & Dixon, Chgo., 1975-77, Hughes Hubbard & Reed, Milw., 1977-81; from assoc. to ptnr. Jenner & Block, Chgo., 1981—. Author: Fiduciary Duty: What Does It Mean?, 1989; co-author Employee Benefits Law, 1987. Mem. Phi Beta Kappa, Omicron Delta Kappa. Republican. Office: Jenner & Block One IBM Plz Fl 4000 Chicago IL 60611-7603

SCOLES, CLYDE SHELDON, library director; b. Columbus, Ohio, Apr. 14, 1949; s. Edward L. and Edna M. (Ruddock) S.; m. Diane Francis, July 14, 1976; children: David, Kevin, Karen, Stephen. BS, Ohio State U., 1971; MLS, U. Mich., 1972. Librarian Columbus Pub. Library, 1972-74; library dir. Zanesville (Ohio) Pub. Library, 1974-78; asst. dir. Toledo-Lucas

County Pub. Library, 1978-85, dir., 1985—. Adj. lectr., libr. bldg. cons. U. Mich.; v.p. bd. dirs. Read for Literacy. Mem. ALA, Ohio Libr. Assn., Ohio Libr. Coun., Toledo C. of C., Com. of 100, Maumee Hist. Soc. Club: Torch (Toledo). Lodge: Rotary.

SCOMMEGNA, ANTONIO, physician, educator; b. Barletta, Italy, Aug. 26, 1931; came to U.S., 1954, naturalized, 1960; s. Francesco Paola and Antonietta (Maresca) S.; m. Lillian F. Sinkiewicz, May 3, 1958; children: Paola, Frank, Roger. B.A., State Lyceum A. Casardi, Barletta, 1947; M.D., U. Bari (Italy), 1953. Diplomate: Am. Bd. Obstetrics and Gynecology, also sub-bd. endocrinology and reprodn. Rotating intern New Eng. Hosp., Boston, 1954-55; resident obstetrics and gynecology Michael Reese Hosp. and Med. Center, Chgo., 1956-59, fellow dept. research human reprodn., 1960-61, research asso., 1961; fellow steroid tng. program Worcester Found. Exptl. Biology, also Clark U., Shrewsbury, Mass., 1964-65; asso. prof. obstetrics and gynecology Chgo. Med. Sch., 1965-69; mem. staff Michael Reese Hosp. and Med. Center, 1961—, attending physician obstetrics and gynecology, 1961—, dir. sect. gynecologic endocrinology, 1965-81; dir. ambulatory care obstetrics and gynecology Mandel Clinic, 1968-69, chmn. dept., 1969-89; attending, chief svc. U. Ill. Chgo. Hosp. and Med. Ctr., 1989-98; trustee Mandel Clinic, 1977-80; prof. dept. ob-gyn. Pritzker Sch. Medicine, U. Chgo., 1969-89; prof., head dept. ob-gyn. Coll. Medicine, U. Ill. Chgo., 1989-98. Author numerous articles in field. Fulbright fellow, 1954-55 Fellow Am. Coll. Obstetricians and Gynecologists, Endocrine Soc., Chgo. Inst. Medicine, Am. Gynecol. and Obstet. Soc.; mem. AMA, Ill., Chgo. med. socs., Am. Fertility Soc., Chgo. Gynecol. Soc. (sec. 1976-79, pres. 1981-82), Soc. Study Reprodn., AAAS, Soc. for Gynecologic Investigation. Home: 1023 W Vernon Park Pl Apt E Chicago IL 60607-3447 E-mail: anmis@uic.edu.

SCORZA, SYLVIO JOSEPH, religion educator; b. Zürich, Switzerland, Mar. 21, 1923; came to U.S., 1929; s. Joseph Peter and Helena Christina (Kopp) S.; m. Phyllis Joan VanSetters, June 6, 1952; children: Christine Marie, Philip Joseph, John Forrest. AA, Woodrow Wilson Jr. Coll., 1942; AB, Hope Coll., 1945; BD, Western Theol. Sem., Holland, Mich., 1953; ThD, Princeton Theol. Sem., 1956; PhD, U. Ill., 1972. Ordained to ministry Ref. Ch. in Am., 1955. Stated supply pastor Hickory Bottom Charge, Loysburg, Pa., 1957-58; prof. religion Northwestern Coll., Orange City, Iowa, 1959-90, prof. emeritus, 1990—. Vis. prof. Lancaster (Pa.) Theol. Sem., 1956-57, Western Theol. Sem., Holland, Mich., 1958-59; v.p. Ref. Ch. in Am., N.Y.C., 1988-89, pres., 1989-90, moderator, exec. com., 1990-91; mem. Iowa Bd. Law Examiners, 1997—. Co-editor: Concordance to the Greek and Hebrew Text of Ruth, The Computer Bible, Septuagint series, Vols. XXX, XXX-B, 1988-89; contbr. articles to profl. jours. County del. Iowa Dems., Ft. Dodge, 1984. Recipient Disting. Alumnus award Hope Coll., 1989, Homecoming Honors award Northwestern Coll. N Club, 1990, Handicapped Person of Siouxland award Siouxland Com. for the Handicapped, 1990, Gov.'s award Iowa Commn. of Persons with Disabilities, 1990, Victory award Nat. Rehab. Hosp., 1991, Disting. Alumnus award Western Theol. Sem., 2002. Mem. Internat. Orgn. for Septuagint and Cognate Studies, Smithsonian Instsn., Nat. Geog. Soc., Iowa State Chess Assn. (v.p. 1984-85, dir. postal tournament 1987-97). Avocations: chess, bridge. Home and Office: 520 2nd St SW Orange City IA 51041-1728 E-mail: scorza@nwciowa.edu.

SCOTT, BRUCE A. otolaryngologist; b. Louisville, Sept. 30, 1961; m. Christy Scott; 3 children. MD, U. Tex., 1987. Diplomate Am. Bd. Otolaryngology. Intern Sealy Hosp.-U. Galveston, 1987-88; resident in otolaryngology and head and neck surgery U. Tex. Med. Br., Galveston, 1988-92; fellow in facial plastic and reconstructive surgery U. Tex. Health Sci. Ctr., Houston, 1992-93; pvt. practice Lousiville. Tee-ball, baseball coach, basketball coach. Mem. AMA (bd. trustees, com. on membership, nominating com., AMA Found., mem. resident physician sect. governing coun., chairperson, young physician sect. governing coun., del. to ho. of dels. 1997, 98, mem. surg. caucus exec. com., reference com., mem. women in medicine adv. panel, Outreach Awards). Avocations: golfing, flying radio control planes. Office: AMA 515 N State St Chicago IL 60610-4325 also: 225 Abraham Flexner Way Ste 401 Louisville KY 40202-1850

SCOTT, DEBORAH EMONT, curator; b. Passaic, N.J. d. Harold and Rhoda (Baumgarten) Emont; m. George Andrew Scott, June 4, 1983; children: Meredith Suzanne, Diana Faith. BA, Rutgers U., Livingston Coll., 1973; MA, Oberlin Coll., 1979. Asst. curator Allen Meml. Art Mus., Oberlin, Ohio, 1977-79; curator collections Memphis Brooks Mus. Art, 1979-83; curator The Nelson-Atkins Mus. Art, Kansas City, 1983—, chief curator, 1998—. Project dir. Kansas City Sculpture Pk., 1986-01. Author: (catalogue) Alan Shields, 1983, (essay) Jonathan Borofsky, 1988, (essay) Judith Shea, 1989, (interview) John Ahearn, 1990, (essay) Gerhard Richter, 1990, (essay) Kathy Muehlemann, 1991, (essay) Nate Fors, 1991, (essay) Julian Schnabel, 1991, (essay) Louise Bourgeois, 1994, (essay) Joel Shapiro, 1995, (essay) Lewis deSoto, 1996, (catalogue) Ursula von Rydingsvard, 1997; contbr.: Celebrating Moore: Works from the Collection of the Henry Moore Foundation, Selected by David Mithinson, 1998, Modern Sculpture at The Nelson-Atkins Museum of Art: An Anniversary Celebration, 1999; (CD ROM) Masterworks for Learning: A College Collection Catalogue, Allen Memorial Art Museum, Oberlin College, 1998. Office: Nelson-Atkins Mus Art 4525 Oak St Kansas City MO 64111-1818

SCOTT, DELBERT LEE, state legislator; Rep. Mo. State Ho. Reps. Dist. 119. Home: PO Box 147 700 W 7th St Lowry City MO 64763-9550 Office: Mo Ho of Reps State Capitol Jefferson City MO 65101

SCOTT, JIM, radio personality; b. Bridgeport, Conn. Radio host 700 WLW, Cin., 1984—. Active United Way, The Wellness Cmty. Office: 700 WLW 1111 St Gregory St Cincinnati OH 45202*

SCOTT, JOHN E. state legislator; b. Charleston, Mo., July 24, 1939; Mem. Mo. Ho. Reps., Jefferson City, 1971-76, Mo. Senate from 3rd dist., Jefferson City, 1977—. Office: Mo Senate State Capitol Rm 416 Jefferson City MO 65101

SCOTT, JOHN EDWARD SMITH, lawyer; b. St. Louis, Aug. 6, 1936; s. Gordon Hatler and Luella Margarite (Smith) S.; m. Beverly Joan Phillips, Dec. 17, 1960; 1 dau., Pamela Anne. AB, Albion Coll., 1958; JD, Wayne State U., 1961. Bar: Mich. 1961, U.S. Dist. Ct. (ea. dist.) Mich. 1962, U.S. Dist. Ct. (we. dist.) Mich. 1970, U.S. Tax. Ct. 1979, U.S. Ct. Appeals (6th cir.) 1964, U.S. Supreme Ct. 1966. Law clk. Supreme Ct. Mich., Lansing, 1961-62; assoc. Dickinson, Wright, Moon, Van Dusen & Freeman, Detroit, 1962-69, ptnr., 1970—. Adj. prof. U. Detroit Law Sch., 1967-71. Supreme Ct. appointee State Bar Rep. Assembly, Detroit, 1972-77; mayor City of Pleasant Ridge, Mich., 1973-81; commr. Mich. Appellate Defender Commn., Detroit, 1979—, chmn., 1992—; hearing referee Mich. Civil Rights Commn., Detroit, 1974-80; chmn. Detroit Legal Aid & Defender Commn., 1972-77; chmn. case flow mgmt. com. Mich. Supreme Ct., 1989-90. Fellow Am. Coll. Trial Lawyers, Internat. Soc. Barristers, Internat. Acad. Trial Lawyers; mem. ABA (chmn. trial evidence com. sect. litigation 1988-91), Am. Bd. Advs., Am. Bar Found., Internat. Assn. Def. Counsel, Mich. Bar Found., Detroit Golf Club, Order of Coif (hon.). Office: Dickinson Wright PLLC 500 Woodward Ave Ste 4000 Detroit MI 48226-3416

SCOTT, KAREN BONDURANT, consumer catalog company executive; b. East Orange, N.J., June 4, 1946; d. Walter James and Wanda (French) Schmidt; m. Ian James Anderson, May 12, 1982; children: Steven, Michael. BS, U. Mass., 1968; MBA, Northwestern U., 1977. Bus. analyst Dun & Bradstreet, N.Y.C., 1968-69; asst. mgr. Shay Med. Employment, Chgo., 1970-72; mgr. recruitment Michael Reese Med. Ctr., 1972-76; brand mgmt., new bus. devel., dir. mergers & acquisitions Kraft Foods, Inc., Glenview, Ill., 1977-95; pres. Chelsea & Scott dba One Step Ahead, Lake Bluff, 1987—. Sec.-treas. adv. bd. Lincolnshire (Ill.) Nursery Sch., 1987-89; co-leader Boy Scouts Am., Lincolnshire, 1991; Lake Forest cmty. task force mem., NAWBO. Mem. Juvenile Product Mfrs. Assn. (new product judge 1992-99, speaker nat. catalog conf.). Office: Chelsea & Scott Ltd 75 Albrecht Dr Lake Bluff IL 60044-2226

SCOTT, MARTHA G. state legislator; b. Ware Shoals, S.C., Nov. 10, 1935; d. Harold and Pearl (Wardlaw) Smith; children: Marion Jr., Deborah Ann Gilmore. Student, Highland Park Jr. Coll., 1952-54; DHH, Tenn. Sch. Religion, 1990; DHL, Urban Bible Inst., Detroit, 1994. With Mich. Bell Telephone Co., 1960-86; rep. Mich. Ho. of Reps. Mem. Mich. State Dem. Ctrl. Com., 1974-82; commr. Wayne County Bd. Commrs., 1977-80, chairwoman Human Resources Com., 1978-80; vice chairwoman Wayne County Civil Svc. Commn., 1980-82; pres. Highland Park City Coun., 1984-87; mayor City of Highland Park, 1988; Dem. precinct del. 1st Congl. Dist.; bd. dirs. Nat. Coun. Alcoholism and Other Dependencies, 1979, Detroit Osteopathic Hosp., 1990; vice chairwoman Mich. Women in Mcpl. Govt.; founding mem. Nat. Polit. Congress Black Women; adv. bd. Met. Region Bus. Alliance; vol. Residential Care Alternatives. Recipient Plaque Highland Park Sch. Bd., 1977, Nat. Polit. Congress of Black Women award, 1981, Resolution, Wayne County Bd. Commrs., 1981, Wayne County Auditors, 1981, Dollars and Sense Mag. award, 1989, Spl. Achievement award Amvets, Golden Heritage award for excellence in svc., 1988, Cmty. Svc. award Knoxville Coll. Alumni, 1988. Mem. Gamma Phi Delta. Office: Michigan House of Reps State Capitol Lansing MI 48909

SCOTT, NORMAN LAURENCE, engineering consultant; b. Meadow Grove, Nebr., Oct. 17, 1931; s. Laurence Ray Scott and Ruth Louise Braun; m. Joan Culbertson, Jan. 21, 1956; 1 child, Douglas Jay. BS in Civil Engring., U. Nebr., 1954. Registered profl. engr., Ill., Fla., Md., Minn., Va., Tex.; registered structural engr., Ill. Sales engr. R.H. Wright & Son, Ft. Lauderdale, Fla., 1956-58; mgr. Wright of Palm Beach, West Palm Beach, 1958-59; exec. sec. Prestressed Concrete Inst., Chgo., 1959-63; gen. mgr. Wiss, Janney, Elstner & Assoc., Northbrook, Ill., 1963-66; pres., chmn. The Consulting Engrs. Group Inc., Mt. Prospect, 1966—. 1st lt. USAF, 1954-56. Mem. ASCE (life), Am. Concrete Inst. (hon., pres. 1983-84, Henry C. Turner medal 1993), Ill. Soc. Profl. Engrs. (pres. North Shore chpt. 1962). Republican. Home: 701 Chatham Dr Glenview IL 60025-4403 Office: The Consulting Engrs Group 55 E Euclid Ave Mount Prospect IL 60056-1283

SCOTT, NORMAN ROSS, electrical engineering educator; b. N.Y.C., May 15, 1918; s. George Norman and Lillias B.H. (Ogg) S.; m. Marjorie M. Fear, Apr. 6, 1950; children: Mari, George, Ian, Charles. BS, MS, MIT, 1941; PhD, U. Ill., 1950. Asst. prof. elec. engring. U. Ill., Urbana, 1946-50; asst. prof. to prof. elec. engring. U. Mich., Ann Arbor, 1951-87, assoc dean Coll. Engring., 1965-68, dean Dearborn Campus, 1968-71, prof. emeritus of elec. engring. and computer sci., 1987—. Cons. Nat. Cash Register Co., Dayton, 1956-65; mem. math. and computer sci. rsch. adv. com. AEC, Washington, 1961-63. Editor-in-chief IEEE Trans. on Computers, N.Y.C., 1961-65; author: Analog and Digital Computer Technology, 1959, Electronic Computer Technology, 1970, Computer Number Systems and Arithmetic, 1985. Maj. U.S. Army, 1941-46. Fellow IEEE. Home: 2260 Gale Rd Ann Arbor MI 48105-9512 Office: U Mich Eecs Dept Ann Arbor MI 48109

SCOTT, ROBERT LEE, speech educator; b. Fairbury, Nebr., Apr. 19, 1928; s. Walter Everett and Ann Maria (Jensen) S.; m. Betty Rose Foust, Sept. 13, 1947; children— Mark Allen, Janet Lee, Paul Matthew. B.A., U. No. Colo., 1950; M.A., U. Nebr., 1951; Ph.D., U. Ill., 1955. Asst. prof. speech U. Houston, 1953-57; asst. prof. U. Minn., 1957-59, assoc. prof., 1959-63, prof., 1963-2000, prof. emeritus, 2000—, chair dept. speech communication, 1971-89, chair dept. Spanish and Portuguese, 1992-94, dir. Sch. Journalism and Mass Comm., 1995-97. Author: Rhetoric of Black Power, 1969, Moments in the Rhetoric of the Cold War, 1970; contbr. articles to profl. jours. Recipient Teaching award Coll. of Liberal Arts, U. Minn., 1981. Mem. Nat. Comm. Assn. (editor Quar. Jour. Speech 1971-74, Winans-Wichelns Rsch. award 1970, Charles H. Woolbert Rsch. award, 1981, Douglas-Ehninger Disting. Scholar award 1989, Disting. Scholar of Assn. 1992), Ctrl. States Speech Assn., Internat. Soc. for Study of Rhetoric. Office: U Minn Dept Speech Communication Minneapolis MN 55455-0194 E-mail: scott033@umn.edu.

SCOTT, SAMUEL C. food products executive; B in Engring., Fairleigh Dickinson U., 1966, MBA. With Corn Products Internat., Bedford Park, Ill., 1973-89, pres. corn products, 1989-95, pres. corn refining, 1995-97, pres., COO, 1997—. Office: Corn Products Internat 6500 S Archer Ave Bedford Park IL 60501

SCOTT, THEODORE R. lawyer; b. Mount Vernon, Ill., Dec. 7, 1924; s. Theodore R. and Beulah (Flannigan) S.; children: Anne Laurence, Sarah Buckland, Daniel, Barbara Gomon. AB, U. Ill., 1947, JD, 1949. Bar: Ill. 1950. Law clk. to judge U.S. Ct. Appeals, 1949-51; pvt. practice Chgo., 1950—; assoc. Spaulding Glass, 1951-53, Loftus, Lucas & Hammand, 1953-58, Ooms, McDougall, Williams & Hersh, 1958-60; ptnr. McDougall, Hersh & Scott, Chgo., 1960-87; of counsel Jones, Day, Reavis & Pogue, 1987-97, Rockey, Milnamow & Katz, 1998—. 2nd lt. USAAF, 1943-45. Decorated Air medal. Fellow Am. Coll. Trial Lawyers; mem. ABA, Ill. Bar Assn., Chgo. Bar Assn., 7th Cir. Bar Assn. (past pres.), Legal Club Chgo., Law Club Chgo., Patent Law Assn. Chgo. (past pres.), Union League Club, Exmoor Country Club (Highland Park, Ill.), Phi Beta Kappa. E-mail: tsb24nav2aol.com. Home: 1569 Woodvale Ave Deerfield IL 60015-2350

SCOTT, WALTER, JR. construction company executive; b. 1931; BS, Colo. State U., 1953. With Peter Kiewit Sons, Inc., Omaha, 1953—, mgr. Cleve. dist., 1962-64, v.p., 1964, exec. v.p., 1965-79, chmn. bd. dirs., pres., CEO, 1979-97, dir., chmn. level 3 comm., 1997, chmn. emeritus, 1997—; also pres. Joslyn Art Mus., 1987-97. Served with USAF, 1954-56. Office: Peter Kiewit Sons Inc 1000 Kiewit Plz Omaha NE 68131-3302 also: Joslyn Art Mus 2200 Dodge St Omaha NE 68102-1208

SCOTT, WALTER DILL, management educator; b. Chgo., Oct. 27, 1931; s. John Marcy and Mary Louise (Gent) S.; m. Barbara Ann Stein, Sept. 9, 1961; children: Timothy Walter, David Frederick, Gordon Charles. Student, Williams Coll., 1949-51; BS, Northwestern U., 1953; MS, Columbia U., 1958. Cons. Booz, Allen & Hamilton, NYC, 1956—58; assoc. Glore, Forgan & Co., 1958—63, ptnr. Chgo., 1963-65; pntr. Lehman Bros, 1965-72, sr. ptnr., 1972-73, also bd. dirs.; assoc. dir. econs. and govt. Office Mgmt. and Budget, Washington, 1973-75; sr. v.p. internat. and fin. Pillsbury Co., Mpls., 1975-78, exec. v.p., 1978-80, also bd. dirs.; pres., CEO, Investors Diversified Svcs., Inc., 1980-84; group mng. dir. Grand Met. PLC, 1984-86, also bd. dirs.; chmn. Grand Met USA, 1984-86; prof., sr. Austin fellow Kellogg Sch. Mgmt., Northwestern U., Evanston, Ill., 1988—. Bd. dirs., vice chmn. Intermatic, Inc. Bd. dirs. Chgo. Cmtys. in Schs., Leadership for Quality Edn. Lt. (j.g.) USN, 1953-56. Home: 55 Meadowview Dr Northfield IL 60093-3547 Office: Northwestern U Kellog Sch Mgmt 2001 Sheridan Rd Evanston IL 60208-0814 E-mail: wds@kellogg.northwestern.edu.

SCOTT, WILLIAM PAUL, lawyer; b. Staples, Minn., Nov. 8, 1928; m. Elsie Elaine Anderson, Feb. 7, 1968; children: Jason Lee, William P., Mark D., Brian D., Scott; stepchildren: Thomas J. (dec.), Terri L. Weeding-Berg. ALA, U. Minn., 1949; BSL, St. Paul Coll. Law, 1952, JD, 1954. Bar: Minn. 1954. Atty., right of way divsn. Minn. Hwy Dept., 1945-52, civil engr., traffic and safety divsn., 1953-55; practice law Arlington, Minn., 1955-61, Gaylord, 1963-67; sr. ptnr. Scott Law Offices and predecessors, Pipestone, 1967—. Probate, juvenile judge Sibley County, Minn., 1956-61; Minn. pub. examiner, 1961-63; county atty. Sibley County, 1963-68, city atty., Pipestone, 1979-2002. Sibley County Rep. chmn., 1961. Served with USMCR, 1946-50, from 2d lt. to lt. col. USAF Res., 1950-88, ret. Recipient George Washington Honor medal Freedoms Found., 1970, 72. Mem. TROA, VFW, DAV, Minn. Bar Assn., Mensa, Am. Legion, Res. Officers Assn. Home: PO Box 689 Pipestone MN 56164-0689 Office: Park Plz Offices Pipestone MN 56164 E-mail: scottlaw@rconnect.com.

SCOTTI, MICHAEL JOHN, JR. medical association executive; b. N.Y.C., Oct. 30, 1938; s. Michael John and Florence (Ellis) S.; m. Susan Faye Suit, Aug. 25, 1961; children: Michael John III, Pamela Anne, Jennifer Beth. BS, Fordham Coll., 1960; MD, Georgetown U., 1965; postgrad., Indsl. Coll., Washington, 1982-83. Diplomate Am. Bd. Internal Medicine, Am. Bd. Family Practice; CAQ Geriat. Commd. 2d lt. U.S. Army, 1963, advanced through grades to maj. gen., 1990; dir. residency program Dept. Family Practice, Ft. Gordon, Ga., 1976-79; family practice cons. Surgeon Gen., Washington, 1979-80; dir. Grad. Med. Edn. U.S. Army, 1980-82; comdr. army hosp. Ft. Polk, La., 1983-86; dir. quality assurance Army Med. Dept., Washington, 1986-88, dir. profl. svcs., 1988-90; comdg. gen. European 7th Med. Comd, Heidelberg, Fed. Republic Germany, 1990-95; ret. maj. gen., 1995; v.p. AMA, Chgo., 1996—. Assoc. prof. Georgetown U. Sch. Medicine, 1986; chmn. Def. Med. Standardization, Ft. Detrick, Md., 1988-90; prof. Uniformed Svcs. U., Bethesda, Md., 1990. Health cons. Nat. PTA, Chgo., 1976-79. Named Person of Yr. Phi Delta Kappa, 1976. Fellow: ACP, Am. Acad. Family Physicians (vice spkr. 1988—90, apkr., bd. dirs. 1990—92); mem.: AMA (v.p. med. edn. 1995—2000, sr. v.p. profl. stds. 2000—). Office: AMA 515 N State St Chicago IL 60610-4325 E-mail: michael_scotti@ama-assn.org.

SCOVANNER, DOUGLAS, retail company executive; BS, Washington and Lee U., 1977; MBA, U. Va., 1979. With Coca-Cola Enterprises and affiliates, Atlanta, 1980-92, v.p., treas., 1989-92; sr. v.p. fin. Fleming Cos., Oklahoma City, 1992-94; CFO, sr. v.p. fin. Target Corp. (formerly Dayton Hudson Corp.), Mpls., 1994—. Office: Dayton Hudson Corp 777 Nicollet Mall Fl 13 Minneapolis MN 55402-2055

SCOVILLE, JAMES GRIFFIN, economics educator; b. Amarillo, Tex., Mar. 19, 1940; s. Orlin James and Carol Howe (Griffin) S.; m. Judith Ann Nelson, June 11, 1962; 1 child, Nathan James. BA, Oberlin Coll., 1961; MA, Harvard U., 1963, PhD, 1965. Economist ILO, Geneva, 1965-66; instr. econs. Harvard U., Cambridge, Mass., 1964-65, asst. prof., 1966-69; assoc. prof. econs. and labor and indsl. relations U. Ill.-Urbana, 1969-75, prof., 1975-80; prof. indsl. rels. Indsl. Rels. Ctr., U. Minn., Mpls., 1979—, dir., 1979-82, dir. grad. studies, 1990-97. Cons. ILO, World Bank, U.S. Dept. Labor, Orgn. for Econ. Cooperation and Devel., AID; labor-mgmt. arbitrator. Author: The Job Content of the US Economy, 1940-70, 1969, Perspectives on Poverty and Income Distribution, 1971, Manpower and Occupational Analysis: Concepts and Measurements, 1972, (with A. Sturmthal) The International Labor Movement in Transition, 1973, Status Influences in 3rd World Labor Markets, 1991. Mem. Am. Econ. Assn., Indsl. Rels. Rsch. Assn. (v.p. internat. sect. 1998, pres. 1999), Internat. Indsl. Rels. Assn. Office: U Minn Ind Rels Ctr 3-289 CSOM Minneapolis MN 55455 E-mail: jscoville@csom.umn.edu.

SCOVILLE, JOSEPH G. federal magistrate, judge; b. 1949; BA with high honors, Mich. State U., 1971; JD magna cum laude, U. Mich., 1974. Bar: Ill. 1974, U.S. Dist. Ct. (no. dist.) Ill. 1974, Mich. 1976, U.S. Dist. Ct. (we. dist.) Mich. 1976, U.S. Supreme Ct. 1981. Assoc. McDermott, Will & Emery, Chgo., 1974-76; ptnr. Warner, Norcross & Judd, Grand Rapids, Mich., 1976-88; magistrate judge U.S. Dist. Ct. (we. dist.) Mich., 1988—. Mem. Fed. Bar Assn., Mich. State Bar, Grand Rapids Bar Assn. Office: US Dist Ct We Dist Mich 602 Fed Bldg 110 Michigan St NW Grand Rapids MI 49503-2313 Fax: (616) 456-2074. E-mail: scoville@miwd.uscourts.gov.

SCOZZIE, JAMES ANTHONY, chemist; b. Erie, Pa., Nov. 3, 1943; AB, Gannon Coll., 1965; MS, Case Western Res. U., 1968, PhD in Chemistry, 1970. Jr. rsch. chemist ctrl. rsch. dept. Lord Corp., 1965; rsch. chemist Diamond Shamrock Corp., 1970-72, sr. rsch. chemist, 1972-76, rsch. supr. pharmaceutics, 1976-78, group leader agrl. chemistry, 1978-81, assoc. dir. agrl. chemistry rsch., 1981-83; dir. agrl. chemistry rsch. SDS Biotech Corp., 1983-85, dir. corp. rsch., 1985—; pres. Ricerca, Inc., Painesville, Ohio, 1986-2000, Ricerca LLC, Painesville, 2000—. Chmn. bd. trustees State of Ohio Edison Biotechnology Ctr.; bd. governance Edison Biotechnology Inst. Mem. Am. Chem. Soc. Achievements include research in structure and chemistry of peptide antibiotics, synthesis of biologically active compounds, pesticides, process studies of organic compounds, commercial evaluation, nutrition and animal health, herbicides, plant growth regulants, cardiovascular agents and anti-inflammatory agents. Office: Ricerca LLC PO Box 1000 7528 Auburn Rd Painesville OH 44077-9603

SCRIMSHAW, SUSAN CROSBY, dean; PhD in Anthropology, Columbia U., 1974. Dean U. Ill. Sch. Pub. Health, Chgo., 1995—; prof. Sch. Pub. Health UCLA, 1974-94, assoc. dean, 1988-94. Recipient Margaret Mead award, 1985. Fellow AAAS; mem. Inst. Medicine-Nat. Acad. Sci., Am. Anthropology Assn., Soc. Applied Anthropology, Nat. Soc. Med. Anthropology (pres. 1985). Office: Sch of Pub Health U Ill Chicago 2121 W Taylor St # Mc922 Chicago IL 60612-7260

SCRIVEN, JOHN G. retired lawyer, chemical company executive; Bar: Mich. 1993. Sr. staff counsel Dow Europe S.A., 1981-83; gen. counsel Dow Chem. Co., Midland, Mich., 1983-86, v.p., gen. counsel, 1986-2000, v.p., gen. counsel, sec., 1986-2000; ret., 2000. Office: Dow Chem Co 2030 Dow Ctr Midland MI 48674-0001

SCRIVEN, L. E(DWARD), chemical engineering educator, scientist; b. Battle Creek, Mich., Nov. 4, 1931; s. L. Edward and Esther Mabel (Davis) S.; m. Dorene Bates Hayes, June 19, 1952; children: Ellen Dorene, Teresa Ann, Mark Hayes. BS, U. Calif., Berkeley, 1952; PhD, U. Del., 1956. Rsch. engr. Shell Devel. Co., Emeryville, Calif., 1956-59; asst. prof. chem. engring. and fluid mechanics U. Minn., Mpls., 1959-62, assoc. prof., 1962-66, prof., 1966-89, Regents' prof., 1989—, assoc. dept. head, 1975-78, program dir. Ctr. Interfacial Engring., 1988-90. Cons. in fields; advisor to Humboldt Found., Fed. Republic of Germany; vis. com. to chem. engring. MIT, sci. assoc. Jet Propulsion Lab., 1977, 79; tech. expert UN Indsl. Devel. Orgn., Vienna, Austria, 1979-88; exec. com. on chem. engring. frontiers NRC, 1984-87; mem. NRC Bd. on Chem. Scis. and Tech., 1987-92, chmn., 1992; mem. NRC Commn. on Phys. Scis., Math. and Applications, 1994—; sci. adv. com. Packard Found., 1988—. Editor: Physico-chemical Hydrodynamics (V.G. Levich), 1992; assoc. editor Jour. Fluid Mechanics, 1970-75; adv. editor Jour. Coll. Interfluid Sci., Physics of Fluids, L.Am. Jour. Chem. Engring. and Applied Chemistry, Internat. Jour.

Numerical Methods in Fluid Mechanics; contbr. numerous articles to sci. jours.; patentee in field. Recipient chem. engring. award Am. Soc. Engring. Edn., 1968, Minn. Achievement award, 1989, Murphree award Am. Chem. Soc., 1990; named Fairchild disting. scholar Calif. Inst. Tech., 1989; Guggenheim fellow, 1969-70, fellow Minn. Supercomputer Inst., 1984—. Mem. NAE, Am. Inst. Chem. Engrs. (mem. nat. program. com. 1964-69, Colburn award 1960, Walker award 1977, Tallmadge award 1992, Founders award 1997), Am. Phys. Soc., Soc. Petroleum Engrs., Gordon Rsch. Confs., Chem. Soc. (Faraday div.), Soc. Indsl. and Applied Math., Soc. Rheology. Achievements include research in capillarity, fluid mechanics and coating processes, porous media, cold-stage electron microscopy, microstructured fluids and interfaces, origins of pattern and form, supercomputer-aided analysis. Office: Univ Minn 151 Amundson Hall 421 Washington Ave SE Minneapolis MN 55455-0373

SCRIVNER, THOMAS WILLIAM, lawyer; b. Madison, Wis., Sept. 10, 1948; s. William H. and Jane (Gehrz) S.; m. Meredith Burke, Aug. 16, 1980; children: Allison, David. AB, Duke U., 1970, MAT, 1972; JD, U. Wis., 1977. Assoc. Michael, Best & Friedrich LLP, Milw., 1978-85, ptnr., 1985—. Mem. ABA, Wis. Bar Assn., Milw. Bar Assn. (labor sect.), Corp. Practice Inst. (pres. 1989-92). Episcopalian. Home: 4626 N Cramer St Milwaukee WI 53211-1203 Office: Michael Best & Friedrich LLP 100 E Wisconsin Ave Ste 3300 Milwaukee WI 53202-4108

SCRUGGS, STEVEN DENNIS, real estate consultant; b. St. Louis, June 6, 1946; s. Edward B. and Janet W. (Hunt) S.; m. Kristen A. Weiler, June 29, 1968; children: Brian, Brendan, Erin. BSEE, Purdue U., 1968. Registered profl. engr., Ill.; lic. real estate broker, N.Y., N.J.; registered securities prin. NASD; lic. pvt. pilot. Mktg. rep. IBM, Chgo., 1968-77, mktg. mgr., 1977-79, adminstrv. asst. to v.p. White Plains, N.Y., 1979-80, br. mgr., 1980-81; assoc. LaSalle Ptnrs., Inc., N.Y.C., 1981-83, v.p., 1983-85, Edward S. Gordon Co., Inc., N.Y.C., 1985-87, sr. v.p., 1987-89; dir. Jones Lang Wootton USA, 1989-91, sr. dir., 1992—. Vice chmn. Day Care Ctr. of New Canaan, Conn., 1979-84; bd. dirs. Advocates of Edn. of Gifted, New Canaan, 1984-89; coach New Canaan Soccer Assn., 1984-90, pres., bd. dirs., 1987-89. Mem. Woodway Club. Republican. Presbyterian. Avocations: skiing, golf, tennis, running, aviation. Home: 2734 N Mildred Ave Fl 3 Chicago IL 60614-1418 Office: Grubb & Ellis 2215 Sanders Rd 4th Fl Northbrook IL 60062

SCULFIELD, TONY, radio personality, comedian; Weekday morning show radio host, weekend afternoon radio host Sta. WGCI-FM, Chgo. Comedian (comedy shows) HBO Russell Simmons' Def Comedy All Star Jam , BET Comic View , (numerous other comedy acts). Office: WGCI 332 S Michigan Ave Chicago IL 60604*

SCURRY, BRIANA COLLETTE, soccer player; b. Mpls., Sept. 7, 1971; BS in Polit. Sci., U. Mass., 1995. Goalkeeper U.S. Women's Nat. Soccer Team, Chgo. Named Nat. Goalkeeper of Yr. Mo. Athletic Club Sports Found., 1993, 2d Team All-Am., 1993, Gold medal Atlanta Olympics, 1996; World Cup 1999. Office: US Soccer Fedn US Soccer House 1801 S Prairie Ave Chicago IL 60616-1319

SEAGREN, ALICE, state legislator; b. 1947; m. Fred Seagren; 2 children. BS, SE Mo. State U. Mem. Minn. Ho. of Reps., 1993—. Active Bloomington (Minn.) Sch. Bd., 1989-92. Mem. Bloomington C. of C. (bd. dirs. 1990-92), Phi Gamma Nu, Alpha Chi Omega. Republican. Home: 9730 Palmer Cir Bloomington MN 55437-2017 Office: Minn Ho of Reps State Capital Building Saint Paul MN 55155-0001 E-mail: rep.alice.seagren@house.leg.state.mn.us.

SEAL, RICHARD C. marketing executive; BS, U. Cincinnati, 1971. Kroger Co.; Market Audits, 1972-76; Burke Mktg. Svcs., 1976-80, v.p., regional mgr., 1980-86; ptnr. Market Decisions, 1986; mng. ptnr., CEO Market Decisions (acquird ACNielsen's Testing Svcs. Divsn.); pres. ACNielsen Market Decisions, 1999—. Bd. mem. UCATS. Office: AC-Nielsen Market Decisions 312 Plum St Cincinnati OH 45202-2697

SEALL, STEPHEN ALBERT, lawyer; b. South Bend, Ind., Oct. 24, 1940; s. Stephen Henry and Mildred Rita (MacDonald) S.; m. Barbara Ann Halloran, June 25, 1966; children: John Paul, Edward Andrew, Ann Marie. BA, Purdue U., 1963; postgrad., Cornell U. Grad. Sch. Bus. Adminstrn., 1963; LLB, U. Notre Dame, 1966. Bar: Ind. 1966, U.S. Claims Ct. 1973, U.S. Tax Ct. 1968, U.S. Ct. Appeals (6th cir.) 1980, U.S. Ct. Appeals (7th cir.) 1969, U.S. Supreme Ct. 1973. Assoc. Thornburg, McGill, Deahl, Harman, Carey & Murray, South Bend, 1966-71; ptnr. Barnes & Thornburg and predecessor firm Thornburg, McGill, Deahl, Harman, Carey & Murray, 1972—, vice chmn. and mgmt. com., mng. ptnr. South Bend office, 1985—2001. Spkr. in field. (Mem. editl. bd.) Notre Dame Law Rev., 1964—66. Mem. Mayor's Com. on Downtown Devel., South Bend, 1975-77, Mayor's Com. on Utilization of Downtown Bldgs., South Bend, 1988-96; trustee Project Future, South Bend, 1986-2002; exec. com. Meml. Hosp. South Bend, Inc., 1999—; dir. Meml. Health Found., 1992-98, Meml. Health Sys., 1997—, United Way of St. Joseph County, Inc., 1992-98, Conv. and Tourism Industry Coun., 1994-2000. Fellow Am. Coll. Tax Counsel, Am. Bar Found., Ind. Bar Found.; mem. ABA (taxation sect.), Ind. State Bar Assn. (chmn. taxation sect. 1977-78), Summit Club (chmn. 1976-77), Morris Park Country Club (bd. dirs., sec. 1998-2001). Democrat. Roman Catholic. Avocations: golf, softball, weightlifting. Home: 17705 Waxwing Ln South Bend IN 46635-1328 Office: Barnes & Thornburg 600 1st Source Bank Ctr 100 N Michigan St Ste 600 South Bend IN 46601-1632

SEAMAN, IRVING, JR. banker; b. Milw., July 14, 1923; s. Irving and Anne (Douglas) S.; m. June Carry, June 24, 1950; children: Peter Stewart, Marion Carry, Irving Osborne, Anne Douglas. BA, Yale U., 1944. With Continental Ill. Nat. Bank & Trust Co., Chgo., 1947-61, v.p., 1959-61; pres., chief exec. officer, dir. Nat. Boulevard Bank, Chgo., 1961-65, chmn. exec. com., chief exec. officer, dir., 1966-76; vice chmn. bd., dir. Sears Bank and Trust Co., Chgo., 1976-77, pres., chief operating officer, dir., 1977-82; sr. cons. Burson-Marsteller, Chgo., 1982-94. Chmn. bd. Associated Bank Chgo., 1985—. Mem. Northwestern U. Assn.; life mem. bd. dirs. Lake Forest Hosp.; bd. dirs. United Way of Chgo., 1975-89, pres., 1979; bd. dirs. United Way/Crusade of Mercy, 1980-89, 94-95, vice chmn., 1980-81; trustee Chgo. Symphony Orch., 1987—. Lt. (j.g.) USNR, WWII. Mem. Commonwealth Club, Econ. Club, Chgo. Club, Comml. Club, Racquet Club, Onwentsia Club, Winter Club, Old Elm Club (Highland Park, Ill.), Shoreacres Club (Lake Bluff, Ill.), Augusta Nat. Golf Club (Ga.), Marsh Landing Club (Fla.), Sawgrass (Fla.) Country Club. Home: 946 Elmtree Rd Lake Forest IL 60045-1410 Office: Assoc Bank Chgo 200 E Randolph St Chicago IL 60601-6436

SEAMAN, JEROME FRANCIS, actuary; b. Oak Park, Ill., Nov. 4, 1942; s. William Francis and Bernice Florence (Haughey) S.; m. Jacquelyn Ann Robinson, Aug. 22, 1970; children: Carolyn, John. BA, U. Notre Dame, 1964; MA, Northwestern U., 1991. Asst. actuary Combined Ins. Co. of Am., Chgo., 1966-73; v.p., actuary United Equitable Life Ins. Co., Skokie, 1975-77; mgr. Peat Marwick Mitchell & Co., Chgo., 1973-75, 77-78; nat. dir. actuarial svcs. Arthur Young & Co., 1978-83; pres., cons. actuary Jerome F. Seaman & Assocs., Evanston, 1983—. Dir. Polysystems, Inc., Chgo., 1987-91. Contbr. articles to profl. jours. Recipient Commendation for Svc. Pres. Ronald Reagan, 1982. Fellow Soc. of Actuaries, Conf. of Cons. Actuaries; mem. Am. Acad. Actuaries (task force on risk based capital health orgns. 1993-95). Democrat. Unitarian Universalist. Avocations: running, hiking, classical music, opera, baseball. Home: 2107A Sherman Ave Evanston IL 60201-6116 Office: Jerome F Seaman & Assocs 2107 A Sherman Ave Evanston IL 60201-6116 E-mail: jfseaman@hotmail.com.

SEAMAN, WILLIAM CASPER, retired news photographer; b. Grand Island, Nebr., Jan. 19, 1925; s. William H. and Minnie (Cords) S.; m. Ruth Witwer, Feb. 14, 1945; 1 son, Lawrence William. Grad. high sch. Photographer Leschinsky Studio, Grand Island; news photographer Mpls. Star & Tribune, 1945-82; ret., 1982. Recipient Pulitzer prize, 1959; also awards Nat. Headliners Club; also awards Nat. Press Photographers Assn.; also awards Inland Daily Press Assn.; also awards Kent State U.; also awards Mo. U.; also awards Local Page One; State A.P. contest; Silver Anniversary award Honeywell Photog. Products, 1975 Mem. Nat. Press Photographers Assn., Sigma Delta Chi. Home: 8206 Virginia Cir S Minneapolis MN 55426-2458

SEARLES, LYNN MARIE, nurse; b. Cherryvale, Kans., Oct. 29, 1949; d. Darrell Eugene and Beva Caroline (Waller) Stringer; m. Martin Dale Searles, Aug. 23, 1970; children: Jeremy Dale, Michelle Le Anne. Assoc. in Fine Arts, Labette Cmty. Jr. Coll., Parsons, Kans., 1969, ADN, 1970. RN, Kans., Calif. Evening med.-surg. charge nurse Coffeyville (Kans.) Meml. Hosp., 1970-72, med.-surg. head nurse, 1972-73, relief evening house supr. and emergency rm. nurse, 1974, head nurse recovery rm., 1974-81; head nurse recovery rm., ambulatory care unit Coffeyville Meml. Med. Ctr., 1981-83, head nurse recovery rm., ambulatory care unit and surgery, 1983-84; dir. family planning, rural home health aide and multi phasic screening clinics, AIDS edn. and counseling Jefferson County Health Dept., Oskaloosa, Kansas, 1984-87; nurse III, health facility surveyor Lawrence dist. Kans. Dept. Health and Environ., Lawrence, Kans., 1988—. Mem. Nazarene Healthcare Fellowship, Kans. Pub. Health Assn., Am. Soc. Post Anesthesia Nurses (charter mem.). Republican. Nazarene Ch. Avocations: needlecraft, gardening, interior decorating. Office: Kans Dept Health and Environment 808 W 24th St Lawrence KS 66046-4417

SEARLS, EILEEN HAUGHEY, retired lawyer, librarian, educator; b. Madison, Wis., Apr. 27, 1925; d. Edward M. and Anna Mary (Haughey) S. BA, U. Wis., 1948, JD, 1950, MS in LS, 1951. Bar: Wis. 1950. Cataloger Yale U., 1951-52; instr. law St. Louis U., 1952-53, asst. prof., 1953-56, assoc. prof., 1956-64, prof., 1964-2000, law libr., 1952-2000. Chmn. Coun. Law Libr. Consortia, 1984-90; sec. Bd. of Conciliaton and Arbitration, Archdiocese of St. Louis, 1986-98. Named Woman of Yr. Women's Commn., St. Louis U., 1986. Mem. ABA, ALA, Wis. Bar Assn., Bar Assn. Met. St. Louis, Am. Assn. Law Librs. (Marian Gould Gallagher Disting. Svc. award 1999), Mid Am. Assn. Law Librs. (pres. 1984-86), Mid Am. Law Sch. Libr. Consortium (chmn. 1980-84), Southwestern Assn. Law Librs., Altrusa Club. Office: 3700 Lindell Blvd Saint Louis MO 63108-3412

SEASE, GENE ELWOOD, public relations company executive; b. Portage, Pa., June 28, 1931; s. Grover Chauncey and Clara Mae (Over) S.; m. Joanne D. Cherry, July 20, 1952; children: David Gene, Daniel Elwood, Cheryl Joanne. A.B., Juniata Coll., 1952; B.D., Pitts. Theol. Sem., 1956, Th.M., 1959; Ph.D., U. Pitts., 1965, M.Ed., 1958; LL.D., U. Evansville, 1972, Butler U., 1972; Litt.D., Ind. State U., 1974; DD, U. Indpls., 1989. Ordained to ministry United Methodist Ch., 1956; pastor Grace United Meth. Ch., Wilkinsburg, Pitts., 1952-63; conf. dir., supt. Western Pa. Conf. United Meth. Ch., Pitts., 1963-68; lectr. grad. faculty U. Pitts., 1965-68; mem. staff U. Indpls., 1968-89, asst. to pres., 1968-69, pres., 1970-88, chancellor, 1988-89, pres. emeritus, 1989—; chmn. Sease, Gerig & Assocs., Indpls., 1989—. Bd. dirs. Indpls. Life Ins. Co., Bankers Life Ins. Co. of N.Y. Author: Christian Word Book, 1968; also numerous articles. Pres. Greater Indpls. Progress Com., 1972-75, Marion County Sheriff's Merit Bd.; mem. Ind. Scholarship Commn.; cons. Time Warner; bd. dirs. Indpls. Conv. Bur., Ind. Law Enforcement Tng. Acad., 500 Festival, Crossroads coun. Boy Scouts Am., Community Hosp. Indpls., St. Francis Hosp.; chmn. Ind. State Fair Commn. Mem. Internat. Platform Assn., English Speaking Union, Japan-Am. Soc. Ind., Ind. C. of C. (bd. dirs.), Indpls. C. of C. (bd. dirs.), Ind. Schoolmen's Club, Ind. State Fair Commn., Econ. Club of Indpls. (bd. dirs.), Skyline Club (bd. dirs.), Phi Delta Kappa, Alpha Phi Omega, Alpha Psi Omega. Clubs: Mason (Indpls.) (33 deg., Shriner), Kiwanian. (Indpls.), Columbia (Indpls.).

SEATON, EDWARD LEE, newspaper editor and publisher; b. Manhattan, Kans., Feb. 5, 1943; s. Richard Melvin and Mary (Holton) S.; m. Karen Mathisen, Sept. 4, 1965; children: Edward Merrill, John David. AB cum laude, Harvard U., 1965; postgrad., U. Cen., Quito, Ecuador, 1965-66, U. Mo., 1966-67. Staff writer Courier-Jour., Louisville, 1968-69; editor-in-chief, pub. Manhattan Mercury, 1969—. Bd. dirs., officer 8 other newspaper and broadcasting affiliates; mem. adv. com. Knight Internat. Press Fellowship Program; mem. Pulitzer Prize bd., 1992-01, chmn., 2001—; mem. Columbia U., Cabot Awards Bd. Contbr. articles to profl. jours. Chmn. Alfred M. Landon lecture patrons Kans. State U.; chmn. Latin Am. Scholarship Program Am. Univs., Cambridge, Mass., 1986-87. Decorated comendador Order of Christopher Columbus (Dominican Republic); Fulbright scholar, 1965; recipient Cabot prize Columbia U., 1993. Mem. Am. Soc. Newspaper Editors (pres. 1998-99), Inter-Am. Press Assn. (pres. 1989-90), Internat. Ctr. Journalists (bd. dirs. 1990-2001), Internat. Press Inst., Kans. C. of C. and Industry (pres. 1987), Fly Club (Harvard U.). Avocations: tennis, cooking. Office: 318 N 5th St Manhattan KS 66502-5910

SEATON, VAUGHN ALLEN, retired veterinary pathology educator; b. Abilene, Kans., Oct. 11, 1928; m. Clara I. Bertelrud; children: Gregory S., Jeffrey T. BS, DVM, Kans. State U., 1954; MS, Iowa State U., 1957. Pvt. practice, Janesville, Wis., 1954; instr. pathology Vet. Diagnostic Lab. Iowa State U., Ames, 1954-57, from asst. to assoc. prof. pathology Vet. Disgnostic Lab., 1957-64, prof., head Vet. Diagnostic Lab., 1964-94. Lab. coord. regional emergency animal disease eradication orgn. Animal and Plant Health Inspection Svc. USDA, 1974—; mem. rsch. com. Iowa Beef Industry Coun., 1972-85; mem. adv. bd. Iowa State Water Resources Rsch. Inst., 1973-80; cons. several orgns. Co-author: (monographs) Feasibility Study of College of Veterinary Medicine, 1972, Veterinary Diagnostic Laboratory Facilities-State of New York, 1970; bd. dirs. Iowa State U. Press, 1985-88, mem. manuscript com., 1982-85; contbr. articles to profl. jours. Trustee Ames Pub. Libr., 1979-85; mem. Iowa State Bd. Health, 1971-77, v.p., 1976-77; bd. dirs. Masonic Edn. Found., 1985-88. Mem. AVMA, Am. Assn. Vet. Lab. Diagnosticians (bd. govs. 1973-88, pres. 1968, E.P. Pope award 1980), Am. Coll. Vet. Toxicologists, U.S. Animal Health Assn., Iowa Vet. Med. Assn. (pres. 1971), North Ctrl. Assn. Vet. Lab. Diagnosticians, Western Vet. Conf. (exec. bd. 1986-90, v.p. 1994, pres.-elect 1995, pres. 1996), World Assn. Vet. Lab. Diagnosticians (pres. 1980-86), Ames C. of C. (bd. dirs. 1970-73), Phi Kappa Phi, Phi Zeta (pres. 1964), Alpha Zeta, Gamma Sigma Delta. Office: Iowa State U Coll Vet Medicine Vet Diagnostic Lab Ames IA 50011-0001

SEBELIUS, KATHLEEN GILLIGAN, state commissioner; b. Cin., May 15, 1948; d. John J. and Mary K. (Dixon) Gilligan; m. Keith Gary Sebelius, 1974; children: Edward Keith, John McCall. BA, Trinity Coll., 1970; MA in Pub. Adminstrn., U. Kans., 1977. Cert. ins. agt., Kans. Dir. planning Ctr. for Cmty. Justice, Washington, 1971-74; spl. asst. Kans. Dept. Corrections, Topeka, 1975-78; mem. Kans. Ho. of Reps., 1987-95; ins. commr. State of Kans., 1995—. Founder Women's Polit. Caucus; precinct committeewoman, 1980-86; mayor-elect, Potwin, 1985-87; exec. com. Nat. Assn. Ins. Commrs., Kans. Health Care Commn.; appointed Presdl. adv. commn. consumer protection and quality in Health Care Industry, 1997. Mem. Common Cause (state bd., nat. gov. bd. 1975-81), Nat. Assn. Ins. Commrs. (chair), Kans. Trial Lawyers Assn. (dir. 1978-86). Democrat. Roman Catholic. Home: 317 SW Greenwood Ave Topeka KS 66606-1229

SECREST, PATRICIA K. state legislator; Rep. Mo. State Ho. Reps. Dist. 93. Home: 723 Country Heights Ct Ballwin MO 63021-5623 Office: Mo Ho of Reps State Capitol Bldg 701 W Capitol Ave Rm 101A Jefferson City MO 65101-1556

SEDELMAIER, JOHN JOSEF, filmmaker; b. Orrville, Ohio, May 31, 1933; s. Josef Heinrich and Anne Isabel (Baughman) S.; m. Barbara Jean Frank, June 6, 1965; children: John Josef, Nancy Rachel, Adam Frederich. BFA, Art Inst. Chgo. at U. Chgo., 1955. Dir. art Young and Rubicam, Chgo., 1955-61; dir. art, assoc. creative dir. Clinton E. Frank, 1961-64; dir. art, producer J. Walter Thompson, 1964-67; pres. Sedelmaier Film Prodns., 1967—. Spkr. British Design & Art Direction Pres. Lectr. SEries, London, 1998. Retrospective exhibits Mus. Broadcast Communications, Chgo., 1988, Mus. Broadcasting, L.A., 1991, Mus. TV and Radio, N.Y.C., 1992. Recipient Golden Ducat award for short film MROFNOC Mannheim Film Festival, 1968, Golden Gate award for short film Because That's Why, San Francisco Film Festival, 1969, 82 Clio awards, 1968-92, numerous Gold, Silver and Bronze Lion awards Cannes Film Festival, 1972-90, Gold Hugo award Chgo. Film Festival, 1976, 91, 2d Ann. IDC Creative award, Chgo., 1980, Internat. Broadcasting award for world's best TV comml., 1980, 86, Clio award for dir. of yr., 1981, London Internat. Advt. awards, 1986-88, numerous awards Internat. Festival of N.Y., 1984-93, Ann. Achievement award Assn. Ind. Comml. Producers, 1988; named Advt. Person of Yr., Chgo. Advt. Club, 1984, Jewish Communicator of Yr., 1985; named one of 50 Pioneers & Visionaries Who Made TV America's Medium, Advt. Age Mag., 1995; profiled in Communication Arts mag., Mar. 1976, Print mag., Jan. 1982, Fortune mag., June 1983, Newsweek mag., Nov. 1986, numerous others; featured on 60 Minutes, 48 Hours; subject of cover story Esquire mag., Aug. 1983; included in Arts & Entertainment's Top 10 Greatest Commls. of All Time, 1999; inducted The Art Dirs. Hall Fame, 2000. Office: Sedelmaier Film Prodns Inc 858 W Armitage Ave # 267 Chicago IL 60614-4329

SEDERBURG, WILLIAM ALBERT, former state senator, educator; b. Chadron, Nebr., Aug. 1, 1947; s. Marion E. and Viola A. (Shalender) S.; m. Joyce I. Witte, July 29, 1972; children: Matthew E., Karl A. BS, Mankato State Coll., 1969; MA, Mich. State U., 1972, PhD, 1974. Faculty dept. polit. sci. Mich. State U., East Lansing, 1973-75; dir. rsch. Ho. Rep. Office, Lansing, 1975-78, exec. dir., 1978; mem. Mich. Senate, 1979-95; pres. Ferris State U., Big Rapids, Mich., 1995—. Mem. appropriations com., 1983-95, chmn. higher edn. and tech. com., health policy com., 1987-95, Mich. Capitol com., 1989-95. Contbr. articles to profl. jours. Bd. dirs. Luth. Social Svcs. Mich. NSF fellow, 1970-73. Mem. Phi Beta Kappa, Kappa Delta Pi. Republican. Office: Ferris State U 901 S State St Big Rapids MI 49307-2295

SEDGWICK, SALLY BELLE, publishing company executive; b. Chgo., July 6, 1947; d. William Morton and Dorothy Hyde (Dunlap) Price; m. Roger Stephen Sedgwick, Sept. 7, 1968 (div.); children: Peter, Andrew. BA, Lawrence U., 1968; MFA, U. Alaska, 1974; MA, Gen. Theol. Sem., N.Y.C., 1986; DMin, Grad. Theol. Found., Donaldson, Ind., 1996. Instr. Lake Region Jr. Coll., Devils Lake, N.D., 1974-77; dir. Carousel Creative Arts Program, Oakes, 1978-80; pricing analyst Orgn. Resources Counselors, N.Y.C., 1981-85; exec. dir. Ch. Periodical Club, 1985-90; assoc. dir. Forward Movement Publs., Cin., 1990—. Bd. mem. Fountain Sq. Fools, Cin., 1992-95; cons. Episcopal Diocese N.D., 1974-80. Mem. Episcopal Communicators, Nat. Network Lay Profls. Episcopalian. Office: Forward Movement Publs 412 Sycamore St Ste 3 Cincinnati OH 45202-4195

SEDLAK, ROBERT, academic administrator; Prof. spl. edn., dir. Office Rsch. U. Wis.-Stout, Menomonie, asst. to dean Sch. Ed. and Human Svcs., 1983—85, asst. dean rsch., 1985—88, assoc. vice chancellor, provost, vice chancellor, 1999—. Office: U Wis-Stout Office of Provost 303 Adminstrn Bldg 712 Broadway Menomonie WI 54751-0790

SEEBERT, KATHLEEN ANNE, international sales and marketing executive; d. Harold Earl and Marie Anne (Lowery) S. MA, U. Notre Dame, 1976; MM, Northwestern U., 1983. Registered commodity rep. Publs. editor ContiCommodity Svcs., Inc., Chgo., 1977-79, supr. mktg., 1979-82; dir. mktg. MidAm. Commodity Exch., 1982-85; internat. trade cons. to Govt. of Ont. Can., 1985-90; dir. mktg. and program devel. Internat. Orientation Resources, 1990-94; v.p. Am. Internat. Group, 1995-97; dir. KPMG Peat Marwick LLP, 1997-98; cons. Watson Wyatt & Co., 1999—. Guest lectr. U. Dayton, U. Notre Dame, Northwestern U., Kellogg Alumni Chgo., French-Am. C. of C., Internat. Employee Relocation Coun., Soc. Intercultural Educators, Trainers and Rschrs., ASTD, Ill. CPA Soc., SBA, KPMG Peat Marwick, Pricewaterhousecoopers, Ernst & Young, Nat. Fgn. Trade Coun., William M. Mercer, Inc., Minn. Employee Relocation Coun., MRA, CRC, Chgo. Relocation Coun., Ky. Relocation Coun., Chgo.-Midwest Credit Mgmt. Assn. Nat. bd. dirs. U. Dayton. Mem. Futures Industry Assn. Am. (treas.), Greater Cin. C. of C., Notre Dame Club Chgo., Kellogg Mgmt. Club Chgo. Republican. Roman Catholic. Office: 303 W Madison St Ste 2400 Chicago IL 60606-3395

SEEDER, RICHARD OWEN, infosystems specialist; b. Chgo., May 4, 1947; s. Edward Otto and Betty Jane (Reamer) S. BA, Trinity U., 1969; M in Mgmt., Northwestern U., 1979; MS, DePaul U., 1993. Programmer, analyst R.R. Donnelley & Sons Co., Chgo., 1972-76, project mgr., 1977-80; mgr. systems devel. Joint Commn. Accreditation of Healthcare Orgns., 1980-84, dir. mgmt. info. systems, 1985-89; dir. info. svcs., 1989-92; v.p. AApex Info. Systems., Skokie, Ill., 1992—. Cons. Internat. Printworks, Newton, Mass., 1981-82. Served to 1st lt. U.S. Army, 1969-71, Korea. Mem. Assn. MBA Execs., Healthcare Info. and Mgmt. Systems Soc., Am. Mgmt. Assn., Mensa. Club: Northwestern U. Mgmt. Avocations: sports, gardening. Home: 2224 Maple Ave Northbrook IL 60062-5208 Office: AApex Info Systems 9230 Lotus Ave Skokie IL 60077-1150

SEEGER, RONALD L. lawyer; b. Prairie Farm, Wis., June 10, 1930; s. John M. and Mildred G. (Moen) S.; m. Theresa A. Seeger, Sept. 3, 1955; children: Mark, Scott, John, Lynn, Eric. BA, U. Wis., 1951; JD, U. Minn., 1956. Bar: Minn. 1956, U.S. Dist. Ct. 1957, U.S. Supreme Ct. 1983. Pres. Dunlap & Seeger (was Michaels, Seeger, Rosenblad & Arnold), Rochester, Minn., 1956—. Counsel, City of Rochester Charter Commn., 1962-74, chmn., 1971-72; pres. Legal Assistance of Olmsted County, 1973-76; bd. dirs., v.p. Legal Assistace Minn., 1972-74; trustee, chmn. Gamehaven area Boy Scout Found., 1974-76; trustee Rochester Area Found.; dir. Minn. Lawyers Mutual. With U.S. Army, 1951-53, Korea. Fellow Am. Bar Found.; mem. ABA (ho. of dels. 1974-80, 92-96, bd. govs. 1991-95), Minn. State Bar Assn. (bd. govs. 1974-85, pres. 1983-84, Lifetime Svc. award 1997), Minn. Bar Found. (dir.), Minn. Legal Cert. Bd. (chmn. 1985-90). Home: 2924 Salem Point Dr SW Rochester MN 55902-1305 Office: PO Box 549 Rochester MN 55903-0549

SEEGERS, LORI C. lawyer; b. Miami Beach, Fla., June 17, 1955; BA cum laude, U. Pa., 1977; JD, Fordham U., 1982. Bar: N.Y. 1983, Ill. 2002, U.S. Dist. Ct. (so. dist.) N.Y. 1983. Ptnr. Anderson, Kill & Olick, P.C., N.Y.C.; gen. counsel PPM Am., Inc. Contbr. articles to profl. jours. Mem. ABA, N.Y. State Bar Assn. (sect. banking, corp. and bus. law), Assn. of Bar of City of N.Y. Office: PPM Am Inc Ste 1200 225 W Wacker Dr Chicago IL 60606-1276 E-mail: lori.seegers@ppmamerica.com.

SEEHAUSEN, RICHARD FERDINAND, architect; b. Indpls., Mar. 17, 1925; s. Paul Ferdinand and Melusina Dorothea (Nordmeyer) S.; m. Phyllis Jean Gates, Dec. 22, 1948; children: Lyn, Dirk. Student, DePauw U., 1943-44, Wabash Coll., 1944, State U. Iowa, 1944; BArch, U. Ill., 1949. Registered profl. arch. Ptnr. Johnson, Kile, Seehausen & Assocs., Inc. archs., engrs., Rockford, Ill., 1955-82, pres., 1974-82, Richard F. Seehausen-Arch., Inc., Rockford, 1983—. Mem. com. jail planning and constrn. stds. Bur. Detention Facilities, Ill. Dept. Corrections, 1970-73; analyst Dept. Def., 1962-66; analyst Fed. Fall-Out Shelter, 1962—. Prin. works include No. Ill. U. Ctr., Harrison Hall, Lorado Taft, Oreg., also Health Svc. Bldg., Winnebago County Courthouse, Rockford, St. Mark Luth. Ch., Christ Meth. Ch., 1st Presbyn. Ch., Rochelle, Ill., Forest Hills Free Ch., Rockford, Messiah Luth. Ch., Rock Falls, Ill., Ch. of the Nazarene, Freeport, Ill., McHenry County Ct. House, Woodstock, Ill., Stephenson County Courthouse, Freeport, Ogle County Pub. Safety Bldg., Oreg., DeKalb H.S., Page Park Spl. Edn. Sch., Rockford, Oak Crest Retirement Ctr., Sycamore/DeKalb, Ill., Social Security bldgs., Racine, Sheboygan, Oshkosh and Janesville, Wis., Freeport YWCA Bldgs., renovation Carroll County Ct. House, DeKalb Area Retirement Ctr., Old Winnebago County Courthouse, Rockford, Rockford Mut. Ins. Home Office Bldg., Court Street Meth. Ch., Rockford, Willows Personal Care Ctr., others. Bd. dirs. Rockford Boys Club, Lincoln Pk. Boys Club, past dir.; trustee Emmanuel Luth. Ch., Rockford, 1989-92; mem. Nat. Trust Hist. Preservation, 2000—. Served with USN, 1943-45, USNR, 1945-47, lt. USAF, 1949-55. Mem. AIA (dir. No. Ill. chpg. 1966-68, 75-77, pres. chpt. 1978-79), Ill. Coun. of Am. Inst. Archs., U. Ill. Alumni Assn., Mason (Shriner), Kiwanian, Forest Hills Country Club (gov. 1970-72), Saddle Brooke Country Club, Lamdba Chi Alpha. Lutheran. Office: Richard F Seehausen Arch Inc 65297 E Emerald Ridge Dr Tucson AZ 85739-1434 E-mail: dicknjean@worldnet.att.net.

SEEKELY, MARTINS, retail company executive; BS in Acctg., John Carroll U. CPA. Contr. Boston Distributors, Inc.; asst. contr. Phar-Mor, Inc., Youngstown, Ohio, 1993-97, v.p., contr., 1997-2000, v.p., CFO, 2000—. Office: 20 Federal Plz W Youngstown OH 44503-1420

SEELER, RUTH ANDREA, pediatrician, educator; b. N.Y.C., June 13, 1936; d. Thomas and Olivia (Patten) S. BA cum laude, U. Vt., 1959, MD, 1962. Diplomate Am. Bd. Pediatrics, Am. Bd. Pediatric Hematology/Oncology. Intern Bronx (N.Y.) Mcpl. Hosp., 1962—65; pediats. hematology/oncology fellow U. Ill., 1965—67; dir. pediatric hematology/oncology Cook County Hosp., 1967—84; prof. pediatrics and pediatric edn. Coll. Medicine U. Ill., Chgo., 1984—; assoc. chief pediatrics Michael Reese Hosp., 1990—97, acting chief pediatrics, 1997—99; pediatrician St. Anthony's Hosp./U. Ill. Coll. Medicine, 1999—2001. Course coord. pediatrics Nat. Coll. Advanced Med. Edn., Chgo., 1987-96; mem. subboard Pediatric Hematology/Oncology, Chapel Hill, 1990-95. Mem. editl. bd. Am. Jour. Pediatric Hematology/Oncology, 1985-95. Founder camp for hemophiliacs Hemophilia Found., Ill., 1973—2000, med. dir., pres., 1981—85; jr. and sr. warden, treas. Ch. Our Saviour, Chgo., 1970—92, 2002—. Mem.: Phi Beta Kappa, Gamma Phi Beta Found. (trustee 1994—2000, 2000—). Avocations: triathalons, biking, swimming. Office: U Ill Coll Medicine Pediats M/C 856 840 S Wood St Chicago IL 60612-7317

SEGAL, MINDY, chef; Grad., Kendall Coll. Pastry asst. Ambria, Chgo.; pastry chef Charlie Trotter's, Gordon, Chgo., Marche, Chgo., Spago, Chgo., MK the Restaurant, Chgo. Developed dessert menus Mia Francesca, Harvest on Huron, Thyme. Office: 868 N Franklin Chicago IL 60610

SEGERLIND, LARRY J. agricultural engineering educator; Prof. dept. agrl. engring. Mich. State U. Mem. Am. Soc. Agrl. Engrs. (A.W. Farrall Young Educator award 1976, Paper award, Massey-Ferguson medal 1996) Office: Mich State U Rm 205 AW Farrall Hall East Lansing MI 48824-1323 E-mail: segerlin@gr.msu.edu.

SEGUI, DAVID, professional baseball player; b. Kansas City, Kans., July 19, 1966; Baseball player Balt. Orioles, 1990-93, N.Y. Mets, 1994-95, Mont. Expos, 1995-97, Seattle Mariners, 1998-99, Toronto Blue Jays, 1999, Tex. Rangers, 2000, Cleve. Indians, 2000. Office: Cleve Indians 2401 Ontario St Cleveland OH 44115*

SEIDMAN, DAVID N(ATHANIEL), materials science and engineering educator; b. N.Y.C., July 5, 1938; s. Charles and Jeanette (Cohen) S.; m. Shoshanah Cohen-Sabban, Oct. 21, 1973; children: Elie, Ariel, Eytan. BS, NYU, 1960, MS, 1962; PhD, U. Ill., Urbana, 1965. Postdoc. assoc. Cornell U., Ithaca, N.Y., 1964-66, asst. prof. materials sci. and engring., 1966-70, assoc. prof. materials sci. and engring., 1970-76, prof. materials sci. and engring., 1976-85, Northwestern U., Evanston, Ill., 1985-96, Walter P. Murphy prof. materials sci. and engring., 1996—. Vis. prof. Technion, Haifa, 1969, Tel-Aviv U., Ramat-Aviv, 1972; Lady Davis vis. prof. Hebrew U., Jerusalem, 1978, 80-81, prof. materials sci., 1983-85; vis. scientist C.E. de Grenoble, 1981, C.N.E.T.-Meylan, 1981, C.E. de Scalay, 1989, U. Goettingen, 1989, 92; sci. cons. Argonne (Ill.) Nat. labs., 1985-94. Mem. editl. bd., editor spl. issues (jour.) Interface Sci., 1993—2001, editor-in-chief, 2002—, mem. editl. bd. Materials Sci. Forum , 1996—; contbr. numerous articles to profl. jours. Recipient Max Planck Rsch. prize Max-Planck-Gesellschaft and the A. von Humboldt-Stiftung, 1993; Guggenheim fellow, 1972-73, 80-81, Humboldt fellow, 1989, 92; named chair for phys. metallurgy Gordon Conf., 1982. Fellow Am. Phys. Soc., TMS (mem. fellows award com. 2002–, Hardy Gold medal 1967); mem. AAAS, Am. Soc. Metals Internat., Am. Ceramic Soc., Materials Rsch. Soc., Microscopy Soc. Am., A. von Humboldt Soc. Am., Internat. Field-Emission Soc. (mem. steering com. 1997—, pres. 2000—), Böhmische Phys. Soc. Democrat. Jewish. Achievements include research in microstructural evolution, internal interfaces, atomic-scale imperfections in metals and semiconductors, and electron microscopy. Home: 9056 Tamaroa Ter Skokie IL 60076-1928 Office: Northwestern U MS&E Dept MLSB Evanston IL 60208-3108 E-mail: d-seidman@northwestern.edu.

SEIFERT, SHELLEY JANE, human resources specialist; b. Aug. 12, 1954; BS in Consumer Econs. and Journalism, U. Mo., 1976; MBA in Fin. with honors, U. Louisville, 1980. Fin. analyst Nat. City Bank, Ky., 1979-81, compensation analyst, 1981-85, mgr. compensation, 1985-86, mgr. compensation, recruiting and tng., 1986-91; mgr. compensation and devel. Nat. City Corp., Cleve., 1988-91, human resource dir., 1991-94, sr. v.p., corp. human resource dir., 1994—. Spkr. in field. Recipient Woman of Distinction award YMCA. Mem. Urban League (bd. dirs., chair employment com., Ohio labor adv. com.). Office: Nat City Corp Nat City Ctr 1900 E 9th St Cleveland OH 44114-3401

SEIFFERT, RONALD J. bank executive; BAS in Fin. and Econs., Washington U., St. Louis, 1979; grad. with honors, Stonier Sch. Banking, 1994. With Huntington Bancshares, Inc., Columbus, Ohio, 1981—, exec. v.p., exec. dir. comml. svcs., vice chmn., 1996—. Trustee, mem. fin. com. Cleve. State U.; mem. adv. coun. Ctr. for Internat. Bus. Edn. and Rsch., Max M. Fisher Coll. Bus.; trustee Ohio Dominican Coll., Columbus Mus. Art. Mem. Bankers Roundtable. Office: 41 S High St Columbus OH 43287-0001

SEIGLER, DAVID STANLEY, botanist, chemist, educator; b. Wichita Falls, Tex., Sept. 11, 1940; s. Kenneth R. and Floy M. (Wilkinson) S.; m. Janice Kay Cline, Jan. 20, 1961; children: Dava, Rebecca. BS in Chemistry, Southwestern (Okla.) State Coll., 1961; PhD in Organic Chemistry, U. Okla., 1967. Postdoctoral assoc. USDA No. Regional Lab., Peoria, Ill., 1967-68; postdoctoral fellow dept. botany U. Tex., Austin, 1968-70; asst. prof. botany U. Ill., Urbana, 1970-76, assoc. prof., 1976-79, prof. botany, 1979—, head dept. plant biology, 1988-93. Curator U. Ill. Herbarium, 1993—. Author: Plant Secondary Metabolism, 1999; editor: Crop Resources, 1977, Phytochemistry and Angiosperm Phylogeny, 1981; contbr. numerous articles to profl. jours. Recipient Fulbright Hays Lecturer award Fulbright Commn., Argentina, 1976, (alternate) Germany, 1995-96, study award Deutsche Akademischer Austauschdienst, Germany, 1995, Rupert Barneby award N.Y. Bot. Garden, 1997. Mem. Phytochem. Soc. N.Am. (pres. 1988-89), Bot. Soc. Am., Am. Chem. Soc., Am. Soc. Plant Taxonomists, Internat. Soc. Chem. Ecology (pres. 1990-91). Mem. Assembly of God Ch. Avocation: genealogy. Home: 510 W Vermont Ave Urbana IL 61801-4931 Office: U Ill Dept Plant Biology 265 Morrill Hall 505 S Goodwin Ave Urbana IL 61801-3707 E-mail: d-seigler@uiuc.edu.

SEILHAMER, RAY A. bishop; Bishop United Brethren in Christ, 1994—. Office: United Brethren in Christ 302 Lake St Huntington IN 46750-1264

SEILS, WILLIAM GEORGE, lawyer; b. Chgo., Aug. 9, 1935; s. Harry H. and Hazel C. (Sullivan) S.; m. Evelyn E. Oliver, Sept. 8, 1956; children: Elizabeth Ann, Ellen Carol, Eileen Alison. A.B., J.D., U. Mich., 1959. Bar: Ill. bar 1959. Since practiced in, Chgo.; ptnr. Arvey, Hodes & Costello & Burman, 1968-87; gen. counsel, sec., sr. v.p. Richardson Electronics, Ltd., LaFox, Ill., 1986—. Contbr. articles to profl. jours.; asst. editor: Mich. Law Rev, 1958-59. Mem. Ill. Bar Assn., Order of Coif. Office: Richardson Electronics Ltd PO Box 393 40w267 Keslinger Rd Lafox IL 60147-0393 E-mail: wgs@rell.com.

SEIREG, ALI A(BDEL HAY), mechanical engineer; b. Arab Republic of Egypt, Oct. 26, 1927; came to U.S., 1951, naturalized, 1960; s. Abdel Hay and Aisha Seireg; m. Shirley Marachowsky, Dec. 24, 1954; children: Mirette Elizabeth LaFollette, Pamela Aisha Terry. BSME, U. Cairo, 1948; PhD, U. Wis., 1954. Lectr. Cairo U., 1954-56; staff adv. engr. Falk Corp., Milw., 1956-59; assoc. prof. theoretical and applied mechanics Marquette U., 1959-64, prof., 1964-65; prof. emeritus (Kaiser chair) mech. engring. U. Wis., Madison, 1965—; Ebaugh Prof. U. Fla., Gainesville, 1986—. Cons. in field.; chmn. U.S. council Internat. Fedn. Theory of Machines, 1974-94; co-chmn. 5th World Congress of Theory of Machines, 1979, 1st USSR-USA Conf. on Composite Materials, 1989. Author: Mechanical Systems Analysis, 1969, Biomedical Analysis of Musculoskeletal Structure for Medicine and Sports, 1989, Optimized Motion Planning, 1994, The Kinematic Geometry of Gearing, 1995, Optimizing the Shape of Mechanical Elements, 1997, Friction and Lubrication in Mechanical Design, 1998; editor: Computers in Mechanical Engring.; editor in chief SOMA, Engineering for the Human Body, 1986-90; contbr. articles to profl. jours. Recipient Kuwait prize for sci., 1987. Fellow ASME (Richards Meml. award 1973, Machine Design award 1978, Design Automation award 1990, chmn. div. design engring. 1977-78, chmn. computer tech. 1978-81, policy bd. comm. 1978-80, policy bd. gen. engring. 1979-80, chmn. Century II Internat. Computer Tech. Conf. 1980, founding chmn. computer engring. div. 1980-81, v.p. systems and design 1981-85, sr. v.p., chmn. council on engring. 1985-90, pres. Gen. Rsch. Inst. 1984—), Am. Soc. Engring. Edn. (George Westinghouse award 1970), Soc. Exptl. Stress Analysis, Am. Inst. Med. and Biol. Engring. (founding fellow), Am. Gear Mfg. Assn. (E. P. Connell award 1974), Automation Research Council; mem. Chinese Mech. Engring. Soc. (hon.), USSR Acad. Sci. (fgn.), Russian Acad. Sci. (fgn.), Yugoslav Acad. Engring. (fgn.). Office: 1513 University Ave Madison WI 53706-1539 E-mail: aaseireg@facstaff.wisc.edu.

SEIWALD, ROBERT J. retired inventor; b. Ft. Morgan, Colo., Mar. 26, 1925; BS in Chemistry, U. San Francisco; PhD in Organic Chemistry, St. Louis U., 1954. Prof. organic chemistry U. San Francisco, 1957-89; ret., 1989. Inducted Nat. Inventors Hall of Fame, 1995. Office: Nat Inventors Hall of Fame 221 S Broadway St Akron OH 44308-1505

SELBY, DIANE RAY MILLER, fraternal organization administrator; b. Lorain, Ohio, Oct. 11, 1940; d. Dale Edward and Mildred (Ray) Miller; m. David Baxter Selby, Apr. 14, 1962; children: Elizabeth, Susan, Sarah. BS in Edn., Ohio State U., 1962. Sec. Kappa Kappa Gamma Frat., Columbus, Ohio, 1962-63, editor, 1972-86; tchr. Hilliard (Ohio) High Sch., 1963-65; exec. dir. Mortar Bd., Inc. Nat. Office, Columbus, Ohio, 1986—. Editor The Key of Kappa Kappa Gamma Frat, 1972-86 (Student Life award, 1983, 84, 85). Founding officer Community Coordinating Bd., Worthington, Ohio, 1983; pres. PTA Coun., Worthington, 1984, Worthington Band Boosters, 1985; sec., treas. Sports and Recreation Facilities Bd., Worthington, 1986—; mem. sustaining com. Jr. League Columbus, 1991-93, docent Kelton House, 1979—. Mem. Mortar Bd., Inc., Twig 53 Children's Hosp. (assoc.), Assn. Coll. Honor Soc. (mem. exec. com. 1999-2001, chmn. bylaws com.), Ladybugs and Buckeyes, Kappa Kappa Gamma (House Bd. vp. 1997-2000). Republican. Lutheran. E-mila. Home: 6750 Merwin Pl Columbus OH 43235-2838 Office: Mortar Bd Inc 1200 Chambers Rd Ste 201 Columbus OH 43212-1754 E-mail: selby.1@osu.edu.

SELBY, MYRA CONSETTA, state supreme court justice; b. Bay City, Mich., July 1, 1955; d. Ralph Irving and Archie Mae (Franklin) Selby; m. Bruce Curry; 2 children. BA with honors, Kalamazoo (Mich.) Coll., 1977; JD, U. Mich., 1980. Bar: D.C. 1980, Ind. 1983, U.S. Dist. Ct. (so. dist.) 1983, Ct. Appeals (D.C. cir.) 1984, U.S. Ct. Appeals (8th cir.) 1985. Assoc. Seyfarth, Shaw, Fairweather & Geraldson, Washington, 1980-83; ptnr. Ice, Miller, Donadio & Ryan, Indpls., 1983-93; dir. Ind. Healthcare Policy, 1993-94; assoc. justice Ind. Supreme Ct., 1995-2000; ret., 2000. Bd. dirs. Alpha Nursing Home, Flanner House, Inpls. Ballet Theatre. Mem.: Am. Law Inst. Avocations: soccer, biking, reading, ballet.

SELF, BILL, college basketball coach; b. Okmulgee, Okla., Dec. 27, 1962; m. Cindy Self; children: Lauren, Tyler. BSBA, Okla. State U., 1985, M in Athletic Adminstrn., 1989. Asst. coach U. Kans., 1985-86, Okla. State U., 1986-93; head coach Oral Roberts U., 1993-97, U. Tulsa, 1997-2000, U. Ill., 2000—. Named Don Haskins Coach of Yr., Western Athletic Conf., 2000, John and Nellie Wooden Coach of Yr., Utah Tipoff Club, 2000. Led Tulsa U. to Western Athletic Conf. titles, 1998-2000 and consecutive trips to the NCAA tournament; has been asst. or head coach of ten teams that reached the playoffs, 7 times to the NCAA Tournament and 3 times to the National Invitational Tournament. Office: Men's Basketball Dept Intercollegiate Athlet 1700 S 4th Champaign IL 61820 E-mail: bself@uiuc.edu.

SELF, MADISON ALLEN, finance company executive; b. Ozawkie, Kans., June 30, 1921; s. Benjamin B. and Margaret E. (Allen) S.; m. Lila M. Reetz, Sept. 1, 1943; 1 son, Murray A. B.S. in Chem. Engring, U. Kans., 1943. Engr. York Corp., 1943-44; salesman and researcher Sharples Chems., Inc., 1944-47; with Bee Chem. Co., Lansing, Ill., 1947-84, chmn. bd., chief exec. officer, until 1984; pres. Allen Fin., Inc., 1984—; chmn. bd. dirs. Tioga Internat., Inc., 1989-99. Life trustee Ill. Inst. Tech. Mem. Chief Exec. Orgn., World Pres.'s Orgn., Hinsdale Golf Club. Office: Allen Fin Inc 907 N Elm St Ste 302 Hinsdale IL 60521-3645 E-mail: maself@voyager.net.

SELIGMAN, JOEL, dean; b. N.Y.C., Jan. 11, 1950; s. Selig Jacob and Muriel (Bienstock) S.; m. Friederike Felber, July 30, 1981; children: Andrea, Peter. AB magna cum laude, UCLA, 1971; JD, Harvard U., 1974. Bar: Calif. 1975. Atty., writer Corp. Accountability Rsch. Group, Washington, 1974-77; prof. law Northeastern U. Law Sch., 1977-83, George Washington U., 1983-86, U. Mich., Ann Arbor, 1986-95; dean law U. Ariz., Tucson, 1995-99; dean sch. law Washington U., St. Louis, 1999—. Cons. Fed. Trade Commn., 1979-82, Dept. Transp., 1983, Office Tech. Assessment, 1988-89; chair adv. com. on mkt. info. SEC, 2000-2001; reporter Nat. Conf. of Commrs. on Uniform State Laws, Uniform Securities Act, 2001. Author (with others) Constitutionalizing the Corporation: The Case for the Federal Chartering of Giant Corporations, 1976, The High Citadel: The Influence of Harvard Law School, 1978, The Transformation of Wall Street: A History of the Securities and Exchange Commission and Modern Corporate Finance, 1982, The SEC and the Future of Finance, 1985, (multi-volume) Securities Regulation; contbr. articles to profl. jours. Mem. State Bar Calif., Am. Law Inst. (adv. com., advisor corp. governance project), AICPAs (profl. ethics exec. com. 2000—). Office: Wash U Sch Law CB 1120 1 Brookings Dr Saint Louis MO 63130-4862

SELIG-PRIEB, WENDY, sports team executive; JD, Marquette U., 1988. With broadcasting dept. Milw. Brewers, from 1982; exec. trainee Office of Baseball Commr.; corp. atty. Foley & Lardner, to 1990; gen. counsel Milw. Brewers, 1990-95, v.p., gen. counsel, 1995-98, now pres., CEO, 1998—. Office: care Milw Brewers County Stadium PO Box 3099 Milwaukee WI 53201-3099

SELIGSON, THEODORE H. architect, interior designer, art consultant; b. Kansas City, Mo., Nov. 10, 1930; s. Harry and Rose (Haith) S.; m. Jacqueline Rose, Dec. 27, 1964 (div. 1976). BArch, Washington U., St. Louis, 1953. Registered architect, Mo., Kans. Intern Marshall & Brown, Kansas City, Mo., 1949-54; designer, head design Kivett & Myers, 1954-62; prin. Design Assocs., 1955—, Atelier Seligson, Kansas City, Mo., 1962-64; pres. Seligson, Eggen, Inc., 1964-73, Seligson Assocs., Inc., Architects Planners, Kansas City, 1973-97, Seligson Assocs., Inc., Archs. Planners, Kansas City, 1973-97; prin. Foss, Seligson, Lafferty, 1997—. Vis. lectr. adult edn. U. Mo.-Kansas City, 1958-61, vis. prof. arch., 1989—; tchr., critic Kansas City Art Inst., Mo., 1961-64, 71-72, adj. prof., 1986, 89, 91, 92; adj. prof. Kansas State U., 1991-92, 97; vis. prof. Washington U., St. Louis, 1975, 77, 78, 81, 86, 91, U. Kans., Lawrence, 1978, 79, 80, 91, 92; art cons. Design Assocs., Kansas City, Mo., 1955—. Projects pub. in archtl. jours. V.p. Friends of Art Nelson-Atkins Mus. Art, Kansas City, bd. dirs. 1963-67, chmn. selections com., 1981, vis. curator, 1972, 87; chmn. Capitol Fine Arts Commn. Mo., 1983-90, Kansas City Worlds Fair goals and themes subcom., 1985-90; bd. dirs. Westport Tomorrow, Kansas City, 1980-87, Hist. Kansas City Found., 1984-90; pres. Native Sons of Kansas City, 1989, bd. dirs. 1978-94, Westport Cmty. Coun., 1973-75; bd. govs. Truman Med. Ctr., Kansas City, 1998—. Recipient Urban Design award Kansas City Mcpl. Art Commn., 1968, 74, 78; Nat. Archtl. award Am. Inst. Steel Constrn., 1970; Nat. award ASID/DuPont Corian, 1989. Fellow AIA (Kansas City chpt. pres. 1983, bd. dirs. 1979-84, Design Excellence award 1966, 68, 70, 74, Ctrl. States Regional award 1974, 78, Honor award for outstanding svc. to chpt. and profession 1982-83); mem. Mo. Coun. Archs., Am. Soc. Interior Designers, Nat. Coun. Archtl. Registration Bds. (task analysis adv. com. 1988-90), Soc. Archtl. Historians (pres. 1973-75, bd. dirs. 1994-97). Jewish. Office: Foss Seligson Lafferty 106 W 14th St Kansas City MO 64105-1914

SELLERS, BARBARA JACKSON, federal judge; b. Richmond, Va., Oct. 3, 1940; m. Richard F. Sellers; children: Elizabeth M., Anne W., Catherine A. Attended, Baldwin-Wallace Coll., 1958-60; BA cum laude, Ohio State U., 1962; JD magna cum laude, Capital U. Law Sch., Columbus, Ohio, 1979. Bar: Ohio 1979, U.S. Dist. Ct. (so. dist.) Ohio 1981, U.S. Ct. Appeals (6th cir.), 1986. Jud. law clk. Hon. Robert J. Sidman, U.S. Bankruptcy Judge, Columbus, Ohio, 1979-81; assoc. Lasky & Semons, 1981-82; jud. law clk. to Hon. Thomas M. Herbert, U.S. Bankruptcy Ct., 1982-84; assoc. Baker & Hostetler, 1984-86; U.S. bankruptcy judge So. Dist. Ohio, 1986—. Lectr. on bankruptcy univs., insts., assns. Recipient Am. Jurisprudence prize contracts and criminal law, 1975-76, evidence and property, 1976-77, Corpus Juris Secundum awards, 1975-76, 76-77. Mem. Columbus Bar Assn., Am. Bankruptcy Inst., Nat. Conf. Bankruptcy Judges, Order of Curia, Phi Beta Kappa. Office: US Bankruptcy Ct 170 N High St Columbus OH 43215-2403 E-mail: barbara_sellers@ohsb.uscourts.gov.

SEMONIN, RICHARD GERARD, retired state official; b. Akron, Ohio, June 25, 1930; s. Charles Julius and Catherine Cecelia (Schooley) S.; m. Lennie Stuker, Feb. 3, 1951; children: Cecelia C., Richard G. Jr. (dec.), James R., Patricia R. BS, U. Wash., 1955. With Ill. State Water Survey, Champaign, 1955-91, chief, 1986-91, chief emeritus, 1991—; co-chmn. Ill. Water Rsch. & Land Use Planning Task Force, 1992-94. Adj. prof. U. Ill., 1975-91; chmn. Ill. Low-Level Radioactive Waste Task Group, 1994-96. Contbr. chpts. to books and articles to profl. jours.; co-editor: Atmospheric Deposition, 1983. Staff sgt. USAF, 1948-52. Grantee NSF, 1957-76, U.S. Dept. Energy, 1965-90. Fellow AAAS, Am. Meteorol. Soc. (councilor 1983-86); mem. Nat. Weather Assn. (councilor 1978-81), Weather Modification Assn., Ill. Acad. Scis., Sigma Xi. Roman Catholic. Avocations: Civil War, golf, fishing, genealogy. Home: 1002 Devonshire Dr Champaign IL 61821-6620 Office: Ill State Water Survey 2204 Griffith Dr Champaign IL 61820-7495 E-mail: semonin@uiuc.edu.

SEMPLE, LLOYD ASHBY, lawyer; b. St. Louis, June 7, 1939; s. Robert B. and Isabelle A. S.; m. Cynthia T. Semple, Aug. 26, 1961; children: Whitney, Sarah, Lloyd Jr., Terrell. BA, Yale U., 1961; JD, U. Mich, 1964. Bar: Mich. 1964. Assoc. Dykema Gossett, Detroit, 1964-70, ptnr., 1971—; chmn., 1994—. Councilman, mayor pro tem City of Grosse Pointe Farms, Mich, 1975-83; chmn. bd. trustees Detroit Med. Ctr. Corp.; chmn. bd. dirs. Detroit Zool. Soc.; dir., trustee, sec. Karmanos Cancer Inst. Mem. ABA, Mich. Bar Assn., Detroit Bar Assn., Country Club Detroit, Yondotega Club, Detroit Athletic Club, Yale Club (N.Y.C.), Bohemian Club (San Francisco). Episcopalian. Home: 57 Cambridge Rd Grosse Pointe Farms MI 48236-3004 Office: Dykema Gossett 400 Renaissance Ctr Ste 3500 Detroit MI 48243-1602 E-mail: lsemple@dykema.com.

SENECHAL, ALICE R. judge, lawyer; b. Rugby, N.D., June 25, 1955; d. Marvin William and Dora Emma (Erdman) S. BS, N.D. State U., 1977; JD, U. Minn., 1984. Bar: Minn. 1984, U.S. Dist. Ct. Minn. 1984, N.D. 1986, U.S. Ct. Appeals (8th cir.) 1987. Law clk. U.S. Dist. Judge Bruce M. Van Sickle, Bismarck, N.D., 1984-86; with Robert Vogel Law Office, Grand Forks, 1986—. U.S. magistrate judge, 1990—. Office: Robert Vogel Law Office 106 N 3rd St Ste 202 Grand Forks ND 58203-3703

SENEFF, SMILEY HOWARD, business owner; b. Odon, Ind., June 28, 1925; s. Smiley and Ada Fern (Howard) S.; m. Barbara Jean Daum, July 17, 1950 (div. 1966); children: Nancy Kay Secrest, Cheryl Evans; m. Mary Ann Beeler, Mar. 12, 1966; children: Jill Midtbo, Judy Hiland, Jacalyn Harness, Jennifer Peverill, Donald. Student, Duke U., 1945; BS, Ind. U., 1950. Mem. acctg. staff Armour and Co., Indpls., 1950-52, Chevrolet Comml. Body Co., Indpls., 1952-54; owner, mgr. Seneff Hardware and Appliance, Plainfield, Ind., 1955-66, Catalina Motel, Indpls., 1966-73, Smiley's Pancake and Steak, Indpls., 1972—, Smiley's Car Wash, Indpls., 1972—. Mem. County Zoning Bd., 1959-63; Rep. precinct committeeman, del. to state Rep. conv., 1959-63. Mem. Elks, Rotary (pres.), Masons, Scottish Rite, Shriners. Avocations: golf, swimming, walking. Home: 1115 Woodridge Brownsburg IN 46112 Office: Seneff Inns Inc 1307 S High School Rd Indianapolis IN 46241-3128

SENGUPTA, DIPAK LAL, electrical engineering and physics educator, researcher; b. Bengal, India, Mar. 1, 1931; came to U.S., 1959; s. Jayanta Kumar and Pankajini Sengupta; m. Sujata Basu, Aug. 31, 1962; children: Sumit, Mita. BSc in Physics with honors, Calcutta U., India, 1950, MSc in Radio Physics, 1952; PhD, U. Toronto, Ont., Can., 1958. Assoc. rsch.

physicist dept. elec. engring. U. Mich., Ann Arbor, 1959-63, rsch. physicist, 1965-75, rsch. scientist, prof. dept. elec. engring., 1975-86; asst. prof. dept. elec. engring. U. Toronto, 1963-64; asst. dir. Cen. Electronics Engring. Rsch. Inst., Pilani, India, 1964-65; prof., chmn. dept. elec. engring. and physics U. Detroit Mercy, 1986-95; prof. elec. engring. U. Detroit, Mercy, 1996—. Fulbright vis. lectr. in India, 1992-93; cons. Ford Motor Co., Dearborn, Mich., 1976-77, Battelle Pacific N.W. Labs., Richland, Wash., 1978. Author: Radar Cross Section Analysis and Control, 1991; contbr. articles to profl. jours. Fellow IEEE (life, Contbn. award 1969, recognition awards 1978-79); mem. Internat. Radio Scientists Union (sec. commn. B 1976-78), Sigma Xi, Eta Kappa Nu. Office: U Detroit Mercy Dept Elec Engring 4001 W Mcnichols Rd Detroit MI 48221-3038

SENHAUSER, DONALD A(LBERT), pathologist, educator; b. Dover, Ohio, Jan. 30, 1927; s. Albert Carl and Maude Anne (Snyder) S.; m. Helen Brown, July 22, 1961; children: William, Norman. Student, U. Chgo., 1944-45; BS, Columbia U., 1948, MD, 1951; grad. with honors, U.S. Naval Sch. Aviation Medicine, 1953. Diplomate Am. Bd. Pathology. Intern Roosevelt Hosp., N.Y.C., 1951-52; resident Columbia-Presbyn. Hosp., 1955-56, Cleve. Clinic, 1956-60; instr. in pathology Columbia U., 1955-56; fellow in immuno-pathology Middlesex Hosp. Med. Sch., London, 1960-61; mem. dept. pathology Cleve. Clinic Found., 1961-63; assoc. prof. pathology U. Mo., 1963-65; prof., asst. dean Sch. Medicine U. Mo., 1969-70, dir. teaching labs., 1968-70, prof., vice-chmn. dept. pathology, 1965-75; prof., chmn. dept. pathology Coll. Medicine Ohio State U., 1975-92, chair emeritus, 1992, prof. Sch. Allied Med. Professions, 1975-95; prof. emeritus, 1995—. Dir. labs. Ohio State U. Hosps., 1975-92; pres. Univ. Reference Lab., Inc., 1984-86, CEO, 1986-92; bd. dirs. Columbus area chpt. ARC, 1978-82; cons. in field; WHO-AMA Vietnam med. edn. project mem. U. Saigon Med. Sch., 1967-72; vis. scientist HEW, 1972-73; acting dir. Ctrl. Ohio Regional Blood Ctr., 1976-79. Mem. editorial bd. Am. Jour. Clin. Pathology, 1965-76. With USN, 1945-46; lt. M.C. USNR, Korea, China; now capt. USNR ret. Served with USN, 1945-46; served as lt. M.C. USNR, Korea, China; now capt. USNR, Ret. Recipient Lower award Bunts Ednl. Found., 1960-61 Mem. AAAS, Coll. Am. Pathologists (bd. govs. 1980-86, v.p. 1989-90, pres.-elect 1990-91, pres. 1991-93, immediate past pres. 1993—, Pathologist of Yr. 1994, Hartman award 1998), Am. Soc. Clin. Pathologists, Assn. Pathology Chmn., Am. Assn. Pathology, Internat. Acad. Pathology, Assn. Am. Med. Colls., Am. Assn. Blood Banks, Ohio Soc. Pathologists (gov. 1979, pres. 1987-89), Ohio Hist. Soc., Masons, Sigma Xi. Lutheran. Home: 1256 Clubview Blvd N Columbus OH 43235-1226 Office: 333 W 10th Ave Columbus OH 43210-1239 E-mail: donaldsenhauser@cs.com.

SENHAUSER, JOHN CRATER, architect; b. New Philadelphia, Ohio, Apr. 7, 1947; s. Edwin Crater and Margaret Jean (Huffman) S.; m. Teri A. Schleyer, June 25, 1988. BS in Architecture, U. Cin., 1971. Registered architect, Ohio, Ky. Designer Jones, Peacock, Garn & Ptnrs., Cin., 1971-72; project architect Smith Stevens Architects, 1972-76; project mgr. Herrlinger Enterprises, 1976-79; prin., owner John C. Senhauser, Architect, 1979—. Adj. assoc. prof. Sch. Architecture and Interior Design, U. Cin., 1992-98 Exhibited in group shows at Toni Birckhead Gallery, 1990, Contemporary Arts Ctr., Cin., 1993, 98, Canton (Ohio) Art Inst., 1993; prin. works include residences. Mem. historic conservation bd. City of Cin., 1986-98, chmn. 1998—; mem. urban design rev. bd., 1998—; mem. dean's adv. coun. Coll. Design Architecture Art and Planning U. Cin., 1990; mem. design rev. com. U. Cin., 1997—. Recipient Merit award Builder mag., 1985, 88, 94, 96, 99, Grand award, 1990, Grand Best in Region award Profl. Builder, 1988, 90, Grand award for Best Overall Design, Custom Home Mag., 1996, 97, Merit award, 1990, 94, other awards. Fellow AIA (pres. 1991, Honor award Cin. chpt. 1983, 85, 90, 91, 92, 93, 94, 95, 96, 2000, Merit award 1990, 93, 94); mem. AIA Ohio (bd. dirs., sec. 1997-98, v.p. 1999, pres. 2000, regional dir. nat. bd. dirs. 2001—, Honor award 1985, 90, 91, 93, 94, 99). Office: John C Senhauser Architect 1118 Saint Gregory St Cincinnati OH 45202-1724

SENIOR, RICHARD JOHN LANE, textile rental service executive; b. Datchet, Eng., July 6, 1940; arrived in U.S., 1972, naturalized, 1977; s. Harold Dennis Senior and Jane Lane Dorothy (Chadwick) Senior Rigg; m. Diana Morgan, Dec. 19, 1966; children: Alden, Alicia, Amanda. MA, Oxford U., 1962; MIA, Yale U., 1964. Mgmt. cons. McKinsey & Co., Inc., London, Chgo., 1967-74; pres., CEO Morgan Svcs., Inc., Chgo., 1974—. Bd. dirs. Northwestern Meml. Healthcare, 1992-2001, Northwestern U. Assocs., Northwestern Meml. Found., Ball Hort. Co., Near South Planning Bd.; regional adv. bd. Kemper Ins. Cos., 1994-96. Pres. bd. trustees Latin Sch., Chgo., 1979-83; bd. dirs. Chgo. Crime Commn., 1994-99. Hon. scholar Oxford U. Mem. Uniform and Textile Svc. Assn. (bd. dirs. 1996-99, vice chair 2001—), Textile Rental Svcs. Assn. Am. (pres. 1983-85, dir., mem. exec. com. 1978-86), Racquet Club (mem. bd. govs. 1983-91), Chgo. Club, Glen View Club, Casino (mem. bd. govs. 1991-96, treas. 1993-94), Econ. Club, Yale Club Chgo. (bd. dirs. 1991-95, AYA del. 1992-95), Northwestern U. Assocs. Home: 1500 N Lake Shore Dr Chicago IL 60610-6657 Office: Morgan Svcs Inc 323 N Michigan Ave Chicago IL 60601-3798 E-mail: senior@morganservices.com.

SENIOR, THOMAS BRYAN A. electrical engineering educator, researcher, consultant; b. Menston, Yorkshire, Eng., June 26, 1928; came to U.S., 1957; s. Thomas Harold and Emily Dorothy (Matthews) S.; m. Heather Margaret Golby, May 4, 1957; children— Margaret, David, Hazel, Peter. B.Sc., Manchester U., 1949, M.Sc., 1950; Ph.D., Cambridge U., 1954. Sr. sci. officer Royal Radar Establishment, Malvern, Eng., 1952-57; rsch. scientist U. Mich., Ann Arbor, 1957-69, prof. elec. engring., 1969-84, prof. elec. and computer sci., 1984-98, Arthur F. Thurnau prof., 1990-98, prof. emeritus, 1998—, dir. radiation lab., 1975-87, assoc. chmn. elect. engring. & computer sci. dept., 1984-90, acting chmn., 1987-88, assoc. chmn. acad. affairs, 1991-98. Cons. in field. Author: (with Bowman and Uslenghi) Electromagnetic and Acoustical Scattering by Simple Shapes, 1969; Mathematical Methods in Electrical Engineering, 1986; (with Volakis) Approximate Boundary Conditions in Electromagnetics, 1995; contbr. articles to profl. jours. Fellow IEEE (3d Millennium medal, AP-S Disting. Achievement award 2000); mem. Internat. Sci. Radio Union (chmn. U.S. nat. com. 1982-84, vice chmn. Com. B. 1985-87, chmn. 1988-90, pres. 1996-99, Van der Pol Gold medal 1993). Home: 1919 Ivywood Dr Ann Arbor MI 48103-4527 Office: U Mich Dept Elec Engring Comp S Ann Arbor MI 48109 E-mail: senior@eecs.umich.edu.

SENKLER, ROBERT, insurance company executive; Chmn., pres., CEO Minn. Mutual Life Ins. Co., St. Paul, 1994—. Office: Minn Mutual Life Ins Co 400 Robert St N Saint Paul MN 55101-2015

SENKLER, ROBERT L. insurance company executive; BA, Minn. Duluth Coll., 1979. V.p. Individual Ins. Divsn. Minn. Life Ins. Co., 1987-94, CEO, 1994—. Fellow Soc. Actuaries. Office: 400 Robert St N Saint Paul MN 55101-2015

SENNET, CHARLES JOSEPH, lawyer; b. Buffalo, Aug. 7, 1952; s. Saunders M. and Muriel S. (Rotenberg) S. AB magna cum laude, Cornell U., 1974; JD with high honors, George Washington U., 1979. Bar: Ill. 1979, U.S. Dist. Ct. (no. dist.) Ill. 1979, U.S. Ct. Appeals (7th cir.) 1982, U.S. Ct. Appeals (D.C. cir.) 1993. Assoc. Reuben & Proctor, Chgo., 1979-83; assoc. counsel Tribune Co., 1984-91, sr. counsel, 1991—. Adj. faculty Medill Sch. Journalism, Northwestern U., 1991-94; co-chair Television Music Lic. Com., 1995—. Contbr. articles to profl. jours. Mem. ABA (spkr. 1984-88, 91-97, 2000—, mem. gov. bd. Forum on Comms. Law 1995-98), NATAS, Ill. Bar Assn. (chmn. media law com. 1989-91), Chgo. Bar Assn., Fed. Comms. Bar Assn. Office: Tribune Co 435 N Michigan Ave Chicago IL 60611-4066

SENSENBRENNER, F(RANK) JAMES, JR. congressman; b. Chgo., June 14, 1943; s. F. James and Margaret (Luedke) S.; m. Cheryl Warren, Mar. 26, 1977; children: F. James III, Robert Alan. AB, Stanford U., 1965; JD, U. Wis., 1968. Bar: Wis. 1968, U.S. Supreme Ct. 1972. State rep. Wis. Assembly, Madison, 1969-75; state sen. Wis. Senate, 1975-79; asst. minority leader, 1976-79; mem. U.S Ho. of Reps., Washington, 1979—, chmn. jud. com., 2001—, chmn. sci. com., 1997-2001. Mem. Friends of Milw. Mus., Riverside Nature Ctr. Republican. Episcopalian. Mem. Am. Philatelic Soc., Chenequa Country Club, Capitol Hill Club. Home: PO Box 186 Menomonee Falls WI 53052-0186 Office: 2332 Rayburn House Office Bldg Washington DC 20515-4909*

SERAFYN, ALEXANDER JAROSLAV, retired automotive executive; b. Stare Selo, Ukraine, Mar. 27, 1930; came to U.S., 1949; s. Leon and Ahaphia (Peretiatko) S.; m. Zenia Maria Sylvestruk, July 5, 1958; children: Lesia, Lidia, Myron, Roman. BA, Wayne State U., 1954, MBA, 1960; PhD, Kensington U., 1983. Mgr. fin. analysis Ford (France) S.A., Paris, 1964-66; budget analysis mgr. Ford Motor/Indsl. and Chem. Div., Southfield, Mich., 1967; asst. ops. controller Ford Motor/Paint and Vinyl Ops., Mt. Clemens, 1968, ops. controller, 1969-71; controller Ford South Africa, Port Elizabeth, 1972-73; asst. div. controller Ford Motor/Metal Stamping Div., Dearborn, Mich., 1974-80, Ford Motor/Body and Assembly Ops., Dearborn, 1981-82; bus. plans and adminstrv. mgr. Ford Motor/Mfg. Ops., 1983-84; program mgr. Mazda Ford Motor/Body and Assembly Ops., 1985-90. Bd. dirs. Selfreliance Fed. Credit Union, Warren, Mich. Contbr. articles to profl. jours. Adviser Ukrainian Nat. Assn., 1994-98, auditor 1998—, pres. Detroit dist., 1989—, exec. v.p., 1987-89; treas. Shevchenko Sci. Soc., Detroit, 1989—, v.p., 1997—. Named Ukrainian of Yr., Ukrainian Grads. of Detroit and Windsor, 1980, Disting. Alumnus, Wayne State U. Sch. Bus., 1995. Mem. Acad. Engring. Scis. Ukraine, Ukrainian Engrs. Soc. Am. (sr. mem., bd. dirs. 1991-97), Ukrainian Engring. Soc. (pres. Detroit br. 1978-79), Ukrainian Nat. Assn. (Fraternalist of Yr. award 1991), World Found. Ukrainian Med. Assns. (bd. dirs. 1996—), also others. Republican. Ukrainian Catholic. Avocations: golf, skiing, travel, writing, reading. Home: 2565 Timberwyck Trail Dr Troy MI 48098-4103

SERATTI, LORRAINE M. state legislator; b. Oct. 30, 1949; V.p. Wis. Fedn. Taxpayers Orgn.; pres. Florence County Taxpayers Alliance; Wis. state assemblywoman dist. 36, 1992—. Small bus. owner. Mem. Florence Hist. Soc. Mem. NRA. Address: HC 2 Box 588 Florence WI 54121-9620 Office: Wis Assembly PO Box 8952 Madison WI 53708-8952

SERLIN, MARSHA, waste management service administrator; CEO/pres. Ill. United Scrap Metal, Cicero, 1978—. Recipient Nat. Small Bus. Subcontractor Yr. award, U.S. Small Bus. Adminstrn., 1996. Office: United Scrap Metal Inc 1545 S Cicero Ave Chicago IL 60804-1529

SERNETT, RICHARD PATRICK, lawyer, consultant; b. Mason City, Iowa, Sept. 8, 1938; s. Edward Frank and Loretta M. (Cavanaugh) S.; m. Janet Ellen Ward, Apr. 20, 1963; children: Susan Ellen, Thomas Ward, Stephen Edward, Katherine Anne. BBA, U. Iowa, 1960, JD, 1963. Bar: Iowa 1963, Ill. 1965, U.S. Dist. Ct. (no. dist.) Ill. 1965, U.S. Supreme Ct. 1971. House counsel, asst. sec. Scott, Foresman & Co., Glenview, Ill., 1963-70, sec., legal officer, 1970-80; v.p., law sec. SFN Cos., Inc., 1980-83, sr. v.p., sec., gen. counsel, 1983-85, exec. v.p., gen. counsel, 1985-87; pvt. practice Northbrook, Ill., 1988-90; v.p., sec., gen. counsel Macmillan/McGraw-Hill Sch. Pub. Co., 1990-92; v.p. Bert Early Assoc., Chgo., 1992-93; ptnr. Sernett & Blake, Northfield, Ill., 1993-95; ret., 1995. Mem. U.S. Dept. State Adv. Panel on Internat. Copyright, 1972-75. Chmn. bd. dirs. Iowa State U., Broadcasting Co., 1987-94. Mem. ABA (chmn. copyright div. 1972-73, com. on copyright legis. 1967-68, 69-70, com. on copyright office affairs 1966-67, 79-81, com. on program for revision copyright law 1971-72), Am. Intellectual Property Law Assn., Am. Soc. Corp. Secs., Ill. Bar Assn. (chmn. copyright com. 1971-72), Chgo. Bar Assn., Patent Law Assn. Chgo. (bbd. mgrs. 1979-82, chmn. copyright law com. 1972-73, 77-78), Copyright Soc. U.S.A. (trustee 1972-75, 77-80), North Shore Country Club (Glenview, Ill.), Wyndemere Country Club (Naples, Fla.), Met. Club Chgo. Home: 2579 Fairford Ln Northbrook IL 60062-8101

SERRA, JOE, investment company executive; Pres. Team Mgmt., Dearborn, Mich.; pres., CEO Al Serra Chevrolet, Grand Blanc; pres., COO Saturn Enterprises, Inc., Charlotte, N.C., 1998-99; CEO, chmn. Serra Investments, Grand Blanc, Mich., 1999—. Office: Serra Investments 3118 E Hill Rd Grand Blanc MI 48439-8106

SERRIN, JAMES BURTON, mathematics educator; b. Chgo., Nov. 1, 1926; s. James B. and Helen Elizabeth (Wingate) S.; m. Barbara West, Sept. 6, 1952; children: Martha Helen Stack, Elizabeth Ruth, Janet Louise Sucha. Student, Northwestern U., 1944-46; BA, Western Mich. U., 1947; MA, Ind. U., PhD, 1951; DSc, U. Sussex, 1972; DSc in Engring., U. Ferrara, Italy, 1992; DSc in Math., U. Padova, Italy, 1992. With MIT, Cambridge, 1952-54; mem. faculty U. Minn., Mpls., 1955—, prof. math., 1959-95, Regents prof., 1968—, head Sch. Math., 1964-65; emeritus, 1995. Vis. prof. U. Chgo., 1964, 75, Johns Hopkins U., 1966, U. Sussex, 1967-68, 72, 76, U. Naples, 1979, U. Modena, 1988, Ga. Inst. Tech., 1990. Author: Mathematical Principles of Classical Fluid Mechanics, 1957. Mem. Met. Airport Sound Abatement Council, Mpls., 1969— . Recipient Disting. Alumni award Ind. U., 1979 Fellow AAAS; mem. NAS, Am. Math. Soc. (G.D. Birkhoff prize 1973), Math. Assn. Am., Soc. for Natural Philosophy (pres. 1969-70), Finnish Acad. Sci. and Letters. Home: 4422 Dupont Ave S Minneapolis MN 55409-1739

SERRITELLA, JAMES ANTHONY, lawyer; b. Chgo., July 8, 1942; s. Anthony and Angela (Deleonardis) S.; m. Ruby Ann Amoroso, Oct. 3, 1981. LLD, North Park U., 1996; BA, SUNY-S.I., 1965, Pontifical Gregorian U., Rome, 1966; postgrad., DePaul U., 1966-67; MA, U. Chgo., 1968, JD, 1971. Bar: Ill. 1971, U.S. Dist. Ct. (no. and ea. dist.) Ill. 1971, U.S. Supreme Ct. 1976, U.S. Tax Ct. 1985, U.S. Ct. Appeals (fifth cir.) 1995, U.S. Ct. Appeals (sixth cir.) 1992, U.S. Ct. Appeals (seventh cir.) 1993, U.S. Ct. Appeals (ninth cir.) 1996. Ptnr. Kirkland & Ellis, Chgo., 1978; ptnr. Reuben & Proctor, 1978-86, Mayer, Brown & Platt, Chgo., 1986-97, Burke, Warren, MacKay & Serritella, PC, Chgo., 1997—. Lectr. in field. Contbr. articles to profl. jours. Exec. bd. govt. rels. com. United Way of Chgo., 1979-84; bd. dirs. Child Care Assn. Ill., 1975-79, Lyric Opera Guild, 1979-84; v.p. Comprehensive Community Svcs. of Met. Chgo., 1976-81; chmn. adv. bd. DePaul U. Coll. Law Ctr. Ch./State Studies, 1982—, dean's vis. com., 1982—; trustee Mundelein Coll., 1982-86, St. Xavier Coll., St. Mary of the Lake Sem., 1982-83, Sta. WTTW Chgo. Pub. TV, 1978-81, Loretto Hosp., 1989-91; mem. geriatrics/gerontology steering com. McGaw Med. Ctr. Northwestern U., 1981-82; adv. bd. N.Am. Coll., 1990-92; mem. Bus. Execs. for Econ. Justice, 1988-94, State wide citizens com. on Child Abuse and Neglect, 1988-94; bd. advisors Alzheimer's Ctr. Rush-Presbyn.-St. Luke's Med. Ctr., 1990—; cons. Union of Bulgarian Founds., 1992, Internat. Acad. for Freedom of Religion and Belief, Budapest, Hungary, 1992. Recipient St. Joseph Sem. Rerum Novarum award, 1999. Fellow Am. Bar Found.; mem. ABA, FBA, NCCJ (adv. com. on ch., state and taxation), Am. Assn. homes for Aging, Nat. Health Lawyers Assn., Ill. State Bar Assn. (bd. govs., spl. com. on jud. redistricting), Ill. Bar Found. (charter), Chgo. Bar Assn. (com. on evaluation of jud. candidates), Cath. Lawyers Guild (bd. govs.), Canon Law Soc. Am. (active mem.), Diocesan Attys. Assn. (exec. com.), Nat. Cath. Cemetery Conf., Cath. Health Assn., The Chgo. Club, Econ. Club, Tavern Club. Office: Burke Warren MacKay & Serritella PC IBM Plaza 22nd Fl 330 N Wabash Ave Chicago IL 60611-3603 E-mail: jserritella@burkelaw.com.

SERRITELLA, WILLIAM DAVID, lawyer; b. Chgo., May 16, 1946; s. William V. and Josephine Dolores (Scalise) S. JD, U. Ill., Champaign, 1971. Bar: Ill. 1971, U.S. Dist. Ct. (no. and cen. dists.) Ill. 1972, U.S. Dist. Ct. (ea. and we. dists.) Wis. 1995, U.S. Ct. Appeals (7th cir.) 1974, U.S. Supreme Ct. 1979, U.S. Dist. Ct. (so. dist.) Ind. 1997. Law clk. U.S. Dist. Ct., Danville, Ill., 1971-72; ptnr. Ross & Hardies, Chgo., 1972—. Arbitrator Am. Arbitration Assn. Mem. ABA, Ill. Bar Assn., Chgo. Bar Assn., Nat. Assn. R.R. Trial Counsel (Ill.), Soc. Trial Lawyers, Defense Rsch. Inst., Legal Club, Trial Lawyers Club (Chgo.). Office: Ross & Hardies 150 N Michigan Ave Ste 2500 Chicago IL 60601-7567 E-mail: williamserritella@rosshardies.com.

SERVAAS, BEURT RICHARD, corporate executive; b. Indpls., May 7, 1919; s. Beurt Hans and Lela Etta (Neff) S.; m. Cory Jane Synhorst, Jan. 7, 1950; children: Eric, Kristin, Joan, Paul, Amy. Student, U. Mex., Mexico City, 1938-39; AB, Ind. U., 1940, MD, 1970; postgrad., Purdue U., 1941; D Bus. Mgmt., Ind. Inst. Tech.; LHD (hon.), Butler U. Agt. CIA, China, 1946; v.p. constrn. Vestar Corp., N.Y.C., 1948; founder, chief exec. officer, chmn. bd. No. Vernon Forge, Inc. Rev. Pub. Co., SerVaas Labs., Indpls., 1949—. Chmn. bd. SerVaas, Inc., Indpls. and affiliated cos. Curtis Pub. Co., Forge Mexicana, Edgerton Tool, Dependable Engring., SerVaas Mgmt., SerVaas Rubber, Premier, Indpls. Rubber Co., Bridgeport Brass Co.; bd. dirs. Bank One Ind. Pres. City-County Coun., Indpls.; chmn. Ind. State Commn. Higher Edn., Kirksville Coll. Osteo. Medicine; bd. dirs. Coll. Univ. Corp., Ind. Pub. Health Found., Robert Schuller Ministries; past chmn. bd. dirs. Ind. State Bd. Health, Nat. Fgn. Rels. Commn. With USNR, 1941—45. Decorated Bronze Star, Army Commendation medal; recipient Horatio Alger award, 1980. Mem. NAM, Am. Acad. Achievement (Golden Plate award 1973), Assn. Am. Med. Colls., Ind. C. of C., Indpls. C. of C., Marion County Hist. Soc., Ind. Hist. Soc., Newcomen Soc. N.Am., U.S. Naval Res. Assn., World Future Soc., Am. Legion, Columbia Club, Econ. Club, Indpls. Athletic Club, Indpls. Press Club, Meridian Hills Country Club, Phi Delta Kappa. Presbyterian. Home: 2525 W 44th St Indianapolis IN 46228-3249 Office: Office of the City County Coun 241 City-County Bldg 200 E Washington St Indianapolis IN 46204-3307 also: SerVaas Inc 1000 Waterway Blvd Indianapolis IN 46202-2155

SERVAAS, CORY, health sciences association administrator; Pres., CEO Saturday Evening Post, Indpls. Office: Saturday Evening Post 1100 Waterway Blvd Indianapolis IN 46202-2174

SERVER, GREGORY DALE, state legislator, guidance counselor; b. Mpls., Jan. 27, 1939; 3 children. BA, U. Evansville, Ind., 1962; MS, Ind. State U., 1968, MS, 1970, EdS, 1981. Guidance counselor Cen. High Sch., Evansville, 1976; mem. Ind. Senate from 50th dist., 1973—. Bd. dirs. Sta. WNIN-TV. Mem. New Harmony (Ind.) Commn. Served with USN. Mem. Edn. Commn. of States, Evansville Tchrs. Assn., VFW, Phi Delta Kappa. Republican. Methodist. Home: 5601 Spring Lake Dr Evansville IN 47710-4241 Office: Ind Senate Mems State Capitol Indianapolis IN 46204

SERWER, ALAN MICHAEL, lawyer; b. Detroit, Aug. 31, 1944; s. Bernard Jacob and Marian (Borin) S.; m. Laurel Kathryn Robbert, June 6, 1968; children: David Matthew, Karen Anne. BA in Econs., U. Mich., 1966; JD, Northwestern U., 1969. Bar: Ill. 1969, D.C. 1980, U.S. Dist. Ct. (no. dist.) Ill. 1970, U.S. Ct. Appeals (7th cir.) 1979, U.S. Supreme Ct. 1979, U.S. Ct. Appeals (6th cir.) 1982, U.S. Ct. Appeals (5th cir.) 1983, U.S. Ct. Appeals (11th cir.) 1984, U.S. Ct. Appeals (9th cir.) 1986. Trial atty. U.S. Dept. Labor, Chgo., 1969-78, counsel safety and health, 1978-79; assoc. Haley, Bader & Potts, 1979-82, ptnr., 1983-87; mem. Bell, Boyd & Lloyd, 1987—. Mem. Ill. Bar Assn., Chgo. Bar Assn., Assn. Trial Lawyers Am. Home: 233 Woodland Rd Highland Park IL 60035-5052 Office: Bell Boyd & Lloyd 70 W Madison St Ste 3200 Chicago IL 60602-4244

SERWY, ROBERT ANTHONY, accountant; b. Chgo., Mar. 26, 1950; s. Anthony J. and Bernice (Zubek) S.; m. Margaret A. Smejkal, Aug. 12, 1972; children: Karen, Steven. BS in Engring., U. Ill., 1972; MBA, Northwestern U., 1974. Mgr. cons. Arthur Andersen & Co., Chgo., 1974-83; dir. fin. planning Teepak, Inc., Oak Brook, Ill., 1983-85; sr. mgr. cons. Peat Marwick & Mitchell, Chgo., 1985-86; dir. cons. Warady & Davis, Deerfield, Ill., 1986—. F.C. Austin scholar, 1972. Mem. AICPA, Ill. CPA Soc. Roman Catholic. Avocations: amateur radio, microcomputers, football. Home: 203 Buckingham Ct Grayslake IL 60030-3479 Office: Warady & Davis 108 Wilmot Rd Ste 500 Deerfield IL 60015-5108

SESSIONS, JUDITH ANN, librarian, university library dean; b. Lubbock, Tex., Dec. 16, 1947; d. Earl Alva and Anna (Mayer) S. BA cum laude, Cen. Fla. U., 1970; MLS, Fla. State U., 1971; postgrad., Am. U., 1980, George Washington U., 1983. Head libr. U. S.C., Salkehatchie, 1974-77; dir. Libr. and Learing Resources Ctr. Mt. Vernon Coll., Washington, 1977-82; planning and systems libr. George Washington U., 1981-82, asst. univ. libr. for adminstrn. svcs., acting head tech. svcs., 1982-84; univ. libr. Calif. State U., Chico, 1984-88; univ. libr., dean of libr. Miami U., Oxford, Ohio, 1988—. Cons. Space Planning, SC, 1976, DataPhase Implementation, Bowling Green U., 1982, TV News Study Ctr., George Washington U., 1981; asst. prof. dept. child devel. Mt. Vernon Coll., 1978—81; mem., lectr. U.S.-China Libr. Exch. Del., 1986, 91; lectr., presenter in field; mem. coord. com. OhioLink Adv. Coun., 1995—2001, v.p., 1996—97, chair, 1998—2000; mem. gov. bd. OhioLink, exec. com., 1998—2001; mem. OCLC Users Coun., 1998—2001; convenor Pub. Acad. Libr. Group, 1999—2000. Contbr. articles, book revs. to profl. jours. Trustee Christ Hosp., Cin., 1990-94, Deaconness Gamble Rsch. Ctr., Cin., 1990-94, OhioNet, 1990-94, treas. 1993; bd. dirs. Hamilton (Ohio) YWCA, 1994-98, pres., 1995-96, v.p., 1996-97, 97-98; mem. OCLC user's coun., 1998—. Recipient award for outstanding contbn. D.C. Libr. Assn., 1979; rsch. grantee Mt. Vernon Coll., 1980; recipient Fulbright-Hayes Summer Travel fellowship to Czechoslovakia, 1991. Mem. ALA (Olofson award 1978, councillor-at-large policy making group 1981-94, coun. com. on coms. 1983-84, intellectual freedom com. 1984-88, directions and program rev. com. 1989-91, fin. and audit subcom. 1989-90, mem. exec. bd. 1989-94, mem. del. to Zimbabwe Internat. Book Fair 1997), Assn. Coll. and Rsch. Librs. (editorial bd. Coll. and Rsch. Librs. jour. 1979-84, nominations and appointments com. 1983-85, faculty status com. 1984-86), Libr. and Info. Tech. Assn. (chair legis. and regulation com. 1980-81), Libr. Adminstrn. and Mgmt. Assn. (bd. dirs. libr. orgn. and mgmt. sect. 1985-87), Calif. Inst. Librs. (v.p., pres. elect 1987-88), Mid-Atlantic Regional Libr. Fedn. (mem. exec. bd. 1982-84), Jr. Mems. Round Table (pres. 1981-82), Intellectual Freedom Round Table (sec. 1984-85), Freedom to Read Found. (trustee 1984-88, v.p. 1985-86, treas. 1986-87, pres. 1987-88), Rotary, Beta Phi Mu. Home: 45 Waters Way Hamilton OH 45013-6324 Office: Miami U Edgar W King Oxford OH 45056

SETSER, CAROLE SUE, food science educator; b. Warrenton, Mo., Aug. 26, 1940; d. Wesley August and Mary Elizabeth (Meine) Schulze; m. Donald Wayne Setser, June 2, 1969; children: Bradley Wayne, Kirk Wesley, Brett Donald. BS, U. Mo., 1962; MS, Cornell U., 1964; PhD, Kans. State U., 1971. Grad. asst. Cornell U., Ithaca, N.Y., 1962-64; instr. Kans. State U., Manhattan, 1964-72, asst. prof., 1974-81, assoc. prof., 1981-86, prof., 1986-2001, prof. emeritus, 2001—. Vis. prof. Bogazici U., Istanbul, Turkey, 2000—01. Recipient Rsch. Excellence award Coll. of Human Ecology, Manhattan, 1990. Mem.: Inst. Food Techs. (chmn. sensory evaluation divsn. edn. com. 1989—92, continuing edn. com. 1992—95, sec. product devel. divsn. 1997—99, also other offices), Am. Assn. Cereal Chemists (assoc. editor 1989—93), Kappa Omicron Nu (Excellence for Rsch. award 1987), Sigma Xi, Phi Tau Sigma (Outstanding Food Scientist 1998), Gamma Sigma Delta, Phi Upsilon Omicron, Phi Kappa Phi (Scholar award 1998). E-mail: setser@ksu.edu.

SETSER, DONALD WAYNE, chemistry educator; b. Great Bend, Kans., Jan. 2, 1935; s. Leo Wayne and Velma Irene (Hewitt) S.; m. Carole Sue Schulze, June 2, 1969; children: Bradley Wayne, Kirk Wesley, Brett Donald. BS, Kans. State U., 1956, MS, 1958; PhD, U. Wash., 1961. Asst. prof. Kans. State U., Manhattan, 1963-66, assoc. prof., 1966-68, prof. chemistry, 1968-2000, Alumni Disting. prof. chemistry, 1984-2000, prof. emeritus, 2000—. Vis. prof. U. Grenoble, France, 1981, 84, 87, 91; fisitor Bogazici U., Turkey, 2000. Editor Reactive Intermediates, 1976; contbr. more than 300 articles to profl. jours. Recipient Rank prize electro-optics divsn., 1992. Fellow Am. Phys. Soc.; mem. Am. Chem. Soc. (Midwest award St. Louis sect. 1984). Home: 414 Wickham Rd Manhattan KS 66502-3751 Office: Kans State U Dept Of Chemistry Manhattan KS 66506 E-mail: setserdw@ksu.edu.

SEVERINSEN, DOC (CARL H. SEVERINSEN), conductor, musician; b. Arlington, Oreg., July 7, 1927; m. Emily Marshall, 1980; children—Nancy, Judy, Cindy, Robin, Allen. Ptnr. Severinsen-Akwright Co.; pops condr. The Phoenix (Ariz.) Symphony Orchestra; prin. pops condr. Minn. Orch., 1993. Mem. Ted Fio Rito Band, 1945, Charlie Barnet Band, 1947-49, then with, Tommy Dorsey, Benny Goodman, Norro Morales, Vaughn Monroe; soloist network band: Steven Allen Show, NBC-TV, 1954-55; mem. NBC Orch. Tonight Show, 1962-67, music dir., 1967-92; past host of: NBC-TV show The Midnight Special; recs., RCA Records, including; albums: Brass Roots, 1971, Facets, 1988, The Tonight Show Band, Night Journey. Address: Minn Orch 1111 Nicollet Mall Minneapolis MN 55403-2406 also: c/o William Morris Agency 151 S El Camino Dr Beverly Hills CA 90212-2704 also: c/o The Phoenix Symphony Orch 455 N 3rd St Ste 390 Phoenix AZ 85004-3942

SEVERSON, GLEN ARTHUR, circuit court judge; b. Sioux Falls, S.D., Mar. 9, 1949; s. Arthur and Muriel S.; m. Mary K. Schweitzer, May 24, 1975; children: Thomas, Kathryn. BS, U. S.D., 1972, JD, 1975. Bar: S.D. 1975, U.S. Dist. Ct. S.D., 1976, U.S. Ct. Appeals (8th cir.) 1989, Minn. 1990. Dep. states atty. Beadle County, Huron, S.D., 1975-76; ptnr. Benson, Wehde, Martin & Severson, 1976-82, Fingerson, Severson & Nelson, Huron, 1982-93; cir. ct. judge Sioux Falls, 1993—. City atty. City of Huron, 1977-92; pres. S.D. Mcpl. Attys. Assn., Pierre, 1985. Bd. dirs. S.D. Bd. Water and Natural Resources, Pierre, 1986-92, Huron Area C. of C., 1983-86. Name one of Oustanding Young Men of Am., 1977. Mem. ABA, S.D. Bar Assn., Minn. Bar Assn., S.D. Judges Assn. (pres. 2000-2001). Roman Catholic. Avocations: flying, fishing, hunting, reading. Office: 425 N Dakota Ave Sioux Falls SD 57104-2400

SEVERSON, SALLY, meteorologist; married; 2 children. Student, No. Ill. U., U. Wis., Milw.; BS in Meteorology, Miss. State U. Meteorologist WISN, Milw., 1986—. Vol. Children's Hosp. of Wis. Avocations: hiking, bicycling, astronomy, boating. Office: WISN PO Box 402 Milwaukee WI 53201

SEWELL, ANDREW, music director; m. Mary Anne Sewell; children: Anna, Lydia, Alistair. MMus, U. Mich.; studied with Gustav Meier. Past asst. condr. Memphis Symphony; past resident condr. Toledo Symphony Orch.; music dir. Mansfield (Ohio) Symphony, Wis. Chamber Orch., Madison; music dir., condr. Wichita (Kans.) Symphony Orch., 2000—. Guest condr. orchs. Detroit, Japan, Mex., Can., New Zealand. Recipient Young Achiever's award Australian Guarantee Corp., Star award New Zealand Aotea Performing Arts Trust, 1997. Office: Wichita Symphony Orch 225 W Douglas Ave Ste 207 Wichita KS 67202-3181

SEWELL, JAMES, artistic director; b. Mpls. Student, Sch. Am. Ballet, N.Y.; studied with David Howard. Dancer Am. Ballet Theatre II, N.Y., Eliot Feld Co.; guest artist N.Y.C. Ballet, Zvi Gottheiner and Dancers, Denishawn, Martine van Hamel's New Amsterdam Ballet. Choreographer over 45 ballets in U.S. and Taiwan including Musical Toys, Minn. Orch., Amahl and the Night Visitors, St. Paul Chamber Orch., Aida, Minn. Opera, 1998, (video) Nutcracker: The Untold Story, cmty.-portrait ballets Swans Island, Maine, Akron, Ohio, Chadron, Nebr. Office: James Sewell Ballet 528 Hennepin Ave Minneapolis MN 55403-1810

SEWELL, PHYLLIS SHAPIRO, retail chain executive; b. Cin., Dec. 26, 1930; d. Louis and Mollye (Mark) Shapiro; m. Martin Sewell, Apr. 5, 1959; 1 child, Charles Steven. B.S. in Econs. with honors, Wellesley Coll., 1952. With Federated Dept. Stores, Inc., Cin., 1952-88, research dir. store ops., 1961-65, sr. research dir., 1965-70, operating v.p., research, 1970-75, corp. v.p., 1975-79, sr. v.p., research and planning, 1979-88. Bd. dirs. Lee Enterprises, Inc., Davenport, Iowa, Pitney Bowes, Inc., SYSCO Corp. Bd. dirs. Nat. Cystic Fibrosis Found., Cin., 1963—; chmn. divsn. United Appeals, Cin., 1982; mem. bus. adv. coun. Sch. Bus. Adminstrn., Miami U., Oxford, Ohio, 1982-84; trustee Cin. Cmty. Chest, 1984-94, Jewish Fedn., 1990-92, Jewish Hosp., 1990—; mem. bus. leadership coun. Wellesley Coll., 1990—, Fordham U. Grad. Sch. Bus., 1988-89. Recipient Alumnae Achievement award Wellesley Coll., 1979, Disting. Cin. Bus. and Profl. Woman award, 1981, Directors' Choice award Nat. Women's Econ. Alliance, 1995; named one of 100 Top Corp. Women Bus. Week mag., 1976, Career Woman of Achievement YWCA, 1983, to Ohio Women's Hall of Fame, 1982.

SEWELL, RICHARD HERBERT, historian, educator; b. Ann Arbor, Mich., Apr. 11, 1931; s. Herbert Mathieu and Anna Louise (Broene) Sewell; m. Natalie Paperno, Jan. 13, 1971; 1 child Rebecca Elizabeth. AB, U. Mich., 1953; MA, Harvard U., 1954, PhD, 1962. Asst. prof. No. Ill. U., DeKalb, 1962-64, U. Wis., Madison, 1965-67, assoc. prof., 1967-74, prof, 1974-95, prof. emeritus, 1995—. Vis. lectr. U. Mich., Ann Arbor, 1964—65; adv. bd. Lincoln and Soldiers Inst. Gettysburg Coll., Pa., 1990—. Author: (book) John P. Hale and the Politics of Abolition, 1965, Ballots for Freedom, 1976, A House Divided, 1988; contbr. articles to profl. jours. Lt. (j.g.) USNR, 1954—57. Mem.: Hist. Soc. Wis., So. Hist. Assn., Soc. Civil War Historians, Phi Beta Kappa, Phi Kappa Phi. Avocation: white-water rafting. Home: 2206 Van Hise Ave Madison WI 53705-3822 E-mail: rhsewell@wisc.edu.

SEWRIGHT, CHARLES WILLIAM, JR. mortgage banking advisory services company executive; b. Great Lakes, Ill., Feb. 22, 1946; s. Charles William Sewright Sr. and Selma Joy (Nickerson) Kester; m. Bonnie Joyce Knight, July 2, 1967; children: Kimberly Ann, Traci Lynn, Megan Paige. BS in Acctg., Calif. State U., Long Beach, 1969, MBA, 1974. Fin. analyst aeronautic div. Philco-Ford Corp., Newport Beach, Calif., 1969-73; sr. acctg. analyst Calif. Computer Products, Anaheim, 1973-74; product line controller McGaw Labs. div. Am. Hosp. Supply Corp., Irvine, Calif., 1974-75, div. acctg. mgr., 1975-76, fin. planning dir., 1976-80; v.p., controller critical care div. McGaw Park, Ill., 1980-85; v.p., controller EZ Painter Corp., Milw., 1985-86; v.p. dept. mgr. automotive fin. services secondary mkts. Marine Midland Bank, Buffalo, 1986-87; pres., chief exec. officer Marine Midland Mortgage Corp., 1987-91, Anchor Mortgage Svcs., Inc., Wayne, NJ, 1991-95; exec. v.p., COO Avondale Fed. Savs. Bank, Chgo., 1997—2000; founder, chmn. Quest Advisors, Inc., Northbrook, 1995—. Chair credit com. Am. Employees Fed. Credit Union, McGaw Park, Ill., 1980-85; vice chmn. Bd. Am. Employees Fed. Credit Union, 1981-85; mem. Fannie Mae Adv. Bd., 1990-92; speaker in field; mem. bd. trustees Medaille Coll., 1989-92; dir. Avondale Fed. Savs. Bank. Mem. Nat. Assn. Accts., Inst. of Cert. Mgmt. Accts. (cert.), Mortgage Bankers Assn. Am. (legis. com. 1990—), Mortgage Bankers Assn. Am. (bd. govs. 1990-98), Beta Gamma Sigma, Phi Kappa Phi. Avocation: golf. Office: Quest Advisors Inc 3710 Commercial Ave Ste 5 Northbrook IL 60062 Business E-Mail: csewright@questadvisors.com.

SEXSON, RICHMOND LOCKWOOD, baseball player; b. Portland, Oreg., Dec. 29, 1974; m. Kerry Sexson. 1st baseman Milw. Brewers, 2000—. Achievements include third in Brewers franchise history to hit 40 home runs in a season. Office: Milw Brewers 1 Brewers Way Milwaukee WI 53214*

SEXTON, CAROL BURKE, financial institution executive; b. Chgo., Apr. 20, 1939; d. William Patrick and Katharine Marie (Nolan) Burke; m. Thomas W. Sexton Jr., June 30, 1962 (div. June 1976); children: Thomas W., J. Patrick, M. Elizabeth. BA, Barat Coll., 1961; cert. legal, Mallinckrodt Coll., 1974. Tchr. Roosevelt High Sch., Chgo., 1961-63, St. Joseph's Sch., Wilmette, Ill., 1975-80; dir. Jane Byrne Polit. Com., Chgo., 1980-81; mgr. Chgo. Merc. Exch., 1981-84, sr. dir. govt. and civic affairs, 1984-87, v.p. pub. affairs, 1987-94, exec. v.p. corp. rels., 1995-2001. Mem. internat. trade an investment subcom. Chgo. Econ. Devel. Commn., 1989, 90. Bd. dirs. Chgo. Sister Cities, 1992—2000, Ill. Ambs., 1991—98, pres., 1994—98; bd. dirs., sec. Internat. Press Ctr., 1992—97, chmn. bd., 1994. Mem. Exec.'s Club of Chgo. (bd. dirs.), Chgo. Conv. and Tourism Bur. (sec. 1989-90, exec. com. 1987-2000, chmn.-elect 1990, chmn. 1991-92), Econ. Club of Chgo. Roman Catholic. Avocations: books, gardening, travel, mountain hiking.

SEXTON, MIKE W. state legislator; b. Fort Dodge, Iowa, Aug. 22, 1961; m. Carolyn Sexton; 4 children. AAS in Agrl. Mgmt., Iowa Lakes C.C. Farmer; mem. Iowa Senate from 7th dist., Des Moines, 1998—; vice chair transp. com., mem. state govt. com.; mem. agr. com., mem. edn. com.; mem. small bus., econ. devel., and tourism com. Republican. Presbyterian. Office: State Capitol 9th And Grand Ave Des Moines IA 50319-0001 E-mail: mike_sexton@legis.state.ia.us.

SEXTON, OWEN JAMES, vertebrate ecology educator, conservationist; b. Phila., July 11, 1926; s. Gordon and Elizabeth May (Evans) S.; m. Mildred Lewis Bloomsburg, Apr. 5, 1952; children: Kenneth, Jean, Ann, Carolyn. Student, Sampson Coll., 1947-48; BA, Oberlin Coll., 1951; MA, U. Mich., 1953, PhD, 1956. Sr. teaching fellow Washington U., St. Louis, 1955-56, instr., 1956-57, asst. prof., 1957-62, assoc. prof., 1962-68, prof. vertebrate ecology, 1968-97, dir. Tyson Rsch. Ctr., 1996-99, prof. emeritus, 1998—, dir. emeritus, 2001—. Vis. prof. U. Mich. Biol. Sta., Pellston, 1975-83; cons. UNESCO, 1974-75; adj. curator St. Louis Sci. Ctr., 1986-88. Pres., bd. dirs. Mo. Prairie Found., Columbia, 1968-99; pres. Wild Canid Survival and Research Ctr., St. Louis, 1971-73; sec. Contemporary Art Soc., 1972-73; bd. dirs. Creve Coeur Figure Skating Club, 1982-89; mem. membership com. U.S. Figure Skating Assn., 1987-90. NSF fellow, 1966-67; vis. research fellow U. New Eng., 1984. Fellow Herpetologists League; mem. Am. Soc. Icthyologists and Herpetologists, Ecol. Soc. Am., Soc. Study of Amphibians and Reptiles, Orgn. Tropical Studies (bd. dir. 1976-85). Democrat. Home: 13154 Greenbough Dr Saint Louis MO 63146-3622 Office: Tyson Rsch Ctr PO Box 258 Eureka MO 63025 E-mail: sexton@biology.wustl.edu.

SEYFERTH, VIRGINIA M. public relations executive; b. Detroit; With pub. rels. dept. St. Jude Children's Rsch. Hosp., 1977-79, AMOCO Oil Co., 1979-81, Amway Corp., 1981-84; pres. Seyferth & Assocs., Inc., Grand Rapids, Mich., 1984—. Office: Seyferth & Assocs Inc 110 Ionia Ave NW Grand Rapids MI 49503-3003

SEYHUN, HASAN NEJAT, finance educator, department chairman; b. Ankara, Turkey, May 19, 1954; came to U.S., 1972; s. Niyazi and Serife (Sayilgan) S.; m. Tamara Z. Cleland, Aug. 10, 1992; children: Kent E., Jon C. and Evan G. BEE, Northwestern U., 1976; MA in Econs., U. Rochester, 1981, PhD in Fin., 1984. Elec. engr. Sungurlar, Istanbul, 1976-77; asst. prof. fin. U. Mich., Ann Arbor, 1983-91, assoc. prof., 1991-93, prof., 1993—, Jerome B. and Eilene M. York prof. bus. adminstrn., 1998—, chmn. fin. dept., 1994-95, 97-00. Vis. prof. Koc U., Istanbul, 2000-01, vis. assoc. prof. U. Chgo., 1988-89, 92, Wissenschaftliche Hochschule für Unternehmens führung, Koblenz, Germany, 1994; co-dir. banking and fin. svcs. program, cons. Citibank, Zurich, Switzerland, 1991; cons. Tweedy Brown, N.Y.C., 1993—, Towneley Capital, N.Y.C., 1994—. Mem. Am. Fin. Assn., Western Fin. Assn., European Fin. Assn., Beta Gamma Sigma. Avocations: volleyball, running. Office: U Mich 701 Tappan Ave Ann Arbor MI 48109-1217 E-mail: nseyhun@umiu.edu.

SFIKAS, PETER MICHAEL, lawyer, educator; b. Gary, Ind., Aug. 9, 1937; s. Michael E. and Helen (Thureanos) S.; m. Freida Platon, Apr. 24, 1966; children— Ellen M., Pamela C., Sandra N. BS, Ind. U., 1959; JD, Northwestern U., 1962. Bar: Ill. 1962, U.S. Dist. Ct. (no. dist.) Ill. 1963, U.S. Ct. Appeals (7th cir.) 1963, U.S. Supreme Ct. 1970, U.S. Ct. Appeals (9th cir.) 1976, U.S. Ct. Appeals (3d cir.) 1981, U.S. Ct. Appeals (D.C. cir.) 1984, U.S. Dist. Ct. (cen. dist.) Ill. 1988. Atty. Legal Aid Bur., United Charities Chgo., 1962-63; sr. ptnr. Peterson & Ross, Chgo., 1970-95; chief counsel, assoc. exec. dir. div. legal affairs ADA, 1995—; sr. ptnr. Bell, Boyd & Lloyd, 1996—. Prosecutor Village of LaGrange Park, Ill., 1969-74; mem. rules com. Ill. Supreme Ct., 1975-95, mem. spl. joint com. on discovery rules, 1995; arbitrator Nat. Panel Arbitrators, 1972—; adj. prof. Loyola U. Sch. Law, 1978—; guest lectr. U. Ill. Coll. Dentistry, 1988-95; lectr. corp. counsel inst. Northwestern U. Sch. Law, 1984, lectr. Ray Garret Jr. Corp. and Securities Law Inst., 1996. Co-author: Antitrust and Unfair Competition Practice Handbook, 1996; contbr. articles to profl. jours. Mem. Ill. steering com. Ct. Watching Project, LWV, 1975-77; pres. Holy Apostles Greek Orthodox Ch. Parish Coun., 1987-89; co-pres. Oak Sch. PTO, 1989-90; mem. com. to select sch. supr., dist. 86, DuPage County, Ill., 1993-94. Recipient Maurice Weigle award, Chgo. Bar Found., 1973, Fones award and hon. membership, Conn. Dental Assn., 1998. Fellow Am. Bar Found., Am. Coll. Trial Lawyers, Chgo. Bar Found. (life); mem. ABA (editor in chief Forum Law Jour. sect. ins., negligence and compensation law 1972-76), Ill. Bar Found. (bd. dirs.), Northwestern U. Law Alumni Assn. (1st v.p. 1985-86, pres. 1986-87, Svc. award 1990), Ill. State Bar Assn. (bd. govs. 1970-76, chmn. antitrust law sect. coun. 1986-87), Chgo. Bar Assn. (editl. bd. Chgo. Bar Record 1973-84), Bar Assn. 7th Fed. Cir., Ill. Inst. Continuing Legal Edn. (chmn. profl. antitrust problems program 1976, author program on counseling corps., antitrust and trade regulation), Legal Club Chgo. (sec.-treas, 1984-86, v.p. 1989-90, pres. 1990-91). Office: Bell Boyd & Lloyd 70 W Madison St Ste 3300 Chicago IL 60602-4284 E-mail: P.Sfikas@BellBoyd.com.

SHAAR, H. ERIK, academic administrator; V.p. acad. affairs Shippensburg U. of Pa., until 1986; pres. Lake Superior State U., Sault Sainte Marie, Mich., 1986-92, Minot (N.D.) State U., 1992—. Office: Minot State U Office of Pres 500 University Ave W Minot ND 58707-0002

SHABAZ, JOHN C. judge; b. West Allis, Wis., June 25, 1931; s. Cyrus D. and Harriet T. Shabaz; children: Scott J., Jeffrey J., Emily D., John D. BS in Polit. Sci., U. Wis., 1999; LLB, Marquette U., 1957. Comd. 2d. lt. U.S. Army, 1954; advanced through grades to U.S. Dist. Ct. (we. dist.) Wis.; pvt. practice law West Allis, Wis., 1957—81; mem. Wis. Assembly, 1965—81; judge U.S. Dist. Ct. (we. dist.) Wis., 1981—96, chief judge, 1996—2001. Office: US Dist Ct PO Box 591 Madison WI 53701-0591

SHABICA, CHARLES WRIGHT, geologist, earth science educator; b. Elizabeth, N.J., Jan. 2, 1943; s. Anthony Charles and Eleanor (Wright) S.; m. Susan Ewing, Dec. 30, 1967; children: Jonathan, Andrew, Dana. BA in Geology, Brown U., 1965; PhD, U. Chgo., 1971. Prof. earth sci. Northeastern Ill. U., Chgo., 1971—; disting. prof., 1991; pres. Shabica & Assocs. Coastal Cons., Inc., Northfield, Ill., 1985—. Chmn. bd. dirs. Aesti Corp., 1991-96; rsch. collaborator Nat. Park Svc., 1978-82, 89—; adj. prof. Coll. V.I., St. Thomas, 1980, adj. prof. environ. sci. Northwestern U., Evanston, 1999—; Kellogg fellow Northeastern Ill. U., 1979—; chmn. Task Force on Lake Michigan, Chgo., 1986-89; mem. Chgo. Shoreline Protection Commn., 1987-88; cons. Shedd Aquarium, Chgo., 1991; mem. Ft. Sheridan Commn., 1989-90; bd. dirs. Winnetka (Ill.) Hist. Soc. Editor: (with Andrew A. Hay) Richardson's Guide to the Fossil Fauna of Mazon Creek, 1997. Commr., packmaster Boy Scouts Am., Winnetka, Ill., 1984-88. Coop. Inst. for Limnology and Ecosystems Rsch. Lab. fellow. Mem. Internat. Assn. for Great Lakes Rsch., Am. Shore and Beach Preservation Assn. (bd. dirs., pres. Great Lakes chpt.), Sigma Xi. Home: 326 Ridge Ave Winnetka IL 60093-3842 Office: 550 W Frontage Rd Ste 3400 Northfield IL 60093-1246

SHADID, GEORGE P. state legislator; b. Clinton, Iowa, May 15, 1929; m. Lorraine; two children. Sheriff, Peoria County, Ill., 1976-93; mem. Ill. State Senate Dist. 46, 1993—, mem. judiciary, higher edn. and exec. appts. coms. Office: Ill Senate Mems Rm 309H State Capitol Springfield IL 62706-0001

SHADUR, MILTON IRVING, judge; b. St. Paul, June 25, 1924; s. Harris and Mary (Kaplan) S.; m. Eleanor Pilka, Mar. 30, 1946; children: Robert, Karen, Beth. B.S., U. Chgo., 1943, J.D. cum laude, 1949. Bar: Ill. 1949, U.S. Supreme Ct. 1957. Pvt. practice practice, Chgo., 1949-80; assoc. Goldberg, Devoe & Brussell, 1949-51; ptnr. Shadur, Krupp & Miller and predecessor firms, 1951-80; judge U.S. Dist. Ct. (no. dist.) Ill., Chgo., 1980-92, sr. judge, 1992—. Commr. Ill. Supreme Ct. Character and Fitness, 1961-72, chmn., 1971; gen. counsel Ill. Jud. Inquiry Bd., 1975-80; chmn. adv. com. on evidence rules to Jud. Conf. of U.S., 1999—, mem. adv. com., 1992-99. Editor-in-chief: U. Chgo. Law Rev., 1948-49. Chmn. visiting com. U. Chgo. Law Sch., 1971-76, mem. vis. com., 1989-92, 99—; bd. dirs. Legal Assistance Found. Chgo., 1972-78; trustee Village of Glencoe, 1969-74, Ravinia Festival Assn., 1976-93, exec. com. 1983-93, vice chmn. 1989-93, life trustee, 1994—. Lt. (j.g.) USNR, 1943-46. Fellow Am. Bar Found.; mem. ABA (spl. com. on youth edn. for citizenship 1975-79), Ill. State Bar Assn. (joint com. on rules of jud. conduct 1974), Chgo. Bar Assn. (chmn. legis. com. 1963-65, jud. com. 1970-71, profl. ethics com. 1975-76, sec. 1967-69), Chgo. Council Lawyers, Order of Coif Office: US Dist Ct 219 S Dearborn St Ste 2388 Chicago IL 60604-1800

SHAEVSKY, MARK, lawyer; b. Harbin, Manchuria, China, Dec. 2, 1935; came to U.S., 1938, naturalized, 1944; s. Tolio and Rae (Weinstein) S.; m. Lois Ann Levi, Aug. 2, 1964; children: Thomas Lyle, Lawrence Keith. Student, Wayne State U., 1952-53; BA with highest distinction, U. Mich., 1956, JD with highest distinction, 1959. Bar: Mich. 1959. Law clerk to presiding judge U.S. Dist. Ct., Detroit, 1960-61; assoc. Honigman Miller Schwartz & Cohn, 1961-64; ptnr. Honigman, Miller, Schwartz & Cohn, 1965-69, sr. ptnr., 1969—. Instr. law Wayne State U. Law Sch., Detroit, 1961-64; comml. arbitrator Am. Arbitration Assn., Detroit; bd. dirs. Charter One Fin. Inc., Charter One Bank. Contbr. Wayne State U. Law Rev., U. Mich. Law Rev., 1957-59, asst. editor, 1958-59. Dir. Detroit Mens Orgn. of Rehab. through Tng., 1969-79; mem. exec. bd. Am. Jewish Com., Detroit, 1965-74; trustee Jewish Vocat. Svcs., Detroit, 1973-76; sec., dir. Am. Friends Hebrew Univ., Detroit, 1976-84; mem. capital needs com. Jewish Welfare Fedn., Detroit, 1986-97; trustee William Beaumont Hosp., 1997—, Beaumont Found., 1997—; dir. Shaevsky Family Found., 2000—. With U.S. Army, 1959-60. Burton Abstract fellow, 1959. Mem. ABA, Mich. Bar Assn., Franklin Hills Country Club, Detroit Athletic Club, Order of the Coif, Phi Beta Kappa. Home: The Hills of Lone Pine 4750 N Chipping Gln Bloomfield Hills MI 48302-2390 Office: Honigman Miller Schwartz & Cohn 2290 First National Bldg Detroit MI 48226 E-mail: mzs@honigman.com.

SHAFAI, LOTFOLLAH, electrical engineering educator, research company executive; b. Maragheh, Azarbijan, Iran, Mar. 17, 1941; arrived in Can., 1964; s. Gholam-Hossain and Robab Shafai; m. Fateme Shams Tafreshi, Nov. 6, 1966; children: Cyrus, Leili. BEE, U. Tehran, Iran, 1963; MEE, U. Toronto, Ont., Can., 1966, PhDEE, 1969. Registered profl. engr., Man. Sessional lectr. U. Man., Winnipeg, Can., 1969-70, asst. prof. elec. engring. Can., 1970-73, assoc. prof. Can., 1973-79, prof. Can., 1979—, head. dept. elec. engring. Can., 1987—. Dir. Inst. Tech. Devel., Winnipeg, 1985-88; pres. Cyrus Rsch. Ltd., Winnipeg, 1978—, EMWAVE Tech. Ltd., Winnipeg, 1980—; rsch. dir. Spiroll Kipp Kelly, Winnipeg, 1988—. Co-author: Handbook of Microstrip Antennas, 1989; contbr. over 300 papers to profl. jours. and confs.; patentee antennas Recipient Merit award U. Man., 1969, 84, 88. Fellow IEEE; mem. Profl. Engrs. Man. (Merit award 1983), Sigma Xi (sr. scientist award 1989). Avocations: painting, chess. Home: 604 Kilkenny Dr Winnipeg MB Canada R3T 3E1 Office: U Man Dept Elec Engring Winnipeg MB Canada R3T 2N2

SHAFER, ERIC CHRISTOPHER, minister; b. Hanover, Pa., Apr. 10, 1950; s. B. Henry and Doris M. (Von Bergen) S.; m. Kristi L. Owens, Nov. 24, 1973. BA, Muhlenberg Coll., 1972; MDiv, Hamma Sch. Theology, 1976. Ordained to ministry Luth. Ch. Am., 1976. Pastor Holy Trinity Meml. Luth. Ch., Catasauqua, Pa., 1976-83; asst. to Bishop Northeastern Pa. Synod, Wescosville, 1983-92; staff commn. for fin. support Evang. Luth. Ch. in Am., Chgo., 1988-92, asst. dir. dept. for comm., 1992-93, dir. dept. for comm., 1993—. Contbg. editor The Lutheran mag., 1989-92. Trustee Muhlenberg Coll., Allentown, Pa., 1972-83; chmn. Luth. Film Assn., 1995—; chmn. Comm. Commn., Nat. Coun. Chs. in USA, 1996—, mem. exec. bd., 1996—. Democrat. Avocations: running, computers, photography, travel. Office: Evang Luth Ch in Am 8765 W Higgins Rd Chicago IL 60631-4178 E-mail: eshafer@elca.org.

SHAFFER, ALAN LEE, manufacturing systems company executive; b. Cin., Aug. 10, 1950; s. Stanley Edward and Stella Pauline (Lilly) S.; Sharon Elizabeth Schleicher, Dec. 7, 1973; children: Alex, Kelly, Adam, Molly. ASMechE, U. of Cin., 1971; BS in Applied Sci., Miami U., Oxford, Ohio, 1973. Sales project engr. Cin. Milacron, 1973-77, product mgr., 1977-80, div. mgr., 1980-82, gen. mgr. products, 1982-84, gen. sales mgr., 1984-85, group mgr., 1985-86, group v.p., 1986—. Bd. dirs. Grinding Wheel Inst., Cleve., 1984. Mem. Oak Hills Bd. Edn., Cin., 1986—; chmn. Sch. Tax Levy Campaign, Cin., 1986-87. Office: Cincinnati Milacron Inc 4701 Marburg Ave Cincinnati OH 45209-1025

SHAFFER, ALFRED GARFIELD (TERRY), service organization executive; b. Sunbury, Pa., Jan. 5, 1939; s. Alfred G. and Betty Marjorie (Vogel) Shaffer; m. Nancy Jane Dawson, Aug. 29, 1976. BS, Susquehanna U., 1961. Cert. tchr., Pa. Tchr. Danville (Pa.) Sch. Dist., 1962-69; mgr. club svc. Kiwanis Internat., Chgo., 1969-74, dir. program devel., 1974-81, dir. program svcs. Indpls., 1982-85, dir. spl. svcs., 1985-87, asst. sec. spl. svcs., 1987-88, asst. to internat. sec., 1988-94, exec. dir., 1994—; corp. affairs cons. Nat. Easter Seal Soc., Chgo., 1981-82; adminstr. Circle K Internat., 1982; mem. Pres.'s Com. on Employment of Handicapped, 1983-86. Chmn. adv. coun. 70001 Ltd., Indpls., 1984-86; mem. adv. bd. Salvation Army, Indpls., 1996—; bd. govs. Children's Miracle Network, 2001—. Recipient Gold Key of Svc., Pa. Dist. Key Clubs, 1964, Tablet of Honor Kiwanis Internat. Found., award of gold Indiana Kiwanis. Mem. Am. Soc. Assn. Execs., ACLU, Ind. Civil Liberties Union, Indps. Athletic Club, 500 Festival Assocs., USAC Winners' Cir., Travelers Protective Assn., Kiwanis (pres. Selinsgrove, Pa. 1964, lt. gov. Pa. 1966-67, pres. Chgo. 1970-72, pres. Northwest Indpls. 1991-92, Outstanding Svc. award 1981, Kiwanian of Yr. 1966, 85). Lutheran. Home: 5688 N Broadway St Indianapolis IN 46220-3073 Office: Kiwanis International 3636 Woodview Trce Indianapolis IN 46268-3196 E-mail: agtshaffer@kiwanis.org.

SHAFFER, MICHAEL L. transportation company executive; b. Eldorado, Ill., Dec. 28, 1945; s. L.E. Jim Shaffer and Berniece (Belva) Andrews; m. Mary Elaine Charboneau, Jan. 30, 1970; children: Michelle, James. Dispatcher Atlas Van Lines, Inc., Long Beach, Calif., 1969-73, ops. mgr. Hyattsville, Md., 1973-75, Evansville, Ind., 1975-80, asst. v.p., 1980-84; v.p., gen mgr. Atlas Van Lines Texas, Austin, 1983-84; v.p. ops. Atlas Van Lines, Inc., Evansville, 1984-88, sr. v.p., 1988-90; pres. U.S. Transp. Group, 1991-98; chmn., CEO Atlas Van Lines, Inc., 1998—. With U.S. Army, 1963-65, Vietnam. Roman Catholic. Home: 3599 Crossgate Ct Newburgh IN 47630-9661 Office: Atlas Van Lines Inc 1212 Saint George Rd Evansville IN 47711-2364

SHAFFER, THOMAS LINDSAY, lawyer, educator; b. Billings, Mont., Apr. 4, 1934; s. Cecil Burdette and Margaret Jeanne (Parker) S.; m. Nancy Jane Lehr, Mar. 19, 1954; children: Thomas, Francis, Joseph, Daniel, Brian, Mary, Andrew, Edward. B.A., U. Albuquerque, 1958; J.D., U. Notre Dame, 1961; LL.D., St. Mary's U., 1983. Bar: Ind. 1961. Assoc. Barnes, Hickam, Pantzer, & Boyd, Indpls., 1961-63; prof. law U. Notre Dame, Ind., 1963-80, assoc. dean, 1969-71, dean, 1971-75, Robert and Marion Short prof., 1988-97; Robert and Marion Short prof. emeritus, 1997—; supervising atty. Notre Dame Legal Aid Clinic, 1991—; prof. law Washington and Lee U., 1980-87, Robert E.R. Huntley prof. law, 1987-88. Vis. prof. UCLA, 1970-71, U. Va., 1975-76, U. Maine, 1982, 87, 98, Boston Coll., 1992; bd. dirs. Cornerstone Found.; mem. Ind. Constl. Revision Commn., 1969-70, Ind. Trust Code Study Commn., 1968-71; reporter Ind. Jud. Conf., 1963, 67. Author: Death, Property, and Lawyers, 1970, The Planning and Drafting of Wills and Trusts, 1972, 4th edit., 2001, Legal Interviewing and Counseling, 1976, 3rd edit., 1998, On Being a Christian and a Lawyer, 1981, American Legal Ethics, 1985, Faith and the Professions, 1987, ; co-author: Lawyers, Law Students, and People, 1977, Cases in Legal Interviewing and Counseling, 1980, American Lawyers and Their Communities, 1991, Property Cases, Materials and Problems, 1992, 2nd edit., 1998, Lawyers, Clients, and Moral Responsibility, 1994; co-editor: The Mentally Retarded Citizen and the Law, 1976; contbr. articles to legal jours. Served with USAF, 1953-57. Frances Lewis scholar Washington and Lee U., 1979; recipient Emil Brown Found. Preventive Law prize, 1966, Presdl. citation U. Notre Dame, 1975, St. Thomas More award St. Mary's U., 1983, Law medal Gonzaga U., 1991, Jour. Law and Religion award, 1993. Mem. Ind. State Bar Assn., Jewish Law Assn., Nat. Lawyers Assn. Roman Catholic. Home: 1865 Champlain Dr Niles MI 49120-8935 Office: Notre Dame Legal Aid Clinic 725 Howard St South Bend IN 46617-1529

SHAH, RAJESH K. auto parts manufacturing executive; B, U. Bombay; MBA, Bowling Green U. CPA. Various sr. level positions including v.p., COO Dayton Walther divsn. Varity Corp.; v.p. fin. and planning Kelsey Hayes; dir. fin. Perkins Engine Peterborough, Eng.; v.p., CFO United Techs. Automotives divsn. United Techs. Corp.; exec. v.p., CFO Collins & Aikman Corp.; leader MIS. Office: Collins & Aikman Corp 5755 New King Ct Troy MI 48098

SHAH, SURENDRA POONAMCHAND, engineering educator, researcher; b. Bombay, Aug. 30, 1936; s. Poonamchand C. and Maniben (Modi) S.; m. Dorothie Crispell, June 9, 1962; children: Daniel S., Byron C. BE, B.V.M. Coll. Engring., India, 1959; MS, Lehigh U., 1960; PhD, Cornell U., 1965. Asst. prof. U. Ill., Chgo., 1966-69, assoc. prof., 1969-73, prof., 1973-81; prof. civil engring Northwestern U., Evanston, Ill., 1981—, dir. Ctr. for Concrete and Geomaterials, 1987—, prof. civil engring., 1989—, Walter P. Murphy prof. of engring., 1992—. Cons. govt. agys. and industry, U.S.A., UN, France, Switzerland, People's Republic China, Denmark, The Netherlands; vis. prof. MIT, 1969, Delft U., The Netherlands, 1976, Denmark Tech. U., 1984, LCPC, Paris, 1986, U. Sidney, Australia, 1987; NATO vis. sci. Turkey, 1992; disting. vis. prof. Nat. Singapore U., 1999. Co-author: Fiber Reinforced Cement Composites, 1992, High Performance Concrete and Applications, 1994, Fracture Mechanics of Concrete, 1995; contbr. more than 400 articles to profl. jours.; editor 12 books; mem. editorial bds. 4 internat. jours.; editor-in-chief Jour. Concrete Sci. and Engring. Recipient Thompson award ASTM, Phila., 1983, Disting. U.S. Vis. Scientist awrd Alexander von Humboldt Found., 1989, Swedish Concrete award, Stockholm, 1993, Engring. News Record award of Newsmaker, 1995, Charles Perkow award, 1997. Fellow Am. Concrete Inst. (chmn. tech. com., Anderson award 1989, 99, Henry Crown award 2000), Internat. Union Testing and Rsch. Labs. Materials and Structures (chmn. tech. com. 1989—, mgmt. adv. bd. 1996—, Gold medal 1980); mem. ASCE (past chmn. tech. com., mem. exec. com., mem. adv. bd. 1998—, Richard J. Caroll Meml. Lectr. 2001). Home: 921 Isabella St Evanston IL 60201-1773 Office: Northwestern U Tech Inst Rm A130 2145 Sheridan Rd Evanston IL 60208-0834

SHAHEEN, GERALD L. manufacturing executive; With Caterpillar Inc., Peoria, Ill., 1967—, mng. dir. Geneva, Switzerland, 1995, v.p. engring. products divsn. Peoria, 1995, group pres., 1998—. Office: Caterpillar Inc 100 NE Adams St Peoria IL 61629-0002

SHAIN, IRVING, retired chemical company executive and university chancellor; b. Seattle, Jan. 2, 1926; s. Samuel and Selma (Blockoff) S.; m. Mildred Ruth Udell, Aug. 31, 1947; children: Kathryn A., Steven T., John R., Paul S. BS in Chemistry, U. Wash., 1949, PhD in Chemistry, 1952. From instr. to prof. U. Wis., Madison, 1952-75, vice chancellor, 1970-75, chancellor, 1977-86; provost, v.p. acad. affairs U. Wash., Seattle, 1975-77; v.p. Olin Corp., Stamford, Conn., 1987-92, ret., 1992, also bd. dirs. Mem. tech. adv. bd. Johnson Controls, Inc., Milw., 1980—; trustee Univ. Rsch. Park, Inc., Madison, pres., 1984-86, v.p., 1987—; mem. Nat. Commn. on Superconductivity, 1989-90; mem. CEO bd. advisors Kamahameha Schs., Hawaii, 2002--. Contbr. articles on electroanalytical chemistry to profl. jours. Bd. dirs. Madison Gen. Hosp., 1972-75; v.p. Madison Cmty. Found., 1984-86; mem. CEO adv. bd. Kamehameha Schs./Bishop Estates, 2002-. With U.S. Army, 1943-46, PTO. Fellow AAAS, Wis. Acad. Scis., Arts and Letters; mem. Am. Chem. Soc., Electrochem. Soc., Conn. Acad. Sci. and Engring., Phi Beta Kappa, Sigma Xi, Phi Kappa Phi. Home: 2820 Marshall Ct # 8 Madison WI 53705-2270 E-mail: ishain@facstaff.wisc.edu., i.shain@worldnet.att.net.

SHAKNO, ROBERT JULIAN, hospital administrator; b. Amsterdam, Holland, Aug. 15, 1937; came to U.S., 1939, naturalized, 1944; s. Rudy C. and Gertrude (Loeb) S.; m. Elka Linda Baum, June 30, 1962; children: Steven Lee, Deborah Sue. B.B.A. (scholar 1955), So. Methodist U., 1959; M.H.A., Washington U., St. Louis, 1961. Adminstrv. asst. Mt. Sinai Hosp., Chgo., 1961—63; asso. adminstr. Tex. Inst. Rehab. and Research, Houston, 1963—65; asst. adminstr. Michael Reese Hosp., Chgo., 1965—70, v.p., hosp. dir., 1970—73; asso. exec. dir. Cook County Hosp., Chgo., 1973—75; pres. Hackensack Med. Center, NJ, 1975—85, Mt. Sinai Med. Ctr., Cleve., 1985—96; dir. nat. strategy practice KPMG Peat Marwick, 1996-98; v.p. med. affairs, vice dean sch. of medicine Case Western Res. U., 1998—. Bd. dirs. Ohio Hosp. Inc. Co.; pres. & CEO Jewish FAmile Svc. Cleve., 2000—. Mem. editorial bd. Mgmt. Series, Am. Coll. Healthcare Execs. Mem. Leadership Cleve.; bd. dirs. Premier Hosp. Alliance, chmn., 1994-96; bd. dirs. The New Cleve. Inc., Univ. Circle Inc., Cleve., Cleve. Sight Ctr.; trustee Hope Lodge, Cleve. chpt. Am. Cancer Soc.; chmn. elect, bd. dirs. Jewish Family Svcs.; chmn. social svcs. divsn. United Jewish Appeal, Cleve., 1987-88, chmn. health cabinet, 1990, gen. cochmn., 1990—; chmn. Hosp. Pacesetter campaign United Way, chmn. health svcs. portfolio, 1988-89, oversight commn., 1992-93. Served to 1st lt. USAR, 1960-66. Named Young Adminstr. of Yr., Washington U., 1968 Fellow Am. Coll. Hosp. Adminstrs.; mem. Am. Hosp. Assn. (coun. urban hosps., del. coun. on met. hosps., rep. regional policy bd.), Washington U. Alumni Assn. (past pres.), Greater Cleve. Hosp. Assn. (bd. dirs.), Ohio Hosp. Assn. (bd. dirs.), Cleve. Sight Ctr. (trustee, bd. dirs.), Sigma Alpha Mu (past pres.). Home: 32050 Meadow Lark Way Pepper Pike OH 44124-5508 Office: Case Western Res U Sch Medicine 10900 Euclid Ave Rm T-101 Cleveland OH 44106-1712

SHALLENBURGER, TIM, state official; m. Linda N. Shallenburger. Rep. dist. 1 Kans. Ho. of Reps., speaker; state treas. Topeka, 1999—. Republican. Home: 5109 SW Brentwood Rd Topeka KS 66606-2211 Office: Office Kans State Treas 900 SW Jackson St Rm 201N Topeka KS 66612-1221

SHANAHAN, BRENDAN FREDERICK, professional hockey player; b. Mimico, Ont., Canada, Jan. 23, 1969; Formerly with St. Louis Blues; with Hartford Whalers, 1995-97; forward Detroit Red Wings, Detroit, 1997-. Played in NHL All-Star Game, 1994, 96; named to NHL All-Star First Team, 1993-94. Office: care Detroit Red Wings 600 Civic Center Dr Detroit MI 48226-4408

SHANAHAN, EUGENE MILES, flow measurement instrumentation company executive; b. Great Falls, Mont., Sept. 18, 1946; s. Raymond Eugene and Helen Marjorie (Graham) S.; m. Beverly Ann Braaten, Sept. 8, 1967; children— Bret Allen, Shaun Eugene, Shae Erin B.S. in Mech. Engring., Mont. State U., 1968; M.S., Mont. State U., 1969; M.B.A., Portland State U., 1976. Registered profl. engr., Oreg. Mech. engr. Tektronix, Beaverton, Oreg., 1968-71; mech. engr. Shell Oil Co., Martinez, Calif., 1967; chief mech. project engr. Mears Controls, Beaverton, 1971-76, mktg. mgr., 1976-79; v.p., gen. mgr. Eaton Corp., Beaverton, 1979-87; v.p. Asia Pacific Dieterich Standard (a Fisher-Rosemount Co.), Boulder, Colo., 1987-98; with Rosemount Inc., Chanhassen, Minn. Served with N.G., 1969-75 NSF trainee, 1969 Mem. ASME, Instrumentation Soc. Am., Tau Beta Pi, Phi Kappa Phi, Pi Tau Sigma. Home: 1811 Quebec Ave N Golden Valley MN 55427-4025 Office: Rosemount Inc 8200 Market Blvd Chanhassen MN 55317-9687

SHANAHAN, MICHAEL FRANCIS, manufacturing executive, former hockey team executive; b. St. Louis, Oct. 29, 1939; m. Mary Ann Barrett; children: Megan Elizabeth, Michael Francis Jr., Maureen Patricia. BS in Commerce, St. Louis U.; postgrad., Wash. U., St. Louis; LHD (hon.), St. Louis Rabbinical Coll., 1987. With McDonnell Douglas Automation Co., St. Louis, 1962-73, sales mgr., 1969-71, br. mgr., 1971-72, mktg. dir. cen. region, 1972-73; mktg. v.p. Numerical Control Inc., 1973-74, pres., 1974-79; v.p. Cleve. Pneumatic Co. (formerly Numerical Control Inc.), 1979-82; chmn., chief exec. officer Engineered Air Systems Inc., 1982—; former chmn., ceo St. Louis Blues Hockey Team. Bd. dirs. Engineered Air Systems Inc. (chmn.), St. Louis Blues Hockey Inc. (chmn.); adv. com. Nat. Hockey League; mem. U.S. Senatorial Bus. Adv. Bd.; bd. dirs. Capital Bank and Trust of Clayton, The Graphic Arts Ctr. Inc., Kilo Rsch. Found. (vice chmn.). Bd. dirs. Am. Heart Assn., St. Louis Ambassadors, Catholic Charities of St. Louis, Galway Sister City Com., The Backstoppers, Christmas in St. Louis Found.; nat. bd. dirs. Boys Hope; bd. trustees, pres. coun. St. Louis U.; adv. bd. Safe Kids; hon. bd. Paraquad; hon. chmn. Small Bus. Week in St. Louis, 1989; hon. co-chmn. Veteran's Day Observance and Parade, 1989; co-chairperson AMC Cancer Rsch. Ctr. Community Svc. award. Named St. Louis Ambassador of Yr., 1986, Olivette Businessman of Yr., 1987, St. Louis Bus. Leader of Yr. Coll. Bus. Adminstrn., So. Ill. U. at Carbondale, 1987,Outstanding Philanthropist St. Louis chpt., Nat. Soc. Fund Raising Execs., 1987; recipient Spirit of Life award City of Hope Labor Mgmt., 1987, St. Louis U. Alumni Merit award, 1987, Meritorious Svc. to Sports award MS Soc., 1987, Presdl. Sports award Maryville Coll., 1987, Sales Exec. of Yr. award Sales and Mktg. Execs. of Met. St. Louis, 1988, St. Louis Port Coun.'s Mgmt. Man of the Yr. award Greater St. Louis Area and Vicinity Port Council, Maritime Trades Dept., AFL-CIO, , 1989. Mem. Alzeimer's Disease and Related Disorders Assn. (hon.), St. Louis Counts, Hawthorn Found., St. Louis Club, Mo. Athletic Club, Old Warson Country Club, Boone Valley Country Club. Office: Engineered Support Systems Inc 1270 N Price Rd Saint Louis MO 63132-2316

SHANAHAN, THOMAS M. judge; b. Omaha, May 5, 1934; m. Jane Estelle Lodge, Aug. 4, 1956; children: Catherine Shanahan Trofholz, Thomas M. II, Mary Elizabeth, Timothy F. A.B. magna cum laude, U. Notre Dame, 1956; J.D., Georgetown U., 1959. Bar: Nebr., Wyo. Mem. McGinley, Lane, Mueller, Shanahan, O'Donnell & Merritt, Ogallala, Nebr.; assoc. justice Nebr. Supreme Ct., Lincoln, 1983-93; judge U.S. Dist. Ct. Nebr., Omaha, 1993—. Office: US Dist Ct 111 S 18th Plz Ste 3141 Omaha NE 68102

SHANDS, COURTNEY, JR. lawyer; b. St. Louis, Mar. 17, 1929; s. Courtney and Elizabeth W. (Jones) S.; m. Frances Jean Schellfeffer, Aug. 9, 1952 (div. 1976); children: Courtney III, E.F. Berkley, Elizabeth V.; m. Nancy Bliss Lewis, Oct. 25, 1980. AB, Washington U., St. Louis, 1951; LLB, Harvard U., 1954. Assoc. Thompson and Mitchell, St. Louis, 1954-62, ptnr., 1962-63, Thompson, Walther and Shewmaker, St. Louis, 1963-69, Kohn, Shands, Elbert, Gianoulakis & Giljum, St. Louis, 1970—. Trustee Frank G. and Florence V. Bohle Scholarship Found., Edward Chase Garvey Meml. Found., L.F. Jones Charitable Trust, 1958-60; bd. dirs. St. Louis Fund, 1972—, Law Libr. St. Louis, 1988—, pres. 1995—; bd. dirs. Hope Ednl. & Rsch. Found., 1989—, pres. 1995—, Citizenship Edn. Clearing House, St. Louis, 1985-87, pres. 1986-87, Mark Twain Summer Inst., St. Louis, 1968-89, pres., 1974-79; Andrews Acad., 1989—, v.p., 1989—; pres. com. Goldwater for Pres., Met. St. Louis, 1964, Ea. Mo. chpt. ACLU, 1966-69, nat. bd. dirs. 1969-72. Mem. ABA, Mo. Bar Integrated, Bar Assn. of Met. St. Louis, Selden Soc., Law Libr. Assn. (Mo. sect.), Noonday Club, Racquet Club, St. Louis Club. Republican. Episcopalian. Office: Kohn Shands Elbert 1 Mercantile Ctr Fl 24 Saint Louis MO 63101-1643

SHANE, SANDRA KULI, postal service administrator; b. Akron, Ohio, Dec. 12, 1939; d. Amiel M. and Margaret E. (Brady) Kuli; m. Fred Shane, May 30, 1962 (div. 1972); 1 child, Mark Richard; m. Byrl William Campbell, Apr. 26, 1981 (dec. 1984). BA, U. Akron, 1987, postgrad., 1988-90. Scheduler motor vehicle bur. Akron Police Dept., 1959-62; flight and ops. control staff Escort Air, Inc., Akron and Cleve., 1972-78; asst. traffic mgr. Keen Transport, Inc., Hudson, Ohio, 1978-83; mem. ops. and mktg. staff Shawnee Airways and Essco, Akron, 1983-86; in distbn. U.S. Postal Svc., 1986—. Rec. sec. Affirmative Action Coun., Akron, 1988-90. Asst. art tchr. Akron Art Mus., 1979; counselor Support, Inc., Akron, 1983-84; com. chmn. Explorer post Boy Scouts Am., Akron, 1984-85. Mem. Bus. and Profl. Women's Assn. (pres.), Delta Nu Alpha. Democrat. Roman Catholic. Avocations: painting, sculpting, fabric design. Home: 455 E Bath Rd Cuyahoga Falls OH 44223-2511

SHANK, WILLIAM O. lawyer; b. Hamilton, Ohio, Jan. 11, 1924; s. Horace Cooper and Bonnie (Winn) S.; m. Shirleen Allison, June 25, 1949; children— Allison Kay, Kristin Elizabeth. BA, Miami U., Oxford, O., 1947; JD, Yale, 1950. Bar: Ohio, Ill., U.S. Supreme Ct. Pvt. practice, Hamilton, Ohio, 1951-55, Chgo., 1955—; mem. firm Shank, Briede & Spoerl, Hamilton, Ohio, 1951-55; assoc. Lord, Bissell & Brook, Chgo., 1955-58; atty. Chemetron Corp., 1958-60, sr. atty., 1960-61, gen. atty., asst. sec., 1961-71, sec., gen. counsel, 1971-78; v.p., gen. counsel, sec. Walgreen Co., Deerfield, Ill., 1978-89; ptnr. Burditt & Radzius, Chartered, Chgo., 1989-98; exec. v.p. Internat. Bus. Resources, Inc., 1993—; ptnr. Williams Montgomery & John Ltd., 1998—. Mem. bus. adv. coun. Miami U., Oxford, Ohio, 1975—; arbitrator 19th Jud. Cir., Ill., 1995—; adv. bd. eLawForum, Washington, 1999—. Bd. dirs. Coun. for Cmty. Svcs. Met. Chgo., 1973-77; trustee Libr. Internat. Rels., 1971-78; bd. dirs. Chgo. Civic Fedn., 1984-89, Walgreen Drug Stores Hist. Found., 1990—; mem. Chgo. Crime Commn., 1985-89. 1st lt., pilot 8th Air Force, USAAF, World War II, ETO. Fellow Am. Bar Found. (life); mem. ABA (com. corp. gen. counsel), Ill. State Bar Assn., Chgo. Bar Assn. (chmn. com. on corp. law depts. 1971-72, 89-90), Am. Soc. Corp. Secs. (pres. Chgo. regional group 1983-84, nat. bd. dirs. 1984-87), Yale U. Law Sch. Assn. (past pres. Ill. Alumni, exec. com. New Haven), Walgreen Alumni Assn. (pres. 1992-94), Legal Club (pres. 1979-80), Law Club, Lawyers Club (Chgo.), Univ. Club, Econ. Club, Yale Club of Chgo., Omicron Delta Kappa, Phi Delta Phi, Sigma Chi. Home: 755 S Shore Dr Crystal Lake IL 60014-5530 Office: Williams Montgomery & John Ltd 20 N Wacker Dr Ste 2100 Chicago IL 60606 E-mail: wos@willmont.com.

SHANKEL, DELBERT MERRILL, microbiology and biology educator; b. Plainview, Nebr., Aug. 4, 1927; s. Cecil Wilfred and Gladys Dalton (Dodd) S.; m. Carol Jo Mulford, Sept. 10, 1962; children: Merrill, Jill, Kelley. BA, Walla Walla Coll., 1950; PhD, U. Tex., 1959. Tchr. Walla Walla Coll. Acad., College Place, Wash., 1950-51; instr. San Antonio Coll., 1954-55; asst. prof., assoc. prof. microbiology and biology U. Kans., Lawrence, 1959-68, prof., 1968—, asst. dean, assoc. dean arts and sci., 1966-72, acting dean, 1973, exec. vice chancellor, 1974-80, 86, 90-92, acting chancellor, 1980-81, chancellor, 1994-95, prof. and chancellor emeritus, 1996. Cons., evaluator North Ctrl. Assn. Colls. and Schs., Chgo., 1969-96, commr., 1991-95. Editor: (conf. procs.) Antimutagenesis and Anticarcinogenesis: Mechanisms, Vols. 1-3, 1986, 89, 93; assoc. editor Mutation Rsch., 1992-95. Active numerous civic orgns. With U.S. Army, 1952-54. Named Outstanding Educator award Mortar Bd., U. Kans., 1982, 85, 90, Disting. Alumnus of Yr., Walla Walla Coll., 1989; recipient numerous grants for sci. rsch. Fellow Am. Acad. Microbiology; mem. Am. Soc. for Microbiology (past chmn. edn. com., mem., chmn. numerous coms.), Environ. Mutagen Soc. (chmn. pub. policy com. 1991-93, nat. coun. 1994-97, mem., chmn. numerous coms.), Genetics Soc. Am., Soc. Gen. Microbiology (Gt. Britain), Radiation Rsch. Soc., Sigma Xi (pres. U. Kans. chpt. 1967). Republican. Unitarian. Avocations: sports, music, theater, reading. Office: U Kans 1002 Haworth Hl Lawrence KS 66045-0001 E-mail: shankel@ku.edu.

SHANNON, LYLE WILLIAM, sociology educator; b. Storm Lake, Iowa, Sept. 19, 1920; s. Bert Book and Amy Irene (Sivits) S.; m. Magdaline W. Shannon, Feb. 27, 1943; children: Mary Shannon Will, Robert William, John Thomas, Susan Michelle. BA, Cornell Coll., Mount Vernon, Iowa, 1942; MA, U. Wash., 1947, PhD, 1951. Acting instr. U. Wash., 1950-52; mem. faculty dept. sociology U. Wis., Madison, 1952-62, assoc. prof., 1958-62; prof. sociology U. Iowa, Iowa City, 1962—, chmn. dept. sociology and anthropology, 1962-70, dir. Iowa Urban Community Research Ctr., 1970-91; dir. emeritus, 1991—; prof. emeritus U. Iowa, Iowa City, 1991—. Vis. prof. Portland State U., Wayne State U., U. Wyo., U. Colo. Author: Underdeveloped Areas, 1957, Minority Migrants in the Urban Community, 1973, Criminal Career Continuity: Its Social Context, 1988, Changing Patterns of Delinquency and Crime: A Longitudinal Study in Racine, 1991, Developing Areas, 1995, Socks and Cretin: Two Democats Helping Bill with the Presidency, 1995, Alcohol and Drugs, Delinquency and Crime, 1998; editor: Social Ecology of the Community series, 1974-76. With USNR, 1942-46. Mem. AAAS, Am. Sociol. Assn., Midwest Sociol. Soc., Population Assn. Am., Soc. Applied Anthropology, Am. Soc. Criminology, Phi Beta Kappa. Democrat. Lodge: Kiwanis Home: River Heights Iowa City IA 52240-9147 Office: Univ Iowa W504 Seashore Hall Iowa City IA 52242-1407

SHANNON, MARGARET ANNE, lawyer; b. Detroit, July 6, 1945; d. Johannes Jacob and Vera Marie (Spade) Van De Graaf; m. Robert Selby Shannon, Feb. 4, 1967. Student, Brown U., 1963-65; BA in History, Wayne State U., 1966, JD, 1973. Bar: Mich. 1973. Housing aide City of Detroit, 1967-68; employment supr. Sinai Hosp., Detroit, 1968-69; assoc. gen. counsel regulatory affairs Blue Cross Blue Shield Mich., 1969-80; ptnr. Honigman Miller Schwartz and Cohn, 1980-95, of counsel, 1996—. Nat. Merit scholar, 1963-66. Mem. ABA (vice-chmn. pub. regulation of ins. law com. 1981-82), Mich. State Bar (chmn. health care com. 1991, 92, co-chmn. payor subcom. health law sect.), Nat. Health Lawyers Assn., U. Liggett Sch. Alumni (bd. govs.). Home: 2003 Shorepointe Ln Grosse Pointe Woods MI 48236-1060 Office: Honigman Miller Schwartz and Cohn 2290 First National Bldg Detroit MI 48226-3583 E-mail: mshannon@honigman.com.

SHANNON, MICHAEL EDWARD, retired specialty chemical company executive; b. Evanston, Ill., Nov. 21, 1936; s. Edward Francis and Mildred Veronica (Oliver) S.; m. A. Laura McGrath, July 4, 1964; children: Claire Oliver Mary, Kathryn Ann Elizabeth. BA, U. Notre Dame, 1958; MBA, Stanford U., 1960. With Continental Oil Co., Houston, 1960-62, Gulf Oil Corp., 1962-75, asst. treas., 1970-75; treas. Gulf Oil Co. U.S., Houston, 1970-72, Gulf Oil Co.-Ea. Hemisphere, London, 1972-75, Republic Steel Corp., Cleve., 1975-84, v.p., 1978-82, exec. v.p., 1982-84; exec. v.p., chief fin. officer Ecolab Inc., St. Paul, 1984, chief fin. and adminstrv. officer, 1984-90; pres. ChemLawn Svcs. Corp., Columbus, Ohio, 1988-90; CFO Ecolab Inc., 1990-92, pres. Residential Svcs. Group, 1990-92, vice chmn., chief fin. and adminstrv. officer, 1992-95, chmn. bd., chief fin. and adminstrv. officer, 1996-99. Bd. dirs. Minn. Orchestral Assn., Mpls., chair. Mem. Fin. Execs. Inst., Nat. Assn. Mfrs. (bd. dirs.), Univ. Club, Rolling Rock Club, Mpls. Club, Minikahada Club, Minn. Club. Roman Catholic. Office: Ecolab Inc 370 Wabasha St N Saint Paul MN 55102-1390

SHANNON, PETER MICHAEL, JR. lawyer; b. Chgo., Oct. 13, 1928; s. Peter Michael Sr. and Marian (Burke) S.; m. Anne M. Mueller, April 3, 1969; children: Peter III, Stephen, Heather, Eamon. BA, St. Mary of the Lake, Mundelein, Ill., 1949, MA, 1952, STL, 1953; JCL, Gregorian U., Rome, 1958; JD, U. Calif., Berkeley, 1971. Bar: Calif. 1972, D.C. 1972, Ill. 1988, U.S. Dist. Ct. Md. 1972, U.S. Dist. Ct. D.C. 1972, U.S. Dist. Ct. (no. dist.) Ill. 1988, U.S. Ct. Appeals (1st, 2d, 3d, 4th, 5th, 6th, 7th, 8th, 9th, 10th and D.C. cirs.) 1972-75, U.S. Supreme Ct. 1975. Supervisory atty. litigation U.S. Dept. of Justice, Washington, 1971-75; sr. appellate atty. ICC, 1975-77, dir. enforcement, 1977-80; ptnr. Shannon, et al, 1980-82, Keck, Mahin & Cate, Chgo., 1982-96, Arnstein & Lehr, Chgo., 1996—2001; pvt. practice Peter M. Shannon, Jr., P.C., We. Springs, Fla., 2001—. Author: Energy and Transportation Implications of Ratemaking Policy Concerning Sources of Energy, 1980, Disposition of Real Estate by Religious Institutions, 1987, The Dual Approach of Civil Law Courts to Ecclestical Related Disputes, 1988. Mem. ABA (chmn. transp. com., adminstrv. law and regulatory practice sect. 1984-87, coun. mem. 1988-91), Ill. Bar Assn., Chgo. Bar Assn., Am. Acad. Hosp. Attys., Assn. Transp. Law, Logistics and Policy, Canon Law Soc. (pres. 1965-66), Ctr. for Disability and Elder Law (pres. 1997-99). Office: 4546 Wolf Road Western Springs IL 60558-1562

SHANNON, WILLIAM NORMAN, III, marketing and international business educator, food service executive; b. Chgo., Nov. 20, 1937; s. William Norman Jr. and Lee (Lewis) S.; m. Bernice Urbanowicz, July 14, 1962; children: Kathleen Kelly, Colleen Patricia, Kerrie Ann. BS in Indsl. Mgmt., Carnegie Inst. Tech., 1959; MBA in Mktg. Mgmt., U. Toledo, 1963. Sales engr. Westinghouse Electric Co., Detroit, 1959-64; regional mgr. Toledo Scale, Chgo., 1964-70; v.p. J. Lloyd Johnson Assoc., Northbrook, Ill., 1970-72; mgr. spl. projects Hobart Mfg., Troy, Ohio, 1972-74; corp. v.p. mktg. Berkel, Inc., La Porte, Ind., 1974-79; gen. mgr. Berkel Products, Ltd., Toronto, Can., 1975-78; chmn. Avant Industries, Inc., Wheeling, Ill., 1979-81; chmn., pres. Hacienda Mexican Restaurants, South Bend, Ind., 1978—; chmn. Ziker Shannon Corp., 1982-88, Hacienda Franchising

Group, Inc., South Bend, Ind., 1987—. Assoc. prof. mktg. and internat. bus. St. Mary's Coll., Notre Dame, Ind., 1982—; chmn. Hacienda Franchise Group, Inc., 1987-96, Hacienda Mex. Restaurants Mgmt., Inc., 1994-96; sr. chmn. Hacienda Mex. Restaurants, 1996—; mem. London program faculty, 1986, 89, 92, 94, coord. internat. bus. curriculum, 1989—, mktg. curriculum, 1983, 88, 95—; advisor Coun. Internat. Bus. Devel., Notre Dame, 1991—; mng. dir. Alden & Torch Lake Railway, 1995—. Co-author: Laboratory Computers, 1971; columnist small bus. Bus. Digest mag., 1988—; bd. editors Jour. Bus. and Indsl. Mktg., 1986—; mem. bd. editorial advisors South Bend Tribune Business Weekly, 1990—; contbr. articles to profl. jours. V.p. mktg. Jr. Achievement, South Bend, Ind., 1987-90; pres. Small Bus. Devel. Coun., South Bend., 1987-90; bd. dirs. Ind. Small Bus. Coun., Indpls., 1986—, Mental Health Assn., South Bend, 1987-90, Michiana World Trade Orgn., Internat. Bus. Edn., 1989-91; Entrepreneurs Alliance Ind., 1988-92, Nat. Small Bus. United, Washington, 1989-92, Women's Bus. Initiative, 1986-90, dir. ednl. confs., 1986-90; chmn. bd. trustees, Holy Cross Coll., Notre Dame, Ind., 1987—, chmn. edn. com., 1993—; chmn. St. Joseph County Higher Edn. Coun., 1988-91, Nat. Coun. Small Bus., Washington, 1988—; Midwest region adv. coun. U.S. SBA, 1988-91; at-large mem. U.S. Govt. Adv. Coun. on Small Bus., Washington, 1988-90, 1994—, chmn. Bus. and Econ. Devel. Com., 1988-90, 1994—; vice chmn. Internat. Trade Com., 1994—; mem. nat. adv. coun. Women's Network for Entrepreneur Tng., 1991—; mem., vice chmn. State of Ind. Enterprise Zone Bd., 1991—; elected del. White House Conf. Small Bus., Washington, 1986; bd. dirs. Ind. Small Bus. Devel. Ctrs. Adv. Bd. Named Small Bus. Person of the Yr., City of South Bend, 1987, Small Bus. Advocate of the Yr., State of Ind., 1987, Ind. Entrepreneur Advocate of the Yr., 1988. Mem. Am. Mktg. Assn. (chmn. Mich./Ind. chpt., pres. 1985-86), U.S. Assn. Small Bus. and Entrepreneurship (nat. v.p. for entrepreneurship edn. 1991-92, nat. v.p. entrepreneurship devel. 1992—), Ind. Inst. New Bus. Ventures (mktg. faculty 1987-91), Michiana Investment Network (vice chmn. 1988-91), SBA (adminstrn. adv. coun. 1988—, contbg. editor Our Town Michiana mag. 1988-91), U.S. C. of C., Nat. Coun. Small Bus. (Washington), South Bend C. of C. (bd. dirs. 1987—, vice chmn. membership 1993—), Assn. for Bus. Communications (co-chmn. Internat. Conf. 1986), Univ. Club Notre Dame (vice chmn.), Shamrock Club Notre Dame (exec. dir., trustee 1993—), Rotary. Roman Catholic. Home: 2920 S Twyckenham Dr South Bend IN 46614-2116 Office: Saint Mary's Coll Dept Bus Adminstrn Eco Notre Dame IN 46556

SHANTZ, DEBRA MALLONEE, lawyer; b. Springfield, Mo., Aug. 12, 1963; d. Arnold Wayne and Jean Marie (Pyle) Mallonee; m. Joseph Benjamin Shantz, Dec. 26, 1987; children: Benjamin, Riley. BS, S.W. Mo. State U., 1984; JD, U. Mo., 1988. Ptnr. Farrington & Curtis, P.C., Springfield, 1988-95; corp. counsel John Q. Hammons Hotels, 1995—. Home: 1635 E Delmar St Springfield MO 65804-0207 Office: John Q Hammons Hotels Ste 900 300 John Q Hammons Pkwy Springfield MO 65806 E-mail: debbie.shantz@jqh.com.

SHAO COLLINS, JEANNINE, magazine publisher; married; 1 child. BA in Econs., U. Rochester. Various advt. sales mgmt. positions Woman's Day, N.Y.C., Prevention mag.; N.Y. advt. mgr. Ladies' Home Jour., Meredith Corp., N.Y.C., 1993-95, advt. dir. Better Homes and Gardens, Des Moines, 1995-98, assoc. pub., 1998-99, pub., 1999—, v.p., 2000—. Office: Better Homes and Gardens 1716 Locust Street Des Moines IA 50309-3023

SHAPIRA, DAVID S. food products/retail grocery executive; b. 1942; married B.A., Oberlin Coll., 1964; M.A., Stanford U., 1966. V.p. Giant Eagle, Inc. (formerly Giant Eagle Markets, Inc.), Pitts., 1974-81, pres., 1981-1994, CEO, also bd. dirs.; chmn. & CEO Giant Eagle, Youngstown; chmn. bd. Phar-Mor Inc.

SHAPIRO, BURTON LEONARD, oral pathologist, geneticist, educator; b. N.Y.C., Mar. 29, 1934; s. Nat Lazarus and Fay Rebecca (Gartenhouse) S.; m. Eileen Roman, Aug. 11, 1958; children— Norah Leah, Anne Rachael, Carla Faye. Student, Tufts U., 1951-54; D.D.S., NYU, 1958; M.S., U. Minn., 1962, Ph.D., 1966. Faculty U. Minn. Sch. Dentistry, Mpls., 1962—, assoc. prof. div. oral pathology, 1966-70, prof., chmn. div. oral biology, 1970-79, prof., chmn. dept. oral biology, 1979-88, prof. dept. oral pathology and genetics, 1979-88, dir. grad. studies, mem. grad. faculty genetics, 1966—, prof. dept. oral sci., 1988—, mem. grad. faculty pathobiology, 1979; prof. dept. lab. medicine and pathology U. Minn. Sch. Medicine, 1985—, mem. Human Genetics Inst., 1988—, univ. senator, 1968-72, 88-93; also mem. med. staff U. Minn. Health Scis. Center; exec. com. Grad. Sch. U. Minn., chmn. health scis. policy rev. council, chmn. univ. faculty consultative com., 1988-92; chmn. univ. fin. and planning com. Grad. Sch. U. Minn., 1988. Hon. research fellow Galton Lab. dept. human genetics Univ. Coll., London, 1974; spl. vis. prof. Japanese Ministry Edn., Sci. and Culture, 1983 Mem. adv. editorial bd.: Jour. Dental Research, 1971— ; Contbr. articles to profl. jours. Served to lt. USNR, 1958-60. Am. Cancer Soc. postdoctoral fellow, 1960-62; advanced fellow, 1965-68; named Century Club Prof. of Yr., 1988. Fellow Am. Acad. Oral Pathology, AAAS; mem. Internat. Assn. Dental Research (councilor 1969), Am. Soc. Human Genetics, Craniofacial Biology Soc. (pres. 1972), Sigma Xi, Omicron Kappa Upsilon. Home: 148 Nina St # 2 Saint Paul MN 55102-2160 Office: U Minn Sch Dentistry Dept Oral Sci Minneapolis MN 55455 E-mail: burt@umn.edu.

SHAPIRO, HAROLD DAVID, lawyer, educator; b. Chgo., Apr. 15, 1927; s. Charles B. and Celia (Nierenberg) S.; m. Beatrice Cahn, June 6, 1950; children: Matthew D., Michael Ann, Nicholas J. BS, Northwestern U., Chgo., 1949, JD, 1952. Adminstrv. asst. State of Ill. Dept. Fin., Springfield, 1952; assoc. Sonnenschein Nath & Rosenthal, Chgo., 1953-59, ptnr., 1959—; Edward A. Harriman adj. prof. law Northwestern U., Chgo., 1970—. Sec., bd. dirs. West Side Affordable Housing, Inc., West Side Village, Inc. Trustee, mem. exec. com., sec. Jr. Achievement of Chgo.; bd. dirs. Schwab Rehab. Ctr., Chgo.; pres. Homan & Arthington Found., 1995—96, The Ringer Found., 2000—, Northwestern U. Law Sch. Alumni Assn., Chgo., 1984—85, chmn. dean's adv. coun., 1997—99. Served with Seabees USNR, 1945—50, PTO. Recipient Merit award Northwestern U., 1988. Mem. Ill. Bar Assn., ABA, Chgo. Bar Assn., Chgo. Council Lawyers, Legal Club of Chgo. (pres.), Law Club of Chgo., Order of Coif, Wigmore Key, Standard Club, Met. Club, Cliff Dwellers, Chicago Club, Lake Shore Country Club. Democrat. Jewish. Home: 34 Linden Ave Wilmette IL 60091-2837 Office: Sonnenschein Nath & Rosenthal 8000 Sears Tower 233 S Wacker Dr Ste 8000 Chicago IL 60606-6491

SHAPIRO, JAMES EDWARD, judge; b. Chgo., May 28, 1930; BS, U. Wis., 1951; JD, Harvard U., 1954. Bar: Wis. 1956, U.S. Dist. Ct. (ea. dist.) Wis. 1956, U.S. Ct. Appeals (7th cir.) 1962, U.S. Supreme Ct. 1971. Sole practice, Milw., 1956-57; resident house counsel Nat. Presto Industries, Eau Claire, Wis., 1957-60; ptnr. Bratt & Shapiro, Milw., 1960-64; sole practice, 1964-74; ptnr. Frank, Hiller & Shapiro, 1974-82; judge U.S. Bankruptcy Ct., 1982—, chief judge, 1996-2000. Mem. Bayside Bd. Appeals, Wis., 1969-77; Milw. county ct. commr., 1969-78; dir. Milw. Legal Aid Soc., 1969-77. Served to 1st lt. U.S. Army, 1954-56. Jewish. Office: US Courthouse 140 Fed Bldg 517 E Wisconsin Ave Milwaukee WI 53202-4500 E-mail: james_e_shapiro@wieb.uscourts.gov.

SHAPIRO, LEO J. social researcher; b. N.Y.C., July 8, 1921; m. Virginia L. Johnson, Feb. 9, 1952; children: David, Erik, Owen, Amy. BA, U. Chgo., 1942, PhD, 1952. Survey specialist Fed. Govt. Agy., Washington, 1941-45, Sci. Rsch. Assn., Chgo., 1948-52; prin., founder Leo J. Shapiro and Assocs., 1952-91; pres. Greenhouse, Inc., 1991—2001, SAGE LLC Survival & Growth Enterprise, Chgo., 2002—. Bd. dirs. Field of Flowers, Brand Name Ednl. Found. Fellow U. Chgo., 1949. Fellow Social Sci. Research Council; mem. Am. Sociol. Assn., Phi Beta Kappa.

SHAPIRO, MARK, advertising executive; b. St. Louis, June 7, 1951; s. Harvey and Florley (Schimmel) S.; m. Patricia Suzanne Moore, Nov. 26, 1975; children: Andrew Phillip, Max Manlin. BA in English, Wash. U., 1973; MA in Journalism, U. Mo., 1975. Writer Maritz Inc., St. Louis, 1975-77, assoc. creative dir., 1977-78; creative dir. The Hanley Partnership, 1979-81, sr. v.p., 1981-84; mng. ptnr. The Hermann Group, 1984-86, pres., 1986—, Louis London (formerly The Hermann Group), St. Louis, 1988-90; CEO Louis London, 1990-99; chmn. & CEO Momentum N. Am., St. Louis MO, 1999—. Recipient N.Y. Art Dirs. award, 1982, Print ICA award, 1981-82. Mem. St. Louis Advt. Club, St. Louis Advt. Fed. (Flair award 1982-86, Addys award 1987), NIJADC-St. Louis, Phi Beta Kappa. Office: Momentum 6665 Delmar Blvd Ste 300 Saint Louis MO 63130-4525

SHAPIRO, MARK D. retail executive; With Ernst and Young, Blackman Co., Chemlawn Svcs. Corp.; dir., asst. contr. Consolidated Stores Corp., Columbus, 1992-94, v.p., contr., 1994-2000, sr. v.p., CFO, 2000—. Office: Consolidated Stores Corp 300 Phillipi Rd Columbus OH 43228-0512

SHAPIRO, MATTHEW DAVID, economist, educator; b. Mpls., Apr. 11, 1958; s. Irving and Janet (Reinstein) S.; m. Susan L. Garetz, Oct. 21, 1989; children: Benjamin Avigdor, Molly Kendall. BA summa cum laude, MA, Yale U., 1979; PhD, MIT, 1984. Jr. staff economist Coun. Econ. Advisers, Washington, 1979-80, sr. economist, 1993-94; asst. prof. Yale U., New Haven, 1984-89; assoc. prof. U. Mich., Ann Arbor, 1989-95, prof., 1995—, sr. rsch. scientist, 2000—. Rschr. Nat. Bur. Econ. Rsch., Cambridge, Mass., 1986—; mem. acad. adv. coun. Fed. Res. Bank Chgo., 1995-; mem. com. on nat. stats. NAS, 1999-; mem. Fed. Econ. Stats. Adv. Com., 2000-. Bd. editors Am. Econ. Rev., 1993-96, 00—, co-editor, 1997-00; contbr. articles to profl. jours. Recipient Paul A. Samuelson Cert. of Excellence, TIAA-CREF, 1997; Olin fellow Nat. Bur. Econ. Rsch., Cambridge, 1986-87, Alfred P. Sloan fellow Sloan Found., 1991-93. Mem. Am. Econ. Assn., Econometric Soc., Phi Beta Kappa. Office: U Mich Dept Econs 611 Tappan Ave Ann Arbor MI 48109-1220

SHAPIRO, MICHAEL BRUCE, lawyer; b. Akron, Ohio, 1947; BBA summa cum laude, Kent State U., 1969; JD magna cum laude, U. Mich., 1972. Bar: Mich. 1972. Ptnr. Honigman Miller Schwartz & Cohn, LLP, Detroit. Mem. Nat. Assn. of Real Estate Investment Trusts subcom. on state and local taxes, citizens property tax commn. Mich. Senate, 1986-87. Mem. ABA, Am. Property Tax Counsel, State Bar of Mich., Inst. Property Taxation, Order of the Coif, Beta Alpha Psi, Pi Sigma Alpha, Beta Gamma Sigma. Office: Honigman Miller Schwartz & Cohn 2290 1st Nat Bldg Detroit MI 48226 E-mail: mbs@honigman.com.

SHAPIRO, RICHARD CHARLES, publishing sales and marketing executive; b. Bklyn., May 28, 1936; s. Isidore and Sylvia (Rappaport) S.; m. Marilyn Joyce Bialy, Feb. 17, 1957 (div. 1974); children: Joseph, Scott; m. Francine L. Shaw, Sept. 19, 1975. BS in Edn., Golden State U., 1978, MBA, 1981; PhD in Bus. Adminstrn., Honolulu U., 1987. Lic. real estate broker, Ill. Sales mgr. Coca Cola Bottling Co. of N.Y., 1955-62; affiliate Effective Motivation Assocs./Success Motivation inst., Bethpage, N.Y., 1965-68; v.p. sales, dir. Field Enterprises, Chgo., 1962-78; pres., CEO Snack-In, Inc., Detroit, 1978-82; sr. ptnr. Directions Growth and Strategy Cons., Chgo., 1982-95; v.p. domestic & internat. mktg. & sales Ency., oper. officer Ency. Brit.-Compton's Learning Co., 1991-93, specialist network mktg. & relationship mktg., CEO, pres., bd. dirs.; CEO Am.'s Home Detailing Corp., 1995—, CEO, chmn. bd., 2001—; pres., COO Am.'s Deep Clean Divsn., Deerfield, Ill., 1995—; CEO and chmn. emeritus Am.'s Home Detailing Corp.; instr. grad. studies mktg. mgmt., instr. human resources mgmt. Robert Morris Coll., Chgo., 2001—. Instr. planning Life Underwriter Tng. Coun., L.I., 1965-66; assoc. editor Media Technics Pub. Assn., Lake Forest, 1988; bd. dirs. Master Deep Clean Co., Nat. Video Libr.; spkr. on mktg., sales and leadership; cons. in field; liaison with Chgo. Daily News, Chgo. Sun Times, WFLD-TV; founder Discovery Toy Divsn. Pub.: Real Estate Property Marketing News; author various self-improvement cassettes; writer storyarts; contbr. articles to profl. jours.; author bus. writings, 1993-95. Active Explorers, high schs., youth clubs, 1965-74; founder, pres. Abundance and Goodwill Soc., 1968—. Served with USAF, 1957-60. Recipient Leadership award Am. Sales Masters, 1968, 1999-2000, POPAI-OMA Best Industry Point of Purchase Display and Mktg. award, 1992; named Sales/Mktg. Execs. Leadership Recruiter/Trainer of Decade award. Mem. Salesmen With a Purpose, Chgo. Computer Soc., Effective Motivation Assocs., Deercreek Tennis Club (tchr.). Avocations: wild-water rafting, white-water canoeing, camping, tennis, writing. E-mail: ahd10@yahoo.com.

SHAPIRO, ROBERT B. former food products manufacturing executive; b. N.Y.C., Aug. 4, 1938; s. Moses and Lilly (Langsam) S.; m. Berta Gordon, Mar. 27, 1964; children: James Gordon, Nina Rachel. A.B., Harvard U., 1959; LL.B., Columbia U., 1962. Bar: N.Y. 1963. Assoc. in law Columbia U., 1962-63; atty. firm Poletti Freidin Prashker Feldman & Gartner, N.Y.C., 1963-67; spl. asst. to gen. counsel and undersec. U.S. Dept. Transp., Washington, 1967-69; assoc. prof. law Northeastern U., Boston, 1969-71; asst. prof. law U. Wis., Madison, 1971-72; v.p., gen. counsel Gen. Instrument Corp., N.Y.C., 1972-79, G.D. Searle & Co., Skokie, Ill., 1979-82; pres. NutraSweet Group div. G.D. Searle & Co., 1982-85; chmn., pres., chief exec. officer Nutra Sweet Co. subs. Monsanto, 1985-95, also bd. dirs, 1992—; chmn., CEO Monsanto Co., St. Louis, 1995-2000; chmn. Pharmacia Corp., 2000-2001. Mem. Mass. Gov.'s Transp. Task Force, 1970-71; mem. com. on procedure CAB, 1975-76; mem. bus. adv. com. White House Domestic Policy Rev. on Indsl. Innovation, 1978-79; Nat. Bd.. Trustees Boys Clubs of Am. Recipient John R. Miller award as outstanding corporate mktg. exec., 1984; Outstanding Achievement award Sales and Mktg. Mgmt. Mag., 1984 Mem. Am. Bar Assn. (vice chmn. com. on corp. counsel 1981-82), U.S. C. of C. (council on antitrust policy 1981-82), N.Y. State Bar Assn. Office: Pharmacia Corp 800 N Lindbergh Blvd Saint Louis MO 63167-0001

SHAPIRO, ROBYN SUE, lawyer, educator; b. Mpls., July 19, 1952; d. Walter David and Judith Rae (Sweet) S.; m. Charles Howard Barr, June 27, 1976; children: Tania Shapiro-Barr, Jeremy Shapiro-Barr, Michael Shapiro-Barr. BA summa cum laude, U. Mich., 1974; JD, Harvard U., 1977. Bar: D.C., 1977, Wis., 1979, U.S. Supreme Ct., 1990. Assoc. Foley & Lardner, Washington, 1977-79; ptnr. Barr & Shapiro, Menomonee Falls, Wis., 1980-87; assoc. Quarles & Brady, Milw., 1987-92; ptnr. Michael Best & Friedrich, 1992—. Adj. asst. prof. law Marquette U., Milw., 1979-83; assoc. dir. bioethics ctr. Med. Coll. Wis., Milw., 1982-85, dir., 1985—; asst. prof. bioethics Med. Coll. Wis., 1984-89, assoc. prof. bioethics, 1989-97, prof. bioethics, 1997—, Ursula Von der Ruhr prof. bioethics, 2000—; dir. Wis. Ethics Com. Network, 1987-98, Midwest Ethics Com. Network, 1998—; bd. dirs. Wis. Health Decisions, 1990-93. Mem. editl. bd. Cambridge Quar., 1991—, HEC Forum, 1988-91, Human Rights, 1998—; contbr. articles to profl. jours. Mem. ethics com. St. Luke's Hosp., Milw., 1983—, Elmbrook Meml. Hosp., Milw., 1983-86, Cmty. Meml. Hosp., Menomonee Falls, 1984—, Sinai Samaritan Hosp., Milw., 1986—, Milw. County Mental Health Complex, 1984—, Froedtert Meml. Luth. Hosp., 1985—; mem. subcom. organ transplantation Wis. Health Policy Coun., Madison, 1984, bioethics com., 1986-89; mem. com. study on bioethics Wis. Legis. Coun., Madison, 1984-85; bd. dirs. Jewish Home and Care Ctr., 1994—, chair ethics com., 1994—; chair Bayside Ethics Bd., 1994—; bd. dirs. Milw. area chpt. Girl Scouts U.S., Am. Bioethics Assn., 1995-97, Wis. Perinatal Found., 1996-99, Am. Soc. Bioethics and Humanities, 1997-2000; mem. sec.'s adv. com. on xenotransplantation U.S. Dept. Health and Human Svcs., 2001—. James B. Angell scholar, 1971-72. Mem. ABA (health law sec., vice chair clin. ethics group 1998-2001, individual rights and responsibilities sec., health rights com. chair 1994-99, coun. 1999—, coordinating com. on bioethics and law, chair 1995-99), Nat. Health Lawyers Assn., Am. Hosp. Assn. (bioethics tech. panel 1991-94, spl. com. HIV & practitioners 1991-93), Wis. Bar Assn. (chair Wis. health law sect. 1988-89, individual rights sect. coun. 1987-90), Assn. Women Lawyers, ACLU, Wis. Found. (Atty. of Yr. 1988), Assn. Post-Doctoral Programs in Clin. Neurophysiology (bd. dirs.), Am. Soc. Law, Medicine, and Ethics, Milw. Acad. Medicine (coun. 1992-98, chair bioethics com. 1992-98), Milw. AIDS Coalition (steering com. 1988-91), Am. Soc. Transplant Surgeons (ethics com. 1999—), Internat. Bioethics Assn. (chair task force on ethics coms.), Profl. Dimensions (Golden Compass award 1994), Phi Beta Kappa, others. Home: 9474 N Broadmoor Rd Milwaukee WI 53217-1309 Office: Med Coll Wis Bioethics Ctr 8701 W Watertown Plank Rd Milwaukee WI 53226-3548 E-mail: rshapiro@mcw.edu.

SHAPIRO, STEPHEN MICHAEL, lawyer; b. Chgo., May 3, 1946; s. Samuel H. and Dorothy A. (D'Andrea) S.; m. Joan H. Gately, Oct. 30, 1982; children: Dorothy Henderson, Michael Clifford. BA magna cum laude, Yale U., 1968, JD, 1971. Bar: Ill. 1971, Calif. 1972, D.C. 1991, U.S. Dist. Ct. (no. dist. trial bar) Ill. 1992, U.S. Ct. Appeals (all cirs.), U.S. Supreme Ct. 1975. Law clk. U.S. Ct. Appeals (9th cir.), San Francisco, 1971-72; ptnr., sr. mem. appellate practice Mayer, Brown & Platt, Chgo., 1972-78, 83—; asst. to solicitor gen. U.S. Dept. Justice, Washington, 1978-80, dep. solicitor gen., 1981-82. Trustee Product Liability Adv. Found. Co-author: Supreme Court Practice, 2002; contbr. articles to profl. jours. Mem. ABA, Am. Law Inst., Am. Acad. Appellate Lawyers, Supreme Ct. Hist. Soc., Phi Beta Kappa. Republican. Jewish. Office: Mayer Brown Rowe & Maw 190 S La Salle St Ste 3100 Chicago IL 60603-3441

SHAPO, MARSHALL SCHAMBELAN, lawyer, educator; b. Phila., Oct. 1, 1936; s. Mitchell and Norma (Schambelan) S.; m. Helene Shirley Seidner, June 21, 1959; children: Benjamin, Nathaniel. AB summa cum laude, U. Miami, 1958, JD magna cum laude, 1964; AM, Harvard U., 1961, SJD, 1974. Bar: Fla. 1964, Va. 1977, Ill. 1993. Copy editor, writer Miami (Fla.) News, 1958-59; instr. history U. Miami, 1960-61; asst. prof. law U. Tex., 1965-67, asso. prof., 1967-69, prof., 1969-70; prof. law U. Va., 1970-78, Joseph M. Hartfield prof., 1976-78; Frederic P. Vose prof. Northwestern U. Sch. Law, Chgo., 1978—; of counsel Sonnenschein, Nath & Rosenthal, 1991-2001. Vis. prof. Juristisches Seminar U. Gottingen (Fed. Republic Germany), 1976; cons. on med. malpractice and tort law reform U.S. Dept. Justice, 1978-79; mem. panel on food safety Inst. Medicine, NAS, 1978-79; vis. fellow Centre for Socio-legal Studies, Wolfson Coll., Oxford, vis. fellow of Coll., 1975, Wolfson Coll., Cambridge, 1992, 2001; mem. Ctr. for Advanced Studies, U. Va., 1976-77; cons. Pres.'s Commn. for Study of Ethical Problems in Medicine and Biomed. and Behavioral Rsch., 1980-81; reporter Spl. Com. on Tort Liability System Am. Bar Assn., 1980-84; del. leader People to People Citizen Amb. program delegation to East Asia Tort and Ins. Law, 1986; lectr. appellate judges' seminars ABA, 1977, 83, 90; reporter symposium on legal and sci. perspectives on causation, 1990; advisor Restatement of the Law, Third, Torts: Products Liability, 1992-97. Author: Towards a Jurisprudence of Injury, 1984, Tort and Compensation Law, 1976, The Duty to Act: Tort Law, Power and Public Policy, 1978, A Nation of Guinea Pigs, 1979, Products Liability, 1980, Public Regulation of Dangerous Products, 1980, The Law of Products Liability, 1987, Tort and Injury Law, 1990, 2d edit., 2000, The Law of Products Liability, 2 vols., 2d edit., 1990, 4th edit., 2001, supplements, 1991, 92, 93, 95, 96, 97, 98, 99, Products Liability and the Search for Justice, 1993, (with Helene Shapo) Law School Without Fear, 1996, 2d edit., 2002, Basic Principles of Tort Law, 1999; (with Page Keeton) Products and the Consumer: Deceptive Practices, 1972, Products and the Consumer: Defective and Dangerous Products, 1970, (with D. Jacobson & A.N. Weber) International e-Commerce: Business & Legal Issues, 2001, (with G. Hernandez & others) eBusiness & Insurance, 2001; mem. editl. bd. Jour. Consumer Policy, 1980-88, Products Liability Law Jour.; author: A Representational Theory of Consumer Protection: Doctrine, Function and Legal Liability for Product Disappointment, 1975; mem. adv. bd. Loyola Consumer Law Reporter; contbr. articles to legal and med. jours. NEH sr. fellow, 1974-75 Mem. Am. Law Inst., Am. Assn. Law Schs. (chmn. torts compensation systems sect. 1983-84, torts round table coun. 1970). Home: 1910 Orrington Ave Evanston IL 60201-2910 Office: Northwestern U Sch Law 357 E Chicago Ave Chicago IL 60611-3059

SHAPPIRIO, DAVID GORDON, biologist, educator; b. Washington, June 18, 1930; s. Sol and Rebecca (Porton) S.; m. Elvera M. Bamber, July 8, 1953; children: Susan, Mark. B.S. with distinction in Chemistry, U. Mich., 1951; A.M., Harvard U., 1953, Ph.D. in Biology, 1955. NSF postdoctoral fellow in biochemistry Cambridge U., Eng., 1955-56; rsch. fellow in physiology Am. Cancer Soc.-NRC, U. Louvain, Belgium, 1956-57; mem. faculty U. Mich., Ann Arbor, 1957—, prof. zool. and biology, 1967-99, Arthur F. Thurnau prof., 1989-94, prof. emeritus, 1999—, assoc. chair div. biol. scis., 1976-83, acting chair, 1978, 79, 80, 82, coord. NSF undergrad. sci. edn. program, 1962-67, dir. honors program Coll. Lit. Sci. and Arts, 1983-91. Vis. lectr. Am. Inst. Biol. Scis., 1966-68; reviewer, cons. to pubs. on textbook devel.; reviewer rsch. and ednl. tng. grant proposals NSF, NIH, mem. program site visit teams. Author rsch. on biochemistry and physiology growth, devel., dormancy; invited spkr., rsch. symposia of nat. and internat. orgns. in field. Recipient Disting. Teaching award U. Mich., 1967, Excellence in Edn. award, 1991, Bausch & Lomb Sci. award, 1974; Lalor Found fellow, 1953-55; Danforth Found. assoc. Fellow AAAS; mem. Am. Inst. Biol. Scis. (vis. lectr. 1966-68), Am. Soc. Cell Biology, Biochem. Soc., Soc. Exptl. Biology, Assn. Biol. Lab. Edn., Xerces Soc., Phi Beta Kappa (v.p. U. Mich. chpt. 1995-97, pres. 1997—). Office: U Mich Dept Biology 2014 Natural Sci Bldg Ann Arbor MI 48109-1048

SHARF, STEPHAN, automotive company executive; b. Berlin, Dec. 30, 1920; came to U.S., 1947; s. Wilhelm and Martha (Schwartz) S.; m. Rita Schantzer, June 17, 1951. Degree in Mech. Engring., Tech. U., Berlin, Fed. Republic Germany, 1947. Tool and die maker Buerk Tool & Die Co., Buffalo, 1947-50; foreman Ford Motor Co., 1950-53, gen. foreman, 1953-58; with Chrysler Corp., Detroit, 1958-86, master mechanic Twinsburg stamping plant, 1958-63, mfg. engring. mgr., 1963-66, mrg. prodn. Twinsburg stamping plant, 1966-68, plant mgr. Warren stamping plant, 1968-70, plant mgr. Sterling stamping plant, 1970-72, gen. plants mgr. stamping, 1972-78, v.p. Engine and Casting div., 1978-80, v.p. Power Train div., 1980-81, exec. v.p., mfg., dir., 1981-85, exec. v.p. internat., 1985-86, also bd. dirs.; pres. SICA Corp., Troy, Mich., 1986—. Bd. dirs. Integral Vision Inc. Columnist Ward's Auto World Common Sense mag., 1987—. Bd. dirs. Jr. Achievement, Detroit council Boy Scouts Am.; trustee, v.p. Oakland U. Mem. Soc. Auto Engrs., Detroit Engring. Soc. Club: Wabeek Country. Home: 966 Adams Castle Dr Bloomfield Hills MI 48304-3713 Office: SICA Corp PO Box 623 Troy MI 48099-0623 Office Fax: 248-433-3937. E-mail: SICA@concentric.net.

SHARKEY, LEONARD ARTHUR, automobile company executive; b. Detroit, May 21, 1946; s. Percy and Lillian (Peros) S.; m. Irene Johnson, Aug. 9, 1969 (div. Nov. 1991); children: Michelle, Wesley Tucker (step-son). Cert. pvt. pilot. Tool and diemaker Ford Motor Co., Dearborn, Mich., 1965-85; indsl. hazardous substance educator Ford Motor co., 1985-86, indsl. health, safety and energy control educator, 1987-88, tool and diemaker leader, 1989—; non-fiction author Individual Initiative, Brighton, 1989—. Author: Journey Into Fear (reprinted title Split Decision, 1997), 1995, Hidden Shadows - An Opening to the Windows of the Mind, 1996. Mem. Mich. Rep. Party. Mem. Nat. Geog. Soc., Nat. Rifle Assn.,

Boat U.S., Drummond Island Sportsman's Club, Mich. United Conservation Clubs. Avocations: boating, shooting sports, political awareness studies, Biblical prophetic studies, theater.

SHARKEY, THOMAS DAVID, educator, botanist; b. Detroit, Jan. 28, 1953; s. Robert Hugh and Patricia June (Elliott) S.; m. Paulette Marie Bochnig June 21, 1974; 1 child, Jessa Sung. BS in Biology, Mich. State U., 1974, PhD in Botany and Plant Pathology, 1980. Postdoctoral fellow Australian Nat. U., Canberra, 1980-82; assoc. rsch. prof. Desert Rsch. Inst., Reno, 1982-87; asst. prof. U. Wis., Madison, 1987-88, assoc. prof., 1988-91, prof., 1991—. Assoc. dir. Biolog. Scis. Ctr., Reno, Nev., 1983-87; chmn. dept. botany U. Wis., Madison, 1992-94; dir. Biotron, U. Wis., Madison, 1993—. Editor: Trace Gas Emissions from Plants, 1991, Photosynthesis: Physiology and Metabolism, 2000; contbr. more than 100 articles to profl. peer-reviewed jours. Mem.: AAAS, Internat. Soc. Photosynthesis Rsch., Am. Soc. Plant Biologists. Home: 5901 S Highlands Ave Madison WI 53705-1108 Office: Univ Wis Dept Botany 430 Lincoln Dr Madison WI 53706-1313 E-mail: tsharkey@wisc.edu.

SHARP, ALLEN, federal judge; b. Washington, Feb. 11, 1932; s. Robert Lee and Frances Louise (Williams) S.; children: Crystal Catholyn, Scarlet Frances. Student, Ind. State U., 1950-53; AB, George Washington U., 1954; JD, Ind. U., 1957; MA, Butler U., 1986. Bar: Ind. 1957. Practiced in, Williamsport, 1957-68; judge Ct. of Appeals Ind., 1969-73, U.S. Dist. Ct. (no. dist.) Ind., South Bend, 1973—. Served to JAG USAF, Res. Mem. Ind. Judges Assn., Blue Key, Phi Delta Kappa, Pi Gamma Mu, Tau Kappa Alpha. Republican. Mem. Christian Ch. Club: Mason. Office: US Dist Ct 124 Fed Bldg 204 S Main St South Bend IN 46601-2122

SHARP, PAUL DAVID, institute administrator; b. Youngstown, Ohio, Nov. 3, 1940; s. Robert Henderson and Kathryn (Tadsen)S.; m. Carole G. Graff, Sept. 16, 1967; children: David Allen, Kathryn Sharp Snyder. BA cum laude, Kenyon Coll., Gambier, Ohio, 1962; MPA, Auburn U., 1974. Commd. 2d lt. USAF, 1962, advanced through grades to col., 1983, intelligence officer, 1962-80, comdr. Detachment 1, 7450th Intelligence Squadron Germany, 1980-83, comdr. 480th Reconnaissance Tech. Group Langley AFB, Va., 1983-85, dir. intelligence systems HQ Tactical Air Command, 1985-86, dep. chief intelligence Tactical Air Command, 1986-88; mgr. operational intelligence group Battelle Meml. Inst., Columbus, Ohio, 1988-89, mgr. fgn. tech. assessment group, 1989-91, mgr. intelligence projects/programs, 1991-92, v.p. bus. devel. fgn. sci. and tech., 1992-95, dir. fgn. sci. and tech. programs, 1995-98; dir. Air Force spl. programs Batelle Meml. Inst., 1998-99, mgr. spl. programs office, 1999-2000; mgr. Internat. Tech. Assessments Product Line, 2000—. Student career coun. Kenyon Coll., Columbus, 1992—. Trustee Brandywine Assn., Yorktown, Va., 1987, Chase Assn., Powell, Ohio, 1991. Decorated Legion of Merit. Mem. Nat. Mil. Intelligence Assn., Armed Forces Communications and Electronics Assn., Air Force Assn., Retired Officers Assn., Sigma Pi (pres. Lambda chpt. 1961-62). Republican. Episcopalian. Avocations: golf, woodworking, photography, music. Office: Battelle Meml Inst 505 King Ave Columbus OH 43201-2681

SHARP, RONALD ALAN, English literature educator, author; b. Cleve., Oct. 19, 1945; s. Jack Trier and Florence (Tenenbaum) S.; m. Inese Brutans, June 22, 1968; children: Andrew Janis, James Michael. BA, Kalamazoo Coll., 1967; MA, U. Mich., 1968; PhD, U. Va., 1974. Instr. in English Western Mich. U., Kalamazoo, 1968-70; from instr. to acting pres. Kenyon Coll., Gambier, Ohio, 1970—2002, acting pres., 2002—. Dir. Keats Bicentennial Conf., Harvard U., 1995. Author: Keats, Skepticism and the Religion of Beauty, 1979, Friendship and Literature: Spirit and Form. 1986; translator: Teatro Breve (Garcia Lorca), 1979, editor (with Eudora Welty) The Norton Book of Friendship, 1991, (with Nathan Scott) Reading George Steiner, 1994, (with Robert Ryan) The Persistence of Poetry: Bicentennial Essays on John Keats, 1998, Selected forms of Michael Harper, 2002; co-editor Kenyon Rev., 78-82; contbr. articles to profl. jours. Recipient award for editl. excellence Ohioana Assn., 1980; fellow Nat. Humanities Ctr., 1981, 86, NEH, 1981, 84-87, 93, 94, 96, 98, Ford Found., 1971, Mellon Found., 1980, Danforth Found., 1971, English Speaking Union, 1973, Am. Coun. Learned Socs., 1986. Mem. MLA, NEH (chmn's. adv. group humanities edn. 1987), Wordsworth-Coleridge Assn., Keats-Shelley Assn. Jewish. Home: 11671 Kenyon Rd Mount Vernon OH 43050-8633 Office: Kenyon Coll Office of President Gambier OH 43022

SHARP, WILLIAM J. manufacturing company executive; b. Huntington, W.Va., Nov. 2, 1941; BA in Indsl. Rels., U. Akron, 1964. Prodn. scheduler Goodyear Tire & Rubber Co., Akron, Ohio, 1964, various positions, to supt. prodn. various cities, 1964-79, mgr. prodn. Lawton, Okla., 1979-81, plant mgr., tire prodn. facilities various cities, Luxembourg, France, 1981-83, dir. domestic tire prodn. Akron, 1983-84, dir. European tire prodn. Brussels, 1984-87, v.p. tire mfg. Akron, 1987-91, exec. v.p. product supply, 1991-92, pres., gen. mgr. European region Brussels, 1992-96, pres. global support ops., 1996-99, pres. N.Am. Tire, 1999—. Office: Goodyear Tire & Rubber Co 1144 E Market St Akron OH 44316-0002

SHAUGHNESSY, EDWARD LOUIS, Chinese language educator; b. Sewickley, Pa., July 29, 1952; s. James Francis and Marie Rosalie (Kraus) S.; m. Gina Lynn Look, May 15, 1976 (div. Sept. 1992); m. Elena Valussi, Sept. 6, 1997. BA, U. Notre Dame, 1974; MA, Stanford U., 1980, PhD, 1983. Asst. prof. U. Chgo., 1985-90, assoc. prof., 1990-96, prof., 1996—, Lorraine J. and Herrlee G. Creel prof. of early China. Assoc. editor: Early China, 1985-88, editor, 1988-96; editor: New Sources of Early Chinese History: An Introduction to the Reading of Inscriptions and Manuscripts, 1997, (with Michael Loewe) The Cambridge History of Ancient China: From the Origins of Civilization to 221 R.C., 1999, China Empire and Civilization, 2000; author: Sources of Western Zhou History: Inscribed Bronze Vessels, 1991, I Ching, The Classic of Changes: The First English Translation of the Newly Discovered Second-Century B.C. Mawangdui Manuscripts, 1996, Before Confucius: Studies in the Creation of the Chinese Classics, 1997, (with Robert Poor and Harrie A. Vanderstappen) Ritual and Reverence: Chinese Art at the University of Chicago, 1989, (with Cai Fangpei and James F. Shaughnessy) A Concordance of the Xiaotun Nandi Oracle-Bone Inscriptions, 1988; contbr. essays to books. Andrew W. Mellon fellow for Chinese studies, 1984-85, divsn. of humanities jr. faculty fellow U. Chgo., 1986 Home: 711 S Dearborn St Apt 506 Chicago IL 60605-3819 Office: U Chgo East Asian Langs/Civilizat 1050 E 59th St Chicago IL 60637-1559 E-mail: e-shaughnessy@uchicago.edu.

SHAUGHNESSY, THOMAS WILLIAM, librarian, consultant; b. Pitts., May 3, 1938; s. Martin T. and LaVerne (O'Brien) S.; m. Marlene D. Reuben, Aug. 11, 1968; 1 child, Mark Andrew. AB, St. Vincent Coll., 1961; MLS, U. Pitts., 1964; PhD, Rutgers U., 1970. Asst. dean Rutgers U., New Brunswick, N.J., 1969-71; libr. dir. Rutgers-Newark, 1971-74; assoc. dean U. So. Calif., L.A., 1974-78; asst. libr. dir. U. Houston, 1978-82; libr. dir. U. Mo.-Columbia, 1982-89; univ. libr. and dir. U. Minn., Mpls.-St. Paul, 1989—2002. Rsch. dir. Chgo. Pub. Libr. Survey, 1968-69; cons. U. Tulsa Libr., 1982-83; mem. faculty exch. U.S. Info. Agy., Poland, 1998; bd. trustees O.C.L.C., 1997—. Author: (with Lowell A. Martin) Library Response to Urban Change, 1969, Developing Leadership Skills: A Source Book for Librarians, 1990. U.S. Office Edn. grantee Rutgers U., 1971; fellow Coun. Libr. Resources, 1973, sr. fellow, 1985; recipient Hugh C. Atkinson Meml. award, 1996, Pres.'s award for Outstanding Svc. U. Minn., 2002. Mem. ALA, Assn. Coll. and Rsch. Librs., Assn. Rsch. Librs. (cons. tng. fellow 1981, bd. dirs. 1989-92), Minn. Libr. Assn. Home: 5705 Wycliffe Rd Minneapolis MN 55436-2264 E-mail: tws@umn.edu.

SHAVER, JOAN LOUISE FOWLER, adult education educator; BS in Nursing, U. Alberta, Can., 1966; M in Nursing, U. Wash., 1968-70, PhD in Physiology and Biophysics, 1976. Nursing instr. chair med. surgical prog. Holy Cross Hosp. Sch. Nursing, Calgary, Can., 1966-68; staff nurse Virginia Mason Hosp., Seattle, 1970-71; asst. prof. Sch. Nursing U. Ariz., Tucson, 1976-77; assoc. prof. U. Calgary, Can., 1977-80; asst. prof. Dept. Physiological Nursing U. Wash., Seattle, 1980-85, rsch. affil. Regl. Primate Rsch. Ctr., 1983-86, assoc. prof., 1985-89, chair Dept. Physiological Nusring, 1988-95, prof., 1989-95, prof., chair Dept. Biobehavioral Nursing & Health Systems, 1995-96, co-dir. Ctr. Women's Health Rsch., 1989-96; prof., dean Coll. Nursing U. Ill., Chgo., 1996—, co-dir. Rsch. Core Nat. Ctr. Excellence in Women's Health, 1997—. Mem. editl. bd. Health Care for Women Internat., 1984—, Heart and Lung: The Jour. of Critical Care, 1988-90, Jour. of Applied Nursing Rsch., 1988-91, IMAGE: Jour. Nursing Scholarship, editl. adv. bd. Nursing Rsch., 1997—, Biol. Rsch. for Nursing, 1999—, Jour. Nursing Scholarship, 2000—; contbr. artilces to profl. jours. Abe Miller Meml. scholar Alberta Assn. Registered Nurses, 1968-69; Kathryn McLaggen Meml. fellow Can. Nurses Found., fellow Am. Acad. Nursing Am. Nurses Assn., 1988—. Office: U Ill Coll Nursing 845 S Damen Ave # Mc802 Chicago IL 60612-7350

SHAW, CHARLES ALEXANDER, judge; b. Jackson, Tenn., Dec. 31, 1944; s. Alvis and Sarah S.; m. Kathleen Ingram, Aug. 17, 1969; 1 child, Bryan Ingram. BA, Harris Stowe State Coll., 1966; MBA, U. Mo., 1971; JD, Cath. U. Am., 1974. Bar: D.C. 1975, Mo. 1975, U.S. Ct. Appeals (8th and D.C. cirs.) 1975, U.S. Dist. Ct. (ea. dist.) Mo. 1976, U.S. Ct. Appeals (6th and 7th cirs.) 1976. Tchr. St. Louis Pub. Schs., 1966-69, D.C. Pub. Schs., Washington, 1969-71; law clk. U.S. Dept. Justice, 1972-73, NLRB, Washington, 1973-74, atty., 1974-76; assoc. Lashly, Caruthers, Theis, Rava & Hamel, St. Louis, 1976-80, asst. U.S. atty., 1980-87; judge Mo. Cir. Ct., 1987-94, asst. presiding judge, 1993-94; judge U.S. Dist. Ct., 1994—. Hearing officer Office of the Mayor, Washington, 1973-74; instr. U. Mo., St. Louis, 1980-81. State bd. dirs. United Negro Coll. Fund, St. Louis, 1979-83; trustee St. Louis Art Mus., 1979-82, 89-96; bd. dirs. Arts and Edn. Coun., 1992-96, Metro Golf Assn., 1993-2000, Landmarks Assn., St. Louis, 1980-82. Danforth Found. fellow, 1978-79; Cath. U. Am. scholar, 1971-74. Mem. D.C. Bar Assn., Mo. Bar Assn., Mound City Bar Assn., Bar Assn. Metro. St. Louis, Harris-Stowe State Coll. Alumni Assn. (bd. dirs., Disting. Alumni 1988), Nat. Assn. Guardsmen (sec. St. Louis chpt. 1999-2001), Phi Alpha Delta (svc. award 1973-74), Sigma Pi Phi (pres. St. Louis chpt. 1999-2001). Avocation: golf. Office: 111 S 10th St Saint Louis MO 63102

SHAW, CHARLES RUSANDA, government investigator; b. Detroit, Aug. 17, 1914; s. Leonard George and Harriet (Kratzer) S.; m. Sally Madeline Jock, May 3, 1947 (dec. June 1996); children: Patrick R., Sandra L. Keding (dec.), Janice L., Lisa Keding; stepchildren: Lillian Genna, Ruth Czenkus. Cert., Wicker Sch. of Fine Arts, 1936, Mich. Acad. Advt. Art, 1937; student, Intelligence Corps Sch., 1947. Freelance artist, Detroit, 1936-39; spl. agt. U.S. Army Counter Intelligence Corps, Washington, 1947-48, Office Spl. Investigations, USAF, Washington, 1948-66; pvt. investigator Charles Shaw Assocs., Mt. Clemens, Mich., 1966-84; contract investigator USAF & U.S. Customs Svc., Washington, 1984-94; entrepreneur-inventor neoteric products, patents pending C.R. Shaw Assocs., 1994—. Author: Immaculate Misconception, 1999. Master sgt. U.S. Army, 1939-45, PTO, ETO. Mem. Assn. Former OSI Spl. Agts. (chartered), Acad. Am. Poets. Democrat. Roman Catholic. Avocations: fine arts, photography, gardening, home improvements. Home and Office: 59295 Bates Rd New Haven MI 48048-1728

SHAW, DORIS BEAUMAR, film and video producer, executive recruiter, management consultant; b. Pitts., July 13, 1934; d. Emerson C. and Doris Llorene (Rees) Beaumar; m. Robert Newton Shaw, July 6, 1957. BA summa cum laude, Lindenwood Coll., St. Charles, Mo., 1955. Writer, asst. to pres. Baker Prodns., Benton Harbor, Mich., 1955; asst. prodn. mgr. Condor Films, Inc., St. Louis, 1955-57; chief editor, asst. to v.p. Frederick F. Watson Inc., N.Y.C., 1957-58; v.p. Gen. Pictures Corp., Cleve., 1958-71; dir., editor, unit mgr. Cinecraft Inc., 1971-72; mgr. audio-visual dept. Am. Greetings Corp., 1972-73; proprietor Script to Screen Svcs., Chagrin Falls, Ohio, 1973-76; pres. D & B Shaw, Inc., Chardon, 1976-87, Hudson, 1987—, Execusearch, Inc., Hudson, 1987—, Infosearch Inc., Hudson, 1994—, Cybersearch, Inc., Hudson, 1995—. Film festival judge, tchr. Martha Holden Jennings Found./Hawken Sch., Gates Mills, Ohio, 1970-85; advisor teenage film contests, seminars Cleve. Bd. Edn., 1970-88; contest judge/film and video WVIZ-TV, Channel 25, Parma, Ohio, 1971—; guest lectr. Lindenwood Coll., 1973-80; adj. prof. U. Akron, 1990—; cons. to bus. and industry regarding sales, mktg., bus. mgmt., info. and rsch. svcs., computer multimedia prodn., web page design and devel. Writer, dir., editor, prodr. hundreds of film, video, multi-image, multi-media, audio/visual prodn., radio, TV commls. and programs; contbr. articles to profl. jours. Bd. trustees Ohio Boys Town, Cleve., 1957-68; mem. alumnae coun. Lindenwood Coll., 1973-77; publicity chmn. Geauga County Preservation Soc., 1984-91; active various charitable orgns. Named Outstanding Young Woman of Am., Fedn. of Women's Clubs, 1965, Alumna of Yr. Merit award Lindenwood Coll., 1971; recipient numerous awards and grants for film, video projects including Gold Camera Best Documentary award, 1979. Mem. Soc. Motion Picture and TV Engrs., Info. Film Prodrs. Am., Assn. for Multi Image (charter), Detroit Prodrs. Assn., Internat. TV and Video Assn. (charter), Internat. Comm. Industries Assn., Alpha Epsilon Rho. Republican. Avocations: science, travel, physical fitness, environmental issues, organic horticulture. Office: D & B Shaw Inc PO Box 335 Peninsula OH 44264-0335

SHAW, JOHN, sports association administrator; b. N.Y. 1 dau., Alexandra. BS in Acctg., U. San Diego; JD, NYU. Lawyer, Calif.; acct. Arthur Andersen & Co.; pres. St. Louis Rams, 1980—. Primary advisor to chmn. and owner St. Louis Rams; mem. NFL Mgmt. Coun. Exec. Com. Bd. dirs. Greater St. Louis United Way; mem. Coun. Trustees LEARN, St. Louis. Office: St Louis Rams 1 Rams Way Earth City MO 63045-1525

SHAW, JOHN W. lawyer; b. Mo., 1951; BA, MA, U. Mo., 1973, JD, 1977. Bar: Mo. 1977. Ptnr. Bryan Cave, Kansas City, 1977-92, Lathrop & Norquist, 1983-92, Bryan Cave LLP, 1992-98, Berkowitz Feldmiller Stanton Brandt Williams and Shaw LLP, Kansas City, 1998—. Mem. ABA, Securities Industry Assn. (legal and compliance group), Mo. Bar, Def. Rsch. Inst. (chmn. firearms litigation subcom.), Order of Coif. Office: Berkowitz Feldmiller Stanton Brandt Williams and Shaw LLP Ste 50 500 Two Emmanuel Cleaver Bl Kansas City MO 64112

SHAW, MELVIN PHILLIP, physicist, engineering educator, psychologist; b. Bklyn., Aug. 16, 1936; s. Harry and Yetta (Stutsky) S.; m. Carol Joan Phillips, Sept. 5, 1959 (div. Feb. 1987); children: Adam, Evan; m. Bernetta Berger, May 16, 1987. BS, Bklyn. Coll., 1959; MS, Case Western Res. U., 1963, PhD, 1965; MA, Ctr. for Humanistic Studies, 1988. Research scientist United Techs. Research Labs., E. Hartford, Conn., 1964-68, scientist-in-charge, 1966-70; prof. Wayne State U., Detroit, 1970-96, prof. emeritus, 1997—; adminstrv. dir. Assocs. of Birmingham/Kingswood Hosp., 1991-93. Cons. Energy Conversion Devices, Troy, Mich., 1970-92. Co-author: The Gunn-Hilsum Effect, 1979, The Physics and Applications of Amorphous Semiconductors, 1988, The Physics of Instabilities in Solid State Electron Devices, 1992, Creativity and Affect, 1994. Fellow Am. Phys. Soc.; mem. IEEE (sr.), Am. Psychol. Assn. (assoc.). Avocations: cooking, walking, exercising, traveling.

SHAW, MICHAEL ALLAN, lawyer, mail order company executive; b. Evanston, Ill., July 14, 1940; s. Frank C. and Mabel I. (Peacock) S.; m. Genevieve Schrodt, Aug. 16, 1964; children: M. Ian, Trevor A. BA, Colo. State U., 1962; JD, U. Denver, 1965; MBA, DePaul U., 1969; postgrad., Columbia U., 1970. Bar: Ill. bar 1965. Practiced in, Chgo., 1965-83; asst. counsel, staff asst. to v.p. traffic Jewel Cos., Inc., Melrose Park, Ill., 1965-71; corp. sec., asst. treas., house counsel Wieboldt Stores, Inc., Chgo., 1972-83; pvt. practice law Naperville, Ill., 1983-89; pres. Kingston Korner, Inc., 1983—, Aztec Corp., Naperville, 1989—. Pres. Folk Era Prodns., producers folk music concert series, records, 1985—; editor Folk Music Editor, 1984; contbr. articles to legal jours. Mem. Village Planning Commn., Itasca, Ill., 1973-77; bd. dirs. Crimestoppers, Naperville, 1984—, chmn., 1988-94; session mem. Naperville Lumen Christi United Presbyn. Ch., 1984-85; chmn. bldg. fin. com. Naperville Presbyn. Ch., 1989-93. Mem. Fox Valley Folklore Soc. (bd. dirs. 1991—). E-mails. Home: 6 S 230 Cohasset Rd Naperville IL 60540 Office: Aztec Corp 705 S Washington St Naperville IL 60540-6696 E-mail: allan@folkera.com.

SHAW, ROBERT EUGENE, retired minister, administrator; b. Havre, Mont., Apr. 8, 1933; s. Harold Alvin and Lillian Martha (Kruse) S.; m. Marilyn Grace Smit, June 14, 1957; children: Rebecca Jean, Ann Elizabeth, Mark David, Peter Robert. BA, Sioux Falls Coll., 1955; MDiv, Am. Bapt. Sem. of West, 1958; DD (hon.), Ottawa u., 1976, Judson Coll., 1984. Ordained to ministry Am. Bapt. Chs. U.S.A., 1958. Pastor First Bapt. Ch., Webster City, Iowa, 1958-63, Cmty. Bapt. Ch., Topeka, 1963-68; sr. pastor Prairie Bapt. Ch., Prairie Village, 1968-78; pres., prof. religion Ottawa U., 1978-83; exec. minister Am. Bapt. Chs. Mich, East Lansing, 1983-98; ret., 1998; exec. min. emeritus Am. Bapt. Chs. Mich., 2000—. Mem. gen. bd. Am. Bapt. Chs. U.S.A., Valley Forge, Pa., 1972-80, nat. v.p., 1978-80; nat. v.p. Am. Bapt. Minister Coun., Valley Forge, 1969-72, nat. pres., 1972-75; nat. chair Am. Bapt. Evang. Team, 1988-93; mem. Internat. Commn. on Edn. and Evangelism, Bapt. World Alliance, 1990—; mem. nat. exec. com. Am. Bapt. Adminstrs. Colls. and Univs., 1980-82; vis. prof. Evangelism Ctrl. Bapt. Theol. Sem., Kansas City, 1999-2000. Bd. dirs. Kans. Ind. Coll.s Assn., 1980-82; trustee No. Bapt. Theol. Sem., Lombard, Ill., 1983-98, Kalamazoo Coll., Mich., 1983-92, Judson Coll., Elgin, Ill., 1983-96; dir. Webster City C. of C., 1961-62, Ottawa C. of C., 1980-82. Recipient Firman Early award Disting. ministry to ch. and comty. U. Sioux Falls, 1996.

SHAW, SCOTT ALAN, photojournalist; b. Danville, Ill., 1963; BS in Journalism, So. Ill. U., 1985. Formerly with The Comml. News, Danville; with The Paragould (Ark.) Daily Press, 1985-86; staff photographer The Odessa (Tex.) Am., 1986-89; with St. Louis Sun, 1989-90; now staff photographer The Plain Dealer, Cleve., 1990—. Recipient Pulitzer Prize for spot news photgraphy, 1988. Office: The Plain Dealer 1801 Superior Ave E Cleveland OH 44114-2198

SHAW, STANLEY MINER, nuclear pharmacy scientist; b. Parkston, S.D., July 4, 1935; s. George Henry and Jensina (Thompson) S.; m. Excellda J. Watke, Aug. 13, 1961; children: Kimberly Kay, Renee Denise, Elena Aimee. BS, S.D. State U., 1957, MS, 1959; PhD, Purdue U., 1962. Instr. S.D. State U., 1960-62; asst. prof. bionucleonics Purdue U., West Lafayette, Ind., 1962-66, assoc. prof., 1966-71, prof. nuclear pharmacy, 1971—, head. divsn. nuclear pharmacy, 1990—; acting head Purdue U. Sch. Health Scis., 1990-93. Bd. pharm. spltys. Splty. Council Nuclear Pharmacy, 1978-82. Contbr. articles to profl. jours. Recipient Lederle Pharmacy faculty awards, 1962, 65, Parenteral Drug Assn. Rsch. award, 1970, Henry Heine Outstanding Tchr. award Sch. Pharmacy Purdue U., 1989, 93, 99, Disting. Alumnus award S.D. State U., 1991, Disting. Pharmacy Educator award AACP, 1994. Fellow Acad. Pharmacy Practice (chmn. sect. nuclear pharmacy 1979-80, historian 1981-85, mem.-at-large 1993-95, chmn.-elect 1995-96, chmn. 1996-97, Disting. Achievement award 1998), Am. Soc. Hosp. Pharmacy, Am. Pharm. Assn.; mem. Health Physics Soc., Am. Pharm. Assn. (ho. of dels. 1977, 79, 86, 92, Founder's award, Daniel B. Smith Practice Excellence award 2000), Sigma Xi, Phi Lambda Upsilon, Phi Lambda Sigma, Rho Chi. Home: 7208 W Greenview Dr Battle Ground IN 47920-9732 Office: Purdue U Sch Pharmacy West Lafayette IN 47907-1336

SHAW, WILLIAM, state legislator; b. Fulton, Ark., July 31, 1937; s. McKinley and Gertrude (Henderson) S.; m. Shirley Shaw, 1957; children: Gina, Victor, Shawn, 3 stepchildren. Grad. high sch. Adminstrv. asst. to Alderman Wilson Frost 34th Ward; precinct capt. 24th ward and inspector City of Chgo.; pres. 9th ward Regional Dem. Orgn.; Ill. state rep. Dist. 34, 1983—; mem. appropriations I com. labor and commerce com. Ill. Ho. Reps., exec. and vet. affairs com., registration com., vice chmn. fin. insts. com., chmn. ins. com.; mem. Ill. State Senate Dist. 15, 1993—; asst. dir. Supportive Svcs., Chgo. Mem. Masons, C. of C. Home: 12126 S Perry Ave Chicago IL 60628-6627 Office: Ill Senate Rm 103D State Capitol Springfield IL 62706-0001

SHAW, WILLIAM, broadcast executive; V.p., gen. mgr. WGN Superstation Tribune Co., Chgo., 2002—; pres., CEO Fox TV Sales (subs. Rupert Murdoch's News Corp. Ltd.), NY; v.p. sales Tribune TV. Office: Tribune Co 435 N Michigan Ave Chicago IL 60611

SHAYMAN, JAMES ALAN, nephrologist, educator; b. Chgo., June 14, 1954; s. Benjamin and Chernie (Abrams) S.; children: Rebecca Lynn, David Aaron. AB, Cornell U., 1976; MD, Washington U., St. Louis, 1980. Intern and resident Barnes Hosp., St. Louis, 1980-83; instr. Washington U., 1985-86; asst. prof. U. Mich., Ann Arbor, 1986-92, assoc. prof., 1992-97; prof. internal medicine and pharmacology, 1997—; assoc. chair rsch. programs dept. internal medicine U. Mich., Ann Arbor, 1997—. Mem. Am. Soc. Nephrology, Internat. Soc. Nephrology, Am. Diabetes Assn., Am. Soc. Clin. Investigation, Am. Physiol. Soc., Phi Beta Kappa, Phi Kappa Phi, Alpha Omega Alpha. Achievements include research in renal inositol phosphate metabolism and renal glycolipid metabolism.

SHEA, DANIEL BARTHOLOMEW, JR. English language educator, actor; b. Mpls., Oct. 29, 1936; s. Daniel Bartholomew and Dorothea (Lonergan) S.; m. Kathleen Anne Williams, June 3, 1978; children: Timothy, Matthew, Catherine, Daniel, Emily. B.A. summa cum laude, Coll. St. Thomas, 1958; M.A., Stanford U., 1962, Ph.D., 1966. Teaching asst. Stanford U., 1959-61; instr. to prof. English Washington U., St. Louis, 1962—, chmn. dept., 1978-84, 95-98; acting chair performing arts, prof. drama, 1995. Fulbright-Hays lectr. Univs. of Caen and Nice, France, 1968-69; vis. fellow Clare Hall, U. Cambridge, Eng., 1984-85 Author: Spiritual Autobiography in Early America, 1968, 2d edit., 1988; editorial bd.: Early Am. Lit, 1972-74; sect. editor: Columbia Literary History of the United States; contbr. chpts. to books. Woodrow Wilson fellow, 1958; NEH summer grantee, 1971 Mem. MLA (del. gen. assembly 1977-78), AFTRA, Equity. Home: 6138 Kingsbury Ave Saint Louis MO 63112-1102 Office: Washington Univ Dept of English Saint Louis MO 63130 E-mail: dbshea@artsci.wustl.edu.

SHEA, JAMES F. manufacturing executive; CEO Fairmont Homes, Nappanee, Ind. Office: Fairmont Homes 502 S Oakland Ave Nappanee IN 46550-2332

SHEARER, MARK SMITH, state legislator; b. Burlington, Iowa, Aug. 11, 1952; Student, U. Iowa. Broadcast journalist Stas. KCII, KICR, KCRG, 1968-79; mem., chair Iowa Arts Coun., 1981-88; mem. Iowa House, Des Moines, 1989-92; salesperson U.S. Cellular, 1995-98; comms. cons.; mem. Iowa Senate from 49th dist., Des Moines, 1998—; mem. agr. com., mem. edn. com., mem. human resources com.; ranking com. small bus., econ.

devel., and tourism; mem. appropriations com. Editor: Columbus Gazette, 1979-95. Democrat. Office: State Capitol 9th And Grand Ave Des Moines IA 50319-0001 E-mail: mark.shearer@legis.state.ia.us.

SHEA-STONUM, MARILYN, federal judge; b. 1947; AB, U. Santa Cruz, 1969; JD, Case Western Res. U., 1975. Law clk. to Hon. Frank J. Battisti, Cleve., 1975-76; ptnr. Jones, Day, Reavis & Pogue, 1976-94; bankruptcy judge U.S. Dist. Ct. (no. dist.) Ohio, Akron, 1994—. Mem. Order of Coif. Office: US Bankruptcy Ct No Dist Ohio 240 Fed Bldg 2 S Main St Akron OH 44308-1813 Fax: 330-375-5793.

SHEEDY, PATRICK THOMAS, judge; b. Green Bay, Wis., Oct. 31, 1921; s. Earl P. and Elsie L. (Brauel) S.; m. Margaret P. Mulvaney, Sept. 6, 1952; children: Michael, Mary, Kathleen, Patrick Thomas, Ann, Maureen. BS in Bus. Adminstrn., Marquette U., 1943, JD, 1948; LLM in Taxation, John Marshall Law Sch., 1972. Bar: Wis. 1948. Pvt. practice, Milw., 1948-80; judge Wis. Cir. Ct., 1980-90; chief judge 1st Jud. Dist., 1990-98. Past vice chmn. Archdiocesan Sch. Bd., Milw., chairperson, 1986—. Served to col. USAR, 1942-73. Decorated Legion of Merit. Mem. ABA (state del. 1983-85, 89-92, bd. govs. 1985-88), Wis. Bar Assn. (pres. 1974-75, bd. govs., exec. com.). Roman Catholic. Club: Exchange (pres.).

SHEEHAN, CAROL SAMA, magazine editor; Editor-in-chief Country Home Mag., Des Moines, 1997—. Office: Country Home Magazine 1716 Locust St Des Moines IA 50309-3038

SHEEHAN, JAMES PATRICK, printing company executive, former media company executive; b. Jersey City, June 6, 1942; s. John Patrick and Helen Teresa (Woods) S.; m. Mary Ellen Finnell, July 1, 1967; children: James, Christopher. B.S., Seton Hall U., 1965; M.B.A., Wayne State U., 1973. Contr. Otis Elevator Co. N.Am., Farmington, Conn., 1976-78, dir. mfg. Yonkers, N.Y., 1978-80; v.p., contr,. Pratt & Whitney Aircraft, East Hartford, Conn., 1980-82; sr. v.p. A. H. Belo Corp., Dallas, 1982-84; CFO, A.H. Belo Corp., 1984-86, pres., COO, 1987-93, CEO, 1993-99; pres., CEO, chmn. Goss Graphic Systems, Westmont, Ill., 1999-. Mem. devel. bd. U. Tex.-Dallas, 1985—; bd. dirs. United Way, The Dallas Partnership, The Dallas Morning News Charities; trustee St. Paul Med. Ctr. Found. Served to Lt. (j.g.) USN, 1967-69, Vietnam. Mem. Am. Newspaper Pubs. Assn., So. Newspaper Pubs. Assn. Roman Catholic Avocations: tennis; racquetball; golf; jogging. Office: Goss Graphic Systems 700 Oakmont Ln Westmont IL 60559-5551

SHEFFEL, IRVING EUGENE, psychiatric institution executive; b. Chgo., July 5, 1916; s. Joseph and Jennie (Leibson) S.; m. Beth Silver, Aug. 2, 1942 (dec.); 1 child, Anita (dec.); m. Peggy Shelton, Apr. 6, 1996. A.B., U. Chgo., 1939; M.P.A., Harvard U., 1946; LHD (hon.), Washburn U., 1987. Insp., wage and hour div. Dept. Labor, Chgo., 1940-41; mgmt. and budget analyst VA, Washington, 1946-48; budget analyst U.S. Bur. of Budget, 1948-49; controller, treas. Menninger Found., Topeka, 1949-73, v.p., 1973-93, v.p. emeritus, 1993—. Instr. Menninger Sch. Psychiatry. Bd. dirs. Washburn U. Art Center, 1969— , pres., 1971-73; treas. Karl Menninger lect. series, 1983—. Served to maj. U.S. Army, 1942-45. Fellow Assn. Mental Health Adminstrs. (charter); mem. Am. Soc. Public Adminstrn. (charter), Topeka Opera Soc. (treas. 1985—). Jewish. Home: 1215 SW 29th Ter Topeka KS 66611-2192 Office: PO Box 829 Topeka KS 66601-0829

SHEFFIELD, JOHN WILLIAM, mechanical engineering educator; b. Ft. Worth, May 3, 1950; s. James G. and Sarah E. (Laney) S.; m. Mary White, May 21, 1977; children: Jennifer Marie, Katherine Elaine, Christopher William robert. B of Engring. Sci., U. Tex., 1971; M of Engring. Mechanics, N.C. State U., 1973, PhD in Engring. Sci. and Mechanics, 1975. Sr. analytical engr. Pratt & Whitney Aircraft, United Tech. Corp., East Hartford, Conn., 1975-76, sr. exptl. engr. West Palm Beach, Fla., 1976-78; rsch. asst. prof. of mech. engring. U. Miami, Coral Gables, 1978-80; asst. prof. U. Mo., Rolla, 1980-84, assoc. prof., 1984-89, prof. of mech. and aerospace engring., 1989—. Asst. dir. Indsl. Assessment Ctr., 1994—; asst. editor Internat. Assn. for Hydrogen Energy, 1978-82; assoc. editor Internat. Assn. Hydrogen Energy, 1983—; dir. Office of U. Outreach and Extension, 1997—. Contbr. numerous articles to profl. jours. Mem. ASHRAE (Dist. Svc. award 1991, mem. various coms.), ASME, AIAA, Am. Soc. Engring. Edn., Sigma Xi, Phi Kappa Phi, Tau Beta Pi, Pi Tau Sigma. Home: 11870 Forest Lake Dr Rolla MO 65401-7382 Office: Univ Mo Rolla Dept Mech & Aerospace Engrg 108 USBN Bldg 1 1300 Bishop Rolla MO 65409-0001

SHEFFIELD, LEWIS GLOSSON, physiologist; b. Adel, Ga., Oct. 30, 1957; s. Eugene Davis and Martha Sue (Sinclair) S.; m. Mary Frances Tanner, July 18, 1980. MS, Clemson U., 1980; PhD, U. Mo., 1983. Rsch. asst. Clemson (S.C.) U., 1978-80, U. Mo., Columbia, 1980-83; postdoctoral assoc. Mich. State U., East Lansing, 1983-86; asst. prof. dairy sci. dept. U. Wis., Madison, 1986-91, assoc. prof. dairy sci., 1991—, dir. endocrinology-reproductive physiology program, 1990—. Contbr. articles to profl. jours. Recipient First award NIH, 1988. Mem. Am. Dairy Sci. Assn. (milk synthesis chair 1991-92), Com. on Mammary Gland Biology, Endocrine Soc., Sigma Xi. Achievements include demonstration that epidermal growth factor interacts with estrogen and progesterone to regulate mammary devel. and are working to understand the cellular and molecular basis of that interaction; that prolactin causes a decrease in epidermal growth factor-induced growth responses, which appears to be related to mammary gland differentiation. The molecular regulation of this response is also under investigation. Office: U Wis 864 Animal Scis Bldg 1675 Observatory Dr Madison WI 53706-1205

SHELBY, DON, radio personality; Anchor news at 6 pm and 10 pm Sta. WCCO-TV, Mpls., 1978—; radio host, news anchor Sta. WCCO. Recipient 3 nat. Emmy awards, Columbia-duPont citation, Scripps-Howard award for Excellence, 2 George Foster Peabody awards, Disting. Svc. award, Soc. Profl. Journalist. Office: WCCO Radio 625 2nd Ave S Minneapolis MN 55402*

SHELDON, GILBERT IGNATIUS, clergyman; b. Cleve., Sept. 20, 1926; s. Ignatius Peter and Stephanie Josephine (Olszewski) S. Student, John Carroll U.; M.Div., St. Theol. Sem., 1970; D.Min., St. Mary Sem. and Ohio Consortium of Sems., 1974; HHD, Jesuit U. of Wheeling, 1993; STD, Franciscan U., Steubenville, 1994. Ordained priest Roman Cath. Ch., 1953, bishop, 1976. Assoc. pastor Cleve. Diocese, 1953-64, diocesan dir. propagation of faith, 1964-74; pastor, Episcopal vicar Lorain County, Ohio, 1974-76; aux. bishop Cleve., 1976—; vicar for Summit County, 1979-80, So. Region, 1980-92; bishop Steubenville, 1992—. Bd. dirs. Soc. Propagation of Faith, 1968-74, Diocesan Presbyteral Coun.; instr. theology St. John Coll.; clergy adv. bd. econ. edn. Akron U.; mem. Bishop's Com. Latin Am.; bd. trustees St. Mary Seminary, Diocesan Health Ins. Adv. Bd., Cath. Charities Corp.; former mem. bd. trustees Borromeo Coll.; mem. acad. bd. St, Mary Seminary; bd. dirs. Bishops' Com. Latin Am., adminstrv. com. Nat. Conf. Cath. Bishops/USCC, Nat. Adv. Coun., Bishops' Com. for Missions, Nat. Bd. Soc. for Propagation of Faith; bd. trustees Pontifical Coll. Josephinum. Goals for Greater Akron. Served with USAF, 1944—45. Mem. Nat. Conf. Cath. Bishops (adminstrv. bd. 1985—), Am. Legion, Cath. War Vets., Knights of Columbus, Order of Alhambra., Rotary Club Akron and Steubenville. Club: K.C. Lodge: Rotary (Akron). Avocations: golf, astronomy, photography, history, travel. Office: Diocese of Steubenville PO Box 969 Steubenville OH 43952-5969 E-mail: lnichols@diosteub.org.

SHELDON, INGRID KRISTINA, former mayor of Ann Arbor, bookkeeper; b. Ann Arbor, Mich., Jan. 30, 1945; d. Henry Ragnvald and Virginia Schmidt (Clark) Blom; m. Clifford George Sheldon, June 18, 1966; children: Amy Elizabeth, William David. BS, Eastern Mich. U., 1966; MA, U. Mich., 1970. Cert. tchr., Mich. Tchr. Livonia (Mich.) Pub. Schs., 1966-67, Ann Arbor Pub. Schs., 1967-68; bookkeeper Huron Valley Tennis Club, Ann Arbor, 1978—; acct. F.A. Black Co., 1984-88; coun. mem. Ward II City of Ann Arbor, 1988-92, mayor, 1993-2000. Cmn.r Housing Bd. Appeals, Ann Arbor, 1988-91; vice chmn. fin. and budget com. S.E. Mich. Coun. Govts. Treas. Huron Valley Child Guidance Clinic, Ann Arbor, 1984—, Ann Arbor Hist. Found., 1985—, Parks Adv. Commn., 1987-92, Ann Arbor Planning Commn., 1988-89; excellence com. Ann Arbor Pub. Schs. reorgn., 1985; treas. SOS Cmty. Crisis Ctr., Ypsilanti, Mich., 1987-93; precinct ward city vice chmn. Ann Arbor Rep. City Com., 1978—. Recipient Cmty. Svc. award Ann Arbor Jaycees, 1980, DAR Cmty. Svc. award, 1997; AAUW fellow, 1982. Mem. Mich. Mcpl. League (del. 1989-97, trustee, 1997—, pres. 1999-00), Ann Arbor Women's City Club (chair endowment com. 1989-90, fin. com. 1987-90, treas.), Rotary (former dir. Ann Arbor chpt.), Kappa Delta Pi, Alpha Omnicron Pi. Republican. Methodist. Avocation: musical theatre. Home: 1416 Folkstone Ct Ann Arbor MI 48105-2848 E-mail: aasheldon@aol.com.

SHELDON, TED PRESTON, library dean; b. Oak Park, Ill., July 5, 1942; s. Preston and Marjorie Sheldon; m. Beverly Stebel; children: Kathy, Mark. BA, Elmhurst (Ill.) Coll., 1964; MA, Ind. U., 1965, PhD, 1976; MLS, U. Ill., 1977. Asst. archivist U. Ill., Urbana, 1976-77; reference librarian U. Kans., Lawrence, 1977-79, head collection devel., 1979-81; assoc. dir. libraries SUNY, Binghamton, 1981-83, U. Mo., Kansas City, 1983-85, dean libraries, 1985—. Pres. Mo. Libr. Network Corp., 1991-95. Author: Population Trends, 1976, Kans. Coll. Devel. Policy, 1978, History, Sources Social Science, 1985; co-author: ANSI/ISO/AES audio/video data preservation stds., 1997—. Mem. ALA, Am. Nat. Stds. Inst./Audio Engring. Soc. (joint tech. commn. 1994—), Mus. Libr. Assn., Internat. Assn. Sound Archives, Assn. Recorded Sound Collection (mng. editor jour 1988-95, pub. jour. 1995—, pres. 1996-98, pub. 1996—). Office: U Mo Libraries 5100 Rockhill Rd Kansas City MO 64110-2481

SHELL, OWEN G., JR. retired banker; b. Greenville, S.C., June 19, 1936; s. Owen and Katherine S.; m. Mary Ruth Trammell, Aug. 9, 1980; children: Katherine Sloan, Mary Carroll, Robert Owen, James Walker. BS, U. S.C., 1960; postgrad., Stonier Grad. Sch. Banking, 1971; grad., Advanced Mgmt. Program, Harvard U., 1979. Tech. supt. Deering-Milliken, Inc., 1962-63; v.p. Citizens & So. Nat. Bank S.C., Columbia, 1968-71, sr. v.p., 1971-74, exec. v.p., 1974-79; pres., dir., chief exec. officer First Am. Nat. Bank, Nashville, 1979-86; vice chmn. bd., dir. First Am. Corp., 1979-86; chmn., pres., chief exec. officer Sovran Bank/Tenn., Nashville, 1986-91; pres. Nations Bank of Tenn. (formerly Sovran Bank), 1992-96; pres. asset mgmt. group NationsBank Corp., St. Louis, 1997-99; pres. Asset Mgmt. Bank of Am., 1997—2002; ret., 2002. Bd. dirs. Nashville br. Fed. Res. Bank, Atlanta. Chmn. bd. INROADS/Nashville; chmn. Leadership Nashville, Tenn. Performing Arts Found., Mid. Tenn. coun. Boy Scouts Am., Vanderbilt U. Owen Grad. Sch. Mgmt.; trustee Met. Nashville Pub. Edn.; bd. dirs. Tenn. Bus. Roundtable, Tenn. Tomorrow. Mem.: Assn. Res. City Bankers, Old Sarson Country Club (St. Louis), Harvard Club N.Y.C., Belle Meade Country Club, Omicron Delta Kappa, Kappa Alpha. Presbyterian. Home: 4412 Chickering Ln Nashville TN 37215-4915

SHELLEY, WALTER BROWN, physician, educator; b. St. Paul, Feb. 6, 1917; s. Patrick K. and Alfaretta (Brown) S.; m. Marguerite H. Weber, 1942 (dec.); children: Peter B., Anne E. Kiselewich, Barbara A. (dec.); m. E. Dorinda Loeffel, 1980; children: Thomas R., Katharine D., William L. B.S., U. Minn., 1940, Ph.D., 1941, M.D., 1943; M.A. honoris causa, U. Pa., 1971; M.D. honoris causa, U. Uppsala, Sweden, 1977. Diplomate: Am. Bd. Dermatology (pres. 1968-69, dir. 1960-69). Instr. physiology U. Pa., Phila., 1946-47, asst. instr. dermatology and syphilology, 1947-49, asst. prof. dermatology, 1950-53, assoc. prof., 1953-57, prof., 1957-80, chmn. dept., 1965-80; prof. dermatology U. Ill. Peoria Sch. Medicine, 1980-83; prof. medicine (dermatology) Med. Coll. Ohio, 1983-97, emeritus prof. medicine, 1997—. Instr. dermatology Dartmouth Coll., 1949-50; Regional cons. dermatology VA, 1955-59; mem. com. on cutaneous system NRC, 1955-59, Commn. Cutaneous Diseases, Armed Forces Epidemiological Bd., 1958-61, dep. dir., 1959-61; cons. dermatology Surgeon Gen. USAF, 1958-61, U.S. Army, 1958-61; mem. NRC, 1961-64 Author (with Crissey): Classics in Clinical Dermatology, 1953; author: (with Pillsbury, Kligman) Dermatology, 1956; author: Cutaneous Medicine, 1961; author: (with Hurley) The Human Apocrine Sweat Gland in Health and Disease, 1960; author: (with Botelho and Brooks) The Endocrine Glands, 1969; author: Consultations in Dermatology with Walter B. Shelley, 1972, Consultations II, 1974; author: (with Shelley) Advanced Dermatologic Therapy, 1987; author: Advanced Dermatologic Diagnosis, 1992, A Century of International Dermatological Congresses, 1992, Advanced Dermatogical Therapy II, 2001, Shelley's 77 Skins, 2001; mem. editl. bd. Jour. Investigative Dermatology, 1961—64, Archives of Dermatology, 1961—62, Skin and Allergy News, 1970—93, Excerpta Medica Dermatologica, 1960—, Cutis, 1972—, Jour. Geriatric Dermatol, 1993; assoc. editor: Jour. Cutaneous Pathology, 1972—81; editl. cons. Medcom, 1972—. Served as capt. M.C. AUS, 1944-46. Recipient Spl. award Soc. Cosmetic Chemists, 1955, Hellerstrom medal, 1971, Am. Med. Writers Assn. Best Med. Book award, 1973, Dohi medal, 1981, Rothman medal Soc. for Investigative Dermatology, 1987, Rose Hirschler award, 1990. Master A.C.P.; fellow Assn. Am. Physicians, St. John's Dermatol. Soc. London (hon.); mem. AMA (chmn. residency rev. com. for dermatology 1963-67, chmn. sect. dermatology 1969-71), Assn. Profs. Dermatology (pres. 1972-73), Pacific Dermatol. Assn. (hon.), Am. Dermatol. Assn. (hon., dir., pres. 1975-76), Soc. Investigative Dermatology (hon. pres. 1961-62), Am., Phila. physiol. socs., Brit. Dermatol. Soc. (hon.), Phila. Dermatol. Soc. (pres. 1960-61), Mich. Dermatol. Soc., Ohio Dermatol. Soc. (hon.), Am. Acad. Dermatology (Gold medal 1992, hon. pres. 1971-72), Pa. Acad. Dermatology (pres. 1972-73), Am. Soc. for Dermatologic Surgery, North Am. Clin. Dermatol. Soc. (hon.), Noah Worcester Dermatological Soc., Royal Soc. Medicine; corr. mem. Nederlandse Vereniging Van Dermatologen, Israeli Dermatol. Assn., Finnish Soc. Dermatology, Swedish Dermatol. Soc., French Dermatologic Soc.; fgn. hon. mem. Danish Dermatol. Assn., Japanese Dermatol. Assn., Dermatol. Soc. S.Africa. Home: 21171 W River Rd Grand Rapids OH 43522-9703 Office: Med Coll Ohio 3120 Glendale Ave Toledo OH 43614-2595 Fax: 419-383-6285. E-mail: ancampbell@mco.edu.

SHELTON, KEVIN L. geology educator; Prof. geology U. Mo., Columbia. Recipient Lindgren award Soc. Economic Geologists, 1991. Office: Univ of Missouri Columbia Dept of Geol Scis 303 Geol Scis Bldg Columbia MO 65211-0001

SHELTON, O. L. state legislator; b. Greenwood, Miss., Feb. 6, 1946; s. Obie and Idell (McClung) S.; m. Linda Kay, July 21, 1980; children: Eric, Jaimal, Schron, Kiana. AB, Lincoln U., 1970. Youth specialist Mo. Ext. Svc., St. Louis, 1972-82. Committeeman 4th ward Dem. party, St. Louis, 1988—; vice-chmn. Dem. Party; advisor Ville Area Neighborhood Housing Assn.; active Black Leadership Roundtable, Mary Rydar Homes, Williams Community Sch. Mem. Early Childcare Devel. Corp. Home: 1803A Cora Ave Saint Louis MO 63113-2221 Office: Mo Ho of Reps State Capitol Bldg 201 W Capitol Ave Rm 407B Jefferson City MO 65101

SHELTON, WILLIAM EVERETT, university president; b. Batesville, Miss., Sept. 6, 1944; s. Loyd Taylor and Merle Golden (Barlow) S.; m. Sharon Nordengreen, Apr. 23, 1965; 1 child, William Bradley. BS, Memphis State U., 1967, MA, 1970; EdD, U. Miss., 1975. Tchr. Olive Branch (Miss.) High Sch., 1967-68; prin. Oakland (Tenn.) Elem. Sch., 1968-70; adminstr., instr. N.W. Miss. Jr. Coll., Senatobia, 1970-76; dean for student devel. Henderson State U., Arkadelphia, Ark., 1976-78, v.p., 1978-83, Kent (Ohio) State U., 1983-89; pres. Ea. Mich. U., Ypsilanti, 1989—. Vice chmn. Ohio Pub. TV, 1986-89. Mem. Am. Assn. for Higher Edn., Am. Assn. State Colls. and Univs., Kent Area C. of C. (pres. 1986). Avocations: flying, golf. Office: Ea Mich U 202 Welch Hall Ypsilanti MI 48197-2214

SHEN, SIN-YAN, physicist, conductor, acoustics specialist, music director; b. Singapore, Nov. 12, 1949; came to the U.S., 1969, naturalized, 1984; s. Shao-Quan and Tien-Siu (Chen) S.; m. Yuan-Yuan Lee, Aug. 4, 1973; children: Jia, Jian. BSc, U. Singapore, 1969; MS, Ohio State U., 1970, PhD, 1973. Concert recitalist on Erhu Chinese fiddle, 1963—; instr. math. U. Singapore, 1969; asst. prof. physics Northwestern U., Evanston, Ill., 1974-77, assoc. prof., 1977-81; faculty assoc. Argonne (Ill.) Nat. Lab., 1974-77, scientist, 1977-83, sr. rsch. leader, 1983—. Dir. rsch. Divsn. Natural Resource Mgmt., SUPCON Internat., 1988—; prof. Harvard U., 1989—; meeting series reviewer NSF, Washington, 1981—; coord. Tech. Rev., Argonne, Atlanta, Phoenix, Portland, Oreg., 1983—; dir. Global Warming Internat. Ctr., 1991—, chmn. Internat. Conf. Chgo., 1990-93, San Francisco, 1994-95, Vienna, 1996, Columbia U., N.Y.C., 1997, Hong Kong U. Sci. and Tech., 1998, Yamanashi Inst. Environ. Scis., 1999, Harvard U., 2000, Cambridge U., 2001; Chinese Music Internat. Conf., 1991, 94; advisor Internat. Energy Agy., 1986—, Gas Rsch. Inst., 1984—, SUPCON Internat., 1986—, Nat. Geog., 1986—, Intenrat. Boreal Forest Rsch. Assn., 1991—, Electric Power Rsch. Inst., 1992—, UN Devel. PRogram, 1993—, World Bank, 1994—, U.S. Dept. Energy and U.S. EPA, 1995—; prof. Chinese Acad. Forestry, 1986—; mem. panel on biol. diversity Nat. Acad. Scis., Smithsonian Instn., 1986; chmn. internat. program com. Austrian Acad. Scis., 1995-96, Columbia U., 1996-97, Japan Environ. Agy., 1998-99, Intergovt. Panel on Climate Change, 1999—; music dir. Orch. of Chinese Music Soc. N.Am., 1976—, The Silk & Bamboo Ensemble, 1981—; adv. Ctrl. Traditional Orch., 1984—; del. leader, UN Conf. Environ. and Devel., Rio, 1992; del. chmn. Third All China Arts Festival, Kunmin, 1992; panelist Nat. Endowment for Arts, 1981—, New Eng. Found. for Arts, 1987—, Arts Midwest, 1985—, Ill. Arts Coun., 1982—, Chgo. City Arts, 1990—, Ill. Art's Alliance Found., adv. coun., 1992—, bd. dirs., 1988—, mem. adv. coun. Mid-Am. Arts Alliance, 1992—; tech. adv. Shanghai Nat. Musical Instrument Co., 1985—; adv. West Lake Qin Soc., Hangzhou, China, 1991—. Author: Superfluidity, 1982, Acoustics of Ancient Chinese Bells, 1987, Chinese Music and Orchestration: A Primer om Principles and Practice, 1991, Global Warming Science and Policy, 1992, The Boreal Forests and Global Change, 1993, Global Warming Eludidated, 1994, Chinese Musical Instruments, 1999, Global Warming and Public Health, 1999, China: A Journey through Its Musical Art, 1999, Chinese Music in the 20th Century, 2001; editor-in-chief Chinese Music Internat. Jour., 1978—; mem. internat. editl. bd. World Resource Rev., 1989—, Internat. Boreal Forst Rsch., 1992—, Ency. of Life Support Sys., 1994—; adv. Ency. Brit., 1983—; contbr. over 300 articles to profl. jours.; patentee molten liquids, 1974, 80. Recipient Mich. Heritage award, 1992; Fulbright scholar U.S. State Dept., 1969; merit scholar Govt. Singapore, 1967; named Artistic Treasure Gov. Jim Edgar of Ill., 1998. Mem. AAAS, Am. Phys. Soc., Ops. Rsch. Soc. Am., Acoustical Soc. Am., Chinese Music Soc. N.Am. Achievements include current work on renewable energy and materials techs.; global change and global warming; extreme event index; indsl. sonic techs.; energy policy, planning and economics; acoustics; cultural acoustics. Office: Chinese Music Soc N Am 2329 Charmingfare Dr Downers Grove IL 60517-2910 also: SUPCON Internat PO Box 5275 Woodridge IL 60517-0275

SHEPARD, IVAN ALBERT, securities and insurance broker; b. Springfield, Mass., Sept. 28, 1925; s. Albert Joseph and Mary (Harrigan) S.; m. Miriam Murray, May 20, 1950; children: Kirk, Robin, Mark. BS in Edn., Ohio State U., 1949. Registered rep. Divisional mgr. Confedn. Life, Columbus, Ohio, 1953-62; regional v.p. Western Res. Life, Cleve., 1962-69; v.p. Computer Life-Pan Western, Columbus, 1969-74; ins. broker Shepard and Assocs., Rocky River, Ohio, 1974—. Bd. dirs., v.p., sec. Computer Life Ohio, 1969-72. With U.S. Navy, 1943-45. Home: 29318 Lake Rd Cleveland OH 44140-1321 Office: Shepard and Assocs 20525 Center Ridge Rd Cleveland OH 44116-3424 E-mail: 9281925@msn.com.

SHEPARD, RANDALL TERRY, state supreme court chief justice; b. Lafayette, Ind., Dec. 24, 1946; s. Richard Schilling and Dorothy Ione (Donlen) S.; m. Amy Wynne MacDonell, May 7, 1988; one child, Martha MacDonell. AB cum laude, Princeton U., 1969; JD, Yale U., 1972; LLM, U. Va., 1995; LLD (hon.), U. So. Ind., 1995. Bar: Ind. 1972, U.S. Dist. Ct. (so. dist.) Ind. 1972. Spl. asst. to under sec. U.S. Dept. Transp., Washington, 1972-74; exec. asst. to mayor City of Evansville, Ind., 1974-79; judge Vanderburgh Superior Ct., Evansville, 1980-85; assoc. justice Ind. Supreme Ct., Indpls., 1985-87, chief justice, 1987—. Instr. U. Evansville, 1975-78, Indiana U., 1995, 99 Author: Preservation Rules and Regulations, 1980; contbr. articles to profl. publs. Bd. advisors Nat. Trust for Hist. Preservation, 1980-87, chmn. bd. advisors, 1983-85, trustee, 1987-96; dir. Hist. Landmarks Found. Ind., 1983—, chmn., 1989-92, hon. chmn., 1992—; chmn. State Student Assistance Commn. on Ind., 1981-85; chmn. Ind. Commn. on Bicentennial of U.S. Constn., 1986-91; vice chmn. Vanderburgh County Rep. Ctrl. Com., 1977-80. Recipient Friend of Media award Cardinal States chpt. Sigma Delta Chi, 1979, Disting. Svc. award Evansville Jaycees, 1982, Herbert Harley award Am. Judicature Soc., 1992. Mem. ABA (coun. mem. sect. on legal edn. 1991—, chair sect. on legal edn. 1997—, immediate past chair appellate judges conf. 1997-98), Ind. Bar Assn., Ind. Judges Assn., Princeton Club (N.Y.), Capitol Hill Club (Washington), Columbia Club (Indpls.). Republican. Methodist. Home: 3644 Totem Ln Indianapolis IN 46208-4171 Office: Ind Supreme Ct 304 State House Indianapolis IN 46204-2213*

SHEPARD, W. BRUCE, academic administrator; m. Cyndie Shepard; 1 child Paul. BS in Polit. Sci., MS in Polit. Sci., PhD in Polit. Sci., U. Calif. Prof. polit. sci., provost, v.p. acad. affairs Ea. Oreg. U., Oreg.; chancellor U. Wis., Green Bay, Wis.; mem. faculty dept. polit. sci. Oreg. State U., Oreg. Vis. scientist Population Study Ctr., Seattle; vis. fellow Sch. Comm. and Liberal Studies MItchell Coll. Advanced Edn., Bathurst, Australia. Office: U Wis Office Chancellor 2420 Nicolet Dr Green Bay WI 54311-7001

SHEPHERD, DANIEL MARSTON, executive recruiter; b. Madison, Ind., Apr. 8, 1939; s. Marston Vincent and Edith America (Brunson) S.; m. Bonnie Lynn Brawley, June 27, 1970 (div. Nov. 1987); children: Vincent, David, Christopher, Megan; m. Gail Lenore Sanborn, Oct. 3, 1989; children: Heather, Shannon. BS in Civil Engring., U. Ky., 1962; MBA, Harvard Bus. Sch., 1964. Mfg. and distbn. mgr. Procter & Gamble Co., Staten Island, N.Y., 1966-70; distbn. and ops. mgr. Mattel, Inc., Gardenia, Calif., 1970-73; gen. mgr., dir. ops. Fuqua Industries, Inc., Atlanta, 1973-76; v.p. product/market mgmt. Masonite Corp., Chgo., 1976-78; v.p. Heidrick & Struggles, 1978-82, Lamalie Assocs., Chgo., 1982-86; prin. Sweeney Shepherd Bueschel Provus Harbert & Mummert, 1986-91, Shepherd Bueschel & Provus, Inc., Chgo., 1991—. Capt. U.S. Army, 1964-66. Decorated Army Commendation medal, 1966; recipient Am.'s Top 150 Recruiters award Harper Bus., N.Y.C., 1992. Mem. Assn. Exec. Search Cons., Inc., Harvard Bus. Sch. Club. Republican. Episcopalian. Avocations: coin and art collecting, skiing, baseball, food, wine. Home: 100 Buckboard Pl Pagosa Springs CO 81147 Office: 401 N Michigan Ave Ste 3020 Chicago IL 60611-4257 E-mail: sbp401@aol.com.

SHEPHERD, JOHN THOMPSON, physiologist; b. No. Ireland, May 21, 1919; s. William Frederick and Matilda (Thompson) S.; m. Helen Mary Johnston, July 28, 1945; children: Gillian Mary, Roger Frederick John; m. Marion G. Etzwiler, Apr. 22, 1989. Student, Campbell Coll., Belfast, No. Ireland, 1932-37; MB, BCh, Queen's U., Belfast, 1945, MChir, 1948, MD, 1951, DSc, 1956, DSc (hon.), 1979; MD (hon.), U. Bologna, 1984, U. Gent, 1985. Lectr. physiology Queen's U., 1948-53, reader physiology, 1954-57; assoc. prof. physiology Mayo Found., 1957-62, prof. physiology, 1962—, chmn. dept. physiology and biophysics, 1966-74; bd. govs. Mayo Clinic, 1966-80; trustee Mayo Found., 1969-81, dir. rsch., 1969-77, dir. for edn., 1977-83, chmn. bd. devel., 1983-88; dean Mayo Med. Sch., 1977-83; assoc. dir. Gen. Rsch. Ctr. Mayo Clinic, Rochester, 1992-94. Chmn. U.S. Nat. Com. for the Internat. Union of Physiol. Scis., 1991-95; vis. prof. U. Auckland, New Zealand, 1997; vis. prof. cardiovasc. divsn. U. Minn., 1995; Soma Weiss meml. lectr. Third Internat. Congress WHMA, Pecs, Hungary, 1996. Author, editor: Physiology of the Circulation in Human Limbs in Health and Disease, 1963, Cardiac Function in Health and Disease, 1968, Veins and Their Control, 1975, Human Cardiovascular System, 1979, Handbook of Physiology, The Cardiovascular System Peripheral Circulation and Organ Blood Flow, 1983, Vascular Diseases in the Limbs, 1993, Nervous Control of the Heart, 1996; co-editor: Exercise: Regulation and Integration of Multiple Systems. Handbook of Physiology, 1996; mem. editl. bd. Hypertension, 1973—, Am. Jour. Physiology, Am. Heart Jour., Microvascular Rsch.; cons. editor Circulation Rsch., 1981—; editor-in-chief News in Physiol. Sci., 1988-94; mem. editl. adv. bd. Clin. Autonomic Rsch., 1990—, Jour. Autonomic Nervous Sys., 1994—, Exptl. Physiology, 1994—, Vascular Medicine, 1995—, Internat. Angiology Adv. Com., 1994—, Cardiovasc. Rsch., 1997—; contbr. more than 590 sci. articles to profl. jours. Recipient NASA Skylab Achievement award, 1974, A. Ross McIntyre medal for achievement, 1991; Brit. Med. Assn. scholar, 1949-50, Fulbright scholar, 1953-54; Anglo-French Med. exch. bursar, 1957; Internat. Francqui chair, 1978; Einthoven lectr. 1981, Volhard lectr., 1990. Fellow Am. Coll. Cardiology (hon.), Royal Coll. Physicians (London), Royal Acad. Medicine (Belgium); mem. NAS (space sci. bd. 1973-74, chmn. com. space biology and medicine 1973), Am. Physiol. Soc. (Disting. Svc. award 1990, Ray G. Daggs award 1997), Louis Rapkine Assn., Am. Heart Assn. (dir. 1968—, pres. 1975-76, chmn. vascular medicine and biology task force 1990, hon. fellow coun. clin. cardiology), Physiol. Soc. Gt. Brit., Med. Rsch. Soc. London, Assn. Am. Physicians, Internat. Union of Angiology (hon.), Worldwide Hungarian Med. Acad. (hon.), Rappaport Inst. Israel (sci. adv. bd.), Sigma Xi. Home: 600 4th St SW Rochester MN 55902-3247 Office: Mayo Clinic 1044 Plummer Bldg Rochester MN 55902

SHEPHERD, STEWART ROBERT, lawyer; b. Chgo., Sept. 9, 1948; s. Stewart and LaVina Beatrice (Nereim) S.; m. Margaret Brownell Shoop, Aug. 14, 1970; children: Elisabeth Ashby, Megan Brownell, Blair Stewart. BA, Rockford Coll., 1970; JD, U. Chgo., 1973. Bar: Calif. 1973, U.S. Dist. Ct. (no. dist.) Calif. 1973, Ill. 1976, U.S. Dist. Ct. (no. dist.) Ill. 1976. Assoc. Heller, Ehrman, White & McAuliffe, San Francisco, 1973-75, Hopkins & Sutter, Chgo., 1975-79, ptnr., 1979-96, Sidley & Austin, Chgo., 1996—. Mem. ABA, Order of Coif, Phi Beta Kappa. Office: Sidley & Austin Bank One Plz 425 W Surf St Apt 605 Chicago IL 60657-6139 E-mail: sshepher@sidley.com., smemb@aol.com.

SHEPHERD, TERRY L. health facility administrator; BS, Purdue U.; MBA, Ind. U. V.p., CFO Cardiac Pacemakers, Inc.; dir. bus. devel. med. devices and diagnostics divsn., CFO Lilly Industries, Ltd., U.K.; pres. Hybritech Eli Lilly and Co.; pres. heart valve divsn. St. Jude Med. Inc., St. Paul, 1994, mgr. internat. ops., 1996, pres., CEO, 1999—. Office: St Jude Med Inc 1 Lillehei Plz Saint Paul MN 55117-1761

SHEPHERD, WAYNE, radio personality; b. Lapeer, Mich., Jan. 14; m. Becky Shepherd, 1973; children: Levi, Jennifer. Grad., Cedarville Coll. Radio host of Open Line and Proclaim Sta. WMBI Radio, Chgo. Avocations: snowmobiling, riding ATVs. Office: WMBI 820 N LaSalle Blvd Chicago IL 60610*

SHERBY, KATHLEEN REILLY, lawyer; b. St. Louis, Apr. 5, 1947; d. John Victor and Florian Sylvia (Frederick) Reilly; m. James Wilson Sherby, May 17, 1975; children: Michael R.R., William J.R., David J.R. AB magna cum laude, St. Louis U., 1969, JD magna cum laude, 1976. Bar: Mo. 1976. Assoc. Bryan Cave, St. Louis, 1976-85; ptnr. Bryan Cave LLP, 1985—. Contbr. articles to profl. jours. Bd. dirs Jr. League, St. Louis, 1989-90, St. Louis Forum, 1992-99, pres., 1995-97; chmn. Bequest and Gift Coun. of St. Louis U., 1997-99; jr. warden Ch. of St. Michael and St. George, 1998-2000; bd. dirs. Bistate chpt. ARC, 2000—; bd. trustees St. Louis Sci. Ctr., 2000—. Fellow Am. Coll. Trust and Estate Coun. (regent 1997—), Estate Planning Coun. of St. Louis (pres. 1986-87), Bar Assn. Met. St. Louis (chmn. probate sect. 1986-87), Mo. Bar Assn. (chmn. probate and trust com. 1996-98, chmn. probate law revision subcom. 1988-96). Episcopalian. Home: 47 Crestwood Dr Saint Louis MO 63105-3032 Office: Bryan Cave LLP 1 Metropolitan Sq Ste 3600 Saint Louis MO 63102-2733

SHERE, DENNIS, retired publishing executive; b. Cleve., Nov. 29, 1940; s. William and Susan (Luskay) S.; m. Maureen Jones, Sept. 4, 1965; children: Rebecca Lynn, David Matthew, Stephen Andrew. B.S. in Journalism, Ohio U., 1963, M.S. in Journalism, 1964. Staff writer Dayton (Ohio) Daily News, 1966-69; asst. prof. Sch. Journalism Bowling Green (Ohio) State U., 1969-70; fin. editor Detroit News, 1970-72, city editor, 1973-75; editor Dayton Jour. Herald, 1975-80; pub. Springfield (Ohio) Newspapers Inc., 1980-83, Dayton Newspapers, Inc., 1983-88; gen. mgr. Media Group Moody Bible Inst., 1989—2001; ret., 2001. Served with AUS, 1964-66. Mem. Sigma Alpha Epsilon, Omicron Delta Kappa.

SHERIDAN, JAMES EDWARD, history educator; b. Wilmington, Del., July 15, 1922; s. Phillip Lambert and Ida Alverna (Green) S.; m. Sonia Landy, Sept. 27, 1947; 1 son, Jamy. BS, U. Ill., 1949, MA, 1950; PhD, U. Calif. at Berkeley, 1961. Lectr. Chinese history Stanford U., 1960; mem. faculty Northwestern U., 1961—, prof. history, 1968—, chmn. dept., 1969-74, assoc. dean Coll. Arts and Scis., 1985-89, prof. emeritus, 1992—. Author: Chinese Warlord: The Career of Feng Yu-hsiang, 1966, China: A Culture Area in Perspective, 1970, China in Disintegration: The Republican Era in Chinese History, 1912-1949, 1975, A Community of Caring: An Introduction to Kendal at Hanover, 1998; editor: The Transformation of Modern China series, 1975— . Served to ensign USN, 1941-46. Fulbright fellow France, 1950-51; Ford Found. fellow, 1958-60; grantee Am. Council Learned Socs.-Social Sci. Research Council, 1966-67, 71-72 Home: 80 Lyme Rd Apt 438 Hanover NH 03755-1236 Office: Northwestern Univ Dept History Evanston IL 60201 E-mail: james.e.sheridan@valley.net.

SHERIDAN, PATRICK MICHAEL, finance company executive, retired; b. Grosse Pointe, Mich., Apr. 13, 1940; s. Paul Phillip and Frances Mary (Rohan) S.; m. Diane Lorraine Tressler, Nov. 14, 1986; children: Mary, Patrick, Kelly, Kevin, James. BBA, U. Notre Dame, 1962; MBA, U. Detroit, 1975. Acct. Peat, Marwick, Mitchell & Co., Detroit, 1962-72, audit mgr., 1969-72; exec. v.p. fin. Alexander Hamilton Life Ins. Co., Farmington, Mich., 1973-76; sr. v.p. ops. Sun Life Ins. Co. Am., Balt., 1976-78, exec. v.p., 1978-79; pres. Sun Ins. Services, Inc., 1979-81; pres., chief exec. officer Am. Health & Life Ins. Co., Balt., 1981-85; chief exec. officer Gulf Ins. Co., 1985-86; sr. v.p., chief fin. officer Comml. Credit Co., 1985-86, sr. v.p. audit, 1987; exec. v.p., chief fin. officer Anthem, Inc., Indpls., 1987-99, ret., 1999. Rep. candidate for U.S. Congress, 1972; past pres. Charlesbrooke Cmty. Assn.; past. v.p. Jr. Achievement of Met. Balt., 1984-85; bd. dirs. Goodwill Industries of Balt., 1986, bd. govs. 1994; bd. dirs. Family Svcs. Assn., 1994, Goodwill Industries of Indpls., 1994; mem. adv. coun. Clowes Meml. Hall. Capt. AUS, 1963-65. Recipient various Jaycee awards. Fellow Life Mgmt. Inst.; mem. Am. Mgmt. Assn. (pres.'s assn.), AICPAs, Mich. Assn. CPAs, Md. Assn. CPAs, Am. Soc. CLUs, U.S. Jaycees (treas. 1973-74), Mich. Jaycees (pres. 1971-72), Detroit Jaycees (pres. 1968-69), Balt. C. of C. (bd. dirs.), Mensa, Notre Dame Club, Skyline Club.

SHERLOCK, JOHN MICHAEL, bishop; b. Regina, Sask., Can., Jan. 20, 1926; s. Joseph and Catherine S. Student, St. Augustine's Sem., Toronto, Ont., Can., 1950; student canon law, Catholic U. Am., 1950-52; LLD (hon.), U. Windsor, 1986; DD (hon.), Huron Coll., London, Ont., 1986. Ordained priest Roman Catholic Ch., 1950, bishop, 1974; asst. pastor St. Eugene's, Hamilton, Ont., 1952-59, St. Augustine's, Dundas, 1959-63, Cathedral Christ the King, Hamilton, also, Guelph and Maryhill, Ont., 1950-52; pastor St. Charles Ch., Hamilton, 1963-74; aux. bishop London, 1974-78; bishop Diocese of London, 1978—. Chaplain Univ. Newman Club, McMaster U., Hamilton, 1963-66; pres. Canadian Conf. Cath. Bishops, 1983-85, liaison with U. Chaplains Can. and Pres. Cath. Coll. and Univs.; chmn. social affairs com. commn. Ont. Conf. Cath. Bishops, edn. commn., family life com.; adv. judge for the Regional Marriage Truban, 1954-72. Mem. Wentworth County Roman Cath. Separate Sch. Bd., 1964-74, chmn., 1972-73; chmn. Nat. Cath. Broadcasting Found., 1995—. Fellow honoris cause U.St. Michael's Coll., Toronto, 1994. Address: Chancery Office 1070 Waterloo St London ON Canada N6A 3Y2

SHERMAN, LOUIS ALLEN, biology educator; b. Chgo., Dec. 16, 1943; s. Stanley E. and Sarah R. Sherman; m. Debra Meddoff, June 15, 1969; children: Daniel, Jeff. BS in Physics, U. Chgo., 1965, PhD in Biophysics, 1970. Postdoctoral fellow Cornell U., Ithaca, N.Y., 1970-72; asst. prof. U. Mo., Columbia, 1972-78, assoc. prof., 1978-83, prof., 1983-88, dir. biol. scis., 1985-88; prof., head dept. biol. scis. Purdue U., West Lafayette, Ind., 1989-2000, prof. biol. scis., 1989—. Contbr. articles to profl. jours. NIH fellow, 1965-72; Fulbright Hayes scholar, The Netherlands, 1979-80; NSF travel grantee, Fed. Republic Germany, Japan; grantee NIH, USDA, Dept. Energy. Fellow AAAS, Am. Acad. Microbiology; mem. AAUP, Am. Soc. Microbiology, Am. Soc. Plant Physiology, Biophys. Soc., Plant Molecular Biology Soc. Office: Purdue U Dept Biol Scis Lilly Hall West Lafayette IN 47907

SHERMAN, MICHAEL FRANCIS, professional football coach; b. Norwood, Mass., Dec. 19, 1954; m. Karen Sherman; children: Sarah, Emily, Matthew, Benjamin. Student, Ctrl. Conn. State U., 1974, 76-77. Coach U. Pitts., 1981-82, Tulane, 1983-84; offensive coord. Holy Cross, 1985-88; offensive line coord. Tex. A&M, 1989-93, 95-96, UCLA, 1994; tight ends/asst. offensive line Green Bay Packers, 1997-98, head coach, 2000—; offensive coord. Seattle Seahawks, 1999. Office: care Green Bay Packers PO Box 10628 Green Bay WI 54307-0628 also: Green Bay Packers, Inc 1265 Lombardi Ave. Green Bay WI 54304

SHERMAN, STUART, internist, gastroenterologist; b. New York, N.Y., Feb. 21, 1955; s. Sol and Rhoda (Kaplan) S.; m. Leslie Jane Derus, Oct. 5, 1991; children: Matthew, Benjamin. BA, SUNY, Binghampton, 1977; MD, Washington U., St. Louis, 1982. Diplomate Am. Bd. Internal Medicine. Resident in internal medicine U. Pitts., 1982-85, rsch. fellow, 1985-86; gastroenterology fellow Sch. of Medicine UCLA, 1986-89; therapeutic endoscopy fellow Sch. Medicine Ind. U., 1989-90; asst. prof. medicine and pancreaticobiliary endoscopy UCLA, 1990-92; asst. prof. medicine Ind. U., 1992-95, assoc. prof., 1995—, assoc. prof. radiology, 1996—. Cons. Bard Interventional Products Adv. Panel, Tewksbury, Mass., 1994—. Contbr. articles to profl. jours. Recipient Glaxo Award for excellence in gastroenterology Midwest Am. Fedn. Clin. Rsch., 1993, Young Scholars Rsch. award World Congress of Gastroenterology, L.A., 1994. Fellow Am. Coll. Gastroenterology (mem. editl. bd. Gastrointestinal Endoscopy); mem. ACP, Am. Soc. for Gastrointestinal Endoscopy, Am. Gastroent. Assn. Avocations: traveling, skiing, tennis, golf. Office: Ind U Med Ctr 550 University Blvd Ste 2300 Indianapolis IN 46202-5149 E-mail: ssherman@induni.edu.

SHERMAN, THOMAS WEBSTER, JR. environmental company executive; b. Newark, Oct. 17, 1929; s. Thomas Webster and Myrtle Agnes (Benson) S.; m. Marilyn Margaret Noss, Nov. 15, 1952; children: Susan, Catherine, Thomas, Janet. BS in Engring., U.S. Naval Acad., 1951; MS in Bus. Adminstrn., George Washington U., 1964. Commd 2d lt. USAF, 1951, advanced through grades to col., 1969, retired, 1981; engring. coord. Systems Mgmt. Am., Washington, 1984-85; dir. govt. mktg. Sullair Corp., Michigan City, Ind., 1985-90; pres. Aquacide LLC, 1996—, MGS Technology LLC. Cons. in field; guest lectr. Purdue U. Contbr. articles to profl. jours. Coord. Round Table, Michigan City, 1997; bd. dirs. Mil. Mus., Michigan City, 1996-97, Civil War Club, Michigan City, 1995-97. Decorated DFC. Mem. AAAS, Air Force Assn., Naval Inst., Air Commd. Assn., Partnership for Sustainability with Russia, Nat. Shipbuilding Rsch. Program, Doctors for Disaster Preparedness. Avocations: conversation, reading, golf. Home: 12255 Clipper Dr Woodbridge VA 22192 Office: Aquacide 2 Devonshire Ct Ste 9 Michigan City IN 46360-1584

SHERREN, ANNE TERRY, chemistry educator; b. Atlanta, July 1, 1936; d. Edward Allison and Annie Ayres (Lewis) Terry; m. William Samuel Sherren, Aug. 13, 1966. BA, Agnes Scott Coll., 1957; PhD, U. Fla., Gainesville, 1961. Grad. tchg. asst. U. Fla., Gainesville, 1957-61; from instr. to asst. prof. Tex. Womans U., Denton, 1961-66; rsch. participant Argonne Nat. Lab., 1973-80, 93-94; assoc. prof. chemistry North Cen. Coll., Naperville, Ill., 1966-76, prof., 1976-2001, prof. emeritus, 2001—. Contbr. articles to profl. jours. Ruling elder Knox Presbyn. Ch., 1971—, clk. of session, 1976-94. Mem. Am. Chem. Soc., Am. Inst. Chemists, Sigma Xi, Delta Kappa Gamma, Iota Sigma Pi (nat. pres. 1978-81, nat. dir. 1972-78, nat. historian 1989—). Presbyterian. Office: North Ctrl Coll Dept Chemistry Naperville IL 60566 Office Fax: 630-637-5180. E-mail: ats@noctrl.edu.

SHERRER, GARY, state lieutenant governor; m. Judy Waller, 1965; children: Stuart, Nancy. Grad., Emporia State U. Sec. Kans. Dept. Commerce and Housing, 1995—; lt. gov. State of Kans., 1996—. Vice chmn. Gov.'s Cabinet. Recipient Disting. Alumni award Emporia State U., 1994, award of excellence, 1995, Carl Perkins Humanitarian award, 2000; Toll fellow, 1999. Mem. Nat. Conf. Lt. Govs. (chmn.).

SHERRILL, THOMAS BOYKIN, III, retired newspaper publishing executive; b. Tampa, Fla., Nov. 19, 1930; s. Thomas Boykin Jr. and Mary Emma (Addison) S.; m. Sandra Louise Evans, Dec. 27, 1969; children: Thomas Glenn, Stephen Addison. Circulation dir. Tampa (Fla.) Tribune, 1962-67, Sarasota (Fla.) Herald-Tribune, 1967-75; v.p. circulation The Dispatch Printing Co., Columbus, Ohio, 1975-78, v.p. mktg., 1978-97, bd. dirs., 1977-97; v.p., bd. dirs. Ohio Mag., Inc., 1979-97; ret., 1997. Bd. dirs., past chmn. bd. dirs. Salvation Army; trustee, past chmn. bd. dirs. Better Bus. Bur. Ctrl. Ohio, Inc.; bd. dirs. Ctrl. Ohio Ctr. Econ. Edn.; v.p., trustee Columbus Dispatch Charities; exec. bd. mem. Simon Kenton coun. Boy Scouts Am.; past pres. Wesley Glen United Meth. Retirement Ctr.; pres.'s adv. bd. Meth. Theol. Sch.. With USN, 1951-56. Recipient Disting. Svc. award Editor and Pub. Mag., 1978; named hon. pres. Troy State U., 1979, hon. Ky. Col., 1980, hon. lt. col. aide-to-camp to Gov. State of Ala., 1984. Mem. Internat. Circulation Mgrs. Assn. (pres. 1975, Pres's. award 1989), Internat. Newspaper Mktg. Assn., Ohio Newspaper Assn. (bd. dirs. 1984-97, pres. 1986-88, Pres.'s award 1990), So. Circulation Mgrs. Assn. (life; pres. 1967-68, C.W. Bevinger Meml. award 1972), Audit Bur. Circulations (bd. dirs. 1980-90), Am. Advt. Fedn., Navy League, Ohio Newspapers Found., Ohio Circulation Mgrs. Assn (life; Pres.' award 1989), Columbus Area C. of C., SAR, Internat. Platform Assn., Athletic Club of Columbus, Muirfield Village Country Club, Kiwanis Club of Columbus (life, pres. 1982, George F. Hixon fellow). Republican. Home: 5215 Hampton Ln Columbus OH 43220-2270

SHERRY, PAUL HENRY, minister, religious organization administrator; b. Tamaqua, Pa., Dec. 25, 1933; s. Paul Edward and Mary Elizabeth (Stein) S.; m. Mary Louise Thornburg, June 4, 1957; children: Mary Elizabeth, Paul David. BA, Franklin and Marshall Coll., 1955; ThM, Union Theol. Sem., N.Y.C., 1958, PhD, 1969; hon. doctorate, Ursinus Coll., 1981, Elmhurst Coll., 1990, Defiance Coll., 1991, Lakeland Coll., Sheboygan, Wis., 1991, Reformed Theological Acad., Debrecen, Hungary, 1994, United Theol. Sem. Twin Cities, 1995, Eden Theol. Sem., St. Louis, 2000, Chgo. Theol. Sem., 2000. Ordained to ministry United Ch. of Christ, 1958. Pastor St. Matthew United Ch. of Christ, Kenhorst, Pa., 1958-61, Community United Ch. of Christ, Hasbrouck Heights, N.J., 1961-65; mem. staff United Ch. Bd. Homeland Ministry, N.Y.C., 1965-82; exec. dir. Community Renewal Soc., Chgo., 1983-89; pres. United Ch. of Christ, Cleve., 1989-99, pub. policy cons., 2000—. Mem. gen. bd. Nat. Coun. Chs., N.Y.C., 1989-99; mem. ctrl. com. World Coun. Chs., 1990-99, del. 8th Assembly, Harare, Zimbabwe, 1998, del. 7th Assembly, Canberra, Australia, 1991. Editor: The Riverside Preachers; editor Jour. Current Social Issues, 1968-80; contbr. numerous articles to religious jours.; host weekly radio programs local sta., 1974-78, 84-85, 93-97. Bd. dirs., cons. Nat. Campaign for Jobs and Income Support, 2000—; bd. dirs. Nat. Interfaith Com. for Worker Justice, 2000—. Mem. Soc. Christian Ethics. Democrat. Avocations: reading, hiking, cultural events. Home and Office: 12700 Lake Ave Apt 1612 Lakewood OH 44107- E-mail: psher973@aol.com.

SHERTZER, BRUCE ELDON, education educator; b. Bloomfield, Ind., Jan. 11, 1928; s. Edwin Franklin and Lois Belle S.; m. Carol Mae Rice, Nov. 24, 1948; children: Sarah Ann, Mark Eldon. BS, Ind. U., 1952, MD, 1953, EdD, 1958. Tchr., counselor Martinsville (Ind.) High Sch., 1952-56; dir. div. guidance Ind. Dept. Pub. Instrn., 1956-58; assoc. dir. project guidance of superior students North Central Assn. Coll. and Secondary Sch., 1958-60; asst. prof. Purdue U., 1960—, assoc. prof., 1962-65, prof., 1965-95, head dept. ednl. studies, 1989-95, prof. emeritus of counseling, 1995—. Vis. prof. ednl. psychology U. Hawaii, 1967; Fulbright sr. lectr., Reading, Eng., 1967-68; vis. prof. U. So. Calif. Overseas Grad. Program, 1975, 82; chmn. Nat. Adv. Council for Career Edn., 1976 Author: Career Exploration and Planning 1973, 2d edit., 1976, Fundamentals of Counseling, 3d edit., 1980, Fundamentals of Guidance, 4th edit., 1981, Individual Appraisal, 1979, Career Planning, 3d edit., 1985, also articles. Chmn. bd. trustees Found. Am. Assn. of Counseling and Devel., 1986-87. With AUS, 1946-47. Mem. Am. Counseling Assn. (pres. 1973-74, Disting. Profl. Svc. award 1986). Home: 1620 Western Dr West Lafayette IN 47906-2236 Office: Purdue U Liberal Arts Edn Bldg West Lafayette IN 47907

SHERWIN, BYRON LEE, religion educator, college official; b. N.Y.C., Feb. 18, 1946; s. Sidney and Jean Sylvia (Rabinowitz) S.; m. Judith Rita Schwartz, Dec. 24, 1972; 1 child, Jason Samuel. BS, Columbia U., N.Y.C., 1966; B of Hebrew Lit., Jewish Theol. Sem. of Am., 1966, M of Hebrew Lit., 1968; MA, NYU, 1969; PhD, U. Chgo., 1978; DHL (hon.), Jewish Theol. Sem. Am., 1996. Ordained rabbi, 1970. Prof. Jewish philosophy and mysticism Spertus Coll. Judaica, Chgo., 1970—, v.p. acad. affairs, 1984-2001. Author: Judaism, 1978, Encountering the Holocaust, 1979, Abraham Joshua Heschel, 1979, Garden of the Generations, 1981, Jerzy Kosinski: Literary Alarm Clock, 1981, Mystical Theology and Social Dissent, 1982, The Golem Legend, 1985, Contents and Contexts, 1987, Thank God, 1989, In Partnership with God: Contemporary Jewish Law and Ethics, 1990, No Religion Is an Island, 1991, Toward a Jewish Theology, 1991, How To Be a Jew: Ethical Teachings of Judaism, 1992, The Theological Heritage of Polish Jews, 1995, Sparks Amongst the Ashes: The Spiritual Legacy of Polish Jewry, 1997, Crafting the Soul: Creating Your Life as a Work of Art, 1998, Why Be Good?, 1998, John Paul II and Interreligious Dialogue, 1999, Perché Essere Buonil?, 1999, Per Que Ser Bueno?, 1999, Jewish Ethics for the Twenty-First Century, 2000, Creating an Ethical Jewish Life, 2001; contbr. articles to profl. jours. Recipient Man of Reconciliation award Polish Coun. Christians and Jews, 1992, Presdl. medal, Officer of Order of Merit, Republic of Poland, 1995. Mem. Midwest Jewish Studies Assn. (founding pres.), Am. Philos. Assn., Assn. for Jewish Studies, Rabbinical Assembly, Am. Acad. Religion, The Authors Guild. Republican. Avocations: cooking, book collecting. Office: Spertus Coll Judaica 618 S Michigan Ave Chicago IL 60605-1901 E-mail: bsherwin@spertus.edu.

SHETLAR, JAMES FRANCIS, physician; b. Wichita, Dec. 26, 1944; MD, U. Kans., 1970. Resident in family practice Saginaw County Hosp., 1970-72; staff St. Luke's Gen. Hosp.; asst. clin. prof. Mich. State U. Mem. AMA, Am. Assn. Family Practioners, Mich. Assn. Family Practioners. Office: 163 Churchgrove Rd Frankenmuth MI 48734-1025

SHEVITZ, MARK H. sales promotion and marketing executive; b. Dioles, France, July 10, 1955; came to U.S., 1956; s. Arthur E. and Marilyn (Sigoloff) S. Student, U. Mo., 1973-75, Rockhurst Coll., 1983-84; MBA, Washington U., St. Louis, 1988. Program dir. KFMZ-FM, Columbia, Mo., 1974-81; mgmt. supr. Bernstein-Rein Advt., Kansas City, 1981-84; account supr. The Hermann Group, St. Louis, 1984-86; dir. promotions, food svc. products divsn. Seven-Up Co., 1986-87; pres. Landing Assocs., 1987-88, SJI, Inc., St. Louis, 1988-98, SJI Fulfillment, Inc., St. Louis, 1991—; CEO SJI Inc. Lectr. Washington U., St. Louis, 1988—, Bowling Green (Ohio) State U., 1977-89, Stephens Coll., Columbia, Mo., 1976-89, U. Mo., Columbia, 1975-81. Contbr. articles to profl. jours. Chpt. chmn. March of Dimes, mid.-Mo., 1978-81; mem. devel. bd. Cardinal Glennon Children's Hosp., St. Louis, 1984-88; event chmn. March of Dimes, St. Louis, 1990. Named Entrepreneur of Yr. St. Louis region, 1993. Mem. Assn. Promotion Mktg. Agys. Worldwide (sec./treas. 1998-2000), Porsche Club Am. (pres. St. Louis region 1986). Office: SJI Inc 23 Locust Saint Louis MO 63103 also: SJI Fulfillment Inc 2300 Locust St Saint Louis MO 63103-1512

SHIBILSKI, KEVIN W. state legislator; b. June 28, 1961; married. BS, U. Wis., Stevens Point, 1972. With Portage County Bd. Suprs., 1982-87, Portage County Register Deeds, 1987-95; mem. Wis. Senate from 24th dist, Madison, 1995—. Bd. dirs. Portwage County Red Cross. Mem. Izaak Walton League, Whitetails Unlimited, Ducks Unlimited, Wis. Bowhunters Assn., Lions. Office: Rm 402 PO Box 7882 100 N Hamilton St Madison WI 53707-7882

SHIDELER, SHIRLEY ANN WILLIAMS, lawyer; b. Mishawaka, Ind., July 9, 1930; d. William Harmon and Lois Wilma (Koch) Williams; 1 dau., Gail Shideler Frye. LLB, Ind. U., 1964. Bar: Ind. 1964. Legal sec. Barnes, Hickam, Pantzer & Boyd, Indpls., 1953-63; assoc. Barnes & Thornburg, 1964-70, ptnr., 1971-92, of counsel, 1993—. Participant fund drives Indpls. Symphony, 1968-81, Indpls. Mus. Art, 1969-79, Marion County Libr. Restoration, 1985-88, Goodwill Industries, 1988-89; bd. dirs. Bus. Unit Gals Indpls. Mus. Art, 1973-80; bd. dirs. Indpls. Legal Aid Soc., 1982-93, Cmty. Hosp. Found., 1986-94, Ctrl. Newspapers Found., 1979-99. Fellow Am. Coll. Trust and Estate Counsel, 1981-96; mem. Ind. Bar Assn. (sec. 1975-76, chmn. probate, trust and real property sect. 1982), Nat. Conf. Bar. Founds. (trustee 1988-94), Indpls. Bar Assn. (bd. mgrs. 1968-72, v.p. charge affairs 1972), Ind. Bar Found. (bd. mgrs. 1980-92, sec. 1981-82, treas. 1981-86, v.p. 1986-88, pres. 1988-90), Indpls. Bar Found. (bd. mgrs. 1970-82, sec. 1972-77), Women's Rotary (pres. Indpls. club 1969-71, dir. 1968-79). Home: 2224 Boston Ct Apt C Indianapolis IN 46228-3257 Office: Barnes & Thornburg 11 S Meridian St Ste 1313 Indianapolis IN 46204-3535

SHIELDS, CHARLES W. state legislator; b. Kansas City, Mo., July 25, 1959; m. Brenda Brandt; children: Brandt, Bryce. BA, BS, MA, U. Mo. Project coord. Heartland Health Systems; mem. Mo. State Ho. of Reps., 1990—, minority whip, 1996—. Mem. appropriations/health and mental health com., budget com., elem. and secondary end. com., higher edn. com., automation com. Mo. Ho. of Reps., mem. joint com. on health care rules, joint rules and bills, interim desegregation com. Mem. applications com. United Way; mem. Pony Express coun. Boy Scouts Am.; bd. dirs. Children's Healthcare Clinic; mem. adv. bd. Project Discovery, Mo. Rural Health Assn., Mo. Job Corps Coalition, United Way, Mid-Buchanan Sch. Bd.; co-chair arts fund drive Allied Arts Coun., 1997. Mem. Lions Club (v.p.), Buchanan County Rep. Club. Home: 47 SE Erin Ct Saint Joseph MO 64507-7984

SHIELDS, ROBERT EMMET, merchant banker, lawyer; b. Ridley Park, Pa., May 18, 1942; s. Joseph Leonard and Kathryn J. (Walsh) S.; m. Mary Katherine Reid, July 22, 1967; children: Christopher D., David R., Kevin M., Kathleen. AB, Coll. Holy Cross, 1964; LLB cum laude, NYU, 1967. Bar: Pa. bar 1968. Mem. faculty Boalt Hall Sch. Law U. Calif., Berkeley, 1967-68; assoc. Drinker Biddle & Reath, Phila., 1968-74, ptnr., 1974-94, mng. ptnr., 1979-83, 85-94, head corp. and securities group, 1983-93, CFO, 1993-94; mng. dir., prin., ptnr., COO Questor Gen. Ptnr., L.P., 1995—, Questor Ptnrs. Funds, L.P. and Questor Mgmt. Co., 1995—. Sec. Wallquest Inc. Author: (with Eliot B. Thomas) Federal Securities Act Handbook, 4th edit, 1977; (with Robert H. Strouse) Securities Practice Handbook, 1987. Mem. ABA, Am. Law Inst., Pa. Bar Assn., Phila. Bar Assn. Club: Skyline (Southfield, Mich.). Home: 206 Atlee Rd Wayne PA 19087-3836 Office: Questor Mgmt Co 2000 Town Ctr Ste 2450 Southfield MI 48075-1406 also: 1 Logan Sq Ste 2000 Philadelphia PA 19103-6933 E-mail: rshields@questorfund.com.

SHIELDS, THOMAS CHARLES, lawyer; b. Evergreen Park, Ill., Apr. 26, 1941; s. Thomas James and Adelaide (McElligott) S.; m. Nicoline M. Murphy, Sept. 14, 1974; children: Thomas James II, Nicoline M.E., Suzanne Adelaide, Kerry Anne. AB, Georgetown U., 1963; JD cum laude, Northwestern U., 1966. Bar: Ill. 1966, U.S. Dist. Ct. (no. dist.) Ill. 1966, U.S. Ct. Appeals (7th cir.) 1966, U.S. Tax Ct. 1968, U.S. Supreme Ct. 1977. Assoc. Hopkins & Sutter, Chgo., 1966-73, ptnr., 1973-93; ptnr., chair health law dept. Bell, Boyd & Lloyd, Chgo., 1994—; chief counsel Cath. Health Assn. U.S., St. Louis, 1994—. Mem. adv. bd. Health Law Inst. Loyola U. Sch. Law, Chgo., 1984-89, Health Law Inst. DePaul U. Sch. Law, Chgo., 1985-96; lectr. Ill. Inst. Continuing Legal Edn., 1973; bd. dirs. Ill. Health Facilities Authority, 2000—; trustee Village of Riverside, Ill., 2001--. Contbr. articles to profl. pubs., chpt. to book; mng. editor Northwestern Law Rev., 1965-66. Bd. dir. Cancer Rsch. Found., Chgo., 1987—, Brother Louie and Fannie Roncoli Found., 1994—, Chgo. Zool. Soc., Cath. Charities Chgo.; trustee Village of Riverside, 2001—. Mem.: Chgo. Bar Assn., Ill. Assn. Healthcare Attys. (bd. dir. 1983—89, pres. 1987—88), Ill. Bar Assn., Am. Hosp. Assn. (tax adv. group 1987—90), Am. Soc. Law and Medicine, Am. Health Lawyers Assn. (bd. dir. 1983—91, pres. 1989—90), Mid-Am. Club Chgo., Law Club Chgo., Exec. Club Chgo., Order of Coif. Avocations: skiing, bicycling, golf, tennis. Office: Bell Boyd & Lloyd 3 First Nat Plz Ste 3200 Chicago IL 60602

SHIELDS, THOMAS WILLIAM, surgeon, educator; b. Ambridge, Pa., Aug. 17, 1922; s. John Jr. and Elizabeth (Flanagan) S.; m. Dorothea Ann Thomas, June 12, 1948; children: Thomas William, John Leland, Carol Ann. BA, Kenyon Coll., 1943, DSc (hon.), 1978; MD, Temple U., 1947. Resident surgery Northwestern U. Med. Sch., Chgo., 1949-55, prof. surgery, 1968-92, prof. Emeritus of surgery, 1992—; practice medicine specializing in surgery Chgo., 1956—; chief of surgery VA Lakeside Hosp., 1968-87; chief thoracic surgery VA Lakeside Med. Ctr., 1987-90. Editor: General Thoracic Surgery, 1972, 5th edit., 2000, Bronchial Carcinoma, 1974, Mediastinal Surgery, 1991; assoc. editor Surgery, Gynecology and Obstetrics, Annals of Thoracic Surgery, 1993-2002; mem. editl. bd. Annals of Thoracic Surgery, Lung Cancer; contbr. articles to profl. jours. Served with U.S. Army, 1951-53. Mem. ACS, AMA, Am. Assn. for Thoracic Surgery, Soc. Thoracic Surgery, Central, Western Surg. Assns., Société Internationale de Chirurgie, Soc. for Surgery of Alimentary Tract, Internat. Assn. for Study Lung Cancer, Japanese Assn. Thoracic Surgery (hon.), Pan Pacific Surg. Assn., Phi Beta Kappa, Sigma Xi, Alpha Omega Alpha. Home: 10513 E Cinnabar Ave Scottsdale AZ 85258-4908 Office: Northwestern U Feinberg Sch Medicine Galter 10-105 201 E Huron St Chicago IL 60611

SHIELDS, V. SUE, federal magistrate judge; b. 1939; AB, Ball State U., 1959; LLB, Ind. U., 1961. Atty. Office of the Regional Counsel, IRS, 1961; dept. atty. gen. Office of the Atty. Gen. of Ind., 1962-64; judge Hamilton Superior Ct., 1965-78, Ind. Ct. Appeals, 1978-94; magistrate judge U.S. Dist. Ct. for So. Dist. Ind., Indpls., 1994—. Office: 256 US Courthouse 46 E Ohio St Indianapolis IN 46204-1903

SHIELDS, WILL HERTHIE, football player; b. Fort Riley, Kans., Sept. 15, 1971; m. Senia Shields; 2 children. Degree in comm., U. Nebr. Guard Kansas City Chiefs, 1993—. Named to Pro Bowl, 1996. Office: Kansas City Chiefs 1 Arrowhead Dr Kansas City MO 64129-1651

SHIELY, JOHN STEPHEN, company executive, lawyer; b. June 19, 1952; s. Vincent Robert and Mary Elizabeth (Hope) S.; m. Helen Jane Pauly, Aug. 29, 1981; children: Michael, Erin, Megan. BBA, U. Notre Dame, 1974; JD, Marquette U., 1977; M of Mgmt., Northwestern U., 1990. With Arthur Andersen & Co., Milw., 1977-79, Hughes Hubbard & Reed, Milw., 1979-83, Allen-Bradley Co., Milw., 1983-86, Rockwell Internat. Corp., Milw., 1985-86, Briggs & Stratton Corp., Milw., 1986—, gen. counsel, 1986-90, v.p., gen. counsel, 1990-91, pres., COO, 1994-2001, pres., CEO, 2001—. Bd. dirs. Briggs & Stratton Corp., Marshall & Ilsley Corp., Milw., Quad/ Graphics, Inc., Pewaukee, Wis., 1996—. Mem. Greater Milw. Com., 2000—; chmn. bd., dir. Children's Hosp. of Wis., 1992—; mem. bd. regents Milw. Sch. Engring., 1995—. Mem.: Wis. Mfrs. and Commerce (bd. dirs. 2002—), Assn. for Corp. Growth (past pres., bd. dirs. Wis. chpt. 1988—). Office: Briggs & Stratton Corp PO Box 702 Milwaukee WI 53201-0702

SHIFMAN, MIKHAIL, physicist; b. Riga, Latvia, Apr. 4, 1949; came to U.S., 1990; s. Arkady and Raisa (Yakovich) S.; m. Margarita Pusynya, Apr. 21, 1971; children: Julia, Anya. MA in Theoretical Physics, Moscow Inst. Physics & Tech., Dolgoprudny, Russia, 1972; PhD, Inst. Theoretical Exptl. Phys., Moscow, 1976. From jr. rsch. fellow to sr. rschr. Inst. Theoretical & Exptl. Physics, Moscow, 1976-89; prof. theoretical physics U. Minn., Mpls., 1990—. Lectr. on particle physics and field theory. Author: Vacuum Structure and QCD Sum Rules, 1992, Instantons in Gauge Theories, 1994, ITEP Lectures on Particle Physics and Field Theory, 2 vols., 1999, The Many Faces of the Superworld, 2000, The Supersymmetric World, 2000. Recipient Humboldt Rsch. award Alexander-von-Humboldt Stiftung, Bonn, Germany, 1993, Rsch. award Japan Soc. for Promotion Sci., 1993, 96. Fellow Am. Phys. Soc. (Sakurai prize 1999). Achievements include invention (with others) invisible axion; rsch. in hadronic physics/quantum chromodynamics, SVZ sum rules, heavy-flavor hadrons based on the heavy quark expansions, supersymmetric guage theories in the strong coupling regime. Office: Theoretical Phys Inst Univ Minn 116 Church St SE Minneapolis MN 55455-0149 E-mail: shifman@physics.spa.umn.edu.

SHILLINGSBURG, MIRIAM JONES, English educator, academic administrator; b. Balt., Oct. 5, 1943; d. W. Elvin and Miriam (Reeves) Jones; m. Peter L. Shillingsburg, Nov. 21, 1967; children: Robert, George, John, Alice, Anne Carol. BA, Mars Hill Coll., 1964; MA, U. S.C., 1966, PhD, 1969; BGS, Miss. State U., 1994. Asst. prof. Limestone Coll., Gaffney, S.C., 1969, Miss. State U., 1970-75, assoc. prof., 1975-80, prof. English, 1980-96, assoc. v.p. for acad. affairs, 1988-96, dir. summer sch., 1990-96, dir. undergrad. studies, 1994-96; dean arts and scis. Lamar U., Tex., 1996-99; dean liberal arts and scis. Ind. U., South Bend, 2000—. Simms rsch. prof. U. S.C., 1998; vis. fellow Australian Def. Force Acad., 1989; Fulbright lectr. U. New South Wales, Duntroon, Australia, 1984-85. NEH fellow in residence, Columbia U., 1976-77. Author: Mark Twain in Australasia, 1988; editor: Conquest of Granada, 1988, The Cub of the Panther, 1997; mem. editl. bd. Works of W.M. Thackeray, Miss. Quar.; contbr. articles to profl. jours. and mags. Mem. South Ctrl. 18th Century Soc., Am. Lit. Assn., Sigma Tau Delta, Phi Kappa Phi, Simms Soc. (pres.). E-mail: mimishill@hotmail.com.

SHILTS, NANCY S. automotive executive, lawyer; b. Clinton, Mass., Feb. 10, 1942; BA, Smith Coll., 1963; JD, U. Mich., 1980. Bar: Mich. 1980. Assoc. gen. counsel Fed.-Mogul Corp., Southfield, Mich. Mem. ABA, State Bar Mich. Office: Fed Mogul Corp 26555 Northwestern Hwy Southfield MI 48034-2199

SHIMKUS, JOHN MONDY, congressman; b. Collinsville, Ill., Feb. 21, 1958; s. Gene Louis and Kathleen (Mondy) S.; m. Karen Kay Muth; children: David, Joshua. BS, U.S. Mil. Acad., 1980; MBA, So. Ill. U., Edwardsville, 1997. Advanced through grades to capt. U.S. Army, 1980-86; stationed at U.S. Army Base, Columbus, Ga., 1980-81, 85, served at Bamberg, Germany, 1981-84, stationed at Monterey, Calif, 1985-86; tchr. Metro East Luth. H.S., Edwardsville, Ill., 1986-90; treas. Madison County, 1990-96; mem. U.S. Congress from 20th Ill. dist., 1997—, mem. energy and commerce com. Liaison officer U.S. Mil. Acad., 1987-96; treas. So. Ill. Law Enforcement Commn., 1990-96. Bd. dirs. Sr. Citizen Companion Program, Belleville, Ill., 1991; trustee Collinsville Twp., Ill., 1989-93; Rep. precinct committeeman, Collinsville, 1988—. Maj. USAR. Mem. Nat. Assn. County Treas. and Fin. Officers (bd. dirs.), Ill. County Treas. Assn., Am. Legion Post 365. Lutheran. Home: 504 Sumner Blvd Collinsville IL 62234-1934 Office: US Ho of Reps 513 Cannon HOB Washington DC 20515-1320 also: 3130 Chatham Rd Ste C Springfield IL 62704*

SHIN, HYOUN-WOO, aircraft engineer; Sr. engr. GE Aircraft Engines, Cin. Mem. ASME (Meville Medal 1998). Office: GE Aircraft Engines 1 Neumann Way MD/A411 Cincinnati OH 45215-1915 E-mail: jamie.jewell@ae.ge.com.

SHINDELL, SIDNEY, medical educator, physician; b. New Haven, May 31, 1923; s. Benjamin Abraham and Freda (Mann) S.; m. Gloria Emhoff, June 17, 1945; children: Barbara, Roger, Lawrence, Judith. BS, Yale U., 1944; MD, L.I. Coll. Medicine, 1946; postgrad., Emory U., 1948-49; LLB, George Washington U., 1951. Diplomate Am. Bd. Preventive Medicine in Occupl. Medicine, Am. Bd. General Preventive Medicine. With USPHS, 1947-52; med. dir. Conn. Commn. on Chronically Ill and Aged, 1952-57, Am. Joint Distbn. Com., 1957-59; asst. prof. preventive medicine U. Pitts., 1960-65; dir. Hosp. Utilization Project Western Pa., 1965-66; prof. dept. preventive medicine Med. Coll. Wis., Milw., 1966-93, chmn. dept., 1966-89, dir. Office Internat. Affairs, 1989-93, prof. emeritus, 1993—; exec. dir. Health Svc. Data of Wis., 1967-73. Mem. bd. sci. advisors Am. Coun. Sci. and Health, 1978—87, 1992—, chmn., 1988—92; mem. Nat. Adv. Com. on Occupl. Safety and Health U.S. Dept. Labor, 1982—84; cons. Caribbean Epidemiology Ctr. Pan Am. Health Orgn./WHO, 1988; field edpiemiology tng. program Ctr. Disease Control, Thailand, 1989, Nat. Office Occupl. and Environ. Medicine Royal Thai Ministry of Pub Health, 1990; mem. gov.'s white paper com. on health care reform, Wis., 93; acad. cons. Facilities of Medicine Padjadjaran U., Airlangga U., Indonesia, 1993, 94. Author: Statistics, Science and Sense, 1964, A Method of Hospital Utilization Review, 1966, The Law in Medical Practice, 1966, A Coursebook on Health Care Delivery, 1976; contbr. 120 articles to profl. jours. Trustee Med. Coll. Wis., 1996—; mem. sch. bd. Fox Point-Bayside (Wis.), Sch. Dist., 1970-71; vice chmn. Citizens' Adv. Com. Met. Problems, 1971-72; bd. dirs. Med. Care Evaluation S.E. Wis., 1973-76; trustee Interfaith Caregivers Aliance, 2001--. With AUS, 1943-46. Recipient Frank L. Babbott Meml. award SUNY Health Sci. Ctr., Bklyn., 1996. Fellow Am. Coll. Preventive Medicine (mem. bd. regents 1982-85), APHA, Am. Coll. Occupl. and Environ. Medicine (Pres.'s award 1999), Am. Coll. Legal Medicine; mem. Am. Assn. Health Data Sys. (sec. 1972-73), Assn. Tchrs. Preventive Medicine (dir. 1973-74, pres. 1976-77, spl. recognition award 1992, Duncan Clark award 2002), Assn. Occupl. Health Profls. (pres. 1980-90), Wis. Med. Soc. (mem. coun. on health care financing and delivery, mem. coun. on govt. affairs, mem. ho. of dels., 50 Yr. recognition award 1996, svc. award 2000), Am. Coll. Physician Execs., Internat. Commn. on Occupl. Health, Aircraft Owners and Pilots Assn., Masons, CAP. Home and Office: One Polo Creek Unit 201 2400 Cherry Creek South Drive Denver CO 80209-3251

SHINDLER, DONALD A. lawyer; b. New Orleans, Oct. 15, 1946; s. Alan and Isolene (Levy) S.; m. Laura Epstein, 1969; children: Jay, Susan. BSBA, Washington U., St. Louis, 1968; JD, Tulane U., 1971. Bar: La. 1971, U.S. Dist. Ct. (ea. dist.) La. 1971, U.S. Tax Ct. 1974, Ill. 1975, U.S. Dist. Ct. (no. dist.) Ill. 1975; CPA, La.; lic. real estate broker, Ill. Assoc. Pope, Ballard, Shepard & Fowle, Chgo., 1975-78, Rudnick & Wolfe, Chgo., 1978-81, ptnr., 1981-99; gen. counsel America's Second Harvest Nat. Food Bank Network, 1998-2000; ptnr. Piper Marbury Rudnick & Wolfe, Chgo., 1999—2002, Piper Rudnick, Chgo., 2002—. Seminar lectr. ABA, Chgo. Bar Assn., Ill. Inst. CLE, Profl. Edn. Sys., Inc., Internat. Assn. Corp. Real Estate Execs., Urban Land Inst., Am. Corp. Counsel Assn., Bldg. Owners and Mgrs. Assn., Internat. Assn. of Attys. and Execs. in Corp. Real Estate, others. Contbr. articles on real estate to legal jours. Trustee Glencoe (Ill.) Pub. Libr., 1981-87, pres., 1986-87; alumni bd. govs. Washington U., 1992-93; mem. Glencoe Zoning Commn./Bd. Appeals, 1994-2000. Lt. JAGC, USNR, 1971-75. Mem. ABA, La. State Bar Assn., Chgo. Bar Assn. (com. chmn. 1979-80, 83-84, 90-94, 96-99, editor land trust seminars 1984-96), Urban Land Inst. (mem. steering com. Chgo. dist. coun.), Internat. Assn. Corp. Real Estate Execs. (pres. Chgo. chpt. 1997-98, dir. 1991—), Internat. Assn. Attys. and Execs. in Corp. Real Estate, Union League Club (chair real estate group 1993-96), Order of Coif, Beta Gamma Sigma, Omicron Delta Kappa. Office: Piper Rudnick Ste 1800 203 N La Salle St Ste 1800 Chicago IL 60601-1210 E-mail: donald.shindler@piperrudnick.com.

SHINE, NEAL JAMES, journalism educator, former newspaper editor, publisher; b. Grosse Pointe Farms, Mich., Sept. 14, 1930; s. Patrick Joseph and Mary Ellen (Conlon) S.; m. Phyllis Theresa Knowles, Jan. 24, 1953; children: Judith Ann, James Conlon, Susan Brigid, Thomas Patrick, Margaret Mary, Daniel Edward. BS in Journalism, U. Detroit, 1952; PhD (hon.), Cleary Coll., 1989, Siena Heights Coll., 1995, U. Mich., 1995, U. Detroit Mercy, 1996, Ctrl. Mich. U., 1996. Mem. staff Detroit Free Press, 1950-95, asst. city editor, 1963-65, city editor, 1965-71, mng. editor, 1971-82, sr. mng. editor, 1982-89, pub., 1990-95; prof. journalism Oakland U., Rochester, Mich., 1995—. Host, moderator Detroit Week in Rev., Sta. WTVS-TV, 1981-89, host Neal Shine's Detroit, 1989-91. Trustee, vice chmn. bd. trustees Youth for Understanding, 1973-75, chmn., 1975-78; mem. bd. for student publs. U. Mich.; bd. dirs. Children's Hosp., Econ. Club Detroit, Detroit Renaissance, New Detroit, Inc., Detroit Symphony Orch., Detroit Inst. Arts, Detroit Hist. Soc., United Way of Southeastern Mich., Met. Detroit Conv. and Visitors Bur., Operation ABLE, Detroit Press Club Found. With U.S. Army, 1953-55. Inducted Mich. Journalism Hall of Fame, 1990. Mem. Am. Soc. Newspaper Editors, Am. Newspapers Pubs. Assn., Mich. Press Assn. (bd. dirs. 1990-95), AP Mng. Editors, Sons of Whiskey Rebellion (comdr.-in-chief 1979—), Inc. Soc. Irish-Am. Lawyers, Detroit Press Club (charter, bd. govs. 1966-89, sec. 1957-68, v.p. 1969-71, pres. 1971-73). Home: 11009 Harbor Place Dr Saint Clair Shores MI 48080-1527 also: Carraig Rinn 13240 Crystal Beach Rd Pointe aux Roches ON Canada N0R 1N0

SHIPLEY, LARRY, food products executive; Asst. to pres. IBP Inc., Dakota City, Nebr., 1989, sr. v.p. corp. devel., exec. v.p. corp. devel., CFO, 1997—; pres. IBP Enterprises, 1997—. Office: IBP Inc Ste 830 800 Stevens Port Dr North Sioux City SD 57049

SHIPLEY, TONY L(EE), software company executive; b. Elizabethton, Tenn., July 19, 1946; s. James A. and Edith J. (Crowder) S.; m. Lynda Anne Jenkins, Nov. 19, 1971; children: Blake Alan, Sarah Robyn. BS in Indsl. Engring., U. Tenn., 1969; MBA, U. Cin., 1975. Indsl. engr. Monsanto Co., Pensacola, Fla., 1969-72; mktg. mgr. SDRC, Cin., 1972-76; v.p. sales and mktg. Anatrol Corp., 1977-81; pres. Entek Sci. Corp., 1981-96; pres., CEO Entek IRD Internat. Corp., 1996-2000. Bd. dir. Ohio IT Alliance, ABT Corp., RM Waste, Ohio IT Alliance, CHMack. Named Small Bus. Person of Yr., Greater Cin. C. of C., 1994, Entrepreneur of Yr. in Cin., No. Ky. Region, 1996. Mem. ASME, The Exec. Com., Soc. Automotive Engrs., Greater Cin. Software Assn. (pres. 1996-97, chmn. 1997-99, bd. dirs.), Greater Cin. C. of C., Leadership Class XVIII, Terrace Park (Ohio) Country Club (bd. dirs.). Republican. Avocations: golf, family activities, fishing. Home: 7825 Calderwood Ln Cincinnati OH 45243-1319 E-mail: tshipley@fuse.net.

SHIRBROUN, RICHARD ELMER, veterinarian, cattleman; b. Coon Rapids, Iowa, Oct. 22, 1929; s. Francis Clyde and Clara Mable (Bell) S.; m. Treva Margaret Teter (div.), Sept. 9, 1951; children: Randal Mark, Camille Leean, James Bradley; m. Wava Lynne Frank, Nov. 11, 1989. DVM, Iowa State U., 1952. Owner, vet. Shirbroun Vet. Med. Ctr., Coon Rapids, 1955-2001; trust rep. Am. Vet. Med. Assn., Chgo., 2001—. Lt. USAF, 1952-55. Mem. AVMA (trustee 1982-2000), Am. Assn. Bovine Practitioners (bd. dirs. 1982-1990, Excellence Preventive Medicine award 1987), Am. Assn. Swine Practitioners, Iowa Vet. Med. Assn. (pres. 1981, Pres.' award 1985), Soc. for Theriogenology, N.Am. Limousin Found. (founding mem. 1968), Nat. Cattlemen Assn., Iowa Cattlemen Assn., Am. Legion, Rotary (pres. Coon Rapids 1965). Republican. Methodist. Home: 32104 Millard Circle Warrenville IL 60555-3988 Office: Am Vet Med Assn 55 E Jackson PO Box 1629 Chicago IL 60690-1629 E-mail: rshirbroun@mackparker.com.

SHIRLEY, VIRGINIA LEE, advertising executive; b. Kankakee, Ill., Mar. 24, 1936; d. Glenn Lee and Virginia Helen (Ritter) S. Student, Northwestern U., 1960-61. With prodn. control dept. Armour Pharm., Kankakee, 1954-58; exec. sec. Adolph Richman, Chgo., 1958-61; mgr. media dept. Don Kemper Co., 1961-63, 65-69; exec. sec. Playboy mag., 1964-65; exec. v.p. SMY Media inc., 1969-96, CEO, chmn. bd., 1996-2000, CEO, 2000—. Mem. Tavern Club. Home: 1502-J S Prairie Ave Chicago IL 60605-2856 Office: SMY Media Inc 333 N Michigan Ave Chicago IL 60601-3901

SHIVELY, DANIEL JEROME, retired transportation executive; b. Akron, Ohio, Sept. 2, 1924; s. Richard Miles and Josephine (Pellicer) S.; m. Pamela Marion Kurfess, July 31, 1954; children: Jennifer, Laurie, Thomas. Grad., U.S. Mcht. Marine Acad., King's Point, N.Y., 1945. Chief officer (tanker) Trinidad Corp., N.Y.C., 1946-51; co-owner, mgr. Shively Bros. Jersey Farm, Quaker City, Ohio, 1952-54; staff asst. Gulf Oil Corp., Phila., 1955-57; distbn. coord. Standard Oil Co., Cleve., 1957-73; budget coord. BP Oil Co., Wilmington, Del., 1973-79; mgr. mktg. budget and planning Standard Oil Co., Cleve., 1979-85; owner, mgr. Shively & Assocs., 1985-88. Served to lt. (j.g.) USNR, 1945-61. Mem. Transp. Practitioners Assn. (exec. com. 1984-90, pres. local chpt. 1984-85), Kings's Point Club (treas. N.E. Ohio chpt. 1989-94, sec. 1999—), KC (chancellor 1986, dep. grand knight 1987-91). Republican. Roman Catholic. Avocations: farming, sailing. Home: 21347 Erie Rd Rocky River OH 44116-2133

SHIVELY, WILLIAM PHILLIPS, political scientist, educator; b. Altoona, Pa., Mar. 31, 1942; s. Arthur and Ruth Shively; m. Barbara Louise Shank, Aug. 29, 1964; children: Helen, David. B.A., Franklin and Marshall Coll., 1963; Ph.D., U. N.C., 1968. Mem. faculty U. Oreg., Eugene, 1967-68, Yale U., 1968-71; mem. faculty U. Minn., Mpls., 1971—, prof. polit. sci., 1979—, provost arts, scis. & engring., 1995-97. Author: Craft of Political Research, 1974, 5th edit., 2001, Research Process in Political Science, 1985, Power and Choice, 1986, rev. edit., 1989, 7th edit., 2001, Comparative Governance, 1995, Cross-Level Inference, 1995; editor Am. Jour. Polit. Sci., 1977-79; contbr. articles on elections and voting to profl. jours. Home: 1572 Northrop St Saint Paul MN 55108-1322 Office: U Minn Dept Polit Sci 1414 Social Scis Tower Minneapolis MN 55455 E-mail: shively@polisci.umn.edu.

SHIVLEY, ALBERT J. food products executive; Mgr. Am. Pride Co-op, Brighton, Colo.; chmn. Farmland Industries, Inc., Kansas City, Mo., 1992—. Office: Farmland Industries Inc 3315 N Oak Traffic Way Kansas City MO 64116-0005

SHNIDER, BRUCE JAY, lawyer; b. Lansing, Mich., Oct. 16, 1950; s. Harold A. and Raynor (Seidner) Shnider; m. Patricia Lynn Strandness, Dec. 28, 1973; 1 child Ruth Strandness. AB magna cum laude, Dartmouth Coll., 1972; MPP, JD magna cum laude, Harvard U., 1977. Bar: Minn. 1977, U.S. Dist. Ct. Minn. 1977, U.S. Tax Ct. 1978, U.S. Ct. Appeals (8th cir.) 1980, U.S. Supreme Ct. 1981. Asst. to dir. Mich. Dept. Commerce, Lansing, 1972-73; law clk. United Mineworkers Am. Health/Retirement Funds, 1975; summer assoc. Robins, Davis & Lyon, Mpls., 1976; assoc. Dorsey & Whitney, 1977-82, ptnr., 1983—; chmn. diversity com., 1990-93; chmn. tax practice group, 1994-98. Bd. dirs. Minn. Justice Found., Mpls., 1989—91. Mem.: ABA, Hennepin County Bar Assn., Minn. State Bar Assn. Home: 1908 James Ave S Minneapolis MN 55403-2831 Office: Dorsey & Whitney 50 S 6th St Ste 1500 Minneapolis MN 55402-1498 E-mail: shnider.bruce@dorseylaw.com.

SHOAFF, THOMAS MITCHELL, lawyer; b. Ft. Wayne, Ind., Aug. 21, 1941; s. John D. and Agnes H. (Hanna) S.; m. Eunice Swedberg, Feb. 7, 1970; children: Andrew, Nathaniel, Matthew-John. BA, Williams Coll., 1964; JD, Vanderbilt U., 1967. Bar: Ind. 1968. Assoc. Isham, Lincoln & Beale, Chgo., 1967-68; ptnr. Baker & Daniels, Ft. Wayne, Ind., 1968—. Bd. dirs. Weaver Popcorn Co., Inc., Ft. Wayne, Dreibelbiss Title Co., Inc., Ft. Wayne, Am. Steel Investment Corp., Ft. Wayne. Bd. dirs. McMillen Found., Ft. Wayne, Wilson Found., Ft. Wayne. Mem. ABA, Allen County Bar Assn., Ind. State Bar Assn. Presbyterian. Avocations: golf, sailing. Office: Baker & Daniels 111 E Wayne St Ste 800 Fort Wayne IN 46802-2603

SHOAFSTALL, EARL FRED, entrepreneur, consultant; b. Des Moines, Jan. 26, 1936; s. Ralph Paul and Josephine E. (Carnes) S.; m. Sharon I. Vannoy, Mar. 21, 1962 (div. 1980); children: Michael E., Angela R.; m. Carlene Christenson, Dec. 11, 1980; 1 child, Trace Herman. BA, MBA, Drake U., 1962. Enlisted USAF, Des Moines, 1954, advanced through grades to sgt., 1961, resigned, 1962; underwriter Hawkeye Security Ins., Des Moines, 1962-65; mgr., owner B & B Transfer and Storage Inc., West Des Moines, Iowa, 1965-99; cons., owner B & B Mini Storage Inc.,

1975-99. Inventor pressure gage, control valve for air and liquid. Mem. Mason (32 degree), Shriners. Republican. Avocations: flying, golf, hunting, fishing. Home: 12475 Douglas Pkwy Urbandale IA 50323-1813

SHOEMAKER, JOHN CALVIN, aeronautical engineer, engineering company executive; b. Portland, Ind., Dec. 21, 1937; s. Homer Vaughn and Thelora Maxine (Avey) S.; m. Ruby Nell Johnson, Aug. 3, 1957; children: Gena Rebecca, Lora Rachele, John Calvin II; foster child, Jeanine Louise Patterson. BS in Aero. Engring., Ind. Inst. Tech., Ft. Wayne, 1960. Project engr. Wayne Pump Co., Ft. Wayne, 1960-63, Daybrook Ottawa Co., Bowling Green, Ohio, 1963-65; engring. mgr. Globe Wayne div. Dresser Industries, Ft. Wayne, 1965-67; sales engr. Taylor-Newcomb Engring., 1967-74; prin. Shoemaker, Inc., 1974—. Patentee in field. Rep. precinct committeeman, 1984—. Served with USAR, 1960-67. Mem. Am. Inst. Plant Engrs. Lodge: Lions (pres. local chpt. 1972). Avocations: gospel music, ch. choristering, directing choir. Home and Office: 12120 Yellow River Rd Fort Wayne IN 46818-9702

SHOEMAKER, MICHAEL C. state legislator; b. Nipgen, Ohio, July 2, 1945; m. Vicki Shoemaker; children: Michale Todd, Angela Lynn. BS, Capital U., 1967; MEd, Xavier U., Cin., 1973. Tchr. Paint Valley H.S., 1967-70, Waverly H.S., 1970-72, Smith Jr. H.S., 1972-73, Unioto H.S., 1973-77; carpenter, 1977; mem. Ohio Ho. of Reps., Columbus, 1983-97; mem. 17th dist. Ohio Senate, 1997—. Vice chmn. Health & Retirement Com., mem. Edn. Pub. Utilities & Fin. & Appropriations com., mem. Coll. & Univ. com. Named Athletic of Yr. Capital Univ.; recipient Svc. to Edn. award Ohio Univ. 1989, Friend of Edn. award, COTA, 1989. Mem. Bainbridge Hist. Soc., Paint Valley Athletic Boosters, Ross County Farm Bureau, Twp. Trustee and Clerks Assn., Scioto Valley Habitat for Humanity. Home: PO Box 577 Bourneville OH 45617-0577

SHOENER, JERRY JAMES, state legislator; BBA, Nat. Am. U., Rapid City, S.D. Mem. S.D. State Senate, mem. transp. com., chmn., commerce vice chmn., local govt. mem., mem. transp. com., chmn. rules com., mem. legis. exec. bd.; v.p., circulation dir. Rapid City Newspaper. Home: 4012 Clover St Rapid City SD 57702-0252 Office: SD Senate Mems State Capitol Pierre SD 57501

SHORE, THOMAS SPENCER, JR. lawyer; b. Akron, Ohio, Jan. 1, 1939; s. T. Spencer and Harriet G. (Delicate) S.; m. Margaret F. Kudzma, Aug. 12, 1961; children— Thomas Spencer III, John Christopher, Daniel Andrew, Mary Margaret. B.A., Brown U., 1961; J.D., Northwestern U., 1964. Bar: Ohio 1964. Assoc. Taft, Stettinius and Hollister, Cin., 1964-69; asso. Rendigs, Fry, Kiely & Dennis, 1969-71, partner, 1972—. Adj. asst. prof. Chase Law Sch., U. No. Ky. Bd. dirs. United Cerebral Palsy of Cin., 1978— ; bd. dirs., sec. Boys Club Am., Cin.; trustee emeritus Family Svc. of Cin. Area; past pres. Vis. Nurse Assn. of Cin., hon. trustee. Mem. Cin. Bar Assn., Ohio Bar Assn., Am. Bar Assn. Clubs: Cin. Country, Cin. Tennis, Queen City, Webhanet. Home: 3224 Columbia Pkwy Cincinnati OH 45226-1042 Office: 900 Central Trust Tower Cincinnati OH 45202 E-mail: t.shore@rendigs.com.

SHORS, JOHN D. lawyer; b. Ft. Dodge, Iowa, July 21, 1937; s. George A. and Catherine (Shaw) S.; m. Patricia Ann Percival, Oct. 7, 1967; children: John, Tom, Matt, Luke. BSEE, Iowa State U., 1959; JD, U. Iowa, 1964. Bar: Iowa, U.S. Supreme Ct. Assoc. then shareholder Davis, Brown, Koehn, Shors & Roberts, P.C., Des Moines, 1964—. Co-author: Closely Held Corporations in Business and Estate Planning, 1982. Pres. Mercy Hosp. Found., Des Moines, 1981-84; chair Iowa State U. Found., Ames, 1989-92; bd. dirs. Mercy Housing, Denver, 1992—. Cpl. U.S. Army, 1960-61. Recipient Iowa State U. Alumni medal, YLS Merit award Iowa State Bar Assn. Mem. Iowa State Bar Assn. (pres. 1992) Iowa Women Profl. Corp. (Good Guy award 1987), Iowa Rsch. Coun. (bd. dirs. 1994—), Am. Judicature Soc. (bd. dirs. 1974-79), Polk County Bar Assn. (pres. 1986), Rotary (Des Moines chpt.), DM Club, Glenoaks C.C. Republican. Roman Catholic. Office: Davis Brown Koehn Shors & Roberts PC 666 Walnut St Ste 2500 Des Moines IA 50309-3904 E-mail: johnshors@lawiowa.com.

SHORT, MARION PRISCILLA, neurogenetics educator; b. Milford, Del., June 12, 1951; d. Raymond Calistus and Barbara Anne (Ferguson) S.; m. Michael Peter Klein; 1 child, Asher Calistus Klein. BA, Bryn Mawr Coll., 1973; diploma, U. Edinburgh (Scotland), 1975; MD, Med. Coll. Pa., 1978. Diplomate Am. Bd. Psychiatry and Neurology, Am. Bd. Internal Medicine. Intern in internal medicine Hahnemann Med. Coll. Hosp., Phila., 1978-79; med. resident in internal medicine St. Lukes-Roosevelt Hosp., N.Y.C., 1979-81; neurology resident U. Pitts. Health Ctr., 1981-84; fellow in med. genetics Mt. Sinai Med. Ctr., N.Y.C., 1984-86; fellow in neurology Mass. Gen. Hosp., Boston, 1986-90, asst. neurologist, 1990-95; asst. prof. dept. neurology Harvard Med. Sch., 1990-95; asst. prof. dept. neurology, pediat. and pathology U. Chgo., 1995—97, clin. assoc. neurosurgery, 1997—; program dir. genetics, transplantation and clin. rsch. AMA, Chgo., 1997—2002. Cons. Spaulding Rehab. Hosp., Boston. Recipient Clin. Investigator Devel. award NIH, 1988-93.äfellow Inst. Medicine, Chgo., 1999—. Mem. Am. Acad. Neurology, Am. Soc. for Human Genetics, Am. Coll. Med. Genetics. Office: Pediat Neurosurgery U Chgo 5481 S Maryland Ave Chicago IL 60637-4325 E-mail: priscilla_short@ama-assn.org., mpshort@surgery.bsd.uchicago.edu.

SHOTWELL, MALCOLM GREEN, retired minister; b. Brookneal, Va., Aug. 14, 1932; s. John Henry and Ada Mildred (Puckett) S.; m. LaVerne Brown, June 19, 1954; children: Donna (dec.), Paula. BA in Sociology, U. Richmond, 1954; MDiv, Colgate Rochester Div. Sch., 1957; D Ministry, Ea. Bapt. Theol. Sem., 1990; DD (hon.), Judson Coll., 1990. Ordained to ministry Am. Bapt. Ch. in U.S.A., 1957. Student asst. Greece Bapt. Ch., Rochester, N.Y., 1954-57; pastor 1st Bapt. Ch., Cuba, 1957-62, sr. pastor Galesburg, Ill., 1962-71, Olean, N.Y., 1971-81; area minister Am. Bapt. Chs. of Pa. and Del., 1981-90; regional exec. minister Am. Bapt. Chs. of Great Rivers Region, Ill. and Mo., 1990-96; ret., 1997. Mem. Midwest Commn. on Ministry Am. Bapt. Chs. U.S.A., 1990—96, mem. task force for So. Bapt. Am. Bapt. Chs. Relationships, 1990—96; cons. for ch. growth and planning. Author: Creative Programs for the Church Year, 1986, Renewing the Baptist Principle of Associations, 1990; contbg. writer Baptists in the Balance, 1997; rschr., writer, performer: (dramatic monologue) Our Neighbors, the Lincolns: A Clergyman Remembers, 1999—. Trustee No. Bapt. Theol. Sem., Lombard, Ill., 1993-96; mem. gen. exec. coun., 1990-96, regional exec. ministers coun., 1990-96; trustee Judson Coll., 1990—, chmn., 1997-2000, chmn. presdl. search com., 1997-98; bd. dirs. Ctrl. Bapt. Theol. Sem., Kansas City, Kans., 1990-96; sec. bd. dirs. Shurtleff Fund, Springfield, Ill., 1990-96; tchr., libr. Ctrl. Bapt. Ch., Springfield, 1997—; mem. Hist. Commn. Am. Bapts. Ill. and Mo., 1998—; retreat leader in stress mgmt., 1985—; conf., spkr., pulpit supply preacher Bapt. Ch.; mentor ILCS Elem. Sch., Old State Capital Reenactment of Lincoln-Douglas Debates, 1999-2001. Walter Pope Binns fellow William Jewell Coll., 1995. Mem. Ministers Coun. Ill. and Mo., Coun. Ret. Execs.

SHRAUNER, BARBARA WAYNE ABRAHAM, electrical engineering educator; b. Morristown, N.J., June 21, 1934; d. Leonard Gladstone and Ruth Elizabeth (Thrasher) Abraham; m. James Ely Shrauner, 1965; children: Elizabeth Ann, Jay Arthur. BA cum laude, U. Colo., 1956; AM, Harvard U., 1957, PhD, 1962. Postdoctoral researcher U. Libre de Bruxelles, Brussels, 1962-64; postdoctoral researcher NASA-Ames Rsch. Ctr., Moffett Field, Calif., 1964-65; asst. prof. Washington U., St. Louis, 1966-69, assoc. prof., 1969-77, prof., 1977—. Sabbatical Los Alamos (N.Mex.) Sci. Lab., 1975-76, Lawrence Berkeley Lab., Berkeley, Calif., 1985-86; cons. Los Alamos Nat. Lab., 1979, 84, NASA, Washington, 1980, Naval Surface Weapons Lab., Silver Spring, Md., 1984. Contbr. articles on transport in semiconductors, hidden symmetries of differential equations, plasma physics to profl. jours. Fellow Am. Phys. Soc. (sr. divsn. plasma physics, exec. com. 1980-82, 96-98); mem. IEEE (sr. exec. com. of standing tech. com. on plasma sci. and applications 1996-98), AAUP (local sec.-treas. 1980-82), Am. Geophys. Union, Univ. Fusion Assn., Phi Beta Kappa, Sigma Xi, Eta Kappa Nu, Sigma Pi Sigma. Home: 7452 Stratford Ave Saint Louis MO 63130-4044 Office: Washington U 1 Brookings Dr Dept Elec Saint Louis MO 63130-4899 E-mail: bas@ee.wustl.edu.

SHREVE, GENE RUSSELL, law educator; b. San Diego, Aug. 6, 1943; s. Ronald D. and Hazel (Shepherd) S.; m. Marguerite Russell, May 26, 1973. AB with honors, U. Okla., 1965; LLB, Harvard U., 1968, LLM, 1975. Bar: Mass. 1969, Vt. 1981. Appellate atty. and state extradition hearing examiner Office of Mass. Atty Gen., 1968-69; law clk. U.S. Dist. Ct., Dallas, 1969-70; staff and supervising atty. Boston Legal Assistance Project, 1970-73; assoc. prof. Vt. Law Sch., Royalton, 1975-81; vis. assoc. prof. George Washington U., Washington, 1981-83; assoc. prof. law N.Y. Law Sch., N.Y.C., 1983-84, prof., 1984-87; vis. prof. law Ind. U., Bloomington, 1986, prof., 1987-94, Ira C. Batman faculty fellow, 1988-89, Charles L. Whistler faculty fellow, dir. grad. studies, 1992-93, Richard S. Melvin Prof. Law, 1994—. Author: A Conflict of Laws Anthology, 1997; co-author: Understanding Civil Procedure, 2d edit., 1994; mem. editl. bd. Am. Jour. Comparative Law, 1994—, Jour. Legal Edn., 1998—; contbr. numerous articles to legal jours. Mem. Am. Law Inst., Am. Soc. for Pol. and Legal Phil., Assn. Am. Law Schs. (civil procedure sect. chair 1997, conflict of laws sect. chair 1998). Democrat. Episcopalian. Office: Ind U Sch Law Bloomington IN 47405

SHRINER, THOMAS L., JR. lawyer; b. Lafayette, Ind., Dec. 15, 1947; s. Thomas L. Sr. and Margaret (Kamstra); m. Donna L. Galchick, June 5, 1971; children: Thomas L. III, John H. , Joseph P., James A. AB, Ind. U., 1969, JD, 1972. Bar: Wis. 1972, U.S. Ct. Appeals (7th cir.) 1972, U.S. Dist. Ct. (ea. dist.) Wis. 1973, U.S. Dist. Ct. (we. dist.) Wis. 1977, U.S. Supreme Ct. 1978, U.S. Ct. Appeals (8th cir.) 1989, U.S. Ct. Appeals (fed. cir.) 1990. Law clk to Hon. John S. Hastings U.S. Ct. Appeals (7th cir.), Chgo., 1972-73; assoc. Foley & Lardner, Milwaukee, Wis., 1973-79, ptnr., 1979—. Chmn. bd. trustees Cath. Charities of Archdiocese of Milw., 2001—. Fellow Am. Coll. Trial Lawyers; mem. 7th Cir. Bar Assn. (pres. 1993-94), Phi Beta Kappa. Republican. Roman Catholic. Office: Foley & Lardner 777 E Wisconsin Ave Ste 3800 Milwaukee WI 53202-5367 E-mail: tshriner@foleylaw.com.

SHRIVER, DUWARD FELIX, chemistry educator, researcher, consultant; b. Glendale, Calif., Nov. 20, 1934; s. Duward Laurence and Josephine (Williamson) S.; m. Shirley Ann Clark; children: Justin Scott, Daniel Nathan. BS, U. Calif., Berkeley, 1958; PhD, U. Mich., 1961. From instr. to assoc. prof. chemistry Northwestern U., Evanston, Ill., 1961-70, prof., 1970-87, Morrison prof. of chemistry, 1987—, chmn. dept. chem., 1992-95; mem. Inorganic Syntheses Inc., 1974—, pres., 1982-85. Vis. staff mem. Los Alamos (N.Mex.) Nat. Lab., 1976-85, cons., 1985-92; vis. prof. U. Tokyo, 1977, U. Wyo., 1978, U. Western Ont., Can., 1979. Author: The Manipulation of Air-Sensitive Compounds, 1969, edit., 1987; co-author: Inorganic Chemistry, 1990, 2d edit., 1994, 3d edit., 1998; editor-in-chief Inorganic Syntheses, vol. 19, 1979; co-editor: The Chemistry of Metal Cluster Complexes, 1990; editl. bd. Inorganic Synthesis, 1979—, Advances in Inorganic Chemistry, 1986—, Jour. Coordination Chemistry, Inorganic Chimca Acta, 1988—, Chemistry of Materials, 1988-90, 92—, Jour. Cluster Sci., 1990-97, Organometallics, 1993-95; contbr. articles to profl. jours. Alfred P. Sloan fellow, 1967-69; Japan Soc. Promotion of Sci. fellow, 1977; Guggenheim Found. fellow, 1983-84. Fellow AAAS; mem. Am. Chem. Soc. (Disting. Svc. in Inorganic Chemistry award 1987), Royal Soc. Chemistry London (Ludwig Mond lectr. 1989), Electrochem. Soc., Materials Rsch. Soc. (medal 1990). Home: 1100 Colfax St Evanston IL 60201-2611 Office: Northwestern U Dept Chemistry Evanston IL 60208-0001 E-mail: shriver@chem.nwu.edu.

SHRIVER, JOSEPH DUANE, state legislator; b. Arkansas City, Kans., Oct. 13, 1959; s. John Francis and Carolyn Joan (Thornhill) S.; m. Mindi Sue Peterson, 1982; 1 child, Jayme Dawn. AA, Cowley County C.C., 1981. Mem. from dist. 79 Kans. State Ho. of Reps., 1994—, mem. tax and judiciary coms. Mem. Kans. Joint Commn. on Adminstv. Rules and Regulations and Spl. Com. on Motor Fuel Tax, U.s. Dept. Revenue. Recipient Outstanding Svc. award Kans. Dem. Party, 1990. Mem. Arkansas City C. of C. (legis. chmn. 1990-91), Firefighter Relief Assn. (pres. 1991-94), Firefighters Local 2101. Address: PO Box 1324 Arkansas City KS 67005-7324

SHRIVER, PHILLIP RAYMOND, academic administrator; b. Cleve., Aug. 16, 1922; s. Raymond Scott and Corinna Ruth (Smith) S.; m. Martha Damaris Nye, Apr. 15, 1944; children: Carolyn (Mrs. William Shaul), Susan (Mrs. Lester LaVine), Melinda (Mrs. David Williams), Darcy, Raymond Scott II. BA, Yale U., 1943; MA, Harvard U., 1946; PhD, Columbia U., 1954; LittD, U. Cin., 1966; LLD, Heidelberg Coll., 1966, Eastern Mich., 1972, Ohio State U., 1973; DH, McKendree Coll., 1973; DPS, Albion Coll., 1974; LHD, Central State U., 1976, No. Ky. State U., 1980, Miami U., 1984, U. Akron, 1988. Mem. faculty Kent (Ohio) State U., 1947-65, prof. Am. history, 1960-65; dean Coll. Arts and Scis., 1963-65; pres. Miami U., Oxford, Ohio, 1965-81, pres. emeritus, prof. Am. history, 1981-99. Pres. Ohio Coll. Assn., 1974-75; chmn. coun. pres.'s Mid-Am. Conf., 1971-77; chmn. Ohio Bicentennial Commn. for NW Ordinance and U.S. Constn., 1985-89, Ohio Tuition Trust Authority, 1989-92; chmn. coun. pres.'s Nat. Assn. State Univs. and Land Grant Colls., 1975-76, mem. exec. coun., 1976-78. Author: The Years of Youth, 1960, George A. Bowman: The Biography of an Educator, 1963, (with D.J. Breen) Ohio's Military Prisons of the Civil War, 1964, A Tour to New Connecticut: The Narrative of Henry Leavitt Ellsworth, 1985, Miami University: A Personal History, 1998, (with C.E. Wunderlin Jr.) The Documentary Heritage of Ohio, 2000, (with E.F. Puff) The History of Presbyterianism in Oxford, Ohio, 2000. Bd. dirs. Cin. Ctr. Sci. and Industry, 1965-70; trustee Ohio Coll. Library Center, 1968-74; chmn. bd. Univ. Regional Broadcasting, 1975-76, 78-79. Served to lt. (j.g.) USNR, 1943-46, PTO. Decorated Order of Merit Grand Duchy of Luxembourg, 1976; recipient Disting. Acad. Svc. award AAUP, 1965, Gov.'s award 1969, A.K. Morris award, 1974, Ohioana Career medal, 1987, Converse award, 1990, Award of Merit, Am. Assn. for State and Local History, 1993, Bjornson award Ohio Humanities Coun., 2001. Mem. Orgn. Am. Historians, Ohio Acad. History (pres. 1983-84, Disting. Svc. award 1991), Archaeol. Inst. Am., Ohio Hist. Soc. (trustee 1982-91, v.p. 1983-84, pres. 1984-86), Ohio Humanities Council (Bjornson award 2001), Am. Studies Assn., Mortar Board, Phi Beta Kappa, Omicron Delta Kappa, Phi Alpha Theta, Alpha Kappa Psi, Kappa Delta Pi, Phi Eta Sigma, Phi Kappa Phi, Kappa Kappa Psi, Alpha Lambda Delta, Beta Gamma Sigma, Sigma Delta Pi, Alpha Phi Omega, Delta Upsilon (Disting. Alumni Achievement award 1985) Presbyterian. Club: Rotary. Home: 5115 Bonham Rd Oxford OH 45056-1428 Office: Miami U Oxford OH 45056 E-mail: shrivepr@muohio.edu.

SHTOHRYN, DMYTRO MICHAEL, librarian, educator; b. Zvyniach, Ukraine, Nov. 9, 1923; came to U.S., 1950; s. Mykhailo and Kateryna (Figol) S.; m. Eustachia Barwinska, Sept. 3, 1955; children: Bohdar O., Liudoslava V. Student, Ukrainian Free U., Munich, 1947-48, U. Minn., 1954; M.A. in Slavic Studies, U. Ottawa, Can., 1958, B.L.S., 1959, Ph.D. in Slavic Studies, 1970. Slavic cataloger U. Ottawa, 1959; cataloger NRC Can., Ottawa, 1959-60; Slavic cataloger, instr. library adminstrn. U. Ill., Urbana, 1960-64, head Slavic cataloging, asst. prof. library adminstrn., 1964-68, head Slavic cataloging, assoc. prof., 1968-75, head Slavic cataloging, prof., 1975-85, lectr. Ukrainian lit., 1975-91, assoc. Slavic librarian, prof., 1985-95, prof. Ukrainian lit., 1991-95, prof. emeritus, 1995—. Vis. prof. Ukrainian lit. U. Ottawa, 1974; assoc. prof. Ukrainian lit. Ukrainian Cath. U., Rome, 1978— ; prof. Ukrainian lit. Ukrainian Free U., Munich, 1983—, Ukrainian lang. and lit., U. Ill., 1991-95, Ukrainian culture, 1996—; chmn. Ukrainian Research Program U. Ill., 1984—. Editor: Catalog of Publications of Ukrainian Academy of Sciences, 1966, Ukrainians in North America: A Bibliographical Directory, 1975; author: Ukrainian Literature in the U.S.A.: Trends, Influences, Achievements, 1975, The Rise and Fall of Book Studies in Ukraine, 1986, Oleh Kandyba-Olzhych: Bibliography, 1992; editor: Bull. Ukrainian Libr. Assn. Am., 1982-88; mem. editl. bd. Ukrainian Historian, 1985-98, Ethnic Forum, 1985-95, Crossroads, 1986-97, Ukrainian Quar., 1993—, Ukrainian Problems, 1997—, Ukrainian Rev., 1997-99. Counselor Boy Scouts Am., Champaign, Ill., 1967-85; bd. dirs. Ukrainian-Am. Found., Chgo., 1978-87. Recipient Grant Future Credit Union Toronto, 1956, Grant U. Ill., 1977, 1982, Silver medal, Parliament of Can. Librarian, Ottawa, 1959, award, Glorier Soc. Can., 1959, citation plaque, Ukrainian Congress Com. Am., Chgo., 2000, Medal, V. Stefanyk Subcarpathian State U., 2001. Fellow Shevchenko Sci. Soc. (exec. com., M. Hrushevsky medal 1998); mem. ALA (chmn. Slavic and East European sect. 1968-69), Ukrainian Libr. Assn. Am. (pres. 1970-74, 82-87), Ukrainian Acad. and Profl. Assn. (charter, sec. 1985-89, pres. 1989—), I. Franko Internat. Soc. (founding mem., pres. 1978-79, 81-82), Ukrainian-Am. Assn. Univ. Profs. (exec. com. 1981-96), Ukrainian Hist. Assn. (exec. com. 1983-97), Ukrainian Acad. Arts and Scis. in U.S. (exec. com. 1993-98), Ukrainian Congress Com. of Am. Scholarly Coun., Ukrainian Writers' Assn. Slovo, Libr. Congress Assocs. (charter mem.). Ukrainian Catholic. Home: 403 Park Lane Dr Champaign IL 61820-7729 Office: Dept Slavic Langs & Lits 3092 Fgn Langs Bldg 707 S Mathews Ave Urbana IL 61801-3625 E-mail: shtohryn@uiuc.edu.

SHUCK, JERRY MARK, surgeon, educator; b. Bucyrus, Ohio, Apr. 23, 1934; s. James Edwin and Pearl (Mark) S.; m. Linda Wayne, May 28, 1974; children: Jay Steven, Gail Ellen, Kimberly Ann, Lynn Meredith, Steven James. BS in Pharmacy, U. Cin., 1955, MD, 1959, DSc, 1966. Intern Colo. Gen. Hosp., Denver, 1959-60; resident in surgery U. Cin. Integrated Program, 1960-66; mem. faculty dept. surgery U. N.Mex., Albuquerque, 1968-80, prof., 1974-80; Oliver H. Payne prof. dept. surgery Case-Western Res. U., Cleve., 1980—, chmn. dept., 1980-2000, prof. anatomy, 1999—, interim v.p. for med. affairs, 1993-95. Cons. FDA, 1972-77 Contbr. articles to profl. jours. Served to capt. U.S. Army, 1966-68. Mem. ACS, Am. Surg. Assn., Am. Bd. Surgery (bd. dirs., chmn. 1993-94, residency rev. com. for surgery 1994-2000, vice chmn. 1997-2000), Soc. Univ. Surgeons, Am. Ass n. S urgery Trauma, Am. Trauma Soc. (founding mem.), Univ. Assn. Emergency Medicine (founding mem.), Am. Burn Assn. (founding mem.), We. Surg. Assn., Ctrl. Surg. Assn. (pres. 1996-97), Assn. Acad. Surgery, S.W. Surg. Assn., Cleve. Surg. Soc. (pres. 1988-89), Ohio Med. Assn., Acad. Medicine Cleve., Halsted Soc., Surg. Infection Soc. (founding mem.), B'nai B'rith, Jewish Cmty. Ctr. Club, The Temple Club. Democrat. Jewish. Office: Case Western Reserve U Dept Surgery 11100 Euclid Ave Cleveland OH 44106-2602

SHUEY, JOHN HENRY, diversified products company executive; b. Monroe, Mich., Mar. 14, 1946; s. John Henry and Bertha (Thomas) S.; children: Katherine, John Henry, John Joseph Satory. B.S. in Indsl. Engring., U. Mich., 1968, M.B.A., 1970. With Tex. Instruments Co., Dallas, 1970-74; asst. treas. The Trane Co., La Crosse, Wis., 1974-78, treas., 1978-81, v.p., treas., 1981-83, v.p. fin., chief fin. officer, 1983-86; also v.p., group exec. Am. Standard; sr. v.p. and chief fin. officer AM Internat. Inc., Chgo., 1986-91; exec. v.p. Amcast Indsl. Corp., Dayton, Ohio, 1991-93, pres., COO, 1993-95, pres., CEO, 1995—, also chmn. bd. dirs., chmn. bd., pres., CEO, 1997—. Bd. dirs. Cooper Tire and Rubber Co., Findlay, Ohio, EMTEC. Bd. dirs. Wright State Univ. Found., 1996—; bd. trustees Dayton Ballet, 1996—, Ohio Found. of Ind. Colleges, 1994—. Mem. Fin. Execs. Inst. Congregationalist. Office: 7887 Washington Village Dr Dayton OH 45459-3900 also: Elkhart Products Corp 1255 Oak St Elkhart IN 46514-2277

SHUGARS, DALE L. state legislator; b. May 6, 1953; m. Debra; 1 child, Meaghan. BSBA, Western Mich. U. CPA. Mem. Mich. Ho. of Reps. from 47th dist., Lansing, 1991-92, Mich. Ho. of Reps. from 61st dist., Lansing, 1993-94, Mich. Senate from 21st dist., Lansing, 1994—. Chmn. health policy & sr. citizens com. Mich. State Senate, vice chmn. econ. delvel. com., vice chmn. internat. rels. com., vice chmn. regulatory affairs com., mem. fin. com. Vol. Big Brothers and Big Sisters of Kalamazoo. Mem. Lions Club, Rotary, Kalamazoo C. of C. Home: 5315 Angling Rd Portage MI 49024-5602 Address: PO Box 30036 Lansing MI 48909-7536 Office: Mich Senate Mems State Capitol PO Box 30036 Lansing MI 48909-7536

SHUGHART, DONALD LOUIS, lawyer; b. Kansas City, Mo., Aug. 12, 1926; s. Henry M. and Dora M. (O'Leary) Shughart; m. Mary I. Shughart, July 25, 1953; children: Susan C. Hogsett, Nancy J. Goede. AB, U. Mo., Columbia, 1949, JD, 1951. Bar: Mo. 1951, U.S. Dist. Ct. (we. dist.) Mo. 1951, U.S. Tax Ct. 1979. With Shughart, Thompson & Kilroy, PC, Kansas City, Mo., 1951—. Mem. Mo. Motor Carriers Assn. Planned giving com. Rockhurst U.; adv. bd. St. Joseph Hosp. With AC, U.S. Army, 1944-47. Mem. Kansas City Bar Assn. (chmn. bus. orgns. com. 1990-91), Mo. Bar Assn. (chmn. corp. com. 1980-81, 82-83), Lawyers Assn. Kansas City, Am. Judicature Soc., Mo. Orgn. Def. Lawyers (pres. 1971-72), U. Mo. Law Soc., Phi Delta Phi, Sigma Chi. Republican. Roman Catholic. Home: 1242 W 67th Ter Kansas City MO 64113-1941 Office: Shug Thom Kilroy 12 Wyandotte Pla 120 W 12th St Kansas City MO 64105-1917

SHULA, ROBERT JOSEPH, lawyer; b. South Bend, Ind., Dec. 10, 1936; s. Joseph Edward and Bertha Mona (Buckner) S.; m. Gaye Ann Martin, Oct. 8, 1978; children: Deirdre Regina, Robert Joseph II, Elizabeth Martin. BS in Mktg., Ind. U., 1958, JD, 1961. Bar: Ind. 1961. Ptnr. Bingham Summers Welsh & Spilman, Indpls., 1965-82, sr. ptnr., 1982-89; ptnr. Price & Shula, 1989-91, Lowe Gray Steele & Darko, Indpls., 1991—. Mem. faculty Nat. Inst. Trial Advocacy; guest lectr. Brit. Medicine and Law Soc., 1979, Ind. U. Sch. Law; medico-legal lectr. Ind. U. Schs. Medicine, Dentistry, and Nursing. Bd. dirs. Arts Ind., Indpls., 1995-99; pres. Oriental Arts Soc., Indpls., 1975-79, Meridian Women's Clinic, Inc., Indpls.; trustee Indpls. Mus. Art, 1975-78, life trustee, 1984—; bd. dirs. Ind. Repertory Theatre, Indpls., 1982-92, chmn. bd. dirs., pres., 1985-89; pres. Repertory Soc., 1993-96; v.p., bd. dirs. Flanner House of Indpls., Inc., 1977-88, chmn., 1988-99; pres. Internat. Ctr. of Indpls., Inc., 1993-96. Maj. JAGC, USAFR, 1961-65. Recipient Gov.'s award of Sagamore of the Wabash, 1998. Master Am. Inns of Ct.; fellow Internat. Soc. Barristers; mem. ABA, FBA, Ind. Bar Assn., Indpls. Bar Assn., Am. Bd. Trial Advs. (pres. 2000), Am. Law Inst., Am. Coll. Legal Medicine, Def. Trial Counsel Ind. (diplomate), Confrerie Chevaliers du Tastevin, Woodstock Country Club. Democrat. Episcopalian. Home: 7924 Beaumont Green Pl Indianapolis IN 46250-1663 Office: Bank One Ctr 111 Monument Cir Ste 4600 Indianapolis IN 46204-5402 E-mail: bob.shula@lgsd.com.

SHULMAN, CAROLE KAREN, professional society administrator; b. Mpls., Nov. 25, 1940; d. Allen Eldon and Beulah Ovidia (Blomsness) Banbury; m. David Arthur Shulman, Mar. 26, 1962; children: Michael, Krista, Tracy, Robbyn. Student, Colo. Coll., 1958-61, California Coast U., 1983-84. Profl. instr. Rochester (Minn.) Figure Skating Club, 1962-84, dir. skating, 1964-79, cons., 1979—; exec. dir. Profl. Skaters Assn., Rochester, 1984—, master rating examiner, 1971—, world profl. judge, 1976, 79, 87-88. Editor Professional Skater mag., 1984—; prodr. U.S. Open Profl.

Figure Skating Championships, 1987, 89—. Pres. Rochester Arts Council, 1983. Recipient Achievement award Rochester Arts Coun., 1983, Mayor's Medal of Honor, 1997; named triple gold medalist U.S. Figure Skating Assn., Colorado Springs, Colo., 1959, 63, Master Rated Coach Profl. Skaters Assn., 1970, Sr. Rated Coach in Dance Profl. Skaters Assn., 1970. Mem. Am. Harp Soc., Profl. Skaters Assn. (hon., Lifetime Achievement award 1989). Mem. Covenant ch. Avocations: harp, skiing. Office: Profl Skaters Assn Internat 3006 Allegro Park SW Rochester MN 55902-0886

SHULMAN, YECHIEL, engineering educator; b. Tel Aviv, Jan. 28, 1930; came to the U.S., 1950; s. David and Rachel (Chonowski) S.; m. Ruth Danzig, June 29, 1950; children: Elinor D., Ron E., Orna L. BS in Aero. Engring., BS in Bus. and Engring. Adminstrn., MS in Aero. Engring., MIT, 1954, DSc Aero. and Astro., 1959; MBA, U. Chgo., 1973. Assoc. prof. mech. engring. Northwestern U., Evanston, Ill., 1959-67; v.p. adv. engring. Anocut, Inc., Elk Grove Vill., 1967-72; v.p. corp. devel. Alden Press, 1973-84; pres. MMT Environ., Inc., Shoreview, Minn., 1984-87; cons. Shulman Assocs., Mpls., 1987-89; prof. mech. engring. dept. U. Minn., 1989-2000, H. W. Sweatt chair in technol. leadership and dir. ctr. for devel. technol. leadership, 1989-2000, dir. grad. studies mgmt. of tech. program, 1990-2000, prof. emeritus mech. engring. dept., 2000—. Mem. ASME, Internat. Assn. for Mgmt. of Tech. Office: U Minn 109 ME Bldg 111 Church St SE Minneapolis MN 55455-0150

SHUMAN, R. BAIRD, academic program director, writer, English language educator, educational consultant; b. Paterson, N.J., June 20, 1929; s. George William and Elizabeth (Evans) S. A.B. (Trustees scholar), Lehigh U., 1951; M.Ed., Temple U., 1953; Ph.D. (Univ. scholar), U. Pa., 1961; cert. in philology, U. Vienna, Austria, 1954. Tchr. Phila. Pub. Schs., 1953-55; asst. instr. English U. Pa., 1955-57; instr. humanities Drexel U., Phila., 1957-59; asst. prof. English San José (Calif.) State U., 1959-62; asst. prof. English, edn. Duke U., 1962-63, assoc. prof., 1963-66, prof. edn., 1966-77; prof. English, dir. English edn. U. Ill., Urbana-Champaign, 1977-85, dir. freshman rhetoric, 1979-84, coord. Univ. Associates in Rhetoric Program, 1978-84, dir. devel., 1988-93, acting dir. Ctr. for Study of Writing, 1989-90, prof. emeritus, 1993—. Vis. prof. Moore Inst. Art, 1958, Phila. Conservatory Music, 1958-59, Lynchburg Coll., 1965, King Faisal U., Saudi Arabia, 1978, 81, Bread Loaf Sch. English, Middlebury Coll., 1980, East Tenn. State U., Johnson City, 1980, Olivet Nazarene Coll., 1984, 86, 88, U. Tenn., Knoxville, 1987; cons. Ednl. Testing Svc., 1970—, Am. Coll. Testing Svc., 1975-82; cons. in lang. and lit. Coll. Engring., U. Ill., 1980-97, Worldwide Youth in Sci. and Engring., 1995-97; mem. William Inge Nat. Festival Com., 1989—. Author: Clifford Odets, 1962, Robert E. Sherwood, 1964, William Inge, 1965, rev. edit., 1989, Strategies in Teaching Reading: Secondary, 1978, (with Robert J. Krajewski) The Beginning Teacher: A Guide to Problem Solving, 1979, Elements of Early Reading Instruction, 1979, The First R: Strategies in Early Reading Instruction, 1987, rev. edit., 1989, Classroom Encounters: Problems, Case Studies, Solutions, 1989, (with Eric Hobson) Reading and Writing in High School, (with Denny T. Wolfe Jr.) Teaching English Through the Arts, 1990, Resources for Writers, 1992, American drama 1918-1960, 1992, Georgia O'Keeffe, 1993; editor: Nine Black Poets, 1968, An Eye for an Eye, 1969, A Galaxy of Black Writing, 1970, Creative Approaches to the Teaching of English: Secondary, 1974, Questions English Teachers Ask, 1977, Educational Drama for Today's Schools, 1978, Education in the 80's—English, 1980, The Clearing House: A Closer Look, 1984, 70th anniversary issue The Clearing House, 1995, Great American Writers: 20th Century, 13 vols., 2002; exec. editor The Clearing House jour., 1976—; cons. editor Poet Lore, 1977-90, Cygnus, 1978—, Jour. Aesthetic Edn., 1978-82; contbg. editor Reading Horizons, 1975-85; editor quar. column Reading Horizons, 1975-85; editor Trends in English column Ednl. Leadership, 1989-96. Active Nat. Trust Hist. Preservation. NEH researcher Trinity Coll., Dublin, Ireland, 1985 Mem. MLA, Nat. Coun. Tchrs. English (evaluator ERIC Clearing House, com. alt. careers for English profls.), Internat. Fedn. Tchrs. English, Internat. Coun. Edn. of tchrs., Nev. Coun. Tchrs. English, Conf. English Edn. (exec. com. 1976-79), Internat. Reading Assn. (coord. symposium on cultural literacy, Queensland, Australia 1988), Internat. Assn. Univ. Profs. English, Nat. Soc. Study Edn., Am. Fedn. Tchrs., Union Profl. Employees (editor newsletter 1988-92, exec. com. 1988-92). Democrat. Home: PO Box 27647 Las Vegas NV 89126-1647 E-mail: Rbaird@vegasnet.net.

SHUTZ, BYRON CHRISTOPHER, real estate executive; b. Kansas City, Mo., Feb. 16, 1928; s. Byron Theodore and Maxine (Christopher) S.; m. Marilyn Ann Tweedie, Mar. 30, 1957; children: Eleanor S. Gaines, Byron Christopher, Collin Reid, Allison S. Moskow, Lindley Anne Baile. A.B. in Econs, U. Kans., 1949. Ptnr. Herbert V. Jones & Co., Kansas City, Mo., 1953-72; pres. Herbert V. Jones Mortgage Corp., 1967-72, The Byron Shutz Co., Kansas City, 1973—. Dir. 1st Am. Financial Corp., Rothschild's, Inc., Bus. Men's Assurance Co., Faultless Starch, Bon Ami Co. Chmn. bd. trustees U. Kansas City, 1979-81; trustee Pembroke-Country Day Sch., 1974-77, Midwest Rsch. Inst., 1980-89; chmn., bd. govs. Kansas City Art Inst., 1960-62; chmn. bd. dirs. Ctr. for Bus. Innovation, Inc., 1985-87; bd. dirs. Kansas City Crime Commn. 1st lt. USAF, 1951-53. Mem. Mortgage Bankers Assn. Am. (bd. govs. 1966-74), Am. Inst. Real Estate Appraisers. Clubs: Kansas City Country, University, Mercury (pres. 1978-79); Fla. Yacht (Jacksonville), Ocean Reef (Key Largo, Fla.). Home: 1001 W 58th Ter Kansas City MO 64113-1159 Office: 800 W 47th St Kansas City MO 64112-1251 E-mail: arrowrock@aol.com.

SIBBALD, JOHN RISTOW, management consultant; b. Lincoln, Nebr., June 20, 1936; s. Garth E.W. and Rachel (Wright) S.; m. Kathryn J. Costick; children: Allison, John, Wright. BA, U. Nev., 1958; MA, U. Ill., 1964. Office mgr. Hewitt Assocs., Libertyville, Ill., 1964-66; coll. rels. mgr. Pfizer Inc., N.Y.C., 1966-69; pres., CEO Re-Con Systems, 1969-70; v.p. Booz, Allen & Hamilton, 1970-73, Chgo., 1973-75; pres., founder John Sibbald Assocs., Inc., 1975. Mem. Nat. Advisory Coun., Nat. Club Assn. Author: The Career Makers, 1990, 92, The New Career Makers, 1995; pub. Club Leaders Forum; contbr. articles to profl. jours. Capt. AUS, 1958-64. Mem. Mid-Day Club Chgo., St. Louis Club. Episcopalian. Office: 7701 Forsyth Blvd Saint Louis MO 63105-1817

SIBLEY, WILLIS ELBRIDGE, anthropology educator, consultant; b. Nashville, Feb. 22, 1930; s. Elbridge and Elizabeth Reynolds (LaBarre) S.; m. Barbara Jean Grant, June 9, 1956; children: Sheila Katherine, Anthony Grant, Michael David. B.A., Reed Coll., 1951; M.A., U. Chgo., 1953, Ph.D., 1958. Instr. sociology and anthropology Miami (Ohio) U., 1956-58; asst. prof. anthropology U. Utah, 1958-60; from asst. prof. to prof. anthropology Wash. State U., 1960-71; prof. anthropology Cleve. State U., 1971—, chmn. dept., 1971-77, Cleve. (City) faculty fellow, 1987, interim chmn., 1989-90, prof. emeritus, 1990—; sr. program analyst EPA, Washington, 1977-78; Govtl. fellow Am. Coun. on Edn., 1978; Rockefeller Found. vis. prof. anthropology U. Philippines, Quezon City, 1968-69; postdoctoral fellow in society and tech. Carnegie-Mellon U., 1981-82. Fulbright grantee, 1954-55, 64; NIMH grantee, 1959-61; NSF grantee, 1964-71; Nat. Acad. Scis.-NRC travel grantee, 1966; Office Edn., HEW research grantee, 1967 Fellow AAAS, Assn. Profl. Anthropologists (pres. Washington chpt. 1999—), Am. Anthropol. Assn. (treas. 1989-91, alt. dir. Renewable Natural Resources Found., com. on pub. policy 2000-2002), Soc. Applied Anthropology (sec. 1977-80, pres. 1981-82); mem. AAUP (treas. Wash. State U. chpt. 1962-63, v.p. 1963-64, pres. 1965-66, pres. Cleve. State U. chpt. 1979-80, treas. 1980-81, interim pres. 1989-90), ACLU (pres. Pullman chpt. 1963, 66), Ctrl. States Anthropol. Soc. (past mem. exec. bd., treas. 1986-89), Wash. Assn. Profl. Anthropologists, Edgewater Yacht Club (Cleve., commodore 1991), Chesapeake Yacht Club (Shady Side, Md.) (gov. 1999, 2000). Home: PO Box 484 Shady Side MD 20764-0484 Office: Cleve State U Dept Anthropology Cleveland OH 44115 E-mail: shadyside@aol.com.

SICILIANI, ALESSANDRO DOMENICO, conductor; b. Florence, Italy; s. Francesco and Ambra Siciliani; m. Elizabeth Holleque; 1 child, Giacomo Francesco. Student, Giuseppe Verdi Milano Cons., Rome, Santa Cecilia; studied with, Franco Ferrara. Music advisor Columbus Symphony Orch., 1991—, music dir., 1992—. Condr. Nat. Radio Orchs. of Rome and Naples, Symphony of Abruzzi, Palermo Symphony Orch., Cagliari Symphony Orch., Bari Symphony Orch., N.Y. City Opera, Opera Co. of Phila., New Orleans Opera, Ky. Opera, Teatro San Carlo, Naples, Italy, Teatro dell'Opera, Rome, Teatro Massimo, Palermo, Italy, Verdi, Pisa, Italy, also Barcelona, Spain, Marseille, France, Avignon, and Liege; condr. revivals Cavalleria Rusticana, Pagliacci, N.Y. City Opera's revival La Rondine, Am. premiere Schubert's Fierrabras; appeared with Pitts. Symphony, Nat. Symphony, Washington, D.C., Munich Symphony Orch., Cologne Symphony Orch., Dresden Symphony Orch., Stockholm Symphony Orch., Goteborg Symphony Orch., Hong Kong Symphony Orch., Nat. Arts Ctr. Orch. of Ottawa, English Chamber Orch., Symphonia Varsovia, Perugia Chamber Orch., Padova Chamber Orch.; participant festivals including Schleswig-Holstein, Panatenee Pompeiane, Printemps Festival of Praha, Spring Festival in Saratoga Springs, Sagra Musicale Umbra; prin. guest condr. Orch. Teatro Colon, Buenos Aires, Teatro Mcpl. Sao Paulo. Recipient Amerigo Vespucci award, 1992. Office: Columbus Symphony Orch/Ohio Theater 55 E State St Columbus OH 43215-4203 also: Herbert Barrett Mgmt 1776 Broadway Ste 1610 New York NY 10019-2002

SICK, WILLIAM NORMAN, JR. venture capital company executive; b. Houston, Apr. 20, 1935; s. William Norman and Gladys Phylena (Armstrong) S.; m. Stephanie Anne Williams, Sept. 14, 1963; children: Jill Melanie, David Louis. BA, Rice U., 1957, BSEE, 1958. With Tex. Instruments Inc., various locations, 1958-87; exec. v.p. Tex. Instruments, Inc., Dallas, 1982-87; pres. semicondr. products group Tex. Instruments Inc., 1982-86; bd. dirs. Tex. Instruments, Inc., 1985-87; CEO Am. Nat. Can Co., Chgo., 1988-89; also bd. dirs. Am. Nat. Can. Co., 1988-89; mem. exec. com. Pechiney, Paris, 1989; bd. dirs. Pechiney Internat., 1989; vice chmn., bd. dirs. Triangle Industries, N.Y.C., 1988—89; chmn., CEO, Bus. Resources Internat., Winnetka, Ill., 1989—; managing dir. Signature Capital Mgmt., LLC, Northfield, 1997—. Co-founder Metasolv, Dallas; bd. dirs. Acoustic Techs., Mesa, Ariz., VIRxSYS, Gaithersburg, Md.; former chmn. Aware, Bedford, Mass., Power Trends, Warrenville, Ill.; guest lectr. Sophia U., Tokyo, 1973 Trustee, past chmn. Shedd Aquarium, Chgo.; trustee Rice U., 1996—, Santa Fe Inst. Mem. Chgo. Com., Exec. Club Chgo., Glenview Club, Sigma Xi, Tau Beta Pi, Sigma Tau. Episcopalian. Office: Bus Resources Internat PO Box 500 Winnetka IL 60093-0500 E-mail: wsick@sigcap.com.

SIDMAN, ROBERT JOHN, lawyer; b. Cleve., Aug. 4, 1943; s. Charles Frances and Louise (Eckert) S.; m. Mary Mato, July 29, 1967; children: Christa Mary, Alicia Mary. BA, Benedictine Coll., 1965; JD, U. Notre Dame, 1968. Bar: Ohio 1968, U.S. Dist. Ct. (so. dist.) Ohio 1970, U.S. Ct. Appeals (6th cir.) 1971, U.S. Supreme Ct. 1971. Law clk. U.S. Dist. Ct. (so. dist.) Ohio, Columbus, 1968-70; assoc. Mayer, Tingley & Hurd, 1970-75; judge Bankruptcy Ct. U.S. Dist. Ct. (so. dits.) Ohio, 1975-82; ptnr. Vorys, Sater, Seymour & Pease, 1982—. Prof. Ohio State U. Law Sch., Columbus, 1984, 85, 86. Mem. Nat. Conf. Bankruptcy Judges (bd. dirs. 1981-82), Assn. Former Bankruptcy Judges (bd. dirs. 1983-89, treas. 1986-87, pres. 1988-89). Office: Vorys Sater Seymour & Pease PO Box 1008 52 E Gay St Columbus OH 43215-3161 E-mail: rjsidman@vssp.com., rsidman843@aol.com.

SIEBEN, TODD, state legislator; b. Geneso, Ill., July 11, 1945; m. Kay Sieben; children: Rachel, Brandon, Meredith. BS, Western Ill. U., 1967. Commnr. Geneso Park Dist., 1977-87; mem. Henry County Planning Commn., 1978-80, 85-86; Ill. state rep. Dist. 73, 1987-92; vice chmn. fin. inst. com., mem. pub. utilities com. Ill. Ho. Reps., state govt. adminstrn. com., energy, environ. com., natural resources com., aging com., children com., small bus. com.; mem. Ill. State Senate Dist. 37, 1993—. Co-owner, v.p. Sieben Hybrids, Inc. Mem. Am. Legion, Geneso Rotary, VFW, Farm Bur., Masons. Home: 129 S College Ave Geneseo IL 61254-1317 Office: Ill Senate Mems State Capitol Rm 307 Springfield IL 62706-0001

SIEBENBURGEN, DAVID A. airline company executive; b. Cin., Sept. 18, 1947; s. Joseph and Elsie (Diersing) S.; m. Marcia Altieri, Sept. 27, 1974, 1 child, Brian. BBA, Xavier U., 1972. CPA, Ohio. Acct. Arthur Andersen & Co., Ohio, Ohio, 1974—; pres., COO Comair, Inc., Cin., 1984—. Mem. St. James Ch., Cin., 1980—, Community Chest, Cin. Republican. Roman Catholic. Office: Comair Inc PO Box 75106 Cincinnati OH 45275-5106

SIEBERT, CALVIN D. economist, educator; b. Hillsboro, Kans., Feb. 11, 1934; s. Ira and Margaret (Everett) S.; m. Valerie Dawn Nanninga, Feb. 18, 1960; children— Douglas Erik, Derek Christopher. BA, U. Kans., 1958, MA, 1960; PhD in Econs., U. Calif., Berkeley, 1966. Asst. prof. econs. U. Iowa, 1965-68, assoc. prof., 1968-75, prof., 1975—, chmn. dept., 1969-71, 75-79. Rockefeller Found. vis. asso. prof. U. Philippines, 1971-72 Contbr. articles to profl. jours. With U.S. Army, 1954-56. Ford Found. grantee, 1964-65 Mem. Am. Econ. Assn., Phi Beta Kappa. Home: 341 N 7th Ave Iowa City IA 52245-6003 Office: U Iowa Dept Econs S318 Pbb Iowa City IA 52242 E-mail: calvin_siebert@uiowa.edu.

SIEDLECKI, NANCY THERESE, lawyer, funeral director; b. Chgo., May 30, 1954; d. LeRoy John and Dorothy Josephine (Wilczynski) Schielka; m. Jonathan Francis Siedlecki, June 18, 1977; children: Samantha Ann, Abigail Marie. Student Triton Jr. Coll., 1971-73; grad. funeral dir., Worsham Coll., 1974; student Loyola U., Chgo., 1974-76., U. Ill.-Chgo., 1976-77; JD with honors, Chgo.-Kent Coll. Law, 1980. Bar: Ill. 1980. Paralegal in real estate Rosenberg, Savner & Unikel, Chgo., 1974-77; pvt. practice law, Burr Ridge, Ill., 1980—; cons. probate and various small bus. corps., Chgo., 1980—. Mem. ABA, Ill. State Bar Assn., Chgo. Bar Assn. Roman Catholic. Office: 5300 Main St Downers Grove IL 60515-4846

SIEDLER, ARTHUR JAMES, nutrition and food science educator; b. Milw., Mar. 17, 1927; s. Arthur William and Margaret (Stadler) S.; m. Doris Jean Northrop, Feb. 23, 1976; children: William, Nancy Siedler Wilhite, Sandra Siedler Lowman, Roxanne Rose Butler, Randy Rose. BS, U. Wis., 1951; MS, U. Chgo., 1956, PhD, 1959. Chief div. biochemistry and nutrition Am. Meat Inst. Found., Chgo., 1959-64; group leader Norwich (N.Y.) Pharmacal Co., 1964-65, chief physiology sect., 1965-69, chief biochemistry sect., 1969-72; acting dir. div. nutritional scis. U. Ill., Urbana, 1978-81, head dept. food sci., 1972-89, prof. food sci., internal medicine and nutritional scis., 1972-94, prof. emeritus, 1994—. Patentee in field. With USCG, 1945-46, PTO. NIH research grantee, 1960-63; Nat. Livestock and Meat Bd. grantee, 1959-64 Mem. Inst. Food Technologists, Am. Chem. Soc., Am. Soc. Nutritional Scis., Coun. for Agrl. Sci. and Tech., Eagles, Moose, Sigma Xi. Home: 8 Stanford Pl Champaign IL 61820-7620 Office: 382M Ag Eng Sci 1304 W Pennsylvania Ave Urbana IL 61801-4713 E-mail: asiedler@uiuc.edu.

SIEFERS, ROBERT GEORGE, banker; b. Pitts., Aug. 28, 1945; s. George Francis and Idella Alice (Eiler) S.; m. Janice Lynn Kirkpatrick, Mar. 25, 1970; children: Robert Scott, Jillian Stewart B.A., Mt. Union Coll., 1967; M.B.A., Kent State U., 1971; J.D., Cleveland Marshall Law Sch., 1976. Security analyst Nat. City Bank, Cleve., 1971-76, v.p., investment rsch. dir., 1976-80, v.p. adminstrn. and rsch., 1980-82; sr. v.p. corp. planning Nat. City Corp., 1982-85; sr. v.p. corp. banking Nat. City Bank, 1985-86; pres., chief exec. officer Ohio Citizens Bank (affiliate Nat. City Corp.), Toledo, 1986-90; vice chmn., CFO Nat. City Corp., Cleve., 1997—. Bd. dirs. HCR Corp. Bd. trustees Mt. Union Coll. Republican. Presbyterian Club: Chagrin Valley Country. Office: Nat City Corp 1900 E 9th St Cleveland OH 44114-3401 Home: 104 Partridge Ln Chagrin Falls OH 44022-4010

SIEG, STANLEY A. military official; B in Bus. Adminstrn., U. N.Mex., 1970; M in Bus. Adminstrn., U. Okla., 1971; grad., Squadron Officer Sch., 1974, Armed Forces Staff Coll., 1981, Air War Coll., 1987. Commd. 2d lt. USAF, 1970, advanced through grades to brigadier gen., 1998; chief Comdr.'s Mgmt. Rsch. Office, exec. officer to comdr. Hdqs. Air Force Contract Mgmt. Divsn., Kirtland AFB, N.Mex., 1977-81; comdr., DOD plant rep. Def. Contract Adminstrn. Svcs. Plant Rep. Office, ITT, Nutley, N.J., 1981-84; comdr. Air Force Contract Maintenance Ctr., Kimhae Internat. Airport, South Korea, 1984-86; chief item mgmt. divsn. Oklahoma City Air Logistics Ctr., Tinker AFB, Okla., 1987-89; chief sys. and logistics contracting divsn. Office of Asst. Sec. of Air Force for Acquisition, USAF, Washington, 1989-91; inspector gen. Hdqs. Air Force Materiel Command, Wright-Patterson AFB, Ohio, 1993-95; dir. propulsion Oklahoma City Air Logistics Ctr., Tinker AFB, 1995-97; dir. logistics Hdqs. Air Force Materiel Command, Wright-Patterson AFB, 1997—, dir. contracting, 2000—. Decorated Legion of Merit with oak leaf cluster, Def. Meritorious Svc. medal, Meritorious Svc. medal with 2 oak leaf clusters. Office: 4375 HQ AFMC/PK Chidlaw Rd S208 Wright Patterson AFB OH 45433-5006

SIEGAL, BURTON LEE, product designer, consultant, inventor; b. Chgo., Sept. 27, 1931; s. Norman A. and Sylvia (Vitz) S.; m. Rita Goran, Apr. 11, 1954; children: Norman, Laurence Scott BS in Mech. Engring., U. Ill., 1953. Torpedo designer U.S. Naval Ordnance, Forest Park, Ill., 1953-54; chief engr. Gen. Aluminum Corp., Chgo., 1954-55; product designer Chgo. Aerial Industries, Melrose Park, Ill., 1955-58; chief designer Emil J. Paidar Co., Chgo., 1958-59; founder, pres. Budd Engring. Corp., 1959—. Dir. Dur-A-Case Corp., Chgo.; design cons. to numerous corps. Holder more than 125 patents in more than 40 fields including multimemory for power seats and electrified office panel sys., Piezo ink jet valves; contbr. articles to tech. publs. Mem. math., sci. and English adv. bds. Niles Twp. High Schs., Skokie, Ill., 1975-79; electronic cons. Chgo. Police Dept., 1964 Winner, Internat. Extrusion Design Competition, 1975; nominated Presdl. Medal Technology Sen. Paul Simon and Rep. Dan Rostenkowski, 1986; named Inventor of Yr. Patent Law Assn. Chgo., 1986. Mem. ASME, Soc. Plastics Engrs., Soc. Mfg. Engrs., Inventor's Coun., Soc. Automotive Engrs., Pres.'s Assn. Ill.

SIEGAL, RITA GORAN, engineering company executive; b. Chgo., July 16, 1934; d. Leonard and Anabelle (Soloway) Goran; m. Burton L. Siegal, Apr. 11, 1954; children: Norman, Laurence Scott. Student, U. Ill., 1951-53; BA, DePaul U., 1956. Cert. elem. tchr., Ill. Tchr. Chgo. Public Schs., 1956-58; founder, chief exec. officer Budd Engring. Corp., Skokie, Ill., 1959—; founder, pres. Easy Living Products Co., 1960—; pvt. practice in interior design, Chgo., 1968-73; dist. sales mgr. Super Girls, Skokie, 1976. Lectr. Northwestern U., 1983; guest speaker nat. radio and TV, 1979—. Contbr. to profl. jours. Mem. adv. bd. Skokie High Schs., 1975-79; advisor Cub Scouts Skokie coun. Boy Scouts Am., 1975; bus. mgr. Nutrition for Optimal Health Assn., Winnetka, Ill., 1980-82, pres., 1982-84, v.p. med./profl., 1985-93; leader Great Books Found., 1972; founder Profit Plus Investment, 1970; bd. dirs. Noha, Internat. Named Prominent Alumni, Sullivan H.S., 2001; recipient Cub Scout awards, Boy Scouts Am., 1971—72, Nat. Charlotte Danstrom award, Nat. Women of Achievement, 1988, Corp. Achievement award, 1988. Mem. North Shore Women in Mgmt. (pres, 1987-88), Presidents Assn. Ill. (bd. dirs 1990-94, membership chair 1991-93), Inventors Coun., Oriental Art Soc. Chgo. (publicity chair).

SIEGEL, BARRY ALAN, nuclear radiologist; b. Nashville, Dec. 30, 1944; s. Walter Gross Siegel and Lillian B. Ivener; m. Pamela M. Mandel, Aug. 18, 1968 (div. Mar. 1981); children: Peter A., William A.; m. Marilyn J. Siegel, Jan. 29, 1983. AB, Washington U., St. Louis, 1966, MD, 1969. Diplomate Am. Bd. Nuclear Medicine, Am. Bd. Radiology. Intern Barnes Hosp., St. Louis, 1969-70; resident in radiology and nuc. medicine fellow Mallinckrodt Inst. Radiology, Washington U., 1970-73, dir. div. nuc. medicine, 1973—, asst. prof., 1973-76, assoc. prof., 1976-79, prof. radiology, 1979—, assoc. prof. medicine, 1980-83, prof. medicine, 1983—. Dir. Am. Bd. Nuc. Medicine, L.A., 1985-90, sec., 1990; chmn. adv. com. on med. uses of isotopes NRC, Washington, 1990-96; chmn. radiopharm. drugs adv. com. U.S. FDA, Rockville, Md., 1982-85, radiol. devices panel, 1992-95; mem. U.S. Pharmacopeia Adv. Panel on Radiopharms., 1975-2000, Armed Forces Radiobiol. Rsch. Inst., Bethesda; coun. experts, chair Radiopharm. Expert Com., U.S. Pharmacopoeial Conv., 2000—. Author, editor 33 books; contbr. articles to profl. jours., chpts. in books. Maj. USAF, 1974-76. Recipient Commr.'s Spl. citation U.S. FDA, 1988, Honor citation U.S. Pharmacopeial Conv., 1995, 2000. Fellow ACP, Am. Coll. Radiology (vice chmn. commn. on nuc. medicine 1981-93, editor in chief profl. self evaluation program 1988-2002), Am. Coll. Nuc. Physicians; mem. AMA, Am. Roentgen Ray Soc., Assn. Univ. Radiologists, Radiol. Soc. N.Am., Soc. Nuclear Medicine (trustee 1981-85, 87-91), Acad. Molecular Imaging (chair Inst. Clin. PET coun. 2001-). Office: Washington U Mallinckrodt Inst Radiology 510 S Kingshighway Blvd Saint Louis MO 63110-1016 E-mail: siegelb@mir.wustl.edu.

SIEGEL, HOWARD JEROME, lawyer; b. Chgo., July 29, 1942; s. Leonard and Idele (Lehrner) S.; m. Diane L. Gerber; children: Sari D., Allison J., James G. BS, U. Ill., 1963; JD, Northwestern U., 1966. Bar: Ill. 1966, U.S. Dist. Ct. (no. dist.) Ill. 1967. Assoc. Ancel, Stonesifer & Glink, Chgo., 1966-70; ptnr. Goldstine & Siegel, Summit, Ill., 1970-75; sole practice Chgo., 1975-77; pres. Wexler, Siegel & Shaw, Ltd., 1978-82; ptnr. Keck, Mahin & Cate, 1982-95, Neal Gerber & Eisenberg, Chgo., 1995-99; counsel Fagel & Haber, 1999—. Bd. dirs. various corps. Mem.: ABA, Chgo. Bar Assn., Ill. Bar Assn., Twin Orchard Country Club (Long Grove. Ill.). Office: FabelHaberLLC 55 E Monroe 40th Fl Chicago IL 60603 E-mail: hsiegel@fagelhaber.com.

SIEGEL, ROBERT, heat transfer engineer; b. Cleve., July 10, 1927; s. Morris and Mollie (Binder) S.; m. Elaine Jane Jaffe, July 19, 1951; children: Stephen, Lawrence. BS, Case Inst. Tech., 1950, MS, 1951; ScD, MIT, 1953. Heat transfer engr. GE, Schenectady, N.Y., 1953-54; heat transfer analyst Knolls Atomic Power Lab., 1954-55; rsch. scientist NASA Lewis Rsch. Ctr., Cleve., 1955-99; tech. cons., 1999—. Adj. prof. U. Toledo, 1981, 85, 95, adj. prof. mech. engring. U. Akron (Ohio), 1987, adj. prof. mech. engring. Cleve. State U., 1989, 91; mem. adv. coun. U. Akron, 1989-96. Author: Thermal Radiation Heat Transfer, 1972, 4th edit., 2001; tech. editor ASME, 1973-83, AIAA, 1986-98; author numerous sci. papers. With U.S. Army, 1945-47. Recipient Exceptional Sci. Achievement medal NASA, 1986, Space Act award, 1993, ASME-AIChE Max Jakob Meml. award, 1996. Fellow ASME (Heat Transfer Meml. award 1970, Max Jakob Bd. of award 1999-2002), AIAA (Thermophysics award 1993); mem. Sigma Xi, Tau Beta Pi. Jewish. Avocations: ballroom dancing, piano. Home and Office: 3052 Warrington Rd Shaker Heights OH 44120-2425

SIEGLER, MARK, internist, educator; b. N.Y.C., June 20, 1941; s. Abraham J. and Florence (Sternlieb) S.; m. Anna Elizabeth Hollinger, June 4, 1967; children:Dillan, Alison, Richard, Jessica. AB with honors, Princeton U., 1963; MD, U. Chgo., 1967. Diplomate Am. Bd. Internal Medicine. Resident, chief resident internal medicine U. Chgo., 1967-71;

hon. sr. registrar in medicine Royal Postgrad. Med. Sch., London, 1971-72; asst. prof. medicine U. Chgo., 1972-78, assoc. prof. medicine, 1979-85, acting dir. div. gen. internal medicine, 1983-85, dir. MacLean Ctr. Clin. Med. Ethics, 1984—, prof. medicine, 1985—, Lindy Bergman prof., 1997-2000, Lindy Bergman Disting. Svc. prof., 2000—, dir. fellowship tng. program in clin. med. ethics, 1986—. Vis. asst. prof. medicine U. Wis., Madison, 1977; vis. assoc. prof. medicine U. Va., Charlottesville, 1981-82. Co-author: Clinical Ethics, 1981, 2d edit., 1986, 3d edit., 1992, 4th edit., 1998, 5th edit., 2002, An Annotated Bibliography of Medical Ethics, 1988, Institutional Protocols for Decisions About Life-Sustaining Treatment, 1988; co-editor: Changing Values in Medicine, 1985, Medical Innovations and Bad Outcomes, 1987; editl. bd.: Am. Jour. Medicine, 1979—94, editl. bd.: , 1997—, editl. bd.: Archives Internal Medicine, 1979—90, editl. bd.: Bibliography of Bioethics, Jour. Med. Philosophy, 1978—89, editl. bd.: Jour. Med. Philosophy, 1978—89, editl. bd.: Jour. Clin. Ethics , 1989—, editl. bd.: Jour. Med. Ethics (London), 2002—; contbr. articles. Mem. adv. bd. Bioethics Inst., Madrid, Notre Dame Ctr. for Ethics and Culture. Grantee Andrew W. Mellon Found., Henry J. Kaiser Family Found., Pew Charitable Trusts, Field Found. Ill., Ira De Camp Found., Gaylord & Dorothy Donnelley Found.; Phi Beta Kappa vis. scholar, 1991-92, Chirone prize Italian Nat. Acad. Medicine, 1996; mem. NAS Cloning Panel, 2001-02, others. Fellow ACP (human rights com., ethics com. 1985-90), Hastings Ctr.; mem. ACS (ethics com. 1992—), Assn. Am. Physicians, Chgo. Clin. Ethics Program (pres. 1989-90). Office: Univ Chgo MC 6098 MacLean Ctr Clin Med Ethics 5841 S Maryland Ave Chicago IL 60637-1463

SIEGRIST, BRENT, state legislator; b. Council Bluffs, Iowa, Sept. 30, 1952; m. Valerie Siegrist; children: Evan, Harriet. BA, Dana Coll., 1974; postgrad., U. Nebr. Former govt. tchr. Mo. Valley High Sch.; mem. 84th dist. Iowa House of Reps., Des Moines, 1984—, speaker, 1999—. Asst. minority leader 73rd and 74th Gen. Assembly Iowa House of Reps., majority leader 75th and 76th Gen. Assembly, mem. adminstrn. & rules com. Active ISEA, NEA, Bluffs Arts Coun., St. Patrick's Cath. Ch.; past pres. Mo. Valley Edn. Assn.; mem. adv. bd. Ret. Vols. Program, Southwest Iowa Regents Grad. Resource Ctr. Republican. Home: 204 Lori Ln Council Bluffs IA 51503 Office: State Capitol Des Moines IA 50319 E-mail: brent_siegrist@legis.state.ia.us.

SIEKERT, ROBERT GEORGE, neurologist; b. Milw., July 23, 1924; s. Hugo Paul and Elisa (Kraus) S.; m. Mary Jane Evans, Feb. 17, 1951; children: Robert G. Jr., John E., Friedrich A.P. BS, Northwestern U., 1945, MS, 1947, MD, 1948. Diplomate Am. Bd. Psychiatry and Neurology. Instr. anatomy U. Pa., Phila., 1948-49; fellow neurology Mayo Found., Rochester, Minn., 1950-54; cons. Mayo Clinic, 1954-91, head neurology sect., 1966-76, bd. govs., 1973-80, prof. neurology med. sch., 1969-91, prof. emeritus neurology, 1991—. Chmn. Internat. Stroke Conf. Am. Heart Assn., 1976-80. Editor Mayo Clinic Procs., 1982-86; cons. editor Jour. Stroke, 1992-2001; contbr. articles to profl. jours.; described transient cerebral ischemic attacks. Trustee Mayo Found., Rochester, 1973-81, chmn. emeritus com., 1997-98. Served to lt. j.g. M.C., USNR, 1950-52. Recipient Disting. Achievement award, Am. Heart Assn., 1984, Merit award, 1989, Robert G. Siekert Young Investigator award Am. Heart Assn., 1986. Fellow Am. Coll. Physicians; mem. Am. Neurol. Assn., Northwestern U. Med. Sch. Alumni Assn. (Service award 1983), Swiss Neurol. Soc. (corr.), Alpha Omega Alpha. Avocation: philately. Office: Mayo Clinic 200 1st St SW N-10 Rochester MN 55905-0002

SIEKMANN, DONALD CHARLES, accountant; b. St. Louis, July 2, 1938; s. Elmer Charles and Mabel Louise (Blue) S.; m. Linda Lee Knowles, Sept. 10, 1966; 1 child, Brian Charles. BS, Washington U., St. Louis, 1960. CPA, Ohio, Ga. Regional mng. ptnr. Arthur Andersen & Co., Cin., 1960-98. Columnist Cin. Enquirer, 1983-86, Gannett News Services, 1983-86; editor "Tax Clinic" column Tax Advisor mag., 1974-75. Mem. bd. Cin. Zool. Soc., 1985-88; officer, bd. dirs. Cin. Found. for Pub. TV, 1984-88, Cin. Symphony Orch., 1973-85, Cin. Ballet Co., 1973-88, Atlanta Symphony Orch., 1988-91, The Atlanta Opera, 1988-91, Cin. Theatrical Assn., Jewish Hosp., 1993—, Cin. Assn. for Performing Arts, 1992—, Cin. United Way, 1992-99, Cin. Pk. Bd. Found., 1995-98; pres. Greater Cin. Arts and Edn. Ctr., 1996-99; mem. Friends of Sch. for Creative and Performing Arts, 1996-99, Cin. Arts Festival, 1992-96, Ronald McDonald House, 1998—. Mem. AICPA, Ohio Soc. CPAs, Cin. Country Club (trustee 1983-88), Optimists Club (pres. Queen City chpt. 1986). Lutheran. Club: Cin. Country (trustee 1983-88). Home: 5495 Waring Dr Cincinnati OH 45243-3933 Office: Arthur Andersen & Co 425 Walnut St Ste 1500 Cincinnati OH 45202-3946 E-mail: dsiekmann@aol.com.

SIEMER, PAUL JENNINGS, public relations executive; b. St. Louis, Jan. 24, 1946; s. Robert Vincent and Pauline Mary (Nece) S.; m. Susan MacDonald Arnott, Aug. 26, 1967 Student, U. Notre Dame, 1964-67. Reporter South Bend Tribune, Ind., 1967-69; reporter St. Louis Globe-Democrat, 1969-76; account exec. Fleishman-Hillard Inc., St. Louis, 1976-79, v.p., sr. ptnr., 1979-84, exec. v.p., sr. ptnr., 1984-95; ptnr. Stolberg & Siemer Inc., 1995—. Mem. Pub. Relations Soc. Am. Roman Catholic. Home: 2961 Hatherly Dr Saint Louis MO 63121-4551 Office: Stolberg & Siemer Inc 1608 Menard St Saint Louis MO 63104-3702

SIEPMANN, JOERN ILJA, chemistry educator; b. Cologne, Germany, June 28, 1964; came to U.S., 1993; m. Silke Schmid, Mar. 22, 1990; children: Tim Christoph, Ines Vivian. PhD, Cambridge (Eng.) U., 1992. Postdoctoral fellow IBM Zurich Rsch. Lab., Rüschlikon, Switzerland, 1991-92, Koninklijke/Shell Lab., Amsterdam, The Netherlands, 1992-93; rsch. assoc. U. Pa., Phila., 1993-94; asst. prof. chemistry U. Minn., Mpls., 1994-2000, assoc. prof. chemistry, 2000—. Recipient Dreyfus New Faculty award Dreyfus Found., 1994; Alfred P. Sloan Rsch. fellow, 1998. Mem. AIChE, Am. Chem. Soc. Achievements include research on configurational bias Monte Carlo of complex fluids. Office: U Minn Dept Chemistry 207 Pleasant St SE Minneapolis MN 55455-0431

SIERLES, FREDERICK STEPHEN, psychiatrist, educator; b. Bklyn., Nov. 9, 1942; s. Samuel and Elizabeth (Meiselman) S.; m. Laurene Harriet Cohn, Oct. 25, 1970 (div. Aug. 1990); children: Hannah Beth Alterson, Joshua Caleb. AB, Columbia U., 1963; MD, Chgo. Med. Sch., 1967. Diplomate Am. Bd. Psychiatry and Neurology. Intern Cook County Hosp., Chgo., 1967-68; resident in psychiatry Mt. Sinai Hosp., N.Y.C., 1968-69, Chgo. Med. Sch., 1969-71, chief resident, 1970-71; staff psychiatrist U.S. Reynolds Army Hosp., Ft. Sill, Okla., 1971-73; assoc. attending psychiatrist Mt. Sinai Hosp., Chgo., 1973-74; instr. psychiatry Chgo. Med. Sch., North Chicago, 1973—, asst. prof., 1974-78, assoc. prof., 1978-88; prof. Finch U. Health Scis., Chgo. Med. Sch., 1988—, vice chmn., 1990-94, acting chmn., 1994-95, chmn., 1995—2002, chmn. ednl. affairs com., 1983-85, 86-01, residency dir., 1999-2001. Cons. psychiatry Cook County Hosp., 1974-79, St. Mary of Nazareth Hosp., 1979-84, Gt. Lakes Naval Hosp., 1987-90, Jackson Park Hosp., 1987-89, Mt. Sinai Hosp., 1988—, Elgin Mental Health Ctr., 1997—; chief mental health clinic, North Chicago VA Hosp., 1982-85, chief psychiatry svc., 1983-85. Author: (wth others) General Hospital Psychiatry, 1985, Behavioral Science for the Boreds, 1987, rev. 2d edit., 1989, rev. 3d edit., 1993; editor: Clinical Behavioral Science, 1982, Behavioral Science for Medical Students, 1993, USMLE Behavioral Science Made Ridiculously Simple, 1998; editl. bd. Acad. Psychiatry, 2000—; contbr. articles to profl. jours. Coach Glenview (Ill.) Youth Baseball, 1987-89, mgr. 1990 (age 10-12 Glenview World Series winner 1990), Glenview Tennis Club, 1986-90 (3.5 Men's Doubles League winner 1989-90). Maj. M.C., U.S. Army, 1971-73. N.Y.State Regents scholar, 1959-63; NIMH grantee, 1974-83, Chgo. Med. Sch. grantee, 1974-83. Fellow Am. Psychiat. Assn. (coun. edn. and career devel. 1993-95); mem. Am. Coll. Psychiatrists, Ill. Psychiat. Soc. (fellowship com. 1985-99), Columbia Coll. Alumni Secondary Schs. Com., Assn. Dirs. Med. Student Edn. in Psychiatry (exec. coun. 1985-99, chmn. program com. 1987-88, treas. 1989-91, pres-elect 1991-93, pres. 1993-95, immediate past pres. 1995-99), Alliance for Clin. Edn., Am. Assn. Chmn. Depts. Psychiatry, Chgo. Consortium for Psychiat. Rsch. (sec. 1996-97, treas. 1997-99), Am. Assn. Dirs. Psychiat. Residency Tng. (exec. coun. 2000—, chair workforce coalition 2000—), Sigma Xi, Alpha Omega Alpha, Phi Epsilon Pi. Office: Finch U Health Sci Chgo Med Sch 3333 Green Bay Rd North Chicago IL 60064-3037 E-mail: sierlesf@finchcms.edu.

SIERRA-AMOR, ROSA ISABEL, health facility administrator; b. Tampico, Mex., Apr. 28, 1954; Licensure Degree in Clin. Biochemistry, Nat. Autonomous U. Mexico, 1979, MS, 1992, PhD, 1995; postgrad., U. Reading, Eng., 1986. Fellow dept. endocrinology and metabolism Jewish Hosp. and Washington U. Sch. Medicine, St. Louis, 1982; mem. staff dept. nephrology and mineral metabolism, assoc. investigator Nat. Inst. Nutrition Salvador Zubiran, Mexico City, 1978-90; dir. Mineral Metabolism Rsch. Lab., divsn. neonatology Children's Hosp.-U. Cin. Med. Ctr., 1990-96; lab. mgr. Pediat. Bone Rsch. Ctr. Children's Hosp. Med. Ctr., 1996—. Lectr. in field. Contbr. articles to profl. jours. Recipient Ames/Bayer L.Am. award, 1993, award Mexican Coll. Profls. in Chemistry, 1994. Mem.: Spanish Soc. Clin. Chemistry and Molecular Pathology, Iberoamerican Soc. for Rsch. on Bone Metabolism, Nat. Acad. Pharm. Scis. (Mexico), Mexican Assn. Clin. Biochemistry, Am. Assn. for Bone and Mineral Rsch., Am. Assn. for Clin. Chemistry (mem. internat. rels. com. 1992—94, chair OVS membership com. 1994, mem. internat. adv. panel 1994—96, chair exch. program in clin. chemistry OVS 1994—, chair Ohio Valley sect. awards com. 1997—, Internat. Fellowship award 1996, Bernard Katchman ann. award 2001), Mex. Assn. Clin. Biochemistry (mem. congress organizing com. 1986, chair continuing edn. com., mem. sci. program, treas. pediat. maternal, fetal divsn. 1986—, chmn. sci. proc. 8th internat. congress on lab. automation), Internat. Fedn. Clin. Chemistry (alt. rep. to Mexican Assn. Clin. Biochemistry 1992—96, newsletter corr. and reviewer jour. 1992—, mem. sci. program XVII Internat. Congress in Clin. Chemistry 1996—, assoc. mem. com. in metabolic bone disease and bone markers sci. divsn 1996—, mem. at large 1997—99, mem. EB 2000—). Office: Childrens Hosp Med Ctr CRC CH 3d Fl H Bldg 3333 Burnet Ave Cincinnati OH 45229-3039 E-mail: sierr0@chmcc.org.

SIESS, CHESTER PAUL, civil engineering educator; b. Alexandria, La., July 28, 1916; s. Leo C. and Adele (Liebreich) S.; m. Helen Kranson, Oct. 5, 1941; 1 dau., Judith Ann. B.S., La. State U., 1936; M.S., U. Ill., 1939, Ph.D., 1948. Party chief La. Hwy. Commn., 1936-37; research asst. U. Ill., 1937-39; soil engr. Chgo. Subway Project, 1939-41; engr., draftsman N.Y.C. R.R. Co., 1941; mem. faculty U. Ill., 1941—, prof. civil engring., 1955-78, emeritus, head dept. civil engring., 1973-78. Mem. adv. com. on reactor safeguards Nuclear Regulatory Commn., 1968-92, chmn., 1972 Recipient award Concrete Reinforcing Steel Inst., 1956, Alumni Honor award for disting. service in engring. U. Ill., 1985, Disting. Service award NRC, 1987; named to Engring. Hall of Distinction, La. State U., 1979. Mem. ASCE (hon. mem., Rsch. prize 1956, Howard medal 1968, Reese award 1970), Nat. Acad. Engring., Am. Concrete Inst. (pres. 1974-75, Wason medal 1949, Turner medal 1964, hon. mem.), Reinforced Concrete Rsch. coun. (chmn. 1968-80, Boase award 1974), Internat. Assn. Bridge and Structural Engring., Sigma Xi, Tau Beta Pi, Phi Kappa Phi, Omicron Delta Kappa, Gamma Alpha, Chi Epsilon (chap. hon., nat. hon.). Achievements include research in reinforced and prestressed concrete structures and hwy. bridges. Home: 401 Burwash Dr Savoy IL 61874-9215 E-mail: c-siess@uiuc.edu.

SIFFERLEN, NED, university president; m. Joyce Sifferlen; 2 children (twins). BS, U. Dayton, 1963, MS, 1967; EdD, U. Cin., 1974. Instr. bus. techs. Miami Jacobs Jr. Coll., 1963-65; from instr. to asst. prof. to assoc. prof. bus. techs. Sinclair C.C., Dayton, Ohio, 1965-69, dean bus. techs., 1969-79, v.p. for adminstrn., 1979-81, v.p. for instrn., 1981-91, pres., 1997—. Cons. on ednl. programs Am. Coun. on Edn., Washington; workshop presenter on experience-based edn. Am. Tech. Assn., Cin.; chair examining teams for propietary cosmetology schs. Cosmetology Accrediting Commn., Washington; reviewer coll. and univ. ednl. programs Mil. Installation Vol. Edn. Rev., Rota, Spain and Redstone Arsenal, Ala.; presenter experiential edn. concepts Union Coll., Barbourville, Ky; editor Nat. Coun. for Occupl. Edn. Quar. Co-author: (manual) Participative Management Manual; contbr. articles to profl. publs. Sec. Dayton Area Progress Coun.; bd. dirs. Goodwill Industries, Downtown Dayton Assn.; mem. supt.'s adv. com. for vocat. edn. Dayton City Schs.; pres. Nat. Coun. Occupl. Edn., Washington; past pres. coun. chief instrnl. officers Ohio Tech. and C.C. Assn., Columbus; chair various divsn. United Way. Office: Sinclair CC 444 W 3rd St Dayton OH 45402-1421

SIGERSON, CHARLES WILLARD, JR. insurance agency executive; b. Biloxi, Miss., Mar. 6, 1945; s. Charles Willard and Eugenia (Linstad) S.; m. Elizabeth Ann Moss, Dec. 9, 1967; children: Anthea Louise, Andrew Charles. B in Gen. Studies, U. Nebr., Omaha, 1971. Pres., owner Sigerson Ins. Agy., Inc., Omaha, 1973—. Pres. Floyd Rogers Diabetic Found., Lincoln, Nebr., 1981—; mem. Douglas County Stand-by Draft Bd., Omaha, 1982—; chmn. Douglas County Rep. Com., Omaha, 1982-83, 90-93; mem. exec. com. Nebr. Rep. Com., Lincoln, 1982-83, 86-88, 90—; chmn. Nebr. Rep. Party, 1995—. Staff sgt. USAF, 1964-71. Recipient Cosmopolitan of Yr.award I-80 Cosmopolitan Club, 1982, Patrick hodgins award I-80 Cosmopolitan Club, 1983, Legion of Honor ward State Farm Ins. Co., 1984. Mem. Nat. Assn. Health Underwriters, Nat. Assn. Ins. and Fin. Advisors, Soc. Fin. Svc. Profls., Nat. Assn. Life Underwriters, Rotary Internat., Masons, Christian Missionary Alliance. Presbyterian. Avocations: genealogy, antique book and newspaper collecting, coin collecting. Home: 11435 Grand Cir Omaha NE 68164-2109 Office: Sigerson Ins Agy Inc 10766 Fort St Omaha NE 68134-1230

SIGLER, HOLLIS, artist, educator, author; b. Gary, Ind., Mar. 2, 1948; Studied in Florence, Italy, 1968-69; BFA, Moore Coll. Art, 1970, DFA (hon.), 1994; MFA, Sch. Art Inst. Chgo., 1973. Mem. faculty Columbia Coll., Chgo., 1978—, instr. painting and drawing, 1984—. One-woman shows include Akron (Ohio) Art Mus., 1986, S.W. Craft Ctr., San Antonio, 1989, Nat. Mus. Women Arts, Washington, 1991, 93, Printworks Gallery, Chgo., 1991, 93, Priebe Art Gallery, U. Wis., Oshkosh, 1992, Susan Cummins Gallery, Mill Valley, Calif., 1992, 94, Steven Scott Gallery, Balt., 1993, 94, Hartman Ctr. Gallery, Bradley U., Peoria, Ill., 1994, Mus. Contemporary Art, Chgo., 1994, Suburban Fine Arts Ctr., Highland Park, Ill., 1994, Lakeview Mus. Arts and Sci., Peoria, 1994, Decordova Mus. and Sculpture Park, Lincoln, Mass., 1994, Leedy-Voulkos Art Ctr. Gallery, Kansas City, Mo., 1995, Ark. Art Ctr., Little Rock, 1996, Elvehjem Mus. Art., U. Wis., Madison, 1997, Palo Alto Cultural Ctr., Calif., 1998, Carl Hammer Gallery, Chgo., 1998, Printworks Gallery, Chgo., 1999; exhibited in group shows Whitney Mus. Art, N.Y.C., 1981, Walker Art Mus., Mpls., 1982, Mus. Modern Art, N.Y.C., 1984, Corcoran Gallery Art, Washington, 1985, Chgo. Cultural Ctr., 1992, The Drawing Ctr., N.Y.C., 1993, The Contemporary Mus., Honolulu, 1994, Butler Inst. Am. Art, Youngstown, Ohio, 1995, Nat. Mus. Am. Art, Smithsonian, Washington, 1996, Corcoran Sch. of Art and U.S. Senate, Russell Rotunda Gallery, Washington, 1998; represented in permanent collections Mus. Contemporary Art, Chgo., Indpls. Mus. Art, Seattle Art Mus., Madison Art Ctr., High Mus. Art, Atlanta, Nat. Mus. Am. Art, Smithsonian, Nat. Mus. Women in the Arts, Washington, John D. and Catherine T. MacArthur Found., Johns Hopkins Hosp. Oncology Ctr., Balt.; pub.: Hollis Sigler's Breast Cancer Journal, 1999; also others. Recipient cash award Southwestern Ctr. for Contemporary Art, Winston-Salem, N.C., 1987, Childe Hassam purchase award AAAL, 1988; grantee Ill. Arts Coun., 1986, Nat. Endowment for Arts, 1987. Office: Columbia Coll 600 S Michigan Ave Chicago IL 60605-1900

SIGMON, JOYCE ELIZABETH, professional society administrator; b. Stanley, N.C., Oct. 4, 1935; d. Rome Alfred and Pearl Elizabeth (Beal) S. BS, U. N.C., 1971; MA, Loyola U., 1980. Cert. dental asst., assn. exec. Dental asst. Dr. Paul A. Stroup, Jr., Charlotte, N.C., 1953-63; instr. Wayne Tech. Inst., Goldsboro, 1963-65, Ctrl. Piedmont Community Coll., Charlotte, 1965-69; dir. Dental Assisting Edn. ADA, Chgo., 1971-85, asst. sec. Coun. Prosthetics Svcs., 1985-87, mgr. Office Quality Assurance, 1987—90, exec. dir. Aux., 1990-92; dir. adminstrv. activities Am. Acad. of Implant Dentistry, 1993—; exec. sec. Am. Bd. of Oral Implantology/Implant Dentistry, 1993-99. Deacon 4th Presbyn. Ch., 1973-75, elder 1975-77, 88-91, 2002—, trustee, 1991-94; moderator Presbyn. Women in 4th Ch., 1987-91, Stephen min., 1997-99. Mem. Am. Soc. Assn. Execs., Chgo. Soc. Assn. Execs. (chair CAE com. 1991-92), Am. Dental Assts. Assn., N.C. Dental Assn. (pres. 1968-69), Charlotte Dental Assts. Soc. Presbyterian. Home: 260 E Chestnut St Chicago IL 60611-2401 Office: Am Acad Implant Dentistry 211 E Chicago Ave Chicago IL 60611-2637

SIH, CHARLES JOHN, pharmaceutical chemistry educator; b. Shanghai, China, Sept. 11, 1933; s. Paul Kwang-Tsien and Teresa (Dong) S.; m. Catherine Elizabeth Hsu, July 11, 1959; children: Shirley, Gilbert, Ronald. A.B. in Biology, Caroll Coll., 1953; M.S. in Bacteriology, Mont. State Coll., 1955; Ph.D. in Bacteriology, U. Wis., 1958. Sr. research microbial biochemist Squibb Inst. for Med. Research, New Brunswick, N.J., 1958-60; mem. faculty U. Wis.-Madison, 1960—, Frederick B. Power prof. pharm. chemistry, 1978, Hilldare prof., 1987—. Recipient 1st Ernest Volwiler award, 1977; Roussel prize, 1980, Am. Pharm. Assoc. award 1987. Mem. Am. Chem. Soc., Soc. Am. Biol. Chemists, Acad. Pharm. Scis., Soc. Am. Microbiologists. Home: 10 Coyote Ct Madison WI 53717-2736

SIKKEMA, KENNETH R. state legislator; b. Cadillac, Mich., Feb. 10, 1951; s. Peter John and Kathryn Mae (Laarman) S.; m. Carla Chase, Oct. 12, 1985; 1 child, Zachary Chase. BA in History cum laude, Harvard U., 1974; MBA with distinction, U. Mich., 1984. Legis. asst. Mich. Ho. of Reps., Lansing, 1974-75; adminstrv. asst. Mich. State Senate, 1975-79; mktg. mgr. Herman Miller, Inc., Zeeland, Mich., 1984-86; exec. dir. West Mich. Environ. Action, Grand Rapids, 1979-82; mem. Mich. Ho. of Reps., Lansing, 1987-98, Mich. Senate from 31st dist., Lansing, 1999—. Republican. Mem. Reformed Ch. in Am. Home: 4309 Del Mar Ct Grandville MI 49418 Office: State Senate 820 Farnum Bldg Lansing MI 48913-0001 E-mail: senksikkema@senate.state.mi.us.

SIKORA, SUZANNE MARIE, dentist; b. Kenosha, Wis., Dec. 4, 1952; d. Leo F. and Ida A. (Dupuis) S. BS, U. Wis., Parkside, 1975; DDS, Marquette U., 1981. Assoc. Paul G. Hagemann, DDS, Racine, Wis., 1981-84; pvt. practice dentistry, 1984—. Cons. Westview Health Care Ctr., Racine, 1981—89, Lincoln Luth. Home, Racine, 1981—2001, Becker-Shoop Ctr., Racine, 1981—2000, Lincoln Village Convalescent Ctr., Racine, 1986—2000, Lincoln Luth Cmty. Care Ctr., 1989—2000. Mem. ad hoc study com. County Health Dept., Racine, 1982-83. Mem.: ADA, Racine County Dental Soc. (pres.-elect 2001, v.p. 2002), Wis. Dental Assn. (coun. on access preventiona and wellness com. 1984—86, impaired provider program intervenor 1990—2001, del. 1993—, Dental Care for Older Persons award 2000). Office: 1900 Lathrop Ave Racine WI 53405-3707

SIKORSKI, JAMES ALAN, research chemist; b. Stevens Point, Wis., Nov. 9, 1948; s. John Paul and Florence Lucille (Wierzba) S.; m. Jeanne Delaney, Apr. 15, 1968 (div. 1975); 1 child, Christine René; m. Georgina Weber, Nov. 19, 1977. BS, Northeast La. State Coll., 1970; MS, Purdue U., 1976, PhD, 1981. With Monsanto Agrl. Co., St. Louis, 1976-91, sci. fellow, 1987-91, Monsanto Corp. Rsch., St. Louis, 1991-93; sci. fellow med. chem. G.D. Searle R&D, 1994-2000; sci. fellow med. chemistry Pharmacia Discovery Rsch., 2000—. Instr. organic chemistry St. Louis C.C., 1977-78; adj. prof. biochemistry Ctrl. Meth. Coll., 1995-97; invited spkr. tech. presentations and seminars. Contbr. chpts. to books, rev. articles, symposia-in-print and articles to profl. jours.; patentee and co-patentee in field. Mem. AAAS, Am. Chem. Soc. (St. Louis ACS award St. Louis Mo. sect. 1994, Kenneth A. Spencer award Kansas City Mo. sect. 1999, Internat. Soc. Heterocyclic Chemistry. Avocations: hiking, canoeing, skiing, photography, snorkeling. Office: Pharmacia Discovery Rsch 700 Chesterfield Pkwy N Saint Louis MO 63198-0001 E-mail: james.a.sikorski@pharmacia.com.

SILBAJORIS, FRANK RIMVYDAS, Slavic languages educator; b. Kretinga, Lithuania, Jan. 6, 1926; came to U.S., 1949; s. Pranas and Elzbieta (Bagdonaviciute) S.; m. Milda Zamzickaite, Aug. 27, 1955; children: Victoria, Alex BA, Antioch Coll., 1953; MA, Columbia U., 1955; PhD, Columbia U., 1962; D Philology (hon.), Latvian Acad. Scis., Riga, 1991. Instr. to asst. prof. Oberlin Coll., Ohio, 1957-63; assoc. prof. Ohio State U., Columbus, 1963-67, prof. Slavic langs., 1967-91, chmn. dept., 1986-89, prof. emeritus, 1991. Cons. NEH, 1978-79, exchange fellow, USSR, 1977-79; dir. NEH summer seminars, 1975, 77, 83, 84, 86, 88. Author: Russian Versification: The Theories of Trediakovskij, Lomonosov and Kantemir, 1968, Perfection of Exile: Fourteen Contemporary Lithuanian Writers, 1970, Tolstoy's Aesthetics and His Art, 1991, War and Peace. Tolstoy's Mirror of the World, 1995; editor: The Architecture of Reading, 1976, Mind Against the Wall, 1983; contbr. articles to profl. jours. Cons., lectr., organizer cultural events Lithuanian-Am. Community Orgn., 1949—Antioch Coll. scholar, 1950-53; fellow John Hay Whitney Found., 1953-54, Ford Found., 1954-56, Woodrow Wilson Ctr., 1984, IREX, USSR, 1963-64 Mem. Inst. Lithuanian Studies (pres. 1977-82), Assn. Advancement Baltic Studies (pres. 1973-74). Avocations: photography; bicycling; swimming; travel. Home: 4082 Ruxton Ln Columbus OH 43220-4046 also: Ohio State U Dept Slavic Langs Columbus OH 43210 E-mail: silbajoris.1@osu.edu.

SILBERMAN, ALAN HARVEY, lawyer; b. Chgo., Oct. 22, 1940; s. Milton J. and Mollie E. (Hymanson) S.; m. Margaret Judith Auslander, Nov. 17, 1968; children: Elena, Mark. BA with distinction, Northwestern U., 1961; LLB, Yale U., 1964. Bar: Ill. 1964, U.S. Dist. Ct. (no. dist.) Ill. 1966, U.S. Ct. Appeals (7th cir.) 1970, (5th and 9th cir.) 1977, (D.C. cir.) 1979, (4th cir.) 1980, (11th cir.) 1981, (3rd cir.) 1982, (8th and 10th cirs.) 1993, U.S. Supreme Ct. 1978. Law clk. U.S. Dist. Ct., Chgo., 1964-66; assoc. Sonnenschein Nath & Rosenthal, 1964-71, ptnr., 1972—. Mem. antitrust adv. bd. Bur. Nat. Affairs, Washington, 1985—; mem. Ill. Atty. Gen. Franchise Adv. Bd., 1996—. Contbr. articles to profl. jours. Bd. dirs., v.p., sec. Camp Ramah in Wisc., Inc., Chgo., 1966-86, pres., 1986-94; bd. dirs. Nat. Ramah Commn., Inc. of Jewish Theol. Sem. Am., N.Y.C., 1970—, v.p., 1986-94, pres., 1994-99, sr. v.p., 1999—; mem. U.S. del. 33d World Zionist Congress, Jerusalem, 1997. Mem. ABA (chmn. antitrust sect. FTC com. 1981-83, chmn. nat. insts. 1983-85, mem. coun. antitrust sect. 1985-88, fin. officer 1988-90, sect. del. ho. of dels. 1990-92, chmn.-elect 1992-93, chmn. 1993-94), Ill. Bar Assn. (chmn. antitrust sect. 1975-76), Northwestern U. 1851 Soc. (chair 1994-97). Home: 430 Oakdale Ave Glencoe IL 60022-2113 Office: Sonnenschein Nath 233 S Wacker Dr Ste 8000 Chicago IL 60606-6491

SILBERSACK, MARK LOUIS, lawyer; b. Cin., Dec. 27, 1946; s. Joseph Leo and Rhoda Marie (Hinkler) S.; m. Ruth Ann Schwallie, Sept. 7, 1985. AB, Boston Coll., 1968; JD, U. Chgo., 1971. Bar: Ohio 1971, U.S. Dist. Ct.

(so. dist.) Ohio 1973, U.S. Ct. Appeals (6th cir.) 1974, U.S. Supreme Ct. 1975. Atty. Dinsmore & Shohl, Cin., 1971—. Lectr. Ohio CLE Inst., Columbus, 1981-91. Co-author: Managed Care: The PPO Experience, 1990, Information Sharing Among Health Care Providers, 1994. Bd. dirs. United Way, Cmty. Chest, 1985-89, 2001—, chmn. pub. policy com., 1998—; vice-chmn. Ohio United Way, Columbus, 1989-94, chmn. bd. dirs., 1994-96; pres. Hyde Park Neighborhood Coun., Cin., 1989-91, Hyde Park Ctr. for Older Adults, 1989-91; active Cin. Bd. Health, 1991-97, chmn., 1995-97; bd. dirs. Cath. Social Svcs. of S.W. Ohio, 1998--. Mem. ABA, Ohio State Bar Assn. (bd. govs., antitrust sect.), Cin. Bar Assn., Fed. Bar Assn., Hyde Park Golf And County Club. Republican. Roman Catholic. Avocations: reading, travel, theater . Home: 3465 Forestoak Ct Cincinnati OH 45208-1842 Office: Dinsmore & Shohl 1900 Chemed Ctr 255 E 5th St Cincinnati OH 45202-4700

SILBERSTEIN, EDWARD BERNARD, nuclear medicine educator, researcher, oncologist; b. Cin., Sept. 3, 1936; s. Bernard Gumpert and Harriet Louise (Kahn) S.; m. Jacqueline Rose Mervis, Oct. 2, 1988; children: Scott, Lisa. BS magna cum laude, Yale U., 1958; MD, Harvard U., 1962. Intern Cin. Gen. Hosp., 1962-63, resident in internal medicine, 1963-64; resident Univ. Hosps. Cleve., 1966-67; NIH fellow in hematology New Eng. Med. Ctr., Boston, 1967-68; asst. prof. radiol. medicine U. Cin. Med. Ctr., 1968-72, assoc. prof. radiol. medicine, 1972-76, prof. radiol. medicine, 1976—, Eugene L. and Sue R. Saenger prof. radiol. scis., 1998—; chmn. Am. Bd. Nuclear Medicine, Los Angeles. Assoc. dir. E.L. Saenger Radioisotope Lab., 1980—; chmn. Environ. Safety Health Com. Dept. Energy Fernald Facility, 1986-91; mem. U.S. Pharmacopeia Com. of Revision, 1990—; mem. Nat. Coun. on Radiation Protection and Measurement, 1997—; cons. Nuclear Regulatory Commn., 1988—; dir. divsn. nuclear medicine Jewish Hosp., 1976-95; cancer pain panel Agy. for Health Care Planning and Rsch., 1992-93. Author: Differential Diagnosis in Nuclear Medicine, 1984, Bone Scintigraphy, 1984, Diagnostic Patterns in Nuclear Medicine, 1998; contbr. articles to profl. jours. Active Race Rels. Commn. Greater Cin., 1995—2000; trustee Cin. Opera Assn., 1993—; active Jewish Cmty. Rels. Coun., 1992—; trustee Isaac M. Wise Temple, 1992—2000, treas., 1997—2000; bd. dirs. Talbert House, 1969—, Air Pollution Control League, Cin., 1980—95. Capt. U.S. Army, 1964—66. Mem.: Am. Bd. Nuclear Medicine (chmn. 1999), Soc. Nuc. Medicine (sec. 1989—92, bd. dirs. 1989—99, pres. S.E. chpt. 1990—91, chair sci. program 1992—94). Jewish. Avocations: tennis, history of art, archaeology, travel. Office: U Cin Med Ctr Mont Reid Pavilion G026 234 Goodman St Cincinnati OH 45219-2364 E-mail: silbereb@healthall.com.

SILICH, GREG, advertising executive; CFO BCOM3 Group, Chgo. Office: BCOM3 Group 35 W Wacker Dr Chicago IL 60601

SILVER, ALAN IRVING, lawyer; b. St. Paul, Sept. 17, 1949; s. Sherman J. Silver and Muriel (Bernstein) Braverman; m. Janice Lynn Gleekel, July 8, 1973; children: Stephen, Amy. BA cum laude, U. Minn., 1971, JD cum laude, 1975. Bar: Minn. 1975, U.S. Dist. Ct. Minn. 1975, U.S. Dist. Ct. (ea. dist.) Wis. 1975, U.S. Ct. Appeals 8th and 10th cirs.) 1975. Assoc. Doherty, Rumble & Butler, P.A., St. Paul, 1975-80, ptnr. Mpls., 1980-99, Bassford, Lockhart, Truesdell & Briggs, P.A., Mpls., 1999—. Mem. 2d Jud. Dist. Ethics Com., St. Paul, 1985-88, 4th Jud. Dist. Ethics Com., Mpls., 1990-97. Author numerous continuing edn. seminar material. Vol. atty. Legal Assistance Ramsey County, St. Paul, 1975-82; mem. St. Louis Park (Minn.) Sch. Bd., 1993-99, chair, 1995-97; mem. St. Louis Park Human Rights Commn., 1987-91; chmn. site mgmt. coun. Susan Lindgren Sch., St. Louis Park, 1986-93; bd. dirs. Jewish Cmty. Rels. Coun., Anti-Defamation League Minn. and Dakotas, 1987-93, 97—, treas., 1992-93. Mem. ABA, Minn. Bar Assn. (exec. bd. antitrust sect. 1984, litigation chair probate and trust sect.), Hennepin County Bar Assn. Avocations: running, guitar, reading. Home: 4320 W 25th St Minneapolis MN 55416-3841 Office: Bassford Lockhart Truesdell & Briggs PA 3550 Multifoods Tower 33 S 6th St Minneapolis MN 55402-1501 E-mail: alans@bassford.com.

SILVER, DONALD, surgeon, educator; b. N.Y.C., Oct. 19, 1929; s. Herman and Cecilia (Meyer) S.; m. Helen Elizabeth Harnden, Aug. 9, 1958; children: Elizabeth Tyler, Donald Meyer, Stephanie Davies, William Paige. AB, Duke U., 1950, BS in Medicine, MD, 1955. Diplomate Am. Bd. Surgery, Am. Bd. Gen. Vascular Surgery, Am. Bd. Thoracic Surgery. Intern Duke Med. Ctr., 1955-56, asst. resident, 1958-63, resident, 1963-64; mem. faculty Duke Med. Sch., 1964-75, prof. surgery, 1972-75; cons. Watts Hosp., Durham, 1965-75, VA Hosp., Durham, 1970-75, chief surgery, 1968-70; prof. surgery, chmn. dept. U. Mo. VA Med. Ctr., Columbia, 1975-98. Cons. Harry S. Truman Hosp., Columbia, 1975— ; mem. bd. sci. advisers Cancer Research Center, Columbia, 1975— ; mem. surg. study sect. A NIH; dir surg. svcs. U. Mo. Health System, 2001—. Contbr. articles to med. jours., chpts. to books; editorial bds.; Jour. Vascular Surgery, Postgrad. Gen. Surgery, Vascular Surgery. Served with USAF, 1956-58. James IV Surg. traveler, 1977 Fellow ACS (gov. 1995-99), Deryl Hart Soc.; mem. AMA, AAAS, Mo. Med. Assn., Boone County Med. Soc., Internat. Cardiovascular Soc., Soc. Univ. Surgeons, Am. Heart Assn. (Mo. affiliate rsch. com.), Soc. Surgery Alimentary Tract, Assn. Acad. Surgery, So. Thoracic Surg. Assn., Internat. Soc. Surgery, Soc. Vascular Surgery, Am. Assn. Thoracic Surgery, Am. Surg. Assn., Ctrl. Surg. Assn. (pres.-elect 1990-91, pres. 1991-92), Western Surg. Assn., Midwestern Vascular Surg. Soc. (pres. 1984-85), Ctrl. Surg. Assn. Found. (treas. 1992-93, 2d v.p. 1993-94, 1st v.p. 1994-95, pres. 1995-96). Home: 1050 W Covered Bridge Rd Columbia MO 65203-9569 Office: U Mo Med Ctr Dept Surgery N514 Columbia MO 65212-0001 E-mail: Silverd@health.missour.edu.

SILVERMAN, ALBERT JACK, psychiatrist, educator; b. Montreal, Que., Can., Jan. 27, 1925; came to U.S., 1950, naturalized, 1955; s. Norman and Molly (Cohen) S.; m. Halina Weinthal, June 22, 1947; children: Barry Evan, Marcy Lynn. B.Sc., McGill U., 1947, M.D., C.M., 1949; grad., Washington Psychoanalytic Inst., 1964. Diplomate: Am. Bd. Psychiatry and Neurology. Intern Jewish Gen. Hosp., Montreal, 1949-50; resident psychiatry Colo. U. Med. Center, 1950-53, instr., 1953; from assoc. to assoc. prof. psychiatry Duke Med. Center, 1953-63; prof. psychiatry, chmn. dept. Rutgers U. Med. Sch., 1964-70; prof. psychiatry U. Mich. Med. Sch., Ann Arbor, 1970-90, prof. emeritus, from 1990, chmn. dept., 1970-81. Cons. Dept. of Def., 1974—; mem. biol. scis. tng. rev. com. NIMH, 1964-69, chmn., 1968-69, mem. rsch. scientist devel. award com., 1970-75, chmn., 1973-75, mem. merit rev. bd. in behavioral scis. VA, 1975-78, chmn., 1976-78, mem. small grants awards com., 1985-89; bd. mgrs. N.J. Neuropsychiat. Inst., 1965-69; trustee N.J. Fund Rsch. and Devel. Nervous and Mental Diseases, 1965-67; bd. dirs. N.J. Mental Health Assn., 1964-69; mem. behavioral sci. com. Nat. Bd. Med. Examiners, 1978-82, chmn., 1984-87, mem. comprehensive com., 1986-93, task force for nervous system, 1989-91; chmn. task force on Cons. Liaison Psychiat., 1991-92. Cons. editor: Psychophysiology, 1970-74, Psychosomatic Medicine, 1972-87; Contbr. articles in field. Served as capt. M.C. USAF, 1955-57. Fellow Am. Coll. Psychiatry (charter), Am. Psychiat. Assn. (chmn. coun. on med. edn. 1970-75, chair task force on DSM III ednl. materials 1979-81), Am. Acad. Psychoanalysis, Am. Coll. Neuropsychopharmacology; mem. Am. Psychosomatic Soc. (coun. 1964-68, 70-74, pres. 1976-77, vis. scholar com. 1992-96, co-chair program com. 1992-93), N.J. Psychoanalytic Soc. (trustee 1968-70), Assn. Rsch. Nervous and Mental Diseases, N.J. Neuropsychiat. Assn. (coun. 1966-69), Group Advancement Psychiatry (chmn. com. psychopathology 1968-74), Soc. Psychophys. Rsch., Soc. Biol. Psychiatry, Mich. Psychiat. Soc. (coun. 1975-77), Pacific Behavioral Rsch. Found. (v.p. 1999—). Home: Santa Barbara, Calif. Died May 10, 2002.

SILVERMAN, ELLEN-MARIE, speech and language pathologist; b. Milw., Oct. 12, 1942; d. Roy and Bettie (Schlaeger) Loebel; m. Feb. 5, 1967 (div.); 1 child, Catherine Bette. BS, U. Wis., Milw., 1964; MA, U. Iowa, 1967, PhD, 1970. Rsch. assoc. U. Ill., Urbana, 1969-71; asst. prof. speech pathology Marquette U., Milw., 1973-79; assoc. clin. prof. otolaryngology Med. Coll. Wis., 1980—83; assoc. prof. speech pathology Marquette U., 1979-85; pvt. practice speech and lang. pathology, Milw., 1985—. Founder, pres. TSS-The Speech Source, Inc., 1995—. Author, illustrator: Jason's Secret; contbr. articles to profl. jours., chpts. to books. Marquette U. grantee, 1982. Fellow Am. Speech, Hearing, Lang. Assn.; mem. Wis. Speech, Hearing, Lang. Assn., Sigma Xi, Delta Kappa Gamma. Avocations: photography, painting, gardening, writing. E-mail: tsss920499@aol.com.

SILVERMAN, FRANKLIN HAROLD, speech pathologist, educator; b. Providence, Aug. 16, 1933; s. Meyer and Reba (Sack) Silverman; m. Ellen-Marie Loebel, Feb. 1, 1967 (div. Feb. 1981); 1 child Catherine ; m. Evelyn Ellen Chanda, Nov. 13, 1983. BS in Speech, Emerson Coll., 1960; MA, Northwestern U., 1961; PhD, U. Iowa, 1966. Lic. speech-lang. pathologist Wis. Rsch. assoc. U. Iowa, Iowa City, 1965-67; asst. prof. U. Ill., Champaign, 1968-71; assoc. prof. Marquette U., Milw., 1971-77, prof., 1978—; clin. prof. Med. Coll. Wis., Wauwatosa, 1978—. Mem. adv. bd. Wis. Telecomm. Relay Svcs., Madison, 1991—; cons. USAID Palestinian Speech Pathology Tng. Program, Gaza City, 1993—, Joint Centre for Rsch. Prosthetics and Orthotics and Rehab. Programmes, Riyadh, Saudi Arabia, 1995—, Disables Children's Assn., Riyadh, Saudi Arabia, 1998—. Author: Speech, Language, and Hearing Disorders, 1995, Communication for the Speechless, 3d edit, 1995, Stuttering and Other Fluency Disorders, 2d edit., 1996, Computer Applications for Augmenting the Management of Speech, Language and Hearing Disorders, 1997, Research Design and Evaluation in Speech-Language Pathology and Audiology, 4th edit., 1998, Authoring Books and Materials for Students, Academics, and Professionals, 1998, Telecommunication Relay Service Handbook, 1999, Professional Issues in Speech-Language Pathology and Audiology, 1999, Fundamentals of Electronics for Speech-Language Pathologists and Audiologists, 1999, Publishing for Tenure and Beyond, 1999, Self-Publishing Books and Materials for Students, Academics and Professionals, 1999, Second Thoughts About Stuttering, 2000, Teaching for Tenure and Beyond, 2001; contbr. Fellow: Text and Acad. Authors Assn. (sec. 1993—94, pres.-elect 1996, pres. 1997), Am. Speech-Lang.-Hearing Assn. Jewish. Avocation: photography. Home: 5918 Currant Ln Greendale WI 53129-2427 Office: Marquette U Dept Speech Pathology Milwaukee WI 53201-1881

SILVERMAN, HARRY J. pizza delivery company executive; BA, U. Ill. CPA. With Grant Thornton, until 1985; regional contr. Domino's Pizza Inc., Chgo., 1985-88, nat. ops. contr. Ann Arbor, Mich., from 1988, divsnl. v.p. fin., CFO, v.p. fin. and adminstrn., 1993—, now exec. v.p. fin., CFO, treas. Office: 30 Frank Lloyd Wright Dr Ann Arbor MI 48105-9757

SILVERMAN, MARK, publisher; Pub., editor, Detroit News. Office: Detroit News 615 W Lafayette Blvd Detroit MI 48226-3197

SILVERMAN, NORMAN ALAN, cardiac surgeon; b. Boston, Dec. 19, 1946; BA, Dartmouth Coll., 1968; MD, Boston U., 1971. Prof. surgery U. Ill., Chgo., 1980-89; divsn. head Henry Ford Hosp., Detroit, 1989—; prof. surgery Case-Western Res. U., Cleve., 1992—. Contbr. 200 scientific articles to profl. jours. Lt. comdr. USPHS, 1973-75. Fellow Am. Coll. Surgeons, Am. coll. Cardiology, Am. Coll. Chest Physicians. Avocation: sailing. Office: Henry Ford Hosp 2799 W Grand Blvd Detroit MI 48202-2689

SILVERMAN, RICHARD BRUCE, chemist, biochemist, educator; b. Phila., May 12, 1946; s. Philip and S. Ruth (Simon) S.; . Barbara Jean Kesner, Jan. 9, 1983; children: Matthew, Margaret, Philip. BS, Pa. State U., 1968; MA, Harvard U., 1972, PhD, 1974. Asst. prof. Northwestern U., Evanston, Ill., 1976-82, assoc. prof., 1982-86, prof., 1986—, Arthur Andersen teaching & rsch. prof., 1996-98, mem. Inst. Neurosci., 1990—, Charles Deering McCormick prof., 2001—. Cons. Procter and Gamble Co., Cin., 1984, Abbott Labs, North Chicago, 1987, Searle R&D, St. Louis, 1988-90, DuPont, 1991, Dow, 1991, Leytig, Voit & Mayer law offices, 1992—, DowElanco, 1993-95, G.D. Searle, 1995, Affymax, 1995, Kinetik Pharms., 1999, Guilford Pharms., 2001, Activ X Bioscis., 2001, Cytoclonal Pharms., 2001; mem. adv. panel NIH, Bethesda, Md., 1981, 83, 85, 87-91; expert analyst CHEMTRACTS; scientific adv. bd. Influx, Inc., 1998—. Mem. editl. bd.: Jour. Enzyme Inhibition, 1988—2002, mem. editl. bd.: Archives Biochem. & Biophys., 1993—, mem. editl. bd.: Jour. Medicinal Chemistry, 1995—2000, mem. editl. bd.: Enzyme Inhibition and Medicinal Chemistry, 2002—; contbr. articles. Mem. adv. bd. Ill. Math. & Scis. Acad., 1988. With U.S. Army, 1969-71. Recipient Career Devel. award USPHS, 1982-87, E. LeRoy Hall award for tchg. excellence, 1999, Northwestern Alumni Tchg. award, 2000; postdoctoral fellow Brandeis U., Waltham, Mass., 1974-76, DuPont Young Faculty fellow, 1976, Alfred P. Sloan Found. fellow, 1981-85; grantee various govt. and pvt. insts., 1976—. Fellow: AAAS; mem.: Am. Chem. Soc. (nat. elected nominating com. divns. biol. chemistry 1993—96, long-range planning com. divsn. med. chem. 1999—2002), Am. Soc. Biochem. Molecular Biology, Am. Inst. Chemists. Avocations: tennis, family, golf. Office: Northwestern U Dept Chemistry 2145 Sheridan Rd Evanston IL 60208-3113

SILVERMAN, ROBERT JOSEPH, lawyer; b. Mpls., Apr. 4, 1942; s. Maurice and Toby (Goldstein) S.; 1 child, Adam Graham-Silverman; m. Suzanne M. Brown; 1 child, Thomas B. BA, U. Minn., 1964, JD, 1967. Bar: Minn. 1967. Assoc. Dorsey & Whitney, Mpls., 1967-72, ptnr., 1972—2001. Lectr. William Mitchell Coll. Law, St. Paul, 1977-78, Hamline Law Sch., St. Paul, 1990-96, Minn. Continuing Legal Edn., Mpls, 1985-99, Bd. dirs. Courage Ctr., Golden Valley, Minn., 1978-84, 85-95, v.p., 1983-86, pres., 1988-89. With USAR, 1967-73. Mem. ABA, Minn. Bar Assn., Hennepin County Bar Assn., Am. Coll. Real Estate Lawyers. Jewish. Office: Dorsey & Whitney 50 S 6th St Ste 1500 Minneapolis MN 55402-1498 E-mail: silverman.robert@dorseylaw.com.

SILVERS, GERALD THOMAS, publishing executive; b. Cin., Aug. 26, 1937; s. Steve Allen and Tina Mae (Roberts) S.; m. Ann Gregory Woodward, July 25, 1964. BA, U. Ky., 1960. Asst. research svcs. mgr. Cin. Enquirer, 1963-72, research svcs. dir., 1972-74, research dir., 1974-90, v.p. mktg. svcs., 1990-94, v.p. market devel., 1994—. Mem. U. Ky. Devel. Coun., Lexington, 1986—; trustee Neediest Kids of All, 1991—; mem. region 5 exec. com. Ohio Sch. to Work, 1997-2000; mem. corps. com. St. Elizabeth Med. Ctr. Found., 1998; mem. bd. overseers Taft Mus. Art, 1999—, treas., bd. govs., 2002--. 1st lt. U.S. Army, 1960-62. Recipient Thomas H. Copeland award of merit, 1991. Mem. U. Ky. Alumni Assn. Cin. Chpt. (pres. 1985), Newspaper Research Council (pres. 1985,86), Internat. Newspaper Market Assn., Am. Mktg. Assn. Presbyterian. Home: 229 Watch Hill Rd Fort Mitchell KY 41011-1822 Office: Cin Enquirer 312 Elm St Cincinnati OH 45202-2739 E-mail: gsilvers@enquirer.com.

SILVERSTEIN, IRA I. state legislator; m. Debra; 4 children. Grad., Loyola U., 1982, John Marshall Law Sch., 1985. Mem. Ill. Senate from 8th dist., Springfield, 1999—; mem. state govt. ops., judiciary & lic. activities coms. Ill. Senate. Past pres. Northtown Cmty. Coun.; past bd. dirs. Korean Sr. Ctr.; mem. Greek Pan-Hellenic Laconian Orgn.; bd. dirs. Bernard Horwitz Jewish. Cmty. Ctr., Arie Crown Hebrew Day Sch., Akiba Schechter Jewish Day Sch. Democrat. Office: State Capitol Capitol Bldg 105D Springfield IL 62706-0001 also: 6199 N Lincoln Ave Chicago IL 60659

SIM, RICHARD GUILD, business executive; b. Glasgow, Scotland, Sept. 9, 1944; came to U.S., 1970; BSc, Glasgow U., 1965; PhD, Cambridge U., Eng., 1968. Engr. Westinghouse Electric, 1970-71; gen. mgr. Gen. Electric, 1972-85; CEO, chmn. Applied Power, Milw., 1985—; chmn., pres. & CEO APW Ltd., Waukesha, Wis. Bd. dirs. Gehl Co., Wis., IPSCO, Inc., Sask., Can. Office: APW Ltd N22 W23685 Ridgewiew Pkwy W Waukesha WI 53188-1013

SIMECKA, BETTY JEAN, marketing executive; b. Topeka, Apr. 15, 1935; d. William Bryan and Regina Marie (Rezac) S.; m. Alex Pappas, Jan. 15, 1956 (div. Apr. 1983); 1 child, Alex William. Student, Butler County C.C., 1983-85. Freelance writer and photographer, L.A., also St. Marys, Kans., 1969-77; co-owner Creative Enterprises, El Dorado, 1977-83; coord. excursions into history Butler County C.C., 1983-84; dir. Hutchinson (Kans.) Conv. & Visitors Bur., 1984-85; dir. mktg. divsn. Exec. Mgmt., Inc., Wichita, 1985-87; exec. dir. Topeka Conv. and Visitors Bur., 1987-91, pres., CEO, 1991-96; pres. Internat. Connections, Inc., 1996-97, Simecka and Assoc., 1996-99, Pinnacle Prodns., L.L.C., 1997-99; pres., CEO Cultural Exhbns. and Events, L.L.C., 1999—. Dir. promotion El Dorado Thunderboat Races, 1977-78. Contbr. articles to jours. and mags.; columnist St. Marys Star, 1973-79. Pres. El Dorado Art Assn., 1984; chair Santa Fe Trail Bike Assn., Kans., 1988-90; co-dir. St. Marys Summer Track Festival, 1973-81; chair spl. events Mulvane Art Mus., 1990, sec., 1991-92; membership chair, 1993-94, bd. dirs., 1995-96; bd. dirs. Topeka Civic Theater, 1991-96, co-chair spl. events, 1992; Kans. chair Russian Festival Com., 1992-93; vice-chair Kans. Film Commn., 1993-94, chair, 1994; bd. dirs. Kans. Expoctr. Adv. Bd., 1990-96, Brain Injury Assn. Greater Kansas City, Concerned Citizens Topeka, 1998-2000; pres. Kans. Internat. Mus., 1994-96. Recipient Kans. Gov.'s Tourism award Kans. Broadcaster's Assn., 1993, Disting. Svc award City of Topeka, 1995, Hist. Ward Meade Disting. award Topeka Parks & Recreation Dept., 1995; named Kansan of Yr., Topeka Capitol-Jour., 1995, Sales and Mktg. Exec. of Yr., 1995, Internatn. Soroptomists, Topeka chpt., Woman of Distinction, 1996. Mem. Nat. Tour Assn., Sales and Mktg. execs. (bd. dirs. 1991-92), Internat. Assn. Conv. and Visitors Burs. (co-chair rural tourism com. 1994), Am. Soc. Assn. Execs., Travel Industry Assn. Kans. (membership chair 1988-89, sec. 1990, pres. 1991-92, Outstanding Merit award 1994), St. Marys C. of C. (pres. 1975), I-70 Assn. (v.p. 1989, pres. 1990), Optimists (social sec. Topeka chpt. 1988-89). Republican. Methodist. Avocations: writing, painting, photography, masters track. Holder Nat. AAU record for 100-yard dash, 1974. E-mail: exhibition2@bettysimecka.com., bettyj@bettysimecka.com.

SIMES, STEPHEN MARK, pharmaceutical products executive; b. N.Y.C., Nov. 23, 1951; s. Herbert H. and Mimi (Maurer) S.; m. Anita H. Herzog, Aug. 23, 1975. BS in Chemistry, Bklyn. Coll., 1973; MBA in Mktg., NYU, 1980. Sales rep. G.D. Searle and Co., N.Y.C., 1974-78, supr. sales tng. Chgo., 1978-79, dist. sales mgr. N.Y.C., 1979-81, product mgr. Chgo., 1981-82, sr. product mgr., 1982-83, dir. pub. affairs and communications, 1983-84; v.p. Gynex Inc., 1984-88; dir. Gynex Pharms. Inc., Deerfield, 1985-93; pres., dir. Gynex Labs., Chgo., 1985-88; pres., CEO Contracap Inc., Ill., 1988-89, Gynex Pharms., Inc., Chgo., 1989-93, chmn., 1992-93; sr. v.p., dir. Bio-Technology Gen. Corp., 1993-94; pres., CEO, dir. Unimed Pharms., Inc., 1994-97; bd. dirs., CEO, pres. Simes Pharm. Cons., 1997-98. Vice chmn., CEO, pres., BioSante Pharms., Inc., Lincolnshire, Ill., 1998—. Mem. Chgo. Coun. Fgn. Rels., Licensing Exec. Soc. Office: 111 Barclay Blvd Lincolnshire IL 60069 Office Fax: 847-478-9260.

SIMMONS, CHARLES E. state official; Sec. Dept. Corrections, Topeka. Office: Corrections Dept 900 SW Jackson St # 400 Topeka KS 66612-1220

SIMMONS, EMORY G. mycologist, microbiologist, botanist, educator; b. Ind., Apr. 12, 1920; AB, Wabash Coll., 1941; AM, DePauw U., 1946; PhD in Botany, U. Mich., 1950; DSc in Microbiology (hon.), Kasetsart U., Thailand, 1988. Instr. bacteriology & botany DePauw U., Greencastle, Ind., 1946-47; asst. prof. botany Dartmouth Coll., Hanover, N.H., 1950-53; mycologist U.S. Army Natick Labs., 1953-58, head mycology lab., 1958-74; prin. investor Devel. Ctr. Cult Collection of Fungi, 1974-77; prof. botany U. Mass., Amherst, 1974-77, prof. microbiology, 1977-87, ret., 1987; rsch. assoc. Wabash Coll., Crawfordsville, Ind., 1987—. Chmn. adv. com. fungi Am. Type Cult Collection; U.S. rep. Expert Group on Fungus Taxonomy, Orgn. Econ. Coop. & Devel.; rsch. fellow Sec. Army, Thailand Indonesia, 1968-69; adj. prof. U. R.I., 1972-74; mem. exec. bd. U.S. Fedn. Cult Collections, 1974-76, pres., 1976-78; pres., chmn. bd. dirs. Second Internat. Mycology Congress Inc., 1975-78; mem. adv. com. cult collections UN Environ. Program/UNESCO/Internat. Cell Rsch. Orgn., 1977—. Mem AAAS, Mycological Soc. Am. (sec.- treas. 1963-65, v.p. 1966, pres. 1968, Disting. Mycologist award 1990), Brit. Mycological Soc., Internat. Assn. Plant Taxonomists. Achievements include research in taxonomic mycology, taxonomy of Fungi imperfecti, taxonomy and cultural characteristics of Ascomycetes. Office: 717 Thornwood Rd Crawfordsville IN 47933-2760

SIMMONS, LEE GUYTON, JR. zoological park director; b. Tucson, Feb. 20, 1938; s. Lee Guyton and Dorothy Esther (Taylor) S.; m. Marie Annette Geim, Sept. 6, 1959; children: Lee Guyton, Heather, Heidi. Student, Cen. State Coll.; DVM, Okla. State U. Resident veterinarian Columbus Zoo, Powell, Ohio, 1963-66, Henry Doorly Zoo, Omaha, 1966-70, dir., 1970—. Research cons. VA Hosp.; assoc. instr. U. Nebr. Med. Ctr., Omaha; assoc. clin. prof. Creighton U. Sch. Dentistry. Contbr. articles to profl. jours. Bd. dirs. Nebr. State Mus., Lincoln. Served with USAR. Recipient Nat. Idealism award City of Hope, 1979; named Man of Yr., Lions Club, 1978. Fellow AVMA, Am. Assn. Zool. Veterinarians (pres.), Am. Assn. Zool. Parks, Nebr. Vet. Med. Assn. (Veterinarian of Yr. 1979). Lodge: Rotary. Office: Henry Doorly Zoo Office of the Director 3701 S 10th St Omaha NE 68107-2200

SIMMONS, ROBERTA JOHNSON, public relations firm executive; b. St. Louis, June 28, 1947; d. Robert Andrew and Thelma Josephine (Bunch) J.; m. Clifford Michael Simmons, Aug. 10, 1968; children: Andrew Park, Matthew Clay, Jordan Michael. BA, Ind. U., South Bend, 1972. Lic. real estate broker, Ind.; accredited pub. rels. practitioner; mem. Inst. Residential Mktg. Account exec., supr. Juhl Advt., Inc., Mishawaka, Ind., 1971-74, pub. rels. dir., 1974-79, v.p., 1979, v.p., pub. rels. dir. Mishawaka and Indpls., 1984-89; v.p. E.L. Yoder & Assocs., Inc., Granger, Ind., 1979-80; pres. Simmons Communications, Inc., Mishawaka, 1981-82; v.p., gen. mgr. Juhl Bldg. Communications, Inc., South Bend, 1983-84; sr. v.p. Wyse Advt., Inc., Indpls., 1989-90; v.p., pub. rels. dir. Caldwell VanRiper, Inc., 1990-94; v.p. Pub. Rels. Network, 1995—. Contbr. articles to profl. publs. Mem. pub. rels. com. Ind. Adult Literacy Coalition, Indpls., 1989; chairperson pub. rels. com. Crossroads of Am. coun. Boy Scouts Am., Indpls., 1990-91; dep. community info. com. Indpls. C. of C. Infrastructure Study, 1990-91. Mem. PRSA (accredited, mem. counsellors acad., Hoosier chpt. job bank com. 1993—, Nat. Assembly Del., 1996—, v.p. programs, 1997), Nat. Sales Mktg. Coun. (trustee 1991-92), Inst. Residential Mktg. Elder Christian Ch. (Disciples of Christ). Avocations: travel, reading. Office: Pub Rels Network 111 Monument Cir Ste 882 Indianapolis IN 46204-5173

SIMMS, LOWELLE, synod executive; b. Sterling, Colo., June 16, 1931; s. Griffin L. and Irene O. (Geer) S.; m. Lois A. Streeter, Aug. 8, 1959. BA, Park Coll., 1953; MDiv, Union Theol. Sem., 1956. Ordained min. Presbyn. Ch., 1956. Pastor East Trenton Presbyn. Ch., Trenton, N.J., 1957-61, Calvary Presbyn. Ch., Phila., 1961-66; min. of mission First, North, Westminster Chs., Kalamazoo, 1966-69; assoc. exec. Presbytery of Sccoto Valley, Columbus, Ohio, 1969-80; administr. interims Presbytery and

Synods Presbyterian Ch., 1980-83; synod exec. Synod of the Covenant, Columbus, 1993. Avocation: photography. Office: Synod of the Covenant 6172 Busch Blvd Ste 3000 Columbus OH 43229-2564

SIMON, BERNECE KERN, social work educator; b. Denver, Nov. 27, 1914; d. Maurice Meyer and Jennie (Bloch) Kern; m. Marvin L. Simon, Feb. 26, 1939; 1 dau., Anne Elizabeth. B.A., U. Chgo., 1936, M.A., 1942. Social worker Jewish Children's Bur. Chgo., 1938-40, U. Chgo. Hosps. and Clinics, 1940-44; mem. faculty U. Chgo., 1944-81, instr., 1944-48, asst. prof., 1948-60, prof. social casework, 1960—, Samuel Deutsch prof. Sch. Social Service Adminstrn., 1960-81, emeritus, 1981—. Mem. bd. editors 17th Edit. Ency. Social Work, 1975-77, Social Svc. Rev., 1975-99; bd. editors: Social Work, 1978-82, book rev. editor, 1982-87; cons. editor Journal of Social Work Education, 1991-94; contbr. articles to profl. jours., book chpts., monographs. Mem. NASW, Coun. Social Work Edn. (mem. nat. bd., sec. 1972-74), Acad. Cert. Social Workers, Nat. Acads. Practice: Social Work Office: U Chgo Sch of Social Svc Adminstrn 969 E 60th St Chicago IL 60637-2677

SIMON, EVELYN, lawyer; b. N.Y.C., May 13, 1943; d. Joseph and Adele (Holzschlag) Berkman; m. Fredrick Simon, Aug. 18, 1963; children: Amy Jocelyn, Marcie Ann. AB in Physics, Barnard Coll., 1963; MS in Physics, U. Pitts., 1964; JD, Wayne State U., 1978; LLB, Monash U., Melbourne, Australia, 1980. Bar: Mich. 1980, Victoria (Australia) 1981. Supr. engring. Chrysler Corp., Detroit, 1964-72; edn. and profl. mgr. Engring. Soc. Detroit, 1972-78; solicitor Arthur Robinson & Co., Melbourne, 1980-81; sr. atty. Ford Motor Co., Detroit, 1981-89; assoc. gen. counsel Sheller-Globe Corp., 1989-90; v.p. planning, gen. counsel United Techs. Automotive Inc., Dearborn, Mich., 1991-94, v.p. bus. devel. and legal affairs, 1995-96, v.p. Asian bus. devel., 1997-98. Cons. internat. bus. devel., 1998-99. Mem. Mich. Bar Assn. Office: 1787 Alexander Dr Bloomfield Hills MI 48302-1204 E-mail: evelynsimon@prodigy.net.

SIMON, HERBERT, professional basketball team executive; b. Bronx; Grad., CCNY. With Albert Frankel Co., Indpls., 1959; co-founder Melvin Simon and Assocs., Inc., 1959—, pres., 1973—; owner Ind. Pacers (Nat. Basketball Assn.), 1983—. Office: Ind Pacers Market Sq Arena 300 E Market St Indianapolis IN 46204-2603

SIMON, JACK AARON, geologist, former state official; b. Champaign, Ill., June 17, 1919; s. Abraham and Lenore (Levy) S. B.A., U. Ill., 1941, M.S., 1946; postgrad., Northwestern U., 1947-49, D.Sc. (hon.), 1981. Tech. and research asst. Ill. State Geol. Survey, Urbana, 1937-42, asst. to assoc. geologist, 1945-53, geologist, head, coal sect., 1953-67, prin. geologist, 1967-74, asst. chief, 1973-74, chief, 1974-81, prin. scientist, 1981-83. Occasional cons.; asso. prof. dept. metallurgy and mining engring. U. Ill., 1967-74, prof., 1974-77, 80-85, adj. prof. dept. geology, 1979-86. Served with F.A. AUS, 1942-43, F.A., USAAF, 1943-45. Decorated Air Medal with 4 oak leaf clusters; recipient Disting. Svc. award So. Ill. U., Edwardsville, 1982, Coal Day award So. Ill. U., Carbondale, 1982, Alumni Achievement award U. Ill. dept. geology, 1994. Fellow AAAS (sect. E chmn. 1980), Geol. Soc. Am. (chmn. coal geology div. 1962-63, Gilbert H. Cady award 1975, mem. council and exec. com. 1979-81); mem. Am. Assn. Petroleum Geologists (ea. sect. Gordon M. Wood Jr. Meml. award 1991), AIME (chmn. Midwest coal sect. 1966, Percy W. Nicholls award 1981), Am. Inst. Profl. Geologists (v.p. 1973), Am. Mining Congress, Assn. Am. State Geologists (hon.), Ill. Mining Inst. (hon. life; exec. sec.-treas. 1963-68, v.p. 1980-81, pres. 1981-82), Ill. Soc. Coal Preparation Engrs. and Chemists, Ill. Geol. Soc., Ill. Acad. Sci., Soc. Econ. Geologists (councillor 1982-84), B'nai Brith, Sigma Xi. Club: Exchange (Urbana) (pres. 1969). Home: 101 W Windsor Rd # 4204 Urbana IL 61802-6697 E-mail: coaljack@hotmail.com.

SIMON, JOHN BERN, lawyer; b. Cleve., Aug. 8, 1942; s. Seymour Frank and Roslyn (Schultz) S.; children: Lindsey Helaine, Douglas Banning. BS, U. Wis., 1964; JD, DePaul U., 1967. Bar: Ill. 1967. Asst. U.S. atty. U.S. Justice Dept., Chgo., 1967-70, dep. chief civil div., 1970-71, chief civil div., 1971-74; spl. counsel to dir. Ill. Dept. Pub. Aid, 1974-75; legal cons. to Commn. on Rev. of Nat. Policy Toward Gambling, 1975-76; ptnr. firm Friedman & Koven, 1975-85, mem. exec. com., 1983-85; ptnr. firm Jenner & Block, 1986—. Spl. cons. to adminstr. DEA Dept. Justice, 1976-77; counsel to Gov.'s Revenue Study Commn. on Legalized Gambling, 1977-78; spl. counsel Ill. Racing Bd., 1979-80; lectr. tng. seminars and confs.; instr. U.S. Atty. Gen.'s Advocacy Inst., Washington, 1974; lectr. Nat. Conf. Organized Crime, Washington, 1975, Dade County Inst. Organized Crime, Ft. Lauderdale, Fla., 1976; faculty Cornell Inst. Organized Crime, Ithaca, N.Y., 1976, judge Miner Moot Ct. competition Northwestern U., 1971-73; mem. law coun. DePaul U., 1974-83, mem. alumni assn., 1984-85, chmn., 1975-79; adj. prof. DePaul U. Coll. Law, 1977, 81; faculty Practising Law Inst., Chgo., 1984. Contbr. articles to profl. jours. Bd. dirs. Lawyer's Trust Fund of Ill., 1998—, treas., 2000—, Cmty. Film Workshop of Chgo., 1977-90, Friends of Glencoe Parks, 1977-78, sec., 1978-79; mem. nominating com. Glencoe Sch. Bd., 1978-81, chmn. rules com., 1980-81; pres. Glencoe Hist. Soc., 1979-82; mem. Glencoe Zoning Bd. Appeals, Zoning Commn., Sign Bd. Appeals, 1981-86, chmn., 1984-86; mem. Ill. Inaugural Com., 1979, 83, 87, 95; bd. dirs., mem. exec. com. Chgo. World's Fair 1992 Authority, 1983-85; mem. Chancery divsn. task force Spl. Commn. on Adminstrn. of Justice in Cook County, 1985-87; trustee De Paul U., 1990, chair phys. plant and property com., 1992-94, vice chair, 1995—; commr. Ill. Racing Bd., 1990—; gen. trustee Lincoln Acad. Ill., 1993—, regent, 1999—, chancellor, 2001—; mem. Ill. Supreme Ct. Planning and Oversight Com. for Jud. Performance Evaluation Program, 1997-98, 2000—. Recipient Bankcroft-Whitney Am. Jurisprudence award, 1965, 66, Judge Learned Hand Human Rels. award Am. Jewish Com., 1994, award for outstanding svc. to legal profession DePaul U. Coll. Law, 1996, Am. ORT Jurisprudence award, 1999. Mem. ABA (com. on liaison with the judiciary 1983-95), FBA (fed. civil procedure com. 1979-85, chmn. 1985-86, bd. mgrs. 1987-89, chmn. house com. 1989-90, treas. 1990-91, 2d v.p. 1991-92, 1st v.p. 1992-93, pres. 1993-94), Ill. State Bar Assn., Women's Bar Assn., Ill. Police Assn., Ill. Sheriffs Assn., U.S. Treasury Agts. Assn., Chgo. Bar Assn., DePaul U. Alumni Assn. (pres. 1985-87, chmn. spl. gifts com. campaign, chmn. Simon Commn. 1989-91, nat. chair for ann. giving 1991-94), Std. Club. Office: Jenner & Block One IBM Plz 42nd Fl Chicago IL 60611

SIMON, LOU ANNA KIMSEY, academic administrator; V.p. acad. affairs, provost Coll. Human Medicine Mich. State U., 1993—. Office: Mich State U 438 Administration Bldg East Lansing MI 48824-1046

SIMON, MELVIN, real estate developer, professional basketball executive; b. Oct. 21, 1926; s. Max and Mae Simon; m. Bren Burns, Sept. 14, 1972; children: Deborah, Cynthia, Tamme, David, Max. Bs in Acctg., CCNY, 1949, M in Bus., Real Estate, 1983; PhD (hon.), Butler U., 1986, Ind. U., 1991. Leasing spt. Albert Frankel Co., Indpls., 1955-60; pres. Melvin Simon & Assocs., 1960-73, co-chmn. bd. dirs., 1973—; co-owner Ind. Pacers, 1983—. Adv. bd. Wharton's Real Estate, Phila., 1986—. Adv. bd. dean's council Ind. U., Bloomington; bd. dirs. United Cerebral Palsy, Indpls., Muscular Dystrophy Assn., Indpls., Jewish Welfare Found., Indpls.; trustee Urban Land Inst., Internat. Council Shopping Ctrs. Recipient Horatio Alger award Boy's Club Indpls., 1986; named Man of Yr., Jewish Welfare Found., 1980. Democrat. Jewish.

SIMON, MICHAEL ALEXANDER, photographer, educator; b. Budapest, Hungary, June 20, 1936; came to U.S., 1957, naturalized, 1962; s. Miklos and Magda (Schreiber) Stern; m. Carol Susan Winters, Jan. 21, 1961; children: Amy Catherine, Nicholas Andrew. Student, Budapest Tech. U., 1954-56, Pa. State U., 1957-58; MFA in Photography, Rochester Inst. Tech., 1986. Propr. Michael Simon Studio, N.Y.C., 1966-68; mem. faculty Beloit (Wis.) Coll., 1968—, asst. prof. dept. art, 1971-76, chmn. dept. art and art history, 1984-98, assoc. prof., 1976-85, prof., now prof emeritus, 1985-98, 98-; curator photography, now cons. Theodore Lyman Wright Art Center, 1980—. Free-lance photographer, 1958-66, artist-in-residence, Nat. Park Service, Mus. Div., Harpers Ferry, W.Va., 1971, vis. artist, U. Del., Newark, 1974, Sch. of Art Inst. Chgo., 1978; numerous one-man shows of photography, 1964— , latest being, Wright Art Center, Beloit, 1977, 78, Mpls. Inst. Arts, 1979, U. Rochester, 1985; group shows include, Gallery 38A, Beloit Coll., 1974, U. Iowa, Iowa City, 1975, Columbia Coll. Gallery, Chgo., 1975, Mpls. Inst. Arts, 1976, Evanston (Ill.) Art Center, 1978, Purdue U., Lafayette, Ind., 1978, Kohler Art Center, Sheboygan, Wis., 1979, Madison Art Ctr., (Wis.), 1983; represented in permanent collections, Mus. Modern Art, N.Y.C., U. Kans., Lawrence, Mpls. Inst. Arts, Sheldon Meml. Art Gallery, Lincoln, Nebr.; Author: Comparative History of Hungarian Photography, 2000, Wis. Arts Bd. fellow, 1980; Nat. Endowment for Arts grantee, 1980; Mellon Fund. grantee, 1977 Mem. Soc. for Photog. Edn. (chmn. nat. bd. 1979-81, chmn. Midwest region 1973-76), Szechenyi Soc. of Hungary. Achievements include research on history of Hungarian photography, the photographic snapshot. Office: Beloit Coll Dept Art Beloit WI 53511

SIMON, MORDECAI, religious association administrator, clergyman; b. St. Louis, July 19, 1925; s. Abraham M. and Rose (Solomon) S.; m. Maxine R. Abrams, July 4, 1954; children: Ora, Eve, Avrom. BA, St. Louis U., 1947; MA, Washington U., St. Louis, 1952; MHL, Rabbi, Jewish Theol. Sem. Am., N.Y.C., 1952, DD (hon.), 1977. Ordained rabbi, 1952. Rabbi in, Mpls., 1952-56, Waterloo, Iowa, 1956-63; exec. dir. Chgo. Bd. Rabbis, 1963-80, exec. v.p., 1980-95, exec. v.p. emeritus, 1995—. Nat. chaplain Jewish War Vets., 1977-78. Host: (weekly program) What's Nu?, Sta. WGN-TV, 1973-92. With AUS, 1943-46. Recipient citation Jewish War Vets., 1967, Boy Scouts Am., 1966, 74, 88, Chgo. chpt. Am. Jewish Congress, 1973, Chgo. Conf. Jewish Women's Orgns., 1973, Chgo. Bd. Rabbis, 1973, Rabbinical Svc. award of Appreciation, Jewish Theol. Sem. Am., 1988, Raoul Wallenberg Humanitarian award, 1989, citation and commendation Ill. Ho. Reps., 1995, Order of Merit, The Equestrian Order of the Holy Sepulchre of Jerusalem, 1996; Rabbi Mordecai Simon Day proclaimed by Gov. James Edgar, State of Ill., 1995. Mem. Rabbinical Assembly. Home: 621 County Line Rd Highland Park IL 60035-5220 Office: 1 S Franklin St Chicago IL 60606-4609

SIMON, PAUL, former senator, educator, writer; b. Eugene, Oreg., Nov. 29, 1928; s. Martin Paul and Ruth (Troemel) S.; m. Jeanne Hurley, Apr. 21, 1960 (dec. Feb. 20, 2000); children: Sheila, Martin; m. Patricia Derge, May 20, 2001. Student, U. Oreg., 1945-46, Dana Coll., Blair, Nebr., 1946-48; 54 hon. doctorates. Pub. Troy (Ill.) Tribune and 12 other So. Ill. weeklies., 1948-66; mem. Ill. Ho. of Reps., 1955-63, Ill. Senate, 1963-69; lt. gov. Ill., 1969-73; fellow John F. Kennedy Sch. Govt., Harvard U., 1972-73; founded pub. affairs reporting program Sangamon State U., Springfield, Ill., 1972-73; mem. 94th-98th Congresses from 22d and 24th Dists. 94th-98th Congresses from 24th and 22d Dists. Ill., 1975-85; U.S. Senator from Ill., 1985-96; dir. Pub. Policy Inst. So. Ill. U., 1996—. U.S. presdl. candidate, 1987-88. Author: Lovejoy: Martyr to Freedom, 1964, Lincoln's Preparation for Greatness, 1965, A Hungry World, 1966, You Want to Change the World, So Change It, 1971, The Tongue-Tied American, 1980, The Once and Future Democrats, 1982, The Glass House: Politics and Morality in The Nation's Capitol, 1984, Beginnings, 1986, Let's Put America Back to Work, 1986, Winners and Losers, 1989, (with Jeanne Hurley Simon) Protestant-Catholic Marriages Can Succeed, 1967, (with Arthur Simon) The Politics of World Hunger, 1973, Advice and Consent, 1992, Freedom's Champion: Elijah Lovejoy, 1994, The Dollar Crisis (with Ross Perot), 1996, Tapped Out: The Coming World Crisis in Water and What We Can Do About It, 1998, Autobiography of Paul Simon, 1999, (with Michael Dukakis) How to Get Into Politics and Why, 2000. With CIC, AUS, 1951-53. Recipient Am. Polit. Sci. Assn. award, 1957; named Best Legislator by Ind. Voters of Ill., 7 times. Mem. Luth. Human Rels. Assn., Am. Legion, VFW, NAACP, Urban League. Democrat. Lutheran. Office: So Ill U Pub Policy Inst Carbondale IL 62901-4429 E-mail: psimon@siu.edu.

SIMON, PAUL H. newspaper editor; Bur. chief AP, Omaha, 1978—. Office: 909 N 96th St Ste 104 Omaha NE 68114-2508

SIMON, SEYMOUR, lawyer, former state supreme court justice; b. Chgo., Aug. 10, 1915; s. Ben and Gertrude (Rusky) S.; m. Roslyn Schultz Biel, May 26, 1954; children: John B., Nancy Simon Cooper, Anthony Biel. BS, Northwestern U., 1935, JD, 1938; LLD (hon.), John Marshall Law Sch., 1982, North Park Coll., 1986, Northwestern U., 1987. Bar: Ill. 1938. Spl. atty. Dept. Justice, 1938-42; practice law Chgo., 1946-74; judge Ill. Appellate Ct., 1974-80; presiding justice Ill. Appellate Ct. (1st Dist., 3d Div.), 1977, 79; justice Ill. Supreme Ct., 1980-88; ptnr. Piper Marbury Rudnick & Wolfe, Chgo., 1988—. Former chmn. Ill. Low-Level Radioactive Waste Disposal Facility Siting Commn.; former dir. Nat. Gen. Corp., Bantam Books, Grosset & Dunlap, Inc., Gt. Am. Ins. Corp. Mem. Cook County Bd. Commrs., 1961-66, pres., 1962-66; pres. Cook County Forest Preserve Dist., 1962-66; mem. Pub. Bldg. Commn., City Chgo., 1962-67; Alderman 40th ward, Chgo., 1955-61, 67-74; Democratic ward committeeman, 1960-74; bd. dirs. Schwab Rehab. Hosp., 1961-71, Swedish Covenant Hosp., 1969-75. With USNR, 1942-45. Decorated Legion of Merit; recipient 9th Ann. Pub. Svc. award Tau Epsilon Rho, 1963, Hubert L. Will award Am. Vets. Com., 1983, award of merit Decalogue Soc. Lawyers, 1986, Judge Learned Hand award Am. Jewish Com., 1994, Frances Feinberg Meml. Crown award Associated Talmud Torahs of Chgo., 1995, Bill of Rights in Action award Constl. Rights Found., 1997, Civic Contbn. award LWV Chgo., 2000; named to Sr. Citizen's Hall of Fame, City of Chgo., 1989, Hall of Fame Jewish Cmty. Ctrs. Chgo., 1989, Laureate Lincoln Acad. Ill., 1997, Chgo. Coun. Lawyers and the Appleseed Fund Justice Commitment to Justice award, 1998. Mem. ABA, Ill. Bar Assn., Chgo. Bar Assn., Chgo. Hist. Soc., Decalogue Soc. Lawyers (Merit award 1986), Izaak Walton League, Chgo. Hort. Soc., Comml. Club Chgo., Std. Club, Variety Club, Order of Coif, Phi Beta Kappa, Phi Beta Kappa Assocs. Home: 1555 N Astor St Chicago IL 60610-1673 Office: Piper Marbury Rudnick & Wolfe 203 N La Salle St Ste 1800 Chicago IL 60601-1210

SIMONS, DOLPH COLLINS, JR. newspaper publisher; b. Lawrence, Kans., Mar. 11, 1930; s. Dolph Collins and Marie (Nelson) S.; m. Pamela Counseller, Feb. 7, 1952; children: Pamela, Linda, Dolph Collins, Dan. AB, U. Kans., 1951; LLD (hon.), Colby Coll., 1972. Reporter Lawrence Jour.-World, 1953, asso. pub., 1957, pub., 1962—, editor, 1978—, pres., 1969—; reporter The Times, London, 1956, Johannesburg (South Africa) Star, 1958; pres. World Co. Mem. Pulitzer Awards Jury, 1977, 78, 80, 81. Trustee, past pres. William Allen White Found.; trustee Midwest Rsch. Inst., Menninger Found., Nat. Parks and Conservation Assn.; former mem. governing bd. Children's Mercy Hosp., Kansas City, Mo.; trustee, chmn. U. Kans. Endowment Assn.; past bd. dirs. Greater Kansas City Cmty. Found., Commerce Bancshares, Kansas City, Mo.; former trustee The Freedom Forum, Kans. Nature Conservancy. Served to capt. USMRC, 1951-53. Recipient Elijah Parish Lovejoy award, 1972; Fred Ellsworth award for significant service to U. Kans., 1976; Disting. Service citation, 1980 Mem. Newspaper Advt. Bur. (past dir.), Am. Soc. Newspaper Editors, Inland Daily Press Assn. (past dir.), Kans. Press Assn. (past pres., dir.), AP (past dir.), Am. Newspaper Pubs. Assn. (past dir., past nat. sec.), Lawrence C. of C. (past pres., dir.), U. Kans. Alumni Assn. (past pres., dir.), Lawrence Country Club, Kansas City Country Club, Kansas City River Club, Masons, Rotary, Sigma Delta Chi, Phi Delta Theta. Republican. Episcopalian. Home: 2425 Vermont St Lawrence KS 66046-4761 Office: 609 New Hampshire St Lawrence KS 66044-2243 E-mail: dsimonsjr@ljworld.com.

SIMONS, GALE GENE, nuclear and electrical engineer, educator; b. Kingman, Kans., Sept. 25, 1939; s. Robert Earl and Laura V. (Swartz) S.; m. Barbara Irene Rinkel, July 2, 1966; 1 child, Curtis Dean. BS, Kans. State U., 1962, MS, 1964, PhD, 1968. Engr. Argonne Nat. Lab., Idaho Falls, Idaho, 1968-77, mgr. fast source reactor, head exptl. support group, 1972-77; prof. nuclear engring. Kans. State U., Manhattan, 1977—, assoc. dean for rsch., dir. rsch. coun. Coll. Engring., 1988-97, bd. dirs. Rsch. Found., 1988-97, Presdl. lectr., 1983-96, career counselor, 1984-96. Cons. to pvt. and fed. agys., 1983—; bd. dirs. Kans. Tech. Enterprise Corp., Topeka; com. mem. Kans. Gov.'s Energy Policy Com., Topeka, 1992-97; numerous presentations in field; reviewer proposals fed. agys. Contbr. over 100 articles to sci. jours.; patentee radiation dosimeter. Expert witness State of Kans., Topeka, 1986. Fellow AEC, 1964-67; numerous grants from fed. agys., 1979—. Mem. AAAS, IEEE, Am. Nuclear Soc., Health Physics Soc., Am. Soc. for Engring. Edn., Masons, Rotary, Phi Kappa Phi, Tau Beta Pi, Pi Mu Epsilon. Home: 2395 Grandview Ter Manhattan KS 66502-3729 Office: Kans State U Durland Hall Rm 261 Manhattan KS 66506-5103

SIMONSON, BRUCE MILLER, geologist, educator; b. Washington, May 13, 1950; s. Roy Walter and Susan (Miller) S.; m. Sue Mareske, June 28, 1974; children: Joseph Walter, Sonja Anne, Maya Beth. BA with high honors, Wesleyan U., Middletown, Conn., 1972; PhD, Johns Hopkins U., 1982. Field mapper Nat. Geog. Inst., Honduras, 1973-74; instr. dept. geology Oberlin (Ohio) Coll., 1979-81, asst. prof., 1982-85, assoc. prof., 1986-88, prof., 1989—, chmn. dept. geology, 1986-89, 93-97, 2000—. Adj. faculty Case Western Res. U., Cleve., 1983—2000; vis. scientist Geol. Survery Western Australia, summers, 1985—87, 1989, 93; tchr. U.S. Geol. Survey, Reston, Va., 1985, vis. prof., Denver, 1992—93. Contbr. articles to profl. jours. Grantee Nat. Geog. Soc., 1986-89, 93-94, 96-97, 99-2000, NSF, 1977-79, 84, 91-94, Rsch. Corp., 1983, Petroleum Rsch. Fund, 1982-84. Mem.: Meteoritical Soc., Soc. for Sedimentary Geology (sec. Gt. Lakes sect. 1986—90), No. Ohio Geol. Soc., Geol. Soc. Australia, Geol. Soc. Am. Office: Oberlin Coll Dept Geology Oberlin OH 44074-1044 E-mail: bruce.simonson@oberlin.edu.

SIMOVIC, LASZLO, architect; b. O Becej, Yugoslavia, May 11, 1957; s. Mihaly and Eva (Daku) S. BArch, Ill. Inst. Tech., 1982; postgrad., Mass. Inst. Tech., 1984. Architect Marton Sass & Assoc., Chgo., 1974-82, Imre & Anthony Halasz Inc., Boston, 1984-85, Skidmore, Owings & Merrill, N.Y.C., 1985-86, Chgo., 1986-87, Loebl, Schlossman & Hackl, Chgo., 1987-89; pvt. practice, 1989—. Home: 6512 N Artesian Ave Chicago IL 60645-5328 Office Fax: 773-338-2226. E-mail: laszloarch@aol.com.

SIMPKIN, LAWRENCE JAMES, engineering company executive; b. Sault Ste Marie, Mich., Jan. 1, 1933; s. Fred Bernard and Helen Clara (Goetz) S.; m. Agnes Diane L'Huillier, Sept. 3, 1960; children: Lawrence J., Lynn Marie, Dawn Catherine. B.S. in Elec. Engring, Mich. Technol. Inst., 1954; M.S., Wayne State U., 1965. Registered profl. engr., Mich. Engr. Detroit Edison Co., 1957-67, supr. engring. instrumentation, 1967-69, dir. elec. div., 1969-72, dir. engring. research, 1972-75, dir. tech. systems planning, 1975-76, gen. dir. div. services, 1976-82, dir. outage mgmt., 1982-84, dir. nuclear engring., 1985-87, gen. dir. generation engring., 1987-95, engring. cons., 1995—; pres. Sunrise Solutions Inc., 1996—. Lectr. Lawrence Inst. Tech., 1965-72; adj. prof. U. Mich., 1974 Contbr. articles to profl. jours. Served to capt. USAF, 1954-57. Mem. IEEE, Engring. Soc. Detroit, Sigma Xi. Home: 4615 S US 23 Greenbush MI 48738 also: 4615 Us Highway 23 Greenbush MI 48738-9753

SIMPSON, A. W. B. law educator; b. 1931; Fellow Oxford U., Eng., 1955-72; prof. U. Kent, Canterbury, Eng., 1972-84, U. Chgo., 1984-87, U. Mich., Ann Arbor, 1987—. Office: U Mich Law Sch 625 S State St Ann Arbor MI 48109-1215

SIMPSON, JACK BENJAMIN, medical technologist, business executive; b. Tompkinsville, Ky., Oct. 30, 1937; s. Benjamin Harrison and Verda Mae (Woods) S.; m. Winona Clara Walden, Mar. 21, 1957; children: Janet Lazann, Richard Benjamin, Randall Walden, Angela Elizabeth. Student, Western Ky. U., 1954-57; grad., Norton Infirmary Sch. Med. Tech., 1958. Asst. chief med. technologist Jackson County Hosp., Seymour, Ind., 1958-61; chief med. technologist, bus. mgr. Mershon Med. Labs., Indpls., 1962-66; founder, dir., officer Am. Monitor Corp., 1966-77; founder, pres., dir. Global Data, Inc., Ft. Lauderdale, Fla., 1986—. Mng. ptnr. Astroland Enterprises, Indpls., 1968—, 106th St. Assocs., Indpls., 1969-72, Keystones Ltd., Indpls., 1970-82, Delray Rd. Assoc. Ltd., Indpls., 1970-71, Allisonville Assocs. Ltd., Indpls., 1970-82, Grandview Assocs. Ltd., 1977—, Rucker Assocs. Ltd., Indpls., 1974—; mng. ptnr. Raintree Assocs. Ltd., Indpls., 1978—, Westgate Assocs. Ltd., Indpls., 1978—; pres., dir. Topps Constrn. Co., Inc., Bradenton, Fla., 1973-91, Acrovest Corp., Asheville, N.C., 1980—; dir. Indpls. Broadcasting, Inc.; founder, bd. dirs. Bank of Bradenton, 1986-92; founder, CFO Biomass Processing Tech., Inc., West Palm Beach, Fla., 1996—; also bd. dirs. Mem. Am. Soc. Med. Technologists (cert.), Indpls. Soc. Med. Technologists, Fla. Soc. Med. Technologists, Am. Soc. Clin. Pathologists, Am. Assn. Clin. Chemistry, Royal Soc. Health (London), Internat. Platform Assn., Am. Mus. Natural History, Columbia of Indpls. Club, Harbor Beach Surf Club, Fishing of Am. Club, Marina Bay Club (Ft. Lauderdale), Elks. Republican. E-mail: jack_simpson@msn.com.

SIMPSON, JOHN S. former finance executive; Grad., U. Minn.; postgrad., Harvard U., U. Wis., U. Calif. Contr. Seco Electronics-Dana Corp., 1973-76; treas. Indsl. Power Transmission Divsn.-Dana Corp., 1976-78; contr. Perfect Circle Products Divsn.-Dana Corp., 1978-82; dir. internat. fin. Dana Corp., 1982-85; v.p. fin. Warner Electric, 1985-87; pres. Diamond Savs. & Loan, 1987-92, Dana Asia Pacific, 1992-96; v.p. fin., treas. Dana Corp., 1996-97, CFO, 1997-99; ret., 1999. Trustee Siena Heights Coll., Adrian, Mich. Mem. Fin. Execs. Inst. Office: Dana Corp PO Box 1000 Toledo OH 43697-1000

SIMPSON, MICHAEL, metals service center executive; b. Albany, N.Y., Dec. 10, 1938; s. John McLaren Simpson and Constance (Hasler) Ames; m. Barbara Ann Bodtke, Jan. 5, 1963; children: Leslie Ann, Elizabeth S. Wessel. BA, U. Mich., 1965, MBA, 1966. Product mgr. Armour & Co., Chgo., 1966-68; with A.M. Castle & Co., Franklin Park, Ill., 1968—, pres. Hy-Alloy Steels Co. divsn., 1974-79, v.p. Midwestern region, 1977-79, chmn. bd., 1979—, also bd. dirs. Trustee Rush-Presbyn.-St. Luke's Med. Ctr., Chgo., 1978—, mem. exec. com., 1980—, vice chmn., 1991—; trustee Oldfields Sch., Glencoe, Md., 1982-87, 95—, chmn. bd., 1998-2000; bd. dirs. Lake Forest (Ill.) Hosp. Found. and Lake Forest Hosp., 1998—; chmn. bd. overseers Rush U., Chgo., 1996--. Office: AM Castle & Co 3400 N Wolf Rd Franklin Park IL 60131-1319 E-mail: msimpson@amcastle.com.

SIMPSON, VI, state senator; b. L.A., Mar. 18, 1946; d. Lloyd M. and Helen (Chacon) Sentman; m. William D. McCarty; children: Jason, Kristina. Student, Ind. U., Indpls. Asst. to chmn. Com. on Status of Women, Calif., 1974-75; dir. pub. affairs Calif. Parks and Recreation Soc., Sacramento, 1975-77; county auditor Monroe County, Ind., 1980-84; mem. Ind. Senate, Indpls., 1984—; exec. dir. Heritage Edn. Found., 1989—. Editor Equal Rights Monitor mag., 1974-76; syndicated newspaper columnist Know You Rights, 1975-76. Named Fresman Dem. Senator of Yr., Ind.

Broadcasters Assn., 1985, Legislator of Yr., Ind. State Employees Assn., 1985, various legis. awards Sierra Club, Ind. Wildlife Fedn., Isaac Walton League, Ind. Parks and Recreation Assn. Mem. NAACP, AAUW. Methodist. Office: Heritage Edn Found 7821 W Morris St Indianapolis IN 46231-1364 also: Ind Senate Dist 40 200 W Washington St Indianapolis IN 46204-2728

SIMPSON, VINSON RALEIGH, manufacturing company executive; b. Chgo., Aug. 9, 1928; s. Vinson Raleigh and Elsie (Passeger) S.; m. Elizabeth Caroline Matte, Sept. 9, 1950; children: Kathleen Simpson Zier, Nancy Simpson Ignacio, James Morgan. SB in Chem. Engring, MIT, 1950; MBA, Ind. U., 1955. With Trane Co., LaCrosse, Wis., 1950-75, mgr. mktg. services, 1957-64, mgr. dealer devel., 1964-66; mng. dir. Trane Ltd., Edinburgh, Scotland, 1966-67; v.p. internat. Trane Co., LaCrosse, Wis., 1967-68, exec. v.p., 1968-70; exec. v.p., gen. mgr. comml. air conditioning div., 1970-73; pres., 1973-75, Simpson and Co., La Crosse, 1975-76; pres., chief operating officer Marathon Electric Mfg. Corp., Wausau, Wis., 1976-80; chmn., pres., chief exec. officer Marion Body Works, Inc., 1980-93, chmn., 1993—. Bd. dirs. Clintonville Area Found. Past trustee, treas. Fox Valley Tech. Coll.; bd. dir., past pres. Fox Valley Tech. Coll. Found.; past pres., bd. dir. Wausau Area Jr. Achievement; mem. Marion Minutemen; past 20 yr. trustee, chair endowment com. Northland Coll.; past dir. Wis. Mfrs. and Commerce, divsn. Wis. Family Bus. Forum, divsn. Wis. Found. for Ind. Colls. Decorated Korean War Commendation ribbon. Mem. Fire Apparatus Mfrs., Nat. Truck Equipment Assn., Am. Legion, Kappa Kappa Sigma, Alpha Tau Omega, Beta Gamma Sigma (dirs. table). Congregationalist. Lodges: Masons, Shriners, Jesters, Rotary (past. pres. Marion club, Paul Harris fellow). Avocations: running, snorkeling, water skiing, cross country skiing, playing the trombone. Home: 171 Fairway Dr Clintonville WI 54929-1071 Office: Marion Body Works Inc 211 W Ramsdell PO Box 500 Marion WI 54950-0500

SIMPSON, WILLIAM ARTHUR, insurance company executive; b. Oakland, Calif., Feb. 2, 1939; s. Arthur Earl and Pauline (Mikalasic) S.; m. Nancy Doughery Simpson, Mar. 31, 1962; children— Sharon Elizabeth, Shelley Pauline B.S., U. Calif.-Berkeley, 1961; postgrad. Exec. Mgmt. Program, Columbia U. C.L.U. V.p. mktg. Countrywide Life, L.A., 1973-76; v.p. agy. Occidental Life of Calif., 1976-79; pres., CEO Vol. State Life, Chattanooga, 1979-83; exec. v.p. Transam. Occidental Life Ins. Co., L.A., 1983-86, pres., 1986-88, pres., CEO, COO, 1988-90, also bd. dirs.; dir. USLIFE Corp., N.Y.C., 1990—; pres., CEO All Am. Life Ins. Co., Pasadena, Calif., 1990-94, USLIFE Life Ins. div. USLIFE Corp., 1994, USLIFE Corp., 1995-97. Chmn. Franklin Life Ins. Co. Pres. Chattanooga coun. Boy Scouts Am., 1982, bd. dirs., L.A., 1983, v.p., 1983-85, vice-chmn L.A. area, 1989, chmn., 1989; pres. bd. councillors L.A. County Am. Cancer Soc.; trustee Verdugo Hills Hosp. Found. 1st lt. U.S. Army, 1961-64, Ill. Symphony Orch.; bd. dirs. Abraham Lincoln coun. Boy Scouts Am. Mem. Am. Soc. CLUs, Life Ins. Mktg. and Rsch. Assn. (bd. dirs. 1986-89), Ctl. Ill. Ins. Co. (bd. dirs.). Republican. Presbyterian. Lodge: Rotary Avocations: golf; skiing. Office: Franklin Life Ins Co 1 Franklin Sq Springfield IL 62713-0002

SIMPSON, WILLIAM MARSHALL, college administrator; b. Chgo., Aug. 26, 1943; s. Marshall Wayne and Edith Berniece (Smith) S.; m. Joyce Ann Heald, Dec. 23, 1966; children: Katherine, Diane. BA, Monmouth Coll., 1965; MA, Ill. State U., 1968, EdD, 1979. Faculty mem. Carl Sandburg Coll., Galesburg, Ill., 1968-79; dir. community svc. Black Hawk Coll., Kewanee, 1979-82; dir. continuing edn. Olympic Coll., Bremerton, Wash., 1982-85, dir. bus. and engring., 1985-86, assoc. dean instrn., 1986-90; dean of the coll. Marshalltown (Iowa) C.C., 1990-97; v.p. acad. affairs Iowa Valley C.C. Dist., 1992=97; pres. John Wood C.C., Quincy, Ill., 1997—. Pres. Adult Edn. Dirs. of Wash., 1984-85; dir. Nat. Coun. Instrnl. Adminstrs., 1986-88; cons. evaluator North Cen. Assn. Colls. and Schs., 1992—; mem. adv. coun. Iowa Youth Apprenticeship, 1993-95. Contbr. articles to profl. jours. Elder First Presbyn. Ch., Galesburg, 1976-79, pres. trustees, 1980-82; elder Cen. Kisap Presbyn. Ch., Bremerton, 1983-86, Marshalltown First Presbyn. Ch., 1993-96; campaign cabinet mem. Marshalltown United Way, 1990, 92, bd. dirs., 1991-97, allocation chair, 1992-93, v.p., 1994-95, pres. 1995-96; mem. adv. com. dept. ednl. adminstrn., Ill. State U., 1991-94; Gov.'s adv. bd. on Literacy, 2000—; bd. dirs. Quincy YMCA, 2001—. Named one of Outstanding Young Men in Am., 1971, Regional Person of Yr. Nat. Coun. on Community Svcs. and Continuing Edn., 1985; NEH grantee, 1975; League for Innovation in the C.C. Exec. Leaership Inst., Class of 1993, Iowa Assn. fo Bus. and Insdustry Leadership Iowa Class of 1994-95. Mem.: Quincy Rotary Club (pres. 2002—), Sigma Phi Epsilon, Phi Delta Kappa. Office: 1301 S 48th St Quincy IL 62305-8736

SIMS, BETTY, state legislator; b. St. Louis, Dec. 15, 1935; Mem. Mo. Senate from 24th dist., Jefferson City, 1994—. Active United Way, Girl Scout Coun., Jr. League Girls, Inc., 1972—. Office: Mo State Mems Rm 226 State Capitol Bldg Jefferson City MO 65101

SINCLAIR, VIRGIL LEE, JR. judge, writer; b. Canton, Ohio, Nov. 10, 1951; s. Virgil Lee and Thelma Irene (Dunlap) S.; children: Kelly, Shannon; m. Janet Brahler Sinclair. BA, Kent State U., 1973; JD, U. Akron, 1976; postgrad., Case Western Res. U., 1939. Adminstr. Stark County Prosecutor's Office, Canton, 1974-76; mem. faculty Walsh Coll., 1976-78; asst. pros. atty. Stark County, 1976-77; ptnr. Amerman Burt Bones Co. LPA, 1976-91, Buckingham, Doolittle and Burroughs Co., L.P.A., Canton, 1991-95; judge Stark County Common Pleas Ct., 1995—, adminstrv. judge, 1996, presiding judge, 1999. Mem. faculty Ohio Jud. Coll., 1991—, lead faculty, 1998—; mem. legal adviser Mayor's Office, City of North Canton, Ohio, 1978-79; referee Stark County Family Ct., Canton, 1981, Canton Mcpl. Ct., 1991—; spl. referee Canton Mcpl. Ct., 1985-86. Author: Law Enforcement Officers' Guide to Juvenile Law, 1975, Lawy Manual of Juvenile Law, 1976, Handling Capital Punishment Cases, 1998, Ohio Jury Institutions, Capital Punishment Approved, Jury Instructions, 2000; editor: U. Akron Law Rev.; contbr. to Ohio Family Law, 1983, also articles to profl. jours. Mem. North Canton Planning Comm., 1979-82; bd. mgrs. North Canton YMCA, 1976—, Camp Tippecanoe, Ohio, 1981—; profl. adviser Parents Without Partners, 1980—; spl. sep. Stark County Sheriff Dept., 1983—; trustee Palace Theatre Assn., Canton, 1983—. Recipient Disting. Service award U.S. Jaycees, 1984; named to Hall of Distinction, Plain Local Schs., 1999, Jud. Hall of Fame, U. Akron Sch. Law, 2000. Mem. ABA, Ohio Bar Assn., Stark County Bar Assn. (lects. 1984), Ohio Trial Lawyers Assn., Assn. Trial Lawyers Am., Nat. Dist. Attys. Assn., Akron Law Sch. Alumni Assn. (trustee), Jaycees, Elks, Eagles, Masons, Delta Theta Phi (bailiff 1976, nat. key winner 1975-76). Republican. Methodist.

SINCOFF, MICHAEL Z. human resources and marketing professional; b. Washington, June 28, 1943; s. Murray P. and Anna F. (Jaffe) S. m. Kathleen M. Dunham, Oct. 9, 1983. BA, U. Md., 1964, MA, 1966; PhD, Purdue U., 1969. Instr. U. Tenn., Knoxville, 1968; asst. prof. Ohio U., Athens, 1969-74, dir. Ctr. for Comm. Studies, 1969-76, assoc. prof., 1974-76; vis. prof. U. Minn., St. Paul, 1974; dir. personnel devel. Hoechst-Celanese Corp. (formerly Celanese Corp.), N.Y., 1976-79; dir. employee comm. The Mead Corp., Dayton, Ohio, 1979-81, dir. edn., tng., 1981-83; assoc. dean Sch. of Bus. Adminstrn. Georgetown U., Washington, 1983-84; v.p. human resources ADVO, Inc. (formerly ADVO-Sys., Inc.), Hartford, Conn., 1984-87; v.p. human resources, corp. officer DIMAC Direct Inc., St. Louis, 1987-88; sr. v.p. human resources and adminstrn., sr. corp. officer DIMAC Mktg. Corp. (parent of DIMAC Direct Inc.), 1988-97, also sec., asst. treas., exec. com., 1988-97; sr. v.p. human resources, exec. corp. officer Brooks Fiber Properties, Inc. (now Brooks WorldCom), 1997-98; pres., CEO Michaelson Group Ptnrs., Dayton, Ohio, 1998—. Vis. prof. Wright State U., Dayton, Ohio, 1999—; assoc. grad. faculty mem. Ctrl. Mich. U., Mt. Pleasant, 1999—. Author, editor human resources sect. Am. Mgmt. Assn. Mgmt. Handbook, 3d edit., 1994; author approximately 50 books and articles; mem. edtl. adv. bd. Jour. Applied Comm. Rsch., 1991-97. Life mem. Internat. Comm. Assn. (bus. mgr.-exec. sec. 1969-73, fin. com. 1982-85); mem. Am. Mgmt. Assn. (human resources coun. 1990-2000), Printing Industries of Am. (employer resources group 1989-97).

SINDLINGER, VERNE E. bishop; Bishop Lincoln Trails Synod, Indpls.; exec. SYNOD, 1994. Office: Presbyterian Church USA 1100 W 42d St Ste 220 Indianapolis IN 46208-3345

SINES, RAYMOND E. former state legislator; m. Suanne Sines; children: Stephanie, Amanda, Victoria. Student, Lakeland Coll., Aldenson-Broadus Coll. Mem. Ohio Ho. of Reps., Columbus, 1993-97; state rep. Ohio Dist. 69, 1993; owner Sines & Sons, Inc., Painesville, Ohio. Bd. dirs. Humane Soc. Mem. Am Legion, United Way, C. of C., Farm Bureau, Ahtletic Assocs. Home: 4287 Harper St Perry OH 44081-9744 Office: 2481 N Oak Ridge Rd Painesville OH 44077

SINGER, ELEANOR, sociologist, editor; b. Vienna, Austria, Mar. 4, 1930; came to U.S., 1938; d. Alfons and Anna (Troedl) Schwarzbart; m. Alan Gerard Singer, Sept. 8, 1949; children: Emily Ann, Lawrence Alexander BA, Queens Coll., 1951; PhD, Columbia U., 1966. Asst. editor Am. Scholar, Williamsburg, Va., 1951-52; editor Tchrs. Coll. Press, N.Y.C., 1952-56, Dryden-Holt, N.Y.C., 1956-57; rsch. assoc., sr. rsch. assoc., sr. rsch. scholar Columbia U., 1966-94; sr. rsch. scientist Inst. for Social Rsch. U. Mich., Ann Arbor, 1994—, acting assoc. dir., 1998-99, assoc. dir., 1999—2002; editor Pub. Opinion Quar., N.Y.C., 1975-86. Author: (with Carol Weiss) The Reporting of Social Science in the Mass Media, 1988, (with Phyllis Endreny) Reporting On Risk, 1993; editor: (with Herbert H. Hyman) Readings in Reference Group Theory and Research, 1968, (with Stanley Presser) Survey Research Methods: A Reader, 1989; contbr. articles to profl. jours. Mem. Am. Assn. Pub. Opinion Rsch. (pres. N.Y.C. chpt. 1983-84, pres. 1987-88, Exceptionally Disting. Achievement award 1996), Am. Sociol. Assn., Am. Statis. Assn. Office: U Mich Inst Social Rsch PO Box 1248 Ann Arbor MI 48106-1248 E-mail: esinger@isr.umich.edu.

SINGER, J. DAVID, political science educator; b. Bklyn., Dec. 7, 1925; s. Morris L. and Anne (Newman) S.; m. C. Diane Macaulay, Apr., 1990; children: Kathryn Louise, Eleanor Anne. BA, Duke U., 1946; LLD (hon.), Northwestern U., 1983; PhD, NYU, 1956. Instr. NYU, 1954-55, Vassar Coll., 1955-57; vis. fellow social relations Harvard U., 1957-58; vis. asst. prof. U. Mich., Ann Arbor, 1958-60, sr. scientist Mental Health Research Inst., 1960-82, assoc. prof., 1964-65, prof. polit. sci., 1965—, coordinator World Politics Program, 1969-75, 81-90; vis. prof. U. Oslo and Inst. Social Research, 1963-64, 90, Carnegie Endowment Internat. Peace and Grd. Inst. Internat. Studies, Geneva, 1967-68, Zuma and U. Mannheim (W. Ger.), 1976, Grad. Inst. Internat. Studies, Geneva, 1983-84; U. Groningen, The Netherlands, 1991; Nat. Chengchi U., Taiwan, 1998. Author: Financing International Organization: The United Nations Budget Process, 1961, Deterrence, Arms Control and Disarmament: Toward a Synthesis in National Security Policy, 1962, rev. 1984, (with Melvin Small) The Wages of War, 1816-1965: A Statistical Handbook, 1972, (with Susan Jones) Beyond Conjecture in International Politics: Abstracts of Data Based Research, 1972, (with Dorothy La Barr) The Study of International Politics: A Guide to Sources for the Student, Teacher and Researcher, 1976, Correlates of War I and II, 1979, 80, (with Melvin Small) Resort to Arms: International and Civil War, 1816-1980, 1982, Models, Methods, and Progress: A Peace Research Odyssey, 1990, (with Paul Diehl) Measuring the Correlates of War, 1998, (with D. Geller) Nations at War, 1998; monographs; contbr. articles to profl. jours.; mem. editorial bd. ABC: Polit. Sci. and Govt., 1968-84, Polit. Sci. Reviewer, 1971— , Conflict Mgmt. and Peace Sci., 1978— , Etudes Polemologigues, 1978—, Internat. Studies Quar., 1989—, Jour. Conflict Resolution, 1989—, Internat. Interactions, 1989—. With USNR, 1943-66. Ford fellow, 1956; Ford grantee, 1957-58; Phoenix Meml. Fund grantee, 1959,, 1981-82; Fulbright scholar, 1963-64; Carnegie Corp. research grantee, 1963-67; NSF grantee, 1967-76, 1986-89, 1992-94; Guggenheim grantee, 1978-79 Mem. Am. Polit. Sci. Assn. (Helen Dwight Reid award com. 1967, 95, chmn. Woodrow Wilson award com., chmn. nominating com. 1970), Internat. Polit. Sci. Assn. (chmn. conflict and peace rsch. com. 1974—), World Assn. Internat. Rels., Internat. Soc. Polit. Psychology, Internat. Soc. Rsch. on Aggression, Social Sci. History Assn., Peace Sci. Soc., Internat. Peace Rsch. Assn. (pres. 1972-73), Consortium on Peace Rsch., Fedn. Am. Scientists (nat. coun. 1991-95), Union Concerned Scientists, Arms Control Assn., Internat. Studies Assn. (pres. 1985-86), Com. Nat. Security, Am. Com. on East-West Accord, World Federalist Assn. Office: U Mich Dept Polit Sci Ann Arbor MI 48104

SINGH, RAJENDRA, mechanical engineering educator; b. Dhampur, India, Feb. 13, 1950; came to U.S., 1973; s. Raghubir and Ishwar (Kali) S.; m. Veena Ghungesh, June 24, 1979; children: Rohit, Arun. BS with honors, Birla Inst., 1971; MS, U. Roorkee, India, 1973; PhD, Purdue U., 1975. Grad. instr. Purdue U., West Layfayette, Ind., 1973-75; sr. engr. Carrier Corp., Syracuse, N.Y., 1975-79; asst. prof. Ohio State U., Columbus, 1979-83, assoc. prof., 1983-87, prof., 1987—, Donald D. Glower chair in engring., 2001—. Adj. lectr. Syracuse (N.Y.) U., 1977-79; pres.-elect, bd. dirs., v.p. tech. activities Inst. of Noise Control Engring., pres.-elect, 2002; gen. chmn. Nat. Noise Conf., Columbus, 1985; leader of U.S. delegation to India-U.S.A. Symposium on Vibration and Noise Engring., 1996; vis. prof. U. Calif., Berkeley, 1987-88; pres. Inter-Noise 2002 Congress; chmn. India-USA Symposium on Vibration and Noise, 2001; cons., lectr. in field. Author: Emerging Trends in Vibration and Noise Engineering, 1996; contbr. over 240 articles to profl. jours.; guest editor jours. Recipient Gold medal U. Roorkee, 1973, R. H. Kohr Rsch. award Purdue U., 1975, Excellence in Tchg. award Inst. Noise Control Engring., 1989, Rsch. award Ohio State U., 1983, 87, 91, 96, 2001, Educator of Yr. award GM Tech. Edn. Program, 1998. Fellow ASME, Acoustical Soc. Am.; mem. Soc. Auto Engring., Inst. Noise Control Engring.(cert.), Am. Soc. Engring. Edn. (George Westinghouse award 1993). Achievements include patent for rolling door; development of new analytical and experimental techniques in machine dynamics, acoustics, vibration and fluid control. Home: 4772 Belfield Ct Dublin OH 43017-2592 Office: Ohio State U 206 W 18th Ave Columbus OH 43210-1189 E-mail: singh.3@osu.edu.

SINGHVI, SURENDRA SINGH, finance and strategy consultant; b. Jodhpur, Rajasthan, India, Jan. 16, 1942; came to U.S., 1962, naturalized 1986; s. Rang Raj and Ugam Kanwar (Surana) S.; m. Sushila Bhandari, July 7, 1965; children: Seema, Sandeep. B in Commerce, Rajasthan U., 1961; MBA, Atlanta U., 1963; PhD, Columbia U., 1967. CPA, Cert. Mgmt. Acct. Asst. prof. fin. Miami U., Oxford, Ohio, 1967-69, assoc. prof., 1969-70; adj. prof. fin., 1970-95; fin. mgr. ARMCO Inc., Middletown, Ohio, 1970-79, asst. treas., 1979-83, gen. fin. mgr., 1983-86; v.p. and treas. Edison Bros. Stores, Inc., St. Louis, 1986-90; pres. Singhvi & Assocs., Inc., Dayton, Ohio, 1990—. Bd. dirs. Columbia Indsl. Sales Corp., Hauer Music Co., Oasis Property Inc., Keystone Industries Ltd., Om Hospitality, Inc. Author: Planning for Capital Investment, 1980; co-editor: Frontiers of Financial Management, 4th edit., 1984, Global Finance 2000-A Handbook of Strategy and Organization (The Conference Board), 1996; contbr. over 90 articles to profl. jours. Bd. trustees South Ctrl. Ohio Minority Bus. Coun., 2000—. Recipient Chancellor's Gold medal Rajasthan U., Ahimsa (Non-Violence) award Fedn. Jaina Assns. in N.Am., 1999. Mem. Inst. Mgmt. Accts. (Bayer Silver medal 1978), Fin. Execs. Inst., Fin. Mgmt. Assn., Asian Am. Hotel Owners Assn., Asian Indian Am. Bus. Group in S.W. Ohio (pres. 1997, 98), Dayton Minority Supplier Devel. Coun. (dir. 1997—, chmn. 2000), Rotary (dir. internat. program Middletown chpt. 1973-86, Dayton chpt. 1995—, treas., dir. 2001—), India Club (pres. Dayton chpt. 1980). Avocations: swimming, kanasta, travel, hiking, writing. Home: 439 Ridge Line Ct Dayton OH 45458-9564 Office: Singhvi and Assocs Inc 515 Windsor Park Dr Dayton OH 45459-4112 E-mail: ssinghvi@att.net.

SINGLETON, MARVIN AYERS, state legislator, otolaryngologist; b. Baytown, Tex., Oct. 7, 1939; s. Henry Marvin and Mary Ruth Singleton. BA, U. of the South, 1962; MD, U. Tenn., 1966. Diplomate Am. Bd. Otolaryngology. Intern City of Memphis Hosps., 1966-67; resident in surgery Highland Alameda City Hosp., Oakland, Calif., 1967-68; resident in otolaryngology U. Tenn. Hosp., Memphis, 1968-71; fellow in otolaryngic pathology Armed Forces Inst. Pathology, Washington, 1971; fellow in otologic surgery U. Colo. at Gallup (N.Mex.) Indian Med. Ctr., 1972; practice medicine specializing in otolaryngology/allergies Joplin, Mo., 1972—. Founder, operator Home and Farm Investments, Joplin, 1975—, staff mem. Freeman Hosp., St. John's Hosp., Joplin, Oakhill Hosp.; cons. in otolaryngology Mo. Crippled Children's Service, Santa Fe R.R.; pres. Ozark Mfg. Co., Inc., Joplin. Mem. Internat. Arabian Racing Bd., 1983-88; mem. Mo. State Senate, 1990—; del. Rep. Nat. Conv., 1988, 92. Served with USNG, 1966-72. Fellow Am. Coll. Surgery, Am. Acad. Otolaryngologic Allergy (past pres.), Am. Assn. Clin. Immunology & Allergy; mem. AMA (Mo. del.), Mo. State Med. Assn., Sthn. Med. Assn., Jasper County Med. Assn., Coun. Otolaryngology, Mo. State Allergy Assn., Ear Nose & Throat Soc. Mo. (past pres.), Joplin C. of C., Masons (32d degree), Sigam Alpha Epsilon, Phi Theta Kappa, Phi Chi. Methodist. Home: 4476 Five Mile Rd Seneca MO 64865-8357 Office: 114 W 32nd St Joplin MO 64804-3701 E-mail: DocSingleton@fivemileranch.com.

SINHA, KUMARES CHANDRA, civil engineering educator, researcher, consultant; b. Calcutta, India, July 12, 1939; s. Amares Chandra and Asha Rani (Mitra) S.; m. Anne Elizabeth Kallina; children: Shohini Sarah, Rahul Norman, Nabina Justine, Arjun Daniel, Ishan Edmund. BSCE, Jadavpur U., 1961; diploma in town and regional planning, Calcutta U., 1964; MSCE, U. Conn., 1966, PhD, 1968. Registered profl. engr., Ind. Asst. engr. Pub. Works Dept., West Bengal, Calcutta, 1961-64; asst. prof. civil engring. Marquette U., Milw., 1968-72, assoc. prof., dir. urban transp. program, 1972-74; assoc. prof. civil engring. Purdue U., West Lafayette, Ind., 1974-78, prof., 1978—, assoc. dir. Ctr. Pub. Policy, 1978-79, head transp. and urban engring., 1981—. Vis. prof. MIT, Cambridge, 1980, U. Roorkee, India, 1981; systems engring. cons. Southeastern Wis. Regional Planning Commn., Waukesha, 1969-76; cons. Ind. Transp. Assn. Inc., Indpls., 1985, UN Devel. Program, India, 1985, Chinese Ministry of Communications, Beijing, 1986, World Bank, 1988—. Author or co-author over 200 tech. publs. on transp. engring. and mgmt. Recipient Fred Burggraff award Transp. Research Bd., Washington, 1972; 50 research grants and contracts NSF, U.S. Dept. Transp., Ind. Dept. Transp., 1968—. Fellow ASCE (chmn. urban transp. div. 1982-83, Frank M. Masters award 1986), Inst. Transp. Engrs. (chmn. tech. coms. 1978-84); mem. Am. Inst. Cert. Planners, Am. Pub. Works Assn., Am. Soc. Engring. Edn. Hindu. Avocations: reading. Home: 2224 Miami Trl West Lafayette IN 47906-1924 Office: Purdue Univ Sch Civil Engring West Lafayette IN 47907

SINHA, SUNIL KUMAR, physicist; b. Calcutta, India, Sept. 13, 1939; came to U.S., 1965; s. Sushil Kumar and Romola Sinha; m. Lonny Linde Olsen, Jan. 27, 1962; children: Arjun, Ranjan. BA in Natural Scis., Cambridge U., Britain, 1960, PhD in Physics, 1964. Vis. scientist Bhabha Atomic Rsch. Ctr., Trombay, India, 1965; asst. prof. physics dept. Iowa State U., Ames, 1966-69, assoc. prof., 1969-71, prof. physics, 1972-75; sr. physicist Argonne (Ill.) Nat. Lab., 1975-82; sr. rsch. assoc. Corp. Rsch., Exxon Rsch., Annandale, N.J., 1982-95; assoc. dir. exptl. facilities divsn. Advanced Photon Source Argonne (Ill.) Nat. Lab., 1995-2001; prof. physics U. Calif., San Diego, 2001—. Chmn. U. Chgo. Rev. Com. for Materials Scis. Div., Argonne (Ill.) Nat. Lab., 1990; past chmn. Argonne Intense Pulsed Neutron Source Rev. Com., 1987-91; chmn. Div. Condensed Matter Physics Fellowship Com. of Am. Phys. Soc., 1990-91, Oak Ridge Nat. Small Angle Scattering Ctr. Rev. Com., 1986-89. Editor: Ordering in Two Dimensions, 1980, Spin Waves and Magnetic Excitations, 1990; contbr. articles to profl. jours. Recipient Dept. Energy Rsch. Achievement award, 1981, Ernest Orlando Lawrence Meml. award, 1996, Arthur H. Compton award Advanced Photon Source, 2000; Guggenheim fellow, 1982. Fellow AAAS, Am. Phys. Soc.; mem. Materials Rsch. Soc., Am. Crystallographic Assn. Achievements include rsch. in antiferromagnetism in High Tc materials by neutron diffraction; theory of diffuse X-ray scattering from surfaces. Office: Argonne Nat Lab 9700 Cass Ave Argonne IL 60439-4803

SINOR, DENIS, Orientalist, educator; b. Kolozsvar, Hungary, Apr. 17, 1916; s. Miklos and Marguerite (Weitzenfeld) S.; m. Eugenia Trinajstic (dec.); children: Christophe (dec.), Sophie. BA, U. Budapest, 1938; MA, Cambridge (Eng.) U., 1948; doctorate (hon.), U. Szeged, Hungary, 1971. Attache Centre National de la Recherche Scientifique, Paris, 1939-48; univ. lectr. Altaic studies Cambridge U., 1948-62; prof. Uralic and Altaic studies and history Ind. U., Bloomington, 1962-81, disting. prof. Uralic and Altaic studies and history, 1975-86, disting. prof. emeritus Uralic and Altaic studies and history, 1986—, chmn. dept. Uralic and Altaic studies, 1963-1981, dir. Lang. and Area Ctr., 1963-88, dir. Asian studies program, 1965-67, dir. Asian Studies Rsch. Inst., 1967-79, dir. Rsch. Inst. for Inner Asian Studies, 1979-1981, 85-86. Sec. gen. Permanent Internat. Altaistic Conf., 1961—; rsch. project dir. U.S. Office Edn., 1969-70; sec. Internat. Union Orientalists, 1954-64; vis. prof. Institut Nat. des Langues et Civilizations Orientales, Paris, spring 1974; scholar-in-residence Rockefeller Found. Study Ctr., Bellagio, 1975; vice chmn. UNESCO Commn. for History Civilization Cen. Asia, 1981—, mem. consultative com. UNESCO Silk Rd. Project, 1990-97; summer seminar dir. NEH, 1988. Author: Orientalism and History, 1954, History of Hungary, 1959, Introduction a l'ètude de l'Eurasie Centrale, 1963, Aspects of Altaic Civilization, 1963, Inner Asia, 1968, Inner Asia and Its Contacts with Medieval Europe, 1977, Tanulmányok, 1982, Essays in Comparative Altaic Linguistics, 1990, Studies in Medieval Inner Asia, 1997; editor, contbr.: Modern Hungary, 1977, Studies in Finno-Ugric Linguistics, 1977, Uralic Languages, 1988, Essays on Uzbek History, Culture and Languages, 1993, Cambridge History of Early Inner Asia, Handbook of Uralic Studies, Jour. Asian History, Ind. U. Uralic and Altaic Series; mem. am. edtl. rev. bd. Britannica-Hungarica. Served with Forces Françaises de l'Intérieur, 1943-44; with French Army, 1944-45. NEH grantee, 1981, 87, 88; recipient Jubilee prize U. Budapest, 1938, Barczi Geza Meml. medal, 1981, Gold medal Permanent Internat. Altaistic Conf., 1982, 1996, Arminius Vambery Meml. medal, 1983, The Thomas Hart Benton Mural Medallion, Hungarian Order of Star, 1986, UNESCO Avicenna medal, 1998; Am. Philos. Soc. Research grantee, 1963; Am. Council Learned Soc. research grantee, 1962; Guggenheim fellow, 1968-69, 1981-82, Amer. Oriental Soc. Med. of Hon., 1999. Fellow Körösi Csoma Soc. (hon.); mem. Royal Asiatic Soc. (hon. sec. 1954-64, Denis Sinor medal for Inner Asian Studies named in his honor 1992), Am. Oriental Soc. (pres. Midwest br. 1968-70, nat. pres. 1975-76, medal of honor 1999), Assn. Asian Studies, Am. Hist. Soc., Soc. Asiatique (hon.), Tibet Soc. (pres. 1969-74), Mongolia Soc. (pres. 1987-94), Correspondant de l'Académie des inscriptions et belles lettres (Paris), Hungarian Acad. Scis. (hon.), Acad. Europaea (fgn.), Deutsche Morgenlandische Gesellschaft, Suomalais-Ugrilaisen Seura (hon.), Soc. Uralo-Altaica (v.p. 1964-94, hon.), Internat. Union Oriental and Asian Studies (v.p. 1993—), Cosmos Club Washington, Explorers Club N.Y.C., United

Oxford and Cambridge Club London. Home: 5581 E Lampkins Ridge Rd Bloomington IN 47401-8674 Office: Indiana U Dept Ctrl Eurasian Studies Goodbody Hall Bloomington IN 47405

SIPES, CONNIE W. state legislator, educator; b. New Albany, Ind., Aug. 6, 1949; m. Stephen Sipes; children: Cassie, Zachary. BS, Ind. U.-S.E., 1971, MS in Edn., 1975, MS in Adminstrn., 1991. Prin. Fairmont Elem. Sch., New Albany, Ind., 1991—; mem. Ind. Senate from 46th dist., Indpls., 1997—; mem. edn. com., mem. pension and labor com.; ranking minority elections com.; mem. transp. and interstate coop. com. Mem. Dem. Women's Club. Recipient Woman of Achievement award BPW, 1986. Mem. LWV, Ind. State Prins. Assn., Nat. Assn. Elem. Prins. Avocation: running. Office: 200 W Washington St Indianapolis IN 46204-2728

SIPES, KAREN KAY, newspaper editor; b. Higginsville, Mo., Jan. 8, 1947; d. Walter John and Katherine Marie (McLelland) Heins; m. Joel Rodney Sipes, Sept. 24, 1971; 1 child, Lesley Katherine. BS in Edn., Ctrl. Mo. State U., 1970. Reporter/news editor Newton Kansan, 1973—76; sports writer Capital-Jour., Topeka, 1976—83, spl. sects. editor, 1983—85, editl. page editor, 1985—92, mng. editor/features, 1992—2002, asst. editl. page editor, 2002—. Co-chair Mayor's Commn. on Literacy, Topeka, 1995-96; mem. Act Against Violence Com., Topeka, 1995-96, Mayor's Task Force on Race Rels., 1998; mem. planning com. Leadership Greater Topeka, 1997; Great Am. Cleanup, 1999-2001, ERC/Resource and Referral, 2001—; mem. Martin Luther King Living the Dream Bus. Ptnrs. Com., 2001--. Mem. Ctrl. Mo. State U. Alumni Assn. (bd. dirs. 1996-2002, v.p. 1999, pres. 2000). Avocations: music, gardening, art. Office: The Capital-Journal 616 SE Jefferson St Topeka KS 66607-1194 E-mail: critterkaren@aol.com., ksipes@cjonline.com.

SIPFLE, DAVID ARTHUR, retired philosophy educator; b. Pekin, Ill., Aug. 29, 1932; s. Karl Edward and Louis Adele (Hinners) S.; m. Mary-Alice Slauson, Sept. 4, 1954; children: Ann Littlefield (dec.), Gail Elizabeth. BA in Math., Philosophy magna cum laude, Carleton Coll., 1953; MA, Yale U., 1955, PhD, 1958. Instr. philosophy Robert Coll., Istanbul, Turkey, 1957-58, Am. Coll. for Girls, Istanbul, 1957-60; asst. prof. Carleton Coll., Northfield, Minn., 1960-67, assoc. prof., 1967-70, chmn. dept., 1968-71, 89-92, prof., 1970-92, William H. Laird prof. philosophy and liberal arts, 1992-98. Vis. fellow Wolfson Coll., Cambridge U., 1975-76. Translator: (with Mary-Alice Sipfle) Emile Meyerson, The Relativistic Deduction: Epistemological Implications of the Theory of Relativity, 1985, Explanation in the Sciences, 1991; contbr. articles to profl. jours. NEH Younger Humanist fellow, Nice, France, 1971-72, NSF Sci. Faculty fellow, Cambridge, Eng., 1975-76; Carleton Coll. Faculty Devel. grantee, 1981-83, 86-87. Mem. Am. Philos. Assn., Metaphysical Soc. Am., Philosophy of Sci. Assn. Avocation: cross country skiing. Office: Carleton Coll 1 N College St Northfield MN 55057-4001 E-mail: dsipfle@carleton.edu.

SIROTKA, MIKE, professional baseball player; b. Chgo., May 13, 1971; Baseball player Chgo. White Sox, 1995—. Office: Chgo White Sox 333 W 35th St Chicago IL 60616

SISKE, ROGER CHARLES, lawyer; b. Starkville, Miss., Mar. 2, 1944; s. Lester L. and Helen (Cagan) S.; m. Regina Markunas, May 31, 1969; children: Kelly, Jennifer, Kimberly. BS in Fin. with honors, Ohio State U., 1966; JD magna cum laude, U. Mich., 1969. Bar: Ill. 1969. Assoc. Sonnenschein Nath & Rosenthal, Chgo., 1969-78, ptnr., 1978—. Chmn. nat. employee benefits and exec. compensation dept. Served to capt. U.S. Army, 1970-71. Decorated Bronze Star. Fellow Am. Coll. Employee Benefits Counsel (charter); mem. ABA (past chmn. tax sect. employee benefits com., past chmn. joint com. on employee benefits and exec. compensation and bus. law sect., employee benefits and exec. compensation com.), Chgo. Bar Assn. (past chmn. employee benefits com., mem. exec. coun. of tax com.), past chmn. employee benefits coun. ISBA, Order of Coif (editor law review), Phi Alpha Kappa. Republican. Office: Sonnenschein Nath Rosenthal 233 S Wacker Dr Ste 8000 Chicago IL 60606-6491

SIVE, REBECCA ANNE, public affairs company executive; b. N.Y.C., Jan. 29, 1950; d. David and Mary (Robinson) S.; m. Clark Steven Tomashefsky, June 18, 1972. BA, Carleton Coll., 1972; MA in Am. History, U. Ill., Chgo., 1975. Asst. to chmn. of pres.' task force on vocations Carleton Coll., Northfield, Minn., 1972; asst. to acquisitions librarian Am. Hosp. Assn., Chgo., 1973; rsch. asst. Jane Addams Hull House, 1974; instr. Loop Coll., 1975, Columbia Coll., Chgo., 1975-76; cons. Am. Jewish Com., 1975, Ctr. for Urban Affairs, Northwestern U., Evanston, Ill., 1977, Ill. Consultation on Ethnicity in Edn., 1976, MLA, 1977; dir. Ill. Women's History Project, 1975-76; founder, exec. dir. Midwest Women's Ctr., Chgo., 1977-81; exec. dir. Playboy Found., 1981-84; v.p. pub. affairs/pub. rels. Playboy Video Corp., 1985; v.p. pub. affairs Playboy Enterprises, Inc., Chgo., 1985-86; pres. The Sive Group, Inc., 1986—. Guest speaker various edn. orgns., 1972— ; instr. Roosevelt U., Chgo., 1977-78; dir. spl. projects Inst. on Pluralism and Group Identity, Am. Jewish Com., Chgo., 1975-77; cons. Nat. Women's Polit. Caucus, 1978-80; bd. dirs. NOVA Health Systems, Woodlawn Community Devel. Corp.; trainer Midwest Acad.; mem. adv. bd. urban studies program Associated Colls. Midwest; proposal reviewer NEH Contbr. articles to profl. jours. Commr. Chgo. Park Dist., 1986-88; mem. steering com. Ill. Commn. on Human Rels., 1976; mem. structure com. Nat. Women's Agenda Coalition, 1976-77; del.-at-large Nat. Women's conf., 1977; mem. Ill. Gov.'s Com. on Displaced Homemakers, 1979-81, Ill. Human Rights Com., 1980-87, Ill. coordinating com., Internat Womens Yr.; coord. Ill. Bicentennial Photog. Exhbn., 1977; mem. Ill. Employment and Tng. Coun.; mem. employment com. Ill. Com. on Status of Women; bd. dirs. Nat. Abortion Rights Action League and NARAL Found., Ill. div. ACLU, Midwest Women's Ctr. Recipient award for outstanding community leadership YWCA Met. Chgo., 1979, award for outstanding community leadership Chgo. Jaycees, 1988. Home: 1235 N Astor St Apt 3N Chicago IL 60610-5213 Office: The Sive Group Inc 1235 N Astor St Chicago IL 60610-5213

SIX, FRED N. state supreme court justice; b. Independence, Mo., Apr. 20, 1929; AB, U. Kans., 1951, JD with honors, 1956; LLM in Judicial Process, U. Va., 1990. Bar: Kans. 1956. Asst. atty. gen. State of Kans., 1957-58; pvt. practice Lawrence, Kans., 1958-87; judge Kans. Ct. Appeals, 1987-88; justice Kans. Supreme Ct., Topeka, 1988—. Editor-in-chief U. Kans. Law Review, 1955-56; lectr. on law Washburn U. Sch. Law, 1957-58, U. Kans., 1975-76. Served with USMC, 1951-53; USMCR, 1957-62. Recipient Disting. Alumnus award U. Kans. Sch. Law, 1994. Fellow Am. Bar Found. (chmn. Kans. chpt. 1983-87); mem. ABA (jud. adminstrn. divsn.), Am. Judicature Soc., Kans. Bar Assn., Kans. Bar Found., Kans. Law Soc. (pres. 1970-72), Kans. Inn of Ct. (pres. 1993-94), Order of Coif, Phi Delta Phi. Office: Kans Supreme Ct 374 Kansas JudICIAL Center 301 SW 10th Ave Topeka KS 66612-1502 E-mail: fsix@kscourts.org.

SKAGGS, BILL, state legislator; b. Sylacanga, Ala., Jan. 24, 1942; Student, Ctrl. Mo. State U. Rep. Mo. State Ho. Reps. Dist. 34, 1983-93, Mo. State Ho. Reps. Dist. 31, 1993—. Home: 3613 N Park Ave Kansas City MO 64116-2831 Office: Mo Ho of Reps State Capitol Jefferson City MO 65101

SKELTON, ISAAC NEWTON, IV (IKE SKELTON), congressman; b. Lexington, Mo., Dec. 20, 1931; s. Isaac Newton and Carolyn (Boone) S.; m. Susan B. Anding, July 22, 1961; children: Ike, Jim, Page. AB, U. Mo., 1953, LLB, 1956. Bar: Mo. 1956. Pvt. practice, Lexington; pros. atty. Lafayette County, Mo., 1957-60; spl. asst. atty. gen. State of Mo., 1961-63; mem. Mo. Senate from 28th dist., 1971-76, 95th-107th Congresses from 4th Mo. Dist., 1977—, ranking minority mem. ho. armed svcs. com., mem. intelligence com. Active Boy Scouts Am. Mem. Phi Beta Kappa, Sigma Chi. Democrat. Mem. Christian Ch. Clubs: Masons, Shriners, Elks. Home: 6754 Towne Lane Rd Mc Lean VA 22101-2935 Office: US Ho of Reps 2206 Rayburn House Ofc Bldg Washington DC 20515-0001*

SKIBNIEWSKI, MIROSLAW JAN, engineering educator, management researcher; MEng, Warsaw Tech. U., 1981; MS, Carnegie-Mellon U., 1983, PhD, 1986; cert. in advanced studies, Harvard U. Grad. Sch. Edn., 2000. Staff engr. engrng. dept. Pitts. Testing Lab., 1981-82; rsch. and tchg. asst. dept. civil engrng. Carnegie-Mellon U., Pitts., 1982-86; asst. prof. Sch. Civil Engrng. Purdue U., West Lafayette, Ind., 1986-90, assoc. prof. Sch. Civil Engrng., 1990-95, prof. Sch. Civil Engrng., 1995—, asst. exec. v.p. acad. affairs, 1997-2001, assoc. provost Ind., 2001—. Vis. sr. rsch. scientist divsn. bldg., constrn. and engrng. Commonwealth Scientific and Indsl. Rsch. Orgn., Melbourne, Australia, 1992; vis. rsch. prof. Inst. Mechanized Constrn. and Rock Mining, Warsaw, 1993; rsch. engr. Robotics Ctr. Constrn. Engrng. Rsch. Lab. U. S. Arm. Corps. of Engrs., Champaign, Ill., 1993; presenter workshops. Editor-in-chief constrn. techs. and engrng. Automation in Constrn.; guest editor Microcomputers in Civil Engrng.; mem. editl. bd. Internat. Jour. Cont. Engirng. Edn. and Lifelong Learning, Real Estate Valuation and Investment, Constrn. Mgmt. and Econs., Constrn. Rsch. jours.; contbr. articlest to over 100 profl. jours., chpts. to books. Recipient Best Paper award Am. Soc. Engring. Edn., 1991; named Presdl. Young Investigator NSF, 1987-92. Mem. ASCE Ind. gel. dist. 9 coun. 1986-91) mem. control group aerospace divsn. tsk force on constrn. robotics 1987-89, constrn. rsch. coun. 1987—, expert sys. and artificial intelligence com. 1987—, data base and info. ech. com. 1988—, com. on field sensing and robotics in civil engring. 1990— (Walter L. Huber Civil Engrng. Rsch. prize 1998), Internat. Assn. Automation and Robotics in Constrn. (founding mem., co-dir. 1991—, chmn. newsletter com. 1993-95 chmn. Comms. Com. 1997, v.p. 1990-2000, pres. 2000—), Internat. Coun. Bldg. Rsch. Studies and Documentation (Mem. W-75 working commn. on conrstrn. equipment and mechanization 1989-96, task group on computer-aided learning in constrn. and property, W-89 commn. on bldg. rsch. and edn. 1993— TG27 Task Group on Human Machine Technologies in Constrn.), Internat. Coun. on Tall Bldgs. and Urban Habitat (co-chmn. com. 65 robots and tall bldgs. 1991—, mem. com. on applications of emerging techs 1994-95) Internat. Stds Orgn. (U.S. rep. on behalf of Am. Nat. Stds. Inst. to tech. com. on constrn., machinery and equipment 1994—) Constrn. Industry Inst., Sigma Xi. Achievements include development of a decision support system for managing a fleet of construciton robotics, a computerized constructabilty review system for advanced construction technologies applications. Office: Purdue U Sch Civil Engring 1294 Civil Engineering Rm 1245 West Lafayette IN 47907-1294 also: 232 Hovde Hall Adminisrn West Lafayette IN 47907-1073 Fax: (765) 494-0644. E-mail: mirek@purdue.edu.

SKILES, JAMES JEAN, electrical and computer engineering educator; b. St Louis, Oct. 16, 1928; s. Coy Emerson and Vernetta Beatrice (Maples) S.; m. Deloris Audrey McKenney, Sept. 4, 1948; children: Steven, Randall, Jeffrey. BSEE, Washington U., St. Louis, 1948; MS, U. Mo.-Rolla, 1951; PhD, U. Wis., 1954. Engr. Union Electric Co., St. Louis, 1948-49; instr. U. Mo.-Rolla, 1949-51; prof. elec. engring. U. Wis., Madison, 1954-89, prof. emeritus, 1989—, chmn. Dept. Elec. Engring., 1972-79, dir. Univ. Industry Rsch. program, 1972-75, dir. Energy Rsch. Ctr., 1975-95. Cons. in field Contbr. articles to profl. jours. Mem. Monona Grove Dist. Schs. Bd., Wis., 1961-69; mem. adv. com. Wis. Energy Office, Madison, 1979-80, Wis. Pub. Service Commn., 1980-81. Recipient Wis. Electric Utilities Professorship in Energy Engring. U. Wis., 1975-89; recipient Benjamin Smith Reynolds Teaching award, 1980, Kiekhofer Teaching award, 1955, Acad of Elec. Engring. award U. Mo.-Rolla, 1982 Mem. IEEE (sr.), Am. Soc. Engring. Edn. Home: 8099 Coray Ln Verona WI 53593-9073 Office: Univ of Wisconsin Dept Elec & Computer Engring 1415 Engineering Dr Madison WI 53706-1607 E-mail: skiles@engr.wisc.edu.

SKILLING, RAYMOND INWOOD, lawyer; b. Enniskillen, U.K., July 14, 1939; s. Dane and Elizabeth (Burleigh) S.; m. Alice Mae Welsh, Aug. 14, 1982; 1 child by previous marriage, Keith A. F. LLB, Queen's U., Belfast, U.K., 1961; JD, U. Chgo., 1962. Solicitor English Supreme Ct. 1966. Bar: Ill 1974. Assoc. Clifford-Turner (now Clifford Chance), London, 1963-69, ptnr., 1969-76; exec. v.p., chief counsel Aon Corp. (and predecessor cos.), Chgo., 1976—. Bd. dirs. Aon Corp. (and predecessor cos.). Commonwealth fellow, U. Chgo., 1961-62, Bigelow teaching fellow U. Chgo. Law Sch., 1962-63; Fulbright scholar U.S. Ednl. Commn., London, 1961-63; recipient McKane medal Queen's U., Belfast, 1961. Mem. ABA, Ill. Bar Assn., Chgo. Bar Assn., The Casino Chgo., Chgo. Club, Econ. Club Chgo., Racquet Club Chgo., Bucks Club London, The Carlton Club London, The City of London Club. Office: Aon Corp 200 E Randolph Chicago IL 60601

SKILLING, THOMAS ETHELBERT, III, meteorologist, meteorology educator; b. Pitts., Feb. 20, 1952; s. Elizabeth Clarke. Student, U. Wis., 1970-74; Dr. Humanities (hon.), Lewis U., Romeoville, Ill., 1995. Meteorologist Sta. WKKD-AM-FM, Aurora, Ill., 1967-70, Sta. WLXT-TV, Aurora, 1969-70, Sta. WKOW-TV, Madison, Wis., 1970-74, Sta. WTSO, Madison, 1970-74, Sta. WTLV-TV, Jacksonville, Fla., 1974-75, Sta. WITI-TV, Milw., 1975-78, Sta. WAUK, Waukesha, Wis., 1976-77, Sta. WGN-TV, Chgo., 1978—. Weather forecaster Wis. Farm Broadcast Network, Madison, 1970-74; weather cons. Piper, Jaffray & Hopwood, Madison, 1972-74; instr. meteorology Columbia Coll., Chgo., 1982-92, Adler Planetarium, Chgo., 1985-86. Prodr. weather page Chgo. Tribune. Vol. Chgo. chpt. Muscular Dystrophy Assn. Recipient Emmy award for "It Sounded Like a Freight Train," 1991, "The Cosmic Challenge," 1994, Peter Lisagor awards for weather spls. aired on WGN, 1991, 93, Pub. Svc. award NOAA-Nat. Weather Svc., 1998. Fellow Am. Meteorol. Soc. (v.p. Chgo. chpt. 1985-86, TV Seal of Approval, Outstanding Svc. award 1997), Nat. Weather Assn., Soc. Profl. Journalists, Chgo. Acad. TV Arts and Scis. Avocations: hiking, cross country skiing. Home: 6033 N Sheridan Rd Apt 31C Chicago IL 60660-3048 Office: Sta WGN-TV 2501 W Bradley Pl Chicago IL 60618-4701

SKILLMAN, BECKY SUE, state legislator; b. Bedford, Ind., Sept. 26, 1950; d. Jack Delmar and Catherine Louise (Flinn) Foddrill; m. Stephen E. Skillman, 1969. Dep. recorder Lawrence County, 1971-76, county recorder, 1977-84; clerk Lawrence County crct. ct., 1985—; mem. Ind. Senate from 44th dist., 1992—. Co-dir. Lawrence County Young Reps., 1973-78; co-chmn. State Young Reps. Conv., 1975, 77; vice chmn. Lawrence County Rep. Ctrl. Com. Office: Ind Senate Dist 44 200 W Washington St Indianapolis IN 46204-2728

SKILLMAN, THOMAS GRANT, endocrinology consultant, former educator; b. Cin., Jan. 7, 1925; s. Harold Grant and Faustina (Jobes) S.; m. Elizabeth Louise McClellan, Sept. 6, 1947; children: Linda, Barbara. B.S., Baldwin-Wallace Coll., 1946; M.D., U. Cin., 1949. Intern Cin. Gen. Hosp., 1949-50, resident, 1952-54; instr. medicine U. Cin., 1952-57; asst. prof. medicine Ohio State U., Columbus, 1957-61, dir. endocrinology and metabolism Coll. Medicine, 1967-74, Ralph Kurtz prof. endocrinology, 1974-81, prof. emeritus, 1981—, cons. to v.p. med. affairs, 1981—. Asso. prof. medicine Creighton U., Omaha, 1961-67 Editor: Case Studies in Endocrinology, 1971; Contbr. numerous articles to med. jours. Served with USNR, 1943-45; 1950-52, Korea. Recipient Golden Apple award Student Am. Med. Assn., 1966 Mem. Am. Diabetes Assn., Central Soc. Clin. Investigation, Am. Fedn. for Clin. Research, Alpha Omega Alpha. Club: Ohio State Golf (Columbus). Home: 4179 Stoneroot Dr Hilliard OH 43026-3023 Office: Ohio State U Hosps McCampbell Hall 485 Columbus OH 43210

SKILTON, JOHN SINGLETON, lawyer; b. Washington, Apr. 13, 1944; s. Robert Henry and Margaret (Neisser) S.; m. Carmen Fisher, Jan. 28, 1967; children: Laura Anne, Susan Elizabeth, Robert John. BA, U. Wis., 1966, JD, 1969. Bar: Wis. Supreme Ct. 1969, U.S. Dist. Ct. (ea. and we. dists.) Wis. 1969, U.S. Ct. Appeals (7th cir.) 1969, U.S. Supreme Ct. 1989, U.S. Ct. Appeals (Fed. cir.) 1991. Law clk. 7th Cir. Ct. Appeals, Milw., 1969-70; assoc. Foley & Lardner, 1970-77, ptnr. Madison, Wis., 1977-2000; shareholder Heller, Ehrman, White & McAuliffer, Washington, 2000—. Bd. visitors U. Wis. Law Sch., Madison, 1982-90, chmn., 1988-89; chair Wis. Fed. Nominating Commn., 1994; mem. Gov.'s Task Force on Bus. Ct., 1994-95; pres. Wis. Law Found., 2000—. Fellow Am. Bar Found., Am. Coll. Trial Lawyers, Internat. Acad. Trial Lawyers; mem. ABA (chmn. standing com. on delivery of legal svcs. 1996-2000, chmn. consortium legal svcs. and pub. 2000—), Am. Law Inst., Am. Acad. Appellate Lawyers, 7th Cir. Bar Assn. (pres. 1985-86, chmn. 7th cir. adv. com. on rules 1994—), State Bar Wis. (pres. 1995-96, Pres.'s award of excellence 1989, Sinykin award for publ svc. 1996), Western Dist. Wis. Bar Assn. (pres. 1992-93), Western Dist. Adv. Group (chmn. 1991), Wis. Law Found. (pres.-elect 1997-99), James E. Doyle Am. Inn of Ct. (coun. 1992-94), Am. Inns of Ct. Found. (trustee 1995-98), U. Wis. Law Alumni Assn. (bd. dirs. 1991-97, pres. 1993-95). Home: 8 N Prospect Ave Madison WI 53705-3936 Office: 10 E Main St Madison WI 53703-3331

SKINDRUD, RICK, state legislator; b. Sept. 15, 1944; Bd. dirs. Dane County, Wis.; planning commn. Town of Primrose; assemblyman Wis. State Dist. 79, 1993—. Former dairy farmer; chmn. State Affairs Com., Consumer Affairs Com., Colo. Land Conservation Com., Colo. Extension Com. Past pres. Mt. Vernon Park Assn. Mem. Govs. Coun. on Tourism. Address: 1261 La Follette Rd Mount Horeb WI 53572-2930 Office: Wis Assembly PO Box 8952 Madison WI 53708-8952

SKINNER, CALVIN L., JR. state legislator; b. Easton, Md., June 11, 1942; s. Calvin L. Sr. and Eleanor (Stevens) S.; m. Robin Meredith Geist, 1977 (div.); m. Michele M. Giangrasso, 1990; children: Alexandra, Steven. BA, Oberlin Coll., 1964; MPA, U. Mich., 1971. Treas. McHenry County, 1966-70; mem. Ill. Ho. of Reps., Springfield, 1973-81, 93—. Rep. candidate for comptr. State of Ill., 1982; precinct committeeman Algonquin (Il.) Rep. Com., 1986—; mem. Ill. AIDS Adv. Cou., 1988-92, 93-97. Mem. McHenry County Defenders. Home: 275 Meridian St Crystal Lake IL 60014-5411

SKINNER, JAMES LAURISTON, chemist, educator; b. Ithaca, N.Y., Aug. 17, 1953; s. G. William and Carol (Bagger) S.; m. Wendy Moore, May 31, 1986; children: Colin Andrew, Duncan Geoffrey. AB, U. Calif., Santa Cruz, 1975; PhD, Harvard U., 1979. Rsch. assoc. Stanford (Calif.) U., 1980-81; from asst. prof. to prof. chemistry Columbia U., N.Y.C., 1981-90; Hirschfelder prof. chemistry, dir. Theol. Chemistry Inst. U. Wis., Madison, 1990—. Vis. scientist Inst. Theol. Physics U. Calif., Santa Barbara, 1987; vis. prof. physics U. Jos. Fourier, Grenoble, France, 1987, U. Bordeaux (France), 1995. Contbr. articles to profl. jours. Recipient Fresenius award Phi Lambda Upsilon, 1989, Camille and Henry Dreyfus Tchr.-Scholar award, 1984, NSF Presdl. Young Investigator award, 1984, Humboldt Sr. Scientist award, 1993; NSF grad fellow, 1975, NSF post-doctoral fellow, 1980, Alfred P. Sloan Found. fellow, 1984, Guggenheim fellow, 1993. Mem. AAAS, Am. Chem. Soc., Am. Phys. Soc. Achievements include fundamental research in condensed phase theoretical chemistry. Office: U Wis Dept Chemistry Theoretical Chem Inst 1101 University Ave Madison WI 53706-1322

SKINNER, MARY JACOBS, lawyer; BA cum laude, Harvard U., 1978; JD, Northwestern U., 1981. Bar: Ill. 1981, D.C. 1990, U.S. Supreme Ct. 1990. Parliamentarian Ill. Ho. of Reps., Springfield, 1983, counsel to spkr., 1983-85; ptnr. Sidley & Austin, Chgo. Intern White House, 1979. Former trustee RAdcliffe Coll.; participant leadership coun. Greater Chgo. Fellowship Program, 1984. Named One of Forty under 40 Most Outstanding Leaders in Chco., Crain's Chgo. Bus. Mem.. Harvard Alumni Assn. (bd. dirs.), Radcliffe Coll. Alumni Assn. (past pres.). Office: Sidley & Austin 1 S First National Plz Chicago IL 60603-2000 Fax: 312-853-7036.

SKINNER, SAMUEL K. transportation executive; BS in Acctg., U. Ill., 1960; JD, DePaul U., 1966; numerous hon. degrees. Bar: Ill.; jet-cert. pilot. Various sales and mgmt. positions IBM Corp., 1960-68; with U.S. Atty. for No. Dist. Ill., 1968-75; U.S. atty. Dept. of Justice, 1975—77; sr. litigation and regulatory ptnr. Sidley & Austin, Chgo., 1977-89; chmn. Regional Transp. Authority, 1985-89; U.S. Sec. of Transp., CEO Dept. Transp., 1989—91; chief of staff Pres. George Bush, 1991-92; pres. Commonwealth Edison Co., 1993—98, Unicom Corp., 1993—98; co-chmn. Hopkins & Sutter, 1998—2000, chmn., pres., CEO, 2000—; pres. USFreightways Corp., Chgo., 2000—. Active Northwestern Meml. Hosp., Ill. Econ. Devel. Bd., George Bush Presdl. Libr. Found. With U.S. Army, 1960-61. Mem.: Comml. Club, Econ. Club. Office: 8550 W Bryn Mawr Ave Chicago IL 60631

SKINNER, THOMAS, broadcasting and film executive; b. Poughkeepsie, N.Y., Aug. 17, 1934; s. Clarence F. and Frances D. S.; m. Elizabeth Burroughs, June 22, 1957; children: Kristin Jon, Karin Anne, Erik Lloyd. BS, SUNY, Fredonia, 1956; MA, U. Mich., 1957, PhD, 1962. Instr. speech U. Mich., 1960; assoc. prof., exec. producer dept. broadcasting San Diego State U., 1961-66; asst. mgr. Sta. WITF-TV, Hershey, Pa., 1966-70; v.p. Sta. WQED-TV, Pitts., 1970-72; exec. v.p., COO QED Communications Inc. (WQED-TV, WQED-FM, Pittsburgh mag., WQEX-TV), 1972-93; founder, pres., exec. prodr. Windrush Assocs., 1993—; v.p. Programming Resolution Prodns., Burlington, Vt., 1996—; asst. dir. Inland Seas Edn. Assn., 2000—. Exec. prodr.: spls. and series including (for PBS) Nat. Geog. spls. Planet Earth, The Infinite Voyage, Conserving America, (for TBS) Pirate Tales, (for A&E) Floating Palaces, California and the Dream Seekers, The Story of Money, (for Discovery) Battleship, The Secret World of Air Freight. Recipient award as exec. prodr. DuPont Columbia, 1979, Oscar award as dir. Acad. Motion Picture Arts and Scis., 1967, Emmy award as exec. prodr. Nat. Acad. TV Arts and Scis., 1979, 83-84, 86-87, Peabody award as exec. prodr., 1980, 86. Episcopalian.

SKLARSKY, CHARLES B. lawyer; b. Chgo., June 13, 1946; s. Morris and Sadie (Brenner) S.; m. Elizabeth Ann Hardzinski, Dec. 28, 1973; children: Jacob Daniel, Katherine Gabrielle, Jessica Leah. AB, Harvard U., 1968; JD, U. Wis., 1973. Bar: Wis. 1973, Ill. 1973, U.S. Dist. Ct. (no. dist.) Ill. 1973, U.S. Ct. Appeals (7th cir.) 1978, U.S. Ct. Appeals (2nd cir.) 1986. Asst. states atty. Cook County, Chgo., 1973-78; asst. U.S. atty. U.S. Dist. Ct. (no. dist.) Ill., 1978-86; ptnr. Jenner & Block, 1986—. Mem. ABA, Am. Coll. Trial Lawyers, Chgo. Bar Assn. Office: Jenner & Block One IBM Plz Chicago IL 60611-3586

SKOCHELAK, SUSAN E. college dean; BS, Mich. Tech. U., 1975, MS in Biol. Sci., 1977; MD, U. Mich., 1981; MPH, U. N.C., 1986. Diplomae Am. Bd. Family Medicine. Intern, resident family medicine U. N.C.-N.C. Meml. Hosp., Chapel Hill, 1977-81; assoc. dean Academic Affairs U. Wis., Madison, 1993—. Cons. in field; assoc. prof. U. Wis. Author: (with others) Preceptor Education Project, Handbook for Clerkship Directors. Mem. Wis. Rural Health Dev. Council, Consortium Primary Care in Wis.; co-dir. Wis. Area Health Edn. Sys. Recipient National award Patient Care mag.,

1997. Mem. AMA, Soc. Tchrs. Family Medicine, Assn. Am. Med. Colls., Am. Med. Women's ssn., ACPHE. Office: Univ Wisconsin Med School 1300 University Ave Madison WI 53706-1510

SKOGLUND, WESLEY JOHN, state legislator; b. Mpls., June 9, 1945; s. John and Edith Peterson S.; m. Linda; children: Anne, Jenny. BA, U. Minn., 1967. Park commr. Hennepin County, Minn., 1974-75; Minn. State rep. Dist. 62B, 1975—; personnel-employee rels. Control Data Corp., 1967-75; businessman. Chmn. ins. com. and fin. inst. com., Nat. Conf. of Ins. Legislators, Nat. Conf. of State Legislators; mem. capitol area archtl. and planning bd.; legis. audit com. and judiciary coms; mem. edn. and ways and means coms. Active YMCA, Bicentennial Commn., Hennepin County Study Group, Adoptive Families of Am. Recipient Anti-Smoking Group awards, Hennepin County award, Airport Noise Control award, United Way awards. Office: 251 State Office Bldg Saint Paul MN 55155-0001

SKOGMAN, DALE R. retired bishop; Bishop No. Great Lakes Synod, Marquette, Mich.; ret., 1999. Address: 7784 Summit 1955 Dr Gladstone MI 49837-2455

SKOIEN, GARY, real estate company executive; BS cum laude, Colgate U., 1976; M Pub. Policy with honors, U. Mich., 1978. Asst. to James R. Thompson Gov. of Ill., Springfield, 1980-83; exec. dir. Ill. Capital Devel. Bd., 1983-90; sr. v.p., COO retail divsn. PGI (name now Prime Retail Inc.), 1991-92; exec. v.p., COO Prime Group, Inc., 1991—; chmn. bd., pres., CEO Horizon Group, Inc., Chgo., 1998—. Bd. dirs. Civic Fedn.; vice-chmn. bd. trustees No. Ill. U. Mem. Chicagoland C. of C. (bd. dirs.). Office: Horizon Group Inc 77 W Wacker Dr Ste 4200 Chicago IL 60601-1604

SKOLNIK, DAVID ERWIN, financial analyst; b. Cleve., Oct. 31, 1949; s. Marvin and Ruth (Kovit) S.; m. Linda Susan Pollack, Mar. 31, 1973; children: Carla Denise, Robyn Laurel. BS in Acctg., Ohio State U., 1971. CPA, Ohio. Chief acct. Gray Drug Fair, Cleve., 1976-82, mgr. acctg. systems, 1982-84; fin. systems analyst Soc. Corp., 1984, fin. systems officer, 1984-86, fin. systems rsch. officer, 1986-90, sr. fin. systems officer, 1990-91, strategic rsch. officer, 1991-92; mgmt. acctg. officer Keycorp, 1992-96, asst. v.p., 1996—. Scoutmaster Boy Scouts Am., Cleve., 1971-77; coach Girls Softball League, South Euclid, Ohio, 1989-97. Mem. AICPAs, Ohio Soc. CPAs, Am. Inst. Banking, Am. Mgmt. Assn., Tau Epsilon Phi. Jewish. Avocations: golf, bowling, home repairs. Home: 33892 Hanover Woods Trl Solon OH 44139-4473 Office: Keycorp 127 Public Sq Cleveland OH 44114-1306

SKORTON, DAVID JAN, academic administrator, internist, educator; b. Milw., Nov. 22, 1949; s. Samuel and Pauline (Millstein) Skorton; 1 child Joshua Samuel. BA, Northwestern U., 1970; MD, Northwestern U., Chgo., 1974. Diplomate Nat. Bd. Med. Examiners, Am. Bd. Internal Medicine, Am. Bd. Cardiovascular Disease. Resident UCLA, 1974-77, fellow in cardiology, 1977-80, chief resident in medicine, 1978-79, adj. asst. prof., 1978-80; instr. medicine U. Iowa, Iowa City, 1980-81, asst. prof., 1981-84, asst. prof. elec. and computer engrng., 1982-84, assoc. prof. medicine and elec. and computer engring., 1984-88, prof. medicine, elec. and computer engrng. and biomed. engrng., 1988—; acting dir., then dir. div. gen. internal medicine U. Iowa Coll. Medicine, 1985-89, assoc. chmn. for clinical programs, 1989-92, v.p. for rsch. and external rels., 1992—. Dir. ochocardiology lab. VA Med. Ctr., Iowa City, 1980—89; mem. internat. and coop. projects study sect. NIH, 1988—92, chmn., 1990—92; lectr. in field numerous sci. sessions, nat. and internat. meetings; manuscript reviewer maj. jours. in field. Editor: (book) Cardiac Imaging and Image Processing, 1986, Cardiac Imaging, 1990, Cardiac Imaging, 2d edit., 1996; contbr. articles and abstracts to profl. jours., chapters to books. Named Intern-of-Yr., UCLA, 1975; recipient Rsch. Assoc. Career Devel. award, VA, 1981—84, Rsch. Career Devel. award, Nat. Heart Lung & Blood Inst., 1984—89; scholar Regents', UCLA, 1967—68. Fellow: ACP, Am. Physiol. Soc., Am. Heart Assn., Am. Coll. Cardiology; mem.: AAAS, Internat. Soc. Adult Congenital Cardiac Disease, Assn. Univ. Cardiologists, Am. Soc. Echocardiography. Jewish. Office: U Iowa VP for Rsch & External Rels 201 Gilmore Hall Iowa City IA 52242-1320 E-mail: david-skorton@uiowa.edu.

SKROMME, ARNOLD BURTON, educational writer, engineering consultant; b. Zearing, Iowa, Apr. 1, 1917; s. Austin and Belle (Holmedal) S.; m. Lois Lucille Fausch, Sept. 14, 1940; children: Roger, Keith, Deborah, Erik. Agrl. Engr., Iowa State U., 1941. Engr. Firestone Tire & Rubber Co., Akron, Ohio, 1941-45, Auto Splty. Mfg., St. Joseph, Mich., 1945-46; rsch. engr. Pineapple Rsch. Inst., Honolulu, 1946-50; asst. chief engr. John Deere, Ottumwa, Iowa, 1950-55; chief engr. John Deer Spreader Works, East Moline, Ill., 1955-70; mgr. value engring. John Deere Harvester Works, 1970-84; writer and cons., 1984—. Cons. to corps., 1984—. Author The 7-Ability Plan, 1989; The Cause and Cure of Dropouts, 1998; holder 44 patents. Chmn. Citizens Adv. Com., Moline, 1964-66. Mem. Am. Soc. Agrl. Engrs. (v.p. 1965-68, Honor Roll 1997). Lutheran. Avocation: research on children's education. Home: 2605 31st St Moline IL 61265-5309

SKROWACZEWSKI, STANISLAW, conductor, composer; b. Lwow, Poland, Oct. 3, 1923; came to U.S., 1960; s. Pawel and Zofia (Karszniewicz) S.; m. Krystyna Jarosz, Sept. 6, 1956; children: Anna, Paul, Nicholas. Diploma faculty philosophy, U. Lwow, 1945; diploma faculties composition and conducting, Acad. Music Lwow, 1945, Conservatory at Krakow, Poland, 1946; L.H.D., Hamline U., 1963, Macalester Coll., 1972; L.H.D. hon. doctorate, U. Minn. Guest condr. in, Europe, S.A., U.S., 1947—; Composer, 1931—; pianist, 1928—; violinist, 1934—; condr., 1939—; permanent condr., music dir. Wroclaw (Poland) Philharmonic, 1946-47, Katowice (Poland) Nat. Philharmonic, 1949-54, Krakow Philharmonic, 1955-56, Warsaw Nat. Philharmonic Orch., 1957-59, Minnesota Orch., 1960-79; prin. condr., mus. adviser Halle Orch., Manchester, Eng., 1984-91; musical advisor St. Paul Chamber Orchestra, 1986-87. First symphony and overture for orch. written at age 8, played by Lwow Philharm. Orch., 1931. Composer: 4 symphonies Prelude and Fugue for Orchestra (conducted first performance Paris), 1948, Overture, 1947 (2d prize Szymanowski Concours, Warsaw 1947); Cantiques des Cantiques, 1951, String Quartet, 1953 (2d Prize Internat. Concours Composers, Belgium 1953), Suite Symphonique, 1954 (first prize, gold medal Composers Competition Moscow 1957), Music at Night, 1954, Ricercari Notturni, 1978 (3d prize Kennedy Center Friedheim Competition, Washington), Concerti for Clarinet and Orch., 1980, Violin Concerto, 1985, Concerto for Orch., 1985, Fanfare for Orch., 1987, Sextett for Oboe, Violin, Viola, Orchestra, 1980, String Trio for Violin, Viola, 1990, Triple Concerto for Violin, Clarinet, Piano, Orchestra, 1992, Fantasie per Tre (Flute, Oboe, Cello), 1993, Chamber Concerto, 1993, Passacaglia Immaginaria for Orch., 1995, Musica a Quattro for Clarinet, Violin, Viola, Cello, 1998; also music for theatre, motion pictures, songs and piano sonatas, English horn concerto; rec. by Mercury, Columbia, RCA Victor, Vox, EMI, Angel. Recipient nat. prize for artistic activity Poland, 1953; First prize Santa Cecilia Internat. Concours for Condrs., Rome, 1956, Comdr. Cross, Polonia Restituta, 1999. Mem. Union Polish Composers, Internat. Soc. Modern Music, Nat. Assn. Am. Composers-Condrs., Am. Music Center. Office: Orch Hall 1111 Nicollet Mall Minneapolis MN 55403-2406 Fax: 216-473-7384.

SKULINA, THOMAS RAYMOND, lawyer; b. Cleve., Sept. 14, 1933; s. John J. and Mary B. (Vesely) S. AB, John Carroll U., 1955; JD, Case Western Res. U., 1959, LLM, 1962. Bar: Ohio 1959, U.S. Supreme Ct. 1964, ICC 1965. Ptnr. Skulina & Stringer, Cleve., 1967-72, Riemer Oberdank & Skulina, Cleve., 1978-81, Skulina, Fillo, Walters & Negrelli, 1981-86, Skulina & McKeon, Cleve., 1986-90, Skulina & Hill, Cleve., 1990-97; atty. Penn Ctrl. Transp. Co., 1960-65, asst. gen. atty., 1965-78, trial counsel, 1965-76; with Consol. Rail Corp., 1976-78; pvt. practice Cleve., 1997—. Tchr. comml. law Practicing Law Inst., N.Y.C., 1970; practicing labor arbitrator Fed. Mediation and Conciliation Svc., 1990—; arbitrator Mcpl. Securities Rulemaking Bd., 1994-98, N.Y. Stock Exch., 1995—, NASD, 1996—; mediator NASD, 1997—, AAA Comml., 1997—; mediator vol. panel EEOC, 1997-99, contract panel, 1999-2000, v.p., 2000—, contract, 2001—; arbitrator Better Bus. Bur., 2000—. Contbr. articles to legal jours. Income tax and fed. fund coord. City of Warrensville Heights, Ohio, 1970-77; spl. counsel City of North Olmstead, Ohio, 1971-75, spl. counsel to Ohio Atty. Gen., 1983-93, Cleve. Charter Rev. Commn., 1988; pres. Civil Svc. Commn., Cleve., 1977-86, referee, 1986—; fact-finder State Employees Rels. Bd., Ohio, 1986—; hearing officer Human Resource Commn., Summit County, Ohio, 2000—. With U.S. Army, 1959. Mem. ABA (R.R. and motor carrier com. 1988-96, jr. chmn. 1989-96, alt. dispute resolution com. 1998—), FBA, Assn. Conflict Resolution, Cleve. Bar Assn. (grievance com. 1987-93, chmn. 1997-98, trustee 1993-96, ADR com. 1997—), Ohio Bar Assn. (bd. govs. litigation sect. 1986-98, negligence law com. 1989-96, ethics and profl. responsibility com. 1990-91, alt. dispute resolution com. 1996—), Am. Arbitration Assn. (practicing labor arbitrator 1987—), Nat. Assn. R.R. Trial Counsel, Internat. Assn. Law and Sci., Pub. Sector Labor Rels. Assn., Internat. Indsl. Rels. Rsch. Assn. Democrat. Roman Catholic. Home: 3162 W 165th St Cleveland OH 44111-1016 Office: 24803 Detroit Rd Cleveland OH 44145-2553 E-mail: tskulina@aol.com.

SKWARCZYńSKI, HENRYK ADAM (HENRYK SKWAR), writer; b. Łódź, Poland, Aug. 13, 1952; came to U.S., 1980; s. Zdzislaw and Stanislawa Ewa (Laszczyk) S.; m. Eglé Juodvalkis, Sept. 2, 1989 MA, U. Warsaw, 1977; postgrad., Polish Acad. Sci., 1978-80, Sorbonne U. Freelance writer, N.Y.C., 1980-81, Voice of Am., Washington, 1981-82; instr. Defense Lang. Inst., Monterey, Calif., 1982-84; staff writer Libertas, Paris, 1984-86; free-lance writer Radio Free Europe, Munich, 1987-95; writer Chgo., 1995—. Author: Man in a Cleft, 1979, The Anguish of Becoming American, 1989, Sweeney Among the Nightingales, 2000, The Straw Sea, 2002; editor-in-chief: Ephemeron, 1974—75; contbr. short stories to mags. Activist Solidarity Movement, 1980-89. Rotary Club grantee, 1982, Hoover Inst. grantee, 1985. Avocation: travel in Africa.

SKYES, GREGORY, food products executive; New products mktg. mgr. Hillshire Farm & Kahn's, 1984; pres., CEO Ball Park Brands, 1995; mgr. State Fair Foods, Best Kosher; v.p. Sara Lee Foods, Chgo.; pres., CEO Sara Lee Foods Retail. Office: Sara Lee Corp 3 First National Plz Chicago IL 60602-4260

SLADE, ROY, artist, college president, museum director; b. Cardiff, U.K., July 14, 1933; came to U.S., 1967, naturalized, 1975; s. David Trevor and Millicent (Stone) S. N.D.D., Cardiff Coll. Art, 1954; A.T.D., U. Wales, 1954; D of Arts, Art Inst. So. Calif., 1994. Tchr. art and crafts Heolgam High Sch., Wales, 1956-60; lectr. art Clarendon Coll., Nottingham, Eng., 1960-64; sr. lectr. fine art Leeds Coll. Art, Eng., 1964-67; prof. painting Corcoran Sch. Art, Washington, 1967-68, assoc. dean, 1969-70, dean, 1970-77; dir. Corcoran Gallery of Art, 1972-77; pres., dir. Cranbrook Acad. Art, Bloomfield Hills, Mich., 1977-94. Sr. lectr. Leeds Coll. Art, England, 1968—69; vis. Boston Mus. Fine Arts, 1970; dir. emeritus Cranbrook Art Mus., 2000—. Exhibited one-man shows Howard Roberts Gallery, Cardiff, Wales, 1958, New Art Ctr., London, 1960, U. Birmingham, 1964, 69, Herbert Art Gallery and Mus., Coventry, 1964, Va. State Art League, 1967, Mus. of Arts and Crafts, Columbus, Ga., 1968, Jefferson Place Gallery, Washington, 1968, 70, 72, 73, Park Sq. Gallery, Leeds, 1969, St. Mary's Coll., Md., 1971, Guelph U., Ont., Can., 1971, Hood Coll., 1974, Pyramid Gallery, Washington, 1976, Robert Kidd Gallery, 1981, 92, Herman Miller, Inc., Mich., 1985; group shows in U.K., Washington, Can.; represented in permanent collections Arts Council Gt. Brit., Contemporary Art Soc., Nuffield Found., Ministry of Works, Eng., Brit. Embassy, Washington, Brit. Overseas Airways Corp., U. Birmingham, Wakefield City Art Gallery, Clarendon Coll., Cadbury Bros., Ltd., Eng., Lord Ogmore, Local Edn. Authorities. Mem. D.C. Commn. on Arts.; bd. dirs. Artists for Environment Found., Nat. Assn. Schs. Art; chmn. Nat. Council Art Adminstrs., 1981. Served with Brit. Army, 1954-56. Decorated knight 1st class Order of White Rose (Finland), Royal Order of Polar Star (Sweden); recipient award Welsh Soc., Phila., 1974, Gov.'s Arts Orgn. award, 1988; Fulbright scholar, 1967-68. Mem. Nat. Soc. Lit. and Arts, AIA (hon. Detroit chpt.), Assn. Art Mus. Dirs. (hon.). Home: #C1009 880 Mandalay Ave Clearwater FL 33767 E-mail: roy.slade@worldnet.att.com.

SLANSKY, JERRY WILLIAM, investment company executive; b. Chgo., Mar. 8, 1947; s. Elmer Edward and Florence Anna (Kosobud) S.; m. Marlene Jean Cannella, Jan. 29, 1950; children: Brett Matthew, Blake Adam. BA, Elmhurst Coll., 1969; MA, No. Ill. U., 1971. Mktg. rep. Bantam Book Co., Chgo., 1972-73, Charles Levy Circulating Co., Chgo., 1973-76; account exec. Merrill Lynch, 1976-77, CIBC-Oppenheimer & Co., Inc., Chgo., 1977—, asst. v.p., 1978, v.p., 1979, sr. v.p., 1981, mng. dir., 1986, ptnr., 1986—. Bd. dirs. Lake Geneva (Wis.) Beach Assn., 1987—, Glen Ellyn Youth Ctr., Glenbard West H.S., pres., 1998-99; mem. bus. affairs com. Presbytery of Chgo., 1999—. Mem. Nat. Assn. Securities Dealers (arbitrator 1988—), N.Y. Stock Exch., Chgo. Bd. Options, Am. Arbitration. Assn, Omaha C. of C. Presbyterian. Avocations: swimming, water skiing, golf, snow skiing. Office: CIBC-Oppenheimer 311 S Wacker Dr Chicago IL 60606-6627

SLATOPOLSKY, EDUARDO, nephrologist, educator; b. Buenos Aires, Argentina, Dec. 12, 1934; (parents Am. citizens); married, 1959; 3 children. BS, Nat. Coll. Nicolas Avellaneda, 1952; MD, U. Buenos Aires, 1959. Postdoctoral renal USPHS, renal divsn., Dept. Internal Medicine Washington U. Sch. Medicine, 1963-65, instr. med. nephrology, 1965-67, from asst. prof. to assoc. prof. medicine dept. nephrology, 1967-75; dir. Chromalloy Am. Kidney Ctr., Washington U. Sch. medicine, St. Louis, 1967-97, co-dir. renal divsn., 1972-97, prof. medicine, nephrology dept., 1975—, Joseph Friedman Prof. renal disease medicine, 1991—. Adv. mem. regional med. program, renal program sch. medicine Washington U., 1970-75; chmn. transplantation com. Barne Hosp., 1975—; fellow com. Kidney Found. Ea. Mo. and Metro.-E., 1978; mem. adv. com. artificial kidney-chronic uremia program NIH, 1978-90, rep. Latin-Am. nephrology, 1983-88; mem. study sect. Gen. Med., NIH, 1984-88. Recipient Frederick C. Bartter award 1991. Mem. AAAS, Am. Fedn. Clin. Rsch., Internat. Soc. Nephrology, Am. Soc. Nephrology, Endocrine Soc., Sigma Xi. Achievements include pathogenesis and treatment of secondary hyparathyroidism and bone disease in renal failure; studies conducted at both levels: clinical, on patients maintained on chronic dialysis and on animals with experimentally induced renal feilure; detailed studies of the effects of calcitriol on PTH MRNA and the extra-renal production of calcitriol by macrophages; vitro studies in primary culture of bovine parathyroid cells used to understand the mechanisms that control the secretion of PTH. Office: Washington U Chromalloy Am Kidney Ctr PO Box 8126 Saint Louis MO 63156-8126

SLAUGHTER ANDREW, ANNE, lawyer; b. Evansville, Ind., Sept. 23, 1955; d. Owen L. and Marjorie (Specht) Slaughter; m. Joseph J. Andrew, Sept. 9, 1989. BA, Georgetown U., 1977; JD cum laude, Ind. U., 1983. Bar: Ind. 1983, U.S. Dist. Ct. (so. dist.) Ind. Ptnr. Baker & Daniels, Indpls. Adj. prof. environ. law Ind. U. Sch. Law, Indpls. Editor-in-chief Ind. U. Law Rev., 1982-83; contbr. articles to profl. jours. Bd. dirs. Nature Conservancy, 1997—, Ind. Natural Resources Found., 1994—; mem. Indpls. Pub. Sch. Found. Com., 1997—; mem. Brownfield Remediation Adv. Com., 1997—. Mem. ABA (chair state and regional environ. coop. com. 1996-98), Ind. Bar Assn. (chair environ. law sect. 1992-93), Ind. C. of C. (govt. affairs commn.). Office: Baker & Daniels 300 N Meridian St Ste 2700 Indianapolis IN 46204-1782

SLAVENS, THOMAS PAUL, library science educator; b. Cincinnati, Iowa, Nov. 12, 1928; s. William Blaine and Rhoda (Bowen) S.; m. Cora Pearl Hart, July 9, 1950; 1 son, Mark Thomas. BA, Phillips U., 1951; MDiv, Union Theol. Sem., 1954; MA, U. Minn., 1962; PhD, U. Mich., 1965. Ordained to ministry Christian Ch., 1953. Pastor First Christian Ch., Sac City, Iowa, 1953-56, Sioux Falls, S.D., 1956-60; librarian Divinity Sch., Drake U., Des Moines, 1960-64; teaching fellow Sch. Info., U. Mich., Ann Arbor, 1964-65; instr. U. Mich., 1965-66, asst. prof., 1966-69, assoc. prof., 1969-77, prof., 1977—. Vis. prof. U. Minn., 1967, U. Coll. of Wales, 1978, 80, 93; vis. scholar U. Oxford, Eng., 1980; adv. bd. Marcel Dekker Inc., N.Y.C., 1982—; cons. Nutrition Planning Abstracts-UN, N.Y.C., 1977-79. Author-editor: Library Problems in the Humanities, 1981, (with John F. Wilson) Research Guide to Religious Studies, 1982, (with W. Eugene Kleinbaur) Research Guide to History of Western Art, 1982, (with Terrence Tice) Research Guide to Philosophy, 1983, Theological Libraries at Oxford, 1984, (with James Pruett) Research Guide to Musicology, 1985, The Literary Adviser, 1985, A Great Library through Gifts, 1986, The Retrieval of Information, 1989, Number One in the U.S.A.: Records and Wins in Sports, Entertainment, Business, and Science, 1988, 2d edit., 1990, Doors to God, 1990, Sources of Information for Historical Research, 1994, Introduction to Systematic Theology, 1992, Reference Interviews Questions and Materials, 3d edit., 1994. Served with U.S. Army, 1946-48. Recipient Warner Rice Faculty award U. Mich., 1975; H.W. Wilson fellow, 1960; Lilly Endowment fellow Am. Theol. Library Assn., 1963. Mem. ALA (chmn. coms. 1964—), Assn. Libr. and Info. Sci. Edn. (pres. 1972), Beta Phi Mu. Office: University of Michigan School of Information 550 E University Ave Ann Arbor MI 48109-1092 E-mail: tslavens@umich.edu.

SLAVIN, CRAIG STEVEN, management and franchising consultant; b. Tucson, Sept. 7, 1951; s. Sidney and Eileen (Gilbert) S.; m. Carol Lynn Haft, Aug. 30, 1982; children: Carly Blair, Samantha Illyna. Student, U. Ariz., 1969073, U. Balt., 1978. Dir. franchising and sales Evelyn Wood Reading Dynamics, Walnut Creek, Calif., 1974-75; dir. franchising Pasquale Food Co., Birmingham, Ala., 1975-77; exec. v.p. Franchise Concepts, Flossmoor, Ill., 1977-80; pres. Franchise Architects, Chgo., 1980-88; mng. dir. franchise practice Arthur Andersen & Co., 1988-91; chmn. Franchise Architects, Bannockburn, Ill., 1991—. Founder, bd. dirs. Franchise Broadcast Network, Riverwoods, 1991—; founder Franchise Success System, 1991, The Original Franchise Match, 1992. Author: Complete Guide to Self-Employment in Franchising, 1991, Franchising for the Growing Company, 1993, AMACON, The Franchising Handbook. Mem. ABA (faculty), Am. Arbitration Assn., Internat. Franchise Assn., Nat. Assn. Info. Suppliers, Water Quality Assn., Inst. Mgmt. Cons., Coun. Franchise Suppliers (adv. bd. dirs.), Nat. Restaurant Assn. Avocations: golf, chess, saltwater fish. Office: Franchise Architects 2275 Half Day Rd Ste 350 Bannockburn IL 60015-1277

SLAVIN, PETER L. hospital administrator; AB Harvard U., 1979, MD Harvard U., 1984, MBA Harvard U., 1990. Chief med. officer Mass. Gen. Hosp.; med. dir. Mass. Gen. Physicians Orgn.; pres. Barnes-Jewish Hosp., St. Louis, 1997-99; chair., CEO Mass. Gen. Physicians Orgn., Boston, 1999—. Address: Mass Gen Hosp BUL 208 55 Fruit St Boston MA 02114-2622

SLAVIN, RAYMOND GRANAM, allergist, immunologist; b. Cleve., June 29, 1930; s. Philip and Dinah (Baskind) S.; m. Alberta Cohrt, June 10, 1953; children: Philip, Stuart, David, Linda. A.B., U. Mich., 1952; M.D., St. Louis U., 1956; M.S., Northwestern U., 1963. Diplomate: Am. Bd. Internal Medicine, Am. Bd. Allergy and Immunology (treas.). Intern U. Mich. Hosp., Ann Arbor, 1956-57; resident St. Louis U. Hosp., 1959-61; fellow in allergy and immunology Northwestern U. Med. Sch., 1961-64; asst. prof. internal medicine and microbiology St. Louis U., 1965-70, assoc., 1970-73, prof., 1973—, dir. div. allergy and immunology, 1965—. Mem. NIH study sect., 1985-89; cons. U.S. Army M.C. Contbr. numerous articles to med. publs.; editorial bd.: Jour. Allergy and Clin. Immunology, 1975-81, Tice Practice Medicine, 1973-84, Jour. Club of Allergy, 1978-80. Chmn. bd. Asthma and Allergy Found. Am., 1985-88. With M.C., U.S. Army, 1957-59. Grantee NIH, 1967-70, 84—, Nat. Inst. Occpl. Safety and Health, 1974-80. Master: ACP; fellow: Am. Acad. Allergy and Immunology (exec. bd., historian, pres. 1983—84); mem.: AAAS, Central Soc. Clin. Research, Am. Assn. Immunologists. Democrat. Jewish. Home: 631 E Polo Dr Saint Louis MO 63105-2629 Office: 1402 S Grand Blvd Saint Louis MO 63104-1004 E-mail: slavinrg@slu.edu.

SLAY, FRANCIS G. mayor; b. St. Louis; s. Francis R. and Anna Slay; m. Kim Slay; children: Francis Jr., Katherine. Law degree, Saint Louis U. Sch. Law, 1980; postgrad in political sci., Quincy Coll. , Ill., 1977. Mayor City of St. Louis, 2001—; pvt. lawyer 20 yrs.; law clerk Judge Paul J. Simon, Mo. Court Appeals , 1981; ptnr. Guilfoil, Petzall & Shoemake. Mem. St. Louis Bd. Alderman, 1995, elected pres. Office: City Hall Rm 200 1200 Mrk St Saint Louis MO 63103*

SLAYMAKER, GENE ARTHUR, public relations executive; b. Kenton, Ohio, Sept. 15, 1928; s. Edwin Paul and Anna Elizabeth (Grable) S.; divorced; children: Jill Brook, Scott Wood, Leslie Beth; m. Julie Ann Graff, Feb. 3, 1979; 1 adopted child, Peter Fredric Bannon II; stepchildren: Jennifer Elizabeth Nash, David Frank Nash. B.A. in Radio Journalism, Ohio State U. Announcer, reporter WLWC-TV, Columbus, Ohio, 1951-52; anchor, reporter WKBN-AM-FM-TV, Youngstown, 1952-56, KYW-TV, Cleve., 1956-60; editor news Sta. WFBM-AM-FM-TV, Indpls., 1960-68; pres., founder Slaymaker & Assocs. Pub. Rels., 1969—; dir. news, sports, pub. affairs WTLC-FM and WTUX-AM, Indpls., 1976-92; community rels. liaison Marion County Pros. Atty. Office, 1993. Pres., founder Slaymaker and Assocs., Indpls., 1969—. Mambo dancer (movie) Going All the Way, 1996. Past bd. dirs. Park-Tudor Father's Assn.; mem. Meridian Kessler Neighborhood Assn., pres., 1968-69. Recipient Disting. Service award (2). Mem. Ind. AP Broadcasters Assn. (awards), UPI (awards), Nat. Fedn. Press Women, Soc. Profl. Journalists (awards Ind. chpt., bd. dirs., chpt. pres. 1991-92, Radio-TV News Dirs. Assn. (region bd. dirs. 1987-91), Indpls. Press Club, Woman's Press Club Ind., Players Club, Lambs Club (pres. 2000—). Democrat. Clubs: Nat. Headliners, Unity. Avocations: writing, painting, singing, gardening, tennis. Home: 5161 N Washington Blvd Indianapolis IN 46205-1071 Office: Slaymaker Assoc 5161 N Washington Blvd Indianapolis IN 46205-1071

SLEIK, THOMAS SCOTT, lawyer; b. La Crosse, Wis., Feb. 24, 1947; s. John Thomas and Marion Gladys (Johnson) S.; m. Judith Mattson, Aug. 24, 1968; children: Jennifer, Julia, Joanna. BS, Marquette U., 1969, JD, 1971. Bar: Wis. 1971, U.S. Dist. Ct. (we. dist.) Wis. 1971. Assoc. Hale Skemp Hanson Skemp & Sleik, La Crosse, 1971-74, ptnr., 1975—. State pres. Boy Scouts Am., 1981-83, bd. dirs. Gateway Area Coun., 1973-99, pres., 1980-81; trustee La Crosse Pub. Libr., 1981—; bd. dirs. Children's Mus. of LaCrosse, Greater La Crosse Area United Way, 1985-92, campaign chmn., 1986, pres., 1987; mem. Sch. Dist. La Crosse Bd. Edn., 1973-77, v.p., 1977; Festmaster, Oktoberfest (LaCross Festivals Inc.), 2001, trustee, 2001--. Fellow Am. Acad. Matrimonial Lawyers (pres. Wis. chpt. 1999-2000); mem. ABA, State Bar Wis. (bd. govs. 1987-94, pres. 1992-93, spkr. litigation sect. and family law seminars), La Crosse County Bar Assn. Roman Catholic. Home: 4082 Glenhaven Dr La Crosse WI 54601-7503

Office: Hale Skemp Hanson Skemp & Sleik 505 King St Ste 300 La Crosse WI 54602-1927 E-mail: tss@halesstemp.com.

SLEMMONS, ROBERT SHELDON, architect; b. Mitchell, Nebr., Mar. 12, 1922; s. Matthew Garvin and K. Fern (Borland) S.; m. Dorothy Virginia Herrick, Dec. 16, 1945; children: David (dec.), Claire, Jennifer, Robert, Timothy. AB, U. Nebr., 1947, BArch, 1948. Draftsman Davis & Wilson, Archs., Lincoln, Nebr., 1947-48; chief designer, project arch. Office of Kans. State Arch., Topeka, 1948-54; assoc. John A. Brown, Arch., 1954-56; ptnr. Brown & Slemmons, Arch., 1956-69; v.p. Brown-Slemmons-Krueger, Archs., 1969-73; owner Robert S. Slemmons, A.I.A. & Assocs., Archs., 1973—. Cons. Kans. State Office Bldg. Commn., 1956-57; lectr. in design U. Kans., 1961; bd. dirs. Kaw Valley State Bank & Trust Co., Topeka, 1978-92. Prin. archtl. works include Kans. State Office Bldg., 1954, Topeka Presbyn. Manor, 1960-74, Meadowlark Hills Ret. Cmty., 1979, Shawnee County Adult Detention Facility, 1985. Bd. dirs. Topeka Civic Symphony Soc., 1950-60, Midstates Ret. Cmtys., Inc., 1986-92, Topeka Festival Singers; cons. Ministries for Aging, Inc., Topeka, 1984-97; mem. Topeka Bd. Bldg. and Fire Appeals, Kans., 1977-97, Com. for Employer Support of the Guard and Res. With USNR, 1942-48. Mem. AIA (Topeka pres. 1955-56, Kans. dir. 1957-58, com. on housing, com. for hist. resources), Internat. Conf. Bldg. Ofcls., Topeka Art Guild (pres. 1950), Am. Corrections Assn., Kans. Coun. Chs. (dir. 1961-62), Shawnee County Hist. Soc., Greater Topeka C. of C. (sr. coun.), Downtown Topeka Inc. (v.p. 1992-99), Topeka, Shawnee County Libr. (dir. friends of the libr.), St. Andrews Soc. (pres.), SAR (pres. state soc., pres. chpt.), Soc. of Antiquaries of Scotland (fellow), U. Nebr. Alumni Assn. (life), Band Alumni Assn., Kiwanis (pres. 1966-67), Topeka Knife and Fork Club. Presbyterian (elder, deacon, chmn. trustees). Office: Slemmons Assocs Archs 534 S Kansas Ave Ste 140 Topeka KS 66603-3473 E-mail: bpresource@webtv.net.

SLICHTER, CHARLES PENCE, physicist, educator; b. Ithaca, N.Y., Jan. 21, 1924; s. Sumner Huber and Ada (Pence) S.; m. Gertrude Thayer Almy, Aug. 23, 1952 (div. Sept. 1977); children: Sumner Pence, William Almy, Jacob Huber, Ann Thayer; m. Anne FitzGerald, June 7, 1980; children: Daniel Huber, David Pence AB, Harvard U., 1946, MA, 1947, PhD, 1949; DSc (hon.), U. Waterloo, 1993; LLD (hon.), Harvard U., 1996. Rsch. asst. Underwater Explosives Rsch. Lab., Woods Hole, Mass., 1943-46; faculty U. Ill., Urbana, 1949—, prof. physics, 1955-97, prof. Ctr. for Advanced Study, 1968-97, prof. chemistry, 1986-97, rsch. prof. physics, 1997—, prof. emeritus, 1997—. Morris Loeb lectr. Harvard U., 1961; mem. Pres.'s Sci. Adv. Com., 1964-69, Com. on Nat. Medal Sci., 1969-74, Nat. Sci. Bd., 1975-84, Pres.'s Com. Sci. and Tech., 1976 Author: Principles of Magnetic Resonance, 1963, 3d edit., 1989; Contbr. articles to profl. jours. Former trustee, mem. corp. Woods Hole Oceanog. Instn.; mem. Harvard Corp., 1970-95. Recipient Langmuir award Am. Phys. Soc., 1969, Buckley prize, 1996; Alfred P. Sloan fellow, 1955-61. Fellow AAAS, Am. Phys. Soc., Internat. Electron Paramagnetic Resonance Soc.; mem. NAS (Comstock prize 1993), Am. Acad. Arts and Scis., Am. Philos. Soc., Internat. Soc. Magnetic Resonance (pres. 1987-90, Trienniel prize 1986). Home: 61 Chestnut Ct Champaign IL 61822-7121

SLINGER, MICHAEL JEFFERY, law library director; b. Pitts., Apr. 12, 1956; s. Maurice and Mary Helen (Kengerski) S.; m. Cheryl Blaney, Apr. 19, 1980; children: Rebecca, Sarah. BA, U. Pitts., 1978; M Librianship, U. S.C., 1979; JD, Duquesne U., 1984. Reference libr. Duquesne U. Sch. Law, Pitts., 1983-84; rsch. libr. U. Notre Dame (Ind.) Sch. Law, 1984-85, head rsch. svcs., 1985-86, assoc. dir. pub. svcs., 1986-90; law libr. dir., assoc. prof. law Suffolk U. Sch. Law, Boston, 1990-93, law libr. dir., prof. law, 1994-95; law libr. dir., prof. law, assoc. dean Cleve. State U., 1995—. Contbr. articles to profl. jours., chpt. to book. Mem. ABA, ALA, Am. Assn. Law Librs., Am. Assn. Law Schs. (exec. bd. sect. on law librs. 1993-94), New Eng. Law Libr. Consortium (treas. 1992-95), Ohio Regional Assn. Law Librs. (v.p. 1987-88, pres. 1988-89, Pres. award 1989). Avocations: reading, sports, family. Office: Cleveland-Marshall Coll Law Law Libr 1801 Euclid Ave Cleveland OH 44115-2223

SLOAN, DAVID W. lawyer; b. Rahway, N.J., June 23, 1941; s. Harper Allen and Margaret (Walker) S.; m. Margaret J. Neville, Oct. 23, 1965; children: Matthew A., John S. AB, Princeton U., 1963; MS, Stanford U., 1965; JD, Harvard U., 1970. Bar: Calif. 1971, Ohio 1974. Assoc. Brobeck, Phleger & Harrison, San Francisco, 1970-73; assoc. and ptnr. Burke, Haber & Berick, Cleve., 1973-83; ptnr. Jones, Day, Reavis & Pogue, 1983—. Adj. prof. law Case Western Reserve U., 1975. Vol. Peace Corps., Turkey, 1965-67; sr. warden St. Paul's Episcopal Ch., Cleveland Heights, 1993-96. Mem. ABA (former council mem. sect. on science and technology, bus. law sect., intellectual property law sect.), Ohio Bar Assn., Cleve. Bar Assn., Computer Law Assn., Princeton Assn. No. Ohio (pres. 1990-94), Sigma Xi, Alzheimer's Assn. (former trustee and v.p.). Office: Jones Day Reavis & Pogue North Point 901 Lakeside Ave E Cleveland OH 44114-1190

SLOAN, HUGH WALTER, JR. automotive industry executive; b. Princeton, N.J., Nov. 1, 1940; s. Hugh Walter and Elizabeth (Johnson) S.; m. Deborah Louise Murray, Feb. 20, 1971; children: Melissa, Peter, Jennifer, William. A.B. in History with honors, Princeton U., 1963. Staff asst. to Pres. U.S., White House, Washington, 1969-71; treas. Pres. Nixon's Re-election Campaign, 1971; spl. asst. to pres. Budd Co., Troy, Mich., 1973-74, exec. asst. internat., 1974-77, mgr. corp. mktg., 1977-79; pres., gen. mgr. Budd Can. Inc., Kitchener, Ont., 1979-85; pres. automotive The Woodbridge Group, Troy, Mich., 1985-98, dep. chmn., 1998—. Bd. dirs. Woodbridge Foam Corp., Mfrs. Life Ins. Co., Wescast Industries, Virtek Vision Internat. Inc. Gov. Jr. Achievement of Can.; bd. govs. Cranbrook Schs.; bd. dirs. The Cmty. House; pres., bd. dirs. Deerwood Found.; dir. Beaumont Found. Lt. USNR, 1963—65. Recipient Outstanding Bus. Leader award Wilfrid Laurier U., 1987. Mem. World Pres. Orgn., Automotive Parts Mfrs. Assn. (past chmn.), Am. Soc. Employers (dir., past chmn./pres.), Original Equipment Suppliers Assn. (dir.), Automotive Market Rsch. Coun. (past pres.)., Bloomfield Hills (Mich.) Country Club. Republican. Office: Woodbridge Group 2500 Meijer Dr Troy MI 48084-7146

SLOAN, JUDI C. former physical education educator; b. Kansas City, Mo., July 17, 1944; d. Oscar H. Wilde and Florance (Janes) Wilde Graupner; m. Richard J. Sloan; children: Blake, Tracy. BS in Phys. Edn., No. Ill. U., 1966, postgrad.; MS in Phys. Edn., Ind. U., 1970; postgrad., U. Ill., DePaul U., Loyola U., Nat. Louis U. Tchr. phys. edn., coach Niles West High Sch., Skokie, Ill., 1966-99. Former coach gymnastics, tennis; coach cross-country; coop. tchr.; creator, dir. Galibo Gymnastics Show, 1968-75; founder, co-chair staff wellness com., Niles Township Sch. Dist., 1988—, curriculum coun., 1988-91; creator phys. mgmt. course, sophomore health and fitness program, evening children's, summer girls' gymnastics programs; co-dir. Indian Cross Country Invitational, Niles West Gymnastics Invitational; adv. com. cross country Ill. High Sch. Assn. Recipient All-Am. High Sch. Gymnastics Coach award U.S. Gymnastics Fedn., 1981, award of Honor Nat. Sch. Pub. Rels. Assn., 1990, Ill. Disting. Educator award, 1992; Named Ill. Tchr. Yr., 1992-93. Mem. AAHPERD, Am. Fedn. Tchrs., Nat. Assn. Secondary Physical Edn., Nat. Coaches Fedn., Ill. Fedn. Tchrs., Ill. Assn. Heatlh, Phys. Edn., Recreation, Dance (Outstanding Phys. Edn. award 1986), Nat. Assn. Girls' and Women's Sports, Ill. Track and Cross Country Coaches Assn., Ill. Girls' Coaches Assn. Office: Niles West High Sch 5701 Oakton St Skokie IL 60077-2681

SLOANE, SCOTT, radio personality; Radio host WSPD, Toledo; radio personality 700 WLW, Cin. Office: 700 WLW 111 St Gregory St Cincinnati OH 45202

SLOGOFF, STEPHEN, anesthesiologist, educator; b. Phila., July 7, 1942; s. Israel and Lillian (Rittenberg) S.; m. Barbara Anita Gershman, June 2, 1963; children: Michele, Deborah. AB in Biology, Franklin and Marshall Coll., 1964; MD, Jefferson Med. Coll., 1967. Diplomate Am. Bd. Med. Examiners, Am. Bd. Anesthesiology (jr. assoc. examiner 1977-80, sr. assoc. examiner 1980-81, bd. dirs. 1981-93, pres. 1989-90, joint coun. on in-tng. exams, vice chmn. 1983-86, chmn. 1986-92). Intern Harrisburg (Pa.) Hosp., 1967-68; resident in anesthesiology Jefferson Med. Coll. Hosp., 1968-71; chief anesthesia sect. U.S. Army, Brooke Army Med. Ctr., Fort Sam Houston, Tex., 1971-74; staff anesthesiologist Baylor Coll. Medicne, Houston, 1974-75; attending cardiovascular anesthesiologist U. Tex. Health Sci. Ctr., 1974-93, clin. asst. prof., 1977-81, clin. assoc. prof., 1981-85, clin. prof., 1985-93; prof., chmn. dept. anesthesiology Loyola U., Chgo., 1993—; sr. v.p. for clin. affairs Loyola U. Health Sys., 1999—; dean, Strich Sch. Medicine Loyola U., Chgo., 1999—. Chmn. rsch com., co-dir. rsch. labs Tex. Heart Inst., Houston, 1990-93. Contbr. articles to profl. jours. Trustee Loyola U. Health Sys., Chgo., 1996—; chmn. Loyola U. Physicians Found., 1995-99. Mem. Am. Soc. Anesthesiologists, Alpha Omega Alpha. Avocations: tennis, jogging. Office: Loyola U Med Ctr Office of Dean 2160 S 1st Ave Maywood IL 60153-3304

SLORP, JOHN S. academic administrator; b. Hartford, Conn., Dec. 5, 1936; Student, Ocean Coll., Calif., 1956, Taft Coll., 1961; BFA Painting, Calif. Coll. Arts and Crafts, 1963, MFA Painting, 1965. Grad. tchr. U. N.D., Grand Forks, 1964; in house designer Nat. Canner's Assn., Berkeley, Calif., 1965; faculty Md. Inst. Coll. Art, Balt., 1965-82, chmn. Found. Studies, 1972-78; faculty Emma Lake program U. Sask., Can., 1967-68, 70; selection, planning group for Polish Posters Smithsonian Instn., Md. Inst. Coll. Art, Warsaw, Poland, 1977; planner, initiator visual arts facility, curriculum Balt. High Sch. Arts, 1979-81; adjudicator Arts Recognition and Talent Search, Princeton, N.J., 1980-82; mem. Commn. Accredation Nat. Assn. Schs. Art and Design, 1985-88; pres. Memphis Coll. Art, 1982-90, Mpls. Coll Art and Design, 1990—. Com. Advanced Placement Studio Art Ednl. Testing Svc., Princeton, N.J., 1975-82; chair Assn. Memphis Area Colls. and Univs., 1986-88. Prodr. film A Romance of Calligraphy; calligrapher various brochures, manuscripts, album covers, children's books. Mem. Hotel adv. com. City of Memphis and Shelby County Convention Hotel, 1982; adv. bd. Memphis Design Ctr.; bd. trustees Opera Memphis, 1985—, ART Today Memphis Brooks Mus., 1988—. Avocations: painting, calligraphy, computer graphics. Office: Mpls Coll Art Design Office of President 2501 Stevens Ave Minneapolis MN 55404-4347

SLY, WILLIAM S. biochemist, educator; b. East St. Louis, Ill., Oct. 19, 1932; MD, St. Louis U., 1957. Intern, asst. resident ward medicine Barnes Hosp., St. Louis, 1957-59; clin. assoc. nat. heart inst. NIH, Bethesda, Md., 1959-63, rsch. biochemist, 1959-63; dir. divsn. med. genetics, dept. medicine and pediatrics, sch. medicine Washington U., St. Louis, 1964-84, from asst. prof. to prof. medicine, 1964-78, from asst. prof. to prof. pediatrics, 1967-78, prof. pediatrics, medicine and genetics, 1978-84; prof. biochemistry and pediat. St. Louis U., 1984—, chmn. Edward A. Doisy dept. biochemistry-molecular biology, 1984—. Vis. physician Nat. Heart Inst., 1961-63, pediatric genetics clinic U. Wis., Madison, 1963-64; Am. Cancer Soc. fellow lab. enzymol Nat. Ctr. Sci. Rsch., Gif-sur-Yvette, France, 1963, dept. biochemistry and genetics U. Wis., 1963-64; attending physician St. Louis County Hosp., Mo., 1964-84; asst. physician Barnes Hosp., St. Louis, 1964-84, St. Louis Children's Hosp., 1967-84; genetics cons. Homer G. Philips Hosp., St. Louis, 1969-81; mem. genetics study sect. divsn. rsch. grants NIH, 1971-75; mem. active staff Cardinal Glennon Children's Hosp., St. Louis, 1984—; mem. med. adv. bd. Howard Hughes Med. Inst., 1989-92. Recipient Merit award NIH, 1988; named Passano Found. laureate, 1991; Travelling fellow Royal Soc. Medicine, 1973. Mem. NAS, AMA, AAAS, Am. Soc. Human Genetics (mem. steering com. human cell biology program 1971-73, com. genetic counseling 1972-76), Am. Soc. Clin. Investigation, Am. Chem. Soc., Genetics Soc. Am., Am. Soc. Microbiology, Soc. Pediatric Rsch., Sigma Xi. Achievements include research on lysosomal enzyme replacement in storage diseases, inherited carbonic anhydrase deficiencies, and hereditary hemochromatosis. Office: St Louis U Med Sch Dept Biochemistry 1402 S Grand Blvd Saint Louis MO 63104-1004

SMALE, JOHN GRAY, diversified industry executive; b. Listowel, Ont., Can., Aug. 1, 1927; s. Peter John and Vera Gladys (Gray) S.; m. Phyllis Anne Weaver, Sept. 2, 1950; children: John Gray, Jr., Catherine Anne, Lisa Beth, Peter McKee. BS, Miami U., Oxford, Ohio, 1949; LLD (hon.), Kenyon Coll., Gambier, Ohio, 1974, Miami U., Oxford, Ohio, 1979; DSc (hon.), DePauw U., 1983; DCL (hon.), St. Augustine's Coll., 1985; LLD (hon.), Xavier U., 1986. With Vick Chem. Co., N.Y.C., 1949-50, Bio-Rsch., Inc., N.Y.C., 1950-52; asst. brand mgr. Procter & Gamble Co., 1952-54, brand mgr., 1954-58, assoc. advt. mgr., 1958-63, mgr. advt. dept. toilet goods divsn., 1963-66, mgr. toilet goods divsn., 1966-67, v.p. toilet goods divsn., 1967-68, v.p. bar soap and household cleaning products divsn., 1968-69, v.p. packaged soap and detergent divsn., 1969-70, v.p. group exec., 1970-72, mem. bd. dirs., 1972, exec. v.p., 1973-74, pres., 1974-81, pres., chief exec., 1981-86, chmn. of bd., chief exec., 1986-90, chmn. exec. com. of bd. of dirs., 1990-95; chmn. GM, 1992-95, chmn. exec. com., 1995-2000, chmn. bd. dirs., 1996-2000, chmn. exec. com., 1996-2000, also bd. dirs.; ret., 2000. Bd. dirs. Rand McNally. Emeritus trustee Kenyon Coll. With USNR, 1945-46. Mem. Comml. Club, Queen City Club, Cin. Country Club. Office: Procter & Gamble PO Box 599 Cincinnati OH 45201-0599

SMALL, ERWIN, veterinarian, educator; b. Boston, Nov. 28, 1924; Cert., Vt. State Sch. Agr., 1943; BS, U. Ill., 1955, DVM, 1957, MS, 1965. Diplomate: Am. Coll. Vet. Internal Medicine, Am. Coll. Vet. Dermatology. Intern Angell Meml. Animal Hosp., Boston, 1957-58; with U. Ill. Coll. Vet. Medicine, Urbana, 1958-92, prof. vet. clin. medicine, 1968-92, assoc. dean alumni and public affairs, chief of medicine, 1970-84, asst. dept. chmn., 1989-92, prof. emeritus, assoc. dean alumni and pub. affairs, 1992—. Contbr. articles to profl. jours. Served with USMC, 1944-46, 50-51, PTO. Recipient Nat. Gamma award Ohio State U., 1971, Ill. State VMA Svc. award, 1973, Nat. Zeta award Auburn U., 1974, Bustad Companion Animal Veterinarian award, 1993, Disting. Svc. award U. Ill. Alumni Assn., 1995; named Outstanding Tchr., Nordens Labs., 1967, Outstanding Educator, 1973, Outstanding Faculty Mem., Dad's Assn. U. Ill., 1990, Veterinarian of Yr., Mass. Soc. for Prevention Cruelty to Animals, 1993; recipient recognition for svc. with USMC War Dog Platoon, War Dog Meml., Quantico, Va., 2001, ISUMA Pres. award, 2002. Fellow Am. Coll. Vet. Pharmacology and Therapeutics; mem. AVMA (chmn. coun. edn. 1981-82, chmn. program com. 1983-87, Pres.'s award 1992, AVMA award 1998), Am. Animal Hosp. Assn. (award 1983, Midwest Region Svc. award 1989), Am. Coll. Vet. Dermatology (pres.), Internat. Vet. Symposia (pres.), Am. Assn. Vet. Clinics (pres., Faculty Achievement award 1992), Ill. Vet. Med. Polit. Action Com. (past chmn.), Chgo. Vet. Med. Assn. (lifetime achievement award 1997), Am. Coll. Vet. Internal Medicine (Robert W. Kirk award 1997), Coll. of Vet. Med. Alumni Assn. (Vet. Med. Achievement award 1997), Am. Legion, VFW, Moose, Omega Tau Sigma (pres. 1971-79), Phi Zeta, Gamma Sigma Delta. Republican. Jewish. Office: Vet Med Adminstrn U Ill Coll Vet Medicine Urbana IL 61802 Home: # A 1815 W Kirby Ave Champaign IL 61821-5410 E-mail: esmall@cvm.uiuc.edu.

SMALL, JOYCE GRAHAM, psychiatrist, educator; b. Edmonton, Alta., Can., June 12, 1931; came to U.S., 1956; d. John Earl and Rachel C. (Redmond) Graham; m. Iver Francis Small, May 26, 1954; children: Michael, Jeffrey. BA, U. Sask., Saskatoon, Can., 1951; MD, U. Man., Alta., Can., 1956; MS, U. Mich., 1959. Diplomat Am. Bd. Psychiatry and Neurology, Am. Bd. Electroencephalography. Instr. in psychiatry Neuropsychiat. Inst. U. Mich., Ann Arbor, 1959-60; instr. in psychiatry med. sch. U. Oreg., Portland, 1960-61, asst. prof. in psychiatry med. sch., 1961-62; asst. prof. in psychiatry sch. of medicine Washington U., St. Louis, 1962-65; assoc. prof. in psychiatry sch. of medicine Ind. U., Indpls., 1965-69, prof. psychiatry sch. of medicine, 1969—. Mem. initial rev. groups NIMH, Washington, 1972-76, 79-82, 87-91; assoc. mem. Inst. Psychiat. Rsch., Indpls., 1974—. Mem. editl. bd. Quar. Jour. Convulsive Therapy, 1984, Clin. EEG, 1990, and more than 150 publs. in field; contbr. articles to profl. jours. Rsch. grantee NIMH, Portland, Oreg., 1961-62, St. Louis, 1962-64, Indpls., 1967—, Epilepsy Found., Dreyfus Found., Indpls., 1965; recipient Merit award NIMH, Indpls., 1990. Fellow Am. Psychiat. Assn., Am. EEG Soc. (councillor 1972-75, 1982); mem. Soc. Biol. Psychiatry, Cen. Assn. Electroencephalographers (sec., treas. 1967-68, pres. 1970, councillor 1971-72), Sigma Xi. Office: Larue D Carter Meml Hosp 2601 Cold Spring Rd Indianapolis IN 46222-2202

SMALL, MELVIN, history educator; b. N.Y.C., Mar. 14, 1939; s. Herman Z. and Ann (Ashkinazy) S.; m. Sarajane Miller, Oct. 23, 1958; children: Michael, Mark. BA, Dartmouth Coll., 1960; MA, U. Mich., 1961, PhD, 1965. Asst. prof. history Wayne State U., Detroit, 1965-68, assoc. prof., 1968-76, prof., 1976—, chmn. dept. history, 1979-86. Vis. prof. U. Mich., Ann Arbor, 1968, Marygrove Coll., Detroit, 1971, Aarhus (Denmark) U., 1972-74, 83, Windsor (Ont., Can.) U., 1977-78. Author: Was War Necessary, 1980, Johnson, Nixon and the Doves, 1988, Covering Dissent, 1994, Democracy and Diplomacy, 1996, The Presidency of Richard Nixon, 1999, Antiwarriors, 2002; co-author: Wages of War, 1972, Resort to Arms, 1982; editor: Public Opinion and Historians, 1970; co-editor: International War, 1986, Appeasing Fascism, 1991, Give Peace a Chance, 1992; mem. editl. bd. Internat. Interactions, 1987-91, Peace and Change, 1989—; restaurant critic Detroit Metro Times, 1982-95; history book reviewer Detroit Free Press, 1988-95. Mem. hon. bd. Swords into Plowshares Mus., 1992—, mem. bd. Abraham Lincoln Brigade Archives, 1998—. Recipient Disting. Faculty award Mich. Assn. Governing Bds., 1993; Am. Coun. Learned Socs. fellow, 1969; Stanford Ctr. for Advanced Study fellow, 1969-70; grantee Am. Coun. Learned Socs., 1983, Johnson Libr., 1982, 88, Can. Govt., 1987; NATO rsch. fellow, 1996. Mem. Coun. on Peace Rsch. in History (nat. coun. 1986-90, pres. 1990-92), Am. Hist. Assn., Atlantic Coun. (acad. assoc.), Orgn. Am. Historians, Soc. for Historians of Am. Fgn. Rels. (Warren Kuehl prize 1989). Home: 1815 Northwood Blvd Royal Oak MI 48073-3919 Office: Wayne State U Dept History 3119 Fab Detroit MI 48202 E-mail: M.Small@Wayne.edu.

SMALLEY, WILLIAM EDWARD, bishop; b. New Brunswick, N.J., Apr. 8, 1940; s. August Harold and Emma May (Gleason) S.; m. Carole A. Kuhns, Sept. 12, 1964; children: Michelle Lynn, Jennifer Ann. BA in Sociology, Lehigh U., 1962; MDiv, Episcopal Theol. Sch., 1965; MEd, Temple U., 1970; D of Ministry, Wesley Theol. Sem., 1987. Ordained to ministry Episcopal Ch., 1965, bishop, 1989; oblate Order of St. Benedict. Vicar St. Peter's Episcopal Ch., Plymouth, Pa., 1965-67, St. Martin-in-the-Fields Ch., Nuangola, 1965-67; rector All Saints' Episcopal Ch., Lehighton, 1967-75; fed. program adminstr. Lehighton Area Schs., 1970-72; rector Episcopal Ministry of Unity, Palmerton, Pa., 1975-80, Ch. of Ascension, Gaithersburg, Md., 1980-89; bishop Episcopal Diocese Kans., Topeka, 1989—. Pres. Gaithersburg (Md.) Pastoral Counseling Inc., 1986-89; bd. dirs. Washington Pastoral Counseling, 1988-89; chmn. Turner House Inc., Kansas City, Kans., 1989—, Episcopal Social Svcs., Wichita, Kans., 1989—; bd. dirs. Christ Ch. Hosp., Topeka, 1989—, St. Francis Acad., Atchison, Kans., 1989—; v.p. Province VII, The Episcopal Ch., 1993-95, pres. Province VII, 1995—; pres. Province VII House of Bishops; mem. Ch. Deployment Bd., vice chair, 1997-2000; chair Presiding Bishop's Coun. Advice; mem. joint nominating com. for Presiding Bishop; pres. Friends of Topeka and Shawnee County Pub. Libr., 1998-2000. Mem. Omicron Delta Kappa. Democrat. Avocations: gardening, swimming, cross-stitching, reading. Address: 833 SW Polk St Topeka KS 66612-1620

SMARR, LARRY LEE, science administrator, educator, astrophysicist; b. Columbia, Mo., Oct. 16, 1948; s. Robert L. Jr. and Jane (Crampton) S.; m. Janet Levarie, June 3, 1973; children: Joseph Robert, Benjamin Lee. BA, MS, U. Mo., 1970; MS, Stanford U., 1972; PhD, U. Tex., 1975. Rsch. asst. in physics U. Tex., Austin, 1972-74; lectr. dept. astrophys. sci. Princeton U., 1974-75; rsch. assoc. Princeton U. Obs., 1975-76; rsch. affiliate dept. physics Yale U., New Haven, 1978-79; asst. prof. astronomy dept. U. Ill., Urbana, 1979-81, asst. prof. physics dept., 1980-81, assoc. prof. astronomy and physics dept., 1981-85, prof. astronomy and physics dept., 1985—; dir. Nat. Ctr. for Supercomputing Applications, Champaign, Ill., 1985—, Nat. Computational Sci. Alliance, 1997—. Cons. Lawrence Livermore Nat. Lab., Calif., 1976—, Los Alamos (New Nex.) Nat. Lab., 1983—; mem. Commn. on Phys. Sci., Math. and Resources, NRC, Washington, 1987-90, commn. on Geoscience, Environ. and Resources, 1990—, adv. panel on Basic Rsch. in the 90's Office Tech. Assesment, 1990—. Editor: Sources of Gravitational Radiation, 1979; mem. editoral bd. Science mag., 1986-90; contbr. over 50 sci. articles to jours. in field. Co-founder, co-dir. Ill. Alliance to Prevent Nuclear War, Champaign, 1981-84. Recipient Fahrney medal Franklin Inst., Phila., 1990; NSF fellow Stanford U., 1970-74, Woodrow Wilson fellow, 1970-71, Lane Scholar U. Tex., Austin, 1972-73, jr. fellow Harvard U., 1976-79, Alfred P. Sloan fellow, 1980-84. Fellow Am. Phys. Soc.; mem. NAE, AAAS, Am. Astron. Soc., Govt. Rsch. Roundtable U. Ind. Avocations: marine aquarium, gardening. Office: NCSA at UIUC 605 E Springfield Ave Champaign IL 61820-5518

SMEDINGHOFF, THOMAS J. lawyer; b. Chgo., July 15, 1951; s. John A. and Dorothy M. Smedinghoff; m. Mary Beth Smedinghoff. BA in Math., Knox Coll., 1973; JD, U. Mich., 1978. Bar: Ill. 1978, U.S. Dist. Ct. (no. dist.) Ill. 1978. Assoc. McBride, Baker & Coles and predecessor McBride & Baker, Chgo., 1978-84, ptnr., 1985-99, Baker & McKenzie, Chgo., 1999—. Adj. prof. computer law John Marshall Law Sch., Chgo.; chair Ill. Commn. on Electronic Commerce and Crime, 1996—; mem. U.S. Del. to UN Commn. on Internat. Trade Law. Author: Online Law, 1996. Mem. ABA (chair electronic commerce divsn. 1995—). Office: Baker & McKenzie 130 E Randolph St Ste 3700 Chicago IL 60601-6342 E-mail: smedinghoff@bakernet.com.

SMERZ, NANCY, entrepreneur; Chair Air Comfort Corp., Broadview, Ill. Office: Air Comfort Corp 2550 Braga Dr Broadview IL 60155-3987

SMETANA, MARK, food products executive; CFO Eby-Brown Co., Naperville, Ill. Office: 280 Shuman Blvd Ste 280 Naperville IL 60563-2578

SMILEY, WYNN RAY, nonprofit corporation executive; b. Danville, Ill., May 18, 1961; s. Arthur Glen and Lois Jean (Lawrence) S. BS in Agriculture Comms., U. Ill., 1983. Asst. prodr. Sta. WCIA-TV, Champaign, Ill., 1982-83, news prodr., 1983-87, gen. assignments reporter, 1987-91, host, anchor news show, 1988-99; founder, owner, pres. Advisory Inc., Indpls., 1989—, CEO, 1997—; dir. communications Alpha Tau Omega Nat. Hqrs., 1991-98. Facilitator Leadershape Inc., Champaign, 1990—. Editor: The Positive Experience, 1992, 96, 2000; pub. Live Life Intentionally!, 1996; prodr. (CD-ROM) Live Life Intentionally!, 1996. Chmn. bd. Am. Cancer Soc., Champaign, 1991-93; bd. dirs., sec. Meadowbrook Cmty. Ch., 1994-98; bd. fraternity affairs, U. Ill., 1993—; mem. Grace Cmty. Ch. Mem. Assembly of God. Avocations: running, outdoor ropes course guide. Office: ATO 12th Fl One N Pennsylvania St Indianapolis IN 46204

SMITH, ADRIAN DEVAUN, architect; b. Chgo., Aug. 19, 1944; s. Alfred D. and Hazel (Davis) S.; m. Nancy L. Smith, Aug. 17, 1968; children: Katherine, Jason. Student, Tex. A&M U., 1962-66; BArch, U. Ill., Chgo., 1969. Registered architect, Ill., Ohio, N.J., N.Y., Mass., Iowa, Md., Conn., D.C., Fla., Ind., Mo., R.I., Tex. Design ptnr. Skidmore, Owings, & Merrill, Chgo., 1967—, ptnr., 1980—, CEO, 1994-96. Vis. faculty Sch. Architecture, U. Ill., Chgo., 1984; chmn. U. Ill. Sch. Archtl. Alumni Assn., AIA Jury on Inst. Honors; adv. jury AIA gold metal and architecture firm award, 2000; chmn. Skidmore Owings Merrill Found., 1990-95; pres. Chgo. Ctrl. Area, 1998-99; bd. dirs. Greater State Street Coun.. trustee; bd. govs. Sch. Art Inst. Chgo., 1999—; cons. and lectr. in field. Designer numerous projects including Jin Mao Tower (World's Tallest Mixed-Use Project), Shanghai, China (Nat. AIA award for interiors 2000), Banco de Occidente, Guatemala City (CCAIA Interior Architecture award 1981, NAIA Honor award 1982), United Gulf Bank, Manama, Bahrain (Progressive Architecture award 1984, CCAIA Disting. Bldg. award 1988, NAIA Honor award 1988, CCAIA Disting. Detail Honor award 1989), 222 N. LaSalle, Chgo., (Disting. Bldg. award CCAIA 1988), Art Inst. Chgo. 2d Fl. Galleries (CCAIA Disting. Bldg. award 1987), Rowes Wharf, Boston (Build Am. award 1988, Build Mass. award 1989, ULI award 1989, PCI Profl. Design award 1989, CCAIA Hon. award 1998, Nat. AIA Honor award 1994), AT&T Corp. Ctr., Chgo. (recipient Gold Metal Ill. Ind. Masonry award), NBC Tower (Chgo. Sun Times Bldg. of Yr. award 1989, CCAIA Disting. Bldg. award 1990, PCI Design award 1989), 75 State St. Boston (Archtl. Woodwork Inst. award 1989, Nat. Comml. Builder's Coun. Merit award 1990, Bldg. Stone Inst. Tucker Archtl. award 1990), Arthur Anderson Tng. Ctr. (Masonry award 1988), St. Charles, Ill., USG Hdqs., Chgo., Heller Internat. Tower, Chgo., State St. Renovation (spl. achievement award 1997, AIA honor award urban design 1998) designer numerous other fgn. projects including: Monterey Cultural Ctr., Mex., 1978; hdqurs. Banco de Occidente, Guatemala City, 1978 (AIA Nat. Honor award Bus. Interior Design award Guatemala 1981, CCAIA Interior Architecture award 1982, NAI A Honor award), Canary Wharf Fin. Ctr., London, Eng., 1988, 10 Ludgate (CCAIA 1994 Honor award), 100 Ludgate, London, 1992, Aramco Hdqs. Dharan Saudi Arabia, Tower Palace III, Seoul, Korea, 7 South Dearborn Tower, Chgo. (world's tallest), McGraw Hill European Headquarters, Canary Wharf (DS4), CSFB European Headquarters, Canary Wharf (DSI), Morgan Stanley Headquarters for Europe (HQI), Canary Wharf; contbr. articles to profl. jours.; subject numerous pubs. in architecture. Mem. com. Task Force for New City Plan, Chgo., Light Up Chgo., Cen. Area Com. Task Force Chgo.; chmn. Senator Richard A. Newhouse Bldg. Competition Jury, 1982, Progressive Architecture Design Jury, 1985; bd. dirs. State St. Coun. Recipient U. Ill. Alumni Achievement award. Fellow AIA (mem. Young Architects Award Design Jury, 1987, Mich. Jury 1988, Disting. Bldg. award 1990), Royal Inst. Brit. Architects, Archtl. Registration Coun., U.K., Nat. Coun. Archtl. Registration Bds., Architecture Soc. of Art Inst. Chgo., Chgo. Arch. Found. (bd. dirs.), Chgo. Archtl. Club, Urban Land Found. (bd. trustees) University Club, Arts Club. Home: 1100 W Summerfield Dr Lake Forest IL 60045-1545 Office: Skidmore Owings & Merrill LLP 224 S Michigan Ave Ste 1000 Chicago IL 60604-2592

SMITH, ADRIAN J.R. management company executive; b. Liverpool, Eng. married; 4 children. Grad., Liverpool Law Sch., 1966. With Procter & Gamble Ltd., 1966-79; v.p. European consumer ops. Ecolab Inc., Minn., 1979-90; pres. Ecolab Can. Ltd.; with Arthur Andersen and Co., 1990-96; CEO Grant Thornton LLP, Chgo., 1996; ptnr. Skidmore, Owings & Merrill LLP. Mem. Am. Bus. Conf. Bd. dirs. March of Dimes, Chgo., Montessori Sch., Lake Forest, Chgo. Sinfonietta. Office: Skidmore Owings & Merrill LLP 800 One Prudential Plz 244 S Michigan Ave Ste 1000 Chicago IL 60604

SMITH, ADRIAN M. state legislator, real estate agent; b. Scottsbluff, Nebr., Dec. 19, 1970; BS in Mktg. Edn., U. Nebr., 1993, postgrad., Portland State U. Legis. page Nebr. Legislature, 1992; mem. Nebr. Legislature from 48th dist., Lincoln, 1998—; staff internat., mktg. specialist Nebrs. Gov.'s Office, 1992; rsch. asst. U. Nebr. Found., 1992-93; educator, staff devel. project mgr. Ednl. Svc. Unit 13, 1994-97; real estate agt., mktg. specialist Buyers Realty, 1997—. Mem. Scotts Bluff County Bd. Realtors. Mem. Gering City Coun., 1994-98, We. Nebr. Regional Airport Ops. Bd., Scotts Bluff County Visitors Adv. Com., 1995-96, N. Platte Valley Hist. Soc., Riverside Zool. Soc., Wyo-Braska Mus. Natural History, Calvary Meml. Evang. Free Ch., Farm and Ranch Mus. Assn.; chmn. land use task force Vision 2020; bd. dirs. Twin Cities Devel. Mem. Scottsbluff Kiwanis Club (bd. dirs. Camp Kiwanis). Home: 2035 10th St Gering NE 69341-2417 Office: State Capitol Dist 48 PO Box 94604 Rm 1523 Lincoln NE 68509

SMITH, AKILI, professional football player; b. Aug. 21, 1975; Student, U. Oreg. Football player Cin. Bengals, 1999—. Office: Cin Bengals 1 Paul Brown Stadium Cincinnati OH 45202

SMITH, ALMA WHEELER, state legislator; b. Aug. 6, 1941; BA, U. Mich. Legis. coord. Senator Lane Pollack; mem. Mich. Senate from 18th dist., Lansing, 1995—; mem. appropriations com. Mem. South Lyon (Mich.) Bd. Edn.

SMITH, ARTHUR LEE, lawyer; b. Davenport, Iowa, Dec. 19, 1941; s. Harry Arthur Smith and Ethel (Hoffman) Duerre; m. Georgia Mills, June 12, 1965 (dec. Jan. 1984); m. Jean Bowler, Aug. 4, 1984; children: Juliana, Christopher, Andrew. BA, Augustana Coll., Rock Island, Ill., 1964; MA, Am. U., 1968; JD, Washington U., St. Louis, 1971. Bar: Mo 1971, DC 1983. Telegraph editor Davenport Morning Democrat, 1962-64; ptnr. Peper Martin Jensen Maichel & Hetlage, 1971-95, Husch & Eppenberger, St. Louis, 1995—. Arbitrator Nat Asn Security Dealers, 1980—, Am Arbit Asn, 1980—. Columnist: St Louis Lawyer. Lt USN, 1964—68. Mem.: ABA, Bar Asn Metropolitan St Louis (chmn law mgt comt 1993—96, chair technology comt 1996—99, Pres's award Exceptional Serv 1995), P Buckley Moss Soc (dir 1994—, vpres 1998—2000, exec vpres 2001—), Mo Bar Asn (chair admin law comt 1995—97, vice-chair ins programs comt 1981—83, vice-chair antitrust comt 1981—83), DC Bar Asn (chmn law practice mgt 1990—91), Order Coif. Home: 1320 Chesterfield Estate Dr Chesterfield MO 63005-4400 Office: Husch & Eppenberger 190 Carondelet Plz Ste 600 Saint Louis MO 63105-3441 E-mail: arthur.smith@husch.com.

SMITH, BARBARA JEAN, lawyer; b. Washington, Jan. 9, 1947; d. Harry Wallace and Jean (Fraser) S.; m. Philip R. Chall, July 13, 1991; children: Brian C.S. Brown, Craig F.S. Brown, Amy E. Spiers, Carrie A. Chall. BA, Old Dominion Coll., 1968; MBA, Pepperdine U., 1974; JD, Case Western Res. U., 1977. Bar: Ohio 1977. Assoc. Squire, Sanders & Dempsey, Cleve., 1977-88, ptnr., 1988-93; shareholder McDonald, Hopkins, Burke & Haber Co., L.P.A., 1993—. Bd. editors Health Law Jour. of Ohio, 1989-95; contbr. articles to health jours. and periodicals. Trustee Urban Community Sch., Cleve., 1984-86, Alzheimer's Assn. Greater Cleve., 2000—. Mem. Ohio Women's Bar Assn. (pres. 1994-95), Cleve. Bar Assn. (pres. 1998-99, trustee 1992-95, chair health law sect. 1991-92), Am. Health Lawyers Assn., Ohio State Bar Assn. (health law com. 1991—), Soc. Ohio Hosp. Attys. Democrat. Mem. United Ch. of Christ. Avocations: reading, hiking. Home: 416 Fairway Vw Chagrin Falls OH 44023-6718 Office: McDonald Hopkins Burke & Haber 2100 Bank One Ctr 600 Superior Ave E Cleveland OH 44114-2653 E-mail: bsmith@mhbh.com.

SMITH, BILL, advertising and marketing executive; V.p. advt. and mktg. Meijer, Inc., Grand Rapids, Mich., 1987—. Office: Meijer Inc 2929 Walker Ave NW Grand Rapids MI 49544-9428

SMITH, C. LEMOYNE, publishing company executive; b. Atkins, Ark., Sept. 15, 1934; s. Cecil Garland and Salena Bell (Wilson) S.; m. Selma Jean Tucker, May 23, 1964; 1 child, Jennifer Lee B.S., Ark. Tech. U., 1956; M.Ed., U. Ark., 1958. Tchr. pub. schs., Little Rock, 1956-58; instr. bus. adminstrn. Ark. Tech. U., Russellville, 1958-60; sales rep. South-Western Pub. Co., Cin., 1960-67, editorial staff, 1967-82, pres., chief exec. officer, 1982-90, chmn., 1990-91, ret., 1991. Bd. dirs. Cin. Council on World Affairs, 1983-95. Mem. Nat. Bus. Edn. Assn., Delta Pi Epsilon Republican. Presbyterian. Avocations: bridge, travel, golf. Office: South-Western Pub Co 5191 Natorp Blvd Mason OH 45040-7980 E-mail: lemselm@aol.com.

SMITH, CARL BERNARD, education educator; b. Feb. 29, 1932; s. Carl R. and Elizabeth Ann (Lefeld) S.; m. Virginia Lee Cope, Aug. 30, 1958; children: Madonna, Anthony, Regina, Marla. BA, U. Dayton, 1954; MA, Miami U., Oxford, Ohio, 1961; PhD, Case Western Res. U., 1967. Tchr. Cathedral Latin H.S., Cleve., 1954-57; customer corr. E.F. MacDonald Co., Dayton, 1958-59; tchr. Kettering (Ohio) H.S., 1959-61; editor Reardon Baer Pub. Co., Cleve., 1961-62; tchr., rschr. Case Western Res. U., 1962-65, Cleve. Pub. Schs., 1966-67; asst. prof. edn. Ind. U., Bloomington, 1967-69, assoc. prof., 1970-72, prof., 1973—99, prof. emeritus, 1999—. Dir. ERIC Ctr., 1988—, Family Literacy Ctr., 1990—; pres. Grayson Bernard Pub. Co., 1988—, Am. Family Learning Corp., 1996—. Author: Reading Instruction through Diagnostic Teaching (Pi Lambda Theta Best Book in Edn. award 1972), Getting People to Read, 1978; sr. author: Series r, 1983, New View, 1993, Teaching Reading and Writing Together, 1984, Connect! Getting Your Kids to Talk to You, 1994, World History A Resource Book, 1995, Self-Directed Learner Curriculum, 1998, (videotape) Make a Difference, 1996, Improving Your Child's Writing Skills, 1999, Gotcha Grandpa, 2000, Talk to Your Children About Books, 2001. Pres. Bd. Edn., St. Charles Sch., Bloomington, 1976-80. Recipient Sch. Bell award NEA, 1967, Literacy award Ind. State Reading Assn., 1997. Mem. ASCD, Internat. Reading Assn., Nat. Coun. Tchrs. of English, Am. Ednl. Rsch. Assn., Phi Delta Kappa. Republican. Roman Catholic. Home: 401 Serena Ln Bloomington IN 47401-9226 Office: ERIC Clearinghouse Smith Rsch Ctr Bloomington IN 47405 E-mail: smith2@indiana.edu.

SMITH, CAROLE DIANNE, lawyer, editor, writer, product developer; b. Seattle, June 12, 1945; d. Glaude Francis and Elaine Claire (Finkenstein) S.; m. Stephen Bruce Presser, June 18, 1968 (div. June 1987); children: David Carter, Elisabeth Catherine. AB cum laude, Harvard U., Radcliffe Coll., 1968; JD, Georgetown U., 1974. Bar: Pa. 1974. Law clk. Hon. Judith Jamison, Phila., 1974-75; assoc. Gratz, Tate, Spiegel, Ervin & Ruthrouff, 1975-76; freelance editor, writer Evanston, Ill., 1983-87; editor Ill. Inst. Tech., Chgo., 1987-88; mng. editor LawLetters, Inc., 1988-89; editor ABA, 1989-95; product devel. dir. Gt. Lakes divsn. Lawyers Coop. Pub., Deerfield, Ill., 1995-96; product devel. mgr. Midwest Market Ctr. West Group, 1996-97; mgr acquisitions, bus. and fin. group CCH, Inc., Riverwoods, 1997—. Author Jour. of Legal Medicine, 1975, Selling and the Law: Advertising and Promotion, 1987; (under pseudonym Sarah Toast) 77 children's books and stories, 1994-2002; editor The Brief, 1990-95, Criminal Justice, 1989-90, 92-95 (Gen. Excellence award Soc. Nat. Assn. Pubs. 1990, Feature Article award-bronze Soc. Nat. Assn. Pubs. 1994), Franchise Law Jour., 1995; editor-in-chief The Brief, ABA Tort and Ins. Practice Sect., 1998-2000; mem. editl. bd. The Brief, ABA Tort and Ins. Practice Sect., 1995-2000. Dir. Radcliffe Club of Chgo., 1990-93; mem. parents council Latin Sch. Chgo., 1995-96. Mem. ABA. Office: CCH Inc Bus and Fin Group 2700 Lake Cook Rd Riverwoods IL 60015-3867 E-mail: smithca@cch.com.

SMITH, DAVID BRUCE, lawyer; b. Moline, Ill., May 9, 1948; s. Neal Schriever and Barbara Jean (Harris) S.; children: Neal, Stephanie. BSME, U. Iowa, 1970; JD, U. Tex., 1973. Bar: Tex. 1973, Wis. 1975. Patent examiner U.S. Patent and Trademark Office, Washington, 1973-74; atty. Nilles & Kirby S.C., Milw., 1974-76, Globe-Union, Inc., Milw., 1976-77; atty., intellectual property practice coord. Michael Best & Friedrich, 1978—. Co-chair Intellectual Property Com. of Lex Mundi. Pres. Milw. County coun. Boy Scouts Am., Milw., 1994-95. Mem. ABA, Am. Intellectual Property Law Assn., State Bar Wis., Wis. Intellectual Property Law Assn., Ozaukee Country Club, Milw. Club. Office: Michael Best & Friedrich 100 E Wisconsin Ave Ste 3300 Milwaukee WI 53202-4108 E-mail: dbsmith@mbf-law.com.

SMITH, DAVID JAMES, corporate lawyer; Asst. sec. Archer Daniels Midland, Decatur, Ill., 1988-97, asst. gen. counsel, 1995-97, v.p., sec., gen. counsel, 1997—2001, sr. v.p., sec., gen. counsel, 2002—. Office: Archer Daniels Midland Co 4666 E Faries Pkwy Decatur IL 62526-5666

SMITH, DAVID JOHN, JR. plastic surgeon; b. Indpls., Feb. 20, 1947; s. David John and Carolyn (Culp) S.; m. Nancy Loonsten, June 7, 1975; children: Matthew, Peter, Hadley. BA, Wesleyan U., 1969; MD, Ind. U., 1973. Diplomate Am. Bd. Plastic Surgery. Resident Emory U.-Grady Hosp., Atlanta, 1973-78; resident Ind. U. Med. Ctr., Indpls., 1978-80; Christine Kleinert fellow in hand surgery, 1979; asst. prof. surgery Ind. U. Sch. Medicine, 1980-84; assoc. prof. of surgery Wayne State U. Sch. Medicine, 1984-87; assoc. prof. plastic surgery, surgery sect. head U. Mich. Med. Ctr., Ann Arbor, 1987-92, prof. surgery sect. head, 1992—2001. Mem. Residency Rev. Com. for Plastic Surgery, 1992-2000, vice chmn., 1994, chmn. 1996-99. Mem. editl. bd. Jour. of Surg. Rsch., 1989-95, Annals of Plastic Surgery, 1992—, assoc. editor, 1994—, Yearbook of Hand Surgery, 1989—; guest reviewer Surgery, 1988—, Plastic and Reconstructive Surgery, 1988—; contbr. articles to profl. jours. Recipient numerous grants. Fellow ACS (many coms.), Soc. Univ. Surgeons, Am. Assn. Plastic Surgeons, Am. Surg. Assn., Am. Bd. Plastic Surgeons (vice chmn. 1997-98, chair-elect 1998-99, chmn. oral exam 1995-97, chmn. 1999-2000), Assn. for Acad. Surgery, Western Surg. Assn., Ctrl. Surg. Assn., Am. Soc. for Surgery of the Hand, Am. Soc. Plastic Surgeons, Plastic Surgery Ednl. Found. (bd. dirs. 1988-99, treas. 1994, v.p., pres.-elec., pres., chair nominating com. 1997-98), Plastic Surgery Rsch. Coun., Am. Burn Assn. (chmn. com. on organization and delivery of burn care 1995-98), Am. Burn Life Support Nat. Faculty, Am. Assn. for Hand Surgeons (pres. 1994), Assn. Acad. Chmn. Plastic Surgery (pres.-elect 1997, pres. 1998-99, chmn. nominating com. 1999-2000). Home: 769 Heatherway St Ann Arbor MI 48104-2731 Office: U Mich Med Ctr 2130 Taubman Health Ctr 1500 E Medical Center Dr Ann Arbor MI 48109-0005

SMITH, DAVID WALDO EDWARD, pathology and gerontology educator, physician; b. Fargo, N.D., Apr. 3, 1934; s. Waldo Edward and Martha (Althaus) S.; m. Diane Leigh Walker, June 18, 1960. BA, Swarthmore Coll., 1956; MD, Yale U., 1960. Intern, asst. resident, research fellow pathology Yale U. Med. Sch., 1960-62; research assoc. lab. molecular biology Nat. Inst. Arthritis and Metabolic Diseases, 1962-64, investigator lab. exptl. pathology, 1964-67; assoc. prof. pathology and microbiology Ind. U. Med. Sch., 1967-69; prof. pathology Northwestern U. Med. Sch., 1969—, dir. Ctr. on Aging, 1988—, prof. emeritus, 2000—. Guest investigator Internat. Lab. Genetics and Biophysics, Naples, Italy, 1969; mem. ad hoc biochemistry study sect. NIH, 1974-75, mem. pathobiol. chemistry study sect., 1975-79, cons., 1982; sabbatical leave NIH, 1986-87; chmn. NIH Conf. on Gender and Longevity: Why Do Women Live Longer Than Men?, 1987. Author: Human Longevity, 1993, also research papers, chpts. in books.; editorial bd. Yale Jour. Biology and Medicine, 1957-60. Sr. surgeon USPHS, 1958-67. Recipient Career Devel. award NIH, 1968-69 Mem. AAAS, Am. Soc.for Investigative Pathology, Am. Soc. for Biochem. and Molecular Biology, Gerontol. Soc. Am., Sigma Xi, Alpha Omega Alpha. Home: 1212 N Lake Shore Dr Apt 33 Chicago IL 60610-2371 Office: Northwestern U Med Sch Dept Pathology 303 E Chicago Ave Chicago IL 60611-3072

SMITH, DONALD E. banker; b. Terre Haute, Ind., Nov. 4, 1926; s. Henry P. and Ruth I. (Bius) S.; m. Mary F. Ryan, June 25, 1947; children: Virginia Lee, Sarah Jane. Student, Ind. U., 1945-47, Ind. State U., 1947-48. Chmn. Deep Vein Coal Co., Terre Haute, Ind., 1947—; with R.J. Oil Co., Inc., 1948—; chmn. Princeton Mining Co., Terre Haute, 1947—; pres. Terre Haute Oil Corp., 1947—; chmn. of bd. Terre Haute 1st Nat. Bank, 1969—; pres., CEO 1st Fin. Corp., Terre Haute, 1969—. Trustee Ind. State U.; bd. mgrs. Rose-Hulman Inst. Tech., 1978—; treas. Terre Haute Econ. Devel. Commn., 1981—; mem. Ind. Econ. Devel. Coun. Mem. Terre Haute C. of C. (bd. dirs. 1982—), Elks, Country Club of Terre Haute. Home: 94 Allendale Terre Haute IN 47802-4751 Office: Terre Haute First Nat Bank One First Financial Pla PO Box 540 Terre Haute IN 47808-0540

SMITH, DONALD EUGENE, healthcare facility management administrator owner; b. Mishawaka, Ind., Oct. 15, 1936; s. Ernest Hartmann and Lucile Emma (Krumanaker) S.; m. Nancy Mae Jaffke, Sept. 2, 1961; children: Adam, Reid, Lynn. AB, Wabash Coll., 1959; MBA, U. Chgo., 1963. Adminstrv. resident Ind. U. Med. Ctr., 1960-61; assoc. dir. Ind. U. Hosps., 1966-72; pres. Henderson & Smith Corp., Indpls., 1978—. Lectr. in health adminstrn. Ind. U., 1965-66, adj. asst. prof. in health adminstrn., 1966-78; ptnr. Carmel (Ind.) Care Ctr., Countryside Manor, Anderson, Ind., Dearborn Enterprises, Lawrenceburg, Ind., Rawlins House, Pendleton, Ind., Manor House of Carmel, Ind.; chmn. Ind. State Bd. Registration and Edn. Health Facility Adminstrs., 1969-82. Bd. dirs. Ind. U. Med. Ctr. Fed. Credit Union, 1965-68, Ind. Blue Cross, 1966-71; med. ctr. chmn. United Fund Drive, 1962-65; sec. Carmel (Ind.) Classic, 1979, v.p., 1981, pres., 1982-83; bd. trustees Wabash Coll., 1986—, mem. exec. com., 1986—, chmn. capital campaign drive, 1987-91, mem. long range planning com., 1985; active Hamilton County Rep. Fin. Com., 1990—. Fellow ACHS; mem. Am. Health Care Assn., Ind. Health Care Assn., Wabash Coll. Alumni Assn., U. Chgo. Hosp. Adminstrn. Alumni Assn., Woodland Country Club, Vero Beach Country Club. Office: Henderson & Smith Corp 10333 N Meridian St Ste 250 Indianapolis IN 46290-1144

SMITH, DONALD NICKERSON, food service executive; b. Can., Sept. 12, 1940; came to U.S., 1946, naturalized, 1956; s. Fred Raymond and Hazel (Nickerson) S.; m. Beverley Thorell, Dec. 1961 (div.); children: Jeffrey, Stacy, Darby; m. Angela Dangerfield, Mar. 8, 1984. BA, U. Mont., 1962; D in Bus. Adminstrn. (hon.), Upper Iowa U., 1980. Sr. exec. v.p., sr. ops. officer McDonald's Corp., Oak Brook, Ill., 1964-77; pres., chief exec. officer Burger King Corp., Miami, 1977-80; sr. v.p., pres. food svc. div. PepsiCo, Inc., Purchase, N.Y., 1980-83; pres., chief exec. officer Chart House, Inc. (name changed to Diversifoods, Inc.), Itasca, Ill., 1983-85; chmn., chief exec. officer Tenn. Restaurant Co., 1985—; chmn., pres., CEO Friendly Holding Corp., Wilbraham, Mass. With USMCR, 1957-65. Named Adman of the Yr., Advt. Age mag., 1979.

SMITH, DURET S. physician, medical educator; b. Palo Alto, Calif. m. Dorothy Hughes; children: Darrah, Erica. Grad. magna cum laude, Syracuse U., 1973; MD, SUNY, Buffalo, 1977. Resident in gen. and orthop. surgery SUNY Health Scis. Ctr., Syracuse; fellow in hand surgery U. N. Mex., Tucson; pres. med. staff Lakewood (Ohio) Hosp., chmn. dept. orthop. surgery; pvt. practice Cleve. Mem. faculty Case Western Res. U. Sch. Medicine, Uniformed Svcs. U. Health Scis. Bd. trustees Lakewood Hosp. Rear adm. M.C., USNR.

SMITH, FRANK EARL, retired association executive; b. Fremont Center, N.Y., Feb. 4, 1931; s. Earl A. and Hazel (Knack) S.; m. Caroline R. Gillin, Aug. 14, 1954; children— Stephen F., David S., Daniel E. B.S., Syracuse U., 1952. With Mellor Advt. Agy., Elmira, N.Y., 1954-55; asst. mgr. Elmire Assn. of Commerce, 1955-56; retail dept. mgr. C. of C., Binghamton, N.Y.; mgr. Better Bus. Bur., Broome County, 1956-60; exec. v.p. C. of C., Chemung County, Elmira, 1960-65, Schenectady County (N.Y.) C. of C., 1965-69, Greater Cin. C. of C., 1969-78; pres. Greater Detroit C. of C., 1978-95. Dir. Presbyn. Devel. Corp. Detroit, Inc. 1995—. Served to 1st lt. USAF, 1952-54. Named Young Man of Yr. Jr. C. of C. Elmira, 1964 Mem. C. of C. Execs. Mich., Am. C. of C. Execs. (past chmn.), N.Y. State C. of C. Execs. (past pres.), Ohio C. of C. Execs. (past pres.), C. of C. of U.S. (past bd. dirs., past chmn. nat. bd. regents, Inst. for Orgn. Mgmt.). Presbyterian. Home: 173 Windwood Pointe Dr Saint Clair Shores MI 48080

SMITH, FREDERICK COE, retired manufacturing executive; b. Ridgewood, N.J., June 3, 1916; s. Frederick Coe and Mary (Steffee) S.; m. Ruth Pfeiffer, Oct. 5, 1940; children: Frederick Coe, Geoffrey, Roger, William, Bart. B.S., Cornell U., 1938; M.B.A., Harvard U., 1940. With Armstrong Cork Co., Lancaster, Pa., 1940-41; with Huffy Corp., Dayton, Ohio, 1946-86, pres., chief exec. officer, 1961-72, chmn., chief exec. officer, 1972-76, chmn., 1976-78, chmn. exec. com., 1979-86. Former chmn. Sinclair C.C. Found.; past chmn. nat. bd. dirs. Planned Parenthoo Fedn-.;former dir. Internat. Parenthood Fedn.; past chmn. Dayton Found.; trustee emeritus Alan Gutmacher Inst., Ohio United Way; past chmn. employment and tng. com. Gov.'s Human Investment Coun. Lt. col. USAAF, 1941-46. Decorated Legion of Merit. Fax: 937-225-9932.

SMITH, FREDERICK ROBERT, JR. social studies educator, educator; b. Lynn, Mass., Sept. 19, 1929; s. Frederick Robert and Margaret Theresa (Donovan) S. m. Mary Patricia Barry, Aug. 28, 1954; children: Brian Patrick, Barry Frederick, Brendan Edmund. A.B., Duke U., 1951; M.Ed., Boston U., 1954; Ph.D., U. Mich., 1960. Tchr. social studies public, Jackson, Mich., 1954-58; instr. Eastern Mich. U., 1959, U. Mich., 1959-60; mem. faculty Sch. Edn., Ind. U., Bloomington, 1960-94, prof., 1969-94, chmn. social studies edn., 1965-69, chmn. secondary edn. dept., 1969-72, chmn. dept. curriculum and instrn., 1983-84, assoc. dean adminstrn. and devel., 1975-78, dir. external rels., 1991-94; dir. devel. Bloomington campus and annual giving Ind. U. Found., 1984-90; prof. emeritus retired, 1994. Vis. prof. U. Wis., summer 1967, U. Hawaii, summer 1972 Co-author: New Strategies and Curriculum in Social Studies, 1969, Secondary Schools in a Changing Society, 1976; co-editor 2 books. Bd. overseers St. Meinrad Coll. and Sem., 1991-98, trustee, 1995-97; treas. Bloomington Pk. and Recreation Found., 1996-98; bd. dirs. Monroe County YMCA, 1995-2002. With USAF, 1951-53. Recipient Booklist award Phi Lambda Theta, 1965, 69 Mem. Ind. Coun. Social Studies (pres. 1968-69), Phi Delta Kappa, Kappa Sigma, Phi Kappa Phi. Roman Catholic. Home: 2306 E Edgehill Ct Bloomington IN 47401-6839 Office: Indiana Univ Sch of Edu Rm 3032 Bloomington IN 47405

SMITH, GARY LEE, lawyer; b. Seymour, Ind., June 24, 1961; s. Adam Donald and Noretta Joyce (Johnston) S.; m. Carol Stith, May 19, 1990. BA, Ind. U., 1984, JD, 1988. Bar: Ind. 1988, U.S. Dist. Ct. (no. and so. dists.) Ind. 1988. Assoc. Beck and Harrison, P.C., Columbus, Ind., 1988-90; pros. atty. Jennings County, North Vernon, 1991—. State of Ind. scholar, 1980. Mem. Ind. Bar Assn., Jennings County Bar Assn. (pres. 1990—), Am. Trial Lawyers Assn., Ind. Trial Lawyers Assn., NRA, Moose, Optimists (charter). Democrat. Baptist. Avocations: fishing, firearms, softball, coin collector. Office: Jennings County Office of Prosecutor Courthouse Annex Vernon IN 47282

SMITH, GEORGE CURTIS, judge; b. Columbus, Ohio, Aug. 8, 1935; s. George B. and Dorothy R. Smith; m. Barbara Jean Wood, July 10, 1963; children: Curtis, Geoffrey, Elizabeth Ann. BA, Ohio State U., 1957, JD, 1959. Bar: Ohio 1959, U.S. Dist. Ct. (so. dist.) Ohio 1987. Asst. city atty. City of Columbus, 1959-62; exec. asst. to Mayor of Columbus, 1962-63; asst. atty. gen. State of Ohio, 1964; chief counsel to pros. atty. Franklin County, Ohio, 1965-70; pros. atty., 1971-80; judge Franklin County Mcpl.

Ct., Columbus, 1980-85, Franklin County Common Pleas Ct., 1985-87. Mem. 2003 Ohio Bicentennial Com.; mem. Ohio Supreme Ct. Coun. on Victims Rights; judge in residence Law Sch. U. Cin.; chair Fed. Ct. Case Settlement Svc.; faculty Ohio Jud. Coll., Litig. Practice Inst.; chmn., Fed. Bench-Bar Conf.; lectr. ABA Anti-Trust Sec.; alumni spkr. law graduation Ohio State U.; pres. Young Rep. Club; chmn. Perry Group, Put-in-Bay, 2002; exec. com. Franklin County Rep. Party, 1971-80. Elder Presbyn. Ch. Recipient Superior Jud. Svc. award Supreme Ct. Ohio; recipient Outstanding Pub. Svc. award Fr. Co. Rep. Orgn., 2001. Mem. Ohio Pros. Attys. Assn. (pres., Ohio Pros. of Yr. Award of Hon. Leadership award), Columbus Bar Assn., Columbus Bar Found., Columbus Athletic Club (pres., dir.), Lawyers Club of Columbus (pres.), Masons (33d degree), Shriners. Office: 85 Marconi Blvd Columbus OH 43215-2823

SMITH, GLEE SIDNEY, JR. lawyer; b. Rozel, Kans., Apr. 29, 1921; s. Glee S. and Bernice M. (Augustine) S.; m. Geraldine B. Buhler, Dec. 14, 1943; children: Glee S., Stephen B., Susan K. AB, U. Kans., 1943, JD, 1947. Bar: Kans. 1947, U.S. Dist. Ct. 1951, U.S. Supreme Ct. 1973, U.S. Ct. Mil. Appeals 1988. Ptnr. Smith Burnett & Larson, Larned, Kans., 1947—. Of counsel Barber, Emerson et. al., Lawrence, Kans., 1992—, Kans. state senator, 1957-73, pres. Senate, 1965-73; mem. Kans. Bd. Regents, 1975-83, pres., 1976; bd. govs. Kans. U. Law Soc., 1967—; mem. Kans. Jud. Coun., 1963-65; county atty. Pawnee County, 1949-53; mem. bd. edn. Larned, 1951-63; Kans. commr. Nat. Conf. Commn. on Uniform State Laws, 1963—; bd. dirs. Nat. Legal Svcs. Corp., 1975-79. Served to 1st lt. U.S. Army Air Corps, 1943-45. Recipient disting. svc. award U. Kans. Law Sch., 1976; disting. svc. citation U. Kans., 1984. Fellow Am. Coll. Probate Counsel, Am. Bar Found.; mem. ABA (bd. of govs. 1987-90, chmn. ops. com. 1989-90, exec. com. 1989-90, chmn. task force on solo and small firm practitioners 1990-91, chmn. com. on solo and small firm practitioners 1992-94, chmn. task force on applying fed. legis. to congress 1994-96), Kans. Bar Assn. (del. to ABA ho. of dels. 1982-92, bd. govs. 1982-92, leadership award 1973, medal of distinction 1993), Southwest Kans. Bar Assn., Am. Jud. Soc., Kiwanis, Masons, Rotary. Republican. Presbyterian. Home: 4313 Quail Pointe Rd Lawrence KS 66047-1966 E-mail: gsmith@eagle.cc.ukans.edu.

SMITH, GLORIA RICHARDSON, nursing educator; b. Chgo., Sept. 29, 1934; BSN, Wayne State U., 1955; MPH, U. Mich., 1959; cert., UCLA, 1971; MA in Anthropology, U. Okla., 1977; PhD, Union for Experimenting Colls. and Univs., 1979; D Honoris Causa (hon.), U. Cin., 1992. Pub. health nurse Detroit Vis. Nurse Assn., 1955-56, sr. pub. health nurse, 1957-58, asst. dist. office supr., 1959-63; asst. prof. nursing Tuskegee Inst. Sch. Nursing, Ala., 1963-66, Albany (Ga.) State Coll., 1966-68; cons. nurse home health care Okla. State Health Dept., 1968-70, medicare nurse cons., 1970-71; asst. prof. U. Okla. Coll. Nursing, Oklahoma City, 1971-73, assoc. prof. and interim dean, 1973-75; state health dir. Mich. Dept. Pub. Health, 1983-88; prof., dean Coll. Nursing Wayne State U., 1988-91; coord., program dir. in health WK Kellogg Found., 1991-95, v.p. programs in health, 1995—. Chair Mich. Task Force on Nursing Issues, 1989-90, Nat. Commn. on Nursing Shortage, 1990-91; cons. on nursing Colo. Commn. Higher Edn., 1990, U. N.C., 1990; mem. adv. com. nursing Okla. State Regents for Higher Edn., 1973-83; cons. VA Hosp., 1975-77, HEW, 1977-78, U. Mich. External Rev. Sch. Nursing, 1980. Contbr. articles on health care and nursing edn. to profl. pubs. Mem. Mayor's Com. to Study In-Migrants, Detroit, 1963; bd. dirs. St. Peter Claver Cmty. Credit Union, 1961-63, YMCA, Oklahoma City, 1972-76, Better Homes Found. for Homeless, 1986—; mem. steering com. Kellogg Fellowship Internat. Program in Health, 1985-89; mem. study com. health care for homeless Inst. Medicine, 1987-88. Recipient Outstanding Svc. award Franklin Settlement, 1963, Disting. Alumni award Wayne State U., 1984, Disting. Scholar award Am. Nurses Found., 1987—. Mem. Nat. League Nursing (dir. from 1979), Am. Nurses Assn. (mem. commn. on nursing edn. 1978-82), Okla. League Nursing, Midwest Alliance in Nursing (dir. 1977-80), Black Pers. (exec. com. 1974-76), Am. Assn. Colls. Nursing (exec. com. from 1976), Nat. Black Nurses Assn. (dir. 1972-78), Okla. State Nurses Assn. (Nurse of Yr. 1972), Am. Assn. for Higher Edn., Okla. State Assn. for Black Pers. in Higher Edn. (rec. sec. 1976-78), Am. Acad. Nursing (governing coun. 1983-85), Assn. State and Territorial Health Officers, Am. Pub. Health Assn., Okla. Pub. Health Assn., Sigma Gamma Rho (Outstanding Sigma of Yr. 1963), Sigma Theta Tau.

SMITH, GORDON HOWELL, lawyer; b. Syracuse, N.Y., Oct. 26, 1915; s. Lewis P. and Maud (Mixer) S.; m. Eunice Hale, June 28,1947; children: Lewis Peter, Susan S. Rizk, Catherine S. Maxson, Maud S. Daudon. B.A., Princeton U., 1932-36; LL.B., Yale U., 1939. Bar: N.Y. 1939, Ill. 1946. Asso. Lord, Day & Lord, N.Y.C., 1939-41, Gardner, Carton & Douglas, Chgo., 1946-51; partner Mackenzie, Smith & Michell, Syracuse, 1951-53, Gardner, Carton & Douglas, 1954-57, 60-85, of counsel, 1986-96, retired ptnr., 1996—. Sec., dir. Smith-Corona, Inc., 1951-54, v.p., Syracuse, 1957-60 Bd. dirs. Rehab. Inst. Chgo., chmn., 1974-78, 83-86; bd. dirs. United Way Met. Chgo., 1962-85. Served to lt. comdr. USNR, 1941-46. Mem. Am. Soc. Corporate Secs., Am., Ill., Chgo. bar assns. Clubs: Comml., Law, Econ., Legal, Chgo., Old Elm (Chgo.). Home: 1302 N Green Bay Rd Lake Forest IL 60045-1108 Office: 321 N Clark St Ste 3400 Chicago IL 60610-4717 E-mail: gsmith1302@aol.com.

SMITH, GREGORY ALLGIRE, college administrator; b. Washington, Mar. 31, 1951; s. Donald Eugene and Mary Elizabeth (Reichert) Smith; m. Susan Elizabeth Watts, Oct. 31, 1980; 1 child David Joseph Smith-Watts. BA, The Johns Hopkins U., 1972; MA, Williams Coll., Williamstown, Mass., 1974. Adminstrv. asst. Washington Project for the Arts, 1975; intern Walker Art Ctr., Mpls., 1975—76; asst. devel. officer The Sci. Mus. of Minn., St. Paul, 1977; asst. dir. Akron (Ohio) Art Inst., 1977—80; asst. to dir. Toledo Mus. Art, 1980—82, asst. dir. adminstrn., 1982—86; exec. v.p. Internat. Exhbns. Found., Washington, 1986—87; dir. The Telfair Mus. Art, Savannah, Ga., 1987—94, Art Acad. of Cin., 1994—98, pres., 1998—. Trustee Greater Cin. Consortium of Colls. and Univs., vice chmn., 2001—; trustee Assn. Ind. Colls. of Art and Design. Mem.: Coll. Art Assn., Ohio Found. on the Arts (v.p. 1981—83, trustee 1981—84), Assn. Art Mus. Adminstrs. (founder 1984—85), Am. Assn. Mus. (surveyor mus. assessment program 1988—), Rotary (dir. Cin. club 2000—01, sec.-treas. 2001—02, pres. 2002—03), Univ. Club. Avocation: collecting arts and crafts movement objects, landscape design, gardening.. Home: 8380 Springvalley Dr Cincinnati OH 45236-1356 Office: Art Acad of Cin 1125 Saint Gregory St Cincinnati OH 45202-1799 E-mail: gasmith@artacademy.edu.

SMITH, GREGORY SCOTT, medical researcher, educator; b. Troy, N.Y., Mar. 22, 1955; s. Oney Percy and Gloria Ann (Tetrault) S. BS in Biology, LeMoyne Coll., 1977; MS in Physiology, U. Tex. Houston, 1989, PhD in Physiology, 1993. From rsch. asst. to rsch. assoc. Surgery U. Tex. Med. Sch., Houston, 1979-90, postdoctoral fellow Pathology, 1993-94, asst. prof. surgery and pathology, 1994-95; assoc. prof. surgery and anatomy St. Louis U. Sch. Medicine, 1996—. Contbr. chpts. in books and articles to profl. jours. Head usher Braeburn Presbyn. Ch., Houston, 1987-95; judge Houston Sci. and Engring. Fair, 1993-95. Mem. Am. Physiol. Soc., Gastroenterology Rsch. Group, Am. Gastroenterology Assn., Shock Soc., Am. Assn. Lab. Animal Sci., Am. Assn. Anatomy. Republican. Avocations: woodworking, fishing, cooking.

SMITH, HAROLD B. manufacturing executive; b. Chgo., Apr. 7, 1933; s. Harold Byron and Pauline (Hart) S. Grad., Choate Sch., 1951; BS, Princeton U., 1955; MBA, Northwestern U., 1957. With Ill. Tool Works, Inc., Chgo., 1954—, exec. v.p., 1968-72, pres., 1972-81, vice chmn., 1981, chmn. exec. com., 1982—, also bd. dirs. Bd. dirs. W.W. Grainger, Inc., No. Trust Corp.; trustee Northwestern Mut. Life Ins. Co. Mem. Rep. Nat. Com., 1976-99; chmn. Ill. Rep. Com., 1993-99; del. Rep. Nat. Conv., 1964, 76, 88, 92, 96, 2000; bd. dirs. Adler Planetarium, Boys and Girls Clubs Am., Northwestern U., Rush-Presbyn.-St. Luke's Med. Ctr., Newberry Libr. Clubs: Chicago, Commercial, Commonwealth, Economic, Northwestern, Princeton (Chgo.). Office: Ill Tool Works Inc 3600 W Lake Ave Glenview IL 60025-5811

SMITH, HARVEY, social science research administrator; Dir. Social Sci. Rsch. Inst. No. Ill. U., De Kalb, Ill., 1993—. Office: No Ill U Social Sci Rsch Inst Dekalb IL 60115 E-mail: hsmith@niu.edu.

SMITH, HENRY CHARLES, III, symphony orchestra conductor; b. Phila., Jan. 31, 1931; s. Henry Charles Jr. and Gertrude Ruth (Downs) S.; m. Mary Jane Dressner, Sept. 3, 1955; children— Katherine Anne, Pamela Jane, Henry Charles IV. BA, U. Pa., 1952; artist diploma, Curtis Inst. Music, Phila., 1955. Solo trombonist Phila. Orch., 1955-67; condr. Rochester (Minn.) Symphony Orch., 1967-68; assoc. prof. music Ind. U., Bloomington, 1968-71; resident condr., ednl. dir. Minn. Orch., Mpls., 1971-88; prof. music U. Tex., Austin, 1988-89, Frank C. Erwin Centennial Prof. of Opera, 1988-89; music dir. S.D. Symphony, Sioux Falls, 1989-2001; prof. Ariz. State U., Tempe, 1989-93, prof. emeritus, 1993—. Vis. prof. U. Tex., Austin, 1987-88; founding mem. Phila. Brass Ensemble, 1956—; music dir. World Youth Symphony Orch., Interlochen, Mich., 1981-96. Composer 5 books of solos for trombone including Solos for the Trombone Player, 1963, Hear Us As We Pray, 1963, First Solos for the Trombone Player, 1972, Easy Duets for Winds, 1972; editor 14 books 20th century symphonies lit. Served to 1st lt. AUS, 1952-54. Recipient 3 Grammy nominations, 1967, 76, 1 Grammy award for best chamber music rec. with Phila. Brass Ensemble, 1969. Mem. Internat. Trombone Assn. (dir.), Am. Symphony Orch. League, Music Educators Nat. Conf., Am. Guild Organists, Am. Fedn. Musicians, Tubist Universal Brotherhood Assn., Acacia Fraternity. Republican. Congregationalist. Home: 8032 Pennsylvania Rd S Bloomington MN 55438-1135

SMITH, HERALD ALVIN, JR. transportation executive; b. Beaconsfield, Iowa, Dec. 23, 1923; s. Herald Alvin and Iva Viola (Briggeman) S.; m. Miriam Gayle Armstrong, Oct. 5, 1946; children: Sharon Konchar, John, Susan Johnson, Jim. Student, U. Iowa, 1942-43, Coe Coll., Cedar Rapids, Iowa, 1944-45. Pres., chmn. bd. CRST, Inc., Cedar Rapids, 1955-77, chmn. bd., chief exec. officer, 1977-83; chmn. bd. CRST Internat., Inc., 1983—. Chmn. bd., pres. Crest Microfilm, Inc., Cedar Rapids, 1980—. Mem. Gov.'s Blue Ribbon Task Force on Transp., Iowa, 1982; trustee Regional Transit Authority, Cedar Rapids, 1967-78; campaign mgr. United Way, 1973-74; bd. dirs. CMC Colls. Associated, 1979, Cornell Coll., Mt. Vernon, Iowa, 1979-87, Four Oaks Treatment Ctr., 1986—. Mem. Am. Trucking Assn., Inc. (interstate carriers conf. 1st v.p. 1980-81, pres. 1981-82, chmn. 1982-83), Iowa Motor Truck Assn. (pres., chmn. bd. 1978-79, exec. bd. 1979—). Avocations: tennis, sailing, running a resort. Office: CRST Internat Inc 3930 16th Ave SW Cedar Rapids IA 52404-2332

SMITH, IAN CORMACK PALMER, biophysicist; b. Winnipeg, Man., Can., Sept. 23, 1939; s. Cormack and Grace Mary S.; m. Eva Gunilla Landvik, Mar. 27, 1965; children: Brittmarie, Cormack, Duncan, Roderick. BS, U. Man., 1961, MS, 1962; PhD, Cambridge U., England, 1965; Filosophie Doktor (hon.), U. Stockholm, 1986; DSc (hon.), U. Winnipeg, 1990; Diploma Tech. (hon.), Red River Coll., 1996; DSc (hon.), Brandon U., 2001. Fellow Stanford U., 1965-66; mem. rsch. staff Bell Tel. Labs., Murray Hill, N.J., 1966-67; rsch. officer divsn. biol. scis. NRC, Ottawa, 1967-87, dir. gen., 1987-91; dir.-gen. Inst. Biodiagnostics, Winnipeg, 1992—; adj. prof. chemistry and biochemistry Carleton U., 1973-90, U. Ottawa, 1976-92; adj. prof. chemistry, physics and anatomy U. Man., 1992—; adj. prof. biophysics U. Ill., Chgo., 1974-80. Allied scientist Ottawa Civic Hosp., 1985—, Ottawa Gen. Hosp., 1989-98, Ont. Cancer Found., 1989-91, St. Boniface Hosp., 1992—, Health Scis. Ctr., 1993—, Econ. Tech. Innovation Coun., Man., 1994-98, mem. exec. com., 1995-98, Man. Health Rsch. Coun., 1995—, mem. exec. com. 1996-98, chmn. 1998—; bd. dirs. ENSIS Growth Fund, DIASPEC Holdings, IMRIS Inc., Magnetic Resonance for Vets., Novadaq, Inc., Spectex PTY; mem. adv. bd. Loeb Inst., Ottawa, 1999—, Keystone Ventures, 1999-2002, Western Life Scis. Fund, 2002--. Contbr. 400 chpts. in books, articles in field to profl. jours. Bd. govs. U. Man., 2000—; mem. Premier's Econ. Adv. Bd., Man., 2001--; mem. adv. bd. Can. Inst. for Cancer Rsch., 2001—, Smart Winnipeg, 2000—, Can. Inst. Cancer Rsch., 2001—, Western Life Scis. Growth Fund, 2002—; premier Manitoba Adv. Coun., 2002—. Recipient Barringer award Can. Spectroscopy Soc., 1979, Herzberg award, 1986, Organon Teknika award Can. Soc. Clin. Chemists, 1987, Sr. Scientist award Sigma Xi, 1995. Fellow Chem. Inst. Can. (Merck award 1978, Labatt award 1984), Royal Soc. Can. (Flavelle medal 1996), Soc. Magnetic Resonance Medicine (exec. com. 1989-94); mem. Internat. Coun. Sci. Unions (gen. com. 1993-98), Chem. Inst. Can., Biophys. Soc., Can. Biochem. Soc. (Ayerst award 1978), Biophys. Soc. Can. (pres. 1992-94), Internat. Union Pure and Applied Biophysics (coun. 1993—, v.p. 1996-99, 2002--), U. Man. Alumni Assn. (bd. dirs. 1994-2000, v.p. 1997-98, pres. 1998-99). Office: Inst Biodiagnostics Winnipeg MB Canada R3B 1Y6 E-mail: ian.smith@nrc.ca.

SMITH, JAMES ALBERT, lawyer; b. Jackson, Mich., May 12, 1942; s. J. William and Mary Barbara (Browning) S.; m. Lucia S. Santini, Aug. 14, 1965; children: Matthew Browning, Aaron Michael, Rachel Elizabeth. BA, U. Mich., 1964, JD, 1967. Bar: Mich. 1968, U.S. Dist. Ct. (ea. dist.) Mich., U.S. Ct. Appeals (6th and D.C. cirs.), U.S. Supreme Ct. Assoc. Bodman, Longley & Dahling, Detroit, 1967-75, ptnr., 1975—. Mem. panel Atty. Discipline Bd., Wayne County, Mich., 1987—; arbitrator Am. Arbitration Assn., 1975—; mem. Banking Commrs. com. on Contested Case Adminstrn., 1978. Mem. pro bono referral group Call For Action, Detroit, 1982—. Mem. ABA, State Bar Mich., Detroit Bar Assn. Roman Catholic. Avocations: sailing, travel. Office: Bodman Longley & Dahling 100 Renaissance Ctr Ste 34 Detroit MI 48243-1001

SMITH, JAMES WARREN, pathologist, microbiologist, parasitologist; b. Logan, Utah, July 5, 1934; s. Kenneth Warren and Nina Lou (Sykes) S.; m. Nancy Chesterman, July 19, 1958; children: Warren, Scott. BS, U. Iowa, 1956, MD, 1959. Diplomate Am. Bd. Pathology. Intern Colo. Gen. Hosp., Denver, 1959-60; resident U. Iowa Hosps., Iowa City, 1960-65; asst. prof. pathology U. Vt., Burlington, 1967-70; prof. pathology Ind. U., Indpls., 1970-98, chmn. dept. pathology and lab. medicine, 1992-98, Nordshow prof. of lab. medicine, 1997-98, prof. emeritus, 1998—. Contbr. articles to profl. jours. Served to lt. comdr. USN, 1965-67. Recipient Outstanding Contbn. to Clin. Microbiology award South Ctrl. Assn. Clin. Microbiology, 1977. Fellow Coll. Am. Pathologists (chmn. mcirobiology resource com. 1981-85); mem. AMA, Infectious Disease Soc. Am., Am. Soc. Investigative Pathology, Royal Soc. Tropical Medicine and Hygiene, Am. Soc. Clin. Pathology, Am. Soc. Microbiology, Am. Soc. Tropical Medicine and Hygiene, U.S.-Can. Acad. Pathology, Assn. Pathology Chairs, Binford Dammin Soc. Infectious Disease Pathologists, Soc. Protozoologists. Home: 4375 Cold Spring Rd Indianapolis IN 46228-3327 Office: Ind U Med Ctr 635 Barnhill Dr Rm A128 Indianapolis IN 46202-5126

SMITH, JAY LAWRENCE, planning company executive; b. Detroit, June 10, 1954; s. Paul Edward Smith and Gloria D. Lawrence; m. Janice Irene Acheson, May 21, 1978; children: Kevin Hamilton, Travis Jay. Student, Oakland U., 1972-75. CFP. Asst. tng. dir. Equitable Cos., Troy, Mich., 1978-81; pres. JLS Fin. Planning Corp., Oxford, 1978—. Adj. faculty Oakland U., Rochester, Mich., 1986-87; commentator TV show Your Money and You, 1987. Cons. Practicing Fin. Planning, 1990; contbr. articles to profl. jours. Mem. Internat. Assn. Fin. Planning (v.p. 1985-87, bd. dirs. 1987-89), Inst. Cert. Fin. Planners (bd. dirs. 1988-90), Inst. Cert. Fin. Planners-Mich. (pres. 1992-93), Fin. Profl. Adv. Panel, Internat. Bd. Cert. Fin. Planners, Rotary (bd. dirs. 1984-86, treas. 1985-87, pres. Oxford 1992-93). Republican. Methodist. Avocations: skiing, music, raquetball. Office: Investment Mgmt & Rsch Inc PO Box 4 28 S Washington St Oxford MI 48371-4985

SMITH, JOAN H. retired women's health nurse, educator; b. Akron, Ohio; d. Joseph A. and Troynette M. (Lower) McDonald; m. William G. Smith; children: Sue Ann, Priscilla, Timothy. Diploma, Akron City Hosp., 1948; BSN in Edn., U. Akron, 1972, MA in Family Devel., 1980. Cert. in inpatient obstetric nursing. Mem. faculty Akron Gen. Med. Ctr. Sch. Nursing, 1964; former dir. obstet. spl. procedures Speakers Bur., Women's Health Ctrs. Akron Gen. Med. Ctr., 1988; ret., 1990. Cons., speaker women's health care. Mem. Assn. Women's Health, Obstet. and Neonatal Nursing (charter, past sec.-treas., past vice chmn. Ohio sect., chmn. program various confs.). Home: 873 Kirkwall Dr Copley OH 44321-1751

SMITH, JOHN FRANCIS, JR. automobile company executive; b. Worcester, Mass., Apr. 6, 1938; s. John Francis and Eleanor C. (Sullivan) S.; children: Brian, Kevin; m. Lydia G. Sigrist, Aug. 27, 1988; 1 stepchild, Nicola. B.B.A., U. Mass., 1960; M.B.A., Boston U., 1965. Fisher Body div. mgr. Gen. Motors Corp., Framingham, Mass., 1961-73, asst. treas N.Y.C., 1973-80, comptroller Detroit, 1980-81, dir. worldwide product planning, 1981-84; pres., gen. mgr. Gen. Motors Can., Oshawa, Ont., Can., 1984-85; exec. v.p. Gen. Motors Europe, Glattbrugg, Switzerland, 1986-87, pres. Switzerland, 1987-88; exec. v.p. internat. ops. Gen. Motors Corp., Detroit, 1988-90, vice chmn. internat. ops., 1990, bd. dirs., mem. fin. com., 1990-98, pres., COO, 1992-98; CEO, pres., 1992-98; chmn. bd., CEO, pres. Gen. Motors Corp., Detroit, 1996-98; chmn. bd., CEO Gen Motors Corp., 1998-2000; chmn. bd General Motors Corp., 1996—. Pres.'s coun. Global Strategy Bd.; bd. dirs. EDS, Hughes Electronics Corp., Gen. Motors Acceptance Corp.; mem. Bus. Roundtable Policy Com.; mem. U.S. Japan Bus. Coun., Am. Soc. Corp. Execs.; mem. Bd. of Detroit Renaissance; bus. coun. Meml. Sloan-Kettering Cancer Ctr.; bd. dirs. Procter & Gamble Co. Mem. chancellor's exec. com. U. Mass., dir.; trustee United Way S.E. Mich., New Am. Revolution, Boston U. Mem. Am. Soc. Corp. Execs., Am. Auto Mfrs. Assn. (bd. dirs.), Econ. Club Detroit (bd. dirs.), Beta Gamma Sigma (pres.), Dirs. Table. Roman Catholic. Office: GM 100 Renaissance Ctr Detroit MI 48265-0001 also: Globe Hdqs at Renaissance PO Box 100 100 Renaissance Ctr Detroit MI 48243-1001

SMITH, JOHN FRANCIS, materials science educator; b. Kansas City, Kans., May 9, 1923; s. Peter Francis and Johanna Teresa (Spandle) S.; m. Evelyn Ann Ross, Sept. 1, 1947 (dec. July 1994); children— Mark Francis, Letitia Ann Smith Harder; m. Eileen R. Ross, Apr. 12, 1997. BA with distinction, U. Mo.-Kansas City, 1948; PhD, Iowa State U., 1953. Grad. asst. Iowa State U., Ames, 1948-53, faculty and research scientist 1953-88, dept. chmn., div. chief Ames Lab., 1966-70. Cons. Tex. Instruments, Inc., Dallas and Attleboro, Mass., 1958-63, Argonne Nat. Lab., Ill., 1964-70, Iowa Hwy. Commn., Ames, Los Alamos Nat. Lab., N.Mex., 1984-88, bur. standards Nat. Inst. Standards and Tech., Gaithersburg, Md., 1988-91, Sandia Nat. Lab., Albuquerque, N.M., 1991-92, ASM Internat., Cleve., 1992—. Patentee ultrasonic determination of texture in metal sheet and plate, lead-free solder; author: Phase Diagrams of Binary Vanadium Alloys; Hellcats Over the Philippine Deep; co-author: Thorium: Preparation and Properties, 1975; editor: Calculation of Phase Diagrams and Thermochemistry of Alloy Phases, 1978; editor Jour. Phase Equilibria; contbr. articles to profl. publs. Mem. former comdr. Ames-Boone Squadron CAP, 1970-75. With USN, 1942-46, PTO, comdr. USNR, 1946-64. Decorated Air medal with star; recipient Disting. Svc. award CAP, Maxwell AFB, Ala., 1979, faculty citation Iowa State U. Alumni Assn., Ames, 1977. Fellow Am. Inst. Chemists, ASM (chmn. Des Moines chpt. 1966); mem. AIME, Materials Rsch. Soc., Am. Legion, Silent Knights, Inc. (trustee 1980-96), Exptl. Aircraft Assn., Alpha Sigma Mu (trustee 1984-86). Roman Catholic. Avocation: flying. Home: 2919 S Riverside RR 5 Box 343 Ames IA 50010-9520 Office: Iowa State U Ames Lab 136F Wilhelm Hall Ames IA 50010

SMITH, JOHN M. trucking executive; b. 1948; Degree in econs., Cornell Coll., 1971; MBA, Cornell U., 1974. With CRST Internat. Inc., Cedar Rapids, Iowa, 1971—, pres., CEO, 1987—. Named Regional Entrepreneur of the Yr., 1992. Mem. Am. Trucking Assn. (exec. com.), ITCC. Office: CRST Internat Inc 3930 16th Ave SW Cedar Rapids IA 52404-2332

SMITH, JOHN ROBERT, physicist, department chairman; b. Salt Lake City, Oct. 1, 1940; married; 2 children. BS, Toledo U., 1962; PhD in Physics, Ohio State U., 1968. Aerospace engr. surface physics Lewis Rsch. Ctr. NASA, 1965-68; sr. rsch. physicist, head surface and interface physics group Gen. Motors, Warren, Mich., 1972-80, sr. staff scientist, head solid state physics group, 1980-86, prin. rsch. scientist rsch. lab., 1986-99, head engineered surfaces program, 1995-99; group mgr. mfg. process Delphi Rsch. Labs, Shelby, 1999—. Adj. prof. dept. physics U. Mich., 1983—. Air Force Office Sci. Rsch., Nat. Rsch. Coun. fellow U. Calif., 1970-72. Fellow Am. Phys. Soc. (David Adler Lectureship award in field of materials sci. 1991); mem. Am. Vacuum Soc., Sigma Xi. Achievements include research in the theory and experiment of solid surfaces, electronic properties, magnetic properties and chemisorption, adhesion, metal contact electronic structure, defects and universal features of bonding in solids, as well as manufacturing processes including machining and coatings. Office: M/C 483-478-107 51786 Shelby Pkwy Shelby Township MI 48315-1786

SMITH, KEITH, protective services official; Fire chief City of Indpls.; liaison 2001 World Police & Fire Games, Indlpls. Office: 2001 World Police & Fire Games 39 Jackson Pl Indianapolis IN 46225-1050

SMITH, K(ERMIT) WAYNE, computer company executive; b. Newton, N.C., Sept. 15, 1938; s. Harold Robert and Hazel K. (Smith) S.; m. Audrey M. Kennedy, Dec. 19, 1958; 1 son, Stuart W. BA, Wake Forest U., 1960; MA, Princeton U., 1962, PhD, 1964; postgrad., U. So. Calif., 1965; LLD (hon.), Ohio U., 1992; LHD (hon.), Ohio State U., 1998. Instr. Princeton U., 1963; asst. prof. econs. and polit. sci. U.S. Mil. Acad., 1963-66; spl. asst. to asst. sec. def. for sys. analysis Washington, 1966-69; program mgr. def. studies RAND Corp., Santa Monica, Calif., 1969-70; dir. program analysis NSC, Washington, 1970-72; group v.p. planning Dart Industries, L.A., 1972-73, group pres. resort devel. group, 1973-76; exec. v.p. Washington Group, Inc., 1976-77; mng. ptnr. Coopers & Lybrand, Washington, 1977-80, group mng. ptnr., 1980-83; chmn., CEO World Book, Inc., 1983-86; prof. Wake Forest U., 1986-88, 2000—; CEO OCLC Online Computer Libr. Ctr., Inc., Dublin, 1989-98, pres. emeritus, 1998—. Sr. cons. Dept. Def., Dept. State, NSC, NASA, Dept. Energy, OMB, GAO; bd. dirs. Nat. City Bank, K. Wayne Smith and Assocs., OCLC Info Dimensions, Inc.; con. prof. (hon.) Tsinghua U., Beijing, 1996; chmn. Rainbow Care For Kids Found., 1999-2000. Author: How Much is Enough? Shaping the Defense Program, 1961-69, 1971; editor: OCLC 1967-97: Thirty Years of Furthering Access to the World's Information, 1998; contbr. articles to profl. jours. Mem. vis. com. Brookings Instn., Washington, 1971-79; mem. bd. visitors Wake Forest U., 1974-78, 82-90, chmn. bd. visitors, 1976-78, trustee, 1991-95, 96-2000, 2001—; mem. bd. visitors Def. Sys. Mgmt. Coll., 1982-85, Lenoir Rhyne Coll., 1988-94, Mershon Ctr. Ohio State U., 1990-92, Columbus Assn. for Performing Arts, 1991-95, U. Pitts. Sch. Libr. and Info. Sci., 1992-95; mem. bd. visitors Bowman Gray Bapt. Hosp. Med. Ctr., 1992-95, chmn. bd. visitors, 1993-95. Danforth fellow, Woodrow Wilson fellow Princeton U., 1962. Mem. ALA (hon., life), Coun. Fgn. Rels., Internat. Inst. Strategic Studies, Inst. Internat. Edn., Coun. Higher

Edn., Am. Assn. Higher Edn., Am. Soc. Info. Sci., Chgo. Club, Lakes Golf and Country Club, Capital Club, Phi Beta Kappa, Omicron Delta Kappa, Kappa Sigma. Methodist. Home: 2606 Sigmon Dairy Rd Newton NC 28658-8607 Office: Online Computer Libr Ctr Inc 6565 Frantz Rd Dublin OH 43017-5308

SMITH, L. DENNIS, academic administrator; m. Suzanne Smith. BS in Zoology and Chemistry, Ind. U., 1959, PhD, 1964. With Ind. U., 1963—64, Argonne Nat. Lab., 1964—69; mem. faculty Purdue U., Ind., 1969—87, head dept. biol. scis., 1980—87; mem. faculty, dean Sch. Biol. Scis. U. Calif., Irvine, 1987—90, acting chancellor, 1982—93, exec. vice chancellor, 1990—94; pres. U. Nebr., Lincoln, 1994—. Mem. bd. sci. counselors Nat. Inst. Child Health and Human Devel., 1990—95; mem. space sci. bd. NRC, 1984—91, chmn. com. on space biology and medicine, 1986—91. Bd. dirs. Nebr. Arts Coun., Nebr., Nebr. Indsl. Competitiveness Alliance. Mem.: AAAS, Soc. Devel. Biology, Am. Soc. Biochemistry and Molecular Biology, Am. Soc. Microbiology, Am. Soc. Cell Biology, Internat. Soc. Devel. Biology, Nebr. C. of C. and Indsutry, U.S. Coun. on Competitiveness, Nat. Assn. Sys. Heads, Nat. Assn. Governing Bds., Assn. State Colls. and Univs., Nat. Assn. State Univs. and Land-Grant Colls., Assn. Am. Univs., Am. Coun. Edn., Bus.-Higher Edn. Forum. Office: U Nebr Office of Pres Varner Hall 3835 Holdrege Lincoln NE 68583

SMITH, LEROY HARRINGTON, JR. mechanical engineer, aerodynamics consultant; b. Balt., Nov. 3, 1928; s. Leroy Harrington and Edna (Marsh) S.; m. Barbara Ann Williams, July 7, 1951; children: Glenn Harrington, Bruce Lyttleton, Cynthia Ann. BS in Engring., Johns Hopkins U., 1949, MS, 1951, Dr. Engring., 1954. Compressor aerodynamacist Gen. Electric Co., Cin., 1954-61, mgr. turbomachinery devel., 1961-68, mgr. compressor & fan design tech., 1968-75, mgr. turbomachinery aerodynamics tech., 1975-92, cons. technologist Turbomachinery Aerodynamics, 1992-94, cons., 1994—. Contbr. articles to ASME Trans. Recipient Perry T. Egbert Jr. awards, 1969, 83, Charles P. Steinmetz award, 1987 Gen. Electric Co. Fellow ASME (Gas Turbine award 1981, 87, R. Tom Sawyer award 1987, Aircraft Engine Tech. award 1993, ISABE award 2001); mem. NAE, Ohio River Launch Club. Achievements include patents for 12 in field. Office: GE Aircraft Eng Mail Drop A411 1 Neumann Way Cincinnati OH 45215-1915 E-mail: leroy.smith@ae.ge.com.

SMITH, LEWIS DENNIS, academic administrator, educator; b. Muncie, Ind., Jan. 18, 1938; s. Thurman Lewis and Dorothy Ann (Dennis) S.; m. Suzanne F. Metcalfe; children: Lauren Kay, Raymond Bradley. AB, Ind. U., 1959, PhD, 1964. Asst. embryologist Argonne (Ill.) Nat. Lab., 1964-67, assoc. biologist, 1967-69; assoc. prof. Purdue U., West Lafayette, Ind., 1969-73, prof. biology, 1973-87, assoc. head dept. biol. scis., 1979-80, head dept., 1980-87; prof. dept. devel. and cell. U. Calif., Irvine, 1987-94, dean Sch. Biol. Scis., 1987-90, exec. vice chancellor, 1990-94; pres. U. of Nebr., 1994—. Instr. embryology Woods Hole (Mass.) Marine Biology Lab., summers 1972, 73, 74, mem. Space Sci. Bd., Washington, 1984-91; chmn. Space Biology and Medicine, Space Sci. Bd., 1986-91; mem. cell biology study sect. NIH, Bethesda, Md., 1971-75; chmn., 1977-79, bd. sci. counselors Nat. Inst. Child Health and Human Devel., 1990-95, chmn. 1992-95; mem. space biology peer rev. bd. AIBS, 1980-85. Guggenheim fellow, 1987. Mem. Am. Soc. Biochemistry and Molecular Biology, AAAS, Internat. Soc. for Devel. Biology, Soc. for Devel. Biology, Am. Soc. Cell Biology, Am. Soc. for Microbiology. Home: 2524 Wilderness Ridge Rd Lincoln NE 68516 Office: 3835 Holdrege St Lincoln NE 68503-1435

SMITH, LOUIS, sports association administrator; m. Sharon Smith; 4 children. BSEE, U. Mo., Rolla; MBA, Rockhurst Coll.; postgrad., U. Kans. Assoc. engr. to asst. gen. mgr. AlliedSignal Inc., Kansas City, Mo., 1966-86, v.p. prodn. ops. Bendix Aerospace Sector Arlington, Va., 1986-88; v.p. mfg. AlliedSignal Aerospace Co., Torrance, Calif., 1988-89; asst. gen. mgr., adminstrn. AlliedSignal Inc., Kansas City, 1989-90, pres., 1990-95; pres., COO, bd. dirs. Ewing Marion Kauffman Found., 1995—. Bd. dirs. Western Resources, Commerce Bank Kansas City. Bd. dirs. Kansas City Royals, Greater Kansas City C. of C., Midwest Rsch. Inst., Civic Coun. Greater Kansas City, The Learning Exch.; mem. exec. com. Kansas City Area Devel. Coun., Rockhurst Coll. Bd. Trustees; mem. numerous coms. U. Mo.-Rolla, U. Kans.; ;past chmn. corp. devel. coun., mem. Acad. Elec. Engring. U. Mo.-Rolla; adv. bd. U. Kans. Sch. Engring. On Board of Directors of KC Royals since 1992. Office: Kansas City Royals Kauffman Stadium PO Box 419969 Kansas City MO 64141-6969

SMITH, MARGARET, state legislator; b. Chgo. m. Fred J. Smith; 2 sons, (dec.). Student, Tenn. State U. Mem. Ill. Ho. of Reps., 1981-83, Ill. Senate dist. 12, 1983—. Trustee Chgo. Bapt. Inst. Democrat. Office: State Senate State Capital Rm 103A Springfield IL 62706-0001 Address: 4949 N Melvina Ave Chicago IL 60630-2907

SMITH, MARGARET TAYLOR, volunteer; b. Roanoke Rapids, N.C., May 31, 1925; d. George Napoleon and Sarah Luella (Waller) T.; m. Sidney William Smith Jr., Aug. 15, 1947; children: Sarah Smith, Sidney William Smith III, Susan Smith, Amy Smith. BA in Sociology, Duke U., 1947. Chair emeritus bd. trustees Kresge Found., Troy, Mich., 1985—; chmn. Nat. Coun. for Women's Studies Duke U., N.C., 1986—, chmn. Trinity Bd. Visitors, 1988-98; chair emeritus. Chmn. bd. visitors Wayne State U. Med. Sch., 1993; bd. dirs., mem. exec. com. Detroit Med. Ctr. Recipient the Merrill-Palmer award Wayne State U., Detroit, 1987, Zimmerman award Gtr. Detroit Health Coun., Athena award C. of C., 1998, Women of Achievement award Mich. Women's Fedn., 1999, disting. svc. award Wayne State U., 1999; named disting. alumna award Duke U. Mem. The Village Club, Internat. Women's Forum, Pi Beta Phi, Phi Beta Kappa. Methodist. E-mail: sidmyth@aol.com.

SMITH, MARJORIE AILEEN MATTHEWS, museum director; b. Richmond, Va., Aug. 19, 1918; d. Harry Anderson and Adelia Charlotte (Howland) Matthews; m. Robert Woodrow Smith, July 23, 1945 (dec. Mar. 1992). Pilot lic., Taneytown (Md.) Aviation Svc., 1944, cert. CAA navigation ground sch. instr., 1945. Founder, editor, pub. Spinning Wheel, Taneytown, 1945-63; v.p. Antiques Publs., Inc., 1960-68; pres. Prism Inc., 1968-78; mus. dir. Trapshooting Hall of Fame, Vandalia, Ohio, 1976-2000, mus. dir. emeritus, 2001—, sec., 1993-99. Co-author: Handbook of Tomorrow's Antiques, 1954; contbr. articles to profl. publs. Sec. Balt. area coun. Girl Scouts USA, 1950. Named to All-Am. Trapshooting team Sports Afield mag., 1960, 61; inductee Trapshooting Hall of Fame, 1998. Mem. Nat. League Am. Pen Women, Amateur Trapshooting Assn. (life), Internat. Assn. Sports Mus. and Halls of Fame (bd. dirs. 1993-94, W.R. Schroeder Disting. Svc. award 1999). Lutheran. Avocations: duplicate bridge, trapshooting, antiques collecting.

SMITH, MAURA ABELN, lawyer; b. Reading, Pa., Oct. 3, 1955; d. Henry Joseph and Lynn (Blashe) Abeln; children: Gwendolyn Casebeer, Karl Casebeer; m. Steven A. Smith, Dec. 18, 1999. AB, Vassar Coll., 1977; M Philosophy, Oxford U., 1979; JD, U. Miami, 1982. Bar: Fla. 1982. Assoc. Steel, Hector & Davis, Miami, 1981-87; ptnr. Baker & McKenzie, 1987-91; v.p., gen. counsel GE Co./Plastics, Pittsfield, Mass., 1991-98; sr. v.p., gen. counsel, sec. Owens Corning, Toledo, 1998-2000, chief restructuring officer, sr. v.p., gen. counsel, sec., 2000—. Rhodes scholar, Oxford, Eng., 1977; John M. Olin fellow in law and econs., Olin Found., 1979-82. Mem. Elfun, Phi Beta Kappa. Avocations: skiing, horseback riding, tennis, golf. E-mail: maura.abelnsmith@owenscorning.com.

SMITH, MICHAEL JAMES, industrial engineering educator; b. Madison, Wis., May 12, 1945; s. James William and Ruth Gladys (Murphy) S.; m. Patricia Ann Bentley, June 22, 1968; children: Megan Colleen, Melissa Maureen. BA, U. Wis., 1968, MA, 1970, PhD, 1973. Rsch. analyst Wis. Dept. Industry Labor, Madison, 1971-74; rsch. psychologist Nat. Inst. for Occupational Safety and Health, USPHS, Cin., 1974-84; prof. U. Wis., Madison, 1984—. Owner, prin. M.J. Smith Assocs. Inc., Madison, 1991—. Contbr. articles to profl. jours. Mem. APA, Inst. Indsl. Engrs. (sr.), Human Factors Soc., Assn. Computer Machinery, Am. Soc. Testing and Measurement. Avocation: tennis. Home: 6719 Shamrock Glen Cir Middleton WI 53562-1144 Office: U Wis Dept Indsl Engring Human Factors Rsch Lab 1513 University Ave Madison WI 53706-1539

SMITH, MICHAEL KENT, state legislator; b. Canton, Ill., May 23, 1966; m. Donna Shaw. BA, Bradley U., 1988. Legis. asst. to Rep. Thomas J. Homer Ill. State Ho. of Reps., Springfield, 1986-92, mem. from dist. 91, 1994—, mem. agr., mem. consumer protection, mem. elem. and secondary sch. com., mem. judiciary criminal law com. Trustee Graham Hosp.; field coord. Dukakis/Bentsen Presdl. Campaign, 1988; precinct committeeman Dem. Com., 1984—; chmn. Fulton County Dem. Ctrl. Com., 1990—; trustee Canton Twp., 1991-94; citizen's advocate Ill. Atty. Gen., Peoria, 1992-95. Mem. Canton Area C. of C. (past pres.), Am. Heart Assn., Dem. County Chmn.'s Assn. (v.p. 1992—). Office: Ill Ho of Reps Rm 2068L State Capitol Springfield IL 62706-0001 Address: # 301 45 E Side Sq Canton IL 61520-2603

SMITH, MIKE, professional sports team executive; b. Potsdam, NY; Asst. coach NY Rangers, 1976—77; with Winnipeg Jets, Canada, 1979—94, gen. mgr. Canada, 1988; cons. Chgo. Blackhawks, 1995—97, mgr. hockey ops., 1999, gen. mgr., 2000—; asst. gen. mgr. Toronto Maple Leafs, Canada, 1979—99. Office: United Ctr 1901 W Madison St Chicago IL 60612

SMITH, MORTON EDWARD, ophthalmology educator, dean; b. Balt., Oct. 17, 1934; BS, U. Md., 1956, MD, 1960. Bd. cert. Ophthalmology Bd.; lic. physician Mo., Md., Wis. Rotating intern Denver Gen. Hosp., 1960-61; resident, nat. inst. of neorol. diseases and blindness fellow in opthalmology Washington U. Sch. Medicine-Barnes Hosp., 1961-63; NIH spl. fellow in ophthalmic pathology Armed Forces Inst. of Pathology, Washington, 1964; chief resident, instr. ophthalmology Washington U. Sch. Medicine, St. Louis, 1965-66, instr. ophthalmology, 1966-67, asst. prof. ophthalmology and pathology, 1967-69, assoc. prof. ophthalmology and pathology, 1969-75, prof. ophthalmology and pathology, 1975—, asst. dean, 1978-91, assoc. dean, 1991-96, prof. emeritus, assoc. dean emeritus, 1996—; prof. ophthalmology U. Wis., Madison, 1995-2001. Vis. scholar Eye Inst., Columbia Presbyn. Med. Ctr., N.Y.C., 1966; prof./lectr. Montefiore Hosp., Pitts., 1969, U. Ark., 1970, 77, 80, 82, 84, 86, 88, U. Fla., 1972, 81, U. Tex. and Lackland AFB, San Antonio, 1973, U. Colo., 1974, 82, U. Mo., 1974, 79, 80, 88, So. Ill. U., Springfield, 1974, U. Md., 1975, Montreal (Can.) Gen. Hosp., 1975, U. Wis., 1976, 87, 93, U. Pitts., 1977, 83, 87, U. Iowa, 1977, 87, Cleve. Clinic, 1978, Colo. Ophthalmol. Soc., 1978, Brooke Army Hosp., San Antonio, 1979, Wills Eye Hosp., Phila., 1980, USPHS Hosp., San Francisco, 1981, U. Calif., Davis, 1981, Sinai Hosp., Balt., 1985, 89, 94, U. Calif., San Diego, 1985, Tufts U., Boston, 1985, Cornell U., N.Y.C., 1988, U. Wash., Seattle, 1990, Brown U., Providence, 1990, Vanderbilt U., Nashville, 1991, Duke U., Durham, N.C., 1992; Chandler lectr. Harvard U., 1988; The Lois A. Young-Thomas Meml. lectr. U. Md., 1991; Braley lectr. U. Iowa, 1993; Havener Meml. lectr. Ohio State, 1994. Editor pathology sect.: Perspectives in Ophthalmology, 1977; mem. editl. bd. Ophthalmic Plastic & Reconstructive Surgery, 1986-90; contbr. articles to profl. jours. With USAR M.C., 1958-66. Scholar U. Md., 1958, 59. Fellow Am. Acad. Ophthalmology (ophthalmic pathology com. 1977-83, chmn. ophthalmic com. 1979-83, Honor award for svc. 1981, Sr. Honor award 1992); mem. AMA, Am. Bd. Ophthalmology (diplomate, bd. dirs. 1992—), Assn. for Rsch. in Vision and Ophthalmology (chmn. sect. pathology ann. meeting 1971), Am. Assn. Ophthalmic Pathologists (pres. 1977-80), Assn. Am. Med. Colls. (group med. edn. 1985—), Mo. Med. Assn., Mo. Ophthalmol. Soc., Verhoeff Soc., Theobald Soc., St. Louis Med. Soc., St. Louis Ophthalmol. Soc., Soc. Med. Coll. Dirs. for Continuing Med. Edn., Alpha Omega Alpha (sec.-treas. Wash. U. chpt. 1993-95). Office: PO Box 8096 Saint Louis MO 63156-8096 E-mail: smithm@vision.wustl.edu.

SMITH, MURRAY THOMAS, transportation company executive; b. Hudson, S.D., 1939; s. Rex D. and Frances M. Smith; m. Diane R. Cramer, Dec. 4, 1959 (div. June 1994); children: Lisa B., Thomas M., Amy R.; m. Donna Thomas Kjonaas, Jan. 1995. V.p. Overland Express Inc., Indpls., 1978-82; v.p. ops. R.T.C. Transp. Inc., Forest Pk., Ga., 1982-83; with Midwest Coast Transport L.P., Sioux Falls, S.D., 1983—, sr. v.p., 1983-84; pres. Midwest Coast Transport L.P., 1984-89, prin., pres., chief exec. officer, 1989—, also bd. dirs.; pres. Willis Shaw Express, Elm Springs, Ark., 1999—. Bd. dirs. Interstate Carrier Conf., Nat. Perishable Logistics Assn. Bd. dirs. Sioux Valley Hosp., 1991-2000, United Way, Sioux Falls, 1991-2000. Office: Midwest Coast Transport LP 1600 E Benson Rd Sioux Falls SD 57104-0822 E-mail: smithm@mct-comcar.com.

SMITH, NANCY HOHENDORF, sales and marketing executive; b. Detroit, Jan. 30, 1943; d. Donald Gerald and Lucille Marie (Kopp) Hohendorf; m. Richard Harold Smith, Aug. 21, 1978 (div. Jan. 1984). BA, U. Detroit, 1965; MA, Wayne State U., 1969. Customer rep. Xerox Corp., Detroit, 1965-67, mktg. rep. Univ. Microfilms subs. Ann Arbor, Mich., 1967-73, mktg. coord., 1973-74, mgr. dir. mktg., 1975-76, mgr. mktg. Can., 1976-77, major account mktg. exec. Conn., 1978-79, New Haven, 1979-80, account exec. State of N.Y. N.Y.C., 1981, N.Y. region mgr. customer support Greenwich, Conn., 1982, N.Y. region sales ops. mgr., 1982, State of Ohio account exec. Columbus, 1983, new bus. sales mgr. Dayton, Ohio, 1983, major accounts sales mgr., 1984, info. systems sales and support mgr., quality specialist Detroit, 1985-87, new product launch mgr., ops. quality mgr., 1988, dist. mktg. mgr., 1989-92, major accounts sales mgr., 1992—; graphics arts industry sales mgr., 1998—. Reg. graphic arts industry cons. mgr., 1999. Named to Outstanding Young Women of Am., 1968, Outstanding Bus. Woman, Dayton C. of C., 1984, Women's Inner Circle of Achievement, 1990. Mem. NAFE, Am. Mgmt. Assn., Women's Econ. Club Detroit, Detroit Inst. Arts Founders' Soc., Detroit Hist. Soc., Detroit Hist. Soc. Republican. Roman Catholic. Avocations: interior decorating, reading, music, art. Home: 6462 West Oaks Dr West Bloomfield MI 48324-3269 Office: Xerox Corp 300 Galleria Officentre Southfield MI 48034-4700

SMITH, NICK, congressman, farmer; b. Addison, Mich., Nov. 5, 1934; s. LeGrand John and Blanche (Nichols) S.; m. Bonnalyn Belle Atwood, Jan. 1, 1960; children: Julianna, Bradley, Elizabeth, Stacia. BA, Mich. State U., 1957; MS, U. Del., 1959. Radio & TV farm editor Sta. WDEL, Wilmington, Del., 1957-59; radio editor Sta. KSWD, Wichita Falls, Tex., 1959-60; capt. intelligence USAF, 1959-61; mem. twp. bd. Somerset Twp., Addison, 1962-68; asst. dep. adminstr. USDA, Washington, 1972-74; state rep. Mich. Ho. of Reps., Lansing, 1978-82; state senator Mich. State Senate, 1982-92; mem. U.S. Congress from 7th Mich. dist, 1993—, mem. agr., sci., and internat. rels. coms. Chmn. Mich. Senate Agrl. Com., 1982-92, Mich. Senate Corrections Appropriation Com., 1984-90, Mich. Senate Mil. Affairs Com., 1984-90, Mich.Senate Fin. Com., 1990-92 Del. Am. Assembly on World Population & Hunger, Washington, 1973; nat. del. on U.S.-Soviet Cooperation and Trade, 1991; former trustee Somerset Congl. Ch. Capt. USAF, 1959-61. Fellow Kellogg Found., 1965; named Hon. FFA State Star Farmer, 1987, SCF Conservator of Yr. Hillsdale County, 1988. Mem. Mich. Farm Bur. (bd. dirs.), Jackson C. of C., Mich. State U. Alumni Club, Masons. Republican. Office: US House of Reps 2305 Rayburn House Office Bldg Washington DC 20515*

SMITH, ORTRIE D. judge; b. Jonesboro, Ark., 1946; m. Christine Wendel, 1968; children: Casey, Angie, Mikki, B.J. BA, U. Mo., 1968, JD with distinction, 1971. Bar: Mo., 1971. Ptnr. Ewing, Smith & Hoberock, Nevada, Mo., 1971-95; judge western dist. U.S. Dist. Ct., Kansas City, 1995—. Adj. prof. Sch. Law, U. Mo.-Kansas City, 1999; bd. dirs. Mo. Inst. Justice, Inc.; spkr. in field. Bd. trustees U. Mo.-Kansas City Law Sch. Found., 1997—; treas. Vernon County (Mo.) Dems., 1982-95; pres. bd. dirs. region 9 coun. Mo. Sch. Bds. Assn., 1990; pres. Nevada Cmty. Betterment, 1981, Cmty. Coun. Perfomring Arts, 1980, Vernon County chpt. Am. Red Cross, 1976; trustee Mo. Bar Ctr., 1991-92. Recipient award appreciation Mo. Jud. Conf. Master Ross T. Roberts Inn of Ct.; fellow Am. Bar. Found., Mo. Bar Found. (trustee); mem. ABA (vice chmn. trial evidence com. litig. sect., Ho. Dels. 1993-97), Mo. Bar Assn. (pres. 1991-92, chmn. fin. com., bd. govs. 1978-93, mem. Young Lawyers Counsel 1975-82, exec. com. young Lawyers Counsel 1978-82, exec. com. Mo. Bd. Govs., Tom Cochran Cmty. Svc. award Young Lawyers Sect.), Vernon County Bar Assn. (sec.-treas. 1972-75), Am. Law Inst., Bench and Robe Honor Soc. (pres. 1983), Nevada Rotary Club (Citizen of Yr. award), Vernon County C. of C. (pres. 1975), Nevada Jaycees (Key Man of Yr.). Office: US Dist Ct 400 E 9th St Ste 7652 Kansas City MO 64106-2675

SMITH, OZZIE (OSBORNE EARL SMITH), retired professional baseball player; b. Mobile, Ala., Dec. 26, 1954; m. Denise Jackson, Nov. 1, 1980; children: Osborne Earl Jr., Dustin Cameron. Grad., Calif. State Poly. U., San Luis Obispo. Shortstop San Diego Padres Baseball Club, Nat. League, 1977-82, St. Louis Cardinals Baseball Club, Nat. League, 1982-96; baseball analyst St. Louis Cardinals Sta. KPLR, St. Louis, 1997—. Player Nat. League All-Star Team, 1981-92, 94, All-Star Team Sporting News, 1982, 84-87, World Series Championship Team, 1982; recipient Most Valuable Player award Nat. League Championship Series, 1985, Gold Glove award, 1980-92, Silver Slugger award, 1987. Avocations: jazz, word puzzles, backgammon. Office: KPLR-TV/WB-11 Station 4935 Lindell Blvd Saint Louis MO 63108-1587

SMITH, PAUL LETTON, JR. geophysicist; b. Columbia, Mo., Dec. 16, 1932; s. Paul Letton and Helen Marie (Doersam) S.; m. Mary Barbara Noel; children: Patrick, Melody, Timothy, Christopher, Anne. BS in Physics, Carnegie Inst. Tech., 1955, MSEE, 1957, PhD in Elec. Engring., 1960. From instr. to asst. prof. Carnegie Inst. Tech., Pitts., 1955-63; sr. engr. Midwest Rsch. Inst., Kansas City, Mo., 1963-66; from rsch. engr. to sr. scientist and group head Inst. Atmospheric Scis., S.D. Sch. Mines and Tech., Rapid City, 1966-81; vis. prof. McGill U., Montreal, Que., Can., 1969-70; chief scientist Air Weather Svc. USAF, Scott AFB, Ill., 1974-75; dir. Inst. Atmospheric Scis., S.D. Sch. Mines and Tech., Rapid City, 1981-96, prof. emeritus, 1996—. Lectr. Tech. Svc. Corp., Silver Spring, Md., 1972-91; vis. scientist Alberta Rsch. Coun., Edmonton, Can., 1984-85; dir. S.D. Space Grant Consortium, Rapid City, 1991-96; Fulbright lectr. U. Helsinki, 1986. Contbr. over 60 articles to profl. jours. Fellow Am. Meteorol. Soc. (Editor's award 1992); mem. IEEE (life, sr.), Weather Modification Assn. (Thunderbird award 1995), Sigma Xi. Home: 2107 9th St Rapid City SD 57701-5315 E-mail: psmith@ias.sdsmt.edu.

SMITH, PHILIP G. state legislator; b. Louisiana, Mo., Oct. 4, 1946; m. Andrea K. Smith; children: Andrew Gentry, James Lyndon. BS, N.E. Mo. State U., 1968; JD, U. Mo., 1972. Atty.; rep. Mo. State Ho. Reps. Dist. 11. Mem. Rotary Club, Elks, Masons, Mo. Alumni Assn., Mo. State U. Alumnus Assn. Home: PO Box 486 Louisiana MO 63353-0486 Office: Mo Ho of Reps State Capitol Jefferson City MO 65101

SMITH, RALPH ALEXANDER, cultural and educational policy educator; b. Ellwood City, Pa., June 12, 1929; s. J.V. and B. V. S.; m. Christiana M. Kolbe, Nov. 16, 1955. A.B., Columbia Coll., 1954; M.A., Teachers Coll., Columbia U., 1959, Ed.D., 1962. Faculty, art history and arts edn. Kent (Ohio) State U., 1959-61, Wis. State U., Oshkosh, 1961-63, SUNY, New Paltz, 1963-64; faculty edn. and art edn. U. Ill., Urbana-Champaign, 1964—, also prof. cultural and ednl. policy & aesthetic edn., prof. emeritus, 1996—. First Italo DeFrancesca Meml. lectr. Kutztown State U., 1974, Leon Jackman Meml. lectr., Perth, Australia, 1985, Dean's lectr. Coll. Fine Arts and Comm., Brigham Young U., 1985, Dunbar lectr. Millsaps Coll., 1993; John Landrum Bryant lectr. Harvard U., 1999; disting. vis. prof. Ohio State U., 1987; sr. scholar Coll. Edn. U. Ill., 1991. Author: (with Albert William Levi) Art Education: A Critical Necessity, 1991; founder, editor Jour. Aesthetic Edn., 1966-2000; editor: Aesthetics and Criticism in Art Education, 1966, Aesthetic Concepts and Education, 1970, Aesthetics and Problems of Education, 1971, Regaining Educational Leadership, 1975, Cultural Literacy and Arts Education, 1991; contbg. editor: Arts Edn. Policy Rev., 2001--; co-author: Research in the Arts and Aesthetic Education: A Directory of Investigators and Their Fields of Inquiry, 1978, Excellence in Art Education: Ideas and Initiatives, 1987, The Sense of Art: A Study in Aesthetic Education, 1989; editor: Discipline-Based Art Education, 1989, (with Alan Simpson) Aesthetics and Arts Education, 1991, (with Bennett Reimer) The Arts, Education and Aesthetic Knowing, 1992, (with Ronald Berman) Public Policy and the Aesthetic Interest, 1992, General Knowledge and Arts Education, 1994, Excellence II: The Continuing Quest Art Education, 1995, Online Bibliography: Discipline Based Art Education, 1997, Readings in Discipline-Based Art Education: A Literature of Educational Reform, 2000. With Med. Svc. U.S. Army, 1954—57. Recipient spl. merit recognition Coll. Edn., U. Ill., 1975, Disting. lectr. Studies in Art Edn. award, 1991. Fellow Nat. Art Edn. Assn. (Disting., Manuel Barkan Meml. award 1973, Nat. Educator award 2000); mem. Coun. Policy Studies in Art Edn. (first exec. sec. 1978-82), Ill. Art Edn. Assn. (Disting.). Home: 2909 Heathwood Ct Champaign IL 61822-7659 Office: 361 Education 1310 S 6th St Champaign IL 61820-6925

SMITH, RALPH EDWARD, psychology assistant; b. Bellfountaine, Ohio, May 19, 1953; s. Ralph Raymond and Virginia (Picklesimer) S.; m. Melody Lee Welbaum Smith, Sept. 3, 1988. B of Gen. Studies, Ohio U., 1980; MS in Edn., U. Dayton, 1987. Houseparent Roweton Boys Ranch, Chillicothe, Ohio, 1974-86, social worker, 1981-82; employment counselor Ross County Community Action, 1980-81, 83; social worker Roweton Residential Ctr., 1986-87; psychology asst. Ross Correctional Inst., 1988-89, 97—, Chillicothe Correctional Inst., State of Ohio, 1989-97. Pres. H.Y.S. Fed. Credit Union, Chillicothe, 1981-86. Vol. Ross County Community Action, Inc., Chillicothe, 1983-87, commodity distbn. vol. Mem. Sons of Union Veterans, Sons and Daughters of Pioneer Rivermen. Avocations: music, film, books. Office: Ross Correctional Institution PO Box 7010 Chillicothe OH 45601-7010

SMITH, RAYMOND THOMAS, anthropology educator; b. Oldham, Lancashire, Eng., Jan. 12, 1925; s. Harry and Margaret (Mulchrone) S.; m. Flora Alexandrina Tong, June 30, 1954; children: Fenela, Colin, Anthony. B.A., Cambridge (Eng.) U., 1950, M.A., 1951, Ph.D., 1954. Sociol. research officer govt., Brit. Guiana, 1951-54; research fellow U. W.I., 1954-59; prof. sociology U. Ghana, 1959-62; sr. lectr. sociology, prof. anthropology U. West Indies, 1962-66; prof. anthropology U. Chgo., 1966-95, prof. emeritus, 1995—, chmn. dept. anthropology, 1975-81, 84-85, 94-95. Vis. prof. U. Calif.-Berkeley, 1957-58, McGill U., Montreal, 1964-65; mem. com. on child devel. rsch. and pub. policy NRC, 1977-80; dir. Caribbean Consortium Grad. Sch., 1985-86. Author: The Negro Family in British Guiana, 1956, British Guiana, 1962, 2d edit., 1980, Kinship and Class In The West Indies, 1988, The Matrifocal Family, 1996; co-author:

Class Differences in American Kinship, 1978; editor: Kinship Ideology and Practice in Latin America, 1984; contbr. articles to profl. jours. Co-investigator urban family life project U. Chgo., 1986-90. Served with RAF, 1943-48. Guggenheim fellow, 1983-84 Fellow Am. Anthrop. Assn.; mem. Assn. Social Anthropologists. Office: Univ Chicago Dept Anthropology 1126 E 59th St Chicago IL 60637-1580 E-mail: r-smith@uchicago.edu.

SMITH, RICHEY, chemical company executive; b. Akron, Ohio, Nov. 11, 1933; s. Thomas William and Martha (Richey) S.; m. Sandra Cosgrave Roe, Nov. 25, 1961; children: Mason Roe, Parker Richey. Grad. The Hotchkiss Sch.; BS, U. Va., 1956. Asst. to pres. Sun Products Corp., Barberton, Ohio, 1960-64, v.p., 1964-67, gen. mgr., dir., 1967-69, chmn., CEO, 1969-76; prin. A.T. Kearney Co., Cleve., 1977-87; chmn., CEO Richey Industries, Inc., Medina, Ohio, 1987—. Bd. dirs. Jaite Packaging, Inc. Exec. com. Gt. Trail coun. Boy Scouts Am.; chmn. capital funds dr. Summit County Planned Parenthood; trustee, found. pres. Old Trail Sch., Barberton Citizens Hosp., Medina County Arts Coun., Akron Regional Devel. Bd.; treas. Friends of Metro Park; found. trustee, vestryman St. Paul's Episcopal Ch.; corp. bd. Cleve. Mus. of Art; bd. govs. The Hotchkiss Sch. Lt. USNR, 1957—67. Mem. Bluecoats, Navy League (pres. Akron coun. 1972-73), Young Pres. Orgn., Portage Country Club (bd. dirs.), Mayflower Club, Sawgrass Club (Fla.) Farmington Club (Charlottesville, Va.), Rotary (trustee Akron 1974-75), Chi Psi (pres.). Home: 721 Delaware Ave Akron OH 44303-1303 Office: PO Box 928 910 Lake Rd Medina OH 44256-2453 E-mail: rsmith@richeyind.com.

SMITH, ROBERT FREEMAN, history educator; b. Little Rock, May 13, 1930; s. Robert Freeman and Emma Martha Gottlieb (Buerkle) S.; m. Alberta Vester, Feb. 1, 1951 (dec. 1985); children: Robin Ann, Robert Freeman III; m. Charlotte Ann Coleman, Sept. 9, 1985. BA, U. Ark., 1951, MA, 1952; PhD, U. Wis., Madison, 1958. Instr. U. Ark., Fayetteville, 1953; asst. prof. Tex. Luth. Coll., Seguin, 1958-62; assoc. prof. U. R.I., Kingston, 1962-66, U. Conn., Storrs, 1966-69; prof. history U. Toledo, 1969-86, disting. univ. prof., 1986—. Vis. prof. U. Wis., Madison, 1966-67. Author: The United States and Cuba: Business and Diplomacy 1917-1960, 1961 (Tex. Writers' Roundup award 1961), What Happened in Cuba: A Documentary History of U.S.-Cuban Relations, 1963, The United States and Revolutionary Nationalism in Mexico, 1916-1932, 1973 (Ohio Acad. History award 1973), The Era of Caribbean Intervention, 1890-1930, 1981, The Era of Good Neighbors, Cold Warriors, and Hairshirts, 1930-82, 1983, The Caribbean World and the United States: Mixing Rum & Coca-Cola, 1994; contbr. to numerous publs. Retired Col. 7th Hist. Detachment, Ohio Mil. Res. 1st lt. U.S. Army, 1953-55. Knapp fellow in history U. Wis., 1957; Tom L. Evans rsch. fellow Harry S. Truman Libr., Independence, Mo., 1976-77, Mexican Ministry Fgn. Rels. fellow, 1991-92. Mem. Soc. Historians of Am. Fgn. Rels., Soc. Mil. History, U.S. Naval Inst., Ohio Acad. History, So. Hist. Assn., Orgn. Am. Historians, Assn. U.S. Army, State Guard Assn. of U.S., Am. Legion, Masons, Scottish Rite, Shriners, Army Hist. Found., Inst. Land Warfare, Sons of Confederate Vets., Phi Beta Kappa, Phi Alpha Theta. Episcopalian. Avocation: photography. Home: 4110 Dunkirk Rd Toledo OH 43606-2217 Office: U Toledo Dept History Toledo OH 43606

SMITH, ROBERT HUGH, former engineering construction company executive; b. Wichita, Kans., Dec. 29, 1936; s. Richard Lyon and E. Eileen (O'Neal) S.; m. Melinda Louise Fitch, Sept. 26, 1959 (div. Dec. 1969); children: Robert Blake, Thomas Hugh; m. Margaret Anne Moseley, Dec. 11, 1971; 1 child, Steven Richard. BS, Kans. State U., 1959; MS, U. Kansas, 1964, PhD, 1970. Sr. process engr. FMC Corp., Lawrence, Kans., 1959-64; rsch. engr. Phillips Petroleum Co., Bartlesville, Okla., 1964-66; group leader Standard Oil of Ohio, Warrenville Heights, Ohio, 1966-67; sr. rsch. assoc., group leader Atlantic Richfield, Plano, Tex., 1970-80; regional mgr., sr. mgr., sales mgr. Fluor Daniel, Houston and Marlton, N.J., 1980-90; v.p., gen. mgr. Badger Design & Construction, Tampa, Fla., 1990-93; exec. v.p., COO Process divsn. Black & Veatch, Overland Park, 1993-2000. Patentee in the field; contbr. to profl. jours. Adv. bd. dept. chem. engring, coll. of engring. U. Kans., Lawrence, 1993—; mem. adv. bd. coll. engring. Kans. State U., 1998—. Recipient Disting. Svc. award Kans. State U., 1998; named into Engring. Hall of Fame Kans. State, Chem. and Petroleum Engring. Hall of fame, U. Kans., 2000. Fellow AIChE (chmn., vice chmn., sec. Dallas chpt. 1962—, Engr. of Yr. award Dallas chpt. 1980, exec. bd. Engr. and Cons. Contracting divsn.), Phi Lambda Upsilon, Sigma Xi. Avocations: tennis, sailing, skiing, reading.

SMITH, ROY ALLEN, United States marshal; b. Columbus, Ohio, Sept. 29, 1946; s. Chester Allen and Frances (Goff) S.; m. Janet Lee Coldicott, Aug. 13, 1967 (dec. Apr. 13, 1999); 2 children. BS in Secondary Edn., Ohio U., 1971, PhD in Ednl. Leadership, 1993; MS, Ea. Ky. U., 1980. Dep. sheriff Pike County, Ohio, 1969-71, chief probation officer, 1973-77; state probation parole officer Ohio Parole Authority, 1972-73; U.S. marshal so. dist. Ohio U.S. Marshal's Office, 1977-81, 94—; chief dep. sheriff Richland County, Ohio, 1981; dir. Pike County Dept. Human Svcs., 1981-94. Tech. advisor ct. security com. Ohio Supreme Ct., security advisor. With USMC, 1964-68. Recipient Nat. Def. medal, Vietnam Def. Ribbon, Vietnamese Campaign medal with 2 stars, Vietnam unit Cross of Gallantry, Presdl. Navy unit Citation, 1966, Good Conduct medal. Mem. U.S. Marshals Svc. (dir.'s adv. com., past chair), Fin./Human Resources Allocation Com., Chillicothe, York Rite Bodies (Aladdin Shrine Temple), Orient Lodge, Order of Ea. Star (Waverly chpt.), Am. Legion (life). Methodist. Avocations: Tom Clancy novels, pistol shooting, helping young people into college.

SMITH, SAM, columnist, author; b. Bklyn., Jan. 24, 1948; s. Leon and Betty (Pritzker) S.; m. Kathleen Ellen Rood, Jan. 24, 1976; 1 child, Connor. BBA in Acctg., Pace U., N.Y.C., 1970; MA in Journalism, Ball State U., Muncie, Ind., 1974. Acct. Arthur Young & Co., N.Y.C., 1970-72; reporter Ft. Wayne (Ind.) News Sentinal, Ft. Wayne, 1973-76, States News Svc., Washington, 1976-79; press sec. U.S. Senator Lowell Weicker Jr., 1979; writer/reporter Chgo. Tribune, 1979-90, columnist, 1991—. Commentator ESBN Radio. Author: The Jordan Rules, 1991, Second Coming, 1995; contbg. writer (magazine) ESPN Mag.; contbr. articles. With USAR, 1970-76. Named Ball State U. Journalism Alumnus of Yr.; named to Ball State U. Journalism Hall of Fame, 2002; recipient Journalism awards, AP, UPI, Sigma Delta Chi, Sports Local Emmy award, WGN-TV. Mem.: Basketball Writers Assn. (pres. 1998—). Office: Chicago Tribune 435 N Michigan Ave Chicago IL 60611-4066

SMITH, SAMUEL, JR. state legislator; m. Diane Taylor; children: Emerald, Danielle. Grad., Worsham Coll. Mortuary Sci. Pres. Div. Funeral Home, Inc.; mem. Ind. Senate from 2nd dist., Indpls., 1998—. Mem. Magic City Consistory, Gary, Ind., Mahomet Temple, E. Chgo., Mt. Herman Bapt. Ch., E. Chgo. Mem. Nat. Funeral Dirs. Assn., Nat. Funeral Dirs. and Morticians Assn., Lakeside Lodge, Gary Shriners. Avocation: reading. Office: State House Dist 2 200 W Washington St Indianapolis IN 46204-2728 also: PO Box 3812 East Chicago IN 46312-1312 E-mail: s2@ai.org.

SMITH, SCOTT CLYBOURN, media company executive; b. Evanston, Ill., Sept. 13, 1950; s. E. Sawyer and Jerolanne (Jones) S.; m. Martha Reilly, June 22, 1974; children— Carolyn Baldwin, Thomas Clybourn B.A., Yale U., 1973; M.Mgmt., Northwestern U., 1976. Comml. banking officer No. Trust Co., Chgo., 1973-77; fin. planning mgr. Tribune Co., 1977-79, asst. treas., 1979-81, treas., 1981-82, v.p., treas., 1982-84, v.p. fin., 1984-89, sr. v.p., chief fin. officer, 1989-91, sr. v.p. for devel., 1991-93; pres., CEO, pub. Sun Sentinel Co., Ft. Lauderdale, Fla., 1993-97; pres., pub., CEO Chgo. Tribune Co., 1997—. Episcopalian. Clubs: Glen View (Golf, Ill.), Lauderdale Yacht Club, Fort Lauderdale Country Club. Office: Chgo Tribune Co 435 N Michigan Ave Chicago IL 60611-4066

SMITH, SHARMAN BRIDGES, state librarian; b. Lambert, Miss. BS, Miss. U. for Women, Columbus, 1972; MLS, George Peabody Coll., Nashville, 1975. Head libr. Clinton (Miss.) Pub. Libr., 1972-74; asst. dir. Lincoln-Lawrence-Franklin Regional Libr., Brookhaven, Miss., 1975-77, dir., 1977-78; info. svcs. mgr. Miss. Libr. Commn., Jackson, 1978-87, asst. dir. libr. ops., 1987-89, dir. libr. svcs. div., 1989-92, exec. dir., 2001—; state libr. State Libr. of Iowa, Des Moines, 1992—2001. Recipient Iowa Computer Using Educators Friend of Edn. award, 1995, Iowa Libr. Assn. Mem. of Yr. award, 1996. Office: Miss Libr Commn PO Box 10700 1221 Ellis Ave Jackson MS 39289-0700

SMITH, STAN VLADIMIR, economist, financial service company executive; b. Rhinelander, Wis., Nov. 16, 1946; s. Valy Zdenek and Sylvia Smith; children: Cara, David. BS in Ops. Research, Cornell U., 1968; MBA, U. Chgo., 1972, PhD in Econs., 1997. Diplomate Am. Bd. Disability Analysts. Lectr. U. Chgo., 1973; economist bd. govs. Fed. Res. System, Washington, 1973-74; staff economist First Nat. Bank of Chgo., 1974; assoc. December Group, Chgo., 1974-77; founding pres. Seaquest Internat., 1977-85; mgr., ptnr. Ibbotson Assocs., 1981-85; pres. Corp. Fin. Group, Ltd., 1985—. Expert econ. witness in field; adj. prof. Coll. Law DePaul U., Chgo. Author: Economic/Hedonic Damages, 1990; founding editor Stocks, Bonds, Bills and Inflation yearbook, 1983-2001; bd. editors Jour. Forensic Economics, 1990-2001; also contbr. articles in field. Founder, exec. dir. Inst. for Value of Life, 1996. Fellow Allied Chem., 1967, John McMullen Trust, 1969; grantee Ford Found., 1972, U.S. Fed. Res., 1973. Fellow Am. Coll. Forensic Examiners (bd. cert.); mem. Am. Econ. Assn., Am. Fin. Assn., Nat. Assn. Forensic Econs. (v.p. 2000—), Nat. Acad. Econ. Arbitrators (founder 1989—), Am. Arbitration Assn. (arbitrator 1994-96), Nat. Future Assn. (arbitrator), Am. Bd. Forensic Examiners, Am. Acad. Econ. and Fin. Experts, Soc. Litigation Economists (bd. govs. 1999--), Alpha Delta Phi. Office: Corp Fin Group Ste 600 1165 N Clark St Chicago IL 60610-7861 E-mail: stan@CFG-Economics.com.

SMITH, STEVE C. lawyer, state legislator; b. Hutchinson, Minn., Nov. 29, 1949; s. Charles H. and Laura G. Smith; married; 1 child, Ryan. BA, U. Minn., 1972; JD, Oklahoma City U., 1975. City coun. mem. City of Mound, Minn., 1984-86, mayor, 1986-90; state rep. Minn. Ho. of Reps., St. Paul, 1990—. Served with U.S. Army, 1971-75. Republican. Home: 2710 Clare Ln Mound MN 55364-1812 Office: 353 State Office Bldg Saint Paul MN 55155-0001

SMITH, STEVEN J. communications company executive; b. Milw., Apr. 10, 1950; married; 2 children. BA in Communication Arts, U. Wis., 1972; Cert. Advanced Mgmt. Program, Harvard U., 1995. Advt. salesperson Sta. WTMJ-AM, subs. Jour. Comm., Milw., 1976; gen. mgr. Sta. WKTI-FM, 1980-83; v.p., gen. mgr. WTMJ-AM and WKTI-FM, subs. Jour. Comm., 1983-85, KTNV-TV, ABC-TV affiliate, Las Vegas, 1985; pres. Jour. Broadcast Group Inc. subs. Jour. Comm., 1987-92, Jour. Comm., 1992—, COO, 1996—, CEO, chmn., 1998—. Trustee Faye McBeath Found., Med. Coll. of Wis., Boys and Girls Club of Greater Milw.; bd. dirs. YMCA of Greater Milw., United Performing ArtsFund, Milw. Met. Assn. of Commerce; co-chair Safe & Sound, Milw.; past chmn. bd. dirs. Am. Heart Assn. of Wis. Mem. Wis. Broadcasters Assn. (past bd. dirs.), Milw. Area Radio Stas. (past pres.).

SMITH, TEFFT WELDON, lawyer; b. Evanston, Ill., Nov. 18, 1946; s. Edward W. and Margery T. (Weldon) S.; m. Nancy Jo Smith, Feb. 25, 1967; children: Lara Andrea, Tefft Weldon II. BA, Brown U., 1968; JD, U. Chgo., 1971. Bar: Ill. 1971, U.S. Supreme Ct. 1977. Sr. litigation ptnr. Kirkland & Ellis, Chgo., 1971—, ptnr.-in-charge competition and antitrust practice group. Mem. adv. bd. Bur. Nat. Affairs Antitrust and Trade Regulation Reporter; instr. trial advocacy. Contbr. numerous articles on trial practice and antitrust issues to law jours. Mem. ABA (litigation sect., antitrust law sect.), Econ. Club, Univ. Club, Mid-Am. Club, Sea Pines Country Club (Hilton Head, S.C.). Avocations: squash, Ferraris, sculpture. Office: Kirkland & Ellis 200 E Randolph St Fl 54 Chicago IL 60601-6636 also: 655 15th St NW Washington DC 20005-5701

SMITH, TERRY LYNN, information scientist; b. La Porte, Ind., Dec. 8, 1944; s. Paul F. and Ferne R. (Eplett) S.; m. Mary Jo Hartley, Jan. 31, 1970; children: Todd Alan, Timothy Eric. BS, Butler U., 1968. Programmer LTV Steel Co., East Chicago, Ind., 1971-74; systems analyst Allis Chalmers Co., Harvey, Ill., 1974-76; mgr. finished inventory La Salle Steel Co., Hammond, Ind., 1976-80; internal cons. Wheelabrater-Frye Co., Harvey, 1980-82; dir. mgmt. info. systems Trailmobile, Inc., Chgo., 1982-83; prin., cons. Ernst and Young, 1983-86; sr. mgr. KPMG Peat Marwick, 1986-88; prin. Ernst and Young, 1988—, CSC Cons., 1988-90, Mfg. Mgmt. Assocs., Oakbrook, Ill., 1992-96; sr. prin. Tech. Solutions Co., Chgo., 1996—. Mem. client strategy com., Ernst and Young, Chgo., 1986, peer rev. team, Orange County, Calif., 1986. Mem. Com. for Strategic Ednl. Planning Lake Cen. Ind. Sch., 1987, 88. Served as sgt. U.S. Army, 1968-71. Mem. Am. Prodn. and Inventory Control Soc. (edn. com. 1981, cert.), Data Processing Mgmt. Assn., Spl. Interest Group for Cert. Data Processors, Assn. Inst. Cert. Group Computer Profls. (cert.). Republican. Methodist. Club: East Bank (Chgo.). Avocations: tennis, basketball, softball, reading autobiographies. Home: 8752 Lantern Dr Saint John IN 46373-9316 Office: TSC 205 N Michigan Ave Chicago IL 60601-5927 E-mail: mjhtostm@jorsm.com.

SMITH, VERNON G. education educator, state representative; b. Gary, Ind. BS, Ind. U., 1966, MS, 1969, EdD, 1978; postgrad., Ind.U.-Purdue U., 1986-90. Tchr. Gary Pub. Schs. Systems, 1966-71, resource tchr., 1971-72; asst. prin. Ivanhoe Sch., Gary, 1972-78; prin. Nobel Sch., 1978-85, Williams Sch., Gary, 1985-92; part-time counselor edn. div. Ind. U. N.W., 1967-69, adj. lectr., 1987-92, asst. prof., 1992—; mem. Ind. Ho. of Reps., Indpls., 1990—. Columnist Gary Crusader, 1969-71; speaker Devel. Tng. Inst., 1986—. Author: (with D. McClam) Building Bridges Instead of Walls—History of I.U. Dons, Inc., 1979; also articles. Mem. Gary City Coun., 1972-90; precinct committeeman Gary Dem. Com., 1972-92; founder, chmn. Gary City-wide Festival Com.; bd. dirs. N.W. Ind. Urban League; founder, pres. I.U. Dons, Inc.; past pres. Gary Cmty. Mental Health Bd.; v.p. Gary Common Coun., 1982, 85-87, pres., 1976, 83-84, 88; past mem. bd. dirs. Little League World series; founder, past sponsor Youth Ensuring Solidarity, Young Citizens' League; chmn. Ind. Commn. on Status of Black Males, 1992—; mem. Gov.'s Commn. for Drug-Free Ind., 1990—. Recipient citation in edn. Gary NAACP, 1970, Good Govt. award Gary Jaycees, 1977, Outstanding Svc. award Gary Young Dems., 1979, Businessman of Yr. award Gary Downtown Mchts., 1979, Bd. Dirs. Svcs. award Gary Cmty. Health Ctr., 1982, G.O.I.C. Dr. Leon H. Sullivan award, 1982, Gary Jaycees Youth award, 1983, Info Newspaper Outstanding Citizen of N.W. Ind. and Info. Newspaper's Outstanding Educator award, 1984, Post Tribune Blaine Marz Tap award, 1984, Gary Cmty. Sch. Corp. Speech Dept. Recognition award, 1984, Gary Cmty. Mental Health Ctr.'s 10th Yr. Svc. award, 1985, Roosevelt H.S. Exemplary Svc. award, 1985, Gary Crusader 25th Anniversary award, 1986, Purdue U. Ednl. Opportunity Programs Black History Svc. award, 1986, Educator Par Excellence award Williams Sch., 1987, Black Woman Hall of Fame Found. Success award, 1987, Black Women Hall of Fame Bethune-Tubman-Truth award, 1987, Our Lady of Perpetual Help Ch. Hon. Mem. award, 1987, Gary Educator of Christ Adminstr. Leadership award, 1988, NBC-LEO Appreciation award, 1988, Omega Psi Phi Citizen of Yr., 1989, Omicron Rho chpt. Appreciation award, 1991, Gary Cmty. Schs. Presenters award, 1991, Mr. G.'s Svc. award, 1991, Appreciation award Ind. Assn. Chiefs Police, 1992, Meth. Hosp., 1992, Bros. Keeper, 1992, Svc. award Ind. Assn. Elem. and Mid. Sch. Prins., 1992, I.U. N.W. Alumni Assn. Divsn. of Edn. Disting. Educator award, 1992, N.W. Ind. Black Expo's Sen. Carolyn Mosby Above and Beyond award, 1995, In the Bethune Tradition award Nat. Coun. Negro Women, 1996, Citizen of Yr. award NASW, 1997, Appreciation award Ind. chpt., 1997. Mem. NAACP (life), Ind. Assn. Sch. Prins., No. Ind. Assn. Black School Educators (founder), Ind. U. N.W. Alumni Assn. (life, Disting. Educator award 1992), Phi Delta Kappa (25 Yr. award), Omega Psi Phi (life, Omega Man of Yr. award 1974, Citizen of Yr. award 10th dist. 1989, appreciation award Omicron Rho chpt. 1991). Baptist. Home: PO Box M622 Gary IN 46401-0622 Office: Ind U NW 3400 Broadway # 339 Gary IN 46408-1101

SMITH, VERONICA LATTA, real estate corporation officer; b. Wyandotte, Mich., Jan. 13, 1925; d. Jan August and Helena (Hulak) Latta; m. Stewart Gene Smith, Apr. 12, 1952; children: Stewart Gregory, Patrick Allen, Paul Donald, Alison Veronica, Alisa Margaret Lyons, Glenn Laurence. BA in Sociology, postgrad., U. Mich., 1948. Tchr. Coral Gables (Fla.) Pub. Sch. System, 1949-50; COO Latta Ins. Agy, Wyandotte, 1950-62; treas. L & S Devel. Co., Grosse Ile, Mich., 1963-84; v.p. Regency Devel., Riverview, 1984—. Active U. Mich. Bd. Regents, 1985-92, regent emeritus, 1993—; mem. Martha Cook Bd. Govs., U. Mich., pres., 1976-78; del. Rep. County Conv., Grand Rapids, Mich., 1985, 87, 89, 91, 92, 94, 96, Lansing, Mich., 1996, Detroit, 1986, 88, 90, 92, 97; mem. pres. adv. com. Campaign for Mich., 1992-97, mem. campaign steering com., 1992-97. Mem. Mich. Lawyers Aux. (treas. 1975, chmn. 1976, 77, 78, 79), Nat. Assn. Ins. Women (cert.), Faculty Women's Club U. Mich. (hon.), Radrick Farms Golf Club (Ann Arbor), Pres.'s Club U. Mich., Investment Club (pres. 1976, sec. 1974-75, treas. 1975-76), Alpha Kappa Delta. Home: 22225 Balmoral Dr Grosse Ile MI 48138-1403

SMITH, VIRGIL CLARK, state legislator; b. Detroit, July 4, 1947; s. Virgil Columbus and Eliza (Boyer) S.; m. Evelyn Owens (div.); children: Virgil Kai, Adam Smith; m. Elizabeth Ann Little. BA in polit. sci., Mich. State U., 1969; JD, Wayne State U., 1972. Legal advisor various community groups, Detroit, 1972-73; supervising atty. Wayne County Legal Svcs., 1973-74; sr. asst.corp. counsel law dept. City of Detroit, 1974-75; mem. Mich. State Ho. Reps., 1976-88, Mich. State Senate, 1988—. Mem. Appropriations Comm. Mem. Nat. Caucus Black State Legislators, Nat. Caucus of State Legistlators, Mich. Legis. Black Caucus (2d chair 1991-92). Democrat. Avocations: golf, swimming, bowling, skiing. Office: State Senate PO Box 30036 Lansing MI 48909-7536 Address: 475 Keelson Dr Detroit MI 48215-3076

SMITH, WAYNE ARTHUR, export company executive; b. Detroit, Jan. 28, 1945; s. Edson Alvin Smith and Helen Margaret (Hofer) McKnight. PhB, Wayne State U., 1966, JD, 1969. Bar: Mich. 1969, U.S. Dist. Ct. (ea. dist.) Mich. 1969, U.S. Ct. Appeals (6th cir.) 1970. V.p. R.G. Corace, P.C., Detroit, 1970-76; pvt. practice, 1976-80; pres. Tech. Pers. Svcs. of Mich., Ltd., Royal Oak, Mich., 1980-81; v.p. McRae Energy Resources, Inc., Harper Woods, 1981-82; pres. Diversified Energy Corp. and subs., Deckerville, 1982—. Mem. ABA, State Bar of Mich., World Trade Club, Can. Legion, Elks (P.E.R. 1990-91, Elk of Yr. Royal Oak chpt. 1992-93). Republican. Avocation: charitable activities. Office: Diversified Energy Corp PO Box 580 Deckerville MI 48427-0580

SMITH, WILBUR LAZEAR, radiologist, educator; b. Warwick, N.Y., Oct. 11, 1943; s. Wilbur and Betty (Norris) S.; m. Rebecca Rowlands, June 19, 1965; children: Jason, Daniel, Joanna, Noah, Ethan, Jacob. BA, SUNY, Buffalo, 1965, MD, 1969. Diplomate Am. Bd. Radiology, Am. Bd. Pediatrics, Am. Bd. Pediatric Radiology. Intern, then resident Buffalo Children's Hosp., 1969-71; resident in pediatric radiology Cin. Gen. and Children's Hosp., 1971-74; asst. prof. pediatrics and radiology Ind. U., Indpls., 1975-78, assoc. prof., 1978-80, acting dir. pediatric radiology, 1979-80; assoc. prof. U. Iowa, Iowa City, 1980-82, prof., 1982—, dir. med. edn. in radiology, 1980-86, vice chmn. dept. radiology, 1986-94, interim head, 1994-96, dir. pediatric radiology, 1980-92; chmn. dept. radiology Henry Ford Health Sys., Detroit, 1998-99; prof. radiology Wayne State U., 2000—; staff radiologist Mich. Children's Hosp., 2000—. Vice chmn. radiology for academics Wayne State U., 2001; radiology residency dir. Wayne State U. Radiology, 2001. Assoc. editor Gastrointestinal Imaging in Pediatrics, Acad. Radiology, 1992—; exec. assoc. editor Acad. Radiology, 1997-2000, assoc. editor, 2000—; contbr. articles to profl. jours. Mem. equity adv. com. Iowa City Sch. Bd., 1983-87. Served with USAR, 1969-77. Fellow Am. Acad. Pediatrics, Am. Coll. Radiology; mem. AMA, Radiol. Soc. N.Am., Iowa Radiol. Soc. (pres. 1987-88), Assn. Univ. Radiologists (pres. 1995-96), Soc. Pediat. Radiology (treas. 1995-98, rep. coun. Acad. Socs. of AAMC 1996—). Quaker. Avocation: photography. Home: 10124 Lasalle Blvd Huntington Woods MI 48070-1162 Office: Children's Hosp of Mich Dept Pediat Imaging 3901 Beaubien St Detroit MI 48201-2119 E-mail: wsmith@dmc.org.

SMITH, WILLIAM G. transportation executive; Chmn., pres., CEO Smithway Motor Xpress Corp., Ft. Dodge, Iowa, 1993—. Office: Smithway Motor Xpress Corp 2031 Quail Ave Fort Dodge IA 50501-8511 Fax: 515-576-8794.

SMITHBURG, WILLIAM DEAN, food manufacturing company executive, retired; b. Chgo., July 9, 1938; s. Pearl L. and Margaret L. (Savage) S.; children: Susan, Thomas. BS, DePaul U., 1960; MBA, Northwestern U., 1962. With Leo Burnett Co., Chgo., 1961-63, McCann-Erickson, Inc., Chgo., 1963-66; various positions Quaker Oats Co., 1966-71, v.p., gen. mgr. cereals and mixes divsn., 1971-75, pres. food divsn., 1975-76, exec. v.p. U.S. grocery products, 1976-79, pres., COO, 1979-81, CEO, 1981-97, also bd. dirs. Served with USAR, 1959-60. Roman Catholic. Office: Quaker Oats Co 676 N Michigan Ave Ste 3860 Chicago IL 60611-2837

SMITHEY, DONALD LEON, airport authority director; b. St. Louis, Aug. 31, 1940; children: Kelly, Jill. Student, St. Ambrose Coll., 1962; BS in Bus. Mgmt., So. Ill. U., 1966; postgrad., U. Mo., St. Louis, 1973-74. Asst. ops. dispatcher Ozark Airlines, 1971-72; transp. analyst Olin Corp., 1972-78, cost acct., 1978-80; commr. St. Louis Regional Airport Authority, 1971-80, chmn., 1974-80, airport dir., 1980-83; asst. dir. Cedar Rapids Mcpl. Airport, 1983-85; dir. adminstrn. Omaha Airport Authority, 1985-87, dep. exec. dir., 1987-89, exec. dir., 1989—. With USN Air Res. 1963-66, USN, 1966-68. Mem. Am. Assn. Airport Execs. (Great Lakes chpt.), Airports Coun. Internat., Iowa Airport Exec. Assn. (past pres.), Ill. Pub. Airports Assn. (past v.p.), Exptl. Aircraft Assn., Omaha Rotary Club, Masonic Lodge (Bethalto, Ill.), Tangier Shrine (Omaha), Quiet Birdmen Assn., Silver Wings Fraternity. Office: Omaha Airport Authority 4501 Abbott Dr Omaha NE 68110-2698

SMITS, RIK, retired professional basketball player; b. The Netherlands, Aug. 23, 1966; m. Candice Smits; children: Jasmine, Derrik. Grad., Marist Coll., 1988. Center Ind. Pacers, 1988—. Named to NBA All-Rookie First Team, 1998. Avocations: Roadrunner cartoon memorabilia, rebuilding old cars. Office: Ind Pacers 300 E Market St Indianapolis IN 46204-2603

SMOKVINA, GLORIA JACQUELINE, nursing educator; b. East Chicago, Ind., July 29, 1937; Diploma in nursing, St. Margaret Hosp. Sch. Nursing, 1959; BSN, DePaul U., 1964; MSN, Ind. U., 1966; PhD in Nursing, Wayne State U., 1977. RN, Ind. Staff and charge nurse surgical units St. Catherine Hosp., East Chgo., Ind., 1959-61, charge nurse surgical units, 1962-64; asst. head nurse ICU El Camino Hosp., Mountain View, Calif., 1961-62; instr. nursing South Chgo. Community Hosp., Chgo., 1964-65; asst. prof. med.-surgical nursing U. Evansville, Ind., 1966-70;

assoc. prof. nursing Purdue U. Calumet, Hammond, 1970-80, prof. nursing, 1980—, acting head dept. nursing, 1986-87, head dept. nursing, 1987—, head sch. nursing, 1996—, dean schs. of profl. programs, 1996—2002, dean Sch. of Nursing, 2002—. Bd. dir. Health East Chgo. Cmty. Bd., St. Catherine Hosp.; cons. ICU St. Catherine Hosp., 1971, 74, 77, 79, 81, staff nurse, 71, 74, 77, 79, 81; cons. Vis. Nurses Assn., 1979, 80, Klapper, Issac & Parish Law Firm, Indpls., 1995; mem. adv. com. Vis. Nurse Assn. of NW Ind., 1977—; mem. Statewide Task Force on Nursing in Ind., 1987—; mem. Health E. Chgo. Task Force, 1996—; peer reviewer Coll. Nursing Valparaiso U., Ind., 1989; mem. gov. bd. St. Margaret Mercy Healthcare Ctrs. Inc., 1992—, chair quality svcs. com., 1992—, v.p., 1998—2001; mem. gov. bd. Sisters of St. Francis Regional Bd.; expert witness in several cases. Contbr. chpt. to Normal Aging: Dimensions of Wellness, 1986, Medical-Surgical Nursing, 1981; contbr. articles to profl. jours.; numerous rsch. projects. Mem. planning com. Lake County Health Fair, 1975, 77, nursing chair, 1978-80; chmn. nominations com. Ind. League for Nursing, 1995—; mem. adv. bd. Horizon Career Coll., Merriville, Ind., 1994—; mem. adv. com. Community Ctr. Devel. Corp., Hammond, 1993—, Three City Empowerment Zone E. Chgo., Gary and Hammond, 1994-95, grad. edn. Ind. U. Purdue U., 1981-85, Westhaysen Med. Edn. Trust Com. Calument Nat. Bank, Hammond, 1987—; mem. panel Healthy E. Chgo., 1994-96; mem. Community Health Assn., 1979-84; v.p. Am. Heart Assn. N.W. Ind. affiliate, 1984-87, mem. edn. com. 1982-87; bd. dirs. Our Lady of Mercy Hosp., Dyer, Ind., 1989-92, Health Adv., 1979-82; bd. dirs. Am. Heart Assn. Ind. affiliate, 1981-87, chair community programs, 1982-87; bd. dirs. Lakeshore Health Care System, 1988-89, quality assurance com. Grantee HHS, 1983-85, 84, 85-88, 90—, Helene Fuld Health Trust, 1989, 92, 93-94, Pub. Health Svc., 1989-90, 1990-91, Meth. Hosp., 1993-98; recipient Meritorious Svc. award Am. Cancer Soc. of N.W. Ind., 1979, Lake Area United Way, 1979, Cert. of Recognition Am. Heart Assn., 1983-84, Med. and Sci. Disting. Program award, 1985. Mem. AACN, N.W. Ind. Orgn. Nurse Execs., Nurse Exec. Resource Group (U. Chgo.), Nat. League for Nursing, Ind. Deans and Dirs. of AD, BS and Higher Degree Programs, Nurse Exec. Forum, Wayne State Alumni Assn., St. Margaret Alumni Assn. (v.p. program com., chmn. scholarship com.), Ind. U. Alumni Assn., Mu Omega (chpt. commitment award 1994, chair fin. com. 1991—), Sigma Theta Tau (hon.). Office: Purdue U Calumet 2200 169th St Hammond IN 46323-2068 E-mail: smokvina@calumet.purdue.edu.

SMOTHERS, ANN ELIZABETH, museum director; b. Chgo., Dec. 20, 1946; With adminstn. Mercy Hosp., Iowa City, 1982-85; asst. dir. Old Capital Mus., 1985-95, dir., 1995—. Recipient Hon. Achievement for Women award YWCA, 1996. Mem. Altrusa. Office: Old Capitol Mus Univ Iowa 24 Old Capitol Iowa City IA 52242 E-mail: ann.smothers@niowa.edu.

SMUCKER, RICHARD K. food company executive; Pres. The J.M. Smucker Co., 1986—. Office: 1 Strawberry Ln Orrville OH 44667-1241

SMUCKER, TIMOTHY P. food company executive; Chmn. The J.M. Smucker Co., 1984—. Office: 1 Strawberry Ln Orrville OH 44667-1241

SMYNTEK, JOHN EUGENE, JR. editor; b. Buffalo, Aug. 24, 1950; BA, U. Detroit, 1972. Asst. instr. Mich. State U., East Lansing, 1981; features editor Free Press, Detroit, 1985-92; dir. online svcs. and dir. libr. Free Press Plus, 1992-95, spl. features and syndicate editor, 1995—; asst. instr. U. Detroit Mercy, 2000—. Vis. fellow in journalism Duke U., 1988; profl. student publs. advisor U. Detroit Mercy, 1992—94; bd. visitors Wayne State U. Coll. Fine, Performing and Comm. Arts, 2001—. Recipient Fine Arts Reporting award, Detroit Press Club, 1985. Roman Catholic. Office: Detroit Free Press 600 W Fort St Detroit MI 48226-2706 E-mail: smyntek@freepress.com.

SNADER, JACK ROSS, publishing company executive; b. Athens, Ohio, Feb. 25, 1938; s. Daniel Webster and Mae Estella (Miller) S.; m. Sharon Perschnick, Apr. 4, 1959; children: Susan Mae, Brian Ross. BS, U. Ill., 1959. Cert. mgmt. cons. With mktg. Richardson-Merrell, Cin., 1959-65, Xerox Corp., N.Y.C., 1965-67, Sieber & McIntyre, Chgo., 1967-69; pres. Systema Corp., Northbrook, Ill., 1969—. Author Systematic Selling, 1987, The Sales Relationship, 1988. Mem. ASTD, Instrnl. Sys. Assn., Inst. of Mgmt. Cons., Am. Mgmt. Assn. Office: Systema Corporation Ste 240 633 Skokie Blvd Northbrook IL 60062-2824 E-mail: jrsnader@systema.com.

SNEED, MICHAEL (MICHELE SNEED), columnist; b. Mandan, N.D., Nov. 16, 1943; d. Richard Edward and June Marie (Ritchey) S.; m. William J. Griffin, Sept. 16, 1978; 1 child, Patrick B.S., Wayne State U., 1965. Tchr. Barrington High Sch., Ill., 1965-66; legis. asst. Congressman Ray Clevenger, 1966-67; reporter City News Bur., Chgo., 1967-69, Chgo. Tribune, 1969-86, columnist, 1981-86; pres. sec. Mayor Jane Byrne, Chgo., 1979; gossip columnist Chgo. Sun-Times, 1986—. Co-editor Chgo. Journalism Rev., 1971-72 Vice pres. No. Mich. U. chpt. Young Democrats, 1962 Roman Catholic. Club: Women's Athletic Avocation: gardening. Office: Chgo Sun-Times Inc 401 N Wabash Ave Chicago IL 60611-5642

SNELL, BRUCE M., JR. retired judge; b. Ida Grove, Iowa, Aug. 18, 1929; s. Bruce M. and Donna (Potter) Snell; m. Anne Snell, Feb. 4, 1956; children: Rebecca, Brad. AB, Grinnell Coll., 1951; JD, U. Iowa, 1956. Bar: Iowa 1956, N.Y. 1958. Law clk. to presiding judge U.S. Dist. Ct. (no. dist.) Iowa, 1956-57; asst. atty. gen., 1961-65; judge Iowa Ct. Appeals, 1976-87; justice Iowa Supreme Ct., Des Moines, 1987—2001; ret., 2001. Comments editor: Iowa Law Rev. Mem.: ABA, Am. Judicature Soc., Iowa State Bar Assn., Order Coif. Methodist. Home: PO Box 192 Ida Grove IA 51445-0192

SNELL, JOHN RAYMOND, civil engineer; b. Suzhou, China, Dec. 9, 1912; (parents Am. citizens); s. John A. and Grace (Birkett) S.; m. Florence Moffett, Dec. 8, 1939; children: Chica Dorothea, Karen Snell Dailey, Martha E. Snell Rood, John Raymond Jr., David Moffett. BE, Vanderbilt U., 1934; MS, U. Ill., 1936; DSc, Harvard U., 1939. Registered profl. engr., Mass., Mich., Ohio, Ill., Ind., La. Wis., N.Y., Tex. Fla., Idaho, Oreg., Ont., Can.; cert. san. engr.; diplomate Am. Acad. Environ. Engrs. Instr. civil engring. Hangchow U., 1934-35; with Water Supply Fed. Pub. Works Dept., Venezuela, 1939-40; design engr. Metcalf & Eddy, also Fay Spofford and Thorndyke, Stone & Webster, Boston, 1941-42; san. engr., head water and sewage sect. 1st Svc. Command, 1946; assigned UNRA restoration water, sewage, solid wastes 5 no. provinces China San. Engring. Services Inc., 1945-46; project engr. Burns & Kenerson, Boston, 1947; pres., chief engr. Engring. Svcs. Inc., 1948-51; lectr. MIT, 1949-51; prof., head dept. civil and san. engring. Mich. State U., 1951-55; owner John R. Snell & Assocs., 1956; sr. prin. Mich. Assocs., cons. engrs., 1956-60; pres. John R. Snell Engrs. Inc., 1960-75, Snell Environ. Group, 1975-80, hon. chmn. bd., spl. cons., 1980-88; joint venturer Snell-Republic Assocs. Ltd., Lahore, West Pakistan, 1961-80; with Assoc. Architects & Engrs., Dacca, Bangladesh, 1965-80; pres. Caribbean Devel. Corp. and subs. Gen. Shrimp Ltd., Belize, 1984-92. Sr. adj. scientist Mich. Biotech. Inst., 1990—; 1994 guest of China-Suzhou Hosp. 110 Aniv.; solid waste cons. Xiaogan Recycling Treatment Utilization of Organics, Peoples Republic of China, 1995—; founder Trans Mich. Waterway Inc., S.W. Waterway (Ont.) Ltd., N.Y.; spl. cons. on ast high rate compost plant to Govt. of Japan, 1955-56; cons. in Orient, WHO, 1956; chmn. bd. Bootstrap Internat. Inc., 1972; chmn. bd. Save Our Spaceship/nc.NFP 2001 (to abate pollution, sustainability and population control); expert witness on over 50 ct. cases. Author: Toward a Better World, 1997, trans. into Chinese, 1999, 12 sects. Environment Engineering Handbook; co-author: Municipal Solid Waste Disposal; contbr. articles to profl. jours.; patentee in composting field. Maj. USPHS, 1945-47. Recipient Prescott Eddy award, 1944. Mem. Nat., Mich. (life) socs. profl. engrs., Am. Water Works Assn., Hwy. Rsch. Bd., ASTM, ASCE, Am. Pub. Works Assn., Water Pollution Control Fedn. (life), Mich. Engring. Soc. (life), Cons. Engrs. Coun. (past dir.), Cons. Engrs. Assn. Mich. (past pres.), Inter-Am. Assn. San. Engrs., World Aquaculture Soc., Composters Inc. (pres. Worldwide Techs. Inc. East Lansing 1980—), Rotary, Tau Beta Pi, Chi Epsilon. Home and Office: 918 Rosewood Ave East Lansing MI 48823-3127 Fax: 517-351-3929. E-mail: snelljo@pilot.msu.edu.

SNELL, RICHARD A. equipment manufacturing company executive; b. 1942; BA, Union Coll., Albany, N.Y.; MBA, U. Pa. Brand mgmt. position Procter & Gamble, Cin.; various sr. positions, including v.p. maktg. SmithKline Beecham; exev. v.p. Quaker State Corp., until 1986; various positions Tenneco, Inc., 1987-96, in charge automotive retail bus., sr. v.p., head Walker Mfg. divsn., until 1993, pres., CEO Tenneco Automotive, 1993-96; chmn., CEO, pres. Fed.-Mogul Corp., Southfield, Mich., 1996—. Bd. dirs. Schneider Nat. Nat. bd. dirs. Big Bros. Am.; bd. dirs. United Way Cmty. Svcs. Mem. Equipment Mfrs. Assn. (past chmn.). Office: Fed-Mogul Corp 26555 Northwestern Hwy Southfield MI 48034-2199

SNIDER, LAWRENCE K. lawyer; b. Detroit, Dec. 28, 1938; s. Ben and Ida (Hertz) S.; m. Maxine Bobman, Aug. 12, 1962; children: Stephanie, Suzanne. BA, U. Mich., 1960, JD, 1963. Bar: Mich. 1964, Ill. 1991. Ptnr. Jaffe, Snider, Raitt & Heuer, Detroit, 1968-91, Mayer, Brown & Platt, Chgo., 1991—. Mem. Nat. Bankruptcy Conf., Am. Coll. Bankruptcy, 1991—. Contbr. articles to profl. jours. Mem. Mich. Coun. for the Arts, 1990-91. Avocations: photography, collections. Office: Mayer Brown & Platt 190 S La Salle St Ste 3100 Chicago IL 60603-3441

SNODDY, ANTHONY L. manufacturing executive; Degree in indsl. tech., Ea. Mich. U., 1973. Mem. staff materials and purchasing mgmt. GE Corp., 1973-91; pres. Exemplar Mfg. Co., 1991—. Office: 506 S Huron St Ypsilanti MI 48197-5455

SNODDY, JAMES ERNEST, education educator; b. Perrysville, Ind., Oct. 6, 1932; s. James Elmer and Edna May (Hayworth) S.; m. Alice Joanne Crowder, Aug. 15, 1954; children: Ryan Anthony, Elise Suzanne. BS, Ind. State U., 1954; MEd, U. Ill., 1961, EdD, 1967. Tchr. Danville (Ill.) Pub. Schs., 1954-57, prin., 1961-64; instr. U. Ill., Champaign, 1965-67; prof. edn. Mich. State U., East Lansing, 1967-72, 78-96, chmn. dept. elem. and spl. edn., 1972-78, ret., 1996, prof. emeritus, 1997—; dir. Program CORK, 1978-82. With U.S. Army, 1955-57. Mem. Am. Assn. for Adult and Continuing Edn., Commn. of Profs. of Adult and Continuing Edn. Methodist. Home: 1926 Creek Lndg Haslett MI 48840-8704 Office: Mich State U 419 Erickson Hall East Lansing MI 48824-1034 E-mail: jsnoddy@pilot.msu.edu.

SNOEYINK, VERNON L. civil engineer, educator; BS in Civil Engring., U. Mich., 1984, MS in Sanitary Engring., 1966, PhD in Water Resource Engring., 1968. Asst. prof. sanitary engring. U. Ill., Urbana, 1969-73, from assoc. prof. to prof. environ. engring., 1973—, Ivan Racheff Prof. Environ. Engring. Mem. NAE. Office: U Ill Dept Civil Engring Newmark Civil Engring Lab 205 N Mathews Ave Urbana IL 61801

SNOW, JOEL ALAN, research director; b. Brockton, Mass., Apr. 1, 1937; s. George H. Jr. and Mary W. (Sproul) S.; m. Laetitia Harrer, June 29, 1957 (div. 1983); children: Jonathan E., Nicholas H.; m. Barbara Kashian, Feb. 7, 1992; stepchildren: James, Alexander. BS in Physics, U. N.C., 1958; MA in Physics, Washington U., St. Louis, 1963, PhD in Physics, 1967. Fellow Ctr. Advanced Study U. Ill., Champaign, 1967-68; program dir. for theoretical physics NSF, Washington, 1968-70, head office of interdisciplinary rsch., 1969-71, dep. asst. dir. for sci. and tech., rsch. applications, 1971-74, dir. office of planning and resources mgmt., 1974-76, dir. div. of policy rsch. and analysis, 1976; sr. policy analyst, office of sci. and tech. policy Exec. Office of the Pres., 1976-77; assoc. dir. for rsch. policy U.S. Dept. Energy, 1977-81, dir. sci. and tech. affairs, 1981-88; assoc. v.p. for rsch. Argonne Nat. Lab., U. Chgo., 1988-92; dir. Inst. for Phys. Rsch. and Tech. Iowa State U., Ames, 1993-98, prof. elec. and computer engring., 1993—, prof. polit. sci., 1998-2000, exec. assoc. dir. Internat. Inst. Theoret./Applied Physics, 1998—. Rsch. assoc. dept. physics U. Ill., Urbana, 1967-68; instr. physics and electronics U.S. Navy Nulcear Power Shc., New London, Conn., 1958-61; sci. tech. organizer Pres.'s Conf. on Superconductivity, 1987, NSF program rsch. applied to nat. needs, 1971, designer, mgr., founder NSF program interdisciplinary rsch. relevant to problems of society, 1969. Contbr. over 130 articles to mags. and profl. jours. Lt. (j.g.) USN, 1958-61. Recipient Meritorious Svc. award NSF, 1972, Meritorious award William A. Jump Found., 1973, Arthur S. Fleming award Downtown Jaycees, 1974; NSF postdoctoral fellow Ctr. for Advanced Study U. Ill., 1967-68; NSF fellow, 1963-65. Fellow AAAS, Am. Phys. Soc.; mem. IEEE, Am. Chem. Soc., Am. Nuc. Soc., World Future Soc., Sigma Xi, Phi Beta Kappa, Phi Kappa Phi. Achievements include pioneering devel. of federal programs in environment, solar and geothermal energy and energy conservation, sustainable development; fed. programs in technology transfer to industry; developed collaborations between univ., govt. and industry; fostering internat. collaboration in sci., engring. and edn. Office: IITAP/Iowa State U 2318 Howe Hall Ames IA 50011-0001 E-mail: jasnow@iastate.edu.

SNOWBARGER, VINCE, former congressman; b. Kankakee, Ill., Sept. 16, 1949; s. Willis Edward and Wahnona Ruth (Horger) S.; m. Carolyn Ruth McMahon, Mar. 25, 1972; children: Jeffrey Edward, Matthew David. BA in History, So. Nazarene U., 1971; MA in Polit. Sci., U. Ill., 1974; JD, U. Kans., 1977. Bar: Kans. 1977, U.S. Dist. Ct. Kans. 1977, Mo. 1987. Instr. Mid-Am. Nazarene Coll., Olathe, Kans., 1973-76; ptnr. Haskin, Hinkle, Slater & Snowbarger, 1977-84, Dietrich, Davis, Dicus et al, Olathe, 1984-88, Armstrong, Teasdale, Schafly & Davis, Overland Park, Kans., 1989-92; Holbrook, Heaven & Fay, P.C., Merriam, 1992-94; ptnr. Snowbarger & Veatch LLP, Olathe, 1994-96; mem. 105th Congress from 3rd Kans. dist., 1997-99; exec. dir. Kans. Assn. Am. Educators, 2000—01. Mem. Kans. Legislature, Topeka, 1985-96; majority leader Ho. of Reps., 1993-96; mem. Olathe Planning Commn., 1982-84, Leadership Olalthe; divsn. chmn. United Way, Olathe, 1985-88, chmn. citizen rev. com., 1991-95. Mem. Olathe Area C. of C. (bd. dirs. 1984). Republican. Nazarene. Avocation: politics. Home: 7902 Oak St Dunn Loring VA 22027-1017 E-mail: vincesnowbarger@netscape.net.

SNYDER, ARLEN DEAN, actor; b. Rice, Kans., Mar. 5, 1933; s. Glenn Arlen and Sylvia Thelma (Guiot) S.; m. Angela Thornton, Jan. 7, 1970 (div. July 1976); m. Joanne Elizabeth Burke, May 8, 1983; 1 child, Kimble Burke. BA in Theater, U. Tulsa, 1957; MA in Theater, U. Iowa, 1959. Facilities designer Diamond Circle Theatre, Durango, Colo., 1961, ptnr., mgr., actor, 1961-63. Instr. dept. cinema Hunter Coll., N.Y.C., 1975-76. Dir.: (plays) Under Milkwood, 1974, Miss Pete, 1975; appeared in motion pictures including Yanks, 1978, Heartbreak Ridge, 1986, Bird, 1987, Internal Affairs, 1989, Marked For Death, 1990, Mommy's Day, 1996; recurring roles (TV series) Dallas, TV 101, Eisenhower & Lutz, Designing Women; guest appearances (TV series) Hart to Hart, M*A*S*H, Murder She Wrote, Benson, Dynasty, Private Benjamin, St. Elsewhere, Quantum Leap, Trial By Jury, others; appeared in theatrical plays including The Candy Apple, 1970, Trial of the Catonsville Nine, 1972, Big Broadcast on E. 53rd, 1973, One World at a Time, 1973, The Poison Tree, 1974, 75, Streamers, 1976, The Trip Back Down, 1977, Curse of the Starving Class, 1978, Better Living, 1989, Mr Rickey Calls A Meeting, 1992; starred in TV series including Secret Storm, 1966-68, As The World Turns, 1968-69, Dear Detective, 1979, The Texas Rangers/Pilot, 1981, Trauma Center, 1983, One Life to Live, 1984, Macgruder and Loud/Pilot, 1984; starred in movies for TV viewing including Young Love, First Love, 1979, Attica, 1979, Red Flag, 1980, RFK, 1981, Bus Stop, 1982, Night Partners, 1983, North & South Book II, 1986, The Oliver North Story, 1989, Frog Girl, 1989, Terror in Copper Valley, 1989, The Beach Boys' Story, 1990, Willing To Kill: The Texas Cheerleader Story, 1992, Cora Unashamed, PBS, 1999; recs. for Iowa's Books for the Blind and Handicapped. Bd. dirs. San Fernando Valley (Calif.) Arts Coun., 1987-88, mem. bd. advisors, 1989-90, pres., 1991. With U.S. Army, 1953-55. Named Leading Male Performer, L.A. Weekly, Matrix Theatre, 1989. Mem. AFTRA, SAG (bd. dirs. 1991), Actors' Equity Assn., The Players' Club (bd. dirs. 1974-76), Theta Alpha Phi. Democrat. Avocations: set design, political history, farming, cabinet making. Office: 4580 Broadway Ste 4D New York NY 10040 E-mail: arlen@adsturtlehouse.com.

SNYDER, BILL, football coach; m. Sharon Snyder; children: Sean, Ross, Shannon, Meredith, Whitney. BA, William Jewell Coll., 1963; MA, Ea. N.Mex. U., 1965. Asst. coach Indio (Calif.) H.S., 1964—66, head coach, 1969—73; grad. asst. U. So. Calif., 1966—67; offensive coord. football, head swimming coach Austin Coll., Sherman, Tex., 1979; coach U. Iowa, 1979—89; head football coach Kans. State U., Manhattan, 1989—. Coached in numerous bowl games, including Copper, Aloha, Holiday, Cotton, Fiesta, Alamo. Named Nat. Coach of Yr., Walter Camp Found., Bobby Dodd Coach of Yr. Found., Paul "Bear" Bryant Award, Schutt Sports Group, ESPN, 1991, CNN, 1994, AP, 1990, 1991, 1993. Mem.: Am. Football Coaches Assn. (mem. rules com., mem. ethics com.). Office: Vanier Football Complex 2102 Kimball Ave Manhattan KS 66502

SNYDER, CAROLYN ANN, education educator, librarian; b. Elgin, Nebr., Nov. 5, 1942; d. Ralph and Florence Wagner. Student, Nebr. Wesleyan U., 1960-61; BS cum laude, Kearney State Coll., 1964; MS in Librarianship, U. Denver, 1965. Asst. libr. sci. and tech. U. Nebr., Lincoln, 1965-67, asst. pub. svc. libr., 1967-68, 70-73; pers. libr. Ind. U. Librs., Bloomington, 1973-76, acting dean of univ. librs., 1980, 88-89, assoc. dean for pub. svcs., 1977-88, 89-91, interim devel. officer, 1989-91; adminstrv. army libr. Spl. Svcs. Agy., Europe, 1968-70; dean libr. affairs So. Ill. U., Carbondale, 1991-2000, prof., 2000—. Team leader Midwest Univs. Consortium for Internat. Activities-World Bank IX project to develop libr. system and implement automation U. Indonesia, Jakarta, 1984-86; libr. devel. cons. Inst. Tech. MARA/Midwest Univs. Consortium for Internat. Activities Program in Malaysia, 1985; ofcl. rep. EDUCAUSE, 1996-2000; mem. working group on scholarly comm. Nat. Commn. on Librs. and Info. Sci., 1998-2000; dir. found. rels. So. Ill. U., Carbondale, 2002-. Editor Library and Other Academic Support Services for Distance Learning, 1997; contbr. chpt. to book and articles to profl. jours. Active Humane Assn. Jackson County, 1991—, Carbondale Pub. Libr. Friends, 1991—. Cooperative Rsch. grant Coun. on Libr. Resources, Washington, 1984. Mem. ALA (councilor 1985-89, Bogle Internat. Travel award 1988, H.W. Wilson Libr. Staff devel. grant 1981), Libr. Adminstrn./Mgmt. Assn. (pres. 1981-82), Com. on Instnl. Coop./Resource Sharing (chair 1987-91), Coalition for Networked Info. (So. Ill. U. at Carbondale rep. 1991-2000), Coun. Dirs. State Univ. Librs. in Ill. (chair 1992-93, 99-2000), Coun. on Libr. and Info. Resources Digital Leadership Inst. Steering Com. (Assn. Rsch. Librs. rep. 1998-2000), Ill. Assn. Coll. and Rsch. Librs. (chair Ill. Bd. Higher Edn. liaison com. 1993-94), Ill. Network (bd. dirs.), Ind. Libr. Assn. (chair coll./univ. divsn. 1982-83), U.S. Grant Assn. (bd. dirs. 1992—), Ill. Libr. Computer Sys. Orgn. (policy coun. 1992-95, 96-2000), Nat. Assn. State Univs. and Land-Grant Colls. (commn. on info. tech. and its distance learning and libr. bds. 1994-96), NetIllinois (bd. dirs. 1994-96), OCLC Users Coun. (elected rep. 1995-98), Big 12 Plus Libr. Consortium (chair 1997-98), Nat. Commn. on Librs. and Info. Sci. Working Group on Scholarly Comms., Assn. Rsch. Libr. (vis. program officer 2000—01). Avocations: antiques, theater, movies. Office: So Ill U Morris Libr Carbondale IL 62901-6632

SNYDER, GEORGE EDWARD, lawyer; b. Battle Creek, Mich., Feb. 7, 1934; s. Leon R. and Edith (Dullabahn) S.; m. Mary Jane Belt, July 27, 1957 (div. Sept. 23, 1982); children: Sara Lynn, Elizabeth Jane; m. Claudia Gage Brooks, Feb. 25, 1984 B.S., Mich. State U., 1957; J.D., U. Mich., 1960. Bar: Mich. 1961, U.S. Dist. Ct. (we. and ea. dists.) Mich. 1961. With Gen. Electric Co., 1957-58; assoc. firm Miller, Johnson, Snell & Commisky, Grand Rapids, 1960-62, Goodenough & Buesser, Detroit, 1962-66; partner firm Buesser, Buesser, Snyder & Blank, Detroit and Bloomfield Hills, 1966-85, Meyer, Kirk, Snyder & Lynch PLLC, Bloomfield Hills, 1985—. Chmn. bd. dirs. Bill Knapps Mich., Inc., 1998-2000. Chmn. E. Mich. Environ. Action Council, 1974-78; pub. mem. inland lakes and streams rev. com. Mich. Dept. Natural Resources, 1975-76. Served as 2d lt. AUS, 1957. Fellow Am. Acad. Matrimonial Lawyers (pres. Mich. chpt. 1991-92), Am. Coll. Family Trial Lawyers, Am. Bar Found., Internat. Acad. Matrimonial Lawyers, Mich. Bar Found; mem. ABA, Am. Judicature Soc., Am. Arbitration Assn. (panel arbitrators), State Bar Mich. (chmn. family law com. 1968-72, mem. rep. assembly 1972-78, chmn. rules and calendar com. 1977-78, mem. family law sect. coun. 1973-76, environ. law sect. coun. 1980-85, prepaid legal svcs. com. 1973-82, com. on judicial selection 1974, com. on specialization 1976-82), Detroit Bar Assn. (chmn. family law com. 1966-68), Oakland County Bar Assn., Delta Upsilon (chmn. trustees, alumni chpt. dep. 1965-70), Tau Beta Pi, Pi Tau Sigma, Phi Eta Sigma. Episcopalian. Clubs: Detroit Athletic, Birmingham (Mich.) Athletic. Home: 32965 Outland Trl Bingham Farms MI 48025-2555 Office: Meyer Kirk Snyder & Lynch PLLC Ste 100 100 W Long Lake Rd Bloomfield Hills MI 48304-2773 E-mail: gsnyder@meyerkirk.com.

SNYDER, HARRY COOPER, retired state senator; b. July 10, 1928; Student, Wilmington Coll., Ohio U. Mem. Ohio State Senate, Columbus, 1979-96; ret., 1996; chmn. edn. and retirement com. Ohio State Senate, Columbus. Former mem. exec. com. Ohio Sch. Bds. Assn.; commr. Ohio High Speed Rail Devel. Authority; mem. Edn. Commn. of the States; chmn. Ohio Retirement Study Commn.; chmn. Legis. Office on Edn. Oversight; ad hoc mem. State Bd. Edn., Ohio Bd. Regents; mem. Jobs for Ohio Grads.; founder Clinton County Family Y; mem. Clinton County Bd. Edn. Recipient Outstanding Legis. Svc. award Citizens United for Responsible Edn., Ohio Ret. Tchrs. Assn., Ohio Coalition for Edn. of Handicapped Children, Ohio Assn. Civil Trial Attys., Guardian of Small Bus. award Nat. Fedn. Ind. Bus., Outstanding Contbr. to Edn. in Ohio award Ohio Confedn. Tchr. Edn. Orgn., Disting. Govtl. Svc. award Ohio Coun. Pvt. Colls. and Schs., Legis. of Yr. Ohio Sch. and Transit Assn. Mem. Am. Legis. Exch. Coun. (edn. com., Outstanding State Legis.-Jefferson award), Nat. Conf. State Legislatures (state/fed. assembly, edn. and job tng. com., assembly of legislature, edn. com.), Rotary Club (pres.), Great Oaks Task Force. Republican. Methodist. Avocations: reading, gardening, sailing. Home: 6508 Spring Hill Dr Hillsboro OH 45133-9209

SNYDER, JEAN MACLEAN, lawyer; b. Chgo., Jan. 26, 1942; d. Norman Fitzroy and Jessie (Burns) Maclean; m. Joel Martin Snyder, Sept. 4, 1964; children: Jacob Samuel, Noah Scot. BA, U. Chgo., 1963, JD, 1979. Bar: Ill. 1979, U.S. Dist. Ct. (no. dist.) Ill. 1979, U.S. Ct. Appeals (7th cir.) 1981. Ptnr. D'Ancona & Pflaum, Chgo., 1979-92; prin. Law Office of Jean Maclean Snyder, 1993-97; trial counsel The MacArthur Justice Ctr. U. Chgo. Law Sch., 1997—. Contbr. articles to profl. jours. Mem.: Lawyers for the Creative Arts (bd. dirs. 1995—97), ACLU of Ill. 1996—99, ABA (mem. coun. on litigation sect. 1989—92, editor-in-chief Litigation mag. 1987—88, co-chair First Amendment and media litigation com. 1995—96, co-chair sect. litigation task force on gender, racial and ethnic bias 1998—2001, standing com. on strategic comms. 1996—2001). Office: The MacArthur Justic Ctr Univ of Chgo Law Sch 1111 E 60th St Chicago IL 60637-2776 E-mail: jean_snyder@law.uchicago.edu .

SNYDER, LEWIS EMIL, astrophysicist, educator; b. Ft. Wayne, Ind., Nov. 26, 1939; s. Herman Lewis and Bernice (McKee) S.; m. Doris Jean Selma Lautner, June 16, 1962; children: Herman Emil, Catherine Jean. BS, Ind. State U., 1961; MA, So. Ill. U., 1964; PhD, Mich. State U., 1967. Research assoc. Nat. Radio Astronomy Obs., Charlottesville., Va., 1967-69; prof. astronomy dept. U. Va., Charlottesville, 1969-73, 74-75; vis. fellow Joint Inst. for Lab. Astrophysics, U. Colo., Boulder, 1973-74; prof. astronomy dept. U. Ill., Urbana, 1975—. Co-editor: Molecules in the Galactic Environment, 1973; contbr. articles to sci. jours. NASA-Am. Soc. Engring. Edn. summer fellow, 1972, 73; Alexander von Humboldt Found. sr. U.S. scientist award, 1983-84. Mem. AAAS, Astron. Soc. Pacific, Am. Phys. Soc., Am. Astron. Soc., Internat. Astron. Union, Union Radio Scientifique Internationale, Alexander von Humboldt Assn. Am. Lutheran. Office: U Ill 1002 W Green St Urbana IL 61801-3074

SNYDER, PETER M. medical educator, medical researcher; BA in Biology summa cum laude, Luther Coll., 1984; MD, U. Iowa, 1989. Diplomate Am. Bd. Internal Medicine, Am. Bd. Cardiovasc. Disease. Resident in internal medicine U. Tex., Dallas, 1989—92; fellow in cardiovasc. diseases Dept. Internal Medicine U. Iowa Hosp. & Clinics, Iowa City, 1992—96, asst. prof. Dept. Internal Medicine, 1996—2000, assoc. prof. internal medicine and physiology and biophysics, 2000—. Contbr. articles to profl. jours. Recipient Clinician Scientist award, 1996, Katz Basic Sci. award, 1998; fellow Student Rsch., U. Iowa, 1985, Student, Am. Heart Assn., 1987—88. Mem.: ACP, Alpha Omega Alpha. Achievements include research in sodium channel structure and function. Office: U Iowa Coll of Medicine Dept Internal Medicine 200 Hawkins Dr Iowa City IA 52242-1009

SNYDER, ROBERT LYMAN, materials scientist, educator; b. Plattsburgh, N.Y., June 5, 1941; s. George Michael and Dorothy (Lyman) M.; m. Sheila Nolan, Sept. 1, 1963; children: Robert N., Kristina M. BA, Marist Coll., 1963; PhD, Fordham U., 1968. Postdoctoral fellow NIH U. Pitts., 1968; NRC fellow NASA Elec. Rsch. Ctr., Cambridge, Mass., 1969; asst. prof. ceramic sci. Alfred (N.Y.) U., 1970-77, assoc. prof., 1977-83, prof., 1983-96, dir. Inst. Ceramic Superconductivity, 1987-96; prof., chmn. dept. materials sci. and engring. Ohio State U., Columbus, 1996—. Vis. prof. Lawrence Livermore (Calif.) Lab., 1977, 78, U.S. Nat. Bur. Stds., Gaithersburg, Md., 1980, 81, Siemens AG Ctrl. Rsch. Labs., Munich, 1983, 91; invited prof. U. Rennes, France, 1995. Author: Introduction to X-Ray Powder Diffractometry, 1996; author, editor 8 books; contbr. chpts. to books and over 220 articles to profl. jours. Deputy mayor Village of Alfred, 1973-77; pres. Alfred Vol. Fire Co., 1979-88. Recipient Chancellor's award SUNY, 1980, numerous research grants; named Faculty Exch. scholar SUNY, 1978-96. Fellow Am. Ceramic Soc. (Outstanding Educator award 1999), Am. Soc. Metals; mem. NAS (U.S. nat. com. on crystallography 1991-95), Nat. Inst. Ceramic Engrs., Am. Crystallography Assn. (chmn. applied crystallography div. 1988-92), Materials Rsch. Soc., Ceramic Ednl. Coun., Internat. Ctr. Diffraction Data (bd. dirs. 1986-92, elected chmn. bd. dirs. 1996-2000), Internat. X-ray Analysis Soc. (pres. 2000-2001), Edward Orton Jr. Ceramic Found. (bd. dirs. 1996—), Alfred and Allegany County Fire Assn., Sigma Xi, Phi Kappa Phi. Democrat. Achievements include numerous patents for practical superconductors. Home: 8500 Stonechat Loop Dublin OH 43017-8625 Office: Ohio State U Dept Materials Sci and Engring Columbus OH 43209-2885

SNYDER, THOMAS J. automotive company executive; With Delco Remy divsn. of GM Corp., 1962-94, product mgr. heavy duty systems; pres., CEO, dir. Delco Remy Internat., Inc., Anderson, Ind., 1994—. Bd. dirs. St. John's Health Systems. Office: Delco Remy Internat Inc 2902 Enterprise Dr Anderson IN 46013

SO, FRANK S. educational association administrator; b. Youngstown, Ohio, Apr. 25, 1937; BA cum laude, Youngstown U., 1959; MA, Ohio State U., 1961. Dir. planning and cmty. devel. City of Harvey, Ill., 1964-67; cons. advisor to village mgr. Village of Flossmoor, 1980-96; exec. dir. Am. Planning Assn., Chgo., 1996—. Adj. prof. Govs. State U., University Park, Ill.; spkr. in field. Editor-in-chief: The Practice of Local Government Planning, 3 edits., The Practice of State and Regional Planning; contbr. articles to profl. jours. Vol. planning career advisor to Peace Corps. Mem. Am. Planning assn., Am. Inst. Cert. Planners, Lambda Alpha Internat. Office: Am Planning Assn 122 S Michigan Ave Ste 1600 Chicago IL 60603-6190

SOAVE, ANTHONY, business executive; Pres., CEO Soave Enterprises, Detroit. Office: Soave Enterprises 3400 E Lafayette St Detroit MI 48207-4962

SOBEL, ALAN, electrical engineer, physicist; b. N.Y.C., Feb. 23, 1928; s. Edward P. and Rose (Naftalison) S.; m. Marjorie Loebel, June 15, 1952; children: Leslie Ann, Edward Robert. BSEE, Columbia U., 1947, MSEE, 1949; PhD in Physics, Poly. Inst. Bklyn., 1964. Lic. Profl. Engr., N.Y. and Ill. Asst. chief engr. The Electronic Workshop, N.Y.C., 1950-51; head, functional engr. Fairchild Controls Corp., 1951-56; project engr. Skiatron Electronics and TV Corp., 1956-57; sr. rsch. engr. Zenith Radio Corp., Glenview, Ill., 1964-78; v.p. Lucitron inc., Northbrook, 1978-87, pres., 1987; pvt. practice cons. Evanston, 1988—; v.p. Machine Vision and Control Internat. Inc., 1994—, LightWave Technologies Corp., 2000—. Asst., instr. Poly. Inst. Bklyn.,1957-64; mem. program coms. SID Internat. Symposium, Internat. Display Rsch. Conf., 1970—. Inventor: 14 patents on various display and electron devices; author 55 papers on electronics, physics, electronic displays, etc.; editor Jour. Soc. Info. Display, 1991—99; adv. editor Info. Display Mag.; assoc. editor: IEEE Trans. on Electron Devices, N.Y., 1970-77. Mem. Democratic Party of Evanston. NSF fellow, 1959, 60. Fellow Soc. Info. Display; mem. IEEE (sr., life), SPIE, Am. Phys. Soc., Sigma Xi. Democrat Home and Office: 633 Michigan Ave Evanston IL 60202-2552

SOBEL, HOWARD BERNARD, osteopath, educator; b. N.Y.C., May 15, 1929; s. Martin and Ella (Sternberg) S.; m. Ann Louise Silverbush, June 16, 1957 (dec. May 1978); children— Nancy Sobel Schumer, Janet Sobel Medow, Robert; m. Irene S. Miller, June 8, 1980; stepchildren— Avner Saferstein, Daniel Saferstein, Naomi Saferstein A.B., Syracuse U., 1951; D.O., Kansas City Coll. Osteopathy and Surgery, 1955. Intern Zieger Osteo. Hosp., Detroit, 1955-56; gen. practice osteo. medicine Redford Twp., Mich., 1956-74, Livonia, 1974—. Chief of staff Botsford Gen. Hosp., Farmington, Mich., 1978; mem. faculty Mich. State U. Coll. Osteo. Medicine, 1969— , clin. assoc. prof. family practice, 1973— ; mem. exec. and med. adv. coms. United Health Orgn. Mich.; mem. Venereal Disease Action Com., Mich.; apptd. to asst. impaired osteo. physicians Mich., 1983 Mem. Am. Osteo. Assn. (ho. of dels. 1981—), Mich. Assn. Osteo. Physicians and Surgeons (ho. of dels.), Am. Coll. Osteo. Rheumatologists, Coll. Am. Osteo. Gen. Practitioners, Osteo. Gen. Practice Mich., Wayne County Osteo. Assn. (pres.) Jewish Home: 6222 Northfield Rd West Bloomfield MI 48322-2431 Office: 28275 5 Mile Rd Livonia MI 48154-3944

SOBKOWICZ, HANNA MARIA, neurology researcher; b. Warsaw, Poland, Jan. 1, 1931; came to U.S., 1963; d. Stanislaw and Jadwiga (Ignaczak) S.; m. Jerzy E. Rose, Mar. 12, 1972. B.A., Girls State Lyceum, Gilwice, Poland, 1949; M.D, Med. Acad., Warsaw, 1954, Ph.D., 1962. Intern. 1st Internal Med. Clinic Med. Acad., Warsaw, 1954-55; resident 1st Internal Med. Clinic, Med. Acad., 1955-59, Neurol. Clinic, Med. Acad., 1959, jr. asst., 1959-61, sr. asst., 1961-63; research fellow neurology Mt. Sinai Hosp., N.Y.C., 1963-65; Nat. Multiple Sclerosis Soc. fellow Columbia U., 1965-66; asst. prof. neurology U. Wis., Madison, 1966-72, assoc. prof., 1972-79, prof., 1979—. Contbr. articles to profl. jours. NIH research grantee, 1968— Mem. Internat. Brain Rsch. Orgn., Assn. Rsch. in Otolaryngology, Soc. Neurosci., Internat. Soc. Devel. Neurosci. (editorial bd. 1984—), Electron Microscopy Soc. Am. Office: U Wis Dept Neurology 1300 University Ave Madison WI 53706-1510

SOBOL, LAWRENCE RAYMOND, lawyer; b. Kansas City, Mo., May 8, 1950; s. Haskell and Mary (Press) S.; m. Maureen Patricia O'Connell, May 29, 1976; children: David, Kevin. BBA, U. Tex., 1972; JD, U. Mo., 1975. Bar: Mo. 1975, U.S. Dist. Ct. (ea. dist.) Mo. 1975. Gen. counsel, gen. ptnr. Edward D. Jones & Co., Maryland Heights, Mo., 1975—. Allied mem. N.Y.C. Stock Exchange, 1977—; sec. Lake Communications Corp., Conroe, Tex., 1984-86, LHC Inc., EDJ Holding Co. Inc., Unison Capital Corp., 1990—, Cornerstone Mortgage Investment Group, 1987-92; sec., bd. dirs. Cornerstone Mortgage Inc., St. Louis, 1986; v.p., bd. dirs. Tempus Corp., St. Louis, 1984—. Omar Robinson Meml. scholar U. Mo., 1974-75. Mem. ABA (securities law com. 1982—), Met. St. Louis Bar Assn. (securities law sect.), Nat. Assn. Securities Dealers (dist. bus. com., registered prin. officer, nat. arbitration com. 1991—), Securities Industry Assn. (fed. regulation securities com. 1987-88), Persimmon Woods Country Club, Lake Las Vegas South Shore Country Club, Phi Eta Sigma. Republican. Avocations: tennis, golf. Office: Edward D Jones & Co 12555 Manchester Rd Saint Louis MO 63131-3729

SOBRERO, KATHRYN MICHELE, soccer player; b. Pontiac, Mich., Aug. 23, 1976; Student in bus., U. Notre Dame, 1994—. Mem. U.S. Nat. Women's Soccer Team, 1995—; mem. U.S. Under-20 Nat. Team, 1993—, including Nordic Cup, 1994, championship team 1997 (as overage player). Named Defensive Most Valuable Player NCAA Final Four, 1995; on cover of (mag.) Soccer Am., 1995. Office: US Soccer Fedn 1801-1811 S Prairie Ave Chicago IL 60616

SOBTI, ARUN, telecommunications executive; BS in Electronics, Punjab Engring. Coll., India; MSEE, PhD in Elec. Engring., U. Kans. Gen. mgr. mobile computing products divsn. Motorola, v.p. R&D cellular infrastructure group, v.p., dir. solutions engrs. global telecom solutions group; sr. v.p., pres. residential broadband group ADC Telecom., Minnetonka, Minn., 1999—. Contbr. articles to profl. jours. Achievements include 18 patents in field. Office: ADC 12501 Whitewater Dr Minnetonka MN 55343-9498

SOBUS, KERSTIN MARYLOUISE, physician, physical therapist; b. Washington, June 16, 1960; d. Earl Francis and Dolores Jane (Gill) G.; m. Paul John Jr., March 10, 1990; children: Darlene Marie, Julieann Marie. BS in Phys. Therapy summa cum laude, U. N.D., 1981, MD, 1987. Clinic instr. pediatric physical therapy U.N.D. Sch. Medicine, Grand Forks, 1981-83; pediat. phys. theraist child evaluation-treatment program Med. Rehab. Ctr., 1981-83, med. dir. program, 1997—; asst. prof. dept. pediatrics, asst. prof. dept. physical medicine and rehab. U. Ark. for Med. Scis., Little Rock, 1992-96; resident in internal medicine Sinai Hosp. Balt., 1987-88; resident in phys. medicine and rehab. Johns Hopkins program Sinai Hosp., Balt., 1988-91; pediatric rehab. clin. and rsch. fellow Alfred I. DuPont Inst., Wilmington, Del., 1991-92; pediatric pysiatrist Altru Health System, Grand Forks, 1997—. Contbr. articles to med. jours. Mem. Am. Acad. Cerebral Palsy and Devel. Medicine, Alpha Omega Alpha Honor Soc. Home: 1548 30th Ave NE Manvel ND 58256-9793 Office: Altru Health Sys PO Box 6002 1300 S Columbia Rd Grand Forks ND 58201-4012

SOCHEN, JUNE, history educator; b. Chgo., Nov. 26, 1937; d. Sam and Ruth (Finkelstein) S. B.A., U. Chgo., 1958; M.A., Northwestern U., 1960, Ph.D., 1967. Project editor Chgo. Superior and Talented Student Project, 1959-60; high sch. tchr. English and history North Shore Country Day Sch., Winnetka, Ill., 1961-64; instr. history Northeastern Ill. U., 1964-67, asst. prof., 1967-69, assoc. prof., 1969-72, prof., 1972—. Author: The New Woman, 1971, Movers and Shakers, 1973, Herstory: A Woman's View of American History, 1975, 2d edit., 1981, Consecrate Every Day: The Public Lives of Jewish American Women, 1981, Enduring Values: Women in Popular Culture, 1987, Cafeteria America: New Identities in Contemporary Life, 1988, Mae West: She Who Laughs Lasts, 1992, From Mae to Madonna: Women Entertainers in 20th Century America, 1999; editor: Women's Comic Visions, 1991; contbr. articles to profl. jours. Nat. Endowment for Humanities grantee, 1971-72 Office: Northeastern Ill U 5500 N Saint Louis Ave Chicago IL 60625-4679 E-mail: j-sochen@neiu.edu.

SOCOL, MICHAEL LEE, obstetrician, gynecologist, educator; b. Chgo., Oct. 3, 1949; s. Joseph and Bernice (Bofman) S.; m. Donna Kaner, Dec. 17, 1972. BS, U. Ill., 1970; MD, U. Ill., Chgo., 1974. Diplomate Am. Bd. Ob-Gyn., Am. Bd. Maternal-Fetal Medicine. Resident obstetrics and gynecology U. Ill. Hosp., Chgo., 1974-77; clin. rsch. fellow dept. obstetrics and gynecology L.A. County-U. So. Calif. Med. Ctr., 1977-79; assoc. attending physician Northwestern Meml. Hosp., Chgo., 1980-86, attending physician dept. ob-gyn., 1986—; co-dir. Northwestern Perinatal Ctr., 1987—; head maternal-fetal medicine, chief obstetrics Northwestern U. Med. Sch., 1987—, dir. maternal-fetal medicine fellowship program, 1987-99, asst. prof. obstetrics and gynecology, 1979-84, assoc. prof., 1984-92, prof., 1992—. Vice chmn. dept. ob-gyn Northwestern Meml. Hosp., Chgo., 1992—. Author: (with others) Clinical Obstetrics and Gynecology, 1982, 1984, Diagnostic Ultrasound Applied to Obstetrics and Gynecology, 1987, Principles and Practice of Medical Therapy in Pregnancy, 1992; peer reviewer Am. Jour. Obstetrics and Gynecology, 1980—, Obstetrics and Gynecology, 1984—; contbr. numerous articles to profl. jours. Fellow Am. Coll. Ob-Gyn., Soc. Maternal-Fetal Medicine, Ctrl. Assn. Ob-Gyn., Chgo. Gynecol. Soc., Soc. for Gynecol. Investigation, Am. Gynecol. and Obstetrical Soc.; mem. AMA, Assn. Profs. of Gynecology and Obstetrics, Ill. State Med. Assn., Chgo. Med. Soc. Avocation: marathon running. Office: 333 E Superior St Ste 410 Chicago IL 60611-3015

SOCOLOFSKY, JON EDWARD, banker; b. Chgo., Mar. 27, 1946; s. E. E. and Jane C. (Ward) S.; married; 1 child, Brian Edward. BA, DePauw U., 1968; MBA, Ind. U., 1970. Auditor No. Trust Co., Chgo., 1970-79, v.p., 1979-86, sr. v.p., 1986—. Pres. Cass Sch. Dist. # 63, Darien, Ill., 1987-93. Mem. Internat. Ops. Assn. Republican. Congregationalist. Avocations: water skiing, volleyball, motorcycles. Office: The Northern Trust Co 50 S La Salle St Chicago IL 60603-1003

SODERBERG, LEIF G. electronics company executive; BA, Harvard Coll.; MS in Mgmt., MIT. Various positions ending with ptnr. McKinsey & Co., Cleveland and Scandinavia, 1978-93; head bus. strategy Land Mobile Products Sector, Network Svcs. Bus. Motorola, 1993-94, v.p., gen. mgr. Network Svcs. and Bus. Strategies Group Ill., 1994—, sr. v.p. Systems Solutions Group, 1998—. Mem. Clearnet's Nominating Com. Office: Motorola 1301 E Algonquin Rd Schaumburg IL 60196-1078

SOERGEL, KONRAD HERMANN, physician; b. Coburg, Germany, July 27, 1929; came to U.S., 1954, naturalized, 1962; s. Konrad Daniel and Erna Henrietta (Schilling) S.; m. Rosina Klara Rudin, June 24, 1955; children: Elizabeth Ann, Karen Theresa, Marilyn Virginia, Kenneth Thomas. M.D., U. Erlangen, Germany, 1954, Dr. med., 1958. Intern Bergen Pines County Hosp., Paramus, N.J., 1954-55; resident in pathology West Pa. Hosp., Pitts., 1955-56; rsch. asst. U. Erlangen, Germany, 1956-57; resident in medicine Mass. Meml. Hosp., Boston, 1957-58; fellow in gastroenterology Boston U. Med. Sch., 1958-60, instr., 1960-61; mem. faculty Med. Coll. Wis., Milw., 1961—, prof. medicine, 1969—, prof. physiology, 1993—, chief sect. gastroenterology, 1961-93. Chmn. gastroenterology and clin. nutrition study sect. NIH, 1979-80 Contbr. articles to profl. jours., chpts. to books. Recipient Research Career Devel. award USPHS, 1963-72; Alexander von Humboldt Found. sr. fellow, 1973-74 Mem. Am. Gastroenterol. Assn., Am. Soc. Clin. Investigation, Am. Assn. Physicians, German Soc. for Digestive and Metabolic Disorders (hon.), Ger. Soc. Internal Medicine (hon.). Home: 14245 Hillside Rd Elm Grove WI 53122-1677 Office: Med Coll Wis 9200 W Wisconsin Ave Milwaukee WI 53226-3522 E-mail: ksoergel@mcw.edu.

SOETEBER, ELLEN, journalist, newspaper editor; b. East St. Louis, Ill., June 14, 1950; d. Lyle Potter and Norma Elizabeth (Osborn) S.; m. Richard M. Martins, Mar. 16, 1974. BJ, Northwestern U., 1972. Edn. writer, copy editor Chgo. Today, 1972-74; reporter Chgo. Tribune, 1974-76, asst. met. editor, 1976-84, assoc. met. editor, 1984-86, TV and media editor, 1986, met. editor, 1987-89, assoc. mng. editor for met. news, 1989-91, dep. editor editorial page, 1991-94; mng. editor South Fla. Sun-Sentinel, Ft. Lauderdale, 1994-2001; editor St. Louis Post-Dispatch, 2001—. Fellow journalism U. Mich., Ann Arbor, 1986-87. Office: The St Louis Post-Dispatch 900 N Tucker Blvd Saint Louis MO 63101 E-mail: esoeteber@post-dispatch.com.

SOGG, WILTON SHERMAN, lawyer; b. Cleve., May 28, 1935; s. Paul P. and Julia (Cahn) S.; m. Saralee Frances Krow, Aug. 12, 1962 (div. July 1975); 1 child, Stephanie; m. Linda Rocker Lehman, Dec. 22, 1979 (div. Dec. 1990); m. Nancy Rosenfield Walsh, June 2, 1991. AB, Dartmouth Coll., 1956; JD, Harvard U., 1959; postgrad., London Grad. Sch. Bus. Studies, 1974-76. Bar: (Ohio) 1960, (Fla) 1970, (U.S. Tax Ct.) 1961, (U.S. Supreme Ct.) 1969. Assoc. Gottfried, Ginsberg, Guren & Merritt, 1960-63, ptnr., 1963-70, Guren, Merritt, Feibel, Sogg & Cohen, Cleve., 1970-84; of counsel Hahn, Loeser, Freedheim, Dean and Wellman, 1984-85; ptnr. Hahn Loeser & Parks LLP, 1986-2000; of counsel McCarthy, Lebit, Crystal & Liffman Co., 2001—. Trustee, pres. Cleve. Jewish News; adj. prof. Cleve. State Law Sch., 1960—; lectr. Harvard U. Law Sch., 1978-80. Author: (with Howard M. Rossen) new and rev. vols. of Smith's Review Legal Gems series, 1969—; editor: Harvard Law Rev.; contbr. articles to profl. jours. Trustee Jewish Cmty. Fedn. of Cleve., 1966-72; bd. overseers Cleveland Marshall Coll. Law, Cleve. State U., 1969—, vis. com. Coll. Bus. Adminstrn., 1996-00; mem. U.S. and State of Ohio Holocaust commns. Fulbright fellow U. London, 1959-60. Mem. Ohio Bar Assn., Fla. Bar Assn., Germany Philatelic Soc., Oakwood Club, Union Club, Chagrin Valley Hunt, Phi Beta Kappa. Home: PO Box 278 Gates Mills OH 44040-0278 Office: McCarthy Lebit Crystal & Liffman 1800 Midland Bldg 101 W Prospect Ave Cleveland OH 44115-1088 E-mail: wss@mccarthylebit.com.

SOKOL, DAVID L. energy services provider company executive; b. 1957; BSCE, U. Nebr., Omaha, 1978; hon. doctoral degree, Bellevue (Nebr.) U. With Citycorp, Henningson, Durham and Richardson, Inc.; pres., CEO, bd. dirs. Ogden Projects, Inc.; chmn., CEO, MidAm. Energy Holdings Co. (successor to CalEnergy Co., Inc.), Des Moines, 1991—, pres., from 1991. Co-chmn. for Campaign Nebr., U. Nebr. Found.; mem. Met. Omaha Conv., Sports and Entertainment Authority; bd. dirs. Creighton U., Coll. World Series Omaha, Inc., Omaha Airport Authority, Strategic Command Consultation Co., Joslyn Art Mus., River City Roundup and Rodeo, Nebr. Easter Seal Soc., Mt. Michael Abbey H.S., Archdiocese of Omaha, Girls, Inc., Mid-Am. coun. Boy Scouts Am., United Way Midlands.; bd. govs. Knights of Ak-Sar-Ben Mem.. Del. Assn. Profl. Engrs., Neb. Soc. Profl. Engrs. Office: MidAm Energy Holdings Co 666 Grand Ave Des Moines IA 50309-2506

SOKOL, JOHN S. insurance executive; BA, Denison U.; MBA, Vanderbilt U. Officer Chem. Bank N.Y.; v.p. investments Bancins. Corp., Columbus, Ohio, 1993-96, exec. v.p., 1996-99, pres., 1999—, Ohio Indemnity Co. Chmn. Custom Title Svcs. Trustee Ctrl. Ohio Transit Authority. Mem. Consumer Credit Ins. Assn. Office: Bancins Corp 20 E Broad St Fl 4 Columbus OH 43215-3416

SOKOL, ROBERT JAMES, obstetrician, gynecologist, educator; b. Rochester, N.Y., Nov. 18, 1941; s. Eli and Mildred (Levine) S.; m. Roberta Sue Kahn, July 26, 1964; children: Melissa Anne, Eric Russell, Andrew Ian. BA with highest distinction in Philosophy, U. Rochester, 1963, MD with honors, 1966. Diplomate Am. Bd. Ob-Gyn (assoc. examiner 1984-86), Sub-Bd. Maternal-Fetal Medicine. Intern Barnes Hosp., Washington U., St. Louis, 1966-67, resident in ob-gyn., 1967-70, asst. in ob-gyn., 1966-70, rsch. asst., 1967-68, instr. clin. ob-gyn., 1970; Buswell fellow in maternal fetal medicine Strong Meml. Hosp.-U. Rochester, 1972-73; fellow in maternal-fetal medicine Cleve. Met. Gen. Hosp.-Case Western Res. U., Cleve., 1974-75, assoc. obstetrician and gynecologist, 1973-83, asst. prof. ob-gyn., 1973-77; asst. program dir. Perinatal Clin. Rsch. Ctr., 1973-78, co-program dir., 1978-82, program dir., 1982-83, acting dir. obstetrics, 1974-75, co-dir., 1977-83, assoc. prof., 1977-81, prof., 1981-83, assoc. dir. dept. ob-gyn., 1981-83; prof. ob-gyn. Wayne State U., Detroit, 1983-2000, disting. prof., 2000—, chmn. dept. ob-gyn., 1983-89, mem. grad. faculty dept. physiology, 1984—, interim dean Med. Sch., 1988-89, dean, 1989-99, pres. Fund for Med. Rsch. and Edn., 1988—99, disting. prof. ob-gyn, 2000—; chief ob-gyn. Hutzel Hosp., 1983-89; interim chmn. med. bd. Detroit Med. Ctr., 1988-89, chmn. med. bd., 1989-99, sr. v.p. med. affairs, 1992-99, trustee, 1990-99; past pres. med. staff Cuyahoga County Hosps.; mem. profl. adv. bd. Educated Childbirth Inc., 1976-80; dir. C.S. Mott Ctr. for Human Growth and Devel., 1983-89, 99—. Sr. Ob cons. Symposia Medicus; cons. Grant Planning Task Force Robert Wood Johnson Found., Nat. Inst. Child Health and Human Devel., Nat. Inst. Alcohol Abuse and Alcoholism, Ctr. for Disease Control, NIH, Health Resources and Services Adminstrn., Nat. Clearinghouse for Alcohol Info., Am. Psychol. Assn.; mem. alcohol psychosocial research rev. com. Nat. Inst. Alcohol Abuse and Alcoholism, 1982-86; mem. ob/gyn adv. panel U.S. Pharmacopeial Conv., 1985-90, adv. com. on policy Am. Jour. Ob-Gyn., 1999-, internat. adv. bd. Karmanos Cancer Inst., Detroit, Mich., 2002-; mem. clin. rsch. task force Assn. Am. Med. Colls., 1998-2000. Mem. internat. editorial bd. Israel Jour. Obstetrics and Gynecology; reviewer med. jours.; mem. editorial bd. Jour. Perinatal Medicine; editor-in-chief Interactions: Programs in Clinical Decision-Making, 1987-90; researcher computer applications in perinatal medicine, alcohol-related birth defects, perinatal risk and neurobehavioral devel.; contbr. articles to profl. jours. Mem.Pres.'s leadership coun. U. Rochester, 1976—80; mem. exec. com. bd. trustees Oakland Health Edn. Program (OHEP), 1987—2000, permanent trustee, 2000—, U. Rochester, 1986—. Maj. M.C. USAF, 1970—72. Mem.: APHA, ACOG (chmn. steering com. drug and alcohol abuse contract 1986—87, rep. ctr. for disease control & prevention task force 2000—, editor-in-chief ACOG Update 2001—), NAS (Inst. of Medicine, com. to study fetal alcohol syndrome 1994—96), AMA, Soc. Physicians Reproductive Choice and Health, World Assn. Perinatal Medicine, Internat. Soc. Computers in Obstetrics, Neonatology, Gynecology (v.p. 1987—89, pres. 1989—92), Soc. for Neuroscis. (Mich. chpt.), Am. Med. Soc. on Alcoholism and Other Drug Dependencies, Am. Gynecol. and Obstet. Soc., Neurobehavioral Teratology Soc., Soc. Perinatal Obstetricians (pres.-elect 1987—88, pres. 1988—89, v.p., achievement award 1995), Rsch. Soc. Alcoholism, Cen. Assn. Obstetricians-Gynecologists (pres.-elect 1997—99, pres. 1999—2000), Detroit Acad. Medicine (pres.-elect 1999—2001, pres. 2001—02), Wayne County Med. Soc., Mich. Med. Soc., Royal Soc. Medicine, Assn. Profs. Gyn.-Ob, Perinatal Rsch. Soc., Soc. Gynecologic Investigation, Am. Med. Informatics Assn., Chgo. Gyn. Soc. (hon.), Detroit

Physiol. Soc. (hon.), Polish Gynecologists World Club, Alpha Omega Alpha, Sigma Xi, Phi Beta Kappa. Republican. Jewish. Home: 7921 Danbury Dr West Bloomfield MI 48322-3581 Office: Wayne State U CS Mott Ctr for Human Growth and Devel Detroit MI 48201 E-mail: rsokol@moose.med.wayne.edu.

SOKOL, SI, insurance company executive; b. Columbus, Ohio, Dec. 22, 1927; s. Nathan and Rose (Klyst) S.; student Ohio State U., 1949-52; m. Barbara, June 29, 1958; children— John, James, Carla. Exec. v.p. Beverlee Dr. Ins., Columbus, Ohio, 1949-62; partner DeWitt, Sokol & Co., Columbus, 1962-70; pres., chmn. Ohio Indemnity Co., Columbus, 1970— , Bancinsurance Corp., Columbus, 1970— ; pres. Community Venture, Columbus, 1975-81; dir. Dollar Savs. & Loan, Columbus, Am. Savs. & Loan, Cin.; prin. owner Si Sokol & Assos.; pres. Westford Group, Inc., 1980—; chmn. Am. Legal Pub. Co., 1988—; mergers and acquisitions cons., Columbus. Clubs: Athletic (Columbus); Cincinnati. Home: 2346 Fishinger Rd Columbus OH 43221-1251 Office: PO Box 182138 Columbus OH 43218-2138

SOKOLOF, PHIL, industrialist, consumer advocate; b. Omaha, Dec. 14, 1922; s. Louis and Rose (Jacobson) S.; m. Ruth Rosinsky, June 1, 1947 (dec. Feb. 1982); children: Steven, Karen Sokolof Javitch. Grad. H.S., Omaha, 1939. Founder, CEO Phillips Mfg. Co., Omaha, 1955-92; founder, pres. Nat. Heart Savers Assn., 1985—. Author: Bridge Philosophy, 1971; contbg. editor N.Y. Times, 1991; featured in Time mag., Mar. 1990, in Journal of American Medicine, Dec. 1990 as catalyst of American public's cholesterol consciousness; contbg. ed. Sunday New York Times, 1991. Designated by Congress hon. co-sponsor 1990 Nutrition Labeling and Edn. Act; conducted Poisoning of Am. nat. media campaigns against major food processors for high cholesterol, high fat content in foods, 1988-93 (citation FDA 1993); activist in lowering fat content Nat. Sch. Lunch Program; conducted, funded $1 million Nutrition Facts sweepstakes quiz to educate pub. regarding nutrition food labels, 1994; ran nat. advt. campaign promoting skim milk and alerting Ams. that 2% milk is not low fat, 1995; ran nat. advt. campaigns advising pub. of lifesaving cholesterol-lowering drugs, 1996, 98; pioneered citywide cholesterol testing in U.S., 1985-88, testing over 200,000 people in 16 states; created, won congl. approval designating Apr. as Nat. Know Your Cholesterol Month, 1987, Cholesterol Kills pub. svc. announcements featured on over 1000 TV stas., 1987—; nat. spokesperson of danger of cholesterol and saturated fats in food products which promote heart disease; ran most expensive pub. svc. announcement in TV history-$2.5 million ad on Super Bowl urging Ams. take breakthrough cholesterol-lowering drugs, 2000. Named Person of Week, ABC News, Mar. 15, 1991; recipient Food & Drug Admin. Commr's. Spl. Achievement citation, 1993, C. Everett Koop Health Advocate award Am. Hosp. Assn., 1994, Am. award Norman Vincent Peale Found., 1997. Mem. Am. Contract Bridge League (life master), King Solomon's Cir. philanthropy,1990 (charter). Office: Nat Heart Savers Assn 9140 W Dodge Rd Omaha NE 68114-3322

SOKOLOFF, STEPHEN PAUL, lawyer; b. Mt. Kisco, N.Y., July 27, 1953; s. Martin A. and Vivienne A. (Albam) S.; m. Amy H. Newberry, May 28, 1976 (div. 1980); m. Freddi Diann Killebrew, Sept. 3, 1981. BA, Pace U., 1978; JD, U. Mo., 1979. Bar: Mo. 1979, U.S. Tax Ct. 1981, U.S. Dist. Ct. (ea. dist.) Mo. 1985. Asst. pros. atty. Dunklin County, Kennett, Mo., 1979-84; assoc. Law Office of Stephen R. Sharp, 1979-84; ptnr. Hilfiker & Sokoloff, Malden, Mo., 1984-87, Sharp & Sokoloff, Kennett, 1987-90, Sokoloff & Tinsley, Kennett, 1991—. City atty. City of Kennett, 1987-91, City of Clarkton (Mo.), 1986—, City of Holcomb (Mo.), 1989—; pros. atty. Dunkin County, 1990—; treas. Delmo Housing Corp., Lilbourn, Mo., 1986—; instr. bus. law S.E. Mo. State U., Cape Girardeau, 1980-82; mem. U. Mo. Bd. Advocates; spl. asst. U.S. atty. Ea. Dist. Mo., 1991—. Contbg. author: Missouri Criminal Law Enforcement Handbook, 1978. Trustee, Dunklin County Youth Devel. Project, Kennett, 1985-88; pres. Dunklin County Probation Community Adv. Bd., Kennett, 1985-86. Mem. ABA, Assn. Trial Lawyers Am., Mo. Assn. Trial Attys., Dunklin County Bar Assn. (sec.-treas. 1988—), Nat. Dist. Attys. Assn., Mo. Assn. Pros. Attys. (chair edn. com. 1990), Semo Little Theater Inc. (pres., bd. dirs. 1988—), Kennett Country Club, Kennett Optimist Club (pres. 1988-90), Eagles, Phi Delta Phi. Avocations: painting, bonsai, cooking, golf, art collecting. Home: 301 N Everett St Kennett MO 63857-1872 Office: Sokoloff & Tinsley Donklin County Courtho Kennett MO 63857

SOKOLOV, RICHARD SAUL, real estate company executive; b. Phila., Dec. 7, 1949; s. Morris and Estelle Rita (Steinberg) S.; m. Susan Barbara Saltzman, Aug. 13, 1972; children: Lisa, Anne, Kate. BA, Pa. State U., 1971; JD, Georgetown U., 1974. Assoc. Weinberg & Green, Balt., 1974-80, ptnr., 1980-82; v.p., gen. counsel The Edward J. DeBartolo Corp., Youngstown, Ohio, 1982-86, sr. v.p. devel., gen. coun., 1986-94; pres., CEO DeBartolo Realty Corp., 1994-96; pres., COO Simon DeBartolo Group, Indpls., 1996-98; pres, COO Simon Property Group, 1998—. Mem. investment com. Jewish Fedn., Youngstown, 1992—; trustee U. Wis.-Madison Ctr. for Urban Land Econs. Rsch., Youngstown/Mahoning Valley United Way. Alumni fellow Pa. State U., 2000. Mem. Internat. Coun. Shopping Ctrs. (trustee 1994—, chmn. 1998-99), Urban Land Inst. (assoc.). Office: Simon Property Group 115 W Washington St Ste 1465 Indianapolis IN 46204-3464

SOLAND, NORMAN R. corporate lawyer; b. Duluth, Minn., Oct. 17, 1940; m. Carol A. Isaacson, Aug. 29, 1964; children: Kirk, Lisa, Kari, Chad. BA, U. Minn., 1963; JD, Am. Univ., 1972. Bar: Minn. 1973. Analyst CIA, 1963-73; assoc. Thompson, Hessian, Fletcher, McKasy & Soderberg, Thompson, Fletcher, Stone & Morse, 1973-79; corp. counsel Nash-Finch Co., Mpls., 1979-84, asst. sec., counsel, 1984-86, sec., gen counsel, 1986-88, v.p., sec. & gen. counsel, 1988-98, sr. v.p., sec., gen. counsel, 1998—. Mem. ABA, Minn. State Bar Assn., Hennepin County Bar Assn., Am. Corp. Counsel Assn. Office: Nash Finch Co PO Box 355 Minneapolis MN 55440-0355

SOLARO, ROSS JOHN, physiologist, biophysicist; b. Wadsworth, Ohio, Jan. 9, 1942; s. Ross and Lena (Chuppa) S.; m. Kathleen Marie Cole, Sept. 18, 1965; children: Christopher, Elizabeth. BS, U. Cin., 1965; PhD, U. Pitts., 1971. Asst. prof. Med. Coll. Va., Richmond, 1973-77; assoc. prof. pharmacology and physiology U. Cin., 1977-81, prof. pharmacology and cell biophysics, 1981-85, prof. physiology, 1981-88; prof. physiology, head U. Ill., Chgo., 1988—, disting. univ. prof., 1998—. Sec. gen. Internat. Soc. Heart Rsch., 1989-93, sec./treas., 1995-98, pres., 1999, assoc. chair dept. physiology; chmn. exptl. cardiovasc. study sect. NIH, 1990-92; vice-chmn. physiology U. Cin., 1987-88. Editor: Protein Phosphorylation in Heart Muscle, 1986; contbr. articles to profl. jours. including Nature, Jour. Biol. Chemistry, Circulation Rsch. Chmn. rsch. coun. Am. Heart Assn., Met. Chgo., 1990-92. Grantee NIH, 1977—, Fogarty fellow, 1986; Brit. Am. Heart fellow Am. Heart Assn., 1974-75; Sr. Internat. fellow U. Coll. London, 1987. Mem. Am. Physiol. Soc. (chmn. subgroup), Am. Soc. Pharm. Exptl. Therapeutics, Biosphys. Soc. (chmn. subgroup 1983-84). Office: U Ill at Chgo MC901 Physiology & Biophysics 835 S Wolcott Ave Chicago IL 60612-7340

SOLBERG, ELIZABETH TRANSOU, public relations executive; b. Dallas, Aug. 10, 1939; d. Ross W. and Josephine V. (Perkins) Transou; m. Frederick M. Solberg Jr., Mar. 8, 1969; 1 son, Frederick W. BJ, U. Mo., 1961. Reporter Kansas City (Mo.) Star, 1963-70, asst. city editor, 1970-73; reporter spl. events, documentaries Sta. WDAF-TV, Kansas City, Mo., 1973-74; prof. dept. journalism Park Coll., 1975-76, advisor, 1976-79; mng. ptnr. Fleishman-Hillard Inc., then exec. v.p., sr. ptnr., gen. mgr. Kansas City br., now regional pres., sr. ptnr., gen. mgr.; also pres. Fleishman-Hillard/Can. Mem. Kansas City Commn. Planned Indsl. Expansion Authority, 1974-91; bd. dirs. Kansas City Life Ins. Co., Ferrellgas. Mem. long range planning com. Heart of Am. coun. Boy Scouts Am., 1980-82, bd. dirs., 1986-89; mem. Clay County (Mo.) Devel. Commn., 1979-88; bd. govs. Citizens Assn., 1975—; mem. exec. com. bd. Kansas City Area Devel. Coun., 1989-96, co-chair, 1991-93; trustee Pembroke Hill Sch., 1987-93, U. Kansas City, 1990—, exec. com., 1992—, Midwest Rsch. Inst., 1995—; bd. dirs. Greater Kansas City Cmty. Found. and Affiliated Trusts, 1996—, Starlight Theatre, 1996—; regent Rockhurst Coll., 1984-96; active Bus. Coun., Nelson Gallery Found., Nelson-Atkins Mus. Art, 1990—; bd. dirs. Civic Coun. Greater Kansas City, 1992—; mem. Jr. League Kansas City. Recipient award for contbn. to mental health Mo. Psychiat. Assn., 1973, Arthur E. Lowell award for excellence in orgn. comm. Kansas City/IABC, 1985, Kansas City Spirit award Gillis Ctr., 1994. Mem. Pub. Rels. Soc. Am. (nat. honors and awards com., co-chmn. SilverAnvil com. 1983, Silver Anvil award 1979-82, chair nat. membership com. 1989-91, assembly del.-at-large 1995-96), Counselor's Acad. (exec. com. 1991-92), Mo. C. of C. Pub. Rels. Coun., Greater Kans. City C. of C. (chair 1994-95, bd. exec. com.), Pi Beta Phi, River Kansas City Club, Carriage Club, Ctrl. Exch. Club. Office: Fleishman Hillard Inc 2405 Grand Blvd Ste 700 Kansas City MO 64108-2522

SOLBERG, JAMES JOSEPH, industrial engineering educator; b. Toledo, May 27, 1942; s. Archie Norman and Margaret Jean (Olsen) S.; m. Elizabeth Alice Snow, May 28, 1966; children: Kirsten Kari, Margaret Elizabeth. BA, Harvard U., 1964; MA, MS, U. Mich., 1967, PhD, 1969. Asst. prof. U. Toledo, 1969-71; assoc. prof. Purdue U., West Lafayette, Ind., 1971-81, prof., 1981—, dir. engring. rsch. ctr., 1986—. Author: Operations Research, 1976 (Book of the Yr. 1977); contbr. over 100 articles to profl. jours. Mem. NAE, Inst. Indsl. Engrs. (Disting. Rsch. award 1982), Soc. Mfg. Engrs., AAAS. Achievements include invention of CAN-Q which is a method for predicting performance of manufacturing systems used by hundreds of companies. Office: Purdue U Sch Industrial Engineering West Lafayette IN 47907-1287

SOLBERG, KENNETH R. state legislator; b. Minot, N.D., Jan. 10, 1940; m. Chris; children: Tom, Brad, Stacy. Mem. N.D. Senate from 7th dist., Bismark, 1991—; mem. judiciary, agr., transp., joint constn. rev. coms. N.D. Senate, mem. appropriations com. Owner, mgr. Rugby Livestock Sales, 1965—. Mem. Rugby City Coun., 1966-72; bd. dirs. Regional Selective Svc., 1980, Good Samaritan Hosp., 1981-87, pres., 1985-86, chmn. health found., 1988; alt. del. Nat. Rep. Conv., 1988. Recipient DSA award N.D. Jaycees, 1965. Mem. Eagles Club, Am. Legion, Stockmens Assn. (bd. dirs. 1985), Cattlemen's Assn., Rugby C. of C. Home: 207 Sunset Ln Rugby ND 58368-2510 Office: ND Senate State Capitol Bismarck ND 58505

SOLBERG, LOREN ALBIN, state legislator, secondary education educator; b. Blackduck, Minn., Nov. 3, 1941; s. Albin Andy and Mabel Ethel (Bergen) S.; m. Joan Maxine Olsen, Aug. 9, 1969; children: Sean, John, Previn, Kjirstin. BS, Bemidji (Minn.) State U., 1965, MS, 1974; MPA, Harvard U., 1990. Tchr. math. Ind. Sch. Dist. 316, Coleraine, Minn., 1965—; mem. Minn. Ho. of Reps., St. Paul, 1983—. Instr. math. Itasca C.C., Grand Rapids, Minn., 1981-83; instr. computer sci. Harvard U., Cambridge, Mass., 1988. Mayor City of Bovey, Minn., 1970-82. Democrat. Lutheran. Home: 115 Fifth Ave Bovey MN 55709-0061 Office: Minn Ho of Reps State Office Bldg Saint Paul MN 55155-0001

SOLBERG, WINTON UDELL, history educator; b. Aberdeen, S.D., Jan. 11, 1922; s. Ole Alexander and Bertha Georgia (Tschappat) S.; m. Ruth Constance Walton, Nov. 8, 1952; children— Gail Elizabeth, Andrew Walton, Kristin Ruth. A.B. magna cum laude, U. S.D., 1943, LHD (hon.), 1987; student, Biarritz (France) Am. U., 1946; A.M., Harvard, 1947, Ph.D., 1954. Instr., then asst. prof. social scis. U.S. Mil. Acad., 1951-54; instr., then asst. prof. history Yale U., 1954-58; fellow Pierson Coll., 1955-58, Morse fellow, 1958; James Wallace prof. history Macalester Coll., 1958-62; vis. prof. U. Ill., 1961-62, assoc. prof. history, 1962, prof., 1967—, chmn. dept. history, 1970-72. Research fellow Ctr. Study History of Liberty in Am., Harvard U., 1962-63; summer research scholar Henry E. Huntington Library, San Marino, Calif., 1959; dir. Coe Found. Am. Studies Inst., summers 1960-62; lectr., cons. Army War Coll., 1959-62; lectr. U.S. Command and Gen. Staff Sch., 1963-64; Fulbright lectr. Johns Hopkins U. Bologna, 1967-68, Moscow (USSR) State U., 1978, U. Calcutta India, 1993; vis. prof. Konan U., Kobe, Japan, 1981; USIA Lectr., Korea and Malaysia, 1985, Korea, 1992. Author: The Federal Convention and the Formation of the Union of the American States, 1958, The Constitutional Convention and the Formation of the Union, 1990, The University of Illinois, 1867-1894, 1968, Redeem the Time: The Puritan Sabbath in Early America, 1977, History of American Thought and Culture, 1983, Cotton Mather, The Christian Philosopher, 1994, The University of Illinois, 1894-1904: The Shaping of the University, 2000; also articles. Mem. Ill. Humanities Council, 1973-75; sec. Council on Study of Religion, 1981-85. Served to maj. inf. AUS, 1943-46, 51-54; lt. col. U.S. Army Res. Recipient Faculty Achievement award Burlington No. Found., 1986, Disting. Teaching award U. Ill. Coll. Liberal Arts and Scis., 1988; NEH sr. fellow, 1974-75; NSF research grantee, 1981-82 Mem. Am. Hist. Assn., So. Hist. Assn., Orgn. Am. Historians, Am. Studies Assn. (pres. Mid-Am. 1985-86), Am. Soc. Ch. History (pres. 1985-86), AAUP (chpt. pres. 1965-66, mem. council 1969-72, 1st v.p. 1974-76), Phi Beta Kappa. Episcopalian. Home: 8 Lake Park Rd Champaign IL 61822-7101 Office: U Ill History Dept Urbana IL 61801 E-mail: wsolberg@uiuc.edu.

SOLED, KATHLEEN A. airline company executive; Degree in criminal justice, St. Anselm Coll.; grad., Rutgers U. Law Sch. Sole practice law, until 1992; sr. atty. Trans World Airlines Inc., St. Louis, 1992-98, sr. v.p., gen. counsel, 1998—. Office: One City Ctr 515 N 6th St Saint Louis MO 63101-1842

SOLGANIK, MARVIN, real estate executive; b. Chgo., Nov. 7, 1930; s. Harry and Dora (Fastoff) S.; m. Judith Rosenberg, Sept. 11, 1960; children: Randall, Janet, Robert. BBA, Case Western Res. U., 1952. Real estate broker, Cleve., 1950-65, Herbert Laronge Inc., 1965-68; sr. v.p. real estate Revco D.S., Inc., Twinsburgh, Ohio, 1968—, corp. dir., 1974—; guest lectr. Cleve. State U., Case Western Res. U., Cuyahoga Community Coll., Ohio No. U., Cleve. Real Estate Bd. Adj. prof., Ohio No. U. Vol. jewish Welfare Fund, Shaker heights, Ohio; chmn. capital and budget coms. Jewish Fedn.; chmn. Agnon Sch. Bdlg. Com.; bd. dirs. Bellfair-J.C.B.-Home for Emotionally Disturbed Children, Visconsi Cos. Recipient Appreciation award Am. Soc. Real Estate Appraisers, Akron-Cleve. chpt., 1971 Mem. Nat. Assn. Corp. Real Estate Officers, Internat. Council Shopping Ctrs. Office: D S Revco 22925 Holmwood Rd Shaker Heights OH 44122-3005

SOLICH, FRANK, coach; b. Cleve., Sept. 8, 1944; s. Frank Solich Sr.; m. Pamela Solich; children: Cindy, Jeff. BS, U. Nebr., 1966, MEd, 1972. Coach football, runningbacks U. Nebr., Lincoln, head coach football, freshman, head coach football. Office: U Nebr 221 S Stadium Lincoln NE 68588*

SOLIMAN, SAM, gas, oil and chemical industry executive, investment company executive; BS in chemical engring., Texas A&M Univ., 1984. Assoc. McKinsey & Co., 1993—95; CFO Koch Industries, 2000—02; pres. Koch Investment Group, 2001—. Lt. USN, 1984—89. Office: Koch Industries 20 E Greenway Plaza Houston TX 77046 E-mail: solimans@kochind.com.

SOLOMON, DAVID EUGENE, engineering company executive; b. Milton, Pa., June 22, 1931; s. Oren Benjamin and Bernardine Claire Solomon; m. Joyce Marie Hoffman, June 24, 1950; children: Timothy, Melissa, Daniel. AB, Susquehanna U., 1958; MS, Bucknell U., 1960; MBA, Ea. Mich. U., 1974. Sr. engr. Westinghouse Electric Corp., Balt., 1959-65; rsch. engr. U. Mich., 1965-67; chief engr. Electro-Optics divsn. Bendix Corp., 1967-72; v.p. ops. KMS Fusion, Inc., Ann Arbor, Mich., 1972-85; pres., CEO Solohill Engring. Inc., 1985—. Bd. dirs. Ann Arbor Engring. Inc., SoloHill Labs. Inc. Patentee in field. With USN, 1950-55. Fellow IEEE. Office: 4220 Varsity Dr Ann Arbor MI 48108-2241 E-mail: solomon@ic.net.

SOLOMON, RANDALL LEE, lawyer; b. Dayton, Ohio, June 8, 1948; BA summa cum laude, Wright State U., 1970; JD, Case Western Res. U., 1973. Bar: Ohio 1973, U.S. Dist. Ct. (no. dist.) Ohio 1973, U.S. Ct. Appeals (6th cir.) 1973, U.S. Ct. Appeals (fed. cir.) 1988. Ptnr. Baker & Hostetler, Cleve. Speaker in field. Fellow Am. Coll. Trial Lawyers; mem. ABA (mem. litigation, tort and ins. practice sects., mem. toxic and hazardous substances and environ. law coms.), Ohio State Bar Assn., Cleve. Bar Assn. (chair litigation sect. 1991-92), Nat. Inst. Trial Advocacy (mem. nat. session 1978), Def. Rsch. Inst., Anthony J. Celebrezze Inn. of Ct. (master). Office: Baker & Hostetler LLP 3200 Nat City Ctr 1900 E 9th St Ste 3200 Cleveland OH 44114-3475 E-mail: rsolomon@bakerlaw.com.

SOLON, SAM GEORGE, state legislator; b. Duluth, Minn., June 25, 1931; s. Nick and Demitra (Stasinopooulos) S.; m. Carole Wedan, 1958 (div.); m. Paula Korhonen, 1974 (div.); children: Jon, Nicholas, Chris, Dina, Vicki; m. Yvonne Prettner, 1996. BS, U. Minn., 1958. Minn. State rep. Dist. 7, 1971-72, Minn. State sen., 1973—2001; ret. tchr. Duluth Bd. Edn. Chmn. com. and consumer protection com.; mem. edn., higher edn. divsn., family svc., health care and family svc. fin. divsn. and rules and adminstrn. coms. Mem. VFA, Eagles, Am. Hellenic Edn. Progressive Assn., Am. Legion, Moose, Duluth Hall of Fame Com. Died Dec. 28, 2001.

SOLOSKI, JOHN, journalism and communications educator; AB cum laude, Boston Coll., 1974; MA in journalism, Univ. Iowa, 1976, PhD, 1978. Copy editor, reporter Iowa City Press Citizen, 1977-78; instr. Univ. Iowa, 1977-78, asst. prof. sch. journalism and mass communication, 1978-84, assoc. prof. sch. journalism and mass communication, 1984-85, assoc. prof., head of grad. studies, 1985-92, prof., head of grad. studies, 1992-94, prof., acting dir., 1994-95, prof. sch. of journalism and mass communication, 1995-96, prof., dir. sch. of journalism and mass communication, 1996—, prof. law, 1996—. Con. Ottumwa Courier, 1976-77, Iowa City Press-Citizen, 1976-77; speaker in field; vis. prof. Univ. Tech., Sydney, Australia, 1995. Co-author: Reforming Libel Law, 1992, Libel and the Press: Myth and Reality, 1987; contbr. numerous articles to profl. jours.; editor: Journalism and Communication Monographs, 1994—. Recipient Soc. of Profl. Journalists Disting. Svc. award, 1988; numerous rsch. grants. Office: Univ Iowa Sch Journalism Iowa City IA 52242

SOLOVY, JEROLD SHERWIN, lawyer; b. Chgo., Apr. 10, 1930; s. David and Ida (Wilensky) S.; m. Kathleen Hart; children: Stephen, Jonathan. BA, U. Mich., 1952; LLB, Harvard U., 1955. Bar: Ill. 1955. Assoc. Jenner & Block, Chgo., 1955-63, ptnr., 1963—, chmn., 1991—. Chmn. Spl. Commn. on Adminstrn. Justice in Cook County, 1984-91, Ill. Supreme Ct. Spl. Commn. on Adminstrn. of Justice, 1992-93, Criminal Justice Project of Cook County, 1987-91. Mem. Cook County Jud. Adv. Council, Chgo., 1975-77, 82-89, chmn., 1989-91; trustee U.S. Supreme Ct. Hist. Soc., 1993—. Fellow Am. Coll. Trial Lawyers; mem. ABA, Chgo. Bar Assn., Ill. State Bar. Assn., Am. Law Inst. Clubs: Standard; Lake Shore Country (Chgo.). Office: Jenner & Block 1 E IBM Plz Ste 4400 Chicago IL 60611-5698 E-mail: jsolovy@jenner.com.

SOLOWAY, ALBERT HERMAN, medicinal chemist; b. Worcester, Mass., May 29, 1925; s. Bernard and Mollie (Raphaelson) S.; m. Barbara Berkowicz, Nov. 29, 1953; children: Madeleine Rae, Paul Daniel, Renee Ellen. Student, U.S. Naval Acad., 1945-46; BS, Worcester Poly. Inst., 1948; PhD, U. Rochester, 1951. Postdoctoral fellow Nat. Cancer Inst. at Sloan-Kettering Inst., N.Y.C., 1951-53; research chemist Eastman Kodak Co., Rochester, N.Y., 1953-56; asst. chemist Mass. Gen. Hosp., Boston, 1956-61, asso. chemist, 1961-73; asso. prof. med. chemistry Northeastern U., 1966-68, prof. medicinal chemistry, chmn. dept., 1968-71, prof. medicinal chemistry and chemistry, chmn. dept. medicinal chemistry and pharmacology, 1971-74; dean Coll. Pharmacy and Allied Health Professions, 1975-77; dean Coll. Pharmacy Ohio State U., Columbus, 1977-88, prof. medicinal chemistry, 1977-98, Kimberly prof. pharmacy, 1997-2000, dean, prof. emeritus, 1998—. Author rsch. in medicinal chemistry, boron neutron capture therapy of cancer. Recipient Disting. Achievements in Boron Sci. award Boron USA, 1994. Fellow AAAS, Acad. Pharm. Soc.; mem. AHS, Am. Chem. Soc., Am. Assn. Coll. Pharmacy, Am. Assn. Cancer Rsch. Office: Ohio State U 500 W 12th Ave Columbus OH 43210-1214 E-mail: soloway.1@osu.edu.

SOLSO, THEODORE M. manufacturing executive; m. Denny; 3 children. BA, DePauw U., 1969; MBA, Harvard U., 1971. Asst. to v.p. personnel Cummins Engine Co., Inc., Columbus, Ind., 1971, exec. dir. personnel, 1977-80, v.p. spl. engine markets, 1984-86, v.p. mktg., 1986-88, v.p., gen. mgr. engine bus., 1988-92, exec. v.p. opers., 1992-95, COO, 1994-00, pres., 1995-00, chmn., CEO, 1999—; dir. adminstrn. CAEMI Cummins., Brazil; v.p., mng. dir. Holset Engring. Co., Ltd. (Cummins' U.K. subs.), 1980-84. Bd. dirs. Ashland, Inc., Cyprus Amax Minerals, Inc. Bd. trustees DePauw U.; bd. advisors U. Mich. Sch. Bus.; past bd. dirs. Heritage Fund Bartholomew County, Ind.; chmn. campaign Bartholomew County United Way; bd. dirs. Otter Creek Golf Course, Columbus, Ind. Mem. Mfrs. Alliance (bd. trustees). Office: Cummins Engine Co Inc 500 Jackson St Columbus OH 43206-1353

SOMER, THOMAS JOSEPH (T.J. SOMER), police officer, lawyer; b. Chicago Heights, Oct. 13, 1953; m. Cynthia Flamini; 2 children. BA, Nat. Louis U., 1987; JD, John Marshall Law Sch., 1991. Republican candidate for U.S. House, 2d dist., Ill., 1996. Roman Catholic.

SOMERS, K(ARL) BRENT, consumer products company executive; b. Logan, Utah, Aug. 4, 1948; s. W. Karl and Beth (Johnson) S.; m. Kathryn Lenhart, Aug. 8, 1978; children: Anne Marie, Mary Margaret, Andrew, Robert, Maren. BS, Utah State U., 1972; MBA, Brigham Young U., 1975. Fin. analyst U.S. Shoe Corp., Cin., 1975-80, dir. corp. fin. planning, 1979-83, asst. treas., 1983-85; v.p. fin. Cin. Shoe Co., 1985-86; treas, Precision Lenscrafters, 1986-87, dir. fin. and acctg., 1987, chief fin. officer/v.p. fin. and acctg., 1987-90; chief fin. officer/v.p. fin. U.S. Shoe Corp., 1990—; sr. exec. v.p., CFO KeyCorp, Cleve. Office: Key Corporation 127 Public Sq Cleveland OH 44114-1306

SOMMER, ANNEMARIE, pediatrician; b. Königsberg, Prussia, Federal Republic Germany, Jan. 1, 1932; came to U.S., 1955; d. Heinrich Otto and Maria Magdalena (Kruppa) S. BA, Wittenberg U., Springfield, Ohio, 1960; MD, Ohio State U., 1964. Diplomate Am. Bd. Pediat., Am. Bd. Med. Genetics. Intern Grant Hosp., Columbus, Ohio, 1964-65; resident in pediat. Children's Hosp., 1965-67; NIH fellow in med. genetics, 1968-70; from asst. prof. pediatrics to assoc. prof. Coll. Medicine Ohio State U., Columbus, 1975-97, prof., 1997-99, chief genetics div., 1984-98. Mem. adv. bd. Heinzerling Found., Columbus, 1980—; bd. dirs. Regional Genetics Ctr., Columbus. Contbr. articles to profl. jours. Com. mem. Ohio Prevention MR/DD Coalition, Columbus, 1987; bd. dirs. Franklin County Bd. Health, Columbus, 1985—. Fellow Am. Acad. Pediatrics, Am. Bd.

Med. Genetics, Am. Coll. Med. Genetics (founder); mem. Ctrl. Ohio Pediatric Soc., Midwest Soc. for Pediatric Research, Dublin (Ohio) Hist. Soc. Lutheran. Home: 4700 Brand Rd Dublin OH 43017-9530 Office: Ohio State Coll Medicine Sect Human and Molecular Genetics 700 Childrens Dr Columbus OH 43205-2664

SOMMER, HOWARD ELLSWORTH, textile executive; b. Kansas City, Mo., May 1, 1918; s. Frederick H. and Edna O. (Olsen) S.; m. Sarah Scott McElevey, June 20, 1942; children: Scott E., Paul F. BA magna cum laude, Dartmouth Coll., 1940, degree in engring. (hon.), 1997; MBA, Harvard U., 1942. Cert. mgmt. cons. With Wolf & Co. CPAs, Chgo., 1946-76, chmn. mng. group, 1960-76; dir. Jockey Internat., Kenosha, Wis., 1959—, sr. v.p., chmn. audit com., 1979-89. Author: Procedural Routine for a Business Audit, 1947; also articles. Counsellor, Chgo. chpt. Boy Scouts Am.; vestryman, warden Episcopalian ch. Lt. col. AUS, 1942-46. Decorated Bronze Star; Croix de Guerre with palms; Medaille de la Reconnaissance (France) Mem. ASME, Assn. Cons. Mgmt. Engrs. (cert. of Award 1956, v.p. 1970-72), Inst. Mgmt. Cons. (cert. mgmt. cons., past dir.), Univ. Club (pres., dir. Chgo. chpt. 1959-61), Indian Hill Club, Harvard Bus. Sch. Club (dir. Chgo. chpt. 1958-59), North Shore Cotillion Club, Dartmouth Club, Halter Wildlife Club, Masons (32 degree), Shriners, Phi Beta Kappa, Chi Phi.

SOMMERS, DAVID LYNN, architect; b. Salem, Ohio, June 17, 1949; s. Carl Ervin and Jean (Mohr) S. BArch, Kent State U., 1974. Registered architect, Ohio. Designer, draftsman Rice & Stewart, Architects, Painesville, Ohio, 1974-76; assoc. architect Prentiss Brown Assoc., Kent, 1977-81; project architect Edward W. Prusak, Assoc., Ravenna, 1982-83; pvt. practice Kent, 1983—. Mem. archtl. adv. com. Kent Planning Commn., 1985—; mem. Franklin Twp. Bd. Zoning Appeals; bd. bldg. appeals, City of Kent Bldg. Dept.; bd. dirs. Townhall II Drug and Crisis Intervention Ctr., Kent, 1986. Named one of Outstanding Young Men of Am., 1979-81. Mem. AIA (pres. Akron chpt. 1991—), Archs. Soc. Ohio, Jaycees (pres. Kent chpt. 1981-82, Jaycee of Yr. 1980, Keyman of Yr. 1981), Rotary (bd. dirs. 1994-96). Office: 136 N Water St # 208 Kent OH 44240-2450

SOMMESE, ANDREW JOHN, mathematics educator; b. N.Y.C., May 3, 1948; s. Joseph Anthony and Frances (Lia) S.; m. Rebecca Rooze DeBoer, June 7, 1971; children: Rachel, Ruth. BA in Math., Fordham U., 1969; PhD in Math., Princeton U., 1973. Gibbs instr. Yale U., New Haven, 1973-75; asst. prof. Cornell U., Ithaca, N.Y., 1975-79; assoc. prof. U. Notre Dame, Ind., 1979-83, prof. of math., 1983—, chair dept. math., 1988-92, Vincent J. Duncan and Annamarie Micus Duncan chair math., 1994—. Mem. Inst. for Advanced Study, Princeton, N.J., 1975-76; guest prof. U. Bonn, Germany, 1978-79; guest rschr. Max Planck Inst. for Math., Bonn, 1992-93; cons. GM Rsch., Warren, Mich., 1986-97. Editor: Manuscripta Mathematica jour., 1986-93, Advances in Geometry, 2000;mem. editl. bd. Milan Jour. Math., 2002; contbr. articles to profl. publs. Recipient Rsch. award for Sr. U.S. Scientists Alexander Von Humboldt found., 1993; A.P. Sloan Found. rsch. fellow, 1979. Mem. Am. Math. Soc., Soc. for Indsl. and Applied Math., Phi Beta Kappa. Office: U Notre Dame Dept Math Notre Dame IN 46556 E-mail: sommese@nd.edu.

SONDEL, PAUL MARK, pediatric oncologist, educator; b. Milw., Aug. 14, 1950; s. Robert F. and Audrey J. (Dworkus) S.; m. Sherie Ann Katz, Jan. 1, 1973; children: Jesse Adam, Beth Leah, Elana Rose, Jodi Zipporah. BS with honors, U. Wis., 1971, PhD in Genetics, 1975; MD magna cum laude, Harvard Med. Sch., Boston, 1977. Diplomate Nat. Bd. Med. Examiners, Am. Bd. Pediatrics; lic. physician, Wis. Postdoctoral rsch. fellow Harvard Med. Sch., Boston, 1975-77; intern in pediatrics U. Minn. Hosp., Mpls., 1977-78; resident in pediatris U. Wis. Hosp. and Clinics, Madison, 1978-80; asst. prof. pediatrics, human oncology and genetics U. Wis., 1980-84, assoc. prof., 1984-86, prof. pediatrics, human oncology and genetics, 1987—, head divsn. pediatric hematology/oncology, program leader, 1990—; assoc. dir. U Wisc. Cancer Ctr., 1996-99. Sub-fellow pediatric oncology; Midwest Children's Cancer Ctr., Milw., 1980; vis. scientist dept. cell biology Weizmann Inst. Sci., Rehovot, Israel, 1987; chmn. immunology com. Children's Cancer Group 1990—; mem. cancer ctr. rev. com. Nat. Cancer Inst., 1997—. Sr. editor Clin. Cancer Rsch., 1996-99; mem. editl. bd. Jour. Immunology, 1985-87, Jour. Nat. Cancer Inst., 1987—, Jour. Biol. Response Modifiers, 1990—, BLOOD, 1992—, Natural Immunity, 1992—; contbr. articles to Jour. Exptl. Mediacine, Jour. Immunology, Cellular Immunology, Immunol. Revs., Med. Pediatric Oncology, Wis. State Med. Jour., Jour. Biol. Response Modifiers, Jour. Pediatrics, Jour. Clin. Oncology, Jour. Clin. Investigation, and others. State of Wis. Regents scholar, 1968; J.A. and G.L. Hartford Found. fellow, 1981-84. Mem. Am. Assn. Immunologists, Am. Assn. Clin. Histocompatibility Typing, Am. Fedn. Clin. Rsch., Am. Soc. Pediatric Hematology/Oncology, Am. Assn. Cancer Rsch., Am. Soc. Transplant Physicians, Am. Soc. Clin. Oncology, Am. Acad. Pediatrics, Leukemia Soc. Am. (bd. dirs. Wis. chpt. 1987-90 Achievements include patent for Typing Leukocyte Antigens; research on clinical and immunological effects of human recombinant Interleukin-2 and monoclonal antibodies. Home: 1114 Winston Dr Madison WI 53711-3161 Office: U Wis K4/448 Clin Sci Ctr 600 Highland Ave Madison WI 53792-3284 E-mail: pmsondel@facstaff.wisc.edu.

SONDERBY, SUSAN PIERSON, federal judge; b. Chgo., May 15, 1947; d. George W. and Shirley L. (Eckstrom) Pierson; m. James A. De Witt, June 14, 1975 (dec. 1978); m. Peter R. Sonderby, Apr. 7, 1990. AA, Joliet (Ill.) Jr. Coll., 1967; BA, U. Ill., 1969; JD, John Marshall Law Sch., 1973. Bar: Ill. 1973, U.S. Dist. Ct. (cen. and so. dists.) Ill. 1978, U.S. Dist. Ct. (no. dist.) Ill. 1984, U.S. Ct. Appeals (7th Cir.) 1984. Assoc. O'Brien, Garrison, Berard, Kusta and De Witt, Joliet, 1973-75, ptnr., 1975-77; asst. atty. gen. consumer protection div., litigation sect. Office of the Atty. Gen., Chgo., 1977-78, asst. atty. gen., chief consumer protection divsn. Springfield, 1978-83; U.S. trustee for no. dist. Ill. Chgo., 1983-86; judge U.S. Bankruptcy Ct. (no. dist.) Ill., 1986—, chief fed. bankruptcy judge, 1998—. Mem. law faculty Fed. Judicial Tng. Ctr., Practising Law Inst., U.S. Dept. Justice, Nat. Bankruptcy Inst., Ill. Continuing Edn.; adj. faculty De Paul U. Coll. Law, Chgo., 1986; spl. asst. atty. gen., 1972—78; past mem. U.S. Trustee adv. com.; consumer adv. coun. Fed. Res. Bd.; past sec. of State Fraudulent I.D. com. Dept. of Ins. Task Force on Improper Claims Practices; former chair pers. rev. bd., mem. task force race and gender bias U.S. Dist. Ct.; jud. conf. planning com. 7th Cir. Jud. Conf.; former mem. Civil Justice Reform Act Adv. Com., Ct. Security com.; mem. Adminstrv. Office of the U.S. Cts. Bankruptcy Judges Adv. Group. Contbr. articles to profl. jours. Mem. Fourth Presbyn. Ch., Art Inst. Chgo.; past mem. Westminster Presbyn. Ch., Chgo. Coun. of Fgn. Rels.; past bd. dirs. Land of Lincoln Coun. Girl Scouts U.S.; past mem. individual guarantors com. Goodman Theatre, Chgo.; past chair clubs and orgns. Sangamon County United Way Capital campaign; past bd. dirs., chair house rules com. and legal subcom. Lake Point Tower; past mem. Family Svc. Ctr., Aid to Retarded Citizens, Henson Robinson Zoo. Named Young Career Woman, Bus. and Profl. Women; recipient Spl. Achievement award, Dept. Justice, 1984, Disting. Svc. Alumni award, Joliet Jr. Coll., 1987, Disting. Alumni award, John Marshall Law Sch., 1988, Dir.'s award, Exec. Office U.S. Trustee, Leadership award, Internat. Orgn. Women Execs., Outstanding Svc. to Bench, Am. Bankruptcy Inst., 1990. Fellow: Am. Coll. Bankruptcy (circuit admissions com.); mem.: ATLA, Comml. Law League Am. (former exec. coun. mem., bankruptcy and insolvency sect., coord. with nat. conf. bankruptcy judges com.), Nat. Conf. Bankruptcy Judges (co-chair ednl. program com. conf. 2001, liaison with bankruptcy rev. commn. com.), 7th Cir. Bar Assn. (former treas., judicial conf. planning com.), Fed. Bar Assn. (hon.), Am. Bankruptcy Inst., Fed. Bar Assn., Chgo. Archtl. Found., John Marshall Law Sch. Alumni Assn. (bd. dirs.), Nordic Law Club (past legisl. com.), Lawyers Club Chgo. (hon.), Abraham Lincoln Marovitz Inn of Ct. (master, former pres., membership com.). Avocations: travel, flying, interior decorating. Office: US Bankruptcy Ct 219 S Dearborn St Ste 638 Chicago IL 60604-1702

SONDEREGGER, THEO BROWN, psychology educator; b. Birmingham, Ala., May 31, 1925; d. Ernest T. and Vera M. (Sillox) Brown; children: Richard Paul, Diane Carol, Douglas Robert. BS, Fla. State U., 1946; MA in Chemistry, U. Nebr., 1948, MA in Exptl. Psychology, 1960; PhD in Clin. Psychology, U. Nebr., 1965. Lic. psychologist, Calif; clin. lic., cert. Nebr. Asst. prof. U. Nebr. Med. Ctr., Omaha, 1965-71, Nebr. Wesleyan U., Lincoln, 1965-68, U. Nebr., Lincoln, 1968-71, assoc. prof., 1971-76, prof., 1976-94; ret., 1994; prof. emeritus, 1995—. Vol. assoc. prof. U. Nebr. Med. Ctr., 1972-77, courtesy prof. med. psychology, 1977-95. Editor: Nebr. Symposium on Motivation, 1974, 84, 91, Problems of Perinatal Drug Dependence: Research and Clinical Implications, 1986, Neurobehavioral Toxicology and Teratology vol. 8, 1988-89, Problems of Perinatal Drug Dependence, 1979, 82, 84, Feminist Therapy Interchange, 1988-89, 91, Perinatal Substance Abuse: Research and Clinical Implications, 1992, Agendas for Aging, 1994-97. Mem. grant rev. coms. Nat. Inst. Drug Abuse, 1983-84, 85, 91-94. Tribute to Women award Lincoln YMCA, 1985, named Outstanding Rsch. Scientist Nebr. Chpt. Sigma Xi, 1991, Outstanding Contbn. to Status of Women, U N-L Chancellors Commn. on Status of Women, 1994, Pound Howard Disting. Career Achievement award, 1996. Fellow: AAAS, Am. Psychol. Soc., Am. Psychol. Assn.; mem.: Region V Adv. Coun. on Drugs, Fetal Alcohol (bd. dir. child guidance ctr. 1997—, bd. dir. UN-L emeriti assoc. 1999—2001), Soc. Neuroscis., Nebr. Psychol. Assn. (pres. 1972), Internat. Soc. Psychoneuroendocrinology, Internat. Soc. Devel. Psychobiology, Midwestern Psychol. Assn., Advanced Feminist Therapy Inst., Altrusa YWCA, Sigma Xi 1986, Phi Beta Kappa (sec. Nebr. chpt. 1974). Avocations: painting, photography.

SONDERMAN, JOE R. news executive; Bur. chief St. Louis Met. Network News, 1995—. Office: 8251 Maryland Ave Ste 108 Clayton MO 63105-3659

SONNEDECKER, GLENN ALLEN, pharmaceutical historian, pharmaceutical educator; b. Creston, Ohio, Dec. 11, 1917; s. Ira Elmer and Letia (Linter) S.; m. Cleo Bell, Apr. 3, 1943; 1 child, Stuart Bruce. BS, Ohio State U., 1942; MS, U Wis., 1950, PhD, 1952; Dr. Sci. honoris causa, Ohio State U., 1964, Phila. Coll. Pharmacy and Sci., 1989; PharmD honoris causa, Mass. Coll. Pharmacy, 1974. Lic. pharmacist. Mem. editorial staff Sci. Service, Washington, 1942-43; editor Jour. Am. Pharm. Assn. (practical pharmacy edit.), 1943-48; asst. prof. U. Wis., 1952-56, asso. prof., 1956-60, prof., 1960-81, Edward Kremers prof., 1981-86; sec. Am. Inst. History of Pharmacy, 1949-57, dir., 1957-73, 81-85, hon. dir. life, chmn. bd., 1988-89; editor-in-chief RPh, 1978-80. Sec., bd. dirs. Friends of Hist. Pharmacy, 1945-49; chmn. Joint Com. on Pharmacy Coll. Librs., 1960-61; U.S. del. Internat. Pharm. Fedn., 1953, 55, 62; U.S. rep. to Mid. East Pharm. Congress, Beirut, 1956; sec. sect. history of pharmacy and biochemistry Pan-Am. Congress Pharmacy and Biochemistry, 1957. Co-author books; contbr. to pharm. and hist. publs. Recipient Edward Kremers award (for writings), 1964, Nat. award Rho Chi, 1967, Schelenz plaquette German Soc. for History of Pharmacy, 1971, Remington honor medal Am. Pharm. Assn., 1972, Urdang medal, 1976, Folch Andreu prize, Spain, 1985, Profile award Am. Found. Pharm. Edn., 1994; Am. Found. fellow, 1948-52, Guggenheim fellow, 1955, Fulbright Rsch. scholar, Germany, 1955-56. Mem. Am. Pharm. Assn. (life mem.; sec. sect. history of pharmacy 1949-50, vice chmn. 1950-51, chmn. 1951-52, rsch. assoc. 1964-65, chmn. joint task force with Acad. Pharm Scis. 1985, hon. chmn. bd. trustees 1985), Internat. Acad. History Pharmacy (1st v.p. 1970-81, pres. 1983-91, hon. pres. 1991—), Am. Assn. History of Medicine (exec. coun. 1966-69), Internat. Gesellschaft fur Geschichte der Pharmazie (exec. bd. 1965-89), hon. mem. socs. for history of pharmacy of Italy, Benelux, pan-Arab, Spain; mem. Sigma Xi, Rho Chi (mem. nat. exec. coun. 1957-59), Phi Delta Chi. Unitarian. Home: 2030 Chadbourne Ave Madison WI 53705-4047 Office: Univ Wis Sch of Pharmacy 777 Highland Ave Madison WI 53705-2222

SONNENSCHEIN, HUGO FREUND, academic administrator, economics educator; b. N.Y.C., Nov. 14, 1940; s. Leo William and Lillian Silver Sonnenschein; m. Elizabeth Gunn, Aug. 26, 1962; children: Leah, Amy, Rachel. AB, U. Rochester, 1961; MS, Purdue U., 1963, PhD, 1964, PhD (hon.) , 1996; PhD (hon.) , Tel Aviv U., 1993; D (hon.) , U. Autonoma Barcelona, Spain, 1994; PhD (hon.) , Lake Forest Coll., 1995, North Ctrl. Coll., 2001, U. Chgo., 2002. Faculty dept. econs. U. Minn., 1964—70, prof., 1968—70; prof. econs. U. Mass., Amherst, 1970—73, Northwestern U., 1973—76, Princeton (N.J.) U., 1976—87, Class of 1926 prof., 1987—88, provost, 1991—93; dean, Thomas S. Gates prof. U. Pa. Sch. Arts & Scis., Phila., 1988—91; pres. U. Chgo., 1993—2000, Hutchinson disting. prof., pres. emeritus, 2000—. Vis. prof. U. Andes, Columbia, 1965, Tel Aviv U., 1972, Hebrew U., 1973, U. Paris, 1978, U. Aix-en-Provence, France, 1978, Stanford U., 1984—85; bd. dirs. Van Kampen Mutual Funds. Editor: Econometrica, 1977—84; mem. editl. bd.: Jour. Econ. Theory, 1972—75, mem. editl. bd.: Jour. Math. Econs., 1974—, mem. editl. bd.: SIAM Jour., 1976—80; contbr. articles to profl. jours. Trustee U. Rochester, 1992—, U. Chgo., 1993—. Fellow, Social Sci. Rsch. Coun., 1967—68, NSF, 1970—, Ford Found., 1970—71, Guggenheim Found., 1976—77. Fellow: Econometric Soc. (pres. 1988—89), Am. Acad. Arts and Scis.; mem.: NAS, Am. Philos. Soc.

SONS, LINDA RUTH, mathematics educator; b. Chicago Heights, Ill., Oct. 31, 1939; d. Robert and Ruth (Diekelman) S. AB in Math., Ind. U., 1961; MS in Math., Cornell U., 1963, PhD in Math., 1966. Tchg. asst. Cornell U., Ithaca, N.Y., 1961-63, instr. math., summer 1963, rsch. asst., 1963-65; asst. prof. math. No. Ill. U., De Kalb, 1965-70, assoc. prof., 1970-78, prof., 1978—, presdl. tchg. prof. DeKalb, 1994-98, disting. tchg. prof., 1998—. Vis. assoc. prof. U. London, 1970-71; dir. undergrad. studies math. dept. No. Ill. U., 1971-77, exec. sec. univ. coun., 1978-79; chair faculty fund No. Ill. U. Found., De Kalb, 1982—. Author: (with others) A Study Guide for Introduction to Mathematics, 1976, Mathematical Thinking in a Quantitative World, 1990; contbr. articles to profl. jours. Mem. campus ministry com. No. Ill. Dist. Luth. Ch./Mo. Synod, Hillside, 1977—2001; mem. ch. coun. Immanuel Luth. Ch., DeKalb, 1978—85, 1987—89; pres. Luth. Women's Missionary League, 1974—87; bd. dirs., treas. DeKalb County Migrant Ministry, 1967—78. NSF Rsch. grantee, 1970-72, 74-75; recipient 1988 Award for Disting. Svc. of Ill. Sect. of the Math Assn. Am., 1991 Award for Excellence in Coll. Teaching of Ill. Coun. Tchrs. Math. Mem. Am. Math. Soc., Assn. for Women in Math., Math. Assn. Am. (mem. nat. bd. govs. 1989-92, mem. com. undergrad. program in math. 1990-96, chmn. coun. on awards 1997—, Disting. Svc. to Ill. Sect. award 1988, Disting. Coll. or Univ. Tchg. of Math. Sect. award 1995, Cert. Meritorious Svc. nat. award 1998), Ill. Sect. Math. Assn. (v.p. sect., pres.-elect, pres., then past pres. 1982-87, bd. dirs. 1989-92), London Math. Soc., Phi Beta Kappa (pres. No. Ill. assn. 1981-85), Sigma Xi (past. chpt. pres.). Achievements include research in mathematics education and research in classical complex analysis--especially value distribution for meromorphic functions with unbounded characteristic in the unit disc. Office: No Ill U Dept Math Scis Dekalb IL 60115

SOPRANOS, ORPHEUS JAVARAS, manufacturing company executive; b. Evanston, Ill., Oct. 4, 1935; s. James Javaras and Marigoula (Papalexatou) S.; m. Angeline Buches, Dec. 31, 1959; children— Andrew, Katherine. AB, MBA, U. Chgo., 1957. Mgmt. trainee Ford Motor Co., Chgo., 1958-59; with Amsted Industries, 1959—, dir. bus. research, 1966-70, treas., 1970-80, v.p., 1980—; pres. Amsted Internat., 1991-93, corp. v.p., 1993-2000, ret. Served with U.S. Army, 1958, 61-62. Mem. Univ. Club (Chgo.), Skokie Country Club. Clubs: Univ. (Chgo.), Skokie Country, Mid-Am.

SORBO, ALLEN JON, actuary, consultant; b. Blue Earth, Minn., Aug. 7, 1953; m. Karen Lee Anderson, June 5, 1982; children: Matthew Allen, Sunny Lynn. BA, Gustavus Adolphus Coll., 1975; MS, U. Wis., 1976. Cons. Stennes and Assocs., Mpls., 1976-78, Towers Perrin Forster and Crosby, Mpls., 1978-86, prin., 1986-87; prin.-in-charge health care actuarial svcs. Ernst and Whinney, Chgo., 1987-89; prin. Tillinghast, Towers, Perrin, Mpls., 1989-94; prin. and mgr. Towers Perrin Integrated Health Systems Cons., 1995-98; v.p. actuarial and underwriting svcs. Oxford Health Plans, Inc., Trumbull, Conn., 1998—. Mem. Am. Acad. Actuaries, Soc. Actuaries. Republican. Avocations: golf, skiing, fitness. Office: Oxford Health Plans Inc 48 Monroe Turnpike Trumbull CT 06611 E-mail: asactuary@aol.com.

SORENSEN, CHARLES W. academic administrator; V.p. acad. affairs Winona (Minn.) State U., until 1988; chancellor U. Wis., Stout, 1988—. Office: U Wis-Stout Office of Chancellor Menomonie WI 54751

SORENSEN, W. ROBERT, clergy member, church administrator; BA, Concordia Coll., Moorhead, Minn., 1956; MDiv, Luther Theol. Sem., 1959; PhD, U. Iowa, 1978. Exec. dir. Divsn. Higher Edn. and Schs., Evang. Luth. Ch. in Am., Chgo., 1988. Office: Evangelical Lutheran Church Am 8765 W Higgins Rd Chicago IL 60631-4101

SORTWELL, CHRISTOPHER T. food products executive; MBA, U. Chgo. With McKinsey & Co.; dir. corp. planning and devel. Stroh Brewery Co., 1985, v.p. corp. planning and devel., CFO, sr. v.p., 1990-96, CFO, exec. v.p., 1996—; exec. v.p., CFO, sec. Aurora Foods Inc., St. Louis, 2000—. Office: Aurora Foods Inc 11432 Lackland Rd Saint Louis MO 63146

SOSA, SAMUEL (SAMMY SOSA), professional baseball player; b. San Pedro de Macoris, Dominican Republic, Nov. 12, 1968; With Tex. Rangers, 1989; outfield Chgo. Cubs, 1989—. Selected to N.L All-Star Team, 1995, 98; 66 Homeruns in 1998 2nd only to Mark McGwire all time homeruns; lead major leagues in RBI, runs and total bases (416), 1998; RBI total 4th highest in NL history, 1998; record for new major league baseball record for homeruns in a single month (21), 1998; single season club record of 35 homeruns at Wrigley Field, 1998; named Player of Month of June, 1998; winner Roberto Clemente award for outstanding svc. to cmty. Major League Baseball, 1998. Office: Chgo Cubs 1060 W Addison St Chicago IL 60613-4383*

SOSVILLE, DICK, sales and marketing executive; V.p. sales and mktg. The Dow Chem. Co., Midland, Mich., v.p. engring. plastics, 1997—. Office: The Dow Chem Co 2030 Dow Ctr Midland MI 48674-0001

SOTELINO, GABINO, chef; b. Vigo, Spain; Mem. staff Hotel Ritz, Madrid, Plaza Athanee, Paris, Koons Hotel, Switzerland, Hilton Internat. Hotels, Montreal Expo., Madison Hotel, Washington; exec. chef Capitol Hill Restaurants, Le Perrouquet, Chgo.; head chef The Pump Room, 1980; owner, chef Ambria, 1980—, Un Grande Cafe, Chgo., 1981—, Cafe Ba-Ba-Reeba!, Chgo., 1985—, Mon Ami, Chgo., 1998—. Named Chef of Yr., Chefs of Am., 1990; recipient Perrier-Jouet Chef of Midwest award, James Beard Found., 1997, Medalla Merito Nacional os Fpain, 1990, Academie Culinaire de France. Mem.: Euro-Toque Inc. (pres. U.S. chpt.), Grand Master Chefs Assn. (nat. chmn.), Commanderie des Corden Bleus de France. Office: Ambria 2300 N Lincoln Park W Chicago IL 60614

SOTIR, MARK, automotive rental executive; B in Econs., Amherst Coll.; MBA, Harvard U. Group mktg. mgr. Coca-Cola Co.; sr. v.p. worldwide mktg. Budget Rent-A-Car Corp., 1997-98, pres., 1999-2000; v.p. ops. and reservations Budget Group, Inc., Daytona Beach, Fla., 1998-99, pres. worldwide reservation svcs., 1999-2000, pres. N.Am. vehicle rental ops., pres., COO, 2000—. Office: Budget Group Inc 4225 Naporville Rd Lisle IL 60532

SOUDER, MARK EDWARD, congressman; b. Ft. Wayne, Ind., July 18, 1950; s. Edward Getz and Irma (Fahling) S.; m. Diane Kay Zimmer, July 28; children: Brooke Diane, Nathan Elias, Zachary. BS, Ind. U., Ft. Wayne, 1972; MBA, U. Notre Dame, 1974. Mgmt. trainee Crossroads Furniture Co., Houston, 1974; mktg. mgr. Gabberts Furniture & Studio, Mpls., 1974-76; mktg. mgr., exec. v.p. Souder's Furniture & Studio, Grabill, Ind., 1976-80, pres., 1981-84; econ. devel. liaison for U.S. Rep. Dan Coats, from 1983; mem. U.S. Congress from Ind. 4th Dist., 1995—. Mem. edn. and workforce com., govt. reform and oversight com., small bus. com., natural resources com. Publicity chmn. Grabill County Fair, 1977—; advisor Dan Coats for Congress Com., 1980-81; mem. Ind. Area Devel. Coun.; mem. bus. alumni adv. com. Ind. U.-Ft. Wayne. Mem. Midwest Home Furnishings Assn. (dir. 1976-84, past treas., exec. v.p.), Ft. Wayne, Grabill C. of C., Allen County Hist. Soc., Alumni Assn. Ind. U. at Ft. Wayne (dir., past pres.), Alumni Assn. U. Notre Dame. Republican. Mem. Apostolic Christian Ch. Home: 13733 Ridgeview Ct Grabill IN 46741 Office: US House Reps 1227 Longworth House Office Building Washington DC 20515-0001*

SOUKUP, BETTY A. state legislator; b. Clarksburg, W.Va. m. Robert Soukup; 3 children. AS in Bus. Mgmt., BA in Comms. Arts. Mem. Iowa Senate from 15th dist., Des Moines, 1998—; mem. agr. com., mem. appropriations com.; mem. small bus., econs. devel. and tourism com. Iowa Senate, Des Moines, mem. ways and means com. Democrat. Office: State Capitol 9th And Grand Ave Des Moines IA 50319-0001 E-mail: betty_soukup@legis.state.ia.us.

SOURDIFF, GERALD, retired insurance company executive; CFO Luth. Bros., Mpls., 60 2001. Office: Luth Bros 625 4th Ave S Minneapolis MN 55415-1624

SOUTAS-LITTLE, ROBERT WILLIAM, mechanical engineer, educator; b. Oklahoma City, Feb. 25, 1933; s. Harry Glenn and Mary Evelyn (Miller) Little; m. Patricia Soutas, Sept. 3, 1982; children: Deborah, Catherine, Colleen, Jennifer, Karen. B.S. in Mech. Engring, Duke U., 1955; M.S., U. Wis., 1959, Ph.D., 1962. Design engr. Allis Chalmers Mfg. Co., Milw., 1955-57; instr. mech. engring. Marquette U., 1957-59; instr. U. Wis., Madison, 1959-62, asst. prof., 1962-63, Okla. State U., 1963-65; prof. Mich. State U., 1965—, chmn. dept. mech. engring., 1972-77, chmn. dept. biomechanics, 1977-90; dir. biomechanics evaluation lab., 1989—. Cons. A. C. Electronics Co., Ford Motor Co., CBS Research Lab., B. F. Goodrich Co.; lectr. AID, India, 1965 Author: Elasticity, 1973, Engineering Mechanics: Statics, 1999, Engineering Mechanics: Dynamics, 1999; contbr. articles to profl. jours. Vice pres. Okemos (Mich.) Sch. Bd., 1967-72; mem. Meridian Twp. (Mich.) Charter Commn., 1969-70, Meridian Twp. Zoning Bd. Appeals, 1969-71. Recipient award for excellence in instrn. engring. students Western Electric Co., 1970-71, Disting. Faculty award, 1996; NSF grantee, 1964-69, 79, NIH grantee, 1973-75, 79—. Fellow ASME; mem. Soc. Engring. Sci., Am. Soc. Biomechanics, Internat. Soc. Biomechanics, N.Am. Soc. Clin. Gait and Movement Analysis, Sigma Xi, Pi Tau Sigma, Ta Beta Pi. Home: 187 S Highland Dr Leland MI 49654-1143 Office: PO Box 1143 Leland MI 49654-1143 E-mail: soutas@egr.msu.edu.

SOUTHERN, ROBERT ALLEN, lawyer; b. Independence, Mo., July 17, 1930; s. James Allen and Josephine (Ragland) S.; m. Cynthia Agnes Drews, May 17, 1952; children: David D., William A., James M., Kathryn S. O'Brien. B.S. in Polit. Sci., Northwestern U., 1952, LL.B., 1954. Bar: Ill. 1955. Assoc. Mayer, Brown & Platt, Chgo., 1954-64, ptnr., 1965-96, mng. ptnr., 1978-91, L.A., 1991-96; CEO So. Assocs., Gurnee, Ill., 1997—. Editor in chief Northwestern U. Law Rev., 1953-54. Trustee, v.p., gen. counsel LaRabida Children's Hosp. and Rsch. Ctr., Chgo., 1974-89; trustee Kenilworth (Ill.) Union Ch., 1980-88; pres. Joseph Sears Sch. Bd., 1977-79; trustee Rush-Presbyn.-St. Luke's Med. Ctr., 1983-91, life trustee, 1991—; bd. dirs. Boys and Girls Clubs Chgo., 1986-91; governing mem. Orchestral Assn. Chgo., 1988-93. With U.S. Army, 1955-57. Mem. ABA, Chgo. Bar Assn., Lawyers Club Chgo., Order of Coif, Indian Hill Club, Chgo. Club. Office: 7600 Bittersweet Dr Gurnee IL 60031-5110 E-mail: rsouthern2@earthlink.net.

SOUTHGATE, MARIE THERESE, physician, editor; b. Detroit, Apr. 27, 1928; d. Clair and Josephine Marie (Hoefeyzers) S. BS, Coll. St. Francis, 1948, LLD (hon.), 1974; MD, Marquette U., 1960. Duplomate Nat. Bd. Med. Examiners. Rsch. editor Ill. Inst. Tech. Rsch. Inst., Chgo., 1951-55; intern St. Mary's Hosp., San Francisco, 1960-61; sr. editor Jour. of AMA, Chgo., 1962-75, dep. editor, 1975-88, sr. contbg. editor, 1988—. Mem. editorial bd. Forum, from 1978; mem. ad hoc com. on biol. scis. Ill. Bd. Huigher Edn., 1969-70; mem. ad hoc com. on lay deacons Archdiocese Chgo., 1973; trustee Coll. St. Francis, from 1978. Editor-in-chief Marquette Med. Rev., 1959-60. Mem. AMA, AAAS, Am. Med. Women's Assn. (v.p Chgo. chpt. 1967-68, mem. continuing med. edn. com. from 1978), Coun. Biology Editors. Office: JAMA 515 N State St Chicago IL 60610-4325

SOUTHWICK, DAVID LEROY, geology researcher; b. Rochester, Minn., Aug. 30, 1936; m. 1959; 3 children. BA, Carleton Coll., 1958; PhD in Geology, Johns Hopkins U., 1962. Geologist U.S. Geol. Survey, 1962-68; asst. prof. to prof. geology Macalester Coll., 1968-77; sr. geologist Minn. Geol. Survey, St. Paul, 1977-89, asst. dir., rsch. assoc., 1989-93, acting dir., 1993-94, dir., 1994—. Adj. assoc. prof. U. Minn., 1983-94, prof., 1994—. Fellow Geol. Assn. Can., Geol. Soc. Am.; mem. Am. Geophys. Union. Office: Minnesota Geological Survey 2642 University Ave W Saint Paul MN 55114-1057 E-mail: south002@tc.umn.edu.

SOVEY, WILLIAM PIERRE, manufacturing company executive; b. Helen, Ga., Aug. 26, 1933; s. Louis Terrell and Kathryn Bell (White) S.; m. Kathryne Owen Doyle, Dec. 28, 1958; children: Margaret Elizabeth, John Todd. B.S.I.E., Ga. Inst. Tech., 1955; grad., Advanced Mgmt. Program, Harvard U., 1976. Gen. mgr. automotive div. Atwood Vacuum Machine Co., Rockford, Ill., 1963-68; v.p. internat. A.G. Spalding & Bros., Inc., Chicopee, Mass., 1968-71; pres. Ben Hogan Co. div. AMF Inc., Ft. Worth, 1971-77, corp. v.p., group exec. indsl. products group Stamford, Conn., 1977-79, pres., chief operating officer, dir. White Plains, N.Y., 1982-85; pres., chief operating officer Newell Rubbermaid Inc., Freeport, Ill., 1986-92, CEO, 1992-97, 2000—, also bd. dirs. Served with USN, 1955-58. Home: PO Box 31102 Sea Island GA 31561-1102 Office: Newell Rubbermaid 29 E Stephenson St Freeport IL 61032

SOZEN, METE AVNI, civil engineering educator; b. Turkey, May 22, 1930; m. Joan Bates; children: Timothy, Adria, Ayshe. BCE, Roberts Coll., Turkey, 1951; MCE, U. Ill., 1952, PhD in Civil Engring., 1957; hon. doctorate, Bogazici U., Istanbul, Turkey, 1988, Janus Pannonius U., Pecs, Hungary, 1998. Registered structural engr., Ill. Jr. engr. Kaiser Engrs., Oakland, Calif., 1952; structural engr. Hardesty and Hanover, N.Y.C., 1953; research asst. civil engring. U. Ill., Urbana, 1953-55, research assoc., 1955-57, asst. prof. civil engring., 1957-59, assoc. prof., 1959-63, prof., 1963-94, Purdue U., 1994—. Cons. problems related to earthquake-resistant constrn. VA, various firms Europe, S.Am., U.S., UNESCO, UN Devel. Programs; cons. criteria for mass housing projects P.R.; adv. com. structural safety VA, rsch. project NSF, Applied Tech. Coun., Los Alamos and Sandia Nat. Labs.; chief investigator various NSF contracts and grants. Contbr. over 125 tech. papers, monographs, procs., reports to profl. jours.; presenter numerous papers to profl. meetings U.S.A, Japan, Italy, India, Turkey, Mexico. Recipient Drucker award U. Ill., 1986, Howard award, 1987, Boase award, 1988, Parlar Sci. and Tech. prize Mid. East Tech. U., Ankara, Turkey, 1995, ASEE Gen. Electric Sr. Rsch. award, 1997, Ill. Sect. Structural Group Lifetime Achievement award, 1998. Mem. NAE, ASCE (hon., Rsch. prize 1963, Raymond C. Reese award 1971, 94, Moiseiff award 1972, Howard award 1987, Raymond C. Reese Rsch. award 1994), Am. Concrete Inst. (Kelly award 1975, Bloem award 1985, Lindau award 1993), Am. Arbitration Assn. (nat. panel) Seismological Soc. Am., Swedish Royal Acad. Engring. Office: Purdue Univ Sch Civil Engring 1284 Civil Engineering West Lafayette IN 47907-1284 E-mail: sozen@ecn.purdue.edu.

SPADA, ROBERT F. state legislator; b. Cleveland, OH; BS, Cleveland State Coll.; MBA, Baldwin Wallace Coll. Business owner, accountant; mem. Ohio Senate from 24th dist., Columbus, 1999—. Mem. Parma Heights City Coun., Parma Area C. of C. Republican. Office: Senate Bldg 24 Dist 1st Fl Rm 143 Columbus OH 43215

SPAETH, NICHOLAS JOHN, lawyer, former state attorney general; b. Mahnomen, Minn., Jan. 27, 1950; AB, Stanford U., 1972, JD, 1977; BA, Oxford U., Eng., 1974. Bar: Minn. 1979, U.S. Dist. Ct. (Minn.) 1979, U.S. Ct. Appeals (8th cir.) 1979, N.D. 1980, U.S. Dist. Ct. (N.D.) 1980, U.S. Supreme Ct. 1984. Law clk. U.S. Ct. Appeals (8th cir.), Fargo, N.D., 1977-78; law clk. to Justice Byron White U.S. Supreme Ct., Washington, 1978-79; pvt. practice, 1979-84; atty. gen. State of N.D., Bismarck, 1984-93; ptnr. Dorsey & Whitney, Fargo, 1993-99, Oppenheimer, Wolff & Donnelly, Mpls., 1999, Cooley Godward, Palo Alto, 1999—. Adj. prof. law U. Minn., 1980-83. Rhodes scholar, 1972-74. Democrat. Roman Catholic. Office: 5200 Metcalf Ave Overland Park KS 66202-1265

SPAGNOLO, JOSEPH A., JR. state agency administrator; b. Mar. 16, 1943; BS, Fairleigh Dickinson U., 1965, MAT, 1966; EdD, U. Va., 1971. Tchr. Henrico High Sch., Henrico County, Va., 1966-67; asst. prin. Burford Jr. High Sch., Charlottesville, 1968-69; prin. Providence Jr. High Sch., Chesterfield County, 1968-69; asst. supt. Henrico County Sch., 1971-73; supt. schs. Lynchburg, Va., 1973-90; supt. pub. instrn. Commonwealth of Va., Richmond, 1990-94; superintendent Ill. State Dept. of Edn., Chgo., 1994-98, asst. to chief edn. officer, 1998—; supt. Virtual Learning Sys., Schaumburg, Ill. Mem. Coun. Early Childhood Edn. and Day Care, 1988-90, New Standards Governing Bd., 1990—, Coun. Chief State Sch. Officers, 1990—, Edn. Commn. of States, 1990—. Bd. dirs. U. Va. Edn. Found., 1990—; me. Gov.'s Commn. Ednl. Opportunities for all Virginians, 1990—. Recipient Lamp of Knowledge award for contbns. pub. edn. Va. Assn. Secondary Sch. Prins., 1993, Outstanding Contbn. to Elem. Edn. Va. Assn. Elem. Sch. Prins., 1993, Leadership award Va. Assn. Supervision and Curriculum Devel., 1992, Brotherhood award NCCJ, 1990, Disting. Alumnus award Sch. Edn. U. Va., 1990. Mem. Assn. Supervision and Curriculum Devel., Am. Assn. Sch. Adminstrs., Va. Assn. Sch. Adminstrs. Office: Virtual Learning Sys 1430 N Meacham Rd Schaumburg IL 60173-4808

SPALTY, EDWARD ROBERT, lawyer; b. New Haven, Oct. 1, 1946; s. Kermit and Elinor (Phelan) Turgeon; m. Suzy Clune; children: Thomas John, Kathlene Tess. AB, Emory U., 1968; JD, Columbia U., 1973. Bar: Mo 1975, US Dist Ct (we dist) Mo 1975, US Ct Claims 1977, US Supreme Ct 1994, Nebr 1997, Kans 1998, US Ct Appeals (8th cir) 1984, US Ct Appeals (10th cir) 1999. Assoc. Webster & Sheffield, N.Y.C., 1973-74; mng. atty. Armstrong Teasdale LLP, Kansas City, Mo., 1991-2001. Contbr. articles to profl jours. Chmn bd dirs Mo Easter Seals, 1990—92; various positions Nat Easter Seal Soc, former chmn rules, agenda and resolutions comt, former chmn membership and orgn structure comt house dels, chmn bylaws comt; founding mem Heartland Franchise Asn. With U.S. Army, 1968—70. Mem.: ABA (litigation sect, franchising forum comt), Am Arbit Asn (nat panel comt arbitrators 1987), Int Relations Coun Kansas City, Def Research Inst, Mo Orgn Def Attys, Lawyers Asn Kansas City, Kansas City Metropolitan Bar Asn (chmn atnitrust and franchise law comt, co-chair 14th and 16h ann Nat Franchise Law Inst), Mo Bar Asn (civil rules and procedures comt), German-Am CofC (vpres Kansas City chpt), Nat Golf Club Kansas City (founder), Phi Delta, Pi Sigma Alpha, Sigma Nu. Home: 13703 NW 73rd St Parkville MO 64152-1120 Office: Armstrong Teasdale LLP 2345 Grand Blvd Ste 2000 Kansas City MO 64108-2617 Business E-Mail: espalty@armstrongteasdale.com.

SPANGLER, DOUGLAS FRANK, state legislator; m. Mary Clare Spangler. BS, Kans. State U., 1985; MPA, U. Kans., 1993. Small bus. owner; mem. from dist. 36 Kans. State Ho. of Reps., Topeka. Dem. precinct committeeman, Wyco Dem. Ctrl. Com., 1986-88. Address: 3024 N 54th St Kansas City KS 66104-2117 Office: Kans Ho of Reps State House Topeka KS 66612

SPANOGLE, ROBERT WILLIAM, marketing and advertising company executive, association administrator; b. Lansing, Mich., Nov. 13, 1942; s. William P. and Mary A. (Lenneman) S.; m. Ruth Ann Long, Jan. 14, 1967; children: John Paul Stephen Donald, Amy Lynn. AA, Lansing C.C., 1969; BA, Mich. State U., 1971; postgrad., U. Pa., 1985. Cons. Nat. League Cities, Washington, 1971-72, Am. Legion, Indpls., 1972-75, dir. membership, 1975-79, exec. dir. Washington, 1975-81, nat. adjutant, 1981—; chmn. HP Direct, Inc., Indpls., 1985—, chmn. exec. com. Washington, 1989—. Mem. individual investors adv. com. N.Y. Stock Exch., N.Y.C., 1989-92. Bd. govs. USO, Washington, 1986-92, Childrens Miracle Network, 2001—; trustee St. Mary of the Woods Coll., Terre Haute, Ind., 1991-2001; treas. Civil War Battle Flags Commn. State of Ind., Indpls., 1994—; sec. 500 Festival Assocs., Indpls., 1985-91; mem. Vet.'s Day Coun., Indpls., 1989; bd. dirs. Indpls. Athletic Club, 1989-93, Crossroads Coun. Boy Scouts Am., 1985-92. With U.S. Army, 1962-65. Mem. Am. Legion of Mich. (Hon. Comdr. 1985), Kiwanis (exec. com. 1989-92). Roman Catholic. Avocations: golf, hunting, reading. Home: 7420 Killarney Dr Indianapolis IN 46217-5472 Office: Am Legion 700 N Pennsylvania St Indianapolis IN 46204-1129

SPANSKY, ROBERT ALAN, computer systems analyst, retired; b. Hamtramck, Mich., July 29, 1942; s. Harry Joseph and Alicia Eileen (Kossak) S. BS, U. Detroit, 1964, MBA, 1967. Asst. br. mgr. Nat. Bank Detroit, 1965-67, sr. asst. br. mgr., 1969-71; computer programmer Ford Motor Co., Dearborn, Mich., 1972-76, sys. analyst, project leader, 1976-99; ret., 1999. Active in food delivery to elderly Focus Hope, Detroit, 1990—2001; chmn. 75th anniversary reunion dinner dance St. Matthew Parish, 2002. Sgt. U.S. Army, 1967—69, Vietnam. Recipient Disting. Svc. award Alpha Kappa Psi, 1967, 83, 91, 25-Yr. Svc. award Alpha Kappa Psi/Ford Motor Co., 1987, 97. Mem. Assn. MBAs, Econ. Club Detroit Roman Catholic. Avocations: coin collecting, stamp collecting, landscaping. Home: 5574 Haverhill St Detroit MI 48224-3245 E-mail: rspansky@msn.com.

SPARBERG, MARSHALL STUART, gastroenterologist, educator; b. Chgo., May 20, 1936; s. Max Shane and Mildred Rose (Haffron) S.; m. Eve Gaymont Enda, Mar. 15, 1987. BA, Northwestern U., 1957, MD, 1960. Intern Evanston Hosp., Ill., 1960-61; resident in internal medicine Barnes Hosp., St. Louis, 1961-63; fellow U. Chgo., 1963-65; practice medicine specializing in gastroenterolgy Chgo., 1967—; asst. prof. medicine Northwestern U., 1967-72, assoc. prof., 1972-80, prof. medicine, 1980—; instr. Wash. U., St. Louis, 1961-63, U. Chgo., 1963-65. Author: Ileostomy Care, 1969, Primer of Clinical Diagnosis, 1972, Ulcerative Colitis, 1978, Inflammatory Bowel Disease, 1982; contbr. numerous articles to profl. jours. Pres. Fine Arts Music Found., 1974-76, Crohn's Disease and Colitis Found. of Am., pres. Ill. chpt., 1994-97; bd. dirs. Lyric Opera Guild, 1974-94, Chamber Music Soc. North Shore Chgo., 1984—; physician to Chgo. Symphony Orch., 1981-97. With USAF, 1965-67. Named Outstanding Tchr. Northwestern U. Med. Sch., 1972 Mem. AMA, ACP, Am. Gastroent. Assn., Am. Coll. Gastroent. (bd. govs.), Chgo. Med. Soc., Chgo. Soc. Internal Medicine, Chgo. Soc. Gastroenterology (pres.), Chgo. Soc. Gastrointestinal Endoscopy (pres.) Office: 676 N Saint Clair St Ste 1525 Chicago IL 60611-2862

SPARKS, BILLY SCHLEY, lawyer; b. Marshall, Mo., Mar. 1, 1923; s. John and Clarinda (Schley) S.; m. Dorothy O. Stone, May 14, 1946; children: Stephen Stone, Susan Lee Sparks Raben Taylor, John David. AB, Harvard U., 1945, LLB, 1949. Bar: Mo. 1949. Ptnr. Langworthy, Matz & Linde, Kansas City, Mo., 1949-62, Linde, Thomason, Fairchild, Langworthy, Kohn & Van Dyke, Kansas City, 1962-91; ret., 1991. Mem. Mission (Kans.) Planning Coun., 1954-63; treas. Johnson County (Kans.) Dem. Ctrl. Com., 1958-64; candidate for rep. 10th Dist., Kans., 1956, 3d Dist., 1962; mem. Dist. 100 Sch. Bd., 1964-68, pres., 1967-69; mem. Dist. 512 Sch. Bd., 1969-73, pres., 1971-72; del. Dem. Nat. Conv., 1964; ; mem. Kans. Civil Svc. Commn., 1975-90. Lt. USAAF, 1944-46. Mem. ABA, Mo. Bar Assn., Kansas City Bar Assn., Law Assn. Kansas City, Harvard Law Sch. Assn. Mo. (past dir.), Nat. Assn. Sch. Bds. (mem. legis. com. 1968-73), St. Andrews Soc., Harvard Club (v.p. 1953-54), The Kansas City (Mo.) Club, Milburn Golf and Country Club, Am. Legion, Kansas City C. of C. (legis. com. 1956-82), Mem. Christian Ch. Home and Office: 8517 W 90th Ter Shawnee Mission KS 66212-3053

SPARKS, DONALD EUGENE, interscholastic activities association executive; b. St. Louis, May 26, 1933; s. Lloyd Garland and Elsie Wilma (Finn) S.; m. Gloria Helle, Sept. 22, 1951; children: Robert, Michael, Donna Lyn. BS in Edn., Truman State Univ., 1956, MA, 1959, postgrad., 1962-63. Cert. tchr. and principal, Mo. High sch. coach, athletic dir. The Parkway Sch. Dist., Chesterfield, Mo., 1959-77; assoc. dir. Mo. High Sch. Activity Assn., Columbia, 1977-81; asst. dir. Nat. Fedn. State High Sch. Assns., Kansas City, Mo., 1981-98, retired, 1998. Recipient spl. Nat. Athletic Dir.'s and Nat. Coach and Nat. Ofcl. citations Nat. Fedn. State High Sch. Assns., 1972; named to Truman State U. Athletics Hall of Fame, 1996, Greater St. Louis Athletics Hall of Fame, 1978. Mem. Nat. Interathletic Adminstrs. Assn. (Disting. Service award 1979). Home: 20 Whispering Sands Dr Sarasota FL 34242-1665 Office: Nat High Sch Athletics Hall of Fame 2000 PO Box 690 Indianapolis IN 46206-0690

SPARKS, RICHARD EDWARD, aquatic ecologist; b. Kingston, Pa., Apr. 19, 1942; s. Raymond Earl and Marjory Bernice (Coffey) S.; m. Ruth Marie Cole, Dec. 30, 1966; children: Amelia Mary, Carolyn Denise. BA, Amherst Coll., 1964; MS, U. Kans., 1968; PhD, Va. Poly. Inst., 1971. Instr. Meth. Tchr. Tng. Coll., Uzuakoli, Nigeria, 1964-66; rsch. assoc. Va. Poly. Inst. and State U., Blacksburg, 1971-72; asst. aquatic biologist Ill. Natural History Survey, Champaign, 1972-77, assoc. aquatic biologist, 1977-80, aquatic biologist, 1980—. Contbr. articles to profl. jours.; author and co-author 11 spl. publs. and refereed symposia. Mem. Ill. Chpt. Am. Fisheries Soc. (pres. 1980, north cen. div. exec. com. 1980), Sigma Xi. Achievements include research in how the flood regulates and enhances biological productivity in large floodplain rivers. Home: RR 1 Ipava IL 61441-9801 Office: Ill Natural History Survey River Rsch Lab PO Box 590 Havana IL 62644-0590

SPARKS, WILLIAM SHERAL, retired seminary librarian; b. Alden Bridge, La., Oct. 30, 1924; s. Fred DeWitt and Truda (Bradford) S.; m. Joy Eleanor Young, Aug. 8, 1947; 1 child, David Frederick. AB, Phillips U., 1946; MDiv, Christian Theol. Sem., 1949; ThM, Iliff Sch. of Theology, 1955, ThD, 1957; MA, U. Denver, 1962. Pastor chs., 1950-60; asst. libr. Kans. Wesleyan U., Salina, 1962-66; dir. libr. and info. svcs. St. Paul Sch. of Theology, Kansas City, Mo., 1966-93, ret., 1993. Horowitz Found. fellow Hebrew Union Coll.-Jewish Inst. of Religion, 1949-52. Mem. Am. Theol. Libr. Assn.

SPARLING, PETER DAVID, dancer, dance educator; b. Detroit, June 4, 1951; s. Robert Daniel and Emily Louise (Matthews) S. BFA, Juilliard Sch., N.Y.C., 1973. Dancer José Limón Co., N.Y.C., 1971-73; co. instr. London (Eng.) Contemporary Dance Theatre, 1983-84; prin. dancer Martha Graham Dance Co., N.Y.C., 1973-87; asst. prof. dance U. Mich., Ann Arbor, 1984-87, chmn. dance dept., assoc. prof., 1987-94, prof. of dance, 1994—. Artistic dir. Peter Sparling Presents Solo Flight, N.Y.C., 1977-82, Peter Sparling Dance Co., N.Y.C., 1980-84; co-dir. Ann Arbor Dance Works, 1984-94; artistic dir. Dance Gallery/Peter Sparling & Co., 1993—; guest choreographer Victorian Coll. Arts, 1981, 84, Dance Uptown, Am. Ballet Theatre II, Cloud Dance Theatre, Taiwan, Ballet Gulbenkian, Lisbon, Utah Repertory Dance Theatre, Joseph Holmes Dance Theatre, Corning Dances, Fla. State U., Danza Una, Costa Rica. Choreographer Divining Rod, 1973, Little Incarnations, 1974, Three Farewells, 1977, Suite to Sleep, 1978, A Thief's Progress or The Lantern Night, 1979, Excursions of Chung Kuei, 1978, Nocturnes for Eurydice, 1978, Once in a Blue Moon, 1978, Herald's Round, 1979, Hard Rock, 1979, What She Forgot He Remembered, 1979, Sitting Harlequin, 1979, In Stride, 1979, Elegy, 1979, The Tempest, 1980, Orion, 1980, Landscape with Bridge, 1980, Nocturnes, Modern Life, Bright Bowed River, A Fearful Symmetry, Alibi, Rounding the Square, De Profundis, Rondo, Wings, Witness, The Boy Who Played With Dolls, Jealousy, Bride of Grand Prairie, Travelogue, The Four Seasons, New Bach, Popular Songs, Johnny Angel, Unfinished, The Pursuit of Happiness, Sonata, Philistines, Seven Enigmas, Berliner Mass, Ask/Tell; contbr. poetry to Mich. Quarterly Rev. Louis Horst Meml. scholar Juilliard Sch., 1973; Nat. Endowment for the Arts fellow 1971, 79, 83; grantee U. Mich., 1985-86, 89, 96-97, Mich. Coun. for the Arts, 1986, 93-98; faculty fellow U. Mich. Inst. for Humanities, 1996-97; recipient Choreographer's award Mich. Dance Assn., 1988, Artist's award Arts Found. Mich., 1989, 1997. Office: Univ of Michigan Dept of Dance 1310 N University Ct Ann Arbor MI 48109-1037

SPARROW, EPHRAIM MAURICE, mechanical engineering scientist, educator; b. Hartford, Conn., May 27, 1928; s. Charles and Frieda (Gottlieb) S.; m. Ruth May Saltman, Nov. 2, 1952; 1 child, Rachel Bernarr. BS, MIT, 1948, MS, 1949; MA, Harvard Coll., 1950, PhD, 1956; Doutor Honoris Causa, U. Brazil, 1967. Heat transfer specialist Raytheon Mfg. Co., 1952-53; rsch. specialist Lewis Rsch. Ctr., NASA, Cleve., 1953-59; prof. mech. engring. U. Minn., 1959—, Inst. prof., 1994—, chmn. fluid dynamics program, 1968-80, Morse alumni disting. tchg. prof., 1980—. Program dir. NSF, 1986-87, dir. chem., biochem. and thermal engring. divsn., 1986-88; vis. prof., chief AID mission U. Brazil, 1966-67; adv. prof. Xi'an Jiaotong U., 1984—; cons. in field, 1960—; pres. 1st Brazilian Symposium on Heat Transfer and Fluid Mechanics, 1966; mem. solar energy panel Fed. Coun. on Sci. and Tech., 1972; U.S. sci. committeeman 5th Internat. Heat Transfer Conf., 1973-74. Author: (with R.D. Cess) Radiation Heat Transfer, 1966, 2nd edit., 1978; editor: Handbook of Numerical Heat Transfer, Advances in Numerical Heat Transfer; hon. mem. editorial bd. Internat. Jour. Heat Mass Transfer, 1964—, Internat. Comm. in Heat Mass Transfer, 1975—; sr. editor Jour. Heat Transfer, 1972-80; editor Series in Computational and Phys. Processes in Mechanics and Thermal Scis., 1980—; chmn. editorial adv. bd. Numerical Heat Transfer, 1978—; contbr. over 560 tech. articles to profl. jours. Recipient Ralph Coates Roe award Am. Soc. Engring. Edn., 1978, Outstanding Teaching award U. Minn., 1985, Fed. Engr. of Yr. award NSF, 1988, Sr. Rsch. award Am. Soc. Engring. Edn., 1989, Horace T. Morse award for outstanding contbns. to undergraduate teaching, 1993, Disting. Tchg. award Acad. Disting. Tchrs., U. Minn., 1997, 99, Donald Q. Kern award, Am. Inst. Chemical Engrs., 1999; named George Hawkins Disting. lectr. Purdue U., 1985. Fellow ASME (Meml. award for outstanding contbn. to sci. heat transfer 1962, Max Jakob award for eminent contbn. 1976, Centennial medal 1980, Disting. Svc. award heat transfer div. 1982, Charles Russ Richards Meml. award 1985, Worcester Reed Warner medal 1986, 50th Anniversary award heat transfer div. 1988, Disting. lectr. 1986-91, 93-94); mem. NAE, Biomed. Engring. Soc. (faculty advisor 1994—), Sigma Xi (Monie A. Ferst medal for contbn. to rsch. through edn. 1993), Pi Tau Sigma. Home: 2105 West Hoyt Ave Saint Paul MN 55108-1314 Office: U Minn Dept Mech Engring Minneapolis MN 55455-0111 E-mail: esparrow@umn.edu.

SPARROW, HERBERT GEORGE, III, lawyer, educator; b. Ft. Bragg, N.C., May 26, 1936; s. Herbert George and Virginia (Monroe) S.; m. Nancy Woodruff, Mar. 4, 1962; children: Amy Winslow, Edward Harrison, Herbert G. IV, Alison Kidder. AB cum laude, Princeton U., 1958; JD, U. Mich., 1961. Bar: Mich. 1961, Calif. 1964, D.C. 1979, U.S. Ct. Claims 1982, U.S. Tax Ct. 1983, U.S. Ct. Mil. Appeals 1962, U.S. Supreme Ct. 1976. Assoc. Dickinson Wright PLLC, Detroit, 1965-70, ptnr., 1970—. Adj. prof. Detroit Coll. Law, 1977—. Author numerous articles environ. law.; speaker in field. Bd. dirs. Family Life Edn. Coun., Grosse Pointe, Mich., 1982-88, Adult Well-Being Svcs., Inc., Detroit, 1995—. Capt. JAGC, U.S. Army, 1962-65. Mem. ABA, Mich. Bar Assn. (rep. assembly 1979-85, environ. law sect. coun. 1985-91), Calif. Bar Assn., D.C. Bar Assn., Detroit Bar Assn., Am. Arbitration Assn. (panel arbitrators 1975—), Mich. State Bar Found. (fellow 1989—), Environment Law Inst. (assoc.), Phi Delta Phi (pres. Kent Inn Assn., Ann Arbor 1985-97). Office: Dickinson Wright PLLC 500 Woodward Ave Ste 4000 Detroit MI 48226-3416

SPATZ, D(ONALD) DEAN, chemical executive; b. Montclair, N.J., Mar. 20, 1944; s. Donald and Narosonia Spatz; m. Ruth Carol Neiman, June 29, 1968; children: Mark Jeffrey, Sharon Virginia. AB, Dartmouth Coll., 1966, B in Engring., 1967, M in Engring., 1968. Registered profl. chem. engr. Mgr. engring. Aqua Tech., Inc., Minnetonka, Minn., 1968-69; chmn., CEO, founder Osmonics, Inc., 1969—. Bd. dirs. SI Technologies, Inc., Seattle, Sigma Aldrich Corp., St. Louis. Recipient Putnam Food award, 1975, Innovation in Materials Reclamation award Indsl. Equipment News, 1982, Chem. Equipment Energy award Chem. Equipment Mag., 1982, Chem. Processing Vaaler award Chem. Processing Mag., 1984; Minn. Entrepeneur of Yr. in High Tech./Med. Field, 1991. Mem.: ASTM, AIChE, N.Am. Membrane Soc., Am. Desalting Assn., Am. Electroplaters Soc., Am. Waterworks Assn., Am. Chem. Soc., World Pres. Orgn. Avocations: skiing, boating, scuba diving, golf, tennis. Office: Osmonics Inc 5951 Clearwater Dr Minnetonka MN 55343-8995 Business E-Mail: dspatz@osmonics.com.

SPAULDING, DAN, public relations executive; BA, MA, U. Mich. Commd. USN; aide, pub. affairs officer to comdr. Tng. Command U.S. Pacific Fleet, San Diego, 1969-72; news anchor/prodr./reporter Staf. WFRV-TV, Green Bay, Wis., Sta. WEYI-TV, Flint-Saginaw, Mich.; mem. faculty U. Wis., Green Bay; news dir. Sta. KOMU-TV, Columbia, Mo., Sta. WOTV-TV 8; with Seyferth & Assocs., Inc., Grand Rapids, Mich., 1989-94, exec. v.p., 1994—. Active West Mich. Environ. Action Com.; mem. bd., exec. com., chiar Ctmy. Wide Care Com., Heart of West Mich. United Way. Mem. Pub. Rels. Soc. Am. (accredited). Office: Seyferth & Assocs Inc Rockford Ctr 110 Ionia Ave NW Grand Rapids MI 49503-3003

SPEAR, ALLAN HENRY, state senator, historian, educator; b. Michigan City, Ind., June 24, 1937; s. Irving S. and Esther (Lieber) S. BA, Oberlin Coll., 1958, LLD (hon.), 1997; MA, Yale U., 1960, PhD, 1965. Lectr. history U. Minn., Mpls., 1964-65, asst. prof., 1965-67, assoc. prof., 1967-2000; mem. Minn. State Senate, St. Paul, 1973-2000, chmn. jud. com., 1983-93; chmn. crime prevention com., 1993-2000; pres. Minn. State Senate, 1883-2000. Vis. prof. Carleton Coll., Northfield, Minn., 1970, Stanford U., Palo Alto, Calif., 1970. Author: Black Chicago, 1967. Mem. Internat. Network Gay and Lesbian Offcls., Com. on Suggested State Legislation of Coun. of State Govts. Mem. Dem. Farm Labor Party. Avocations: cooking, travel, reading, classical music. Home: 2429 Colfax Ave S Minneapolis MN 55405-2942 Office: Minn State Senate 120 State Capitol Saint Paul MN 55155-0001

SPEAR, THOMAS TURNER, history educator; b. Coral Gables, Fla., Dec. 23, 1940; BA, Williams Coll., 1962; MA, U. Wis., 1970, PhD, 1974; postgrad., Sch. Oriental and African Studies, 1976-77. Sr. lectr. La Trobe U., Melbourne, Australia, 1973-80; Charles R. Keller prof. Williams Coll., Williamstown, Mass., 1981-92; prof. U. Wis., Madison, 1993—, dir. African studies program, 1995-98, chair dept. history, 2001—. Reviewer NEH, Social Sci. Rsch. Coun./Am. Coun. Learned Socs., Am. Philos. Soc. Author: The Kaya Complex: A History of the Mijikenda Peoples of the Kenya Coast to 1900, 1978, Kenya's Past: An Introduction to Historical Method in Africa, 1981, (with Derek Nurse) The Swahili: Reconstructing the History and Language of and African Soc., 800-1500, 1985, Mountain Farmers: Moral Economics of Land and Agricultural Development in Arusha and Meru, 1997; editor: (with Richard Waller) Being Maasai: Ethnicity and Identity in East Africa, 1993, (with Isaria N. Kimambo) East African Expressions of Christianity, 1999; editor Jour. of African History, 1997-2001; contbr. articles to profl. jours. Grantee Williams Coll., 1984, 87-89, 91-92, NEH, 1984, Am. Coun. Learned Socs., 1982, La Trobe U., 1976-77; recipient A.C. Jordan prize U. Wis., 1972, Fgn. Area fellowship Social Sci. Rsch. Coun./Am. Coun. Learned Socs., 1970-72, Coll. Tchrs. fellowship NEH, 1987-88, Guggenheim fellowship, 1995-96, U. Wis., 1995—. Mem. Am. Hist. Soc. (contbr. Guide to Hist. Lit.), African Studies Assn., African Studies Assn. Australia (founder, exec. sec. 1978-80), Internat. African Inst. Office: U Wis Dept History 3211 Humanities 455 N Park St Madison WI 53706-1405

SPEARS, KENNETH GEORGE, chemistry educator; b. Erie, Pa., Oct. 23, 1943; BS, Bowling Green State U., 1966; MS, PhD in Phys. Chemistry, U. Chgo., 1970. NIH predoctoral fellow U. Chgo., 1968-70; NRC-NOAA postdoctoral fellow NOAA, Boulder, Colo., 1970-72; prof. dept. chemistry Northwestern U., 1972—, mem. biomedical engring. dept., 1987—. Bd. editors The Rev. Scientific Instruments, 1980-83; conbtr. articles to profl.jours. Alfred P. Sloan Found. fellow, 1974-76. Fellow AAAS; mem. Am. Phys. Soc., Am. Chem. Soc. Office: Northwestern U Dept Chemistry 2145 Sheridan Rd Evanston IL 60208-3113 E-mail: k-spears@northwestern.edu.

SPEARS, MARIAN CADDY, dietetics and institutional management educator; b. East Liverpool, Ohio, Jan. 12, 1921; d. Frederick Louis and Marie Caddy Spears-Ralston; m. Sholto M. Spears, May 29, 1959; m. Joseph D. Ralston, May 29, 1998. BS, Case Western Res. U., 1942, MS, 1947; PhD, U. Mo., 1971. Chief dietitian Bellefaire Children's Home, Cleve., 1942-53; head dietitian Drs. Hosp., 1953-57; assoc. dir. dietetics Barnes Hosp., St. Louis, 1957-59; asst. prof. U. Ark., Fayetteville, 1959-68; assoc. prof. U. Mo., Columbia, 1971-75; prof., head dept. hotel, restaurant, instn. mgmt. and dietetics Kans. State U., Manhattan, 1975-89. Cons. dietitian small hosps. and nursing homes; cons. dietetic edn. Author: Foodservice Organizations Textbook, 4th edit., 2000, Foodservice Procurement Textbook, 1st edit., 1998, 99; contbr. articles to profl. jours. Recipient Kans. State U. Advancement award, 1997. Mem. Am. Dietetic Assn. (Copher award 1989), Am. Sch. Foodsvc. Assn., Food Systems Mgmt. Edn. Coun., Soc. Advancement of Foodsvc. Rsch., Nat. Restaurant Assn., Coun. Hotel, Restaurant, Inst. Mgmt. Edn., Manhattan C. of C., Sigma Xi, Gamma Sigma Delta, Omicron Nu, Phi Kappa Phi. Home: 1522 Williamsburg Dr Manhattan KS 66502-0408 Office: Kans State U 105 Justin Hall Manhattan KS 66506-1400

SPECHT, JAMES E. agronomist, educator; b. Scottsbluff, Nebr., Sept. 12, 1945; s. Henry W. and Lydia (Marsh) S.; m. Pamela S. Hammers, May 31, 1969. BS, U. Nebr., 1967; MS, U. Ill., 1971; PhD, U. Nebr., 1974. Rsch. assoc. dept. agronomy U. Nebr., Lincoln, 1974, asst. prof., 1974-80, assoc. prof., 1980-85, prof., 1985—. Mem. editorial bd. Crops Sci., 1983-86, Field Crops Rsch. Jour., 1987-90. Contbr. numerous articles to profl. jours; presenter many rsch. lectures, 1975-85. Sgt. US Army, 1969-71, Vietnam. Recipient, Agronomic Acheivement award American Society of Agronomy, 1994. Fellow AAAS, Crop Sci. Soc. Am., Am. Soc. Agronomy. Democrat. Avocations: travel, investments, reading, computers. Office: Univ Nebr Plant Sci Rm 279 PO Box 830915 Lincoln NE 68583-0915

SPECK, SAMUEL WALLACE, JR. state official; b. Canton, Ohio, Jan. 31, 1937; s. Samuel Wallace Sr. and Lois Ione (Schneider) S.; m. Sharon Jane Anderson, Jan. 20, 1962; children: Samuel Wallace III, Derek Charles. BA, Muskingum Coll., 1959; postgrad., U. Zimbabwe, Harare, 1961; MA, Harvard U., 1963, PhD, 1968. Prof. polit. sci. Muskingum Coll., New Concord, Ohio, 1964-83, asst. to pres., 1986-87, exec. v.p., 1987, acting pres., 1987-88, pres., 1988-99; assoc. dir. Fed. Emergency Mgmt. Agy., 1983-86; mem. Ohio Ho. of Reps., 1971-76; state senator from Ohio 20th Dist., 1977-83; dir. Dept. Natural Resources, mem. Gov's. cabinet State of Ohio, 1999—. Bd. dirs. Camco Fin. Corp., Cambridge, Ohio, Advantage Savs. Bank; pres. Eastern Ohio Devel. Alliance, 1990-92; Fund for Improvement of Postsecondary Edn., 1990-92, chmn. 1991. Contbr.: Southern Africa in Perspective, 1972; also numerous articles on African and Am. govt. and pub. policy. Bd. dirs. Ohio Tuition Trust Authority, 1991-93, Internat. Ctr. for Preservation Wild Animals, Lake Erie Commn., 1999—, Ohio Water Resources Coun., 1999—; mem. Great Lakes Commn., 1999—, Ohio Power Siting Bd., 1999—. Recipient Outstanding Legislator award VFW/DAV/Am. Legion, Conservation Achievement award State of Ohio. Mem. Assn. Ind. Colls. and Univs. of Ohio (chmn. 1992-94). Republican. Presbyterian. Home: 240 Greenbriar Ct Worthington OH 43085-3055 Office: Dir OH Dept of Natural Resources 1930 Belcher Dr # D-3 Columbus OH 43224-1392

SPECTOR, DAVID M. lawyer; b. Rock Island, Ill., Dec. 20, 1946; s. Louis and Ruth (Vinikour) S.; m. Laraine Fingold, Jan. 15, 1972; children: Rachel, Laurence. BA, Northwestern U., 1968; JD magna cum laude, U. Mich., 1971. Bar: Ill. 1971, U.S. Dist. Ct. (no. dist.) Ill. 1971, U.S. Ct. Appeals (7th cir.) 1977, U.S. Ct. Appeals (4th cir.) 1984, U.S. Dist. Ct. (cen. dist.) Ill. 1984. Clk. Ill. Supreme Ct., Chgo., 1971-72; ptnr., assoc. Isham, Lincoln & Beale, 1972-87; ptnr. Mayer, Brown & Platt, 1987-97, Hopkins & Sutter, Chgo., 1997-2001, Schiff, Hardin & Waite, Chgo., 2001—. Chmn. ABA Nat. Inst. on Ins. Co. Insolvency, Boston, 1986; co-chmn. ABA Nat. Inst. on Internat. Reins.: Collections and Insolvency, N.Y., 1988; chmn. ABA Nat. Inst. on Life Ins. Co. Insolvency, Chgo., 1993; spkr. in field. Editor: Law and Practice of Insurance Company Insolvency, 1986, Law and Practice of Life Insurer Insolvency, 1993; co-editor: Law and Practice of International Reinsurance Collections and Insolvency, 1988; contbr. articles to profl. jours. Mem. ABA (chair Nat. Inst. on Life Insurer Insolvency 1993), Chgo. Bar Assn., Lawyer's Club of Chgo. Office: Schiff Hardin & Waite 6600 Sears Tower Chicago IL 60606 Home: 1418 Lake Shore Dr Chicago IL 60611 E-mail: dspector@schiffhardin.com.

SPECTOR, GERSHON JERRY, physician, educator, researcher; b. Rovno, Poland, Oct. 20, 1937; came to U.S., 1949; naturalized, 1956; m. Patsy Carol Tanenbaum, Aug. 28, 1965. BA, Johns Hopkins U., 1960; MD cum laude, U. Md., 1964. Intern Beth Israel Hosp., Boston, 1964-65; resident in surgery Sinai Hosp., Balt., 1965-66; resident in otolaryngology Mass. Eye and Ear Infirmary, Boston, 1966-69, Peter Bent Brigham Hosp., Boston, 1968-69; teaching fellow in otolaryngology Harvard U. Med. Sch., 1968-69; assoc. physician Ill. Crippled Children's Svc., Carbondale, 1971; mem. faculty Washington U. Med. Sch., St. Louis, 1971—, assoc. prof. otolaryngology, 1974-76, prof., 1976—; chief dept. otolaryngology St. Louis County Hosp., 1971-77. Mem. staff Washington U. Med. Ctr., Barnes Hosp.; dir. temporal bone bank, 1971-81; guest examiner Am. Bd. Otolaryngology, 1975-77; rsch. cons. neurosci. group, G.D. Searle Pharm. Corp. Mem. editl. bd. Laryngoscope, 1978, editor-in-chief, 1984-94; contbr. articles to med. jours. With U.S. Army, 1969-71. Hancock scholar, 1962. Fellow ACS; mem. AAAS, AMA, Am. Acad. Ophthalmology and Otolaryngology (Honor award 1979), St. Louis Med. Soc., St. Louis County Med. Soc., Am. Coun. Otolarygology, St. Louis Ear, Nose and Throat Club (pres. 1986), So. Med. Assn., Deafness Rsch. Found., Pan. Am. Assn. Otorhinolaryngology and Broncho Esophagology, Am. Soc. Head and Neck Surgery, Soc. Univ. Otolaryngologists, Am. Laryngological, Rhinological and Otological Soc. (Edmund Prince Fowler award 1974), Am. Soc. Cell Biology, Electron Microscopy Soc., N.Y. Acad. Scis., Am. Assn. Anatomists, Am. Acad. Facial Plastic and Reconstructive Surgery, Am. Neuro-Otology Soc., Gesellschaft fur Neurootologie und Aequilibrimoetrie A.V., Barany Soc., Am. Radium Soc., Assn. Acad. Surgery, Am. Fedn. Clin. Oncologic Socs., Am Otological Soc., Acoustical Soc. Am., Soc. for Neurosci., Internat. Skull Base Soc. (founding), Brazilian Skull Base Soc. (hon.), Centurion Club, Alpha Omega Alpha, Psi Chi. Home: 7365 Westmoreland Dr Saint Louis MO 63130-4241 Office: Washington U Med Sch Saint Louis MO 63110 E-mail: spectorg@msnotes.wustl.edu.

SPEER, NANCY GIROUARD, health care administrator; b. Mankato, Minn., Sept. 14, 1941; d. Jared and Katherine (Schmitt) How; m. Robert L. Girouard, Aug. 29, 1964 (dec. Mar. 1983); children: Robert James Girouard, Mark Jared Girouard; m. David J. Speer, Dec. 21, 1985 (dec. Aug. 1999). BA, Wellesley Coll., 1963; MA in Tchg., Wesleyan U., 1965; cert. mgmt., Smith Coll., 1985. Tchr. secondary sch. Bunnell H.S., Stratford, Conn., 1964-65; tchr., class advisor Lincoln Sch., Providence, 1965-69; substitute tchr. Mankato, 1972-74; pub. info. dir. City of Mankato, 1974-78; univ. editor, dir. pub. affairs forum Mankato State U., 1978-79; comms. mgr. Humphrey Inst., U. Minn., Mpls., 1980-83, dir. external rels., 1983-87, dir. devel. and external rels., 1987-95; dir. devel. Breck Sch., 1996-2000; v.p. Abbott Northwestern Hosp., 2000—02, Planned Parenthood of Minn. and S.D., 2002—. Mem. steering com. Minn. Meeting, Mpls., 1990-96. Contbr. articles to mags. and periodicals; photographer for publs. and newspapers. Bd. dirs. Minn. Newspaper Found., St. Paul, 1985-91, chairperson, 1990-91, bd. dirs., vice-chairperson Cabrini House, Mpls., 1993-97; bd. dirs., sec. Minn. Ctr. for Book Arts, Mpls., 1990-97; bd. dirs. Minn. Landmark Ctr., St. Paul, 1994-2000; dir. Minn. Women's Campaign Fund, Mpls., 1994-2000, co-pres. bd., 1997; bd. dirs. Loft Lit. Ctr., 2000—; vice chair Metropolitan Airport Commn., 1999—, v. chmn. 2001—; mem. Leadership Mpls., Mpls. C. of C., 1982. Bush Leader fellow, 1985-87. Avocations: literature, nature, books.

SPEICHER, CARL EUGENE, pathologist; b. Carbondale, Pa., Mar. 21, 1933; s. William Joseph and Elizabeth Marcella (Connolly) S.; m. Mary Louise Walsh, June 21, 1958; children: Carl E. Jr., Gregory, Erik. BS in Biology, King's Coll., 1954; MD, U. Pa., 1958; primary course in aeroship medicine, Sch. of Aerospace Medicine, Brooks AFB, Tex., 1969. Diplomate Am. Bd. Pathology. Intern U. Pa. Hosp., Phila., 1958-59, resident, 1959-63; chief lab. svcs. USAF Hosp., London, Eng., 1963-66, USAF Med. Ctr. Wright Patterson, Dayton, Ohio, 1966-70; dir. clin. labs. and chmn. dept. pathology Wilford Hall USAF Med. Ctr., San Antonio, 1971-77; prof. dept. pathology Ohio State U., Columbus, 1977—2000, vice chair dept. pathology, 1992—2000, prof. emeritus dept. pathology, 2000—; dir. clin. svcs. Ohio State U. Med. Ctr., 1977—2000; dir. clin. lab. Stoneridge Med. Ctr., Ohio State U., 2000—. Co-author: Choosing Effective Laboratory Tests, 1983; author: (book) The Right Test, 1990, 3d edit., 1998. Col. USAF, 1963-77. Decorated Legion of Merit, 1977, USAF; fellowship in med. chemistry SUNY, Syracuse, 1970-71. Mem. AMA (Physicians Recognition award), Ohio Soc. Pathologists, Ctrl. Ohio Soc. Pathologists, Royal Soc. of Medicine (Eng.), Coll. of Am. Pathologists, Am. Soc. Clin. Pathologists, Alpha Omega Alpha. Office: Ohio State U Med Ctr 410 W 10th Ave Columbus OH 43210-1228

SPELLMIRE, GEORGE W. lawyer; b. Oak Park, Ill., June 10, 1948; Student, Brown U.; BA, Ohio State U., 1970; JD, De Paul U., 1974. Bar: Ill. 1974, U.S. Dist. Ct. (no. dist.) Ill. 1974, U.S. Tax Ct. 1984, U.S. Ct. Appeals (7th cir.) 1984, U.S. Supreme Ct. 1994. Ptnr. Hinshaw & Culbertson, Chgo., 1982-98, D'Ancona & Pflaum, Chgo., 1998—. Author: Attorney Malpractice: Prevention and Defense, 1988; co-author: Accounting, Auditing and Financial Malpractice, 1998, Accountants' Legal Liability Guide, 1990, Illinois Handbook on Legal Malpractice, 1982, Associates Primer for the Prevention of Malpractice, 1987. Mem. ABA, Am. Coll. Trial Lawyers, Soc. Trial Lawyers, Fed. Trial Bar, Internat. Assn. Def. Counsel (legal malpractice com., def. counsel practice mgmt. com.), Ill. State Bar Assn., Chgo. Bar Assn., Trial Lawyers Club Chgo. Office: D'Ancona & Pflaum 111 E Wacker Dr Ste 2800 Chicago IL 60601-4209

SPELSON, NICHOLAS JAMES, engineering executive, retired; b. Oak Park, Ill., Sept. 10, 1923; s. James and Constance (Rellos) S. BS in Mech. Engring., Ill. Inst. Tech., Chgo., 1947. Mech. engr. pvt. industry, Chgo., 1947-60; mech. engr. USAF, 1960-65, Def. Logistics Agy., Dept. of Def., Chgo., 1965-82; br. chief ops. Def. Logistics Agy.-Def. Contract Adminstrn. Svcs. Region, 1982-90; br. chief quality assurance engring. Def. Logistics Agy.-Def. Contracts Dist., 1990-94. With U.S. Army, 1943-45. Mem. Am. Legion, Hellenic Profl. Soc. Ill. Greek Orthodox. Avocations: golf, travel.

SPENCE, MARY LEE, historian, educator; b. Kyle, Tex., Aug. 4, 1927; d. Jeremiah Milton and Mary Louise (Hutchison) Nance; m. Clark Christian Spence, Sept. 12, 1953; children: Thomas Christian, Ann Leslie. BA, U. Tex., 1947, MA, 1948; PhD, U. Minn., 1957. Instr., asst. prof. S.W. Tex. State U., San Marcos, 1948-53; lectr. Pa. State U., State College, 1955-58; mem. faculty U. Ill., Urbana-Champaign, 1973—, asst. prof., assoc. prof., 1973-81, 81-89, prof. history, 1989-90, prof. emerita, 1990—. Editor (with Donald Jackson) The Expeditions of John Charles Fremont, 3 vols., 1970-84, (with Clark Spence) Fanny Kelly's Narrative of Her Captivity Among the Sioux Indians, 1990, (with Pamela Herr) The Letters of Jessie Benton Fremont, 1993, The Arizona Diary of Lily Fremont, 1878-1881, 1997; contbr. articles to profl. jours. Mem. Children's Theater Bd., Urbana-Champaign, 1965-73. Grantee Nat. Hist. Pub. and Records Commn., Washington, 1977-78, 87-90, Huntington Libr., 1992; recipient Excellent Advisor award Liberal Arts and Sci. Coll./U. Ill., 1986. Mem. Western History Assn. (pres. 1981-82), Orgn. Am. Historians, Phi Beta Kappa (exec. sect. Gamma chpt. 1985-89, pres. 1991-92), Phi Alpha Theta. Episcopalian. Home: 1107 S Foley St Champaign IL 61820-6326 Office: U Ill Dept History 810 S Wright St Urbana IL 61801-3644 E-mail: c-spence@uiuc.edu.

SPENCER, C. STANLEY, insurance company executive; b. Canton, Pa., Sept. 24, 1940; s. Clarence N. and Maude E. (Phipps) S.; m. Carol M. Vest, Aug. 23, 1962; children: Greg, Mike. BS in Agrl. Engring., Pa. State U., 1961. Regional sales mgr. W.T. Grant Co., N.Y.C., 1966-76; engr. Hoover Well Service, Zion, Ill., 1976-80, Nielson Iron Works, Racine, Wis., 1980-82; spl. agent Prudential Ins. Co., 1982-84, div. mgr., from 1984; v.p. legal dept. Am. Family Mut. Ins. Co., Madison, Wis. Recipient 1st Place Barbershop Chorus award, Racine, 1984, Kenosha, 1985, Manitowoc, 1986, 1st Place Barbershop Quartet award, Kenosha, Wis., 1986. Mem. Life Underwriters Assn. (v.p. 1985-86), Soc. for the Preservation and Encouragement of Barber Shop Quartet Singing in Am. (pres. Racine 1984-85). Republican. Club: Toastmasters (1st Place 1985). Home: 6234 Larchmont Dr Racine WI 53406-5120 Office: American Family Mutual Insurance Company 6000 American Pkwy Madison WI 53783-0001

SPENCER, DAVID JAMES, lawyer; b. Altadena, Calif., June 23, 1943; s. Dorcy James and Dorothy Estelle (Pingry) S.; m. Donna Rae Blair, Aug. 22, 1965; children: Daniel, Matthew. BA, Rocky Mountain Coll., 1965; JD, Yale U., 1968. Bar: Minn. 1968, U.S. Dist. Ct. Minn. 1968, U.S. Ct. Appeals (8th cir.) 1970. Mem. firm Briggs and Morgan, P.A., Mpls. and St. Paul, 1968—. Contbg. author 10 William Mitchell Law Rev., 1984; contbr. articles to profl. jours. Trustee Rocky Mountain Coll., Billings, Mont., 1980-01; bd. dirs. Reentry Svcs., Inc., 1993—, River Valley Arts Coun., 1996-01, Stillwater Area Arts Ctr. Alliance, 1998-01, Homeward Bound, Inc., 1999—; pres., bd. dirs. St. Croix Friends of Arts, Stillwater, Minn., 1981-84; bd. dirs. Valley Chamber Chorale, Stillwater, 1989-92; v.p. Minn. Jaycees, St. Paul, 1974; elder Presbyn. Ch. Recipient Silver Key St. Paul Jaycees, 1974; Disting. Svc. award Rocky Mountain Coll., 1981, Outstanding Svc. award, 1988, Disting. Achievement award, 1992. Fellow Am. Coll. Real Estate Lawyers; mem. ABA, Minn. Bar Assn., Ramsey County Bar Assn., Stillwater Country Club, Stillwater Sunrise Rotary Club (bd. dirs. 1997-99). Presbyterian. Avocations: trout fishing, golf, singing. Home: 10135 Waterfront Dr Woodbury MN 55129 Office: Briggs & Morgan 2200 First Nat Bank Bldg 332 Minnesota St Ste W2200 Saint Paul MN 55101-1396 E-mail: dspencer@briggs.com.

SPENCER, DONALD SPURGEON, historian, academic administrator; b. Anderson, Ind., Jan. 29, 1945; s. Thomas E. and Josephine (Litz) S.; m. Pamela Sue Roberts, June 19, 1965; 1 chld, Jennifer Wynne. BA, Ill. Coll., 1967; PhD, U. Va., 1973. Asst. prof. history Westminster Coll., Fulton, Mo., 1973-76, Ohio U., Athens, 1976-77; from asst., assoc. to full prof., assoc. dean, asst. provost U. Mont., Missoula, 1977-90; provost SUNY, Geneseo, 1990-93; pres. Western Ill. U., Macomb, 1994—. Author: Louis Kossuth and Young America, 1978, The Carter Implosion: Jimmy Carter and the Amateur Style of Diplomacy,1989; contbr. articles to jours. in field. With U.S. Army, 1968-71, Korea. Woodrow Wilson Found. fellow, 1968; Danforth Found. univ. teaching fellow, 1971. Mem. Phi Beta Kappa. Congregationalist. Office: W Ill Univ Office of the President Sherman Hall Macomb IL 61455 Home: 124 Links Of Leith Williamsburg VA 23188-7461

SPENCER, GARY L. state government lawyer; b. Amboy, Ill., Sept. 4, 1949; s. W. Leslie and Mabel E. (Smith) S.; m. Julie A. Swanson, Mar. 14, 1987; children: Erin, Elizabeth, Nichole, Nathan. BS, Ill. State U., Normal, 1971; JD, Drake U., 1979. Bar: Ill. 1979, U.S. Dist. Ct. (no. dist.) Ill. 1981. Asst. state's atty. Whiteside County, Morrison, Ill., 1979-81, state's atty., 1981—. Mem. Ill. State Bar Assn., Whiteside County Bar Assn., Kiwanis Club Moarrison (2d v.p. 1993—). Methodist. Avocation: boating. Office: Whiteside County Courthouse 200 E Knox St Morrison IL 61270-2819

SPENCER, RICHARD HENRY, lawyer; b. Kansas City, Mo., Nov. 29, 1926; s. Byron Spencer and Helen Elizabeth (McCune) Hockaday; m. Barbara G. Rau, Aug. 2, 1952 (div. 1955); 1 child, Christina G. Cuevas; m. Katherine Graham, Dec. 28, 1957; children: Elisabeth M., Katherine S. Rivard. BS in Engring., Princeton U., 1949; LLB, U. Mo., 1952. Bar: Mo. 1952, U.S. Dist. Ct (we. dist.) Mo. 1955. Assoc. Spencer, Fane, Britt & Browne, Kansas City, 1952-59, ptnr., 1959-94; ret. ptnr., 1995—. Co-author: Fiduciary Duties, Rights and Responsibilities of Directors, 1985. Sec., bd. dirs. Met. Performing Arts Fund, Kansas City, 1984—; trustee Barstow Sch., Kansas City, 2002--. Mem. ABA, Mo. Bar Assn., Lawyers Assn. Kansas City, Kansas City Club (pres. 1974), Kansas City Country Club (pres. 1986), Rotary. Republican. Episcopalian. Avocations: hunting, golf, traveling. Home: 77 Le Mans Ct Shawnee Mission KS 66208-5230 Office: Spencer Fane Britt & Browne 1400 Commerce Bank Bldg 1000 Walnut St Kansas City MO 64106-2140

SPENDLOVE, STEVE DALE, broadcast executive; b. L.A., Calif., July 20, 1955; V.p. and gen. mgr. KSAS, Wichita, Kans., 1992-96, WFTC-TV, Mpls., 1996—. Mem. Minn. Broadcasters Assn. (bd. dirs.), TV Music License Fee Com. (bd. dirs.). Office: WFTC-TV 1701 Broadway St NE Minneapolis MN 55413-2638

SPERELAKIS, NICHOLAS, SR. physiology and biophysics educator, researcher; b. Joliet, Ill., Mar. 3, 1930; s. James and Aristea (Kayadakis) S.; m. Dolores Martinis, Jan. 28, 1960; children: Nicholas Jr., Mark (dec.), Christine, Sophia, Thomas, Anthony. BS in Chemistry, U. Ill., 1951, MS in Physiology, 1955, PhD in Physiology, 1957. Teaching asst. U. Ill., Urbana, 1954-57; instr. Case Western Res. U., Cleve., 1957-59, asst. prof., 1959-66, assoc. prof., 1966; prof. U. Va., Charlottesville, 1966-83; Joseph Eichberg prof. physiology Coll. Medicine U. Cin., 1983-96, chmn. dept., 1983-93, Eichberg prof. emeritus, 1996—. Cons. NPS Pharm., Inc., Salt Lake City, 1988-95, Carter Wallace, Inc. Cranbury, N.J., 1988-91; vis. prof. U. St. Andrews, Scotland, 1972-73, U. San Luis Potosi, Mex., 1986, U. Athens, Greece, 1994; Rosenblueth prof. Centro de Investigacion y Avanzades, Mex., 1972; mem. sci. adv. com. several internat. meetings, edit. bds. numerous sci. jours. Co-editor: Handbook of Physiology: Heart, 1979; editor: Physiology and Pathophysiology of the Heart, 1984, 2d edit., 1988, 3rd edit., 1994, 4th edit., 2000, Calcium Antagonists: Mechanisms of Action on Cardiac Muscle and Vascular Smooth Muscle, 1984, Cell Interactions and Gap Junctions, vols. I and II, 1989, Frontiers in Smooth Muscle Research, 1990, Ion Channels in Vascular Smooth Muscle and Endothelial Cells, 1991, Essentials of Physiology, 1993, 2d edit., 1996, Cell Physiology Source Book, 1995 (Outstanding Acad. Book, Choice Am. Libr. Assn. 1996, 98), 3d edit., 2001, Electrogenesis of Biopotentials, 1995; assoc. editor Circulation Rsch., 1970-75, 75-80, Molecular Cellular Cardiology; regional editor Current Drug Targets, 2000-2002; contbr. articles to profl. jours. Lectr. Project Hope, Peru, 1962. Sgt. USMC, 1951-53, Res., 1953-59. Recipient Disting. Alumnus award Rockdale (Ill.) Pub. Schs., 1958; U. Cin. Grad. fellow, 1989; NIH grantee, 1959-99. Mem. IEEE, Engring. in Medicine and Biology, Am. Physiol. Soc. (chair steering com. sect. 1981-82), Biophys. Soc. (coun. 1990-93), Am. Soc. Pharmacology and Exptl. Therapeutics, Internat. Soc. Heart Rsch. (coun. 1980-89, 92-98), Am. Hellenic Ednl. Progressive Assn. (pres. Charlottesville chpt. 1980-82), Ohio Physiol. Soc. (pres. 1990-91), Phi Kappa Phi. Independent. Greek Orthodox. Avocations: ancient coins, stamp collecting. Office: U Cin Coll Medicine 231 Bethesda Ave Cincinnati OH 45229-2827

SPERLICH, HAROLD KEITH, automobile company executive; b. Detroit, Dec. 1, 1929; s. Harold Christ and Elva Margaret (Stoker) S.; m. Polly A. Berryman, May 22, 1976; children: Sue, Scott, Terry L.; stepchildren: Laurie, Brian, Scott, Colleen. B.S. in Mech. Engring, U. Mich., 1951, M.B.A., 1961. With Aluminum Co. Am., 1951-54; v.p. car ops. Ford Motor Co., Detroit, 1957-77; v.p. product planning and design Chrysler Motors Corp., Highland Park, Mich., 1977-78, group v.p. engring., product devel., 1978-81, pres. N.Am. ops., 1981-84, pres., 1984-88, also dir. Active Detroit Community Fund. Served with USNR, 1954-57. Presbyterian. Club: Orchard Lake (Mich.) Country. Home: 3333 W Shore Dr Orchard Lake MI 48324-2372 Office: Chrysler Motors Corp 12000 Chrysler Dr Detroit MI 48288-0001

SPERLING, JAC, professional sports team executive; CEO Minn. Wild Minn. Hockey Ventures Group, St. Paul, 1997—; ptnr. Hogan & Hartson, Washington. Office: 317 Washington St Saint Paul MN 55102

SPERO, KEITH ERWIN, lawyer, educator; b. Cleve., Aug. 21, 1933; s. Milton D. and Yetta (Silverstein) S.; m. Carol Kohn, July 4, 1957 (div. 1974); children: Alana, Scott, Susan; m. Karen Weaver, Dec. 28, 1975. BA, Western Res. U., 1954, LLB, 1956. Bar: Ohio 1956. Assoc. Sindell, Sindell & Bourne, Cleve., 1956-57, Sindell, Sindell, Bourne, Markus, Cleve., 1960-64; ptnr. Sindell, Sindell, Bourne, Markus, Stern & Spero, 1964-74, Spero & Rosenfield, Cleve., 1974-76, Spero, Rosenfeld & Bourne, LPA, Cleve., 1977-79, Spero & Rosenfield Co. LPA, 1979—. Tchr. bus. law U. Md. overseas div., Eng., 1958-59; lectr. Case-Western Res. U., 1965-69; instr.; nat. panel arbitrators Am. Arbitration Assn. Author: The Spero Divorce Folio, 1966, Hospital Libaiblity for Acts of Professional Negligence, 1979. Trustee Western Res. Hist. Soc., 1984—2000, exec. com., 1992—2000; v.p., chmn. libr. display and collections com. Western Res. Hist. Soc, 1992—95, chmn. history mus. com., 1995—99; commodore Dugway Creek Yacht Club, 1985—87; bd. dirs. Vail Valley Inst., 2000—. 1st lt. UAGC USAF, 1957—60, capt. Res. USAF, 1960—70. Fellow Am. Acad. Matrimonial Lawyers; mem. ABA, Ohio Bar Assn., Cleve. Bar Assn., Cuyahoga County Bar Assn., Ohio Acad. Trial Lawyers (pres. 1970-71), Assn. Trial Lawyers Am. (state committeeman 1971-75, bd. govs. 1975-79, sec. family law litigation sect. 1975-76, vice-chmn. 1976-77, chmn. 1977-79), Am. Bd. Trial Advs., Order of Coif, Masons, Phi Beta Kappa, Zeta Beta Tau, Tau Epsilon Rho. Jewish. (trustee, v.p. congregation 1972-78). Office: 440 Leader Bldg E 6th and Superior Cleveland OH 44114-1214 E-mail: keith@vail.net.

SPERZEL, GEORGE E., JR. personal care industry executive; b. 1951; BS in Bus. Adminstrn./Mgmt., U. Louisville, 1977. With General Electric Co., 1977-93; v.p., CFO Andrew Jergens Co., Cin., 1993-2000, Kao Am. Inc., Wilmington, Del., 1995-2000; svp and CFO Alliant Exchange, Inc., 2000—. Office: Alliant Exchange Inc One Parkway North Deerfield IL 60015

SPICE, DENNIS DEAN, venture capitalist, consultant; b. Rochester, Ind., Feb. 7, 1950; s. Donnelly Dean and Lorene (Rhodes) S.; m. Linda Kay Buehler, Oct. 1, 1971; children: Kristie Lorene, Danielle Deanne. AA, SUNY, Albany, 1974; BA, Ea. Ill. U., 1978; MBA, U. Ill., Urbana, 1985. Employee benefits mgr. Ea. Ill. U., Charleston, 1977-80; disbursements officer State Univs. Retirement Sys., Champaign, Ill., 1980-81, asst. dir. adminstrn., 1981-85, assoc. exec. dir., 1985-90, exec. dir., 1991-95; pres., chmn. Instnl. Advisors, Ltd., 1995—. Chmn. Rockwell Rhode Assocs. Inc., 1998—; mng. mem. Open Prairie Ventures, Champaign, 1997; sec. bd. dirs. HarVestco Agrl. Properties, Agrarian Mgmt. LLC.; mem. adv. Ea. Ill. U. Sch. Tech.; bd. dirs. Nims Assocs., Inc.; mem. adv. bd. dept. gen. engring. U. Ill. Staff sgt. USMC, 1968-77, Vietnam. Paul Harris fellow. Mem. Econ. Club Chgo. Office: Open Prairie Ventures 115 N Neil St Ste 209 Champaign IL 61820-4083 E-mail: dspice@ia-ltd.com.

SPICER, HOLT VANDERCOOK, retired speech and theater educator; b. Pasadena, Calif., Feb. 1, 1928; s. John Lovely and Dorothy Eleanor (Clause) S.; m. Marion Arel Gibson, Aug. 16, 1952; children: Mary Ellen, Susan Leah, Laura Alice, John Millard. BA, U. Redlands, 1952, MA, 1957; PhD, U. Okla., 1964. From instr. speech and theatre to prof. S.W. Mo. State Coll., 1952-93, emeritus prof., 1993—, head dept. speech and theatre, 1967-71, dean Sch. Arts and Humanities, 1971-85. Chmn. Dist. 4 Nat. Debate Tournament Com., 1955, 58, 64, 68 Vestryman Episcopalian Ch., 1981—85, 1998—2001; bd. dirs. Springfield (Mo.) Cmty. Ctr., 1981—. Named Debate Coach of Decade U.S. Air Force Acad., 1965, Holt V. Spicer Debate Forum, 1988; recipient Alumni Achievement award in Speech and Debate U. Redlands, 1991, Alumni award of appreciation S.W. Mo. State U., 1996; team won CEDA Nat. Debate championship, 1992. Mem.: AAUP, Am. Forensic Assn., Speech Communication Assn. Episcopalian. Home: 2232 E Langston St Springfield MO 65804-2646 E-mail: holtspicer9@mchsi.com.

SPIEGEL, S. ARTHUR, federal judge; b. Cin., Oct. 24, 1920; s. Arthur Major and Hazel (Wise) S.; m. Louise Wachman, Oct. 31, 1945; children: Thomas, Arthur Major II, Andrew, Roger Daniel. BA, U. Cin., 1942, postgrad., 1949; LLB, Harvard U., 1948. Assoc. Kasfir & Chalfie, Cin., 1948-52; assoc. Benedict, Bartlett & Shepard, 1952-53, Gould & Gould, Cin., 1953-54; ptnr. Gould & Spiegel, 1954-59; assoc. Cohen, Baron, Druffel & Hogan, 1960; ptnr. Cohen, Todd, Kite & Spiegel, 1961-80; judge U.S. Dist Ct. Ohio, 1980—; sr. status, 1995—. Served to capt. USMC, 1942-46 Mem. ABA, FBA, Ohio Bar Assn., Cin. Bar Assn., Cin. Lawyers Club. Democrat. Jewish. Office: US Dist Ct 838 US Courthouse 5th Walnut St Cincinnati OH 45202

SPINA, ANTHONY FERDINAND, lawyer; b. Chgo., Aug. 15, 1937; s. John Dominic and Nancy Maria (Ponzio) S.; m. Anita Phyllis De Orio, Jan. 28, 1961; children: Nancy M. Spina Okal, John D., Catherine M. Spina Samatas, Maria J. Spina Samatas, Felicia M. BS in Social Sci., Loyola U., Chgo., 1959; JD, DePaul U., 1962. Bar: Ill. 1962. Assoc. Epton, Scott, McCarthy & Bohling, Chgo., 1962-64; pvt. practice Elmwood Park, Ill., 1964-71; pres. Anthony & Spina, PC, 1971-84, Spina, McGuire & Okal, PC, Elmwood Park, 1985—. Codifier Rosemont Village Ordinances, 1971, Elmwood Park Bldg. Code, 1975, Leyden Twp. Codified Ordinances, 1987. Mem. Elmwood Pk. Bldg. Code Planning Commn. Bd. Appeals; bd. dirs. Sheridan Carrol Charitable Works Fund, 1994—; atty. Leyden Twp., Ill., 1969—89, Village of Rosemont, 1971; counsel for Pres. and dir. Cook County Twp. Ofcls. Ill., 1975—96; counsel for exec. dir. Ill. State Assn. Twp. Ofcls., 1975—96; counsel Elmwood Park Village Bd., 1967—89, Norwood Park St. Lighting Dist., 1988—, various Cook County Twps. including DuPage, 1980—82, Maine, 1981—97, Norwood Park, 1982—, Wayne, 1982—84, Berwyn Twp., 1997—99, Hanover Twp., 1997, Cook County Hwy. Commrs. Traffic Fine Litigation, 1974—96, 1999—2001, Hanover Twp. Mental Health Bd., 1991—, Glen Edens Assn., 1994—99, Berwyn Twp. Mental Health Bd., 1997—. Recipient Lacodaire medal, Deans Key Loyola U., Loyola U. Housing awards, 1965, 71, 76; Appreciation award Cook County Twp. Ofcls., av rating Martindale-Hubbel. Mem. ABA, Ill. Bar Assn., Chgo. Bar Assn., West Suburban Bar Assn. Cook County (past chmn. unauthorized practice law sect.), Am. Judicature Soc., Justinian Soc., Lawyers Ill. State Twp. Attys. Assn. (past v.p., pres. 1982-86, dir. 1996-99, dir. emeritus 1999—), Nat. Inst. Town and Twp. Attys. (past v.p., pres. 1993-95, Ill. del.), Montclare/Leyden C. of C., Edgebrook C. of C. (past bd. dirs.), Nat. Assn. Italian Am. Lawyers, Joint Civic Com. Chgo. (exec. com.), World Bocce Assn. (dir.), St. Rocco Soc. Simbario, KC (scribe, trustee, past Grand Knight, bldg. corp. dir. 1967-99), Calabresi in Am. Orgn. (bd. dirs. 1991—), Fra Noi Ethnic Publ. (dir. 1995—), Blue Key, Delta Theta Phi, Tau Kappa Epsilon, Pi Gamma Mu. Roman Catholic. Office: 7610 W North Ave Elmwood Park IL 60707-4100 E-mail: spinalaw@aol.com.

SPINDLER, GEORGE S. lawyer, retired oil industry executive; BCE, Ga. Inst. Tech., 1961; JD, DePaul U., 1966. Bar: Ill. 1966. Asst. gen. counsel, patents and licensing Amoco Corp., Chgo., 1979-81, gen. mgr. info. svcs., 1981-85, v.p. planning and adminstrn., 1985-87, assoc. gen. counsel 1987-88, dep. gen. counsel, 1988-89, v.p., gen. counsel, 1989-92, sr. v.p., gen. counsel, 1992-95, sr. v.p. law and corporate affairs, 1995-99; ret., 1999. Office: 200 E Randolph Dr PO Box 2106C Chicago IL 60690-2106

SPINELL, RICHARD E. financial services company executive; Ptnr. Mid-Am. Asset Mgmt., Inc., Oakbrook Terrace, Ill., 1993—. Office: Mid-Am Asset Mgmt Inc 2 Mid-Am Plz Ste 330 Oakbrook Terrace IL 60181

SPINNATO, JOSEPH ANTHONY, II, obstetrician; b. Ketchikan, Alaska, May 10, 1949; s. Joseph Anthony and Ann S.; m. Diane Dusak, Apr. 26, 1969; children: Joseph Anthony III, Mark Andrew, Julie Anne. BS, U. Dayton, 1970; MD, U. Louisville, 1974. Diplomate Am. Bd. Obstetricians and Gynecologists. Resident on ob/gyn U. Louisville, 1974-77; asst. prof. ob/gyn Sch. Medicine Tex. Tech U., Lubbock, 1979-82; nutrition intern Montreal (Can.) Diet Dispensary, 1980; fellow in maternal-fetal medicine U. Tenn. Ctr. for Health Scis., Memphis, 1982-84, clin. instr. dept. ob/gyn, 1982-84; assoc. prof. divsn. maternal-fetal medicine dept. ob/gyn Coll. Medicine U. South Ala., 1984-88; dir., prof. divsn. maternal-fetal medicine dept. ob/gyn. Sch. Medicine/U. Louisville, 1988-99; prof., vice chair dept. ob/gyn. U. Cin., 2000—. Mem. ob/gyn staff Lubbock Gen. Hosp., 1979-82, City of Memphis Hosps., 1982-84, U. South Ala. Med. Ctr., Mobile, 1984-88, Norton Hosp., Louisville, 1988-99, U. Louisville Hosp., 1988-99; mem. birth defects adv. com., human resources dept. Commonwealth of Ky., 1992; dir. maternal transport Norton Hosp., 1988-93, dir. women's reproductive testing ctr., 1988-96; dir. improved pregnancy outcome project U. Louisville, 1988-93, 96-99; dir. Fetal Rev. Bd., 1990-92; dir. perinatology Christ Hosp. Cin.; presenter, lectr., rschr. in field. Spl. reviewer jours. in field; contbr. articles, abstracts to profl. publs. Dir. teenage parent program Emerson Sch., Louisville, 1988-92, 96—. Lt. comdr. Med. Corps USN, 1977-79. Nutrition intern March of Dimes, 1980; grantee Smith Kline French Labs., 1986, NIH, 1986, NKC Cmty. Trust Fund, 1988, 95-96, WHAS Crusade for Children, 1989-90, 92, 98, Ky. Human Resources Dept., 1990, 93-94; recipient Outstanding Tchr. award, 1991, 93, APGO Excellence in Tchg. award U. Louisville, 1994. Mem. Am. Coll. Obstetricians and Gynecologists, Assn. Profs. of Gynecology and Obstetrics (Excellence in Tchg. award 1994), Soc. Perinatal Obstetricians, Soc. for Maternal-Fetal Medicine, Nat. Perinatal Assn., Jefferson County Med. Soc., Louisville Obgyn Soc., Am. Inst. Ultrasound in Medicine. Avocations: tennis, golf, music, basketball. Office: U Cin PO Box 670526 Cincinnati OH 45267-0526 E-mail: spinnaja@ucmail.uc.edu.

SPIOTTA, RAYMOND HERMAN, editor; b. Bklyn., Feb. 24, 1927; s. Michael Joseph and Olga Elizabeth (Schmidt) S.; m. Maria Theresa Attanasio, Apr. 17, 1949; children: Robert, Michael, Ronald, Mark, Sandra. B.M.E., Pratt Inst., 1953. Mfg. engr. Arma div. Am. Bosch Arma Corp., Garden City, N.Y., 1948-53; mng. editor Machinery mag., N.Y.C., 1953-65; editor Machine and Tool Blue Book, Wheaton, Ill., 1965-89; editorial dir. Machine and Tool Blue Book & Mfg. Systems, Carol Stream, 1989-90; cons. editor Cutting Tool Engring., Northbrook, 1992-95; acquisitions editor Hanser Gardner Publs., Cin., 1995-97, ret., 1997. Contbr. to Am. Peoples Ency. Yearbook; contbr. articles to profl. jours. Mem. DuPage County (Ill.) area council Boy Scouts Am., 1966-73. Served with AC USNR, 1944-48. Mem. Numerical Control Soc. of AIM-Tech., Soc. Am. Value Engrs., Soc. Mfg. Engrs., Am. Inst. Indsl. Engrs., Robotics Internat., Computer and Automated Sys. Assn. Roman Catholic. Home and Office: 1484 Aberdeen Ct Naperville IL 60564-9796 E-mail: r-mspiotta@mindspring.com.

SPIOTTO, JAMES ERNEST, lawyer; b. Chgo., Nov. 25, 1946; s. Michael Angelo and Vinnetta Catherine (Henninger) S.; m. Ann Elizabeth Humphreys, Dec. 23, 1972; children: Michael Thomas, Mary Catherine, Joan Elizabeth, Kathryn Ann. AB, St. Mary's of the Lake, 1968; JD, U. Chgo., 1972. Bar: Ill. 1972, U.S. Dist. Ct. (no. dist.) Ill. 1973, U.S. Ct. Appeals (3rd and 7th cir.) 1974, U.S. Supreme Ct. 1978, U.S. Ct. Appeals (9th cir.) 1984, U.S. Dist. Ct. (so. dist.) Calif. 1984. Exclusionary rule study-project dir. Law Enforcement Assistance Agy. Grant, Chgo., 1972; law clk. to presiding justice U.S. Dist. Ct., 1972-74; assoc. Chapman and Cutler, 1974-80, ptnr., 1980—. Chmn. program on defaulted bonds and bankruptcy Practising Law Inst., 1982—, chmn program on troubled debt financing, 1987— Author: Defaulted Securities, 1990; contbr. numerous articles to profl. jours. With USAR, 1969-75. Mem. Assn. Bond Lawyers, Soc. Mcpl. Analysts, Law Club of City of Chgo., Union League, Econs. Club Chgo. Roman Catholic. Office: Chapman and Cutler 111 W Monroe St Ste 1700 Chicago IL 60603-4006

SPIRES, ROBERT CECIL, foreign language educator; b. Missouri Valley, Iowa, Dec. 1, 1936; s. Roy C. and Ellen M. (Epperson) S.; m. Roberta A. Hyde, Feb. 2, 1963; children: Jeffrey R., Leslie Ann. BA, U. Iowa, 1959, MA, 1963, PhD, 1968. Asst. prof. Ohio U., Athens, 1967-69; asst. prof. dept. Spanish and Portuguese U. Kans., Lawrence, 1969-72, assoc. prof., 1972-78, prof., 1978—, chmn. dept., 1983-92. Author: La novela española, 1978, Beyond the Metafictional Mode, 1984, Transparent Simulacra, 1988, Post-Totalitarian Spanish Fiction, 1996; contbg. editor SigloXX/20th Century; editl. bd. Jour. of Interdisciplinary Literary Studies, 1993—, Ind. Jour. of Hispanic Lit., 1992—. Served with U.S. Army, 1959-61. NEH fellow, 1981-82, U.S.-Spain Joint Com. fellow, 1985-86, Hall Ctr. for Humanities fellow, 1992, Program Cultural Coop. fellow, 1993. Mem. Revista de Estudios Hispánicos (editorial bd. 1985—), Anales de Literatura Contemporánea (editorial bd. 1981—), Letras Peninsulares (editorial bd. 1987—), MLA (del. assembly 1989-91), MLA 20th Century Spain (exec. com. 1983-89), 20th Century Spanish Assn. Am. (v.p. 1989-92). Home: 2420 Orchard Ln Lawrence KS 66049-2710 Office: U Kans Dept Spanish & Portuguese Lawrence KS 66045-0001 E-mail: rspires@ukans.edu.

SPIRES, ROBERTA LYNN, small business owner; b. Gary, Ind., Sept. 4, 1952; d. Merle Russell and Kathryn Dias (Felts) Harris; m. Richard John Badovinich, Aug. 16, 1975 (div. 1989); m. Patrick Robert Spires, Mar. 14, 1992; 1 child, Zachary Robert. Grad. h.s., Griffith, Ind. Dep. clk. U.S. Bankruptcy Ct., Gary, 1970-80, chief dep. clk., 1980-97; owner, mgr. Spl. Touch, personal shopping svc., Griffith, 1997—; owner Specialized Secretarial Svcs., Highland, Ind., 1997-99, Special Touch Typing Svc., Griffith, 1999—. Mem. Fed. Ct. Clks. Assn., FBA (cert., lectr.). Democrat. Roman Catholic. Avocations: water skiing, boating, sewing, handcrafts, reading. Home and Office: 719 N Rueth Dr Griffith IN 46319-3817 E-mail: RSpires799@aol.com.

SPITZER, ALAN, automotive executive; Student, Baldwin Wallce Coll. Gen. mgr. Dodge dealership Spitzer Mgmt. Inc., Ohio, dealer, operator, CEO Elyria, 1990—, also chmn. bd. dirs. Mem. nat. dealer coun. Ford Motor Co., Chrysler Corp.; mem. Key Bank USA Dealer Adv. Bd. Office: Spitzer Mgmt Inc 150 E Bridge St Elyria OH 44035-5219

SPITZER, JOHN BRUMBACK, lawyer; b. Toledo, Mar. 6, 1918; s. Lyman and Blanche (Brumback) S.; m. Lucy Ohlinger, May 10, 1941 (dec. Oct. 13, 1971); children: John B., Molly (Mrs. Edmund Frost), Lyman, Adelbert L.; m. Vondah D. Thornbury, July 3, 1972 (dec. Nov. 2001); stepchildren: Vondah, Barbara, James R. Thornbury. Grad., Phillips Andover Acad., 1935; BA, Yale U., 1939, LLB, 1947. Bar: Ohio 1947. Law clk. to U.S. Supreme Ct. Justice Stanley Reed, 1947-48; ptnr. Marshall, Melhorn, Cole, Hummer & Spitzer, Toledo, 1955-86, Hummer & Spitzer, Toledo, 1986-89; with Hummer Legal Svcs. Corp., Perrysburg, Ohio, 1990—. Pres. Spitzer Box Co., 1955-63; v.p. Spitzer Bldg. Co., 1960-91, pres. 1992—. Pres. Toledo Symphony Orch., 1956-58, v.p., sec., 1958-86. Maj. AUS, World War II. Mem.: Belmont Country Club. Congregationalist. Home: 29620 Gleneagles Rd Perrysburg OH 43551-3530 Office: Hummer Legal Svcs Corp 4841 Monroe St Ste 205 Toledo OH 43623-4352 E-mail: h/sc@accessToledo.com.

SPLINTER, WILLIAM ELDON, agricultural engineering educator; b. North Platte, Nebr., Nov. 24, 1925; s. William John and Minnie (Calhoun) Splinter; m. Eleanor Love Peterson, Jan. 10, 1952 (dec. Jan. 1999); children: Kathryn Love, William John, Karen Ann, Robert Marvin; m. Elizabeth Butters Calhoun, Feb. 9, 2002. BS in Agrl. Engring., U. Nebr., 1950; MS in Agrl. Engring., Mich. State U., 1951, PhD in Agrl. Engring., 1955. Instr. agrl. engring. Mich. State U., East Lansing, 1953-54; assoc. prof. biology and agrl. engring. N.C. State U., Raleigh, 1954-60, prof. biology and agrl. engring., 1960-68; from prof., chmn. dept. agrl. engring. to interim dean U. Nebr., Lincoln, Nebr., 1968—2001; interim dean Coll. of Engring. and Tech., 2001—. Cons. engr. Mem. exec. bd. Am. Assn. Engring. Socs.; hon. prof. Shengyang (People's Republic of China) Agrl. U. Contbr. articles to tech. jours.; patentee in field. Vol. dir. L.F. Larsen Tractor Mus. Served with USNR, 1946-51. Recipient Massey Ferguson gold medal, 1978, John Deere gold medal, 1995, Kiwanis award for disting. svc., 1994; named to Nebr. Hall of Agrl. Achievement; named Disting. Alumni, U. Nebr.-Lincoln, 2000. Recipient George Howard-Louise Pound award, 2001. Fellow AAAS, Am. Soc. Agrl. Engrs. (pres., adminstrv. council, found. pres., Presdl. citation 1999); mem. Nat. Acad. Engring., Soc. Automotive Engrs., Am. Soc. Engring. Edn., Nat. Soc. Profl. Engrs., Sigma Xi, Sigma Tau, Sigma Pi Sigma, Pi Mu Epsilon, Gamma Sigma Delta, Phi Kappa Phi, Beta Sigma Psi. Home: 4801 Bridle Ln Lincoln NE 68516-3436 Office: U Nebr W181 Nebraska Hall 2000 N 35th St Lincoln NE 68588-0501 E-mail: wsplinter1@ual.edu.

SPODEK, BERNARD, early childhood educator; b. Bklyn., Sept. 17, 1931; s. David and Esther (Lebenbaum) S.; m. Prudence Debb, June 21, 1957; children: Esther Yin-ling, Jonathan Chou. BA, Bklyn. Coll., 1952; MA, Columbia U., 1955, EdD, 1962. Cert. early childhood edn. tchr., N.Y. Tchr. Beth Hayeled Sch., N.Y.C., 1952-56, N.Y. City Pub. Schs., Bklyn., 1956-57, Early Childhood Ctr., Bklyn. Coll., 1957-60; asst. prof. elem. edn. U. Wis.-Milw., 1961-65; assoc. prof. early childhood edn. U. Ill., Champaign, 1965-68, prof. dept. curriculum and instrn., 1968-97, dir. dept. grad. programs, 1986-87, chair dept., 1987-89, dir. hons. program, Coll. Edn., 1984-86, mem. faculty Bur. Ednl. Rsch., 1981-85, prof. emeritus, 1997—; adv. prof. Hong Kong Inst. of Edn., 1999-2001. Dir. insts. Nat. Def. Edn. Act, 1965-67, dir. experienced tchr. fellowship program, 1967-69, co-dir. program for tchr. trainers in early childhood edn., 1969-74; vis. prof. Western Wash. State U., 1974, U. Wis., Madison, 1980; vis. scholar Sch. Early Childhood Studies, Brisbane (Australia) Coll. Advanced Edn., Delissa Inst. Early Childhood Studies, S. Australia Coll. Advanced Edn., 1985, Beijing Normal U., Nanjing Normal U., E. China Normal U., Shangai, People's Republic China, 1986; rsch. fellow Kobe U., Japan, 1996; adj. prof. Queensland (Australia) U. Tech., 2000. Author or co-author 31 books including: (with others) A Black Studies Curriculum for Early Childhood Eduication, 1972, 2d edit., 1976, Teaching in the Early Years, 1972, 3d edit., 1985, Early Childhood Education, 1973, Studies in Open Education, 1975 (Japanese trans.), Early Childhood Education: Issues and Perspectives, 1977, (with Nir-Janiv and Steg) International Perspectives on Early Childhood Education, 1982 (Hebrew trans.), with Saracho and Lee (Mainstreaming Young Children, 1984, (with Saracho and Davis) Foundations of Early Childhood Education, 1987, 2d edit. (Japanese trans.), 1991, (with Saracho) Right from the Start, 1994 (Chinese and Korean translations), Dealing with Individual Differences in the Early Childhood Classroom, 1994; editor: Handbook of Research in Early Childhood Education, 1982, Today's Kindergarten, 1986, (with Saracho and Peters) Professionalism and the Early Childhood Practitioner, 1988, (with Saracho) Early Childhood Teacher Education, 1990, Issues in Early Childhood Curriculum, 1991, Educationally Appropriate Kindergarten Practices, 1991, Issues in Childcare, 1992, Handbook of Research on the Education of Young Children (Portuguese translation), 1993, (Portuguese tranls.) (with Saracho), Language and Literacy in Early Childhood Education, 1993; (with Safford and Saracho) Early Childhood Special Education, 1994; (with Garcia, McLaughlin & Saracho) Meeting the Challenge of Cultural and Linguistic Diversity, 1995, (with Saracho) Issues in Early Childhood Educational Evaluation and Assessment, 1996, (with Saracho) Multiple Perspectives on Play in Early Childhood Education, 1998, (With Saracho and Pellegrino) Issues in Early Childhood Educational Research, 1998, (with Saracho) Contemporary Perspectives in Early Childhood Curriculum, 2002, (with Saracho) Contemporary Perspectives in Early Childhood Language and Literacy, 2002; series editor Yearbook in Early Childhood Education, early childhood edn. publs., 1971-79; guest editor Studies in Ednl. Evaluation, 1982, Early Education and Child Development, 1995; also contbr. chpts to books, articles to profl. jours. Mem. Am. Ednl. Rsch. Assn. (chair early childhood and child devel. spl. interest group 1983-84, publs. com. 1984-86), Nat. Assn. Edn. Young Children (sec. 1965-68, bd. govs. 1968-72, pres. 1976-78, editorial adv. bd. 1972-76, book rev. editor, 1972-74, cons. editor, 1985-87 Young Children jour., mem. tchr. edn. commn. 1981-88, chair commn. on appropriate edn. 4-5 yr. old children, 1984-85, cons. editor Early Childhood Rsch. Quar. 1987-90), Nat. Soc. for Study of Edn. (1972 yearbook com.). Office: U Ill Dept Curriculum & Instrn 1310 S 6th St Champaign IL 61820-6925 E-mail: b-spodek@uiuc.edu.

SPOHN, HERBERT EMIL, psychologist; b. Berlin, Germany, June 10, 1923; s. Herbert F. and Bertha S.; m. Billie M. Powell, July 28, 1973; children: Jessica, Madeleine. B.S.S., CCNY, 1949; Ph.D., Columbia U., 1955. Research psychologist VA Hosp., Montrose, N.Y., 1955-60, chief research sect., 1960-64; sr. research psychologist Menninger Found., Topeka, 1965-80, dir. hosp. research, 1979-94, dir. research dept., 1981-94; ret., prof. emeritus for rsch., 1994—. Mem. mental health small grant com. NIMH, 1972-76, mem. treatment assessment rev. com., 1983-86, chmn. 1986-87. Author: (with Gardner Murphy) Encounter with Reality, 1968; assoc. editor: Schizophrenia Bull, 1970-87, 91—; contbr. articles to profl. jours. Served with AUS, World War II. USPHS grantee, 1964— Fellow Am. Psychopath. Assn.; mem. AAAS, N.Y. Acad. Sci., Soc. Psychopath. Research, Phi Beta Kappa, Sigma Xi. Office: Menninger Found PO Box 829 Topeka KS 66601-0829 E-mail: hspohn@prodigy.net.

SPOHR, ARNOLD THEODORE, artistic director, choreographer; b. Rhein, Sask., Can., Dec. 26, 1927; Student, Winnipeg (Can.) Tchrs. Coll., 1942-43; Assocs., Royal Conservatory Music, Toronto, Can.; cert., Royal Acad. Dance; LLD (hon.), U. Man., Can., 1970, U. Winnipeg, 1984; DFA (hon.), U. Victoria, Can., 1987. Cert. tchr. pub. schs. Tchr. piano, 1946-51; prin. dancer Winnipeg Ballet (now Royal Winnipeg Ballet), 1945-58, artistic dir., tchr. dance, 1958-88, artistic dir. emeritus, 1988—; choreographer, performer Rainbow Stage Sta. CBC-TV, 1957-60; dir. dept. dance Nelson Sch. Fine Arts, 1964-67; artistic dir. dept. dance Banff Sch. Fine Arts, 1967-81. Bd. dirs. Can. Theatre Centre; vice chmn. Bd. Dance Can.; adjudicator Can. Council, Can. Dance Tchrs. Assn., N.Y. Internat. Ballet Competitions. Choreographer Ballet Premier, 1950, Intermede, 1951, E Minor, 1959, Hansel and Gretal, 1960, also 18 musicals for Rainbow Stage. Decorated Order of Can., 1970; recipient Centennial medal Govt. of Can., 1967, Manitoba's Order of Buffalo, 1969, Molson prize, 1970, Can. Actor's Equity Assn. Champagne award, 1979, Dance mag. Ann. award, 1981, Diplome D'honneur Can. Conf. of Arts, 1983, Can. Tourism medal, 1985, Royal Bank award, 1987. Mem. Dance in Can. Assn. (bd. dirs., Can. Dance award 1986). Office: Canada's Royal Winnipeg Ballet 380 Graham Ave Winnipeg MB Canada R3C 4K2

SPOKANE, ROBERT BRUCE, biophysical chemist; b. Cleve., Aug. 5, 1952; s. Herbert and Marjorie Ellen (Firsten) S.; m. Linda Carol Wright, June 20, 1976; children: Lea, Hannah, Tara. BS in Chemistry, Ohio U., 1975; MS in Biophys. Chemistry, U. Colo., 1978, PhD in Biophys. Chemistry, 1981. Cert. full cave diver. Teaching asst. dept. Chemistry, U. Colo., Boulder, 1975-77, rsch. asst., 1977-81; staff scientist Procter &

Gamble Co., Cin., 1981-84; rsch. scientist Dept. Neurophysiology, Children's Hosp., 1984-90, YSI Co., Rsch. Ctr., Yellow Springs, Ohio, 1990—. Cons. Synthetic Blood Internat., Yellow Springs, 1992. Contbr. articles to profl. jours. Rescuer, treas. Boulder Emergency Squad, 1980; rescue diver Kitty Hawk Scuba, Dayton, Ohio, 1992. Recipient Merck Index award Ohio U., 1975. Mem. Am. Chem. Soc., N.Y. Acad. Sci., Am. Physiol. Soc., Nat. Speleological Soc. (cave diving sect.), Sigma Xi. Achievements include research in implantable glucose sensors; oxygen tonometer for peritoneal oxygen measurements; interferant removal system for biosensors for methanol, ethanol, glutamate, and glutamine, optical carbon dioxide sensor, water chemistry in submerged caves. Home: 1715 Garry Dr Bellbrook OH 45305-1362 Office: YSI Co 1725 Brannum Ln Yellow Springs OH 45387-1107 E-mail: rspokane@ysi.com.

SPONG, DOUGLAS K. public relations executive; B in English, Iowa State U. With Colle & McVoy, sr. v.p., mng. dir., also bd. dirs.; mng. ptnr. Carmichael Lynch Spong, 1990—. Office: Carmichael Lynch Spong Pub Rels 800 Hennepin Ave Minneapolis MN 55403-1817

SPOOR, WILLIAM HOWARD, food company executive; b. Pueblo, Colo., Jan. 16, 1923; s. Charles Hinchman and Doris Field (Slaughter) S.; m. Janet Spain, Sept. 23, 1950; children: Melanie G., Cynthia F., William Lincoln. BA, Dartmouth Coll., 1949; postgrad., Denver U., 1949, Stanford U., 1965. Asst. sales mgr. N.Y. Export divsn. Pillsbury Co., 1949-53; mgr. N.Y. office Pillsbury Co., 1953-62, v.p. export divsn., 1962-68, v.p., gen. mgr. internat. ops., 1968-73, CEO, 1973-85, also bd. dirs., chmn. exec. com., 1987, pres., CEO, 1988, past chmn. bd. dirs. Bd. dirs. Coleman Co. Mem. regional export expansion coun. Dept. Commerce, 1966-74; bd. dirs. exec. Coun. Fgn. Diplomats, 1976-78; mem. bd. visitors Nelson A. Rockefeller Ctr., Dartmouth Coll., 1992-95; Minn. Orchestral Assn., United Negro Coll. Fund, 1973-75; chmn. Capitol City Renaissance Task Force, 1985; trustee Mpls. Found., 1985-92; mem. sr. campaign cabinet Carlson Com. U. Minn., 1985; mem. corps. rels. com. Nature Conservancy, 1985; mem. Nat. Cambodia Crisis Com., pres. pvt. sector Dept. Transp. task force, 1982, pres. pvt. sector survey on cost control, 1983; chmn. YWCA Tribute to Womwn in Internat. Industry. 2d lt. inf. U.S. Army, 1943-46. Recipient Golden Plate award, Am. Acad. Achievement, Disting. Bus. Leadership award, St. Cloud State U., Miss. Valley World Trade award, Outstanding Achievement award, Dartmouth Coll., Horatio Alger award, 1986, Medal of Merit, U.S. Savs. Bond Program; honored with William H. Spoor Dialogues on Leadership, Dartmouth Coll., honored Fair Player Minn. Women's Polit. Caucus, 1989. Mem. Grocery Mfrs. Am. (treas. 1973-84), Nat. Fgn. Trade Coun., Minn. Hist. Soc. (mem. exec. com. 1983, bd. dirs.), Minn. Bus. Partnership, River Club N.Y.C., Woodhill Country Club, Lafayette Club (Wayzata, Minn.), Mpls. Club (bd. govs. 1985, pres. 1986), Gulf Stream Bath and Tennis Club, Delray Beach Yacht Club, Gulf Stream Golf Club, Old Baldy Club (Saratoga, Wyo.), Alta Club (Salt Lake City), Phi Beta Kappa. Home: 622 Ferndale Rd W Wayzata MN 55391-9628 Office: 4900 IDS Ctr Minneapolis MN 55402

SPORE, KEITH KENT, newspaper executive; b. Milw., May 29, 1942; s. G. Keith and Evelyn A. (Morgan) S.; divorced; children: Bradley, Julie, Justine; m. Kathy Stokebrand. BS in Journalism, U. Wis., Milw., 1967. City editor Milw. Sentinel, 1977-81; asst. mng. editor/news Milw. Jour. Sentinel, 1981-89, mng. editor, 1989-91, editor, 1991-95, editl. page editor, 1995, pres., 1995—, pub., 1996—. Author: (novels) The Hell Masters, 1977, Death of a Scavenger, 1980. With U.S. Army, 1961-64. Recipient Freedom of Info. award Soc. Profl. Journalists, 1995; named Mass Comms. Alumnus of Yr., U. Wis.-Milw., 1994. Mem. Greater Milw. Com. Office: Milw Jour Sentinel PO Box 661 Milwaukee WI 53201-0661 E-mail: kspore@onwis.com.

SPRANDEL, DENNIS STEUART, management consulting company executive; b. Little Falls, Minn, June 1, 1941; s. George Washington and Lucille Margaret (Steuart) S. AB, Albion Coll., 1963; MEd, U. Ariz., 1965; PhD, Mich. State U., 1973. Grad. tchg. asst. U. Ariz., Tucson, 1964-65; dir. athletics Owen Grad. Ctr., Mich. State U., East Lansing, 1965-68; prof., dir. student tchg. Mt. St. Mary's Coll., 1968-70; exec. dir. Mich. AAU, 1974-81, mem. numerous nat. coms., 1974-81; mem. U.S. Olympic Com., 1974-77; pres., chmn. bd. Am. Sports Mgmt., Ann Arbor, 1976—, Am. SportsVision, 1981—, Am. Sports Rsch., 1977—, Sprandel Group, 1984—; pres. Nat. Sports & Entertainment, Inc., 1984—; with Sprandel Assocs., 1984—, registered rep., 1988—, pres., 1996—, Sprandel Portfolio Mgmt., 2000—. Fin. advisor Prudential Preferred, 1988-95; bd. dirs. Nat. Golden Gloves, 1980—, bd. trustees, 1986, Port Huron TV Project, 1985—; pres. Detroit Golden Gloves Charities; pres. adminstrv. bd. Detroit Golden Gloves, 1985—; bd. dirs. Mich. Sports Hall of Fame, 1976—; cons. in field. Contbr. articles to profl. jours. Recipient Detroit Striders award, 1978, Emerald award, 1979, World TaeKwonDo award, 1979, Detroit Spl. Olympics award, 1978, Cmty. Svc. award Mich. State U., 1985. Mem. Am. Soc. Assn. Execs., Nat. Assn. Phys. Edn. in Higher Edn., AAHPER, Nat. Recreation and Pks. Assn., Nat. Assn. Life Underwriters, Internat. Boxing Fedn., N.Am. Boxing Fedn., U.S. Boxing Assn., World Boxing Assn., World Boxing Coun., Nat. Assn. for Girls and Women in Sport, Psi Chi. Home: 219 Hutchinson Big Rapids MI 49307-1715 Office: Sprandel & Assocs PO Box 6047 Ann Arbor MI 48106-6047 E-mail: dennwins@aol.com.

SPRANG, MILTON LEROY, obstetrician, gynecologist, educator; b. Chgo., Jan. 15, 1944; s. Eugene and Carmella (Bruno) S.; m. Sandra Lee Karabelas, July 16, 1966; children: David, Christina, Michael. Student, St. Mary's Coll., 1962-65; MD, Loyola U., 1969. Diplomate Am. Bd. Ob-gyn; Nat. Bd. Med. Examiners; CME accreditation. Intern St. Francis Hosp., Evanston, Ill., 1969-70, resident, 1972-75, sr. attending physician, 1985—; assoc. attending phsycian Evanston Hosp., 1975-79, attending physician, 1980-84, sr. attending physician, 1985—, v.p. med. staff, 1990-91, pres.-elect, 1991-92, pres., 1992-93; also bd. dirs., 1991-94; sec. exec. com. Evanston Hosp., 1993-94; chmn. ob-gyn Cook County Grad. Sch. Medicine, Chgo., 1983-91. Instr. Northwestern U. Med. Sch., Chgo., 1975-78, asst. prof., 1984-95, assoc. prof., 1995—; pres. Northwestern Healthcare Network Physician Leadership, 1994; lectr. acad. and civic groups OB-Gyn. Nat. Ctr. Advanced Med. Edn., 1991—; bd. dirs. Ill. Found. Med. Rev.; bd. trustees Ill. State Ins. Svcs., 1992—, chair, 1998-2000; bd. govs. Ill. State Med. Inter-Inst. Exch., 1987-92. Editor: Profl. Staff News, 1992-93; chmn. editorial bd. Jour. Chgo. Medicine, 1986-91; contbr. articles to profl. jours. Bd. dirs. Am. Cancer Sooc., chmn. profl. edn. com. North Shoore unit, 1982-85; bd. dirs. Chgo. Community Info. Network, 1994-95; mem. Nat. Rep. Congrl. Com., 1981—, Ill. Med. Polit. Action Com.; bd. advisors Nat. Youth Leadership Forum on Medicine, Chgo., 1998-. With USN, 1970-72. Fellow: ACOG (chmn. Ill. sect. 1975—76), ACS, Am. Soc. Colposcopy and Cervical Pathology; mem.: AMA (Physician Recognition award 1977, 1980, 1983), Chgo. Found. Med. Care (med. care evaluation and edn. com. 1980—83, nominating com. 1980—84, practice guidelines com. 1984), Ednl. and Scientific Found. (bd. dirs. 1994—98), Chgo. Med. Soc. (adv. com. advt. stds. 1978—84, physician's rev. com. 1980—85, exec. coun. north suburban br. 1981—82, trustee ins. bd. 1982—, v.p. 1984—85, chmn. 1985, 1985, nominating com. 1985—, exec. coun. north suburban br. 1986, treas. 1986—89, chmn. fin. com. 1986—89, trustee 1986—92, sec. 1989—90, pres.-elect 1990—91, chmn. bd. trustees 1990—91, pres. 1991—92, immediate past pres. 1992—93, chmn. ethical rels. com. 1994—, counselor), Ill. Med. Soc. (del. to AMA 1987—, govt. affairs com. 1988—, chmn. reference com. 1989, chmn. fin. com. 1992—94, sec.-treas. 1994—96, chmn. bd. trustees 1996—98, chmn. bylaws com. 1998—99, pres.-elect 1999—2000, 1999—2000, vice chair delegation 2001—02, immediate past pres. 2001—02, chair delegation 2003—, bd. trustees 2002—), Physician Benefit Trust (chmn. fin. com. 1993—2002). Roman Catholic. Avocations: reading, raising fish, swimming. Home: 4442 Concord Ln Skokie IL 60076-2606 Office: AGSO 1000 Central St Evanston IL 60201-1777

SPRENGER, GORDON M. hospital administrator; b. Albert Lea, Minn., Apr. 30, 1937; Bachelors degree, St. Olaf Coll., 1959; masters degree, U. Minn., 1961. Registrar USAF Hosp., Hamilton AFB, Calif., 1961-64; with St. Luke's Hosp., Milw., 1964-67, Northwestern Hosp., Mpls., 1967-71; exec. v.p. Abbott-Northwestern Hosp., 1971-75, pres. ceo., 1975-88, LifeSpan, 1982-92; exec. ofcr HealthSpan, 1992-94; chief exec. ofcr Allina Health, 1994-. Prof. U. Minn., 1976—; acad. lectureship; preceptor. Mem. ACHE and AHA; Affiliated Hosp. Srvs: Past Sec. Bd mem., 1971-74; Council of Community Hosp., chair. 1980-81; Governor's Task Force on Nursing, 1981; Health Political Action Comm. of Minn., chair. 1981; Minn. Hosp. Assoc. Governmntl Relations Comm., chair. 1979, bd mem, 1978-81, exec. comm. treas., 1981; chair. elect, Minn. Hosp. Assoc., 1982; MMI Cos bd mem, currently vice chair., preceptor and faculty mem., U of Minn. Hosp. and Health Care Admin., 1982 bd of Minnehaha Acad.; disting. alumnus, St. Olaf Coll., mem. bd of regents; Voluntary Hosp. of Amer., past chair., mem. Medtronics, Inc., bd of dirs., 1991-; mem. St. Paul Cos., bd of dirs. Office: Allina Health System 5601 Smetana Dr PO Box 9310 Minneapolis MN 55440-9310

SPRIESER, JUDITH A. food products company executive; BA in Linguistics, MBA in Fin., Northwestern U. CPA, Ill., 1982. Comml. banker Harris Bank, Chgo., 1974-81; dir. treasury ops. Esmark, 1981-84; asst. treas. internat. Nalco Chem. Co., 1984-87; asst. treas. corp. fin. Sara Lee Corp., 1987-90; sr. v.p., CFO Sara Lee Bakery N.Am., 1990-93, pres., CEO, 1993-94; sr. v.p., CFO Sara Lee Corp., 1994-99, CEO, Foods and Food Svc., 2000-2001; CEO Transora, Chgo., 2001—. Bd. dirs. USG Corp. Bd. dirs. Hinsdale Hosp. Found.; trustee Northwestern U. Mem. AICPA, Chgo. Network, Young Pres. Orgn., Chgo. coun. Fgn. Rels., Econ. Club, Conf. Bd. Coun. Fin. Execs. Office: 547 W Jackson Blvd Ste 900 Chicago IL 60661-5717

SPRIESTERSBACH, DUANE CARYL, academic administrator, speech pathology/audiology services professional, educator; b. Pine Island, Minn., Sept. 5, 1916; s. Merle Lee and Esther Lucille (Stucky) Spriestersbach; m. Bette Rae Bartell, Aug. 31, 1946; children: Michael Lee, Ann. BEd, Winona State Tchrs. Coll., 1939; MA, U. Iowa, 1940, PhD, 1948. Asst. dir. pers. rels. Pacific Portland Cement Co., San Francisco, 1946-47; prof. speech pathology U. Iowa, Iowa City, 1948-89, prof. emeritus, 1989—, dean. Grad. Coll., v.p. ednl. devel. and rsch., 1965-89, v. pres. and dean emeritus, 1989—, acting pres., 1981-82; v.p. ops. Breakthrough, Inc., Oakdale, 1993-94; cons., 1994—. Com. mem. Nat. Inst. Neurol. Disease and Blindess; chmn. dental tng. com. Nat. Inst. Dental Rsch., 1967—72, chmn. spl. grants rev., 1978—82; chmn. bd. dirs. Midwest Univs. Cons. Internat. Activities, Columbus, 1978—87. Author: (book) Psychosocial Aspects of Cleft Palate, 1973; author: (with others) Diagnostic Methods in Speech Pathology, 1978; co-editor: Cleft Palate and Communication, 1968, Diagnosis in Speech Language Pathology, rev. edit., 1999, The Way It Was: The University of Iowa 1964-1989, 1999. Pres. Iowa City Cmty. Theater, 1964, 1977, 1983. Served to lt. col. U.S. Army, 1941—46, ETO. Decorated Bronze Star; fellow Nat. Inst. Dental Rsch., 1971. Fellow: AAAS; mem.: Midwestern Assn. Grad. Schs. (chmn. 1979—80), Am. Cleft Palate Assn. (pres. 1961—62, disting. svc. award), Am. Speech and Hearing Assn. 1965, (honor award), Assn. Grad. Schs. 1979—80, Cosmos Clug (Washington), Mortar Bd., Sigma Xi. Home: 2 Longview Knoll NE Iowa City IA 52240-9148 Office: Univ Iowa M212 Oakdale Hall Iowa City IA 52242-5000 E-mail: duane-spriestersbach@uiowa.edu.

SPRING, TERRI, political organization executive; BA, U. Wis., 1975. 2d vice chair Dem. Party—Wis., Madison, 1994-97, state chair, 1997; legis. asst. State Senate, 1996-00; state chair Dem. Party-Wis., 2000—. Mem. Assn. State Dem. Chairs. Office: 222 State St Ste 400 Madison WI 53703-2273

SPRINGER, DENIS E. former railroad executive; m. Roselyn Springer; 4 children. BSEE, U. Notre Dame; MBA, U. Chgo. With Arthur Andersen & Co., Gould, Inc., Brown, Boveri Electric Inc.; dir. fin. Santa Fe Industries, Ft. Worth, 1982-84, asst. v.p. vin., 1984-88, v.p. fin., 1988-91, v.p., treas., CFO, 1991-92, sr. v.p., CFO, 1992-95, Burlington Northern Santa Fe Corp., Ft. Worth, 1995-99; bd. dirs. Webmodal Inc., Lombard, Ill. Mem. nat. adv. bd. Chase Manhattan Bank. Bd. dirs. Jr. Achievement of chgo.; mem. Coll. of Commerce adv. coun. DePaul U., Chgo. Mem. AICPAs, Ill. Soc. CPAs, Fin. Execs. Inst. Office: Webmodal Inc Ste 3610 150 N Michigan Ave Chicago IL 60601-7569

SPRINGER, JERRY, television talk show host; b. London, 1944; came to U.S. BA in Polit. Sci., Tulane U.; JD, Northwestern U., 1968. Presdl. campaign aide Sen. Robert F. Kennedy; elected mem. at large Cin. Coun., 1971-77; elected mayor Cin., 1977; polit. reporter, commentator WLWT-TV, 1982-84, anchor, mng. editor, 1984-93; host The Jerry Springer Show, 1991—. Author Ringmaster, 1998; video collection Jerry Springer: Too Hot for TV. On-site reporter Cin. Reaches Out; mem. adv. bd. Audrey Hepburn Hollywood for Children Fund; co-host Stars Across America Muscular Dystrophy Labor Day Telethon; v.p. bd. Nat. Muscular Dystrophy Assn.; founder scholarship fund Kellman Sch., Chgo. Recipient 7 Emmy awards for nightly news commentaries; named Best Anchor Cin. Mag. 5 times. Achievements include top rated daytime talk show series in the U.S. Office: Jerry Springer Show 454 N Columbus Dr Fl 2 Chicago IL 60611-5514

SPROGER, CHARLES EDMUND, lawyer; b. Chgo., Feb. 18, 1933; s. William and Minnette (Weiss) Sproger. BA (David Himmelblau scholar), Northwestern U., 1954, JD, 1957. Bar: Ill. 1957. Practiced in, Chgo., 1958—; assoc. Ehrlich & Cohn, 1958-63, Ehrlich, Bundesen, Friedman & Ross, 1963-72; partner Ehrlich, Bundesen, Broecker & Sproger, 1972-77; pvt. practice, 1977—. Mem. adv. com. curriculum Ill. Inst. Continuing Legal Edn., Chgo., 1976— ; v.p. Mediation Coun. of Ill., 1986-87; arbitration panelist for Cir. Ct. Cook County, 1990—. Editor: Family Lawyer, 1962-63; contbr. articles to legal publs. Mediator Pastoral Psychotherapy Inst., 1982-86. Fellow Am. Acad. Matrimonial Lawyers (bd. examiners 1972-86, chmn. Law Day U.S.A. 1975); mem. ABA, Ill. Bar Assn. (chmn. coun. family law 1970-71), Chgo. Bar Assn. (matrimonial law com. 1958—), Am. Arbitration Assn. (divorce mediation com. 1983—), Decalogue Soc., U. Mich. Club Chgo. (pres. 1988-89), Phi Alpha Delta. Address: 2800 W Birchwood Ave Chicago IL 60645-1218

SPURRIER-BRIGHT, PATRICIA ANN, professional society administrator; b. El Paso, Tex., Feb. 27, 1943; d. James Ray and Lucile Gray (Lafferty) Spurrier; m. Martin Oliver Bright, Sept. 18, 1964 (div. 1967); 1 child, James R. Student, Frederick Coll., 1962-64. Planning technician Reston Va, Inc./Gulf Reston, Inc., 1966-75; adminstrv. asst. Gulf Oil, Tulsa, 1975-79; planner Conde Engring., El Paso, Tex., 1979-82; adjutant U.S. Horse Cavalry Assn., Ft. Bliss, 1983-91; exec. dir. U.S. Cavalry Assn., Ft. Riley, Kans., 1991—, sec., 1991—. Sec. U.S. Cavalry Meml. Found., Fort Riley, 1994—; trustee Spurrier Trust, El Paso, 1990—; mem. Bigheart Cemetery Found., Barnsdale, Okla., 1989—; bd. dirs. 1st Kans. Territorial Capital. Editor The Cavalry Jour., 1990—. Mem. U.S. Army Daus. Republican. Avocations: research, painting, genealogy. Home: 1517 Leavenworth St Manhattan KS 66502-4154 Office: US Cavalry Assn PO Box 2325 Fort Riley KS 66442-0325 E-mail: cavalry@flinthills.com.

SPYERS-DURAN, PETER, librarian, educator; b. Budapest, Hungary, Jan. 26, 1932; came to U.S., 1956, naturalized, 1964; s. Alfred and Maria (Almasi-Balogh) S-D; m. Jane F. Cumber, Mar. 21, 1964; children: Kimberly, Hilary, Peter. Certificate, Free U. Budapest, 1955; M.A. in L.S, U. Chgo., 1960; Ed.D., Nova S Ea. U., 1975. Profl. asst. libr. adminstrn. div. ALA, Chgo., 1961-62; assoc. dir. librs., assoc. prof. U. Wis., 1962-67; dir. librs., prof. Western Mich. U., 1967-70; dir. librs., prof. libr. sci. Fla. Atlantic U., 1970-76; dir. libr. Calif. State U., Long Beach, 1976-83; prof. libr. and info. sci., dir. libr. Wayne State U., Detroit, 1983-86, dean, prof. libr. and info. sci. program, 1986-95, dean and prof. emeritus, 1995—; cons. Spyers-Duran Assocs., 1995—; acting univ. libr. Nova Southeastern U., Ft. Lauderdale, Fla., 1996-97. Vis. prof. State U. N.Y. at Geneseo, summers 1969-70; cons. publs., libr. and info. scis.-related enterprises; chmn. bd. internat. confs., 1970—. Author: Moving Library Materials, 1965, Public Libraries - A Comparative Survey of Basic Fringe Benefits, 1967; editor: Approval and Gathering Plans in Academic Libraries, 1969, Advances in Understanding Approval Plans in Academic Libraries, 1970, Economics of Approval Plans in Research Libraries, 1972, Management Problems in Serials Work, 1973, Prediction of Resource Needs, 1975, Requiem for the Card Catalog: Management Issues in Automated Cataloging, 1979, Shaping Library Collections for the 1980's, 1981, Austerity Management in Academic Libraries, 1984, Financing Information Systems, 1985, Issues in Academic Libraries, 1985; mem. editorial bd. Jour. of Library Adminstration, 1989-95. Mem. Kalamazoo County Library Bd., 1969-70; Bd. dirs. United Fund. Reciient G. Flint Purdy award for outstanding contbns. Wayne State U., 1999. Mem. ALA, Mich. Libr. Assn., Internat. Fed. Libr. Assns., Assn. Info. Sci., Fla. Libr. Assn., Calif. Libr. Assn., Fla. Assn. Community Colls., Boca Raton C. of C., U. Chgo. Grad. Libr. Sch. Alumni Club (pres. 1973-75), Solinet Mich. Libr. Consortium (founder charter bd. mem. 1973—, bd. dirs. 1973-76), Detroit Area Libr. Network (pres. bd. dirs. 1985-95), Mich. Ctr. for Book (pres. 1988-89), Am. Soc. Info. Sci., Assn. Libr. and Info. Sci. Edn. Republican. Methodist. Home: 7295 Maidencane Ct Largo FL 33777-4900 Office: Wayne State Univ Librs Detroit MI 48202 E-mail: PSpyers@aol.com.

SQUIRES, JOHN HENRY, judge; b. Oct. 21, 1946; married; five children. AB cum laude, U. Ill., 1968, JD, 1971. Bar: Ill. 1971, U.S. Dist. Ct. (cen. dist.) Ill. 1972, U.S. Tax Ct. 1978. Assoc. Brown, Hay & Stephens, Springfield, Ill., 1971-76, ptnr., 1977-87; judge U.S. Bankruptcy Ct. No. Dist. Ill. ea. divsn., 1988—2001, reappointed, 2002—. Trustee in bankruptcy, 1984-87; adj. prof. law John Marshall Law Sch., Chgo., 1994, DePaul U., Chgo., 1995-96; lectr. Am. Bankruptcy Inst., Sangamon County Bar Assn., Winnebago County Bar Assn., Chgo. Bar Assn., Ill. Inst. CLE, Comml. Law League Am., DuPage County (Ill.) Bar Assn. Mem. Nat. Conf. Bankruptcy Judges, Am. Bankruptcy Inst., Fed. Bar Assn., Am. Bus. Club, Union League Club Chgo. Office: US Bankruptcy Ct No Dist Ill Ea Div 219 S Dearborn St #676 Chicago IL 60604-1702

SQUIRES, VERNON T. lawyer; b. 1935; BA, Williams Coll.; LLB, Harvard U. Bar: Ill., 1960. V.p., sec. and gen. counsel The Service Master Co., Downers Grove, Ill. Mem. ABA. Office: The Service Master Co One Service Master Way Downers Grove IL 60515-1700

SROGE, MAXWELL HAROLD, marketing consultant, publishing executive; b. N.Y.C., Oct. 9, 1927; s. Albert N. and Goldie (Feldman) S.; children: Roberta, David, Marc, Sarah. Student, CCNY, 1946-48, NYU, 1948, New Sch. Social Research, 1948. Dir. sales Bell & Howell Co., Chgo., 1950-60, dir. prodn. planning, 1961-62, pres. Robert Maxwell div., 1962-63; pres. Maxwell Sroge Co., Inc., Chgo., 1965—, Telespond, Inc., Chgo., 1971—, Maxwell Sroge Pub., Inc., Chgo., 1976—. Chmn. JUF Comm. Industry, 1974-75, Transatlantic Catalogue Corp.; chmn. Direct Mktg. Svcs., Inc.; pub. Non-Store Mktg. Report, Inside Leading Mail Order Houses, Mail Order Industry Ann. Report, Best in Catalogs, How to Create Successful Catalogs, The Catalog Marketer, 101 Ideas for More Profitable Catalogs; bd. dirs. Tools Direct, DMSI; chmn. Telespond Inc. Mem. New Ill. Com., 1965; speakers bur. Percy for Gov., 1964, Citizens for Percy, 1972; co-chmn. Percy for Pres. Exploratory Com., 1974; mem. regional adv. bd. Nat. Jewish Hosp., 1974-75; mem. devel. com. WTTW-Channel 11, 1975-76, NCCJ; founder Save the Tarryall, Inc., 1982. Served with USNR, World War II. Mem. Direct Mail Mktg. Assn. (Gold Mail Box award 1978, Internat. Gold Carrier Pigeon award 1979), Nat. Retail Merchants Assn., Retail Advt. Conf., World Futures Soc. E-mail: msroge@catalog-news.com.

STABENOW, DEBORAH ANN, senator, former congresswoman; b. Gladwin, Mich., Apr. 29, 1950; d. Robert Lee and Anna Merle (Hallmark) Greer; children: Todd Dennis, Michelle Deborah. BS magna cum laude, Mich. State U., 1972, MSW magna cum laude, 1975. With spl. svcs. Lansing (Mich.) Sch. Dist., 1972-73; county commr. Ingham County, Mason, Mich., 1975-78; state rep. State of Mich., Lansing, 1979—, state senator, 1990-94; mem. 103rd-106th Congress from Mich. 8th dist. U.S. Ho. Reps. Founder Ingham County Women's Commn.; co-founder Council Against Domestic Assault. Recipient Service to Children award Council for Prevention of Child Abuse and Neglect, 1983, Disting. Service to Mich. Families award Mich. Council Family Relations, 1983, Outstanding Leadership award Nat. Council Community Mental Health Ctrs., 1983, Snyder-Kok award Mental Health Assn. Mich., Awareness Leader of Yr. award Awareness Communications Team Developmentally Disabled, 1984, Communicator of Yr. award Woman in Communications, 1984, Lawmaker of Yr. award Nat. Child Support Enforcement Assn., 1985, Disting. Service award Lansing Jaycees, 1985, Disting. Service in Govt. award Retarded Citizens of Mich., 1986, Boxing Glove award Nat. Com. to Preserve Social Security and Medicare, 1999, Home Health Hero Nat. Assn. for Home Care, 1999, Friend of Farm Bur. Mich. Farm Bur., 1999, Leadership award Nat. Coun. of Space Grant Dirs., 1998, Outstanding Achievement Nat. Farmers Union, 1998, Legislator of Yr. award Nat. Multiple Sclerosis Soc., 1992, Assn. for Children's Mental Health, 1991, Mich. Assn. of Vol. Adminstrs., 1989, Citizens Alliace to Uphold Spl. Edn., 1989, Recognition award State 4-H Alumni, 1991, Cmty. award Mich. Mental Health, 1988; named One of Ten Outstanding Young Ams. Jaycees, 1986. Mem. NAACP, Lansing Regional C. of C., Delta Kappa Gamma. Office: US Senate 702 Hart Washington DC 20510 also: US Senate 702 Hart Senate Office Bldg Washington DC 20510 E-mail: senator@stabenow.senate.gov.

STACK, JOHN WALLACE, lawyer; b. Chgo., May 30, 1937; s. Wallace and Irma Evelyn (Anderson) S.; divorced; children: James Randolph, Linnea Claire, Theodore. BBA, U. Wis., 1960; JD, U. Calif., Berkeley, 1963. Bar: Ill. 1963, D.C. 1972, U.S. Ct. Appeals (7th cir.) 1963, U.S. Supreme Ct. 1972. Assoc. Pattishall, McAuliffe & Hofstetter, Chgo., 1963-64, Winston & Strawn, Chgo., 1964-70, ptnr., 1970-99; ret., 1999; adminstrv. law judge City of Evanston, Ill. Contbg. editor U. Calif. Law Rev., 1963. Mem. ABA (antitrust sect.), Am. Arbitration Assn., W Club of U. Wis. (Madison), Order of Coif, Phi Delta Phi, Beta Gamma Sigma. Republican. Lutheran. Avocations: sports, gardening, reading. Home: 2906 Lincoln St Evanston IL 60201-2047 Office: Winston & Strawn 40th Fl 35 W Wacker Dr Fl 40 Chicago IL 60601-1614

STACK, STEPHEN S. manufacturing company executive; b. DuPont, Pa., Apr. 25, 1934; s. Steve and Sophie (Baranowski) Stasenko; m. Lois Sims Agnew, May 25, 1996. BSME, Case Western Res. U., 1956; postgrad., Syracuse Univ. reg. profl engr., Ill. Mech. engr. Kaiser Aluminum, Erie, PA, 1956-58; instr. Gannon Univ., 1958-60, Syracuse U., NY, 1960-61; engrg. supr. A.O. Smith Corp., Erie and Los Angeles, 1961-66; gen. mgr. Am. Elec. Fusion, Chgo., 1966-67; mgr.new products Maremont Corp., 1967-69; dir. market planning Gulf and Western Ind., Bellwood, IL, 1969-71; mgmt. and fin. cons. Stack & Assocs., Chgo., 1971-76; pres.

Seamcraft, Inc., 1976—. Mem. Ill. Legis. Small Bus. Conf., 1980, Gov.'s Small Bus. Adv. Commn., 1984-94, Ill. State House Conf. on Small Bus., 1984, 86, 99; chmn. West Cell, 1988-2000, Bridge Pers. Svcs. Corp., 1989—; vice pres. Ind. Bus. Assn. Ill., 1993-94; mem. small bus. adv. counc. Fed. Res. Bank of Chgo., 1989-91, Nat. Fedn. Ind. Bus. mem. 1980—, del. White House Conf. on Small Bus., 1986, pres. Chgo. Marine Heritage Soc., 1999—, mem. Navy League of the U.S., 1991—, del. Congl. Small Bus. Summit, 1998, 2000, 2002; with Ill. Small Bus. Leadership Coun., 2000—. Treas. Sem. Townhouse Assn., 1993-94; active Lincoln Park Conservation Assn., Sheffield Neighbors Assn.; mem. adv. coun., DePaul U. Coll. Commerce, 2000—. Recipient Am. Legion awd., 1948, Case Western Res. U. Honor key, 1956, Easgle Scout awd., 1949. Mem. Ill. Mfrs. Assn. (bd. dirs. 1986-98, vice chmn. 1995-98), Small Mfrs. Action Couns. (vice chmn. 1986-87, chmn. 1988-89), Mfrs. Polit. Action Com. (exec. com. 1987-98, vice chmn. 1993-95, chmn. 1995-98), Am. Mgmt. Assn., Pres. Assn., Blue Key, Beta Theta Pi, Theta Thau, Pi Delta Epsilon. Clubs: Chgo. Yacht, East Bank Club, Capitol Hill (Wash.), Fullerton Tennis (pres. 1971-79, treas. 1979-83, bd. dirs. 1983-86), Lake Shore Ski (v.p. 1982, 91), Lincoln Park Tennis Assn., Oak Park Tennis Club. Patentee in liquid control and metering fields. Office: 932 W Dakin St Chicago IL 60613-2922

STACKHOUSE, DAVID WILLIAM, JR. retired furniture systems installation contractor; b. Cumberland, Ind., Aug. 29, 1926; s. David William and Dorothy Frances (Snider) S.; B.S., Lawrence Coll., Appleton, Wis., 1950; m. Shirley Pat Smith, Dec. 23, 1950; 1 son, Stefan Brent. Indsl. designer Globe Am. Co., Kokomo, Ind., 1951-53; product designer, chief engr. Midwest Foundry & Workwall divsn. L.A. Darling Co., Bronson, Mich., 1954-66; contract mgr. Brass Office Products, Indpls., 1966-73; mfrs. rep., Nashville, Ind., 1973-78; mktg. exec. Brass Office Products, Inc., Indpls., 1978-80; office furniture systems installation contractor, 1980-92; creator This Great House, The Story of This Home, 1995; founder Half-High Hill Prodns., Inc., 1996. Served with USNR, 1944-46; Beta Theta Pi. Anglican. Clubs: Lions, Masons, Shriners. Patentee interior structural systems. E-mail: davenpat@bloomington.in.us. Home: 4617 N Helmsburg Rd Nashville IN 47448-8227

STADELMANN, EDUARD JOSEPH, plant physiologist, educator, researcher; b. Graz, Austria, Sept. 24, 1920; s. Eduard Joseph and Josefa (Eigner) S.; m. Ok Young Lee, Mar. 22, 1975. BS, Bundesrealgymnasium, Graz, Austria, 1939; PhD, U. Innsbruck, Austria, 1953; Pvt. Docent, U. Freiburg, Switzerland, 1957; PhD (hon.), Agrl. U. Vienna, 1989. Sr. asst. U. Freiburg, 1962-63; rsch. assoc. U. Minn., Mpls., 1963, asst. prof., 1964-66, assoc. prof., 1966-72, prof. hort. sci., 1972-91, prof. emeritus, 1991—. Muellhaupt Scholar in Biology, Ohio State U., 1958-59; Humboldt Found. awardee, 1974-75; Fulbright award, Coun. Internat. Exchange, 1979-80, 87-88. Mem. Am. Inst. Biology, Am. Soc. Plant Physiologists, German Bot. Soc., Swiss Bot. Soc., Sigma Xi. Roman Catholic. Office: Univ Minn Dept Hort Sci 1970 Folwell Ave Saint Paul MN 55108-6007 E-mail: estadelm@tc.umn.edu.

STADTHERR, MARK A. chemical engineer, educator; B in Chem. Engring., U. Minn., 1972; PhD in Chem. Engring., U. Wis., 1976. Faculty U. Ill., Urbana-Champaign, 1976-95; chem. engring. faculty U. Notre Dame, Ind., 1996—. Presenter in field. Contbr. articles to profl. jours. Recipient Xerox award for engring. rsch., 1982, Computing in Chem. Engring. award AIChE, 1998; named GTE Emerging scholar lectr. U. Notre Dame, 1986. Achievements include research on advanced computational strategies for process engineering, application of interval analysis to chemical engineering problems, environmentally conscious process design. Office: Dept Chem Engring Univ Notre Dame Notre Dame IN 46556 Fax: 219-631-8366. E-mail: markst@nd.edu.

STADTMUELLER, JOSEPH PETER, federal judge; b. Oshkosh, Wis., Jan. 28, 1942; s. Joseph Francis and Irene Mary (Kilp) S.; m. Mary Ellen Brady, Sept. 5, 1970; children: Jeremy, Sarah. B.S. in Bus. Adminstrn., Marquette U., 1964, J.D., 1967. Bar: Wis. 1967, U.S. Supreme Ct. 1980. With Kluwin, Dunphy, Hankin and McNulty, 1968-69; asst. U.S. atty. Dept. Justice, Milw., 1969-74, 1st asst. U.S. atty., 1974-75; with Stepke, Kossow, Trebon and Stadtmueller, Milw., 1975-76; asst. U.S. atty. Dept. Justice, 1977-78, dep. U.S. atty., 1978-81, U.S. atty., 1981-87; judge U.S. Dist. Ct. (ea. dist.) Wis., Milw., 1987—, chief judge, 1995—2002. Mem. 7th Cir. Jud. Coun., 1995—2002. Recipient Spl. Commendation award Atty. Gen. U.S., 1974, 80. Mem. ABA, State Bar Wis. (bd. govs. 1979-83, exec. com. 1982-83), Am. Law Inst., Fed. Judges Assn. (bd. dirs. 1995—, sec. 2001-). Republican. Roman Catholic. Club: University (Milw.). Office: 471 US Courthouse 517 E Wisconsin Ave Milwaukee WI 53202-4500

STAFFORD, ARTHUR CHARLES, medical association administrator; b. Cleve., May 10, 1947; s. Charles Arthur and Florence Mildred (Hovey) S.; m. Patricia Anne Cz, Dec. 20, 1991. BS, Kent State U., 1977; MBA, Lake Erie Coll., 1984. Med. tech. VA, Cleve., 1977-81, supr. med. tech., 1981-97; lab. mgr. Univ. Hosps. Health System Meml. Hosp. of Geneva, 1998-99; instr. Lake Erie Coll., Painesville, 1980-82, Cuyahoga C.C., Cleve., 1988-91; mgr. customer svc. Giant Eagle Supermarket, Madison, 2001—. Pres. Kent State U. Veterans Assn., 1974, mem. Kent State U Budget Review Com., 1975. Contbr. articles to profl. jour. Mem. Am. Legion, 1974, VFW, 1973. With USN, 1968-72. Mem.: Rock and Roll Hall of Fame, Founders Club. Republican. Avocations: genealogy, computers, antiques, chess, cooking. Home: 2193 Chimney Ridge Dr Madison OH 44057-2588 E-mail: czstafford@ncweb.com.

STAFFORD, EARL, conductor; Artistic dir. Saskatoon (Sask., Can.) Symphony Orch., 1997—. Began piano studies at age 8; profl. and solo debut with Thunder Bay Symphony at age 10; studied at Faculty of Music, U. Toronto, with Milton Kaye in N.Y.C., at Paris Conservatory with Franco Ferrara and Aldo Ciccolini; joined Royal Winnipeg Ballet as prin. pianist, 1975, appointed assoc. music dir., 1982, now music dir. and condr.; also music dir. dance div. Banff Ctr. Fine Arts. Orchestrator numerous ballets for Royal Winnipeg Ballet, including Five Tangos, Bluebird Pas De Deux, Giselle Pas De Deux, Tchaikovsky Pas De Deux, Nuages; guest condr. various Can. orchs. including Vancouver Symphony, Calgary Philharmonic, Regina Symphony, Winnipeg Symphony, Saskatoon Symphony Orch., Nat. Arts Ctr. Orch., Thunder Bay Symphony. Recipient Gold medal for accompanying, Internat. Ballet Competition, Varna, Bulgaria, 1980. Office: EML Internat Artist Mgmt Inc 219 Baseline Rd East London ON Canada N6C 2N6 also: Saskatoon Symphony Ste 203 Delta Bessborough Hotel Saskatoon SK Canada S7K 3G8

STAFFORD, FRANK PETER, JR. economics educator, consultant; b. Chgo., Sept. 17, 1940; s. Frank Peter and Ida Gustava (Tormala) S.; m. Lilian Elisabeth Lundin, Aug. 8, 1964; children: Craig Peter, Jennifer Elisabeth, Christine Anna BA, Northwestern U., 1962; MBA, U. Chgo., 1964, PhD, 1968. Asst. prof. econs. U. Mich., 1966-71, assoc. prof., 1971-73, 74-75, prof., 1976—, chmn. dept. econs., 1980—, rsch. scientist Inst. Social Rsch., 1995—, chair budget study com., 1995—, assoc. dir. Inst. for Social Rsch., 2000—. Vis. assoc. prof. Grad. Sch. Bus.-Stanford U., 1973-74; spl. asst. for econ. affairs U.S. Dept. Labor, Washington, 1975-76; vis. prof. dept. econs. U. Saarlandes, Fed. Republic Germany, 1986; faculty rsch. assoc. Inst. Social Rsch., Ann Arbor, 1979—; vis. scholar Indsl. Inst. for Econs. and Social Rsch., Stockholm, 1979, 83, 90, Worklife Study Ctr., Stockholm, 1988, 90; Tinbergen Found. prof. U. Amsterdam, 1992, 94; panel mem. Social Sci. Rsch. Coun., N.Y.C., 1979—; rsch. assoc. Nat. Bur. Econ. Rsch., Cambridge, Mass., 1983—; prof. econs. Tinbsrgne Found. U. Amsterdam, 1992; vis. scholar U. Stockholm, 1994. Author, editor: Time Use Goods and Well Being, 1986, Studies in Labor Market Behavior: Sweden and the United States, 1981; mem. editorial bd.: Am. Econ. Rev., 1976-78; contbr. articles to profl. jours. Dir. Panel Study of Income Dynamics, 1995—. Grantee NSF, 1973, 80, 95—, NICHD, 1995—, Nat. Ins. on Aging, 1999—. Mem. Am. Econs. Assn. Home: 3535 Daleview Dr Ann Arbor MI 48105-9686 Office: U Mich Dept Econs Lorch Hall Rm 312 Ann Arbor MI 48105

STAFFORD, LORI, reporter; b. Birmingham, Ala. m. Jeff Stafford. Student, Auburn U., U. Ala.; MA, Northwestern U. Mem. staff TV sta., Reno, Cin., Chattanooga, Evansville, Ind.; reporter WISN, Milw. Office: WISN PO Box 402 Milwaukee WI 53201-0402

STAGE, RICHARD LEE, consultant, retired utilities executive; b. Byesville, Ohio, Nov. 5, 1936; s. Clifford Earl Stage and Evelyn Virginia (Nunley) Rolston; m. Joan Eleanor Bednarz, Feb. 1, 1958; 1 child, Julie Marie. B in Mgmt., Malone Coll., 1987. Fleet office supr. Ohio Power Co., Canton, 1954-77; supr. automotive acctg. and leasing Am. Electric Power, 1977-83, dir. fleet mgmt. Columbus, 1983-95; fleet mgmt. cons., Canton, 1995—. Mem. Soc. Automotive Engrs. (chmn. utilities com. 1988-89, exec. com.), Edison Electric Inst. (fleet mgmt. com. 1983-95), Masons. Republican. Avocations: golf, woodworking. Home and Office: 1329 Davis St SW Canton OH 44706-4503 E-mail: rlstage@sssnet.com.

STAGEBERG, ROGER V. lawyer; B of Math. with distinction, U. Minn., 1963, JD cum laude, 1966. Assoc. Mackall, Crounse & Moore, Mpls., 1966-70, ptnr., 1970-86; shareholder and officer Lommen, Nelson, Cole & Stageberg, P.A., 1986—. Co-chmn. joint legal svcs. funding com. Minn. Supreme Ct., 1995-96. Mem. U. Minn. Law Rev. Bd. dirs. Mpls. Legal Aid Soc., 1970—, treas., 1973, pres., 1977, dir. of fund, 1980—, chmn. of fund, 1998-2000; chmn. bd. trustees Colonial Ch. of Edina, 1975, chmn. congregation, 1976, pres. found., 1978; officer, trustee Mpls. Found, 1983-88. Mem. Minn. State Bar Assn. (numerous offices and coms., pres. 1994), Hennepin County Bar Assn. (chmn. securities law sect. 1979, chmn. attys. referral svc. com. 1980, sec. 1980, treas. 1981, pres. 1983), Order of Coif. Office: Lommen Nelson Cole & Stageberg PA 1800 IDS Center 80 S 8th St Minneapolis MN 55402-2100 E-mail: roger@lommen.com.

STAGGERS, KERMIT LEMOYNE, II, history and political science educator, state legislator, municipal official; b. Washington, Nov. 2, 1947; s. Kermit LeMoyne and Christine Ruby (Scherich) S.; m. June Ann Wenda, Aug. 22, 1970; children: Ayn Kristen, Kyle Lee. BS, U. Idaho, 1969, MA, 1975; PhD, Claremont Grad. U., 1986. Instr. history Troy (Ala.) State U., 1975-76, U. Idaho, Moscow, 1977, Northwestern Coll., Orange City, Iowa, 1979-80, Coll. Lake County, Grayslake, Ill., 1981-82; lectr. history Chapman Coll., Orange, Calif., 1979, U. Md.-Europe, Heidelberg, Germany, 1988-89; vis. instr. history Trinity Internat. U., Deerfield, Ill., 1980; ad. instr. history Coll. St. Francis, Joliet, 1982; prof. history and polit. sci. U. Sioux Falls (S.D.), 1982—; mem. S.D. Senate, Pierre, 1995—2002, Sioux Falls City Coun., 2002—. Lectr. Diplomatic Acad. Ukrainian Fgn. Ministry and Nat. U. Kiev-Mohyla Acad., 2001; expert analyst on polit. and social issues for local radio and TV. Contbr. to profl. publs. Chair Senate Transp. Com., 1997-99. Capt. USAF, 1970-76. Recipient Guardian Small Bus. award Nat. Fedn. Ind. Bus., 1996; Malone Faculty fellow, 1993. Mem. Orgn. Am. Historians, Great Plains Polit. Sci and Pub. Affairs Assn. (pres. 2000-01), Conf. on Faith and History, Federalist Soc., Fulbright Assn., Hist. Soc., Kiwanis, Phi Alpha Theta, Phi Kappa Phi. Republican. Avocations: book collecting, travel. Home: 1135 S Walts Ave Sioux Falls SD 57105-0543 Office: U Sioux Falls Dept History/Polit Sci 1101 W 22nd St Sioux Falls SD 57105-1699 E-mail: kermit.staggers@usiouxfalls.edu.

STAGLIN, GAREN KENT, computer service company executive, venture capitalist; b. Lincoln, Nebr., Dec. 22, 1944; s. Ramon and Darlene (Guilliams) S.; m. Sharalyn King, June 8, 1968; children: Brandon Kent, Shannon King. BS in Engring. with honors, UCLA, 1966; MBA, Stanford U., 1968. Assoc. Carr Mgmt. Co., N.Y.C., 1971-75; v.p. Crocker Nat. Bank, San Francisco, 1975-76; dir. fin. Itel Corp., 1976-77, pres. ins. services divsn., 1977-79; corp. v.p., gen. mgr. ADP Automotive Svcs. Group, San Ramon, Calif., 1978-91; chmn., CEO Safelite Glass Corp., Columbus, Ohio, 1991-97, chmn., 1998-2000; owner Staglin Family Vineyard, Rutherford, Calif., 1985—; pres., CEO, eOne Global L.L.C., Napa, 2000—. Bd. dirs. Certive Corp., Specialized Bicycle Corp., Dashboard Enterprises, Quick Response Svcs., Inc., 1st Data Corp. Bd. dirs. Peralta Hosp. Cancer Inst., 1977-78, Berkeley Repertory Theatre, 1979-85; trustee Justin Sienna H.S., Napa, Calif., 1995-2000; chmn. major gifts program East Bay region Stanford (Calif.) U., 1989-92; mem. adv. bd. Stanford Bus. Sch., 1995-2000; chmn. 75th anniversary campaign Stanford Grad. Sch. Bus., 1998-2000; chmn. capital campaign, pres. bd. trustees Am. Ctr. Wine, Food and Arts, Napa, Calif., 1998—. Lt. USN, 1968-71. Recipient Gold Spike award, Stanford U., 2000. Mem. Stanford Assocs. (bd. govs. 1985-92), World Pres. Orgn., Internat. Inst. Soc. (bd. govs. 1985-92). Democrat. Lutheran. Home: PO Box 680 1570 Bella Oaks Ln Rutherford CA 94573 E-mail: gstaglin@coveglobal.com.

STAIR, CHARLES WILLIAM, former service company executive; b. Ida Grove, Iowa, Oct. 21, 1940; s. Frderic Cleveland and Eunice (Carlson) S.; m. Patricia Ellen Gramley, June 15, 1963; children: Kerry John, Andrew Charles, Melissa Kathrine. BA, Wheaton Coll., 1963. Coordinating mgr. The ServiceMaster Co., Downers Grove, Ill., 1963-65, regional ops. mgr., 1966-68, area ops. mgr., 1969-70, div. v.p., 1971, exec. v.p., 1972-73, div. pres., 1974-75, group v.p. east group, 1976-77, group pres. east group, 1978-79, group pres. west group, 1980-82, group pres. cen. group, 1983-85, exec. v.p. healthcare/edn., 1986, exec. v.p. mgmt. svcs., 1987-88, also bd. dirs., exec. v.p., chief oper. officer mgmt. svcs., 1989-90, pres., chief ops. officer mgmt. svcs., 1990-2000; ret., 2000. Exec. chmn. bd. dirs. Tyndale House Pubs. Inc., Wheaton. Republican. Avocations: tennis, golfing, fishing, hunting. Home: 25w487 Plamondon Rd Wheaton IL 60187-7364 Office: ServiceMaster Co 1 ServiceMaster Way Downers Grove IL 60515-1700

STALEY, HENRY MUELLER, manufacturing company executive; b. Decatur, Ill., June 3, 1932; s. Augustus Eugene, Jr. and Lenore (Mueller) S.; m. Violet Lucas, Feb. 4, 1955; children— Mark Eugene, Grant Spencer. Grad., Governor Dummer Acad., 1950; B.S. in Psychology, Northwestern U., 1954, M.B.A. in Finance, 1956. Salesman Field Enterprises, Chgo., 1953; salesman A.E. Staley Mfg. Co., 1951, mgmt. trainee, 1956-57, ins. mgr., 1957-59, asst. treas., 1959-65, treas., asst. sec., 1965-73, v.p., treas., asst. sec., 1973-77, v.p. bus. and econ. analysis, 1977-87, also dir., 1969-85; pvt. investor Decatur, 1987—. Dir. Staley Continental, Inc., 1985-88. Crusade chmn. Macon County unit Am. Cancer Soc., 1964-65, mem. bd. dirs., 1965-71, vice chmn. bd., 1965-66, chmn. bd., 1966-69; bd. dirs. United Way Decatur and Macon County, 1972-74; mem. adv. council Millikin U., 1968-91, chmn. adv. coun., 1970-71; mem. Decatur Meml. Hosp. Devel. Council, 1969-71, mem. finan. com., bd. dirs., 1970-79, mem. long-range planning com., 1976-77, mem. devel. and community relations com., 1977-78. Mem. Decatur C. of C. (dir. 1967-72), Sigma Nu. Clubs: Decatur, Decatur Country. Home and Office: 276 N Park Pl Decatur IL 62522-1952 also: 74 Ironwood Ln Lahaina HI 96761-9062

STALEY, ROBERT W. mechanical engineer, electric company executive; b. 1935; BSME, Cornell U., 1958, MBA, 1959. Dir. corp. devel. Trane Co., 1960-75; v.p. corp. tech. Emerson Electric Co., St. Louis, 1975-77, internat. v.p., 1977-78, chief fin. officer, sr. v.p. fin., 1978-81, sr. v.p., group v.p., 1981-83, exec. v.p., 1983-88, vice chmn., 1988—, also bd. dirs. Capt. U.S. Army, 1959-66. Office: Emerson Electric Co 8100 W Florissant Ave Saint Louis MO 63136-1494

STALEY, WARREN, food products company executive; b. Springfield, Ill., May 14, 1942; BS in Elec. Engring., Kans. State U., 1965; MS in Bus. Adminstrn., Cornell U., 1967. With Cargill, Inc., Mpls., 1969—, pres. for N.Am. and Latin Am., to 1998, pres., COO, 1998, pres., CEO, 1999—, chmn., 2000—, also bd. dirs. Chmn. Cargill Found.; bd. dirs. U.S. Bancorp. Bd. dirs. United Way, Minn. Pvt. Coll. Coun. Office: Cargill Inc PO Box 9300 Minneapolis MN 55440-9300

STALL, ALAN DAVID, packaging company executive; b. Moose Jaw, Sask., Can., June 14, 1951; came to U.S., 1982; s. Joel and Evelyn (Schwartz) S.; m. Carol I. Johnston; children: Jeffrey, Jennifer, Michael, Timothy. BSME, U. Sask., 1973; MBA, Lewis U., 1986. Registered profl. engr., Ont. Devel. engr. DuPont Can., North Bay, Ont., 1973-76; project engr. Union Carbide Corp. Can., Lindsay, 1976-79, engring. mgr., 1979-82; mgr. shirring rsch. Union Carbide Corp., Chgo., 1982-85; dir. engring. tech. Viskase Corp., 1985-90, v.p. engring., 1990-95; gen. mgr. Kuko Corp., Gross-Gerau, Germany, 1995-98; pres. Films Casings Tech. Inc., Woodridge, Ill., 1996—; gen. mgr. Alfacel Inc., 1998—. Patentee breathable plastic, shirring apparatus, sausage stuffing machine, cellulose casings, cellulose regeneration. Rotary bus. exchange fellow, London, 1982. Mem. Engring. Inst. Can., Can. Soc. Mech. Engrs., Soc. Plastics Engrs., Assn. Profl. Engrs., Ont., Am. Mensa, Can. Club Chgo. Home: 23W540 James Way Naperville IL 60540-9552 Office: Alfacel Inc PO Box 5415 Woodridge IL 60517-0415

STALLMEYER, JAMES EDWARD, engineer, educator; b. Covington, Ky., Aug. 11, 1926; s. Joseph Julius and Anna Catherine (Scheper) S.; m. Mary Katherine Davenport, Apr. 11, 1953; children: Cynthia Marie, James Duncan, Michael John, Catherine Ann, John Charles, Gregory Edward. BS, U. Ill., 1947, MS, 1949, PhD, 1953. Jr. engr. So. Ry. System, 1947; research asst. U. Ill., Urbana, 1947-49, research asso., 1951-52, asst. prof. civil engring, 1952-57, assoc. prof., 1957-60, prof., 1960-91, prof. emeritus, 1991—. Cons. on structural problems various indsl. and govt. agys. Author: (with E.H. Gaylord Jr.), Design of Steel Structures; editor: (with E.H. Gaylord Jr.) Structural Engineering Handbook; contbr. to Shock and Vibration Handbook. Served with USN, 1944-46. Standard Oil fellow, 1949-51; recipient Adams meml. award, 1964, Everitt award for teaching excellence, 1981 Mem. ASCE, Am. Concrete Inst., Am. Ry. Engring. Assn., ASTM, Am. Welding Soc., Am. Soc. Metals, Soc. Exptl. Stress Analysis, Scabbard and Blade, Sigma Xi, Chi Epsilon, Sigma Tau, Tau Beta Pi, Phi Kappa Phi. Republican. Roman Catholic. Club: KC. Office: Newmark Civil Engring 205 N Mathews Ave Urbana IL 61801-2350

STALLWORTH, ALMA GRACE, former state legislator; Grad., Highland Park Community Coll., 1956; student, Wayne State U., 1956. Mem. Mich. Ho. of Reps., Lansing, 1970-74, 81-96; dep. dir. Hist. Dept. City of Detroit, 1975-78, job developer, 1978-79. Mem. exec. com. Nat. Conf. State Legislatures, 1986-89. Commr. Wayne County Charter, Detroit, 1978-79, Martin Luther King Commn., Detroit, 1987; chairperson bd. dirs. task force on infant mortality Mich. Legislature, 1987; pres. Nat. Black Child Devel. Inst., Detroit; vol. United Negro Coll. Fund, 1987—; founder, adminstr. Black Caucus Found. of Mich., 1987—. Recipient cert. of appreciation Mich. Dept. Edn., 1986, Advs. award Mich. Health Mothers, Health Babies Coalition, 1987; named Woman Leader in Pub. Health, Mi ch. Assn. Local Pub. Health, 1987, Woman of Yr., Minority Women's Network, 1988. Mem. NAACP, Nat. Conf. State Legislators (exec. commr. 1986), Nat. Black Caucus State Legislators, (sec. women's caucus), Mich. Legis. Black Causus (chair 1987), Alpha Kappa Alpha. Democrat. Clubs: Cameo, Top Ladies of Distinction. Home: 19793 Sorrento St Detroit MI 48235-1149

STALLWORTH, SAM, television executive; b. Washington, Sept. 4, 1946; BS in Mktg., U. Ala., 1968. V.p. sales CBS on TV, N.Y.C., 1975-95; v.p., gen. mgr. WSYX-TV, Columbus, Ohio, 1995—. Mem. RTNDA, NAD, United Way. Office: WSYX TV 1261 Dublin Rd Columbus OH 43215-7000

STAMOS, JOHN JAMES, judge; b. Chgo., Jan. 30, 1924; s. James S. and Katherine (Manolopoulos) S.; m. Helen Voutiritsas, Sept. 3, 1955 (dec. 1981); children— James, Theo, Colleen, Jana; m. Mary Sotter, March 21, 1986. LL.B., DePaul U., 1948. Bar: Ill. 1949. Since practiced in, Chgo.; asst. corp. counsel City Chgo., 1951-54; asst. states atty. Cook County, 1954-61; chief criminal div. States Attys. Office, 1961-64, 1st asst. states atty., 1964-66, states atty., 1966-68; judge Appellate Ct. of State of Ill., 1968-88; Judge Ill. Supreme Ct., Springfield, 1988-90; ret., 1990; of counsel Stamos and Trucco, Chgo., 1991—. Served with AUS, 1943-45.

STANALAJCZO, GREG CHARLES, computer and technology company executive; b. 1959; Degree, Oakland U. With CDI Computer Svcs., Inc., Troy, Mich., 1986-95, pres., 1993-95; exec. v.p., COO, owner Trillium Teamologies, Inc., Royal Oak, 1996—. Office: Trillium Teamologies Inc 219 S Main St Ste 300 Royal Oak MI 48067-2611 E-mail: greg_stano@cs.com.

STANDEN, CRAIG CLAYTON, newspaper executive; b. Camden, N.J., Oct. 3, 1942; s. Charles Raymond and Maxine Jeanette (Lundgren) S.; m. Marcia Claire Peterson, Feb. 10, 1968; children: Kimberly Ruth, Charles Arthur. B.A., Denison U., 1964; M.B.A., Northwestern U., 1966. Assoc. product mgr. Gen. Foods Corp., White Plains, N.Y., 1969-73; dir. mktg. services R.J. Reynolds Tobacco Co., Winston-Salem, N.C., 1973-80; pres. Newspaper Advt. Bur., N.Y.C., 1980-90; v.p. mktg. and advt. Scripps Howard, Cin., 1990—. Mem. Leadership Cin., 1992-93; bd. dirs. ARC, Cin. Chpt., 1993—, Jr. Achievement, 1993—. Mem. Pres. Assn. Advt. Coun. N.Y.C. (dir. 1981—), Media Advt. Partnership for Drug Free Am. (bd. dirs. 1986-89), Country Club of Darien (Conn., bd. dirs. 1989-90), Kenwood Country Club (Cin.), Ivy Hills Country Club (Cin.). Home: 6280 Shawnee Pines Dr Cincinnati OH 45243-3150 Office: Scripps Howard 312 Walnut St Ste 2800 Cincinnati OH 45202-4040

STANDISH, SAMUEL MILES, oral pathologist, college dean; b. Campbellsburg, Ind., July 6, 1923; s. Irvin Arthur and Etta May (Smedley) S.; m. Gertrude Elizabeth Eberle, Aug. 6, 1949; children— Nancy Jo, Linda Sue. D.D.S., Ind. U., 1945, M.S., 1956. Diplomate: Am. Bd. Oral Pathology (dir. 1973-80), Am. Bd. Forensic Odontology. Practice dentistry, specializing in oral pathology, Indpls., 1948-58; mem. faculty Sch. Dentistry Ind. U., 1958-88, emeritus prof. oral pathology, 1967-88, chmn. div. clin. oral pathology, 1967-77, asst. dean sch., 1969-74, asso. dean, 1974-88. Cons. Nat. Cancer Inst., 1969-73, Nat. Bd. Dental Examiners, 1966-74, ADA, 1971-77. Author: (with others) Oral Diagnosis/Oral Medicine, 1978, Maxillofacial Prosthetics: Multidisciplinary Practice, 1972, Outline of Forensic Dentistry, 1982. Served with USNR, 1945-47. Fellow Am. Acad. Oral Pathology (pres. 1972-73); mem. ADA, Internat. Assn. Dental Research, Am. Acad. Forensic Sci., Sigma Xi, Omicron Kappa Upsilon, Xi Psi Phi. Home: 4548 Manning Rd Indianapolis IN 46228-2768 Office: Ind U Sch Dentistry Indianapolis IN 46202

STANFIELD, REBECCA, radio personality; b. Newport Beach, Calif. Grad. Broadcast Journalism and History, U. Southern Calif. Assignment editor, sr. reporter Sta. KRCR-TV, Redding, Calif.; gen. assignment reporter Cable 12 News , Brooklyn Park; freelance writer Fox TV, Mpls.; news anchor Sta. WCCO Radio. Navigator Great Am. Race. Office: WCCO 625 2nd Ave S Minneapolis MN 55402*

STANGE, JAMES HENRY, architect; b. Davenport, Iowa, May 25, 1930; s. Henry Claus and Norma (Ballhorn) S.; m. Mary Suanne Peterson, Dec. 12, 1954; children: Wade Weston, Drew Dayton, Grant Owen. BArch, Iowa State U., 1954. Registered architect, Iowa, Nebr., Kans., Mo., Okla. Designer Davis & Wilson, Lincoln, Nebr., 1954-62, v.p., 1962-68; v.p., sec. Davis, Fenton, Stange, Darling, 1977-92, pres., 1976—93, chmn., 1978—94. Mem. State Bd. Examiners for Engrs. and Architects, 1989-92, chmn. region V NCARB, 1991. Prin. works include Dorsey Labs., 1960, East H.S., Lincoln, 1966, Lincoln Gen. Hosp., 1967, Lincoln Airport Terminal, Sq. D Mfg. Plant, Lincoln, Bryan Meml. Hosp. (masterplans and additions), 1970, 80, 90, Bryan Ambulatory Care Ctr. Med. Office Bldg., Same Day Surgery Conf. Ctr., Parking Garage, 1993-95, Nebr. Wesleyan Theatre, Lincoln, Hasting (Nebr.) YMCA, various structures U. Nebr., Lincoln, ctr. and br. offices Am. Charter Fed. Savs. & Loan, S.E. H.S. (addition), 1984, U. Nebr. Animal Sci. Bldg., 1987, Beadle Ctr., UNL, 1991, Carriage Park Parking Garage, 1995. Pres. Lincoln Ctr. Assn., 1979; bd. dirs. Capitol Assn. Retarded Citizens, 1968-72, 94—, pres., 1970; chmn. United Way Campaign, 1986, chmn. bd., 1988; chmn. Bryan Hosp. Found. Endowment Com., 1988-90; bd. dirs. Delta Dental, 1987-92, Downtown Lincoln Assn., 1985-94, steering com., 1989, v.p. Nebr. Jazz Orch., 1995, pres., 1997, Nebr. Art Assn., 1996-99; mem. mayor's com. Study Downtown Redevel., 1989, pub. bldg. commn., masterplan rev. com., 1994; deacon First Presbyn. Ch., 1960, chmn. bd. trustees, 1968-90, elder, 1972-87, 97-99, chmn. property com., 1998-00. Recipient Honor award Conf. on Religious Architecture-First Plymouth Ch. Addition, 1969, also numerous state and nat. awards from archtl. orgns. Mem. AIA (Nebr. bd. dirs. 1964-65, treas. 1965, sec. 1966, v.p. 1967, pres. Nebr. 1968, mem. com. on architecture for health 1980-94, Regional Design award 1976, 88, 96), Am. Assn. Health Planners, Interfaith Forum on Religion, Art, Architecture, Lincoln C. of C. (bd. dirs. 1982), Exec. Club (pres. 1972), Crucible Club, 12 Club, Hillcrest Country Club (pres. 1977), Lincoln U. Club (sec. 1992, bd. dirs. 1991-97, pres. 1995, 96). Avocations: travel, photography, golf. Home: 3545 Calvert St Lincoln NE 68506-5744 Office: Davis Design 211 N 14th St Lincoln NE 68508-1616 E-mail: JimSustange@aol.com.

STANGE, KURT C. medical educator; MD, Albany Med. Coll., 1983; PhD, U. N.C., 1989. Diplomate Am. Bd. Family Practice, Am. Bd. Preventive Medicine. Prof. family medicine, epidemiology, biostatistics, oncology and sociology Case Western Reserve U., Cleve.; physician, tchr., rschr. dept. family medicine U. Hosps. Cleve.; assoc. dir. prevention, control and population rsch. Ireland Cancer Ctr. at U. Hosps. Cleve. and Case Western Reserve U. Mem. Inst. Medicine, Rsch. Assn. Practicing Physicians. Office: Case Western Reserve U Sch Medicine Dept Family Medicine 10900 Euclid Ave Cleveland OH 44106-1712 also: Dept Family Medicine U Circle Rsch Ctr 11001 Cedar Ave Ste 306 Cleveland OH 44106-3043 Fax: 216-368-4348. E-mail: kcs@po.cwru.edu.

STANLEY, ELLEN MAY, historian, consultant; b. Dighton, Kans., Feb. 3, 1921; d. Delmar Orange and Lena May (Bobb) Durr; m. Max Neal Stanley, Nov. 5, 1939; children: Ann Y. Stanley Epps, Janet M. Stanley Horsky, Gail L. Stanley Peck, Kenneth D., Neal M., Mary E. Stanley McEniry. BA in English and Journalism, Ft. Hays (Kans.) State U., 1972, MA in History, 1984. Pvt. practice local/state historian, cons., writer local history, Dighton, 1973—; cons. genealogy, 1980—. Vice chmn. State Preservation Bd. Rev., Kans., 1980-87; area rep. Kans. State Mus. Assn., 1978-84. Author: Early Lane County History: 12,000 B.C.–A.D. 1884, 1993, Cowboy Josh: Adventures of a Real Cowboy, 1996, Early Lane County Development, 1999, Golden Age, Great Depression and Dust Bowl, 2001; contbr. Precinct woman com. Alamota Township, Kans., 1962-86; mem. Dem. State Affirmative Action Com., 1975. Recipient hon. mention for photography Ann. Christian Arts Festival, 1974, Artist of Month award Dane G. Hansen Mus., 1975. Mem. Kans. State Hist. Soc. (pres. 1990-91), Lane County Hist. Soc. (sec. 1970-78). Methodist. Avocations: fossil hunting, walking, photography, antiques. Home: 100 N 4th Dighton KS 67839 Office: 110 E Pearl St Dighton KS 67839

STANLEY, HUGH MONROE, JR. lawyer; b. Ft. Lewis, Wash., Oct. 25, 1944; s. Hugh Monroe Sr. and Rita (McHugh) S.; m. Patricia Page, Aug. 17, 1968; children: Allison Michelle, Matthew Monroe, Trevor Marshall. BA magna cum laude, U. Dayton, 1966; JD, Georgetown U., 1969. Bar: Ohio 1969, U.S. Ct. Appeals (6th cir.) 1983, U.S. Supreme Ct. 1979. Assoc. Arter & Hadden, Cleve., 1969-76, ptnr., 1976—, chmn. litigation dept., 1983-96. Staff editor Georgetown Law Jour., bd. editors. Fellow Am. Bar Found., Bar Assn. Greater Cleve., Am. Coll. Trial Lawyers, Internat. Acad. Trial Lawyers, Internat. Soc. Barristers, Nat. Assn. R.R. Trial Counsel; mem. ABA, Fed. Bar Assn., Def. Rsch. Inst., Cleve. Assn. Civil Trial Attys., Ohio Assn. Civil Trial Attys. Republican. Roman Catholic. Avocation: reading. Office: Arter & Hadden 1100 Huntington Bldg 925 Euclid Ave Ste 1100 Cleveland OH 44115-1475

STANTON, KATHRYN, retail bookstores/educ products and services executive; b. Nov. 29, 1954; BS in Acctg., U. Ill., 1976; MBA, U. Chgo., 1996. CPA, Ill. From auditor to mgr. Arthur Anderson, Chgo., 1976-81, mgr., 1981-86; from controller to v.p. finance, CFO Follett Corp., Chgo., River Grove, Ill., 1986-97, v.p. finance, CFO River Grove, 1997—. Bd. dirs. Mus. Sci. and Industry, Chgo. Mem. Am. Inst. CPAs, Financial Exec. Inst., Ill. CPA Soc., Chgo. Council Foreign Rels. Office: Follett Corp 2233 N West St River Grove IL 60171-1895 Fax: 708-452-9347.

STANTON, R. THOMAS, lawyer; b. Moline, Ill., 1943; BA, Knox Coll., 1965; postgrad., Harvard U.; JD, Northwestern U., 1969. Bar: Ohio 1969, N.Y. 1982. Mng. ptnr. Squire Sanders & Dempsey, Cleve. Mem. Order of Coif. (chmn. mgmt. com.). Office: Squire Sanders & Dempsey 4900 Key Tower 127 Public Sq Ste 4900 Cleveland OH 44114-1304 Fax: 216-479-8780.

STANTON, ROGER D. lawyer; b. Oct. 4, 1938; s. George W. and Helen V. (Peterson) S.; m. Judith L. Duncan, Jan. 27, 1962; children: Jeffrey B., Brady D., Todd A. AB, U. Kans., 1960, JD, 1963. Bar: Kans. 1963, U.S. Dist. Ct. Kans. 1963, U.S. Ct. Appeals (10th cir.) 1972, U.S. Supreme Ct. 1973. Assoc. Stanley, Schroeder, Weeks, Thomas & Lysaught, Kansas City, 1968-72, Weeks, Thomas & Lysaught, Kansas City, 1969-80, also bd. dirs., chmn. exec. com., 1981-82, Stinson, Mag & Fizzell, Kansas City, 1983-96, chmn. products practice group, also bd. dirs., 1993-95; ptnr. Berkowitz, Feldmiller, Stanton, Brandt, Williams & Shaw, Prairie Village, Kans., 1997—. Chmn. bd. editors Jour. Kans. Bar Assn., 1975-83; contbr. articles to profl. jours. Active Boy Scouts Am., 1973-79; pres. YMCA Youth Football Club, 1980-82; co-chmn. Civil Justice Reform Act com. Dist. of Kans., 1991-95; bd. dirs. Kans. Appleseed Found., 2000—. Fellow Am. Coll. Trial Lawyers (state chmn. 1984-86); mem. Internat. Assn. Def. Counsel, Exec. com., 1994-99 East Kansas/West Miss. Chpt., Am. Bd. Trial Adv., Def. Rsch. Inst. (state co-chmn. 1979-90, Exceptionl Performance award 1979), Kans. Bar Assn. (Pres.'s award 1982), Johnson County Bar Found. (pres., trustee), Chmn. Bench/Bar Com. of Johnson Co. Bar Assn., Kans. Assn. Def. Counsel (pres. 1977-78), Kans. Inn. Ct., U. Kans. Sch. Law Alumni Assn. (bd. dirs. 1972-75, 2001-), U. Kans. Kansas City Alumni (bd. dirs. 2001--). Office: Berkowitz Feldmiller Stanton Brandt Williams & Stueve 4121 W 83rd St Ste 227 Prairie Village KS 66208

STANTON, THOMAS MITCHELL, lawyer, educator; b. Vicksburg, Miss., Sept. 30, 1922; s. John Francis and Hazel Florence (Mitchell) S.; m. Jean Aldrich Herron, Oct. 31, 1953; children: Lucinda S. Duddy, Amy S. Conklin, Thomas Herron. BS, Harvard U., 1943, JD, 1948. Bar: Ohio 1949, Wis. 1962. Pvt. practice law, Cin., 1949-56; corp. atty. Kroger Co., 1957-61; with Kimberly-Clark Corp., Neenah, Wis., 1962-86, v.p., gen. counsel, 1971-84, v.p., internat. counsel, 1985-86, ret., 1986; pvt. practice law Neenah, 1987—. Trustee Friends of Bronze Age Archeology in the Aegean Area. Capt. AUS, 1943-46. Mem. ABA, Wis. Bar Assn., Am. Corp. Counsel Assn. (internat. legal affairs com.), North Shore Golf Club, Univ. Club. Home: 390 Park St Menasha WI 54952-3428 Office: 101 W Canal St Ste 25 Neenah WI 54956-3093

STAPLES, DANNY LEW, state legislator; b. Eminence, Mo., Apr. 1, 1935; s. Harvey R. and Edna O.(Smith) S.; m. Barbara Ann Salisbury, 1966; children: Jeannine Shaffer Spurgin, Janet Shaffer, Robin Staples, Joe Shaffer, Richard Staples. Student, Southwest Mo. State U., 1952-54, Ark. State U., 1954. Mem. Mo. Ho. Reps., 1977-82, Mo. Senate Dist. 20, 1983—. Mem. Sigma Pi. Democrat. Methodist. Office: Rte 3 Box 18 Eminence MO 65466 also: State Senate State Capitol Building Jefferson City MO 65101-1556

STAPLES, THORI YVETTE, former soccer player; b. Balt., Apr. 17, 1974; Student in sports mgmt., N.C. State U. Asst. women's soccer coach Va. Poly. Inst. and State U. Mem. silver medal U.S. squad, 1993 World Univ. Games, Buffalo, N.Y.; mem. 3d-place U.S. team FIFA Women's World Cup, Sweden, 1995; alternate U.S. Olynmpic Team, 1996; 1994 NSCAA All-Am., 3-time All-Atlantic Coast Conf. and All-South Region selection for N.C. State U. Wolfpack; Gold medalist heptathlon, Nat. Amateur Athletic Union Jr. Olympics, 1991, 92; winner N.C. state championships in long jump, 400-meter dash, 800-meter run. Nominated Mo. Athletic Club Nat. Player of Yr., 1994, 95; named ACC Rookie of Yr., 1994; 5-yr. player Columbia (Md.) Crusaders. Office: US Soccer Fedn 1801-1811 S Prairie Ave Chicago IL 60616

STAPLETON, JAMES HALL, statistician, educator; b. Royal Oak, Mich., Feb. 8, 1931; s. James Leo and Dorothy May (Hall) S.; m. Alicia M. Brown, Apr. 3, 1963; children: James, Lara, Sara. B.A., Eastern Mich. U., 1952; M.S., Purdue U., 1954, Ph.D., 1957. Statistician Gen. Electric Co., 1957-58; asst. prof. stats. and probability Mich. State U., East Lansing, 1958-63, assoc. prof., 1963-72, prof., 1972—, chmn. dept., 1968-75, grad. dir., 1985—. Cons. Gen. Telephone Co. of Ind.; vis. prof. U. Philippines, 1978-79 Mem. USS-Mich. Swim Com., AAU, 1976-84, chmn., 1976-78; mem. Mich. AAU Exec. Bd., 1976-81. NSF fellow, 1966-67 Mem. Inst. Math. Stats., Am. Statis. Assn. Office: Mich State U Dept Statistics East Lansing MI 48823

STARK, GEORGE ROBERT, health science association administrator; b. N.Y.C., July 4, 1933; s. Jack and Florence (Israel) S.; m. Mary Susan Beck, Aug. 19, 1956; children: Robert Braden, Janna Elizabeth. BA in Chemistry, Columbia Coll., N.Y.C., 1955; PhD in Chemistry, Columbia Coll., 1959. Rsch. assoc., asst. prof. Rockefeller U., N.Y.C., 1959-63; asst. prof. dept. biochemistry Stanford (Calif.) U., 1963-66, assoc. prof., 1966-71, prof., 1971-83; sr. scientist Imperial Cancer Rsch. Fund, London, 1983-85, asst. dir. rsch., 1985-89, assoc. dir. rsch., 1989-92; chair Lerner Rsch. Inst. Cleve. Clinic Found., 1992—. Reilly lectr. Notre Dame U., 1972; mem. physiol. chemistry study sect. NIH, 1974-77, study sect. Am. Cancer Soc., 1981-83; mem. European Molecular Biology Orgn. Coun., 1990; mem. sci. com. Cancer Rsch. Campaign, 1990-92 Mem. editl. bd. Jour. Biol. Chemistry, 1970-75, Cell, 1983-88, European Molecular Biology Orgn. Jour., 1990-93; contbr. over 180 articles to profl. jours. including European Molecular Biology Orgn. Jour., Jour. Biol. Chemistry, Molecular Cellular Biology, Nature, Oncogene, Proceedings of the Nat. Acad. Scis., among others. Trustee Cleve. Playhouse, 1993—. Guggenheim fellow, 1970-71, Josiah Macy, Jr. fellow, 1977-78; Yamagiwa-Yoshida Study grantee Internat. Union Against Cancer, 1981; named H.A. Sober Meml. lectr. Am. Soc. Biol. Chemists. Fellow Royal Soc.; mem. NAS, Am. Soc. Biochemistry Molecular Biology (rep. U.S. nat. com. biochemistry 1995—), European Molecular Biology Orgn. Achievements include discoveries in enzyme chemisry, interferon signaling and mammalian genetics; contributions to methodology in protein chemistry and molecular biology. Home: 2900 W Park Blvd Shaker Heights OH 44120-1812 Office: Cleve Clinic Found 9500 Euclid Ave Cleveland OH 44195-0001

STARK, HENRY, technology educator; BSEE, CCNY, 1961; MSEE, Columbia U., 1964, D in Engring. Sci., 1968. Project engr. Bendix Corp., 1961—62; rsch. engr. Columbia U., N.Y.C., 1962—69; assoc. prof. Yale U., New Haven, 1970—77; prof. Rensselaer Poly. Inst., Troy, NY, 1977—87; prof., chmn. dept. Ill. Inst. Technology, Chgo., 1988—97; Bodine disting. prof. elec. and computer engring. Co-author: Modern Electrical Communications: Theory and Systems, 1979, Probability, Random Processes and Estimation Theory for Engineers, 1986, Modern Electrical Communications: Analog, Digital and Optical Systems, 1988, Probability, Random Processes and Estimation Theory for Engineers, 1994, Vector Space Projections: A Numerical Approach to Signal and Image Processing, Neurol Nets and Optics, 1998; editor: Applications of Optical Fourier Transforms, 1981, Image Recovery: Theory and Practice, 1987; co-editor: Signal Processing Methods for Audio, Images and Telecommunications, 1995; contbr. articles to profl. jours., chapters to books. Grantee, NSF. Fellow: IEEE, Optical Soc. Am. (Ester Hoffman Beller prize 2000). Office: Ill Inst Technology Dept Elec/Computer Engring 3301 S Dearborn Chicago IL 60616 E-mail: eestark@ece.iit.edu.

STARK, JOAN SCISM, education educator; b. Hudson, N.Y., Jan. 6, 1937; d. Ormonde F. and Myrtle Margaret (Kirkey) S.; m. William L. Stark, June 28, 1958 (dec.); children: Eugene William, Susan Elizabeth, Linda Anne, Ellen Scism; m. Malcolm A. Lowther, Jan. 31, 1981. B.S., Syracuse U., 1957; M.A. (Hoadly fellow), Columbia U., 1960; Ed.D., SUNY, Albany, 1971. Tchr. Ossining (N.Y.) High Sch., 1957-59; free-lance editor Holt, Rinehart & Winston, Harcourt, Brace & World, 1960-70; lectr. Ulster County Community Coll., Stone Ridge, N.Y., 1968-70; asst. dean Goucher Coll., Balt., 1970-73, asso. dean, 1973-74; assoc. prof., chmn. dept. higher postsecondary edn. Syracuse (N.Y.) U., 1974-78; dean Sch. Edn. U. Mich., Ann Arbor, 1978-83, prof., 1983-2001, prof. and dean emeritus, 2001—; dir. Nat. Ctr. for Improving Postsecondary Teaching and Learning, 1986—91. Editor: Rev. of Higher Edn., 1991-96; contbr. articles to various publs. Leader Girl Scouts U.S.A., Cub Scouts Am.; coach girls Little League; dist. officer PTA, intermittently, 1968-80; mem. adv. com. Gerald R. Ford Library, U. Mich., 1980-83; trustee Kalamazoo Coll., 1979-85; mem. exec. com. Inst. Social Research, U. Mich., 1979-81; bd. dirs. Mich. Assn. Colls. Tchr. Edn., 1979-81. Mem. Am. Assn. for Higher Edn., Am. Ednl. Rsch. Assn. (Div. J. Rsch. award 1998), Assn. Study Higher Edn. (dir. 1977-79, v.p. 1983, pres. 1984, Rsch. Achievement award 1992, svc. award 1998, Disting. Career award 1999), Assn. Innovation Higher Edn. (nat. chmn. 1974-75), Assn. Instl. Rsch. (disting. mem., Sidney Suslow award 1999), Assn. Colls. and Schs. Edn. State Univs. and Land Grant Colls. (dir. 1981-83), Acctg. Edn. Change Commn., Phi Beta Kappa, Phi Kappa Phi, Sigma Pi Sigma, Eta Pi Upsilon, Lambda Sigma Sigma, Phi Delta Kappa, Pi Lambda Theta.

STARK, PATRICIA ANN, psychologist, educator; b. Ames, Iowa, Apr. 21, 1937; d. Keith C. and Mary L. (Johnston) Moore. BS, So. Ill. U., Edwardsville, 1970, MS, 1972; PhD, St. Louis U., 1976. Counselor to alcoholics Bapt. Rescue Mission, East St. Louis, Ill., 1969; rschr. alcoholics Gateway Rehab. Ctr., 1972; psychologist intern Henry-Stark Counties Spl. Edn. Dist. and Galesburg State Rsch. Hosp., Ill., 1972-73; instr. Lewis and Clark C.C., Godfrey, 1973-76, asst. prof., 1976-84, assoc. prof., 1984, coord. child care svcs., 1974-84; mem. staff dept. psychiatry Meml. Hosp., St. Elizabeth's Hosp., 1979-2001; supr. various workshops in field, 1974-84. Supr. various workshops in field, 1974-84; dir. child and family svc. Collinsville Counseling Ctr., 1977-82; clin. dir., owner Empas-Complete Family Psychol. and Hypnosis Svcs., Collinsville, 1982—; cons. cmty. agys., 1974—; mem. adv. bd. Madison County Coun. on Alcoholism and Drug Dependency, 1977-80. Mem. APA, Ill. Psychol. Assn., Midwestern Psychol. Assn., Nat. Assn. Sch. Psychologists, Am. Soc. Clin. Hypnosis, Internat. Soc. Hypnosis. Office: 2802 Maryville Rd Maryville IL 62062

STARK, SUSAN R. film critic; b. N.Y.C., July 9, 1940; d. Albert A. and Lillian H. (Landau) Rothenberg; m. Allan F. Stark, June 26, 1968 (div. 1983); children: Allana Fredericka, Paula-Rose. B.A., Smith Coll., 1962; M.A.T., Harvard U., 1963. Film critic Detroit Free Press, 1968-79, Detroit News, 1979—. Mem. Phi Beta Kappa Office: Detroit News 615 W Lafayette Blvd Detroit MI 48226-3197

STARKMAN, GARY LEE, lawyer; b. Chgo., Sept. 2, 1946; s. Oscar and Sara (Ordman) S. AB, U. Ill., 1968; JD cum laude, Northwestern U., 1971. Bar: Ill. 1971, U.S. Dist. Ct. (no. dist.) Ill. 1972, U.S. Ct. Appeals (7th cir.) 1972, U.S. Supreme Ct. 1974, Trial Bar U.S. Dist. Ct. (no. dist.) Ill. 1982, U.S. Ct. Appeals (3d cir.) 1984, U.S. Ct. Appeals (D.C. cir.) 1984. Asst. U.S. Atty. No. Dist. Ill., 1971-75; gen. counsel, dir. rsch. Citizens for Thompson Campaign Com., 1975-77; counsel to Gov. of Ill., 1977-81; ptnr. Ross & Hardies, Chgo., 1990—; admissions com. U.S. Dist. Ct. (no. dist.) Ill., 1982-90. Co-author: (textbook) Cases and Comments on Criminal Procedure, 1974, 5th edit., 1998; contbr. articles to profl. jours.; reviewer in field. Chmn. state agys. divsn. Jewish United Fund Met. Chgo., 1978-81; chmn. Ill. Racing Bd., 1991-96; bd. dirs. Internat. Assn. Racing Commn., 1992-94; cmty. adv. bd. Jr. League Chgo., 1979-83. Recipient John Marshall award for appellate litigation Atty. Gen. U.S., 1974, Nat. Svc. award Tau Epsilon Phi, 1968; named one of Ten Outstanding Young Citizens, Chgo. Jr. C. of C., 1978. Mem. ABA (litigation sect.), Chgo. Bar Assn. (constl. law com.), Decalogue Soc., Northwestern U. Law Alumni Assn. Office: Ross & Hardies 150 N Michigan Ave Ste 2500 Chicago IL 60601-7567 E-mail: gary.starkman@rosshardies.com.

STARRETT, FREDERICK KENT, lawyer; b. Lincoln, Nebr., May 23, 1947; s. Clyde Frederick and Helen Virginia (Meyers) Starrett; m. Linda Lee Jensen, Jan. 19, 1969; children: Courtney, Kathryn, Scott. BA, U. Nebr., 1969; JD, Creighton U., 1976. Bar: Nebr 1976, Kans 1977, US Dist Ct Nebr 1976, US Dist Ct Kans 1977, US Ct Appeals (8th and 10th cirs) 1983, Mo 1987, US Dist Ct (we dit) Mo 1987, US Supreme Ct 1993. Pvt. practice law, Great Bend, Kans., 1976-77, Topeka, 1977-86; ptnr. Miller, Bash & Starrett, P.C., Kansas City, Mo., 1986-90, Lathrop Norquist & Miller, 1990-91, Lathrop and Norquist, Overland Park, Kans., 1991-95, Lathrop & Gage L.C., Overland Park, 1996—. Judicial nominating comnr 10th Judicial Dist, 2000—. Lt (jg) USNR, 1969—72. Mem.: ABA, Mo Orgn Def Lawyers, Def Research Inst (state rep Kans 1998—2001), Am Bd Trials Advs (pres Kans chpt 1997), Kans Bar Asn (pres litigation sect 1985—86), Civitan Club (pres 1985—86, Distinguished Pres Award 1985—86). Democrat. Presbyterian. Avocations: aviation, scuba diving. Office: Lathrop & Gage LC Bldg 82 10851 Mastin Blvd Ste 1000 Shawnee Mission KS 66210-2007 E-mail: fstarrett@lathropgage.com.

STARZEL, ROBERT F. business executive; BS, Ariz. State U.; JD, Harvard U. Sr. v.p. corp. rels. Union Pacific Corp., Omaha, 1997—. Office: Union Pacific Corp 1416 Dodge St Omaha NE 68179-0001

STASHOWER, DAVID L. advertising executive; Chmn., CEO Liggett-Stashower Inc., Cleve. Active Cleve. Play House, Cleve. Opera. Inducted into Cleve. Advt. Club Hall of Fame, 1986. Mem. Am. Assn. Advt. Agys. (nat. sec./treas., trustee pension & profit sharing plans), Advt. & Mktg. Internat. Network, Ohio Motorists Assn., Cleve. Advt. Club, Neighborhood Ctrs. Assn. Office: Liggett-Stashower Inc 1228 Euclid Ave Cleveland OH 44115-1831

STATES, DAVID JOHNSON, biomedical scientist, physician; b. Boston, July 12, 1953; m. Angel W. Lee, Sept. 1, 1979. BA, Harvard Coll., 1975; MD, PhD, Harvard U., 1983. Diplomate Am. Bd. Internal Medicine. Staff scientist Nat. Magnel Lab. MIT, Cambridge, 1983-84; resident and intern in internal medicine U. Calif., San Diego, 1984-86; staff fellow NIH, Bethesda, Md., 1986-89; sr. staff fellow Nat. Ctr. Biotechnology Info. Nat. Libr. Medicine, 1989-92; dir., assoc. prof. inst. biomedical computing Washington U., St. Louis, 1992—. Lt. Comdr. USPHS, 1990—. Mem. AAAS, Am. Fedn. Clin. Rsch., Intenrat. Soc. Computational Biology. Office: Washington Univ Inst Biomedical Computing Campus Boc 8036 Saint Louis MO 63110

STATKUS, JEROME FRANCIS, lawyer; b. Hammond, Ind., June 13, 1942; s. Albert William and Helen Ann (Vaicunas) S.; children: Wesley Albert, Nicholas Jerome. BA, So. Ill. U., 1964; JD, U. Louisville, 1968; MA, U. Wyo., 1974. Bar: Wyo. 1971, U.S. Dist. Ct. Wyo. 1971, Wis. 1989, D.C. 1977, U.S. Ct. Claims 1973, U.S. Supreme Ct. 1974, U.S. Ct. Appeals (10th cir.) 1973, U.S. Ct. Appeals (7th cir.) 1992. Law clk. U.S. Dist. Ct., So. Dist. Ill., Peoria, 1968-69; asst. atty. gen. State of Wyo., Cheyenne, 1971-75; legis. asst. to U.S. Senator Clifford Hansen Washington, 1975-76; asst. U.S. atty. U.S. Dept. Justice, Dist. of Wyo., 1976-77; sole practice Cheyenne, 1978-79; assoc. Horisky, Bagley & Hickey, 1979-81; ptnr. Rooney, Bagley, Hickey Evans & Stratkus, 1981-88; exec. dir. Wyo. State Bar, 1988-89; trustee Village of Germantown, Wis., 1991-93; office share Ladewig and Rechlicz, 1990-93; pvt. practice Douglas, Wyo., 1993-96; asst. pub. defender State of Wyo., 1993-96. Pres. Ret. Sr. Vol. Program, Cheyenne, 1982-83; treas. Pathfinder (drug rehab.), Cheyenne, 1982-85; bar commr. 1st Jud. Dist., 1985-87; mem. Future Milw., 1991; chair Waukesha County Devel. Disability Adv. Coun., 1996—; mem. Washington County Econ. Devel. Com. Served with USNR, 1969-70. Mem. Wyo. Bar Assn., D.C. Bar Assn., Wis. State Bar Assn., Wyo. Trial Lawyers Assn. (bd. dirs. 1984-85), KC, VFW. Republican. Roman Catholic. Office: W156N 11340 Pilgrim Rd Germantown WI 53022 Home: Apt 912 9301 N 76th St Milwaukee WI 53223-1071

STAUBER, MARILYN JEAN, retired secondary and elementary school; b. Duluth, Minn., Feb. 5, 1938; d. Harold Milton and Dorothy Florence (Thompson) Froehlich; children: Kenneth D. and James H. Atkinson; m. Lawrence B. Stauber Sr., Jan. 11, 1991. BS in Edn., U. Minn., Duluth, 1969, MEd in Math., 1977. Cert. elem. and secondary reading tchr., remedial reading specialist, devel. reading tchr., reading cons. Sec. div. vocat. rehab. State Minn., Duluth, 1956-59; sec. Travelers Ins. Co., 1962-66; lead tchr. Title 1 reading and math. Proctor, Minn., 1969-98. Mem. choirs and Choral Soc. John Duss Music, chairperson Outreach, Forbes Meth. Ch., proctor. Mem. NEA, VFW, Internat. Reading Assn., Nat. Reading Assn., Minn. Arrowhead Reading Coun., Elem. Coun. (pres. 1983-84, 86-87), Proctor Fedn. Tchrs. (recert. com. 1980—, treas. 1981-86), Proctor Edn. Assn. (chairperson recert. com.), Am. Legion, Phi Delta Kappa. Home: 6713 Grand Lake Rd Saginaw MN 55779-9782

STAUFFER, STANLEY HOWARD, retired newspaper and broadcasting executive; b. Peabody, Kans., Sept. 11, 1920; s. Oscar S. and Ethel L. (Stone) S.; m. Suzanne R. Wallace, Feb. 16, 1945 (div. 1961); children: Peter, Clay, Charles; m. Elizabeth D. Priest, July 14, 1962 (div. 1991); children: Elizabeth, Grant; m. Madeline A. Sargent, Nov. 27, 1992. AB, U. Kans., 1942; DHL (hon.), Washburn U., 2001. Assoc. editor Topeka State Jour., 1946-47; editor, pub. Santa Maria (Calif.) Times, 1948-52; rewrite and copy editor Denver Post, 1953-54; staff mem. AP (Denver bur.), 1954-55; exec. v.p. Stauffer Publs., Inc., 1955-69; gen. mgr. Topeka Capital-Jour., 1957-69; pres. Stauffer Comm., Inc., 1969-86, chmn., 1986-92. Bd. dirs., chmn. Morris Comm. Fnd. Past pres. Topeka YMCA; past chmn. adv. bd. St. Francis Hosp.; past chmn. Met. Topeka Airport Authority; trustee William Allen White Found., Menninger Found., Midwest Rsch. Inst., Washburn U. Endowment Assn. With USAAF, 1942-45. Named Chpt. Boss of Yr. Am. Bus. Women's Assn., 1976, Outstanding Kans. Pub. Kappa Tau Alpha, 1980, Legion of Honor De Molay, Topeka Phi of Yr., 1971 Mem. Kans. Press Assn. (past pres.), Inland Daily Press Assn. (past dir.), Air Force Assn. (past pres. Topeka), Kans. U. Alumni Assn. (past dir.), Kans. C. of C. and Industry (past chmn.), Def. Orientation Conf. Assn., Topeka Country Club, Top of the Tower Club, Garden of the Gods Club, La Quinta (Calif.) Country Club, Masons (32d deg.), Arab Shrine, Phi Delta Theta (past chpt. pres.), Sigma Delta chi (past chpt. pres.). Episcopalian (past sr. warden).

STAVITSKY, ABRAM BENJAMIN, immunologist, educator; b. Newark, May 14, 1919; s. Nathan and Ida (Novak) S.; m. Ruth Bernice Okney, Dec. 6, 1942; children: Ellen Barbara, Gail Beth. AB, U. Mich., 1939, MS, 1940; PhD, U. Minn., 1943; VMD, U. Pa., 1946. Research fellow Calif. Inst. Tech., 1946-47; faculty Case Western Res. U., 1947—, prof. microbiology, 1962—, prof. molecular biology and microbiology, 1983-89, emeritus, 1989; mem. expert com. immunochemistry WHO, 1963-83; mem. microbiology fellowship com. NIH, 1963-66; mem. microbiology test com. Nat. Bd. Med. Examiners, 1970-73; chmn. microbiology test com. Nat. Bd. Podiatry Examiners, 1978-82. Mem. editl. bd. Jour. Immunological Methods, 1979-88, Immunopharmacology, 1983-96. Vice pres. Ludlow Community Assn., 1964-66. Fellow AAAS; mem. Am. Assn. Immunologists, Am. Soc. Microbiology, Sigma Xi. Home: 14604 Onaway Rd Cleveland OH 44120-2845 Office: 2119 Abington Rd Cleveland OH 44106-2333

STAVROPOULOS, WILLIAM S. chemical executive; b. Bridgehampton, N.Y., May 12, 1939; m. Linda Stavropoulos; children: S. William, Angela D. BA in Pharm. Chemistry, Fordham U.; PhD in Medicinal Chemistry, U. Washington. Rsch. chemist in pharm. rsch. Dow Chem. Co., Midland, Mich., 1967, rsch. chemist for diagnostics product rsch., 1970, rsch. mgr. diagnostics product rsch., 1973, bus. mgr. diagnostics product rsch., 1976, bus. mgr. polyolefins, 1977, dir. mktg. plastics dept., 1979; comml. v.p. Dow Chem. Co. Latin Am., Coral Gables, Fla., 1980; pres. Dow Latin Am., 1984; comml. v.p., basics and hydrocarbons Dow Chem. Co. U.S.A., Midland, 1985-87, group v.p., 1987-90; pres. Dow U.S.A., 1990—; v.p. The Dow Chemical Co., 1990; sr. v.p. The Dow Chem. Co., 1991, pres., 1992, pres., CEO, bd. dirs., 1993-2001, chmn., 2001—. Bd. dirs. Dow Corning Corp., The Dow Chem. Co., Marion Merrel Dow Inc.; CEO Essex Chem Corp, 1988-92. Office: Dow Chem Co 2030 Dow Ctr Midland MI 48674-0001

STAY, BARBARA, zoologist, educator; b. Cleve., Aug. 31, 1926; d. Theron David and Florence (Finley) S. A.B., Vassar Coll., 1947; M.A., Radcliffe Coll., 1949, Ph.D., 1953. Entomologist Army Research Center, Natick, Mass., 1954-60; vis. asst. prof. Pomona Coll., 1960; asst. prof. biology U. Pa., 1961-67; asso. prof. zoology U. Iowa, Iowa City, 1967-77, prof., 1977—. Fulbright fellow to Australia, 1953; Lalor fellow Harvard U., 1960 Mem. Soc. Comparative and Integrative Biology, Am. Inst. Biol. Scis., Am. Soc. Cell Biology, Entomol. Soc. Am., Iowa Acad. Scis., Sigma Xi. Office: U Iowa Dept Biological Scis Iowa City IA 52242

STAYTON, THOMAS GEORGE, lawyer; b. Rochester, Minn., May 1, 1948; m. Barbara Joan Feck, Aug. 8, 1970; children: Ryan, Megan. BS, Miami U., Oxford, Ohio, 1970; JD, U. Mich., 1973. Bar: Ind. 1973, U.S. Dist. Ct. (so. dist.) Ind. 1973, U.S. Ct. Appeals (7th cir.) 1977. Ptnr. Baker & Daniels, Indpls., 1973—. Recipient Sagamore of the Wabash Gov. of Ind., 1988. Mem. ABA, Ind. State Bar Assn., Indpls. Bar Assn. Club: Indpls. Athletic. Office: Baker & Daniels 300 N Meridian St Ste 2700 Indianapolis IN 46204-1782 E-mail: tstayton@bakerd.com.

STEADMAN, DAVID WILTON, retired museum official; b. Honolulu, Oct. 24, 1936; s. Alva Edgar and Martha (Cooke) S.; m. Kathleen Carroll Reilly, Aug. 1, 1964; children: Alexander Carroll, Kate Montague. B.A., Harvard U., 1960, M.A.T., 1961; M.A., U. Calif.-Berkeley, 1966; Ph.D., Princeton U., 1974. Lectr. Frick Collection, N.Y.C., 1970-71; asst. dir., acting dir., assoc. dir. Princeton U. Art Mus., 1971-73; dir. galleries Claremont Colls., (Calif.), 1974-80; art cons. Archtl. Digest, L.A., 1974-77; rsch. curator Norton Simon Mus., Pasadena, Calif., 1977-80; dir. Chrysler Mus., Norfolk, Va., 1980-89, Toledo Mus. Art, Ohio, 1989-99; ret., 2000. Author: Graphic Art of Francisco Goya, 1975, Works on Paper 1900-1960, 1977, Abraham van Diepenbeeck, 1982. Chester Dale fellow Nat. Gallery Art, Washington, 1969-70 Mem. Coll. Art Assn., Am. Assn. Mus. Dirs. Episcopalian.

STEADMAN, JACK W. professional football team executive; b. Warrenville, Ill., Sept. 14, 1928; s. Walter Angus and Vera Ruth (Burkholder) S.; m. Judy Tewksbury, Oct. 17, 1998; children: Thomas Edward, Barbara Ann, Donald Wayne. B.B.A., So. Methodist U., 1950. Accountant Hunt Oil Co., Dallas, 1950-54; chief accountant W.H. Hunt, 1954-58, Penrod Drilling Co., Dallas, 1958-60; gen. mgr. Dallas Texans Football Club, 1960-63, Kansas City Chiefs Football Club, 1963-76, exec. v.p., 1966-76, pres., 1976-88; also chmn. bd., 1988—. Chmn. benefit com. NFL; chmn. Hunt Midwest Enterprises, Inc., Kansas City; former dir. Commerce Bank of Kansas City, Pvt. Industry Coun.; former chmn. Full Employment Coun. Former bd. dirs. Children's Mercy Hosp., bd. dirs. Civic Council, Starlight Theatre Assn., Kansas City, Am. Royal Assn.; pres. Heart of Am. United Way, 1981; adv. trustee Research Med. Ctr., Kansas City; trustee Midwest Research Inst.; mem. First Bapt. Ch. of Raytown; past chmn. C. of C. of Greater Kansas City. Recipient Kans. Citian of Yr. award, 1988. Mem. Indian Hills Country Club, Kansas City Club (pres. 1988), 711 Inner, River, Carriage, Man-of-the-Month Fraternity. Home: 6436 Wenonga Ter Shawnee Mission KS 66208-1732 Office: Kansas City Chiefs 1000 Walnut St Ste 1528 Kansas City MO 64106-2174 also: Kansas City Chiefs Football Club, Inc 1 Arrowhead Drive Kansas City MO 64129

STEARNS, NEELE EDWARD, JR. investment executive; b. Chgo., Apr. 2, 1936; s. Neele Edward Sr. and Grace (Kessler) S.; m. Bonnie Ann Evans; children: Katherine Stearns Sprenger, Kendra Stearns Drozd. BA magna cum laude, Carleton Coll., 1958; MBA with distinction, Harvard U., 1960. Audit staff Arthur Andersen Co., 1962-66, audit mgr., 1966-67; asst. gen. mgr. internat. divsn. Imperial-Eastman Corp., 1967-68; asst. treas. Allied Products Corp., 1968-69, treas., 1969-72; v.p. Henry Crown (Ill.) and Co., 1972-75, v.p., controller, 1975-79; exec. v.p., COO, Henry Crown and Co., 1979-86; pres., CEO, CC Industries, Inc., Chgo., 1986-95; chmn. exec. com. Barnes Internat., Inc., Northbrook, 1996-99; chmn. Wallace Computer Svcs., Inc., 2000, Fin. Investments Corp., Chgo., 2001—. Dir. Maytag Corp., 1989—, Wallace Computer Svcs., Inc., 1990—, Footstar, Inc., 2000—. Trustee Evanston Northwestern Healthcare. Mem. Commercial Club Chgo., Econ. Club Chgo., Country Club Fla., Chgo. Club, OldElm Club, Skokie Country Club, Phi Beta Kappa. Office: Financial Investments Corp 405 N Wabash River Plz 2E Chicago IL 60611

STEARNS, ROBERT LELAND, curator; b. L.A., Aug. 28, 1947; s. Edward Van Buren and Harriett Ann (Hauck) S.; m. Sheri Roseanne Lucas, Oct. 2, 1982 (div. 1994); children: Marissa Hauck, Caroline Lucas. Student, U. Calif., San Diego, 1965-68, BFA, 1970; student, Calif. Poly. State U., San Luis Obispo, 1968. Asst. dir. Paula Cooper Gallery, N.Y.C., 1970-72; prodn. asst. Avalanche Mag., 1972; dir. Kitchen Ctr. for Video/Music, 1972-77, Contemporary Arts Ctr., Cin., 1977-82; dir. performing arts Walker Art Ctr., Mpls., 1982-88; dir. Wexner Ctr. for Arts, Columbus, Ohio, 1988-92; mem. Wexner Ctr. Found., 1990-92; dir. Stearns & Assocs./Contemporary Exhbn. Svcs., Ohio, 1992—2000; sr. prgm. dir. Arts Midwest, Minneapolis, 1998—. Adj. prof. dept. art, assoc. dean Coll. Art, Ohio State U., Columbus, 1988-92; lectr. Sch. of the Art Inst. Chgo., 2002; cons. McKnight Found., St. Paul, 1978, Jerome Found., 1978-79; chmn. Artists TV Workshop, N.Y.C., 1976-77; bd. dirs., chmn. Minn. Dance Alliance, Mpls., 1983-88; bd. dirs. Haleakala, Inc., N.Y.C.; mem. various panels Nat. Endowment for Arts, Washington, 1977-91; mem. pub. arts policy Greater Columbus Arts Coun., 1988-90; adv. coun. Bklyn. Acad. Music, 1982-84, Houston Grand Opera, 1991-93. Author, editor: Robert Wilson: Theater of Images, 1980, Photography and Beyond in Japan, 1995; author: Mexico Now: Point of Departure, 1997, Robert Wilson: Scenografie e Installazioni, 1997, Illusions of Eden: Visions of the American Heartland, 2000, Aspirations: Toward a Future in the Middle East, 2001, Staking Middle Ground: Recent Pictures from Central Europe and the American Midwest, 2002, Staking Middle Ground: Central Europe and Middle America, 2002; editor: Dimensions of Black, 1970; exec. editor: Breakthroughs, 1991; author and editor numerous catalogues. Decorated chevalier Order of Arts and Letters (France); Jerome Found. travel grantee, 1986, Japan Found. travel grantee, 1991. E-mail: arts2020@aol.com.

STEBBINS, DONALD J. car parts manufacturing company executive; V.p., treas., asst. sec. Lear Corp., Southfield, Mich., sr. v.p., CFO, treas., 1997—. Office: Lear Corp 21557 Telegraph Rd Southfield MI 48034

STEC, JOHN ZYGMUNT, real estate executive; b. Stalowawola, Poland, Jan. 21, 1925; Came to U.S.A. 1947. s. Valenty and Maria (Madej) S. m. Wanda G. Baca, Oct. 13, 1956; children: David, Maria, Monica. Student, Poland, 1941-44, Kent St. U., Oh., 1965-66, student, 1966-67. Cert. Master of Corporate Real Estate. With The Singer Co., Cleve., 1952-54, dis. mgr., 1954-60, sales supr., 1960-67, dir. real estate Detroit and Chgo., 1967-73; v.p. Fabri Center of Am., Beachwood, Ohio, 1973—; sr. v.p. real estate Fabri-Centers of Am., Inc., 1987—. With U.S. Army 1950-52 With U.S. Army, 1950-52. Mem. Nat. Assoc. of Corporate Real Estate (speaker, organizer 1974-77, audit Com. 1977-79, bd. dirs. 1970-82, Outstanding Achievement award 1982). Chagrin Valley Club. Repulican. Roman Catholic. Avocations: swimming, hiking, reading. Home: 725 Sagewood Dr Chagrin Falls OH 44023-6733 Office: JoAnn Stores Inc 5555 Darrow Rd Hudson OH 44236-4011 E-mail: johnstec@jo-annstores.com.

STECHER, KENNETH W. financial corporation executive; Sr. v.p., CFO, treas. Cin. Fin. Corp., 1999. Office: 6200 S Gilmore Rd Fairfield OH 45014-5141

STECK, THEODORE LYLE, biochemistry and molecular biology educator, physician; b. Chgo., May 3, 1939; s. Irving E. and Mary L. S.; children: David B., Oliver M. B.S. in Chemistry, Lawrence Coll., 1960; M.D., Harvard U., 1964. Intern Beth Israel Hosp., Boston, 1964-65, fellow, 1965-66; research assoc. Nat. Cancer Inst., NIH, Bethesda, Md., 1966-68, Harvard U. Med. Sch., Boston, 1968-70; asst. prof. medicine U. Chgo., 1970-74, asst. prof. biochemistry and medicine, 1973-74, assoc. prof., 1974-77, prof., 1977-84, chmn. dept. biochemistry, 1979-84, prof. biochemistry and molecular biology, 1984—, chair environ. studies program, 1993—. Office: 920 E 58th St Chicago IL 60637-5415

STECKO, PAUL T. packaging company executive; With Internat. Paper Co.; pres., CEO Tenneco Packing, 1993-96, COO, 1997-98, pres., COO, 1998-99; CEO, chmn. bd. Packaging Corp. of Am., Lake Forest, Ill., 1999—. Bd. dirs. Tenneco, Am. Forest and Paper Assn., State Farm Mut. Ins. Co. Office: Packaging Corp of Am 1900 W Field Ct Lake Forest IL 60045-4828

STEEL, DUNCAN GREGORY, physics educator; b. Cleve., Jan. 11, 1951; s. Robert John and Mildred (Graham) S.; children: Adam, Benjamin. BA, U. N.C., 1972; MS, U. Mich., 1973, 75, PhD, 1976. Physicist Exxon Rsch. and Engring., Linden, N.J., 1977-78, Hughes Rsch. Labs., Malibu, Calif., 1975-85; prof. U. Mich., Ann Arbor, 1985—; sr. rsch. scientist Inst. Gerontology Sch. Medicine, U. Mich., 1986—, sr. rsch. scientist biophys. rsch. divsn., 1992—, Peter S. Fuss prof. engring., 1999—, area chair optical scis., dir. optical scis. lab., 1989—. Topical editor Jour. Optical Soc., Washington, 1986-92. Contbr. articles to profl. jours. Guggenheim fellow, 1999. Fellow IEEE, Optical Soc. Am., Am. Phys. Soc. Achievements include development of first phase conjugate laser;development of first high resolution nonlinear laser spectroscopy of semiconductor heterostructures;research in of collision induced resonances in atoms;research in low noise (below the standard quantum limit) room temperature semiconductor lasers;of first demonstration of coherence optical control and wave function engineering in quantum dots;of first demonstration of wave function engineering;first deimonstration quantum entanglement in a single quantum dot;demonstration of in vitro tryptophan phosphorescence for studies of protein structure in solution;discovery of of structural annealing in proteins during protein folding. Office: U Mich Physics Dept 500 E University Ave Ann Arbor MI 48109-1120

STEELE, BRENT E. state legislator; m. Sally Steele. BS, JD, Ind. U. Atty. Steele, Steele, McSoley & McSoley; mem. Ind. State Ho. of Reps. Dist. 65, mem. agr. and rural devel. com., mem. cts. and criminal code com., mem. judiciary com., vice-chmn. fin. inst. com. Vice precinct committeeman, Ind.; former pres. Bedford City Planning Bd.; mem. Rep. Ctr. Fin. Com. Mem. Lions Club. Office: Ind Ho of Reps State Capitol Indianapolis IN 46204

STEELE, GLENN DANIEL, JR. surgical oncologist; b. Balt., June 23, 1944; m. Diana; 1 child, Joshua; m. Lisa; children: Kirsten, Lara. AB magna cum laude, Harvard Coll., 1966; MD, NYU, 1970; PhD, Lund U., Sweden, 1975. Intern, then resident Med. Ctr. U. Colo., Denver, 1970-76; fellow NIH in immunology Univ. Lund, Sweden, 1973-75; asst. surgeon Sidney Farber Cancer Inst., Boston, 1976-78; cons. surgeon Boston Hosp. for Women, 1977-80; clin. assoc. surgical oncology Sidney Farber Cancer Inst., 1978-79; jr. assoc. in surgery Peter Bent Brigham Hosp., Boston, 1976-82; instr. surgery Med. Sch. Harvard, 1976-78; asst. prof. surgery Med. Sch. Harvard Coll., 1978-81; asst. physician surgical oncology Sidney Farber Cancer Inst., 1979-82; assoc. prof. surgery Med. Sch. Harvard Coll., 1981-84; surgeon Brigham & Women's Hosp., 1982-84; assoc. physician surgical oncology Dana-Farber Cancer Inst., 1982-84, physician surg. oncology, 1984-95; chmn. dept. surgery, deaconess Harvard Surg. Svc. New England Deaconess Hosp., Boston, 1985-95; William V. McDermott prof. surgery Med. Sch. Harvard Coll., 1985-95; prof. Univ. Chgo., 1995—, dean biological scis. divsn. and Pritzker Sch. Medicine, 1995—, v.p. medical affairs Pritzker Sch. Medicine, 1995—; chair. Am. Bd. Surgery, Phila., 1999-. Assoc. editor Jour. of Clin. Oncology, 1986—, Jour. of Hepatobiliary-Pancreatic Surgery, 1993—; mem. editorial bd. Annals of Surgery, Annals of Surg. Oncology, British Jour. of Surgery, Surgery, Surgical Oncology; contbr. numerous articles to profl. jours. Recipient NIH fellow 1973-75, Am. Cancer Soc. fellow 1972-73, 76-79, various other rsch. grants. Fellow Am. Coll. Surgeons (chmn. patient care and rsch. com. commn. on cancer 1989-91, mem. bd. govs. 1991-95, chmn. commn. on cancer 1991-93, mem. exec. com. commn. on cancer 1992-93); mem. Am. Assn. Immunologists, Am. Bd. Surgery (dir. 1993-98, vice-chmn. 1998—), Ill. Surgical Soc., Am. Bd. Med. Specialties, Am. Soc. Clin. Oncology, Am. Surg. Assn., Assn. Program Dirs. in Surgery, Assn. for Surgical Edn., Internat. Fedn. Surg. Colls., Internat. Surg. Group, Soc. Surg. Oncology (treas. 1994-97, v.p. 1997, pres.-elect 1998), New England Cancer Soc., and numerous other mems. Office: Univ Chicago 5841 S Maryland Ave # Mc1000 Chicago IL 60637-1463

STEELE, JAMES L. researcher; Rschr. USDA-ARS, Manhattan, Kans. Fellow Am. Soc. Agrl. Engrs. Office: US Grain Mktg Rsch Lab USDA-ARS CMPRC 1515 College Ave Manhattan KS 66502-2736

STEELE, JOHN WISEMAN, retired pharmacy educator; b. Motherwell, Scotland, May 27, 1934; emigrated to Can., 1958; s. James F. H. and Janet H. M. (Ogilvie) S.; m. Muriel Grace Gribbon, Dec. 27, 1958; children: Colin, Alison, Graham, Alistair. B.Sc. in Pharmacy (hon.), U. Glasgow, 1955, Ph.D., 1959. Lectr. pharmacy U. Man. (Can.), Winnipeg, 1958-59, asst. prof., 1959-63, assoc. prof., 1963-68, prof., 1968-96, dean Faculty Pharmacy, 1981-92, dean emeritus, 1995-96; ret., 1996. Mem. Man. Pharm. Assn. (Centennial award 1980), Royal Soc. Chemistry (London) (assoc.), Winnipeg Lawn Tennis Club. Home: 61 Agassiz Dr Winnipeg MB Canada R3T 2K9 Office: University of Manitoba Faculty of Pharmacy Winnipeg MB Canada R3T 2N2

STEELE, MICHAEL A. real estate investment/financial executive; BS in Acctg., St. Joseph's Coll., Ind.; postgrad., U. Ill. Sr. v.p., regional dir. Rubloff Inc., Chgo.; with Equity Office Properties, 1992—, exec. v.p. real estate ops., chief investment officer, 1998—, head corp. and property real estate ops. Office: Equity Office Properties Trust 2 N Riverside Plz Ste 2100 Chicago IL 60606

STEELE, WILLIAM M. career military officer; b. July 24, 1945; Commd. 2d lt. U.S. Army, advanced through grades to lt. gen., 1996—, comdg. gen. Office: Combined Arms Center 415 Sherman Ave Fort Leavenworth KS 66027-2300

STEELMAN, SARAH, state legislator; Mem. Mo. State Senate, 1998—, mem. civil and criminal jurisprudence com., chair commerce and environment com., mem. edn. com., vice chair judiciary com., vice chair pub. health and welfare com. Republican. Home: 11820 Springhouse Ln Rolla MO 65401 Office: 900 Pine St Rolla MO 65401 also: State Capitol Bldg Rm 433 Jefferson City MO 65101 Fax: 573-751-2745.

STEEN, LYNN ARTHUR, mathematician, educator; b. Chgo., Jan. 1, 1941; s. Sigvart J. and Margery (Mayer) S.; m. Mary Elizabeth Frost, July 7, 1940; children: Margaret, Catherine. BA, Luther Coll., 1961; PhD, MIT, 1965; DSc (hon.), Luther Coll., 1986, Wittenberg U., 1991, Concordia Coll., Minn., 1996. Prof. math. St. Olaf Coll., Northfield, Minn., 1965—. Vis. scholar Inst. Mittag-Leffler, Djursholm, Sweden, 1970-71; writing fellow Conf. Bd. Math. Sci., Washington, 1974-75; exec. dir. Math. Sci. Edn. Bd., Washington, 1992-95. Author: Counterexamples in Topology, 1970, Everybody Counts, 1989; editor: Mathematics Today, 1978, On the Shoulders of Giants, 1990, Math. Mag., 1976-80, Why Numbers Count, 1997, Mathematics and Democracy, 2001; contbg. editor: Sci. News, 1976-82. NSF Sci. faculty fellow, 1970-71, Danforth Found. grad. fellow, 1961-65. Fellow AAAS (sec. math. sect. 1982-88); mem. Am. Math. Soc., Math. Assn. Am. (pres. 1985-86, Disting. Svc. award 1992), Coun. Sci. Soc. Pres. (chmn. 1989), Sigma Xi (Bd. Dirs. Spl. award 1989). Home: 716 Saint Olaf Ave Northfield MN 55057-1523 Office: St Olaf Coll Dept of Math Northfield MN 55057 E-mail: steen@stolaf.edu.

STEENLAND, DOUGLAS, lawyer; Sr. v.p., gen. counsel, sec. Northwest Airlines Inc., St. Paul, exec. v.p., chief corp. officer. Office: Northwest Airlines Inc 5101 Northwest Dr Saint Paul MN 55111-3027

STEER, ROBERT L. food products executive; V.p., CFO Seaboard Corp., Shawnee Mission, Kans. Office: Seaboard Corp 9000 W 67th St Shawnee Mission KS 66202

STEFANIAK, NORBERT JOHN, business administration educator; b. Milw., Jan. 12, 1921; s. Peter Stephen and Mary Ann (Schlaikowski) S.; m. Elizabeth Jean Horning, Aug. 27, 1949; children— John, Mary, Jane, Beth, Joel, Peter, James, Thomas, Anne, Jean. B.B.A., U. Wis., 1948, M.B.A., 1950, Ph.D., 1960. C.P.A. Instr. U. Wis., Milw., 1950-53; treas., controller Wauwatosa (Wis.) Realty Co., 1953-56; prof. bus. adminstrn. U. Wis., Milw., 1957-75, prof. emeritus. Author: Real Estate Marketing, monograph and articles in field. Past commr. West Allis (Wis.) Planning Commn.; bd. dirs. Internat. Exch. Found.-Poland and Milw. County, Wis.; condemnation commr. Milw. County; bd. review City of West Allis, Wis. With USAAF, WWII. Named Polish-Am. Man of Yr., Polish Nat. Alliance (Milw. Soc.), 1990. Mem. Am. Real Estate and Urban Econs. Assn. (past pres.), Wis. Realtors Assn. (past dir.), Wis. Real Estate Exam. Bd. (past vice chmn.), Am. Soc. Real Estate Counselors (emeritus), Polish Nat. Alliance. Home: 865 S 76th St Milwaukee WI 53214-3026 E-mail: walker@milwpc.com.

STEFANSSON, BALDUR ROSMUND, retired plant scientist, educator; BSA, U. Manitoba, 1950, MSc, 1952, PhD, 1966, ScD (hon.), 1997, U. Iceland, 2000. Rsch. assoc. Dept. Plant Sci., U. Manitoba, 1952-66, assoc. prof., 1966-74, prof., 1974-86, prof., sr. scholar, 1986—, prof. emeritus, 1987—; prof. emeritus Faculty of Agrl. and Food Scis. U. Man., Winnipeg, Can. Contbr. articles to profl. jours. Recipient Royal Bank award, 1975, Queen's Jubilee medal, 1977, Grindley medal, 1978, H.R. MacMillan Laureate in Agr., 1980, Agronomy Merit award, 1980, CSP Foods Canola award, 1981, Man. Inst. Agrologists Disting. Agrologist award, 1981, Can. Barley and Oilseed Conf. award, 1982, GCIRC Internat. Award for Rsch. in Rapeseed, 1987, McANSH award, 1989, Commemmorative Medal for the 125th Anniversary of the Confedn. of Can., 1992, Wolf Found. Prize in Agr., 1998, Order of the Buffalo Hunt, 1998, Order of Man., 2000, Icelandic Order of the Falcon, 2000. Fellow Agrl. Inst. of Can.; mem. Am. Contract Bridge League, Swedish Seed Assn., Manitoba Inst. of Agrologists (hon. life), Can. Seed Growers Assn. (hon. life, Manitoba stock seed distbn. com. Manitoba br.), others. Achievements include pioneering research in breeding rapeseed leading to the development of canola oil. Home: 915 Crescent Dr Winnipeg MB Canada R3T 1X6 Office: U Man Agr and Food Scis Dep 222 Agriculture Bldg Winnipeg MB Canada R3T 2N2

STEFFAN, MARK THIEL, lawyer; b. Algona, Iowa, Nov. 27, 1956; s. Willard Henry and Dorothy (Thiel) S.; m. Becky Sue Veld, Feb. 14, 1984; children: Camorah, John, Michael. BA, Mankato State U., 1979; JD, U. Minn., 1987. Bar: Minn. 1988, U.S. Dist. Ct. Minn. 1989. Pvt. practice, Windom, Minn., 1989-90; atty. County of Jackson, 1990—. Instr. Southwestern Tech. Coll., Jackson, 1990-94, mem. adv. bd., 1990-94; instr. Jackson County Law Enforcement, 1990-94. Graduation speaker DARE Program, Jackson, 1991-94; advisor Mock Trial Program, Jackson, 1991-94; presenter Wellness Day, Jackson, 1994. Mem. ABA, Nat. Dist. Attys. Assn., Minn. State Bar Assn., Ptnrs. in Prevention. Office: Jackson County Atty PO Box 374 Jackson MN 56143-0374

STEFFEN, ALAN LESLIE, entomologist; b. Ansonia, Ohio, Feb. 27, 1927; s. Henry William and Maude Moiselle (DuBois) S.; m. Genevieve Carlyle, Dec. 27, 1950 (dec. Jan. 6, 1989); m. Doris Mae Rable, Jan. 20, 1990. AB, Miami U., 1948; MSc in Entomology, Ohio State U., 1949; diploma, Malaria Tng. Ctr., 1959; postgrad., WHO, Sri Lanka and The Philippines, 1967, 68. Registered profl. entomologist. Malaria specialist Agy. for Internat. Devel., Jakarta, Indonesia, 1959-65, chief malaria advisor Kathmandu, Nepal, 1966-72, Addis Ababa, Ethiopia, 1972-76, Kathmandu, 1976-78, Islamabad, Pakistan, 1978-80; malaria specialist Ctr.

Disease Control, Songkhla, Thailand, 1965-66; tropical disease cons. Ill., 1981—. Cons. U.S. AID, Port Au Prince, Haiti, 1981, WHO, Geneva, 1981—, Tifa, Ltd., Millington, N.J., 1982, John Snow, Inc., Boston, 1984, Vector Biology and Control Project, Arlington, Va., 1986. Mem. Nature Conservancy, Washington, 1986-88. With U.S. Army, 1945-46, ETO. Recipient Meritorious Honor award U.S. Dept. State, 1972. Fellow Royal Soc. Tropical Medicine; mem. Entomol. Soc. Am., Am. Registry Profl. Entomologists, Nat. Assn. Ret. Fed. Employees (life), Am. Fgn. Svc. Assn., Ohio State Alumni Assn. (life), VFW. Avocations: stamp collecting, study of Asian art. Home and Office: 3666 E Cromwell Ln Springfield MO 65802-2487

STEFFES, DON CLARENCE, state senator; b. Olpe, Kans., Jan. 13, 1930; s. William A. and Marie M. (Dwyer) S.; m. Janie L. Steele, Oct. 10, 1953; children: Michael, Steve, David, Andrew, Nancy, Terrence, Jennifer. BS, Kans. State Tchrs. Coll., 1952, MS, 1958. Mgr. Abilene C. of C., Kans., 1955-57; mem. staff Topeka C. of C., 1957-60; mgr. McPherson C. of C., Kans., 1960-65; exec. v.p. Kans. Devel. Credit Corp., Topeka, 1965-68, McPherson Bank & Trust, 1968-73; pres., CEO BANK IV McPherson (formely McPherson Bank & Trust), 1973-91; mem. Kans. State Senate, Topeka, 1992—; chmn. Fin. Instns. and Ins. Cos., 1996—. Chair joint com. on arts and culture Kans. State Senate, 1997—. Mem. Kans. Main St. Adv. Counsel, Topeka, 1978-82; pres., bd. dirs. Mingenback Found., McPherson, Kans., 1970—; vice chmn. Nat. Commn. Agrl. Fin., Washington, 1987-89; v.p. McPherson Indsl. Devel. Co., 1970-75. Named Man of Yr. McPherson Coll., 1989. Mem. Kans. Bankers Assn. (pres. 1985), KC. Roman Catholic. Home: 1008 Turkey Creek Dr Mcpherson KS 67460-9763

STEFFY, MARION NANCY, state agency administrator; b. Fairport Harbor, Ohio, Sept. 23, 1937; d. Felix and Anna (Kosaber) Jackopin; 1 child, Christopher C. BA, Ohio State U., 1959; postgrad., Butler U., 1962-65, Ind. U., 1983. Exec. sec. Franklin County Mental Health Assn., Columbus, Ohio, 1959-61; caseworker Marion County Dept. Pub. Welfare, Indpls., 1961-63, supr., 1963-66, asst. chief supr., 1966-73; dir. divsn. pub. assistance Ind. Dept. Pub. Welfare, 1973-77, asst. adminstr., 1977-85; regional adminstr. Adminstrn. Children and Families Ill. Dept. Health and Human Svcs., Chgo., 1985-98; nat. dir. Performance Intitiative, 1998—. Lectr. Ball State U., Lockyear Coll., Ind. U. Grad. Sch. Social Work; mem. Ind. Devel. Disabilities Coun., 1979-81, Ind. Cmty. Svc.s Adv. Coun., 1978-81; Ind. Child Support Adv. Coun., 1976-82, Welfare Svc. League, 1968—; chmn. rules com. Ind. Health Facilities Coun., 1974-81. Chmn. Lawrence Twp. Roundtable, 1983—. Mem. Nat. Assn. State Pub. Welfare Adminstrs., Am. Pub. Welfare Assn., Network of Women in Bus. Roman Catholic.

STEGALL, MARK D. surgeon, medical educator; b. Lubbock, Tex., June 24, 1957; BA, Harvard Coll., 1979; postgrad., Trinity Coll., Oxford (Eng.), 1979; MD, Columbia U., 1984. Diplomate Am. Bd. Surgery. Resident in surgery Presbyn. Hosp., N.Y.C., 1984-91; post-doctoral rsch. scientist Columbia U., 1987-89; fellow in transplantation U. Wis., Madison, 1991-93; asst. prof. surgery, dir. pancreas and islet transplantation U. Colo., Denver, 1993-98; dir. kidney and pancreas transplantation surgery Mayo Clinic, Rochester, 1998—. Assoc. prof. surgery Mayo Med. Sch., 1998—. Post-Doctoral Rsch. fellow N.Y. State Diabetes Fund, 1987-88; recipient NIH-NIAID Individual Nat. Rsch. Svc. award, 1988-89, Upjohn prize N.Y. State Transplantation Soc., 1988. Mem. Am. Soc. Transplant Surgeons (Upjohn award 1989, Ortho Faculty Devel. award 1995), Soc. Univ. Surgeons, Assn. Acad. Surgery. Office: Mayo Clinic Campus Box C-318 200 1st St SW Rochester MN 55905-0002

STEGER, EVAN EVANS, III, retired lawyer; b. Indpls., Oct. 24, 1937; s. Charles Franklin and Alice (Hill) S.; m. Suzy Gillespie, July 18, 1964; children: Cynthia Anne, Emily McKee. AB, Wabash Coll., 1959; JD, Ind. U., 1962. Bar: Ind. 1962, U.S. Dist. Ct. (so. dist.) Ind. 1962, U.S. Ct. Appeals (7th cir.) 1972, U.S. Tax Ct. 1982, U.S. Supreme Ct. 1982. Assoc. Ice, Miller, Donadio and Ryan and predecessor firm Ross, McCord, Ice and Miller, Indpls., 1962-69, ptnr., 1970-96, mng. ptnr., 1996-99, ret., 1999. Fellow Am. Coll. Trial Lawyers. Democrat. Presbyterian. Office: Ice Miller Box 82001 1 American Sq Indianapolis IN 46282-0020 E-mail: esteger565@aol.com.

STEGER, JOSEPH A. university president; Formerly sr. v.p. and provost U. Cin., pres., 1984—. Office: U Cin PO Box 210063 Cincinnati OH 45221-0063

STEHMAN, FREDERICK BATES, gynecologic oncologist, educator; b. Washington, July 20, 1946; s. Vernon Andrew and Elizabeth Coats (Bates) S.; m. Helen Sellinger, July 17, 1971; children— Christine Renee, Eileen Patricia, Andrea Kathleen, Lara Michelle. A.B., U. Mich., 1968, M.D., 1972. Diplomate Am. Bd. Ob-gyn. Resident in ob-gyn. U. Kans. Med. Ctr., Kansas City, 1972-75, resident in surgery, 1975-77; fellow in gynecol. oncology UCLA, 1977-79; asst. prof., attending staff Ind. U. Med. Ctr., Indpls., 1979-83, assoc. prof., 1983-87, prof., 1987—, chief gynecol. oncology, 1984-88, interim chmn., 1992-94, chair 1994—; chief ob-gyn service Wishard Meml. Hosp., Indpls., 1987-95. Author: (with B.J. Masterson and R.P. Carter) Gynecologic Oncology for Medical Students, 1975; also articles. Nat. Cancer Inst. grantee, 1981-89. Fellow Am. Coll. Obstetricians and Gynecologists, ACS (chpt. dir. 1984-92); mem. AMA, Am. Soc. Clin. Oncology, Am. Cancer Soc., Am. Gynecology and Obstetrics Soc., Ind. Med. Assn., Assn. Profs. Gynecology and Obstetrics, Central Assn. Obstetricians and Gynecologists, Gynecol. Oncology Group, K.E. Krantz Soc., Marion County Med. Soc., Soc. Gynecol. Oncologists, Western Assn. Gynecol. Oncologists, Phi Chi. Office: Ind U Med Ctr 550 University Blvd # 2440 Indianapolis IN 46202-5149

STEIL, GEORGE KENNETH, SR. lawyer; b. Darlington, Wis., Dec. 16, 1924; s. George John and Laura (Donahoe) S.; m. Mavis Elaine Andrews, May 24, 1947; children: George Kenneth, John R., MIchelle Steil Bryski, Marcelaine Steil-Zimmermann. Student, Platteville State Tchrs. Coll., 1942-43; JD, U. Wis., Madison, 1950. Bar: Wis. 1950, U.S. Tax Ct. 1971, U.S. Dist. Ct. (western dist.) Wis. 1950. Assoc. J. G. McWilliams, Janesville, 1950-53; ptnr. McWilliams and Steil, 1954-60, Brennan, Steil, Basting & MacDougall, Janesville, 1960-72; pres. Brennan, Steil, Basting & MacDougall (S.C., and predecessor), 1972—. Lectr. law U. Wis., 1974; bd. dirs. Acuity Ins. Co., Sheboygan, Wis., Blain Supply Inc., Blain's Farm & Fleet Stores, 1993-00; trustee, bd. dirs. Roman Cath. Diocese of Madison; mem. Wis. Supreme Ct. Bd. Atty. Profl. Responsibility, 1982-87, chmn., 1984-87; chmn. Gov.'s Adv. Coun. Jud. Selection, State of Wis., 1987-92; chmn. Wis. Lottery Bd., 1987-90; bd. dirs. Acuity Bank, SSB, Tomah, Wis., chmn. 2000—. Bd. dirs. St. Coletta Sch. for Exceptional Children, Jefferson, Wis., 1972-76, 78-84, 86-89, chmn., 1982-83; bd. regents U. Wis., 1990-97, pres., 1992-94; bd. dirs. U. Wis. Hosp. Authority, 1996—; bd. dirs., chair U. Wis. Med. Found., 1996-99. Recipient Disting. Svc. award U. Wis. Law Alumni, 1991, Cath. Leadership awrd Diocese of Madison, 1998; named Knight of St. Gregory, Pope John Paul II, 1997. Fellow Am. Bar Found. (life), Am. Coll. Trust and Estate Counsel; mem. ABA, Jamesville Area C. of C. (pres. 1970-71), State Bar Wis. (pres. 1977-78), Wis. Bar Found. (bd. dirs. 1976—, Charles L. Goldberg Disting. Svc. award 1990). Roman Catholic. Home: 2818 Cambridge Ct Janesville WI 53545-2797 Office: 1 E Milwaukee St Janesville WI 53545 Fax: 608-756-9000. E-mail: gkss@bsbmlaw.com.

STEIL, GLENN, state legislator; b. Aug. 29, 1940; AAS, Davenport Coll.; BSBA, Aquinas Coll. Bus. owner; mem. Mich. Senate from 30th dist., Lansing, 1995—; mem. appropriations and legis. coun. coms.; vice chmn. govt. ops. com. Office: Mich State Senate State Capitol PO Box 30036 Lansing MI 48909-7536

STEIN, ERIC, retired law educator; b. Holice, Czechoslovakia, July 8, 1913; came to U.S., 1940, naturalized, 1943; s. Zikmund and Hermina (Zalud) S.; m. Virginia Elizabeth Rhine, July 30, 1955. JUD, Charles U., Prague, Czechoslovakia, 1937; JD, U. Mich., 1942; Dr. honoris causa, Vrije U., Brussels, 1978, U. Libre, 1979, West-Bohemian U., Pilsen, Czech Republic, 1997. Bar: Ill. 1946, D.C. 1953. Practiced law, Prague, 1937; with State Dept., 1946-55; acting dep. dir. Office UN Polit. Affairs, 1955; mem. faculty U. Mich. Law Sch., Ann Arbor, 1956, prof. internat. law and orgn., 1958-76, Hessel E. Yntema prof. law, 1976-83, emeritus prof., 1983—; co-dir. internat. legal studies, 1958-76; dir., 1976-81. Vis. prof. Stanford Law Sch., 1956, 77, Law Faculties, Stockholm, Uppsala and Lund, Sweden, 1969, Inst. Advanced Legal Studies U. London, 1975, U. Ariz., 1991, 92; lectr. Hague Acad. Internat. Law, summer 1971; vis. lectr. European U. Inst., Florence, Italy, 1983, Beijing, Shanghai, Wuhan, 1986, U. Tokyo, Kyoto, 1986, Coll. of Europe, Bruges, Pontificia, Madrid, 1988; Jean Monnet prof. European U. Inst., Florence, Italy, 1991, Henry Morris lectr. Kent Coll. of Law, Chgo., 1992, Jeanne Kiewit Taylor disting. vis. lectr. U. Ariz., winter 1993; adviser U.S. delegation UN Gen. Assembly, 1947-55; mem. adv. panel, cons. Bur. European Affairs, State Dept., 1966-73; cons. U.S. rep. for trade negotiations, 1979; vice chmn. com. Atlantic studies Atlantic Inst., 1966-68; mem. adv. council Inst. European Studies, Free U., Brussels, Belgium, 1965-70; mem. U.S. Com. for Legal Edn. Exchange with China, 1983-91; lectr. Acad. of European Law, Florence, Italy 1990. Author: (with others) American Enterprise in the European Common Market-A Legal Profile, vols. I, II, 1960, (with H.K. Jacobson) Diplomats, Scientists and Politicians: The United States and the Nuclear Test Ban Negotiations, 1966, Harmonization of European Company Law: National Reform and Transnational Coordination, 1971, Impact of New Weapons Technology on International Law-Selected Aspects, 1971, Un Nuovo Diritto per l'Europa, 1991, Czecho Slovakia: Ethnic Conflict, Constitutional Fissure, Negotiated Breakup, 1997, Czech translation, 2000, Thoughts From a Bridge: A Retrospective of Writings on New Europe and American Federalism, 2000; editor: (with Peter Hay) Law and Institutions in the Atlantic Area Readings, Cases and Problems, 1967, (with Peter Hay and Michel Waelbroeck) European Community Law and Institutions in Perspective, 1976; co-author, co-editor: Courts and Free Markets-Perspectives From the United States and Europe, 1982; bd. editors: Am. Jour. Internat. Law, 1965—; mem. adv. bd. Common Market Law Rev., 1964—, Legal Issues of European Integration, 1974—, Rivista di Diritto Europeo, 1978—, Columbia Jour. East European Law, 1994—, Columbia Jour. European Law, 1994—; contbr. articles to profl. jours. Mem. Internat. Com. for Revision Czechoslovak Constn., 1990-92. With AUS, 1943-46. Decorated Bronze Star, Order Italian Crown, Italian Mil. Cross; Guggenheim fellow, 1962-63; Social Sci. Rsch. Coun. grantee; Rockefeller Found. scholar-in-residence, 1965, 73; Alexander von Humboldt Stiftung awardee, 1982; fellow Inst. Advanced Study, Berlin, 1984-85, IREX rsch. grant, 1995. Mem. ABA (co-chmn. European law com. 1982, mem. coun. sect. on internat. law and practice 1983-84), Internat. Law Assn., Coun. Fgn. Rels., Am. Soc. Internat. Law (exec. coun. 1954-57, bd. rev. and devel. 1965-67, 70-75, hon. v.p. 1982—2000), Brit. Inst. Internat. and Comparative Law, Internat. Acad. Comparative Law (assoc., Medal of Merit, First Degree Outstanding Scholarly Achievement). Home: 2649 Heather Way Ann Arbor MI 48104-2850 E-mail: steine@umich.edu.

STEIN, RICHARD PAUL, lawyer; b. New Albany, Ind., Sept. 2, 1925; s. William P. and Lillian M. (Russell) S.; m. Mary Charlotte Key, June 22, 1959; children: Richard Paul, William, Patricia. Student, Miligan (Tenn.) Coll., 1943-44, Duke, 1944-45; J.D., U. Louisville, 1950. Bar: Ind., 1950. With labor relations Goodyear Engring. Co., Charlestown, Ind., 1952-54; ptnr. Naville & Stein, New Albany, 1954-61; pros. atty. 52d Jud. Circuit Ind., 1956-61; U.S. atty. So. Dist. Ind., 1961-67; chmn. Pub. Service Commn. of Ind., 1967-70; legis. counsel Eli Lilly Co., Indpls., 1970-74; v.p. pub. affairs Pub. Service Co. Ind., 1974-90; atty., pub. affairs cons., 1990-98; of counsel Stewart, Irwin, 1999—. Dir. Indpls. Indians; Co-counsel New Albany-Floyd County Bldg. Authority, 1960-62; mem. State Bd. Tax Commrs. Adv. Bd., Jud. Study Commn. Sec. New Albany Dist. Dem. Com., 1956-61; chmn. New Albany United Way, 1957. Served to lt. USNR, 1943-46, 50-51; lt. Res. Named Floyd County Young Man of Yr. Floyd County Jr. C. of C., 1955, Outstanding Young Man of Yr. New ALbany Jaycees, 1958. Mem. Ind. Bar Assn., Marion County Bar Assn., Ind. Prosecutors Assn. (pres. 1960-61), Ind. Electric Assn. (dir.), Am. Legion, Plum Creek Country Club, Skyline Club, K.C. Roman Catholic. Avocations: tennis, golf, reading. Home: 12414 Medalist Pkwy Carmel IN 46033-8933

STEIN, ROBERT ALLEN, legal association executive, law educator; b. Mpls., Sept. 16, 1938; s. Lawrence E. and Agnes T. (Brynildson) S.; m. Sandra H. Stein; children: Linda Stein Routh, Laura Stein Conrad, Karin Stein O'Boyle. BS in Law, U. Minn., 1960, JD summa cum laude, 1961; LLD (hon.), Uppsala U., Sweden, 1993. Bar: Wis. 1961, Minn. 1967. Assoc. Foley, Sammond & Lardner, Milw., 1961-64; prof. U. Minn. Law Sch., Mpls., 1964-77; assoc. dean U. Minn., 1976-77, v.p. adminstrn. and planning, 1978-80; dean U. Minn. Law Sch., 1979-94; faculty rep. men's intercollegiate athletics U. Minn., 1981-94; of counsel Mullin, Weinberg & Daly, PA, Mpls., 1970-80, Gray, Plant, Mooty, Mooty & Bennett, Mpls., 1980-94; exec. dir., COO ABA, Chgo., 1994—. Vis. prof. UCLA, 1969-70, U. Chgo., 1975-76; commr. Uniform State Laws Commn. Minn., 1973—; v.p. Nat. Uniform Laws Com., 1991-93, exec. comm., 1991—, sec., 1997—; acad. fellow Am. Coll. Trusts and Estates Counsel, 1975—; vis. scholar Am. Bar Found., Chgo., 1975-76; trustee Gt. No. Iron Ore Properties, 1982—, Uniform Laws Found., 1992—; advisor Restatement of Law Second, Property, 1977—, Restatement of Law Trusts (Prudent Investor Rule), 1989-90, Restatement of Law Third, Trusts, 1993—; chmn. bd. dirs. Ednl. Credit Mgmt. Corp., 1993—; bd. dirs. Fiduciary Counselling Inc. Author: Stein on Probate, 1976, 3d edit., 1995, How to Study Law and Take Law Exams, 1996, Estate Planning Under the Tax Reform Act of 1976, 2d edit, 1978, In Pursuit of Excellence: A History of the University of Minnesota Law School, 1980, contbr. articles to profl. jours. Founding bd. dirs. Park Ridge Ctr., 1985-95; co-chair Gov.'s Task Force on Ctr. for Treatment of Torture Victims, 1985, bd. dirs., 1985-87. Fellow Am. Bar Found (bd. dirs. 1987-94), Am. Coll. Tax Counsel; mem. ABA (coun. sect. of legal edn. and admission to bar 1986-91, vice chairperson 1991-92, chair-elect 1992-93, chair 1993-94), Internat. Acad. Estate and Trust Law (academician), Am. Judicature Soc. (bd. dirs. 1984-88), Am. Law Inst. (coun. mem. 1987—, exec. com. 1993—), Minn. Bar Assn. (bd. govs. 1979-94, exec. coun., probate and trust law sect. 1973-77), Hennepin County Bar Assn. Home: 990 N Lake Shore Dr Apt 7A Chicago IL 60611-1342 Office: American Bar Assn 750 N Lake Shore Dr Chicago IL 60611-4497

STEINBERG, ARTHUR G(ERALD), geneticist; b. Port Chester, N.Y., Feb. 27, 1912; s. Bernard Aaron and Sarah (Kaplan) S.; m. Edith Wexler, Nov. 22, 1939; children: Arthur E., Jean E. Strimling. B.S., CCNY, 1933; M.A., Columbia U., 1934, Ph.D. (Univ. fellow), 1941. Mem. genetics dept. McGill U., Montreal, Que., Can., 1940-44; chmn. dept. genetics Fels Research Inst., asso. prof. genetics Antioch Coll., Yellow Springs, Ohio, 1946-48; cons. divsn. biometry and med. stats. Mayo Clinic, Rochester, Minn., 1948-52; geneticist Children's Cancer Research Found. and research asso. Children's Hosp., Boston, 1952-56; prof. biology Case We. Res. U., Cleve., 1956-72, asst. prof. human genetics, dept. preventive medicine, 1956-60, asso. prof., 1960-70, prof. human genetics, dept. reproductive biology, 1970—, Francis Hobart Herrick prof. biology, 1972-82, emeritus, 1982—, prof. human genetics, dept. medicine, 1975-82. Lectr. genetics dept. orthodontics Harvard Sch. Dental Medicine, 1956-58; dir. heredity clinic Lakeside Hosp., Cleve., 1958-76; vis. prof. Albert Einstein Med. Coll., N.Y.C., 1962, 64, 66, Ind. U., Bloomington, 1972, N.Y. St. Sch. Medicine, 1977; XIIth Ann. Raymond Dart lectr. U. Witwatersrand, Johannesburg, S.Africa, 1975; mem. permanent com. to arrange Internat. Congresses Human Genetics; mem. med. adv. bd. Cystic Fibrosis Found. Cleve., 1957-69; mem. sci. adv. bd. Nat. Cystic Fibrosis Research Found., 1961-63; cons. to expert adv. panel on human genetics WHO, 1961, mem. expert adv. panel, 1965-85; mem. research adv. com. United Cerebral Palsy Found., 1962-65; mem. med. adv. bd. Nat. Genetics Found., 1966-68, chmn., 1968-80; dir. WHO Collaborating Centre for Reference and Research on Genetic Factors of Human Immunoglobulins, 1966-78; cons. study of diabetes in Pima Indians NIH, 1970—. Editor: Am. Jour. Human Genetics, 1956-61; sr. editor: Progress in Med. Genetics, 1960-83; mem. internat. bd. editors: Human Genetics Abstracts, 1962— ; cons. editor: Transfusion, 1964— ; contbg. editor: Vox Sanguinis, 1965-79; contbr. articles to sci. jours. Bd. dirs. Cleve. Zoo; mem. Cleve. Inst. Art, Cleve. Mus. Art, Cleve. Health Mus., Mus. Natural History. Fellow Australian Acad. Sci. (sr.), AAAS; mem. Am. Soc. Human Genetics (pres. 1964, dir. 1954-66), Genetics Soc. Am., Am. Assn. Immunologists, Japanese Soc. Human Genetics (hon.), Societe Francaise d'Anthropologie et d'Ecologie Humaine (fgn. mem. sci. counsel 1972), Sigma Xi. Home: Judson Manor #610 1890 E 107th St Cleveland OH 44106-2235 Office: Dept Biology Case Western Res U Cleveland OH 44106 E-mail: agaz@po.cwru.edu.

STEINBERG, GREGG MARTIN, financial and management consultant, investment banker; b. Columbus, Ind., Mar. 26, 1962; s. Jerry H. and Sharla C. (Waitzman) S.; m. Stacy A. Schneider, Nov. 6, 1988; 2 children. BSBA, U. Ariz., 1982; M in Mgmt., Am. Grad. Sch. Internat. Mgmt., Glendale, Ariz., 1984. V.p. fin. Bera Hotels Ltd., Phoenix, 1984-85; gen. mgr. Les Jardains Hotel, 1985-87; asst. dir., sr. negotiator GVA Mergers & Acquisitions, 1987-88; pres. Gregg M. Steinberg Ltd., Phoenix and Chgo., 1987—; prin. Berger, Goldstein Capital Group, Inc., Chgo., 1989-91; pres. Internat. Profit Assocs., 1992—, Integrated Bus. Analysis, Toronto, 1994—. Bd. dirs., chmn. N.W. com. Jewish Coun. for Youth Svcs., Chgo., 1989-92; bd. dirs. J.C.C., 1997—. Avocations: golf, squash. Office: Integrated Business Analysis 40 King St W Ste 4900 Toronto ON Canada M5H 4A2

STEINBERG, MORTON M. lawyer; b. Chgo., Feb. 13, 1945; m. Miriam C. Bernstein, Aug. 25, 1974; children: Adam Michael, Shira Judith. AB with honors, U. Ill., 1967; JD, Northwestern U., 1971. Bar: Ill. 1971, DC 1994, Colo. 1995, U.S. Dist. Ct. (no. dist.) Ill. 1971, U.S. Dist. Ct. Colo. 1998, U.S. Ct. Appeals (7th cir.) 1971, U.S. Supreme Ct. 1974. Assoc. Caffarelli & Wiczer, Chgo., 1971-73, Arnstein, Gluck, Lehr, Barron & Milligan, Chgo., 1974-76, ptnr., 1977-86, Piper, Rudnick and predecessor, 1986—. Speaker in field. Sr. editor Jour. Criminal Law and Criminology, Northwestern U., 1969-71. Chmn. Chgo. region Leaders Tng. Fellowship, 1962-63; bd. dirs. Camp Ramah in Wis., Inc., Chgo., 1974—, sr. v.p., 1992-94, pres. 1994—, bd. dirs., pres. Ramah Day Camp, Inc., Chgo., 2001-; bd. dirs., v.p. Camp Ramah in Wis. Endowment Corp., 1993—; bd. dirs. North Suburban Synagogue Beth-El, Highland Park, Ill, 1978—, corp. sec., 1983-87, pres. 1989-91, chmn. bd. trustees, 1991-93, trustee, 1991—; mem. Nat. Ramah Commn., 1987—, v.p., 1994—; bd. dirs. Found. Conservative Judaism in Israel, 1985-90; Midwest region bd. dirs. United Synagogue of Conservative Judaism, 1989-91, 94—; mem. editor's cir. Jewish Forward Newspaper, 1997-2000; trustee Am. Jewish Hist. Soc., 1998—; charter mem. U.S. Holocaust Meml. Mus., 1992; pro bono counsel Frank Lloyd Wright Preservation Trust, Oak Park, Ill., 1996—. Served with USAR, 1969-75. Recipient Youth Leadership award Nat. Fedn. Jewish Men's Clubs, N.Y.C., 1963; cert. of merit U.S. Dist. Ct. Fed. Defender Program, Chgo., 1969. Mem. ABA, Internat. Wine Law Assn., D.C. Br, Std. Club, Ill. State Bar Assn., Chgo. Bar Assn. Jewish. Home: 1320 Lincoln Ave S Highland Park IL 60035-3459 Office: Piper Rudnick Ste 1800 203 N La Salle St Chicago IL 60601-1225 E-mail: morton.steinberg@piperrudnick.com.

STEINBERG, SALME ELIZABETH HARJU, university president, historian; b. N.Y.C. d. Johan Edward and Jenny Lydia (Peltonen) Harju; m. Michael Stephen Steinberg, Sept. 15, 1963; children: William, Katharine Lovisa. BA, Hunter Coll., 1960; MA, CCNY, 1962; PhD, Johns Hopkins U., 1971. Lectr. history Goucher Coll., Towson, Md., 1971-72; asst. prof. history Northwestern U., Evanston, Ill., 1972-75; prof. Northeastern Ill. U., Chgo., 1975-83, chmn. dept., 1983-87, assoc. provost then acting provost, 1987-92, provost, v.p. for acad. affairs, 1992-95, pres., 1995—. Author: Reformer in the Marketplace: Edward W. Bok and The Ladies' Home Journal, 1979; also articles. Mem. bd. for theol. edn. Episcopal Ch., 1994—; trustee Seabury-Western Theol. Sem., 1996—. Recipient 14th ann. award of appreciation Asian Am. Coalition Chgo., 1997; named to Hunter Coll. Hall of Fame, 1997; tchr. grantee Danforth Found., 1967-68. Episcopalian. Avocations: opera, theatre. Office: Northeastern Ill U Office of President 5500 N Saint Louis Ave Chicago IL 60625-4679

STEINDLER, HOWARD ALLEN, lawyer; b. Cleve., June 12, 1942; s. Sidney and Lois Jean (Rosenberg) S.; children: Rebecca, Allison, Daniel. BS, Miami U., Oxford, Ohio, 1964; JD, Ohio State U., 1967. Bar: Ohio 1967. Mem. firm Benesch, Friedlander, Coplan & Aronoff, Cleve., 1967—. Pres. bd. trustees Cleve. Scholarship Program, 1987-97, trustee, 1997—; trustee Downtown Cleve. Partnership, Inc., The Ratner Sch. Office: Benesch Friedlander Coplan & Aronoff 2300 BP Tower 200 Public Sq Cleveland OH 44114-2371 E-mail: hsteindler@bfca.com.

STEINDLER, MARTIN JOSEPH, chemist; b. Vienna, Austria, Jan. 3, 1928; came to U.S., 1938; s. J.P. and M.G. S.; m. Joan Long, Aug. 16, 1952; children: M.H., T.P. PhB, U. Chgo., 1947, BS, 1948, MS, 1949, PhD, 1952. Chemist Argonne (Ill.) Nat. Lab., 1953-74, sr. chemist, 1974—, assoc. dir. div. chem. engring., 1978-84, dir. chem. tech. div., 1984-93, sr. tech. advisor, 1993—. Mem. adv. com. on nuclear waste NRC, Washington, 1988-96, chmn. 1995; adminstrv. judge ASLBP, 1973-90. Contbr. articles to profl. pubs.; patentee in field. Pres. Matteson-Park Forest (Ill.) Sch. Bd., 1959-78. Recipient Disting. Performance medal U. Chgo., 1992, Meritorious Svc. award for Scientific Excellence, U.S. NRC, 1996. Mem. AAAS, Am. Nuclear Soc., Am. Inst. Chem. Engrs. (Robert E. Wilson award 1990), Sigma Xi. Office: Argonne Nat Lab 9700 Cass Ave Argonne IL 60439-4803

STEINEGER, CHRIS, state legislator; b. Kansas City, Kans., Jan. 8, 1962; m. Shari Wilson. BS, Kans. State U., 1986; MS, U. Kans., 1992. Staff asst. U.S. Rep. Jim Slattery, 1987-88; stock broker, 1988-90; tax auditor Kans. Dept. Revenue, 1993-95; devel. dir. Cross-Lines Coop. Coun., 1995—; mem. Kans. State Senate, 1996—, mem. assessment and tax com., commerce com., elections and local govt. com. Bd. pres. Grinter Place Friends; bd. mem. Kaw Valley Arts and Humanities, Wyandotte County Hist. Soc.; bd. sec. Kans. Dem. Leadership Coun. Com., Inc.; treas. Southside Dem. Club; v.p. Mid-County Dem. Club. Democrat. Office: 51 S 64th St Kansas City KS 66111 also: State Capitol Rm 523-S Topeka KS 66612 E-mail: steineger@senate.state.ks.us.

STEINEGER, MARGARET LEISY, non-profit organization officer; b. Newton, Kans., Feb. 8, 1926; d. Ernest Erwin and Elva Agnes (Krehbiel) L.; m. John Francis Steineger, Dec. 2, 1949; children: John Steineger III, Cindy Blair, Melissa, Chris. B., So. Meth. U., 1947; M. in Social Work, U. Kans., 1949. County vice-chair United Way, Kansas City, Kans., 1960-61;

bd., sec., treas. Wyandotte County Bar Aux., 1960-63; bd. Jr. League of Kansas City, 1962-66, County Coun. PTA, Wyandotte County, 1963-66, KCK Friends of the Arts, Kansas City, 1974-77; pres. Grinter Place Mus. Friends, Kans., 1977-78; bd. Kaw Valley Arts Coun., Kansas City, 1982-86; commr. Landmarks Commn., 1985-87; bd. Arts with the Handicapped, Wyandotte County, 1986—. Bd. dirs. Kans. Arts Adv. Bd., Grinter Place Friends, Kans., Tri-County Tourism Coun., Kans. V.p. Kans. Legis. Wives, Topeka, 1975-76; bd. dirs. KCK Friends of the Libr., Kansas City, 1984—, Shepherd's Ctr., 1996—; founder Wyandotte County Libr., 1963-64, Creative Experiences, Kansas City, 1967; commr. Kans. Arts Commn., 1965-85; mem. Kaw Valley Arts and Humanities Bd., 1988-92; mem. adv. bd. Parents as Tchrs., 1992-99; mem. Kansas City Ballet Guild.; bd. dirs. Shepherd's Ctr., 1996—. Recipient Humanities award Kans. Com. for the Humanities, 1989; named Citizen of Yr. Kansas City, Kans., 1978. Mem. Kappa Kappa Gamma (C.C. Endowment Bd. 1989—). Democrat. Methodist. Avocations: skiing, sailing, inventing. Home: 6400 Valleyview Ave Kansas City KS 66111-2013 Office: Security Bank Building Ste 600 Kansas City KS 66101

STEINER, PETER OTTO, economics educator, dean; b. N.Y.C., July 9, 1922; s. Otto Davidson and Ruth (Wurzburger) S.; m. Ruth E. Riggs, Dec. 20, 1947 (div. 1967); children: Mary Catherine, Alison Ruth, David Denison; m. Patricia F. Owen, June 2, 1968. A.B., Oberlin Coll., 1943; M.A., Harvard, 1949, Ph.D., 1950. Instr. U. Calif., Berkeley, 1949-50, asst. prof. econs., 1950-57; assoc. prof. U. Wis., Madison, 1957-59, prof., 1959-68; prof. econs. and law U. Mich., Ann Arbor, 1968-91, prof. emeritus, 1991—, chmn. dept. econs., 1971-74, dean Coll. Lit., Sci. and Arts, 1981-89. Vis. prof. U. Nairobi, Kenya, 1974—75; cons. U.S. Bur. Budget, 1961—62, Treasury Dept., 1962—63, various pvt. firms, 1952—. Author: An Introduction to the Analysis of Time Series, 1956, (with r. Dorfman) The Economic Status of the Aged, 1957, (with R.G. Lipsey) Economics, 10th edit., 1993, On the Process of Planning, 1968, Public Expenditure Budgeting, 1969, Mergers: Motives, Effects, Policies, 1975, Thursday Night Poker: Understand, Enjoy and Win, 1996; contbr. articles to profl. publs. Served to lt. USNR, 1944-46. Social Sci. Research Council Faculty Research fellow, 1956; Guggenheim fellow, 1960; Ford Faculty Research fellow, 1965 Mem. Am. Econ. Assn., Econometric Soc., AAUP (chmn. com. Z 1970-73, pres. 1976-78) Home: 502 Heritage Dr Ann Arbor MI 48105-2556 Office: U Mich Law Sch 625 S State St Ann Arbor MI 48109-1215 E-mail: psteiner@umich.edu.

STEINGASS, SUSAN R. lawyer; b. Cambridge, Mass., Dec. 18, 1941; BA in English Lit., Denison U., 1963; MA in English Lit. with honors, Northwestern U., 1965; JD with honors, U. Wis., 1976. Bar: Wis. 1976, U.S. Dist. Ct. Wis. 1976. Instr. dept. English La. State U., 1965-66, Calif. State Coll., L.A., 1966-68, U. Wis., Stevens Point, 1968-72; law clk. Hon. Nathan S. Heffernan Wis. Supreme Ct., 1976-77; ptnr. Stafford, Rosenbaum, Reiser and Hansen, 1977-85; judge Dane County Cir. Ct., Wis., 1985-93; ptnr. Habush, Habush & Rottier, S.C., Madison, 1993—. Lectr. civil procedure, environ. law, evidence, trial advocacy Law Sch., U. Wis., 1981—; instr. Nat. Inst. for Trial Advocacy, 1987—, Nat. Jud. Coll., 1993—. Note and comment editor Wis. Law Rev., 1974-76; co-editor: Wisconsin Civil Procedure Before Trial, 1994, The Wisconsin Rules of Evidence: A Courtroom Handbook, 1998—. Chairperson Wis. Equal Justice Task Force, 1989-91. Named Wis. Trial Judge of Yr. Am. Bd. Trial Advocates, 1992. Fellow Wis. Bar Found.; mem. ATLA, ABA (ho. dels. 2000—), Am. Bar Found., Am. Law Inst., Am. Adjudicature Soc. (bd. dirs., v.p.), Wis. Bar Assn. (pres. 1998-99), Wis. Law Alumni Assn. (bd. dirs., v.p.), Wis. Acad. Trial Lawyers, Wis. Equal Justice Fund (pres.), Dane County Bar Assn., Order of the Coif. Office: Habush Habush Davis & Rottier SC 150 E Gilman St Ste 2000 Madison WI 53703-1481 E-mail: ssteinga@habush.com.

STEINGER, CHRIS, state legislator; b. Kansas City, Jan. 8, 1962; m. Shari Steinger. BS, Kans. State U., 1986; MS, U. Kans., 1992. Stock broker, 1988-90; tax auditor Kans. Dept. Rev., 1993-95; devel. dir. Cross-Lines Coop. Coun., 1995—; mem. Kans. Senate, Topeka, 1996—, mem. assessment and tax. commerce com., mem. elections and local govt. com., mem. pub. health and welfare com., ranking minority mem., mem. joint com. on legis. post audit com., mem. joint com. on health care reform com. Staff asst. U.S. Rep. Jim Slattery, 1987-88; v.p. Mid-County Dem. Club; bd. pres. Grinter Pl. Friends; bd. dirs. Kaw Valleys Arts and Humanities, Wyandotte County Hist. Soc.; bd. sec. Kans. Dem. Leadership Coun.; treas. Southside Dem. Club. Office: 300 SW 10th Ave Topeka KS 66612-1504

STEINGRABER, FREDERICK GEORGE, management consultant; b. Mpls., July 7, 1938; s. Frederick F. and Evelyn (Luger) S.; m. Veronika Agnes Wagner, Aug. 9, 1974; children: Karla, Frederick. BS, Ind. U., 1960; MBA, U. Chgo., 1964. Cert. mgmt. cons. Internat. banker Harris Trust, Chgo., 1960-61; with comml. loan and credit No. Trust Co., 1964—68; assoc. A.T. Kearney, 1969—72, prin., 1972—, officer/ptnr., 1972—, pres., COO, 1981—82, CEO, 1983—2000, chmn. bd., 1983—2000, also bd. dirs. Bd. dirs. Continental AG, Maytag Corp., John Hancock Fin. Trend Funds; bd. mem. Inst. for Ill. , 1986. Chief crusader United Way Crusade of Mercy, Chgo., 1983—90; divsn.chmn., bd. dirs.l Ill. Coalition, 1989; fin. rsch. aand adv. com. City of Chgo., 1989—; mem., past chmn. dean's adv. coun. U. Ind. , Bloomington, 1985—; bd. dirs. Ind. U. Cound.; mem. coun. Grad. Sch. Bus. U. Chgo.; mem. Northwestern U. Assocs., Evanston, Ill.; exec. com. Mid. Am. Com., 1985—; mem. Chgo. Com. , 1994—; bd. dirs. Northwestern Healtcare Network, 1989—96, Children's Meml. Hosp., Chgo., 1985—. Recipient Disting. Alumnus award U. Chgo., 1996, Disting. Corp. Exec. award U. Chgo., 1996, Disting. Corp. and Comm. Leadership award Am. Jewish Com., 1998, Disting. Alumnus award Ind. U., 2000. Mem. NAM (bd. dirs.), Inst. Mgmt. Cons., Chgo. Coun. Fgn. Rels. (bd. dirs., chair devel. com.), Ill. State C. of C. (bd. dirs. 1982-88, exec. com. 1984-88, chmn. Ill. Alliance for Econ. Initiatives), Exec. Club Chgo., Acad. Alumni Fellows Ind. U. (award), Chgo. Club, Econ. Club (bd. dirs.), Comml. Club, Met. Club, Glenview Club, Beta Gamma Sigma, others. Home: 615 Warwick Rd Kenilworth IL 60043-1149 Office: AT Kearney Inc 222 W Adams St Ste 2500 Chicago IL 60606-5307

STEINMETZ, DONALD WALTER, former state supreme court justice; b. Milw., Sept. 19, 1924; B.A., U. Wis., 1949, J.D., 1951. Bar: Wis. 1951. Individual practice law, Milw., 1951-58; asst. city atty., 1958-60; 1st asst. dist. atty. County of Milw., 1960-65; spl. asst. atty. gen. State of Wis., 1965-66; judge Milw. County Ct., 1966-80; justice Wis. Supreme Ct., 1980-99. Chmn. Wis. Bd. County Judges; sec.-treas. Wis. Bd. Criminal Ct. Judges; mem. State Adminstrv. Commn. Cts., Chief Judge Study Com., Study Com. for TV and Radio Coverage in Courtroom, Wis. Council on Criminal Justice. Mem. ABA, Wis. Bar Assn., Am. Judicature Soc.

STEINMETZ, JON DAVID, mental health executive, psychologist; b. N.Y.C., June 4, 1940; s. Lewis I. and Rose (Josefsberg) S.; m. Jane Audrey Hilton, Dec. 24, 1964; children: Jonna Lynn, Jay Daniel. BA, NYU, 1962; MA, Bradley U., 1963. Lic. psychologist, Ill. Intern in psychology Galesburg (Ill.) State Rsch. Hosp., 1963-64; staff psychologist Manteno (Ill.) State Hosp., 1964-68, program dir., 1968-70, asst. dir., 1970-72; dep. dir. Manteno Mental Health Ctr., 1972-80, Tinley Park (Ill.) Mental Health Ctr., 1980-88; dir. Chgo. Read Mental Health Ctr., 1988-91; ret., 1991. Clin. dir. Jane Addams Hull House Assn., 1992-98. Trustee Village of Park Forest, Cook and Will Counties, Ill.; officer, bd. dirs. various civic orgns., Park Forest. Home: 200 Hickory St Park Forest IL 60466-1016

STEINMETZ, JOSEPH EDWARD, neuroscience and psychology educator; b. Marine City, Mich., Jan. 6, 1955; s. James Robert and Catherine Elizabeth (Gould) S.; m. Sandra Sue Bieth, Aug. 8, 1975; children: Jacob Joseph, Adam Benjamin. BS, Cen. Mich. U., 1977, MA, 1979; PhD, Ohio U., 1983. NIMH postdoctoral fellow Stanford (Calif.) U., 1983-85, rsch. assoc., 1985-87; from asst. prof. to prof. neurosci. Ind. U., Bloomington, 1987-95, prof., chair psychology, 1995—. Cons. editor: Behavior Research Methods, Instruments and Computer Jour., 1989—, Behavior Neuroscience, 1993—; contbr. numerous articles to profl. jours. NIMH grantee, 1988; recipient Troland Rsch. award NAS, 1996. Fellow Am. Psychol. Soc. (charter, bd. dirs. 1997—); mem. Internat. Brain Rsch. Orgn., Soc. for Neurosci., Sigma Xi. Democrat. Roman Catholic. Home: 3681 Lauren Ln Bloomington IN 47404-9206 Office: Program in Neural Sci Ind U Dept Psychology Bloomington IN 47405-6801

STEINMETZ, MARK S. broadcast executive; Pres., gen. mgr. Sta. KQRS-AM-FM, Mpls.; group pres. ABC, 1998—. Office: Sta KQRS 917 Lilac Dr N Minneapolis MN 55422-4615

STEINMETZ, RICHARD, geologist, petroleum company executive; b. Cuxhaven, Germany, Aug. 3, 1932; s. Carl Steinmetz and Florence (Beaver) Faust; m. Janet Elaine Berkshire, Aug. 21, 1954; children—Charles, Carolyn, Christopher. B.A. with honors, Princeton U., 1954; M.S., Pa. State U., Pa., 1957; Ph.D., Northwestern U., 1962. Asst. prof. geology Tex. Christian U., Ft. Worth, 1967-71; staff research scientist Amoco Research Ctr, Tulsa, 1971-77; sr. staff geologist Amoco Prodn. Co., Denver, 1977-80, regional cons. geologist, New Orleans, 1980-83, regional geologist, 1983-84, asst. mgr. geology, 1984-87, sr. cons. gealogist, Chgo., 1987—. Contbr. articles to profl. jours. Mem. AAAS, Am. Assn. Petroleum Geologists (editor 1983-85), Soc. Petroleum Engrs. Republican. Presbyterian. Clubs: Princeton (Chgo.) (Tulsa) (pres. 1975-76). Avocations: hiking; skiing; travel. Home: 260 E Chestnut St Chicago IL 60611-2401

STEINMILLER, JOHN F. professional basketball team executive; b. Mt. Prospect, Ill. m. Corinne Steinmiller; children: John Henry, Mary Kate. V.p. bus. ops. Milw. Bucks, 1977—. Bd. dirs. M.W. Athletes Against Childhood Cancer Fund, Milw. Big Bros.-Big Sisters, Metro Milw. YMCA, Milw. Convention Visitors Bur.; mem. Greater Milw. Com. Recipient Contardi Commitment award MACC Fund, 1991, Vol. of Yr. award YMCA, 1996. Office: Milw Bucks 1001 N 4th St Milwaukee WI 53203-1314 E-mail: jsteinmiller@milwaukeebucks.com.

STELLA, VALENTINO JOHN, pharmaceutical chemistry educator; b. Melbourne, Victoria, Australia, Oct. 27, 1946; came to U.S., 1968; s. Giobatta and Mary Katherine (Sartori) S.; m. Mary Elizabeth Roeder, Aug. 16, 1969; children: Catherine Marie, Anne Elizabeth, Elise Valentina. B of Pharmacy, Victorian Coll. Pharmacy, Melbourne, 1967; PhD, U. Kans., 1971. Lic. pharmacist, Victoria. Pharmacist Bendigo (Victoria) Base Hosp., 1967-68; asst. prof. Coll. Pharmacy U. Ill., Chgo., 1971-73; from asst. prof. to assoc. prof. to prof. Sch. Pharmacy U. Kans., Lawrence, 1973-90, Univ. disting. prof., 1990—. Dir. Ctr. for Drug Delivery Rsch.; cons. to 15 pharm. cos., U.S, Japan, Europe. Co-author: Chemical Stability of Pharmaceuticals, 2d edit., 1986; co-editor: Prodrugs as Novel Drug Delivery Systems, 1976, Directed Drug Delivery, 1985, Lymphatic Transport of Drugs, 1992; author numerous papers, revs., abstracts. Fellow AAAS, Am. Assn. Pharm. Scientists, Am. Acad. Pharm. Scientists. Roman Catholic. Achievements include 16 U.S. patents; rsch. in application of phys./organic chemistry to the solution of pharm. problems. Office: U Kans West Campus Dept Pharm Chemistry 2095 Constant Ave Lawrence KS 66047-3729 Home: 1135 W Campus Rd Lawrence KS 66044-3115

STELLAR, ARTHUR WAYNE, educational administrator; b. Columbus, Ohio, Apr. 12, 1947; s. Fredrick and Bonnie Jean (Clark) S. BS, Ohio U., 1969, MA, 1970, PhD, 1973. Tchr. Athens (Ohio) City Schs., 1969-71; curriculum coord., tchr. Belpre (Ohio) City Schs., 1971-72; prin. elem. schs., head tchr. learning disabilities South-Western City Schs., Grove City, Ohio, 1972-76; dir. elem. edn. Beverly (Mass.) Pub. Schs., 1976-78; coord. spl. projects and systemwide planning Montgomery County Pub. Schs., Rockville, Md., 1978-80; asst. supt. Shaker Heights (Ohio), 1980-83; supt. schs. Mercer County Pub. Schs., Princeton, W.Va., 1983-85, Oklahoma City Pub. Schs., 1985-92, Cobb County, Ga., 1992-93; dep. supt. Boston Pub. Schs., 1993-95, acting supt., 1995-96; supt. Kingston (N.Y.) Sch. Dist., 1996—2001; pres., CEO High/Scope Ednl. Rsch. Found., Ypsilanti, Mich., 2001—. Adj. prof. Lesley Coll., Cambridge, Mass., 1976-78; adj. faculty Harvard U., 1992-93. Author: Educational Planning for Educational Success, Effective Schools Research: Practice and Promise; editor: Effective Instructional Management; cons. editor, book rev. editor Jour. Ednl. Pub. Rels.; mem. editl. bd. Jour. Curriculum & Supervision, Reading Today's Youth; contbr. articles to profl. jours. Bd. govs. Kirkpatrick Ctr.; mem. Oklahoma City Com. Econ. Devel.; founding bd. dirs. Oklahoma Alliance Against Drugs, Oklahoma Zool. Soc. Inc.; selected for Leadership Oklahoma City, 1986; bd. dirs. Leadership Oklahoma City, ARC; bd. dirs. Okla. Centennial Sports Inc., Rip Van Winkle Coun. BSA; mem. Oklahoma Acad. for State Goals, State Supt.'s Adv. Coun.; mem. clin. experiences adv. com. U. Okla. Coll. Edn.; trustee Arts Coun. Oklahoma City, Omniplex Sci. and Arts Mus., Oklahoma City Area Vocat.-Tech. Dist. 22 Found.; mem. Urban Ctr. Ednl. Adv. Bd., U.S. Dept. Edn. Urban Supt. Network, Coun. Great City Schs. Bd., Urban Edn. Clearing House Adv. com., U. Okla. Adminstrn. cert. program com., Cmty. Literacy Coun. Bd.; chmn. bd. dirs. Langston U.; chairperson United Way Greater Okla., Sch. Mgmt. Study Group, Okla. Reading Coun. (Okla. literacy coun. reading award 1-89), Oklahoma City PTA; bd. dirs. Oklahoma County chpt. ARC, Jr. Achievement Greater Oklahoma City Bd., Oklahoma State Fair Bd., Horace Mann League Bd., 1993-2000, v.p. 2000-01, pres.-elect, 2001-2002, pres. 2002-; v.p. Last Frontier Coun. Bd.; v.p. N.Y. State PTA, 1996-2000, Kingston Chpt. Rip Van Winkle Coun., Boy Scouts Am., 1996-2001, membership chmn., 1996-97; exec. bd. Nat. Dropout Prevention Ctr. Network, 1998—; mem. curriculum com. N.Y. State Coun. Sch. Supts., 1996-2001; bd. dirs. Friends Historic Kingston, 1996-2001, Friends Senate House, Kingston, 1996-2001. Recipient Silver Beaver award, Boy Scouts Am., 1990, Amb. award, Horace Mann League, 1995, 1996, 1997, 1998, 1999, 2000, 2001, 2002; fellow, Charles Kettering Found. IDEA, 1976, 1978, 1980, NEH, Danforth Found., 1987—88. Mem. ASCD (exec. coun., pres.-elect 1993-94, pres. 1994-95, rev. coun. 1997-2002), Mass. ASCD, Ohio ASCD, Okla. ASCD (Publ. award 1989), N.Y. ASCD, Internat. Soc. Ednl. Planning, Nat. Soc. Study Edn., Nat. Planning Assn., Nat. Assn. Gifted Children (life), Nat. Coun. Tchrs. English (life), Music Educators Nat. Conf. (life), Nat. Orgn. Legal Problems Edn., Nat. Policy Bd. Ednl. Adminstrn., Am. Assn. Sch. Adminstrs. (life, Leadership for Learning award 1991), Coll. Bd. Advanced Placement Spl. Recognition award 1991, Nat. Assn. Elem. Sch. Prins. (life), Am. Edn. Fin. Assn., Nat. Assn. Edn. Young Children (life), Nat. Sch. Pub. Rels. Assn. (Honor award 1991), Am. Mus. Natural Hist. (assoc.), World Coun. Curriculum and Instrn. (life, bd. dirs. N.Am. chpt. 1996-2000, pres. 2000—), Coun. Basic Edn., Ohio Assn. Elem. Sch. Adminstrs., Buckeye Assn. Sch. Adminstrs., Ohio U. Coll. Edn. (disting. alumnus award 1991), Okla. Assn. Sch. Adminstrs., Mass. Assn. Sch. Adminstrs., Okla. Coalaition Pub. Edn., Okla. Commn. Ednl. Leadership, Urban Area Supts. (Okla. br.), Ohio U. Alumni Assn. (nat. dir. 1975-78, pres. Ctrl. Ohio chpt. 1975-76, pres. Mass. chpt. 1976-78, life mem. trustee's acad.), World Future Soc. (life) Greater Oklahoma City C. of C. (bd. dirs.), Oklahoma Heritage Assn., H eritage Hills Assn. (bd. dirs.), Victorian Soc. (New England chpt.), Nat. Eagle Scout Assn., Aerospace Found. (hon. bd. dirs.), PLATO, Learning, Inc. (bd. dirs.), Am. Bus. Card Club, Coca Cola Collectors Club, Internat. Club, Mgmt. Consortium (bd. advisors), Rotary (Boston), Tau Kappa Epsilon Alumni Assn. (regional officer Mass. 1976-78, named Alumni Nat. Hall of Fame 1986, Nat. Alumnus of Yr. 1993, Excellence in Edn. award 1993), Kappa Delta Pi (life, advisor Cen. Okla. chpt., nat. publs. com.), Phi Delta Kappa (life). Methodist.

STELLATO, LOUIS EUGENE, lawyer; b. 1950; BBA, U. Tex., 1972; JD, U. Pitts., 1977; LLM, Temple U., 1979. Bar: PA. 1977. With Touche Ross & Co., 1979-81; with tax dept. Sherwin-Williams Co., 1981-87; sr. corp. counsel The Sherwin-Williams Co., 1987-90, asst. secy. and corp. dir. of taxes, 1990-91, v.p., gen. counsel, sec., 1991—. Office: Sherwin Williams Co 101 Prospect Ave NW Cleveland OH 44115-1075

STEMMONS, RANDEE SMITH, lawyer; b. Springfield, Mo., July 15, 1958; d. Robert Lee and Connie (Smith) S. BA, William Woods Coll., 1980; JD, U. Mo., 1983. Bar: Mo. 1983, U.S. Dist. Ct. (we. dist.) Mo., 1983. Ptnr. Stemmons & Stemmons, Mt. Vernon, Mo., 1983—. V.p. Democratic Alliance, Springfield, 1984—; mem. adv. bd. Hospice. Recipient Profl. Responsibility award Am. Jurisprudence, 1983. Mem. ABA, Assn. Trial Lawyers Am., Mo. Assn. Trial Lawyers, 39th Judicial Cir. Bar Assn. (pres. 1984—), Student Bar Assn. (v.p. 1982-83), Mt. Vernon C. of C. (bd. dirs., v.p. 1984-87, pres. 1987), Order of the Coif, Phi Delta Phi. Democrat. Presbyterian. Home: 520 E Center St Mount Vernon MO 65712-1208 Office: 101 E Dallas St Mount Vernon MO 65712-1401

STEMPEL, GUIDO HERMANN, III, journalism educator; b. Bloomington, Ind., Aug. 13, 1928; s. Guido Hermann Jr. and Alice Margaret (Menninger) S.; m. Anne Elliott, Aug. 30, 1952; children: Ralph Warren, Carl William, Jane Louise. Student, Carnegie Tech., 1945-46; AB in Journalism, Ind. U., 1949, AM in Journalism, 1951; PhD in Mass Communication, U. Wis., 1954. Sports editor Frankfort (Ind.) Times, 1949-50; instr., asst. prof. Sch. Journalism, Pa. State U., University Park, 1955-57; from assoc. prof. to prof. Dept. Journalism, Cen. Mich. U., Mt. Pleasant, 1957-65; assoc. prof. Sch. Journalism, Ohio U., Athens, 1965-68, prof., 1968-82, Disting. prof., 1982-97, dir., 1972-79, Disting. prof. emeritus, 1997—. Rsch. cons. Ohio Newspaper Assn., Columbus, 1985—; chmn. rsch. com. Coll. Media Advisors, 1963-69, 79-84; mem. adv. bd. dept. comm. arts U. West Fla., 1987—; survey coord. Scripps Howard News Svc., 1992—. Co-author: The Media in the 1984 and 1988 Presidential Campaigns, 1991; assoc. editor, Newspaper Rsch. Jour., 1992-2001; co-editor Web Jour. of Mass Comm. Rsch., 1997—; editor, co-author: The Practice of Political Communication, 1994; co-editor, co-author: Research Methods in Mass Communications, 1981, 2d edit., 1989, The Media in the 1984 and 1988 Presidential Campaigns, 1991; co-editor: Historical Dictionary of Political Communication in the United States, 1999; editor: Journalism Quar., 1972-89; contbr. articles to profl. jours. Mem. bd. visitors Def. Info. Sch., Ft. Meade, 1985-96. Recipient Chancellor's award U. Wis., 1977. Mem. Assn. for Edn. in Journalism and Mass Communication (chmn. rsch. com. 1968-71; Eleanor Blum award 1989, Trayes tchr. of yr. award 1997, Disting. Svc. award 1999), Soc. Profl. Journalists, Rotary (pres. Athens unit 1984-85). Democrat. Methodist. Home: 7 Lamar Dr Athens OH 45701-3730 Office: Ohio Univ Sch of Journalism Athens OH 45701 E-mail: stempel@ohio.edu.

STEMPEL, ROBERT C. automobile manufacturing company executive; b. 1933; BSME, Worcester Polytech Inst., 1955, PhD, 1977; MBA, Mich. State U., 1970. Sr. detailer chassis design dept. Oldsmobile div. GM, Detroit, 1958-62. Sr. designer, 1962-64, transmission design engr., 1964-69, motor engr., 1969-72, asst. chief engr., 1972-73, spl. asst. to pres., 1973-74, chief engines and components engr. Chevrolet div., 1974-75, dir. engring., 1975-78, corp. v.p. and gen. mgr. Pontiac div., 1978-80, corp. v.p. European passenger car ops., Fed. Republic Germany, 1980-82, corp. v.p., gen. mgr. Chevrolet div., 1982-84, corp. v.p., group exec. Buick-Oldsmobile-Cadillac Group, 1984-86, corp. exec. v.p. Worldwide Truck & Bus Group, Overseas Group, 1986-87, corp. pres., chief operating officer, 1987-90, chmn., chief exec. officer, 1990-92, chmn., Energy Conversion Devices, Inc., Troy, Mich. Served with U.S. Army, 1956-58. Mem. NAE. Office: Energy Conversion Devices Inc 1675 W Maple Rd Troy MI 48084

STEMPL, ROBERT C. energy company executive; b. 1932; Pres. GM Corp., 1987-90, chmn., CEO, 1990-92; mem. bd. mgrs. GM Ovonic; chmn. Ovonic Battery; sr. bus. and tech. advisor to chmn. Energy Conversion Devices, Inc., Troy, Mich., chmn. bd. dirs., exec. dir., 1999—. Bd. dirs. United Solar and Ovonyx, Alliance Bd. of Ovonic Media, Southwall Technologies, Inc.; mem. mgmt. com. Texaco Ovonic Fuel Cell Co., Bekaert ECD Solar Systems; others. Office: Energy Conversion Devices Inc 2956 Waterview Dr Rochester MI 48309

STENBERG, DONALD B. state attorney general; b. David City, Nebr., Sept. 30, 1948; s. Eugene A. and Alice (Kasal) Stenberg; m. Susan K. Hoegemeyer, June 9, 1971; children: Julie A., Donald B. Jr., Joseph L., Abby E. BA, U. Nebr., 1970; MBA, JD cum laude, Harvard U., 1974. Bar: Nebr. 1974, U.S. Dist. Ct. Nebr. 1974, U.S. Ct. Appeals (fed. cir.) 1984, U.S. Ct. Claims 1989, U.S. Ct. Appeals (8th cir.) 1989, U.S. Supreme Ct. 1991. Assoc. Barlow, Watson & Johnson, Lincoln, Nebr., 1974—75; ptnr. Stenberg and Stenberg, 1976—78; legal counsel Gov. of Nebr., 1979—82; sr. prin. Erickson & Sederstrom, 1983—85; pvt. practice, 1985—90; atty. gen. State of Nebr., 1991—. Mem.: Phi Beta Kappa. Republican. Office: Office of Atty Gen 2115 State Capitol Lincoln NE 68509-8000

STENEHJEM, BOB, state legislator; m. Kathy; 4 children. Degree, Bismarck State Coll. Mem. N.D. Senate from 30th dist., Bismark, 1992—; mem. human svc. com. N.D. Senate, chmn. transp. com. Mem. NRA, Elks, Ducks Unlimited, N.Am. Boone and Crockett Club. Home: 7475 41st St SE Bismarck ND 58504-3200 Office: ND State Senate State Capitol Bismarck ND 58505

STENEHJEM, WAYNE KEVIN, state attorney general, lawyer; b. Mohall, N.D., Feb. 5, 1953; s. Martin Edward and Marguerite Mae (McMaster) Stenehjem; m. Tama Lou Smith, June 16, 1978 (div. Apr. 1984); 1 child Andrew Stenehjem ; m. Beth D. Bakke, June 30, 1995. AA, Bismarck (N.D.) Jr. Coll., 1972; BA, U. N.D., 1974, JD, 1977. Bar: N.D. 1977. Ptnr. Kuchera & Stenehjem, Grand Forks, ND, 1977—2000; spl. asst. atty. gen. State of N.D., 1983—87, atty. gen., 2000—; mem. N.D. Ho. Reps. , 1976—80, N.D. State Senate, 1980—2000, pres. pro tempore, 1998—99. Chmn. Senate Com. on Social Svcs., 1985—86, Senate Com. on Judiciary, 1995—2000, Interim Legis. Judiciary Com., 1995—2000, Legis. Coun., 1995—2000; mem. Nat. Conf. Commrs. on Uniform State Laws, 1995—, Gov.'s Com. on Juvenile Justice. Bd. dirs. N.D. Spl. Olympics, 1985—89; chmn. Dist. 42 Reps., Grand Forks, 1986—88; bd. dirs. Christus Rex Luth. Ch., pres., 1985—86. Named Champion of People's Right to Know, Sigma Delta Chi, 1979, N.D. Friend of Psychology, N.D. Psychol. Assn., 1990; named one of Outstanding Young Man of N.D, Jaycees, 1985; recipient Excellence in County Govt. award, N.D. Assn. Counties, 1991. Mem.: Grand Forks County Bar Assn., N.D. State Bar Assn. (Legis. Svc. award 1995). Home: 1216 Crestview Ln Bismarck ND 58501 Office: Office of the Atty Gen State Capitol Bldg 600 E Boulevard Ave Bismarck ND 58505

STENGER, SARAH, chef; Grad., Dumas Pere Cooking Sch.; studied with chef Pierre Orsi, Pierre Orsi restaurant, Lyons, France. From apprentice to chef The Dining Room, Ritz-Carlton hotel, Chgo., 1984—. Founder Women Chefs of Chgo. Named U.S. winner, Prix Culinaire Internat. Pierre Taittinger competition, Paris, 1991, Rising Star Chef of the Yr. in Am., James Beard Found., 1994, Best Chef of the Midwest, 1998. Office: Ritz-Carlton 106 E Pearson St Chicago IL 60611

STEP, EUGENE LEE, retired pharmaceutical company executive; b. Sioux City, Iowa, Feb. 19, 1929; s. Harry and Ann (Keiser) S.; m. Hannah Scheuermann, Dec. 27, 1953; children: Steven Harry, Michael David, Jonathan Allen. BA in Econs., U. Nebr., 1951; MS in Acctg. and Fin., U. Ill., 1952. With Eli Lilly Internat. Corp., London and Paris, 1964-69, dir. Elanco Internat. Indpls., 1969-70, v.p. marketing, 1970-72, v.p. Europe, 1972; v.p. mktg. Eli Lilly and Co., 1972-73, pres. pharm. div., 1973-86, exec. v.p., 1986—. Bd. dirs. Scios Cell-Genesys, Guidant Corp. 1st lt. U.S. Army, 1953-56. Mem. Pharm. Mfrs. Assn. (bd. dirs. 1980-92, chmn. 1989-90), Internat. Pharm. Mfrs. Assn. (pres. 1991-92). Home: PO Box 8997 Rancho Santa Fe CA 92067-8997

STEPAN, FRANK QUINN, chemical company executive; b. Chgo., Oct. 24, 1937; s. Alfred Charles and Mary Louise (Quinn) S.; m. Jean Finn, Aug. 23, 1958; children: Jeanne, Frank Quinn, Todd, Jennifer, Lisa, Colleen, Alfred, Richard. AB, U. Notre Dame, 1959; MBA, U. Chgo., 1963. Salesman Indsl. Chems. div. Stepan Chem. Co., Northfield, Ill., 1961-63, mgr. internat. dept., 1964-66, v.p. corporate planning, 1967-69, v.p., gen. mgr., 1970-73, pres., 1973-84; pres., chmn., CEO Stepan Co., 1984-99, chmn., CEO, 1999—, also bd. dirs. Mem. liberal arts council Notre Dame U., South Bend, Ind., 1972—; bd. dirs. Big Shoulders, Chgo. 1st lt. AUS, 1959-61. Mem. Chem. Mfrs. Assn. (bd. dirs.), Soap and Detergent Assn. (bd. dirs., exec. com., chmn.), Ill. Bus. Roundtable (policy com., sec.), Econ. Club Chgo., Exmoor Country Club, Bob O'Link Golf Club, Everglades Club, Sailfish Club Fla. Home: 200 Linden St Winnetka IL 60093-3862 Office: Stepan Co Edens & Winnetka Rds Northfield IL 60093

STEPHAN, ALEXANDER FRIEDRICH, German language and literature educator; b. Lüdenscheid, Fed. Republic Germany, Aug. 16, 1946; came to U.S., 1968; s. Eberhard and Ingeborg (Hörnig) S.; m. Halina Konopacka, Dec. 15, 1969; 1 child, Michael. MA, U. Mich., 1969; PhD, Princeton U., 1973. Instr. German Princeton U., N.J., 1972-73; from asst. prof. to prof. German UCLA, 1973-85; prof. German U. Fla., Gainesville, 1985-2000, chmn., 1985-93; prof. German, Ohio Eminent Scholar, mem. Mershon Ctr., Ohio State U., 2000—. Author: (literature critiques) Christa Wolf, 1976, Die deutsche Exilliteratur, 1979, Christa Wolf (Forschungbericht), 1981, Max Frisch, 1983, Anna Seghers im Exil, 1993, Im Visier dem FBI, paperback edit 1998, English translation Cañon Communazis, 2000, 1995, Vanna Seghers: Das siebte Kreuzi Welt und Wirkung eines Romans, 1997; editor: Peter Weiss: Die Asthetik des Widerstands, 1983, 3d edit., (literature critiques) Exili Literatur und die Künste, 1990, Exil-Studien, 1993—, Christa Wolf: The Author's Dimension , 1993—, 2d edit., 1995—, Themes and Structures,Uwe Johnson: Speculations about Jakob and Other Writings, 2000; co-editor: Studies in GDR Culture and Society, 1981—90, Schreiben in Exil, 1985, The New Sufferings of Young Werther and Other Stories from the GDR, 1997; editor: (biography) Peter Weiss Jahrbuch, 1994; co-prodr.: (documentaries) In Visier des FBI, 1995; co-editor: Rot Brauu Brecht Dialogs, 2000, (Book of Essays) Nationalsozialimus und Stalinismus bei Brecht und Zeitgenossen, 2000; co-prodr.: (documentaries) Das FBI und Marlene Dietrich, 2000, Das FBI und Brecht's Telephone, 2001, Exilauten und der CIA, 2002, Thomas Mann und der CIA, 2002. Humboldt Found. fellow, 1988, 94, 98-99, 2002-03, Guggenheim Found. fellow, 1989, VG Wort fellow, 1992, UCLA faculty fellow, 1984; grantee Feuchtwanger Meml. Libr., 1998, Internat. Rsch. and Exchs. Bd., 1993, German Acad. Exch. Svcs., 1993, 97, NEH, 1974, 84, 97, Am. Coun. Learned Socs., 1976-77, 84, Sch. Theory and Criticism, 1978, Am. Philos. Soc., 1979, 81, 92, Weichmann Stiftung, 1998. Mem.: German PEN, Internat. Anna Seghers Soc., Soc. for Exile Studies, Internat. Lion Feuchtwanger Soc. Office: Ohio State U Dept Germanic Lang/Lit 314 Dieter Cunz Hall Columbus OH 43210-1229

STEPHAN, KENNETH C. state supreme court justice; b. Omaha, Oct. 8, 1946; m. Sharon Ross, Apr. 19, 1969; children: Alissa Potocnik, Karen Borchert, Charles. BA, U. Nebr., 1968, JD with high distinction, 1972. Bar: Nebr. Former pvt. practice atty., 1973-97; judge Nebr. Supreme Ct., Lincoln, 1997—. With U.S. Army, 1969—71. Mem.: Am Col Trial Lawyers (jud fellow), Lincoln Bar Asn (former trustee), Nebr State Bar Asn (former chmn young lawyers sect, former mem house delegs). Office: Nebr Supreme Ct State Capitol Bldg Rm 2211 PO Box 98910 Lincoln NE 68509-8910 E-mail: kstephan@nsc.state.ne.us.

STEPHENS, HARRY, state legislator; b. Winfield, July 14, 1942; m. Sharron Stephens; 2 children. BA in Edn., MS in Edn., Emporia State U.; PhD, U. No. Colo., 1975. Mem. Kans. Senate, Topeka, 1999—, ranking mem. agr. com., mem. assessment and tax. com., mem. energy and natural resources com., mem. joint spl. claims against the state com., mem. transp. and tourism com. Democrat. Lutheran. Office: 300 SW 10th Ave Rm 401-s Topeka KS 66612-1504

STEPHENS, NORMAN L. former academic administrator; b. Hinsdale, Ill. m. Laurie Stephens; 4 children. Doctorate, U. Fla., 1971. Various positions including faculty mem., dean coll. sys. St. Petersburg Jr. Coll., Pinellas County, Fla.; founding provost Brandon (Fla.) campus Hillsborough C.C.; v.p. acad. svcs. Lincoln Land C.C., Springfield, Ill., 1990-92, pres., 1992-99. Active comty. svc. orgns. and programs. Fellow U. Fla., 1971. Office: Lincoln Land C C 5250 Shepherd Rd Springfield IL 62703-5402

STEPHENS, PAUL ALFRED, dentist; b. Muskogee, Okla., Feb. 28, 1921; s. Lonny and Maudie Janie (Wynn) S.; m. Lola Helena Byrd, May 7, 1950; children: Marsha Stephens Wilson, Paul Alfred Jr., Derek M. BS cum laude, Howard U., 1942, DDS, 1945. Instr. dentistry Howard U., Washington, 1945-46; gen practice dentistry Gary, Ind., 1947—; chmn. bd. Assocs. Med. Ctr., Inc. Sec. Gary Ind. Sch. Bldg. Corp., 1967-85; pres. Bd. Health, 1973-81; Ind. State Bd. Dental Examiners, 1975-83. Mem. adv. bd. Ind. U.-Purdue U. Calumet Campus, 1973; bd. dirs. Urban League Northwest Ind.; pres. Gary Ednl. Devel. Found., 1990—. With AUS, 1942-44. Fellow Internat. Coll. Dentists, Acad. Dentistry Internat., Acad. Gen. Gen. Dentistry (pres. chpt. 1973, nat. chmn. dental care com. 1977, Midwestern v.p., nat. bd. dirs. 1984-89, v.p. 1990-91, pres. 1992-93), Am. Coll. Dentists; mem. ADA, Nat. Dental Assn., N.W. Ind. Dental Assn. (bd. dirs., pres. 1976-77, Disting. Svc. award 1993), Am. Soc. Anesthesia in Dentistry, Am. Acad. Radiology, Gary C. of C., Alpha Phi Alpha (pres. Gary Ednl. Found. 1988, pres. Gary Ednl. Devel. Found. 1990—), Acad. Gen. Dentistry (pres. 1992-93). Baptist. Home: 1901 Taft St Gary IN 46404-2759 Office: 2200 Grant St Gary IN 46404-3439

STEPHENS, RONALD EARL, state legislator; b. East St. Louis, Ill., Feb. 19, 1948; s. Earl Evered and Velma Juanita (Wills) S.; m. Karen Kay Angleton, 1975; children: Wendi, Chad, Kent, Tod, Molly. BS, St. Louis Coll. of Pharmacy. Pres., CEO Stephens Pharmacy, Inc., 1975, Freedom Pharmacy, Inc., 1982; pres. Caseyville Township Rep., Ill., 1980-82, trustee, 1981-82; Ill. state rep. Dist. 110, 1985-89, 93—. Rep. candidate Ill. House, 1982. Decorated Purple Heart, Bronze Star. Mem. Nat. Pharmacists Assn., Lions, Jaycees (state dir. 1982), Shriners, Kiwanis, Kappa Psi (Man of Yr. 1980). Office: Ill House of Reps Rm 2003-G State Capitol Springfield IL 62706-0001 Address: 535 Edwardsville Rd Ste 110 Troy IL 62294-1399

STEPHENS, THOMAS M(ARON), education educator; b. Youngstown, Ohio, June 15, 1931; s. Thomas and Mary (Hanna) S.; m. Evelyn Kleshock, July 1, 1955. BS, Youngstown Coll., 1955; MEd, Kent State U., 1957; EdD, U. Pitts., 1966. Lic. psychologist, Ohio. Tchr. Warren (Ohio) public schs., 1955-57, Niles (Ohio) public schs., 1957-58; psychologist Montgomery County, Ohio, 1958-60; dir. gifted edn. Ohio Dept. Edn., Columbus, 1960-66; assoc. prof. edn. U. Pitts., 1966-70; prof. edn. Ohio State U., 1970—, chmn. dept. exceptional children ., 1972-82, chmn. dept. human services edn., 1982-87, assoc. dean Coll. Edn., 1987-92, prof., 1987-92, prof. emeritus, 1992—; clin. prof. edn. U. Dayton, Ohio, 1993—; exec. dir. Sch. Study Coun. Ohio, Columbus, 1993—. Mem. Higher Edn. Consortium for Spl. Edn., chmn., 1976-77; pub., pres. Cedars Press, Inc. Author: Directive Teaching of Children with Learning and Behavioral Handicaps, 2d edit, 1976, Implementing Behavioral Approaches in Elementary and Secondary Schools, 1975, Teaching Skills to Children with Learning and Behavioral Disorders, 1977, Teaching Children Basic Skills: A Curriculum Handbook, 1978, 2d edit., 1983, Social Skills In The Classroom, 1978, 2d edit., 1991, Teaching Mainstreamed Students, 1982, 2d edit., 1988, Social Behavior Assessment Scale, 1991; dir.: Jour. Sch. Psychology, 1965-75, 80—; exec. editor: The Directive Tchr.; assoc. editor: Spl. Edn. and Tchr. Edn., Techniques, Behavioral Disorders, Spl. Edn. and Remedial Edn.; contbr. articles to profl. jours. Named to Ohio State U. Coll. of Edn. Hall of Fame, 1999; U.S. Office of Edn. fellow, 1964-65. Mem. APA, NASP (charter), State Dirs. for Gifted (pres. 1962-63), Coun. for Exceptional Children (gov., Tchr. Educator of Yr. tchr. edn. divsn. 1985), Coun. Children with Behavioral Disorders (pres. 1972-73). Home: 551 E Cooke Rd Columbus OH 43214-2813 Office: Sch Study Coun of Ohio 4807 Evanswood Dr # 300 Columbus OH 43229-6294

STEPHENSON, ROBERT BAIRD, energy company executive; b. Washington, Jan. 20, 1943; s. Orlando Worth and Martha Ann (Kostelak) S.; m. Sheryl Ann Fish, Jan. 10, 1967; children: Brie Danielle, Eric Baird. BS in Mech. Engring., Purdue U., 1965; MS in Nuclear Engring., U. Mich., 1970, MBA, 1972. Engr. Jersey Nuclear Co., Inc., Boston, 1972-74; engr., mgr. Exxon Nuclear Co., Inc., Richland, Wash., 1974-80; mng. dir. Exxon Nuclear GmbH, Lingen, Fed. Rep. Germany, 1980-83; mktg., sales staff Exxon Nuclear Co., Inc., Bellevue, Wash., 1983-85, v.p. adminstn., 1986, v.p. comml. div., 1987; pres., chief exec. officer, chmn. EPID, Inc., San Jose, Calif., 1985-86; pres., chief exec. officer Advanced Nuclear Fuels Corp., Bellevue, Wash., 1988-91; pres. CEO Siemens Nuclear Power Corp., 1991-92; pres., CEO, Siemens Power Corp., Milw., 1992—, also bd. dirs. Bd. regents Milw. Sch. Engring. Lt. USN, 1965-70. Mem. Am. Nuclear Soc. Avocations: sailing, boating, golf. Office: Siemens Power Corp 6682 W Greenfield Ave # 209 Milwaukee WI 53214-4960

STEPHENSON, VIVIAN M. former retail executive; B Math., NYU; MBA, U. Havana. Mgmt. positions Rand Info. Sys., Occidental Petroleum Corp., Assoc. Credit Burs. Svcs., Inc.; dir. info. sys. devel. Mervyn's, 1989-90, v.p. MIS, 1990-94, sr. v.p., 1994-95; sr. v.p., chief info. officer Dayton Hudson Corp., Mpls., 1995-2000; exec. v.p., chief info. officer Target Corp., —2000; ret., 2000. Bd. dirs. MobiNetrix Sys. Inc.; mem. info. sys. customer adv. coun. IBM; mem. Tandem Americas Customer Coun. Chair bd. dirs. San Francisco AIDS Found.; mem. Nat. Retail Fedn. Info. Sys. Bd. Mem. Calif. C. of C. Office: Target Corp 1000 Nicollet Mall Minneapolis MN 55403-2467

STERN, CARL WILLIAM, JR. management consultant; b. San Francisco, Mar. 31, 1946; s. Carl William and Marjorie Aline (Gunst) S.; m. Karen Jaffe, Sept. 7, 1966 (div. Mar. 1972); 1 child, David; m. Holly Drick Hayes, Mar. 21, 1985; children: Kenneth, Matthew. BA, Harvard U., 1968; MBA, Stanford U., 1974. Cons. Boston Cons. Group, Inc., Menlo Park, Calif., 1974-77, mgr., 1977-78, London, 1978-80, v.p. Chgo., 1980-87, sr. v.p., 1987-97, pres., CEO, 1998—. Lt. USNR, 1968-71. Office: Boston Consulting Group Inc 200 S Wacker Dr Ste 2700 Chicago IL 60606-5846

STERN, EDWARD, performing company executive; Producing artistic dir. Cin. Playhouse in the Park. Office: Cincinnati Playhouse in the Park PO Box 6537 Cincinnati OH 45206-0537

STERN, GEOFFREY, lawyer, disciplinary counsel; b. Columbus, Ohio, Nov. 29, 1942; s. Leonard J. and Anastasia (Percin) S.; m. Barbara Shnider; children: Emily Staheli, Elizabeth; stepchildren: Courtney, Jennifer, Brian Feuer. Student, Williams Coll., 1960-63; BA cum laude, Ohio State U., 1965, JD summa cum laude, 1968. Bar: Ohio 1968. Assoc. Alexander, Ebinger, Holschuh & Fisher, Columbus, Ohio, 1968-72; ptnr. Folkerth, Calhoun, Webster & O'Brien, 1972-80, Arter & Hadden, Columbus, 1980-93; disciplinary counsel Supreme Ct. of Ohio, 1993-97; counsel Kegler, Brown, Hill & Ritter, Columbus, 1997-2000, dir., 2000—. Nat. coordinating counsel for asbestos litigation Combustion Engring. Inc. and Basic, Inc., 1985-93; lectr. on legal ethics and profl. responsibility; mem. Spl. Commn. to Review Ohio Ethics Rules, 1995-98, Spl. Commn. on Legal Edn., 1995-98; mem. symposium on ethics and Chinese legal sys., Shanghai, 1998; keynote spkr. Faith and Law Symposium, 1999; spl. investigator Bd. Commrs. Character and Fitness Ohio Supreme Ct., 1998. Sr. editor Ohio State Law Jour., 1967-68. Pres. Bexley (Ohio) City Coun., 1977-80, mem., 1973-80, mem. Bexley Civil Svc. Commn., 1983-85; v.p., trustee Creative Living, Columbus, 1981-89, Ohio Citizens Com. for Arts, Columbus, 1982-88; mem. Nat. Def. Com. on Asbestos in Bldgs. Litigation, 1986-92; pub. mem. Ohio Optical Dispensers Bd., Columbus, 1978-82. Recipient Am. Jurisprudence Evidence award Ohio State U. Coll. Law, 1967. Fellow Am. Bar Found., Columbus Bar Found., Ohio State Bar Found.; mem. Ohio State Bar Assn. (com. on legal ethics and profl. conduct, sec. 1981-90, vice chmn. 1990-92, chmn. 1992-93), Columbus Bar Assn. (profl. ethics com. 1975-86, 90-93, Liberty Bell award for Cmty. and Profl. Svc. 1998), Order of Coif, Phi Beta Kappa, Pi Sigma Alpha. Home: 278 Crossing Crk N Columbus OH 43230-6108 Office: Kegler Brown Hill & Ritter 65 E State St Ste 1800 Columbus OH 43215-4213 E-mail: gstern@kbhr.com.

STERN, GERALD DANIEL, poet; b. Pitts., Feb. 22, 1925; s. Harry and Ida (Barach) S.; m. Patricia Miller, Sept. 12, 1952 (div.); children: Rachel, David. BA, U. Pitts., 1947; MA, Columbia U., 1949. English tchr., prin. Lake Grove (N.Y.) Sch., 1951-53; English tchr. Victoria Dr. Secondary Sch., Glasgow, Scotland, 1953-54; English instr. Temple U., Phila., 1956-63; assoc. prof. English Indiana (Pa.) U. of Pa., 1963-67; prof. English Somerset (N.J.) County Coll., 1968-82; prof. English, Writers' Workshop, U. Iowa, Iowa City, 1982-96. Lectr. Douglas Coll., New Brunswick, N.J., 1968; vis. poet Sarah Lawrence Coll., Bronxville, N.Y., 1978, U. Pitts., 1978; vis. prof. Columbia U., N.Y.C., 1980, Bucknell U., Lewisburg, Pa., 1988, NYU, 1989, 91, Princeton U., 1989; Fanny Hurst prof. Washignton U., St. Louis, 1985; Coal chair creative writing U. Ala., Tuscaloosa, 1984. Author: (poetry) Pineys, 1971, The Naming of Beasts, 1972, Rejoicings: selected Poems 1966-72, 1973, Lucky Life, 1977 (Lamont Poetry selection 1977, Nat. Book Critics Cir. award for poetry nominee 1978), The Red Coal, 1981 (Melville Caine award Poetry Soc. Am. 1982), Paradise Poems, 1984, Lovesick, 1987, Two Long Poems, 1990, Leaving Another Kingdom: Selected Poems, 1990, Bread Without Sugar, 1992, Odd Mercy, 1995, This Time: New and Seleced Poems, 1998 (Nat. Book award); (essays) Selected Essays, 1988. Guggenheim fellow, 1980, Am. Acad. Poets fellow, 1993; NEA grantee to be master poet for Pa. 1973-75, Creative Writing grantee, 1976, 81, 87, State of Pa. Creative Writing grantee, 1979; recipient Gov. award for excellence in arts State of Pa., 1980, Bess Hokin award Poetry, 1980, Bernard F. Connor's award Paris Rev., 1981, Am. Poetry Rev. award, 1982, Jerome J. Shestack Poetry prize Am. Poetry Rev., 1984, Ruth Lilly prize, 1996. Fellow Acad. Am. Poets. Office: U Iowa 436 EPB Iowa City IA 52242

STERN, GRACE MARY, former state legislator; b. Holyoke, Mass., July 10, 1925; d. Frank McLellan and Marguerite M. (Nason) Dain; m. Charles H. Suber, June 21, 1947 (div. 1959); children: Ann, Peter, Thomas, John; m. Herbert L. Stern, May 13, 1962; stepchildren: Gwen, Herbert III, Robert. Student, Wellesley Coll., 1942-45; LLD (hon.), Shimer Coll., 1984. Asst. supr. Deerfield Twp., Lake County, Ill., 1967-70; county clk. Lake County, Ill., 1970-82; mem. Ill. Ho. of Reps., Springfield, 1984-92, Ill. State Senate, 1993-95. Author: With a Stern Eye, 1967, Still Stern, 1969. Candidate lt. gov. State of Ill., 1982. Democrat. Presbyterian. Home: 140 S Dearborn St Ste 1400 Chicago IL 60603-5208

STERN, LEO G. lawyer; b. Mpls., Apr. 10, 1945; s. Philip J. and June I. (Monasch) S.; m. Christine E. Lamb, June 29, 1968; children: Alison M., Zachary A. BA, U. Calif., Davis, 1967; JD cum laude, U. Minn., 1970. Bar: Minn. 1970, U.S. Dist. Ct. Minn. 1971, Calif. 1971, U.S. Ct. Appeals (6th, 7th and 8th cirs.) 1985, U.S. Supreme Ct. 1993, Wis. 1999; cert. mediator and arbitrator, Minn. Ptnr. Cox, King & Stern, Mpls., 1970-77, Wright, West & Diessner, Mpls., 1977-84, Fredrikson & Byron, P.A., Mpls., 1984—. Mem. Minn. Bar Assn. (governing coun. environ. and natural resources law sect. 1989-95, governing coun. litigation sect. 1995-99), Am. Arbitration Assn. (arbitrator, mediator). Avocations: sailing, jogging. Home: 206 Central Ave S Wayzata MN 55391-1818 Office: Fredrikson & Byron PA 1100 International Ctr 900 2nd Ave S Minneapolis MN 55402-3314 E-mail: lstern@fredlaw.com.

STERN, LOUIS WILLIAM, marketing educator, consultant; b. Boston, Sept. 19, 1935; s. Berthold Summerfield Stern and Gladys (Koch) Cohen (deceased); m. Rhona L. Grant; children: Beth Ida, Deborah Lynn. A.B., Harvard U., 1957; M.B.A. in Mktg, U. Pa., 1959; Ph.D. in Mktg, Northwestern U., 1962. Mem. staff bus. research and consumer mktg. sects. Arthur D. Little, Inc., Cambridge, Mass., 1961-63; from asst. prof. bus. orgn. to prof. Ohio State U., Columbus, Ohio, 1963—70, prof. mktg., 1970—73; from A. Montgomery Ward prof. mktg. to prof. emeritus Northwestern U., 1975—2001, John D. Gray disting. prof. mktg., 2001—; on leave as exec. dir. Mktg. Sci. Inst., Cambridge, Mass., 1983-85; Thomas Henry Carroll Ford Found. vis. prof. Harvard U. Grad. Sch. Bus. Adminstrn., 1984-85. Mem. staff Nat. Commn. on Food Mktg., Washington, 1965-66; vis. assoc. prof. bus. adminstrn. U. Calif., Berkeley, 1969-70; guest lectr. York U., U. Minn., U. Ky., UCLA, Ohio State U., U. N.C., Duke U., U. Wis., U. Pitts., U. Chgo., MIT, U. Mich., U. Pa., Cornell U., U. Mo., Norwegian Sch. Econs. and Bus. Adminstrn.; faculty assoc. Hernstein Inst., Vienna, Austria, 1976-77, Mgmt. Centre Europe, 1988-96; faculty assoc. Gemini Cons. Inc., Montvale, N.J., 1977-96, mem. midwest adv. bd., 1989-94; Xerox research prof. Northwestern U., 1981-82; cons. to FTC, 1973, 80; vis. scholar U. Calif., Berkeley, 1997-2001; mem. faculty adv. bd. CSC Index, 1997-98. Author: Distribution Channels: Behavioral Dimensions, 1969, (with Frederick D. Sturdivant and others) Managerial Analysis in Marketing, 1970, Perspectives in Marketing Management, 1971, (with John R. Grabner, Jr.) Competition in the Marketplace, 1970, (with Anne T. Coughlan, Erin Anderson and Adel I. El-Ansary) Marketing Channels, 6th edit., 2001, (with Thomas L. Eovaldi) Legal Aspects of Marketing Strategy: Antitrust and Consumer Protection Issues, 1984; (with Adel I. El-Ansary and James R. Brown) Management in Marketing Channels, 1989; mem. editl. bd. Jour. Mktg. Rsch., 1976-82, Jour. Mktg., 1979-83, Mktg. Letters, 1988-94; contbr. articles on mktg. to profl. jours. Mem. exec. com. Northwest Area Coun. on Human Rels., Columbus, 1971—72. Rsch. grantee: Ohio State U., 1964-73, Mktg. Sci. Inst., 1976-77, 88-90, 92-94; recipient Harold H. Maynard award best article Jour. Mktg., 1980; named Mktg. Educator of Yr. Sales and Mktg. Execs. Internat., 1989, also Chgo. chpt. 1990, Outstanding Profl. of Yr. award, 1992, and named One of Top 6 Profs. in Kellogg Sch., Northwestern U., Grad. Mgmt. Assocs., 1984-94, (named 6 times Outstanding Prof. Exec. Masters Program), One of Top 12 Tchrs. in U.S., Bus. Week. Mem. AAUP, Am. Mktg. Assn. (mem. program com. educators conf. 1971, chmn. com. 1978, Paul D. Converse award 1986, Richard D. Irwin Disting. Mktg. Educator of Yr. 1994), Hellenic Inst. Mktg. (hon.), Beta Gamma Sigma. Home: 522 Church St Apt 2D Evanston IL 60201-4575 Office: Northwestern U JL Kellogg Sch Mgmt Dept Mktg Evanston IL 60208-2001 E-mail: lwstern@kellogg.northwestern.edu.

STERN, RICHARD GUSTAVE, writer, educator; b. N.Y.C., Feb. 25, 1928; s. Henry George and Marion (Veit) S.; m. Gay Clark, Mar. 14, 1950 (div. Feb. 1972); children: Christopher Holmes, Kate Macomber, Andrew Henry, Nicholas Clark; m. Alane Rollings, Aug. 9, 1985. BA, U. N.C., 1947; MA, Harvard U., 1950; PhD, State U. Iowa, 1954. Mem. faculty U. Chgo., 1955—, prof. English, 1965—, Helen Regenstein prof. English, 1990—. Author: Golk, 1960, Europe and Up and Down with Baggish and Schreiber, 1961, In Any Case, 1962, Teeth, Dying and Other Matters, 1964, Stitch, 1965, 1968: A Short Novel, An Urban Idyll, Five Stories and Two Trade Notes, 1970, The Books in Fred Hampton's Apartment, 1973, Other Men's Daughters, 1973, Natural Shocks, 1978, Packages, 1980, The Invention of the Real, 1982, A Father's Words, 1986, The Position of the Body, 1986, Noble Rot: Stories, 1949-88, 1989 (book of yr. award Chgo. Sun-Times 1990), Shares and Other Fictions, 1992, One Person and Another, 1993, A Sistermony, 1995 (Heartland award, nonfiction book of year), Pacific Tremors, 2001, What Is What Was, 2002; editor: Honey and Wax, 1966. Recipient Longwood Found. award, 1960, Friends of Lit. award, 1963, fiction award Nat. Inst. Arts and Letters, 1968; Nat. Coun. Arts and Humanities fellow, 1967-68, Carl Sandburg award for fiction, 1979, Arts Coun. awards, 1979, 81, Am. Acad. and Inst. of Arts and Letters medal of Merit for Novel, 1985; Rockefeller fellow, 1965, Guggenheim fellow, 1973-74. Fellow Ctr. Advanced Studies in the Behavioral Scis.; mem. Am. Acad. Arts and Scis. Office: U Chgo Dept English Chicago IL 60637 E-mail: rstern@midway.uchicago.edu.

STERNBERG, PAUL, retired ophthalmologist; b. Chgo., Dec. 18, 1917; s. David M. and Sarah (Kopeka) S.; m. Dorie Betty Feitler, Dec. 24, 1949; children— Daniel P., Patricia F., Paul, Susan P., David. BS, Northwestern U., 1938, MD, 1940. Intern Michael Reese Hosp., Chgo., 1940-41, resident ophthalmology, Ill. Eye & Ear Infirmary U. Ill.; spl. fellow ophthalmology Cornell U. Med. Center, N.Y. Hosp., Wilmer Inst. Johns Hopkins, 1941-44; practice medicine, specializing in ophthalmology Chgo., from 1945. Attending ophthalmologist Cook County Hosp., Michael Reese Hosp., Highland Park (Ill.) Hosp., Louis Weiss Meml. Hosp.; prof. ophthalmology Chgo. Med. Sch., U. Ill. Med. Sch. Contbr. sci. articles to med. and ophthal. jours. Trustee Art Inst. Chgo. Fellow A.C.S.; mem. Assn. for Research in Ophthalmology, Am. Assn. Ophthalmology, Am. Acad. Ophthalmology, Chgo. Ophthal. Soc., Pan-Am. Congress Ophthalmology, Merit Country Club, Standard Club, Lake Shore Country Club. Home: 359 Surfside Pl Glencoe IL 60022-1723 Office: 225 W Washington St Ste 2150 Chicago IL 60606-3483

STERNER, FRANK MAURICE, industrial executive; b. Lafayette, Ind., Nov. 26, 1935; s. Raymond E. and Maudelene M. (Scipio) S.; m. Elsa Y. Rasmusson, June 29, 1958; children: Mark, Lisa. BS, Purdue U., 1958, MS, 1959, PhD, 1962. Sr. staff specialist Gen. Motors Inst., Flint, Mich., 1962-63; dir. personnel and orgnl. research Delco Electronics, Milw., 1963-66, dir. personnel devel. and research, 1966-68; partner Nourse & Sterner, Inc., Milw., 1968-69; pres., 1969-73; assoc. dean, prof. Krannert Grad. Sch. of Mgmt., Purdue U., West Lafayette, Ind., 1973-79; v.p. human resources mgmt. Johnson Controls, Inc., Milw., 1979-89; pres., chief exec. officer E.R. Wagner Mfg. Co., 1989—; pres., owner Ridgeway Devel. Inc., Milw., 1993—. Bd. dirs. Wausau Homes, Inc., E.R. Wagner Mfg. Co., Ridgeway Devel. Inc. Mem. rsch .com. Am. Lung Assn., Wis.; mem. Greater Milwaukee Com., 1997—; bd. dirs. Children's Hosp. of Wis. Found. Club: Reamer. Home: 1440 E Standish Pl Milwaukee WI 53217-1958 Office: ER Wagner Mfg Co 4611 N 32nd St Milwaukee WI 53209-6000 E-mail: frank.sterner@erwagner.com.

STERNLIEB, LAWRENCE JAY, marketing professional, writer; b. Akron, Ohio, Aug. 19, 1951; s. Max and Mollie (Atleson) S. BA in English, BA in Sociology, Kent State U., 1974, MA in Sociology, 1977. Lic. social worker, Ohio. Social program specialist State of Ohio, Cleve., 1976-79; sr. mktg. exec. Xerox Corp., 1979-82; nat. acct. mgr. NCR Corp., Independence, Ohio, 1983-85; sr. acct. mgr. McDonnell Douglas Corp., 1985-87; sr. mktg. rep. Prime Computer Inc., 1987-90; acct. exec. GE Cons. Svcs., 1990-94; sr. sales and mktg. exec. Decarlo, Paternite and Assoc., 1994-96; major acct. mgr. General DataComm, Inc., Cleve., 1996—. Instr. Cuyahoga C.C., Cleve., 1980-81, 92. Author: Barry Storm, 1995. Mem. Cleve. Playhouse. Avocations: acting, modeling, writing, sports, physical fitness. Home: 950 Tollis Pkwy Apt 610 Broadview Heights OH 44147

STERNSTEIN, ALLAN J. lawyer; b. Chgo., June 7, 1948; s. Milton and Celia (Kaganove) S.; m. Miriam A. Dolgin, July 12, 1970 (div. July 1981); children— Jeffery A., Amy R.; m. Beverly A. Cook, Feb. 8, 1986; children: Cheryl L., Julia S. B.S., U. Ill., 1970; M.S., U. Mich., 1972; J.D., Loyola U., 1977. Bar: Ill. 1977, U.S. Dist. Ct. (no. dist.) Ill. 1977, U.S. Dist. Ct. (no. dist.) Ohio 1977, U.S. Dist. Ct. (ea. dist) Mich. 1986, U.S. Dist. Ct. (we. dist.) Mich. 1990, U.S. Ct. Customs and Patent Appeals 1978, U.S. Ct. Appeals (7th cir.) 1979, U.S. Ct. Appeals (Fed. cir.) 1982. Patent agent Sunbeam Corp., Oak Brook, Ill., 1972-76; ptnr. Neuman, Williams, Anderson & Olson, Chgo., 1976-84; div. patent counsel Abbott Labs., North Chgo., Ill., 1984-87; ptnr. Brinks Hofer Gilson & Lione, Chgo., 1987—, mng. ptnr., 1996-99; adj. prof. of law John Marshall Law Sch., 1989-90, DePaul Univ., 1990-92, Univ. Ill., 1992—; lectr. Nat. Sci. and Tech. Devel. Agy. Chunlangkon U., Bangkok, Thailand, 1994; arbitrator Cir. Ct. Cook County, Ill., 1996—. Co-author: Designing an Effective Intellectual Property Compliance Program; contbr. article to profl. jour. Legal advisor Legal Aid Soc., Chgo., 1974-76, Pub. Defender's Office, Chgo., 1974. Teaching fellow U. Mich., 1971-72; research grantee U. Mich., U.S. Air Force, 1971-72. Mem. ABA, Chgo. Bar Assn., Patent Law Assn. of Chgo. (com. chmn. 1982), Am. Intellectual Property Law Assn., Licensing Execs. Soc., Tau Beta Pi, Sigma Tau, Sigma Gamma Tau, Phi Eta Sigma. Jewish. Office: Brinks Hofer Gilson & Lione Ste 3600 455 N Cityfront Plaza Dr Chicago IL 60611-5599

STETLER, DAVID J. lawyer; b. Washington, Sept. 6, 1949; s. C. Joseph and Norine (Delaney) S.; m. Mary Ann Ferguson, Aug. 14, 1971; children: Brian, Christopher, Jennifer. BA, Villanova U., 1971, JD, 1974. Bar: U.S. Supreme Ct. 1978, Ill. 1988, U.S. Ct. Appeals (7th cir.) 1988, U.S. Ct. Appeals (3d cir.) 1992, U.S. Dist. Ct. (ctrl. dist.) 1994, U.S. Ct. Appeals (8th cir.) 1994. Atty. IRS, Washington, 1974-79; spl. atty. tax divsn. Dept. Justice, 1975-79; asst. atty. U.S. Atty.'s Office, Chgo., 1979-88, dep. chief spl. prosecutions div., 1985-86, chief criminal receiving and appellate divsns., 1986-88; ptnr. McDermott, Will & Emery, 1988-98; prin. Stetler & Duffy, Ltd., 1998—. Lectr. Atty. Gen. Trial Advocacy Inst., Washington, 1977—. Fellow Internat. Soc. Barristers, Am. Coll. Trial Lawyers; mem. ABA (chmn. midwest subcom. White Collar Crime com. 1991-93), Wong Sun Soc. San Francisco. Office: 140 S Dearborn St Chicago IL 60603-5202

STEVENS, DAN, state legislator; b. Feb. 23, 1950; m. Barbara; four children. Student, U. Minn. Mem. Minn. Senate from 17th dist., St. Paul, 1993—; bus. mgr.; farmer. Office: Minn State Members 100 Constitution Ave Saint Paul MN 55155-1232

STEVENS, JANE, advertising executive; Exec. v.p., exec. media dir. Bernstein-Rein Advertising Inc, Kansas City, Mo., 1990—. Office: Bernstein-Rein Advertising Inc 4600 Madison Ave Ste 1500 Kansas City MO 64112-3016

STEVENS, MARK, banker; b. Chgo., May 24, 1947; s. Joseph K. and Phoebe (Copeland) S.; m. Joyce Sue Skinner, Aug. 22, 1970; children: Mark Benjamin, Katherine Joyce. BA, W.Va. U., 1969, JD, 1972. V.p. Continental Ill. Nat. Bank & Trust Co., Chgo., 1972-79, No. Trust Co., Chgo., 1979-81; pres., CEO, No. Trust Bank Fla., Sarasota, 1981-87, chmn., pres., CEO, 1987-96; exec. v.p. No. Trust Co. & No. Trust Corp., 1996-98, pres. personal fin. svcs., 1998—. Pres. No. Trust Fla. Corp., Miami, 1987-96, chmn., 1996—. Trustee Ctr. Fine Arts, 1988-94, 1988-94, Miami Children's Hosp. Found., 1993-96, South Fla. Performing Arts Ctr. Found., 1993—, U. Miami, 1994, Beacon Coun., 1990—; mem. U. Miami Citizens Bd., 1988-89, Young Pres.'s Orgn., 1988—; bd. dirs. Miami Coalition and Task Force, 1988—, New World Symphony, 1991—; charter mem. Coun. of 100 Fla. Internat. Univ. Found., 1990—; hon. bd. dirs. Audubon House; mem. Orange Bowl Com., 1994. Mem. Young Pres. Orgn., Riviera Country Club, Miami Club. Office: The No Trust Co 50 S Lasalle St Chicago IL 60603-1006

STEVENS, PAUL, newspaper editor; Bur. chief AP, Kansas City, Mo., 1980—. Office: 215 W Pershing Rd Kansas City MO 64108-4317

STEVENS, PAUL EDWARD, lawyer; b. Youngstown, Ohio, July 22, 1916; s. Raymond U. and Mary Ann (Pritchard) S.; m. Janet L. Weisert, Mar. 9, 1946; 1 son, Mark O. LL.B., Ohio State U., 1941. Bar: Ohio 1941. Practiced in, Youngstown, 1941—; ptnr. Green, Schiavoni, Murphy & Stevens, 1962-71, Burdman, Stevens & Gilliland, 1971-75, Stevens & Toot, 1976-77, Paul E. Stevens Co., 1977—. Prof. law Youngstown Coll. Sch. Law, 1946-60; gen. counsel Animal Charity League of Ohio, 1965—; sec.-treas. CASTLO Community Improvement Corp., 1986—. Trustee Poland Twp., Ohio, 1960-69; Republican candidate for U.S. Congress, 1959; dist. adminstrv. asst. Congressman Charles J. Carney, 19th Ohio dist., 1970-80; pres. Welsh Nat. Gymanfa Ganu Assn., 1988-90. With AUS, 1942-46. Mem. ABA, Ohio Bar Assn. (chmn. membership com. 1955), Mahoning County Bar Assn. (pres. 1953-54), Mahoning County Planning Assn. (chmn. 1990-98). Unitarian. Home: 7191 N Lima Rd Youngstown OH 44514-3749 Office: 780 Boardman Canfield Rd Youngstown OH 44512-4344

STEVENS, PAUL G., JR. brokerage house executive; b. 1944; With Saul Lerner Co., N.Y.C., 1968-71, Lombard Street Inc., N.Y.C., 1971-72, Ragner Option Corp., N.Y.C., 1975-89, Am. Stock Exch., N.Y.C., 1989—, pres., COO, treas.; pres. Options Clearing Corp., Chgo., 1989—. Office: Options Clearing Corp 440 S La Salle St Ste 2400 Chicago IL 60605-1028

STEVENS, ROBERT JAY, magazine editor; b. Detroit, July 25, 1945; s. Jay Benjamin and Louise Ann (Beyreuther) S.; m. Dahlia Jean Conger, Aug. 15, 1970; children— Sandra Lee, Julie Ann. Student, Huron (S.D.) Coll., 1963-66, Wayne State U., 1968-71. Sr. staff writer Automotive News, Detroit, 1968-71; editor Excavating Contractor mag., Cummins Pub. Co., Oak Park, Mich., 1971-78, Chevrolet's Pro Jour., Sandy Corp., Southfield, 1978—79, Cars and Parts mag., Cars and Parts Corvette mag. Amos Press, Sidney, Ohio, 1979—; truck editor Automotive Design & Devel. mag., 1971-78. Lectr., speaker in field. Author articles, poems. Served with AUS, 1966-68, Vietnam. Decorated Air medal, Bronze star, Commendation medal; recipient Alphomega Publs. award, 1965—, Robert F. Boger Meml. award for outstanding constrn. journalism, 1975, U.L.C.C. nat. editl. award, Am. Pub. Works Assn., 1978, Moto award for outstanding automotive journalism, Internat. Automotive Media Conf., 1997, 1998, 1999, 2000, 2001, Best of Divsn. award, 2001, Folio mag. Editl. Excellence award, 2001. Mem. Detroit Auto Writers (past dir.), Internat. Motor Press Assn., Antique Automobile Club Am. Republican. Presbyterian. Home: 653 Ridgeway Dr Sidney OH 45365-3432 Office: PO Box 482 911 Vandemark Rd Sidney OH 45365 E-mail: bstevens@carsandparts.com.

STEVENS, THOMAS CHARLES, lawyer; b. Auburn, N.Y., Oct. 17, 1949; s. Alice (Kerlin) S.; m. Christine Eleanor Brown, June 2, 1973; children: Erin, Leigh, Timothy. BA, SUNY, Albany, 1971; JD, Duke U., 1974. Bar: Ohio 1974. Mng. ptnr. Thompson, Hine & Flory, Cleve., 1991-96; vice-chmn., chief adminstrv. officer, sec. KeyCorp., 1996—. Trustee Greater Cleve. Growth Assn., 1993-96, Greater Cleve. Roundtable, 1993—, Playhouse Sq. Found., 1998—; active Leadership Cleve., 1992-93, Young Audiences, 1999—, 1999 United Way Campaign. Mem. ABA, Cleve. Bar Assn., Am. Soc. Corp. Secs., Nisi Prius. Office: KeyCorp 127 Public Sq Cleveland OH 44114-1306 E-mail: thomas_stevens@keybank.com.

STEVENS, TONY, radio station official, radio personality; b. Jersey City, June 7, 1955; s. Baldassare and Josephine Frances (Costanza) Restivo; m. Maria Ciliberti, July 31, 1976 (div.); children: Anthony Jr., Paul; m. Geri Suzanne Hastert, Oct. 24, 1987; 1 child, Nicholas. BA in Comm., U. Mo., Kansas City, 1985. Profl. musician, Kansas City, Mo., 1974—; owner Wizards Arcade, Independence, 1982-85; news dir. Sta. KBSM, Blue Springs, 1984-85; program dir. Sta. KCKM, Kansas City, Kans., 1985-87; on air personality, music dir., asst. program dir. Sta. KFKF, Mo., 1984—. Music cons. Sta. WLLR, Davenport, Iowa, 1990—; featured writer Country Star mag., 1990. Hon. chmn. Multiple Sclerosis Soc., Kansas City, Mo., 1991-92. Roman Catholic. Avocations: collecting records, softball. Office: Sta KFKF 4917 Grand Ave Ste 600 Kansas City MO 64112

STEVENSON, ADLAI EWING, III, lawyer, former senator; b. Chgo., Oct. 10, 1930; s. Adlai Ewing and Ellen (Borden) S.; m. Nancy L. Anderson, June 25, 1955; children: Adlai Ewing IV, Lucy W., Katherine R., Warwick L. Grad., Milton Acad., 1948; A.B., Harvard U., 1952, LL.B., 1957. Bar: Ill. 1957, D.C. 1977. Law clk. Ill. Supreme Ct., 1957-58; assoc. Mayer, Brown & Platt, Chgo., 1958-66, ptnr., 1966-67, 81-83, of counsel, 1983-91; treas. State of Ill., 1967-70; U.S. senator from Ill., 1970-81; chmn. SC&M Internat. Ltd., Chgo., 1991-95, pres., 1995-98, chmn. of bd., 1998—. Mem. Ill. Ho. of Reps., 1965-67; Dem. candidate for gov. of Ill., 1982, 86. Capt. USMCR, 1952-54. Office: 20 N Clark St Ste 750 Chicago IL 60602

STEVENSON, DAN CHARLES, state legislator; m. Dawn Stevenson. Student, Calumet Coll. Steelworker Inland Steel Co.; mem. Ind. State Ho. of Reps. Dist. 11, mem. labor and employment com., mem. local govt. and pub. safety com. Mem. Jaycees, Ind. Young Dems. (former pres.), Hessville Dem. Club. Office: Ind House of Reps State Capitol Indianapolis IN 46204

STEVENSON, FRANK J. soil scientist, educator; b. Logan, Utah, Aug. 2, 1922; m. Leda Jensen; children: Mark, Diana, Frank E. BS, Brigham Young U., 1949; PhD, Ohio State U., 1952. Now prof. emeritus U. Ill., Urbana. Recipient Agron Rsch. award, 1980, Soil Sci. Rsch. award Soil Sci. Soc. Am., 1983, Bouyoucos Soil Sci. Disting. Career award, 1991, Wolf Found. Agr. award, 1995. Soil Sci. Soc. Agron, Internat. Soil Sci. Soc. Office: U Illinois Dept NRES Urbana IL 61801

STEVENSON, HAROLD WILLIAM, psychology educator; b. Dines, Wyo., Nov. 19, 1924; s. Merlin R. and Mildred M. (Stodick) S.; m. Nancy Guy, Aug. 23, 1950; children: Peggy, Janet, Andrew, Patricia. BA, U. Colo., 1947; MA, Stanford U., 1948, PhD, 1951; DS (hon.), U. Minn., 1996. Asst. prof. psychology Pomona Coll., 1950-53; asst. to asso. prof. psychology U. Tex., Austin, 1953-59; prof. child devel. and psychology, dir. Inst. Child Devel., U. Minn., Mpls., 1959-71; prof. psychology, fellow Center for Human Growth and Devel., U. Mich., Ann Arbor, 1971—; dir. program in child devel. and social policy U. Mich., 1978-93. Adj. prof. Tohoku Fukushi Coll., Japan, 1989—, Peking U., 1990—, Inst. Psychology Chinese Acad. Scis.; mem. tng. com. Nat. Inst. Child Health and Human Devel., 1964-67; mem. personality and cognition study sect. NIMH, 1975-79; chmn. adv. com. on child devel. Nat. Acad. Scis.-NRC, 1971-73; exec. com. div. behavioral scis. NRC, 1969-72; mem. del. early childhood People's Republic of China, 1973, mem. del. psychologists, 1980; mem. vis. com. Grad. Sch. Edn., Harvard U., 1979-86; fellow Center Advanced Studies in Behavioral Scis., 1967-68, 82-83, 89-90. Recipient J.M. Cattell Fellow award in applied psychology Am. Psychol. Soc., 1994, William James Fellow award, 1995, Quest award Am. Fedn. Tchrs., 1995. Fellow Am. Acad. Arts and Scis., Nat. Acad. Edn.; mem. APA (pres. divsn. devel. psychology 1964-65, G. Stanley Hall award 1988, Bronfenbrenner award 1997, Dist. Sci. award Applications of Psychology 1997), Soc. Rsch. Child Devel. (mem. governing coun. 1961-67, pres. 1969-71, chmn. long-range planning com. 1971-74, mem. social policy com. 1977-85, mem. internat. affairs com. 1991-94, Disting. Rsch. award 1993), Internat. Soc. Study Behavioral Devel. (mem. exec. com. 1972-77, pres. 1987-91), Phi Beta Kappa, Sigma Xi. Home: 1030 Spruce Dr Ann Arbor MI 48104-2847 E-mail: hstevens@umich.edu.

STEVENSON, JAMES LARAWAY, communications engineer, consulting; b. Detroit, Oct. 25, 1938; s. Joseph Morley and Kittie Harriet (Laraway) S.; m. Jeanie Lorraine Minkstein, Aug. 7, 1965; children: Amy Jean, Brian Morley. AAS, U.S. Armed Forces Inst., 1958; BSEE, MIT, 1960, MSEE, 1962. Cert. master radio and telecommunications engr. FCC. With USN Mercury Space Project, 1957-63, Office of Naval Rsch., 1962—63; engr. Sta. WBCM-FM, Bay City, Mich., 1964-65; chief engr. Sta. WCRM, Clare, 1965-66, Sta. WSMA, Marine City, 1966; engr. Sta. WWJ-AM-FM-TV, Detroit, 1966-79; owner, mgr. Twin Oaks Comms. Engring. (name now Twin Oaks Comms. Engring. P.C.), North Branch, 1972—. Charter pilot, flight & ground instr. G. B. DuPont Co., Almont Marlette Aviation Inc., 1977-82; cons. electronics engr. various cos., 1968—; expert legal witness, 1968—; mem. corp. edn. dean's adv. coun. Colls. Bus. Adminstr., Sci., Engring. & Tech., Saginaw Valley State U., 1997—. Contbr. articles to profl. jours. Sr. div. judge Detroit Met. Sci. and Engring. Fair, 1975—, Mich. State Sci. & Engring. Fair, 2000—; spl. awards judge Intel Internat. Sci. & Engring. Fair, Detroit, 2000; search & rescue pilot, mission comdr., capt. Mich. wing CAP, 1961-81; cubmaster Pack 457 Boy Scouts Am., North Branch, 1983-85; mem. adv. bd. jacknabbit.com., Issaquah, Wash., 1999-2001; hon. state chmn. bus. adv. coun. Rep. Congl. Com., 2002-. Recipient appreciation award CAP, 1980, North Branch Area Schs., 1985, Century award Boy Scouts Am., 1984 Mem. AIAA, IEEE (sr., chmn. N.E. Mich. sect. 1987-88, 95—, bd. dirs. 1984—), NSPE, Am. Soc. for Engring. Edn. (profl. mem.), Nat. Assn. Radio Telecomm. Engrs. (sr.), Am. Inst. Physics (assoc.), Mich. Soc. Profl. Engrs. (flint chpt.), Saginaw Valley Engring. Coun. (chmn. 1990-91, 2000-01, sec.-treas. 1992-95, Outstanding Leadership award 1991, 2001), Engring. Soc. Detroit (profl.), Profl. Activities Coun. Engrs. (chmn. U.S. activities bd. 1985—), Nat. Pilots Assn. (sr. pilot citation, safe pilot award 1978), Aircraft Owners and Pilots Assn., North Branch C. of C. (charter), Am. Legion, Lions (pres. North Br. club 1990-91), Radio Club Am. Avocations: computers, amateur radio, flying. Office: Twin Oaks Comms Engring PC 2465 Johnson Mill Rd PO Box 340 North Branch MI 48461-0340

STEVENSON, JO ANN C. federal bankruptcy judge; b. 1942; AB, Rutgers U., 1965; JD cum laude, Detroit Coll. Law, 1979. Bar: Mich. 1979. Law clk. to Vincent J. Brennan, Mich. Ct. Appeals, Detroit, 1979; law clk. to Cornelia G. Kenendy, U.S. Ct. Appeals for 6th Cir., 1980; assoc. Hertzberg, Jacob & Weingarten, P.C., 1980-87; judge U.S. Bankruptcy Ct., Grand Rapids, Mich., 1987—. Office: US Bankruptcy Ct PO Box 3310 Grand Rapids MI 49501-3310

STEVENSON, JUDY G. instrument manufacturing executive; Bookeeper Magnetrol, Naperville, Ill., 1964-65, accounting supr./mgr., 1965-76, treas./admin. v.p., 1967-75, pres., 1975-78, owner, 1978—. Bd. trustees N. Ctrl. Coll.; established Harold E. Meiley, Judy G. Stevenson, African Scholarship Funds; supports Naperville Heritage Soc., Edward Hosp., the Riverwalk, Millennium Carillon Found., Good Samaritan Hosp., DuPage Intergenerational Village. Recipient YWCA Businesswoman Yr. DuPage Co., 1985, YWCA Outstanding Woman Leader DuPage Co., 1997, Top 500 Woman-Owned Businesses, Working Woman Mag., 1998. Mem. Chief Exec. Officers Club, Nat. Assn. Women Bus. Owners, Nat. Assn. Female Execs., Eastern Star. Avocations: gardening, gourmet cooking, music, ballet, horses. Office: Magnetrol Internat 5300 Belmont Rd Downers Grove IL 60515-4499

STEVENSON, KENNETH LEE, chemist, educator; b. Ft. Wayne, Ind., Aug. 1, 1939; s. Willard Henry and Luella Marie (Meyer) S.; m. Virginia Grace Lowe, Dec. 26, 1959 (dec. Mar. 1991); children: Melinda Anne, Jill Marie; m. Carmen Ramona Kmety, May 9, 1992. B.S., Purdue U., 1961, M.S., 1965; Ph.D., U. Mich., 1968. Tchr. Ladoga High Sch., Ind., 1961-63; tchr. Central High Sch., Pontiac, Mich., 1963-65; prof. chemistry Ind.-Purdue U., Ft. Wayne, 1968—, chmn. dept. chemistry, 1979-86, 87—, acting dean Sch. Sci. and Humanities, 1986-87. Sabbatical visitor Solar Energy Research Inst., Golden, Colo., 1980; vis. faculty N.Mex. State U., Las Cruces, 1975-76 Author: Charge Transfer Photochemistry of Coordination Compounds, 1993, also numerous rsch. papers. Mem. Am. Chem. Soc. (chmn. Northeastern Ind. sect. 1978-79, Chemist of Yr. 1979, 93), Inter-Am. Photochem. Soc., Phi Kappa Phi, Sigma Xi. Office: Ind U-Purdue U Dept Chemistry Fort Wayne IN 46805 E-mail: stevenso@ipfw.edu.

STEVENSON, ROBERT BENJAMIN, III, prosthodontist, writer; b. Topeka, Feb. 13, 1950; s. Robert Benjamin and Martha (McClelland) S.; m. Barbara Jean Sulick, June 6, 1975; children: Jody Ann, Robert Woodrow. BS, U. Miami, Coral Gables, Fla., 1972; DDS, Ohio State U., 1975, MS, MA, cert. in prosthodontics splty. tng., Ohio State U., 1980. Practice dentistry specializing in prosthodontics, Columbus, Ohio, 1981—; clin. asst. prof. Ohio State U., 1981-87, 98—. Chmn. oral cancer com. Columbus Dental Soc., 1981-85, Am. Cancer Soc., Columbus, 1985-97; trustee Ohio Divsn, 1997-2000; vol. dentist Provodencialis Ctr., Turks and Chicos Islands, Brit. West Indies, 1982-87. Editor Columbus Dental Soc. Bull., 1981-87, 89-92; assoc. editor Ohio State U. Dental Alumni Quar., 1982—, Am. Med. Writer's Assn. Ohio Newsletter, 1983-86, Ohio State Journalism Alumni Assn. Newsletter, 1986-88, alumni spotlight editor, 1995—; assoc. editor Jour. Prosthetic Dentistry, 1987-92; mem. edtl. coun. Jour. Prosthetic Dentistry; inventor intraoral measuring device. Vol. Am. Cancer Soc., Columbus, 1982—, Gahanna and Reynoldsburg, Ohio, 1983, 84; fundraiser Columbus council Boy Scouts of Am., 1984; Served to capt. USAF, 1975-78. Mem. ADA, Am. Coll. Prosthodontists, Ohio Dental Assn. (alt. del. 1982-89, del. 1990-92, 97—, editor new products newsletter 1988-97), Carl Boucher Prosthodontic Conf. (editor 1987-92, sec. 1992-98, treas. 1998—), Procrastinator's Club Am, Columbus Downtown Quarterback Club. Avocations: playing electric organ, golf, music, reading. Home: 1300 Southport Cir Columbus OH 43235-7642 Office: Riverview Profl Village 3600 Olentangy River Rd Columbus OH 43214 E-mail: stevenson.113@osu.edu.

STEVENSON, WARREN HOWARD, mechanical engineering educator; b. Rock Island, Ill., Nov. 18, 1938; s. Joseph Howard and Camilla Irene (Darnall) S.; m. Judith Ann Fleener, June 7, 1959; children: Kathleen, Kevin, Kent. BSME, Purdue U., 1960, MSME, 1963, PhD, 1965. Engr. Martin Co., Denver, 1960-61; rsch. asst., instr. Purdue U., West Lafayette, Ind., 1961-65, asst. prof., 1965-68, assoc. prof., 1968-74, prof., 1974—, asst. dean engring., 1992-97, assoc. dean engring., 1997—. Guest prof. U. Karlsruhe, Germany, 1973-74; vis. prof. Ibaraki U., Hitachi, Japan, 1993; mem. tech. conf. coms. various profl. groups. Editor: Laser Velocimetry and Particle Sizing, 1979; mem. editorial bd. Jour. Laser Applications, 1988-98; contbr. articles to profl. jours.; patentee in field. U.S. sr. scientist Alexander von Humboldt Found., Fed. Republic Germany, 1973. Fellow Laser Inst. Am. (bd. dirs. 1984—, pres. 1989); mem. ASME, Optical Soc. Am. Avocations: sailing, photography. Office: Purdue U Sch Mech Engring Engring Adminstrn West Lafayette IN 47907

STEWARD, DAVID L. technology company executive; Founder, CEO World Wide Tech., Maryland Heights, Mo., 1990—. Named 14th Best Am. Entrepreneur, Success Mag., 1998, Minority Small Bus. Person of Yr., Small Bus. Adminstrn., 1997, 98. Office: World Wide Tech Inc 127 Weldon Pkwy Maryland Heights MO 63043-3108

STEWARD, WELDON CECIL, architecture educator, architect, consultant; b. Pampa, Tex., Apr. 7, 1934; s. Weldon C. and Lois (Maness) S.; m. Mary Jane Nedbalek, June 9, 1956; children: Karen A., W. Craig. Cert. in architecture and planning, Ecole des Beaux Arts, Fontainebleu, France, 1956; B.Arch., Tex. A&M U, 1957; M.S. in Architecture, Columbia U., 1961; LHD (hon.), Drury Coll., 1991. Registered architect, Tex., Nebr. Designer Perkins & Will, Architects, White Plains, N.Y., 1961-62; asst. prof. architecture Tex. A&M U., College Station, 1962-67, assoc. chmn. Sch. Architecture, 1966-69, assoc. dean, prof. Coll. Environ. Design, 1969-73; dean, prof. Coll. Architecture U. Nebr., Lincoln, 1973-2000, emeritus dean, prof. arch. and planning, 2000—; founding pres. Joslyn Castle Inst. Sustainable Cmtys., Omaha, 1996—; W. Cecil Steward dist. chair sustainable arch. U. Nebr., Lincoln, 2000—02. Adj. prof. Sch. Arch. U. Hawaii, 1999—; ednl. cons. People's Republic of China, 1979--; project dir. Imo State U. Planning, Nigeria, 1981-88; vis. prof. Tong ji U., Shanghai, 1984; hon. prof. N.W. Inst. Architects Engrs., Xian, 1989; specialist Design USA, USSR, 1990; co-chmn. nat. coordination com. AIA Nat. Coun. Archtl. Registration Bd. Intership, Washington, 1980-81; bd. visitors Drury Coll., 1980-97, Coll. Arch. U. Miami, Fla., 1993-96, Judson Coll., 1998-2000; mem. nat. design rev. bd. GSA, Washington, 1994—; mem. founding bd. dirs. East/West Pacific Arch., U. Hawaii, 1995—; vice chmn. Design Futures Coun., Reston, Va., 1995—; sr. fellow Design Futures Coun., 1999. Designer, Quinnipiac Elem. Sch., New Haven, Conn., 1961 (Am Assn. Sch. Adminstrs. Exhibit 1969), J.J. Buser Residence, Bryan, Tex., 1969, Steward Urban Residence, Lincoln, Nebr., 1994. Mem. Lincoln Architects, Engrs. Selection Bd., 1979-88; mem. Nat. Com. for U.S.-China Rels., N.Y.C., 1981—, Nebr. Capitol Environ. Commn., 1989-97; bd. dirs. Downtown Lincoln Assn., 1996—, KZUM Pub. Radio, 1997-2001; mem. Lincoln Planning Commn., 1996—; bd. dirs. Lincoln Children's Mus., 1996-2001; profl. adviser nat. design competition Wick Alumni Ctr., Lincoln, 1981; steering com. Internat. Coun. Tall Bldgs., 1992-96. Named Disting. Alumnus, Tex. A&M U., 1998; Grad. fellow Columbia U., 1960 Mem. AIA (pres. Brazos chpt. 1969, chmn. profl. devel. com. 1979, bd. dirs. 1979-90, dir. Cen. States 1987-90, nat. pres. 1991-92, Coll. of Fellows 1983, Tri-Nat. com. 1991--, Nebr. Gold medal 1997, nat. AIA/ACSA Topaz award for excellence in architecture 1999); mem. Am. Planning Assn. (chair Dubai Internat. award for sustaining cmty. 2000), Nebr. Soc. Architects (bd. dirs. 1977-2000), Archtl. Found. Nebr. (bd. dirs. 1981-94, treas. 1981-94), Assn. Collegiate Schs. Architecture (bd. dirs. 1975-79), Nat. Archtl. Accrediting Bd. (bd. dirs. 1986-89, pres. 1988-89), Kazakhstan Union Architecture, Assn. Siamese Architects, Royal Inst. Canadian Architects, Fedn. Mexican Achitects, Japan Inst. Architects (hon.), Tau Sigma Delta (medal 1999), Phi Kappa Phi, Phi Beta Delta. Home: 125 N 11th St Lincoln NE 68508-3605 Office: U Nebr Coll Architecture Lincoln NE 68588 E-mail: csteward1@unl.edu.

STEWART, ALBERT ELISHA, safety engineer, industrial hygienist; b. Urbana, Mo., Dec. 20, 1927; s. Albert E. and Maurine (Lighter) S.; m. Elizabeth O. Tice, May 31, 1958 (div.); children: Sheryl E., Mical A. BA, U. Kans., 1949; MS, U. Mo., 1958, MBA, 1970; PhD, Western States U., 1984. Registered profl. engr., Calif., cert. safety engr., cert. indsl. hygenist. Sales engr. Kaiser Aluminum and Chem. Co., Toledo, 1949-56; tchr. Kansas City (Mo.) Pub. Schs., 1959-65; indsl. hygienist Bendix Corp., Kansas City, 1960-65; safety adminstr. Gulf R&D, Merriam, Kans., 1968-71; sr. indsl. hygienist USDOL-OSHA, Kansas City, 1971-77; pres. Stewart Indsl. Hygiene, 1977—. Adj. prof. Cen. Mo. State U. Mem. Boy Scouts Am. With U.S. Army, 1950-53. Mem. Am. Indsl. Hygiene Assn., Am. Chem. Soc., Am. Acad. Indsl. Hygiene, Am. Soc. Safety Engrs., Am. Welding Soc., Nat. Mgmt. Assn., Nat. Sci. Tchrs. Assn., Adminstrv. Govt. Soc., Am. Legion Post 596, DAV, ARC, Alpha Chi Sigma. Episcopalian. Avocations: fishing, golf, travel.

STEWART, FRASER, agronomist; b. Winnipeg, Can. BSA in Animal Sci., U. Manitoba, 1961; MS in Animal Nutrition, N.D. State U., 1963. Agronomist Manitoba Agrl, Can. Office: Manitoba Agrl 20 1st St S Beausejovr MB Canada

STEWART, J. DANIEL, air force official; b. Savannah, Ga., June 20, 1941; s. Benjamin F. and Bessie L. (Edenfield) S.; m. Rebecca M. Smith; children: Daniel, Laura. BS in Aero. Engring., Ga. Inst. Tech., 1963, MS in Aero. Engring., 1965, PhD in Aero. Engring., 1967; M. in Mgmt. Sci., Stanford U., 1979. Mem. tech. staff applied mechanics divsn. Aerospace Corp., El Segundo, Calif., 1967-74; br. chief tech. divsn. Air Force Rocket Propulsion Lab., Edwards AFB, 1974-78, asst. for R&D mgmt., 1979-81; divsn. chief Air Force Armament Divsn., Eglin AFB, Fla., 1981-83; dir. drone control program office 3246 Test Wing, 1983-85, joint dir. US/Allied munitions program office, 1985-86; tech. dir. rsch./devel./acquisitions Air Force Armament Divsn., 1986-88; asst. to comdr. Air Force Munitions Divsn., 1988-90; tech. dir. Air Force Devel. and Test Ctr., 1990-93, exec. dir., 1993-98, Air Armament Ctr., Eglin AFB, Fla., 1998-99, Air Force Materiel Command, Wright-Paterson AFB, Ohio, 1999—. Mem. policy coun. Scientist and Engr. Career Program, Randolph AFB, Tex., 1994—, chmn. career devel. panel, 1994-96. Bd. dirs. Internat. Found. for Telemetering, Woodland Hills, Calif., 1991-95; mem. engring. adv. bd. U. Fla., Gainesville, 1988—; mem. citizens adv. com. U. West Fla., Pensacola, 1991—; mem. civilian exec. adv. bd. Air Force Materiel Command, 1990—, also former chmn.; mem. curricular adv. com. Def. Test and Evaluation Profl. Inst., 1991—. Recipient Presdl. Meritorious Rank award Pres. of U.S., 1993. Mem. Air Force Assn. (Lewis H. Brereton award 1994), Sr. Exec. Assn., Am. Def. Preparedness Assn., Internat. Test and Evaluation Assn. (Cross medal 1994), Assn. of Old Crows, Fed. Exec. Inst. Alumni, Gulf Coast Alliance for Tech. Transfer. Avocations: tennis, golf, fishing. Office: Air Force Materiel Command 4375 Chidlaw Rd Wright Patterson AFB OH 45433

STEWART, JAMES BREWER, historian, writer, college administrator; b. Cleve., Aug. 8, 1940; s. Richard Henry and Marion Elizabeth (Brewer) S.; m. Dorothy Ann Carlson; children: Rebecca Ann, Jennifer Lynn. BA, Dartmouth Coll., 1962; PhD, Case Western Res. U., 1968. Asst. prof. history Carrol Coll., Waukesha, Wis., 1968-69, Macalester Coll., St. Paul, 1969-79, James Wallace prof. history, 1979—, provost, 1986-89. Cons. Am. Coun. of Learned Socs., N.Y.C., 1988-92. Author: Joshua R. Giddings & the Tactics of Radical Politics, 1970, Holy Warriors: Abolitionists & Slavery, 1976, rev. editon 1997, Liberty's Hero: Wendell Phillips, 1986 (Best Biography award, Soc. Midland Authors 1986), William Lloyd Garrison and the Challenge of Emmancipation, 1992, To Heal the Scourge of Prejudice: The Life and Writings of Hosea Easton, 1999, Race and the Construction of the Republican State, 2000. Rsch. fellow NEH, 1973, Am. Coun. Learned Socs., 1984. Mem. Am. Hist. Assn., Orgn. Am. Historians (nom. com. 1988-92), Soc. Historians of the Early Republic (exec. com. 1987-94, editl. bd. 1999—). Avocations: camping, gardening, furniture restoration. Home: 1924 Princeton Ave Saint Paul MN 55105-1523 Office: Macalester Coll Dept Of History Saint Paul MN 55105 E-mail: stewart@macalester.edu.

STEWART, JOHN HARGER, music educator; b. Cleve., Mar. 31, 1940; s. Cecil Tooker and Marian (Harger) S.; m. Julia Wallace, Aug. 14, 1977; children: Barbara, Cecily Bronwen. BA, Yale U., 1962; MA, Brown U., 1972; cert., New Eng. Conservatory, 1965. With various operas including Santa Fe Opera, N.Y.C. Opera, Met. Opera, U.S. and Europe, 1965—; lectr. Mt. Holyoke Coll., South Hadley, Mass., 1988-90; dir. vocal activities Washington U., St. Louis, 1990—; dir. Friends of Music. Office: Washington U Campus Box 1032 One Brookings Dr Saint Louis MO 63130-4899

STEWART, MELBOURNE GEORGE, JR. physicist, educator; b. Detroit, Sept. 30, 1927; s. Melbourne George and Ottilie (Tuholke) S.; m. Charlotte L. Ford, Jan. 23, 1954; children— Jill K., John H., Kevin G. A.B., U. Mich., 1949, M.S., 1950, Ph.D., 1955. Research assoc. dept. physics AEC, Ames Lab., Iowa State U., 1955-56, asst. prof., 1956-62, assoc. prof., 1962-63; prof. Wayne State U., Detroit, 1963-94, prof. emeritus, 1994—, chmn. dept. physics, 1963-73, assoc. provost for faculty relations, 1973-86; hon. research fellow Univ. Coll., London, 1986-87,93. Editorial bd.: Wayne State U. Press, 1969-73. Served with AUS, 1946-47. Mem. Am. Phys. Soc., AAAS, Sigma Xi, Phi Beta Kappa. Home: 415 Bournemouth Rd Grosse Pointe Farms MI 48236-2817 Office: Dept Physics Wayne State U Detroit MI 48202

STEWART, RICHARD DONALD, internist, educator, biographer; b. Lakeland, Fla., Dec. 26, 1926; s. LeRoy Hepburn and Zoa Irene (Hachet) S.; m. Mary Leeuw, June 14, 1952; children: R. Scot, Gregory D., Mary E. AB, U. Mich., 1951, MD, 1955, MPH, 1962; MA, U. Wis. Milw., 1979; PhD in English, U. Wis., Milw., 1997. Diplomate Am. Bd. Internal Medicine, Am. Bd. Med. Toxicology, Acad. Toxicol. Scis. Intern Saginaw (Mich.) Gen. Hosp., 1955-56; resident U. Mich. Med. Ctr., Ann Arbor, 1959-62; dir. med. rsch. sect. Dow Chem. Co., Midland, Mich., 1962-66; staff physician Midland Hosp., 1962-66; assoc. prof. preventive medicine Med. Coll. Wis., Milw., 1966-68, prof., chmn. dept. environ. medicine, 1969-78, adj. prof. dept. pharmacology and toxicology, 1978—. Cons. Children's Hosp. Wis., 1989-93, Internal Medicine St. Mary's Hosp., Racine, Wis., 1983-93; prof., dir. med. toxicology fellowship Dept. Emergency Medicine Milw. Regional Med. Ctr., 1989-91; sr. attending staff, 1967-90; staff Internal Medicine St. Luke's Hosp., Racine, 1983-93; med. dir. Poison Control Ctr. Southeastern Wis., 1989-93; corp. med. advisor S.C. Johnson & Son, Inc., Racine, 1971-78, corp. med. dir., 1978-89. Mem. adv. med. staff Milw. Fire Dept., 1975—. Cadet USAF, 1945-46. Fellow ACP, Am. Coll. Occuptl. Medicine, Am. Acad. Clin. Toxicology, Acad. Toxicological Scis.; mem. AMA, Soc. Toxicology, Wis. State Med. Soc., Racine Acad. Medicine, Rotary Internat., Phi Theta Kappa, Phi Kappa Phi, Sigma Tau Delta. Avocations: history of medicine, wilderness hiking, literature, creative writing, inventing medical devices, including hollow fiber artificial kidney. Home and Office: 5337 Wind Point Rd Racine WI 53402-2322

STEWART, S. JAY, automotive company executive; b. Pineville, W.Va., Sept. 18, 1938; s. Virgil Harvey and Lena Rivers (Repair) S.; m. Judith Ann Daniels, June 3, 1961; children: Julie Annette, Jennifer Amy, Steven Jay. BSChemE, U. Cin., 1961; MBA, W.Va. U., 1966. Various positions in engring., mfg., mktg. Monsanto Co., St. Louis, 1961-73; dir. mktg. Ventron Corp. subs. Thiokol, Inc., Beverly, Mass., 1973-77, gen. mgr., 1977-79; pres. Dynachem Corp. subs. Thiokol, Inc., Tustin, Calif., 1979-82; group v.p. Thiokol Corp., Newtown, Pa., 1982; group v.p. splty. chems. Morton Internat., Inc. (formerly Morton Thiokol, Inc.), Chgo., 1983-86, pres., chief oper. officer, 1986-94, also bd. dirs., 94—; chmn. bd., CEO, 1994—; chmn. Autolive, Inc., Stockholm, Sweden, 2001—. Mem. Household Internat. Inc., Autoliv, Inc.; trustee Rush Presbyn.-St. Luke's Med. Ctr., Chgo., 1987—; Trustee Mus. Scis. and Industry; mem. exec. comm., Soc. Chem. Industry. Recipient Disting. Alumnus award U. Cin., 1984. Mem. Am. Chem. Soc., Am. Inst. Chem. Engrs., Chem. Mfrs. Assn. (bd. dirs. 1984-87, 94), Comml. Devel. Assn., Chem. Mktg. Assn. (bd. dirs. 1990), Comml. Club Chgo., The Chgo. Club, Econ. Club Chgo. Republican. Methodist. Office: Autolive Inc Klarabergsciadukten 70 Sec E Box 70381 SE 10724 Stockholm Sweden

STEWART, TODD I. military officer; BSCE, Mich. Technol. U., 1968; MS in Engring. Adminstrn., So. Meth. U., 1971; disting. grad., Squadron Officer Sch., 1974; PhD in Mgmt., U. Nebr., 1980; disting. grad., Air Command and Staff Coll., 1982; grad., Air War Coll., 1989. Commd. 2d lt. USAF, 1968, advanced through grades to brigadier gen., 1995; chief of programs 4683d Air Base Group, Thule Air Base, Greenland, 1971-72; civil engring. staff officer Hdqs. Strategic Air Command, Offutt AFB, Nebr., 1972-77; assoc. prof. mgmt. Grad. Sch. Sys. and Logistics Air Force Inst. Tech., Wright-Patterson AFB, Ohio, 1977-81; chief programs divsn., dep. dir. programs dir. engring./svc. Hdqs. U.S. Air Forces in Europe, Ramstein Air Base, West Germany, 1982-85; comdr. 36th Civil Engring. Squadron, Bitburg Air Base, West Germany, 1985-88; dir. plans and programs Office of Civil Engr. Hdqs. USAF, Washington, 1989-91, dep. civil engr. Office of Civil Engr., 1991-94; command civil engr. Hdqs. Air Edn. and Tng. Command, Randolph AFB, Tex., 1994-95, Hdqs. Air Force Materiel Command, Wright-Patterson AFB, 1995—; maj. gen. USAF. Decorated Legion of Merit, Meritorious Svc. medal with 3 oak leaf clusters; recipient Curtina ward Soc. Mil. Engrs., 1988, Newman medal Soc. Mil. Engrs., 1993. Office: HQ AFMC/XP 4375 Chidlaw Rd Wright Pat OH 45433-5066

STEWART III, JAMES OTTIS, football player; b. Morristown, Tenn., Dec. 27, 1971; m. Jennifer Stewart; 1 child Alyssa Stewart. Degree in sports mgmt., U. Tenn. Football player Jacksonville Jaguars, 1995—2000, Detroit Lions, 2000—. Achievements include became only the 4th Lion to ever rush for 1,000 yards in a single season; rushed for 10 touchdowns in his first year in Detroit;his 11 total touchdowns (including one receiving) also tied him for the 3d highest mark among NFC runnning backs;in NFL record books as 1 of 5 players in league history to rush for five touchdowns in a game (vs. Phila., Oct. 12, 1997).*

STIEFF, JOHN JOSEPH, legislative lawyer, educator; b. Indpls., Feb. 28, 1952; s. James Frederick and Mary Therese (Bisch) S.; m. Dusty Lee-Ann Warner, Apr. 21, 1989; stepchildren: Robert Franklin Russell, E.I. Annie Russell. BA with Distinction, Ind. U., 1973, JD, 1977. Bar: Ind. 1977. Sr. atty. Office of Bill Drafting & Rsch., Legislative Svcs. Agy., Indpls., 1977-86; dep. dir. and asst. revisor of statutes Office of Code Revision, Legislative Svcs. Agy., 1986-92, dir. and revisor of statutes, 1992—. Adj. prof. law Ind. Univ., Bloomington, 1985-86; instr. continuing legal edn. Ind. Gen. Assembly, Indpls., 1987-96; faculty mem. Nat. Conf. State Legislatures, Denver, Colo., 1988-89; supervising atty. program on law and state govt. Ind. U. Sch. Law, Indpls., 2001—; assoc commr. Nat. Conf. Commrs. on Uniform State Laws, Chgo., 1993—. Editor in chief: (books) The Acts of Indiana, 1986—, The Indiana Code, 1993—; ast. editor, The Indiana Code, 1986-92. Poetry instr. Gage Inst. for Gifted Children, Indpls., 1982-86. Named Hoosier Scholar, Indiana Commn. for Higher Edn., 1970-73. Mem. Writer's Ctr. of Indpls. (founding mem.), Ind. U. Varsity Club. Avocations: travel, phtography, writing poetry, Am. blues music. Home: 7707 Windy Hill Way Indianapolis IN 46239-8749 Office: Legislative Svcs Agy Office Code Revision 1 N Capitol Ave Ste 420 Indianapolis IN 46204-2097

STIEGEL, MICHAEL ALLEN, lawyer; b. Greenfield, Mass., Sept. 15, 1946; s. Sid James and Ida Eleanor (Solomon) S.; m. Marsha Palmer, Sept. 10, 1983. BA, U. Ariz., 1968; JD cum laude, Loyola U., Chgo., 1971. Bar: Ill. 1971, U.S. Dist. Ct. Ill. 1971, U.S. Ct. Appeals (7th cir.) 1971, U.S. Ct. Appeals (6th cir.) 1975, U.S. Supreme Ct. 1975, Wis. 1985, Fla. 1987. Law clk. to fed. judge U.S. Dist. Ct. Ill., Chgo., 1971-72; assoc. Arnstein & Lehr, 1972-78, ptnr., 1978-82, equity ptnr., 1982-85, dir. trial dept., 1985-87, mng. ptnr., 1985-98. Vice chmn. exec. com., 1987-98; adj. prof. law Northwestern U.; faculty Nat. Inst. Trial Advocacy Equity, La. State U. Trial Advocacy Program, 1995. Contbr. articles to profl. jours. Mem. fin. com. Lynn Martin for Senate, Ill., 1989-90. Recipient Cert. of Appreciation, Nat. Safety Coun., Chgo., 1987, Cert. of Distinction, Chgo. Bar Assn., 1975. Mem. ABA (sects. on litigation and labor and employment law, vice chmn. trial evidence com. litigation sect. 1990-91, co-chmn. trial evidence com. 1991-95, lawyers conf. standards for admissibility of technologically sophisticated evidence com., co-chair nat. CLE programs 1995-97, coun. 1997-2000, budget officer 2000—, litigation sect. advisor, uniform laws commn., drafting com. on Model Punitive Damages Act), Ill. Bar Assn., Fla. Bar Assn., Wis. Bar Assn., Chgo. Social Clubs, East Bank Club. Avocations: sports, reading, horse racing syndications. Office: Michael Best & Friedrich 401 N Michigan Ave Ste 1900 Chicago IL 60601-1635

STIEHL, WILLIAM D. federal judge; b. 1925; m. Celeste M. Sullivan; children: William D., Susan M. Student, U. N.C., 1943-45; LLB, St. Louis U., 1949. Pvt. practice, 1952-78; ptnrs. Stiehl & Hess, 1978-81; ptnr. Stiehl & Stiehl, 1982-86; judge, former chief judge U.S. District Court, (so. dist.) Ill., East Saint Louis, 1986—. Spl. asst. atty. gen. State of Ill., 1970-73. Mem. bd. Belleville Twp. High Sch. and Jr. Coll., 1949-50, 54-56, pres., 1956-57, Clair County, Ill., county civil atty., 1956-60. Mem. Ill. State Bar Assn., St. Clair County Bar Assn. Office: US Dist Ct 750 Missouri Ave East Saint Louis IL 62201-2954

STIER, MARY, publishing executive; m. Jeff Stier; 2 children. Grad. in comm., broadcasting, U. Iowa. Sr. group pres. Gannett Midwest Newspaper Group, 1982—; pres., pub., regional pres., sr. group pres. Reno Gazette-Jour., 1985; adv. mgr. Iowa City Press-Citizen, adv. dir., pres., pub., 1987; v.p. Ctrl. Region Newspaper Divsn. , 1990, pres. Midwest group, 1993; pres., pub., regional v.p., group pres. Rockford Register Star, 1991—2000; pres., pub. The Des Moines Register, 2000—; pres., pub., regional v.p. Binghamton (N.Y.) Press & Sun-Bulletin. Mem.: The Greater Des Moines Partnership, Am. Press Inst., Iowa Newspaper Assn., Newspaper Assn. Am., Phi Beta Kappa. Office: Des Moines Register PO Box 957 Des Moines IA 50304-0957 Address: 715 Locust St Des Moines IA 50309*

STIFLER, VENETIA CHAKOS, dancer, choreographer, dance educator; b. Chgo., Feb. 27, 1950; d. Theodore and Ruth (Pastirsky) Chakos; m. John G. Stifler, Jan. 28, 1972 (dec. 1977); m. Michael Hugos, 1994. BA, U. Ill., Chgo., 1983; MFA equivalency, Union Inst., Cin., 1987, PhD, 1992. Tchr. workshops Urban Gateways, Chgo., 1977; tchr. Chgo. Dance Ctr., 1971-78, Smith Coll., Northampton, Mass., 1975, Wilson Coll., Chambersburg, Pa., 1984; gusest tchr., artistic dir. composition/improvisation U. Wis., Madison, 1980-81, 85, 87; tchr. modern, jazz and ballet Venetia Stifler & Concert Dance, Inc., Chgo., 1978—; tchr. choreography workshop Bell Elem. Sch., 1987; tchr./artist in residence Mundelein Coll., 1982-90; asst. prof., chair dance program Northeastern Ill. U., 1987—; tchr. modern technique So. Ill. U., Carbondale, 1975. Lectr. Mundelein Coll., Chgo., 1983, 84, 85, 86, Mayor's Office of Spl. Events, Chgo., 1980program dir. and choreogrpaher spl. programs Chgo. Symphony Orch., 1985, 87; pres. bd. dirs. Chgo. Dance Arts Coalition, 1983-85; adv. dance panel Ill. Arts Coun., 1983-85, Chgo. Office of Fine Arts, 1983-86; guest speaker Chgo. Office of Fine Arts, 1987; choreographer Sears Fashion Files, BoMay Prodns., 1983, 84, 86; prodn. asst. Audio Visual Prodns., 1970-71; artistic dir. Ruth Page Dance Series, 1992—; centennial dir. Ruth Page Found. Centennial, 1999; exec. dir. Ruth Page Found., 2001. Choreographer Between Us, 1991, Magic Spaces, 1985, 86, Fugues, 1981, 82, Corporate Cases, 1988, Private places, 1987, Bell School Scrimmage, 1987, Blessings, 1986, Don't Dance with Your Back to the Moon, 1986, Imagery & Concept in the Dances of Venetia Stifler, 1985, Rhymes, 1984, Arriving at Onion, 1984, Pulse, 1983, Haiku, 1982, Mundelein Madness, 1981, Solo Crane, 1981, Tales of a Winter's Night, 1980, Jackson Park-Howard, 1979, La Gaite Parisienne (opera), 1976, Chicago Sketches, 1995, Veils, 1996, Over Weight Over Wrought Over You, 1997, Three German Songs, 1999, Shenandoah. Recipient Ruth Page award; named for Outstanding Artistic Achievement, Chgo. Dance Coalition, 1985. Avocations: voice, film, art. Office: Northeastern Ill U 5500 N Saint Louis Ave Chicago IL 60625-4679 E-mail: venetia@ruth.

STIGLER, STEPHEN MACK, statistician, educator; b. Mpls., Aug. 10, 1941; s. George Joseph and Margaret (Mack) S.; m. Virginia Lee, June 27,1964; children: Andrew, Geoffrey, Margaret, Elizabeth. BA, Carleton Coll., 1963; PhD, U. Calif., Berkeley, 1967. Asst. prof. U. Wis., Madison, 1967-71, assoc. prof., 1971-75, prof., 1975-79, U. Chgo., 1979—; chmn. dept., 1986-92; Ernest DeWitt Burton Disting. Svc. prof. U. Chgo., 1992—. Trustee Ctr. for Advanced Study in the Behavioral Scis., Stanford, Calif., 1986-92, 93-99, 2000—, chmn., 1995-99, 2002--. Author: The History of Statistics, 1986, Statistics on the Table, 1999; contbr. articles to jours. in field. Guggenheim Found. fellow, 1976-77; Ctr. for Advanced Study in Behavioral Scis. fellow, 1978-79. Fellow AAAS, Am. Acad. Arts and Scis. (mem. coun. 1995-99), Inst. Math. Stats. (Neyman lectr. 1988, pres. 1993-94), Am. Statis. Assn. (editor Jour. 1979-82, Outstanding Statistician award Chgo. chpt. 1993), Royal Statis. Soc. (Fisher lectr. 1986); mem. Internat. Statis. Inst. (mem. coun. 1999—, pres.-elect 2001—), Statis. Soc. Can., Bernoulli Soc., History of Sci. Soc., Brit. Soc. for History Sci., Quadrangle Club, Sigma Xi, Phi Beta Kappa. Office: U Chgo Dept Statistics 5734 S University Ave Chicago IL 60637-1514

STILLE, LEON E. state legislator; b. Olive, Mich., Nov. 21, 1939; m. Zinnie; four children. BS, Mich. State U. Market rep., mgr. IBM, 1966-92; mayor Ferrysburg, Mich.; mem. Mich. Ho. of Reps. from 89th dist., Lansing, 1993-94; Rep. asst. whip, 1993-94; mem. Mich. Senate from 32nd dist., Lansing, 1995—. Chair regularity subcom. 1993-94, transportation subcom., 1993-94; mem. higher edn. subcom., 1993-94, gen. govt. subcom., 1993-94. Mem. Rotary. Home: PO Box 511 Spring Lake MI 49456-0511 Office: Mich State Senate State Capitol PO Box 30036 Lansing MI 48909-7536

STILLMAN, NINA GIDDEN, lawyer; b. N.Y.C., Apr. 3, 1948; d. Melvin and Joyce Audrey (Gidden) S. AB with distinction, Smith Coll., 1970; JD cum laude, Northwestern U., 1973. Bar: Ill. 1973, U.S. Dist. Ct. (no. dist.) Ill. 1973, U.S. Dist. Ct. (ea. dist.) Wis. 1979, U.S. Dist. Ct. (no. dist. trial bar) Ill. 1983, U.S. Ct. Appeals (7th cir.) 1974, U.S. Supreme Ct. 1981, U.S. Dist. Ct. (ctrl. dist.) Ill. 1994, U.S. Dist. Ct. (ea. dist.) Tex., 1996, U.S. Dist. Ct. (Colo.), 1999, U.S. Dist. Ct. (ND) 2002. Assoc. Vedder, Price, Kaufman & Kammholz, Chgo., 1973-79, ptnr., 1980—. Adv. bd. occupational health and safety tng. program U. Mich., Ann Arbor, 1980-83; adj. faculty Inst. Human Resources and Indsl. Rels., Loyola U., Chgo., 1983-86, bd. advisors, 1986—. Author: (with others) Women, Work, and Health: Challenge to Corporate Policy, 1979, Occupational Health Law: A Guide for Industry, 1981, Employment Discrimination, 1981, Personnel Management: Labor Relations, 1981, Occupational Safety and Health Law, 1988; contbg. author: Occupational Medicine: State of the Art Reviews, 1996; contbr. articles to profl. jours. Legal advisor, v.p. Planned Parenthood Assn. Chgo., 1979—81; sec. jr. governing bd. Chgo. Symphony Orch., 1983; trustee Merit Sch. Music, 2000—, vice chmn. bd. trustees, 2001—. Recipient Svc. award Northwestern U., 1994. Mem.: ABA (occupl. safety and health law com. 1978—), Human Resources Mgmt. Assn. Chgo. (bd. dirs. 1986—88, officer), Am. Inns of Ct. (v.p. Wigmore chpt. 1988—89), Chgo. Bar Assn. (chmn. labor and employment law com. 1986—87), Northwestern U. Sch. Law Alumni Assn. (pres. 1991—92), Univ. Club Chgo. (bd. dirs. 1988—2001, sec. 1999—2000, v.p. 2000—01), The Chgo. Com., Econ. Club Chgo., Lawyers Club, Smith Coll. Club Chgo. (pres. 1972). Avocations: travel, reading, the arts, collecting art. Office: Vedder Price Kaufman & Kammholz 222 N La Salle St Ste 2600 Chicago IL 60601-1100

STINE, ROBERT HOWARD, pediatrician; b. Nov. 1, 1929; s. Harry Raymond and Mabel Eva (Newhard) S.; m. Lois Elaine Kihlgren, Oct. 22, 1960; children: Robert E., Karen E., Jonathan N. BS in Biology, Moravian Coll., 1952. Diplomate Am. Bd. Pediatrics, Am. Subbd. Pediatric Allergy, Cojoint Bd. Allergy and Immunology. Intern St. Luke's Hosp., Bethlehem, Pa., 1960-61, resident in surgery, 1961-62; physician Jefferson Med. Coll., Phila., 1956-60; resident in pediatrics U. N.Y., Syracuse, 1962-64; resident in allergy Robert A. Cooke Inst. Allergy Roosevelt Hosp., N.Y.C., 1964-65; clin. instr. pediatrics U. Ill., Chgo., 1965-71; mem. courtesy staff Proctor Community Hosp., Peoria, Ill., 1966-77, mem. active staff, 1977—, chmn. dept. medicine, 1988—; pres. elect. med. staff, 1990-91; pres. med. staff, 1991-92; mem. teaching staff St. Francis Hosp., Peoria, 1969—; clin. instr. pediatrics Rush-Presbyn. St. Luke's Hosp., Chgo., 1971—. Lt. (j.g.), USN, 1953-56. Fellow Am. Acad. Pediatrics, Am. Acad. Allergy Asthma and Immunology, Am. Coll. Allergy and Asthma, Am. Assn. Cert. Allergists; mem. Ill. Soc. Allergy and Clin. Immunology, Peoria Med. Soc. (pres.-elect 1993, pres. 1994), Christian Med. and Dental Soc. Home: 105 Hollands Grove Ln Washington IL 61571-9623 Office: 6615 N Big Hollow Rd Peoria IL 61615-2450

STINEHART, ROGER RAY, lawyer; b. Toledo, Jan. 27, 1945; s. Forrest William and Nettie May (Twyman) S.; m. Martha Jean Goodnight, Sept. 19, 1970; children: Amanda Jean, Brian Scott. BS, Bowling Green (Ohio) State U., 1968; JD, Ohio State U., 1972. Bar: Ohio 1972. Fin. analyst Gen. Electric, Detroit, 1968-69; assoc. Gingher & Christensen, Columbus, Ohio, 1972-76, ptnr., 1976-80; sr. v.p., gen. counsel, sec. G.D. Ritzy's, Inc., 1983-85; ptnr. Jones, Day, Reavis & Pogue, 1980-83, 85—. Adj. prof. law Capital U., Columbus, 1976-79; mem. adv. com. Ohio securities divsn. Dept. Commerce, Columbus, 1979—; fellow Columbus Bar Found., 1992—; adv. bd. The Entrepreneurship Inst., 1992-95. Contbr. Ohio State U. Coll. Law Jour., 1970-72. Gen. counsel, trustee Internat. Assn. Rsch. on Leukemia and Related Diseases, 1975—; v.p., trustee Hospice of Columbus, 1978-80; trustee Cen. Ohio chpt. Leukemia Soc. of Am., Columbus, 1983-93, v.p., 1985-87; trustee Ohio Cancer Rsch. Assocs., Columbus, 1983—, v.p., 1990—. With USMCR, 1963-68. Mem. ABA (bus. law com., franchise law com.), Ohio State Bar Assn. (corp. law com., franchise law com.), Columbus Bar Assn. (securities law com., chmn. 1981-83, bus. law com., franchise law com.), Rotary Club (Columbus), Sigma Tau Delta, Beta Gamma Sigma. Home: 2155 Waltham Rd Columbus OH 43221-4149 Office: Jones Day Reavis & Pogue 1900 Huntington Ctr Columbus OH 43215-6103

STINES, FRED, JR. publisher; b. Newton, Iowa, Mar. 16, 1925; s. Fred and Nella (Haun) S.; m. Dorothy G. McClanahan, Sept. 5, 1953 (dec.); children: Steven, Scott, Ann; m. Mary K. Devin, Sept. 12, 1989. B.C.S., U. Iowa, 1949. With Meredith Corp., Des Moines, 1949-90, sales promotion and mdse. mgr., 1955-63, advt. dir., 1963-66, pub., 1966-73, pub. dir. mag. div., 1973-76, v.p., gen. mgr. books and newspapers, 1976-83, sr. v.p., 1983-87, pres. book pub., 1986-90, corp. v.p. spl. projects, 1988-90; pres., prin. Concepts in Mktg., 1990—. Cert. instr. Dale Carnegie courses, 1958-63. Bd. dirs. Des Moines Ballet Assn., North Am. Outdoor Group, Mpls., 1992-95; bd. dirs., v.p. Jr. Achievement of Ctrl. Iowa. Served with AUS, 1946-49. Named Farm Marketing Man of Year, 1972 Mem. Future

Farmers Am. Found. (nat. chmn. 1971), Rotary Internat., Des Moines Golf and Country Club, Phi Gamma Delta (sect. chief 1983, nat. bd. dirs. 1985-89), Alpha Kappa Psi, Alpha Delta Sigma. Club: Des Moines Golf and Country (dir., pres. 1981, pres. Ednl. Found.).

STINSON, KENNETH E. construction company executive; b. Chgo, May 24, 1946; BS in Civil Engring., U. Notre Dame; MS in Civil Engring., Stanford U. Pres. Kiewit Constrn. Group Inc., Omaha, 1992-93, chair., pres, 1993-96; chmn., CEO Peter Kiewit Sons' Inc., 1996-. Office: Peter Kiewit Sons Inc 1000 Kiewit Plaza Omaha NE 68131

STIRITZ, WILLIAM P. food company executive; b. Jasper, Ark., July 1, 1934; s. Paul and Dorothy (Bradley) S.; m. Susan Ekberg, Dec. 4, 1972; children: Bradley, Charlotte, Rebecca, Nicholas. B.S., Northwestern U., 1959; M.A., St. Louis U., 1968. Mem. mktg. mgmt. staff Pillsbury Co., Mpls., 1959-62; staff Gardner Advt. Co., St. Louis, 1963; with Ralston Purina Co., 1963-97, pres., CEO, chmn., 1981-97; chmn., CEO Agribrands Internat., 1997—. Bd. dirs. Am. Freightways, Angelica Corp., Ball Corp., Boatmen's Bancshares, Inc., Gen. Am. Life Ins. Co., May Dept. Stores, S.C. Johnson & Son, Reins. Group Am., Vail Resorts; bd. dirs., chmn. Ralston Purina, Ralcorp; chmn. Westgate Equity Group, LLC. With USN, 1954-57. Office: AgriBrands Internat Ste 650 1401 S Brentwood Blvd Saint Louis MO 63144-1465

STIRLING, ELLEN ADAIR, retail executive; b. Chgo., June 21, 1949; d. Volney W. and Ellen Adair (Orr) Foster; m. James P. Stirling, June 6, 1970; children: Elizabeth Ginevra, Diana Leslie, Alexandra Curtiss. Student, U. Chgo., 1970-71; BA, Wheaton Coll., Norton, Mass., 1971; postgrad., U. London, 1974. Pres., CEO, The Lake Forest Shop, 1986—. Bd. dirs. Lake Forest Bank and Trust. Founder, v.p. aux. bd. Art Inst. Chgo., 1972-91; dir. Friends of Ryerson Woods, 1992—; mem. women's bd. Lyric Opera, Chgo., 1992—, Lake Forest Coll., 1989—; mem. adv. bd. Hope C. McCormick Costume Ctr., Chgo. Hist. Soc.; trustee Nat. Louis U., 1999—. Mem. Onwentsia Club, Racquet Club, Chgo. Club. Office: The Lake Forest Shop 165 E Market Sq Lake Forest IL 60045

STIRLING, JAMES PAULMAN, investment banker; b. Chgo., Mar. 30, 1941; s. Louis James and Beverly L. (Paulman) S.; m. Ellen Adair Foster, June 6, 1970; children— Elizabeth Ginevra, Diana Leslie, Alexandra Curtiss. A.B., Princeton U., 1963; M.B.A., Stanford U., 1965. Chartered fin. analyst. Vice pres. corp. fin. Kidder, Peabody & Co. (now UBS Warburg PaineWebber), N.Y.C. and Chgo., 1965-71, 84-86, sr. v.p. corp. fin., 1987—; dir. internat. investments Sears Roebuck Co., Chgo. and London, 1971-75, 77-84; asst. to sec. U.S. Dept. Commerce, Washington, 1976-77. Chmn. bd. Northwestern Meml. Mgmt. Corp., Chgo., 1989—; trustee Northwestern Meml. Hosp., Chgo., 1985—. Pres. jr. bd. Chgo. Symphony, 1968—70; mem. exec. coun. Chgo. Metropolis 2020; trustee Chgo. Symphony, 1970—75, Tchrs. Acad. for Math. Sci., 1991—95. Mem. Investment Analysts Soc., Bond Club of Chgo., Nat. Econ. Hon. Soc. Clubs: Chicago, Racquet (Chgo.); Onwentsia (Lake Forest, Ill.) Office: UBS Warburg PaineWebber 125 S Wacker Dr Ste 2710 Chicago IL 60606-4302

STITH, LAURA DENVIR, judge; b. St. Louis, Oct. 30, 1953; BA magna cum laude, Tufts U., 1975; JD magna cum laude, Georgetown U., 1978. Law clk. to Hon. Robert E. Seiler, Mo. Supreme Ct., 1978—79; assoc. Shook, Hardy & Bacon, Kansas City, Mo., 1979—84, ptnr., 1984—94; judge. Mo. Ct. Appeals (we. dist.), 1994—2001; judge Supreme Ct. Mo., 2001—. Office: PO Box 150 Jefferson City MO 65102*

STOCK, ANITA See **SCHERER, ANITA**

STOCK, LEON MILO, chemist, educator; b. Detroit, Oct. 15, 1930; s. J.H. Frederick and Anna (Fischer) S.; m. Mary K. Elmblad, May 6, 1961; children: Katherine L., Ann V. BS in Chemistry, U. Mich., 1952; PhD in Chemistry, Purdue U., 1959. Instr. U. Chgo., 1958-61, asst. prof., 1961-65, assoc. prof., 1965-70, prof. dept. chemistry, 1970-96, master Phys. Scis. Collegiate div., 1970-96, prof. emeritus dept. chemistry, 1997—, assoc. dean div. Phys. Scis., 1976-81, assoc. dean, 1976-81, chmn. dept. chemistry, 1985-88; faculty assoc. Argonne (Ill.) Nat. Lab., 1984-85, joint appointment chemistry div., 1985-96, dir. chemistry div., 1988-95. Exploratory rsch. assoc. Elec. Power Rsch. Inst., 1989; adv. bd. Ctr. for Applied Rsch., U. Ky., 1990-95; Brown lectr. Purdue U., 1992; Given lectr. Pa. State U., 1995; cons. Westinghouse Hanford Co., 1995-96, Phillips Petroleum Co., 1964-95, Amoco Oil Co., 1989-95, Argonne Nat. Lab., 1995—, Pacific N.W. Nat. Lab., 1996—, Fluor Daniel Hanford Co., 1996—; faculty assoc. Wash. State U., 1997—. Recipient L.J. and H.M. Quantrell prize, 1974, H.H. Storch award Am. Chem. Soc., 1987. Mem. NAS (energy engring. bd.), Am. Chem. Soc. (com. on sci. 1990-92), Coun. of Gordon Rsch. Confs. (chmn. Gordon Conf. on Fuel Sci. 1983), NRC (mem. panel on coop. rsch. in fossil energy 1984, energy engring. bd. 1984-90, mem. panel on strategic petroleum rsch. 1985, panel on rsch. needs of advanced process tech. 1992-93), Ill. Coal Bd. (program panel 1986-90, panel on prodn. techs. for transp. fuels 1990, editl. bd. Jour. Organic Chemistry 1981-86, Energy and Fuels, 1986-96, mem. panel on new strategy for safety issue resolution at Hanford, 1996, mem. panel rsch. needs radiation chemistry, 1998). Office: Argonne Nat Lab Chem Divsn Argonne IL 60439

STOCKGLAUSNER, WILLIAM GEORGE, accountant; b. St. Louis, Dec. 25, 1950; s. William George and Mary Virginia (Lopez) S.; m. Vickie Kay Mackler, Nov. 17, 1973 (div. Dec. 1999); children: Tyson Marshall, Jacob Cameron. BS summa cum laude, Columbia (Mo.) Coll., 1985. CPA, Mo. Staff acct. Wright-Price Inc., Jefferson City, Mo., 1974-77, Williams-Keepers CPAs, Columbia, 1977-81, supr. acctg. svc., 1981-85, auditor, 1985-86; acct. Don Landers & Co. CPAs, 1986-89, ptnr., 1990-99; founder, pres. William. G. Stockglausner CPA, PC, 1999—; ptnr. Ashland Manor Properties, 2001—. Coach Daniel Boone Little League, Columbia, 1986-90, 94-99, Diamond Coun., 1994-99, Columbia Soccer Club, 1988-90, 94-2000, divsn. coord., 1991-92; campaign vol. United Way, 1991-94, 97-98; fin. adv. com. City of Columbia, 1996—. Mem. AICPA, Mo. Soc. CPAs (tech. standards rev. com. 1989-90), Lions (sec. Columbia club 1983-85, bd. dirs. 1986-88). Republican. Roman Catholic. Avocations: fishing, photography, running, music/guitar, mem. Low-Water Crossing bluegrass band. Office: 601 W Nifong Blvd Ste 1E Columbia MO 65203-6804 Personal E-mail: wstock138@aol.com. E-mail: wstock139@worldnet.att.net.

STOCKING, GEORGE WARD, JR. anthropology educator; b. Berlin, Dec. 8, 1928; came to U.S., 1929; s. George Ward and Dorothé Amelia (Reichhard) S.; m. Wilhelmina Davis, Aug. 19, 1949 (div. 1965); children: Susan Hallowell, Rebecca, Rachel Louise, Melissa, Thomas Shepard; m. Carol Ann Bowman, Sept. 29, 1968. BA, Harvard U., 1949; PhD, U. Pa., 1960. From instr. to assoc. prof. history U. Calif., Berkeley, 1960-68; assoc. prof. anthropology and history U. Chgo., 1968-74, prof. anthropology, 1974—, Stein-Freiler Disting. Svc. prof., 1990—, prof. emeritus, 2000—, dir. Fishbein Ctr. for History Sci. and Medicine, 1981-92. Vis. prof. U. Minn., Mpls., 1974, Harvard U., Cambridge, Mass., 1977, Stanford U., Palo Alto, Calif., 1983, U. Ill., Urbana, 1999. Author: Race, Culture and Evolution, 1968, Victorian Anthropology, 1987, The Ethnographer's Magic, 1992, After Tylor, 1995, Delimiting Anthropology, 2001; author, editor: The Shaping of American Anthropology, 1974; editor History of Anthropology, 1983-97. Active labor union and radical polit. activity, 1949-56. Fellow Ctr. for Advanced Study in Behavioral Scis., 1976-77, John Simon Guggenheim Meml. Found., 1984-85, Inst. for Advanced Study, 1992-93; Getty Ctr. for History of Art and Humanities scholar, 1988-89, Dibner Inst., MIT, 1998. Fellow Am. Anthropol. Assn. (Franz Boas award 1998), Am. Acad. Arts and Scis.; mem. Royal Anthropol. Inst. (Huxley medal 1993), History Sci. Soc. Avocation: needlepoint. Office: Univ Chicago Dept Anthropology 1126 E 59th St Chicago IL 60637-1580 E-mail: g-stocking@uchicago.edu.

STOCKLOSA, GREGORY A. printing company executive; BS, U. Mich.; M in Mgmt., Northwestern U. Fin. staff Kraft Gen. Foods, Inc.; asst. treas. global corp. fin. R.R. Donnelley & Sons Co., Chgo., 1993-94, v.p., treas., 1994-99, v.p., corp. contr., 1999-2000, acting CFO, 2000, exec. v.p., CFO, 2000—. Office: RR Donnelley Sons Co 77 W Wacker Dr Chicago IL 60601-1696

STOECKER, DAVID THOMAS, banker; b. St. Louis, June 8, 1939; s. John Garth and Marie (Zahler) S.; m. Ann E. Conrad, Aug. 18, 1962; children— Lisa Ann, Susan Jane. B.S., Ind. U., 1963. Sr. v.p. comml. loans Mercantile Trust Co. N.Am., St. Louis, 1965-80; pres. Gravois-Merc. Bank, 1980-87; pres., chief exec. officer Bank of South County, 1987-95; chmn. bd., pres., CEO Ctrl. West End Bank, 1996—. Served to 1st lt. AUS, 1963-65. Mem. Robert Morris Assos. (pres. St. Louis 1980) Methodist. Club: Sunset Country. Office: 415 Debaliviere Saint Louis MO 63112

STOERMER, EUGENE FILMORE, biologist, educator; b. Webb, Iowa, Mar. 7, 1934; s. Edward Filmore and Agnes Elizabeth (Ekstrand) S.; m. Barbara Purves Ryder, Aug. 13, 1960; children: Eric Filmore, Karla Jean, Peter Emil. BS, Iowa State U., 1959, PhD, 1963. Assoc. rsch. scientist, rsch. scientist U. Mich., Ann Arbor, 1965-79, assoc. prof., 1979-85, prof., 1985—. Editl. advisor Jour. Paleolimonology. Contbr. over 200 articles to profl. jours. Fellow Acad. Natural Scis., Phila., 1980; recipient Darbaker prize, Bot. Soc. Am., 1993. Mem. Phycological Soc. Am. (pres. 1988-89), Internat. Assn. for Diatom Rsch. (pres. 1992-94). Home: 4392 Dexter Ave Ann Arbor MI 48103-1636 Office: U Mich Ctr for Great Lakes Ann Arbor MI 48109 E-mail: stoermer@umich.edu.

STOHLER, MICHAEL JOE, dentist; b. Anderson, Ind., Mar. 26, 1956; s. Herbert Warren and Mary Jo (Philbert) S.; m. Mary Anne Poinsette, May 16, 1981; children: James Lawrence, Maria Christine, Benjamin Joseph. Student, Lake-Sumter C.C., Leesburg, Fla., 1974-76; BS, Ball State U., 1978; DDS, Ind. U., 1982. Gen. practice dentistry, Anderson, 1982—. Fellow Acad. Gen. Dentistry; mem. ADA, Ind. Dental Assn., East Ctrl. Dental Assn., Madison County Dental Assn., Acad. Gen. Dentistry, Acad. Dentistry for Handicapped, Ind. U. Alumni Assn. (life), Rotary (sgt.-at-arms Anderson Suburban chpt. 1986), Psi Omega. Avocations: snow and water skiing, scuba, sky diving, computers. Home: 2829 W Ridge Ln Anderson IN 46013-9749 Office: 2012 E 53rd St Anderson IN 46013-3102 E-mail: mstohler@aol.com.

STOHR, DONALD J. federal judge; b. Sedalia, Mo., Mar. 9, 1934; s. Julius Leo and Margaret Elizabeth (McGaw) Stohr; m. Mary Ann Kuhlman, July 31, 1957; 5 children. BS, St. Louis U., 1956, JD, 1958. Bar: Mo. 1958, U.S. Dist. Ct. (ea. dist.) Mo. 1958, U.S. Ct. Appeals (8th cir.) 1966, U.S. Supreme Ct. 1969. Assoc. Hocker Goodwin & MacGreevy, St. Louis, 1958-63, 66-69; asst. counselor St. Louis County, 1963-65, counselor, 1965-66; U.S. atty. Ea. Dist. Mo., St. Louis, 1973-76; ptnr. Thompson & Mitchell, 1969-73, 76-92; judge U.S. Dist. Ct. (ea. dist.) Mo., 1992—. Mem. ABA, Mo. Bar Assn., Am. Judicature Soc., St. Louis Met. Bar Assn. Office: 111 S 10th St Rm 16.182 Saint Louis MO 63102

STOKAN, LANA J. LADD, state legislator; b. El Dorado, Ark., Sept. 5, 1958; children: Garrett, Adair. BA, MA in Secondary Edn. and History, So. Ill. U. Rep. dist. 76 State of Mo. Office: 625 Wilshire Dr Florissant MO 63033-3824 also: State Capital Rm 305A Jefferson City MO 65101

STOKES, KATHLEEN SARAH, dermatologist, educator; b. Springfield, Mass., Oct. 18, 1954; d. John Francis and Margaret Cecelia (MacDonnell) Stokes; m. William Walter Greaves; children: Ian R., Spenver W., Malcolm W. BS, U. Utah, 1978, MS, 1980; MD, Med. Coll. Wis., 1987. Diplomate Am. Bd. Dermatology. Intern in internal medicine Med. Coll. Wis., Milw., 1987-88, resident in dermatology, 1988-90, chief resident, 1990-91, asst. clin. prof. dermatology, 1991—; pvt. practice, 1991—. Contbr. articles to med. jours., including Critical Care Medicine, Jour. Pediatric Dermatology. Named A Top Physician, Milw. mag., 1996, 00. Fellow Am. Acad. Dermatology, Milw. Acad. Medicine; mem. AMA, Wis. Dermatol. Soc., Women's Dermatologic Soc., Tempo, Alpha Omega Alpha. Office: Affiliated Dermatologists 2300 N Mayfair Rd Milwaukee WI 53226-1505

STOKES, LOUIS, former congressman, lawyer; b. Cleveland, Ohio, Feb. 23, 1925; s. Charles and Louise (Stone) S.; m. Jeanette Francis, Aug. 21, 1960; children: Shelley, Louis C., Angela, Lorene. Student, Case Western Res. U., 1946-48; JD, Cleve. Marshall Law Sch., 1953; 26 hon. doctorate degrees, 1953-2001. Bar: Ohio 1953. Mem. 91st-105th Congresses from 11th (formerly 21st) Ohio dist., Washington, 1969-99; sr. counsel Squire, Sanders and Dempsey, 1999—. Former ranking minority mem. appropriations subcom. on Vets. Affairs, HUD & Ind. Agys.; sr. vis. scholar Mandel Sch. Applied Social Scis. Case Western Res. U., 1999—. Polit. analyst, WEWS TV, Cleve. Served with AUS, 1943-46. Recipient numerous awards for civic activities including Distinguished Service award Cleve. br. NAACP; Certificate of Appreciation U.S. Commn. on Civil Rights. Fellow Ohio State Bar Assn.; mem. Am., Cuyahoga County, Cleve. bar assns., Nat. Assn. Def. Lawyers Criminal Cases Fair Housing (dir.), Norman's Minor Bar Assn., Urban League, Citizens League, John Harlan Law Club, ACLU, Am. Legion, Kappa Alpha Psi. Clubs: Masons (Cleve.). Office: Squire Sanders & Dempsey 1201 Pennsylvania Ave Washington DC 20044-0407 Address: 127 Public Square Cleveland OH 44114-1304 E-mail: lstokes@ssd.com.

STOKES, PATRICK T. brewery company executive; b. Washington, 1942; married. BS, Boston Coll., 1964; MBA, Columbia U., 1966. Fin. analyst Shell Oil Co., 1966-67; v.p. materials acquisitions Anheuser-Busch Cos. Inc., St. Louis, 1979-81, v.p., group exec., 1981—; pres. Anheuser-Busch Inc., 1990—; COO Campbell Taggart Inc. (subs. Anheuser-Busch Cos. Inc.), Dallas, 1986-90, CEO, 1990—; pres. Anheuser-Busch Inc.; chmn. Anheuser-Busch Internat.; CEO, sen. exec. v.p. Anheuser-Busch Cos. Inc., 2000—. Served to 1st lt. U.S. Army, 1967-69. Office: Anheuser-Busch Co Inc 1 Busch Place Saint Louis MO 63118-1852

STOKES, RODNEY, state agency administrator; Dir. Mich. Pks. and Recreation Divsn., Lansing, 1996—. Office: Mich Pks & Recreation Divsn PO Box 30028 Lansing MI 48909-7528 Fax: 517-335-4242.

STOKSTAD, MARILYN JANE, art history educator, curator; b. Lansing, Mich., Feb. 16, 1929; d. Olaf Lawrence and Edythe Marian (Gardiner) S. BA, Carleton Coll., 1950; MA, Mich. State U., 1953; PhD, U. Mich., 1957; postgrad., U. Oslo, 1951-52; LHD (hon.), Carleton Coll., 1997. Instr. U. Mich., Ann Arbor, 1956-58; mem. faculty U. Kans., Lawrence, 1958—, assoc. prof., 1961-66, prof., 1966-80, Univ. Disting. prof. art history, 1980-94, Judith Harris Murphy disting. prof. art, 1994—, dir. mus. art, 1961-67, research assoc., summers 1965-66, 67, 71, 72; assoc. dean Coll. Liberal Arts and Scis., U. Kans., 1972-76; research curator Nelson-Atkins Mus. Art, Kansas City, Mo., 1969-80, consultative curator medieval art, 1980—. Bd. dirs. Internat. Ctr. Medieval Art, 1972-75, 81-84, 88-96, v.p., 1990-93, pres., 1993-96, sr. advisor, 1996-97; cons., evaluator North Ctrl. Assn. Colls. and Univs., 1972—, commr.-at-large, 1984-89. Author: Santiago de Compostela, 1978, The Scottish World, 1981, Medieval Art, 1986, Art History, 1995, rev. edit., 1999, Art: A Brief History, 2000. Recipient Disting. Service award Alumni Assn. Carleton Coll., 1983, Kans. Gov.'s Arts award, 1997; Fulbright fellow, 1951-52; NEH grantee, 1967-68 Fellow AAUW; mem. AAUP (nat. coun. 1972-75), Archeol. Inst. Am. (pres. Kans. chpt. 1960-61), Midwest Coll. Art Conf. (pres. 1964-65), Coll. Art Assn. (bd. dirs. 1970-80, pres. 1978-80), Soc. Archtl. Historians (chpt. bd. dirs. 1971-73). E-mail: stokstad@ku.edu.

STOLAR, HENRY SAMUEL, lawyer; b. St. Louis, Oct. 29, 1939; s. William Allen and Pearl Minnette (Schukar) S.; m. Mary Goldstein, Aug. 26, 1962 (dec. Nov. 1987); children: Daniel Bruce, Susan Eileen; m. Suzanne Chapman Jones, June 2, 1989. AB, Washington U., 1960; JD, Harvard U., 1963. Bar: Mo. 1963, U.S. Supreme Ct. 1972. Assoc. then ptnr. Hocker, Goodwin & MacGreevy, St. Louis, 1963-69; v.p., sec., gen. counsel LaBarge Inc., 1969-74; from v.p., assoc. gen. counsel then sr. exec. v.p., gen. counsel, sec. Maritz Inc., 1974—. Sec., bd. dirs. New City Sch. Inc., St. Louis, 1968-75, Ctrl. West End. Assn., 1993-2000; mem. St. Louis Bd. Aldermen, 1969-73, Bd. Freeholders City and County St. Louis, 1987-88; bd. dirs. Forest Park Forever, Inc., 1991—. Mem. ABA, Mo. Bar, Bar Assn. Met. St. Louis, Triple A Club, Phi Beta Kappa. Home: 59 Kingsbury Pl Saint Louis MO 63112-1824 Office: Maritz Inc 1375 N Highway Dr Fenton MO 63099-0001

STOLL, JOHN ROBERT, lawyer, educator; b. Phila., Nov. 29, 1950; s. Wilhelm Friedrich and Marilyn Jane (Kremser) S.; m. Christine Larson, June 24, 1972; children: Andrew Michael, Michael Robert, Meredith Kirstin, Alison Courtney. BA magna cum laude, Haverford Coll., 1972; JD, Columbia U., 1975. Bar: Ind. 1975, U.S. Dist. Ct. (no. and so. dists.) Ind. 1975, U.S. Ct. Appeals (7th cir.) 1978, U.S. Dist. Ct. (no. dist.) Ill. 1980, (so. dist.) N.Y. 1993, Ill. 1981, N.Y. 1989. Atty. Barnes & Thornburg, South Bend, Ind., 1975-80, Mayer, Brown & Platt, Chgo., 1980—. Adj. prof. law Northwestern U., Chgo., 1985—, DePaul U., Chgo., 1987; lectr. in bus. St. Mary's Coll., Notre Dame, Ind., 1977-78. Contbr. articles to profl. jours. Mem. ABA, Ind. State Bar Assn., Am. Bankruptcy Inst., Phi Beta Kappa. Office: Mayer Brown & Platt 190 S La Salle St Ste 3100 Chicago IL 60603-3441

STOLL, ROBERT W. principal; Prin. Harrison (Ohio) Elem. Sch., 1989—. Recipient Elem. Sch. Recognition award U.S. Dept. Edn., 1989-90. Office: Harrison Elem Sch 600 Broadway Harrison OH 45030-1323

STOLL, STEVE M. state legislator; b. St. Louis, Apr. 3, 1947; m. Kathleen Woods; children: Emily, Laura, Amy, Andrew. Student, S.E. Mo. State U., 1965-67; BA, U. Mo., 1970, postgrad., 1979. Tchr., 1078-93; mem. Mo. Ho. of Reps. from 103d dist., Jefferson City, 1993-98, Mo. Senate from 22nd dist., Jefferson City, 1998—. Mem. Appropriations, Natural and Econ. Resources, Edn., Labor, Profl. Registration, Licensing and Budget Coms. Mo. Ho. of Reps. Councilman Ward II, Crystal City, Mo., 1983, 85, 87, 89, 91, Mayor Pro Tem, 1987-92. Mem. KC, Am. Legion. Democrat. Home: 716 Richard Dr Festus MO 63028-1077

STOLL, WILHELM, mathematics educator; b. Freiburg, Germany, Dec. 22, 1923; arrived in U.S., 1960; s. Heinrich and Doris (Eberle) S.; m. Marilyn Jane Kremser, June 11, 1955; children: Robert, Dieter, Elisabeth, Rebecca. Ph.D. in Math, U. Tübingen, Fed. Republic Germany, 1953, habilitation, 1954. Asst. U. Tübingen, 1953-59, dozent, 1954-60, ausserplanmässiger prof., 1960; vis. lectr. U. Pa., 1954-55; temp. mem. Inst. Advanced Study, Princeton, 1957-59; prof. math. U. Notre Dame, 1960-88, Vincent J. Duncan and Annamarie Micus Duncan prof. math., 1988-94, prof. emeritus, 1994—, chmn. dept., 1966-68, co-dir. Ctr. for Applied Math., 1992. Vis. prof. Stanford U., 1968-69, Tulane U., 1973, U. Sci. and Tech., Hefei, Anhui, People's Republic of China, summer, 1986; adviser Clark Sch., South Bend, Ind., 1963-68; Japan Soc. Promotion Sci. fellow, vis. prof. Kyoto U., summer 1983. Publs. in field. Fellow: AAAS. Achievements include research complex analysis several variables. Home: 54763 Merrifield Dr Mishawaka IN 46545-1519 Office: U Notre Dame Dept Math Notre Dame IN 46556

STOLZ, BENJAMIN ARMOND, foreign language educator; b. Lansing, Mich., Mar. 28, 1934; s. Armond John and Mabel May (Smith) S.; m. Mona Eleanor Seelig, June 16, 1962; children: Elizabeth Mona, John Benjamin. A.B., U. Mich., Ann Arbor, 1955; certificat, U. Libre de Bruxelles, Belgium, 1956; A.M., Harvard U., 1957, Ph.D., 1965. Mem. faculty U. Mich., 1964-2001, prof. Slavic langs. and lits., 1972-2001, chmn. dept., 1971-85, 89-91; prof. emeritus, 2001—. Cons. in field. Editor: Papers in Slavic Philology, 1977, Studies in Macedonian Language, Literature, and Culture, 1995; co-editor: Oral Literature and the Formula, 1976, Cross Currents, 1982-85, Language and Literary Theory, 1984, Mich. Slavic Publs., 1990—; co-editor, translator: (Konstantin Mihailovic): Memoirs of a Janissary, 1975; contbr. articles to profl. pubs. Served to lt. (j.g.) USNR, 1957-60. Recipient Orion E. Scott award humanities U. Mich., 1954, Fulbright scholar, 1955-56; Fgn. Area fellow Yugoslavia, 1963-64; Fulbright-Hays rsch. fellow Eng. and Yugoslavia, 1970-71; grantee Am. Coun. Learned Socs., 1968-70, 73, Internat. Rsch. and Exchs. Bd., 1985, 87, Woodrow Wilson Ctr., 1992. Mem. Am. Assn. Advancement Slavic Studies, Am. Assn. Tchrs. Slavic and East European Langs., Huron Valley Tennis Club, Phi Beta Kappa, Phi Kappa Phi, Delta Upsilon. Democrat. Home: 3423 Riverbend Dr Ann Arbor MI 48105 Office: Univ Mich 3040 MLB Ann Arbor MI 48109

STOLZER, LEO WILLIAM, bank executive; b. Kansas City, Mo., Oct. 14, 1934; s. Leo Joseph and Lennie Lucille (Hopp) S.; m. Eleanor Katherine Griffith, Aug. 17, 1957; children: Joan Ellen Stolzer Bolen, Mary Kevin Stolzer Giller. BS in Acctg., Kans. State U., 1957. Teller Union Nat. Bank & Trust Co., Manhattan, Kans., 1960-62, asst. cashier, 1962-63, asst. v.p., 1963-64, v.p., 1964-69, exec. v.p., 1969-72, pres., 1972-80, chmn., CEO, 1980-95; chmn., 1995—. Bd. dirs. Commerce Bankshares Inc., Commerce Bank-Manhattan; chmn., CEO Griffith Lumber Co., Cmty. Bancorporation of N.Mex., Inc. Trustee, past treas., past vice-chair Kans. State U. Found.; trustee Midwest Rsch. Inst.; chmn. Riley County Savs. Bond. Capt. USAF, 1957-60. Recipient Disting. Service award Manhattan Jr. C. of C., 1968, Kans. State U. Advancement award. Fellow Coll. Bus. Adminstrn. Alumni; mem. Am. Bankers Assn. (past treas., past exec. com., past bd. dirs.), Assn. U.S. Army (bd. dirs. Ft. Riley Ctl. Kans. chpt., past chair), Kans. U. Alumni Assn. (devel. com.), Newcomen Soc. in N.Am. (past Kans. chmn.), KC, Beta Theta Pi. Avocation: skiing. Office: Commerce Bank 727 Poyntz Ave Manhattan KS 66502-0118

STONE, ALAN, container company executive; b. Chgo., Feb. 5, 1928; s. Norman H. and Ida (Finkelstein) S.; children: Christie-Ann Stone Weiss, Joshua. B.S.E., U. Pa., 1951. Trainee, salesman Stone Container Corp., Chgo., 1951-53, dir. mktg. service, 1954-64, gen. mgr., regional mgr., 1964-72, sr. v.p. adminstrn., gen. mgr. energy div., 1972—, also dir., sr. v.p. purchasing and transp.; pres. North La. and Gulf R.R./Ctrl. La. and Gulf R.R., 1985-92, Atlanta St. Andrews and Bay Line R.R., 1992-94, Abbeville-Grimes R.R., 1992-94, Apache R.R., 1992-94. Bd. dirs., exec. com. Stone Container Corp., 1960—; cons. Chgo. Mfg.; pres. No. La. Gulf Railroad, 1985, Ctrl. La. Gulf Railroad, 1985. Pres. Jewish Vocat. Svc., Chgo., 1975-77; v.p. Sinai Temple, Chgo., 1977-84; bd. dirs. Jewish Fedn. Chgo.; vice chmn. Roycemore Sch., Evanston, Ill., 1982-87; pres. Emergency Fund for Needy People, 1993—; trustee Brewster Acad., Wolfeboro, N.H.; vol. exec. for overseas needs Citizen's Democracy Corps; vol. cons. for non-profit agys., schs. and librs. Exec. Svc. Corps., 1992—; bd. dirs. Gastrointestinal Rsch. Found., Intermodal Transp. Inst., U. Denver, 1997—. Mem. Standard Club, Tavern Club, Bryn Mawr Country Club,

Tamarisk Country Club, Long Boat Key Club, Beta Alpha Psi, Phi Eta Sigma, Zeta Beta Tau. Avocations: golf, sports, reading. Office: Stone Container Corp 645 N Michigan Ave Ste 800 Chicago IL 60611-3775 E-mail: stonealan@msn.com.

STONE, ALAN JAY, retired college administrator; b. Ft. Dodge, Iowa, Oct. 15, 1942; s. Hubert H. and Bernice A. (Tilton) S.; m. Jonieta J. Smith; 1 child, Kirsten K. Stone Morlock. BA, Morningside Coll., 1964; MA, U. Iowa, 1966; MTh, U. Chgo., 1968, DMin, 1970; PhD (hon.), Kyonggi U., Korea, 1985; LLD, Stillman Coll., 1991, Sogong U., Korea, 1992, Alma Coll., 2001; HHD, Morningside Coll., 2001. Admissions counselor Morningside Coll., Sioux City, Iowa, 1964-66; dir. admissions, asso. prof. history George Williams Coll., Downers Grove, Ill., 1969-73; v.p. coll. relations Hood Coll., Frederick, Md., 1973-75; v.p. devel. and fin. affairs W.Va. Wesleyan Coll., Buckhannon, 1975-77; dir. devel. U. Maine, 1977-78; pres. Aurora (Ill.) U., 1978-88, Alma (Mich.) Coll., 1988-2000; pres., CEO Alzheimer's Assn., Chgo., 2001—02; ret., 2002. Home: 28897 N 94th Pl Scottsdale AZ 85262 E-mail: stone5613@earthlink.net.

STONE, BERNARD LEONARD, vice mayor, alderman, lawyer; b. Chgo., Nov. 24, 1927; s. Sidney and Rebecca (Spinka) S.; m. Lois D. Falk, Aug. 28, 1949 (dec.); children: Robin, Jay, Ilana, Lori. JD, John Marshall Law Sch., 1952. Alderman, 50th Ward City Coun. City of Chgo., 1973—; vice mayor City of Chgo., 1998—. Chmn. com. on bldgs., City of Chgo. Del. North Town Community Coun., 1963—, bd. dirs.; zoning chmn. Hood Ave. Civic Improvement Assn., 1954-58; dist. leader Am. Cancer Soc., 1959; bd. dirs. Congregation Ezras Israel, 1958—, Bernard Horwich Jewish Community Ctr., 1974-78, Assoc. Talmud Torahs, 1983—, Chgo. Assn. Retarded Citizens, 1979—; bd. govs. Bonds for Israel, 1972—; past campaign chmn. govt. agys. div. Jewish United Fund, 1978-79; commr. N.E. Ill. Planning Commn., 1977-83; mem. Cook County Commn. on Criminal Justice, 1977-82. Mem. ABA, Ill. Bar Assn., Decalogue Soc. of Lawyers, Am. Legion, Devon-NT Bus. and Profl. Assn., B'nai B'rith (1st pres. Jacob M Arvey Pub. Svc. Lodge), West Rogers Park Lodge, Jewish War Vets. (past state judge adv., post comdr.). Office: City of Chgo City Hall 121 N La Salle St Rm 203 Chicago IL 60602-1204

STONE, GEOFFREY RICHARD, law educator, lawyer; b. Nov. 20, 1946; s. Robert R. and Shirley (Weliky) S.; m. Nancy Spector, Oct. 8, 1977; children: Julie, Mollie. BS, U. Pa., 1968; JD, U. Chgo., 1971. Bar: N.Y. 1972. Law clk. to Hon. J.S. Kelly Wright U.S. Ct. Appeals (D.C. cir.), 1971-72; law clk. to Hon. William J. Brennan, Jr. U.S. Supreme Ct., 1972-73; asst. prof. U. Chgo., 1973-77, assoc. prof., 1977-79, prof., 1979-84, Harry Kalven Jr. disting. svc. prof., 1984—, dean Law Sch., 1987-93, provost, 1994—2002. Author: Constitutional Law, 1986, 4th edit., 2001, The Bill of Rights in the Modern State, 1992, The First Amendment, 1999, Eternally Vigilant: Free Speech in the Modern Era, 2001; editor The Supreme Ct. Rev., 1991—; contbr. articles to profl. jours. Bd. dirs. Ill. divsn. ACLU, 1978-84; bd. advisors Pub. Svc. Challenge, 1989; bd. govs. Argonne Nat. Lab., 1994—. Fellow AAAS; mem. Chgo. Coun. Lawyers (bd. govs. 1976-77), Assn. Am. Law Schs. (exec. com. 1990-93), Legal Aid Soc. (bd. dirs. 1988), Order of Coif. Office: U Chgo 1111 E 60th St Chicago IL 60637-5418

STONE, HARRY H. business executive; b. Cleve., May 21, 1917; s. Jacob and Jennie (Kantor) Sapirstein; m. Lucile Tabak, Aug. 10, 1960; children: Phillip, Allan, Laurie (Mrs. Parker), James Rose, Douglas Rose. Student, Cleve. Coll., 1935-36. With Am. Greetings Corp., Cleve., 1936—, v.p., 1944-58, exec. v.p., 1958-69, vice chmn. bd., chmn. finance com., chmn audit com., 1969-78, now dir., 1944—. Mem. Ofcl. U.S. Mission to India and Nepal, 1965; cons. U.S. Dept. Commerce, U.S. Dept. State; adviser U.S. del. 24th session UN Econ. Commn. for Asia and Far East, Canberra, Australia, 1968; cons. Nat. Endowment for Arts, Nat. Council on Arts. Treas. Criminal Justice Co-ordinating Council., 1968-82; trustee emeritus Brandeis U., also univ. fellow. Mem. Rotary (hon. pres.). Office: The Courtland Group Inc 1621 Euclid Ave Ste 1600 Cleveland OH 44115-2195

STONE, HERBERT MARSHALL, architect; b. N.Y.C., July 12, 1936; s. Irving and Rose (Gelb) S.; m. Linda Ann Baskind, May 30, 1960; children: Ian Howard, Matthew Lloyd. BArch, Pratt Inst., N.Y.C., 1958, postgrad., 1958-59. Registered architect, N.Y., Iowa, Kans., Ill., Wis., Minn. Designer Henry Dreyfuss Indsl. Design, N.Y.C., 1960-63; architect Max O. Urbahn Architect, 1963-66; project architect Brown Healey Bock, P.C., Cedar Rapids, Iowa, 1966-73; ptnr. Brown Healey Stone & Sauer, 1973—, pres., 1994—. Guest lectr. U.S. Inst. Theatre Tech., Seattle, 1978; speaker on design of pub. librs. ALA Nat. Conv., Miami, Fla., 1994. Prin. works include Strayer-Wood Theatre, 1978, KUNI radio sta. U. No. Iowa, 1978, Cedar Rapids Pub. Libr., 1984, Greenwood Terr. Sr. Citizen Housing, 1986, Iowa State Hist. Mus., 1988, Nat. Hot Air Balloon Mus., 1988 (Spectrum Ceramic Tile Grand award 1989), Student Ctr. Grinnell Coll., 1992, Hall of Pride, Iowa H.S. Athletic Assn., 1995. Pres. Cedar Rapids Trust for Hist. Preservation, 1981—; bd. dirs. Art in Pub. Places Com., Cedar Rapids, 1988, Cedar Rapids/Marion Arts Coun., 1988, Jane Boyd Community House, Cedar Rapids, 1988; mem. Cedar Rapids Hist. Commn. Mem. AIA, Am. Mus. Assn. Avocations: bicycling, skiing, reading, ceramics. Home: 3411 Riverside Dr NE Cedar Rapids IA 52411-7405 Office: Brown Healey Stone & Sauer PC 800 1st Ave NE Cedar Rapids IA 52402-5002

STONE, JACK, religious organization administrator; Sec., hdqs. ops. officer Ch. of the Nazarene, Kansas City, Mo., 1991—. Office: Ch of Nazarene 6401 The Paseo Kansas City MO 64131-1213

STONE, JAMES ROBERT, surgeon; b. Greeley, Colo., Jan. 8, 1948; s. Anthony Joseph and Dolores Concetta (Pietrafeso) S.; m. Kaye Janet Friedman, May 16, 1970; children: Jeffrey, Marisa. BA, U. Colo., 1970; MD, U. Guadalajara, Mex., 1976; MBA, Madison U., 2002. Diplomate Am. Bd. Surgery, Am. Bd. Surg. Critical Care, Am. Bd. Forensic Medicine. Intern Md. Gen. Hosp., Balt., 1978-79; resident in surgery St. Joseph Hosp., Denver, 1979-83; pvt. practice Grand Junction, 1983-87; staff surgeon, dir. critical care Va. Med. Ctr., 1987-88; dir. trauma surgery and critical care, chief surgery St. Francis Hosp., Colorado Springs, Colo., 1988-91; pvt. practice Kodiak, Alaska, 1991-92; with Summit Surg. Assocs., 1992-96; asst. dir. trauma Tristate Trauma System, Erie, Pa., 1996-99; med. dir. LifeStar Aeromed, 1997-99; dir. trauma, sr. assoc. physician, med. dir. emergency svcs. ISJ Mayo Health, 1999—2001; clin. prof. surgery U. Minn. Med. Sch., Mpls., 1999—2001, dir. trauma/EMS med. dir., sr. assoc.; gen., thoracic and vasc. surgery Caylor-Nickel Clinic, 2001—. Asst. clin. prof. surgery U. Colo. Health Sci. Ctr., Denver, 1984-96; pres. Stone Aire Cons., Grand Junction, 1988—; owner, operator Jjnka Ranch, Flourissant, Colo.; spl. advisor CAP, wing med. officer, 1992-96; advisor med. com. unit, 1990-92; advisor Colo. Ground Team Search and Rescue, 1994-96. Contbr. articles to profl. jours.; inventor in field. Bd. dirs. Mesa County Cancer Soc., 1988-89, Colo. Trauma Inst., 1988-91. Colo. Speaks out on Health grantee, 1988; recipient Bronze medal of Valor Civil Air Patrol. Fellow Denver Acad. Surgery, Southwestern Surg. Congress, Am. Coll. Chest Physicians, Am. Coll. Surgeons (trauma com. Colo. chpt.), Am. Coll. Critical Care; mem. Am. Coll. Physician Execs., Soc. Critical Care (task force 1988—), Assn. Air Med. Physicians. Roman Catholic. Avocations: horse breeding, hunting, fishing. Office: Caylor-Nickel Clinic 1 Caylor Nickel Sq Bluffton IN 46714

STONE, JOHN MCWILLIAMS, JR. electronics executive; b. Chgo., Nov. 4, 1927; s. J. McWilliams and Marion (Jones) S.; m. Cheryl Johansen Cullison, Dec. 18, 1976; children: Jean Stone, Lee Stone Nelson, John III (dec.), Michael (dec.), Shannon Bergman, Tamra Stone. BA, Princeton U., 1950. Salesman A.B. Dick Co., Milw., 1950-51; prodn. supr. Dukane Corp., St. Charles, Ill., 1951-56, exec. v.p., 1956-62, pres., 1962-70, pres., chmn. bd., 1970—, chmn. bd., pres., CEO, 1991-97. Trustee The Elgin (Ill.) Acad. (recipient Elgin medal 1984, emeritus 1985—), Phillips Exeter (N.H.) Coun., 1985—, Three Rivers Coun. Boy Scouts Am., St. Charles; mem. Delnor Cmty. Hosp. Men's Found., St. Charles. Named Exec. of Yr. Valley chpt. Profl. Secs. Internat., Aurora, 1981. Mem. Commonwealth Club of Chgo., Econ. Club of Chgo., Princeton Club of Chgo., Execs. Club of Chgo., Dunham Woods Riding Club (pres. 1967-68, 78-79, 89-90). Republican. Episcopalian. Avocation: tennis. Home: PO Box 755 Wayne IL 60184-0755 Office: Dukane Corp 2900 Dukane Dr Saint Charles IL 60174-3395

STONE, JOHN TIMOTHY, JR. writer; b. Denver, July 13, 1933; s. John Timothy and Marie Elizabeth (Briggs) S.; m. Judith Bosworth Stone, June 22, 1955; children: John Timothy III, George Williams. Student, Amherst Coll., 1951-52, U. Mex., 1952; BA, postgrad., U. Miami, 1955, U. Colo., 1959-60. Sales mgr. Atlas Tag, Chgo., 1955-57; br. mgr. Household Fin. Corp., 1958-62; pres. Janeff Credit Corp., Madison, Wis., 1962-72, Recreation Internat., Mpls., 1972-74, Continental Royal Svcs., N.Y.C., 1973-74; dir. devel. The Heartlands Group/Tryon Mint, Toronto, Ont., Can., 1987-89; spl. cons. Creative Resources Internat., Madison, 1988-90, Pubs. Adv. Group, 1990—; spl. cons. art and antiques Treasure Hunt Assocs., 1994—. Bd. dirs. Madison Credit Bur., Wis. Lenders' Exch. Author: Mark, 1973, Going for Broke, 1976, The Minnesota Connection, 1978, Debby Boone So Far, 1980, (with John Dallas McPherson) He Calls Himself "An Ordinary Man", 1981, Satiacum, The Chief Who's Winning Back the West, 1981, Runaways, 1983, (with Robert E. Gard) Where the Green Bird Flies, 1984, The Insiders Guide to Buying Art, 1993, Anyone's Treasure Hunt, 1995; syndicated columnist The Great American Treasure Hunt, 1983-87. Served with CIC, U.S. Army, 1957-59. Mem. Minarani Club, African First Shotters Club, Sigma Alpha Epsilon. Presbyterian. Office: Pubs Adv Group 1009 Starlight Dr Madison WI 53711-2724

STONE, RANDOLPH NOEL, law educator; b. Milw., Nov. 26, 1946; s. Fisher and Lee Della Stone; m. Cheryl M. Bradley; children: Sokoni, Rahman, Marisa, Lee Sukari. BA, U. Wis., Milw., 1972; JD, Madison, 1975. Bar: D.C., 1975, Wis. 1975, Ill. 1977. Staff atty. Criminal Def. Consortium of Cook County, Chgo., 1976-78; clin. fellow U. Chgo. Law Sch., 1977-80; ptnr. Stone & clark, Chgo., 1980-83; staff atty., dep. dir. Pub. Defender Svc. for D.C., Washington, 1983-88; pub. defender Cook County Pub. Defender's Office, Chgo., 1988-91; lectr. U. Chgo. Law Sch., 1990, clin. prof. law, dir. Mandel Legal Aid Clinic, 1991—. Adj. prof. Ill. Inst. Tech. Chgo.-Kent Coll. Law Sch., 1991, bd. overseers, 1990; lectr. law Harvard U., 1991—; mem. Ill. Bd. Admissions to the Bar, 1994—; bd. dirs. The Sentencing Project, 1986—; instr. trial advocacy workshop Harvard Law Sch., 1985-89. Adv. bd. Neighborhood Defender Svc. (Harlem), N.Y.C. Reginald Heber Smith fellow Neighborhood Legal Svcs. Program, Washington, 1975-76. Mem. ABA (sect. criminal justice coun. 1989-95, chair 1993, commn. domestic violence 1994-97), Ill. State Bar Assn. (sect. criminal justice coun. 1989-92), Chgo. Bar Assn. (bd. dirs. 1990-92), Nat. Legal Aid and Defender Assn. (def. com. 1988-96). Office: U Chgo Law Sch Mandel Legal Aid Clinic 6020 S University Ave Chicago IL 60637-2704

STONE, ROGER WARREN, container company executive; b. Chgo., Feb. 16, 1935; s. Marvin N. and Anita (Masover) S.; m. Susan Kesert, Dec. 24, 1955; children: Karen, Lauren, Jennifer. BS in Econs., U. Pa., 1957. With Stone Container Corp., Chgo., 1957-98, dir., 1968-77, v.p., gen. mgr. container divsn., 1970-75, pres., COO, 1975-79, pres., CEO, 1979-83, chmn. bd., CEO, 1983-98; pres., CEO Smurfit-Stone Container Corp., 1998-99; chmn., CEO Box USA, Northbrook, Ill., 1999—. Bd. dirs. McDonald's Corp. Past trustee Glenwood (Ill.) Sch. for Boys; trustee Chgo. Symphony Orch. Assn.; fellow Lake Forest (Ill.) Acad.; mem. bd. overseers Wharton Sch. Bus., U. Pa.; mem. adv. coun. Econ. Devel.; bd. dirs. Lyric Opera of Chgo. Named Best or Top CEO in firm's industry Wall Street Transcript, 1981-86; recipient Top CEO award in Forest and Paper Specialty Products Industry, Fin. World Mag., 1984, Bronze award in Paper and Packaging Category, 1996. Mem. Am. Forest and Paper Assn. (chmn. bd. 1985-86, bd. dirs), Chief Execs. Orgn., Corrugated Industry Devel. Corp. (past pres.), Inst. Paper Sci. and Tech. (former trustee), The Chgo. Com., Mid-Am. Com., Chgo. Coun. Fgn. Rels., Standard Club, Tavern Club, Comml. Club, Econ. Club, Lake Shore Country Club. Republican. Office: Box USA 2100 Sanders Rd Ste 200 Northbrook IL 60062

STONE, STEVEN MICHAEL, sports announcer, former baseball player; b. Cleve., July 14, 1947; BS in Edn., Kent State U. Baseball player San Francisco Giants, 1971-72, Chgo. Cubs, 1974-76, Chgo. White Sox, 1977-78, Balt. Orioles, 1979-82; baseball announcer WGN Continental Broadcasting Co., Chgo., 1982—; owner restaurant Scottsdale, Ariz. Recipient Cy Young award Am. League, 1980 Achievements include being a mem. Am. League All-Star Team, 1980. Office: WGN TV 2501 W Bradley Pl Chicago IL 60618-4718

STONE, SUSAN A. lawyer; BA summa cum laude, Yale U., 1983; JD cum laude, Harvard U., 1987. Bar: Calif. 1987, U.S. Dist. Ct. (no. dist.) Calif. 1987, U.S. Ct. Appeals (9th cir.) 1987, U.S. Dist. Ct. (ctrl. dist.) Calif. 1988, Ill. 1990, U.S. Dist. Ct. (no. dist.) Ill. 1990, U.S. Ct. Appeals (7th cir.) 1990. Asst. U.S. atty. U.S. Dept. Justice, L.A.; law clk. to Judge William J. Orrick, U.S. Dist. Ct. for No. Dist. Calif.; ptnr. Sidley & Austin, Chgo. Former adj. prof. trial practice DePaul U. Coll. Law, Chgo. Named one of Top Young Litigators Under 40, Ill. Legal Times. Mem. Ill. Bar Assn., Calif. State Bar, Phi Beta Kappa. Office: Sidley & Austin 1 S First National Plz Chicago IL 60603-2000 Fax: 312-853-7036. E-mail: sstone@sidley.com.

STONEMAN, WILLIAM, III, physician, educator; b. Kansas City, Mo., Sept. 8, 1927; s. William and Helen Louise (Bloom) S.; m. Elizabeth Johanna Wilson, May 19, 1951; children: William Laurence, Sidney Camdon (dec.), Cecily Anne Erker, Elizabeth Wilson, John Spalding. Student, Rockhurst Coll., 1944-46; B.S., St. Louis U., 1948, M.D., 1952. Diplomate: Am. Bd. Surgery, Am. Bd. Plastic Surgery. Intern Kansas City Gen. Hosp., 1952-53; resident in surgery St. Louis U., 1953-57, resident in plastic surgery, 1957-59, mem. faculty, 1959—, assoc. prof. surgery, assoc. prof. community medicine, 1975-84, prof. surgery, community medicine, 1984-94, prof. surgery, community medicine emeritus, 1994, assoc. dean Sch. Medicine, 1973-76; exec. assoc. dean St. Louis U. (Sch. Medicine), 1976-82, dean, 1982-95, dean emeritus, 1995—, assoc. v.p. med. ctr., 1983-95. Mem. adj. faculty Washington U. Sch. Medicine, St. Louis, 1968-74; chief exec. officer Bi-State Regional Med. Program, 1968-74; bd. dirs. St. Louis Office Mental Retardation/Developmentally Disabled Resources, 1980-82, Combined Health Appeal of Mo., 1990-94. Editor: Parameters, 1976-94 ; contbr. articles on plastic surgery, health care delivery planning to profl. jours. Served with AUS, 1946-47. Fellow ACS; mem. AMA (chmn. sect. on med. schs. 1987-88, sect. alt. del. 1989-91, del. 1992-94), Mo. Med. Assn., Mem. St. Louis Met. Med. Soc., St. Louis Surg. Soc., Am. Soc. Plastic and Reconstructive Surgeons, Midwestern Assn. Plastic Surgeons. [f[]oman Catholic. Clubs: University. Office: St Louis U Sch Medicine 1316 Carr Lane Ave Saint Louis MO 63104-1011 E-mail: stoneman@slu.edu.

STONER, GARY DAVID, cancer researcher; b. Bozeman, Mont., Oct. 25, 1942; married; 2 children. BS, Mont. State U., 1964; MS, U. Mich., 1968, PhD in Microbiol., 1970. Asst. rsch. scientist U. Calif., San Diego, 1970-72, assoc. rsch. scientist, 1972-75; cancer expert Nat. Cancer Inst., 1976-79; assoc. prof. pathology Med. Coll. Ohio, 1979-83; prof. pathology, 1983-92; prof. preventive medicine and pathology Ohio State U., Columbus, 1992—, assoc. dir. Ctr. for Molecular and Environ. Health, 1993—, assoc. dir. basic rsch. Comp Cancer Ctr, 1994—, prof., chmn. divsn. environ. health scis. Sch. Pub. Health, 1995—. Cons. Nat. Heart Lung & Blood Inst., 1974—, EPA, 1979—, Nat. Cancer Inst., 1979—, Nat. Toxicol. Program, 1981—; lectr. W. Alton Jones Cell Sci. Ctr., 1978—; mem. study sect. NIH, 1980-88, Am. Cancer Soc., Ohio, 1982—, Am. Cancer Soc., Nat., 1995—. Grantee Nat. Cancer Inst., EPA, U.S. Army R & D Command. Mem. AAAS, Soc. Toxicology, Am. Assn. Cancer Rsch., Am. Assn. Pathologists, Am. Soc. Cell Biology, Internat. Soc. Cancer Chrmopre. Achievements include research in carcinogenesis in human and animal model respiratory and esophagal tissues, carcinogen metabolism, mutagenesis, in vitro transformation of epithelial cells chemoprevention. Office: Ohio State U Sch Pub Health 1148 CHRI 300 W 10th Ave Columbus OH 43210-1240

STOOKEY, GEORGE KENNETH, research institute administrator, dental educator; b. Waterloo, Ind., Nov. 6, 1935; s. Emra Gladison and Mary Catherine (Anglin) S.; m. Nola Jean Meek, Jan. 15, 1955; children: Lynda, Lisa, Laura, Kenneth. A.B. in Chemistry, Ind. U., 1957, M.S.D., 1962, Ph.D. in Preventive Dentistry, 1971. Asst. dir. Preventive Dentistry Research Inst., U. Ind., Indpls., 1968-70; assoc. dir. Oral Health Research Inst., U. Ind., 1974-81, 99—, dir., 1981-99; assoc. prof. preventive dentistry Ind. U. Sch. Dentistry, 1973-78, prof., 1978-98, disting. prof., 1998—, assoc. dean rsch., 1987-97, 00-01, acting dean, 1996, assoc. dean acad. affairs, 1997-98, exec. assoc. dean, 1998-2000. Cons. USAF, San Antonio, 1973—, ADA, Chgo., 1972—, Nat. Inst. Dental Rsch., Bethesda, Md., 1978-82, 91-95. Author: (with others) Introduction to Oral Biology and Preventive Dentistry, 1971, Preventive Dentistry for the Dental Assistant and Dental Hygienist, 1977, Preventive Dentistry in Action, 1972ä 8ä (Meritorious award 1973); contbr. more than 245 articles to profl. jours. Mem. Internat. Assn. for Dental Research, European Orgn. Caries Research, Am. Assn. Lab. Animal Sci. Republican. Office: Oral Health Research Inst 719 Indiana Ave Indianapolis IN 46202-6100 E-mail: gstookey@iupui.edu.

STOOKSBURY, WALTER ELBERT, insurance company executive; b. Harriman, Tenn., June 19, 1940; s. Maurice Claude and Thelma Marie (Dyer) S.; m. Mary Evelyn Farmer, Dec. 21, 1964; children: Kevin, Andrew. BS, U. Tenn., 1962. Tchr. Anderson County Schs., Clinton, Tenn., 1963-67; agt. Horace Mann Ins. Co., Springfield, Ill., 1967-68, agy. mgr., 1968-70, zone v.p., 1970-77, v.p. casualty div., 1977-92, sr. v.p. casualty div., 1992—, exec. v.p. property & casualty divsn., 1992—, also bd. dirs. Bd. dirs. Allegiance Ins. Co., Allegiance Life Ins. Co., Assn. and Consumer Mktg. Svc. Corp., Educators Life Ins. Co. Am., Horace Mann Svc. Corp., Sr. Mktg. Ins. Svc. Corp., Tchrs. Ins. Co. Mem. Am. Assn. Ins. Svcs. (bd. dirs., exec. dir. 1980—), Sangamo Club. Methodist. Avocations: golf, antique cars. Home: 3210 Victoria Dr Springfield IL 62704-1045 Office: Horace Mann Educators Corp 1 Horace Mann Plz Springfield IL 62715

STORANDT, MARTHA, psychologist; b. Little Rock, June 2, 1938; d. Farris and Floy (Montgomery) Mobbs; m. Duane Storandt, Dec. 15, 1962; 1 child, Eric AB, Washington U., St. Louis, 1960, PhD, 1966. Lic. psychologist, Mo. Staff psychologist VA, Jefferson Barracks, Mo., 1967-68; asst. prof. to prof. Washington U., St. Louis, 1968—. Mem. nat. adv. council on aging Nat. Inst. on Aging, 1984-87; editor-in-chief Jour. Gerontology, 1981-86 Author: Counseling and Therapy with Older Adults, 1983; co-author: Memory, Related Functions and Age, 1974; co-editor: The Clinical Psychology of Aging, 1978, The Adult Years: Continuity and Change, 1989, Neuropsychological Assessment of Dementia and Depression in Older Adults: A Clinician's Guide, 1994. Recipient Disting. Service award Mo. Assn. Homes for the Aging, 1984. Fellow APA (pres. divsn. 20 1979-80, council rep. 1983-84, 86-88, Disting. Sci. Contbn. award divsn. adult devel. and aging 1988, Master Mentor award divsn. adult devel. and aging 2000), Gerontol. Soc. Am. Office: Washington U Dept Psychology Saint Louis MO 63130

STORB, URSULA BEATE, molecular genetics and cell biology educator; b. Stuttgart, Germany; came to U.S., 1966; d. Walter M. Stemmer and Marianne M. (Kämmerer) Nowara. MD, U. Freiburg, Germany, 1960. Asst. prof. dept. microbiology U. Wash., Seattle, 1971-75, assoc. prof., 1975-81, prof., 1981-86, head. div. immunology, 1980-86; prof. dept. molecular genetics and cell biology U. Chgo., 1986—. Mem. editl. bd. Immunity, Current Opinion in Immunology, Internat. Immunology, Immunol. Revs.; contbr. articles to sci. jours. Grantee NIH, NSF, Am. Cancer Soc., 1973—. Fellow Am. Acad. Arts and Scis.; mem. Assn. Women in Sci., Am. Assn. Immunologists. Office: U Chgo 920 E 58th St Chicago IL 60637-5415 E-mail: stor@midway.uchicago.edu.

STORK, DONALD ARTHUR, advertising executive; b. Walsh, Ill., June 17, 1939; s. Arthur William and Katherine Frances (Young) S.; m. Joanna Gentry, June 9, 1962; 1 child, Brian Wesley. BS, So. Ill. U., 1961; postgrad., St. Louis U., 1968-69. With Naegele Outdoor Advtsg., Mpls. and St. Louis, 1961-63; acct. exec. Richard C. Lynch Advtsg., 1963-64; media exec. Gardner Advtsg. co., 1964-69; v.p. mktg. Advanswers Media/Programming, 1975-79; pres. Advanswers divsn. Wells/BDDP, N.Y.C., 1979-98; pres. Advanswers unit Omnicom, St. Louis, 1998—2002, pres. PHD unit, 2002—. Bd. dirs. Trailblazers, Inc.; corp. devel. St. Louis Art Mus., 1999. Pres. Signal Hill Sch. Assn. Parents Tchrs. Capt. Mo. Air N.G., 1961-67. Recipient Journalism Alumnus of Yr. award So. Ill. U., Alumni Achievement award. Mem. St. Louis Advtsg. Club, Mensa, Mo. Athletic Club, St. Clair Country Club (bd. dirs. 2001), Alpha Delta Sigma (Aid to Advtg. Edn. award). Home: 27 Symonds Dr Belleville IL 62223-1905 Office: Advanswers PHD 10 S Broadway Saint Louis MO 63102-1712 E-mail: dstork@advanswersPHD.com.

STORY, KENDRA, wholesale distribution executive; CFO Am. Bldrs. & Contrs. Supply Co., Inc., Beloit, Wis. Office: Am Bldrs & Contrs Supply One ABC Pkwy Beloit WI 53511 Office Fax: (608) 362-6215.

STOUT, GLENN EMANUEL, retired science administrator; b. Fostoria, Ohio, Mar. 23, 1920; AB, Findlay U., 1942, DSc, 1973. Sci. coord. NSF, 1969-71; asst. to chief Ill. State Water Survey, Champaign, 1971-74; prof. Inst. Environ. Studies, Urbana, Ill., 1973-94, dir. task force, 1975-79; dir. Water Resources Ctr. U. Ill., 1973-94; rsch. coord. Ill.-Ind. Sea Grant Program, 1987-94; emeritus, 1994—. Mem. Ill. Gov.'s Task Force on State Water Plan, 1980-94; bd. dirs. Univ. Coun. Water Resources, 1983-86, chmn. internat. affairs, 1989-92; mem. nomination com. for Stockholm Water Prize, 1994-96. Contbr. articles to profl. jours. Bd. govs. World Water Coun., 1996-98. Mem. Am. Water Resources Assn., Internat. Water Resources Assn. (sec. gen. 1985-91, v.p. 1992-94, exec. dir. 1984-95, pres. 1995-97), Am. Meteorol. Soc., Am. Geophys. Union, N.Am. Lake Mgmt. Soc., Ill. Lake Mgmt. Assn. (bd. dirs. 1985-88), Am. Water Works Assn., Kiwanis (pres. local club 1979-80, lt. gov. 1982-83), Sigma Xi (pres. U. Ill. chpt. 1985-86). Home: 920 W John St Champaign IL 61821-3907 Office: Intl Water Resource Assn 1101 W Peabody Dr Urbana IL 61801-4723 E-mail: g-stout@uiuc.edu.

STOUT, MAYE ALMA, educator; b. Reliance, S.D., Mar. 3, 1920; d. Jesse Wilbur and Susie Maude (Fletcher) Moulton; m. Dennis William Stout, Jan. 6, 1943; children: Perry Wilbur, David Jay. BA, Dakota Wesleyan U., Mitchell, S.D., 1969. Tchr. Rural Lyman County Sch., Iona/Oacoma, S.D., 1939-42, Vivian (S.D.) Pub. Sch., 1942, Rural Lyman County Sch., Reliance, S.D., 1944-45, Reliance Cons. Dist., 1945-46,

49-51, Ft. Pierre (S.D.) Ind. Sch. Dist., 1954-67, Kadoka (S.D.) Ind. Sch., 1967-82; ret. Asst. editor: Jackson/Washabaugh County History 2, 1989; contbr. articles to publications. Pres. Kadoka Community Betterment Assn., 1987. Mem. Am. Legion Aux. (dist. pres. 1985-89, chmn. com. Dept. Fgn. Rels. 1990-91, dept. chmn. constitution and by-laws com. 1992-93). Republican. Methodist. Avocations: reading, crocheting, travel. Address: PO Box 231 Kadoka SD 57543-0231 E-mail: mastout@gwtc.net.

STOVALL, CARLA JO, state attorney general; b. Hardner, Kans., Mar. 18, 1957; d. Carl E. and Juanita Joe (Ford) Stovall. BA, Pittsburg (Kans.) State U., 1979; JD, U. Kans., 1982, MPA , 1993. Bar: Kans. 1982, U.S. Dist. Ct. Kans. 1982. Pvt. practice, Pitts., 1982—85; atty. Crawford County, 1984—88; gov. Kans. Parole Bd., Topeka, 1988—94; atty. gen. State of Kans., 1995—. Lectr. law Pittsburg State U. , 1982—84; pres. Gilston Internat. Mktg., Inc., 1988—. Mem. bd. govs. U. Kans. Sch. Law; Nat. Ctr. Missing and Exploited Children; Am. Legacy Found.; Nat. Crime Prevention Coun.; Coun. State Govts.; mem. bd. govs. Kans. Children's Cabinet; pres. NAAG, 2001—02, chmn. exec. com. midwest region, sexually violent predator com., 1995—96; Bd. dirs., sec. Pittsburg Family YMCA, 1983—88. Named Outstanding Atty. Gen., Nat. Assn. Attys. Gen., 2001, Topeka Fraternal Order of Police's Amb. to Law Enforcement; recipient Champion award, Campaign Tobacco Free Kids, 2002, Adam Walsh Children's Fund Rainbow award, Nat. Ctr. Missing and Exploited Children, 2001, Kelley-Wyman award, Nat. Assn. Attys. Gen., 2001, Person of the Yr., Kans. Peace Officer Assn.'s Law Enforcement, Morton Baud Allied Profl. award, Nat. Orgn. Victim Assistance, Father Ken Czillinger award, Nat. Parents Murdered Children, Disting. Svc. to Kans. Children award, Kans. Children's Svc. League, Woman of Achievement award, Miss Kans. Pageant. Mem.: NAAG (pres. 2001—02), AAUW (bd. dirs. 1983—87), ABA, Bus. and Profl. Women Assn. (Young Careerist award 1984), Nat. Coll. Dist. Attys., Kans. County and Dist. Attys. Assn., Crawford County Bar Assn. (sec. 1984—85, v.p. 1985—86, pres. 1986—87), Kans. Bar Assn., Kans. Assn. Commerce and Industry (Leadership Kans. award 1983), Pittsburg Area C. of C. (bd. dirs. 1983—85, Leadership Pitts. award 1984), Pittsburg State U. Alumni Assn. 1983—88. Republican. Methodist. Avocations: travel, photography, tennis. Home: 3561 SW Mission Ave Topeka KS 66614-3637 Office: Atty Gen Office Meml Hall 120 SW 10th Ave Fl 2 Topeka KS 66612-1597*

STOWELL, JOSEPH, III, academic administrator; Pres. Moody Bible Inst., Chgo., 1987—. Office: Moody Bible Inst 820 N La Salle Dr Chicago IL 60610-3263 also: Sta WKES-FM PO Box 8888 Saint Petersburg FL 33738-8888

STOWERS, JAMES EVANS, JR. investment company executive; b. Kansas City, Mo., Jan. 10, 1924; s. James Evans Sr. and Laura (Smith) S.; m. Virginia Ann Glasscock, Feb. 4, 1954; children: Pamela, Kathleen, James Evans III, Linda. A.B., U. Mo., 1946, B.S. in Medicine, 1947. Chmn. bd. Am. Century Investment Mgmt. Inc., Am. Century Cos., Inc.; Am. Century Group of Mutual Funds, Kansas City, 1958—. Author: Why Waste Your Money on Life Insurance, 1967, Principles of Financial Consulting, 1971, Yes, You Can....achieve financial independence, 1992. Co-founder, chmn. Stowers Inst. for Med. Rsch., Kansas City, 1995—. Capt. USAAF, 1943-45; with USAFR, 1945-57. Mem. Kansas City C. of C., Sigma Chi Republican. Office: Am Century Svcs 4500 Main St Kansas City MO 64111-1816

STOWERS, JAMES W., III, data processing company executive; b. 1958; With Twentieth Century Svcs., Kansas City, Mo., 1979—, pres.; CEO Am. Century Cos. Office: Am Century Investments 4500 Main St Kansas City MO 64111-1816

STRAIN, JAMES ARTHUR, lawyer; b. Alexandria, La., Oct. 11, 1944; s. William Joseph and Louise (Moore) S.; m. Cheryl Sue Williamson, Aug. 19, 1967; children: William Joseph, Gordon Richard, Elizabeth Parks. BS in Econs., Ind. U., 1966, JD, 1969. Bar: Ind. 1969, U.S. Dist. Ct. (so. dist.) Ind. 1969, U.S. Ct. Appeals (7th cir.) 1972, U.S. Supreme Ct. 1975, U.S. Ct. Appeals (5th cir.) 1978. Instr. Law Sch. Ind. U., Indpls., 1969-70; law clk. to Hon. John S. Hastings 7th Cir. Ct. Appeals, Chgo., 1970-71; assoc. Cahill, Gordon & Reindel, N.Y.C., 1971-72; law clk. to Hon. William H. Rehnquist U.S. Supreme Ct., Washington, 1972-73; assoc. Barnes, Hickam, Pantzer & Boyd, Indpls., 1973-75; ptnr. Barnes, Hickam, Pantzer & Boyd (name changed to Barnes & Thornburg), 1976-96, Sommer & Barnard, PC, Indpls., 1996—. Adj. asst. prof. law Ind. U. Sch. Law, 1986-92. Mem., bd. dirs. The Penrod Soc., Indpls., 1976—, Indpls. Symphonic Choir, 1988-91, Festival Music Soc., Indpls., 1990-96. Mem. 7th Cir. Bar Assn. (meetings chmn. Ind. chpt. 1979-88, portraits 1988-89, bd. govs. 1989—, 1st v.p. 1995, pres. 1996). Avocations: photography, music. Office: Sommer & Barnard PC 4000 Bank One Tower 111 Monument Cir Ste 4000 Indianapolis IN 46204-5198 E-mail: strain@sommerbarnard.com.

STRANG, JAMES DENNIS, editor; b. Ashtabula, Ohio, June 23, 1945; s. Delbert Devoe and Mildred Edith (Green) S.; m. Margaret Florence Littell, Aug. 25, 1974; children: Megan Lisbeth, Amy Colleen, Benjamin Jefferson. BS in Journalism, Kent State U., 1969. Cert. firearms instr. Reporter The Star-Beacon, Ashtabula, Ohio, 1966, The Record-Courier, Kent, 1966-69, The Cleve. Press, 1969-71; cons. Tom Rall & Assocs., Washington, 1971-72; reporter, editor The Plain Dealer, Cleve., 1973-75, assoc. editor, 1975—. Instr. journalism Lorain County C.C., Elyria, Ohio, 1973-74. Recipient Nat. Comdrs. award DAV, 1980, Best Editorial award AP Soc. Ohio, 1988. Mem. Nat. Conf. Editorial Writers, Soc. Profl. Journalists, Nat. Rifle Assn. (life). Unitarian-Universalist. Avocation: shooting sports. Office: The Plain Dealer 1801 Superior Ave E Cleveland OH 44114-2198

STRANG, RUTH HANCOCK, pediatric educator, pediatric cardiologist, priest; b. Bridgeport, Conn., Mar. 11, 1923; d. Robert Hallock Wright and Ruth (Hancock) S. BA, Wellesley Coll., 1944, postgrad., 1944-45; MD, N.Y. Med. Coll., 1949; MDiv, Seabury Western Theol. Sem., 1993. Diplomate Am. Bd. Pediat.; ordained deacon Episc. Ch., 1993, priest, 1994. Intern Flower and Fifth Ave. Hosp., N.Y.C., 1949-50, resident in pediat., 1950-52; mem. faculty N.Y. Med. Coll., 1952-57; fellow cardiology Babies Hosp., 1956-57, Harriet Lane Cardiac Clinic, Johns Hopkins Hosp., Balt., 1957-59, Children's Hosp., Boston, 1959-62; mem. faculty U. Mich., Univ. Hosp., Ann Arbor, 1962-89, prof. pediatrics, 1970-89, prof. emeritus, 1989—; priest-in-charge St. Johns Episcopal Ch., Howell, Mich., 1994—. Dir. pediat. Wayne County Gen. Hosp., Westland, Mich, 1965-85; mem. staff U. Mich. Hosps.; mem. med. adv. com. Wayne County chpt. Nat. Cystic Fibrosis Rsch. Found., 1966-80, chmn. med. adv. com. nat. found., Detroit, 1971-78; cons. cardiology Plymouth (Mich.) State Home and Tng. Sch., 1970-81. Author: Clinical Aspects of Operable Heart Disease, 1968; contbr. numerous articles to profl. jours. Mem. citizen's adv. coun. Juvenile Ct., Ann Arbor, 1968—76; mem. med. adv. bd. Ann Arbor Continuing Edn. Dept., 1968—77; v.p. Am. Heart Assn. Mich. , 1989, pres., 1991; bd. dirs. Livingston Cmty. Hospice, 1995—99, Emrich Episcopal Conf. Ctr., 1998—; mem. Diocesan Com. for World Relief, Detroit, 1970—72; trustee Episcopal Med. Chaplaincy, Ann Arbor, 1971—96; mem. bishop's com. St. Aidan's Episc. Ch., 1966—69, sec., 1966—68, vestry, 1973—76, 1978—80, 1984—86, 1990—91, sr. warden, 1975—76, 1978, 1986, 1990; del. Episc. Diocesan Conv., 1980, 1991; mem. Congl. Life Circle Episcopal Diocese Mich., 1995—2001, mem. loans and grants com., 1995—99, mem. com. on reference ann. diocesan conv., 1995-98, chmn., 1996; mem. Diocese Mich. Clergy Family Project, 1996—98; co-dean Huron Valley area coun. Diocese Mich., 1998—2000; bd. trustees Ecumenical Theol. Sem., 1996—, chair acad. affairs com., 2000—; mem. Congl. Devel. Commn., 2001—. Mem. AMA, Am. Acad. Pediat., Am. Coll. Cardiology, Mich. Med. Soc., Washtenaw County Med. Soc., N.Y. Acad. Medicine, Am. Heart Assn., Women's Rsch. Club (membership sec. 1966-67), Ambulatory Pediat. Assn., Am. Assn. Child Care in Hosps., Am. Assn. Med. Colls., Assn. Faculties of Pediat. Nurse Assn./Practitioners Programs (pres. 1978-81, exec. com. 1981-84), Episc. Clergy Assn. Mich., Northside Assn. Ministries (pres. 1975, 76, 79-80). Home: 4500 E Huron River Dr Ann Arbor MI 48105-9335 E-mail: sjec@cac.net.

STRANGHOENER, LARRY W. manufacturing company executive; BS, St. Olaf Coll., Northfield, Minn.; MBA, Northwestern U. CFA. Investment analyst Dain Bosworth, Mpls.; with Honeywell, Inc., 1983—; dir. corp. fin. planning/bus. analysis, asst. treas. Honeywell Centra, Germany, dir. investor rels., dir. mktg./internat. sales Germany; v.p. fin. Honeywell Indsl. Automation and Control, Phoenix; v.p. bus. devel. Honeywell, Inc., Mpls., v.p., CFO, 1997-99. Office: 101 Columbia Rd Morristown NJ 07960-4640

STRASSMANN, W. PAUL, economics educator; b. Berlin, July 26, 1926; s. Erwin Otto and Ilse (Wens) S.; m. Elizabeth Marsh Fanck, June 27, 1952; children— Joan, Diana, Beverly B.A. magna cum laude, U. Tex., Austin, 1949; M.A., Columbia U., 1950; Ph.D., U. Md., 1956. Econ. analyst Dept. Commerce, 1950-52; instr. U. Md., 1955; mem. faculty Mich. State U., East Lansing, 1956—, assoc. prof. econs., 1959-63, prof., 1963—. Sr. research dir. ILO, Geneva, 1969-70, 73-74; cons. World Bank, AID Author: Risk and Technological Innovation, 1959, Technological Change and Economic Development, 1968, The Transformation of Housing, 1982, (with Jill Wells) The Global Construction Industry, 1988. Served with USN, 1944-46 Mem. Am. Econ. Assn., Latin Am. Studies Assn., Am. Real Estate and Urban Econs. Assn., Assn. Evolutionary Econs., European Housing Rsch. Network, Phi Beta Kappa. Office: Mich State Univ Dept Econs East Lansing MI 48824 E-mail: strassm@msu.edu.

STRATTON, EVELYN LUNDBERG, state supreme court justice; b. Bangkok, Feb. 25, 1953; came to U.S., 1971 (parents Am. citizens); d. Elmer John and Corrine Sylvia (Henricksen) Sahlberg; children: Luke Andrew, Tyler John; m. Jack A. Lundberg. Student, LeTourneau Coll., Longview, Tex., 1971-74; AA, U. Fla., 1973; BA, U. Akron, 1976; JD, Ohio State U., 1978. Bar: Ohio 1979, U.S. Dist. Ct. (so. dist.) Ohio 1979, U.S. Ct. Appeals (6th cir.) 1983. Assoc. Hamilton, Kramer, Myers & Cheek, Columbus, 1979-85; ptnr. Wesp, Osterkamp & Stratton, 1985-88; judge Franklin County Ct. Common Pleas, 1989-96; justice Ohio State Supreme Ct., 1996—. Vis. prof. Nat. Jud. Coll., 1997—; spkr. legal seminars. Contbr. articles to profl. jours. Trustee Ohio affiliate Nat. Soc. to Prevent Blindness, 1989—, bd. dirs., trustee Columbus Coun. World Affairs, 1990-99, chmn. bd. dirs., 1999—; bd. dirs., trustee Dave Thomas Adoption Found., 1996—, ArChSafe Found., 1997—; mem. women's bd. Zephyrus League Cen. Ohio Lung Assn., 1989—; mem. Alliance Women Cmty. Corrections, 1993—. Recipient Gold Key award LeTourneau Coll., Gainesville, Fla., 1974, Svc. commendation Ohio Ho. of Reps., 1984, Scholar of Life award St. Joseph's Orphanage, 1998. Mem. ABA, ATLA, Columbus Bar Assn. (bd. govs. 1984-88, 90—, lectr.), Ohio Bar Assn. (jud. adminstrv. and legal reform com., coun. dels. 1992-96, Ohio Cmty. Corrections Orgn. (trustee 1995—), Columbus Bar Found. (trustee 1986-91, officer, sec. 1986-87, v.p. 1987-88), Am. Inns of Ct., Women Lawyers Franklin County, Phi Alpha Delta (pres. 1982-83). Office: Supreme Ct Ohio 30 E Broad St Fl 3 Columbus OH 43215*

STRATTON, JULIUS AUGUSTUS, psychologist, consultant; b. Norfolk, Va., July 9, 1924; s. Julius Augustus and Annie (Thornton) S. BS, Hampton U., Va., 1947; MEd, Cornell U., 1957; postgrad., Harvard U., 1966-67, U. Chgo., 1965. Instr., chmn. dept. counseling Roosevelt High Sch., Gary, Ind., 1952-68; assoc. faculty Ind. U. N.W., 1971-74; research dir. Gary Sch. Corp., 1968-76; v.p. Cornell Urban Cons., Chgo., 1976—. Author: Nonintellectual Factors Associated with Academic Achievement, 1957; contbr. articles to profl. jours. Mem. Nat. Coun. Tchrs. of Math., Assn. for Measurement and Evaluation in Counseling & Devel., Alpha Phi Alpha, Phi Delta Kappa, Sigma Gamma Mu. Democrat. Episcopalian. Avocations: opera, art, computer telecommunications.

STRATTON, STEVEN F. real estate executive; m. Sarah Stratton. Degree in fin., U. Ill. Mng. prin. corp. svcs. Tanguay-Burke-Stratton, Chgo., 1987—. Past. bd. dirs. St. Joseph's Hosp. Celebrity Golf Invitational; mem. bd. dirs. St. Joseph Found., LaSalle St. Coun.; active Anti-Defamation League Chgo. Recipient Tenant Rep. of Yr. award Chgo. Sun Times, 1993. Mem. Chgo. Office Leasing Brokers Assn. (past bd. dirs., COLBY Teamwork award 1996), Chgo. Real Estate Orgn., Chgo. Bd. Realtors. Office: Tanguay Burke Stratton 321 N Clark St Ste 900 Chicago IL 60610-4765

STRATTON-CROOKE, THOMAS EDWARD, financial consultant; b. N.Y.C., June 28, 1933; s. Harold and Jeanne Mildred (Stifft); children: Karen, John Ryland; m. Suzanne Williams, Oct. 21, 1989. Student, Hunter Coll., 1951-52; BS in Marine Engrng. and Transp., U.S. Maritime Acad., 1952-56; student, Washington U., St. Louis, 1961; MBA in Internat. Mktg., Banking and Fin., NYU, 1967. Commd. ensign USN, 1956, advanced through grades to lt., 1957; with Goodyear Internat. Corp., Akron, Ohio, 1960-63, Esso Internat., N.Y.C., 1958-60; dir. market info. and devel. Hotel Corp. Am., Boston, 1964-68; with Continental Grain Co., N.Y.C., 1968-72; dir. charter contracts Conoco, Stamford, Conn., 1973-75; cons. A. T. Kearney, Cleve., 1976-81; investment banker E. F. Hutton, 1981-83, AG Edwards and Sons, Inc., Cleve., 1983-89; sr. fin. advisor, registered investment advisor, asst. v.p., sr. fin. cons. Merrill Lynch, 1989—. Chmn. Indsl. Devel. Resch. Coun., Atlanta, 1970, Indsl. Devel. Resch. Coun., Snow Mass, Colo., 1971; lectr. bus. U. R.I., Kingston, 1968-70, tchr. Bus. Coll. Internat., 1986-89. Contbr. articles to profl. jours. Mem. Findley Lake (N.Y.) Hist. Soc.; mem. Nat. Task Force Reps. for Pres. Reagan, Cleve., 1982—. Officer (ret.) USN. Mem. Naval Res. Officers Assn., Naval Res. Assn., Great Lakes Hist. Soc., Soc. Naval Architects/Engrs., Navy League, Civil War Roundtable, NYU Alumni Assn., U.S. Coast Guard Club (Cleve.), Univ. Club, Circumnavigators Club (life), Internat. Shipmasters Assn., Propeller Club, Army Club, Navy Club, French Creek Hist. Soc., Town Club (Jamestown, N.Y.), Masons, Shriners, Cleve. City Club, Kings Point Alumni Assn., Civil War Round Table, U.S. Merchant Marine Acad. Avocations: sailing, skiing, bird watching, gardening, sports car enthusiast. Office: Merrill Lynch One Cleveland Ctr 1375 E 9th St Cleveland OH 44114-1798 E-mail: tommyesc@aol.com.

STRAUCH, JOHN L. lawyer; b. Pitts., Apr. 16, 1939; s. Paul L. and Delilah M. (Madison) S.; m. Gail Lorraine Kohn, Dec. 5, 1991; children: Paul L., John M., Lisa E. BA summa cum laude, U. Pitts., 1960; JD magna cum laude, NYU Sch. Law, 1963. Law clk. to Judge Sterry Waterman U.S. Ct. Appeals (2d cir.), St. Johnsbury, Vt., 1963-64; assoc. Jones, Day, Reavis & Pogue, Cleve., 1964-70, ptnr., 1970—, mem. adv. com., partnership com., chmn. litigation group. Mem. Statutory Com. on Selecting Bankruptcy Judges, Cleve., 1985-88; mem. lawyers com. Nat. Ctr. for State Cts. Editor-in-chief: NYU Law Rev., 1962-63; contbr. chpt. to book. Pres., trustee Cleve. Task Force on Violent Crimes, 1985-88; trustee Legal Aid Soc., Cleve., 1978, Cleve. Greater Growth Assn., 1985-86, Citizens Mental Health Assembly, 1989-90, lawyers com. Nat. Ctr. for State Cts., 1989—. Fellow Am. Coll. Trial Lawyers (life); mem. ABA, Ohio Bar Assn., Cleve. Bar Assn. (trustee 1980-83, pres. 1985-86), Fed. Bar Assn. (trustee Cleve. chpt. 1978-79, v.p. Cleve. chpt. 1979-80), Sixth Fed. Jud. Conf. (life), Ohio Eighth Jud. Conf. (life), Order of Coif, Inns of Ct., Oakmont Country Club, The Country Club, Kiawah Island Club, Phi Beta Kappa. Home: 28149 N Woodland Rd Cleveland OH 44124-4522 Office: Jones Day Reavis & Pogue N Point 901 Lakeside Ave E Cleveland OH 44114-1190

STRAUS, KATHLEEN NAGLER, education administrator, consultant; b. N.Y.C., Dec. 3, 1923; d. Maurice and Mildred (Kohn) Nagler; m. Everet M. Straus, May 29, 1948 (dec. Nov. 1967); children: Peter R., Barbara L. BA in Econs., Hunter Coll., 1944; postgrad., Columbia U., 1944-45, Am. U., 1946-47, Wayne State U., 1976-78. Various positions, 1944-50, 66; dep. dir. Model Neighborhood Agy., City of Detroit, 1968-70; dir. social svcs. Southeastern Mich. Coun. Govts., Detroit, 1970-74; staff coord. Edn. Task Force, 1974-75; exec. dir. People and Responsible Orgns. for Detroit, 1975-76; staff dir. edn. com. Mich. Senate, Lansing, 1976-79; assoc. exec. dir. Mich. Assn. Sch. Bds., 1979-86; dir. community rels. and devel. Ctr. for Creative Studies, Detroit, 1986-87, pres., 1987-91; mem. Mich. Bd. Edn., 1992—. Mem. Mich. Bd. for Pub. Jr. and C.C.s, Lansing, 1980-92, v.p., 1989, pres., 1991; cons. Met. Columbus (Ohio) Schs. Com., 1975-76; mem.. steering com. Mich. Edn. Seminars, 1979-86; mem. Adv. Com. on Higher Edn. Needs in S.W. Mich., 1971-72, Ad Hoc Com. on Equal Access to Higher Edn., 1970-71, Citizens Action Com. on Sch. Fin. Contbr. articles to profl. jours. Active numerous civic orgns.; vice chmn. downtown br. Met. Detroit YWCA, 1970-74; bd. dirs. Citizens for Better Care, Inc., 1973-78; mem. edn. com. New Detroit, Inc., 1972—; trustee Detroit Sci. Ctr., Inc., 1975—; founder, pres. Mich. Tax Info. Coun., 1982—; v.p. bd. dirs. Univ. Cultural Ctr. Assn., 1986-91; trustee Comprehensive Health Planning Coun. Southeastern Mich., 1977-78; mem. Wayne County Art and History Commn., 1988; co-chmn. Nat. Arts Program, 1987-88. Recipient Amity citation Congress, Detroit, 1966, Disting. Community Svc. award Am. Jewish Com., 1988, Disting. Community Svc. award Common Coun., Detroit, 1976, resolution Mich. Ho. of Reps., 1986, Mich. Senate, 1988, Educator of Yr. Wayne State U., 1999, Disting. Warrior award Detroit Urban League, 2000; named to Mich. Edn. Hall of Fame, 1997; inducted into Mich. Women's Hall of Fame, 2000. Mem. LWV (pres. Detroit 1961-63), Alpha Chi Alpha.. Democrat. Avocations: travel, theater, concerts. Home: 8801 Kingswood St Detroit MI 48221-1569 Office: State Bd Edn PO Box 30008 Lansing MI 48909-7508

STRAUS, LORNA PUTTKAMMER, biology educator; b. Chgo., Feb. 15, 1933; d. Ernst Wilfred and Helen Louise (Monroe) Puttkammer; m. Francis Howe Straus II, June 11, 1955; children: Francis, Helen, Christopher, Michael. BA magna cum laude, Radcliffe Coll., 1955; MS, U. Chgo., 1960, PhD, 1962. Rsch. assoc. dept. anatomy U. Chgo., 1962-64, instr., 1964-67, asst. prof., 1967-73, assoc. prof., 1973-87, prof., 1987—, asst. dean, then dean students Coll., 1967-82, dean admissions Coll., 1975-80, univ. marshal, 1999—. Trustee Radcliffe Coll., Cambridge, Mass., 1973-83; chmn. Cmty. Found., Mackinac Island, Mich., 1994—. Recipient silver medal Coun. for Advancement and Support Edn., 1987. Mem.: North Ctrl. Assn. (commr. 1998—, pres.-elect 2001—), Harvard U. Alumni Assn. (bd. dirs. 1980—83), Phi Beta Kappa. Avocations: travel, gardening. Home: 5642 S Kimbark Ave Chicago IL 60637-1606 Office: U Chgo 5845 S Ellis Ave Chicago IL 60637-1476 E-mail: l-straus@uchicago.edu.

STRAUSBAUGH, JEFFREY ALAN, lawyer; b. Lima, Ohio, Nov. 24, 1956; s. Stanley L. Strausbaugh and Margaret E. (Ebersole) Rutter; m. Sue Ann Webb, Nov. 29, 1975; children: Erin, Erica, Emily, Stanley, Sarah. BA, Defiance (Ohio) Coll., 1983; JD, U. Toledo, 1985. Bar: Ohio 1986. Supr., driver Webb Bros. Trucking & Excavating, Defiance, Ohio, 1975_83; ptnr. Ryan, Borland, Snavely & Strausbaugh, 1986-90; pvt. practice, 1990—. Chmn. Defiance County Rep. Cen. and Exec. Coms., 1988—; pres. Defiance County Young Reps., 1987. Mem. ABA, Ohio Bar Assn., NW Ohio Bar Assn., Defiance County Bar Assn., Rotary. Republican. Office: 414 W 3rd St Defiance OH 43512-2137

STRAUSS, JAMES LESTER, investment sales executive; b. Indpls., Aug. 24, 1944; s. Lester H. and Rosalie (Grossman) S. BS, Ind. U., 1966; MBA, Columbia U., 1968. CPA, Ohio. Acct. Deloitte & Touche, Dayton, Ohio, 1975-79, Main Hurdman, Cin., 1979-83; mng. exec. Royal Alliance Assocs., Inc., 1983—. Gen. securities prin. Nat. Assn. Securities Dealers; trustee Judah Touro Cemetary Assn.; speaker in field. With USAR, 1968-74. Mem. Am. Inst. CPA's, Ohio Soc. CPA's, Alliance Francaise, Mensa, Cin. Racquet Club. Republican. Home: 3435 Golden Ave # 604 Cincinnati OH 45226-2020 Office: Royal Alliance Assocs Inc 414 Walnut St Ste 502 Cincinnati OH 45202-3913

STRAUSS, JOHN STEINERT, dermatologist, educator; b. New Haven, July 15, 1926; s. Maurice Jacob and Carolyn Mina (Ullman) Strauss; m. Susan Thalheimer, Aug. 19, 1950; children: Joan Sue, Mary Lynn. BS, Yale U., 1946, MD, 1950. Intern U. Chgo., 1950-51; resident in dermatology U. Pa., Phila., 1951-52, 54-55, fellow in dermatology, 1955-57, instr., 1956-57; mem. faculty Boston U. Med. Sch., 1958-78, prof., 1966-78; head dept. dermatology U. Iowa, Iowa City, 1978-98, prof. dermatology, 1978-00, prof. emeritus, 2000—. Mem. editl. bd.: Archives of Dermatology, 1970—79, mem. editl. bd.: Jour. Am. Acad. Dermatology, 1979—89, mem. editl. bd.: Jour. Investigative Dermatology, 1977—82; contbr. articles to profl. jours. With USNR, 1952—54. Fellow James H. Brown Jr., 1947—48, USPHS, 1955—57; grantee. Fellow: Am. Acad. Dermatology (pres.); mem.: Internat. Com. Dermatology 1992—97, Internat. League Dermatol. Socs. 1992—97, 18th World Congress Dermatology, Am. Bd. Med. Spltys. (exec. com. 2001—), Coun. Med. Splty. Socs. (pres.), Am. Fedn. Clin. Rsch., Ctrl. Soc. Clin. Rsch., Assn. Am. Physicians, Am. Dermatol. Assn. (sec., pres.), Am. Bd. Dermatology (bd. dirs., assoc. exec. dir., pres., exec. cons.), Dermatology Found. (pres.), Soc. Investigative Dermatology (sec.-treas., pres.). Achievements include research in in sebaceous glands and pathogenesis of acne. Office: U Iowa Hosp & Clinics Dept of Dermatology 200 Hawkins Dr # BT2045-1 Iowa City IA 52242-1009

STRAUSS, WILLIAM VICTOR, lawyer; b. Cin., July 5, 1942; s. William Victor and Elsa (Lovitt) S.; m. Linda Leopold, Nov. 9, 1969; children: Nancy T., Katherine S. AB cum laude, Harvard U., 1964; JD, U. Pa., 1967. Bar: Ohio 1967. Pres. Security Title and Guaranty Agy., Inc., Cin., 1982—, Strauss & Troy, Cin., 1995—. Trustee Cin. Psychoanalytic Inst., 1990—, Cin. Contemporary Arts Ctr., 1997—. Mem. ABA, Nat. Assn. Office and Indsl. Parks, Ohio State Bar Assn., Cin. Bar Assn., Ohio Land Title Assn. Home: 40 Walnut Ave Wyoming OH 45215-4350 Office: Strauss & Troy Fed Res Bldg 150 E 4th St Fl 4 Cincinnati OH 45202-4018

STREETER, JOHN WILLIS, information systems manager; b. Topeka, Sept. 3, 1947; s. Jack and Edith Bernice (Vowels) S.; m. Nancy Ann Buck, June 15, 1968 (div. 1985); children: Sarah Beth, Timothy Paine; m. Linda Lea Wenrich Weisbender, Sept. 13, 1986; stepchildren: Michael Leon Weisbender II, Debra Ann Weisbender Johnson, Dawn Marie Weisbender. BS in Computer Sci., Kans. State U., 1973, MBA in Mgmt., 1974; postgrad., Harvard U., 1992. Computer programmer U.S.M.C., 1965-70, Kans. State U., Manhattan, 1970-74; cons., mgr., prin. Am. Mgmt. Systems, Inc., Arlington, Va., 1974-83; systems planning analyst Fed. Nat. Mortgage Assn., Washington, 1983-85; assoc. dir. computing and telecomm. Kans. State U., Manhattan, 1985-91, dir. info. systems, 1991—. Mem. State of Kans. Info. Tech. Adv. Bd., 1997-98. Author: Streeter Genealogy, 1985. Staff sgt. USMC, 1965-70. Recipient Navy Achievement medal in data processing Sec. Navy, 1971. Mem. IEEE, SR, KC, IEEE Computer Soc., Assn. for Computing Machinery, Am. Inst. Cert. Computer Profls., Educause, Inc. (Kans. State U. voting mem. rep. 1987—), Streeter Family Assn. (bd. dirs. 1988—, v.p. 1990-95), Am. Legion. Republican. Roman Catholic. Avocations: genealogy, history, book collecting. Home: 6765 Salzer Rd Wamego KS 66547-9636 Office: Kans State U Info Sys 2323 Anderson Ave Ste 215 Manhattan KS 66502-2912

STREETMAN, JOHN WILLIAM, III, museum official; b. Marion, N.C., Jan. 19, 1941; s. John William, Jr. and Emily Elaine (Carver) S.;

children: Katherine Drake, Leah Farrior, Burgin Eaves. BA in English and Theatre History, Western Carolina U., 1963; cert. in Shakespeare studies, Lincoln Coll., Oxford (Eng.) U., 1963. Founding dir. Jewett Creative Arts Ctr., Berwick Acad., South Berwick, Maine, 1964-70; exec. dir. Polk Mus. Art, Lakeland, Fla., 1970-75; dir. Mus. Arts and Sci., Evansville, Ind., 1975—; chmn. mus. adv. panel Ind. Arts Commn., 1977-78. Mem. Am. Assn. Museums, Assn. Ind. Museums (bd. dirs.) Episcopalian. Office: Evansville Mus Arts & Scis 411 SE Riverside Dr Evansville IN 47713-1037

STREFF, WILLIAM ALBERT, JR. lawyer; b. Chgo., Aug. 12, 1949; s. William Albert Streff Sr. and Margaret (McKeough) Streff Fisher; m. Kathleen Myslinski, Sept. 29, 1984; children: Amanda, William III, Kimberly. BSME, Northwestern U., 1971, JD cum laude, 1974. Bar: Ill. 1974, U.S. Dist. Ct. (no. dist.) Ill. 1974, U.S. Dist. Ct. (no. dist.) N.Y. 1987, U.S. Dist. Ct. (no. dist.) Calif. 1988, U.S. Ct. Appeals (7th cir.) 1980, U.S. Ct. Appeals (9th cir.) 1988, U.S. Ct. Appeals (fed. cir.) 1982. Legal writing instr. Law Sch. Northwestern U., Chgo., 1973-74; assoc. Kirkland & Ellis, 1974-80, ptnr., 1980—. Lectr. Ill. Inst. Continuing Legal Edn., 1984; adj. prof. Northwestern U. Law Sch., 1992-94, 97-99, Chgo. Kent-IIT Law Sch., 1998, John Marshall Law Sch., 2000. Contbr. articles to profl. jours. Mem. adv. bd. Ill. Inst. Tech./Chgo.-Kent, 1983-86; trustee Northwestern U., Evanston, 1984-86, mem. vis. com. Law Sch., Chgo., 1988-94. Mem. ABA. Office: Kirkland & Ellis 200 E Randolph Dr Chicago IL 60601-6636

STREIBEL, BRYCE, state senator; b. Fessenden, N.D., Nov. 19, 1922; s. Reinhold M. and Frieda I. (Broschat) S.; m. June P. Buckley, Mar. 23, 1947; 1 child, Kent. Attended U. N.D., Grand Forks; BS, San Francisco State Coll., 1947. Engr. U.S. Govt., Napa, Calif., 1943-46; dir. Martin Funeral Home, Stockton, 1946-55; owner Streibel Twin Oaks Farm, Fessenden, N.D., 1955—; state sen. State of N.D., Bismarck, 1981—, pres. pro tempore, 1995, state rep., 1957-75, majority leader, 1966-74. Author: Pathways Through LIfe, 1983. Chmn. N.D. Legis. Coun., Bismarck, 1969-75; councilman Town of Fessenden, 1976-84; former pres. 20-30 Internat. Group, Sacramento, trustee, 1952-54; dir. World Coun., Sacramento, 1951-53; bd. dirs. U. N.D. Fellows, Grand Forks, 1982-86; pres. Fessenden Airport Authority, 1980—; mem. N.D. Bd. Higher Edn., 1977-81; chmn. N.D. adv. commn. U.S. Commn. on Civil Rights, 1988-93. Recipient Sioux award U. N.D. Alumni Assn., 1976, Benefactor award U. N.D. Found., 1982, William Budge award, 1983, Outstanding Svc. award Jaycees, 1988, Nat. Barn Again Farm Heritage award, 1996; named Outstanding Alumnus Theta Chi, 1987. Mem. N.D. Centennial Farm, Commodore N.D. Mythical Navy, Masons (Master), Elks, Kiwanis, Shriners, Farm Bur. Republican. Baptist. Avocations: golf, philately. Home and Office: 226 2nd St N Fessenden ND 58438-7204 Office: PO Box 467 Fessenden ND 58438-0467

STREICHER, JAMES FRANKLIN, lawyer; b. Ashtabula, Ohio, Dec. 6, 1940; s. Carl Jacob and Helen Marie (Dugan) S.; m. Sandra JoAnn Jennings, May 22, 1940; children: Cheryl Ann, Gregory Scott, Kerry Marie. BA, Ohio State U., 1962; JD, Case Western Res. U., 1966. Bar: Ohio 1966, U.S. Dist. Ct. (no. dist.) Ohio 1966. Assoc. Calfee, Halter & Griswold, Cleve., 1966-71, ptnr., 1972—. Bd. dirs. The Mariner Group Inc., Ft. Myers, Fla., Spectra-Tech Inc., Stamford, Conn., Mid Am. Consulting; mem. Divsn. Securities Adv. Bd., State of Ohio; lectr. Case Western Res. U., Cleve. State U.; mem. pvt. sector com. John Carroll U. Trustee Achievement Ctr. for Children, Western Reserve Hist. Soc., Make-A-Wish Found. Endowment. Mem. ABA, Fed. Bar Assn., Ohio State Bar Assn., Assn. for Corp. Growth, Ohio Venture Assn., Greater Cleve. Bar Assn. (founding chmn. corp., banking, bus. law sect.), Ohio State U. Alumni Assn., Case Western Res. U. Alumni Assn., Newcomen Soc., Bluecoats Club (Cleve.), Mayfield Country (bd. dirs. 1985-89), Union Club, The Pepper Pike Club, Beta Theta Pi, Phi Delta Phi. Roman Catholic. Republican. Fax: 216-241-0816. E-mail: j.streich@calfee.com.

STREIFFER, JENNY, former soccer player; b. Metairie, La., May 25, 1978; Student, U. Notre Dame. Alternate U.S. Women's Olympic Soccer Team, 1996; mem. 1997 U-20 Nat. Team (Nordic Cup championship, Denmark), scoring winning goal; midfielder Notre Dame, NCAA championship freshman yr., undefeated regular season sophomore yr. Named Big East Rookie of Yr. and NSCAA 3d Team All-Am., freshman yr., U. Notre Dame. Office: US Soccer Fedn 1801-1811 S Prairie Ave Chicago IL 60616

STREIT, MICHAEL J. judge; b. Sheldon, Iowa; married; 1 child. BA, U. Iowa, 1972; grad., U. San Diego Sch. Law, 1975. Cert.: (U.S. Ct. Appeals) 1996. Asst. atty. Lucas County, atty.; dist. ct. judge, 1983; Supreme Ct. justice Iowa State Supreme Ct., 2001—. Mem.: Blackstone Inn of Ct., Supreme Ct. Jud. Tech. Com., Iowa Jud. Inst., Judges Assn. Edn. Com., Supreme Ct. Edn. Adv. Com. Office: State House Des Moines IA 50319*

STRENSKI, JAMES B. communications executive; b. Jan. 2, 1930; m. Jane E.; 5 children. Grad., Marquette U. Pub. info. officer USN, NATO; with Pub. Communications Inc., Chgo.; chmn., chief exec. officer Pub. Communications Inc, Tampa, Fla. Cons. to nonprofit, health care and social agys., pub. and pvt. corps., fin. and acad. instns.; lectr. to industry groups, trade assns., bus. orgns. Contbr. more than 70 articles on pub. rels. to jours. in field. Mem. Tampa Jesuit High Sch. Found., Tampa Downtown Partnership Bd., Hillsborough County Affordable Housing Com., Bus. Adv. Coun., Coll. of Journalism of Marquette U.; bd. dirs. Chgo. Leadership Coun. for Met. Open Communities, Tampa Goodwill Industries-Suncoast; program chmn. Tampa Pkwy. Assn.; pub. rels. chmn. Paint Your Heart Out, Tampa, U. Tampa Bd. Fellows. Mem. Worldcom Group, Inc. (founder, exec. com.). Office: Public Communications Inc 35 E Wacker Dr Chicago IL 60601-2103*

STRETCH, JOHN JOSEPH, social work educator, management and evaluation consultant; b. St. Louis, Feb. 24, 1935; s. John Joseph and Theresa Carmelita (Fleming) S.; children: Paul, Leonmarie, Sylvan, Adrienne, Sharonalice; m. Barbara Ann Stewart, Mar. 16, 1985; children: Margaret, Thomas. AB, Maryknoll Coll., Glen Ellyn, Ill., 1957; MSW, Washington U., St. Louis, 1961; PhD, Tulane U., 1967; MBA, St. Louis U., 1980. Lic. clin. social worker, 1990. Instr. Tulane U., 1962-67, asst. prof., 1967-69; assoc. prof. social work St. Louis U., 1969-72, prof., 1972—87, asst. dean Sch. Social Service, 1976-87, dir. doctoral studies, 1976-94, dir. MSW. program, 1985-86, bd. dirs., mem. exec. com. Ctr. for Social Justice, mem. instnl. rev. bd. Sch. Social Svc., 1987—92; dir. rsch. Social Welfare Planning Coun. Met. New Orleans, 1962-69. Cons. to United Way Met. St. Louis, Cath. Charities of Archdiocese of St. Louis, Cath. Svcs. for Children and Youth, Full Achievement, Mo. Province of S.J., Cath. Commn. on Housing, Cath. Family Svcs., Youth Emergency Svcs., Mo. State Dept. Social Svcs., U. Mo. Extension Svc., St. Joseph's Home for Boys, Marian Hall Ctr. for Adolescent Girls, Boys Town-Girls Town of Mo., A World of Difference, Anti Defamation League of B'nai Brith, Prog. Youth Ctr., Foster Care Coalition of Greater St. Louis, Rankin-Jordan Children's Rehab. Hosp., 1999-2000, Old Man River; expert witness on homeless U.S. House Select Com. on Families, Children and Youth, 1987; mem. resource spl. task force on homeless Office of Sec. U.S. Dept. Housing and Urban Devel., 1989; survey design cons. U.S. Office of The Insp. Gen., 1990; methodology expert on homelessness U.S. Census Bur., 1989; expert homeless policy General Acctg. Office hearings, 1992; chair Mo. Assn. for Social Welfare Low Income Housing, 1982—; mem., chmn. St. Louis Low Income Housing Preservation Com., 1985—; mem. Comprehensive Housing Affordabiltiy Strategies (CHAS) Mo. Statewide Planning Group, Missouri Housing Devel. CHAS citizen's com., State of Mo. Affordable House Task Force, Mo. Housing Devel. Corp., 1998—, Mo. Inst. of Psychiatry, 1995, Univ. City sch. dist., 1990; mgmt. cons. People's Issues Task Force Agricultural div. Monsanto Chemical Inc., 1992, Nat. Conf. of Christians and Jews, regional office, 1990-92; vis. prof. Nat. Catholic U. of Am. Sch. of Soc. Svcs., 1991, 92, U. Bristol, England, 1992, U. Calif. Sch. of Pub. Health, Berkeley, 1990; cons. Mo. Speaker of the Ho. statewide legislative task force, 1990-92, Russian Am. Summer U., 2000; statewide grant project reviewer emergency shelter grant program Mo. Dept. Social Svcs., 1989—, chair, 2002; homeless svcs. grant reviewer City of St. Louis, 1996-97. Editl. bd. Social Work, 1968-74, Health Progress, 1988—01; manuscript referee Jour. Social Svc. Rsch., 1977-99; mgmt. and evaluation content referee Wadsworth Press, Human Svcs. Press, Allyn and Bacon Press; editor, contbr. books and profl. jours. and books. Bd. dirs. Beyond Housing, Inc. 1985—, pres. bd. dirs., 1993-95; bd. Housing Comes First, 1997—; mem. Mo. Assn. Social Welfare, 1980—, DuBourg Soc. of St. Louis U., 1988; bd. mem. St. Louis U. Ctr. for Social Justice, 1990—; mem. Salvation Army Family Haven, 1987, mem. adv. bd., 1988-92; chmn. United Way of Greater St. Louis venture grant com., 1988-91, mem. allocation com., 1985-95, mem. process and rev. com., 1991-93, inter-orgnl. priorities com., 1991-93; mem. leadership coun. Success By Six, 1990—; organizer Mo. State Nat. Coalition for the Homeless; appointee St. Louis U. Instl. Representation nat. Jesuits social Concern Group, 1993—; mem. exec. and support tng. group, St. Louis U., 1987—92; mem. instnl. rev. bd. Institutional Rev. Bd., St. Louis U. Med. Ctr., 1996-98. NIMH Career Leadership Devel. fellow, 1965-67, Fed. Ednl. grantee Ill. Sch. Sys., 2002; recipient Scholar of Yr. award Sch. Social Svc., St. Louis U., 1987; named Vol. of Yr. Ecumenical Housing Prodn. Corp., 1990; Presdl. scholar Sch. Social Svc., 1992. Mem. AAUP (St. Louis U. chpt. exec. com. 1990—, pres. 1994—), ACLU, Acad. Cert. Social Workers (charter mem.), Nat. Assn. Social Workers, Mo. Assn. for Social Welfare (bd. dirs., Outstanding State-Wide Mem. of Yr. 1987), Coun. on Social Work Edn., Common Cause, Amnesty Internat., Nat. Consumer's Union (com. on vital and health stats.), U.S. Census Bur. (subcom. on health stats. for minorities and other spl. populations of U.S. 1988—). Democrat. Roman Catholic. Home: 9100 Litzsinger Rd Saint Louis MO 63144-2214 Office: 3550 Lindell Blvd Saint Louis MO 63103-1021

STREVEY, GUY DONALD, insurance company executive; b. Norcatur, Kans., Mar. 8, 1932; s. Guy Ross Strevey and Maxine Elizabeth (Johnson) Gruse.; m. Irene Franklyn Corey Nov. 7, 1953; children: Richard A., Janet E. Bolte, Philip E., Melinda K. Halverson. BS, Okla. A&M U., 1953. Cert. CFP, CLU, ChFC. Agt. Penn Mut. Life Ins. Co., Tulsa, 1955-62, regional mgr., 1958-62, gen. agt. Omaha, 1962-69, agt., 1969—; ptnr. Strevey and Assocs., 1979—; agt. Various Cos., 1979—; registered rep. Hornor, Townsend & Kent, Inc., 1985—. Bd. dirs. Citipower LLC: A Del. Corp.; cons. Appalachian Gas Assocs. I-XII. Deacon Hillcrest Bapt. Ch., Omaha, 1960, Westside Bapt. Ch., Omaha, 1978, chmn., 1979-81. 1st It. U.S. Army, 1953-55. Mem. NAIFA (Nat. Quality award 1970-94), Soc. Fin. Svc. Profls., Nat. Assn. Ins. & Fin. Advisors, Million Dollar Roundtable (life), F.P.A. Assoc. (pres. 1997—, chmn. bd. 1998-99, named Mem. of Yr. 2002). Republican. Avocations: sports, traveling. Home: 3518 S 106th St Omaha NE 68124-3614 Office: Strevey & Assocs 11422 Miracle Hills Dr Ste 508 Omaha NE 68154-4420

STREVEY, TRACY ELMER, JR. army officer, surgeon, physician executive; b. Shorewood, Wis., Apr. 24, 1933; s. Tracy Elmer and Margaret (Rees) S.; m. Victoria Crowley (div.); children: Virginia Ann, Tracy Elmer III, Andrew Victor; m. Elizabeth Sommers; children: Stephanie Jean, James Sommers. Student, Pomona Coll., 1951-54; MD, U. So. Calif., 1958; student, Armed Forces Staff Coll., 1970-71, U.S. Army War Coll., 1977-78. Diplomate Am. Bd. Surgery, Am. Bd. Thoracic Surgery. Intern Los Angeles County Gen. Hosp., 1958-59; commd. officer U.S. Army, 1959, advanced through grades to maj. gen., 1983; resident in gen. surgery Letterman Gen. Hosp., San Francisco, 1962-66; resident in thoracic and cardiovascular surgery Walter Reed Gen. Hosp., Washington, 1968-70; comdg. officer 757 Med. Detachment OA, Ludwigsburg, Germany, 1959-61; ward officer orthopaedic svc. 75th Sta. Hosp., Stuttgart, Fed. Republic Germany, 1961-62; chief profl. svc., chief surgery 85th Evacuation Hosp., Qui Nhon, Vietnam, 1967; comdg. officer 3d Surg. Hosp., Dong Tam, Vietnam, 1967-68; asst. chief thoracic and cardiovascular surgery service Fitzsimons Army Med Ctr., Denver, 1971-73, chief thoracic and cardiovascular surgery service, 1973-75; asst. dir. med. activities and dir. Profl. Edn. Gorgas Hosp., Panama Canal Zone, 1975-77; chief dept. surgery Walter Reed Army Med. Ctr., Washington, 1978-81; comdr. Brooke Army Med. Ctr., Ft. Sam Houston, Tex., 1981-83, Tripler Army Med. Ctr., Hawaii, 1983-86, U.S. Army Health Svcs. Command, San Antonio, 1986-88; ret. U.S. Army, 1988; CEO Nassau County Med. Ctr., 1988-93; pres., CEO N.Y. Hosp Med. Ctr. Queens, N.Y.C., 1993-94; v.p. N.Y. Hosp. Care Network, 1994-95; v.p. for med. affairs Sisters of Mercy Health Sys., St. Louis, 1995-99; cons., 1999—. Asst. clin. prof. surgery U. Colo. Med. Ctr., Denver, 1973-75; prof. surgery Uniformed Services U. Health Scis., Bethesda, 1978— , vice chmn. dept. surgery, 1978-81 Contbr. articles to profl. jours. Mem. reg. bd. Am. Heart Assn. Decorated D.S.M., Legion of Merit with 2 oak leaf clusters, Meritorious Service medal with 2 oak leaf clusters, Purple Heart, Army Commendation Medal for Valor, Vietnam Cross of Gallantry with Palm; recipient Outstanding Service award U. So. Calif. Med. Alumni Assn., 1983 Fellow ACS, Am. Coll. Chest Physicians, Am. Coll. Cardiology, Am. Coll. Physician Execs. (disting.); mem. Assn. Mil. Surgeons U.S., Soc. Thoracic Surgeons, Western Thoracic Surg. Assn., Am. Assn. Thoracic Surgery, Masons. Avocations: ham radio; scuba diving; golf; computer science. Home and Office: 1509 Woodgate Dr Saint Louis MO 63131-4724

STRICKLAND, ARVARH EUNICE, history educator; b. Hattiesburg, Miss., July 6, 1930; s. Eunice and Clotiel (Marshall) S.; m. Willie Pearl Elmore, June 17, 1951; children: Duane Arvarh, Bruce Elmore. BA, Tougaloo Coll., 1951; MA, U. Ill., 1953, PhD, 1962. Tchr. Hattiesburg Schs., 1951-52; instr. Tuskegee Inst., 1955-56; prin. supr. Madison County Schs., Canton, Miss., 1956-59; asst. prof. history Chgo. State U., 1962-65, assoc. prof. history, 1965-68, prof., 1968-69, U. Mo., Columbia, 1969-96, prof. emeritus, 1996—, chmn. dept. history, 1980-83, interim dir. black studies program, 1994-96, sr. faculty assoc., Office of V.P. acad. affairs, 1987-88, assoc. v.p. acad. affairs, 1989-91. Author: History of the Chicago Urban League, 1966, reprint, 2001, (with Reich and Biller) Building the United States, 1971, (with Reich) The Black American Experience to 1877, 1974, The Black American Experience since 1877, 1974; editor: Working with Carter G. Woodson, (with Lorenzo J. Greene) The Father of Black History: A Diary, 1928-1930, 1989, Selling Black History for Carter G. Woodson: A Diary, 1930-33, 1996, (with Robert E. Weems) The African American Experience: A Historiographical and Bibliographical Guide, 2000. Commr. Planning and Zoning, Columbia, Mo., 1977-80, Boone County Home Rule Charter, 1982, Mo. Peace Officers Standards and Tng. Commn., 1988-89; co-chmn. Mayors Com. to Commemorate Contbns. of Black Columbians, Columbia, 1981; mem. exec. subcom. Mayor's Ad Hoc Election '82 Com., 1982; bd. dirs. Harry S. Truman Library Inst., 1987-96. Recipient Disting. Svc. award Ill. Hist. Soc., 1957, Byler Disting. Prof. award U. Mo., 1994, St. Louis Am.'s Educator of Yr. award, 1994, Disting. Faculty award U. Mo.-Columbia Alumni Assn., 1995, Tougaloo Coll. Alumni Hall of Fame, 1995, Alumni Achievement U. Ill. Coll. Liberal Arts and Scis., 1997, Disting. Svc. award State Hist. Soc. Mo., 1997. Mem. Orgn. Am. Historians, Am. Hist. Assn., Assn. Study Afro-Am. Life and History (Carter Godwin Woodson Scholars medallion 1999), So. Hist. Assn., State Hist. Soc. Mo. (Disting. Svc. award 1997), Boone County Hist. Soc. (bd. dirs. 1998—, 2d v.p. 1999), Kiwanis, Alpha Phi Alpha, Phi Alpha Theta (internat. v.p. 1991-93, pres. 1994-95, chair adv. bd. 1996-97, Disting. Svc. award 1997). Democrat. Methodist. E-mail: stricklandamissouri.edu. Home: 4100 Defoe Dr Columbia MO 65203-0252 Office: U Mo Dept History 101 Read Hall Columbia MO 65211-7500

STRICKLAND, HUGH ALFRED, lawyer; b. Rockford, Ill., May 3, 1931; s. Hugh and Marie (Elmer) S.; m. Donna E. McDonald, Aug. 11, 1956; children: Amy Alice, Karen Ann. A.B., Knox Coll., 1953; J.D., Chgo. Kent Coll. Law, 1959. Bar: Ill. 1960. Partner firm McDonald, Strickland & Clough, Carrollton, Ill., 1961—; asst. atty. gen., 1960-67; spl. asst. gen., 1967-69; pres. McDonald Title Co. Mem. Greene County Welfare Svcs. Com., 1963—, Ill. Heart Assn., 1961-65; trustee Thomas H. Boyd Meml. Hosp., 1972-95. With AUS, 1953-55. Recipient award for meritorious service Am. Heart Assn., 1964 Fellow Ill. Bar Found. (charter); mem. ABA, Ill. Bar Assn., Greene County Bar Assn. (past pres.), Southwestern Bar Assn. (past pres.), Ill. Def. Counsel, Am. Judicature Soc., Def. Rsch. Inst., Elks Club, Westlake Country Club (v.p. 1968-70, dir.), Big Sand Lake Country Club, Phi Delta Theta, Phi Delta Phi. Methodist. Home: 827 7th St Carrollton IL 62016-1421 Office: 524 N Main St PO Box 71 Carrollton IL 62016-1027 Fax: 217-942-3178. E-mail: has3@irtc.net., lawyers@irtc.net.

STRICKLAND, TED, congressman, clergyman, psychology educator, psychologist; b. Lucasville, Ohio, Aug. 4, 1941; m. Frances Smith. BA in History, Asbury Coll., 1963; MDiv, Asbury Seminary, 1967; PhD in Psychology, U. Ky., 1980. Clergyman; dir. social svcs. Ky. Meth. Home; consulting psychologist Southern Ohio Correctional Facility, 1985-92, 94-96; prof. psychology Shawnee State U., 1988-92, 94-96; mem. U.S. Congress from 6th Ohio dist., Washington, 1993-94, 97—; mem. energy and commerce com. Mem. numerous coms. in fields of: edn. and labor, post-secondary edn. and tng., labor standards, occupational health and safety, small bus., rural enterprise, exports and environ. Democrat. Office: US Ho of Reps 336 Cannon House Office Bldg Washington DC 20515-3506*

STRICKLER, IVAN K. dairy farmer; b. Carlyle, Kans., Oct. 23, 1921; s. Elmer E. and Edna Louise (James) S.; m. Madge Lee Marshall, Aug. 7, 1949; children— Steven Mark, Thomas Scott, Douglas Lee. B.S., Kans. State U., 1947. Owner, mgr. dairy farm, Iola, Kans., 1947—; tchr. farm tng. to vets. World War II, 1947-54; judge 1st and 2d Nat. Holstein Show, Brazil, 1969-70, Internat. Holstein Show, Buenos Aires, 1972, Nat. Holstein Show, Ecuador, 1978, 10th Nat. Holstein Show, Brazil, 1980, Holstein Show, Australia, Mex. and Argentina, 1981, Lang Lang, 1984, Adelaide (Australia) Royal Show, 1987; pres Mid-America Dairymen, Inc., Springfield, MO, 1981—. Appointed chmn. Nat. Dairy Bd., 1985-90; dairy leader 4-H Club, 1962-75; dir. Iola State Bank; rep. U.S. Internat. Dairy Symposium, 1994, Belo Horinzote, Brazil. Author: Wholly Cow We Did It, 1996 (Centennia Honor roll 1997). Trustee Allen County Community Jr. Coll.; mem. agr. edn. and rsch. com. Kans. State U. (recipient Medallion-highest honor, 2000), U.S. Agrl. Trade and Devel. Mission, Algeria and Tunisia, 1989. With USN, 1942-46, PTO. Recipient Silver award Holstein Friesian Assn. Brazil, 1969, Top Dairy Farm Efficiency award Ford Found., 1971, Master Farmer award Kans. State U. and Kans. Assn. Commerce and Industry, 1972, Gold award Holstein Friesian Assn. Argentina, 1972, Richard Lynng award Nat. Dairy Bd., 1990, award of merit Gamma Sigma Delta, 1987, Alumni medallion Kans. State U., 1999; named Man of Yr. World Dairy Exposition, 1978; portrait in Dairy Hall of Fame Kans. State U., 1974; Guest of Hon. Nat. Dairy Shrine, 1985; selected First Dairy Leader of Yr., 1996; inductee Kans. Co-op Hall of Fame, 1999. Mem. Mid Am. Dairymen (sec. corporate bd. 1971-81, pres. 1981-95), Holstein Friesian Assn. Am. (nat. dir. 1964-72), Dairy Shrine (nat. dir. 1971-81), United Dairy Industry Assn. (dir. 1971-79), Nat. Holstein Assn. Am. (pres. 1979-80), Alpha Gamma Rho (highest honor 1989, Hall of Fame 1998). Mem. Christian Ch. (elder, bd. dirs.). Club: Nat. Dairy Shrine (pres. 1978). Home: PO Box 365 Iola KS 66749-0365 Office: Mid America Dairymen Inc 3253 E Chestnut Expy Springfield MO 65802-2584

STRIEFSKY, LINDA A(NN), lawyer; b. Carbondale, Pa., Apr. 27, 1952; d. Leo James and Antoinette Marie (Carachilo) S.; m. James Richard Carlson, Nov. 3, 1984; children: David Carlson, Paul Carlson, Daniel Carlson. BA summa cum laude, Marywood Coll., 1974; JD, Georgetown U., 1977. Bar: Ohio 1977. Assoc. Thompson Hine LLP (formerly Thompson, Hine & Flory), Cleve., 1977-85, ptnr., 1985—. Loaned exec. United Way N.E. Ohio, Cleve., 1978; trustee Cleve. Pub. Radio. Mem. ABA (real estate fin. com. 1980-87, vice chmn. leader liability com. 1993-97, mem. non-traditional real estate fin. com. 1987—), Am. Bar Found., Am. Coll. Real Estate Lawyers (bd. govs. 1994-98, treas. 1999), Internat. Coun. Shopping Ctrs., Nat. Assn. Office and Indsl. Parks, Urban Land Inst. (chmn. Cleve. dist. coun. 1996-2000), Cleve. Real Estate Women, Ohio Bar Assn. (bd. govs. real property sect. 1985-97), Greater Cleve. Bar Assn. (chmn. bar applicants com. 1983-84, exec. coun. young lawyers sect. 1982-85, chmn. 1984-85, mem. exec. coun. real property sect. 1980-84, Merit Svc. award 1983, 85), Pi Gamma Mu. Democrat. Roman Catholic. Home: 2222 Delamere Dr Cleveland OH 44106-3204 Office: Thompson Hine LLP 3900 Key Ctr 127 Public Square Cleveland OH 44114-1216 E-mail: linda.striefsky@thompsonhine.com.

STRIER, KAREN BARBARA, anthropologist, educator; b. Summit, N.J., May 22, 1959; d. Murray Paul and Arlene Strier. BA, Swarthmore Coll., 1980; MA, Harvard U., 1981, PhD, 1986. Lectr. anthropology Harvard U., Cambridge, Mass., 1986-87; asst. prof. Beloit (Wis.) Coll., 1987-89, U. Wis., Madison, 1989-92, assoc. prof., 1992-95, prof., 1995—, dept. chair, 1994-96. Panel mem. U.S. Dept. Edn., Washington, 1989—92. Author: (book) Faces in the Forest, 1999, Primate Behavioral Ecology, 2000; co-author: Planning, Purposing, and Presenting Science Effectively; mem. editl. bd.: Internat. Jour. Primatology, 1990—, mem. editl. bd.: Primates, 1991—, mem. editl. bd.: Yearbook of Phys. Anthropology. Recipient Presdl. Young Investigator award, NSF, 1989—94. Fellow: Am. Anthropol. Assn.; mem.: AAAS (coun. del. anthropology sect. 1998—2000), Animal Behavior Soc., Internat. Primatologcial Soc., Am. Assn. Phys. Anthropologists. Office: U Wis Dept Anthropology 5403 Social Sci Bldg 1180 Observatory Dr Madison WI 53706-1320 E-mail: kbstrier@facstaff.wisc.edu.

STRIMBU, VICTOR, JR. lawyer; b. New Philadelphia, Ohio, Nov. 25, 1932; s. Victor and Veda (Stancu) S.; m. Kathryn May Schrote, Apr. 9, 1955 (dec. 1995); children: Victor Paul, Michael, Julie, Sue; m. Marjorie Bichsel, Oct. 23, 1999. BA, Heidelberg Coll., 1954; postgrad., Western Res. U., 1956-57; JD, COlumbia U., 1960. Bar: Ohio 1960, U.S. Supreme Ct. 1972. With Baker & Hostetler LLP, Cleve., 1960—, ptnr., 1970—. Bd. dirs. North Coast Health Ministry; mem. Bay Village (Ohio) Bd. Edn., 1976-84, pres., 1978-82; mem. indsl. rels. adv. com. Cleve. State U., 1979—, chmn., 1982, 98; mem. Bay Village Planning Commn., 1967-69; life mem. Ohio PTA; mem. Greater Cleve. Growth Assn.; trustee New Cleve. Campaign, 1987-94—, North Coast Health Ministry, 1989-2001, Heidelberg Coll., 1996—; mem. indsl. rels. adv. com. Cleve. State U., 1979—, chmn., 1982,1999, vice chmn., 1998. With AUS, 1955-56. Mem. ABA, Ohio Bar Assn., Greater Cleve. Bar Assn., Ohio Newspaper Assn. (minority affairs com. 1987-90), Ct. of Nisi Prius Club, Cleve. Athletic Club, The Club at Soc. Ctr. Republican. Presbyterian. Office: Baker & Hostetler LLP 3200 National City Ctr 1900 E 9th St Ste 3200 Cleveland OH 44114-3475

STRINGER, EDWARD CHARLES, state supreme court justice; b. St. Paul, Feb. 13, 1935; s. Philip and Anne (Driscoll) S.; m. Mary Lucille Lange, June 19, 1957 (div. Mar. 1991); children: Philip, Lucille, Charles, Carolyn; m. Virginia L. Ward, Sept. 10, 1993. BA, Amherst Coll., 1957; LLD, U. Minn., 1960. Bar: Minn. Ptnr. Stringer, Donnelly & Sharood, St. Paul, 1960-69, Briggs & Morgan, St. Paul, 1969-79; sr. v.p., gen. counsel Pillsbury Co., Mpls., 1980-82, exec. v.p., gen. counsel, 1982-83, exec. v.p., gen. counsel, chief adminstrv. officer, 1983-89; gen. counsel U.S. Dept.

Edn., Washington, 1989-91; chief of staff Minn. Gov. Arne H. Carlson, 1992-94; assoc. justice Minn. Supreme Ct., St. Paul, 1994—. Mem. ABA, Minn. State Bar Assn., Ramsey County Bar Assn. (sec. 1977-80), Order of Coif, Mpls. Club. Congregationalist. Home: 712 Linwood Ave Saint Paul MN 55105-3513 Office: Minn Judicial Center 25 Constitution Ave Saint Paul MN 55155-1500

STROBECK, CHARLES LEROY, real estate executive; b. Chgo., June 27, 1928; s. Roy Alfred and Alice Rebecca (Stenberg) S.; m. Janet Louise Halverson, June 2, 1951; children: Carol Louise, Nancy Faith, Beth Ann, Jane Alison, Jean Marie. BA, Wheaton (Ill.) Coll., 1949. Mgr. Sudler & Co., Chgo., 1949-50, ptnr., 1951-63; chmn. bd. Strobeck, Reiss & Co., 1964-82; pres. Strobeck Real Estate, 1983-94, chmn. bd. dirs., 1994—. Bd. dirs. Am. Slide-Chart Corp., Carol Stream, 1971—. Bd. dirs. YMCA, Ill. Humane Soc., 1982—; pres. Chgo. Youth Ctrs., 1981-83, bd. dirs., 1985—; trustee Wheaton Sanitary Dist., 1976-91. Mem. Inst. Real Estate Mgmt. (pres. 1970-71), Am. Soc. Real Estate Counselors, Mental Health Assocs. Greater Chgo. (bd. dirs.), Am. Arbitration Assn., Chgo. Club, Chgo. Golf Club (bd. dirs. 1984-86), Union League Club (pres. 1975-76), Mid-Am. Club, Laurel Oak Country Club, Long Boat Key Club, Mill Creek Club, Lambda Alpha. Republican. Home: 642 Maplewood Dr Wheaton IL 60187-8067 Office: 104 S Michigan Ave Chicago IL 60603-5902

STROBEL, MARTIN JACK, lawyer, motor vehicle and industrial component manufacturing and distribution company executive; b. N.Y.C., July 4, 1940; s. Nathan and Clara (Sorgen) S.; m. Hadassah Orenstein, Aug. 15, 1965; children: Gil Michael, Karen Rachel. BA, Columbia U., 1962; JD, Cleve. Marshall Law Sch., 1966; completed advanced bus. mgmt. program, Harvard U., 1977. Bar: Ohio bar 1966. Counsel def. contract adminstrn. services region Def. Supply Agy., Cleve., 1966-68; with Dana Corp., Toledo, 1968—, gen. counsel, 1970—, dir. govt. relations, 1970-71, asst. sec., 1971—, v.p., 1976—, sec., 1982—. Mem. ABA, Fed. Bar Assn., Machinery and Allied Products Inst., Ohio Bar Assn., Toledo Bar Assn. Office: Dana Corp PO Box 1000 Toledo OH 43697-1000

STROBEL, PAMELA B. lawyer; b. Chgo., Sept. 9, 1952; BS highest honors, U. Ill., 1974, JD cum laude, 1977. Bar: Ill. 1977, U.S. Dist. (ctrl. and no. dists.) Ill. 1977, U.S. Ct. Appeals (7th cir.) 1981, U.S. Claims Ct. 1983, U.S. Ct. Appeals (fed. cir.) 1985. Ptnr. Sidley & Austin, Chgo., 1988-93; exec. v.p. Commonwealth Edison Co., 1993—. Mem. Kappa Tau Alpha (staff 1975-77). Office: Commonwealth Edison Co PO Box 767 Chicago IL 60690-0767

STRODE, GEORGE K. sports editor; b. Amesville, Ohio, Nov. 10, 1935; s. Mac and Edith M. (Murphey) S.; m. Jennifer Lanning (div. 1973); m. Ruth E. Wingett, July 15, 1973. BJ, Ohio U., 1958. Sports editor Zanesville (Ohio) Times Reporter, 1958, Athens (Ohio) Messenger, 1958-62; sports reporter Dayton (Ohio) Daily News, 1962-63, Columbus (Ohio) Citizen Jour., 1963-69; Ohio sports editor AP, Columbus, 1969-85; sports editor Columbus Dispatch, 1985—, exec. sports editor, 1999—. Mem. Ohio AP Sports Writers Assn. (v.p. 1984—), U.S. Golf Writers Assn., U.S. Harness Writers Assn. (pres. Ohio chpt. 1968-69). Republican. Methodist. Avocations: golfing, horse racing. Office: Columbus Dispatch 34 S 3rd St Columbus OH 43215-4241

STRODEL, ROBERT CARL, lawyer; b. Evanston, Ill., Aug. 12, 1930; s. Carl Frederick and Imogene (Board) S.; m. Mary Alice Shonkwiler, June 17, 1956; children: Julie Ann, Linda Lee, Sally Payson. BS, Northwestern U., 1952; JD, U. Mich., 1955. Bar: Ill. 1955, U.S. Supreme Ct. 1970; diplomate Am. Bd. Profl. Liability Attys., Am. Bd. Forensic Examiners; cert. civil trial specialist Am. Bd. Trial Advocacy. Mem. firm Davis, Morgan & Witherell, Peoria, Ill., 1957-59; pvt. practice, 1959-69; prin. Strodel, Kingery & Durree Assoc., Ill., 1969-92, Law Offices of Robert C. Strodel, Ltd., Peoria, 1992—; asst. state's atty., 1960-61; instr. bus. law Bradley U., 1961-62; lectr. Belli seminars, 1969-87. Mem. U.S. Presdl. Commn. German-Am. Tricentennial, 1983; lectr. in trial practice and med.-legal litigation. Author: Securing and Using Medical Evidence in Personal Injury and Health-Care Cases, 1988; contbr. articles to profl. jours. Gov. appointee Ill. Dangerous Drugs Adv. Coun., 1970-71; gen. chmn. Peoria-Tazewell Easter Seals, 1963, Cancer Crusade, 1970; pres. Peoria Civic Ballet, 1969-70; mem. Mayor's Commn. on Human Rels., 1962-64; chmn. City of Peoria Campaign Ethics Bd., 1975; chmn., builder City of Peoria Mil. Svcs. Meml. Plaza Project, 1998; Peoria County Rep. Sec., 1970-74; campaign chmn. Gov. Richard Ogilvie, Peoria County, 1972, Sen. Ralph Smith, 1970; treas. Michel for Congress, 1977-94, campaign coord., 1982; bd. dirs. Crippled Children's Ctr., 1964-65, Peoria Symphony Orch., 1964-68. Served with AUS, 1956-64. Decorated Officer's Cross of Order of Merit (Fed. Republic Germany), 1984; named Outstanding Young Man Peoria Peoria Jr. C. of C., 1963. Mem. ATLA (bd. govs. 1987-96), ABA, Ill. Trial Lawyers Assn. (bd. mgrs. 1985—), Ill. Bar Assn. (Lincoln awards for legal writing 1961, 63, 65), Am. Inns of Ct. (charter master of bench, Lincoln Inn-Peoria, Ill.), Civil Justice Found. (pres., charter founder, trustee 1986—), Masons, Scottish Rite. Club: Mason, Scottish Rite. Office: 927 Commerce Bank Peoria IL 61602 E-mail: stro927@aol.com.

STROGER, TODD H. state legislator; b. Chicago, IL, Jan. 14, 1963; BA, Xavier U., 1988; postgrad., DePaul U., 1991. Adminstrv. asst. Chgo. Park Dist.; jury supr. Cook County Jury Commn.; statistician Office of Chief Judge Cook County Cir. Ct.; 2nd v.p. Young Dems. of Ill.; mem. for dist. 31 Ill. Ho. of Reps., 1990—. Home: 8534 S Cottage Grove Chicago IL 60619-6527 Office: Ill Ho of Reps State Capitol Springfield IL 62706-0001

STROHMAIER, THOMAS EDWARD, designer, educator, photographer; b. Cin., Aug. 26, 1943; s. Charles Edward and Margaret Mary (Meyers) S.; m. Margaret Ann Haglage, June 7, 1980; children: Paige Maura, Edward Michael, Phoebe Greer, Michael Thomas. BFA, U. Cin., 1969, MFA, 1973. Asst. prof. design U. Cin., 1973—; City Outreach Program, 1975-76; instr. in design U. Dayton, 1976-80, asst. prof. design, 1980-83; pres. Strohmaier Design, Cin., 1983—. Cons. City Arts Corp., Cin., 1977-78, City Beautiful Program, Dayton, 1982; adj. prof. design U. Cin., 1983—, mem. lecture outreach program, 1995, developed digital design program in photography, 1999-2000. Designer urban wall projects Ohio Arts Council, Columbus, 1974, Corbet award, Cin., 1977; patentee in field. U. Dayton grantee, 1980. Mem. Contemporary Arts Ctr., Design, Architecture, Art and Planning Alumni Com., Internat. Freelance Photographers Orgn., Associated Photographers Internat., U. Cin. Decade Club. Republican. Roman Catholic. Club: Decade. Avocations: running, cycling. Home: 7311 Redondo Ct Cincinnati OH 45243-1247 Office: Strohmaier Design 5274 Ridge Ave Cincinnati OH 45213-2542 E-mail: tesmah80@aol.com., strohmaier@queencity.com.

STROM, LYLE ELMER, federal judge; b. Omaha, Jan. 6, 1925; s. Elmer T. and Eda (Hanisch) Strom; m. Regina Ann Kelly, July 31, 1950 (dec.); children: Mary Bess, Susan Frances(dec.) , Amy Claire, Cassie A., David Kelly, Margaret Mary, Bryan Thomas. Student, U. Nebr., 1946-47; AB, Creighton U., 1950, JD cum laude, 1953. Bar: Nebr. 1953. Assoc. Fitzgerald, Brown, Leahy, Strom, Schorr & Barmettler and predecessor firm, Omaha, 1953-60, ptnr., 1960-63, gen. trial ptnr., 1963-85; judge U.S. Dist. Ct. Nebr., 1985-87, chief judge, 1987-94, sr. judge, 1995—. Adj. prof. law Creighton U., 1959-95, clinical prof., 1996—; mem. com. pattern jury instrns. and practice and proc. Nebr. Supreme Ct., 1965-91; spl. legal counsel Omaha Charter Rev. Commn., 1973; chair gender fairness task force U.S. Ct. Appeals (8th cir.), 1993-97. Exec. com. Covered Wagon Coun. Boy Scouts Am., 1953—57, bd. trustees, exec. com. Mid-Am. Coun., 1988—; chmn. bd. trustees Marian H.S., 1969—71; mem. pres. coun. Creighton U., 1990—. Fellow Am. Coll. Trial Lawyers, Internat. Acad. Trial Lawyers; mem. Nebr. Bar Assn. (ho. of dels. 1978-81, exec. coun. 1981-87, pres. 1989-90), Nebr. Bar Found. (bd. trustees 1998—), Omaha Bar Assn. (pres. 1980-81), Am. Judicature Soc., Midwestern Assn. Amateur Athletic Union (pres. 1976-78), Rotary (pres. 1993-94), Alpha Sigma Nu (pres. alumni chpt. 1970-71). Republican. Roman Catholic. Office: US Dist Ct Roman Hruska Courthouse 111 S 18th Plz Ste 3190 Omaha NE 68102

STROM, ROGER, radio personality; m. Mary Strom; 2 children. Farm broadcaster, Waterloo, Iowa, Rochester, Minn., Oshkosh, Wis., Fargo, ND; farm dir. Country Day syndicated TV show, Sta. WCCO Radio, Mpls., 1988—. Spkr. in field. Master of ceremonies Princess Kay Coronation. Recipient Chem Agra award for Farm Broadcasting Excellence, Farm Bur. Communicator award. Avocation: do it yourselfer. Office: WCCO 625 2nd Ave S Minneapolis MN 55402*

STROME, STEPHEN, distribution company executive; b. Lynn, Mass., June 20, 1945; s. David and Rose (Cantor) S.; m. Phyllis Ruth Fields, Jan. 14, 1967; children: Michael, Rochelle. BA, Hillsdale (Mich.) Coll., 1967; MBA, Wayne State U., 1968. Trainee KMart Corp., Detroit, 1968-69, mgr. work measurement Troy, Mich., 1970-73; mgr. tng., edn. Fruehauf Corp., Detroit, 1974-76, regional mgr. labor relations, 1976-78; dir. ops. Handleman Co., Clawson, Mich., 1978-80, account exec., 1980-82, v.p. computer software div. Troy, 1983-85, pres. computer software/video div., 1986-87, exec. v.p., 1987-89, exec. v.p., chief oper. officer, 1990, pres., CEO, 1991-2001, chmn., CEO, 2001—. Home: 4597 Kiftsgate Bnd Bloomfield Hills MI 48302-2331 Office: Handleman Co 500 Kirts Blvd Troy MI 48084-4142

STRONG, JOHN DAVID, insurance company executive; b. Cortland, N.Y., Apr. 12, 1936; s. Harold A. and Helen H. Strong; m. Carolyn Dimmick, Oct. 26, 1957; children: John David, Suzanne. BS, Syracuse U., 1957; postgrad., Columbia U., 1980. With Kemper Group, 1957-90, Kemper Corp., 1990-96, Empire sales divsn. mgr., 1972-74, CEO, 1988-93, chmn. bd., 1989-93; vice chmn. Millikin Assocs., 1993-96, chmn., 1996; exec. v.p., dir. Facilitators, Inc., 1995-98. Mem. adv. coun. Sch. Bus., Millikin U., 1975-79, 84—; bd. dirs. United Way of Decatur and Macon County, Ill., 1976-83, campaign chmn., 1978-79, pres. bd. dirs., 1979-81; pres. United Way of Ill., 1981-83; bd. dirs. DMH Commn. Svcs. Corp., 1985-97, chmn., 1988-90; bd. dirs. Decatur-Macon County Econ. Devel. Found., 1983-88, DMH Health Systems, 1987-94, Richland C.C. Found., 1987-90, Symphony Orch. Guild of Decatur, 1992-96, DMH Found., 1988-97; bd. dirs. Ill. Ednl. Devel. Found., 1983-90, pres., 1986-87; bd. dirs. Decatur Meml. Hosp., 1985-94, vice chmn., 1988, chmn., 1990-92; bd. dirs. Ctrl. Ill. Health Assocs., Inc., 1994, vice chmn., 1994-96; mem. steering com. Decatur Advantage, 1981-93, pres., 1988-93. Capt. USAR, 1958-69. Mem. Metro Decatur C. of C. (bd. dirs. 1977-80, chmn. 1983-84), Decatur Club (bd. dirs. 19080-83, pres. 1983), Country Club of Decatur (bd. dirs. 1993-99, pres. bd. 1995-97), Alpha Kappa Psi. E-mail: jack@strongs.net.

STROSS, JEOFFREY KNIGHT, physician, educator; b. Detroit, May 2, 1941; s. Julius Knight and Molly Ellen (Fishman) S.; m. Ellen Nora Schwartz, May 22, 1965; children: Wendy, Jonathan. BS in Pharmacy, U. Mich., 1962, MD, 1967. Diplomate Am. Bd. Internal Medicine. Intern Univ. Mich. Hosp., Ann Arbor, 1967-68, resident in internal medicine, 1971-73; instr. internal medicine U. Mich., 1973-74, asst. prof., 1974-79, assoc. prof., 1979-87, prof., 1987—. Cons. Merck Sharp Dohme Co., West Point, Pa., 1982—, U.S. Dept. State, Washington, 1976—. Contbr. numerous articles to med. jours. Served to maj. USAF, 1969-71. Nat. Heart, Lung and Blood Inst. grantee, 1975—. Fellow ACP; mem. Soc. for Gen. Internal Medicine (regional chmn. 1984-86). Jewish. Home: 824 Asa Gray Dr Ann Arbor MI 48105-2853 Office: U Mich Med Sch 3119 Taubman Ann Arbor MI 48109-0376 E-mail: jstross@umich.edu.

STROTHER, JAY D. legal editor; b. Wichita, Kans., May 31, 1967; m. Cynthia L. Mehnert, Sept. 7, 1991; children: Garrett, Claire. BA, U. Tulsa, 1989. Editor U.S. Jr. C. of C., Tulsa, 1990-93, Assn. Legal Adminstrs., Vernon Hills, Ill., 1993—; editor-in-chief Legal Mgmt. Mag. Author: ALA News. Mem. Am. Soc. Assn. Execs., Soc. Nat. Assn. Publs. (bd. dirs. Chgo. chpt.), Internat. Assn. Bus. Communicators (bd. dirs., suburban v.p. 1994-95), Am. Soc. Bus. Press Editors. Office: Assn Legal Adminstrs 175 E Hawthorn Pkwy Vernon Hills IL 60061-1463 E-mail: jstrother@alanet.org.

STROUCKEN, ALBERT P.L. chemical company executive; Exec. v.p. industrial chemicals divsn. Bayer Corp.; gen. mgr. inorganic chemicals divsn. Bayer AG; chmn., pres./CEO H.B. Fuller Co., St. Paul, 1998—. Office: HB Fuller Co 1200 Willow Lake Blvd Saint Paul MN 55110

STROUD, HERSCHEL LEON, retired dentist; b. Peabody, Kans., Sept. 21, 1930; Student, U. Kans., 1948-50; BS, U. Mo., Kansas City, 1952; OD cum laude, Ill. Inst. Tech., 1954; DDS magna cum laude, U. Mo., Kansas City, 1961. Diplomate Nat. Dental Bd. Officer, founder Topeka Dental Lab., Inc., 1971; ptnr. Gage Ctr. Dental Group, P.A., Topeka, 1979-98. Pres., bd. dirs. Delta Dental Ins. of Kans. Corp., 1974-92; mem. dental staff St. Francis Hosp. and Med. Ctr., Topeka, 1963—, C.F. Menninger Meml. Hosp., Topeka, 1964—; cons., lectr. civil war medicine. Contbr. articles to profl. publs.; co-partner Kings of Swing Big Band. Vesteryman St. David's Episcopal Ch., 1966-68, composer/dir. Jubilee Mass, dir. Rejoice folk mass, 1967-74, mem. choir; dir. music for blessing of animals Friends of Topeka Zoo, 1983—; mem. U. Kans. Alumni Marching Band; founder/dir. Kans. U. Pep Band, Topeka Club; re-enactor surgeon Maj. Frontier Brigade, 1st Fed. Divsn., Union Army, Civil War, officer Kans. City Civil War Round Table. With USNR, 1950-54; capt. USAF, 1954-57, USAR, 1957-70. Fellow Am. Coll. Dentists, Internat. Coll. Dentists; mem. Soc. Preservation Oral Health (bd. dirs. 1965, exec. sec.-treas. 1966-70), Kans. State Dental Assn. (chmn. coun. on dental care plans 1972-76, state peer rev. com. 1974-76), Am. Dental Assn., Chgo. Dental Soc., Midwest Soc. Peridontology, Am. Prosthodontic Soc., Am. Equilibration Soc., Acad. Gen. Dentistry, Am. Pain Soc., Soc. for Preservation Barbership Quartet Singing Am. (chorus dir.), Rip Chords babershop quartet, Shawnee Yacht Club, Masons, Shriner, Associated Club Spkrs of Am., Knife and Fork Club Inc., Tau Kappa Epsilon, Tau Kappa Nu, Xi Psi Phi. Avocations: scuba diving, snow skiing, sailboat racing, marching band. Home: 3640 SW Drury Ln Topeka KS 66604-2550

STROUD, RHODA M. elementary education educator; Tchr. Webster Magnet Elem. Sch., St. Paul. Apptd. mem. Minn. Bd. Edn. for State of Minn. Recipient State Tchr. of Yr. Elem. award Minn., 1992. Office: Webster Magnet Elem Sch 707 Holly Ave Saint Paul MN 55104-7126

STROUP, KALA MAYS, state higher education commissioner; BA in Speech and Drama, U. Kans., 1959, MS in Psychology, 1964, PhD in Speech Comm. and Human Rels., 1974; EdD (hon.), Mo. Western State Coll., 1996; LHD (hon.), Harris-Stowe State Coll., 2000. V.p. acad. affairs Emporia (Kans.) State U., 1978-83; pres. Murray State U., Ky., 1983-90, S.E. Mo. State U., Cape Girardeau, 1990-95; commr. higher edn., mem. gov.'s cabinet State of Mo., Jefferson City, 1995—. Pres. Mo. Coun. on Pub. Higher Edn.; mem. pres.'s commn. NCAA; cons. Edn. Commn. of States Task Force on State Policy and Ind. Higher Edn.; adv. bd. NSF Directorate for Sci. Edn. Evaluation; adv. com. Dept. Health, Edn. and Welfare, chair edn. com.; citizen's adv. coun. on state of Women U. S. Dept. Labor, 1974-76. Mem. nat. exec. bd. Boy Scouts Am., nat. exploring com., former chair profl. devel. com., mem. profl. devel. com., exploring com., Young Am. awards com., 1986-87, north ctrl. region strategic planning com., bd. trustees, nat. mus. chair; mem. Gov.'s Coun. on Workforce Quality, State of Mo.; bd. dirs. Midwestern Higher Edn. Commn.; chair ACE Leadership Commn.; mem. bd. visitors Air U.; v.p. Missourians for Higher Edn.; mem. bd. St. Francis Med. Ctr. Found., 1990-95, Cape Girardeau C. of C., 1990-95, U. Kans. Alumni Assn.; pres. Forum on Excellence, Carnegie Found.; adv. bd. World Trade Ctr., St. Louis, Svc. Mems. Opty. Colls., 1997—; mem. Mo. Higher Edn. Loan Authority, 1995—, depts. econ. devel. & agrl. Mo. Global Partnership, 1995—, Mo. Tng. & Employment Coun., 1995—, Concordia U. Sys. Advancement Cabinet, State Higher Edn. Exec. Officers, 1995—, mem. com. workforce edn. and tng., 1996; bd. govs. Heartland's Alliance Minority Participation, 1995—; chair, mem. workforce devel. com. NPEC coun. U.S. Office of Edn., 1997—; bd. dirs. Midwestern Higher Edn. Com. Distributed Learning Workshop, 1998—, Dept. Natural Resources Minority Scholarship Adv. Bd.; chair Show Me Results sub-cabinet Educated Missourians; mem. Pub. Policy Initiative Stakeholder Com., 1999—; mem. Coun. Higher Edn. transfer and pub. interest com.; mem. access/diversity com. State Higher Edn. Exec. Officers; trustee, mem. adv. coun. Assn. Governing Bds. of Univs. and Colls. Ctr. for Pub. Edn., 2000—. ACE fellow; recipient Alumni Honor Citation award U. Kans., Award Distinction Profl. Black Men's Club, S.E. Mo., 1990, Dist. Svc. to Edn. award Harris-Stowe State Coll., 1996; named to U. Kans. Womans Hall of Fame, Ohio Valley Conf. Hall of Fame, 1997. Mem. Am. Assn. State Colls. and Univs. (past bd. dirs., mem. Pres.'s Commn. on Tchr. Edn., Task Force on Labor Force Issues and Implications for the Curriculum), Mortar Board, Phi Beta Kappa, Omicron Delta Kappa, Phi Kappa Phi, Rotary (found. Ednl. awards com.). Office: Mo Dept Higher Edn 3515 Amazonas Dr Jefferson City MO 65109-6821

STRUBEL, ELLA DOYLE, advertising and public relations executive; b. Chgo., Mar. 14, 1940; d. George Floyd and Myrtle (McKnight) D.; m. Richard Craig G'sell, Apr. 26, 1969 (div. 1973); m. Richard Perry Strubel, Oct. 23, 1976; stepchildren: Douglas Arthur, Craig Tollerton. BA magna cum laude, U. Memphis, 1962; MA, U. Ill., 1963. Staff asst. Corinthian Broadcasting Co., N.Y.C., 1963-65; dir. advt. and pub. rels. WANE-TV, Ft. Wayne, Ind., 1965-66; asst. dir. advt. WBBM-TV, Chgo., 1966-67, mgr. sales promotion, 1967-69, dir. advt. sales promotion and info. svcs., 1969-70; dir. pub. rels. Walthaw Watch Co., 1973-74; mgr. advt. promotion and pub. rels. WMAQ-TV, 1974-76; v.p. corp. rels. Kraft, Inc., Glenview, 1985-87; sr. v.p. corp. affairs Leo Burnett Co., Inc., Chgo., 1987-92, exec. v.p., 1992-98; mng. dir. EllaQuent Designs, 2002—. Bd. dirs. Parson Group. Mem. vis. com. U. Chgo. Harris Sch. Pub. Policy; pres. women's bd. Rehab. Inst. Chgo., 1982—84; chair Chgo. Network, 1994—95; bd. dirs. Rehab. Inst. Chgo., 1998—2001, Chgo. Pub. Libr. Found., Athena Found. Named Outstanding Woman in Comms. in Chgo., YWCA, 1995, one of 100 Most Influential Women in Chgo., Crain's Chgo. Bus., 1996, Who's Who in Chgo. Bus., 2001. Mem. Casino Club, Econ. Club. Democrat. Presbyterian. Home: 55 W Goethe St Chicago IL 60610-7406 Office: 737 N Michigan Ave Ste 1405 Chicago IL 60611-6654 E-mail: estrubel@aol.com.

STRUBEL, RICHARD PERRY, company executive; b. Evanston, Ill., Aug. 10, 1939; s. Arthur Raymond and Martha (Smith) S.; m. Linda Jane Freeman, Aug. 25, 1961 (div. 1974); children: Douglas Arthur, Craig Tollerton; m. Ella Doyle G'sell, Oct. 23, 1976. B.A., Williams Coll., 1962; M.B.A., Harvard U., 1964. Assoc. Fry Cons., Chgo., 1964-66, mng. prin., 1966-68; with N.W. Industries, Inc., 1968-83, v.p. corp. devel., 1969-73, group v.p., 1973-79, exec. v.p., 1979-83, pres., 1983; chmn. bd., pres. Buckingham Corp., N.Y.C., 1972-73; pres., chief exec. officer Microdot Inc., Chgo., 1983-94; mng. dir. Tandem Ptnrs. Inc., 1990-99; pres., COO, dir. UNext Inc., Deerfield, 1999—. Trustee Mut. Funds of The No. Trust Co., Chgo., and various mutual funds of Goldman Sachs Asset Mgmt., N.Y.C.; bd. dirs. Gildan Activewear, Inc., Montreal, Que., Can. Trustee U. Chgo.; bd. dirs. Children's Meml. Hosp., Children's Meml. Med. Ctr.; chair vis. com. Divinity Sch., U. Chgo.; adv. bd. Martin Marty Ctr. Mem. Casino Club, Chicago Club, Comml. Club, Racquet Club of Chicago, Commonwealth Club, Econ. Club. Presbyterian. Office: UNext Inc Ste 150 500 Lake Cook Rd Deerfield IL 60015

STRUGGLES, JOHN EDWARD, management consultant; b. Wilmette, Ill., Nov. 29, 1913; s. William George and Sarah Adell (Chambers) S.; m. Dorothy Eloise Goetz, Oct. 23, 1937; 1 child, John Kirk. Student, Miami U., Oxford, Ohio, 1932-34. Supt. Consol. Biscuit Co., Chgo., 1934-37; sales rep. Pillsbury Mills, 1937-41; various personnel and operating positions Montgomery Ward & Co., Chgo., Kansas City, Denver, 1941-50, v.p. personnel, 1950-53; co-founder, co-chmn. Heidrick & Struggles, Inc., Chgo., 1953—. With USNR, World War II. Republican. Home: 505 Sheridan Rd Winnetka IL 60093-2639 Office: Heidrick Struggles Inc 233 S Wacker Dr Chicago IL 60606-6306

STRUNK, ROBERT CHARLES, physician; b. Evanston, Ill., May 29, 1942; s. Norman Wesley and Marion Mildred (Ree) S.; m. Juanita; children: Christopher Robert, Alix Elizabeth. BA in Chemistry, Northwestern U., 1964, MS in Biochemistry, MD, Northwestern U., 1968. Lic. MD, Ariz., Colo., Mass., Mo. Resident in pediatrics Cin. Children's Hosp., 1968-70; pediatrician Newport (R.I.) Naval Hosp., 1970-72; rsch. fellow in pediatrics Harvard Med. Sch., Boston, 1972-74; asst. prof. pediatrics U. Ariz. Health Sci. Ctr., Tucson, 1974-78; dir. clin. svcs. Nat. Jewish Ctr. for Immunology and Respiratory Med., Denver, 1978-87; sabbatical leave Boston Children's Hosp., 1984-85; dir. divsn. allergy and pulmonary medicine Children's Hosp., St. Louis, 1987-98; pediatrician Barnes and Allied Hosp., 1987—; prof. pediatrics Washington U. Sch. Medicine, 1987—. Recipient Allergic Disease Acad. award Nat. Inst. Allergy and Infectious Disease of NIH. Mem. Am. Acad. Allergy and Immunology, Am. Thoracic Soc. Office: Washington U Sch Med Dept Pediatrics 1 Childrens Pl Saint Louis MO 63110-1002

STRUTHERS, MARGO S. lawyer; BA, Carleton Coll., 1972; JD cum laude, U. Minn., 1976. Atty., shareholder Moss & Barnett, P.A. and predecessor firms, Mpls., 1976-93; ptnr. Oppenheimer Wolff & Donnelly, LLP, 1993—. Mem. Am. Health Lawyers Assn., Minn. State Bar Assn (bus. law sect., former chair nonprofit com., former chair and former mem. governing coun. health law sect.). Office: Oppenheimer Wolff & Donnelly LLP Plaza VII 45 S 7th St Ste 3300 Minneapolis MN 55402-1614 E-mail: mstruthers@oppenheimer.com.

STRUYK, ROBERT JOHN, lawyer; b. Sanborn, Iowa, May 17, 1932; s. Arie Peter and Adriana (VerHoef) S.; m. Barbara Damon, Sept. 7, 1963; children: Arie Franklin, Damon Nicholas, Elizabeth Snow. BA, Hope Coll., 1954; MA, Columbia U., 1957; LLB, U. Minn., 1961. Bar: Minn., U.S. Dist. Ct. Minn. Secondary tchr. Indianola (Iowa) Pub. Schs., 1957-58; assoc., then ptnr. Dorsey & Whitney, Mpls., 1961—. Episcopalian. Clubs: Mpls., Minikahda. Office: Dorsey & Whitney 220 S 6th St Ste 2200 Minneapolis MN 55402-1498

STUART, JAMES, banker, broadcaster; b. Lincoln, Nebr., Apr. 11, 1917; s. Charles and Marie (Talbot) S.; m. Helen Catherine Davis, July 24, 1940; children: Catherine, James, William Scott. BA, BS, U. Nebr., 1940, HHD (hon.), HHD (hon.), DHL (hon.), U. Nebr., 1990. Chmn. bd. Stuart Mgmt. Co.; mng. ptnr. Stuart Enterprises; chmn. exec. com., bd. dirs. Nat. Bank Commerce, Lincoln; pres. Stuart Found. Founder, trustee Nebr. Human Resources Rsch. Found., 1948—; trustee Bryan Meml. Hosp., 1952-58, U. Nebr. Found., 1956—, Nebr. U. Endowment Fund for Disting. Tchrs.;

mem. Lincoln Found., 1955—, Lincoln Sch. Bd., 1961-64, pres., 1964; chmn. bd. trustees 1st Plymouth Ch., Lincoln, 1956; pres. Lincoln Community Chest, 1960. With AUS, 1942-45. Recipient Disting. Svc. award U. Nebr., 1961, Alumni Achievement award, 1980; named Nebraskan of Yr., Lincoln Rotary Club, 1997. Mem. U. Nebr. Alumni Assn. (past pres.), Lincoln U. Club, Country Club of Lincoln, Gitchigami Club (Duluth, Minn.), Sunrise Country Club (Rancho Mirage, Calif.), Thunderbird Country Club. Home: 2801 Bonacum Dr Lincoln NE 68502-5723 Office: 1248 O St Ste 852 Lincoln NE 68508

STUART, ROBERT, container manufacturing executive; b. Oak Park, Ill., Aug. 3, 1921; s. Robert S. and Marie (Vavra) Solinsky; m. Lillian C. Kondelik, Dec. 5, 1962 (dec. May 1978); m. Lila Winterhoff Peters, May 21, 1982. BS, U. Ill., 1943; LLD, U. Ill., Chgo., 1982. Sec.-treas., gen. mgr. Warren Metal Decorating Co., 1947-49; asst. to gen. mgr. Cans, Inc., 1950-52; asst. to v.p., then v.p. Nat. Can Corp., Chgo., 1953-59, exec. v.p., 1959-63, pres., 1963-69, chief exec., 1966-69, chmn. bd., chief exec. officer, 1969-73, chmn. bd., 1973-83, chmn. fin. com., 1983, mem. corp. devel. com., until 1986, chmn. emeritus, 1986—. Past pres., bd. dirs. Corp. Responsibility Group of Greater Chgo. Past pres., bd. dirs. Chgo. Crime Commn.; dir. Nat. Crime Prevention Coun.; founding chmn. Nat. Minority Supplier Devel. Coun., 1972-73, Lloyd Morey Scholarship Fund: Freedoms Found. at Valley Forge, trustee; bd. assocs. Chgo. Theol. Sem.; life trustee Ill. Masonic Med. Ctr.; mem. adv. bd. Salvation Army, Broader Urban Involvement and Leadership Devel.; chmn. emeritus World Federalist Assn.; past pres., trustee Cen. Ch. Chgo. Congregationalist; chmn. emeritus Assn. to Unite the Democracies; numerous other civic activities. Capt. AUS, 1943-46. Mem. Chgo. Club, Comml. Club, Yacht Club, Little Ship Club (London), Mason (32 degree, Red Cross of Constantine), Rotary (past pres. Chgo. club, past dist. gov.), Alpha Kappa Lambda (past nat. pres.). Office: 3351 Ridge Rd Lansing IL 60438-3119

STUART, WILLIAM CORWIN, federal judge; b. Knoxville, Iowa, Apr. 28, 1920; s. George Corwin and Edith (Abram) S.; m. Mary Elgin Cleaver, Oct. 20, 1946; children: William Corwin II, Robert Cullen, Melanie Rae, Valerie Jo. BA, State U. Iowa, 1941, JD, 1942. Bar: Iowa 1942. Pvt. practice, Chariton, 1946-62; city atty., 1947-49; mem. Iowa Senate from, Lucas-Wayne Counties, 1951-61; justice Supreme Ct. Iowa, 1962-71; judge U.S. Dist. Ct., So. Dist. of Iowa, Des Moines, 1971-86, sr. judge, 1986—. With USNR, 1943-45. Recipient Outstanding Svc. award Iowa Acad. Trial lawyer, 1987, Iowa Trial Lawyers Assn., 1988, Spl. award Iowa State Bar Assn., 1987, Disting. Alumni, U. Iowa Coll. Law, 1987. Mem. ABA, Iowa Bar Assn., Am. Legion, All For Iowa, Order of Coif, Omicron Delta Kappa, Phi Kappa Psi, Phi Delta Phi. Presbyterian. Club: Mason (Shriner). Home: 216 S Grand St Chariton IA 50049-2139

STUBBLEFIELD, ROBERT F. travel agency executive; married Judy Stubblefield; children: Matt, Rob, Kaarin, Erik. BSBA, U. Nebr. Enlisted U.S. Army, served to inf. capt., ret.; former asst. gen. merchandise mgr. Brandeis & Co.; pres. AAA, Omaha, 1976—. Active Nebr. Spl. Olympics; mem. North Hill Hunt Club; bd. dirs. numerous civic bds.; active Mid-Am. Coun. Boy Scouts. Office: AAA 10703 J St Omaha NE 68127-1023

STUBBS, JERALD D. career military officer; BA, U. Ga., 1967; JD, Harvard Law Sch., 1970. Commd. USAF, advanced through grades to brigadier gen., 1999; asst. staff judge advocate Elec. Sys. Divsn., Hanscom AFB, Mass., 1970-73; dep. staff judge advocate 21st Composite Wing, Elmendorf AFB, Alaska, 1973-76, 314th Mil. Airlift Wing, Little Rock AFB, 1978-80; trial atty. Air Force Contract Trial Team, Wright-Patterson AFB, Ohio, 1980-84; staff judge advocate 51st Tactical Fighter Wing, Osan Air Base, South Korea, 1984-86; chief adminstrn. law HQ USAF, Pentagon, 1986-89; staff judge advocate Warner Robins Air Logistics Ctr, Robins AFB, Ga., 1990-92; dep. staff judge advocate HQ Air Force Materiel Command, Wright-Patterson AFB, 1992-95; staff judge advocate HQ U.S. Space Command Air Force Space Command, Peterson AFB, Colo., 1995-96; comdr. Air Force Legal Svcs. Agy., Bolling AFB, D.C., 1996-99; staff judge advocate HQ Air Force Materiel Command, Wright-Patterson AFB, 1999—. Office: HQ AFMC/JA 4225 Logistics Ave Ste 23 Wright Patterson AFB OH 45433-5769

STUDDERT, ANDREW PAUL, air transportation executive; married; 3 children. BS, San Francisco State U., 1979. Various exec. positions First Interstate Bancorp, L.A., exec. v.p.; sr. v.p. info. svcs. divsn., chief info. officer United Airlines, Chgo., sr. v.p. fleet ops., 1997—99, COO, 1999—. Office: UAL Corp and United Airlines World Hqrs PO Box 66100 Chicago IL 60666-0100

STUDER, WILLIAM JOSEPH, library educator; b. Whiting, Ind., Oct. 1, 1936; s. Victor E. and Sarah G. (Hammersley) S.; m. Rosemary Lippie, Aug. 31, 1957; children: Joshua E., Rachel Marie. BA, Ind. U., 1958, MA, 1960, PhD (Univ. fellow), 1968. Grad. asst. divsn. libr. sci. Ind. U., 1959-60, reference asst., 1960-61; spl. intern Libr. of Congress, 1961-62, reference libr., sr. bibliographer, 1962-65; dir. regional campus librs. Ind. U., Bloomington, 1968-73, assoc. dean univ. librs., 1973-77; dir. librs. Ohio State U., Columbus, 1977-2000, prof. emeritus libr. sci., 2000—, coord. univ. oral history program, 2001—. Mem. Libr. Svcs. and Constrn. Act Adv. Com. of Ind., 1971-76, Adv. Coun. on Fed. Libr. Programs in Ohio, 1977-85, chmn., 1980-81; adv. coun. Libr. Svcs. and Tech. Act, 1997-99; mem. ARL Office Mgmt. Studies Adv. Com., 1977-81, ARL Task Force on Nat. Libr. Network Devel., 1978-83, chmn., 1981-83, com. on preservation, 1985-88, vice-chmn., 1989-90, chmn., 1990-91, task force on scholarly comm., 1983-87, com. stats. and measurement, 1993-99, chmn., 1997-98; network adv. com. Libr. of Congress, 1981-88; libr. study com. Ohio Bd. Regents, 1986-87; steering com. Ohio Libr. and Info. Network (Ohio Link), 1987-90; vice-chmn. Ctr. Rsch. Librs., 1993-94, chmn., 1994-95, sec., chmn. membership com., 1990-93; adv. coun. Ohio Link Libr., 1990-2000, chmn., 1991-92, policy adv. coun., governing bd., 1991-92. Contbr. articles to profl. jours. Trustee On Line Computer Libr. Ctr. Inc., 1977-78; del. On Line Computer Libr. Ctr. Users Coun., 1983-91; rsch. librs. adv. com. OnLine Computer Libr. Ctr., 1989-95, vice-chmn., chmn.-elect, 1993-94, chmn., 1994-95; bd. dirs. Ohio Network of Librs. Ohionet, 1977-87, chmn., 1980-82, 86-87, treas., 1983-86; mem. Columbia U. Sch. Library Svc. Conservation Programs, vis. com., 1987-90; nat. adv. coun. to commn. on preservation and access, 1989-92; treas. Monroe County (Ind.) Mental Health Assn., 1968-76; budget rev. com. United Way, 1975-77; bd. dirs. Mental Health Assn. Recipient citation for participation MARC Insts., 1968-69; Louise Maxwell award Ind. U., 1978 Mem. ALA, Ohio Libr. Assn. (bd. dirs. 1980-83), Assn. Coll. and Rsch. Librs. (bd. dirs. 1977-81, com. on activities model for 1990, 1981-82, chmn. libr. sch. curriculum task force 1988-89), Acad. Libr. Assn. Ohio, Torch Club (pres. 1993-94), Phi Kappa Phi (pub. rels. officer 1982-83, sec. 1983-85), Phi Eta Sigma, Alpha Epsilon Delta., Beta Phi Mu. Home: 724 Olde Settler Pl Columbus OH 43214-2924 Office: Ohio State U William Oxley Thompson Meml Libr 1858 Neil Ave Columbus OH 43210-1286 E-mail: studer.2@osu.edu.

STUEBE, DAVID CHARLES, steel products manufacturing company executive; b. Racine, Wis., May 29, 1940; s. Edwin C. Stuebe and Henrietta (Dryanski) Stuebe Tunnell; m. Joy L. Laughlin, Aug. 23, 1986; children: David C., Kelly Ann, Ginger, Kelly Catherine, Jon. BBA, U. Notre Dame, 1962. C.P.A., Ill. Audit mgr. Arthur Andersen, Chgo., 1962-75; v.p.-fin. School Products div. Schering Plough Inc., 1975-76, 80; pres. Arno Adhesives div. Schering Plough Inc., 1976-79; v.p. fin.-adminstrn. Carpetland, Merrillville, Ind., 1980-81; v.p. fin. MSL Industries, Inc., Lincolnwood, Ill., 1981-84, chmn. Oak Brook, 1982—, pres., chief exec. officer, 1984-87, also bd. dirs.; chmn., chief exec. officer Laughlin & Flynn, Inc., Barrington, 1987-88; pres., chief exec. officer Auto Specialties Mfg. Co., Benton Harbor, Mich., 1988—. Vice pres., bd. dirs. Ill. Assn. Retarded Citizens, Chgo., 1971-75 Mem. Ill. Soc. CPA's, Am. Inst. CPA's, Turnabout Mgmt. Assn. Club: Met. (Chgo.). Office: Hon Industries Inc 414 E 3rd St PO Box 1109 Muscatine IA 52761-7109 Home: 22620 Forest Ridge Dr Lakeville MN 55044-8004

STUECK, WILLIAM NOBLE, small business owner; b. Elmhurst, Ill., May 20, 1939; s. Otto Theodore and Anna Elizabeth (Noble) S.; m. Martha Lee Hemphill Stueck, June 2, 1963; children: Matthew Noble, Erika Lee. BS, U. Kans., 1963. Owner, pres. Suburban Lawn & Garden, Inc., Overland Park, Kans., 1953—. Chmn. bd. Mark Twain Bank South, Kansas City., Mo., 1984—. Bd. dirs. Ronald McDonald House, Kansas City; ambassador Am. Royal, Kansas City, 1983. Mem. Am. Assn. Nurserymen, Mission Valley Hunt Club (master 1986—), Leavenworth Hunt Club, Saddle & Sirloin Club. Office: PO Box 480200 Kansas City MO 64148-0200 also: Suburban Lawn & Garden Inc 13635 Wyandotte St Kansas City MO 64145-1516

STUELAND, DEAN THEODORE, emergency physician; b. Viroqua, Wis., June 24, 1950; s. Theodore Andrew and Hazel Thelma (Oftedahl) S.; m. Marlene Ann McClurg, Dec. 30, 1972; children: Jeffrey, Michael, Nancy, Kevin. BSEE, U. Wis., 1972, MSEE, 1973, MD, 1977; MPH, Med. Coll. Wis., 1997. Diplomate Am. Bd. Internal Medicine, Am. Bd. Geriatric Medicine, Am. Bd. Emergency Medicine; cert. in addictions medicine, cert. med. rev. officer. Resident Marshfield (Wis.) Clinic, 1977-80, emergency physician, dir. emergency svc., 1981-93; emergency physician Riverview Hosp., Wisconsin Rapids, Wis., 1980-81. Med. dir. Nat. Farm Medicine Ctr., Marshfield, 1986—, alcohol and other drug abuse unit St. Joseph's Hosp., Marshfield, 1988-99; exec. com. Marshfield Clinic, 1989-91, 93-95, treas., 1993-95, v.p., 1997—, ACLS state affiliate faculty Am. Heart Assn., 1984-98, nat. faculty, 1992-97; mem. emergency med. svcs. adv. bd. State of Wis., 1994-97, ECC com., 1998—. Contbr. articles to profl. jours. Charter mem., pres. Hewitt (Wis.) Jaycees, 1984; bd. dirs. Northwood County chpt. ARC, 1988-95, Wood County Partnership Coun., 1993-98. Fellow ACP, Am. Coll. Emergency Physicians (bd. dirs. Wis. chpt. 1984-90, v.p. 1990-91, pres. 1991-92, counselor 1993-98), Am. Coll. Preventive Medicine; mem. Biomed. Engring. Soc. (sr. mem.), Am. Soc. Addictions Medicine. Mem. Missionary Alliance Ch. (bd. govs., treas. 1991-97).

STUFFLEBEAM, DANIEL LEROY, education educator; b. Waverly, Iowa, Sept. 19, 1936; s. LeRoy and Melva Stufflebeam; m. Carolyn T. Joseph; children: Kevin D., Tracy Smith, Joseph. BA, State U. Iowa, 1958; MS, Purdue U., 1962, PhD, 1964; postgrad., U. Wis., 1965. Prof., dir. Ohio State U. Evaluation Ctr., Columbus, 1963-73; prof. edn. Western Mich. U. Evaluation Ctr., Kalamazoo, 1973-99, dir., 1973—; Beula McKee prof. edn. Western Mich. U., 1997—. Author monographs and 15 books; contbr. chpts. to books, articles to profl. jours. Served with U.S. Army, 1960. Recipient Paul Lazersfeld award Evaluation Rsch. Soc., 1985, Jason Millman award Consortium for Rsch. on Ednl. Accountability and Tchr. Evaluation, 1999. Mem. Am. Ednl. Rsch. Assn., Nat. Coun. on Measurement in Edn., Am. Evaluation Assn. Baptist. Office: Western Michigan Univ The Evaluation Ctr Kalamazoo MI 49008-5237 Fax: 616-387-5923. E-mail: daniel-stufflebeam@umich.edu.

STUHAN, RICHARD GEORGE, lawyer; b. Braddock, Pa., July 1, 1951; s. George and Pauline Madeline (Pavlocik) S.; m. Mary Ann Cipriano, Aug. 23, 1975; children: Brendan George, Sara Katherine, Brian Christopher, Caitlin Emily. BA summa cum laude, Duquesne U., 1973; JD, U. Va., 1976. Bar: Va. 1976, D.C. 1977, U.S. Ct. Appeals (D.C. cir.) 1977, U.S. Ct. Appeals (4th cir.) 1977, U.S. Claims Ct. 1979, U.S. Supreme Ct. 1980, U.S. Ct. Appeals (3d cir.) 1981, U.S. Ct. Appeals (11th cir.) 1982, U.S. Dist. Ct. (no. dist.) Ohio 1985, Ohio 1986. Assoc. Arnold & Porter, Washington, 1976-84; of counsel Jones, Day, Reavis & Pogue, Cleve., 1984-86, ptnr., 1987—. Mem. Va. Law Review, 1974-76. Recipient Gold Medal for Gen. Excellence, Duquesne U., 1973, Mem. Order of Coif. Democrat. Roman Catholic. Avocations: tennis, swimming, basketball, home repair. Home: 2865 Falmouth Rd Shaker Heights OH 44122-2838 Office: Jones Day Reavis & Pogue 901 Lakeside Ave Cleveland OH 44114-1190 E-mail: RGSTUHAN@JONESDAY.COM.

STUHR, ELAINE RUTH, state legislator; b. Polk County, Nebr., June 19, 1936; m. Boyd E. Stuhr, 1956; children: Cynthia (Stuhr) Zluticky, Teresa (Stuhr) Robbins, Boyd E., Jr. BS, U. Nebr. Tchr. jr. and sr. vocat. h.s. Nebr. schs.; senator Nebr. Unicameral, Lincoln, 1994—; farmer Bradshaw, Nebr. Former asst. instr. U. Nebr., Lincoln; participant farmer to farmer assignment to Russia with Winrock, Internat., 1993, to Lithuania with Vol. Overseas Coop. Asistance, 1993; former pres. Agrl. Womens Leadership Network; former mem. bd. dirs. Feed Grains Coun., Nebr. Corn Bd.; agrl. adv. com. for Congressman Doug Bereuter. Past pres., bd. dirs. Found. for Agrl. Edn. and Devel.; former mem. exec. com. and bd. dirs. Agrl. Coun. Am.; nat. pres. Women Involved in Farm Econs., state pres.; mem. adv. com. Nebr. Extension Sv.; bd. dirs. Nebr. Family Comty. Leadership Program; past chmn. Nebr. Agrl. Leadership Coun. Office: Nebr State Capitol Dist # 24 Lincoln NE 68509 E-mail: estuhr@unicam.state.ne.us.

STUKEL, JAMES JOSEPH, academic administrator, mechanical engineering educator; b. Joliet, Ill., Mar. 30, 1937; s. Philip and Julia (Mattivi) S.; m. Mary Joan Helpling, Nov. 27, 1958; children: Catherine, James, David, Paul. B.S. in Mech. Engring, Purdue U., 1959; M.S., U. Ill., Urbana-Champaign, 1963, Ph.D., 1968. Research engr. W.Va. Pulp and Paper Co., Covington, Va., 1959-61; mem. faculty U. Ill., Urbana-Champaign, 1968—, prof. mech. engring., 1975—, dir. Office Coal Research and Utilization, 1974-76, dir. Office Energy Research, 1976-81, dir. pub. policy program Coll. Engring., 1981-84, assoc. dean Coll. Engring. and dir. Expt. Sta., 1984-85; dean Grad. Coll., vice chancellor for research U. Ill. at Chgo., 1985-86, exec. vice chancellor, vice chancellor academic affairs, 1986-91, interim chancellor, 1990-91, chancellor, 1991-95, pres., 1995—. V.p. Chgo. Tech. Park Corp., 1985-88. pres., 1990-91; exec. sec. midwest Consortium Air Pollution, 1972-73, chmn. bd. dirs., 1973-75; mem. adv. bd. regional studies program Argonne (Ill.) Nat. Lab., 1975-76; adv. com. Energy Resources Commn., 1976; chmn. panel on dispersed electric generating techs. Office Tech. Assessment, U.S. Congress, 1980-81; chmn. rev. adv. bd. tech. rev. dist. heating and combined heat and power systems Internat. Energy Agy, OECD, Paris, 1982-83; cons. in field. Contbr. articles to profl. jours. Pres. parish council Holy Cross Roman Cath. Ch., Urbana, 1967-68. Mem. ASCE (State-of-the-Art of Civil Engring. award 1975), ASME, AAAS, Sigma Xi, Phi Kappa Phi, Pi Tau Sigma. Home: 2650 N Lakeview Ave Apt 1610 Chicago IL 60614-1819 Office: 364 Henry Adm Bldg M/C 346 Urbana IL 61801

STUMPF, DAVID ALLEN, pediatric neurologist; b. L.A., May 8, 1945; s. Herman A. and Dorothy F. (Davis) S.; children: Jennifer F., Kaitrin E.; m. Elizabeth Dusenbery, Feb. 2, 1989; children: Todd Coleman, Shilo Walker. BA, Lewis and Clark Coll., 1966; MD cum laude, PhD, U. Colo., 1972. Pediatric intern Strong Meml. Hosp., Rochester, N.Y., 1972-73, resident, 1973-74; resident in neurology Harvard Med. Sch., Boston, 1974-77; dir. pediatric neurology U. Colo. Health Sci. Ctr., Denver, 1977-85; chief neurology Children's Meml. Hosp., Chgo., 1985-89; chmn. neurology, Benjamin and Virginia T. Boshes prof. Northwestern U., 1989-98, prof. neurology and pediatrics, 1999—; pres. and CEO Oyxis, LLC, 1999—. Mem. sci. adv. com. Muscular Dystrophy Assn., 1981-87; bd. dirs. North-Western Meml. Corp., Chgo. Mem. editl. bd. Neurology, 1982-87; contbr. articles to sci. jours. Recipient Lewis and Clark Coll. Disting. Alumni award, 1991; NIH grantee, 1979-84; Muscular Dystrophy Assn. grantee, 1977-89; March of Dimes grantee, 1983-85. Fellow Am. Acad. Neurology; mem. Child Neurology Soc. (counsellor 1982-84, pres. 1985-87), Am. Neurol. Assn., Am. Pediatric Soc., Soc. Pediatric Rsch., Internat. Child Neurology Assn. (v.p. 1998—). Presbyterian. Office: 540 Judson Ave Evanston IL 60202-3084 Mailing: Northwestern U Dept Neurology Abbott Hall 710 N Lakeshore Dr Chicago IL 60611-3006 Office Fax: 800-701-9821. E-mail: david@stumpf.org.

STUMPF, LEROY A. state legislator; b. May 29, 1944; m. Carol; three children. BA, St. Paul Seminary; MPA, Syracuse U. Former Minn. State rep.; mem. Minn. Senate from dist. 1, St. Paul, 1982—; farmer. Chmn. higher edn. divsn.; co-chmn. edn. mem. edn. funding divsn.; mem. fin., govt. ops. and reform and rules and adminstrn. coms. Office: 428 Riverside Ave Thief River Falls MN 56701-3521 also: State Senate State Capital Building Saint Paul MN 55155-0001

STUPAK, BART T. congressman, lawyer; b. Feb. 29, 1952; m. Laurie Ann Olsen; children: Ken, Bart Jr. (dec.). AA in Criminal Justice, Northwestern Mich. C.C., Traverse City, 1972; BS in Criminal Justice, Saginaw Valley State Coll., 1977; JD, Thomas M. Cooley Law Sch., 1981. Patrolman Escanaba City Police Dept., 1972-73; state trooper Mich. Dept. State Police, 1973-84; instr. State Police Tng. Acad., 1980-82; atty., 1981-84, Hansley, Neiman, Peterson, Beauchamp, Stupak, Bergman P.C., 1984-85; ptnr. Stupak, Bergman, Stupak P.C., 1985-88; mem. Mich. Ho. of Reps., 1989-90; prin. Bart T. Stupak P.C., 1991—; mem. 103rd-106th Congresses from 1st Mich. dist., 1993—. Mem. commerce subcom. on health & environment. Nat. committeeman Boy Scouts Am., coach Menominee Youth Baseball Assn., Little League; active Wildlife Unltd., Menominee Woods and Streams Assn., Menominee County Hist. Soc.; adv. com. Bay Pines Juv. Detection Ctr. Mem. Nat. Rifle Assn., Sons of the Am. Legion, Knights of Columbus, Elks Club, State Employees Retirees Assn., fin. com. Holy Spirit Catholic Ch. Democrat. Office: US Ho of Reps 2348 Rayburn Ho Office Bldg Washington DC 20515-0001 E-mail: stupak@mail.house.gov.*

STURGEON, JOHN ASHLEY, insurance company executive; b. Alliance, Alaska; B degree, Midland Luth. Coll., 1962. Ptnr. Arthur Andersen & Co., 1962—82; exec. v.p., gen. comptroller The Mutual of Omaha Ins. Cos., Omaha, 1982—97, pres., 1997—98, pres., COO, 1998—; pres. United World Life Ins. Co., 1997—. Bd. dirs. Kirkpatrick, Pettis, Smith, Polian Inc., 1983—, Companion Life Ins. Co., 1984—, United World Life Ins. Co., 1990—, The Omaha Indemnity Co., 1993—, Mut. of Omaha Structured Settlement Co., 1995—, KFS Corp., 1996—, Mut. of Omaha Holdings, Inc., 1997—, Mut. of Omaha Ins. Co., 1997—, Mut. of Omaha Life Ins. Co., 1997—, Health Ins. Assn. Am., 1998—, Creighton U., 2000—, Mut. of Omaha Investor Svcs., Inc., 2000—; chmn. Omaha Property and Casualty Ins. Co., 1996—, Innowave Inc., 1998—. Consultation com. U.S. Strategic Command; bd. trustees Mid-Am. Coun. Boy Scouts Am. Mem.: Nebr. Soc. CPA's, Am. Inst. CPA's. Office: The Mutual of Omaha Ins Co Mutual of Omaha Plz Omaha NE 68175

STURGESS, GEOFFREY J. aeronautical research engineer; Aero. and mech. rsch. engr. Innovative Scientific Solutions, Inc., Beavercreek, Ohio. Recipient Energy Systems award AIAA, 1994. Home: 1747 Lesourd Dr Beavercreek OH 45432-2478 Office: 2766 Indian Ripple Rd Dayton OH 45440-3638

STURTZ, W. DALE, state legislator; m. Fay Sturtz. Grad., Nat. Sheriffs Inst., FBI Acad. Sheriff LaGrange County, Ind., 1980-90; investigator, legal adminstr. Yoder Law Offices, 1990—; mem. from 52d dist. Ind. State Ho. of Reps., 1992—, chmn. judiciary com., mem. agr., natural resources/rural devel. com., mem. cts. and criminal codes com. Mem. Nat. Sheriffs Inst., Fraternal Order of Police, Meridian Sun Lodge, Exch. Club, Scottish Rite. Home: 2770 N 200 E Lagrange IN 46761-9154 Office: Ind House of Reps State Capitol Indianapolis IN 46204

STYNES, STANLEY KENNETH, retired chemical engineer, educator; b. Detroit, Jan. 18, 1932; s. Stanley Kenneth and Bessie Myrtle (Casey) S.; m. Marcia Ann Meyers, Aug. 27, 1955; children: Peter Casey, Pamela Kay, Suzanne Elizabeth. B.S., Wayne State U., 1955, M.S., 1958; Ph.D., Purdue U., 1963. Lab. asst. U. Chgo., 1951; instr. Purdue U., 1960-63; asst. prof. chem. engring. Wayne State U., Detroit, 1963-64, assoc. prof., 1964-71, prof., 1971-92, dean engring., 1972-85, prof. emeritus, 1992—. Dir. Energy Conversion Devices, Inc., Troy, Mich., MacMedia; cons. Schwayder Chem. Metallurgy Co., 1965, chemistry dept. Wayne State U., 1965—66, Claude B. Schneible Co., Holly, Mich., 1968. Contbr. engring. articles to profl. jours. Mem. coun. on environ. strategy S.E. Mich. Coun. Govts., 1976—81; sec.-treas. Mich. Ednl. Rsch. Info. Triad; trustee Sci. Ctr. Met. Detroit, 1980—92; mem. ops. com. MACTV, 2000; bd. dirs. Program for Minorities in S.E. Mich., Sci. and Engring. Fair of Met. Detroit, pres., 1983; bd. dirs. Midwest Program for Minorities in Engring., Friends of Herrick Dist. Libr. Ford Found. fellow, 1959-63; DuPont fellow, 1962-63; Wayne State U. faculty research fellow, 1964-65 Fellow: AIChE (past chmn. Detroit sect.), Mich. Soc. Profl. Engrs. (pres. 1987—88), Engring. Soc. Detroit (past bd. dirs.); mem.: Adult Learning Inst. (bd. dirs. 1994—99), Engring. Sci. Devel. Found. (pres. 1992—94), Am. Chem. Soc., Phi Lambda Upsilon, Omicron Delta Kappa, Tau Beta Pi, Sigma Xi. Presbyterian. Home: 145 Columbia #609 Holland MI 49423-2980 E-mail: stynes@macatawa.org.

SUAREZ, BENJAMIN, consumer products company executive; Pres., CEO Suarez Corp. Office: Suarez Corp 7800 Whipple Ave NW Canton OH 44767-0002

SUAREZ, RAY, city official; b. Yauco, P.R., Oct. 26, 1946; m. Marta. Coord. CETA program Dept. Streets & Sanitation, Chgo., 1974, asst. commr., 1974-91; alderman of the 31st ward City of Chgo., 1991—, chmn. com. on housing and real estate. Chair human rels. com. Chgo. City Coun., 1994—, budget and govt. ops. com., bldgs. com., rules & ethics com., fin. com., spl. events and cultural affairs com., zoning, transportation & pub. ways com., 1994. Served in USMC, Vietnam. Mem. Caballeros de San Juan (pres.), Lions. Office: 31st Ward 4502 W Fullerton Ave Chicago IL 60639-1934

SUDBRINK, JANE MARIE, sales and marketing executive; b. Sandusky, Ohio, Jan. 14, 1942; niece of Arthur and Lydia Sudbrink. BS, Bowling Green State U., 1964; postgrad. in cytogenetics, Kinderspital-Zurich, Switzerland, 1965. Field rep. Random House and Alfred A. Knopf Inc., Mpls., 1969-72, Ann Arbor, Mich., 1973, regional mgr. Midwest and Can., 1974-79, Can. rep., mgr., 1980-81; psychology and ednl. psychology adminstrv. editor Charles E. Merrill Pub. Co. div. Bell & Howell Corp., Columbus, Ohio, 1982-84; sales and mktg. mgr. trade products Wilson Learning Corp., Eden Prairie, Minn., 1984-85; fin. cons. Merrill Lynch Pierce Fenner & Smith, Edina, 1986-88; sr. editor Gorsuch Scarisbrick Pubs., Scottsdale, Ariz., 1988-89; regional mgr. Worth Publs., Inc. - von Holtzbrinck Pub. Grp., N.Y.C., 1997-98; mktg. assoc. Harcourt Brace Coll. Pubs., Northbrook, Ill., 1997-98, cons. midatlantic region, 1998—; mktg. assoc. W.W. Norton & Co., Ill., Ind., Ohio, 1998—. Lutheran. Home and Office: 3801 Mission Hills Rd Northbrook IL 60062-5729 E-mail: jsudbrink@wwnorton.com.

SUDHOLT, TOM, radio personality; 1 child Kate. Radio host Classic 99, St. Louis. Avocations: history, astronomy, meteorology. Office: Classic 99 85 Founders Ln Saint Louis MO 63105

SUELFLOW, AUGUST ROBERT, historian, educator, archivist; b. Rockfield, Wis., Sept. 5, 1922; s. August Henry and Selma Hilda (Kressin) S.; m. Gladys I. Gierach, June 16, 1946; children: August Mark, Kathryn Lynn Du Bois. BA, Concordia Coll., Milw., 1942; BDiv, MDiv, Concordia Sem., St. Louis, 1946, fellow, 1947, STM, 1947; DivD, Concordia Sem., Springfield, Ill., 1967. Asst. curator Concordia Hist. Inst., St. Louis, 1946-48, dir., 1948-95, cons., 1995-97; guest lectr. Concordia Sem., St. Louis, 1952-69, 74-75, adj. prof., 1975—; asst. pastor Luther Meml. Ch., Richmond Heights, Mo., 1948-56, Mt. Olive, St. Louis, 1958-75; archivist Western Dist. Luth. Ch.-Mo. Synod, 1948-66, archivist Mo. Dist., 1966-87, 88-95; instr. Washington U., St. Louis, 1967-82. Inst. Mem. Am. Assn. Museums, Nat. Trust for Hist. Preservation, Soc. Am. Archivists, Orgn. Am. Historians, Western History Assn., Luth. Hist. Conf. Lutheran. Author: A Preliminary Guide to Church Records Depositories, 1969, Religious Archives: An Introduction, 1980, Heart of Missouri, 1954; cons., contbr. Luth. Cyclopedia, 1975; contbr. Moving Frontiers, 1964, Ency. of the Luth. Ch., 1965, The Luths. in N.Am., 1975, C.F.W. Walther: The American Luther, 1987; mng. editor Concordia Hist. Inst. Quar., 1950-95, assoc. editor., 1950—; Archives & History: Minutes and Reports, 1952-89; editor: Directory of Religious Hist. Depositories in America, 1963, Microfilm Index and Bibliography, vol. I, 1966, vol. II, 1978, Luth. Hist. Conf. Essays and Reports, 1964-92; series editor: Selected Writings of C.F.W. Walther, 6 vols., 1981; vol. editor, translator: Walther's Convention Essays, vol. III, 1981; sec., mem. editorial com. Concordia Jour., 1976-81; mem. editorial/adv. com. Luth. Higher Edn. in N.Am., 1980; mem. editorial com., contbr. Moving Frontiers, 1964. Office: 7249 Northmoor Dr Saint Louis MO 63105-2109

SUGAR, RONALD D. aerospace executive; BSEE summa cum laude, UCLA, 1968, MS, 1969, PhD, 1971. Dir. advanced R & D programs TRW Inc., Cleve., 1981-83, chief engr., dep. program mgr. Milstar Satellite payload program, 1983-87, v.p., gen. mgr. space comms. divsn., 1987-92, v.p. strategic bus. devel. space and def. sector, 1992-94, exec. v.p., CFO, 1994-96, exec. v.p., gen. mgr. automotive electronics group, 1996-98, exec. v.p. spl. projects, 1998-99, pres., COO space and info. sys. sector, 1999-2000; pres. & COO Litton Industries, Inc., Woodland Hills, Calif., 2000—. Office: Litton Industries 21240 Burbank Blvd Woodland Hills CA 91367-6675

SUGARBAKER, EVAN R. nuclear science research administrator; b. Mineola, N.Y., Nov. 17, 1949; married, 1985; 1 child. BA, Kalamazoo Coll., 1971; PhD in Physics, U. Mich., 1976. Rsch. assoc. nuclear structural rsch. lab. U. Rochester (N.Y.), 1976-78; vis. asst. prof. physics U. Colo., 1978-80; asst. prof. physics Ohio State U., Columbus, 1981-86, assoc. prof. physics, 1986-94, prof. physics, 1994—, vice chmn. dept., 2001—. Co-prin. investigator NSF grant, 1981-88, 95—, prin. investigator, 1988-95; bd. dirs. Los Alamos Meson Physics Facility Users Group, Inc., 1990-92; cons. Los Alamos Nat. Lab., 1991-94. Mem. AAAS, Am. Phys. Soc., Am. Assn. Physics Tchrs. Office: Dept Physics Ohio State U 174 W 18th Ave Columbus OH 43210-1106

SUGDEN, RICHARD LEE, pastor; b. Compton, Calif., Apr. 13, 1959; s. L. Fred Sugden and Nancy Jane (Motherwell) Coulter; m. Rebecca Lynn Travis, June 1981; children: Richard Lee II, Ryan Leon, Rachel Lynn, Lawrence Fred, Nicole Irene. BA, Pensacola (Fla.) Christian Coll., 1981. Ordained pastor, 1985. Assoc. pastor Chippewa Lake Bapt. Ch., Medina, Ohio, 1981-84; dir., evangelist Victory Acres Christian Camp, Warren, 1985; asst. pastor Bible Bapt. Temple, Campbell, 1985-93; missionary evangelist Sugden Evang. Ministries, Struthers, 1993—. Del. pastors' sch. 1st Bapt. Ch., Hammond, Ind., 1982—. Author: Philippians on Your Level, 1990, James on Your Level, 1991, I Timothy On Your Level, 1991. Founder, dir. Penn-Ohio Bapt. Youth Fellowship. Mem. Christian Law Assn., Buckeye Ind. Bapt. Fellowship. Republican. Avocations: gardening, home improvements. Home and Office: Sugden Evang Ministries 71 Harvey St Struthers OH 44471-1538 E-mail: ricsugden@juno.com.

SUHRE, RICHARD L. transportation company executive; Pres. Cassens Transport Co., Edwardsville, Ill., 1994—. Office: Cassens Transport Co 145 N Kansas St Edwardsville IL 62025-1770

SUHRHEINRICH, RICHARD FRED, judge; b. 1936; BS, Wayne State U., 1960; JD cum laude, Detroit Coll. Law, 1963, LLM, 1992, U. Va., 1990. Bar: Mich. Assoc. Moll, Desenberg, Purdy, Glover & Bayer, 1963—67; asst. prosecutor Macomb County, 1967; ptnr. Rogensues, Richard & Suhrheinrich, 1967; assoc. Moll, Desenberg, Purdy, Glover & Bayer, 1967—68; ptnr. Kitch, Suhrheinrich, Saurbier & Drutchas, 1968—84; judge U.S. Dist. Ct. (ea. dist.) Mich., Detroit, 1984—90, U.S. Ct. Appeals (6th Cir.), Lansing, 1990—. Mem.: Ingham County Bar Assn., State Bar Mich. Office: US Ct Appeals 6th Cir USPO & Fed Bldg 315 W Allegan St Rm 241 Lansing MI 48933-1514

SULKIN, HOWARD ALLEN, college president; b. Detroit, Aug. 19, 1941; s. Lewis and Vivian P. (Mandel) S.; m. Constance Annette Adler, Aug. 4, 1963; children— Seth R., Randall K. PhB, Wayne State U., 1963; MBA, U. Chgo., 1965, PhD, 1969; LHD (hon.), De Paul U., 1990. Dir. program rsch., indsl. rels. ctr. U. Chgo., 1964-72; dean Sch. for New Learning, De Paul U., Chgo., 1972-77; v.p. De Paul U., 1977-84; pres. Spertus Inst. Jewish Studies, 1984—. St. Paul's vis. prof. Rikkyo U., Tokyo, 1970—; cons., evaluator North Central Assn., Chgo., 1975—. Contbr. articles to profl. jours. Sec.-treas. Grant Park Cultural and Ednl. Cmty., Chgo., 1984—; bd. dirs. Chgo. Sinai Congregation, 1972—, pres., 1980-83; bd. dirs. S.E. Chgo. Commn., 1980—, United Way, 1984—, Crusade of Mercy United Way, 1990—; bd. dirs., chmn. Parliament of World's Religions, 1989—. Mem. The Standard Club, Tavern Club. Office: Spertus Inst of Jewish Studies 618 S Michigan Ave Chicago IL 60605-1901

SULLIVAN, ALFRED DEWITT, academic administrator; b. New Orleans, Feb. 2, 1942; s. Dewitt Walter and Natalie (Alford) S.; m. Marilyn Janie Hewitt, Sept. 1, 1962 (div. May 1989); children: Alan, Sean; m. Dorothy Madeleine Hess, Apr. 1993. BS, La. State U., 1964, MS, 1966; PhD, U. Ga., 1969. Asst. prof. Va. Poly. Inst. and State U., Blacksburg, 1969-73; assoc. prof., then prof. Miss. State U., Starkville, 1973-88; dir. Sch. Forest Resources Pa. State U., University Park, 1988-93; dean coll. natural resources U. Minn., St. Paul, 1993—. Contbr. articles to profl. jours. Fellow Am. Coun. on Edn., 1987-88, NDEA fellow U. Ga., 1966-69; assoc. Danforth Found., 1981. Mem. Soc. Am. Foresters. Office: U Minn 235 Natural Resources Adminstrn Bldg 2003 Upper Buford Cir Saint Paul MN 55108-6146

SULLIVAN, AUSTIN PADRAIC, JR. diversified food company executive; b. Washington, June 26, 1940; s. Austin P. and Janet Lay (Patterson) Sullivan; m. Judith Ann Raab, June 1, 1968 (dec. Jan. 1995); children: Austin P. Sullivan III, Amanda, Alexander; m. Marie Elise de Golian, Aug. 1, 1997; children: Lauren Gibbons, Georgia Gibbons, Samuel Gibbons. AB cum laude, Princeton U., 1964. Spl. asst. to dep. dir. N.J. Office Econ. Opportunity, Trenton, 1965-66; prof. staff mem. Com. on Edn. and Labor, U.S. Ho. of Reps., Washington, 1967-71, legis. dir., 1971-76; dir. govt. relations Gen. Mills, Inc., Mpls., 1976-78, v.p., corp. dir. govt. relations, 1978-79, v.p. pub. affairs, 1979-93, v.p. corp. comms. and pub. affairs, 1993-94, sr. v.p. corp. rels., 1994—. Lectr. fed. labor market policies Harvard U., 1972—76, Boston U., 1972—76. Bd. dirs., exec. com. Guthrie Theatre, Mpls., 1978—84, Minn. Citizens for the Arts, 1980—83, Urban Coalition Mpls., 1978—80; chmn. Pub. Affairs Coun., 1993—94, Gov.'s Coun. on Employment and Tng., 1976—82; mem. Nat. Commn. on Employment and Tng., 1979—81; co-chmn. Gov.'s Commn. on Dislocated Workers, 1988—89; trustee Minn. Pub. Radio, 1999—; bd. advisors Min. C. of C., bd. dirs., 1993—99; mem. U.S. Sec. Agr. Adv. Com. on Agrl. Biotech., 2000—; bd. advisors Dem. Leadership Coun., 1996—. With1959 USMC, 1957. Fellow Eleanor Roosevelt fellow in interracial rels., 1964—65. Mem.: Grocery Mfrs. Assn. (govt. affairs coun. 1991—, chmn. biotech. task force 1999—, co-chmn. bus. roundtable fiscal policy coord. com. 2001—), Coun. of Pub. Affairs Execs. (chmn. 1989—90), Conf. Bd., Medica (bd. dirs. 2001—), GreaterMpls. C. of C. (exec. com. 1980—86, 1990—93, bd. dirs.), Mpls. Club (bd. govs. 2001—). Home: 17830 County Rd 6 Minneapolis MN 55447-2905 Office: Gen Mills Inc One Gen Mills Blvd Minneapolis MN 55426

SULLIVAN, BARRY, lawyer; b. Newburyport, Mass., Jan. 11, 1949; s. George Arnold and Dorothy Bennett (Furbush) S.; m. Winnifred Mary Fallers, June 14, 1975; children: George Arnold, Lloyd Ashton. AB cum laude, Middlebury Coll., 1970; JD, U. Chgo., 1974. Bar: Mass. 1975, Ill. 1975, Va. 1995, U.S. Dist. Ct. (no. dist.) Ill. 1976, U.S. Ct. Appeals (7th cir.) 1976, U.S. Ct. Appeals (10th cir.) 1977, U.S. Ct. Appeals (11th cir.) 1986, U.S. Ct. Appeals (5th and 9th cirs.) 1987, U.S. Ct. Appeals (fed. cir.) 1993, U.S. Ct. Appeals (DC cir.) 1994, U.S. Ct. Appeals (4th cir.) 1997, U.S. Supreme Ct. 1978. Law clk. to judge John Minor Wisdom U.S. Ct. Appeals (5th cir.), New Orleans, 1974-75; assoc. Jenner & Block, Chgo., 1975-80; asst. to solicitor gen. of U.S. U.S. Dept. of Justice, Washington, 1980-81; ptnr. Jenner & Block, Chgo., 1981-94, 2001—; prof. law Washington and Lee U., Lexington, Va., 1994-2001, dean, 1994-99, v.p., 1998-99; Fulbright prof. U. Warsaw, Poland, 2000—01; lectr. in law U. Chgo., 2001—. Vis. fellow Queen Mary and Westfield Coll., U. London, 2001; spl. asst. atty. gen. State of Ill., 1989—90; lectr. in law Loyola U., Chgo., 1978—79; adj. prof. law Northwestern U., Chgo., 1990—92, Chgo., 1993—94, vis. prof., 1992—93; Jessica Swift Meml. lectr. in constnl. law Middlebury Coll., 1991. Assoc. editor U. Chgo. Law Rev., 1973-74; contbr. articles to profl. jours. Trustee Cath. Theol. Union at Chgo., 1993—; mem. vis. com. Irving B. Harris Grad. Sch. Public Policy Studies U., Chgo., 2001—; mem. vis. com. U. Chgo. Divinity Sch., 1987—2001; mem. adv. panel Fulbright Sr. Specialist Program, 2001—. Yeats Soc. scholar, 1968; Woodrow Wilson fellow, Woodrow Wilson Found., 1970. Mem. ABA (chmn. coord. com. on AIDS 1988-94, mem. standing com. on amicus curiae briefs 1990-97, mem. coun. of sect. of individual rights and responsibilities 1993-98, mem. sect. of legal edn. com. on law sch. adminstrn. 1994-98, chair sect. legal edn. com. on professionalism 1999-2000), Va. Bar Assn., Va. State Bar (chair sect. on edn. of lawyers 1998-99), Bar Assn. 7th Fed. Cir. (vice chmn. adminstrv. justice com. 1985-86), Am. Law Inst., Chgo. Bar Assn., Ill. State Bar Assn., Lawyers Club Chgo., Phi Beta Kappa. Democrat. Roman Catholic. Home: 5555 S Everett Apt A1-2 Chicago IL 60637 Office: Jenner & Block One IBM Plz Chicago IL 60611 E-mail: bsullivan@jenner.com.

SULLIVAN, BERNARD JAMES, accountant; b. Chgo., June 25, 1927; s. Bernard Hugh and Therese Sarah (Condon) S.; m. Joan Lois Costello, June 9, 1951; children: Therese Lynn Scanlan, Bernard J., Geralyn M. Snyder. BSC, Loyola U., Chgo., 1950. CPA, Ill. Staff Bansley and Kiener, Chgo., 1950-66, ptnr., 1966-82, mng. ptnr., 1982—. Bd. dirs. Associated Acctg. Firms, Internat.; exec. com. Moore Stephens and Co., U.S.A., 1984—, Arbitrator Nat. Assn. Security Dealers. Served with USN, 1945-46. Mem. Am. Inst. CPA's, Ill. Soc. CPA's, Govt. Fin. Officer Assn., Internat. Found. Employee Benefit Plans, Delta Sigma Pi. Clubs: Beverly Country (Chgo.), Metropolitan (Chgo.). Lodges: Elks, K.C. Avocations: golf, sports, travel. Home: 9636 S Kolmar Ave Oak Lawn IL 60453-3214 Office: Bansley & Kiener 125 S Wacker Dr Ste 1200 Chicago IL 60606-4496 E-mail: bsullivan@bk-cpa.com.

SULLIVAN, BILL M. church administrator; USA/Can. Mission/Evangelism dept. dir. Church of the Nazarene, Kansas City, Mo., 1980. Office: Church of Nazarene 6401 The Paseo Kansas City MO 64131-1213

SULLIVAN, CHARLES A. food products executive; BBA, U. Toledo, 1959. With Seven-Up Co., Los Angeles, 1966-70; v.p. strategic planning Pepsi-Cola Co., 1966-70; pres. Seven Up of Ind.; with Westinghouse Electric Corp., 1970-79; pres. Can. Dry of New Eng. subs. Norton Simon Co., 1979-82; sr. v.p. pres. Merita div. Am. Bakeries Co. subs. BCA Corp., N.Y.C., 1982-86; exec. v.p. BCA Corp.; pres., exec. v.p. Merita div. Am. Bakeries Co., 1986-89; pres., CEO, Interstate Bakeries Corp., 1989-90, CEO and chmn., 1991—; pres., CEO, Interstate Brands Corp., 1989-90. Office: Interstate Brands Corp PO Box 419627 Kansas City MO 64141-6627 also: Interstate Brands Corp 12 E Armour Blvd Kansas City MO 64111-1202

SULLIVAN, DANIEL JOSEPH, theater critic; b. Worcester, Mass., Oct. 22, 1935; s. John Daniel and Irene Ann (Flagg) S.; m. Helen Faith Scheid, 1965; children: Margaret Ann, Benjamin, Kathleen. AB, Holy Cross Coll., 1957; postgrad., U. Minn., 1957-59, U. So. Calif., 1964-65, Stanford U., 1978-79. Reporter Worcester Telegram, Mass., 1957, Red Wing Republican Eagle, Minn., 1959, St. Paul Pioneer Press, 1959-61; music and theater critic Mpls. Tribune, 1962-64; comedy writer Dudley Riggs' Brave New Workshop, 1961-64; arts reporter/theater reviewer N.Y. Times, 1965-68; theater critic L.A. Times, 1969-90. Dramaturg Eugene O'Neill Theatre Ctr., Waterford, Conn., 1972-73, 93-98; instr. O'Neill Critics Inst., Waterford, 1977-92, assoc. dir., 1993-98, dir., 1999—; adj. prof. U. Minn., Mpls., 1990—; juror theater panel Nat. Endowment for Arts, 1983; juror Pulitzer Prize for Drama, 1985, 89, 92; pres. L.A. Drama Critics Circle, 1970-71, Ctr. for Arts Criticism, St. Paul, 1992-95. Mem. Am. Theater Critics Assn. (founding). Fax: 612-827-4254. E-mail: Sulli008@umn.edu.

SULLIVAN, DAVE, state legislator; b. Chgo., Dec. 29, 1964; m. Dru; 4 children. BA in Polit. Sci., Marquette U. Mem. Ill. Senate, Springfield, 1999—, mem. lic. activities com., environ. & energy com. V.p., precinct capt. Maine Twp. Regular Rep. Orgn.; exec. asst. intergovtl. affairs Sec. of State George H. Ryan, 1992-98; cons. several Ill. campaigns. Republican. Office: State Capitol Capitol Bldg M108 Springfield IL 62706-0001 also: 800 E Northwest Hwy Ste 102 Mount Prospect IL 60056-3457

SULLIVAN, DENNIS JAMES, JR. hospitality and music executive; b. Jersey City, Feb. 23, 1932; s. Dennis James and Mary Theresa (Coyle) S.; m. Constance Rosemary Shields, Jan. 31, 1953; children: Denise Sullivan Morrison, Mary Agnes Sullivan Wilderotter, Colleen Sullivan Bastkowski, Andrea Sullivan Doelling. AB, St. Peters Coll., 1953; postgrad., U. Md., 1955; MBA, U. Pa., 1973. Various line and staff positions N.J. Bell, 1955-61, N.Y. Telephone Co., 1961-64, 67-68, AT&T, N.Y.C., 1964-67, 68-76, dir. mktg., 1972-74, asst. v.p., 1974-76; v.p. mktg. Ohio Bell Telephone Co., Cleve., 1976-78; v.p. consumer info. services AT&T-Am. Bell, Parsippany, N.J., 1978-83; exec. v.p. Cin. Bell Telephone Co., 1983-84, pres., 1984-87, also bd. dirs.; exec. v.p., chief fin. officer Cin. Bell Inc., 1987-93; exec. founder Dan Pingor Pub. Rels., 1993-2000; pres., CEO Gaylord Entertainment, Nashville, 2000—. Bd. dirs. Fifth Third Bancorp & Bank, Anthem Ins. Co., Kalthoff Internat. Author: Videotex, IEE Nat. Conf., 1981. Bd. dirs. Boy Scouts, Cin. Bd. Edn., 1993-97; gen. chmn. United Way, 1990—. Lt. (j.g.) USN, 1953-55, ret. comdr. USNR, 1976. Mem. Fin. Exec. Inst., Commonwealth Club, Cin. Country Club, Queen City Club, Legatus, Metropolitan Club. Roman Catholic. Office: Gaylord Entertainment Pinger Bldg One Gaylord Dr Nashville TN 37214 E-mail: dennissullivan@gaylordentertainment.com.

SULLIVAN, DENNIS W. power systems company executive; b. Chgo., 1938; Grad., Purdue U., 1960, Case Western Res. U., 1969. Exec. v.p. Parker Hannifin Corp., Cleve., 1981—, bd. dirs., 1983—. Bd. dirs. Soc. Bat. Bank. Office: Parker Hannifin Corp 6035 Parkland Blvd Cleveland OH 44124-4141

SULLIVAN, E. THOMAS, dean; b. Amboy, Ill., Dec. 4, 1948; s. Edward McDonald and Mary Lorraine (Murphy) S.; m. Susan A. Sullivan, Oct. 2, 1971. BA, Drake U., 1970; JD, Ind. U., Indpls., 1973. Bar: Ind. 1973, Fla. 1974, D.C. 1975, Mo. 1980. Law clk. to Judge Joe Eaton, U.S. Dist. Ct. for So. Dist. Fla., Miami, 1973-75; trial atty. U.S. Dept. Justice, Washington, 1975-77; sr. assoc. Donovan, Leisure, Newton & Irvine, 1977-79; prof. law U. Mo., Columbia, 1979-84; assoc. dean, prof. Washington U., St. Louis, 1984-89; dean U. Ariz. Coll. Law, Tucson, 1989-95; William S. Pattee prof. law, dean U. Minn. Law Sch., Mpls., 1995—. Fellow Am. Bar Found.; mem. Am. Law Inst., Am. Econ. Assn. Home: 180 Bank St SE Minneapolis MN 55414-1042 Office: U Minn Law Sch Walter F Mondale Hall Office 381 229 19th Ave S Minneapolis MN 55455

SULLIVAN, EDWARD, periodical editor; b. Sharon, Pa., 1956; BA in Journalism, Johns Hopkins U., 1979. From news editor to mg. pubis. Am. Soc. Quality Control, 1979-87; acquisitions editor Panel Publishers, 1987-89; editor Trade Press Pub., Milw., 1989—. Office: Trade Press Pub Bldg Operating Mgmt Mag 2100 W Florist Ave Milwaukee WI 53209-3721

SULLIVAN, FRANK, JR. state supreme court justice; b. Mar. 21, 1950; s. Frank E. and Colette (Cleary) S.; m. Cheryl Gibson, June 14, 1972; children: Denis M., Douglas S., Thomas R. AB cum laude, Dartmouth Coll., 1972; JD magna cum laude, Ind. U., 1982; LLM, U. Va., 2001. Bar: Ind. 1982. Mem. staff Office of U.S. Rep. John Brademas, 1974-79, dir. staff, 1975-78; with Barnes & Thornburg, Indpls., 1982-89; budget dir. State of Ind., 1989-92; exec. asst. Office of Gov. Evan Bayh, 1993; assoc. justice Ind. Supreme Ct., 1993—. Mem. ABA, Ind. State Bar Assn., Indpls. Bar Assn. Home: 6153 N Olney St Indianapolis IN 46220-5166 Office: State House Rm 321 Indianapolis IN 46204-2728

SULLIVAN, FRANK C. company executive; BA, U. N.C., 1983. Various comml. lending corp. fin. 1st Union Nat. Bank and Harris Bank, 1983-87; regional sales mgr. AGR Co. RPM Group, Inc., 1987-89, dir. corp. devel., 1989-91, v.p., 1991-93, CFO, 1993-98, exec. v.p., 1998-99, pres., 1999—. Morehead scholar, 1983. Office: 2628 Pearl Rd Medina OH 44256-7623

SULLIVAN, JAMES GERALD, business owner, postal letter carrier; b. Bad Axe, Mich., Sept. 13, 1935; s. John Thomas and Frances Eugena (O'Henley) S.; m. Florence Marie Tack, Sept. 12, 1959; children: Kevin Michael, Kathleen Marie. Student, U. Detroit, 1957-58, Highland Park Coll., 1959-60. Owner Jerry's Barber Shop, Kinde, Bad Axe, Mich., 1963-66, 79—; purchasing agt. Thumb Elec. Coop., Ubly, 1966-79, Walbro Corp., Cass City, 1979-80; sales rep. Thumb Blanket, Bad Axe, 1980-81, Sta. WLEW, Bad Axe, 1981-82; regional mgr. Pri Am. Fin. Svcs., 1985—; treas. Colfax Twp., 1979-90; rural letter carrier U.S. Postal Svc., 1982-98, ret., 1998. Loss clk., Toplis & Harding Wagner & Gliddon, Detroit, 1959-61; inventory control clk., Carrick Products Co., Royal Oak, Mich., 1957-59. Pres., Huron County (Mich.) Twp. Assn., 1988-90; leader Boy Scouts Am., Bad Axe,1975-77. Served in U.S. Army, 1954-56. Mem. Huron County Rural Letter Carriers Assn. (pres. 1990—), Armed Forces Vets. Club of the Nat. Rural Letter Carriers Assn. (Mich. divsn., state sec. 1999—), Am. Legion, 4-H Club (pres. 1948-50), Lions (pres. 1979-80), Cmty. Club (pres. 1976-77), KC (mem. coun. #1546), Ushers Club Sacred Heart Ch. Republican. Roman Catholic. Avocations: gardening, golf, swimming, snowmobiling, fishing. Home: 122 W Richardson Rd Bad Axe MI 48413-9108

SULLIVAN, JAMES STEPHEN, bishop; b. Kalamazoo, July 23, 1929; s. Stephen James and Dorothy Marie (Bernier) S. Student, St. Joseph Sem.; BA, Sacred Heart Sem.; postgrad., St. John Provincial Sem. Ordained priest, Roman Cath. Ch., 1955, consecrated bishop, 1972. Assoc. pastor St. Luke Ch., Flint, Mich., 1955-58, St. Mary Cathedral, Lansing, 1958-60, sec. to bishop, 1960-61; assoc. pastor St. Joseph (Mich.) Ch., 1961-65, sec. to bishop, 1965-69; assoc. pastor Lansing, 1965; vice chancellor, 1969-72; aux. bishop, vicar gen. Diocese of Lansing, 1972-85, diocesan consultor, 1971-85; bishop Fargo, N.D., 1985—. Pres. World Apostolate Fatima; episc. liaison Cath. Mktg. Network; nat. episcopal liaison to the Cath. Cursillo Movement. Mem. Nat. Conf. Cath. Bishops. Office: Chancery Office PO Box 1750 1310 Broadway Fargo ND 58102-2639

SULLIVAN, LAURA PATRICIA, lawyer, insurance company executive; b. Des Moines, Oct. 16, 1947; d. William and Patricia S. BA, Cornell Coll., Iowa, 1971; JD, Drake U., 1972. Bar: Iowa 1972. Various positions Ins. Dept. Iowa, Des Moines, 1972-75; various legal positions State Farm Mut. Auto Ins. Co., Bloomington, Ill., 1975-81, sec. and counsel, 1981-88, v.p., counsel and sec., 1988—; v.p., sec., dir. State Farm Cos. Found., 1985—; sec. State Farm Lloyd's, Inc., 1987—; v.p., counsel and sec. State Farm Fire and Casualty Co., 1988—, State Farm Gen. Ins. Co., 1988—, also bd. dirs.; v.p. counsel, sec., dir. State Farm Life and Accident Assurance Co.; v.p. counsel, sec. State Farm Annuity and Life Assurance Co., State Farm Life Ins. Co.; dir. State Farm Indemnity Co., Bloomington, Ill., 1995—; sec., dir. State Farm Fla. Ins. Co., 1998—. Bd. dirs. Ins. Inst. for Hwy. Safety, Nat. Conf. Ins. Guaranty Funds, chmn., 1995-97. Trustee John M. Scott Indsl. Sch. Trust, Bloomington, 1983-86, Cornell Coll., 1999—; bd. dirs. Scott Ctr., 1983-86, Bloomington-Normal Symphony, 1980-85, YWCA of McLean County, 1993-95; chmn. Ins. Inst. for Hwy. Safety, 1987-88. Mem. ABA, Iowa State Bar Assn., Am. Corp. Counsel Assn., Am. Soc. Corp. Secs. Office: State Farm Mut Automobile Ins Co 1 State Farm Plz Bloomington IL 61710-0001

SULLIVAN, MARCIA WAITE, lawyer; b. Chgo., Nov. 30, 1950; d. Robert Macke and Jacqueline (Northrop) S.; m. Steven Donald Jansen, Dec. 20, 1975; children: Eric Spurlock, Laura Macke, Brian Northrop. BA, DePauw U., 1972; JD, Ind. U., 1975. Assoc. Arnstein, Gluck, Weitzenfeld & Minow, Chgo., 1975-76; ptnr. Greenberger and Kaufmann, 1976-86, Katten Muchin Zavis Rosenman, Chgo., 1986—. Adj. prof. Kent Coll. Law, Ill. Inst. Tech., Chgo., 1991—94; pres. Chgo. Real Estate Exec. Women, 2000—01. Mem. ABA, Chgo. Bar Assn., Am. Land Title Assn. (lender's coun.). Avocations: bicycling, cross country skiing, gardening, camping. Office: Katten Muchin Zavis Rosenman 525 W Monroe St Ste 1600 Chicago IL 60661-3693

SULLIVAN, MICHAEL FRANCIS, III, executive; b. DuBois, Pa., Mar. 11, 1948; s. Michael F. and Mary Jane (Borger) S.; m. Janice Marie Calame, May 30, 1969 (dec.); children: Courtney, Shannon, Michael IV; m. Rosa Leigh Gillespie, Aug. 16, 1997. BS in English & Speech, Bowling Green State U., 1969; MEd in Curriculum Devel., Wright State U., 1971; EdD in Instructional Technology, Va. Polytech Inst. & State U., 1976. Specialist in instructional design Md. State Dept. Edn., Balt., 1974-80, asst. state supt. in instructional technology, 1980-86; sr. edn. cons. UNISYS Corp., Bluebell, Pa., 1986-87, product mktg. mgr., 1987-88, dir. strategic planning and devel., 1988-90; exec. dir. Agy. for Instructional Technology, Bloomington, Ind., 1990—. Contbr. articles to profl. jours. Office: Agency for Instructional Tech Box A Bloomington IN 47402

SULLIVAN, MICHAEL PATRICK, food service executive; b. Dec. 5, 1934; s. Michael Francis and Susan Ellen (Doran) S.; m. Marilyn Emmer, June 27, 1964; children: Katherine, Michael, Maureen, Bridget, Daniel,

Thomas. BS, Marquette U., 1956; JD, U. Minn., 1962. Bar: Minn. 1962, U.S. Dist. Ct. Minn. 1962, U.S. Supreme Ct. 1975, U.S. Ct. Appeals (8th cir.) 1978. Assoc. Gray, Plant, Mooty, Mooty & Bennett, Mpls., 1962-67, ptnr., 1968-87, mng. ptnr., 1976-87; pres., CEO Internat. Dairy Queen, Inc., 1987-2001, chmn. bd., 2001—. Bd. dirs. The Valspar Corp., Allianz Life Ins. Co. N.Am., Opus Corp.; instr. U. Minn. Law Sch., 1962-67; lectr. continuing legal edn.; spl. counsel to atty. gen. Minn., 1971-79, 82-84; bd. dirs. Met. Mpls.YMCA, chmn. bd. dirs., 1997-99; pres. Uniform Law Commn., 1987-89. Contbr. articles to profl. jours. Bd. regents St. John's U., 2000; bd. dirs. YMCA Met. Mpls.; bd. trustees St. Paul Sem. Served with USN, 1956-59. Mem. ABA (ho. of dels., 1984-89), Minn. Bar Assn. (gov. 1974-86), Hennepin County Bar Assn. (pres. 1978-89), Am. Bar Found., Am. Law Inst., Am. Arbitration Assn. (bd. dirs.), Order of Coif. Roman Catholic. Office: Internat Dairy Queen 7505 Metro Blvd Minneapolis MN 55439-3020

SULLIVAN, PAUL F. career officer; b. Wellesley, Mass. m. Ann Sullivan; children: Shane, Morgan. BS with distinction, U.S. Naval Acad., 1970; MS in Ocean Engring., MIT, 1975; postgrad., Nuclear Power Sch. Commd. ensign USN, 1970, advanced through grades to rear adm.; supply officer USS Caiman; various engring. assignments USS Dace; engr. officer USS George C. Marshall; exce. officer USS Richard B. Russell; commdr. USS Birmingham, Pearl Harbor, Hawaii, USS Fla., Bangor, Wash.; mem. tactical analysis group COMSUBDEVRON 12; dep. commdr. tng. & ops. COMSUBDERVON 17; dep. dir. current ops. Ops. Directorate Joint Staff, Washington; commdr. Submarine Group 9, Silverdale, Wash., now rear admiral. Decorated Def. Superior Svc. Medal, Legion Merit award, 2 Meritorious Svc. Medals, 3 Navy Commendation Medals, 3 Navy Achievement Medals. Office: Dir Ops and Logistics 901 Sac Blvd Ste Ba3 Offutt A F B NE 68113-5455

SULLIVAN, PEGGY (ANNE), librarian, consultant; b. Kansas City, Mo., Aug. 12, 1929; d. Michael C. and Ella (O'Donnell) S. AB, Clarke Coll., 1950; MS in L.S., Cath. U. Am., 1953; Ph.D. (Tangley Oaks fellow, Higher Edn. Act Title II fellow), U. Chgo., 1972. Children's public librarian, Mo., Md., Va., 1952-61; sch. library specialist Montgomery County (Md.) public schs., 1961-63; dir. Knapp Sch. Libraries Project, ALA, 1963-68, Jr. Coll. Library Info. Ctr., 1968-69; asst. prof. U. Pitts., 1971-73; dir. Office for Library Personnel Resources, ALA, Chgo., 1973-74; dean of students, assoc. prof. Grad. Library Sch., U. Chgo., 1974-77; asst. commr. for extension services Chgo. Public Library, 1977-81; dean Coll. Profl. Studies, No. Ill. U., DeKalb, 1981-90; dir. univ. librs. No. Ill. U., 1990-92; exec. dir. ALA, 1992-94; assoc. Tuft & Assocs., 1995-98; dean Grad. Sch. Libr. and Info. Sci. Rosary Coll., 1995-97. Instr. grad. libr. edn. programs, 1958-73, UNESCO cons. on sch. librs., Australia, 1970; trustee Clarke Coll., 1969-72; sr. ptnr. Able Cons., 1987-92; cons. in field. Author: The O'Donnells, 1956, Many Names for Eileen, 1969, Problems in School Media Management, 1971, Carl H. Milam and the American Library Association, 1976, Opportunities in Library and Information Science, 1977, Realization: The Final Report of the Knapp School Libraries Project, 1968; co-author: Public Libraries: smart Practices in Personnel, 1982. Mem.: ALA, Assn. for Libr. and Info., Ill. Libr. Assn., Cath. Libr. Assn., Carlton Club. Roman Catholic. Home and Office: 2800 N Lake Shore Dr Apt 816 Chicago IL 60657-6202 E-mail: sullivanp@iopener.net., sullivanp2@mindspring.com.

SULLIVAN, THOMAS CHRISTOPHER, coatings company executive; b. Cleve., July 8, 1937; s. Frank Charles and Margaret Mary (Wilhelmy) S.; m. Sandra Simmons, Mar. 12, 1960; children: Frank, Sean, Tommy, Danny, Kathleen, Julie. B.S., Miami U., Oxford, Ohio, 1959. Div. sales mgr. Republic Powdered Metals, Cleve., 1961-65, exec. v.p., 1965-70; pres., chmn. bd. RPM, Inc., Medina, Ohio, 1971-78, chmn. bd. and CEO, 1978—. Bd. dirs. Pioneer Standard Electronics, Inc., Cleve., Nat. City Bank, Cleve., Cleve. Clinic Found., Huffy Corp., Dayton, Ohio, Kaydon Corp., Ann Arbor, Mich. Trustee emeritus Culver (Ind.) Ednl. Found.; trustee Cleve. Tomorrow; bd. advisors Urban Cmty. Sch., Cleve., Malachi House, Cleve.; trustee City Year Cleve. Lt. (j.g.) USNR, 1959-60. Mem.: Nat. Assn. Securities Dealers (bd. govs. 1986—88, long-range strategic planning com.), Nat. Paint and Coatings Assn. (chmn. bd., CEO). Roman Catholic. Office: RPM Inc 2628 Pearl Rd Medina OH 44256-7623

SULLIVAN, THOMAS PATRICK, lawyer; b. Evanston, Ill., Mar. 23, 1930; s. Clarence M. and Pauline (DeHaye) S.; children: Margaret Mary, Timothy Joseph, Elizabeth Ann; m. Anne Landau. Student, Loras Coll., Dubuque, Iowa, 1947-49; LL.B. cum laude, Loyola U., Chgo., 1952. Bar: Ill. 1952, Calif. 1982, N.Mex., 1997. Asso. firm Jenner & Block, Chgo., 1954-62, partner, 1963-77, 81—; U.S. atty. for No. Dist. Ill., Chgo., 1977-81. Contbr. articles to profl. jours. Served with U.S. Army, 1952-54. Decorated Bronze Star.; Recipient medal of excellence Loyola U. Law Sch., 1965; Ill. Pub. Defender Assn. award, 1972, Justice John Paul Stevens award, 2000. Fellow Am. Coll. Trial Lawyers; mem. Am., Ill., Fed. Seventh Circuit, Chgo. bar assns., Fed. Bar Assn., Am. Law Inst., Am. Judicature Soc., Chgo. Council Lawyers. Office: Jenner & Block 1 Ibm Plz Fl 4100 Chicago IL 60611-5697 E-mail: tsullivan@jenner.com.

SULLIVAN, THOMAS PATRICK, academic administrator; b. Detroit, July 8, 1947; s. Walter James and Helen Rose (Polosky) S.; m. Barbara Jean Fournier, Aug. 9, 1968; children: Colleen, Brendan. BA in English, U. Dayton, 1969; M. Edn. and Adminstrn., Kent State U., 1971; postgrad., U. Mich., 1988. Tchr. Resurection Elem. Sch., Dayton, Ohio, 1968-69; administr. residence hall Kent (Ohio) State U., 1969-71; program mgr. residence hall Ea. Mich. U., Ypsilanti, 1971-73, adminstrv. assoc., 1973-76, dir. housing, 1976-83; assoc. provost Wayne County Community Coll., Belleville, Mich., 1983-84, dir. budget and mgmt. devel. Detroit, 1984-85, sr. v.p. acad. affairs, acting provost, 1985-86, acting exec. dean Belleville, 1986-88, dir. budget and mgmt. devel. Detroit, 1988-89; pres. Cleary Coll., Ypsilanti, 1989—. Part-time instr. English and math. Schoolcraft Coll., Livonia, Mich., 1980-90. Home: 9835 Whisperwood Ln Brighton MI 48116-8859 Office: Cleary Coll 3601 Plymouth Rd Ann Arbor MI 48105-2659

SUMICHRAST, JOZEF, illustrator, designer; b. Hobart, Ind., July 26, 1958; s. Joseph Steven and Stella Sumichrast; m. Susan Ann Snyder, June 22, 1972; children— Kristin Ann, Lindsey Ann Student, Am. Acad. Art, Chgo. Illustrator Stevens Gross, Chgo., 1971-72; illustrator Eaton & Iwen, 1972-73, Graphique, Chgo., 1973-74; pres. Jozef Sumichrast, Deerfield, Ill., 1975—. Author, illustrator: Onomatopoeia, Q is For Crazy; exhbns. include: 200 Years of Am. Illustration, N.Y. Hist. Soc. Mus., Chgo. Hist. Soc., Finland Lath Mus., Library of Congress, Los Angeles County Mus. Art, Md. Inst. Graphic Art, State Colo. Community Coll., Tokyo Designers Gakiun Coll.; represented in permanent collections: Soc. Illustrators, Chgo. Hist. Soc., Milw. Art Dirs. Club, Phoenix Art Dirs. Club, Columbia Coll., U. Tex., contbr. numerous articles to profl. periodicals. Recipient award for children's book Chgo. Book Clinic, 1978; Gold medal Internat. Exhibition of Graphic Arts, Brazil, 1981; Gold medal Chgo. Artist Guild, 1980, 81; Silver medal N.Y. Art Dirs. Club, 1983; numerous others Mem. Soc. Illustrators

SUMMERS, DAVID ARCHIBALD, research mining engineer, educator and director; b. Newcastle-on-Tyne, Eng., Feb. 2, 1944; married, 1972; 2 children. BSc, U. Leeds, 1965, PhD in Mining, 1968. Asst. prof. mining U. Mo., Rolla, 1968-74, assoc. prof. mining, 1974-77, prof. mining, 1977-80, prof., 1980—, sr. investor Rock Mech. & Explosives Rsch. Ctr., 1970-76, dir. Rock Mech. & Explosives Rsch. Ctr., 1976-84, dir. High Pressure Water Jet Lab., 1984—; dir. Rock Mech. & Explosives Rsch. Ctr. Recipient Rock Mechanics award Soc. Mining, Metallurgy & Exploration, 1993. Fellow Brit. Inst. Mining Engrs., Brit. Inst. Mining and Metallurgy, Brit. Tunneling Soc., Cleaning Equipment Mfr. Assn., Water Jet Technol. Assn. (pres. 1986-87); mem. ASME, Am. Inst. Mining, Metall. and Petroleum Engrs., Brit. Hydromech. Rsch. Assn. (hon.). Achievements include research in water jet cutting, surface energy of rock and minerals, novel methods of excavation, cavitation at high pressure, coal mining, geothermal development, strata control. Home: 808 Cypress Dr Rolla MO 65401-3804 Office: U Mo High Pressure Waterjet Lab Rock Mech Facility #116 1006 Kingshighway St # 116 Rolla MO 65409-0001

SUMMERS, DON, state legislator; Rep. dist. 2 State of Mo. Office: Rte 4 Box 209 Unionville MO 63565-9273 also: Mo Ho of Reps State Capitol Jefferson City MO 65101

SUMMERS, VANESSA, state legislator; m. Nicholas T. Barnes. Grad., Mid-Am. Coll. Funeral Svcs. State rep., mem. aged & aging, pub. policy, ethics, vet. affairs & urban affairs coms., chmn. interstate coop. com. Ind. Ho. of Reps., Indpls., 1991—; funeral dir. Summers Funeral Chapel. Named one of Top Ladies of Distinction. Mem. Alpha Kappa Alpha, Alpha Mu Omega. Democrat. Office: 1140 Brook Ln Indianapolis IN 46202-2255

SUMMERS, WILLIAM B. brokerage house executive; b. 1950; With McDonald & Co. Investments Inc., Cleve., 1971—; pres., CEO and chmn. McDonald & Co. Securities, 1983—; now chmn., CEO McDonald Investment Inc., A Keycorp Co. Office: McDonald Investment Inc A Keycorp Co 800 Superior Ave E Cleveland OH 44114-2601

SUMMERS, WILLIAM B., JR. investment company executive; Pres., CEO McDonald & Co. Securities, Cleve. Office: McDonald & Co Securities 800 Superior Ave E Ste 2100 Cleveland OH 44114-2604

SUMNER, DAVID SPURGEON, surgery educator; b. Asheboro, N.C., Feb. 20, 1933; s. George Herbert and Velna Elizabeth (Welborn) S.; m. Martha Eileen Sypher, July 25, 1959; children: David Vance, Mary Elizabeth, John Franklin. BA, U. N.C., 1954; MD, Johns Hopkins U., 1958. Diplomate Am. Bd. Surgery; cert. spl. qualification gen. vascular surgery. Intern Johns Hopkins Hosp., Balt., 1958-59, resident in gen. surgery, 1960-61, U. Wash. Sch. Medicine, Seattle, 1961-66; clin. investigator in vascular surgery VA Hosp., 1967, 70-73; asst. surgery U. Wash. Sch. Medicine, 1961-66, instr. surgery, 1966-70, asst. prof. surgery, 1970-72, assoc. prof. surgery, 1972-75; prof. surgery, chief sect. peripheral vascular surgery So. Ill. U. Sch. Medicine., Springfield, 1975-84, Disting. prof. surgery, chief sect. peripheral vascular surgery, 1984-98, disting. prof. emeritus, 1998. Staff surgeon Seattle VA Hosp., 1973-75, Univ. Hosp., Seattle, 1973-75, St. John's Hosp., Springfield, 1975-98, Meml. Med. Ctr., Springfield, 1975-98; mem. VA Merit Review Bd. Surgery, 1975-78; mem. vascular surgery rsch. award com. The Liebig Found., 1990-95, chmn., 1994; bd. dirs. Am. Venous Forum Found., 1993-95; vis. prof. Cook County Hosp., Chgo., 1971, Washington U., St. Louis, 1976, U. Tex., San Antonio, 1978, Wayne State U., Detroit, 1978, U. Ind., Indpls., 1979, Ea. Va. Med. Sch., Norfolk, 1979, Case-Western Res. U., Cleve., 1980, U. Chgo., 1981, U. Manitoba, Winnipeg, Can., 1983, others; dist. lectr. Yale U., 1982; guest examiner Am. Bd. Surgery, St. Louis, 1982, assoc. examiner, 1989; lectr. in field. Author: (with D.E. Strandness Jr.) Ultrasonic Techniques in Angiology, 1975, Hemodynamics for Surgeons, 1975; (with R.B. Rutherford, V. Bernhard, F. Maddison, W.S. Moore, M.O. Perry) Vascular Surgery, 1977; (with J.B. Russell) Ultrasonic Arteriography, 1980; (with F.B. Hershey, R.W. Barnes) Noninvasive Diagnosis of Vascular Disease, 1984; (with R.B. Rutherford, G. Johnson Jr., R.F. Kempczinski, W.S. Moore, M.O. Perry, G.W. Smith) Vascular Surgery, 3d edit., 1989; (with A.N. Nicolaides) Investigation of Patients With Deep Vein Thrombosis and Chronic Venous Insufficiency, 1991; (with R.B. Rutherford, G. Johnson, K.W. Johnston, R.F. Kempczinski, W.C. Krupski, W.S. Moore, M.O. Perry, A.J. Comerota, R.H. Dean, P. Gloviczki, K.H. Johansen, T.S. Riles, L.M. Taylor Jr.) Vascular Surgery, 4th edit., 1995; (with K.A. Myers, A.N. Nicolaides Lower Limb Ischaemia, 1997; author 150 chpts. to books; mem. editl. bd. Vascular Diagnosis and Therapy, 1980-84, Appleton Davies, Inc., 1983—, Jour. Soc. of Non-Invasive Vascular Tech., 1987—, Jour. Vascular Surgery, 1987-97; series editor Introduction to Vascular Tech., 1990—; mem. exec. editl. com. Phlebology, 1987-91; mem. Internat. Editl. Adv. Bd., 1991-2000; mem. editl. com. Internat. Angiology, 1992—; contbr. over 150 articles to profl. jours. Lt. col. U.S. Army, 1967-70. Fellow in surg. rsch. Johns Hopkins U. Sch. Medicine, 1959-60, Am. Cancer Soc., Inc. fellow, 1965-66; Appleton-Century Crofts scholar, 1956, Mosby scholar, 1958. Fellow Am. Coll. Surgeons (Wash. chpt. 1971-75, Ill. chpt. counselor 1981-83), Cyprus Vascular Soc. (hon.); mem. AMA, Soc. Univ. Surgeons, Soc. Vascular Surgery (constn. and by-laws com. 1983, Wiley Fellowship com. 1990), Internat. Soc. Cardiovascular Surgery (N.Am. chpt. program com. 1985-88), Am. Surg. Assn., Am. Heart Assn. (stroke coun., cardiovascular surgery coun. 1978), Soc. Noninvasive Vascular Tech. (hon.), Vascular Surgery Biology Club, Am. Venous Forum (organizing com. 1987, founding mem. 1988, chmn. membership com. 1988-91, treas. 1992-95, pres. elect 1998, pres. 1999-2000), Cardiovascular Sys. Dynamics Soc., Internat. Soc. Surgery, Vascular Soc. So. Africa (hon.), North Pacific Surg. Assn., Ctrl. Surg. Assn., Midwestern Vascular Surg. Soc. (counselor 1977-79, pres.-elect 1980-81, pres. 1981-82), So. Assn. for Vascular Surgery, Ill. Heart Assn., Ill. Med. Soc., Ill. Surg. Soc., Chgo. Surg. Soc., Seattle Surg. Soc., Sangamon County Med. Soc., Henry N. Harkins Surg. Soc., Harbinger Soc., Phi Eta Sigma, Phi Beta Kappa, Sigma Xi, Alpha Omega Alpha. Presbyterian. Achievements include research in surgical hemodynamics and noninvasive methods for diagnosing peripheral vascular disease. Avocations: painting, sailing, history, computers. Home: 2324 W Lake Shore Dr Springfield IL 62707-9521 Office: So Ill U Sch Medicine Dept Surgery 701 N 1st St Ste D346 Springfield IL 62702 E-mail: dsumner1@aol.com.

SUMNER, WILLIAM MARVIN, anthropology and archaeology educator; b. Detroit, Sept. 8, 1928; s. William Pulford Jr. and Virginia Friel (Umberger) S.; m. Frances Wilson Morton, June 21, 1952 (div. 1975): children: Jane Cassell, William Morton; m. Kathleen A. MacLean, Apr. 7, 1989. Student, Va. Mil. Inst., 1947-48; B.S., U.S. Naval Acad., 1952; Ph.D., U. Pa., 1972. Dir. Am. Inst. Iranian Studies, Tehran, Iran, 1969-71; asst. prof. Ohio State U., Columbus, 1971-73, assoc. prof., 1974-80, prof. anthropology, 1981-89, prof. emeritus, 1989—; dir. Oriental Inst., prof. Near Eastern langs. and civilizations U. Chgo., 1989-98. Dir. excavations at Tal-e Malyan (site of Elamite Anshan) sponsored by Univ. Mus., U. Pa., 1971— ; v.p. Am. Inst. Iranian Studies, 1983-86. Contbr. chpts. to books, articles and essays to profl. jours. Served to lt. comdr. USN, 1952-64. Grantee NSF, 1975, 76, 79, NEH, 1988. Office: Univ Chgo Oriental Inst 1155 E 58th St Chicago IL 60637-1540 E-mail: sumner.1@osu.edu.

SUND, JEFFREY OWEN, retired publishing company executive; b. Bklyn., June 19, 1940; children: Catherine, Meredith. BA, Dartmouth Coll., 1962. Sales rep. Prentice-Hall, Englewood Cliffs, N.J., 1967-73, Houghton Mifflin, Boston, 1973-74, coll. div. editor, 1974-77, editor-in-chief, 1977-86, v.p., editorial dir., 1986-89; pres., chief exec. officer Richard D. Irwin, Burr Ridge, Ill., 1989-96; pres. McGraw-Hill Higher Edn., 1996-2000; ret. Lt. USN, 1962-66.

SUNDAY, JACK, radio personality; Midday weekday radio host Sta. KFGO-AM, Fargo, ND. Office: KFGO 1020 25th St S Fargo ND 58103*

SUNDBERG, MARSHALL DAVID, biology educator; b. Apr. 18, 1949; m. Sara Jane Brooks, Aug. 1, 1977; children: Marshall Isaac, Adam, Emma. BA in Biology, Carleton Coll., 1971; MA in Botany, U. Minn., 1973, PhD in Botany, 1978. Lab. technician Carleton Coll., Minn., 1973-74; teaching asst. U. Minn., Mpls., 1974-76, rsch. asst., 1976-77; adj. asst. prof. Biology U. Wis., Eau Claire, 1978-85, mem. faculty summer sci. inst., 1982-85; instr. La. State U., Baton Rouge, 1985-88, asst. prof. Biology, 1988-91, coord. dept. Biology, 1988-93, assoc. prof. Biology, 1991-97; prof., chair divsn. biol. scis. Emporia State U., 1997—. Author: General Botany Laboratory Workbook, 5th revision, 1984, General Botany 1001 Laboratory Manual, 1986, General Botany 1002 Laboratory Manual, 1987, Biology 1002 Correspondence Study Guide, 1987, Boty 1202: General Botany Laboratory Manual, 1988, Biol 1208: Biology for Science Majors Laboratory Manual, 1988, 2d edit., 1989, Instructor's Manual for J. Mauseth, Introductory Botany, 1991; contbr. articles to profl. jours. Judge sci. fairs, La. schs., 1985—; coach Baton Rouge Soccer Assn., 1991-96; asst. scoutmaster Boy Scouts Am., 1991-97, scoutmaster, 1998—. Brand fellow U. Minn., 1976-77, Faculty Grants scholar U. Wis., 1984-85. Fellow Linnaean Soc. London; mem. NSTA, AAAS, Am. Inst. Biol. Scis. (coun. mem. at large 1992-95, edn. com. 1994-95, 98—), Assn. Biology Lab. Edn., Bot. Soc. Am. (chmn. teaching sect. 1985-86, workshop com. teaching sect. 1983-84, slide exchange/lab. exchange teaching sect. 1980-89, edn. com. 1991, 92, Charles H. Bessey award 1992, editor Plant Sci. Bull. 2000—), Internat. Soc. Plant Morphologists, Nat. Assn. Biology Tchrs. (Outstanding 4-Yr. Coll. Tchr. award 1997), Soc. Econ. Botany, The Nature Conservancy, Sigma Xi (sec. 1982-84, 93-95, v.p. 1984-85, 96-97). Home: 1912 Briarcliff Ln Emporia KS 66801-5404 Office: Emporia State U Divsn Biol Scis 1200 Commercial St Emporia KS 66801-5087

SUNDERMAN, DUANE NEUMAN, chemist, research institute executive; b. Wadsworth, Ohio, July 14, 1928; s. Richard Benjamin and Carolyn (Neuman) S.; m. Joan Catherine Hoffman, Jan. 31, 1953; children: David, Christine, Richard. BA, U. Mich., 1949, MS, 1954, PhD in Chemistry, 1956. Researcher Battelle Meml. Inst., Columbus, Ohio, 1956-59, mgr., 1959-69, assoc. dir., 1969-79, dir. internat. programs, 1979-84; sr. v.p. Midwest Rsch. Inst., Kansas City, Mo., 1984-90, exec. v.p., 1990-94, Golden, Colo., 1990-94. Dir. Nat. Renewable Energy Lab., Golden, Colo., 1990-94, dir. emeritus, 1994—. Contbr. numerous articles to profl. jours. Bd. dirs. Mid-Ohio chpt. ARC, 1982-83, U. Kansas City, 1985-90, Mo. Corp. for Sci. and Tech., Jefferson City, 1986-90; vice chmn. bd. Colo. Energy Sci. Ctr., 2000-01. Mem. AAAS, Am. Chem. Soc. Republican. Presbyterian. Avocation: computers. E-mail: dsunderm@columbus.rr.com.

SUNDQUIST, ERIC JOHN, American studies educator; b. McPherson, Kans., Aug. 21, 1952; s. Laurence A. and Frances J. (Halene) S.; m. Tatiana Kreinine, Aug. 14, 1982; children: Alexandra, Joanna, Ariane. BA, U. Kans., 1974; MA, Johns Hopkins U., 1976, PhD, 1978. Asst. prof. English Johns Hopkins U., Balt., 1978-80, U. Calif., Berkeley, 1980-82, assoc. prof., 1982-86, prof. English, 1986-89, UCLA, 1989-97, chair dept. English, 1994-97; dean Judd A. and Marjorie Weinberg Coll. Arts and Scis. Northwestern U., Evanston, Ill., 1997—. Vis. scholar U. Kans., 1985, dir. Holmes grad. seminar, 1993; dir. NEH Summer Seminar for Coll. Tchrs., U. Calif., Berkeley, 1986, 90, UCLA, 1994; cons. Calif. Coun. for Humanities, 1986-87; prof. Bread Loaf Sch. English, Middlebury (Vt.) Coll., 1987, 89, Sante Fe, 95; mem. fellowship com. Newberry Libr., 1987, 88, 92; dir. NEH Summer Seminar for Secondary Sch. Tchrs., Berkeley, 1988; vis. prof. UCLA, 1988; Andrew Hilen vis. prof. U. Wash., 1990; Lamar Meml. lectr. in so. states Mercer U., 1991; Gertrude Conaway Vanderbilt prof. English Vanderbilt U., Nashville, 1992-93; mem. fellowship cons. Nat. Humanities Ctr., 1992, 93; acad. specialist in Am. studies Tel Aviv U., 1994; mem. adv. bd. Colloquium for the Study of Am. Culture, Claremont (Calif.) Grad. Sch. & Huntington Libr., 1994—. Author: Home as Found: Authority and Genealogy in Nineteenth-Century American Literature, 1979 (Gustave Arlt award Coun. Grad. Schs. in U.S. 1980), Faulkner: The House Divided, 1983, The Hammers of Creation: Folk Culture in Modern African-American Fiction, 1992, To Take the Nations: Race in the Making of American Literature, 1993 (Christian Gauss award Phi Beta Kappa 1993, James Russell Lowell award MLA 1993, Choice Outstanding Acad. Book 1994); co-author: Cambridge History of American Literature, Vol. II, 1995; editor: American Realism: New Essays, 1982, New Essays on Uncle Tom's Cabin, 1986, Frederick Douglass: New Literary and Historical Essays, 1990, Mark Twain: A Collection of Critical Essays, 1994, Cultural Contexts for Ralph Ellison's Invisible Man, 1995, Oxford W.E.B. DuBois Reader, 1996; mem. adv. bd. Studies in Am. Lit. and Culture, 1987-90, gen. editor, 1991-97; mem. editl. bd. Am. Lit. History, 1987—, Ariz. Quar., 1987—; assoc. editor Am. Nat. Biography, 1990—; cons. The Libr. of Am., 1992—; consulting reader African-Am. Rev., 1992—; contbr. articles to profl. jours. Am. Coun. Learned Socs. fellow, 1981, NEH fellow, 1989-90, Guggenheim fellow, 1993-94 (declined). Mem. MLA (chair adv. coun. Am. lit. sect. 1994, mem. exec. com. divsn. 19th Century Am. lit. 1994-97), Am. Studies Assn. (chair John Hope Franklin Prize com. 1993, mem. nat. coun. 1994-97, mem. fin. com. 1995-97, and other coms.), Am. Lit. Assn., Orgn. Am. Historians, So. Hist. Assn., So. Am. Studies Assn. (mem. exec. com. 1993-97), Phi Beta Kappa. Office: Northwestern U Coll Arts and Scis 1918 Sheridan Rd Evanston IL 60208-0847

SUPPELSA, MARK, newscaster, reporter; b. Milw. B Broadcast Comms., Marquette U., 1984. Weekend anchor, reporter Sta. WFRV-TV, Green Bay, Wis., 1984—87; anchor, reporter Sta. KSTP-TV, 1987—90, co-anchor 10 pm newscast, 1990—93; with NBC 5, Chgo., 1993—, weekend anchor, reporter, co-anchor early afternoon newscasts, now anchor 4:30 pm and 5 pm newscast. Recipient Regional award, AP, award, Soc. Profl. Journalists, Chgo. Emmy, 1995—96. Office: NBC 454 N Columbus Dr Chicago IL 60611*

SURFACE, CHUCK L. state legislator; b. Webb City, Mo., Feb. 5, 1944; s. Hubert Basil and Hazel (Ulmer) S.; m. Sherry Louzader, 1978; children: Jason, Christi, Kimberly. BS, So. State Coll., 1969. Agt. Shelter Ins., 1970—; mem. Mo. Ho. of Reps. from 129th dist., 1985—. Mem. Joplin (Mo.) Zoning and Planning Commn., 1977-82, chmn., 1981-82; mem. Joplin City Coun., 1982-85. Mem. Am. Legion, Sertoma, Mo. So. State Coll. Alumni Assn. (past bd. dirs.), Jaycees (past pres. Joplin chpt.), Elks. Republican. Home: 2401 W 29th St Joplin MO 64804-1425 Office: Mo House of Reps State Capitol Jefferson City MO 65101

SURI, JASJIT S. research scientist; BS in Computer Engring., Regional Engring. Coll., Bhopal, India, 1988; MS, U. Ill., Chgo., 1991; PhD in Elec. Engring., U. Wash., 1997. Lectr. dept. electronic and computer engring. Regional Engring. Coll., Bhopal, 1988-89; rsch. asst. biomed. visualization dept. U. Ill., Chgo., 1989-90; rsch. programmer image sci. group IBM Palo Alto (Calif.) Sci. Ctr., summer 1990-91; rsch. assoc. U. Wash., Seattle, 1992-97; rsch. software engr. radiation treatment planning group Siemens Med. Sys., Calif., 1991-92; rsch. scientist Gammex Inc., Middleton, Wis., 1997, Sch. Medicine, U. Wis., Madison, 1997; rsch. scientist software devel. TSI, N.Y., 1997; rsch. staff scientist image guided surgery dept. Image Processing and Computer Graphics Picker Internat., Cleve., 1999—. With Bharat Heavy Elec. Ltd., Bhopal, summer 1986, Larson & Tubro Ltd., Bombay, India, summer 1987, Nat. Info. Tech. Ltd., Bhopal, summer 1987; presenter in field; mem. Mayo Clinic Procs., Rochester, Minn.; mem. rev. com. Internat. Conf. in Pattern Analysis and Applications, Plymouth, Eng., 1998. Author: (with others) Model Based Segmentation, 2d. rev. edit., 2000; mem. rev. bd. bd. Radiology, Jour. Computer Assisted Tomography, Internat. Jour. Pattern Analysis and Applications, Internat. Conf. Pattern Analysis and Applications; contbr. more than 75 articles. to profl. jours.; patentee in field. Scholar Regional Engring. Coll., 1985-88 Mem. IEEE, Assn. Computing Machinery, Artificial Intelligence, Optical

Engring. Soc. Am., Engring. in Medicine and Biology Soc. (mem. editl. bd.), Am. Assn. Artificial Int., USENIX-Tcl/Tk. Office: Marconi Med Sys MR Clin Sci Rsch Divsn 595 Minor Rd Cleveland OH 44143 E-mail: jsuri@mr.marcoimed.com.

SURLES, CAROL D. academic administrator; b. Pensacola, Fla., Oct. 7, 1946; d. Elza Allen and Versy Lee Smith; divorced; children: Lisa Surles, Philip Surles. BA, Fisk U., 1968; MA, Chapman Coll., 1971; PhD, U. Mich., 1978. Personnel rep. U. Mich., Ann Arbor, 1973-78, vice-chancellor-adminstrn. Flint, 1987-89; exec. asst. to pres., assoc. v.p. for human resources U. Ctrl. Fla., Orlando, 1978-87; v.p. acad. affairs Jackson State U., Miss., 1989-92; v.p. adminstrn. and bus. Calif. State U., Hayward, 1992-94; pres. Tex. Woman's U., Denton, 1994-99, Ea. Ill. U., Charleston, 1999—. Trustee Pub. Broadcasting Ch. 24, Orlando, 1985-87; bd. dirs. First State Bank, Denton, Tex., Tex.-N.Mex. Power Co., TNP-Enterprise. Recipient Outstanding Scholar's award Delta Tau Kappa, 1983. Mem. AAUW, Am. Assn. Colls. and Univs., Golden Key Honor Soc., Mortar Bd. Soc., Dallas Citizens' Coun., Dallas Women's Found., Coun. of Pres. (Austin, Tex.), Phi Kappa Phi, Alpha Kappa Alpha. Methodist. Avocation: playing piano and oboe. Office: Ea Ill U 600 Lincoln Ave Charleston IL 61920-3011

SURSA, CHARLES DAVID, banker; b. Muncie, Ind., Nov. 5, 1925; s. Charles Vaught and Ethel Fay (Schukraft) S; m. Mary Jane Palmer, Feb. 2, 1947; children: Ann Elizabeth, Janet Lynne, Charles Vaught, Laura Jane. BSChemE, Purdue U., 1946; MBA, Harvard, 1948. Executive NBD Bank N.A. (formerly Summit Bank, Indsl. Trust & Savings), Muncie, Ind., 1946-51, pres., 1951-80, chmn. bd., pres., 1980-88, chmn. bd., CEO, 1988-90, chmn. bd., 1990-94, chmn. emeritus, 1994—. Bd. dirs. Old Rep. Life Ins. Co., Chgo., Home Owners Life Ins. Co., Chgo., Old Rep. Internat. Corp., Chgo., Ball Meml. Hosp., Inc., Old Rep. Ins. Co., Greensburg, Pa., Internat. Bus. & Merc. Ins. Group, Chgo., Am. Bus. & Merc. Reassurance Co., Chgo., bd. dirs., pres. Com. Svcs. Coun. of Del. County, 1973-74. Treas. Muncie Symphony Assn., 1949-62, pres., 1962-72, 2d v.p., 1978-80, dir., 1991-97; bd. dirs., pres. The Cmty. Found. of Muncie and Del. County, Inc., 1985-97. Recipient Outstanding Young Man award Ind. Jr. C. of C., 1956, Hon. Jaycees award, 1974. Mem. Ind. Banker's Assn., Ind. Pres.'s Orgn. (treas. 1980-86), Delaware County C. of C., Ind. State C. of C., Muncie C. of C. (pres. 1959-60), Rotary (pres. 1964-65), Delaware Country Club (pres., bd. dirs. 1964), Elks, Phi Gamma Delta. Republican. Presbyterian. Home: 3410 W University Ave Muncie IN 47304-3970

SURYANARAYANAN, RAJ GOPALAN, researcher, consultant, educator; b. Cuddalore, Tamil Nadu, India, Apr. 19, 1955; came to U.S., 1985; s. Natesan and Pushpa (Subramanian) Rajagopalan; m. Shanti Venkateswaran, Nov. 24, 1985; children: Priya Mallika Sury, Meera Sindu Sury. B in Pharmacy, Banaras Hindu U., Varanasi, India, 1976, M in Pharmacy, 1978; MS, U. BC, Vancouver, Can., 1981, PhD, 1985. Mgmt. trainee Indian Drugs and Pharms. Ltd., Rishikesh, India, 1978; supr. Roche Products, Bombay, India, 1979; tchg. asst. U. B.C., Vancouver, Can., 1979, 82-83; asst. prof. pharmaceutics U. Minn., Mpls., 1985-92, assoc. prof., 1992-99, prof., 1999—, dir. grad. studies, 1994-98. Cons. numerous pharm. cos. in U.S., 1987—. Contbr. articles to profl. jours.; patentee quantitative analysis of intact tablets. Recipient numerous grants for rsch., U.S., 1985—. Mem. Am. Assn. Pharm. Scientists, Am. Assn. Colls. Pharmacy. Hindu. Avocations: Tamil literature, sports. Home: 1861 Moore St Saint Paul MN 55113-5530 Office: U Minn Coll of Pharmacy 308 Harvard St SE Minneapolis MN 55455-0353 E-mail: surya001@tc.umn.edu.

SUSANKA, SARAH HILLS, architect; b. Bromley, Kent, England, Mar. 21, 1957; d. Brian and Margaret (Hampson) Hills; m. Lawrence A. Susanka, July 4, 1980 (div. May 1984); m. James Robert Larson, Sept. 4, 1988 (div. Jan. 2000). BArch, U. Oreg., 1978; MArch, U. Minn., 1983. Registered architect. Founding prin. Mulfinger, Susanka, Mahady & Ptnrs., Mpls., 1983-99; founder Susanka Studios, Raleigh, NC, 1999—. Author: The Not So Big House, 1998; columnist Fine Homebuilding mag. Author: The Not So Big House, 1998, Creating the Not So Big House, 2000; columnist Fine Homebuilding mag. Mem. AIA. Office: 2600 Salisbury Pln Raleigh NC 27613-4331 E-mail: ssuanka@notsobighouse.com.

SUSLICK, KENNETH SANDERS, chemistry educator; b. Chgo., Sept. 16, 1952; s. Alvin and Edith Suslick. BS with honors, Calif. Inst. Tech., 1974; PhD, Stanford U., 1978. Rsch., teaching asst. Stanford (Calif.) U., 1974-78; chemist Lawrence Livermore (Calif.) Lab., 1974-75; asst. prof. U. Ill., Urbana, 1978-84, assoc. prof., 1984-88, prof. of chemistry, 1988—, Alumni Rsch. Scholar prof., 1995-97; prof. Beckman Inst. for Advanced Sci. and Tech., 1989-92; prof. of materials sci. and enging. U. Ill., 1993—, William H. and Janet Lycan prof. chemistry, 1997—; founder, CEO ChemSensing, Inc., 2001—. Vis. fellow Balliol Coll., Inorganic Chemistry Lab., Oxford (Eng.) U., 1986; cons. in field. Editor: High Energy Processes in Organometallic Chemistry, 1987, Ultrasound: Its Chemical, Physical and Biological Effects, 1988, Comprehensive Supramolecular Chemistry, vol. 5, 1996; co-editor: Sonochemistry and Sonoluminescence, 1999; editl. bd. Ultrasonics, 1992-96, Ultrasonic Sonochemistry, 1996—; patentee isotope separation by photochromatography, protein microspheres, drug delivery, blood substitutes, smell-seeing, artificial olfaction; contbr. articles to profl. jours. Fellow DuPont Found., 1979-80, Sloan Found., 1985-87; recipient Rsch. Career Devel. award NIH, 1985-90, NSF Spl. Creativity award 1992-94, Material Rsch. Soc. medal, 1994. Fellow AAAS, Am. Acoustical Soc. Royal Soc. Arts, Mfrs. and Commerce (Silver medal 1974); mem. Am. Chem. Soc. (chmn. sect. 1987-89, Nobel Laureate Signature award 1994). Avocations: sculpting, folk music. Office: U Ill Dept Chemistry 600 S Mathews Ave Urbana IL 61801-3602 E-mail: ksuslick@uiuc.edu.

SUSMAN, MILLARD, geneticist, educator; b. St. Louis, Sept. 1, 1934; s. Albert and Patsy Ruth S.; m. Barbara Beth Fretwell, Aug. 18, 1957; children: Michael K., David L. A.B., Washington U., St. Louis, 1956; Ph.D., Calif. Inst. Tech., 1962. With microbial genetics research unit Hammersmith Hosp., London, 1961-62; asst. prof. genetics U. Wis., Madison, 1962-66, assoc. prof., 1966-72, prof., 1972—2002, prof. emeritus, 2002—, chmn. lab. genetics, 1971-75, 77-86, assoc. dean med. sch., 1986-95, acting dean Sch. Allied Health Professions, 1988-90, vice dean med. sch., 1994-95, spl. advisor to the dean med. sch., 1995; dir. Ctr. for Biology Edn., Madison, 1996—2002. Phage course instr., Cold Spring Harbor, N.Y., 1965; v.p. scis., Wis. Acad. Scis., Arts and Letters, 2000—. Co-author: Life on Earth, 2d edit., 1978, Human Chromosomes: Structure, Behavior, Effects, 3d edit., 1992; contbr. articles to sci. jours. Mem Genetics Soc. Am., AAAS, Sigma Xi, Phi Beta Kappa, Phi Eta Sigma, Omicron Delta Kapp. Home: 2707 Colgate Rd Madison WI 53705-2234 Office: 507 Genetics Blvd Madison WI 53706 E-mail: msusman@factstaff.wisc.edu.

SUSSMAN, ARTHUR MELVIN, law educator, foundation administrator; b. Bklyn., Nov. 17, 1942; m. Rita Padnick; children: Eric, Johanna. BS, Cornell U., 1963; JD magna cum laude, Harvard U., 1966. Bar: N.Y. 1967, Ill. 1970. Assoc. atty. Cahill, Gordon, Reindel & Ohl, N.Y.C., 1966-67; from assoc. atty. to ptnr. Jenner & Block, Chgo., 1970-77; legal counsel So. Ill. U., Carbondale, 1977-79; gen. counsel, v.p. U. Chgo., 1979-84, gen. counsel, v.p. adminstrn., 1984-2001, lectr. law Grad. Sch. Bus., 1986-94, master Broadview Hall, 1986-87, resident master Woodward Ct., 1987-92, bd. dirs. Lab. Schs., 1985-01; law school lecturer, 1998—; v.p. & sec. John D and Catherine T MacArthur Found., 2001—. Exec. dir. Borman Commn., U.S. Mil. Acad., 1976; chmn., bd. dirs. Ency. Brit., Inc., 1995-96; presenter in field. Contr. articles to profl. jours. Mem. Ill. Sec. of State's Com. on Not-for-Profit Corp. Act, 1984-85; chair regional selection panel Harry S. Truman Scholarship Found.; bd. dirs. Chapin Hall for Children, 1986—. Capt. JAGC, U.S. Army, 1967-70. Fulbright fellow, London, 1987. Mem. Nat. Assn. Coll. and Univ. Attys., Am. Coun. Edn. Office: The MacArthur Foundation 140 S Dearborn St Chicago IL 60603 E-mail: asussman@macfound.org.

SUSTER, RONALD, judge, former state legislator; b. Cleveland, Oct. 31, 1942; s. Joseph and Frances (Pryatel) S.; m. Patricia Hocevart, 1974; children: Jennifer, Joseph, Michael. BA, Western Res. Univ., 1964, JD, 1967. Lawyer, 1967; asst. law dir. City of Cleveland, 1967; asst. county prosecutor Cuyahoga, Ohio, 1968-71; law dir. City of Highland Heights, 1976-80; asst. atty. gen. Ohio, 1971-80; legal adv. Euclid Dem. Exec. Com., 1975-76; state rep. Ohio Dist. 19, 1981-92, Ohio Dist. 14, 1993; judge Common Pleas Ct. of Cuyahoga County, 1995—. Mem. Labor-Mgmt. Rels. subcom., chmn. ethics com. 1983-84, chmn. Civil & Comml. Law com., 1985-87; chmn. Fin. Inst. Com., 1987; exec. com. mem. Cuyahoga County Dem., 1974-78. Mem. Am. Fedn. of State, County & Mcpl. Employees, Fraternal Order of Police Auxiliary, Northern Ohio Patrolmen Benevolent Assn., Internat. Assn. Firefighters, Am. Arbit Assn. Home: 18519 Underwood Ave Cleveland OH 44119-2927 Office: 1200 Ontario St Cleveland OH 44113-1678

SUTER, ALBERT EDWARD, manufacturing company executive; b. East Orange, N.J., Sept. 18, 1935; s. Joseph Vincent and Catherine (Clay) S.; m. Michaela Sams Suter, May 28, 1966; children: Christian C., Bradley J., Allison A. BME, Cornell U., 1957, MBA, 1959. Pres., chief exec. officer L.B. Knight & Assocs., Chgo., 1959-79; v.p. internat. Emerson Electric Co., St. Louis, 1979-80, pres. motor div., 1980-87, group v.p., 1981-83, exec. v.p., 1983-87, vice chmn., 1987; pres., chief operating officer, dir. Firestone Tire & Rubber Co., Akron, Ohio, 1987-88; pres., chief operating officer Whirlpool Corp., Benton Harbor, Mich., from 1988; exec. v.p. Emerson Electric Co., St. Louis, until 1990, pres., COO, 1990-92, sr. vice chmn., COO, 1992-97; CAO, 1999—2001; ret. sr. advisor, COO Emerson Electric Co., St. Louis, 2001. Bd. dirs. Furniture Brands Internat. Bd. dirs. Jr. Achievement Nat. Bd., Colorado Springs, Colo., Jr. Achievement Miss. Valley, St. Louis Sci. Ctr. Bd.; chmn. Torch div. St. Louis chpt. United Way, 1982-86. Mem. Glenview (Ill.) Country Club, St. Louis Club, Old Warson Country Club , Log Cabin Club. Republican. Episcopalian. Office: Emerson Electric Co PO Box 4100 Saint Louis MO 63136-8506

SUTERA, SALVATORE PHILIP, mechanical engineering educator; b. Balt., Jan. 12, 1933; s. Philip and Ann (D'Amico) S.; m. Celia Ann Fielden, June 21, 1958; children: Marie-Anne, Annette Nicole, Michelle Cecile. B.S. in Mech. Engring, Johns Hopkins, 1954; postgrad., U. Paris, 1955-56; M.S., Calif. Inst. Tech., 1955; Ph.D., Cal. Inst. Tech., 1960; M.A. (hon.), Brown U., 1965. Asst. prof. mech. engring. Brown U., Providence, 1960-65, asso. prof., 1965-68, exec. officer div. engring., 1966-68; prof. dept. mech. engring. Washington U., St. Louis, 1968-97, chmn. dept., 1968-82, 86-97, Spencer T. Olin prof. engring. and applied sci., 1997—, prof. biomed. engring., 1997—. Vis. prof. U. Paris VI, 1973. Assoc. editor: Jour. Biomech. Engring., 1993-97; mem. editorial bd. Circulation Rsch., 1975-82. Pres. St. Louis-Lyon Sister Cities, Inc., 2000—. Fulbright fellow Paris, 1955; recipient Nat. Marconi Sci. award UNICO, 1999. Fellow ASME, Am. Inst. of Med and Biol. Engring. (founding); mem. Biomed. Engring. Soc. (bd. dirs. 1997-2000), Internat. Soc. Biorheology, N.Am. Soc. Biorheology (pres.-elect 1986-89, pres. 1989-90), Am. Soc. Artificial Internal Organs, Am. Soc. Engring. Edn., AAAS (Lindbergh award St. Louis sect. 1988), AIAA, Tau Beta Pi, Pi Tau Sigma. Republican. Roman Catholic. Achievements include research in fluid mechanics, heat transfer, blood flow, rheology of suspensions. Home: 830 S Meramec Ave Saint Louis MO 63105-2539 E-mail: sps@biomed.wustl.edu.

SUTHERLAND, DONALD GRAY, retired lawyer; b. Houston, Jan. 19, 1929; s. Robert Gray and Elizabeth (Cunningham) S.; m. Mary Reynolds Moodey, July 23, 1955; children: Stuart Gray, Elizabeth Dana. BS, Purdue U., 1954; LLB, Ind. U., Bloomington, 1954. Bar: Ind. 1954, U.S. Dist. Ct. (so. dist.) Ind. 1954, U.S. Tax Ct. 1956, U.S. Ct. Claims 1957, U.S. Ct. Appeals (7th cir.) 1981, U.S. Ct. Appeals (3d cir.) 1984, U.S. Ct. Internat. Trade 1987, U.S. Supreme Ct. 1987. Assoc. IceMiller, Indpls., 1954-64, ptnr., 1965-98, ret., 1998. Practitioner in residence Ind. U. Sch. of Law, Bloomington, 1987; trustee, pres. Pegasus Funds, Detroit, 1992-99; trustee, chmn. bd. dirs., pres. Bison Money Market Fund., Indpls., 1982-92. Contbr. articles to numerous profl. jours. Bd. dirs., v.p. Japan-Am. Soc. of Ind., Inc., Indpls., 1988-97; bd. dirs. Conner Prairie Inc., Fishers, Ind., 1988-97, v.p., 1989-90, chmn. bd., 1990-93; tennis ceremonies 10th Pan-Am. Games, Indpls., 1987; bd. dirs. The Children's Bur. Indpls., 1962-73, v.p., 1968-70, pres., 1970-72; bd. dirs. Orchard Country Day Sch., Indpls., 1970-73, Episc. Cmty. Svcs., Indpls., 1965-73, v.p., 1968, pres., 1969; trustee United Episc. Charities, Indpls., 1970-71, pres., 1971. With USMC, 1946-48. Mem.: Econ. Club (bd. dirs. Ind. chpt. 1988—94), Contemporary Club, Woodstock Club. Republican. Avocations: golf, tennis, opera. Office: Ice Miller Donadio & Ryan 1 American Sq Indianapolis IN 46282-0020

SUTHERLAND, JOHN STEPHEN, lawyer; b. Ft. Scott, Kans., July 24, 1950; s. Carl Mason and Mary Jane (Harryman) S.; m. Maureen Elaine Boyle, Nov. 30, 1985; children: Ian, Ryan, Patrick. AA Data Procession, Johnson County C.C., Overland Park, Kans., 1982; BA History, Baker U., 1972; JD, Washburn U., 1975. Bar: Kans., Mo.; U.S. Dist. Ct. (fed. dist.) Kans., U.S. Dist. Ct. (we. dist.) Mo. Pvt. practice, Kansas City, Kans., 1975—. Office: Bank Midwest 5th & Minnesota Kansas City KS 66117-1094

SUTTER, BRIAN, former professional hockey coach; Left wing St. Louis Blues, NHL, head coach, 1988-92, Boston Bruins, NHL, 1992-95. Office: Boston Bruins 1 Accolyn Way Ste 250 Boston MA 02114-1389

SUTTER, WILLIAM PAUL, lawyer; b. Chgo., Jan. 15, 1924; s. Harry Blair and Elsie (Paul) S.; m. Helen Yvonne Stebbins, Nov. 13, 1954; children: William Paul, Helen Blair Sutter Doppelheuer. AB, Yale U., 1947; JD, U. Mich., 1950. Bar: Ill. 1950, Fla. 1977, U.S. Supreme Ct. 1981. Assoc. Hopkins & Sutter (and predecessors), Chgo., 1950-57, ptnr., 1957-89, of counsel, 1989—2001. Mem. Ill. Supreme Ct. Atty. Registration Commn., 1975-81 Contbr. articles on estate planning and taxation to profl. jours. Chmn. Winnetka Caucus Com., 1966-67; pres., trustee Lucille P. Markey Charitable Trust, 1983-98; precinct capt. New Trier Twp. (Ill.) Rep. party, 1960-68; asst. area chmn. New Trier Rep. Orgn., 1968-72; trustee Gads Hill Center, pres., 1962-70, chmn., 1971-80; trustee Northwestern Meml. Hosp., 1983-98, life trustee, 1998—; bd. dirs. Chgo. Hort. Soc., 1982—; mem. dean's coun. Sch. Medicine, Yale U., 1991—; bd. visitors Waisman Ctr., U. Wis., 1996-2002; corr. sec. Yale U. Class of 1945, 1990—. Served to 1st lt. AUS, 1943-46. Fellow Am. Bar Found., Am. Coll. Trust and Estate Counsel (bd. regents 1977-83, exec. com. 1981-83); mem. ABA (ho. dels. 1972-81, chmn. com. on income estates and trusts, taxation sect. 1973-75), Ill. Bar Assn. (bd. govs. 1964-75, pres. 1973-74), Chgo. Bar Assn. (chmn. probate practice com. 1963-64), Am. Law Inst., Internat. Acad. Estate and Trust Law, Am. Judicature Soc., Ill. LAWPAC (pres. 1977-83), Order of Coif, Phi Beta Kappa, Phi Delta Phi, Chi Psi, Mid-Day Club, Indian Hill Club, Gulf Stream Golf Club, Country Club Fla., Ocean Club (Fla.) (bd. govs. 1993-99, sec. 1993-97, pres. 1997-99), Lawyers Club Chgo. Episcopalian. also: Two Par Club Cir Village of Golf 96 Woodley Rd Winnetka IL 60093 Office: Foley & Lardner 3 First Nat Pl Chicago IL 60602 E-mail: wpsutter@aol.com.

SUTTIE, JOHN WESTON, biochemist; b. La Crosse, Wis., Aug. 25, 1934; married; 2 children. BS, U. Wis., 1957, MS, 1958, PhD, 1960. Fellow biochemist Nat. Inst. Med. Rsch, England, 1960-61; asst. prof. to assoc. prof. U. Wis., Madison, 1961-69, prof., 1969—2001, prof. nutrition sci., 1988-97. Bd. agrl. Nat. Rsch. Ctr., 1996—2001. Assoc. editor Jour Nutrition, 1991-97; editor Jour. Nutrition, 1997—. Mem. NAS, Am. Soc. Expl. Biology and Medicine, Am. Soc. Biochemistry and Biology, Am. Soc. for Nutrition Scis. (Osborne and Mendel award award 1980, Mead Johns award 1974), Internat. Soc. Thrombosis and Hemostasis (Hemostasis Career award 1989), Am. Soc. Clin. Nutrition. Office: U Wis Dept Biochemistry Madison WI 53706-1544 E-mail: suttie@biochem.wisc.edu.

SUTTLE, DEBORAH S. state legislator; b. Charleston, W.Va., Dec. 28, 1945; m. James H. Suttle, June 4, 1966; children: Virginia Adele, Amber Karolyn. BS, W.Va. U., 1967; postgrad., U. Nebr., Omaha, 1989-91. Former RN; mem. Nebr. Legislature from 10th dist., Lincoln, 1997—. Vol. Douglas County election commr.; mem. United Meth. Ch., Omaha, League Women Voters, 1980—, Voices for Children; former mem. Omaha 2000 Task Force, Pulling Ams. Communities Together, Omaha Pub. Sch. Supt. Adv. Com., Nebr. Partnership Com., Douglas County Corrections Adv. Com.; mem. various PTA's, Omaha, 1976-93; former pres. LWV for Greater Omaha, 1991-93, Laura Dodge Elem. Parent-Tchr. Assn., 1978-79; vol. lobbyist Omaha PTA/PTSA Coun., 1980-91, Nebr. PTA, 1986-89; v.p. Optimist Internat., 1995-96; vol. lobbyist Nebr. LWV, 1994-96; vol. lobbyist, bd. dirs. PRIDE-Omaha, 1984-96. Mem. Nebr. Nurses' Assn. also: 402-479-0910. Home: 6054 Country Club Oaks Pl Omaha NE 68152-2009 Office: State Capitol Dist 10 PO Box 94604 Rm 1000 Lincoln NE 68509 Fax: 402-571-6901.

SUTTON, BETTY, state legislator; married. BA, Kent State Univ., 1985; JD, Univ. Akron, 1990. Coun.-at-larte Barberton City Coun., 1990-91; v.p. Summit County Coun., 1991-92; state rep. Ohio Dist. 47, 1993—. Vice chmn. Judiciary & Criminal Justice Com., mem. Civil & Comml. Law, Ways & Means, Ins. Pub. Utilities & Elec. Twp. Com. Recipient Outstanding Performance in Const. Law Fed. Bar Assn., 1989, Am. Jurisprudence award, 1989. Mem. ABA, Akron Child Guidance Adv. Coun., Assn. Trial Lawyers Am., Ohio Acad. Trial Lawyers, Summit County Trial Lawyers, Fed. Dem. Women. Office: Ohio Ho of Reps State House Columbus OH 43215 Home: 13488 Walnut Trce Chardon OH 44024-9302

SUTTON, GREGORY PAUL, obstetrician, gynecologist; b. Tokyo, Dec. 12, 1948; (parents Am. citizens); s. Vernon S. And Vonna Lou (Streeter) S.; m. Judith Craigie Holt, June 26, 1977; children: Anne Craigie, James Streeter. BS in Chemistry with honors, Ind. U., 1970; MD, U. Mich., 1976. Diplomate Am. Bd. of Ob/Gyn. Prof. gynecol. oncology Ind. U. Sch. Medicine, Indpls., 1986-97; Mary Fendrich Hulman prof. Gynecologic Oncology Ind. U. Sch. Med., 1997-2000; prof. gynecologic oncology St. Vincent Hosp. and Health Svcs., 2000—01. Cancer Clin. fellow Am. Cancer Soc., Phila., 1981-83; recipient Career Devel. award Am. Cancer Soc., 1986-89. Fellow: Am. Coll. Obstetrics and Gynecology (chair Ind. sect.); mem.: Hoosier Oncology Group, Soc. of Gynecologic Oncologists, Bayard Carter Soc., Ind. State Med. Soc., Marion County Med. Soc., Gynecologic Oncology Group (cert. Spl. Competence in Gynecologic Oncology 1985). Avocations: swimming, cycling, woodworking, sailing. Office: 2001 W 86th St Indianapolis IN 46260-1902 Fax: (317) 338-4312. E-mail: gsutton@stvincent.org.

SUTTON, LYNN SORENSEN, librarian; b. Detroit, July 31, 1953; d. Leonard Arthur Edward and Dorothy Ann (Steele) Sorensen. AB, U. Mich., 1975, MLS, 1976. Dir. Med. Libr. South Chgo. Cmty. Hosp., 1976-77; corp. dirs. librs. Detroit-Macomb Hosp. Corp., Detroit, 1977-86; dir. librs. Harper Hosp., 1987-88; dir. Sci. and Engring. Libr. Wayne State U., 1989-95, dir. undergrad. libr., 1996—. Cons. Catherine McAuley Health Sys., Ann Arbor, Mich., 1993. Contbr. articles to profl. jours. Mem. ALA, Assn. Coll. and Rsch. Librs. (budget and fin. com. 1995—), Mich. Health Scis. Librs. Assn. (pres. 1987-88), Met. Detroit Med. Libr. Group (pres. 1983-84), Phi Beta Kappa, Beta Phi Mu. Office: Wayne State U Undergrad Libr Detroit MI 48202-3918

SUTTON, PETER ALFRED, former archbishop; b. Chandler, Que., Can., Oct. 18, 1934; BA, U. Ottawa, 1960; MA in Religious Edn, Loyola U., Chgo., 1969. Ordained priest Roman Catholic Ch., 1960, bishop, 1974; oblate of Mary Immaculate; high sch. tchr. St. Patricks, Ottawa, Ont., 1961-63, London (Ont.) Cath. Cen. Sch., 1963-74; bishop of Labrador-Schefferville, Que., Can., 1974-86; archbishop Missionary Diocese of Keewatin-Le Pas, Man., 1986, apptd. coadjustor archbishop, 1986-98, archbishop, 1986-98. Mem. Can. Conf. Cath. Bishops, mem. social affairs commn.; mem. Western Cath. Conf. of No. Bishops, Man. Bishops; Canadian accompanying Bishop L'Arche Internat. (homes for mentally handicapped), 1983—. Contbr. religious articles to newspapers. Address: PO Box 270 108 1st St W The Pas MB R9A 1K4 Canada

SUTTON, RAY SANDY, lawyer, company executive; b. Springfield, Mo., Sept. 4, 1937; AB, S.W. Mo. State U., 1959; postgrad., U. Mo., 1959-60; JD, Washburn U., 1966; grad., U.S. Command/Gen. Staff Coll., 1975. With Ross, Wells & Barnett, Kansas City, Brenner, Lockwood & O'Neal, Kansas City, J.F. Pritchard Co., Kansas City; legal asst. Interstate Brands, 1971-76, legal dir., 1976-77, v.p., gen. counsel, 1977-85; v.p. parent co. Interstate Bakeries Corp., Kansas City, Mo., 1979—, corp. sec., 1985—. Col. AUSR, 1960-62; ret. Mem. ABA, Am. Corp. Counsel Assn., Am. Soc. Corp. Secs., Kans. City Met. Bar Assn., Mo. Bar Assn., Lawyers Assn. Kansas City-Mo., Res. Officers Assn., Masons, Phi Alpha Delta. Office: 12 E Armour Blvd Kansas City MO 64111-1202

SUZUKI, HIDETARO, violinist; b. Tokyo, June 1, 1937; came to U.S., 1956; s. Hidezo and Humi (Sakai) S.; m. Zeyda Ruga, May 16, 1962; children: Kenneth Hideo, Nantel Hiroshi, Elina Humi. Diploma, Toho Sch. Music, Tokyo, 1956, Curtis Inst. Music, 1963. Prof. violin Conservatory Province Que., Quebec, 1963-79, Laval U., Quebec, 1971-77, Butler U., Indpls., 1979—. Concertmaster Que. Symphony Orch., 1963-78, Indpls. Symphony Orch., 1978—; performed as concert violinist Can., U.S., Ea. and Western Europe, Cuba, Japan, S.E. Asia, India, USSR 1951-; guest condr. orchs. in numerous concerts, broadcasts, 1968—; mem. jury Mont. Internat. Competition, 1979, Internat. Violin Competition, 1979, Internat. Violin Competition of Indpls., 1982, 86, 90, 94; artistic dir. Suzuki and Friends chamber music series, 1980—; rec. artist. Office: Indpls Symphony Orch 45 Monument Cir Indianapolis IN 46204-2907

SUZUKI, ISAMU, microbiology educator, researcher; b. Tokyo, Aug. 4, 1930; emigrated to Can., 1962; s. Jisaku and Michie (Baba) S.; m. Yumiko Kanehira, May 16, 1962; children: Kenji, Miyo, Kohji. B.Sc.Agr., U. Tokyo, 1953; Ph.D., Iowa State U., 1958. NIH postdoctoral fellow Western Res. U., 1958-60; instr. Inst. Applied Microbiology, U. Toyko, 1960-62; asst. prof. mcirobiology U. Man., Winnipeg, Canada, 1964—66, assoc. prof., 1966—69, prof., 1969—99, head. dept., 1972—85, sr. scholar, 1999—2000, prof. emeritus, 2000—. Contbr. articles on sulfur-oxidizing bacteria, chemoautotrophic bacteria, mechanism of inorganic oxidation to sci. jours. NRC of Can. postdoctoral fellow, 1962-64. Mem. AAAS, Can. Soc. Microbiologists, Am. Soc. Microbiology, Can. Soc. Biochem. and Molecular Cell Biology, Sigma Xi Office: U Manitoba Dept Microbiology Winnipeg MB Canada R3T 2N2 E-mail: isuzuki@cc.umanitoba.ca.

SUZUKI, TSUNEO, molecular immunologist; b. Nagoya, Aichi, Japan, Nov. 23, 1931; s. Morichika and Toshiko (Kita) S.; widowed; children: Riichiro, Aijiro, Yozo. BS, U. Tokyo, 1953, MD, 1957; PhD, U. Hokkaido, 1967. Asst. prof. U. Kans. Med. Ctr., Kansas City, 1970-79, assoc. prof., 1979-83, prof., 1983—, interim chair, 1994-98. Mem. NIH Study Sect., Washington, 1983-87. Contbr. articles to profl. jours. Postdoctoral fellows

U. Wis., 1963-66, 69-70, U. Lausanne, Switzerland, 1966-67, U Toronto, 1969; recipient Fulbright Travel award, 1962, Sr. Investigator award, U. Kans. Med. Ctr., 1990. Mem. Am. Assn. Immunologists, Am. Soc. Biological Chemists (Travel award 1988). Home: 3620 W 73rd St Prairie Village KS 66208-2903 Office: U Kans Med Ctr/Dept Microbiology Rm 3025 Wahl Hall West 3901 Rainbow Blvd Kansas City KS 66160-0001

SVÄRD, N. TRYGVE, electrical engineer; b. Gothenburg, Sweden; came to U.S., 1973; s. Owe V. and Berit S. (Heden) S.; children: Michael, Stefan. BEE, Gothensburg U., Sweden, 1966. Registered profl. engr. Engr. Volvo Car Div., Gothenburg, 1969-73; from project engr., sr. sect. engr. to program mgr. Honeywell Inc., Mpls., 1973-90; sr. program mgr., internat. programs Alliant Techsystems, Inc., 1990-99; ret., 1999. Pres. Nord Mark Inc., Mpls, 1986-- Sgt. Swedish Coast Arty., 1967-68. Mem. Am. Swedish Inst. Republican. Home and Office: 12075 48th Ave N Minneapolis MN 55442-2129

SVEC, HARRY JOHN, chemist, educator; b. Cleve., June 24, 1918; s. Ralph Joseph and Lilian Josephine (Pekarek) S.; m. Edna Mary Bruno, Oct. 27, 1943; children— Mary, Peter, Katherine, Jan, Thomas, Jeanne, Benjamin, Daniel, Lillian. BS, John Carroll U., 1941; PhD in Phys. Chemistry, Iowa State U., 1949. Asst. chemist Iowa State U., 1941-43; rsch. assoc. Inst. Atomic Rsch., 1946-50, asst. prof. chemistry, 1950-55, assoc. prof., 1955-60, prof., 1960-83, emeritus prof. chemistry, 1983—, Disting. prof. in scis. and humanities emeritus, 1978—; assoc. chemist Ames Lab., 1950-55; chemist Ames Lab., Dept. Energy, 1955-60, sr. chemist, 1960-85, program dir., 1974-85, assoc. scientist, 1983—. Jr. chemist Manhattan Project, Iowa State Coll., 1943-46; cons., lectr. in field. Author lab. manual in phys. chemistry; contbr. numerous articles to profl. publs.; founding editor: Internat. Jour. Mass Spectrometry and Ion Processes, 1968-86. NSF grantee, 1972-82; EPA grantee, 1974-81; AEC grantee, 1950-74; ERDA grantee, 1974-77; Dept. Energy grantee, 1977-87; Am. Water Works Assn. grantee, 1977-79 Fellow: AAAS, The Chem. Soc.; mem.: ASTM, Am. Soc. Mass Spectroscopy (charter, v.p. 1972—74, pres. 1974—76), Geochem. Soc., Am. Chem. Soc. (emeritus), Alpha Chi Sigma (cons. 1985—), Phi Lambda Upsilon, Alpha Signa Nu, Sigma Xi. Roman Catholic. Home: 2427 Hamilton Dr Ames IA 50014-8203 Office: Iowa State U 1605 Gilman Hall Ames IA 50014-8203

SVEDJAN, KEN, state legislator; m. Lorrtta; 1 child. BS, MS, U. N.D. Mem. from dist. 17 N.D. Ho. of Reps., 1991—; pres. Altru Health Found. Pres. United Health Found.; chmn. bd. Third St. Clinic. With U.S. Army, 1968-70. Recipient Disting. Svc. award Am. Diabetes Assn. Mem. Rotary Internat. (bd. dirs.), Grand Forks C. of C., Elks. Republican. Home: 4697 Harvest Cir Grand Forks ND 58201-3502 Office: ND House of Reps State Capitol Bismarck ND 58505

SVEEN, GERALD O. state legislator; m. Ruth Ellen; 3 children. Student, U. N.D., Temple U. Retired dentist; mayor Bottineau, 12 yrs.; mem. N.D. Ho. of Reps., 1993—, mem. edn., transp. coms. Pres. Internat. Peace Garden. With USAF, WWII and Korea. Recipient Cmty. Svc. award. Mem. Am. Legion, Lions, Oak Creek Cemetery Assn. (pres.). Republican. Presbyterian. Home: 411 5th St E Bottineau ND 58318-1403 Office: ND House of Reps State Capitol Bismarck ND 58505 E-mail: gsveen@state.nd.us.

SVETLOVA, MARINA, ballerina, choreographer, educator; b. Paris, May 3, 1922; came to U.S. from Australia, 1940; d. Max and Tamara (Andreieff) Hartman. Studies with Vera Trefilova, Paris, 1930-36, studies with L. Egorova and M. Kschessinska, 1936-39; studies with A. Vilzak, N.Y.C., 1940-57; D honoris causa, Fedn. Francaise de Danse, 1988. Ballet dir. So. Vt. Art Ctr., 1959-64; dir. Svetlova Dance Ctr., Dorset, Vt., 1965-95; prof. ballet dept. Ind. U., Bloomington, 1969-92, prof. emeritus, 1992—, chmn. dept., 1969-78. Choreographer Dallas Civic Opera, 1964-67, Ft. Worth Opera, 1967-83, San Antonio Opera, 1983, Seattle Opera, Houston Opera, Kansas City Performing Arts Found. Ballerina original Ballet Russe de Monte Carlo, 1939-41; guest ballerina Ballet Theatre, 1942, London's Festival Ballet, Teatro dell Opera, Rome, Nat. Opera, Stockholm, Sweden, Suomi Opera, Helsinki, Finland, Het Nederland Ballet, Holland, Cork Irish Ballet, Paris Opera Comique, London Palladium, Teatro Colon, Buenos Aires, others; prima ballerina Met. Opera, 1943-50, N.Y.C. Opera, 1950-52; choreographer: (ballet sequences) The Fairy Queen, 1966, L'Histoire du Soldat, 1968; tours in Far East, Middle East, Europe, S.Am., U.S.; performer various classical ballets Graduation Ball; contbr. articles to Debut, Paris Opera. Mem. Am. Guild Mus. Artists (bd. dirs.), Conf. on Ballet in Higher Edn., Nat. Soc. Arts and Letters (nat. dance chmn.) Office: 2100 E Maxwell Ln Bloomington IN 47401-6119

SVIGGUM, STEVEN ARTHUR, farmer, state representative; b. Minn., Sept. 15, 1951; m. Debra Beegh; children: Hans, Erik, Marit. BA in Math., St. Olaf Coll., 1973. Tchr. math., coach Belgrade (Minn.) High Sch., 1973-77, West Concord (Minn.) High Sch., 1977-78; farmer, 1973—; state rep. State of Minn., 1992—, speaker of the ho., 1999—. Bd. dirs. Riverview Manor, Inc., Wanamingo, Minn.; Rep. caucus leader Minn. Ho. of Reps., St. Paul, 1992—. Recipient Hutchinson award Am. Assn. for Mentally Retarded, 1991, Recognition of Disting. Svc. award Minn. Assn. Rehab. Facilities and Minn. Devel. Achievement Ctr. Assn., 1991, Champion of Small Bus. award Nat. Fedn. Ind. Bus. Minn., 1991; named Legislator of Yr., Assn. Retarded Citizens, 1986. Mem. Kenyon (Minn.) Lions, Kenyon Sportsmen's Club. Lutheran. Avocations: baseball, basketball, coaching. Home: 42490 60th Ave Kenyon MN 55946-3224 Office: 463 State Office Bldg Saint Paul MN 55155-0001 E-mail: rep.steve.sviggum@house.leg.state.mn.us.*

SWAIMAN, KENNETH FRED, pediatric neurologist, educator; b. St. Paul, Nov. 19, 1931; s. Lester J. and Shirley (Ryan) S.; m. Phyllis Kammerman Sher, Oct. 1985; children: Lisa, Jerrold, Barbara, Dana. BA magna cum laude, U. Minn., 1952, BS, 1953, MD, 1955; postgrad., 1956-58. Diplomate Am. Bd. Psychiatry and Neurology, Am. Bd. Pediatrics, Am. Bd. Psychiatry and Neurology with Spl. Competence in Child Neurology. Intern Mpls. Gen. Hosp., 1955-56; resident in pediatrics, fellow in pediatrics to chief resident U. Minn. Hosp., 1956-58, spl. fellow in pediatric neurology, 1960-63, dir. pediatric neurology tng. program, 1968-94, various to interim head dept. neurology, 1994-96; chief pediatrics U.S. Army Hosp., Ft. McPherson, Ga., 1958-60; asst. prof. pediatrics, neurology U. Minn. Med. Sch., Mpls., 1963-66, prof., dir. pediatric neurology, 1969-96, mem. internship adv. coun. exec. faculty, 1966-70, interim head dept. neurology, 1994-96; postgrad. fellow pediatric neurology Nat. Inst. Neurologic Diseases and Blindness, 1960-63, assoc. prof., 1966-69. Cons. pediatric neurology Hennepin County Gen. Hosp., 1963—, Mpls., St. Paul-Ramsey Hosp., St. Paul Children's Hosp., Mpls. Children's Hosp.; vis. prof. numerous univs. including Loyola U., 1982, U. N.Mex., 1982, U. Ind. Med. Sch., 1983, U. Kyushu, Shiga, Nagoya, Tokyo, 1985, Driscoll Children's Hosp., Corpus Christi, Tex., 1986, Inst. Nacional de Pediatria, Mexico City, 1986, U. de Concepion, Chile, 1989, Beijing U. Med. Sch., 1989, Xian Med. U., China, 1989, Children's Hosp. of Mich., Detroit, 1990, Hong Kong Child Neurology Soc., 1995, Tartu, Estonia, 1997, Krem, Austria, 1997, Santiago, Chile, 1997, Kaunas, Lithuania, 1998, ICNA Ednl. Seminar, Tartu, 1998, Montevideo, Uruguay, 1999, others; lectr. in field; guest worker NIH, NICHD, Bethesda, Md., 1978-79, 79-81. Author: (with Francis S. Wright) Neuromuscular Diseases in Infancy and Childhood, 1969, Pediatric Neuromuscular Diseases, 1979, (with Stephen Ashwal) Pediatric Neurology Case Studies, 1978, 2d edit., 1984, Pediatric Neurology: Practice and Principles, 1989, 3d edit., 1999; editor: (with John A. Anderson) Phenylketonuria and Allied Metabolic Diseases, 1966, (with Francis S. Wright) Practice Pediatric Neurology, 1975, 2d edit., 1982; mem. editorial bd.: Annals of Neurology, 1977-83, Neurology Update, 1977-82, Pediatric Update, 1977-85, Brain and Devel. (Jour. Japanese Soc. Child Neurology), 1980—, Neuropediatrics (Stuttgart), 1982-92; editor-in-chief: Pediatric Neurology, 1984—; contbr. articles to sci. jours. Chmn. Minn. Gov.'s Bd. for Handicapped, Exceptional and Gifted Children, 1972-76; mem. human devel. study sect. NIH, 1976-79, guest worker, 1978-81. Served to capt. M.C. U.S. Army, 1958-60. Fellow Am. Acad. Pediatrics, Am. Acad. Neurology (rep. to nat. coun. Nat. Soc. Med. Rsch.); mem. Soc. Pediatric Rsch., Ctrl. Soc. Clin. Rsch., Ctrl. Soc. Neurol. Rsch., Internat. Soc. Neurochemistry, Am. Neurol. Assn., Minn. Neurol. Soc., AAAS, Midwest Pediatric Soc., Am. Soc. Neurochemistry, Child Neurology Soc. (1st pres. 1972-73, Hower award 1981, Founder's award 1996, chmn. internat. affairs com., 1991-96, mem. long range planning com. 1991-97, chmn. fin. com. 1995—), Internat. Assn. Child Neurologists (exec. com. 1975-79, chmn. global edn. com. 1996-99), Profs. of Child Neurology (1st pres. 1978-80, mem. nominating com. 1986-92), Japanese Child Neurology Soc. (Segawa award 1986, mem. nominating com. 1986-92, chair internat. affairs com. 1991—, mem. long range planning com. 1991-98), Soc. de Psiquiatria y Neurologia de la Infancia y Adolescencia, Internat. Child Neurology Assn. (chair internat. edn. com. 1996-99), Lithuanian Child Neurology Soc. (hon., pres. 2000—), Child Neurology Found. (pres. 2000—), Phi Beta Kappa, Sigma Xi. Office: U Minn Med Sch Dept Pediatric Neurology 1821 University Ave W Saint Paul MN 55104-2801 also: UMHC Box 486 420 Delaware St SE Minneapolis MN 55455-0374 E-mail: pncomm@uswet.net.

SWAIN, DENNIS MICHAEL, lawyer; b. Jackson, Mich., June 15, 1948; s. Donald Elliot and Rose Therese (Flynn) S.; m. Jacque Lee Wallace, Mar. 20, 1971; 1 child, Jason Patrick. BA, Mich. State U., 1974; JD, Thomas M. Cooley Law Sch., 1978. Bar: Mich. 1979, U.S. Dist. Ct. (we. dist.) Mich. 1983. Assoc. Law Office of Zerafa P.C., Elk Rapids, Mich., 1978-81; ptnr. Gockerman & Swain, Manistee, 1981-85; pros. atty. Manistee County, 1985—. Instr. West Shore Community Coll., Scottville, Mich., 1985—, bd. dirs. law enforcement adv. bd.; bd. chmn. Region 10 Detectives, Manistee, 1985—. Fellow Mich. Bar Found.; mem. ABA, Mich. Bar Assn. (rep. state assembly 1983—), Manistee County Bar Assn. (pres. 1985-86), Assn. Trial Lawyers Am., Pros. Attys. Assn. of Mich., Nat. Dist. Attys. Assn. Republican. Episcopalian. Lodge: Elks. Avocations: hunting, fishing, skiing, shooting. Home: 13767 Lakeside Ave Bear Lake MI 49614-9615 Office: Manistee County Prosecutor 402 Maple St Manistee MI 49660-1617

SWANEY, THOMAS EDWARD, lawyer; b. Detroit, Apr. 25, 1942; s. Robert Ernest and Mary Alice (Slinger) S.; m. Patricia Louise Nash, Sept. 9, 1967; children: Julia Bay, Mary Elizabeth, David Paul. AB, U. Mich., 1963, JD, 1967; postdoctoral, London Sch. Econs., 1967-68. Bar: Ill. 1968. From assoc. to ptnr. Sidley & Austin, Chgo., 1968—. Bd. dirs. Corey Steel Co., Cicero, Ill., Gertrude B. Nielsen Child Care & Learning Ctr., Northbrook, Ill., Ward C. Rogers Found., Chgo. Trustee H. Earl Hoover Found., Glencoe, Ill., 1986—, RF Found., Chgo., 1992—; trustee, bd. pres. 1st Presbyn. Ch., Evanston, Ill., 1984-87, 96-98; bd. dirs. Lakeland Conservancy, Minocqua, Wis., 1987—; vol. sch. dists., Chgo., 2000—. Mem. ABA, Ill. State Bar Assn., Chgo. Bar Assn., Legal Club Chgo. Office: Sidley & Austin Bank One Plz 425 W Surf St Apt 605 Chicago IL 60657-6139

SWANK, DARRYL, agricultural products executive; CFO Purina Mills, St. Louis. Office: Purina Mills PO Box 66812 Saint Louis MO 63166-6812

SWANSON, ALFRED BERTIL, orthopaedic and hand surgeon, inventor, educator; b. Kenosha, Wis., Apr. 16, 1923; s. O.P. and Esther (Person) S.; children: Karin Louise, Miles Raymond; m. Genevieve de Groot, Dec. 27, 1969; 1 son, Eric Alfred. B.S., U. Ill., 1944, M.D., 1947. Diplomate: Am. Bd. Orthopaedic Surgery. Intern St. Luke's Hosp., Chgo., 1947; spl. tng. orthopaedic surgery Ill. Crippled Children's Hosp. Sch., 1948, St. Luke's Hosp., 1949, Northwestern U. Med. Sch., 1950, Ind. U. Med. Center, 1951; practice medicine specializing in orthopaedic/hand surgery Grand Rapids, Mich., 1954—; chief hand surgery fellowship, orthopaedic research dir. Blodgett Meml. Hosp.-Spectrum Health East, 1962—; dir. Grand Rapids Orthopaedic Surgery Residency Tng. Program. Chief of staff Mary Free Bed Children's Hosp. and Orthopaedic Center, Juvenile Amputee Clinic, 1963-65, 67-68, 73-78; prof. surgery Mich. State U., Lansing; chmn. Grand Rapids Internat. Symposium on Implant Orthoplasty, 1970-92; nat. and internat. lectr. in field. Author: Implant Resection Arthroplasty in the Hand and Extremities, 1973; Contbr. numerous sci. articles and exhibits in field; producer teaching films. Served with USNR, 1944-45; served to capt. M.C. AUS, 1952-54. Decorated medal of Honor South Vietnam, 1967; recipient Profl. Medicine award Mich. Internat. Council, 1977; recipient Resolution of Tribute State of Mich., 1986, Order of Merit Orthopaedic Research Soc., 1982, 89, 91, Disting. Service in Health Care award Hosp. Council West Mich., 1984, Nat. Vol. Service Citation Arthritis Found., 1984, U. Ill. Alumni Achievement award, 1985, Orthopaedic Overseas Spl. award for personal service and recruitment of orthopaedic and hand surgery vols. for South Vietnam and Peru, Disting. Svc. award Arthritis Found., 1990, Cert. of Appreciation, Operation Desert Storm, U.S. Dept. VA, 1991; named prof. h.c. Orthopedic Alumni of Shriners Hosp. Crippled Children Mexico City Fellow A.C.S.; mem. Am. Med. Writers Assn., AMA (Disting. Service award 1966, 69, Sci. Achievement award 1996), Am. Acad. Orthopaedic Surgeons (Kappa Delta award 1982), Pan Am. Med. Assn., Pan Pacific Surg. Assn., Assn. Mil. Surgeons, Am. Acad. Cerebral Palsy, Brit. Club Surgery of Hand, Italian Soc. Surgery of Hand, Brazilian, Colombian, South African, Japanese, Argentinian, S. Am., Caribbean Hand socs., Internat. Fedn. Socs. Surgery Hand (sec.-gen. 1978-83, pres. 1983-89, historian 1989—, Pioneer in Hand Surgery award 1995), Groupe d'Etude de la Main, Am. Assn. Hand Surgeons, Am. Soc. Surgery Hand (pres. 1979-80), Am., Clin., Mich., Lamplighter's orthopaedic socs., Am. Orthopaedic Assn., Am. Orthopaedic Foot Soc., Am. Soc. Plastic and Reconstructive Surgeons, Peruvian Soc. Plastic and Reconstructive Surgeons, Mich. Med. Soc. (Disting. Service award 1966, Nat. Pres.'s award 1979, 84, Cmty. Svc. award 1993), Assn. Orthopaedic Chairmen, European Rheumatoid Arthritis Surg. Soc., Norwegian Soc. Rheumatoid Surgery, Ga. Orthopaedic Soc., Fla. Orthopaedic Soc., Ark. Orthopaedic Soc., Orthopaedic Letters Club, Brazilian, Latin Am., Chilean, Columbian, Internat., Argentinian, Peruvian, Belgian, Turkish socs. Orthopaedic Surgery and Traumatology, Internat. Soc. Rehab. Disabled, Rheumatoid Arthritis Surg. Soc., Soc. Am. Inventors, Soc. Biomaterials, Internat. coll. Surgeons, Internat. Soc. Orthopaedic and Traumatology Rsch., Internat. Soc. Prosthetics and Orthotics Alternative Methods Internat. Stability (founder, chmn. 1983—), Internat. Trees Corps (founder, chmn. 1983—), Airplane Owners and Pilots Assn., Mid Mich. Soaring Soc., World Affairs Council Western Mich. (chmn. numerous coms.), Blythefield Country Club, Peninsular Club (Grand Rapids), Rotary, many others. Congregationalist. Achievements include inventing implants for replacement arthritic joints. Home: 2945 Bonnell Ave SE Grand Rapids MI 49506-3131 Office: Blodgett Hosp Profl Bldg 1900 Wealthy St SE Grand Rapids MI 49506-2969

SWANSON, DAVID HEATH, agricultural company executive; b. Aurora, Ill., Nov. 3, 1942; s. Neil H. and Helen J. (McKendry) S.; m. Carolyn Breitinger; children: Benjamin Heath, Matthew Banford. B.A., Harvard U., 1964; M.A., U. Chgo., 1969. Account exec. 1st Nat. Bank Chgo., 1967-69; dep. mgr. Brown Bros. Harriman & Co., N.Y.C., 1969-72; treas. Borden, Inc. Internat., 1972-75; v.p., treas. Continental Grain Co., 1975-77, v.p., CFO, 1977-79, gen. mgr. European div., 1979-81, exec. v.p. and gen. mgr. World Grain div., 1981-83, corp. sr. v.p., chief fin. and adminstrv. officer, 1983-86, group pres., 1985-86; pres., CEO Cen. Soya, Ft. Wayne, Ind., 1986-93; chmn., CEO Explorer Nutrition Group, N.Y.C., 1994-96; pres., CEO, Countrymark, Inc., Indpls., 1996-98. Mem. adv. bd. U.S. Export-Import Bank, 1985-86; bd. dirs. Fiduciary Trust Internat., Conrail. Founding bd. dirs. Internat. Policy Coun. on Agr. and Trade; mem. adv. bd. Purdue U. Agr. Sch.; mem. Gov.'s Econ. Devel. Ind. Bd.; bd. govs. Exec. Coun. on Fgn. Diplomats and U.S. Agr. Libr.; gov. Found. for U.S. Constn. Mem. Coun. Fgn. Rels., Nat. Assn. Mfrs. (bd. dirs.), Ind. C. of C. (bd. dirs.), Am. Alpine Club (bd. dirs.), Links Club, Racquet and Tennis Club, Explorers Club (bd. dirs., sec., pres.), Millbrook Golf and Tennis. Republican. Congregationalist. Office: PO Box 609 Bangall NY 12506-0609

SWANSON, DON RICHARD, university dean; b. L.A., Oct. 10, 1924; s. Harry Windfield and Grace Clara (Sandstrom) S.; m. Patricia Elizabeth Klick, Aug. 22, 1976; children— Douglas Alan, Richard Brian, Judith Ann. BS, Calif. Inst. Tech., 1945; MA, Rice U., 1947; PhD, U. Calif., Berkeley, 1952. Physicist U. Calif. Radiation Lab., Berkeley, 1947-52, Hughes Research and devel. Labs., Culver City, Calif., 1952-55; research scientist TRW, Inc., Canoga Park, 1955-63; prof. Grad. Library Sch., U. Chgo., 1963-92, dean, 1963-72, 77-79, 86-90, prof. bio-sci. coll. divsn. and divsn. humanities, 1992-96, prof. emeritus, 1996—. Mem. Sci. Info. Council, NSF, 1960-65; mem. toxicology info. panel Pres.'s Sci. Advisory Com., 1964-66; mem. library vis. com. Mass. Inst. Tech., 1966-71; mem. com. on sci. and tech. communication Nat. Acad. Scis., 1966-69 Editor: The Intellectual Founds. of Library Education, 1965, The Role of Libraries in the Growth of Knowledge, 1980; co-editor: Operations Research: Implications for Libraries, 1972, Management Education: Implications for Libraries and Library Schools, 1974; mem. editorial bd.: Library Quarterly, 1963-93; contbr.: chpt. to Ency. Brit, 1968—; sci. articles to profl. jours. Trustee Nat. Opinion Research Center, 1964-73; Research fellow Chgo. Inst. for Psychoanalysis, 1972-76. Served with USNR, 1943-46. Recipient Award of Merit Am. Soc. for Info. Sci. and Tech., 2000. Mem. Am. Soc. for Info. Sci., Am. Assn. Artificial Intelligence. Home: 5468 S Ingleside Ave Chicago IL 60615-5062 Office: U Chgo Divsn Humanities 1010 E 59th St Chicago IL 60637-1512 E-mail: d-swanson@uchicago.edu.

SWANSON, DONALD FREDERICK, retired food company executive; b. Mpls., Aug. 6, 1927; s. Clayton A. and Irma (Baiocchi) S.; m. Virginia Clare Hannah, Dec. 17, 1948; children— Donald Frederick, Cynthia Hannah Lindgren, Janet Clare Webster. B.A., U. Minn., 1948. With Gen. Mills, Inc., 1949-85, div. v.p., dir. marketing flour, dessert and baking mixes, 1964-65, v.p., gen. mgr. grocery products div., 1965-68, v.p., corporate adminstrn. officer consumer foods group, fashion div., transp. and purchasing depts., advt. and marketing services, 1969, exec. v.p. craft, game and toy group, fashion group, direct marketing group, travel group, dir., 1968-76, sr. exec. v.p. consumer non-foods, 1976-85, chief financial officer, 1977-79, sr. exec. v.p. restaurants and consumer non-foods, 1980-81, vice chmn. restaurants and consumer non-foods, 1981-85. Ret. chmn. bd. Soo Line Corp. Served with AUS, 1946-47. Mem. Lafayette Club, Mpls. Club, Wayzata Country Club, Royal Poinciana Golf Club, Phi Kappa Psi. Home: 2171 Gulf Shore Blvd N Apt 504 Naples FL 34102-4685 Office: 641 Lake St E Wayzata MN 55391-1760

SWANSON, PATRICIA KLICK, foundation administrator; b. St. Louis, May 8, 1940; d. Emil Louis and Patricia (McNair) Klick; 1 child, Ivan Clatanoff. BS in Edn., U. Mo., 1962; postgrad., Cornell U., 1963; MLS, Simmons Coll., 1967. Reference librarian Simmons Coll., Boston, 1967-68, U. Chgo., 1970-79, sr. lectr. Grad. Library Sch., 1974-83, 86-88, head reference service, 1979-83, asst. dir. for sci. libraries, 1983-93, acting asst. dir. for tech. svcs., 1987-88, assoc. provost, 1993-98; program officer MacArthur Found., 1999—. Project dir. Office Mgmt. Svcs., Assn. Rsch. Librs., 1982-83; speaker in field; cons. on libr. mgmt., planning and space. Author: Great is the Gift that Bringeth Knowledge: Highlights from the History of the John Crerar Library, 1989; contbr. articles to profl. jours. Office: John D and Catherine T MacArthur Found 140 S Dearborn St Ste 1100 Chicago IL 60603-5202

SWANSON, ROY ARTHUR, classicist, educator; b. St. Paul, Apr. 7, 1925; s. Roy Benjamin and Gertrude (Larson) S.; m. Vivian May Vitous, Mar. 30, 1946; children: Lynn Marie (Mrs. Gerald A. Snider), Robin Lillian, Robert Roy (dec.), Dyack Tyler, Dana Miriam (Mrs. Jon Butts). BA, U. Minn., 1948, BS, 1949, MA, 1951; PhD, U. Ill., 1954. Prin. Maplewood Elementary Sch., St. Paul, 1949-51; instr. U. Ill., 1952-53, Ind. U., 1954-57; asst. prof. U. Minn., Mpls., 1957-61, assoc. prof., 1961-64, acting chmn. classics, 1963-64, prof. classics, chmn. comparative lit., 1964-65; prof. English Macalester Coll., St. Paul, 1965-67, coord. humanities program, 1966-67; prof. comparative lit. and classics U. Wis.-Milw., 1967—, prof. English, 1990-96, chmn. classics dept., 1967-70, 86-89, chmn. comparative lit., 1970-73, 76-83, coord. Scandinavian studies program, 1982-96. Cons. St. Paul Tchrs. Sr. High Sch. English, 1964 Author: Odi et Amo: The Complete Poetry of Catullus, 1959, Heart of Reason: Introductory Essays in Modern-World Humanities, 1963, Pindar's Odes, 1974, Greek and Latin Word Elements, 1981, The Love Songs of the Carmina Burana, 1987, Pär Lagerkvist: Five Early Works, 1989; editor Minn. Rev., 1963-67; Classical Jour., 1966-72; contbr. articles to profl. jours. With AUS, 1944-46. Decorated Bronze Star; recipient Disting. Teaching award U. Minn., 1962, Disting. Teaching award U. Wis.-Milw., 1974, 91, 99. Mem. Am. Philol. Assn., Am. Comparative Lit. Assn., Modern Lang. Assn., Soc. for Advancement Scandinavian Study, Phi Beta Kappa (pres. chpt. 1975-76). Home: 11618 N Bobolink Ln Mequon WI 53092-2804 Office: U Wis French/Italian/Comp Lit PO Box 413 Milwaukee WI 53201-0413 E-mail: rexroy333@aol.com., rexcy@uwm.edu.

SWANSON, WAYNE HAROLD, lawyer; b. Aitkin, Minn., May 6, 1943; s. Edwin and Alma (Sundholm) Swanson; m. Joanne Maxine Case, June 22, 1968; children: Tamara K., Scott E. BA, U. Minn., 1967; JD, William Mitchell Coll. Law, St. Paul, 1974. Bar: Minn. 1974, U.S. Dist. Ct. Minn. 1983. Asst. county atty., then asst. pub. defender Polk County, Crookston, Minn., 1974-78, county atty., 1979—; pvt. practice, 1976—. Chmn. adv. bd. Tri-County Cmty. Corrections; mem. Northwestern Minn. Ednl. Improvement Assn. Mem.: ABA, Riverview Hosp. Assn., 14th Dist. Bar Assn., Minn. State Bar Assn., Crookston C. of C., Minakwa Country Club, Crookston Gun Club (bd. dirs.), Lions, Eagles. Lutheran. Home: RR 2 Box 195B Crookston MN 56716-9648 Office: 223 E 7th St Crookston MN 56716-1477

SWANSTROM, THOMAS EVAN, economist; b. Green Bay, Wis., May 17, 1939; s. Alfred Enoch and Elizabeth Nan (Thomas) S.; m. Nancy Anne Roche; children: Amy, Scott. Student, U. Notre Dame, 1957-59; BA, U. Wis., 1962, MA, 1963; postgrad., Am. U., 1963-66. Economist, U.S. Bur. Labor Statistics, Washington, 1963-66. Dir. research Population Ref. Bur., Washington, 1966-68; economist Sears, Roebuck & Co., Chgo., 1968-70, market analyst, 1970-72, mgr. catalog research, 1972-75, asst. mgr. econ. research, 1974-80, chief economist, 1980-90; pres. Consumer Econs., Chgo., 1991—; mem. bus. research adv. council Bur. Labor Stats.; adj. prof. Lake Forest Grad. Sch. Mgmt. Contbr. articles to industry publs. Mem. Nat. Assn. Bus. Economists, Conf. Bus. Economists. E-mail: tevanswan@aol.com.

SWANTON, VIRGINIA LEE, writer, publisher, bookseller; b. Oak Park, Ill., Feb. 6, 1933; d. Milton Wesley and Eleanor Louise (Linnell) S. BA, Lake Forest (Ill.) Coll., 1954; MA in English Lit., Northwestern U., 1955; cert. in acctg., Coll. of Lake County, Ill., 1984. Editorial asst. Publs. Office, Northwestern U., Evanston, Ill., 1955-58; reporter Lake Forester, Lake Forest, 1959; editor Scott, Foresman & Co., Glenview, Ill., 1959-84; copy editor, travel coord. McDougal Littell/Houghton Mifflin, Evanston, 1985-94; sr. bookseller B. Dalton Bookseller, Lake Forest, Ill., 1985—; author, pub. Gold Star Publ. Svcs., 1994—. Contbr. articles to profl. jours.; pub. local interest and ref. works. Mem. bd. deacons First Presbyn. Ch. of Lake Forest; former sec. bd. dirs., newsletter editor Career Resource Ctr., Inc., Lake Forest; current events discusssion vol. Lake Forest/Lake Bluff Sr. Ctr. Mem. Deerpath Art League, Chgo. Women in Pub., Lake Forest/Lake Bluff Hist. Soc. Presbyterian. Avocation: gardening. Office: Gold Star Publ Svcs PO Box 125 Lake Forest IL 60045-0125

SWARTZ, B(ENJAMIN) K(INSELL), JR. archaeologist, educator; b. L.A., June 23, 1931; s. Benjamin Kinsell and Maxine Marietta (Pearce) S.; m. Cyrilla Casillas, Oct. 23, 1966; children: Benjamin Kinsell III, Frank Casillas. AA summa cum laude, L.A. City Coll., 1952; BA, UCLA, 1954, MA, 1958; PhD, U. Ariz., 1964. Curator Klamath County Mus., Oreg., 1959-61, rsch. assoc., 1961-62; asst. prof. anthropology Ball State U., Muncie, Ind., 1964-68, assoc. prof., 1968-72, prof., 1972-2001, prof. emeritus, 2001—. Vis. sr. lectr. U. Ghana, 1970-71; exch. prof. U. Yaounde, Cameroon, 1984-85; field rschr. N.Am. and West Africa; mem. exec. bd., pres. Am. Com. to Advance the Study of Petroglyphs and Pictographs; rep. to Internat. Fedn. Rock Art Orgns.; bd. dirs. Coun. Conservation Ind. Archaeology; mem. adv. bd. Am. Com. for Preservation of Archaeol. Collections. Contbr. revs. and articles to profl. jours.; author books, monographs in field, including: West African Culture Dynamics, 1980, Indiana's Prehistoric Past, 1981, Rock Art and Posterity, 1991, Procs. of Ist Internat. South African Rock Art Assn. Conf., 1991. Klamath County chmn. Oreg. Statehood Centennial, 1959. With USN, 1954-56. Fellow AAAS, Ind. Acad. Sci.; mem. Current Anthropology (assoc.), Soc. Am. Archaeology, Internat. Com. Rock Art, Sigma Xi, Lambda Alpha (nat. coun., exec. sec.). Home: 805 W Charles St Muncie IN 47305-2235 E-mail: 01bkswartz@bsuvc.bsu.edu.

SWARTZ, DONALD EVERETT, television executive; b. Mpls., Mar. 7, 1916; s. Albert L. and Sara (Shore) S.; m. Helen Gordon, Mar. 24, 1940; children: Stuart, Lawrence, Gary. Grad. high sch. Owner Ind. Film Distbrs., 1940-53, Tele-Film Assocs., 1953-57; pres., gen. mgr. KMSP-TV, Mpls., 1957-79; pres. United TV, Inc. (subs. 20th Century Fox Film Corp. until 1981); operating KMSP-TV, KTV4, Salt Lake City, KBHK-TV, San Francisco KMOL-TV, San Antonio; CEO United Television, Inc., Mpls., 1979-85; cons. KMOL-TV, 1985—; founder Tele-Video Assocs., 1985—, Tele-Video Entertainment, 1985—; owner/mgr. Donald Investment Co., 1989—. Vice pres. Twin City Broadcast Skills Bank (scholarship program), St. Paul Arts and Sci. Inst.; pres. U. Minn. Heart Hosp.; mem. Gov.'s Commn. Bicentennial; bd. dirs. Mpls. United Jewish Fund and Council; Mem. Mpls. Inst. Arts, Mpls., St. Paul chambers commerce, Minn. Orch. Assn., Citizens League. Named Minn. Pioneer Broadcaster of Yr., 1992, charter mem. Hall of Fame, Panck Mus. of Broadcasting, 2001; recipient Silver Bride trophy, Nat. Acad. Arts and Scis., 2000. Mem.U. Minn Alumni Assn., Press Club (Mpls.), Advt. Standard Club (Mpls.), Hillcrest Country Club (St. Paul), Variety Club, Mission Hills Country Club (Rancho Mirage, Calif.), Oak Ridge Country Club (Mpls.), B'nai B'rith. Jewish (pres. temple). Home: 2221 Youngman Ave Saint Paul MN 55116-3055 Office: Ste 224 10505 Wayzata Blvd Minnetonka MN 55305 Fax: (763) 952-0661.

SWARTZ, JACK, chamber of commerce executive; b. Nov. 24, 1932; s. John Ralph and Fern (Cave) S.; m. Nadine Ann Langlois, Aug. 4, 1956; children: Dana, Shawn, Tim, Jay. AA, Dodge City C.C., 1953; student, St. Mary of Plains Coll., 1953-55, 58; BBA, Washburn U., 1973, BA in Econs., 1974. V.p. D.C. Terminal Elevator Co., Dodge City, Kans., 1957-65; exec. v.p. Kans. Jaycees, Hutchinson, 1965-68, Kans. C. of C. and Industry, Topeka, 1968-82; pres. Nebr. C. of C. and Industry, Lincoln, 1982—. Past chmn., bd. regents U.S. C. of C. Inst. U. Colo. With U.S. Army, 1955-57. Named Outstanding Local Pres. in State, Kans. Jaycees, 1961, Outstanding Young Man of Yr., Dodge City Jaycees, 1961, Outstanding State V.P., U.S. Jaycees, 1962, Outstanding Nat. Dir., 1963. Mem. Am. Soc. Assn. Execs. (cert.), Am. Chamber Commerce Execs. (bd. dirs., cert.), Nebr. Chamber Commerce Execs. (sec.-treas.), Nebr. Soc. Assn. Execs. (past pres.), Nebr. Fedn. Bus. Assns. (pres. 1986-88), Nebr. Thoroughbred Breeders Assn. (bd. dirs.), Washburn U. Alum. (bd. dirs.), Rotary. Republican. Roman Catholic. Home: 625 W Gibraltar Ln Phoenix AZ 85023-5243

SWARTZ, THOMAS R. economist, educator; b. Phila., Aug. 31, 1937; s. Henry Jr. and Elizabeth (Thomas) S.; m. Jeanne Marie Jourdan, Aug. 12, 1961; children: Mary Butler, Karen Miller, Jennifer, Anne, Rebecca. BA, LaSalle U., 1960; MA, Ohio U., 1962; PhD, Ind. U., 1965. Asst. prof. U. Notre Dame, Ind., 1965-70, assoc. dept. chair, 1968-70, assoc. prof., 1970-78, acting dir. grad. studies, 1977-78, prof. econs., 1978—82, dir. program econ. policy, 1982-85; resident dir. U. Notre Dame London Program, 1990-91, U. Notre Dame Austraulia Program, Fremantle, 1996. Vis. prof. U. Notre Dame London Program 1982, 85, 90-91, 2001; dir. London Summer Program, 2001--; fiscal cons. Ind. Commn. State Tax, Indpls., 1965-68, also spl. tax cons., 1971-81, City of South Bend, Ind., 1972-75. Co-editor: The Supply Side, 1983, Changing Face of Fiscal Federalism, 1990, Urban Finance Under Siege, 1993, Taking Sides, 10th edit., 2000, America's Working Poor, 1995; contbr. articles to profl. jours. Bd. dirs. Forever Learning Inst., South Bend, Ind., 1988-93; mem. steering com. Mayor's Housing Forum, South Bend, 1989-95; chair Com. Svcs. Block Grant, South Bend, 1985-90, Econ. Devel. Task Force, South Bend, 1985. Rsch. fellow Nat. Ctr. Urban Ethnic Affairs, 1979-85; recipient Danforth Assoc. award Danforth Found., 1972-86, Tchg. award Kanzajian Found., 1974; rsch. grantee Mellon Found., 1998—. Fellow Inst. Ednl. Initiatives. Democrat. Roman Catholic. Avocation: racquetball. Office: U Notre Dame Dept Econs 414 Decio Hall Notre Dame IN 46556-5644 E-mail: swartz.i@end.edu.

SWARTZBAUGH, MARC L. lawyer; b. Urbana, Ohio, Jan. 3, 1937; s. Merrill L. and Lillian K. (Hill) S.; m. Marjory Anne Emhardt, Aug. 16, 1958 (deceased May 20, 2000); children: Marc Charles, Kathleen Marie, Laura Kay. BA magna cum laude, Wittenberg Coll., 1958; LLB magna cum laude, U. Pa., 1961. Bar: Ohio 1961, U.S. Dist. Ct. (no. dist.) Ohio 1962, U.S. Claims Ct. 1991, U.S. Ct. Appeals (6th cir.) 1970, U.S. Ct. Appeals (3d cir.) 1985, U.S. Ct. Appeals (Fed. cir.) 1995, U.S. Supreme Ct. 1973. Law clk. to judge U.S. Ct. Appeals (3d cir.), Phila., 1961-62; assoc. Jones, Day, Reavis & Pogue, Cleve., 1962-69, ptnr., 1970-98; ret., 1998; cons., 1998—. Note editor U. Pa. Law Rev., 1960-61; co-author: Ohio Legal Ethics, 2001. Co-chmn. Suburban Citizens for Open Housing, Shaker Heights, Ohio, 1966; v.p. Lomond Assn., Shaker Heights, 1965-68; trustee The Dance Ctr., Cleve., 1980-83; amb. People to People Internat., 1986; chmn. legal divsn. Cleve. campaign United Negro Coll. Fund, 1989-96. Mem. ABA (litigation sect., sr. lawyers divsn.), Fed. Bar Assn., Ohio Bar Assn., Cleve. Bar Assn., Order of Coif, Beta Theta Pi. Democrat. Avocations: poetry, painting, music, skiing, photography. Office: Jones Day Reavis & Pogue N Point 901 Lakeside Ave E Cleveland OH 44114-1190

SWARTZENDRUBER, DALE, soil physicist, educator; b. Parnell, Iowa, July 6, 1925; s. Urie and Norma (Kinsinger) S.; m. Kathleen Jeanette Yoder, June 26, 1949; children: Karl Grant, Myra Mae, John Keith, David Mark. BS, Iowa State U., 1950, MS, 1952, PhD, 1954. Instr. sci. Goshen (Ind.) Coll., 1953-54; asst. soil scientist U. Calif., Los Angeles, 1955-56; assoc. prof. soil physics Purdue U., West Lafayette, Ind., 1956-63, prof., 1963-77; prof. soil physics U. Nebr., Lincoln, 1977-98, prof. emeritus soil physics, 1998—. Vis. prof. Iowa State U., 1959, Ga. Inst. Tech., 1968, Hebrew U. Jerusalem at Rehovot, 1971, Griffith U., Brisbane, Australia, 1989-90, Centre for Environ. Mechanics, CSIRO, Canberra, Australia, 1990; vis. scholar Cambridge (Eng.) U., 1971. Contbr. articles on soil physics to profl. jours.; assoc. editor: Soil Sci. Soc. Am. Proc., 1965-70; mem. editorial bd. Geoderma (Amsterdam), 1975-93; editor: Soil Sci., 1976-98. Fellow Soil Sci. Soc. Am. (Soil Sci. award 1975, Editors' citation for excellence in manuscript rev. 1993, Soil Sci. Disting. Svc. award 2001), Am. Soc. Agronomy; mem. Am. Geophys. Union, Internat. Union Soil Sci., Am. Sci. Affiliation, Sigma Xi, Phi Kappa Phi, Gamma Sigma Delta. Mennonite. Achievements include research in water infiltration into soil, validity of Darcy's equation for water flow in soils, measurement of water and solid content in soils, mathematical solutions to problems of water flow in saturated and unsaturated soils. Home: 1400 N 37th St Lincoln NE 68503-2016 Office: U Nebr E Campus Dept Agronomy and Horticulture 246 Keim Hall Lincoln NE 68583 E-mail: agrohort@unl.edu.

SWEARER, WILLIAM BROOKS, lawyer; b. Hays, Kans. Grad., Princeton U., 1951; law degree, U. Kans., 1955. Bar: Kans. 1955. Pvt. practice, Hutchinson, Kans., 1955—; ptnr. Martindell, Swearer & Shaffer, LLP, 1955—. Mem. Kans. Bd. Discipline for Attys., 1979-92, chmn., 1987-92. With U.S. Army, 1952-53, Korea. Mem. ABA (ho. of dels. 1995-2000), Am. Bar Found. (state chair 1998—), Kans. Bar Assn. (pres. 1992-93, various offices, mem. coms.), Kans. Assn. Sch. Attys. (pres. 1989-90), Reno County Bar Assn. Office: PO Box 1907 Hutchinson KS 67504-1907 E-mail: wbs@martindell-law.com.

SWEENEY, ASHER WILLIAM, state supreme court justice; b. Canfield, Ohio, Dec. 11, 1920; s. Walter William and Jessie Joan (Kidd) S.; m. Bertha M. Englert, May 21, 1945; children: Randall W., Ronald R., Garland A., Karen M. Student, Youngstown U., 1939-42; LL.B., Duke U., 1948. Bar: Ohio 1949. Practiced law, Youngstown, Ohio, 1949-51; judge adv. gen. Dept. Def., Washington, 1951-65; chief Fed. Contracting Agy., Cin., 1965-68; corp. law, 1968-77; justice Ohio Supreme Ct., Columbus, 1977—. Democratic candidate for Sec. of State Ohio, 1958. Served with U.S. Army, 1942-46; col. Res. 1951-68. Decorated Legion of Merit, Bronze Star; named to Army Hall of Fame Ft. Benning, Ga., 1981 Mem. Ohio Bar Assn., Phi Delta Phi. Democrat. Home: 6690 Drake Rd Cincinnati OH 45243-2706 Office: Ohio Supreme Ct 30 E Broad St Fl 3D Columbus OH 43215-3414

SWEENEY, EMILY MARGARET, prosecutor; b. Cleve., May 2, 1948; d. Mark Elliot and Neydra (Ginsburg) Mirsky; m. Patrick Anthony Sweeney, Dec. 30, 1983; 1 child, Margaret Anne. BA, Case Western Res. U., 1970; JD, Cleve. Marshall Coll. Law, 1981. Bar: Ohio 1981. Tchr. English Cleve. Pub. Schs., 1970; plant mgr. Union Gospel Press Pub. Co., Cleve., 1971-73; publ. specialist Cleve. State U., 1973-82; asst. U.S. atty. Dept. Justice, Cleve., 1982—; now U.S. atty., 1993—. Precinct committeeman, Woodmere, Ohio, 1978; mem. Atty. Gen.'s Adv. Com. U.S. Attys., 1993—96, 1998—99, chmn. office mgmt. and budget subcom., 1993—2001, mem. asset forfeiture, civil issues, controlled substances and drug demand reduction, LECC/victim witness subcoms., 1993—2001; chmn. law enforcement coord. com. No. Dist. Ohio, 1993—. Recipient Eddy award for graphic design, 1977, Spl Achievement award U.S. Dept. Justice, 1985. Mem.: Fed. Bar Assn. Democrat. Office: US Atty's Office 1800 Bank One Ctr 600 Superior Ave E Ste 1800 Cleveland OH 44114-2600

SWEENEY, FRANCIS E. state supreme court justice; b. Jan. 26, 1934; married; 4 children. BSBA, Xavier U., 1956; JD, Cleve.-Marshall Law Sch., 1963. Profl. football player Ottawa Rough Riders, Ont., Can., 1956-58; mem. legal dept. Allstate Ins. Co., Cleve., 1958-63; asst. prosecuting atty. Cuyahoga County, 1963-70; judge Cuyahoga County Ct. of Common Pleas, 1970-88; judge (8th cir.) U.S. Ct. Appeals, 1988-92; justice Ohio Supreme Ct., Columbus, 1992—. With U.S. Army, 1957-58. Recipient Legion of Honor award Xavier U., 1956, Outstanding Jud. Svc. award Ohio Supreme Ct., 1972-85, Alumnus of Yr. award Xavier U., 1977. Office: Ohio Supreme Ct 30 E Broad St Fl 3 Columbus OH 43215-0001*

SWEENEY, JAMES RAYMOND, lawyer; b. Chgo., Feb. 19, 1928; s. John Francis and Mae J. (McDonald) S.; m. Rhoda W. Davis, May 15, 1987; children from previous marriage: Margaret Elizabeth, John Francis, Thomas Edward. B.S., U. Notre Dame, 1950; J.D., Northwestern U., 1956. Bar: Ill. 1956. With firm Schroeder, Hofgren, Brady & Wegner, Chgo., 1956-61; ptnr. Hofgren, Wegner, Allen, Stellman & McCord, 1962-71, Coffee, Wetzel, Sweeney, Chgo., 1971-72, Coffee & Sweeney, 1972-76, Mason, Kolehmainen, Rathburn & Wyss, Chgo., 1976-82, McWilliams, Mann, Zummer & Sweeney, 1983-86, Mann, McWilliams, Zummer, & Sweeney, 1986-89, Lee, Mann, Smith, McWilliams & Sweeney, 1989-91, Lee, Mann, Smith, McWilliams, Sweeney & Ohlson, 1991—; dir. ctr. intellectual property law John Marshall Law Sch., 1998—. Commr. for disbarment matters Ill. Supreme Ct., 1963-73; mem. hearing div. Atty. Registration and Discipline Commn., 1974-77, chmn. commn. 1983-90; chmn. Ctr. for Intellectual Property Law adv. bd. John Marshall Law Sch., 1997-99. Bd. dirs., sec. Highland Park (Ill.) Hosp., 1972-79. Served as lt. (j.g.) USN, 1950-53; lt. comdr. Res. ret. Mem. ABA (coun. patent, trademark and copyright sect., sec. 1978-82), Ill. State Bar (assembly 1990-96), Chgo. Bar Assn. (sec. 1977-79), Bar Assn. 7th Cir., Intellectual Property Law Assn. Chgo., Patent Law Assn. Chgo. (pres. 1974), The Lawyers Club, Skokie (Ill.) Country Club, Union League Club. Home: 505 N Lake Shore Dr Chicago IL 60611-3427 Office: Lee Mann Smith McWilliams Sweeney & Ohlson 209 S La Salle St Ste 410 Chicago IL 60604-1203 also: John Marshall Law Sch 315 S Plymouth Ct Chicago IL 60604-3969 E-mail: 7Sweeney@jmls.edu.

SWEENEY, MIKE, professional baseball player; b. Orange, Calif., July 22, 1973; Baseball player Kansas City (Mo.) Royals, 1995—. Office: Kansas City Royals PO Box 419969 Kansas City MO 64141-6969*

SWEENEY, THOMAS LEONARD, chemical engineering educator, researcher; b. Cleve., Dec. 12, 1936; s. Patrick and Anne (Morrin) S.; m. Beverly Marie Starks, Dec. 30, 1961; children: Patrick E., Thomas J., Michael S., Kevin E. BS, Case Inst. Tech., 1958, MS, 1960, PhD, 1962; JD, Capital U., Columbus, Ohio, 1974. Bar: Ohio 1974, U.S. Supreme Ct. 1978. Registered profl. engr., Ohio. Asst. prof. then assoc. prof. chem. engring. The Ohio State U., Columbus, 1963-73, prof., 1973-94, assoc. v.p. rsch., 1982-94, acting v.p. rsch. and grad., 1989-91, emeritus prof., assoc. v.p., 1995—; pres. The Ohio State U. Research Found., 1989-91, exec. dir., 1988-94. Mem. Ohio Hazardous Waste Facility Bd., Columbus, 1984-93; asst. v.p., dir. office rsch., prof. chem. engring. U. Notre Dame, 1994—; mem. bd. dirs. Children's Hosp. Rsch. Found., Columbus, 1990-94; cons. numerous orgns. Editor: Hazardous Waste Management, 1982, Management of Hazardous and Toxic Waste, 1985; contbr. articles to profl. jours. Mem. Am. Inst. Chem. Engrs. (exec. com., cen. Ohio sect., 1970-72), Am. Chem. Soc., Am. Soc. for Engring. Edn. (chmn. environ. engring. div., 1973-74, mem. coun. govtl. rels. bd. dirs., 1993—). Roman Catholic. Office: U Notre Dame Rsch Office 511 Main Building Notre Dame IN 46556-5602

SWEET, ARTHUR, orthopedist; b. Chgo., Aug. 30, 1920; s. Mandel and Yetta (Spector) S.; m. Natalie Levy, Feb. 21, 1964; 1 child, Margaret Helaine. BS, U. Ill., 1941; MD, 1944. Diplomate Am. Bd. Orthopaedic Surgery. Instr. Northwestern U., 1947-52; mem. staff Decatur (Ill.) Meml. Hosp., 1954—, St. Mary's Hosp., Decatur, 1954—; cons. Wabash Hosp. Assn., 1954—; instr. U. Ill., 1972—; pres. med. staff St. Mary's Hosp., Decatur, Ill. Capt. M.C., U.S. Army, 1946-48, 51-53, Korea. Mem. Acad. Orthopaedic Surgery, Decatur Club. Jewish. Avocation: amateur radio operator. Home: 245 N Park Pl Decatur IL 62522-1951

SWEET, CHARLES WHEELER, retired executive recruiter; b. Chgo., June 11, 1943; s. Charles Wheeler and Alice Naomi (Grush) Sweet; m. Joy Ann Weidernmiller, Mar. 23, 1968; children: Charles III, Kimberly Ann, Rebecca Townsend. AB, Hamilton Coll., Clinton, N.Y., 1965; MBA, U. Chgo., 1968. Salesman Procter & Gamble, Chgo., 1965-67; with pers. Ford, Dearborn, Mich., 1968-69, R.R. Donnelley, Chgo., 1969-72; exec. recruiter A.T. Kearney Inc. Exec. Search, 1972—87, pres., 1987-99, chmn., 2000—01; ret., 2001. Bd. dirs. Gt. Bank Algonquin. Chmn. bd. dirs., exec. advisor No. Ill. U., 1979—88; bd. dirs. Rehab. Inst. Chgo., 1987—. Mem.: Assn. Exec. Search Cons., Barrington Hills Country Club (bd. dirs. 1993—96). Avocations: tennis, bridge. Home: 92 Meadow Hill Rd Barrington IL 60010-9601

SWEET, CYNTHIA RAE, small business owner; b. Oelwein, Iowa, Apr. 4, 1958; d. Garth Wayne and Shirley Jean (Bond) Huffman; m. Stanton Logan Sweet, May 30, 1981; children: Ashley Anne, Devin Logan, Tyler Bond. BA with honors, U. No. Iowa, 1979. Office mgr. Midway Devel. Corp., Cedar Falls, Iowa, 1979-84; adminstrv. asst. D.T.S., Inc., 1984—, Montessori Sys. Sch., Cedar Falls, 1995—2002; owner Sweet Press, 2002—. Author: Nuts and Bolts - How to Build a Bell Program, 1986, The Rottink Family of the Netherlands, 1986, Silver Celebration: A History of the Sturgis Falls Celebration, 2000; co-author: The Descendants of John Bond, 1992, David Elliott, Loyalist, and his Descendants, 1995, The Life and Family of Rev. Joshua Sweet, 2001; editor annual Sturgis Falls Celebration Program Book, 1996—. Adminstrv. asst. Sturgis Falls Celebration, Inc., Cedar Falls, 1987—; music dir. handbell program First United Meth. Ch., Cedar Falls, 1979-95. Home and Office: 1116 Washington St Cedar Falls IA 50613-3070

SWEET, PHILIP W. K., JR. former banker; b. Mt. Vernon, N.Y., Dec. 31, 1927; s. Philip W.K. and Katherine (Buhl) S.; m. Nancy Frederick, July 23, 1950; children— Sandra H., Philip W.K. III, David A.F. AB, Harvard U., 1950; MBA, U. Chgo., 1957. Pres., dir. The No. Trust Co., Chgo., 1975-81; chmn., chief exec. officer No. Trust Corp., 1981-84. Alderman City of Lake Forest, Ill., 1972-74; vis. com. U. Chgo. Grad. Sch. Bus.; trustee Chgo. Zool. Soc., past chmn. 1988-93; life trustee Rush-Presbyn.-St. Luke's Med. Ctr.; vestryman Episc. Ch., 1971-74, 86-89. Mem. Soc. Colonial Wars (gov. Ill. chpt. 1978-80), Chgo. Sunday Evening Club (trustee, chmn. 1997-2000), Econ. Club, Comml. Club, Chgo. Club, Commonwealth Club (past pres.), Old Elm Club (Highwood, Ill.), Onwentsia Club (v.p., gov.), Shoreacres Club (past pres. Lake Bluff).

SWEET, STUART C. pediatrician; BS in Chemistry with highest distinction, U. Mich., 1981, MD with distinction, PhD, U. Mich., 1989. Resident in pediatrics St. Louis Children's Hosp., 1990-93, fellow in pediatric pulmonology, 1993-96; fellow pediatric pulmonology dept. pediatrics Wash. U. Med. Sch. Mem. physicians adv. com. St. Louis Children's Hosp. Contbr. articles to profl. pubis. Burton L. Baker Cancer Rsch. fellowship Mich. Cancer Inst., 1986-87. Mem. Phi Beta Kappa. Office: Wash U Sch Medicine Dept Pediatrics One Children's Pl Saint Louis MO 63110-1093

SWEETS, HENRY HAYES, III, museum director; b. Lexington, Ky., May 8, 1949; s. Henry Hayes Jr. and Elizabeth (Keith) S.; m. Nancy Riley, Jan. 28, 1984; children: Amy Louisa, Henry Hayes IV. BS in Chemistry, U. Ill., 1971, MEd., 1973; MA in History, U. Del., 1978. Tchr. Scotch Plains (N.J.)-Fanwood High Sch., 1972-74, Byron (Ill.) High Sch., 1974-76; mus. dir. Mark Twain Mus., Hannibal, Mo., 1978—. Author: A Sesquicentennial History of the Hannibal, Missouri Presbyterian Church; editor The Fence Painter. Bd. dirs. Becky Thatcher coun. Girl Scouts U.S., 1984-88; mem. bd. edn. Hannibal, Mo. Pub. Schs., 1991—. Mem. Nat. Trust for Hist. Preservation. Methodist. Office: Mark Twain Home and Mus 208 Hill St Hannibal MO 63401-3316

SWENSON, DALE, state legislator; b. Wichita, K.S., Mar. 2, 1957; m. Roberta Swenson. Mem. from dist. 97 Kans. State Ho. of Reps., Topeka, 1994—. Address: 3351 S McComas St Wichita KS 67217-1158 Office: Kans House of Reps State House Topeka KS 66612

SWENSON, DOUGLAS, state legislator; b. Aug. 1945; m. Sandie; two children. BS, Gustavus Adolphus Coll.; JD, William Mitchell Coll. Minn. State Rep. Dist. 51B, 1987-2000; atty.; judge Pine County Dist. Ct., Pice City, Minn., 2000—. Mem. edn., health and human svc., judiciary, environ. and natural resources and local govt. and met. affairs coms. Home: 9429 Jewel Lane Ct N Forest Lake MN 55025-9169 Office: Pine County Courthouse 315 6th St Pine City MN 55063-1620

SWENSON, GEORGE WARNER, JR. electronics engineer, radio astronomer, educator; b. Mpls., Sept. 22, 1922; s. George Warner and Vernie (Larson) S.; m. Virginia Laura Savard, June 26, 1943 (div. 1970); children: George Warner III, Vernie Laura, Julie Loretta, Donna Joan; m. Joy Janice Locke, July 2, 1971. BS, Mich. Coll. Mining and Tech., 1944, E.E., 1950; MS, MIT, 1948; PhD, U. Wis., 1951. Asso. prof. elec. engring. Washington U., St. Louis, 1952-53; prof. U. Alaska, 1953-54; asso. prof. Mich. State U., 1954-56; faculty U. Ill., Urbana, 1956—, prof. elec. engring. and astronomy, 1958-88, prof. emeritus, 1988—, acting head dept. astronomy, 1970-72, head dept. elec. and computer engring., 1979-85. Dir. Vermilion River Obs., 1968-81; vis. scientist Nat. Radio Astronomy Obs., 1964-68; cons. to govt. agys. and other sci. bodies; sr. rsch. assoc. U.S. Army Constrn. Engring. Rsch. Lab., 1988—; adj. prof. elec. engring. Mich. Technol. U., 1996—. Author: Principles of Modern Acoustics, 1953, An Amateur Radio Telescope, 1980; co-author: Interferometry and Synthesis in Radio Astronomy, 1986, 2d edit., 2001; contbr. articles to profl. jours. 1st lt. signal corps U.S. Army, WWII. Recipient citation for disting. service to engring. U. Wis., 1984; Guggenheim fellow, 1984-85 Fellow IEEE, AAAS; mem. NAE, Am. Astron. Soc., Internat. Sci. Radio Union (U.S. nat. com. 1965-67, 80-82), Internat. Astron. Union, Inst. Noise Control Engring. (cert.), Sigma Xi, Eta Kappa Nu, Tau Beta Pi, Phi Kappa Phi. Achievements include chairing conceptual design group which produced the concept/proposal for the Very Large Array of National Radio Astronomy Observatory; designed and built two large innovative radio telescopes for the University of Illinois. Home: 1107 Kenwood Rd Champaign IL 61821-4718 Office: U Ill 328 CSL 1308 W Main St Urbana IL 61801-2307

SWENSON, HOWARD, state legislator, farmer; b. Dec. 20, 1930; m. Jane Swenson; 5 children. Farmer, Nicollet, Minn.; mem. Minn. Ho. of Reps., St. Paul, 1994—. Independent-Republican.

SWENSON, LYLE W. protective services official; U.S. marshal U.S. Marshal's Svc., Sioux Falls, S.D., 1997—. Mem. Nat. Sheriffs' Assn. (sec.), S.D. Peace Officers Assn. (past pres.), S.D. Sheriffs's Assn. (past pres.). Office: US Marshal Svc Fed Bldg 400 S Phillips Ave Rm 216 Sioux Falls SD 57104-6851

SWERDLOW, MARTIN ABRAHAM, physician, pathologist, educator; b. Chgo., July 7, 1923; s. Sol Hyman and Rose (Lasky) Swerdlow; m. Marion Levin, May 19, 1945; children: Steven Howard, Gary Bruce. Student, Herzl Jr. Coll., 1941-42; BS, U. Ill., 1945; MD, U. Ill., Chgo., 1947. Diplomate Am Bd Pathology. Intern Michael Reese Hosp. and Med. Center, Chgo., 1947-48, resident, 1948-50, 51-52, mem. staff, 1974—, chmn. dept. pathology, v.p. acad. affairs, 1974-90; pathologist Menorah Med Ctr, Kansas City, Mo., 1954—57. Asst prof, pathologist Univ Ill Col Med , Chicago, 1957—59, assoc prof, 1959—60, clin prof, 1960—64, prof, pathologist, 1966—72, assoc dean, prof pathology, 1970—72; prof pathology, chmn Univ Mo, Kansas City, 1972—74; prof pathology Univ Chicago, 1975—89, Geever prof, head pathology emeritus, 1993—; mem comt standards Chicago Health Sys Agency, 1976—. With MC U.S. Army, 1944—45. Recipient Alumnus of the Yr Award, Univ Ill Col Med, 1973, Instructorship Award, Univ Ill, 1960, 1965, 1968, 1971, 1972. Mem.:

AMA, Inst Med, Am Soc Dermatopathology, Am Acad Dermatology, Int Acad Pathology, Col Am Pathologists, Am Soc Clin Pathologists, Chicago Pathology Soc (pres 1980—). Jewish. Office: U Ill Coll Medicine Dept Pathology 1819 W Polk St Chicago IL 60612-7331 E-mail: maswerdl@vic.edu.

SWIBEL, STEVEN WARREN, lawyer; b. Chgo., July 18, 1946; s. Morris Howard and Gloria Swibel; m. Leslie S. Swibel; children: Deborah, Laura. BS, MIT, 1968; JD, Harvard U., 1971. Bar: Ill. 1971, U.S. Dist. Ct. (no. dist.) Ill. 1971, U.S. Tax Ct. 1973, U.S. Ct. Appeals (7th cir.) 1981. Assoc. Sonnenschein Carlin Nath & Rosenthal, Chgo., 1971-78, ptnr., 1978-84, Rudnick & Wolfe, 1984-93, Schwartz, Cooper, Greenberger, Krauss Chartered, Chgo., 1993—. Adj. prof. taxation Ill. Inst. Tech. Kent Coll. Law, Chgo., 1989—; lectr. in field; contbr. articles to profl. jours. Ednl. counselor MIT, 1979—; bd. dirs. MIT Alumni Fund, 1992-95, Ragdale Found., 1987-00, treas, 1987-92; bd. dirs. Kids In Danger, 1998—. Recipient Lobdell Disting. Svc. award MIT Alumni Assn., 1989. Mem. ABA (com. partnerships sect. taxation), Ill. Bar Assn., Chgo. Bar Assn. (fed. taxation com., exec. subcom. 1984—, chmn. subcom. on real estate and partnerships 1986-87, vice-chmn. 1988-89, chmn. 1990), Met. Club, MIT Club (dir. Chgo. chpt. 1980-91, 96—, sec. 1980-87, pres. 1987-89), Sigma Xi, Tau Beta Pi, Eta Kappa Nu. Office: Schwartz Cooper Greenberger & Krauss Chartered 180 N La Salle St Ste 2700 Chicago IL 60601-2757 E-mail: swibel@alum.mit.edu.

SWIFT, EDWARD FOSTER, III, investment banker; b. Chgo., Nov. 1, 1923; s. Theodore Philip I and Elizabeth (Hoyt) S.; m. Joan McKelvy, July 2, 1947; children: Theodore Philip II, Edward McKelvy, Lockhart McKelvy, Elizabeth Hoyt; m. Carol Coffey Whipple, June 21, 1968. Grad., Hotchkiss Sch., 1941; BA, Yale U., 1945. With Esmark, Inc. (formerly Swift & Co.), 1947-75, asst. to v.p. charge meat packing plants, 1958, asst. v.p., 1958-59, v.p. for provisions, fgn., casings and storage, 1959-64, exec. v.p., 1964-75; vice-chmn. Chgo. Corp., 1975-79; vice chmn. Bacon, Whipple & Co., Chgo., 1980-84; mng. dir. A.G. Becker Paribas Inc., 1984-85; with E.F. Hutton and Co., 1985-87; mng. dir. Shearson Lehman Hutton Inc, 1987-92. Bd. dirs. Santa Fe Pacific Pipelines, Inc. Chmn. So. Ind. chpt. United Negro Coll. Fund, 1956; trustee Northwestern U., Evanston, Ill.; bd. dirs. Northwestern Meml. Hosp., Chgo. Served to capt. U.S. Army, 1942-46. Mem. Chgo. Assn. Commerce and Industry (bd. dirs.), Scroll and Key, Chgo. Club, Racquet Club, Econ. Club, Valley Club, Comml. Club, Onwentsia Club, Old Elm ClubBirnam Wood Golf Club, Aurelian Honor Soc. Home: 1500 N Astor St Chicago IL 60610-1635 Office: 70 W Madison St Ste 1400 Chicago IL 60602-4267

SWIGER, ELINOR PORTER, lawyer; b. Cleve., Aug. 1, 1927; d. Louie Charles and Mary Isabelle (Shank) Porter; m. Quentin Gilbert Swiger, Feb. 5, 1955; children: Andrew Porter, Calvin Gilbert, Charles Robinson. BA, Ohio State U., 1949, JD, 1951. Bar: Ohio 1951, Ill. 1979. Sr. assoc. Robbins, Schwartz, Nicholas, Lifton & Taylor, Ltd., Chgo., 1979—. Author: Mexico for Kids, 1971, Europe for Young Travelers, 1972, The Law and You, 1973 (Literary Guild award), Careers in the Legal Professions, 1978, Women Lawyers at Work, 1978, Law in Everday Life, 1977. Mem. Northfield Twp. (Ill.) Bd. Edn., 1976-83; mem. Glenview (Ill.) Fire and Police Commn., 1976-86; chmn. Glenview Zoning Bd. Appeals, 1987-97. Mem. Ill. Coun. Sch. Attys. (past chmn.), Women Bar Assn. Ill., Chgo. Bar Assn. (chmn. legis. exec. com. 1990-92), Soc. Midland Authors. Republican. Home: 1933 Burr Oak Dr Glenview IL 60025 Office: Robbins Schwartz Nicholas Lifton & Taylor 20 N Clark St Ste 900 Chicago IL 60602-4115

SWIGERT, JAMES MACK, lawyer; b. Carthage, Ill., Sept. 25, 1907; s. James Ross and Pearl (Mack) S.; m. Alice Francis Titcomb Harrower, July 7, 1931 (dec. 1990); children: Oliver, David Ladd, Sally Harper (Mrs. Hamilton). Student, Grinnell Coll., 1925-27; SB, Harvard U., 1930, LLB, 1935. Bar: Ill. 1935, Ohio 1937. With Campbell, Clithero & Fischer, Chgo., 1935-36, Taft, Stettinius & Hollister, Cin., 1936—, ptnr., 1948-79, sr. ptnr. and chmn. exec. com., 1979-85, of counsel, 1985—. Dir., mem. exec. com. Union Cen. Life Ins. Co., 1963-79; dir., chmn. audit com. Philips Industries, 1975-82. Author articles on labor rels. and labor law. Bd. dirs. Cin. Symphony Orch., 1976-78; trustee, chmn. exec. com. Am. Music Scholarship Assn., 1987-92. Republican. Presbyterian. Clubs: Queen City (past dir.), Cincinnati Country (past v.p., dir.), Queen City Optimists (past pres.), Tennis (past pres.), Recess (past pres.), Harvard Law (past pres.) (Cin.). Home: 2121 Alpine Pl Cincinnati OH 45206-2690 Office: 1800 Star Bank Ctr Cincinnati OH 45202 E-mail: swigert@taftlaw.com.

SWINGLE, HARRY MORLEY, JR. prosecutor; b. Cape Girardeau, Mo., Apr. 21, 1955; s. Harry Morley and Alberta (Pointer) S.; m. Candace Ann Ely, Aug. 1, 1980; children: Olivia Ann, Veronica Candace. AB in English, U. Mo., 1977, JD, 1980. Bar: Mo., U.S. Dist. Ct. (ea. and we. dists.) Mo. 1980. Intern to presiding justice Mo. Supreme Ct., Jefferson City, spring 1980; assoc. Spradling & Spradling, Cape Girardeau, 1980-82; asst. pros. atty. Cape Girardeau County, 1982-86, pros. atty., 1987—. Guest instr. Mo. Hwy. Patrol Tng. Acad., Jefferson City, 1980, 90, Mo. Judicial Coll., 1994—, Mo. Prosecuting Atty.'s Assn., 1992—, Kansas Dist. Atty.'s Assn., 1994, Iowa Dist. Atty.'s Assn., 1995; guest lectr. criminal justice dept. S.E. Mo. State U., Cape Girardeau, 1986—. Contbr. chpt. to Criminal Practice in Missouri, 1989, 96; contbr. articles to profl. publs. Bd. dirs. Cape River Heritage Mus., Cape Girardeau, 1982-84; pres. Firends of Pub. Libr., Cape Girardeau, 1984. Mem. Nat. Assn. Trial Lawyers, Nat. Dist. Attys. Assn., Mo. Pros. Attys. Assn., Cape Girardeau County Bar Assn. Republican. Methodist. Avocations: reading and writing fiction, reading history, running, bridge. Home: 226 N Sunset Blvd Cape Girardeau MO 63701-5216 Office: Office of Prosecuting Atty Courthouse 100 Court St Jackson MO 63755-1875

SWINNEY, CAROL JOYCE, secondary education educator; Langs. tchr. Hugoton (Kans.) High Sch., 1972-98; dir. distance learning S.W. Plains Regional Svcs. Ctr., Kans., 1998—. Named Kans. Tchr. of Yr., Disney for Lang. Tchr. of Yr., 1993, Milken Nat. Educator, 1992. Office: PO Drawer 1010 Sublette KS 67877-1010

SWITZ, ROBERT E. telecommunications executive; BS in Mktg. and Econs., Quinnipiac Coll.; MBA in Fin., U. Bridgeport. Sr. fin. mgmt. staff PepsiCo., AMF, Olin Corp.; v.p. European ops., ventures and fin. Burr-Brown Corp., Tucson, 1988-94; CFO ADC Telecom., Mpls., 1994—, sr. v.p., 1997—. Bd. dirs. Hickory Tech. Corp., Mpls. Youth Trust. Office: ADC Telecom Inc 12501 Whitewater Dr Minnetonka MN 55343-9498

SWITZER, JON REX, architect; b. Shelbyville, Ill., Aug. 22, 1937; s. John Woodrow and Ida Marie (Vadalabene) S.; m. Judith Ann Heinlein, July 7, 1962; 1 child, Jeffrey Eric. Student, U. Ill., 1955-58; BS, Millikin U., 1972; MA, U. Ill., Springfield, 1981. Registered architect Ill., Mo., Ohio, Colo.; registered interior designer, Ill. Architect Warren & Van Praag, Inc., Decatur, Ill., 1970-72; prin., 1972-81, Bloomington, Ill., 1981-83; architect Hilfinger, Asbury, Cufaude, Abels, 1983-84; ptnr. Riddle/Switzer, Ltd., 1984-86; with bldg., design and constrn. div. State Farm Ins. Cos., 1986-89; architect The Riddle Group, 1989-91; prin. J. Rex Switzer, Architect, 1991—. Elder Presbyn. Ch., 1996. With U.S. Army, 1958-61. Mem. AIA (pres. Bloomington chpt. 1983, Decatur chpt. 1976, v.p. Ill. chpt. 1986-87, sec. 1985, treas. 1984), Am. Archtl. Found., Chgo. Architecture Found., Nat. Trust Hist. Preservation, Frank Lloyd Found., Decatur C. of C. (merit citation 1974, merit award 1979), Am. Legion, Masons (32d degree). Republican. Presbyterian. Avocations: swimming, hunting, fishing, reading, drawing, travel. Home: 9 Mary Ellen Way Bloomington IL 61701-2014 Office: 2412 E Washington St Ste 6A Bloomington IL 61704-1613

SWITZER, ROBERT LEE, biochemistry educator; b. Clinton, Iowa, Aug. 26, 1940; s. Stephen and Elva Delila (Allison) S.; m. Bonnie George, June 13, 1965; children: Brian, Stephanie. BS, U. Ill., 1961; PhD, U. Calif., Berkeley, 1966. Research fellow Lab. Biochemistry, Nat. Heart Inst., Bethesda, Md., 1966-68; asst. prof. biochemistry U. Ill., Urbana, 1968—73, assoc. prof., 1973—78, prof. biochemistry and basic med. scis., 1978—2002, prof. emeritus, 2002—, dept. head, 1988—93. Mem. biochemistry study sect. NIH, 1985-89, chmn., 1987-89; guest prof. U. Copenhagen, 1995; mem. microbial physiology and genetics study sect., NIH, 1998-2000. Author: (with Liam F. Garrity) Experimental Biochemistry, 3rd rev. edit., 1999; mem. bd. editors Jour. Bacteriology, 1977-82, 85— , Archives Biochemistry and Biophysics, 1977-98, Jour. Biol. Chemistry, 1980-85; contbr. articles to profl. jours. NSF predoctoral fellow, 1961-66; NIH postdoctoral fellow, 1966-68; Guggenheim fellow, 1975 Mem. Am. Soc. for Biochemistry and Molecular Biology, Am. Soc. Microbiology, Am. Chem. Soc., AAAS, Sigma Xi. Home: 404 W Michigan Ave Urbana IL 61801-4948 Office: U Ill Dept Biochemistry 600 S Mathews Ave Urbana IL 61801-3602 E-mail: rswitzer.@uiuc.edu.

SWOBODA, LARY JOSEPH, state legislator; b. Luxemburg, Wis., May 28, 1939; s. Joseph Francis and Catherine Magdalene (Daul) S.; m. Janice Marie Hendricks, Nov. 16, 1968. BS in Speech and Edn., U. Wis., Milw., 1963, MS in Polit. Sci., 1965, EdS, 1988; PhD in Ednl. Adminstrn., U. Wis., Madison, 1999. Cert. ednl. specialist. Tchr. speech and English, So. H.S., Brussels, 1963-67; tchr. civics and govt. Luxemburg Schs., 1967-70; mem. Wis. State Assembly, Madison, 1970—; chmn. adminstrv. rules com. Wis. Ho. of Reps., 1993—; exec. dir. Wis. Nat. and Cmty. Svc. Bd.; prin. Oneida Nation Elem. Sch. Active Dem. County Unit. Mem. Luxemburg C. of C., KC, Lions, Phi Eta Sigma, Kappa Delta Pi, Phi Kappa Phi, Phi Delta Kappa. Roman Catholic. Avocations: reading, attending concerts, drama. Home: 197 Church Rd Luxemburg WI 54217-1363 Office: Wis Nat and Cmty Svc Bd Madison WI 53703-3213

SYKES, CHARLIE, radio personality; 3 children. Reporter The Jour., Milw.; editor-in-chief Milw. Mag.; radio host 620 AM WTMJ. Author: Dumbing Down Our Children: Why American Children Feel Good About Themsleves but Can't Read, Write or Add, Profscam? Professors and the Demise of Higher Education, The End of Privacy, A Nation of Victims: The Decay of the American Character, The Hollow Men: Politics and Corruption in Higher Education. Nominee Pulitzer prize. Office: WTMJ 720 E Capital Dr Milwaukee WI 53212*

SYKES, DIANE S. state supreme court justice; b. Milw. children: Jay, Alexander. B, Northwestern U., 1980; JD, Marquette U., 1984. Reporter Milw. Jour.; law clk. to Hon. Terence T. Evans; assoc. Whyte & Hirschboeck S.C.; judge Milw. County Ct., 1992, Wis. Supreme Ct., Madison, 1999—. Office: Wis Supreme Ct PO Box 1688 Madison WI 53702*

SYKES, GREGORY, food products executive; New products mktg. mgr. Hillshire Farms & Kahn's, 1984; pres., CEO Ball Park Brands, 1995, State Fair Foods, Best Kosher, Ball Park and Hillshiar Farm & Kahn's groups; v.p. Sara Lee Corp., Chgo.; pres., CEO Sara Lee Foods Retail. Office: Sara Lee Corp 3 First National Plz Chicago IL 60602-4260

SYKES, VERNON L. state legislator; b. Oct. 2, 1951; m. Barbara Sykes; children: Stancy, Emilia. BS, Ohio Univ., 1974; MS, Wright State Univ., 1980; MPA, Harvard Univ., 1986. Planner, rsch. & eval., asst. Fiscal Officer Summit Coun. Criminal Justice Com., Akron, Ohio, 1976-79; city councilman, 1980-83; Ohio State Rep. Dist. 42, 1983-92, Dist. 44, 1993—; chmn. Interstate Coop Com.; real estate agt. Clarence K. Allen Realty, Akron, 1982. Mem. Ohio Housing Fin. Agy., Econ. Devel. & Small Bus, Financial Inst., Econ. Affairs & Fed. Rels., Transp. & Urban Affairs Com., mem. jt. Com. on Agy. Rule Rev; tchr. Akron Bd. Edn., Ohio, 1974-75, sr. mgmt. specialist United Neighborhood Coun. Inc., Akron, 1975-76; instr. Univ. Akron & Southern Ohio Coll., 1980; pres. Harvard Group, 1987, mem. BancOne Cmty. adv. bd., 1996—. Named Legis. of Yr. Nat. Assn. Social Workers, 1986. Mem. Akron Pvt. Indsl. Coun., Akron Cmty. Action Agy., Western Econ. Assn. Internat. Cuyahoga Valley Assn. Home: 615 Diagonal Rd Akron OH 44320-3011 Office: Ohio House of Reps State House Columbus OH 43215

SYKORA, BARBARA ZWACH, state legislator; b. Tracy, Minn., Mar. 5, 1941; d. John M. and Agnes (Schueller) Zwach; m. Robert G. Sykora, 1965; children: Mona, John, Kara, Mary. BA, St. Catherine Coll., 1963. Tchr. Springfield (Mass.) Sch., 1963-64, Roseville (Minn.) Sch., 1964-66; mem. Minn. Ho. of Reps., St. Paul, 1994—. Bd. dirs. Beacon Bank. Vice chmn. 2d Congl. Dist. Rep. Com., Minn., 1978-82; chmn. 6th Congl. Dist. Rep. Com., 1982-86, 2d congl. dist. Senator Durenberger Campaign, 1980-82, Senator Pillsbury Campaign, Wayzata, Minn., 1980; chair Ind. Rep. State Com., Minn., 1987-93; dist. dir. Office Congressman Rod Grams, 1993-94; bd. dirs. Animal Humane Soc. Hennepin County, Minn. Acad. Excellence Found.; chair Family and Early Childhood Edn. Com., 1999-2002; chair Legis. Commn. on IEcon. Status of Women, 2001—. Mem. Excelsior C. of C., Hopkins/Minnetonka Rotary. E-mial. E-mail: bsykora@uswestmail.net.

SYKORA, HAROLD JAMES, military officer; b. Tripp, S.D., Mar. 10, 1939; s. James J. and Mary (Tucek) S.; m. Patricia Ann Friedrich, Dec. 26, 1962; children: Montgomery James, Gina Marie. BS, U. S.D., 1961, MA in Math., 1965; postgrad., U. Wis., 1971-72, Indsl. Coll. Armed Forces, Ft. McNair, Washington, 1987-88. Math. tchr. Mitchell (S.D.) Sr. H.S., 1961-64, 65-71, 72-74; commd. U.S. Army; advanced through grades to maj. gen.; with U.S. Army Command and Gen. Staff Coll., Ft. Leavenworth, Kans., 1974-75; exec. officer hdqs. 147th F.A. S.D. N.G., Pierre, 1975-80; tng. officer hdqrs. S.D. N.G., Rapid City, 1980-83, chief of staff, 1983-87, adj. gen., 1988-98; pvt. practice def. industry cons., 1998—. Bd. dirs. Am. Sys. Corp., Inc., Am. Sys. Internat. Alumni Achievement award U. S.D., 1996. Mem. N.G. Assn. S.D. (pres. 1979-80), N.G. Assn. U.S. (chmn. fire support task force 1998—), Am. Legion, Assn. U.S. Army, Adjutant's Gen. Assn. U.S. (sec. 1991-97, Army res. forces policy com. 1992-97, chmn. Army res. forces policy com. 1995-97), Rapid City Area C. of C. Republican. Roman Catholic. Home and Office: 5204 Pinedale Hts Rapid City SD 57702-2079 E-mail: sykorajh@aol.com.

SYLVESTER, RONALD CHARLES, newspaper writer; b. Springfield, Mo., Feb. 10, 1959; s. Edgar Donald and Barbara Jean (Hedgecock) S.; m. Angela Sylvester; children: Christian Alexander, Lauryn Ayiana. Sports writer Springfield (Mo.) News-Leader, 1976-88, entertainment writer, 1988-96, gen. assignment news reporter, 1996—. Mem. media panel Leadership Music, Nashville, 1993. Author: Branson: On Stage in the Ozarks, 1994; contbr. articles to New Country Music, Gannett News Svc., Colliers Ency. Bd. dirs. Entertainers Guild of Branson, Mo., 1993-94. Recipient Media award Mo. Pub. Health Assn., 1998, 99. Mem. Soc. of Profl.. Journalists. Mem. Christian Ch. (Disciples of Christ). Avocations: music, reading, outdoor recreation. Office: Springfield News-Leader 651 N Boonville Ave Springfield MO 65806-1039

SYMENS, PAUL N. state legislator, farmer; b. Marshall County, S.D., July 15, 1943; m. Faye Bovendam; 5 children. AA, Northwestern Coll., Iowa, 1993. Mem. S.D. Senate from 1st dist., Pierre, 1987-94, 97—. Mem. S.D. Farmers Union, Marshall County Farmers Union. Democrat. Presbyterian. Office: State Capitol Bldg 500 E Capitol Ave Pierre SD 57501-5070 also: 41547 105th St Amherst SD 57421

SYMMONDS, RICHARD EARL, gynecologist; b. Greensburg, Mo., Mar. 19, 1922; s. Emmett E. S. A.B., Central Coll., Fayette, Mo., 1943; M.D., Duke U., 1946; M.S. in Ob-Gyn, U. Minn., 1953. Intern Los Angeles County Hosp., 1946, resident in Ob-Gyn, 1950-53, resident in gen. surgery, 1954-56; practice medicine specializing in gen. surgery Rochester, Minn., 1958—; mem. faculty Mayo Clinic, 1953—, prof. gynecologic surgery, 1960—, chmn. dept., 1970-84, chmn. emeritus, 1984—. Contbr. articles to profl. jours. Served with USN, 1947-49. Fellow A.C.S.; mem. Am. Gynecol. Soc., Am. Assn. Obstetricians and Gynecologists, Soc. Pelvic Surgeons, Soc. Gynecologic Oncologists, Am. Coll. Obstetricians and Gynecologists. Office: 200 1st St SW Rochester MN 55905-0001

SYTSMA, FREDRIC A. lawyer; b. Grand Rapids, Mich., Jan. 12, 1944; BA, Mich. State U., 1964; JD, U. Mich., 1968. Bar: Mich. 1968. Mem. Varnum, Riddering, Schmidt & Howlett, Grand Rapids. Fellow Am. Coll. Trust and Estate Counsel; mem. ABA, State Bar Mich. (mem. coun. probate and estate planning sect. 1977—, chmn. 1986-87), Grand Rapids Bar Assn. Office: Varnum Riddering Schmidt & Howlett PO Box 352 333 Bridge St NW Grand Rapids MI 49501-0352 E-mail: fasytsma@varnumlaw.com.

SYVERSON, DAVE, state legislator; b. Chgo., June 29, 1957; m. Shirley Syverson. Student, Rock Valley Coll. Mem. Ill. State Senate, Dist. 34; ptnr. Market Ins. Group. Mem. Rockford Boys and Girls Club; bd. govs. Luth. Social Svc. Recipient Humanitarian award Office Internat. Conf., 1994, Activator award Famr Bur., Voice of Employer award; named Freshman Legislator of Yr. Hosp. Assn. Home: 6757 Flower Hill Rd Rockford IL 61114-6636 Office: Ill Senate State Capitol Springfield IL 62706-0001

SZABO, BARNA ALADAR, mechanical engineering educator, mining engineer; b. Martonvasar, Hungary, Sept. 21, 1935; came to U.S., 1967, naturalized, 1974; s. Jozsef and Gizella (Ivanyi) S.; m. Magdalin Gerstmayer, July 23, 1960; children: Mark, Nicholas. B.A.Sc., U. Toronto, Ont., Can., 1962; M.S., SUNY, Buffalo, 1966, Ph.D., 1968; D. honoris causa, U. of Miskolc, Hungary, 1998. Registered profl. engr., Mo. Mining engr. Internat. Nickel Co. Can., 1960-62; engr. Acres Cons. Services Ltd., Niagara Falls, Can., 1962-66; instr. SUNY, Buffalo, 1966-68; mem. faculty Washington U., St. Louis, 1968—, prof. mech. engring., 1974—, Albert P. and Blanche Y. Greensfelder prof., 1975—, dir. Ctr. Computational Mechanics, 1977-92; chmn. engring. software Rsch. and Devel., Inc., 1989—. Author: (with Ivo Babuska) Finite Element Analysis, 1991; contbr. articles to profl. jours. Fellow U.S. Assn. Computational Mechanics (founding mem.); mem. ASME, Hungarian Acad. Sci., Soc. Engring. Sci. Home: 48 Crestwood Dr Clayton MO 63105-3033 Office: PO Box 1129 Saint Louis MO 63188-1129 E-mail: szabo@me.wustl.edu.

SZAREK, STANISLAW JERZY, mathematics educator; b. Ladek Zdroj, Poland, Nov. 13, 1953; came to U.S., 1980, naturalized, 1994; s. Mieczyslaw and Bronislawa (Brzezinska) S.; m. Malgorzata Chwascinska, June 22, 1980 (separated 1996); children: Martina, Natalia; 1 stepchild, Olga. M in Math., Warsaw (Poland) U., 1976; PhD in Math. Scis., Polish Acad. Scis., Warsaw, 1979. Rsch. asst. Math. Inst. Polish Acad. Scis., Warsaw, 1976-79, rsch. fellow, 1979-83; asst. prof. Case Western Res. U., Cleve., 1983-87, prof., 1987—, chair math. dept., 1994-96; prof. U. Paris, 1996—. Vis. positions U. Ill., Urbana, 1980, Ohio State U., Columbus, 1981, U. Tex., Austin, 1981-83, Inst. des Hautes Etudes Scientifiques, Bures-Sur-Yvette, France, 1986-89, U. Paris, 1990, 92, 95, Math. Scis. Rsch. Inst., Berkeley, Calif., 1996. Contbr. articles to profl. jours. Recipient Prize of Sci. Sec., Polish Acad. Scis., 1979; rsch. grantee NSF, 1983—, U.S.-Israel Binat. Sci. Found., 1993-97; Sloan fellow Alfred P. Sloan Found., 1986-88. Mem. Am. Math. Soc. Avocations: skiing, sailing, diving, bridge, travel. Office: Case Western Res U Dept of Math Cleveland OH 44106 E-mail: sjs13@po.cwru.edu.

SZCZEPANSKI, SLAWOMIR ZBIGNIEW STEVEN, lawyer; b. Lodz, Poland, Mar. 9, 1948; s. Wladyslaw and Janina Szczepanski; m. Cynthia Ellen Weagley, Sept. 30, 1972; children: Christine, Diana. BS in Chem. Engring., Rensselaer Poly. Inst., 1971; MS in Chem. Engring., Rensselaer Poly. Inst., 1972; JD, Union U., Albany, N.Y., 1975. Bar: N.Y. 1976, D.C. 1976, Ill. 1977, U.S. Dist. Ct. (no. dist.) Ill. 1977, U.S. Ct. Appeals (fed. cir.) 1988. Atty. Philips Petroleum Co., Washington, 1975-77; from assoc. to ptnr. Willian, Brinks, Hofer, Gilson & Lione, Chgo., 1977-95; of counsel Arnold White and Durkee, 1996-99; shareholder Jenkens & Gilchrist, 2000—. Author: Licensing in Foreign and Domestic Operations, 1985-98; editor (legal periodical) Licensing Law and Business Report, 1986-98; contbr. articles to profl. jours. Mem. ABA, ATLA, Am. Intellectual Property Law Assn., Internat. Assn. Protection Indsl. Property, Nat. Advocates Soc., Licensing Execs. Soc. Intellectual Property Law Assn. Chgo., Univ. Club. Avocations: tennis, sailing. Home: 641 W Willow St Apt 107 Chicago IL 60614-5176 Office: Jenkens & Gilchrist Ste 2600 225 W Washington St Chicago IL 60606-3416 Fax: (312) 425-3909. E-mail: sszczepanski@jenkens.com.

SZEWCZYK, ALBIN ANTHONY, engineering educator; b. Chgo., Feb. 26, 1935; s. Andrew Aloysius and Jean Cecelia (Wojcik) S.; m. Barbara Valerie Gale, June 16, 1956; children: Karen Marie Knop, Lisa Anne, Andrea Jean Simpson, Terese Helen Sinka. BS, U. Notre Dame, 1956, MS, 1958; PhD, U. Md., 1961. Staff engr. Northrop Aircraft Corp., Hawthorne, Calif., 1956-57; grad. asst. U. Notre Dame, Ind., 1957-58, asst. prof. engring., 1962-65, assoc. prof., 1965-67, prof., 1967—, chmn. dept., 1978-88; research asst. U. Md., College Park, 1958-61, postdoctoral researcher, 1961-62; mem. tech. staff Aerospace Corp., El Segundo, Calif., 1962. Cons. Argonne (Ill.) Nat. Lab., 1968-80, Miles Lab., Elkhart, Ind., 1983-88, Chung Shan Inst. Sci. and Tech., Taiwan, 1987-89; vis. prof. Imperial Coll., London, 1989, 99, Kernforschungzentrum, Karlsruhe, Germany, 1990. Editor: Development in Mechanics, 1971. Fellow ASME, AIAA (assoc.); mem. AAAS, Am. Phys. Soc., Am. Soc. Engring. Edn., N.Y. Acad. Sci., Sigma Xi, Pi Tau Sigma, Sigma Gamma Tau. Roman Catholic. Club: South Bend Country (bd. dirs. 1982-89, pres. 1986-88). Avocations: golfing, model railroading. Home: 17331 Willowbrook Dr South Bend IN 46635-1750 Office: U Notre Dame Dept Aero & Mech Engring Notre Dame IN 46556

SZEWS, CHARLES, transportation executive; BBA, U. Wis., Eau Claire. CPA. With Ernst & Young; v.p., contr. Fort Howard Corp., Green Bay, Wis.; v.p., CFO Oshkosh (Wis.) Truck Corp., 1996-97, exec. v.p., CFO, 1997—. Office: Oshkosh Truck Corp 2307 Oregon St Oshkosh WI 54902

SZYBALSKI, WACLAW, molecular geneticist, educator; b. Lwów, Poland, Sept. 9, 1921; came to U.S., 1950, naturalized, 1957; s. Stefan and Michalina (Rakowska) S.; m. Elizabeth Hunter, Feb. 5, 1955; children: Barbara A. Szybalski Sandor, Stefan H. BSChemE, Politechnika Lwów, 1944; MSChemE, Politechnika Slaska, Gliwice, Poland, 1945; DSc, Inst. Tech., Gdańsk, Poland, 1949; Ph.D. (hon.), U. Marie Curie, Lublin, Poland, 1980, U. Gdańsk (Poland), 1989, Inst. of Tech., Gdańsk, 2001; PhD (hon.) (hon.) , Med. U. Gdansk, Poland, 2000, Inst. Tech., Gdansk, 2001. Asst. prof. Inst. Tech., Gdańsk, 1945—50; staff Cold Spring Harbor (N.Y.) Biol. Labs., 1951—55; asst. prof. Inst. Microbiology, Rutgers U., New Brunswick, N.J., 1955-60; prof. oncology McArdle Lab., U. Wis.-Madison, 1960—. Mem. recombinant DNA adv. com. (RAC) NIH, 1974-78; Wendel H. Griffith meml. lectr. St. Louis U., 1975; Raine vis. prof. U. Western

Australia, Perth, 1997. Author numerous papers, revs., abstracts and books in field; editor-in-chief: Gene, 1976-96, hon. and founding editor-in-chief, 1996—; mem. editorial bd. other jours. Recipient Karl A. Forster lecture award U. Mainz, 1970, A. Jurzykowski Found. award in biology, 1988, Hilldale award in biology U. Wis., 1994, Gold G.J. Mendel Hon. medal for merit in biol. scis. Acad. Scis. of Czech Republic, 1995; Cogene lectr. Internat. Union Biochem., Nairobi, 1987, Cairo, 1988, Harare, Zimbabwe, 1989. Mem. AAAS, Am. Soc. Biochemists, Genetic Soc. Am., Am. Soc. Microbiologists (chmn. virology divsn. 1972-74, chmn. divsn. IV 1974-75), European Molecular Biology Orgns. (lectr. 1971, 76), Polish Soc. Microbiologists (hon.), Italian Soc. Exptl. Biology (hon.), Polish Med. Alliance (hon.), Polish Acad. Scis. (fgn. mem.). Home: 1124 Merrill Springs Rd Madison WI 53705-1317 Office: U Wis McArdle Lab Madison WI 53706 E-mail: szybalski@oncology.wisc.edu.

SZYMONIAK, ELAINE EISFELDER, retired state senator; b. Boscobel, Wis., May 24, 1920; d. Hugo Adolph and Pauline (Vig) Eisfelder; Casimir Donald Szymoniak, Dec. 7, 1943; children: Kathryn, Peter, John, Mary, Thomas. BS, U. Wis., 1941; MS, Iowa State U., 1977. Speech clinician Waukesha (Wis.) Pub. Sch., 1941-43, Rochester (N.Y.) Pub. Sch., 1943-44; rehab. aide U.S. Army, Chickasha, Okla., 1944-46; audiologist U. Wis., Madison, 1946-48; speech clinician Buffalo Pub. Sch., 1948-49, Sch. for Handicapped, Salina, Kans., 1951-52; speech pathologist, audiologist, counselor, resource mgr. Vocat. Rehab. State Iowa, Des Moines, 1956-85; mem. Iowa Senate, 1989—2000; ret., 2000. Bd. dir. On With Life, Terrace Hill Found. Adv. bd. Iowa State Inst. for Social and Behavioral Health; mem. Child Care Resource and Referral Cmty. Empowerment Bd., Greater Des Moines Coun. for Internat. Understanding, United Way, 1987—88, Urban Dreams, Iowa Maternal and Child Health com.; pres. Chrysalis Found., 1997; mem. City-County Study Commn.; bd. dirs. On with Life; Mem. Des Moines City coun., 1978—88; bd. dirs. Nat. League Cities, Washington, 1982—84, Civic Ctr., House of Mercy, Westminster House, Iowa Leadership Consortium, Iowa Comprehensive Health Assn. Named Woman of Achievement, YWCA, 1982, Visionary Woman, 1993, Young Women's Resource Ctr., 1989; named to Iowa Women's Hall of Fame, 1999; named Des Moines Woman of Influence, Bus. Record, 2000. Mem. Am. Speech Lang. and Hearing Assn., Iowa Speech Lang. and Hearing Assn. (pres. 1977-78), Nat. Coun. State Legislators (fed. state com. on health, adv. com. on child protection), Women's Polit. Caucus, Nexus (pres. 1981-82, mem. Supreme Ct. Select Com.), Wellmark Found. (adv. bd.). Avocations: reading, traveling, swimming, whitewater rafting. Home: 2116 44th St Des Moines IA 50310-3011 E-mail: ElaineSzy@aol.com.

TAAM, RONALD EVERETT, physics and astronomy educator; b. N.Y.C., Apr. 24, 1948; s. Lawrence and Julia (Louie) T.; m. Rosa Wen Mei Yang, Oct. 19, 1974; children: Jonathan, Alexander. BS, Poly. Inst., N.Y.C., 1969; MA, Columbia U., 1971, PhD, 1973. Postdoctoral fellow U. Calif., Santa Cruz, 1973-76, vis. faculty Berkeley, 1976-78; asst. prof. Northwestern U., Evanston, Ill., 1978-83, assoc. prof., 1984-86, prof. physics and astronomy, 1986—, chmn. physics and astronomy, 1995-98. Fellow Am. Phys. Soc.; mem. Am. Astron. Soc., Royal Astron. Soc., Internat. Astron. Union. Office: Dept Physics and Astronomy Northwestern U 2145 Sheridan Rd Evanston IL 60208-0834 E-mail: r-taam@northwestern.edu.

TABACZYNSKI, RON, state legislator; m. Mary Tabaczynski. AA, BA, Calumet Coll., St. Joseph. Legis. asst. House Dem. Caucus, 1988-90; mem. from 1st dist. Ind. State Ho. of Reps., 1992-98; govt. cons. SRI, Inc., Indpls. Mem. commerce and econ. devel. com., elections and apportionment com., ins., corps. and small bus. com., environ. affairs com., labor com. Formerly Dem. Precinct Committeeman; del. Dem. State Conv. Mem. N.W. Ind. World Trade Coun., Hammond Mohawks Conservation Club, FDR Club, Elks, KC. Home: 550 141st St Hammond IN 46327-1249 Office: SRI Inc 8082 Dash St Indianapolis IN 46250

TABATABAI, M. ALI, chemist, biochemist; b. Karbala, Iraq, Feb. 25, 1934; BS, U. Baghdad, 1958; MS, Okla. State U., 1960; PhD in Soil Chemistry, Iowa State U., 1965. Rsch. assoc. soil biochemistry Iowa State U., Ames, 1966-72, from asst. prof. to assoc. prof., 1972-78, prof. soil chemistry and biochemistry, 1978—. Cons. Electric Power Rsch. Inst., Palo Alto, 1978-83. Fellow AAAS, Am. Inst. Chemists, Am. Soc. Agronomy (Soil Sci. rsch. award 1992), Soil Sci. Soc. Am., Iowa Acad. Sci. (Disting. scientist, Disting. fellow); mem. Coun. Agrl. Sci. and Tech., Am. Chem. Soc., Am. Soc. Microbiology, Am. Soc. Agronomy, Soil Sci. Soc. Am., Assn. Univ. Profs., Iowa Acad. Sci., Gamma Sigma Delta (Alumni award of merit Iowa Beta chpt. 1993), Sigma Xi, Phi Kappa Phi. Achievements include research in soil enzymology and chemistry of sulfur, nitrogen and phosphorus in soils, nutrient cycling in the environment. Office: Iowa State U Sci & Tech Dept Agronomy Ames IA 50011-0001 E-mail: malit@iastate.edu.

TABER, MARGARET RUTH, electrical engineering technology educator, electrical engineer; b. St. Louis, Apr. 29, 1935; d. Wynn Orr and Margaret Ruth (Feldman) Gould Stevens; m. William James Taber, Sept. 6, 1958 B of Engring. Sci., BEE, Cleve. State U., 1958; MS in Engring., U. Akron, 1967; EdD, Nova Southeastern U., 1976; postgrad., Western Res. U., 1959-64. Registered profl. engr., Ohio; cert. engring. technologist. From engring. trainee to tng. dir. Ohio Crankshaft Co., Cleve., 1954-64; from instr. elec.-electronic engring. tech. to prof. Cuyahoga C.C., 1964-79, chmn. engring. tech., 1977-79; assoc. prof. elec. engring. tech. Purdue U., West Lafayette, Ind., 1979-83, prof., 1983-2000, prof. emeritus, 2000—. Lectr. Cleve. State U., 1963-64; mem. acad. adv. bd. Cleve. Inst. Electronics, 1981—; cons. in field. Author: (with Frank P. Tedeschi) Solid State Electronics, 1976; (with Eugene M. Silgalis) Electric Circuit Analysis, 1980; (with Jerry L. Casebeer) Registers, 1980; (with Kenneth Rosenow) Arithmetic Logic Units, 1980, Timing and Control, 1980, Memory Units, 1980; 6809 Architecture and Operation, 1984, Programming I: Straight Line, 1984; contbr. articles to profl. jours. Bd. dirs. West Blvd. Christian Ch., deaconess, 1974-77, elder, 1977-79; deacon Federated Ch., 1981-84, 86-89, Stephen Leader, 1988—; mem. Cancer Support Group; vol. Lafayette Reading Acad., 1992—; ednl. resource vol., vol. tchr. Sunburst Farm Rainbow Acres, Inc., Ariz., 1988—. Recipient Helen B. Schleman Gold Medallion award Purdue U., 1991, The Greater Lafayette Cmty. Survivorship award, 1994, Outstanding Alumni award U. Akron Coll. Engring., 1994, Disting. Alumni award, Cleve. State U., 2002; Margaret R. Taber Microcomputer Lab. named in her honor Purdue U., 1991; NSF grant, 1970-73, 78. Fellow Soc. Women Engrs. (counselor Purdue chpt. 1983-94, Disting. Engring. Educator award 1987); mem. IEEE (life sr.), Am. Cancer Soc. (co-chair svc. and rehab com. 1992-94, vol. coord. CanSurmount 1993-98, chair Cmty. Connections, mem. Resource, Info. and Guidance CoreTeam, 1994-98, v.p. Tippecanoe bd. dirs. 1996-98, relay for life hon. chair 1999), Am. Bus. Women's Assn. (ednl. chmn. 1964-66), Am. Soc. Engring. Edn., Am. Tech. Edn. Assn., Tau Beta Pi (hon.), Phi Kappa Phi. Avocations: robotics; camping; housekeeping. Home: 3036 State Rd 26 W West Lafayette IN 47906-4743 Office: Purdue U Elec Engring Tech Dept Knoy Hall Tech West Lafayette IN 47907

TABIN, JULIUS, patent lawyer, physicist; b. Chgo., Nov. 8, 1919; s. Sol and Lillian (Klingman) T.; m. Johanna Krout, Sept. 7, 1952; children: Clifford James, Geoffrey Craig. B.S., U. Chgo., 1940, Ph.D. in Physics, 1946; LL.B., Harvard U., 1949. Bar: Calif., D.C. 1949, Ill. 1950. Jr. physicist metall. lab. U. Chgo., 1943-44; physicist Los Alamos Sci. Lab. (U. Calif.), N.Mex., 1944-45, Argonne Nat. Lab., AEC, Chgo., 1946; staff mem., group supr. Inst. Nuclear Studies, Mass. Inst. Tech., 1946-49; patent examiner U.S. Patent Office, Washington, 1949-50; asso. firm Fitch, Even, Tabin & Flannery, Chgo., 1950-52; mem. firm Fich, Even, Tabin & Flannery, 1952—. Lectr. U. Chgo., 1959 Mem. Am., D.C., Calif., Ill., Chgo. bar assns., Sigma Xi. Home: 162 Park Ave Glencoe IL 60022-1352 Office: 120 S La Salle St Chicago IL 60603-3403

TABLER, BRYAN G. lawyer; b. Louisville, Jan. 12, 1943; s. Norman Gardner and Sarah Marie (Grant) T.; m. Susan Y. Beidler, Dec. 28, 1968 (div. June 1987); children: Justin Elizabeth, Gillian Gardner; m. Karen Sue Strome, July 24, 1987. AB, Princeton U., 1969; JD, Yale U., 1972. Bar: Ind. 1972, U.S. Dist. Ct. (so. dist.) Ind. 1972, U.S. Dist. Ct. (no. dist.) Ind. 1976, U.S. Ct. Appeals (7th cir.) 1976, U.S. Supreme Ct. 1976. Assoc. Barnes & Thornburg, Indpls., 1972-79, ptnr., chmn. environ. law dept., 1979-94; v.p., gen. counsel, sec. IPALCO Enterprises, Inc., 1994—; sr. v.p., gen. coun., sec. Indpls. Power & Light Co., 1994—. Mem. exec. com. Environ. Quality Control, Inc., Indpls., 1985-97. Mem. Indpls. Mus. of Art, 1972—; bd. dirs. Indpls. Symphony Orch., 1995—. 1st lt. U.S. Army, 1964-68, Vietnam. Mem. ABA, Ind. Bar Assn., Bar Assn. of the 7th Cir., Indpls. Bar Assn. Avocation: golf. Home: 137 Willowgate Dr Indianapolis IN 46260-1471 Office: Indpls Power & Light Co One Monument PO Box 1595 Indianapolis IN 46206-1595

TABLER, NORMAN GARDNER, JR. lawyer; b. Louisville, Oct. 15, 1944; s. Norman Gardner and Marie (Grant) T.; m. Dawn Carla Martin, May 6, 1989; 1 child, Rachel Ann Ayres-Tabler. BA, Princeton U., 1966; MA, Yale U., 1968; JD, Columbia U., 1971. Bar: Ind. 1971, U.S. Dist. Ct. (so. dist.) Ind. 1971. Assoc. Baker & Daniels, Indpls., 1971-77, ptnr., 1978-96; sr. v.p. corp. affairs, gen. counsel, chief compliance officer, sec. Clarian Health Ptnrs., Inc., 1996—. Adj. prof. Ind. U. Law Sch., Indpls., 1984-88; mem. adv. com. Ctr. for Law and Health, Ind. U., Indpls., 1987-91; mem. antitrust task force Ind. Dept. Health, 1993-94; lectr. Ind. U. Law Sch., 1992-96. Bd. dirs. Ind. Repertory Theatre, Inc., Indpls., 1984-97, Indpls. Art Ctr., 1988-93, chmn., 1989-92; bd. dirs. Indpls. 500 Festival, 1992-98, Brickyard 400 Festival, 1993-98, Found. of Indy Festivals, 1995-98, Indy Festivals, 1995-98; bd. dirs. Indpls. Pub. Broadcasting, 1992—, chmn., 1997-2001; mem. Ind. Sec. of State's Com. on Revision of Ind. Nonprofit Corp. Act, 1989-92, Ind. Ednl. Fin. Authority, 1989-93; mem. Ind. Recreational Devel. Commn., 1993—, vice chmn., 2002; mem. Medicaid Task Force Ind. Commn. Health Policy, 1990-92, Ind. Commn. on CLE, 1999—; mem. nat. bd. lay reps. PBS, 1997—. Mem. ABA (health care com. sect. antitrust law, health law sect.), Ind. Bar Assn. (health law sect.), Indpls. Bar Assn. (health law sect.), Am. Health Lawyers Assn. (com. on antitrust, com. on fraud and abuse, self-referrals and false claims, in-house counsel com. and tchg. hosps., acad. med. ctrs. com.), Ind. Health and Hosp. Assn. (com. on hosp. governance 1999—), Ind. U. Parents Assn., Ind. U. Parents Ann. Fund (nat. chmn. 1995-98), U.S. Squash Racquets Assn., Princeton Alumni Assn. Ind. (pres. 1988-97), Indpls. Athletic Club (bd. dirs. 1994-2000), Skyline Club (bd. govs. 1992—), Princeton Club N.Y., Lawyers Club (Indpls.), Five Seasons Country Club (Indpls.). Methodist. Avocations: reading biographies, squash. Address: General Counsel & Senior VP Legal Dept Clarian Health Partners Inc PO Box 1367 Indianapolis IN 46206-1367

TACHA, DEANELL REECE, federal judge; b. Jan. 26, 1946; BA, U. Kans., 1968; JD, U. Mich., 1971. Spl. asst. to U.S. Sec. of Labor, Washington, 1971—72; assoc. Hogan & Hartson, 1973, Thomas J. Pitner, Concordia, Kans., 1973—74; dir. Douglas County Legal Aid Clinic, Lawrence, 1974—77; assoc. prof. law U. Kans., 1974—77, prof., 1977—85, assoc. dean, 1977—79, assoc. vice chancellor, 1979—81, vice chancellor, 1981—85; judge U.S. Ct. Appeals (10th cir.), Denver, 1985—; U.S. sentencing commr., 1994—98; chief judge U.S. Ct. Appeals (10th cir.), Denver, 2001—. Office: US Ct Appeals 10th Cir 643 Massachusetts St Ste301 Lawrence KS 66044-2292

TACKER, WILLIS ARNOLD, JR. medical educator, researcher; b. Tyler, Tex., May 24, 1942; s. Willis Arnold and Willie Mae (Massey) T.; m. Martha J. McClelland, Mar. 18, 1967; children: Sarah Mae, Betsy Jane, Katherine Ann. BS, Baylor U., 1964, MD, PhD, 1970. Lic. physician, Ind., Alaska, Tex. Intern Mayo Grad. Sch. Medicine Mayo Clinic, Rochester, Minn., 1970-71; pvt. practice Prudhoe Bay, Alaska, 1971; instr. dept. physiology Baylor Coll. Medicine, Houston, 1971-73, asst. prof. dept. physiology, 1973-74; clin. prof. family medicine Ind. U. Sch. Medicine, West Lafayette, Ind., 1981—; vis. asst. prof. Biomed. Engring. Ctr., Purdue U., 1974-76, assoc. prof. Sch. Vet. Medicine, 1976-79; assoc. dir. William A. Hillenbrand Biomed. Engring. Ctr., Purdue U., 1980-93, prof. Sch. Vet. Medicine, 1979—, acting dir., 1991-93; exec. dir. Hillenbrand Biomed. Engring. Ctr., 1993-95. Vis. rsch. fellow Sch. Aerospace Medicine, Brooks AFB, San Antonio, 1982; with Corp. Sci. and Tech., State of Ind., 1985-88; presenter, cons. in field. Author: Some Advice on Getting Grants, 1991; co-author: Electrical Defibrillation, 1980; author: (with others) Handbook of Engineering and Medicine and Biology, 1980, Implantable Sensors for Closed-Loop Prosthetic Systems, 1985, Encyclopedia of Medical Devices and Instrumentation, 1988, (with others) Defibrillation of the Heart, 1994; contbr. numerous articles to profl. jours. Chmn. bd. dirs. Assn. Advancemnt Med. Instrumentation Found., Arlington, Va., 1987-95. Mem. Am. Heart Assn. (bd. dirs. Ind. affiliate 1975-81, med. edn. com. 1975-81, pub. health edn. com. 1975-81, chmn. ad hoc com. CPR tng. for physicians 1976-77, rsch. review com. 1988-90), Am. Physiol. Soc., Ind. State Med. Assn., Tippecanoe County Med. Soc., Assn. Advancement Med. Instrumentation (chmn. various coms., bd. dirs. 1981-84, pres. 1985-86), Am. Men and Women Sci., Alpha Epsilon Delta, Beta Beta Beta, Soc. Sigma Xi. Achievements include research in biomedical engineering, cardiovascular physiology, medical education, emergency cardiovascular care, motor evoked potentials, skeletal muscle ventricle; patents for an apparatus and method for measurement and control of blood pressure, electrode system and method for implantable defibrillators, pressure mapping system with capacitive measuring pad. Office: Purdue U Lynn Hall West Lafayette IN 47907 E-mail: tacker@vet.purdue.edu.

TADDIKEN, MARK, state legislator; b. Clay Center, Kans., Jan. 27, 1950; m. Debra Taddiken; children: Tawnya, Bria, Shawn. BS, Ft. Hays State U., 1972. Mem. Kans. State Senate, 2000, vice chair natural resources com., mem. agr. com., assessment and taxation com., utilities com. Sec., treas. Riverdale Cemetery Dist., 1993—; mem. Clay County Ext. Coun., 1997—. Mem. Farmers Coop Shipping Assn. (pres. 1980's), Lower Rep. Water Users Assn. (v.p. 1991—), Kans. Soybean Assn. (v.p. 1994—), Bluestem Rural Electric Cooperative (pres. 1994—). Republican. Episcopalian. Office: 2614 Hackberry Rd Clifton KS 66937 Fax: 785-926-3210. E-mail: taddiken@senate.state.ks.us.

TAFF, GERRY, reporter; With WFAA-TV, Dallas, WJRT-TV, Flint, Mich., WTNH-TV, New Haven; news anchor WISN 12, Milw., 1979—. Recipient spl. medallion, S.W. Journalism Forum. Office: WISN PO Box 402 Milwaukee WI 53201-0402

TAFLOVE, ALLEN, electrical engineer, educator, researcher, consultant; b. Chgo., June 14, 1949; s. Harry and Leah T.; m. Sylvia Hinda Friedman, Nov. 6, 1977; children: Michael Lee, Nathan Brent. BS with highest distinction, Northwestern U., 1971, MS, 1972, PhD, 1975. Assoc. engr. IIT Rsch. Inst., Chgo., 1975-78, rsch. engr., 1978-81, sr. engr., 1981-84; assoc. prof. Northwestern U., Evanston, 1984-88, prof., 1988—, Charles Deering McCormick prof., 2000—; master Lindgren/Slivka Residential Coll. Sci. & Engring., 2000—. Co-author: Computational Electromagnetics: Integral Equation Approach, 1993; author: Computational Electrodynamics: The Finite-Difference Time-Domain Method, 1995, 2d edit., 2000; editor: Advances in Computational Electrodynamics: The Finite-Difference Time-Domain Method, 1998; contbr. 12 book chpts. and over 80 articles to profl. jours.; patentee in field. Fellow: IEEE. Achievements include pioneer of finite-difference time-domain method in computational electromagnetics. Office: Northwestern U Dept Elec and Comp Engring 2145 Sheridan Rd Evanston IL 60208-0834 E-mail: taflove@ece.northwestern.edu.

TAFT, BOB, governor; b. Jan. 8, 1942; m. Hope Taft; 1 child, Anna. BA, Yale U., 1963; MA, Princeton U., 1967; JD, U. Cin., 1976. Pvt. practice; mem. Ohio Ho. of Reps., Columbus, 1976-80; commr. Hamilton County, Ohio, 1981-90; sec. of state State of Ohio, Columbus, 1991-99, gov., 1999—. Office: 30th Fl 77 S High St Fl 30 Columbus OH 43215-6117*

TAFT, SETH CHASE, retired lawyer; b. Cin., Dec. 31, 1922; s. Charles Phelps and Eleanor K. (Chase) T.; m. Frances Prindle, June 19, 1943; children: Frederick, Thomas, Cynthia, Tucker. B.A., Yale U., 1943, LL.B., 1948. Bar: Ohio 1948. Assoc. Jones, Day, Reavis & Pogue, Cleve., 1948-59, ptnr., 1959-88. Mem. Cuyahoga County (Ohio) Bd. Commrs., 1971-78, pres., 1977-78; mem. Cuyahoga County Charter Commn., 1958-59; Rep. candidate for mayor of Cleve., 1967, for gov. of Ohio, 1982; pres. Fedn. for Community Planning, Cleve., 1986-89, Cleve. Internat. Program, 1990-94; chmn. Substance Abuse Initiative Greater Cleve., 1989—; chmn. Coun. Internat. Programs USA, 1999—; chmn. Cleve. Coun. World Affairs, 2000—. With USNR, 1943-46. Home: 6 Pepper Ridge Rd Cleveland OH 44124-4904 Office: Jones Day Reavis & Pogue 901 Lakeside Ave E Cleveland OH 44114-1190 E-mail: sethtaft@aol.com.

TAFT, SHELDON ASHLEY, lawyer; b. Cleve., Mar. 2, 1937; s. Kingsley Arter and Louise Parsons (Dakin) T.; m. Rebecca Sue Rinehart, Dec. 26, 1962; children: Mariner R., Ashley A., Curtis N. BA, Amherst Coll., 1959; LLB, Harvard U., 1962. Bar: Ohio 1962. Assoc. Vorys, Sater, Seymour & Pease, Columbus, Ohio, 1965-69, 71-73, ptnr., 1974—2001, of counsel, 2002—; chief legal counsel Pub. Utilities Commn. Ohio, 1969-71. Ohio bd. advisors Chgo. Title Ins. Co., 1967-98. Rep. candidate for justice Ohio Supreme Ct., 1974; trustee Opera Columbus, 1989—, pres., 1991-93, life trustee, 1995—. 1st lt. USAF, 1963-65. Mem. ABA (pub. utilities sect.), Ohio State Bar Assn. (pres. pub. utilities com. 1984-87), Columbus Bar Assn. (pub. utilities com.), Ohio Camera Collectors Soc. (pres. 1985-87), Rocky Fork Hunt and Country Club, Capital Club, 41 Club. Congregationalist. Avocation: camera collecting. Home: 27 Sessions Dr Columbus OH 43209-1440 Office: Vorys Sater Seymour & Pease PO Box 1008 52 E Gay St Columbus OH 43216-1008

TAGATZ, GEORGE ELMO, retired obstetrician, gynecologist, educator; b. Milw., Sept. 21, 1935; s. George Herman and Beth Elinore (Blain) T.; m. Susan Trunnell, Oct. 28, 1967; children: Jennifer Lynn, Kirsten Susan, Kathryn Elizabeth. A.B., Oberlin Coll., 1957; M.D., U. Chgo., 1961. Diplomate Am. Bd. Obstetricians and Gynecologists, Am. Bd. Reproductive Endocrinology (examiner, bd. reproductive endocrinology 1976-79). Rotating intern Univ. Hosps. of Cleve., 1961-62, resident in internal medicine, 1962-63; resident in ob-gyn U. Iowa, 1965-68; sr. research fellow in endocrinology U. Wash. dept. obstetrics and gynecology, 1968-70; asst. prof. ob-gyn U. Minn. Med. Sch., 1970-73, assoc. prof., 1973-76, prof., 1976-2000, ret., 2000, asst. prof. internal medicine, 1970-73, dir. div. reproductive endocrinology, 1974-92. Mem. fertility and maternal health adv. com. FDA, USPHS, HHS, 1982-86; cons. in field, 1986-87. Ad hoc editor: Am. Jour. Ob-Gyn, Fertility and Sterility; contbr. articles to profl. publs. Served with M.C. U.S. Army, 1963-65. Mem. AMA, Minn., Hennepin County med. socs., Minn. Obstet. and Gynecol. Soc., Am. Coll. Ob-Gyn (subcom. on reproductive endocrinology 1979-82), Endocrine Soc., Am. Fertility Soc., Central Assn. Obstetricians and Gynecologists, U. Iowa Ob-Gyn Alumni Soc. Home: 5828 Long Brake Trl Minneapolis MN 55439-2622 Office: U Minn Hosps & Clinic PO Box 395 Minneapolis MN 55455

TAGGART, DAVID D. company executive; Chmn., CEO Crouse Cartage Co., Lenexa, Kans., 1994—. Office: Crouse Cartage Co 8245 Nieman Rd Lenexa KS 66214-1508

TAGGART, THOMAS MICHAEL, lawyer; b. Sioux City, Iowa, Feb. 22, 1937; s. Palmer Robert and Lois Allette (Sedgwick) T.; m. Dolores Cecilia Baroway Renfro, Jan. 4, 1963; children: Thomas Michael Jr., Theodore Christopher; m. Mary Ann Gribben, Feb. 7, 1976. BA, Dartmouth Coll., 1959; JD, Harvard U., 1965. Bar: Ohio 1965, U.S. Dist. Ct. (so. dist.) Ohio 1967, U.S. Dist. Ct. (no. dist.) Ohio 1981, U.S. Supreme Ct. 1997. Ptnr. Vorys, Sater, Seymour & Pease, Columbus, Ohio, 1965—. Lectr. Ohio Legal Ctr. Inst., Ohio Mfrs. Assn., Capital U. Ctr. for Spl. and Continuing Legal Edn. Capt. USMC, 1959-63. Mem. ABA, Ohio Bar Assn. (bd. govs. 1991-99, liability ins. com. 1996-97, 99-00, pres. 1997-98, trustee Found. 1996-98, 2000—, chair commn. on jud. evaluations 2000, Ohio Bar medal 1999), Columbus Bar Assn. (bd. govs., pres. 1989-90), Ohio Assn. Civil Trial Attys., Am. Arbitration Assn., Columbus Area C. of C. Methodist. Home: 145 Stanbery Ave Columbus OH 43209-1465 Office: Vorys Sater Seymour & Pease 52 E Gay St Columbus OH 43215-3161

TAI, CHEN-TO, electrical engineering educator; b. Soochow, China, Dec. 30, 1915; came to U.S., 1943; m. Chia Ming Shen, Apr. 28, 1941; children: Arthur, Bing, Julie, David, James. BSc, Tsing Hua U., Beijing, 1937; DSc, Harvard U., 1947. Rsch. fellow Harvard U., Cambridge, Mass., 1947-49; sr. rsch. scientist Stanford Rsch. Inst., Palo Alto, Calif., 1949-54; assoc. prof. Ohio State U., Columbus, 1954-56, prof., 1960-64, Tech. Inst. Electronics, Brazil, 1956-60, U. Mich., Ann Arbor, 1964-86, prof. emeritus, 1986—. Author: Dyadic Green's Functions, 1971, 2d edit., 1994, Generalized Vector and Dyadic Analysis, 1991, 2d edit., 1997; contbr. numerous articles to profl. jours. Fellow IEEE (life, Centennial award 1985, Heinrich Hertz medal 1998); mem. U.S. Nat. Acad. Engring. Home: 1155 Arlington Blvd Ann Arbor MI 48104-4023 Office: Univ of Mich Dept EECS Ann Arbor MI 48109 E-mail: ctnming@aol.com., tai@eecs.umich.com.

TAIGANIDES, E. PAUL, agricultural and environmental engineer, consultant; b. Polymylos, Macedonia, Greece, Oct. 6, 1934; s. Pavlos Theodorou and Sophia ((Elezidou) T.; m. Maro Taiganides, Dec. 25, 1961; children: Paul Anthony, Tasos E., Katerina. BS in Agri. Engring., U. Maine, 1957; MS in Soil and Water Engring., Iowa State U., 1961, D of Environ. Engring., 1963. Cert. engr., Iowa, Colo. Rsch. assoc., asst. prof. Iowa State U., Ames, 1957-65; prof. Ohio State U., Columbus, 1965-75; mgr., chief tech. adviser UN, FAO, Singapore, Singapore, 1975-84, mgr., chief engr. Singapore, 1984-85, mgr., chief tech. adviser Kuala Lumpur, Malaysia, 1985-87; mgr., owner EPT Cons., Columbus, 1987—. Cons. EPD/Hong Kong, 1988-92, WHO, UN, Denmark, Poland, Czechoslovakia, 1972-75, Internat. Devel. Rsch. Ctr., Can., China, Asian, 1984-89, NAE, Thailand, 1990, FAO, Malaysia, Foxley & Co., Nu-Tek Foods; environ. advisor to Bertam Devel. Corp., Kuala Lampur, Malaysia, 1992—; waste cons. to U.S. Feed Grains Coun., Taiwan, Malaysia, 1992, Venezuela, 1993; pres. Fan Engring., (US) Inc., 1991—, Red Hill Farms, Ohio, 1992—. Author: (video) Waste Resources Recycle, 1985, Pig Waste Treatment and Recycle, 1992; editor: Animal Wastes, 1977; co-editor Agricultural Wastes/ Biological Wastes, 1979; contbr. articles to profl. jours. Bd. govs., v.p. Singapore Am. Sch., Singapore, 1978-83; clergy-leity congress Greek Orthodox Ch., Houston, 1974. Recipient rsch. awards EPA, 1971-75, Water Resources Inst., 1968-73; rsch. grantee UNDP, FAO, IDRC, GTZ, Asean, 1975-88. Fellow Am. Soc. Agrl. Engrs. (chmn. dept., A.W. Farral award 1974), Am. Assn. Environ. Engrs. (diplomate); mem. Am. Soc. Engring. Edn. (div. chmn.), Singapore Lawn Tennis Assn. (v.p. 1980-84), Am. Club (mgmt. com. 1980-85), Sigma Xi. Greek Orthodox. Avocations: tennis, classical music, folk dancing. Home and Office: 1800 Willow Forge Dr Columbus OH 43220-4414

TAIT, ROBERT E. lawyer; b. Lima, Ohio, Sept. 3, 1946; s. Robert and Helen (Smith) T.; m. Donna G. Dome, June 22, 1968; children: Heather, Jennifer, Robert. BA, Kenyon Coll., 1968; JD, U. Mich., 1973. Bar: Ohio 1973, U.S. Dist. Ct. (so. dist.) Ohio. 1976, U.S. Dist. Ct. (no. dist.) Ohio 1976, U.S. Dist. Ct. Md. 1980, U.S. Ct. Appeals (6th cir.) 1981, U.S. Supreme Ct. 1982. Ptnr. Vorys, Sater, Seymour & Pease, LLP, Columbus, Ohio, 1973—. Staff counsel Govs. Select Com. on Prevention Indsl. Accidents, Columbus, 1977-78. Served with U.S. Army, 1969-70. Fellow Columbus Bar Found.; mem. ABA (litigation sect., products liability com.), Ohio Bar Assn. (worker's compensation com.), Columbus Bar Assn. (workers compensation and professionalism coms.), Def. Rsch. Inst. (workers compensation com.), Columbus Def. Assn., Assn. Def. Trial Attys. (exec. com. 1991-94, treas., 2002-), Fedn. Def. and Corp. Counsel. Clubs: Capital, Columbus Country. Home: 2045 Wickford Rd Columbus OH 43221-4223 Office: Vorys Sater Seymour & Pease PO Box 1008 52 E Gay St Columbus OH 43215-3161

TAKAHASHI, JOSEPH S. neuroscientist, educator; b. Tokyo, Dec. 16, 1951; s. Shigeharu and Hiroko (Hara) T.; m. Barbara Pillsbury Snook, June 28, 1985; children: Erika S., Matthew N. BA, Swarthmore (Pa.) Coll., 1974; PhD, U. Oreg., 1981. Pharmacology rsch. assoc. NIMH, NIGMS, Bethesda, Md., 1981-83; asst. prof. Northwestern U., Evanston, Ill., 1983-87, assoc. chmn. neurobiology and physiology, 1988-96, assoc. prof. neurobiology and physiology, 1987-91, prof. neurobiology and physiology, 1991-96, Walter and Mary Elizabeth Glass prof. life scis., 1996—, acting assoc. dir. Inst. for Neurosci., 1988-95; investigator Northwestern U. Howard Hughes Med. Inst., 1997—. Active NIMH Psychobiology and Behavior Rev. Com., 1988-92; mem. Nat. Mental Health Adv. Coun., 1997—; mem. neurosci. adv. com. Klingenatein Fund, 1999—. Assoc. editor Neuron; mem. adv. bd. Jour. Biol. Rhythms, 1984—; contbr. over 120 articles to profl. jours. Grantee Bristol-Myers Squibb, 1995—; recipient Alfred P. Sloan award A.P. Sloan Found., 1983-85, Searl Scholars award Chgo. Cmty. Trust, 1985-88, Merit award NIMH, 1987, Honma prize in Biol. Rhythms Honma Found., 1986, Presdl. Young Investigator award NSF, 1985-90, 6th C.U. Ariens Kappers award Netherlands Soc. for Advancement Nat. Scis., Medicine and Surgery, 1995. Fellow Am. Acad. Arts and Sci.; mem. Am. Soc. Human Genetics, Genetics Soc. Am., Soc. Neurosci., Soc. for Rsch. on Biol. Rhythms (adv. bd. 1986—), Mammalian Genome Soc. Achievements include discovery of the expression of circadian oscillations in cells from vertebrates; and identification of first circadian clock gene in mice. Office: Northwestern U Howard Hughes Med Inst 2153 N Campus Dr Evanston IL 60208-0877

TALBOT, EMILE JOSEPH, French language educator; b. Brunswick, Maine, Apr. 12, 1941; s. Joseph Emile and Flora Talbot; m. Elizabeth Mullen, Aug. 6, 1966; children: Marc, Paul. BA, St. Francis Coll., Biddeford, Maine, 1963; MA, Brown U., 1965, PhD, 1968. Instr. French U. Ill., Urbana, 1967-68, asst. prof., 1968-73, assoc. prof., 1973-86, prof., 1986—, head dept. French, 1988-94. Author: (book) Stendhal and Romantic Esthetics, 1985, Stendhal Revisited, 1993, Reading Nelligan, 2002; editor: La Critique Stndhalienne, 1979; assoc. editor: Quebec Studies, 1993—96, rev. editor: The French Rev., 1979—82, rev. editor: Quebec Studies, 1988—93, mem. editl. bd.: Nineteenth-Century French Studies, 1986—, mem. editl. bd.: La Revue Francophone, 1990—96, mem. editl. bd.: Etudes Francophones, 1996—. Decorated chevalier Ordre des Palmes Académiques (France); fellow, Ctr. Advanced Study U. Ill., 1973, Assoc., 1988, NEH, 1973—74, Camargo Found., France, 1976. Mem.: MLA, Am. Coun. Quebec Studies (v.p. 1995—97, pres. 1997—99), Assn. Can. Studies in U.S., Am. Assn. Tchrs. French. Roman Catholic. Office: U Illinois Dept French 707 S Mathews Ave Urbana IL 61801-3625 E-mail: ejtalbot@uiuc.edu.

TALBOT, PAMELA, public relations executive; b. Chgo., Aug. 10, 1946; BA in English, Vassar Coll., 1968. Reporter Worcester, Mass. Telegram and Gazette, 1970-72; account exec. Daniel J. Edelman, Inc., Chgo., 1972-74, account supr., 1974-76, v.p., 1976-78, sr. v.p., 1978-84, exec. v.p., gen. mgr., 1984-90; pres. Edelman West, 1990-95; pres., COO Edelman U.S., 1995—. Office: Edelman Pub Rels 200 E Randolph Dr Ste 6300 Chicago IL 60601-6436 E-mail: pam.talbot@edelman.com.

TALENT, JAMES M. former congressman, lawyer; b. St. Louis, Oct. 18, 1956; m. Brenda Lyons, 1984; children: Michael, Kathleen Marie, Christine. BA in Polit. Sci., Washington U., 1978; JD, U. Chgo. Law Sch., 1981. Law clk. 7th Ct. Appeals, 1981-82; adj. prof. law, 1982-84; mem. Mo. State Ho. Reps., 1984-93; minority leader, 1989-93; mem. 103rd-106th Congresses from 2nd Mo. Dist., 1993—2001, mem. edn. and the workforce com., armed svcs. com., chmn. small bus. com. Legislative Achievement award Mo. Hosp. Assn., 1989. Mem. Mo. Bar Assn. (Award for significant contbns. to adminstrv. justice 1989), Mo. C. of C. (Spirit of Enterprise award 1990), Order of the Coif. Republican. Office: US Ho Reps 1022 Longworth Hob Washington DC 20515-0001

TALLACKSON, HARVEY DEAN, state legislator, real estate and insurance salesman; b. Grafton, N.D., May 15, 1925; s. Arthur J. and Mabel R. (McDougald) T.; m. Glenna M. Walstad, Aug. 4, 1946; children: Lynda, Thomas, Debra, Amy, Laura. Grad. h.s., Park River, N.D. Grain and potato farmer, Grafton, 1946-68; ins. agt. Tallackson Ins., 1968—; mem. N.D. Senate, Bismark, 1976—; real estate salesman Johnson Real Estate, Grafton, 1982—. Chmn. appropriation com. N.D. Senate, 1987-93. Bd. dirs. Nodak Rural Electric Coop., Grand Forks, N.D., 1965—; bd. dirs. Minnkota Power Coop., Grand Forks, 1979—, pres., 1990—. Recipient Pub. Svc. award N.D. Lignite Coun., 1989; named Outstanding Young Farmer by Area Chamber of Walsh & Pembina Counties, 1951-52. Mem. Nat. Coun. Ins. Legislatures (mem. exec. com. 1985—, pres. 1996-97), Lions (pres. 1977-79), Masons. Democrat. Lutheran. Avocations: golf, curling, travel, reading. Office: Tallackson Ins & Real Estate 53 W 5th St Grafton ND 58237-1468

TALLCHIEF, MARIA, ballerina; b. Fairfax, Okla., Jan. 24, 1925; d. Alexander Joseph and Ruth Mary (Porter) T.; m. Henry Paschen, Jr., June 3, 1956; 1 child, Elise. DFA (hon.), Lake Forest (Ill.) Coll., Colby Coll., Waterville, Maine, 1968, Ripon Coll., 1973, Boston Coll., Smith Coll., 1981, Northwestern U., Evanston, Ill., 1982, Yale U., 1984, St. Mary-of-the-Woods (Ind.) Coll., 1984, Dartmouth Coll., 1985, St. Xavier Coll., 1989, U. Ill., 1997. Ballerina Ballet Russe de Monte Carlo, 1942-47; with N.Y.C. Ballet Co., 1947-65, prima ballerina, 1947-60; founder Chgo. City Ballet, 1979; now ballet dir. Lyric Opera Chgo., 1979—. Prima ballerina Am. Ballet Theatre, 1960; founder Sch. Chgo. Ballet. Guest star, Paris Opera, 1947, Royal Danish Ballet, 1961; created roles in Danses Concertantes, 1944, Night Shadow, 1946, Four Temperaments, 1946, Orpheus, 1948, The Firebird, 1949, Bourée Fantastique, 1949, Capriccio Brillante, 1951, Á la Françaix, 1951, Swan Lake, 1951, Caracole, 1952, Scotch Symphony, 1952, The Nutcracker, 1954, Allegro Brillante, 1956, The Gounod Symphony, 1958; appeared in films Presenting Lily Mais, 1943, Million Dollar Mermaid, 1953. Named Hon. Princess Osage Indian Tribe, 1953; recipient Disting. Service award U. Okla., 1972, award Dance mag., 1960, Jane Addams Humanitarian award Rockford Coll., 1973, Order of Lincoln award 1974, Bravo award Rosary Coll., 1983, award Dance Educators Am., 1956, Achievement award Women's Nat. Press Club, 1953, Capezio award, 1965, Leadership for Freedom award Roosevelt U. Scholarship Assn., 1986, Kennedy Ctr. honor, 1996, Nat. medal of Arts, Pres. Clinton, 1999; named to Nat. Women's Hall of Fame, 1996, Internat. Women's Forum Hall of Fame, 1997. Mem. Nat. Soc. Arts and Letters. Office: Lyric Opera Ballet 20 N Wacker Dr Ste 860 Chicago IL 60606-2874

TALLENT, WILLIAM HUGH, chemist, research administrator; b. Akron, Ohio, May 28, 1928; s. Charles Othar and Agnes Annette (Johnson) T.; m. Joy Anne Redfield, Aug.23, 1952; children: Elizabeth Ann, Cinda Marie, Raymond Charles. BS, U. Tenn., 1949, MS, 1950; PhD, U. Ill., 1953. Chemist Nat. Heart Inst., Bethesda, Md., 1953-57, G.D. Searle & Co., Skokie, Ill., 1957-64; head new crops evaluation investigations Agr. Rsch. Svc., USDA, Peoria, 1964-69, chief indsl. crops lab., 1969-74, asst. dir., 1974-75, ctr. dir. No. Regional Rsch. Ctr., 1975-83, regional adminstr. N.E. region, 1983-84, asst. adminstr. Washington, 1984-94, tech. transfer advisor Beltsville, Md., 1994—. Editor Jour. Am. Oil Chemists Soc., 1998-2001. Recipient Merit award Gamma Sigma Delta, 1979, Presdl. Rank award for Sr. Execs., 1988, NASA Tech. 2002 award for lifetime achievement in tech. transfer, 1992. Mem. AAAS, Am. Oil Chemists' Soc., Am. Chem. Soc., Soc. Econ. Botany. Home and Office: 831 West Side Dr Iowa City IA 52246-4309 Fax: 319-354-4059.

TALLET, MARGARET ANNE, theatre executive; b. Binghamton, N.Y., Feb. 14, 1953; d. George Francis and Wilma Ann (Wagner) T.; m. Peter A., Myks, July 6, 1991. BA, St. Mary's Coll./U. Notre Dame, 1975; MBA, SUNY, 1979. Asst. dir. Parrish Art Mus., Southampton, N.Y., 1979-81; assoc. dir. devel. Detroit Inst. Arts Founders Soc., 1981-92; v.p. Franco Pub. Rels. Group, Detroit, 1992-96; pres. Music Hall Ctr. for the Performing Arts, 1996—. Bd. dirs. Aid for AIDS Rsch., 1987-92, Detroiters at Heart, 1992—; mktg. com. Mich. Cancer Found., Detroit, 1992—, Cultural adv. comm. city of Detroit, Adv. bd.:Arts Serve MI. Mem. Pub. Rels. Soc. Am. Roman Catholic. Office: Music Hall Ctr for Performing Arts 350 Madison St Detroit MI 48226-2290

TALLEY, ROBERT COCHRAN, medical school dean and administrator, cardiologist; b. May 26, 1936; m. Katherine Ann Plocar; children: Andrew, Katherine, David. BS, U. Mich., 1958; MD, U. Chgo., 1962. Diplomate Nat. Bd. Med. Examiners (mem. medicine com. 1984-88, com. chair 1988-93), Am. Bd. Internal Medicine, subsplty. cardiovascular diseases. Asst. prof., dept. physiology and medicine U. Tex. Med. Sch., San Antonio, 1969-71, head, sect. cardiovascular diseases, 1971-75, assoc. prof., dept. medicine, 1971-75; acting chief medicine VA Hosp., 1974, chief cardiology service, 1973-75; chmn. dept. internal medicine U. S.D. Sch. Medicine, Sioux Falls, 1975-87, Freeman prof. medicine, 1984-87, interim v.p., dean, 1986-87, v.p., dean, 1987—. Mem. Liaison Com. on Med. Edn., 1998—; mem. adminstrn. bd., coun. of deans Assn. Am. Med. Colls., 1999-2000. Contbr. 33 articles to med. jours. Served to surgeon USPHS, 1966-68. Tchg. scholar Am. Heart Assn. U. Chgo., 1972-75; Outstanding Tchr. and Clinician award U. Tex., San Antonio, 1969-70, Ann. Tchg. award for Best Clin. Instr., U. Tex., San Antonio, 1971-72, Anton Hyden Disting. Prof. award. U. S.D. Sch. Medicine, 1979, Faculty Recognition award U. S.D. Sch. Medicine, 1981. Fellow ACP, Am. Coll. Cardiology; mem. AMA, Am. Heart Assn. (bd. dirs. Dakota affiliate), Am. Fedn. Clin. Rsch. Home: 1305 Cedar Ln Sioux Falls SD 57103-4512 Office: U SD Sch Medicine 1400 W 22nd St Sioux Falls SD 57105-1505

TALMAGE, LANCE ALLEN, obstetrician/gynecologist, career military officer; b. Vandergrift, Pa., Feb. 23, 1938; s. Guy Wesley and Martha Lois (Bradstock) T.; m. Diana Elizabeth Heywood, June 23, 1962; children: Tamara, Lance Jr., Tenley. BS in Chem. Engring., U. Toledo, 1960; MD, U. Mich., 1964. Flight surgeon 24th Infantry Divsn. U.S. Army, Europe, 1966-69; resident U. Mich. Med. Ctr., Ann Arbor, 1969-73; clin. prof. Med. Coll. Ohio, Toledo, 1987—2000; med. dir. Ctr. for Women's Health, 1987—. Brigadier gen. 112th Med. Brigage Ohio Army Nat. Guard, Columbus, 1995-97; pres. med. staff Toledo Hosp., 1989-91, chair dept. Ob-gyn., 1979-86; pres. Toledo Lucas County Acad. Medicine, 1994-95; mem. Toledo Hosp. Found. Bd., 2000—; mem. adv. com. Promedia Bd. of Trustees; bd. trustees Accreditation Assn. Ambulatory Health Care, 2000—. Cabinet mem. United Way, Toledo, 1994-96; hon. chmn. March of Dimes Mothers-March, Toledo, 1989; pres. Ottawa Hills (Ohio) Athletic Boosters, 1986-88, team physician, 1981—. Named to, Ohio Vets. Hall Fame, 2001; recipient Garde Nationale Trophy, Ohio Army Nat. Guard, 1998, Outstanding Team Physician, 2002. Fellow Am. Coll. Surgeons, Am. Coll. Obstetricians & Gynecologists (dist. chair 1996-99, v.p. 2000—); mem. AMA (mem. ho. of dels.), Ohio State Med. Assn. (pres. 1998-99), Kiwanis, Pi Kappa Phi Alumni Assn., U. Toledo Alumni Assn. (bd. trustees 1996—, pres. 2000-01), Lucas County Domestic Violence Task Force. Republican. Lutheran. Office: The Toledo Hosp 2142 N Cove Blvd Toledo OH 43606 E-mail: latalmage@voyager.net.

TAMBRINO, PAUL AUGUST, college president; m. Faye M. Thompson; children: Paul, Jeffrey, Mark, Lauren. BA, Cen. Coll., Pella, Iowa, 1958; postgrad., Am. Inst. Banking, N.Y.C., 1958-59; MS, Hofstra U., 1966; EdD, Temple U., 1973. Cert. quality transformation cons. Group acturial supr. N.Y. Life Ins. Co., N.Y.C., 1960-64; tchr. acctg. and bus. N. Babylon (N.Y.) Sr. High Sch., 1964-68; instr. econs. and acctg. coord. Ursinus Coll., Collegeville, Pa., 1968-70; asst. prof. acctg. and edn. Hofstra U., Hempstead, N.Y., 1970-78; dean bus. and art div. Northampton County C.C., Bethlehem, Pa., 1978-83; coll. dean Warren County C.C., Washington, 1984-91; pres., CEO Iowa Valley C.C. Dist., Marshalltown, 1991—. Cons. N.J. Dept. Higher Edn., 1989—, Pfizer, Inc., N.Y.C., 1974-78, John Wiley & Sons, 1984, Union Coll., 1982, Verbatim, Inc.,m 1974-78, McGraw-Hill, 1967-74. Contbr. chpt. to Accountants Encyclopedia, 1978; revised Careers and Opportunities in Accounting, 1978; contbr. articles to profl. jours. 1st lt. USAR, 1959-65. Mem. Rotary Internat., C. of C., Beta Alpha Psi, Delta Pi Epsilon. Home: 2515 Reyclif Dr Marshalltown IA 50158-2351 Office: Iowa Valley CC Dist Marshalltown IA 50158

TAMM, ELEANOR RUTH, retired accountant; b. Hansell, Iowa, July 20, 1921; d. Horace Gerald and Sibyl (Armstrong) Wells; m. Roy C. Tamm, Oct. 18, 1941 (dec. Jan. 1980); children: Larry LeRoy, Marilyn Ruth Tamm-Schmitt. Grad., Am. Soc. Travel Agts., Inc., 1970; student, Iowa Cen. C.C., 1983, 85; grad., Inst. Children's Lit., 1994. Tchr. Howard County Rural Sch., Riceville, 1939-41; bookkeeper, cashier Cen. States Power and Light Co., Elma, Iowa, 1941-42; office supr. J.C. Penney Co., Goldsboro, N.C., 1942-44, bookkeeper West Palm Beach, Fla., 1945; head teller Iowa State Bank, Clarksville, Iowa, 1955-69; office and group mgr. Allen Travel Agy., Charles City, 1969-81, tour conductor, tour organizer and planner, 1971-81; office mgr. Arora Clinics, P.C., Fonda, Iowa, 1986-90; freelance collaborator on children's books Clarksville, 1989—. Author: Flight to the Everlands, 1993, Firm Foundations, 1996, Adventure Down Under, 2001. Leader Girl Scouts U.S.A., Clarksville, 1946-47; tchr. St. John Luth. Ch., Clarksville, 1946-66, ch. sec., 1954-66, sec.-treas. Altar Guild, 1993-94; United Fund sec.-treas. Clarksville Cmty. Fund, 1956-66; sec.-treas. Clarksville Band Boosters, 1964-66. Lutheran. Avocations: reading, music, writing, decorating, designing and sewing fashions. Home: 408 E 3rd St Fonda IA 50540-0425

TAMMEUS, WILLIAM DAVID, journalist, columnist; b. Woodstock, Ill., Jan. 18, 1945; s. W. H. and Bertha H. (Helander) T.; m. Marcia Bibens, Nov. 29, 1996; children: Lisen, Kate; stepchildren: Christopher L. Johnston, Daniel Bednarczyk, Kathryn Bednarczyk, David Bednarczyk. BJ, U. Mo., Columbia, 1967; postgrad., U. Rochester, 1967-69. Reporter Rochester (N.Y.) Times-Union, 1967-70; reporter Kansas City (Mo.) Star, 1970-77, Starbeams columnist, 1977—; syndicated columnist N.Y. Times News Svc., 1989-99, Knight Ridder/Tribune Info. Svcs., 2000—. Author: A Gift of Meaning, 2001; editor-at-large Presbyn. Outlook, 1993; contbg. editor Mo. Life mag., 1980-81; commentator Sta. KCPT-TV, 1979-90. Co-recipient Pulitzer prize for gen. local reporting of Hyatt Regency Hotel disaster, 1982, recipient 1st pl. opinion-editl. divsn. Heart of Am. award Kansas City Press Club, 1991, 93, 1st pl. column divsn., 1994, 1st pl. award for best column/humor divsn. Mo. Press Assn., 1997, Best In-Depth Reporting on Religion award Am. Acad. Religion, 2001. Mem. Nat. Soc. Newspaper Columnists (v.p. 1990-92, pres. 1992-94, 1st pl. items divsn. Writing award 1992, 3d place humor writing, 1999, 2000), Soc. Profl. Journalists. Presbyterian. Office: 1729 Grand Blvd Kansas City MO 64108-1413 E-mail: tammeus@kcstar.com.

TAN, HUI QIAN, computer science and civil engineering educator; b. Tsingtao, China, June 12, 1948; s. Dumen Tan and Ruifan Rao; m. Ren Zhong, June 16, 1994; children: William W., Danny D. BA, Oberlin Coll., 1982; MS, Kent State U., 1984, PhD, 1986. Asst. prof. computer sci. and civil engring. U. Akron, Ohio, 1986-89, assoc., 1990—; rsch. prof. Kent (Ohio) State U., 1987. Contbr. articles to profl. jours. Grantee NASA, 1987—, 91—, NSF, 1988-92. Mem. IEEE Computer Soc., Assn. for Computing Machinery, SIGSAM Assn. for Computing Machinery, Phi Beta Kappa. Avocations: classical music, history, literature, swimming, cycling.

TAN, JAMES, internist, educator; b. Aug. 3, 1938; married. AA, U. Philippines, 1960, MD, 1965. Diplomate in internal medicine and infectious disease Am. Bd. Internal Medicine; cert. physician, Ohio. Intern Philippine Gen. Hosp., Manila, 1964-65, resident in internal medicine, 1965-67; tng. Bangkok, 1967-68; fellow in infectious diseases U. Cin. Coll. Medicine, 1968-71; mem. staff U. Cinn. Med. Ctr., other Cin. hosps., 1971-74; active staff Summa Health System, 1975—; prof. medicine Northeastern Ohio Univs. Coll. Medicine, Rootstown, 1979—, vice chmn. dept. internal medicine, 1993—, chmn. infectious disease sect., 1977—; chmn. dept. of programs Summa Health Sys., Akron, Ohio, 1992—. Contbr. articles to profl. jours.; reviewer for jours. Fellow Am. Coll. Chest Physicians, Infectious Disease Soc. Am. (sec. Ohio 1994—), ACP-Am. Soc. Internal Medicine (master, gov. Ohio chpt. 1995-99); mem. Am. Soc. for Microbiology, Ohio Med. Soc., Soc. for Hosp. Epidemiologists, Assn. Program Dirs. in Internal Medicine, Alpha Omega Alpha. Office: Summa Health Sys 75 Arch St Ste 303 Akron OH 44304-1432 E-mail: tanj@summa-health.org.

TANDON, RAJIV, psychiatrist, educator; b. Kanpur, India, Aug. 3, 1956; came to U.S., 1984; s. Bhagwan Sarup and Usha (Mehrotra) T.; m. Chanchal Nammi Vohra; children: Neeraj, Anisha, Gitanjali. Student, St. Xavier's Coll., Bombay, India, 1974; BS, All India Inst., New Delhi, 1980; MD, Nat. Inst. of MH, India, 1983. Sr. resident Mental Health and Neuro-Scis., India, 1983-84; resident U. Mich. Hosps., Ann Arbor, 1984-87, attending psychiatrist, 1987-2000. Dir. schizophrenia program, dir. hosp. svcs. divsn. U. Mich., Ann Arbor, 1987—2000, assoc. prof., 1993—99, prof., 1999—; cons. Lenawee County Cmty. Mental Health, Adrian, Mich., 1985—99. Author: Biochemical Parameters of Mixed Affective States; Negative Schizophrenic Symptoms: Pathophysiology and Clinical Implications; contbr. more than 120 articles to profl. jours. Recipient Young Scientist's award Biennial Winter workshop on Schizophrenia, 1990, 92, Travel award Am. Coll. Neuropsychopharmacology/Mead, 1990, Rsch. Excellence award Am. Assn. Psychiatrists from India, 1993, Sci. award, Best Drs. in Am. award, 1994-98, Gerald Klerman award for outstanding rsch. by a Nat. Alliance for Rsch. in Schizophrenia and Depression young investigator, 1995, FuturPsych award CINP, 1997. Mem. Am. Psychiat. Assn. (Wisniewski Young Psychiatrist Rschr. award 1993), World Fedn. Mental Health, Soc. for Neurosci., N.Y. Acad. Scis., Soc. Biol. Psychiatry, Mich. Psychiat. Soc. Democrat. Hindu. Office: U Mich Med Ctr Dept Psychiatry Box 0120 1500 E Medical Center Dr # 9C Ann Arbor MI 48109-0005

TANG, CYRUS, investment company executive; CEO, pres., chmn. Tang Industries, Mt. Prospect, Ill. Office: 1650 W Jefferson Ave Trenton MI 48183-2136 Address: Tang Industries 3773 Howard Hughes Pkwy Ste 350N Las Vegas NV 89109

TANGUAY, MARK H. company executive; Mng. prin. Tanguay-Burke-Stratton, Chgo., 1987—. Office: Tanguay-Burke-Stratton 321 N Clark St Ste 900 Chicago IL 60610-4765

TANK, ALAN, trade association administrator; BA in Animal Sci., Iowa State U. Field dir. Iowa Pork Prodrs. Assn., 1980; mem. staff Congressman Jim Leach, Wash.; lobbyist; v.p. pub. policy Nat. Pork Prodrs. Council, Des Moines, 1991, chief exec. officer. Office: National Pork Producers Council 1776 NW 114th St Clive IA 50325-7000

TANNER, HELEN HORNBECK, historian, consultant; b. Northfield, Minn., July 5, 1916; d. John Wesley and Frances Cornelia (Wolfe) Hornbeck; m. Wilson P. Tanner, Jr., Nov. 22, 1940 (dec. 1977); children: Frances, Margaret Tanner Tewson, Wilson P., Robert (dec. 1983) AB with honors, Swarthmore Coll., 1937; MA, U. Fla., 1949; PhD, U. Mich., 1961. Asst. to dir. pub. rels. Kalamazoo Pub. Schs., 1937-39; with sales dept. Am. Airlines Inc., N.Y.C., 1940-43; teaching fellow, then teaching asst. U. Mich., Ann Arbor, 1949-53, 57-60, lectr. extension svc., 1961-74, asst. dir. Ctr. Continuing Edn. for Women, 1964-68; project dir. Newberry Libr., Chgo., 1976-81, rsch. assoc., 1981-95, sr. rsch. fellow, 1995—. Expert witness in Indian treaty litigation, 1963—; dir. D'Arcy McNickle Ctr. for Indian History, 1984-85; cons., expert witness Indian treaties; mem. Mich. Commn. Indian Affairs, 1966-70 Author: Zespedes in East Florida 1784-1790, 1963, 89, General Green Visits St. Augustine, 1964, The Greeneville Treaty, 1974, The Territory of the Caddo Tribe of Oklahoma, 1974, The Ojibwas, 1992; editor: Atlas of Great Lakes Indian History, 1987, The Settling of North America: An Atlas, 1995. NEH grantee, 1976, fellow, 1989; ACLS grantee, 1990. Mem. Am. Soc. Ethnohistory (pres. 1982-83), Am. Hist. Assn., Conf. L.Am. History, Soc. History Discoveries, Chgo. Map Soc., Fla. Hist. Soc., Hist. Soc. Mich. Home: 5178 Crystal Dr Beulah MI 49617-9618 Office: The Newberry Libr 60 W Walton St Chicago IL 60610-3380 E-mail: hhtanner@aol.com.

TANNER, JIMMIE EUGENE, college dean; b. Hartford, Ark., Sept. 27, 1933; s. Alford C. and Hazel Ame (Anthony) T.; m. Carole Joy Yant, Aug. 28, 1958; children— Leslie Allison, Kevin Don. BA, Okla. Baptist U., 1955; MA, U. Okla., 1957, PhD, 1964. Assoc. prof. English, Franklin Coll., Ind., 1964-65; prof. English, Okla. Bapt. U., Shawnee, 1958-64, 65-72; v.p. acad. affairs Hardin-Simmons U., Abilene, Tex., 1972-78, La. Coll., Pineville, 1978-80; dean William Jewell Coll., Liberty, Mo., 1980-97, prof. English, 1997—, interim pres., 1993-94. Contbr.: The Annotated Bibliography of D.H. Lawrence, Vol. 1, 1982, Vol. 2, 1985. Mem. Shawnee Sch. Bd., 1966-72; mem. edn. commn. So. Bapt. Conv., 1967-72. So. Fellowships Fund fellow, 1960-61; Danforth fellow, 1962-63. Democrat. Baptist. Avocations: tennis; photography. E-mail: tanner@william.jewell.edu Home: 609 Lancelot Dr Liberty MO 64068-1023 Office: William Jewell Coll Liberty MO 64068

TANNER, MARTIN ABBA, statistics and human oncology educator; b. Highland Park, Ill., Oct. 19, 1957; s. Meir and Esther Rose (Bauer) T.; m. Anat Talitman, Aug. 14, 1984; 1 child, Noam Ben. BA, U. Chgo., 1978, PhD, 1982. Asst. prof. stats. and human oncology U. Wis., Madison, 1982-87, assoc. prof., 1987-90; dir. lab., prof. and dept. chair biostatistics U. Rochester, 1990-94; prof. dept. statistics Northwestern U., 1994—. Cons. Kirkland & Ellis, 1980-82; mem. Nat. Inst. Allergy and Infectious diseases study sect., 1994-98; reviewer NIH, NSF, VA. Assoc. editor Jour. Am. Stat. Assn., 1987-99; editor Jour. of Am. Statis. Assn., 1999—; contbr. articles to profl. jours. Recipient New Investigator Rsch. award NIH, 1984, Mortimer Spiegelman award Am. Pub. Health Assn., 1993; NSF grantee, 1983, 95, NIH grantee, 1986—. Fellow Royal Statis. Soc., Am. Statis.

Assn. (Continuing Edn. Excellence award); mem. AAAS, Mensa, Sigma Xi. Avocations: classical guitar, medieval poetry. Office: Northwestern U 2006 Sheridan Rd Evanston IL 60208-0852 E-mail: mat132@nwu.edu.

TANNER, RALPH M. state legislator; b. Jefferson County, A.L., Dec. 10, 1926; m. Judith Tanner. B.A., Birmingham-Southern Coll., 1954, M.A., 1967; PhD, U. Ala., 1967. Rep. dist. 10 Kans. Ho. of Reps., 1994—. Republican. Office: Kans Ho of Reps Rm 426 - S Topeka KS 66612

TAPLETT, LLOYD MELVIN, human resources management consultant; b. Tyndall, S.D., July 25, 1924; s. Herman Leopold and Emiley (Nedvidek) T.; m. Patricia Ann Sweeney, Aug. 21, 1958; children: Virginia Ann, Sharon Lorraine, Carla Jo, Carolyn Patricia,m Catherne Marie, Colleen Elizabeth. BA, Augustana Coll., 1949; MA, U. Nebr., 1958; postgrad., S.D. State U., U. S.D., U. Iowa, Colo. State U. Accredited personnel dir.; prof. human resources; cert. tchr. & counselor. Tchr. Sioux Falls (S.D.) pub. schs., 1952-69; with All-Am. Transport co., Sioux Falls, 1969-78, Am. Freight System, Inc., Overland Park, Kans., 1978-79; dir. human resources & pub. rels., corp. affirmative action Chippewa Motor Freight, Inc., Sioux Falls, 1979-80; human resources & mgmt. cons., 1980-81; mgr. Sioux Falls Job Svcs., 1981-85, Pioneer Enterprises, Inc., 1985-86; ops. mgr. ATE Environ., Inc., 1986-88; cons. Royal River Casino, 1988-90; acad. dean Huron U., Sioux Falls, 1990-97; instr. econs. Coll. Bus., 1992—. Chmn. Chippewa Credit Union; mem. adv. bd. dirs. Nelson Labs., Sioux Dalls, 1981-82; evening mgmt. instr. Nat. Coll., Sioux Falls, 1981-90, chmn. adv. com., 1984—, Huron U., 1990-97, S.F. Washington High Sch. Sports Heritage, 1989-98. Contbr. articles to nat. mags. Past bd. dirs. Jr. Achievement, United Way, Sioux Vocat. Sch. Handicapped; past mem. Gov.'s Adv. Bd. Cmty. Adult Manpower Planning; chmn. bus. edn. adv. com. Sioux Falls Pub. Schs., 1982-85; chmn. adv. com. South East Area Vocat. Sch., 1982-85; mem. alumnae bd. Augustana Coll., 1985-88; commencement spkr. Capt. USMC, 1943-46, 50-52, WWII, Korea. Recipient VFW Commendation award, 1990, Liberty Bell award S.D. Bar Assn., 1967, Sch. Bd. award NEA/Thom McAn Shoe Corp., 1966, S.D. Unsung Heroes Edn. Recognition award Sta. KSFV-TV, 1998; named Boss of Yr., Sioux Falls, 1977. Mem. NEA (life, Pacemaker award), Am. Soc. Personnel Adminstrn. (accredited personnel mgr., life, S.D. dist. dir. 1980-84), Am. Trucking Assn. (mem. pub. rels. coun.), S.D. Edn. Assn. (life), Sioux Falls Personnel Assn. (past pres.), Sales & Mktg. Club Sioux Falls, Sioux Falls Traffic Club, VFW (life, Nat. Polit. Action Recognition award 1990), Am. Legion, Toastmasters (past gov. dist. 41, Disting. Toastmaster award, Outstanding Toastmaster award dist. 41, Hall of Fame 1977), Elks. Republican. Roman Catholic.

TARASZKIEWICZ, WALDEMAR, physician; b. Wilno, Poland, July 6, 1936; came to U.S., 1979; s. Michal Taraszkiewicz and Nina (Lutomska) Dylla; m. Teresa Barbara Szwarc, Oct. 15, 1966. MD, Med. Acad., Gdansk, Poland, 1961, internal medicine specialty, 1967, internal medicine specialty II, 1972. Diplomate Am. Bd. Family Practice. Family physician Out Patient Clinic, Sopot, Poland, 1962—64; resident doctor U. Hosp., Gdansk, 1965—71; allergist Clinic of Allergy, 1965—75; physician Cardiology Dept., 1971—75, Hôpital Civil, Telagh, Algeria, 1975—79; surg. asst. Hinsdale (Ill.) Hosp., 1979—82; resident physician St. Mary of Nazareth Hosp., Chgo., 1982—85, emergency room physician, 1984—85; family practice medicine Brookfield, 1985—88, Westmont, 1988—89, Chgo., 1987—; med. dir. Winston Manor Nursing Home, 1989—90; clin. asst. prof. U. Ill. Med. Coll., 1994—. Sr. asst. dept. cardiology Univ. Hosp., Gdansk, 1971-75; mem. adminstrv. com., pres. med. staff Hôpital Civil, Telagh, 1976-79. Contbr. articles to profl. jours. Recipient Bronze medal Polski Zwiazek Wedkarski, 1970, cert. 3d place, 1971. Fellow Am. Acad. Family Practice; mem. AMA (continuing edn. award), Ill. Med. Soc., Chgo. Med. Soc. (practice mgmt. com.), World Med. Assn., Am. Acad. Allergy and Immunology, Am. Coll. Allergy and Immunology, Polish Med. Alliance, N.Y. Acad. Scis. Avocations: art collecting, fishing. Office: Jefferson Park Med Bldg 4811 N Milwaukee Ave Ste 130 Chicago IL 60630-2157 E-mail: waldemar_taraszkiewicz@yahoo.com.

TARDY, MEDNEY EUGENE, JR. retired otolaryngologist, facial plastic surgeon; b. Scottsburg, Ind., Dec. 3, 1934; MD, Ind. U., 1960. Diplomate Am. Bd. Otolaryngology (v.p. 1993, pres. 1994). Intern Tampa Gen. Hosp., 1960—61; resident in otolaryngology U. Ill. Hosp., 1963—67, fellow head, neck and plastic surgery, 1967—68; otolaryngologist St. Joseph Hosp., Chgo.; prof. clin. otolaryngology U. Ill.; pvt. practice Chgo.; dir. divsn. facial plastic and reconstructive surgery U. Ill.; prof. clin. otolaryngology Ind. U. Med. Ctr., Indpls.; pvt. practice Chgo.; ret. Bd. govs. Chgo. Symphony Orch., Hubbard St. Dance Co., Chgo. Mem.: Soc. Univ. Otolaryngologists, Am. Rhinol. Soc., Am. Laryngol. Soc., Am. Acad. Otolaryngology-Head and Neck Surgery (past pres.), Am. Acad. Facial Plastic and Reconstructive Surgery, ACS. Office: 2913 N Commonwealth Ave Ste 430 Chicago IL 60657-6238

TARNOVE, LORRAINE, medical association executive; b. Atlantic City, July 26, 1947; d. Leonard Robert Tarnove and Jeanne Tarnove Yudkin; m. Steven B. Friedman, June 1, 1969; children: K. Brooke, Ari-Benjamin. BA, U. Md., 1969. Pres. Lorraine Tarnove Consulting, Columbia, Md., 1985-93; exec. dir. Am. Med. Dirs. Assn. Contbr. chpt. to book. Office: AMDA 10840 Little Patuxent #760 Columbia MO 21044

TARONJI, JAIME, JR. lawyer; b. N.Y.C., Nov. 20, 1944; s. Jaime and Ruth T.; m. Mary Taronji, May 16, 1970; children: Ian A., Mark N., Nicole V. BA, George Washington U., 1972; JD, Georgetown U., 1976. Bar: Va. 1977, DC 1978, Ohio 1996. Asst. to dep. staff dir. U.S. Commn. on Civil Rights, Washington, 1972-76; trial atty. FTC, 1976-79; antitrust counsel Westinghouse Electric Corp., Pitts., 1979-81; group legal counsel Dana Corp., Toledo, 1982-88; v.p., gen. counsel Packaging Corp. Am. subs. Tenneco, Evanston, Ill., 1988-95; law v.p. NCR Corp., Dayton, 1996-99; v.p., gen. counsel, sec. Dayton Superior Corp., 1999—. Adv. bd. mem. Corp. Counsel Inst., Georgetown U. Law Ctr. Author: The 1970 Census Undercount of Spanish Speaking Persons, 1974; editor: Puerto Ricans in the U.S., 1976. Capt. M.I., U.S. Army, 1965-70, Vietnam. Mem. ABA (antitrust sect.), Am. Corp. Counsel Assn., Minority Corp. Counsel Assn., Hispanic Nat. Bar Assn. (mem. adv. bd.), Georgetown Law Ctr.'s Corp. Counsel Inst. Democrat. Roman Catholic. Home: 5 Grandon Rd Dayton OH 45419-2548 Office: Ste 130 7777 Washington Village Dr Dayton OH 45459-3976 E-mail: jimtaronji@daytonsuperior.com.

TARPY, THOMAS MICHAEL, lawyer; b. Columbus, Ohio, Jan. 4, 1945; s. Thomas Michael and Catherine G. (Sharshal) T.; m. Mary Patricia Canna, Sept. 9, 1967; children: Joshua Michael, Megan Patricia, Thomas Canna, John Patrick. AB, John Carroll U., 1966; JD, Ohio State U., 1969. Bar: Ohio 1969, U.S. Dist. Ct. (so. dist.) Ohio 1972, U.S. Dist. Ct. (no. dist.) Ohio 1974, U.S. Ct. Appeals (6th cir.) 1982, U.S. Supreme Ct. 1997. Assoc. Vorys, Sater, Seymour & Pease LLP, Columbus, 1969-76, ptnr., 1977-85, 87—; v.p. Liebert Corp., 1985-87. Chmn. Columbus Graphics Commn., 1980; mem. Columbus Area Leadership Program, 1975. With U.S. Army, 1969-75. Fellow Coll. Labor and Employment Lawyers; mem. ABA, Ohio Bar Assn., Columbus Bar Assn. Office: Vorys Sater Seymour & Pease LLP PO Box 1008 52 E Gay St Columbus OH 43215-3161

TARUN, ROBERT WALTER, lawyer; b. Lake Forest, Ill., Sept. 1, 1949; s. Donald Walter and Bonnie Jean (Cruickshank) T.; m. Helen J. McSweeney, May 1, 1987; children: Abigail Esch, Tyler Vincent, Parker Donald, Aimée Dakota. AB, Stanford U., 1971; JD, DePaul U., 1974; MBA, U. Chgo., 1982. Bar: Ill. 1974, Calif. 1975, U.S. Dist. Ct. (no. dist.) Ill. 1974, U.S. Dist. Ct. (we. dist.) Ark. 1986, U.S. Dist. Ct. (so. dist.) Ind. 1995, U.S. Dist. Ct. (no. dist.) Calif. 1995, U.S. Dist. Ct. (ea. dist.) Mich. 1996, U.S. Dist. Ct. (ea. dist.) Wis. 2000, U.S. Dist. Ct. (ctrl. dist.) Ill. 2001, U.S. Ct. Appeals (7th cir.) 1975, U.S. Ct. Appeals (5th cir.) 1992, U.S. Ct. Appeals (3d cir.) 1993, U.S. Ct. Appeals (Fed. cir.) 1995, U.S. Ct. Appeals (9th and 11th cirs.) 1996, U.S. Supreme Ct. 1978. Asst. atty. gen. State of Ill., Chgo., 1974-76; asst. U.S. atty. U.S. Dept. Justice, 1976-79, dep. chief criminal div., 1979-82, exec. asst. U.S. atty. no. dist. Ill., 1982-85; ptnr. Reuben & Proctor, 1985-86, Isham, Lincoln & Beale, Chgo., 1986-88, Winston & Strawn, Chgo., 1988—. Lectr. in law U. Chgo., 2001—; adj. prof. Northwestern U. Sch. Law, 1999—2001, lectr. criminal law parctice, 2000—01; instr. Atty. Gen.'s Advocacy Inst., Washington, 1980—85, Nat. Inst. Trial Advs., 1990. Author (with Dan K. Webb): Corporate Internal Investigations, 1993—2002. Bd. dirs. Chgo. Ctrl. Area Com., 1994—. Fellow Am. Coll. Trial Lawyers (mem. fed. criminal procedure com. 1993—, admission to fellowship com. 1997-2000); mem. ABA (white collar crime inst. 1997—, planning com.), Bar Assn. San Francisco, Chgo. Bar Assn., Nat. Assn. Criminal Def. Lawyers, U. Chgo. Grad. Sch. Bus. Alumni Assn. (bd. dirs. 1986), Racquet Club, Wong Sun Soc. (San Francisco), Kenilworth Club, H.O.G. (Black Hills chpt.), Chgo. Stanford Assn. Presbyterian. Avocations: architecture, screenplays, forensic science. Office: Winston & Strawn 35 W Wacker Dr Ste 4700 Chicago IL 60601-1614 Home: 219 Leicester Rd Kenilworth IL 60043-1244

TARVESTAD, ANTHONY M. medical board executive; BA magna cum laude, Winona State U., 1973; JD, William Mitchell Coll. of Law, 1977. Exec. dir. Am. Bd. Physical Medicine and Rehab. Named Super Lawyer Minn. Jour. Law and Politics, 1994. Mem. Am. Coll. Healthcare Execs., Am. Health Laywers Assn., ABA, Am. Arbitration Assn. (arbitrator), Minn. State Bar. Assn. Office: Am Bd PM&R 21 1st St SW Ste 674 Rochester MN 55902-3007

TATAR, JEROME F. business products executive; V.p., operating officer Mead Corp., Dayton, Ohio, 1994, pres., chmn., CEO, pres., 1997—. Office: Mead Corp Courthouse Plz NE Dayton OH 45463-0001

TATE, PHIL, state legislator; b. Mar. 21, 1946; m. Nancy Cassity; 1 child, Aaron Phillip. BS, U. Mo. Oil jobber; mem. Mo. Ho. of Reps. from 3d dist.; dir. bus. expansion and attractions Dept. Econ. Devel., Jefferson City, Mo. Vice chmn. Misc. Bill and Resolution Com. Mo. Ho. of Reps., mem. Agr., Appropriations, Health and Mental Health, Edn., Legis. Rsch. Coms. Mem. Jaycees, Rotary. Democrat. Home: 901 W Grand St Gallatin MO 64640-1610 Office: Dept Econ Devel PO Box 118 Jefferson City MO 65102-0118

TATHAM, RON, marketing executive; BBA, U. Texas, Austin; MBA, Texas Tech U; PhD, U. Ala. CEO Burke Inc. Mem. Mktg. Rsch. Adv. Bd. U. Ga., U. Tex. at Arlington; adv. bd. U. Wis.; presenter in field. Co-author: Multivariate Data Analysis, 4th edition, 1994; contbr. articles to prof. jours. Office: Burke Inc 805 Central Ave Fl 5 Cincinnati OH 45202-5747

TAUB, RICHARD PAUL, social sciences educator; b. Bklyn., Apr. 16, 1937; s. Martin Glynn and Frances (Israel) T.; m. Doris Susan Leventhal, Aug. 14, 1961 (dec. Feb. 1996); children: Neela Robin, Zachariah Jacob; m. Betty G. Farrell, June 21, 2000. BA, U. Mich., 1959; MA, Harvard U., 1962, PhD in Social Relations, 1966. Asst. prof. sociology Brown U., Providence, 1965-69; from asst. prof. to Paul Klapper prof. of social scis. U. Chgo., 1969—, assoc. dean Coll. of Univ., 1982-86, chmn. com. on human devel., 2000—. Adv. bd. Neighborhood Preservation Initiative, 1993-2000; chair adv. bd. Nat. Comty. Devel. Initiative, 1991-95; dir. South Ark. Rural Devel. Study, 1988—; Disting. visitor Mac Arthur Found., 1998. Author: Community Capitalism, Bureaucrats Under Stress, (with D. Garth Taylor and Jan Dunham) Paths of Neighborhood Change, (with Doris L. Taub) Entrepreneurship in India's Small Scale Industries; editor: (with Doris L. Taub) American Society in Tocqueville's Time and Today; co-editor Studies of Urban Soc., 1978—; contbr. articles to profl. jours. Chmn. bd. St. Thomas the Apostle Sch., Chgo., 1983-86; bd. dirs. Hyde Park Kenwood Cmty. Conf., Chgo., 1972-75; bd. seminary Coop Bookstore, Chgo., 1994—; chair com. on human devel., U. Chgo., 2000—. Angell scholar U. Mich., 1956; Woodrow Wilson fellow Harvard U., 1959-60, W.E.B. DuBois Inst. fellow, 1997-98; grantee Am. Inst. Indian Studies, Ford Found., MacArthur Found., NSF, Wieboldt Found., Nat. Inst. Justice. Mem. Am. Sociol. Assn., Midwest Sociol. Soc., Assn. for Asian Studies. Avocations: bicycling, music. Office: Univ Chgo 5730 S Woodlawn Ave Chicago IL 60637 E-mail: rpt2@uchicago.edu.

TAUB, ROBERT ALLAN, lawyer; b. Denver, Nov. 25, 1923; s. Clarence Arthur and Mary Frances (Jones) T.; m. Doris Irene Schroeder, Dec. 22, 1945; children: Amanda, Jonathan, Barbara. BA, U. Chgo., 1944, JD, 1947. Bar: Ill. 1947. Legal staff Marshall Field & Co., Chgo., 1947-50; mgr. exec. compensation Ford Motor Co., Dearborn, Mich., 1950-63, asst. sect., 1963-74, dir. corp. affairs planning, 1974-98. Pres. Dearborn Community Arts Council, 1971-72; trustee Internat. Mus. Photography, George Eastman House, Rochester, N.Y., 1976—, chmn., 1979-82; mem. adv. bd. U. Mich. Dearborn, 1980—, Met. Mus. Art, N.Y.C., 1987—; trustee Henry Ford Hosp., Detroit, 1983—; chmn. Dearborn Pub. Libr., 1986—; bd. dirs., mem. exec. com., chmn. fin. com., Health Alliance Plan, 1992—. Mem. ABA, Ill. Bar Assn, Art Inst. Chicago, 1998—. Presbyterian. Home: 1824 Hawthorne St Dearborn MI 48128-1448 E-mail: rataub@mediaone.net.

TAUBMAN, ROBERT S. real estate developer; b. Detroit, Dec. 27, 1953; s. A. Alfred and Reva (Kolodney) T.; m. Julie Reyes, Aug. 27, 1999; 1 child, Alexander Alfred. BS in Econs., MA, Boston U. With Taubman Co. Inc., Bloomfield Hills, Mich., 1976—, exec. v.p., 1984—, exec. v.p., chief oper. officer, 1988-90; pres. chief exec. officer, 1990—. Bd. dirs. Taubman Ctrs. Inc., Comerica, Inc., Sotheby's Holdings, Inc., fashionmall.com. Chmn. Mich. campaign drive UNCF; bd. dirs. Beaumont Hosp.; trustee Cranbrook Ednl. Cmty. Mem. Nat. Sssn. Real Estate Investment Trusts (bd. govs.), Real Estate Roundtable (bd. dirs.), Urban Land Inst. (trustee, chmn. Detroit regional dist. coun.). Office: Taubman Co Inc 200 E Long Lake Rd Bloomfield Hills MI 48304-2360

TAUREL, SIDNEY, pharmaceutical executive; b. Casablanca, Morocco, Feb. 9, 1949; came to U.S., 1986; s. Jose and Marjorie (Afriat) T.; m. Kathryn H. Fleischmann, Mar. 22, 1977; children: Alexis, Patrick, Olivia. BSBA, Ecole des Hautes Etudes Commerciales, Paris, 1969; MBA, Columbia U., 1971. Mktg. assoc. Eli Lilly Internat. Corp., Indpls., 1971-72; mktg. planning mgr. Eli Lilly Do Brasil Limitada, Sao Paulo, Brazil, 1972-75, gen. mgr. Brazil, 1982-83; mgr. pharm. ops. Eastern Europe Eli Lilly und Elanco Gesmbh, Vienna, Austria, 1976; sales mgr. pharm. Eli Lilly France SA, Paris, 1977-79, mktg. dir. pharm., 1980-81; v.p. Europe Lilly European ops., London, 1984-85; exec. v.p. Eli Lilly Internat. Corp., Indpls., 1986, pres., 1986-91, exec. v.p. pharm. divsn., 1991-93; exec. v.p. Eli Lilly and Co., 1993—, pres. pharm. divsn., 1993—, bd. dirs., 1993—; pres., COO Eli Lilly & Co., 1996-98, CEO, 1998—. Chmn. Eli Lilly & Co., 1999—; bd. dirs. McGraw-Hill, Cies, IBM, ITT Industries; bd. overseers Columbia Bus. Sch. Bd. dirs. RCA Tennis Championships. Recipient Ellis Island medal of honor, 2000; named to Order Knight of the French Legion of Honor, 2000. Mem. Pharm. Rsch. and Mfrs. Assn. Avocations: tennis, music. Office: Eli Lilly and Co Lilly Corporate Ctr Indianapolis IN 46285 E-mail: staurel@lilly.com.

TAUSCHER, JOHN WALTER, retired pediatrician, emeritus educator; b. LaSalle, Ill., Feb. 3, 1929; s. John Robert and Ella (Danz) Tauscher; m. Mary Claire Cline, June 19, 1954 (dec. 1989); children: Michael, John, Claire, Mark, Matthew; m. Delphine Bonanni, Oct. 26, 1991. BS, U. Ill., 1952, MD, 1954. Diplomate Am. Bd. Pediatrics. Intern Cook County Hosp., Chgo., 1954-55; resident in pediatrics Hurley Med. Ctr., Flint, Mich., 1958-60; practice medicine specializing in pediatrics, 1960-75; assoc. prof. human devel. Coll. Human Medicine, Mich. State U., East Lansing, 1975-80, prof. pediatrics and human devel., 1980-94, prof. emeritus, 1994; ret., 1994. V.p. After Hours Pediatric Care, P.C., Flint, 1972-87; chmn. pediatrics Hurley Med. Ctr., 1980-90, dir. pediatric edn., dir. primary care pediatrics, 1991-94; dir. clin. svcs. Mott Children's Health Ctr., 1981-85, v.p. health affairs, 1985-91. Served with USAF, 1955-58 Recipient Outstanding Teaching award Coll. Human Medicine, Mich. State U., 1977, 84, 85, Clin. Instr. of Yr. award St. Joseph Hosp., 1977, Disting. Community Faculty award Mich. State U., 1989. Mem. AMA, Genesee County Med. Soc. (pres. 1990), Mich. State Med. Soc., Northeastern Mich. Pediatric Soc., Am. Acad. Pediatrics Roman Catholic. Home: 1069 Rayna Dr Davison MI 48423-2845 also: 1010 Ibis Ct Bradenton FL 34209-7323

TAVARES, CHARLETA B. former state legislator; Student, Spelman Coll., Ohio State U. Mem. Ohio Ho. of Reps., Columbus, 1993-98; council mem. City of Columbus, OH. Mem. Met. Human Svc. Commn. Vol. Huckleberry House, Literacy Initiative. Recipient award Black Students in Comm. Ohio State U., 1992, Ctrl. Comty House award, 1992, Pub. Children's Svc. Assn. award, 1993; named Franklin County Dem. Women's Club Sweetheart, 1993. Mem. LWV, Far East Dem. Women's Club, Columbus Area Women's Polit. Caucus, Coalition of 100 Black Women.

TAVLIN, MICHAEL JOHN, computer software company executive; b. Lincoln, Nebr., Dec. 16, 1946; BEd, Oklahoma City U., 1970; JD, U. Nebr., 1973; LLM in Taxation, Washington U., St. Louis, 1977. Bar: Nebr. 1973, Mo. 1974. Ptnr. Nelson & Harding, Lincoln, 1973-77; sr. tax. mgr. Deloitte & Touche, Lincoln and Tulsa, 1979-84, PriceWaterhouseCoopers, Tulsa, 1984-86; v.p., treas., sec. Aliant Comm. Inc. and subs., Lincoln, 1986-99; sr. v.p., CFO, treas., sec. Interactive Intelligence, Inc. and subs., Indpls., 1999—2001; CFO, gen. counsel Speedway Motors, Inc., Lincoln, 2001—. Bd. dirs. Cmty. Health Endowment, Lincoln, 1998, Woods Charitable Fund, Lincoln, 2000. Named Disting. Alumnus Oklahoma City U., 1995. Office: Speedway Motors Inc PO Box 81906 Lincoln NE 68501

TAYLOR, ALLEN M. community foundation executive; b. Cedar Rapids, Iowa, Dec. 22, 1923; AB, Princeton U., 1946; LLB, Yale U., 1949. Bar: Wis. Assoc. Foley & Lardner, Milw., 1949-57, ptnr., 1957-88, sr. ptnr., 1988-93, of counsel, 1993; chmn., CFO The Chipstone Found., 1994—. Vice-chmn., bd. dirs. The Lynde and Harry Bradley Found.; bd. dirs. Stark Hosp. Found., Med. Coll. Wis. Health Policy Inst.; adv. bd. dirs. Med. Coll. Wis. Mem. The Greater Milw. Found.; chmn. capital fund drive Milw. Symphony Orch.; steering com. Pabst Theatre Reconstruction Campaign. With USMC, 1942-45. Mem. ABA, Wisconsin Bar Assn., Assn. Bank Holding Cos. (past chmn. lawyers com.), Milw. Country Club (past pres., sec., bd. dirs.), The Milw. Club, Cap and Gown Princeton, Princeton Club N.Y. Home: 2825 E Newport Ave Milwaukee WI 53211-2922 Office: The Chipstone Found Ste 3090 777 E Wisconsin Ave Milwaukee WI 53202-5302

TAYLOR, ANDREW C. rental leasing company executive; b. 1947; Degree, Denver U., 1970. With Enterprise Rent-A-Car, St. Louis, 1972—, pres., CEO. Office: Enterprise Rent-A-Car 600 Corporate Park Dr Saint Louis MO 63105-4204

TAYLOR, ANNA DIGGS, judge; b. Washington, Dec. 9, 1932; d. Virginius Douglass and Hazel (Bramlette) Johnston; m. S. Martin Taylor, May 22, 1976; children: Douglass Johnston Diggs, Carla Cecile Diggs. BA, Barnard Coll., 1954; LLB, Yale U., 1957. Bar: D.C. 1957, Mich. 1961. Atty. Office Solicitor, Dept. Labor, W, 1957-60; asst. prosecutor Wayne County, Mich., 1961-62; asst. U.S. atty. Eastern Dist. of Mich., 1966; ptnr. Zwerdling, Maurer, Diggs & Papp, Detroit, 1970-75; asst. corp. counsel City of Detroit, 1975-79; U.S. dist. judge Eastern Dist. Mich. Detroit, 1979—. Hon. chair, trustee United Way Cmty. Found., S.E. Mich., Detroit Inst. Arts; co-chair, vol. Leadership Coun.; trustee Henry Ford Health Sys., Cmty. Found. for S.E. Mich. Mem. Fed. Bar Assn., State Bar Mich., Wolverine Bar Assn. (v.p.), Yale Law Assn. Episcopalian. Office: US Dist Ct 740 US Courthouse 231 W Lafayette Blvd Detroit MI 48226-2700

TAYLOR, CLIFFORD WOODWORTH, state supreme court justice; b. Delaware, Ohio, Nov. 9, 1942; s. Alexander E. and Carolyn (Clifford) T.; m. Lucille Taylor; 2 children. BA, U. Mich., 1964; JD, George Washington U., 1967. Asst. prosecuting atty. Ingham County, 1971-72; ptnr. Denfield, Timmer & Taylor, 1972-92; judge Mich. Ct. of Appeals, 1992-97, Supreme Ct. Justice, 1997—. Mem. standing com. on professionalism Mich. State Bar, 1992. Bd. dirs. Mich. Dyslexia Inst., 1991—, Friends of the Gov.'s Residence, 1991—; mem. St. Thomas Aquinas Ch. With USN, 1967-71. Fellow Mich. State Bar Found.; mem. Mich. Supreme Ct. Hist. Soc., Federalist Soc., Cath. Lawyers Guild, State Bar. Home: 9760 Sunny Point Dr Laingsburg MI 48848 Office: Mich Supreme Ct PO Box 300052 Lansing MI 48909*

TAYLOR, COLLETTE, public relations executive; Sr. v.p. human resources Golin/Harris Comms., Inc., Chgo., 1998, chief adminstrv. officer, 1998—. Office: Golin/Harris Comms Inc 111 E Wacker Dr Chicago IL 60601-3713

TAYLOR, DORIS DENICE, physician, entrepreneur, oncology consultant; b. Indpls., Sept. 19, 1955; d. Eugene and Mary Catherine (Ryder) T. BA, U. Minn., 1976, cert. behavior analyst, 1977, MD, 1983; BS, Purdue U., 1979. Diplomate Nat. Bd. Med. Examiners. Pvt. practice Locumtenens, 1989—; mng. dir. Sebree-Watkins-Ovbokhan Meml. Cancer Fund, Indpls. Pres., CEO Taylors of Indy Corp., Indpls.; oncologic svcs. cons. and developer; del. People to People Amb. Programs, 2002; CEO One Bed One Chair Charitable Found., Indpls. Lange scholar, U. Minn., 1980, Joseph Collins Found. scholar, 1980-81, Nat. Med. Fellowship scholar, 1980-81. Mem. AMA, Am. Soc. for Therapeutic Radiology and Oncology, Am. Soc. Clin. Oncologists, People to People Amb. Programs (del. 2002). Office: PO Box 11278 Fargo ND 58106-1278 E-mail: locumradonc@aol.com.

TAYLOR, GLEN, printing and graphics company executive, professional sports team executive; State senator Minnesota Senate, 1980-90; chmn. Taylor Corp., Mankato, Minn.; owner Minnesota Timberwolves, Minneapolis, 1994—. Office: Taylor Corp 1725 Roe Crest Dr Mankato MN 56003-1807 also: Minnesota Timberwolves Target Ctr 600 1st Ave N Minneapolis MN 55403-1416

TAYLOR, JACK C. rental and leasing company executive; b. 1922; With Lindburg Cadillac, St. Louis, 1944-50, Forrest Cadillac, St. Louis, 1951-56; chmn. bd. Enterprise Rent-A-Car, 1980—. With USN, ret. Office: Enterprise Rent-A-Car 600 Corporate Park Dr Saint Louis MO 63105-4204

TAYLOR, JEFF, reporter, editor; Reporter Kansas City Star, Detroit Free Press. Recipient Pulitzer Prize for nat. reporting, 1992, Sigma Delta Chi award. Office: Detroit Free Press Metro Desk 600 W Lafayette Blvd Detroit MI 48226-2703

TAYLOR, J(OCELYN) MARY, museum administrator, zoologist, educator; b. Portland, Oreg., May 30, 1931; d. Arnold Llewellyn and Kathleen Mary (Yorke) T.; m. Joseph William Kamp, Mar. 18, 1972 (dec.); m. Wesley Kingston Whitten, Mar. 20, 2001. B.A., Smith Coll., 1952; M.A., U. Calif., Berkeley, 1953, Ph.D., 1959. Instr. zoology Wellesley Coll., 1959-61, asst. prof. zoology, 1961-65; assoc. prof. zoology U. B.C.,

1965-74; dir. Cowan Vertebrate Mus., 1965-82, prof. dept. zoology, 1974-82; collaborative scientist Oreg. Regional Primate Research Ctr., 1983-87; prof. (courtesy) dept. fisheries and wildlife Oreg. State U., 1984-95; dir. Cleve. Mus. Nat. History, 1987-96, dir. emerita, 1996—. Adj. prof. dept. biology Case Western Res. U., 1987-96. Assoc. editor Jour. Mammalogy, 1981-82. Contbr. numerous articles to sci. jours. Trustee Benjamin Rose Inst., 1988-93, Western Res. Acad., 1989-94, U. Circle, Inc., 1987-96, The Cleve. Aquarium, 1990-93, Cleve. Access to the Arts, 1992-96; corp. bd. Holden Arboretum, 1988-98, The Cleve. Mus. Natural History, 1996—, The Catlin Gabel Sch., 1998-2000, The Inst. for the Northwest, 1999—. Recipient Lake County Environ. award, Lake county metro parks.; Fulbright scholar, 1954-55; Lalor Found. grantee, 1962-63; NSF grantee, 1963-71; NRC Can. grantee, 1966-84; Killam Sr. Rsch. fellow, 1978-79 Mem. Soc. Women Geographers, Am. Soc. Mammalogists (1st v.p. 1978-82, pres. 1982-84, Hartley T. Jackson award 1993, hon. mem. 2001), Australian Mammal Soc., Cooper Ornithol., Assn. Sci. Mus. Dirs. (v.p. 1990-93), Rodent Specialist Group of Species Survival Commn. (chmn. 1989-93), Sigma Xi. Home: 2718 SW Old Orchard Rd Portland OR 97201-1637 E-mail: taylorjm@teleport.com.

TAYLOR, JOEL SANFORD, retired lawyer; b. Hazleton, Pa., Oct. 8, 1942; s. Robert Joseph and Alice Josephine (Sanford) T.; m. Donna Rae Caron, Mar. 26, 1967; children: Jason, Adam, Jeremy. BA, Swarthmore Coll., 1965; LLB, Columbia U., 1968. Bar: N.Y. 1969, U.S. Ct. Appeals (2d cir.) 1970, U.S. Dist. Ct. (no. dist.) Ohio 1974, U.S. Supreme Ct. 1974, U.S. Dist. Ct. (so. dist.) Ohio 1975, U.S. Ct. Appeals (6th cir.) 1975, U.S. Dist. Ct. (ea. dist.) Ky. 1979. Law clk. hon. Constance B. Motley U.S. Dist. Ct., N.Y.C., 1968-69; assoc. Paul, Weiss, Rifkind, Wharton & Garrison, 1969-72; exec. asst. Ohio Office of Budget & Mgmt., Columbus, Ohio, 1972-74; asst. atty. gen. Ohio Atty. Gen., 1974-83, chief counsel, 1983-91; ptnr. Dinsmore & Shohl, 1991-2000; fin. dir. City of Columbus, 2000—. Pres. Ohio Sundry Claims Bd., Columbus, 1972-74, Ohio State Controlling Bd., Columbus, 1973-74; mem., bd. trustees Ohio State Tchrs. Retirement Sys., Columbus, 1986-91, Solid Waste Authority Ctrl. Ohio, 2001—. Trustee Franklin County Solid Waste Authority, 2001—. Mem. Govt. Fin. Officers Assn., Columbia Law Alumni Assn., Ohio Sierra Club, Nat. Wildlife Fedn., Nature Conservany. Office: City Hall 90 W Broad St Columbus OH 43215-9000 E-mail: jstaylor@cmhmetro.net.

TAYLOR, KATHLEEN (CHRISTINE), physical chemist, researcher; b. Cambridge, Mass., Mar. 16, 1942; d. John F. and Anna M. (Maloney) T. BA in Chemistry, Douglass Coll., New Brunswick, N.J., 1964; PhD in Phys. Chemistry, Northwestern U., 1968. Postdoctoral fellow U. Edinburgh, Scotland, 1968-70; assoc. sr. rsch. chemist Gen. Motors Rsch. Labs., Warren, Mich., 1970-74, sr. rsch. chemist, 1974-75, asst. phys. chemistry dept. head, 1975-83, environ. sci. dept. head, 1983-85, phys. chemistry dept. head, 1985-96; physics and phys. chemistry dept. head Gen. Motors Global Rsch. & Devel. Operations, 1995-98, materials and protesses dir., 1998—2002. Recipient Mich. Sci. Trailblazer award Detroit Sci. Ctr., 1986. Fellow AAAS, mem. NAE, Am. Chem. Soc. (Garvan medal 1989), Materials Rsch. Soc. (treas. 1984, 2d v.p. 1985, 1st v.p. 1986, pres. 1987), Soc. Automotive Engrs., The Catalysis Soc., Sigma Xi.

TAYLOR, KENNETH NATHANIEL, publishing executive, writer; b. Portland, Oreg., May 8, 1917; s. George Nathaniel and Charlotte Bodwell (Huff) T.; m. Margaret Louise West, Sept. 13, 1940; children: Becky, John, Martha, Peter, Janet, Mark, Cynthia, Gretchen, Mary Lee, Alison. BA, Wheaton Coll., 1938, DLitt (hon.), 1965; student, Dallas Theol. Sem., 1940-43; ThM, No. Bapt. Theol. Sem., 1944; DLitt (hon.), Trinity Evang. Div. Sch., 1972; LHD (hon.), Huntington Coll., 1974, Taylor U., 1989. With Moody Press (pub. protestant religious lit.), Chgo., 1947-63, dir., 1948-62, Moody Lit. Mission (prodn. and distbn. lit.), 1948-62; pres. Tyndale House Publishers, 1963-84, chmn. bd., 1984—, Coverdale House Pubs., London, Eng., 1969-79. Pres. Tyndale House Found., 1964-79, bd. dirs., 1964—; dir. Inter-Varsity Christian Fellowship, 1956-59, Evang. Lit. Overseas, 1951-70, Short Terms Abroad, 1963-77; pres. Living Bibles Internat., Wheaton, Ill., 1968-77, internat. pres., 1977-90, internat. chmn. emeritus, 1990-92; chmn. Unilit., Inc., Portland, 1972-73 Author: Is Christianity Credible, 1946, Living Letters: The Paraphrased Epistles, 1962; juveniles Stories for the Children's Hour, 1953, Devotions for the Children's Hour, 1954, I See, 1958 (reprinted as Small Talks About God, 1995), Bible in Pictures for Little Eyes, 1956, Lost on the Trail, 1959, Romans for the Children's Hour, 1959; Living Prophecies - The Minor Prophets Paraphrased, 1965, Living Gospels, 1966, Living Psalms and Proverbs With the Major Prophets Paraphrased, 1967, The Living New Testament, 1967, Almost 12, 1968, revised, 1995, Living Lessons of Life and Love, 1968, Living Books of Moses, 1969, Living History of Israel, 1970, The Living Bible, 1971, Taylor's Bible Story Book, 1970, The Lord Is My Strength, 1975; juveniles What High School Students Should Know About Creation, 1983, What High School Students Should Know About Evolution, 1983, Big Thoughts for Little People, 1983, Giant Steps for Little People, 1985, Wise Words for Little People, 1987, Next Steps for New Christians (originally How To Grow), 1989, My First Bible in Pictures, 1989 (ann. Angel award 1990, Platinum Book award 1990), The Good Samaritan, 1989, Jesus Feeds A Crowd, 1989, The Lost Sheep, 1989, The Prodigal Son, 1989; Good News for Little People, 1991 (ann. Angel award 1992), My Life, A Guided Tour, 1991, Daniel and the Lions' Den, 1992, Noah's Ark, 1992, Family-Time Bible in Pictures, 1992, A Boy Helps Jesus, 1994, The Good Neighbor, 1994, Noah Builds a Boat, 1994, A Very Special Baby, 1994, The Story of Noah's Ark, 1994, Small Talks About God, 1995, Everything a Child Should Know About God, 1996; co-editor: The Bible for Children, 1990 (ann. Angel award 1991); pub. The Christian Reader, 1964-92, Have a Good Day, 68—; co-author: My First Bible Words: A Kid's Devotional, 1998, Right Choices, 1999, Family Devotions With Children, 1999, A Child's First Bible, 2000. Bd. dirs. Christian Libr. Svc., 1972-75, InterSkrift forlage Aktiebolag, Sweden, Internat. Bible Soc., 1992-94; trustee Living Bible Found., Fuller Theol. Sem.; mem. adv. bd. Internat. Bible Reading Assn. Recipient citation Layman's Nat. Bible Com., 1971; award Religious Heritage Am., 1972; disting. svc. citation Internat. Soc. Christian Endeavor, 1973; Nelson Bible award, 1973; Better World award VFW Aux., 1974; disting. pub. svc. award 1974; Recognition award Urban Ministries, Inc., 1977; Svc. award Wheaton Coll. Alumni Assn., 1977; Crusader award Wheaton Coll., 1979; Gutenberg award Chgo. Bible Soc., 1981; Internat. Christian Edn. Assn. award, 1983, Disting. Svc. to Family award Wheaton Coll. Alumni Assn.; Inducted into DuPage County Heritage Gallery, 1983; named Man of Yr. Com. Internat. Goodwill, 1983; recipient 1st Ann. Lit. award Evang. Lit. Overseas, 1983; Svc. award YFC/USA, 1984; Gold Medallion Achievement award Evang. Pubs. Assn., 1984; named to Christian Booksellers Hall of Fame, 1989; recipient Ann. James DeForest Murch award Nat. Assn. Evangelicals, 1995, Annual Golden Word award Internat. Bible Soc., 1996. Evangelical Christian Publ. Assn. awd. for leadership, example, integrity, creativity, and passion for communicating the Word of God, 1997. Mem. Wheaton Coll. Scholastic Honor Soc., Wheaton Coll. Alumni Assn. (Disting. Svc. to Family award 2000). Home: 1515 E Forest Ave Wheaton IL 60187-4469 Office: 351 Executive Dr Carol Stream IL 60188-2420

TAYLOR, KOKO, singer; Albums include The Earthshaker, from the Heart of a Woman, I Got What It Takes, Queen of the Blues, 1985, Koko Taylor, 1987, Live From Chicago: An Audience with the Queen, 1987, Teaches Old Standard New Tricks, Jump for Joy, 1990, What It Takes: The Chess Years, 1991, Force of Nature, 1994. Office: Alligator Records care Nora Kinnally PO Box 60234 Chicago IL 60660-0234

TAYLOR, MARK DOUGLAS, publishing executive; b. Geneva, Jan. 16, 1951; s. Kenneth Nathaniel and Margaret Louise (West) T.; m. Carol E. Rogers, May 28, 1973; children: Jeremy Peter, Kristen Elizabeth, Margaret Louise, Rebecca Cynthia, Stephen Rogers. BA, Duke U., 1973. Exec. dir. Tyndale House Found., Wheaton, Ill., 1973-78; v.p. Tyndale House Pubs., 1978-84, pres., chief exec. officer, 1984—. Dir. Living Bibles Internat. U.S., Naperville, Ill., 1972-92; bd. trustees Taylor U., 1998—. Author The Complete Book of Bible Literacy, 1992. Mem. Wheaton Liquor Control Commn., 1986—, chmn., 1994—; chmn. bd. dirs. Outreach Cmty. Ctr., 1986-93. Mem. Internat. Bible Soc. (bd. dirs. 1992-96). Office: Tyndale House Publishers Inc PO Box 80 Wheaton IL 60189-0080

TAYLOR, MICHAEL ALAN, psychiatrist; b. N.Y.C., Mar. 6, 1940; s. Edward D. and Clara D. T.; m. Ellen Schoenfield, June 28, 1963; children— Christopher, Andrew. B.A., Cornell U., 1961; M.D., N.Y. Med. Coll., 1965. Intern Lenox Hill Hosp., N.Y.C., 1965-66; resident N.Y. Med. Coll., 1966-69, asst. prof. psychiatry, 1971-73; asso. prof. SUNY Med. Sch., Stony Brook, 1973-76; prof. psychiatry Univ. Health Scis., Chgo. Med. Sch., 1976—, dept., 1976-94. Author: The Neuropsychiatric Mental Status Examination, 1981; sr. author: General Hospital Psychiatry, 1985, The Neuropsychiatric Guide to Modern Everyday Psychiatry, 1993, The Fundamentals of Neuropsychiatry, 1999; editor-in-chief Neuropsychiat., Neuropsychology and Behavioral Neurology Jour.; also numerous articles. Served to lt. comdr. M.C. USNR, 1969-71. Grantee NIMH, 1971-73; Grantee Ill. Dept. Mental Health, 1976-81; VA grantee, 1985-93. Mem. Am. Psychopath. Assn. Office: FUHS Chgo Med Sch 3333 Green Bay Rd North Chicago IL 60064-3037

TAYLOR, RAY, state senator; b. Steamboat Rock, Iowa, June 4, 1923; s. Leonard Allen and Mary Delilah (Huffman) T.; m. Mary Allen, Aug. 29, 1924; chidlren: Gordon, Laura Rae Taylor Hansmann, Karol Ann Taylor Rogers, Jean Lorraine Taylor Mahl. Student, U. No. Iowa, 1940-41, Baylor U., 1948-49. Farmer, Steamboat Rock, Iowa, 1943—; mem. Iowa Senate, 1973-95. Bd. dirs., sec. Am. Legis. Exch. Coun., 1979-94; sec. Hardin County Farm Bur., 1970-72; mem. Iowa divsn. bds. Am. Cancer Soc.; chmn. Am. Revolution Bicentennial com.; mem. Steamboat Rock Cmty. Sch. Bd., 1955-70; coord. Rep. youth, 1968-72; chmn. bd. Faith Bapt. Bible Coll.; pres. Eldora Area Chamber and Devel. Coun., 1998—2001; mem. Eldora Indsl. Corp., 1998—; pres. Am. Coun. Christian Chs.; chmn. Iowans for Responsible Govt.; bd. dirs. Iowans for Tax Relief, 1995—; chmn. Steamboat Rock Schoolhouse Com., 2000—. Named Guardian of Small Bus. NFIB/Iowa, 1989-90, for outstanding support for good govt. and accessible, affordable health care in Iowa, Iowa Physician Asst. Soc., 1991; Ind. Bapt. fellow of the Midwest, Christian Patriots, 1994, Hon. alumnus Faith Bapt. Bible Coll. & Theol. Sem., 1995; recipient Contenders award Am. Coun. Christian Chs., 1991, Legislator of Yr. award Iowa Soc. of Friends, 1991-92. Mem. Wildlife Club, Eldora Rotary (v.p. 2001). Baptist. Home: 31363 185th St Steamboat Rock IA 50672-8107 E-mail: raymaryt@netins.net.

TAYLOR, ROBERT HOMER, quality assurance professional, pilot; b. Rochester, N.Y., Mar. 18, 1922; s. C. Gilbert and Josephine Mary (Woodward) T.; m. Mignon Jane Beight, Aug. 1945; children: Robert Jr., Douglas Beight, Scott Woodward, Sondra Lee. BSME, Case Western Res. U., 1947. Commd. 2d lt. USAF, 1944, advanced through grades to lt. col., 1975; v.p., gen. mgr. Taylor Corp., 1947-53; mgr. quality assurance Spectra Physics Laserplane, Dayton, Ohio, 1976-89; pres., gen. mgr. CON-AV Corp., Tipp City, 1989—, pres., sec., 1990—. Chief quality assurance staff on NASA Mercury Booster for USAF, Cape Canaveral, Fla., 1961-63; mgr. nuc. tng. weapons devel. USAF Weapons Lab., 1964-67; CAT I test mgr. F-111, 1967-68; instr. pilot C-7, tng. officer, Vietnam, 1969; project element monitor T-43, attache, A-37, C-130 aircraft, Pentagon, 1970-74; br. chief WPAFB, 1974-75. Advisor Aero Scis. Alternatives, Tipp City, 1990—. Lt. col. CAP, Vietnam. Decorated Air medal with three oak leaf clusters, DFC; named to Aviation Hall of Fame, 1986. Mem. VFW, Exptl. Aircraft Assn., Flying Angels, Inc. (pres. 1991), Vets. Am., Masons, Beta Theta Pi (Case chpt. pres. 1942), Theta Tau, Early Birds. Episcopalian. Avocations: boating, flying, fishing, refurbishing antique aircraft. Home: 5855 Us Route 40 Tipp City OH 45371-9419 Office: CON-AV Corp 5855 Us Route 40 Tipp City OH 45371-9419

TAYLOR, ROGER LEE, lawyer, academic administrator; b. Canton, Ill., Apr. 6, 1941; s. Ivan and Pauline Helen (Mahr) T.; m. E. Anne Zweifel, June 13, 1964. BA, Knox Coll., 1963; JD cum laude, Northwestern U., 1971. Bar: Ill. 1971, U.S. Dist. Ct. (no. dist.) Ill. 1971, U.S. Dist. Ct. (no. dist.) Tex. 1975, U.S. Ct. Appeals (7th cir.) 1972, U.S. Ct. Appeals (5th and 11th cirs.) 1981, U.S. Supreme Ct. 1975. Assoc. Kirkland & Ellis, Chgo., 1971-78, ptnr., 1978—; pres. Knox Coll., Galesburg, 2002—. Trustee Knox Coll., interim pres. 2002. Mem. ABA, Chgo. Coun. Lawyers, Friends of the Parks (bd. dirs.), Order of Coif, Univ. Club, Mid-Am. Club Chgo., Soangetaha Country Club (Galesburg, Ill.). Office: Knox College Galesburg IL 61401

TAYLOR, RONALD LEE, academic administrator; b. Urbana, Ill., Nov. 11, 1943; s. Lee R. and Katherine L. (Becker) Taylor; m. Patricia D. Fitsimmons, Mar. 10, 1973; children: Jamie, Lara, Meredith, Dana. AB, Harvard U., 1966; MBA, Stanford U., 1971. Asst. contr. Bell & Howell, Chgo., 1971-73; pres. DeVry Inc./Keller Grad. Sch., 1973—. Bd. dirs. La Petite Acad., Inc.; mem. Commn. Ednl. Credit and Credentials, 1997—2000, Commn. Govt. and Pub. Affairs, 2001—. Pres. Hinsdale (Ill.) Sch. Bd., 1983—91; com. chmn. Ill. Bd. Higher Edn., Springfield, 1985—; mem. mgmt. bd. Stanford U. Sch. Bus. Mem.: Am. Coun. Edn., Ill. C. of C. (edn. com. 1987—, bd. dirs.). Office: DeVry Inc 1 Tower Ln Ste 1000 Hinsdale IL 60181-4663 E-mail: rtaylor@devry.com.

TAYLOR, S. MARTIN, utilities executive; BS, Western Mich. U., 1964; JD, Detroit Coll. Law, 67. Dir. Mich. Employment Security Commn., 1971—84, Mich. Dept. Labor, 1983—89; pres. New Detroit Inc.; v.p. corp. and public affairs Detroit Edison (now DTE Energy Co.), 1989—2001, sr. v.p. human resources and corp. affairs. Bd. regents U. Mich., Ann Arbor, 1996—; chmn. Detroit's Future; mem., former chmn. Citizen's Rsch. Coun.; mem. Detroit Urban League; pres. Detroit Zool. Commn.; chmn. mayoral campaign Mayor Dennis Archer; former bd. dirs. Marygrove Coll., Detroit Symphony Orch., Karmanos Cancer Inst. Democrat. Office: 2000 2d Ave Ste 2428 Detroit MI 48226-1279

TAYLOR, SCOTT, radio personality; Radio host KUDL, Westwood, Kans. Office: KUDL 4935 Belinder Shawnee Mission KS 66205

TAYLOR, STEPHEN LLOYD, food toxicologist, educator, food scientist; b. Portland, Oreg., July 19, 1946; s. Lloyd Emerson and Frances Hattie (Hanson) T.; m. Susan Annette Kerns, June 23, 1973; children: Amanda, Andrew. BS in Food Sci. Tech., Oreg. State U., 1968, MS in Food Sci. Tech., 1969; PhD in Biochemistry, U. Calif., Davis, 1973. Research assoc. U. Calif., Davis, 1973-74, research fellow, 1974-75; chief food toxicology Letterman Army Inst., San Francisco, 1975-78; asst. prof. food toxicology U. Wis., Madison, 1978-83, assoc. prof., 1983-87; head dept. food sci. technology, dir. Food Processing Ctr. U. Nebr., Lincoln, 1987—. Cons. in field, 1978—. Contbr. articles to profl. jours. Fellow: Inst. Food Technologists (divsn. chmn. 1981—82, sect. chmn. 1984—85, exec. com. 1988—91), Nat. Acad. Scis. (bd. food and nutrition), Nat. Inst. Environ. Health Sco.; mem.: Soc. Toxicology, Am. Chem. Soc., Am. Acad. Allergy, Asthma and Immunology. Democrat. Presbyterian. Home: 941 Evergreen Dr Lincoln NE 68510-4131 Office: U Nebr Dept Food Sci Tech Lincoln NE 68583-0919 E-mail: staylor@unl.edu.

TAYLOR, STEVE HENRY, zoologist; b. Inglewood, Calif., Mar. 18, 1947; s. Raymond Marten and Ardath (Metz) T.; 1 child, Michael Travis; m. Sarah Margaret Young, May 14, 1993. BA in Biology, U. Calif.-Irvine, 1969. Animal keeper Los Angeles Zoo, 1972-75, assoc. curator, 1975-76; children's zoo mgr. San Francisco Zoo, 1976-81; zoo dir. Sacramento Zoo, 1981-88; dir. Cleve. Met. Zoo, 1989—. Bd. dirs. Sacramento Soc. Prevention Cruelty to Animals, 1983-87, Sacramento Red Cross, 1988-89, Conv. and Visitor Bur. of Greater Cleve., 1995—, Leadership Cleveland Class 1997; mem. admissions com. United Way, 1999. Recipient Robert P. Bergman Impact award Convention & Visitors Bur. Greater Cleve., 2000. Fellow Am. Assn. Zool. Parks and Aquariums (infant care diet advisor 1979, 85, bd. dirs. 1987-93, pres. 1991-92, chmn. pub. edn. com. 1987-89, bd. regents, mgmt. sch., chmn. accreditation com. 1998, 99, Outstanding Svc. award 1979, 85, 88, 89, 91, 95, 98, 99, 2001); mem. Conservation Breeding Specialist Group, World Assn. Zoos and Aquariums, The Wilds (bd. dirs. Ohio club), Sierra Club, Audubon Soc. Democrat. Home: 1265 Elmwood Rd Rocky River OH 44116-2236 Office: Cleveland Metroparks Zoo 3900 Wildlife Way Cleveland OH 44109-3132 E-mail: sht@clevelandmetroparks.com.

TAYLOR, WILLIAM, state legislator; Mem. from dist. 63 Ohio State Ho. of Reps., 1995—. Address: 100 Eastwood Dr Norwalk OH 44857-1105 Office: Ohio Ho of Reps State House Columbus OH 43215

TEAGAN, JOHN GERARD, newspaper executive; b. Detroit, Sept. 23, 1947; s. Stanley John and Margaret Suzanne (Sullivan) T.; m. Carla Kay Eurich, Sept. 13, 1975; 1 child, Elizabeth Margaret. B.B.A., U. Notre Dame, 1969. C.P.A., Mich. Audit supr. Ernst & Whinney (C.P.A.s), Detroit, 1969-73; acctg. mgr. Detroit Free Press, 1973-77, treas., controller, 1977-83, v.p. fin., treas., 1983-89, v.p., bus. mgr., 1989—. Adv. bd. Providence Hosp., Southfield, Mich., 1984-93, sec., 1989, vice chmn. 1990, chmn., 1991; trustee Grosse Pointe (Mich.) Acad., 1990-96, Children's Home Detroit, Grosse Pointe, 1997—; bd. dirs., treas. Free Press Charities, Inc.; bd. dirs. Providence Hosp. and Med. Ctrs., Southfield, 1998—; Metro Detroit bd. dirs. Am. Heart Assn., 1999—; bd. dirs. Boysville of Mich., Inc., 2001—' cmty. adv. bd. Knight Found., 2002—. Mem. AICPA, Internat. Newspaper Fin. Execs., Mich. Assn. CPAs, Grosse Pointe Yacht Club. Roman Catholic. Office: Detroit Free Press Inc 600 W Fort St Detroit MI 48226-2706 E-mail: teagan@freepress.com.

TEASDALE, KENNETH FULBRIGHT, lawyer; b. St. Louis, Nov. 8, 1934; s. Kenneth and Ann (Fulbright) T.; m. Elizabeth Driscol Langdon, June 13, 1964; children: Caroline, Doug, Cindy. AB, Amherst Coll., 1956; LLB, Washington U., St. Louis, 1961. Bar: Mo. 1961. Atty. antitrust div. U.S. Dept. Justice, Washington, 1961-62; asst. counsel Dem. Policy Com. U.S. Senate, 1962-63, gen. counsel Dem. Policy Com., asst. to majority leader, 1963-64; assoc. Armstrong, Teasdale, Kramer & Vaughan, St. Louis, 1964-67, ptnr., 1967-86; mng. ptnr. Armstrong, Teasdale, Schlafly & Davis, 1986-93, chmn. of firm, 1993—. Trustee United Way Greater St. Louis, Sci. Ctr. St. Louis, St. Louis Art Mus. ; trustee, chmn. bd. regents St. Louis U.; mem. nat. coun. Washington U. Law Sch., 1988—. Mem. ABA, Bar Assn. Mo., Bar Assn. St. Louis, Racquet Club, Noonday Club, Old Warson Country Club. Episcopalian. Office: Armstrong Teasdale Schlafly & Davis Metropolitan Sq Saint Louis MO 63102-2733

TEATER, DOROTHY SEATH, retired county official; b. Manhattan, Kans., Feb. 11, 1931; d. Dwight Moody and Martha (Stahnke) Seath; m. Robert Woodson Teater, May 24, 1952; children: David Dwight, James Stanley, Donald Robert, Andrew Scott. BS, U. Ky., 1951; MS, Ohio State U., 1954. Home econs. tchr. Georgetown (Ky.) City Schs., 1951-53; extension specialist Ohio Coop. Extension, Columbus, 1967-73; consumer affairs adminstr. City of Columbus, 1974-79, Bank One Columbus NA, 1980-85; councilmember Columbus City Coun., 1980-85; commr. Franklin County, Columbus, Ohio, 1985-2000; ret. Mem. Columbus Met. Area Cmty. Action Orgn.; mem. adv. bd. Ohio Housing Trust; chairwoman Franklin County Children's Cabinet. Bd. dirs. BBB; mem. hon. adv. bd. Girl Scouts. Recipient Outstanding Alumnus award U. Ky., 1989, Women of Achievement award YWCA, 1995, Disting. Svc. award Ohio State U., 1997; named Disting. Alumni, Ohio State U., 1977. Mem. County Commrs. Assn. Ohio (pres. 1994), Columbus Met. Club, Greater Columbus C. of C. (Columbus award 1997). Republican. Methodist. Avocations: gardening, sewing.

TEETERS, JOSEPH LEE, mathematician, consultant; b. Caney, Kans., Dec. 10, 1934; s. Jesse L. and Marie (Tapper) Teeters; m. Janet L. Hamm, June 18, 1984; children: Jeffrey, Susan, Christopher. Student, Colo. Sch. Mines, 1956, U. Kans., 1957; MA in Math., U. No. Colo., 1960, EdD in Math., 1968. Cert. secondary sch. tchr., Colo., Ill., hazard waste profl., OSHA. Exploration geologist Ohio Oil Co., Rawlings, Wyo., 1956-57; instr. Stout State U., Menomonie, Wis., 1960-62; asst. prof. Baker U., Baldwin City, Kans., 1962-65; temp. instr. U. No. Colo., Greeley, 1965-68; asst. prof. Western State Coll., Gunnison, Colo., 1968-69; prof. U. Wis., Eau Claire, 1969-88; cons. assoc. Delphi Data, Corona, Calif., 1989-98; ind. mathematician and cons., Lake Zurich, Ill., 1998—. Land surveying cons. Donaldson Engring., Menomonie, 1960-62; land boundary cons. ACLU, Eau Claire, 1974; lectr., spkr., cons. in field. Author: Creating Escher-Type Drawings, 1977; designer tessellation art; contbr. cover designs for profl. pubis. Active Forest Lake (Ill.) Cmty. Assn., 1990—; sr. citizen trainer Marathon Challenge, St. Louis, 1994; mem. Golden Colo. Civic Orch., 1956; unicyclist Kans. State Sunflower State Games. Grantee NSF, 1965, U. New Orleans, 1987. Mem. Internat. Assn. for Math. Geology, Internat. Platform Assn., Stanton County Kans. Hist. Assn., No Man's Land Hist. Soc., Santa Fe Trail Assn., Kans. Trails Assn., Am. Volkssport Assn. (triathlete), Colo. Sch. of Mines Assn., Tiblow Trailblazers (sports cons. 1994—), Sherman County Kans. Hist. Soc., Kappa Kappa Psi, Sigma Gamma Epsilon, Phi Delta Kappa. Achievements include creation of magnetic fishing tool for small sand screen well openings, designing and development of motion activated vortiginous reflector system(s) for bicycles, creation of a multi-function recursive algorithm which yields (with each use) a unique random lottery number ball quick-pick selection result, and two successful completions of the Boston Marathon as well as six other 26.2 mile running events. Avocations: raising St. Bernards, designing birdhouses, planning and building full size windmills. Home and Office: 21635 W Ravine Rd Lake Zurich IL 60047-8890

TEICHNER, BRUCE A. lawyer; b. Chgo. BA, U. Iowa, 1981; JD, De Paul U., 1985; MBA, U. Chgo., 1997. Legal writing tchg. asst. Coll. Law De Paul U., Chgo., 1982-83; assoc. coun. Allstate Ins. Co., Northbrook, Ill. Mem. writing staff De Paul Law Rev., 1983-85; contbr. articles to profl. jours. Mem. ABA, Chgo. Bar Assn. (corp. law coms.), Am. Corp. Counsel Assn. (assoc. counsel), Phi Beta Kappa. Office: Allstate Ins Co 3075 Sanders Rd Ste G5A Northbrook IL 60062-7127 E-mail: bteichner@allstate.com.

TEICHNER, LESTER, management consulting executive; b. Chgo., Apr. 21, 1944; s. Ben Bernard and Eva Bertha (Weinberg) T.; m. Barbara Rae Bush, Jan. 30, 1966 (div. Aug. 1969); m. Doris Jean Ayres, Jan. 31, 1980; children: Lauren Ayres, Caroline Ayres. BSEE, U. Ill., 1965; MBA in Mktg. and Fin., U. Chgo., 1969. Sales engr. Westinghouse Electric Corp., Chgo., 1965-69; v.p. ops. Intec Inc., 1969-74; pres., CEO The Chgo. Group Inc., 1974—, also bd. dirs., 1974—. Bd. dirs. Strategic Processing Inc., N.Y.C., Dees Communications Ltd., Vancouver, B.C., Maxcor Mfg. Co., Colorado Springs; CEO, bd. dirs. Axcess Worldwide Ltd., Coal Gasification, Inc., Chgo.; guest lectr. U. Chgo. Grad. Sch. Bus., 1982-95. Co-inventor U.S. patent electronic marketplace; contbr. articles to profl. publs. Mem. The Chgo. Forum, 1976—; bd. dirs. Am. Israeli C. of C. Mem. Am. Mgmt.

Assn., Am. Mktg. Assn., Midwest Planning Assn. (bd. dirs. 1981). Republican. Jewish. Avocations: comml. renovation, astronomy, skiing, venture capital investment. Home: 2230 N Seminary Ave Chicago IL 60614-3507 Office: The Chgo Group Inc 744 N Wells St Chicago IL 60610-3521

TEITELBAUM, STEVEN LAZARUS, pathology educator; b. Bklyn., June 29, 1938; s. Hyman and Rose Leah (Harnick) T.; m. Marilyn Ruth Schaffner; children: Caren Beth, Aaron Michael, Rebecca Lee. BA, Columbia U., 1960; MD, Washington U., St. Louis, 1964. Intern Washington U. Sch. Medicine, St. Louis, 1964-65, 3d. yr. asst. resident, ACS clin. fellow, 1967-68; intern NYU, 1965-66, 2d yr. resident, 1966-67; assoc. pathologist Jewish Hosp. at Washington U. Med. Ctr., St. Louis, 1969-89, pathologist-in-chief, 1987-96; assoc. pathologist Barnes-Jewish Hosp., 1986—; pathologist St. Louis Shriners Hosp. for Crippled Children, 1986—; Wilma and Roswell Messing prof. pathology Washington U. Sch. Medicine, St. Louis, 1987—. Mem. Othopedics and Musculoskeletal Study Sect. NIH, 1983-87. Contbr. numerous sci. articles to med. jours., 1965—, 12 chpts. to med. books and texts, 1976—; mem. editorial bd. Calcified Tissue Internat., 1980-85, 89-91, Human Pathology; mem. bd. assoc. editors Jour. Orthopaedic Rsch., Jour. Cellular Biochemistry. Mem. Am. Soc. Clin. Investigation, Assn. Am. Physicians, Am. Acad. Orthopaedic Surgeons (Ann Doner Vaughan Kappa Delta award 1988), Paget's Disease Found. (adv. panel), Am. Soc. for Bone and Mineral Rsch. (pres. 1993, William F. Neuman award 1998), Fed. Am. Soc. Expl. Biology (bd. dirs. 1997—, pres. 2002--). Office: Washington U Sch Medicine 216 S Kingshighway Blvd Saint Louis MO 63110-1026 E-mail: teitelbs@medicine.wustl.edu.

TEITELMAN, RICHARD BERTRAM, judge; b. Phila., Sept. 25, 1947; s. Nathan and May B. (Schreibman) T. BA in Math., U. Pa., 1969; JD, Washington U., St. Louis, 1973. Bar: Mo. 1974. Pvt. practice, St. Louis, 1974-75; staff atty. Legal Svcs. Ea. Mo., 1975-76, mng. atty., 1976-80, exec. dir., gen. counsel, 1980—; judge Mo. Ct. Appeals (ea. dist.), 1997—2000, Supreme Ct., 2002—. Bd. dirs., Citizens for Mo.'s Children, St. Louis, 1988—. Recipient Durward K. McDaniel award, Am. Coun. of Blind, 1986. Mem. ABA, Mo. Bar, Bar Assn. Met. St. Louis (pres. 1989-90; award of merit, young lawyers sect., 1985), Mound City Bar Assn., Lawyers Assn., St. Louis, Women Lawyers' Assn. Greater St. Louis, St. Louis County Bar Assn., Am. Blind Lawyers Assn., St. Louis Bar Found., Am. Judicature Soc. (bd. dirs. 1986—), Leadership St. Louis. Office: Legal Svcs Ea Mo 625 N Euclid Ave Saint Louis MO 63108-1660*

TELFER, MARGARET CLARE, internist, hematologist, oncologist; b. Manila, The Philippines, Apr. 9, 1939; came to U.S., 1941; d. James Gavin and Margaret Adele (Baldwin) T. BA, Stanford U., 1961; MD, Washington U., St. Louis, 1965. Diplomate Am. Bd. Internal Medicine, Am. Bd. Hematology, Am. Bd. Oncology; lic. Ill., Mo. Resident in medicine Michael Reese Hosp., Chgo., 1968, fellow in hematology and oncology, 1970, assoc. attending physician, 1970-72, dir. Hemophilia Ctr., 1971—, interim dir. div. hematology and oncology, 1971-74, 81-84, 89—, attending physician, 1972—, Rush-Presbyn. St. Luke's Hosp., 1999—, Olympia Fields (Ill.) Hosp., 1999—, Cook County Hosp., Chgo., 2000—; asst. prof. medicine U. Chgo., 1975-80, assoc. prof. medicine, 1980-85, assoc. prof. clin. medicine, 1985-89; assoc. prof. medicine U. Ill., Chgo., 1990-2001, Rush U., Chgo., 2001—. Mem. med. adv. bd. Hemophilia Found. Ill., 1971, chmn., 1972—83, lectr. annual symposium, 1978—84; mem. med. adv. bd. State of Ill. Hemophilia Program; dir. hematology-oncology fellowship program Michael Reese Hosp., 1971—75, 1981—84, 1989—2000, lectr. and mem. numerous coms.; lectr. Cook County Grad. Sch. Medicine, 1980—85, U. Chgo., ARC. Contbr. articles to profl. jours. Fellow ACP; mem. Am. Soc. Clin. Oncology, Am. Assn. Med. Colls., Am. Soc. Hematology, World Fedn. Hemophilia, Blood Club (Chgo.), Thrombosis Club (Chgo.). Office: Florsheim Bldg 29th & Ellis Chicago IL 60616

TEMKIN, HARVEY L. lawyer; b. Madison, Wis., Jan. 1, 1952; s. Joe L. and Sylvia (Libanoff) T.; m. Barbara Jean Myers, June 13, 1976; children: James, Daniel, Eli. BA, U. Wis., 1974; JD, U. Ill., 1978. Bar: Wis. 1978. Assoc. Foley & Lardner, Madison, 1978—83; prof. Tulane Law Sch., New Orleans, 1983-87; ptnr. Foley & Lardner, Madison, 1987—2002, Reinhart Boerner Van Deuren, s.c., Madison, 2002—. Lectr. U. Wis. Law Sch., 1990-93; mem. U.S. Senator Feingold's Bus. Adv. Group. 1st v.p. Hillel Found., Madison, 1982-83, bd. dirs., 1987-95; chmn. edn. com. Beth Israel Synagogue, Madison, 1980-82; chmn. Downtown Madison, Inc., 1989-91; chmn. Jewish edn. panel Madison Jewish Community Coun., 1993-98. Fellow Am. Coll. Real Estate Lawyers; mem. ABA (real property probate and trust sect., reporter significant legis. panel 1983-85, significant lit. panel 1985-87). Home: 2313 Sugar River Rd Verona WI 53593-8741 Office: Reinhart Boerner Van Deuren 22 East Mifflin St PO Box 2018 Madison WI 53701-2018 E-mail: htemkin@reinhartlaw.com.

TEMPLE, WAYNE CALHOUN, historian, writer; b. nr. Richwood, Ohio, Feb. 5, 1924; s. Howard M. and Ruby March (Calhoun) T.; m. Lois Marjorie Bridges, Sept. 22, 1956 (dec. Apr. 1978); m. Sunderine Wilson, Apr. 9, 1979; 2 stepsons, James C. Mohn, Randy E. Mohn. AB cum laude, U. Ill., 1949, AM, 1951, PhD, 1956. Rsch. asst. history U. Ill., 1949-53, tchg. asst., 1953-54; curator ethnohistory Ill. State Mus., 1954-58; editor-in-chief Lincoln Herald, Lincoln Meml. U., 1958-73, assoc. editor, 1973—, also dir. dept. Lincolniana, dir. univ. press, John Wingate Weeks prof. history, 1958-64; with Ill. State Archives, 1964—, now chief dep. dir. Lectr. U.S. Mil. Acad., 1975; sec.-treas. Nat. Lincoln-Civil War Council, 1958-64; mem. bibliography com. Lincoln Lore, 1958—; hon. mem. Lincoln Sesquicentennial Commn., 1959-60; advisory council U.S. Civil War Centennial Commn., 1960-66; maj. Civil War Press Corps, 1962—; pres. Midwest Conf. Masonic Edn., 1985. Author: Indian Villages of the Illinois Country: Historic Tribes, 1958, rev. edits., 1966, 77, 87, Lincoln the Railsplitter, 1961, Abraham Lincoln and Others at the St. Nicholas, 1968, Alexander Williamson-Tutor to the Lincoln Boys, 1971, (with others) First Steps to Victory: Grant's March to Naples, 1977, Lincoln and Grant: Illinois Militiamen, 1981, Stephen A. Douglas: Freemason, 1982, Lincoln as a Lecturer, 1982, By Square and Compasses: The Building of Lincoln's Home and Its Saga, 1984, Lincoln's Connections with the Illinois and Michigan Canal, 1986, Dr. Anson G. Henry: Personal Physician to the Lincolns, 1988, Abraham Lincoln: From Skeptic to Prophet, 1995, Thomas and Abraham Lincoln as Farmers, 1996, Alexander Williamson: Friend of the Lincolns, 1998, By Square and Compass: Saga of the Lincoln Home, 2002; co-author: Illinois's Fifth Capitol: The House that Lincoln Built, 1988; contbg. author: Capitol Centennial Papers, 1988; editor: Campaigning with Grant, 1961, 72, The Civil War Letters of Henry C. Bear, 1961; 71 radio scripts A. Lincoln 1809-1959, Indian Villages of the Illinois Country: Atlas Supplement, 1975; editorial advisory bd. Am. Biog. Inst., 1971— , Ency. Indians of Ams., 1973— ; contbr. articles to profl. jours., encys. Sponsor Abraham Lincoln Bay, Washington Nat. Cathedral; mem. Ill. State Flag Commn., 1969—; trustee, regent Lincoln Acad. Ill., 1970-82; bd. govs. St. Louis unit Shriners Hosps. for Crippled Children, 1975-81; mem. commissioning com., hon. crew mem. and plank owner USS Springfield submarine, 1990—; hon. crew mem. USS Abraham Lincoln aircraft carrier, 1989—. With U.S. Army, 1943-46, gen. Res. (ret.). Decorated Bronze Star Medal, Silver Citizenship medal SAR, 1993, Literary Merit Gold medal Ill. Lodge of Rsch., 1993; recipient Order of Arrow Boy Scouts Am., 1957, Scouters award, 1960, Scouter's Key, also medallion, 1967, Lincoln medallion Lincoln Sesquicentennial Commn., 1960, award of Achievement U.S. Civil War Centennial Commn., 1965, Algernon Sydney Sullivan medallion, 1969, Distinguished Service award Ill. State Hist. Library, 1969, 77, I.H. Duval Distinguished Service award, 1971, legion of honor Internat. Supreme Council, Order of De Molay, 1972, Disting. Service award Civil War Round Table of Chgo., 1983, 91, Cert. Excellence Ill. State Hist. Soc., 1985, Archbishop Richard Chenevix Trench award, 1999;Lincoln Diploma Honor, Lincoln Meml. U., Harrogate, Tenn., 1963, Lifetime Achievement award 2001; named Hon. Ky. Col., Marshal of Okla. Territory. Fellow Royal Soc. Arts (life); mem. Lincoln Group D.C. (hon.), U. Ill. Alumni Assn., Ill. State Hist. Soc., Board of Advisors, The Lincoln Forum, Ill. Profl. Land Surveyors Assn., Ill. State Dental Soc. (citation plague 1966), Res. Officers Assn., Lincoln Fellowship of Wis., NRA (endowment), Iron Brigade Assn. (hon. life), Mil. Order Loyal Legion U.S. (hon. companion), Mil. Order Fgn. Wars U.S., Masons (33 degree, Meritorious Svc. award, Red Cross of Constantine, grand rep. from Grand Lodge of Colo.), Shriners, K.T., Kappa Delta Pi, Phi Alpha, Phi Alpha Theta (Scholarship Key award), Chi Gamma Iota, Tau Kappa Alpha, Alpha Psi Omega, Sigma Pi Beta (Headmaster), Sigma Tau Delta (Gold Honor Key award for editorial writing), Zeta Psi. Presbyterian (elder). Home: 1121 S 4th Street Ct Springfield IL 62703-2200 Office: Ill State Archives Springfield IL 62756-0001

TEMPLETON, ALAN ROBERT, biology educator; b. Litchfield, Ill., Feb. 28, 1947; s. John Smith and Lois Arlene (McCormick) T.; m. Bonnie A. Altman, Dec. 20, 1969; children: Jeremy Alan, Jeffrey Alan. BA, Washington U., 1969; MS in Stats., PhD in Genetics, U. Mich., 1972. Jr. fellow Mich. Soc. Fellows, Ann Arbor, 1972-74; asst. prof. U. Tex., Austin, 1974-77; assoc. prof. Washington U., St. Louis, 1977-81, prof., 1981—, Charles Rebstock prof. biology, 2001—. Cons. St. Louis Zool. Park, 1979—; founding mem., dir. Soc. for Conservation Biology, 1985—. Editor: Theoretical Population Biology, 1981-91; mem. editorial bd. Molecular Phylogenetics & Evolution, 1991—, Brazilian Jour. of Genetics, 1991-97, Genetics and Molecular Biology, 1998—; assoc. editor Am. Naturalist, 2002-; contbr. numerous article to profl. jours. Grantee NSF, 1974-80, 90—, NIH, 1980—, Nixon Griffis Fund for Zool. Rsch., 1986-87, Burroughs Welcome Fund for Functional Genomics, 2000—. Fellow AAAS; mem. Soc. for Study Evolution (v.p. 1982, pres. 1996-97), Genetics Soc. Am., Soc. Conservation Biology (bd. dirs. 1985-88), Nature Conservancy (trustee Mo. chpt. 1988—, v.p. 1996-2000). Avocations: hiking, caving, music, ethnomusicology, scuba diving. Office: Washington U Dept Biology Saint Louis MO 63130-4899

TEMPLETON, JOHN ALEXANDER, II, coal company executive; b. Chgo., Mar. 31, 1927; s. Philip Henry and Florence (Moore) T.; m. Norma Frazier, Aug. 10, 1949; children: Lori, Linda, Leslie, Sally. BS, Ind. U., 1950. Agt. Conn. Mut. Life Ins. Co., Terre Haute, Ind., 1949-51; ptnr. Miller, Templeton, Scott Ins. Agy., 1951-64, elected chmn., 1994, also bd. dirs.; pres. Sherwood Templeton Coal Co., Inc., Indpls., 1968—, also bd. dirs. Bd. dirs. Plumb Supply Co., Des Moines, Dicksons, Inc., Seymour, Ind., Mchts. Nat. Bank Terre Haute. Chmn. Vigo County Goldwater for Pres. Com., 1964; trustee Union Hosp., 1968—, v.p., 1975—, chmn. bd. dirs., 1986-91; bd. dirs. Ind. State U. Found., 1970—; trustee U. Evansville, 1974-77; v.p., trustee Ind. Asbury Towers, Greencastle, 1980-83. With U.S. Army, 1946-48. Mem. Ind. Assn. Ins. Agts. (pres. 1959-60), Ind. Coal Assn. (bd. dirs.), Lynch Coal Ops. Reciprocal Assn., Interstate Coal Conf., Ind. C. of C. (bd. dirs. 1981-95), Ind. U. Alumni Assn. (exec. coun. 1983-86), Masons, Elks. Republican. Methodist.

TEMPLIN, KENNETH ELWOOD, paper company executive; b. Mason City, Nebr., Jan. 26, 1927; s. Otto Rudolph and Marianna (Graf) T.; m. Harriet Elaine Ressel, Aug. 24, 1951; children: Steven, David, Daniel, Benjamin, Elizabeth. B.S. in Bus. Adminstrn, U. Nebr., 1950; M.B.A., Wayne State U., 1961. Fin. analyst Ford Motor Co., 1950-54; fin. analyst, corp. staff Chrysler Corp., 1955-60, div. controller marine engine div., 1961-63, gen. sales mgr., 1964-65; v.p. Marsh and Templin, N.Y.C., 1966-69; v.p., gen. mgr. operating group Saxon Industries, 1970-79, group v.p., 1979-82, sr. v.p., c.o.o., 1982-85; v.p.-converting Paper Corp. Am., Wayne, Pa., 1985-86; exec. v.p. Quality Park Products Inc., St. Paul, 1986-88, 1986-88, pres., 1988-96, ret., 1996. Mem. exec. com. Single Service Inst., 1971-79 Regional chmn. Minn. devel. com. Nat. Multiple Sclerosis Soc., 1970-71; co-pres. Home and Sch. Assn., Bernardsville, N.J., 1975-76; bd. dirs. West Hennepin Counseling Svcs., Inc., 1996-2000, Brain Injury Assn. Minn., 1997-2001; mem. Svc. Corps Ret. Execs. (SCORE), 1996—, chmn. Mpls. chpt., 1999-2000; bd. dirs. Hennepin History Mus., 2000—. With U.S. Army, 1945-47, 50-51. Mem. Envelope Mfrs. Assn. Am. (postal affairs com. 1989-96, fin. com. chmn. 1994-95, bd. dirs. 1990-91, 93-95). Presbyterian. E-mail: templink@aol.com.

TENHOUSE, ART, state representative, farmer; b. Dec. 27, 1950; m. Sharon Roberts; children: Kate, Andy, Adam. BS in Agrl. Sci., Econs., U. Ill., 1973, MBA in Fin. Acctg., 1974. CPA, Ill. Cash mgr. DeKalb (Ill.) Inc.; ptnr. Four-Ten Famrs; state rep. 96th dist. State of Ill., 1989—. Chmn. Ho. Rep. Conf.; past chmn. Pub. Sfaety Appropriations Com.; bd. dirs. U. Ill. Coll. Agr. Alumni Assn.; instr. agrl. credit and fin. John Wood C.C. Burton Twp. clk., 1981-89; chmn. Adams County Farm Bur. Polit. Involvement Fund, 1988-89; 4-H leader Burton Flyers 4-H Club; treas. Farm Bur., Adams County, 1983-85, state utility spl. study com., 1986, legis. chmn., 1985-89, past. pres., v.p., 1985-89. Home: PO Box 1161 Quincy IL 62306-1161 Office: Rep Art Tenhouse 640 Maine St Quincy IL 62301-3908

TENNEFOS, JENS JUNIOR, retired state senator; b. Fargo, N.D., Feb. 15, 1930; s. Jens Peterson and Iva M. (Gilbraith) T.; m. Jeanne P. Quamme, 1960; children: Daniel J., David A., Judie A., Mary J. Student, N.D. State U., 1947-49. Pres. Tennefos Constrn., 1951-74, Tennefos Enterprises, 1975-96; mem. N.D. Ho. of Reps., 1974-76, N.D. Senate, 1977-96, chmn. fin. and taxation com., mem. transp. com., pres. pro tempore, 1995-97. Past chmn., bd. trustees Constrn. Employees Pension, Trust and Health and Welfare Plan, capitol ground com., 1976-95. Featured in front page picture and article Modern Hwy. Mag., 1960, Local Guide Mag., 1980. Bd. regents Oak Grove Luth. H.S., 1970—, also v.p.; bd. dirs. Friendship, Heritage Hjemkosmst Interpretive Ctr., 1998—. Mem. Assn. Gen. Contractors N.D. (hon., past pres., Disting. Svc. Citation 1969), Elks, Am. Legion, Sons of Norway, Masons, Sigma Alpha Epsilon. Home: 310 8th St S Apt 304 Fargo ND 58103-1867

TENNYSON, JOSEPH ALAN, engineering executive; b. St. Paul, May 28, 1958; s. Walter Arnold and Carol Jean (Hauenstein) T.; m. Patricia Ann Jordan, Aug. 29, 1981; children: Alexa Jordan, Ryley Joseph. BSBA, AA in Lib. Arts, U. Minn., 1981. Fin. planner K.A. Richard & Assocs., St. Paul, 1981-83; reporting analyst Control Data Corp., Mpls., 1983-84, systems analyst, 1984-85, fin. analyst, 1985-86; dir. ops. Michaud, Cooley, Erickson, 1986-89, corp. sec., 1986—, v.p. fin. and adminstrn., 1989-93, prin., 1993—. Bd. dirs. Compas. Mem. Leadership Mpls., 1988-89; bd. dirs. United Arts Partnership Fund, 1996-98, Wolf Ridge Environ. Learning Ctr., 1999-2000; mem. assembly com. on intercollegiate athletics U. Minn., 1994-97; trustee Minnatonka Found. for Excellence, 2000—. Mem. Mpls. Club, U. Minn. Alumni Assn. (nat. bd. dirs. 1995-97), Sigma Chi (Grand Consul citation 1983, L.G. Balfour award 1981), Omicron Delta Kappa, Order of Omega. Avocations: computers, fly fishing, golf. Office: Michaud Cooley Erickson 333 S 7th St Ste 1200 Minneapolis MN 55402-2422 Home: 20260 Excelsior Blvd Excelsior MN 55331-8731

TEPHLY, THOMAS ROBERT, pharmacologist, toxicologist, educator; b. Norwich, Conn., Feb. 1, 1936; m. Joan Bernice Clifcorn, Dec. 17, 1960; children: Susan Lynn, Linda Ann, Annette Michele. B.S., U. Conn., 1957; Ph.D., U. Wis., 1962; M.D., U. Minn., 1965. Research asst. U. Wis., Madison, 1957-62, instr., 1962; asst. prof. U. Mich., Ann Arbor, 1965-69, assoc. prof., 1969-71; prof. pharmacology U. Iowa, Iowa City, 1971—. Contbr. articles to profl. jours. Rsch. scholar Am. Cancer Soc., 1962-65; recipient John Jacob Abel award, 1971, Kenneth P. Dubois award, 1992; Fogarty sr. internat. fellow NIH, 1978; rsch. grantee NIH, 1966—. Mem. Am. Soc. Pharmacology and Exptl. Therapeutics, Soc. Toxicology, AAAS, Am. Soc. Biochem. Molecular Biologists. Home: 6 Lakeview Dr NE Iowa City IA 52240-9142 Office: U Iowa Dept Pharmacology 2-452 BSB Iowa City IA 52242

TERKEL, STUDS (LOUIS TERKEL), writer, interviewer; b. N.Y.C., May 16, 1912; s. Samuel and Anna (Finkel) T.; m. Ida Goldberg, July 2, 1939; 1 son, Dan. PhB, U. Chgo., 1932, JD, 1934. Disting. Scholar in Residence, Chgo. Hist. Soc., 1998—. Stage appearances include Detective Story, 1950, A View From the Bridge, 1958, Light Up the Sky, 1959, The Cave Dwellers, 1960; moderator: (TV program) Studs Place, 1950-53, (radio programs) Wax Museum, 1945— (Ohio State Univ. award 1959, UNESCO Prix Italia award 1962), Studs Terkel Almanac, 1952—, Studs Terkel Show, Sta. WFMT-FM, Chgo.; master of ceremonies Newport Folk Festival, 1959, 60, Ravinia Music Festival, 1959, U. Chgo. Folk Festival, 1961, others; panel moderator, lectr., narrator films; author: (books) Giants of Jazz, 1957, Division Street: America, 1967, Hard Times: An Oral History of the Great Depression, 1970, Working: People Talk about What They Do All Day and How They Feel About What They Do, 1974 (Nat. Book award nomination 1975), Talking to Myself: A Memoir of My Times, 1977, American Dreams: Lost and Found, 1980, The Good War: An Oral History of World War II (Pulitzer prize in nonfiction 1985), Chicago, 1986, The Great Divide: Second Thoughts On The American Dream, 1988, Race: How Blacks and Whites Think and Feel About the American Obsession, 1992, Coming of Age, 1995, My American Century, 1997; (play) Amazing Grace, 1959; also short stories. Named Communicator of Yr. U. Chgo. Alumni Assn., 1969; recipient Nat. Humanities Medal, 1997. Office: Chgo Hist Soc Clark St at North Ave Chicago IL 60614

TERNBERG, JESSIE LAMOIN, pediatric surgeon; b. Corning, Calif., May 28, 1924; d. Eric G. and Alta M. (Jones) T. A.B., Grinnell Coll., 1946, Sc.D. (hon.), 1972; Ph.D., U. Tex., 1950; M.D., Washington U., St. Louis, 1953; Sc.D. (hon.), U. Mo., St. Louis, 1981. Diplomate: Am. Bd. Surgery. Intern Boston City Hosp., 1953-54; asst. resident in surgery Barnes Hosp., St. Louis, 1954-57, resident in surgery, 1958-59; research fellow Washington U. (Sch. Medicine), 1957-58; practice medicine specializing in pediatric surgery St. Louis, 1966—; instr., trainee in surgery Washington U., 1959-62, asst. prof. surgery, 1962-65, assoc. prof., 1965-71, prof. surgery in pediatrics, 1975-96, prof. surgery, 1971-96, chief div. pediatric surgery, 1972-90, prof. emeritus, 1996—; mem. staff Barnes Hosp., 1974-90, pediatric surgeon in chief, 1974-90, mem. operating room com., 1971-90, mem. med. adv. com., 1975-90. Mem. staff Children's Hosp., dir. pediatric surgery, 1972-90. Contbr. numerous articles on pediatric surgery to profl. jours. Trustee Grinnell Coll., 1984—. Recipient Alumni award Grinnell Coll., 1966, Faculty/Alumni award Washington U. Sch. Medicine, 1991, 1st Aphrodite Jannopaulo Hofsommer award, 1993. Fellow ACS, AAAS; mem. SIOP, Am. Pediatric Surg. Assn., We. Surg. Assn. (2d v.p. 1984-85), St. Louis Med. Soc., Soc. Surgery of the Alimentary Tract, Am. Acad. Pediatrics, Soc. Pelvic Surgeons (v.p. 1991-92), Brit. Assn. Paediatric Surgeons, Assn. Women Surgeons (disting. mem. 1995), Mo. State Surg. Soc., St. Louis Surg. Soc. (pres. 1980-81), St. Louis Pediatric Soc., Soc. Surg. Oncology, Pediatric Oncology Group (chmn. surg. discipline 1983-96), St. Louis Childrens Hosp. Soc. (pres. 1979-80), St. Louis Met. Med. Soc. (hon., councilor, trustee), Barnes Hosp. Soc., Phi Beta Kappa, Sigma Xi, Iota Sigma Pi, Alpha Omega Alpha. Office: St Louis Childrens Hosp 1 Childrens Pl Saint Louis MO 63110-1002 E-mail: ternbergj@msnotes.wustl.edu.

TERNUS, MARSHA K. state supreme court justice; b. Vinton, Iowa, May 30, 1951; BA, U. Iowa, 1972; JD, Drake U., 1977. Bar: Iowa 1977, Ariz. 1984. With Bradshaw, Fowler, Proctor & Fairgrave, Des Moines, 1977—93; justice Iowa Supreme Ct., 1993—. Editor-in-chief: Drake Law Rev., 1976—77. Mem.: Polk County Bar Assn. (pres. 1984—85), Order of Coif, Phi Beta Kappa. Office: Iowa Supreme Ct State Capital Bldg Des Moines IA 50319-0001*

TERP, DANA GEORGE, architect; b. Chgo., Nov. 5, 1953; s. George and June (Hansen) T.; m. Lynn Meyers, May 17, 1975; children: Sophia, Rachel. BA in Architecture, Washington U., St. Louis, 1974; postgrad., Yale U., 1975-76; MArch, Washington U., 1977. Registered architect, Ill., Calif., Fla. Architect Skidmore Owings & Merrill, Chgo., 1976, 1978-84, Terp Meyers Architects, Chgo., 1984—; prin. Arquitectonica Chgo. Inc., 1986—. Exhibited in group shows at Moming Gallery, Chgo., 1980, Printers Row Exhibit, 1980, Frumkin Struve Gallery, Chgo., 1981, Chgo. Art Inst., 1983; pub. in profl jours. including Progressive Architecture, Los Angeles Architect; work featured in various archtl books; exhibited 150 Yrs. of Chgo. Architecture. Bd. dirs. Architecture Soc. Art Inst. Chgo. Recipient hon. mention Chgo. Townhouse Competition, 1978, award Progressive Architecture mag., 1980, Archtl. Record Houses, 1989, GLOBAL Architecture Ga. Houses/26, 1989, Casa Vogue, 1989, 2d place award Burnham Prize Competition, 1991. Office: Terp Meyers Architects Inc 919 N Michigan Ave Ste 2402 Chicago IL 60611-1664

TERP, THOMAS THOMSEN, lawyer; b. Fountain Hill, Pa., Aug. 12, 1947; s. Norman T. and Josephine (Uhran) T.; m. Pamela Robinson; children: Stephanie, Brian, Adam; step-children: Taylor Mefford, Grace Mefford. BA, Albion (Mich.) Coll., 1969; JD, Coll. of William and Mary, 1973. Bar: Ohio 1973, U.S. Dist. Ct. (so. dist.) Ohio 1973, U.S. Ct. Appeals (6th cir.) 1973, U.S. Supreme Ct. 1979. Assoc. Taft, Stettinius & Hollister, Cin., 1973-80, ptnr., 1981—. Bd. dirs. Starflo Corp., Orangeburg, S.C., Attorneys' Liability Assurance Soc., Ltd., Hamilton, Bermuda, ALAS, Inc., Chgo. Editor-in-chief William & Mary Law Rev., 1972-73; mem. bd. editors Jour. of Environ. Hazards, 1988—, Environ. Law Jour. of Ohio, 1989—. Mem. Cin. Athletic Club, Coldstream Country Club, Epworth Assembly (Ludington, Mich.), Lincoln Hills Golf Club (Ludington), Queen City Club. Avocations: tennis, golf, travel. Office: 1800 Firstar Tower 425 Walnut St Cincinnati OH 45202 E-mail: terp@taftlaw.com.

TERRY, LEE R. congressman, lawyer; b. Omaha, Jan. 29, 1962; s. Leland R. Terry; m. Robyn L. Terry, Feb. 14, 1992; 1 child, Nolan E. BS, U. Nebr., 1984; JD, Creighton U., Omaha, 1987. Bar: Nebr. 1987, U.S. Dist. Ct. Nebr. 1987. Staff atty. Schrempp & Salerno, Omaha, 1987-92; ptnr. Schrempp, Salerno & Terry, 1992-93, Terry & Kratville, Omaha, 1993-98; mem. U.S. Congress from 2d Nebr. dist., 1999—; former mem. banking and fin. svcs. com.; former mem. govt. reform and oversight com.; former mem. transport and infrastructure com.; mem. energy and commerce com. Co-author: Trying the Soft Tissue Case in Nebraska, 1995. Mem. Omaha City Coun., 1991—, pres., 1995-97; chair elect Am. Diabetes Assn., Great Plains, 1996-97, chair Nebr. area, 1997-99. Named One of Ten Outstanding Young Omahans, Omaha Jaycees-C. of C., 1994. Mem. Nebr. Assn. Trial Attys. (dir. 1995—), Suburban Rotary. Republican. Methodist. Avocations: travel, playing, spending time with family. Office: Ho Reps 1513 Longworth House Office Bldg Washington DC 20515-0001 Home: 35 Spyglass Pt Valley NE 68064-9325*

TERRY, LEON CASS, neurologist, educator; b. Dec. 22, 1940; s. Leon Herbert and Zella Irene (Boyd) T.; m. Suzanne Martinson, June 27, 1964; children: Kristin, Sean. Pharm. D., U. Mich., 1964; MD, Marquette U., 1969; PhD, McGill U., 1982; MBA, U.D. Fla., 1994. Diplomate Am. Bd. Psychiatry and Neurology, Am. Bd. Med. Mgmt. Intern U. Rochester, N.Y., 1969-70; staff assoc. NIH, 1970-72; resident in neurology McGill U., Montreal, Que., Can., 1972-75; MRC fellow, 1975-78; assoc. prof. U. Tenn., Memphis, 1978-81; prof. neurology U. Mich., Ann Arbor, 1981-89; assoc. prof. physiology, 1982-89; asst. chief neurology VA Med. Ctr., Ann Arbor, 1982-89; prof. neurology and physiology, chmn. dept. neurology

Med. Coll. of Wis., Milw., 1989-2000. Dir. clin neurosci. ctr. and multiple sclerosis clinic, Med. Coll. Wis.; assoc. dean for amb. care, 1996-98; vice chief of staff Froedtert Hosp., 1994-97; chief of staff, 1997-98; chief med. officer cenegenics, 1997-98. Contbr. articles to profl. jours, chpts. to books. Served to lt. comdr. USPHS, 1970-72. NIH grantee, 1981-92; VA grantee, 1980-92; VA Clin. Investigator award, 1980-81. Mem. AMA, Am. Soc. Clin. Investigation, Cen. Soc. Clin. Investigation, Am. Neurol. Assn., Am. Coll. Physician Execs. (vice chmn. academic health ctr. soc. 1994-95, chair, 1995-98, leader forum health care delivery 1995-98), Am. Coll. Healthcare Execs., Endocrine Soc., Am. Acad. Neurology, Internat. Soc. Neuroendocrinilogy, Internat. Soc. Psychoeuroendocrinilogy, Soc. Neurosci., Soc. Rsch. Biol. Rhythms, Milw. Acad. Physicians, Wis. Neurol. Assn., Wis. State Med. Soc. (del.-elect 1995-96), Med. Soc. Milw. County, Milw. Neuropsychiatric Soc. (pres.-elect.). Avocations: pilot, skiing, scuba diving, computers. Office: Med Coll Wis Dept Neurology Froedtert Hosp 9200 W Watertown Plank Rd Milwaukee WI 53226-3557 E-mail: cass@ross-terry.com., cass@megapathdsl.com.

TERRY, RICHARD EDWARD, public utility holding company executive; b. Green Bay, Wis., July 7, 1937; s. Joseph Edward and Arleen (Agamet) T.; m. Catherine Lombardo, Nov. 19, 1966; children— Angela, Edward BA, St. Norbert's Coll., West DePere, Wis., 1959; LLB, U. Wis., 1964; postgrad., Harvard U., 1986. Assoc. Ross & Hardies, Chgo., 1964-72; atty. Peoples Energy Corp., 1972-79, asst. gen. counsel, 1979-81, v.p., gen. counsel, 1981-84; exec. v.p. People's Energy Corp., Peoples Gas Light & Coke Co. and North Shore Gas Co., 1984-87, pres., COO, 1987-90, chair, CEO, 1990—. Bd. dirs. Peoples Energy Corp., Peoples Gas Light, North Shore Gas Co., Harris Bankcorp, Harris Trust & Savs., Amsted Industries. Bd. dirs. Mus. Sci. & Ind., 1991—, Inst. Gas Tech., 1987—, Ill. Coun. on Econ. Edn., 1987—, Big Shoulders, 1991—; mem. Chgo. Area Ctrl. Com., 1991—; mem. bus. adv. coun. Chgo. Urban League, 1991—; prin. Chgo. United, 1991—; trustee St. Xavier U., 1989—, St. Norbert Coll., 1982—, DePaul U., 1992—. 1st lt. U.S. Army, 1959-61. Mem. Am. Gas Assn. (bd. dirs. 1991—), Nat. Petroleum Coun., Chgo. C. of C. (bd. dirs. 1988—), Univ. Club, Mid-Am. Club, Chgo. Club, Econ. Club, Comml. Club Chgo. (mem. civic com. 1991—). Avocations: golf, fishing, reading. Office: Peoples Energy Corp 130 E Randolph St Chicago IL 60601-6207

TERRY, ROBERT BROOKS, lawyer; b. Kansas City, Mo., July 7, 1956; s. Frank R. and Susan S. (Smart) T.; m. Penny Susan Kanterman, July 2, 1987; children: Ryan, Kevin, Erin. Student, Vanderbilt U., 1974-75; BS in Acctg., U. Mo., 1978, JD, 1981. Bar: Mo. 1981, U.S. Dist. ct. (we. dist.) Mo. 1981, U.S. ct. Appeals (8th and 10th cirs.) 1983. Assoc. Spencer, Fane, Britt & Browne, Kansas City, Mo., 1981—; v.p., gen. counsel Farmland Industries, Inc., 1993—. Mem. ABA, Kansas City Mo. Bar Assn., Lawyers' Assn. Kansas City, Order of Coif. Avocation: baseball. Home: 4952 W 132nd Ter Leawood KS 66209-3460 Office: Farmland Industries Inc PO Box 7305 3315 N Oak Trfy Kansas City MO 64116-2798

TERSCHAN, FRANK ROBERT, lawyer; b. Dec. 25, 1949; s. Frank Joseph and Margaret Anna (Heidt) T.; m. Barbara Elizabeth Keily, Dec. 28, 1974; 1 child, Frank Martin. BA, Syracuse U., 1972; JD, U. Wis., 1975. Bar: Wis. 1976, U.S. Dist. Ct. (ea. and we. dists.) Wis. 1976, U.S. Ct. Appeals (7th cir.) 1979, U.S. Ct. Appeals (10th cir.) 1989, U.S. Supreme Ct. 1992. From assoc. to ptnr. Frisch, Dudek & Slattery Ltd., Milw., 1975-88; ptnr. Slattery and Hausman Ltd., 1988-94, Terschan & Steinle Ltd., Milw., 1994-96, Terschan, Steinle & Ness, Milw., 1996—. Treas., sec. Ville du Park Homeowners Assn., Mequon, Wis., 1985-86; cub scout packmaster pack 3844 Boy Scouts Am., 1989-90, asst. scoutmaster Troop 865, 1991-93. Mem. ABA, Am. Bd. Trial Advocates, Wis. Bar Assn., Milw. Bar Assn., Assn. Trial Lawyers Am., Wis. Acad. of Trial Lawyers (bd. dirs. 1996—), 7th Cir. Bar Assn. (judicial conduct adv. com. 2002—), Order of Coif. Republican. Lutheran. Avocations: swimming, coin collecting, reading, outdoor activities. Home: 10143 N Lake Shore Dr Mequon WI 53092-6109 Office: 2600 N Mayfair Rd Ste 700 Milwaukee WI 53226-1314 E-mail: terstein@execpc.com

TERWILLEGER, GEORGE E. state legislator; m. Jackie Johnson; children: DeWayne, DeLanna, DeAnna. AA, Xavier Univ. Trustee Hamilton Twp., 1969-74; state rep. Ohio Dist. 2, 1996—. Mem. Nat. Land Use com., Nat. Assn. Towns & Townships, County Commn. Assn.; vice chair Clinton Warren Counties Solid Waste Policy com., chair County Reg. Planning Com. Corp. dir. spl. svc. Otterbein Homes, Lebanon, Ohio; treas. Watchdog. Named County Clerk of Yr. Mem. Scottish Rite Club (pres.), County Assn. of Trustees (pres.), Warren County Bd. Realtors (dir., pres.). Home: 10609 Rochester Cozaddale Rd Goshen OH 45122-9607 Office: Ohio Ho of Reps State House Columbus OH 43215

TERWILLIGER, ROY W. state legislator; b. June 20, 1937; m. Mary Lou; three children. BS, U. S.D.; MA, U. Iowa. Mem. Minn. Senate from 42nd dist., St. Paul, 1992—; banker. Home: 6512 Navaho Trl Edina MN 55439-1138 Office: Minn Senate State Capitol Saint Paul MN 55155-0001

TESANOVICH, PAUL, state legislator; b. Jan. 29, 1952; Grad., Mich. Tech. U. Rep. Dist. 110 Mich. Ho. of reps., 1995—, mem. appropriations com.

TETLOCK, PHILIP E. behavioral scientist, psychology educator; b. Toronto, Ont., Can., Mar. 2, 1954; BA with honors, U. B.C., 1975, MA in Psychology, 1976; PhD in Psychology, Yale U., 1979. Asst. prof. dept. psychology U. Calif., Berkeley, 1979-84, assoc. prof. dept. psychology, 1984-87, prof. psychology, adj. prof. bus. adminstrn., 1987-96, disting. prof., 1992-96, rsch. psychologist Survey Rsch. Ctr., 1980-95, dir. Inst. Personality and Social Rsch., 1988-95; Harold E. Burtt prof. psychology and polit. sci. Ohio State U., 1996—. V.p. Internat. Soc. Polit. Psychology, 1991-93; fellow Ctr. for Advanced Study in the Behavioral Scis., 1993-94. Author: (with P.M. Sniderman and R. Brody) Reasoning About Politics: Explorations in Political Psychology, 1991, (with P. Sniderman, J. Fletcher, P. Russell) The Clash of Rights: Liberty, Equality, and Legitimacy in Liberal Democracy, 1996; co-editor: Psychology and Social Policy, 1991, Learning in U.S. and Soviet Foreign Policy, 1991, Behavior, Society and Nuclear War, vol. 1, 1989, vol. 2, 1991, vol. 3, 1993, Prejudice, Politics, and the American Dilemma, 1993, Counterfactual Thought Experiments in World Politics, 1996, Umaking the West: Counterfactual Explorations of Alternative Histories, 2000; contbr. chpts. to books and articles to profl. jours. Recipient Gold medal B.C. Psychol. Assn., 1975, Gov.-Gen.'s Gold medal Award for Undergrad. Acad. Excellence, 1975, Disting. Sci. award for early career contbn. to social psychology Am. Psychol. Assn., 1986, Erik H. Erikson award Internat. Soc. Polit. Psychology, 1987, prize for behavioral sci. rsch. AAAS, 1988, Woodrow Wilson Book award Am. Polit. Sci. Assn., 1992, Nevitt Sanford award for disting. profl. contbns. to polit. pscyhology Internat. Soc. Polit. Psychology, 1997; Yale U. fellow, 1976-77, Can. Coun. doctoral fellow, 1977-79, Regent's jr. faculty fellow U. Calif., Berkeley, summer 1983, MacArthur fellow in internat. security; Walter C. Koerner scholar, 1974-75. Office: Ohio State U Dept Psychology 1885 Neil Ave Columbus OH 43210-1222 Fax: 614-292-5601. E-mail: tetlock.1@osu.edu.

TETTLEBAUM, HARVEY M. lawyer; m. Ann Safier; children: Marianne, Benjamin. AB, Dartmouth Coll., 1964; JD, AM in History, Washington U. Sch. Law, 1968. Asst. dean Washington U. Sch. Law, 1969-77; asst. atty. gne., chief counsel Consumer Protection and Anti-Trust Div., 1970-77; pvt. practice Jefferson City, Mo., 1977-90; mem., chmn. health law practice group Husch & Eppenberger, LLC, 1990—. Contbr. articles to profl. jours. Treas. Mo. Rep. State Com., 1976—; v.p. Moniteau County R-1 Sch. Dist. Bd., 1991-95, pres., 1995-96; mem. Calif. R-1 Sch. Bd., 1990-96, v.p., 1993-95, pres., 1995-96. [e]m. Am. Health Lawyers Assn. (bd. dirs. 1993-99, co-chair long-term care and the law program 1993-2001, chair 2001—, chair long-term care and law program 2001—, chair long term care substantive law com. 1997-2001), Mo. Bar Assn. (health and hosp. law com., chmn. adminstrv. law com., vice chair delivery of legal svc. com., Mo. statewide legal svc. com.), Am. Health Care Assn. (legal subcom. 1994—). Home: 56295 Little Moniteau Rd California MO 65018-3069 Office: Husch & Eppenberger LLC Monroe House Ste 300 235 E High St PO Box 1251 Jefferson City MO 65102-1251

TETZLAFF, THEODORE R. lawyer; b. Saukville, Wis., Feb. 27, 1944; AB magna cum laude, Princeton U., 1966; LLB, Yale U., 1969. Bar: Ind. 1969, D.C. 1969, Ill. 1974. Legis. asst. to Congressman John Brademas, 1970; exec. dir. Nat. Conf. Police Community Rels., 1970-71; acting dir. U.S. Office Legal Svcs., Office Econ. Opportunity, Washington, 1972-73; counsel, Com. Judiciary U.S. Ho. of Reps., 1974; v.p., legal and external affairs Cummins Engine Co., 1980-82; gen. coun. Tenneco, Inc., Greenwich, Conn., 1992-99; ptnr. Jenner & Block, Chgo., 1976—80, 1982—2001; mng. ptnr. McGuireWoods LLP, 2002—. Bd. dirs. Continental Materials Corp., Chgo. Pres. Chgo. area Found. Legal Svcs., 1983—; commr. Pub. Bldg. Commn. Chgo., 1990—. Reginald Heber Smith fellow, 1969-70. Mem. ABA (chair sect. litigation 1991-92), Ill. State Bar Assn., Ind. State Bar Assn., D.C. Bar. Office: McGuireWoods LLP Suite 4400 77 West Wacker Dr Chicago IL 60601

THACH, WILLIAM THOMAS, JR. neurobiology and neurology educator; b. Okla. City, Jan. 3, 1937; s. William Thomas and Mary Elizabeth T.; m. Emily Ransom Otis, June 30, 1963 (div. 1979); children: Sarah Brill, James Otis, William Thomas III. AB in Biology magna cum laude, Princeton U., 1959; MD cum laude, Harvard U., 1964. Diplomate Am. Bd. Psychiatry and Neurology (in Neurology). Intern Mass. Gen. Hosp., Boston, 1964-65, asst. residency, 1965-66; staff assoc. physiology sect. lab. clin. sci. NIMH, Bethesda, Md., 1966-69; neurology resident, clin. and rsch. fellow Mass. Gen. Hosp., 1969-71; from asst. prof. neurology to assoc. prof. neurology Yale U. Sch. Medicine, New Haven, 1971-75; assoc. prof. neurobiology and neurology dept. anatomy and neurobiology Washington U. Sch. Medicine, St. Louis, 1975-80, prof. neurobiology and neurology dept. anatomy and neurobiology, 1980—, chief divsn. neurorehab. dept. neurology, 1992—. Acting dir. Irene Walter Johnson Rehab. Inst. Washington U. Sch. Medicine, 1989-91, dir., 1991-92; attending neurologist Barnes Hosp., med. dir. dept. rehab.; attending neurologist Jewish Hosp., St. Louis Regional Hosp.; bd. sci. counselors NINCDS, 1988-92; mem. NIH Study Sect. Neurology A, 1981-85. Assoc. editor Somatosenory and Motor Research; contbr. numerous articles to profl. jours. Fulbright grantee U. Melbourne, Australia, 1959-60; NIH grantee, 1971— Mem. Physiol. Soc., Am. Acad. Neurology, Soc. Neurosci., Am. Neurol. Assn., Am. Soc. Neurorehab., Phi Beta Kappa, Sigma Xi, Alpha Omega Alpha. Achievements include research on brain control of movement and motor learning, roles of the basal ganglia and the cerebellum in health and disease. Home: 7520 Clayton Rd Saint Louis MO 63117-1418 Office: Washington Univ Dept Anatomy & Neurobiol 600 S Euclid Ave Dept Anatomy& Saint Louis MO 63110-1010

THADEN, EDWARD CARL, history educator; b. Seattle, Apr. 24, 1922; s. Edward Carl and Astrid (Engvik) T.; m. Marianna Theresia Forster, Aug. 7, 1952. BA, U. Wash., 1944; student, U. Zurich, Switzerland, 1948; PhD, U. Paris, 1950. Instr. Russian history Pa. State U., 1952-55, asst. prof., 1955-58, assoc. prof., 1958-64, prof., 1964-68, prof. emeritus, 1992—. Vis. prof. Ind. U., 1957, U. Marburg, 1965, U. Ill., Urbana, 1980, U. Halle, Germany, 1988, U. Helsinki, Finland, 1990; prof. U. Ill., Chgo., 1968—, chmn. dept. history, 1971—73; editl. cons. Can. Rev. Studies in Nationalism, 1973—78; vis. rsch. scholar USSR Acad. Scis., 1975, 88, 90; project prin. rschr. Ford Found., 1975—78; U.S. rep. Internat. Congress of Hist. Scis., 1980; project dir. NEH grant, 1980—82. Author: Conservative Nationalism in Nineteenth-Century Russia, 1964, Russia and the Balken Alliance of 1912, 1965, Russia Since 1801: The Making of a New Society, 1971, Russia's Western Borderlands, 1710-1870, 1984, Interpreting History: collected Essays on Russia's Relations with Europe, 1990, Essays in Russian and East European History: Festschrift in Honor of Edward C. Thaden, 1995, The Rise of Historicism in Russia, 1999; co-author, editor: Russification in the Baltic Provinces and Finland, 1955-1914, 1981; co-author, co-editor: Finland and the Baltic Provinces in the Russian Empire, 1984; mem. editorial bd. Jour Baltic Studies, 1984-93, assoc. editor, 1987-93, East European Quarterly, 1998—. Served to lt. (j.g.) USNR, 1943-46. Carnegie Inter-Univ. Com. travel grantee to USSR, 1956; Fulbright rsch. grantee Finland, 1957-58, Germany, 1965, Poland and Finland, 1968; Soc. Sci. Rsch. Coun. grantee, 1957; Am. Coun. Learned Socs. grantee, 1963, 65-66; fellow Woodrow Wilson Internat. Ctr. for Scholars, 1980 Mem. Am. Assn. for Advancement Slavic Studies (pres. Midwest br. 1975-76, exec. sec. 1980-82), Chgo. Consortium for Slavic and Ea. European Studies (pres. 1982-84), Baltische Historische Kommission, Göttingen (corr. mem. 1985—), Commn. Internat. des Etudes Historiques Slaves (v.p. 1985-95, pres. 1995-2000, pres.d'honneur 2000—). Office: U Ill Dept History 913 UH (M/C 198) 601 S Morgan St Chicago IL 60607-7100

THALDEN, BARRY R. architect; b. Chgo., July 5, 1942; s. Joseph and Sibyl (Goodwin) Hechtenthal; m. Irene L. Mittleman, June 23, 1966 (div. 1989); 1 child, Stacey; m. Kathyn McKnight, Sept. 1996. BArch, U. Ill., 1965; M in Land Architecture, U. Mich., 1969. Landscape architect Hellmuth, Obata, Kassebaum, St. Louis, 1969-70; dir. landscape architecture PGAV Architects, 1970-71; pres. Thalden Corp. Architects, 1971—; ptnr. Thalden-Boyd Architects. Prin. works include Rock Hill Park, 1975 (AIA award, 1977), Wilson Residence, 1983 (AIA award), Nat. Bowling Hall of Fame, 1983 (St. Louis RCGA award, 1984), Village Bogey Hills (Home Builders award, 1985, St. Louis ASLA award, 1994), St. Louis U. Campus Mall (St. Louis ASLA award, 1989), Horizon Casino Resort, Lake Tahoe, Nev., St. Louis Airport's Radisson Hotel, Lady Luck, Treasure Bay, Palace Casinos, Biloxi, Miss., Boomtown Casino, New Orleans, Pres. Casino on the Admiral, St. Louis, Plaza of Champions, Busch Stadium, Ho Chunk Casino, Wisconsin Dells (ABC award Best Bldg. in Wis., 2000), Potowatomi Casino, Milw., Terrible's Casino, Las Vegas. Bd. dirs. St. Louis Open Space Coun., 1973—83, St. Louis Art., Ednl. Coun.; bd. trustees Las Vegas Art Mus.; apptd. Mo. Lands Architect Coun., 1990—94. Named Architect of Yr. Builder Architect mag., 1986. Fellow Am. Soc. Landscape Architects (nat. v.p. 1979-81, pres. St. Louis chpt. 1975, trustee 1976-79, nat. conv. chair 1991); mem. AIA, World Future Soc. (pres. St. Louis chpt. 1984-94, keynote conf. spkr. 1995). Avocations: painting, gardening, tennis, guitar. Home: 2204 Chatsworth Ct Henderson NV 89074-5307 Office: Thalden Corp 7777 Bonhomme Ave Ste 2200 Saint Louis MO 63105-1911

THAMAN, MICHAEL H. building material systems executive; BSEE, BS in Computer Sci., Princeton U. V.p. Mercer Mgmt. Cons., N.Y.C.; dir. corp. devel. Owens Corning, 1992-94, plant mgr. Toronto insulation facility, 1994-96, gen. mgr. OEM solutions group, 1996-97, v.p., pres. engineered pipe systems bus. Brussels, 1997-99, v.p., pres. exterior systems bus., 1999-2000, CFO, 2000—. Office: Owens Corning Dept 2-D One Owens Corning Pkwy Toledo OH 43659

THANE, RUSSELL T. state legislator; b. Denver, July 14, 1926; s. Joseph and Bernice (Steere) T.; m. Betty Jo Chowning, 1952; children: Ronald, Kathleen. Degree, N.D. State Sch. Sci., 1949, N.D. State U., 1955. Dir. Home Mutual Ins. Co., Wahpeton, 1968—; mem. N.D. Senate from 25th dist., Bismark, 1971—; asst. majority floor whip N.D. Senate, 1981-82, mem. appropriations com., chmn. human svc., mem. interim adv. com. on intergovt. rels. Farmer; dir. Red River Valley Beet Growers, 1969—. Precinct committeeman 25th dist., N.D., 1964-70; mem. adv. bd. N.D. State Sch. Sci. Drug and Alcohol Prevention, Wahpeton Cmty. Devel. Corp., State Hosp. Mem. N.D. Cattle Feeders Assn. (sec.-treas. 1964-70), Zagal Shrine, Elks, Masons, Eagles, Am. Legion (life), Farm Bur. Office: Rte 1 Box 142 Wahpeton ND 58075-9801 also: ND Senate State Capitol Bismarck ND 58505 Home: 7660 178th Ave SE Wahpeton ND 58075-9615

THARALDSON, GARY DEAN, hotel developer and owner; b. Valley City, N.D., Oct. 17, 1945; BA in Phys. Edn., Valley City State U.; postgrad., N.D. State U. Tchr., Leonard, N.D.; ins. agt., agy. owner, 1969-89; owner of 340 hotels, Valley City, 1982; pres. Tharaldson Enterprises, Fargo, N.D., 1982—. Office: Tharaldson Enterprises 1202 Westrac Dr Fargo ND 58103-2344

THEEN, ROLF HEINZ-WILHELM, political science educator; b. Stadthagen, Germany, Feb. 20, 1937; came to U.S., 1956, naturalized, 1962; s. Walter and Gertrud (Tysper) T.; m. Norma Lee Plunkett, June 14, 1959; children: Tanya Sue, Terrell René. BA magna cum laude, Manchester Coll., 1959; MA, cert. with high distinction Russian and East European Inst., Ind. U., 1962, PhD, 1964. From asst. prof. to assoc. prof. Iowa State U., 1964-70; assoc. prof. polit. sci. Purdue U., West Lafayette, Ind., 1971-73, prof., 1974—. Dir. Purdue U.-Ind. U. study program U. Hamburg, 1980-81; translator, editor U.S. Joint Publs. Rsch. Svc. Author: Lenin: Genesis and Development of a Revolutionary, 1973, 74, 79; co-author: Comparative Politics: An Introduction to Seven Countries, 1992, 4th edit., 2000; editor, translator: The Early Years of Lenin (N. Valentinov), 1969; editor: The USSR First Congress of People's Deputies: Complete Documents and Records, 4 vols., 1991; contbr. articles to profl. jours., chpts. to books. Recipient Wilton Park award Iowa State U., 1971; Fgn. Area Tng. fellow Russian and East European Inst., 1962-64; grantee Am. Philos. Soc., Inter Univ. Com., Joint Com. Slavic Studies, Fulbright grantee, 1995; NEH sr. fellow, 1974-75, rsch. fellow Kennan Inst. Advanced Russian Studies, Woodrow Wilson Internat. Ctr. for Scholars, 1976, Ctr. Humanistic Studies fellow Purdue U., 1982, 88, 91. Mem. Am. Polit. Sci. Assn., Am. Assn. Advancement Slavic Studies, Am. Acad. Social and Polit. Sci. Mem. Ch. of the Brethren. Home: 717 Orchard Dr Lafayette IN 47905-4435 Office: Purdue U Dept Polit Sci Liberal Arts/Edn Bldg 2221 West Lafayette IN 47907-1363 Home (Winter): 6415 Midnight Pass Rd Unit 611 Sarasota FL 34242 E-mail: Theen@polscipurdue.edu.

THELEN, BRUCE CYRIL, lawyer; b. St. Johns, Mich., Nov. 24, 1951; BA, Mich. State U., 1973; JD, U. Mich., 1977. Bar: N.Y. 1978, Mich. 1980, Ill. 1992. Assoc. Dewey, Ballantine, Bushby, Palmer & Wood, N.Y.C., 1977-80; ptnr. Dickinson, Wright, Moon, Van Dusen & Freeman, Detroit, 1981-83, Dickinson Wright PLLC, Detroit, 1984—. Mem. U.S. Dept. Commerce-Mich. Dist. Export Coun., 1995—. Contbr. articles to profl. jours. Mem. allocation panel, mem. spkrs. bur., chmn. rsch. and info. svcs. com., mem. strategic planning com. and comty. leaders coun. United Way Cmty. Svcs., 1987—; mem. state of Mich. Task Force on Internat. Trade, Lansing, 1990; mem. Detroit Com. on Fgn. Rels., Greater Detroit-Windsor Japan Am. Soc. Decorated Order of Merit (Fed. Rep. Germany). Mem. N.Y. Bar Assn. (mem. internat. law sect.), State Bar Mich. (chmn. internat. law sect. 1990-91), Internat. Bar Assn., Am. Soc. Internat. Law, Ill. Bar Assn. (internat. law sect.), Internat. Inst. Detroit (bd. dirs. 1997-99, v.p. 1999-2000), French-Am. C. of C. of Detroit, German Am. C. of C. of Midwest (bd. dirs. 1992—, pres. Mich. chpt. 1994—), Mich. Israel C. of C. (bd. dirs. 1997-01), Greater Detroit C. of C. (chmn. European mission com. 1991-92, 95, export com. 1992-95, Leadership Detroit VIII program 1986-87), World Trade Club and Internat. Bus. Coun. (exec. com. 1992—), Internat. Bridge, Coun. Mentors, Wayne State U., Econ. Club Detroit, Detroit Athletic Club. Office: Dickinson Wright PLLC 500 Woodward Ave Ste 4000 Detroit MI 48226-3416

THEOBALD, THOMAS CHARLES, banker; b. Cin., May 5, 1937; m. Gigi Mahon, Jan. 1987 AB in Econs., Coll. Holy Cross, 1958; MBA in Fin. with high distinction, Harvard U., 1960. With Citibank, N.A. div. Citicorp, 1960-87; vice-chmn. Citicorp, N.Y.C., 1982-87; CEO, chmn. Continental Bank Corp., Chgo., 1987-94; chmn. bd. dirs. Continental Bank N.A., 1987-94; ptnr. Blair Capital Ptnrs, LLC, 1994—. Bd. dir. Xerox Corp., Jones, Lang LaSalle US Realty Income & Growth Fund, Anixter Internat., Liberty Funds, Mac Arthur Found., MONY Group. Trustee Northwestern U. Office: William Blair Capital Partners 227 N Monroe Ste 3500 Chicago IL 60606-5307

THIBODEAU, GARY A. academic administrator; b. Sioux City, Iowa, Sept. 26, 1938; m. Emogene J. McCarville, Aug. 1, 1964; children: Douglas James, Beth Ann. BS, Creighton U., 1962; MS, S.D. State U., 1967, MS, 1970, PhD, 1971. Profl. service rep. Baxter Lab., Inc., Deerfield, Ill., 1963-65; tchr., researcher dept. biology S.D. State U., Brookings, 1965-76, asst. to v.p. for acad. affairs, 1976-80, v.p. for adminstrn., 1980-85; chancellor U. Wis., River Falls, 1985-2000; sr. v.p. acad. affairs U. Wis. Sys., 2000—01. Mem. investment com. U. Wis., River Falls Found.; trustee W. Cen. Wis. Consortium U. Wis. System; bd. dirs. U. Wis. at River Falls Found.; mem. Phi Kappa Phi nat. budget rev. and adv. comm., Phi Kappa Phi Found. investment comm., comm. on Agrl. and Rural Devel., steering commn. Coun. of Rural Colls. and Univs., Joint Coun. on Food and Agrl. Scis., USDA. Author: Basic Concepts in Anatomy and Physiology, 1983, Athletic Injury Assessment, 1994, Structure and Function of the Body, 1996, The Human Body in Health and Disease, 1996, Textbook of Anatomy and Physiology, 1996. Mem. AAAS, Sigma Xi, Phi Kappa Phi, Gamma Sigma Delta, Gamma Alpha. Office: U Wis 116 N Hall River Falls WI 54022

THIEMANN, CHARLES LEE, banker; b. Louisville, Nov. 21, 1937; s. Paul and Helen (Kern) T.; m. Donna Timperman, June 18, 1960; children: Laura Gerette, Charles Lee, Rodney Gerard, Jeffrey Michael, Matthew Joseph. BA in Chemistry, Bellarmine Coll., 1959; MBA, Ind. U., 1961, DBA, 1963. Mem. rsch. dept. Fed. Res. Bank, St. Louis, 1963-64; with Fed. Home Loan Bank, Cin., 1964—, sr. v.p., then exec. v.p., 1974, pres., 1976—. Past chmn. bd. dirs. Office Fin.; trustee Fin. Instns. Retirement Fund; past mem. First Step Home. Bd. dirs. Habitat for Humanity Internat., Bellarmine U. Named Bellarmine Coll. Alumnus of Yr., 1999. Mem. Rotary Club, Queen City Club. Roman Catholic. Office: Fed Home Loan Bank 221 E 4th St Ste 1000 Cincinnati OH 45202-5139

THIES, RICHARD BRIAN, lawyer; b. Chgo., Dec. 14, 1943; s. Fred W. and Loraine C. (Mannix) T.; m. Anita Marie Rees, Aug. 5, 1972; children: Emily Marie, Richard Clarke. BA, Miami U., 1966; JD, Loyola U., 1974. Bar: (Ill. 1974), 1989 (U.S. Tax Ct.). Assoc. Wilson & McIlvaine, Chgo., 1974-78; assoc.-ptnr. Isham, Lincoln & Beale, 1978-88; ptnr. Wildman, Harrold, Allen & Dixon, 1988—, mem. exec. com., 1999—. Bd. govs. Chgo. Heart Assn., 1980-87, exec. com., 1982-87; bd. dirs. Juvenile Protective Assn., Chgo., 1984—; v.p. Samaritan Counseling Ctr., Evanston, 1989-94, pres., 1994. Mem. ABA, Chgo. Bar Assn., Chgo. Estate Planning Coun. Avocations: coaching children's sports, photography, music. Home: 305 Driftwood Ln Wilmette IL 60091-3441 Office: Wildman Harrold Allen & Dixon 225 W Wacker Dr Chicago IL 60606-1229

THIESENHUSEN, WILLIAM CHARLES, agricultural economist, educator; b. Waukesha, Wis., Feb. 12, 1936; s. Arthur Henry and Myrtle O. (Honeyager) T.; children— James Waring, Kathryn Hague, Gail Ann. BS, U. Wis., 1958, MS, 1960, PhD, 1965; M.P.A. (Danforth Found. fellow),

Harvard U., 1962, postgrad., 1968-69. Instr. agrl. extension U. Wis., Madison, 1959-61; exec. asst. Land Tenure Center and Instituto de Economia Universidad de Chile research team in, Santiago, 1963-65, asst. prof. agrl. econs., 1965-68, asso. prof. agrl. econs., 1971-72, asso. prof. agrl. journalism, 1968-72, prof. agrl. journalism and agrl. econs., 1972—. Dir. Land Tenure Ctr., 1971-75, 94-98, prof. emeritus Agrl. Applied Econs., 1998—; asst. prof. econs. U. Wis., Milw., 1966-67; prof. agrl. econs. Escuela Nacional de Agricultura, Chapingo, Mex.; under AID contract, summer 1965; vis. prof. Universidad Autonoma de Madrid, Fulbright Program, 1977; cons., condr. seminars in field; Fulbright-Hays lectr., 1965, 72. Author: Chile's Experiments in Agrarian Reform, 1966, Reforma Agraria en Chile: Experimentos en Cuatro Fundos de la Iglesia, 1968, Broken Promises: Agrarian Reform and the Latin American Campesino, 1995; editor: Searching for Agrarian Reform in Latin America, 1989; mem. editl. bd. Latin Am. Rsch. Rev., Pakistan Devel. Rev.; contbr. articles to profl. jours. Served with USAR, 1960. Recipient award for best article Am. Jour. Agrl. Econs., 1969; Alpha Zeta nat. fellow, 1957; U. Wis. fellow, 1956; Harvard U. Adminstrn. fellow, 1962 Mem. Am. Agrl. Econs. Assn., Am. Econ. Assn., Latin Am. Studies Assn., Council Internat. Exchange Scholars (chmn. com. econs. selection 1979-80), Inter-Am. Found. (selection bd.), Wis. Acad. Scis., Arts and Letters, Phi Kappa Phi, Alpha Zeta, Sigma Delta Chi. Unitarian. Office: U Wis Land Tenure Ctr 1357 University Ave Madison WI 53715-1054 E-mail: wthiesen@facstaff.wisc.edu.

THIMESCH, DANIEL J. state legislator; m. Ruth A. Thimesch. Contractor; mem. from dist. 93 Kans. State Ho. of Reps., Topeka. Address: 30121 W 63rd St S Cheney KS 67025-8775 Office: Kans House of Reps State House Topeka KS 66612

THIMMIG, DIANA M. lawyer; b. Germany, May 5, 1959; BA cum laude, John Carroll U., 1980; JD, Cleve. State U., 1982. Bar: Ohio 1983, U.S. Dist. Ct. (no. dist.) Ohio 1983, U.S. Ct. Appeals (6th cir.) 1983, U.S. Supreme Ct. 1983, U.S. Ct. Appeals (3d cir. 1996); cert. Am. Bankruptcy Bd. for Consumer and Bus. Bankruptcy. Ptnr. Arter & Hadden, Cleve. Contbr. articles to profl. jours. Hon. consul of Germany, 1988—; trustee Geauga United Way Svcs. Coun., 1992-96, Altenheim, 1992-97, Legal Aid Soc., 1998—, Internat. Svcs. Ctr., 1998—, Cuyahoga County Bar Assn., 1995—. Mem. Women's City Club Cleve. (pres. 1995-97). Office: Arter & Hadden 1100 Huntington Bldg 925 Euclid Ave Ste 1100 Cleveland OH 44115-1475

THISTED, RONALD AARON, statistician, educator, consultant; b. L.A., Mar. 2, 1951; s. Dale Owen and Barbara Jean (Walker) T.; m. Linda Jeane Soder, Dec. 30, 1972; 1 child, Walker. BA, Pomona Coll., 1972; PhD, Stanford U., 1977. Asst. prof. statistics U. Chgo., 1976-82, assoc. prof. statistics, 1982-92, assoc. prof. anesthesia and critical care, 1989-92, prof. stats. and anesthesia and critical care, 1992—, prof. health studies, 1996—, chmn. health studies, 1999—. Co-dir. Clin. Rsch. Training Program, 1999—. Author: Elements of Statistical Computing, 1988; contbr. over 70 articles to profl. jours. Fellow AAAS, Am. Statis. Assn.; mem. Assn. for Computing Machinery, Inst. for Math. Stats., Soc. for Clin. Trials. Office: U Chgo MC 2007 5841 S Maryland Ave Chicago IL 60637-1463

THOMAN, HENRY NIXON, lawyer; b. Cin., May 5, 1957; s. Richard B. and Barbara (Lutz) Thoman; m. Anne Davies, May 25, 2002; children: Victoria E., Nicholas B. BA, Duke U., 1979; JD, U. Chgo., 1982. Bar: Ohio 1982, U.S. Dist. Ct. (so. dist.) Ohio, 1982. With Taft, Stettinius & Hollister, Cin., 1982-88; sr. atty. John Morrell & Co., 1988-90; sr. counsel Chiquita Brands Internat. Inc., 1990-91, corp. planner, 1991-92; sr. dir. CTP ops. Chiquita Brands, Inc., 1993-94, chief adminstrv. officer Armuelles divsn., 1994-95; corp. counsel The Loewen Group, Covington, Ky., 1995-97; asst. chief counsel, asst. v.p. The Midland Co., Amelia, Ohio, 1997-99; v.p. orgnl. devel. Kendle Internat. Inc., 1999-2000, v.p. complementary ops., 2000—02; pvt. atty., 2002—. Mem. counselors com. U.S. Swimming, Colo., 1983-89; bd. dirs. Friends of Cin. Parks, 1990-93, 96-98, Starshine Children's Hospice, 1996-99, Cinci. Aquatic Club, 1997—, Kids Helping Kids, 2000—, Mariemont Aquatic Club, v.p., 1992-93; pres. Club Atletico Y Socialde Chiriqui, 1994-95. Mem. Ohio State Bar, Cin. Bar Assn. E-mail: ccdsauc@fusc.net.

THOMAN, MARK EDWARD, pediatrician; b. Chgo., Feb. 15, 1936; s. John Charles and Tasula Mark (Petrakis) T.; m. Theresa Thompson, 1984; children: Marlisa Rae, Susan Kay, Edward Kim, Nancy Lynn, Janet Lea, David Mark. AA, Graceland Coll., 1956; BA, U. Mo., 1958, MD, 1962. Diplomate Am. Bd. Pediat., Am. Coll. Toxicology (examiner). Intern U. Mo. at Columbia, 1962—63; resident in pediat. Blank Meml. Children's Hosp., Des Moines, 1963—65; cons. in toxicology USPHS, Washington, 1965—66; chief dept. pediat. Shiprock (N.Mex.) Navajo Indian Hosp., 1966—67; dir. N.D. Poison Info. Ctr.; also practice medicine specializing in pediat. Quain & Ramstad Clinic, Bismarck, ND, 1967—69; dir. Iowa Poison Info. Ctr., Des Moines, 1967—69; mem. pediat. exec. com. Broadlawns Med. Ctr., 1969—2000, pres. med. staff, 2000—01. Accident investigator FAA, 1976—, sr. aviation examiner, 1977—2000; sr. cons. in field; lectr. aviation seminars, 1977—; mem. faculty U. Osteo. Sci. & Health, 1969—2000, dir. cystic fibrosis clin., 1973—82; dir. Mid-Iowa Drug Abuse Program, 1972—76; mem. med. adv. bd. La Leche League Internat., 1965—; pres. Medic-Air Ltd., 1976—; chief med. officer Broadlawns Med. Ctr , Des Moines, 2000—02. Editor-in-chief AACTION, 1975-90. Bd. dirs. Polk County Pub. Health Nurses Assn., 1969-77, Des Moines Speech and Hearing Ctr., 1974-79, Ecumenical Coun. Iowa, 1990-99; bd. govs. Mo. U. Sch. Medicine Alumni, 1988—, pres., 1997-99; elder mem. Cmty. of Christ Ch. With USMCR, 1954-59; lt. comdr. USPHS, 1965-66; capt. USNR, 1988-96, ret. 1996; dir. Dept. Health Svcs. USNR. Recipient N.D. Gov.'s award of merit, 1969, Cystic Fibrosis Rsch. Found. award, 1975, Am. Psychiat. Assn. Thesis award, 1962. Fellow Am. Coll. Med. Toxicology (diplomate 1996); mem. AMA (del. 1970-88), APHA, NRA (life), Assn. Am. Physicians & Surgeons (chief of staff, pres. Broadlawns Polk County Med. Ctr. 2000—), Polk County Med. Soc., Iowa State Med. Assn., Aerospace Med. Assn., Res. Officers Assn., Civil Aviation Med. Assn., Soc. Adolescent Medicine, Inst. Clin. Toxicology, Internat. Soc. Pediat., Am. Acad. Pediat. (chmn. accident prevention com. Iowa chpt. 1975-2000), Cystic Fibrosis Club, Am. Acad. Clin. Toxicology (trustee 1969-90, pres. 1982-84), Am. Assn. Poison Control Ctrs., Am. Coll. Physician Execs., U.S. Naval Inst., Flying Physicians Club, Aircraft Owners and Pilots Assn, Nat. Pilots Assn. (Safe Pilot award), Hyperion Field and Country Club. Republican. Home: 6896 NW Trail Ridge Dr Johnston IA 50131-1322 Office: PO Box 349 Johnston IA 50131-0349 E-mail: paro1795@aol.com., mthoman@broadlawns.org.

THOMAS, ALAN, candy company executive; b. Evansburg, Pa., Jan. 1, 1923; s. William Roberts and Letta (Garrett) T.; m. Marguerite Atria, July 1, 1972; children: Garrett Lee, Michael Alan, Randall Stephen, Brett Eliot. BS, Pa. State U., 1949; MS, U. Minn., 1950, PhD, 1954. Instr. Temple U., Phila., 1950-51, U. Minn., St. Paul, 1951-54; rsch. asst. Bowman Dairy Co., Chgo., 1954-56; rsch. project mgr. M&M Candies divsn. Mars, Inc., Hackettstown, N.J., 1956-60, product devel. mgr., 1961-64, chocolate rsch. dir., 1964; v.p. rsch. & devel. Mars Candies, Chgo., 1964-67, v.p. rsch. & devel. M&M/Mars divsn. Hackettstown, 1967-77, v.p. sci. affairs, 1977-78; gen. mgr. Ethel M, Las Vegas, 1978-83; cons., 1985; sr. cons. Knechtel Rsch. Scis., Inc., Skokie, Ill., 1984; v.p. tech. Ferrara Pan Candy Co., Forest Park, Ill., 1986-92; cons., 1993—. Chmn. coun. industry liaison panel Food and Nutrition Bd., Nat. Acad. Scis./NRC, 1972-73; adv. U.S. del. Codex Alimentarius Com. on Cocoa and Chocolate Products, 1967-78. Served to 1st lt. inf. AUS, 1942-46. Recipient rsch. award Nat. Confectioners Assn. U.S., 1971. Mem. Grocery Mfrs. Am. (chmn. tech. com. 1975-76), Chocolate Mfrs. Assn. (chmn. FDA liaison com. 1975-77), Inst. Food Technologists, Am. Assn. Candy Technologists, Gamma Sigma Delta, Phi Kappa Phi. Home: 2005 Sedona Morning Dr Las Vegas NV 89128-8484 Office: Ferrara Pan Candy Co 7301 Harrison St Forest Park IL 60130-2016

THOMAS, CHRISTOPHER YANCEY, III, surgeon, educator; b. Kansas City, Mo., Oct. 27, 1923; s. Christopher Yancey and Dorothea Louise (Engel) T.; m. Barbara Ann Barcroft, June 27, 1946; children— Christopher, Gregg, Jeffrey, Anne Student, U. Colo., 1942-44; M.D., U. Kans., 1948. Diplomate Am. Bd. Surgery. Intern U. Utah Hosp., Salt Lake City, 1948-49; resident in surgery Cleve. Clinic Found., 1949-52; pvt. practice specializing in surgery Kansas City, Mo., 1954-89. Mem. staff St. Luke's Hosp., chief surgery, 1969-70; mem. staff Children's Mercy Hosp.; clin. prof. surgery U. Mo., Kansas City Med. Sch.; pres. St. Luke's Hosp. Edn. Found., 1977-83, Med. Plaza Corp., 1977-79; pres. Midwest Organ Bank, 1977-82. Editor IMTRAC investment adv. letter, 1978-2000. Served to capt. M.C., U.S. Army, 1952-54 Fellow ACS; mem. AMA, Southwestern Surg. Congress, Central Surg. Assn., Mo. State Med. Soc., Kansas City Surg. Soc. (pres. 1968), Jackson County Med. Soc. (pres. 1971) Republican. Methodist. Club: Kansas City Country. Home: 50 Coventry Ct Shawnee Mission KS 66208-5225 Office: 4121 W 83d St Ste 147 Shawnee Mission KS 66208 E-mail: barbtommy@aol.com.

THOMAS, DALE E. lawyer; b. New Rochelle, N.Y., Jan. 25, 1947; AB summa cum laude, Princeton U., 1969; MDiv, Yale Divinity Sch., 1973; JD, Yale U., 1974. Bar: Ill. 1975. Law clerk U.S. Ct. Appeals 2d cir., 1974-75; ptnr. Sidley & Austin, Chgo., 1980—. Mem. ABA, Ill. State Bar Assn., Chgo. Bar Assn., Phi Beta Kappa. Office: Sidley & Austin Bank One Plz 425 W Surf St Apt 605 Chicago IL 60657-6139

THOMAS, DUKE WINSTON, lawyer; b. Scuddy, Ky., Jan. 25, 1937; s. William E. and Grace T.; m. Jill Staples, Oct. 24, 1964; children: Deborah L., William E. II, Judith A. BSBA, Ohio State U., 1959, JD, 1964. Bar: Ohio 1964, U.S. Dist. Ct. Ohio 1966, U.S. Ct. Appeals (3d cir.) 1971, U.S. Ct. Appeals (6th cir.) 1972, U.S. Supreme Ct. 1973, U.S. Ct. Appeals (7th cir.) 1979. Ptnr. Vorys, Sater, Seymour and Pease, LLP, Columbus, Ohio, 1964—. Bd. dirs. Ohio Bar Liability Ins. Co., Frontstep, Inc. Fellow Internat. Soc. Barristers, Am. Coll. Trial Lawyers (chmn. Ohio joint select com. on jud. compensation 1987), Am. Bar Found. (life), Ohio Bar Found., Columbus Bar Found.; mem. ABA (ho. of dels. 1985—, state del. 1989-95, bd. govs. 1995-98), Ohio Bar Assn. (pres. 1985), Columbus Bar Assn. (pres. 1978), Pres.'s Club Ohio State U., The Golf Club, Worthington Hills Country Club, Columbus Athletic Club. Home: 2090 Sheringham Rd Columbus OH 43220-4358 Office: Vorys Sater Seymour & Pease LLP PO Box 1008 52 E Gay St Columbus OH 43215-3161 E-mail: dwthomas@vssp.com.

THOMAS, E.J. state legislator; b. Dec. 7, 1951; s. Eddie James III and Alice (Layne) T. BS, Ohio State Univ.; MA, Ball State Univ. Dep. asst. legis & adminstrn. Gov. James A. Rhodes, Ohio; state rep. Dist. 28, 1985-92, Dist. 27, 1993; mem. coord. Am. Legis. Exchange Coun., Ohio, 1996—; Ohio House Rep., 1996-98. Mem. Ways & Means Ins. Fin. Inst. & Human Resources Com., Select Com. of Child Abuse & Juvenile Justice, Capital Sq. Renovation Hazardous Waste & Landfill Study Com. Indigent Care Task Force; at-large commn. appt. Mayor Moody & Rinehart, Clintonville Area Com.; dir. corp. affairs Security Group; v.p. bus. devel. G.W. Ganning & Assocs.; aviation cons. Treas. Watchdog, 1986, 88, 90. With Ohio Air Nat. Guard, Pub. Affairs officer Air Force, 1976-80. Recipient Vol. of Yr. Columbus Symphony Orchestra, 1988. Mem. Columbus Bd. Realtors, Nat. Guard Assn., Lions, Shriner, Scottish Rite, Am. Legion. Home: 4866 Rustic Bridge Rd Columbus OH 43214-2034

THOMAS, EVELYN B. agricultural products supplier; Sec., treas., bookkeeper Brandt Fertilizer, Pleasant Plains, Ill., 1953—; co-owner Har Brand, 1963-67, Brandt Chemical, 1967; sec./treas. Brandt Consolidated, Pleasant Plains, Ill. Office: Brandt Consolidated PO Box 277 Pleasant Plains IL 62677-0277 Fax: 217-626-1927. E-mail: bcadmin@brandtconsolidated.com.

THOMAS, FRANK EDWARD, professional baseball player; b. Columbus, Ga., May 27, 1968; Student, Auburn U. With Chgo. White Sox, 1990—. Named to Sporting News All-Star Coll. All Am. team, 1989; Sporting News All-Star team, 1991, 93-94; recipient Silver Slugger award, 1991, 93, 94; mem. Am. League All-Star Team, 1993-95; recipient Am. League MVP award, 1994; named Major League Player of Yr., Sporting News, 1993. Office: Chgo White Sox Comiskey Park 333 W 35th St Chicago IL 60616-3651*

THOMAS, FREDERICK BRADLEY, lawyer; b. Evanston, Ill., Aug. 13, 1949; s. Frederick Bradley and Katherine Kidder (Bingham) T.; m. Elizabeth Maxwell, Oct. 25, 1975; children: Bradley Bingham, Stephens Maxwell, Rosa Macaulay. AB, Dartmouth Coll., 1971; JD, U. Chgo., 1974. Bar: Ill. 1974. Law clk. to hon. judge John C. Godbold U.S. Ct. Appeals (5th cir.), Montgomery, Ala., 1974-75; assoc. Mayer, Brown, Rowe & Maw, Chgo., 1975—80, ptnr., 1981—. Bd. dirs. St. Gregory Episcopal Sch., 1989—; bd. trustees La Rabida Children's Hosp., 1990—; bd. mgrs. YMCA Met. Chgo., 2002--. Mem. ABA, Chgo. Council Lawyers. Republican. Episcopalian. Office: Mayer Brown Rowe & Maw 190 S La Salle St Ste 3100 Chicago IL 60603-3441 E-mail: fthomas@mayerbrown.com.

THOMAS, ISIAH LORD , III, former professional basketball player, basketball team executive; b. Chgo., Apr. 30, 1961; Grad. in Criminal Justice, Ind. U., 1987. With Detroit Pistons, 1981-94; v.p. Toronto Raptors, 1994-97, now v.p. basketball ops., owner, exec. v.p., 1996-97; sportscaster N.B.C. Sports, N.Y.C., 1997-00; head coach Indiana Pacers, Indianapolis, 2000—. Mem. U.S. Olympic Basketball Team, 1980, NBA Championship Teams, 1989-90. Named to All-Star team, 1982-93, All NBA First Team, 1984, 85, 86; recipient All-Star team MVP award, 1984, 86, NBA Playoff MVP award, 1990, NBA Finals MVP, 1990. Named to NBA All-Rookie team 1982. Address: Indiana Pacers 125 S Pennsylvania St Indianapolis IN 46204-3610

THOMAS, JOHN, mechanical engineer, research and development; b. Tiruvalla, Kerala, India, Jan. 2, 1946; came to U.S., 1974; s. Munnencheril Varghese and Rachel (Mathai) T.; m. Mary Parapat Varghese, Apr. 28, 1975; children: Joel George, Sayana Rachel. BSc in Mech. Engring., Birla Inst. Tech., Ranchi, India, 1969; MA Sc in Mech. Engring., U. Waterloo, Ont., Can., 1974. Registered profl. engr., Wis. Lectr. mech. engring. U. Kerala, India, 1970-71; design engr. Combustion Engring., Inc., Springfield, Ohio, 1974-76; mech. engr. Ingersoll-Rand Co., Painted Post, N.Y., 1977-80; engr. Allis-Chalmers Corp., Milw., 1980-82; pvt. practice engring. cons., 1982-84; sr. tech. devel. engr. Cross & Trecker divsn. Kearney & Trecker Corp., 1984-87; prin. John Thomas & Assocs., Brookfield, Wis., 1988-90; sr. product engr. N.W. Water Group, Pub. Ltd. Corp., Waukesha, 1989-94; pres. Thomas Products Co., Brookfield, 1995—; staff engr. Milsco Mfg. Co. unit of Jason Inc., Milw., 1997—. Patentee in field. Mem. Am. Soc. Mech. Engrs., U. Waterloo Alumni Assn. Mem. Mar Thoma Syrian Ch. of Malabar. Avocation: photography. Home: 18330 Benington Brookfield WI 53045-5419 Office: Thomas Products Co PO Box 401 Brookfield WI 53008-0401

THOMAS, JOHN KERRY, chemistry educator; b. Llanelli, Wales, May 16, 1934; came to U.S., 1960; s. Ronald W. and Rebecca (Johns) T.; m. June M. Critchley, Feb. 28, 1959; children: Delia, Roland, Roger. BS, U. Manchester, Eng., 1954, PhD, 1957, DSc, 1969. Rsch. assoc. Nat. Rsch. Coun. Can., Ottawa, 1957-58; sci. officer Atomic Energy. U.K., Harwell, Eng., 1958-60; rsch. assoc. Argonne (Ill.) Nat. Lab., 1960-70; prof. chemistry U. Notre Dame, Ind., 1970-82, Nieuwland prof. chemistry, 1982—. Author: Chemistry of Excitation at Interfaces, 1984; mem. editorial bd. Macromolecules Langmuir, Jour. of Colloid and Interface Soc. Recipient of Rsch. Awd., 1994, Radiation Rsch, Am. Chem. Soc. award in Colloid or Surface Chemistry, 1994. Fellow Royal Soc. Chemistry; mem. Am. Chem. Soc. (award in colloids and surface 1994), Radiation Rsch. Soc. (editorial bd. jours., Rsch. award 1972, 94), Photochem. Soc. Home: 17704 Waxwing Ln South Bend IN 46635-1327 Office: Univ Notre Dame Dept Chemistry Notre Dame IN 46556

THOMAS, JOHN THIEME, management consultant; b. Detroit, Aug. 21, 1935; s. John Shepherd and Florence Leona (Thieme) T.; m. Ellen Linden Taylor, June 27, 1959; children: Johnson Taylor, Evan Thurston. BBA, U. Mich., 1957, MBA, 1958. Mfg. dept. mgr. Procter & Gamble Co., Cin., 1958-60, brand mgr., 1960-63; sr. cons. Glendinning Cos. Inc., Westport, Conn., 1964-66, v.p. London, 1967-69, exec. v.p. Westport, 1970-74, also bd. dirs.; exec. v.p., chief operating officer Ero Industries, Chgo., 1974-76; v.p. Lamalie Assocs. Inc., 1977-81; pres. Wilkins & Thomas Inc., 1981-87; ptnr. Ward Howell Internat., 1987—, mng. dir., cons. practice, 1992-98, chief of staff, 1995-98; also bd. dirs.; cons. ret. LAI Ward Howell, Chgo., 1999—, El Jefe, Thomas Ent. Inc., 1999. Exec. dir. Proctor & Gamble Alumni Assn., Chgo., 1981—. Pub. Procter & Gamble Mfg. Alumni directory, 1981—; author articles in profl. jours. Chmn. bd. dirs. Winnetka (Ill.) Youth Orgn., 1986—; bd. dirs. No. Ill. Girl Scouts Coun., 2002—; selector Winnetka Town Coun., 1978, 1980, 1984, Winnetka Caucus Exec. Com., 1997—2001. Mem. Nat. Assn. Corp. & Profl. Recruiters, Assn. Exec. Search Cons., Am. Soc. Pers. Adminstrn. Club: Fairfield (Conn.) Hunt (treas. 1971-74). Avocations: gardening, music, playing tuba. Home and Office: 525 Ash St Winnetka IL 60093-2601 E-mail: enjthomas@aol.com.

THOMAS, LLOYD BREWSTER, economics educator; b. Columbia, Mo., Oct. 22, 1941; s. Lloyd B. and Marianne (Moon) T.; m. Sally Leach, Aug. 11, 1963; 1 child, Elizabeth. AB, U. Mo., 1963, AM, 1964; PhD, Northwestern U., 1970. Instr. Northwestern U., Evanston, Ill., 1966-68; asst. prof. econs. Kan. State U., Manhattan, 1968-72, assoc. prof., 1974-81, prof., 1983—; asst. prof. Fla. State U., Tallahassee, 1973-74. Vis. prof. U. Calif., Berkeley, 1981-82, U. Del., 1993, U. Ind., Bloomington, 1997-98; prof., chair dept. econs. U. Idaho, 1989. Author: Money, Banking and Economic Activity, 3d edit., 1986, Principles of Economics, 2d edit, 1993, Principles of Macroeconomics, 2d edit,, 1993, Principles of Microeconomics, 2d edit, 1993, Money, Banking and Financial Markets, 1997; contbr. articles to profl. jours. Mem. Am. Econs. Assn., Midwest Econs. Assn., So. Econs. Assn., Western Econs. Assn., Phi Kappa Phi. Avocations: tennis, classical music. Home: 1501 N 10th St Manhattan KS 66502-4607 E-mail: lbt@ksu.edu.

THOMAS, MARGARET JEAN, clergywoman, religious research consultant; b. Detroit, Dec. 24, 1943; d. Robert Elcana and Purcella Margaret (Hartness) T. BS, Mich. State U., 1964; MDiv, Union Theol. Sem., Va., 1971; DMin, San Francisco Theol. Sem., 1991. Ordained to ministry United Presbyn. Ch., 1971. Dir. rsch. bd. Christian edn. Presbyn. Ch. U.S., Richmond, Va., 1965-71, dir. rsch. gen. coun. Atlanta, 1972-73; mng. dir. rsch. div. support agy. United Presbyn. Ch. U.S.A., N.Y.C., 1974-76, dep. exec. dir. gen. assembly mission coun., 1977-83; dir. N.Y. coordination Presbyn. Ch. (U.S.A.), 1983-85; exec. dir. Minn. Coun. Chs., Mpls., 1985-95; synod exec. Synod of Lakes and Prairies Presbyn. Ch. (U.S.A.), Bloomington, Minn., 1995—. Mem. Permanent Jud. Commn., Presbyn. Ch. (U.S.A.), 1985-91, moderator, 1989-91, mem. adv. com. on constn., 1992-98, moderator, 1997-98, mem. synod exec. forum, 1995—, mem. coop. com. on partnership funding, 1997-98, chair, 1998, gen. assembly coun., 2000—; sec. com Contbr. articles to profl. jours. Active alumni bd. Union Theol. Seminary Va., 1980-85; mem. adv. panel crime victims svcs. Hennepin County Atty.'s Office, 1985-86, Police and Cmty. Rels. Task Force, St. Paul, 1986; mem. adv. panel Hennepin County Crime Victim Coun., 1990-93, chair 1990-93; bd. dirs. Minn. Foodshare, 1985-95, Minn. Coalition on Health, 1986-92, Minn. Black-on-Black Crime Task Force, 1988, Twin Cities Coalition Affordable Health Care, 1986-87, Presbyn. Homes of Minn., 1995—, Clearwater Forest, Deerwood, Minn., 1995-96; co-chmn. Minn. Interreligious Com., 1988-95; bd. dirs. Abbott Northwestern Pastoral Counseling Ctr., 1988-91, chair 1990-91; chaplains adv. panel, Immortal Chaplains Found., 1999—. Recipient Human Rels. award Jewish Community Rels. Coun./Anti-Defamation League, 1989, Gov.'s Cert. of Commendation for Women's Leadership, 1993. Mem. NOW (Outstanding Woman of Minn. 1986). Mem. Democrat-Farm-Labor Party. Office: Synod of Lakes and Prairies Presbyn Ch USA 8012 Cedar Ave S Bloomington MN 55425-1204

THOMAS, MARLIN ULUESS, industrial engineering educator, academic administrator; b. Middlesboro, Ky., June 28, 1942; s. Elmer Vernon and Helen Lavada (Banks) T.; m. Susan Kay Stoner, Jan. 18, 1963; children: Pamela Claire Thomas Davis, Martin Phillip. BSE, U. Mich., Dearborn, 1967; MSE, U. Mich., Ann Arbor, 1968, PhD, 1971. Registered profl. engr., Mich. Asst. and assoc. prof. dept. ops. rsch. Naval Postgrad. Sch., Monterey, Calif., 1971-76; assoc. prof. systems design dept. U. Wis., Milw., 1976-78; mgr. tech. planning and analysis vehicle quality-reliability Chrysler Corp., Detroit, 1978-79; prof. dept. indsl. engring. U. Mo., Columbia, 1979-82; prof. indsl. engring., chmn. dept. Cleve State U., 1982-88, acting dir. Advanced Mfg. Ctr., 1984-85; prof., chmn. indsl. engring. Lehigh U., Bethlehem, Pa., 1988-93; prof., head Sch. Indsl. Engring. Purdue U., West Lafayette, Ind., 1993-98; dir. Inst. Interdisciplinary Engring. Studies, 1998—. Program dir. NSF, Washington, 1987-88. Contbr. numerous articles on indsl. engring. and ops. rsch. to profl. jours. With USN, 1958-62; capt. USNR, 1971—. Named Outstanding Tchr., U. Mo. Coll. Engring., 1980, Coll. Man of Yr, Cleve. State U. Coll. Engring., 1985, Disting. Alumnus of Yr., U. Mich.-Dearborn, 1996. Fellow Inst. Indsl. Engrs. (pres.-elect), Am. Soc. for Quality; mem. Ops. Rsch. Soc. Am., Am. Soc. for Engring. Edn., Soc. Am. Mil. Engrs., VFW. Office: Inst Interdisciplinary Engring Studies Purdue Univ 1293 Potter Engineering Ctr West Lafayette IN 47907-1293 Fax: 765-494-2351.

THOMAS, PAMELA ADRIENNE, special education educator; b. St. Louis, Oct. 28, 1940; d. Charles Seraphin Fernandez and Adrienne Louise (O'Brien) Fernandez Reeg; divorced, 1977; m. Alvertis T. Thomas, July 22, 1981. BA in Spanish and EdS, Maryville U., 1962; Cert. EdS, U. Ky., 1966-67; MA in Edn., St. Louis U., 1974. Cert. learning disabilities, behavior disorders, educable mentally retarded, Spanish, Mo. Tchr. Pawnee Rock Kans. Sch., 1963-64; diagnostic tchr. Frankfort State Hosp. Sch., Ky., 1964-67; spl. edn. tchr. St. Louis City Pub. Schs., 1968-71, itinerant tchr., 1971-73, ednl. strategist, 1973-74, elem. level resource tchr., 1974-78, secondary resource tchr., dept. head, 1978—, head dept. spl. edn., 1978—, resource tchr., 1998—, dept. head, 1998; ret., 2000. Co-author: Sophomore English Resource for Credit Curriculum Handbook, 1991. Co-author: Teaching Foreign Language to Handicapped Secondary Students, 1990. Pres. Council for Exceptional Children, local chpt. #103, 1982-83, Mo. Division of Mentally Retarded, 1985-87. Mem. Alpha Delta Kappa (St. Louis chpt. pres. 1982-84). Avocations: traveling, reading, swimming, theatre, handicrafts. Home: 4534 Ohio Ave Saint Louis MO 63111-1324

THOMAS, PHILIP STANLEY, economist, educator; b. Hinsdale, Ill., Oct. 23, 1928; s. Roy Kehl and Pauline (Grafton) Thomas; m. Carol Morris, Dec. 27, 1950; children: Lindsey Carol, Daniel Kyle, Lauren Louise, Gay Richardson. BA, Oberlin Coll., 1950; MA, U. Mich., 1951, PhD, 1961; postgrad., Delhi U., 1953-54. Instr. U. Mich., 1956-57; asst.

prof. Grinnell (Iowa) Coll., 1957-63, assoc. prof., 1963-65; assoc. prof. econs. Kalamazoo Coll., 1965-68, prof. econs., 1968-94, prof. emeritus, 1994—. Econ. advisor Pakistan Inst. Devel. Econs., 1963—64, USAID, 1965—68, 1971, Planning Commn., Pakistan, 1969—70, Ctrl. Bank Swaziland, 1974—75, Ministry Planning, Kenya, 1980—81, Kenya, 1983—85, 1986—88, Ministry Fin., Swaziland, 1990, Kenya, 91, Kenya, 92, Ministry Indsl. Devel., Sri Lanka, 1997, Res. Bank Malawi, 1998—99, Jordan-U.S. Bus. Partnership, 2000—01. Contbr. articles to profl. jours. Mem. alumni coun. Oberlin Coll., 1961—63, 1974—76, 1983—86, 1995—2001. Fellow Overseas, Ford Found., 1953—54; scholar Fulbright. Mem.: Am. Econs. Assn., Phi Beta Kappa. Home and Office: 313A S Shabwasung St Northport MI 49670-9604 E-mail: pcthomas@traverse.net.

THOMAS, R. DAVID, food services company executive; b. Atlantic City, July 2, 1932; s. R. and Olivia (Sinclair) T.; m. I. Lorraine Buskirk, May 21, 1954; 5 children. Student pub. schs. Past owner, mgr. Ky. Fried Chicken Franchise; founder, chmn. bd. Wendy's Internat., Inc. (parent co. Wendy's Old Fashioned Hamburgers restaurants), Columbus, Ohio, from 1969, also Dublin, Ohio., now sr. chmn. bd., founder, 1981—. Bd. dirs. Children's Hosp., Columbus, Ohio, St. Jude Children's Research Hosp., Memphis; founder Dave Thomas Found. for Adoption. Served with U.S. Army. Recipient Horatio Alger award, 1979 Mem. Ohio Restaurant Assn., Nat. Restaurant Assn. (dir.) Club: Ohio Commodores. Office: Wendy's Internat Inc PO Box 256 4288 W Dublin Granville Rd Dublin OH 43017-1442

THOMAS, RICHARD LEE, banker; b. Marion, Ohio, Jan. 11, 1931; s. Marvin C. and Irene (Harruff) T.; m. Helen Moore, June 17, 1953; children: Richard L., David Paul, Laura Sue. BA, Kenyon Coll., 1953; postgrad. (Fulbright scholar), U. Copenhagen, Denmark, 1954; MBA (George F. Baker scholar), Harvard U., 1958. With First Nat. Bank Chgo., 1958—, asst. v.p., 1962-63, v.p., 1963-65; v.p., gen. mgr. First Nat. Bank Chgo. (London br.), 1965-66; v.p. term loan divsn. First Nat. Bank, Chgo., 1968; sr. v.p., gen. mgr. First Chgo. Corp., 1969-72, exec. v.p., 1972-73, vice chmn. bd., 1973-75, pres., 1975-92, chmn., pres., CEO, 1992-95; chmn. First Chgo. NBD Corp., 1995-96, ret. chmn., 1996. Bd. dirs. Sara Lee Corp., Sabre Holdings Corp., IMC Global Inc., PMI Group Inc., EXELON Corp. Trustee, past chmn. bd. trustees Kenyon Coll., Chgo. Symphony Orch.; trustee Rush-Presbyn.-St. Luke's Med. Ctr., Northwestern U. With AUS, 1954-56. Mem. Chgo. Coun. Fgn. Rels., Sunningdale Golf Club (London), Econ. Club (past pres.), Comml. Club (past chmn.), Chgo. Club, Casino Club, Mid-Am. Club, Indian Hill Club (Winnetka, Ill.), Old Elm Club (Highland Park, Ill.), Phi Beta Kappa, Beta Theta Pi. Office: First Chgo NBD Corp 1 Bank One Plz, Ste. IL1-0518 Chicago IL 60670-0001 E-mail: richard_l_thomas@bankone.com.

THOMAS, RICHARD STEPHEN, financial executive; b. Mason City, Iowa, June 5, 1949; s. H. Idris and Mildred (Keen) T.; m. Pamela Jane Chipka, Sept. 11, 1982. AA, No. Iowa C.C., 1969; BA, U. No. Iowa, 1971, BLS, 1991; MBA, U. Calif., Berkeley, 1991. Cost acct. Boise Cascade, Mason City, Iowa, 1971-72, cost acct. mgr. Shippensburg, Pa., 1973-74; staff acct. Grumman Corp., Williamsport, 1974-76; acctg. mgr. Pullman Power Products, 1976-79; treas, controller Schweizer Dipple Inc., Cleve., 1979-87; treas., corp. controller Langenau Mfg. Co., 1987-92, chief fin. officer, 1987-92; sec.-treas. World Trade Wins Inc., 1987-92; v.p. fin. and CFO Norris Bros, Co., Inc., 1992—. Mem. employer adv. com. Ohio Job Svc., Greater Cleve. Growth Assn., Westlake Ohio Sch. Bd. Mem. Inst. Mgmt. Accts. (contr.'s coun. 1985), Constrn. Fin. Mgmt. Assn. (pres. 1995—, state dir., nat. dir.), Am. Coun. for Constrn. Edn. (accreditation and standards com. 1996—, fin. comm. 1997-98), Constrn. Industry Liason Comm. (chmn.), Cleve. Treas.'s Assn., Cleve. Engring. Soc., Associated Builders and Contractors, Constrn. Employers Assn., Econ. Club Indpls., Cleve. World Trade Assn., Masons (local treas. 1984), York Rite Bodies, City Club of Cleve., Phi Beta Lambda. Republican. Avocations: skiing, photography, sailing. Home: 1663 Settlers Reserve Way Westlake OH 44145-2042 Office: Norris Bros Co Inc 2138 Davenport Ave Cleveland OH 44114-3791 E-mail: rsthomas49@aol.com.

THOMAS, ROBERT LEIGHTON, physicist, researcher; b. Dover-Foxcroft, Maine, Oct. 10, 1938; s. Tillson Davis and Ruth (Leighton) T.; m. Sandra Evenson, June 23, 1962; 1 child, Stephen Leighton. AB, Bowdoin Coll., 1960; PhD, Brown U., 1965. Rsch. assoc. Wayne State U., Detroit, 1965-66, from asst. to assoc. prof. physics, 1966-76, prof. physics, 1976—, dir. Inst. for Mfg. Rsch., 1986—. Chmn. Gordon Rsch. Conf. in Nondestructive Evaluation, 1991-92. Assoc. editor Rsch. in Nondestructive Evaluation; contbr. more than 150 articles to sci. jours. Fellow Am. Phys. Soc.; mem. Acad.Scholars, Sigma Xi (chpt. pres. 1990-91). Achievements include patents for Thermal Wave Imaging Apparatus, for Vector Lock-in Imaging System for Single Beam Interferometer, and for Confocal Optical Microscope. Office: Wayne State U Inst for Mfg Rsch Detroit MI 48202

THOMAS, ROBERT R. judge; b. Rochester, N.Y., Aug. 7, 1952; m. Maggie Thomas; 3 children. BA in govt., U. Notre Dame, 1974; JD, Loyola U., 1981. Cir. ct. judge DuPage County, 1988, acting chief judge, 1989—94; judge Appellate Ct. Second Dist., 1994—2000; Supreme Ct. justice Ill. State Supreme Ct., 2000—. Mem.: DuPage County Bar Assn., Acad. All-Am. Hall of Fame (life NCAA Silver Ann. Award 1999). Office: Bldg A Rm 207A 1776 S Naperville Rd Wheaton IL 60187*

THOMAS, STEPHEN PAUL, lawyer; b. Bloomington, Ill., July 30, 1938; s. Owen Wilson and Mary Katherine (Paulsen) T.; m. Marieanne Sauer, Dec. 7, 1963 (dec. June 1984); 1 child, Catherine Marie; m. Marcia Aldrich Toomey, May 28, 1988; 1 child, Ellen Antonia. BA, U. Ill., 1959; LLB, Harvard U., 1962. Bar: Ill. 1962; cert. naturalist Morton Arboretum, 2001. Vol. Peace Corps, Malawi, Africa, 1963-65; assoc. Sidley & Austin, Chgo., 1965-70, ptnr., 1970-2000. Lectr. on law Malawi Inst. Pub. Adminstrn., 1963-65. Pres. Hyde Park-Kenwood Cmty. Conf., Chgo., 1988-90; trustee Chgo. Acad. for Arts, 1991—, chmn., 1992-97; bd. dirs. Union League Civic and Arts Found., Chgo., 1999—. Recipient Paul Cornell award Hyde Park Hist. Soc., 1981. Mem. ABA, Chgo. Bar Assn., Chgo. Fedn. of Musicians, Lawyers Club of Chgo., Union League Club Chgo., Chgo. Literary Club. Democrat. Roman Catholic. Avocations: jazz piano playing, naturalist studies. Home: 9765 S Longwood Dr Chicago IL 60643-1610 Office: Sidley Austin Brown & Wood 55 W Monroe St Chicago IL 60603-5001 E-mail: sthomas@sidley.com.

THOMASON, LARRY, state official; b. Jefferson City, Mo., Oct. 31, 1948; m. Diane Bush, 1978; 1 child, Sarah. BS, Ark. State U. Mem. Mo. Ho. of Reps. from 163d dist., 1988-98; dir. Mo. Hwy. Reciprocity Commn., 1998—. Mem. Agr.-Bus., Appropriations, Comm., Transp. Coms. Mo. Ho. of Reps.; cons. econ. devel.; mem. adv. bd. Internat. Bus. Inst. S.E. Mo. State U., Dyersburg C.C. Assoc. dir. Mo. Indsl. Devel. Commn.; active S.E. Mo. Regional Growth Assn., Hwy. 412 Corridor Assn. Mem. Kennett C. of C. (exec. dir.), Am. Legion, Lions. Democrat. Home: PO Box 523 Kennett MO 63857-0523

THOME, JAMES J. financial executive; Exec. v.p., COO BHA Group Holdings Inc., 1993—. Office: 8800 E 63d St Kansas City MO 64133

THOME, JIM, professional baseball player; b. Peoria, Ill., Aug. 27, 1970; Player Cleve. Indians, 1991—. Office: Cleve Indians 2401 Ontario St Cleveland OH 44115*

THOMOPULOS, GREGS G. consulting engineering company executive; b. Benin City, Nigeria, May 16, 1942; s. Aristoteles and Christiana E. (Ogiamien) T.; m. Patricia Walker, Sept. 4, 1966 (div. 1974); 1 child, Lisa; m. Mettie L. Williams, May 28, 1976; children: Nicole, Euphemia. BSCE with highest distinction, U. Kans., 1965; MS in Structural Enging., U. Calif., Berkeley, 1966; PhD (hon.), Teikyo Marycrest U., 1996. Sr. v.p. internat. div. Stanley Cons., Inc., Muscatine, Iowa, 1978-84, sr. v.p. project divsn., 1984-87; pres., CEO Stanley Consultants, Inc., 1987—; exec. v.p. SC Co., Inc., 1992-98; pres., COO, 1998-99; pres., CEO, 2000—; also bd. dirs. SC Co., Inc., Muscatine; chmn., CEO Stanley Environ., Inc., Chgo., 1991—, also bd. dirs.; chmn., CEO SC Power Devel., Inc., 1992—. Chmn., CEO Stanley Design-Build, Inc., 1995—; bd. dirs. Stanley Cons., Inc., Muscatine, Wellmark, Inc., Blue Cross Blue Shield Iowa and S.D., 1999—. Mem. adv. bd. Coll. Engring. U. Iowa, 1992-2000, Hydraulics Inst., 2000—. Fellow ASCE, Am. Cons. Engring. Coun.; mem. NSPE, 33 Club (pres. 1987), Rotary. Presbyterian. Avocations: tennis, computers, music. Home: 75 Shagbark Ct Iowa City IA 52246-2786 Office: Stanley Cons Inc 225 Iowa Ave Muscatine IA 52761-3765 E-mail: thomopulos@home.com., :thomopulosg@stanleygroup.com.

THOMPSON, BASIL F. ballet master; b. Newcastle-on-Tyne, Eng., 1937; came to U.S., 1958; Grad., Royal Acad. Dance; studies with, David Lichine, Tania Riabouchinska; student, Sch. Classical. Ballet, 1958-60. Dancer Covent Garden Opera Co., Sadler Wells Opera Co., London, 1954-55, Royal Ballet Eng., London, 1955-58; instr. ballet and character Eugene Loring Sch. Ballet, L.A., 1958-60, Al Gilber Sch. Ballet, L.A., 1958-60; instr. ballet Michael Panaieff Sch. Ballet, 1958-60; soloist Am. Ballet Theatre, N.Y.C., 1960-67; ballet master Joffrey Ballet Co., 1967-79; ballet master, choreographer N.J. Ballet Co., West Orange, 1979-80; mem. faculty ballet and character N.J. Ballet Sch., Morristown/West Orange, 1979-80; ballet master Milw. Ballet, 1981-86, also artistic head; ballet master Pa. and Milw. Ballet; apptd. artistic dir. Milw. Ballet, spring 1995; now prof. dance U. Iowa, Iowa City. Guest ballet instr. Internat. Ballet Inst., Aix-en-Provence, France, 1980; guest instr. character Am. Ballet Co. Sch., 1981. Roles include (prin.) Billy the Kid, Sleeping Beauty, Graduation Ball, La Sylphide, Moon Reindeer, Peter and The Wolf, Three Cornered Hat, others, (soloist) Rodeo, Fall River Legend, Fire Bird, Coppelia, Swan Lake, Cinderella, La Boutique Fantastic, Undertow, others (opera) Aida; guest appearances include for Dame Margo Fontayne Royal Acad. Gala, Pres. John F. Kennedy, Pres. Lyndon B. Johnson, L.A. Civic Light Opera, Michael Panaieff Ballet Theatre; TV appearances include Bell Telephone Hour Spectacular prodn. Graduation Ball, NBC prodn. Sleeping Beauty and Cinderella; Broadway prodns. On a Clear Day You Can See Forever, Tavarich, Happiest Girl in the World; choreographer La Traviata. Office: Univ of Iowa Dept Dance 107 W Hoalsey Iowa City IA 52240 E-mail: basil-thompson@uiowa.edu., BASIL34@juno.com.

THOMPSON, BERTHA BOYA, retired education educator, antique dealer and appraiser; b. New Castle, Pa., Jan. 31, 1917; d. Frank L. and Kathryn Belle (Park) Boya; m. John L. Thompson, Mar. 27, 1942; children: Kay Lynn Thompson Koolage, Scott McClain. BS in Elem. & Secondary Edn., Slippery Rock State Coll., 1940; MA in Geography and History, Miami U., 1954; EdD, Ind. U., 1961. Cert. elem. and secondary edn. tchr. Elem. tchr., reading specialist New Castle (Pa.) Sch. System, 1940-45; tchr., chmn. social studies Talawanda Sch. System, Oxford, Ohio, 1954-63; assoc. prof. psychology and geography, chair edn. dept. Western Coll. for Women, 1963-74; assoc. prof. edn., reading clinic Miami U., 1974-78, prof. emeritus, 1978—; pvt. antique dealer, appraiser, 1978—. Contbr. articles to profl. jours. Mem. folk art com. Miami U. Art Mus., Oxford, 1974-76; mem. adv. com. Smith libr., Oxford Pub. Libr., 1978-81. Mem. AAUP, Nat. Coun. Geographic Edn. (exec. bd. dirs. 1966-69), Nat. Soc. for Study Edn., Assn. Am. Geographers, Soc. Women Geographers, Nat. Coun. for the Social Studies, Pi Lambda Theta, Zeta Tau Alpha, Pi Gamma Mu, Gamma Theta Upsilon, Kappa Delta Pi. Avocations: antique collecting, reading, travel, tennis. Home: 6073 Contreras Rd Oxford OH 45056-9708

THOMPSON, CHARLES MURRAY, lawyer; b. Childress, Tex., Oct. 13, 1942; s. Walter Lee and Lois S. (Sheehan) T.; children: Murray McKay, McLean Ann. BS with honors, Colo. State U., 1965; JD cum laude, U. S.D., 1969, LLD (hon.), 1995. Bar: S.D. 1969, U.S. Dist. Ct. S.D. 1969, U.S. Ct. Claims 1989, U.S. Ct. Appeals (8th cir.) 1972, U.S. Supreme Ct. 1973. Ptnr. May, Adam, Gerdes & Thompson, Pierre, S.D., 1969—. Spkr. at trial lawyer and state bar seminars; bd. dirs. Bank West, Pierre, S.D.; dir. Delta Trust, Pierre. Editor S.D. Law Rev., 1969 Pres. S.D. Council Sch. Attys., 1984-86. Fellow Am. Bar Found. (chmn. 1991-92, bd. dirs. 1989-92), Coll. Law Practice Mgmt., Am. Coll. Trial Lawyers; mem. ABA (ho. of dels. 1978—, bd. govs. 1983-86), ATLA, Am. Bd. Trial Advs., Am. Counsel Assn., Am. Judicature Soc. (bd. dirs. 1981-85), Am. Bar Endowment (bd. dirs. 1991—, v.p. 1998—), Nat. Conf. Bar Pres.'s (exec. coun. 1986-94, pres. 1992-93), State Bar S.D. (pres. young lawyers sect. 1974-75, pres. 1986-87), S.D. Bar Found. (pres. 1991), S.D. Trial Lawyers Assn. (pres. 1980-81), Jackrabbit Bar Assn. (chancellor 1981-82), Kiwanis (pres. local club 1977). Democrat. Avocations: flying, ranching. Home and Office: PO Box 160 Pierre SD 57501-0160

THOMPSON, CLIFTON C. retired chemistry educator, university administrator; b. Franklin, Tenn., Aug. 16, 1939; s. Clifton C. and Ruby M. (Moore) T.; m. Sarah Ellen Gaunt, Dec. 1, 1978; children: Brenda Kay, Victoria Lea. BS, Middle Tenn. State U., 1961; PhD, U. Miss., 1964. Asst. prof. Rutgers U., New Brunswick, N.J., 1965, Marshall U., Huntington, W.Va., 1965-66; assoc. prof. Middle Tenn. State U., Murfreesboro, 1966-68, Memphis State U., 1968-74; prof. chemistry, dept. head, dean Coll. Sci. and Math., dir. Ctr. for Sci. Rsch., assoc. v.p. for grad. studies and rsch. S.W. Mo. State U., Springfield, 1974-96, prof. emeritus, 1996—; prof. chemistry Cen. Mich. U., Mt. Pleasant, 1996-98. Rsch. assoc. U. Tex., Austin, 1964-65; rschr. Oak Ridge Nat. Lab., 1968; cons. Mid-South Research Assocs., Memphis, 1969-71; mem. med. tech. rev. com. Nat. Accrediting Agy. for Clin. Lab. Sci., Chgo., 1974-80; vis. prof. So. Ill. U., Carbondale, 1995. Author: Ultraviolet-Visible Absorption Spectroscopy, 1974; contbr. articles to profl. jours. Mem. health care com. Springfield C. of C., 1978-79, mem. econ. devel. com., 1983-89; bd. dirs. United Hebrew Congregation, Springfield, 1983-86, United Hebrew Found., Inc., 1994-96. NSF fellow, 1961-64; Sigma Xi grantee-in-aide, 1970; NSF sr. fgn. scientist grantee, 1971; NSF coop-coll. sch. sci. grantee, 1972; Higher Edn. Applied Projects grantee, 1987-90. Mem. Am. Chem. Soc., Royal Soc. Chemistry, Sigma Xi, Phi Kappa Phi. Jewish. Office: SW Mo State U Dept Chemistry Springfield MO 65804 E-mail: thompson@biip.net.

THOMPSON, ERIC THOMAS, retail executive; b. Warren, Ohio, July 19, 1962; s. Thomas Leroy Thompson; Eugene (stepfather) and Georgia Kay (Rex) Stafani; m. Susan E. Robertson, 1988; children: Sara Rebecca, Eric Thomas Jr., Katlyn Grace. Student., Youngstown State U., 1981, 83-84, Kent State U., 1982. Outside sales rep., disc jockey WTCL Radio Sta., Warren, Ohio, 1979-80; disc jockey WOKG, 1981-82, WMGZ, Sharon, Pa., 1982-83; sales rep. Custom Sound Co., Warren, Ohio, 1983-86, Litco Internat., Youngstown, 1986-88; admissions rep. Bryant and Stratton Bus. Inst., Cleve., 1988-89; broker Argent Diamond & Gems, Charlotte, N.C., 1983; asst. sales mgr. Gene and Sons Jewelers, Warren, 1986-87; mgr. sales ops. Internat. Graphics Co., Cleve., 1988-89; network coord. The Ohio Desk Co., 1989-90; account executive Alco Office Furniture, 1989-91; high sch. admissions rep. Nat. Edn. Ctr., 1992-93; small bus. owner, operator, ptnr. Satolli Carpet Floor Covering, Warren, Ohio, 1993—, Hometown Mattress and Futon, Warren, 2000—; ptnr., owner/operator Mahoning Ave. Manufactured Housing Cmty., 1997-2000; cable TV talk show host Falls Focus Cmty. Program, 1995-96; v.p., treas. Northeast Ohio Realty Investors, Inc., Warren, 1996—. Disc jockey WSOM-WQXK, Salem, Ohio, 1980-82; comedian, magician, 1981—; host (TV weekly program) Newton Falls Focus, 1995-96; ptnr. Real Estate Holdings Mahoning, 1997-2000; owner, distbr. EcoQuest Internat. Host, Bus. Connections radio show WRRO, Warren; contbr. articles to bus. publs., newspapers and mags. Firefighter and EMT, Newton Falls Fire and Rescue Dept., 2000—; pres. Brooklyn (Ohio) Rep. Club, 1990-93, treas., 1992; team capt. spl. project Am. Heart Assn. N.E. Ohio, 1992; vol. Shoes for Kids, 1991-93, Child Care Task Force, Brooklyn, 1991-93; mem. Greater Cleve. Holiday Lighting Com., 1991-93; st. capt. Mayor's Com. on Recycling, Brooklyn, 1990-93; bd. mem. Trumbull County Govt. Affairs Com., 1996-99; cons. Jr. Achievement, Cleve., 1991-93; mem. Rock and Roll Hall of Fame and Mus. Task Force, Clean-Land Ohio Task Force; dir., com. mem. Newton Falls Bus. Comty. Expo, 1994-96; dir. Broad St. Merchants Group, 1994-95; co-dir., advisor Newton Falls United Meth. Youth Group, 1996-98; bd. trustees Newton Falls United Meth. Ch., 1995-98, liturgist, lay spkr., 1995-2000; mem. bd. July 4th Com., 1995—; mem. Youngstown-Warren Ohio Better Bus. Bur., 1993—, Crescendo Club/Band Boosters, 1997-2002; youth coach Newton Falls (Ohio) Hot Stove Baseball, 1994—; vol. Newton Falls Cmty. Car Show, 1995—, Newton Falls All-Weather Track Com., 1999, Newton Falls Athletic Boosters, 1997—; dir., cubmaster pack 67 Greater Western Res. coun. Newton Falls Boy Scouts, 1997-99; mem. Friends of the Newton Falls Libr., 1995-99; mem. Ohio H.S. Athletic Assn., varsity/jr. varsity baseball umpire, 1998—; ofcl. Continental Am. Baseball Assn., umpire, 1998—; youth league coord., exec. com. Newton Falls Babe Ruth Youth Baseball/Softball Assn., 1998—, umpire in chief, 1999—, Little League Invitational Tournament, Trumbull County, Ohio, 2000. Recipient Outstanding Leadership award Brooklyn Rep. Club, 1990, Coun. of Sml. Bus. Outstanding Effort award, 1991, Comty. Leadership & Bus. Success award U.S. Congress, 1997, Home Town Hero award Cub Scouts/Boy Scouts, 1999; inducted as umpire Am. Youth Baseball Hall of Fame, 2000. Mem. Greater Cleve. Growth Assn. (Outstanding Vol. Svc. award 1991, 93), Greater Cleve. Coun. Smaller Enterprises, Ind. C. of C., Cleve. Zool. Soc., Internat. Customer Svc. Assn., Sale and Mktg. Execs., N.E. Ohio Floor Covering Assn., Eagles Bus. and Profl. Orgn., Internat. Brotherhood Magicians, Soc. Am. Magicians, Fellowship Christian Magicians, Eagles, Soc. Am. Baseball Rsch. (umpire and rules history com. 1999—), Newton Falls C. of C. (pres. 1994, 95, 96, bd. dirs. 1993-96, Disting. Svc. Honor Leadership award 1995), N.E. Ohio Floor Covering Assn., Youngstown Warren C. of C., Kiwanis Club (v.p. 1994-95, chmn. program com. Newton Falls chpt. 1993-94, July 4th festivities com. 1995), Warren Civic Music Assn., Bus. Connections (bd. dirs. 1998), Trumbull County Interscholastic Umpires Assn. (h.s. ofcl. 1998—), Ohio H.S. Athletic Assn. Methodist. Avocations: stand up comedy, magic and illusion, travel, reading. Home: 315 Marshall St Newton Falls OH 44444-1426 Office: 367 High St NE Warren OH 44481-1246

THOMPSON, HERBERT STANLEY, neuro-ophthalmologist; b. Shansi, China, June 12, 1932; arrived in U.S., 1949, naturalized, 1955; s. Robert Ernest and Ellen Thompson; m. Delores Lucille Johnson, June 27, 1953; children: Geoffrey, Peter, Kenneth, Philip, Susan. Student, Methodist Coll., Belfast, No. Ireland, 1947—49; BA, U. Minn., 1953, MD, 1961; MS, U. Iowa, 1966. Diplomate Am. Bd. Ophthalmology (assoc. examiner 1972-88, bd. dirs. 1989-96, chmn. ABO 1996). Intern U. Iowa, Iowa City, 1961—62, resident in ophthalmology, 1962—66; fellow in pupillography Columbia Coll. Physicians and Surgeons, 1962; fellow in clin. neuro-ophthalmology U. Calif., San Francisco, 1966—67; prof. ophthalmology U. Iowa, Iowa City, 1976—97, emeritus prof., 1997—, dir. neuro-ophthalmology unit, 1967—97; practice medicine specializing in neuro-ophthalmology Iowa City, 1967—97. Editor: Topics in Neuro-ophthalmology, 1979; assoc. editor: Am. Jour. Ophthalmology, 1981—84, book rev. editor: , 1984—91, cons.: Stedman's Med. Dictionary, 26th edit. Served with AUS, 1954-55. Recipient rsch. career devel. award, NIH, 1968—72; fellow spl. fellow, 1966—67. Fellow: N.Am. Neuro-ophthalmol. Soc., Am. Acad. Ophthalmology; mem.: Cogan Ophthalmic History Soc. (Charles Snyder lectr. 1995), Am. Ophthalmol. Soc. Avocation: research on movements of the pupil of human eye. Office: U Iowa Dept Ophthalmology Iowa City IA 52242

THOMPSON, HOLLEY MARKER, lawyer, marketing professional; b. Jamestown, N.Y., Jan. 30, 1947; d. Burdette James and Mary (Novitske) Marker; children: Jennifer Kristen Simos, Kendra Elise Blair, Jennifer Lynn, Stephanie Lynn; m. Lawrence D. Thompson. AAS, Jamestown C.C., 1966; BS, Ohio U., 1969; MA, W.Va. U., 1974, JD, 1980. Bar: W.Va. 1980, U.S. Dist. Ct. (so. dist.) W.Va. 1980, Pa. 1982, U.S. Dist. Ct. (we. dist.) Pa. 1982. Tchr. math. various pub. schs., Santa Ana (Calif.), Lakewood (N.Y.) and Morgantown (W.Va.), 1970-77; atty. for students W.Va. U., Morgantown, 1980; assoc. libr., lectr. W.Va. U. Coll. Law, 1980-83; assoc., libr. Jackson, Kelly, Holt & O'Farrell, Charleston, W.Va., 1983-86; cons. Hildebrandt, Inc., Somerville, N.J., 1986-94; v.p. mktg., assn. markets profl. rels. Lexis Nexis, Dayton, Ohio, 1994—. Spkr. in field. Contbr. articles to profl. jours. Mem. ABA, Spl. Libr. Assn., Am. Assn. Law Libs., N.J. Assn. Law Libs., Legal Mktg. Assn., Phi Delta Phi. Office: Lexis Nexis 9443 Springboro Pike Miamisburg OH 45342 E-mail: holley.thompson@lexisnexis.com.

THOMPSON, JAMES ROBERT, JR. lawyer, former governor; b. Chgo., May 8, 1936; s. James Robert and Agnes Josephine (Swanson) T.; m. Jayne Carr, 1976; 1 child, Samantha Jayne. Student, U. Ill., Chgo., 1953-55, Washington U., St. Louis, 1955-56; J.D., Northwestern U., 1959. Bar: Ill. 1959, U.S. Supreme Ct. 1964. Asst. state's atty., Cook County, Ill., 1959-64; assoc. prof. law Northwestern U. Law Sch., 1964-69; asst. atty. gen. State of Ill., 1969-70; chief criminal div., 1969; chief dept. law enforcement and pub. protection, 1969-70; 1st asst. U.S. atty. No. Dist. Ill., 1970-71, U.S. atty., 1971-75; counsel firm Winston & Strawn, Chgo., 1975-77, ptnr., chmn. exec. com., 1991—; gov. Ill., 1977-91. Chmn. Pres.' Intelligence Oversight Bd., 1989—93; adv. bd. Fed. Emergency Mgmt. Agy., 1991—93; bd. govs. Chgo. Bd. Trade; bd. dirs. FMC Corp., FMC Techs., Inc., Jefferson Smurfit Group, PLC, Prime Retail Inc., Hollinger Internat., Inc., Prime Group Realty Trust, Navigant Consulting Inc., Maximus, Inc., Chgo. Mus. Contemporary Art, Lyric Opera Chgo., Econ. Club Chgo., Civic Com., Comml. Club Chgo., Execs. Club Chgo. Co-author: Cases and Comments on Criminal Justice, 2 vols, 1968, 74, Criminal Law and Its Adminstration, 1970, 74. Chmn. Ill. Math. and Sci. Acad. Found.; chmn. Rep. Gov.'s Assn., 1982, Nat. Gov.'s Assn., Midwest Gov.'s Assn., Coun. Gt. Lakes Gov.'s, 1985. Mem. ABA, Ill. Bar Assn., Chgo. Bar Assn. Republican. Office: Winston & Strawn 35 W Wacker Dr Ste 4200 Chicago IL 60601-1695

THOMPSON, LEE (MORRIS THOMPSON), lawyer; b. Hutchinson, Kans., Nov. 29, 1946; s. Morris J. and Ruth W. (Smith) T.; m. M. Susan Morgan, May 26, 1974; children: Deborah, Erin, Andrew, Christopher. BA, Wichita State U., 1968; MA, Emporia State U., 1970; JD, George Washington U., 1974. Bar: Kans., 1974, U.S. Dist. Ct. Kans., 1974, U.S. Ct. Appeals (10th cir.) 1976, U.S. Supreme Ct., 1978. Instr., lectr. Emporia (Kans.) State U., 1969-70; lctr. in speech George Washington U., Washington, 1970-71; asst. to Senator James Pearson, 1971-75; assoc. Martin, Pringle, et al., Wichita, Kans., 1976-78, ptnr., 1979-89; U.S. atty. for dist. of Kans., Dept. Justice, 1990-93; ptnr. Triplett, Woolf & Garrets, LLC, 1993—2001; mng. mem. Thompson Stout & Goering LLC, 2001—. Treas. Kansans for Kassebaum, Wichita, 1978-88; mem. Kans. State Rep. Cen. Com., Topeka, 1978-79, 88-90; candidate U.S. Ho. of Reps., Kans., 1988; chmn. civil issues subcom. Atty. Gen.'s Adv. Com. of U.S. Attys., 1992-93. Mem. Kans. Bar Assn. (pres. criminal law sect. 1994-95). Methodist. Office: Thompson Stout & Goering LLC 100 N Broadway Ste 710 Wichita KS 67202 E-mail: Lthompson@tslawfirm.com.

THOMPSON, MARGARET M. physical education educator; b. Merrifield, Va., Aug. 1, 1921; d. Lesley L. and Madeline (Shawen) T. B.S., Mary Washington Coll., 1941; M.A., George Washington U., 1947; Ph.D., U. Iowa, 1961. Tchr., supr. phys. edn. Staunton (Va.) City Schs., 1941-44; tchr. jr. high sch. phys. edn. Arlington County, Va., 1944-47; instr. women's phys. edn. Fla. State U., Tallahassee, 1947-51; instr., asst. prof., assoc. prof. phys. edn. Purdue U., Lafayette, Ind., 1951-65, dir. gross motor therapy lab., 1963-65; assoc. prof. phys. edn. U. Mo., Columbia, 1965-68, prof., 1968-71, dir. Cinematography and Motor Learning Lab. Dept. Health and Phys. Edn., 1965-71; prof. phys. edn. U. Ill., Champaign-Urbana, 1971-87, prof. emeritus, 1987—. Vis. prof. Escola de Educacão Fisica, U. de São Paulo, Brazil, 1985; vis. prof. phy. edn. Inst. Bioscis. de Rio Claro, U. Estadual Paulista, Brazil, 1991. Author: (with Barbara B. Godfrey) Movement Pattern Checklists, 1966, (with Chappelle Arnett) Perceptual Motor and Motor Test Battery for Children, 1968, (with Barbara Mann) An Holistic Approach to Physical Education Curriculum: Objectives Classification System for Elementary Schools, 1977, Gross Motor Inventory, 1976, revised edit., 1980, Developing the Curriculum, 1980, Setting the Learning Environment, 1980, Sex Stereotyping and Human Development, 1980; also film strips, articles. Mem. AAHPER, Internat. Assn. Phys. Edn. and Sports for Coll. Girls and Women. Home and Office: 1311 Wildwood Ln Mahomet IL 61853-9770 E-mail: mmthomps@uiuc.edu.

THOMPSON, MARY EILEEN, chemistry educator; b. Mpls., Dec. 21, 1928; d. Albert C. and Blanche (McAvoy) T. BA, Coll. St. Catherine, 1953; MS, U. Minn., 1958; PhD, U. Calif., Berkeley, 1964. Tchr. math. and sci. Derham Hall H.S., St. Paul, 1953-58; mem. faculty Coll. of St. Catherine, 1964-69, prof. chemistry, 1969-2000, chmn. dept., 1969-90, prof. emeritus, 2000—. Project dir. Women in Chemistry, 1984-98. Contbr. articles to profl. jours. Mem. AAAS, Am. Chem. Soc. (chmn. women chemists com. 1992-94, award for encouraging women into chem. scis. careers 1997), Coun. Undergrad. Rsch. (councillor 1991-96), N.Y. Acad. Scis., Chem. Soc. London, Sigma Xi, Phi Beta Kappa (senator 1997—). Democrat. Roman Catholic. Achievements include research interests in Cr(III) hydrolytic polymers, kinetics of inorganic complexes, Co(III) peroxo/superoxo complexes. Office: Coll of St Catherine 2004 Randolph Ave Saint Paul MN 55105-1750 E-mail: methompson@stkate.edu., MTHOM17349@aol.com.

THOMPSON, MORLEY PUNSHON, textile company executive; b. San Francisco, Jan. 2, 1927; s. Morley Punshon and Ruth (Wetmore) T.; m. Patricia Ann Smith, Jan. 31, 1953 (dec.); children: Page Elizabeth Tredennick, Morley Punshon; m. Katharine Shaw Wallace. AB, Stanford U., 1948; MBA, Harvard U., 1950; JD, Chase Law Sch., 1969; LLD, Xavier U., 1981. CPA, Ohio. Chmn. Stearns Tech. Textiles Co., Cin., 1985—, Stearns Can., Inc., Cin., 1985—. Bd. dirs. Cin. Inst. Fine Arts. Lt. Supply Corps USNR, 1952-54. Mem. Beta Theta Pi. Office: 100 Williams St Cincinnati OH 45215-4602

THOMPSON, NANCY P. state legislator; b. Sioux Falls, S.D., Oct. 26, 1947; m. James Thompson, July 4, 1970; children: Kevin, Matthew, Cynthia, Joseph. BA, Creighton U., 1969, MA, 1982. Dist. staff mem. U.S. Rep. John Cavanaugh; dep. chief of staff Gov. Ben Nelson; former tchr.; mem. Nebr. Legislature from 14th dist., Lincoln, 1997—. Former exec. dir. Omaha Cmty. Partnership; mem. Sarpy County Bd. Commrs. Home: 1302 Western Hills Dr Papillion NE 68046-7036 Office: State Capitol Dist 14 PO Box 94604 Rm 1117 Lincoln NE 68509-4604 E-mail: nthompson@unicam.state.ne.us.

THOMPSON, NORMAN WINSLOW, surgeon, educator; b. Boston, July 12, 1932; s. Herman Chandler and Evelyn Millicent (Palmer) T.; m. Marcia Ann Veldman, June 12, 1956; children: Robert, Karen, Susan, Jennifer. BA, Hope Coll., 1953; MD, U. Mich., 1957; MD (hon.), U. Linköping, Sweden, 1995. Diplomate Am. Bd. Surgery. From intern to prof. emeritus surgery U. Mich., Ann Arbor, Mich., 1957—2001, prof. emeritus surgery, 2001—. Contbr. articles to profl. jours. Trustee Hope Coll., Holland, Mich., 1973-88. Fellow Royal Australasian Coll. Surgeons (hon.), Royal Coll. Physicians and Surgeons of Glasgow; mem. ACS (gov. 1979-85), Ctrl. Surg. Assn., Western Surg. Assn. (1st v.p. 1992-93, pres. 1994-95), F.A. Coller Surg. Soc. (pres. 1986), Am. Surg. Assn., Am. Thyroid Assn., Soc. Surg. Alimentary Tract, Internat. Assn. Endocrine Surgeons (pres. 1989-91), Internat. Soc. Surgeons (v.p. 1995—), Am. Assn. Endocrine Surgeons (pres. 1980-81, 81-82), Royal Soc. Medicine, Brit. Assn. Endocrine Surgeons, Assn. French Endocrine Surgeons, Scandanvian Surg. Soc., Soc. Surg. Oncology, Turkish Assn. Endocrine Surgeons, Alpha Omega Alpha. Home: 465 Hillspur Rd Ann Arbor MI 48105-1048 Office: U Mich Med Ctr 2920 Taubman Bldg Ann Arbor MI 48109 Fax: 734 936 5830. E-mail: normant@umich.edu.

THOMPSON, RICHARD L. manufacturing executive; B in Engring., Stanford U. V.p. engring. divsn. Caterpillar Inc., 1990-95, group pres., 1995—. Office: Caterpillar Inc 100 NE Adams St Peoria IL 61629-0002

THOMPSON, RICHARD LLOYD, pastor; b. Lansing, Mich., May 8, 1939; s. Lloyd Walter and Gladys V. (Gates) T.; m. Dianne Lee Tuttle, Nov. 14, 1958; children: Matthew, Beth Anne, Douglas. BA, Azusa Pacific U., 1969; MDiv, Concordia Theol. Sem., 1973; DD, Concordia U., Mequon, Wis., 1997. Aerospace industry test engr. Hycon Mfg. Co., Monrovia, Calif., 1961-69; pastor Trinity Luth. Ch., Cedar Rapids, Iowa, 1973-84, Billings, Mont., 1984-94, Good Shepherd Luth. Ch., Watertown, Wis., 1994—2001. Chmn. mission com. Iowa E. dist. Luth. Ch. Mo. Synod, 1979-81, 2nd v.p. Iowa dist. E., Cedar Rapids, 1981-84, bd. mgr. Concordia plans, St. Louis, 1983-86, bd. dirs., St. Louis, 1986-98, chmn. bd. dirs., 1992-98, mem. commn. on theology and ch. rels., 2001; served on various task forces and coms. dealing with structure and vision setting for chs. at local, dist. and nat. level, 1975—. Mem. Nat. Exch. Club, Cedar Rapids, 1982-84, Billings, 1986. With USN, 1957-61. Mem. Kiwanis. Avocations: attending auctions, yard work, travel, exercise activity. E-mail: rlt50@hotmail.com.

THOMPSON, RICHARD THOMAS, academic administrator; b. Buffalo, Oct. 11, 1939; m. Nancy A. Streeter, July 29, 1959; children: Elizabeth Thompson Grapentine, Richard Thomas Jr., David Bryant. BA, Ea. Mich. U., 1961, MA, 1963; LLD (hon.), Walsh Coll., 2000. Cert. tchr., Mich. Tchr. Warren (Mich.) Consol. Sch., 1961-66; dean, pres. Highland Lake campus Oakland C.C., Union Lake, Mich., 1966-75, pres. Orchard Ridge campus Farmington, 1975-84, v.p. Bloomfield, 1984-88, vice chancellor, 1988-91, chancellor, 1996—, pres. Auburn Hills campus. Arbitrator Better Bus. Bur., Detroit, 1987—; bd. dirs., past chair Providence Hosp., Southfield, Mich., 1988—; cons. examiner N. Ctrl. Assn. Commn. on Higher Learning, 1988—. Contbr. articles to profl. jours. Pres. Oakway Symphony Orch., Livonia, Mich., 1981-85; chair Oakland Literacy coun., Pontiac, Mich., 1988—, Recipient Leadership award Oakland County C. of C., 1987, Tricounty Disting. Svc. award Detroit Coll. Bus., 1996, Shirley B. Gordon award of Distinction Phi Theta Kappa Internat., 2001. Mem. Phi Delta Kappa. Home: 625 E Commerce St Milford MI 48381-1723 Office: Oakland Community Coll 2480 Opdyke Rd Bloomfield Hills MI 48304-2223

THOMPSON, ROBERT DOUGLAS, computer science educator, banker, consultant; b. Van Wert, Ohio, Apr. 2, 1944; s. Ernest Clinton and Gertrude Marcele (McBride) T.; m. Gail Joyce Knudson; children: Linda Marie Temple, Cheryl Elizabeth Christensen, Mark Robert. BS summa cum laude, Huntington Coll., 1966; MA, Mich. State U., East Lansing, 1967; student, Wright State U., 1974-90, Bowling Green State U., 1984, U. Dayton, 1985. Cert. tchr., Ohio. Office sec. United Brethren in Christ Denomination Ch., Huntington, Ind., 1963-66; grad. research asst. Mich. State U., East Lansing, 1966-67; instr. Wright State U. Lake Campus, Celina, Ohio, 1976, 93-97, Tri Star Career Compact, Celina, 1984-96; ptnr. Thompson Painting and Carpentry, Rockford, Ohio, 1969-95; tchr., dept. head, tech. coord. St. Henry (Ohio) Consol. Local Schs., 1967-97; asst. v.p., br. mgr. Peoples Bank Co., Rockford, Ohio, 1997—. Author, photographer numerous newspaper articles, 1974—, Business Professionals of America Ohio Association Handbook, 1989. Bd. dirs., pres., v.p. Oscar Figert Guidance Clinic, 1972-75; pres. Mercer County Mental Health Clinic, 1975; fin. chmn. Coldwater United Meth. Ch., 1982-90, 2000—, chmn. adminstrv. bd., 1994-99, lay leader, 1998--; solicitor Coldwater Combined Charities, 1982, 85; PRIDE evaluation svc. rep. State Dept. Edn., 1973, 78; troop treas. Coldwater area Boy Scouts Am., 1989-92; mem. office tech. adv. bd. Wright State U.-Lake Campus, Celina, Ohio, 1991—; gen. chairperson Rockford Combined Charities, 1997-2001; exec. officer Rockford Citizen Crime Awareness, 1998—; trustee Shanes Park, 1999—, Rockford Carnegie Libr., 1999—, v.p. 2001, pres. 2002; pres. Leota Braun Charitable Found., Inc., 2002--. Named super advisor Ohio Office Edn. Assn., 1983, 84, 85; recipient proclamation of excellence, Ohio State Dept. Edn. Mem. NEA, Am. Vocat. Assn., Bus. Profl. Am. (advisor 1973-97, star advisor and honor advisor award), Ohio Bus. Tchrs. Assn. (state exec. bd. 1976-77, 93-98, state conv. chmn. 1995, Western Ohio Bus. Tchr. of Yr. award 1983, 91, 95, Ohio Bus. Tchr. of Yr. 1995, Editor of Publs. 1996-98), Ohio Edn. Assn., St. Henry Edn. Assn. (local pres. 1970-72), Wabash Valley Dartball Assn. (sec. 1978-79, 87-88), Rockford (Ohio) C. of C. (treas. 1998—), Lions (Rockford chpt. v.p. 2001—), Delta Pi Epsilon. Republican. Avocations: travel, computers, choir singing. Home: 405 S Main St PO Box 242 Rockford OH 45882-0242 Office: Peoples Bank Co PO Box 475 101 N Main St Rockford OH 45882-8118 E-mail: rthompson@pbcbank.com.

THOMPSON, ROBY CALVIN, JR. orthopedic surgeon, educator; b. Winchester, Ky., May 1, 1934; s. Roby Calvin and Mary Davis (Guerrant) T.; m. Jane Elizabeth Searcy, May 2, 1959; children: Searcy Lee, Roby Calvin, III, Mary Alexandria. BA, Va. Mil. Inst., 1955; MD, U. Va., 1959. Diplomate Am. Bd. Orthopaedic Surgery (mem. bd. 1983). Intern Columbia Presbyn. Med. Center, N.Y.C., 1959-60, asst. resident, then resident in orthopedic surgery, 1963-67; instr. orthopaedic surgery Coll. Phys. and Surg. Columbia U., 1967-68; mem. faculty Med. Sch. U. Va., 1968-74, prof. orthopaedic surgery, vice chmn. dept. Med. Sch., 1973-74; prof., chmn. dept. Med. Sch. U. Minn., 1974-95; chief med. officer U. Minn. Health Sys., 1995-96, v.p. clin. and acad. affairs, 1996—. Mem. merit rev. bd. VA, 1977-80; mem. study sect. on applied physiology and orthopedics NIH, 1980-83; adv. council mem. NIH, Nat. Inst. Arthritis, Musculoskeletal Disease and Skin, 1987-91. Trustee Jour. Bone and Joint Surgery, 1988-94, chmn. bd. trustees, 1991-94; contbr. articles to med. jours. Capt. M.C. USAR, 1960-61. Grantee John Hartford Found., NIH Mem. ACS, Orthopaedic Rsch. and Edn. Found. (bd. trustees 1990-96), Am. Acad. Orthopaedic Surgeons (bd. dirs. 1975-76, 83-90, pres. 1986), Orthopaedic Rsch. Soc. (pres. 1978), Am. Orthopaedic Assn., Musculoskeletal Tumor Soc. (pres. 1988-89), U. Va. Med. Alumni Assn. (bd. dirs. 1979-84), Woodhill Club (Wayzata). Republican. Presbyterian. Office: U of Minn PO Box 501 420 Delaware St SE Minneapolis MN 55455-0374

THOMPSON, ROGER G., JR. career military officer, retired; b. Dec. 19, 1944; BS, US Military Acad., 1966; MBA, Syracuse U., 1977. Exec. officer Battery D, 1st Bn., 73rd Arty., 1st Armored Divsn., Fort Hood, TX, 1966-67, comdr., 1968; S-2 Battery B, 2nd Bn., 321st Arty., 3rd Brigade, 82nd Airborne Divsn., US Army, Vietnam, 1968, comdr., 1968-69; exec. officer, later asst. S-3 (Operations), later S-1 (Personnel), 3rd Bn., 76th Arty., 3rd Inf. Divsn., US Army, Europe, 7th Army, 1969-71; chief Plans and Ops. Divsn. G-4 (Logistics), 3rd Inf. Divsn., US Army Europe and 7th Army, Germany, 1971-72; asst. instr., later stud. Transp. Officer Advanced Course, Fort Eustis, VA, 1972-73; tng. ofcr. US Army Transp. Sch., 1973-74; comdr. 872th Transp. Co., 24th Transp. Bn., 7th Transp. Group, 1974-75; combat devel. staff officer US Army Transp. Sch., 1975-76; comdr. 37th Transp. Command, US Army Europe and Seventh Army, Germany, 1989-91; dep. comdr. for combat devel. US Army, Fort Lee, VA, 1991-92; dir. ops. and support Office of Asst. Sec. of Army (Fin. Mgmt.), Wash., D.C., 1992-93; dep. chief of staff for res. mgmt. US Army Material Command, Alexandria, VA, 1993-94; comdg. gen. Military Traffic Mgmt. Command, Falls Church, 1994-96; dep. asst. sec. of Army for Budget Office of Asst. Sec. of Army for Fin. Mgmt. and Comptroller, Wash., D.C., 1996-97; commd. 2d lt. U.S. Army, advanced through grades to lt. gen., 1997—. Recipient Disting. Svc. medal, Legion of Merit (with two oak leaf clusters), Bronze Star medal, Meritorious Svc. medal (with 6 oak leaf clusters), Army Commendation medal (with 2 oak leaf clusters), Parachutist Badge, Ranger Tab, Army Staff Identification Badge. Office: US Transp Command 508 Scott Dr Rm 339 Scott Air Force Base IL 62225-5313

THOMPSON, RONALD L. manufacturing company executive; BBA, U. Mich.; MS, PhD, Mich. State U. Chmn., CEO Evaluation Techs., Inc.; chmn. bd. dirs., pres. GR Group Inc., 1980—; chmn., CEO Midwest Stamping and Mfg. Co. (subs. of GR Group Inc.), Bowling Green, Ohio. Mem. faculty Old Dominion U., Va. State Coll., U. Mich.; bd. dirs. Mcdonnell Douglas Corp. Recipient Nat. Minority Entrepreneur of Yr. award U.S. Dept. Commerce, 1989, Disting. Svc. to Edn. award Harris-Stowe State Coll., 1991, disting. Cmty. Svc. award So. Ill. U., Edwardsville, 1990. Office: Midwest Stamping Inc 3455 Briarfield Blvd Ste A Maumee OH 43537-9503

THOMPSON, RONELLE KAY HILDEBRANDT, library director; b. Brookings, S.D., Apr. 21, 1954; d. Earl E. and Maxine R. (Taplin) Hildebrandt; m. Harry Floyd Thompson II, Dec. 24, 1976; children: Clarissa, Harry III. BA in Humanities magna cum laude, Houghton Coll., 1976; MLS, Syracuse U., 1976; postgrad., U. Rochester, 1980, 81; cert., Miami U., 1990. Libr. asst. Norwalk (Conn.) Pub. Libr., 1977; elem. libr. Moriah Cen. Schs., Port Henry, N.Y., 1977-78; divsn. coord. pediat. gastroenterology and nutrition U. Rochester (N.Y.) Med. Ctr., 1978-81, cons., pediat. housestaff libr. com., 1980-81; dir. Medford Libr. U. S.C., Lancaster, 1981-83; dir. Mikkelsen Libr., Libr. Assocs., Ctr. for Western Studies, mem. libr. com. Augustana Coll., Sioux Falls, S.D., 1983—, adminstrv. pers. coun., 1989-94, 97—. Presenter in field. Contbr. articles to profl. jours. Mem. Sioux Falls Cmty. Playhouse, S.D. Symphony, Sioux Falls Civic Fine Arts Assn.; advisor pers. dept. City of Sioux Falls. Recipient leader award YWCA, 1991; Gaylord Co. scholar Syracuse U., 1976; named S.D. Libr. of Yr., 1998. Mem. ALA, AAUW, Assn. Coll. and Rsch. Librs. (nat. adv. coun. coll. librs. sect. 1987—), Mountain Plains Libr. Assn. (chair acad. sect., nominating com. 1988, pres. 1993-94), S.D. Libr. Assn. (chair interlibr. coop. task force 1986-87, pres. 1987-88, chair recommended minimum salary task force 1988, chair local arrangements com. 1989-90), S.D. Libr. Network (adv. coun. 1986—, exec. com. 1992-96, 1998-2000, chair adv. coun. 1994-96, 98-2000). Office: Augustana Coll Mikkelsen Libr 29th & Smt Sioux Falls SD 57197-0001 E-mail: ronelle_thompson@augie.edu.

THOMPSON, SETH CHARLES, retired oral and maxillofacial surgeon; b. Whittemore, Mich., Aug. 12, 1927; s. Seth Charles and Annie Ernestine (Washburn) T.; m. Effie Valore Garland, Jan. 20, 1954; children: Seth Charles III, David Garland. BS, Mich. State U., 1949; DDS, U. Mich., 1952, MS, 1959. Pvt. practice oral and maxillofacial surgery, Midland, Mich., 1959-94; ret., 1994. Discoverer surgical treatment for trigeminal neuralgia, 1976. Bd. dirs. Midland (Mich.) Christian Sch., 1971-72, Inst. for Achievement of Human Potential, Midland, 1970-71. Served to capt. USAF, 1953-55. Fellow Am. Assn. Oral and Maxillofacial Surgery; mem. ADA, Mich. Dental Assn., Mich. Assn. Oral and Maxillofacial Surgery, Midland County Med. Soc. Republican. Baptist. Avocations: hunting, fishing, travel, woodworking. Home and Office: 2728 W Parish Rd Midland MI 48642-9601

THOMPSON, STANLEY B. church administrator; Pres., CEO, dir. The Free Meth. Found., Spring Arbor, Mich.; chmn., CEO, dir. King Trust Co., N.A.; chmn., dir. Free Meth. Found. Office: Free Methodist Foundation PO Box 580 Spring Arbor MI 49283-0580 E-mail: sbthompson@kingtrust.org.

THOMPSON, STEPHEN ARTHUR, sales consultant; b. Englewood, N.J., Jan. 24, 1934; s. Stephen Gerard and Doris Lillian (Evans) T.; m. Joan Frances O'Connor, May 12, 1955 (div. 1978); children: Stephen Andrew, Craig Allen, David John; m. Sandra Rene Fingernut, May 27, 1979. BS, Ohio State U., 1961. Physicist Rocketdyne div. North Am. Aviation, Canoga Park, Calif., 1961-62, Marquardt Corp., Van Nuys, 1962-63; mem. tech. staff Hughes Rsch. Labs., Malibu, 1963-69; editor Electronic Engr. mag. Chilton Co., L.A., 1969-72, in advt. sales Instruments and Controls Sys., mag., 1972-77; regional advt. sales Design News mag. Cahners Pub. Co., 1977-84, sales mgr. Design News mag. Newton, Mass., 1984-87, pub. Design News mag., 1987-95, group. pub. mfg. group, 1989-93, sr. v.p. integrated mktg., 1993-94, gen. mgr. Boston divsn., 1995-96, gen. mgr. mfg. mktg. divsn., 1995-97, sr. v.p. tng., 1996-97; gen. mgr. OEM/processing group Advanstar Comms., Cleve., 1997-99; sales training cons. Bentleyville, Ohio, 1999-2000. Founder Design News Engring. Edn. Found., Newton, 1991-97; pub. Design News Mag., 1994-95; group pub. Mfg. Group. Author: Basketball for Boys, 1970; contbr. articles to Jour. Spacecraft/Rockets, 1966. Club leader YMCA, Canoga Park, 1963-78; active PTA, Canoga Park, 1961-80; bd. dirs. Chatsworth (Calif.) High Booster Club, 1972-80. 1st lt., jet fighter pilot USAF, 1952-58. Mem. Bus. Profl. Advt. Assn. (Golden Spike award 1980, 81, 82, 83), L.A. Mag. Reps. Assn. (life), Nat. Fluid Power Assn., BPA Internat. (bd. dirs.). Achievements include patents for ion source, system and method for ion implantation of semiconductors. Office: 7500 Old Oak Blvd Cleveland OH 44130-3343

THOMPSON, THEODORE ROBERT, pediatric educator; b. Dayton, Ohio, July 18, 1943; s. Theodore Roosevelt and Helen (Casey) J.;m. Lynette Joanne Shenk; 1 child, S. Beth. BS, Wittenberg U., 1965; MD, U. Pa., 1969. Diplomate Am. Bd. Pediatrics (Neonatal, Perinatal Medicine). Resident in pediat. U. Minn. Hosp., Mpls., 1969-72, chief resident in pediat., 1971-72, fellow neonatal, perinatal, 1974-75, asst. prof., 1975-80, dir. divsn. neonatology and newborn intensive care unit, 1977-80, assoc. prof., 1980-85, prof., 1985—, co-dir. Med. Outreach, 1988-91, med. dir. med. outreach, 1991-00, assoc. chief of pediat., 1988—; med. dir. outreach U. Minn. Physicians, 1992—, dir. clin. edn. med. students, 1999—. Editor: Newborn Intensive Care: A Practical Manual, 1983. Bd. dirs. Life Link III, St. Paul, 1987—; cons. Maternal and Child Health, Minn. Bd. Health, 1975-94; bd. dirs. Minn. Med. Found., 1995-99. With USPHS. 1972-74. Fellow: Am. Acad. Pediats.; mem.: Gt. Plains Orgn. for Perinatal Health Care (Sioux Falls, SD Kunshe award 1989). Lutheran. Office: MMC 39 420 Delaware St SE Minneapolis MN 55455-0374 E-mail: thomp005@umn.edu.

THOMPSON, THOMAS ADRIAN, sculptor; b. Sidney, Mont., Aug. 28, 1944; s. Vernon Eugene and Helen Alice (Torstenson) T.; m. M. Aileen Braun, June 7, 1968; children: Blair C., Meghann C. BA, Concordia Coll., 1966; postgrad., Mich. State U., 1968-69, Oakland U., 1970-72. Art tchr. Carman Ainsworth Sch. Dist., Flint, Mich., 1966-98; ret., 1998. Chmn. Flint Art Curriculum Com., 1980. Mem. adv. bd. Mich. Equine Artists; mem. Gand Blanc Arts Coun. Mem. NEA, Nat. Art. Edn. Assn., Mich. Art Edn. Assn. (liaison mem.), Internat. Arabian Horse Assn., Arabian Horse Registry. Lutheran. Avocations: painting, sculpture, golf. Home: 1120 Old Town Ct Grand Blanc MI 48439-1622 E-mail: TaThomps@hotmail.com.

THOMPSON, TOMMY GEORGE, federal agency administrator, former governor; b. Elroy, Wis., Nov. 19, 1941; s. Allan and Julia (Dutton) T.; m. Sue Ann Mashak, 1969; children: Kelli Sue, Tommi, Jason. BS in Polit. Sci. and History, U. Wis., 1963, JD, 1966. Polit. intern U.S. Rep. Thomson, 1963; legis. messenger Wis. State Senate, 1964-66; sole practice Elroy and Mauston, Wis., 1966-87; mem. Dist. 87 Wis. State Assembly, 1966-87, asst. minority leader, 1972-81, floor leader, 1981-87; self-employed real estate broker Mauston, 1970—; gov. State of Wis., 1987-2001; Secy Dept HHS, Washington, 2001—. Alt. del. Rep. Nat. Conv., 1976; chmn. Intergovtl. Policy Adv. Commn. to U.S. Trade Rep.; chmn. Natl. Govs. Assn., 1995-96, mem. nat. govs. assn. exec. com.; chmn. bd. dirs., Amtrak, 1998-99. Served with USAR. Recipient med. award for Legis. Wis. Acad. Gen. Practice, Thomas Jefferson Freedon award Am. Legis. Exchange Coun., 1991, Most Valuable Pub. Official award City and State Mag., 1991, Governance award Free Congress Found., 1992, Governing Mag. Public Ofcl. of the Year, 1997, recipient Horatio Alger Awd., 1998, USA Mex. C of C, Good Neighbor Awd., 1999. Mem. ABA, Wis. Bar Assn., Rep. Govs. Assn., Phi Delta Phi. Roman Catholic. Office: Dept HHS Office of the Secy 200 Independence Ave SW Washington DC 20201-0004 Office Fax: 202-690-7203.*

THOMPSON, VERN, state senator; b. Maddock, N.D., Aug. 23, 1956; m. Cindy; one child, Will. City councilman; supr.; rep. N.D. State, 1989-91, state senator, 1997—. Recipient N.D. Weekly N.D. POl. Figure of the Yr., 1995, Minnewaukan Citizen of the Yr., 1996. Democrat. Office: Dist 12 111 East B Street Minnewaukan ND 58351*

THOMPSON, WADE FRANCIS BRUCE, manufacturing company executive; b. Wellington, New Zealand, July 23, 1940; came to U.S., 1961, naturalized, 1990. m. Angela Ellen Barry, Jan. 20, 1967; children: Amanda and Charles (twins). B in Commerce, Cert. Acctg., Victoria U., Wellington, 1961; MSc, NYU, 1963. Dir. diversification Sperry & Hutchinson, N.Y.C., 1967-72; v.p. Texstar Corp., 1972-77; chmn. Hi-Lo Trailer Co., Butler, Ohio, 1977—; chmn., pres., chief exec. officer Thor Industries Inc., Jackson Center, 1980—. Trustee Mystic Seaport Mus., Conn., 1984—; trustee Wade F.B. Thompson Charitable Found. Inc., 1985—, Mcpl. Art Soc., N.Y.C., 1993—, Seventh Regiment Armory Conservancy, N.Y.C., 1997—; founder The Drive Against Prostate Cancer. Mem. Union Club, N.Y. Yacht Club (N.Y.C.). Avocations: tennis, collecting contemporary art. Office: Thor Industries Inc PO Box 629 Jackson Center OH 45334-0629

THOMPSON, WILLIAM EDWARD, state official; b. Lima, Ohio, Apr. 17, 1948; s. Richard Edward and Claudine (Burt) T.; m. Kay Swick, 1974; children; Marshall Burt, Kendra Lea, Parker Sherman. BS, Ohio State Univ., 1972. Mem. Ohio Ho. of Reps., 1987-97; chairperson Indsl. Commn. of Ohio, Columbus, 1997—. V.p. Thompson Seed Farm, Inc., 1977; mem. extension adv. com. Mem. Ohio Seed Improvement Assn., Ohio Seed Dealers Assn., Agrl. Genetic Rsch. Assn., Masonic Lodge, Ohio Farm Bureau, Phi Kappa Psi. Home: 4960 Defiance Trl Delphos OH 45833-9666 Office: 30 W Spring St # L-30 Columbus OH 43215-2241

THOMPSON, WILLIAM MOREAU, radiologist, educator; b. Phila., Oct. 20, 1943; s. Charles Moreau and Aileen (Haddon) T.; m. Judy Ann Seel, July 27, 1968; children: Christopher Moreau, Thayer Haddon. BA, Colgate U., 1965; MD, U. Pa., 1969. Diplomate Am. Bd. Radiology. Intern Case Western Res. U., Cleve., 1969-70; resident in radiology Duke U., Durham, N.C., 1972-75; asst. prof. Duke U. Med. Ctr., 1976-77, assoc. prof., 1977-82, prof. radiology, 1982-86; prof., chmn. dept. radiology, Vilhelmina and Eugene Gedgared chair in Radiology U. Minn. Hosp. and Clinic, Mpls., 1986-2000, prof. radiology, dir. imaging rsch., 2000-01;

prof. radiology Duke U. Med. Ctr., 2001—. Contbr. chpts. to books and articles to profl. jours. Served with USPHS, 1970-72. Recipient James Picker Found. Scholar in Acad. Medicine award, 1975-79, Disting. Scientist award, Armed Forces Inst. Pathology, Washington, 2001-02; R&D grantee VA, 1977-86. Fellow Am. Coll. Radiology; mem. AMA, Radiology Soc. N.Am. (program chmn. 1994-97), Minn. Med. Soc., Am. Roentgen Ray Soc., Assn. Univ. Radiologists (pres. 1989-90, Gold medal 2001), Soc. Gastrointestinal Radiology (pres. 1994-95, Cannon medal 2001), Assn. Program Dirs. (pres. 1995, Achievement award 2001), Soc. Chairs of Acad. Radiology Depts. (pres. 1997-98), Sigma Xi. Republican. Presbyterian. Home: 225 Galway Dr Chapel Hill NC 27517-6558 Office: PO Box 3808 Durham NC 27702-3808

THOMSON, JAMES ADOLPH, medical group practice administrator; b. Kansas City, Mo., Feb. 25, 1924; s. Edward Wilkins and Gladys Lucile (Opperman) T.; m. Patricia Jane Herron, Jan. 24, 1943; children: Linda Lee Thomson Schwartz, Kenneth Leroy, James Howard. BBA, Rockhurst U., Kansas City, 1950. Cost acct. Std. Brands, Inc., Kansas City, 1950-52; asst. comptr. Menorah Med. Ctr., 1952-56; comptr. Holzer Hosp. and Clinic, Gallipolis, Ohio, 1956-63; adminstr. Oberlin (Ohio) Clinic, Inc., 1963-71; adminstr. and treas. Thompson, Brumm & Knepper Clinic, Inc., St. Joseph, Mo., 1971-80; bus. mgr. Cin. Neurol. Assocs., Inc., 1980-89, ret., 1989. Cons. med. groups, Ohio, 1968-70. V.p. St. Joseph (Mo.) Area C. of C., 1976-78; pres. Oberlin Health Commn., 1968-69; bd. dirs. St. Joseph Sheltered Workshop, 1978-80. Served with M.C. U.S. Army, 1943-46, ETO. Recipient Disting. Svc. award St. Joseph Area C. of C., 1979. Fellow Am. Coll. Med. Group Adminstrs.; mem. Am. Assn. Hosp. Accts. (charter, pres. 1954-56), Mo. Med. Group Mgmt. Assn. (charter, pres. 1978-79), Med. Group Mgmt. Assn., Ohio Med. Group Mgmt. Assn., Cin. Med. Group Mgmt. Assn. (pres. 1983-84), Rotary (pres. Oberlin and St. Joseph), Lions (pres. 1962-63), KC, Masons, Shriners, Am. Legion. Republican. Episcopalian. Avocations: woodworking, gardening, golf.

THOMSON, STEVE, radio personality; b. St. Paul; m. Michele Thomson, 1989; 2 children. Student, U. Minn., Brown Inst. With radio stas., Montevideo, Minn., Sioux Falls, SD; with WCCO Radio, Mpls., 1997—, weekend afternoon radio host, 1998, announcer. Avocations: golf, reading. Office: WCCO 625 2nd Ave S Minneapolis MN 55402*

THORESON, LAUREL, state legislator; m. Betty Thoreson; 3 children. Rep. N.D. Ho. of Reps., Bismarck, 1994—. Mem. human svc. and govt. and vet. affairs com. N.D. Ho. of Reps. Mem. Amvets. Office: ND House of Reps State Capitol Bismarck ND 58505

THORNBURGH, RON E. state official; b. Burlingame, Kans., Dec. 31, 1962; m. Annette Thornburgh. Student, Washburn U., 1985. Dep. asst. sec. of state, then asst. sec. of state State of Kans., Topeka, 1985-87, sec. of state, 1995—; asst. sec. of state Sec. of State's Office, 1991-95, sec. of state, 1995—. Vice chairperson blue ribbon panel on ethical conduct State of Kans., 1989. Mem. Kids Voting Kans. Exec. Com.; mem. adv. com. United Way. Toll fellow Henry Toll Fellowship Program, 1995. Mem. Washburn U. Alumni Bd., 20/30 Club Internat. Methodist. Office: Sec of State Statehouse 300 SW 10th Ave Fl 2D Topeka KS 66612-1504

THORNE-THOMSEN, THOMAS, lawyer; b. El Dorado, Kans., Oct. 22, 1949; s. Fletcher and Barbara (Macoubrey) T.-T. BA, Vanderbilt U., 1972; JD, U. Colo., 1976; LLM in Taxation, NYU, 1983. Bar: Colo. 1976, Ga. 1977, Ill. 1983. Law clk. to Chief Judge Alfred A. Arraj U.S. Dist. Ct. Colo., Boulder, 1976-77; assoc. Alston & Bird, Atlanta, 1977-82; assoc., ptnr. Keck, Mahin & Cate, Chgo., 1983-95; ptnr. Schiff, Harden & Waite, 1995-98, Applegate & Thorne-Thomsen, Chgo., 1998—. Bd. dirs. Century Place Devel. Corp., Chgo., 1989—, Sutherland Neighborhood Devel. Corp., Chgo., 1989—, South Shore Neighborhood Devel. Crop. Chgo. 1990—, Argyle Neighborhood Devel. Corp., Chgo., 1991—, Heartland Alliance for Human Rights and Human Need, 1995—, Howard Brown Health Ctr., Chgo., 1991-94; com. mem. Chgo.'s Comprehensive Housing Affordability Strategy, Chgo., 1992—; mem. bond leverage trust fund task force Ill. Housing Authority, 1993. Mem. ABA, Colo. State Bar Assn., Ill. State Bar Assn., Ga. State Bar Assn. Avocations: jogging, biking, swimming, boating, horses. Home: 233 E Wacker Dr Apt 606 Chicago IL 60601-5106 Office: Applegate & Thorne-Thomsen 322 S Green St Ste 412 Chicago IL 60607-3544

THORNTON, JERRY SUE, community college president; BA, MA, Murray (Ky.) State U.; PhD, U. Tex.; DHL, Coll. St. Catherine, St. Paul. Tchr. jr. high sch., Earlington, Ky., Murray H.S., Triton Coll., RiverGrove, Ill., dean arts ans scis.; pres. Lakewood C.C., White Bear Lake, Minn., 1985-92, Cuyahoga C.C., Cleve., 1992—. Bd. dirs. Nat. City Bank, Applied Indsl. Techs. Author books, book chpts. and articles. Bd. dirs. Greater Cleve. Growth Assn., Greater Cleve. Roundtable, Urban League of Greater Cleve., United Way Svcs., Rock and Roll Hall of Fame and Mus., Cleve. Found. Mem. Alpha Kappa Alpha. Office: Cuyahoga CC Office of Pres 700 Carnegie Ave Cleveland OH 44115-2833

THORNTON, JOHN T. corporate financial executive; b. N.Y.C., Oct. 22, 1937; s. John T. and Catherine (Burke) T.; m. Patricia C. Robertson; children: Kevin, Brian, Vincent, Elizabeth, Monica. BBA, St. John's U., 1959, JD, 1972. Bar: N.Y.; CPA. Auditor Peat, Marwick, Mitchell & Co., N.Y.C., 1961-67; asst. controller Texasgulf Inc., Stamford, Conn., 1967-81, v.p., controller, 1981-84; sr. v.p., controller Norwest Corp., Mpls., 1984-87, exec. v.p., chief fin. officer, 1987-97. Bd. dirs. Exel., Ltd., Stock Exch. Listed Co. Office: Norwest Ctr 6th & Marquette Minneapolis MN 55479-0001

THORNTON, THOMAS NOEL, publishing executive; b. Marceline, Mo., Apr. 23, 1950; s. Bernard F. and Helen F. (Kelley) T.; m. Cynthia L. Murray, Nov. 26, 1971; children: T. Zachary, Timothy. B.J., U. Mo., 1972. Asst. to editor Universal Press Syndicate, Kansas City, Mo., 1972, v.p., 1974, dir. mktg., 1976; v.p., dir. mktg. Universal Press Syndicate and Andrews McMeel Pub., Kansas City, 1976-87; pres., COO Andrews McMeel Pub., 1987—. Bd. dirs. Andrews McMeel Universal. Office: Universal Press Syndicate 4520 Main St Ste 700 Kansas City MO 64111-7701 E-mail: tthornton@amuniversal.com.

THORPE, NORMAN RALPH, lawyer, automobile company executive, retired air force officer; b. Carlinville, Ill., Oct. 17, 1934; s. Edwin Everett and Imogene Midas (Hayes) T.; m. Elaine Frances Pritzman, Nov. 1, 1968; children: Sarah Elizabeth, Carrie Rebecca. AB in Econs., U. Ill., 1956, JD, 1958; LLM in Pub. Internat. Law, George Washington U., 1967. Bar: Ill. 1958, Mich. 1988, U.S. Supreme. Ct. 1969. Commd. 2d lt. USAF, 1956, advanced through grades to brig. gen., 1983; legal advisor U.S. Embassy, Manila, 1969-72; chief internat. law hdqrs. USAF, Washington, 1972-77; staff judge adv. 21st Air Force, McGuire AFB, N.J., 1977-80, USAF Europe, Ramstein AB, Fed. Republic Germany, 1980-84; comdr. Air Force Contract Law Ctr., Wright-Patterson AFB, Ohio, 1984-88, ret., 1988; mem. legal staff, group counsel GM Def. and Power Products Gen. Motors Corp., Detroit, 1988—. Legal advisor Dept. of Def. Blue Ribbon Com. on Code of Conduct, 1975; USAF del. Internat. Aero. and Astronautical Fedn., Budapest, 1983; adj. prof. U. Dayton Sch. Law, 1986-87; partnership counsel U.S. Advanced Battery Consortium, Legal Advisor U.S. Coun. Automotive Rsch., Chrysler Corp., Ford Motor Co., GM, 1990—. Contbr. articles to profl. jours. Staff mem. Commn. on Police Policies and Procedures, Dayton, 1986; trustee Dayton Philharm. Orch., 1987-88. Recipient Disting. Svc. medal Legion of Merit. Mem. ABA (chmn. com. internat. law sect. 1977-80, coun. mem. pub. contract law sect. 1986-88, chmn. com. pub. contract law sect. 1988-95, chair-elect pub. contract law sect. 2000-01, vice chair 1999-2000, chair-elect 2000-01, chair 2001-02), Air Force Assn., Dayton Coun. on World Affairs, Army/Navy Club, Detroit Econ. Club. Republican. Avocations: music, piano, gardening. Home: 498 Abbey Rd Birmingham MI 48009-5618 Office: 300 Renaissance Ctr Detroit MI 48243-1401

THORSEN, MARIE KRISTIN, radiologist, educator; b. Milw., Aug. 1, 1947; d. Charles Christian and Margaret Josephine (Little) T.; M. James Lawrence Troy, Jan. 7, 1978; children: Katherine Marie, Megan Elizabeth. BA, U. Wis., 1969; MBA, George Washington U., 1971; MD, Columbia Coll. Physicians and Surgeons, 1977. Diplomate Am. Bd. Radiology. Intern. Columbia-Presbyn. med. Ctr., N.Y.C., 1977-78, resident dept. radiology, 1978-81; asst. prof. radiology Med. Coll. Wis., 1982-84, assoc. prof., 1984-89, prof., 1989-94; dir. computed tomography Waukesha Meml. Hosp., 1994—. Contbr. articles to profl. jours. Fellow computed body tomography Med. Coll. Wisc., Milw, 1981-82; Am. Coll. Radiology, Radiol. Soc. N. Am. E-mail: mkthoren@aol.com.

THORSON, JOHN MARTIN, JR. electrical engineer, consultant; b. Armstrong, Iowa, Dec. 16, 1929; s. John Martin and Hazel Marguerite (Martin) T.; m. Geraldine Carol Moran, Apr. 21, 1956 (dec. 1975); children— John Robert, James Michael; m. Lee Houk, Sept. 24, 1977 B.S.E.E., Iowa State U., 1951. Transmission engr. No. States Power Co., Mpls., 1953-58, system operation relay engr., 1962-74, telephone engr. Minot, N.D., 1958-62; utility industry mktg. mgr. Control Data Corp., Mpls., 1974-77, product/program mgr. utilities, 1977-84, sr. cons. energy mgmt. systems, 1984-90; pres. Thorson Engrs., Inc., Chanhassen, Minn., 1991—. Inductive coordination cons. SNC Corp., Oshkosh, Wis., 1985—; tech. cons. Power Technologies, Inc., Schenectady, N.Y., 1991—, Control Corp., Osseo, Minn., 1992-93, Control Data, Plymouth, Minn., 1991-92, Hathaway, Denver, 1992-93, Scottish Hydro-Electric, PLC, Perth, Scotland, 1992—, NRG Energy Inc., Mpls., 1993—, Stanford Rsch. Inst., 1995—, Univ. Online, Inc., 1995—, GE, 1996—, No. States Power Co., 1998-2000, Siemens, 2000—; head U.S. nat. com. Internat. Electrotech. Com., TC57, 1985-2001. Contbr. tech. papers to profl. jours. Dist. commr. Boy Scouts Am., Minn., 1954-58, 64-65, coun. commr. N.D., Mont., 1959-62; mem. coun. St. Philip Luth. Ch., Wayzata, Minn., 1968-69; county del. Rep. Com., Chanhassen, Minn., 1980-82. 1st lt. USAF, 1951-53. Recipient Alumni Service award Iowa State U., 1972 Fellow IEEE (life mem., bd. dirs. 1981-82, dir. region 4, 1981-82, mem. U.S. activities bd. 1981-82, regional activities bd. 1981-82, Centennial medal 1984); mem. Internat. Conf. on Large High Voltage Electric Sys. (Atwood assoc. 2000), Iowa State U. Alumni Assn. (v.p., pres. 1963-66). Independent. Avocations: canoeing, back packing, mountain climbing. Home and Office: 7320 Longview Cir Chanhassen MN 55317-7905

THORSTENSON, TERRY N. construction equipment company executive; b. Rugby, N.D., Apr. 1, 1938; s. Marvin Byron and Inez (Blessum) T.; m. Carol Trigg, Nov. 26, 1960; 1 child, Craig. BSME, U. N.D., 1959. Tng., sales, field rep. Caterpillar, Inc., Peoria, Ill., 1959-64, dist. rep., gen. supr., 1965-69, asst. sales mgr., 1969-74, mng. dir. sales, 1974-85, mgr. mktg. and engring devel., 1985-97; mgr. corp. pub. affairs and human resources Caterpillar, 1997-99, dir. corp. pub. affairs, 1999—. Elder Westminster Presbyn. Ch., Peoria, 1979-81. Served to 2d lt., U.S. Army ROTC. Mem. Machinery and Allied Products Inst. (mem. mktg. council). Club: Peoria Country. Avocations: golf, tennis. Office: Caterpillar Inc 100 NE Adams St Peoria IL 61629-0002

THRASH, PATRICIA ANN, educational association administrator; b. Grenada, Miss., May 4, 1929; d. Lewis Edgar and Weaver (Betts) T. BS, Delta State Coll., 1950; MA, Northwestern U., 1953, PhD, 1959; cert. Inst. Edn. Mgmt., Harvard U., 1983; EdD (hon.) , Vincennes U., 1997; DHL, Drake U., 1997, Adrian Coll., 1998. Tchr. high sch. English, Clarksdale, Miss., 1950-52; head resident Northwestern U., 1953-55, asst. to dean women, 1955-58, asst. dean women, 1958-60, lectr. edn., 1959-65, dean women, 1960-69, assoc. prof. edn., 1965-72, assoc. dean students, 1969-71; asst. exec. sec. Commn. on Instns. Higher Edn., North Central Assn. Colls. and Schs., 1972-73, assoc. exec. dir., 1973-76, assoc. dir., 1976-87, exec. dir., 1988-96; exec. dir. emeritus, 1997—. Mem. adv. panel Am. Coun. on Edn., MIVER program evaluation mil. base program, 1991-94; mem. nat. adv. panel Nat. Ctr. Postsecondary Tchg., Learning & Assessment, 1991-95. Author (with others): Handbook of College and University Administration, 1970; contbr. articles to ednl. jours. Bd. dirs. Delta State U. Found., 2000—. Mem. Nat. Assn. Women Deans and Counselors (v.p. 1967-69, pres. 1972-73), Ill. Assn. Women Deans and Counselors (sec. 1961-63, pres. 1964-66), Am. Coll. Pers. Assn. (editl. bd. jour. 1971-74), Coun. Student Pers. Assns. in Higher Edn. (program nominations com. 1974-75, adv. panel Am. Coll. Testing Coll. Outcome Measures project 1977-78, staff Coun. on Postsecondary Accreditation project for evaluation nontraditional edn. 1977-78, mem. editl. bd. Jour. Higher Edn. 1975-80, guest editor Mar.-Apr. 1979, co-editor NCA Quar. 1988—, vice-chair regional accrediting dirs. group 1993, exec. com. Nat. Policy Bd. for Higher Edn. Inst. 1993-95), Mortar Bd. (hon.), Phi Delta Theta, Pi Lambda Theta, Alpha Psi Omega, Alpha Lambda Delta. Methodist. Home: 2337 Hartrey Ave Evanston IL 60201-2552

THUNE, JOHN, congressman; b. Murdo, S.D., Jan. 7, 1961; m. Kimberley Thune; children: Brittany, Larissa. BBA, MBA, U. S.D. Legis. asst. Senator James Abdnor, 1985-87; dep. staff dir. to the ranking rep. Senate Small Bus. Com., 1987-89; exec. dir. South Dakota Rep. Party, 1989-91; state railroad dir. Gov. George Mickelson, 1991-93; exec. dir. S.D. Mcpl. League, 1993-96; mem. U.S. Congress from S.D., 1997—. Mem. agr. com., transp. and infrastructure com., small bus. com. Avocations: basketball, pheasant hunting.*

THURBER, JOHN ALEXANDER, lawyer; b. Detroit, Nov. 9, 1939; s. John Levington and Mary Anne (D'Agostino) T.; m. Barbara Irene Brown, June 30, 1962; children: John Levington II, Sarah Jeanne. AB in History, U. Mich., 1962, JD, 1965. Bar: Ohio 1965, Mich. 1968. Assoc. Hahn, Loeser and Parks, Cleve., 1965-67, Miller, Canfield, Paddock and Stone, Birmingham, Mich., 1967-73; sr. mem. Miller, Canfield, Paddock and Stone, P.L.C., Troy, 1974—. Treas. Birmingham Community House, 1971-73; pres. Birmingham Village Players, 1983-84; bd. dirs. Oakland Parks Found., Pontiac, Mich., 1984—, pres., 1989-92; mem. capital com. Lighthouse Found.; trustee Oakland Land Conservancy. Avocations: reading, theater, walking, sports. Office: Miller Canfield Paddock & Stone PLC 840 W Long Lake Rd Ste 200 Troy MI 48098-6358 E-mail: thurberj@millercanfield.com.

THURBER, PETER PALMS, lawyer; b. Detroit, Mar. 23, 1928; s. Cleveland and Marie Louise (Palms) T.; m. Ellen Bodley Stites, Apr. 16, 1955; children: Edith Bodley, Jane Chenoweth, Thomas, Sarah Bartlett B.A., Williams Coll., 1950; J.D., Harvard U., 1953. Bar: Mich., 1954. Ptnr. Miller, Canfield, Paddock and Stone, Detroit, 1953-93, of counsel, 1994—. Trustee McGregor Fund, Detroit, 1979—. Bd. dirs. Detroit Symphony Orch., Inc., 1974-93; trustee Community Found. for Southeastern Mich., 1990-2000, Coun. Mich. Founds., 1991-2000. With U.S. Army, 1953-55. Fellow Am. Bar Found.; mem. ABA, Mich. Bar Assn. Roman Catholic. Club: Country of Detroit (Grosse Pointe Farms, Mich.) Avocations: reading; traveling; athletics. Home: 28 Provencal Rd Grosse Pointe Farms MI 48236-3038 Office: Miller Canfield Paddock & Stone 150 W Jefferson Ave Ste 2500 Detroit MI 48226-4416

THURSBY, JERRY GILBERT, economics educator, consultant; b. Camp Le Jeune, N.C., Aug. 6, 1947; s. Gilbert Earl and Mary Kathleen (Bailey) T.; m. Marie Sloan Currie, Mar. 11, 1972; children: James, Mary. AB, U. N.C., 1969, PhD, 1975. Asst. prof. Syracuse (N.Y.) U., 1975-78; from asst. to assoc. prof. Ohio State U., Columbus, 1978-88; prof. Purdue U., West Lafayette, Ind., 1988-01; prof. econs., chmn. dept. Emory U., Atlanta, 2001—. Contbr. articles to profl. jours. With U.S. Army, 1969-71. edu. Home: 910 Springdale Rd NE Atlanta GA 30306-4620 Office: Emory U Dept Econs Rich Meml Bldg Atlanta GA 30322 E-mail: jthursb@emory.

THURSTON, STEPHEN JOHN, pastor; b. Chgo., July 20, 1952; s. John Lee and Ruth (Hall) T.; m. Joyce DeVonne Hand, June 18, 1977; children: Stephen John II, Nicole D'Vaugh, Teniece Rael, Christian Avery Elijah. BA in Religion, Bishop Coll., 1975; Hon. degree, Chgo. Baptist Inst., 1986. Co-pastor New Covenant Missionary Bapt. Ch., Chgo., 1975-79, pastor, 1979—. Third v.p. Nat. Bapt. Conv. Am., mem. exec. com. Christian Edn. Congress; pres. Ill. Nat. Bapt. State Conv.; mem. Christian Fellowship Dist. Assn.; lectr. various orgns.; instr. New Covenant Bapt. Ch., Fellowship Bapt. Ch. Co-chmn. religious affairs div. People United to Save Humanity (PUSH); bd. dirs. nat. alumni assn. Bishop Coll.; active NAACP; trustee, fin. chmn. Chgo. Bapt. Inst. Mem. Broadcast Ministers Alliance, Bapt. Ministers Conf. Chgo. (Ministerial Pioneer award). Club: Bishop Coll. (Chgo.). Office: New Cov Miss Baptist Church 740 E 77th St Chicago IL 60619-2553

THURSWELL, GERALD ELLIOTT, lawyer; b. Detroit, Feb. 4, 1944; s. Harry and Lilyan (Zeitlin) T.; m. Lynn Satovsky, Sept. 17, 1967 (div. Aug. 1978); children: Jennifer, Lawrence; m. Judith Linda Bendix, Sept. 2, 1978 (div. May 1999); chldren: Jeremy, Lindsey. LLB with distinction, Wayne State U., 1967. Bar: Mich. 1968, N.Y. 1984, D.C. 1985, Colo. 1990, Ill. 1992, U.S. Dist. Ct. (ea. dist.) Mich. 1968, U.S. Ct. Appeals (7th cir.) 1968, U.S. Supreme Ct. 1994. Student asst. to U.S. Atty. Eas. Dist. Mich., Detroit, 1966; assoc. Zwerdling, Miller, Klimist & Maurer, 1967-68; st. prnt. The Thurswell Law Firm, Southfield, Mich. Arbitrator Am. Arbitration Assn., Detroit, 1969—; mediator Wayne County Cir. Ct., Mich., 1983—, Oakland County Cir. Ct. Mich., 1984—, also facilitator, 1991; twp. atty. Royal Oak Twp., Mich., 1982—; lectr. Oakland County Bar Assn. People's Law Sch., 1988. Pres. Powder Horn Estates Subdivsn. Assn., West Bloomfield, Mich., 1975, United Fund, West Bloomfield, 1976. Arthur F. Lederly scholar Wayne State U. Law Sch., 1965; Wayne State U. Law Sch. grad. profl. scholar, 1965, 66. Mem. ATLA (treas. Detroit met. chpt. 1986-87, v.p. 1989-90, pres. 1991-93), Mich. Bar Assn. (investigator/arbitrator grievance bd., atty. discipline bd., chmn. hearing panel), Mich. Trial Lawyers Assn. (legis. com. on govtl. immunity 1984), Detroit Bar Assn. (lawyer referral com., panel pub. adv. com. jud. candidates), Oakland County Bar Assn., Skyline Club (Southfield). Office: The Thurswell Law Firm 1000 Town Ctr Ste 500 Southfield MI 48075-1221

THYEN, JAMES C. furniture company executive; b. Jasper, Ind., 1943; BS, Xavier U., 1965; MBA, Ind. U., 1967. With Kimball Internat. Inc., Jasper, 1967—, sr. exec. v.p., treas., 1982—, also bd. dirs. Home: 1440 W Schuetter Rd Jasper IN 47546-9545 Office: Kimball Internat Inc 1038 E 15th St Jasper IN 47546-2225

TIAHRT, W. TODD, congressman, former state senator; b. Vermillion, S.D., June 15, 1951; s. Wilbur E. and Sara Ella Marcine (Steele) T.; m. Vicki Lyn Holland, Aug. 14, 1976; children: Jessica, John, Luke. Student, S.D. Sch. Mines & Tech., Rapid City, 1969-72; BA, Evangel Coll., 1975; MBA, S.W. Mo. State U., 1989. Property estimator Crawford & Co., Springfield, Mo., 1975-78; project engr. Zenith Electronics, 1978-81; cost engr. Boeing, Wichita, Kans., 1981-94, proposal mgr., 1991-94; state senator State of Kans., Topeka, 1993—95; mem. U.S. Congress from 4th Kans. dist., Washington, 1995—; mem. appropriations com., 1997—. Chmn. 4th dist. Rep. party, 1990-92; exec. com. Kans. Rep. party, 1990-92, nat. security com., sci. com. Mem. Pachyderm (bd. dirs. 1991-92), Delta Sigma Phi. Republican. Home: 1329 Amity St Goddard KS 67052-9133 Office: 401 Cannon HOB Washington DC 20515-1604*

TIBBLE, DOUGLAS CLAIR, lawyer; b. Joliet, Ill., May 26, 1952; BA, DePaul U., 1974; JD, Syracuse U., 1977, MPA, 1978. Bar: Ill., U.S. Dist. Ct. (no. dist.) Ill., U.S. Ct. Appeals (7th cir.), U.S. Supreme Ct. Ptnr. McBride, Baker & Coles, Oakbrook Terrace, Ill., 1996—. Mem. ABA, DuPage County Bar Assn., Chgo. Bar Assn. Office: McBride Baker & Coles 1 Mid America Plz Ste 1000 Oakbrook Terrace IL 60181-4710 E-mail: tibble@mbc.com.

TIBERI, PAT, state legislator; m. Denice Tiberi. BA, Ohio State Univ. Asst. dist. mgr. Congressman John Kasich; rep. from dist. 26 Ohio Ho. Reps., 1993—2001, majority fl. leader, mem. ins. and vets. affairs coms.; mem. U.S. Congress from 12th Ohio dist., 2001—. Pres. Windsor Terrace Learning Ctr. Mem. adv. bd. Columbus chpt. ARC, Columbus Italian Cultural Ctr.; past pres. Forest Park Civic Assn.; former rep. Northland Community Coun.; pres., co-founder Windsor Terrace Learning Ctr. Recipient Pres.'s award Northland Cmty. Coun., Vet. Admin Commendation award, Svc. award Am. Red Cross, Watchdog of Treas. award United Conservatives of Ohio. Mem. Sons of Italy. Home: 5208 Honeytree Loop W Columbus OH 43229-4631 Office: 508 Cannon Ho Office Bldg Washington DC 20515*

TICE, MIKE, professional football coach; b. Bayshore, NY, Feb. 2, 1959; m. Diane Tice; children: Adrienne, Nathan. Student, U. Md., 1977—80. Tight end Seattle Seahawks, 1981—88, 1990—91, Washington Redskins, 1989, Minn. Vikings , Eden Prairie, 1992—93, 1995, coach tight ends, 1996, offensive line coach, 1997—2001, asst. head head coach, 2001, head coach, 2002—. Office: Minn Vikings 9520 Vikings Dr Eden Prairie MN 55344

TIEDJE, JAMES MICHAEL, microbiology educator, ecologist; b. Newton, Iowa, Feb. 9, 1942; married, 1965; 3 children. BS, Iowa State U., 1964; MS, Cornell U., 1966, PhD in Soil Microbiology, 1968. From asst. prof. to prof. Mich. State U., 1968-78, disting. prof., 1991—; dir. sci. and tech. ctr. microbial ecology NSF, 1988—. Vis. assoc. prof. U. Ga., 1974-75; cons. NSF, 1974-77; vis. prof. U. Calif. Berkeley, 1981-82; mem. biotech. sci. adv. com. EPA, 1986-89, chair sci. adv. coun. GPA, 1988-90. Editor: Applied Microbiology, 1974—, editor-in-chief, 1980-86. Recipient Carlos J. Finley prize, UNESCO, 1993. Mem. AAAS, Am. Soc. Agronomy (Soil Sci. award 1990), Internat. Inst. Biotech., Am. Soc. Microbiology (award in applied and environ. microbiology 1992), Soil Sci. Soc. Am., Ecol. Soc. Am., Internat. Soc. Soil Sci. (chair soil biology divsn.). Achievements include research in dentrification, microbial metabolism of organic pollutants, and molecular microbiol. ecology. Office: Michigan State U Microbial Ecology Ctr 540 Plant & Soil Scis Bldg East Lansing MI 48824-1325

TIEFENTHAL, MARGUERITE AURAND, school social worker; b. Battle Creek, Mich., July 23, 1919; d. Charles Henry and Elisabeth Dirk (Hoekstra) Aurand; m. Harlan E. Tiefenthal, Nov. 26, 1942; children: Susan Ann, Daniel E., Elisabeth Amber, Carol Aurand. BS, Western Mich. U., 1941; MSW, U. Mich., 1950; postgrad., Coll. of DuPage, Ill., 1988-90. Tchr. No. High Sch., Flint, Mich., 1941-44, Cen. High Sch., Kalamazoo, 1944-45; acct. Upjohn Co., 1945-48; social worker Family Svc. Agy., Lansing, Mich., 1948-50, Pitts., 1950-55; sch. social worker Gower Sch. Dist., Hinsdale, Ill., 1962-70, Hinsdale (Ill.) Dist. 181, 1970-89, cons., 1989—; sch. social worker Villa Park (Ill.) Sch. Dist. 45, 1989; addictions counselor Mercy Hosp., 1990-92; asst. prof. sch. social work, liaison to pub. schs. Loyola U., Chgo., 1990-98, ret., 1998. Field instr. social work interns U. Ill., 1979-88; impartial due process hearing officer; mem. adv. com. sch. social work Ill. State Bd. Edn. approved programs U. Ill. and George Williams Coll.; speaker Nat. Conf. Sch. Social Work, Denver, U. Tex. Joint Conf. Sch. Social Work in Ill.; founder Marguerite Tiefenthal Symposium for Ill. Sch. Social Work Interns. Co-editor The School Social Worker and the Handicapped Child: Making P.L. 94-142 Work; sect. editor: Sch. Social Work Quarterly, 1979. Sec. All Village Caucus Village of Western Springs, Ill., mem. village disaster com.; deacon Presbyn. Ch. Western Springs, Sunday sch. tchr., mem. choir; instr. Parent Effectiveness, Teacher Effectiveness, STEP; trainer Widowed Persons Service Tng. Program for Vol. Aides AARP. Recipient Ill. Sch. Social Worker of Yr., 1982. Mem. Nat. Assn. Social Workers (chmn. exec. council on social work in schs.), Ill. Assn. Sch. Social Workers (past pres., past conf. chmn., conf. program chmn.), Ladies Libr. Assn., Sch. Social Workers Supervisors Group (del. to Ill. Commn. on Children), Programs. for Licensure of Social Work Practice in Ill., Ladies Libr. Assn. (Kalamazoo), LWV, DKG, PEO. Avocation: sewing. Home: 4544 Grand Ave Western Springs IL 60558-1545 also: 3151 West B Ave Plainwell MI 49080

TIEKEN, ROBERT W. tire manufacturing company executive; b. Decatur, Ill., May 6, 1939; married; 2 children. BS, Ill. Wesleyan U. With GE Co., mem. corp. audit staff; mgr. fin. ops. GE Nuclear Energy, GE Transp. Sys.; with GE Aerospace, v.p. fin. and info. tech.; corp. v.p. GE Co., 1988; corp. v.p. fin. Martin Marietta, Bethesda, Md.; v.p. fin. Utah Internat., Inc.; exec. v.p., CFO Goodyear Tire and Rubber Co., Akron, Ohio, 1994—. Office: Goodyear Tire and Rubber Co 1144 E Market St Akron OH 44316-0002

TIEMEYER, CHRISTIAN, conductor; m. Pattie Farris; children: Jeanie, Hank, Elisa. Grad., Peabody Conservatory; D of Musical Arts, Cath. U. of Am. Assoc. condr. Dallas Symphony, 1978-83; interim artistic dir., prin. guest condr. Omaha Symphony; music dir. Cedar Rapids Symphony, 1982—; founder Symphony Sch. of Music, 1986. Chmn. string and conducting faculties U. Utah; faculty Brigham Young U.; founding condr. Snowbird Summer Arts Inst.; founder Bear Lake Music Festival, 1992; guest condr. Preucil Orch. Prin. cellist Utah Symphony. Avocations: fly fishing, boating, outdoor activities. Office: Cedar Rapids Symphony Orch 205 2nd Ave SE Cedar Rapids IA 52401-1213

TIEN, H. TI, biophysics and physiology educator, scientist; b. Beijing, China, Feb. 01; came to U.S., 1947; s. Fang-cheng and Wen-tsun (Chow) T.; children: Stephen, David, Adrienne, Jennifer; m. Angelica Leitmannova, 1992. B.Sc., U. Nebr., 1953; Ph.D., Temple U., 1963. Chem. engr. Allied Chem. Corp., Phila., 1953-57; med. scientist Eastern Pa. Psychiat. Inst., 1957-63; assoc. prof. Northwestern U., Boston, 1963-66, Mich. State U., East Lansing, 1966-70, prof. biophysics, 1970—, chmn. dept., 1978-82. Cons. Hungarian Acad. Sci., Szeged, 1975-76; rsch. prof. Acad. Sinica, Beijing, 1978; cons. prof. Sichuan U., 1984—; cons. Tianjin Econ. Tech. Devel. Area, China; external dir. Ctr. Interface Scis., Slovak Tech. U., Slovakia; cons. prof. Jilin U., Peoples Republic China; frequent lectr. many countries. Author: Bilayer Lipid Membranes, 1974; co-author: Membrane Biophysics, 2000; contbr. chpts. to books. Research grantee NIH, 1964—, NSF, 1978, Dept. Energy, 1980-83, U.S. Naval Rsch. Office, 1985—. Mem. AAAS, Biophys. Soc. (council 1972-75), Nat. Inst. Peer Reviewer Achievements include research in membrane biophysics, bioelectrochemistry, photobiology, solar energy conversion via semiconductor septum electrochemical photovoltaic cells (SC-SEP); biomolecular electronic devices. Office: Mich State U Physiology Dept Giltner Hall East Lansing MI 48824 E-mail: tien@msu.edu.

TIERNEY, GORDON PAUL, real estate broker, genealogist; b. Ft. Wayne, Ind., Oct. 17, 1922; s. James Leonard and Ethele Lydia (Brown) T.; m. Carma Lillian Devine, Oct. 17, 1946; 1 child, Paul N. Student, Ind. U., 1940-41, Cath. U. Am., 1941-42; coll. tng. detachment, Clemson U., 1943. Br. mgr. Bartlett-Collins Co., Chgo., 1956-84; prin., broker Kaiser-Tierney Real Estate, Inc., Palatine, Ill., 1984-89; pres. Tierney Real Estate, Newburgh, Ind. Author: Burgess/Bryan Connection, 1978; assoc. editor Colonial Genealogist Jour., 1976-85. Served in USAC, 1943-45, China. Decorated Legion of Honor; named Ky. Col. Fellow Am. Coll. Genealogists (pres. 1977-2000); mem. SAR (v.p. gen. 1984-85, genealogist gen. 1981-83, Silver and Bronze medals 1978-80, Patriot medal 1976, Meritorious Svc. award 1983, Minutemen award 1984), Huguenot Soc. Ill. (state pres. 1978-80), Huguenot Soc. S.C., Nat. Huguenot Soc., Huguenot Soc. Ind. (pres. 1993-95), Nat. Geneal. Soc., Ind. Hist. Soc., Soc. Ind. Pioneers, First Families Ohio, Ohio Geneal. Soc., Va. Geneal. Soc., Md. Geneal. Soc., Augustan Soc., Gen. Soc. War 1812 (state pres. 1985), Sons. and Daus. Pilgrims, Descs. Old Plymouth Colony, Mil. Order Stars and Bars, Soc. Descs. Colonial Clergy, Sons of Union Vets., Sons of Confederate Vets., Pioneer Wis. Families, Welcome Soc. Pa., Pa. Geneal. Soc., Nat. Soc. Archivists, Soc. Colonial Wars in Ill., Soc. Colonial Wars in Ind. (gov. 1992-94), Soc. Colonial Wars in Commonwealth Ky. (life), Sons of Am. Colonists (nat. v.p. 1971-74), Mil. and Hospitalier Order St. Lazarus of Jerusalem, Clan Johnston/e in Am., Order Descs. Ancient Planters, Hump Pilots Assn., Nat. Bd. Realtors, Ill. Bd. Realtors, Sword Bunker Hill, Tri-State Geneal. Soc., Jamestowne Soc., Baronial Order Magna Charta, Royal Order Scotland, Masons, Shriners, Rolling Hill Country Club, Legion of Honor (comdr. 2001—). Republican. Presbyterian. Home and Office: 8766 Hanover Dr Newburgh IN 47630-9327

TIERNEY, MICHAEL EDWARD, lawyer; b. N.Y., July 16, 1948; s. Michael Francis and Margaret Mary (Creamer) T.; m. Alicia Mary Boldt, June 6, 1981; children: Colin, Madeleine. BA, St. Louis U., 1970, MBA, JD, St. Louis U., 1978. Bar: Mo. Assoc., law clk. Wayne L. Millsap, PC, St. Louis, 1977-80; staff atty. Interco. Inc., 1980-83; textile divsn. counsel Chromalloy Am. Corp., 1984-87; v.p., sec. P.N. Hirsch & Co., 1983-84; sr. counsel, asst. sec. Jefferson Smurfit Corp., 1987-92, v.p., gen. counsel, sec., 1993-99, Kinexus Corp., St. Louis, 1999—. Adv. bd. St. Louis Area Food Bank, 1980—. U.S. Army Security Agy., 1970-73. Mem. Racquet Club St. Louis, Old Warson Country Club. Republican. Roman Catholic. Avocations: sailing, squash. Home: 10 Twin Springs Ln Saint Louis MO 63124-1139 Address: Kinexus Corp 18500 Edison Ave Chesterfield MO 63005-3629

TIGERMAN, STANLEY, architect, educator; b. Chgo., Sept. 20, 1930; s. Samuel Bernard and Emma Louise (Stern) T.; m. Margaret I. McCurry; children: Judson Joel, Tracy Leigh. Student, MIT, 1948-49; BArch, Yale U., 1960, MArch, 1961. Archtl. draftsman firm George Fred Keck, Chgo., 1949-50, Skidmore, Owings and Merrill, Chgo., 1957-59, Paul Rudolph, New Haven, 1959-61, Harry Weese, Chgo., 1961-62; partner firm Tigerman & Koglin, 1962-64; prin. firm Stanley Tigerman & Assos., 1964-82; ptnr. Tigerman Fugman McCurry, 1982-88, Tigerman McCurry, 1988—. Prof. architecture U. Ill.-Chgo., 1967-71, 80-93, dir. Sch. Architecture, 1985-93; vis. lectr. Yale U., 1974, Cornell U., Ithaca, N.Y., 1963, Cooper Union, 1970, U. Calif. at Berkeley, 1968, Cardiff (Wales) Coll., 1965, Engring. U., Bangladesh, 1967; chmn. AIA com. on design, coordinator exhbn. and book Chicago Architects, 1977; Charlotte Shepherd Davenport prof. architecture Yale U., 1979; architect-in-residence Am. Acad. in Rome, 1980; vis. prof. architecture Harvard U., 1982; William Henry Bishop Chair. prof. architecture Yale U., 1984, Sarrinen prof., 1993; dir. post-professional grad. program U. Ill.-Chgo.; co-founder Archeworks, Design Lab., Chgo., 1993; mem. adv. com. Princeton U., 1997. Prin. works include The Ounce of Prevention Educare Ctr., Chgo., Fukuoka Apt. Complex, Japan, The Power House, Zion, Ill., The Chgo. Children's Adv. Ctr.; author: Versus, 1982, Architecture of Exile, 1988, Stanley Tigerman: Buildings and Projects, 1966-89, 1989; contbr. , , , , articles;exhibitions include Venice Biennale, 1976, 1980, Calif. Condition, 1982; , author essay;exhibitions include Chicago Architecture, The New Zeitgeist: In Search of Closure, 1989, 1989; author: (catalog) Chicago Architecture, The New Zeitgeist: In Search of Closure, 1989. Pres. Yale Arts Assn., 1969-70; mem. advisory com. Yale Archtl. Sch., 1976—; bd. dirs. Bangladesh Found. Served with USN, 1950-54. Recipient Alpha Rho Chi medal, Yale, 1961, Archtl. Record award, 1970, Masonry award, 1974, Masonry gold medal, 1974, Alumni Art award, Yale U., 1985, Design award for Art Inst. Chgo. Schinkel Exhbn., Am. Soc. Interior Designers, 1995, Humanitarian award, Holocaust Meml. Found. Ill., 2001; grantee Advanced Studies in Fine Art, Graham Fedn., 1965. Fellow AIA (chmn. com. design 1976-77, adv. com., Disting. Svc. award Chgo. chpt. 1983, Chgo. Honor awards 1977-79, Nat. Honor award 1982, 84, 87, 91, 98, Nat. Modern Income Housing award 1970, Nat. Homes for Better Living award 1974, 75, Ill. award 1976, Nat. award of Merit 1970, 74, 75, named to Hall of Fame 1990, Disting. Bldg. award for pvt. residence Chgo. chpt. 1991, Chgo. Interior Archtl. Award of Excellence 1981, 83, 87, 91, 92, Nat. Interior Archtl. Award of Excellence 1992-93, Chgo. Disting. Bldg. award 1971, 73, 75, 77, 79, 81, 82, 84, 85, 86, 91, 94, Italian Ceramic Tile Design award 1995, Fukuoka Urban Beautification award 1995, 6 citations of merit Chgo. chpt. 1994, Interior Design award for A.I.C. Schinkel Exhibit 1996, Chgo. Interior Architecture award 1997, Chgo. Chpt. Arch. award 1998, Nat. Interior Architecture award 1998, Louis Sullivan award 2000); mem. Arts Club of Chgo., Yale Club of N.Y.C., Century Assn. Club, Phi Kappa Phi. Office: Tigerman & McCurry Ltd 444 N Wells St Ste 206 Chicago IL 60610-4522

TILL, CHARLES EDGAR, nuclear engineer; b. Can., June 14, 1934; BE, U. Sask., Can., 1956, MS, 1958; PhD in Reactor Physics, U. London, 1960. Jr. rsch. officer physics Nat. Rsch. Coun. Can., 1956-58; reactor physicist Can. Gen. Electric, 1961-63; asst. physicist Argonne (Ill.) Nat. Lab., 1963-65, assoc. physicist, 1965-66, sect. head exp devel. sect., 1966-68, head critical exp anal sect., 1966-72, mgr. zero power reactor program, 1968-72, assoc. dir. applied physics divsn., 1972-73, dir. applied physics, 1973-80, assoc. lab. dir. engring. rsch., 1980-97, sr. counsellor to lab. dir., 1998; ret., 1998. Mem. NAE, Am. Nuc. Soc. (Cisler award 1995), Nat. Acad. Rsch. Office: Argonne Nat Lab 9700 Cass Ave Bldg 208 Argonne IL 60439-4842

TILLER, THOMAS C. manufacturing executive; BA, MIT, 1983; MBA, Harvard U., 1991; M in Mech. Engring., U. Vt. Engr. GE, 1983; mgr. GE Appliances; v.p., gen. mgr. GE Silicones; pres., COO Polaris Industries Inc., Mpls., 1998—. Office: Polaris Industries Inc 2100 Highway 55 Hamel MN 55340-9770

TILLSON, JOHN BRADFORD, JR. newspaper publisher; b. Paris, Dec. 21, 1944; s. John Bradford Sr. and Frances (Ragland) T.; m. Patricia Hunt, June 14, 1966 (div. June 1978); children: John, Karen; m. Cynthia Wornom, Oct. 10, 1981. BA, Denison U., Granville, Ohio, 1966. Reporter Charlotte (N.C.) News, 1969-71, Dayton (Ohio) Daily News, 1971-76, city editor, 1977-80, asst. mng. editor, 1980-82, mng. editor features, 1982-84; editor Dayton Daily News and Jour. Herald, 1984-88, pub., 1988—; pres., CEO Cox Pub., 1996—. Lectr. Am. Press Inst., Reston, Va., 1980-84. Chair Inventing Flight/2003 Com., 1998—; mem. Centennial of Flight Commn., 1998—; chair Miami Valley Econ. Devel. Coalition, 1999—; pres. Dayton Art Inst., 1990-96; chair Alliance for Edn., 1992-94. Mem. Oio Newspaper Assn. (treas. 2000—), Newspaper Assn. Am. Episcopalian. Office: Cox Ohio Pub 45 S Ludlow St Dayton OH 45402-1810

TIMBERLAKE, CHARLES EDWARD, history educator; b. South Shore, Ky., Sept. 9, 1935; s. Howard Ellis and Mabel Viola (Collier) T.; m. Patricia Alice Perkins, Dec. 23, 1958; children: Mark Brewster, Daniel Edward, Eric Collier BA, Berea Coll., 1957; Calif. State Teaching Credential, Claremont Grad. Sch., 1958, MA, 1962; PhD, U. Wash., 1968. Tchr. Barstow H.S., Calif., 1959-60, Claremont City Sch.., 1960-61; tchg., rsch. asst. U. Wash., Seattle, 1961-64; asst. prof. history U. Mo., Columbia, 1967-73, assoc. prof., 1973-81, prof., 1981—, Byler disting. prof., 1996, chmn. dept., 1996—2000, asst. dir. Honors Coll., 1988-90. Exch. prof. Moscow State U., 1985, U. Manchester, England, 1987—88; hon. prof. history Lanzou U., China, 1991; dir. edn. svcs. Leisure Voyages, 1992—2000; vis. prof. Joensuu (Finland) U., 1996, 98, 2000. Author: The Fate of Russian Orthodox Monasteries and Convents Since 1917, 1995; editor: Essays on Russian Liberalism, 1972, Detente: A Documentary Record, 1978, Religious and Secular Forces in Late Tsarist Russia, 1992, Profiles of Finland series, 1991-94, (microfiche) The St. Petersburg Collection of Zemstvo Publs., 1992—; contbr. chpts. to books, articles to profl. jours. Mem. Citizens Alliance for Progress, Columbia, Mo., 1969—75, pres., 1969—70; founding mem. High Edn. Rescue Operation, 1983—91; mem. Columbians Against Throw-Aways, 1980—83. Fgn. Area fellow, 1965-66, fellow Internat. Rsch. and Exchs. Bd., 1971, 95, 2001, Am. Coun. Learned Socs., 1978-79, Fulbright-Hays fellow, 1995; grantee NEH, 1972, 79, 87. Mem. Am. Assn. Advancement Slavic Studies (bd. dirs. 1980-82, 84-86, chmn. council regional affiliates 1981-82, 85-86, chmn. permanent membership com. 1981-84), Western Slavic Conf., Am. Hist. Assn. (exec. council Conf. on Slavic and East European History 1987-89), Central Slavic Conf. (sec.-treas. 1967-68, pres. 1968-69, 76-77, 83-84, 88-89, 2001-02, exec. bd. 1972— , custodian archive 1972—), Mo. Conf. History (pres. 1992, sec.-treas. 1996-2000), State Hist. Soc. Mo., Fulbright Assn. (pres. Mo. chpt. 1997-2000). Avocations: hiking, travel. Home: 9221 S Rt N Columbia MO 65203-9312 Office: U Mo Dept History Columbia MO 65211-0001 E-mail: timberlakec@missouri.edu.

TIMKEN, W. ROBERT, JR. manufacturing company executive; b. 1938; married B.A., Stanford U., 1960; M.B.A., Harvard U., 1962. With Timken Co. (formerly The Timken Roller Bearing Co.), Canton, Ohio, 1962—, asst. v.p. sales, 1964-65, dir. corp. devel., 1965-68, v.p., 1968-73, vice-chmn. bd., chmn. fin. com., 1973-75, chmn. bd., chmn. fin. com., 1975—, chmn. exec. com., 1983—, also dir. Office: Timken Co 1835 Dueber Ave SW Canton OH 44706-2798

TIMM, MIKE, state legislator; m. Sonia Timm; 4 children. Student, Minot (N.D.) State U. Pres., mgr. Timm Moving & Storage Co.; mem. N.D. Ho. of Reps. from 5th dist., 1973-85, 89—. Chmn. Fin. & Taxation Com. N.D. Ho. of Reps., mem. Transp. Com., spkr. of the house, 1997—. Named Outstanding Jaycee, 1965. Mem. Elks, Eagles, Moose, Am. Legion, Lions. Republican. Home: PO Box 29 Minot ND 58702-0029

TIMM, ROGER K. lawyer; b. Bay City, Mich., May 21, 1947; BS, U. Mich., 1969; JD, Harvard U., 1972. Bar: Mich. 1972. Mem. Dykema Gossett, Detroit. Mem. ABA, State Bar Mich. Office: Dykema Gossett 400 Renaissance Ctr Detroit MI 48243-1668 E-mail: rtimm@dykema.com.

TIMMONS, GERALD DEAN, pediatric neurologist; b. Rensselaer, Ind., June 1, 1931; s. Homer Timmons and Tamma Mildred (Spall) Rodgers; m. Lynne Rita Matrisciano, May 29, 1982; 1 child, Deanna Lynne; children from previous marriage: Jane Christina Timmons Mitchell, Ann Elizabeth, Mary Catherine. AB, Ind. U., 1953, MD, 1956. Diplomate Am. Bd. Psychiatry and Neurology. Intern Lima (Ohio) Meml. Hosp., 1956-57; resident Ind. U. Hosp., Indpls., 1957-59, 61-62; instr. neurology dept. Ind. U., 1962-64; practice medicine specializing in psychiatry and neurology, 1962-64; practice medicine specializing in pediatric neurology Akron, Ohio, 1964—; chief pediatric neurology Children's Hosp. Med. Ctr., 1964—; chmn. neurology subcouncil Coll. Medicine Northeastern Ohio Univs., Rootstown, 1978-99. Sr. examiner Am. Bd. Neurology and Psychiatry. Contbr. articles to profl. and scholarly jours. Served to capt. USAF, 1959-61. Mem. Summit County Med. Soc., Ohio Med. Soc., AMA, Am. Acad. Pediatrics, Am. Acad. Neurology (practice com. 1980-86, sec. child neurology sect. 2000—), Child Neurology Soc. (chmn. honors and awards com. 1978-88), Am. Soc. Internal Medicine, Am. Electroencephalographic Soc. Republican. Methodist. Office: Akron Pediatric Neurology 300 Locust St Ste 460 Akron OH 44302-1804

TIMPANO, ANNE, museum director, art historian; b. Osaka, Japan, June 17, 1950; d. A.J. and Margaret (Smith) T. BA, Coll. William and Mary, 1972; MA, George Washington U., 1983. Program mgmt. asst. Nat. Mus. Am. Art, Washington, 1977-86; dir. The Columbus (Ga.) Mus., 1986-93, DAAP Galleries, U. Cin., 1993—. Grant reviewer Inst. Mus. Svcs., Washington, 1988—, Ga. Coun. for Arts, Atlanta, 1988-91. Mem. 1992 Quincentenary Commn., Columbus, 1987-92. Recipient David Lloyd Kreeger award George Washington U., 1980. Mem. Am. Assn. Mus. (surveyor mus. assessment program), Assn. of Coll. and Univ. Mus. and Galleries, Coll. Art Assn., Midwest Mus. Conf. Roman Catholic. Home: 85 Pleasant Ridge Ave Fort Mitchell KY 41017-2861 Office: U Cin PO Box 210016 Cincinnati OH 45221-0016 E-mail: anne.timpano@uc.edu.

TIMPTE, ROBERT NELSON, secondary school educator; b. Mpls., Dec. 4, 1925; s. Oscar William and Mildred Marie (Nelson) T. BS in Edn., U. Minn., 1949, postgrad., 1955-73; MA in History, U. Iowa, 1956. Jr. high english, social studies tchr. Bloomington (Minn.) Pub. Schs., 1955-63, secondary schs. social studies coord., 1963-65, K-12 social studies coord., 1965-73, jr. high sch. social studies tchr., 1973-85. Condr. insvc. in field. Editor curriculum guides and catalogs Bloomington K-12 Social Studies Guides, 1963-73, Human Rels. Guide: Inter and Intracultural Education, 1974; creator Realia (Material Culture Kits) Asia and Africa, 1966-73. Cons. Human Rights Commn., Bloomington, 1970—73; City Hall tour guide City of Bloomington, 1963—73; treas., bd. dirs. Hidden Village Townhomes, Golden Valley, Minn. India Inst. grant, 1966; recipient Omar Bonderud Human Rights award Bloomington Human Rights Commn., 1974, WCCO Radio Good Neighbor award, 1974. Mem. Am. Fedn. Tchrs., Minn. Ret. Tchrs. Assn., Minn. Coun. for Social Studies (treas., conv. arrangements chmn.). Democrat. Avocations: travel, the Arts, American Indian culture research.

TINDER, JOHN DANIEL, federal judge; b. Indpls., Feb. 17, 1950; s. John Glendon and Eileen M. (Foley) T.; m. Jan M. Carroll, Mar. 17, 1984 B.S., Ind. U., 1972, J.D., 1975. Bar: Ind. 1975, U.S. Dist. Ct. (so. dist.) Ind., U.S. Ct. Appeals (7th cir.), U.S. Supreme Ct. Asst. U.S. atty. Dept. of Justice, Indpls., 1975-77; pub. defender Marion County Criminal Ct., 1977-78; chief trial dep. Marion County Pros. Office, 1979-82; litigation counsel Harrisone Moberly, 1982-84; U.S. atty. U.S. Dist. Ct. (so. dist.) Ind., 1984-87, judge, 1987—. Adj. prof. Ind. U. Sch. of Law, Indpls., 1980— ; mem. Supreme Ct. Character & Fitness Com., Ind., 1982— Co-founder Turkey Trot Invitational Race, Indpls., 1980 Recipient Cert. of Appreciation award Bur. Alcohol, Tobacco & Firearms, Indpls., 1976; Service award Marion County Prosecutor, Indpls., 1981 Mem. ABA, Ind. State Bar Assn. (dir. criminal justice sect. 1984—), Indpls. Bar Assn., 7th Circuit Ct. Bar Assn., Fed. Bar Assn. Republican. Roman Catholic. Office: US Dist Ct 304 US Courthouse 46 E Ohio St Indianapolis IN 46204-1903

TINKER, H(AROLD) BURNHAM, chemical company executive; b. St. Louis, May 16, 1939; s. H(arold) Burnham and Emily (Barnicle) T.; m. Barbara Ann Lydon, Feb. 20, 1965; children: Michael B., Mary K., Ann E. BS in Chemistry, St. Louis U., 1961; MS in Chemistry, U. Chgo., 1964, PhD in Chemistry, 1966. Sr. research chemist Monsanto, St. Louis, 1966-69, research specialist, 1969-73, research group leader, 1973-77, research mgr., 1977-81; tech. dir. Mooney Chems., Inc., Cleve., 1981-90, v.p. rsch. and devel., 1991-94; v.p. corp. devel., 1994—. Patentee in field; contbr. article to profl. jours. Mem. scis. adv. coun. U. Akron, 1995—. Mem. Am. Chem. Soc. (chmn. bd. St. Louis sect. 1978-79), Cleve. Assn. Rsch. Dirs. (v.p. 1989, pres. 1990, bd. dirs. 1991—). Roman Catholic. Avocation: computers. Home: 2889 Manchester Rd Cleveland OH 44122-2570 Office: OM Group Inc 50 Public Sq Ste 3500 Cleveland OH 44113-2204 E-mail: burn.tinker@omqi.com.

TINKER, JOHN HEATH, anesthesiologist, educator; b. Cin., May 18, 1941; s. Leonard Henry and Georgia (Reeves) T.; m. Martha Iuen (div. Jan., 1989); children: Deborah H. Lynne, Karen Sue, Juliette Kay; m. Bonnie Howard, Mar. 18, 1989. BS magna cum laude, U. Cin., 1964, MS summa cum laude, 1968. Diplomate Am. Bd. Anesthesiology (sr. examiner 1976—). Surg. intern, resident Harvard Med. Sch., Peter Bent Brigham Hosp., Boston, 1969-70, resident in anesthesiology, 1970-72; cons. anesthesiology Mayo Clinic, Rochester, Minn., 1974-83, chief cardiovascular anesthesiology, 1978-83; prof. anesthesiology U. Iowa Coll. Medicine, Iowa City, 1983-97, chmn. dept., 1983-97; prof., chmn. anesthesiology U. Nebr., Med. Ctr., Omaha, 1997—. Mem. pharm. scis. rev. com., NIH, Bethesda, Md., 1986—; dir. Matrix Med. Inc., Orchard Park, N.Y., 1988—; frequent guest lectr. Author: Controversies in Cardiopulmonary Bypass, 1989 (monograph award Soc. Cardiovascular Anesthsiologists); editor: Anesthesia and Analgesia, Jour. Internat. Anesthesiology Rsch. Soc., 1983—; contbr. over 185 articles to profl. jours. Maj. U.S. Army, 1972-74. NIH grantee, 1977-87. Fellow Royal Coll. Surgeons Australia; mem. Am. Soc. Anesthesiologists (active numerous coms. 1972—), Soc. Cardiovascular Anesthesiologists, Assn. Univ. Anesthetists. Avocations: fishing, golf, modeling ships and airplanes. Office: U Nebr 984455 Nebr Med Ctr Omaha NE 68198-0001

TINSMAN, MARGARET NEIR, state legislator; b. Moline, Ill., July 14, 1936; d. Francis Earl and Elizabeth (Lourie) Neir; m. Robert Hovey Tinsman Jr., Feb. 21, 1959; children: Robert Hovey III, Heidi Elizabeth, Bruce MacAlister. BA in Sociology, U. Colo., 1958; MSW, U. Iowa, 1974. Health care coord. Community Health Care, Inc., Davenport, Iowa, 1975-77; assoc. dir. Scott County Info., Referal, and Assistance Svc., 1977-79; county supr. Scott County Bd. Suprs., 1978-89; mem. Iowa Senate from 21st dist., Des Moines, 1989—, asst. minority leader, 1992—96. Chair Iowa Adv. Commn. on Inter-govt. Rels., 1982—84; U.S. country rep. to the German-Am. Symposium German Marshall Plan, 1983; commr. Iowa Dept. Elder Affairs, Des Moines, 1983—89. Chairperson Planning Com. Quad City United Way, Davenport; bd. dirs. Bi-State Met. Planning Commn., Davenport, 1981-89, Quad City Devel. Group, Davenport, 1988-90. Named Iowa Social Worker of Yr., NASW, 1978. Mem. Am. Lung Assn. (bd. dirs. 1989—), Davenport C. of C. (local/state govt. com. 1989—), Nat. Assn. Legislators, Nat. Assn. of Counties (bd. dirs. 1984-89, pres. Women Ofcl. 1984-89), Iowa State Assn. of Counties (bd. dirs. 1983-89, chair), Jr. League (sustaining mem. 1989), Vol. Action Ctr. (pres. 1989). Republican. Episcopalian. Avocations: tennis, golf, sailing, water and snow skiing. Home: 3055 Red Wing Ct Bettendorf IA 52722-2185 Office: 3541 E Kimberly Rd Davenport IA 52807-2552

TINSTMAN, DALE CLINTON, food products company consultant; b. Chester, Nebr., May 19, 1919; s. Clinton Lewis and Elizabeth Golashin (Gretzinger) T.; m. Jean Sundell, Oct. 1, 1942; children: Thomas C., Nancy Tinstman Remington, Jane C. Tinstman Kramer. BS, U. Nebr., 1941, JD, 1947. Bar: Nebr. 1947. Asst. sec., asst. mgr. investment dept. First Trust Co., Lincoln, Nebr., 1947-48; v.p., asst. treas. Securities Acceptance Corp., Omaha; fin. v.p., treas. Ctrl. Nat. Ins. Group, 1958-60; pres., treas. Tinstman & Co., Inc., Lincoln, 1960-61; exec. v.p. First Med Am., Inc., 1961-68, pres., 1968-74, fin. cons., 1974—; pres., dir. Iowa Beef Processors, Inc., 1976-77, vice chmn., 1977-82, co-chmn., 1982-83, dir., cons., 1983—; chmn., dir. Eaton Tinstman Druliner, Inc., 1983—2000. Bd. dirs. IBP, Inc.; past chmn. Nebr. Investment Coun. Trustee, chmn. U. Nebr. Found.; trustee Lincoln Found., Nebr. Coun. Econ. Edn. Served with USAAF

TIPTON, DANIEL L. religious organization executive; Gen. supt. Churches of Christ in Christian Union, Circleville, Ohio, 1990—. Office: Chs of Christ in Christian Union Box 30 1426 Lancaster Pike Circleville OH 43113-9487

TISHLER, WILLIAM HENRY, landscape architect, educator; b. Baileys Harbor, Wis., June 22, 1936; s. William John and Mary Viola (Sarter) T.; m. Betsy Lehner, Sept. 23, 1961; children: William Phillip, Robin Elizabeth. BS in Landscape Architecture, U. Wis., 1960; M in Landscape Architecture, Harvard U., 1964. Urban planner City of Milw., 1961-62; mem. faculty dept. landscape architecture U. Wis., Madison, 1964—; assoc. Hugh A Dega & Assocs. (Landscape Archs.), 1964-66; prin. Land Plans Inc. (Land and Hist. Preservation Planning Cons.), Madison, 1966—. Advisor emeritus Nat. Trust for Hist. Preservation; bd. dirs. The Hubbard Ednl. Trust. Author: American Landscape Architecture: Designers and Places, 1989, Midwestern Landscape Architecture, 2000; contbr. articles to profl. jours. With C.E., U.S. Army, 1960. Recipient Design Arts Program award NEA, 1981, Hawthorn award Friends of The Clearing, 1997, Outstanding Educator award Coun. Educators in Landscape Architecture, 1998; Attingham (Eng.) Program fellow Soc. Archtl. Historians, 1980; Dumbarton Oaks sr. fellow, 1990. Fellow Am. Soc. Landscape Archs. (Horace Cleve. vis. prof. U. Minn. 1993, nat. merit award 1971, 97, 99, honor award 1980, 89, Wis. chpt. Lifetime Achievement award 2000); mem. Assn. Preservation Tech., Wis. Acad. Arts, Letters and Scis., Pioneer Am. Soc. (Henry Douglas award) , Hist. Madison (hon.), Vernacular Architecture Forum (past pres.), Madison Trust for Hist. Preservation, Alliance for Hist. Landscape Preservation (founder), The Clearing Landscape Inst. (founder, dir.), Phi Kappa Phi, Sigma Lambda Alpha, Sigma Nu. Lutheran. Home: 3925 Regent St Madison WI 53705-5222 Office: U Wis Dept Landscape Architecture Dept Landscape Architecture Madison WI 53706 E-mail: wtishler@facstaff.wisch.edu.

TITLEY, LARRY J. lawyer; b. Tecumseh, Mich., Dec. 9, 1943; s. Leroy H. and Julia B. (Ruesink) T.; m. Julia Margaret Neukom, May 23, 1970; children: Sarah Catherine, John Neukom. BA, U. Mich., 1965, JD, 1972. Bar: Va. 1973, Mich. 1973. Assoc. Hunton & Williams, Richmond, Va., 1972-73, Varnum, Riddering, Schmidt & Howlett, Grand Rapids, Mich., 1973—. Trustee Friends Pub. Mus., 1985—94; bd. dirs. Pub. Mus. Found., 1988—97, pres., 1992—95; bd. dirs. Camp Optimist YMCA, 1993—98, Peninsular Club, 1994—, pres., 1997. Mem. ABA, Mich. Bar Assn., Grand Rapids Bar Assn. Home: 520 Roundtree Dr NE Ada MI 49301-9707 Office: Varnum Riddering Schmidt & Howlett Bridgewater Pl PO Box 352 Grand Rapids MI 49501-0352 E-mail: ljtitley@vrsh.com.

TITLEY, ROBERT L. lawyer; b. Tecumseh, Mich., Dec. 15, 1947; AB, U. Mich., 1970; JD, Duke U., 1973. Bar: Wis. 1973, Mich. 1974. Ptnr. Quarles & Brady, Milw. Mem. editorial bd. Duke Law Jour., 1972-73. Mem. State Bar Mich., State Bar Wis., Order of Coif. Office: Quarles & Brady 411 E Wisconsin Ave Milwaukee WI 53202-4497

TITUS, JACK L. pathologist, educator; b. South Bend, Ind., Dec. 7, 1926; s. Loren O. and Rutha B. (Orr) T.; m. Beverly Harden, June 18, 1949; children— Jack, Elizabeth Ann Titus Engelbrecht, Michael, Matthew, Joan, Marie Titus Davis. B.S., Notre Dame U., 1948; M.D., Washington U., St. Louis, 1952; Ph.D., U. Minn., 1962. Practice medicine, Rensselaer, Ind., 1953-57; fellow in pathology U. Minn., 1957-61; assoc. prof. pathology Mayo Grad. Sch., Rochester, Minn., 1961-72; prof. pathology Mayo Med. Sch., 1971-72, coordinator pathology tng. programs, 1964-72; W.L. Moody Jr. prof., chmn. dept. pathology Baylor Coll. Medicine, Houston, 1972-87; chief pathology service Meth. Hosp., 1972-87; pathologist-in-chief Harris County Hosp. Dist., 1972-87; chmn. dept. pathology Med. Ctr. Hosp., Conroe, Tex., 1982-87, Woodlands Community Hosp., 1984-87; dir. registry for cardiovascular diseases United Hosp., 1987-95, 97—, sr. cons. registry, 1996-97, dir., 1997—; prof. pathology U. Minn., 1987—. Adj. prof. pathology Baylor Coll. Medicine, 1987—; sr. cons. in pathology U. Tex. System Cancer Ctr., Houston, 1974—. Mem. editl. bd. Circulation, 1966-72, Am. Heart Jour., 1972-77, Modern Pathology, 1987-95, Human Pathology, 1988—, Am. Jour. of Cardiovascular Pathology, 1987-94, Cardiovascular Pathology, 1991—, Advances in Pathology, 1998--; contbr. articles to med. jours. Served with U.S. Army, 1945-47. Recipient Billings gold medal AMA, 1968, Hoektoen gold medal, 1969, Disting. Achievement award Soc. Cardiovascular Pathology, 1993, Scholarly Achievement award Houston Soc. Clin. Pathology, 1993. Mem. Internat. Acad. Pathology, Am. Assn. Pathologists, Am. Soc. Clin. Pathologists, AAAS, AMA, Am. Heart Assn., Coll. Am. Pathologists, Minn. Med. Assn., Minn. Heart Assn., Minn. Soc. Clin. Pathologists, Minn. Acad. Medicine (pres. 1998-99), Ramsey County Med. Soc., Soc. for Cardiovascular Pathology (pres. 1995-97), Sigma Xi, Alpha Omega Alpha. Methodist. Office: 333 Smith Ave N Ste 4625 Saint Paul MN 55102-2518 E-mail: jtitus@allina.com.

TKACHUK, KEITH, professional hockey player; b. Melrose, Mass., Mar. 28, 1972; With Phoenix Coyotes formerly Winnipeg (Canada) Jets, 1992—. Named to Hockey East All-Rookie team, 1990-91, NHL All-Star second team, 1994-95, Sporting News All-Star team, 1996. Office: St. Louis Blues Savvis Center Saint Louis MO 63103*

TOALE, THOMAS EDWARD, school system administrator, priest; b. Independence, Iowa, Aug. 30, 1953; s. Francis Mark and Clara R. (DePaepe) T. BS in Biology, Loras Coll., 1975, MA in Ednl. Adminstrn., 1986; MA in Theology, St. Paul Sem., 1980; PhD in Ednl. Adminstrn., U. Iowa, 1988. Ordained priest Roman Cath. Ch., 1981; cert. tchr., prin., supt., Iowa. Tchr. St. Joseph Key West, Dubuque, Iowa, 1975-77, Marquette High Sch., Bellevue, 1981-84, prin., 1984-86; assoc. supt. Archdiocese of Dubuque, 1986-87, supt. schs., 1987—. Assoc. pastor St. Joseph Ch., Bellevue, 1981-84; pastor Sts. Peter and Paul Ch., Springbrook, Iowa, 1984-86, St. Peter, Temple Hill, Cascade, Iowa, 1986—. Mem. Nat. Cath. Edn. Assn. (pres., chief adminstrn. Cath. edn.). Office: Archdiocese of Dubuque 1229 Mount Loretta Ave Dubuque IA 52003-7826

TOAN, BARRETT A. executive; BA, Kenyon Coll.; MBA, U. Pa. Commr. divsn. social svcs. State of Ark.; dir. dept. social svcs. State of Mo.; exec. dir. Sanus Health Plan of St. Louis; pres., CEO Express Scripts, Maryland Heights, Mo., 1989—. Names Entrepreneur of Yr. Inc. Mag., 1994. Office: Express Scripts 14000 Riverport Dr Maryland Heights MO 63043-4827

TOBACCOWALA, RISHAD, marketing professional; b. Bombay, India, 1959; BA in Maths., U. Bombay, 1979; MBA, U. Chgo., 1982. Media buyer Leo Burnett USA, Chgo., 1982-84, account supr., 1984-92, v.p., account dir. direct mkg., 1992-94, dir. interactive mktg., 1994-96; pres. Giant Step, 1996; now v.p., acct. dir. interactive mktg. Leo Burnett USA, exec. v.p. Starcom IP, 2000—. Office: Leo Burnett USA 35 W Wacker Dr Chicago IL 60601-1614

TOBIAS, CHARLES HARRISON, JR. lawyer; b. Cin., Apr. 16, 1921; s. Charles Harrison and Charlotte (Westheimer) T.; m. Mary J. Kaufman, June 15, 1946; children— Jean M., Thomas Charles, Robert Charles. B.A. cum laude, Harvard U., 1943, LL.B., 1949. Bar: Ohio 1949. Assoc. firm Steer, Strauss and Adair, Cin., 1949-56; ptnr. firm Steer, Strauss, White and Tobias, 1956-90; mem. Kepley MacConnell & Eyrich, 1990-93; mediator U.S. Ct. Appeals (6th crct.), 1993—. Bd. dirs. Cin. City Charter Com., 1955-75; mem. Wyoming (Ohio) City Council, 1972-77, vice mayor, 1974-77; bd. govs., past chmn. Cin. Overseers, Hebrew Union Coll.-Jewish Inst. Religion; pres. Met. Area Religious Coalition of Cin., 1977-80, Jewish Fedn. Cin., 1972-74; mem. nat. bd. govs. Am. Jewish Com., 1981-87. With USN, 1943-46. Mem. Cin. Bar Assn., Losantiville Country Club. Office: US Ct Appeals Potter Stewart US Courthse 5th and Walnut St Cincinnati OH 45202 Home: 2115 Evergreen Ridge Dr Cincinnati OH 45215-5713

TOBIAS, PAUL HENRY, lawyer; b. Cin., Jan. 5, 1930; s. Charles H. and Charlotte (Westheimer) T.; 1 child, Eliza L. AB magna cum laude, Harvard U., 1951, LLB, 1958. Bar: Mass. 1958, Ohio 1962. Assoc. Stoneman & Chandler, Boston, 1958-61, Goldman & Putnick, Cin., 1962-75; ptnr. Tobias, Kraus and Torchia, 1976—. Instr. U. Cin. Law Sch., 1975-77. Author: Litigating Wrongful Discharge Claims, 1987; co-author: Job Rights and Survivor Strategies, a Handbook for Terminated Employees, 1997; contbr. articles to profl. jours. Mem. Cin. Bd. of Park Commrs., 1973-81, Cin. Human Rels. Commn., 1980-84, Cin. Hist. Conservation Bd., 1990-91. With U.S. Army, 1952-54. Mem. ABA, Nat. Employment Lawyers Assn. (founder), Nat. Employee Rights Inst. (chmn.; editor-in-chief Employee Rights quar. 2000—), Ohio State Bar Assn., Cin. Bar Assn. (past chmn. legal aid com.), Phi Beta Kappa. Home: 15 Hill And Hollow Ln Cincinnati OH 45208-3317 Office: Tobias Kraus Torchia 911 Mercantile Libr Bldg Cincinnati OH 45202

TOBIAS, RANDALL LEE, retired pharmaceutical company executive; b. Lafayette, Ind., Mar. 20, 1942; m. Marilyn Jane Salyer, Sept. 2, 1966 (dec. May 1994); children: Paige Noelle, Todd Christopher; m. Marianne Williams, July 15, 1995; stepchildren: James Russell Ullyot, Kathryn Lee Ullyot. BS in Mktg., Ind. U., 1964; LLD (hon.), Galuedette U.; D of Engrng. (hon.), Rose Hulman Inst. Tech., Sagamore of the Wabash, Ind.; LLD (hon.), Ind. U., 1997. Numerous positions Ind. Bell, 1964-77, Ill. Bell, 1977-81; v.p. residence mktg. sales and service AT&T, 1981-82, pres. Am. Bell Consumer Products, 1983, pres. Consumer Products, 1983-84, sr. v.p., 1984-85; chmn., CEO AT&T Comm., N.Y.C., 1985-91, AT&T Internat., Basking Ridge, N.J., 1991-93; vice chmn. bd. AT&T, N.Y.C., 1986-93; chmn., CEO Eli Lilly & Co., Indpls., 1993-98, chmn. emeritus, 1999. Bd. dirs. Kimberly-Clark, Knight-Ridder, Phillips Petroleum. Chmn. bd. trustees Duke U.; trustee Colonial Williamsburg Found.; bd. govs. Indpls. Mus. Art; bd. dirs. Indpls. Symphony Orch., Ind. U. Found. (hon.), Econ. Club Indpls. Named one of Top 25 Mgrs. of Yr., Bus. Week, 1997, Family Champion, Working Mothers Mag., 1997. Mem. Bus. Coun., Indpls. Corp. Cmty. Coun., Coun. Fgn. Rels., Meridian Hills Country Club (Indpls.), Woodstock Club (Indpls.), Columbia Club (Indpls.), Athletic Club (Indpls.), Univ. Club (Indpls.), Amwell Valley Conservancy (N.J.), Theta Chi. Avocations: skiing, fly fishing, shooting. Office: Eli Lilly & Co 500 E 96th St Ste 110 Indianapolis IN 46240-3733

TOBIN, PATRICK JOHN, dermatologist; b. Bay City, Mich., Sept. 20, 1938; s. John Howard and Dorothy Ida (De Matio) T.; m. Suzanne Lane Bumstead, Apr. 11, 1959; children: Jennifer Lane, Suzannah Lane, Benjamin Lane. AS, Bay City Jr. Coll., 1958; MD, U. Mich., 1964. Diplomate Am. Bd. Dermatology. Intern Munson Med. Ctr., Traverse City, Mich., 1964-65, mem. active staff, 1970—; resident Univ. Hosp., Ann Arbor, 1965-68. Lt. comdr. USN, 1968-70. Fellow Am. Acad. Dermatology; mem. Mich. State Med. Soc., AMA, Am. Soc. for Dermatologic Surgery, Alpha Omega Alpha, Grand Traverse Yacht Club (commodore 1977), Grand Traverse Ski Club (pres. 1975). Avocations: skiing, cycling, sailing, travel, reading. Home: 7777 Truesdale Ln Traverse City MI 49686-1667 Office: Northwestern Mich Dermatol 550 Munson Ave Traverse City MI 49686-3580

TOBIN, THOMAS F. lawyer; b. Chgo., Apr. 12, 1929; BSS, John Carroll U., 1951; JD, Loyola U., 1954. Bar: Ill. 1954. Ptnr. Connelly Robert and McGivney, Chgo. Office: Connelly Robert and McGivney 1 N Franklin St Ste 1200 Chicago IL 60606-3447

TOCCO, JAMES, pianist; b. Detroit, Sept. 21, 1943; s. Vincenzo and Rose (Tabbita) T.; 1 child, Rhoya. Prof. music Ind. U., Bloomington, 1977-91; eminent scholar, artist-in-residence U. Cin. Coll.-Conservatory Music, 1991—; prof. Musikhochschule, Lübeck, Ger., 1990—; artistic dir. Great Lakes Chamber Music Festival, 1994—. Debut with orch., Detroit, 1956, since performed with symphony orchs. including Chgo. Symphony, Los Angeles Philharmonic, Cin. Symphony, Detroit Symphony, Nat. Symphony, Balt. Symphony, Atlanta Symphony, Denver Symphony, Montreal Symphony, London Symphony, London Philharm., BBC Orch., Berlin Philharm., Moscow Radio-TV Orch., Amsterdam Philharmonic, Munich Philharmonic, Bavarian Radio Orch., Royal Concertebouw Orch., also recitals, U.S. and abroad, and performances, CBS and NBC networks; guest performer, White House; Recs. include the complete preludes of Chopin, collected piano works of Leonard Bernstein, complete piano works of Charles Tomlinson Griffes, 4 piano sonatas of Edward MacDowell, selected piano works of Aaron Copland, complete Bach-Liszt organ transcriptions, piano works of John Corigliano. Recipient Bronze medal Tchaikovsky Competition, Moscow 1970, Bronze medal Queen Elisabeth of Belgium Competition, Brussels 1972, 1st prize Piano Competition of Americas, Rio de Janeiro 1973, 1st prize Munich Internat. Competition 1973. Office: U Cin Coll Conservatory Musi Cincinnati OH 45221-0001

TODD, JOHN JOSEPH, lawyer; b. St. Paul, Mar. 16, 1927; s. John Alfred and Martha Agnes (Jagoe) T.; m. Dolores Jean Shanahan, Sept. 9, 1950; children: Richard M., Jane E., John P. Student, St. Thomas Coll., 1944, 46-47; B.Sci. and Law, U. Minn., 1949, LL.B., 1950. Bar: Minn. bar 1951. Practice in, South St. Paul, Minn., 1951-72; partner Thuet and Todd, 1953-72; asso. justice Minn. Supreme Ct., St. Paul, 1972-85; sole practice West St. Paul, 1985-92; of counsel Brenner & Glassman Ltd., Mpls., 1992-99, Orme & Assoc., Eagan, Minn., 1999—. Served with USNR, 1945-46. Mem. state bar assns., VFW. Home: 6689 Argenta Trl W Inver Grove Heights MN 55077-2208 Office: Orme & Associates 3140 Neil Armstrong Blvd Eagan MN 55121-2273 E-mail: jtodd@ormelaw.com., jjbtodd@aol.com.

TODD, ROBERT FRANKLIN, III, oncologist, educator; b. Granville, Ohio, Apr. 16, 1948; m. Susan Erhard, 1977; children: Currier Nathaniel, Andrew Joseph. AB, Duke U., 1970, PhD, 1975, MD, 1976. Diplomate Am. Bd. Internal Medicine. Intern Peter Bent Brigham Hosp., Boston, 1976-77, resident, 1977-78; fellow in oncology Sidney Farber Cancer Inst., 1978-80; clin. fellow in medicine Harvard Med. Sch., 1978-81; postdoctoral fellow divsn. tumor immunology Sidney Farber Cancer Inst., 1979-81; asst. prof. medicine Harvard Med. Sch., 1981-84; assoc. prof. internal medicine U. Mich., Ann Arbor, 1984-88, assoc. prof. cellular and molecular biology, 1985-88, assoc. dir. divsn. hematology-oncology internal medicine, 1987-91, prof. internal medicine, 1988—, assoc. chair for rsch. dept. internal medicine, 1989-91, assoc. chair dept. internal medicine, 1991-93, chief divsn. hematology-oncology dept. internal medicine, 1993—, assoc. v.p. rsch., 1999—, Frances and Victor Ginsberg prof. hematology/oncology, 1999—. Attending physician U. Mich. Hosps., 1984—; chmn. hematology/oncology subsplty chpt. Ctrl. Soc. for Clin. Rsch., 1995-97. Contbr. numerous articles to profl. jours.; patentee in field. Mem.: The Microcirculatory Soc., Am. Soc. for Clin. Investigation, S.W. Oncology Group, Ctrl. Soc. for Clin. Rsch. (councilor 1997—, pres. 2001—), Am. Fedn. for Clin. Rsch. (councilor midwest chpt. 1986—89), Am. Soc. Hematology, Soc. Leukocyte Biology (councilor 1996—99), Am. Soc. Clin. Oncology, Am. Assn. for Cancer Rsch., Am. Assn. Immunologists, ACP, Alpha Omega Alpha, Phi Beta Kappa. Office: U of Mich Med Sch 1500 E Med Ctr Dr 7216 CCGC Ann Arbor MI 48109-0948

TODD, WILLIAM MICHAEL, lawyer; b. Cleve., Dec. 13, 1952; s. William Charles and Jennie Ann (Diana) T. BA, U. Notre Dame, 1973; JD, Ohio State U., 1976. Bar: Ohio 1976, U.S. Dist. Ct. (so. dist.) Ohio 1977, U.S. Supreme Ct. 1987. Assoc. Porter, Wright, Morris & Arthur, Columbus, Ohio, 1976-82, ptnr., 1983-93, Squire, Sanders & Dempsey, Columbus, 1993—. Trustee Callvac Svcs., Columbus, 1985-91, pres. 1988. Mem. ABA (governing com. forum on health law 1988-91), Ohio Bar Assn., Columbus Bar Assn., Am. Soc. Med. Assn. Counsel, Am. Bd. Trial Advocates, Ohio Soc. Healthcare Attys. (pres. 1999-2000), Am. Health Lawyers Assn., Worthington Hills Country Club, Columbus Athletic Club. Roman Catholic. Avocations: music, recreational sports. Office: Squire Sanders & Dempsey 41 S High St Columbus OH 43215-6101

TOELKES, DIXIE E. state legislator; m. Roger Toelkes. Educator; mem. from dist. 53 Kans. State Ho. of Reps., Topeka. Address: 3811 SE 33rd Ter Topeka KS 66605-3077 Office: Kans House of Reps State House Topeka KS 66612

TOFTNER, RICHARD ORVILLE, engineering executive; b. Warren, Minn., Mar. 5, 1935; s. Orville Gayhart and Cora Evelyn (Anderson) T.; m. Jeanne Bredine, June 26, 1960; children: Douglas, Scott, Kristine, Kimberly, Brian. BA, U. Minn., 1966; MBA, Xavier U., 1970. Registered environ. assessor, Calif. Sr. economist Federated Dept. Stores, Inc., Cin., 1967-68; dep. dir. EPA, Washington and Cin., 1968-73; mgmt. cons. environ. affairs, products and mktg., 1973-74; prin. PEDCo Environ., Cin., 1974-80; trustee PEDCo trusts, 1974-80; pres. ROTA Mgmt., Inc., Cin., 1980-82; gen. mgr. CECOS, 1982-85; cons., 1985—; v.p. Smith, Stevens & Young, 1985-88; real estate developer, 1980—. Pres., CEO Toxitrol Internat., Inc., 1988-89; dir. Environ. Svcs. Belcan Engrng. Group, Inc., Cin., 1989-92; prin. exec. cons. Resource Mgmt. Internat., Inc., 1994—; adj. prof. environ. engring. U. Cin., 1975-86; lectr. Grad. fellowship rev. panel Office of Edn., 1978-79; advisor, cabinet-level task force Office of Gov. of P.R., 1973; pvt. investor, 1991—; bd. dirs. EnviroAudit Svcs., Inc., pres., CEO, 1992—; mem. legis. com. Ohio Chem. Coun., 1995—; v.p. environ. engring. CSA Architects & Engrs., 1996-2001; client svc. mgr. Weston Environ. Cons., 2001—; subcom. Nat. Safety Coun., 1972; mem. exec. environ. briefing panels Andersen Consulting, 1991-92; nominee commr. PUCO, Ohio; chmn. Cin. City Waste Task Force, 1987-88; co-chair Hamilton County Resource Recovery Com., 1989—. Contbr. articles on mgmt. planning and environ. to periodicals, chpts. to books; inventor, developer Toxitrol Waste Minimization; inventor EnviroAudit. With AUS, 1954-57. Mem. USTA, Nat. Registry Environ. Profl. Rep., Engring. Soc. Cin., Assn. Corp. Environ. Execs., Cin. C. of C., Global Assn. Corp. Environ. Execs. (charter), U.S. Tennis Assn. Republican. Lutheran. Home: 9175 Yellowwood Dr Cincinnati OH 45251-1948 Office: 4100 Executive Park Dr Ste 11 Cincinnati OH 45241-4026

TOIRAC, S(ETH) THOMAS, software engineering executive, consultant; b. Ft. Wayne, Ind., May 17, 1951; s. Florent D. and Dorothy M. (Lee) T.; m. Martha J. Rife, Dec. 20, 1969 (div. 1979); m. Linda Diane Benecke, Aug. 2, 1987 (div. 1999); children: Kristina M., Danielle Shari, Anthony David. Student, Grace Coll., 1970. Computer operator United Telephone Co., Warsaw, Poland, 1968-69; programmer-analyst GTE Data Svcs., Ft. Wayne, 1970-76, systems programmer, 1976-79, systems supr., 1979-82; mgr. software N.Am. Van Lines, 1982-84, dir. computing svcs., 1984-90; founder, exec. dir. Pioneer Missionary, Inc., 1990-94; CFO Pillar Pub., New Carlisle, Ind., 1990-94; exec. v.p. Kessington Network, Indpls., 1990-91; info. mgmt. cons., 1991-95; sr. consulting engr. Lexis-Nexis, Inc., Dayton, Ohio, 1995-98, mgr. devel. svcs., 1998—2001, mgr. sys. support, 2001—. Chmn. GTE Tech. Adv. Group, 1978-79; cons. in field. Sec.-treas. bd. dirs. Greater Ft. Wayne Crime Stoppers, 1986-91; lay min. Wesleyan Meth. Ch., Ft. Wayne, 1974-75; mem. Share, Inc., 1976-81. Republican. Avocations: photography, personal computers. E-mail: tom.toirac@lexis-nexis.com.

TOLBERT, NATHAN EDWARD, biochemistry educator, plant science researcher; b. Twin Falls, Idaho, May 19, 1919; s. Edward and Helen (Mills) T.; m. Evelynne Cedarlund, June 21, 1952 (dec. Nov. 1963); children— Helen, Carol, James; m. Eleanor Dalgleish, June 22, 1964 BS in Chemistry, U. Calif., Berkeley, 1941; PhD in Biochemistry, U. Wis., 1950. Prof. biochemistry Mich. State U., East Lansing, 1958-89, prof. emeritus, 1989—. Editor: Biochemistry of Plants, Vol. 1, 1980; editor 3 sci. jours.; contbr. numerous papers, revs., abstracts to profl. publs.; patentee in field Served to capt. USAF, 1943-45, PTO Named disting. prof. Mich. State U., 1963, Mich. Scientist of Yr., 1985; Fulbright fellow, 1969; grantee NSF, NIH Mem. Nat. Acad. Sci., Am. Soc. Plant Physiology (pres. 1983-84, Stephen Hale award 1980), Am. Soc. Biol. Chemists, Am. Chem. Soc., Nat. Acad. Sci. Avocation: travel. Office: Mich State U Dept Biochemistry East Lansing MI 48824

TOLCHINSKY, PAUL DEAN, organization design psychologist; b. Cleve., Sept. 30, 1946; s. Sanford Melvin and Frances (Klein) T.; m. Laurie S. Schermer, Nov. 3, 1968 (div. Jan. 1982); m. Kathy L. Dworkin, June 19, 1988; children: Heidi E., Dana M. BA, Bowling Green State U., 1971; PhD, Purdue U., 1978. Asst. br. mgr., tng. instr. Detroit Bank and Trust, 1971-73; mgr. tng. and devel. nuclear divsn. Babcock and Wilcox Co., Barberton, Ohio, 1973-75; internal cons. food products divsn. Gen. Foods Corp., West Lafayette, Ind., 1975-77; grad. tchg. asst. Krannert Grad. Sch. Mgmt. Purdue U., 1975-78; asst. prof. mgmt. Coll. Bus. Adminstrn. Fla. State U., Tallahassee, 1978-79, U. Akron, Ohio, 1979-81; pres. Performance Devel. Assocs., Cleve., 1975—; ptnr. Dannemiller Tyson Assocs., 1994-99; mng. ptnr. Performance Devel. Assocs., 2000—. Contbr. articles to profl. publs. Bd. dirs. Temple Tiferth Israel, Cleve., 195. With U.S. Army, 1966-69, Vietnam. Mem. APA, Acad. Mgmt. Democrat. Jewish. Avocations: running, travel. Office: Performance Devel Assocs 50 Fox Glen Rd Moreland Hills OH 44022

TOLIA, VASUNDHARA K. pediatric gastroenterologist, educator; b. Calcutta, India; came to U.S., 1975; d. Rasiklal and Saroj (Kothari) Doshi; m. Kirit Tolia, May 30, 1975; children: Vinay, Sanjay. MBBS, Calcutta U., 1968-75. Intern, resident Children's Hosp. Mich., Detroit, 1976-79, fellow, 1979-81, dir. pediat. endoscopy unit, 1984-90, dir. pediat. gastroenterology and nutrition, 1990—; instr. Wayne State U., 1981-83, asst. prof., 1983-91, assoc. prof., 1991-97, prof., 1997—. Mem. editl. bd. Inflammatory Bowel Diseases, 1999— Am. Jour. Gastroenterology, 1999, Rev. of World Lit. in Pediatrics, 1999—; contbr. articles to profl. jours. Named Woman of Distinction, Mich. chpt. Crohn's and Colitis Found. Am., 1991. Fellow Am. Coll. Gastroenterology (chair ad-hoc com. pediat. gastroenterology 1998-2000), Am. Acad. Pediats.; mem. Am. Gastroenterology Assn., N.Am. Soc. Pediat. Gastroenterology and Nutrition, Soc. Pediat. Rsch. Office: Children's Hosp of Mich 3901 Beaubien St Detroit MI 48201-2119

TOLL, DANIEL ROGER, corporate executive, civic leader; b. Denver, Dec. 3, 1927; s. Oliver W. and Merle D'Aubigne (Sampson) T.; m. Sue Andersen, June 15, 1963; children: Daniel Andersen, Matthew Mitchell. AB magna cum laude (Pyne prize), Princeton U., 1949; MBA with distinction, Harvard U., 1955. With Deep Rock Oil Corp., Tulsa, 1949-51, asst. mgr. product supply and distbn.; with Helmerich & Payne, 1955-64, roughneck, landman, exploration mgr., pipeline constrn. mgr., v.p. fin., 1961-64; with Sunray DX Oil Co., 1964-69, treas., v.p. corp. planning and devel.; v.p. Sun Oil Co., 1969; with Walter E. Heller Internat. Corp., Chgo., 1970-85, sr. v.p. fin., dir., 1970-80, pres., dir., 1980-85, corp. and civic dir., 1985—. Bd. dirs. Mallinckrodt, Inc. (formerly IMCERA Group Inc.), Kemper Nat. Ins. Co., Lincoln Nat. Income Fund, Inc., Lincoln Nat. Convertible Securities, Inc. Vice chmn. Tulsa Cmty. Chest, 1964-66; v.p., bd. dirs. Tulsa Opera, 1960-69; bd. dirs. Tulsa Little Theatre, 1963-69, Internat. House, Chgo., 1984-87; bd. dirs. Inroads, Inc., 1973-95, nat. vice chmn., 1982-95; bd. dirs. Chgo. Area coun. Boy Scouts Am., 1976-94, pres., 1981-83; mem. Kenilworth (Ill.) Sch. Bd. Dist. 38, 1975-81, pres.,

1978-81; bd. dirs., mem. exec. com., chmn. fin. and hosp. affairs coms. Evanston (Ill.) Northwestern Healthcare, Inc., 1982—; bd. dirs. Chgo. Met. Planning Coun., 1989—, pres., 1991-94; bd. dirs. Northwestern Healthcare Network, Inc., 1995-99; trustee Princeton U., 1990-94. Lt. (j.g.) USNR, 1951-52. Baker scholar Harvard U., 1955. Mem. Chgo. Assn. Commerce and Industry (bd. dirs. 1979-86), Chgo. Club, Comml. Club, Econ. Club, Harvard Bus. Sch. Club (past pres., bd. dirs. 1971-91), Indian Hill Club (bd. govs. 1987-90), Princeton Club (past pres., bd. dirs. 1985—), Phi Beta Kappa. Home: 1005 Mount Pleasant Rd Winnetka IL 60093-3614 Office: Ste 300 560 Green Bay Rd Winnetka IL 60093-2242

TOLL, PERRY MARK, lawyer, educator; b. Kansas City, Mo., Oct. 28, 1945; s. Mark Irving and Ruth (Parker) T.; m. Mary Anne Shottenkirk, Aug. 26, 1967; children: Andrea Lynne, Hillary Anne. BS in Polit. Sci. and Econs., U. Kans., 1967, JD, 1970. Bar: Mo. 1970 1970, U.S. Dist. Ct. (we. dist.) Mo. 1970, U.S. Tax. Ct. 1979, U.S. Supreme Ct. 1979. With Shughart, Thomson & Kilroy P.C., Kansas City, 1970—, pres., 1995—, chmn. bus. dept., 1999—. Asst. prof. deferred compensation U. Mo., Kansas City, 1979-83; bd. dirs., pres. Heart of Am. Tax Inst., Kansas City, 1975-87. Mem., chmn. Prairie Village (Kans.) Bd. Zoning Appeals, 1977-95. Mem. ABA, Mo. Bar Assn., Nat. Health Lawyers Assn., Am. Agr. Law Assn., Mo. Merchants and Mfrs. Assn., Greater Kansas City Med. Mgrs. Assn., Lawyers Assn. Kansas City, East Kans. Estate Planning Coun. (bd. dirs., pres.), Phi Kappa Tau (bd. dirs. Beta Theta chpt.). Office: Shughart Thomson & Kilroy 12 Wyandotte Plz 120 W 12th St Ste 1500 Kansas City MO 64105-1929

TOLL, SHELDON SAMUEL, lawyer; b. Phila., June 6, 1940; s. Herman and Rose (Ornstein) T.; m. Roberta Darlene Pollack, Aug. 11, 1968; children: Candice Moore, John Maitland, Kevin Scott. Bar: Pa. 1967, Mich. 1972, Ill. 1990, Tex. 1990, U.S. Dist. Ct. (ea. dist.) Pa. 1968, U.S. Ct. Appeals (3d cir.) 1970, U.S. Supreme Ct. 1971, Mich. 1972, U.S. Dist. Ct. (ea. dist.), U.S. Ct. Appeals (6th cir.) 1973, U.S. Ct. Appeals (5th cir.) 1978, U.S. Dist. Ct. (no. dist.) Calif. 1986, U.S. Ct. Appeals (9th cir.) 1987, U.S. Dist. Ct. (ea. dist.) Wis. 1989. Assoc. Montgomery, McCracken et al, Phila., 1967-72; sr. ptnr. Honigman Miller Schwartz and Cohn, Detroit, 1972—. Panelist Bankruptcy Litigation Inst., N.Y.C., 1984—. Author: Pennsylvania Crime Codes, 1972, Bankruptcy Litigation Manual, 1988. Bd. dirs. Southeastern Mich. chpt. ARC, Detroit. Mem. Fed. Bar Assn. (past pres. Detroit chpt.), ABA, Pa. Bar Assn., Phila. Bar Assn., Detroit Bar Assn., Am. Bankruptcy Inst. (cert. bus. bankruptcy law specialist), Franklin (Mich.) Hills Country Club, Phi Beta Kappa. Democrat. Jewish. Office: Honigman Miller Schwartz & Cohn 2290 1st National Bldg Detroit MI 48226

TOLLEFSON, BEN C. state legislator, retired utility sales manager; b. Minot, N.D., June 14, 1927; s. Ben K. and Hannah G. (Espeseth) T.; m. Lila R. Adams, Apr. 11, 1949; children: Robb, LuAnn, David, Richard. Student, Minot State U., 1946-48. Advt. salesman Minot Daily News, 1956-57; utility salesman No. States Power Co., Minot, 1957-72, sales mgr., 1972-89; retired, 1989; advisor Ctrl. Venture Capital, Minot, 1990-95; mem. N.D. Ho. of Reps., Bismark, 1984-99, N.D. Senate from 38th dist., Bismark, 2001—. Pres. Minot Jaycees, 1957. Served with USN, 1945-47. Recipient Clara Barton Svc. award Am. Red Cross, 1969; named one of Outstanding Young Men Am., Minot Jaycees, 1958, State Ofcl. Yr., Nat. Assn. Home Builders, 1992. Mem. Kiwanis (Minot lt. gov. 1973, Outstanding Lt. Gov. 1973), Elks. Republican. Lutheran. Avocations: hunting, public speaking. Home: 500 Twenty Fourth St NW Minot ND 58701

TOLLESTRUP, ALVIN VIRGIL, physicist; b. Los Angeles, Mar. 22, 1924; s. Albert Virgil and Maureen (Petersen) T.; m. Alice Hatch, Feb. 26, 1945 (div. Nov. 1970); children: Kristine, Kurt, Eric, Carl; m. Janine Cukay, Oct. 11, 1986. BS, U. Utah, 1944; PhD, Calif. Inst. Tech., 1950. Mem. faculty Calif. Inst. Tech., Pasadena, 1950-77, prof. physics, 1968-77; scientist Fermi Nat. Lab., Batavia, Ill., 1977-93; co-spokesman CDF Collaboration, 1977-93. Co-developer superconducting magnets for Tevatron, Fermi Lab. Served to lt. (j.g.) USN, 1944-46. NSF fellow; Disting. Alumni award Calif. Inst. Tech., 1993. Fellow AAAS, NAS, Am. Phys. Soc. (R.R. Wilson prize 1989, Nat. medal for tech. 1989). Democrat. Office: Fermi Nat Lab PO Box 500 Batavia IL 60510-0500

TOMAC, STEVEN WAYNE, state legislator, farmer; b. Hettinger, N.D., Nov. 23, 1953; s. Robert and Betty Ann (Schmidt) T. BS, N.D. State U., 1976. Loan officer Bank of N.D., Bismarck, 1976-79; v.p. 1st Southwest Bank, Mandan, N.D., 1979-80; dir. mktg. N.D. Dept. Agr., Bismarck, 1980-81; exec. dir. N.D. Grain Growers, 1981-86; rodeo clown PRCA, Colorado Springs, 1971—; farmer/rancher St. Anthony, N.D., 1982—; mem. N.D. Ho. of Reps., Bismarck, 1986-90, N.D. Senate from 31st dist., Bismarck, 1990—. Mem. Accredited Rural Appraisers, Am. Soc. Farm Mgrs. and Rural Appraisers (appraiser 1981—). Democrat. Roman Catholic. Home: 2498 59th St Saint Anthony ND 58566-9640 Office: ND Senate 600 E Boulevard Ave Bismarck ND 58505-0660

TOMAIN, JOSEPH PATRICK, dean, law educator; b. Long Branch, N.J., Sept. 3, 1948; s. Joseph Pasquale and Bernice M. (Krzan) T.; m. Kathleen Corcione, Aug. 1, 1971; children: Joseph Anthony, John Fiore. AB, U. Notre Dame, 1970; JD, George Washington U., 1974. Bar: NJ, Iowa. Assoc. Giordano & Halleran, Middletown, N.J., 1974-76; from asst. to prof. law Drake U. Sch. Law, Des Moines, 1976-83; prof. law U. Cin. Coll. Law, 1983—, acting dean, 1989-90, dean, 1990—, Nippert prof. law, 1990—. Vis. prof. law U. Tex. Sch. Law, Austin, 1986-87. Author: Energy Law in a Nutshell, 1981, Nuclear Power Transformation, 1987; co-author: Energy Decision Making, 1983, Energy Law and Policy, 1989, Energy and Natural Resources Law, 1992, Regulatory Law and Policy, 1993, 2d edit., 1998, Energy, The Environment and the Global Economy, 2000. Bd. trustees Ctr. for Chem. Addictions Treatment, Cin., Vol. Lawyers for Poor, Cin.; mem. steering com. BLAC/CBA Round Table, Cin.; chair KnowledgeWorks Found. Served with USAR, 1970-76. Mem. ABA, Am. Law Inst., Ohio State Bar Assn. (del.), Cin. Bar Assn. (bd. trustees). Roman Catholic. Home: 3009 Springer Ave Cincinnati OH 45208-2440 Office: U Cin Coll Law Office Dean PO Box 210040 Cincinnati OH 45221-0040 E-mail: joseph.tomain@uc.edu.

TOMAR, RUSSELL HERMAN, pathologist, educator, researcher; b. Phila., Oct. 19, 1937; s. Julius and Ethel (Weinreb) T.; m. Karen J. Kent, Aug. 29, 1965; children: Elizabeth, David. BA in Journalism, George Washington U., 1959, MD, 1963. Diplomate Am. Bd. Pathology, Am. Bd. Allergy and Immunology, Am. Bd. Pathology, Immunopathology. Intern Barnes Hosp., Washington U. Sch. Medicine, 1963-64, resident in medicine, 1964-65; asst. prof. medicine SUNY, Syracuse, 1971-79, assoc. prof., 1979-88, assoc. prof. microbiology, 1980-84, prof., 1984-88, asst. prof. pathology, 1974-76, assoc. prof., 1976-83, prof., 1983-88, dir. immunopathology, 1974-88, attending physician immunodeficiency clinic, 1982-88, acting dir. microbiology, 1977-78, 82-83, interim dir. clin. pathology, 1986-87; prof. pathology and lab. medicine U. Wis. Ctr. for Health Scis., Madison, 1988—; dir. div. lab medicine U. Wis., 1988-95, dir. immunopathology and diagnostic immunology, 1995-98, prof. preventive medicine, 1999—; chair dept. pathology Cook County Hosp., Chgo., 1999—. Past mem. numerous coms. SUNY, Syracuse, U. Wis., Madison; mem. exec. com., chair and med. cons. AIDS Task Force Cen. N.Y., 1983-88. Assoc. editor Jour. Clin. Lab. Analysis; contbr. articles, rev. to profl. jours. Mem. pub. health com. Onondaga County Med. Soc., 1987-88. Lt. comdr. USPHS, 1965-67. Allergy and Immunology Div. fellow U. Pa. Fellow Coll. Am. Pathologists (diagnostics immunology rsch. com. 1993—, stds. com. 1995-97, commn. on clin. pathology 1997—), Am. Soc. Clin. Pathology (com. on continuing edn. immunopathology 1985-91, pathology data presentation com. 1976-79), Am. Acad. Allergy (penicillin hypersensitivity com. 1973-77); mem. AAAS, Am. Assn. Immunologists, Am. Assn. Pathology, Acad. Clin. Lab. Physicians and Scientists (com. on rsch. 1979-81, chairperson immunology 1979), Clin. Immunology Soc. (clin. lab. immunology com., chair coun. 1991-96). Office: Cook County Hosp Dept Pathology 627 S Wood St Ste 229 Chicago IL 60612-3810 Fax: 312-633-3364. E-mail: rtomar@hektoen.org.

TOMASKY, SUSAN, corporate officer; b. Morgantown, W.Va., Mar. 29, 1953; m. Ron Ungvarsky; 1 child, Victoria. BA cum laude, Univ. Ky., 1974; JD (hons.), George Washington Univ., 1979. Staff mem. House Com. Interstate and Fgn. Commerce, Washington, 1974—76; with FERC's Office of Gen. Counsel., 1979—81; assoc. Van Ness, Feldman & Curtin, 1981—86; ptnr. Van Ness, Feldman & Curtis, 1986—93; gen. coun. Federal Energy Regulatory Commn., 1993—97; 1997ptnr. 1998Hogan & Harts, 1997-98; senior v.p., gen. coun. & Sec. Am. Electric Power Svc. Corp., Columbus, Ohio, 1998—2000, exec. v.p., gen. counsel, sec., 2000—01, exec. v.p., CFO, 2001—02. Staff mem. George Washington U. Law Rev., 1979. Trustee Columbus Symphony Orch., Columbus Sch. for Girls; co-chair Keystone Energy Bd. Mem. Greater Columbus C. of C., Phi Beta Kappa.

TOMBLINSON, JAMES EDMOND, architect; b. Flint, Mich., Feb. 12, 1927; s. Carl and Edna Ethel (Spears) T.; m. Betsy Kinley, Sept. 26, 1959; children: Amy Lisa, John Timothy (dec.). B.Arch., U. Mich., 1951. Draftsman firms in, Detroit, 1951-53, Flint, 1953-54, 56-57, San Francisco, 1955-56; field engr. Atlas Constructors, Morocco, 1952-53; architect Tomblinson, Harburn, & Assocs., Inc. (and predecessors), Flint, 1958—, pres., 1969-95; chmn. bd. Tomblinson, Harburn & Assocs., Inc. (and predecessors), 1995—; chmn. Mich. Bd. Registration Architects, 1975-77; sec. Mundy Twp. Planning Commn., 1974-85, Grand Blanc Planning Commn., City of Mich., 1985—; chmn., 1988—. Pres. Flint Beautification Commn., 1968-69; bd. dirs. Grand Blanc Beautification Commn., 1969-84; founding mem. bd. dirs. Flint YMCA, 1969-75, chmn. camp com., 1971-75; founding mem. bd. dirs. Flint Environ. Action Team, 1971-77, v.p., 1971-73; elder First Presbyn. Ch. Flint, 1983, trustee, 1986-99; exec. com. Tall Pine council Boy Scouts Am., 1975— ; bd. dirs. New Paths, pres., 1985-86, 94—; trustee Grand Blanc Cmty. Found., 1997—. Served with AUS, 1945-46. Recipient various civic service awards. Fellow AIA; mem. Mich. Soc. Architects, Flint Area C. of C. Clubs: Greater Flint Jaycees (dir. 1957-63, v.p. 1963), Flint City, U. Mich. (pres. Flint chpt. 1980—). Lodge: Rotary (pres. 1984-85). Home: 686 Applegate Ln Grand Blanc MI 48439-1669 Office: THA Architects Engrs 817 E Kearsley St Flint MI 48503-2076

TOMITA, TADANORI, neurosurgeon, educator; b. Osaka, Japan, Nov. 19, 1945; s. Tadao and Noriko (Ikeda) T.; m. Kathryn Morley, June 28, 1980; children: Tadaki M., Kenji W., Dan Y. MD, Kobe (Japan) U., 1970. Diplomate Am. Bd. Neurol. Surgery, Am. Bd. Pediat. Neurosurgery. Attending neurosurgeon Children's Meml. Hosp., Chgo., 1981—, dir. Brain Tumor Ctr., 1984—. Prof. Northwestern U. Med. Sch. Contbr. articles to profl. jours. Recipient Sherry Kallick award Northwestern Meml. Hosp., 1979, Frank Notides award Children's Meml. Hosp., Chgo., 1980. Fellow ACS, Am. Acad. Pediatrics; mem. Am. Assn. Neurol. Surgeons, Congress Neurorol. Surgeons, Am. Soc. Pediatric Neurosurgery, Soc. Pediatric Neurosurgery. Office: Childrens Meml Hosp 2300 N Childrens Plz Chicago IL 60614-3394

TOMKINS, ANDY, state commissioner education; BA, East Ctrl. State U., 1969; MEd, Emporia State U., 1973; PhD, U. Kans., 1977. Tchr. Kans. High Schs.; prin., supr. Kans. Sch. Dist.; dean sch. edn. Pitts. State U.; commr. edn. Kans. State Dept. Edn., Topeka, 1996—. Recipient Kans. Supr. Yr. award, 1991-92. Office: Kansas State Dept Education 120 SE 10th Ave Topeka KS 66612-1103

TOMKOVICZ, JAMES JOSEPH, law educator; b. L.A., Oct. 10, 1951; s. Anthony Edward and Vivian Marion (Coory) T.; m. Nancy Louise Abboud, June 27, 1987; children: Vivian Rose, Michelle Evelene, Henry James. BA, U. So. Calif., 1973; JD, UCLA, 1976. Bar: Calif. 1976, U.S. Dist. Ct. (so. dist.) Calif., U.S. Ct. Appeals (9th and 10th cirs.), U.S. Supreme Ct. Law clk. to Hon. Edward J. Schwartz, San Diego, 1976-77; law clk. to Hon. John M. Ferren Washington, 1977-78; atty. U.S. Dept. Justice, 1979-80; assoc. prof. law U. Iowa, Iowa City, 1982-86, prof., 1986—. Vis. prof. U. Iowa, Iowa City, 1981, U. Mich., Ann Arbor, 1992; adj. prof. UCLA, 1981-82. Author: (casebook) Criminal Procedure, 4th edit. (with W. White), 2001, (book) The Right to the Assistance of Counsel, 2002; (outline) Criminal Procedure, 1997; contbr. articles to profl. jours. Mem. Order of Coif, Phi Beta Kappa. Democrat. Roman Catholic. Avocations: running, softball, creative writing. Office: U Iowa Coll Law Melrose & Byngton Iowa City IA 52242 E-mail: james-tomkovicz@uiowa.edu.

TOMLINSON, JOSEPH ERNEST, manufacturing company executive; b. Sycamore, Ill., Apr. 22, 1939; s. Bernie Gilbert and Elizabeth Lowe (Hoffman) T.; m. Judith Ann Worst, Sept. 20, 1969; children: Mark Joseph, Amy Ann. BS in Acctg., U. Ill., 1962. CPA. Staff acct. Price Waterhouse and Co., Chgo., 1962-65, sr. acct., 1965-69, audit mgr. Indpls., 1969-74; corp. contr. Inland Paperboard and Pkg., 1974-82; v.p., treas., contr. Inland Container Corp., 1982—. Congl. chmn. Carmel Luth. Ch., Ind., 1983-86, v.p., 1988-91; mem. bd. dirs. Luth. Child and Family Svcs., Indpls., 1994-97. With Ill. N.G. 1963-69. Mem. Fin. Execs. Inst. (treas. Indpls. chpt. 1986-87, sec. 1987-88, 2d v.p. 1988-89, 1st v.p. 1989-90, pres. 1990-91). Republican. Club: Crooked Stick Golf. Home: 2204 Mason Point Pl Wilmington NC 28405-5276 Office: Inland Paperboard and Pkg Inc 4030 Vincennes Rd Indianapolis IN 46268-3007

TOMLINSON, ROBERT (BOB TOMLINSON), state legislator; b. Linclon, NE, May 6, 1957; m. Carole Tomlinson. BSE, Kansas U., 1980; MLA, Baker U., 1987. Special svcs. teacher Shawnee Mission AEP, Kans., 1985—; Kans. state rep. Dist. 24, 1993—. Spl. svc. tchr. Address: 5722 Birch Roeland Park KS 66205

TOMLJANOVICH, ESTHER M. state supreme court justice; b. Galt, Iowa, Nov. 1, 1931; d. Chester William and Thelma L. (Brooks) Moeller-ing; m. William S. Tomljanovich, Dec. 26, 1957; 1 child, William Brooks. AA, Itasca Jr. Coll., 1951; BSL, St. Paul Coll. Law, 1953, LLB, 1955. Bar: Minn. 1955, U.S. Dist. Ct. Minn. 1958. Asst. revisor of statutes State of Minn., St. Paul, 1957-66, revisor of statutes, 1974-77, dist. ct. judge Stillwater, 1977-90; assoc. justice Minn. Supreme Ct., St. Paul, 1990-98. Mem. adv. bd. women offenders Minn. Dept. Corrections, 1999—; mem. leadership com. So. Minn. Legal Svcs. Corp., 1999—. Former mem. North St. Paul Bd. Edn., Maplewood Bd. Edn., Lake Elmo Planning Commn.; trustee William Mitchell Call Law, 1995—, Legal Rights Ctr., 1995—, pres., 1999; trustee So. Minn. Legal Svcs. Corp.; bd. dirs. Itasca C.C. Found., 1996—, Medica Health Ins. Co., 2001—. Recipient Centennial 2000 award William Mitchell Coll; named one of One Hundred Who Made a Difference William Mitchell Coll. Law Mem. Minn. State Bar Assn., Bus. and Profl. Women's Assn. St. Paul (former pres.), Minn. Women Laywers (founding mem.). Office: Supreme Ct MN 423 Minnesota Judicial Center 25 Constitution Ave Saint Paul MN 55155-1500

TOMPKINS, CURTIS JOHNSTON, university president; b. Roanoke, Va., July 14, 1942; s. Joseph Buford and Rebecca (Johnston) T.; m. Mary Katherine Hasle, Sept. 5, 1964; children: Robert, Joseph, Rebecca. BS, Va. Poly. Inst., 1965, MS, 1967; PhD, Ga. Inst. Tech., 1971. Indsl. engr. E.I. DuPont de Nemours, Richmond, Va., 1965-67; instr. Sch. Indsl. and Systems Engrng., Ga. Inst. Tech., Atlanta, 1968-71; assoc. prof. Colgate Darden Grad. Sch. Bus. Adminstrn., U. Va., Charlottesville, 1971-77; prof., chmn. dept. indsl. engrng. W.Va. U., Morgantown, 1977-80, dean Coll. Engrng., 1980-91; pres. Mich. Technol. U., Houghton, 1991—, also bd. dirs. Mem. engrng. accreditation commn. Accreditation Bd. for Engrng. and Tech., 1981-86; mem. exec. bd. Engrng. Deans Coun., 1985-89, vice chmn., 1987-89; mem. engrng. adv. com., chmn. of planning com. NSF, 1988-91, chm. Mich. Univs. pres. coun., 1996-98; bd. dirs. Oak Ridge Assoc. Univs., 1996-99, Mich. Technologies, Inc., 1998-99; Pres. Coun. Assn. Governing bds. 1996—, Gov's. Workforce Commn., 1996-2002; mem. engrng. adv. bd. U. Cin., 1996-99 Author: (with L.E. Grayson) Management of Public Sector and Nonprofit Organizations, 1983, (with others) Maynard's Industrial Engineering Handbook, 1992; contbr. chpt. to Ency. of Profl. Mgmt, 1978, 83. Co-chmn. W.Va. Gov.'s Coun. on Econ. Devel.; bd. dirs. Pub. Land Corp. W.Va., 1980-89; mem. faculty Nat. Acad. Voluntarism, United Way Am., 1976-91; mem. Morgantown Water Commn., 1981-87, Morgantown Utility Bd., 1987-91; mem. steering com. W.Va. Conf. on Environ., 1985-89; chmn. Monogalia County United Way, 1989-90; campaign chmn. Copper Country United Way, 1995-96. Named to Com. of 100 Va. Tech. Coll., Disting. Alumni Acad. dept. indsl. engring; recipient Frank and Lillian Gilbreth Indsl. Engring. award Inst. Indsl. Engrs., 1998. Fellow Inst. Indsl. Engrs. (life mem., trustee 1983-90, pres. 1988-89), Am. Soc. Engring. Edn. (pres. 1990-91), Mich. Soc. Profl. Engrs.; mem. Am. Assn. Engring. Soc. (bd. govs. 1987-90, exec. com. 1987-90, sec.-treas. 1989-90), Jr. Engring. Tech. Soc. (bd. dirs. 1988-91), Nat. Soc. for Sci., Tech. and Society (bd. dirs. 1991-94), Internat. Hall of Fame of Sci. and Engring. (hon. trustee), Ga. Tech. Coll. Engring. Disting. Alumni Acad., Ga. Tech. Sch. Indsl. and Sys. Engring. Disting. Alumni Acad., W.Va. U. Dept. Indsl. Engring. Disting. Alumni Acad. (hon.), Mich. C. of C. (bd. dirs 1997—), Blue Key (hon.), Sigma Xi, Phi Kappa Phi, Tau Beta Pi, Alpha Pi Mu. Methodist. Home: 21680 Woodland Rd Houghton MI 49931-9746 Office: Mich Technol U 1400 Townsend Dr Houghton MI 49931-1200 E-mail: curt@mtu.edu.

TOMPSON, MARIAN LEONARD, professional society administrator; b. Chgo., Dec. 5, 1929; d. Charles Clark and Marie Christine (Bernardini) Leonard; m. Clement R. Tompson, May 7, 1949 (dec. 1981); children: Melanie Tompson Kandler, Deborah Tompson Frueh, Allison Tompson Fagerholm, Laurel Tompson Davies, Sheila Tompson Doucet, Brian, Philip. Student public and parochial schs., Chgo. and Franklin Park, Ill. Co-founder La Leche League (Internat.), Franklin Park, 1956, pres., 1956-80, dir., 1956—, pres. emeritus, 1990—; exec. dir. Alternative Birth Crisis Coalition, 1981-85; co-founder, pres., exec. dir. AnotherLook, Inc., 2001—. Cons. WHO; bd. dirs. N.Am. Soc. Psychosomatic Ob-Gyn, Natural Birth and Natural Parenting, 1981-83; mem. adv. bd. Nat. Assn. Parents and Profls. for Safe Alternatives in Childbirth, Am. Acad. Husband-Coached Childbirth; mem. adv. bd. Fellowship of Christian Midwives; mem. profl. adv. bd. Home Oriented Maternity Experience; guest lectr. Harvard U. Med. Sch., UCLA Sch. Pub. Health, U. Antioquia Med. Sch., Medellín, Columbia, U. Ill. Sch. Medicine, Chgo., U. W.I., Jamaica, U. N.C., Nat. Coll. of Chiropractic, Am. Coll. Nurse Midwives, U. Parma, Italy, Inst. Psychology, Rome, Rockford (Ill.) Sch. Medicine, Northwestern U. Sch. Medicine, NGO Forum/4th World Conf. on Women, Beijing; mem. family com. Ill. Commn. on Status of Women, 1976-85; mem. perinatal adv. com. Ill. Dept. Pub. Health, 1980-83; mem. adv. bd. Internat. Nutrition Comm. Svc., 1980—; bd. cons. We Can, 1984—; exec. adv. bd. United Resources for Family Health and Support, 1985-86; mem. internat. adv. coun. World Alliance of Breast Feeding Action, 1996. Author: (with others) Safe Alternatives in Childbirth, 1976, 21st Century Obstetrics Now!, 1977, The Womanly Art of Breastfeeding, 6th edit., 1997, Five Standards for Safe Childbearing, 1981, But Doctor, About That Shot..., 1988, The Childbirth Activists Handbook, 1983; author prefaces and forwards in 11 books; columnist La Leche League News, 1958-80; columnist People's Doctor Newsletter, 1977-88, mem. adv. bd., cons., 1988-92; assoc. editor Child and Family Quar., 1967—; mem. med. adv. bd. East West Jour., 1980—; also articles. Mem. adv. bd. Shelters for Healthy Environments, 1998, The Beginning Project, 2000. Recipient Gold medal of honor Centro de Rehabilitacao Nossa Senhora da Gloria, 1975, Night of 100 Stars III Achiever award Actors Fund Am., 1990, N.Y. Soc. Ethical Culture Ethical Humanist award, 1999, 100 Women Making a Difference Today's Chgo. Woman. Mem. Nat. Assn. Postpartum Care Svcs. (adv. bd.), Chgo. Cmty. Midwives (adv. bd.), World Alliance for Breast Feeding Action (mem. internat. adv. coun. 1997). Office: 1400 N Meacham Rd Schaumburg IL 60173-4808 E-mail: mt@anotherlook.org.

TOMSICH, ROBERT J. heavy machinery manufacturing executive; Chmn. Blaw Knox Corp., Pitts.; pres., chmn. Nesco, Inc., Cleve. Office: Nesco 6140 Parkland Blvd Cleveland OH 44124-4187

TONACK, DELORIS, elementary school educator; Elem. tchr. math. and sci. Goodrich Jr. High Sch., 1996—. Recipient Nebr. State Tchr. of Yr. award math./sci., 1992. Office: Sci Focus Program 1222 S 27th St Lincoln NE 68502-1832

TONDEUR, PHILIPPE MAURICE, mathematician, educator; b. Zurich, Switzerland, Dec. 7, 1932; came to U.S., 1964, naturalized, 1974; s. Jean and Simone (Lapaire) T.; m. Claire-Lise Ballansat, Dec. 20, 1965. PhD, U. Zurich, 1961. Rsch. fellow U. Paris, 1961-63; lectr. math. U. Zurich, 1963-64, U. Buenos Aires, 1964, Harvard U., Cambridge, Mass., 1964-65, U. Calif., Berkeley, 1965-66; asso. prof. Wesleyan U., Middletown, Conn., 1966-68; assoc. prof. U. Ill., Urbana, 1968-70, prof., 1970—, chair dept. math., 1996-99. Chmn. NSF Divsn. Math. Sci. U. Ill., Urbana, Ill., 1999-2002; vis. prof. Auckland U., 1968, Eidg. Techn. Hochschule U. Heidelberg, 1973, U. Zurich, 1982, U. Rome, 1984, Ecole Polytechnique, Paris, 1987, U. Santiago de Compostela, 1987, Max Planck Inst., 1987, U. Leuven, Belgium, 1990, Keio U., Yokohama, Japan, 1993; assoc. mem. Ctr. Advanced Study U. Ill., 1977-78, 91-92. Contbr. articles to profl. jours. Recipient fellowships Swiss Nat. Sci. Found., fellowships Harvard U., fellowships U. Ill. Mem. Am. Math. Soc., Schweiz Math. Gesellschaft, Société Math. de France, Soc. for Indsl. and Appl. Math., Math. Assn. of Am. Office: U Ill Math Dept Urbana IL 61801

TONGUE, WILLIAM WALTER, economics and business consultant, educator emeritus; b. Worcester, Mass., May 24, 1915; s. Walter Ernest and Lena (Brown) T.; m. Beverly Harriet Cohan, Dec. 26, 1936; children—Barbara Tongue Duggan, Kathleen Tongue Alligood. A.B., Dartmouth, 1937, M.C.S., 1938; Ph.D., U. Chgo., 1947. Jr. acct. Price, Waterhouse & Co. (C.P.A.'s), N.Y.C., 1938; instr. Coe Coll., Cedar Rapids, Iowa, 1941-42; spl. cons. OSS, 1942; fin. economist Fed. Res. Bank Chgo., 1942-44; economist Jewel Companies, Inc., Chgo., 1944-64; prof. econs. and finance U. Ill. Chgo. , 1965-80. Prof. emeritus, 1980—; econ. cons. LaSalle Nat. Bank, Chgo., 1968-91; mem. com. CNA Fin. Separate Fund B.; dir. St. Joseph Light & Power Co., Mo., 1965-86; trustee Signode Employees' Savs. and Profit Sharing Trust Fund, 1980-89. Author articles; contbr.: to books including How We Can Halt Inflation and Still Keep Our Jobs, 1974. Bd. dirs., v.p. rsch. and stats. Chgo. Assn. Commerce and Industry, 1968-69. Mem. Nat. Assn. Bus. Economists (pres. 1962-63), Conf. Bus. Economists, Am. Statis. Assn. (pres. Chgo. chpt. 1951-52), Econ. Club Chgo., Investment Analysts Assn. Chgo., Inst. Chartered Fin. Analysts (chartered fin. analyst 1963), Midwest Fin. Assn. (pres. 1972-73). Home and Office: 1220 Village Dr Apt 427 Arlington Heights IL 60004-8123 E-mail: williamTongue@msn.com.

TONN, ROBERT JAMES, retired entomologist; b. Watertown, Wis., June 23, 1927; s. Harry James and Elise (Foogman) T.; m. Noemi C. Tonn; children: Sigrid M., Monica E. BS, Colo. State U., 1949, MS, 1950; MPH, Okla. Med. Sch., 1963; PhD, Okla. State U., 1959. Rsch. assoc La. State U., Costa Rica/New Orleans, 1961-63; dir. Taunton Field Sta., Taunton, Mass., 1963-65; chief PMO unit WHO, various locations, 1965-87. Adj. prof. of parasitology U. Tex.-El Paso, 1988—; cons. USAID/VBC, 1987—. Contbr. numerous articles to profl. jours. Mem. Am. Soc. Tropical Medicine, Soc. Vector Ecology (pres. 1984), Am. Mosquito Control Assn., U.S./ Mex. Border Health Assn., Royal Soc. Tropical Medicine and Hygiene, Masons. Congregationalist. Home: 4247 Winchester Rd Las Cruces NM 88011 E-mail: stonn@zianet.com.

TOOHEY, BRIAN FREDERICK, lawyer; b. Niagara Falls, N.Y., Dec. 14, 1944; s. Matthew and Marilyn (Hoag) T.; m. Mary Elizabeth Monihan; children: Maureen Elizabeth, Matthew Sheridan, Margaret Monihan, Mary Catherine, Elizabeth Warner. BS, Niagara U., 1966; JD, Cornell U., 1969. Bar: N.Y. 1969, N.Mex. 1978, Ohio 1980. Ptnr. Cohen, Swados, Wright, Hanifin & Bradford, Buffalo, 1973-77; pvt. practice Santa Fe, 1977-79; of counsel Jones, Day, Reavis & Pogue, Cleve., 1979-80, ptnr., 1981—. Mem. Citizens League Greater Cleve., 1982—. Lt. JAG Corps, USNR, 1970-73. Mem. ABA, N.Y. State Bar Assn., State Bar N.Mex., Ohio State Bar Assn., Greater Cleve. Bar Assn. Roman Catholic. Home: 25 Pepper Creek Dr Cleveland OH 44124-5279 Office: Jones Day Reavis & Pogue N Point 901 Lakeside Ave E Cleveland OH 44114-1190 E-mail: bftoohey@jonesday.com.

TOOHEY, JAMES KEVIN, lawyer; b. Evanston, Ill., July 16, 1944; s. John Joseph and Ruth Regina (Cassidy) T.; m. Julie Marie Crane, Nov. 1, 1969 (div. Aug. 1977); children: Julie Colleen, Jeanne Christine; m. Anne Margaret Boettingheimer, May 28, 1983; children: James Robert, Kevin John, Casey Anne. BBA, U. Notre Dame, 1966; JD, Northwestern U., 1969. BAr: Ill. 1969, U.S. Dist. Ct. (no. dist.) Ill. 1971, U.S. Dist. Ct. (ctrl. dist.) Ill. 1991, U.S. Ct. Appeals (7th cir.) 1973, U.S. Ct. Appeals (8th cir.) 1975, U.S. Supreme Ct. 1988. Assoc. Taylor, Miller, Magner, Sprowl & Hutchings, Chgo., 1970-71; asst. U.S. Atty. Office U.S. Atty., 1971-74; assoc. Ross, Hardies, O'Keefe, Babcock & Parsons, 1974-77; ptnr. Ross & Hardies, 1978—. Mem. St. Mary of the Wood Parish Coun., 1999—. Mem. Ill. State Bar Assn., Soc. Trial Lawyers, Assn. Advancement of Automotive Medicine, Ill. Assn. Def. Attys., Trial Lawyers Club Chgo., Edgebrook Sauganash Athletic Assn. (bd. dirs., commr. 1993-96; softball, baseball, and basketball coach). Office: Ross & Hardies 150 N Michigan Ave Ste 2500 Chicago IL 60601-7567 E-mail: james.toohey@rosshardies.com.

TOOKER, GARY LAMARR, electronics company executive; b. Shelby, Ohio, May 25, 1939; s. William Henry and Frances Ione (Melick) T.; m. Diane Rae Kreider, Aug. 4, 1962; children: Lisa, Michael. B.S.E.E., Ariz. State U., 1962. With Motorola Inc., Phoenix, 1962—, v.p., gen. mgr. internat. semicondr. div., 1980-81, v.p., gen. mgr. semicondr. products sector, 1981-82, sr. v.p., gen. mgr. semicondr. products sector, 1982-83, exec. v.p., gen. mgr. semicondr. products sector, 1983-86, sr. exec. v.p., chief corp. staff officer Ill., 1986-88, sr. exec. v.p., chief operating officer, 1988-90, pres., chief oper. officer, 1990-93, chief exec. officer, 1993—, also bd. of dirs., vice chmn., CEO, now chmn. Mem. engring. adv. council Ariz. State U., Tempe, 1982-86. Bd. dirs. Scottsdale (Ariz.) Boys Club, 1980-86, Jr. Achievement Chgo., 1988—; chief crusader, major. corp. group United Way, Chgo., 1988—; mem. alumni bd., mem. Found. bd. Ariz. State U., 1991—. Named Outstanding Alumni of Yr., Ariz. State U., 1983. Mem. IEEE, Am. Mgmt. Assn., Semicondr. Industry Assn. (bd. dirs. 1981-86, chmn. bd. 1982-86), Ariz. Assn. Industries (bd. dirs. 1981-86), Am. Electronics Assn. (bd. dirs. 1988—, chmn. bd. 1991), Econ. Club of Chgo., Elec. Mfrs. Club. Republican. Office: Motorola Inc 1303 E Algonquin Rd Schaumburg IL 60196-1079

TOOMAJIAN, WILLIAM MARTIN, lawyer; b. Troy, N.Y., Sept. 26, 1943; s. Leo R. and Elizabeth (Gundrum) T.; children: Andrew, Philip. AB, Hamilton Coll., 1965; JD, U. Mich., 1968; LLM, N.Y.U., 1975. Bar: N.Y. 1968, Ohio 1978. Mem. firm Cadwalader, Wickersham & Taft, N.Y.C., 1971-77, Baker & Hostetler, Cleve., 1977—. Served to lt. USCG, 1968-71. Mem. ABA, Ohio Bar Assn., Cleve. Bar Assn., Cleve. Tax Club. Home: 3582 Lytle Rd Cleveland OH 44122-4908 Office: Baker & Hostetler 3200 National City Ctr 1900 E 9th St Ste 3200 Cleveland OH 44114-3475

TOPEL, DAVID GLEN, agricultural studies educator; b. Lake Mills, Wis., Oct. 24, 1937; BS, U. Wis., 1960; MS, Kans. State U., 1962; PhD, Mich. State U., 1965. Assoc. prof. animal sci. and food tech. Iowa State U., Ames, 1967-73, prof. animal sci. and food tech., 1973-79, dean Coll. Agr., 1988-2000, dir. agr. and home econs. experiment sta., 1988-2000, M.E. Ensminger chair animal sci., 2000—; prof., head dept. Auburn U., 1979-88, M.E. Ensminger endowed chair animal sci., 2000—. Cons., presenter, lectr. in field; mem. Gov. of Iowa's Sci. Adv. Coun., 1990-2000, Gov. of Iowa's Livestock Revitalization Task Force, 1993-98; chair Gov.'s Environ. Agr. Com., 1994; mem. Iowa Corn Promotion Bd.; mem. faculty Royal Vet. and Agrl. U., Denmark, 1971-72, 90; vis. prof. Nat. Taiwan U., 1972. Author: The Pork Industry - Problems and Progress, 1968. Secretariat World Food Prize, Iowa State U., Ames, 1991-96. Fulbright-Hays scholar Royal Vet. and Agrl. U., 1971-72; recipient award of merit Knights of Ak-Sar-Ben, 1973, Commr.'s award Agrl. Commr. Republic of China, 1977, disting. Achievement award Block and Bridle Club, 1979, Ala. Cattlemen's Assn.,1 984, Hon. State Farmer Degree, Ala., 1986, Harry L. Rudnick Educator's award Nat. Assn. Meat Purveyors, 1989, USDA Honor award, 1999, Hon. Prof. award Gyöngyös Coll., Hungary, 2000; named hon. prof. Ukrainian State Agrl. U., 1993. Fellow Am. Soc. Animal Sci. (Disting. Rsch. award in meat sci. 1979); mem. Am. Meat Sci. Assn., Inst. Food Tech., Iowa Crop Improvement Assn., Extension and Tchg. (pres. North Ctrl. Region 1992), Nat. Assn. State Univs. and Land-Grant Colls. (chair bd. agr. 1993, mem. commn. on food, environ. and renewable resources 1992-99), Ukrainian Acad. Agrl. Scis., Sigma Xi (Outstanding Achievement award Iowa chpt. 1993), Alpha Zeta, Gamma Sigma Delta (Internat. award). Presbyterian. Avocations: fishing, golf. Home: 2630 Meadow Glen Rd Ames IA 50014-8239 Office: Iowa State U Coll Agriculture 2374 Kildee Hall Ames IA 50011-0001

TOPILOW, CARL S. symphony conductor; b. Jersey City, N.J., Mar. 14, 1947; s. Jacob Topilow and Pearl (Roth) Topilow Josephs; m. Shirley; 1 child, Jenny Michelle. B.Mus., Manhattan Sch. of Mus., 1968, M.Mus., 1969. Exxon/Arts Endowment Condr. Denver Symphony Orch., 1976-79, asst. condr., 1979-80; mus. dir. Denver Chamber Orch., 1976-81, Denver Youth Orch., 1977-80, Grand Junction Symphony, Colo., 1977-80, Nat. Repertory Orch., Breckenridge, Colo., 1978—; dir. orchs. Cleve. Inst. Mus., 1981—, condr. Summit Brass 1986—, Cleve. Pops Orch., 1995—. Recipient Conducting fellowship Nat. Orch. Assn., N.Y.C., 1972-75, Aspen Mus. Festival, Colo., 1976; winner 1st place Balt. Symphony Conducting Competition, Md., 1976. Office: Cleve Inst Music 11021 East Blvd Cleveland OH 44106-1705

TOPINKA, JUDY BAAR, state official; b. Riverside, Ill., Jan. 16, 1944; d. William Daniel and Lillian Mary (Shuss) Baar; 1 child, Joseph Baar. BS, Northwestern U., 1966. Features editor, reporter, columnist Life Newspapers, Berwyn and LaGrange, Ill., 1966-77; with Forest Park (Ill.) Rev. and Westchester News, 1976-77; coord. spl. events dept. fedn. comm. AMA, 1978-80; rsch. analyst Senator Leonard Becker, 1978-79; mem. Ill. Ho. of Reps., 1981-84, Ill. Senate, 1985-94; treas. State of Ill., Springfield, 1995—. Former mem. judiciary com., former chmn. senate health and welfare com.; former mem. fin. instn. com.; former co-chmn. Citizens Coun. on Econ. Devel.; former co-chmn. U.S. Commn. for Preservation of Am.'s Heritage Abroad, serves on legis. ref. bur.; former mem. minority bus. resource ctr. adv. com. U.S. Dept. Transp.; former mem. adv. bd. Nat. Inst. Justice. Founder, pres., bd. dirs. West Suburban Exec. Breakfast Club, from 1976; chmn. Ill. Ethnics for Reagan-Bush, 1984, Bush-Quayle 1988; spokesman Nat. Coun. State Legislatures Health Com.; former mem. nat. adv. coun. health professions edn. HHS; mem., GOP chairwoman Legis. Audit Commn. of Cook County; chmn. Riverside Twp. Regular Republican Orgn., 1994—. Recipient Outstanding Civilian Svc. medal, Molly Pitcher award, Abraham Lincoln award, Silver Eagle award U.S. Army and N.G. Office: Office of Ill State Treasurer 100 W Randolph St Ste 15-600 Chicago IL 60601-3232

TOPLIKAR, JOHN M. state legislator; m. Dianne Lee. Kans. state rep. Dist. 15, 1993—. Bus. owner, carpenter. Home: 507 E Spruce St Olathe KS 66061-3356

TORDOFF, HARRISON BRUCE, retired zoologist, educator; b. Mechanicville, N.Y., Feb. 8, 1923; s. Harry F. and Ethel M. (Dormandy) T.; m. Jean Van Nostrand, July 3, 1946; children: Jeffrey, James. B.S., Cornell U., 1946; M.A., U. Mich., 1949, Ph.D., 1952. Curator Inst. of Jamaica, Kingston, 1946-47; instr. U. Kans., 1950-52, asst. prof., 1952-57, assoc. prof., 1957; asst. prof. U. Mich., 1957-59, assoc. prof., 1959-62, prof., 1962-70; former dir. Bell Mus. Natural History; prof. ecology U. Minn., Mpls., 1970-91, dean coll. biol. scis., 1986-87. Contbr. articles in ornithology to profl. jours. Served with USAF, 1942-45. Decorated D.F.C., 17 Air medals. Fellow Am. Ornithologists Union (pres. 1978-80); mem. Nature Conservancy (chmn. bd. Minn. chpt. 1975-77), Wilson Ornithol. Soc. (editor 1952-54), Cooper Ornithol. Soc. Office: 100 Ecology 1987 Upper Buford Cir Saint Paul MN 55108-1051 Home: 189 11th St Lake Placid FL 33852-9460 E-mail: tordoff@ecology.umin.edu.

TORF, PHILIP R. lawyer, pharmacist; b. Chgo., Aug. 4, 1952; m. Donna Torf; 3 children. BS, U. Ill., 1976; JD, John Marshall Law Sch., 1984. Dem. candidate 10th dist. Ill. U.S. House of Reps., 1996. Jewish.

TORGERSEN, TORWALD HAROLD, architect, designer; b. Chgo., Sept. 2, 1929; s. Peder and Hansine Malene (Hansen) T.; m. Dorothy Darlene Peterson, June 22, 1963. B.S. in Archtl. Engring. with honors, U. Ill., 1951. Lic. architect Ill., D.C., real estate broker, Ill., interior designer, Ill.; registered architect Nat. Coun. Archtl. Registration Bds. Ptnr. Coyle & Torgersen (Architects-Engrs.), Washington, Chgo. and Joliet, Ill., 1955-56; project coord. Skidmore, Owings & Merrill, Chgo., 1956-60; corp. architect, dir. architecture, constrn. and interiors Container Corp. Am., 1960-86; prin. in charge of orgn. and adminstrn. Jack Train Assocs. Inc., 1987-88; cons. Torwald H. Torgersen, AIA, FASID, 1988—. Guest lectr. U. Wis. Capt. USNR, 1951-82. Recipient Top Ten Design award Factory mag., 1964 Fellow Am. Soc. Interior Designers; mem. AIA, Naval Res. Assn., Ill. Naval Militia, Am. Arbitration Assn., Am. Soc. Mil. Engrs., Paper Industry Mgmt. Assn. (hon.), Sports Car Club Am., Nat. Eagle Scout Assn. Club: 20 Fathoms. Home and Office: 3750 N Lake Shore Dr Chicago IL 60613-4238

TORGERSON, JAMES PAUL, energy company executive; b. Cleve., Nov. 30, 1952; s. Alfred Paul and Alice Marie (Kola) T.; m. Mary Ann Gadzinski, Sept. 9, 1978; children: Paul David, Beth Ann. BBA in Acctg., Cleve. State U., 1977; postgrad., So. Meth. U., 1980-81. Sr. budget acct. Diamond Shamrock Corp., Cleve., 1977-79, fin. planning supr., 1979, fin. staff analyst Dallas, 1979-80, sr. fin. analyst, 1980-81, planning analyst Lexington, Ky., 1981-83, mgr. planning and devel., 1983-86, gen. mgr. planning systems, 1986—, v.p., Development Dallas; exec. v.p., Chief Adminstrv. Officer and CFO Washington Energy Co., Seattle; v.p. and CFO Puget Sound Energy, Inc.; CFO and treas. DPL, Inc., Dayton, OH, 1998—. Republican. Roman Catholic. Avocations: golf, aerobics. Home: 2202 Burgandy Dr Carrollton TX 75006-4324 Office: DPL Inc Courthouse Plaza SW Dayton OH 45402

TORGERSON, JIM, state legislator; m. Analene Torgerson; 4 children. BS, Minot State U. Operator restaurant and marina, Ray, N.D.; mem. from dist. 2 N.D. State Ho. of Reps., Bismarck, 1993-98, mem. edn. and natural resources coms. Office: HC 1 Box 22 Ray ND 58849-9615

TORGERSON, KATHERINE P. diversified business media company executive; Now v.p. human resources and exec. adminstrn. Penton Media, Inc., Cleve., with. Office: Penton Media Inc Ste 316 1300 E 9th St Cleveland OH 44114-1503

TORGERSON, LARRY KEITH, lawyer; b. Albert Lea, Minn., Aug. 25, 1935; s. Fritz G. and Lu (Hillman) T. BA, Drake U., 1958, MA, 1960, LLB, 1963, JD, 1968; MA, Iowa U., 1962; cert., The Hague Acad. Internat. Law, The Netherlands, 1965, 69; LLM, U. Minn., 1969, Columbia U., 1971, U. Mo., 1976; PMD, Harvard U., 1973; EdM, 1974. Bar: Minn. 1964, U.S. Dist. Ct. Minn. 1964, Wis. 1970, Iowa 1970, U.S. Dist. Ct. (no. dist.) Iowa 1971, U.S. Tax Ct. 1971, U.S. Supreme Ct. 1972, U.S. Dist. Ct. (ea. dist.) Wis. 1981, U.S. Ct. Appeals (8th cir.) 1981. Asst. corp. counsel 1st Bank Stock Corp. (88 Banks), Mpls., 1963-67, 1st Svc. Corp. (27 ins. agys., computer subs.), Mpls., 1965-67; v.p., trust officer Nat. City Bank, 1967-69; sr. mem. Torgerson Law Firm, Northwood, Iowa, 1969-87; trustee, gen. counsel Torgerson Farms, 19677—, Redbirch Farms, Kensett, Iowa, 1987—, Sunburst Farms, Grafton, 1987—, Gold Dust Farms, Bolan, 1988—, Torgerson Grain Storage, Bolan, 1988—, Indian Summer Farms, Bolan, 1991—, Sunset Farms, Bolan, 1992—, Sunrise Farms, Grafton, 1994—. CEO, gen. counsel Internat. Investments, Mpls., 1983-96, Transoceanic, Mpls., 1987-96, Torgerson Capital, Northwood, 1996—, Torgerson Investments, Northwood, 1984—, Torgerson Properties, Northwood, 1987—, Torgerson Ranches, Sundance, Wyo., 1998—, Hawaiian Investments Unltd., Maui, Hawaii, 1998—, Internat. Investments Unltd., San Pedro, Belize, 1999—. Recipient All-Am. Journalism award Thomas Arkle Clark Outstanding Achievement award, 1958, Dennis E. Brumfield Outstanding Achievement award, 1958, Johnny B. Guy Outstanding Leadership award, 1958; named to Outstanding Young Men of Am., U.S. Jaycees; Hagen scholar, Honor scholar. Mem. ABA, Am. Judicature Soc., Iowa Bar Assn., Minn. Bar Assn., Wis. Bar Assn., Hennepin County Bar Assn., Mensa, Drake Student-Faculty Coun., Drake Student Alumni Coun. (chmn.), Jaycees, Harvard Bus. Sch. Study (pres., exec. com., univ. editor in chief), Psi Chi, Circle K (pres. local chpt.), Phi Alpha Delta, Omicron Delta Kappa (pres. local chpt.), Pi Kappa Delta (pres. local chpt.), Alpha Tau Omega (pres. local chpt., Silver Bullet Outstanding Leadership award, 1965, 66), Pi Delta Epsilon (founder, chpt. pres.), Alpha Kappa Delta, Alpha Scholastic Hon. (U. editor-in-chief), Harvard Bus. Sch. Exec. Com. (U. editor-in-chief). Lutheran.

TORNABENE, RUSSELL C. communications executive; b. Gary, Ind., Sept. 18, 1923; s. Samuel Tornabene and Marion LaVorci Roush; m. Audrey F. Shankey, June 21, 1952; children: Joseph, Leigh, David, Lynn. A.A., Gary Jr. Coll., 1941, 46-47; B.A., Ind. U., 1949, M.A., 1950. Radio, TV newswriter WRC-AM-TV, Washington, 1951-55; network supr. NBC Network News, 1955-61, network gen. mgr. NYC, 1961-75; v.p. NBC News, 1975-81; exec. officer Soc. Profl. Journalists, Chgo., 1981-87; Midwest dir. Exec. TV Workshop, 1987-96; pres. Russell Communications Cons., 1996—. Bd. dirs. LifeLine Pilots. Contbr. articles on news to mags. and newspapers Mem. N.Y. Catholic Archdiocese Sch. Bd., N.Y.C., 1972 Recipient Disting. Service award, Sigma Delta Chi, 1949; Ernie Pyle scholar, 1949 Mem. Acad. TV Arts and Scis., Radio TV News Dirs. Assn. Club: Overseas Press (former v.p.) Avocation: photography. Office: 626 Sheridan Sq Apt 2 Evanston IL 60202-4749

TOSCANO, JAMES VINCENT, medical institute administration; b. Passaic, N.J., Aug. 8, 1937; s. William V. and Mary A. (DeNigris) T.; m. Sharon Lee Bowers; children: Shawn Truelson, Lauren Bjorklund, David Brendan, Dania Toscano Miwa. A.B. summa cum laude, Rutgers Coll., 1959; M.A., Yale U., 1960. Lectr. Wharton Sch., U. Pa., 1961-64; chief opinion analyst Pa. Opinion Poll, 1962-64; mng. dir. World Press Inst., St. Paul, 1964-68, exec. dir., 1968-72; dir. devel. Macalester Coll., St. Paul, 1972-74; v.p. resource devel. and public affairs Mpls. Soc. Fine Arts, 1974-79; pres. Minn. Mus. Art, 1979-81; exec. v.p. Park Nicollet Med. Found., 1981-95; corp. sec. Park Nicollet Clinic, 1983-86; sr. v.p. Am. Med. Ctrs., Inc., 1985-87; exec. v.p. Park Nicollet Inst., Mpls., 1996—. Adj. prof. sch. of mgmt. U. St. Thomas, 1989—; co-chair prin. practices nonprofit excellence com. MCN, 1994-98. Author: The Chief Elected Official in the Penjerdel Region, 1964; co-author, co-editor: The Integration of Political Communities, 1964. Bd. dirs., exec. com., sec., World Press Ins., 1972—; bd. dirs., chmn. Southside Newspaper Mpls., 1975-79; chmn. com. to improve student behavior St. Paul Pub. Schs., 1977-79; bd. dirs. Planned Parenthood St. Paul, 1965-72, Mpls. Action Agy., 1976-79; emeritus dir. Help Enable Alcoholics Receive Treatment; mem. St. Paul Heritage Preservation Commn., 1979-82, vice chmn., 1981; mem. Citizens Adv. Com. on Cable Commn.; bd. dirs. Citizens League, 1980, Park Nicollet Med. Found., 1981-95, Park Nicollet Inst., 1996—2000, African-Am. Culture Ctr., 1979-82, Am. Composers Forum, 1981-85, St. Paul Chamber Orch., 1976-80, 83-89, United Theol. Sem., 1985-88; dir. emeritus Minn. Citizens for the Arts; bd. dirs., mem. exec. com., chmn. Med. Alley Assn., 1986-96; mem. task force on tech. assessment Med. Alley, 1992-93; mem. health affairs adv. com. Acad. Health Ctr. U. Minn., 1988-95; bd. dirs. Mother Cabrini House, 1985-92, Minn. Civil Justice Coalition, 1987-91, also chmn.; chmn. Gov.'s Task Force on Health Care Promotion, 1985-86, mem. Gov.'s Com. Promotion Health Care Resources, 1986-87; chmn. bd. Minn. Fin. Counseling Svcs., Inc., 1990-93; mem. task force cost effectiveness Med. Alley, 1994-95; bd. dirs. Meml. Blood Bank, 1995—2001, mem. exec. com., 1996—; bd. dirs. Bakken Mus., 1997—, Stevens Square Cmty. Orgn., 1997-99, Rainbow Rsch., Inc., 2002-. Woodrow Wilson Nat. fellow, 1960. Mem. Minn. Newspaper Found. (bd. dirs. 1987-92), Minn. Coun. Nonprofits (bd. dirs. 1989-95, 97—, bd. mem. Plymouth Music series 1993-96, alt. Minn. Healthcare Commn., 1993-95, mem. Minn. Healthcare Commn., 1995-97, chair task force on med. edn. and rsch. costs 1994-96; mem. com. on med. rsch. and edn. costs, 1996—, chair 1996-99; liaison health tech. adv. com. 1993-97; pres. bd. dirs. Summit Ave Residential Preservation Assn., 2000—), Skylight Club, Informal Club. Address: 1982 Summit Ave Saint Paul MN 55105-1460 Office: Pk Nicollet Inst 3800 Park Nicollet Blvd Minneapolis MN 55416-2527 E-mail: Toscaj@ParkNicolkt.com., jvt2@attbi.com.

TOSHACH, CLARICE OVERSBY, real estate developer, former computer executive; b. Firbank, Westmoreland, Eng., Nov. 21, 1928; came to U.S., 1955; d. Oliver and Nora (Brown) Oversby; m. Daniel Wilkie Toshach, July 30, 1965 (dec. Aug. 1992); 1 child, Duncan Oversby Toshach; 1 child from previous marriage, Paul Anthony Beard. Textile designer Storeys of Lancaster, Eng., 1949-55; owner, operator Broadway Lane, Saginaw, Mich., 1956-70; pres., owner Clarissa Jane Inc., 1962-70, Over-Tosh Computers, Inc. dba Computerland, Saginaw and Flint, Mich., 1983-95; mgr., ptnr. Mich. Comml. Devel. L.L.C., Saginaw, 1995—. Trustee Saginaw Gen. Hosp., 1977-83, Home for the Aged, 1978-80; bd. dirs. Vis. Nurse Assn., pres., 1981-83; bd. dirs. Hospice of Saginaw, Inc., v.p., 1981-83; mem. long range planning com. United Way of Saginaw, 1982-83; cmty. advisor Jr. League of Saginaw, 1982-83; pres. Saginaw Gen. Hosp. Aux., 1972-82, pres., 1976-77.

TOSTE, ANTHONY PAIM, chemistry educator, researcher; b. Mountain View, Calif., June 26, 1948; BS in Chemistry with honors, Santa Clara (Calif.) U., 1970; PhD in Biochemistry and Chemistry, U. Calif., Berkeley, 1976. Rsch. fellow Cardiovascular Rsch. Inst., San Francisco, 1977-79; rsch. scientist Battelle Meml. Inst. Pacific N.W. Nat. Lab., Richland, Wash., 1980-88; asst. prof. S.W. Mo. State U., Springfield, 1988-94, assoc. prof., 1994-99, full prof., 1999—. Cons. Mitsubishi Metal Corp., Tokyo, 1984-87, Dow Chem., Tex., 1994-96; presenter in field. Contbr. articles to jours. in field, cmty. svc. presentations. Bd. dirs. Mid Columbia Arts Coun., Richland, 1987-88, Bot. Soc. S.W. Mo., Springfield, 1997—; pres. bd. dirs. Springfield Sister Cities Assn., 1993-96; co-founder, leader Internat. Friendship Delegations to Japan, 1996, 99, 2001. Rsch./equipment grantee NSF, 1990; recipient Diverse Cmty. award Sister Cities Internat., Boston, 1996. Mem. Am. Chem. Soc. (treas. Ozark sect. 1989-91, chmn.-elect 2000, chmn. 2000-01), Am. Nuc. Soc. (Best Poster award 1987), Assn. Ofcl. Analytical Chemists (program chair 1986, 90), Mo. Acad. Sci. (program chair 1997, 2002). Avocations: picture framing, collecting fine art, woodworking, reading, cinema. Home: 2113 E Woodhaven Pl Springfield MO 65804-6767 Office: SW Mo State U Dept Chemistry 901 S National Ave Springfield MO 65804-0088 E-mail: anthonytoste@smsu.edu.

TOUHILL, BLANCHE MARIE, university chancellor, history-education educator; b. St. Louis, July 1, 1931; d. Robert and Margaret (Walsh) Van Dillen; m. Joseph M. Touhill, Aug. 29, 1959. BA in History, St. Louis U., 1953, MA in Geography, 1954, PhD in History, 1962. Prof. history and edn. U. Mo., St. Louis, 1965-73, assoc. dean faculties, 1974-76, assoc. vice chancellor for acad. affairs, 1976-87, vice chancellor, 1987-90, chancellor, 1991—. Bd. dirs. Boatmen's Nat. Bank of St. Louis, Barnes-Jewish Christian Health Hosps. Conglomerate. Author: William Smith O'Brien and His Irish Revolutionary Companions in Penal Exile, 1981, The Emerging University UM-St. Louis, 1963-83, 1985; editor: Readings in American History, 1970, Varieties of Ireland, 1976; adv. editor Victorian Periodicals Rev. Bd. dirs. Sister City Internat., Am. Coun. Fgn. Rels., St. Louis Forum, Network Bd., Mo. State Hist. Soc., 1989—, Mo. Bot. Garden, 1980, St. Louis Symphony Soc., 1993—. Named Outstanding Educator St. Louis chpt. Urban League, 1976; recipient Leadership award St. Louis YWCA, 1986. Mem. Nat. Assn. State Univs. and Land Grant Colls. (exec. com. 1988—), Am. Com. on Irish Studies (pres. 1991—), Phi Kappa Phi, Alpha Sigma Lambda. Office: U Mo-St Louis Office of the Chancellor 8001 Natural Bridge Rd Saint Louis MO 63121-4401

TOURLENTES, THOMAS THEODORE, psychiatrist; b. Chgo., Dec. 7, 1922; s. Theodore A. and Mary (Xenostathy) T.; m. Mona Belle Land, Sept. 9, 1956; children: Theodore W., Stephen C., Elizabeth A. BS, U. Chgo., 1945, MD, 1947. Diplomate Am. Bd. Psychiatry and Neurology (sr. examiner 1964-88, 90). Intern Cook County Hosp., Chgo., 1947-48; resident psychiatry Downey (Ill.) VA Hosp., 1948-51; practice medicine specializing in psychiatry Chgo., 1952, Camp Atterbury, Ind., 1953, Ft. Carson, Colo., 1954, Galesburg, Ill., 1955-71; staff psychiatrist Chgo. VA Clinic, 1952; clin. instr. psychiatry Med. Sch., Northwestern U., 1952; dir. mental hygiene consultation service Camp Atterbury, 1953-54, Ft. Carson, 1953-54; asst. supt. Galesburg State Research Hosp., 1954-58, supt., 1958-71; dir. Comprehensive Community Mental Health Ctr. Rock Island and Mercer Counties; dir. psychiat. services Franciscan Hosp., 1971-85; chief mental health services VA Outpatient Clinic, Peoria, Ill., 1985-88; clin. prof. psychiatry U. Ill., Chgo. and Peoria, 1955—; preceptor in hosp. adminstrn. State U. Iowa, Iowa City, 1958-64. Councilor, del. Ill. Psychiat. Soc.; chmn. liaison com. Am. Hosp. and Psychiat. Assns., 1978-79, chmn. Quality Care Bd., Ill. Dept. Mental Health, 1995-97. Contbr. articles profl. jours. Mem. Gov. Ill. Com. Employment Handicapped, 1962-64; zone dir. Ill. Dept. Mental Health, Peoria, 1964-71; mem. Spl. Survey Joint Commn. Accreditation Hosps.; chmn. Commn. Cert. Psychiat. Adminstrs., 1979-81; pres. Knox-Galesburg Symphony Soc., 1966-68; bd. dirs. Galesburg Civic Music Assn., pres., 1968-70; chair Knox county United Way Campaign, 1989; pres. Civic Art Ctr., 1990-92. Capt. M.C. AUS, 1952-54. Fellow

AAAS, AMA, Am. Psychiat. Assn. (chair hosp. and cmty. psychiatry award bd. 1989-90), Am. Coll. Psychiatrists, Am. Coll. Mental Health Adminstrs.; mem. Ill. Med. Soc. (chmn. aging com. 1968-71, coun. on mental health and addictions 1987-89), chair mental health substance abuse com. 1987-89), Ill. Psychiat. Soc. (pres. 1969-70), Am. Pub. Health Assn., Soc. Biol. Psychiatry, Ill. Hosp. Assn. (trustee 1968-70), Am. Coll. Hosp. Adminstrs., Assn. for Rsch. Nervous and Mental, Am. Assn. Psychiat. Adminstrs. (pres. 1980), Ctrl. Neuorpsychiat. Assn. (pres. 1988-89). Home and Office: 138 Valley View Rd Galesburg IL 61401-8524 E-mail: tourlentes@gallatinriver.net.

TOWNE, JONATHAN BAKER, vascular surgeon; b. Youngstown, Ohio, Jan. 10, 1942; m. Sandra Green Towne, Aug. 24, 1963; children: Timothy, Heidi, Crista. BS, U. Pitts., 1963; MD, U. Rochester, N.Y., 1967. Intern in surgery U. Mich., Ann Arbor, 1967-68, resident I, 1968-69; resident II, III, IV U. Nebr., Omaha, 1969-72; chief gen. surgery USAF Hosp., Vandenberg AFB, Calif., 1972-74; asst. prof. surgery Med. Coll. Wis., Milw., 1975-79, assoc. prof., 1979-84, prof., 1984—, chair vascular surgery, 1984—. Editor: (book) Complications Vascular Surgery, 1980, Complications Vascular Surgery, II, 1985, Complications Vascular Surgery, III, 1991. Mem.: Wis. Surg. Soc. (pres. 1991—92), Assn. Program Dirs. Vascular Surgery 1997—98, Ctrl. Surg. Assn. (recorder 1992—97, pres.-elect 2001), Soc. Vascular Surgery (sec. 1994—98, pres.-elect 1999, pres. 2000). Avocation: photography. Office: Med Coll Wis 9200 W Wisconsin Ave Milwaukee WI 53226-3522 E-mail: jtowne@mcw.edu.

TOWNSEND, EARL C., JR. lawyer, writer; b. Indpls., Nov. 9, 1914; s. Earl Cunningham and Besse (Kuhn) T.; m. Emily Macnab, Apr. 3, 1947 (dec. Mar. 1988); children: Starr, Vicki M., Julia E. (Mrs. Edward Goodrich Dunn Jr.), Earl Cunningham III, Clyde G. Student, De Pauw U., 1932-34; AB, U. Mich., 1936, JD, 1939. Bar: Ind. 1939, Mich. 1973, U.S. Supreme Ct. 1973, U.S. Ct. Appeals (4th, 5th, 6th, 7th cirs.), U.S. Dist. Ct. (no. and so. dists.) Ind., U.S. Dist. Ct. (ea. dist.) Va., U.S. Dist. Ct. (ea. dist.) Mich. Sr. ptnr. Townsend & Townsend, Indpls., 1941-64, Townsend, Hovde & Townsend, Indpls., 1964-84, Townsend & Townsend, Indpls., 1984—. Dep. prosecutor, Marion County, Ind., 1942-44; radio-TV announcer WIRE, WFBM, WFBM-TV, Indpls., 1940-53, 1st TV announcer Indpls. 500 mile race, 1949, 50; Big Ten basketball referee, 1940-47; lectr. trial tactics U. Notre Dame, Ind. U., U. Mich., 1968-79; chmn. faculty seminar on personal injury trials Ind. U. Sch. Law, U. Notre Dame Sch. Law, Valparaiso Sch. Law, 1981; mem. Com. to Revise Ind. Supreme Ct. Pattern Jury Instrns., 1975-83; lectr. Trial Lawyers 30 Yrs. Inst., 1986; counsel atty gen., 1988-92. Author: Birdstones of the North American Indian, 1959; editor: Am. Assn. Trial Lawyers Am. Jour., 1964-88; contbr. articles to legal and archeol. jours.; composer (waltz) Moon of Halloween. Trustee Cathedral High Sch., Indpls., Eiteljorg Mus. Am. Indian and Western Art, Cale J. Holder Scholarship Found. Ind. U. Law Sch.; life trustee, bd. dirs., mem. fin. and bldg. coms. Indpls. Mus. Art; life trustee Ind. State Mus.; founder, dir. Meridian St. Found.; mem. dean's coun. Ind. U.; founder, life fellow Roscoe Pound/Am. Trial Lawyers Found., Harvard U.; fellow Meth. Hosp. Found. Recipient Ind. Univ. Writers Conf. award, 1960, Hanson H. Anderson medal of honor Arsenal Tech. Schs., Indpls., 1971; named to Coun. Sagamores of Wabash, 1969; Rector scholar, 1934, Ind. Basketball Hall of Fame; hon. chief Black River-Swan Creek Saginaw-Chippewa Indian tribe. Fellow Internat. Acad. Trial Lawyers, Internat. Soc. Barristers, Ind. Bar Found. (life trustee, disting. fellow award); mem. ASCAP, ABA (com. on trial techniques 1964-76, aviation and space 1977—), Assn. Trial Lawyers Am. (v.p.), Ind. State Bar Assn. (Golden Career award 1989), Indpls. Bar Found. (disting. charter 1986), Ind. Trial Lawyers Assn. (pres. 1965, pres. Coll. Fellows 1984-90, Lifetime Achievement award 1992), Am. Bd. Trial Advs. (diplomate, pres. Ind. chpt. 1980-86), Am. Arbitration Assn. (nat. arbitrators panel), Am. Judicature Soc., State Bar of Mich. (Champion of Justice award 1989), Roscommon County Bar Assn., 34th Jud. Cir. Bar Assn., Bar Assn. 7th Fed. Cir. (bd. govs. 1966-68), Mich. Trial Lawyers Assn., Soc. Mayflower Descendants (gov. 1947-49), Ind. Hist. Soc., Marion County/Indpls. Hist. Soc. (bd. dirs.), U. Mich. Pres. Club, U. Mich. Victors Club (founder, charter mem.), Trowel and Brush Soc. (hon.), Genuine Indian Relic Soc. (founder, pres., chmn. frauds com.), The Players Club, Key Biscayne Yacht Club, Columbia Club, Masons (33 degree), Shriners, Delta Kappa Epsilon, Phi Kappa Phi. Republican. Methodist. Avocations: art, Indian relics. Home: 5008 N Meridian St Indianapolis IN 46208-2624

TOWNSEND, JAMES DOUGLAS, accountant; b. Kokomo, Ind., May 20, 1959; s. Lemon Dale and Diamond Sue (Turner) T.; m. Ariane Antonia Atkins, May 7, 1983 (div. July 1992); 1 child, Bradley Alan; m. Mildred Ann Kurtz, Oct. 18, 1992; children: Heather Marie, Tyler Neil. Student, Ind. U., 1977, Ind. State U., 1977-78; BS in Acctg. summa cum laude, Ball State U., 1980. CPA, Ind., Colo.; cert. mgmt. acct. Acctg. intern Chevrolet Motor Div. Gen. Motors Corp., Muncie, Ind., 1979; staff acct. Price Waterhouse, Indpls., 1980-83, sr. acct., 1983-85, mgr., 1985-88, sr. mgr., 1988-89; contr. Raffensperger, Hughes & Co., Inc., 1989-92, asst. treas., 1991-95, asst. v.p., 1991-92, v.p. fin., 1992-95; sr. v.p., chief adminstrv. officer Nat City Investments, Inc., 1995-99; pres. Fin. Mgmt., Inc., 1994—; sr. v.p. Madison Ave. Capital Group LLC, 1999-2000; CFO Colo.'s Ocean Journey, 2000-01, exec. v.p., COO, 2001—; pres., CEO Colo.'s Ocean Journey , 2001—. Coord. Seek Program Ind. U., Indpls., 1985-86; cons. project bus. Jr. Achievement, Indpls., 1986; treas., asst. sec. Sagamore Funds Trust, 1991-94; treas. Raffensberger Hughes Capitol Corp., 1991-94, RHGP, Inc., 1993-95. Baseball coach Pike Twp. (Ind.) Youth League, 1986-87; cubmaster Pike Twp. Coun. Boy Scouts Am., 1987-88; mem. Pike Twp. Sch. Bd., 1988-92, v.p., 1989-90, pres., 1990-92; bd. dirs. Project I-Star, 1992-94, Crooked Creek Villages Homeowners Assn., 1998-99; fin. com. Highlands Ranch Cmty. Assn., 2000—. Fellow Life Mgmt. Inst.; mem. AICPA, Inst. Mgmt. Accts., Ind. CPA Soc. (vice chmn. edn. com. 1988-89, chmn. 1989-90, chmn. govt. rels. com. 1999), Colo. Soc. CPAs, Indpls. C. of C. (SKLA exec. coun. 1992-94), Swallow Hill Music Assn. Republican. Avocations: bowling, golf, guitar, chess. Home: 10011 S Heywood Ln Highlands Ranch CO 80130-8860

TOWNSEND, ROBERT J. lawyer; b. Charlotte, Mich., Nov. 11, 1938; s. Robert Wright and Rhea Lucille (Jennings) T.; m. Thea E. Kolb, Aug. 1, 1964; children: Melissa, Bradley. BA, Mich. State U., 1960; LLB, Harvard U., 1963. Bar: Ohio 1964, U.S. Dist. Ct. (so. dist.) Ohio 1964, U.S. Ct. Appeals (6th cir.) 1971, U.S. Supreme Ct. 1992. Assoc. Taft, Stettinus & Hollister, Cin., 1963-72, ptnr., 1972—. Dir. Employers Resource Assn., Cin., 1989—. With U.S. Army, 1963-64, 68-69. Office: 1800 Firstar Tower 425 Walnut St Cincinnati OH 45202-3923 E-mail: townsend@taftlaw.com.

TOWSON, THOMAS D. securities trader; b. 1954; Grad., Western Mich. U., 1977. With Pacific Investment, Chgo., 1977-78, Conti Securities, Chgo., 1978-80, Thomson Mc Kinnon Securities, Chgo., 1980-82, Gelber Group Inc., 1982—; exec. v.p. Gelber Group, Chgo., 1986—. Office: Gelber Group 141 W Jackson Blvd Ste 2150 Chicago IL 60604-2981

TRACI, DONALD PHILIP, retired lawyer; b. Cleve., Mar. 13, 1927; m. Lillian Traci Calafiore; 11 children. BS cum laude, Coll. of the Holy Cross, Worcester, Mass., 1950; JD magna cum laude, Cleve. State U., 1955; LLD (hon.), U. Urbino, Italy, 1989. Bar: Ohio 1955, U.S. Dist. Ct. (no. and so. dists.) Ohio 1955, U.S. Ct. Appeals (3d, 6th and 7th cirs.), U.S. Dist. Ct. (we. and ea. dists.) Pa., U.S. Supreme Ct. 1965. Ptnr. Spangenberg, Shibley, Traci, Lancione & Liber, Cleve., 1955-94; ret., 1994—. Lectr. York U., Toronto, Ont., Can., Case Western Res. U., Cleve. Marshall Law Sch., U. Mich., Akron U., U. Cin., Ohio No. U., Harvard U. Trustee Cath. Charities Diocese of Cleve., past pres. Bd. Cath. Edn.; former chmn. bd. regents St. Ignatius H.S., Cleve.; mem. pres.'s coun. Coll. of Holy Cross; Eucharist min. St. Rose of Lima Ch. With USN, 1945-46. Fellow Am. Coll. Trial Lawyers, Internat. Acad. Trial Lawyers (past pres.), Am. Bd. Trial Advocacy; mem. ABA, ATLA (trustee Lambert Chair Found., lectr. trial practice), Ohio State Bar Assn. (lectr. trial practice), Ohio Acad. Trial Lawyers (past chmn. rules seminar, lectr. trial practice), Cuyahoga County Bar Assn. (lectr. trial practice), Cleve. Acad. Trial Lawyers (lectr. trial practice), Trial Lawyers for Pub. Justice (sustaining founder), Cleve. Bar Assn. (chmn. Advocacy Inst., trustee, CLE com., jud. selection com., spl. justice ctr. com., fed. ct., common pleas ct. and ct. appeals com., pres. 1986), Jud. Conf. U.S. 6th Cir. Ct. (life), Jud. Conf. 8th Jud. Dist. Ohio life), Knights of Malta, Knights of Holu Sepulchre of Jerusalem, Delta Theta Phi. Home: 12700 Lake Ave Apt 505 Lakewood OH 44107-1547

TRACY, ALLEN WAYNE, management consultant; b. Windsor, Vt., July 25, 1943; s. J. Wayne and Helen (Bernard) T.; m. Karla Noelte, Dec. 14, 1969; children: Tania, Tara. BA, U. Vt., 1965; MBA cum laude, Boston U., 1974. Retail salesman Exxon Corp., Boston, 1965-72; mgr. mfg. Leonard Silver Mfg. Co., Inc., 1974-78, v.p. ops., 1979-81; pres. OESM Corp., N.Y.C., 1978-81; pres., bd. dirs. Gold Lance Inc., Houston, 1981-91; v.p. ops. Town & Country Corp., 1989-92; sr. v.p. L.G. Balfour Co., 1990-92; asst. to pres. Syratech Corp., Boston, 1993; dir. ops. Goldman-Kolber Co., Inc., Norwood, Mass., 1994; exec. v.p., COO, George H. Fuller & Son Co., Inc., Pawtucket, R.I., 1994-97; COO, BioMatrix Techs., Inc., Lincoln, 1997-98; mgmt. cons. IPA, Buffalo Grove, Ill., 1998—. Bd. dirs. Verilyte Gold, Inc., L.G. Balfour Co., Inc. Mem. Ashland Bd. Selectmen, 1977-78; chmn. Ashland Study Town Govt. Com., 1976-77; vice chmn. ch. coun. Federated Ch. Ashland, 1979-80, chmn., 1981; bd. dirs. Nottingham Forest Civic Assn., 1886. With U.S. Army, 1965-68. Mem. Nottingham Forest Club (bd. dirs. Houston 1986), Beta Gamma Sigma. Home: 455 Prospect St Seekonk MA 02771-1503 Office: IPA 1250 Barclay Blvd Buffalo Grove IL 60089-4500

TRACY, JAMES DONALD, historian, educator; b. St. Louis, Feb. 14, 1938; s. Leo W. and Marguerite M. (Meehan) T.; m. Nancy Ann McBride, Sept. 6, 1968 (div. 1993); children: Patrick, Samuel, Mary Ann; m. Suzanne K. Swan, May 2, 1997. BA, St. Louis U., 1959; MA, Johns Hopkins U., 1960, Notre Dame U., 1961; PhD, Princeton U., 1967. Instr. U. Mich., 1964-66; instr. to prof. history U. Minn., Mpls., 1966—, dept. chmn., 1988-91. Vis. prof. U. Leiden, Netherlands, spring 1987, U. Paris IV, 2001. Author: Erasmus: The Growth of a Mind, 1972, The Politics of Erasmus: A Pacifist Intellectual and His Political Milieu, 1979, True Ocean Found; Paludanus' Letters on Dutch Voyages to the Kara Sea, 1980, A Financial Revolution in the Habsburg Netherlands: Renten and Renteniers in the County of Holland, 1515-1565, 1985, Holland under Habsburg Rule: The Formation of a Body Politic, 1506-1566, 1990, Erasmus of the Low Countries, 1996, Europe's Reformations, 1450-1650, 1999, Emperor Charles V, Impresario of War, 2002; editor: Luther and the Modern State in Germany, 1986, The Rise of Merchant Empires: Long Distance Trade in the Early Modern Era, 1350-1750, 1990, The Political Economy of Merchant Empires: Long Distance Trade and State Power in the Early Modern World, 1991, (with T.A. Brady and H.A. Oberman) Handbook of European History in the Late Middle Ages, Renaissance and Reformation, Vol. 1, 1994, Vol. 2, 1995, City Walls: The Urban Enceinte in Global Perspective, 2000; mem. editl. bd. Sixteenth Century Jour., 1979—; co-editor Jour. Early Modern History, 1997-2000, editor, 2000—. Guggenheim fellow, 1972-73; NEH summer grantee, 1977, 85; Fulbright rsch. grantee, Belgium, 1979, Netherlands, 1980; resident fellow Netherlands Inst. for Advanced Studies, 1993-94. Mem. Am. Cath. Hist. Soc. (pres. 1999-00), Soc. Reformation Rsch. (pres. 1995-97), 16th Century Studies Conf. (pres. 1985-86). Republican. Roman Catholic. Home: 757 Osceola Ave # 2 Saint Paul MN 55105-3327 Office: U Minn 614 Social Sci Bldg Minneapolis MN 55455 E-mail: tracy001@tc.umn.edu.

TRADER, JOSEPH EDGAR, orthopedic surgeon; b. Milw., Nov. 2, 1946; s. Edgar Joseph and Dorothy Elizabeth (Senzig) T.; m. Janet Louise Burzycki, Sept. 23, 1972 (div. Nov. 1987); children: James, Jonathan, Ann Elizabeth; m. Rhonda Sue Schultz, May 26, 1990. Student, Marquette U., 1964-67; MD, Med. Coll. Wis., 1971. Diplomate Am. Bd. Orthopaedic Surgery. Emergency rm. physician columbia, St. Joseph's Hosps., Milw., 1972-76; orthopaedic surgeon Orthopaedic Assn., Manitowoc, Wis., 1978—. Mem. exec. com. Holy Family Meml. Med. Ctr., Manitowoc, 1985-96, chief-of-staff, 1994-96, ethics com., 1995—, chair instnl. rev. com. Former pres., bd. dirs. Holy Innocents Mens Choir; county del. State Med. Soc. Charitable Sci. and Edn. Found. Fellow Am. Acad. Orthopaedic Surgeons (orthopaedic rsch. and edn. found. state com.), ACS; mem. AMA, Wis. State Med. Soc., Wis. Orthopaedic Soc., Midwest Orthopaedic Soc., Milw. Orthopaedic Soc., Phi Delta Epsilon, Psi Chi, Crown & Anchor. Roman Catholic. Club: Manitowoc Yacht. Avocations: singing, piano, scuba diving, tennis, skiing, sailing. Home: 1021 Memorial Dr Manitowoc WI 54220-2242 Office: Orthopaedic Assocs 501 N 10th St Manitowoc WI 54220-4039

TRAFICANT, JAMES A., JR. former congressman; b. Youngstown, Ohio, May 8, 1941; s. James A. and Agnes T. Traficant; m. Patricia Coppa; children: Robin, Elizabeth B.S., U. Pitts., 1963, M.S., 1973, Youngstown State U., 1976. Exec. dir. Mahoning County Drug Program, Ohio, 1971-81; sheriff Mahoning County, 1981-85; mem. U.S. Congress from 17th Ohio dist., Washington, 1985—2002; mem. transp. and infrastructure com., ranking Dem. oversight and investigations subcom. Office: US House of Reps Office of House Members 2446 Rayburn Bldg Ofc Washington DC 20515-3517*

TRAISMAN, HOWARD SEVIN, pediatrician; b. Chgo., Mar. 18, 1923; s. Alfred Stanley and Sara (Sevin) T.; m. Regina Gallagher, Feb. 29, 1956; children: Barry D. Lifschultz, Edward S., Kenneth N. BS in Chemistry, Northwestern U., 1943, MB, 1946, MD, 1947. Intern Cook County Hosp., Chgo., 1946-47; resident in pediatrics Children's Meml. Hosp., 1949-51, attending physician div. endocrinology, 1951—; mem. faculty Med. Sch. Northwestern U., Evanston, Ill., 1951—, prof. pediatrics, 1973—, pres., 1999—. Author articles in field, chpts. in books. Capt. M.C. AUS, 1943-46, 47-49. Recipient Northwestern U. Alumni Merit award, 1995. Mem. Am. Diabetes Assn. (Disting. Service award 1976), Am. Pediatric Soc., Am. Acad. Pediatrics, Endocrine Soc., Lawson Wilkins Pediatric Endocrine Soc., AMA, Midwest Soc. Pediatric Research, Ill. Med. Soc., Chgo. Pediatric Soc., Chgo. Med. Soc., Inst. Medicine Chgo. Democrat. Jewish. Office: 1325 Howard St Evanston IL 60202-3766 Fax: 847-869-4330.

TRAMBLEY, DONALD BRIAN, lawyer; b. Anna, Ill., Aug. 31, 1967; s. Donald Ralph and Nona June (Brimm) T.; m. Michelle Lynne Pierson, Dec. 26, 1991; children: Kirsten Elizabeth Marie, Brian Andrew. BA, So. Ill. U., 1990; JD, Miss. Coll. Sch. Law, 1993. Bar: U.S. Dist. Ct. (so. dist.) Ill. Pub. defender Union County Cir. Ct., Jonesboro, Ill., 1994-96; state's atty. Johnson County Cir. Ct., Vienna, 1996—. Pres. Nazarene World Missionary Soc., Anna, 1995—, Rep. Booster Club, Vienna, 1995—. Mam. ABA, ATLA, Ill. State Bar Assn. Avocations: reading, parenting, Christian fellowship. Office: Johnson County State's Atty PO Box 1257 Vienna IL 62995-1257

TRAMONTO, RICK, chef; b. Rochester, NY; m. Gale Gand. Grill/saute cook The Scotch & Sirloin; chef Strathallen; garde-mgr. chef Tavern on the Green; chef Gotham Bar & Grill, Aurora, Avanzare, Chgo., The Pump Room, Chgo., Scoozi!, Chgo., Charlie Trotter's, Chgo., Stapleford Park Hotel, London; owner, chef Tru, Chgo., 1999—, Brasserie T., Chgo. Appeared on Oprah TV program. Named one of Am.'s rising Star Chefs, Robert Mondavi, 1995; named to Ten Best New Chefs, Food & Wine, 1994. Office: 676 N St Clair St Chicago IL 60611

TRAN, NANG TRI, electrical engineer, physicist; b. Binh Dinh, Vietnam, Jan. 2, 1948; came to the U.S., 1979, naturalized, 1986; s. Cam Tran and Cuu Thi Nguyen; m. Thu-Huong Thi Tong, Oct. 14, 1982; children: Helen, Florence, Irene, Kenneth. BSEE, Kyushu Inst. Tech., Kitakyushu, Japan, 1973, MSEE, 1975; PhD in Materials Sci./Solid State Device, U. Osaka Prefecture, Sakai, Japan, 1979. Rsch. assoc. U. Calif. Irvine, 1979; engr., rsch. scientist Sharp Electronics, Irvine, 1979-80; sr. rsch. scientist Arco Solar Industries, Chatsworth, Calif., 1980-84; sr. rsch. specialist, group leader 3M Co., St. Paul, 1985-96; staff scientist Imation Corp., Oakdale, Minn., 1996—; exec. Khanti Inc. Adj. prof. Inst. Tech., U. Minn., Mpls.; cons., lectr. Japan industry mgmt.; reviewer NSF. Author: (poetry) My Journey; contbr. articles to profl. jours.; inventor direct digital x-rays, transparent conducting zinc oxide doped with group III elements, thin film transistors on flexible substrate, structured phosphors; patentee in field. Mem. tech. com. various internat. confs. Recipient R&D awards, Photonic Cir. Excellence award; fellow, Govt. South Vietnam, Japan, USAID, Rotary Internat., 1968—79. Mem. IEEE (sr.), Japan Soc. Applied Physics, N.Y. Acad. Scis. Achievements include patents for;research in different types of thin film displays;research in amorphous silicon solar cells;research in image sensors;research in solid state memory;research in photoconductors;research in CD;research in high density data storage media;research in transparent conducting oxide films. Office: Imation Corp Materials Media Devel 1 Imation Pl Discovery 1D-20 Oakdale MN 55128-3414 E-mail: nttran@imation.com.

TRANK, DOUGLAS MONTY, rhetoric and speech communications educator; b. Lincoln, Nebr., Sept. 8, 1944; s. Walter John and Hazel Elaine (Stegeman) T.; children: Heather Nicole, Jessica Celeste; m. Christine Marie Quinn, 1992. BA in English, U. Nebr., Kearney, 1967, MS in Comm., 1970; PhD in Comm., U. Utah, 1973. Tchr. Ogallala (Nebr.) High Sch., 1967-70; teaching fellow in communications U. Utah, Salt Lake City, 1970-72; prof. communications Old Dominion U., Norfolk, Va., 1972-74; prof. rhetoric and edn. U. Iowa, Iowa City, 1974—, chmn. rhetoric dept., 1984-89, 2001—. Chmn. bd. control athletics, faculty senate, mem. ednl. policy com., faculty adv. com., faculty assembly, exec. com. U. Iowa. Author 3 books; editor Communication Edn., 1993-96; assoc. editor Communication Studies; contbr. numerous articles to profl. jours. Recipient Admiral award Ace Adventures, Inc., Iowa, 1987, Hemingway prize, 1992. Mem. Speech Communication Assn., Iowa Communication Assn. (pres. 1980-82, editor 1977-81, mem. jour. editorial bd.), Cen. States Communication Assn. (pres. 1990-91), Fedn. Iowa Speech Orgns. (pres. 1977-79), Iowa City Optimist Club (dir. 1982-89, pres. 1987-88). Democrat. Avocations: ice sailing, hunting, fishing, canoeing. Office: U Iowa Dept Rhetoric Iowa City IA 52242 E-mail: douglas-trank@uiowa.edu.

TRAPP, JAMES MCCREERY, lawyer; b. Macomb, Ill., Aug. 11, 1934; BA, Knox Coll., 1956; JD, U. Mich., 1961. Bar: Ill. 1961. Ptnr. McDermott, Will & Emery, Chgo., 1961-98, sr. counsel, 1998—. Chmn. Ill. Inst. Continuing Legal Edn., 1978-79, bd. dirs., 1980-86, pres., 1984-85. Fellow Am. Coll. Trust and Estate Coun. (Ill. chmn. 1980-83, nat. regent 1983—, treas. 1989-90, sec. 1990-91, v.p. 1991-92, pres.-elect 1992-93, pres. 1993-94, exec. com. 1986-94), Am. Bar Found., Ill. Bar Found.; mem. ABA, Ill. State Bar Assn., Chgo. Bar Assn. (chair trust law com. 1972-73, com. on coms. 1972-74), Internat. Acad. Estate and Trust Law, Am. Law Inst. (pres.), Chgo. Estate Planning Coun. Office: McDermott Will & Emery 227 W Monroe St Ste 3100 Chicago IL 60606-5096

TRASK, THOMAS EDWARD, religious organization administrator; b. Brainard, Minn., Mar. 23, 1936; m. Shirley Burkhart; children: Kimberly, Bradley, Todd, Tom. BA, North Ctrl. Bible Coll., 1956, DDiv (hon.), 1994. Ordained min. Assemblies of God, 1958. Pastor First Assembly of God, Hibbing, Minn., 1956-60, pastor Vicksburg, Mich., 1960-64; Mich. dist. youth Sunday sch. dir. Assembly of God, 1964-68; pastor First Assembly of God, Saginaw, Mich., 1968-73, Brightmoor Tabernacle, Southfield, 1976-88; supt. Mich. Dist. Coun., Dearborn, 1973-76; gen. treas. The Gen. Coun. Assemblies of God, Springfield, Mo., 1988-93, gen. supt., 1993—. Co-author: Back to the Altar: A Call to Spiritual Awakening, 1994, Back to the Word, A Call to Biblical Authority, 1996, The Battle: Defeating the Enemies of Your Soul, 1997, The Blessing: Experiencing the Power of the Holy Spirit Today, 1998, The Choice: Embracing God's Vision in the New Millennium, 1999, The Fruit of the Spirit, 2000, Ministry for a Lifetime, 2001. Office: Assemblies of God 1445 N Boonville Ave Springfield MO 65802-1894

TRAUDT, MARY B. elementary education educator; b. Chgo., Jan. 1, 1930; d. Lloyd Andrews Haldeman and Adele Eleanor (MacKinnon) Haldeman-Oliver; m. Eugene Peter Traudt, Dec. 6, 1952 (dec.); 1 child, Victoria Jean. BS, Cen. Mich. U., 1951; MA, Roosevelt U., 1978; postgrad., U. Ill., 1982. Asst. editor Commerce Clearing House, Chgo., 1951-53; tchr. Cleve. Elem. Sch., 1954-56, Chgo. Sch. System, 1956-57, Community Consolidated # 54, Hoffman Estates, Ill., 1957-64, Avoca Elem. Sch., Wilmette, 1964—; ret., 1995. Recipient Computer award Apple Computer Co. Mem. NEA (life), Ill. Assn. of Ret. Tchrs. (life), North Shore Assn. of Ret. Tchrs. (life), Avoca Edn. Assn. (v.p. 1986-91), Alpha Psi Omega. Presbyterian. Avocations: reading, sewing, music, travel, gardening. Home: 1 W Superior St Apt 1601 Chicago IL 60610

TRAUTH, JOSEPH LOUIS, JR. lawyer; b. Cin., Apr. 22, 1945; s. Joseph L. and Margaret (Walter) T.; m. Barbara Widmeyer, July 4, 1970; children: Jennifer, Joseph III, Jonathan, Braden, Maria. BS in Econs., Xavier U., 1967; JD, U. Cin., 1973. Bar: Ohio 1973, U.S. Dist. Ct. (so. dist.) Ohio 1973, U.S. Ct. Appeals (6th cir.) 1973, U.S. Supreme Ct. 1988, Ky. 2000. Ptnr. Keating, Muething & Klekamp, PLL, Cin., 1973-80, Keating, Muething & Klekamp, Cin., 1980—. Speaker real estate law, 1974—. Contbr. articles to real estate publs. Mem. Rep. Leadership Coun., Cin., 1987—, Parish Coun., Cin., 1990. Mem. Cin. Bar Assn. (grievance com., real estate com., negligence com.). Roman Catholic. Avocations: running, tennis, reading. Office: Keating Muething & Klekamp 1800 Provident Tower 1 E 4th St Ste 1400 Cincinnati OH 45202-3717 E-mail: jtrauth@kmklaw.com.

TRAUTMANN, THOMAS ROGER, history and anthropology educator; b. Madison, Wis., May 27, 1940; s. Milton and Esther Florence (Trachte) T.; m. Marcella Hauolilani Choy, Sept. 25, 1962; children: Theodore William, Robert Arthur. BA, Beloit Coll., 1962; PhD, U. London, 1968. Lectr. in history Sch. Oriental and African Studies, U. London, 1965-68; asst. prof. history U. Mich., Ann Arbor, 1968-71, assoc. prof., 1971-77, prof., 1977—, Richard Hudson rsch. prof., 1979, prof. history and anthropology, 1984—, chmn. dept. history, 1987-90, Steelcase rsch. prof., 1993-94, dir. Inst. Humanities, Mary Fair Croushore prof. humanities, 1997—2002, Marshall D. Sahlins coll. prof. history and anthropology, 1997—. Author: Kautilya and the Arthasastra, 1971, Dravidian Kinship, 1981, Lewis Henry Morgan and the Invention of Kinship, 1987; author: (with K.S. Kabelac) The Library of Lewis Henry Morgan, 1994; author: (edit. with Diane Owen Hughes) Time: Histories and Ethnologies, 1995, Aryans and British India, 1997; author: (edit. with Maurice Godelier and Franklin Tjon Sie Fat) Transformations of Kinship, 1999; editor: Comparative Studies in Society and History, 1997—; contbr. articles on India, kinship and history of anthropology. Sr. Humanist fellow NEH, 1984. Mem. Am. Anthrop. Assn., Assn. Asian Studies, Am. Inst. Indian Studies (mem. exec. com. trustee, sr. rsch. fellow in India 1985, 97), Phi Beta Kappa. Office: U Mich Dept History Ann Arbor MI 48109-1003

TRAVIS, DAVID M. state legislator; b. Pawtucket, R.I., Sept. 21, 1948; s. Gideon and Jessie (Campbell) T.; married. BA, U. Wis., 1970; MA, U. Wis. Adminstrv. asst. Wis. State Legis., 1971-72; analyst Senate Dem.

Caucus, 1972-73, dir., 1973-78; mem. Joint Fin. Com.; Wis. state assemblyman dist. 81, 1978—. Majority leader; chmn. rules com.; mem. orgn. com., Joint Com. on Employ Rels. and Spl. Com. on Reapportionment; del. Dem. Nat. Conv., 1980; instr. polit. sci. Mem. Northside Comty. Coun., Eastmorland and Elvehjem Comty. Assn. Home: 4229 Mandrake Rd Madison WI 53704-1653

TRAVIS, DEMPSEY JEROME, real estate executive and developer; b. Chgo., Feb. 25, 1920; s. Louis and Mittie (Strickland) T.; m. Moselynne Hardwick, Sept. 17, 1949. B.A., Roosevelt U., 1949; grad., Sch. Mortgage Banking, Northwestern U., 1969; D.Econs., Olive Harvey Coll., 1974; D.B.A. (hon.), Daniel Hale Williams U., Chgo., 1976; PhD (hon.), Kennedy-King Coll., 1982; DHL (hon.), Governor State U., 2001. Cert. property mgr.; cert. real estate counselor. Pres. Travis Realty Co., Chgo., 1949—, Urban Rsch. Press, 1969—. Author: Don't Stop Me Now, 1970, An Autobiography of Black Chicago, 1981, An Autobiography of Black Jazz, 1983, An Autobiography of Black Politics, 1987, Real Estate is the Gold in Your Future, 1988, Harold: The People's Mayor, 1989, Racism: American Style a Corporate Gift, 1990, I Refuse to Learn to Fail, 1992, Views From the Back of the Bus During World War II and Beyond, 1995, The Duke Ellington Primer, 1996, The Louis Armstrong Odessey: From Jazz Alley to America's Jazz Ambassador, 1997, Racism: Revolves Like a Merry Go 'Round: 'Round 'n 'Round It Goes, 1998, They Heard a Thousand Thunders, 1999, The Life and Times of Redd Foxx, 1999, The Victory Monument: The Beacon of Chicago's Bronzeville, 1999, J. Edgar Hoover's FBI Wired the Nation, 2000, The FBI Files on the Tainted and the Damned. Trustee Northwestern Meml. Hosp., Chgo., Chgo. Hist. Soc., Auditorium Theater, Chgo., Roosevelt U.; bd. dirs. Columbia Coll. With AUS, 1942-46. Recipient award Soc. Midland Authors, 1982, Chgo. Art Deco Soc., 1985, The Human Rights award The Gustavus Myers Ctr. for Study of Human Rights in N.Am., 1995, Humanitarian award Kennedy-King Coll., 1997, Art Deco award, 1983, Soc. Midland Authors award for nonfiction, 1981; named to Jr. Achievement Chgo. Bus. Hall of Fame, 1995; named embedded in sidewalk of Bronzeville Walk of Fame, Chgo; inductee Internat. Literary Hall of Fame, Chgo. State U., 2000. Mem. United Mortgage Bankers Assn. Am. (pres. 1961-74), Dearborn Real Estate Bd. (pres. 1957-59, 70-71), Nat. Assn. Real Estate Brokers (1st v.p. 1959-60), Inst. Real Estate Mgmt., Soc. Profl. Journalists, Soc. Midland Authors (pres. 1988-90), NAACP (pres. Chgo. 1959-60), Econs. Club, Forty Club Chgo., Assembly Club, Cliff Dwellers, The Caxtons Club. Office: Travis Realty Co 840 E 87th St Chicago IL 60619-6298 E-mail: travisDT88@aol.com.

TRAYNOR, DANIEL M. state representative; Postgrad in law, U.N.D., 1997. Lic.: N.D. (Law). Elected state chmn. N.D. Rep. party, 2001—; law clerk N.D. Supreme Court. District 15 chmn.; vol. Political Campaigns, 1988; dir. N.D. Rep. Party Election, 1992; mem., delegate rules com. Rep. Nat. Convention, Phila., 2000. Republican. Office: PO Box 1917 Bismarck ND 58502-1917*

TRAYNOR, JOHN THOMAS, JR. state legislator, lawyer; b. Devils Lake, N.D., June 14, 1955; s. John Thomas and Kathryn Jane (Donovan) T. BA, U. N.D., 1977, JD, 1980. Bar: N.D. 1980, U.S. Dist. Ct. N.D. 1980. Assoc. Traynor & Rutten, Devils Lake, 1980-82; ptnr. Traynor, Rutten & Traynor, 1982—; mem. N.D. Senate from 15th dist., Bismark, 1990—. Mcpl. judge, Devils Lake, 1983-84; dir. 1st Ins. Agy., Devils Lake, 1984—. Editor Law Rev., U. N.D., 1979-80. Bd. dirs. Cmty. Devel. Corp., Devils Lake, 1983—, treas., 1984; pres. Lake Region Devel. Corp., Devils Lake, 1983-84, bd. dirs., 1983—. Recipient Book award Am. Jurisprudence, 1980. Mem. ABA, N.D. Bar Assn., N.E. Jud. Dist. Bar Assn., Lake Region Bar Assn. (pres. 1980-83), Devils Lake C. of C. (dir. 1982—), Jaycees, Rotary, KC, Elks (officer 1982—). Republican. Roman Catholic. Home: PO Box 838 Devils Lake ND 58301-0838 Office: Traynor Rutten & Traynor 509 5th St Devils Lake ND 58301-2571

TREADWAY, JOSEPH L. state legislator; b. St. Louis, Mar. 23, 1947; m. Marlene Kroeger, 1982; 2 children. Diploma, Forest Pk. C.C. Office mgr.; real estate broker; mem. Mo. Ho. of Reps. from 96th dist., 1983—. Mem. C. of C. Democrat. Home: 1456 Telegraph Rd Lemay MO 63125-2532

TRECKELO, RICHARD M. lawyer; b. Elkhart, Ind., Oct. 22, 1926; s. Frank J. and Mary T.; m. Anne Kosick, June 25, 1955; children: Marla Treckelo Buck, Mary Treckelo Lucchesi. AB, U. Mich., 1951, JD, 1953. Bar: Ind. 1953, U.S. Dist. Ct. (no. and so. dists.) Ind. Pvt. practice, Elkhart, 1953-70; ptnr. Barnes and Thornburg, Elkhart, South Bend, others, 1971-91, of counsel, 1992—. Sec. Skyline Corp., Elkhart, 1959-94, bd. dirs., 1961-91. Bd. dirs. Elkhart Gen. Hosp. Found., Elkhart Park Found.; co-chmn. Elkhart Constl. Bicentennial Commn. Served with USAF, 1945-46. Mem. ABA, Elkhart City Bar Assn. (pres. 1975), Ind. Bar Assn., Elkhart County Bar Assn., Pres.'s Club (U. Mich.), Christiana Country Club, Michiana Club (chmn., U. Mich. Elbel Scholarship award), Rotary. Republican. Office: Barnes & Thornburg 121 W Franklin St Ste 200 Elkhart IN 46516-3200

TREDWAY, THOMAS, college president; b. North Tonawanda, N.Y., Sept. 4, 1935; s. Harold and Melanya (Scorby) T.; m. Catherine Craft, Jan. 12, 1991; children: Daniel John, Rebecca Elizabeth. BA, Augustana Coll., 1957; MA, U. Ill., 1958; BD, Garrett Theol. Sem., 1961; PhD, Northwestern U., 1964. Instr. history Augustana Coll., Rock Island, Ill., 1964-65, asst. prof., 1965-69, assoc. prof., 1969-71, prof., 1971—, v.p. acad affairs, 1970-75, pres., 1975—. Vis. prof. ch. history Waterloo Lutheran Sem., 1967-68 Mem. Phi Beta Kappa, Omicron Delta Kappa Lutheran. Office: Augustana Coll Office of President 639 38th St Rock Island IL 61201-2210

TREE, DAVID L. advertising agency executive; Formerly sr. v.p., creative dir. D'Arcy Masius Benton & Bowles, Inc., N.Y.C.; vice chmn. Campbell Mithun Esty, Mpls., 1989—. Office: Campbell Mithun Esty 222 S 9th St Ste 2600 Minneapolis MN 55402-3389

TREFFERT, DAROLD ALLEN, psychiatrist, author, hospital director; b. Fond du Lac, Wis., Mar. 12, 1933; s. Walter O. and Emma (Leu) T.; m. Dorothy Marie Sorgatz, June 11, 1955; children: Jon, Joni, Jill, Jay. B.S., U. Wis., 1955, M.D., 1958. Diplomate: Am. Bd. Psychiatry and Neurology. Resident in psychiatry U. Wis. Med. Sch., 1959-62, assoc. clin. prof. psychiatry, 1965—; chief children's unit Winnebago (Wis.) Mental Health Inst., 1962-64, supt., 1964-79, Central State Hosp., Waupun, Wis., 1977-78; dir. Dodge County Mental Health Center, Juneau, 1964-74; mem. staff St. Agnes Hosp., Fond du Lac, 1963—; exec. dir. Fond du Lac County Mental Health Center, 1979-92. Chmn. Controlled Substances Bd. Wis.; mem. critical health problems com. Wis. Dept. Pub. Instrn., med. examining bd. State of Wis. Author: Extraordinary People: Understanding Savant Syndrome, 1989, re-issued, 2000, edits. in U.S., U.K., Italy, Japan, The Netherlands, Sweden; autism cons. (movie) Rainman, 1988. Fellow Am. Coll. Psychiatrists; mem. AMA, Wis. Med. Soc. (pres. 1979-80), Wis. Psychiat. Assn. (pres.), Am. Assn. Psychiat. Adminstrs. (pres.), Alpha Omega Alpha. Home: W 4065 Maplewood Ln Fond Du Lac WI 54935-9562 Office: 430 E Division St Fond Du Lac WI 54935-4560 E-mail: dtreffert@pol.net.

TREINAVICZ, KATHRYN MARY, software engineer; b. Nov. 25, 1957; d. Ralph Clement and Frances Elizabeth (O'Leary) T. BS, Salem State Coll., Mass., 1980. Tchr. Brockton Pub. Schs., 1980-81; instr. Quincy CETA Inc., Mass., 1981-82; programmer Systems Architects Inc., Randolph, 1982; programmer analyst Dayton, Ohio, 1982-84; sr. programmer analyst System Devel. Corp., 1984-86; project mgr. Unisys Inc., 1986-87; software engr. Computer Scis. Corp. (formerly Systems & Applied Corp. 1988), 1987-89; project mgr. Computer Sci. Corp. (formerly Atlantic Rsch. Corp. 1994), Fairborn, Ohio, 1989-96; dept. mgr., 1996-98; sr. test analyst, 1998—. Mem. NAFE. Democrat. Roman Catholic. Avocations: Steven King novels, needlepoint, knitting, crocheting.

TRENBEATH, THOMAS L. state legislator, lawyer; b. Neche, N.D., July 23, 1948; m. Rose Trenbeath; children: Ian, Britta. BS, U. N.D., 1970, JD, 1978. Underwriting atty. Chgo. Title Ins. Co., Denver, 1981-84; v.p. Ticro Title Ins. Co., 1984-86; ptnr. Fleming, DuBois & Trenbeath, Attys., 1986-97; city adminstr., atty., 1997—; mem. N.D. Senate from 10th dist., Bismark, 2001—. Mem. ct. svcs. adminstrn. com. N.D. Supreme Ct., 1995—; dir. Red River Regional Coun., 1999—. Capt. USAR, 1971-78. Mem. N.D. Assn. Mcpl. Power Sys. (v.p. 1999—), N.D. Bar Assn., N.D. Humanities Coun. Republican. Lutheran. Office: PO Box 361 Cavalier ND 58220-0361 E-mail: rosentom@polarcomm.com., ttrenbea@state.nd.us.

TRENEFF, CRAIG PAUL, lawyer; b. Columbus, Ohio, July 16, 1952; s. Christ and Marlene Sue (Bach) T.; m. Loraine Marsh Treneff, July 12, 1986. BA, Ohio State U., 1974; JD, Capital U., 1981. Bar: Ohio 1981, U.S. Dist. Ct. (so. dist.) Ohio 1982. Legis. asst. Ohio House Rep., Columbus, 1974-81; law clk. Ohio Supreme Ct., 1981-83; assoc. Morrow, Gordon & Byrd, Newark, 1983-84; counsel atty. Teaford, Rich & Dorsey, Columbus, 1984-85; ptnr. Schottenstein, Treneff & Williams, 1985-97, Treneff & Williams, Columbus, 1997-2001; prin. Craig P. Treneff Law Office, 2001—. Del. coord. Gore for Pres., Ohio, 1988; mgr. Franklin County Treas. campaign, 1988; rsch. coord. Brown for Ohio Sec. campaign, 1982, 90, Franklin County Pres. campaign, 1980' treas. Ohioans with Sherrod Brown; pres. bd. trustees Directions for Youth; mem. Zoning Bd. Appeals, Westerville, Ohio, 1990-95, 96; chmn. Planning Commn., Westerville, Ohio, 1996—. Fellow Am. Acad. Matrimonial Lawyers; mem. ABA, Columbus Bar Assn., Ohio Bar Assn. (bd. cert. family rels. law specialist). Democrat. Lutheran. Home: 148 Executive Ct Westerville OH 43081-1474 Office: Treneff & Williams 555 S Front St Ste 320 Columbus OH 43215-5668 E-mail: cptreneff@cs.com.

TREPPLER, IRENE ESTHER, retired state senator; b. St. Louis County, Mo., Oct. 13, 1926; d. Martin H. and Julia C. (Bender) Hagemann; student Meramec Community Coll., 1972; m. Walter J. Treppler, Aug. 18, 1950; children: John M., Steven A., Diane V. Anderson, Walter W. Payroll chief USAF Aero. Chart Plant, 1943-51; enumerator U.S. Census Bur., St. Louis, 1960, crew leader, 1970; mem. Mo. Ho. of Reps., Jefferson City, 1972-84; mem. Mo. Senate, Jefferson City, 1985-96; chmn. minority caucus, 1991-92. Active Gravois Twp. Rep. Club, Concord Twp. Rep. Club; alt. del. Rep. Nat. Conv., 1976, 84; mem. Mo. Adv. Coun. on Hist. Preservation, 1998—; gov. apptd. Mo. Adv. Coun. on Hist. Preservation, 1998—. Recipient Spirit of Enterprise award Mo. C. of C., 1992, appreciation award Mo. Med. Assn., Nat. Otto Nuttli Earthquake Hazard Mitigation award, 1993, Disting. Legislator award Cmty. Colls. Mo., 1995; named Concord Twp. Rep. of Yr., 1992. Mem. Nat. Order Women Legislators (rec. sec. 1981-82, pres. 1985), Nat. Fedn. Rep. Women. Mem. Evangelical Ch.

TRESTMAN, FRANK D. distribution company executive; b. Mpls., Sept. 3, 1934; s. Saul and Rose (Hyster) T.; m. Carol Lynn Wasserman, Apr. 3, 1960; children— Lisa Ellen, Jill Susan B.B.A. with high distinction, U. Minn., 1955. Exec. v.p., treas. Napco Industries, Inc., Mpls., 1965-74, pres., dir., 1974-84; chmn, CEO Mass Merchandisers, Inc., Hopkins, Minn., 1984-86; pres. Trestman Enterprises, Golden Valley, 1987—. Bd. dirs. Best Buy Co., Mpls., Western Container Corp., Mpls., Insignia Systems, Inc., T.C.F. Industries, Metris Cos., Inc.; ptnr. Avalon Real Estate Group., Mpls., Camir Investment Co., Mpls. Mem. bd. govs. Mt. Sinai Hosp., Mpls., 1978-91, Abbott Northwestern Hosp., 1993—; chmn. bd. trustees Mpls. Fedn. Endowment Fund; bd. dirs. Harry Kay Found. With USN, 1957-58. Mem. Oak Ridge Country Club (Hopkins). Jewish. Home: 11629 Cedar Pass Minnetonka MN 55305-2971 Office: Trestman Enterprises 5500 Wayzata Blvd Ste 1045 Minneapolis MN 55416-1241

TRESTON, SHERRY S. lawyer; BA, Dominican U., 1972; MS, Purdue U., 1973; MBA, U. Chgo., 1979; HD with honors, DePaul U., 1983. Bar: Ill. 1983. With trust dept. 1st Nat. Bank Chgo.; with sys. dept. Sears Bank & Trust Co., Chgo.; with planning dept. Fed. Res. Bank; assoc. Sidley & Austin, ptnr. Trustee Dominican U. Office: Sidley & Austin 1 S First National Plz Chicago IL 60603-2000 Fax: 312-853-7036.

TREUMANN, WILLIAM BORGEN, university dean; b. Grafton, N.D., Feb. 26, 1916; s. William King and Dagny Helen (Borgen) T.; m. Mildred Elizabeth Jenkins, Aug. 14, 1948; children— Richard Roy, Robert Evan, Beverly Kay. B.S., U. N.D., 1942; M.A., U. Ill., 1944, Ph.D., 1947. Teaching asst. chemistry U. Ill., 1942-45, teaching asst. math., 1945-46, vis. prof., summers 1948-50; from asst. prof. to prof. chemistry N.D. State U., 1946-55; mem. faculty Minn. State U. Moorhead, 1960—, prof. chemistry, 1962—, asso. dean acad. affairs, 1968-70, dean faculty math. and sci., 1970—. Contbr. to profl. jours. Research Corp. Am. grantee, 1954; Minn. U. Bd. grantee, 1967 Fellow Am. Inst. Chemists; mem. Am. Chem. Soc., Am. Assn. U. Profs., Minn. Acad. Sci., Fedn. Am. Scientists, Phi Beta Kappa, Sigma Xi. Home: One 2nd St S Apt 5-204 Fargo ND 58103-1921 Office: Math Dept Moorhead State U Moorhead MN 56560

TREVES, SAMUEL BLAIN, geologist, educator; b. Detroit, Sept. 11, 1925; s. Samuel and Stella (Stork) T.; m. Jane Patricia Mitroy, Nov. 24, 1960; children: John Samuel, David Samuel. BS, Mich. Tech. U., 1951; postgrad., U. Otago, New Zealand, 1953-54; MS, U. Idaho, 1953; PhD, Ohio State U., 1959. Geologist Ford Motor Co., 1951, Idaho Bur. Mines and Geology, 1952, Otago Catchment Bd., 1953-54; mem. faculty U. Nebr., Lincoln, 1958—, prof. geology, 1966—, chmn. dept., 1964-70, 74-89, assoc. dean Coll. Arts and Scis., 1989-96. Curator geology Nebr. State Mus., 1964—; participant expdns. to Antarctica and Greenland, 1960, 61, 63, 65, 70, annually 72-76. Rsch. and pubis. on geology of igneous and metamorphic rocks of Idaho, New Zealand, Mich., Antarctica, Nebr., Can., Greenland with emphasis on origin of Precambrian granite complexes and basaltic volcanic rocks. Fulbright scholar U. Otago, New Zealand, 1953-54. Fellow Geol. Soc. Am.; mem. Am. Mineral Soc., Am. Geophys. Union, Sigma Xi, Tau Beta Pi, Sigma Gamma Epsilon. Home: 1710 B St Lincoln NE 68502-1524

TREVOR, ALEXANDER BRUEN, computer company executive; b. N.Y.C., Apr. 12, 1945; s. John B. Jr. and Evelyn (Bruen) T.; m. Ellen Ruth Armstrong, Sept. 21, 1974; children: Anne Wood, Alexander Jay Bruen. BS, Yale U., 1967; MS, U. Ariz., 1971. Rsch. asst. U. Ariz., Tucson, 1971; systems analyst CompuServe Inc., Columbus, Ohio, 1971-73, dir. systems, 1973-74, v.p., 1974-81, exec. v.p., chief tech. officer, 1981-96, also bd. dirs., 1985-96; pres. Nuvocom, Inc., 1996—. Bd. dirs. Applied Innovation, Inc., Dublin, Ohio, CMHC Sys., Dublin. Author (software program) CB Simulator, 1980. Trustee Trudeau Inst., Saranac Lake, N.Y., Aviation Safety Inst., Worthington, Ohio, Wellington Sch., Upper Arlington, Ohio. 1st lt. Signal Corps, U.S. Army, 1968-70, Vietnam. Decorated Bronze Star. Mem. IEEE, SAR (N.Y.), Union Club (N.Y.). Republican. Episcopalian. Office: Box 340876 Worthington OH 43234-0876

TRIANDIS, HARRY CHARALAMBOS, psychology educator; b. Patras, Greece, Oct. 16, 1926; s. Christos Charalambos and Louise J. (Nikokavouras) T.; m. Pola Fotitch, Dec. 23, 1966; 1 child, Louisa. B.Engring., McGill U., 1951; M.Commerce, U. Toronto, Ont., Can., 1954; Ph.D., Cornell U., 1958; Doctorate (hon.), U. Athens, Greece, 1987. Asst. prof. U. Ill., Champaign, 1958-61, assoc. prof., 1961-66, prof. psychology, 1966-97; cons. USIA, 1970-75, NSF, 1968-75; prof. emeritius, 1997—. Author: Attitudes and Attitude Change, 1971, The Analysis of Subjective Culture, 1972, Varieties of Black and White Perception of the Social Environment, 1975, Interpersonal Behavior, 1977, Culture and Social Behavior, 1994, Individualism and Collectivism, 1995; editor: Handbook of Cross-Cultural Psychology, Vol. 1-6, 1980-81, Handbook of Industrial and Organizational Psychology, Vol. 4, 1994; editorial cons.; Jour. Personality and social Psychology, 1963-71, Jour. Applied Psychology, 1970-79, Sociometry, 1971-74, Jour. Cross-Cultural Psychology, 1974—, others. Chmn. fgn. grants com. Am. Psychol. Found., 1968-90. Sr. fellow Ford Found., 1964-65; Guggenheim fellow, 1972-73; grantee USPHS, 1956-60, 62; grantee Office Naval Research, 1960-68, 80-85; grantee Social and Rehab. Service, HEW, 1968-73; grantee Ford Found., 1973-75; recipient award Interam. Soc. Psychology, 1981 Mem. Soc. for Psychol. Study of Social Issues (pres. 1975-76), Internat. Assn. Cross-Cultural Psychology (pres. 1974-76), Interam. Soc. Psychology (pres. 1985-87), Soc. for Exptl. Social Psychology (chmn. 1972-74), Soc. for Personality and Social Psychology (pres. 1976-77), Internat. Assn. Applied Psychology (pres. 1990-94). Home: 1 Lake Park Rd Champaign IL 61822-7101 Office: 603 E Daniel St Champaign IL 61820-6232

TRICK, TIMOTHY NOEL, electrical and computer engineering educator, researcher; b. Dayton, Ohio, July 14, 1939; s. Edmund Louis and Roberta Elizabeth (Heckel) T.; m. Dorothe Lee Jacobs, Feb. 18, 1958; children: Patricia, Michael, Thomas, William, Gregory, Andrew. BSEE, U. Dayton, 1961; MSEE, Purdue U., 1962, PhD, 1966. Instr. Purdue U., West Lafayette, Ind., 1963-65; asst. prof. elec. and computer engring. U. Ill., Urbana, 1965-70, assoc. prof., 1970-75, prof., 1975—, dir. Coordinated Sci. Lab., 1984-86, head dept. elec. and computer engring., 1985-95. Author: Introduction to Circuit Analysis, 1978. Fellow AAAS, IEEE (bd. dirs. 1986-89, v.p. publs. 1988-89, Guillemin-Cauer award 1976, Centennial medal 1984, Meritorious Svc. award 1987); mem. Circuits and Sys. Soc. of IEEE (pres. 1979, Van Valkenburg award 1994), Am. Soc. Engring. Edn. Avocations: hiking, camping. Office: U Ill Dept Elec & Computer Engring 1406 W Green St Urbana IL 61801-2918

TRIENENS, HOWARD JOSEPH, lawyer; b. Chgo., Sept. 13, 1923; s. Joseph Herman and Myrtle (Wilsberg) T.; m. Paula Miller, Aug. 27, 1946; children: John, Thomas, Nancy. BS, Northwestern U., 1945; JD, 1949. Bar: Ill. 1949, N.Y. 1980, U.S. Dist. Ct. (no. dist.) Ill. 1949, U.S. Dist. Ct. (so. and ea. dists.) N.Y. 1980, U.S. Ct. Appeals (2d, 3d, 7th, 8th, 10th, 11th and D.C. cirs.), U.S. Supreme Ct. 1954. Assoc. firm Sidley, Austin, Burgess & Harper, Chgo., 1949-50; law clk. to Chief Justice Vinson, 1950-52; assoc. Sidley, Austin, Burgess & Smith, Chgo., 1952-56; ptnr. Sidley Austin Brown & Wood, 1956—; v.p., gen. counsel AT&T, 1980-86. Trustee Northwestern U., 1967—. With USAAF, 1943-46. Mem. ABA, Ill. Bar Assn., Chgo. Bar Assn., N.Y. State Bar Assn., Am. Coll. Trial Lawyers, Lawyers Club (Chgo.), Chgo. Club, Casino Club (Chgo.), Mid-Day Club, Skokie Country Club, Shoreacres Club, Glen View Club (Golf, Ill.), Met. Club (Washington), Old Elm Club, Sigma Chi. Democrat. Home: 690 Longwood Ave Glencoe IL 60022-1761 Office: Sidley Austin Brown & Wood Apt 605 425 W Surf St Chicago IL 60657-6139 E-mail: htrienens@sidley.com.

TRIGG, PAUL REGINALD, JR. lawyer; b. Lewistown, Mont., Mar. 25, 1913; s. Paul Reginald and Opal Stella (Fay) T.; m. Helen Ruth Leake, Dec. 25, 1938; children: Paul Reginald III, Mary Adra; m. Mary Helen Wood, Apr. 8, 2000. BA, Grinnell Coll., 1935; JD, U. Mich., 1938. Bar: Mich. 1938. Practiced law in, Detroit; ptnr. Dykema, Gossett (and predecessor), 1938—. Mem. ABA, Mich. Bar Assn., Detroit Bar Assn. Clubs: Detroit Country, Yondotega.

TRIM, DONALD ROY, consulting engineer; b. Saginaw, Mich., June 23, 1937; s. Roy E. and Agnes (Kontranowski) T.; m. Dorothy Mae Franek, Aug. 11, 1962; children: Jeffrey D., Gregory S., Christopher M. BS in Civic Engring., U. Mich., 1959. Registered profl. engr., Mich., Ohio, Fla.; registered land surveyor, Mich. Engr. Francis Engring., Saginaw, 1959-64, Edwin M. Orr, Inc., Dearborn, Mich., 1964-66; pres. Wade-Trim Group, Plymouth, 1966-96, CEO, 1996-99, chmn., 1999—. V.p. Plymouth Canton Basketball Assn., 1980-84; bd. govs. Greater Mich. Found., Lansing, 1983-85. Mem. Nat. Soc. Profl. Engrs., Cons. Engrs. Coun. Mich. (dir. 1972-73, Pres. 1983-84), Am. Cons. Engrs. Coun. (v.p. 1986-88, pres. 1998-99), Am. Waterworks Assn. Roman Cath. Office: Wade-Trim Group 400 Monroe St Ste 310 Detroit MI 48226-2962 E-mail: dtrim@wadetrim.com.

TRIMBLE, STEVE, state legislator; b. Dec. 1942; two children. BA, So. Meth. U.; postgrad., U. Chgo. Minn. State rep. Dist. 67B, 1987—; tchr. Vice-chmn. capital investments com.; chmn. regulation of industries and energy; mem. environ. and natural resources, rules and legislation adminstrn., environ. fin. coms. Office: 485 State Office Bldg Saint Paul MN 55155-0001

TRIPLEHORN, CHARLES A. entomology educator, insects curator; b. Bluffton, Ohio, Oct. 27, 1927; s. Murray E. and Alice Irene (Lora) T.; m. Wanda Elaine Neiswander, June 12, 1949 (dec. Nov. 1985); children: Bradley Alyn, Bruce Wayne; m. Linda Sue Parsons, July 11, 1987. B.Sc., Ohio State U., 1949, M.S., 1952; Ph.D., Cornell U., 1957. Asst. prof. entomology U. Del., Newark, 1952-54; teaching asst. entomology Cornell U., Ithaca, N.Y., 1954-57; asst. prof. entomology Ohio Agrl. Research and Devel. Ctr., Wooster, Ohio, 1957-61, Ohio State U., Columbus, 1961-62, assoc. prof. entomology, 1962-66, prof. entomology, 1966-92, prof. emeritus, 1992—. Econ. entomologist U.S. AID/Brazil, Piracicaba, Sao Paulo, 1964-66; vis. curator Field Mus. Natural History, Chgo., 1974, Can. Nat. Collection, Ottawa, Ont., 1977, Am. Mus. Natural History, N.Y.C., 1982, U. Mich., 1989, U. Ariz., 1989, Nat. Mus. of Natural History, 1998, Cornell U., 1999, Colo. State U., 2000, Brigham Young U., 2000. Co-author: Introduction to the Study of Insects, 6th edit., 1989. Cubmaster Boy Scouts Am., Wooster, Ohio, 1959-60, scoutmaster, Columbus, 1971-72; football coach Upper Arlington Football Assn., Ohio, 1968-71 Grantee Am. Philos. Soc., 1963, NSF, 1979, 85, 92. Mem. Entomol. Soc. Am. (pres. 1985), Coleopterists Soc. (pres. 1976), Royal Entomol. Soc. London, Entomol. Soc. Washington, Sigma Xi, Gamma Sigma Delta Republican. Methodist. Club: Wheaton (pres.) Avocations: sports; music; reading; writing. Home: 3943 Medford Sq Hilliard OH 43026-2219 Office: Mus Biol Diversity Div Insects The Ohio State University 1315 Kinnear Rd Columbus OH 43212-1157 E-mail: triplehorn.1@osu.edu.

TRIPP, MARIAN BARLOW LOOFE, retired public relations company executive; b. Lodgepole, Nebr., July 26; d. Lewis Rockwell and Cora Dee (Davis) Barlow; m. James Edward Tripp, Feb. 9, 1957; children: Brendan Michael, Kevin Mark. BS, Iowa State U., 1944. Writer Dairy Record, St. Paul, 1944-45; head product promotion divsn., pub. rels. dept. Swift & Co., Chgo., 1945-55; mgmt. supr., v.p. pub. rels. J. Walter Thompson Co., N.Y.C. and Chgo., 1956-76, v.p. consumer affairs Chgo., 1974-76; pres. Marian Tripp Communications Inc., 1976-94. Mem. Am. Inst. Wine and Food, Confriere de la Chaine des Rotisseriers (officer Chgo. chpt.), Mayflower Soc., Daughters of the Am. Revolution. Episcopalian. Office: 100 E Bellevue Pl Chicago IL 60611-1157 E-mail: mbtripp.@aol.com.

TROLANDER, HARDY WILCOX, engineering executive, consultant; b. Chgo., June 2, 1921; s. Elmer Wilcox and Freda Marie (Zobel) T.; m. Imogen Davenport, July 3, 1946 (dec.); children: Megan, Patricia. BS in Engring., Antioch Coll., 1947. Instr. Antioch Coll., Yellow Springs, Ohio, 1947-48; co-founder, CEO Yellow Springs Instrument Co., Inc., 1948-86.

Dir., co-founder Cook Design Ctr., Dartmouth Coll., Hanover, N.H., 1975-88; bd. dirs. Deban Inc., Yellow Springs, Camax Tool co., Arvada, Colo.; mem. evaluation panel Inst. Basic Stds., Nat. Bur. Stds., 1977-79. Contbr. articles to profl. jours.; patentee in field. Co-founder, trustee Yellow Springs Community Found., 1974-83; trustee Autioch Coll., 1968-74, chmn. bd., 1972-74; trustee Engring. and Sci. Found., Dayton, 1982-96, Engrs. Club Dayton Found., 1994—, Engring. and Sci. Hall of Fame, 1994—; mem. adv. bd. Coll. Engring. and Computer Sci. Wright State U., 1993—; bd. dirs. united Way Greater Dayton Area, 184-92. 1st lt. USAF, 1943-46. Named Outstanding Engr., Dayton Affiliate Socs., 1967, 89. Fellow Dayton Engrs. Club, Am. Inst. for Med. and Biol. Engring.; mem. ACLU, Nat. Acad. Engring., Am. Inst. Biol. Scis. (bioinstrumentation adv. , coun. 1969-75), Internat. Orgn. of Legal Metrology (tech. advisor, sec. 1975-82), Amnesty Internat. Democrat. Home and Office: 1475 President St Yellow Springs OH 45387-1326

TROST, EILEEN BANNON, lawyer; b. Teaneck, N.J., Jan. 9, 1951; d. William Eugene and Marie Thelma (Finlayson) Bannon; m. Lawrence Peter Trost Jr., Aug. 27, 1977; children: Lawrence Peter III, William Patrick, Timothy Alexander. BA with great distinction, Shimer Coll., 1972; JD cum laude, U. Minn., 1976. Bar: Ill. 1976, U.S. Dist. Ct. (no. dist.) Ill. 1976, Minn. 1978, U.S. Tax Ct. 1978, U.S. Supreme Ct. 1981. Assoc. McDermott, Will & Emery, Chgo., 1976-82, ptnr., 1982-93; v.p. No. Trust Bank Ariz. N.A., Phoenix, 1993-95; ptnr. Sonnenschein Nath & Rosenthal, Chgo., 1995—. Mem. Am. Coll. Trust and Estate Coun., Minn. Bar Assn., Internat. Acad. Estate and Trust Law, Chgo. Estate Planning Coun. Roman Catholic. Office: Sonnenschein Nath & Rosenthal 8000 Sears Tower Chicago IL 60606 E-mail: etrost@sonnenschein.com.

TROTMAN, ALEXANDER J. retired automobile manufacturing company executive; b. Middlesex, Eng., July 22, 1933; married. MBA, Mich. State U., 1972. Various positions Ford Motor Co., 1951—, Ford of Britain, 1955-67; dir. car prodn. planning office Ford of Europe, 1967-69; spl. assignment advanced car prodn. planning dept. Ford USA, 1969-70, mgr. product planning dept. Lincoln-Mercury divsn., 1970-71, dir. mktg. staff sales planning office, 1971-72, exec. dir. product planning, product planning and rsch., 1972-75, chief car planning mgr., car prodn. devel. group, 1975-77, exec. dir. ops. planning, 1977-78, asst. gen. mgr. truck and recreational products ops., 1978-79; v.p. truck ops. Ford of Europe, 1979-83; pres. Ford Asia-Pacific Inc., 1983-84, Ford of Europe, Inc., 1984-88; exec. v.p. N.Am. Auto Ops., 1988-93; pres. Ford Auto Group, 1993. Bd. dirs. Ford Motor Co., IBM Corp., Armonk, N.Y., Imperial Chem. Industries, London, N.Y. Stock Exch., N.Y.C.; adv. com. mem. Chase Internat. Knighted by Queen of Eng., 1996. Officer RAF, 1951-55. Mem. Am.-China Soc., U.S. China Bus. Coun., U.S.-Japan Bus. Coun., Bus. Roundtable, Bus. Coun. Office: Ford Motor Co One American Rd Dearborn MI 48126-2798

TROTTER, CHARLIE, chef; Degree in polit. sci., U. Wis., 1982. Owner, chef Charlie Trotter's, Chgo. Author: Charlie Trotter's, Charlie Trotter's Vegetables, Charlie Trotter's Seafood, Charlie Trotter's Desserts, Charlie Trotter's Meat and Game, Kitchen Sessions with Charlie Trotter, Gourmet Cooking for Dummies; (host): (tv series) Kitchen Sessions with Charlie Trotter. Recipient Grand award, Wine Spectator, Best Restaurant in U.S., 2000. Office: Charlie Trotter's 816 W. Armitage Ave Chicago IL 60614

TROTTER, DONNE E. state legislator, hospital administrator; b. Cairo, Jan. 30, 1950; s. James and Carita (Caldwell) T.; m. Rose Zuniga; 4 children. BA, U. Chgo., 1976, Chgo. State U.; MJ, Loyola U. Sch. Law. Sr. hosp. adminstr. Cook County Hosp., Chgo., 1981—; house rep. Ill. Ho. of Reps., Springfield, 1988-93; state senator Ill. Senate, 1993-. State rep. State of Ill., Chgo., 1988—; vice-chmn. Health Care Commn., Ill. Gen. Assembly, 1991, mem. human svcs. com., 1988—, mem. minority caucus. Adv. bd. mem. 8th Ward Region Dem., 1983—; mem. Ill. Black United Front. Mem. APHA, Ill. Pub. Health Assn., Nat. Assn. of Health Care Adminstrs., Nat. Conf. State Legislators, Nat. Conf. Black State Legislators. Office: 417 Capitol Bldg Springfield IL 62706-0001 Address: 8704 S Constance Ave Ste 324 Chicago IL 60617-2756

TROTTER, THOMAS ROBERT, lawyer; b. Akron, Ohio, Apr. 11, 1949; s. Fred and Josephine (Dalcy) T. BA, Ohio U., 1971; JD, Tulane U., 1975. Bar: Ohio 1975, D.C. 2000, U.S. Dist. Ct. (no. dist.) Ohio 1975. Assoc. Squire, Sanders & Dempsey, Cleve., 1975-80; mem. Buckingham, Doolittle & Burroughs, Akron, 1980—. Chair taxation and legis. com. Akron Regional Devel. Bd., 1988-95. Trustee Akron Symphony Orch., 1984-93, Cascade CDC, Inc., Akron, 1983—, Akron-Summit Solid Waste Mgmt. Authority, 1994-97; trustee Weathervane Cmty. Playhouse, 1996—, pres., 1999-2001. Mem. ABA, Ohio Bar Assn. (chair local govt. law com.), Akron Bar Assn., Nat. Assn. Bond Lawyers, Sigma Alpha Epsilon. Democrat. Home: 589 Avalon Akron OH 44320-2048 Office: Buckingham Doolittle & Burroughs PO Box 1500 50 S Main St Akron OH 44308-1828 E-mail: ttrotter@bdblaw.com.

TROUPE, CHARLES QUINCY, state legislator; b. St. Louis, May 12, 1936; Qiploma, Nat. Inst. Electronics & Tech, Denver. Elec. contrator; mem. Mo. Ho. of Reps. from 63d dist., 1978-82, Mo. Ho. of Reps. from 62d dist., 1982—. Chmn. Appropriations, Social Svc. and Corrections Coms. Mo. Ho. of Reps., mem. Budget, Banks & Fin. Instns., Local Govt. Accounts, Ops. and Fin Coms.; mem. Mo. Legis. Black Caucus. V.p. Local 788 ATU. Democrat. Home: PO Box 150019 Saint Louis MO 63115-8019

TROUT, MICHAEL GERALD, airport administrator; b. Apr. 16, 1959; B in Urban Adminstrn. with honors, U. Mich., 1993, MPA, 1996. Owner, operator Arrow Video, 1985-90; airport planning cons. GTA, 1990-93; prin. aviation planner SEMCOG, 1993-96; dep. dir. Detroit City Airport, 1996-2000; dep. dir. maintenance ops. Flint (Mich.) Bishop Airport, 2000—. Mgr. Whatley Farm Domino's Farms, 1989. Mem. Am. Assn. Airport Execs., Am. Planning Assn., Am. Inst. Cert. Planners, Am. Soc. Pub. Adminstrn., Mich. Assn. Airport Execs. Office: Fliint Bishop Airport G 3425 W Bristol Rd Flint MI 48507

TROY, DANIEL PATRICK, former state legislator, county official; b. Cleveland, Ohio, May 6, 1948; s. John Edward and Marjorie (Farrell) T. BA in Polit. Sci., U. Dayton, 1970. City councilman Ward I, Willowick, Ohio, 1972-77, coun. pres., 1980-82; pres. Lake County Coun. Govt., 1975-78; committeeman Lake County Dem. Com., 1976; Ohio State Rep. Dist. 60., 1983-92, Dist. 70, 1993-97; del. Dem. Nat. Conv., 1984; pres., bd. dirs. Lake County (Ohio) Commrs., Painesville. Tech. Kahoe Air Balance Co., 1967-74; prof. Balance Co., 1975-80, proj. engr., 1980. Recipient Legis. Svc. award, 1983-84, Ohio Sea grant Disting. Svc. award, 1988, Legis. Leadership award Ohio Coalition for Edn. Handicapped Children, 1989, 91, Voc. Edn. Person of Yr. award, 1989, Ohio Edn. Broadcasting award, 1983, Friends of Cmty. Coll. Excellence award, 1994. Mem. AFL, East Side Irish-Am. Club. Home: 31600 Lakeshore Blvd Willowick OH 44095-3522

TROYER, LEROY SETH, architect; b. Middlebury, Ind., Nov. 23, 1937; s. Seth and Nancy (Miller) T.; m. Phyllis Eigsti, May 24, 1958; children: Terry, Ronald, Donald. BArch, U. Notre Dame, 1971. Founder, pres., CEO LeRoy Troyer and Assocs., South Bend, 1971; sr. ptnr. The Trouer Group, Inc. (formerly LeRoy Troyer and Assocs.), Mishawaka, Ind., 1988—; pres. Southfield, Inc., 1988—. Bd. dirs. Lead Devel., Inc. Author numerous documents; contbr. numerous papers and articles to publs. Past pres., chair Environic Found. Internat., Inc.; bd. dirs. Habitat for Humanity Internat. Americus, Ga., 1987-93, Coun. of Christian Colls. and Univs., 1991-96, Habitat for Humanity St. Joseph County, Ind., 1992-99, 2001—; bd. dirs. Bethel Coll., 1988-97, Mishawaka, Housing Devel. Corp., South Bend, CONNECT, South Bend; bd. dirs., exec. com. Fourth Freedom Forum Internat., 1996—; bd. dirs. Evangelicals for Social Action, Wynnewood, Pa., 1997—; chmn. Miracle of Nazareth Internat. Found., 2000–. Recipient numerous local, state and nat. awards and honors. Fellow AIA (practice mgmt. com., chmn. 1983-84), Ind. Soc. Architects, Mennonite Econ. Devel. Assn. Internat. (chmn. bd. 1987-91). Avocations: photography, travel, reading, art, woodworking. Home: 1442 Deerfield Ct South Bend IN 46614-6429 Office: The Troyer Group Inc 550 Union St Mishawaka IN 46544-2346 E-mail: leroy@troyergroup.com.

TROZZOLO, ANTHONY MARION, chemistry educator; b. Chgo., Jan. 11, 1930; s. Pasquale and Francesca (Vercillo) T.; m. Doris C. Stoffregen, Oct. 8, 1955; children: Thomas, Susan, Patricia, Michael, Lisa, Laura. BS, Ill. Inst. Tech., 1950; MS, U. Chgo., 1957, PhD, 1960. Asst. chemist Chgo. Midway Labs., 1952-53; assoc. chemist Armour Rsch. Found., Chgo., 1953-56; tech. staff Bell Labs., Murray Hill, N.J., 1959-75; Charles L. Huisking prof. chemistry U. Notre Dame, 1975-92, Charles L. Huisking prof. emeritus, 1992—; asst. dean U. Notre Dame Coll. Sci., 1993-98; P.C. Reilly lectr. U. Notre Dame, 1972, Hesburgh Alumni lectr., 1986, Disting. lectr. sci., 1986. Vis. prof. Columbia U., N.Y.C., 1971, U. Colo., 1981, Katholieke U. Leuven, Belgium, 1983, Max Planck Inst. für Strahlenchemie, Mülheim/Ruhr, Fed. Republic Germany, 1990; vis. lectr. Academia Sinica, 1984, 85; Phillips lectr. U. Okla., 1971; C.L. Brown lectr. Rutgers U., 1975; Sigma Xi lectr. Bowling Green U., 1976, Abbott Labs., 1978; M. Faraday lectr. No. Ill. U., 1976; F.O. Butler lectr. S.D. State U., 1978; Chevron lectr. U. Nev., Reno, 1983; J. Crano lectr. U. Akron, 2000; plenary lectr. various internat. confs.; founder, chmn. Gordon Conf. on Organic Photochemistry, 1964; trustee Gordon Rsch. Confs., 1988-92; cons. in field. Assoc. editor Jour. Am. Chem. Soc., 1975-76; editor Chem. Revs., 1977-84; editorial adv. bd. Accounts of Chem. Rsch., 1977-85; cons. editor Encyclopedia of Science and Technology, 1982-92; contbr. articles to profl. jours.; patentee in field. Fellow AEC, 1951, NSF, 1957-59; named Hon. Citizen of Castrolibero, Italy, 1997; recipient Pietro Bucci prize U. Calabria/Italian Chem. Soc., 1997. Fellow AAAS, Am. Inst. Chemists (Student award 1950), N.Y. Acad. Scis. (chmn. chem. scis. sect. 1969-70, Halpern award in photochemistry 1980), Inter-Am. Photochemical Soc.; mem. AAUP, Am. Chem. Soc. (Disting. Svc. award St. Joseph Valley sect. 1979, Tex. lectr. 1975, Pacific Coast lectr. 1981, Coronado lectr. 1980, 93, 98, N.Y. state lectr. 1993, Hoosier lectr. 1995, Ozark lectr. 1995, Rocky Mountain lectr. 1996, Tex. Coast lectr. 1996, Osage lectr. 1998), Sigma Xi. Roman Catholic. Home: 1329 E Washington St South Bend IN 46617-3340 Office: U Notre Dame Dept Chemistry-Biochemistry Notre Dame IN 46556-5670

TRUCANO, MICHAEL, lawyer; b. Washington, May 28, 1945; s. Peter Joseph and Fern Margaret (Bauer) T.; m. Doreen E. Struck, 1969; children: Michael, David. BA, Carleton Coll., 1967; JD, NYU, 1970. Assoc. Dorsey & Whitney, Mpls., 1970-75, ptnr., 1976—, head of office, 2000—. Office: Dorsey & Whitney LLP Ste 1500 50 S 6th St Minneapolis MN 55402-1498 E-mail: trucano.mike@dorseylaw.com.

TRUCE, WILLIAM EVERETT, chemist, educator; b. Chgo., Sept. 30, 1917; s. Stanley C. and Frances (Novak) T.; m. Eloise Joyce McBroom, June 16, 1940; children: Nancy Jane, Roger William. BS, U. Ill., 1939; PhD, Northwestern U., 1943. Mem. faculty Purdue U., 1946-88, prof. chemistry, 1956-88, prof. chemistry emeritus, 1988—, asst. dean Grad. Sch., 1963-66. Mem. numerous univ. dept. and profl. coms.; chmn. various profl. meetings; exec. officer Nat. Organic Symposium, 1961; chmn. Gordon Rsch. Conf. on Organic Reactions and Processes; cons. in field. Co-author book; contbr. articles to profl. jours., chpts. to books. Guggenheim fellow Oxford U., 1957 Mem. Am. Chem. Soc., Phi Beta Kappa (sec. Purdue chpt.), Sigma Xi (pres. Purdue chpt.). Achievements include research in new methods of synthesis, devel. new kinds of compounds and reactions. Home: 220 Hopi Pl Boulder CO 80303-3533 Office: Purdue U Dept Chemistry West Lafayette IN 47907 E-mail: etruce@bouldernews.infi.net.

TRUCKSESS, H.A., III, company executive; CFO, sr. v.p., Treasurer Yellow Corp., Overland Park, Kans. Office: 10990 Rob Ave PO Box 7563 Overland Park KS 66207-0563

TRUCKSIS, THERESA A. retired library director; b. Hubbard, Ohio, Sept. 1, 1924; d. Peter and Carmella (DiSilverio) Pagliastotti; m. Robert C. Trucksis, May 29, 1948 (dec. May 1980); children: M. Laura, Anne, Michele, Patricia, David, Robert, Claire, Peter; m. Philip P. Hickey, Oct. 19, 1985 (dec. May 1993). BS in Edn., Youngstown Coll., 1945; postgrad., Youngstown State U., 1968-71; MLS, Kent State U., 1972. Psychometrist Youngstown (Ohio) Coll., 1946-49; instr. ltd. svc. Youngstown State U., 1968-71; libr. Pub. Libr. Youngstown & Mahoning County, Youngstown, 1972-73, asst. dept. head, 1973-74, asst. dir., 1985-89, dir., 1989-97, NOLA Regional Libr. System, Youngstown, 1974-85. Contbr. articles to profl. jours. Mem. bd. Hubbard Sch. Dist., 1980-85. Mem. ALA, Ohio Libr. Assn. (bd. dirs. 1979-81), Pub. Libr. Assn. Address: 133 Viola Ave Hubbard OH 44425-2062

TRUDEAU, GARRETSON BEEKMAN (GARRY TRUDEAU), cartoonist; b. N.Y.C., 1948; m. Jane Pauley, June 14, 1980; children: Ross and Rachel (twins), Thomas. BA, Yale U., 1970, MFA, 1973, DHL, 1976. Syndicated cartoonist, writer. Creator: comic strip Doonesbury; syndicated nationwide comic strip; author: Still a Few Bugs in the System, 1972, The President is a Lot Smarter Than You Think, 1973, But This War Had Such Promise, 1973, Call Me When You Find America, 1973, Guilty, Guilty, Guilty, 1974, Joanie, 1974, The Doonesbury Chronicles, 1975, What Do We Have for the Witnesses, Johnnie?, 1975, Dare to Be Great, Ms. Caucus, 1975, Wouldn't A Gremlin Have Been More Sensible?, 1975, We'll Take it From Here, Sarge, 1975, Speaking of Inalienable Rights, Amy..., 1976, You're Never Too Old for Nuts and Berries, 1976, An Especially Tricky People, 1977, As the Kid Goes For Broke, 1977, Stalking the Perfect Tan, 1978, Any Grooming Hints for Your Fans, Rollie?, 1978, Doonesbury's Greatest Hits, 1978, But The Pension Fund was Just Sitting There, 1979, We're Not Out of the Woods Yet, 1979, A Tad Overweight, but Violet Eyes to Die For, 1980, And That's My Final Offer!, 1980, The People's Doonesbury, 1981, He's Never Heard of You, Either, 1981, In Search of Reagan's Brain, 1981, Ask for May, Settle for June, 1982, Unfortunately, She Was Also Wired for Sound, 1982, Adjectives Will Cost You Extra, 1982, Gotta Run, My Government is Collapsing, 1982, The Wreck of the Rusty Nail, 1983, You Give Great Meeting, Sid, 1983, Guess Who Fish Face, 1983, It's Supposed to be Yellow Pinhead: Selected Cartoons From Ask For May, Settle For June, Vol. I, 1983, Do All Birders Have Bedrooms, 1983, Farewell to Alms, 1984, Doonesbury Dossier: The Reagan Years, 1984, Doonesbury: A Musical Comedy, 1984, Check Your Egos at the Door, 1985, That's Doctor Sinatra, You Little Bimbo, 1986, Death of a Party Animal, 1986, Doonesbury Deluxe: Selected Glances Askance, 1987, Downtown Doonesbury, 1987, Calling Dr. Whoopee, 1987, The Doonesbury Desk Diary 1988, 1987, Talking Bout My G-G-Generation, 1988, We're Eating More Beets, 1988, Read My Lips, Make My Day, Eat Quiche & Die! A Doonesbury Collection, 1989, Small Collection, 1989, The Doonesbury Stamp Album, 1990, 1990, Recycled Doonesbury: Second Thoughts on a Gilded Age, 1990, You're Smokin' Now, Mr. Butts! A Doonesbury Book, 1990, Welcome to Club Scud: A Doonesbury Book, 1991, Action Figure: The Life and Times of Doonesbury's Uncle Duke, 1992, The Portable Doonesbury, 1993, In Search of Cigarette Holder Man: A Doonesbury Book, 1994, Doonesbury Nation, 1995, Flashbacks: Twenty-five Years of Doonesbury, 1995; co-author: Tales From the Margaret Mead Taproom, 1979; plays include: Doonesbury, 1983, Rapmaster Ronnie, A Partisan Review (with Elizabeth Swados), 1984 Pulitzer Prize for Editorial Cartooning, 1975.

TRUE, RAYMOND STEPHEN, writer, editor, analyst, consultant; b. Lowell, Mass., June 29, 1934; s. Sylvester Raymond and Madeline Rose (Farrell) T.; m. Doreen Therese Jambrosek BA, U. Chgo., 1961, MBA, 1968, postgrad., 1968-69. Commd. 2nd lt. USAF, 1953, advanced through grades to col., 1980; master navigator U.S. Air Force Reserve, Chgo., 1957-77; regional cons. U.S. Bur. Census, 1970-71; dir. operations U.S. Air Force Reserve, Milw., 1977-80, base civil engr., 1980-87, chief planning analyst, 1987-89; owner Classic Comics Libr., 1990—. Fire marshall Milw. County, 1980-87, chmn. membership Reserve Officers Assn., Wash. 1975-78. Editor Classics Newsletter, 1971-75. Precinct committeeman, Libertyville, Ill., 2000—; pres. ROA chpt. 61, 2000-02; chmn. Rep. Assembly Lake County, 2001-. Mem. Air Force Assn., Grad. Sch. Bus. Exec. Council U. Chgo. Roman Catholic. Avocations: philately, antique books, videophile. Address: 839 Terre Dr Libertyville IL 60048-1649 E-mail: raymon8844@aol.com.

TRUE, STEVE, radio personality; Student, U. Wis. Radio host 1130 WISN, Greenfield, Wis., 1989—. Office: WISN Radio 12100 W Howard Ave Greenfield WI 53228*

TRUHLAR, DONALD GENE, chemist, educator; b. Chgo. , Feb. 27, 1944; s. John Joseph and Lucille Marie (Vancura) T.; m. Jane Teresa Gust, Aug. 28, 1965; children: Sara Elizabeth, Stephanie Marie. BA in Chemistry summa cum laude, St. Mary's Coll., Winona, Minn., 1965; PhD in Chemistry, Calif. Inst. Tech., 1970. Asst. prof. chemistry and chem. physics U. Minn., Mpls., 1969—72, assoc. prof., 1972—76, prof., 1976—93, Inst. of Tech. prof., 1993—98, Inst. of Tech. disting. prof., 1998—, Lloyd H. Reyerson prof., 2002—. Cons. Los Alamos Sci. Lab.; vis. fellow Joint Inst. for Lab. Astrophysics, 1975-76; sci. dir. Minn. Supercomputer Inst., 1987-88, dir., 1988—. Editor Theoretical Chemistry Accounts (Theoretica Chemica Acta), 1985-98, Computer Physics Comms., 1986—, Topics Phys. Chemistry, 1992-99, Understanding Chem. Reactivity, 1990-92; mem. editorial bd. Jour. Chem. Physics, 1978-80, Chem. Physics Letters, 1982—, Jour. Phys. Chemistry, 1985-87, Understanding Chem. Reactivity, 1993—, Advances in Chem. Physics, 1993—, Internat. Jour. Modern Physics C, 1994—, IEEE Computational Sci. and Engring., 1994-98, Internat. Jour. Quantum Chemistry, 1996-2000, Computing in Science and Engineering, 1999—, Physics Chem. Comm., 2001—; assoc. editor Theoretical Chemistry Accounts, 1998-2001, chief adv. editor, 2002–. Ruhland Walzer Meml. scholar, 1961-62; John Stauffer fellow, 1965-66, NDEA fellow, 1966-68, Alfred P. Sloan Found. fellow, 1973-77; grantee NSF, 1971—, NASA, 1987-95, U.S. Dept. Energy, 1979—, NIST, 1995-98. Fellow AAAS, Am. Phys. Soc.; mem. Am. Chem. Soc. (sec.-treas. theoretical chemistry subdivsn. 1980-89, councilor 1985-87, assoc. editor jour. 1984—, Award for computers in chem. and pharm. rsch. 2000). Achievements include research, numerous publications in field. Home: 5033 Thomas Ave S Minneapolis MN 55410-2240 Office: U Minn 207 Pleasant St SE Minneapolis MN 55455-0431 E-mail: truhlar@umn.edu.

TRUJILLO, ANGELINA, endocrinologist; b. Long Beach, Calif. BA in Psychology, Chapman Coll., 1974; postgrad., U. Colo., 1974-75, MD, 1979. Resident in internal medicine Kern Med. Ctr., Bakersfield, Calif., 1979-82; fellow in endocrinology UCLA, Sepulveda, 1982-84, chief resident dept. internal medicine, 1985-86; chief diabetes clinic Sepulveda (Calif.) VA Med. Ctr., 1986-89; physician specialist Olive View Med. Ctr., Sylmar, Calif., 1989; chief divsn. endocrinology U. S.D. Sch. Medicine, Sioux Falls, 1990—2001; ACOS R&D Royal C. Johnson VA Med. Ctr., 1998—2001. Adj. instr. UCLA, 1982-84, adj. asst. prof. medicine, 1985-89, clin. asst. prof. family medicine, 1994-2001; asst. prof. U. S.D. Sch. Medicine, 1990-94, assoc. prof., 1994—, assoc. dir. internal medicine residency program, 1992-95; spkr. in field. Pub. spkr. in diabetes, women and heart disease. Grantee NIH, 1986-89, Am. Diabetes Assn., 1985-87, Pfizer, Inc., 1990-91, Nat. Heart, Lung, and Blood Inst., 1994—, Bristol-Myers Squibb, 1994-2001 Mem. ACP, Am. Fedn. Clin. Rsch. (med. sch. rep., endo/metabolism subspecialty coun.), Am. Soc. Hypertension, Am. Diabetes Assn., Assn. Program Dirs. in Internal Medicine, Assn. Clerkship Dirs. in Internal Medicine, S.D. State Med. Assn., Seventh Dist. Med. Soc., Wilderness Med. Soc. (mem. environ. coun.). Office: U SD Sch Med 1400 W 22nd St Sioux Falls SD 57105-1505

TRURAN, JAMES WELLINGTON, JR. astrophysicist, educator; b. Brewster, N.Y., July 12, 1940; s. James Wellington and Suzanne (Foglesong) T.; m. Carol Kay Dell'Acy, June 26, 1965; children— Elaina Michelle, Diana Lee, Anastasia Elizabeth. B.A. in Physics, Cornell U., 1961; M.S. in Physics, Yale U., 1963, Ph.D. in Physics, 1966. Postdoctoral rsch. assoc. NAS-NRC Goddard Inst. Space Studies, NASA, N.Y.C., 1965-67; asst. prof. physics Belfer Grad. Sch. Sci., Yeshiva U., 1967-70; rsch. fellow in physics Calif. Inst. Tech., 1968-69; assoc. prof. Belfer Grad. Sch. Sci., Yeshiva U., 1970-72, prof., 1972-73; prof. astronomy U. Ill., Urbana, 1973-91; sr. vis. fellow, Guggenheim Meml. Found. fellow Inst. Astronomy, U. Cambridge, Eng., 1979-80; trustee Aspen Ctr. Physics, 1979-85, 91-93, 96-99, v.p., 1985-88; assoc. U. Ill. Ctr. for Advanced Study, 1979-80, 86-87; prof. astronomy astrophysics U. Chgo., 1991—. Alexander von Humboldt-Stiftung sr. scientist Max-Plank Inst., Munich, Germany, 1986-87, 94; Beatrice Tinsley vis. prof. U. Tex., Austin, 1999. Contbr. articles to profl. jours.; co-editor: Nucleosynthesis, 1968, Nucleosynthesis— Challenges and New Developments, 1985, Nuclear Astrophysics, 1987, Type Ia Supernovae: Theory and Cosmology, 2000, Cosmic Chemical Evolution, 2002; editor: Physics Letters B, 1974-80. Co-recipient Yale Sci. and Engring. Assn. annual award for advancement basic or applied sci., 1980 Fellow AAAS, Am. Phys. Soc.; mem. Am. Astron. Soc., Am. Phys. Soc., Internat. Astron. Union. Home: 210 Wysteria Dr Olympia Fields IL 60461-1202 Office: U Chgo Dept Astronomy Astrophysics 5640 S Ellis Ave Chicago IL 60637-1433

TRUSCHKE, EDWARD F. medical association administrator; Formerly with Xerox Corp; past exec. dir. BankAm. Found.; past sr. v.p. social policy, chmn. social policy com., sec. pub. policy com. to bd. dirs., head social policy dept. BankAm. Corp.; pres. Alzheimer's Assn., Chgo., 1994—. Office: Alzheimers Assn 919 N Michigan Ave Ste 1000 Chicago IL 60611-1696

TRUSKOWSKI, JOHN BUDD, lawyer; b. Chgo., Dec. 3, 1945; s. Casimer T. and Jewell S. (Kirk) T.; m. Karen Lee Sloss, Mar. 21, 1970; children: Philip K., Jennifer B. BS, U. Ill., 1967; JD, U. Chgo., 1970. Bar: Ill. 1970, U.S. Dist. Ct. (no. dist.) Ill. 1970, U.S. Tax Ct. 1977. Assoc. Keck, Mahin & Cate, Chgo., 1970-71, 74-78, ptnr., 1978-97, Lord, Bissell & Brook, Chgo., 1997—. Author, editor Callaghan's Federal Tax Guide, 1987. Lt., USNR, 1971-74. Mem. ABA, Ill. State Bar Assn., Chgo. Bar Assn. Republican. Presbyterian. Avocations: model railroading, stamp collecting. Home: 251 Kimberly Ln Lake Forest IL 60045-3862 Office: Lord Bissell & Brook Harris Bank Bldg 115 S Lasalle St Chicago IL 60603-3801

TRUTTER, JOHN THOMAS, consulting company executive; b. Springfield, Ill., Apr. 18, 1920; s. Frank Louis and Frances (Mischler) T.; m. Edith English Woods II, June 17, 1950 (dec.); children: Edith English II, Jonathan Woods. BA, U. Ill., 1942; postgrad., Northwestern U., 1947-50, U. Chgo., 1947-50; LHD (hon.), Lincoln Coll., 1986. Various positions Ill. Bell, Chgo., 1946-58, gen. traffic mgr., from asst. v.p. pub. rels. to gen. mgr., 1958-69, v.p. pub. rels., 1969-71, v.p. operator svcs., 1971-80, v.p.

community affairs, 1980-85; mem. hdqs. staff AT&T, N.Y.C., 1955-57; pres. John T. Trutter Co., Inc., Chgo., 1985—; pres., CEO Chgo. Conv. and Visitors Bur., 1985-88; pres. Chgo. Tourism Coun., 1988-90; v.p. Profl. Impressions Media Group, Inc., 1998-2000, prof. emeritus, 2001. Mem. adv. bd. The Alford Group, Chgo., 1984—, Bozell-Worldwide, Chgo., 1994-96; chancellor Lincoln Acad. of Ill., 1985-2001. Co-author: Handling Barriers in Communication, 1957, The Governor Takes a Bride, 1977 Past chmn., life trustee Jane Addams Hull House Assn.; chmn. United Cerebral Palsy Assn. Greater Chgo., 1967-95, hon. chmn., 1995—, chmn. Canal Corridor Assn., 1991-99; bd. dirs. Chgo. Crime Commn., Abraham Lincoln Assn., Lyric Opera Chgo.; v.p. English Speaking Union, 1989-91, bd. govs., 1980—; chmn. bd. City Colls. Chgo. Found., 1987-91; past chmn. Children's Home and Aid Soc. Ill.; v.p. City Club Chgo.; treas. Chgo. United, 1970-85; mem. Ill. Econ. Devel. Commn., 1985; past presiding co-chmn. NCCJ; numerous others; bd. govs. Northwestern U. Libr. Coun., 1984—; trustee Lincoln (Ill.) Coll., 1987-90, Mundelein Coll., 1988-91; mem. sch. problems coun. State Ill. Assembly, 1985-91, spl. commn. on adminstrn. of justice in Cook County, 1986-92; founding chmn. adv. coun. Evanston Hist. Soc., 1995-98. Lt. col. U.S. Army, 1945. Decorated Legion of Merit; recipient Laureate award State of Ill., 1980, Outstanding Exec. Leader award Am. Soc. Fundraisers, Humanitarian of Yr. award, Jane Addams award The Hull House Assn., 1991, Nat. Infinitec award for individual leadership in assistive technology for disabled people, 1997, Jack Brickhouse award for outstanding svcs., 2000. Mem. Pub. Rels. Soc. Am., Sangamon County Hist. Soc. (founder, past pres.), Ill. State Hist. Soc. (pres. 1985-87), Coun. on Ill. History (chmn. 1991—), U. Ill. Alumni Assn. (bd. dirs. 1990-94), Tavern Club, Econ. Club, Mid-Am. Club, Alpha Sigma Phi (Nat. Merit Achievement award 1994), Phi Delta Phi. Fax: 847-441-0582.

TRYLOFF, ROBIN S. food products executive; BS, U. Mich.; MS, U. Chgo. Office: 3 First Nat Plz Chicago IL 60602-4260

TSALIKIAN, EVA, physician, educator; b. Piraeus, Greece, June 22, 1949; came to U.S., 1974; d. Vartan and Arousiak (Kasparian) T.; m. Arthur Bonfield, Apr. 8, 2000. MD, U. Athens, 1973. Rsch. fellow U. Calif., San Francisco, 1974-76; resident in pediats. Children's Hosp., Pitts., 1976-78, fellow in endocrinology, 1978-80; rsch. fellow Mayo Clinic, Rochester, Minn., 1980-83; asst. prof. pediats. U. Iowa, 1983-87, assoc. prof. pediats., 1987—, dir. pediat. endocrinology, 1988—. Fellow Juvenile Diabetes Found., 1978-80, Heinz Nutrition Found., 1980-81; recipient Young Physician award AMA, 1977. Mem. Am. Diabetes Assn. (mem. bd. mid Am. sect.), Endocrine Soc., Soc. Pediat. Rsch., Lawson Wilkins Soc. for Pediat. Endocrinology, Internat. Soc. Pediat. and Adolescent Diabetes. Home: 206 Mahaska Dr Iowa City IA 52246-1606 Office: U Iowa Dept Pediatrics 2856 JPP Iowa City IA 52242

TSAO, GEORGE T. chemical engineer, educator; b. Nanking, China, Dec. 4, 1931; married; 3 children. BSc, Nat. Taiwan U., 1953; MSc, U. Fla., 1956; PhD in Chem. Engring., U. Mich., 1960. Asst. prof. physics Olivet Coll., 1959-60; chem. engr. Merck & Co., Inc., 1960-61; rsch. chemist TVA, 1961-62; sect. leader hydrolisys and fermentation, rsch. dept. Union Starch & Refining Co. divsn. Miles Labs., Inc., 1962-65, asst. rsch. dir., 1965-66; from assoc. prof. to prof. chem. engring. Iowa State U., 1966-77; prof. chem. engring. Purdue U., West Lafayette, Ind., 1977—, dir. Lab. Renewable Resources Engring., 1978-99. Recipient John Ericsson award Dept. Energy, 1989. Mem. AIChE, Am. Chem. Soc., Am. Soc. Engring. Edn. Office: Purdue U Lab Renewable Resources Engring 1295 Potter Dr West Lafayette IN 47906-1333

TSOULFANIDIS, NICHOLAS, nuclear engineering educator, university official; b. Ioannina, Greece, May 6, 1938; came to U.S., 1963; s. Stephen and Aristea (Ganiou) T.; m. Zizeta Koutsombidou, June 21, 1964; children: Stephen, Lena. BS in Physics, U. Athens, Greece, 1960; MS in Nuclear Engring., U. Ill., 1965, PhD in Nuclear Engring., 1968. Registered profl. engr., Mo. Prof. nuclear engring. U. Mo., Rolla, 1968—, vice chancellor acad. affairs, 1985-86, assoc. dean for rsch. Sch. Mines and Metallurgy, 1989—. Sr. engr. Gen. Atomic Co., San Diego, 1974-75; researcher Cadarache France, 1986-87. Author: Measurement and Detection of Radiation, 1984, 2d edit. 1995; co-author: Nuclear Fuel Analysis and Management, 1990; editor: Nuclear Technology, 1997, 2nd edit., 1999. Mem. Am. Nuclear Soc. (chmn. radiation protection shielding div. 1987-88), Health Physics Soc., Nat. Soc. Profl. Engring., Rotary. Office: U of Mo Rolla Dept Nuc Engring 1870 Miner Cir Dept Nuc Rolla MO 65409-0001

TSUBAKI, ANDREW TAKAHISA, theater director, educator; b. Chiyoda-ku, Tokyo, Japan, Nov. 29, 1931; s. Ken and Yasu (Oyama) T.; m. Lilly Yuri, Aug. 3, 1963; children: Arthur Yuichi, Philip Takeshi. BA in English, Tokyo Gakugei U., Tokyo, Japan, 1954; postgrad. in Drama, U. Saskatchewan, Saskatoon, Canada, 1958-59; MFA in Theatre Arts, Tex. Christian U., 1961; PhD in Speech & Drama, U. Ill., 1967. Tchr. Bunkyo-ku 4th Jr. High Sch., Tokyo, 1954—58; instr., scene designer Bowling Green (Ohio) State U., 1964—68; asst. prof. speech & drama U. Kans., Lawrence, 1968—73, assoc. prof., 1973—79; vis. assoc. prof. Carleton Coll., Northfield, Minn., 1974; lectr. Tsuda U., Tokyo, 1975; vis. assoc. prof. theatre Tel-Aviv (Israel) U., 1975—76; vis. prof. theatre Mo. Repertory Theatre, Kansas City, Mo., 1976, Nat. Sch. Drama, New Delhi, 1983; prof. theatre, film, east Asian Languages and Cultures U. Kans., Lawrence, 1979—2000, prof. emeritus, 2000—. Dir. Internat. Theatre Studies Ctr., U. Kans., Lawrence, 1971-2000, Operation Internat. Classical Theatre, 1988—; Benedict disting. vis. prof. Asian studies Carleton Coll., 1993; area editor Asian Theatre Jour., U. Hawaii, Honolulu, 1982-94; chmn. East Asian Langs. and Cultures, U. Kans., Lawrence, 1983-90; mem. editl. bd. Studies in Am. Drama, Oxford, Miss., 1985-88. Dir. plays Kanjincho, 1973, Rashomon, 1976, 96, King Lear, 1985, Fujito and Shimizu, 1985, Hippolytus, 1990, Busu and the Missing Lamb (Japan) 1992, Suehirogari and Sumidagawa, 1992, 93, Tea, 1995; choreographed Antigone (Greece), 1987, Hamlet (Germany), 1989, The Resistible Rise of Arturo Ui, 1991, Man and the Masses (Germany), 1993, The Children of Fate (Hungary), 1994, The Great Theatre of the World (Germany); editor Theatre Companies of the World, 1986; contbg. author to Indian Theatre: Traditions of Performance, 1990; contbr. 7 entries in Japanese Traditional plays to the Internat. Dictionary of Theatre, vol. 1, 1992, vol. 2, 1994. Recipient World Univ. Svc. Scholarship U. Saskatchewan, 1958-59, University fellow U. Ill., 1961-62, Rsch. fellow The Japan Found., 1974-75, 90, Rsch. Fulbright grantee, 1983. Fellow Coll. Am. Theatre (elected 2002); mem. Am. Theatre Assn., Asian Theatre Program (chair 1976-79), Assn. for Asian Studies, Assn. Kans. Theatres., Assn. Kans. Theatres U/C Div. (chmn. 1980-82), Assn. for Theatre in Higher Edn., Assn. for Asian Performance. Democrat. Buddhist. Avocations: Ki-Aikido (4th Dan), photography, travel. Home: 924 Holiday Dr Lawrence KS 66049-3005 E-mail: atsubaki@ku.edu.

TUAN, DEBBIE FU-TAI, chemistry educator; b. Kiangsu, China, Feb. 2, 1930; came to U.S., 1958; d. Shiau-gien and Chen (Lee) T.; m. John W. Reed, Aug. 15, 1987. BS in Chemistry, Nat. Taiwan U., Taipei, 1954, MS in Chemistry, 1958, Yale U., 1960, PhD in Chemistry, 1961. Rsch. fellow Yale U., New Haven, 1961-64; rsch. assoc. U. Wis., Madison, 1964-65; asst. prof. Kent (Ohio) State U., 1965-70, assoc. prof., 1970-73, prof., 1973—; vis. scientist Yeshiva U., N.Y.C., summer 1966; rsch. fellow Harvard U., Cambridge, 1969-70; vis. scientist SRI Internat., Menlo Park, Calif., 1981; rsch. assoc. Cornell U., Ithica, N.Y., 1983. Vis. prof. Acad. Sinica of China, Nat. Taiwan U. and Nat. Tsing-Hwa U., summer 1967, Ohio State U., 1993, 95. Contbr. articles to profl. jours. Recipient NSF Career Advanced award, 1994—; U. Grad. fellow Nat. Taiwan U., 1955-58, F.W. Heyl-Anon F fellow Yale U., 1960-61, U. Faculty Rsch. fellow Kent State U., 1966, 68, 71, 85; Pres. Chiang's scholar Chinese Women Assn., 1954, 58, Grad. scholar in humanity and scis. China Found., 1955. Mem. Am. Chem. Soc., Am. Phys. Soc., Sigma Xi. Office: Kent State U Chemistry Dept Williams Hl Kent OH 44242-0001

TUCKER, DON EUGENE, retired lawyer; b. Rockbridge, Ohio, Feb. 3, 1928; s. Beryl Hollis and Ruth (Primmer) T.; m. Elizabeth Jane Parke, Aug. 2, 1950; children: Janet Elizabeth, Kerry Jane, Richard Parke. B.A., Aurora Coll., 1951; LL.B., Yale, 1956. Bar: Ohio 1956. Since practiced in, Youngstown, Ohio; asso. Manchester, Bennett, Powers & Ullman, 1956-62, ptnr., 1962-73, of counsel, 1973-87; gen. counsel Comml. Intertech Corp., Youngstown, 1973-75, v.p., gen. counsel, 1975-83, also dir., sr. v.p., gen. counsel, 1983-87, sr. v.p., 1987-93; ret., 1993. Solicitor Village of Poland, Ohio, 1961-63; former chmn. bd., pres., trustee United Cerebral Palsy Assn., Youngstown and Mahoning County; trustee Mahoning County Tb and Health Assn.; former trustee, pres. Indsl. Info. Inst.; former pres., trustee Ea. Ohio Lung Assn.; trustee, former chmn. Cmty. Corp.; trustee, former pres. Butler Inst. Am. Art. With USMCR, 1946-48, 51-53. Mem. Ohio Bar Assn., Mahoning County Bar Assn. (pres. 1972, trustee 1970-73), Youngstown Area C. of C. (chmn. bd. dirs. 1979). Methodist. Home: 6005 Martins Point Rd Kitty Hawk NC 27949-3819 Office: Comml Intertech Corp PO Box 239 Youngstown OH 44501-0239

TUCKER, FREDERICK THOMAS, electronics company executive; b. Herkimer, N.Y., May 27, 1940; s. Edmond and Martha R. (Rich) T.; m. Mary McDonald; children: Michael, Lisa. BSEE, Rochester Inst. Tech., 1963. Coop. student designer Delco Products divsn. Gen. Motors, Rochester, N.Y., 1960-65; salesman Motorola, N.Y., N.J., Conn., 1965-70, from prodn. engr. to v.p. divsn. ops. Phoenix, 1970-79, v.p., gen. mgr. power products divsn., 1981-84, v.p., gen. mgr. bipolar i.c. divsn., 1984-87, corp. v.p., asst. gen. mgr. automotive and indsl. electronics group Ill., 1987-88, sr. v.p., gen. mgr. Northbrook, 1988-92, exec. v.p., gen. mgr. automotive and inds. electronics group, 1992-93, exec. v.p., gen. mgr. automotive, energy and controls group, 1993-97, exec. v.p., pres., gen. mgr. automotive, energy, components sector, 1997-98, exec. v.p., pres. automotive, component, computer & energy sector, 1998, exec. v.p., dep. to chief exec. office, 1998—. Patentee in field. Bd. dirs. Jr. Achievement Chgo.; trustee Rochester Inst. Tech., 1986. Named Distinq. Alumnus Coll. Engring., Rochester Inst. Tech., 1983, Outstanding Alumnus Rochester Inst. Tech., 1997; Alumni Honor Roll of Excellence, Rochester Inst. Tech., 1986. Mem. Intelligent Transp. Soc. Am. (chmn. bd. 1993). Republican. Lutheran. Office: Motorola Inc 1303 E Algonquin Rd Schaumburg IL 60196-1079

TUCKER, JOHN MARK, librarian, educator; s. Paul Marlin and Edith T.; m. Barbara Ann Wilson, Mar. 22, 1968. BA, David Lipscomb Coll., 1967; MLS, George Peabody Coll. Tchrs., 1968, specialist in edn., 1972; PhD, U. Ill., 1983. Head libr. Freed-Hardeman Coll., Henderson, Tenn., 1968-71; reference libr. Wabash Coll., Crawfordsville, Ind., 1973-79, Purdue U., West Lafayette, 1979-82, asst. prof. libr. sci., 1979-85, assoc. prof. libr. sci., 1985-89, sr. reference libr. Humanities, Social Sci. and Edn. Libr., 1982-90, prof. libr. sci., 1989—, libr. Humanities, Social Sci. and Edn. Libr., 1990—. Grantee com. on instnl. coop. NEH, 1991-94. Co-editor: Reference Services and Library Education, 1983, User Instruction in Academic Libraries, 1986, American Library History, 1989; editor: Untold Stories: Civil Rights, Libraries and Black Librarianship, 1998; editl. bd.: Dictionary of American Library Biography, 2002; contbr. articles to profl. publs. Thomas S. Wilmeth grantee for innovative excellence, 1988, Frederick B. Artz rsch. grantee Oberlin Coll. Archives, 1991; Coun. on Libr. Resources rsch. fellow, 1990. Mem. ALA (chair Libr. History Round Table 1993-94), SCV, Assn. for Bibliography of History, Assn. Coll. and Rsch. Librs., Disciples of Christ Hist. Soc., Soc. for Historians of the Gilded Age and Prog. Era, So. Hist. Assn., Friends of Univ. Ill. Libr., Phi Kappa Phi, Beta Phi Mu. Democrat. Mem. Chs. of Christ. Home: 1055 Southernview Dr S Lafayette IN 47909-3797 Office: Purdue U Humanities Social Sci & Edn Libr 1530 Stewart Ctr West Lafayette IN 47907-1530 E-mail: jmark@purdue.edu.

TUCKER, KEITH A. investment company executive; b. 1945; BBA, U. Tex., 1967, JD, 1970. With KPMG Peat Marwick, Dallas, 1970-85, Stephens, Inc., Little Rock, 1985-87, Trivest Inc., Miami, Fla., 1987-91; dir. Waddell & Reed Inc., Shawnee Mission, Kans., 1989—, vice chmn., 1991—, chmn. Office: Waddell & Reed Inc 6300 Lamar Ave Shawnee Mission KS 66202-4200

TUCKER, MICHAEL, elementary school principal; Prin. Grace Abbott Elem. Sch., Omaha, 1982—. Recipient Elem. Sch. Recognition award U.S. Dept. Edn., 1989-90. Office: Grace Abbott Elem Sch 1313 N 156th St Omaha NE 68118-2371

TUCKER, RAYMOND A. chemical company executive; Various positions Bayer Corp., Pitts., 1968-99, sr. v.p. inorganics products; CFO, treas. HB Fuller Co., St. Paul, 1999—. Office: HB Fuller Co 1200 Willow Lake Bvld Saint Paul MN 55110

TUCKER, WATSON BILLOPP, lawyer; b. Dobbs Ferry, N.Y., Nov. 16, 1940; s. Watson Billopp and Mary (Prema) T.; children: Robin, Craig, Christopher, Alexander, John. BS, Northwestern U., Evanston, Ill., 1962; JD magna cum laude, Northwestern U., 1965. Bar: Ill. 1965, U.S. Dist. Ct. (no. dist.) Ill. 1966, U.S. Supreme Ct. 1971, U.S. Dist. Ct. (no. dist.) N.Y. 1976, U.S. Ct. Appeals (2d, 3d, 5th, 6th, 7th, and 9th cirs.). Ptnr. Mayer, Brown & Platt, Chgo., 1972-99, Smith Tucker & Brown, DeKalb, Ill., 1999—. Fellow Am. Coll. Trial Lawyers. Office: Smith Tucker & Brown 115 N 1st St Dekalb IL 60115-3201 E-mail: wbtucker@smithtuckerbrown.com.

TUCKMAN, BRUCE WAYNE, educational psychologist, educator, researcher; b. N.Y.C., Nov. 24, 1938; s. Jack Stanley and Sophie Sylvia (Goldberg) T.; children: Blair Z., Bret A. BS, Rensselaer Poly. Inst., 1960; MA, Princeton U., 1962, PhD, 1963. Rsch. assoc. Princeton (N.J.) U., 1963; rsch. psychologist Naval Med. Rsch. Inst., Bethesda, Md., 1963-65; assoc. prof. edn. Rutgers U., New Brunswick, N.J., 1965-70; prof., 1970-78; dir. Bur. Rsch. and Devel.-Rutgers U., New Brunswick, 1975-78; dean Coll. Edn. Baruch Coll., CUNY, 1978-82; sr. rsch. fellow CUNY, 1982-83; dean Coll. Edn. Fla. State U., Tallahassee, 1983-86, prof., 1983—98; prof. dir. acad. learning lab. Ohio State U., Columbus, 1998—. Author: Preparing to Teach the Disadvantaged, 1969 (N.J. Assn. Tchrs. of English Author's award 1969), Conducting Educational Research, 1972, 5th rev. edit., 1999 (Phi Delta Kappa Rsch. award 1973), Evaluating Instructional Programs, 1979, 2d rev. edit., 1985, Analyzing and Designing Educational Research, 1979, Effective College Management, 1987, Testing for Teachers, 1988; (novel) Long Road to Boston, 1988, Educational Psychology: From Theory to Application, 1992, 96, 98, 2002, Learning and Motivation Strategies: Your Guide to Success, 2002. Rsch. dir. Task Force on Competency Stds. Trenton, N.J., 1976. N.Y. State Regents scholar, 1956; Kappa Nu grad. scholar, 1960; NIMH predoctoral fellow, 1961, 62; Rutgers U. faculty study fellow, 1974-75 Fellow APA, Am. Psychol. Soc.; mem. Am. Ednl. Rsch. Assn. Office: 250B Younkin Success Ctr 1640 Neil Ave Columbus OH 43201-2333

TUCKNER, MICHELLE, newscaster; b. Hudson, Wis. BS in Journalism/Broadcast News, U. Kans. Weekend news reporter KTKA, Topeka; anchor/reporter WEAU-TV Channel 13, 2000—. Recipient award, Kans. Assn. Broadcasters, William Randolph Hearst Journalism awards; scholar, Assn. for Women in Sports Media, 1999. Office: WEAU PO Box 47 Eau Claire WI 54702

TUCKSON, REED V. academic administrator; Pres. Charles R. Drew U., L.A.; sr. v.p. profl. stds. AMA, Chgo., 1998—. Office: AMA 515 N State St Chicago IL 60610-4325

TULLY, ROBERT GERARD, lawyer; b. Dubuque, Iowa, Sept. 7, 1955; s. Thomas Alois and Marjorie May (Fosselman) T. BA, U. Notre Dame, 1977; postgrad., U. Notre Dame, London, summer 1979; JD, Drake U., 1981. Bar: Iowa 1981, U.S. Dist. Ct (no. and so. dists.) Iowa 1981, U.S. Ct. Appeals (8th cir.) 1981, U.S. Supreme Ct. 1986. Assoc. Verne Lawyer & Assocs., Des Moines, 1981-93, Michael J. Galligan Law Firm; ptnr. Galligan, Tully, Doyle & Reid P.C., 1993—. Bd. dirs. Dubuque Lumber Co., sec., treas., 1984-87; lectr. Nat. Collegiate Mock Trial Drake U., Des Moines, 1984-93, atty., coach, 1985-93; bd. counselors Drake U. Law Sch., 1986-92, chmn. alumni rels. com. Contbr. articles to profl. jours. Com. mem. Dubuque County Dem. party, 1976-78, Polk County Dem. party, 1982-83, 87-89, 92—, del. state convs., 1988, chmn. IA Dem. Party, 1999—; bd. dirs. nat. Coun. Alcoholism and Other Drug Dependencies for Des Moines Area, pres. 1985-92; mem. nat. commn. on future of Drake U.; Dem. candidate for U.S. Congress 2d Dist., 1998; chmn. Iowa Dem., 1999-2001. Fellow Iowa Acad. Trial Lawyers (compiler various profl. publs.); mem. ABA, ATLA (state del. 1991—, bd. govs. 1993—, mem. key peron com.), Iowa Bar Assn. (Uniform Jury Instructions rules com., young lawyers sect., com. legal svcs. for elderly chmn. fed. practice com., law related edn. com.), Assn. Trial Lawyers Iowa (pres. 1992-93, pres.-elect 1991-92, v.p. legis. 1988-91, bd. govs. 1985—, Outstanding Key Person 1983-84, 91-92, chmn. key person com. 1985-88), Polk County Bar Assn. (bd. dirs. 1993—, grievance com.), Iowa Citizens Action Network (bd. dirs. 1989-98), Blackstone Inn of Ct., Notre Dame Club of Des Moines (pres. 1981-83), Drake Student Bar Assn. (pres. 1980-81), Phi Alpha Delta. Roman Catholic. Home: 4315 Greenwood Dr Des Moines IA 50312 Office: Galligan Tully Doyle and Reid PC 300 Walnut St Des Moines IA 50309-2249 E-mail: rtully@galliganlaw.com.

TUMA, JOHN, former state legislator, lawyer; b. Sept. 25, 1962; m. Wendy Tuma; 1 child. BA, Mankato State U.; JD, U. Minn. Bar: Minn. Mem. Minn. Ho. of Reps., St. Paul, 1994—. Independent-Republican.

TUNHEIM, JAMES RONALD, state legislator, farmer; b. Drayton, N.Dak., June 6, 1941; s. Olaf and Grace (Doran) T.; m. Diana Lee Rojas, 1964; children: Christopher Alan, Aaron Cory, Nicolle Anne. Student, Thief River Falls Vocat. Sch., 1959-61. Owner, mgr. James Tunheim Farms, Kennedy, Minn., 1964—; mem. Minn. Ho. of Reps., St. Paul, 1982—. Vice chmn. commerce and econ. devel. tourism divsn., mem. regulated industry, edn., ethics, and transp. coms. Treas. Kennedy (Minn.) Sch. Dist., 1975; del. Minn. Dem. Conv., 1978; past chmn. Kittson County (Minn.) Dem.-Farmer-Labor Com.; mem. bd. Maria Luth. Ch., 1975. Mem. Nat. Rural Water Assn., Minn. Rural Water Assn. (bd. dirs. 1978), Lions, Masons, Shriners (sec., treas.). Office: Minn Ho of Reps 509 State Office Bldg Saint Paul MN 55155-1206

TUNHEIM, JERALD ARDEN, academic administrator, physics educator; b. Claremont, S.D., Sept. 3, 1940; s. Johannes and Annie Tunheim; children: Jon, Angie, Alec. BS in Engring. Physics, S.D. State U., 1962, MS in Physics, 1964; PhD in Physics, Okla. State U., 1968. Vis. scientist Sandia Corp., Albuquerque, 1970-71, Ames (Iowa) AEC Labs., 1972; asst. prof. S.D. State U., Brookings, 1968-73, assoc. prof., 1973-78, prof., 1978-80, prof., head physics dept., 1980-85; dean Ea. Wash. U., Cheney, 1985-87; pres. Dakota State U., Madison, S.D., 1987—. Bd. dirs. NSF Systemic Initiative, Nat. Skill Stds. Bd., 1998—. Co-author: Elementary Particles and Unitary Symmetry, 1966, Quantum Field Theory, 1966; contbr. articles to profl.jours. Bd. dirs. Lake Area Improvement Corp. Grantee USDA, 1987-88, S.D. Govt. Office Edn. Devel., 1988-89, U.S. Dept. Edn., Eisenhower Program, 1985-86, 87-90, 92-93, 95-96, U.S. Dept. Edn. Math. and Sci. Program, 1989-92; named Tchr. of Yr. S.D. State U., 1972. Mem. NSPE, Am. Phys. Soc., Am. Assn. Physics Tchrs., Madison C. of C. (bd. dirs. 1990—), Rotary. Republican. Lutheran. Office: Dakota State U Office of President 820 N Washington Ave Madison SD 57042-1799 E-mail: Jerald.Tunheim@dsu.edu.

TUNHEIM, KATHRYN H. public relations executive; b. Sacred Heart, Minn., 1956; BA in Polit. Sci., U. Minn., 1979. Staff asst. U.S. Senator Wendell Anderson, 1977-79; mgr., bus. planning NCR Comten, 1979-81; corp. pub. rels. mgr. Honeywell, 1981-84, dir. corp. pub. rels., 1985-86; v.p. pub. rels. and internal comm. Honeywell Inc., 1987-90; pres., CEO Tunheim Santrizos, Mpls., 1990—. Office: Tunheim Santrizos 1100 Riverview Tower 8009 34th Ave S Minneapolis MN 55425-1608

TUPPER, LEON F. manufacturing company executive; BS in Indsl. Psychology, Wayne State U.; MS in Indsl. Psychology, U. Mich.; postgrad., Dartmouth U. Tng. mgr. Am. Motors Corp., Detroit, 1972-77, buyer/procurement specialist, 1977-83, sr. buyer interior trim group, 1983-86, purchasing mgr. interior trim group, 1986-88; sales mgr. steering divsn. Sheller-Globe Corp., Toledo, 1984-88; dir. sales and engring. Gilreath Mfg., Inc., Howell, Mich., 1988-91, pres., CEO, owner, 1991—. Trustee Cleary Coll., Ypsilanti, Mich.; treas., trustee High/Scope Edn. Rsch. Found.; bd. trustees Rehab. Inst. of Mich., Detroit Med. Ctr.; bus. sch. bd. exec. advisors Wayne State U.; mem. friends of the Detroit Area Pre-Coll. Engring. Program, Nat. Conf. for Cmty. Justice, 100 Black Men of Detroit. Office: Gilreath Manufacturing Inc 15565 Northland Dr W Ste 812 Southfield MI 48075-5325 also: PO Box 408 Howell MI 48844-0408 Fax: 248-728-1753.

TURANO, DAVID A. lawyer; b. Ashtabula, Ohio, Sept. 9, 1946; s. Egidio A. and Mary Agnes (Bartko) T.; m. Karen J. Emmel, Aug. 29, 1970; children: Aaron, Thad, Bethen, Kyle. BS, Kent State U., 1968; JD, Ohio State U., 1971. Bar: Ohio 1971. Staff atty. The Pub. Utilities Commn. Ohio, Columbus, 1971-72; assoc., then ptnr. George, Greek, King, McMahon and Mcconnaughey, 1972-79; ptnr. Baker & Hostetler, 1979-96, Harris, Carter, Mahota, Turano & Mazza, Columbus, 1996-97, Harris, Turano & Mazza, Columbus, 1997—. Mem. ABA, Ohio State Bar Assn., Columbus Bar Assn., Transp. Lawyers Assn. Roman Catholic. Office: Harris Turano & Mazza 941 Chatham Ln Ste 201 Columbus OH 43221-2416

TURKEVICH, ANTHONY LEONID, chemist, educator; b. N.Y.C., July 23, 1916; s. Leonid Jerome and Anna (Chervinsky) T.; m. Ireene Podlesak, Sept. 20, 1948; children: Leonid, Darya. B.A., Dartmouth Coll., 1937, D.Sc., 1971; Ph.D., Princeton U., 1940. Research assoc. spectroscopy physics dept. U. Chgo., 1940-41; asst. prof., research on nuclear transformations Enrico Fermi Inst. and chemistry dept., 1946-48, assoc. prof., 1948-53, prof., 1953-86, James Franck prof. chemistry, 1965-70, Distinguished Ser. prof., 1970-86, prof. emeritus, 1986. War research Manhattan Project, Columbia U., 1942-43, U. Chgo., 1943-45, Los Alamos Sci. Lab., 1945-46; Participant test first nuclear bomb, Alamagordo, N.Mex., 1945, in theoretical work on and test of thermonuclear reactions, 1945— , chem. analysis of moon, 1967— ; cons. to AEC Labs.; fellow Los Alamos Sci. Lab., 1972— Del. Geneva Conf. on Nuclear Test Suspension, 1958, 59. Recipient E.O. Lawrence Meml. award AEC, 1962; Atoms for Peace award, 1969 Fellow Am. Phys. Soc.; mem. N.Y. Acad. Sci. (Pregel award 1988), AAAS, Am. Chem. Soc. (nuclear applications award 1972), Am. Acad. Arts and Scis. Mem. Russian Orthodox Greek Cath. Ch. Clubs: Quadrangle, Cosmos. Home: Apt 1021 160 Kendal Dr Lexington VA 24450-1792

TURLEY, MICHAEL ROY, lawyer; b. St. Louis, Mar. 7, 1945; s. W. Richard and Mary Jeanne (Ogle) T.; m. Patricia Ederle, Aug. 21, 1968; children: James, Alisyn. AB, Princeton U., 1967; JD, Mo. U., 1970. Bar: Mo. 1970, U.S. Dist. Ct. (ea. dist.) Mo. 1975. Assoc. Lewis, Rice & Fingersh (formerly Lewis & Rice), St. Louis, 1970-71, 74-80, ptnr., 1980—. Mem. Jefferson County Planning and Zoning Commn., 1987—2000; bd. dirs., sec.-treas. Ctr. for Emerging Techs. Mem. ABA, Mo. Bar Assn., St. Louis Met. Bar Assn., Princeton Club. Episcopalian. Office: Lewis Rice & Fingersh 500 N Broadway Ste 2000 Saint Louis MO 63102-2147 E-mail: mturley@lewisrice.com.

TURNBULL, ANN PATTERSON, special educator, consultant, research director; b. Tuscaloosa, Ala., Oct. 19, 1947; d. H. F. and Mary (Boone) Patterson; m. H. Rutherford Turnbull III, Mar. 23, 1974; children: Jay, Amy, Kate. BS in Edn., U. Ga., 1968; MEd, Auburn U., 1971; EdD, U. Ala., 1972. Asst. prof. U. N.C., Chapel Hill, 1972-80; prof., co-dir. Beach Ctr. U. Kans., Lawrence, 1980—. Cons. Dept. Edn., Washington, 1987—, Australian Soc. for Study of Intellectual Disability, Adelaide and Washington, 1990. Author: Free Appropriate Public Education, 2000, Exceptional Lives: Special Education in Today's Schools, 2001, Families, Professionals and Exceptionality, 2001. Recipient Rose Kennedy Internat. Leadership award, Kennedy Found., 1990, 20th Century award in Mental Retardation, 1999; Joseph P. Kennedy Jr. Found. fellow, 1987-88. Mem.: Internat. League Socs. for Persons with Mental Handicaps (com. chair 1986—90), The Arc-U.S. (named Educator of Yr. 1982), Am. Assn. on Mental Retardation (bd. dirs. 1986—88, v.p. 2001, pres.-elect 2002). Democrat. Avocations: travel, exercise. Home: 1636 Alvamar Dr Lawrence KS 66047-1714 Office: Univ Kans Beach Ctr 3136 1200 Sunnyside Dr Lawrence KS 66045-7534 E-mail: aturnbull@ku.edu.

TURNBULL, H. RUTHERFORD , III, law educator, lawyer; b. N.Y.C., Sept. 22, 1937; s. Henry R. and Ruth (White) T.; m. Mary M. Slingluff, Apr. 4, 1964 (div. 1972); m. Ann Patterson, Mar. 23, 1974; children: Jay, Amy, Katherine. Grad., The Kent (Conn.) Sch., 1955; BA, Johns Hopkins U., 1959; LLB with hon., U. Md., 1964; LLM, Harvard U., 1969. Bar: Md., N.C. Law clerk to Hon. Emory H. Niles Supreme Bench Balt. City, 1959-60; law clerk to Hon. Roszel C. Thomsen U.S. Dist. Ct. Md., 1962-63; assoc. Piper & Marbury, Balt., 1964-67; prof. Inst. Govt. U. N.C., Chapel Hill, 1969-80, U. Kans., Lawrence, 1980—. Prof. spl. edn., courtesy prof. law U. Kans. Editor-in-chief Md. Law Review. Cons., author, lectr., co-dir. Beach Ctr. on Families and Disability, U. Kans.; pres. Full Citizenship Inc., Lawrence, 1987-93; spl. staff-fellow U.S. Senate subcom. on disability policy, Washington, 1987-88; bd. dirs. Camphill Assn. N.Am., Inc., 1985-87; trustee Judge David L. Bazelon Ctr. Mental Health Law, 1993-2000, chmn., 1999—. With U.S. Army, 1960-65. Recipient Nat. Leadership award Nat. Assn. Pvt. Residential Resources, 1988, Nat. Leadership award Internat. Coun. for Exceptional Children, 1996, Nat. Leadership award Am. Assn. on Mental Retardation, 1997, Century award Nat. Trust for Hist. Preservation in Mental Retardation, 1999; named Nat. Educator of Yr., ARC, 1982; Public Policy fellow Joseph P. Kennedy, Jr. Found., 1987-88. Fellow Am. Assn. on Mental Retardation (pres. 1985-86, bd. dirs. 1980-86); mem. ABA (chmn. disability law commn. 1991-95), U.S.A. As sn. for Retarded Citizens (sec. and dir. 1981-83), Assn. for Persons with Severe Handicaps (treas. 1988, bd. dirs. 1987-90), Nat. Assn. Rehab. Rsch. and Tng. Ctrs. (chair govt. affairs com. 1990-93), Internat. Assn. Scientific Study of Mental Deficiency, Internat. League of Assns. for Persons with Mental Handicaps, Johns Hopkins U. Alumni Assn. (prs. N.C. chpt. 1977-79). Democrat. Episcopalian. Home: 1636 Alvamar Dr Lawrence KS 66047-1714 Office: U Kans 3111 Haworth Hall 1200 Sunnyside Ave Lawrence KS 66045-7534 E-mail: Rud@ku.edu.

TURNER, ARTHUR L. state legislator; b. Chgo., Dec. 2, 1950; m. Rosalyn Turner; 2 children. BS, Ill. State U.; MS, Lewis U. Ill. state rep. Dist. 9, 1981—; vice chmn. consumer protection, higher edn. Ill. Ho. Reps., ins., labor and com. revenue, chmn. housing com., health care, ins. com., dep. majority leader; treas. Ill. Minority Caucus, 1987—. Exec. com. Nat. Conf. of Black State Legislators, 1987-89; mem. housing com. Nat. Conf. of State Legislators, 1987-89; mem. NCSL, Reapportionment Task Force, 1988—; vice chmn. edn. com., 1989—. Mem. Lawndale Cmty. Econ. Devel. Corp.; active Operation Brotherhood, YMCA. Mem. NAACP, Urban League. Home: 2102 S Avers Ave Chicago IL 60623-2467 Office: Ill House of Reps State Capitol Springfield IL 62706-0001

TURNER, BARBARA A. dance company executive; b. Louisville; BA, U. Ky.; MA, U. Louisville. Dir. devel. Ballet Internat., Indpls., now mng. dir. Office: Ballet Internat 502 N Capitol Ave Ste B Indianapolis IN 46204-1204

TURNER, EVAN HOPKINS, retired art museum director; b. Orono, Maine, Nov. 8, 1927; s. Albert Morton and Percie Trowbridge (Hopkins) T.; m. Brenda Winthrop Bowman, May 12, 1956; children: John, Jennifer. A.B. cum laude, Harvard U., 1949, M.A., 1950, Ph.D., 1954; hon. degree, Swarthmore Coll., Sir George Williams U., Cleve. State U.; Case Western Res. U., 2001. Head docent svc. Fogg Mus., Cambridge, Mass., 1950-51; curator Robbins Art Collection of Prints, Arlington, 1951; teaching fellow fine arts Harvard U., 1951-52; lectr., research asst. Frick Collection, N.Y.C., 1953-56; gen. curator, asst. dir. Wadsworth Atheneum, Hartford, Conn., 1956-59; dir. Montreal Mus. Fine Arts, Que., Can., 1959-64, Phila. Mus. Art, 1964-77, Ackland Art Mus., 1978-83, Cleve. Mus. Art, 1983-93. Adj. prof. art history U. Pa., U. N.C., Chapel Hill, 1978-83; disting. vis. prof. Oberlin Coll., 1993-95. Author: Ray K. Metzker: Photographs, 2001. Recipient Chevalier L'Ordre Arts Lettres. Mem. Assn. Art Mus. Dirs., Coll. Art Assn. Am., Am. Mus. Assn., Century Assn. Club. Home: 2125 Cypress St Philadelphia PA 19103-6507

TURNER, FRED L. fast food company executive; b. 1933; married. B.S., Drake U., 1954. With McDonald's Corp., Oak Brook, Ill., 1956—, exec. v.p., 1967—68, pres., chief adminstrv. officer, 1968—73, CEO, 1973—87, chmn., 1977—90, now sr. chmn., 1990, also bd. dirs., 1968—. Bd. dirs. Baxter Internat. Inc., Aon Corp. W.W. Grainger, Inc. US Army, 1954-56. Office: McDonald's Corp One Kroc Dr Oak Brook IL 60523

TURNER, HAROLD EDWARD, education educator; b. Hamilton, Ill., Nov. 22, 1921; s. Edward Jesse and Beulah May (White) T.; m. Catherine Skeeters, Apr. 5, 1946; children: Michele Turner Nimerick, Thomas, Barbara Turner McMahon, Krista Turner Landgraf. A.B., Carthage Coll., 1950; M.S., U. Ill. - Urbana, 1951, Ed.D. (George Peabody fellow), 1956. Tchr. Taylorville (Ill.) Jr. H.S., 1951-52, Moline (Ill.) Jr. H.S., 1952-54; dir. elem. edn. Jefferson County, Colo., 1955-57; prin. Jefferson County H.S., 1957-60; asst. prof. edn. North Tex. State U., Denton, 1960-63; asst. supt. curriculum Sacramento City Schs., 1963-66; assoc. prof., chmn. dept. curriculum and instrn. U. Mo., St. Louis, 1966-69, prof., 1971-85, prof. emeritus, 1985—, chmn. dept. adminstrn., founds., secondary edn., 1977-78, dept. chmn., 1983-85. Vis. prof. Adams State Coll., Alamosa, Colo., 1959, U. Ga., Athens, 1981-82; adj. prof. NYU, 1965, U. Ill., 1980; cons. various sch. dists., Tex., Mo.; spl. cons. Mo. State Dept. Edn., 1973. Author: (with Adolph Unruh) Supervision for Change and Innovation, 1970; contbr. articles to profl. jours. Served with USNR, 1942-46. Mem. Profs. Supervision. Presbyterian (elder). Home: 685 S La Posada Cir # 1202 Green Valley AZ 85614 E-mail: gazvk@aol.com.

TURNER, HARRY EDWARD, lawyer; b. Mt. Vernon, Ohio, Dec. 25, 1927; s. Paul Hamilton and Harriett (Krafft) T.; m. Shirley Marilyn Eggert, July 8, 1950; children: Harry Edward, Thomas Frederick (dec. Mar. 1995). B.A., Baldwin Wallace Coll., 1951; J.D., Ohio No. U., 1954. Bar: Ohio 1954, U.S. Supreme Ct. 1966. Practice in Mt. Vernon, 1954—; state rep. Ohio Gen. Assembly, 1973-85; solicitor Mt. Vernon, 1958-62. Prosecutor Mt. Vernon Municipal Ct., 1955-58 Mem. Mt. Vernon City Sch. Bd., 1964-70, pres., 1965-70; trustee Ohio Sch. Bd. Assn., 1968-70, Hannah Browning Home, 1987—, Sta. Break/Commn. on Planning Svcs., 1989-95; mem. Knox County Pub. Defender Commn., 1987-91. With USN, 1946-47. Mem. Ohio State Bar Assn., Knox County Bar Assn. (pres. 1970), Alpha Sigma Phi, Sigma Delta Kappa. Republican. Lutheran. Home: 1575 Yauger Rd Apt 15 Mount Vernon OH 43050-8299 Office: 118 E High St Mount Vernon OH 43050-3443

TURNER, JOHN, company executive; Exec. v.p. The LTV Corp., Cleve., 1999—. Office: The LTV Corp PO Box 6778 Cleveland OH 44101-1778

TURNER, JOHN GOSNEY, insurance company executive, director; b. Springfield, Mass., Oct. 3, 1939; s. John William and Clarence Oma (Gosney) T.; m. Leslie Corrigan, June 23, 1962; children: John Fredric, Mary Leslie, James Gosney, Andrew William. B.A., Amherst Coll., 1961; student, Advanced Mgmt. Program, Harvard U., 1980. Assoc. actuary Monarch Life Ins. Co., Springfield, Mass., 1961-67; group actuary Northwestern Nat. Life Ins. Co., Mpls., 1967-75, sr. v.p. group, 1975-79, sr. v.p., chief actuary, 1979-81, exec. v.p., chief actuary, 1981-83, pres., chief operating officer, 1983—; chmn., CEO Northwestern Nat. Life Ins. Co. (now ReliaStar Fin. Corp.), 1993—. Dir. NWNL Reins. Co., NWNL Gen. No. Life, North Atlantic Life Ins. Co. N.Y. Trustee Abbott-Northwestern Hosps., Evans Sch. Found.; chmn. Minn. Trustees of the Evans Scholars Found. Fellow Soc. Actuaries; mem. Am. Acad. Actuaries, Western Golf Assn. (dir.), Minn. Golf Assn. Club: Minikahda (Mpls.).

TURNER, JOHN W. state legislator; b. Lincoln, Ill., 1956; m. Kimberly Turner; 1 child, Jack. BA, U. Ill., 1978; JD, DePaul U., 1981. Pub. defender Logan County, 1984-87, state atty., 1988-94; mem. Blue Ribbon Com., Firearm Transfer Inquiry Program, 1992—; Ill. state rep. Dist. 90, 1994—; atty. Kavanagh, Scully Sudow, White & Frederick PC, 1981-82, Turner & Rossi, 1982-87. Bd. dirs. Lincoln YMCA, chmn. fin. com.; active Lincoln Jaycees. Mem. Logan County Tri-Police Assn., Elks, Phi Beta Kappa, Phi Kappa Phi. Office: Wallace Computer Svcs Inc 4600 Roosevelt Rd Hillside IL 60162-2034 also: Ill House of Reps State Capitol Springfield IL 62706-0001

TURNER, LEE, travel company executive; b. 1952; BS, Worcester Polytechnic Inst., 1974; MBA, Dartmouth, 1976. With Baxter Healthcare, Deerfield, Ill., 1976-79, 82-87, Southeastern Pub. Svc. Co., Miami Beach, Fla., 1979-82; exec. v.p. BTI Ams., Inc., Northbrook, Ill., 1987-98; CFO WorldTravel Ptnrs., 1998—. Office: WorldTravel Ptnrs 400 Skokie Blvd Fl 8 Northbrook IL 60062-2816

TURNER, MICHAEL STANLEY, astrophysics educator; b. L.A., July 29, 1949; s. Paul Joseph and Janet Mary (Lindholm) T.; m. Terri Lee Shields, Aug. 1978 (div. Sept. 1980); m. Barbara Lynn Ahlberg, Sept. 10, 1988; children: Rachel Mary, Joseph Lucien. BS in Physics, Calif. Inst. Tech., 1971; MS in Physics, Stanford U., 1973, PhD in Physics, 1978. Enrico Fermi fellow U. Chgo., 1978-80, from asst. to assoc. prof. physics and astronomy and strophysics, 1980-85, prof., 1985—, chmn. dept. astronomy and astrophysics, 1997—, Bruce V. and Diana M. Rauner Disting. Svc. prof., 1998—; scientist Fermi Nat. Accelerator Lab., Batavia, Ill., 1983—. Trustee Aspen (Colo.) Ctr. Physics, 1984—97, pres., 1989—93; Halley lectr. Oxford U., 1994; Klopsteg lectr. Am. Assn. Physics Tchrs., 1999; Neils Bohr lectr. Copenhagen U., 2001. Author: (with E.W. Kolb) The Early Universe, 1990; contbr. over 200 articles to profl. jours. Bd. trustees Ill. Math. Sci. Acad., 1998—. Sloan fellow A.P. Sloan Found., 1983-88, W. Paul fellow Bonn U., 2000. Fellow Am. Acad. Arts and Scis., Am. Phys. Soc. (mem. exec. bd. 1992-94, chmn. publ. oversight com. 1993-94, chmn. nominating com. 1999-2000, Lilienfeld prize 1997); mem. NAS (NRC astronomy astrophysics survey com. 1998-2000, chair NRC com. Physics of Universe, 2000-02), Am. Astron. Soc. (Helen B. Warner prize 1984), Internat. Astron. Union, Sigma Xi. Office: U Chgo Astron & Astrophysics Ctr 5640 S Ellis Ave Chicago IL 60637-1433 E-mail: mturner@oddjob.uchicago.edu.

TURNER, PAUL ERIC, state legislator; m. Cyndy Rush. BS, Taylor U., 1975. Pres., CEO Family Sales Co. & T-3 Investments, Gas City, Ind.; mem. Ind. State Ho. of Reps. Dist. 32, 1982-86, 1994—, mem. elec. and apportionment com., mem. ways and means com. Former state chmn. Am. Legis. Exch. Coun.; mem. small bus. adv. coun. Fed. Res. Bank. Active State Enterprise Zone. Mem. Am. Pyrotechnics Assn., Taylor U. Trojan Club (bd. mem.), Gas City C. of C. (bd. mem.). Office: Ind House of Reps State Capitol Indianapolis IN 46204

TURNER, ROBERT EUGENE, infosystems specialist; b. Ft. Thomas, Ky., July 25, 1962; s. Clarence Eugene and Peggy Anna Mary (Lepper) T. BS in Mathematics, Northern Ky. U., 1985. Programmer Western-So. Life Ins., Cin., 1986, programmer-analyst, 1987-89; sr. program analyst, 1989—. Music dir. High Ave. Bapt. Tabernacle, Ft. Thomas, 1989—. Democrat. Office: Western-So Life Ins 400 Broadway St Cincinnati OH 45202-3312

TURNER, ROBERT LLOYD, state legislator; b. Columbus, Miss., Sept. 14, 1947; s. Roosevelt and Beatrice (Hargrove) T.; m. Gloria Harrell; children: Roosevelt, Robert, Ryan. BS, U. Wis., Racine, 1976. Mgr. French Quarter Restaurant, Racine, 1989; legislator Wis. State Assembly, Madison, 1990—, mem. transp. com. bldg. commn., mem. ways and means com., labor com., fin. institutions com.; minority vice chmn. caucus, highway com. Br. sales mgr. ETG Temporaries, Inc., Racine, 1989—; pub. Communicator News, Racine, 1989—; v.p. Racine Raider Football Team. State chmn. Dem. Black Polit. Caucus, Madison; pres. Bd. Health, Racine; chmn. Wis. State Elections Bd., Madison, 1990; adj. chmn. Racine City Coun., 1976—; chair Econ. Devel. Com., Racine; regional dir. Badger State Games, Racine; active Pvt. Industry Coun. Southeastern Wis., 1988-89, bd. dirs. Racine County Youth Sports Assn.; active Racine Juneteenth Day Com., bd. advisors Big Bros./Big Sisters. Sgt. USAF, 1967-71, Vietnam. Decorated Commendation medal; named Man of Yr. 2d Missionary Bapt. Ch., 1983. Mem. Urban League (pres. bd. dirs.), NAACP (2d v.p.), VFW, Vietnam Vets. Am. (life mem.), Am. Legion, Masons (supreme coun. 33rd degree), Shriners. Home: 36 Mckinley Ave Racine WI 53404-3414 Office: Wis Assembly PO Box 8953 Madison WI 53708-8953

TURNER, RONALD L. information services executive; BS in Aerospace Engring., U. Tenn.; MS in Engring., U. Fla., MIT. Sys. command USAF, 1968—73; with Martin Marietta, 1973—87; pres., CEO GEC Marconi Electronic Sys., 1987—93; chmn., pres., CEO Ceridian Corp., Mpls., 1993—. Bd. dir. Ceridian Corp., FLIR Sys., Inc., Minn. Bus. Partnership, Minn. Mtg.; v.chmn. Electronic Industries Alliance. Office: Ceridian Corp 3311 E Old Shakopee Rd Minneapolis MN 55425-1640

TURNER, WILLIAM V. bank executive; b. Aug. 13, 1932; m. Ann Turner; children: Julie Ann Brown, Joseph William. BS in Bus. and Pub. Adminstrn., U. Mo., 1956. Regional sales and credit mgr. Kraft Foods Co., 1956-60; chief mgmt. assistance sect. Small Bus. Adminstrn., 1961-68; v.p. comml. and consumer lending, exec. v.p., pres., CEO Citizens Bank, 1966-74; pres. Greater So. Bank, Springfield, Mo., 1974-97, chmn., CEO, 1997-99, chmn., 1999—. Dir., vice chmn. Fed. Home Loan Bank Des Moines; dir. Fed. Savs. and Loan Adv. Coun., Washington; com. mem. U.S. Savs. and Loan League, Mo. Savs. and Loan League. Pres. Springfield Area C. of C., Springfield Bapt. Hosp.; pres., mem. Springfield R-12 Sch. Dist.; chmn. Greene County Cancer Crusade, Boy Scouts Am., Campaign Fund Dr. for Mental Retardation; bd. mem. Greene County ARC; dir., pres. Am. Cancer Soc., Greene County; dir., pres. Cox Health Sys. Bd. Dirs.; trustee, chmn. Pres. Club, Drury Coll.; trustee Ozarks Playgrounds Assn., Springfield Boy's Club, S.W. Bapt. Coll.; bd. mem. Springfield Girls Club; dir. Cmty. Found.; treas. exec. com. YMCA; mem. Pub. Safety Com., Mayor's Commn. on Human Rights; chmn. Better Bus. Bur. S.W. Mo. Recipient Civic Contbr. award North Springfield Betterment Assn., Springfieldian award, 1979. Office: Great So Bank PO Box 9009 Springfield MO 65808-9009

TUROW, SCOTT F. lawyer, writer; b. Chgo., Apr. 12, 1949; s. David D. and Rita (Pastron) Turow; m. Annette Weisberg, Apr. 4, 1971; 3 children. BA magna cum laude, Amherst Coll., 1970; MA, Stanford U., 1974; JD cum laude, Harvard U., 1978. Bar: Ill. 1978, U.S. Dist. Ct. (no. dist.) Ill. 1978, U.S. Ct. Appeals (7th cir.) 1979. Asst. U.S. atty. U.S. Ct. Appeals (7th dist.), Chgo., 1978—86; ptnr. Sonnenschein Nath & Rosenthal, 1986—. E.H. Jones lectr. Stanford U., 1972—75. Author: One L.: An Inside Account of Life in the First Year at Harvard Law School, 1977, Presumed Innocent, 1987, The Burden of Proof, 1990, Pleading Guilty, 1993, The Laws of Our Fathers, 1996, Personal Injuries, 1999; contbr. articles to profl. jours. Mem.: Chgo. Coun. Lawyers, Chgo. Bar Assn. Office: Sonnenschein Nath Rosenthal 233 S Wacker Dr Ste 8000 Chicago IL 60606-6491

TUSHMAN, J. LAWRENCE, wholesale distribution executive; Ptnr., mgr. Sherwood Food Distbrs., Detroit. Office: Sherwood Food Distributors 18615 Sherwood St Detroit MI 48234-2813

TUTEN, RICHARD LAMAR, professional football player; b. Perry, Fla., Jan. 5, 1965; BS in Econs., Fla. State U., 1986. Mem. Phila. Eagles, 1989, Buffalo Bills, 1990; punter Seattle Seahawks, 1991-98, St. Louis Rams, 1999—. Named to NFL Pro Bowl, 1994. Office: St Louis Rams One Rams Way Saint Louis MO 63045

TUTTLE, WILLIAM MCCULLOUGH, JR. history educator; b. Detroit, Oct. 7, 1937; s. William McCullough and Geneva (Duvall) T.; m. Linda Lee Stumpp, Dec. 12, 1959 (div.); children: William McCullough III, Catharine D., Andrew S.; m. Kathryn Nemeth, May 6, 1995. BA, Denison U., 1959; MA, U. Wis., 1964, PhD, 1967. Faculty mem. U. Kans., Lawrence, 1967—, prof. history, 1975-2000, intra-univ. prof., 1982-83; sr. fellow in So. and Negro history Johns Hopkins U., 1969-70; Charles Warren fellow Harvard U., Cambridge, Mass., 1972-73; vis. prof. U. Sc., Columbia, 1980; assoc. fellow Stanford Humanities Ctr., 1983-84; rsch. assoc. U. Calif., Berkeley, 1986-88; prof. Am. Studies U. Kans., Lawrence, 2000—. Vis. scholar Radcliffe Coll., 1993-94. Author: Race Riot: Chicago in the Red Summer of 1919, 1970, 2d edit., 1996, W.E.B. Du Bois, 1973, (with David M. Katzman) Plain Folk, 1982, (with others) A People and A Nation, 1982, 6th edit., 2001, "Daddy's Gone to War": The Second World War in the Lives of America's Children, 1993; contbr. chpts. to books, numerous articles to profl. jours. Dem. precinct committeeman, Lawrence, 1980-90. Lt. USAF, 1959-62 Recipient Merit award Am. Assn. for State and Local History, 1972; Younger Humanist fellow NEH, 1972-73, Guggenheim fellow, 1975-76, NEH fellow, 1983-84, rsch. fellow Hall Ctr., 1990, Kemper fellow for tchg. excellence, 1998; grantee Evans, 1975-76, Beveridge, 1982, NEH, 1986-89. Mem. Soc. Am. Historians (elected), Am. Hist. Assn., Orgn. Am. Historians, Am. Studies Assn., Assn. for Study of African Am. Life and History, Lawrence Trout Club, Golden Key (hon.), Omicron Delta Kappa, Phi Beta Delta, Phi Gamma Delta. Home: 713 Louisiana St Lawrence KS 66044-2339 Office: U Kans Dept Am Studies Lawrence KS 66045-0001 E-mail: tuttle@ku.edu.

TWADDLE, ANDREW CHRISTIAN, sociology educator; b. Hartford, Conn., Apr. 21, 1938; s. Paul Holmes and Ruth Bridenbaugh (Christian) T.; m. Sarah A. Wolcott, June 15, 1963; children: Lisa, Kristin. AB, Bucknell U., 1961; MA, U. Conn., 1963; PhD, Brown U., 1968. Instr. sociology Coll. of Holy Cross, Worcester, Mass., 1966-67; instr. preventive medicine Harvard U. Med. Sch., Boston, 1967-69; asst. prof. sociology and community medicine U. Pa., Phila., 1969-71; assoc. prof. sociology and family and community medicine U. Mo., Columbia, 1971-74, prof. sociology, 1974-2000, chmn. dept., 1988-93, prof. emeritus sociology, 2000—. Guest prof. U. Göteborg, Sweden, 1978-79; Fulbright rsch. fellow Linköping U., Sweden, 1993; guest rschr. Uppsala U., Sweden, 1993; vis. prof. Colby Coll., 2000. Author: Sickness Behavior and the Sick Role, 1979; co-author: A Sociology of Health, 1987, Disease, Illness and Sickness, 1994, Salvaging Medical Care, 1994, Health Care Reform in Sweden 1980-1994, 1999. Chair Columbia Bd. Health, 1980-83, Noel P. Gist Internat. Affairs Seminar; co-chair Citizens for Dem. Govt.; health chair Columbia/Boone County LWV. Recipient John Kosa Meml. prize Pergamon Press, Eng., 1974. Mem. Internat. Sociol. Assn., Am. Sociol. Assn., Midwest Sociol. Soc., Muleskinners Club (v.p. 1985-87, 94-95), Soc. Advancement Scandinavian Studies. Democrat. Unitarian-Universalist. Avocations: genealogy, sailing, poetry. Home: 597 Ocean Point Rd Columbia MO 65203-2823 Office: U Mo Dept Sociology 109 Sociology Columbia MO 65211-0001 E-mail: twaddlea@missouri.edu., ansar@gwi.net.

TYER, TRAVIS EARL, library consultant; b. Lorenzo, Tex., Oct. 23, 1930; s. Charlie Earl and Juanita (Travis) T.; m. Alma Lois Davis, Nov. 6, 1951; children: Alan Ross, Juanita Linn. BS, Abilene Christian U., 1952; BLS, U. North Tex., 1959; AdM in LS, Fla. State U., 1969, postgrad., 1969-71. Librarian, tchr. pub. schs., Gail, Lubbock, and Seminole, Tex., 1952-61; with Dallas Pub. Library, 1961-66, coordinator young adult services, 1962-66; library dir. Lubbock Pub. Library, 1966, Lubbock City-County Libraries, 1967-68; grad. library sch. faculty-state personnel coordinator Emporia (Kans.) State U., 1971-72; sr. cons. profl. devel. Ill. State Library, Springfield, 1972-80; exec. dir. Great River Libr. Sys., Quincy, Ill., 1980-94; cons. pub. rels. and comm. Alliance Libr. Sys., 1994-97; ind. libr. cons., 1997—. Lectr. summer workshops Tex. Woman's U., U. Okla., U. Utah, Fla. State U., U. North Tex.; adj. faculty U. Mo., 1986-89; cons. in field; mem. adv. com. Ill. State Libr., 1984-87, 93-96; pres. Resource Sharing Alliance West Ctrl. Ill., Inc., 1981-94, sec., 1994-97; pres. Ill. Libr. System Dirs. Orgn., 1992-94. Contbr. articles to library jours. Inductee U. North Tex. Libr. and Info. Sci. Hall of Fame, 1990. Mem. ALA, Ill. Libr. Assn., Ill. Ctr. for the Book, Friends of Librs. U.S.A., U. North Tex. Sch. Libr. and Info. Sci. (life), Friends Lubbock City-County Librs. (life), Ill. Sch. Libr. MEdia Assn. Democrat. Mem. Ch. of Christ. Home and Office: 2008 S Arrowood Ct Quincy IL 62305-8961

TYLER, SEAN, radio personality; Radio personality KPRS, Kanss City, Mo. Office: Charter Broadcast Group 11131 Colorado Ave Kansas City MO 64137

TYLER, W(ILLIAM) ED, finance company executive; b. Cleve., Nov. 3, 1952; s. Ralph Tyler and Edith (Green) Kauer; m. Vickie Sue Boggs, Feb. 7, 1976; children: Stacia Leigh, Adam William. BS in Elec. Engring., Ind. Inst. Tech., 1974; MBA, Ind. U., 1977; postgrad., Harvard U., 1981; postgrad. in bus., Baruch U., 1988. From electronic engr. to exec. v.p. R.R. Donnelley & Sons Co., Warsaw, 1974—95, exec. v.p & chief tech. officer, 1995—2001; CEO, pres. Moore Corp. Ltd., 2001—, Willoughby Capitol, Lake Forest, Ill., 2001—. E-mail: edtyler1@aol.com.

TYLER, WILLIAM HOWARD, JR. advertising executive, educator; b. Elizabethton, Tenn., May 21, 1932; s. William Howard and Ethel Margaret (Schueler) T.; m. Margery Moss, Aug. 31, 1957; children: William James, Daniel Moss. Student, Iowa State U., 1950-52, U. Iowa, 1952; AB in Lit.,

BJ in Advt., U. Mo., 1958, MA in Journalism, 1966. Advt. mgr. Rolla (Mo.) Daily News, 1958-59; instr. sch. journalism U. Mo., Columbia, 1959-61; copy writer, then v.p. copy dir. D'Arcy Advt. Agy., St. Louis, 1961-67; writer, producer, creative supr. Gardner Advt. Co., 1967-69; sr. v.p., creative dir. D'Arcy, McManus, Masius, 1969-77; exec. v.p., creative dir. Larson Bateman Advt. Agy., Santa Barbara, Calif., 1977-80; v.p. advt. Pizza Hut, Inc., Wichita, Kans., 1980-82; v.p., creative dir. Frye-Sills/Y&R, Denver, 1980; exec. v.p., creative dir. Gardner Advt. Co., St. Louis, 1982-88; exec. v.p., ptnr., creative dir. Parker Group, 1988-91; pres. Tylertoo Prodns., 1991—. Assoc. prof. St. Louis U., 1993—. Mng. editor St. Louis Advt. Mag., 1992-95. Trustee Blackburn Coll., Carlinville, Ill., 1983—84; bd. advisors U. Mo. Journalism Sch., 1986—91. Named AAF 9th Dist. Educator of Yr., 1998. Mem. U. Mo. Alumni Assn. (bd. dirs. 1969-70), Advt. Club Greater St. Louis, Golden Key (hon.), Mensa, Kappa Tau Alpha (hon.). Episcopalian. Office: Saint Louis U Dept Comm 3733 W Pine Blvd Saint Louis MO 63108-3305 E-mail: tylerwh@slu.edu.

TYLEVICH, ALEXANDER V. sculptor, architect, educator; b. Minsk, Belarus, Sept. 12, 1947; came to U.S., 1989; s. Wulf Tylevich and Asia Klebanova; m. Poline M. Dvorkin, Jan. 22, 1981; children: Alexei, Katherine. BA in Arch., Minsk Archtl. Inst., 1965; MA in Arch., Byelorussian Poly. Inst., Minsk, 1971. Prin., sr. arch. Minskprojekt, 1971-84; artist, arch. Fine Arts Found., Minsk, 1984-89; sculptor-arch. Tylevich Arts, St. Paul, 1989—. Prin. works include Vincentian Letter sculpture, DePaul U., Chgo., Blue Springs.Net, Blue Springs, Mo., Letters of Creation, Wayzata, Minn., Montessori's Vision: Through the Eyes of a Child, Lake Country Sch., Mpls., Tree of Life, U. Minn., Mpls., Sculpture Anoka Ramsey C.C., Coon Rapids, Minn. (suspended recognition), Resurrection, Ch. of St. Stephen, Anoka, Minn., Madonna and Child, The Ch. of St. Mary, Alexandria, Minn., Gateway to Belief/Point of Belief, St. Mary's U., Winona, Minn., Thomas Becket, The Cath. Cmty. of Thomas Becket, Eagan, Minn., Tribute to Erich Mendelsohn, FORECAST Pub. Artwork, St. Paul, Zenon Possis, North Meml. Hosp., Mpls., Winona Tech. Coll. Aviation Facility (Minn. Percent for Art in Pub. Pls. program), North Shore Synagogue, Syosset, N.Y., Mt. Zion Temple, St. Paul, St. Paul Sem., St. Joseph Abbey, St. Benedict, La., Mepkin Abbey, S.C., master plan for Ctr. of Minsk, Minsk City Govt. Bldg., Subway Sta., Minsk, pvt. collections, exhibited in group shows at Monumental Art of Byelorussia, Minsk, 1989, Sacred Image, Sacred Text, Nat. Jewish Mus., Washington, 1993, Harvard U. Grad. Sch. Design New Eng., 1993, St. John's U., Collegeville, Minn. Grantee Minn. Met. Regional Arts Coun., 1991, Howard B. Brin Arts Endowment, 1991, FORECAST Pub. Artworks, 1993. Fellow Archtl. Assn. USSR. Home: 1937 Highland Pkwy Saint Paul MN 55116-1350 E-mail: tyleart@aol.com.

TYLKA, GREGORY L. plant pathologist, educator; BS in Biology, California U. Pa., 1983, MS in Biology, 1985; PhD in Plant Pathology, U. Ga., 1990. Asst. prof. dept. plant pathology Iowa State U., Ames, 1990-95, assoc. prof. dept. plant pathology, 1995—. Recipient Prodn. Rsch. award United Soybean Bd., 1998. Mem. Agronomy Soc. Am., Am. Phytopathol. Soc. (Excellence in Ext. award 1999), Am. Soybean Assn., Iowa Soybean Assn., Helminthological Soc. Washington, Soc. Nematologists, Soil Sci. Soc. Am., Sigma Xi, Beta Beta Beta (Outstanding Alumnus award 1992), Gamma Sigma Delta. Achievements include research on the effects of cultural practices and soybean resistance and tolerance on soybean cyst nematode population densities and soybean yields. Office: Iowa State U Dept Plant Pathology 321 Bessey Hall Ames IA 50011 Fax: 515-294-3851. E-mail: gltylka@iastate.edu.

TYNER, HOWARD A. publishing executive, newspaper editor, journalist; b. Milw., May 30, 1943; s. Howard Arthur and Katharine Elizabeth Tyner; m. Elizabeth Jane Adams, May 3, 1969; children: Sophie Elizabeth, Ian Adams. BA, Carleton Coll., 1965; MSJ, Northwestern U., 1967. Sports editor Chippewa Herald-Telegram, Chippewa Falls, Wis., 1965-66; fgn. corr. UPI, Europe, 1967-77; with Chgo. Tribune, 1977—, fgn. corr., 1982-85, fgn. editor Chgo., 1985-88, asst. mng. editor, 1988-90, dep. mng. editor, 1990-92, assoc. editor, 1992-93, v.p., editor, 1993—. Mem. adv. bd. Alfred Friendly Press Fellowships, Washington, 1988—; mem. exec. bd. World Press Inst., 1994—. Mem. Am. Soc. of Newspaper Editors (mem. found. bd. 1994—), Am. Press Inst. (bd. dirs. 1997—), Found. for Am. Comms. (adv. bd. 1997—). Home: 2700 Park Pl Evanston IL 60201-1337 Office: Chgo Tribune Co 435 N Michigan Ave Chicago IL 60611-4066

TYNER, NEAL EDWARD, retired insurance company executive; b. Grand Island, Nebr., Jan. 30, 1930; s. Edward Raymond and Lydia Dorothea (Kruse) T.; children: Karen Tyner Redrow, Morgan. BBA, U. Nebr., 1956. Jr. analyst Bankers Life Nebr., Lincoln, 1956-62, asst. v.p. securities, 1962-67, v.p. securities, treas., 1967-69, fin. v.p., treas., 1970-72, sr. v.p. fin., treas., 1972-83, pres., chief exec. officer, 1983-87, chmn., pres., chief exec. officer, 1987-88, chmn., CEO, 1988-95; pres. Net Cons., Paradise Valley, Ariz., 1995—. Bd. dir. Union Bank & Trust Co. Trustee U. Nebr. Found., Lincoln Found.; bd. govs. Nebr. Wesleyan U. Capt. USMC, 1950-54, Korea. Fellow: CFAs; mem.: Omaha/Lincoln Soc. Fin. Analysts, Mountain Shadows Golf Club. Lutheran. Avocations: tennis, computers. Office: 8225 N Golf Dr Scottsdale AZ 85253-2716

TYNER, WALLACE EDWARD, economics educator; b. Orange, Tex., Mar. 21, 1945; s. Richard D. and Jeanne (Gullahorn) T.; m. Jean M. Young, May 2, 1970; children: Davis, Jeffrey. BS in Chemistry, Tex. Christian U., 1966; MA in Econs., U. Md., 1972, PhD in Econs., 1977. Vol. Peace Corps., India, 1966-68, math, sci., ednl. skill desk chief, 1968-70; grad. teacher asst. U. Md., Balt., 1971-73; assoc. scientist Earth Satellite Corp., Washington, 1973-74; rsch. assoc. Cornell U., Ithaca, N.Y., 1974-77; asst. prof., assoc. prof. natural resource econs. and policy Purdue U., West Lafayette, Ind., 1977-84, prof., asst. dept. head, 1983-88, dept. head, 1989—. Cons. UN Food and Agrl. Orgn., Rome, Office Tech. Assessment, Washington, U.S. Dept. Interior, Washington, OECD, Paris, World Bank, Washington, USDA, Washington. Author: Energy Resources and Economic Development in India, 1978, A Perspective on U.S. Farm Problems and Agricultural Policy, 1987. Mem. Am. Assn. Agrl. Economists, Am. Econs. Assn., Internat. Assn. Agrl. Economist, Sigma Xi, Gamma Sigma Delta. Home: 116 Arrowhead Dr West Lafayette IN 47906-2105 Office: Purdue U Krannert Bldg West Lafayette IN 47907-1145 E-mail: wtyner@purdue.edu.

TYREE, ALAN DEAN, clergyman; b. Kansas City, Mo., Dec. 14, 1929; s. Clarence Tillman and Avis Ora (Gross) T.; m. Gladys Louise Omohundro, Nov. 23, 1951; children: Lawrence Wayne, Jonathan Tama, Sharon Avis. BA, U. Iowa, 1950; postgrad., U. Mo.-Columbia, 1956-58, U. Mo.-Kansas City, 1961-62. Ordained to ministry Cmty. of Christ, 1947. Appointee min., Lawrence, Kans., 1950-52; mission adminstr. (Mission Sanito), French Polynesia, 1953-64; regional adminstr. Denver, 1964-66; mem. Council Twelve Apostles, Independence, Mo., 1966-82, sec., 1980-82, mem. First Presidency, 1982-92; ret. First Presidency, 1992; pastor East 39th Street Congregation Cmty. of Christ, Independence, 2000—02. Mem. Joint Coun. and Bd. Appropriations, 1966-92; originator music appreciation broadcasts Radio Tahiti, 1962-64, Mission Sanito Radio Ministry, 1960-64; instr. Music/Arts Inst., 1992—, Met. C.C.'s, 1994—. Editor: Cantiques des Saints French-Tahitian hymnal, 1965, Exploring the Faith: A Study of Basic Christian Beliefs, 1987; mem. editing com.: Hymns of the Saints, 1981; author: The Gospel Graced by a People: A Biography of Persons in Tahiti, 1993, Evan Fry: Proclaimer of Good News, 1995, Priesthood: For Other's Sake, 1996, God: Getting to Know the Unknown, 1998. Bd. dirs. Outreach Internat. Found., 1979-82, mem. corp. body, 1982-92; mem. corp. body Independence Regional Health Ctr., 1982-92, v.p., 1983-92, bd. dirs., 1984-93; mem. bd. publs. Herald House, 1984-92; mem. corp. body Restoration Trail Found., 1982-92; chmn. Temple Art Com., 1988-94; bd. dirs. Independence Symphony Orch., 1992-96, pres., 1995-96; mem. human rels. commn. city of Independence, 1995-97, chmn., 1996-97. Recipient Elbert A. Smith Meml. award for publ. articles, 1968, 72 Mem. Phi Beta Kappa, Phi Eta Sigma. Home and Office: 3408 S Trail Ridge Dr Independence MO 64055 E-mail: tyree@mail.com.

TYREE, JAMES C. insurance company executive; b. 1957; Grad., Ill. State U., 1979. With Mesirow Ins. Svcs. Inc., Chgo., 1980—, CEO, chmn., CEO, 1994—. Office: Mesirow Ins Svcs Inc 350 N Clark St Chicago IL 60610-4712

TYRRELL, THOMAS NEIL, former metal processing executive; b. Valdosta, Ga., Feb. 5, 1945; s. Thomas W. and Marilynn (Bowler) T.; children from previous marriage: Tracey, Torrey, Taryn; m. Diane Montague, 1995. BA in Bus. Adminstra., Elmhurst Coll., 1967; LLD (hon.), Baldwin-Wallace Coll., 1992. Sales loop trainee Bethlehem (Penn.) Steel Corp., 1967; gen. product sales person Bethlehem Steel Sales Office, Greensboro, N.C., 1968-73; product specialist Bethlehem Steel Corp., 1973-78; v.p. mktg. Raritan River Steel, Perth Amboy, N.J., 1978-86; CEO Am. Steel & Wire Corp., Cuyahoga Hgts., Ohio, 1986-94; vice chmn., CAO Birmingham (Ala.) Steel Corp., 1994-96; pres., ceo Bar Technologies, Inc., 1996-98; ceo Republic Engineered Steels, Akron, Ohio, 1998-99; ceo. Republic Technologies Intl.(merger USS/KOBE, Bar Technologies & Republic Engineered Steels), 1999-00. Bd. dirs. Birmingham Steel Corp. Contbr. articles to profl. jours. Vol. Leadership Cleve., 1987, Baldwin Wallace Coll., 1989—, Elmhurst Coll., 1990—, Ohio Valley Corridor Commn. emeritus, 1990—. Named Entrepreneur of Yr. Northeast Ohio, Venture Inc. mag., 1988; recipient Register award for Bus. and Commerce, Esquire mag., 1988. Mem. Wire Assn. Internat., Cold Finished Bar Inst., Am. Wire Producers Assn., Indsl. Fastener Inst., Concrete Reinforced Steel Inst., Am. Inst. Steel Engrs., Summit Club (Birmingham), Old Overton C. of C. Roman Catholic. Avocations: running, fishing, scuba diving, weight training. Office: Republic Technologies Intl 3770 Embassy Pkwy Akron OH 44333-8367

TYSON, EUGENE, state legislator; b. Omaha, July 26, 1931; m. Barbara Tyson, Apr. 7, 1956 (dec.); children: Ann, Claire, Catherine, Elizabeth, Brian, Joseph. Grad., Creighton U., 1958. Collection mgr. loan ctr. First Nat. Bank Omaha, 1960-68; controller Vulcraft div. Nucor Corp., 1968-73; controller Nucor Steel, 1973-77, sales mgr., 1977-95; mem. Nebr. Legislature from 19th dist., Lincoln, 1996—. Former mem. Norfolk City Coun., Norfolk Planning Commn., Norfolk Libr. Bd. With USAF, 1950-54. Mem. N.E. Nebr. Shooting Assn. (pres.). Home: 2406 Norfolk Ave Norfolk NE 68701-3522 Office: State Capitol Dist 19 PO Box 94604 Rm 1021 Lincoln NE 68509-4604

TYSON, KIRK W. M. management consultant; b. Jackson, Mich., July 2, 1952; s. George Carlton and Wilma Marion (Barnes) T.; m. Terri Lynn Long, Mar. 25, 2000. BBA, Western Mich. U., 1974; MBA, DePaul U., Chgo., 1982. CPA, Ill.; cert. mgmt. cons. Bus. cons. Arthur Andersen & Co., Chgo., 1974-84; v.p. cons. First Chgo. Corp., 1984; chmn. Kirk Tyson Internat., 1984-2000; pres. Corp. Growth Assocs., Chgo., 2001—. Author: Business Planning, 1982, Business Intelligence: Putting It All Together, 1986, Competitor Intelligence: Manual and Guide, 1990, Competition in the 21st Century, 1996, The Complete Guide to Competitive Intelligence, 1998 2d rev. edit. 2002. Pres., Chgo. Jr. Assn. Commerce and Industry Found., 1977-79; active Easter Seals Soc., 1977, Am. Blind Skiing Found., 1977-78, Jr. Achievement, 1976-77, United Way Met. Chgo., 1979-80, Urban Gateways, 1975; Rep. precinct committeeman Downers Grove Twp., 1985-88; treas. St. Charles H.S. Football Booster club, 1994-95. Fellow Soc. Competitive Intelligence Profls.; mem. Rotary Club of Chgo., Alpha Kappa Psi (Disting. Alumni Svc. award 1974-86). Office: Corporate Growth Assocs 30 South Wacker Dr Ste 2200 Chicago IL 60606-7456 E-mail: kirk.tyson@kirktyson.com.

TYSON, ROBERT, state legislator; b. Ottawa, Kans., Sept. 29, 1940; m. Linda Tyson; 2 children. Grad., Ottawa U. Rancher, Linn County; airline pilot TWO, 1966-92; mem. Kans. Senate from 12th dist., Topeka, 1997—. Mem. Young Reps.; mem. com. Ottawa Franklin County; chmn. Bob Dole's 1st U.S. Senate Campaign; mem. Prairie View United Sch. Dist. Mem. Am. Hereford Assn., Kans. Livestock Assn. (Kans. Environ. Stewardship award 1992), Kans. Farm Bur., Ottawa C. of C. Republican. Office: 300 SW 10th Ave Rm 136N Topeka KS 66612-1504

TYSOR, RONALD W. retail executive; CFO Federated Dept. Stores, Inc., Cin., federated vice chmn. fin., real estate, 1990—. Mem. Federated Direct; pres., COO Campeau Corp., 1989. Office: Federated Dept Stores 7 W 7th St Cincinnati OH 45202

TZAGOURNIS, MANUEL, physician, educator, university administrator; b. Youngstown, Ohio, Oct. 20, 1934; s. Adam and Argiro T.; m. Madeline Jean Kalos, Aug. 30, 1958; children: Adam, Alice, Ellen, Jack, George. B.S., Ohio State U., 1956, M.D., 1960, M.S., 1967. Intern Phila. Gen. Hosp., 1960-61; resident Ohio State U., Columbus, 1961-63, chief med. resident, 1966-67, instr., 1967-68, asst. prof., 1968-70, assoc. prof., 1970-74, prof., 1974—, asst. dean Coll. Medicine, 1973-75, assoc. dean, med. dirs. hosps., 1975-80, v.p. health svcs., dean of medicine, 1981-95, v.p. health scis., 1995-99; pvt. practice endocrinology, 1967—; mem. staff Ohio State U. Hosps./James Cancer Hosp. & Rsch. Ctr. Mem. Coalition for Cost Effective Health Services Edn. and Research Group State of Ohio, 1983 Contbg. author: textbook Endocrinology, 1974, Clinical Diabetes: Modern Management, 1980; co-author: Diabetes Mellitus, 1983, 88; contbr. chpts. to books. Citation Ohio State Senate Resolution No. 984, 1989. Capt. U.S. Army, 1962-64; bd. trustees Hellenic Coll./Holy Cross. Recipient Homeric Order of Ahepa Cleve. chpt., 1976, Phys. of Yr. award Hellenic Med. Soc. N.Y., 1989; citations Ohio State Senate and Ho. of Reps., 1975, 83 Mem. AMA, Am. Red Cross (past chair, bd. dirs. ctrl. Ohio 1996—), Assn. Am. Med. Colls., Columbus Med. Assn., Deans' Coun. Mem. Greek Orthodox Ch. Home: 4335 Sawmill Rd Columbus OH 43220-2243 Office: Ohio State U Coll Medicine 1024 Cramblett Hall 456 W 10th Ave Columbus OH 43210-1238

UBER, LARRY R. transportation executive; BA, Pa. State U. With Ingersoll-Rand, 1967-90, pres. Prodn. Equipment Group, 1990-95, pres. Constrn. and Mining Group, 1995-98; pres., CEO, N.Am. Van Lines, Fort Wayne, Ind., 1998—. Office: NAm Van Lines 5001 Us Highway 30 W Fort Wayne IN 46818-9701

UCHIDA, HIROSHI, diagnostic equipment company executive; BA, Brown U.; MA, PhD, Harvard U. Sr. mgmt. positions Arthur D. Little, Bain Cons.; v.p., gen. mgr. Asia-Pacific region Dade Behring, Deerfield, Ill., 1997-99, pres. Asia divsn., 1999—.

UCKO, DAVID ALAN, museum director; b. N.Y.C., July 9, 1948; s. Lawrence L. and Helen H. Ucko; m. Barbara Alice Clark, Aug. 13, 1977; 1 child Aaron. BA, Columbia Coll., N.Y.C., 1969; PhD, MIT, 1972. Asst. prof. chemistry Hostos C.C., CUNY, Bronx, 1972-76, Antioch Coll., Yellow Springs, Ohio, 1976-79, assoc. prof. chemistry, 1979; rsch. coord. Mus. Sci. and Industry, Chgo., 1979-80, dir. sci., 1981-87, v.p., 1986-87; dep. dir. Calif. Mus. Sci. and Industry, L.A., 1987-90; pres. Kansas City (Mo.) Mus., 1990-2000, Sci. City at Union Sta., 1999-2000; exec. dir. Koshland Sci. Mus. and Sci. Outreach, NAS, Washington, 2001—02; guest faculty mus. mgmt. program U. Colo., Boulder, Colo., 2001—. Rsch. assoc., assoc. prof. dept. edn. U. Chgo., 1982—87; adj. staff scientist C. F. Kettering Rsch. Lab., Yellow Springs, 1977—79. Author: (book) Basics for Chemistry, 1982, Living Chemistry, 2d edit.; contbr. articles to profl. jours.; host, prodr. (radio program) Science Alive!, 1983—87, developer numerous mus. exhibits. Apptd. Nat. Mus. Svcs. Bd., 1996; v.p., bd. dirs. Heritage League, Greater Kansas City, 1991—92; mem. Mid. Am. Regional Coun. Regional Amenities Task Force, Kansas City, 1990—96; trustee Mus. Without Walls, 1996—2000, Sci. Pioneers, 2000; bd. dirs. Cultural Alliance Greater Kansas City, 1995—98. Recipient Up and Comers award, Jr. Achievement Mid.-Am., 1992; fellow Woodrow Wilson, 1969, NIH postdoctoral, 1972; grantee, NSF, NEH, U.S. Dept. Edn., Ill. Humanities Coun., 1976—88. Fellow: AAAS (at large sect. Y 1987—93); mem.: Greater Kansas City C. of C. (edn. com. 1993—96), Assn. Sci. Tech. Ctrs. (publs. com. 1984—94, chmn. 1988—94, ethics com. 1994—95, legis. com., chmn. 1996—2000), Phi Lambda Upsilon, Sigma Xi, Alpha Sigma Nu (hon.). Home: 2528 Queen Anne's Ln NW Washington DC 20037

UECKER, BOB, actor, radio announcer, former baseball player, TV personality; b. Milw., Jan. 26, 1935; m. Judy Uecker. Major league baseball player Milw. Braves, Nat. League, 1962, 63; major league baseball player St. Louis Cardinals, 1964, 65, Phila. Phillies, 1966-67, Atlanta Braves, 1967; radio-TV announcer Milw. Brewers, 1971—; commentator ABC Monday Night Baseball, 1976-82; commentator playoff and world series NBC Baseball, 1994-98. Host War of the Start, Bob Ueckers Wacky World of Sports, Saturday Night Live; guest Tim Conway show, Who's the Boss, Peter Marshall Show; appeared in Fatal Instinct. Co-star TV series Mr. Belvedere, ABC-TV, 1985—; guest TV appearances include Late Night with David Letterman, The Tonight Show, Midnight Special, LateLine, 1998; also numerous commls.; author: Catcher in the Wry, 1985; films include: Major League, 1989, Major League 2, 1994, (voice over) Homeward Bound II: Lost in San Francisco, 1996, Major League: Back to the Minors, 1998, Andre the Giant: Larger Than Life, 1999. Recipient Big B.A.T. award Baseball Assistance Team, 1995; inducted Wis. Performing Artists Hall of Fame, 1993, Wis. Broadcasters Assn. Hall of Fame, 1994, Wis. Sports Hall of Fame, 1998. Office: Milw Brewers Baseball Club Milw County Stadium 1 Brewers Way Milwaukee WI 53214-3651

UHDE, THOMAS WHITLEY, psychiatry educator, psychiatrist; b. Louisville, Jan. 6, 1948; s. George Irwin and Maurine U.; m. Marlene Ann Kraus, Oct. 22, 1977; children: Miles August, Katherine Kraus. BS, Duke U., 1971; MD, U. Louisville, 1975. Postdoctoral fellow Yale U., New Haven, 1975-79, chief resident clin. rsch. unit, 1979; rsch. fellow NIMH, 1979-81; pvt. practice in psychiatry Bethesda, Md., 1979-93; clin. adminstr. sect. psychobiology BPB, NIMH, ADAMHA, 1979-80, chief unit on anxiety and affective disorders, 1982-89, chief 3-West clin. rsch. unit, 1980-90, chief sect. on anxiety and affective disorders, 1989-93; asst. clin. prof. Uniformed Svcs. U. Health Scis., 1982-85, assoc. clin. prof. uniformed svcs., 1985-91, clin. prof. psychiatry, 1991—; attending staff Clin. Ctr. NIH, 1982-93; chmn. dept. psychiatry Detroit Receiving Hosp. and Harper Hosp., 1994-98; psychiatrist in chief Detroit Med. Ctr., 1993—2001; clin. prof. Uniformed Svcs. U. Health Scis. Sch. Medicine, Bethesda, 1991—; chmn. dept. psychiatry and behavioral neuroscis. Wayne State U. Sch. Medicine , Detroit, 1993—2001; prof. dept. pharmacology Wayne State U. Sch. of Medicine , 1993—. Prof., psychiatry and behavioral neuroscis. dept., Wayne State U. Sch. Medicine, 1993-, assoc. dean rsch. and grad. programs, 1999-2001; asst. dean neuroscis., 2001-; mem. sci. adv. com. Bethesda, Md., 1990—; cons. Rsch. Scientist Devel. Rev. Com., HHS, ADAMHA, 1983—, Career Devel. Program Awards Com., VA, Washington, 1986, Primary Care Rsch. Program, ADAMHA, 1988; exec. bd. Anxiety Disorders Assn. Am., 1991-93, 99-, chair sci. adv. bd., Rockville, Md., 1991-93. Editor-in-chief (jour.) Anxiety; editor-in-chief Depression and Anxiety; mem. editl. bd. Actualities Medicales Internationales en Psychiatrie, 1983, Jour. Affective Disorders, 1986, Jour. Anxiety Disorders, 1987-95, Biol. Psychiatry, 1998—; contbr. more than 300 sci. articles to profl. jours. Capt. USPHS, 1979-93. Recipient The Ackerly award, 1975, Nat. Rsch. Svc. award, 1979, A.E. Bennet Neuropsychiat. Rsch. Found. award, Brain, Body & Mind award USPHS, Recognition award ADAA; Am. Coll. Neuropsychopharmacology travel fellow. Mem. Am. Coll. Neuropsychopharmacolgoy, Am. Coll. Psychiatry, Am. Soc. of Clin. Psychopharmacology, Internat. Brain Rsch. Orgn., Sleep Rsch. Soc. Office: Wayne State Sch Medicine 42011 St Antoine St 9B UHC Detroit MI 48201-2153

UHLMANN, FREDERICK GODFREY, commodity and securities broker; b. Chgo., Dec. 31, 1929; s. Richard F. and Rosamond G. (Goldman) U.; m. Virginia Lee Strauss, July 24, 1951; children: Richard, Thomas, Virginia, Karen, Elizabeth. B.A., Washington and Lee U., 1951. Ptnr. Uhlmann Grain Co., Chgo., 1951-61; v.p. Uhlmann & Co., Inc., 1961-65; sr. v.p. H. Hentz & Co., 1965-73, Drexel Burnham Lambert Inc., Chgo., 1973-84; exec. v.p., gen. bus. futures Dean Witter Reynolds Inc., 1984-85; sr. v.p., mgr. commodity dept. Bear, Stearns & Co., Inc., 1985-88; exec. v.p. Rodman & Renshaw, Inc., 1988-95; sr. v.p. LIT-Divsn. of First Options Inc., Chgo., 1995-98; chmn. Chgo Bd. Trade, 1973-74; sr. v.p., exec. dir. MAN Internat., 1998—. Ptnr. Uhlmann Investments, LLC. Trustee Highland Park Hosp., Ill.; bd. dirs. Dist. 113 H.S. Found., 1990—, Mt. Sanai Hosp. Inst., Chgo., 1999—. Mem. Nat. Futures Assn. (dir. 1981—, vice chair 1998—), Futures Industry Assn. (bd. dirs., chmn. 1975-76), Futures Industry Inst. (bd. dirs.). Clubs: Lake Shore Country (Glencoe, Ill.) (dir.); Standard (Chgo.). Home: 783 Whiteoaks Ln Highland Park IL 60035-3656 E-mail: fgu73@aol.com.

UICKER, JOSEPH BERNARD, retired engineering company executive; b. Mar. 29, 1940; s. John Joseph and Elizabeth Josephine (Flint) U.; m. Mary Catherine Howze, June 5, 1965 (div. Oct. 1971); children: Patricia, Suzzane; m. Janet Ann Ballman, Sept. 22, 1973. BSME, U. Detroit, 1963, MS, 1965. Registered profl. engr., Mich. Engr. Smith Hinchman & Grylls, Detroit, 1964-72, chief mech. engr. health facilities, 1972-73, asst. dir. health facilities, 1973-75, v.p., dir. mech. engring., 1975-82, v.p., dir. profl. staff, 1983-2000; also bd. dirs.; ret., 2000. Dir. Smith Group, Detroit, 1984-2000. Capt. U.S. Army, 1966—67. Mem. NSPE, ASME, ASHRAE, Soc. Am. Mil. Engrs., Engring. Soc., Athletic Club. Avocations: golf, photography, gardening. Home: 15250 Knolson St Livonia MI 48154-4736 E-mail: juicker@ameritech.net.

ULABY, FAWWAZ TAYSSIR, electrical engineering and computer science educator, research center administrator; b. Damascus, Syria, Feb. 4, 1943; came to U.S. 1964; s. Tayssir Kamel and Makram (Ard) U.; children: Neda, Aziza, Laith. BS in Physics, Am. U. Beirut, 1964; MSEE, U. Tex., 1966, PhDEE, 1968. Asst. prof. elec. and computer engring. U. Kans., Lawrence, 1968-71, assoc. prof., 1971-76, prof., 1976-84; prof. elec. engring. and computer sci. U. Mich., Ann Arbor, 1984—, dir. NASA Ctr. for Space Terahertz Tech., 1988—, Williams Disting. prof., 1993—, v.p. for rsch., 1999—. Author: Microwave Remote Sensing, Vol. 1, 1981, Vol. 2, 1982, Vol. 3, 1986, Radar Polarimetry, 1990. Recipient Kuwait prize in applied scis. Govt. of Kuwait, 1987, NASA Group Achievement award, 1990. Fellow IEEE (gen. chmn. internat. symposium 1981, Disting. Achievement award 1983, Centennial medal 1984); mem. IEEE Geosci. and Remote Sensing Soc. (exec. editor jour., pres. 1979-81), Internat. Union Radio Sci., Nat. Acad. Engring. Avocations: flying kites, racketball. Office: U Mich 3228 EECS 1301 Beal Ave Ann Arbor MI 48109-2122

ULETT, GEORGE ANDREW, psychiatrist; b. Needham, Mass., Jan. 10, 1918; s. George Andrew and Mabel Elizabeth (Caswell) U.; m. Pearl Carolyn Lawrence; children: Richard Carlton, Judith Anne, Carol Lynn. BA in Psychology, Stanford U., 1940; MS in Anatomy, U. Oreg., 1943, PhD in Anatomy, MD, U. Oreg., 1944. Diplomate Am. Bd. Psychiatry and Neurology. Asst. psychiatrist Barnes Hosp., St. Louis, 1950-64; med. dir.

Malcolm Bliss Hosp., 1951-61; dir. Mo. Dept. Mental Health, Jefferson City, Mo., 1962-72; prof., chair Mo. Inst. Psychiatry, St. Louis, 1964-73; dir. psychiatry Deaconess Hosp., 1973-94; interim dir. Mo. Inst. of Mental Health, 1990-91, assoc. dir. for policy and ethics, 1991-94; clin. prof. dept. family and cmty. medicine St. Louis U. Sch. Medicine, 1995-98. Mem. adv. coun. Mental Health Assn. St. Louis, 1965-66, 69-70, mem. profl. adv. com., 1965; chair health and hosp. com. Health & Welfare Coun. St. Louis, 1960; mem. alcohol rev. com., psychopharmacology study sect., alcoholism study sect., 1993, grants rev. com. for alternative medicine NIMH, Rockville, Md.; prof. psychiatry Washington U. Sch. Medicine, St. Louis, 1956-61; clin. prof. psychiatry St. Louis U. Sch. Medicine, 1981-89, U. Mo. Sch. Medicine, 1990—. Author 10 books, including The Biology of Acupuncture, 2001; contbr. over 270 articles to profl jours. Capt. U.S. Air Force, 1946-47. Recipient Ann. award Mo. Assn. for Mental Health, 1966, Recognition award, 1970, AMA Honorable Mention award Foster Com. Exhibit, 1974, Pax Mundi Fellowship award for profl. excellence, 1989; named hon. mem. Turkish Coll. Neuropharmacology, 1969. Fellow Am. Psychiat. Assn.; mem. Am. Soc. Acupuncture (past pres.), Am. Soc. of Med. Psychiatry (past pres.), Mo. Acad. Psychiatry (past pres.). Office: Mo Inst Mental Health 5400 Arsenal St Saint Louis MO 63139-1400 E-mail: gulett@earthlink.net.

ULLIAN, JOSEPH SILBERT, philosophy educator; b. Ann Arbor, Mich., Nov. 9, 1930; s. Hyman Benjamin and Frieda G. (Silbert) U. AB, Harvard U., 1952, AM, 1953, PhD, 1957. Instr. philosophy Stanford U., Calif., 1957-58; asst. prof. philosophy Johns Hopkins U., Balt., 1958-60; vis. asst. prof. philosophy U. Pa., Phila., 1959-60, rsch. assoc. in linguistics, 1961-62; vis. asst. prof. philosophy U. Chgo., 1962-63; asst. prof. U. Calif., Santa Barbara, 1964-66; assoc. prof. Washington U., St. Louis, 1965-70, prof., 1970—. Lectr. U. Calif., Berkeley, 1961; cons. Rsch. Directorate System Devel. Corp., Santa Monica, Calif., 1962-70. Co-author: The Web of Belief, 1970, 2d edit., 1978; contbr. articles to profl. jours. Mem. Am. Philos. Assn., Assn. for Symbolic Logic (exec. com. 1974-77), Am. Soc. for Aesthetics, Phi Beta Kappa. Democrat. Avocations: sports, theatre, music. Home: 984 Tornoe Rd Santa Barbara CA 93105-2229 Office: Washington U Dept Philosophy 1 Brookings Dr Saint Louis MO 63130-4899

ULLMAN, NELLY SZABO, statistician, educator; b. Vienna, Austria, Aug. 11, 1925; came to U.S., 1939; d. Viktor and Elizabeth (Rosenberg) Szabo; m. Robert Ullman, Mar. 20, 1947 (dec.); children: Buddy, Wiliiam John, Martha Ann, Daniel Howard. BA, Hunter Coll., 1945; MA, Columbia U., 1948; PhD, U. Mich., 1969. Rsch. assoc. MIT Radiation Lab, Cambridge, Mass., 1945; instr. Polytechnic Inst. of Bklyn., 1945-63; from asst. prof. to prof. Ea. Mich. U., Ypsilanti, 1963—2002, prof., 2002—. Author: Study Guide To Actuarial Exam, 1978; contbr. articles to profl. jours. Mem. Am. Math. Assn., Am. Assn. Univ. Profs. Office: Ea Mich Univ Dept Emath Ypsilanti MI 48197 E-mail: mth_ullman@online.emich.edu.

ULMER, EVONNE GAIL, health science facility executive; b. Bagley, Minn., Sept. 12, 1947; d. John Ferdinand and Elsie Mabel (McCollum) Lundmark; m. G. Bryan Ulmer, Jan. 11, 1969; 1 child, G. Bryan. Diploma, St. Luke's Hosp., Duluth, Minn., 1968; BS, St. Joseph's Coll., N. Windam, Maine, 1981; MHA, U. Minn., 1984; JD, T.M. Cooley Law Sch., Lansing, Mich., 1997. Bar: Mich. 1997. Staff nurse Baton Rouge Gen., 196970, St. Luke's Hosp., Duluth, Minn., 1968-69, 71-72; asst. adminstr. Hickory Heights Care Ctr., Metarie, La., 1972-73; asst. head nurse Eisenhower Hosp., Colorado Springs, Colo., 1973-74; dir. pt. care svcs. St. Vincent's Gen. Hosp., Leadville, 1974-78; insvc., quality assurance dir. Watsatch Hosp., Heber City, Utah, 1979; adminstr. Prospect Park Living Ctr., Estes Park, Colo., 1982-84; asst. adminstr. Estes Park Med. Ctr., 1979-84; CEO Weston Co. Hosp. and Manor, Newcastle, Wyo., 1984-92, Ionia (Mich.) County Meml. Hosp., 1992—; pres. Ionia County Health Sys., 1995—. Mem. Am. Hosp. Assn. Chgo. (trustee 1998-01, past tech. small and rural governing coun., past del. region and policy bd., past chair small and rural governing com., mem. leadership com.), Medicare Geog. Reclassification Rev. Bd., Mich. Health and Hosp. Assn. (bd. dirs.). Republican. Lutheran. Home: 536 Skyview Dr Ionia MI 48846-9776 Office: Ionia County Meml Hosp Ionia MI 48846 E-mail: evonneulmer@hotmail.com.

ULMER, JAMES HOWARD, potter; b. Carrington, N.D., Oct. 12, 1945; s. James Francis and Lois Adelle (Wolf) U.; m. Ann Cecile Gerlach, May 28, 1977; children: Jesse Gerlach, Matthew James. BSBA, N.D. State U., 1969; MS, U. N.D., 1973. Geologist UND Engring. Sta., Grand Forks, N.D., 1974-76; potter Stoneware by Jim Ulmer, Frazee, Minn., 1972—. Dir. Lake Region Arts Coun., Fergus Falls, Minn., 1990-92; dir. intern program U.N.D., Grand Forks, 1976-93, Moorhead (Minn.) State U., 1976-93. Author of poems. Mem. Mich. Guild Artists, Minn. Craft Coun. Home and Office: 15158 330th Ave Frazee MN 56544-8810 E-mail: ulmerstoneware@yahoo.com.

ULMER, MELVILLE PAUL, physics and astronomy educator; b. Washington, Mar. 12, 1943; s. Melville Jack and Naomi Louise (Zinkin) U.; m. Patricia Elifson, Dec. 28, 1968; children: Andrew Todd, Jeremy John, Rachel Ann. BA, Johns Hopkins U., 1965; PhD, U. Wis., 1970. Asst. research U. Calif., San Diego, 1970-74; astrophysicist Harvard Smithsonian Ctr. for Astrophysics, Cambridge, Mass., 1974-76; asst. prof. Dept. Physics and Astronomy, Northwestern U., Evanston, Ill., 1976-82, assoc. prof., 1982-87, dir. astrophysics program, 1982—, prof., 1987—; dir. Lindheimer and Dearborn Obs. Northwestern U., 1982—. Co-investigator on Gamma Ray Ob. experiment and Orbiting Solar Ob. 7. Contbr. articles to profl. jours. Fellow Am. Phys. Soc.; mem. Am. Astron. Soc., Soc. Photo-optical Instrumentation Engrs., Internat. Astron. Union. Home: 2021 Noyes St Evanston IL 60201-2556 Office: Northwestern U Dearborn Obs 2131 Sheridan Rd Evanston IL 60208-0832

ULRICH, ROBERT GENE, judge; b. St. Louis, Nov. 23, 1941; s. Henry George Ulrich and Wanda Ruth (Engram) Webb; m. JoAnn Demark, July 3, 1965; children— Jill Elizabeth, Jane Ashley B.A., William Jewell Coll., 1963; J.D., U. Mo., Kansas City, 1969, LLM, 1972, U. Va., 2001. Bar: Mo. 1969. Assoc. Von Erdmannsdorff, Voigts & Kuhlman, North Kansas City, Mo., 1969—72; pvt. practice Raytown, 1972; asst. U.S. atty. Dept. Justice, Kansas City and Springfield, 1973-76, 78-81; ptnr. Pine & Ulrich, Warrensburg, 1976-77; litigation atty. Shifran, Treiman, et al., Clayton, 1977-78; U.S. atty. We. Dist. Mo., Kansas City, 1981-89; judge Mo. Ct. Appeals (we. dist.), 1989—, chief judge, 1996-98. Mem. U.S. Atty. Gen.'s Econ. Crime Council, 1983-89 , Atty. Gen.'s Adv. Com. of U.S. Attys., 1983-89, chmn. 1986-89, adv. com. U.S. Ct. Appeals (8th cir.), 1983-86. Appointed mem. steering com. Protect our Children Campaign, Gov. of Mo., chmn. legis. subcom., 1985; mem. resource bd., personnel mgmt. bd. Dept. Justice, 1985-89; trustee Liberty Meml. Assn., 1989—; vice chmn. Orgn. Crime Drug Enforcement Task Force Nat. Program, Dept. Justice, 1987-89. Col. USMCR, 1963-66. Mem.: U. Mo.-Kansas City Alumni Assn. (v.p. 1997—98, pres. 1998—2001), U. Mo.-Kansas City Law Found., U. Mo.-Kansas City Law Sch. Alumni Assn. (v.p. 1994—95, pres. 1995—96), Marine Corps Res. Officers' Assn. (exec. councillor 1986—87), Kansas City Met. Bar Assn., Mo. Bar Assn., Inst. Jud. Adminstrn., Am. Judicature Soc. Office: Missouri Ct Appeals 1300 Oak St Kansas City MO 64106-2904

ULRICH, ROBERT J. retail discount chain stores executive; b. 1944; Grad., U. Minn., 1967, Stanford U., 1978. Chmn., chief exec. officer, dir. Dayton Hudson Corp.; with Dayton Hudson Corp. (now Target Corp.), Mpls., 1967—, exec. v.p. dept. stores divsn., 1981-84, pres. dept. stores divsn., 1984-87, chmn., CEO Target stores divsn., 1987-93, dir., 1993—; chmn, CEO Target Corp. (formerly Dayton Hudson Corp.), 1994—. Office: Target Corp 1000 Nicollet Mall Minneapolis MN 55403-2467

ULRICH, WERNER, patent lawyer; b. Munich, Germany, Mar. 12, 1931; came to U.S., 1940, naturalized, 1945; s. Karl Justus and Grete (Rosenthal) U.; m. Ursula Wolff, June 28, 1959; children— Greta, Kenneth. B.S., Columbia U., 1952, M.S. (NSF fellow 1952-53), 1953, Dr.Engring. Sci., 1957; M.B.A., U. Chgo., 1975; J.D., Loyola U., Chgo, 1985. Bar: Ill., 1985. With AT&T Bell Labs, Naperville, Ill., 1953-95; head electronic switching dept. AT&T Bell Labs., 1964-68; dir. Advanced Switching Tech., 1968-77, head maintenance architecture dept., 1977-81; sr. atty. Intellectual Property Law Orgn., 1981-95. Vis. lectr. U. Calif., Berkeley, 1966-67 Inventor of over 20 telecommunications inventions; patentee electronic switching systems. Fellow IEEE; mem. ABA, Ill. State Bar Assn., Am. Intellectual Property Law Assn., Tau Beta Pi, Beta Gamma Sigma. Office: 434 Maple St Glen Ellyn IL 60137-3826

ULSENHEIMER, DEAN, English language educator; b. Cleve., Dec. 20, 1941; s. Lon Sherwood and Mary Dorothy (Kupstas) U.; m. Sharon Lee Williams, Dec. 27, 1963 (div. June 1980); children: Cathi, Chris, Shelley, Scott.; m. Monica Joan Rigo, Aug. 10, 1984. BS in Edn., Ohio U., Athens, 1964; postgrad., John Carroll U., 1969-70, Kent State U., 1979. Cert. secondary sch. tchr. Tchr. English South Amherst (Ohio) Schs., 1964-66; project engr. Otto Konigslow Mfg. Co., Cleve., 1966-67; tchr. English Cardinal Schs., Middlefield, Ohio, 1967-80, Shaw High Sch., East Cleveland, 1980-92; instr. English Cuyahoga Community Coll., Cleve., 1980—, Lakeland Community Coll., Mentor, Ohio, 1984—. Owner, cons. Power Reading, Power Writing; cons. NASA Lewis Rsch. Ctr., The East Ohio Gas Co., Centerior Energy, Owens Corning Inc., STERIS Corp.; cons. mgmt. devel. program Lubrizol Corp., Wickliffe, Ohio, 1987—; spkr. Lakeland C.C. Spkrs. Bur., Mentor, 1988—; hon. poetry intern NEH, Hiram Coll., 1977. Author: Easy Writing, 1977, Sentence Analysis, 1977, Communication Problems, 1978, Short Story Starters, 1980. Mem. NEA, Am. Cons. League, Ohio Edn. Assn., East Cleveland Edn. Assn., Greater Cleve. Growth Assn., Coun. Smaller Bus. Ent. Roman Catholic. Avocations: tennis, golf, phys. fitness. Home and Office: 6691 Morley Rd Concord OH 44077-5924

UMANS, ALVIN ROBERT, manufacturing company executive; b. N.Y.C., Mar. 11, 1927; s. Louis and Ethel (Banner) U.; m. Nancy Jo Zadek, June 28, 1953 (div.); children: Kathi Lee Umans Lind, Craig Joseph; m. Madeleine Sayer, Sept. 21, 1985; 1 child, Valentine Brett. Student, U. Rochester, 1945. Sales mgr. Textile Mills Co., Chgo., 1954-56; regional sales mgr. Reflector Hardware Corp., Melrose Park, Ill., 1956-58, nat. sales mgr., 1959-62, v.p., 1962-65, pres., treas., dir., 1965-92; pres., CEO RHC/Spacemaster Corp., 1992-97, chmn., CEO, 1997—. Chmn., bd. dirs. Goer Mfg. Co., Inc., Charleston, S.C.; chmn., dir. Discovery Plastics, Oreg., Morgan Marshall Industries, Inc., Ill., Capitol Hardware, Inc., Ill.; chmn., dir. Spartan Showcase Inc., Mo.; v.p., dir. Adams Comm., Chgo.; bd. dirs. Monroe Comm., Chgo.; chmn., treas., dir. Spacemaster Corp., Del. Trustee Mt. Sinai Hosp. Med. Ctr., Chgo., 1970—, chmn. bd., 1987-89; trustee Schwab Rehab. Hosp., Chgo., 1987—, chmn. bd., 1987-89; trustee Sinai Health Sys., Chgo., 1993—, chmn., 1995-97; mem. Cook County Bur. Adv. Com., 1994—; trustee Driehaus Mutual Funds, 1996—; bd. dirs. Milton & Rose Zadek Fund, 1965-78; governing bd. mem. Cinema/Chgo., 1988-89. Served with AUS, 1945-46. Mem. Nat. Assn. Store Fixture Mfrs. (dir. 1969-70), World Pres.'s Orgn., Chgo. Pres.'s Orgn. Club: Standard (Chgo.). Home: 132 E Delaware Pl Chicago IL 60611-1445 Office: RHC/Spacemaster Corp 1400 N 25th Ave Melrose Park IL 60160-3001 E-mail: arumans@rhcspacemaster.com.

UMBARGER, DWAYNE, state legislator; b. Chanute, Kans., Aug. 2, 1952; m. Toni Umbarger. AA, Neosho C.C., 1972; student, Pittsburg State U. Rural mail carrier U.S. Postal Svc., 1984-86; mem. Kans. Senate from 14th dist., Topeka, 1996—; mem. agr. com., mem. commerce com., mem. edn. com.; mem. joint com. on children and families com. Mem. site coun. Thayer Pub. Schs.; bd. dirs. Thayer Christian Ch.; mem. Neosho County Farm Bur.; mem. Hidden Haven Christian Camp Bd. Republican. Office: 300 SW 10th Ave Topeka KS 66612-1504

UNAKAR, NALIN JAYANTILAL, biological sciences educator; b. Karachi, Sindh, Pakistan, Mar. 26, 1935; came to U.S., 1961; s. Jayantilal Virshankar and Malati Jaswantrai (Buch) U.; m. Nita Shantilal Mankad; children: Rita, Rupa. BS, Gujerat U., Bhavnagar, India, 1955; MSc, Bombay U., 1961; PhD, Brown U., 1965. Research asst. Indian Cancer Research Ctr., Bombay, 1955-61; USPHS trainee in biology Brown U., Providence, 1961-65; research assoc. in pathology U. Toronto, Ont., Can., 1965-66; asst. prof. biology Oakland U., Rochester, Mich., 1966-69, assoc. prof., 1969-74, prof., chmn. biology dept., 1974-87, prof., 1974-2000, prof. emeritus, 2000—, adj. prof. biomed. scis., 1984—. Mem. coop. cataract research group Nat. Eye Inst., Bethesda, Md., 1977—; mem. visual scis. study sect. NIH, Bethesda, 1982-86, mem. cataract panel, 1980—. Mem. vis. bd. Lehigh U., Bethlehem, Pa., 1986-89. Grantee Nat. Cancer Inst., NIH, 1967-70, Nat. Eye Inst., NIH, 1976-97. Mem. AAAS, Am. Soc. Cell Biology, Assn. Rsch. in Vision and Ophthalmology, Sigma Xi. Home: 2822 Rhineberry Rd Rochester Hills MI 48309-1912 Office: Oakland U Dept Of Biol Scis Rochester MI 48309

UNANUE, EMIL RAPHAEL, immunopathologist; b. Havana, Cuba, Sept. 13, 1934; married, 1965; 3 children. B.Sc., Inst. Secondary Edn., 1952; M.D., U. Havana Sch. Medicine, Cuba, 1960; M.A., Harvard U., 1974. Assoc. exptl. pathology Scripps Clin. and Research Found., 1960-70; intern in pathology Presbyn. Univ. Hosp., Pitts., 1961-62; research fellow in exptl. pathology Scripps Clin. and Research Found., 1962-65; research fellow immunology Nat. Inst. Med. Research, London, 1966-68; from asst. prof. to assoc. prof. pathology Harvard U. Med. Sch., Boston, 1971-74, prof., 1974-77, Mallinckrodt prof. immunopathology, 1977—; prof., chmn. dept. pathology Washington U. Sch. Medicine, St. Louis, 1988—. Recipient T. Duckett Jones award, Helen Hay Whitney Found., 1968, Park-Davis award, Am. Soc. Exptl. Pathology, 1973, Albert Lasker Award for Basic Med. Rsch., 1995. Office: Washington U Sch Medicine Dept Pathology and Immunology Box 8118 Saint Louis MO 63110-1093

UNDERHEIM, GREGG, state legislator; b. Aug. 22, 1950; BS, U. Wis., La Crosse, 1972. Former mem. Winnebago County Bd.; former congl. aide; Wis. state assemblyman dist. 54, 1987—. Former h.s. tchr. Home: 1652 Beech St Oshkosh WI 54901-2808 Office: Wis Assembly PO Box 8952 Madison WI 53708-8952

UNDERHILL, ROBERT ALAN, consumer products company executive; b. Columbus, Ohio, June 9, 1944; s. Robert Alan and Grace Ruth (Smith) U.; m. Lynn Louise Stentz, Oct. 18, 1963 (dec. Dec. 1997); children: Robert Alan III, Richard Louis; m. Lynn Carol Riviere, July 4, 1998. Student, Case Western Res. U., 1962-64, Ohio State U., 1965. With tech. svc. dept. Gen. Tire & Rubber Co., Akron, Ohio, 1966-69; quality control engr. Edmont-Wilson Co., Canton, 1969-70; mgr. quality assurance Pharmaseal Labs., Massillon, 1970-72; mgr. R&D Internat. Playtex Corp., Paramus, N.J., 1972-78; from mgr. to dir. R&D Kimberly-Clark Corp., Neenah, Wis., 1978-83, v.p. R&D, 1983-93, sr. v.p. R&D, sr. tech. officer, 1994-99; trustee United Health Group, 1994-99, exec. com., vice-chmn., 1997-99, chmn. compensation com., 1994-99; pres. Tech. Solutions, Inc., Appleton, Wis., 1999—. Trustee Novus Health Group, 1993—94; bd. dirs. Appleton (Wis.) Med. Ctr., 1993—96; trustee Thedacare, 1999—, chmn., 2000—01. Patentee (U.S. and fgn.) med. device; mem. editl. bd. Revs. in Process Chemistry and Engring. jour. Mem. exec. bd. Bay Lakes Coun. Boy Scouts Am., 1988-92; bd. dirs. Outagamie County (Wis.) chpt. ARC, 1993-99, chmn. nominations com., 1993-99, mem. exec. com., 1994-99, sec., 1994-99; bd. dirs. Cmty. Blood Ctr., Appleton, Wis., 1996-2001, chmn., 1999-2000; bd. dirs. Cmty. Found. Fox Valley Region, 1997—, vice-chmn. 1998—; bd. dirs. Silver Lake Coll., Manitowoc, Wis., 1998-2000; corp. bd. dirs. U. Wis. Med. Sch. Fox Valley Family Practice Residency Program, 1998—; mem. rsch. adv. com. Inst. Paper Sci. and Tech., 1998-99; trustee Lawrence U., 1998-2001; bd. dirs. Appleton Med. Ctr. Found., 1999—, United Way Fox Cities, 2000—, Goodwill of North Ctrl. Wis., Inc., 2000—, Vis. Nurse Assn. Cmty. Hospice Found., 2001—; active 1st Congl. Ch., Appleton; mem. dean's adv. coun. U. Mo. Coll. Engring., Columbia, 1999-2001. Mem. AAAS, N.Y. Acad. Scis., Am. Assn. Blood Banks (stds. com. 1997-99), Svc. Corps. Ret. Execs., Rotary Internat., Riverview Country Club, Appleton Rotary Club, Butte des Morts Country Club, Pi Delta Epsilon. Republican. Avocations: stock market investment analysis, travel. Home and Office: 2525 W Prospect Ave Appleton WI 54914-8718 E-mail: rau@athenet.net.

UNDERWOOD, ROBERT LEIGH, venture capitalist; b. Paducah, Ky., Dec. 31, 1944; s. Robert Humphreys and Nancy Wells (Jessup) Underwood; m. Susan Lynn Doscher, May 22, 1976; children: Elizabeth Leigh, Dana Whitney, George Gregory. BS with gt. distinction, Stanford U., 1965, MS, 1966, PhD, 1968; MBA, Santa Clara U., 1970. Rsch. scientist, project leader Lockheed Missiles & Space Co., Sunnyside, Calif., 1967—71; spl. asst. for engring. scis. Office Sec., Dept. Transp., Washington, 1971—73; sr. mgmt. assoc. Office Mgmt. and Budget, Exec. OFfice Pres., 1973; with TRW Inc., L.A., 1973—79, dir. retail nat. accts., 1977—78, dir. product planning and devel., 1978—79; pres., CEO OMEX, Santa Clara, 1980—82; v.p. Heizer Corp., Chgo., 1979—85, No. Trust; pres. No. Capital Corp., Chgo., 1985—86; mng. ptnr. ISSS Ventures, 1986—88; founding ptnr. N.Am. Bus. Devel. Co., Chgo., 1988—. Dir. various pvt. and pub. portfolio cos. MECC, 1991—96; trustee Burridge Mut. Funds, 1996—98. Contbr. articles to profl. jours. Mem. sch. bd. Avoca Dist. 37, 1990—99, v.p., 1996—99; mem. adv. bd. Leavy Sch. Bus. and Adminstrn. Santa Clara U., 1995—; elder Presbyn. Ch., 1978—79. Fellow, NASA, NSF; scholar, Alcoa. Mem.: IEEE, Indian Hill Club (Winnetka, Ill.), Manasquan River Yacht Club (Brielle, NJ), Union League Chgo., Chgo. Club, Beta Gamma Sigma, Tau Beta Pi, Phi Beta Kappa, Sigma Xi. Home: 59 Woodley Rd Winnetka IL 60093-3748 Office: 135 S La Salle St Chicago IL 60603-4159

UNGAR, IRWIN ALLAN, botany educator; b. N.Y.C., Jan. 21, 1934; s. Isidore and Gertrude (Fageles) U.; m. Ana Celia Del Cid, Aug. 10, 1959; children: Steven, Sandra, Sharon. BS, CCNY, 1955; MA, U. Kans., Lawrence, 1957, PhD, 1961. Instr. U. R.I., Kingston, 1961-62; asst. prof. Quincy Coll., Ill., 1961-66, Ohio U., Athens, 1966-69, assoc. prof., 1969-74, prof. botany, 1974—, chmn. dept. botany, 1984-89. Dir. Dysart Woods Lab., 1985—99, Environ. Studies Program, 1991—95; vis. prof. dept. plant scis. and vis. fellow Wolfson Coll., Oxford (Eng.) U., 1990—91; panelist Nat. Sea Grant Program, 1984; grant proposal reviewer NSF, 1980—2002. Contbr. articles to profl. jours.; manuscript reviewer Am. Jour. Botany, Internat. Jour. Plant Scis. NSF grantee, 1974-76, 76-78, 80-83, 94-95, 98-2001; rsch. grantee Petroleum Environ. Rsch. Forum, 1992-96. Fellow Ohio Acad. Sci.; mem. AAAS, Am. Inst. Biol. Scis., Bot. Soc. Am., Ecol. Soc. Am., Sigma Xi. Home: 44 Walker St Athens OH 45701-2252 Office: Ohio Univ Dept Of Botany Athens OH 45701 E-mail: ungar@ohio.edu.

UNGARETTI, RICHARD ANTHONY, lawyer; b. Chgo., May 25, 1942; s. Dino Carl and Antoinette (Calvetti) U.; children: Joy A., Paul R. BS, DePaul U., 1964, JD, 1970. Bar: Ill. 1970, U.S. Dist. Ct. (no. dist.) Ill. 1970, U.S. Supreme Ct. 1980. Assoc. Kirkland & Ellis, Chgo., 1970-74; ptnr. Ungaretti & Harris, 1974—. Mem. adv. coun. DePaul Coll. Law, Chgo., 1988. Mem. ABA, Chgo. Bar Assn., Ill. State Bar Assn., Internat. Coun. Shopping Ctrs., Am. Coll. Real Estate Lawyers, Justinian Soc., Urban Land Inst. (assoc.), Lamda Alpha Avocations: golf, fishing, hunting. Office: Ungaretti & Harris 3500 Three First Nat Plz Chicago IL 60602 E-mail: raungaretti@uhlaw.com.

UNIKEL, EVA TAYLOR, interior designer; b. Hungary; arrived in Can., 1956; came to U.S., 1967; d. Istvan Domolky and Lea Maria (Koszegi) Coan; m. Alan L. Unikel; 1 child, Renee Christine; m. June 26, 1993. BS, So. Ill. U., 1972. Dir. mktg. Lococo Design, St. Louis, 1982-83; project mgr., nat. dir. mktg. hosp. div. Hotel Restaurant Planners div. Profl. Interiors, 1983-87; founder Interior Solutions Inc., Hinsdale, Ill., 1987—. Mem. AIA (assoc.), Nat. Assn. Women Bus. Owners, Am. Soc. Interior Design (chairperson 1984-86), Nat. Assn. Indsl. Office Pks., Bldg. Owners and Mgrs. Assn., Internat. Interior Design Assn. Roman Catholic. Office: 500 E Ravine Rd Hinsdale IL 60521-2449

UNSER, AL, retired professional auto racer, racing official; b. Albuquerque, May 29, 1939; s. Jerry H. and Mary C. (Craven) U.; m. Wanda Jesperson, Apr. 22, 1958 (div.); children: Mary Linda, Debra Ann, Alfred; m. Karen Barnes, Nov. 22, 1977 (div.). Auto racer U.S. Auto Club, Speedway, Ind., 1964-94. Achievements include placing 3d in nat. standings, 1968, 2d in 1969, 77, 78, 1st in 1970, 4th in 1976; winner Indpls. 500, 1970, 71, 78, 87, Pocono 500, 1976, 78, Ont. 500, 1977, 78; placed 3d in U.S. Auto Club Sports Car Club Am. Formula 5000, 1975, 2d place, 1976; Internat. Race of Champions champion, 1978; 2d pl. Indpls. Motor Speedway, 1983; CART/PPG Indy Car champion, 1983, 85. Office: IRL 4567 W 16th St Indianapolis IN 46222-2513

UNTENER, KENNETH E. bishop; b. Detroit, Aug. 3, 1937; Ed., Sacred Heart Sem., Detroit, St. John's Provincial Sem., Plymouth, Mich., Gregorian U., Rome. Ordained priest Roman Cath. Ch., 1963, ordained bishop, 1980. Bishop Diocese of Saginaw, Mich., 1980—. Office: Chancery Office 5800 Weiss St Saginaw MI 48603-2762

UOTILA, URHO ANTTI KALEVI, geodesist, educator; b. Pöytyä, Finland, Feb. 22, 1923; came to U.S., 1951, naturalized, 1957; s. Antti Samuli and Vera Justina (Kyto) U.; m. Helena Vanhakartano, Aug. 6, 1949; children: Heidi, Kirsi, Elizabeth, Julie, Trina, Caroline. B.S., Finland's Inst. Tech., 1946, M.S., 1949; Ph.D., Ohio State U., 1959. Surveyor, geodesist Finnish Govt., 1944-46, 46-51; geodesist Swedish Govt., 1946; research asst. Ohio State U., 1952-53, research assoc., 1953-58, research supr., 1959-88, lectr. in geodesy, 1955-57, asst. prof., 1959-62, assoc. prof., 1962-65, chmn. dept. geodetic sci., 1964-84, prof., 1965-89, chmn., prof. emeritus, 1989—. Mem. Solar Eclipse Expdn. to Greenland, 1954; Mem. adv. panel on geodesy U.S. Coast and Geodetic Survey, Nat. Acad. Sci., 1964-66; mem. geodesy and cartography working group, space sci. steering com. NASA, 1965-67, mem. geodesy/cartography working group, summer conf. lunar exploration and sci., 1965, mem. geodesy and cartography adv. subcom., 1967-72; mem. ad hoc com. on N.Am. datum div. earth scis. Nat. Acad. Scis.-N.A.E., 1968-70; bd. dirs. Internat. Gravity Bur., France, 1975-83; mem. com. on geodesy Nat. Acad. Scis., 1975-78 Mem. editorial adv. com.: Advances in Geophysics, 1968-77; Contbr. articles to profl. jours., encys. Served with Finnish Army, 1942-44. Recipient Kaarina and W.A. Heiskanen award, 1962, Apollo Achievement award NASA, 1969, Disting. Svc. award Surveyor's Inst. Sri Lanka, Earle J. Fennell award Am. Congress on Surveying and Mapping, 1989. Fellow Am. Geophys. Union (v.p. geodesy sect. 1964-68, pres. 1968-70), Am. Congress Surveying and Mapping (nat. dir. 1970-73, 2d v.p. 1977-78, pres.-elect 1978-79, pres. 1979-80), Internat. Assn. Geodesy (pres. spl. study group 5.30 1967-71, pres. sect. V 1971-75, exec. com. 1971-79); mem. Am. Assn. Geodetic Surveying (pres. 1984-86), Am. Soc. Photogrammetry, Can. Inst. Surveying, Univs. Space Research Assn. (trustee 1973-75), Finnish Nat. Acad.

Scis. (fgn.), Profl. Land Surveyors Ohio (hon.), Ala. Soc. Profl. Land Surveyors (hon.), Tenn. Assn. Profl. Surveyors (hon.) Achievements include: research in geometric geodesy, phys. geodesy and statis. analysis of data. Home: 4329 Shelbourne Ln Columbus OH 43220-4243 Office: Ohio State U 2070 Neil Ave Columbus OH 43210-1226

UPATNIEKS, JURIS, retired optical engineer; b. Riga, Latvia, May 7, 1936; arrived in U.S., 1951; s. Karlis and Eleonora (Jegers) Upatnieks; m. Ilze Induss, July 13, 1968; children: Ivars, Ansis. BSEE, U. Akron, Ohio, 1960; MSEE, U. Mich., 1965. Rsch. asst., then rsch. assoc. Willow Run Labs. U. Mich., Ann Arbor, 1960-69; rsch. engr. Inst. Sci. and Tech., U. Mich., 1969-72, Environ. Rsch. Inst. Mich., Ann Arbor, 1973-93; sr. engr. Applied Optics, 1993—2001; ret., 2001. Lectr. elec. engring. dept. U. Mich., 1971—73, adj. assoc. prof. elec. engring. and computer sci. dept., 1974—2001, adj. rsch. scientist dept. mech. engring. and applied mechanics, 1996—2001. Contbr. articles to profl. jours. 2d lt. U.S. Army, 1961—62. Recipient Holley medal, ASME, 1976, Inventor of the Yr. award, Assn. Advancement Invention and Innovation, 1976. Fellow: Latvian Acad. Sci. (Grand medal 1999), Acad. Soc. Austrums, Soc. Photographic Instrumentation Engrs. (Robert Gordon award 1965), Optical Soc. Am. (R. W. Wood prize 1975), Am. Latvian Assn. Achievements include patents in field. Office: Applied Optics 2662 Valley Dr Ann Arbor MI 48103-2748 E-mail: upatnks@ic.net.

UPBIN, HAL JAY, consumer products executive; b. Bronx, N.Y., Jan. 15, 1939; s. David and Evelyn (Sloan) U.; m. Shari Kiesler, May 29, 1960; children: Edward, Elyse, Danielle. BBA, Pace Coll., 1961. CPA, N.Y. Tax sr. Peat, Marwick, Mitchell & Co., N.Y.C., 1961-65; tax mgr. Price Waterhouse & Co., 1965-71; dir. taxes Wheelabrator-Frye Inc., 1971-72, treas., 1972-74; pres. Wheelabrator Fin. Corp., 1974-75; v.p., chief fin. officer Chase Manhattan Mortgage and Realty Trust (became Triton Group Ltd. 1980), 1975-76, pres., 1976-78, pres., chmn., 1978-83, also dir.; chmn., pres., dir. Isomedics, 1983-85; chmn., pres. Fifth Ave. Cards, Inc., Fifth Retail Corp., Ashley's Stores, Ashley's Outlet Stores, 1984-88; bd. dirs. Stacy Industries, 1984-88; vice chmn. Am. Recreation Products, St. Louis, 1985-88, vice chmn., pres., 1988—, chmn., 1992—; v.p. corp. devel., chmn. acquistion com. Kellwood Co., Chesterfield, 1990—, exec. v.p. corp. devel., chmn. acquisition com., 1992—, pres., COO, 1994—, pres., COO, dir., 1995-97, pres., CEO, 1997—, also bd. dirs., chmn. Alumni advisor to bd. trustees Pace U.; past pres. Jewish Temple. Mem. AICPA, N.Y. State Soc. CPA's, Franklin Jaycees (v.p.). Home: 625 S Skinker Blvd Saint Louis MO 63105-2301 Office: Kellwood Co PO Box 14374 Saint Louis MO 63178-4374 E-mail: HJU@kellwood.com.

UPHOFF, JAMES KENT, education educator; b. Hebron, Nebr., Sept. 1, 1937; s. Ernest John and Alice Marie (Dutcher) U.; m. Harriet Lucille Martin, Aug. 6, 1962; 1 child, Nicholas James. BA, Hastings Coll., 1959; MEd, U. Nebr., 1962, EdD, 1967. Tchr. Walnut Jr. H.S., Grand Island, Nebr., 1959-65, dept. chmn., 1962-65; instr. dept. edn. U. Nebr., Lincoln, 1965-66; curriculum intern Bellevue (Nebr.) Pub. Schs., 1966-67; asst. prof. edn. Wright State U., Dayton, Ohio, 1967-70, assoc. prof., 1970-75, prof. edn., 1975—, co-dir. pub. edn. religion studies ctr., 1972-75, dean br. campuses, 1974-79, dir. lab. experiences, 1982-91, chmn. dept. tchr. edn., 1994-97, dir. coll. student svcs., 1994-97, dir. profl. field experiences, prof. emeritus, 1997—, assoc. dir. Ctr. for Tchg. and Learning, 1999—. Vis. prof. U. Dayton, 1968-69, 98, 99. Author: (with others) Summer Children: Ready or Not for School, 4th edit., 1986, School Readiness and Transition Programs: Real Facts from Real Schools, 1990, 2d edit., 1995; editor: Dialogues on Development Curriculum K and I, 1987, Changing to a Developmentally Appropriate Curriculum-Successfully: 4 Case Studies, 1989; bi-weekly columnist Oakwood Register newspapers, the Kettering-Oakwood Times andthe Centerville-Bellbrook Times; weekly commentator on edn. WYSO-FM Pub. Radio. Bd. dirs. pub. edn. fund Dayton Found., 1985-97; mem. Luth. Ch. coun., 1987-90, chair, 1988-90; mem. Oakwood City Schs. Bd. Edn., 1989—, v.p., 1994-95, pres., 1996, 97, 99—. Phi Delta Kappa scholar, 1969; Malone fellow in Arab Islamic studies, 1989. Mem. ASCD (dir. 1974-79, editor early childhood network 1989-98, editor and facilitator pub. edn. and religion network 1992—), Western Ohio Edn. Assn. (pres. 1974-75, exec. com. 1979-85), Assn. Tchr. Educators, Assn. Childhood Edn. Internat., Ohio Assn. Supervision and Curriculum Devel. (v.p. 1972-73), Nat. Coun. Social Studies, Ohio Coun. Social Studies, Ohio Sch. Bds. Assn. (chair rules com. 1993-94, mem. policy and legislation com. 1994—, Achievement award 1995, 96, 98, bd. trustees 1996—, exec. com. 1998-99, pres.-elect 2000, pres. 2001), Nat. Assn. Edn. Young Children, Dayton Area Coun. Social Studies (pres. 1970-71, 85-87), Ohio Assn. Edn. Young Children (com. chair 1992-95), Dayton Assn. for Young Children (exec. bd. 1988-94), LWV Greater Dayton (edn. dir. 1981-85), Ohio Coun. Chs. (edn. com. 1973-75), Optimists Club (pres. 1983-85, sec.-treas. 1988-99), Phi Delta Kappa (chpt. pres. 1983-84, 98—, chpt. advisor 1988-94, area 5 coord. 2001—), Kappa Delta Pi. Republican. Home: 150 Spirea Dr Dayton OH 45419-3409 Office: Wright State U CTL 023 Library Dayton OH 45435 E-mail: james.uphoff@wright.edu.

UPTON, FREDERICK STEPHEN, congressman; b. St. Joseph, Mich., Apr. 23, 1953; s. Stephen E. and Elizabeth Brooks (Vial) U.; m. Amey Richmond Rulon-Miller, Nov. 5, 1983; 2 children. BA in Journalism, U. Mich., 1975. Staff asst. to Congressman David A. Stockman, Washington, 1976-81; legis. asst. Office Mgmt. and Budget, 1981-83, dep. dir. legis. affairs, 1983-84, dir. legis. affairs, 1984-85; mem. U.S. Congress from 6th Mich. dist., 1987—; mem. edn. and the workforce com., energy and commerce com. Mem. commerce com. Field mgr. Stockman for Congress, St. Joseph, 1975; campaign mgr. Globensky for Congress, St. Joseph, 1981. Republican. Office: US House of Reps 2333 Rayburn Hob Washington DC 20515-0001*

URBAN, FRANK HENRY, retired dermatologist, state legislator; b. St. Louis, May 24, 1930; s. Frank and Helen Gertrude (Zingsheim) U.; m. Lois Elaine Thurwachter, June 18, 1954 (dec. 1991); children: James, Barbara, Michael, Mark, David, Bruce, John; m. Kathryn Calvert Bloomberg, Nov. 28, 1992. BS in Med. Sci., U. Wis., 1951, MD, 1954; MS, U. Minn., 1960. Diplomate Am. Bd. Dermatology. Intern Beaumont Army Hosp., El Paso, 1954-55; resident Mayo Clinic, Rochester, Minn., 1957-60; pvt. practice dermatology Wauwatosa, Wis., 1960-93; asst. clin. prof. Med. Coll. Wis., 1964—; mem. Wis. State Assembly, Madison, 1989—. Trustee Village Bd. of Elm Grove, Wis., 1985-87, pres., 1987-89; bd. dirs. ARC of Greater Milw.; pres. Friends U. Wis.-Milw. Sch. Edn., 1995—, bd. dirs.; hon. mem. Potawatomi coun. Boy Scouts Am., pres., 1974-76. Recipient Silver Beaver award East Cen. Region Boy Scouts Am., 1972, Silver Antelope award, 1979, Civic Leadership award State Med. Soc. Wis., 1990, Disting. Svc. award U. Wis. Med. Sch. Alumni Assn., 1991. Fellow Am. Acad. Dermatology; mem. Wis. Dermatol. Soc. (pres. 1969-70), Wis. State Med. Soc. (dir. 1987-92, 93—), Milw. County Med. Soc. (caucus chmn. 1987-92, pres.-elect 1992-93, pres. 1993-94), Brookfield C. of C. (Outstanding Mem. award 1992). Republican. Roman Catholic. Avocations: walking, photography, toy trains, music. Office: State Capitol PO Box 8953 Madison WI 53708-8953

URBOM, WARREN KEITH, federal judge; b. Atlanta, Dec. 17, 1925; s. Clarence Andrew and Anna Myrl (Irelan) U.; m. Joyce Marie Crawford, Aug. 19, 1951; children: Kim Marie, Randall Crawford, Allison Lee, Joy Renee. AB with highest distinction, Nebr. Wesleyan U., 1950, LLD (hon.), 1984; JD with distinction, U. Mich., 1953. Bar: Nebr. 1953. Mem. firm Baylor, Evnen, Baylor, Urbom, & Curtiss, Lincoln, Nebr., 1953-70; judge U.S. Dist. Ct. Nebr., 1970—; chief judge U.S. Dist. Ct. Dist. Nebr., 1972-86, sr. judge, 1991—. Mem. com. on practice and procedure Nebr. Supreme Ct., 1965-95; mem. subcom. on fed. jurisdiction Jud. Conf. U.S., 1975-83; adj. instr. trial advocacy U. Nebr. Coll. Law, 1979-90; bd. dirs. Fed. Jud. Ctr., 1982-86; chmn. com. on orientation newly apptd. dist. judges Fed. Jud. Ctr., 1986-89; mem. 8th Cir. Com. on Model Criminal and Civil Jury Instrns., 1983—; mem. adv. com. on alternative sentences U.S. Sentencing Com., 1989-91. Contbr. articles to profl. jours. Trustee St. Paul Sch. Theology, Kansas City, Mo., 1986-89; active United Methodist Ch. (bd. mgrs., bd. global ministries 1972-76, gen. com. on status and role of women, 1988-96, gen. conf. 1972, 76, 80, 88, 92, 96, 2000); pres. Lincoln YMCA, 1965-67; bd. govs. Nebr. Wesleyan U., chmn. 1975-80. With AUS, 1944-46. Recipient Medal of Honor, Nebr. Wesleyan U. Alumni Assn., 1983. Fellow Am. Coll. Trial Lawyers; mem. ABA, Nebr. Bar Assn. (ho. of dels. 1966-70, Outstanding Legal Educator award 1990), Lincoln Bar Assn. (Liberty Bell award 1993, pres. 1968-69), Kiwanis (Disting. Svc. award 1993), Masons (33 deg.), Am. Inns of Ct. (Lewis F. Powell Jr. award for Professionalism and Ethics 1995). Methodist. Home: 4421 Ridgeview Dr Lincoln NE 68516-1516 Office: US Dist Ct 586 Fed Bldg 100 Centennial Mall N Lincoln NE 68508-3859 E-mail: urbom1@aol.com.

URLACHER, BRIAN, football player; b. May 25, 1978; Attended, Univ. New Mex. Linebacker Chgo. Bears, 2000—. Office: Halas Hall 1000 Football Dr Lake Forest IL 60045*

URLACHER, HERBERT, state legislator; b. New England, N.D., Dec. 30, 1931; m. Claire Urlacher; 5 children. Farmer, rancher; mem. N.D. State Ho. of Reps., Bismarck, 1989-91, N.D. Senate from 36th dist., Bismarck, 1992—. Pres. Stark County Sch. Officers, N.D. Water Users, West River Joint Water Resource Bd.; past pres. ch. coun. St. Mary's Ch.; bd. dirs. Water Resources Bd. N.D.; mem. Stark County Water Resource Bd.; mem. adv. bd. State Water Commn. Mem. KC, Elks. Office: ND State Capitol 600 E Boulevard Ave Bismarck ND 58505-0660 also: 3320 94th Ave SW Taylor ND 58656-9643

URSHAN, NATHANIEL ANDREW, minister, church administrator; b. St. Paul, Aug. 29, 1920; s. Andrew David and Mildred (Hammergren) U.; m. Jean Louise Habig, Oct. 1, 1941; children: Sharon, Annette, Nathaniel, Andrew. Student, Columbia U., 1936-39; DTh (hon.), Gateway Coll. Evangelism, 1976. Ordained to ministry United Pentecostal Ch. Internat. Evangelist, 1941-44; assoc. pastor Royal Oak, Mich., 1944-46, N.Y.C., 1947-48, Indpls., 1948-49; pastor Calvary Tabernacle, 1949-78; presbyter Ind. Dist. United Pentecostal Chs., 1950-77; asst. gen. supt. United Pentecostal Ch. Internat., 1971-77, gen. supt. Mo., 1978—; chancellor Urshan Grad. Sch. of Theology, Florissant, 2002. Host radio show Harvestime, 1961-78, 81—; chaplain Ind. Ho. of Reps., 1972. Author: Consider Him, 1962, These Men Are Not Drunk, 1964, Book of Sermons of the Baptism of the Holy Spirit, 1968, Major Bible Prophecy, 1971. Mem. internat. com. YMCA, 1958-79, bd. dirs. Indpls. chpt. 1961-79, world service chmn. Region L., 1969-71; chmn. Heart Fund Campaign, 1968-69; mem. screening com. Marion County Reps., Ind., 1973-74; chmn. Ministerial Com. of Richard Lugar for May of Indpls., 1968, William Hudnut for Mayor, 1975; bd. dirs. Little Red Door, Cancer Soc. Indpls., 1974-77. Recipient gold and brass medallion Heart Fund., Indpls., 1968-69; Nathaniel A. Urshan Day named in his honor, Nov. 3, 1979, Mayor Hudnut, Indpls. Mem. Indpls. Ministerial Assn. Office: United Pentecostal Ch Internat 8855 Dunn Rd Hazelwood MO 63042-2212

URSU, JOHN JOSEPH, lawyer; b. 1939; BA, U. Mich., 1962, JD, 1965. Bar: Mich. 1966, Ky. 1970, Minn. 1972. Trial atty. FTC, 1965-67; staff mem. Pres.'s Commn. on Civil Disorders, 1967; advisor to commr. FTC, 1968-69; legal counsel GE, 1969-72; divsn. atty. 3M, 1972-74, sr. atty., 1974-76, assoc. counsel, 1976-81, asst. gen. counsel, 1981-86, assoc. gen. counsel, 1986-90, dep. gen. counsel, 1990-92, gen. counsel, 1992-93, v.p. legal affairs & gen. counsel, 1993-96, sr. v.p. legal affairs and gen. counsel, 1997—. Adj. faculty William Mitchell Coll. Law, 1978-82. Office: 3M Gen Offices 3M Ctr Bldg 220-14W-07 Saint Paul MN 55144-1000

USHER, PHYLLIS LAND, state official; b. Winona, Miss., Aug. 29, 1944; d. Sandy Kenneth and Ruth (Cottingham) Land; m. William A. Usher (dec. Dec. 1993). BS, U. So. Miss., 1967; MS, U. Tenn., 1969; postgrad., Purdue U., Ind. U., Utah State U. Libr. Natchez (Miss.) - Adams County Schs., 1967-68; materials specialist Fulton County Bd. Edn., Atlanta, 1969-71; cons. divsn. instructional media Ind. Dept. Pub. Instrn., Indpls., 1971-74, dir. divsn., 1974-82, dir. fed. resources and sch. improvement, 1982-85; acting assoc. supt. Ind. Dept. Edn., 1985, sr. officer Ctr. Sch. Improvement, 1985-96, asst. supt., 1996—. Pres. bd. dirs. INCOLSA, mcpl. corp., 1980-82; pres., owner Usher Funeral Home, Inc.; pres. NU Realty Corp.; mem. task force sch. Libraries Nat. Commn. Libraries and Info. Sci.; cons. in field. Bd. dirs. Hawthorne Cmty. Ctr.; mem. Gov. Inst. Conf. Children and Youth Task Force. Recipient citation Internat. Reading Assn., 1975; Title II-B fellow, U. Tenn., 1968-69. Mem. ALA, Nat. Assn. State Ednl. Media Profls., West Deanery Bd. Edn., Indpls. Archdiocese, Delta Kappa Gamma. Office: State House Rm 229 Indianapolis IN 46204-2728

UTSCHIG, THOMAS S. federal judge; Bankruptcy judge U.S. Dist. Ct. (we. dist.) Wis., Eau Claire, 1986—. Office: 500 S Barstow St Eau Claire WI 54701-3657

UTT, GLENN S., JR. motel investor, former biotech and pharmaceutical industry company executive; b. Neodesha, Kans., Aug. 7, 1926; s. Glenn S. and Reba Pauline (White) U.; m. Mary Lou Ford, Aug. 8, 1948; 1 child, Jan A. BSEE, BSBA, Kans. State U., 1949; MBA, Harvard U., 1951. Salesman Drexel Furniture Co., N.C., 1951-55; v.p. Booz Allen & Hamilton, Chgo. and Zurich, Switzerland, 1955-62; exec. v.p. Abbott Labs., North Chicago, Ill., 1962-83, also dir., ret., 1983. Chmn. bd. Janmar Enterprises, Minocqua, Wis., Marjan Inc., Houghton, Mich., U.P. Hotel Group Inc., Houghton. Co-author: Lalique Perfume Bottles, 1990. Alderman City of Lake Forest, Ill., 1972-76, chmn. recreational bd., 1975-78; mem. exec. com. Lake County Republican Fedn., Waukegan, Ill., 1974-83. With USN, 1944-46, USAF (res.), 1949-53. Mem.: Beta Theta Pi. Avocations: antiques, objects of art. Home: PO Box 810 Houghton MI 49931

VADNER, GREGORY A. state agency administrator; b. Indpls., Mar. 24, 1951; s. Clyde H. and Marilyn (Whickcar) V.; m. Frances A. Woods, May 21, 1983; 1 child, Ariel. BA, DePauw U., 1974; MPA, U. Mo., 1984. Mgr. A&W Root Beer Restaurant, DeSoto, Mo., 1974; photographer Chromalloy Photog. Industries, St. Louis, 1974-75; caseworker Mo. Div. Family Svcs., Hillsboro, 1975-79, income maintenance supr., 1979, county dir. I Centerville, 1979-80, county dir. II Mexico, 1980-85, county dir. IV St. Joseph, 1985-87, income maintenance supr. V Kansas City, 1987-88, dep. dir. Jefferson City, 1988; dir. Mo. Divsn. Med. Svcs. Mem. Am. Pub. Welfare Assn., Nat. Eligibility Workers Assn., Reform Orgn. for Welfare. Lutheran. Avocations: photography, trout fishing, tennis. Home: 1105 Schumate Chapel Rd Jefferson City MO 65109-0585 Office: Mo Divsn Med Svcs PO Box 6500 Jefferson City MO 65102-6500

VAIL, THOMAS VAN HUSEN, retired newspaper publisher and editor; b. Cleve., June 23, 1926; s. Herman Lansing and Delia (White) V.; m. Iris W. Jennings, Sept. 15, 1951; children: Siri Jennings, Thomas Van Husen, Jr. A.B. in Politics cum laude, Princeton U., 1948; H.H.D. (hon.), Wilberforce U., 1964; L.H.D., Kenyon Coll., 1969, Cleve. State U., 1973. Reporter Cleve. News, 1949-53, polit. editor, 1953-57; with Cleve. Plain Dealer, 1957-91, v.p., 1961-63, pub., editor, 1963-91, pres., 1970-91; dir. AP, 1968-74; ret., 1991. Bd. dirs. Greater Cleve. Growth Assn.; bd. dirs., past pres. Cleve. Conv. and Visitors Bur.; mem. Nat. Adv. Commn. on Health Manpower; presdl. apptd. to U.S. Adv. Commn. on Info., Pres.'s Commn. for Observance 25th Anniversay UN; trustee No. Ohio region NCCJ, Nat. Brotherhood Week chmn., 1969; trustee Cleve. Coun. World Affairs; fellow Cleve. Clinic Found.; former mem. Downtown Cleve. Corp.; former mem. distbn. com. Cleve. Found.; chmn., founder New Cleve. Campaign; trustee, founder Cleve. Tomorrow; former trustee Com. Econ. Devel.; former mem. Pres.'s Adv. Coun. on Pvt. Sector Initiatives; participant Nat. Conf. Christians and Jews. Lt. (j.g.) USNR, 1944-46. Recipient Nat. Human Relations award, 1970, Cleve. Man of Year award Sales and Mktg. Execs. Cleve., 1976, Ohio Gov.'s award, 1982, Downtown Bus. Council recognition award Greater Cleve. Growth Assn., 1983, award Nat. Conf. Christians and Jews, 1970, award Mt. Vernon Adv. Com., 1994. Mem. Nat. Assn. Profl. Journalists (Lifetime Hall of Fame), Am. Newspaper Pubs. Assn., Am. Soc. Newspaper Editors, Soc. Profl. Journalists, Kirtland Country Club (Willoughby, Ohio), Sand Ridge Golf Club (Chardon, Ohio), Cypress Point Club (Pebble Beach, Calif.), Bohemian Club (San Francisco), Chagrin Valley Hunt Club (Gates Mills, Ohio), Links Club (N.Y.C.). Episcopalian. Home: L Ecurie 14950 County Line Rd Hunting Valley Chagrin Falls OH 44022 Office: 29225 Chagrin Blvd Ste 200 Pepper Pike OH 44122-4632

VAINSCHTEIN, ARKADY, physics educator; b. Novokuznetsk, Russia, Feb. 24, 1942; MS in Physics, Novosibrisk U., 1964; Budker U., 1968. Prof. physics Novosibirsk, 1983-89; dir. theoretical physics inst. U. Minn., 1993-96, mem. theoretical physics inst., 1990—, Gloria Lubkin prof. physics, 1990—. Vis. prof. U. Minn., 1989-90. Mem. Am. Phys. Soc. Office: U Minn Sch Physics & Astronomy 116 Church St SE Minneapolis MN 55455-0149

VALADE, ALAN MICHAEL, lawyer; b. Berwyn, Ill., Jan. 26, 1952; s. Merle F. and Vera M. Valade; m. June 17, 1978. Student, Oakland C.C., 1970—72; BA, U. Mich., 1974; JD, Wayne State U., 1977; LLM in Taxation, NYU, 1978. Bar: Mich. 1978, Fla. 1987. Assoc. Kemp, Klein, Endelman & Beer, Southfield, Mich., 1978-79; shareholder Valade, MacKinnon & Higgins, P.C., Detroit, 1979-84, Schwendener & Valade, P.C., Mason, 1985-91; ptnr. Honigman Miller Schwartz and Cohn LLP, Lansing, 1991—. Co-author: The Michigan Single Business Tax, 1991; contbr. articles to profl. jours. Fellow Mich. State Bar Found.; mem. ABA, State Bar Mich. (chmn. state and local tax com. 1991, tax. coun. 1989-92), State Bar Fla. Office: Honigman Miller Schwartz and Cohn LLP 222 N Washington Sq Ste 400 Lansing MI 48933-1800

VALADE, GARY C. automobile company executive; b. Detroit, Oct. 13, 1942; BSEE, Mich. State U., 1966, MBA, 1968. Mgmt. trainee, budget and profit analyst Chrysler Corp., Auburn Hills, Mich., 1968-74, budget and acctg. supr. Huber Avenue Foundry, 1974-76, fin. specialist enging and casting divsn., 1976-78, contr. Jefferson and Hamtramck assemblies, 1978-80, mgr. product analysis and cost planning, 1980-84, asst. contr. corp. fin. control, 1984-90, v.p., corp. contr., 1990-91, v.p. corp. pers., 1992-93, exec. v.p., CFO, 1993—; exec. v.p. global procurement and supply Daimler Chrysler Corp. Trustee Henry Ford Health Sys., Adrian Coll., Chrysler Corp. Fund; mem. corp. coun. Interlochen Ctr. for Arts; chmn. Mich. Colls. Found. Mem. Mich. State U. Eli Broad Coll. Bus. Alumni Assn. (bd. dirs.). Office: Daimler Chrysler Corp 1000 Chrysler Dr Auburn Hills MI 48326-2766

VALANDRA, PAUL, state legislator; m. Cheryl Valandra; four children. Student, Black Hills State U., U. S.D., Oglala Lakota Coll. Former state senator dist. 28 State of S.D., state senator dist. 27, 1993—. Mem. com. health and human svcs. S.D. State Senate; tribal adminstr. Seargant, US Marine Corps, 1972-75. Mem. Rosebud Sioux Tribal Council, 1993— Democrat. Home: PO Box 909 Mission SD 57555-0909 Office: SD State Senate State Capitol Pierre SD 57501

VALDIVIA, HECTOR HORACIO, medical educator; b. Loreto, Mex., Aug. 23, 1958; married. MD, Nat U. Mex., 1982, PhD, 1987. Teaching asst. Nat. U. Mex. Sch. Medicine, Mexico City, 1980-86; rsch. assoc. Baylor Coll. Medicine, Houston, 1986-89; assoc. scientist U. Wis. Sch. Medicine, Madison, 1989-92; rsch. asst. prof. U. Md. Med. Sch., Bapt., 1992-94; asst. prof. dept. physiology U. Wis. Med. Sch., Madison, 1994-99, assoc. prof. dept. physiology, 1999—. Lectr. and researcher in field. Contbr. articles to profl. jours., chpts. to books. Cystic Fibrosis Found. fellow, 1989-91. Mem. Am. Heart Assn. (scintific coun. 1995—), Biophys. Soc. U.S.A. Office: U Wis Med Sch Dept Physiology 1300 University Ave Madison WI 53706-1510

VALERIO, JOSEPH MASTRO, architectural firm executive, educator; b. Dec. 26, 1947; m. Linda A. Searl; children: Joseph Jr., Anthony. BArch, U. Mich., 1970; MArch, UCLA, 1972. Registered architect, Wis., Ill., Ind., Mo., Calif., Tex., Ariz., Minn., Ala., Iowa, Ind., Md., Mich., Okla., Ga., Mass., N.Y., Va., Utah; cert. Nat. Coun. Archtl. Registration Bds. Pres. Chrysalis Corp. Architects, 1970-85; assoc. prof. U. Wis., 1973-86; design dir. Swanke Hayden Connell Architects, 1985-86; v.p. architecture A. Epstein and Sons, Inc., 1986-88; pres. Valerio-Assocs. Inc., 1988-94; prin. Valerio Dewalt Train Assocs., Inc., Chgo., 1994—. Speaker Ariz. State U., UCLA, U. Ariz., U. Cin., others; cons. USG Interiors, Formica Corp., AAAS, NAS, NEA: vis. critic and lectr. in field. Prin. works include corp., high-tech. indsl., retail, health and residential bldgs.; author: Movie Palaces, 1983; (monograph) Joe Valerio, 1999; editor: Architectural Fabric Structures, 1985; featured in Inside Architecture, Domestic Interiors, 1997, New Am. Apt., 1997, Internat. Interiors, 1997, Lofts/Living and Working Spaces, 1999. Mem. exec. bd. men's coun. Mus. Contemporary Art, 1989-91; mem. exec. bd. Contemporary Arts Coun., 1994-96 (pres. 1999). Recipient Honor awards Wis. Soc. Architects, 1975, 81, 84, 85, Gov.'s Award for Design Excellence, State of Mich., 1979, Gold medal Inst. Bus. Designers, 1988, Design award Progressive Architecture, 1991, Architectural Record Interiors award 1993, 95, 96, Disting. Interior award Inst. Bus. Designers, Chgo., 1993; honored by Emerging Voices series Archtl. League N.Y., 1984, Met. Home mag., Interiors mag. Fellow AIA (programs chmn. design com. Chgo. chpt. 1990, mem. long range planning com. 1992, chair nat. com. on design 1997, Nat. Honor award 1981, 93, Interiors award Chgo. chpt. 1988, 90, 92, 95-97, 99, 2000, 01, Disting. Bldg. award 1991, 93, Nat. Interior Honor award 1993, 96, Divine Detail award 1999, 2001), Chgo. Architecture Club (pres. 1994). Office: Valerio Dewalt Train Assocs 500 N Dearborn St Fl 9 Chicago IL 60610-4900

VALERIO, MICHAEL ANTHONY, financial executive; b. Detroit, Sept. 20, 1953; s. Anthony Rudolph and Victoria (Popoff) V.; m. Barbara Ann Nabozny, Oct. 8, 1983. BA, U. Mich., Dearborn, 1975. CPA, Mich. Jr. acct. Carabell, Bocknek CPA's, Southfield, Mich., 1975-76; sr. acct. Purdy, Donovan & Beal, CPA's, Detroit, 1976-77; mgr. Bucytnck & Co., CPA's, Southfield, 1978-79; controller Transcontinental Travel, Harper Woods, Mich., 1979-80; exec. v.p. Holland Cons., Inc., Detroit, 1980-85; controller, CFO SLC Recycling Industries, Inc., Warren, Mich., 1985-98; owner Pinnacle Fin. Consulting, PLLC, Livonia, 1994—. Mem. AICPA, Mich. Soc. CPAs, Acctg. Rsch. Found. Roman Catholic. Office: Pinnacle Fin Consulting PLLC 33300 Five Mile Rd Ste 102 Livonia MI 48154-3074

VALINE, DELMAR EDMOND, SR. corporate executive; b. Edwardsville, Ill., May 2, 1919; s. Edward and Clara Louise (Schon) V.; m. Geraldine Goley, Aug. 26, 1939; children: Jayne M. Valine Klein, Linda L. Valine Hay, Delmar E. Jr. Student, Summer Bus. Coll., 1939. Purchasing agt. Swift and Co., Nat. Stockyards., Ill., 1937-58; asst. to pres. St. Louis Nat. Stock Yards Co., Nat. Stockyards, 1958-60; exec. v.p. St. Louis Livestock Mkt. Found., 1960-64; exec. sec. Nat. Museum of Transport, St. Louis; v.p. First Ill. Bank, East St. Louis, Ill., 1967-81; bd. chairman

Southwest Regional Port Dist., 1961—. Bd. dirs. First Ill. Bank, East St. Louis, 1982—, Target 2000, East St. Louis, 1977—, Inland Rivers Port and Terminals 1987—, Port of Metropolitan St. Louis, 1975—, sec., treas. Gateway Ctr. Metropolitan St. Louis, 1976—; exec. v.p. East Side Associated Industries, East St. Louis, 1990—. Mayor village of Dupo, Ill., 1945-49, mem. sch. bd. dist. 193, Dupo, 1955-56, Selective Service bd., East St. Louis, 1950-55; mem. Fed. Agy. Adv. Com., 1964-70; commr. Southwestern Ill. Planning Comm., 1976—. Recipient Medallion award, Boys Club Am., 1969. Mem. U.S. C. of C., Rotary (past pres.), Boys Club, Mo. Athletic Club, Royal Order of Jesters. Republican.

VALK, ROBERT EARL, corporate executive; b. Muskegon, Mich., Aug. 21, 1914; s. Allen and Lulu (Schuler) V.; m. Ann Parker, August 9, 1941 (div. July 1959); children: James A., Sara C.; m. Alice Melick, Dec. 29, 1960 (dec. 1999); children: Marie, Susan. B.S. in Mech. Engring, U. Mich., 1938. With Nat. Supply Co., 1938-55, plant mgr., 1945-48, works mgr. Toledo, Houston and Gainesville, Tex., 1949-55; asst. v.p. prodn. Electric Auto-Lite Co., Toledo, 1956, v.p., group exec. gen. products, 1956-60; gen. mgr. mfg. automotive div. Essex Internat., Inc., 1960-66, v.p. corp., gen. mgr. automotive div., 1966-74; pres. ITT Automotive Elec. Products Div., 1974-80; v.p. ITT N.Am. Automotive Ops. Worldwide, 1980-86; chmn. Chamberlin, Davis, Rutan & Valk, 1986—. Trustee Henry Ford Health Care Sys., Detroit. Bd. dirs. Ecumenical Theological Ctr. Mem. Am. Soc. Naval Engrs., Soc. Automotive Engrs., Am. Ordnance Assn., Am. Mgmt. Assn., Air Force Assn., Am. Mfrs. Assn., Wire Assn., Nat. Elec. Mfrs. Assn., Engring. Soc. Detroit. Republican. Episcopalian. Clubs: Country (Detroit), Renaissance Club, Yondotega, Economics (Detroit); Grosse Pointe, Bay View Yacht; Little Harbor (Harbor Springs, Mich., Question Club. Home: 80 Renaud Rd Grosse Pointe Shores MI 48236-1742 Office: 21 Kercheval Ave Ste 270 Grosse Pointe Farms MI 48236-3633

VALLIERE, ROLAND EDWARD, performing company executive; b. Pawtucket, R.I., Oct. 3, 1954; s. Roland Edgar and Anita Alice (Dubois) V.; m. Stacey Lyn Rein, June 3, 1984 (separated). MusB, New England Conservatory, 1978; MFA, Brandeis U., 1984. Regional mgr. Syracuse (N.Y.) Symphony, 1984-86; gen. mgr. N.H. Symphony, Manchester, 1986-89; exec. dir. Hudson Valley Philharmonic, Poughkeepsie, N.Y., 1989-92, Omaha Symphony, Nebr., 1992-95, Kansas City Symphony, Mo., 1995—. Presenter Am. Symphony Orchestra League, Washington, 1987, 90. Office: Kansas City Symphony 1020 Central St Ste 300 Kansas City MO 64105-1663

VAN AKEN, WILLIAM J. construction executive; b. 1954; Grad., South Utah State Coll., 1984, Case Western Res. U., Cleve., 1990. Pvt. practice as contractor, Cedar City, Utah, 1976-83; with Sam W. Emerson Co., Cleve., 1983—, pres., treas., 1990—. Office: Sam W Emerson Co 3365 Richmond Rd Ste 200 Cleveland OH 44122-4178

VAN ALLEN, JAMES ALFRED, physicist, educator; b. Mt. Pleasant, Iowa, Sept. 7, 1914; s. Alfred Morris and Alma E. (Olney) Van A.; m. Abigail Fithian Halsey, Oct. 13, 1945; children: Cynthia Schaffner, Margot Cairns, Sarah Trimble, Thomas, Peter. BS, Iowa Wesleyan Coll., 1935; MS, U. Iowa, 1936, PhD, 1939; ScD (hon.), Iowa Wesleyan Coll., 1951, Grinnell Coll., 1957, Coe Coll., 1958, Cornell Coll., Mt. Vernon, Iowa, 1959, U. Dubuque, 1960, U. Mich., 1961, Northwestern U., 1961, Ill. Coll., 1963, Butler U., 1966, Boston Coll., 1966, Southampton Coll., 1967, Augustana Coll., 1969, St. Ambrose Coll., 1982, U. Bridgeport, 1987; DHL (hon.), Johns Hopkins U., 1999. Rsch. fellow, physicist dept. terrestial magnetism Carnegie Instn., Washington, 1939-42; physicist, group and unit supr. applied physics lab. Johns Hopkins U., 1942, 46-50; organizer, leader sci. expdns. study cosmic radiation Peru, 1949, Gulf of Alaska, 1950, Arctic, 1952, 57, Antarctic, 1957; prof. physics, head dept. U. Iowa, Iowa City, 1951-85, Carver prof. physics, emeritus, 1989-92, Regent disting. prof., 1992—; now prof. emeritus. Regents fellow Smithsonian Instn., 1981; rsch. assoc. Princeton U., 1953-54; mem. devel. group radio proximity fuze Nat. Def. Rsch. Coun., OSRD; pioneer high attitude rsch. with rockets, satellites and space probes. Author: Origins of Magnetospheric Physics, 1983, First to Jupiter, Saturn and Beyond, 1981; 924 Elementary Problems and Answers in Solar System Astronomy, 1993; contbg. author: Physics and Medicine of Upper Atmosphere, 1952, Rocket Exploration of the Upper Atmosphere; editor: Scientific Uses of Earth Satellites, 1956, Cosmic Rays, the Sun, and Geomagnetism: The Works of Scott E. Forbush, 1993; acting editor Jour. Geophys. Rsch.-Space Physics, 1991-92; contbr. numerous articles to profl. jours. * Lt. comdr. USNR, 1942-46, ordnance and gunnery specialist, combat observer. Recipient Physics award Washington Acad. Sci., 1949, Space Flight award Am. Astronautical Soc., 1958, Louis W. Hill Space Transp. award Inst. Aero. Scis., 1959, Elliot Cresson medal Franklin Inst., 1961, Golden Omega award Elec. Insulation Conf., 1963, Iowa Broadcasters Assn. award, 1964, Fellows award of merit Am. Cons. Engrs. Coun., 1978, Nat. Medal of Sci., 1987, Vannevar Bush award NSF, 1991, Gerard P. Kuiper prize Am. Astron. Soc. 1994, Nansen award and prize Norwegian Acad. Sci. and Letters, 1990; named comdr. Order du Merit Pour la Recherche et l'Invention, 1964; Guggenheim Found. rsch. fellow, 1951. Fellow Am. Rocket Soc. (C.N. Hickman medal devel. Aerobee rocket 1949), IEEE, Am. Phys. Soc., Am. Geophys. Union (pres. 1982-84, John A. Fleming award 1963, William Bowie medal 1977); mem. NAS, AAAS (Abelson prize 1986), Iowa Acad. Sci., Internat. Acad. Astronautics (founding), Am. Philos. Soc., Am. Astron. Soc., Royal Astron. Soc. U.K. (Gold medal 1978), Royal Swedish Acad. Sci. (Crafoord prize 1989), Am. Acad. Arts and Scis., Cosmos Club, Sigma Xi (Procter prize 1987), Gamma Alpha. Presbyterian. Achievements include discovery of radiation belts around earth. Office: Univ Iowa Dept Physics and Astronomy 701 Van Allen Hall Iowa City IA 52242-1403 E-mail: james-vanallen@uiowa.edu.

VAN ANDEL, JAY, direct selling company executive; b. Grand Rapids, Mich., June 3, 1924; s. James and Nella (Vanderwoude) Van A.; m. Betty J. Hoekstra, Aug. 16, 1952; children: Nan, Stephen, David, Barbara. Student, Pratt Jr. Coll., 1945, Calvin Coll., 1942, 46, Yale, 1943-44; DBA (hon.), No. Mich. U., 1976, Western Mich. U., 1979, Grand Valley State U., 1992; LLD (hon.), Ferris State Coll., 1977, Mich. State U., 1997. Co-founder, sr. chmn., owner Amway Corp., Ada, Mich.; founder Van Andel Edn. and Med. Rsch., Grand Rapids. U.S. amb., commr. gen. Genoa Expo '92, 1992 World's Fair marking 500th Anniversary of Columbus Journey to Am.; chmn. bd. Amway Internat., Amway Hotel Corp., Amway Environ. Found., Nutrilite Products, Inc.; chmn. Ja-Ri Corp., Ada, Mich.; mem. adv. coun. Am. Private Edn. Participant White Ho. Conf. Indsl. World Ahead, 1972; chmn. Mich. Rep. fin. com., 1975-81; Founding chmn. Right Place Com., Grand Rapids, Mich.; mem. adv. council Nat. 4H Found.; trustee Hillsdale (Mich.) Coll., Citizens Rsch. Coun. Mich., Hudson Inst., Indpls. and Washington; dir. Jamestown Found., Gerald R. Ford Found.; bd. dirs., trustee, treas. Washington, Heritage Found., Washington; pres. Van Andel Found.; co-chmn. Mich. Botanic Garden Capital Campaign; founding chmn. Citizen's Choice, Washington; former bd. dirs. BIPAC, Washington, former chmn. Netherlands-Am. Bicentennial Commn; former mem. bd. govs. USO World. Served to 1st lt. USAAF, 1943-46. Knighted Grand Officer of Orange-Nassau, The Netherlands; recipient Disting. Alumni award Calvin Coll., 1976, Golden Plate award Am. Acad. Achievement, Gt. Living Am. award and Bus. and Profl. Leader of the Yr. award Religious Heritage Am., George Washington medal of Honor Freedom Found., Gold medals Netherland Soc. of Phila. and N.Y.C., Disting. Citizen award Northwood Inst., Patron award Mich. Found. for Arts, 1982, Achievement award UN Environment Programme, 1989, UN Environment Programme Achievement award Amway, 1989, Adam Smith Free Enterprise award Am. Legis. Exchange Coun., 1993, Disting. Svc. award Rotary Grand Rapids, Gold Medal Netherlands Soc. N.Y., Edison Achievement award Am. Mktg. Assn., 1994, named Bus. Person Yr. Econ. Club Grand Rapids, 1990, Clare Booth Luce award, Heritage Found., 1998, Jr. Ach. Nat. Bus. Hall of Fame, 1998, Donald Porter Humanitarian award YMCA Heritage Club, 1999; named to Grand Rapids Bus. Hall of Fame; World fellow Duke of Edinburgh's award. Mem. Sales and Mktg. Execs. Internat. Acad. Achievement (charter), Direct Selling Assn. (bd. dirs., hall of fame), U.S. C. of C. (past chmn. bd.), Right Place Com. (founding chmn.), de Tocqueville Soc. (former chmn.), Nat. Chamber Found. (dir.), Mensa Soc. USA, Peninsular Club, Cascade Hills Country Club, Lotus Club, Capitol Hill Club (Washington), Macatawa Bay Yacht Club (Holland, Mich.), Le Mirador Country Club (Switzerland), Econ. Club (Grand Rapids), Omicron Delta Kappa (hon.) Mem. Christian Reformed Ch. (elder). Home: 7186 Windy Hill Dr SE Grand Rapids MI 49546-9745 Office: Amway Corp 7575 Fulton St E Ada MI 49355-0001

VAN ANDEL, STEVE ALAN, business executive; b. Ada, Mich., Oct. 9, 1955; BLS in Econs. and Bus., Hillsdale Coll., 1978; MBA in MKtg., Miami U., Oxford, Ohio, 1979. V.p. mktg. Amway Corp., Worldwide, chmn. exec. com. policy bd.; vice chmn. Amway Japan Ltd.; chmn. Amway Asia Pacific Ltd., Amway Corp., Ada, now CEO. Dir. Met. Found., Operation Enterprise-AMA; bd. dirs. Met. Hosp., Mich. Nat. Bank Corp., Ctr. for Internat. Pvt. Enterprises; mem. dean's adv. bd. Seidman Sch. of Bus. Bd. dirs. Grand Rapids John Ball Soc., Amway Environmental Found. Mem. U.S. C. of C. (bd. dirs.). Office: Amway Corp 7575 Fulton St E Ada MI 49355-0001

VANBEBBER, GEORGE THOMAS, federal judge; b. Troy, Kans., Oct. 21, 1931; s. Roy Vest and Anne (Wenner) V.; m. Alleen Sara Castellani. AB, U. Kans., 1953, LLB, 1955. Bar: Kans. 1955, U.S. Dist. Ct. Kans. 1955, U.S. Ct. Appeals (10th cir.) 1961. Pvt. practice, Troy, 1955-58, 1961-82; asst. U.S. atty. Topeka, Kansas City, Kans., 1958-61; county atty. Doniphan County, Troy, 1963-69; mem. Kans. House of Reps., 1973-75; chmn. Kans. Corp. Commn., Topeka, 1975-79; U.S. magistrate, 1982-89; judge U.S. Dist. Ct., Kansas City, Kans., 1989-95, chief judge, 1995-2001. Mem. ABA, Kas. Bar Assn. Episcopalian. Office: US Dist Ct 529 US Courthouse 500 State Ave Kansas City KS 66101-2403

VAN BOKKELEN, JOSEPH SCOTT, prosecutor; b. Chgo., June 7, 1943; s. Robert W. and W. Louise (Reynolds) Van B.; m. Sally Wardall Huey, Aug. 14, 1971; children— Brian, Kate. B.A., U. Ind., 1966, J.D., 1969. Bar: Ind. 1969, U.S. Dist. Ct. (so. dist.) Ind. 1969, U.S. Dist. Ct. (no. dist.) Ind. 1973, U.S. Ct. Appeals (7th cir.) 1973, U.S. Supreme Ct. 1973. Dep. atty. gen. State of Ind., Indpls., 1969-71, asst. atty. gen., 1971-72; asst. U.S. atty. No. Dist. Ind., Hammond, 1972-75; ptnr. Goldsmith, Goodman, Ball & Van Bokkelen, Highland, Ind., 1975— ; U.S. atty. Ind. No. Dist., 2001-. Recipient Outstanding Asst. U.S. Atty. award U.S. Dept. Justice, 1974. Mem. ABA, Fed. Bar Assn., Ind. Bar Assn., Criminal Def. Lawyers Assn. Home: 9013 Indianapolis Blvd Highland IN 46322-2502 Office: 1001 Main St Ste A Dyer IN 46311-1234

VAN BRUNT, MARCIA ADELE, social worker; b. Chgo., Oct. 21, 1937; d. Dean Frederick and Faye Lila (Greim) Slauson; children: Suzanne, Christine, David. Student, Moline (Ill.) Pub. Hosp. Sch. Nursing, 1955—57; BA with disting. scholastic record, U. Wis., Madison, 1972, MSW (Fed. tng. grantee), 1973. Social worker divsn. cmty. svcs. Wis. Dept. Health Social Svcs., Rheinlander, 1973, regional adoption coord., 1973—79, chief adoption and permanent planning no. region, 1979—83, asst. chief direct svcs. and regulation no. region, 1983—84; adminstr., clin. social worker No. Family Svcs., Inc., 1984—. Counselor, psychotherapist, pub. spkr., cons. in field of clin. social work. Home: 5264 Forest Ln Rhinelander WI 54501-7900 Office: Northern Family Services Inc 5 W Frederick St PO Box 237 Rhinelander WI 54501-0237 E-mail: barmar@newnorth.net.

VAN BUREN, ABIGAIL (JEANNE PHILLIPS), columnist, lecturer; b. Minneapolis, Minnesota, Apr. 10, 1942; d. Morton and Pauline (Friedman) Phillips. Student, Morningside Coll., Sioux City, 1936-39; Litt.D. (hon.), Morningside Coll., 1965; L.H.D. (hon.), U. Jacksonville, Fla., 1984. Vol. worker for causes of better mental health Nat. Found. Infantile Paralysis; tng. Gray Ladies, ARC, 1939-56; pres. Minn.-Wis. council B'nai B'rith Aux., 1945-49; columnist Dear Abby San Francisco Chronicle, 1956, McNaught Syndicate, 1956-74, Chgo. Tribune Syndicate, 1974-80, Universal Press Syndicate, 1980—; syndicated U.S., Brazil, Mex., Japan, Philippines, Fed. Republic Germany, India, Holland, Denmark, Can., Korea, Thailand, Italy, Hong Kong, Taiwan, Ireland, Saudi Arabia, Greece, France, Dominican Republic, P.R., Costa Rica, U.S. Virgin Islands, Bermuda, Guam. Host radio program The Dear Abby Show, CBS, 1963-75; life-time cons. Group for Advancement Psychiatry, 1985— Author: Dear Abby, 1957 (also translated into Japanese, Dutch, German, Spanish, Danish, Italian, Finnish), Dear Teen Ager, 1959, Dear Abby on Marriage, 1962, The Best of Dear Abby, 1981, reissued, 1989, Dear Abby on Planning Your Wedding, 1988, Where Were You When President Kennedy Was Shot?: Memories and Tributes to a Slain President as Told to Dear Abby, 1993. Mem. nat. adv. council on aging NIH, HEW, 1978-81; hon. chairwoman 1st Nat. Women's Conf. on Cancer, Am. Cancer Soc., Los Angeles, 1979; mem. public adv. council Center for Study Multiple Gestation, 1981; trustee, mem. adv. bd. Westside Community for Ind. Living, 1981; bd. dirs. Guthrie Theatre, Mpls., 1970-74; charter mem. Franz Alexander Research Found., Los Angeles; charter trustee Armand Hammer United World Coll. of Am. West; bd. dirs. Am. Fedn. for Aging Research Inc.; mem. nat. bd. Goodwill Industries, 1968-75; nat. chmn. Crippled Children Soc., 1962; founding mem. The Amazing Blue Ribbon 400; hon. chmn. Easter Seal campaign Nat. Soc. Crippled Children and Adults, Washington, 1963; del. to Democratic Nat. Conf. from Calif., 1964; Calif. del. White House Conf. on Children and Youth, 1974; non. life mem. Concern for Dying-Am. Ednl. Council; mem. White House Conf. on Physically Handicapped, 1976, NIH, 1976; mem. adv. council Suicide Prevention Ctr., Los Angeles, 1977; mem. com. on aging HHS, 1977-82; council sponsor Assn. Vol. Sterilization, 1981; mem. Women's Trusteeship, 1980; sponsor Mayo Found., Rochester, 1982; bd. dirs. Lupus Found. Am., 1983; mem. adv. com. Ams. for Substance Abuse Prevention, 1984; participant XIII Internat. Congress Gerontology, N.Y.C., 1985; mem. adv. bd. Young Writer's Contest Found., 1985; bd. dirs. Am. Found. for AIDS Research, 1985— ; mem. adv. bd. Nat. Council for Children's Rights, Washington, 1988; mem. adv. bd. San Diego Hospice, 1990; mem. adv. bd. Rhonda Fleming Mann Clinic for Women's Comprehensive Care, 1991; mem. Scripps Rsch. Coun. Recipient Times Mother of Yr. award, L.A., 1958; Golden Kidney award, L.A., 1960; Sarah Coventry award, Miami, 1961; Woman of Yr. award Internat. Rotary Club, Rome, 1965; award NCCJ, St. Louis, 1968; award for disting. svc. to sightless Internat. Lions Club, Dallas, 1972; Nat. Planned Parenthood award, 1974, Dinting. Svc. award Suicide Prevention Ctr., San Mateo, Calif., 1975; Good Samaritan award Salvation Army, San Francisco, 1970; Margaret Sanger award for outstanding svcs. in mental health So. Psychiat. Assn., 1974; Robert T. Morse writer's award Am. Psychiat. Assn., 1977; Tex. Gov.'s award in recognition of exceptional svc. to youth of Am. for Ops. Peace of Mind, 1979; Humanitarian award Gay Acad. Union, L.A., 1979, Braille Inst. So. Calif., 1981, Gay and Lesbian Cmty. Svcs. Ctr., 1984; pub. Awareness trophy for Living Will, Soc. for Right to Die, 1983; citation of commentation Simon Weisenthal Found., 1984; Internat. Image in Media award Gay Fathers Coalition, 1985; 1st ann. Woman of Yr. Humanitarian award Rainbow Guild of Amy Karen Children's Cancer Clinic, Cedars-Sinai Med. Ctr., L.A. 1985; Pub. Svc. award Nat. Kidney Found., 1985, John Rock award Ctr. Population Options, 1986, Serve Am. award Ladies Auxiliary VFW, 1986, Genesis award Fund for Animals, 1986, Disting. Svc. award Inst. Studies Destructive Behavior and Suicide Prevention Ctr., 1986, Citizen of Yr. award Beverly Hills, Calif. C. of C., 1988, Humanitarian award Nat. Coun. on Alcoholism, 1988, Helen B. Taussig medal Internat. Socs. for the Right to Die with Dignity, 1988, Media award So. Psychiat. Soc., 1988, Disting. Achievement award Nat. Assn. to Advance Fat Acceptance, 1988, Hand to Hand award Episc. Charities San Francisco, 1989, Nat. Media award for print Nat. Down Syndrome Congress, 1991, Sec.'s award for excellence in comm. HHS, 1992, Dove award Assn. Retarded Citizens, 1992, Civic award Alzheimer's Assn., 1996, Founders award Westside Ctr. Ind. Living, 1996, Disting. Contbns. to Journalism award Nat. Press Found., 1997, Person of Vision award Prevent Blindness Am., 1998, Gift of Life award Ariz. Kidney Found., 1999, Generations for Choice awards Planned Parenthood of L.A., 1999; named Hon. Dir. Found. for Craniofacial Deformities, 1988. Mem. Women in Communications (hon.), Am. Coll. Psychiatrists (hon. life mem.), Nat. Coun. Jewish Women (hon. life mem.), Newspapers Features Council, Soc. Profl. Journalists, Nat. Orgn. Women, "Women For", Nat. Com. Preserve Social Security and Medicare, Korean War Vets. Assn. (hon.), L.A. World Affairs Coun., Sigma Delta Chi. Office: Universal Press Syndicate 4520 Main St Ste 700 Kansas City MO 64111-7701

VAN CLEAVE, WILLIAM ROBERT, international relations educator; b. Kansas City, Mo., Aug. 27, 1935; s. Earl Jr. and Georgiana (Offutt) Van C.; children: William Robert II, Cynthia Kay. BA in Polit. Sci. summa cum laude, Calif. State U., Long Beach, 1962; MA in Govt. and Internat. Rels., Claremont (Calif.) Grad. Sch., 1964, PhD, 1966. Political scientist Stanford U., 1964-67; mem. faculty U. So. Calif., 1967-87, prof. internat. rels., 1974-87, dir. def. and strategic studies ctr., 1971-87; prof., dept. head, dir. Ctr. for Def. and Strategic Studies Southwest Mo. State U., 1987—; sr. rsch. fellow Hoover Instn. Stanford U., 1981-97. Chmn. Strategic Alternatives Team, 1977-90; acting chmn. Pres.'s Gen. Adv. Com. on Arms Control, 1981-82; spl. asst. Office Sec. Def., mem. Strategic Arms Limitation Talks (SALT) delegation, 1969-71; mem. B team on Nat. Intelligence Estimates, 1976; mem. exec. panel, bd. dirs. Com. Present Danger, 1980-93; dir. transition team Dept. Def., 1980-81; sr. nat. security advisor to Ronald Reagan, 1979-80; mem. nat. security affairs adv. council Republican Nat. Com., 1979-89; research council Fgn. Policy Research Inst., Inst. Fgn. Policy Analysis; co-dir. Ann. Internat. Security Summer Seminar, Fed. Republic Germany, 1981-98; trustee Am. com. Internat. Inst. Strategic Studies, 1980—; vis. prof. U.S. Army Advanced Russian Inst., Garmisch, Fed. Republic Germany, 1978-79; chmn. adv. bd. Internat. Security Coun., 1991-96; cons. in field, mem. numerous govt. adv. coms. Co-author: Strategic Options for the Early Eighties: What Can Be Done?, 1979, Tactical Nuclear Weapons, 1978, Nuclear Weapons, Policies, and the Test Ban Issue, 1987, Strategy and International Politics, 2000; author: Fortress USSR, 1986; mem. bd. editors Global Affairs. Co-chmn. Scholars for Reagan, 1984; mem. exec. coun., dir. NCAA rels. Haka Bowl, NCAA Postseason Football Bowl. With USMC, 1953-61. Recipient Freedom Found. award, 1976, Outstanding Contbn. award Air War Coll., 1979, award teaching excellence U. So. Calif., 1980, 86; named Outstanding Prof. U. So. Calif., 1977, Disting. Alumnus Claremont Colls., 1978; Woodrow Wilson fellow, 1962, NDEA fellow, 1963-65. Mem. Internat. Inst. Strategic Studies (U.S. com., bd. trustees). Home: 8226 E Panther Hollow Ln Rogersville MO 65742-8386 Office: Dept Def and Strategic Studies Southwest Mo State U Southwest Mo State U Springfield MO 65804-0095

VAN CLEVE, WILLIAM MOORE, lawyer; b. Mar. 17, 1929; s. William T Van Cleve and Catherine (Baldwin) Moore Van Cleve; m. Georgia Hess Dunbar, June 27, 1953; children: Peter Dunbar, Robert Baldwin, Sarah Van Cleve Van Doren, Emory Basford. Grad., Phillips Acad., 1946; AB in Econs., Princeton U., 1950; JD, Washington U., St. Louis, 1953, LLD (hon.), 2001. Bar: Mo. 1953. Assoc. Dunbar and Gaddy, St. Louis, 1955-58; ptnr. Bryan Cave LLP (and predecessor firm), 1958-2000, chmn., 1973-94, sr. counsel., 2001—. Bd. dirs. Emerson Electric Co. Trustee Washington U., 1983—, vice chmn. bd. trustees, 1988-93, 95-2000, chmn., 1993-95, mem. exec. com., 1985—; pres. Eliot Soc., 1982-86; chmn. Law Sch. Nat. Coun., 1986-93; commr. St. Louis Sci. Ctr., 1993-2000, bd. trustees, 2001—; bd. dirs., Parents As Tchrs. Nat. Ctr., 1991—, pres., 1997-2000. Mem. ABA, Bar Assn. Met. St. Louis, Mound City Bar Assn., St. Louis County Bar Assn., Order of Coif (hon.). Democrat. Episcopalian. Clubs: Princeton (pres. 1974-75), Noonday (pres. 1985), St. Louis Country, Bogey (pres. 1990-91), Round Table (St. Louis) Home: 8 Dromara Rd Saint Louis MO 63124-1816 Office: Bryan Cave LLP 211 N Broadway Fl 36 Saint Louis MO 63102-2750 E-mail: wmvancleve@bryancave.com.

VANDE KROL, JERRY LEE, architect; b. Oskaloosa, Iowa, Oct. 5, 1949; s. Glen Vande Krol and Nola Fern (Monsma) Emmert; m. Constance Louise Wood, May 30, 1970; children: Sarah Lynn, Rachel Ann, Molly Jayne. BArch, Iowa State U., 1972. Registered architect, Iowa. Designer City of Akron, Ohio, 1972-76; architect Brooks Borg and Skiles, Des Moines, 1976-90; founder VOV Architecture and Design, P.C., 1990—. Recipient Merit Design award Ohio Chpt. Soc. Landscape Architects, 1977. Mem. AIA (Iowa chpt., Design award 1984, 90, regional chpt. Design award 1985, 91, 97), Ctrl. Iowa Archs. Republican. Mem. Brethren Ch. Avocations: music, classical guitar, reading, golf. Office: Vov Architecture Design Ste 250 108 3rd St Des Moines IA 50309-4758

VANDELL, KERRY DEAN, real estate and urban economics educator; b. Biloxi, Miss., Jan. 8, 1947; s. Benedict Sandy and Eleanor Ruby (Lenhart) V.; m. Deborah Ann Lowe, May 16, 1970; children: Colin Buckner, Ashley Elizabeth. BA, MME, Rice U., 1970; M City Planning, Harvard U., 1973; PhD, MIT, 1977. Assoc. engr. Exxon Co., USA, Houston, 1970-71; asst. prof. So. Meth. U., Dallas, 1976-80, assoc. prof., 1980-86, prof., chmn. dept., 1986-89; prof. real estate and urban land econs., chm. dept. U. Wis., Madison, 1989-93, dir. Ctr. for Urban Land Econs. rsch., 1989—, Tiefenthaler chairholder, 1996—; exec. dir. Bolz Ctr. Arts Adminstrn., 2000—. Vis. assoc. prof. Harvard U., Cambridge, Mass., 1985-86; vis. prof. U. Calif., Berkeley, 1988-89, U. Hong Kong, 1997; bd. dirs. Park Bank, Madison, U. Rsch. Pk., Chrisken Realty Trust. Mem. editl. bd. Jour. Real Estate Fin. and Econs., 1989—, Land Econs., 1989—, Jour. Property Rsch., 1989-94; contbr. numerous articles on mortgage default risk, neighborhood dynamics, econs. of architecture, and appraisal theory to profl. jours. Fellow Homer Hoyt Advanced Studies Inst. (faculty 1989—, bd. dirs.); mem. Urban Land Inst., Am. Real Estate and Urban Econs. Assn. (2nd v.p. 1989, 1st v.p. 1990, pres. 1991, co-editor jour. 1991-96). Episcopalian. Home: 3301 Topping Rd Madison WI 53705-1436 Office: U Wis Sch Bus 975 University Ave Madison WI 53706-1324 E-mail: kvandell@bus.wisc.edu.

VAN DELLEN, H. TODD, state legislator; b. Apr. 24, 1964; m. Dana Lynn; three children. BBA, U. N.D.; JD, U. Minn. Minn. State rep. Dist. 34B, 1993—; corp. counsel EBP Health Plans, Inc. Named Best First Term Mem., State House of Reps., Politics in Minn. newsletter. Home: 14615 43rd Ave N Plymouth MN 55446-2786 Office: Minn House Standing Com State Capitol Saint Paul MN 55155-0001

VAN DEMARK, RUTH ELAINE, lawyer; b. Santa Fe, May 16, 1944; d. Robert Eugene and Bertha Marie (Thompson) Van D.; m. Leland Wilkinson, June 23, 1967; children: Anne Marie, Caroline Cook. AB, Vassar Coll., 1966; MTS, Harvard U., 1969; JD with honors, U. Conn., 1976; MDiv, Luth Sch. Theology, Chgo., 1999. Bar: Conn. 1976, Ill. 1977, U.S. Dist. Ct. Conn. 1976, U.S. Dist. Ct. (no. dist.) Ill., U.S. Ct. Appeals (7th cir.) 1984, U.S. Supreme Ct. 1983; ordained to ministry, Luth Ch., 1999. Instr. legal rsch. and writing Loyola U. Sch. Law, Chgo., 1976-79; assoc. Wildman, Harrold, Allen & Dixon, 1977-84, ptnr., 1985-94; prin. Law Offices of Ruth E. Van Demark, 1995—; pastor Wicker Park Luth. Ch., 1999—. Mem.

rules com. Ill. Supreme Ct., 1999—, chair appellate rules subcom., 1996—; mem. dist. ct. fund adv. com. U.S. Dist. Ct. (no. dist.) Ill., 1997—. Assoc. editor Conn. Law Rev., 1975-76. Bd. dirs. Lutheran Soc. Svcs. Ill., 1998—, sec., 2000—02, chmn., 2002-; mem. adv. bd. Horizon Hospice, Chgo., 1978—, YWCA Battered Women's Shelter, Evanston, Ill., 1982-86; del.-at-large White House Conf. on Families, L.A., 1980; mem. alumni coun. Harvard Divinity Sch., 1988-91; vol. atty. Pro Bono Advocates Chgo., 1982-92, bd. dirs., 1993-99, chair devel. com., 1993; bd. dirs. Friends of Pro Bono Advocates Orgn., 1987-89, New Voice Prodns., 1984-86, Byrne Piven Theater Workshop, 1987-90, Luth. Social Svcs. Ill. (sec., 2000—), 1998—; founder, bd. dirs. Friends of Battered Women and Their Children, 1986-87; chair 175th Reunion Fund Harvard U. Div. Sch., 1992. Mem. ABA, Ill. Bar Assn., Conn. Bar Assn., Chgo. Bar Assn., Appellate Lawyers Assn. Ill. (bd. dirs. 1985-87, treas. 1989-90, sec. 1990-91, v.p. 1991-92, pres. 1992-93), Women's Bar Assn. Ill., Jr. League Evanston (chair State Pub. Affairs Com. 1987-88, Vol. of Yr. 1983-84), Chgo. Vassar Club (pres. 1979-81), Cosmopolitan Club (N.Y.C.). Home: 2046 W Pierce Ave Chicago IL 60622-1946 Office: 225 W Washington St Ste 2200 Chicago IL 60606-3408 E-mail: revlaw@msn.com.

VANDENBROUCKE, RUSSELL JAMES, theatre director, writer, educator; b. Chgo., Aug. 16, 1948; s. Arthur C. Sr. and Ardelle (Barker) V.; m. Mary Allison Dilg, Sept. 7, 1974; children: Aynsley Louise, Justin Arthur. BA, U. Ill., 1970; MA, U. Warwick, Coventry, Eng., 1975; MFA in Drama, Yale U., 1977, DFA in Drama, 1978. Asst. literary mgr. Yale Repertory Theatre, New Haven, 1977-78; lit. mgr., dramaturg Mark Taper Forum, Los Angeles, 1978-85; assoc. producing dir. Repertory Theatre St. Louis, 1985-87; artistic dir. Northlight Theatre, Evanston, Ill., 1987-98. Vis. prof. Yale U., 1978, La. State U., 1981, U. Calif.-San Diego, 1983, Middlebury Coll., 1985, Washington U., 1986; adj. assoc. prof. Northwestern U., 1987-2001; prof., chair theater arts U. Louisville, 2001—. Author: Truths the Hand Can Tough: The Theatre of Athol Fugard, 1985, The Theatre Quotation Book: A Treasury of Insights and Insults, 2001; editor: Contemporary Australian Plays; play adapted for radio and stage: Los Alamos Revisited, 1984, play adapted for radio and stage: , 1987, play adapted for tv: Eleanor: In Her Own Words, 1985, play adapted from Truman Capote: Holiday Memories, 1991, adapted play: Feiffer's America, 1988, adapted play: An Enemy of the People, 1991, adapted play: Atomic Bombers, 1997; dir.: (plays) Feiffer's America, 1988, Eleanor: In Her Own Words, 1990, Lucky Lindy, Love Letters on Blue Paper, 84 Charing Cross Rd, Three Women Talking, Smoke on the Mountain, The White Rose, Betrayal, My Other Heart, Later Life, Hedda Gabler, Bubbe Meises, Valley Song, Fires in the Mirror, The Glass House, Philoctetes, Blood Knot, Atomic Bombers, Proof, Humana Festival, Snapshot, (play for radio): Three Women Talking; contbr. articles. Recipient L.A. Drama Critics Cir. award, 1984, Spl. Actors Equity Assn. award, 1990; Fulbright sr. scholar, Australia, 1996. Avocation: basketball. E-mail: russ.van@aya.yale.edu.

VAN DEN HENDE, FRED J(OSEPH), human resources executive; b. Chgo., Sept. 28, 1953; s. Maurice Everett and Alice Helen (Davey) Van Den H.; m. Sharon Joyce Kucharski, Oct. 4, 1975; children: John Michael, Karen Michelle. BA, DePaul U., 1975; grad., U. Wash. Sch. Exec. Dev., 1981; MS, Nat. Louis U., 1998. Cert. sr. profl. human resources. Asst. v.p. human resources Land of Lincoln Savs. and Loan, Berwyn, Ill., 1977-84; v.p. human resources Uptown Fed. Bank FSB, Niles, 1984-88; dir. human resources Archdiocese of Chgo., 1988—; adj. faculty Grad. Sch. Mgmt. and Bus. Nat. Louis U., 1998—. Mem. Savs. Assn. Pers. Adminstrn., Berwyn, 1977-84; part-time instr. Inst. Fin. Edn., Chgo., 1984-90, Moraine Valley C.C., Palos Hills, Ill., 1984-90. Sch. bd. treas. St. Rene Sch., Chgo., 1981; sch. bd. mem. St. Daniel the Prophet Sch., Chgo., 1986-88, 93-95, sch. bd. chmn., 1988-89; boy scout leader St. Daniel Parish, Chgo., 1987-94. Recipient Oustanding Achievement in the Field of Athletics award St. Rita H.S. Alumni Assn., Chgo., 1991; Athletic scholar DePaul U., Chgo., 1971-75. Mem. Nat. Assn. Ch. Pers. Adminstrs., Soc. for Human Resource Mgmt. (mem. sch.-to-work com. 1998—), Ill. State C. of C. (human resources com. 1979—, healthcare com. 1998—), Inst. Internat. Human Resources, Am. Mgmt. Assn. (Chicago Area Tng. Coun. 2001—). Roman Catholic. Avocations: camping, fishing, coaching youth sports teams, horseback riding. Home: 5130 S Mulligan Ave Chicago IL 60638-1316 Office: Archdiocese of Chgo 155 E Superior St Chicago IL 60611-2911 E-mail: fvandenhende@archdiocese-chgo.org.

VANDER AARDE, STANLEY BERNARD, retired otolaryngologist; b. Orange City, Iowa, Sept. 26, 1931; s. Bernard John and Christina (Luchtenberg) Vander A.; m. Agnes Darlene De Beer, June 19, 1956; children: Paul, David, Debra, Mary. BA, Hope Coll., 1953; MD, Northwestern U., 1957. Diplomate Am. Bd. Otolaryngology. Intern Cook County Hosp., Chgo., 1957-59; resident in otolaryngology Northwestern U. Hosp., 1966-70; mem. staff Mary Lott Lyles Hosp., Madanapalle, India, 1961-66, 71-87, Affiliated Med. Clinic, Willmar, Minn., 1987-95, ret., 1995. Served to capt., USAF, 1959-60. Fellow ACS, Am. Bd. Otolaryngology, Am. Acad. Otolaryngology. Republican. Mem. Reformed Church in America. Home: 708 2nd St SE Apt 112 Orange City IA 51041-2165 Office: Affiliated Med Clinic 101 Willmar Ave SW Willmar MN 56201-3556

VANDERBEKE, PATRICIA K. architect; b. Detroit, Apr. 3, 1963; d. B. H. and Dolores I. VanderBeke. BS in Architecture, U. Mich., 1985, MArch, 1987. Registered arch., Ill. Archtl. intern Hobbs & Black, Assocs., Ann Arbor, Mich., 1984-86, Fry Assocs., Ann Arbor, 1988; arch. Decker & Kemp Architecture/Urban Design, Chgo., 1989-92; prin., founder P. K. VanderBeke, Arch., 1992—. Mem. adv. com. dept. arch., Triton Coll. Contbr. photographs and articles to Inland Arch. mag.; contbr. photographs to AIA calendar. Chair recycling com. Lake Point Tower Condo. Assn., Chgo., 1990—, chair. ops. com., 1993; mem. benefit com. The Renaissance Soc., U. Chgo., Redmoon Theater, Chgo. George S. Booth travelling fellow, 1992. Mem. AIA (participant 1st ann. leadership inst. 1997, 1st place nat. photog. contest award 1992, hon. mention 1994, membership com. Chgo. chpt.), Chgo. Archtl. Club, hon. mention 2000 Burnham Prize Competition, The Cliff Dwellers (mem. arts com.). Office: 155 W Burton Pl Apt 16 Chicago IL 60610-1326

VANDER LAAN, MARK ALAN, lawyer; b. Akron, Ohio, Sept. 14, 1948; s. Robert H. and Isabel R. (Bishop) Vander L.; m. Barbara Ann Ryzenga, Aug. 25, 1970; children: Aaron, Matthew. AB, Hope Coll., 1970; JD, U. Mich., 1972. Bar: Ohio 1973, U.S. Dist. Ct. (so. dist.) Ohio 1973, U.S. Ct. Appeals (6th cir.) 1978, U.S. Supreme Ct. 1981. Assoc. Dinsmore, Shohl, Coates & Deupree, Cin., 1972-79; ptnr. Dinsmore & Shohl, 1979—. Chair litig. dept., 2001—, spl. counsel Ohio Atty. Gen.'s Office, 1983—; spl. prosecutor State of Ohio, 1985-94; city solicitor City of Blue Ash, Ohio, 1987—, City of Silverton, Ohio, 1999—; trustee Cin. So. Railway, 1994—, pres., 1999—; trustee, chair Grassroots Leadership Acad., 1997—. Mem. Cin. Human Rels. Commn., 1980-86; mem. Leadership Cin. Class XIII, 1989-90; trustee Legal Aid Soc. of Cin., 1981-94, pres., 1988-90. Mem. ABA, Ohio Bar Assn., Cin. Bar Assn. (ethics com. 1983—), Sixth Cir. Jud. Conf. (life), Potter Stewart Inn of Ct. (master), Queen City Club. Office: Dinsmore & Shohl 1900 Chemed Ct 255 E 5th St Cincinnati OH 45202-4700

VAN DER MARCK, JAN, art historian; b. Roermond, The Netherlands, Aug. 19, 1929; s. Everard and Anny (Finken) van der Marck; m. Ingeborg Lachmann, Apr. 27, 1961 (dec. 1988); m. Sheila Stamell, May 24, 1990. BA, U. Nijmegen, The Netherlands, 1952, MA, 1954, PhD in Art History, 1956; postgrad., U. Utrecht, The Netherlands, 1956-57, Columbia U., 1957-59. Curator Gemeentemuseum, Arnhem, Netherlands, 1959-61; asst. dir. fine arts Seattle World's Fair, 1961-62; curator Walker Art Center, Mpls., 1963-67; dir. Mus. Contemporary Art, Chgo., 1967-70; assoc. prof. art history U. Wash., 1972-74; dir. Dartmouth Coll. Mus. and Galleries, 1974-80, Center for Fine Arts, Miami, 1980-85; curator 20th century art, chief curator Detroit Inst. Arts, 1986-95, consultative curator, 1998—. Author: (book) Romantische Boekillustratie in Belgie, 1956, George Segal, 1975, Arman, 1984, Bernar Venet, 1988, The Art of Contemporary Bookbinding, 1997, Art and the American Experience, 1998, Lucio Pozzi, 2001; contbr. articles to art jours., essays to catalogues. Fellow Pierpont Morgan Libr. Decorated officer Order Arts and Letters, knight Order of Orange Nassau; fellow Netherlands Orgn. Pure Rsch., 1954—55, Rockefeller Found., 1957—59, Aspen Inst., 1974, 1994, Vis. Sr., Ctr. Advanced Study in Visual Arts, 1986. Mem.: Les Amis de la Reliure Originale, Assn. Internat. Bibliophilie, Internat. Art Critics Assn., Grolier Club.

VANDER MOLEN, THOMAS DALE, lawyer; b. Ann Arbor, Mich., Oct. 30, 1950; s. John and Eleanor Ruth (Driesens) Vander M.; m. Judith P. Wrahlstad, June 16, 2001; children from previous marriage: Laura, David, Eric. BA, Calvin Coll., 1972; JD magna cum laude, Harvard U., 1975. Bar: Minn. 1976, U.S. Dist. Ct. Minn. 1981, U.S. Claims Ct. 1983, U.S. Tax Ct. 1977, U.S. Ct. Appeals 1988. Law clk. to judge U.S. Ct. Appeals-First Cir., Boston, 1975-76; assoc. Dorsey & Whitney, Mpls., 1976-81; ptnr. Dorsey & Whitney LLP, 1982—, gen. counsel, 1993—2001. Mem. editorial bd. Harvard Law Rev., 1973-75. Presbyterian. Office: Dorsey & Whitney LLP 50 South 6th St Minneapolis MN 55402

VANDERPOOL, WARD MELVIN, management and marketing consultant; b. Oakland, Mo., Jan. 20, 1918; s. Oscar B. and Clara (McGuire) V.; m. Lee Kendall, July 7, 1939. MEE, Tulane U. V.p. charge sales Van Lang Brokerage, Los Angeles, 1934-38; mgr. agrl. div. Dayton Rubber Co., Chgo., 1939-48; pres., gen. mgr. Vee Mac Co., Rockford, Ill., 1948—; pres., dir. Zipout, Inc., 1951—, Wife Saver Products, Inc., 1959—. Chmn. bd. Zipout Internat., Kenvan Inc., 1952—, Shevan Corp., 1951—, Atlas Internat. Corp.; pres. Global Enterprises Ltd., Global Assos. Ltd.; chmn. bd. dirs. Am. Atlas Corp., Atlas Chem. Corp., Merzat Industries Ltd.; trustee Ice Crafter Trust, 1949—; bd. dirs. Atlas Chem. Internat. Ltd., Kenlee Internat., Ltd., Shrimp Tool Internat. Ltd.; mem. Toronto Bd. Trade; chmn. bd. dirs. Am. Atlas Corp., Am. Packaging Corp. Mem. adv. bd. Nat. Security Council, congl. adv. com. Heritage Found.; mem. Rep. Nat. Com., Presdl. Task Force, Congrl. Adv. Com. Hon. mem. Internat. Swimming Hall of Fame. Mem. Nat. (dir. at large), Rock River (past pres.), sales execs., Sales and Mktg. Execs. Internat. (dir.), Am. Mgmt. Assn., Rockford Engring. Soc., Am. Tool Engrs., Internat. Acad. Aquatic Art (dir.), Am. Inst. Mgmt. (pres. council), Am. Ordnance Assn., Internat. Platform Assn., Heritage Found., Ill. C. of C., Jesters Club, IAA Swim Club, Elmcrest Country Club, Pyramid Club, Dolphin Club, Marlin Club, Univ. Club, Athletic Club, Oxford Club, Masons (consistory), Shriners, Elks. Home: 374 Parkland Dr SE Cedar Rapids IA 52403-2031 also: 40 Richview Rd # 308 Toronto ON Canada M9A 5C1 also: 704 Park Center Dr Santa Ana CA 92705-3563 Office: PO Box 1972 Cedar Rapids IA 52406-1972 also: 111 Richmond St W Ste 318 Toronto ON Canada M5H 1T1

VAN DER VOO, ROB, geophysicist; b. Zeist, The Netherlands, Aug. 4, 1940; arrived in U.S., 1970; s. Maximiliaan and Johanna Hendrika (Baggerman) Van der V.; m. Tatiana M. C. Graafland, Mar. 26, 1966; children— Serge Nicholas, Bjorn Alexander. B.S., U. Utrecht, Netherlands, 1961, M.S., 1965, Ph.D., 1969. Rsch. asst. U. Utrecht, 1964-65, rsch. assoc., 1965-69, sr. rsch. assoc., 1969-70; vis. asst. prof. U. Mich., Ann Arbor, 1970-72, asst. prof., 1972-75, assoc. prof., 1975-79, prof. geophysics, 1979—, chmn., 1981-88, 91-95, Arthur F. Thurnau prof., 1994-97, dir. honors program, Coll. Lit., Sci. & the Arts, 1998—2003. Guest prof. ETH, Zurich, Switzerland, 1978, Kuwait U., 1979, Utrecht U. and Delft U. Tech., 1997-98. Author: Paleomagnetism of the Atlantic, Tethys and Iapetus Oceans, 1993; contbr. articles to profl. jours. Recipient Russell award, U. Mich., 1976, Disting. Faculty Achievement award, 1990, Benjamin Franklin medal in Earth Scis., 2001. Mem. Geol. Soc. Am., Am. Geophys. Union, Geologische Vereinigung (W.Ger.), Royal Acad. Scis. (Netherlands), Royal Norwegian Soc. Scis. and Letters, Sigma Xi, Phi Kappa Phi. Home: 2305 Devonshire Rd Ann Arbor MI 48104-2703 Office: U Mich 4534 CC Little Bldg Ann Arbor MI 48109-1063 E-mail: voo@umich.edu.

VANDER WILT, CARL EUGENE, banker; b. Ottumwa, Iowa, Aug. 17, 1942; s. John Adrian and Wilma (Hulsbos) V W.; m. Carol Anne Szymanski, Jan. 29, 1977; children— Dirk Francis, Neal Adrian BS, Iowa State U., 1964, PhD, 1968; grad. Advanced Mgmt. Program, Harvard U., 1986. Research economist Fed. Res. Bank, Chgo., 1970-73, asst. v.p., 1973-74, v.p., 1974-79, sr. v.p., 1979-84, sr. v.p., chief fin. officer, 1984—. Mem., bd. dirs. Goodwill Industries of Southeastern Wis., Met. Chgo., Chgo. Bd. Roosevelt U. Served to capt. U.S. Army, 1968-70. Mem. Chgo. Coun. Fgn. Rels., Execs. Club Chgo. (dir., chmn. reception com.), Banker's Club Chgo., Econ. Club Chgo. Home: 656 Locust St Winnetka IL 60093-2012 Office: Fed Res Bank 230 S La Salle St Chicago IL 60604-1496

VANDEUSEN, BRUCE DUDLEY, company executive; b. Lorain, Ohio, Aug. 20, 1931; s. Clarence Elmer and Margaret (Richards) VanD.; m. Ann Marie Groves, Aug. 17, 1957; children: David Bruce, Elizabeth Ann. Janet Marie. B.A., Ohio Wesleyan U., 1952; M.S., U. Mich., 1958, Ph.D., 1971; M.A.E., Chrysler Inst. Engring., Highland Park, Mich., 1958. Registered profl. engr., Mich. Fellow Ohio State U., Columbus, 1953-54; student engr. Chrysler Corp., Highland Park, 1956-58, sr. research scientist, 1958-67; chief engr. Chrysler Def., Inc., Center Line, Mich., 1967-79, mgr. advanced devel., 1979-82; dir. advanced devel. Gen. Dynamics, Warren, 1982-87, program dir., 1987-93; pres. Edn. Svcs., Birmingham, 1994—. Contbr. numerous articles to profl. publs.; patentee electronic cirs. Trustee Birmingham Bd. Edn., Mich., 1976-88, pres., 1979-84, 87-88; trustee Birmingham Community House, 1981-87. Mem. Soc. Automotive Engrs. (chmn. sci. engring. activity 1967-69, Arch T. Colwell award 1968). Republican. Methodist. Home: 4173 Chatfield Ln Troy MI 48098-4327 Office: Edn Svcs PO Box 170 Birmingham MI 48012-0170 E-mail: BVD@EducationServicesInc.com., Vandeus@yahoo.com.

VAN DE VYVER, SISTER MARY FRANCILENE, academic administrator; b. Detroit, Sept. 6, 1941; d. Hector Joseph and Irene Cecilia (Zygailo) V. BA, Madonna Coll., 1965; MEd, Wayne State U., 1970, PhD, 1977. Joined Sisters of St. Felix of Cantalice, Roman Cath. Ch., 1959. Tchr. Ladywood High Sch., 1967-71, Gabriel Richard H.S., 1971-74; adminstrv. asst. to pres. Madonna Coll., Livonia, Mich., 1974-75, acad. dean, 1975-76; now pres. Madonna U. Office: Madonna U Office of President 36600 Schoolcraft Rd Livonia MI 48150-1176

VANDEWALLE, GERALD WAYNE, state supreme court chief justice; b. Noonan, N.D., Aug. 15, 1933; s. Jules C. and Blanche Marie (Gits) VandeW. BSc, U. N.D., 1955, JD, 1958. Bar: N.D., U.S. Dist. Ct. N.D. 1959. Spl. asst. atty. gen. State of N.D., Bismarck, 1958-75, 1st asst. atty. gen., 1975-78; justice N.D. Supreme Ct., 1978-92, chief justice, 1993—. Mem. faculty Bismarck Jr. Coll., 1972-76; mem. Nat. Ctr. for State Cts. Rsch. adv. coun.; mem. fed.-state jurisdiction com. Jud. Conf. of the U.S. Editor-in-chief N.D. Law Rev, 1957-58. Active Bismarck Meals on Wheels Recipient Sioux award U. N.D., 1992, Ednl. Law award N.D. Coun. Sch. Attys., 1987, Love Without Fear award Abused Adult Resource Ctr., 1995, N. Dakota State Bar Assoc. Dist. Service Award, 1998. Mem. ABA (co-chmn. bar admissions com. 1991-99, mem. coun. sect. legal edn. and admissions, chmn. coun. sect. legal edn. and admissions), State Bar Assn. N.D., Burleigh County Bar Assn., Conf. of Chief Justices (past pres., bd. dirs. 1996-98, chmn. fed.-state tribal rels. com.), Am. Contract Bridge League, Order of Coif, N.D. Jud. Conf. (exec. com.), Elks, KC, Phi Eta Sigma, Beta Alpha Psi (Outstanding Alumnus award Zeta chpt. 1995), Beta Gamma Sigma, Phi Alpha Delta. Roman Catholic. Office: ND Supreme Ct State Capitol 600 E Boulevard Ave Bismarck ND 58505-0530 E-mail: gvandewalle@ndcourts.com.

VAN DINE, HAROLD FORSTER, JR. architect, artist; b. New Haven, Aug. 28, 1930; s. Harold Forster and Marguerite Anna (Eichstedt) Van D.; m. Maureen Kallick, Mar. 1, 1983; children by previous marriage: Rebecca Van Dine, Stephanie Van Dine Natale, Gretchen Van Dine Natale. BA, Yale Coll., 1952; MArch, Yale Sch. Arch., 1958. Registered architect. Designer Minoru Yamasaki & Assocs., Detroit, 1958-60; chief designer Gunnar Birkerts & Assocs., 1960-67; prin. Straub, Van Dine & Assocs., Troy, Mich., 1967-80; chief architecture and design officer Harley Ellington Design, Southfield, 1980-95; archtl. cons. Birmingham, 1995—. V.p. Fields, Devereaux, HEPY, L.A., 1984-95. Prin. works include Mcpl. Libr., Troy, Mich., campuses for Oakland (Mich.) Community Coll., North Hills Ch., Troy, First Ctr. Office Plaza, chemistry bldgs at. U. Mich. and Ind. U., G.M.F. Robotics Hdqrs., Flint Ink Rsch. and Devel. Ctr., Comerica Bank Ops. Ctr., Christ the King Mausoleum, Chgo., Resurrection Mausoleum, Staten Island, Mich. Biotech Inst., Ford Sci. Rsch. Labs, Fetzer Inst. Hdqrs. and Retreat Ctr., Cen. Mich. U. Music Sch., Oakland U. Sci. Techs. Bldg., Corning (N.Y.) Credit Union. Bd. dirs. Cultural Coun. Birmingham/Bloomfield, 1990-99. Served to lt. (j.g.) USN, 1952-55 Recipient Book award AIA, 1958, Excellence in Architecture Silver medal AIA, 1958, Gold medal Detroit chpt. AIA, 1987, Mich. Soc. of Architects gold medal, 1991, over 50 major design awards; William Wirt Winchester travelling fellowship Yale U. Sch. Architecture, 1958; elect. to AIA Coll. Fellows, 1979. Mem. Pewabic Soc. (bd. dirs. 1983—) Home: 1000 Stratford Ln Bloomfield Hills MI 48304-2930 E-mail: harryv@mediaone.net., jmrandhv@got.com.

VANDIVER, DONNA, public relations executive; BJ, MBA in Mgmt. Pres. Vandiver Group, St. Louis. Bd. dirs. Am. Heart Assn.; mem. adv. bd. Pky. Edn. Found. Named Small Bus. Person of the Yr. SBA, 1998; recipient Quest award Nat. Fedn. Press Women, 1999. Mem. Nat. Assn. Women Bus. Owners (Bd. dirs. St. Louis chpt., Disting Women Bus. Owner of the Yr. award 1999), Assn. Corp. Growth, St. Louis Press Club, Downtown St. Louis Partnership, St. Louis Regional Commerce and Growth Assn., Media Club. Office: Vandiver Group 10411 Clayton Rd Saint Louis MO 63131-2928

VAN DYKE, CLIFFORD CRAIG, retired banker; b. Ft. Madison, Iowa, June 23, 1929; s. Charles Clifford and Frances Mary (Butterwick) Van D.; m. Edith Ellicott Powers, Aug. 4, 1951 (dec. Oct. 1980); children: Carol Elizabeth, Deborah Ellicott, Jill Anne, Lisa Ellicott. BA, Knox Coll., 1951; MBA, Harvard U., 1955. Asst. v.p. Nat. Bank of Detroit, 1962-65, v.p., 1965-76; pres. Peoples Nat. Bank & Trust Co. of Bay City, Mich., 1976-78, chmn. bd., pres., 1979-86; chmn. bd., pres., chief exec. officer New Ctr. Bank Corp., Bay City, 1986; chmn. First of Am. Bank-Bay City, N.A., 1987-89; sr. v.p. First of Am. Bank-Mid Mich. N.A., 1990-94; ret., 1994. Trustee Kantzler Found., Bay City, 1979—; bd. dirs., pres. Bay County Growth Alliance, 1987—. 1st lt. U.S. Army, 1951-53, Korea. Mem. Bay City Country Club, Saginaw Valley Torch Club, Rotary. Republican. Unitarian. Office: Bay County Growth Alliance PO Box 369 Bay City MI 48707-0369 E-mail: bcga@concentric.net.

VAN DYKE, THOMAS WESLEY, lawyer; b. Kansas City, Mo., May 12, 1938; s. Harold Thomas and Elizabeth Louise (Barritt) Van D.; m. Sharon Edgar, Jan. 30, 1960; children: Jennifer Van Dyke Winters, Jeffrey. BA, U. Kans., 1960; JD, U. Mich., 1963. Bar: Mo. 1963, Kans. 1983. Atty. SEC, Washington, 1963-64; legal asst. to commr. Hamer E. Budge, 1964-65; from assoc. to ptnr. Linde Thomson Langworthy Kohn & Van Dyke, P.C., Overland Park, Kans., 1965-91. Co-chmn. ALI-ABA Tax and Bus. Planning Seminar, 1987-96; mem. securities adv. panel Sec. of State of Mo., 1984-89. Mem. ABA (fed. regulation securities com. bus. law sect. 1982-2002, negotatiated acquisitions com. 1989-2002), Kans. Bar Assn., Mo. Bar Assn. (corp. banking and bus. law com., chmn. full com. 1983-84, past chmn. securities law subcom.), Carriage Club (bd. dirs. 1986-89). Republican. Avocations: tennis, golf, reading. Office: Bryan Cave LLP 7500 College Blvd Ste 1100 Overland Park KS 66210-4097

VAN DYKE, WILLIAM GRANT, manufacturing company executive; b. Mpls., June 30, 1945; s. Russell Lawrence and Carolyn (Grant) Van D.; m. Karin Van Dyke; children: Carolyn Julie, Colin Grant, Alexander Grant, Stephanie Joyce. BA in Econs., U. Minn., 1967, MBA, 1972. V.p., CFO Northland Aluminum Co., Mpls., 1977-78; controller Donaldson Co., Inc., 1978-80, v.p. controller, 1980-82, v.p., CFO, 1982-84, v.p., gen. mgr. indsl. group, 1984-94, pres., COO, 1994-96, chmn., pres., CEO, 1996—, also bd. dirs. Bd. dirs. Graco Inc. Served to lt. U.S. Army, 1968-70, Vietnam. Mem. Kappa Sigma Alumni Assn. Avocations: running; bicycling. Office: Donaldson Co Inc 1400 W 94th St Minneapolis MN 55431-2370

VAN ENGEN, THOMAS LEE, state legislator; b. Sioux Center, Iowa, Mar. 28, 1953; s. Leo Herman and Dolores (Nelma) Van E.; m. Rosalyn Faye Vander Plaats, 1979; children: Matthew Thomas, David James, Jeremy Lee. BA, Dordt Coll., Sioux Center, 1979. Lic. social worker, Minn.; lic. pvt. pilot. Chair dist. 15 Minn. Ho. of Reps., St. Paul, 1992-94, mem., 1994-98; life and health ins. agt. Am. United Life Ins. Co. and Blue Cross Blue Shield Minn., 1997-98; devel. cons. Terwisscha Construction, Willmar, 1998—. Del. Rep. dist. and state convs., 1984-2000, Minn. Rep. Ctrl. Com., 1989-2000; chmn. Pipestone County Com., Minn., 1988-89, Kandiyohi County Com., 1991-93; co-chmn. dist. 15 Minn. Senate, 1990-92, chmn., 1992-94; candidate for Minn. Ho. of Reps., 1992; chmn. edn. com. Cmty. Christian Sch. Bd., 1990-94; elder Christian Reformed Ch., 1985-88, 96-99, 2001—, handicapped children and adults, 1978-82, 2001—, chem. dependency counselor, 1982-94. With U.S. Army, 1972-74. Mem. CAP (mission pilot 1996—, moral leadership officer 2000—, squadron comdr. 2000—), Am. Legion, Kiwanis. E-mail: tve@tds.net.

VAN ERON, KEVIN JOSEPH, organizational development consultant, psychologist; b. Hutchinson, Kans., Apr. 9, 1957; s. Kenneth J. and Meriam J. (Buller) Van Eron; m. Ann M. Schwartz, Jan. 1, 1984. B in Gen Studies, U. Md., 1980; MA, Ill. Sch. Profl. Psychology, 2000. Chartered life underwriter. Dist. rep. Aid Assn. for Luths., Appleton, Wis., 1980-83, dist. mgr., 1983-84, gen. agt., 1984-87, gen. mgr., 1987-91, v.p., mem. field svcs., 1992, sr. v.p., mem. field svcs., 1993-95, sr. v.p. creating mem. relationships, 1996-97; prin. Potentials, Chgo., 1997—. Mem. APA, Jungian Inst. Democrat. Avocations: traveling, reading, hiking. Home and Office: 195 N Harbor Dr Apt 3706 Chicago IL 60601-7534 E-mail: kjvaneron@aol.com.

VAN GELDER, MARC CHRISTIAAN, retail executive; b. Amsterdam, The Netherlands, May 21, 1961; s. Bob Frits and Maria Johanna (Van Teeseling) Van G.; m. Karah L. Henry, July 7, 1990; children: Alexander F., Robert H. M of Econs., Erasmus U., Rottendam, The Netherlands, 1986; MBA, U. Pa., 1990. Asst. v.p. Drexel-Burnham Lambert, N.Y.C., 1986-88; assoc. McKinsey & Co., Amsterdam, 1990-96; dir. bus. devel. Ahold, Netherlands, 1996—98; v.p. supply chain mgnt. The Stop & Shop Supermarket Company, 1998—99, sr. v.p., logistics & supply chain mgnt., 1999-2000; pres. & CEO Peapod Inc., Skokie, IL, 2000—. Author: Venture Capital Market , 1985. Mem. Wharton Alumni Club The Netherlands (pres. 1991—). Avocations: skiing, horseback riding, playing squash, arts. Office: Peapod Inc 9933 Woods Dr Ste 375 Skokie IL 60077-1057

VAN GILDER, JOHN CORLEY, neurosurgeon, educator; b. Huntington, W.Va., Aug. 14, 1935; s. John Ray and Sarah Pool (Corley) Van G.; m. Kerstin Margarita Olesson, Mar., 1965; children: Sarah, John, Rachel, David. BA, W.Va. U., 1957, BS, 1959; MD, U. Pitts., 1961. Diplomate Am. Bd. Neurol. Surgery. (examiner 1976, 79, 84). Intern Pa. Hosp., Phila., 1961, asst. resident in surgery, 1964-65, Wilkes-Barre (Pa.) Hosp., 1962; asst. resident neurosurgery Barnes Hosp., St. Louis, 1966-68, sr. resident, 1968-69; instr. neurosurgery Yale U. Sch. Medicine, New Haven, 1970, asst. prof., 1970-73, assoc. prof., 1973-76; prof. neurosurgery U. Iowa, Iowa City, 1976—, chmn. div. neurosurgery, 1976—, exec. com. dept. surgery, 1978-81. Fellow neurosurgery Wash. U. Sch. Medicine, St. Louis, 1965 -66, instr., 1966; attending neurosurgeon VA Hosp., New Haven, 1970-73, cons. 1973-76; assoc. to attending neurosurgeon Yale-New Haven Med. Ctr., 1970-76; cons. VA Hosp., Iowa City, 1976—; neurol. surg. cons. Vets. Affairs Hdqrs., Washington; mem. clin. coordinating com. U. Iowa Cancer Ctr., 1979—; presenter numerous papers at profl. meetings., confs., symposia; vis. prof. U. Tenn., 1984, Tufts U. Med. Ctr., Boston, 1986, U. Tex., San Antonio, 1987, U. Mich., Ann Arbor, 1988, People's Republic China at Hunan Med. Coll., Beijing Neurol. Inst., Tianjin Med. Coll. Hosp., Tiantan Xili, Xian Gen. Hosp., 2d Mil. Coll., Shanghai, Suzhou Med. Coll. Shanghai, 1985, USSR at Burdenk Inst., Kiev Neurol. Inst., Leningrad Neurol. Soc., 1989, Western Reserve U., Cleve., 1993, Yale U., New Haven, Conn., 1994, U. Wash., Seattle, 1997, Mayo Clinic, 1998, U. Calif., San Francisco, 1998, Ind. U., 1999. Author: (with others): Principles of Surgery, 2d edit., 1973, Brief Textbook of Surgery, 1976, Aneurysmal Subarachnoid Hemorrhage, 1981, Operative Meurosurgical Techniques, Indications, Methods, and Results, 1982, Sports Medicine, 1982, Neurosurgery, 1982, Clinical Neurosurgery, 1982, Operative Neurosurgical Technique, Vol. II, 1982, 88, Vol. III, 1995, Current Therapy in Neurosurgical Surgery, 1985, 2d edit. , 1987, Craniovertebral Junction Abnormalities, 1987, Decision Making in Neurological Surgery, 1987, Neurological Surgery, 3d edit., 1988, Anterior Cervical Spine Surgery, 1993, Brain Surgery: Complication Avoidance and Management, 1993, Neurosurgical Emergencies, 1994, Techniques of Spinal Fusion and Instrumation, 1995, Somatic Gene Therapy, 1995, Infections in Neurological Surgery, 1999; contbr. numerous articles and abstracts to profl. jours.; co-author teaching films; mem. editorial bd. Neurosurgery jour., 1978-84. Capt. USAF, 1962-64. Grantee NIH, 1973-78, Nat. Cancer Inst., 1980-88. Fellow: ACS (membership com. Iowa dist. #1 1983—); mem.: AMA, Am. Bd. Neurol. Surgery (dir. 1992—98, chmn. 1997—98, residency rev. com.-neurol. surgery 1995—2001, neurosurgery chmn. 1999—2001), Am. Acad. Neurol. Surgery (v.p. 1995—), Midwest Surg. Assn., Soc. Neurol. Surgeons (chmn. membership com. 1986—87, treas. 1991—, pres 1997—98, treas. 1991—96, pres. 1997), Iowa-Midwest Neurosurg. Soc. 1978—79, Johnson County Med. Soc. (program com. 1984—88, chmn. 1985—86), Iowa Med. Soc., Neurol. Soc. Am. (long range planning com. 1984—, v.p. 1985, pres. 1998—99), Rsch. Soc. Neurol. Surgeons, Am. Assn. Neurol. Surgeons (awards com. 1986—87, bd. dirs. 1986—90, chmn. 1987—88), Congress Neurol. Surgeons (resident placement com. 1970), Am. Physiol. Soc., Ga. Neurosurg. Soc. (hon.), Sigma Xi. Home: 330 S Summit St Iowa City IA 52240-3220 Office: U Iowa Hosps & Clinics Dept Neurosurgery 200 Hawkins Dr Iowa City IA 52242-1009

VAN HAAFTEN, TRENT, lawyer; BA in Politics and Bus., Lake Forest Coll., 1987; JD with honors, Drake Law Sch., 1990. Lic. to practice law, Ind., Iowa. Chief dep. prosecuting atty., Posey County, Ind., 1991-93; prosecuting atty., 1995—. Mem. Posey County Dem. Party; pres., coach Wildcat Cub Football. Mem. Nat. Dist. Attys. Assn., Evansville Bar Assn., Posey County Bar Assn. Office: PO Box 721 PO Box 721 Mount Vernon IN 47620-0721

VAN HANDEL, MICHAEL J. staffing company executive; Sr. v.p., CFO, sec.-treas. Manpower, Inc., Milw., 1994—. Office: Manpower Inc 5301 N Ironwood Rd. Milwaukee WI 53217-4982

VAN HARLINGEN, DALE, physics educator; Assoc. prof. physics U. Ill., Urbana. Recipient Oliver E. Buckley Condensed-Matter Physics prize, 1998. Mem. Am. phys. Soc. Office: U Ill The Materials Rsch Lab 104 S Goodwin Ave Urbana IL 61801-2902

VANHARN, GORDON LEE, college administrator and provost; b. Grand Rapids, Mich., Dec. 30, 1935; s. Henry and Edna (Riemersma) VanH.; m. Mary Kool, June 12, 1958; children: Pamela L., Mark L., Barbara A. BA, Calvin Coll., 1957; MS, U. Ill., 1959, PhD, 1961. Asst. prof. biology Calvin Coll., Grand Rapids, 1961-68, prof., 1970-82, acad. dean, 1982-85, provost, 1985-94, sr. v.p., provost, 1994-96, prof. interdisciplinary studies, 1996-99, prof. emeritus, 1999—. Assoc. prof. biology Oberlin Coll., Ohio, 1968-70; assoc. physiologist Blodgett Meml. Med. Ctr., Grand Rapids, 1970-76; rsch, assoc. U. Va., Charlotteville, 1975-76. Contbr. articles to profl. jours. Mem. sci. adv. com. Gerald R. Ford, 1972-73; mem. rsch. and rev. com. Blodget Hosp., 1978-84; pres. bd. Grand Rapids Christian Sch. Assn., 1982-85; v.p. Christian Schs. Internat., 1987-93; mem Grand Rapids Pub. Sch. Bd., 1996—; bd. dirs. Pine Rest Found., 1997—; trustee Van Andel Edn. Inst., 2000—. Grass Found. fellow, 1969. Mem. Phi Kappa Phi. Mem. Christian Reformed Ch. Home: 1403 Cornell Dr SE Grand Rapids MI 49506-4103 Office: Calvin Coll 3201 Burton St SE Grand Rapids MI 49546-4301

VAN HIMBERGEN, THOMAS, manufacturing company executive; b. 1948; With Tenneco Automotive, Allied Signal; CFO Fed.-Mogul Corp.; sr. v.p., CFO Deluxe Corp., Donaldson Co., Inc., Mpls., 2000-2001. Office: Donaldson Co Inc 1400 W 94th St Minneapolis MN 55431-2370

VAN HOOSER, DAVID, retired manufacturing executive; CFO, sr. v.p. Owens-Illinois Inc., Toledo. Office: Owens Ill Inc One Seagate Toledo OH 43666

VAN HOUSEN, THOMAS CORWIN, III, architect, designer, builder; b. Oak Park, Ill., Jan. 2, 1927; s. Thomas Corwin and Dorothea (Saunders) Van H.; children: Deborah, Victoria, Constance. BA, Lawrence U., 1951; BArch, U. Minn., Mpls., 1954; MArch in Urban Design, Harvard U., 1962. Registered architect, Minn., Wis. With Ellerbe Assocs., Inc., St. Paul, 1951-61; architect, prin. Progressive Design Assocs., Inc., 1961-71; architect, developer, v.p. Landmark Devel. Corp./Appletree Enterprises, Inc., Bloomington, Minn., 1971-85; architect, developer Mortenson Devel. Co., Mpls., 1985-88; architect, design, bldg. dir. D&B Collaborative, Inc., 1989—. Bldg. official City of North Oaks, Minn., 1964-78; mem. Minn. League of Municipalities-Metro, St. Paul, 1970-72, Gov.'s Open Space Adv. Com., St. Paul, 1972-74. With U.S. Air Force, 1945-47, ETO. Recipient Outstanding House award St. Paul Jaycees, 1958, 62; named finalist (team mem.) Archtl. competition Boston City Hall, 1962. Fellow AIA (nat. bd. dirs. 1985-88, v.p., pres.-elect Minn. chpt. 1994-95, pres. 1995, spl. award 1981, Presdl. citation 1988, 90); mem. N.W. YMCA. Republican. Lutheran. Avocations: tennis, swimming, music.

VAN HOUTEN, JAMES FORESTER, insurance company executive; b. Fullerton, Calif., Jan. 13, 1942; s. James Forester and Lois Evangeline (Trout) V.H.; m. Mary Ann Nelson; children: Kimberly Evangeline, Lori Lynn. BA in English Lit., St. Mary's U.; MBA, Ill. State U. CPCU, CLU. Sales mgr. for Can. Motors Ins. Corp. divsn. GM, Detroit, 1963-74; v.p. sales Volkswagen Group, St. Louis, 1974-78; v.p. personal lines mktg. Wausau Ins. Cos., 1978-80, v.p., chief mktg. officer life and health, 1980-84; v.p., chief mktg. and strategic planning officer Country Cos., Bloomington, Ill., 1984-89; pres., CEO Mut. Svc. Ins. Cos., St. Paul, 1989—. Adj. prof. strategic mgmt. MBA program U. Minn., 1990—, bd. dirs. Strategic Mgmt. Rsch. Ctr., U. Minn. Program leader Youth Black Achievers, St. Paul; mem. exec. bd. arrowhead coun. Boy Scouts of Am., Minn. Assn. Scholars. Mem. Ins. Fedn. Minn. (past chmn. bd.), Minn. Assn. Mutual Ins. Cos. (pres.), Nat. Coop. Bus. Assn. (bd. dirs. and exec. com., chair fin. com.), Minn. Bus. Partnership (bd. dirs., Minn. K-12 edn. com .), Ctr. Am. Experiment Think Tank (bd. dirs., ex com., chair fin. and audit com., treas.). Office: Mut Svc Ins Cos 2 Pine Tree Dr Arden Hills MN 55112-3715

VAN HOUWELING, DOUGLAS EDWARD, university administrator, educator; b. Kansas City, Mo., Sept. 20, 1943; s. Cornelius Donald and Roberta Irene (Olson) Van H.; m. Andrea Taylor Parks, Aug. 28, 1965; children: Robert Parks, Benjamin Parks BS, Iowa State U., Ames, 1965; PhD, Ind. U., 1974. Asst. prof. Cornell U., Ithaca, N.Y., 1970-81, dir. acad. computing, 1978-81; vice provost Carnegie-Mellon U., Pitts., 1981-84, adj. assoc. prof., 1981-84; vice provost, dean, prof. U. Mich., Ann Arbor, 1984-88, prof., 1984—, pres., CEO univ. corp. for advanced internet devel., 1998—. Mem. research adv. com. Online Coll. Library Consortium, Dublin, Ohio, 1984-87; trustee EDUCOM, vice chmn. bd. dirs., 1987-91; Princeton, vice chmn., 1987, council chmn., 1986-87; co-founder Interuniv. Corsortium for Ednl. Computing, 1984; chmn. bd. MERIT computer network, 1986-90, Advanced Network and Svcs., 1990—; state of Mich. del. Midwest Tech. Inst., 1986-87. Contbr. chpts. in books, articles to profl. publs. NSF fellow, 1968; Indiana U. fellow, 1969; CAUSE nat. leadership award, 1986. Mem. Simulation Symposiums (pres. 1971; grants chmn. 1972-75), N.Am. Simulation and Gaming Assn. Home: 920 Lincoln Ave Ann Arbor MI 48104-3508 Office: Univ Corp for Advanced Internet Devel 3025 Boardwalk St Ann Arbor MI 48108-3230

VAN INWAGEN, PETER JAN, philosophy educator; b. Rochester, N.Y., Sept. 21, 1942; s. George Butler and Mildred Gloria (Knudson) van I; m. Margery Bedford Naylor, Mar. 31, 1967 (div. Apr. 1988); 1 child, Elizabeth Core; m. Elisabeth Marie Bolduc, June 3, 1989. B.S., Rensselaer Poly. Inst., 1965; Ph.D., U. Rochester, 1969. Vis. asst. prof. U. Rochester, N.Y., 1971-72; asst. prof. Syracuse U., 1972-74, assoc. prof., 1974-80, prof. philosophy, 1980-95; John Cardinal O'Hara prof. of philosophy U. Notre Dame, South Bend, Ind., 1995—. Vis. prof. U. Ariz., Tucson, 1981; lectr. Oxford U., 2001, U. London, 1998. Author: An Essay on Free Will, 1983, Material Beings, 1990, Metaphysics, 1993, God, Knowledge and Mystery, 1995, The Possibility of Resurrection, 1997, Ontology, Identity, and Modality, 2001; editor: Time and Cause, 1980, Alvin Plantinga, 1985, Metaphysics: The Big Questions, 1998; mem. editl. bd. Jour. Faith and Philosophy, Philos. Perspectives, Nous, Philos. Studies, Jour. of Ethics, Philosophy and Phenomenological Rsch.; contbr. articles to profl. jours. Served to capt. U.S. Army, 1969-71 NEH grantee, 1983-84, 89-90. Mem. Am. Philos. Assn., Soc. Christian Philosophers. Democrat. Episcopalian Home: 52145 Farmington Square Rd Granger IN 46530-6403 Office: U Notre Dame Dept Philosophy South Bend IN 46556-4619 E-mail: peter.vaninwagen.1@nd.edu.

VANLEER, JAMES G. state legislator; m. Gwendolyn Vanleer. BA, Wilberforce U.; MA, Ball State U. Benefits mgr. New Venture Gear, Inc.; mem. Ind. State Ho. of Reps. Dist. 34, mem. environ. affairs com., mem. pub. policy, ethics and vet. affairs com., mem. roads and transp. com., vice chmn. aged and aging com. Mem. Jr. Achievement Coun.; former mem. Muncie (Ind.) Housing Bd. Mem. C. of C. (mem. advocacy and local govt. com.).

VAN LEUVEN, ROBERT JOSEPH, lawyer; b. Detroit, Apr. 17, 1931; s. Joseph Francis and Olive (Stowell) Van Leuven; m. Merri Lee Van Leuven; children: Joseph Michael, Douglas Robert, Julie Margaret. Student, Albion Coll., 1949-51; BA with distinction, Wayne State U., 1953; JD, U. Mich., 1957. Bar: (Mich.) 1957. Since practiced in, Muskegon, Mich.; ptnr. Hathaway, Latimer, Clink & Robb, 1957-68, McCroskey, Libner & Van Leuven, 1968-81, Libner-Van Leuven, 1982—99; ret., 1999. Past mem. coun. negligence law sect. State Bar Mich. Bd. dirs. Muskegon Children's Home, 1965—75. Served with U.S. Army, 1953—55. Fellow: Am. Coll. Trial Lawyers, Mich. Bar Found.; mem.: ATLA, Mich. Trial Lawyers Assn., Muskegon Country Club, Delta Sigma Phi. Home: 410 Ruddiman Dr # 4 Muskegon MI 49445-2795 Office: Libner-Van Leuven 4th Fl Comerica Bank Bldg 801 W Norton Ave Muskegon MI 49441

VAN LUVEN, WILLIAM ROBERT, management consultant; b. Toledo, Feb. 15, 1931; s. Harold Calvin and Ruth Frick (Routson) Van L.; m. Lyda Marie Buchanan Jones, Nov. 15, 1956 (div. Sept. 1960); children: Lynn Chase, Michael Frick; m. Barbara Wilson Ehni, Aug. 17, 1968; children: Eric Finley, Jay Palmer. BBA, U. Toledo, 1957; postgrad., U. Va., 1979. Group gen. mgr. Union Camp Corp., Wayne, N.J., 1961-73, 1979-82; pres.container & carton divs. Clevepak Corp., White Plains, N.Y., 1973-79; v.p., gen. mgr. Jefferson Smurfit Corp., Clayton, Mo., 1982-84; pres. Wm. R. Van Luven & Assocs. Inc., St. Louis, 1984—; exec. dir. Exec. Svcs. Corps of St. Louis. Bd. dirs. Smurfit Industries, Alton, Ill., 1982-84, O'Connor Pharm. Corp., Detroit, 1982-84; pres. Mo. Clippers, Inc. (Great Clips for Hair Franchise), 1988—. Cons. United Way of Greater St. Louis, 1987—; chair United Way Mgmt. Assistance Ctr., 1988-90; dir. Combined Health Appeal, Sherwood Forst Camp, Places for People, Inc., Christian Svc. Ctr. With USN, 1951-53. Recipient Keyman award Toledo C. of C., 1956. Mem. Fibre Box Assn., Composite Can & Tube Inst. (pres. 1979), Paperboard Packaging Council, U.S. Brewers Assn., Racquet Club (St. Louis), Aspetuch Country Club (Weston, Conn.), Univ. Club (St. Louis), Shriner, Sigma Nu. Republican. Episcopalian. Avocations: running, skiing, biking. Home: 2 Portland Ct Saint Louis MO 63108-1291 E-mail: wrvl@aol.com.

VAN METER, ABRAM DEBOIS, lawyer, retired banker; b. Springfield, Ill., May 16, 1922; s. A.D. and Edith (Graham) Van M.; m. Margaret Schlipf, Dec. 1, 1956; children: Andy, Alice, Ann. BS, Kings Point Coll., 1946; JD, Northwestern U., 1948. Bar: Ill. 1949. Ptnr. Van Meter, Oxtoby & Funk, Springfield, 1949—2001; adminstrv. asst. to treas. State of Ill., 1963; v.p. Ill. Nat. Bank, 1964-65, pres., 1965-88, chmn. bd. dirs., 1988-90, also bd. dirs.; chmn. bd. dirs. First of Am.-Springfield, N.A., 1990-93, dir. emeritus, 1993—. Chmn. bd. dirs. Ill. Housing Devel. Authority, 1977—; chmn. bd. trustees So. Ill. U., 1989—; bd. dirs., mem. exec. com. Meml. Med. Ctr. (emeritus). Mem. ABA, Ill. Bar Assn., Sangamon Bar Assn., Chgo. Club, Chgo. Athletic Club, Sangamo Club, Island Bay Yacht Club, Home: 6 Fair Oaks St Springfield IL 62704-3222 Office: Nat City 1 N Old State Capitol Plz Springfield IL 62701-1323

VAN REGENMORTER, WILLIAM, state legislator; m. Cheryl; four children. Mich. jud. com., econ. devel. com., energy com.; chmn. House Rep. Caucus, 84-90. Commr. Ottawa County Bd. Commrs., 1980-82; mem. Mich. Ho. of Reps., 1982-90, Mich. Senate from 22nd dist., Lansing, 1990—. Named legis. of yr. 1985 Mich. Sheriff's Assn., Mich. Assn. Police, 1988, Police Officer's Assn. Mich., 1989; recipient Santarelli award Nat. Orgn. for Victim Assistance, 1985, justice award Found. for Improvement of Justice, 1986, leadership award Nat. Sheriff's Assn., 1987. Home: 6293 Springmont Dr Hudsonville MI 49426-8704 Office: Mich Senate State Capitol PO Box 30036 Lansing MI 48909-7536

VAN SANT, JOANNE FRANCES, academic administrator; b. Morehead, Ky., Dec. 29, 1924; d. Lewis L. and Dorothy (Greene) Van S. BA, Denison U., Granville, Ohio; MA, The Ohio State U.; postgrad., U. Colo. and The Ohio State U.; LLD (hon.), Albright Coll., 1975. Tchr., health and phys. edn. Mayfield, Kentucky High Sch., 1946-48; instr. Denison U., Granville, Ohio, 1948; instr. women's phys. edn. Otterbein Coll., Westerville, 1948-52, assoc. prof., 1955-62, dept. chmn., 1950-62, chmn. div. profl. studies, 1961-65, dean of women, 1952-60, 62-64, dean of students, 1964-93, v.p. student affairs, 1968-93; v.p., dean student affairs emeritus, 1993—; cons. Instnl. Advancement, 1993—. Co-pres. Directions for Youth, 1983-84, pres., 1984-85; bd. dirs. North Area Mental Health, Friendship Village of Columbus, 1996—, pres. bd., 1998—; trustee Westerville Civic Symphony at Otterbein Coll., 1983-88; active numerous other community orgns.; ordained elder Presbyn. Ch., 1967. Named to hon. Order of Ky. Cols., 1957; recipient Focus on Youth award Columbus Dispatch, 1983, Vol. of the Yr. award North Area Mental Health Svcs., 1982, citation Denison U., 1996. Mem. Am. Assn. Counseling and Devel., Ohio Personnel and Guidance Assn., Ohio Assn. Women Deans, Adminstrs., Counselors (treas., exec. bd. 1972-73), Nat. Assn. Student Personnel Adminstrs., Ohio Coll. Personnel Assn., Mortar Bd. (hon.), Zonta Internat. (pres. Columbus, Ohio club 1978-80, dist. gov. 1988-90, internat. svc. chmn. 1996-98, internat. found. bd. 1997-2001), Vocal Arts Resource Network (chair bd. dirs. 1994-96), Cap and Dagger Club, Torch and Key Hon., Order Omega, Alpha Lambda Delta, Theta Alpha Phi, others. Avocations: musical and children's theater production, choreography. Home: 9100 Oakwood Pt Westerville OH 43082-9643 Office: Otterbein Coll Instnl Advancement Westerville OH 43081 Home Fax: 614-882-4038. E-mail: deanvan@aol.com.

VAN SICKLE, BRUCE MARION, federal judge; b. Minot, N.D., Feb. 13, 1917; s. Guy Robin and Hilda Alice (Rosenquist) Van S.; m. Dorothy Alfreda Hermann, May 26, 1943; children: Susan Van Sickle Cooper, John Allan, Craig Bruce, David Max. BSL, JD, U. Minn., 1941. Bar: Minn. 1941, N.D. 1946. Pvt. practice law, Minot, 1947-71; judge U.S. Dist. Ct. N.D., 1971-85, sr. judge, 1985—. Mem. N.D. Ho. of Reps., 1957, 59. Served with USMCR, 1941-46. Mem. ABA, N.D. Bar Assn., N.W. Bar Assn., Ward County Bar Assn., Am. Trial Lawyers Assn., Am. Coll. Probate Counsel, Am. Judicature Soc., Bruce M. Van Sickle Inns of Ct., Masons, Shriners, Elks, Delta Theta Phi. Office: US Dist Ct US Courthouse Rm 428 PO Box 670 Bismarck ND 58502-0670

VANSTROM, MARILYN JUNE CHRISTENSEN, retired elementary education educator; b. Mpls., June 10, 1924; d. Harry Clifford and Myrtle Agnes (Hagland) Christensen; m. Reginald Earl Vanstrom, Mar. 20, 1948; children: Gary Alan, Kathryn June Vanstrom Marinello. AA, U. Minn., 1943, BS, 1946. Cert. elem. tchr., N.Y., Ill. Tchr. Pub. Sch., St. Louis Park, Minn., 1946-47, Deephaven, 1947-50, Chicago Heights, Ill., 1950-52, Steger, 1964, substitute tchr. Dobbs Ferry, N.Y., 1965-72, Yonkers, 1965-92. Mem. Ch. Women, Christ Meml. Luth. Ch. Mem. AAUW (life, pres. So. Westchester br. 1988-90, Ednl. Found. award 1990), Morning Book Club, Evening Book Club (Met. West br. Minn., So. Westchester br. N.Y.), Yonkers Fedn. Tchrs. Democrat. Avocations: painting, sketching, choir, piano, travel. Home: 12300 Marion Ln W Apt 2105 Minnetonka MN 55305-1317

VAN'T HOF, WILLIAM KEITH, lawyer; b. N.Y.C., Feb. 18, 1930; s. William and Nell (DeValois) Van't H.; m. Barbara Marie Rogers, Oct. 6, 1961; children: Sarah Lynn, David Edward. BA, Hope Coll., 1951; LLB, U. Mich., 1954. Bar: Mich. 1954, Conn. 1955, U.S. Dist. Ct. (we. dist.) Mich. 1956, U.S. Ct. Appeals (6th cir.) 1956. Assoc. Gumbart, Corbin, Tyler & Cooper, New Haven, 1954-56; ptnr. McCobb, Heaney & Van't Hof, Grand Rapids, Mich., 1959-72, Schmidt, Howlett, Van't Hof, Smell & Vana, Grand Rapids, 1972-82, Varnum, Riddering, Schmidt & Howlett, Grand Rapids, 1983-99. Mem. faculty Inst. Continuing Legal Edn., Ann Arbor, Mich., 1974-99. Chmn. Mich. Heart Assn., 1973-75; pres. United Way Kent County, 1979-80, hon. life mem., 1986—; chmn. Am. Heart Assn., Dallas, 1989-90. Mem. ABA, State Bar Mich. (grievance and arbitration panel 1970-91, 94-, chmn. com. on coops. and condos. 1982-86), Grand Rapids Bar Assn. (trustee 1965-67), West Mich. Hort. Soc. (pres. 1992-93), Cascade Hills Country Club, Univ. Club. Home: 3508 Windshire Dr SE Grand Rapids MI 49546-3698 Office: Varnum Riddering Schmidt & Howlett 333 Bridge St NW Ste 1700 Grand Rapids MI 49504-5356 E-mail: wkvanthof@varnumlaw.com.

VAN TUYL, CECIL L. investment company executive; Chmn., pres., CEO VT Inc., Merriam, Kans. Office: V T Inc PO Box 795 Shawnee Mission KS 66201-0795

VAN UMMERSEN, CLAIRE A(NN), academic administrator, biologist, educator; b. Chelsea, Mass., July 28, 1935; d. George and Catherine (Courtovich); m. Frank Van Ummersen, June 7, 1958; children: Lynn, Scott. BS, Tufts U., 1957, MS, 1960, PhD, 1963; DSc (hon.), U. Mass., 1988, U. Maine, 1991. Rsch. asst. Tufts U., 1957-60, 60-67, grad. asst. in embryology, 1962, postdoctoral tchg. asst., 1963-66, lectr. in biology, 1967-68; asst. prof. biology U. Mass., Boston, 1968-74, assoc. prof., 1974—76, assoc. dean acad. affairs, 1975-76, assoc. vice chancellor acad. affairs, 1976-78, chancellor, 1978-79, dir. Environ. Sci. Ctr., 1980-82; assoc. vice chancellor acad. affairs Mass. Bd. Regents for Higher Edn., 1982-85, vice chancellor for mgmt. systems and telecommunications, 1985-86; chancellor Univ. System N.H., Durham, 1986-92; sr. fellow New Eng. Bd. Higher Edn., 1992-93; sr. fellow New Eng. Resource Ctr. Higher Edn. U. Mass., 1992-93; pres. Cleve. (Ohio) State U., 1993—2001; v.p., dir. Office of Women Am. Coun. Edn., 2001—. V.p., dir. Women Higher Ed. Am. Coun. Ed.; cons. Mass. Bd. Regents, 1981-82, AGB, 1992—, Kuwait U., 1992-93; asst. Lancaster Course in Ophthalmology, Mass. Eye. and Ear Infirmary, 1962-69, lectr., 1970-93, also coord.; reviewer HEW; mem. rsch. team which established safety stds. for exposure to microwave radiation, 1958-65; participant Leadership Am. program, 1992-93; bd. dirs. Nat. Coun. Sci. Environ., 1998. Mem. N.H. Ct. Systems Rev. Task Force, 1989-90; mem. New Eng. Bd. Higher Edn., 1986-92, mem. exec. com., 1989-92, N.H. adv. coun., 1990-92; chair Rhodes Scholarship Selection Com., 1986-91; bd. dirs. N.H. Bus. and Industry Assn., 1987-90, 90-93; governing bd. N.H. Math. Coalition, 1991-92; exec. com. 21st Century Learning Community, 1992-93; state panelist N.H. Women in Higher Edn., 1986-93; bd. dirs. Urban League Greater Cleve., 1993-2001, mem. strategic planning com., chair edn. com., 1996-99, sec., exec. com., 1997-99; bd. dirs. Great Lakes Sci. and Tech. Ctr., 1993-2001, mem. edn. com., 1995-2001; bd. dirs. Greater Cleve. Growth Assn., 1994-2001, Civic Vision 2000 and Beyond, Cleve., 1997-98; bd. dirs., mem. exec. com. Sci. and Tech. Coun. Cleve. Tomorrow, 1998-99; rep. Northeast Ohio Tech. Coalition, 1999-2001; trustee Ohio Aerospace Inst., 1993-2001, mem. exec. com., 1996-2001; mem. Leadership Cleve. Class '95; strategic planning com. United Way, 1996-2000, chair environtl. scan subcom. 1996-2001; mem. Gov.'s Coun. on Sci. and Tech., 1996-98; mem. leadership devel. com. ACE, 1995-98, mem. women's commn., 1999-2001; mem. Strategy Coun. Cleve. Pub. Schs., 1996-98; bd. dirs. United Way, 1995-2001; co-chair Pub. Sector Campaign, 1997, 98; bd. dirs. NCAA, divsn. 1, mem. exec. com., 1999-2001; mem. Cleve. Sports Commn., 1999-2001; mem. Cleve. Mcpl. Sch. Dist. Bd., 1999-2001; mem. AGB Edn. Trusteeship and Goverance, 2001-; mem. adv. com. Assn. Liaison Officers Adv. Com., 1998-2001. Recipient Disting. Svc. medal U. Mass., 1979, Woman of the Yr. Achievement award YWCA, 1998; Am. Cancer Soc. grantee Tufts U., 1960. Mem. Am. Coun. on Edn. (com. on self-regulation 1987-91), Nat. Conf. Cmty. & Justice (program com.), State Higher Exec. Officers (fed. rels. com., 1986-92, cost accountability task force, exec. com. 1990-92), ACE (com. leadership devel.), Nat. Assn. Sys. Heads (exec. com. 1990-92), Nat. Ctr. for Edn. Stats. (network adv. com. 1989-92), Am. Assn. State Colls. and Univs. (commn. on urban agenda 1996-2001), New Eng. Assn. Schs. and Colls. (commn. on higher edn. 1990-93), North Ctrl. Assn. Schs. and Colls. (evaluator 1993-2001, chair accreditation teams 1986-90), Greater Cleve. Round Table (bd. dirs. 1993-2001, exec. com. 1995), Cleve. Playhouse (trustee 1994-2001), Nat.

Assn. State Univs. and Land Grant Colls. (exec. com. on urban agenda, mem. commn. tech. transfer, state rep. Am. Assn. State Colls. and Univs. (bd. dirs. 1996-99, mem. emerging issues task force 1996-98), Phi Beta Kappa, Sigma Xi. Office: American Coun on Edn One DuPont Cir NW Washington DC 20036-1193 E-mail: claire_van_ummersen@acc.nche.edu.

VAN VALEN, LEIGH, biologist, educator; b. Albany, N.Y., Aug. 12, 1935; s. A. Donald and Eleanor (Williams) Van V.; m. Phebe May Hoff, 1959; children: Katrina, Diana; m. Virginia C. Maiorana, 1974. BA, Miami U., Ohio, 1956; MA, Columbia U., 1957, PhD, 1961. Boese fellow Columbia U., N.Y.C., 1961-62; NATO and NIH fellow Univ. Coll. London, 1962-63; rsch. fellow Am. Mus. Natural History, N.Y.C., 1963-66; asst. prof. anatomy U. Chgo., 1967-71, assoc. prof. evolutionary biology & conceptual founds. sci., 1971-73, assoc. prof. biology & conceptual founds. of sci., 1973-76, prof. biology and conceptual founds. of sci., 1976-88, prof. ecology, evolution, conceptual founds. sci., 1988—; rsch. assoc. dept. geology Field Mus., Chgo., 1971—. Author: Deltatheridia, A New Order of Mammals, 1966, Paleocene Dinosaurs or Cretaceous Ungulates in South America?, 1988, The Origin of the Plesiadapid Primates and the Nature of Purgatorius, 1994; editor: Evolutionary Theory, 1973—, Evolutionary Monographs, 1977—; mem. editl. bd. Jour. Molecular Evolution, 1970-76, Evolución Biológica, 1988—; mem. editl. bd. commentators Behavioral and Brain Scis., 1978—; assoc. editor Evolution, 1969-71. Nat. adv. bd. Voice of Reason, N.Y., 1981—. NIH Rsch. Career Devel. award, 1967-72; NSF grantee, 1963-71. Mem. AAUP (pres. U. Chgo. chpt.), Soc. Study Evolution (v.p. 1973, 80), Am. Soc. Naturalists (v.p. 1974-75), Paleontol. Soc. (councillor 1980-82), Internat. Soc. Cryptozoology (bd. dirs.), Ecol. Soc. Am. Office: Univ Chgo Dept Ecology and Evolution 1101 E 57th St Chicago IL 60637-1503

VAN VYVEN, DALE NULSEN, state legislator; b. Cin., Apr. 20, 1935; s. Richard J. and Vera Nulsen Bennett (Plue) Va V.; m. Anne Saterfield, 1952; children: Pamela S. Van Vyven Seils, Stacey C. Van Vyven Petitt, Margo B. Van Vyven Johnson, Eric; m. Meredith A. Stuart. Student, U. Cin., 1953-66. Packaging engr. Avco Corp., Cin., 1955-66; ins. agt. Dale N. Van Vyven, Sharonville, 1967; clk. of coun. Ohio, 1964-65; councilman at large, 1966-75; pres. of coun. Sharonville, Ohio, 1975-78; Ohio state rep. Dist. 32, 1978—. Del. Rep. Nat. Conv., 1980; chmn. United Conservatives of Ohio, ALEC. nat. chmn. Named Outstanding Legislator Ohio, 1984, 94, Outstanding Am Lgis. Exch. Coun. leader, 1989; recipient Ohio Guardian of Small Bus. award Nat. Fedn. Ind. Bus., 1992. Mem. Cin. Assn. Life Underwriters, Ohio Life Underwriters, Nat. Assn. Life Underwriters, Bus. Assn., Nat. Fedn. Ind. Bus., Kiwanis, Jaycees, Dan Beard Coun. Home: 4799 Fields Ertel Rd Sharonville OH 45241-1759 Office: 11006 Reading Rd Cincinnati OH 45241-1929 also: 910 17th St NW Fl 5 Washington DC 20006-2601 also: 77 S High St Fl 13 Columbus OH 43215-6199

VAN ZANDT, DAVID E. dean; b. Princeton, N.J., Feb. 17, 1953; m. Lisa A. Huestis; children: Caroline, Nicholas. AB summa cum laude, Princeton U., 1975; JD, Yale U., 1981; PhD in Sociology, U. London, 1985. Bar: Ill. Clk. to Hon. Pierre N. Leval U.S. Dist. Ct. (so. dist.) N.Y., 1981-82; clk. to Hon. Harry A. Blackmun U.S. Supreme Ct., Washington, 1982-83; atty. Davis, Polk & Wardwell, 1984-85; mem. faculty Northwestern U. Law Sch., Chgo., 1985—, dean, 1995—. Mem. planning com. Northwestern U. Corporate Counsel Inst., Northwestern U. Corp. Counsel Ctr. Author: Living in the Children of God, 1991; mng. editor Yale Law Jour., 1980-81; contbr. articles to profl. jours. Office: Northwestern U Sch Law Office of Dean 357 E Chicago Ave Chicago IL 60611-3059

VAN ZANDT, TIM, state legislator; Rep. dist. 38 State of Mo., Kansas City. Office: Mo Ho of Reps State Capitol 201 W Capitol Ave Rm 400 Jefferson City MO 65101-1556

VAN ZELST, THEODORE WILLIAM, civil engineer, natural resource exploration company executive; b. Chgo., May 11, 1923; s. Theodore Walter and Wilhelmina (Oomens) Van Z.; m. Louann Hurter, Dec. 29, 1951; children: Anne, Jean, David. B.S., U. Calif., Berkeley, 1944; BS in Naval Sci., Northwestern U., 1944, B.A.S., 1945, M.S. in Civil Engring., 1948. Registered profl. engr., Ill. Pres., Soil Testing Services, Inc., Chgo., 1948-52; pres. Soiltest, Inc., 1948-78, chmn. bd., 1978-80; sec., dir. Exploration Data Cons., Inc., 1980-82; exec. v.p. Cenco Inc., Chgo., 1962-77, vice chmn., 1975-77, also dir., 1962-77. Bd. dirs. Minann, Inc., Testing Sci., Inc., Van Zelst, Inc., Rsch. Park, Inc., Northwestern U., 1992-95, chmn. bd. dirs. Envirotech Svcs., Inc., 1983-85; sec., bd. dirs. Van Zelst, Inc. Wadsworth, Ill., 1983—; pres., bd. dirs. Geneva-Pacific Corp., 1969-83, Geneva Resources, Inc., 1983-91. Treas. Internat. Road Fedn., 1961-64, sec., 1964-79, dir., 1973-88, vice chmn., 1980-87; pres. Internat. Road Edn. Found., 1978-80, 87-88, hon. life bd. dirs., 1988—; bd. dirs. Chgo. Acad. Scis., 1983-86, v.p., 1985-86, hon. dir., 1986—; bd. dirs. Pres.'s Assn., Chgo., 1985-86; mem. adv. bd. Mitchell Indian Mus., Kendall Coll., 1977-94. Lt. (j.g.) USNR, 1942-45. Lt. j.g. USNR, 1944—46. Recipient Service award Northwestern U., 1970, Merit award, 1974, Alumni medal, 1989, Svc. award U. Wis., 1971, La Sallian award, 1975. Mem. ASCE (Chgo. Civil Engr. of Yr., 1988), Nat. Soc. Profl. Engrs., Western Soc. Engrs., Evanston C. of C. (v.p. 1969-73), Ovid Esbach Soc. (pres. 1968-80), Northwestern U. Alumni Assn., Tau Beta Pi, Sigma Xi. Clubs: Economic, North Shore. Achievements include invention of engring. testing equipment for soil, rock, concrete and asphalt; co-invention of Swing-wing for supersonic aircraft. Home: 1213 Wagner Rd Glenview IL 60025-3297 Office: PO Box 126 Glenview IL 60025-0126

VARCHMIN, THOMAS EDWARD, environmental health administrator; b. Chgo., Dec. 5, 1947; s. Arthur William and Laurie Eileen (Allen) V.; m. Beth Virginia Plank, Dec. 16, 1972; children: Jeffrey Thomas, Brian Arthur, Jennifer Beth, Matthew James. B.A., St. Mary's Coll., Winona, Minn., 1969; M.S., Western Ill. U., Macomb, 1977. Registered sanitarian, Wis. Virologist, microbiologist Chgo. Dept. Health, 1974-78; environ. health and safety mgr. Great Atlantic & Pacific Tea Co., Chgo., 1978-79; adminstr. occupational safety and environ. health Nat. Safety Council, 1979-80; mgr. environ. health Lake County Health Dept., Waukegan, Ill., 1980-84, mgr. environ. health and pub. relations, 1984-87; mgr. environ. health Cook County Dept. Pub. Health, Oak Park, 1987-89, asst. dir. environ. health, mgr. intergovtl. rels., 1989-98, dir. environ. health, 1998—. Environ. health cons. Editor: Food and Beverage Newsletter, Hospital and Health Care Newsletter, Trades and Services Newsletter, 1979-80. NSF grantee, 1968-69 Mem. Nat. Environ. Health Assn. (registered environ. health specialist), Ill. Environ. Health Assn. (lic. environ. health practitioner), Nat. Safety Coun., Am. Soc. Microbiology, Anvil Club of Ill., Phi Mu Alpha, Delta Epsilon Sigma. Achievements include research on autumn food habits of game fish, behavioral and phys. devel. of barred owl nestlings in Ill. Office: Cook County Dept Pub Health 1010 Lake St Ste 300 Oak Park IL 60301-1133

VARGA, RICHARD STEVEN, mathematics educator; b. Cleve., Oct. 9, 1928; s. Steven and Ella (Krejcs) V.; m. Esther Marie Pfister, Sept. 22, 1951; 1 dau., Gretchen Marie. BS, Case Inst. Tech. (merged with Case Western Res. U.), 1950; AM, Harvard U., 1951, PhD, 1954; hon. doctorate, U. Karlsruhe, 1991, U. Lille, 1993. With Bettis Atomic Power Lab., Westinghouse Electric Co., 1954-60, adv. mathematician, 1959-60; full prof. math. Case Inst. Tech. (now Case We. Res. U.), 1960-69; Univ. Prof. math. Kent (Ohio) State U., 1969—, dir. rsch. Inst. for Computational Math. Cons. to govt. and industry. Author: Matrix Iterative Analysis, 1962, Functional Analysis and Approximation Theory in Numerical Analysis, 1971, Topics in Polynomial and Rational Interpolation and Approximation, 1982, Zeros of Sections of Power Series, 1983, Scientific Computation on Mathematical Problems and Conjectures, 1990; editor: Numerical Solution of Field Problems in Continuum Physics, 1970, Padé and Rational Approximations: Theory and Applications, 1977, Rational Approximations and Interpolation, 1984, Computational Methods and Function Theory, 1990, Numerical Linear Algebra, 1993; editor-in-chief. Numerische Math., Electronic Transactions Numerical Analysis; mem. editl. bd. Linear Algebra and Applications, Constructive Approximation, Computational Mathematics (China), Numerical Algorithms, Analysis, Electronic Jour. Linear Algebra, Comms. in Applied Analysis. Recipient Rsch. award Sigma Xi, 1965, von Humboldt prize, 1982, Pres.' medal Kent State U., 1981; Guggenheim fellow, 1963; Fairchild scholar, 1974. Home: 7065 Arcadia Dr Cleveland OH 44129-6065 Office: Kent State U Inst Computational Mat Kent OH 44242-0001 E-mail: varga@mcs.kent.edu.

VARMA, ARVIND, chemical engineering educator, researcher; b. Ferozabad, India, Oct. 13, 1947; s. Hans Raj and Vijay L. (Jhanjhee) V.; m. Karen K. Guse, Aug. 7, 1971; children: Anita, Sophia. BS ChemE, Panjab U., 1966; MS ChemE, U. N.B., Fredericton, Can., 1968; PhD ChemE, U. Minn., 1972. Asst. prof. U. Minn., Mpls., 1972-73; sr. research engr. Union Carbide Corp., Tarrytown, N.Y., 1973-75; asst. prof. chem. engring. U. Notre Dame, Ind., 1975-77, assoc. prof., 1977-80, prof., 1980-88, Arthur J. Schmitt prof., 1988—, chmn. dept., 1983-88; dir. Ctr. for Molecularly Engineered Materials, 2000—. Vis. prof. U. Wis., Madison, 1981; Chevron vis. prof. Calif. Inst. Tech., Pasadena, 1982; vis. prof. Ind. Inst. Tech.-Kanpur, 1989, U. Cagliari, Italy, 1989, Italy, 92; vis. fellow Princeton U., 0996; Piercy vis. prof. U. Minn., 2001. Piercy visiting prof., U. of Minn. 2001,Co-author: Mathematical Methods in Chemical Engineering, 1997, Parametric Sensitivity in Chemical Systems, 1999, Catalyst Design, 2001; editor: (with others) The Mathematical Understanding of Chemical Engineering Systems, 1980, Chemical Reaction and Reactor Engineering, 1987; series editor: Cambridge Series in Chemical Engineering, 1996—; contbr. numerous articles to profl. jours. Recipient Tchr. of Yr. award Coll. Engring. U. Notre Dame, 1991, Spl. Presdl. award 1992, R.H. Wilhelm award AIChE, 1993, Burns Grad. Sch. award 1997, E.W. Thiele award AIChE, 1998, Chemical Engring. Lectureship award, ASEE, 2000, Rsch. Achievement award U. Notre Dame, 2001; Fulbright scholar; Indo-Am. fellow, 1988-89, Rschr. achievement award U. of Notre Dame 2001. Home: 52121 N Lakeshore Dr Granger IN 46530-7848 Office: Dept Chem Engrng U Notre Dame Notre Dame IN 46556

VARNER, STERLING VERL, retired oil company executive; b. Ranger, Tex., Dec. 20, 1919; s. George Virgle and Christina Ellen (Shafer) V.; m. Paula Jean Kennedy, Nov. 17, 1945; children: Jane Ann, Richard Alan. Student, Murray State Sch. Agr., 1940, Wichita State U., 1949. With Kerr-McGee, Inc., 1941-45; with Koch Industries, Inc., Wichita, Kans., 1945-90, pres., chief operating officer, 1974-86, vice chmn., 1987-90, chmn. bd. dirs., 1990, now bd. dirs.; ret. Owner Shadow Valley Ranch; bd. dirs. Koch Industries Inc. Mem. Wichita Country Club, Crestview Country Club. Mem. Ch. of Christ. Home: 1515 N Linden Ct Wichita KS 67206-3312 Office: Koch Industries Inc PO Box 2256 411 E 37th St N Wichita KS 67219

VARNEY, RICHARD ALAN, medical center administrator; b. Concord, N.H., July 8, 1950; s. John Berry and Hattie Elizabeth (Harrington) V.; m. Cheryl Suzanne Glaab, Dec. 31, 1983; stepchildren: Alysen Suzanne, Craig Judson. BS in Phys. Edn., U. N.H., 1972; MHA in Health Adminstrn., Baylor U., 1984; diploma, Command and Gen. Staff Coll., 1986. Commd. 2d lt. U.S. Army, 1973, advanced through grades to lt. col., 1991; dep. asst. CEO Cutler Army Hosp., Ft. Devens, Mass., 1973—76; field med. asst. 38th ADA Bde.., Osan Air Base, Republic of Korea, 1977—78; dep. asst. CEO 15th Med. Battalion, Ft. Hood, Tex., 1979—81; adminstrv. resident Ireland Army Hosp., Ft. Knox, Ky., 1982—83; COO, exec. officer U.S. Army Dental Activity, 1983—86; grad. instr. Army-Baylor Healthcare Program, San Antonio, 1986—90; project mgr. Office of the Army Surgeon Gen., Washington, 1990—93; ret. U.S. Army, 1993; office mgr. Aebi, Ginty, Romaker & Sprouse MD's, Inc., Lancaster, Ohio, 1993—2000; dir. gen. internal medicine program The Ohio State U. Med. Ctr., Columbus, 2000—. Mem. Source Selection Evaluation Bd.-Champus Reform, Arlington, Va., 1987; mem. adv. com. for assoc. degree program in med. assisting Ohio U., Lancaster, 1998-2000. Adult leader Boy Scouts Am., Tex., Va. and Ohio, 1988-97; mem. Lancaster City Bd. of Health, 1996-2001, pres. pro tem, 1999-2001; mem. Fairfield County Combined Gen. Health Dist. Bd., 2002--. Decorated Legion of Merit, Order of Mil. Med. Merit award, Expert Field Med. badge; named to Hon. Order Ky. Cols., 1989, Outstanding Young Man of Am., 1982. Fellow Am. Coll. Healthcare Execs.; mem. Ctrl. Ohio Health Adminstrs. Assn., Ohio Med. Group Mgmt. Assn., Mid-Ohio Med. Mgmt. Assn., Profl. Assn. Med. Mgrs., Am. Assn. Procedural Coders, Lancaster Area Soc. for Human Resource Mrmt. (legis. rep. 1998-99, membership chair 1999—), Am. Hosp. Assn., Nat. Eagle Scout Assn., The Ret. Officers Assn., Am. Legion, Fraternal Order of Eagles, Alpha Phi Omega. Avocations: home improvement, music. Home: 1025 E 5th Ave Lancaster OH 43130-3276 Business E-Mail: varney-1@medctr.osu.edu. E-mail: richvarney@buckeyeinternet.com.

VARRO, BARBARA JOAN, retired editor; b. East Chicago, Ind., Jan. 25, 1938; d. Alexander R. and Lottie R. (Bess) V. B.A., Duquesne U., 1959. Feature reporter, asst. fashion editor Chgo. Sun-Times, 1959-64, fashion editor, 1964-76, feature writer, 1976-84; v.p. pub. rels. Daniel J. Edelman Inc., Chgo., 1984-85; v.p. PRB/Needham Porter Novelli, 1985-86; editor Am. Hosp. Assn. News, 1987-94; editor spl. sects. Chgo. Tribune, 1995-2000; ret. Recipient awards for feature writing Ill. AP, 1978, 79, 80 Mem.: PEO.

VASSELL, GREGORY S. electric utility consultant; b. Moscow, Dec. 24, 1921; came to U.S., 1951, naturalized, 1957; s. Gregory M. and Eugenia M. Wasiljeff; m. Martha Elizabeth Williams, Apr. 26, 1957; children: Laura Kay, Thomas Gregory. Dipl. Ing. in Elec. Engring, Tech. U. Berlin, 1951; MBA in Corp. Fin., NYU, 1954. With Am. Electric Power Svc. Corp., Columbus, Ohio, 1951-88, v.p. system planning, 1973-76, dir., 1973-88, sr. v.p. system planning, 1976-88; electric utility cons. Upper Arlington, Ohio, 1988—. Bd. dirs. Columbus & Southern Ohio Electric Co., 1981-88, Cardinal Operating Co.; mem. tech. adv. com. transmission FPC, 1968-70, FERC Task Force on Power Pooling, 1980-81; mem. U.S. com. World Energy Coun. Contbr. articles to profl. jours. Fellow IEEE (life); mem. NAE, Internat. Conf. Large High Voltage Electric Systems, Am. Arbitration Assn., Athletic Club of Columbus. Home and Office: 2247 Pinebrook Rd Columbus OH 43220-4327

VAUGHAN, MICHAEL RICHARD, lawyer; b. Chgo., Aug. 27, 1936; s. Michael Ambrose and Loretta M. (Parks) Vaughan; m. Therese Marie Perri, Aug. 6, 1960; children: Charles Thomas, Susan Enger. Student, U. Ill., 1954-59; LLB, U. Wis., 1962. Bar: Wis. 1962. Chief atty. bill drafting sect. Wis. Legislature, Madison, 1962-68, dir. legis. attys., 1968-72; assoc. Murphy & Desmond, and predecessor, 1972-73, ptnr., 1974—2000. Mem. Commn. Uniform State Laws, 1966—72; cons. Nat. Commn. Marijuana and Drug Abuse, 1971—73; lectr. CLE seminars. Contbr. articles to profl. jours. Warden, vestryman St. Dunstan's Episcopal Ch., 1973—78, 1980—87; mem. Wis. Episcopal Conf., 1972—76. Mem.: ABA, Dane County Bar Assn., State Bar Wis. (dir. govtl. and adminstrv. law sect. 1971—78, mem. interprofl. and bus. rels. com. 1976—89), Nakoma Golf Club, Madison Club, U. Wis. Law Sch. Bencher Soc., Delta Kappa Epsilon. Home: 4714 Lafayette Dr Madison WI 53705-4865 Office: 2 E Mifflin St Ste 800 Madison WI 53701-2038

VAUGHAN, THERESE MICHELE, insurance commissioner; b. Blair, Nebr., June 12, 1956; d. Emmett John and Lonne Kay (Smith) V.; m. Robert Allen Carber, Aug. 14, 1993; 1 child, Kevin Leo Vaughan-Carber. BBA, U. Iowa, 1979; PhD, U. Pa., 1985. CPCU. Asst. prof. Baruch Coll., CUNY, 1986-87; cons. Tillinghast, N.Y.C., 1987-88; dir. ins. ctr. Drake U., Des Moines, 1988-94; ins. commr. State of Iowa, 1994—, dir. dept. commerce, 1996-98. Dir. EMC Ins. Group, Des Moines, 1992-94; trustee Am. Inst. for CPCU, Malvern, Pa., 1996—. Chair Jour. of Ins. Regulation Bd., Kansas City, Mo., 1995-99; co-author: Fundamentals of Risk and Insurance, 1996, 99, Essentials of Insurance: A Risk Management Approach, 1995, 2d edit., 2000; contbr. articles to profl. jours. S.S. Huebner fellow U. Pa., 1979-82; named Outstanding Young Alumnus U. Iowa, 1996. Mem. Nat. Assn. Ins. Commrs. (pres. 2002, v.p. 2001, sec.-treas. 2000, chair Midwest Zone 1996-99), Am. Acad. Actuaries, Soc. Actuaries, Casualty Actuarial Soc., Soc. CPCU, Am. Risk and Ins. Assn., Beta Gamma Sigma, Omicron Delta Epsilon. Avocations: hiking, biking, reading. Home: 4632 Elm St West Des Moines IA 50265-2993 Office: Iowa Ins Divsn 330 Maple St Des Moines IA 50319-0065

VAUGHAN, WORTH EDWARD, chemistry educator; b. N.Y.C., Feb. 1, 1936; s. Royal Worth and Sylvia Marie (Fernholz) V.; m. Diane Marilyn Mayer, Aug. 9, 1969; 1 child, Wayne John B.A., Oberlin Coll., 1957; M.A., Princeton U., 1959, Ph.D., 1960. Asst. prof. chemistry U. Wis.-Madison, 1961-66, assoc. prof., 1967-76, prof., 1977—. Mem. bd. advisors Am. Exchange Bank West Br., Madison, 1983-87. Author: Dielectric Properties and Molecular Behavior, 1969; editor: Digest of Literature on Dielectrics, 1974; translation editor: Dipole Moments of Organic Compounds, 1970; contbr. articles to profl. jours. Mem. Am. Chem. Soc. (pres. Wis. sect. 1968, sec. 1968, 98), Am. Phys. Soc., AAAS, Phi Beta Kappa, Sigma Xi, Alpha Chi Sigma Avocations: canoeing, contract bridge. Home: 501 Ozark Trl Madison WI 53705-2538 Office: Univ Wis 1101 University Ave Madison WI 53706-1322 E-mail: vaughan@chem.wisc.edu.

VAUGHN, EDWARD, state legislator; b. Abbeville, Ala., July 30, 1934; s. Ivory Vaughn and Posie (White) V.; m. Wilma Jean Lathion, 1957; children: Eric, Randall, Sybil, Attallah. BA, Fisk U., 1955; postgrad., U. Ill., 1955-56. Owner/founder Vaughn's Book Store, 1961—, Langston Hughes Theatre, 1975—; rep. Dist. 4 Mich. Ho. of Reps., 1995—. Contbr. articles to profl. jours. Recipient Hon. Citizenship award Republic of Uganda, East Africa, 1974, African Hist. Club award, Detroit, 1977, Great Contbrs. award Wayne County C.C., 1977, Spirit of Detroit award Detroit Common Coun., 1978. Mem. Pan-African Congress U.S., New Directions Inst., Am. Writers league, The New Pioneers.

VAUGHN, JACKIE, III, state legislator; BA, Hillsdale (Mich.) Coll.; MA, Oberlin (Ohio) Coll.; LittB, Oxford U.; LLD (hon.), Marygrove Coll., Detroit, Shaw Coll.; HHD (hon.), Highland Park (Mich.) Community Coll. Tchr. U. Detroit, Wayne State U., Detroit, 1963-64; mem. Mich. Ho. of Reps., Lansing, 1966-78, Mich. Senate, Lansing, 1978—, asst. pres. pro tem, 1978-82, pres. pro tem, 1982-86, assoc. pres. pro tem, 1986—. Past pres. Mich. Young Dems.; chmn. Mich. Dr. Martin Luther King Jr. Holiday commn.; exec. bd. dirs. Detroit NAACP. With USN. Fulbright fellow; recipient Frank J. Wieting Meml. Service award, 1977, Focus and Impact award Cotillion Club, 1980, Outstanding Achievement award Booker T. Washington Bus. Assn., Outstanding Community Service award Charles Stewart Mott Community Coll. and Urban Coalition of Greater Flint, Mich., 1981; named Outstanding State Senator of Yr., Detroit Urban League Guild, 1983, Most Outstanding Legislator of Yr., Washburn-Ilene Block Club, 1983, numerous others. Mem. Am. Oxonian Assn., Fulbright Alumni Assn. Baptist. Home: 19930 Roslyn Rd Detroit MI 48221-1853 Office: Mich Senate State Capitol PO Box 30036 Lansing MI 48909-7536

VAUGHT, LOY, professional basketball player; b. Feb. 27, 1968; Grad., U. Mich., 1990. Forward L.A. Clippers, 1990-98, Detroit Pistons, 1998—. Avocations: movies, reading, sketching, painting, collecting art. Office: c/o Detroit Pistons 2 Championship Dr Auburn Hills MI 48326

VAYO, DAVID JOSEPH, composer, music educator; b. New Haven, Mar. 28, 1957; s. Harold Edward and Joan Virginia (Cassidy) V.; m. Marie-Susanne Langille, 2002; children: Rebecca Lynn, Gordon Francis. MusB, Ind. U., 1980, MusM, 1982; D of Musical Arts, U. Mich., 1990. Prof. Nat. U., Heredia, Costa Rica, 1982-84, Nat. Symphony Youth Sch., San Jose, Costa Rica, 1982-84; asst. prof. music Conn. Coll., New London, 1988-91, Ill. Wesleyan U. Sch. Music, Bloomington, 1991-95, assoc. prof., 1995-2000, prof., 2000—. Resident artist Banff Ctr. for Arts, 1992, 94, Va. Ctr. for Creative Arts, 1994, Centrum, Port Townsend, Wash., 1996; participating composer Internat. Soc. Contemporary Music-World Music Days, Yokohama, 2001, Mexico City, 1993, Internat. Double Reed Festival, Rotterdam, The Netherlands, 1995, Internat. Trombone Festival, 1997. Composer chamber composition Signals, 1997 (commd. by Koussevitzky Music Found. and Orkest de Volharding), Symphony: Blossoms and Awakenings, 1990 (performer St. Louis Symphony, Leonard Slatkin condr. 1993), Septet, 1998 (commd. by Southeastern Composers League), Eight Poems of William Carlos Williams for solo trombonist, 1994 (commd. by St. Louis Symphony), piano trio Awakening of the Heart (commd. Barlow Endowment for Music Composition), 1998; works pub. by MMB Music, Internat. Trombone Assn. Press and A.M. Percussion Publs. John Simon Guggenheim Meml. Found. fellow, 2001; Ill. Arts Coun. fellow, 2000. Mem. ASCAP (awards 1988—), Am. Music Ctr. (copying assistance grantee 1992), Coll. Music Soc. (presenter nat. conf. 1990, 94, 96), Soc. for Electro-Acoustic Music in U.S. (presenter nat. conf. 1989), Soc. Composers (membership chmn. 1990-2000, presenter nat. conf. 1990, 92, 95, 97, 98), Am. Composers Forum. Avocations: athletics, popular music, travel, reading, cooking. Office: Ill Wesleyan U Sch Music PO Box 2900 Bloomington IL 61702-2900 E-mail: dvayo@titan.iwu.edu.

VEALE, TINKHAM, II, former chemical company executive, engineer; b. Topeka, Dec. 26, 1914; s. George W. and Grace Elizabeth (Walworth) V.; m. Harriett Alice Ernst, Sept. 6, 1941; children: Harriett Elizabeth Veale Leedy, Tinkham III, Helen Ernst Veale Gelbach. BS in Mech. Engring., Case Inst. Tech., 1937; LLD, Kenyon Coll., 1981. Registered profl. engr. With Gen. Motors Corp., 1937-38, Avery Engring. Co., 1939, Reliance Electric Co., 1940-41; asst. to pres. Ohio Crankshaft Co., 1942-46; gen. mgr. Tocco Co., 1947-51; pres. Ric Wil Corp., 1952-53, Alco Chem. Corp., 1954-56, dir., 1954-86. Spl. ptnr. Ball Burge & Kraus, investment bankers, 1957-60; chmn. bd. V. and V. Cos., Inc. and subs., Cleve., 1960-65, Alco Standard Corp. and subs., Valley Forge, Pa., 1965-86, Horsehead Industries, Inc. and subs., N.Y.C., 1981—2001, HTV Industries Inc. and subs., Cleve., 1978—; ptnr. Fair Elm Farm, 1948-2000, Kennedy Veale Stable, 1954-2000. Trustee Veale Charitable Found., 1966—. Recipient Silver Bowl award Case Inst. Tech., 1980; recipient Gold Medal Case Inst. Tech., 1982 Mem. Cleve. Engring. Soc., Nat. Soc. Registered Profl. Engrs., Newcomen Soc., Phi Kappa Psi. Home: PO Box 39 Gates Mills OH 44040-0039 Office: HTV Industries Inc PO Box 295 Gates Mills OH 44040-0295

VEBLEN, THOMAS CLAYTON, management consultant; b. Hallock, Minn., Dec. 17, 1929; s. Edgar R. and Hattie (Lundgren) V.; m. Susan Alma Beaver, Sept. 1, 1950 (div. 1971); children: Kari Christen, Erik Rodli, Mark Andrew, Sara Catherine; m. Linda Joyce Eaton, Aug. 30, 1975; 1 child, Kristen Kirby. Student, U. Calif., Santa Barbara, 1950-51; BS, Calif. Poly. U., 1953; MS, Oreg. State U., 1955. Corp. v.p. Cargill, Inc., Wayzata, Minn., 1955-75; spl. asst. Sec. Interior, Washington, 1965; dir. food and agr. SRI Internat., Menlo Park, Calif., 1975-80; pres. Food Sys. Assocs., Inc., Washington, 1980-94; also bd. dirs. Food System Assocs., Inc.; chmn. Enterprise Cons., Inc., 1990—; dir. Georgetown Cons., Inc., 1993-95; convener The Superior Bus. Firm Roundtable, 1993—; chmn. Kirby Ventures LLC, Mpls., 1997—, Wyatt Ventures, LLC, Mpls. Mem. CMC Inst. Mgmt. Cons., 1988—97, pres. Washington chpt., 1991—93. Author:

(with M. Nichols) The U.S. Food System, 1978; (with M. Abel) Creating a Superior National Food System, 1992, The Way of Business, 2000; editor Food System Update, 1986-95. Treas., bd. dirs. White House Fellows Assn., Washington, 1985; trustee Freedom from Hunger Found., Davis, Calif., 1980-99, chmn., 1986-89; bd. dirs. Patterson Sch., U. Ky., Lexington, 1976-99, Am. Near East Refugee Aid, 1994--. Recipient Presdl. Appointment White House Fellows Commn., Washington, 1965. Mem. Coun. on Fgn. Rels., Cato Inst., Cosmos Club. Episcopalian. Avocations: canoeing, gardening. Office: Enterprise Cons Inc 3105 Bloomington Ave South Minneapolis MN 55407 E-mail: superbizrt@aol.com.

VECCHIO, ROBERT PETER, business management educator; b. Chgo., June 29, 1950; s. Dominick C. and Angeline V.; m. Betty Ann Vecchio; Aug. 21, 1974; children: Julie, Mark. BS summa cum laude, DePaul U., 1972; MA, U. Ill., 1974, PhD, 1976. Instr. U. Ill., Urbana, 1973-76; mem. faculty dept. mgmt. U. Notre Dame, 1976—, dept. chmn., 1983-90, Franklin D. Schurz Prof. Mgmt., 1986—. Editor Jour. of Mgmt., 1995-2000. Fellow: APA, Am. Psychol. Soc., Soc. for Indsl. and Orgnl. Psychology; mem.: Midwest Psychol. Assn., Midwest Acad. Mgmt., Decision Scis. Inst., Acad. of Mgmt., Phi Eta Sigma, Delta Epsilon Sigma, Phi Kappa Phi. Home: 16856 Hampton Dr Granger IN 46530-6907 Office: U Notre Dame Dept Mgmt Notre Dame IN 46556

VECCHIOTTI, ROBERT ANTHONY, management and organizational consultant; b. N.Y.C., May 21, 1941; s. R. Lucien and Louise Victoria V.; m. Dorothea Irene Hoban, Oct. 12, 1963; children: John Robert, Rachel Irene, Sara Christine. BS, St. Peter's Coll., 1962; MA, Fordham U., 1964; PhD, St. Louis U., 1973. Lic. psychologist, Mo. Psychologist Testing and Advisement Ctr., NYU, Washington Sq. campus, 1964-65; group psychologist McDonnell Douglas, St. Louis, 1967-76, sr. bus. analyst, 1976-77, mgr. bus. planning, 1977-79; pres. Orgnl. Cons. Svcs., Inc., 1980—. Adj. assoc. prof. mgmt. Maryville Coll., St. Louis, 1975-81. Bd. dirs. Cath. Charities of St. Louis, 1981-86, Cath. Family Svc., 1986-2000, Mental Health Assn. St. Louis, 1989—, Sta. KWMU-FM, 1989-94. With U.S. Army, 1965-67. Mem. APA, Strategic Leadership Forum, Mo. Athletic Club, Rotary (past pres.). Office: Organizational Consulting Svcs Inc 230 S Bemiston Ave Ste 1107 Clayton MO 63105-1907

VECCI, RAYMOND JOSEPH, airline industry consultant; b. N.Y.C., Jan. 22, 1943; s. Romeo John and Mary (Fabretti) V.; m. Helen Cecelia Clampett, Sept. 3, 1967; children: Brian John, Damon Jay. BBA, CCNY, 1965; MBA, NYU, 1967. Adminstrv. asst. Internat. Air Transport Assn., N.Y.C., 1961-66; econ. analyst United Airlines, Chgo., 1967-74; asst. v.p. planning and regulatory affairs Alaska Airlines Inc., Seattle, 1975-76, staff v.p. planning and regulatory affairs, 1976-79, staff v.p. planning, 1979, v.p. planning, 1979-85, exec. v.p., chief operating officer, 1986-90, pres., chief exec. officer, 1990-95, chmn., dir., 1991-95; also chmn., pres., chief exec. officer, dir. Alaska Air Group Inc.; pres. Carnival Airlines, Dania, Fla., 1997; exec. v.p. customer svc. Northwest Airlines, pres. Mich. ops. Served with U.S. Army, 1968-69, Vietnam. Decorated Bronze Star. Roman Catholic.

VEENSTRA, KENNETH, state legislator; b. Tracy, Iowa, Apr. 19, 1939; m. Jan Veenstra; 4 children. CLU, Am. Coll., 1985. Ins. agt. State Farm Ins. Co.; mem. Iowa Ho. of Reps., Des Moines, 1994-98, Iowa Senate from 3rd dist., Des Moines, 1998—; mem. agr. com., mem. edn. com., mem. human resources com.; mem. small bus., econ. devel. and tourism com. Former mem. coun. Cavelry Christian Reformed Ch.; pres. Sioux County Assn. for Retarded Citizens; former bd. dirs. Orange City Christian Sch.; mem. Iowa Farm Bur.; founding bd. dirs. Ronald McDonald House, Iowa City. Mem. Northwestern Assn. Life Underwriters (pres. 1993-94), Nat. Fedn. Ind. Bus., Orange City C. of C. Republican.

VEGA, FRANK J. newspaper publishing executive; Pres., CEO Detroit Newspapers. Office: 615 W Lafayette Blvd Detroit MI 48226-3124

VEGA, SARAH, state official; b. Oak Lawn, Ill., May 7, 1963; d. David and Hilda Maria Vega; m. Leonard A. Sherman, Sept. 8, 1990; children: Marissa and Elizabeth (twins). BA, DePaul U., Chgo., 1985, JD, 1988. Bar: Ill. 1989. Legal advisor, hearing officer Adminstrv. Hearing divsn. Office of Sec. of State, Chgo., 1989-91, enforcement atty., 1989-91; adminstr. Credit Union divsn. Ill. Dept. Fin. Instns., 1991—, dir. Mem. Nat. Assn. Sate of Credit Union Suprs. (chmn. bd. dirs. 1999—), Ill. Women in Govt. Office: Ill Dept Fin Instns 100 W Randolph St Ste 15-7000 Chicago IL 60601-3218

VEIT, GAE, construction executive; CEO, owner Shingobee Builders, Loretto, Minn., 1980—. Recipient Contractor Yr., Am. Public Works Assn., 1994, Supplier Yr., Alliant Techsystems, 1993, Nat. Female Entrepreneur Yr., Dept. Commerce, 1991. Office: Shingobee Builders PO Box 8 Loretto MN 55357-0008 Fax: 612-479-3267.

VELICK, STEPHEN H. medical facility administrator; BS, Wayne State U., 1970, MS, 1980. Mgr. billing Henry Ford Hosp., Detroit, 1970-72, 72-74, mgr. patient svcs., 1974-75, asst. dir. bus., 1975-76, dir. bus. office, 1976-78, assoc. adminstr., 1978-83; exec. dir. Greenfield Health Sys. Corp., 1983-86; chief adminstrv. officer Henry Ford Med. Group, 1986-90; group v.p., COO Henry Ford Hosp., 1990-95, CEO, 1995—. Adv. bd., bd. dirs. various healthcare orgns. Mem. adv. bd. Wayne State U. Coll. Pharmacy & Allied Health; active various cmty. orgns. Mem. Am. Coll. Healthcare Execs. (assoc.), Am. Hosp. Assn. Office: HFH Sys 2799 W Grand Blvd Detroit MI 48202-2608

VELLENGA, KATHLEEN OSBORNE, former state legislator; b. Alliance, Nebr., Aug. 5, 1938; d. Howard Benson and Marjorie (Menke) Osborne; m. James Alan Vellenga, Aug. 9, 1959; children: Thomas, Charlotte Vellenga Landreau, Carolyn Vellenga Berman. BA, Macalester Coll., 1959. Tchr. St. Paul Pub. Schs., 1959-60, Children's Ctr. Montessori, St. Paul, 1973-74, Children's House Montessori, St. Paul, 1974-79; mem. Minn. Ho. of Reps., 1980-94, mem. tax. com. and rules com., 1991—, chmn. St. Paul del., 1985-89, chmn. criminal justice div., 1989-90, chmn. crime and family law div., 1987-88, mem. Dem. steering com., 1987-94, chmn. judiciary, 1991, 92, chmn. edn. fin., 1992-93, 93-94. Mem. St. Paul Family Svcs. Bd., 1994-95; exec. dir. St. Paul/Ramsey County Children's Initiative, 1994-2000. Chmn. Healthstart, St. Paul, 1987-91; mem. Children, Youth and Families Consortium, 1995-99, Macalester Coll. Bd. Alumni, 1995-01; chair Minn. Higher Edn. Svcs. Coun., 2000—; mem. Citizen's League Bd., Minn., 1999—, State Commn. Cmty. Svc., 00—. Mem. LWV (v.p. St. Paul chpt. 1979), Minn. Women Elected Ofcls. (vice chair 1994). Democrat. Presbyterian.

VELTMAN, MARTINUS J. retired physics educator; b. The Netherlands, 1931; PhD, U. Utrecht, The Netherlands, 1963. John D. MacArthur prof. physics U. Mich., Ann Arbor, now prof. emeritus. Recipient High Energy and Particle Physics prize, European Physics Soc., 1993, P.A.M. Dirac Medal and Prize, Internat. Ctr. for Theoretical Physics, 1996, Nobel prize in Physics, 1999. Office: U Mich Dept Physics 2477 Randall Lab 500 E University Ave Ann Arbor MI 48109-1120

VENIT, WILLIAM BENNETT, electrical products company executive, consultant; b. Chgo., May 28, 1931; s. George Bernard and Ida (Schaffel) V.; m. Nancy Jean Carlson, Jan. 28, 1956; children: Steven Louis, Aprilann. Student, U. Ill., Champaign, 1949. Sales mgr. Coronet, Inc., Chgo., 1952-63, pres., chmn. bd. dirs., 1963-74, Roma Wire Inc., Chgo., 1971-74; chmn. bd. dirs. Swing Time #2, 1988-89; pres. Wm. Allen Inc., 1972-74; pres., chmn. bd. dirs. Wraprama Inc., 1988-95, Swag Lite, Inc., 1989—. Pres. William Lamp Co., Inc., 1993, 97, William Wire Co., Inc., 1974-76; chmn. bd. dirs. MSWV, Inc., 1978—, pres. bd. dirs. 1985—; pres. Trio Steel Inc., Chgo., 1987-90; chmn. bd. Chgo. Lamp Works LLB, 1995, 98, chair 1996, 98; CEO Chgo. Chair Works, 1998, 2000, 2001; spl. cons. Roto Products, 1998—, DMSI Inc.; cons. Nu Style Lamp Shade. Patentee Printed-Cir., 1964. With QMC AUS, 1949-52. Avocations: bicycling, golf. Home and Office: 323 Suwanee Ave Sarasota FL 34243-1930 E-mail: LampBill@aol.com.

VENKATA, SUBRAHMANYAM SARASWATI, electrical engineering educator, electric energy and power researcher; b. Nellore, Andhra Pradesh, India, June 28, 1942; came to U.S., 1968; s. Ramiah Saraswati and Lakshmi (Alladi) V.; m. Padma Subrahmanyam Mahadevan, Sept. 3, 1971; children: Sridevi Ramakumar, Harish Saraswati. BSEE, Andhra U., Waltair, India, 1963; MSEE, Indian Inst. Tech., Madras, 1965; PhD, U. S.C., 1971. Registered profl. engr., W.Va., Wash. Lectr. in elec. engring. Coimbatore (India) Inst. Tech., 1965-66; planning engr. S.C. Elec. & Gas Co., Columbia, 1969-70; postdoctoral fellow U. S.C., 1971; instr. elec. engring. U. Mass., Lowell, 1971-72; asst. prof. W.Va. U., Morgantown, 1972-75, assoc. prof., 1975-79; prof. U. Wash., Seattle, 1979-96; prof., chmn. dept. elec. and computer engring. Iowa State U., Ames, 1996—. Cons. Puget Sound Energy Co., Bellevue, Wash., 1980-93, GEC/Alsthom, N.Y.C., 1991-92; series editor, bd. dirs. PWS Pub. Co., 1991-98; affiliate prof. U. Wash., Seattle, 1997—; editor, IEEE Transactions on Power Systems, 1998-2000, IEEE/PES Rev. Letters, 1999—, Internat. Jour. Sys. Author: Introduction of Electrical Energy Devices, 1987; patentee adaptive var compensators, adaptive power quality conditioner, distribution reliability based design software. Advisor Explorers Club, Morgantown, 1976-78; sec. Hindu Temple and Cultural Ctr. Pacific N.W., Seattle, 1990, chmn., 1991, 95; founding chmn. Hindu Temple and Cultural Ctr., Ames, Iowa, 1999—. Recipient W.Va. U. Assocs. award W.Va. U. Found., 1974, 78. Fellow IEEE (best paper award 1985, 88, 91, Outstanding Power Engring. Educator award 1996, chmn. power engring. edn. com. 2000—, Millenneum Medal award 2000)); mem. Conf. Internat. des Grands Reseaux Electriques, IEEE Press for Power Series, 1998—, Sigma Xi, Tau Beta Pi, Eta Kappa Nu, Rotary. Democrat. Avocations: photography, tennis, table tennis. Home: 3109 Sycamore Rd Ames IA 50014-4510 Office: Dept Elec Computer Engring Iowa State U Ames IA 50011-3060 E-mail: venkata@iastate.edu.

VENO, GLEN COREY, management consultant; b. Montreal, Que., Can., Sept. 5, 1951; came to U.S., 1953; s. Corey Elroy and Elsie Milly (Munro) V. BS in Aviation Tech. and Mgmt., Western Mich. U., 1976. Cert. mgmt. cons. Project mgr. The ASIST Corp., Oak Park, Mich., 1978-83; mgr. tech. support J.B. Systems, Inc., Woodland Hills, Calif., 1984-85; mgr. cons. svcs. Mgmt. Tech., Inc., Troy, Mich., 1985-88; v.p. Mgmt. Support Svcs., Inc., Southfield, 1989-90; owner Maintenance Mgmt. Support Svcs., Brighton, 1990—. With U.S. Army, 1969-72, Vietnam. Mem. ASTD, VFW (life), Inst. Mgmt. Cons., Soc. Mfg. Engrs. (sr.), Am. Prodn. and Inventory Control Soc., Inst. Indsl. Engrs., Project Mgmt. Inst., Am. Mgmt. Assn., Am. Soc. Quality, Am. Inst. for Total Productive Maintenance. Avocations: flying, boating, golf. Home: 6397 Kinyon Dr Brighton MI 48116-9581 Office: PO Box 605 Brighton MI 48116-0605 E-mail: gcveno@maintenance-mgmt.com.

VENTURA, JESSE (JAMES JANOS), governor; b. Mpls., July 15, 1951; s. George and Bernice Janos; m. Terry Ventura; children: Tyrel, Jade. Student, North Hennepin C.C. Profl. wrestler, 1973-84; ret.; gov. State of Minn., St. Paul, 1998—. Actor starring in several films including Predator; radio talk show host. Mayor City of Brooklyn Park, Minn., 1990-95; bd. advisors Make a Wish of Minn.; vol. football coach Champlin Park H.S. Served with USN, USNR. Mem. Am. Fedn. of TV and radio Announcers, Screen Actors Guild. Office: Office of the Governor State Capitol Rm 130 Saint Paul MN 55155-0001*

VENTURINI, TISHA LEA, professional soccer player; b. Modesto, Calif., Mar. 3, 1973; Degree in phys. edn., U. N.C. Mem. U.S. Women's Nat. Soccer Team. Recipient Gold medal Centennial Olympic Games, 1996, Silver medal world Univ. Games, 1993, Hermann trophy, 1994; mem. championship team CONCACAF, National, 1994; named Player of Yr. Mo. Athletic Club, 1994. Office: c/o US Soccer Fedn 1801 S Prairie Ave # 1811 Chicago IL 60616-1319

VENZAGO, MARIO, conductor; b. Zurich, Switzerland, 1948; m. Marianne Skansi; children: Mario, Gabriel. Studied with, Hans Swarowsky, Vienna, 1973. Prin. guest conductor Malmo Symphony, Sweden; music dir. Basel Symphony Orch., Heidelberg Opera, 1986—89, Deutsche Kammerphilharmonic, 1989—92, Graz Opera Ho., 1990—95, Euskadi Nat. Opera, Spain, 1998—2001, Ind. Symphony Orch., 2002—. Guest conductor Berlin Philharmonic, Leipzig Gewandhaus Orchetser, London Philharmonic, City of Birmingham Symphony, Orchestre de la Suisse Romande , Tonhalle Orchestra Zurich , Tokyo's NHK Symphony, Berlin's Komische Oper, Salzburg Festival, Hannover Radio-Philharmonie, invited by Kurt Masur, Leipzig, Am. debut Hollywood Bowl, 1988, appeared N.J. Symphony, Ind. Symphony, Fla. Philharmonic, 1988; dir.: Balt. Symphony, 1995 (named artistic dir. symphony's summer festival , 2000); prin. conductor Winterthur City Orch. , Lucerne Opera Ho., Orchestre de la Suisse Romande. Recipient award, Diapason d'or, awards, Grand Prix du Disque, Edison prize. Office: Ind Symphony Orch 45 Monument Cir Indianapolis IN 46204-2919 Office Fax: 317-262-1159. Business E-Mail: iso@indyorch.org.*

VERDOORN, SID, food service executive; b. Albert Lea, Minn., Feb. 11, 1939; s. Cornelius Emery and Gwen (Pickell) V.; m. Carol Joyce Hoekstra, July 3, 1959; children: Jay Richard, Jeffrey Lee, James Dale. Student, Cen. Coll., Pella, Iowa. With sales C.H. Robinson Co., Mpls., 1963-66, mgr. San Francisco, 1966-71, pers. dir. Mpls., 1971-75, v.p., 1975-77, pres., 1977-2000, CEO, 1977—. Bd. dirs. Produce Mktg. Assocs., Newark, United Fruit and Produce, Washington. With U.S. Army, 1959-61. Republican. Avocations: hiking, water sports. Home: 28210 Woodside Rd Excelsior MN 55331-7950 Office: C H Robinson Co Inc 8100 Mitchell Rd Ste 200 Eden Prairie MN 55344-2178

VEREEN, ROBERT CHARLES, retired trade association executive; b. Stillwater, Minn., Sept. 8, 1924; s. George and Leona Lucille (Made) Wihren; m. Rose Catherine Blair, Nov. 5, 1945; children: Robin, Stacy, Kim. Grad. high sch. Mng. editor Comml. West Mag., Mpls., 1946-50, Bruce Pub. Co., St. Paul, 1950-53, Nat. Retail Hardware Assn., Indpls., 1953-59; mng. dir. Liberty Distbrs., Phila., 1959-63; editor Hardware Retailing, Indpls., 1963-80; assoc. pub., dir. communications Nat. Retail Hardware Assn., 1980-84, sr. v.p., 1984-87; Vereen & Assocs., Mgmt., Mktg. Cons., 1987—. Lectr. mgmt. insts.; guest lectr. on distbn. pub.; co-founder U.S.A. Direct; co-founder, ptnr. Eurotrade Mktg., 1988—; ptnr. Hardlines Pers. Finders, 1987—. Author: (with Paul M. Doane) Hunting for Profit, 1965, The Computer Age in Merchandising, 1968, Perpetuating the Family-Owned Business, 1970, The How-To of Merchandising, 1975, The How-To of Store Operations, 1976, A Guide to Financial Management, 1976, Productivity: A Crisis for Management, 1978, Hardlines Rep Report Newsletter, 1984-94, Guidelines to Improve the Rep/Factory Relationships, 1992. Served with AUS, 1943-46. Mem. Am. Soc. Bus. Press Editors (dir., v.p. 1966-70), Soc. Nat. Assn. Publs. (dir., pres. 1970-75, chmn. journalism edn. liaison com. 1976-79), Toastmasters (v.p., treas., sec. 1955-59), Am. Hardware Mfrs. Assn. (co-founder, sec.-treas. Young Execs. Club 1958-.59, 63-65), Hardware-Housewares Packaging Expn. (founder 1960, chmn. com. packaging 1960-62, chmn. judging com. Hardware-Packaging Expn. 1975-78), Packaging Inst., Household Consumer Products Export Coun. (chmn. 1981-83), World-Wide DIY Coun. (exec. sec. 1981-99, dir. emeritus 1999—). Home and Office: 4560 Lincoln Rd Indianapolis IN 46228-6706

VERFAILLIE, HENDRIK A. food products company executive; Joined Monsanto, St. Louis, 1976, pres. former agrl. group, corp. v.p., 1993, exec. v.p., 1995, pres., pres., CEO, 1999—, also bd. dirs. Office: Monsanto 800 N Lindbergh Blvd Saint Louis MO 63167-0001

VERICH, DEMETRIO, lawyer; b. Laona, Wis., June 21, 1932; s. Peter Paul and Annetta (Mariani) V.; m. Mary Therese Rathborne, Nov. 28, 1967; children: Peter, Andrew, Nicole, Matthew, Daniel, John, Joseph. Student, St. Norbert Coll., 1951-52; BS in Engring., U.S. Naval Postgrad. Sch., 1958-60; student, U.S. Naval War Coll., 1964-65; MBA, JD, U. Notre Dame, 1976. Bar: Wis. Commd. ensign USN, 1952; advanced through grades to commdr.; naval aviator USN, 1952-72; cand. for U.S. Congress 8th congl. dist. U. S. Ho. of Reps., 1976; cand. for assembly 36th assembly dist. Wis. State Legislature, 1978, 80; town atty. Laona, 1980-82; pvt. practice in law, 1980—; dist. atty. Forest County, 1990—. Pres. Laona Sch. Bd., 1989-91. Decorated DFC, 1967, Air Medal with seven stars, 1966-67, Purple Heart with two stars, 1966-67. Mem. VFW (commdr. post 6823 1990—), KC (Grand Knight 1982-83). Republican. Roman Catholic. Avocations: private pilot, aircraft homebuilder, hunting. Home: Box 137 RR 1 RR 1 Box 137 Laona WI 54541-9732 Office: Forest County Dist Atty Court House Crandon WI 54520

VERICH, MICHAEL GREGORY, state legislator; b. Warren, Ohio, Dec. 30, 1953; s. Alex and Dolores (Kudrich) V.; m. Aliza Wallace. BA magna cum laude, Bowling Green State Univ., 1976; JD, Univ. Akron, 1981; MPA, Harvard Univ., 1985. Cong. intern U.S. House Rep., Washington, 1987, cong. aide, 1976-77; State rep. Dist 59 Ohio, 1983-92, Dist 66, 1993—; chmn. aging & housing com. Ohio House Rep.; lawyer Wiener, Orkin, Abbate & Suit, 1984—. Mem. employment rels. bd. State of Ohio, Columbus; acad. hist. asst. Bowling Green State Univ., 1975-76. Named Outstanding Young Man of Yr., Edn. Excellence award, Disting. Disabled Vet. award, Legislator of Yr. award. Mem. MENSA, KC, Phi Alpha Theta, ABA, Ohio Bar Assn., Trumbull County Bar Assn. Home: 1460 Central Parkway Ave SE Warren OH 44484-4457 Office: Ohio Ho of Reps 65 E State St Ste 12 Columbus OH 43215-4259

VERING, JOHN ALBERT, lawyer; b. Marysville, Kans., Feb. 6, 1951; s. John Albert and Bernadine E. (Kieffer) V.; m. Ann E. Arman, June 28, 1980; children: Julia Ann, Catherine Ann, Mary Ann. BA summa cum laude, Harvard U., 1973; JD, U. Va., 1976. Bar: Mo. 1976, U.S. Dist. Ct. (we. dist.) Mo. 1976, U.S. Ct. Appeals (10th cir.), 1980, U.S. Ct. Appeals (4th cir.) 1987, Kans. 1990, U.S. Dist. Ct. Kans. 1990; arbitrator, mediator. Assoc. Dietrich, Davis, Dicus, Rowlands, Schmitt & Gorman, Kansas City, Mo., 1976-81, ptnr., 1982—. Editor: U. Va. Law Rev., 1974-76. Bd. dirs. Greater Kansas City YMCA Southwest Dist., 1987. Mem.: Harvard Club (adv. bd. schs. com. Kans. City 1977—2002, v.p. 1981—82, 1992—93, pres. 1994—96, mem. adv. bd. 1996—2002). Democrat. Roman Catholic. Home: 1210 W 68th Ter Kansas City MO 64113-1904 Office: Armstrong Teasdale LLP 2345 Grand Blvd Ste 2000 Kansas City MO 64108-2617 E-mail: jvering@armstrongteasdale.com.

VERMEIL, DICK, professional football coach; m. Carolyn Drake; two sons. Football coach St. Louis Rams, 1997-2000, retired football coach, 2000; pub. spkr. Nationwide Spkrs. Bur., Beverly Hills, Calif., 2000—. Career highlights include: coaching 1999-2000 Super Bowl XXXIV championship season, St. Louis Rams, becoming the oldest coach in NFL history to win a Super Bowl; tv analyst with CBS, ABC. Named Coach of Yr. on four levels, high sch., jr. coll., nat. collegiate Divsn. I, NFL; named first fulltime spl. teams coach in NFL history with Rams, under head coach George Allen, 1969. Office: care/Nationwide Spkrs Bur 120 S El Camino Dr Beverly Hills CA 90212-2730 also: Kansas City Chiefs One Arrowhead Drive Kansas City MO 64129

VERRETT, SHIRLEY, soprano; b. New Orleans, May 31, 1931; d. Leon Solomon and Elvira Augustine (Harris) V.; m. Louis Frank LoMonaco, Dec. 10, 1963; 1 dau., Francesca. AA, Ventura (Calif.) Coll., 1951; diploma in voice (scholarship 1956-61), Juilliard Sch. Music, 1961; MusD (hon.), Coll. Holy Cross, Mass., 1978. CPA, Cert. real estate broker. James Earl Jones disting. univ. prof. voice U. Mich. Sch. Music, 1996—. Mem. adv. bd. Opera Ebony. Recital debut Town Hall, N.Y.C., 1958; appeared as Irina in Lost in the Stars, 1958; orchestral debut Phila. Orch., 1960; operatic debut in Carmen, Festival of Two Worlds, Spoleto, Italy, 1962; debuts with Bolshoi Opera, Moscow, 1963, N.Y.C. Opera, 1964, Royal Opera, Covent Garden, 1966, Maggio Fiorentino, Florence, 1967, Met. Opera, 1968, Teatro San Carlos, Naples, 1968, Dallas Civic Opera, 1969, La Scala, 1970, Vienna State Opera, 1970, San Francisco Opera, 1972, Paris Opera, 1973, Opera Co. Boston, 1976, Opera Bastille, Paris, 1990; guest appearances with all major U.S. symphony orchs.; toured Eastern Europe and Greece with La Scala chorus and orch., 1981; TV debut on Ed Sullivan Show, 1963; TV performances include: Great Performances series, live performance of Macbeth at La Scala, Santuzza in Cavalleria Rusticana; film debut Maggio Musicale, 1989, Macbeth, 1986; rec. artist, RCA, Columbia, ABC (Westminster), Angel Everest, Kapp, Philips Records and Deutsche Grammophon. Recipient Marian Anderson award, 1955, Nat. Fedn. Music Clubs award, 1961, Walter Naumberg award, 1958, Blanche Thebom award, 1960; named Chevalier Arts and Letters (France), 1970, Commandeur, 1984; John Hay Whitney fellow, 1959; Ford Found. fellow, 1962-63; Martha Baird Rockefeller Aid to Music Fund fellow, 1959-61; grantee William Matteus Sullivan Fund, 1959; grantee Berkshire Music Opera, 1956; recipient Achievement award Ventura Coll., 1963, Achievement award N.Y. chpt. Albert Einstein Coll. Medicine, 1975; 2 plaques Los Angeles Sentinel Newspaper, 1960; plaque Peninsula Music Festival, 1963; Los Angeles Times Woman of Yr. award, 1969 Mem. Mu Phi Epsilon. Office: Herbert Breslin Inc 6124 Liebig Ave Bronx NY 10471-1008 also: U Mich Sch Music 1100 Baits Dr Ann Arbor MI 48109-2085

VERSCHOOR, CURTIS CARL, business educator, consultant; b. Grand Rapids, Mich., June 7, 1931; s. Peter and Leonene (Dahlstrom) V.; m. Marie Emilie Kritschgau, June 18, 1952; children— Katherine Anne, Carolyn Marie, John Peter, Carla Michelle. BBA with distinction, U. Mich., 1951, MBA, 1952; EdD, No. Ill. U., 1977. CPA; cert. mgmt. acctg., cert. fin. planner, cert. fraud examiner, cert. internal auditor; chartered fin. cons. Pub. accountant Touche, Ross, Bailey & Smart (C.P.A.'s), 1955-63; with Singer Co., 1963-68, asst. controller, 1965-68; controller Colgate-Palmolive Co., 1968-69; asst. controller bus. products group Xerox Corp., 1969-72; controller Baxter Internat., 1972-73; v.p. finance Altair Corp., Chgo., 1973-74; prof. DePaul U., 1974-94, ledger and quill alumni rsch. prof., 1994—; pres. C.C. Verschoor & Assocs., Inc., 1981—. Part-time instr. Wayne State U., 1955-60; author audit com. briefings. Author: Audit Committee Briefing: Understanding the 21st Century Audit Committee Governance Roles, 2000, Audit Committee Briefing: Facilitating New Audit Committee Responsibilites, 2001; contbg. editor: Jour. Accountancy, 1961-62, Jour. Internal Auditing, 1985—, Strategic Fin.; editl. adv. bd. Acctg. Today, 1991—. Trustee Hektoen Inst. Med. Rsch., Chgo., 1996—. Served with AUS, 1953-55. Recipient Elijah Watts Sells award Am. Inst. C.P.A.'s, 1953 Mem. AICPA, Fin. Execs. Inst., Am. Acctg. Assn., Inst. Mgmt. Accts., Inst. Internal Auditors, Nat. Assn. Corp. Dirs., Beta Gamma Sigma, Beta Alpha Psi, Delta Pi Epsilon, Phi Kappa Phi, Phi Eta Sigma. Home: 231 Wyngate Dr Barrington IL 60010-4840 Office: DePaul Univ One E Jackson Blvd Chicago IL 60604-2287 E-mail: cverscho@condor.depaul.edu.

VER STEEG, CLARENCE LESTER, historian, educator; b. Orange City, Iowa, Dec. 28, 1922; s. John A. and Annie (Vischer) Ver S.; m. Dorothy Ann De Vries, Dec. 24, 1943; 1 child, John Charles. AB, Morningside Coll., Sioux City, Iowa, 1943; MA, Columbia U., 1946, PhD, 1950; LHD, Morningside Coll., 1988. Lectr., then instr. history Columbia U., N.Y.C., 1946-50; mem. faculty Northwestern U., Evanston, Ill., 1950—, prof. history, 1959—, dean grad. sch., 1975-86. Vis. lectr. Harvard U., 1959-60; mem. council Inst. Early Am. History and Culture, Williamsburg, Va., 1961-64, 68-72, chmn. exec. com., 1970-72; vis. mem. Inst. Advanced Study, Princeton, N.J., 1967-68; chmn. faculty com. to recommend Master Plan Higher Edn. in Ill., 1962-64; mem. Grad. Record Exam. Bd., 1981-86, chmn., 1984-86; bd. dirs. Ctr. for Research Libraries, 1980-85, Council Grad. Schs. in U.S., 1983-87; pres. Assn. Grad. Schs., 1984-85; mem. steering com. Grad. Research Project, Consortium on Financing Higher Edn., 1981-85; mem. working group on talent Nat. Acad. Scis., 1984-87; mem. Higher Edn. Policy Adv. Com. to OCLC, Online Computer Library Ctr., 1984-87. Author: Robert Morris, Revolutionary Financier, 1954, A True and Historical Narrative of the Colony of Georgia, 1960, The American People: Their History, 1961, The Formative Years, 1607-1763, 1964 (Brit. edit.), 1965, The Story of Our Country, 1965, (with others) Investigating Man's World, 6 vols., 1970, A People and a Nation, 1971, The Origins of a Southern Mosaic: Studies of Early Carolina and Georgia, 1975, World Cultures, 1977, American Spirit, 1982, rev. edit., 1990; sr. author: Heath Social Studies, 7 Vols., 1991, Planning at Northwestern University in the 1960s, 1993; editor: Great Issues in American History, From Settlement to Revolution 1584-1776, 1969; editl. cons.: Papers of Robert Morris, vols. I-IX, 1973-99; contbr. articles to profl. jours. Served with USAAF, 1942-45. Decorated Air medal with 3 oak leaf clusters; 5 Battle Stars; Social Sci. Research Council fellow, 1948-49, George A. and Eliza Gardner Howard Found. fellow, 1954-55, Huntington Library research fellow, 1955, Am. Council Learned Socs. sr. fellow, 1958-59, Guggenheim fellow, 1964-65, NEH sr. fellow, 1973; Northwestern U. Clarence L. Ver Steeg Professorship established in his honor, 1997. Mem. AAUP, Am. Hist. Assn. (nominating com. 1965-68, chmn. 1967-68, Albert J. Beveridge prize 1952, hon. mention 1991 Eugene Asher Disting. Teaching award), Orgn. Am. Historians (editorial bd. Jour. Am. History 1968-72), So. Hist. Assn. (nominating com. 1970-72). Presbyterian. Home: Apt 229 1100 Pembridge Dr Lake Forest IL 60045-4216 Office: Northwestern Univ Dept History Evanston IL 60208-0001 E-mail: c-ver@nww.edu.

VESCOVI, SELVI, pharmaceutical company executive; b. N.Y.C., June 14, 1930; s. Antonio and Desolina V.; BS, Coll. William and Mary, 1951; m. Elma Pasquinelli, Oct. 16, 1954; children: Mark, James, Anne. Salesman, Upjohn Co., N.Y.C., 1954-59, sales supr.,1959-62, product mgr. U.S. domestic pharm. dir., 1962-65, mgr. mktg. planning internat. div., 1965-71, v.p. Europe, 1971-74, group v.p. Europe, 1975-77, exec. v.p. Upjohn Internat., Inc., Kalamazoo, Mich., 1978-85, pres., gen. mgr., 1975-88, v.p. parent co., 1978-88; adj. prof. mgmt. Western Mich. U., Kalamazoo, 1988-92; chmn. bd. Carrington Labs.; bd. dirs. Centaur Corp. 2d lt. M.C., U.S. Army, 1951-53. Mem. Internat. Pharm. Mfrs. Assn., NYAC (N.Y.). Republican. Roman Catholic. Office: Upjon Internat Co 7000 Portage Rd Kalamazoo MI 49001-0102

VESPER, ROSE, state legislator; m. Lee Vesper; children: Stephanie, Jennifer, Jessica. BA, Xavier U., 1960; MA, Midwestern U., 1967. Past mem. Ohio Valley Regional Devel. Commn., Ohio Water and Sewer Rotary Commn.; pres. Ohio Clermont County Farm Bur.; rep. Ohio State Ho. Reps. Dist. 72. Mem. Nat. Fedn. Rep. Women; chmn. Clermont County Rep. Party, 1990—, Southwestern Ohio Rep. Leadership; owner, operator beef cattle/crop farm. Named Clermont County Farm Woman of Yr., 1988; recipient Disting. Svc. award Ohio Med. Polit. Action Com., 1988, Coop. Ext. Agts. Assn. award, 1990, Frances Boltom award Ohio League Young Reps., 1990. Mem. Richmond Hist. Soc., Clermont, Brown and Clinton County C. of C., State Med. Assn., Farm Bur., Farmers Union. Home: 1174 Watkins Hill Rd New Richmond OH 45157-9504 Office: Ohio Ho of Reps State House Columbus OH 43215

VESTA, RICHARD V. meat packing company executive; b. Dec. 25, 1946; Pres., CEO Packerland Packing, Green Bay, Wis. Office: Packerland Packing PO Box 23000 Green Bay WI 54305-3000

VIAULT, RAYMOND G. food company executive; b. N.Y.C., Sept. 19, 1944; m. Lucille Viault; children: Lisa, Deborah, Russell. Bachelor's degree, Brown U.; MBA, Columbia U. Pres., CEO Kraft Jacobs Suchard, Zurich, Switzerland; CEO Jacobs Suchard A.G. (acquired by Kraft Gen. Foods), 1990-93; pres. Maxwell House Coffee Co. Kraft Gen. Foods, v.p., gen. mgr. desserts divsn.; with Gen. Mills, Mpls., 1996—, responsible for internat. ops., responsible for corp. fin. functions, vice-chmn., 1996—, also bd. dirs. Bd. dirs. Cereal Ptnrs. Worldwide; dir. Willis Corroon Plc. Bd. overseers Columbia Grad. Sch. Bus., N.Y.C.; trustee Lawrenceville Sch., N.J.; bd. dirs. United Way Mpls., Minn. Internat. Ctr., Technoserve. Office: PO Box 1113 One General Mills Blvd Minneapolis MN 55440-1113

VICE, ROY LEE, history educator; b. Lynchburg, Va., Oct. 12, 1950; s. Cline Lowell and Ruth Burchell (Newman) V. BA in History, BS in Physics, Carson-Newman Coll., 1972; MA in History, U. Chgo., 1976, PhD in History, 1984. Lectr. Continuing Edn. program U. Chgo., 1985-86, 87-88, rare books asst. univ. librs., 1986; asst. prof. Pacific Luth. U., Tacoma, 1986-87, Clemson (S.C.) U., 1988-90, Wright State U., Dayton, Ohio, 1990-95, assoc. prof., 1995—. Contbr. articles to profl. jours. Vol. tutor CYCLE Cabrini-Green Projects, Chgo., 1981—86; vol. lectr. LaSalle St. Ch. , 1989—98, 2000—01. With U.S. Army, 1972—74. Mem. Am. Hist. Assn., 16th Century Studies Conf. Democrat. Baptist. Home: 229 E 2nd St Dayton OH 45402-1719 Office: Wright State U Dept History 3640 Colonel Glenn Hwy Dayton OH 45435-0001 E-mail: roy.vice@wright.edu.

VICK, NICHOLAS A. neurologist; b. Chgo., Oct. 3, 1939; MD, U. Chgo., 1965. Diplomate Am. Bd. Neurology. Intern U. Chgo. Hosps., 1965, resident in neurology, 1966-68; fellow in neurology NIH, Bethesda, Md., 1968-70; staff Evanston (Ill.) Hosp., 1975—; prof. neurology Northwestern U. Med. Sch., Evanston, Ill., 1978—. Office: Evanston Hosp Dept Neurology 2650 Ridge Ave Evanston IL 60201-1781

VICKERMAN, JIM, state legislator; b. May 1, 1931; m. Wava; six children. County commr.; mem. Minn. Senate from 22nd dist., St. Paul, 1986—. Chmn. vet. and gen. legis. com.; vice-chmn. health and human svc. com., agr. and rural devel. com., local and urban govt. com, transp. com., vet. and mi. affairs com., health care com., health care and family svc. fin. divsn. com., rules and adminstrn. com., transp. com. and transp. fin. divsn. com.; farmer. Office: RR 2 Box 134 Tracy MN 56175-9430 also: Minn Senate State Capitol Building Saint Paul MN 55155-0001

VICKREY, JENE, state legislator; m. Teresa Vickrey. Kans. state rep. Dist. 6, 1993—. Carpet layer. Address: PO Box 1282 Louisburg KS 66053-1282 also: Kans Ho of Reps State House Topeka KS 66612

VICTOR, JAY, retired dermatologist; b. Detroit, Dec. 4, 1935; s. Ben and Pauline (Meisel) Victor; m. Elana S. Lepler, Mar. 1965 (div. Aug. 1977); children: Pamela C. Victor, Daryl B. Victor; m. Marianne Cook, Sept. 4, 1978; children: Jonah A. Victor, Lauren Victor. BA, U. Mich., 1958, MD, 1962. Diplomate Am. Bd. Dermatology. Intern Henry Ford Hosp., Detroit, 1962-63, resident in dermatology, 1963-66; asst. prof. dermatology Wayne State U. Sch. of Medicine, 1968—; pvt. practice in dermatology Allen Park, 1966—2001; ret., 2001. Mem. active staff Oakwood Hosp., Dearborn, Mich., 1967—, emeritus staff, Mich.; courtesy staff Detroit Med. Ctr., 1967—; cons. Heritage Hosp., Taylor, Mich., 1980—. Fellow: Am. Acad. Dermatology; mem.: AMA, Mich. Dermatology Soc., Wayne County Med. Soc., Mich. State Med. Soc. (del. 1980—). Jewish. Avocations: skiing, running, bicycling, sports.

VICTOR, MICHAEL GARY, lawyer, physician; b. Detroit, Sept. 20, 1945; s. Simon H. and Helen (Litsky) V.; children: Elise Nicole, Sara Lisabeth. Bar: Ill. 1980, U.S. Dist. Ct. (no. dist.) Ill. 1980, U.S. Ct. Appeals (7th cir.) 1981; diplomate Am. Bd. Legal Medicine. Pres. Advocate Adv. Assocs., Chgo., 1982-95; asst. prof. medicine Northwestern U. Med. Sch., 1982—; pvt. practice law Barrington, Ill., 1982—; lectr. U. Ill., Chgo., 1999—. Dir. emergency medicine Loretto Hosp., Chgo., 1980-85, chief. sect. of emergency medicine St. Josephs Hosp., Chgo., 1985-87; v.p. Med. Emergency Svcs. Assocs., Buffalo Grove, Ill., 1989; v.p. MESA Mgmt. Corp.; of counsel Bollinger, Ruberry & Garvey, Chgo. Author: Informed Consent, 1980; Brain Death, 1980; (with others) Due Process for Physicians, 1984, A Physicians Guide to the Illinios Living Will Act, The Choice is Ours!, 1989. Recipient Service awards Am. Coll. Emergency Medicine, 1973-83. Fellow Am. Coll. Legal Medicine (bd. govs. 1996-97, alt. del. to AMA House of Dels. 1996-97), Chgo. Acad. Legal Medicine; mem. Am. Coll. Emergency Physicians (pres. Ill. chpt. 1980, med.-legal-ins. council 1980-81, 83-84), ABA, Ill. State Bar Assn., Am. Soc. Law and Medicine, Chgo. Bar Assn. (med.-legal council 1981-83), AMA, Ill. State Med. Soc. (med.-legal council 1980-86, 88), Chgo. Med. Soc. Jewish. Home and Office: 153 Aberdour Ln Palatine IL 60067-8001 E-mail: mgv@merle.acns.nwu.edu.

VIDAVER, ANNE K. plant pathologist, educator; Grad. with high honors in biology, Russell Sage Coll., 1960; PhD, U. Ind., 1965. Prof., head dept. plant pathology U. Nebr., Lincoln. Recipient Pub. Svc. award Nebr. Agri-Bus. Club, 1977, Sci. award for agrl. excellence Midlands chpt. Nat. Agri-Mktg. Assn., 1991, Sci. award for agrl. excellence Nat. Agri-Mktg. Assn., 1991, Disting. Scientist award Sigma Xi, Lincoln chpt., 2000; N.Y. State Regents scholar, 1956-60; Floyd Fund fellow Ind. U., 1960-61, predoctoral fellow NIH, Ind. U., 1961-65. Fellow AAAS (mem. com. on opportunities in sci. 1998-2000), Am. Phytopathol. Soc. (mem. numerous coms. including mem. phyllosphere microbiology com. 1992-95, mem. ad-hoc com. to develop improved outreach and pub. edn. programs 1993, acting dir. office of pub. affairs and edn. 1995-97, chair nat. plant pathology bd. 1991-2001, award of distinction 1998), Am. Soc. for Microbiology (mem. com. on status of women in microbiology 1987-90, mem. com. on agrl., food and indsl. microbiology 1988-94, chair 1994-2000, others); mem. Am. Inst. Biol. Scis. (exec. dir. screening com. 1992-93, biol. agenda como. 1992-94), Internat. Soc. for Plant Pathology (bacteriology com. 1978-81, taxonomy subcom. 1981-91), Intersociety Consortium for Plant Protection (sec. 1987, pres. 1988), Alliance for the Prudent Use Antibiotics (mem. sci. adv. bd. 1990-2000), H.A. Wallace Inst. for Alternative Agr. (bd. dirs. 1990-96, treas. 1994-95, pres. 1995-97). Office: U Nebr Dept Plant Pathology 406 Plant Scis Hall Lincoln NE 68583 E-mail: avidaveri@unl.edu.

VIDAVER, ANNE MARIE, plant pathology educator; b. Vienna, Austria, Mar. 29, 1938; came to U.S., 1941; d. Franz and Klara (Winter) Kopecky; children: Gordon W.F., Regina M. BA, Russell Sage Coll., 1960; MA, Ind. U., 1962, PhD, 1965. Lectr. U. Nebr., Lincoln, 1965-66, rsch. assoc., 1966-72, asst. prof., 1972-74, assoc. prof., 1974-79, prof. plant pathology, 1979—, interim dir. Ctr. Biotech., 1988-89, 97-00, head dept. plant pathology, 1984-2000; chief scientist USDA's NRICGP, 2000—. Contbr. articles to profl. jours. and books; patentee in field. Recipient Pub. Svc. award Nebr. Agri-Bus., 1977, Sci. award for excellence NAMA, New Orleans, 1991. Fellow AAAS, Am. Phytopath. Soc., Am. Soc. Microbiology; mem. Intersoc. Consortium for Plant Protection, Internat. Soc. Plant Pathology, Alliance for Prudent Use of Antibiotics. Avocations: indoor gardening, reading. Office: U Nebr Dept Plant Pathology Lincoln NE 68583-0722 E-mail: avidaver1@unl.edu.

VIDRICKSEN, BEN EUGENE, food service executive, state legislator; b. Salina, Kans., June 11, 1927; s. Henry and Ruby Mae Vidricksen; m. Lola Mae Nienke, Jan. 20, 1950 (div.); children: Nancy, Janice, Ben, Penelope, Jeffery. AB, Kans. Wesleyan U., 1951. Field supt. Harding Creamery divsn. Nat. Dairy Products, Kearney, Kans., 1951-52, plant mgr. Kraft divsn. O'Neill, Nebr., 1952-59; owner Vidricksen's Food Svc., Salina, 1959—. Cons. in field; mem. Kans. Senate, 1979—, asst. majority leader; chmn. joint bldg. constrn. com., legis. and congl. apportionment com., legis. post audit, econ. devel., transp. and utilities, pub. health and welfare, fed. and state affairs, govtl. orgn., spl. interim com. on efficiency in state govt., 1983; del. White House Conf. on Tourism and Travel, 1995, 96; mem. Hennessy/USAF Worldwide Food Svc. Evaluation Team, 1978, 79. Mem. Salina Airport Authority, 1972-84, chmn., 1976-77; chmn. Rep. Ctrl. Com., County of Saline, Kans., 1974-79; adv. coun. SBA, 1982—, chmn. adv. coun. small bus. devel. ctr.; mem. adv. bd. Salvation Army; past chmn. Salina Conv. and Tourism Bur.; vice chmn. Kans. Turnpike Authority, 1995—. Served with USN, 1945-46. Recipient Salut au Restaurateur award Fla. State U., 1974, Gov.'s Spl. award Kans. Assn. Broadcasters, Guardian award Nat. Fedn. Indep. Bus., 1989, Promotion of Tourism and Travel award Travel Ind. Assn. Kans., 1989, Support of Kans. Nat. Guard award Kans. Adjutant Gen., 1990, Good Citizenship award Kans. Engrng. Soc., 1991, 92, Freedom award NRA, 1994, Kans. Nat. Guard award Excellence, 1997; named Nat. Rep. Legislator of Yr., Nat. Rep. Legislators Assn., 1991, Assoc. of Yr., Am. Womens Bus. Assn., 1992. Mem. USAF Assn., Assn. U.S. Army, Nat. Rep. Legislators Assn., Am. Legis. Exch. Coun., Pan Am. Hwy. Assn. (Internat. Achievement award 1992, Road Buiulders award 1995), North Salina Bus. Assn. (past pres.), Internat. Brdige, Tunnel and Tpke. Assn., Kans. Restaurant Assn. (past pres., Restauranteur of Yr. 1973), Kans. Tourism and Travel Commn., Kans. Film Commn., Nat. Restaurant Assn. (dir. 1977—), Travel Industry Assn. Kans. (dir.), VFW (life), Salina C. of C. (past bd. dirs.), Am. Legion, Optimists, North Salina Lions Club, Elks, Moose, Eagles, Masons (knight commdr. Scottish rite 1994), Shriners. Office: State Senate State Capitol Topeka KS 66612

VIERLING, H. PHILIP, medical device company executive; With Empi, Inc., St. Paul, 1986—, v.p., officer, 1997-99, pres., COO, 1999—. Office: 599 Cardigan Rd PO Box 26500 Saint Paul MN 55126-4099

VIETOR, HAROLD DUANE, federal judge; b. Parkersburg, Iowa, Dec. 29, 1931; s. Harold Howard and Alma Johanna (Kreimeyer) V.; m. Dalia Artemisa Zamarripa Cadena, Mar. 24, 1973; children: Christine Elizabeth, John Richard, Greta Maria. BA, U. Iowa, 1955, JD, 1958. Bar: Iowa 1958. Law clk. U.S. Ct. Appeals 8th Circuit, 1958-59; ptnr. Bleakley Law Offices, Cedar Rapids, Iowa, 1959-65; judge Iowa Dist. Ct., 1965-79, chief judge, 1970-79; U.S. dist. judge U.S. Dist. Ct. for So. Dist. Iowa, Des Moines, 1979-96, chief judge, 1985-92, sr. U.S. dist. judge, 1997—. Lectr. at law schs., legal seminars U.S. and Japan. Contbr. articles to profl. jours. in U.S. and Japan. Served with USN, 1952-54. Mem. ABA, Iowa Bar Assn. (pres. jr. sect. 1966-67), Iowa Judges Assn. (pres. 1975-76), 8th Cir. Dist. Judges Assn. (pres. 1986-88). Office: US Dist Ct 221 US Courthouse 123 E Walnut St Des Moines IA 50309-2035

VIETS, HERMANN, college president, consultant; b. Quedlinburg, Fed. Republic Germany, Jan. 28, 1943; came to U.S., 1949, naturalized, 1961; s. Hans and Herta (Heik) V.; m. Pamela Deane, June 30, 1968; children: Danielle, Deane, Hans, Hillary BS, Polytech. U., 1965, MS, 1966, PhD, 1970. Fellow von Karman Inst., Brussels, 1969-70; group leader Wright-Patterson AFB, Dayton, Ohio, 1970-76; prof. Wright State U., 1976-81; assoc. dean W.Va. U., Morgantown, 1981-83; dean U. R.I., Kingston, 1983-91; pres. Milw. Sch. Engrng., 1991—. Chmn. bd. dirs. Precision Stampings, Inc., Beaumont, Calif., 1977—; bd. dirs. Gehl Co., West Bend, Wis., Astro Med, Inc., West Warwick, R.I., Wenthe-Davidson Engrng. Co., New Berlin, Wis., Max Kade Inst. for German-Am. Studies, Discovery World, Milw. County Rsch. Park Corp.; cons. USAF Aero Propulsion Lab., Dayton, 1976-80, Covington & Burling, Washington, 1976-77; cons. in field. Patentee in aero. field; contbr. numerous articles to profl. jours. Mem. Greater Milw. Com.; dir. Competitive Wis., Gov. Regional H.S. Excellence Co., 1994, Gov.'s Export Strategy Commn., 1994; trustee Pub. Policy Forum. Recipient Tech. Achievement award USAF, 1974, Sci. Achievement award, 1975, Gov.'s Sci. and Tech. award State of R.I., 1987, Goodrich Pub. Svc. award, 1990, Citation R.I. Legislature, 1987, 90, 91, Outstanding Alumnus award aerospace engrng. dept. Poly. U., 1994; Disting. Alumnus Poly. U., 1995, Engr. of Yr. award Engrs. and Scientists of Milw., 1997; named Hon. Citizen Fachhochschule Luebeck, Germany, 1998; postdoctoral fellow NATO, 1969-70, NASA, 1965-69. Fellow AIAA (assoc., acad. affairs com. 1998—, Best Tech. Paper award Allegheny-Pitts. sect. 1982); mem. German Assn. for Luft and Raumfahrt, German-Am. Heritage Soc. (bd. dirs.), Nat. Assn. Independent Coll. and Univ. (bd. dirs.), Am. Soc. Engrng. Edn., Japan-Am. Soc. (bd. dirs. 1994), Soc. Mfg. Engrs., Rotary, Sigma Xi, Phi Kappa Phi, Tau Beta Pi, Sigma Gamma Tau. Avocations: antique automobiles, beer steins, Notgeld currency. Home: 4216 N Lake Dr Shorewood WI 53211-1722 Office: Milw Sch Engring 1025 N Broadway Milwaukee WI 53202-3109

VIETS, ROBERT O. utilities executive; b. Girard, Kans., Dec. 8, 1943; s. Willard O. and Caroline L. (Bollwinkel) V.; m. Karen M. Kreiter, June 13, 1980. BA in Econs., Washburn U., 1965; JD, Washington U., 1969. Bar: Kans. 1966, Mo. 1969, Ill. 1975; CPA, Kans. Auditor Arthur Andersen & Co., St. Louis, 1969-73; mgr. spl. studies Cen. Ill. Light Co., Peoria, 1973-76, mgr. rates and regulatory affairs, 1976-80, asst. v.p., regulatory affairs, 1980-81, v.p. fin. services, 1981-83, v.p. fin. group, 1983-86, sr. v.p., 1988—, Cilcorp, Inc., Peoria, 1986-88; pres., CEO Cilcorp, Inc. and Ctrl. Ill. Light Co., 1988—. Bd. dirs. Consumers Water Co., Lincoln Office Supply, Inc., RLI Corp.; pres., CEO, chmn. bd. QST Enterprises, Inc., 1996—. Chmn. bd. dirs. Meth. Health Svcs., Inc.; trustee Bradley U. Mem. ABA, Ill. Bar Assn., Peoria County Bar Assn., AICPA, Ill. Soc. CPAs. Republican. Lutheran. Lodge: Rotary (bd. dirs. 1985—, pres. 1986-87). Avocation: golf. Home: 11305 N Pawnee Rd Peoria IL 61615-9796 Office: Cilcorp Inc 399 Liberty St Fl 8 Peoria IL 61602-1403

VIGNERON, ALLEN HENRY, theology educator, rector, auxiliary bishop; b. Mt. Clemens, Mich., Oct. 21, 1948; s. Elwin E. and Bernadine K. (Kott) V. AB in Philosophy, Sacred Heart Sem., Detroit, 1970; STL in Fundamental Theology, Pontifical Gregorian U., 1977; PhD in Philosophy, Cath. U. Am., 1987. Ordained deacon Roman Cath. Ch., 1973, ordained priest, 1975, titular bishop, 1996. Assoc. pastor Our Lady Queen of Peace Ch., Harper Woods, Mich., 1975-79; asst. prof. philosophy and theology Sacred Heart Major Sem., Detroit, 1985—; addetto of the secretariat of his Holiness the Pope The Holy See, Vatican City, 1991-94; rector, pres. Sacred Heart Major Sem., Detroit, 1994—; auxiliary bishop Archdiocese of Detroit, 1996—. Adj. prof. theology Pontifical Gregorian U., Rome, 1992-94. Office: Sacred Heart Major Sem 2701 W Chicago Detroit MI 48206-1704

VILIM, NANCY CATHERINE, advertising agency executive; b. Quincy, Mass., Jan. 15, 1952; d. John Robert and Rosemary (Malpede) V.; m. Geoffrey S. Horner, Feb. 16, 1992; children: Matthew Edward Cajda, Megan Catherine Cajda, Margaret Horner. Student, Miami U., Oxford, Ohio, 1970-72. Media asst. Draper Daniels, Inc., Chgo., 1972-74; asst. buyer Campbell Mithun, 1974-75; buyer Tatham, Laird & Kudner, 1975-77; media buyer Adcom, Inc. div. Quaker Oats Corp., 1977-79; media supr. G.M. Feldman, 1979-81; v.p. media dir. Media Mgmt., 1981-83; v.p. broadcast dir. Bozell, Jacobs, Kenyon & Eckhardt, Chgo., 1983-88; v.p., media mgr. McCann-Erickson, Inc., 1989—. Judge 27th Internat. Broadcast Awards, Chgo., 1987. Co-pres. Immaculate Conception Religious Edn. Parents Club, 1995-96. Recipient Media All Star awards Sound Mgmt. Mag., N.Y.C., 1987. Mem. Broadcast Advt. Club Chgo., Mus. Broadcast Communications, NAFE. Office: McCann-Erickson Inc 515 N State St Chicago IL 60610-4325

VILLA-KOMAROFF, LYDIA, molecular biologist, educator, university official; b. Las Vegas, N.Mex., Aug. 7, 1947; d. John Dias and Drucilla (Jaramillo) V.; m. Anthony Leader Komaroff, June 18, 1970. BA, Goucher Coll., 1970; PhD, MIT, 1975; DSc (hon.), St. Thomas U., 1996, Pine Manor Coll., 1997; PhD (hon.), Goucher Coll., 1997. Rsch. fellow Harvard U., Cambridge, 1975-78; asst. prof. dept. microbiology U. Mass. Med. Ctr., Worcester, 1978-81, assoc. prof. dept. molecular genetics micro, 1982-85; assoc. prof. dept. neurology Harvard Med. Sch., Boston, 1986-95; sr. rsch. assoc. neurology Children's Hosp., 1985-95, assoc. dir. mental retardation rsch. ctr., 1987-94; prof. dept. neurology Northwestern U., Evanston, Ill., 1995—, assoc. v.p. rsch., 1995-97, v.p. rsch., 1998—. Mem. mammalian genetics study sect. NIH, 1982-84, mem. reviewers rsch., 1989, mem. neurol. disorders program project rev. com., 1989-94; mem. adv. bd. Biol. Scis. Directorate, NSF, 1994-99; mem. bd. dirs. Nat. Ctr. Genome Rsch., 1995-2000, AAAS, 2000—; mem. adv. coun. Nat. Inst. Neurol. Disorders and Stroke, NIH, 2000—. Contbr. articles and abstracts to profl. jours.; patentee in field. Recipient Hispanic Engr. Nat. Achievement award, 1992, Nat. Achievement award Hispanic Mag., 1996; inducted Hispanic Engr. Nat. Achievement Hall of Fame, 1999; Helen Hay Whitney Found. fellow, 1975-78; NIH grantee, 1978-85, 89-96. Mem. Am. Soc. Microbiology, Assn. for Women in Sci., Soc. for Neurosci., Am. Soc. Cell Biology, Soc. for Advancement Chicanos and Native Ams. in Sci. (founding, bd. dirs. 1987-93, v.p. 1990-93). Office: Northwestern U 633 Clark St Evanston IL 60208-0001 E-mail: LVK@northwestern.edu.

VILLALPANDO, JESSE MICHAEL, state legislator; b. East Chicago, Ind., July 4, 1959; s. Jesse and Rose (Oria) V.; m. Elizabeth Villalpando. BA, Ind. U., 1981, JD, 1984. Bar: Ind. 1984. Atty. Lesniak & Ruff, East Chicago; mem. from 12th dist. Ind. State Ho. of Reps., 1982—. Co-chmn. cts. com.; mem. criminal code, ins. and corps. com., judiciary com., pub. safety com., pub. policy com., ethcis com., vets. affairs com. Named to Ind. State AFL-CIO Honor Roll, 1984. Mem. Ind. State Bar Assn., Griffith Dem. Club, Hammond FDR Club, South Hammond Dem. Club, Mutualista of Gary, Phi Delta Theta. Home: 956 N Griffith Blvd Griffith IN 46319-1514 Office: Ind Ho of Reps State Capitol Indianapolis IN 46204

VILLARS, HORACE SUMNER, retired food company executive, marketing professional; b. San Francisco, Mar. 15, 1931; s. Horace Sumner and Alice Emily (Stacy) V.; m. Patricia Ann Adams, June 15, 1951; children: Rebecca, Thomas, Constance, Laura, Russell. BS, Northwestern U., 1952. With Armour Co., Chgo., 1952-54, Durkee Foods, Chgo., 1954-65; mgr. indsl. sales McCormick & Co., Balt., 1965-68; exec. v.p. Kraft Sesame Corp., Paris, 1968-71; pres. Food Ingredients, Inc., Elk Grove, Ill., 1971-99. Chmn. Sycamore Foods, Inc., Elk Grove, 1987—. Contbg. author: Encyclopedia of Food Technology, 1974, Elements of Food Technology, 1977. Mem. Inst. Food Technologists (exec. com. Chgo. sect. 1974—), Am. Assn. Cereal Chemists, Am. Oil Chemists Soc., Am. Assn. Candy Technologists (chmn. Chgo. sect. 1964-65), Am. Soc. Bakery Engrs. Republican. Avocations: golf, swimming, photography, travel. Home: 820 Acorn Dr Dundee IL 60118-2659

VILLWOCK, DON, farmer, farming association executive; m. Joyce Villwock; children: Sarah, Betsy. Degree in agrl. econs., Purdue U. Farmer; v.p. Ind. Farm Bur, 1998—, Farm Bur. Ins. Cos. Dist. dir., Knox County pres., chmn. state young farmer com., chmn. feed grains com. Ind. Farm Bur., mem. farm bill task force, farm credit task force; mem. feed grains, grain quality, farm credit coms. Am. Farm Bur. Fedn.; state exec. dir. Agrl. Stabilization and Conservation Svc., 1989—93; state agrl. liaison Sen. Richard Lugar; mem. Commn. on 21st Century Prodn. Agr., 1997. Leader 4-H; mem. Purdue Disting. Agrl. Alumnus. Named Sagamore of the Wabash, Friend of Extension. Mem.: Ind. Inst. Agr. (chmn.), Ind. Pork Producers, Ind. Soybean Growers, Ind. Corn Growers. Office: Ind Farm Bur Inc PO Box 1290 Indianapolis IN 46206

VILSACK, THOMAS, governor; b. Dec. 13, 1950; adopted s. Bud and Dolly Vilsack; m. Christie Bell, Aug. 1973; children: Jess, Doug. B.History, Hamilton Coll., Clinton, N.Y., 1972; JD, Union U., 1975. Pvt. practice, Mt. Pleasant, Iowa, 1975—87; senator State of Iowa, 1992-98, gov., 1999—. Mayor City of Mt. Pleasant, 1987-92; bd. dirs. United Way, Mt. Pleasant. Mem. Mt. Pleasant C. of C. (pres.), Rotary (pres.). Office: Office of the Governor State Capitol Bldg Des Moines IA 50319-0001*

VILTER, RICHARD WILLIAM, physician, educator; b. Cin., Mar. 21, 1911; s. William Frederick and Clara (Bieler) V.; m. Sue Potter, Aug. 17, 1935; 1 son, Richard William (dec.). A.B., Harvard U., 1933, M.D., 1937. Diplomate: Am. Bd. Internal Medicine. Intern, resident internal medicine Cin. Gen. Hosp., 1937-42, founding dir. divsn. hematology/oncology, 1945-56, asst. dir. dept. internal medicine, 1953-56, dir., 1956-78; assoc. prof. medicine U. Cin. Coll. Medicine, 1948-56, Gordon and Helen Hughes Taylor prof., 1956-78, prof. medicine on spl. assignment, 1978-81, prof. medicine emeritus, 1981—, asst. dean, 1945-51. Cons. VA, 1947—; cons. hematology Good Samaritan Hosp., Cin.; cons. physician Christ, Drake hosps., Cin.; mem. sci adv. bd. Nat. Vitamin Found., 1953-56; spl. cons. nutrition and anemias in Egypt WHO, 1954; cons. Pan Am. Sanitary Bur. Anemias of Kashiorkor in Guatemala and Panama, 1955; mem. Am. Cancer Soc. Com. on Investigation and Therapy of Cancer, 1960-64, chmn. 1964; chmn. hematology sect. NIH, 1965-69, nat. adv. com. anemia malnutrition Rsch. Ctr. Chiengmai, Thailand, 1967-75. Assoc. editor Jour. Clin. Investigation, 1951-52; contbr. to profl. publs. Recipient Joseph Goldberger award AMA, 1960, Daniel Drake medal U. Cin., 1985, Golden Apple award U. Cin., 1985, award for excellence U. Cin., 1990, Daniel Drake Humanitarian award Acad. Medicine, Cin., 1991, 1st recipient U. Cin. Coll. Medicine Lifetime Tchg. award, 1995; Richard W. and Sue P. Vilter endowed professorship U. Cin. Coll. Medicine est. and funded 1999. Master ACP (past gov. Ohio bd. regents, sec. gen. 1973-78, pres.-elect 1978-79, pres. 1979-80, pres. emeritus 1984); mem. Federated Coun. for Internal Medicine (chmn. 1979-80), Clin. and Climatol. Assn. (v.p. 1982-83), Assn. Am. Physicians, Am. Soc. Clin. Nutrition (pres. 1960-61), Am. Soc. Clin. Investigation, Ctrl. Soc. Clin. Rsch. (coun. mem. 1957-60), Am. Soc. Hematology, Am. Bd. Nutrition, Internat. Soc. Hematology, Cin. Lit. Club (pres. 1990-91), Phi Beta Kappa, Alpha Omega Alpha, Nu Sigma Nu. Home: 5 Annwood Ln Cincinnati OH 45206-1419 Office: U Cin Med Ctr Cincinnati OH 45267-0001 E-mail: vilterr@ucmail.uc.edu.

VINCENT, CHARLES EAGAR, JR. sports columnist; b. Beaumont, Tex., Mar. 24, 1940; s. Charles Eagar and Hazel Ruth (Balston) V.; m. Mary Jacquelyn Bertman, Aug. 8, 1959 (div. Jan. 1969); children: Lisa Marie, Dixie Ann, Charles Joseph, John Patrick; m. Patricia Helene Skinner, Mar. 28, 1970 (div. Apr. 1985); 1 child, Susanna Lee; m. Karen Judith Peterson, Aug. 17, 1985. Student, Victoria Coll., 1958-59. Reporter Victoria (Tex.) Mirror, 1958-59, Taylor (Tex.) Daily Press, 1959-60; sports writer Beaumont (Tex.) Jour., 1960-62; sports editor Galveston (Tex.) Tribune, 1962-63; sports writer San Antonio Express-News, 1963-69, Sandusky (Ohio) Register, 1969-70, Detroit Free Press, 1970-85, sports columnist, 1985-99. Author: Welcome to My World, 1994, Broken Wings, 1998; co-author: (with Richard Bak) The Corner, A Century of Memories at Michigan and Trumbull, 1999. Recipient 4th Pl. award Nat. AP Sports Editors, 1981, 5th Pl., 1989, 92, Sister Mary Leila Meml. award, 1991, Mich. Columnist of Yr. award, 1991, 97; Afro-Am. Night honoree, 1991, Mich. Writer of the Yr. Nat. Sportscasters and Sportswriters, 1998. Mem. Baseball Writers Assn. Am. Avocations: traveling, cooking, geneology. E-mail: Vincentcharlie@hotmail.com.

VINCI, JOHN NICHOLAS, architect, educator; b. Chgo., Feb. 6, 1937; s. Nicholas and Nicolina (Camiola) V. B.Arch., Ill. Inst. Tech., 1960. Registered architect, Ill., Mo., Mich., NCARB. Draftsman Skidmore, Owings, Merrill, Chgo., 1960-61; with City of Chgo., 1961; stencil restorer Crombie Taylor, Chgo., 1961-62; designer Brenner, Danforth, Rockwell, 1962-68; architect Vinci, Inc., 1977-95; ptnr. Vinci/Hamp, Architects, Inc., 1995—; lectr. Roosevelt U., 1969-72, Ill. Inst. Tech., Chgo., 1972-90, adj. prof., 1999. Author: (booklet) Trading Room-Art Inst. Chgo., 1977; contbr. articles to profl. jours.; exhbn. designer. Bd. dirs. Music of Baroque, Chgo., 1976-87, Campbell Ctr. Found.; mem. adv. com. Commn. on Chgo. Archtl. and Hist. Landmarks, 1971-83; exec. sec. Richard Nickel Com, Chgo., 1972—; chmn. Howard Van Doren Shaw Soc., 1994—; internat. arts adv. coun. Wexner Ctr. for the Arts, 1994—. Fellow AIA; mem. Soc. Archtl. Historians, Frank Lloyd Wright Home and Studio Found., Art Inst. Chgo., The Corp. of YADDO, Chgo. Hist. Soc., Arts Club of Chgo. Roman Catholic. Home: 3152 N Cambridge Ave Chicago IL 60657-4613 Office: Vinci/Hamp Architects Inc 1147 W Ohio St Chicago IL 60622-6472

VINEYARD, JERRY D. geologist; b. Dixon, Mo., Mar. 26, 1935; s. Henry and Bessie Florence (Geisler) V.; m. Helen Louise Anderson, Nov. 24, 1960; children: Monica Lynne, Vanessa Anne. BA, U. Mo., 1960, MA, 1963. Registered profl. geologist, Ark., Mo. Lectr. in geology and geography Kansas City (Mo.) Met. Coll., 1961-63; chief publs. and info. Mo. Geol. Survey, Rolla, 1963-79; asst. state geologist Mo. Dept. Natural Resources, 1979-89, dep. state geologist, 1989-98, interstate rivers dir., 1998—. Mem. adv. bd. U. Mo., Columbia, 1982-91. Author: Springs of Missouri, 1978; co-author: Geologic Wonders and Curiosities of Missouri, 1990, Missouri Geology, 1992. Lt. (j.g.) USN, 1958-60. Fellow Cave Rsch. Found., 1998. Fellow Geol. Soc. Am. (Disting. Hydrogeologist 1989); mem. Nat. Speleological Soc. (hon. life mem., bd. dirs., editor jour. 1973), Mo. Speleological Soc. (hon. life mem., founder 1955—), Mo. Acad. Sci. (pres. 1996), Sigma Xi (pres. Mo. chpt. 1974). Baptist. Avocations: photography, woodworking, singing. Home: 4715 N Pheasant Dr Ozark MO 65721-6278 Office: 111 Fairgrounds Rd Rolla MO 65401-2909 E-mail: nrvinej@mail.dnr.state.mo.us.

VINH, NGUYEN XUAN, aerospace engineering educator; b. Yen Bay, Vietnam, Jan. 3, 1930; came to U.S., 1962; s. Nguyen X. and Thao (Do) Nhien; m. Joan Cung, Aug. 15, 1955; children: Alphonse, Phuong, Phoenix, John. PhD in Aerospace Engring., U. Colo., 1965; DSc in Math., U. Paris VI, 1972. Asst. prof. aerospace engring. U. Colo., Boulder, 1965-68; assoc. prof. aerospace engring. U. Mich., Ann Arbor, 1968-72, prof. aerospace engring., 1972—. Vis. lectr. U. Calif., Berkeley, 1967; vis. prof. ecol. nat. sup. aero., France, 1974; chair prof. Nat Tsing Hua U., Taiwan, 1982. Co-author: Hypersonic and Planetary Entry Flight Mechanics, 1980; author: Optimal Trajectories in Atmospheric Flight, 1981, Flight Mechanics of High Performance Aircraft, 1993. Chief of staff Vietnam Air Force, 1957-62. Recipient Mechanics and Control of Flight award AIAA, 1994, Excellence 2000 award USPAACC, 1996. Mem. Internat. Acad. Astronautics, Nat. Acad. Air and Space (France). Achievements include research in ordinary differential equations; astrodynamics and optimization of space flight trajectories; theory of non-linear oscillations. Office: U Mich Dept Aerospace Engring 3001 FXB Bldg Ann Arbor MI 48109-2140

VINING, JOSEPH (GEORGE JOSEPH VINING), law educator; b. Fulton, Mo., Mar. 3, 1938; s. D. Rutledge and Margaret (McClanahan) V.; m. Alice Marshall Williams, Sept. 18, 1965; children: George Joseph IV, Spencer Carter. BA, Yale U., 1959, Cambridge U., 1961, MA, 1970; JD, Harvard U., 1964. Bar: DC 1965. Atty. Office Dep. Atty. Gen., Dept. Justice, Washington, 1965; asst. to exec. dir. Nat. Crime Commn., 1966; assoc. Covington and Burling, Washington, 1966-69; asst. prof. law U. Mich., 1969-72, assoc. prof., 1972-74, prof., 1974-85, Hutchins prof., 1985—. Author: Legal Identity, 1978, The Authoritative and the Authoritarian, 1986, From Newton's Sleep, 1995. NEH sr. fellow, 1982-83, Bellagio fellow Rockfeller Found., 1997. Fellow Am. Acad. Arts and Scis.; mem. ABA, D.C. Bar Assn. Am. Law Inst., Century Assn. Office: U Mich 964 Lega Rsch Ann Arbor MI 48109-1215

VINSON, JAMES SPANGLER, academic administrator; b. Chambersburg, Pa., May 17, 1941; s. Wilbur S. and Anna M. (Spangler) V.; m. Susan Alexander, Apr. 8, 1967; children: Suzannah, Elizabeth. B.A., Gettysburg Coll., 1963; M.S., U. Va., 1965, Ph.D., 1967. Asst. prof. physics MacMurray Coll., Jacksonville, Ill., 1967-71; asso. prof. physics U. N.C., Asheville, 1971-78, prof. physics, 1974-78, chmn. dept. physics, dir. acad. computing, 1974-78; prof. physics, dean Coll. Arts and Scis. U. Hartford (Conn.), 1978-83; v.p. acad. affairs Trinity U., San Antonio, 1983-87; pres. U. Evansville, Ind., 1987-2001, pres. emeritus, 2001—. Computer cons. Contbr. articles to profl. jours. Mem. Am. Phys. Soc., World Future Soc., AAAS, Am. Assn. for Advancement of Humanities, Am. Assn. for Higher Edn., Am. Assn. Physics Tchrs., Phi Beta Kappa, Sigma Xi, Phi Sigma Kappa. Methodist.

VIOLA, DONN J. manufacturing company executive; b. Pa. BSME, Lehigh U. With Volkswagen, Masco Industries; sr. exec. v.p., COO, bd. dirs. Mack Trucks, Inc.; COO N.Am. Donnelly Corp., Holland, Mich., 1996-2001, COO, 2001—. Office: Donnelly Corp 49 W 3d St Holland MI 49423

VIRTEL, JAMES JOHN, lawyer; b. Joliet, Ill., May 15, 1944; BA cum laude, Loras Coll., 1966; JD cum laude, St. Louis U., 1969. Bar: Mo. 1969, Ill. 1969. Atty. Armstrong, Teasdale, Schlafly & Davis (now called Armstrong Teasdale LLP), St. Louis, 1976—. Adj. prof. law St. Louis U., 1995-99; regent Loras Coll., Dubuque, Iowa, 1996—. Editor: St. Louis U. Law Jour., 1968-69. Fellow Am. Coll. Trial Lawyers; mem. Ill. State Bar Assn., Mo. State Bar Assn. Office: Armstrong Teasdale LLP 1 Metropolitan Sq Ste 2600 Saint Louis MO 63102-2740 E-mail: jvirtel@armstrongteasdale.com.

VISCHER, HAROLD HARRY, manufacturing company executive; b. Toledo, Oct. 17, 1914; s. Harry Philip and Hazel May (Patterson) V.; m. DeNell Meyers, Feb. 18, 1938; children: Harold Harry, Robert P., Michael L. B.B.A., U. Toledo, 1937. With Ohio Bell Telephone Co., 1937-38; with Firestone Tire & Rubber Co., Toledo, 1948-61, nat. passenger tire sales mgr., 1953-57, dist. mgr., 1957-61; with Bandag Inc., Muscatine, Iowa, 1961-80; exec. v.p., pres. Bandag Inc. (Rubber and Equipment Sales group), 1975-80; also dir.; pres., gen. mgr. Hardline Internat., Inc., Jackson, Mich., 1980-82; chmn. Tred-X Corp., 1982—. Mem. City Council, Muscatine, 1964-76; chmn., mem. Dist. Export Council Iowa, 1964-81; chmn. Muscatine United Way, 1969-70; mem. adv. bd. Engring. Coll. Iowa State U., 1970-81; mem. Muscatine Light & Water Bd., 1979-80. Elected to Nat. Tire Dealers and Retreaders Assn. Hall of Fame, 1988, to Internat. Tire Retreading and Repairing Hall of Fame, 1990. Mem. Nat. Tire and Retreaders Suppliers Group Assn. (chmn. 1979-80, exec. com. 1977-80), Tire Retread Info. Bur. (exec. com. 1974-81), Am. Retreading Assn. (adv. bd. 1970-72), Retreading Industry Assn., Industry Man of Yr. 1979), Christian Business men's Com., Gideons, Rotary. Republican. Baptist. Home: 13500 Vischer Rd Brooklyn MI 49230-9022 Office: 116 Frost St Jackson MI 49202-2371

VISCLOSKY, PETER JOHN, congressman, lawyer; b. Gary, Ind., Aug. 13, 1949; s. John and Helen (Kauzlaric) V. B.S. in Acctg., Ind. U.-Indpls., 1970; J.D., U. Notre Dame, 1973; LL.M. in Internat. and Comparative Law, Georgetown U., 1983. Bar: Ind., D.C., U.S. Supreme Court. Legal asst. Dist. Atty.'s Office, N.Y.C., 1972; assoc. Benjamin, Greco & Gouveia, Merrillville, Ind., 1973-76, Greco, Gouveia, Miller, Pera & Bishop, Merrillville, 1982-84; assoc. staff appropriations com. U.S. Ho. of Reps., Washington, 1976-80, assoc. staff budget com., 1980-82; mem. U.S. Congress from 1st dist. Ind., 1985—; mem. appropriations com., subcoms. treasury, postal svc., gen. govt. and military constrn. Democrat. Roman Catholic Office: US House of Reps 2313 Rayburn Hob Washington DC 20515-0001

VISEK, WILLARD JAMES, nutritionist, animal scientist, physician, educator; b. Sargent, Nebr., Sept. 19, 1922; s. James and Anna S. (Dworak) V.; m. Priscilla Flagg, Dec. 28, 1949; children: Dianna, Madeleine, Clayton Paul. B.Sc. with honors (Carl R. Gray scholar), U. Nebr., 1947; MSc (Smith fellow in agr.), Cornell U., 1949, Ph.D., 1951; M.D. (Peter Yost Fund scholar), U. Chgo., 1957; DSc (hon.), U. Nebr., 1980. Diplomate Nat. Bd. Med. Examiners, 1960. Grad. asst., lab. animal nutrition Cornell U., 1947-51; AEC postdoctoral fellow Oak Ridge, 1951-52; research assoc., 1952-53; research asst. pharmacology U. Chgo., 1953-57, asst. prof., 1957-61, assoc. prof., 1961-64; rotating med. intern U. Chgo. Clinics, 1957-58, 58-59, 59; prof. nutrition and comparative metabolism, dept. animal sci. Cornell U., Ithaca, N.Y., 1964-75; prof. clin. sci. (nutrition and metabolism) Coll. Medicine and prof. food sci. U. Ill. Coll. Agr., Urbana-Champaign, 1975—; prof. dept. internal medicine U. Ill. Coll. Medicine, 1986-93, prof. emeritus, 1993—. Bd. dirs. Coun. Agriculture, Sci. and Tech., 1994-97; bd. sci. advisors Coun. Sci. and Health, 1994—; Brittingham vis. prof. U. Wis. Madison, 1982-83; Hogan meml. lectr. U. Mo., 1987; mem. subcom. dog nutrition com. animal nutrition NRC-Nat. Acad. Sci., 1965-71; adv. coun. Inst. Lab. Animal Resources, NRC-Nat. Acad. Sci., 1966-69; sub-com. animal care facilitities Survey Inst. Lab. Animal Resources, 1967-70; cons., lectr. in field; mem. sci. adv. com. diet and nutrition cancer program Nat. Cancer Inst., 1976-81; mem. nutrition study sect. NIH, 1980-84; chmn. membership com. Am. Inst. Nutrition-Am. Soc. Clin. Nutrition, 1978-79, 80-83, 85; cons. VA, NSF, indsl. orgns.; Wellcome vis. prof. in basic med. scis. Oreg. State U., 1991-92; bd. sci. counselors USDA, 1989-91. Mem. editl. bd. Jour. Nutrition, 1980-84, editor, 1990-97; mem. editl. bd. Physiol. Rev., 1995—; contbr. articles to profl. jours. Bd. dirs. Coun. for Agrl. Sci. and Tech., 1994-97; active local Boy Scouts Am. Served with AUS, 1943-46. Recipient alumni award Nebr. 4-H, 1967, 97, alumni award U. Chgo., 1997, faculty merit award U. Ill. Coll. Medicine, 1988, Alumni Achievement award U. Nebr., 1997, U. Chgo., 1997; Nat. Cancer Inst. spl. fellow MIT, rsch. fellow Mass. Gen. Hosp., 1970-71; sr. scholar U. Ill., 1988. Fellow AAAS, Am. Inst. Nutrition (Osborne and Mendel award 1985), Am. Soc. Animal Sci. (chmn. subcom. antimicrobials, mem. regulatory agency com. 1973-78); mem. Am. Physiol. Soc., Soc. Pharmacology and Exptl. Therapeutics, Am. Inst. Nutrition (council 1980-83, 85-86), Soc. Exptl. Biology and Medicine, Am. Soc. Clin. Nutrition, Am. Therapeutic Soc., Am. Gastroenterol. Assn., Am. Bd. Clin. Nutrition, Innocents Soc., Fedn. Am. Socs. Exptl. Biology (sci. steering group life scis. rsch. office, adv. com. 1986-92), Am. Bd. Nutrition (bd. dirs.), Am. Soc. Nutritional Scis. (Conrad Elvehjem award 1996), Nat. Dairy Coun. (rsch. adv. com. 1987-91, vis. prof. nutrition program 1981-92), Gamma Alpha (pres. 1948-49), Phi Kappa Phi (pres. 1981-82), Alpha Gamma Rho (pres. 1946-47), Gamma Sigma Delta. Presbyterian (elder). Home: 1405 W William St Champaign IL 61821-4406 Office: U Ill 190 Med Sci Bldg 506 S Mathews Ave Urbana IL 61801-3618 E-mail: w-visek@uiuc.edu.

VISKANTA, RAYMOND, mechanical engineering educator; b. Lithuania, July 16, 1931; came to U.S., 1949, naturalized, 1955; s. Vincas and Genovaite (Vinickas) V.; m. Birute Barbara Barpsys, Oct. 13, 1956; children: Renata, Vitas, Tadas. BSME, U. Ill., 1955; MSME, Purdue U., 1956, PhD, 1960; DEng (hon.), Tech. U. Munich, 1994. Registered profl. engr., Ill. Asst. mech. engr. Argonne (Ill.) Nat. Lab., 1956-59, student rsch. assoc., 1959-60, assoc. mech. engr., 1960-62; assoc. prof. mech. engring. Purdue U., West Lafayette, Ind., 1962-66, prof. mech. engring., 1966-86, Goss disting. prof. engring., 1986—. Guest prof. Tech. U. Munich, Germany, 1976-77, U. Karlsruhe, Germany, 1987; vis. prof. Tokyo Inst. Tech., 1983. Contbr. over 500 tech. articles to profl. jours. Recipient Sr. U.S. Scientist award Alexander von Humboldt Found., 1975, Sr. Rsch. award Am. Soc. Engring. Edn., 1984, Nusselt-Reynolds prize, 1991, Thermal Engring. award for Internat. Activity, Japan Soc. Mech. Engrs., 1994, Alumni award for Disting. Svc. U. Ill.-Urbana-Champaign, 2000; Japan Soc. for Promotion of Sci. fellow, 1983. Fellow ASME (Heat Transfer Meml. award 1976, Max Jakob Meml. award 1986, Melville medal 1988), AIAA (Thermophysics award 1979); mem. AAAS, NAE, Acad. Engring. Scis. Russian Fedn. (fgn.), Lithuanian Acad. Scis. (fgn.), Sigma Xi, Pi Tau Sigma, Tau Beta Pi. Home: 3631 Chancellor Way West Lafayette IN 47906-8809 Office: Purdue Univ 1288 Mechanical Engineering West Lafayette IN 47907-1288 E-mail: rviskanta@earthlink.net., viskanta@ecn.purdue.edu.

VITALE, DAVID J. banker; b. 1946; With First Nat. Bank of Chgo. subs. First Chgo. NBD Corp., 1968—, exec. v.p., 1986—, First Chgo. NBD Corp., 1986—, also bd. dirs., 1992—; vice chmn., pres. First Nat. Bank Chgo., 1995-2001; CEO Chgo. Bd. Trade, 2001—. Office: Chgo Bd Trade 141 W Jackson Blvd Chicago IL 60604-2994

VITALE, GERALD LEE, financial services executive; b. Chgo., Apr. 3, 1950; s. Le Roy Allen and Gilda Leanora (Rasori) V. BS in Psychology, Loyola U., Chgo., 1972. Credit mgr. Mellon Fin., Chgo., 1973-76, Kemper Ins. Co., Chgo., 1976-78; pres., CEO Tribune Employees Credit Union, 1978-96. Pres. NCR Credit Union User Group, Dayton, Ohio, 1984-91; CEO, Gerald Equity Resources, Inc., 1996—; mem. adv. bd. Ill. Gov.'s Credit Union, 1993-98; dir. fin. Rush Cancer Inst., 2000-2001. Co-host Chicagoland Cable (CLTV) TV Fin. Reports, Tribune Broadcasting, 1993-96. Counselor youth motivation Chgo. C. of C. and Industry, 1980-97, mem. adv. bd., 1984-96; counselor Hire the Future, 1988-96; vol. Red Cloud Athletic Assn., 1993-2000, Friends of Providence-St. Mel, 1993—; mem. Chgo. Coun. Fgn. Rels., 1995-98, Nat. Itali an Am. Found., Coun. of 1000, 1995-99, Humane Soc. U.S., 1997—; mem. fin. svcs. com. Exec. Club, City of Chgo., 1993-99; GOP Action Com., 1992-97; mem. Ctr. for Study of Presidency, 1993-97; dep. gov. Am. Biog. Inst., 1993—, Filene Inst., 1992-96; mem. Habitat for Humanity, 1998—, Ill. Arts Alliance, 1996-98; mem. Nat. Assn. Investors Corp., 1999—, Rep. Nat. Com., 1977—; mem. (life) Rep. Nat. Com., 1977—. Mem. Am. Mgmt. Assn., Midwest Assn. Credit Unions (bd. dirs. 1992-96), Nat. Assn. State Chartered Credit Unions (region V dir., bd. dirs. 1995-97), Nat. Assn. Investors (corp. mem. 1999—), Am. Enterprise Inst., Greater Garfield C. of C. (bd. dirs., pres. 1992-95), Monroe Club (bd. dirs. 1995-99), Sky Line Club. Roman Catholic. Avocations: hiking, rowing, long-distance walking. Home: 1636 N Wells St Apt 2410 Chicago IL 60614-6020 Office: GER Inc 1636 N Wells St Apt 2410 Chicago IL 60614-6020 E-mail: gerinc@aol.com.

VITITO, ROBERT J. bank executive; Mgmt. trainee Second Nat. Bank Saginaw, Mich., 1967, various, 1967-86, pres., 1986; pres., chief adminstrv. officer Citizens Banking Corp., Flint, 1994-95, pres., CEO, 1995-99, chmn., 1999—. Office: Citizens Banking Corp 328 S Saginaw St Flint MI 48502-1943

VITTER, DRUE J. state legislator, mayor; b. New Orleans, July 21, 1942; m. Patsy Vitter. Grad., Holy Cross H.S. Mayor Hill City, S.D., 1992—; mem. dist. 30 S.D. Senate, Pierre, 1996—. Mem. Heart Hills Econ. Devel. Com. Mem. No. Mayors Assn., C. of C. and Econ. Devel. Corp., Hill City C. of C. Office: State Capitol Bldg 500 E Capitol Ave Pierre SD 57501-5070

VIVERITO, LOUIS SAMUEL, state legislator; b. Chgo. m. Carolyn Strobl; children: Dean, Diane, Marianne. Mem. Ill. State Senate, 1995—. Mem. Stickney Twp. Dem. Com., 1969—; del. Dem. Nat. Conv., 1972; commr. Met. Sanitary Dist. Greater Chgo., 1980-86; mem. Cook County Zoning Bd. Appeals, 1987-95; local chmn. Chgo. Lung Assn., 1973—. Named Man of Yr., Joint Civic Com. Italian-Am., 1980; inductee Hall of Fame, Valentine Boys & Girls Club, 1987. Mem. VFW (life), Am. Legion (life), Burbank C. of C., Burbank Sertoma Club (founder).

VIZQUEL, OMAR ENRIQUE, professional baseball player; b. Caracus, Venezuela, Apr. 24, 1967; Grad. high sch., Caracus. With Seattle Mariners, 1989-93; shortstop Cleve. Indians, 1993—. Recipient Winner Am. League Golden Glove, 1993-96. Office: Cleve Indians 2401 Ontario St Cleveland OH 44115-4003*

VLCEK, DONALD JOSEPH, JR. food distribution company executive, consultant, business author, executive coach; b. Chgo., Oct. 30, 1949; s. Donald Joseph and Rosemarie (Krizek) V.; m. Claudia Germain Meyer, July 22, 1978 (div. 1983); 1 child, Suzanne Mae; m. Valeria Olive Russell, Nov. 11, 1989; children: James Donald, Victoria Rose. BBA, U. Mich., 1971. Cert. facilitator Adires Inst. Gen. mgr. Popps, Inc., Hamtramck, Mich., 1969-76; pres. Domino's Pizza Distbn. Corp., Ann Arbor, 1978-93, chmn., 1993-94, also bd. dirs.; pres. Don Vlcek & Assocs., Ltd., Plymouth, 1994—; CEO Beaver Buddies, LLC; master franchisee Beaver Tails Can., Inc., Mich., Ind., Ill., Ohio, Wis. Profl. speaker, personal coach, seminar leader, bus. cons., workshop facilitator; trustee Domino's Pizza Ptnrs. Found.; bd. dirs. RPM Pizza Inc., Gulfport, Miss., Dimango Corp., South Lyon, Mich.; sr. v.p. distbn. and tech. Domino's Ohio Commissary, Zanesville; pres. Morel Mountain Corp.; judge 1994 Duck Stamp contest U.S. Dept. Interior, Jr. Fed. Duck Stamp Contest, 1995; bd. dirs. Beaver Tails Can. Author: The Domino Effect, 1992 (Best of Bus. award ALA 1992, Soundview's Top 30 Business books of 1993), SuperVision, 1997, Job Planning and Review System Manual, 1997, 2001; (audio cassette tape series Super Vision; contbr. articles to profl. jours. Bd. dirs. Men's Hockey League of Oak Park, Mich., 1973-78; asst. coach Redford Scorpions Jr. Travel Hockey Team. Named Person of Yr. Bd. Franchises, Boston, 1981; recipient Teal award Ducks Unltd., 1992, State Major Gifts Chmn. award, 1992, 93, State Chmn.'s award, 1992, State Major Gifts award, 1994. Mem. Am. Soc. of Tng. Dirs., Mich. Steelheaders Assn. (life), Ducks Unltd. (life, Domino's Pizza chpt. treas., sponsor, chmn. 1988—, Mich. state bd. dirs., life sponsor, chmn. 1989, 91-92, state trustee 1992-98, hon. trustee 2001—, chmn. exec. com. 1992-94, major gifts chmn. 1993-98, chmn. strategic devel. com. 1994, sponsor in perpetuity Grand Slam Life, Heritage sponsor), Mich. United Conservation Club (life), Whitetails Unltd. (life), Pheasants Forever (life), Midstates Masters Bowling Assn. (bd. dirs. 1976-85), Barton Hills Country Club (golf com., capt. dist. team), U. Mich. Alumni Assn. (life), Domino's Lodge/Drummond Island Wildlife Habitat Found. (pres., chmn. bd.), Vlcek Family Wildlife Found. (pres., chmn. bd.), Elks (life), Die Hard Cubs Fan Club, Greater Detroit C. of C., Profl. Spkrs. Assn. of Mich. (bd. dirs. 1997-99), Mich. Soc. Assn. Execs., Sm. Bus. Assn. Mich., Nat. Spkrs. Assn., Profl. Spkrs. Ill. (profl.), Internat. Coaching Fedn. (cert. master), Am. Soc. Tng. Dirs. Republican. Roman Catholic. Avocations: hunting, fishing, hockey, collecting wildlife art, coins, and sports cards and memorabilia. Home: 9251 Beck Rd N Plymouth MI 48170-3336 Office: Don Vlcek & Assoc Ltd PO Box 701353 Plymouth MI 48170-0963

VOGEL, ARTHUR ANTON, clergyman; b. Milw., Feb. 24, 1924; s. Arthur Louis and Gladys Eirene (Larson) V.; m. Katharine Louise Nunn, Dec. 29, 1947; children: John Nunn, Arthur Anton, Katharine Ann. Student, U. of South, 1942-43, Carroll Coll., 1943-44; B.D., Nashotah House Theol. Sem., 1946; M.A., U. Chgo., 1948; Ph.D., Harvard, 1952; S.T.D., Gen. Theol. Sem., 1969; D.C.L., Nashotah House, 1969; D.D., U. of South, 1971. Ordained deacon Episcopal Ch., 1946, priest, 1948; teaching asst. philosophy Harvard, Cambridge, Mass., 1949-50; instr. Trinity Coll., Hartford, Conn., 1950-52; mem. faculty Nashotah House Theol. Sem., Nashotah, Wis., 1952-71, asso. prof., 1954-56, William Adams prof. philosophical and systematic theology, 1956-71, sub-dean Sem., 1964-71; bishop coadjutor Diocese of West Mo., Kansas City, 1971-72, bishop, 1972-89; rector Ch. St. John Chrysostom, Delafield, Wis., 1952-56; dir. Anglican Theol. Rev., Evanston, Ill., 1964-69; mem. Internat. Anglican-Roman Cath. Consultation, 1970-90, Nat. Anglican-Roman Catholic Consultation, 1965-84, Anglican chmn., 1973-84; mem. Standing Commn. on Ecumenical Relations of Episcopal Ch., 1957-79; mem. gen. bd. examining chaplains Episcopal Ch., 1971-72. Del. Episcopal Ch., 4th Assembly World Council Chruches, Uppsala, Sweden, 1968, and others. Author: Reality, Reason and Religion, 1957, The Gift of Grace, 1958, The Christian Person, 1963, The Next Christian Epoch, 1966, Is the Last Supper Finished?, 1968, Body Theology, 1973, The Power of His Resurrection, 1976, Proclamation 2: Easter, 1980, The Jesus Prayer for Today, 1982, I Know God Better Than I Know Myself, 1989, Christ in His Time and Ours, 1982, God, Prayer and Healing, 1995, Radical Christianity and the Flesh of Jesus, 1995; editor: Theology in Anglicanism, 1985; contbr. articles to profl. jours. Vice chmn. bd. dirs. St. Luke's Hosp., Kansas City, Mo., 1971, chmn., 1973-89. Research fellow Harvard, 1950 Mem. Am. Philos. Assn., Metaphys. Soc. Am., Soc. Existential and Phenomenological Philosophy, Catholic Theol. Soc. Am. Home: 524 W 119th Ter Kansas City MO 64145-1043

VOGEL, CARL M. state legislator; Mem. Mo. Ho. of Reps. from 114th dist. Republican. Home: 311 Constitution Dr Jefferson City MO 65109-5723

VOGEL, CEDRIC WAKELEE, lawyer; b. Cin., June 4, 1946; s. Cedric and Patricia (Woodruff) V. BA, Yale U., 1968; JD, Harvard U., 1971. Bar: Ohio 1972, Fla. 1973, U.S. Tax Ct. 1972, U.S. Supreme Ct. 1975. Ptnr. Vogel, Heis, Wenstrup & Cameron, Cin., 1972-96; sole practice, 1997—. Bd. dirs. Pro Srs., 1994—. Chmn. mem.'s com. Cin. Art Mus., 1987-88; chmn. auction Cin. Hist. Soc., 1985; local pres. English Speaking Union, 1979-81, nat. bd. dirs., 1981; chmn. Keep Cin. Beautiful, Inc., 1994-96; active Bravo! Cin. Ballet, 1989; chmn. Act II Nutcracker Ball, 1987-88; bd. dirs. Merc Libr., 1991-98; bd. dirs. Cin. Preservation Assn., 1990-93, Cin. Opera Guild, 1997-99; vice chmn. Children's Heart Assn. Reds Rally, 1989; bd. dirs. Cin. Country Day Sch., 1983, pres. Alumni Coun. and Ann. Fund, 1983. Mem. Cin. Bar Assn., Fla. Bar Assn., Harvard Law Sch. Assn. Cin. (pres. 1997-99, Heimlich Inst. (trustee 1987—), Yale Alumni Assn. (del. 1984-87), Cin. Yale Club (pres. 1980-81, 96-97), Cincinnatus, The Lawyers Club Cin. (pres. 1995), Harvard Club of Cin. (bd. dirs. 1996-98, pres. 1999-2000). Republican. Home: 2270 Madison Rd Cincinnati OH 45208-2659 Office: 817 Main St Ste 800 Cincinnati OH 45202-2183

VOGEL, NELSON J., JR. lawyer; b. South Bend, Ind., Oct. 13, 1946; s. Nelson J. and Carolyn B. (Drzewiecki) V.; m. Sandra L. Cudney, May 17, 1969; children: Ryan C., Justin M., Nathan J., Lindsey M. BS cum laude, Miami U., Oxford, Ohio, 1968; JD cum laude, U. Notre Dame, 1971. Bar: Ind. 1971, Mich. 1971, U.S. Dist. Ct. (no. dist.) Ind. 1971, U.S. Tax Ct. 1972, U.S. Ct. Appeals (5th cir.) 1975, U.S. Ct. Claims 1980; CPA, Ind. Acct. Coopers & Lybrand, South Bend, 1969-71; assoc. Barnes & Thornburg, 1971-76, ptnr., 1977—. Lectr. U. Notre Dame, South Bend, 1971, 74-80; instr. Ind. U., South Bend, 1971-74; bd. advisors Goshen Coll. Family Bus. Program, 1993-99; vice-chair Barnes & Thornburg, woo1—, mnging. ptnr. (S. Bend office), 2001—; bd. trustees Project Future (St. Joseph Co.), 2002—. Pres. Big Bros., Big Sisters, South Bend, 1978-79; bd. pres. South Bend Regional Mus. Art, 1984-86; mem. ethics com. Meml. Hosp., South Bend, 1986-94. Mem. Nat. Employee Stock Ownership Plan Assn. (sec.-treas. Ind. chpt. 1993-95), Am. Assn. Atty.-CPAs, Nat. Assn. State Bar Tax Sec. (exec. com. 1982-84), Ind. State Bar Assn. (chmn. taxation sect. 1981-82, Citation of Merit 1979), Ind. Assn. Mediators, Mich. Bar Assn. (tax sect.), Ind. State H.S. Hockey Assn., Inc. (bd. dirs. 1998-2001, treas. 1998-2001), Michiana World Affairs Coun. (bd. dirs. 1992-96), Michiana World Trade club (bd. dirs. 1992-96), Mental Health Assn. St. Joseph County (bd. dirs. 1997-2001). Home: 1146 Dunrobbin Ln South Bend IN 46614-2150 Office: Barnes & Thornburg 600 1st Source Bank 100 N Michigan St Ste 600 South Bend IN 46601-1632 E-mail: nvogel@btlaw.com.

VOGEL, THOMAS TIMOTHY, surgeon, health care consultant, lay church worker; b. Columbus, Ohio, Feb. 1, 1934; s. Thomas A. and Charlotte A. (Hogan) V.; m. M.M. Darina Kelleher, May 29, 1965; children: Thomas T., Catherine D., Mark P., Nicola M. AB, Coll. of Holy Cross, 1955; MS, Ohio State U., 1960, PhD, 1962; MD, Georgetown U., 1965. Pvt. practice surgery, Columbus, 1971-2001; chmn. liturgy com., pres. parish coun. St. Catharine Parish, 1971-73; chmn. diocesan adminstrn. com. Diocesan Pastoral Coun., 1972-73, chmn., 1973-75; vice prefect Sodality of Holy Cross, 1953-55; mem. Ohio Bishop's Adv. Coun., Columbus, 1976-79. Clin. asst. prof. surgery Ohio State U., Columbus, 1974—; past trustee Peer Rev. Sys., Inc.; assoc. med. dir. United Health Care, Columbus, 1997-2000; cons. Rehabilitation Svcs.; commr., surveillance utilization rev. mem. Medicaid, State of Ohio; assoc. med. dir. Nationwide Medicare, 1999—. Contbr. articles to profl. jours. Bd. dirs. St. Vincent's Children's Ctr., 1975-83, chmn., 1981-82; past chmn. bd. trustees St. Joseph Montessori Sch. Named Knight of the Holy Sepulchre, 2001; recipient Layman's award, Columbus Ea. Kiwanis, 1972. Mem. ACS, Am. Physiol. Soc., Assn. for Acad. Surgery, Ohio State Med. Assn. (del. 1993—), Sigma Xi, Delta Epsilon Sigma. Roman Catholic. E-mail: vogel.3@osu.edu; vogel+@nationwide.com; Thomas.Vogel@ssq.gov. Home: 247 S Ardmore Rd Columbus OH 43209-1701 Office: 621 S Cassingham Rd Columbus OH 43209-2403 E-mail: vogel.3@osu.edu.

VOGT, ALBERT RALPH, forester, educator, program director; BS in Forest Mgmt., U. Mo., 1961, MS in Tree Physiology, 1962, PhD in Tree Physiology, 1966. Instr. in dendrology U. Mo., Columbia, 1965-66; asst. prof. rsch. tree physiology Ohio State U., 1966-69, assoc. prof., assoc. chmn. rsch. and adminstrn. forestry, 1969-76, prof., chmn. dept. adminstrn. and tchg. forestry, 1976-85; prof., dir. sch. natural resources U. Mo., 1985—. Pres Nat Asn Prof Forestry Schs and Cols, 1998—2000; mem Mo Forest Heritage Initiative, Gov's Task Force Environ Educ, Mo Gov's Energy Coalition, Mo Citizen's Comt Soil, Water, and State Parks; co-chair steering comt 3d Forestry Educ Symp, 1991; co-chair external rev dept forestry So Ill Univ, Carbondale, 1993; co-chair sch forest resources Pa State Univ, 1995; chair external rev forestry Univ Wis, Madison, 1997. Office: U Mo Sch Natural Resources 103C Natural Resources Bldg Columbia MO 65211-0001 E-mail: vogta@missouri.edu.

VOIGHT, JACK C. state official; b. New London, Wis., Dec. 17, 1945; s. Oscar C. and Thelma J. (Hamm) V.; m. Martha J. Wolfe, July 14, 1973; children: Carly, Emily. BS, U. Wis., Oshkosh, 1971. Claims adjuster U.S. F&G Ins. Co., Appleton, Wis., 1971-74; ins. agy. owner Voight Ins. Agy., 1974—; state treas. State of Wis., Madison, 1995—. Bank organizer Am. Nat. Bank, Appleton, 1992-94; real estate broker Voight Realty & Ins., Appleton, 1977-92. Pres. Appleton Northside Bus. Assn., 1982; alderman City Coun., City of Appleton, 1983-83, pres., 1992-93. Sgt. U.S. Army, 1968-70. Decorated Bronze Star; named Citizen of Yr., Appleton Northside Bus. Assn., 1990. Mem. Nat. Assn. State Treas., Midwest State Treass. Assn. (pres. 1996-97), Appleton Noon Optimist Club (pres. 1980). Republican. Presbyterian. Avocations: gardening, politics. Office: State Treas Wis PO Box 7871 Madison WI 53707-7871 E-mail: jack.voight@ost.state.wi.us.

VOINOVICH, GEORGE V. senator, former mayor and governor; b. Cleve., July 15, 1936; m. Janet Voinovich; 3 children. B.A., Ohio U., 1958; J.D., Ohio State U., 1961; LL.D. (hon.), Ohio U., 1981. Bar: Ohio 1961, U.S. Supreme Ct. 1968. Asst. atty. gen. State of Ohio, 1963-64; mem. Ohio Ho. of Reps., 1967-71; auditor Cuyahoga County, Ohio, 1971-76; commr., 1977-78; lt. gov. State of Ohio, 1979; mayor City of Cleve., 1979-89; gov. State of Ohio, 1991-98; U.S. senator from Ohio, 1999—. Pres. Nat. League Cities, 1984-85; trustee U.S. Conf. Mayors; chmn. Midwestern Govs. Conf., 1991-92, Coun. Gt. Lakes Govs., 1992-94. Recipient cert. of Merit award Ohio U., Humanitarian award NCCJ, 1986; named one of Outstanding Young Men in Ohio Ohio Jaycees, 1970; one of Outstanding Young Men in Greater Cleve. Cleve. Jaycees; Disting. Urban Mayor award Nat. Urban Coalition, 1987; named to All-Pro City Mgmt. team City & State Mag., 1987. Mem. Rep. Govs. Assn. (vice chmn. 1991-92, chmn. 1992-93), Nat. Govs. Assn. (chmn. edn. action team on sch. readiness 1991, chmn. child support enforcement work group 1991-92, mem. strategic planning task force 1991-92, mem. human resources com. 1991—, co-chmn. task force on edn. 1992-93, mem. exec. com. 1993—, co-lead gov. on fed. mandates 1993—, chmn. 1997-98), Omicron Delta Kappa, Phi Alpha Theta, Phi Delta Phi. Republican. Office: US Senate 317 Hart Bldg Washington DC 20510-0001*

VOLESKY, RON JAMES, state legislator; b. Bullhead, S.D., July 13, 1954; s. Leonard and Louise (Kleinsasser) V. BA in Govt., Harvard Coll., 1976; MS in Journalism and Mass Communication, S.D. State U., 1977; postgrad., U. S.D. Sch. Law, 1980. Prodr. bicentennial programming S.D. Pub. TV, 1975; news dir., anchorman S.D. Pub. Radio Network, 1976-77; real estate salesman Montgomery Agy., 1978-79; pvt. practice as atty. Volesky Law Offices, Huron, S.D.; ptnr. Churchill, Manolis, Freeman & Volesky; mem. S.D. Ho. of Reps from 23rd dist., Pierre; majority whip S.D. Ho. of Reps, 1983-84, mem. judiciary & transp. coms.; mem. S.D. Senate from 21st dist., 2001—. Bd. dirs. Bank Wessington. Co-author: Who's Who Among the Sioux, 1977. Del. Rep. State Conv., 1978; chmn. Beadle County Rep. Ctrl. Com., S.D., 1979-80. Recipient Citizenship award Huron Am. Legion, 1972; scholar Harvard Club N.Y., 1972-76, Sarah and Pauline Maier scholar Harvard Coll., 1972-76. Mem. Soc. Profl. Journalists, S.D. Trial Lawyers Assn., ABA, Jaycees. Democrat. Home: 592 Dakota Ave S Huron SD 57350-2858 Office: SD House of Reps 356 Dakota Ave S Huron SD 57350-2513

VOLKEMA, MICHAEL A. office furniture manufacturer; Chmn., CEO Meridian Inc., Spring Lake, Mich.; pres., CEO Coro Inc., Zeeland, Herman Miller Inc., Zeeland, 1995—, chmn., 2000—. Office: Herman Miller Inc 855 E Main Ave Zeeland MI 49464-0302

VOLKMER, HAROLD L. former congressman; b. Jefferson City, Mo., Apr. 4, 1931; m. Shirley Ruth Braskett; children: Jerry Wayne, John Paul, Elizabeth Ann. Student, Jefferson City Jr. Coll., 1949-51, St. Louis U. Sch. Commerce and Finance, 1951-52; LL.B., U. Mo., 1955. Bar: Mo. 1955. Individual practice law, Hannibal, 1958—; asst. atty. gen. Mo., 1955; pros. atty. Marion County, 1960-66; mem. Mo. Ho. of Reps., 1966-76; chmn. judiciary com., mem. revenue and econs. com.; mem. 95th-104th Congresses from 9th Mo. Dist., 1977-96; ranking minority mem. agr. subcom. livestock, dairy, & poultry. Served with U.S. Army, 1955-57. Recipient award for meritorious pub. service in Gen. Assembly St. Louis Globe-Democrat, 1972-74 Mem. NRA (bd. dirs., chmn. civil rights ef. fund), Mo. Bar Assn., 10th Jud. Circuit Bar Assn. Roman Catholic. Clubs: KC, Hannibal Lions.

VOLLMER, HOWARD ROBERT, artist, photographer; b. St. Paul, Dec. 16, 1930; s. Herbert Lenard and Elfreida Wilhelmena Elizabeth (Rubbert) V.; m. Velma Martin, Feb. l0, l951; children: Mark David, Lori Lynn. BA, Hamline U., l957; MA, Ariz. State U., l968; postgrad., U. Minn., 1970-85. Screen print rsch. developer 3M Co., St. Paul, l948-5l; tchr. art ESL, St. Paul Pub. Schs., l957-87; corp. product analyst, treas. Gateway Labs., Golden Valley, Minn., 1975-78; owner, photographer, artist Remember Art and Photog. Svcs., White Bear Lake, l980—; owner, photographer, artist, writer Image Concepts, Florence, Ariz. Creator, co-presenter TV program Crafts in Edn., Sta. KTCA-TV, St. Paul, l959. Author, illustrator: Chipmunk Children's Book, 1995. Chmn. White Bear Arts Coun., l975-80; bd. dirs. Florence Gardens Mobile Home Assn. Sgt. USAF, l95l-52. Nat. Experienced Tchrs. Art fellow, l967-68. Mem. Nat. Art Edn. Assn., St. Paul Fedn. Tchrs. Democrat-Farmer-Labor Party. Lutheran. Avocations: nature, hiking, woodworking, collecting stamps. E-mail: hofmiler@casagrande.com.

VOLZ, WILLIAM HARRY, law educator, administrator; b. Sandusky, Mich., Dec. 28, 1946; s. Harry Bender and Belva Geneva (Riehl) V. BA, Mich. State U., 1968; MA, U. Mich., 1972; MBA, Harvard U., 1978; JD, Wayne State U., 1975. Bar: mich. 1975. Atty. pvt. practice, Detroit, 1975-77; mgmt. analyst Office of Gen. Counsel, HEW, Woodlawn, Md., 1977; from asst. to dean Wayne State U., Detroit, 1978—86, dean, 1986—95; dir. Ctr. for Legal Studies Wayne State U. Law Sch., 1996-97. Cons. Merrill Lynch, Pierce, Fenner & Smith, N.Y.C., 1980-93, City of Detroit Law Dept., 1982, Mich. Supreme Ct., Detroit, 1981; ptnr. Mich. CPA Rev., Southfield, 1983-85; expert witness in product liability, comml. law and bus. ethics; pres. Wedgewood Group. Author: Managing a Trial, 1982; contbr. articles to legal jours.; mem. editl. bds. of bus. and law jours. Internat. adv. bd. Inst. Mgmt., I. L'viv, Ukraine, Legal counsel Free Legal Aid Clinic, Inc., Detroitm 1976—, Shared Ministries, Detroit, 1981, Sino-Am. Tech. Exch. coun., China, 1982; chair advt. rev. panel BBB, Detroit, 1988-90; pres. Mich. Acad. Sci., Arts and Letters, 1995-96, 98-2000, bd. dirs.; pres. Common Ground, PLAYERS; bd. dirs. Greater Detroit Alliance Bus., Olde Custodian Fund. Mem.: ABA, The Wedgewood Group (pres.), Players, Amateur Medicant Soc. (commissionaire 1981—85), Harvard Bus. Sch. Club Detroitm, Econ. Club Detroit, Detroit Athletic Club, Beta Alpha Psu, Alpha Kappa Psi, Golden Key. Mem. Reorganized LDS Ch. Home: 3846 Wedgewood Dr Bloomfield Hills MI 48301-3949 Office: Wayne State U Sch Bus Adminstrn Cass Ave Detroit MI 48202 E-mail: w.h.volz@wayne.edu.

VON BERNUTH, CARL W. lawyer, diversified corporation executive; b. Feb. 2, 1944; BA, Yale U., 1966, LLB, 1969. Bar: N.Y. 1970, Pa. 1990. Corp. atty. White & Case, 1969-80; assoc. gen. counsel Union Pacific Corp., N.Y.C., 1980-83, dep. gen. counsel fin. and adminstrn., 1984-88, v.p., gen. counsel Bethlehem, Pa., 1988-91, sr. v.p., gen. counsel, 1991-97, sr. v.p., gen. counsel and sec. Omaha, 1997—. Mem. Am. Corp. Counsel Assn., Practicing Law Inst. Office: Union Pacific Corp 1416 Dodge St Rm 1230 Omaha NE 68179-0001

VON BERNUTH, ROBERT DEAN, agricultural engineering educator, consultant; b. Del Norte, Colo., Apr. 14, 1946; s. John Daniel and Bernice H. (Dunlap) von B.; m. Judy M. Wehrman, Dec. 27, 1969; children: Jeanie, Suzie BSE, Colo. State U., 1968; MS, U. Idaho, 1970; MBA, Claremont (Calif.) Grad. Sch., 1980; PhD in Engring., U. Nebr., 1982. Registered profl. engr., Calif., Nebr. Agrl. product mgr. Rain Bird Sprinkler Mfg., Glendora, Calif., 1974-80; instr. agrl. engring. U. Nebr., Lincoln, 1980-82; from assoc. prof. to prof. U. Tenn., Knoxville, 1982-90; prof. Mich. State U., East Lansing, 1990—, chmn., 1992-96. V.p. Von-Sol Cons., Lincoln, 1980-82; prin. Von Bernuth Agrl. cons., Knoxville, East Lansing, 1982—. Patentee in field. With USNR, 1970-95, Vietnam. Decorated DFC (2); recipient Disting. Naval Grad. award USN Flight Program, Pensacola, Fla., 1970. Fellow Am. Soc. Agrl. Engrs.; mem. ASCE, Irrigation Assn. (Person of Yr. 1994), Naval Res. Assn. Avocations: flying, skiing, antique tractors. Office: Mich State U Dept Agrl Engring 213 Farrall Hall East Lansing MI 48824-1323

VON FURSTENBERG, GEORGE MICHAEL, economics educator, researcher; b. Germany, Dec. 3, 1941; came to U.S., 1961; s. Kaspar Freiherr and Elisabeth Freifrau (von Boeselager) von F.; m. Gabrielle M. Freiin Koblitz von Willmburg, June 9, 1967; 1 child, Philip G. Ph.D., Princeton U., 1967. Asst. prof. econs. Cornell U., Ithaca, N.Y., 1966-70; assoc. prof. econs. Ind. U., Bloomington, 1970-73, prof., 1976-78, Rudy prof. econs., 1983-2000; Robert Bendheim prof. econ. and financial policy Fordham U., N.Y.C., 2000—; sr. staff economist Council Econ. Advisors, Washington, 1973-76; div. chief research dept. IMF, 1978-83. Project dir. Am. Coun. Life Ins., Washington, 1976-78; sr. advisor Brookings Instn., Washington, 1978-90; vis. sr. economist planning and analysis staff Dept. State, Washington 1989-90; Bissell-Fulbright vis. prof. Can.-Am. rels. U. Toronto, 1994-95. Contbg. author, editor: The Government and Capital Formation, 1980, Capital, Efficiency and Growth, 1980, Acting Under Uncertainty: Multidisciplinary Conceptions, 1990, Regulation and Supervision of Financial Institutions in the NAFTA Countries and Beyond, 1997; editor: International Money and Credit: The Policy Roles, 1983; co-author: Learning from the World's Best Central Bankers, 1998; assoc. editor Rev. of Econs. and Stats., 1987-92, Open Econs. Rev., 1997—; contbr. articles to profl. jours. Fulbright grantee to Poland, 1991-92. Mem. N.Am. Econs. and Fin. Assn. (pres. 2000), Am. Econ. Assn. Roman Catholic Avocations: tennis, sailing. Office: Indiana U Dept Economics Wylie Hall Bloomington IN 47405

VONK, HANS, conductor; b. Amsterdam, The Netherlands, June 18, 1942; s. Frans Vonk; m. Jessie Folkerts. Degree in Music, Ignatius Coll., Amsterdam; Degree in Law, City U., Amsterdam, 1964; trained with Franco Ferrara, 1964-66. Condr. Nat. Ballet, Amsterdam, 1966-69; asst. condr. Concertgebouw Orch., 1969-73; condr. Radio Philharm. Orch., Hilversum, The Netherlands, 1973-79; chief condr. Netherlands Opera, Amsterdam, 1976-85, Residentie Orkestra, Den Haag, 1980-91, Staatskapelle, Dresden, Germany, 1985-90; assoc. condr. Royal Philharmonie, London, 1976-79; chief condr. Radio Symphonie Orch., Cologne, Germany, 1991-97; music dir., condr. St. Louis Symphony, 1996—. Prin. guest condr. Netherlands Radio Philharm.; guest condr. l'Orchestre Nat. de France, Oslo Philharmonic, London Symphony, Norddeutsche Rundfunk, London Philharmonic, English Chamber Orch., Phila. Orch., Minn. Orch., Nat. Symphony Orch., Detroit Orch., Montreal Orch., Dallas Orch., Seattle Orch., Cleve. Orch., Boston Symphony Orch., Pitts. Orch., San Francisco Orch., Houston Orch., Balt. Orch., Mostly Mozart Festival Orch.; opera condr. La Scala, Rome, 1980, 88, Netherlands Opera, Dresden State Opera. Recs.: (with Christian Zacharias) 5 Beethoven piano concertos, Mozart overtures, The Nutcracker (Tchaikovsky), Der Rosenkavalier, Schumann symphonies and concertos, Bruckner Symphonies 4 and 6. Office: St Louis Symphony Orch Powell Symphony Hall 718 N Grand Blvd Saint Louis MO 63103-1011 also: care IMG Artists North AM 22 E 71st St New York NY 10021-4975

VON LEHMAN, JOHN, financial executive; BA, U. Dayton. CPA. Acct. Deloitte, Haskins & Sells; v.p., treas., chief acctg. officer The Midland Co., 1980-88, v.p., treas., CFO, 1988—. Address: 7000 Midland Blvd Amelia OH 45102-2608

VON MEHREN, GEORGE M. lawyer; b. Boston, Nov. 2, 1950; s. Arthur Taylor and Joan Elizabeth (Moore) von M.; children: Paige Elizabeth, Reed Carl. AB, Harvard U., 1972, JD, 1977; BA, Cambridge U., Eng., 1974, MA, 1985. Bar: Ohio 1977. Assoc. Squire, Sanders & Dempsey, Cleve., 1977-86, ptnr., 1986—, mem. mgmt. com., 1990-93, co-chmn. internat. litig. practice group, 1998—. Mem. adv. com. U.S. Dist. Ct. (no. dist.) Ohio, 1991-95; del. 59th Conf. of the Sixth Jud. Cir. of the U.S. Co-author: Non-US Firms, How to Enforce Your Foreign Trade Secrets in the US, United States Ligigation Yearbook, 1999; editor: Harvard Law Rev., 1975-77. Trustee Rainbow Children's Mus., 1998—2001, Beck Ctr. for the Arts, 1999—2001. Mem.: Union Club. Office: Squire Sanders & Dempsey 127 Public Sq Ste 4900 Cleveland OH 44114-1304

VON RECUM, ANDREAS F. veterinarian, bioengineer; b. Dillingen, Bavaria, Germany, July 5, 1939; came to U.S., 1971; s. Bogdan Freiherr and Ilse Freifrau (von Rosenberg) von R.; m. Grudrun F. Bredenbröker-Hardt, Oct. 2, 1965; children: Derik F., Vera F., Uta F., Horst F., Thomas F., Elsa F. BS, U. Giessen, 1965; DVM, Free U. Berlin, 1968, PhD, 1969; PhD in Vet. Surgery, Colo. State U., 1974. Practitioner farm animal medicine and surgery, Meitingen, Germany, 1968-69; clin. staff small animal clinic Free U. Berlin (Germany), Coll. Vet. Medicine, 1969-72; rsch. asst. surg. lab. Colo. State U., Coll. Vet. Medicine, Ft. Collins, 1972-74; dir. surg. rsch. lab. Sinai Hosp. Detroit, 1975-77; prof. dept. bioengring. Clemson (S.C.) U., 1978-93, head dept. bioengring., 1982-93; chmn. bioengring. alliance S.C. Coll. Engring., Clemson U., 1984-88; scientific staff Shriners Hosp., Greenville, S.C., 1989-95; prof. Hunter endowed chair bioengring. Clemson U. Coll. Engring., 1993-97; assoc. dean rsch., prof. Ohio State U., Columbus, 1997—. Mem. coll. exec. com. Coll. Vet. Medicine, Free U., Berlin, 1970-71; adj. assoc. prof. comparative surgery Wayne State U. Sch. Medicine, Dept. Comparative Medicine, 1975-77; adj. prof. surgery U. S.C. Sch. Medicine, 1984—, Med. U. S.C., 1987-97; adj. prof. biomaterials Coll. Dentistry, U. Nijmegen, 1993—; chair internat. liaison com. World's Biomaterials Socs., 1996-2000; cons. in field. Editor Jour. Investigative Surg., 1991-97; patentee in field. Recipient Fulbright Scientist award, 1990-91, Alexander von Humboldt Sr. Scientist award, 1990-91; nat. and internat. fellow Biomaterials Sci. and Engring., 1996. Mem. AVMA, Am. Soc. Lab. Animal Practitioners, Blue Ridge Vet. Med. Assn. (pres. 1984), Soc. Biomaterials (asst. editor 1986—, editl. bd. 1983, program chmn. 1990, sec.-treas. 1990-92, pres. 1993-94), Internat. Soc. Artificial Internal Organs, Am. Soc. Artificial Organs, Am. Heart Assn., Acad. Surg. Rsch. (founder 1982, pres. 1982-83, newsletter editor 1982-85), Biomed. Engring. Soc., Am. Soc. Engring. Edn., Assn. Advancement Med. Instrumentation. Presbyterian. Office: Ohio State U Coll Vet Medicine 1900 Coffey Rd Columbus OH 43210-1006 E-mail: vonrecum.1@osu.edu.

VON RHEIN, JOHN RICHARD, music critic, editor; b. Pasadena, Calif., Sept. 10, 1945; s. Hans Walter and Elsa Maryon (Brossmann) von R. AA, Pasadena City Coll., 1965; BA in Eng., UCLA, 1967; BA in Music, Calif. State U., Los Angeles, 1970. Music reviewer Hollywood (Calif.) Citizen-News, 1968-70; music editor and critic, dance critic Akron (Ohio) Beacon Jour., 1971-77; music critic Chgo. Tribune, 1977—; prof. music appreciation Rio Hondo Jr. Coll., Calif., 1970-71. Lectr., TV host, rec. annotator. Author (with Andrew Porter): Bravi; contbr. revs. and articles to , , , , . Music Critics Assn.-Kennedy Center for Performing Arts fellow, 1972, 75; recipient Peter Lisagor award Soc. Profl. Journalists, 1999. Mem. Music Critics Assn. (edn. com., dir. 1988), Ravinia Critics Inst. (dir. 1988). Office: Chgo Tribune Co 435 N Michigan Ave Chicago IL 60611-4066 E-mail: jvonrhein@tribune.com.

VON ROENN, KELVIN ALEXANDER, neurosurgeon; b. Louisville, Dec. 5, 1949; s. Warren George and Catherine Jean (Bauer) Von R.; m. Jamie Hayden, June 24, 1979; children: Erika Marie, Lisa J., Alexander H., Karl G. BS, Xavier U., 1971; MD, U. Ky., 1975. Diplomate Am. Bd. Neurol. Surgery. Instr. neurosurgery Rush-Presbyn. St. Luke's Med. Ctr., Chgo., 1980-83, asst. prof. neurosurgery, 1983—; vice chmn. dept. of neurosurgery Rush-Presbyn. St Luke's Med. Ctr., 2000—; cons. neurosurgery Shriner's Hosp. for Crippled Children, 1988—, attending neurosurgeon, 1990—, dir. neurosurg. resident edn., 1997—; dir. brain tumor clinic Rush Cancer Ctr., 1997—. Lectr. sect. of neurosurgery U. Ill. Coll. Med., 1996, 97, 98, 99, 2000; vol. attending Cook County Hosp., Chgo., 1996; attending neurosurgeon U. Ill., 1997, 98, 99, 2000. Named one of Outstanding Young Men of Am., 1986. Fellow ACS; mem. Congress Neurologic Surgeons, Am. Assn. Neurol. Surgeons, Ill. Neurosurg. Soc. (v.p. 1994-95, pres. 1995-96), Alpha Sigma Nu, Alpha Omega Alpha. Avocations: opera, gardening, fishing. Office: Chgo Inst Neurosurgery and Neurorsch 1725 W Harrison St Ste 1115 Chicago IL 60612-3835

VON TERSCH, LAWRENCE WAYNE, electrical engineering educator, university dean; b. Waverly, Iowa, Mar. 17, 1923; s. Alfred and Martha (Emerson) Von T.; m. LaValle Sills, Dec. 17, 1948; 1 son, Richard George. B.S., Iowa State U., 1943, M.S., 1948, Ph.D., 1953. From instr. to prof. elec. engring. Iowa State U., 1946-56; dir. computer lab. Mich. State U., 1956-83, prof. elec. engring., chmn. dept., 1958-65, assoc. dean engring., 1965-68, dean, 1968-89, dean emeritus, 1989—. Author: (with A. W. Swago) Recurrent Electrical Transients, 1953. Mem. IEEE; mem. Sigma Xi, Tau Beta Pi, Eta Kappa Nu, Phi Kappa Phi, Pi Mu Epsilon Home: 4282 Tacoma Blvd Okemos MI 48864-2734 Office: Michigan State U Coll Engring East Lansing MI 48823 E-mail: vontersc@egr.msu.edu.

VOOGT, JAMES LEONARD, medical educator; b. Grand Rapids, Mich., Feb. 8, 1944; married; 3 children. Student, Calvin Coll., 1962-64; BS in Biological Sci., Mich. Tech. U., 1966; MS in Physiology, Mich. State U., 1968, PhD in Physiology, 1970. Fellow, lectr. dept. physiology U. Calif., San Francisco, 1970-71; asst. prof. dept. physiology and biophysics U. Louisville Sch. Medicine, 1971-77, assoc. prof. dept. physiology and biophysics, 1977; assoc. prof. dept. physiology U. Kans. Sch. Medicine, 1977-82, prof. physiology, 1982—. Assoc. dean rsch. U. Kans. Sch. Medicine, 1982—84, acting chmn. dept. physiology, 1993—2001; vis. prof. Erasmus U., 1985. Mem. editl. bd. Endocrinology, 1984-86, 89-92, Am. Jour. Physiology, 1984-88, Doody's Jour., 1995-98; ad hoc reviewer Neuroendocrinology, Sci., Biology of Reproduction, Life Scis., Jour. Endocrinology, Molecular Cellular Neuroscis., Procs. Soc. Exptl. Biology and Medicine, biochm. endocrinology study sect. NIH, 1992, reproductive endocrinology study sect., 1994-98; reviewer grants NSF; editor sci. procs. Rsch. Week, 1982-83; contbr. over 120 articles to profl. publs., 4 chpts. to books. Grantee NIH, 1972-85, 88—, NSF, 1985-86, 91-94, Ctr. on Aging, 1988, Nat. Inst. Drug Abuse, 1991-93; fellow Japan Soc. Promotion of Sci., 1993; recipient Outstanding Young Alumni award Mich. Tech. Univ., 1974, Honors in Edn., Med. Student Voice, 1990; inducted Mich. Tech. U. Acad. of Scis. and Arts, 2000. Mem. AAAS, Endocrine Soc., Internat. Soc. Neuroendocrinology (charter mem.), Am. Physiol. Soc. (pub. affairs adv. com. 1983-87) Soc. Neuroscis., Phi Kappa Phi, Sigma Xi. Office: Dept Molecular and Integrative Physiology U Kans Med Ctr 3901 Rainbow Blvd Kansas City KS 66160-0001

VOORHEES, HAROLD J., SR. state legislator; s. John and Helena V.; m. Joanne Land; children: Harold Jr., Nancy Baker Voorhees, Karla Vereecken Voorhees. , Grand Rapids (Mich.) Jr. Coll. Councilman-at-large Wyoming (Mich.) City Coun.; mayor Wyoming, Mich.; state rep. Dist. 77 Mich. Ho. of Reps., 1993—; owner, pres. Serv-U-Sweets, Inc., Grandville, Mich., 1996—. Vice chair Local Govt. Com., Mich. Ho. of Reps., 1993—; mem. Ins., Mil. & Vets. Affairs, State Affairs & Transp. Coms., 1993—. V.p. Grandville Srs. Housing Facility, 1996—. Mem. Rotary Club. Home: 5380 Kenowa Ave SW Grandville MI 49418-9507

VOORHEES, JOHN JAMES, dermatologist, department chairman; B.S., Bowling Green U., 1959; M.D., U. Mich., 1963. Intern U. Mich., 1963-64, resident in dermatology, 1966-69, asso. prof. dermatology, 1972-74, prof., 1974—; chief dermatology service Univ. Hosp., Ann Arbor, 1975; chmn. dept. dermatology U. Mich., 1975—. Contbr. articles to profl. jours., chpts. in books. Recipient Taub Internat. Meml. award for psoriasis research, 1973, 86, Henry Russel award U. Mich., 1973; Herzog fellow Am. Dermatol. Assn., 1968-70 Mem. Am. Soc. Clin. Investigation, Am. Soc. Pharmacology and Exptl. Therapeutics, Am. Assn. Pathologists, Central Soc. Clin. Research, Soc. Investigative Dermatology, Dermatology Found., Skin Pharmacol. Soc., Assn. Profs. Dermatology, Am. Soc. Cell Biology, Am. Acad. Dermatology, Am. Dermatol. Assn., Alpha Omega Alpha. Office: U Mich Med Ctr Dept Dermatology 1910 Taubman Health Care Ctr Ann Arbor MI 48109

VORA, MANU KISHANDAS, chemical engineer, quality consultant; b. Bombay, India, Oct. 31, 1945; s. Kishandas Narandas and Shantaben K. (Valia) V., m. Nila Narotamdas Kothari, June 16, 1974; children: Ashish, Anand. BSChemE, Banaras (India) Hindu U., 1968; MSChemE, Ill. Inst. Tech., Chgo., 1970, PhD in ChemE, 1975; MBA, Keller Grad. Sch. Mgmt., Chgo., 1985. Grad. asst. Ill. Inst. Tech., 1969-74; rsch. assoc. Inst. Gas Tech., Chgo., 1976-77, chem. engr., 1977-79, engring. supr., 1979-82; mem. tech. staff AT&T Bell Labs. (now Lucent Techs.), Holmdel, N.J., 1983-84, Naperville, Ill., 1984—; mgr. customer satisfaction, 1990-96, voice of the customer mgr., 1997-2000; pres., CEO Bus. Excellence, Inc., 2000—. Adj. faculty mem. Ill. Inst. Tech., Chgo., part-time, 1993—; spkr. in field. Invited editor Internat. Petroleum Encyclopedia, 1980. Chmn. Save the Children Holiday Fund Drive, 1986-99; trustee Avery Coonley Sch., Downers Grove, Ill., 1987-91; pres., dir. Blind Found. for India, Naperville, 1989—. Recipient Non-Supervisory AA award Affirmative Actions Adv. Com., 1987, 92, 97, Outstanding Contbn. award Asian Am. for Affirmative Actions, 1989, Disting. Svc. award Save the Children, 1990, Ann. Merit award Chgo. Assn. Tech. Socs., 1992. Fellow Am. Soc. Quality Control (standing rev. bd. 1988—, editl. re. bd. 1989, tech. media com. 1989, mixed media rev. bd. 1994, nat. quality month regional planning com. 1989-94, nat. cert. com. 1989-94, chmn. cert. process improvements subcom. 1990-94, testimonial awards 1995, 96, 2001, 02, exec. bd. Chgo. sect., vice chmn. sect. affairs 1993-94, sect. chmn. 1994-95, nat. dir. at large, 1996-98, nat. dir. 1998-2000, v.p. 2000-2002, vice chmn. investing in quality capital campaign, spl. award 1991, Century Club award 1992, Founders' award 1993, Joe Lisy Quality award 1994, Grant medal 2001); mem. Ill. Team Excellence award (chief judge 1993-99, steering com. 1993-99, award). Hindu. Avocations: reading, photography, travel, philanthropic activities. Home: 1256 Hamilton Ln Naperville IL 60540-8373 Office: Bus Excellence Inc PO Box 5585 Naperville IL 60567-5585 E-mail: manuvora@b-einc.com.

VORAN, JOEL BRUCE, lawyer; b. Kingman, Kans., Mar. 24, 1952; s. Bruce H. and Venora M. (Layman) V.; m. Marsha A. Kooser, May 26, 1979; children: Erica, Ben, Ashley. BA, U. Kans., 1974; JD, U. Tex., 1977. Bar: Mo. 1977, U.S. Dist. Ct. (we. dist.) Mo. 1977, U.S. Tax Ct. 1986. From assoc. to ptnr. Lathrop & Gage L.C., Kansas City, Mo., 1977—. Adv. dir. Mark Twain Bank, Kansas City, 1985-89. Bd. dirs. Kansas City YMCA, 1979—; city chmn. Prairie Village (Kans.) Rep. Party, 1985-88; participant Kansas City Tomorrow Project, 1989-90. Mem. ABA, Mo. Bar Assn., Kansas City Met. Bar Assn., Kansas City Lawyers Assn., Delta Tau Delta (bd. dirs., pres. 1977-87; alumni pres. Kansas City chpt. 1989-90), Friends of Art Club. Republican. Roman Catholic. Avocations: tennis, golf, jogging. Home: 2949 W 118th Ter Leawood KS 66211-3047 Office: Lathrop & Gage LC 2345 Grand Blvd Ste 2400 Kansas City MO 64108-2642

VORHOLT, JEFFREY JOSEPH, lawyer, software company executive; b. Cin., Feb. 20, 1953; s. Edward C. and Rita L. (Kinross) V.; m. Marcia Anne Meyer, Apr. 30, 1976; children: Kimberly Anne, Gregory Michael, Karen Michelle. BBA cum laude, U. Cin., 1976; MBA, Xavier U., Cin., 1978; JD, Chase Law Sch., 1983. Bar: Ohio, 1983; CPA, Ohio. Sec., treas. Cin. Bell Info. Systems, Inc., 1983-84, v.p., chief fin. officer, 1984-88, also bd. dirs.; v.p., controller Cin. Bell, Inc., 1988-89; sr. v.p. Cin. Bell Info. Systems, Inc., 1989-91, Cin. Bell Telephone Co., 1991-93; CFO Structural Dynamics Rsch. Corp., Milford, Ohio, 1994—. Voting mem. Cin. Playhouse, 1986—; mem. fin. planning com. ARC, Cin., 1986-89; trustee U. Health Maintenance Orgn., Inc., 1990-93, St. Joseph Infant and Maternity Home, Inc. Mem. ABA, AICPAs, Ohio Bar Assn., Aircraft Owners and Pilots Assn., Cin. Hist. Soc., Bankers Club of Cin. (bd. govs. 1990-97). Avocations: golf, tennis, hiking, photography, running. Office: Structural Dynamics Rsch Corp 2000 Eastman Dr Milford OH 45150-2712 E-mail: jeff.vorholt@sdrc.com.

VORYS, ARTHUR ISAIAH, lawyer; b. Columbus, Ohio, June 16, 1923; s. Webb Isaiah and Adeline (Werner) V.; m. Lucia Rogers, July 16, 1949 (div. 1980); children: Caroline S., Adeline Vorys Cranson, Lucy Vorys Noll, Webb I.; m. Ann Harris, Dec. 13, 1980. BA, Williams Coll., 1945; LLB, JD, Ohio State U., 1949. Bar: Ohio 1949. From assoc. to ptnr. Vorys, Sater, Seymour & Pease LLP, Columbus, 1949-82, sr. ptnr., 1982-93, of counsel, 1993—. Supt. ins. State of Ohio, 1957-59; bd. dirs Vorys Bros., Inc., others. Trustee, past pres. Children's Hosp., Greenlawn Cemetery Found.; trustee, former chmn. Ohio State U. Hosps.; regent Capital U.; del. Rep. Nat. Conv., 1968, 72. Lt. USMCR, World War II. Decorated Purple Heart. Fellow Ohio State Bar, Columbus Bar Assn.; mem. ABA, Am. Judicature Soc., Rocky Fork Headley Hunt Club, Rocky Fork Hunt and Country Club, Capital Club, Phi Delta Phi, Chi Psi. Home: 5826 Havens Corners Rd Columbus OH 43230-3142 Office: Vorys Sater Seymour & Pease LLP PO Box 1008 52 E Gay St Columbus OH 43216-1008

VOSS, ANNE COBLE, nutritional biochemist; b. Richmond, Ind., Aug. 22, 1946; d. James Richard and Helen Lucille (Hoyt) Coble; m. Harold Lloyd Voss, July 20, 1969; children: Daniel, Jordan Matthew, Sarah Georgette. BS, Ohio State U., 1968, PhD, 1984. Registered dietitian. Therapeutic dietitian Johns Hopkins Hosp., Balt., 1968-69; clin. instr. Ohio State U. Hosps., Columbus, 1969-70; clin. dietitian U.S. Army Med. Clinic, Rothwesten, Fed. Republic Germany, 1970-72; clin. rsch. monitor Ross Labs., Columbus, 1978-79; rsch. asst. Ohio State U., 1979-84, rsch. assoc., lectr., 1985-91; mgr. outcomes rsch. Ross Products divsn. Abbott Labs., Ohio, 1992—. Adj. asst. prof. Otterbein Coll., Westerville, Ohio, 1990-93; nutrition advisor Ohio Dental Assn., Columbus, 1977-93, ADA, Chgo., 1987-93; cons. Ohio Bd. Dietetics, Columbus, 1989-93; vis. scientist Rikshospitalet, Oslo, Norway, 1992. Author: Polyunsaturated Fatty Acids and Eicosanoids, 1987; author, editor: Nutrition Perspectives, 1990, 91, 2d edit., 1993; contbr. articles to profl. jours. Mem. exec. bd. Aux. to Ohio Dental Assn., Columbus, 1979-95; bd. dirs. Ohio Dental Polit. Action Com., Columbus, 1989-92, YWCA, Columbus, 1990-93; Gov.'s appointee, chmn. Ohio Bd. Dietetics. Recipient award Clement Found., Westerville, 1991, Disting. Alumni award Ohio State U., 1996; Nutrition Edn. in Tng. grant Ohio Dept. Edn., Columbus, 1978. Mem. Am. Dietetic Assn., Ohio Dietetic Assn., Med. Dietetics Assn. (founding mem., pres., v.p., sec. 1978—), Ohio Coun. Against Health Fraud (founding mem., bd. govs. 1987—), Ohio Nutrition Coun. (exec. bd. 1987-94), Columbus Dietetic Assn., Sigma Xi, Sigma Delta Epsilon (sec. 1985—). Methodist. Avocations: gardening, cooking, sewing, skiing. Home: 1526 Bridgeton Dr Columbus OH 43220-3908 Office: Abbott Labs Ross Products Divsn 625 Cleveland Ave Columbus OH 43215-1754

VOSS, EDWARD WILLIAM, JR. immunologist, educator; b. Chgo., Dec. 2, 1933; s. Edward William and Lois Wilma (Graham) V.; m. Virginia Hellman, June 15, 1974; children: Cathleen, Valerie. A.B., Cornell Coll., Iowa, 1955; M.S., Ind. U., 1964, Ph.D., 1966. Asst. prof. microbiology U. Ill., Urbana, 1967-71, assoc. prof., 1971-74, prof., 1974-98, prof. emeritus, 1999—, adj. prof. dept. vet. pathobiology, 2001—, dir. cell sci. ctr., 1988-94, Coll. Liberal Arts and Scis. Jubilee prof., 1990. Rev. panel on molecular biology-gene structure USDA, Washington, 1985-86, U.S. Dept. Energy Rsch., 1994; panel mem. in biol. scis. NSF Minority Grad. Fellowships, Washington, 1986-88; sci. adv. bd. Biotech. Rsch. and Devel. Corp., 1989—; mem. Peer Review Com. AHA, 1993-96; study sect. innovation grant program for approaches in HIV vaccine rsch. NIH, 1997; adj. prof. U. Hawaii, Manoa, 1999-2001, Coll. Vet. Medicine, 2001-. Author, editor: Fluorescein Hapten: An Immunological Probe, 1984, Anti-DNA Antibodies in SLE, 1988; adv. editor: Immunochemistry, 1975-78, Molecular Immunology, 1980— ; mem. editorial bd.: Applied and Environ. Microbiology, 1979— ; contbr. articles to profl. jours. Apptd. to pres.'s coun. U. Ill. Found., 1995. Served with U.S. Army, 1956-58. NIH fellow, 1966-67, NSF fellow, 1975-77; NIH grantee, 1967—, NSF grantee, 1967—; recipient Disting. Lectr. award U. Ill., 1983; named 1st James R. Martin Univ. scholar, 1994; recipient Exemplary Contbn. award Lupus Found. Am., 1994. Ednl. Aid award E.I. DuPont, 1994, 95. Fellow Am. Inst. Chemists; mem. AAAS, Fedn. Am. Scientists, Am. Assn. Immunologists, Am. Assn. Biol. Chemists, Reticuloendothelial Soc., Am. Lupus Soc. (hon. bd. dirs. Cen. Ill. chpt. 1986—, named to Nat. Lupus Hall of Fame 1988, Cmty. Svc. award 1996), N.Y. Acad. Scis., U.S. Pharmacopeial Conv., Inc., Nat. Geog. Soc., Am. Chem. Soc. (tour speaker 1984-87), Protein Soc., Sigma Xi. Home: 2207 Boudreau Cir Urbana IL 61801-6601 Office: U Ill Dept Microbiology B103 Chem Life Sci Bldg 601 S Goodwin Ave Urbana IL 61801 E-mail: e-voss1@life.uiuc.edu.

VOSS, JACK DONALD, international business consultant, lawyer; b. Stoughton, Wis., Sept. 24, 1921; s. George C. and Grace (Tusler) V.; m. Mary Josephine Edgarton, May 7, 1955; children: Julia, Jennifer, Andrew, Charles. Ph.B., U. Wis., 1943; J.D., Harvard U., 1948. Bar: Ill. 1949, Ohio 1963. From assoc. to ptnr. Sidney & Austin predecessor firm, Chgo., 1948-62; gen. counsel Anchor Hocking Corp., Lancaster, Ohio, 1962-67, v.p., gen. counsel, 1967-72, gen. mgr. internat., 1970-86; pres. Anchor Hocking Internat. Corp., 1972-86; mng. ptnr. Voss Internat., 1986—. Chmn. Internat. Coun. Conf. bd., 1985-87. Mem. Fairfield County Rep. Ctrl. and Exec. Com.; pres. Fairfield Heritage Assn., 1966-69; v.p. Lancaster Community Concert Assn., 1965-73; trustee, chmn. Ohio Info. Com. With USNR, 1943-46, ATO, MTO, PTO. Mem. ABA (internat. law & practice and bus. law sects.), Ohio Bar Assn. (chmn. corp. counsel sect. 1966), Columbus Bar Assn., Chgo. Bar Assn., Fairfield County Bar Assn., Licensing Execs. Soc., Am. Arbitration Assn. (panel mem.), Ctr. for Internat. Comml. Arbitration (panel mem.), Harvard Law Sch. Assn., Ohio Mfrs. Assn. (trustee, v.p. 1970-72), Symposiarch, Alpha Chi Rho. Lutheran. Clubs: Rotary (pres. Lancaster 1968), Racquet (Chgo.); Landsdowne (London). Home: PO Box 0624 Lancaster OH 43130-0624 Office: Voss Internat 212 S Broad St Lancaster OH 43130-4381

VOSS, JERROLD RICHARD, city planner, educator, university official; b. Chgo., Nov. 4, 1932; s. Peter Walter and Annis Lorraine (Hayes) V.; m. Jean Evelyn Peterson, Aug. 21, 1954; children— Cynthia Jean, Tania Hayes. B.Arch., Cornell U., 1955; M. City Planning, Harvard U., 1959; Ph.D. (Bus. History fellow, Univ. fellow, IBM fellow), 1971. Asst. prof. U. Calif., 1960-61; asst. prof., asso. prof. U. Ill., 1961-69; asso. prof. Harvard U., 1969-71; prof. city and regional planning Ohio State U., Columbus, 1971—, chmn. dept. city and regional planning, 1971-79; dir. Ohio State U. (Knowlton Sch. Architecture), 1981-96, prof., 1996-2000, dir., prof. emeritus, 2000—. UN advisor to Govt. Indonesia, 1964-65; social affairs officer UN Secretariat, 1970-71; project mgr. UN Task Force on Human Environment, Thailand, 1975-76; dir. rsch. and devel. UN Ctr. for Human Settlements (Habitat), 1979-81; cons. Ill. Dept. Devel., J.S. Bolles & Assocs., UN Office Tech. Cooperation, UN Devel. Program, AID, Bechtel Nat. Inc., other pvt. and pub. orgns.; mem. external examiners team United Arab U., 1992—. Author: Human Settlements: Problems and Priorities; Contbr. articles to profl. jours. Mem. pub. policy com. Smithsonian Instn., 1970-73; bd. dirs. Champaign County United Community Council, 1965-69, Columbus Theatre Ballet Assn., 1972-75. Served to 1st lt. U.S. Army, 1955-57. Mem. Acad. for Contemporary Problems (asso.), Am. Am. Inst. Planners, Am. Soc. Engring. Edn., Internat. Center for Urban Land Policy (London). Office: 190 W 17th Ave Columbus OH 43210-1320

VOSS, REGIS DALE, agronomist, educator; b. Cedar Rapids, Iowa, Jan. 4, 1931; s. Francis Joseph and Mary Valeria (Womichil) V.; m. Margaret Anne Mitchell, Nov. 24, 1956; children: Lori Anne, John Patrick, David James. BS, Iowa State U., 1952, PhD, 1962. cert. profl. agronomist. Agriculturist Tenn. Valley Authority, Muscle Shoals, Ala., 1962-64; prof. Iowa State U., Ames, 1964-99, prof. emeritus, 1999—. Co-contbr. chpt. to: Fertilizer Technology and Use, 1985, Soil Testing and Plant Analysis, 1990; assoc. editor Jour. Prodn. Agr., 1988-92. Pres. FarmHouse Frat. Alumni Assn. Bd., Ames, 1990. 1st lt. USAF, 1952-56, Korea. Recipient Burlington No. Found. award Iowa State U., 1990, disting. svc. award Iowa State U. Ext., 1996, Iowa Master Farmer Exceptional Svc. award, 1998. Fellow AAAS, Am. Soc. Agronomy (bd. dirs. 1976-78, Agronomic Extension Edn. award 1984, Agronomic Achievement award 1989, Werner L. Nelson award 1992), Soil Sci. Soc. Am. (bd. dirs. 1980-83). Republican. Roman Catholic. Achievements include development of field laboratory for training of crop advisors on diagnosis of crop problems; research on effects of soil amendments on chemical indices and crop yields and economic analysis of crop yield. Office: Iowa State Univ Agronomy Hl Ames IA 50011-0001

VOSS, THOMAS, customer services executive; Sr. v.p. customer svcs. Ameren Corp., St. Louis, 1999—. Office: Ameren Corp One Ameren Plaza 1901 Chouteau Ave Saint Louis MO 63103-3003 Fax: 314-554-3066.

VOWELL, J. LARRY, food equipment manufacturer; With Hussmann Internat., Inc., Bridgeton, Mo., 1959-90, pres., COO, 1990—. Office: Hussmann Internat Inc 12999 Saint Charles Rock Rd Bridgeton MO 63044

VRABLIK, EDWARD ROBERT, import/export company executive; b. Chgo., June 8, 1932; s. Steven Martin and Meri (Korbel) V.; m. Bernice G. Germer, Jan. 25, 1958; children: Edward Robert, II, Scott S. B.S. in Chem. Engring, Northwestern U., 1956; M.B.A., U. Chgo., 1961; postgrad., MIT, 1970. Registered profl. engr., Ill. Dir. indsl. mktg. Eimco Corp., 1956-61; dir. indsl. mktg. and planning Swift & Co., Chgo., 1961-68; v.p., gen. mgr. Swift Chem. Co., 1968-73; pres., chief exec. officer Estech Gen. Chems. Corp., 1973-86; pres. Kare Internat. Inc., 1986—. Pres. Julius and Assocs., Inc., Kare Internat., Inc.; bd dirs. Potash Phosphate Inst., Consol. Fertilizers, Ltd.; mem. mgmt. com. Esmark Inc., Korbel, Inc., Mister Lawn Care, Inc. Author; patentee in field. Bd. dirs., v.p. Northwestern U. Tech. Inst.; trustee Future Farmers Am. Mem. Internat. Superphosphate Mfrs. Assn. (dir.), Am. Inst. Chem. Engrs., Fertilizer Inst. (dir.) Lutheran. Clubs: Butler Nat. (Oak Brook, Ill.). Home: 631 Thompsons Way Palatine IL 60067-4653 Office: 141 W Jackson Blvd Chicago IL 60604-2992

VRAKAS, DANIEL PAUL, state legislator; b. Waukesha, Wis., Oct. 31, 1955; BA, U. Wis., Stevens Point, 1979. Wis. state assemblyman dist. 33, 1990—; chmn. Rep. Caucus. Former restaurant owner. Mem. Am. Cancer Soc.; v.p. connection bd. dirs. Waukesha County Mediation Ctr.; bd. dirs. Waukesha and Washington County Rep. Party. Named Friend of Agr., Wis. Farm Bur., 1992—, Champion of Commerce, Milw. Met. Area C. of C., 1992. Mem. Hartland, Waukesha and Delafield C. of C., Lake Country Rotary. Address: N45w28912 E Capitol Dr Hartland WI 53029-2250

VRANA, VERLON KENNETH, retired professional society administrator, conservationist; b. Seward, Nebr., June 25, 1925; s. Anton and Florence (Walker) V.; m. Elaine Janet Flowerday, June 5, 1949; children: Verlon Rodney, Timothy James, Carolyn Elaine, Jon David. Student, U. Nebr., 1959-62; BBA, George Washington U., 1967, MBA, 1970; mgmt. course, Harvard U., 1979. Field technician Soil Conservation Svc., USDA, Seward, 1948-58, watershed planner, cons. Lincoln, Nebr., 1958-62, mem. pers. staff Washington, 1962-72, dir. pers. div., 1972-76, asst. adminstr. for mgmt., 1976-79, assoc. dep. chief for adminstrn., 1979-80; chief planning div. Nebr. Natural Resources Com., Lincoln, 1980-88; owner-farmer Blue Ridge Farm, Seward, 1980-89; exec. v.p. Soil and Water Conservation Soc., Ankeny, Iowa, 1989-91; pres. Vrana Assocs., Seward, Nebr., 1992—. Bd. dirs., sec. N.E. Natural Resources Dist., York, Nebr., 1988-89; bd. dirs. Cattle Nat. Bank and Trust, Seward; alt. dir. Renewable Natural Resources Foun., Washington, 1989-91. Contbr. articles to jours. in field. Mem. Com. on Ministry Presbyn. Ch. U.S.A., 1986-89, elder, 1970—; vice moderator Homestead Presbytery, 1989; treas. Nebr. Soil and Water Conservation Found., 1992-97; mem. Seward City Coun., 1998—. Recipient N.E. Centennial Grass Seeding award N.E. Centennial Commn., Lincoln, 1967, N.E. Soil Steward award N.E. Natural Resources Commn., Lincoln, 1986. Fellow Soil and Water Conservation Soc. (pres. N.E. Coun. 1986, Presdl. citation 1989), Isaac Walton League (dir. Seward chpt. 1984-89), Nat. Wildlife Fedn. (soil conservationist of yr. award 1987), Seward Grange (officer 1984-89, 92-99), Shriner, Kiwanis (Disting. Pres. Seward chpt. 1996-97). Home and Office: Vrana Assocs 131 N 1st St Seward NE 68434-2130 E-mail: vv21929@alltel.net.

VRATIL, JOHN LOGAN, state legislator, lawyer; b. Great Bend, Kans., Oct. 28, 1945; s. Frank and Althea (Shuss) V.; m. Kathy Hoefer, June 21, 1971 (div. Dec. 1985); m. Anne Whitfill, Mar. 7, 1986 (div. Dec. 1992); m. Teresa Hobbs, Mar. 15, 1996; children: Alison, Andy, Ashley. BS in Edn., U. Kans., 1967; postgrad., U. Southampton, Eng., 1967-68; JD, U. Kans., 1971; postgrad., U. Exeter, Eng., 1972. Bar: Kans. 1971, U.S. Dist. Ct. Kans. 1971, U.S. Ct. Appeals (10th and 8th cirs.) 1975. From assoc. to ptnr. Bennett, Lytle, Wetzler & Winn, Prairie Village, Kans., 1972-83; with Lathrop & Gage, Overland Park, 1983—; mem. Kans. Senate from 11th dist., Topeka, 1999—. Contbr. articles to profl. jours. Mem. recreation commn. Prairie Village, 1982-83, mem. planning commn., 1983-84; v.p. Usher Mansion Hist. Found., Lawrence, Kans., 1990—. Fellow ABA Found.; mem. ABA, Kans. Bar Assn. (pres. 1995-96, gov. 1988-97), Kans. Bar Found. (trustee 1996-2002), Johnson County Bar Assn. (pres. 1979), Kans. Sch. Attys. Assn. (pres. 1985), Overland Park C. of C. (bd. dirs. 1985-94, pres. 1988). Republican. Avocations: sports, hunting, reading. Office: Lathrop & Gage 10851 Mastin Blvd Ste 1000 Overland Park KS 66210-2007 Address: Kansas Senate State Capitol Rm 120-S Topeka KS 66612 E-mail: jvratil@lathropgage.com., vratil@senate.state.ks.us.

VRATIL, KATHRYN HOEFER, federal judge; b. Manhattan, Kans., Apr. 21, 1949; d. John J. and Kathryn Ruth (Fryer) Hoefer; children: Alison K., John A., Ashley A. BA, U. Kans., 1971, JD, 1975; postgrad., Exeter U., 1971-72. Bar: Kans. 1975, Mo. 1978, U.S. Dist. Ct. Kans. 1975, U.S. Dist. Ct. (we. dist.) Mo. 1978, U.S. Dist. Ct. (ea. dist.) Mo. 1985, U.S. Ct. Appeals (8th cir.) 1978, U.S. Ct. Appeals (10th cir.) 1980, U.S. Ct. Appeals (11th dist.) 1983, U.S. Supreme Ct., 1995. Law clk. U.S. Dist. Ct., Kansas City, Kans., 1975-78; assoc. Lathrop Koontz & Norquist, Mo., 1978-83; ptnr. Lathrop & Norquist, 1984-92; judge City of Prairie Village, Kans., 1990-92. Bd. dirs. Kans. Legal Bd. Svcs., 1991-92. Bd. editors Kans. Law Rev., 1974-75, Jour. Kans. Bar Assn., 1992—. Mem. Kansas City Tomorrow (XIV); bd. trustees, shepherd-deacon Village Presbyn. Ch.; nat. adv. bd. U. Kans. Ctr. for Environ. Edn. and Tng., 1993-95; bd. dirs. Kans. Legal Svcs., 1991-92. Fellow Kans. Bar Foun., Am. Bar Found.; mem. ABA (edtl. bd. Judges Jour. 1996—), Am. Judicature Soc., Nat. Assn. Judges, Fed. Judges Assn., Kans. Bar Assn., Mo. Bar Assn., Kansas City Met. Area Bar Assn., Wyandotte County Bar Assn., Johnson County Bar Assn., Assn. Women Judges, Lawyers Assn. Kansas City, Supreme Ct. Hist. Soc., Kans. State Hist. Soc., U. Kans. Law Soc. (bd. govs. 1978-81), Kans. U. Alumni Assn. (mem. Kansas City chpt. alumni bd. 1990-92, nat.

bd. dirs. 1991-96, bd. govs. Adams Alumni Ctr. 1992-95, mem. chancellor's club 1993—, mem. Williams ednl. fund 1993—, mem. Jayhawks for higher edn. 1993-95), Homestead Country Club Prairie Village (pres. 1985-86), Native Sons and Daus of Kans. (life), Rotary, Jr. League Wyandotte and Johnson Counties, Order of Coif, Kans. Inn of Ct. (master 1993—, pres. 1999-2000), Phi Kappa Phi. Republican. Presbyterian. Avocations: cycling, sailing. Office: 511 US Courthouse 500 State Ave Kansas City KS 66101-2403

VREE, ROGER ALLEN, lawyer; b. Chgo., Oct. 2, 1943; s. Louis Gerard and Ruby June (Boersma) V.; m. Lauren Trumbull Gartside, Mar. 29, 1969; children: Jonathan Todd, Matthew David. BA, Wheaton Coll., 1965; MA, Stanford U., 1966, JD, 1969. Bar: Ill. 1969, U.S. Dist. Ct. (no. dist.) Ill. 1969. Assoc. Sidley & Austin, Chgo., 1969—75; ptnr. Sidley Austin Brown & Wood, 1975—. Mem.: ABA, Univ. Club (Chgo.). Office: Sidley Austin Brown & Wood Bank One Plz 10 South Dearborn Chicago IL 60603-2000 E-mail: rvree@sidley.com.

VROUSTOURIS, ALEXANDER, inspector general; b. Chgo., Apr. 24, 1954; BS, Loyola U., 1977; JD, John Marshall Law Sch., 1980. Bar: Ill. Asst. state atty. Cook County State Atty.'s Office, Chgo., 1980-89; inspector gen. Office of the Inspector Gen. City of Chgo., 1989—. Contbr. articles to profl. jours. Mem. Nat. Assn. Inspector Gens., Ill. Bar Assn. Office: City of Chgo Office of the Inspector Gen PO Box 2996 Chicago IL 60654-2996

VRTISKA, FLOYD P. state legislator; b. Oct. 12, 1926; m. Doris Vrtiska; children: Terri Jo, Lori Ann, Kim R. Grad., Table Rock H.S. Commr., chmn. Pawnee County, Nebr., 1973-92; mem. Nebr. Legislature from 1st dist., Lincoln, 1992—; mem. agr., health and human svc. coms. Nebr. Legislature, vice chmn. bus. and labor com. Recipient Ak-Sar-Ben Agr. Achievement award, Outstanding Cmty. Svc. award Peru State Coll., Ak-Sar-Ben Nebr. Farm Bur. award, Appreciation award Table Rock Devel. Corp., County Ofcl. of Yr. award and Pres.'s award Nebr. Assn. County Ofcls., Spl. Svc. award Table Rock Vol. Fire Dept. Office: Unicameral Legislature State Capitol Rm 350 Lincoln NE 68509

VUKAS, RONALD, publishing executive; Exec. v.p. Inst. Real Estate Mgmt., Chgo., 1990—. Office: Inst Real Estate Mgmt 430 N Michigan Ave Chicago IL 60611-4011

VUKOVICH, JOSEPH JOHN, judge; b. Youngstown, Ohio, Sept. 29, 1945; s. Joseph J. and Josephine (Kurdowski) V.; m. Patricia D. Matthews, 1988 (div.); children: Andrew Joseph, Joseph John. BA, Youngstown State U., 1968; JD, U. Akron, 1973. Bar: Ohio. Asst. atty gen. State of Ohio, 1973-77; dep. dir. law City of Youngstown, Ohio, 1978—; rep. dist. 52 Ohio Ho. Reps., Columbus, 1978-92; senator Ohio State Senate, 1993-97; judge State of Ohio 7th Dist. Ct. Appeals, 1997—. Mem. civil and comml. law commn., 1982-84, Ohio Ho. Reps., chmn. ethics com. 1980-82, 88-92. Mem. Easter Seal Soc. Decorated Bronze star U.S. Army; recipient Meritorious Svc. award Ohio Acad. Trial Lawyers, 1981, 87, Commdrs. award Nat. Amvets 1983, Resolution of Merit, Ohio Prosecuting Attys., 1984, Meritorius Service medal U.S. Selective Svc. System, 1986. Mem. ABA, VFW (Legislator of Yr. Ohio 1982), Ohio State Bar Assn., Mahoning County Bar Assn., Cath. War Vets. Am. (Disting. Legislator Ohio 1988), Ohio Appellate Judges Assn. Office: 7th Dist Ct Appeals Mahoning County Courthouse Youngstown OH 44503

WACHENFELD, TIMOTHY H. aeronautical engineering executive; Gen. mgr. Gen. Electric Aircraft Engines, Cin. Recipient Leadership in Quality Mgmt. award AIAA, 1994. Office: GE Aircraft Engines 1 Neumann Way Cincinnati OH 45215-1915

WACHTMAN, LYNN R. state legislator; m. Trudy Wachtman; children: Cory, Aaron. Student, Four County Joint Vocat. Sch. Plant mgr. Culligan Water Conditioning, Napoleon, Ohio; pres. Maumee Valley Bottlers, Inc.; city councilman City of Napoleon, Ohio; dist. 80 rep. Ohio Ho. of Reps., Columbus, 1985-92, dist. 83 rep., 1993-98; dist. 1 rep. Ohio State Senate, 1998—. Recipient Legislator's award Am. Legion Commdrs. Ohio. Mem. Ohio Right to Life, Gideons Internat., Ohio Farm Bur., Ducks Unlimited. Office: Ohio State Senate Rm 040 Ground Fl Columbus OH 43215

WACHTMANN, LYNN R. state legislator; m. Trudy Blue; children: Cory, Aaron. Grad., Four County Joint Vocat. Sch. Owner, pres. Maumee Valley Bottlers, Inc., Napoleon, Ohio; ptnr. Culligan Water Conditioning; former councilman City of Napoleon; mem. Ho. of Reps., Ohio, 1985—98, Ohio Senate from 1st dist., Columbus, 1999—, chmn. health, human svcs. and aging com., mem. energy, natural resources, environment, highways and transp., ins., commerce and labor coms. Vol. fundraiser Crisis Pregnancy Ctrs. of N.W. Ohio, Bryan; vol. Orphan Grain Train; mem. Rep. Ctrl. Com.; Sunday sch. tchr., usher St. Paul Luth. Ch.; bd. dirs. Ohio Water Quality Assn. Named Nat. Legislator of Yr., Am. Legis. Exch. Coun., 1994, State Legislator of Yr., Nat. Retail Fedn., 1996, Legislator of Yr., Am. Legion; recipient Bobcat Legis. award, 1993, Watchdog of the Treasury award, United Conservatives of Ohio, Oustanding Freshman Legislator of Yr. award, 2000, Grad. Wall of Fame award, Four County Joint Vocat. Sch., 1997, Legislator of Yr. Defender of Life award, Ohio Right to Life, 1997, Conservation Legis. award, League of Ohio Sportsmen Nat. Wildlife Fedn., 1997, Guardian of Small Bus. award, Nat. Fedn. Ind. Bus., 1998. Mem.: NRA, Ohio Twp. Assn., Nat. Assn. Sportsman Legislators, Am. Legis. Exch. Coun. (state chmn.), Ohio Right to Life Soc., Gideon's Internat., Ohio Farm Bur., Pheasants Forever, Ducks Unlimited. Republican. Office: Rm # 040 Senate Bldg Columbus OH 43215

WADDEN, RICHARD ALBERT, environmental engineer, educator, consultant, research director; b. Sioux City, Iowa, Oct. 3, 1936; s. Sylvester Francis and Hermina Lillian (Costello) W.; m. Angela Louise Trabert, Aug. 9, 1975; children: Angela Terese, Noah Albert, Nuiko Clare Student, St. John's U., Collegeville, Minn., 1954-56; B.S. in Chem. Engring., Iowa State U., 1959; M.S. in Chem. Engring, N.C. State U., 1962; Ph.D. in Chem. and Environ. Engring., Northwestern U., 1972. Registered profl. engr., Ill.; cert. indsl. hygienist. Engr. Linde Co., Tonnawanda, N.Y., 1959-60, Humble Oil Co., Houston, 1962-65; instr. engring. Pahlavi U. Peace Corps, Shiraz, Iran, 1965-67; tech. adviser Ill. Pollution Control Bd., Chgo., 1971-72; asst. dir. Environ. Health Resource Ctr. Ill., 1972-74; asst. prof. environ. and occupational health scis. Sch. Pub. Health U. Ill.-Chgo., 1972-75, assoc. prof., 1975-79, prof., 1979—, dir., 1984-86, 88-92; dir. Office Tech. Transfer U. Ill. Ctr. for Solid Waste Mgmt. and Resch., 1987-92; dir. indsl. hygiene and hazardous waste tng. programs Occupl. Safety and Health Ctr., U. Ill.-Chgo., Chgo. Vis. scientist Nat. Inst. Environ. Studies, Japan, 1978-79, invited scientist, 1983, 84, 88; cons. air pollution control, health implications of energy devel., indoor air pollution; vis. scholar dept. civil engring. Northwestern U., Evanston, Ill., 1997. Author: Energy Utilization and Environmental Health, 1978, (with P.A. Scheff) Indoor Air Pollution, 1983, Engineering Design for Control of Workplace Hazards, 1987; contbr. numerous articles to profl. publs. Sr. Internat. fellow Fogarty Internat. Ctr.-NIH, 1978-79, 83; WHO fellow, 1984. Mem. AIChE, Am. Chem. Soc., Am. Acad. Environ. Engrs. (diplomate), Am. Acad. Indsl. Hygiene (diplomate), Air and Waste Mgmt. Assn., Am. Indsl. Hygiene Assn., Am. Conf. Govtl. Indsl. Hygienists. Office: U Ill m/c 922 2121 W Taylor St Chicago IL 60612-7260

WADE, EDWIN LEE, author, lawyer; b. Yonkers, N.Y., Jan. 26, 1932; s. James and Helen Pierce (Kinne) W.; m. Nancy Lou Sells, Mar. 23, 1957; children: James Lee, Jeffrey K. BS, Columbia U., 1954; MA, U. Chgo., 1956; JD, Georgetown U., 1965. Bar: Ill. 1965. Fgn. svc. officer U.S. Dept. State, 1956-57; mktg. analyst Chrysler Internat., S.A., Switzerland, 1957-61; intelligence officer CIA, 1961-63; industry analyst U.S. Internat. Trade Commn., 1963-65; gen. atty. Universal Oil Products Co., Des Plaines, Ill., 1965-72; atty. Amsted Industries, Inc., Chgo., 1972-73; chief counsel dept. gen. svcs. State of Ill., Springfield, 1973-75; sr. atty. U.S. Gypsum Co., Chgo., 1975-84; gen. atty. USG Corp., 1985, corp. counsel, 1986, asst. gen. counsel, 1987, corp. sec., 1987-90, corp. sec., asst. gen. counsel, 1990-93; prin. Edwin L. Wade, 1993-95; instr. Roosevelt U., Chgo., 1995-96. Author: (books) Constitution 2000: A Federalist Proposal for the New Century, 2000, Talking Sense at Century's End: A Barbarous Time...Now What?, 2000; editor: Let's Talk Sense, A Pub. Affairs Newsletter, 1994-98. Fellow Chgo. Bar Assn. (life); mem. ABA, Ill. Bar Assn., Am. Philatelic Soc., Royal Philatelic Soc. Can. Home: 434 Mary Ln Crystal Lake IL 60014-7257 Office: Let's Talk Sense Publishing Co PO Box 6716 Chicago IL 60680-6716 E-mail: edwade@mymailstation.com.

WADE, NIGEL, editor in chief; Editor in chief Chgo. Times. Office: Chgo Sun Times 401 N Wabash Ave Chicago IL 60611-5642

WADSWORTH, MICHAEL A. former athletic director, former ambassador; b. Toronto, ON, Canada, 1943; Professional football player Toronto Argonauts, CFL, 1966-70; lawyer, 1971-81; ambassador to Ireland Canadian Foreign Min., 1989-94; athletic dir. U. Notre Dame, 1995—. Home: 51311 Grandoaks Ct Granger IN 46530-8432

WAGGENER, RONALD EDGAR, radiologist; b. Green River, Wyo., Oct. 6, 1926; s. Edgar Fleetwood and Mary Harlene (Hutton) W.; m. Everina Ann Stalker, Aug. 1, 1948; children: Marta, Nancy, Paul, Daphne. Student, Colo. A&M U., 1944; student, Oreg. State U., 1945; BS, U. Nebr., 1949, MS, 1952, PhD, 1957, MD cum laude, 1954, postgrad., 1955-58, St. Bartholomew's, London, 1956-57. Diplomate Am. Bd. Radiology. Intern U. Nebr. Hosp., 1954-55, resident, 1955-56, 57-58; radiation therapist Nebr. Meth. Hosp., Omaha, 1965-70, chmn. cancer com., 1964-89, dir. cancer and radiation therapy, 1964-89, dir. dept. radiology, 1970-89, dir. cancer fellowship program, 1977-89; instr. radiology U. Nebr., 1958, asst. prof., 1959-61, radiation therapist, 1959-65, assoc. prof., 1962-80, clin. assoc. prof., 1981—. Pres. Highland Assocs. Ltd., Omaha, 1977-89; mem. cancer com. Children's Meml. Hosp., Omaha, 1970-89. Contbr. articles to profl. jours. With C.E., U.S. Army, 1944-46. Fellow AEC, 1952-53, Am. Cancer Soc., 1956-57. Fellow Am. Coll. Radiologists; mem. Nebr. Radiology Soc. (pres. 1963-64), Sigma Xi, Alpha Omega Alpha, Phi Nu. Home: PO Box 666 Pinedale WY 82941-0666 Office: 13304 W Center Rd Omaha NE 68144-3453

WAGGONER, SUSAN MARIE, electronics engineer; b. East Chicago, Ind., Sept. 1, 1952; d. Joseph John and Elizabeth Vasilak; m. Steven Richard Waggoner, July 31, 1976; children: Kenneth David, Michael Christopher. AS, Ind. U., 1975, BA in Journalism, 1976, BS in Physics, 1982, M in Pub. Affairs, 1991. Engring. technician Naval Surface Warfare Ctr., Crane, Ind., 1978-82, electronics engr. test and measurement equipment, 1982-91, electronics engr. batteries, 1991—. Recipient Value Engring. Spl. award Dept. of Def., 2000. Mem. AIAA, Am. Soc. Naval Engrs., Fed. Mgrs. Assn., Federally Employed Women, Am. Rose Soc., Am. Hort. Soc., Mensa, Theatre Circle Ind. U., Sigma Pi Sigma. Home: RR 5 Box 387 Loogootee IN 47553-9337 Office: Naval Surface Warfare Ctr 300 Highway 361 Crane IN 47522-5001

WAGLE, SUSAN, state legislator, small business owner; b. Allentown, Pa., Sept. 27, 1953; m. John Thomas Wagle, Apr. 3, 1980; children: Julia Marie, Andrea Elizabeth, John Timothy, Paul Thomas. BA in Elem. Edn. cum laude, Wichita State U., 1979, post grad., 1979-82. Tchr. Chisholm Trail Elem., Kans., 1979-80; tchr. emotionally disturbed, special edn. Price Elem., 1980-82; real estate investor, 1980—; prin. Wichita Bus. Inc., 1983—; mem. Kans. Ho. Reps. from 99th dist., Topeka, 1990, 92, 94-2000; speaker pro tem Kans. Ho. Reps., 1994-2000; mem. Kans. Senate from 30th dist., 2001—. Mem. Am. Legis. Exchange Coun. (state chmn., nat. bd. dirs., Outstanding Legis. of Yr. award 1994), Farm Bur., Nat. Fedn. Ind. Bus., Nat. Restaurant Assn., Wichita Ind. Bus. Assn. Home: 14 N Sandalwood St Wichita KS 67230-6612

WAGNER, ANN, political organization executive; m. Ray Wagner; children: Raymond III, Stephen, Mary Ruth. BSBA, U. Mo., 1984. Dir. ho. and senate redistricting commn. Mo. Reps., 1991, vice chmn., chmn., 1999—; Mo. state exec. dir. Bush/Quayle Campaign, 1992; advisor Ashcroft for Senate Campaign, 1994; 2nd congl. dist. chair Dole for Pres. Campaign, 1996. Vocal Music scholar U. Mo. Office: Mo Rep Party 204 East Dunklin Jefferson City MO 65101

WAGNER, BRUCE STANLEY, marketing professional; b. San Diego, Aug. 1, 1943; s. Robert Sheldon and Janet (Lowther) Wagner; m. Elizabeth Pearsall Winslow, Oct. 4, 1975; children: Sage Elizabeth, Alexander Winslow. BA, Dartmouth Coll., 1965; MBA, U. Pa., 1984. Sr. v.p. Grey Advt., Inc., N.Y.C., 1967-81; exec. v.p., chief oper. officer Campaign '76 Media Comm., Inc., Washington, 1975-76; exec. v.p., bd. dirs. Ross Roy, Inc., Bloomfield Hills, Mich., 1981-91, Ross Roy Group, Inc., Bloomfield Hills, 1991-94; v.p. mktg. and comms. ITT Automotive Inc., Auburn Hills, 1995-99; pres. Wagner & Co., Ltd., Birmingham, 1999—; v.p. mktg. and corp. comms. MSX Internat. Inc., Auburn Hills, 2001—. Mem. parents bd. Bucknell U., pres. parents bd., 1999—2000. Mem.: Am. Assn. Advt. Agys. (bd. govs. ctrl. region 1988—94, chmn., bd. govs. Mich. coun. 1985—86), Wharton Alumni Assn. (chmn. 1983—85), Birmingham Athletic Club, Orchard Lake Country Club, Detroit Athletic Club, Wharton Club Mich. (bd. dirs. 1985—). Home: 975 Arlington Rd Birmingham MI 48009-1684 Office: MSX Internat Inc 22355 W Eleven Mile Rd Southfield MI 48034-4735

WAGNER, BURTON ALLAN, lawyer; b. Milw., June 13, 1941; s. Irwin and Jennie (Oxman) W.; m. Georgia Olchoff, Aug. 29, 1964; children: Andrew, Laura. B.B.A. in Acctg, U. Wis., 1963, J.D., 1966, M.A. in Health Services Adminstrn, 1976. Bar: Wis. 1966. Assoc. legal counsel U. Wis., 1968-74; asst. to vice chancellor, legal counsel U. Wis. Hosps., 1974-77; asst. sec. Wis. Dept. Health and Social Services, 1977-83, adminstr. div. community services, 1979-83; clin. assoc. prof. health adminstrn. U. Wis.; ptnr. Thomas Harnisch & Wagner, Madison, 1983-85, Whyte & Hirschboeck, Madison, 1985-90; ptnr. (of counsel) Katten Muchin and Zavis, 1990-93; ptnr. Reinhart Boerner Van Deuren Norris & Rieselbach, 1993—. Served with USAR, 1966-68, Vietnam. Decorated Bronze Star. Mem. Soc. Law and Medicine, Wis. Bar Assn., Dane County Bar Assn. Jewish. Office: PO Box 2018 Madison WI 53701-2018 E-mail: bwagner@reinhartlaw.com.

WAGNER, CHARLES ALAN, librarian; b. Elkhart, Ind., Apr. 27, 1948; s. Arthur and Lydia M. (Stump) W.; m. Marilynn B. Dray, Aug. 17, 1971; children; Sarah, Wendy. BA, Manchester (Ind.) Coll., 1970; MLA, Ind. U., 1973. Libr. dir. Peru (Ind.) Pub. Libr., 1973—. Contbr. articles in field; cartoons appear in comic books, newspapers, mags. With USAR, ret. Mem. Ind. Library Assn., Plymouth Club Am., Rotary. Address: 102 E Main St Peru IN 46970-2338

WAGNER, DURRETT, former publisher, picture service executive; b. El Paso, Tex., Feb. 27, 1929; s. Francis and Florence (Durrett) W.; m. Betty Jane Brown, June 7, 1951; children— Gordon, Velma, Kendra. B.A., Baylor U., 1950; M.Div., Yale, 1954; postgrad., U. Chgo., 1954-59. Chmn. social sci. div. Kendall Coll., Evanston, Ill., 1959-63, dean, 1963-67; partner v.p.; Swallow Press Inc., Chgo., 1967-92; owner, partner, pres. Hist. Pictures Service, Inc., 1975-92; pres. Bookworks, Inc., 1990—2001. Home: Evanston, Ill. Died Nov. 21, 2001.

WAGNER, JAMES WARREN, engineering educator; b. Washington, July 12, 1953; s. Robert Earl and Bernice (Bittner) W.; m. Debbie Kelley, July 31, 1976; children: Kimberly Renee, Christine Kelley. BSEE, U. Del., 1975; MS, Johns Hopkins U., 1978, PhD, 1984. Electronics engr. U.S. FDA, Washington, 1975-84; asst. prof. Johns Hopkins U., Balt., 1984-88, assoc. prof., 1988-93, prof., 1993-97, chmn. dept. materials sci. and engring., 1993-97; dean Case Sch. Engring. Case Western Res. U., Cleve., 1998-2000, prof. materials sci. and engring., dean Case Sch. Engring., 1998—, provost, 2000-01, interim pres., 2001—. Contbr. articles to profl. jours. Regional v.p. Chesapeake Bay Yacht Racing Assn., Annapolis, Md., 1982; elder Presbyterian Ch. U.S.A. Mem. IEEE, Optical Soc. Am., Materials Rsch. Soc., Laser & Electro-Optics Soc., Biomed. Engring., Am. Soc. for Nondestructive Evaluation, Soc. Exptl. Mechanics (Peterson award 1988), Nat. Materials Adv. Bd. Presbyterian. Achievements include contributions to the field of optical metrology applied to materials characterization, especially advanced holographic and laser-based ultrasonic methods. Office: Case Western Res U 10900 Euclid Ave Cleveland OH 44106-7001

WAGNER, JEFF, radio personality; married. Grad., Marquette U., 1982. Head organized crime task force U.S. Atty.'s Office, 1982—93; atty. pvt. practice, 1993—98; radio host 620 WTMJ, Milw., 1998—. Rep. candidate State Atty. Gen., 1994. Avocations: golf, horse racing. Office: WTMJ 720 E Capital Dr Milwaukee WI 53212

WAGNER, JOSEPH EDWARD, veterinarian, educator; b. Dubuque, Iowa, July 29, 1938; s. Jacob Edward and Leona (Callahan) W.; m. Kay Rose (div. Apr. 1983); children: Lucinda, Pamela, Jennifer, Douglas. DVM, Iowa State U., 1963; MPH, Tulane U., 1964; PhD, U. Ill., 1967. Asst. prof. U. Kans. Med. Ctr., Kansas City, 1967-69; assoc. prof. U. Mo. Coll. Vet. Medicine, Columbia, 1969-72, prof. vet. medicine, 1972—, Curator's prof., 1989—. Cons. Harlan Sprague Dawley, Indpls., 1984—. Author: The Biology and Medicine of Rabbits and Rodents, 1989, 4th edit., 1995. Recipient award of excellence in lab. animal medicine Charles River Found., Wilmington, Mass., 1986. Mem. AMVA, Am. Coll. Lab. Animal Medicine (pres. 1985-86), Am. Assn. Lab. Animal Scis. (pres. 1980-81). Office: U Mo-Coll of Veterinary Medicine Dept of Vet Pathobiology 1600 W Rollins Rd Columbia MO 65211-0001

WAGNER, JOSEPH M. church administrator; Exec dir. Division for Ministry of the Evangelical Lutheran Church in America, Chgo., 1987—. Office: Evangelical Lutheran Church Am 8765 W Higgins Rd Chicago IL 60631-4101

WAGNER, MARK ANTHONY, videotape editor; b. Bethlehem, Pa., Mar. 15, 1958; s. Harry Paul and Theresa Marie (Spadaccia) W.; m. Nancy Susan Davis, Sept. 8, 1984. BA in Comm., Temple U., 1980. Videotape operator Swell Pictures, Chgo., 1983-85; asst. editor Post Pro Video, 1985-88; sr. editor Ave. Edit, 1988-91; editor/post-prodn. supr. WMX Techs., 1992-97; owner Spark Prodns., 1997. Recipient R.L. Jacobs Meml. award Boys' Clubs Am., 1976. Mem. Nat. Amusement Park Hist. Assn., Soc. Comml. Archaeology. Avocations: table tennis, film studies.

WAGNER, MARY KATHRYN, sociology educator, former state legislator; b. Madison, S.D., June 19, 1932; d. Irving Macaulay and Mary Browning (Wines) Mumford; m. Robert Todd Wagner, June 23, 1954; children: Christopher John, Andrea Browning. BA, U. S.D., 1954; MEd, S.D. State U., 1974, PhD, 1978. Sec. R.A. Burleigh & Assocs., Evanston, Ill., 1954-57; dir. resource ctr. Watertown (S.D.) Sr. High Sch., 1969-71, Brookings (S.D.) High Sch., 1971-74; asst. dir. S.D. Com. on the Humanities, Brookings, 1976-90; asst. prof. rural sociology S.D. State U., 1990-96; mem. S.D. Ho. of Reps., 1981-88, S.D. Senate, 1988-92. Mem., pres. Brookings Sch. Bd., 1975-81; chair fund dr. Brookings United Way, 1985; bd. dirs. Brookings Chamber music Soc., 1981-98, Advance and Career Learning Ctr. Named Woman of Yr., Bus. and Profl. Women, 1981, Legislator Conservationist of Yr., Nat. and S.D. Wildlife Fedn., 1988. Mem. Population Assn. Am., Midwest Sociol. Soc., Rural Sociol. Soc., Brookings C. of C. (mem. indsl. devel. com. 1988-98), PEO, Rotary. Republican. Episcopalian. Avocations: reading, gardening, music, golf, bridge. Home: 24497 N Playhouse Rd Keystone SD 57751-6653 E-mail: drswagnerrtmk@aol.com.

WAGNER, MARY MARGARET, library and information science educator; b. Mpls., Feb. 4, 1946; d. Harvey F.J. and Yvonne M. (Brettner) W.; m. William Moore, June 16, 1988; children: Lebohang Y.C., Nora M. BA, Coll. St. Catherine, St. Paul, 1969; MLS, U. Wash., 1973. Asst. libr. St. Margarets Acad., Mpls., 1969-70; libr. Derham Hall High Sch., St. Paul, 1970-71; youth worker The Bridge for Runaways, Mpls., 1971-72; libr. Guthrie Theater Reference and Rsch. Libr., 1973-75; asst. br. libr. St. Paul Pub. Libr., 1975; assoc. prof. dept. info. mgmt. Coll. St. Catherine, St. Paul, 1975—. Del. Minn. Gov.'s Pre-White House Conf. on Librs. and Info. Svcs., 1990; mem. Minn. Pre-White House Program Com., 1989-90, Continuing Libr. Info. and Media Edn. Com. Minn. Dept. Edn., Libr. Devel. and Svcs., 1980-83, 87—; mem. cmty. faculty Met. State U., St. Paul, 1980—; mem. core revision com. Coll. St. Catherine, 1992-93, faculty budget adv. com., 1992-95, faculty pers. com., 1989-92, 2001—, acad. computing com. 1991-96, ednl. policies com., 1998-01; chair curriculum subcom. Minn. Vol. Cert. Com., 1993—. Contbr. articles to profl. jours. Bd. dirs. Christian Sharing Fund, 1976-80, chair, 1977-78. Grantee: U.S. Embassy, Maseru, Lesotho, Africa, Brit. Consulate, Maseru, various founds.; Upper Midwest Assn. for Intercultural Edn. travel grantee Assoc. Colls. Twin Cities. Fellow: Higher Edn Consortia for Urban Affairs (bd. dirs. 1998—); mem.: ALISE (chair internat. rels. com. 2001—), ALA (libr. book fellows program 1990—91), Twin Cities Women in Computing, Minn. Ednl. Media Orgn., Minn. Libr. Assn. (pres. 1981—82, chair continuing edn. com. 1987—90, steering com. Readers Adv. Roundtable 1989—91), Spl. Libr. Assn., Am. Soc. Indexers, Am. Soc. Info. Sci. Office: Coll St Catherine Dept Info Mgmt 2004 Randolph Ave Saint Paul MN 55105-1750 E-mail: mmwagner@stkate.edu.

WAGNER, ROD, library director; b. Oakland, Nebr., Sept. 14, 1948; s. Francis Lynn and Doris Jean (Egbers) W.; m. M. Diane Kennedy, June 14, 1969; children: Jennifer, Brian, James. BA Social Sci. Edn., Wayne (Nebr.) State Coll., 1970; MA Polit. Sci., U. Nebr. Lincoln, 1971; MA Libr. Sci., U. Mo., 1981. Rsch. coord. Nebr. Libr. Commn., Lincoln, 1972, planning, evaluation, rsch. coord., 1972-73, adminstrv. asst., 1973-74, dep. dir., 1974-87, dir., 1988—. Bd. dirs. Nebr. Ctr. for the Book, Nebr. Devel. Network. Mem. state govt. coun. Nebr. Info. Tech. Commn., 1999—. With U.S. Army N.G., 1970-77. Mem. ALA (contbr. yearbook 1981-84), Assn. Specialized and Cooperative Libr. Agys. (bd. dirs. 1998-2000), Nebr. Libr. Assn. (pres.-elect 1993-94, pres. 1994-95), Chief Officers State Libr. Agys., Western Coun. State Librs. (pres. 1992-93). Presbyterian. Home: 3205 W Pershing Rd Lincoln NE 68502-4844 Office: NE Libr Commn 1200 N St Ste 120 Lincoln NE 68508-2023 E-mail: rwagner@nlc.state.ne.us.

WAGNER, THOMAS EDWARD, academic administrator, educator; b. Lexington, Ky., Dec. 6, 1937; s. Thomas Caney and Gaynell (Waggoner) W.; m. Susan Adell Brant, Sept. 3, 1960; children: Brant, Brian, Jennifer. BS, U. Cin., 1962; MA, Miami U., Oxford, Ohio, 1967; EdD, U. Cin, 1973. Tchr. Finneytown Sch. Dist., Cin., 1962-67; admissions officer U. Cin., 1967-70, summer sch. dean, 1970-73, asst. to pres., 1973-74, asst. v.p.,

1974-77, vice provost faculty affairs, 1977-85, sr. vice provost, 1985-91, univ. dean for undergrad. and student affairs, 1987-91, v.p. student affairs and svcs., 1991-94, univ. prof. planning, 1983-2000, univ. prof. emeritus, 2000—. Mem. adv. com. The Collegeboard, N.Y.C., 1989-91. Contbr. articles to profl. jours and chpts. to books. Bd. dirs. Charter Com., Cin., 1985-88, Inroads, Cin., 1990-96, Presbyn. Child Welfare Agy., 1992-98, Buckhorn Children's Ctr., 1992-98; mem. steering com. Cin. Youth Collaborative, 1988-91; active Fernald Citizens Adv. Bd., 1993—. With USAFR, 1955-63. Fulbright fellow, 1992, USIA rsch. fellow, 1997. Fellow Ctr. for Dispute Resolution, Soc. for Values in Higher Edn. Presbyterian. Avocations: reading, sports, photography. Home: 1086 W Galbraith Rd Cincinnati OH 45231-5612 Office: Univ Cin Sch of Planning PO Box 210016 Cincinnati OH 45221-0016

WAGNER, WILLIAM BURDETTE, business educator; b. Oswego, N.Y., Apr. 27, 1941; s. Guy Wesley and Gladys M. (Redlinger) W.; divorced; 1 child, Geoffrey D. BA with highest honors, Mich. State U., 1963; MBA, Ohio State U., 1965, PhD, 1967. Research and teaching asst. Ohio State U., Columbus, 1966-68; prof. mktg. and logistics U. Mo., Columbia, 1969-2000, prof. emeritus, 2000—. Guest prof. mktg. U. Nanjing, China, 1985-87, Prince of Songla U., Hat Yai, Thailand, 1990, 92, 98, 99, Assumption U., Bangkok, 1998-99, U. of Thai C. of C., Bangkok, 1998; vis. prof. bus. Chulalongkorn U., Bangkok, 2000, 2001; expert witness petroleum industry, 1989—; adv. dir. Mo. State Bank, St. Louis, 1981-93. Contbr. articles to profl. jours. Univ. coordinator book procurement program for minorities McDonnell Douglas, St. Louis, 1972—; mem. St. Louis-Nanjing Sister City Com., 1985—; faculty ambassador U. Mo. Alumni Assn., 1987—; mem. speakers bur., high sch. liaison team U. Mo., 1987—; Mizzou Outreach prof., 1987—; bd. dirs. Cen. Mo. Sheltered Enterprises for Handicapped, Columbia, 1985-92. Recipient Civic Svc. award McDonnell Douglas, 1977, Educator of Yr. award Jr. C. of C., 1983, Prof. of Yr. award Coll. of Bus. and Pub. Adminstrn., 1987, Golden Key Honor Soc. Faculty Mem. of Yr. award, 1987, Faculty Mem. of Yr. award Beta Theta Pi, 1990, Prof. of Yr. award Kans. City Alumni Assn., 1990; named Mktg. Prof. of Yr., U. Mo., 1987-88, 89-91; rsch. grantee SBC, Econ. Devel. Adminstrn., U. Mo.; NDEA fellow Ohio State U., 1963-66, William T. Kemper Teaching fellow, 1991, Wakonse Teaching fellow, 1995; Fulbright scholar, Korea, 1992. Mem. Nat. Assn. Purchasing Mgmt., St. Louis Purchasing Mgmt. Assn., Coun. Logistics Mgmt., Nat. Fulbright Assn., Nat. Eagle Scout Assn., Am. Soc. Transp. and Logistics (pres. Mo. chpt. 1974-75, bd. govs. 1970-74, 75-82), Delta Sigma Pi, Beta Gamma Sigma, Omicron Delta Epsilon, Rotary Internat. (Paul Harris fellow), Mo. Athletic Club (St. Louis), Country Club of Mo. (Columbia), Univ. Club (Columbia), Jefferson Club. Methodist. Avocations: bridge, golf, stamp and coin collecting, reading historical novels, jogging. Home: 2401 Bluff Blvd Columbia MO 65201-8613 Office: Univ Mo 214 Middlebush Hall Columbia MO 65211-6100 E-mail: wagnerw@missouri.edu.

WAGNON, JOAN, banker, former mayor; b. Texarkana, Ark., Oct. 17, 1940; d. Jack and Louise (lucas) D.; m. William O. Wagnon Jr., June 4, 1964; children: Jack, William O. III. BA in Biology, Hendrix Coll., Conway, Ark., 1962; MEd in Guidance and Counseling, U. Mo., 1968. Sr. rsch. technician U. Ark. Med. Sch., Little Rock, 1962-64, sr. rsch. asst. Columbia, Mo., 1964-68; tchr. No. Hills Jr. H.S., Topeka, 1968-69, J.S. Kendall Sch., Boston, 1970-71; counselor Neighborhood Youth Corps, Topeka, 1973-74; exec. dir. Topeka YWCA, 1977-93; mem. Kans. Legislature, 1983-94; exec. dir. Kans. Families for Kids, 1994-97; mayor City of Topeka, 1997-2001; pres. Ctrl. Nat. Bank, Topeka, 2001—. Mem. Health Planning Rev. Commn., Topeka, 1984-85. Recipient Service to Edn. award Topeka NEA, 1979, Outstanding Achievement award, Kans. Home Econs. Assn., 1985, Equity in Action award Kans. B & PW Clubs, 1991, Disting. Svc. award Kans. Ct. Svcs. Officers, 1992, Womens Rights Star award NOW, 1994; named Woman of Yr. Mayors Council Status of Women, 1983, named one of Top Ten Legislators Kans. Mag., Wichita, 1986, Legislator of Yr., Kans. NASW, 1989. Mem. Topeka Assn. Human Svc. Execs. (pres. 1981-83), Topekans for Ednl. Involvement (pres. 1979-82), Women's Polit. Caucus (state chair). Democrat. Methodist. Lodge: Rotary. Avocations: music, swimming, boating. Home: 1606 SW Boswell Ave Topeka KS 66604-2729 Office: City Hall 215 SW 7th St Topeka KS 66603-3732

WAGONER, G. RICHARD, JR. automotive company executive; b. Wilmington, Del., Feb. 9, 1953; BS in Econs., Duke U., 1975; MBA, Harvard U., 1977. Analyst in treas.'s office, mgr. Latin Am. financing, dir. Can. and overseas borrowing, dir. capital analysis and investment GM, N.Y., 1977-81, treas. Sao Paulo, Brazil, 1981-84, exec. dir. fin. Brazil, 1984-87, v.p., fin. mgr. Can., 1987-88, group dir. strategic bus. planning Can., 1988-89, v.p. fin. Switzerland, 1989-91, pres. Brazil, 1992-93, head Worldwide Purchasing Group, 1993-94, exec. v.p., pres. North Am. ops., 1994-98, pres., COO, mem. bd. dirs., 1998—, CEO, 2000—. Chmn. bd. visitors Fuqua Sch. Bus. Duke U.; trustee Detroit County Day Sch. Mem. Soc. Automotive Engrs. (mem. VISION 2000 exec. com.). Office: GM Corp 300 Renaissance Ctr Detroit MI 48265-0001

WAGONER, RALPH HOWARD, academic administrator, educator; b. Pitts., May 30, 1938; s. Richard Henry and Charlotte (Stevenson) W.; m. Wilma Jo Staup, Dec. 21, 1961; children: Amanda Jane, Joseph Ryan. AB in Biology, Gettysburg Coll., 1960; MS in Ednl. Adminstrn., Westminster Coll., 1963; PhD, Kent State U., 1967; postgrad., MIT, 1973, Dartmouth Coll., 1979. Prin., tchr., coach Williamsfield (Ohio) Elem. and Jr. High Sch., 1960-62; dir. elem. edn. Pymatuning Valley (Ohio) Local Schs., 1962-64, asst. supt. instrn., 1964-65; acad. counselor, asst. to dean coll. edn. Kent (Ohio) State U., 1965-66, instr. edn., 1966-67; asst. prof. Drake U., Des Moines, 1967-70, assoc. prof., 1970-71, chmn. dept. elem. edn., 1968-70, chmn. dept. tchr. edn., 1970-71, acad. adminstrn. intern Am. Council Edn., Office of Pres., 1971-72, asst. to pres., 1972-77, dir. devel., 1975-77; v.p. pub. affairs and devel., prof. Western Ill. U., Macomb, 1977-87, pres., 1987-93, Augustana Coll., Sioux Falls, S.D., 1993—. Adj. prof. San Francisco Theol. Sem., 1971; mem. senate Drake U., 1968-77; sponsor interhall council Western Ill. U., 197893, mem. BOG/UPI task force on incentives for faculty excellence, co-chmn., faculty mentor, 1985-93; cons. in field. Co-author: (with L. Wayne Bryan) Societal Crises and Educational Response: A Book of Readings, 1969, (with Robert L. Evans) The Emerging Teacher, 1970, (with William R. Abell) The Instructional Module Package System, 1971, Writing Behavioral Objectives or How Do I Know When He Knows, 1971; contbr. articles to profl. jours. Chmn. Mid-Ill. Computer Consortium, 1980, 85, Western Ill. Corridor of Opportunity, 1987-93; mem. Pres.' Regional Adv. Coun., 1977-87; mem. investments com. McDonough County YMCA; mem. exec. com. Macomb Area Indsl. Corp.; trustee Robert Morris Coll., 1983-88, Chgo. and Carthage, Ill., 1983-88; bd. dirs. Ill. Coun. Econ. Edn., 1987-93, McDonough County United Way Dr., 1980-82; bd. trustees The Cornerstone Found. LSS of Ill., 1990-96; mem. Sioux Falls Tomorrow Task Force, 1993-94; bd. dirs. S.D. Symphony, 1993—, Edn. Telecomms. State of S.D., 1993—, Sioux Falls Devel. Found., 1993—, Children's Inn, 1993—, Sioux Valley Physicians Alliance, 1995—, LECNA, 1996—; life trustee Lutheran Social Svcs., 1996—. Recipient Man of Yr. award Andover Rotary Club, 1964, Quax Honor award, 1969-70, Disting. Alumni award Gettysburg (Pa.) Coll., 1991; named McDonough County Citizen of Yr., Elks, 1982. Fellow Am. Coun. Edn. (cons. fund raising 1984-87); mem. Am. Assn. State Colls. and Univs. (com. econ. devel. 1988, com. on athletics 1987), Ednl. Computing Network (chmn. policy bd. 1985-87), Assn. Midcontinent Univs. (coun. dels. 1987-93), Gateway Conf. (coun. dels. 1987-93), Coun. for Advancement and Support of Edn. (discussion leader, speaker, 1975, 77, 80, 84, 86, 91, 92, 93, 94, Citation award 1981, 83, Grand award 1982, Bronze award 1985, Silver award 1986), Macomb C. of C. (exec. com., bd. dirs.), Ill. Chamber Econ. Devel. Policy Task Force, Blue Key (hon.), Omicron Delta Kappa, Phi Eta Sigma (hon.), Phi Mu Alpha. Lutheran. Lodge: Rotary. Home: 2505 S Poplar Dr Sioux Falls SD 57105-4946 Office: Augustana Coll 2001 S Summit Ave Sioux Falls SD 57197-0001

WAGONER, ROBERT HALL, engineering educator, researcher; b. Columbus, Ohio, Jan. 8, 1952; s. Robert H. and Leorra (Schmucker) W.; m. Robyn K. O'Donnell, Aug. 30, 1980; children: Erin A. Wagoner Hansgen, Amy J. BS, Ohio State U., 1974, MS, 1975, PhD, 1976. NSF postdoctoral rschr. U. Oxford, Eng., 1976-77; staff rsch. scientist GM Rsch. Labs., Warren, Mich., 1977-83; assoc. prof. material sci. engring. Ohio State U., Columbus, 1983-86, prof., 1986-98, chmn. dept., 1992-96, prof. engring, 1998—. Maitre de recherche Ecole des Mines de Paris, Sophia Antipolis, France, 1990-91; dir. Ohio State U. Rsch. Found., 1991-94, Ctr. Advt. Materials Mfg. Auto Components, 1994—; trustee Orton Found., 1992-96. Co-author: Fundamentals of Metal Forming, 1997; editor: Novel Techniques in Metal Deformation, 1983, Forming Limit Diagrams, 1989. Recipient Raymond Meml. award AIME, 1981, 83; Disting. Scholar award Ohio State U., 1990, Harrison award for tchg. excellence, 1988; Presdl. Young Investigator award NSF, 1984; NSF postdoctoral fellow Oxford (Eng.) U., 1976. Fellow ASM Internat.; mem. Nat. Acad. Engring., Minerals, Metals and Materials Soc. (pres. 1997-98, dir. 1991-95, Mathewson Gold medal 1988, Hardy Gold medal 1981, v.p. 1996-97, pres. 1997—), Am. Inst. Mining, Metall., and Petroleum Engring. (trustee 1997—). TMS found. (founding mem., trustee 1997—) Achievements include developing SHEET-3 and SHEET-S, sheet forming simulation programs for indsl. use; introducing first quantitative test for plane-tensile work hardening; inventing formability test and friction test. Office: Ohio State U Dept Material Sci Engring 2041 N College Rd Columbus OH 43210-1124

WAHL, RICHARD LEO, radiologist, educator, nuclear medicine researcher; b. Iowa, July 13, 1952; s. Max Henry and Josephine Elizabeth (Hogan) Wahl; m. Sandra K. Moeller, June 28, 1975; children: Daniel, Matthew, Peter, Katherine. BA in Chemistry, Wartburg Coll., 1974; MD, Washington U., St. Louis, 1978. Diplomate Am. Bd. Nuc. Medicine (pres. 1998-), Am. Bd. Radiology. Intern U. Calif., San Diego, 1978—79; resident in radiology Mallinckrodt Inst. Washington U., 1979—82, fellow in nuc. medicine and immunology, 1982—83; asst. prof. U. Mich. Med. Ctr., Ann Arbor, 1983—87, assoc. prof., 1987—90, prof., 1990—; dir. gen. nuc. imaging, dir. radiopharm. program U. Mich. Cancer Ctr., 1999—. Mem. exptl. immunology study sect. NIH, Bethesda, Md., 1990—94; sec. Am. Bd. Nuc. Medicine, 1997, chmn., 98. Editor: textbook; contbr. 200 articles to profl. jours., chpts. to textbooks; holder (30 patents). Recipient Jerome W. Conn rsch. award, U. Mich., 1989; grantee rsch. grantee, NIH, ACS, Dept. of Army. Fellow: Am. Coll. Nuc. Physicians; mem.: AMA, Inst. for Clin. Positron Emission Tomography (bd. dirs., pres. 1996), Am. Assn. for Cancer Rsch., Am. Soc. for Clin. Investigation, Radiol. Soc. N.Am., Soc. Nuc. Medicine (Marc Tetalman award 1986, Berson and Yalow rsch. award 1992, Hounsfield rsch. award 1992). Avocations: reading, sports. Office: Johns Hopkins Outpatient Ctr Divsn Nuclear Medicine 601 N Caroline St Rm 3223 Baltimore MD 21287

WAHLEN, EDWIN ALFRED, lawyer; b. Gary, Ind., Mar. 12, 1919; s. Alfred and Ethel (Pearson) W.; m. Alice Elizabeth Condit, Apr. 24, 1943 (div. 1983); children: Edwin Alfred, Virginia Elizabeth, Martha Anne; m. Elizabeth L. Corey, Nov. 23, 1984. Student, U. Ala., 1936-38; A.B., U. Chgo., 1942, J.D., 1948. Bar: Ill. 1948. Practiced in, Chgo., 1948—; mem. firm Haight, Goldstein & Haight, 1948-55; ptnr. Goldstein & Wahlen, 1956-59, Arvey, Hodes, Costello & Burman (and predecessor), 1959-91, Wildman, Harrold, Allen & Dixon, 1992—. Author: Soldiers and Sailors Wills: A Proposal For Federal Legislation, 1948. Served to 2d lt. AUS, 1942-46. Decorated Silver Star medal, Bronze Star medal. Mem. ABA, Ill. Bar Assn., Chgo. Bar Assn., Order of Coif, Phi Beta Kappa, Phi Alpha Delta. Home: 1250 Breckenridge Ct Lake Forest IL 60045-3875 Office: 225 W Wacker Dr Chicago IL 60606-1224

WAHOSKE, MICHAEL JAMES, lawyer; b. Ripon, Wis., June 4, 1953; children: Jennifer, John. BA with highest honors, U. Notre Dame, 1975, JD summa cum laude, 1978. Bar: Minn. 1978, U.S. Dist. Ct. Minn. 1979, U.S. Ct. Appeals (7th cir.) 1979, U.S. Ct. Appeals (8th and 9th cirs.) 1980, U.S. Ct. Appeals (10th cir.) 1982, U.S. Supreme Ct. 1982, U.S. Ct. Appeals (6th cir.) 1988, U.S. Ct. Appeals (fed. cir.) 1989, U.S. Ct. Appeals (D.C. cir.) 1992, U.S. Ct. Appeals (4th cir.) 1994, U.S. Ct. Appeals (11th cir.) 1996, Supreme Ct. of Winnebago Tribe of Nebr., 1996. Law clk. to judge Luther M. Swygert U.S. Ct. Appeals (7th cir.), Chgo., 1978-79; law clk. to chief justice Warren E. Burger U.S. Supreme Ct., Washington, 1979-80; assoc. Dorsey & Whitney, Mpls., 1980-85, ptnr., 1986—. Adj. prof. law U. Minn., Mpls., 1981-83. Exec. editor U. Notre Dame Law Rev., 1977-78; co-editor: Freedom & Education: Pierce v. Society of Sisters Reconsidered, 1978. Recipient Vol. Recognition award Nat. Assn. Attys. Gen., 1993, Supreme Ct. Reception hons. State and Local Legal Ctr., 1991, 92, 93, 95. Fellow Am. Acad. Appellate Lawyers; mem. ABA (standing com. on Amicus Briefs), FBA, Minn. Bar Assn., Hennepin County Bar Assn., Phi Beta Kappa. Office: Dorsey & Whitney LLP Ste 1500 50 S Sixth St Minneapolis MN 55402-1498

WAINSCOTT, JAMES LAWRENCE, accountant; b. LaPorte, Ind., Mar. 31, 1957; s. James J. and Frances J. (Cunningham) W. BS magna cum laude, Ball State U., 1979; MBA U. Notre Dame, 1987. CPA, Ind.; cert. mgmt. acct.; cert. internal auditor; cert. info. systems auditor; chartered fin. analyst. Sr. auditor Geo. S. Olive & Co., CPAs, Indpls. and Valparaiso, Ind., 1979-82; fin. mgr. Midwest div. Nat. Steel Corp., Portage, Ind., 1982-88, mgr. pension investments, Pitts., 1988-90, asst. treas., asst. sec., Pitts., 1991-92; treas., asst. sec., Mishawaka. Ind., 1993-95, v.p. & treas., AK Steel Holding Corp., Middletown, OH, 1995—, CFO, AK Steel Holding Corp., 1998— ; cons. Edward J. Wainscott, CPA, LaPorte, Ind., 1982—; instr. acctg. Purdue U.-Westville, 1980-82, Valparaiso U., 1980-84. Advisor Jr. Achievement, 1984; vol. Am. Cancer Soc., Valparaiso Income Tax Assistance Program, Valparaiso Community/Univ. Campaign; pres., treas. Midwest Steel Employees Fed. Credit Union; pres. Midwest Steel Employees Assn.; mem. Ball State U. Cardinal Connection; mem. N.W. Ind. Open Housing Council; chmn. dean's adv. council Valparaiso U.; bd. dirs. Youth Svc. Bur. St. Joseph County. Mem. Ind. CPA Soc. (chmn. chpt. activities com. 1985-86, chpt. bd. dirs. 1983-86, chpt. pres. 1984-85, chmn. chpt. task force, Pres. award 1994, state bd. dirs. 1987-90), Nat. Assn. Accts. (chpt. bd. dirs. 1982-86, chpt. pres. 1983-84; Past Pres. award 1984), Am. Inst. CPA's, Inst. Mgmt. Acctg., Inst. Internal Auditors, Inst. Chartered Fin. Analysts, Assn. for Investment Mgmt. and Rsch., Chgo. Soc. Fin. Analysts, U. Notre Dame Exec. MBA Alumni Assn., Mensa, Blue Key, Golden Key, Intertel, Delta Sigma Pi. Roman Catholic. Avocations: music, chess, coin collecting, sports, travel. Home: 11990 Millstone Ct Loveland OH 45140-6220 Office: AK Steel Holding Corp 703 Curtis St Middletown OH 45043

WAINSCOTT, KENT, reporter; b. Des Plaines, Ill. Reporter, anchor WTWO-TV, Terre Haute, Ind.; bur. chief reporter WDTN-TV, Dayton, Ohio; reporter WISN, Milw., 1988—. Recipient award, Clarion, NY Festivals Internat., AP, Wis. Broadcasters Assn., Milw. Press Club, Communicator awards, 5 regional Emmy awards. Office: WISN PO Box 402 Milwaukee WI 53201-0402

WAINTROOB, ANDREA RUTH, lawyer; b. Chgo., Dec. 23, 1952; d. David Samuel and Lees (Carson) W. AB, Brown U., 1975; JD, U. Chgo., 1978. Bar: Ill. 1978, U.S. Dist. Ct. (no. dist.) Ill. 1978, U.S. Dist. Ct. (cen. dist.) Ill. 1996, U.S. Ct. Appeals (7th cir.) 1982, U.S. Supreme Ct. 1989. Assoc. Vedder, Price, Kaufman and Kammholz, Chgo., 1978-84; ptnr. Vedder, Price, Kaufman, 1984-94, Franczek Sullivan, P.C., Chgo., 1994—. Mem. Chgo. Bar Assn., Nat. Coun. Sch. Attys. Home: 5428 S Harper Ave Chicago IL 60615-5506 Office: Franczek Sullivan 300 S Wacker Dr Ste 3400 Chicago IL 60606-6708

WAIT, RONALD A. state legislator; b. Apr. 15, 1944; BS, JD, Drake U.; MBS, MS in Spl. Edn., No. Ill. U. Farm mgr.; mem. Ill. State Ho. of Reps. Dist. 64, 1983-93, Ill. State Ho. of Reps. Dist. 68, 1995—. Bd. dirs. Highland Hosp., Boone County Housing Authority Bd., Janet Wattles Mental Health Bd., United Givers Bd.

WAITE, DENNIS VERNON, investor relations consultant; b. Chgo., Aug. 26, 1938; s. Vernon George and Marie G. Waite; m. Christine Rene Hibbs; 1 child, Kip Anthony. BA, U. Ill., 1968; MS in Journalism, Northwestern U., 1969. Fin. reporter, columnist Chgo. Sun-Times, Chgo., 1969-76; asst. prof. Northwestern U., Evanston, Ill., 1978-79; assoc. prof. Mich. State U., East Lansing, 1979-82; ptnr. Fin. Rels. Bd., Inc., Chgo., 1982-90, sr. ptnr., 1991-97, sr. counselor, 1997—. Reporter, producer econ. affairs Sta. WTTW-TV, Sta. WBBM-TV, Chgo., 1973-76; adj. faculty English, Coll. of DuPage, 1998—. Mem. editorial adv. bd. alumni relations U. Ill., Chgo., 1980-84, 90-94. With USAF, 1956-60, PTO. Rutgers U. fellow, 1972. Mem. Medill Alumni Assn. (bd. dirs. 1989-92). Avocations: reading, writing, study of ancient history. Office: Financial Relations Bd John Hancock Ctr 875 N Michigan Ave Ste 2250 Chicago IL 60611-1805

WAITE, LAWRENCE WESLEY, osteopathic physician, educator; b. Chgo., June 27, 1951; s. Paul J. and Margaret E. (Cresson) W.; m. Courtnay M. Snyder, Nov. 1, 1974; children: Colleen Alexis, Rebecca Maureen, Alexander Quin. BA, Drake U., 1972; DO, Coll. Osteo Medicine and Surgery, Des Moines, 1975; MPH, U. Mich., 1981. Diplomate Nat. Bd. Osteo. Med. Examiners. Intern Garden City Osteo Hosp., Mich., 1975-76; practice gen. osteo. medicine Garden City, 1979-82, Battle Creek, 1982-96, La Crosse, Wis., 1996—; sect. head Onalaska Family Practice, 1999—, coord. rsch., chmn. dept., 1996-99. Cons. Nat. Bd. Examiners Osteo. Physicians and Surgeons, 1981—88, 1998—; chief med. examiner Calhoun County, 1991—93; preceptor U. Wis. Med. Sch., 1997—2000, assoc. clin. prof., 2000—, Mich. State U. Coll. Osteo. Medicine, East Lansing, 1979—97, Lakeview Gen. Osteo. Hosp., Battle Creek, Mich., 1983—87, Des Moines U. Osteo. Med. Ctr., 2001—; mem. profl. adv. coun. Good Samaritan Hosp., Battle Creek, 1982—83; exec. bd. Primary Care Network, 1994—96. Writer TV program Cross Currents Ecology, 1971; editor radio series Friendship Hour, 1971-72 Bd. dirs., La Crosse YMCA, 2000—; bd. dirs., instr. Hospice Support Services, Inc., Westland, Mich., 1981-86; exec. bd. officer Battle Creek Area Urban League, 1987-91; trustee Clearwater Farms Found., Inc., 1999—; vestryman St. Thomas Episcopal Ch., 1990-93; leader Boy Scouts Am. Served to lt. comdr. USN, 1976-79; bd. dirs. Internat. Log Rolling Assn., 2000—. State of Iowa scholar, 1969. Mem. AMA, Population Inst. (population action coun. 1984-99, Am. Pub. Health Assn., Population Inst., Aerospace Med. Assn., Natl. Eagle Scounts Assn. (life), Am. Osteo. Assn., S. Cen. Osteo. Assn. (officer, state del. 1983-96), Am. Acad. Osteopathy, Bermuda Hist. Soc. (life), Wis. Ctr., Academically Talented Youth, Brotherhood St. Andrews (life). Avocations: Geography, medieval history, genealogy. Home: 2110 Evenson Dr Onalaska WI 54650-8772 Office: Gundersen Lutheran 3100 S Kinney Coulee Rd Onalaska WI 54650-8512 E-mail: lwaite@gundluth.org.

WAITE, NORMAN, JR. lawyer; b. Chgo., Mar. 16, 1936; s. Norman and Lavinia (Fyke) W.; m. Jaqueline A. Hurlbutt; children: Leslie Catherine, Lindsay H., Norman III. BA, Yale U., 1958; LLB, Harvard U., 1963. Bar: Ill. 1963. Assoc. Winston & Strawn, Chgo., 1963-69, ptnr., 1969-78, capital ptnr., 1978-99, exec. com., 1978-95, vice chmn., 1989-99. Bd. dirs. Steadman/Hawkins Sports Medicine Found. Lt. (j.g.) USN, 1958-60. Mem. ABA, Chgo. Bar Assn., Cordillera Club (Vail, Colo.), Indian Hill Club (Winnetka, Ill.), Econ. Club, Eagle Springs Club (Vail, Colo.). Republican. Home: 1710 N Burling St Chicago IL 60614-5102 Office: Winston & Strawn 35 W Wacker Dr Ste 4200 Chicago IL 60601-1695

WAJER, RONALD EDWARD, management consultant; b. Chgo., Aug. 31, 1943; s. Edward Joseph and Gertrude Catherine (Rytelny) W.; m. Mary Earlene Hagan, July 5, 1969; children: Catherine, Michael. BSIE, Northwestern U., 1966; MBA, Loyola U., Chgo., 1970. Cert. mgmt. cons. Inst. Mgmt. Cons. Project engring. mgr. Procter & Gamble, Chgo., 1966-67; indsl. engring. mgr. Johnson & Johnson, Bedford Park, Ill., 1967-71; project mgr. Jewel Cos., Franklin Park, 1971-73; divsn. engring. mgr. Abbott Labs., North Chicago, 1973-79; pres. bus. engring. divsn. R.E. Wajer & Assocs., Northbrook, 1979—. Contbr. articles to profl. jours. Sec. Downtown Redevel. Commn., Mt. Prospect, Ill., 1977-78; fundraising vol. Maryville Acad., Des Plaines, 1985—; bd. dirs. Lattof YMCA, Des Plaines, 1994-96; profl. advisor Sch. for New Learning, DePaul U., 1994—; mem. indsl. sector com. Lincoln Found. for Bus. Excellence, 1997-99. Recipient Cmty. Svc. award Chgo. Lighthouse for the Blind, 1989, Cert. of Merit, Village of Mt. Prospect, 1978. Mem. Inst. Indsl. Engrs. (cmty. svc. chmn. 1984), Inst. Mgmt. Cons. (exec. v.p., bd. dirs. 1987-94), Assn. Mgmt. Cons. (ctrl. regional v.p. 1985-87), Midwest Soc. Profl. Cons., Northwestern Club Chgo. Roman Catholic. Office: Bus Engring 5 Revere Dr Ste 200 Northbrook IL 60062-8000 E-mail: rewajer@busnengg.com.

WAKE, MADELINE MUSANTE, nursing educator, university provost; Diploma, St. Francis Hosp. Sch. Nursing, 1963; BS in Nursing, Marquette U., 1968, MS in Nursing, 1971; PhD, U. Wis., Milw., 1986. Clin. nurse specialist St. Mary's Hosp., Milw., 1971-74, asst. dir. nursing, 1974-77; dir. continuing nursing edn. Marquette U., 1977-92, asst. prof., 1977-90, assoc. prof., 1991-99, prof., 2000—, dean Coll. Nursing, 1993—2002, provost, 2002—. Mem. devel. team Internat. Classification for Nursing Practice, Geneva, 1991-99. Chmn. bd. dirs. Trinity Meml. Hosp., Cudahy, Wis., 1991-96. Recipient Profl. Svc. award Am. Diabetes Assn.-Wis. affiliate, 1978, Excellence in Nursing Edn. award Wis. Nurses Assn., 1989; named Disting. Lectr. Sigma Theta Tau Internat., 1991. Fellow Am. Acad. Nursing; mem. ANA, AACN, Am. Orgn. Nurse Execs., Am. Assn. Coll. Nursing (bd. dirs. 1999-2002), Vis. Nurs Assn. wis. (bd. dirs.). Office: Marquette Univ Coll Nursing Milwaukee WI 53201-1881

WAKE, RICHARD W. food products executive; b. 1953; B.S., U of Illinois. With Aurora (Ill.) Eby-Brown Co., Inc., 1975—, co-pres. Ill. Office: 280 Shuman Blvd Ste 280 Naperville IL 60563-2578

WAKE, THOMAS G. food products executive; Co-pres. Eby-Brown Co., Naperville, Ill., now co-chief exec. Office: Eby Brown Co 280 Shuman Blvd Ste 280 Naperville IL 60563-2578

WAKOSKI, DIANE, poet, educator; b. Whittier, Calif., Aug. 3, 1937; d. John Joseph and Marie Elvira (Mengel) W. BA in English, U. Calif., Berkeley, 1960. Writer-in-residence Mich. State U., East Lansing, 1976—, Univ. disting. prof., 1990—. Vis. writer Calif. Inst. Tech., 1972, U. Va., 1972-73, Wilamette U., 1973, Lake Forest Coll., 1974, Colo. Coll., 1974, U. Calif., Irvine, 1974, Macalester Coll., 1975, U. Wis., 1975, Hollins Coll., 1974, U. Wash., 1977, Whitman Coll., 1976, Emory U., 1980-81, U. Hawaii, 1978. Author: books Coins and Coffins, 1962, Discrepancies and Apparitions, 1966, Inside The Blood Factory, 1968, The George Washington Poems, 1967, The Magellanic Clouds, 1969, The Motorcycle Betrayal Poems, 1971, Smudging, 1972, Dancing On The Grave of A Son Of A Bitch, 1973, Trilogy, 1974, Virtuoso Literature For Two and Four Hands,

1976, Waiting For the King of Spain, 1977, The Man Who Shook Hands, 1978, Cap of Darkness, 1980, The Magician's Feastletters, 1982, The Collected Greed: Parts I-XIII, 1984, The Rings of Saturn, 1986, Emerald Ice: Selected Poems 1962-87, 1988 (William Carlos Williams prize 1989), Medea The Sorceress, 1991, Jason the Sailor, 1993, The Emerald City of Las Vegas, 1995, Argonaut Rose, 1998, The Butcher's Apron: New & Selected Poems, 2000. Cassandra Found. grantee, 1970; N.Y. State Cultural Council grantee, 1971-72; Nat. Endowment for Arts grantee, 1973-74; Guggenheim grantee, 1972-73; Fulbright grantee, 1984; Mich. Arts Coun. grantee, 1988; recipient Mich. Arts Found. award, 1989, Disting. Faculty award Mich. State U., 1989, Univ. Disting. Prof., 1990. Office: Mich State U 207 Morrill Hall East Lansing MI 48824-1036 E-mail: dwakoski@aol.com., wakoski@pilot.msu.edu.

WALBERG, HERBERT JOHN, psychologist, educator, consultant; b. Chgo., Dec. 27, 1937; s. Herbert J. and Helen (Bauer) W.; m. Madoka Bessho, Aug. 20, 1965; 1 child, Herbert J. III. BE in Edn. and Psychology, Chgo. State U., 1959; ME in Counseling, U. Ill., 1960; PhD in Ednl. Psychology, U. Chgo., 1964. Instr. psychology Chgo. State U., 1962-63, asst. prof., 1964-65; lectr. edn. Rutgers U., New Brunswick, N.J., 1965-66; asst. prof. edn. Harvard U., Cambridge, Mass., 1966-69; assoc. prof. edn. U. Ill., Chgo., 1970-71, prof., 1971-84, rsch. prof., 1984—, external examiner, 1981. External examiner, 1981; ednl. cons. numerous orgns.; external examiner Monash U., 1974, 76, Australian Nat. U., 1977; speaker in field; former coord. worldwide radio broadcasts on Am. Edn. Voice of Am., USIA, Office Pres. U.S., cons. Ctr. for Disease Control U.S. Pub. Health Svcs., 1985-90. Author, editor 49 books; chmn. editl. bd. Internat. Jour. Ednl. Rsch., 1985—; contbr. over 350 articles to profl. jours., chpts. to books. Mem. Chgo. United Edn. Com., also other civic groups, 1971-86; bd. dirs. Family Study Inst., 1987; chmn. bd. dirs. Heartland Inst., 1995. Nat. Inst. Edn. rsch. grantee, 1973, NSF rsch. grantee, 1974, March of Dimes rsch. grantee, 1976, numerous others. Fellow AAAS, Am. Psychol. Assn., Royal Statis. Soc.; mem. Internat. Acad. Edn. (founding), Am. Ednl. Rsch. Assn., Assn. for Supervision and Curriculum Devel., Brit. Ednl. Rsch. Assn., Nat. Soc. for Study Edn., Evaluation Rsch. Soc., Internat. Acad. Scis., Phi Delta Kappa (Disting. Rsch. award U. Chgo. chpt. 1971, cert. of recognition 1985), Phi Kappa Phi (hon.). Lutheran. Avocation: travel. Home: 180 E Pearson St Apt 3607 Chicago IL 60611-2135 Office: U Ill 1040 W Harrison St Chicago IL 60607-7129

WALCH, TIMOTHY GEORGE, library administrator; b. Detroit, Dec. 6, 1947; s. George Louis Walch and Margaret Mary (Shields) DeSchryver; m. Victoria Irons, June 24, 1978; children: Thomas Emmet, Brian Edward. BA, U. Notre Dame, 1970; PhD, Northwestern U., 1975. Assoc. dir. Soc. Am. Archivists, Chgo., 1975-79; grants analyst Nat. Hist. Publ. Commn., Washington, 1979-81; budget analyst Nat. Archives, 1981-82, editor Prologue, 1982-88; asst. dir. Hoover Presdl. Libr., West Branch, Iowa, 1988-93, dir., 1993—. Author: Catholicism in America, 1989, Pope John Paul II, 1989, Parish School, 1996, others; editor: Herbert Hoover & Harry S Truman, 1992, Immigrant America, 1994, At the President's Side, 1997, Herbert Hoover & Franklin D. Roosevelt, 1998, and others; assoc. editor: U.S. Cath. Historian, 1983—; guest columnist Cedar Rapids Gazette, 1996—. Recipient Journalism award U.S. Cath. Press Assn., 1986, 1st place publ. award Nat. Assn. Govt. Communicators, 1988, U.S. Archivist's award Nat. Archives, 1993, Iowa Gov.'s Vol. award, 1995, 97, Dominican Veritas Forum award, 1996, Rogus Lecture, U. Dayton, 1999. Mem. Orgn. Am. Historians, U.S. Cath. Hist. Soc., Rotary Internat. Home: 65 N Westminster St Iowa City IA 52245-3833 Office: Hoover Presdl Libr PO Box 488 West Branch IA 52358-0488 E-mail: timothy.walch@nara.gov., Twalch47@aol.com.

WALCOTT, ROBERT, healthcare executive, priest; b. Boston, July 31, 1942; s. Robert and Rosamond (Pratt) W.; m. Diane Palmer, Sept. 3, 1966; 1 child, Sara. BA, Coll. of Wooster, 1964; MDiv, Ch. Div. Sch., Berkeley, Calif., 1967; M Healthcare Adminstrn., Ohio State U., 1972. Ordained Episc. priest, 1968. Planning specialist Health Planning and Devel. Coun., Wooster, Ohio, 1972-73, asst. dir., 1974-75, St. Joseph Hosp., Lorain, 1975-78, assoc. dir., 1978-81; CEO, Lakeside Meml. Hosp., Brockport, N.Y., 1981-85; adminstr. Dent Neurologic Inst., Buffalo, 1986-87, Oak Hills Nursing Ctr., Lorain, 1994; pastor Ch. of Transfiguration, Buffalo, 1988-91, St. Michael and All Angels Ch., Uniontown, Ohio, 1991-93; adminstr.-in-tng. Chapel Hill Cmty., Canal Fulton, 1993; interim adminstr. Regina Health Ctr., Richfield, 1994-95; adminstr. Ohio Pythian Sisters Home, Sophia Huntington Parker Home, Medina, 1995-2001, Homestead I and II Nursing Homes, Painesville, Ohio, 2001—. Mem. housing com. Tremont Devel. Corp., Cleve., 1994—, bd. dirs., 1997—; mem. steering com. Habitat for Humanity, Cleve., 1994-97; chair trustees Tremont West Devel. Corp., 2000—. Fellow Am. Coll. Healthcare Execs. Democrat. Avocations: travel, reading. Home: 2173 W 7th St Cleveland OH 44113-3621 Office: Homestead I Nursing Home 164 Liberty Dr Painesville OH 44077 E-mail: homstd@apk.net.

WALD, FRANCIS JOHN, state legislator; b. N.D., Apr. 8, 1935; s. Anton S. and Magdelena (Bosch) W.; m. Sharon Kay Mischel, 1961; children: Kirk James, Mark Allen, Jo Lynn, Laura, Cara, Maria, Michael, Joe. BSBA, U. N.D., 1959. Pres., ins. broker Wald Agy. Inc., Dickinson, N.D., 1973—; mem. from dist. 37 N.D. State Ho. of Reps., Bismarck, 1979-83, 85—, chmn. appropriations, edn. and environ. coms.; speaker of the ho. N.D. State Ho of Reps. Mem. exec. com. Conf. of Ins. Legislators. Recipient Korean Occupation award. Mem. Dickenson C. of C. (past pres.), N.D. Profl. Ins. Agts., Am. Legion, Rotary, KC, Elks, Alpha Tau Omega. Office: 433 7th St E Dickinson ND 58601-4525 Address: 433 7th St E Dickinson ND 58601-4525

WALDBAUER, GILBERT PETER, entomologist, educator; b. Bridgeport, Conn., Apr. 18, 1928; s. George Henry and Hedwig Martha (Gribisch) W.; m. Stephanie Margot Stiefel, Jan. 2, 1955; children: Gwen Ruth, Susan Martha. Student, U. Conn., 1949-50; BS, U. Mass., 1953; MS, U. Ill., Urbana, 1956, PhD, 1960. Instr. entomology U. Ill., Urbana, 1958-60, asst. prof., 1960-65, assoc. prof., 1965-71, prof., 1971—, prof. agrl. entomology Coll. Agr., 1971—, prof. emeritus, 1995—. Sr. scientist Ill. Natural History Survey; vis. scientist ICA, Palmira, Colombia, 1971; vis. sr. scientist Internat. Rice Rsch. Inst., 1978-79; cons. AID, 1985; vis. prof. U. Philippines, 1978-79. Author: Insects Through the Seasons, 1996, The Handy Bug Answer Book, 1998, The Birder's Bug Book, 1998, Millions of Monarchs, Bunches of Beetles, 2000; contbg. author: Insect and Mite Nutrition, 1972, Introduction to Insect Pest Management, 1975, Evolution of Insect Migration and Diapause, 1978, Sampling Methods in Soybean Entomology, 1980, Mimicry and the Evolutionary Process, 1988, Ann. Rev. Entomology, 1991; contbr. numerous articles to profl. jours. Served with AUS, 1946-47, PTO. Grantee Agrl. Rsch. Svc. USDA, 1966-71, 83-90, Nat. Geog. Soc., 1972-74, NSF, 1976-79, 82-90. Mem. AAAS, Sigma Xi, Phi Kappa Phi. Home: 807A Ramblewood Ct Savoy IL 61874-9568 Office: U Ill Dept Entomology 320 Morrill Hall Urbana IL 61801

WALDBAUM, JANE COHN, art history educator; b. Jan. 28, 1940; d. Max Arthur and Sarah (Waldstein) Cohn. BA, Brandeis U., 1962; MA, Harvard U., 1964, PhD, 1968. Rsch. fellow in classical archaeology Harvard U., Cambridge, Mass., 1968-70, 72-73; from asst. prof. to assoc. prof. U. Wis., Milw., 1973-84, prof. art history, 1984—2002, chmn. dept., 1982-85, 86-89, 91-92, adj. prof. anthropology, 2002—. Dorot rsch. prof. W.F. Albright Inst. Archaeol. Rsch., Jerusalem, 1990-91; vis. scholar Hebrew U. Jerusalem, 1989-91. Author: From Bronze to Iron, 1978, Metalwork from Sardis, 1983; author (with others), co-editor: Sardis Report I, 1975; mem. editl. bd. Bull. Am. Schs. Oriental Rsch., 1994-98, Near Eastern Archaeology, 2000—; contbr. numerous articles to profl. jours. Woodrow Wilson Found. fellow, dissertation fellow, 1962-63, 65-66, NEH postdoctoral rsch., Jerusalem, 1989-90; grantee Am. Philos. Soc., 1972, NEH, summer 1975, U. Wis.-Milw. Found., 1983. Mem. Am. Schs. Oriental Rsch., Soc. for Archaeol. Sci., Israel Exploration Soc., Archaeol. Inst. Am. (exec. com. 1975-77, chmn. com. on membership programs 1977-81, nominating com. 1984, chmn. com. on lecture program 1985-87, acad. trustee 1993-98, 1st v.p. 1999—02, pres. 03-, com. profl. responsibilities 1993—, fellowships com. 1993-99, gold medal com. 1993-99, chair 1996-97, mem. Near East Archaeology com. 1993—, chair ann. meeting com. 1999—02, chair regional meetings com. 1999—02, mem. pers. com., governance com., devel. com., fin. com.), W.F. Albright Inst. Archaeol. Rsch. (trustee 1996—, mem. governance com. 1996—), Wis. Soc. Jewish Learning (trustee 1993-99), Milw. Soc. Archaeol. Inst. (bd. dirs. 1973—, pres. 1983-85, 91-95, 97-99), Phi Beta Kappa. Office: U Wis Dept Anthropology PO Box 413 Milwaukee WI 53201-0413 E-mail: JCW@uwm.edu.

WALDECK, JOHN WALTER, JR. lawyer; b. Cleve., May 3, 1949; s. John Walter Sr. and Marjorie Ruth (Palenschat) W.; m. Cheryl Gene Cutter, Sept. 10, 1977; children: John III, Matthew, Rebecca. BS, John Carroll U., 1973; JD, Cleve. State U., 1977. Bar: Ohio 1977. Product applications chemist Synthetic Products Co., Cleve., 1969-76; assoc. Arter & Hadden, 1977-85, ptnr., 1986-88, Porter, Wright, Morris and Arthur, Cleve., 1988-90, ptnr. in charge, 1990-96; ptnr. Walter & Haverfield, 1996—. Bd. advisors Litigation Mgmt., Inc., 2000—. Chmn. Bainbridge Twp. Bd. Zoning Appeals, Chagrin Falls, Ohio, 1984-94; trustee Greater Cleve. chpt. Lupus Found. Am., 1978-91, sec., 1979-86; trustee LeBlond Housing Corp., Cleve., 1990-96, sec., 1996, Univ. Circle, Inc., 1993-97, Fairmount Ctr. for Performing and Fine Arts, Novelty, Ohio, 1993-96, sect., 1994-95; bd. dirs. Geauga County Mental Health Alcohol and Drug Addiction Svc. Bd., Chardon, Ohio, 1988-97, treas., 1991-93, vice-chmn., 1993-95, chmn., 1995-97; mem. bd. advisors Palliative Care Svcs., Cleve. Clinic Cancer Ctr., 1989-91. Mem. Ohio State Bar Assn. (real property sect. bd. govs. 1992), Greater Cleve. Bar Assn. (real property, corp. banking sect, co-chair real estate law inst. 1990, 95, 96). Roman Catholic. Avocations: beekeeping, gardening, jogging. Home: 18814 Rivers Edge Dr W Chagrin Falls OH 44023-4968 Office: Walter & Haverfield 50 Public Square 1300 Terminal Tower Cleveland OH 44113 E-mail: jwaldeck@walterhav.com.

WALDERA, WAYNE EUGENE, crisis management specialist; b. Cayuga, N.D., Mar. 23, 1930; s. Bernard Cyril and Eleanor Nee (Kugler) W.; m. Eva Jenzene Personius, Jan. 13, 1958; children: Anthony, Lori, Mia, Shauna. BSBA, N.D. State U., 1952. With Gamble-Skogmo, 1954-88; pres. Gamble div. Gamble-Skogmo, Mpls., 1972-88; pres., CEO Retail Resource Co., 1988-89, Amdura Corp., Denver, 1989-92, also bd. dirs.; chmn. Sullivan Waldera, Inc., Mpls., 1992-93; prin., CEO Waldera & Co. Inc., 1993—. 1st lt. USAF, 1952-54. Home: 12125 62nd St Waconia MN 55387-9411 Office: Waldera & Co Inc 15500 Wayzata Blvd Ste 604-208 Wayzata MN 55391-1435 E-mail: wwaldera@uswest.net.

WALDMEIR, PETER NIELSEN, journalist; b. Detroit, Jan. 16, 1931; s. Joseph John and Helen Sarah (Nielsen) W.; m. Marilyn C. Choma; children— Peter William, Patti Ann, Lindsey Marilyn, Christopher Norman. Student, Wayne State U., 1949-58. With Detroit News, 1949—, sports columnist, 1962-72, gen. columnist, 1972—. Pres. Old Newsboys Goodfellow Fund, Detroit, 1988. With USMC, 1951-53. Recipient Headliners award Nat. Headliners Club, 1971, SDX Lifetime Achievement award, 2000; named Mich. Sports Writer of Yr., Nat. Sportscasters and Sportswriters, 1967, 69, 71; Heart award Variety Club Internat., 1985; inducted Mich. Journalism Hall of Fame, 2000. Mem. Sigma Delta Chi. Roman Catholic. Office: Detroit News 615 W Lafayette Blvd Detroit MI 48226-3197 E-mail: pwalmeir@aol.com.

WALDRON, KENNETH JOHN, mechanical engineering educator, researcher; b. Sydney, NSW, Australia, Feb. 11, 1943; came to U.S., 1965; s. Edward Walter and Maurine Florence (Barrett) W.; m. Manjula Bhushan, July 3, 1968; children: Andrew, Lalitha, Paul. BEngring., U. Sydney, 1964, M Engring. Sci., 1965, D Engring., 1999; PhD, PhD, Stanford U., 1969. Registered profl. engr., Tex. Acting asst. prof. Stanford (Calif.) U., 1968-69; lectr., sr. lectr. U. NSW, Sydney, 1969-74; assoc. prof. U. Houston, 1974-79; assoc. prof. mech. engring. Ohio State U., Columbus, 1979-81, prof., 1981—, Nordholt prof., 1984—, chmn. dept. mech. engring., 1993—. Co-author: Machines That Walk, 1988, Kinematics, Dynamic and Design of Machinery, 1999; contbr. over 215 articles to profl. jours. and conf. procs. Recipient Robotics Industries Assn. Engelberger award, 1997. Fellow ASME (tech. editor Trans. Jour. Mech. Design 1988-92, Leonardo da Vinci award 1988, Mechanisms award 1990, Machine Design award 1994); mem. Soc. Automotive Engrs. (Ralph R. Teetor award 1977), Am. Soc. for Engring. Edn. Achievements include work on adaptive suspension vehicle project. Office: Ohio State U 2075 B Robinson 206 W 18th Ave Columbus OH 43210-1189

WALENGA, JEANINE MARIE, medical educator, researcher; b. Evergreen Park, Ill., Nov. 21, 1955; d. Eugene Adam and Therese Marie Walenga BS, U. Ill., Chgo., 1978; Diplome d'Etudes Approfondies, U. Paris VI, 1984, PhD, 1987; postgrad., Loyola U., Maywood, Ill., 1981-84. Cert. med. technologist. Med. technologist MacNeal Hosp., Berwyn, Ill., 1978-79; rsch. asst. Loyola U. Med. Ctr., Maywood, 1979-80, hemostasis rsch. lab. supr., 1980-87, co-dir. hemostasis rsch. lab., 1987—, asst. prof. thoracic/cardiovascular surgery/pathology, 1988-94, assoc. prof., 1994-2000, prof., 2000—. Mem. Cardiovascular Inst., Loyola U., 1995—; cons. in field; lectr. in field; observer Nat. Com. for Clin. Lab. Stds., 1988—; del. US Pharmacopeia, 1990—. Contbr. articles to profl. jours. Named Alumnus of Yr., U. Ill., 1990; NHLBI rsch. grantee, 1989—; recipient Investigator Recognition award, 1993. Fellow Am. Coll. Angiology; mem. Internat. Inst. for Thrombosis and Vascular (sec. 1989—), Am. Assn. Pathologists, Am. Soc. Hematology, Internat. Soc. Thrombosis and Hemostasis (sci. and standardization subcoms. control anticoagulation 1990—), Am. Soc. Clin. Pathologists, Am. Heart Assn., Am. Soc. Med. Tech. Avocations: photography, archeology, gardening, birding, travel.

WALENTIK, CORINNE ANNE, pediatrician; b. Rockville Centre, N.Y., Nov. 24, 1949; d. Edward Robert and Evelyn Mary (Brinskele) Finno; m. David Stephen Walentik, June 24, 1972; children: Anne, Stephen, Kristine. AB with honors, St. Louis U., 1970, MD, 1974, MPH, 1992. Diplomate Am. Bd. Pediat., Am. Bd. Neonatal and Perinatal Medicine, cert. cert. physician exec. Certifying Commn. on Med. Mgmt., Am. Coll. Physician Execs. Resident in pediat. St. Louis U. Group Hosps., 1974-76, fellow in neonatalogy, 1976-78; neonatalogist St. Mary's Health Ctr., St. Louis, 1978-79; from co-dir. to dir. neonatal unit St. Louis City Hosps., 1979-85; dir. neonatalogy St. Louis Regional Med. Ctr., 1985-96; asst. prof. pediat. St. Louis U., 1980-94, assoc. clin. prof., 1994-98, assoc. prof. pediat., 1998—2001, prof. pediat., 2001—. Supr. nursery follow up program Cardinal Glennon Children's Hosp., St. Louis, 1979—, neonatologist, physician exec. for managed care and pub. policy, 1997—. Contbr. articles to profl. jours. Mem. adv. com. Mo. Perinatal Program., 1983-86. Fellow Am. Acad. Pediats.; mem. APHA, Mo. Pub. Health Assn. (pres. St. Louis chpt. 1995-96), Mo. Perinatal Assn. (pres. 1983), Nat. Perinatal Assn. (coun. 1984-87), Mo. State Med. Assn., St. Louis Met. Med. Soc. Roman Catholic. Avocations: bridge, baseball, sports. Home: 7234 Princeton Ave Saint Louis MO 63130-3027 Office: Cardinal Glennon Children's Hosp 1465 S Grand Blvd Saint Louis MO 63104-1003 E-mail: walentca@slu.edu.

WALES, ROSS ELLIOT, lawyer; b. Youngstown, Ohio, Oct. 17, 1947; s. Craig C. and Beverly (Bromley) W.; m. Juliana Fraser, Sept. 16, 1972; children: Dod Elliot, James Craig. AB, Princeton U., 1969; JD, U. Va., 1974. Bar: Ohio 1974, U.S. Dist. Ct. (so. dist.) Ohio 1974, U.S. Ct. Appeals (5th cir.) 1979. Assoc. Taft, Stettinius & Hollister, Cin., 1974-81, ptnr., 1981—. Pres. U.S. Swimming, Inc., Colorado Springs, 1979-84, U.S. Aquatic Sports, Inc., Colorado Springs, 1984-88, 94-98. Pres. Cin. Active to Support Edn., 1987-88; chmn. sch. tax levy campaign, Cin., 1987; trustee The Childrens Home Cin., 1987—, v.p., 1995-98, pres., 1998—; bd. sec. Cin. State Tech. and C.C., 1995-98, vice-chmn., 1998-2000, chair 2000-02; pres. Cin. Arts Sch., Inc., 2000-01; sec. Greater Cin. Arts and Edn. Ctr., 1996—; mem. U.S. Anti-Doping Agy., Colo. Springs. Mem. ABA, Ohio Bar Assn., Cin. Bar Assn., Internat. Swimming Fedn. of Lausanne, Switzerland (sec. 1988-92, v.p. 1992-2000). Presbyterian. Office: 1800 Firstar Twr 425 Walnut St Cincinnati OH 45202-3923 E-mail: wales@taftlaw.com.

WALHOUT, JUSTINE SIMON, chemistry educator; b. Aberdeen, S.D., Dec. 11, 1930; d. Otto August and Mabel Ida (Tews) S.; m. Donald Walhout, Feb. 1, 1958; children: Mark, Timothy, Lynne, Peter. BS, Wheaton Coll., 1952; PhD, Northwestern U., 1956. Instr. Wright City Community Coll., Chgo., 1955-56; asst. prof. Rockford (Ill.) Coll., 1956-59, assoc. prof., 1959-66, 81-89, prof., 1989-96, prof. emeritus, 1996—, dept. chmn., 1987-95; cons. Pierce Chem. Co., Rockford, 1968-69; trustee Rockford (Ill.) Coll., 1987-91. Contbr. articles to profl. jours. Mem. Ill. Bd. Edn., 1974-81. Mem. AAUW (Ill. bd. mem. 1985-87), Am. Chem. Soc. (councilor 1993-99), Rockford LWV (bd. dirs. 1983-85), Sigma Xi. Presbyterian. Home: 320 N Rockford Ave Rockford IL 61107-4547 Office: Rockford Coll 5050 E State St Rockford IL 61108-2311

WALI, MOHAN KISHEN, environmental science and natural resources educator; b. Kashmir, India, Mar. 1, 1937; came to U.S., 1969, naturalized, 1975; s. Jagan Nath and Somavati (Wattal) W.; m. Sarla Safaya, Sept. 25, 1960; children: Pamela, Promod. BS, U. Jammu and Kashmir, 1957; MS, U. Allahabad, India, 1960; PhD, U. B.C., Can., 1970. Lectr. S.P. Coll., Srinagar, Kashmir, 1963-65; rsch. fellow U. Copenhagen, 1965-66; grad. fellow U. B.C., 1967-69; asst. prof. biology U. N.D., Grand Forks, 1969-73, assoc. prof., 1973-79, prof., 1979-83, Hill rsch. prof., 1973; dir. Forest River Biology Area Field Sta., 1970-79, Project Reclamation, 1975-83; spl. asst. to univ. pres., 1977-82; staff ecologist Grand Forks Energy Rsch. Lab. U.S. Dept. Interior, 1974-75; prof. Coll. Environ. Sci. and Forestry SUNY, Syracuse, 1983-89, dir. grad. program environ. sci., 1983-85, prof. Sch. Natural Resources, 1990—, dir. Sch. Natural Resources, assoc. dean Coll. Agr., 1990-93; dir. Ohio State U. Environ. Sci. Grad. Program, Columbus, 1994—. Vice chmn. N.D. Air Pollution Adv. Coun., 1981-83; co-chair IV Internat. Congress on Ecology, 1986. Editor: Some Environmental Aspects of Strip-Mining in North Dakota, 1973, Prairie: A Multiple View, 1975, Practices and Problems of Land Reclamation in Western North America, 1975, Ecology and Coal Resource Development, 1979, Ecosystem Rehabilitation-Preamble to Sustainable Development, 1992; co-editor Agriculture and the Environment, 1993; sr. editor Reclamation Rev., 1976-80, chief editor, 1980-81; chief editor Reclamation and Revegetation Rsch., 1982-87; contbr. articles to profl. jours. Recipient B.C. Gamble Disting. Tchg. and Svc. award, 1977. Fellow AAAS, Nat. Acad. Scis. India; mem. Ecol. Soc. Am. (chmn. sect. internat. activities 1980-84), Bot. Ecol. Soc., Can. Bot. Assn. (dir. ecology sect. 1976-79, v.p. 1982-83), Am. Soc. Agronomy, Am. Inst. Biol. Sci. (gen. chmn. 34th ann. meeting), Internat. Assn. Ecolog (co-chmn. IV Internat. Congress Ecology), Internat. Soc. Soil Sci., N.D. Acad. Sci. (chmn. editl. com. 1979-81), Sigma Xi (nat. lectr. 1983-85, pres. Ohio State chpt. 1993-94, pres. Syracuse chpt. 1984-85, Outstanding Rsch. award U. N.D. chpt. 1975). Office: Ohio State U Sch Natural Resources 2021 Coffey Rd Columbus OH 43210-1044

WALICKI, ANDRZEJ STANISLAW, history of ideas educator; b. Warsaw, Poland, May 15, 1930; came to U.S., 1986, naturalized 1993. s. Michal Walicki and Anna (Szlachcinska) Chmielewska; m. Janina Derks, Mar. 10, 1953 (div. June 1970); m. Maria Wodzynska, June 17, 1972 (div. May 1985); children: Malgorzata, Adam; m. Marzena Balicka, July 27, 1985. MA, Warsaw U., 1953; PhD, Polish Acad. Scis., 1957. Asst. prof. Warsaw U., 1958-60, Polish Acad. Scis., Warsaw, 1960-64, assoc. prof., 1964-72, prof., head dept. Inst. Philosophy, 1972-81; sr. rsch. fellow Australian Nat. U., Canberra, 1981-86; O'Neill prof. history U. Notre Dame, Ind., 1986—. Vis. Kratter prof. history Stanford U., 1976. Author: The Slavophile Controversy, 1975, A History of Russian Thought, 1979, Philosophy and Romantic Nationalism, 1982, Legal Philosophies of Russian Liberalism, 1987, Marxism and the Leap to the Kingdom of Freedom: The Rise and Fall of the Communist Utopia, 1995; also 13 others. Recipient award A. Jurzykowski Found., N.Y.C., 1983, Internat. Balzan prize for history Found. Internat. Premio E. Balzan, Milano, Italy, 1998; Rsch. grantee Ford Found., N.Y.C., 1960, vis. fellow All Souls Coll., U. Oxford, 1966-67, 73, Guggenheim fellow J.S. Guggenheim Meml. Found., 1991. Mem. Am. Assn. for Advancement Slavic Studies, Polish Acad. Scis. Roman Catholic. Office: U Notre Dame Dept History Notre Dame IN 46556

WALKER, BRUCE EDWARD, anatomy educator; b. Montreal, Que., Can., June 17, 1926; s. Robinson Clarence and Dorothea Winston (Brown) W.; m. Lois Catherine McCuaig, June 26, 1948; children: Brian Ross, Dianne Heather, Donald Robert, Susan Lois. B.S., McGill U., 1947, M.S., 1952, Ph.D., 1954; M.D., U. Tex. at Galveston, 1966. Instr. anatomy McGill U., 1955-57; asst. prof. anatomy U. Tex. Med. Br., 1957-61, assoc. prof. anatomy, 1961-67; prof. Mich. State U., East Lansing, 1967—, chmn. dept., 1967-75. Contbr. articles to profl. jours. Mem. Am. Assn. Anatomists, Teratology Soc., Am. Assn. for Cancer Research. Office: Mich State U Dept Radiology East Lansing MI 48824

WALKER, DUARD LEE, medical educator; b. Bishop, Calif., June 2, 1921; s. Fred H. and Anna Lee (Shumate) Walker; m. Dorothea Virginia McHenry, Aug. 11, 1945; children: Douglas Keith, Donna Judith, David Cameron, Diane Susan. A.B., U. Calif. - Berkeley, 1943, M.A., 1947; M.D., U. Calif. - San Francisco, 1945. Diplomate Am. Bd. Microbiology. Intern, U.S. Naval Hosp., Shoemaker, Calif., 1945—46; asst. resident internal medicine Stanford U. Service San Francisco Hosp., 1950—52; asso. prof. med. microbiology and preventive medicine U. Wis., Madison, 1952—59, prof. med. microbiology, 1959—88, prof., chmn. med. microbiology, 1970—76, Paul F. Clark prof. med. microbiology, 1977—88, prof. emeritus, 1988—, prof., chmn. med. microbiology, 1981—88. Cons. Naval Med. Rsch. Unit, Gt. Lakes, Ill., 1958—74; mem. microbiology tng. com. Nat. Inst. Gen. Med. Scis., 1966—70; mem. nat. adv. Allergy and Infectious Diseases Coun., 1970—74; mem. adv. com. on blood program rsch. ARC, 1978—79; mem. study group on papovaviridae Internat. Com. on Taxonomy of Viruses, 1976—90; mem. vaccines and related biol. products adv. com. FDA, 1985—89; mem. rev. panel postdoct. rsch. fellowships for physicians Howard Hughes Med Inst., 1990—93. Served to lt. (j.g.) USNR, 1943—46, served to lt. comdr. USNR, 1953—55. Fellow NRC postdoctoral virology, Rockefeller Inst. Med. Rsch., N.Y.C., 1947—49, USPHS immunology, George Williams Hooper Found., U. Calif., San Francisco, 1949—50. Fellow: Infectious Diseases Soc. Am., Am. Acad. Microbiology, Am. Pub. Health Assn.; mem.: Arts and Letters, Wis. Acad. Sics., Am. Soc. Virology, AAUP, Reticulendothelial Soc., Soc. Exptl. Biology and Medicine, AAAS, Am. Soc. Microbiology, Am. Assn. Immunologists, NAS. Home: 618 Odell St Madison WI 53711-1435 Office: U Wis Med Sch 1300 University Ave Madison WI 53706-1510 E-mail: dlwalkel@facstaff.wisc.edu.

WALKER, FRANK DILLING, market research executive; b. Indpls., Dec. 31, 1934; s. Frank D. and Dorothy Mae (Cole) W.; m. Jane Tatman, Aug. 25, 1979; children— Steven F., Leah R. B.A., DePauw U., 1957. Chmn., CEO Walker Group, Indpls., 1960-95, Walker Clin. Evaluations, Inc., Indpls., 1986-95; chmn. Walker Info., 1995—. Bd. dirs. Am. United Life Ins. Co., NBD Ind. Nat. Bank, State Life Ins. Co.; frequent speaker on market rsch. to various groups. Contbr. articles trade publs. Past mem. Indpls. Hist. Preservation Commn.; bd. dirs. Ind. Repertory Theatre, Meth. Hosp., United Way of Greater Indpls.; adv. council Indpls. Mus. Art, Buchanan Counseling Center; former chmn. Central Ind. Better Bus. Bur.; former chmn. Indpls. Econ. Devel. Corp.; trustee Children's Mus. Indpls., Univ. Indpls.; former bd. dirs. Jr. Achievement Central Ind., mem. adv. council; trustee The Children's Mus., YMCA Found.; bd. dirs. Citizens Gas and Coke Utility. With USAF, 1958-60. Mem. Council Am. Survey Research Orgns. (past chmn. bd.), Am. Mktg. Assn. (past pres. Ind. chpt.), Indpls. Sales and Mktg. Execs. Assn. (past pres.), Indpls. C. of C. (past chmn.), Mktg. Rsch. Assn. (hon. life), Sigma Chi. Republican. Methodist. Office: Walker Info Ste 100 3939 Priority Way South Dr Indianapolis IN 46240-3833

WALKER, GEORGE HERBERT, III, investment banking company executive, lawyer; b. St. Louis, Mar. 16, 1931; s. George H. and Mary (Carter) W.; m. Sandra E. Canning, Dec. 23, 1955 (div. Oct. 1962); children: Mary Elizabeth, Wendy, Isabelle; m. Kimberly Gedge, July 27, 1968 (div. Jan. 1977); children: George H. IV, Carter; m. Carol Banta, Feb. 21, 1987. B.A., Yale U., 1953; LL.B., Harvard U., 1956. Bar: Conn. 1956. Gen. ptnr. G.H. Walker & Co. (later G.H. Walker, Laird Inc.), 1961-74; sr. v.p., also bd. dirs. White, Weld & Co. Inc., 1974-75; chmn. bd. dirs. G.H. Walker & Co., 1973-74; exec. v.p. Stifel Nicolaus & Co., 1976-78, pres., CEO, 1978-92, chmn., 1982—, also bd. dirs. Civilian aide to sec. U.S. Army for Ea. Mo., 1973-80; bd. dirs. Laidlaw Corp., Laclede Steel Co., Eck-Adams Corp.; bd. govs. Midwest Stock Exch., 1982-88. Bd. dirs. Downtown St. Louis Inc., 1975-90, chmn., 1984-86; bd. dirs. Webster U., chmn. bd., 1987-92; trustee Mo. Hist. Soc., St. Louis Children's Hosp., 1972-92, Jefferson Nat. Expansion Meml. Assn., 1992; vestryman St. Ann's Ch., Kennebunkport, Maine; mem. Mo. Rep. Ctrl. Com., 1983—; adv. bd. St. Louis Area coun. Boy Scouts Am., 1989—; trustee investment trust Episcopal Diocese of Mo.; hon. bd. dirs. Anti-Drug Abuse Edn. Fund, Inc., 1990—; bd. dirs. St. Louis Zoo, 1992. With USAF, 1956-58. Mem. Rotary (St. Louis club). Home: 19 Portland Pl Saint Louis MO 63108-1203 Office: Stifel Fin Corp 501 N Broadway Saint Louis MO 63102-2102

WALKER, JACK L. environmental scientist; BSEE, MIT, 1962; MSEE, U. Mich., 1967, PhD in Elec. and Computer Engring., 1974. Jr. engr. GE, 1960-61; engr. Bendix Sys. Divsn., 1962-64; rsch. engr. Environ. Rsch. Inst. Mich., Ann Arbor, 1964-79, assoc. dir. radar divsn., 1979-82, dir. infrared and optics divsn., 1982-86, exec. v.p. and dir. tech. ops., 1986-95, v.p., chief scientist, 1995—. Mem. Ind. Surveillance Sci. and Engring. Group, Ballistic Missile Def. Office, Air Force Sci. Adv. Bd.; trustee Consortium for Internat. Earth Sci. Info. Network. Contbr. numerous articles to profl. publs. Recipient decoration for exceptional civilian svc. USAF, 1995. Fellow IEEE (bd. govs. Aerospace and Electronics Sys. Soc., M. Barry Carlton award 1981); mem. NAE. Office: Environ Rsch Inst Mich PO Box 134001 Ann Arbor MI 48113-4001

WALKER, JAMES S. financial executive; Grad., Miami U., Oxford, Ohio. Mgr. Ernst & Young; contr. Park-Ohio Holdings Corp., Cleve., 1983-91, v.p., treas., contr., 1991—. Office: Park-Ohio Holdings Corp 23000 Euclid Ave Cleveland OH 44117-1706

WALKER, JAMES SILAS, academic administrator; b. LaFollette, Tenn., Aug. 21, 1933; s. John Charles and Ruth Constance (Yeagle) W.; m. Nadine Leas Mortenson, May 28, 1954; children: Steven J., David K., Bradley P., Scott C. BA, U. Ariz., 1954; BDiv, McCormick Theol. Sem., 1956; postgrad., U. Basel, Switzerland, 1956-57; PhD, Claremont Grad. U., 1963; LHD, Jamestown Coll., 1999. Ordained to ministry Presbyn. Ch., 1956. Asst. pastor Ctrl. Presbyn. Ch., Denver, 1957-60; prof. Huron Coll., S.D., 1963-66, Hastings (Nebr.) Coll., 1966-75, dir. devel., 1975-79, dean, 1979-83; pres. Jamestown Coll., N.D., 1983—. Adj. faculty mem. Luther Northwestern Theol. Sem., St. Paul, 1984—. Author: Theology of Karl Barth, 1963. Rotary Internat. Found. fellow, 1956-57; Nat. Def. Title IV grantee, 1960-63; named to Claremont Grad. U. Alumni Hall of Fame, 2000. Mem. Assn. Presbyn. Colls. and Univs., Presbytery of Heartland (coun.), Rotary (dist. 563 gov. 1978-79). Republican. Avocations: travel, hunting, photography. Office: Jamestown Coll Office Of Pres # 6080 Jamestown ND 58405-0001 E-mail: jwalker23@kc.rr.com.

WALKER, MARTIN DEAN, specialty chemical company executive; b. 1932; married. BS, GM Inst.; MBA, Mich. State U. With GM, Detroit, 1954-70; v.p. Am. Motors Corp., 1970-72; exec. v.p. Rockwell Internat. Corp., Pitts., 1972-86; chmn., chief exec. officer M.A. Hanna Co., Cleve., 1986—. Office: M A Hanna Co 200 Public Sq Ste 36-5000 Cleveland OH 44114

WALKER, PHILIP CHAMBERLAIN, II, health care executive; b. Big Spring, Tex., July 7, 1944; s. Philip Chamberlain and Mary Catherine (St. John) W.; m. Linda Jane Holsclaw, Jan. 21, 1978; children: Shannon M., Meghan M. BA, Cen. Wash. State Coll., 1970; MS, U. Idaho, 1971. Exec. dir. Multnomah Found. for Med. Care, Portland, Oreg., 1972-81; chief exec. officer Peer Rev. Orgn. for Wash. State, Seattle, 1981-84; dir. Preferred Provider Orgn. devel. Provident Life and Accident, Chattanooga, 1984-88; v.p. Maxicare Health Plans, L.A., 1988-91; v.p., gen. mgr. Maxicare Health Plans Midwest, Chgo., 1991-92; pres. Health Plus, Peoria, Ill., 1992—; CEO, chmn. bd. HCH Adminstrn., 1992-98; sr. v.p. Health Care Horizons, Albuquerque, 1992-98; exec. v.p. Proctor Health Sys., 1998—. Bd. dirs. RMR Group, HCH Adminstrn., Health Care Horizons; cons. to numerous orgns. Contbr. articles to profl. jours. Chmn., bd. dirs. Hult Health Edn. Ctr.; bd. dirs. Cancer Ctr. for Health Living, 2001—. With USAF, 1961—66, Vietnam. Mem.: Creve Coeur Club (bd. govs., sr. v.p.). Office: 5409 N Knoxville Ave Peoria IL 61614

WALKER, ROBERT MOWBRAY, physicist, educator; b. Phila., Feb. 6, 1929; s. Robert and Margaret (Seivwright) W.; m. Alice J. Agedal, Sept. 2, 1951 (div. 1973); children: Eric, Mark; m. Ghislaine Crozaz, Aug. 24, 1973. B.S. in Physics, Union Coll., 1950, D.Sc., 1967; M.S., Yale U., 1951, Ph.D., 1954; Dr honoris causa, Université de Clermont-Ferrand, 1975. Physicist Gen. Electric Research Lab., Schenectady, 1954-62, 63-66; McDonnell prof. physics Washington U., St. Louis, 1966—; dir. McDonnell Center for Space Scis., 1975-99. Vis. prof. U. Paris, 1962—63; adj. prof. metallurgy Rensselaer Poly. Inst., 1958, adj. prof. physics, 1965—66; vis. prof. physics and geology Calif. Inst. Tech., 1972, Phys. Research Lab., Ahmedabad, India, 1981, Institut d'Astrophysique, Paris, 1981, Univ. Libre, Brussels, 2001—; nat. lectr. Sigma Xi, 1984—85; pres. Vols. for Internat. Tech. Assistance, 1960—62, 1965—66, founder, 1960; mem. Lunar Sample Analysis Planning Team, 1968—70; bd. dirs. Univs. Space Rsch. Assn., 1969—71; mem. Lunar Sample Rev. Bd., 1970—72; adv. com. Lunar Sci. Inst., 1972—75; mem. temporary nominating group in planetary scis. Nat. Acad. Scis., 1973—75, bd. on sci. and tech. for internat. devel., 1974—76, com. planetary and lunar exploration, 1977—80, mem. space sci. bd., 1979—82; mem. organizing com. Com. on Space Research-Internat. Astron. Union, Marseille, France, 1984; mem. task force on sci. uses of space sta. Solar System Exploration Com., 1985—86; mem. Antarctic Meteorite Working Group, 1985—92, NASA Planetary Geosci. Strategy Com., 1986—88, European Sci. Found. Sci. Orgn. Com., Workshop on Analysis of Samples from Solar System Bodies, 1990; chmn. Antarctic Meteorite Working Group, 1990—92; mem. cosmic dust allocation com. NASA, 1998; vis. com. dept. terrestial magnetism Carnegie Instn., 1998; vis. com. Max Planck fur Chemie, Mainz, Germany, 1998. Decorated officer de l'Ordre des Palmes Academiques (France); recipient Disting. Svc. award Am. Nuclear Soc., 1964, Yale Engring. Assn. award for contbn. to basic and applied sci., 1966, Indsl. Rsch. awards, 1964, 65; Exceptional Sci. Achievement award NASA, 1970; E.O. Lawrence award AEC, 1971; Antarctic Svc. medal NSF, 1985; NSF fellow, 1962-63; Asteroid 1985 JWI named in his honor, 1999. Fellow AAAS, Am. Phys. Soc., Meteoritical Soc. (Leonard medal 1993), Am. Geophys. Union, Indian Inst. of Astrophycis (hon.); mem. NAS (mem. polar rsch. bd. com. 1995, J. Lawrence Smith medal 1991), Am. Astron. Soc., St. Louis Acad. Scis. (Peter Raven Lifetime Scientific Achievement award 1997). Achievements include research and publs. on cosmic rays, nuclear physics, geophysics, radiation effects in solids, particularly devel. solid state track detectors and their application to geophysics and nuclear physics problems; discovery of fossil particle tracks in terrestrial and extra-terrestrial materials and fission track method of dating; application of phys. scis. to art and archaeology; lab. studies of interplanetary dust and interstellar grains in primitive meteorites. Home: 3 Romany Park Ln Saint Louis MO 63132-4211

WALKER, RONALD EDWARD, psychologist, educator; b. East St. Louis, Ill., Jan. 23, 1935; s. George Edward and Marnella (Altmeyer) W.; m. Aldona M. Mogenis, Oct. 4, 1958; children: Regina, Mark, Paula, Alexis. B.S., St. Louis U., 1957; M.A., Northwestern U., 1959, Ph.D., 1961. Lectr. psychology Northwestern U., 1959-61; faculty dept. psychology Loyola U., Chgo., 1961—, asst., then asso. prof., 1961-68, prof., chmn. dept., 1965—; acting dean Loyola U. (Coll. Arts and Scis.), 1973-74, dean, 1974-80, academic v.p., 1980-81, sr. v.p., dean faculties, 1981-89, exec. v.p., 1989-99. Cons. VA, Chgo., 1965-74; Am. Psychol. Assn.-NIMH; vis. cons., 1969; vis. scientist Am. Psychol. Assn. NSF, 1968; Cook County (Ill.) rep. from Ill. Psychol. Assn., 1969-72; cons.-evaluator North Cen. Assn., 1986-99. Contbr. articles to profl. jours. Trustee St. Francis Hosp., Evanston, Ill., 1986-92, Chgo. Archdiocesan Sems., 1985-97, Loyola Acad., Wilmette, Ill., 1987-93, St. Louis U., 1988-97. Recipient Disting. Psychologist of Yr. award Ill. Psychol. Assn., 1986. Mem. APA (coun. rep. 1970-72), Ill. Psychol. Assn. (chmn. student devel. com. 1965-67, chmn. acad. sec. 1966-67, disting. psychologist of yr. award 1986), Psi Chi, Phi Beta Kappa. Home: Unit 5I 1630 Sheridan Rd Wilmette IL 60091-1835

WALKER, SCOTT KEVIN, state legislator; b. Colorado Springs, Nov. 2, 1967; s. Llewellyn Scott and Patricia Ann (Fitch) W.; m. Tonette Marie Tarantino; children: Matthew David, Alexander Nicholas. Student, Marquette U., 1990. Acct. adminstr. IBM, 1988-90; chmn. 5th congl. dist. Wis. State Rep. Party, 1991-93; assemblyman Wis. State Dist. 14, 1993—. Exec. com. Wis. State Rep. Party, 1991—; chmn. com. elections and constl. law, Wis. State Assembly, 1995—, chmn. com. corrections, 1997—. Fin. devel. specialist ARC, 1990-93; coun. mem. Milw. County Boy Scouts Am. Mem. Wauwatosa Hist. Soc., Wauwatosa Area C. of C. Address: PO Box 8953 Madison WI 53708-8953

WALKER, STEVEN FRANK, management consultant; b. Indpls., Dec. 31, 1957; s. Frank Dilling and Beverly (Trudgen) W.; m. Brenda Anne Brost, July 11, 1986; children: Jack. BS, Boston U., 1980. Acct. R.A. Boston & Co., Boston, 1980-81; staff acct. NEECO, Needham, Mass., 1981-82; sr. project dir. Walker Research Inc., Phoenix, 1982-84, account exec. Walnut Creek, Calif., 1984-85, group mgr. Indpls., 1985-87, v.p. new bus., 1987-88, v.p. new ventures and corp. devel., 1988-95, CEO, 1995-98, 1999—. Bd. dirs. Walker Clin. Evaluations, Indpls., 1989—; lectr. in field. Contbr. articles to profl. ours. Bd. dirs. Boys Clubs of Indpls., 1987—; mem. mktg. com. Indpls. Zoo, 1988; capt. fund raising Indpls. C. of C., 1987-88, Children's Mus., 1986-88; charter mem. Young Leadxers for Mutz, 1988. Mem. Am. Mktg. Assn., Mktg. Research Assn., Advt. Research Found. Republican. Roman Catholic. Avocations: golf, wine, auto racing. Office: Walker Info Inc 3939 Priority Way South Dr Indianapolis IN 46240-3834

WALKER, THOMAS RAY, city aviation commissioner; AB in Art, Dartmouth Coll., 1970; BArch, Ill. Inst. Tech., 1977. Project mgr. Lohan Assocs., 1977-86; v.p. design and constrn. The Chgo. Dock and Canal Trust, 1986-91; exec. dir. Pub. Bldg. Commn. of Chgo., 1991-95; commr. dept. transp. City of Chgo., 1995-99; commr. Chgo. Dept. of Aviation, City of Chgo., 2000—. Prin. works include Soldier Field World Cup renovation, Chgo., Wright Coll. Addition, Chgo. Pub. Schs. capital improvement program, Cityfront Ctr., Chgo., MarketTower Officer Bldg., Indpls., Episcopal Sch. of Dallas Libr./Fine Arts addition, Frito-Lay Nat. Hdqs., Plano, Tex. Vice chmn. Chgo. Area Transp. Study; commr. State St. Commn.; mem. com. Newhouse arch. fellowship program Chgo. Arch. Found.; mem. Chgo. Planning Commn.; mem. selection com. cmty. svc. fellowship Chgo. Cmty. Trust; mem. TRB steering com. Conf. Transp. Issue in Large U.S. Cities; mem. Conf. Minority Transp. Officials; trustee Chgo. Music and Dance Theater; chmn. leadership coun. Met. Open Cmtys.; co-chmn. adv. bd./housing com. Met. Planning Coun. 1st lt. USAF, 1970-72. Mem. Intelligent Transp. Soc. of Am. (bd. dirs.), Nat. Assn. City Transp. Ofcls. (chmn.), Nat. Orgn. Minority Architects, Urban Land Inst., Lambda Alpha Internat. Office: O'Hare Internat Airport Dept of Aviation PO Box 66142 AMF Ohare IL 60666-0142

WALKER, WALDO SYLVESTER, biology educator, academic administrator; b. Fayette, Iowa, June 12, 1931; s. Waldo S. and Mildred (Littele) W.; m. Marie J. Olsen, July 27, 1952 (div.); children: Martha Lynn, Gayle Ann; m. Rita K. White, June 16, 1984. BS cum laude, Upper Iowa U., Fayette, 1953; MS, U. Iowa, 1957, PhD, 1959. Mem. faculty Grinnell (Iowa) Coll., 1958, assoc. dean coll., 1963-65, chmn. div. Natural Scis., 1968-69, dean of adminstrn., 1969-73, exec. v.p., 1973-77, dean coll., 1973-80, provost, 1977-80, exec. v.p., 1980-90, exec. v.p. and treas., 1988-90, v.p. for coll. svcs., 1990-95, prof. biology, 1968-2001, prof. emeritus, 2001—. Research assoc. U. B.C. Dept. of Botany, 1966-67. Author articles on plant physiology, ultrastructural cytology. Served with U.S. Army, 1953-55. Fellow NSF Sci. Faculty, 1966-67; recipient NSF research grants, 1960-63, 68. Mem. Am. Assn. Colls., Am. Conf. Acad. Deans (nat. chmn. 1977-78), Am. Assn. Higher Edn., Sigma Xi. Home: 1920 Country Club Dr Grinnell IA 50112-1130 Address: Grinnell Coll PO Box H2 Grinnell IA 50112-0805 E-mail: walkerws@pcpartner.net.

WALL, CARROLL EDWARD, publishing executive; b. Cherokee, Iowa, Mar. 3, 1942; s. Clifford R. and Mabel B. (Tjossem) W.; m. Mary Ellen Stratton, Sept. 1, 1962; children: Annette, Jannette, Heather, Christopher. B.A. with distinction, U. Iowa, 1964; postgrad. in Chinese mil. history, U. Mich., 1964-65, M.A. in L.S, 1966. Reference librarian U. Mich., Dearborn, 1966-67, head librarian, 1967-84; founder, pub. Pierian Press. (pub. reference books), Ann Arbor, Mich., 1968—. Speaker, cons. in field. Editor: books, the most recent being Author Index to Public Affairs Information Service, 1965-69, 1971; author: books, the most recent being Index to A.L.A.'s Index to General Literature, 1972; contbr. articles to profl. jours.; editor Media Rev. Digest, 1970—, Reference Services Rev., 1972—, Consumers Index, 1972—, Serials Rev., 1975—, Index to Free Periodicals, 1976—, Libr. Hi Tech, 1983—, Libr. Hi Tech News, 1985—, Libr. Hi Tech Bibliography, 1986—, Computer and Office Product Evaluations, 1989—. Mem. exec. com. Mich. region Am. Friends Service Com., 1968-73, Dearborn Hist. Commn., 1971-73; vice chmn., chmn. Fairlane Music Guild, 1971-73; trustee Pittsfield Charter Twp., 1982-89. Recipient Loleta Fyan award Mich. Library Assn., 1971; Ford Found. scholar, 1963 Mem. ALA, Mich. Library Assn. (chmn. acad. div. nominating com. 1971), Assn. Ednl. Communications and Tech., Ednl. Film Library Assn., Phi Beta Kappa, Beta Phi Mu. Office: PO Box 1808 Ann Arbor MI 48106-1808

WALL, LEONARD J. bishop; b. Windsor, Ont., Can., Sept. 27, 1924; Ordained Roman Catholic priest, June 11, 1949; ordained titular bishop of Leptiminus and aux. bishop of Toronto, 1979-92; archbishop of Winnipeg Archdiocese of Winnipeg, 1992—. Office: Archdiocese of Winnipeg 1495 Pembina Hwy Winnipeg MB Canada R3T 2C6

WALL, ROBERT F. lawyer; b. Chgo., Jan. 7, 1952; BA with distinction, Northwestern U., 1973; JD summa cum laude, U. Santa Clara, 1977. Bar: Ill. 1977, U.S. Dist. Ct. (no. dist.) Ill. 1977. Ptnr. Winston & Strawn, Chgo. Mem. editorial bd. M&A and Corp. Control Law Reporter, 1988—. Mem. ABA. Office: Winston & Strawn 35 W Wacker Dr Chicago IL 60601-1695

WALLACE, RICHARD LEE, chancellor; BA in Journalism, Northwestern U., 1958; PhD in Economics, Vanderbilt U., 1965. From instr. to asst. prof. Florida State U., 1961-66; from asst. prof. to prof. U. Mo., Columbia, 1967-77, interim dean Graduate Sch., 1978-79, assoc. dean, 1979-82, interim dean Coll. Arts Scis., 1982-83; assoc. provost Mo. U., 1983-85, from assoc. v.p. to v.p., 1985-89, v.p. Academic Affairs, 1989-96, chancellor, 1996—. Recipient Faculty Svc. award Nat. Continuing Edn. Assn., 1995, J. Rhoads Foster award, 1995, award Northwestern Medill Sch. Journalism, 1998. Mem. Nat. Forum Sys. Chief Academic Officers, Nat. Assn. State Univs. Land-Grant Colls. (chmn. council academic affairs, com. econ. higher edn.). Office: Univ Missouri Columbia Office of the Chancellor 105 Jesse Hall Columbia MO 65211-1050 E-mail: WallaceR@missouri.edu.

WALLACE, RICK, marketing professional; Dir. mktg. and procurement Alliant Foodsvc., Deerfield, Ill., to 1996, v.p. category mgmt., 1996—. Office: Alliant Foodsvc 1 Parkway N Deerfield IL 60015-2532

WALLACE, SAMUEL TAYLOR, health system administrator; b. Blytheville, Ark., Sept. 2, 1943; s. Samuel Edward and Minnie (Taylor) W.; m. Sara Billow, Apr. 30, 1992. B.S., U. Mo., 1965; M.H.A., Washington U., St. Louis, 1970. Asst. administr. Hillcrest Med. Ctr., Tulsa, 1969-75; adminstr. St. Luke's Meth. Hosp., Cedar Rapids, Iowa, 1975-81, pres., 1981-95, Iowa Health Sys., Des Moines, 1995—. Bd. dirs. Vol. Hosp. Am., Dallas, 1982-94, Iowa Golf Charities, 2001-; chmn. bd. dirs. Vol. Hosp. Iowa, Cedar Rapids, 1983-87; bd. dirs. Greater Des Moines Partnershp, 1996—, Physician Mgmt. Resources, 1996—, Health Enterprise of Iowa, 1995—; mem. Cedar Rapids coun. Boy Scouts Am., 1983, Mid-Iowa coun., 1995—. Served to capt. M.S.C. U.S. Army, 1965-68, Vietnam. Recipient Silver Beaver award Boy Scouts Am., 1980, Silver Antelope award, 1992; James E. West fellow, 1994. Fellow Am. Coll. Healthcare Execs. (Iowa bd. regents 1982-84, 88-95, interim gov. Dist. 5 1999-2000); mem. Iowa Hosp. Assn. (dir. 1982-85). Republican. Methodist. Lodge: Rotary (Cedar Rapids pres. 1986-87). Office: Iowa Health Sys 1200 Pleasant St Des Moines IA 50309-1406

WALLACH, JOHN S(IDNEY), library administrator; b. Toronto, Ohio, Jan. 6, 1939; s. Arthur M. and Alice I. (Smith) W.; children: John Michael, Wendy Anne, Bethany Lynne, Kristen Michele; m. Joyce Bapst. B.S. in Edn, Kent State U., 1963; M.L.S., U. R.I., 1968; M.P.A., U. Dayton, 1977. Dir. Mercer County (Ohio) Library, 1968-70, Greene County (Ohio) Library, 1970-77; assoc. dir. Dayton and Montgomery County (Ohio) Library, 1978, dir., treas., 1979—. Bd. dirs. Dayton Mus. Natrual History, Family Svc. Assn., Dayton, Technology Resource Ctr. Served with USN, 1963-68, capt. ret. Mem. ALA, Ohio Libr. Assn. Office: Dayton and Montgomery County Pub Libr 215 E 3d St Dayton OH 45402-2103

WALLACH, MARK IRWIN, lawyer; b. May 19, 1949; s. Ivan A. and Janice (Grossman) W.; m. Karla L. Wallach, 1996; children: Kerry Melissa, Philip Alexander; stepchildren: Daniel Kanter, Rachel Kanter, Adam Kanger BA magna cum laude, Wesleyan U., 1971; JD cum laude, Harvard U., 1974. Bar: Ohio 1974, U.S. Dist. Ct. (no. dist.) Ohio, 1974, U.S. Ct. Appeals (6th cir.) 1985, U.S. Supreme Ct. 1985. Law clk. U.S. Dist. Ct., Cleve., 1974-75; assoc. Baker & Hostetler, 1975-79; chief trial counsel City of Cleve., 1979-81; assoc. Calfee, Halter & Griswold, Cleve., 1981-82, ptnr., 1982—, exec. com., 1997-99. Mem. fed. ct. adv. com. U.S. Dist. Ct. (no. dist.) Ohio, 1991-95; chmn. bd. trustees Ohio Group Against Smoking Pollution, 1986-90; trustee Cleve. chpt. Am. Jewish Com., 1986—, sec. 1989-91, v.p., 1991-95, pres., 1995-97; bd. trustees Citizens League of Greater Cleve., 1978-79, 87-92. Author: Christopher Morley, 1976. Pres. Wesleyan Alumni Club, Cleve., 1983-87, 92—; trustee Lyric Opera, Cleve., 1995—, pres., 1996-98, Ratner Schs., 1994-96; pres. Performing Arts Together, 1997-2001; trustee The Sculpture Ctr., 2001,pres., 2001—; trustee Bellefaire Jewish Children's Bur., 2001—. Mem. ABA, Ohio Bar Assn., Fed. Bar Assn., Cuyahoga County Law Dirs. Assn., The Cleve. Racquet Club, Greater Cleve. Bar Assn., The Club at Soc. Ctr. Avocations: reading, bicycling, space exploration, politics. Home: 2758 Claythorne Rd Shaker Heights OH 44122-1938 Office: Calfee Halter & Griswold 1400 McDonald Investment Ctr 800 Superior Ave E Ste 1800 Cleveland OH 44114-2688 E-mail: mwallach@calfee.com.

WALLER, AARON BRET, III, museum director; b. Liberal, Kans., Dec. 7, 1935; s. Aaron Bret and Juanita M. (Slawson) W.; m. Mary Lou Dooley, Sept. 3, 1959; children: Bret, Mary Elizabeth. BFA, Kansas City Art Inst., 1957; MFA, U. Kans., 1958, postgrad., 1964-67; postgrad. (Fulbright grantee), U. Oslo, 1963-64. Grad. asst. U. Kans., 1957-58; dir. The Citadel Mus., Mil. Coll. S.C., 1957-58, Mus. Art, U. Kans., 1964-71; dept. head public edn. and higher edn. Met. Mus. Art, N.Y.C., 1971-73; dir. Museum Art, U. Mich., Ann Arbor, 1973-80, Meml. Art Gallery, U. Rochester, N.Y., 1980-85, adj. assoc. prof. fine arts dept., 1980-85; assoc. dir. for edn. and pub. affairs J. Paul Getty Mus., Malibu, Calif., 1985-90; dir. Indpls. Mus. Art, 1990—. Assoc. prof. U. Mich., 1973-80; coordinator museum studies program Inst. Fine Arts, NYU, 1971-73; tchr. City Coll. N.Y., 1971-73 Mem. Assn. Art Mus. Dirs. (treas. 1980-81, trustee 1992-94), Intermuseum Conservation Assn. (pres. 1977-78), Am. Assn. Museums (nat. com. on mus. tng. 1976-78, counselor-at-large 1986-89, treas. standing com. on edn. 1990-92), Coll. Art Assn. Office: Indpls Mus Art 1200 W 38th St Ste 2X Indianapolis IN 46208-4196

WALLER, PATRICIA FOSSUM, transportation executive, researcher, psychologist; b. Winnipeg, Man., Can., Oct. 12, 1932; d. Magnus Samuel and Diana Isabel (Briggs) Fossum; m. Marcus Bishop Waller, Dec. 27, 1957; children: Anna Estelle, Justin Magnus, Martha Wilkinson, Benjamin Earl. AB in Psychology cum laude, U. Miami, Coral Gables, 1953, MS in Psychology, 1955; PhD in Psychology, U. N.C., 1959. Lic. psychologist, N.C. Psychology intern VA Hosp., Salem, Va., 1956; psychology instr. Med. Sch. U. N.C., Chapel Hill, 1957; USPHS postdoctoral fellow R.B. Jackson Lab., Bar Harbor, Maine, 1958-60; psychologist VA Hosp., Brockton, Mass., 1961-62; psychology lectr. U. N.C., Chapel Hill, Greensboro, 1962-67, assoc. dir. driver studies Hwy. Safety Rsch. Ctr. Chapel Hill, 1967-89, founding dir. Injury Prevention Rsch. Ctr., 1987-89; dir. Transp. Rsch. Inst. U. Mich., Ann Arbor, 1989-99, sr. rsch. scientist emerita, prof. emerita, 1999—; sr. rsch. scientist Ctr. for Transp. Safety, Tex. Transp. Inst. Tex. A&M U., 2002—. Bd. dirs. Intelligent Transp. Soc. Am., Washington, 1991—99, Traffic Safety Assn. Mich., Lansing, 1991—99; bd. advisors Eno Transp. Found., Inc., Lndnsdowne, Va., 1994—97; chair group 5 coun. Transp. Rsch. Bd. of NRC, Washington, 1992—95; chmn. Task Force Operation Regulations, 1974—76, mem.

study com. devel. ranking rail safety R&D projects, 1980—82, chmn. group 3 coun. operation, safety and maintenance transp. facilities, 1980—83, mem. IVHS-IDEA tech. rev. panel, 1993—2000, chair workshop human factors rsch. in hwy. safety, 1992, chair ad hoc com. environ. activies, 92, mem. task force on elderly drivers, 1990—93, mem. com. vehicle user characteristics, 1983—86, mem. com. planning and adminstrn. of transp. safety, 1986—92, mem. com. alcohol, other drugs and transp., 1986—98, numerous other coms., mem. spl. coms. including Inst. Medicine Dana Award com., 1986—90, com. of 55MPH nat. maximum speed limit, 1983—84; mem. motor vehicle safety rsch. adv. com. Dept. Transp., Washington, 1991—94; reviewer JAMA, Jour. Studies on Alcohol, Jour. of Gerontology, Am. Jour. Pub. Health; apptd. Pres. Coun. Spinal Cord Injury, 1981; apptd. advisor Nat. Hwy. Safety Adv. Com. to Sec. U.S. Dept. Transp., 1979—80, 1980—83, chair nat. motor carrier adv. com., 1997—98; author numerous reports on transp. to govtl. coms. and univs. Author: (with Paul G. Shinkman) Instructor's Manual for Mogan and King: Introduction to Psychology, 1971; author: (with others) Psychological Concepts in the Classroom, 1974, Drinking: Alcohol in American Society—Issues and Current Research, 1978, The American Handbook of Alcoholism, 1982, The Role of the Civil Engineer in Highway Safety, 1983, Aging and Public Health, 1985, Young Driver Accidents: In Search of Solutions, 1985, Alcohol, Accidents and Injuries, 1986, Transportation in an Aging Society: Improving the Mobility and Safety for Older Persons, 1988, Young Drivers Impaired by Alcohol and Drugs, 1988; mem. editorial bd. Jour. Safety Rsch., 1979—; assoc. guest editor Health Edn. Quar., 1989; assoc. editor Accident, Analysis, and Prevention, 1978-84, mem. editorial bd., 1976-87; contbr. articles to profl. jours. Grantee HHS, 1982, 92-97, NIH; named Widmark laureate Internat. Coun. Alcohol, Drugs and Traffic Safety, 1995; Dist. Alumnus Awd., Dept. Psych., UNC Chapel Hill, 1997; recipient James J. Howard Trailblazer award Nat. Assn. of Govs. Hwy. Safety Reps., 1998, Svc. Awd., Intelligent Transportation Soc. of Amer., 1999; World Traffic Soc. Awd., 1999, World Safety Symposium, 1999; Lifetime Acheivement Awd., Mich. Traffic Safety Summit, 1999. Mem. AAAS, APA (Harold M. Hildreth award 1993), APHA (injury control and emergency health svcs. sect., Disting. Career award 1994, transp. rsch. bd., Roy W. Crum award for rsch. contbns. 1995), Assn. for the Advancement of Automotive Medicine (chmn. human factors sect. 1978-80, bd. dirs. 1979-82, pres. 1981-82), Coun. Univ. Transp. Ctrs. (exec. com. 1991-93), Transp. Rsch. Bd., Ea. Psychol. Assn., Sigma Xi. Democrat. Avocations: gardening, reading. Office: 1779 Crawford Dairy Rd Chapel Hill NC 27516 E-mail: pwaller@umich.edu.

WALLER, ROBERT REX, ophthalmologist, educator, foundation executive; b. N.Y.C., Feb. 19, 1937; s. Madison Rex and Sally Elizabeth (Pearce) W.; m. Sarah Elizabeth Pickens, Dec. 27, 1963; children: Elizabeth, Katherine, Robert Jr. BA, Duke U., 1958; MD, U. Tenn., 1963. Diplomate Am. Bd. Ophthalmology (dir. 1982—, vice chmn. 1988-89, chmn. 1989—). Intern City of Memphis Hosps., 1963-64; resident in internal medicine Mayo Grad. Sch. Medicine, Rochester, Minn., 1966-67, resident in ophthalmology, 1967-70, faculty, 1970—; assoc. prof. ophthalmology Mayo Clinic, 1974-78, prof., 1978—; chmn. dept. ophthalmology Mayo Med. Sch., 1974-84, cons., 1970—, bd. govs., 1978-93, chmn., 1988-93; trustee Mayo Found., 1978—, pres., CEO, 1988-98, pres. emeritus, 1999—. Chmn. bd. trustees Healthcare Leadership Coun., Washington, 1999-2001. Contbr. chpts. to books, articles to profl. jours. Elder 1st Presbyn. Ch., Rochester, 1975-78; mem. Rochester Task Force on Pub. Assembly Facilities, 1983-84. Ocuplastic Surgery fellow U. Calif. San Francisco, 1973. Mem. AMA, Minn. State Med. Assn., Zumbro Valley Med. Assn., Am. Acad. Ophthalmology, Am. Ophthalmol. Soc., Orbital Soc., Am. Soc. Ophthalmic Plastic and Reconstructive Surgery, Minn. Acad. Ophthalmology and Otolaryngology, Memphis Country Club, Old Baldy Golf Club, Augusta Nat. Golf Club, Alpha Omega Alpha, Delta Tau Delta. Presbyterian. Avocations: golf, travel, photography, dogs. Home: 199 Greenbriar Dr Memphis TN 38117-3238 E-mail: RWaller@mayo.edu.

WALLERSTEIN, MITCHEL BRUCE, foundation executive; b. N.Y.C., Mar. 8, 1949; s. Melvin Julian and Rita Helen (Nomburg) W.; m. Susan Elyse Perlik, June 29, 1974; children: Matthew, Leah. AB, Dartmouth Coll., 1971; MPA, Syracuse U., 1972; MS, MIT, 1977, PhD, 1978. Assoc. dir. Internat. Food Policy Program MIT, Cambridge, Mass., 1978-83, lectr. dept. polit. sci., 1978-83; asst. prof. dept. polit. sci. Holy Cross Coll., Worcester, 1979-81; assoc. exec. dir. Office Internat. Affairs NAS, Washington, 1983-89; dep. exec. officer NAS, 1989-93; dep. asst. sec. of def. U.S. Dept. Def., 1993-97; disting. rsch. fel. prof. Nat. Def. U., 1998; v.p. John D. and Catherine T. MacArthur Found., Chgo., 1998—. Adj. prof. Sch. Advanced Internat. Studies, Johns Hopkins U., Washington, 1992-98; adj. prof. Sch. Fgn. Svc., Georgetown U., Washington, 1989-93. Author: Food for War - Food for Peace: The Politics of U.S. Food Aid, 1979; author, dir. reports in field including multiple NAS reports on tech. transfer and nat. security. Recipient Sec. Def. medal for Outstanding Pub. Svc., 1997, 98. Mem. AAAS, Internat. Inst. Strategic Studies, Coun. Fgn. Rels. Democrat. Office: John D and Catherine T MacArthur Found 140 S Dearborn St Ste 1100 Chicago IL 60603-5202 E-mail: mwallers@macfound.org.

WALLING, DONOVAN ROBERT, educational book editor; b. Kansas City, Mo., Jan. 9, 1948; s. Donovan Ernest and Dorothy Jane (Goyette) W.; m. Diana Lynn Eveland, Oct. 19, 1968 (dec. 1991); children: Katherine Anne, Donovan David, Alexander James. BS in Edn., Kans. State Tchrs. Coll., 1970; MS, U. Wis., Milw., 1975. Cert. tchr., adminstr., Wis., Ind. Tchr. Sheboygan (Wis.) Area Sch. Dist., 1970-81, 83-86, coord. lang. arts and reading, 1986-91; tchr. Dept. Def. Dependents Schs., Zweibruecken, Germany, 1981-83; dir. instrnl. svcs. Carmel (Ind.)-Clay Schs., 1991-93; dir. publs. and rsch. Phi Delta Kappa Internat., Bloomington, Ind., 1993—. Mem. adj. faculty U. Wis., Oshkosh, 1986-91, Silver Lake Coll., Manitowoc, Wis., 1987-91. Author: Complete Book of School Public Relations, 1982, How To Build Staff Involvement in School Management, 1984, Teachers as Leaders, 1994, Rethinking How Art Is Taught, 2000; also numerous articles. Mem. ASCD, Nat. Coun. Tchrs. English, Internat. Reading Assn., Phi Delta Kappa (v.p. Cen. Ind. chpt. 1992-93). Avocations: writing, painting. Office: Phi Delta Kappa PO Box 789 Bloomington IN 47402-0789 E-mail: dwalling@pdkintl.org.

WALLIS, DEBORAH, curator; M, U. Nebr. Dir., curator Nat. Muss. Roller Skating, Lincoln, Nebr. Office: Nat Mus Roller Skating 4730 South St Ste 2 Lincoln NE 68506*

WALLWORK, WILLIAM WILSON, III, automobile executive; b. Fargo, N.D., Mar. 8, 1961; s. William Wilson Jr.; m. Shannon Wallwork, July 12, 1991. AA in Automotive Mktg., Northwood Inst., 1981; student, San Diego State U., Moorhead State U. Lease rep. Wallwork Lease and Rental, 1984-86; sales mgr. W.W. Wallwork, Inc., Fargo, N.D., 1986-87, v.p., 1987-91, pres., 1991—; v.p. Valley Imports Inc, 1986-91; pres. Valley Imports Inc., 1991—. Vice chmn. Kenworth 20 Group, 1992-93, chmn., 1994-96; mem. PACCAR Chmn.'s Meeting, 1993; mem. Rockwell Internat. Dealer Adv. Bd., 1995-98. Mem. adv. bd. N.D. State U. Coll. Bus. Adminstrn., 1995-2001; mem. Civic Opera Bd., 1999—. Mem. Fargo-Moorhead Automobile Dealers Assn. (v.p. 1986-88, pres. 1988-90, share house bd. 1998—). Avocation: skiing. Office: W W Wallwork Inc PO Box 1819 Fargo ND 58107-1819

WALMER, EDWIN FITCH, lawyer; b. Chgo., Mar. 24, 1930; s. Hillard Wentz and Anna C. (Fitch) W.; m. Florence Poling, June 17, 1952; children: Linda Diane Walmer Dennis, Fred Fitch. BS with distinction, Ind. U., 1952, JD with high distinction, 1957. Bar: Wis. 1957, U.S. Dist. Ct. (ea. dist.) Wis. 1957. Assoc. Foley & Lardner, Milw., 1957-65, ptnr., 1965-90, ret., 1990. Served to 1st lt. U.S. Army, 1952-54. Recipient Cal. C. Chambers award Culver (Ind.) Mil. Acad., 1948. Fellow Am. Coll. Trust and Estate Counsel; mem. Order of Coif, Dairymen's Country Club (Boulder Junction, Wis.), Vineyards Country Club (Naples, Fla.), Phi Eta Sigma, Beta Gamma Sigma. Republican. Congregationalist. Avocations: golf, fishing. Office: Foley & Lardner 777 E Wisconsin Ave Ste 3800 Milwaukee WI 53202-5367

WALROD, DAVID JAMES, retail grocery chain executive; b. Toledo, Dec. 9, 1946; s. Maynard Elmer and Isabella (Soldwish) W.; m. Judith Kay Stevens, Aug. 17, 1968; children— David, Bryant, Marc Student, Michael Owens Coll.; student in food distbn. mgmt. mktg., Toledo U., 1968. With Seaway Food Town, Inc., Maumee, Ohio, 1963—, grocery merchandiser, 1971-74, v.p. supermarket ops., 1974-77, corp. v.p. ops., 1977-80, sr. v.p. ops., 1980-88, exec. v.p., chief oper. officer, 1988—. Bd. dirs. Ohio Grocers Assn. Bd. dirs. Toledo Mud Hens, Riverside Hosp., St. Francis Desales H.S., Toledo, Corp. for Effective Govt., Junior Achievement, Toledo City Parks Commn., Labor Mgmt. Coun., Bishop's Edn. Coun. Cath. Diocese of Toledo; trustee Maumee C. of C. Mem. Brandywine Country Club. Office: Seaway Food Town Inc 1020 Ford St Maumee OH 43537-1898

WALSH, DAVID GRAVES, lawyer; b. Madison, Wis., Jan. 7, 1943; s. John J. and Audrey B. Walsh; married; children: Michael, Katherine, Molly, John. BBA, U. Wis., 1965; JD, Harvard U., 1970. Bar: Wis. Law clk. Wis. Supreme Ct., Madison, 1970-71; ptnr. Walsh, Walsh, Sweeney & Whitney, 1971-86; ptnr.-in-charge Foley & Lardner, 1986—. Bd. dirs. Nat. Guardian Life, Madison, 1981—; lectr. U. Wis., Madison, 1974-75, 77-78. Chmn. State of Wis. Elections Bd., Madison, 1978. Lt. USN, 1965-67, Vietnam. Recipient Disting. Bus. Alumnus award U. Wis. Sch. Bus., 1997. Maple Bluff Country Club (Madison) (pres. 1987). Roman Catholic. Avocations: tennis, golf, fishing. Home: 41 Fuller Dr Madison WI 53704-5962 Office: Foley & Lardner PO Box 1497 Madison WI 53701-1497

WALSH, DONNIE, sports club executive; married; 5 children. Grad., U. N.C.; attended, N.C. Law Sch. Bar: 1977. Assoc. head coach U. N.C.; staff coach Denver Nuggets, head coach, 1979-81; asst. coach Ind. Pacers, 1984-86, exec. v.p., gen. mgr., 1986-92, pres., 1992—. Office: Ind Pacers Market Sq Arena 300 E Market St Indianapolis IN 46204-2603

WALSH, JAMES, retail supermarket executive; CFO Meijer, Grand Rapids, Mich. Office: Meijer 29129 Walker St NW Grand Rapids MI 49544 Office Fax: (616) 453-6067.

WALSH, JOHN CHARLES, metallurgical company executive; b. Indpls., Sept. 8, 1924; s. John Charles and Nell (O'Neil) W.; m. Mary Louise Dreiss, Feb. 5, 1949; children: Michael S., Carolyn Ann, Anne D. B.S., Notre Dame U., 1949. Auditor Herdrich Boggs & Co., Indpls., 1949-50; with P.R. Mallory & Co., Inc., 1949-80; pres. Walgang Co. Inc., Indpls., 1980—. V.p., treas. P.R. Mallory & Co., 1971. Served with USMCR, 1943-45. Mem. Fin. Execs. Inst., Indpls. C. of C., Ind. Hist. Soc., Econ. Club, Notre Dame Club, Rotary. Home: 4974 Shadow Rock Cir Carmel IN 46033-9500 Office: Ste B2 598 W Carmel Dr Carmel IN 46032-2667

WALSH, JOHN E., JR. business educator, consultant; b. St. Louis, Apr. 28, 1927; s. John E. and Ann M. (Narkewicz) W. BS, U.S. Naval Acad., 1950; MBA, Washington U., St. Louis, 1957; DBA, Harvard U., 1960. Asst. prof. Washington U., St. Louis, 1959-60, assoc. prof., 1960-68, prof., 1968-2001, prof. emeritus, 2001—; vis. assoc. prof. Stanford U., 1964-65; vis. prof. INSEAD, Fontainebleau, France, 1970. Mem. exec. com. Econ. Strategy Inst. Author: Preparing Feasibility Studies in Asia, 1971, Guidelines for Management Consultants in Asia, 1973, Planning New Ventures in International Business, 1976, (with others) Strategies in Business, 1978, Management Tactics, 1980, International Business Case Studies: For the Multicultural Market Place, 1994, Joint Authoring: Managing Cultural Differences, 1994. Mem. State of Mo. leadership initiative to former Soviet Union, Poland, Hungary, 1990; mem. coun. Kearny Found., Internat. Ho., Washington U. 1st lt. USAF, 1950-54. Zurn Found. fellow, 1958; Presdl. fellow Am. Grad. Sch. Internat. Mgmt. Mem. Harvard Club N.Y.C. Home: 2301 Gulf of Mexico Dr Apt 24N Longboat Key FL 34228 E-mail: walsh@olin.wustl.edu.

WALSH, JOSEPH, policy analyst, educator, social worker; b. Evanston, Ill., Dec. 27, 1961; m. Laura Jo; 3 children. BA, U. Iowa, 1985; MA, U. Chgo., 1991. Rep. candidate 9th dist. Ill. U.S. House of Reps., 1996. Roman Catholic. Office: 1311 Livingston St Evanston IL 60201-1626

WALSH, LAWRENCE M. state legislator; b. Joliet, Ill., Mar. 3, 1948; m. Irene; 6 children. A in Agrl. & Bus., Joliet Jr. Coll., 1968. Mem. Ill. Senate, Springfield, 1997—, mem. agrl. & conservation com., fin. insts. com. Democrat. Office: State Capitol Capitol Bldg 309-g Springfield IL 62706-0001

WALSH, MATHEW M. corporate executive; CEO, pres. Walsh Group, Inc., Chgo. Office: Walsh Group Inc 929 W Adams St Chicago IL 60607-3021

WALSH, MICHAEL S. lawyer; b. Chgo., Sept. 29, 1951; AB, Colgate U., 1973; MBA, Cornell U., 1975; JD, So. Meth. U., 1978. Bar: Ill. 1978, U.S. Dist. Ct. (no. dist.) Ill. 1978, U.S. Ct. Appeals (fed. cir.) 1983, U.S. Ct. Appeals (9th cir.) 1985. Mem. Jenner & Block, Chgo. Mem. ABA, Fed. Bar Assn., Chgo. Bar Assn., Computer Law Assn. Office: Jenner & Block One IBM Plz Chicago IL 60611-3608 E-mail: mwalsh@jenner.com.

WALSH, PAUL S. food products executive; Chmn., pres., CEO Pillsbury Co., Mpls. Office: Pillsbury Co 200 S 6th St Ste 200 Minneapolis MN 55402-6005

WALSH, THOMAS CHARLES, lawyer; b. Mpls., July 6, 1940; s. William G. and Kathryne M. Walsh; m. Joyce Williams, Sept. 7, 1968; children: Brian Christopher, Timothy Daniel, Laura Elizabeth. BS in Commerce magna cum laude, St. Louis U., 1962, LLB cum laude, 1964. Bar: Mo. 1964, U.S. Dist. Ct. (ea. dist.) Mo. 1964, U.S. Ct. Appeals (8th cir.) 1968, U.S. Supreme Ct. 1971, U.S. Ct. Appeals (6th cir.) 1972, U.S. Ct. Appeals (5th cir.) 1974, U.S. Ct. Appeals (D.C. cir.) 1980, U.S. Ct. Appeals (7th cir.) 1982, U.S. Ct. Appeals (9th cir.) 1987, U.S. Ct. Appeals (4th cir.) 1989, U.S. Ct. Appeals (11th and fed. cirs.) 1992, U.S. Ct. Appeals (2d and 10th cirs.) 1993. Jr. ptnr. Bryan, Cave, McPheeters & McRoberts, St. Louis, 1964-73; ptnr. Bryan, Cave LLP, 1974—, mem. exec. com., 1980-96. Mem. 8th Cir. Adv. Com., 1983-86. Bd. dirs. St. Louis Symphony Soc., 1983-95. With U.S. Army, 1965-66; lt. USNR, 1966-71. Fellow Am. Coll. Trial Lawyers, Am. Acad. Appellate Lawyers; mem. Mo. Bar Assn., St. Louis Bar Assn., Am. Law Inst., Mo. Athletic Club, Bellerive Country Club. Roman Catholic. Office: Bryan Cave LLP 1 Metropolitan Sq 211 N Broadway Saint Louis MO 63102-2733 E-mail: tcwalsh@bryancavellp.com.

WALSH, THOMAS JAMES, state legislator; b. Chgo., July 4, 1960; s. William Dowdle and Barbara Ann (Kennedy) W. BBA, Loras Coll., 1982. Lic. real estate salesperson. From sales rep. to pub. rels. mgr.; mem. Ill. Ho. of Reps, Springfield, 1992-94, Ill. Senate from dist. 22, 1994—. Commr. Met. Water Reclamation Dist. of Greater Chgo., 1988-90, chmn. Engring. com., Health and Pub. Welfare com.; active LaGrange Park Caucus, LaGrange Park Libr., St. Francis Xavier Ch., LaGrange. Mem. Irish Fellowship Club Chgo., Phoenix Soc. of Community Family Svc. and Mental Health Assn., LaGrange Kiwanis, Loras Coll. Alumni Club Chgo. Office: State of Ill 10544 W Cermak Rd Westchester IL 60154-5202

WALTER, KENNETH LUVERNE, retired agricultural facility director; b. Buffalo Lake, Minn., June 20, 1936; s. Clarence Andrew and Ruth (Schafer) W.; m. Nancy Lee Woolard, Jan. 30, 1959; children: Katrina Lynn, Matthew Thomas (dec.), Janelle Mae. BS in Agr., U. Minn., St. Paul, 1963. Sales and tech. rep. Midland Coops. Inc., Mpls., 1963-68; asst. to supt. Agr. Experiment Sta. U. Minn., Rosemount, 1968-90, acting supt. Agr. Experiment Sta., 1990-93, dir. ops. Agr. Experiment Sta., 1993-2000; ret. With USN, 1955-59. Mem. Am. Soc. Agrl. Engrs. E-mail: klwalter@tc.umn.edu.

WALTER, LYNN M. geologist, educator; PhD in Geology, U. Miami, 1983. Prof. geol. scis. U. Mich., Ann Arbor. Recipient Disting. Svc. award Geol. Soc. Am., 1999. Achievements include research on aqueous and solid phase geochemistry of sedimentary systems. Office: U Mich 2534 CC Little Bldg 425 E University Ave Ann Arbor MI 48109-1063 Fax: 734-763-4690. E-mail: lmwalter@umich.edu.

WALTER, ROBERT D. wholesale pharmaceutical distribution executive; b. 1945; BMechE, Ohio U., 1967; MBA, Harvard U., 1970. With Cardinal Foods Inc. (acquired by Roundy's Inc. 1988), Dublin, 1971-88; CEO, chmn. bd. Cardinal Health, Inc., 1979—. Bd. dirs. Bank One Corp., Viacom Inc. Trustee Battelle Meml. Inst., Ohio U. Office: Cardinal Health Inc 7000 Cardinal Pl Dublin OH 43017-1092*

WALTER, ROBERT IRVING, chemistry educator, chemist; b. Johnstown, Pa., Mar. 12, 1920; s. Charles Weller and Frances (Riethmiller) W.; m. Farideh Asghari, Oct. 17, 1973. AB, Swarthmore Coll., 1941; MA, Johns Hopkins U., 1942; PhD, U. Chgo., 1949. Instr. U. Colo., 1949-51, U. Conn., 1953-55; rsch. assoc. Rutgers U., 1951-53; assoc. physicist Brookhaven Nat. Lab., 1955-56; mem. faculty Haverford Coll., 1956-68, prof. chemistry, 1963-68; prof. U. Ill., Chgo., 1968—, prof. emeritus, 1990—. Vis. lectr. Stanford (Calif.) U., winter 1967; acad. guest U. Zurich, 1976; U.S. NAS exch. visitor to Romania, 1982, 88. Mem. Adv. Council Coll. Chemistry, 1966-70. Served with USNR, 1944-46. Grantee U.S. Army Signal Research and Devel. Lab., NIH, NSF, Dept. Energy; NSF fellow, 1960-61 Fellow AAAS; mem. Am. Chem. Soc. (vis. scientist div. chem. edn. 1964-73), Sigma Xi Achievements include special research preparation, proof of structure, chemical and physical properties of stable aromatic free radicals, C1 reactions and mechanisms in heterogeneous catalysis, reactions of porphyrin bases. Home: 2951 Central St Unit 308 Evanston IL 60201-1284 E-mail: mhry@aol.com.

WALTERS, GLEN ROBERT, banker; b. Mpls., Sept. 11, 1943; s. Sterling Thomas and Mildred Eunice (Parkinson) W.; m. Gail Elvira Engelsen, June 11, 1966; children— Nicole Marie, Brent Aaron, Hillary Renee. B.A., U. Minn., Mpls., 1965, postgrad., 1965-67; banking degree, Stonier Grad. Sch. Banking, Rutgers U., New Brunswick, N.J., 1982. Comml. banker 1st Nat. Bank, Mpls., 1967-83, sr. v.p. human resources, 1983-90; sr. v.p. Firstar Bank Minn., 1990-2001, US Bank, Mpls., 2001—. Served to sgt. USNG, 1967-73 Republican. Presbyterian Office: US Bank 9633 Lyndale Ave S Minneapolis MN 55420

WALTERS, JEFFERSON BROOKS, musician, retired real estate broker; b. Dayton, Ohio, Jan. 20, 1922; s. Jefferson Brooks and Mildred Frances (Smith) W.; m. Mary Elizabeth Espey, Apr. 6, 1963 (dec. July 22, 1983); children: Dinah Christine Basson, Jefferson Brooks; m. Carol Elaine Clayton Gillette, Feb. 19, 1984. Student, U. Dayton, 1947. Composer, cornetist, Dayton, 1934—; real estate broker, 1948-88; ret., 1988. Condr., composer choral, solo voice settings of psalms and poetry Alfred Lord Tennyson; composer Crossing the Bar (meml. performances U.S. Navy band), 1961; composer The Yorktown Grand March (Good Citizenship medal SAR, 1988). Founder Am. Psalm Choir, 1965; apptd. deferred giving officer Kettering (Ohio) Med. Ctr., 1982-85. Served with USCGR, 1942-45, PTO, ETO. Mem. SAR (life), Greater Dayton Antique Study Club (past pres.), Dayton Art Inst., Montgomery County Hist. Soc., Masons (32d deg.). Brethren Ch. Home: 4113 Roman Dr Dayton OH 45415-2423

WALTERS, LAWRENCE CHARLES, advertising executive; b. Cin., Apr. 1, 1948; s. Lawrence Simpson and Mary Josephine (Koerner) W.; m. Ann Morley Reifenrath, Jan. 15, 1983. Assoc. in Advt., U. Cin., 1969. Art dir. J. Walter Thompson, Chgo., 1972-78; sr. art dir. Needham Harper and Steers, 1978-81; advt. creative dir. ACOM, Quaker, 1981-83; co. group creative dir. Tatham, Laird, Kudner, 1983-99; exec. creative dir. Euro R.S.C.G. Tatham, 1996—. With the USMC, 1966-69. Democrat. Roman Catholic. Avocations: music writing, white water canoe racing, tennis, water color painting. Office: Euro RSCG Tatham 36 E Grand Ave Chicago IL 60611-3506

WALTERS, RONALD OGDEN, mortgage banker; b. Holcombe, Wis., July 13, 1939; s. Ogden Eugene and Josephine Ann (Hennekens) W.; m. Margaret Ellen Weisheipl, July 14, 1962; children— Laurie, Cheryl, Michael, Patrick Student, U. Wis., 1959-62. Mgr. Thorp Fin., LaCrosse, Wis., 1962-65, regional mgr. Milw., 1965-69, ITT Consumer Fin. Corp., Milw., 1969-74, sr. v.p. Brookfield, Wis., 1974-90, exec. v.p. adminstrn., 1990-92; CEO Ideal Fin. Corp., 1993—, USA Funding Corp., Brookfield, Wis., 1993—. Mem. Wis. Fin. Services Assn. (pres. 1980) Republican. Roman Catholic Avocations: boating, fishing, hunting. Home: 808 Back Bay Rd Delafield WI 53018-1528 also: 17035 W Wisconsin Ave Brookfield WI 53005-5734 E-mail: rowmew@earthlink.net.

WALTERS, ROSS A. federal judge; Magistrate judge U.S. Dist. Ct. (so. dist.) Iowa, 1994—. Office: US Courthouse Rm 440 123 E Walnut St Des Moines IA 50309-2035

WALTHER, JOSEPH EDWARD, health facility administrator, retired physician; b. Indpls., Nov. 24, 1912; s. Joseph Edward and Winona (McCampbell) W.; m. Mary Margaret Ruddell, July 11, 1945 (dec. July 1983); children: Mary Ann Margolis, Karl, Joanne Landman, Suzanne Conran, Diane Paczesny, Kurt. BS, MD, Ind. U., 1936; postgrad., U. Chgo., Harvard U., U. Minn., 1945-47; DSc (hon.), Ind. U., 1997. Diplomate Nat. Bd. Med. Examiners, Am. Bd. Internal Medicine, Am. Bd. Gastroenterology. Intern Meth. Hosp. and St. Vincent Hosp. of Indpls., 1936-37; physician, surgeon U.S. Engrs./Pan Am. Airways, Midway Island, 1937-38; chief resident, med. dir. Wilcox Meml. Hosp., Lihue, Kauai, 1938-39; internist, gastroenterologist Meml. Clinic Indpls., 1947-83, med. dir., pres., chief exec. officer, 1947—; founder, pres. Doctors' Offices Inc., Indpls., 1947—; founder, pres., chief exec. officer Winona Meml. Found. and Hosp. (now Walther Cancer Inst.), 1956—. Clinical asst. prof. medicine Ind. U. Sch. Medicine, Indpls., 1948-93, clin. asst. prof. emeritus, 1993—. Author: (with others) Current Therapy, 1965; mem. edit. rsch. bd. Postgrad. Medicine, 1982-83; contbr. articles to profl. jours. Bd. dirs. March of Dimes, Marion County div., 1962-66, Am. Cancer Soc., Ind. div., 1983-92. Col. USAAF, 1941-47, PTO. Decorated Bronze Star, Silver Star, Air medal; recipient Clevenger award Ind. U. 1989;, Disting. Alumnus award Ind. U. Sch. Med., 1989, Sagamore of Wabash award State of Ind., 1995; Dr. Joseph E. Walther Disting. Physician's award named in honor Winona Meml. Hosp., 1995. Mem. Am. Coll. Gastroenterology (pres. 1970-71, Weiss award 1988), AMA (del. 1970-76), Soc. Cons. to Armed Forces, Ind. Med. Assn., Marion County Med. Assn., Ind. U. Alumni Assn. (life), Hoosier Hundred (charter), Highland Golf and Country Club (hon.),

Waikoloa Golf and Country Club (Hawaii), Indpls. Athletic Club, 702 Club. Republican. Home: 3266 N Meridian St Ste 104 Indianapolis IN 46208-5846 Office: Walther Cancer Inst 3202 N Meridian St Indianapolis IN 46208-4646

WALTMAN, ALFRED ANTHONY, state legislator; m. Sally Waltman; ten children. Grad. high sch. Former state rep. dist. 2 State of S.D., state rep. dist. 3, 1993—. Mem. local govt. and taxation coms. S.D. Ho. of Reps.; farmer, rancher. Democrat. Office: 12277 376th Ave Aberdeen SD 57401-8349

WALTMAN, GLENN C. military officer; BS in Internat. Affairs, USAF Acad., 1975; MA in Psychology, Counseling, Guidance, U. No. Colo., 1981; grad., Squadron Officer Sch., 1981, Air Command and Staff Coll., 1985; disting. grad., Naval War Coll., 1991; MS in Mgmt., Salve Regina U., 1991; MA in Nat. Security/Strategic Studies, Naval War Coll., 1991. Commd. 2d lt. USAF, 1975, advanced through grades to brigadier gen., 1998; staff officer directorate of plans Hdqs. Strategic Air Command, Offutt AFB, Nebr., 1981-84; staff officer, chief nuclear plans and policy br. Hdqs. USAF, The Pentagon, Washington, 1984-88; chief ops. and tng. divsn. 321st Strategic Missile Wing, Grand Forks AFB, N.D., 1988-89; comdr. 448th Strategic Missile Squadron, 1989-90; spl. asst. Supreme Allied Comdr. Supreme Hdqs. Allied Powers Europe, Mons, Belgium, 1991-93; comdr. 45th Ops. Group, Patrick AFB, Fla., 1993-95; dir. logistics Hdqs. Air Force Space Command, Peterson AFB, Colo., 1995; mil. asst. to sec. of Air Force Hdqs. USAF, The Pentagon, Washington, 1995-97; comdr. 341st Space Wing, Malmstrom AFB, Mont., 1997—; brig. gen. dir. intelligence U.S. STRATCOM, Offutt AFB, Nebr. Decorated Def. Superior Svc. medal, Legion of Merit with oak leaf cluster, Meritorious Svc. medal with 2 oak leaf clusters. Office: 901 Sac Blvd Offutt A F B NE 68113-5455

WALTON, RALPH GERALD, psychiatrist, educator; b. Darlington, Eng., Aug. 18, 1942; came to U.S., 1950; s. Kenneth and Paula (Weissman) W.; m. Ellen Paula Liebling, Feb. 15, 1970 (div. 1980); children: Deborah, Rachel; m. Mary Elaine Hultburg, Sept. 27, 1981; children: Lisa, Jonathan. AB, U. Rochester, 1963; MD, SUNY, Syracuse, 1967. Diplomate Am. Bd. Psychiatry and Neurology. Intern Strong Meml. Hosp., Rochester, N.Y., 1967-68, resident in psychiatry, 1968-71; asst. prof. psychiatry Sch. Medicine U. Rochester, 1973-76; chief psychiatry Jamestown (N.Y.) Gen. Hosp., 1976-88; commr. mental health Chautauqua County, Jamestown, 1985-88; chmn. dept. psychiatry Western Res. Care System, Youngstown, Ohio, 1988-98; prof., chmn. dept. psychiatry N.E. Ohio Univs. Coll. of Medicine, Rootstown, 1998—. Med. dir. Profl. Recovery Plus Alcoholic Clinic, Youngstown, 1992—. Contbr. chpt. to: Dietary Phenylalanine and Brain Function, 1988; contbr. foreword to: Katherine It's Time, 1989; contbr. articles to profl. jours., 1972—. Maj. U.S. Army, 1971-73, Panama. Fellow Am. Psychiat. Assn. Jewish. Office: 725 Boardman Canfield Rd Youngstown OH 44512-4380 E-mail: rwalton193@aol.com.

WALTON, ROBERT LEE, JR. plastic surgeon; b. Lawrence, Kans., May 30, 1946; s. Robert L. and Thelma B. (Morgan) W.; m. Elisabeth K. Beahm, Oct. 7, 2000; children: Marc, Morgan, Lindsey. BA, U. Kans., 1968; MD, U. Kans., Kansas City, 1972. Diplomate Am. Bd. Surgery, Am. Bd. Plastic Surgery. Resident in surgery Johns Hopkins Hosp., Balt., 1972-74, Yale-New Haven (Conn.) Hosp., 1974-78; chief of plastic surgery San Francisco Gen. Hosp., 1979-83; prof. and chmn. dept. plastic surgery U. Mass. Med. Ctr., Worcester, 1983-94; prof., chmn dept. plastic surgery U. of Chicago, 1994—. Contbr. articles to profl. jours. Founder Projecto Mira Found. for Handicapped Children, Santurce, P.R., 1990. Mem. Am. Assn. Plastic Surgeons, Am. Coll. Surgeons, Am. Soc. Plastic and Reconstructive Surgery, Am. Soc. Surgery of the Hand, Alpha Omega Alpha. Office: U Chgo Sect Plastic Surgery MC6035 5841 S Maryland Ave Chicago IL 60637-1463 E-mail: rwalton@surgery.bsd.uchicago.edu.

WALTON, STANLEY ANTHONY, III, lawyer; b. Chgo., Dec. 10, 1939; s. Stanley Anthony and Emily Ann (Pouzar) W.; m. Karen Kayser, Aug. 10, 1963; children: Katherine, Anne, Alex. BA, Washington and Lee U., 1962, LLB, 1965. Bar: Ill. 1965, U.S. Dist. Ct. (no. dist.) Ill. 1966, U.S. Ct. Appeals (7th cir.) 1966. Ptnr. Winston & Strawn, Chgo., 1965-89, Sayfarth Shaw Fairweather, Chgo., 1989-96. Trustee Village of Hinsdale (Ill.), 1985-89; bd. dirs. Washington and Lee Law Sch., Lexington, Va., 1975-78, bd. dirs. univ. alumni, 1983-87, pres., 1986-87; bd. dirs. UNICEF, Chgo., 1983; pres. Hinsdale Hist. Soc., 1979-81, 2001—, St. Isaac Jogues PTA, 1980; sec. Hinsdale Cmty. Svc., 2000—; bd. dirs. Hinsdale Ctrl. Found., 2000—. Mem. Ill. State Bar Assn., Phi Alpha Delta, Hinsdale Golf Club. Republican. Roman Catholic. Home and Office: 6679 Snug Harbor Dr Willowbrook IL 60527

WALTZ, JON RICHARD, lawyer, educator, author; b. Napoleon, Ohio, Oct. 11, 1929; s. Richard R. and Lenore (Tharp) W. B.A. with honors in Polit. Sci, Coll. Wooster, 1951; J.D., Yale U., 1954. Bar: Ohio 1954, Ill. 1965. Assoc. Squire, Sanders & Dempsey, Cleve., 1954-64; chief prosecutor City of Willowick (Ohio), 1958-64; assoc. prof. law Northwestern U. Sch. Law, Chgo., 1964-65, prof. law, 1965-98, Edna B. and Ednyfed H. Williams prof. law emeritus; instr. med. jurisprudence Northwestern Med. Sch., 1969-74. Book critic Washington Post, Chgo. Tribune, others; Disting. vis. prof. law Ill. Inst. Tech.-Chgo.-Kent Coll. Law, 1974; lectr. Author: The Federal Rules of Evidence—An Analysis, 1973, Criminal Evidence, 1975, Chinese lang. edits., 1994, 2000, Evidence: A Summary Analysis, 1976, Introduction to Criminal Evidence, 1991, Chinese lang. edit., 1993; co-author: The Trial of Jack Ruby, 1965, Cases and Materials on Evidence, 1968, Principles of Evidence and Proof, 1968, Medical Jurisprudence, 1971, Cases and Materials on Law and Medicine, 1980, Evidence: Making the Record, 1981, Criminal Prosecution in the People's Republic of China and the United States of America: A Comparative Study, 1995; note and comment editor Yale Law Jour., 1953-54; mem. editorial adv. bd. Harcourt Brace Law Group,. 1978—; contbr. numerous articles to profl. jours. Mem. Ill. adv. com. U.S. Commn. on Civil Rights, 1971-74; mem. Ill. Criminal Justice System Policy and Planning Com., 1973-74, Ill. Jud. Inquiry Bd., 1980-88; mem. com. med. edn. AMA, 1982-83; mem. Gov.'s Task Force on Med. Malpractice, 1985; Capt. AUS, 1955-58. Decorated Commendation medal; recipient Disting. Svc. award Soc. Midland Authors, 1972, Disting. Alumni award Coll. Wooster, 1987. Mem. Assn. Am. Law Schs., Order of Coif, Phi Alpha Delta, Pi Sigma Alpha. Presbyterian. Home: 4005 Lakeridge Dr Holland MI 49424-2263

WALTZ, SUSAN, international relations educator; Former chmn. Amnesty Internat., London, England, 1993-98; prof. internat. pub. policy Gerald Ford Sch. Pub. Policy U. Mich., Ann Arbor, 2001—. Office: Ford Sch Public Policy Michigan U 611 Tappan St Ann Arbor MI 48109

WALZER, NORMAN CHARLES, economics educator; b. Mendota, Ill., Mar. 17, 1943; s. Elmer J. and Anna L. Walzer; m. Dona Lee Maurer, Aug. 22, 1970; children: Steven, Mark. BS, Ill. State U., Normal, 1966; MA, U. Ill., 1969, PhD, 1970. Rsch. dir. Cities and Villages Mcpl. Problems Com., Springfield, Ill., 1974-84; vis. prof. U. Ill., Urbana, 1977-78; prof. econs. Western Ill. U., Macomb, 1978—, chmn. dept. econs., 1980-89, dir. Ill. Inst. Rural Affairs, 1988—, interim dean coll. bus. and tech., 1993-95. Author: Cities, Suburbs and Property Tax, 1981, Government Structure and Public Finance, 1984; editor: Financing State and Local Governments, 1981, Rural Community Economic Development, 1991; co-editor: Financing Local Infrastructure in Non Metro Areas, 1986, Financing Economic Development in The 1980s, 1986, Financing Rural Health Care, 1988, Rural Health Care, 1992, Rural Community Economic Development, 1992, Local Economic Development: International Trends and Issues, 1995, Community Visioning Programs: Practice and Principles, 1996, Public-Private Partnerships for Local Economic Development, 1998, Cooperative Approach to Community Economic Development, 2000, Local Government Innovations, 2000, Managing Change During a Transition: Issues Facing the Rural Midwest, 2001, American Midwest: Managing Change in Rural Transition, 2002. Mem. Am. Econs. Assn., Ill. Econs. Assn. (pres. 1979-80), Mid-Continent Regional Sci. Assn. (pres. 1985-86). Office: Western Ill U Ill Inst Rural Affairs 518 Stipes Hall Macomb IL 61455

WAMBOLD, RICHARD LAWRENCE, manufacturing executive company; b. Wilbraham, Mass., Jan. 19, 1952; s. Richard A. and Virginia M. (Reid) W.; m. Patricia Bentley, Aug. 24, 1974; children: Lauren, Carolyn, Robin. BA, U. Tex., 1974, MBA, 1977. From systems cons. to strategic planning mgr. Tenneco, Inc., Houston, 1977-81, asst. to chmn. and chief exec. officer, 1981-84, pres. Tenneco Ventures Inc., 1984-88, v.p. corp. planning and devel., 1988—; exec. v.p., gen. mgr. Internat. Bus. Group, J.I. Case Co., Racine, Wis., 1988—. Mem. Nat. Venture Capital Assn. Avocation: sailing. Office: J I Case 700 State St Racine WI 53404-3392 also: Headquaters 1900 West Field Court Lake Forest IL 60045

WANDER, HERBERT STANTON, lawyer; b. Cin., Mar. 17, 1935; s. Louis Marvin and Pauline (Schuster) W.; m. Ruth Cele Fell, Aug. 7, 1960; children: Daniel Jerome, Susan Gail, Lois Marlene. AB, U. Mich., 1957; LLB, Yale U., 1960. Bar: Ohio 1960, Ill. 1960. Law clk. to judge U.S. Dist. Ct. (no. dist.) Ill., 1960—61; ptnr. Pope Ballard Shepard & Fowle, Chgo., 1961—78, Katten Muchin Zavis Rosenman, Chgo., 1978—. Trustee Michael Reese Found., 1991—; bd. dirs. Tel. & Data Systems, Chgo.; mem. legal adv. com. to the bd. govs. N.Y. Stock Exch., 1989-92; mem. legal adv. bd. Nat. Assn. Securities Dealers, Inc., 1996-99. Editor: (jour.) Bus. Law Today, 1992-93; editor-in-chief: (jour.) The Bus. Lawyer, 1993-94; contbr. numerous articles to profl. jours. Bd. dirs. Jewish Fedn. Met. Chgo., 1972—, pres., 1981-83; bd. dirs. Jewish United Fund, 1972—, pres., 1981-83, chmn. pub. affairs com., 1984-87, gen. campaign chmn., 1993; former regional chmn. nat. young leadership cabinet United Jewish Appeal; vice-chmn. large city budgeting conf. Coun. Jewish Fedns., 1979-82, bd. dirs., 1980—, exec. com., 1983-84. Mem. ABA (sec. bus. law sect. 1992-93, vice-chair 1993-94, chair-elect 1994-95, chair 1995-96, apptd. to commn. on multidisciplinary practice 1998), Ill. State Bar Assn., Chgo. Bar Assn., Yale Law Sch. Assn. (exec. com. 1982-86), Std. Club, Econ. Club, Northmoor Country Club, Phi Beta Kappa. Home: 70 Prospect Ave Highland Park IL 60035-3329 Office: Katten Muchin Zavis Rosenman 525 W Monroe St Ste 1600 Chicago IL 60661-3693 E-mail: hwander@kmzr.com.

WANG, ALBERT JAMES, violinist, educator; b. Ann Arbor, Mich., Nov. 19, 1958; s. James and Lydia (Ebenhoch) Wang; m. Bridget Renee Becker, June 30, 1987 (div. 2000); children: Ona Lenore, Kevin Lewis. MusB, Ind. U., 1979; MusM, U. Mich., 1981; DMA, Am. Conservatory, 1993. Prin. second violin Baton Rouge Symphony Orch., 1981-82; first violin Valcour String Quartet, Baton Rouge, 1981-82, Loyola String Quartet, 1982-83; mem. Lyric Opera Chgo. Orch., 1982—; mem. Orch. Ill., Chgo., 1982-88; prin. 2d violin Internat. Symphony Orch., Port Huron, Mich., 1984; 1st violin Internat. String Quartet, 1984; concertmaster, soloist Chgo. Chamber Orch., 1985-88, Chgo. Philharm., 1985—; mem. Grant Park Symphony Orch., Chgo., 1986-87; concertmaster, soloist Birch Creek Music Festival, Wis., Woodstock (Ill.) Mozart Festival Orch., 1988-90; concertmaster Rockford (Ill.) Symphony Orch., 1990-91, Northwestern Music Festival Orch., 1990—; soloist, concertmaster Pro Musica Orch. of Mauritius, 1992-93; soloist, concertmaster China tour Classical Symphony Orch., 1994, 95; soloist, concertmaster Midwest Symphony Orch., 1995-96; music dir. Baroque Masterplayers, 1994—; soloist, concertmaster Met. Arts Orch., 1995-98. Artist-in-residence St. Clair Coll., Port Huron, 1984, Elgin C.C., 1994—97; lectr. Am. Conservatory Music, Chgo., 1989—92; Fulbright lectr. Francois Mitterand Conservatory of Music, Quatre Bornes, Mauritius, 1992—93; asst. prof. violin Roosevelt U., 1993—2002; adj. prof. violin Wheaton (Ill.) Coll., 1997—2000; adj. asst. prof. violin Moody Bible Inst., Chgo., 1997—2000; v.p. sales and mktg. Music Edn. Publs., Inc., Coral Springs, Fla., 1997—98. Numerous solo, recital and chamber music appearances and master classes throughout U.S., Can., France, Mauritius and China; recs. and broadcasts by Mauritian Nat. Radio and WFMT Chgo. Fine Arts Sta., PBS, Nat. Pub. Radio, and Chinese Nat. Radio and TV; numerous world premieres; recs. on New World Records and with Slavic Projection Ensemble; N.Y. recital debut at Carnegie Hall, 1998; adjudicator for state and nat. music competitions; contbr. articles and revs. to profl. jours. Vol. ARC, Literacy Vols. Am., Chgo. Pub. Librs., United Way; bd. advisors Prism Music Festival, 1984—, Am. Chamber Symphony, 1985, Symphony II, 1993-94. Fulbright grantee, 1992-93; recipient 1st prize Ann Arbor (Mich.) Symphony Competition, 1976, Soc. Am. Musicians Competition, Chgo., 1984, Internat. Concerts Atlantique Competition, N.Y.C., 1989, Chgo. Park Dist. Competition, 1991, 2nd prize Biennial Adult Artist Competition, 1992, Helmuth Fuchs Performance award 1998; selected to Arts Am. Touring Artist Roster, 1993; finalist Lilly Fellows Program in Humanities and the Arts, Valparaiso U., 1994, Harry and Sarah Zelzer Fellowship and prize; recipient Leo Sowerby medal, 1994; Christian Performing Artists' fellow. Mem. ASCAP, Am. Fedn. Musicians, Am. String Tchrs. Assn., Coll. Music Soc., Chamber Music Am., Am. Music Ctr., Music Tchrs. Nat. Assn., Christian Performing Artists' Fellowship. Avocations: powerlifting, fishing, travel, woodworking. Home: 6110 N Glenwood Ave Chicago IL 60660-1804 Office: Lyric Opera Chgo 20 N Wacker Dr Chicago IL 60606-2806 also: Baroque Masterplayers 5528 S Hyde Park Blvd Ste 1102 Chicago IL 60637-2091 E-mail: embrown1@earthlink.net.

WANG, HENRY YEE-NEEN, chemical engineering educator; b. Shanghai, July 22, 1951; came to U.S., 1969; s. T. C. and Aurza Wang; m. Evangeline Yap Cesar, 1983; 1 child, Stephanie. BS, Iowa State U., 1972; MS, MIT, 1974, PhD, 1977. Rsch. asst. MIT, Cambridge, 1972-77; engring. assoc. Merckle & Co., Rahway, N.J., 1977; sr. scientist Schering-Plough, Union, 1978-79; from asst. prof. to assoc. prof. U. Mich., Ann Arbor, 1978-84, prof., 1989—. Disting. sr. scientist Mich. Biotech. Inst., Lansing, 1984—; cons. Hong Kong U. of Sci. and Tech., 1993—. Internat. editor: Jour. Ferm. Biotech., 1991—. Mem. AIChE, Am. Chem. Soc. (councilor 1984-86), Am. Soc. Microbiology, Soc. Indsl. Microbiology. Home: 1215 Bardstown Trl Ann Arbor MI 48105-2816 Office: U Mich Dept Chem Engring Ann Arbor MI 48109

WANKAT, PHILLIP CHARLES, chemical engineering educator; b. Oak Park, Ill., July 11, 1944; s. Charles and Grace Leona (Pryor) W.; m. Dorothy Nel Richardson, Dec. 13, 1980; children: Charles, Jennifer. BS in Chem. Engring., Purdue U., 1966, MS in Edn., 1982; PhD, Princeton U., 1970. From asst. prof. to C.L. Lovell disting. prof. chem. engring Purdue U., West Lafayette, Ind., 1970—, head freshman engring., 1987-95, interim dir. continuing engring. edn., 1996, head interdisciplinary engring., 2000—. Cons. pharm. firm, 1985-94. Author: Large Scale Ads and Chromatog, 1986, Equil Staged Separations, 1988, Rate Controlled Separations, 1990, Teaching Engineering, 1993, The Effective, Efficient Professor, 2002; patentee in field. With AUS, 1962-64. Recipient award in Separations Sci. and Tech., Am. Chem. Soc., 1994. Mem. AIChE, Am. Soc. Engring. Edn. (Union Carbide Lectr. award 1997), Am. Chem. Soc. Avocations: fishing, canoeing, camping. Office: Purdue U Dept Interdisciplinary Engring West Lafayette IN 47907-1292 E-mail: wankat@ecn.purdue.edu.

WANKE, RONALD LEE, lawyer, educator; b. Chgo., June 22, 1941; s. William F. and Lucille (Kleinwachter) W.; m. Rose Klonowski, Oct. 23, 1987. BSEE, Northwestern U., 1964; JD, DePaul U., 1968. Bar: Ill. 1968. Assoc. Wood, Dalton, Phillips, Mason & Rowe, Chgo., 1968-71, ptnr., 1971-84, Jenner & Block, Chgo., 1984--. Lectr. John Marshall Law Sch., Chgo., 1985-94; mem. adv. com. intellectual property program, U. Fla. Coll. Law. Co-author: (book chpt.) International Intellectual Property Law, 1997; contbr. articles to Software Law Jour., 1987, Internat. Legal Strategy, 1995. Mem. ABA, Computer Law Assn., Intellectual Property Law Assn. Chgo. (chmn. inventor svcs. com. 1976, chmn. fed. rules com. 1981). Home: 1806 N Sedgwick St Chicago IL 60614-5306 Office: Jenner & Block 1 E Ibm Plz Fl 4000 Chicago IL 60611-7603

WANSLEY, TY, radio personality; Former news dir. Sta. WBMX-FM, Sta. WJPC-AM; former talk show host Sta. WVON-AM, Sta. WCGI-AM, Sta. WLS-AM/FM, Sta. WJJD-AM; former host, prodr. TV News Mag. Show Urban St.; radio host, info. anchor morning show Sta. WGCI-FM, Chgo. Office: WGCI 332 S Michigan Ave Ste 600 Chicago IL 60604*

WANTLAND, WILLIAM CHARLES, retired bishop, lawyer; b. Edmond, Okla., Apr. 14, 1934; s. William Lindsay and Edna Louise (Yost) W. BA, U. Hawaii, 1957; JD, Okla. City U., 1967; D in Religion, Geneva Theol. Coll., Knoxville, Tenn., 1976; DD (hon.), Nashotah House, Wis., 1983, Seabury-Western Sem., Evanston, Ill., 1983. With FBI, various locations, 1954-59, Ins. Co. of N.Am., Oklahoma City, 1960-62; law clk.-atty. Bishop & Wantland, Seminole, Okla., 1962-77; vicar St. Mark's Ch., 1963-77, St. Paul's Ch., Holdenville, Okla., 1974-77; presiding judge Seminole Mcpl. Ct., 1970-77; atty. gen. Seminole Nation of Okla., 1969-72, 75-77; exec. dir. Okla. Indian Rights Assn., Norman, 1972-73; rector St. John's Ch., Oklahoma City, 1977-80; bishop Episcopal Diocese of Eau Claire, Wis., 1980-99; interim bishop of Navajoland, 1993-94; ret., 1999. Adj. prof. Law Sch. U. Okla., Norman, 1970-78; instr. canon law Nashotah House, 1983-97; mem. nat. coun. Evang. & Cath. Mission, Chgo., 1977-90; mem. Episcopal Commn. on Racism, 1990-92, Episcopal Coun. Indian Ministries, 1990-95, Standing Commn. on Constn. and Canons, 1992-95. Author: Foundations of the Faith, 1982, Canon Law of the Episcopal Church, 1984, The Prayer Book and the Catholic Faith, 1994; The Catholic Faith, The Episcopal Church and the Ordination of Women, 1997; co-author: Oklahoma Probate Forms, 1971; contbr. articles to profl. jours. Pres. Okla. Conf. Mcpl. Judges, 1973; v.p. South African Ch. Union, 1985-95; trustee Nashotah House, Wis., 1981-2000, chmn., 1992-98; bd. dirs. SPEAK, Eureka Springs, Ark., 1983-89; mem. Wis. adv. com. U.S. Civil Rights Commn., 1990-91; mem. support com. Native Am. Rights Fund, 1990—; co-chmn. Luth.-Anglican-Roman Cath. Commn. of Wis., 1989-95; pres. Wis. Episc. Conf., 1995-97. Recipient Most Outstanding Contbn. to Law and Order award Okla. Supreme Ct., 1975, Outstanding Alumnus award Okla. City U., 1980, Wis. Equal Rights Coun. award, 1986, Manitou Ikwe award Indian Alcoholism Coun., 1988, Episcopal Synod Pres.'s award, 1995. Mem. Okla. Bar Assn., Okla. Indian Bar Assn., Living Ch. Found., Oklahoma City Law Sch. Alumni Assn. (pres. 1968), Wis. Coun. Chs. (pres. 1985-86). Democrat. Avocations: canoeing, skin-diving, cross-country skiing. E-mail: puca382@nbo.net.

WANZEK, TERRY MARVIN, state legislator; b. Jamestown, N.D., Mar. 28, 1957; m. Janice Hoffart; 2 children. Farmer, rancher, Cleveland, N.D.; mem. N.D. Senate from 29th dist., Bismarck, 1995—; mem. edn. com. N.D. Senate, 1995—; vice chmn. agr. com. N.D. State Senate, 1995-97; chmn. agr. com., mem. edn. com. N.D. Senate, 1997—. Pres. Stutsman County Farm Bur. Fellow Jamestown Coll.; recipient Agriculturist award Pres.' Agr. Club N.D. State U. Mem. Stutsman County Agrl. Improvement Assn. (pres.), KC, Jamestown C. of C. Home: 404 10th St SW Jamestown ND 58401-4546

WARCH, RICHARD, academic administrator; b. Hackensack, N.J., Aug. 4, 1939; s. George William and Helen Anna (Hansen) W.; m. Margot Lynn Moses, Sept. 8, 1962; children: Stephen Knud, David Preston, Karin Joy. B.A., Williams Coll., 1961; B.D., Yale Div. Sch., 1964; Ph.D., Yale U., 1969; postgrad., U. Edinburgh, 1962-63; H.H.D., Ripon Coll., 1980. Asst. prof. history and Am. studies Yale U., 1968-73, asso. prof., 1973-77; asso. dean Yale Coll.; dir. summer plans Yale U., 1976-77; asso. dir. Nat. Humanities Inst., New Haven, 1975-76; v.p. acad. affairs Lawrence U., Appleton, Wis., 1977-79, pres., 1979—. Cons. Nat. Humanities Faculty; ordained to ministry United Presbyn. Ch. in U.S.A., 1968; dir. Bank One of Appleton. Author: School of the Prophets, Yale College, 1701-1740, 1973; editor: John Brown, 1973. Rockefeller Bros. Theol. fellow, 1961-62 Mem. Am. Studies Assn., Soc. for Values in Higher Edn., Winnebago Presbytery. Club: Rotary. Home: 229 North Park Ave Appleton WI 54911 Office: Lawrence U PO Box 599 Appleton WI 54912-0599

WARD, DAVID, academic administrator, educator; b. Manchester, Eng., July 8, 1938; came to U.S., 1960; s. Horace and Alice (Harwood) W.; m. Judith B. Freifeld, June 11, 1964; children: Michael J.H., Peter F.B. BA, U. Leeds, Eng., 1959; MA, U. Leeds, 1961; MS, U. Wis., 1961, PhD, 1963; LittD, U. Leeds, 1992. Lectr. Carleton U., Ottawa, Ont., Can., 1963-64; asst. prof. Univ. B.C., Vancouver, Can., 1964-66, U. Wis., Madison, 1966-67, assoc. prof., 1967-70, prof., 1970—, chmn. geography dept., 1974-77, assoc. dean Grad. Sch., 1980-88, provost and vice chancellor acad. affairs, Andrew Clark prof. geography, 1989—; chancellor U. Wis. Madison, 1994-2000; pres. Am. Coun. on Edn., 2001—. Mem. exec. com. Argonne (Ill.) Nat. Lab., 1990-93; dir.-at-large Social Sci. Rsch. Coun., 1991-93; mem. Kellogg Commn. on Future of Land Grant Univs.; chair Internet 2, Univ. Consortium on Advanced Network Devel. Author: Cities and Immigrants, 1970, Geographic Perspectives on Americas Past, 1978, Poverty Ethnicity and the American City, 1989, Landscape of Modernity, 1992; contbr. articles to profl. jours. Guggenheim fellow, 1970, Einstein fellow Hebrew U., 1980, Fulbright fellow, Australian Nat. U., 1979. Fellow Am. Acad. Arts and Scis.; mem. Assn. Am. Geographers (pres. 1989). Office: One Dupont Circle NW Washington DC 20036-1193 E-mail: david_ward@ace.nche.edu.

WARD, DAVID ALLEN, sociology educator; b. Dedham, Mass., June 21, 1933; s. Theodore Allen and Jessie Miller (Ketchum) W.; m. Carol Jane Barton, June 10, 1957 (div. 1964); children: Douglas Allen, Andrew Barton; m. Reneé Ellen Light, Mar. 10, 1967. BA, Colby Coll., 1955; PhD, U. Ill., 1960. Asst. prof. Wash. State U., Pullman, 1960-61; asst. research sociologist UCLA, 1961-64; assoc. prof. U. Minn., Mpls., 1965-68, prof., 1968—, chmn. dept. sociology, 1984-88, 92-95. Chmn. Salzburg (Austria) Seminar in Am. Studies, 1977; cons. jud. com. U.S. Ho. Reps., Washington, 1984. Co-author: Women's Prison, 1965, Prison Treatment, 1971; co-editor: Delinquency, Crime and Social Process, 1969, Confinement in Maximum Custody, 1981; editorial cons. Jour. Criminal Law and Criminology, 1968-97. Mem. Mpls. Civilan Police Rev. Bd., 1991-94. Liberal Arts fellow Harvard U. Law Sch., 1968-69; Fulbright research fellow, 1971-72; research fellow Norwegian Fgn. Office, Oslo, 1976. Mem.: Am. Soc. Criminology, Am. Sociol. Assn. (chmn. sect. criminology 1976—77). Office: Univ of Minn Dept of Sociology 909 Social Sci Bldg Minneapolis MN 55455

WARD, DAVID W. state legislator; b. Ft. Atkinson, Wis., Apr. 29, 1953; m. Jean M. Ward, 1975; 1 child, Kevin. BA, U. Wis., Platteville. Past mem. Wis. Milk Mktg. Bd., Ft. Atkinson Sch. Bd.; Wis. state assembly man dist. 37, 1992—. Farmer. Mem. Jefferson County Farm Bur., pres. Address: 3401 County Rd G Fort Atkinson WI 53538 also: Wis Assembly PO Box 8952 Madison WI 53708-8952

WARD, FRANCIS J. marketing and research executive; Founder Product and Comsumer Evaluations, Inc (PACE), 1975-90; CEO MORPACE Internat (merger PACE and Market Opinion Rsch.), Farmington HIlls, MI, 1990—. Office: MORPACE Internat 31700 Middlebelt Rd Ste 0 Farmington Hills MI 48334-2373

WARD, JONATHAN P. communications executive; BSChemE, U. N.H., 1976; grad. advanced mgmt. program, Harvard Bus. Sch. With R.R. Donnelley, 1977—, pres. Merchandise Media and Fin. Svcs. bus. units, mgr. comml. printing operation, v.p., dir. Spartanburg, S.C., mfg. divsn., pres., COO, 1997—. Dir. Metromail Corp., Siegwerk, Inc. USA, Direct Mktg. Assn., Nat. Assn. Mfrs. Trustee Goodman Theatre, Chgo.; dir. Chgo. Youth Ctrs. Office: RR Donnelley & Sons Co Corp Hdqs 77 W Wacker Dr Ste 1900 Chicago IL 60601-1649

WARD, LLOYD D. appliance company executive; m. Lita; 2 sons. BS Engring, Mich. State U., 1970; MBA, Xavier U. Design engr., group leader engring., product devel., operations, advertising Proctor & Gamble Co., 1970-88, gen. mgr. dish care products, 1988; v.p. ops. Pepsi Cola East, 1988-91; pres. Frito-Lay West PepsiCo, 1991-92, pres. Frito-Lay central divsn., 1992-96; exec. v.p., pres. Maytag Appliances, Newton, Iowa, 1996-98, COO, corp. pres., 1998—, CEO, 1999-. Special assignment PepsiCo restaurant internat. bus. Recipient Exec. Yr. award Black Enterprise mag. 1995. Office: 403 W 4th St N Newton IA 50208-3026

WARD, MICHAEL A. property company executive; Exec. v.p., COO Ramco-Gershenson Properties, Southfield, Mich., 1989—. Office: 27600 Northwestern Hwy Ste 200 Southfield MI 48034-8466 E-mail: mward@ramco.gersherson.com.

WARD, PETER ALLAN, pathologist, educator; b. Winsted, Conn., Nov. 1, 1934; s. Parker J. and Mary Alice (McEvoy) Ward. B.S., U. Mich., Ann Arbor, 1958, M.D., 1960. Diplomate Am. Bd. Anat. Pathology, Am. Bd. Immunopathology. Intern Bellevue Hosp., 1960—61; resident U. Mich. Hosp., Ann Arbor, 1961—63; postdoctoral fellow Scripps Clinic, La Jolla, Calif., 1963—65; chief immunobiology br. Armed Forces Inst. Pathology, Washington, 1967—71; prof. dept. pathology, chmn. dept. U. Conn. Health Center, Farmington, 1971—80; prof., chmn. dept. pathology U. Mich., Ann Arbor, 1980—; interim dean U. Mich. Med. Sch., 1982—85, 1st Godfrey D. Stobbe prof. pathology, 1987; Disting. faculty lectr. U. Mich. Biomed. Rsch. Coun., 1989. Cons. VA Hosp., 1980—; mem. rsch. rev. com. NHLBI, NIH, Bethesda, Md., 1978—82, Inst. Medicine/NAS, 1990—; trustee Am. Bd. Pathology, 1988—97, pres., 1996; bd. dirs. Univs. Assoc. for Rsch. and Edn. in Pathology, Inc., 1978—, pres. bd. dirs., 1988—90; chmn., mem. sch. adv. bd. Armed Forces Inst. Pathology, Washington, 1981—83; mem. pathology A study sect. NIH, 1972—76, chmn., 1976—78; pres.-elect U.S./Can. Acad. Pathology, 1991—92, pres., 1992—93; bd. dirs. Inst. Lab. Resources, NRC. Capt. M.C. U.S. Army, 1965—67. Recipient Borden Rsch. award, U. Mich. Med. Sch., Ann Arbor, 1960, R&D and Devel. award, U.S. Army, 1969, Meritorious Civilian Svc. award, Dept. Army, 1970, Parke-Davis award, Am. Soc. Exptl. Pathology, 1971, Rous-Whipple award, Am. Soc. Investigative Pathology, 1996, Gold Headed Cane award, 2000. Fellow: AAAS; mem.: Mich. Soc. Pathologists, Assn. Am. Physicians, Assn. Pathology Chmn., U.S. and Can. Acad. Pathologists (pres. 1993—94), Am. Assn. Immunologists, Am. Soc. Clin. Investigation, Am. Assn. Pathologists 1978—79. Office: 1301 Catherine St Rm M5240 PO Box 602 Ann Arbor MI 48106-0602

WARD, ROSCOE FREDRICK, engineering educator; b. Boise, Idaho, Dec. 5, 1930; s. Roscoe C. W. and Alice E. (Ward); m. Julia Duffy, June 8, 1963; children: Eric R., David C. Student, U. Oreg., 1949-50; B.A., Coll. of Idaho, 1953; postgrad., U. Wash., 1955-57; B.S., Oreg. State U., 1959; M.S., Wash. State U., 1961; Sc.D., Washington U., St. Louis, 1964. Registered profl. engr., Ohio. Asst. prof. civil engring. U. Mo., Columbia, 1963-65, Robert Coll., Istanbul, Turkey, 1965-67; assoc. prof. civil engring. Asian Inst. Tech., Bangkok, Thailand, 1967-68; assoc. prof. civil engring., assoc. dean Sch. Engring. U. Mass., Amherst, 1968-75; prof. Bogazici U., Istanbul, 1974-75; br. chief biomass energy Dept. Energy, Washington, 1975-79; interregional advisor UN/World Bank, N.Y.C., 1979-83; dean Sch. Applied Scis. Miami U., Oxford, Ohio, 1983-88; prof. paper sci. and engring. Sch. Engring. and Applied Scis. Miami U., 1983—. Vis. scientist Csir, Republic of South Africa, 1990-91. Contbr. chpts. to books, articles to profl. jours. Fellow ASCE Home: 4818 Bonham Rd Oxford OH 45056-1423 E-mail: WARDRF@MUOHIO.EDU.

WARD, SHERMAN CARL, III (BUZZ WARD), theater manager; b. Camden, N.J., Apr. 21, 1958; s. Sherman Carl Jr. and Ann Laura (Bodie) W. BA, Princeton U., 1980; MBA, Harvard U., 1986. Contr.'s asst. McCarter Theatre Co., Princeton, N.J., 1977-80; spl. projects analyst Madison Fin. Corp., Nashville, 1980-81, dir. client svcs., 1981-83; tchr. English, vol. rschr. Nan, Thailand, 1983-84; studio ops. Walt Disney Pictures, Burbank, Calif., summer 1985; contr. Coconut Grove Playhouse, Miami, Fla., 1986-87, dir. ops., 1987-88; gen. mgr. Yale Sch. Drama, Yale Repertory Theatre, New Haven, 1988-92; exec. dir. Cin. Playhouse in the Park, 1992—. Recipient Letter of Appreciation, King of Thailand, 1984. Mem. Actor's Equity Assn. Avocations: travel, singing, dancing, golf, volleyball. Office: Cin Playhouse in the Park 962 Mount Adams Cir Cincinnati OH 45202-6023

WARD, THOMAS, food products executive; b. June 9, 1958; Co-CEO, pres. Russell Stover Candies, Kansas City, Mo. Fax: 816-842-5593.

WARD, VERNON GRAVES, internist; b. Palisade, Nebr., Mar. 5, 1928; s. Charles Bennett and Mildred Belle (Graves) W.; m. Eleanore Mae Farstveet, Aug. 28, 1952; children: Margo, Alison, Barry. BA, Nebr. Wesleyan U., 1948; MD cum laude, U. Nebr., Omaha, 1954. Diplomate Am. Bd. Internal Medicine. Instr. in anatomy Columbia U., N.Y.C., 1948-50; intern U. Wis., Madison, 1954-55, resident internal medicine, 1955-58, chief resident, physician, 1957-58; fellow in neurophysiology and psychosomatic medicine U. Okla., Oklahoma City, 1960-61; asst. clin. prof. medicine U. Wis., Madison, 1961-62; pvt. practice internal medicine Kearney, Nebr., 1962-67; asst. prof. U. Nebr. Coll. Medicine, Omaha, 1967-69; assoc. clin. prof. medicine U. Nebr., 1969—; pvt. practice internal medicine, 1969—. Chmn. dept. internal medicine Clarkson Hosp., Omaha, 1976-78, 96-98. Contbr. articles to profl. jours. including JAMA, Nebr. State Med. Jour., Wis. State Med. Jour., Am. Heart Jour., Postgrad. Medicine. Pres. Nebr. chpt. Arthritis Found., 1969-71. Lt. Commdr. USNR, 1958-60. Recipient Cmty. Based Tchg. award ACP-ASIM, 2000; named Hutton Traveling Scholar Coll. of Physicians, 1965. Fellow Am. Coll. Rheumatology; mem. AMA, Nebr. State Med. Soc., Omaha Med. Soc., ACP-Am. Soc. Internal Medicine (Cmty.-Based Tchg. award 2000), Am. Psychosomatic Soc., Nebr. Soc. Internal Medicine (pres. 1980-82, Disting. Internist award 1990), Phi Kappa Phi, Alpha Omega Alpha (pres. Nebr. chpt. 1984-85), Phi Chi (grand sec.-treas. 1986—, co-chmn. nat. conv. Omaha 1953), Phi Kappa Tau. Republican. Lutheran. Home: 302 N 54th St Omaha NE 68132-2813 Office: 201 S Doctor's Bldg Omaha NE 68131

WARD, WILLIAM EDWARD, museum exhibition designer; b. Apr. 4, 1922; s. Edward and Lura Dell (Eckelberry) W.; m. Evelyn Svec, Nov. 12, 1952; 1 child, Pamela. BS, Western Res. U., 1947, MA, 1948; diploma, Cleve. Inst. Art, 1947; postgrad., Columbia U., 1950. Mem. staff edn. Oriental depts. Cleve. Mus. Art, 1947—, designer, 1957—, ret. chief designer; prof. calligraphy and watercolor Cleve. Inst. Art, 1960—; prof., cons. graphic and installation exhbn., design cons. Egyptian Mus., Cairo, 1995—. Exhibited in numerous exhbns. including (with Evelyn Svec Ward) Oaxacan Inspirations: An Exhibition of Collage and Watercolor, 1986, Valley of Oaxaca: Exhibition of Watercolors and Photographs, Folk Art Gallery, Cleve., 1992, Cleve. Playhouse Gallery, 1984, Butler Inst. Am. Art, Salem Ohio Br., 2000; designer George Gund Collection of Western Art Mus., 1972, Firemen's Meml., Cleve., sculpture design, 1968; designer ofcl. seals Case Western Res. U., also Sch. Medicine, 1969; curator Culcon exhbn. Masterpieces of World Art from Am. Museums, Tokyo and Kyoto, Japan, 1976; co-author (catalogue, exhbn.) Folk Art of Oaxaca: The Ward Colection, Cleve Inst. Art, 1987; textile designs in Cleve. Artists Found. collection; represented in permanent collections of Cleve. Mus. of Art, Akron Art Mus., Art Assn. of Cleve. Inst. of Art, Artists Archives Western Res., Cleve. Mem. Internat. Design Conf., Aspen, 1959—; mem. Tridecca Soc. (trustee 1995-98); mem. Fine Arts Adv. Com. City Cleve., 1966-90; mem. mayor's com. for selection of ofcl. seal City of Cleve., 1973, mem. design rev. com., 1991-92. Served with Terrain Intelligence, AUS, 1942-45, S.E. Asia Command. Recipient commn. award City Canvas competition Cleve. Area Arts Coun., 1975, No. Ohio LIVE Achievement award Cleve. Mus. Art, 1987, Hall of Fame award West Tech. Alumni Assn., 1995. Mem. Cleve. Soc. Contemporary Art, Artists Archives of the Western Reserve, Print Club Cleve., Cleve. Artist Found. (exhibiting mem. Beck Ctr. Gallery, Cleve. 1999), Rowfant Club, Women's City Club Cleve. (Arts Prize Spl. citation 1988). Home: 27045 Solon Rd Solon OH 44139-3452

WARDEN, GAIL LEE, health care executive; b. Clarinda, Iowa, May 11, 1938; s. Lee Roy and Juanita (Haley) W.; m. Lois Jean Johnson, Oct. 9, 1965; children: Jay Christopher, Janna Lynn, Jena Marie. BA, Dartmouth Coll., 1960; MHA, U. Mich., 1962. Adminstrv. asst. Blodgett Meml. Hosp., Grand Rapids, Mich., 1962; adj. Dewitt Hosp., Ft. Belvoir, Va., 1963-65; adminstrv. asst. Presbyn.-St. Luke's Hosp., Chgo., 1965-68, asst. to pres., 1968, v.p. adminstrn., 1968-69; exec. v.p. Rush-Presbyn.-St. Luke's Med. Center, 1970-76, Am. Hosp. Assn., Chgo., 1976-81; pres., CEO Group Health Coop. Puget Sound, Seattle, 1981-88, Henry Ford Health System, Detroit, 1988—. Past chmn. Am. Hosp. Assn.; bd. dirs. Comerica Bank; mem. governing coun. Inst. Medicine of NAS. Contbr. articles to profl. jours. Bd. dirs. Robert Wood Johnson Found. Served to capt. AUS, 1965. Named one of Ten Outstanding Young Men in Chgo., Jr. Assn. Commerce and Industry, 1968, Nat. Health Care award B'nai B'rith Internat., 1992, CEO award Am. Hosp. Assn.'s Soc. for Healthcare Planning and Mktg., 1993. Mem. NAS, Am. Coll. Hosp. Adminstrs. (named Young Adminstr. of Yr. 1972), Am. Pub. Health Assn., Am. Healthcare Systems, Alpha Chi Rho. Office: Henry Ford Health System 1 Ford Pl Detroit MI 48202-3450

WARDNER, RICH, state legislator; m. Kayleen Wardner; children: Brant, Cory. Math. and chemistry tchr., football coach Dickinson (N.D.) H.S.; mem. N.D. Senate from 37th dist., Bismarck, 1991—; mem. state and fed. govt. com. N.D. Senate, former vice chmn., chmn. govt. and vet. affairs com., now mem. fin. and taxation com. Office: 1042 12th Ave W Dickinson ND 58601-3654 also: ND Ho of Reps State Capitol Bismarck ND 58505

WARDROP, RICHARD M., JR. steel holding company executive; b. McKeesport, Pa. BS In Metall. Engring., Pa. State U.; postgrad., U. Pitts. Sr. buyer raw materials U.S. Steel Corp., Pitts., 1980-81, supt. flat-rolled products group Gary, Ind., 1991-84, divsn. mgr. for steel prodn., casting and primary rolling, 1984-86, plant mgr. for primary ops., 1986-88, gen. mgr. Mongehela Valley Works, from 1988; corp. v.p. engring. and purchasing Washington (Pa.) Steel Corp; v.p. mfg. AK Steel Holding Corp., Middletown, Ohio, 1992, CEO, chmn., CEO, 1997—; various positions U.S. Steel Corp., 1968-92. Named to Platinum 400 List, Forbes Mag., 1999. Mem. AIME, Am. Soc. Metals Internat. (David Ford McFarland award for achievement in metallurgy Pa. State U. chpt. 1995), Am. Iron and Steel Engrs. Office: AK Steel Holding Corp 703 Curtis St Middletown OH 45043

WARDROPPER, IAN BRUCE, museum curator, educator; b. Balt., May 11, 1951; s. Bruce Wear and Joyce (Vaz) W.; stepmother: Nancy Hélène (Palmer) W.; m. Laurel Ellen Bradley, May 22, 1982 (div. 1996); 1 child, Chloe Bradley; m. Sarah Anne McNear, June 21, 1997. BA, Brown U., 1973; MA, NYU, 1976, PhD, 1985. Asst. curator European sculpture Art Inst. Chgo., 1982-85, assoc. curator European decorative arts and sculpture, 1985-89, Eloise W. Martin curator European decorative arts and sculpture, and classical art, 1989-2001; Iris and B. Gerald Cantor curator in charge dept. European sculpture and decorative arts Met. Mus. Art, N.Y.C., 2001—. Adj. instr. Drew U., NJ, 1982; vis. asst. prof. Northwestern U., Evanston, Ill., 1986, Sch. of Art Inst. Chgo., 1988; guest scholar J. Paul Getty Mus., Malibu, Calif., 1995; Rhoades lectr. U. Chgo., 1997; exhbns. panelist NEA, 1993, creation and presentation panelist, 98, indemnity panelist, 1998—2001. Co-author: European Decorative Arts in the Art Institute of Chicago, 1991, Austrian Architecture and Design beyond Tradition in the 1990s, 1991, News from a Radiant Future: Soviet Porcelain from the Collection of Craig H. and Kay A. Tuber, 1992, Chiseled with a Brush: Italian Sculpture, 1860-1925, from The Gilgore Collections, 1994, From the Sculptor's Hand: Italian Baroque Terracottas from the State Hermitage Museum, 1998; contbr. articles to profl. jours. NEA fellow, 1976-77, Chester Dale fellow Met. Mus. Art, 1978-79; Kress Found. rsch. grantee, Paris, 1979-81, Am. Philos. Soc. grantee, 1991; named Chicagoan of the Yr. in Arts Chicago Tribune, 1994. Mem. Phi Beta Kappa. Office: Met Mus Art 1000 Fifth Ave New York NY 10028-0198 Business E-Mail: Ian.wardropper@Metmuseum.org.

WARE, D. CLIFTON, singer, educator; b. Newton, Miss., Mar. 15, 1937; s. Durward Clifton and Emma Edna (Blount) W.; m. Elizabeth Jean Oldham, June 20, 1958; children: Jon Clifton, David Michael, Stephen Alan. B.A., Millsaps Coll., 1959; MusM, U. So. Miss., 1962; MusD, Northwestern U., 1970. Voice instr. U. So. Miss., Hattiesburg, 1964-69; prof. voice and pedagogy U. Minn., Mpls., 1970—, chmn. Roy A. Schuessler Vocal Arts Ctr., 1970—. Clinician, cons., adjudicator. Author: (book, song collection and video) Voice Adventures, 1988, (text, song collection, audio cassette, CD) Adventures in Singing, 1995, 2d edit., 1998, Basics of Vocal Pedagogy, 1998; made recs. St. Nicolas, 1977, Paul Bunyan, 1988; tenor soloist opera, oratorio, recitals. Mem. Nat. Assn. Tchrs. Singing (pres. Minn. chpt. 1972-73, 81-82, found.d. 1995—), Nat. Opera Assn. (pres. 1978-79), Music Tchrs. Nat. Assn., Pi Kappa Lambda, Phi Kappa Delta, Phi Mu Alpha Sinfonia, Pi Kappa Alha. Avocations: travel, hiking, reading. Home: 1923 3d St NW New Brighton MN 55112-7254 Office: U Minn Sch Music 100 Ferguson Minneapolis MN 55455 E-mail: warex001@tc.umn.edu.

WARE, RICHARD ANDERSON, foundation executive; b. N.Y.C., Nov. 7, 1919; s. John Sayers and Mabelle (Anderson) W.; m. Lucille Henney, Mar. 20, 1942 (div. 1972); children: Alexander W., Janet M., Bradley J., Patricia E.; m. Beverly G. Mytinger, Dec. 22, 1972. BA, Lehigh U., 1941; M in Pub. Adminstrn., Wayne State U., 1943; D in Social Sci. (honoris causa), Francisco Marroquin U., Guatemala, 1988. Research asst. Detroit Bur. Govt. Research, 1941-42; personnel technician Lend-Lease Adminstrn., Washington, 1942-43; research asso. to asst. dir. Citizens Research Council, Detroit, 1946-56; sec. Earhart and Relm Founds., Ann Arbor, Mich., 1951-70, trustee, pres., 1970-84, trustee, pres. emeritus, 1985—. Prin. dep. asst. sec. def. for internat. security affairs, Washington, 1969-70; cons. Office Asst. Sec. Def., 1970-73; dir. Citizens Trust Co., 1970-87. Vice pres. Ann Arbor United Fund and Community Svcs., 1968, pres., 1969; asst. dir. Mich. Joint Legis. Com. on State Reorgn., 1950-52; sec. Gov.'s Com. to Study Prisons, 1952-53; com. to chmn. Ann Arbor City Planning Commn., 1958-67; mem. Detroit Com. on Fgn. Rels., 1971-87; mem. coun. Woodrow Wilson Internat. Center for Scholars, 1977-85; vis. com. div. social scis. U. Chgo., 1977-85; mem. adv. com. The Citadel, 1977-85; mem. adv. coun. internat. studies program Fletcher Sch., Tufts U., 1979-85; trustee Greenhills Sch., 1973-80, Ann Arbor Area Found., 1977-83, Inst. Fgn. Policy Analysis, 1985—, Inst. Polit. Economy, 1985—, Ctr. for Study Social and Polit. Change Smith Coll., 1988—, Pequawket Found., 1989—, Intercollegiate Studies Inst., 1996—; polit. analyst Republican Nat. Com., Washington, 1964; bd. dirs. The Liberty Fund, Inc., Indpls., 1980—, Bd. Fgn. Scholarships, 1984-90, chmn., 1987-89. With USAAF, 1943-46. Recipient Civilian Meritorious Service medal Dept. Def., 1970; Paul Harris fellow Rotary, 1997. Fellow Mont Pelerin Soc.; mem. Govtl. Research Assoc. (trustee, v.p. 1955-56), Am. Polit. Sci. Assn., Ann Arbor Univ. Club, North Conway Country Club, Cosmos Club (Washington), Phi Beta Kappa, Phi Alpha Theta Congregationalist. Home: PO Box 310 Intervale NH 03845-0310 Office: 2200 Green Rd Ste H Ann Arbor MI 48105-1569

WAREHAM, JAMES LYMAN, steel company executive; b. Clinton, Iowa, Oct. 8, 1939; s. Lyman Hugh and Ulainee Maria (Pitts) W.; m. Patricia Josephine Wrubel, June 18, 1966; children: Lisa Jo, Tara Lynn. BSEE, U. Notre Dame, 1961. Various mgmt. positions U.S. Steel-Gary Works, Ind., 1961-69, div. mgr., 1976-79; various mgmt. positions U.S. Steel-Tex. Works, Baytown, 1969-72, U.S. Steel-South Works, Chgo., 1972-76, gen. plant mgr., 1979-84; v.p. engring. U.S. Steel, Pitts., 1984-86; pres., CEO Bliss Salem, Inc., Ohio, 1986-89; pres., COO Wheeling-Pitts. Steel Corp., W.Va., 1989-92, chmn., pres., CEO, 1992-96; pres. AK Steel Holding Corp., Middletown, OH, 1997—. Pres., bd. dirs. Wheeling-Pitts. Corp.; bd. dirs. Bliss-Salem Inc., Wesbanco, Am. Iron and Steel Inst. Area coord. Thompson for Gov., Homewood, Ill., 1978; div. chmn. United Way, Gary, Ind., 1976; gen. chmn., United Way Wheeling, W.Va., 1990; bd. dirs. United Way of Upper Ohio Valley, Wheeling Jesuit Coll., 1989—, Wheeling Hosp., 1990—. Named Small Businessman of Yr. Salem C. of C., 1988, Entrepreneur of Yr. Ernst & Young, Pitts., 1989. Mem. Assn. Iron & Steel Engrs., Inst. Mining & Metall. Engrs., Ohio Steel Industry Adv. Commn., W.Va. Mfg. Assn., Wheeling C. of C. Home: 5279 Pros Dr West Chester OH 45069-1881 Office: AK Steel Holding Corp 703 Curtis St Middletown OH 45043

WAREHAM, JERROLD F. broadcast executive; b. Clinton, Iowa, 1948; s. Lyman H. and Ullainee Wareham. BS, Marquette U., 1970; student, Wharton Sch. Bus. Pres., gen. mgr. Greater Dayton Pub. TV, Ohio, 1985-93; pres., CEO Sta. WVIZ, Cleve., 1993—; chmn. Am.'s Pub. TV Stas., 1997-99. Bd. dirs. PBS. Office: WVIZ 4300 Brookpark Rd Cleveland OH 44134-1124 E-mail: jwareham@wvtl.org.

WARMBROD, JAMES ROBERT, agriculture educator, university administrator; b. Belvidere, Tenn., Dec. 13, 1929; s. George Victor and Anna Sophia (Zimmerman) W.; m. Catharine P. Phelps, Jan. 30, 1965. B.S., U. Tenn., 1952, M.S., 1954; Ed.D. (Univ. fellow), U. Ill., 1962. Instr. edn. U. Tenn., Knoxville, 1956-57; tchr. high sch. Winchester, Tenn., 1957-59; asst. prof. U. Ill., Urbana, 1961-66, assoc. prof., 1966-67; prof. agrl. edn. Ohio State U., Columbus, 1968-95; ret.; Presdl. prof. Ohio State U., Columbus, 1989, Presdl. prof. emeritus, 1995, Disting. univ. prof. emeritus, 1995—, chmn. dept., 1978-86, acting assoc. dean Coll. Agr., 1989, acting v.p. agrl. adminstrn., dean Coll. Agr., 1989-91. Vis. prof. Pa. State U., 1970, U. Minn., 1971, Iowa State U., 1974, La. State U., 1986; vis. scholar Va. Poly. Inst. and State U., 1976, Univ. Coun. Vocat. Edn., 1988-89; mem. com. on agr. in secondary schs. Nat. Acad. Scis., 1985-87 Author: Review and Synthesis of Research on the Economics of Vocational Education, 1968, The Liberalization of Vocat. Education, 1974, (with others) Methods of Teaching Agriculture, 1986, 2d edit. 1993; editor: Agrl. Edn. mag., 1968-71. Served with USAF, 1954-56. Recipient Tchg. award Gamma Sigma Delta, 1977. Fellow Am. Assn. Agrl. Edn.; mem. Am. Vocat. Assn. (v.p. 1976-79, Outstanding Svc. award 1987), Am. Ednl. Rsch. Assn., Am. Vocat. Edn. Rsch. Assn. (pres. 1976), Am. Assn. Tchr. Educators in Agr. (Disting. Svc. award 1974, Disting. lectr. 1974). Home: 3853 Surrey Hill Pl Columbus OH 43220-4778 Office: 2120 Fyffe Rd Columbus OH 43210-1010

WARNER, CHARLES COLLINS, lawyer; b. Cambridge, Mass., June 19, 1942; s. Hoyt Landon and Charlotte (Collins) W.; m. Elizabeth Denny, Aug. 24, 1964; children: Peter, Andrew, Elizabeth. BA, Yale U., 1964; JD cum laude, Ohio State U., 1970. Bar: Ohio 1970. Assoc. Porter, Wright, Morris & Arthur and predecessor, Columbus, 1970-76, ptnr., 1976—, also mgr. labor and employment law dept., 1988-92. Pres. Peace Corps Svc. Coun., Columbus, 1974—76, Old Worthington (Ohio) Assn., 1976—78, Worthington Ednl. Found., 1994—96, Opera Columbus, 1999—2001; chmn. lawyers sect. United Way, 1983—84; mem. alumni adv. coun. Ohio State U.; pres. Alliance for Quality Edn., Washington, 1987—89. Fellow Am. Bar Found., Ohio Bar Found., Columbus Bar Found., Coll. Labor and Employment Lawyers; mem. ABA (subcom. chmn. EEO com. 1986-89, co-chair 2000—, exec. com. Met. Bar Caucus 1992-94, chmn. state & local bar ADR com. 1995-98), Ohio State Bar Assn. (coun. of dels. 1993—, chmn. fed. cts. com. 1992-94), Ohio Met. Bar Assn. (pres. 1991-92), Columbus Bar Assn. (pres. 1991-92, bd. govs. 1982-87, 88-93), FBA, Ohio Assn. Civil Trial Attys. (exec. bd. 1988-97), Ohio State U. Law Alumni Assn. (pres. 1996-97), Nat. Coun. Ohio State U. Coll. Law (pres. 2002—), Capital Club, Yale Club (pres. 1979-81). Avocations: clarinet, singing, tennis. Home: 145 E South St Columbus OH 43085-4129 Office: Porter Wright Morris & Arthur 41 S High St Ste 2800 Columbus OH 43215-6194 E-mail: cwarner@porterwright.com.

WARNER, DON LEE, dean emeritus; b. Norfolk, N.B., Jan. 4, 1934; s. Donald A. and Cleo V. (Slagel) W.; m. Patricia Ann Walker, Feb. 24, 1957; children: Mark J., Scott Lee. BS in Geol. Engring., Colo. Sch. Mines, 1956, MSc in Geol. Engring., 1961; PhD in Engring. Sci., U. Calif., Berkeley, 1964. Registered profl. engr., Mo., geologist, Mo., Miss. Geol. engr. Gulf Oil Corp., Casper, Wyo., 1956, Calif. Exploration Co., Guatemala, 1957-58; civil engr. U.S. Forest Svc., Gunnison, Colo., 1958-59; teaching asst. Colo. Sch. Mines, Golden, 1959-61; rsch. asst. U. Calif., Berkeley, 1962-64; rsch. geologist and engr. U.S. Pub. Health Svc., Cin., 1964-67; chief, earth scis. Ohio Basin Region Fed. Water Pollution Control Adminstrn., 1967-69; prof. geol. engring. U. Mo., Rolla, 1969-92, prof. emeritus geol. engring., 1992—, dean emeritus Sch. Mines and Metallurgy, 1992—, chmn., geol. engring., 1980-81, dean Sch. Mines and Metallurgy, 1981-93. Bd. dirs. Underground Injection Practices Coun., 1985-89; mem. adv. com. to Sec. of Interior for Mineral Resources Rsch., 1985-92. Author: Subsurface Wastewater Injection, 1977. Special award scholarship Colo. Sch. Mines, 1951-56, grad. fellowship Colo. Sch. Mines, 1959-61, rsch. fellowship U. Calif., 1962-64; recipient Best Paper award Am. Water Works Assn., 1971. Fellow Geol. Soc. Am.; mem. Am. Inst. Profl. Geologists (cert.), Am. Assn. Petroleum Geologists, Geol. Soc. Am., Nat. Ground Water Assn. (sci. award 1984, disting. lectr. 1986), Ground Water Protection Coun., Blue Key, Soc. Petroleum Engrs., Scabbard and Blade, Theta Tau, Tau Beta Pi. Avocations: fishing, boating, tennis, golf. Office: U Mo-Rolla Sch Mines and Metallurgy 1870 Miner Cir Rolla MO 65409-0001

WARNER, H. TY, manufacturing executive; s. Harold and Georgia Warner. Student, Kalamazoo Coll. Salesman Dakin Toys, Applause Inc., San Francisco; founder, owner, pres. Ty Inc., Westmont, Ill., 1985—. Office: Ty Inc 280 Chestnut Ave Westmont IL 60559

WARNER, KENNETH E. public health educator, consultant; b. Washington, Jan. 25, 1947; s. Edgar W. Jr. and Betty (Strasburger) W.; m. Patricia A. Hilty, Oct. 1, 1977; children— Peter, Andrew AB, Dartmouth Coll., 1968; MPhil, Yale U., 1970, PhD, 1974. Lectr. dept. health mgmt. and policy Sch. Pub. Health, U. Mich., Ann Arbor, 1972—74, asst. prof., 1974—77, assoc. prof., 1977—83, prof., 1983—, chmn., 1982—88, 1992—95, Richard D. Remington Collegiate prof. pub. health,

1995—2001, dir. Tobacco Rsch. Network, Avedis Donabedian Disting. prof. pub. health, 2001—. Cons., Washington, 1976—95, Office on Smoking and Health, USPHS, Rockville, Md., 1978—, Inst. Medicine, Nat. Acad. Scis., Washington, 1984—, numerous additional pub. and pvt. orgns.; mem. bd. sci. counselors divsn. cancer prevention and control Nat. Cancer Inst., Bethesda, Md., 1985—89. Author: (with Bryan Luce) Cost-Benefit & Cost Effectiveness Analysis in Health Care, 1982; contbr. articles to profl. jours. Trustee Am. Lung Assn., Mich., Lansing, 1982; mem. subcom. on smoking Am. Heart Assn., Dallas, 1983-87; mem. com. on tobacco and cancer Am. Cancer Soc., N.Y.C., 1984-92; bd. dirs. Am. Legacy Found., 1999—. Hon. Woodrow Wilson fellow, 1968; W.K. Kellog Found. fellow, 1980-83; vis. scholar Nat. Bur. Econ. Research, Stanford, Calif., 1975-76; recipient Surgeon Gen.'s medallion Dr. C. Everett Koop, 1989. Fellow Assn. Health Svcs. Rsch.; mem. APHA (leadership award 1990), Am. Econ. Assn., Inst. Medicine, Nat. Assn. Pub. Health Policy, Phi Beta Kappa. Office: U Michigan Dept Health Sch Pub Health Mgmt Policy 109 Observatory St Ann Arbor MI 48109-2029 E-mail: kwarner@umich.edu.

WARNER, KURT, professional football player; b. Wyoming, Vt., Mar. 18, 1961; Student, Pa. State U. With Seattle Seahawks, 1983—; player NFL Pro Bowl, 1984; mem. NFL Pro Bowl Team, 1987, 88. Address: St Louis Rams 1 Rams Way Earth City MO 63045-1523

WARNER, ROBERT MARK, university dean, archivist, historian; b. Montrose, Colo., June 28, 1927; s. Mark Thomas and Bertha Margaret (Rich) W.; m. Eleanor Jane Bullock, Aug. 21, 1954; children: Mark Steven, Jennifer Jane. Student, U. Denver, 1945; B.A., Muskingum Coll., 1949, LL.D. (hon.), 1981; M.A., U. Mich., 1953, Ph.D., 1958; H.H.D. (hon.), Westminster (Pa.) Coll., 1981; L.H.D. (hon.), DePaul U., 1983. Tchr. high sch., Montrose, Colo., 1949-50; lectr. dept. history U. Mich., 1958-66, assoc. prof., 1966-71, prof., 1971-97, prof. emeritus, 1997—, prof. Sch. Info., 1974-97, emeritus, 1997—, dean Sch. Info. and Library Studies, 1985-92, univ. historian, 1992—, interim dir. Univ. Libraries, 1988-90; asst. in rsch. Bentley Hist. Libr., 1953-57, asst. curator, 1957-61, asst. dir., 1961-66, dir., 1966-80; archivist of U.S., 1980-85. Mem. exec. com. Bentley Hist. Libr., 1988—; bd. visitors Sch. Libr. Sci., Case Western Res. U., 1976-80, chmn., 1980-84, Maxwell Sch. Govt., Syracuse U., 1982-87; chmn. Gerald R. Ford Presdl. Libr. Bldg. Com., 1977-79; bd. dirs., sec. Gerald R. Ford Found., 1987—; trustee Woodrow Wilson Internat. Ctr. for Scholars, 1980-85, chmn. fellowship com., 1983-85; chmn. Nat. Hist. Publs. and Records Commn., 1980-85; mem. exec. com. Internat. Coun. on Archives, 1984-88; pres. 2d European Conf. on Archives, 1989; comptroller gen. U.S. Rsch. and Edn. Adv. Com., 1988-2000; rsch. adv. com. Online Computer Libr. Ctr., 1990-93; bd. govs. Clements Libr., 1988-90, 93—, Clark Hist. Libr. Ctrl. Mich. U., 1987—; vis. prof. UCLA, 1993. Author: Chase S. Osborn, 1860-1949, 1960, Profile of a Profession, 1964, (with R. Bordin) The Modern Manuscript Library, 1966, (with C.W. Vanderhill) A Michigan Reader: 1865 to the Present, 1974, (with F. Blouin) Sources for the Study of Migration and Ethnicity, 1979, Diary of a Dream: A History of the National Archives Independence Movement, 1980-1985, 1995. Served with U.S. Army, 1950-52. Recipient Disting. Svc. award Muskingum Coll., 1990, Disting. Svc. award Nat. Hist. Pub. and Records Commn., 1992. Fellow Soc. Am. Archivists; mem. Am. Hist. Assn. (council 1981-85), Orgn. Am. Historians, ALA (council 1986-91), Assn. for Library and Info. Sci. Edn., Presbyn. Hist. Soc. (bd. dirs. 1987-91), Am. Assn. State and Local History, Hist. Soc. Mich. (trustee 1960-66, v.p. 1972-73, pres. 1973-74), Soc. Am. Archivists (mem. council 1967-71, sec., exec. dir. 1971-73, v.p. 1974-75, pres. 1976-77), Am. Antiquarian Soc., Phi Alpha Theta, Beta Phi Mu. Presbyterian. Club: U. Mich. Research. Lodge: Rotary Home: 1821 Coronada St Ann Arbor MI 48103-5066 Office: U Mich Sch Info 550 E University Ave Ann Arbor MI 48109-1092 E-mail: archlib@umich.edu.

WARNER, WILLIAM HAMER, applied mathematician; b. Pitts., Oct. 6, 1929; s. John Christian and Louise (Hamer) W.; m. Janet Louise West, June 29, 1957; 1 dau., Katherine Patricia. Student, Haverford Coll., 1946-48; B.S., Carnegie Inst. Tech., 1950, M.S., 1951, Ph.D., 1953. Research asso. grad. div. applied math. Brown U., Providence, 1953-55; asst. prof. dept. aerospace engring. and mechanics U. Minn., Mpls., 1955-58, asso. prof., 1958-68, prof., 1968-95, prof. emeritus, 1995—. Author: (with L.E. Goodman) Statics, 1963, Dynamics, 1964; contbr. articles to profl. jours. Mem.: Soc. Natural Philosophy, Math. Assn. Am., Soc. Indsl. and Applied Math., Am. Math. Soc. Office: Univ Minn 107 Akerman Hall 110 Union St SE Minneapolis MN 55455-0153 E-mail: warner@aem.umn.edu.

WARNKE, AMY NICHOLLE, state legislator; BA, U. N.D. Rep. Dist. 42 N.D. Ho. of Reps., mem. appropriations com., com. on corrections, chmn. budget sect. on human svcs. Devel. dir. N.D. Cmty. Found.; bd. dirs. Protection and Advocacy Project. Mem.: Kappa Alpha Theta (pres., adv. bd. chmn.). Home: PO Box 12982 Grand Forks ND 58208

WARREN, RICHARD M. experimental psychologist, educator; b. N.Y.C., Apr. 8, 1925; s. Morris and Rae (Greenberg) W.; m. Roslyn Pauker, Mar. 31, 1950. BS in Chemistry, CCNY, 1946; PhD in Organic Chemistry, NYU, 1951. Flavor chemist Gen. Foods Co., Hoboken, N.J., 1951-53; rsch. assoc. psychology Brown U., Providence, 1954-56; Carnegie sr. rsch. fellow NYU Coll. Medicine, 1956-57, Cambridge (Eng.) U., 1957-58, rsch. psychologist applied psychology rsch. unit, 1958-59; rsch. psychologist NIMH, Bethesda, Md., 1959-61; chmn. psychology Shimer Coll., Mt. Carroll, Ill., 1961-64; assoc. prof. psychology U. Wis., Milw., 1964-66, prof., 1966-73, rsch. prof., 1973-75, disting. prof., 1975-95, adj. disting. prof., 1995—. Vis. scientist Inst. Exptl. Psychology, Oxford (Eng.) U., 1969-70, 77-78. Author: (with Roslyn Warren) Helmholtz on Perception: Its Physiology and Development, 1968, Auditory Perception: A New Analysis and Synthesis, 1999; contbr. articles to profl. jours. Fellow APA, Am. Psychol. Soc., Acoustical Soc. Am.; mem. AAAS, Am. Chem. Soc., Am. Speech and Hearing Assn., Sigma Xi. Office: U Wis Dept Psychology Milwaukee WI 53201

WARRICK, PETER, football player; b. Bradenton, Fla., June 19, 1977; Postgrad in political sci., Fla. State Univ. Wide receiver Cin. Bengals, 2001—. Achievements include club record for rushing yards in a season by a wide receiver. Office: Cin Bengals 1 Paul Brown Stadium Cincinnati OH 45202*

WARSHAWSKY, ISIDORE, physicist, consultant; b. N.Y.C., May 27, 1911; s. Morris and Esther (Sherman) W. BS cum laude, CCNY, 1930. Physicist Nat. Adv. Com. Aeronautics, Langley Field, Va., 1930-42, chief instrumentation sect. Cleve., 1942-50; chief instrument rsch. br. Nat. Adv. Com. Aeronautics/ NASA, 1950-72; instrumentation cons. NASA, 1972-90, ret., 1990, disting. rsch. cons. (unsalaried), 1990-95. Author: (textbook) Foundations of Measurement and Instrumentation, 1990; author 10 NACA/NASA tech. reports; contbr. 20 articles to sci. jours. and books. Fellow Instrument Soc. Am.; mem. Am. Phys. Soc., Combustion Inst., Am. Vacuum Soc, Phi Beta Kappa.

WARTELL, MICHAEL ALAN, academic administrator; b. Albuquerque, Nov. 4, 1946; s. Richard H. and Betty D. (Davis) W.; m. Ruth E. Beachy, Dec. 3, 1977; children: Justin Davis, Richard Harrison. BS, U. N.Mex., 1967; MS, Yale U., 1968, PhD, 1971. Asst. prof. chemistry Met. State Coll., 1971-75, assoc. prof., chmn. dept., 1975-78; dean sch. natural scis., prof. chemistry James Madison U., 1979-84; provost, v.p. acad. affairs Humboldt State U., Arcata, Calif., 1984-89, prof. chemistry, 1984-94; chancellor U. Ind. Purdue U., Ft. Wayne, 1994—. Mem. U.S. Army Sci. Bd., 1981-87, participant various study groups on chem. warfare, decontamination, biodefense; cons. U.S. Army, IRT Corp., Sandia Nat. Labs., SRI Internat., JAYCOR, HERO, Boeing Electronics, Battelle; mem. Def. Intelligence Agy. Sci. Adv. Com., 1984—; chmn. bd. visitors Def. Systems Mgmt. Coll., Ft. Belvoir, Va., 1984—, chair, 1985—. Co-author: Engineering Education and A Lifetime of Learning, 1975, Introduction to Chemistry, 1975 (also study guide and lab. guide), Fundamentals of Chemistry, 1980; also articles, reviews, presentations. Bd. dirs. Humboldt State U. Found., 1984—. Fellow Am. Acad. Forensic Scis.; mem. Am. Chem. Soc., Am. Phys. Soc., Am. Assn. Univ. Adminstrs. (evaluation task force 1978-79, standards and rev. com. 1983-84), Sigma Xi, Phi Beta Kappa, Phi Kappa Phi, Kappa Mu Epsilon. Jewish. Office: Ind U Purdue U 2101 E Coliseum Blvd Fort Wayne IN 46805-1445 E-mail: wartell@ipfw.edu.

WASAN, DARSH TILAKCHAND, university official, chemical engineer educator; b. Sarai, Salah, West Pakistan, July 15, 1938; came to U.S., 1957, naturalized, 1974; s. Tilakchand Gokalchand and Ishari Devi (Obhan) W.; m. Usha Kapur, Aug. 21, 1966; children: Ajay, Kern. BSChemE, U. Ill., 1960; PhD, U. Calif., Berkeley, 1965. Asst. prof. chem. engring. Ill. Inst. Tech., Chgo., 1964-67, assoc. prof., 1967-70, prof., 1970—, chmn. dept., 1971-77, 78-87, acting dean, 1977-78, 87-88, v.p. rsch. and tech., 1988-91, provost, 1991—, provost and sr. v.p., 1995-96, v.p., internat. and Motorola chair, 1996—. Cons. Inst. Gas Tech., 1965-70, Chgo. Bridge & Iron Co., 1967-71, Ill. EPA, 1971-72, NSF, 1971, 78-79, 87-89, Nelson Industries, 1976—, B.F. Goodrich Chem. Co., 1976-78, Exxon Rsch. & Engring. Co., 1977-89, Stauffer Chem. Co., 1980-88, ICI Ams., 1988-92; Procter & Gamble lectr. U. Cin. Editor-in-chief Jour. colloid and Interface sci.; mem. publs. bd. Chem. Engring. Edn. Jour.; mem. adv. bd. Jour. Separations Tech., Current Opinion in Colloid and Interface Sci., Jour. of Dispersion Sci. and Tech.; contbr. articles to profl. jours. Recipient Donald Gage Stevens Disting. Lectureship award Syracuse U., 1991, Jakob J. Bikerman Lectureship award Case Western U., 1994, Robert Gilpin Lectr. award Clarkson U., 1995, MacMoran Disting. Lectrureship award Tulane U., 1996, Sidney Ross lectr. award, 1996, Bonnet Dodge Disting. Lectureship award Yale U., 1998, Spl. citation U.S. FDA, 2000. Fellow Am. Inst. Chem. Engrs. (Ernest Thiele award 1989); mem. AAAS, Am. Chem. Soc. (award in colloid chemistry 2000), Soc. Rheology, Am. Soc. Engring. Edn. (Western Electric award 1972, 3M Lectureship award chem. engring. divsn. 1991), Am. Physics Inst., Fine Particles Soc. (pres. 1976-77, Hausner award 1982), Sigma Xi. Home: 8705 Royal Swan Ln Darien IL 60561-8433 Office: Ill Inst Tech 3300 S Federal St Chicago IL 60616-3793 E-mail: wasan@iit.edu.

WASFIE, TARIK JAWAD, surgeon, educator; b. Baghdad, Iraq, July 1, 1946; m. Barina Y. Wasfie, Mar. 11, 1975; children: Giselle, Nissan. BS, Central U., Iraq, 1964; MD, Baghdad Med. Sch., 1970. Cert. gen. surgeon. Surg. rsch. assoc. Sinai Hosp. of Detroit/Wayne State U., 1981-85; clin. fellow Coll. Phys. & Surg., Columbia U., N.Y.C., 1985-91, postdoctoral rsch. scientist, 1987-91; attending surgeon Mich. State U./McLaren Hosp., Flint, 1991—. Contbr. articles to profl. jours. NIH grantee, 1984. Fellow ACS, Internat. Coll. Surgeons; mem. AMA, Mich. State Med. Soc., Flint Acad. Surgeons, Am. Soc. Artificial Internal Organs, Internat. Soc. Artificial Organs, Soc. Am. Gast. Endoscopic Surgeons. Achievements include production of antiidiotypic antibodies and their role in transplant immunology; development of percutenous access device. Home: 1125 Kings Carriage Rd Grand Blanc MI 48439-8715

WASHBURN, DONALD ARTHUR, business executive, private investor; b. Mankato, Minn., Sept. 24, 1944; s. Donald and Geraldine Helen (Pint) W.; m. Christine Carvell, Aug. 24, 1968; children: Timothy, Abigail. BBA with high honors, Loyola U., Chgo., 1971; MBA, Northwestern U., 1973, JD cum laude, 1978. Bar: Ill. 1978. With prodn. mgmt. dept. J.T. Ryerson/Inland Steel, Chgo., 1963-68; asst. to the pres. G.B. Frank, Inc., 1969-70; cons. Intec, Inc., 1970-72; mktg. mgmt., atty. Quaker Oats, Co., 1972-79; sr. cons. Booz, Allen & Hamilton, 1979-80; from corp. v.p. to sr. v.p. Marriott Corp., Washington, 1980-90; sr. v.p. N.W. Airlines, Mpls., 1990-94, exec. v.p., 1994-98; investor, 1998—. Bd. dirs. LaSalle Hotel Properties, Princess House, Inc.; law bd. Northwestern U., alumni adv. bd. Kellogg Grad. Sch.; adv. bd. Spell Capital Partners Fund II, LP, Bank pf Am.-Twin Cities. Contbr. articles to profl. jours. Bd. dir. Hearing & Speech Inst. Mem. ABA, Ill. Bar Assn., Chgo. Bar Assn., Alpha Sigma Nu, Beta Gamma Sigma. Unitarian Universalist.

WASHINGTON, CLEOPHUS (CLEO WASHINGTON), state senator; b. S. Bend, Ind. BA in Polit. Sci., Wabash Coll., 1985; student, U. Iowa; JD, U. Mo., 1988. Pvt. practice; dep. pub. defender St. Joseph County, 1990-96; atty. Weisman, Kimmell & Walton, S. Bend; state senator Ind. Legislature, Indpls., 1996—. Participant Emerging Leadership Conf. Darden Sch. Bus., U. Va.; del. to tour Germany and Romania to study their polit. and econ. sys. Am. Coun. Young Polit. Leaders; founding pres. Leaders and Positive Role Models, Inc. Contbg. author: Bridging the Gaps, 1996. Mem. Ardmore LaSalle Ch. of Christ, S. Bend; 2d dist. city councilman S. Bend, 1991-95, v.p. of coun., chmn. com., city councilman at large, 1995, chmn. pub. safety, chmn. com.; mem. adv. com. Police Officers and Firefighters Pensions and Disability Fund; mem. Nat. Black Caucus Local Elected Ofcls., Minority Parenting Task Force; mem. mentor program Columbia Sch. Law, U. Mo. Fellow Coun. on Legal Edn. Opportunity. Mem. ABA, Nat. Bar Assn., Ind. State Bar Assn., Ind. Trial Lawyers Assn., St. Joseph County Bar Assn. Office: Ind State House Dist 10 200 W Washington St Indianapolis IN 46204-2728 also: 803 W Washington St Apt 3A South Bend IN 46601-1464

WASHKEWICZ, DONALD E. manufacturing executive; V.p. ops. fluid connectors group Parker Hannifin Corp., Cleve., 1994-97, v.p., pres. hydraulics group, 1997-2000, pres., COO, 2000—. Office: Parker Hannifin Corp 6035 Parkland Blvd Cleveland OH 44124-4141

WASIK, JOHN FRANCIS, editor, writer, publisher; b. Chgo., July 2, 1957; s. Arthur Stanley and Virginia Frances (Gray) W.; m. Kathleen Rose. BA in Psychology, U. Ill., Chgo., 1978, MA in Communication, 1988. Sr. editor Consumers Digest Inc., Chgo., 1986—; editor, pub. Conscious Consumer and Co. Newsletters, 1986—. Author: Electronic Business Information Sourcebook, 1987, Green Company Resource Guide, 1992, The Green Supermarket Shopping Guide, 1993, The Investment Club Book, 1995. Mem. Soc. Profl. Journalists, Soc. Environ. Journalists. Office: Consumers Digest Inc 8001 Lincoln Ave # 6 Skokie IL 60077-3695

WASIOLEK, EDWARD, literary critic, language and literature educator; b. Camden, N.J., Apr. 27, 1924; s. Ignac and Mary (Szczesniewska) W.; m. Emma Jones Thomson, 1948; children: Mark Allan, Karen Lee, Eric Wade. B.A., Rutgers U., 1949; M.A., Harvard, 1950, Ph.D., 1955; postgrad., U. Bordeaux, France, 1950-51. Teaching fellow Harvard U., Cambridge, Mass., 1953-54, research fellow Russian Research Ctr., 1952-54; instr. English Ohio Wesleyan U., 1954-55; asst. prof. U. Chgo., 1955-60, assoc. prof. English and Russian, 1960-64, prof. Russian and comparative lit., 1964-69, Avalon prof. comparative lit. and Russian, 1969-76, Disting. Services prof. of English, comparative lit., and Slavic studies, 1976—, chmn. comparative lit. program, 1965-83, chmn. dept. Slavic langs. and lit., 1971-77. Vis. prof. Slavic and comparative lit. Harvard, 1966-67 Author: (with R. Bauer) Nine Soviet Portraits, 1955, Crime and Punishment and the Critics, 1961, Dostoevsky: The Major Fiction, 1964, The Notebooks for Crime and Punishment, 1967, The Brothers Karamazov and the Critics, 1967, The Notebooks for the Idiot, 1968, The Notebooks for the Possessed, 1968, The Notebooks for A Raw Youth, 1969, The Notebooks for the Brothers Karamazov, 1970, The Gambler, with Paulina Suslova's Diary, 1972, Tolstoy's Major Fiction, 1978, Critical Essays on Tolstoy, 1986, Fathers and Sons: Russia at the Crossroads, 1993. Addressed UN on Tolstoy, 1988. With USNR, 1943-46. Recipient Quantrell teaching prize U. Chgo., 1961; Laing Press prize, 1972; Research fellow USSR, 1963; Guggenheim fellow, 1983-84 Mem. Modern Lang. Assn., Phi Beta Kappa, Lambda Chi Alpha. Home: 1832 Butterfield Ln Flossmoor IL 60422-2107 Office: Univ Chicago Dept English Chicago IL 60637 E-mail: e_wasiolek@uchicago.edu.

WASS, WALLACE MILTON, veterinarian, clinical science educator; b. Lake Park, Iowa, Nov. 19, 1929; s. Authur Carl and Esther (Moberg) W.; m. Doreen McCollum, May 31, 1953; children: Karen, Kimberly, Christopher, Kirby. Student, Minn. Jr. Coll., 1947-48; B.S., U. Minn., 1951, D.V.M., 1953, Ph.D., 1961. Diplomate: Am. Coll. Vet. Internal Medicine. Veterinarian Medford Vet. Clinic, Wis., 1953-58; instr. U. Minn. Coll. Vet. Medicine, St. Paul, 1958-63; prof. vet. medicine Iowa State U., Ames, 1964—, head dept. vet. clin. scis., 1964-83, prof., 1983-99, prof. emeritus, 1999—. Cons. U.S. AID, Bogota, Columbia, 1963, U. Yola, Nigeria, 1983; staff veterinarian for med. rsch. sect. Brookhaven Nat. Lab., Upton, N.Y., 1963-64; cons. investigator fur seal harvest U.S. Dept. Commerce, Pribilof Islands, 1971, South Africa, 1974; use of antibiotics in animal feed U.S. FDA, 1972; cons. Farmland Ins. Co., 1971—; spl. cons. Kasetsart U., Bangkok, Thailand, 1974, Min. of Edn., Thailand, 1994. Contbr. articles, papers in field to profl. lit. Chmn. collegiate-ch. paster parish rels. com. United Methodist Ch., 1979, chmn. stewardship and fin. com., 1982. Served to 1st lt. USAF, 1953-55. Mem. AVMA (del. 1973-88), Iowa Vet. Med. Assn., Central Iowa Vet. Med. Assn. (pres. 1977), Am. Assn. Vet. Clinicians (pres. 1971-73), Phi Kappa Phi (sec. 1984-88, Iowa State U. chpt. pres. 1989-90), Phi Zeta, Alpha Zeta, Gamma Sigma Delta Club: Wiltco Flying (sec. 1966-74). Home: 2166 Ashmore Dr Ames IA 50014-7840 Office: Iowa State U Dept Vet Clin Scis Ames IA 50011-0001

WASSERMAN, EDWARD ARNOLD, psychology educator; b. L.A., Apr. 2, 1946; s. Albert Leonard and May (Sabin) W. BA, UCLA, 1968; PhD, Ind. U., 1972. Postdoctoral fellow U. Sussex, Brighton, Eng., 1972; from asst. prof. to prof. psychology U. Iowa, Iowa City, 1972-83, prof., 1983—, Stuit prof. exptl. psychology, 1997—. Pres. faculty senate U. Iowa, 1997-98; vis. scientist CNRS, Marseille, France, 1999. Contbr. articles to profl. jours., chpts. to books; assoc. editor several jours. Bd. dirs. Big Bros., Big Sisters, Johnson County, Iowa, 1982-85 Ind. U. fellow, 1968, U. Iowa fellow, 1975, 82, NAS fellow, former USSR, 1976, James Van Allen Natural Scis. fellow, 1994-95. Fellow APA, Am. Psychol. Soc.; mem. Psychonomic Soc. (governing bd.), Midwestern Psychol. Assn., Phi Beta Kappa. Office: U Iowa Dept Psychology Iowa City IA 52242

WASSERMAN, SHELDON A. state legislator; b. Milw., Aug. 15, 1961; m. Wendy Jo Wolfman; children: Joseph, Lauren, Benjamin. BS, U. Wis., 1983; MD, Med. Coll. Wis., 1987. Assemblyman Wis. State Dist. 22, 1995—. Staff physician Columbia/St. Mary's Hosp., Milw., 1991—, Sinai Hosp., Milw., 1991—. Fellow AGOG; mem. AMA, Wis. Med. Soc., Milw. County Med. Soc., Phi Beta Kappa, Phi Kappa Phi. Address: 3487 N Lake Dr Milwaukee WI 53211-2919 also: Wis Assembly PO Box 8953 Madison WI 53708-8953

WATANABE, AUGUST MASARU, physician, scientist, medical educator, corporate executive; b. Portland, Oreg., Aug. 17, 1941; s. Frank H. and Mary Y. W.; m. Margaret Whildin Reese, Mar. 14, 1964; children: Nan Reiko, Todd Franklin, Scott Masaru. BS, Wheaton (Ill.) Coll., 1963; MD, Ind. U., 1967. Diplomate Am. Bd. Internal Medicine. Intern Ind. U. Med. Center, Indpls., 1967-68, resident, 1968-69, 71-72, fellow in cardiology, 1972-74; clin. asso. NIH, 1969-71; clin. instr. medicine Georgetown U. Med. Sch., Washington, 1970-71; mem. faculty Ind. U. Sch. Medicine, Indpls., 1972—, prof. medicine and pharmacology, 1978—, chmn. dept. medicine, 1983-90; dir. Regenstrief Inst. for Health Care Ind. U. Sch. of Medicine, 1984-90; from v.p. to group v.p. rsch. labs. Eli Lilly & Co., 1990-94, v.p., pres. labs, 1994-95; exec. v.p. sci. and tech. Eli Lilly and Co., 1996—, also bd. dirs., 1994—; dir. Guidant Corp. Mem. pharmacology study sect. NIH, 1979-81, chmn., 1981-83; mem. cardiovasc.-renal adv. com. FDA, 1982-85; mem. com. A, Nat. Heart, Lung and Blood Inst., 1984-88, chmn., 1986-88; cons. to fed. govt. and industry. Contbr. articles to profl. jours.; editorial bds. sci. jours. Dir. Ind. U. Found., 1989—, Indpls. Symphony Orch., 1994—, Regenstrief Found., 1995—, Riley Meml. Assn. NIH grantee, 1972-92. Fellow ACP, Am. Coll. Cardiology, Am. Heart Assn. (councils on clin. cardiology and circulation, research rev. com. Ind. affiliate 1978-82, research and adv. com. North Central region 1978-82, adv. com. cardiovascular drugs 1976-79, chmn. com. 1979-81, chmn. program com. council on basic sci. 1982-84, chmn. com. on sci. sessions programs 1985-88, bd. dirs. 1985-88), Am. Coll. Cardiology (govt. relations com. 1979-81, trustee 1982-87); mem. Am. Fedn. Clin. Research (councilor Midwest sect. 1976-77, chmn.-elect Midwest sect. 1977-78, chmn. sect. 1978-79, chmn. sect. nominating com. 1979-80), Am. Soc. Clin. Investigation, Am. Soc. Clin. Pharmacology and Therapeutics, Am. Soc. Pharmacology and Exptl. Therapeutics (exec. com. div. clin. pharmacology 1978-81), Cardiac Muscle Soc., Central Soc. Clin. Research (councillor 1983-86, pres.-elect 1989, pres. 1990), Internat. Soc. Heart Research, Assn. Am. Physicians, Assn. Profs. of Medicine, Sigma Xi. Office: Eli Lilly & Co Drop Code 1209 Lilly Corp Ctr Indianapolis IN 46285-0001

WATCHORN, WILLIAM ERNEST, venture capitalist; b. Toronto, Ont., Can., Aug. 8, 1943; s. Roy Elgin and Josephine (Swyrida) W.; m. Maureen Emmett, Dec. 28, 1967; 1 child, Meghan. Chartered Acct., Toronto, 1967. Mgr. fin. planning Found. Group of Cos., Toronto, 1968-70; cons. Regional Master Planning Study, Malaysia, 1970-72; controller Selkirk Holdings, Ltd., Toronto, 1972-75; corp. contr. Torstar Corp., 1975-78; v.p. fin. Canwest Capital Corp., Winnipeg, Man., 1978-82; exec. v.p. Kaiser Resources Ltd., Vancouver, B.C., 1982; sr. v.p., CFO, Fed. Industries Ltd., Winnipeg, 1982-88; pres., CEO, Fed. Industries Indsl. Group, 1989-91, Ensis Corp., Inc., Winnipeg, 1991-97; founder, pres., CEO, Ensis Growth Fund Inc., Ensis Mgmt. Inc., 1997—. Bd. dirs. Ensis Mgmt. Inc., Ensis Growth Fund Inc., Winnipeg Airports Authority Inc. Bd. dirs. C.D. Howe Inst., Toronto; dir. Can. Stds. Assn. (CSA); past chmn. Assocs.; faculty mgmt. U. Manitoba. Mem. Can. Inst. Chartered Accts., Fellowship Inst. of Chartered Accts., Man. Inst., Chartered Accts., Ont. Inst. Chartered Accts., Winter Club, St. Charles Country Club. Avocations: squash, golf, tennis. Home: 6453 Southboine Dr Winnipeg MB Canada R3R 0B7 Office: Ensis Growth Fund Inc 200 Graham Ave Ste 1120 Winnipeg MB Canada R3C 4L5

WATERMAN, JOHN M. state legislator; b. Shelburn, Ind., May 13, 1952; m. Cheryl Lynn Waterman. Sheriff Sullivan County; mem. Ind. Senate from 39th dist., 1994—; mem. agr. and small bus. com.; mem. corrections, criminal and civil procedures com.; mem. natural resources com.; mem. pub. policy com. Mem. NRA. Office: Ind Senate State Capitol Indianapolis IN 46204

WATERS, RONALD W. educator, church executive, pastor; b. Kokomo, Ind., July 23, 1951; s. Ronald Lee and Carolyn Elizabeth (Myers) W.; m. Norma Lee Grumbling Waters, June 16, 1973; 1 child, Melinda Ronee Waters. BA magna cum laude, Ashland (Ohio) Coll., 1973; MA in Comms. with high honors, Wheaton (Ill.) Coll., 1975; MDiv with high honors, Ashland (Ohio) Theol. Seminary, 1985; postgrad., Asbury Theol. Seminary, Wilmore, Ky., 1993—2002. Ordained elder Brethren Ch., 1986; lic. minister, 1985-86. Asst. to dir. Bd. of Christian Edn. The Brethren Ch., Ashland, Ohio, 1971-74; mng. editor of publs. Brethren Pub. Co., 1975-78, asst. to dir. and gen. mgr., 1978-80, exec. dir., 1980-82; dir. of Denom. Bus. The Brethren Ch. Nat. Office, 1982-84; cons. in mgmt. and computer applications, 1984-85; pastor Mt. Olive Brethren Ch., McGaheysville, Va., 1985-89; dir. Brethren Ch. Ministries The Brethren Ch. Nat. Office, Ashland, Ohio, 1989-95; asst. prof. evangelism Ashland Theol. Sem., 1996-2001; cons. for evangelism and ch. growth The Brethren Ch. Nat. Office, Ashland, 1996—; pastor Hammond Ave. Brethren Ch., Waterloo, Iowa, 2002—. Bd. dirs. corp. sec. Brethern Printing Co., Ashland, 1989-96; mem. mission bd. Brethren Ch. Southeastern Dist., 1987-89; mem. statement of faith task force Gen. Conf. Brethern Ch., 1981-84, polity com. 1986-91, bd. ref. congl. adv. The Andrew Ctr., Elgin, Ill., 1994-97; founder, tchr. Young Adult Sunday Sch. class Park St Brethern Ch., Ashland, 1990-93; adv. com. Ashland Theol. Sem., 1990-95; mem. evangelism mgmt. team New Life Ministries, Mt. Joy, Pa., 1992-2001; spkr. in field. Author: Promise for the Future, 1993, Leader's Manual for Inviting and Welcoming New People, 1995; editor: The Brethren Evangelist mag., 1975-78, New Beginnings mag., 1995-97; contbg. editor LIFE process, 1998-99; contbr. numerous articles to religious jours.; webmaster, www.newlifeministries-nlm.org, 2000—. Mem. adv. coun. World Relief Corp., Wheaton, Ill., 1990-92; dir. vol. ministries Park St. Brethren Ch., 1998-99; sec.-treas. Ohio dist. Mission Bd., 1996-2001. Mem. Am. Soc. Ch. Growth, Nat. Assn. Brethern Ch. Elders. Avocation: gardening. Office: Hammond Ave Brethren Ch 1604 Hammond Ave Waterloo IA 50702 E-mail: ron@hammondavenuebrethren.com.

WATERS, STEPHEN RUSSELL, state agency administrator; b. Quincy, Ill., Jan. 9, 1954; s. Russell O. and Dorothy Ann (Bartz) W.; m. Nancy K. Morris, Aug. 31, 1974; children: Leslie Ann, Ryan Patrick. BS in Law Enforcement, N.E. Mo. State, 1976. Police officer City of Kirksville, Mo., 1975; adminstrv. asst. to speaker pro-tem Mo. House of Reps., Jefferson City, 1976; investment counselor IDS Mktg., Dubuque, Iowa, 1977-78; dir. legal svcs. Mark Twain Legal Svcs., Canton, Mo., 1978-80; probation and parole officer State of Mo., Hannibal, 1980-84; juvenile officer 2d Jud. Cir., Edina, Mo., 1984-86; rep. Mo. Ho. of Reps., Canton, 1987-94; dir. Mo. divsn. Motor Carrier and R.R. Safety/Dept. Econ. Devel., Jefferson City, 1994—. Chmn. parks City of Canton, 1980-82; alderman City of Canton, 1980-84. Mem. Am. Corrections Assn., Mo. Corrections Assn., N.E. Mo. Peace Officers, Moose, Kiwanis (bd. dirs. Canton chpt. 1979-80), Canton C. of C. (pres. 1979-82). Democrat. Mem. Christian Ch. Avocation: golf. Office: Mo Divsn Motor Carrier/RR Safety Dept Econ Devel PO Box 1216 Jefferson City MO 65102-1216

WATKINSON, PATRICIA GRIEVE, museum director; b. Merton, Surrey, Eng., Mar. 28, 1946; came to U.S., 1972; d. Thomas Wardle and Kathleen (Bredl) Grieve. BA in Art History and Langs. with honors, Bristol U., Eng., 1968. Sec. Mayfair Fine Arts and The Mayfair Gallery, London, 1969-71; adminstr. Bernard Jacobson, Print Pub., 1971-73; freelance exhbn. work, writer Kilkenny Design Ctr., Davis Gallery, Irish Arts Council in Dublin, Ireland, 1975-76; curator of art Mus. Art, Wash. State U., Pullman, 1978-83, dir., 1984-98; exec. dir. Ft. Wayne (Ind.) Mus. Art, 1998—. Asst. prof. art history Wash. State U., Pullman, 1978; mem. adv. bd. Exhibits USA, 1999—. Co-author, co-editor: Gaylen Hansen: The Paintings of a Decade, 1985. Mem. Assn. Am. Colls. and Univ. Mus. and Galleries (western regional rep. 1987-89), Art Mus. Assn. Am. (Wash. state rep. 1986-87), Internat. Coun. Mus. (modern art com. 1986-89), Wash. Mus. Assn. (bd. dirs. 1984-87), Am. Fedn. Arts (western region rep. 1987-89), Wash. Art Consortium (pres. 1993-95), Western Mus. Assn. (bd. dirs. 1996-98), ARTTABLE. Office: Ft Wayne Mus Art 311 E Main St Fort Wayne IN 46802-1997

WATNE, DARLENE CLAIRE, state legislator; b. Minot, N.D., Feb. 11, 1935; d. Charles A. and Anna Marie Widdel (Fjeld) W.; m. Clair A. Watne, Mar. 27, 1954; children: Carmen, Steven, Nancy, Matthew. Court reporting diploma, Minot (N.D.) Bus. Coll., 1975; grad., Real Estate Inst., 1991. Cert. residential real estate specialist, N.D. Exec. sec. Grand Exalted Ruler Elks, Minot, N.D., 1964-75; pres. Bus. Coll., 1974-76; ct. reporter N.W. Judicial Dist., 1976-90; real estate broker Watne Realtors Better Homes & Gardens, 1990-99; mem. N.D. Senate from 5th dist., Bismark, 1994—. Active Joint Civil Svcs. to the Poor, 1995—. Bd. dirs. ARC, Salvation Army, Red Cross; numerous state polit. interim senate coms. Named Minot Woman of Distinction in Bus. and Industry, 1993, Liberty award ND Bar Assn., 2000, named Citizen of Yr. ND Builders Assn., 2001. Republican. Avocations: reading, laking. Home: 520 28th Ave SW Minot ND 58701-7065

WATSON, CATHERINE ELAINE, journalist; b. Mpls., Feb. 9, 1944; d. Richard Edward and LaVonne (Slater) W.; m. Al Sicherman (div.); children: Joseph Sicherman, David Sicherman. B.A. in Journalism, U. Minn., 1967; M.A. in Teaching, Coll. of St. Thomas, 1971. Reporter Mpls. Star Tribune, 1966-72; editor Picture mag., 1972-78, Travel sect., 1978—; editor in chief Galena (Ill.) Gazette, 1990-91. Instr. split rock arts program U. Minn., 1996-2000. Author: Travel Basics, 1984. Contbr. articles to newspapers and travel mags. and books. Recipient Newspaper Mag. Picture Editor's award Pictures of Yr. Competition, 1974, 75, awards for writing and photography Soc. Am. Travel Writers, 1983-2000, Photographer of Yr. award, 1990, Alumna of Notable Achievement award U. Minn. Coll. Liberal Arts, 1994; named Lowell Thomas Travel Journalist of Yr., 1990. Mem. Am. Newspaper Guild, Soc. Am. Travel Writers, Phi Beta Kappa, Alpha Omicron Pi. Office: 425 Portland Ave Minneapolis MN 55488-1511

WATSON, DENNIS WALLACE, microbiology educator, scientist; b. Morpeth, Ont., Can., Apr. 29, 1914; came to U.S., 1938, naturalized, 1946; s. William and Sarah (Verity) W.; m. Alicemay Whittier, June 15, 1941; children: Catherine W., William V. BSA, U. Toronto, 1934; MS, Dalhousie U., 1937; PhD, U. Wis., 1941, DSc (hon.), 1981. Rsch. assoc. U. Wis., 1942, asst. prof., 1946-49; vis. investigator Rockefeller Inst., 1942; investigator Connaught Lab. Med. Rsch. U. Toronto, 1942-44; assoc. prof. U. Minn., Mpls., 1949-52, prof., 1953-63, head dept. microbiology, 1964-84, Regents prof. microbiology, 1980-84, Regents prof. emeritus, 1984—. Vis. prof. Med. Sch. U. Wash., 1950; mem. Commn. Immunization Armed Forces Epidemiology Bd., 1946-59; mem. bd. sci. counselors, div. biol. standards NIH, 1957-59, mem. allergy and immunology study sect., 1954-58; chmn. tgn. grant com. Inst. Allergy and Infectious Diseases, 1964, mem. adv. coun., 1967-71; mem. microbiology panel Office Naval Rsch., 1963-66; vice chmn. Am. Soc. Microbiology Found., 1973; bd. dirs. Nat. Found. Infectious Diseases, 1976-81 Editorial bd. Infection and Immunity, 1971-72; editorial cons. Medcom Faculty Medicine, 1973—. With AUS, 1944-46. Recipient USPHS Research Career award, 1962-64; Spl. research fellow USPHS, 1960-61 Mem. AAAS, Am. Assn. Immunologists, Am. Chem. Soc., Am. Acad. Microbiology (vice chmn. bd. govs. 1967), Am. Soc. Microbiology (pres. 1969, v.p. Found. 1972-73), Internat. Endotoxin Soc. (hon., life), Soc. Exptl. Biology and Medicine (coun. 1977-79, pres. 1976-77), Lancefield Soc., Sigma Xi, Phi Zeta. Home: 2106 Hendon Ave Saint Paul MN 55108-1419 Office: U Minn Med Sch Dept Microbiology PO Box 196 Minneapolis MN 55440-0196 E-mail: watso006@tc.umn.edu.

WATSON, FRANK CHARLES, state legislator; b. St. Louis, July 26, 1945; s. Charles I. and Pauline (Logsdon) W.; m. Susan DeAnn Rasler, 1969; children: Charles Adam, Kathry Melissa. BPharm, Purdue U., 1968. Trustee and supr. Bond County Ctrl. Twp., Greenville, Ill., 1973-77, bd. suprs.; Ill. state rep., 1979-82; mem. Ill. State Senate, Dist. 55, 1983—, minority spokesman, mem. transp. appropriations II, elem. and secondary edn., mem. Ill. adv. coun. on alcoholism and drug abuse, legis. printing unit coms., joint com. on regulation of professions and occupation, citizens assembly coun. on energy resources, agrl. and conservations and revenue coms., asst. majority leader. Owner The Corner Clothing Store, Greenville, Ill., 1971—, Watson Drug Store, 1972—; bd. dirs. Hillview Manor Nursing Home, First Nat. Bank, Salem Nat. Bank; pharmacist. Mem. Phi Gamma Delta. Republican. Office: 950 Fairway Dr Greenville IL 62246-2336 also: Ill Senate State Capitol Springfield IL 62706-0001

WATSON, PATTY JO, anthropology educator; b. Superior, Nebr., Apr. 26, 1932; d. Ralph Clifton and Elaine Elizabeth (Lance) Andersen; m. Richard Allan Watson, July 30, 1955; 1 child, Anna Melissa M.A., U. Chgo., 1956, Ph.D. in Anthropology, 1959. Archaeologist-ethnographer Oriental Inst.-U. Chgo., 1959-60, research assoc., archaeologist, 1964-70; instr. anthropology U. So. Calif., Los Angeles, 1961, UCLA, 1961, L.A. State U., 1961; asst. prof. anthropology Washington U., St. Louis, 1969-70, assoc. prof., 1970-73, prof., 1973—, Edward Mallinckrodt disting. univ. prof., 1993—. Mem. rev. panel NSF, Washington, 1974-76; fellow Ctr. Advanced Study in Behavioral Scis., Stanford, Calif., 1981-82, 91-92. Author: The Prehistory of Salts Cave, Kentucky, 1969, Archaeological Ethnography in Western Iran, 1979; author: (with others) Man and Nature, 1969, Explanation in Archeology, 1971, Archeological Explanation, 1984, Girikihaciyan, A Halafian Site in Southeastern Turkey; author: (editor) Archeology of the Mammoth Cave Area, 1974, Prehistoric Archeology Along the Zagros Flanks, 1983; co-editor: The Origins of Agriculture, 1992, Of Caves and Shell Mounds, 1996. Grantee NSF, 1959-60, 68, 70, 72-74, 78-79, NEH, 1977-78, Nat. Geog. Soc., 1969-75. Fellow Am. Anthropol. Assn. (editor for archaeology 1973-77, Disting. Lectr. award 1994, Disting. Svc. award 1996), AAAS (chair sect. H 1991-92), Cave rsch. Found.; mem. NAS, Am. Acad. Arts and Scis., Am. Philos. Soc., Soc. Am. Archaeology (exec. com. 1974-76, 82-84, editor Am. Antiquity 1984-87, Fryxell medal 1990), Assn. Paleorient (sci. bd.), Nat. Speleological Soc. (hon. life, editorial bd. bull. 1979—, sci. award), Archaeol. Inst. Am. (Gold Medal for Disting. Archaeol. Achievement 1999). Office: Dept Anthropol CB #1114 Washington U Saint Louis MO 63130-4899 E-mail: pjwatson@artsci.wustl.edu.

WATSON, PAULA D. library administrator; b. N.Y.C., Mar. 6, 1945; d. Joseph Francis and Anna Julia (Miksza) De Simone; m. William Douglas Watson, Aug. 23, 1969; children— Lucia, Elizabeth A.B., Barnard Coll., 1965; M.A., Columbia U., 1966; M.S.L.S., Syracuse U., 1972. Reference librarian U. Ill., Urbana, 1972-77, city planning and landscape architecture librarian, 1977-79, head documents library, 1979-81; asst. dir. gen. services U. Ill. Library, 1981-88, acting dir. gen. svcs., 1988-93, dir. ctrl. pub. svcs., 1989-93, asst. univ. libr., 1993-95, dir. electronic info. svcs., 1995—. Contbr. articles to profl. jours. N.Y. State Regents fellow Columbia U., N.Y.C., 1965-66; Council on Library Resources profl. edn. and tng. for librarianship grantee, 1983 Mem. ALA (sec. univ. librs. sect. ALA-Assn. Coll. and Rsch. Librs. 1989-91, com. on instnl. coop., chair pub. svcs. dirs. group, 1997-99, mem. com. inst. coop./OCLC virtual electronic libr. steering com.), Ill. Library Assn. Avocation: gardening. Home: 715 W Delaware Ave Urbana IL 61801-4806 Office: U Ill 246 A Library 1408 W Gregory Dr Urbana IL 61801-3607 E-mail: pdwatson@uiuc.edu.

WATSON, RALPH EDWARD, physician, educator; b. Cin., Apr. 4, 1948; s. John Sherman and Evelyn (Moore) W.; m. Demetria Rencher, Sept. 9, 1972; children: Ralph Edward, Monifa. BS, Xavier U., 1970; MD, Mich. State U., 1976. Diplomate Am. Bd. Internal Medicine; cert. clin. hypertension specialist. Intern U. Cin. Med. Ctr., 1976-77, resident in internal medicine, 1977-79, asst. clin. prof. internal medicine, 1980-88; asst. prof. internal medicine Mich. State U., East Lansing, 1988-94, assoc. prof., 1994—. Attending physician in hypertension clinic Mich. State U., 1988-91, assoc. dir. hypertension clinic, 1991-94, dir. hypertension clinic, 1995—, program dir. transitional yr. residency, 1990-96, assoc. program dir. internal medicine residency; mem. U.S. HHS Office Minority Health Resource Person Network. Fellow ACP, Internat. Soc. Hypertension in Blacks, Am Assn. Black Cardiologists; mem. Nat. Med. Assn., Am. Soc. Internal Medicine, Am. Soc. Hypertension, Xavier U. Alumni Assn., Alpha Omega Alpha. Home: 4199 Shoals Dr Okemos MI 48864-3434 Office: Mich State U 338B Clinical Ctr East Lansing MI 48824-1313

WATSON, RICHARD ALLAN, philosophy educator, writer; b. New Market, Iowa, Feb. 23, 1931; s. Roscoe Richard and Daisy Belle (Penwell) W.; m. Patty Jo Andersen, July 30, 1955; 1 child, Anna Melissa B.A., U. Iowa, 1953, M.A., 1957, Ph.D. in Philosophy, 1961; M.S. in Geology, U. Minn., 1959. Instr. philosophy U. Mich., Ann Arbor, 1961-64; asst. prof. Washington U., St. Louis, 1964-67, assoc. prof., 1967-74, prof., 1974—. Pres. Cave Research Found., Mammoth Cave, Ky., 1965-67; trustee Nat. Parks and Conservation Assn., Washington, 1969-81 Author: The Downfall of Cartesianism, 1966, Under Plowman's Floor, 1978, The Runner, 1981, The Philosopher's Diet, 1985, The Breakdown of Cartesian Metaphysics, 1987, The Philosopher's Joke, 1990, Writing Philosophy, 1992, Niagara, 1993, Caving, 1994, The Philosopher's Demise, 1995, Representational Ideas, 1995, Good Teaching, 1997, Cogito, Ergo Sum: The Life of René Descartes, 2002;(with others) Man and Nature, 1969, The Longest Cave, 1976; editor: Classics in Speleology, 1968-73, Speleologia, 1974-79, Cave Books, 1980—, Jour. History of Philosophy, 1983, Jour. History of Philosophy Monograph Series, 1985-95, Jour. History of Philosophy Book Series, 2001. Served to 1st lt. USAF, 1953-55 NEH grantee, 1975; fellow Ctr. Advanced Study in Behavioral Scis., Stanford, Calif., 1967-68, 81-82, 91-92, Am. Coun. Learned Socs., 1967-68, Princeton Ctr. Internat. Studies, 1975-76, Camargo Found., 1995, Bogliasco Found., 1998. Mem. Nat. Speleological Soc. (hon. life), Am. Philos. Assn., Cave Research Found; fellow AAAS. Office: Washington U Dept Philosophy Saint Louis MO 63130-4899

WATSON, ROBERT R. lawyer; b. Buffalo, Mar. 10, 1944; BA, Wheaton Coll., 1967; JD, U. Chgo., 1972. Bar: Ill. 1972. Law clerk to Hon. Richard W. McLaren U.S. Dist. Ct. (no. dist.), Ill., 1972-74; ptnr. Sidley & Austin, Chgo. Office: Sidley & Austin Bank One Plz 425 W Surf St Apt 605 Chicago IL 60657-6139

WATSON-BOONE, REBECCA A. library and information studies educator, researcher; b. Springfield, Ohio, Mar. 7, 1946; d. Roger S. and Elizabeth Boone; m. Dennis David Ash, 1967 (div. 1975); m. Frederick Kellogg, 1979 (div. 1988); m. Peter G. Watson, May 26, 1989. Student, Earlham Coll., 1964-67; BA, Case Western Res. U., 1968; MLS, U. N.C., 1971; PhD, U. Wis., 1995. Asst. reference libr. Princeton (N.J) U., 1970-76; head cen. reference dept. U. Ariz., Tucson, 1976-83, assoc. dean Coll. Arts and Scis., 1984-89. Loaned exec. Ariz. Bd. Regents, 1988-89; pres. Ctr. for Study of Info. Profls., 1995—2002. Author: Constancy and Change in the Worklife of Research University Librarians, 1998; contbr. articles to profl. jours. Mem. ALA (div. pres. 1985-86, councilor 1988-92), Assn. for Libr. and Info. Sci. Edn., NAFE. Mem. Soc. of Friends. Office: 4721 W Parkview Dr Mequon WI 53092-2022 E-mail: csip@execpc.com.

WATTENBERG, ALBERT, physicist, educator; b. N.Y.C., Apr. 13, 1917; s. Louis and Bella (Wolff) W.; m. Alice von Neumann, May 23, 1992; children from a previous marriage: Beth, Jill, Nina Diane. B.S., Coll. City N.Y., 1938; M.A., Columbia, 1939; Ph.D., U. Chgo., 1947. Spectroscopist Schenley Distilleries, N.Y.C., 1939-42; physicist Manhattan Project, Metall. Lab., Chgo., 1942-46; group leader Argonne Nat. Lab., 1946-50; asst. prof. U. Ill., Urbana, 1950-51, prof. physics, 1958—. Research physicist Mass. Inst. Tech., 1951-58 Recipient award for 1st nuclear reactor Am. Nuclear Soc., 1962; Nuclear Pioneer award Soc. Nuclear Medicine, 1977; NSF fellow U. Rome, 1962-63 Achievements include pioneering controlled nuclear reactor.

WATTERS, LORAS JOSEPH, bishop; b. Dubuque, Iowa, Oct. 15, 1915; s. Martin James and Carolyn R. (Sisler) W. B.A., Loras Coll., Dubuque, 1937; S.T.B., Gregorian U., Rome, Italy, 1940; S.T.L., Cath. U. Am., 1941, M.A., 1947, Ph.D., 1954. Ordained priest Roman Cath Ch., 1941; asst. pastor St. Martin's Ch., Cascade, Iowa, 1941-45; mem. faculty Loras Coll., 1945-56; prin. Loras Acad., Dubuque, 1947-52, head edn. dept., 1954-56; spiritual dir. N.Am. Coll., Rome, 1956-60; dir. Am. Martyrs Retreat House, Cedar Falls, Iowa, 1960-65; aux. bishop of Dubuque, 1965-69; pastor Ch. of Nativity, Dubuque, 1965-69; archdiocesan supt. schs., 1967-69; bishop of Winona, Minn., 1969—. Mem. bishops' com. on priestly formation Nat. Conf. Cath. Bishops, 1970-78, chmn., 1972-75 Office: 55 W Sanborn PO Box 588 Winona MN 55987-0588

WATTERS, RICHARD DONALD, lawyer; b. Midland, Mich., May 3, 1951; s. Donald Wayne and Madalyn Bird (Tinetti) W.; m. Ann Elizabeth Hutchison, May 24, 1975; children: Kelly E., Nathan Paul. BS in Indsl. Engring., Bradley U., 1973; JD cum laude, St. Louis U., 1976. BAr: Mo. 1976, U.S. Dist. Ct. (we. and ea. dists.) Mo. 1976, Ill. 1977, U.S. Ct. Appeals (8th cir.) 1981. Assoc. Lashly & Baer, P.C., St. Louis, 1976-81, ptnr., 1981—, dept. chmn., 1989—. Instr. St. Louis U. Sch. Law, 1977-79. Chmn., pres. United Cerebral Palsy Assn. St. Louis, 1985-88; bd. dirs. Canterbury Enterprises, sheltered workshop, St. Louis, 1988-94, participant Leadership St. Louis, 1988-89; ethics com. DePaul Health Ctr., 1990—. Mem. Am. Health Lawyers Assn., Mo. Soc. Hosp. Attys. (bd. dirs. 1988-94, pres. 1990-91), Mo. Bar Assn. (vice chmn. health and hosp. com. 1988-90), Bar Assn. Metro. St. Louis (co-chmn. med.-legal com.). Republican. Avocation: sailing. Office: Lashly & Baer PC 714 Locust St Saint Louis MO 63101-1699 E-mail: rdwatters@lashlybaer.com.

WATTERSON, BILL, former cartoonist; b. Washington, 1958; s. James and Kathryn W.; m. Melissa Watterson. Grad. polit. sci., Kenyon Coll., 1980. Editorial cartoonist Cincinnati Post, Cincinnati, OH, 1980; syndicated cartoon strip, Calvin and Hobbes Universal Press Syndicate, 1985-95; ret., 1995. Author, illustrator: Calvin and Hobbes, 1987, The Essential Calvin and Hobbes: A Calvin and Hobbes Treasury, 1988, Something Under the Bed is Drooling: A Calvin and Hobbes Collection, 1988, Yukon Ho!, 1989, The Calvin & Hobbes Lazy Sunday Book, 1989, The Authoritative Calvin and Hobbes, 1990, Weirdos from Another Planet!, 1990, The Revenge of the Baby-Sitter, 1991, Scientific Progress Goes "Boink", 1991, Attack of the Deranged Mutant Killer Monster Snow Goons, 1992, Indispensible Calvin and Hobbes: A Calvin and Hobbes Treasury, 1992, The Days are Just Packed, 1993, Homicidal Psycho Jungle Cat: A Calvin & Hobbes Collection, 1994; illustrator The Komplete Kolor Krazy Kat, vol. I, 1990; wrote forward Fox Trot, 1989. Office: Universal Press Syndicate 4900 Main St Fl 9 Kansas City MO 64112-2630

WATTS, EMILY STIPES, English language educator; b. Urbana, Ill., Mar. 16, 1936; d. Royal Arthur and Virginia Louise (Schenck) Stipes; m. Robert Allan Watts, Aug. 30, 1958; children: Benjamin, Edward, Thomas. Student, Smith Coll., 1954-56; A.B., U. Ill., 1958, M.A. (Woodrow Wilson Nat. fellow), 1959, Ph.D., 1963. Instr. English U. Ill., Urbana, 1963-67, asst. prof., 1967-73, assoc. prof., 1973-77, prof., dir. grad. studies dept. English, 1977—; bd. dirs. U. Ill. Athletic Assn., chmn., 1981-83; mem. faculty adv. com. Ill. Bd. Higher Edn., 1984—, vice chmn., 1986-87, chmn., 1987-88. Author: Ernest Hemingway and The Arts, 1971, The Poetry of American Women from 1632 to 1945, 1977, The Businessman in American Literature, 1982; contbg. editor: English Women Writers from the Middle Ages to the Present, 1990; contbr. articles on Jonathan Edwards, Anne Bradstreet to lit. jours. John Simon Guggenheim Meml. Found. fellow, 1973-74 Mem. AAUP, Midwest MLA, Am. Inst. Archaeology, Assn. Lit. Scholars Critics, Authors Guild, Ill. Hist. Soc., The Phila. Soc., Phi Beta Kappa, Phi Kappa Phi. Presbyterian. Home: 1009 W University Ave Champaign IL 61821-3317 Office: U Ill 208 English Bldg 608 S Wright St Urbana IL 61801

WATTS, EUGENE J. state legislator; b. St. Louis, Oct. 17, 1942; s. Eugene H. and Norma (Shaughnessy) W.; children: Julia Brianne, Mackenzie Mulrane. AB, Knox Coll., 1964; MA, Emory U., 1965, PhD, 1969. Senator Ohio State Senate Dist. 16, 1985—, asst. pres. pro temp, chmn. reference and oversight, fin. subcom. on edn., mem. rules, edn., retirement & aging com., mem. fin. inst. and ins. com. Assoc. prof. history, rsch. asst. Ohio State U., 1972—; rsch. fellow Am. Coun. Learned Soc., 1975—. Author: The Social Basis of City Politics, 1978. Decorated Bronze star, Vietnam Campaign ribbon, Vietnam Svc. ribbon; State and Local Govt. fellow NEH, 1978; Fulbright fellow Internat. Exch. of Scholar, 1981; recipient Humanitarian Achievement award Columbia Dispatch Cmty. Svc. award, 1984; named Outstanding Legislator, Am. Legion, Amvets, Cath. War Vets., Disabled Am. Vets., Ohio State Coun. Vietnam Vets. Am., Ohio VFW, Vet. Assn. State Comdrs. and Adjutants, Ohio Assn. Chiefs of Police, Ohio Crime Prevention Assn., Ohio Prosecutors Assn. Mem. Vietnam Vet. Leadership Program (state chmn. 1982-85), Am. Legion, VFW, Fraternal Order of Police Assn., Orgn. Am. Historians, AMVETS. Home: 352 Monterey Dr Dublin OH 43017-1337 Office: State Senate State Capital Columbus OH 43215

WATTS, JOHN RANSFORD, university administrator; b. Boston, Feb. 9, 1930; s. Henry Fowler Ransford and Mary Marion (Macdonald) Watts; m. Joyce Lannom, Dec. 20, 1975; 1 child David Allister. AB, Boston Coll., 1950, MEd, 1965; MFA, Yale U., 1953; PhD, Union Grad. Sch., 1978. Prof., ast. dean Boston U., 1958-74; prof., dean fine arts Calif. State U., Long Beach, 1974-79; dean and artistic dir. The Theatre Sch./Goodman Sch. Drama, DePaul U., Chgo., 1979-99, prof. and dean emeritus, 1999—. Mng. dir. DePaul U. Merle Reskin Theatre, 1988-99; gen. mgr. Boston Arts Festivals, 1955-64; adminstr. Arts Programs at Tanglewood, 1966-69; producing dir. Theatre Co. of Boston, 1973-75. Chmn. Mass. Coun. on Arts and Humanities, 1968-72; bd. dirs., v.p. Long Beach Pub. Cofp. for the Arts, 1975-79; mem. theatre panel Ill. Arts Coun., 1981-90. With U.S. Army, 1953-55. Recipient Lifetime Achievement award Joseph Jefferson Com., Chgo., 2000. Mem. Mass. Ednl. Comms. Commn., Am. Theatre Asasn., Nat. Coun. on Arts in Edn., Met. Cultural Alliance, U.S. Inst. Theatre Tech., League Chgo. Theatres, Chgo. Internat. Theatre Festival, St. Botolph Club (Boston), Univ. Club (Chgo.), Phi Beta Kappa, Phi Kappa Phi.

WATTS, ROBERT ALLAN, publisher, lawyer; b. July 4, 1936; s. Richard P. and Florence (Hooker) W.; m. Emily Stipes, Aug. 30, 1958; children: Benjamin H., Edward S., Thomas J. Student, DePauw U., 1954-55; BA, U. Ill., 1959, JD, 1961. Bar: Ill. 1961. Assoc. Stipes Pub. Co., Champaign, Ill., 1962-67, ptnr., editor, 1967—. Treas. Planned Parenthood, 1976-80; mem. Pres.'s Coun., U. Ill., 1980-82; pres. Friends of Libr., U. Ill., 1980-82; bd. dirs. local United Way, 1972-81, City of Champaign Libr. Found., 1993—. Mem. Ill. Bar Assn., U. Ill. Found., Nat. Acad. Arts (bd. dirs. 1983-89), Champaign Country Club, Saugatuck Yacht Club (commodore), Lake Shore Bath & Tennis Club (pres. 1983-85). Home: 1009 W University Ave Champaign IL 61821-3317 Office: Stipes Publishing Co 204 W University Ave Champaign IL 61820-3912

WAX, NADINE VIRGINIA, retired banker; b. Van Horne, Iowa, Dec. 7, 1927; d. Laurel Lloyd and Viola Henrietta (Schrader) Bobzien; divorced; 1 child, Sharlyn K. Wax Munns. Student, U. Iowa, 1970-71; grad. Nat. Sch. Real Estate and Fin., Ohio State U., 1980-81. Jr. acct. McGladrey, Hansen, Dunn (now McGladrey-Pullen Co., CPAs), Cedar Rapids, Iowa, 1944-47; office mgr. Iowa Securities Co. (now Wells Fargo Mortgage Co.), 1954-55; asst. cashier Mchts. Nat. Bank (now U.S. Bancorp.), 1956-75; asst. v.p. Mchts. Nat. Bank (now U.S. Bancorp), 1976-78, v.p., 1979-90; ret., 1990. Vol. St. Luke's Hosp. Aux., Cedar Rapids, 1981—85, SCORE,

1999—2002; bd. dirs., v.p. Kirkwood C.C. Facilities Found., 1970—2002; bd. dirs., treas. Kirkwood C.C., 1984—91; trustee Indian Creek Nature Ctr., Cedar Rapids, 1974—2002, pres., 1980—81; mem. Linn County Regional Planning Commn., 1982—92, Cedar Rapids-Marion Fine Arts Coun., 1994—97; bd. suprs. Compensation Commn. for Condemnation, 1987—92; bd. dirs. Am. Heart Assn., Cedar Rapids, 1983—94; mem. Iowa Employment and Tng. Coun., Des Moines, 1982—83. Recipient Outstanding Woman award Cedar Rapids Tribute to Women and Industry, 1984. Mem. Fin. Women Internat. (state edn. chmn. 1982-83), Am. Inst. Banking (bd. dirs. 1968-70), Soc. Real Estate Appraisers (treas. 1978-80), Linn. County Bankers Assn. (pres. 1979-80), Cedar Rapids Bd. Realtors, Cedar Rapids C. of C. (bus.-edn. com. 1986-91), Cedar Rapids Country Club. Independent. Lutheran. Avocations: travel, reading, walking. Home: 147 Ashcombe SE Cedar Rapids IA 52403-1700

WAXLER, BEVERLY JEAN, anesthesiologist, physician; b. Chgo., Apr. 11, 1949; d. Isadore and Ada Belle (Gross) Marcus; m. Richard Norman Waxler, Dec. 24, 1972; 1 child, Adam R. BS in Biology, No. Ill. U., 1971; MD, U. Ill., Chgo., 1975. Diplomate Am. Bd. Anesthesiology, Am. Bd. Pathology. Intern dept. pathology Northwestern U., Chgo., 1975-76, resident, 1976-79; instr. Rush Presbyn. St. Luke's Med. Ctr., 1979-81; asst. prof. pathology Loyola U., Maywood, Ill., 1981-84; resident dept. anesthesiology Cook County Hosp., Chgo., 1984-87, attending anesthesiologist, 1987—; clin. asst. prof. U. Ill., 1988-95; asst. prof. Rush Med. Coll., 1996—. Contbr. papers to Tissue and Cell. Recipient B.B. Sankey Anesthesia Advancement award Internat. Anesthesia Rsch. Soc., 1989; Nat. Rsch. Svc. award fellow Nat. Cancer Inst., 1980; grantee Varlen Corp., 1982. Mem. AAAS, Internat. Anesthesia Rsch. Soc., Am. Soc. Anesthesiologists, Sigma Xi. Achievements include research in effects of anesthetics on the lung. Office: Cook County Hosp Chicago IL 60612

WAXMAN, DAVID, physician, university consultant; b. Albany, N.Y., Feb. 7, 1918; s. Meyer and Fannie (Strosberg) W.; m. Jane Zabel; children: Gail, Michael, Dan, Ann, Steve, Abby. B.S., Syracuse U., 1942, M.D., 1950. Intern Grace Hosp., Detroit, 1950-51; resident in medicine, fellow in cardiology Kans. U. Med. Ctr., Kansas City, 1958-61, instr. internal medicine, 1961-64; asst. prof. internal medicine Kans. City Med. Ctr., 1964-69, assoc. prof., 1969-77, prof., 1977—, dir. dept. medicine outpatient service, 1970-74, asst. dean, 1970-71, assoc. dean for student affairs, 1971-72, dean of students, 1972-74, vice chancellor for students, 1974-76, vice chancellor, 1976-77, exec. vice chancellor, 1977-83, spl. cons. to chancellor for health affairs, 1983-94; ret. Nat. cons. to surgeon gen. USAF. Contbr. articles to med. jours. Mem. Kans. State Bd. Healing Arts, 1984-88. Maj. gen. USAFR ret. Decorated D.S.M., Legion of Merit with one oak leaf cluster. Fellow ACP, Alpha Omega Alpha; mem. Kans. Med. Soc., Soc. Med. Cons. to the Armed Forces. Office: Kans U Med Ctr 39th and Rainbow Blvd Kansas City KS 66103

WAXSE, DAVID JOHN, judge; b. Oswego, Kans., June 29, 1945; s. I. Joseph and Mary (Poole) W.; m. Linda Schilling (div.); children: Rachel, Ryan, Rebecca; m. Judy Pfannenstiel, May 29, 1982; 1 child, Elayna. BA, U. Kans., 1967; teaching cert., Columbia U., 1968, JD, 1971. Bar: Kans. 1971, U.S. Ct. Appeals (10th cir.) 1971, U.S. Supreme Ct. 1975, U.S. Ct. Appeals (8th Cir.) 1998. Dean of students Intermediate Sch. 88, N.Y.C., 1968-70; spl. edn. tchr. Peter Cooper Sch., 1970-71; assoc. Payne & Jones, Olathe, Kans., 1971-74, ptnr., 1974-84; of counsel Shook, Hardy & Bacon, Overland Park, 1984-86, ptnr., 1986-95; shareholder Shook, Hardy & Bacon P.C., 1993-95; ptnr. Shook, Hardy & Bacon L.L.P., Kans., 1995-99; shareholder Shook, Hardy & Bacon P.C., 1993-95, v.p., asst. gen. counsel, 1995-99; U.S. magistrate judge Kansas City, 1999—. Mcpl. judge City of Shawnee, Kans., 1974-80; atty. City of DeSoto, Kans., 1972-79; adj. prof. U. Kans. Sch. Law, Lawrence, 1981-82; mem. juv. code adv. com. Kans. Jud. Coun., 1979-83, guardianship adv. com., 1982-83, atty. fees adv. com., 1986-87; mem. Civil Justice Reform Act Adv. Com., U.S. Dist. Ct. for Dist. Kans., 1991-95; mem. Kans. Commn. on Jud. Qualifications, 1992-99, vice-chmn. 1994-97, chair, 1997-99; v.p. Kans. Legal Svcs., Inc., 1980-82, pres., 1985-87; bd. advisors Kans. Coll. Advocacy, 1979-80; bd. trustees, lawyers' com. Civil Rights Under Law, 1997-99. Author: (with others) Kansas Employment Law, 1985, Litigating Employment Law Cases, 1987, Kansas Employment Law Handbook, 1991, supplements, 1992, 95, Kansas Annual Survey, 1990—. Mem. Kan. Gov.'s Adv. Com. on Criminal Justice, 1974-77; mem. Kans. Justice Commn., 1997-99; gen. counsel Western Mo. Dist. ACLU, 1976-78, 86-97, v.p., 1983-86, nat. bd. dirs., 1979-86, 91-99, chmn. children's rights com., 1980-86; mem. AIDS Pol. Network, 1987-99, med. treatment issues com., 1991-96, constn. com., 1991-99; mem. med./tech. com. AIDS Coun. Greater Kans. City, 1986-98, ethics com. consortium Midwest Bioethics Ctr., 1990—; bd. dirs. Parents Anonymous Kans., 1978-83, pres., 1979; bd. dirs., mem. fin. com. Kans. Com. for Prevention Child Abuse, 1980-83. Fellow Am. Bar Found., Kans. Bar Found.; mem. ABA (chmn. children's rights com. and family law sects. 1985-86, mem. ho. of dels. 2000—, professionalism com. 2000—), Am. Judicature Soc. (bd. dirs. 1997—, adv. com. for ctr. for judicial conduct 1997—), Kans. Bar Assn. (chmn. legal aid com. 1978-83, bd. govs. 1988—, v.p. 1996-97, pres.-elect 1997-98, pres. 1998-99, mem. ABA ho. dels. 2000—, Pres.' Outstanding Svc. award 1982), Kans. City Met. Bar Assn., Johnson County Bar Assn. (chmn. legal aid com. 1975-82, 92-96). Office: U S Courthouse 500 State Ave Rm 219 Kansas City KS 66101-2400 E-mail: judge_waxse@ksd.uscourts.gov.

WAY, KENNETH L. motor vehicle seat manufacturing company executive; b. 1939; BS, Mich. State U., 1961, MBA, 1971. V.p. Lear Siegler, Inc., Southfield, Mich., 1966-88; chmn., CEO Lear Corp., 1988-2000. With USAF, 1962-66. Office: Lear Corp 21557 Telegraph Rd Southfield MI 48034-4248

WEAKLAND, REMBERT G. archbishop; b. Patton, Pa., Apr. 2, 1927; s. Basil and Mary (Kane) W. AB, St. Vincent Coll., Latrobe, Pa., 1948, DD (hon.), 1963, LHD (hon.), 1987; MS in Piano, Juilliard Sch. Music, 1954; grad. studies sch. music, Columbia U., 1954-56, PhD in Musicology, 2000; LHD (hon.), Duquesne U., 1964, Belmont Coll., 1964, Cath. U. Am., 1975, Xavier U., Cin., 1988, DePaul U., 1989, Loyola U., New Orleans, 1991, Villanova U., 1992, Dayton U., 1993, Marian Coll., Fond du Lac, Wis., 1995, St. Anselm Coll., Manchester, N.H., 1996, St. Norbert Coll., De Pere, Wis., 1996, U. San Francisco, 1997, Scholastica Coll., 1998; HHD (hon.), St. Ambrose U., Davenport, 1990, Aquinas Inst. Theology, St. Louis, 1991, St Mary's Coll., Notre Dame, Ind., 1994; LLD (hon.), Cardinal Stritch Coll., Milw., 1978, Marquette U., 1981, Loyola U., Chgo., 1986, U. Notre Dame, 1987, Mt. Mary Coll., Milw., 1989, John Carroll U., Cleve., 1992, Fairfield U., 1994; D of Sacred Music (hon.), St. Joseph's Coll., Rensselaer, Ind., 1979; DST (hon.), Jesuit Sch. Theology, Berkeley, Calif., 1989, St. John's U., Collegeville, Minn., 1991, Santa Clara U., 1991, Yale U., 1993; DD (hon.), Lakeland Coll., Sheboygan, 1991, Ill. Benedictine Coll., Lisle, Ill., 1992, Regis Coll., Toronto, 1993, Trinity Coll., Hartford, 1996, Trinity Lutheran Sem., Columbus, Ohio, 1998; D of Ministry (hon.), Catholic Theol. Union, Chgo., 1999. Joined Benedictines, Roman Cath. Ch., 1945, ordained priest, 1951. Mem. faculty music dept. St. Vincent Coll., 1957-63, chmn., 1961-63, chancellor chmn. of bd. of Coll., 1963-67; elected co-adjutor archabbot, 1963; abbot primate Benedictine Confederation, 1967-77; archbishop of Milw., 1977—. Mem. Ch. Music Assn. Am. (pres. 1964-66), Am. Guild Organists. Office: PO Box 070912 Milwaukee WI 53207-0912

WEATHERWAX, THOMAS K. state legislator; b. Cedar Rapids, Iowa, Oct. 22, 1942; s. Richard G. and Alyce (Kelly) W.; m. Kay A. Weatherwax, 1972; children: Michelle, Kris Chauncey, Kevin, Steve, David, Craig. AA, Cedar Rapids Bus. Coll., 1962; student, ICS Correspondence Sch., 1963-64, U. Ky. From cost acct. to sec.-contr. Wilson & Co., Oklahoma City, 1961-78; sec.-contr. Erny's Fertilizer Svc., Waiton, Ind., 1978—; bus. chmn. LEDC Indsl. Park; mem. Ind. Ho. of Reps., 1984-88, Ind. Senate from 18th dist., 1988—; chmn. transp. & interstate coop. com., local govt. financing subcom.; mem. agr. & small bus. com., commerce & consumer affairs com. Ind. State Senate. Sec. Logansport Area Devel. Corp., 1979-85; gen. chmn. United Way, 1979; mem. Hosp. Cmty. Rels. Bd., pres., 1981-83; Iron Horse Fetival gen. chmn. C. of C., 1983; mem. 21st Century com. Coun. State Govts., Nat. Conf. State Legislatures, Energy & Transp.; bd. dirs. Logansport Econ. Devel. Found., Logansport Area Devel. Corp.; mem. Grissom Cmty. Coun.; advisor Ind. Acad. Competitions Excellence; former pres. Meml. Hosp. Cmty. Rels. Bd., bd. dirs. Sangralea Valley Boys' Home; mem. steering com. Hoosier Heartland Corridor. Recipient John Tipton award Cass County Commrs., 1979, Ind. Small Bus. Champion award, Merit award Ind. Assn. Nurserymen, Guardian award Nat. Fedn. Ind. Bus., 1992, Small Bus. Champion award Ind. State C. of C., 1993, Frank M. McHale Econ. Devel. award, 1995, Nat. Rep. Legis. of Yr. award Nat. Rep. Legs. Assn., 1995, Govt. Leader of Yr. Ind. C. of C., 1995; named Outstanding Freshman Legislator, 10th Gen. Assembly, 1985. Mem. Masons (32 deg.), Shriners. Home: 3012 Woodland Dr Logansport IN 46947-1357 Office: Ind Senate State Capitol Indianapolis IN 46204

WEAVER, ARTHUR LAWRENCE, physician; b. Lincoln, Nebr., Sept. 3, 1936; s. Arthur J. and Harriet Elizabeth (Walt) W.; m. JoAnn Versemann, July 6, 1980; children: Arthur Jensen, Anne Christine. BS (Regents scholar) with distinction, U. Nebr., 1958; MD, Northwestern U., 1962; MS in Medicine, U. Minn., 1966. Intern U. Mich. Hosps., Ann Arbor, 1962-63; resident Mayo Grad. Sch. Medicine, Rochester, Minn., 1963-66; practice medicine specializing in rheumatology and internal Lincoln, 1968—; med. dir. Arthritis Ctr. Nebr., 1968—. Mem. staff Bryan Meml. Hosp., chmn. dept. rheumatology, 1976-78, 82-85, 89-91, vice-chief staff, 1984-87; bd. dirs. Bryancare (PHO), 1995-96, chmn. fin. com., 1995-96; mem. courtesy staff St. Elizabeths Hosp., Lincoln Gen. Hosp.; mem. cons. staff VA Hosp.; chmn. Juvenile Rheumatoid Arthritis Clinic, 1970-88; asst. prof. dept. internal medicine U. Nebr., Omaha, 1976-88, assoc. prof., 1988-95, prof., 1995—; med. dir. Lincoln Benefit Life Co., Nebr., 1972-90; bd. dirs. Lincoln Mutual Life Ins. Co., 1994—, med. dir., 1995—; mem. adv. com. Coop. Systematic Studies in Rheumatic Diseases III; bd. dirs. M.G.I. Pharma Inc.; bd. dirs. Internat. Rheumatology Network. Editl. bd. Nebr. Med. Jour., 1982-96; contbr. articles to med. jours. Bd. dirs. Nebr. chpt. Arthritis Found., 1969—; mem. tech. cons. panel for rheumatology Harvard Resource Based Relative Value Study; trustee U. Nebr. Found., 1974—. Served to capt., M.C., U.S. Army, 1966-68. Recipient Outstanding Nebraskan award U. Nebr., 1958, C.W. Boucher award, 1958; Philip S. Hench award Rheumatology, Mayo Grad. Sch. Medicine, 1966, Founders award Arthritis Found., Nebr. chpt., 1997. Diplomate Am. Bd. Internal Medicine, Am. Bd. Rheumatology. Fellow ACP (Nebr. council 1983-85, Laureate award Nebr. chpt. 1996), Am. Rheumatism Assn. (com. on rheumatologic practice 1983-87, pres.-elect Ctrl. region 1983-84, pres. Ctrl. region 1984-85), Am. Coll. Rheumatology (master 2001); mem. AMA, Am. Coll. Rheumatology (1st Paulding Phelps award 1989, bd. dirs. 1985-96, planning com. 1987-96, exec. com. 1991-96, sec. 1991-93, pres. rsch. and edn. found. 1991-93, 2nd v.p. 1993-94, 1st v.p., pres. elect 1994-95, pres. 1995-96, chmn. nominating com. 1996-97), Am. Soc. Internal Medicine (coord. com. physical payment svcs. 1988-93), Nebr. Soc. Internal Medicine (Internist of Yr., 1988), Nebraska Rheumatism Assn., Nebr. Med. Assn., Lancaster County Med. Soc., Mayo Grad. Sch. Medicine Alumni Assn., U. Mich. Med. Sch. Alumni Assn., U. Minn. Med. Sch. Alumni Assn., Arthritis Health Professions Assn. (com. on practice 1984-87), Nat. Soc. Clin. Rheumatology (program chairperson 1986-87, 88, exec. com. 1987-92), Midwest Cooperative Rheumatic Disease Study Group (chmn. exec. com. 1986-92), Arthritis Found. (nat. mem., profl. del.-at-large 1987-88, 89, 90, 95-96, Nat. Vol. Svc. citation, 1988, blue ribbon rsch. com. 1995-96, Founder award 1997), Phi Beta Kappa, Sigma Xi, Alpha Omega Alpha, Pi Kappa Epsilon, Phi Rho Sigma. Republican. Presbyterian. Home: 9914 Weavers Point Rd Pequot Lakes MN 56472-6472 Office: 2121 S 56th St Lincoln NE 68506-2111

WEAVER, DAVID HUGH, journalism educator, communications researcher; b. Hammond, Ind., Dec. 23, 1946; s. David W. and Josephine L. Weaver; m. Gail Shriver, June 28, 1969; children: Quinn David, Lesley Jo. BA, Ind. U., Bloomington, 1968, MA, 1969; PhD, U. N.C., 1974. Copy editor The Post-Tribune, Gary, Ind., 1968; wire editor, reporter The Courier-Tribune, Bloomington, 1968; wire editor The Chapel Hill Newspaper, N.C., 1973; asst. prof. journalism Ind. U., Bloomington, 1974-78, assoc. prof., 1978-83, prof., 1983-88, Roy W. Howard prof. Ind., 1988—. Author: Videotex Journalism, 1983; co-author: Newsroom Guide to Polls and Surveys, 1980, 90, Media Agenda-Setting, 1981, The American Journalist, 1986 (award Soc. Profl. Journalists 1987), 2d edit., 1991, The Formation of Campaign Agendas, 1991, Contemporary Public Opinion, 1991, The American Journalist in the 1990's, 1996 (award Soc. Profl. Journalists 1997); co-editor: Communication and Democracy, 1997; editor: The Global Journalist, 1998. Lt. U.S. Army, 1969-71. Fellow Midwest Pub. Opinion Rsch. (pres. 1986-87), Internat. Comm. Assn.; mem. Assn. for Edn. in Journalism and Mass Comm. (pres. 1987-88, Krieghbaum award 1983), Soc. Prof. Journalists. Avocations: guitar, music. Office: Ind U Sch Journalism Ernie Pyle Hall Bloomington IN 47405-7108

WEAVER, DONNA RAE, company executive; b. Chgo., Oct. 15, 1945; d. Albert Louis and Gloria Elaine (Graffis) Florence; m. Clifford L. Weaver, Aug. 20, 1966; 1 child, Megan Rae. BS in Edn., No. Ill. U., 1966, EdD, 1977; MEd, De Paul U., 1974. Tchr. H.L. Richards High Sch., Oak Lawn, Ill., 1966-71, Sawyer Coll. Bus., Evanston, 1971-72; asst. prof. Oakton Community Coll., Morton Grove, 1972-75; vis. prof. U. Ill., Chgo., 1977-78; dir. devel. Mallinckrodt Coll., Wilmette, Ill., 1978-80, dean, 1980-83; campus dir. Nat.-Louis U., Chgo., 1983-90, dean div. applied behavioral scis., 1985-89; dean Coll. Mgmt. and Bus., 1989-90; pres. The Oliver Group, Inc., Kenilworth, Ill., 1993-97; mng. ptnr. Le Miccine, Gaiole-in-Chianti, Tuscany, Italy, 1996—. Cons. Nancy Lovely and Assocs., Wilmette, 1981-84, North Ctrl. Assn., Chgo., 1982-90. Contbr. articles to Am. Vocat. Jour., Ill. Bus. Edn. Assn. Monograph, Nat. Coll. Edn.'s ABS Rev., Nat. View. Mem. Ill. Quality of Work Life Coun., 1987-90, New Trier Twp. Health and Human Svcs. Adv. Bd., Winnetka, Ill., 1985-88; bd. dirs. Open Lands Project, 1985-87, Kenilworth (Ill.) Village House, 1986-87. Recipient Achievement award Women in Mgmt., 1981; Am. Bd. Master Educators charter disting. fellow, 1986. Mem. Nat. Bus. Edn. Assn., Delta Pi Epsilon (past pres.). Avocations: reading, traveling, decorating. Office: 505 N Lake Shore Dr Apt 4010 Chicago IL 60611-3619

WEAVER, ELIZABETH A. state supreme court justice; b. New Orleans; d. Louis and Mary Weaver. BA, Newcomb Coll.; JD, Tulane U. Elem. tchr. Glen Lake Cmty. Sch., Maple City, Mich.; French tchr. Leelanau Sch., Glen Arbor; pvt. practice; law clk. Civil Dist. Ct., New Orleans; atty. Coleman, Dutrey & Thomson; atty., title specialist Chevron Oil Co.; probate and juvenile judge Leelanau County, Mich., 1975—86; judge Mich. Ct. of Appeals, 1987—94; justice Mich. Supreme Ct., Lansing, 1995—. Chief justice Mich. Supreme Ct., 1999—2000; instr. edn. dept. Ctr. Mich. U.; mem. Mich. Com. on Juvenile Justice, Nat. Conv. State Adv. Groups on Juvenile Justice for U.S.; chair Gov.'s Task Force on Children's Justice, Trial Ct. Assessment Commn., Office Juvenile Justice and Delinquency Prevention; jud. adv. bd. mem. Law and Orgnl. Econs. Ctr. U. Kans.; treas. Children's Charter of Cts. of Mich. Chairperson Western Mich. U. CLE Adv. Bd.; mem. steering com. Grand Traverse/Leelanau Commn. on Youth; mem. Glen Arbor Twp. Zoning Bd.; mem. charter arts north Leelanau County; mem. citizen's adv. coun. Arnell Engstrom Children's Ctr.; mem. cmty. adv. com. Pathfinder Sch. Treaty Law Demonstration Project; active Grand Traverse/Leelanau Mental Health Found. Named Jurist of Yr., Police Officers Assn. of Mich.; named one of five Outstanding Young Women in Mich., Mich. Jaycees; recipient Eastern award, Warren Easton Hall of Fame. Fellow: Mich. State Bar Found.; mem.: ABA, Antrim County Bar Assn., Leelanau County Bar Assn., Grand Traverse County Bar Assn., La. Bar Assn., Nat. Coun. Juvenile and Family Judges, Mich. Bar Assn. (chair CLE adv. bd., chair crime prevention ctr., chair juvenile law com.), Delta Kappa Gamma (hon.). Office: Mich Supreme Ct 3300 Grandview Plz 10850 E Traverse Hwy Traverse City MI 49684-1364

WEAVER, FRANKLIN THOMAS, retired newspaper executive; b. Johnstown, N.Y., Oct. 11, 1932; s. Edwin K. and Bertha J. (Wendt) W.; children: Thomas, James, Michael, David, Tammy, Kelly, Anna; m. Joyce W. Phelps, Oct. 23, 1991. B.A. with high honors in Journalism, Mich. State U., 1954. Advt. sales rep. Grand Rapids Press, Mich., 1955-64; controller Muskegon (Mich.) Chronicle, 1964-66; mgr. Bay City (Mich.) Times, 1966-73, Jackson (Mich.) Citizen Patriot, 1973-84, pub., 1984—99; ret. Mem. Newspapers Assn. Am., Mich. Press Assn. (pres. 1991), Ella Sharp Mus. (pres. 1995-96), Greater Jackson C. of C., Jackson Country Club. Office: Jackson Citizen Patriot 214 S Jackson St Jackson MI 49201-2282

WEAVER, RICHARD L., II, writer, speaker, educator; b. Hanover, N.H., Dec. 5, 1941; s. Richard L. and Florence B. (Grow) W.; m. Andrea A. Willis; children: R. Scott, Jacquelynn Michelle, Anthony Keith, Joanna Corinne. AB, U. Mich., 1964, MA, 1965; PhD, Ind. U., 1969. Asst. prof. U. Mass., 1968-74; assoc. prof. speech communication Bowling Green State U., 1974-79, prof., 1979-96, dir., basic speech communication course, 1974-96. Vis. prof. U. Hawaii-Manoa, 1981-82, Bond U., Queensland, Australia, 1990, St. Albans, Melbourne, Australia, 1990, Western Inst., Perth, Australia, 1990. Author: (with Saundra Hybels) Speech/Communication, 1974, 2d edit., 1979, Speech/Communication: A Reader, 1975, 2d edit., 1979, Speech/Communication: A Student Manual, 1976, 2d edit., 1979, Understanding Interpersonal Communication, 1978, 2d edit., 1981, 3d edit., 1984, 4th edit., 1987, 5th edit., 1990, 6th edit., 1993, 7th edit., 1996, (with Raymond K. Tucker, Cynthia Berryman-Fink) Research in Speech Communication, 1981, Foundations of Speech Communication: Perspectives of a Discipline, 1982, Speech Communication Skills, 1982, Understanding Public Communication, 1983, Understanding Business Communication, 1985, Understanding Speech Communication Skills, 1985, Readings in Speech Communication, 1985, (with Saundra Hybels) Communicating Effectively, 1986, 2d edit., 1989, 3d edit., 1992, 4th edit., 1995, 5th edit., 1998, 6th edit., 2001, Skills for Communicating Effectively, 1985, 2d edit., 1988, 3d edit., 1991, 4th edit., 1993, rev. edit., 1995, (with Howard W. Cotrell) Innovative Instructional Strategies, 1987, 2d edit., 1988, 3d edit., 1989, 4th edit., 1990, 5th edit., 1992, 6th edit., 1993, (with Curt Bechler) Listen to Win: A Guide to Effective Listening, 1994, Study Guide to Accompany Communicating Effectively, 1995, 2d edit., 1998, Essentials of Public Speaking, 1996, 2d edit., 2001. Mem. emeritus Nat. Comm. Assn., Ctrl. States Speech Assn., Ohio Speech Assn. Home and Office: 9583 Woodleigh Ct Perrysburg OH 43551-2669 E-mail: WeaverII@wcnet.org.

WEAVER, STANLEY B. state senator; b. Harrisburg, Ill., May 23, 1925; m. Mary Smith; children: Blake, Sherry. Student, Mich. State Coll., U. Ill.; grad., Ind. Coll. Mortuary Sci. Ptnr. Weaver-Henderson Funeral Home, Urbana, Ill.; former mem. Ill. Ho. of Reps.; now mem. Ill. Senate; mayor Urbana, 1957-69. Active various civic orgns. Served with USAAF, WWII. Republican. Office: 329 Capitol Bldg Springfield IL 62706-0001 Address: 1717 Philo Rd Ste 17B Urbana IL 61802-6099

WEAVER, TIMOTHY ALLAN, lawyer; b. Elkhart, Ind., Nov. 30, 1948; s. Arthur and Joan Lucile (Yoder) W.; m. Catherine Anne Power, Nov. 23, 1974; children: Daniel Timothy, Christopher Matthew, David Colwell. AB, Brown U., 1971; JD, U. Ill., 1974. Bar: Ill. 1974, Wis. 1999, U.S. Dist. Ct. (no. dist.) Ill. 1975, U.S. Ct. Appeals (7th cir.) 1975, U.S. Dist. Ct. (no. dist. trial bar) Ill. 1982, U.S. Dist. Ct. (ea. dist.) Wis. 1999. Asst. pub. defender Cook County Pub. Defender, Chgo., 1974-75; trial atty. Chgo. Transit Authority, 1975-78; assoc. Philip E. Howard Ltd., Chgo., 1978, Pretzel & Stouffer, Chartered, Chgo., 1978-82, ptnr., 1982—. Editor: Medical Malpractice, 1989, 92, 96; contbr. chpts. to books. Mem. ABA, Ill. State Bar Assn., Ill. Assn. Def. Trial Counsel, State Bar of Wis., Civil Trial Counsel of Wis., The Lawyers Club of Chgo. Office: Pretzel & Stouffer One S Wacker Dr #2500 Chicago IL 60606 E-mail: tweaver@pretzel-stouffer.com.

WEBB, DAN K. lawyer; b. Macomb, Ill., Sept. 5, 1945; s. Keith L. and Phyllis I. (Clow) W.; student Western Ill. U., 1963-66; J.D., Loyola U., 1970; m. Laura A. Buscemi, Mar. 15, 1973; children— Jeffrey, Maggie, Michael, Melanie. Bar: Ill. 1970. Chief spl. prosecutions div. U.S. Atty.'s Office, Chgo., 1970-76; ptnr. firm Cummins, Decker & Webb, Chgo., 1976-79; dir. Ill. Dept. Law Enforcement, Chgo., 1979-80; ptnr. Pierce, Webb, Lydon & Griffin, Chgo., 1980-81; U.S. atty., Chgo., 1981-84; ptnr. Winston & Strawn, Chgo., 1984— ; instr. John Marshall Law Sch., 1975— , Loyola U. Sch. Law, 1980— . Vice chmn. Met. Fair and Expn. Authority, 1978— ; bd. advisers Mercy Hosp. and Med. Ctr.; mem. Chgo. Council on Arson. Recipient spl. commendation award U.S. Justice Dept., 1975; named 1 of 10 Outstanding Young Chicagoans, Chgo. Jaycees, 1979. Mem. ABA, Ill. Bar Assn., Chgo. Bar Assn., Fed. Bar Assn., Legal Club Chgo., Execs. Club Chgo. Republican. Home: 15w151 87th St Burr Ridge IL 60527-6389 Office: Winston & Strawn 35 W Wacker Dr Ste 4200 Chicago IL 60601-1695

WEBB, DAVID ALLEN, writer; b. Beloit, Wis. s. Charles Webb and Marion Cecelia (Doud) Michaels. BS in Agrl. Journalism, U. Wis., 1981. Asst. mgr. Nature Food Ctrs., Eau Claire, Wis., 1993-95; mgr. Gen. Nutrition Ctr., 1995-96. Cons. Tab Books, Inc., Blue Ridge Summit, Pa., 1983-85. Author: Growing Fruits & Berries, 1983, Practical Landscaping & Lawn Care, 1985, Making Potpourri, Colognes and Soaps-102 Natural Recipies, 1988, Easy Potpourri, 1992, (novel) Kong Forest, 1999, Edwardian Summer, 1999. Recipient Editor's Choice award for poems, 1998-2000; Carnegie Fund for Authors grant, 1985; named to Internat. Poetry Hall of Fame, 1998. Avocations: gardening, reading, travel.

WEBB, MARTHA JEANNE, author, speaker, film producer; b. Grinnell, Iowa, Oct. 26, 1947; d. Frederick Winfield and Helen (Potter) W.; m. Bruce A. Clark; children: Marjorie, Paula, David. Student, St. Cloud State U., 1965-67, U. Minn., 1967-69, Coll. of St. Catherine, 1979-81. Personnel, pub. relations, drug abuse edn. NIH, 1967-77; account services Doremus & Co., Mpls., 1977-79; v.p. adminstrn. Webb Enterprises, Inc., 1979-81; v.p. Russell-Manning Prodns., 1981-86; pres. Clark Webb, Inc., 1986-92. Pres. Minn. Film Bd., 1986-87, BCW Corp., 1988—. Author: Dress Your House for Success, 1997, Finding Home, 1998; co-prodr. Hubert H. Humphrey: A Passion for Justice, Whitney Mus., 1998. Recipient Summit awards, 1999, Distinction Communicator awards, 1998, Silver award Internat. Film and TV Festival of N.Y., 1983, 84, 85, 86, 87, Golden Eagle award CINE Festival, 1985, Gold award Telly Awards, 1987.

WEBB, O. GLENN, retired farm supplies company executive; b. 1936; married B.S., U. Ill., 1957; Ph.D., So. Ill. U., 1973. With Growmark, Inc., Bloomington, Ill., 1965—, sec., 1968-72, v.p., 1972-80, pres., from 1980, chmn., 1980—, also dir. Trustee, chmn. Am. Inst. Coop.; dir. St. Louis Farm Credit Banks, Farmers Export Co., Nat. Coop. Refinery Assn., Ill. Agr. Leadership Found.; trustee Grad. Inst. Coop. Leadership. Home: 365 Webbtown Rd Tunnel Hill IL 62991

WEBB, PAUL, physician, researcher, consultant, educator; b. Cleve., Dec. 2, 1923; s. Monte F. and Barbara (Webb) Bourjaily; m. Eileen Whalen, Mar. 13, 1948; children: Shaun P., Paul S. Womacks. BA, U. Va., 1943, MD, 1946; MS in Physiol., U. Wash., 1951. Asst. prof. physiol. U. Okla. Sch. Medicine, Oklahoma City, 1952-54; chief environ. sect. Aeromed. Lab., Wright-Patterson AFB, Ohio, 1954-58; prin. assoc. Webb Assocs., Yellow Springs, 1959-82; vis. scientist INSERM, Paris, 1983; vis. prof. U. Limburg, Maastricht, The Netherlands, 1986, U. Uppsala, Sweden, 1988-89; clin. prof. Wright State U. Sch. Medicine, Dayton, Ohio, 1980—. Cons. aerospace and undersea medicine, energy balance and thermal physiology, Yellow Springs, 1980—. Author: Human Calorimeters, 1985; contbr. articles to profl. jours. Village councilman Village of Yellow Springs, Ohio, 1969-75; mem. Air Force Scientific Adv. Bd., Washington, 1984-88. Recipient Ely award Human Factors Soc., 1972. Fellow Aerospace Med. Assn. (Aerospace Indsl. Life Scis. Assn. award 1969), Am. Inst. Med. and Biol. Engring.; mem. Am. Physiol. Soc., Am. Soc. for Clin. Nutrition, Undersea Med. Soc. (oceaneering internat. award 1979, pres. 1980-81). Home and Office: 370 Orton Rd Yellow Springs OH 45387-1321

WEBB, RODNEY SCOTT, judge; b. Cavalier, N.D., June 21, 1935; s. Chester and Aylza (Martin) W.; m. Betty M. Lykken, Aug. 31, 1957; children: Sharon, Crystal, Todd, Wade, Susan. BS, U. N.D., 1957, JD, 1959. Bar: N.D. 1959, U.S. Dist. Ct. N.D. 1965, U.S. Ct. Appeals (8th cir.) 1981. Assoc. Ringsak, Webb, Rice & Metelman, Grafton, N.D., 1959-81; state's atty. Walsh County, 1966-74; mcpl. judge City of Grafton, 1975-81; spl. asst. atty. gen. State of N.D., 1970-81; U.S. atty. U.S. Dist. Ct. N.D., Fargo, 1981-87, judge, 1987—, chief judge, 1993—. Judge; b. Cavalier, N.D., June 21, 1935; s. Chester and Aylza (Martin) W.; m. Betty M. Lykken, Aug. 31, 1957; children: Sharon, Crystal, Todd, Wade, Susan. BS, U. N.D., 1957, JD, 1959. Bar: N.D. 1959, U.S. Dist. Ct. N.D. 1965, U.S. Ct. Appeals (8th cir.) 1981. Assoc. Ringsak, Webb, Rice & Metelman, Grafton, N.D., 1959-81; state's atty. Walsh County, Grafton, 1966-74; mcpl. judge City of Grafton, 1975-81; spl. asst. atty. gen. State of N.D., 1970-81; U.S. atty. Dist. of N.D., Fargo, 1981-87, judge U.S. Dist. Ct. N.D., 1987—, Fargo, chief judge, 1996—. Col. JAG, N.D. Army N.G., ret. Mem. N.D. State Attys. Assn. (past pres.). Lutheran. Col. JAG, N.D. Army N.G., ret. Mem. N.D. State Attys. Assn. (past pres.). Lutheran. Office: US Dist Ct 655 1st Ave N Ste 410 Fargo ND 58102-4952

WEBB, THOMAS EVAN, biochemistry educator; b. Edmonton, Alta., Can., Mar. 4, 1932; came to U.S., 1970, naturalized, 1978; s. Donald John and Sarah Jane (McMinis) W.; m. Ellen Adair Armstrong, Sept. 4, 1961; children: Linda Carol, Sharon Laura. BS, U. Alta., 1955, MS, 1957; PhD, U. Toronto, 1961. Rsch. assoc. Nat. Rsch. Coun., Ottawa, Can., W. Wis., Madison, 1963-65; 1961-63; asst. prof. biochemistry U. Man. (Can.), Winnipeg, 1965-66; asst. prof. McGill U., Montreal, Que., Can., 1966-70, acting dir. cancer unit. Can., 1969-70; assoc. prof. med. biochemistry Ohio State U., Columbus, 1970-74, prof., 1974-95, prof. emeritus, 1995—. Contbr. numerous articles on biochemistry of cancer to profl. jours. Grantee NIH/Nat. Cancer Inst., 1970-95; fellow Air Force Office Sci. Rsch., 1982. Mem. Am. Soc. Biol. Scientists, Am. Assn. Cancer Research, AAAS, Sigma Xi Office: Ohio State U Dept Molecular and Cellular Biochemistry 1645 Neil Ave Columbus OH 43210-1218 E-mail: TWebb74669@aol.com.

WEBB, THOMAS IRWIN, JR. lawyer, director; b. Toledo, Sept. 16, 1948; s. Thomas Irwin and Marcia Davis (Winters) W.; m. Polly S. DeWitt, Oct. 11, 1986; 1 child, Elisabeth Hurst. BA, Williams Coll., 1970; postgrad., Boston U., 1970-71; JD, Case Western Res. U., 1973. Bar: Ohio. Assoc. Shumaker, Loop & Kendrick, Toledo, 1973-79, ptnr., 1979—, chmn. corp. law dept., 1992-94, mgmt. com., 1994-99. Dir. Calphalon Corp., 1990-98, Yark Automotive Group, Inc. Coun. mem. Village of Ottawa Hills, Ohio, 1979-85, adviser Ohio divsn. Securities, 1979-85, commr. of taxation, Village of Ottawa Hills, Ohio, 1999—; bd. dirs. Kiwanis Youth Found. of Toledo, 1982—, Toledo Area Regional Transit Authority, 1989-91, Arts Commn. Greater Toledo, 1993—, exec. com., 1994-99, v.p., 1994-96, pres., 1996-97; bd. dirs. Jr. Achievement of Northwestern Ohio, Inc., 1992—, Lourdes Coll. Found., 1995-01, Toledo Orch. Assn., 1999—, Med. Coll. Ohio, 2001—, Lourdes Coll., 2001—. Mem. ABA, Ohio Bar Assn. (corp. law com. 1989—), Toledo Bar Assn., Northwestern Ohio Alumni Assn. of Williams Coll. (pres. 1974-83), Toledo-Rowing Found. (trustee 1985-2001), Toledo Area C. of C. (trustee 1991-98, exec. com. 1993-98, fin. com. 1993—), Order of Coif, Crystal Downs Country Club, Toledo Country Club, The Toledo Club (trustee 1984-90, pres. 1987-90), Williams Club N.Y., Crystal Lake Yacht Club. Republican. Episcopalian. Office: Shumaker Loop & Kendrick 1000 Jackson St Toledo OH 43624-1573

WEBB, THOMAS J. utilities executive; b. Alexandria, Va., Oct. 3, 1952; m. Donna; 3 children. B in Fin. with honors, George Mason U.; MBA. Various fin. mgmt. positions Ford Motor Co. and subs.; controller Electronics divsn., Large Front-Wheel Drive Vehicle Ctr.; CFO Visteon Corp.; chief fin. info. officer Ford Motor Co.; exec. v.p., CFO Kellogg Co., Battle Creek, Mich., 2000—02; CFO CMS Energy, Dearborn, 2002—. Bd. dirs. Conix, Can., Hall Climate Control, Korea, Halla Electronics, Korea, Samcor, South Africa, Yan Feng, China, Toledo (Ohio) Molding and Die, Climate Sys., India, others. Office: CMS Energy Fairlane Plaza S Ste 1100 330 Town Center Dr Dearborn MI 48126*

WEBB, WILLIAM DUNCAN, lawyer, mediator; b. Dayton, Ohio, Feb. 14, 1930; s. Herbert Henry and Dorothy (Chamberlain) W.; m. Nancy Helen Regester, June 12, 1953; children: Joseph Chamberlain (dec.), Mary Helen, Nancy Katherine, Sarah Elizabeth, Lucy Ellen. AB, U. Mich., 1952, JD, 1956. Bar: Mo. 1956, Kans. 1958, U.S. Supreme Ct. 1969. Assoc. Stinson, Mag, Thomson, McEvers & Fizzell, Kansas City, Mo., 1956-58; sec. Kansas City (Mo.) Power & Light Co., 1960-78, asst. treas., 1969-78, asst. v.p. communications, 1978-79, asst. v.p. fed. affairs, 1979-84; v.p. investments Paine Webber, 1984-98. Legal counsel Fellowship of Christian Athletes. Mem. city coun. Roeland Park, Kans., 1960-62; chmn. Kansas City Myasthenia Gravis Found., 1965-67; bd. dirs. Boys Club of Kansas City, Mo., 1969-74, Greater Kansas City YMCA, Greater Kansas City chpt. ARC; chmn. bd. councilors Avila Coll., 1969-70; trustee, asst. sec., 1970-89; bd. dirs. Rural Water Dist. # 7, Johnson County, Kans., 1992-94. Mem. Internat. Maine-Anjou Assn. (dir., sec.-treas. 1969-76), Theta Delta Chi, Phi Alpha Delta. Presbyterian. Home and Office: 37000 W 155th St Gardner KS 66030-9617 E-mail: webb37ooo@aol.com.

WEBBER, E. RICHARD, JR. judge; b. Kahoka, Mo., June 4, 1942; m. Peggy Washle, July 6, 1968; children: Erin, Nicki. BS in Bus. Adminstrn., U. Mo.-Columbia, 1964, JD, 1967. Pvt. practice, Mo., 1967-79; cir. judge 1st Jud. Cir., 1979-95; judge ea. dist. Mo. U.S. Dist. Ct., Saint Louis, 1995—. Former chair Presiding Judges' Exec. Com., Supreme Ct. Coms. adopting case processing time standards & implementing family ct. Elder Memphis Presbyn. Ch.; past pres. Law Sch. Alumni Assn. U. Mo., Coun. Family & Juvenile Ct. Judges; former mem. Nat. Task Force Child Support Enforcement. Mem. ABA, Mo. Bar Assn. (former chair jud. adminstrn. divsn., co-chair gender fairness implementation com.), Mo. Trial Judges Assn. (past pres.). Office: 111 S 10th St Saint Louis MO 63102

WEBER, ARNOLD ROBERT, academic administrator; b. N.Y.C., Sept. 20, 1929; s. Jack and Lena (Smith) W.; m. Edna M. Files, Feb. 7, 1954; children: David, Paul, Robert. B.A., U. Ill., 1951; M.A., Ph.D. in Econs., MIT, 1958. Instr., then asst. prof. econs. MIT, 1955-58; faculty U. Chgo. Grad. Sch. Bus., 1958-69, prof. indsl. relations, 1963-69; asst. sec. for manpower Dept. Labor, 1969-70; exec. dir. Cost of Living Council; also spl. asst. to Pres. Nixon, 1971; Gladys C. and Isidore Brown prof. urban and labor econs. U. Chgo., 1971-73; former provost Carnegie-Mellon U.; dean Carnegie-Mellon U. (Grad. Sch. Indsl. Adminstrn.), prof. labor econs. and pub. policy, 1973-80; pres. U. Colo., Boulder, 1980-85, Northwestern U., Evanston, Ill., 1985-95, chancellor, 1995-98, pres. emeritus, 1998—. Cons. union, mgmt. and govt. agys., 1960—; cons. Dept. Labor, 1965; mem. Pres.'s Adv. Com. Labor Mgmt. Policy, 1964, Orgn. Econ. Coop. and Devel., 1987; vice chmn. Sec. Labor Task Force Improving Employment Svcs., 1965; chmn. rsch. adv. com. U.S. Employment Svc., 1966; assoc. dir. OMB Exec. Office of Pres., 1970—71; chmn. Presdl. R.R. Emergency Bd., 1982; trustee Com. for Econ. Devel., Nat. Multiple Sclerosis Soc.; bd. dirs. Aon Corp., Burlington No./Santa Fe, Inc., Tribune Corp., Deere & Co., Diamond Tech. Ptnrs. Inc.; asst. sec. manpower U.S. Dept. Labor, 1969—70. Contbr. articles to profl. jours. Trustee Aspen Inst. Laureate, Lincoln Acad. Ill.; Ford Found. Faculty Rsch. fellow, 1964-65. Mem. Am. Acad. Arts and Scis., Indsl. Rels. Rsch. Assn., Nat. Acad. Pub. Adminstrn., Comml. Club Chgo. (pres., civic com. 1995-2000), Econ. Club Chgo. (pres. 1995-97), Phi Beta Kappa. Jewish Office: Northwestern U Office of Pres Emeritus 555 Clark St 209 Evanston IL 60208-0805 E-mail: arnold-weber@nwu.edu.

WEBER, ARTHUR, magazine executive; b. Chgo., Feb. 1, 1926; s. Philip and Mary (Arlinsky) W.; m. Sylvia Zollinger, Aug. 19, 1950; children—Randy, Lori. Student, Ill. Inst. Tech., 1943-44; BSEE, Northwestern U., 1946. Elec. design engr. Corn Products Refining Co., 1946-48, Naess & Murphy, archs. and engrs., Chgo., 1949-51, Ford Motor Co., 1952-53, Skidmore, Owings & Merill, Chgo., 1954-57, Shaw, Metz & Dolio, Chgo., 1958-59; pres. Consumers Digest mag., 1959—; pub. Money Maker mag. (name changed to Your Money mag., 1991), 1979-97, pres., 1997—; pub. U. Chgo. Better Health Letter, 1995-96, pres., 1997—. Served with USNR, 1944-46.

WEBER, DANIEL E. association executive; b. Chgo., July 6, 1940; BS in Bus. Mgmt., DePaul U., 1962. Asst. to exec. dir. Am. Oil Chemists Soc., Chgo., 1962-67; administrv. mgr. Inst. Food Tech, 1967-69, dir. conv. svcs., 1969-79, dir. mktg. and meetings, 1979-91; exec. dir. Inst. Food Technologists, 1991-99, exec. v.p., CEO, 1999—. Chmn. 25th Anniversary Com. City of Rolling Meadows, 2 term ind. mem. city coun., chmn. every major com., street dedicated "Weber Drive"; officer Crusade of Mercy; bd. dirs., treas., v.p. Northwest Mental Health Assn., Disting. Svc. award. Named Meeting Planner of Yr. Assn. Conv. Ops. Mgmt., 1990. Mem. Internat. Assn. Exposition Mgrs. (charter cert. exposition mgr., v.p. 1987, pres. 1988, nat. bd. mem., chair Midwestern chpt., awards com. 1998—, chair scholarship com. 2000), Nat. Assn. Exposition Mgrs. (bd. dirs., officer, pres. 1988, v.p. 1987, cert. exposition mgr.), Am. Soc. Assn. Execs., Trade Show Bur. (bd. dirs. 1987—), Coun. Engring. and Sci. Soc. Exec. (conv. liaison coun. del. 1980-81, program chmn. meetings, expositions), Profl. Conv. Mgmt. Assn. (bd. dirs. 1992, 93), Conv. Liaison Coun. (task force on reorganization), Chgo. Soc. Assn. Execs. (chmn. directory advt., chmn. membership svcs. com., chmn. awards com.). Avocation: golf. Office: Inst of Food Techs 525 W Van Buren St Ste 1000 Chicago IL 60607-3814 E-mail: info@ift.org.

WEBER, GEORGE, oncology and pharmacology researcher, educator; b. Budapest, Hungary, Mar. 29, 1922; came to U.S., 1959; s. Salamon and Hajnalka (Arvai) W.; m. Catherine Elizabeth Forrest, June 30, 1958; children: Elizabeth Dolly Arvai, Julie Vibert Wallace, Jefferson James. BA, Queen's U., 1950, MD, 1952; MD (hon.), U. Chieti, Italy, 1979, Med. Faculty, Budapest, 1982, U. Leipzig, Fed. Republic of Germany, 1987, Tokushima (Japan) U., 1988, Kagawa (Japan) U., 1992. Rsch. assoc. Montreal Cancer Inst., 1953-59; prof. pharmacology Ind. U. Sch. Medicine, Indpls., 1959—; dir. Lab for Exptl. Oncology Sch. Medicine, Ind. U., 1974—; Milan Panič prof. oncology Ind. U., 1994—, Wellcome prof., 1995—; prof. Lab. for Exptl. Oncology Sch. Medicine, Ind. U., 1974-90, disting. prof. Lab. for Exptl. Oncology, 1990—. Chmn. study sect. USPHS, Washington, 1976-78; sci. adv. com. Am. Cancer Soc., N.Y.C., 1972-76, 94—, Damon Runyon Fund, N.Y.C., 1971-76; mem. U.S. Nat. Com., Internat. Union Against Cancer, Washington, 1974-80, 90-94, NAS, Washington, 1974-80, 90-94, U.S. Army Med. Rsch. & Breast Cancer Rsch. Program, 1996-97; prof. Brit. cancer campaign U. Oxford, Oxford, Eng., 2001; vis. prof. U. Bologna, Italy, 2001-02. Editor: Advances in Enzyme Regulation, Vols. 1-43, 1962—; assoc. editor Jour. Cancer Rsch., 1969-80, 82-89. Recipient Alecce Prize for cancer rsch. Tiberine Acad., Rome, 1971, Best Prof. award Student AMA, Indpls., 1966, 68, G.F. Gallanti prize for enzymology Internat. Soc. Clin. Chemists, 1984, Outstanding Investigator award Nat. Cancer Inst., NIH, 1986-94, Semmelweis medal & diploma Budapest, Hungary, 2001, medal Gastroenterological Soc., Aliga, Hungary, 2001, Prestigious External Award Recognition Ind. U., Indpls., Ind., 2002. Mem. Am. Soc. for Pharmacology and Exptl. Therapeutics, Am. Assn. Cancer Rsch. (G.H.A. Clowes award 1982), Russian Acad. Sci. (hon.), Hungarian Cancer Soc. (hon.), Hungarian Acad. Scis. (hon.), Acad. Scis. Bologna (Italy) (hon.). Home: 7307 Lakeside Dr Indianapolis IN 46278-1618 Office: Ind U Sch Medicine Lab Exptl Oncology 699 West Dr Indianapolis IN 46202-5119

WEBER, GLORIA RICHIE, retired minister, retired state legislator; married; 4 children. BA, Washington U., St. Louis; MA, MDiv, Eden Theol. Sem. Ordained to ministry Evang. Luth. Ch. Am., 1974. Family life educator Luth. Family and Children's Svcs. Mo.; mem. Mo. Ho. of Reps., 1993-94. Mo. state organizer, dir. comm. Mainstream Voters C.A.R.E., 1995. Editor: Interfaith Voices for Peace and Justice, 1996—. Exec. dir. Older Women's League, 1990—95. Named Woman of the Yr., Variety Club, 1978, Woman of Worth, Older Women's League, 1993; recipient Woman of Achievement award, St. Louis Globe-Dem., 1977, Unselfish Cmty. Svc. award, St. Louis Sentinel Newspaper, 1985, Faith in Action award, Luth. Svcs. St. Louis, 1994. Mem.: Phi Beta Kappa. Democrat. Office: 475 E Lockwood Saint Louis MO 63119 Fax: 314-892-1225. E-mail: gloriaweber8@netscape.net.

WEBER, HANNO, architect; b. Barranquilla, Colombia, Sept. 24, 1937; came to U.S., 1952; s. Hans and Ester (Oks) W. BA magna cum laude, Princeton U., 1959, MArch, 1961. Registered architect, Ill., Fla., Mo., Pa., N.J., Va. Urban designer, research assoc. Guayana project MIT and Harvard U., Caracas, Venezuela, 1961-63; project architect Paul Schweikher Assocs., Pitts., 1963-67; asst. prof. architecture Princeton U., 1967-73; assoc. prof. architecture Washington U., St. Louis, 1973-80; sr. design architect, studio head, assoc. Skidmore, Owings & Merrill, Chgo., 1980-83; prin. Hanno Weber & Assocs., 1984—. Vis. lectr. Escuela Nacional de Arquitectura Universidad Nacional de Mex., 1975; rsch. assoc. Rsch. Ctr. Urban and Environ. Planning, Princeton, N.J., 1967-70; project dir. The Cmty. Design Workshop, Washington U. Sch. Architecture, St. Louis, 1973-78; prof. architecture U. Wis., Milw., 1983—. Contbr. articles to profl. jours. Mem. Pres.'s Commn. on Education of Women Princeton U., 1968-69. Fellow NEH, 1970, Graham Found., 1973; 1st prize winner Flagler Dr. Waterfront Master Plan design competition, West Palm Beach, Fla., 1984; 1st prize winner Mcpl. Ctr. design competition, Leesburg, Va., 1987; finalist Okla. City Meml. Internat. design competition, 1997; Chgo. AIA Disting. Bldg. award Citation of Merit, Altamira, Terrace, Highland Park, Fla., 1987. Mem. AIA (Urban Design award Mcpl. Govt. Ctr., Leesburg, Va., 1992, Chgo. AIA Interior Architecture award citation of merit, Mcpl. Govt. Ctr., Leesburg, 1992), The Arch. Assn., Phi Beta Kappa. Office: Hanno Weber & Assocs 417 S Dearborn St Chicago IL 60605-1120 E-mail: weber@hannoweber.com.

WEBER, HERMAN JACOB, federal judge; b. Lima, Ohio, May 20, 1927; s. Herman Jacob and Ada Minola (Esterly) W.; m. Barbara L. Rice, May 22, 1948; children: Clayton, Deborah. BA, Otterbein Coll., 1949; JD summa cum laude, Ohio State U., 1951. Bar: Ohio 1952, U.S. Dist. Ct. (so. dist.) Ohio 1954. Ptnr. Weber & Hogue, Fairborn, Ohio, 1952-61; judge Fairborn Mayor's Ct., 1956-58; acting judge Fairborn Mcpl. Ct., 1958-60; judge Greene County Common Pleas Ct., Xenia, Ohio, 1961-82, Ohio Ct. Appeals (2d dist.), Dayton, 1982-85, U.S. Dist. Ct. (so. dist.) Ohio, Cin., 1985—. Chmn. Sixth Cir. Dist. Judges Conf., 1988, Ohio Jud. Conf., Columbus, 1980-82; pres. Ohio Common Pleas Judges Assn., Columbus, 1975. Vice-mayor City of Fairborn, 1955-57, council mem., 1955-59. Served with USNR, 1945-46. Office: US Dist Ct 801 100 E 5th St Cincinnati OH 45202-3905

WEBER, JAY, radio personality; b. Wis. B English, Boradcast and Print Journalism, U. Wis., 1988. Cert. tchr. Wis. Anchor, reporter WTDY AM, Madison, Wis., 1988—90; radio host 1130 WISN, Greenfield, 1990—. Office: WISN Radio 12100 W Howard Ave Greenfield WI 53228*

WEBER, KENNETH J. hotel executive; b. 1946; With Arthur Young & Co., N.Y.C., 1968-71, ITT-Grinnell Corp., Providence, 1971-73, Farmbest Foods Internat., Jacksonville, 1973-74; regional contr. Marriott Corp., Washington, 1974-76, group contr., 1976-77, divsn. contr., 1977-79, pres., CEO Farrell's Ice Cream divsn., 1983-86; exec. v.p., CFO Isaly Co., Pitts., 1979-80; v.p., contr. Country Kitchens Internat. divsn. Carlson Cos., Inc., Mpls., 1980-81; sr. v.p. Poppin Fresh Restaurant divsn. Pillsbury Co., 1981-83; sr. v.p., corp. contr. Red Lion Hotels Corp., Vancouver, Wash., 1987-92; sr. v.p., CFO Omni Hotels Corp., Hampton, N.H., 1992—; also v.p., treas. Omni Ctr. Corp., Richmond, Va. Office: 3750 E Turtle Hatch Rd Springfield MO 65809-4143

WEBER, MARK F. medical executive; MS, Wash. U., St. Louis, 1981. Pres., CEO St. John's Mercy Med. Ctr., 1995—. Office: 615 S New Ballas Rd Saint Louis MO 63141-8221

WEBER, RANDY, publishing executive; Assoc. pub. Consumers Digest and Your Money mags., pub., 1993—. Office: Consumers Digest 6th Fl 8001 Lincoln Ave Fl 6 Skokie IL 60077-3695

WEBER, ROBERT CARL, lawyer; b. Chester, Pa., Dec. 18, 1950; s. Robert Francis and Lucille (Nobili) W.; m. Linda Brediger, June 30, 1972; children: Robert F., Mary Therese, David P., Joseph T. BA cum laude, Yale U., 1972; JD, Duke U., 1976. Bar: Ohio 1976, U.S. Dist. ct. (no. dist.) Ohio 1976, U.S. Ct. Claims 1980, U.S. Ct. Appeals (6th cir.) 1981, U.S. Ct. Appeals (5th cir.) 1995. Assoc. Jones, Day, Reavis & Pogue, Cleve., 1976-83, ptnr., 1983—. Bd. dirs. United Way Svcs. of Cleve., 1992—. Fellow Am. Coll. Trial Lawyers; mem. Ohio Bar Assn., Am. Law Inst., Product Liability Adv. Coun., Cleve. Bar Assn. (chmn. jud. selection com. 1985-86, trustee 1990-93, pres.-elect 1994-95, pres. 1995-96), Jud. Conf. for 8th Jud. Dist. Ohio (life), Order of Coif. Roman Catholic. Office: Jones Day Reavis & Pogue 901 Lakeside Ave E Cleveland OH 44114-1190 E-mail: rcweber@jonesday.com.

WEBER, ROBERT R. state legislator; b. Nov. 19, 1925; m. Shirley V. Roe, 1948; children: Mary, Anthony, Kathleen, William. State rep. dist. 6 State of S.D., state rep. dist. 4, 1993—. Mem. agriculture and natural resources and local govt. coms. S.D. Ho. of Reps.; farmer, rancher. Supr. Twp. Sch. Bd. Mem. S.D. Farmer's Union (state dir.), Nat. Farmers Orgn., Am. Agriculture Assn., K.C. Republican. Office: SD Ho of Reps State Capitol Pierre SD 57501 Home: 16955 US Highway 212 Clear Lake SD 57226-5141

WEBER, SHARI, state legislator; b. Owatonna, Minn., July 1, 1953; m. Marvin E. Weber. Student, St. John;s Acad. and Coll., Moorhead State U. Dir. downtown devel. Herington (Kans.) Main St. Program, Herington, Kans., 1993-97; rep. Dist. 68 Kans. State Ho. of Reps., Topeka. Address: 934 Union Rd Herington KS 67449-8605

WEBER, STEVEN A. religious organization executive; BSBA, U. Wis. Chartered life underwriter. Actuary, 2d v.p. corp. sys. svcs., v.p. corp. technology Aid Assn. Lutherans, Appleton, 1975—, sr. v.p. mktg. Wis. Bd. dirs. Harbor House shelter, Appleton; treas. Appleton Area Coun. Chs. Fellow Soc. Actuaries; mem. Am. Acad. Actuaries. Office: Aid Assn Lutherans 4321 N Ballard Rd Appleton WI 54913-7729

WEBER, WALTER JACOB, JR. engineering educator; b. Pitts., June 16, 1934; Sc.B., Brown U., 1956; M.S.E., Rutgers U., 1959; A.M., Harvard, 1961, Ph.D., 1962. Registered profl. engr. Diplomate Am. Acad. Environ. Engrs. Engr. Caterpillar Tractor Co., Peoria, Ill., 1956-57; instr. Rutgers U., 1957-59; engr. Soil Conservation Service, New Brunswick, N.J., 1957-59; research, teaching asso. Harvard, 1959-63; faculty U. Mich., Ann Arbor, 1963—, prof., chmn. water resources program, 1968-91, The Earnest Boyce Disting. Prof. of Engring., 1987-94, The Gordon Maskew Fair and Earnest Boyce Disting. U. Prof., 1994—; dir. Inst. Environ. Scis., Engring. & Tech. Great Lakes & Mid-Atlantic Hazardous Substance Rsch. Ctr. Internat. cons. to industry, govt. Author: (with K.H. Mancy) Analysis of Industrial Wastewaters, 1971, Physicochemical Processes for Water Quality Control, 1972, (with F.A. DiGiano) Process Dynamics in Environmental Systems, 1996, Environmental Systems and Processes-Principles, Modeling and Design, 2001; editor, author: (with E. Matijevic) Adsorption from Aqueous Solution, 1968; contbr. numerous articles and chpts. to tech. and profl. jours. and books. Recipient Disting. Faculty awards U. Mich., 1967, 78, Rsch. Excellence award, 1980, Stephen S. Attwood award, 1977; Disting. Faculty award Mich. chpt. Assn. Gov. Bds. of State Univs., 1989; Disting. Scientist award U.S. EPA, 1991; Athalie Richardson Irvine Clarke prize Nat. Water Rsch. Inst., 1996. Mem. NAE, Am. Acad. Environ. Engrs. (Diplomate 1975, Gordon Maskew Fair award, 1995), Am. Chem. Soc. (cert. of merit 1962, F.J. Zimmerman award 1982), Am. Inst. Chem. Engrs., ASCE (Rudolph Hering medal 1980, Thomas R. Camp award 1982, Simon W. Freese award 1984, G. Brooks Earnest award 1985), Am. Water Works Assn. (life, Acad. Achievement awards 1981, 89, A.P. Black Rsch. award 1991), Assn. Environ. Engring. Profs. (Disting. Faculty award 1968, NALCO rsch. award 1979, Engring. Sci. rsch. award 1984, Outstanding Publ. award 1989, Disting. Lectr. award 1990), Internat. Assn. for Water Pollution Rsch. and COntrol (Founders Outstanding Publ. award 1987, 92), Water Pollution Control Fedn. (John R. Rumsey Meml. award 1975, Willard F. Shepard award 1980, Thomas R. Camp medal 1988, Gordon Maskew Fair medal 1990), Tau Beta Pi, Sigma Xi, Chi Epsilon, Delta Omega. Home: PO Box 7775 Ann Arbor MI 48107-7775 Office: U Mich Coll Engring Environ Engring Program Ste 181 EWRE Bldg Ann Arbor MI 48109-2125 E-mail: wjwjr@umich.edu.

WEBER, WENDELL WILLIAM, pharmacologist; b. Maplewood, Mo., Sept. 2, 1925; s. Theodore William and Flora Ann (Holt) W.; m. La Donna Tavis, Sept. 29, 1952; children— Jane Holt, Theodore Wendell. AB, Central Coll., 1945; PhD in Phys. Chemistry, Northwestern U., 1950; MD, U. Chgo., 1959. Diplomate Am. Bd. Pediatrics; lic. Mich., N.Y., Calif. Asst. prof. chemistry U. Tenn., Knoxville, 1949-51; mem. ops. research staff U.S. Army Chem. Center, Edgewood, Md., 1951-55; successively instr., asst. prof., asso. prof., prof. pharmacology N.Y. U. Sch. Medicine, N.Y.C., 1963-74; prof. U. Mich., Ann Arbor, 1974-98, Disting. lectureship in Biomedical Rsch., 1993, emeritus prof., 1998—; Disting. lectureship Ctr. for Environ. Genetics U. Cin., 1997. Mem. pharmacology-toxicology com. NIH, 1969-73, rev. coms., 1968— Mem. editl. bd. Bioessays, 1984-91, Pharmacogenetics, 1990—; author: Pharmacogenetics, 1997, The Acetylator Genes and Drug Response, 1987. NIH spl. fellow, 1962-65; research grantee, 1967—; recipient Career Scientist awards N.Y.C. Health Research Council, 1965-70, 70-74 Fellow N.Y. Acad. Scis.; mem. Am. Soc. Pharmacology and Therapeutics, Am. Chem. Soc., Am. Soc. Human

Genetics, Soc. Toxicology (hon.), AAAS, Sigma Xi, Phi Lambda Upsilon. Achievements include research specialty in pharmacogenetics. Home: 14 Geddes Hts Ann Arbor MI 48104-1724 Office: Dept Pharmacology U Mich Ann Arbor MI 48109-0632 E-mail: wwweber@umich.edu.

WEBSTER, JAMES RANDOLPH, JR. physician; b. Chgo., Aug. 25, 1931; s. James Randolph and Ruth Marian (Burtis) W.; m. Joan Burchfield, Dec. 28, 1954; children: Susan, Donovan, John. B.S., U. Chgo.-Northwestern U., 1953; M.D., M.S., Northwestern U., 1956. Diplomate: Am. Bd. Internal Medicine (sub bd. pulmonary disease and geriatrics). Intern Phila. Gen. Hosp., 1956-57; resident in medicine Northwestern U., 1957-60, NIH fellow in pulmonary disease, 1962-64; chief medicine Northwestern Meml. Hosp., Chgo., 1976—88; prof. medicine Northwestern U. Med. Sch., 1977—2002, chief gen. med. sect. Dept. Medicine, 1987-88; chief exec. officer Northwestern Med. Group Practice, 1978-88; dir. Buehler Ctr. on Aging Northwestern U. Med. Ctr., 1988-2000. Chief staff Northwestern Meml. Hosp., 1988-90. Contbr. chpts. to books, articles to med. jours. Capt. U.S. Army, 1960-62. Recipient Outstanding Clin. tchr. award Northwestern U. Med. Sch., 1974, 77, 84, 86, Alumni Merit award Northwestern U., 1979, Henry P. Russe-Inst. of Medicine award for exemplary compassion in health care, 1997, Aeschulapian award as Physician of Yr., Anti Defamation League, 1998. Master: ACP (gov. for Ill. 1988—92, chair sub-com. on aging 1993, Clayppole award 1994); mem.: Ill. Geriatrics Soc. (pres. 1992—94, chair Ill. ad hoc com. to defend health care), Am. Geriatrics Soc., Inst. Medicine Chgo. (pres. 2002—), Alpha Omega Alpha. Home: Apt 6C 227 E Delaware Pl Chicago IL 60611-7758 Office: Buehler Ctr on Aging Ste 601 750 N Lake Shore Dr Chicago IL 60611-4403 E-mail: j.webster@northwestern.edu.

WEBSTER, JOHN GOODWIN, biomedical engineering educator, researcher; b. Plainfield, N.J., May 27, 1932; s. Franklin Folger and Emily Sykes (Boody) W.; m. Nancy Egan, Dec. 27, 1954; children: Paul, Robin, Mark, Lark BEE, Cornell U., 1953; MSEE, U. Rochester, 1965, PhD, 1967. Engr. North American Aviation, Downey, Calif., 1954-55; engr. Boeing Airplane Co., Seattle, 1955-59, Radiation Inc., Melbourne, Fla., 1959-61; staff engr. Mitre Corp., Bedford, Mass., 1961-62, IBM Corp., Kingston, N.Y., 1962-63; asst. prof. elec. engring. U. Wis., Madison, 1967-70, assoc. prof. elec. engring., 1970-73, prof. elec. and computer engring., 1973-99, prof. biomed. engring., 1999—. Author: (with others) Medicine and Clinical Engineering, 1977, Sensors and Signal Conditioning, 1991, 2d edit., 2001, Analog Signal Processing, 1999; editor: Medical Instrumentation: Application and Design, 1978, 1998, Clinical Engineering: Principles and Practices, 1979, Design of Microcomputer-Based Medical Instrumentation, 1981, Therapeutic Medical Devices: Application and Design, 1982; Electronic Devices for Rehabilitation, 1985; Interfacing Sensors to the IBM-PC, 1988, Encyclopedia of Medical Devices and Instrumentation, 1988, Tactile Sensors for Robotics and Medicine, 1988, Electrical Impedance Tomography, 1990, Teaching Design in Electrical Engineering, 1990, Prevention of Pressure Sores, 1991, Design of Cardiac Pacemakers, 1995, Design of Pulse Oximeters, 1997, The Measurement Instrumentation, and Sensors Handbook, 1999, Encyclopedia of Electrical and Electronics Engineering, 1999, Mechanical Variables Measurement, 2000, Minimally Invasive Medical Technology, 2001. Recipient Rsch. Career Devel. award NIH, 1971-76; NIH fellow, 1963-67; recipient Western Electric Fund award Am. Soc. Engring. Edn., 1978, Best Reference Work award, 1999, Theo C. Pilkington Outstanding Educator award, 1994, IEEE-EMBS Career Achievement award, 2001. Fellow IEEE (3d Millenium medal 2000, Career achievement award 2001), Am. Inst. Med. and Biol. Engring., Inst. Physics, Instrument Soc. Am. (Donald P. Eckman Edn. award 1974), Assn. for Advancement Med. Instrumentation (Found. Laufman-Greatbatch prize 1996). Office: Univ Wis Dept Biomed Engring 1415 Engineering Dr Madison WI 53706-1607 E-mail: webster@engr.wisc.edu.

WEBSTER, LESLIE TILLOTSON, JR. pharmacologist, educator; b. N.Y.C., Mar. 31, 1926; s. Leslie Tillotson and Emily (de Forest) W.; m. Alice Katharine Holland, June 24, 1955; children— Katharine White, Susan Holland Webster Van Drie, Leslie Tillotson III, Romi Anne. B.A., Amherst Coll., 1947, Sc.D. (hon.), 1982; student, Union Coll., 1944; M.D., Harvard U., 1948. Diplomate: Am. Bd. Internal Medicine. Rotating intern Cleve. City Hosp., 1948-49, jr. asst. resident in medicine, 1949-50; asst. resident medicine Bellevue Hosp., N.Y.C., 1952-53; research fellow medicine Harvard and Boston City Hosp. Thorndike Meml. Lab., 1953-55; from demonstrator to instr. medicine Sch. of Medicine Western Res. U., 1955-60; research assoc. to sr. instr. biochemistry Case Western Res. U. Sch. Medicine, 1959-60, asst. prof. medicine, 1960-70, asst. prof. biochemistry, 1960-65, asst. prof. pharmacology, 1965-67, asso. prof., 1967-70, prof. pharmacology, 1976-92, chmn. pharmacology dept., 1976-91, prof. pharmacology dept. emeritus, 1992, prof. medicine, 1980-86. Prof., chmn. pharmacology dept. Northwestern U. Med. and Dental Sch., 1970-76; dir. med. scientist tng. program Case Western Res. U. Sch. Medicine, 1979-92. Served to lt. med. corps. USNR, 1950-52. Russell M. Wilder fellow Nat. Vitamin Found., 1956-59; Sr. USPHS Research fellow, 1959-61; Research Career Devel. awardee, 1961-69; Macy faculty scholar, 1980-81 Mem. ACP (life), Central Soc. Clin. Rsch. Coalition (emeritus), Am. Soc. Clin. Investigation (emeritus), Am. Soc. Biochemistry and Molecular Biology (emeritus), Assn. Med. Sch. Pharmacology (emeritus), Am. Soc. Pharmacology and Exptl. Therapeutics (emeritus), Alpha Omega Alpha (hon.). Home: 12546 Cedar Rd No 4 Cleveland Heights OH 44106-3294 Office: Univ Hosps of Cleve Rainbow Babies and Childrens Hosp 2074 Abington Rd Cleveland OH 44106-2602 E-mail: itwjr@aol.com.

WEBSTER, LOIS SHAND, association executive; b. Springfield, Ill., Sept. 25, 1929; d. Richings James and C. Odell (Gilbert) S.; m. Terrance Ellis Webster, Feb. 12, 1954 (dec. July 1985); children: Terrance Richings, Bruce Douglas, Andrew Michael. BA, Millikin U., 1951; cert. in libr. tech., Coll. Du Page County, Glen Ellyn, Ill., 1974; postgrad. libr. sci., No. Ill. U., 1977-82. Exec. asst. Am. Nuclear Soc., La Grange Park, Ill., 1973—. Contbr. articles and book chpts. to profl. publs. Field dir. Springfield coun. Girl Scouts U.S., 1951-54; libr. advisor Du Page County coun. Girl Scouts U.S., 1973-74. Recipient Octave J. Du Temple award Am. Nuclear Soc., 1989. Mem. Spl. Librs. Assn. (divsn. chmn. 1984-85, chmn. by-laws com. 1987-89, bd. dirs. 1989-92, sec. 1990-91, visioning com. 1992—), Coun. Engring. and Sci. Soc. Execs., Am. Soc. Assn. Execs., Met. Chgo. Libr. Assembly (bd. dirs. 1982-85). Avocations: travel, genealogy. Home: 5383 Newport St Lisle IL 60532-4126 Office: Am Nuclear Soc 555 N Kensington Ave La Grange Park IL 60526-5535

WEBSTER, STEPHEN BURTIS, physician, educator; b. Chgo., Dec. 3, 1935; s. James Randolph Webster and Ruth Marion (Burtis) Holmes; m. Katherine Griffith Webster, Apr. 4, 1959; children: David Randolph, Margaret Elizabeth, James Lucian. BS, Northwestern U., 1957, MD, 1960. Diplomate Am. Bd. Dermatology (bd. dirs. 1992—, v.p. 1997-98, pres.). Intern Colo. Gen. Hosp., Denver, 1960-61; resident Walter Reed Gen. Hosp., Washington, 1962-65; staff physician Henry Ford Hosp., Detroit, 1969-71, Gundersen Clinic, La Crosse, 1971—; assoc. clin. prof. U. Wis., Madison, 1976—; clin. prof. U. Minn., Mpls., 1978—. Lt. col. U.S. Army, 1962-69. Fellow Am. Acad. Dermatology (sec.-treas. 1985-88, pres. 1991); mem. AMA, Am. Dermatol. Assn. (pres. 1996-97), Am. Bd. Dermatology (v.p. 1997-98, pres. 1999-2000, assoc. exec. dir. 2001—), Wis. Med. Soc., La Crosse County Med. Soc., Soc. Investigative Dermatology, Alpha Omega Alpha. Republican. Congregationalist. Avocations: bagpipes, model R.R. Home: N2062 Wedgewood Dr E La Crosse WI 54601-7175 Office: Gundersen Clinic Ltd 1836 South Ave La Crosse WI 54601-5494

WEDL, ROBERT J. state agency commissioner; BEd, MEd, St. Cloud State U. From acting commr. to asst. commr. Minn. Dept. Children, Families, Learning, St. Paul, commr., 1996—. Address: State Dept of Chidren, Families 1500 Highway 36 W Saint Paul MN 55113-4035

WEEKLY, JOHN WILLIAM, insurance company executive; b. Sioux City, Iowa, June 21, 1931; s. John E. Weekly and Alyce Beatrice (Preble) Nichols; children: John William Jr., Thomas Patrick, Michael Craig, James Matthew, Daniel Kevin. Grad. high sch., Omaha. V.p. First Data Resources, Inc., Omaha, 1969-74, Mut. of Omaha/United of Omaha Ins. Co., Omaha, 1974-81, sr. exec. v.p., 1981-87, pres., COO, 1987-95, vice chmn., pres., COO, 1995, vice chmn., pres., CEO, 1996-97, vice chmn., CEO, 1997, chmn., CEO, 1998—. Chmn. bd. dirs. Companiion Life Ins. Co., Mutual Omaha Investor Svcs., Inc., United World Life Ins. Co.; bd. dirs. Innowave, Inc., Kirkpatrick Pettis, Omaha Property and Casualty Ins. Co., Midwest Express Airlines, Inc., 1995—, Cabelas, Inc., 2000—. Bd. govs. Ak-Sar-Ben, 2001—; Bd. dirs. Omaha Zool. Soc. , 1992, Avera St. Luke's Hosp., 1999. Mem.: Greater Omaha C. of C. (bd. dirs. 1991—96), Health Ins. Assn. Am. 1992—96, (chmn. 1996), Am. Coun. Life Ins. (bd. dirs. 1995—98, 2001—). Avocations: fishing, golf, hunting. Office: Mut Omaha Ins Co Mutual Omaha Plz Omaha NE 68175-0001

WEEKS, A. RAY, real estate company executive; Co-chmn., pres., COO Duke-Weeks Realty Corp., Indpls., 1994—. Office: Duke-Weeks Realty Corp Ste 100 600 E 96th St Indianapolis IN 46240-3792

WEEKS, STEVEN WILEY, lawyer; b. Topeka, Mar. 7, 1950; s. Glen Wiley and Grace Aileen (West) W.; m. Lee Nordgren, Aug. 1, 1974 (div. 1985); 1 child, Kirstin Nordgren. BS summa cum laude, Washburn U., 1972; JD cum laude, Harvard U., 1977. Bar: Ohio. Project leader Nat. Sanitation Found., Ann Arbor, Mich., 1972; engr. Kans. Dept. Health and Environ., Topeka, 1972-74; ptnr. Taft, Stettinius & Hollister, Cin., 1977—. Dir. The Myers Y. Cooper Co., Cin.; adj. faculty Chase Coll. Law, 1987-88. Mem. adv. com. prosecuting atty., Hamilton County, Cin., 1992; mem. Hamilton County Rep. Ctrl. Com., 1994—. Mem. Ohio State Bar Assn., Cin. Bar Assn. Republican. Methodist. Avocations: computers, golf. Home: 3641 Michigan Ave Cincinnati OH 45208-1411

WEERTMAN, JOHANNES, materials science educator; b. Fairfield, Ala., May 11, 1925; s. Roelof and Christina (van Vlaardingen) W.; m. Julia Ann Randall, Feb. 10, 1950; children: Julia Ann, Bruce Randall. Student, Pa. State Coll., 1943-44; BS, Carnegie Inst. Tech. (now Carnegie Mellon U.), 1948, DSc, 1951; postgrad., Ecole Normale Superieure, Paris, 1951-52. Solid State physicist U.S. Naval Rsch. Lab., Washington, 1952-58, cons., 1960-67; sci. liaison officer U.S. Office Naval Rsch., Am. Embassy, London, 1958-59; faculty Northwestern U., Evanston, Ill., 1959—, prof. materials sci. dept., 1961-68, chmn. dept., 1964-68, prof. geol. scis. dept., 1963—, Walter P. Murphy prof. materials sci. and engring. emeritus, 1999—. Vis. prof. geophysics Calif. Inst. Tech., 1964, Scott Polar Rsch. Inst., Cambridge (Eng.) U., 1970-71, Swiss Fed. Inst. Reactor Rsch., 1986; cons. Cold Regions Rsch. and Engring. Lab., U.S. Army, 1960-75, Oak Ridge (Tenn.) Nat. Lab., 1963-67, Los Alamos (N.Mex.) Sci. Lab., 1967—; co-editor materials sci. books MacMillan Co., 1962-76. Author: Dislocation Based Fracture Mechanics, 1996, (with Julia Weertman) Elementary Dislocation Theory, 1964, 2d edit., 1992; mem. editorial bd. Metal. Trans., 1967-75, Jour. Glaciology, 1972—; assoc. editor Jour. Geophys. Rsch., 1973-75, 2000-01; contbr. articles to profl. jours. With USMC, 1943-46. Honored with naming of Weertman Island in Antarctica.; Fulbright fellow, 1951-52; recipient Acta Metallurgica gold medal, 1980; Guggenheim fellow, 1970-71 Fellow Am. Acad. Arts and Scis., Am. Soc. Metals, Am. Phys. Soc., Geol. Soc. Am., Am. Geophys. Union (Horton award 1972, AIME Mathewson Gold medal 1977); mem. AAAS, NAE, Am. Inst. Physics, Internat. Glaciol. Soc. (Seligman Crystal award 1983), Arctic Inst., Am. Quaternary Assn., Explorers Club, Fulbright Assn., Sigma Xi, Tau Beta Pi, Phi Kappa Phi, Alpha Sigma Mu, Pi Mu Epsilon. Home: 834 Lincoln St Evanston IL 60201-2405 Office: Northwestern U Materials Sci Dept Evanston IL 60208-0001 E-mail: j-weertman2@nwu.edu.

WEERTMAN, JULIA RANDALL, materials science and engineering educator; b. Muskegon, Mich., Feb. 10, 1926; BS in Physics, Carnegie-Mellon U., 1946, MS in Physics, 1947, DSc in Physics, 1951. Physicist U.S. Naval Rsch. Lab., Washington, 1952-58; vis. asst. prof. dept. materials sci. and engring. Northwestern U., Evanston, Ill., 1972-73, asst. prof., 1973-78, from asst. prof. to assoc. prof., 1973-82, prof., 1982-99, Walter P. Murphy prof., 1989, chmn. dept., 1987-92, asst. to dean grad. studies and rsch. Tech. Inst., 1973-76, Walter P. Murphy prof. emeritus, 1999—. Mem. various NRC coms. and panels. Co-author: Elementary Dislocation Theory, 1964, 1992, also pub. in French, Japanese and Polish; contbr. numerous articles to profl. jours. Mem. Evanston Environ. Control Bd., 1972-79. Recipient Creativity award NSF, 1981, 86; Guggenheim Found. fellow, 1986-87. Fellow Am. Soc. Metals Internat., Minerals, Metals and Materials Soc. (leadership award 1997); mem. ASTM, NAE, Am. Acad. Arts and Scis., Am. Phys. Soc., Materials Rsch. Soc., Soc. Women Engrs. (disting. engring. educator award 1989, achievement award 1991). Home: 834 Lincoln St Evanston IL 60201-2405 Office: Northwestern U Dept Material Sci & Engring 2225 N Campus Dr Evanston IL 60208-0876 E-mail: jrweertman@northwestern.edu.

WEESE, BENJAMIN HORACE, architect; b. Evanston, Ill., June 4, 1929; s. Harry Ernest and Marjorie (Mohr) W.; m. Cynthia Rogers, July 5, 1963; children: Daniel Peter, Catharine Mohr. B.Arch., Harvard U., 1951, M.Arch., 1957; cert., Ecole des Beaux Arts, Fontainebleau, France, 1956. Assoc., Harry Weese & Assocs., Architects, Chgo., 1957-77; prin. Weese Langley Weese, 1977—. Co-founder, pres. Chgo. Arch. Found., Glessner House, Chgo., 1966— Trustee Graham Found. for Advanced Studies in Fine Arts, 1988—, pres. 1995-99; mem. Commn. Chgo. Landmarks, 1998—. Fellow AIA; mem. Nat. Council Archtl. Registration Bds. Home: 2133 N Hudson Ave Chicago IL 60614-4522 Office: Weese Langley Weese Ltd 9 W Hubbard St Chicago IL 60610-4630 E-mail: bweese@wlwltd.com.

WEESE, CYNTHIA ROGERS, architect, educator; b. Des Moines, June 23, 1940; d. Gilbert Taylor and Catharine (Wingard) Rogers; m. Benjamin H. Weese, July 5, 1963; children: Daniel Peter, Catharine Mohr. B.S.A.S., Washington U., St. Louis, 1962; B.Arch., Washington U., 1965. Registered architect, Ill. Pvt. practice architecture, Chgo., 1965-72, 74-77; draftsperson, designer Harry Weese & Assocs., 1972-74; prin. Weese Langley Weese Ltd., 1977—; design critic Ball State U., Muncie, Ind., Miami U., Oxford, Ohio, 1979, U. Wis.-Milw., 1980, U. Ill.-Chgo., 1981, 85, Iowa State U., Ames, 1982, Washington U., St. Louis, 1984, U. Ill., Champaign, 1987-92, Kans. State U., 1992; dean sch. architecture Washington U., St. Louis, 1993—. Bd. regents Am. Architecture Found., 1990-93; bd. mem. Landmarks Commn. St. Louis.; mem. Mayor's Task Force Downtown Now, St. Louis, 1997—. Recipient Alpha Rho Chi award Washington U., 1965, Met. Chgo. YWCA Outstanding Achievement award, 1990. Mem. AIA (bd. dirs. Chgo. chpt. 1980-83, v.p. 1983-85, 1st v.p. 1986-87, pres. 1987-88, regional dir. 1990-92, Disting. Bldg. awards 1977, 81-83, 86, 91, 95, Interior Architecture award 1981, 90, 92, nat. v.p. 1993, chmn. urban design task force St. Louis 2004 1997—), AIA/ACSA Coun. on Archtl. Rsch. (chair 1991-92), AIA Found. (pres. Chgo. chpt. 1988-89), Soc. Archtl. Historians (bd. dirs. 1992-94), Chgo. Women in Architecture, Chgo. Network, Nat. Inst. Archtl. Edn. (bd. dirs. 1988-90), Chgo. Archtl. Club (pres. 1988-89), Washington U. Sch. Architecture Alumni (nat. coun. 1988-93), Lambda Alpha. Democrat. Clubs: Arts, Chgo. Archtl. Office: Washington U Sch Architecture PO Box 1079 Saint Louis MO 63188-1079

WEFALD, JON, university president; b. Nov. 24, 1937; s. Olav and Walma (Ovrum) W.; m. Ruth Ann; children— Skipp, Andy. B.A., Pacific Lutheran U., Tacoma, 1959; M.A., Wash. State U., Pullman, 1961; Ph.D., U. Mich., Ann Arbor, 1965. Teaching asst. Wash. State U., Pullman, 1959—61; teaching fellow U. Mich., Ann Arbor, 1961—64; assoc. prof. Gustavus Adolphus Coll., St. Peter, Minn., 1965—70; commnr. agr. State of Minn., St. Paul, 1971—77; pres. Southwest State U., Marshall, 1977—82; chancellor Minn. State Univ. System, St. Paul, 1982—86; pres. Kans. State U., Manhattan, 1986—. Author: A Voice of Protest: Norwegians in American Politics 1890-1917, 1971. Mem. Mid-Am. Internat. Agri-Trade Council (pres. 1974-75), Midwest Assn. State Depts. of Agr. (sec.treas. 1976-77), U.S. Dept. Agr. Joint Council on Food and Agrl. Scis. Office: Kans State U Office of Pres 110 Anderson Hall Manhattan KS 66506-0100

WEFALD, SUSAN, state commissioner; m. Robert O. Wefald; children: Sarah, Kathryn, Tom. BA, U. Mich., 1969; postgrad., U. N.D. Licensed social worker; cert. consumer credit counselor. Elected mem. Bismarck Pub. Sch. Bd., pres.; commr. N.D. Pub. Svc. Commn. Mem. Energy Conservation Com., Com. Consumer Affairs Nat. Assn. Regulatory Utility Commrs.; sec. Mid Am. Regulatory Commn. Violinist, charter mem. Bismarck-Mandan Symphony Orch.; pres. Sakakawea Girl Scout Coun.; bd. dirs. Mo. Slope United Way. Office: ND Pub Svc Commn 600 E Boulevard Ave Bismarck ND 58505-0660 Fax: 701-328-2410.

WEG, JOHN GERARD, physician; b. N.Y.C., Feb. 16, 1934; s. Leonard and Pauline M. (Kanzleiter) W.; m. Mary Loretta Flynn, June 2, 1956; children: Diane Marie, Kathryn Mary, Carol Ann, Loretta Louise, Veronica Susanne, Michelle Celeste. BA cum laude, Coll. Holy Cross, Worcester, Mass., 1955; MD, N.Y. Med. Coll., 1959. Diplomate: Am. Bd. Internal Medicine. Commd. 2nd lt. USAF, 1958, advanced through grades to capt., 1967; intern Walter Reed Gen. Hosp., Washington, 1959-60; resident, then chief resident in internal medicine Wilford Hall USAF Hosp., Lackland AFB, Tex., 1960-64, chief pulmonary sect., 1964-66, chief inhalation sect., 1964-66, chief pulmonary and infectious disease service, 1966-67; resigned, 1967; clin. dir. pulmonary disease div. Jefferson Davis Hosp., Houston, 1967-71; from asst. prof. to assoc. prof. medicine Baylor U. Coll. Medicine, 1967-71; assoc. prof. medicine U. Mich. Med. Sch. Univ. Hosp., Ann Arbor, 1971-74, prof., 1974—2001, prof. emeritus, 2001—. Physician-in-charge pulmonary div., 1971-81, physician-in-charge pulmonary and critical care med. div., 1981-85; cons. Ann Arbor VA, 1971—, Wayne County Gen. hosps., 1971-84; mem. adv. bd. Washtenaw County Health Dept., 1973—; mem. respiratory and nervous system panel, anesthesiology Sect. Nat. Ctr. Devices and Radiol. Health, FDA, 1983—, chmn., 1985-88. Contbr. med. jours., reviewer, mem. editorial bds. Decorated Air Force Commendation medal; travelling fellow Nat. Tb and Respiratory Disease Assn., 1971; recipient Aesculpaius award Tex. Med. Assn., 1971 Fellow Am. Coll. Chest Physicians (chmn. bd. govs. 1976-79, gov. Mich. 1975-79, chmn. membership com. 1976-79, prof.-in-residence 1972—, chmn. critical care coun. 1982-85, chmn. ethics com. 1998), Am. Coll. Chest Physicians and Internat. Acad. Chest Physicians (exec. council 1976-82, pres. 1980-81), ACP (chmn. Mich. program com. 1974); mem. AAAS, Am. Fedn. Clin. Rsch., AMA, Am. Thoracic Soc. (sec.-treas. 1974-76), Am. Assn. Inhalation Therapy, Air Force Soc. Internists and Allied Specialists, Soc. Med. Consultants to Armed Forces, Internat. Union Against Tb, Mich. Thoracic Soc. (pres. 1976-78), Mich. Lung Assn. (dir., Bruce Douglas award 1981), Am. Lung Assn., Rsch. Club U. Mich., Assn. Advancement Med. Instrumentation, Central Soc. Clin. Rsch., Am. Bd. Internal Medicine (subsplty. com. on pulmonary disease 1980-86, critical care medicine test com. 1985-87, critical care medicine policy com. 1986-87), N.Y. Med. Coll. Alumni Assn. (medal of honor 1990), Alpha Omega Alpha. Home: 3060 Exmoor Rd Ann Arbor MI 48104-4132 Office: B I H 245 Box 0026 1500 E Medical Center Dr Ann Arbor MI 48109-0005 E-mail: jweg@umich.edu.

WEGMAN, MYRON EZRA, physician, educator; b. Bklyn., July 23, 1908; s. Max and Nettie (Finkelstein) W.; m. Isabel Howe, July 4, 1936 (dec. Jan. 1997); children: Judith (Mrs. John A. Hirst), David Howe, Jane (Mrs. David D. Dunatchik), Elizabeth Gooding (Mrs. Ralph A. Petersen) (dec.). AB, CCNY, 1928; MD cum laude, Yale U., 1932; MPH, Johns Hopkins U., 1938. Diplomate Am. Bd. Preventive Medicine, Am. Bd. Pediatrics (ofcl. examiner). Intern, asst. resident, resident in pediatrics New Haven Hosp., 1932-36; instr. pediatrics Yale U., 1933-36; state pediatrician Md. State Health Dept., 1936-41; asst. prof. child hygiene Sch. Tropical Medicine, San Juan, P.R., 1941-42; dir. rsch. and tng. in child health, dir. sch. health N.Y.C. Health Dept., 1942-46; instr. pediatrics and lectr. pub. health adminstrn. Johns Hopkins U., 1939-46; asst. prof. pediatrics and pub. health Cornell U., 1942-46; asst. prof. pub. health Columbia U., 1940-46; prof. pediatrics, head dept. La. State U., 1946-52; pediatrician-in-chief Charity Hosp., New Orleans, 1946-52; prof. pub. health Sch. Pub. Health, U. Mich., Ann Arbor, 1960-74, dean, 1960-74, dean emeritus, 1974—; prof. pediatrics U. Mich. Med. Sch., 1961-78, prof. emeritus, 1978—, chmn. div. health sci., 1970-74; John G. Searle prof. pub. health, 1974-78; emeritus, 1978—. Chief divsn. edn. and tng. Pan-Am. San. Bur., Regional Office for Ams., WHO, 1952-56; sec.-gen. Pan-Am. San. Bur., WHO Regional Office, 1957-60; vis. prof. U. Malaya, 1974, Centro Universitario de Salud Publica, U. Autónoma Madrid, 1990—, U Cin., 1993; external examiner Nat. U. Singapore, 1983; cons. Internat. Sci. and Tech. Inst., 1986—, Sch. Pub. Health, Zaire, 1987, Schs. Pub. Health, Indonesia, 1988; coord. Mich.-Madrid Sch. Pub. Health collaboration, 1990—. Editor: Public Health in the People's Republic of China, 1973; mem. editl. bd. Revista Mexicana de Salud Publica, 1990—. Pres. Assn. Schs. Pub. Health, 1963—66, Comprehensive Health Planning Coun., S.E. Mich., 1970—74; trustee Pan-Am. Health and Edn. Found., 1970—85, 1986—92, 1994—2000, pres., 1984—85, chmn. devel. com., 1991—2000, v.p., 1996—2000; trustee Nat. San. Found., 1969—84, emeritus trustee, 1984—; pres. Physicians for Social Responsibility, Ann Arbor, 1987—92; mem. com. on carcinogenesis of pesticides NAS, 1977—79, com. on advanced study in China, 1978—82; chmn. Task Force in Nat. Immunization Policy HEW, 1975—76; adv. com. Kellogg Nat. Fellowship Program, 1982—; rsch. adv. com. Resources for Future, 1978—84; spl. cons. State U. System Fla., 1982—87; mem. com. on prevention ctrs. CDC, 1986—94. Recipient Man of Yr. award CCNY, 1955; Clifford G. Grulee award Am. Acad. Pediatrics, 1958; Townsend Harris medal CCNY, 1961; Bronfman prize Am. Public Health Assn., 1967; Disting. Service award Mich. Public Health Assn., 1974; Walter P. Reuther award for disting. service United Auto Workers, 1974; Sedgwick medal Am. Pub. Health Assn., 1974; Outstanding Alumnus award Johns Hopkins Sch. Hygiene, 1982; Disting. Service award Delta Omega Soc., 1982; Spes Hominum award Nat. Sanitation Found., 1986, Disting. Alumnus award Yale U. Med. Sch., 1987; Spl. award Korean Soc. Preventive Medicine, 1989. Fellow AAAS, Royal Soc. Health (hon.); mem. Am. Pediatric Soc., Soc. Pediatric Rsch., Am. Acad. Pediatrics (E.H. Christopherson award 1997), Am. Assn. World Health (v.p. 1979-82, 85-88, pres. 1982-84), Am. Pub. Health Assn. (chmn. exec. bd. 1965-70, pres. 1971-72), Fedn. Assn. Schs. Health Professions (1st pres. 1968-70), Soc. Exptl. Biol. and Medicine, Peruvian, Eduadorian, Argentinian Pediatric Socs. (hon.), P.R. Pub. Health Assn. (hon.), Sigma Xi, Alpha Omega Alpha, Delta Omega, Phi Kappa Phi, Phi Beta Kappa (hon.). Club: Cosmos (Washington). Home: 1200 Earhart Rd Ann Arbor MI 48105-2768 Office: Sch Public Health U Mich Ann Arbor MI 48109-2029 E-mail: wegman@umich.edu.

WEHLING, ROBERT LOUIS, household products company executive; b. Chgo., Nov. 27, 1938; s. Ralph Joseph and Rita Helen (Casey) W.; m. Carolyn Thierry Harmon, July 5, 1958; children: Susan, Mary, Jennifer, Linda, Karen, Sandra. BA magna cum laude, Denison U., 1960; LHD (hon.), U. Cin., 1998. Brand asst. Procter & Gamble Co., Cin., 1960, 63-64, asst. brand mgr., 1964-66, brand mgr., 1966-70, assoc. advt. mgr., 1970-74, advt. mgr. bar soap and household cleaning products div., 1974-77, div. mgr. gen. advt., 1977-84, assoc. gen. advt. mgr., 1984-87, gen. mktg. svcs. mgr., 1987-88, v.p. mktg. svcs., 1988-90, v.p. pub. affairs, 1990-94, sr. v.p. advt., market rsch. and pub. affairs, 1994-99, sr. v.p. advt., market rsch. and govt. rels., 1994-99, global mktg., market rsch., consumer and market knowledge and govt. rels. officer, 1999—. Mem. edn. task force Bus. Roundtable, 1990—; mem. Advt. Coun. Bd. (vice chmn. 1994-96, chmn. 1997-98, hon. chair 1998-99). Pres. March of Dimes, Cin., 1981-84; mem. allocations com. Fine Arts Fund, Cin., 1987—; bd. dirs. Just Say No Internat., 1991-93; co-founder with USA Today, Coalition on Edn. Initiatives, 1991—; mem. Mayor's Commn. on Children, 1992—; vice chmn. Downtown Cin., Inc.; exec. com. Cin. Youth Collaborative; trustee United Way Cin., Ohio Schs. Devel. Corp.; bd. dirs. Edn. Excellence Partnership; participant Gov.'s Edn. Mgmt. Coun.; mem. Hamilton county Family and Children First Coun., 1993-94, Greater Cin. C. of C. (trustee 1994-97, chmn. Blue Chip campaign 1994-97, chmn. 1998); numerous other civic activities. Named Citizen of Yr., City of Wyoming, 1986, One of 200 Greater Cincinnatians, Cin. Bicentennial Commn., 1988; recipient award Nat. Coun. Negro Women, 1989, Field of Svc. Organization award United Way, 1991, Chairman's award Marketing Assn. of Am., 1991, Madison Square Boys and Girls Club award, 1991, Disting. Svc. award Ohio Assn. Colls. for Tchr. Edn., 1993, award Coun. for Acad. Excellence, 1994, U.S. Dept. Edn., 1994, The Seasongood Good Govt. award 1994, Nat. Vol. of Yr. Elaine Whitelaw award March of Dimes, 1994, Ohio Gov.'s award, 1995, Beech Acres Children's Advocate award, 1995, Nat. Govs.' Assn. Disting. Svc. award, 1995, Community Hero Torchbearer for the 1996 Olympic Torch Relay, 1996; Bob Wehling Vol. of Yr. award named in his honor March of Dimes Southwestern Ohio chpt., 1993, numerous others. Mem. Assn. Nat. Advertisers (Robert V. Goldstein award for Disting. Svc. 1993), Advt. Coun. (campaign dir. 1988—), Greater Cin. C. of C. (trustee, exec. com.), Queen City Club, Commonwealth Club, Phi Beta Kappa. Republican. Methodist. Avocations: running, reading, education, children's issues. Office: Procter & Gamble Co 1 Procter And Gamble Plz Cincinnati OH 45202-3393

WEHRBEIN, ROGER RALPH, state legislator; b. Lincoln, Nebr., Aug. 18, 1938; s. Ralph Jennings and Vivian Lucille (Johns) W.; m. Jeanene Arlene Markussen, Oct. 7, 1961; children: Douglas, David. BS in Animal Scis., U. Nebr., 1960. Farmer, livestock feeder Breeze Valley Farms Inc., Plattsmouth, Nebr., 1962—; mem. Nebr. Legislature from 2nd dist., Lincoln, 1987—. Chair appropriations com. 1995—; bd. dirs. Lincoln Fed. Land Bank Assn., AG Builders of Nebr. Bd. dirs. Leadership-Edn.-Action-Devel. (LEAD), Lincoln, 1988-94. Capt. U.S. Army, 1961-62. Named to Nebr. Hall of Agrl. Achievement, 1988, honoree, 1999; U. Nebr. Block and Bridle Club honoree, 1993. Mem. Nebr. Cattlemen's Assn. (pres. 1985), Nebr. Pork Producers, Ag-Bldrs. Nebr., Toastmasters (pres. Plattsmouth chpt. 1983), Am. Legion, Nebr. Farm Bur., Rotary (pres. Plattsmouth chpt. 1983), Masons, Kiwanis (Outstanding Farmer Omaha 1985). Republican. Presbyterian. Avocations: reading, travel, agriculture. Home: 5812 Highway 66 Plattsmouth NE 68048-7488

WEHRLE, LEROY SNYDER, economist, educator; b. St. Louis, Feb. 5, 1932; s. Fred Joseph and Eleanor (Snyder) W.; m. JoAnn Griffith, Aug. 29, 1959; children— Chandra Lee, Lon Joseph. B.S., Washington U., St. Louis, 1953; M.A. in Econs, Yale, 1956, Ph.D. with honors, 1959. Asst. instr. Yale, 1958-59; with econ. sect. AID mission to Laos, 1960-61; sr. staff economist President's Council Econ. Advisers, 1961-62; spl. econ. adviser to U.S. Ambassador Unger, Vientiane, 1962; dep. dir. AID mission to Laos, 1963-64; asst. dir. AID mission, also econ. counsellor to U.S. ambassador, Saigon, 1964-67; asso. dir. AID Mission, Saigon, 1964-67; dept. asst. adminstr. Vietnam, AID, Dept. State, 1967-68; univ. fellow Harvard, 1968-69; sr. fellow Brookings Instn., 1969-70; dir. Ill. Inst. for Social Policy, Springfield, 1970-72; aide to Lt. Gov. Paul Simon, 1972; prof. economics Sangamon State U., 1972-88; founding ptnr., chief exec. officer Health Econs. and Mkt. Analysis Inc., Springfield, 1987-94; pres. Health-care Cost Analysis, Inc., 1994—. Chmn. bd. Tie Collar, Ltd. Mem. spl. study group Alliance Progress, 1962; mem. Rockefeller Latin Am. Mission, 1969; chmn. study team world food and nutrition study Nat. Acad. Sci., 1976-77. Served with AUS, 1953-55. Recipient William A. Jump meml. award, 1966 Home and Office: 2001 S Bates Ave Springfield IL 62704-3304 E-mail: wehrle@springnet1.com.

WEHRWEIN, AUSTIN CARL, newspaper reporter, editor, writer; b. Austin, Tex., Jan. 12, 1916; s. George S. and Anna (Ruby) W.; m. Judith Oakes, 1950; children: Sven Austin, Paul, Peter, Joanna Judith. A.B., U. Wis., 1937; LL.B., Columbia U., 1940; student, London Sch. Econs., 1948. Reporter Washington Bur., UP, 1941-43, 46-48; information specialist E.C.A., London, Copenhagen, Oslo, Stockholm, 1948-51; financial writer Milw. Jour., 1951-53; staff corr. Time, Inc., Chgo., 1953-55; reporter Chgo. Sun-Times, 1955-56, fin. editor, 1956-57; chief Chgo. bur. N.Y. Times, 1957-66; editorial writer Mpls. Star, 1966-82. Editor The Observer, 1984-87. Served with USAAF, 1943-45; mem. staff Stars and Stripes 1945-46, Shanghai, China. Recipient Pulitizer prize for internat. reporting, 1953; Disting. Journalism award U. Wis., 1963; cert. of merit ABA Gavel competition, 1968, 80; Gavel award, 1969, 71 Home and Office: 2309 Carter Ave Saint Paul MN 55108-1640

WEIDENAAR, DENNIS JAY, economics educator; b. Grand Rapids, Mich., Oct. 4, 1936; s. John and Jennie (Beukema) W.; m. Kristin Andrews, July 14, 1943; children: Kaarin Jaye, John Andrews. AB, Calvin Coll., Grand Rapids, 1958; MA, U. Chgo., 1961; PhD, Purdue U., 1969. Asst. prof. econs. Purdue U., West Lafayette, Ind., 1966-72, assoc. prof., 1972-77, prof., 1977-83; interim dean Krannert Sch. of Mgmt., 1983-84, assoc. dean, 1984-99; dean Krannert Grad. Sch. Mgmt., 1990-99, prof. econs., 1999—. Cons. TRW, B.F. Goodrich, Ea. Panhandle; bd. dirs. Lafayette Ins. Co. Author: Economics. Contbr. articles to profl. jours. Bd. dirs. Ind. Coun. on Econ. Edn., Lafayette, 1974-83, Lafayette Ins. Co. Recipient The Leavey Awd for Excellence in Pvt. Enterprise Edn., Freedom's Found., Valley Forge, 1983, Distinguished Service Awd., Joint Council on Econ. Edn., N.Y., 1986, Golden Key Nat. Honor Soc., 1985. Mem. Rotary, Delta Sigma Pi, Beta Gamma Sigma (bd. dirs., pres. 2002--), Phi Delta Kappa. Presbyterian. Home: 217 Rosebank Ln West Lafayette IN 47906-8614 Office: Purdue U Krannert Sch Mgmt West Lafayette IN 47907

WEIDENBAUM, MURRAY LEW, economist, educator; b. Bronx, N.Y., Feb. 10, 1927; s. David and Rose (Warshaw) Weidenbaum; m. Phyllis Green, June 13, 1954; children: Susan, James, Laurie. BBA, CCNY, 1948; MA, Columbia U., 1949; MPA, Princeton U., 1954, PhD, 1958; LLD, Baruch Coll., 1981, U. Evansville, 1983, McKendree Coll., 1993. Fiscal economist Bur. Budget, Washington, 1949—57; corp. economist Boeing Co., Seattle, 1958—62; sr. economist Stanford Rsch. Inst., Palo Alto, Calif., 1962—63; mem. faculty Washington U., St. Louis, 1964—, prof., chmn. dept. econs., 1966—69, Mallinckrodt prof., 1971—, dir. Ctr. for Study Am. Bus., 1974—81, Washington U., St. Louis, 1982—95; chmn. Ctr. for Study Am. Bus. Washington U., 1995—2000; asst. sec. econ. policy Treasury Dept., 1969—71; chmn. Coun. of Econ. Advs., 1981—82; hon. chmn. Weidenbaum Ctr. on the Economy, Govt. and Pub. Policy, St. Louis, 2001—. Chmn. rsch. adv. com. St. Louis Regional Indsl. Devel. Corp., 1965—69; exec. sec. Pres.'s Com. on Econ. Impact of Def. and Disarmament, 1964; mem. U.S. Fin. Investment Adv. Panel, 1970—72; cons. various firms and instns.; chmn. U.S. Commn. to Rev. the Trade Deficit, 1999—2000. Author: Federal Budgeting, 1964, Modern Public Sector, 1969, Economics of Peacetime Defense, 1974, Economic Impact of the Vietnam War, 1967, Government-Mandated Price Increases, 1975, The Future of Business Regulation, 1980, Rendezvous With Reality: The American Economy After Reagan, 1988, Rendezvous With Reality: The American Economy After Reagan, paperback edit., 1990, Business, Government, and the Public, 1990, Small Wars, Big Defense, 1992, The Bamboo Network, 1996, Business and Government in the Global Marketplace, 1999; mem. editl. bd.: Publius, 1971—, mem. editl. bd.: Jour. Econ. Issues, 1972—75, mem. editl. bd.: Challenge, 1974—81, mem. editl. bd.: , 1983—, mem. editl. bd.: Business and the Contemporary World, 1997—2000. With U.S. Army, 1945. Named Banbury fellow, Princeton U., 1952—54; named to Free Market Hall of Fame, 1983; recipient Alexander Hamilton medal, U.S. Dept. Treasury, 1971, Disting. Writer award, Georgetown U., award for disting. tchg., Freedoms Found., 1980, award for best book in econs., Assn. Am. Pubs., 1992. Fellow: Assn. for Pvt. Enterprise Edn. (Adam Smith award 1986), City Coll. Alumni Assn. (Townsend Harris medal 1969), Soc. Tech. Comm., Nat. Assn. Bus. Economists, Cosmos. Office: Washington Univ Weidenbaum Ctr 1 Brookings Dr Saint Louis MO 63130-4899

WEIDENTHAL, MAURICE DAVID (BUD WEIDENTHAL), educational administrator, journalist; b. Cleve., Nov. 26, 1925; s. William and Evelyn (Kolinsky) W.; m. Grace Schwartz, Apr. 14, 1957; 1 child, Susan Elizabeth Weidenthal Saltzman. B.A., U. Mich., 1950. Mem. staff Cleve. Press, 1950-81, editorial writer, 1950-51, asst. city editor, 1956-58, edn. editor, 1958-81; v.p. public affairs Cuyahoga Community Coll. Dist., Cleve., 1981-88; dir. Urban Colls. Project RC-2000, Tempe, Ariz., 1989—. Editor The Urban Report, Cleve., 1989—. Mem. pub. affairs com. Greater Cleve. Growth Assn., 1981-88; mem. bd. advisors Coun. for Advancement and Support of Edn., 1981-88, Nat. Coun. Mktg. and Pub. Rels., 1981—; alt. bd. dirs. St. Vincent Quadrangle, 1983-88; trustee Hebrew Free Loan Assn., 1975-86. With AUS, 1944-45. Decorated Air medal. Mem. Edn. Writers Assn., Soc. Profl. Journalists, (bd. dirs.), Cleve. City Club (bd. dirs. 1969-76), Cleve. Press Club. Home: 25858 Fairmount Blvd Cleveland OH 44122-2214 Office: 4250 Richmond Rd Cleveland OH 44122-6104 E-mail: u2w@aol.com., bud.weidenthal@tri-c.cc.oh.us.

WEIGERT, ANDREW JOSEPH, sociology educator; b. N.Y.C., Apr. 8, 1934; s. Andrew Joseph and Marie Teresa (Kollmer) W.; m. Kathleen Rose Maas, Aug. 31, 1967; children: Karen Rose, Sheila Marie. BA, St. Louis U., 1958, PhL, 1959, MA, 1960; BTh, Woodstock (Md.) Coll., 1964; PhD, U. Minn., 1968. NIMH trainee U. Minn., Mpls., 1965-67; asst. prof. sociology U. Notre Dame, Ind., 1968-72, assoc. prof., 1972-76, prof., 1976—, chmn. dept., 1980-84, 88-89. Vis. assoc. prof. Yale U., New Haven, 1973-74; participant nat. and regional profl. meetings. Co-author: Family Socialization, 1974, Interpretive Sociology, 1978, Society and Identity, 1986; author: Everyday Life, 1981, Social Psychology, 1983, Life and Society, 1983, Mixed Emotions, 1991, Self, Interaction, and Natural Environment, 1997; adv. editor various sociology jours.; contbr. numerous articles to profl. jours., chpts. to books. Recipient tchg. awards, 1999, 2002; NSF grantee, 1969. Avocation: woodlot and prairie management. Office: U Notre Dame Dept Sociology Notre Dame IN 46556

WEIGHT, DOUG, professional hockey player; b. Warren, Mich., Jan. 21, 1971; Student, Lake Superior State Coll., Mich. Center N.Y. Rangers, 1990-93; traded Edmonton Oilers, 1993, center, 1993—. Named to CCHA All-Rookie team, 1989-90, NCAA All-Am. West 2d team, 1990-91, CHA All-Star 1st team, 1990-91; selected for NHL All-Star Game, 1996.*

WEIHING, JOHN LAWSON, plant pathologist, state senator; b. Rocky Ford, Colo., Feb. 26, 1921; s. Henry John and Clara Adele (Krull) W.; m. Shirley Ruth Wilkerson, Aug. 18, 1948; children: Lawson James, Martin Roy, Adell Ann, Warren John. BS in Agronomy, Colo. State U., 1942; MSc in Agronomy, U. Nebr., 1949, PhD in Botany and Plant Pathology, 1954. Instr. plant pathology U. Nebr., Lincoln, 1950-54, asst. prof., 1954-56, assoc. prof., 1956-60, prof., 1960-61, 62-64, 66-71, prof., interim chmn. plant pathology dept., 1961-62, prof., dir. Panhandle Rsch. and Extension Ctr. Scottsbluff, 1971-84, with Alumni Office, Panhandle Found. Scottsbluf, 1984-86; prof., chmn. plant sci. dept. Ataturk U., Erzurum, Turkey, 1964-66; mem. dist. 48 Nebr. Legislature, Lincoln, 1987-91. Cons. Am. Hydrponics Systems, Inc., Grapevine, Tex., 1969-72. Creator U. Nebr. TV series Backyard Farmer, The Equation of Nature, 1959-60. Campaign chmn. United Way, Scottsbluff and Gering, Nebr., 1978. Lt. U.S. Army, 1942-46. Recipient Honor award Soil Conservation Soc. Am., 1982, Merit award Gamma Sigma Delta, 1977, Disting. Svc. award Nebr. Turfgrass Found., 1982, Nebr. Coop. Extension, 1970; named to Nebr. Hall Agrl. Achievement, 1987. Mem. Am. Phytopathol. Soc. (chmn. nat. extension com. 1963, pres. north cen. dir. 1971-72), AAAS, Am. Inst. Biol. Scis., Nebr. State Hist. Soc. (trustee 1992—), Scottsbluff/Gering United C. of C. (pres. 1980-81), Rotary (bd. dirs. 1977-80), Elks. Republican. Presbyterian. Avocation: archeology. Home: 1605 Holly Dr Gering NE 69341-1954

WEIKART, DAVID POWELL, educational research foundation administrator; b. Youngstown, Ohio, Aug. 26, 1931; s. Hubert James and Catherine (Powell) W.; m. Phyllis Saxton, Aug. 24, 1957; children: Cynthia, Catherine, Jennifer, Gretchen. AB, Oberlin Coll., 1953, DSc (hon.), 1992; PhD, U. Mich., 1966. Cert. sch. psychologist, Mich. Dir. spl. svcs. Ypsilanti (Mich.) Pub. Schs., 1957-70; pres. High Scope Ednl. Rsch. Found., Ypsilanti, 1970-2000, pres. emeritus, 2001—. Dir. High Scope Inst., 1991, Netherlands, 1995, Ireland, 1999, U.K. Author: Young Children in Action, 1979, Changed Lives, 1984, Challenging the Potential, 1992, Significant Benefits, 1993, Educating Young Children, 1995, 2d edit., 2002, Lasting Difference, 1997; editor: How Nations Serve Young Children, 1991, Families Speak, 1994, What Should Young Children Learn, 1999. Mem., Nat. Commn. on Children, 1990-93. 1st lt. USMC, 1953-55. Recipient Lela Rowland award Nat. Mental Health Assn., Washington, 1987. Mem. Nat. Assn. for Edn. of Young Children (Lifetime Achievement award 1999). Avocation: camping. E-mail: davew@highscope.org.

WEIKEL, MALCOLM KEITH, healthcare company executive; b. Shamokin, Pa., Mar. 9, 1938; s. Malcolm J. and Marian Eleanor (Faust) Weikel; m. Barbara Joan Davis, Dec. 17, 1960; children: Richard, Kristin. BSc, Phila. Coll. Pharmacy and Sci., 1960; MSc, U. Wis., 1962, PhD, 1966. Mgr. Roche Labs., 1966—70; commr. health svcs. HEW, Washington, 1970—77; v.p. Am. Med. Internat., 1978—82, pres., CEO, 1982—84; exec. v.p., COO, Manor Healthcare Corp., Silver Spring, Md., 1984—86; exec. v.p. Health Care & Retirement Corp., Toledo, 1986—88, sr. exec. v.p., COO, 1988—98, sr. exec. v.p., 1998—. Recipient Sec.'s Spl. citation, HEW, 1975, 1977. Mem.: Am. Health Care Assn. (v.p. 1990—, chmn. multifacility group 1990—93). Office: Health Care & Retirement Corp PO Box 10086 Toledo OH 43699-0086

WEIL, CASS SARGENT, lawyer; b. N.Y.C., Nov. 6, 1946; s. Theodore and Ruth Frances (Sargent) W. BA, SUNY, Stonybrook, 1968; JD cum laude, William Mitchell Coll. of Law, 1980. Bar: Minn. 1980, U.S. Dist. Ct. Minn. 1980, U.S. Ct. Appeals (8th cir.) 1980, Wis. 1984, U.S. Ct. Appeals (7th cir.) 1984; cert. bankruptcy law specialist, consumer and bus. Am. Bd. Certification. Assoc. J.R. Kotts & Assoc., Mpls., 1980-81, Wagner, Rutchick & Trojack, St. Paul, 1981-83; ptnr. Zohlmann & Weil, Wilmar, Minn., 1983, Peterson, Franke & Riach, P.A., St. Paul, 1983-91, O'Connor & Hannan, Mpls., 1991-94, Moss & Barnett, P.A., Mpls., 1994—. Editor: Minn. Legal Forms, Bankruptcy, 1983, 87, 91, 92, 93. Recepient Leading Am. Atty. award Am. Rsch. Corp., 1994, 96, 98, 2000, Minn. Top Lawyers Mpls. St. Paul Mag., 1998. Mem. Minn. Bar Assn. (vice chmn. bankruptcy sect. 1984-88, chairperson 1988-89), Wis. Bar Assn., Am. Bankruptcy Inst., Turnaround Mgmt. Assn., Comml. Law League Am., Order of Barristers. Democrat. Jewish. Office: Moss & Barnett PA 4800 Wells Fargo Ctr Minneapolis MN 55402 also: 90 S 7th St Ste 4800 Minneapolis MN 55402 Business E-Mail: weilc@moss-barnett.com.

WEIL, D(ONALD) WALLACE, business administration educator; b. Cleve., July 20, 1923; s. Laurence J. and Carol S. (Wallace) W.; m. Jane A. Bittel, Dec. 29, 1947; children— John Wallace, Charles Andrew, Margaret Jane, Carol Wyn. B.A., Oberlin Coll., 1947; J.D., Willamette U., 1950. Pres. James Foundry Corp., Fort Atkinson, Wis., 1960-70; faculty bus. adminstrn. U. Wis., Eau Claire, 1971-74, chmn. dept. bus. adminstrn., 1974-77, prof., 1985—; pres. Diversified Industries, Inc., St. Louis, 1977-81, UHI Corp., Los Angeles, 1981-85. Dir. U.H.I. Corp. Diversified Industries, Inc., St. Louis, Sales Investments, Mgmt. Inc., Elmwood, Wis., Jane B. Inc., Eau Claire Served with AUS, 1942-45. Mem. Am. Security Council, Nat. Council Small Bus. Mgmt. Devel., Phi Kappa Phi, Beta Gamma Sigma. Republican. Congregationalist. Home: 1530 Canfield St Eau Claire WI 54701-4018 Office: U Wis-Eau Claire Dept Bus Adminstrn Eau Claire WI 54701

WEIL, JOHN WILLIAM, technology management consultant; b. N.Y.C., Feb. 3, 1928; s. Frank Leopold and Henrietta Amelia (Simons) W.; m. Joan Leatrice Landis, June 15, 1950; children— Nancy Ellen, Linda Jill. BS, MIT, 1948; PhD, Cornell U., 1953. Various positions in nuclear reactors and computers Gen. Electric Co. (various locations), 1953-70; v.p. advanced systems and tech. Honeywell Info. Systems, Inc., Waltham, Mass., 1970-74; v.p., chief tech. officer Bendix Corp., Southfield, Mich., 1974-77, sr. v.p., chief tech. officer, 1977-83; v.p. advanced tech. and engring. Allied Corp., 1983; pres. Modular Bio Systems, Inc., 1983-85, Weil Assocs., Inc., Bloomfield Hills, Mich., 1985-97. Founder Met. Detroit Sci. and Engring. Coalition, 1977, sec., 1977-80, pres., 1980-82; chmn. Mich. Biotech. Inst., 1981-85, trustee, 1985-92; mem. Army Sci. Bd., 1982-84. Contbr. articles to prof. jours. AEC fellow, 1950-51 Home and Office: 218 Guilford Rd Bloomfield Hills MI 48304-2737 E-mail: johnww@weilhome.com.

WEIL, ROLF ALFRED, economist, university president emeritus; b. Pforzheim, Germany, Oct. 29, 1921; came to U.S., 1936, naturalized, 1944; s. Henry and Lina (Landauer) W.; m. Leni Metzger, Nov. 3, 1945; children: Susan Linda, Ronald Alan. B.A., U. Chgo., 1942, Ph.D., 1950; D. Hebrew Letters, Coll. Jewish Studies, 1967; L.H.D., Loyola U., 1970; D.H.L., Bowling Green State U., Ohio, 1986; LHD, Roosevelt U., 1988. Rsch. asst. Cowles Commn. for Rsch. in Econs., 1942-44; rsch. analyst Ill. Dept. Revenue, 1944-46; mem. faculty Roosevelt U., Chgo., 1946—, prof. fin. and econs., also chmn. dept. fin., 1954-65, dean Coll. Bus. Adminstrn., 1957-64, acting pres., 1965-66, pres., 1966-88, pres. emeritus, 1988—. Past pres. Selfhelp Home for the Aged, Chgo.; cons. to non-profit orgns., 1988—. Author: Through these Portals-from Immigrant to College President, 1991; contbr. articles on fin. Bd. dirs. trustees Roosevelt U., Selfhelp of Chgo., Inc. Mem. Am. Econ. Assn., Cliff Dwellers Club. E-mail: rweil@roosevelt.edu.

WEIL, ROMAN LEE, accounting educator; b. Montgomery, Ala., May 22, 1940; s. Roman L. and Charlotte (Alexander) W.; children: Alexis Cherie, Charles Alexander Roman, Lacey Lorraine. BA, Yale U., 1962; MS in Indsl. Adminstrn, Carnegie-Mellon U., 1965, PhD in Econs., 1966. CPA, CMA, Ill. From instr. to prof. U. Chgo., 1965-93, Sigmund E. Edelstone prof. acctg., 1993-97, V. Duane Rath prof. acctg., 1997—, dir. Dir.'s Coll., 1998—; Mills B. Lane prof. indsl. mgmt. Ga. Inst. Tech., 1974-76; mem. adv. com. replacement cost implementation SEC, 1976-77. Prof. acctg. Stanford (Calif.) U., 1984, prof. econs., 1985, prof. law, 1990-96; prof. acctg. and law NYU Sch. Law, 1985; mem. adv. coun. Fin. Acctg. Stds., 1989-94; mem. task force on consolidations Fin. Acctg. Stds. Bd., 1984-89, mem. task force on discounting, 1989-99, mem. task force on fin. instruments, 1994-98, mem. adv. coun., 1989-94; dir. Dir.'s Coll., 1999-; co-founder Dir.'s Summit, 2002-. Author: Fundamentals of Accounting, 1975, Financial Accounting, 10th edit., 2002, Accounting: The Language of Business, 10th edit., 1998, Inflation Accounting, 1976, Replacement Cost Accounting, 1976, Managerial Accounting, 1979, 7th edit., 2000, Litigation Svcs. Handbook, 3d edit., 2001; editor: Handbook of Modern Accounting, 1977, 3rd edit., 1983, Handbook of Cost Accounting, 1980, Acctg. Rev., 1974-79, Fin. Analysts Jour., 1980-88. NSF grantee, 1967-81 Mem. AICPA, Ill. Soc. CPAs, Am. Econ. Assn., Inst. Mgmt. Scis., Nat. Assn. Accts. (cert. mgmt. acct.), Am. Acctg. Assn., Inst. Managerial Acctg., Assembly Am. Collegiate Schs. Bus. (acctg. accreditation com. 1987-88), Oenonomy Soc. (co-chmn.). Home: 1540 N Dearborn Pkwy Chicago IL 60610-1402 Office: U Chgo Grad Sch Bus 1101 E 58th St Chicago IL 60637-1511 E-mail: roman.weil@gsb.uchicago.edu.

WEILAND, CHARLES HANKES, lawyer; b. Billings, Mont., Feb. 19, 1921; s. George Michael and Elizabeth (Hankes) W. A.B. cum laude, Johns Hopkins U., 1942; J.D., Harvard U., 1948. Bar: Ill. 1949, U.S. Dist. Ct. (no. dist.) Ill. 1949, U.S. Ct. Appeals (7th cir.) 1949, U.S. Supreme Ct. 1968. Assoc. Lord, Bissell & Brook, Chgo., 1948-55, ptnr., 1956-83. Chmn. Cook County Inquiry Bd., Supreme Ct. Ill. Atty. Regis. and Disciplinary Commn., 1974-75 Served with AUS, 1942-46. Mem. Ill. Bar Assn., Chgo. Bar Assn. Republican. Club: The Lawyers Club of Chgo.

WEILAND, GALEN FRANKLIN, state legislator; s. Joseph Franklin and Ida Lucille (Dunn) W.; m. Ruth Arlene Howland; children: Terry Dean, Teresa Jean. Student, Highland C.C., 1957-58. Kans. state rep. Dist. 49, 1991—. Asst. mgr. Bendena Grain Co. Mem. Elks, Masons. Address: PO Box 217 Bendena KS 66008-0217

WEILER, JEFFRY LOUIS, lawyer; b. N.Y.C., Dec. 31, 1942; s. Kurt and Elaine (Kabb) W.; m. Susan Karen Goodman, June 8, 1964; children: Philip K., June M. BS, Miami U., Oxford, Ohio, 1964; JD, Cleve. State U., 1970. Bar: Ohio 1970, Fla. 1981; CPA, Ohio 1968. Acct. Meaden & Moore, CPAs, Cleve., 1964-65; IRS agt. U.S. Dept. Treasury, 1965-70; assoc. Ulmer & Berne, 1970-71; ptnr. Benesch, Friedlander, Coplan & Aronoff, LLP, 1971—. Adj. assoc. prof. Cleve.-Marshall Coll. Law, Cleve. State U., 1980-87. Contbr. to profl. pubs. Fellow Am. Coll. Trust and Estate Counsel; mem. ABA (sect. taxation, estate and gift tax subcom.), Ohio State Bar Assn. (bd. govs. estate planning trust and probate law sect. 1999—), Cleve. Estate Planning Inst. (chmn. 1980), Cleve. Tax Inst. (chmn. 1983), Cleve. Bar Assn. (treas. 1993-96, trustee 1988-91), Tax Club of Cleve. (sec. 1996-97, v.p. 1997-99, pres. 1999-2000). Avocations: photography, sailboat racing, ice skating. Home: 24714 Maidstone Ln Beachwood OH 44122-1614 Office: Benesch Friedlander Coplan & Aronoff LLP 2300 BP Tower 200 Public Sq Cleveland OH 44114-2301 E-mail: jweiler@bfca.com.

WEIMER, DAVID LEE, educator; b. Buffalo, May 23, 1950; s. Leo Nickolas and Dorthy May (Tates) W.; m. Melanie Frances Manion, June 7, 1990. BS in Engring and BA in Urban Studies, U. Rochester, 1973; M of Pub. Policy, U. Calif., 1975, MA in stats., 1976, PhD, 1978. Grad, intern office rsch. and stats. Social Security Adminstrn., 1974; teaching asst. grad. sch. pub. policy U. Calif., Berkeley, 1975-76; instr. dept. polit. sci. U. Rochester (N.Y.), 1977-78, asst. prof., 1978-82; economist office of policy, planning and analysis U.S. Dept. Energy, 1980-81; assoc. prof. U. Rochester, 1982-86, deputy dir. pub. policy analysis program, 1982-89, prof. polit. sci., pub. policy analysis, 1986-2000; prof. dept. polit. sci. Robert M. La Follette Sch. Pub. Affairs U. Wis., Madison, 2000—. Chevron disting. vis. prof. faculty bus. adminstrn. Simon Fraser U., 1986; disting. vis., prof. Robert M. La Follette Inst. Pub. Affairs U. Wis., Madison, 1989-90; disting. pub. policy lectr. pub. policy program U. N.C., Chapel Hill, 1992; vis. prof. dept. polit. sci. and pub. adminstrn. Peking U., 1993; found. dir. Ctr. For Pub. Policy Studies LIngnan Coll., Hong Kong,

1994-95. Author: Improving Prosecution? The Inducement and Implementation of Innovations for Prosecution Management, 1980, The Strategic Petroleum Reserve: Planning, Implementation and Analysis, 1982, Policy Analysis and Economics: Developments, Tensions, Prospects, 1991; co-editor: Oil Price Stocks, Market Response and Contingency Planning, 1984, Responding to International Oil Crises, 1988, Policy Analysis: Concepts and Practice, 3d edit., 1999, Instl. Design, 1995, Cost Benefit Analysis, 1996, Political Economy of Property Rights, 1997, Organizational Report Cards, 1999; editor Jour. Policy Analysis and Mgmt., 1985-89; author articles. Dir. U.S. Go Congress, Rochester, 1991. Bridging fellow Dept. Pharmacology and Toxicology U. Rochester, 1983. Mem. Assn. Pub. Policy Analysis and Mgmt., Am. Soc. Pub. Adminstrn., Am. Polit. Sci. Assn., Am. Econ. Assn., Am. Risk and Ins. Assn., Am. Go Assn., Phi Beta Kappa. Avocation: Go (Asian game). Office: Robert M La Follette Sch Pub Affairs U Wis Dept Polit Sci Madison WI 53706

WEINBERG, DAVID B. investor; b. Chgo., Feb. 19, 1952; s. Judd A. and Marjorie (Gottlieb) W.; m. Lynne Ellen Mesirow, July 6, 1980. AB cum laude, Harvard U., 1974; JD, Georgetown U., 1977. Bar: Ill. 1977, U.S. Dist. Ct. (no. dist.) Ill. 1977, U.S. Ct. Appeals (7th cir.) 1978. Law clerk to Hon. William G. Clark Supreme Ct. Ill., 1977-79; assoc. Lord, Bissell & Brook, Chgo., 1979-84, ptnr., 1985-89, Mayer, Brown & Platt, Chgo., 1989-96; chmn., CEO Judd Enterprises, Inc., 1996—; pres. Digital BandWidth LLC, 1996—; dir. NFR Security, Inc., Rockville, Md., 2001—. Ill. Supreme Ct. com. Profl. Responsibility, Chgo., 1984-94, chmn. subcom. lawyers certification. Chmn. bd. trustees Ravinia Festival Assn., Highland Park, Ill., 1998—2001; vice chmn. bd. trustees Northwestern U., 1999—. Mem. Chgo. Club, Standard Club Chgo. (d ir. 1988-90), Econ. Club Chgo., Lake Shore Country Club, Arts Club Chgo., Comml. Club Chgo., Civic Com. Office: Judd Enterprises Bank One Plz 21 S Clark St Ste 3140 Chicago IL 60603-2090

WEINBERG, EUGENE DAVID, microbiologist, educator; b. Chgo., Mar. 4, 1922; s. Philip and Lenore (Bergman) W.; m. Frances Murl Izen, Sept. 5, 1949; children— Barbara Ann, Marjorie Jean, Geoffrey Alan, Michael Benjamin. B.S., U. Chgo., 1942, M.A., 1948, Ph.D., 1950. Instr. dept. microbiology Ind. U., Bloomington, 1950-53, asst. prof., 1953-57, asso. prof., 1957-61, prof., 1961—, head microbiology sect., med. sci. program, 1978—. Served with AUS, 1942-45. Mem. AAAS, Am. Soc. Microbiology. Office: Ind U Biology Dept Jordan Hall Bloomington IN 47405 Fax: 812-855-6705. E-mail: eweinber@indiana.edu.

WEINBERG, RONALD ELLIOTT, newspaper, retail and manufacturing executive; b. Memphis, Sept. 25, 1941; s. Lew and Emily (Van Stavoren) W.; m. Anne Weil, Aug. 2, 1965; children: Ronald Jr., Wendy. AB, Harvard U., 1963, MBA, 1965. Pres. Weinberg Capital Corp., Cleve., 1980—; chmn. SunMedia Corp., 1986—, New West, Cleve., 1988—, Hawk Corp., Cleve., 1989—. Chmn. Cleve. chpt. Young Pres. Orgn., 1987-88. Avocations: jogging, golf. Office: Hawk Corp 200 Public Sq Ste 30-5000 Cleveland OH 44114

WEINBERG, SYLVAN LEE, cardiologist, educator, author, editor; b. Nashville, June 14, 1923; s. Abraham J. and Beatrice (Kottler) W.; m. Joan Hutzler, Jan. 29, 1956; children: Andrew Lee, Leslie. BS, Northwestern U., 1945, MD, 1948. From intern to resident, fellow Michael Reese Hosp., Chgo., 1947-51; attending physician Good Samaritan Hosp., Dayton, Ohio, 1953-99, chief of cardiology, 1966-99, founding dir. coronary care unit, 1967-99; clin. prof. medicine Wright State U., 1975—; dir. med. edn. Dayton Heart Hosp., 2000—. Former panelist Med. Affairs, nat. TV; pres. Weinberg Marcus Cardiomed. Group, Inc., 1970-99; pres. Arts & Comms. Internat., Inc., 1995—. Author: An Epitaph for Merlin and Perhaps for Medicine, 1983, The Golden Age of Medical Science and the Dark Age of Health Care Delivery, 2000; founding editor Dayton Medicine, 1980—, Heart & Lung, 1972-87; chief med. editor: Med. Comms. Resources, Inc., 1999—; contbr. articles to profl jours. Capt. U.S. Army, 1951-53, Korea. Recipient Army Commendation medal, Richard A. DeWall MD award for excellence in cardiology, Am. Heart Assn., 2001, Outstanding Pub. Svc. award, Ohio State Senate, 1980. Fellow ACP (Ohio Laureate award 1997), Am. Coll. Cardiology (editor in chief jour. ACCEL 1985-2000, pres. 1993-94), Am. Coll. Chest Physicians (pres. 1984); mem. Montgomery County Med. Soc. (pres. 1980). Avocations: writing, travel, golf. Home: 4555 Southern Blvd Dayton OH 45429-1118 Office: Dayton Heart Hosp 707 S Edwin Moses Blvd Dayton OH 45408 E-mail: slwjal@aol.com.

WEINBERGER, MILES M. physician, pediatric educator; b. McKeesport, Pa., June 28, 1938; divorced; 4 children; m. Leslie Kramer, Aug. 22, 1992. A.B., U. Pitts., 1960, M.D., 1965. Diplomate Am. Bd. Pediatrics, Am. Bd. Allergy and Immunology, Am. Bd. Pediatric Pulmonology. Intern U. Calif. Med. Ctr., San Francisco, 1965-66, pediatric resident, 1965-67; research assoc NIH, Bethesda, Md., 1967-69; allergy and pulmonary fellow U. Colo., Denver, 1969-71; staff Ross Valley Med. Clinic, Greenbrae, Calif., 1971-73; clin. pharmacology fellow U. Colo., Denver, 1973-75; divsn. dir. U. Iowa, Iowa City, 1975—. Cons. D.C.Hosp. for Sick Children, 1967-69, allergy and immunology Family Practice Program, Sonoma County Community Hosp., U. Calif. Sch. Medicine, 1972-73; clin. instr. pediatrics Georgetown U. Sch. Medicine, Washington, 1967-69; staff pediatrician part-time West Side Neighborhood Health Ctr., Denver, 1970-71; pediatric sr. staff mem. Nat.Jewish Hosp. and Research Ctr., 1973-75; clin. asst. U. Colo. Med.Ctr., 1974-75; assoc. prof. pediatrics, chmn. pediatric allergy and pulmonary div. U. Iowa Coll. Medicine, 1975-80, assoc. prof. pharmacology, 1975-79, dir. Cystic Fibrosis Ctr., 1977—, prof. pediatrics, 1980—, dir. pediatric allergy and pulmonary div., 1975—. Author: Managing Asthma, 1990; contbr. numerous articles to profl. jours., chpts. to books, also audio-visual materials, commentaries, pub. letters and presentations in field Recipient Clemens von Pirquet award Am. Coll. Allergy, 1974; grantee NIH, 1980-85, Cystic Fibrosis Ctr., Pharm. Mfrs. Assn. Fellow Am. Acad. Pediatrics (allergy sect. 1972, sect. on clin. pharmacology and therapeutics 1978, diseases of chest 1978); mem. Am. Acad. Allergy, Am. Soc. Clin. Pharmacology and Therapeutics, Soc. for Pediatric Rsch., Am. Thoracic Soc. (pres. Iowa Thoracic Soc. 1992-93), Camp Superkids of Iowa (adv. bd. 1981—), Am. Lung Assn. (pediatric pulmonbary ctr. task force com. 1984-86). Home: 7 Cottage Grove Dr NE Iowa City IA 52240-9171 Office: U Iowa Dept Pediatrics Iowa City IA 52242 E-mail: miles-weinberger@uiowa.edu.

WEINBERGER, MYRON HILMAR, medical educator; b. Cin., Sept. 21, 1937; s. Samuel and Helen Eleanor (Price) W.; m. Myrna M. Rosenberg, June 12, 1960; children: Howard David, Steven Neal, Debra Ellen. BS, Ind. U., Bloomington, 1959, MD, 1963. Intern Ind. U. Med. Ctr., Indpls., 1963-64, resident in internal medicine, 1964-66, asst. prof. medicine, 1969-73, assoc. prof., 1973-76, prof., 1976—, dir. Hypertension Research Ctr., 1981—; USPHS trainee in endocrinology and metabolism Stanford U. Med. Ctr., Calif., 1966-68, USPHS spl. fellow in hypertension, 1968-69. Contbr. articles to profl. jours. Recipient Tigerstedt award Am. Soc. Hypertension, 1996, Page-Bradley Lifetime Achievement award Am. Heart Assn. Coun. for High Blood Pressure Rsch., 1999. Fellow ACP, Am. Coll. Cardiology, Am. Coll. Nutrition, Am. Soc. for Clin. Pharmacology and Therapeutics; mem. AAAS, Am. Fedn. Clin. Research, AMA, Am. Heart Assn. (lifetime achievement award coun. for high blood pressure rsch. 1999), Am. Soc. Nephrology, Internat. Soc. Nephrology, Central Soc. Clin. Research, Endocrine Soc., Internat. Soc. Hypertension, Soc. for Exptl. Biology and Medicine Home: 135 Bow Ln Indianapolis IN 46220-1023 Office: Ind U Hypertension Research Ctr 541 Clinical Dr Indianapolis IN 46202-5233 E-mail: mweinbe@iupui.edu.

WEINBLATT, CHARLES SAMUEL, university administrator, employment consultant; b. Toledo, Dec. 23, 1952; s. Morris and Clara (Volk) W.; m. Frances Barbara Auslander, Aug. 12, 1973; children: Brian J., Lauren M. BA, U. Toledo, 1974. Cert. edn. and tng. counselor, Ohio. Psychiat. counselor St. Vincent Hosp., Toledo, 1974-77; vocat., rehab. counselor Goodwill Industries, 1977-85; employment cons., pvt. practice, 1985—; tng. counselor UAW Chrysler, Perrysburg, Ohio, 1987; dir. divsn. orgn. devel. and leadership U. Toledo, 1988—. Employment svcs. cons. Employers' Assn. Toledo, 1985-90; outplacement cons. Toledo Pub. Schs., 1986; spkr. in field of labor and mgmt. rels., employee involvement. Author: Job Seeking Skills for Students, 1987. Mem. Toledo Vision Com., 1989-90. Recipient Quality Improvement award Chrysler, 1987, cert. Am. Inst. Banking, 1989. Mem. ASTD, Ohio Continuing Higher Edn. Assn., Toledo Area Human Resource Assoc., World Future Soc. Jewish. Avocations: music, sports, gardening. Home: 5118 Brenden Way Sylvania OH 43560-2223 Office: U Toledo Seagate Campus 401 Jefferson Ave Toledo OH 43604-1063 E-mail: cweinbl@utnet.utoledo.edu.

WEINBROT, HOWARD DAVID, English educator; b. Bklyn., May 14, 1936; s. William and Rose (Shapiro) W. BA, Antioch Coll., Yellow Springs, Ohio, 1958; MA with honors (Woodrow Wilson fellow 1959, grad. fellow 1959-63), U. Chgo., 1959, PhD, 1963. Teaching fellow U. Chgo., 1962-63; instr. English Yale U., 1963-66; asst. prof., then assoc. prof. U. Calif., Riverside, 1966-69; mem. faculty U. Wis., Madison, 1969—, prof. English, 1972-84, Ricardo Quintana prof., 1984-87, Vilas prof., 1987—. Andrew Mellon vis. prof. Inst. Advanced Studies, Princeton, N.J., 1993-94. Author: The Formal Strain, 1969, Augustus Caesar in Augustan England, 1978, Alexander Pope and the Traditions of Formal Verse Satire, 1982, Essays on 18th-Century Satire, 1988, Britannia's Issue, 1993; also numerous articles, revs.; editor: New Aspects of Lexicography, 1972, Northrop Frye and 18th Century Studies; co-editor: The 18th Century: A Current Bibliography for 1973, 1975, Poetry in English, An Anthology, 1987, Eighteenth-Century Contexts, 2001. Fellow Inst. for Advanced Studies, Princeton, N.J., 1993-94, 2001; Guggenheim fellow, 1988-89. Mem. Am. Soc. 18th Century Studies (mem. editl. bd. 1977-80, exec. com. 96-99), Johnsonians, Johnson Soc. (sec.-treas. 1970-75, v.p. 2000—), Midwest Am. Soc. Eighteenth Century Studies, Eighteenth Century Scottish Studies. Home: 1505 Wood Ln Madison WI 53705-1456 Office: U Wis Dept English 600 N Park St Madison WI 53706-1403 E-mail: weinbrot@facstaff.wisc.edu.

WEINER, ANDREW MARC, electrical engineering educator; b. Boston, July 25, 1958; s. Jason and Geraldine Hannah (Aronson) W.; m. Brenda Joyce Garland, Apr. 1, 1989. SB in Elec. Engring., MIT, 1979, SM, 1981, ScD, 1984. Mem. tech. staff Bellcore, Red Bank, N.J., 1984-89, dist. mgr., 1989-92; prof. elec. engring. Purdue U., West Lafayette, Ind., 1992—. Assoc. editor IEEE Jour. Quantum Electronics, 1988-94; adv. editor Optics Letters, 1989-94, topical editor, 1995-98; assoc. editor: IEEE Photonics Tech. Letters, 1994-95. Fannie and John Hertz Found. grad. fellow, 1979-84. Fellow Optical Soc. Am. (tech. coun. 1988-91, Adolph Lomb award 1990), IEEE (Traveling Lectr. award Lasers and Electro-optics Soc. 1988-89, bd. Govs. Lasers and Electro-optics Soc. 1997—), Am. Soc. Engring. Edn. (Curtis W. McGraw award 1997), Internat. Commn. for Optics (ICO-97 prize). Avocations include invention of techniques for manipulating the shapes of ultrashort laser pulses; pioneering studies of ultrafast nonlinear optics. Office: Purdue U Sch Elec & Computer Engring West Lafayette IN 47907-1285

WEINER, GEORGE JAY, internist; b. Plainview, N.Y., Mar. 1, 1956; m. Teresa Emily Wilhelm, July 30, 1983; children: Aaron, Miriam, Nathan. BA, Johns Hopkins U., 1978; MD, Ohio State U., 1981. Resident in internal medicine Med. Coll. Ohio, Toledo, 1981-85; hematology/oncology fellow U. Mich., Ann Arbor, 1985-89; asst. prof. medicine U. Iowa, Iowa City, 1989-94, assoc. prof., 1994-99, prof., 1999—, dir. Cancer Ctr., 1998—. Achievements include devel. of new approaches to cancer immunotherapy. Office: Univ of Iowa 5970 JPP Iowa City IA 52242

WEINER, GERALD ARNE, stockbroker; b. Chgo., Dec. 20, 1941; s. Irwin S. and Lilyan (Stock) W.; m. Barbara I. Allen, June 18, 1967; children: Rachel Anne, Sara Naomi. BSS, Loyola U., Chgo., 1964; student, U. Vienna, 1962-63; MS, Georgetown U., 1966; postgrad., Ind. U., 1966-72, S.E. Asian Areas Cert., 1967. Pacification specialist AID, Laos, 1965; instr. polit. sci. Loyola U., Chgo., 1970-72; asst. v.p. A.G. Becker & Co., 1973-78; sr. v.p. Oppenheimer & Co., 1978-83, J. David Securities, Inc., Chgo., 1983-84, Morgan Stanley Dean Witter, Chgo., 1984—. Exec. edn. for securities industry Wharton Sch. Bus. U. Pa., 1988-90. Trustee Highland Park Police Pension Fund. Mucia fellow, 1969. Mem. Midwest Bonsai Soc., Elgin Bonsai Group, Multiplex Club. Democrat. Jewish. Office: Morgan Stanely 70 W Madison St Ste 300 Chicago IL 60602-4278

WEINFURTER, DANIEL JOSEPH, business services executive; b. Milw., Apr. 16, 1957; s. Joseph Thomas and Betty E. (Stanton) W.; m. Martha Marie Brennan, May 14, 1983; children: Amy Jordan, Andrea Taylor. BSBA, Marquette U., 1979, MBA, 1984; postgrad., George Washington U., 1984-85. Account rep. Gen. Electric Info. Svcs., Milw., 1979-81, sr. account rep., 1982-84, project mgr. Rockville, Md., 1984-86; acting regional sales mgr. Gen. Electric Corp., Morristown, N.J., 1986, dist. sales mgr. Bensonville, Ill., 1986-87; regional sales mgr. Intelogic Trace, Inc., Schaumburg, 1987-89, area sales mgr., 1989; dir. bus. devel. Alternative Resources Corp., Lincolnshire, 1989-90, v.p. ops., 1990-93; pres. Alternative Resources Corp. Ventures, 1993—; CEO Parson Group, Chig., 1995—. Ad-hoc com. Riverwoods (Ill.) Village Coun., 1990—; mem. YMCA. Democrat. Roman Catholic. Avocations: running, raquetball, bicycling, golf, reading. Home: 201 Cumberland Ave Kenilworth IL 60043-1169 Office: Alternative Resources Corp 300 Tri State Internat Lincolnshire IL 60069

WEINGEIST, THOMAS ALAN, ophthalmology educator; b. N.Y.C., Jan. 28, 1940; s. Samson and Fausta (Haim) W.; m. Carol Perera, Mar. 19, 1963 (div. Aug. 1977); children: Aaron P., Rachel; m. Catherine McGregor, Aug. 18, 1977; children: Robert M., David M. BA, Earlham Coll., 1963; PhD, Columbia U., 1969; MD, U. Iowa, 1972. Resident in ophthalmology U. Iowa, 1972-75, fellow in retina, 1976, asst. prof. ophthalmology, 1976-80, assoc. prof., 1980-83, prof., 1983—, prof., head dept. ophthalmology, 1986—. DeVoe lectr. Columbia U., 2001. Mem. editl. bd. Documenta Ophthalmologica, The Netherlands, 1989-94, Ophthalmology World News, 1994-96; med. editor Argus/Ophthalmology's World News, 1996-98; med. editor EyeNet mag., 1999-2001. Fellow: Am. Acad. Ophthalmology (editl. bd. jour. 1982—, assoc. sec. for self-assessment 1988—93, sec. continuing edn. 1993—, trustee 1993—, sr. sec. clin. edn. 1994—, pres. 2002—, Honor award 1979, Sr. Honor award 1989); mem.: Assn. Univ. Profs. Ophthalmology (bd. dirs., pres. 1995), Am. Medico-Legal Found., Vitreous Soc., Retina Soc., Macula Soc. Avocations: photography, tennis. Home: 3 Heather Ct Iowa City IA 52245-3226 Office: U Iowa Dept Ophthalmology Iowa City IA 52242

WEINHAUER, BOB, professional sports team executive; b. N.Y.C., May 23, 1939; m. Sue Robin Weinhauer; children: Jodie, Jamie, Kristen, Keri, Robert; 1 stepchild, Michelle. Diploma in phys. edn. and health, SUNY, Cortland, 1961. Coach various h.s., N.Y.C., 1961-72; asst. coach U. Pa., Phila., 1972-77, head coach, 1977-82, Ariz. State U., 1982-85, Detroit Spirits, 1985-86; scout Phila. 76ers, 1987-88, dir. player pers., asst. coach, 1988-90, asst. gen. mgr., 1990-91; asst. coach Atlanta Hawks, 1991-93, Minn. Timberwolves, 1993-94; v.p. basketball ops. Houston Rockets, 1994-96; asst. coach Milw. Bucks, 1996-97, gen. mgr., 1997—. Named to SUNY Cortland Hall of Fame, 1995, Massapequa (N.Y.) H.S. Hall of Fame, 1997. Office: c/o Milw Bucks 1001 N 4th St Milwaukee WI 53203-1314

WEINHOLD, VIRGINIA BEAMER, interior designer; b. Elizabeth, N.J., June 21, 1932; d. Clayton Mitchell and Rosemary (Behrend) Beamer; divorced; children: Thomas Craig, Robert Scott, Amy Linette. BA, Cornell U., 1955; BFA summa cum laude, Ohio State U., 1969; MA in Design Mgmt., Ohio State U., 1982. Freelance interior designer, 1969-72; interior designer, dir. interior design Karlsberger and Assocs. Inc., Columbus, Ohio, 1972-82; assoc. prof. dept. design Ohio State U., 1982—, grad. studies chairperson, 1986-89, 1995-96; lectr. indsl. design Ohio State U., 1972, 79-80. Trustee Found. for Interior Design Edn. and Rsch., 1991-97. Mem. Inst. Bus. Designers (chpt. treas. 1977-79, nat. trustee 1979-81, nat. chmn. contract documents com. 1979-84, chpt. pres. 1981-83), Constrn. Specifications Inst., Interior Design Educator's Coun. (nat. treas. 1989-93), Interior Design Educator's Coun. Found. (nat. treas. 1992-94), Illuminating Engring. Soc. (chpt. v.p. 1997-98), AIA (assoc.), Internat. Interior Design Assn. (nat. dir. 1994-97). Prin. works include Grands Rapids (Mich.) Osteo. Hosp., Melrose (Mass.) Wakefield Hosp., Christopher Inn, Columbus, John W. Galbreath Hdqrs., Columbus, Guernsey Meml. Hosp., Cambridge, Ohio, Trinity Epis. Ch. and Parish House, Columbus, Hale Hosp., Haverhill, Mass., Ohio State U. Dept. Indsl. Design Lighting Lab., others. Author: IBD Forms and Documents Manual, Interior Finish Materials for Health Care Facilities, Subjective Impressions: Lighting Hotels and Resturants, 1989, Effects of Lighting on The Perception of Interior Spaces, 1993. Home: 112 Glen Dr Columbus OH 43085-4010 Office: Ohio State U Dept Design 128 N Oval Mall Columbus OH 43210-1318

WEINKAUF, MARY LOUISE STANLEY, clergywoman; b. Eau Claire, Wis., Sept. 22, 1938; d. Joseph Michael and Marie Barbara (Holzinger) Stanley; m. Alan D. Weinkauf, Oct. 12, 1962 (dec. Nov. 2000); children: Stephen, Xanti. BA, Wis. State U., 1961; MA, U. Tenn., 1962, PhD, 1966; MDiv, Luth. Sch. Theology, Chgo., 1993. Grad. asst., instr. U. Tenn., 1961-66; asst. prof. English Adrian Coll., 1966-69; prof., head dept. English Dakota Wesleyan U., Mitchell, S.D., 1969-89; instr. Columbia Coll., 1989-91. Pastor Calvary Evang. Luth. Ch., Siloa Luth. Ch., Ontonagon Faith, White Pine, Mich., Gowrie, Iowa. Author: Hard-Boiled Heretic, 1994, Sermons in Science Fiction, 1994, Murder Most Poetic, 1996. Trustee The Ednl. Found., 1986-90; bd. dirs. Ontonagon County Habitat for Humanity, 1995-97; mem. bd. Luth. Campus Ministry for Wis. and Upper Mich., 1996—. Mem. AAUW (divsn. pres. 1978-80), Nat. Coun. Tchrs. English, S.D. Coun. Tchrs. English, Sci. Fiction Rsch. Assn., Popular Culture Assn., Milton Soc., S.D. Poetry Soc. (pres. 1982-83), Delta Kappa Gamma (pres. local chpt., mem. state bd. 1972-89, state v.p. 1979-83, state pres. 1983-85), Sigma Tau Delta, Pi Kappa Delta, Phi Kappa Phi. E-mail: woodwork@nnex.net.

WEINKOPF, FRIEDRICH J. lawyer; b. Bautsch, Germany, Feb. 17, 1930; Referendar, U. Marburg, Germany, 1954; LLM, U. Pa., 1958; JD, Chgo.-Kent Coll. Law, 1967. Bar: Ill. 1967. Ptnr. Baker & McKenzie, Chgo. Office: Baker & McKenzie 1 Prudential Plz 130 E Randolph St Fl 3600 Chicago IL 60601-6315

WEINREICH, GABRIEL, physicist, minister, educator; b. Vilnius, Lithuania, Feb. 12, 1928; came to U.S., 1941, naturalized, 1949; s. Max and Regina (Szabad) W.; m. Alisa Lourié, Apr. 19, 1951 (dec. 1970); m. Gerane Siemering Benamou, Oct. 23, 1971; children: Catherine, Marc, Daniel, Rebecca, Natalie. AB, Columbia U., 1948, MA, 1949, PhD, 1954. Ordained priest Episcopal Ch., 1986. Mem. staff Bell Telephone Labs., Murray Hill, N.J., 1953-60; mem. faculty U. Mich., Ann Arbor, 1960—, prof. physics, 1964-95; prof. emeritus, 1995—; Collegiate prof. U. Mich., 1974-76. Adj. min. St. Clare's Episcopal ch., Ann Arbor, 1985-90; rector St. Stephen's Episcopal Ch., Hamburg, Mich., 1993-96. Author: Solids: Elementary Theory for Advanced Students, 1965, Fundamental Thermodynamics, 1968, Notes for General Physics, 1972, Geometrical Vectors, 1998; editor: Mechanics of Musical Instruments, 1995. Recipient Disting. Teaching award U. Mich., 1968, Klopsteg award Am. Assn. Physics Tchrs., 1992, Internat. medal French Acoustical Soc., 1992. Fellow Acoustical Soc. Am. (assoc. editor Jour. 1987-89). Home: 754 Greenhills Dr Ann Arbor MI 48105-2718 Office: Randall Lab U Mich Ann Arbor MI 48109-1120 E-mail: weinreic@umich.edu.

WEINRICH, ALAN JEFFREY, occupational hygienist; b. Passaic, N.J., Aug. 24, 1953; s. Erwin Hermann and Ann Elizabeth Weinrich; m. Nina Kathryn Hooker, Jan. 14, 1983; 1 child, Sheena Elizabeth Rochelle. BS with high honors, Rutgers U., 1975; MS, U. Iowa, 1988, postgrad., 1988-89. Cert. Am. Bd. Indsl. Hygiene, cert. environ. trainer Nat. Environ. Tng. Assn. Indsl. hygienist Tenn. Dept. Labor, Nashville, 1975-78; health info. specialist occupl. health program U. Tenn., Memphis, 1980-82; vol. tchr. Internat. Sch. Moshi, Tanzania, 1982-84; sr. rsch. asst. agrl. medicine rsch. facility U. Iowa, Iowa City, 1985-89; sr. indsl. hygienist PSI Energy, Inc., Plainfield, Ind., 1989-92; asst. dir. health & safety programs environ. mgmt. and edn. Purdue U., West Lafayette, 1992-94; assoc. dir. tech. affairs Am. Conf. Govtl. Indsl. Hygienists, Cin., 1994-97, dir. tech. affairs, 1997-99, dir. scientific affairs, 1999—. Co-editor book supplements: Documentation of the Threshold Limit Values and Biological Exposure Indices, 1996-98; editor, author ACGIH newsletter Today!; developer, editor CD-Rom publ. TLVs and Other Occupational Exposure Values. Mem. healthy cities com. Butler-Tarkington Neighorhood Assn., Indpls., 1992-94; mem. Greenways Com., City of Wyoming, Ohio. Mem. Am. Acad. Indsl. Hygiene, Am. Conf. Govtl. Indsl. Hygienists, Am. Indsl. Hygiene Assn. (v.p. Mid-South sect. 1981-82, bd. dirs. Iowa-Ill. sect. 1987-89, bd. dirs. Ind. sect. 1991-94, pres. Ind. sect. 1994-95), Internat. Occupl. Hygiene Assn., Am. Soc. Assn. Execs. Avocations: bicycling, family, reading, walking, softball. Office: Am Conf Govtl Indsl Hygienists 1330 Kemper Meadow Dr Cincinnati OH 45240-4147 E-mail: science@ACGIH.org.

WEINSTEIN, JAY A. social science educator, researcher; b. Chgo., Feb. 23, 1942; s. Lawrence E. and Jacqueline L. (Caplan) W.; m. Diana S. Staffin, Sept. 16, 1961; m. Marilyn L. Schwartz, Nov. 25, 1972; children— Liza, Bennett. AB, U. Ill., 1963, PhD, 1973; MA, Washington U., St. Louis, 1965. Teaching fellow U. Ill., Urbana, 1963-64; teaching asst. McGill U., Montreal, Que., Can., 1966-68; instr. Sir George Williams U., Can., 1967-68; lectr. Simon Fraser U., Vancouver, B.C., Can., 1968; asst. prof. North Central Coll., Naperville, Ill., 1970-71, U. Iowa, 1973-77; prof. social sci. Ga. Inst. Tech., Atlanta, 1977-86; head dept. sociology Eastern Mich U., 1986-90, faculty rsch. fellow, 1990-91; grantee ednl. devel. project USIA-Soros Found., Albania, 1992—; dir. Applied Rsch. Unit, 1996—. Cons. World Bank Study Social and Econ. Vulnerability in Albania, 1997, World Bank Study on Closing the Vulnerability Gap, Albania, 1997—98; project dir. Ea. Mich.-U-Ypsilanti Cmty. Outreach Partnership Ctr.; cons. pvt. and pub. agencies; rschr. in field. Author: Madras: An Analysis of Urban Ecological Structure in India, 1974, Demographic Transition and Social Change, 1976, Sociology-Technology: Foundations of Postacademic Social Science, 1982, The Grammar of Social Relations: The Major Essays of Louis Schneider, 1984; editor: Paradox and Society, 1986; (with Vinod Tewari and V.L.S. Prakash Rao) Indian Cities: Ecological Perspectives, Social and Cultural Change: Social Science for a Dynamic World, 1997, 1987, The Holocaust: A Sociological Analysis, 1997, Demography: The Science of Population, 2000; Studies in Comparative International Development, 1978-88; mem. editorial bd. Social Development Issues, 1977-85; specialized contbr. Calcutta Mcpl.

Gazette, 1979—; editor: Social and Cultural Change, 1974-75; ed. Michigan Soc. Review, 1997—, editorial reviewer Jour. Asian Studies, Social Devel. Issues, Tech. and Culture, Am. Sociologist, Technol. Forecasting and Social Change; contbr. chpts. to book, articles to profl. jours. Recipient Charles Horton Cooley award for outstanding contbns. to sociology in Mich., 1998; Fulbright prof. Ahmedabad, India, 1975-76, Hyderabad, India, 1981-82; grantee Ga. Tech. Found., 1981-82, World Order Studies Course, 1994-97, State of Mich. Rsch. Excellence Fund; Steinberg fellow, 1967. Mem. Am. Sociol. Assn., Soc. for Applied Sociology (v.p. 1998—, mem. exec. bd. 2000—), Mich. Sociol. Assn. (pres. 1988-89, v.p. 1994-95), Sigma Xi. Jewish Office: Eastern Mich U Sociology Dept Ypsilanti MI 48197 E-mail: weinst@aol.com.

WEINSTEIN, MICHAEL ALAN, political science educator; b. Bklyn., Aug. 24, 1942; s. Aaron and Grace (Sosin) W.; m. Deena Schneiweiss, May 31, 1964. B.A. summa cum laude, NYU, 1964; M.A. in Polit. Sci., Case Western Res. U., 1965, Ph.D., 1967. Asst. prof. polit. sci. Case Western Res. U., summer 1967, Va. Poly. Inst., 1967-68; asst. prof. Purdue U., 1968-70, assoc. prof., 1970-72, prof., 1972—; Milward Simpson disting. prof. polit. sci. U. Wyo., 1979. Author: (with Deena Weinstein) Living Sociology, 1974, The Polarity of Mexican Thought, 1976, The Tragic Sense of Political Life, 1977, Meaning and Appreciation, 1978, The Structure of Human Life, 1979, The Wilderness and the City, 1982, Unity and Variety in the Philosophy of Samuel Alexander, 1984, Finite Perfection, 1985, Culture Critique: Fernand Dumont and New Quebec Sociology, 1985, (with Helmut Loiskandl and Deena Weinstein) Georg Simmel's Scopenhauer and Nietzsche, 1986; (with Deena Weinstein) Deconstruction as Cultural History/The Cultural History of Deconstruction, 1990, La Déconstruction un Jeu Symbolique, 1990, (with Deena Weinstein) Georg Simmel: Sociological Flâmeur/Bricoleur, 1991, Photographic Realism as a Moral Practice, 1992, (with Deena Weinstein) Postmodern(ized) Simmel, 1993, (with Arthur Kroker) Data Trash: The Theory of the Virtual Class, 1994, Culture/Flesh: Explorations of Postcivilized Modernity, 1995, Peter Vierecki Reconciliation and Beyond, 1997, East/West: Globalizing Civilization, 2000; mem. editorial bd. Humanitas, Social Philosophy Rsch. Book Series. Recipient Best Paper prize Midwest Polit. Sci. Assn., 1969; Guggenheim fellow, 1974-75; Rockefeller Found. humanities fellow, 1976; fellow Center Humanistic Studies, Purdue U., 1981 Mem. Phi Beta Kappa. Home: 800 Princess Dr West Lafayette IN 47906-2038 Office: Dept Polit Sci Purdue U West Lafayette IN 47907

WEINSTOCK, JOEL VINCENT, immunologist; b. Detroit, Mar. 21, 1948; s. Herman and Esther B. (Frazein) W.; m. Allison Lee Rose, July 15, 1979; children: Lisa, Jeffrey, Andrew. BS, U. Mich., 1969; MD, Wayne State U., 1973. Diplomate Am. Bd. Internal Medicine, subspeciality gastroenterology; lic. physician, Mich., Iowa. Straight med. intern Univ. Hosp., Ann Arbor, Mich., 1973-74, resident internal medicine, 1974-76, fellow gastroenterology dept. internal medicine, 1976-78; asst. prof. internal medicine Wayne State U. Sch. Medicine, Detroit, 1978-83, assoc. prof., 1983-86, adj. assoc. prof. dept. immunology and microbiology, 1983-86, vice chief divsn. gastroenterology, 1984-86; assoc. prof., dir. gastroenterology divsn. U. Iowa, Iowa City, 1986-91, prof., dir., 1991—, dir. Ctr. Digestive Diseases, 1990—, dir. divsn. gastroenterology-hepatology, 1986—. Mem. exec. bd. Crohn's and Colitis Found. Am., N.Y.C., 1993—, mem. tng. awards rev. com., 1991-93, chmn., 1993—; chief sect. gastroenterology Hutzel Hosp., Detroit, 1978-84, dir. endoscopy unit, 1978-84, dir. nutritional support svc., 1980-84; vice chief gastroenterology dept. medicine Wayne State U. Sch. Medicine, 1984-86; dir. gastroenterology subspecialty unit Harper Hosp., Detroit, 1984-86, vice-chief gastroenterology, 1984-86; mem. sci. adv. ang grant rev. com. Crohn's and Colitis Found. Am., 1987—; mem. NIH Task force for developing nat. agenda for IBD rsch., 1989; mem. Lederle award selection com., 1989; mem. study sect. NIH Core Ctr. Rev. Com., 1990, 92; mem. abstract rev. com. ASCI, 1990; vis. prof. Washington U., St. Louis, 1990, U. Tex., Houston, 1991, Cleve. Clinic, 1992, U. Md., Balt., 1993; participant various conferences and meetings; mem. Digestive Diseases Ctr. Planning Com., 19886—; mem. Adult TPN Subcom., 1986—; chmn. coord. com. Ctr. Digestive Diseases, 1986—; mem. grant rev. coms. NIH, 1980—; mem. gastroenterology subspecialty coun. CSCR, 1993—. Mem. editl. bd. Autoimmunity Forum: Gastroenterology Edit., 1989-92; mem. internat. adv. bd. Alimentary Pharmacology and Therapeutics, 1990—; sect. editor Jour. Inflammatory Bowel Disease, 1994; reviewer Am. Jour Gastroenterology, Jour. Clin. Investigation, Jour. Immunology, Jour. Clin. Immunology, Gastroenterology, Digestive Diseases and Scis.; contbr. articles to profl. jours., chpts. to books. Rsch. grantee NIH, 1982—, Sandoz Pharm., 1993, Marion Merrell Dow, 1994, Centocor, 1995. Mem. AAAS, Am. Inst. Nutrition, Am. Soc. Clin. Nutrition, Ctrl. Soc. Clin. Rsch., Am. Soc. Gastrointestinal Endoscopy, Am. Assn. Study Liver Disease, Am. Fedn. Clin. Rsch., Am. Assn. Immunologists, Ileitis and Colitis Found. Am., Am. Soc. Clin. Investigation, Clin. Immunology Soc., Am. Gastroenterological Assn. (rsch. com. 1987-90, chmn. task force rsch. fellowship awards 1989-90, program evaluation com. 1990—), Midwest Gut Club (councillor 1990—), Alpha Omega Alpha. Achievements include research in elucidaiton of immunoregulatory circuits that control granulomatous inflammation; characterization of how neurokines help control inflammatory responses; avocations: stamp collecting, reading, gardening, exercising, child rearing. Office: U Iowa College of Med Internal Medicine 4607JCP 200 Hawkins Dr Iowa City IA 52242-1009

WEINTRAUB, JOSEPH BARTON, publishing executive; b. Phila., Dec. 2, 1945; s. George and Edith (Lubner) W.; m. Denise Waters, June 14, 1974. BA, U. Pitts., 1966; MA, U. Chgo., 1967, PhD, 1973. Assoc. faculty U. Ind., Gary, Ind., 1970-74; mktg. specialist journalism div. U. Chgo. Press, 1974-75, sr. copywriter journalism div., 1975-78; periodical specialist ABA, Chgo., 1978-80, mktg. mgr., 1980-92, dir. publ. planning, 1992-97, dir. book publ., 1997-99; mgr. dir. mktg. U. Chgo. Press, 1999—. Mktg. cons. Teachers Coll. Record, N.Y.C., 1977-79, Repertoire Internat. de la Litterature de l'Art, N.Y.C., 1977-79, Am. Lung Assn., 1980-82. Writer You, 2000; contbr. essays, translations, plays, poems, short fiction to lit. revs. and small press anthologies. Recipient award Ill. Art Coun., Barrington Art Coun. Mem. Phi Beta Kappa. Avocations: writing, language study. Office: U Chgo Press 1427 E 60th Street Chicago IL 60637-5418

WEINTRAUB, NEAL L. medical educator, cardiologist; Student, Tulane u., 1977-80, MD, 1984. Diplomate Am. Bd. Internal Medicine, Am. Bd. Cardiovasc. Diseases. Resident Emory U., Atlanta, 1984-86, U. Ill., Urbana-Champaign, 1986-87, clin. instr. medicine Coll. Medicine, 1987-88, asst. clin. prof. medicine Coll. Medicine, 1988-90; staff physician VA Med. Ctr., Danville, Ill., 1987-90, St. Louis, 1990-91; asst. prof. medicine Sch. Medicine St. Louis U., 1990-95, postdoctoral fellow clin. pharmacology, 1992-94; asst. cardiology divsn. U. Iowa Coll. Medicine, Iowa City, 1995-97, assoc. prof. cardiology, 1997—. Contbr. articles to profl. jours. Recipient Travel award Am. Coll. Cardiology/Bristol-Myers Squibb, 1994, Clinician Scientist award Am. Heart Assn., 1996. Mem. Alpha Omega Alpha. Achievements include research in vascular biology and physiology and lipid biochemistry. Office: U Iowa Coll Medicine CV Div Dept Internal Medicine 200 Hawkins Dr Iowa City IA 52242-1009

WEINZAPFEL, JONATHAN, public relations executive, congressional aide; b. Evansville, Ill., Nov. 16, 1965; BA, Ind. U., 1988; MA, Georgetown U., 1993. Dem. candidate 8th dist. Ind. U.S. House of Reps., 1996. Roman Catholic. Office: Weinzapfel for Congress PO Box 6630 Evansville IN 47719-0630

WEIR, BRYCE KEITH ALEXANDER, neurosurgeon, neurology educator; b. Edinburgh, Scotland, Apr. 29, 1936; came to U.S., 1992; s. Ernest John and Marion (Stewart) W.; m. Mary Lou Lauber, Feb. 25, 1976; children: Leanora, Glyncora, Brocke. BSc, McGill U., Montreal, Que., Can., 1958, MD, CM, 1960, MSc, 1963. Diplomate Am. Bd. Neurol. Surgery, Nat. Bd. Med. Examiners. Intern Montreal Gen. Hosp., 1960-61; resident in neurosurgery Neurological Inst., Montreal, 1962-64, 65-66, N.Y. Neurol. Inst., N.Y.C., 1964-65; neurosurgeon U. Alta., Edmonton, Can., 1967-92, dir. div. neurosurgery Can., 1982-86, Walter Anderson prof., chmn. dept. surgery Can., 1986-92; surgeon-in-chief U. Alta. Hosps., 1986-92; Maurice Goldblatt prof. surgery and neurology U. Chgo., 1992—2002, dir. Brain Rsch. Inst., 1993—2001, 20interim dean biol. scis. divsn. and Pritzker Sch. Medicine, v.p. med. affairs, 2001—02. Past pres. V Internat. Symposium on Cerebral Vasospasm; mem. neurology A study sect. NIH, 1991—93; invited speaker at over 135 profl. meetings; vis. prof. over 68 univs., including Yale U., Cornell U., Columbia U., Duke U., U. Toronto, U. Calif., San Francisco; over 18 named lectureships, including White lectr. , Harvard U.; over 16 named lectureships, including Gainey lectr., Mayo Clinic. Author: Aneurysms Affecting the Nervous System, 1987, Subarachnoid Hemorrhage-Causes and Cures, 1998, Cerebral Vasospasm, 2001; co-editor: Primer on Cerebrovascular Diseases, 1997; mem. editl. bd. Jour. Neurosurgery, chmn. bd, 1993—94, mem. editl. bd. Neurosurgery Quar., Jour. Cereborvascular Disease, Neurosurgery; contbr. over 265 articles to med. jours. Named Officer of the Order of Can., 1995. Fellow: ACS, Royal Coll. Surgeons Can., Royal Coll. Surgeons Edinburgh (hon.); mem.: Interurban Neurosurg. Soc. (chmn.), Nat. Acad. Scis., Inst. Medicine, Soc. Neurol. Surgsons (Grass gold medal 1992), Japan Neurosurg. Soc. (hon.), Am. Acad. Neurol. Surgeons, James. IV Assn. Surgeons, Am. Surg. Assn. Achievements include contributions to the understanding of cerebral vasospasm and the surgical management of intracranial aneurysms. Office: U of Chgo Pritzker Sch of Medicine 5841 S Maryland Ave Chicago IL 60637-1463

WEIR, MORTON WEBSTER, retired academic administrator, educator; b. Canton, Ill., July 18, 1934; s. James and Frances Mary (Johnson) W.; m. Cecelia Ann Rumler, June 23, 1956; children: Deborah, Kevin, Mark. AB, Knox Coll., 1955; MA, U. Tex., 1958, PhD, 1959. Rsch. assoc., asst. prof. child devel. U. Minn., Mpls., 1959; asst. prof. child devel. U. Ill., Urbana, 1960-64, assoc. prof., 1964-68, prof., 1968-93, prof. emeritus, 1993—, head dept. psychology, 1969-71, vice chancellor acad. affairs, 1971-79, v.p. acad. affairs, 1988-88, chancellor, 1988-93, chancellor emeritus, 1993—, sr. found. rep., 1993-99; dir. Boys Town Center Study Youth Development, 1979-80. Contbr. numerous articles to profl. jours. Trustee Knox Coll., 1984—, chmn., 1995-99; trustee Menninger Found., 1993—; dir. RHR Internat. Co., 1986—. With AUS, 1960. NSF Predoctoral fellow, 1957-59 Fellow AAAS; mem. Soc. Rsch. in Child Devel. (chmn. bd. publs. 1971, chmn. fin. com. 1993-95), Sigma Xi, Phi Beta Kappa, Phi Kappa Phi.

WEIS, MERVYN J. physician, gastroenterologist; b. Chgo., June 9, 1940; s. Theodore A. and Anita (Stavins) W.; m. Myra Rubenstein, Nov. 26, 1966 (dec. Nov. 1990); children: Jonathan Mandel, Sari Tova; m. Anita Kaplan Sherbet, Oct. 1992. BA, Northwestern U., 1961, MD, 1965. Diplomate Am. Bd. Internal Medicine. Intern in internal medicine Michael Reese Hosp. and Med. Ctr., Chgo., 1965-66, resident in internal medicine, 1966-67, 69-70, attending physician, 1972-78; fellow in gastroenterology Northwestern U. Med. Ctr., 1970-72; attending physician Ravenswood Hosp., 1979-83, St. Francis Hosp., Evanston, Ill., 1984-88, Rush North Med. Ctr., Skokie, 1985-91, Louis A. Weiss Meml. Hosp., Chgo., 1972—, chmn. divsn. medicine, 1987-89, pres. med. staff, 1989-93, mem. bd. govs., 1987—. Cons. in gastroenterology VA Rsch. Hosp., Chgo., 1972-80 Contbr. articles to profl. jours. Capt. U.S. Army, 1967-69. Fellow ACP, Am. Coll. Gastroenterology, Am. Gastroenterologic Soc.; mem. AMA, Ill. State Med. Soc., Chgo. Soc. Gastroenterology, Chgo. Med. Soc., Am. Gastroenterol. Assn. (diplomate). Avocations: golf, jogging, computers. Office: 4640 N Marine Dr Ste C 6100 Chicago IL 60640-5719

WEISBACH, LOU, advertising executive; Pres., CEO, founder Ha-Lo Industries, Inc., Niles, Ill., 1972-99, chmn., 1999—. Office: HALO Industries Inc 5800 W Touhy Ave Niles IL 60714

WEISBERG, HERBERT FRANK, political science educator; b. Mpls., Dec. 8, 1941; s. Nathan R. and Jean (Schlessinger) W.; m. Judith Ann Robinson, Dec. 16, 1979; 1 child, Bryan Bowen. BA, U. Minn., 1963; PhD, U. Mich., 1968. Asst. prof. polit. sci. U. Mich., Ann Arbor, 1967-73, assoc. prof. polit. sci., 1973-74, Ohio State U., Columbus, 1974-77, prof. polit. sci., 1977—. Author: Central Tendency and Variation, 1992; co-author: Theory Building and Data Analysis, 1984, Controversies in Voting Behavior, 2001, Survey Research Polling and Data Analysis, 1996, Classics in Congressional Politics, 1999; editor: Political Science: Science of Politics, 1985, Democracy's Feast: Elections in America, 1995; co-editor Am. Jour. Polit. Sci., 1979-82, Great Theatre: The American Congress in the 1990's, 1998, Reelection 1996: How Americans Voted, 1999. Mem.: Am. Polit. Sci. Assn. (program chmn. 1983), Midwest Polit. Sci. Assn. (pres. 2001—02), Phi Kappa Phi, Pi Sigma Alpha, Phi Beta Kappa. Home: 742 Gatehouse Ln Columbus OH 43235-1732 Office: Ohio State U Dept Polic Sci 2140 Derby Hall 154 N Oval Mall Columbus OH 43210-1330

WEISBERG, LOIS, arts administrator, city official; Commr. Chgo. Dept. Cultural Affairs, 1989—. Office: Chicago Cultural Center 78 E Washington St Chicago IL 60602-4816

WEISKITTEL, RALPH JOSEPH, real estate broker; b. Covington, Ky., Jan. 1, 1924; s. Nelson I. and Hilda (Nieman) W.; m. Audrey Bushelman, June 19, 1948; children— Thomas, Carol Anne, Barbara Jane. Eve. student, Xavier U., Cin., 1946-47. Mem. staff Cin. Enquirer, 1942-43, 45—, home sect. editor, 1958-63, bus. editor, 1963-77; v.p. corp. markets Koetzle Corp. (Realtors), 1977-79; v.p. Devitt and Assocs. (Realtors), 1979-90; v.p. sales and mktg. Toebben Cos., 1990-91; sr. v.p. The Chelsea-Moore Co., 1991-94; v.p. sales Cline Realtors, Cin., 1994-2001; comml. broker Huff Realty, Ft. Mitchell, Ky., 2001—. Dir. New Comty. Developers, Inc. Mem. city council, Ft. Wright, Ky., 1960-68; mem. St. Agnes Parish Council, 1974-77; mem. bishop's adv. council Diocese of Covington. Served with AUS, 1943-46. Mem. Nat. Assn. Real Estate Editors, Soc. Am. Bus. Writers. Club: Cin. Athletic. Home: 1571 St Anthony Dr Covington KY 41011-3752 Office: Huff Realty 250 Grandview Dr Fort Mitchell KY 41017

WEISMAN, GARY ANDREW, biochemist; b. Bklyn., June 18, 1951; s. Joseph Herman and Elaine (Melman) W.; m. Sandra Kay Hille, Aug. 4, 1979; children: Laura Joanne, Pamela Michelle, Veronica Evelyn. BS, Polytechnic U., 1972; postgrad., U. Bordeaux, France, 1972-74; PhD, U. Nebr., 1980. Postdoctoral rsch. assoc. Cornell U., N.Y.C., 1980-85; asst. prof. U. Mo., Columbia, 1985-92, assoc. prof., 1992-98, prof., 1998—. Spl. reviewer NIH; reviewer NSF, Jour. Membrane Biology and Eur. Jour. Cancer, Am. Jour. Physiology. Contbr. articles to profl. jours. Grantee USDA, 1987—, NIH, 1988—, CF Found., 1994—, Am. Diabetes, 1995—. Mem. AAAS, Am. Chem. Soc., Am. Soc. Biochem. and Molecular Biology, Am. Diabetes Assn., Am. Heart Assn., N.Y. Acad. Scis. Home: 1804 University Ave Columbia MO 65201-6004 Office: U Mo Dept Biochemistry M121 Med Scis Bldg Columbia MO 65212-0001 E-mail: weismang@missouri.edu.

WEISMAN, JOEL, nuclear engineering educator, engineering consultant; b. N.Y.C., July 15, 1928; s. Abraham and Ethel (Marcus) W.; m. Bernice Newman, Feb. 6, 1955; 1 child, Jay (dec.) B.Ch.E., CCNY, 1948; M.S., Columbia U., 1949; Ph.D., U. Pitts, 1968. Registered profl. engr., N.Y. Plant engr. Etched Products, N.Y.C., 1950-51; from jr. engr. to assoc. engr. Brookhaven Nat. Lab., Upton, N.Y., 1951-54; from engr. to fellow engr. Westinghouse Nuclear Energy Systems, Pitts., 1954-59, from fellow engr. to mgr. thermal and hydraulic analysis, 1960-68; sr. engr. Nuclear Devel. Assocs., White Plains, N.Y., 1959-60; assoc. prof. nuclear engring. U. Cin., 1968-72, prof. nuclear engring., 1972-96, dir. nuclear engring. program, 1977-86, dir. lab. basic and applied nuclear research, 1984-94, prof. emeritus nuclear engring., 1996—. Co-author: Thermal Analysis of Pressurized Water Reactors, 1970, 2d edit., 1979, 3rd edit., 1996, Introduction to Optimization Theory, 1973, Modern Power Plant Engineering, 1985; editor: Elements of Nuclear Reactor Design, 1977, 2d edit., 1983; contbr. tech. articles to profl. jours.; patentee in field. Mem. Cin. Environ. Adv. Council, 1976-78; mem. Cin. Asian Art Soc., 1977—, v.p., 1980-82, pres., 1982-84; mem. exec. bd. Air Pollution League Greater Cin., 1980-90. Sr. NATO fellow, Winfrith Lab., U.K. Atomic Energy Authority, 1972; sr. fellow Argonne Nat. Lab., Ill., 1982; NSF research grantee, 1974-78, 82-85, 86-89; recipient Dean's award U. Cin. Coll. Engring., 1987. Fellow Am. Nuclear Soc. (v.p. Pitts. sect. 1957-58, mem. exec. com. thermal-hydraulics div. 1989-92); mem. Am. Inst. Chem. Engrs., Sigma Xi Democrat. Jewish Avocation: Japanese art. Home: 3419 Manor Hill Dr Cincinnati OH 45220-1522 Office: U Cin Dept Mech Ind & Nuclear Engr Cincinnati OH 45221-0001

WEISMANTEL, GREGORY NELSON, management consultant and software executive; b. Houston, Sept. 8, 1940; s. Leo Joseph and Ellen Elizabeth (Zudis) W.; m. Marilyn Ann Fanger, June 18, 1966; children: Guy Gregory, Christopher Gregory, Andrea Rose. BA in English, U. Notre Dame, 1962; MBA in Internat. Bus., Loyola U., Chgo., 1979. With mgmt. staff Gen. Foods Corp., White Plains, N.Y., 1966-80; pres., chief exec. officer Manor House Foods, Inc., Addison, Ill., 1980-82, Weismantel & Assocs., Downers Grove, 1982-84; v.p. perishable div. Profl. Marketers, Inc., Lombard, 1984-86, group v.p. sales and mktg. services, dir. corp. strategy, 1986-87; v.p. mng. prin. CPG Industry, Louis A. Allen Assoc. Inc., Palo Alto, Calif., 1987-88; pres., chief exec. officer The Vista Tech. Group, Ltd., St. Charles, Ill., 1989-2000, chmn. bd., 2001—. Bd. dirs. Epicurean Foods, Ltd., Chgo.; pres., CEO The Vista Tech. Group, Ltd., The Vista Mgmt. Group. Chmn. fin. St. Edward's High Sch. Jubilee, Elgin, Ill., 1982-85; bd. dirs. Dist. 301 Sch. Bd., Burlington, Ill., 1980-84, St. Edward's Found., Elgin, 1982—. Capt. U.S. Army, 1962-66. Recipient ICP/Chgo. Software Assoc. Re-Engring. award, 1994-96; State of Ill. grantee, 1989, Build Ill. Investment Fund. Mem. Grocery Mfg. Sales Execs., Chgo. Software Assn., Chg. C. of C. (small bus. com.). Roman Catholic. Clubs: Merchandising Execs., Food Products, Am. Mktg. (Chgo.).

WEISS, CHARLES ANDREW, lawyer; b. Perryville, Mo., Jan. 24, 1942; s. Wallace Francis and Iola Francis Weiss; m. Marie Suzanne Desloge, June 10, 1972; children: Christopher, Robert, Julie, Anne. BJ with highest honors, U. Mo., 1964, AB in History, 1965; JD cum laude, Notre Dame U., 1968. Bar: Mo. 1968, U.S. Dist. Ct. (ea. dist.) Mo. 1968, U.S. Ct. Appeals (8th cir.) 1968, U.S. Supreme Ct. 1972, U.S. Ct. Appeals (9th cir.) 1974, U.S. Ct. Appeals (2d cir.) 1977, U.S. Ct. Appeals (5th cir.) 1992. Law clk. to chief judge U.S. Ct. Appeals (8th cir.), 1968; ptnr. Bryan Cave, St. Louis, 1969—. Lectr. St. Louis U. Law Sch., 1970-73. Supr. Red Cross Water Safety Program, Perry County, Mo., 1962-64; dir. Neighborhood Youth Corps., Perry County, 1965-66; pres. Perry County Young Democrats Club, 1965-67; committeeman Boy Scouts Am., 1982-86. Fellow Am. Coll. Trial Lawyers; mem. ABA (ho. of dels. 1986—), Met. Bar Assn. St. Louis (pres. 1984-85), Mo. Bar Assn. (bd. govs. 1985, v.p. 1994-95, pres.-elect 1995-96, pres. 1996-97), Mo. Athletic Club (St. Louis), The Riverlands Assn., Inc. (pres. 1991-93), Jefferson Nat. Parks Assn. (chmn. 1993-2000), Notre Dame Club St. Louis (dir. 1983—), Notre Dame Law Assn. (dir., pres. 1997—). Roman Catholic. Office: Bryan Cave 211 N Broadway Saint Louis MO 63102-2733

WEISS, ERWIN, greeting card company executive; V.p. mktg. and sales Rust Craft, Can., pres., Plus Mark, Inc., 1989; v.p. adminstrv. svcs. Carlton Cards Ltd., Can.; sales rep. Am. Greetings Corp., Cleve., 1977, sr. v.p. consumer products, 1991—. Bd. dirs. Diabetes Assn. Greater Cleve.; grad. leadership Cleve. program Greater Cleve. Growth Assn.; active various charitable orgns., Cleve. Office: Am Greetings Corp 1 American Rd Cleveland OH 44144-2301

WEISS, GERHARD HANS, German language educator; b. Berlin, Aug. 6, 1926; came to U.S., 1946; s. Curt Erich and Gertrud (Grothus) W.; m. Janet Marilyn Smith, Dec. 27, 1953; children: John Martin, Susan Elizabeth Weiss Spencer, James David. BA, Washington U., St. Louis, 1950, MA, 1952; PhD, U. Wis., 1956. Prof. German U. Minn., Mpls., 1956—, assoc. dean, 1967-71, 79, chmn. dept. German, 1987-95, interim dir. Ctr. Austrian Studies, 1999-2001. Mem. German-Am. Textbook Commn., Braunschweig, Fed. Republic Germany, 1985-88. Author: Begegnung mit Deutschland, 1970; editor: Unterrichtspraxis, 1975-80, Minn. Monographs in the Humanities, 1964-70; contbr. articles to profl. jours. Served to lt. col. USAR, 1946-75. Recipient Cross Merit, Fed. Republic Germany, 1982. Mem. MLA, Am. Assn. Tchrs. German (pres. 1982-83, cert. of merit 1981, Disting. German Educator award 1991, elected hon. mem. 1995), German Studies Assn. (v.p. 1997-98, pres. 1999-00), Am. Coun. Tchg. Fgn. Langs. (Nelson Brooks award 1987). Methodist. Home: 4101 Abbott Ave S Minneapolis MN 55410-1004

WEISS, JAMES MOSES AARON, psychiatrist, educator; b. St. Paul, Oct. 22, 1921; s. Louis Robert and Gertrude (Simon) W.; m. Bette Shapera, Apr. 7, 1946; children: Jenny Anne Weiss Ford, Jonathan James. AB summa cum laude, U. Minn., 1941, ScB, 1947, MB, 1949, MD, 1950; MPH with high honors, Yale U., 1951. Diplomate: Am. Bd. Psychiatry and Neurology (examiner 1963-83). Teaching asst. psychology St. Thomas Coll., St. Paul, 1941-42; intern USPHS Hosp., Seattle, 1949-50; resident, fellow psychiatry Yale Med. Sch., 1950-53; from instr. to asst. prof. psychiatry Washington U., St. Louis, 1954-60; mem. faculty U. Mo., 1959—, First Prof. psychiatry, 1961—, founding chmn. dept., 1960-91, prof. community medicine, 1971—, univ. prof. emeritus, 1991—. Vis. prof. Inst. Criminology, Cambridge (Eng.) U., 1968-69, All-India Inst. Med. Scis. and U. Malaya, 1984; internat. cons., 1958— ; founding co-chmn. Asian-Am. Consortium on Psychiat. Disorders, 1986—; Kohler disting. lectr. St. Louis U., 1988. Author numerous articles in field; editor, co-author: Nurses, Patients, and Social Systems, 1968; corr. editor: Jour. Geriatric Psychiatry, 1967-93; founding editor, chmn. bd. Jour. Operational Psychiatry, 1970-90; editorial advisor Community Mental Health Jour., 1979-87; trustee Mo. Rev., 1982-83. Mem. adv. bd. Mo. Probation and Parole, 1st pres., 1995-97. Served with M.C., AUS, 1942-46, PTO; to capt. M.C., AUS, 1953-54. Decorated Philippine Liberation medal, 1945; recipient Sir Henry Wellcome award, 1955, Israeli bronze medal, 1963, Basic Books award, 1974, Disting. Service commendation Nat. Council Community Mental Health Ctrs., 1982, 83, 86, Guhleman award for Clin. Excellence U. Mo., 1987, Hon. Achievement award U.Mo., 1991, Disting. Svc. award VA, 1991; named Chancellor's Emissary U. Mo., 1979, Alumnus Magnus award, St. Thomas U., 1992; faculty fellow Inter-Univ. Council, 1958, sr. research fellow Am. Council Edn. and NSF, 1984 Found. fellow Royal Coll. Psychiatrists; fellow Royal Soc. Medicine, Am. Psychiat. Assn. (life), Am. Pub. Health Assn. (life), Am. Coll. Preventive Medicine (emeritus), AAAS, Am. Coll. Psychiatrists (life), Am. Assn. Psychoanalytic Physicians (hon.); mem. Assn. Mil. Surgeons U.S. (hon. life), Assn. Western Profs. Psychiatry (chmn. 1970-71), Mo. Acad. Psychiatry (1st pres. 1966-67), Mo. Psychiat. Assn. (life, pres. 1987-88), Assn. de Methodologie et Documentation en Psychiatrie, Mil. Order World Wars,

Phi Beta Kappa, Sigma Xi, Psi Chi, Alpha Omega Alpha, Alpha Epsilon Sigma, Gamma Alpha. Clubs: Scholars (Cantab.); Wine Label (London); Univ. (Columbia). Achievements include research on suicide, homicide, antisocial behavior, aging, social psychiatry. Home: Crow Wing Farm RR 2 Box 2 Columbia MO 65201-9802 Office: U Mo Dept Psychiatry Columbia MO 65212-0001 E-mail: doxbj@aol.com.

WEISS, JOSEPH JOEL, consulting company executive; b. Newark, July 27, 1931; s. Harry H. and Belle (Sass) W.; m. Leah Kneller, Apr. 10, 1954 (div. 1961); children: Sara, Daniel; m. Carol Lynn Seegott, Sept. 29, 1967; children: Laura, John. BSBA, Rutgers U., 1953, MBA, 1958. Dist. mgr. N.J. Bell Telephone Co., 1955-61; asst. comptroller ITT P.R. Telephone Co., San Juan, 1964-68; sr. cons. N.Y.C., 1968-71; v.p. data services Rio De Janeiro, 1971-74; dir. ops. N.Y.C., 1975-80; v.p. Control Data Corp., Rio De Janeiro, 1974-75; exec. v.p., chief adminstrv. officer Burger King Corp., Miami, 1980-89; chief oper. officer Goode, Olcott, Knight & Assocs., Coral Gables, Fla., 1989-90; pres. Contraband Detection Internat., Miami, 1990-92; sr. v.p. Seegott Inc., Streetsboro, Ohio, 1992—. Bd. dirs. Sta. WPB-TV. Pres. Civic Betterment Assn., Franklin Twp., N.J., 1961; trustee U. Miami Citizens Bd., 1987—; bd. dirs. Boy Scouts Am., 1982—. Recipient Strategic Planning Achievement award Boy Scouts Am., 1985. Mem. Hist. Soc. Fla. (bd. dirs. 1986—). Republican. Presbyterian. Club: Fisher Island. Avocations: oil painting, tennis. Home: 8216 Chagrin Rd Chagrin Falls OH 44023-4746 Office: Seegott Inc 10040 Aurora Hudson Rd Streetsboro OH 44241-1620

WEISS, MORRY, greeting card company executive; b. Czechoslovakia, 1940; m. Judith Stone. Grad., Wayne State U. Salesman, field mgr. Am. Greetings Corp., Cleve., 1961-66, advt. mgr., 1966-68, v.p., 1969-73, group v.p. mktg. and sales, 1973-78, formerly chief operating officer, from 1978, pres., 1978-92, also bd. dirs., chief exec. officer, 1987—, chmn., 1992—. Office: Am Greetings Corp 1 American Rd Cleveland OH 44144-2301

WEISS, ROBERT FRANCIS, former academic administrator, religious organization administrator, consultant; b. St. Louis, Aug. 27, 1924; s. Frank L. G. and Helen M. (Beck) W. B.A., St. Louis U., 1951, Ph.L., M.A., St. Louis U., 1953, S.T.L., 1961; Ph.D., U. Minn., 1964. Joined Soc. of Jesus, 1946; ordained priest Roman Catholic Ch., 1959; tchr. Rockhurst High Sch., Kansas City, Mo., 1953-56; adminstrv. asst. to pres. St. Louis U., 1961-62; asst. dean Rockhurst Coll., Kansas City, Mo., 1964-66, dean, v.p., asst. prof. edn., 1966-72, pres., 1977-88, St. Louis U. High Sch., 1973-77, interim pres., 1992; asst. for higher edn. and continuing formation Mo. Province S.J., St. Louis, 1989-92, 97—, treas., 1992—. Mem. Commn. on Govtl. Rels., Am. Coun. Edn., 1985-87; bd. dirs. Kansas City Regional Coun. for Higher Edn., 1978-88, Boys Hope Girls Hope, 1977—. Contbr. chpts. to books, articles to profl. jours. Trustee St. Louis U., 1973-87, 91—, Loyola U., New Orleans, 1973-82, 85-88, United Student Aid Funds, Inc., 1977-94, U. San Francisco, 1987-99, Marymount Coll., Salina, Kans., 1986-88, St. Louis U. H.S., 1989-99, Fontbonne Coll., St. Louis, 1973-77, Sacred Heart Program, Radio and TV Apostolate, St. Louis, 1990-96, pres., 1992-96, bd. dirs, 2000—; bd. dirs. Creighton U., Omaha, 1981-97, Our Little Haven, 1992—, St. Elizabeth Acad., St. Louis, 1997—, Loyola Acad. St. Louis, 2000—. 1st sgt. U.S. Army, 1943-46. Decorated Bronze Star. Mem. Am. Assn. for Higher Edn., Rainbow Divsn. Vets. Assn. (nat. chaplain 1976-84, 88-90, pres.-elect 1990-91, pres. 1991-92, assoc. nat. chaplain 1992—), Alpha Sigma Nu, Alpha Phi Omega. Home and Office: 4511 W Pine Blvd Saint Louis MO 63108-2109 E-mail: treasurer@jesuits-mis.org.

WEISS, ROBERT ORR, speech educator; b. Kalamazoo, Apr. 8, 1926; s. Nicholas John and Ruth (Orr) W.; m. Ann Lenore Lawson, Sept. 16, 1951; children: Elizabeth Ann, John Lawson, James Robert, Virginia Lenore. BA, Albion Coll., 1948; MA, Northwestern U., 1949, PhD, 1954. Instr. speech Wayne State U., Detroit, 1949-51; instr. pub. speaking Northwestern U., Evanston, Ill., 1954-55; mem. faculty DePauw U., Greencastle, Ind., 1955—, H.B. Gough prof. speech, 1965-97, head comm. arts and scis., 1963-78, 85-86, 93. Author: Public Argument, 1995; editor: Speaker and Gavel, 1968-75, Speaking Across the Curriculum, 1990—; co-editor: Current Criticism, 1971; contbr. articles to profl. jours. Served with AUS, 1945-46. Recipient Fred C. Tucker Disting. Career award, 1995, Lifetime award, Nat. Ednl. Debate Assn., 1997, Presdl. citation Nat. Communication Assn., 1999. Mem. AAUP (pres. DePauw U. chpt. 1961-62), Nat. Communication Assn. (legis. assembly 1966-68), Am. Forensic Assn. (sec.-treas. 1958-59), Ctrl. States Communication Assn., Internat. Communication Assn., Phi Beta Kappa, Delta Sigma Rho-Tau Kappa Alpha (nat. v.p. 1981-83, pres. 1983-85), Sigma Nu. Home: 722 Highridge Ave Greencastle IN 46135-1402 E-mail: robertweiss@depauw.edu.

WEISSMAN, MICHAEL LEWIS, lawyer; b. Chgo., Sept. 11, 1934; s. Maurice and Sue (Goldberg) Weissman; m. Joanne Sherwin, Dec. 19, 1961; children: Mark Douglas, Greg Steven, Scott Adam, Brett Anthony. Student White scholar, U. Chgo., 1951-52; BS in Econs, Northwestern U., 1954; MBA in Acctg., U. Pa., 1956; JD, Harvard U., 1958; postgrad. Fulbright scholar, U. Sydney, Australia, 1958-59, Hague Acad. Internat. Law, 1959. Bar: D.C. 1958, Ill. 1959. Asst. prof. bus. law Roosevelt U., Chgo., 1959-61; pvt. practice, 1959—; mem. firm Aaron, Aaron, Schimberg & Hess, 1969-78; sr. ptnr. Boorstein & Weissman, 1978-82, Weissman, Smolev & Solow, 1982-88, Foley & Lardner, 1988-92, McBride Baker & Coles, Chgo., 1992—; exec. v.p., gen. counsel Bridgeview Bank Group. Asst. prof. Roosevelt U., 1960—62; adj. prof. law John Marshall Law Sch., 2001—02; lectr. Lake Forest (Ill.) Coll., 1979—80; chmn. Banking Group, Union League Club Chgo.; panelist Robert Morris Assocs., Banking Law Inst., Midwest Fin. Conf., Greater O'Hare Assn., Miss. Law Inst., Bank Lending Inst., Chgo. Assn. Commerce and Industry, State of Art Seminars, Infocast Inc., SBA, Fed. Res. Bank Chgo., Lenders Ednl. Inst., Bank Adminstrn. Inst. Found., Lender's Forum. Author: (book) Lender Liability, 1988, Commercial Loan Documentation and Secured Lending, 1990, How to Avoid Career-Ending Mistakes in Commercial Lending, 1996, The Lender's Edge, 1997; mem. editl. bd.: Commercial Damages, 1985—; contbr. articles to profl. jours. Mem. adv. bd. Affective Disorders Clinic, U. Ill. Med. Sch., 1979—81. Scholar White, U. Chgo., 1951—52, Fulbright, U. Sydney, 1958—59. Mem.: ABA, Robert Morris Assn., Comml. Fin. Assn. Ednl. Found. (adv. bd.), Turnaround Mgmt. Assn. (steering com. Chgo. chpt.), Harvard Law Soc. Ill., Assn. Comml. Fin. Attys. (bd. dirs.), Ill. Inst. CLE 1989—2000, (chmn. 2001—), Ill. Bankers Assn. (mem. com. bank counsel 1987—88, vice chmn. 1988—89), Chgo. Bar Assn., Ill. Bar Assn., Beta Alpha Psi. Home: 2067 Old Briar Rd Highland Park IL 60035-4245 Office: McBride Baker & Coles 500 W Madison St Ste 4000 Chicago IL 60661-2511 also: Bridgeview Bank Group 1740 N Halsted St Chicago IL 60614 Business E-Mail: weissman@bridgeviewbank.com. E-mail: weissman@mbc.com.

WEIST, WILLIAM BERNARD, lawyer; b. Lafayette, Ind., Dec. 23, 1938; s. Bernard Francis and Frances Loretta (Doyle) W.; m. Rosemary Elaine Anderson, Apr. 30, 1963; children: Sean M., Cynthia A. BBA, U. Notre Dame, 1961; JD, U. Louisville, 1970. Bar: Ky. 1971, Ind. 1971, U.S. Dist. Ct. (no. and so. dists.) Ind. 1971. Bank examiner Fed. Res. Bank, St. Louis, 1966-67; Trust officer Citizens Fidelity Bank, Louisville, 1967-71; pvt. practice Fowler, Ind., 1971—. Bd. dirs. Benton Fin. Corp., Fowler, Fowler State Bank; pros. atty. 76th Jud. Cir., Benton County, Ind., 1975-98. Capt. USAF, 1961-65. Fellow Ind. Bar Found. (charter mem.),; mem. Ind. State Bar Assn., Ind. Prosecuting Attys. Assn. (pres. 1979), Ind. Prosecuting Attys. Coun. (chmn. 1989), Nat. Dist. Attys. Assn. (bd. dirs.), Columbia Club (Indpls.), Elks, KC. Avocations: golf, reading. Home: 1000 E 5th St Fowler IN 47944-1520 Office: Weist Bldg Grant Ave Fowler IN 47944-0101

WEITZMAN, ROBERT HAROLD, investment company executive; b. Chgo., July 15, 1937; s. Nathan and Selma Weitzman; m. Marilynn Beth Felzer, Sept. 5, 1965; children— Joshua C., Eliza S. B.A. in Bus., Econs., Grinnell Coll., 1959; J.D., DePaul U., 1963. Bar: Ill 1963. Vice pres. Weitzman Enterprises, Chgo., 1955-63; assoc. Lissner, Rothenberg, Reif & Barth, 1963-68; real estate counsel Continental Ill. Nat. Bank and Trust Co., 1968-74; v.p., group head Continental Ill. Investment Trust, 1974-76; founding ptnr. Group One Investments, 1977—. Lectr. in field. Editor: Real Estate Finance Handbook, 1979. Contbr. articles to profl. jours. Trustee, advisor Weitzman Found., 1963-77, mng. trustee, 1978— ; cons., advisor Ill. chpt. Big Bros. Am. Orgn., 1969-72; trustee The Wis. Real Estate Investment Trust, 1980, 81. Recipient Outstanding Young Man Am. award U.S. Jaycees, 1973 Mem. Ill. Bar Assn., Chgo. Bar Assn., Nat. Assn. Rev. Appraisers and Mortgage Underwriters (charter mem. cert. rev. appraiser designation), Real Estate Securities and Syndication Inst. (bd. dirs. Ill. chpt. 1982-90, pres. 1984, regional v. p. 1988, specialist in real estate securities designation 1988, chmn. nat. com. on continuing edn. 1989, 90). Real Estate Investment Assn. (founding mem., Nat. bd. dirs. 1990—, exec. com. nat assn. and Ill. chpt. 1990—, chmn. nat. com. for advanced edn., 1990-95, nat. pres. 1996-98, nat. chmn. 1999—, specialist in real estate investment designation 1990), Am. Inst. Banking, Internat. Coll. Real Estate Cons. Profls., Internat. Real Estate Bd. Home: 535 Carriage Way Deerfield IL 60015-4534 Office: Group One Investments 77 W Washington St Ste 1005 Chicago IL 60602-2805 E-mail: r.weitzman@g1invest.com.

WEJCMAN, LINDA, state legislator; b. Dec. 1939; m. Jim. Student, Iowa State U. Minn. State rep. Dist. 61B, 1991—; cons. Mem. local govt. and met. affairs com., energy, health and human svcs., housing and judiciary coms. Home: 3203 5th Ave S Minneapolis MN 55408-3248 Office: Minn Ho of Reps 203 State Capital Bldg Saint Paul MN 55155-0001

WELCH, DAVID WILLIAM, lawyer; b. St. Louis, Feb. 26, 1941; s. Claude LeRoy Welch and Mary Eleanor (Peggs) Penney; m. Candace Lee Capages, June 5, 1971; children: Joseph Peggs, Heather Elizabeth, Katherine Laura. BSBA, Washington U., St. Louis, 1963; JD, U. Tulsa, 1971. Bar: Okla. 1972, Mo. 1973, U.S. Dist. Ct. (we. dist.) Mo. 1973, U.S. Dist. Ct. (ea. dist.) Mo. 1974, U.S. Ct. Appeals (8th cir.) 1977, U.S. Ct. Appeals (7th cir.) 1991. Contract adminstr. McDonnell Aircraft Corp., St. Louis, 1965-66; bus. analyst Dun & Bradstreet Inc., Los Angeles, 1967-68; atty. U.S. Dept. Labor, Washington, 1972-73; ptnr. Moller Talent, Kuelthau & Welch, St. Louis, 1973-88, Lashly & Baer, St. Louis, 1988-96, Armstrong Teasdale LLP, St. Louis, 1996—. Author: (handbook) Missouri Employment Law, 1988; contbr. book chpts. Missouri Bar Employer-Employee Law, 1985, 87, 89, 92, 94, Missouri Discrimination Law, 1999; co-editor: Occupational Safety and Health Law, 1996. Mem. City of Creve Coeur Ethics Commn., 1987-88, Planning and Zoning Commn., 1988-96; bd. dirs. Camp Wyman, Eureka, Mo., 1982—, sec., 1987-88, 2nd v.p. 1988-89, 1st v.p. 1990-92, pres., 1992-94. Mem. ABA, Fed. Bar Assn., Mo. Bar Assn., Okla. Bar Assn., St. Louis Bar Assn., Kiwanis (bd. dirs. St. Louis 1979—, sec. 1982-83, 93-94, v.p. 1983-84, 88-90, 92-93, Man of Yr. award 1985). Democrat. Mem. Christian Ch. (Disciples of Christ). Avocations: travel, landscaping, music. Home: 536 N Mosley Rd Saint Louis MO 63141-7633 Office: Armstrong Teasdale 1 Metropolitan Sq Ste 2600 Saint Louis MO 63102-2740

WELCH, MARTIN E., III, retail executive; b. Detroit, June 25, 1948; m. Anne Welch; children: Michele, James, Mary Beth, Brian. BS in Acctg., U. Detroit-Mercy, 1970, MBA, 1973. Audit mgr. Arthur Young & Co., Detroit, 1970-77; dir. mktg. acctg. Fruehauf divsn. Fruehauf Corp., 1977-82; mgr. corp. acctg. Chrysler Corp., Highland Park, Mich., 1982-83, asst. contr., 1983-86, gen. auditor, 1987-88, asst. treas., 1988-91; CFO Chrysler Can., Windsor, Ont., 1986-87; sr. v.p., CFO Federal-Mogul corp., Southfield, Mich., 1991-95; exec. v.p., CFO Kmart Corp, Troy, 1995—. Nat. adv. bd. Chase Manhattan Bank. Bd. dirs. Penske Auto Centers, LLC; past pres. Bus. Sch. Adv. Bd., U. Detroit-Mercy. Mem. Conf. Bd. (coun. fin. execs.), Fin. Execs. Inst. (bd. dirs. Detroit chpt.). Office: K Mart Corp 3100 W Big Beaver Rd Troy MI 48084-3163

WELCH, MICHAEL JOHN, chemistry educator, researcher; b. Stoke-on-Trent, Staffordshire, Eng., June 28, 1939; came to U.S., 1965; s. Arthur John W. and Mary (Welch); m. Teresa Jean Conocchiolli, Apr. 22, 1967 (div. 1979); children: Colin, Lesley. B.A., Cambridge U., Eng., 1961; M.A., Cambridge U., 1964; Ph.D., London U., 1965. Asst. prof. radiation chemistry in radiology Washington U. Sch. Medicine, St. Louis, 1967-70, assoc. prof., 1970-74; assoc. prof. dept. chemistry Washington U. Sch., 1971-75, prof. dept. chemistry, 1978—; prof. radiology Washington U. Sch. Medicine, 1991—, prof. molecular biology and pharmacology, 1993—; prof. biomed. engrng. program Washington U., 1996; co-dir. Mallinckrodt Inst. Dir. radiol. scis. dept. Washignton U., 1990—; mem. diagnostic radiology study sect. NIH, 1986-89, chmn., 1989-91; mem. sci. adv. com. Whitaker Found., 1995—. Author: Introduction to the Tracer Methods, 1972; editor: Radiopharmaceuticals and Other Compounds Labeled with Shortlived Radionuclides, 1977; assoc. editor Jour. Nuclear Medicine, 1989—; contbr. chpts. to books, more than 400 articles to profl. jours. Recipient Georg Charles de Hevesy Nuclear Medicine Pioneer award, 1992; scholar St. Catharine Coll. Cambridge U., 1958-61. Mem. Soc. Nuclear Medicine (trustee, pres. 1984, Paul C. Aebersold award 1980, de Hevesy Nuclear Pioneer award 1992), Radiopharm. Sci. Coun. (pres. 1980-81), Am. Chem. Soc. (St. Louis award 1988, award for nuclear chemistry 1990, Mid-West award 1991), Chem. Soc. London, Radiation Rsch. Soc., Inst. Medicine, Sigma Xi Office: Washington U Sch Medicine Edward Mallinckrodt Inst Radiology 510 S Kingshighway Blvd Saint Louis MO 63110-1016 E-mail: welchm@mir.wustl.edu.

WELCH, PATRICK DANIEL, state legislator; b. Chgo., Dec. 12, 1948; s. William C. and Alice W. Student, So. Ill. U., 1970; JD, Chgo. Kent Coll. Law, 1974. Bar: Ill. 1974. Pvt. practice, Peru, Ill., 1974—; mem. Ill. Senate, 1983—. Asst. minority leader, 1993—; former chmn. energy and environ. com.; nat. del., mem. credentials com. Dem. Nat. Conv., 1976, del., 1980, 84, 88, 92, 96; precinct committeeman Peru Dem. Party, 1976-86; del. Dem. Nat. Mid-Term Conf., 1978, 82; committeeman Ill. Dem. Cen. Com., 1978—; mem. exec. com., 1983—; mem. Peru Citizens' Svc. Orgn.; vice chmn. Ill. Dem. Party, 1990-94, chmn. party platform com., 1994. Recipient Disting. Svc. award Ill. Bicentennial Commn., 1976. Mem. Ill. Bar Assn., La Salle County Bar Assn. Office: Ill State Senate State Capitol Rm 218 Springfield IL 62706-0001

WELCH, ROBERT THOMAS, state legislator; b. Berlin, June 8, 1958; s. William and Betty (Baudhuin) W.; m. Jeanne M. Piechowski, Dec. 30, 1978; children: Adam, Sarah, Peter. AAS, Madison Area Tech. Coll., 1980; student, Lawrence U., 1976-78, U. Wis., Stevens Point, 1978. Surveyor Kiedrowski Engring., Stevens Point, Wis., 1981, Welch Land Surveying, Redgranite, 1982—; mem. Wis. Assembly, Madison, 1985-93, Wis. Senate from 14th dist., Madison, 1995—. Chmn. Council on Migrant Labor, Assembly Rep. Caucus; mem. assembly coms. on employment and tng., rules, elections, adminstrv. rules, orgn. Treas. Waushara County Rep., 1983-84, active State Rep. Platform Co., 1984, chmn. platform com., 1988; 4-H leader. Named one of Outstanding Young Men Am., Montgomery, Ala., 1985, 86, 87. Mem. Green Lake Ripon Area Bd. Realtors. Roman Catholic. Home: PO Box 523 Redgranite WI 54970-0523 Office: State Capitol PO Box 7882 Madison WI 53707-7882

WELGE, DONALD EDWARD, food manufacturing executive; b. St. Louis, July 11, 1935; s. William H. and Rudelle (Fritze) W.; m. Mary Alice Childers, Aug. 4, 1962; children: Robert, Tom. B.S., La. State U., 1957. With Gilster-Mary Lee Corp., Chester, Ill., 1957—, pres., gen. mgr., 1965—. Dir. Buena Vista Bank of Chester; pres. Buena Vista Bankcorp. Former chmn. St. John's Luth. Bd. Edn. 1st lt. Transp. Corp, U.S. Army, 1958-63. Named So. Ill. Bus. Leader of Yr. So. Ill. U., 1988. Mem. Perryville C. of C. (pres. 1989), Chester, Ill. C. of C. (past pres.), Alpha Zeta, Phi Kappa Phi. Republican. Lutheran. Home: 5 Knollwood Dr Chester IL 62233-1416 Office: Gilster Mary Lee Co PO Box 227 Chester IL 62233-0227

WELKER, WALLACE IRVING, neurophysiologist, educator; b. Batavia, N.Y., Dec. 17, 1926; Ph.D. in Psychology, U. Chgo., 1954. Mem. faculty U. Wis. Med. Sch., 1957—, prof. neurophysiology, 1965-90, emeritus prof., 1990—. Served with AUS, 1945-47. Sister Kenny Found. scholar, 1957-62; recipient NIH Career Devel. award, 1962-67 Mem. Am. Anat. Soc., Neurosci. Soc. Office: 1802 Fordem Ave Apt 14 Madison WI 53704-7116

WELL, IRWIN, language educator; b. Cin., Apr. 16, 1928; s. Sidney and Florence (Levy) W.; m. Vivian Max, Dec. 27, 1950; children: Martin, Alice, Daniel. BA, U. Chgo., 1948, MA, 1951; PhD, Harvard U., 1960; D (hon.), Nevsky Inst., Petersburg, Russia, 1999. Teaching fellow Harvard U., Cambridge, Mass., 1955-58; asst. prof. Brandeis U., Waltham, 1958-65; assoc. prof. Northwestern U., Evanston, Ill., 1966-70, prof. Russian, Russian Lit., 1970—. Pres., mem. bd. dirs. Am. Coun. Tchrs. of Russian., Washington, 1967—. Author numerous books in field; contbr. articles to scholarly jours. Recipient Pushkin medal Internat. Assn. of Russian Profs. Jewish. Avocations: music, singing. Office: Northwestern U Slavic Dept Evanston IL 60208-0001

WELLER, GERALD C. congressman; b. Streator, Ill., July 7, 1957; Degree in Agriculture, U. Ill., 1979. Aide to U.S. Congressman Tom Corcoran, 1977-78; aide to U.S. Sec. of Agriculture John R. Block, 1981-85; active family farm, 1985-88; rep. State of Ill., 1988-94; mem. 104th-106th Congresses from 11th Ill. dist., 1994—; asst. majority whip; mem. ways and means com. Rep. House Republican steering com.; mem. Newt Gingrich's policy com.; exec. com. NRCC, House Banking Com., House Veterans Affairs Com., House Transp. and Infrastructure Com. Mem. 1st Christian Ch. of Morris, Ill. Mem. Nat. Republican Legis. Assn. (nominated Legislator of Yr.). Office: US House Reps 1210 Longworth HOB Washington DC 20515-1311*

WELLIN, THOMAS, music director; m. Annette Wellin; children: Claire, Christopher, Patrick. BMus summa cum laude, Ind. U.; MMus, U. Maine; postgrad., Acad. Mus. Chigiana, Siena, Italy; studied with Julius Herford, Ruggiero Ricci, Franco Rerrara, Gustav Meier. Music dir., condr. Bismarck (N.D.)-Mandan Symphony Orch., 1990—. Guest condr. Fargo-Moorhead Symphony; lectr. in field. Condr. summer concerts Pops on the Prairie, New Year's Eve Viennese Gala, Dickinson State U., I-94 Music Festival, Beulah, N.D., 4th of July Spectacular on State Capitol Mall, (CD) Vivaldi's The Four Seasons. Performing Artists fellow N.D. Coun. Arts. Office: Bismarck-Mandan Symphony Orch PO Box 2031 Bismarck ND 58502-2031

WELLINGTON, JEAN SUSORNEY, librarian; b. East Chicago, Ind., Oct. 23, 1945; d. Carl Matthew and Theresa Ann Susorney; m. Donald Clifford Wellington, June 12, 1976; 1 child, Evelin Patricia. BA, Purdue U., 1967; MA in LS, Dominican U., River Forest, Ill., 1969; MA, U. Cin., 1976. Head Burnam Classical Libr. U. Cin., 1970—. Compiler: Dictionary of Bibliographic Abbreviations Found in the Scholarship of Classical Studies and Related Disciplines, 1983. Mem. Art. Librs. Soc. N.Am. (chair Ohio br. 1984-85). Office: U Cin Classics Libr PO Box 210191 Cincinnati OH 45221-0191

WELLINGTON, ROBERT HALL, manufacturing company executive; b. Atlanta, July 4, 1922; s. Robert H. and Ernestine V. (Vossbrinck) W.; m. Marjorie Jarchow, Nov. 15, 1947; children: Charles R., Robert H., Christian J., Jeanne L. BS, McCormack Sch. of Engring. and Applied Scis. (formerly Northwestern Tech. Inst.), 1944; MSBA, MBA, U. Chgo., 1958. With Griffin Wheel Co., 1946-61; v.p. parent co. Amsted Industries, Inc., Chgo., 1961-74, exec. v.p., 1974-80, pres., chief exec. officer, 1981-88, chmn. bd., chief exec. officer, 1988-90. Served to lt. USN, 1943-46. Office: Amsted Industries Inc 205 N Michigan Ave Fl 44 Chicago IL 60601-5927

WELLIVER, WARREN DEE, lawyer, retired state supreme court justice; b. Butler, Mo., Feb. 24, 1920; s. Carl Winfield and Burdee Marie (Wolfe) W.; m. Ruth Rose Galey, Dec. 25, 1942; children: Gale Dee (Mrs. William B. Stone), Carla Camile (Mrs. Dayton Stone), Christy Marie. BA, U. Mo., 1945; JD, U. Mo., 1948. Bar: Mo. 1948. Asst. pros. atty. Boone County, Columbia, 1948-54; sr. ptnr. Welliver, Atkinson and Eng, 1960-79; tchr. law Law Sch. U. Mo., 1948-49; mem. Mo. Senate, 1977-79; justice Supreme Ct. Mo., Jefferson City, 1979-89. Mem. Gov. Mo. Adv. Coun. Alcoholism and Drug Abuse, chmn. drug coun., 1970-72; chmn. Task Force Revision Mo. Drug Laws, 1970-71; liaison mem. coun. Nat. Inst. Alcoholism and Alcohol Abuse, 1973-76; mem. Cen. Regional Adv. Coun. Comprehensive Psychiat. Svcs., 1990-92. Bd. dirs. Nat. Assn. Mental Health, 1970-76, regional v.p., 1973-76; pres. Mo. Assn. Mental Health, 1968-69, Stephens Coll. Assocs., 1965-79; pres. Friends of Libr., U. Mo., 1976, bd. dirs., 1979-92; chmn. Dem. Com., 1954-64; hon. fellow Harry S. Truman Libr. Inst., 1979—; bd. dirs. Supreme Ct. Hist. Soc., 1982—; vice chair adv. bd. U. Mo. Multiple Sclerosis Inst., 1992—; bd. curators Stephen's Coll., 1980-92. With USNR, 1941-45. Recipient Disting. Alumni medal and award U. Mo., 1994. Fellow Am. Coll. Trial Lawyers, Am. Bar Found., Mo. Bar Found.; mem. ABA, Mo. Bar Assn. (pres. 1967-68), Boone County Bar Assn. (pres. 1970), Am. Judicature Soc., Am. Legion (past post comdr.), Multiple Sclerosis Soc. (Gateway chpt. bd. dirs. 1986-92), Order of Coif, Country Club of Mo., Columbia Country Club (past pres.). Home: 3430 Woodrail Ter Columbia MO 65203-0926

WELLS, JONATHAN, state legislator; m. Justina Wells. Kans. state rep. Dist. 84, 1993—. Address: 830 N Madison St Wichita KS 67214-3357

WELLS, LESLEY B. judge; b. Muskegon, Mich., Oct. 6, 1937; d. James Franklin and Inez Simpson Wells; m. Charles F. Clarke, Nov. 13, 1998; children: Lauren Elizabeth, Caryn Alison, Anne Kristin, Thomas Eliot. BA, Chatham Coll., 1959; JD cum laude, Cleve. State U., 1974; cert., Nat. Jud. Coll., 1983, 85, 87, cert., 89. Bar: Ohio 1975, U.S. Dist. Ct. (no. dist.) Ohio 1975, U.S. Supreme Ct. 1989. Pvt. practice, Cleve., 1975; ptnr. Brooks & Moffet, 1975-79; dir., atty. ABAR Litigation Ctr., 1979-80; assoc. Schneider, Smeltz, Huston & Ranney, 1980-83; judge Ct. of Common Pleas, 1983-94, U.S. Dist. Ct. (no. dist.) Ohio 6th Cir., Cleve., 1994—. Adj. prof. law and urban policy Cleve. State U., 1979-82. Editor, author: Litigation Manual, 1980. Past pres. Cleve. Legal Aid Soc.; legal chmn. Nat. Women's Polit. Caucus, 1981-82; chmn. Gov.'s Task Force on Family Violence, Ohio, 1983-87; mem. biomed. ethics com. Case Western Res. U. Med. Sch., 1985-94; mem. N.W. Ordinance U.S. Constn. Commn., Ohio, 1986-88; master Burton Inn of Ct., 1989—, counselor, 1993, pres., 1998-99; trustee Rosemary Ctr., 1986-92, Miami U., 1988-92, Urban League Cleve., 1989-90, Chatham Coll., 1989-94. Recipient Superior Jud. award Supreme Ct. Ohio, 1983, J. Irwin award Womenspace, Ohio, 1984, award Womens City Club, 1985, Disting. Alumna award Chatham Coll., 1988, Alumni Civic Achievement award Cleve. State U., 1992, Golden Gavel award Ohio Judges Assn., 1994, Outstanding Alumni award Cleve. Marshall Law Alumni Assn., 1994, Greater Cleve. Achievement award YWCA, 1995. Mem. ABA (coun. litigation sect. 1996-99), Am. Law Inst.,

Ohio Bar Assn., Ohio Womens Bar Assn., Cleve. Bar Assn. (Merit Svc. award 1983), Cuyahoga County Bar Assn., Nat. Assn. Women Judges, Philos. Club Cleve. Office: 338 US Courthouse 201 Superior Ave E Cleveland OH 44114-1201

WELLS, RICHARD A. manufacturing company executive; BSBA, U. Wis., Madison, 1960; cert. in data processing, U. Wis., Milw. CPA, Wis. With Kohler (Wis.) Co., sr. v.p. fin., CFO, 1979-1999, also mem. exec. com., pension investment com., bd. dirs. Office: Kohler Co 444 Highland Dr Kohler WI 53044-1500

WELLS, SAMUEL ALONZO, JR. surgeon; b. Cuthbert, Ga., Mar. 16, 1936; s. Samuel Alonzo and Martha Steele W.; m. Barbara Anne Atwood, Feb. 13, 1964; children: Sarah, Susan. Student, Emory U., 1954—57, M.D., 1961. Intern Johns Hopkins Hosp., Balt., 1961—62, resident in internal medicine, 1962—63; asst. resident in surgery Barnes Hosp., St. Louis, 1963—64; resident in surgery Duke U., Durham, NC, 1966—70; guest investigator dept. tumor biology Karolinska Inst., Stockholm, 1967—68; asst. prof. surgery Duke U., Durham, NC, 1970—72, assoc. prof., 1972—76, prof., 1976—81; clin. assoc. surgery br. Nat. Cancer Inst., NIH, Bethesda, Md., 1964—66, sr. investigator surgery br., 1970—72, cons. surgery br., 1975—; prof., chmn. dept. surgery Washington U., St. Louis, 1981—98; dir. ACS, Chgo., 1998—99, dir. Ctr. Clin. Trials and Evidence-Based Medicine, 1999—. Dir. Duke U. Clin. Rsch. Ctr., 1978—81; prof. surgery Duke U. Sch. Medicine, 2000—. Mem. editl. bd.: Annals of Surgery, 1975—93, Mem. editl. bd.: Surgery, 1975—93, Mem. editl. bd.: Jour. Surg. Rsch., 1981—93, editor in chief : World Jour. Surgery, 1983—92, editor in chief : Current Problems in Surgery, 1989—. Pres. GM Cancer Rsch. Found., 1996—. Mem.: ACS (bd. regents 1989—98, residency rev. com. for surgery 1987—93, chmn. 1991—93, vice chmn. 1995—, exec. dir. 1998—, group chmn. oncology group 1998—), Soc. Surg. Oncology (pres. 1993—94), Halsted Soc. 1987, Nat. Cancer Adv. Bd., Inst. of Medicine of NAS, Am. Soc. Clin. Investigation, Soc. Clin. Surgery (treas. 1980—86, v.p. 1986—88, pres. 1988—90), Soc. Univ. Surgeons (exec. coun. 1976—78), Am. Surg. Assn. (recorder, mem. coun. 1986—91, pres. 1995—96), Am. Bd. Surgery (exec. com. 1986—89, vice chmn. 1987—88, chmn. 1988—89, diplomate, bd. dirs.), Alpha Omega Alpha. Office: Dept Surgeryurgeons Box 17969 Duke U Sch Medicine Durham NC 27715

WELLS, STEVEN WAYNE, lawyer; b. Ft. Walton Beach, Fla., Sept. 8, 1960; s. H. Wayne and Shirley A. W.; m. Lisa Stieler, May 20, 1983; Robert, James, Jessica. BA in Comm., Mich. State U., 1982; JD with distinction, Detroit Coll. of Law, 1985. Bar: Mich. Asst. prosecutor Oakland County, Pontiac, Mich., 1985-88; mng. ptnr. Schnelz, Bondy & Wells, PC, Troy, 1988-93; shareholder, mng. ptnr. Cross Wrock, PC, Detroit, 1993-99; prin. shareholder Schnelz, Wells, Monaghan & Wells PC, Birmingham, Mich., 1999—. Lectr., presenter in field. Contbr. articles to State Bar Jour. Pres. Bloomfield Village Bd. Fellow Mich. Bar Assn.; ABA, ATLA, Detroit Bar Assn., Mich. Trial Lawyers Assn., Nat. Dist. Attys. Assn. Avocations: golf, tennis, coaching youth baseball, soccer. Address: 255 S Old Woodward Ave Ste 200 Birmingham MI 48009-6184

WELLSTONE, PAUL, senator; b. Arlington, Va., July 21, 1944; s. Leon and Minnie W.; m. Sheila Wellstone, 1963; children: David, Marcia, Mark. BA, U. N.C., 1965, PhD Polit. Sci., 1969. Tchr. Carleton Coll., Minn.; U.S. senator from Minn., 1991—. Mem. U.S. Senate coms. small bus., energy and natural resources, Indian affairs, labor and human resources, Senate Dem. policy com., chmn. subcom. rural economy and family farming; mem. com. fgn. rels., 1997—; mem. com. health, edn., labor & pensions, 1991—; ranking mem. fgn. rels. subcom. on Near Eastern and South Asian affairs, health, education, labor and pensions subcom. on employment safety and tng. Author: How the Rural Poor Got Power, Powerline. Dir. Minn. Community Energy Program. Office: US Senate 136 Hart Senate Office Bldg Washington DC 20510-0001*

WELNETZ, DAVID CHARLES, human resources executive; b. Antigo, Wis., Apr. 12, 1947; s. Francis P. and Marquette A. (Stengl) W.; m. Mary L. McCulley, Aug. 25, 1973; children: Andrew, Timothy. BS in Biology, U. Wis., Stevens Point, Wis., 1969; MS in Indsl. Rels., U. Wis. Madison, 1975. Mgr. coll. recruitment tng. Rexnord Inc., Milw., 1975-77, personnel mgr. Sarasota, Fla., 1977-80, corp. dir. employee rels. Milw., 1980-83; sr. cons. The Thompson Group, Brookfield, Wis., 1983-87, v.p., 1987-91; pres. Thompson Cons., 1991—. Adv. bd. SUNY, Buffalo, 1982-88; bd. dirs. Matarah Industries. Bd. dirs. Outplacement Internat., 1996—; bd. dirs. Matarah Ind., 1994—, Lutheran Social Svcs., Milw. Ctr. for Independence. Recipient Bronze Star U.S. Army, 1972. Mem. Pers. Indsl. Rels. Assn. (program com. 1988-91, chmn. pers. rsch. 1980-82), Human Resources Planning Soc., Human Resources Mgmt. Assn. Roman Catholic. Home: N54W 38928 Islandale Dr Oconomowoc WI 53066-2101 Office: Thompson Cons Ltd 17700 W Capitol Dr Brookfield WI 53045-2006

WELSH, KELLY RAYMOND, lawyer, former telecommunications company executive; b. Chgo., July 6, 1952; s. Raymond J. and Mary Jane (Kelly) W.; m. Ellen S. Alberding, June 28, 1985; children: Katherine A., Julia S. AB cum laude, Harvard U., 1974, JD magna cum laude, 1978; MA, Sussex U., Eng., 1975. Assoc. Mayer, Brown & Platt, Chgo., 1979-85, ptnr., 1985-89; corp. counsel City of Chgo., 1989-93; v.p., assoc. gen. counsel Ameritech Corp., Chgo., 1993-96, exec. v.p., gen. counsel, 1996-99; ret., 1999. Chmn. Met. Pier and Exposition Authority, Chgo., 1994—. Mem. ABA, Chgo. Bar Assn., Chgo. Coun. Lawyers, Chgo. Coun. Fgn. Rels. (mem. Chgo. com.), Legal Club Chgo. Office: Ameritech Corp 30 S Wacker Dr Fl 39 Chicago IL 60606-7413

WELSH, MICHAEL JAMES, medical educator, biophysicist, educator; b. Marshalltown, Iowa, Dec. 22, 1948; Student, Loras Coll., 1967-69; BS, U. Iowa, 1970, MD, 1974. Intern and resident internal medicine U. Iowa Coll. Medicine, Iowa City, 1974-77; clin. fellow internal medicine U. Calif. San Francisco, 1977-78; rsch. fellow cardiovasc. rsch. unit U. Calif., San Francisco, 1978-79; rsch. fellow physiology and cell biology U. Tex., Houston, 1979-80; asst. prof. medicine U. Iowa Coll. Medicine, Iowa City, 1981-84, assoc. prof. medicine, 1984-87, prof. medicine, 1987—, prof. physiology and biophysics, 1989—. Cons. VA Hosp., Iowa City, 1981—; investigator Howard Hughes Med. Inst., U. Iowa., Iowa City, 1989—. Contbr. chpts. to books and numerous articles to profl. jours. Recipient Doris F. Tulcin Cystic Fibrosis Rsch. award, 1992, Paul di Sant-Agnese Disting. Sci. Achievement award, 1993. Mem. Am. Fedn. for Clin. Rsch., Am. Physiol. Soc., Am. Thoracic Soc. (J. Burns Amberson award 1994), Iowa Thoracic Soc. Office: Howard Hughes Med Inst 500 EMRB Univ Iowa Coll Medicine Iowa City IA 52242

WELSH, ROBERT K. religious organization executive; Pres. Coun. on Christian Unity, Indpls., 1999. Office: Coun on Christian Unity PO Box 1986 Indianapolis IN 46206-1986

WELSHIMER, GWEN R. state legislator, real estate broker, appraiser; b. Poughkeepsie, N.Y., Nov. 5, 1935; d. Freanor Ralph and Beulah M. (Reedy) Grant; m. Billy L. Blake (div. 1979); children: Donald E., Jerry A.; m. Robert E. Welshimer (dec. 1996). Student, Kans. State U., 1953-54; cert., Jones Real Estate Coll., Colorado Springs, Colo., 1975. Cert. real estate appraiser, 1993. Exec. sec. Coll. Bd. Trustees, Bellevue, Wash., 1967-69; exec. sec. to chmn. bd. dirs. Garvey Industries, Wichita, Kans., 1969-73, adminstrv. asst. pers. and pub. affairs, 1969-73; copywriter Walter Drake & Sons, Colorado Springs, 1973-75; real estate agt. UTE Realty, 1975-76; newspaper pub., owner Black Forrest News, 1976-79; real estate broker, appraiser Gwen Welshimer Real Estate, Wichita, 1979—; coord. Epic Real Estate Sch., 1988—; legislator Kans. Ho. of Reps., Topeka, 1990—; mem. bus., commerce and labor, ethics and elections, health and human svcs., new economy nat. conf. state legislatures cultural and econ. devel. com., 2001—; mem joint health care reform legis. oversight com., 2001—. Dem. precinct committeewoman, Wichita; bd. dirs. United Meth. Urban Ministries, Wichita, 1990—, Counseling & Mediation Ctr., Wichita, Great Plains Comprehensive Agriculture & Med. Inst. Mem.: Women Dems., Lions Club Internat. Democrat. Methodist. Home: 6103 Castle Dr Wichita KS 67218-3601 Office: Kans Ho of Reps State Capitol Topeka KS 66612

WEN, SHIH-LIANG, mathematics educator; b. Peoples Republic of China; came to U.S., 1959; s. S.W. and C.F. (Hsiao) W.; m. Liang Tao; children: Dennis, Andy, Jue, Nannan. BS, Nat. Taiwan U., Taipei, 1956; MS, U. Utah, 1961; PhD, Purdue U., 1968. Assoc. research engr. The Boeing Co., Seattle, 1961-63; with dept. math. Ohio U., Athens, 1968—, successively asst. prof., assoc. prof. and prof., chmn. dept. math., 1985-93. Rsch. analyst Applied Math Rsch. Lab. USAF, Wright-Patterson AFB, Ohio, summer, 1972; vis. rsch. scientist Courant Inst. Math. Scis. NYU, 1978-79; hon. prof. Jiangxi U., People's Republic of China, 1985; disting. vis. prof. Lanzhou U., People's Republic of China, 1989. Mem. Am. Math. Soc., Soc. for Indsl. and Applied Math., Math. Assn. Am. Avocations: fishing, bridge, music. Office: Ohio Univ Dept Of Math Athens OH 45701

WENDEL, SHIRLEY ANNE, college dean; Diploma, St. Mary's Hosp. Sch. Nursing, 1970; AA, Penn Valley Cmty. Coll., 1972; BSN, Avila Coll., 1974; MN, U. Kans., 1980; PhD, Kansas State U., 1998, U. Kans., 1999. Staff nurse St. Mary's Hosp., Kans. City, Kans., 1970-74, Unity Hosp., Fridley, Minn., 1974-76; nursing instr. Kans. City Kans. Cmty. Coll., 1976-80, dean nursing edn., 1980-98, dean of nursing and allied health, 1998—. Mem. adv. com. Johnson County Cmty. Coll. nursing program, Avila Coll. nursing program, Mid Am. Nazarene Coll. nursing program; asst. Den Mother Cub Scouts, 1985-87; active Annual Health Fair. Mem. Nat. League Nursing, Kans. Assoc. Degree Nursing Educators, Collegiate Nurse Educators Greater Kans. City, Sigma Theta Tau. Home: 12100 W 141st St Shawnee Mission KS 66221-2902 Office: Kansas City Kansas Community College 7250 State Ave Kansas City KS 66112-3003 E-mail: swendel@toto.net.

WENDEL, W. HALL, JR. automotive manufacturer; b. Washington, Jan. 17, 1943; m. Deborah Wendel, 1967; 1 child, Amy. BS, U.S. Naval Acad., 1966; MBA, Harvard U., 1972. Sales adminstr. E-Z-Go Golf Carts, 1973-74, nat. sales mgr., 1974-77; v.p. sales, mktg. Polaris E-Z-Go, Medina, Minn., 1977-80, pres., 1980-81; pres., CEO Polaris Industries L.P., 1981-99, chmn., 1999—. Office: Polaris Industries Inc 2100 Hwy 55 Medina MN 55340

WENDT, GARY CARL, finance company executive; b. Portage, Wis., Mar. 13, 1942; s. Walter Carl and Dorothy Mae (Neesam) W.; children: Sarah, Rachel. BS in Civil Engring., U. Wis., 1965; MBA, Harvard U., 1967. V.p. La. Co. Inc., Houston, 1967-71, Diversified Advisor, Miami, 1971-75, GE Credit Corp., Stamford, Conn., 1975-84, COO, 1984-86; pres., CEO GE Capital Svcs. (formerly Gen. Electric Credit Corp.), 1986—; CEO, chmn., Conseco, Inc., Carmel, IN, 2000—. Trustee Boy's and Girl's Club of Stamford, past campaign chmn. capital fund campaign; past chmn. Stamford United Way; chmn. Conn. Bus. Edn. Coun.; trustee Outward Bound USA; chmn. corp. adv. com. Fairfield County Community Found. Recipient of His Royal Highness Prince Philips award, 1996, Corporate award for Outstanding Svs., to Outward Bound, Stamford Vol. Ctr Heart of Gold Soc. award, Herbert Hoover Humaniarian award, The Boys and Girl Club of Am., 1994, Recipirnt of The Nat. Ethnic Coalition Org. Ellis Island Medal, 1993, Recipient of the SACIA Walter H. Wheeler Jr. Business Leadership award, 1993, Disting Svs. Citation from The Coll. Engring. at U. Wis., Recipient of The Nat. Conf. of Christian and Jews Nat. Human Rels. award, 1990, Recipient of The Outward Bound Corp. Leadership award, 1990, The SACIA Excalibur Leadership award, 1990, Regional Plan Assn. Leadership award, 1990. Mem. Southwestern Area Commerce and Industry Assn. of Conn. (bd. dirs., past chmn.), The Regional Plan Assn. (mem. bd., past chmn.), mem nat. bd of governors, Boys and Girls Club of Am., mem. bd., of govs. for United Way of Tri State. Office: Conseco Inc 11825 N Pennsylvania St Carmel IN 46032

WENGER, RONALD DAVID, surgeon; b. Phila., May 1, 1944; s. Christian Showalter and Helen Grace (Heisey) W.; m. Judith Kay Anderson, Jan. 24, 1970; children: Clayton, Lera. BA, Ohio Wesleyan U., 1966; MD, Case Western Res. U., 1970. Diplomate Am. Bd. Surgery. Intern U. Oreg. Med. Sch., Portland, 1970-71; fellow Mayo Clinic Surgery Dept., Rochester, Minn., 1973-77; clin. prof. surgery U. Wis. Med. Sch., Madison, 1977—; pvt. practice, 1977—; asst. chief surgery St. Mary's Hosp., 1980-00; chief surgery Dean Med. Ctr., 1988-93. Mem. ACS (also Wis. chpt.), AMA, SAGES, Wis. State Med. Soc., Madison Surg. Soc., Wis. Surg. Soc., Soc. for Surgery of Alimentary Tract. Avocations: skiing, bicycling, sailing, travel, reading. Home: 726 Farwell Dr Madison WI 53704-6032 Office: 1912 Atwood Ave Madison WI 53704-5221

WENK, DANIEL N. landmark site administrator; Supt. Mt. Rushmore Nat. Meml., Keystone, S.D. Office: Mt Rushmore Nat Meml PO Box 268 Keystone SD 57751-0268

WENNLUND, LARRY, former state legislator, lawyer; b. DeKalb, Ill., Oct. 31, 1941; s. Donald F. and Gertrude Wennlund; m. Shirley Ann Major, 1963; children: Jayna, Donald Cass, Joelle, Kara. BA, U. Ill., 1964; JD, John Marshall Law Sch., 1968. Mem. Ill. Ho. of Reps., Springfield, 1987-97; mem. transp. and motor vehicles, jud. I, jud. II Ill. Ho. Reps., registration and regulation, labor and commerce coms., elections com., spl. com., conflicts of interest, asst. floor leader, mem. joint com. on adminstrv. rules, asst. majority leader; pvt. practice law New Lenox, Ill. Named Legislator of Yr. Ill. State Attys. Assn., 1988, Ill. Environ. Coun., 1987-89, Ill. Hosp. Assn., 1988, Friend of Agrl. award Agrl. Assn. Activator, 1988, 89; recipient Legislative award Ill. Assn. of Ophthalmology, 1989, Legislative Leadership award Ill. Assn. Recyclers. Mem. New Lenox C. of C., Mokena C. of C., Frankfort C. of C., Lions. Home: 1234 N Cedar Rd New Lenox IL 60451-1273

WENSITS, DAVID L. aerospace executive; b. Sept. 19, 1947; AAS in Aviation Maintenance, Purdue U., 1968, BS in Indsl. Supervision, 1970. Supportability mgr. Rolls-Royce Corp., Indpls., 1970—. With U.S. Army, 1971-73. Recipient Aerospace Maintenance award AIAA, 1996. Office: Rolls-Royce Corp, SPEED Code S27C PO Box 420 Indianapolis IN 46206-0420 E-mail: david.l.wensits@rolls-royce.com., daveewensits@comcast.net.

WENSITS, JAMES EMRICH, newspaper editor; b. South Bend, Ind., Oct. 8, 1944; s. John Andrew and Melva Mae (Betz) W.; m. Wendy Anne Reygaert, June 12, 1965; children: Cheryl Wensits Lightfoot, John, Kristin Wensits Hough, Amy; m. Catherine Marie Palmer Pope, Nov. 27, 1987 (dec. Sept. 1996); 1 stepchild, Christina Pope; m. Carol Schaal, Oct. 19, 1998. BA in Journalism, Purdue U., 1966. Reporter South Bend Tribune, 1966-92, assoc. editor, 1992—. Office: South Bend Tribune 225 W Colfax Ave South Bend IN 46626-1001

WENSTRUP, H. DANIEL, chemical company executive; b. Cin., Sept. 27, 1934; s. Carl D. and Lucille (Cahill) W.; m. Eileen O'Brien, Nov. 24, 1956; children: Gary, Julie, Patrick, Kevin, Katy, Greg. BSBA, Xavier U., 1956. Sales rep. Chemcentral Corp., Cin., 1958-66, sales mgr. Detroit, 1966-72, gen. mgr., 1972-75, v.p. regional mgr., 1975-82, v.p. dir. mktg. Chgo., 1982-86, pres., 1986—, pres., CEO, 1988-99, bd. dirs., chmn. of bd., 1998; ret., 1999. Bd. dirs. Prove Quim S.A. de C.V. Mem., supporter Mus. Sci. Industry, Chgo., 1991—, Ravinia Chgo. Symphony, 1991—, adv. com. Gov. Edgar. 1st lt. U.S. Army, 1956-58. Mem. Chem. Mfrs. Assn. (dir. 1990-92), Chem. Industry Coun. Ill. (dir. 1989-93, pres., chmn.), Nat. Paint & Coatings Assn., Nat. Petroleum Refiners Assn., Ill. Mfrs. Assn., Ill. C. of C., Medinah Country Club, Oak Brook Tennis Club, Am. Cancer Soc., NACD Edn. Found. (trustee). Republican. Roman Catholic. Avocations: golf, tennis, jogging, reading, theatre.

WENTWORTH, JACK ROBERTS, business educator, consultant; b. Elgin, Ill., June 11, 1928; s. William Franklin and Elizabeth (Roberts) W.; m. Rosemary Ann Pawlak, May 30, 1956; children: William, Barbara Student, Carleton Coll., 1946-48; BS, Ind. U., 1950, MBA, 1954, DBA, 1959. Coord. displays Cadillac divsn., Gen. Motors Corp., Detroit, 1954-56; asst. prof. bus., assoc. dir. research Sch. of Bus. Ind. U., Bloomington, 1957-60, assoc. prof., dir. rsch., 1960-70, prof., 1970-93, chmn. MBA program, 1970-76, chmn. dept., faculty rep. NCAA, 1978-85, dean Sch. of Bus., 1984-93, Arthur M. Weimer prof., 1993-97, Arthur M. Weimer prof. emeritus, 1997—. Mktg. cons., Bloomington, 1960—; bd. dirs. Kimball Internat., Jasper, Ind. Editor: (monograph) Marketing Horizons, 1965; exec. editor Bus. Horizons, 1960-70 Served to 1st lt. USAF, 1950-53 Recipient Teaching award MBA Assn., 1973, 78, 81, 84, 85, Svc. award Assn. for Bus. and Econ. Rsch., 1983. Mem. Am. Mktg. Assn. (v.p. 1971-73), Grad. Mgmt. Admissions Coun. (chmn. bd. trustees 1977-78), Univ. Club, Masons, Beta Gamma Sigma (pres. Alpha of Ind. chpt. 1971-72, bd. govs. 1986-98, nat. pres. 1994-96). Republican. Methodist. Avocations: athletic events; travel; bicycling; model railroading; magic. Office: Indiana Univ Sch Bus Bloomington IN 47405

WENTWORTH, RICHARD LEIGH, editor; b. Concord, N.H., July 6, 1930; s. Leigh Mayhew and Yvonne Regina (Wilcott) W.; m. Marlene McClenning, June 9, 1950; children— Douglas, John, Elizabeth, James B.A., U. Okla., 1956. Editorial asst. U. Okla. Press, 1957-58; asst. editor U. Wis. Press, 1958-59; mgr. sales and promotion La. State U. Press, 1959-62, asst. dir., 1962-63, dir., 1963-70; assoc. dir., editor U. Ill. Press, Urbana, 1970-79, dir. Champaign, 1979-99, editor, 1999—. Contbr. articles to pub. and sports jours. Served with USAF, 1948-52 Mem. Assn. Am. Univ. Presses (dir. 1966, 77-79), Orgn. Am. Historians, Ill. Hist. Assn., Abraham Lincoln Assn. Democrat Home: 808 W Springfield Ave Champaign IL 61820-4725 Office: U Ill Press 1325 S Oak St Champaign IL 61820-6903

WENTZ, JANET MARIE, state legislator; b. McClusky, N.D., July 21, 1937; d. Charles G. and Martha (Schindler) Neff; m. Thomas Arthur Wentz, 1957; children: Elizabeth, Karin, Thomas. Student, Westmar Coll., 1955-57, U. Minn., 1960-62, Minot State Coll., 1967-70. Registered securities rep.; mem. from dist. 3 N.D. State Ho. of Reps., Bismarck, 1975—, vice chmn., then chmn. appropriations com. Bd. dirs. Ind. Peace Gardens; mem. Commn. on Status of Women in N.D. United Meth. Ch., rep. N.D. Conf. Chs., 1973—; mem. Ct. Svc. Adminstrn. Com.; mem. N.D. Displaced Homemaker Program, Souris Valley Humane Soc. Mem. LWV, PEO, Orgn. Women Legislators, Nat. Assn. Securities Dealers, Minot C. of C. Office: 505 8th Ave SE Minot ND 58701-4764 also: ND House of Reps Office Of House Mems Bismarck ND 58505

WENTZ, WILLIAM HENRY, JR. aerospace engineer, educator; b. Wichita, Kans., Dec. 18, 1933; BS in Mech. Engring. cum laude, Wichita State U., 1955, MS in Aeronautical Engring., 1961; PhD in Engring. Mechanics, U. Kans., 1969. Lic. profl. engr., Kans. Liaison engr. Beech Aircraft, 1952-53; propulsion engr. Boeing Co., Wichita, Kans., 1955; instr. mech. engring. Wichita State U., 1957-58; aerodynamicist Boeing Co., Wichita, 1958-63; from asst. prof. to assoc. prof. aeronautical engring. Wichita State U., 1963-75, prof. aeronautical engring., 1975-83, Gates-Learjet prof. aeronautical engring., 1983-86, disting. prof. aerospace engring., 1986-98, dir. Ctr. Basic and Applied Rsch. Inst. Aviation Rsch., 1986-89, exec. dir. Nat. Inst. Aviation Rsch., 1988-97; sr. fellow Nat. Inst. Aviation Rsch., 1997-98; disting. prof. emeritus aerospace engring., exec. dir. emer. Nat. Inst. Aviation Rsch., 1999; ret. Dir. rsch. projects Boeing Co., 1960, 61, NASA, 1964-66, 66-68, 70-71, 71-83, 86-87, 86-88, 82-87, Dept. of Def., 1986-88, Kans. Tech. Enterprise Corp., 1988-96, FAA, 1986-96. Contbr. articles to profl. jours. With USAF, 1955-57. Recipient Disting. Engr. Svc. award Wichita State U., 1999, Kans. Aviation Honors award Gov. Bill Graves, 1999; Sci. Faculty fellow NSF, 1967-68. Fellow AIAA (assoc., past chmn. Wichita sect., Outstanding advisor student chpt. 1964, 65, 70, Gen. Aviation award 1981, Engr. of Yr. award Wichita sect. 1992, Engr. of Yr. award Region V 1991-92; mem. Soc. Automotive Engrs. (Ralph R. Teeter award 1973), Sigma Gamma Tau, Tau Beta Pi.

WENZEL, STEPHEN G. state legislator; b. Little Falls, Minn., Dec. 7, 1946; s. Mr. and Mrs. Anthony W. BS, St. Cloud State U. Congrl. intern Sen. Walter F. Mondale, 1967—; pres. St. Cloud State YDFL; chmn. Morrison County Dem.-Farm-Labor Com., 1968-70; Minn. State rep. Dist. 12B, 1972, 74, 76—. Mem. 7th Dist. and Minn. Dem. Farmer-Labor Party; chmn. agr. com.; mem. edn., ins. labor mgmt. rels., environ., nat. resources coms.; del. Dem. Nat. Mid-Term Conf., 1978—; adj. instr. polit. sci. Brainerd C.C., Minn. Active Minn. Citizens Concerned for Life, Morrison County Farmers Union. Mem. K.C., Jaycees. Office: Minn Ho of Reps 389 State Office Bldg Saint Paul MN 55155-0001

WERBA, GABRIEL, public relations consultant; b. Paris, Feb. 28, 1930; came to U.S., 1941; s. Aron and Dina (Lewin) W.; m. Barrie Celia Sakolsky, June 1, 1952; children: Dean Steffen, Annmarie Alexandra Bragdon. BA in Journalism, U. Tex., 1948; postgrad., NYU Grad. Sch. Bus., 1948-49, NYU Sch. Law, 1961-62. Account exec. Harold C. Meyers & Co., N.Y.C., 1959-61; dir. pub. rels. and advt. Yardney Electric Corp., 1961-63, 57-59; sr. assoc. Shiefman & Assocs., Detroit, 1963-66; account exec. Merrill Lynch, 1966-70; exec. v.p. Shiefman Werba & Assocs., 1970-73; sr. v.p., exec. v.p., pres., chief oper. officer Anthony M. Franco, Inc., 1973-88; pres., chief exec. officer The Werba Group, Inc. and Gabriel Werba and Assocs., Inc., 1988-94; prin. Durocher, Dixson, Werba, L.L.C., 1994—. Bd. dirs. Erudite Corp., Detroit. Contbr. articles to profl. jours. Bd. dirs. Oakland Citizens League, Detroit, 1970-93, Detroit Symphony Orch. Hall, Detroit Chamber Winds, 1985-91, The Common Ground Sanctuary, Royal Oak, Mich., The Attic Theatre, Detroit, 1989-93, The Children's Ctr., Detroit, mem. strategic planning com., chmn. comm. com., bd. dirs., 1989-95, adv. bd., 1995-96, bd. dirs., 1996—; bd. dirs. NATAS, Detroit, 1993-98, The Jewish Cmty. Coun. Met. Detroit, 1989-95, Margaret W. Montgomery Hosp., 1993-95, adv. bd. 1988-93; mem. comm. com. Detroit Inst. Arts, 1986-92, exhibits com., 1990-2001. Named to, PRSA-Detroit Hall of Fame, 2002. Mem. Nat. Investor Rels. Inst. (past dir., pres. Detroit chpt., spkr., panelist), Pub. Rels. Soc. Am. (bd. dirs. Detroit chpt. 1988-94, pres. 1992-93, past treas. Detroit Counselors' sect., sect. coun., past nat. chmn. fin. sect., spkr., panelist), Fin. Analysts Soc. Detroit (past chmn. pub. info. com.), Am. Mensa (bd. dirs. 1975-91, nat. chmn. 1979-83), Internat. Mensa (bd. dirs. 1979-83, 85-93), Adcraft Club. Avocations: art collecting, concerts, theater. Home: # 202 23090 Halsted Rd Farmington Hills MI 48335-3748 Office: Durocher Dixson Werba LLC 16th Floor Buhl Bldg 535 Griswold St Detroit MI 48226-3604 E-mail: werba@ddwpr.com.

WERGIN, GARY, radio personality; Radio host Sta. WHO-AM, Des Moines. Office: WHO Radio 1801 Grand Ave Des Moines IA 50309*

WERNER, BILL, communication media executive; Capitol bur. chief UP Internat., Mpls., 1998—. Office: UP Internat 331 S 11th St Minneapolis MN 55404-1006

WERNER, CLARENCE L. transportation executive; b. 1937; Asst. mgr. Larson Grain Co., Omaha, 1958-61; with Bus. Motor Express, Inc., 1961-62, Werner Enterprises, Inc., Omaha, 1956-82, pres., 1982-84, chmn. bd. dirs., CEO, 1984—. Office: Werner Enterprises Inc I-80 Highway 50 Omaha NE 68138

WERNER, LAWRENCE H. editor; BA in Journalism, Mich. State U., 1969. Reporter Courier-Jour., 1969-78; asst. features editor (Louisville) Courier-Jour., 1978-79; bus. editor Grand Rapids (Mich.) Press, 1979; consumer reporter Detroit Free Press, 1979-81; mng. editor features and sports Buffalo Courier-Express, 1981-82; features editor Dallas Times Herald, 1982-83; asst. mng. editor bus. Star Tribune, Mpls., 1983-95, reader involvement editor, 1995—. Mem. Soc. Am. Bus. Editors and Writers (past pres.). Avocations: coaching youth soccer, traveling, reading. Office: Star Tribune 425 Portland Ave Minneapolis MN 55488-0002 E-mail: werner@startribune.com.

WERNER, R(ICHARD) BUDD, retired business executive; b. Lorain, Ohio, Aug. 27, 1931; s. Paul Henry and Bessie Marie (Budd) W.; m. Janet Sue Kelsey, Aug. 28, 1932; children: Richard Budd Jr., David Kelsey, Mary Paula. BS in Commerce, Ohio U., 1953. CPA, Ohio. Sr. auditor Arthur Andersen & Co., Cleve., 1955-59; various fin. positions Glidden Co., 1959-65; v.p., asst. treas. Harshaw divsn. Kewanee Oil Co., 1965-72; v.p. fin., treas. Weatherhead Co., 1973-77; v.p. finance, treas. Hauserman, Inc., 1977-81; v.p. fin., CFO SPX Corp., Muskegon, Mich., 1981-94, sr. v.p. planning and devel., 1994-95; exec. in residence coll. of bus. Ohio U., Athens, 1995—. Mem. Lakewood (Ohio) City Coun., 1972-73; mem. North Muskegon (Mich.) Sch. Bd., 1981-85; bd. mem. Appalachian Cmty. Vis. Nurse Assn., Hospice, Health Svc. Inc., 1999—, ACENET Ventures, Inc., 2000—. Lt. Q.M.C., U.S. Army, 1953-55. Mem. Fin. Execs. Inst., Athletic Club Columbus, Ohio. Office: Ohio U Copeland Hall Athens OH 45701

WERT, CHARLES ALLEN, metallurgical and mining engineering educator; b. Battle Creek, Iowa, Dec. 31, 1919; s. John Henry and Anna (Spotts) W.; m. Lucille Vivian Mathena, Sept. 5, 1943; children: John Arthur, Sara Ann. B.A., Morningside Coll., Sioux City, 1941; M.S., State U. Iowa, 1943, Ph.D., 1948. Mem. staff Radiation Lab., Mass. Inst. Tech., 1943-45; instr. physics U. Chgo., 1948-50; mem. faculty U. Ill. at Urbana, 1950—, prof., 1955, head dept. metall. and mining engring., 1967-86, prof. emeritus, 1989. Cons. to industry. Author: Physics of Metals, 1970, Opportunities in Materials Science and Engineering, 1977; also articles.; Cons. editor, McGraw Hill Book Co. Recipient sr. scientist award von Humboldt-Stiftung. Fellow Am. Phys. Soc., Am. Soc. Metals, AAAS, AIME; mem. Sigma Xi. Home: 1708 W Green St Champaign IL 61821-3721 Office: U Ill Metallurgy & Mining Bldg Urbana IL 61801 E-mail: wert@staff.uiuc.edn.

WERT, LARRY, broadcast executive; m. Julie Wert; 4 children. BA Journalism, U. Wis. With Leo Burnett Advt., ABC-TV; local sales mgr. Sta. WLS-TV, Chgo., ABC-TV Nat. Sales, N.Y.C., Chgo., Sta. KABC-TV, L.A.; pres. Evergreen Media Corp., Chgo.; pres., gen. mgr. Evergreen's The Loop and AM 1000; sr. v.p. Chancellor Media Corp., Chgo.; pres., gen. mgr. Sta. WMAQ-TV, 1998—. Mem. adv. coun. Columbia Coll. Chgo. TV Dept.; elected bd. dirs. Jr. Achievement, Chgo.; bd. dirs. Children's Brittle Bone Found., Cath. League Charities, Chicagoland C. of C., Jim Shorts Children's Charities; hon. bd. dirs., mem. nominating com. RAINBOWS; bd. trustees Fenwick H.S., Oak Park, Ill. Named Hon. Chmn., 11th Ann. Have a Heart for Sickle Cell Anemia benefit, 1998; recipient Gift of Life award, 1998, Responding to Cmty. Standards of Broadcasting award, Cosmopolitan C. of C., 1998, Dante award, Joint Civic Com. Italian Ams., 2000. Office: NBC 454 N Columbus Dr Chicago IL 60611*

WERTHEIM, SALLY HARRIS, academic administrator, dean, education educator; b. Cleve., Nov. 1, 1931; d. Arthur I. and Anne (Manheim) Harris; m. Stanley E. Wertheim, Aug. 6, 1950; children: Kathryn, Susan B., Carole J. BS, Flora Stone Mather Coll., 1953; MA, Case Western Res. U., 1967, PhD, 1970. Cert. elem. and secondary edn. tchr., Ohio. Social worker U. Hosps., Cleve., 1953-54; tchr. Fairmount Temple Religious Sch., 1957-72; from mem. faculty to dir. planning & assessment John Carroll U., 1969—99; dir. planning and assessment John Carrol U., 1999—. Cons. in field; cons. Jennings Found., Cleve.; chmn. sch. com. Cleve. Commn. on Higher Edn., 1987-99. Contbr. articles to profl. jours. Sec. Cuyahoga County Mental Health Bd., Cleve., 1978—82; pres. Montefiore Home for Aged, 1987—90; bd. dirs. Mt. Sinai Med. Ctr., 1984—93, Cleve. Edn. Fund, 1992—94; chair edn. com. Cleve. Found. Commn. on Poverty, 1988—93, Cleve. Cmty. Bldg. Initiative, 1993—95, United Way Svcs., 1994—2001; trustee Mt. Sinai Health Care Found., 1998, Gerson Found., 1998, Miller Found., 1998, Begun Found., 2001, Mandel Found., 2001; pres. Jewish Family Svc. Assn., Cleve., 1974—77; v.p. Jewish Cmty. Fedn., 1988—91, pres., 1994—97, trustee, 1992—. Named One of 100 Most Influential Women, Cleve. mag., 1983, One of 29 Most Influential Women, Cleve. Mag., 1997; recipient award John Carroll U., Curtis Miles award for cmty. svc., 1997; grantee Jennings Found., 1984-87, Cleve. and Gund Found., 1987-90, Lilly Found., 1988; S.H. Wertheim scholarship and edn. excellence award established John Carroll U., 1997. Mem. Am. Assn. Colls. for Tchrs. Edn. (bd. dirs. 1982-85), Ohio Assn. Colls. for Tchrs. Edn. (pres. 1981-83), Coun. of Grad. Schs. Avocations: flower arranging, travel, antiques. Office: John Carroll U Planning & Assessment Cleveland OH 44118

WERTZ, KENNETH DEAN, real estate executive; b. Oklahoma City, July 14, 1946; s. Walter K. and Kathryn L. (Moore) W.; children: Adam Troy, Kirsten Paige. B.S. in Acctg., Okla. State U., 1968, M.S. in Acctg. and Econs., 1969; JD, U. San Francisco, 1978. CPA, Okla., Calif; lic. real estate broker, Okla. Sr. acct. Deloitte, Haskins & Sells, San Francisco, 1969-70, 71-75; v.p. acquisitions, mng. dir. Landsing Corp., Menlo Park, Calif., 1975-86; pres. Detrick Salsberry Mgmt. Inc., Tulsa, 1987-88; v.p. asset mgmt. Corporex Co., Cin., 1989-90; exec. v.p. real estate Brunner Cos., Dayton, Ohio, 1990-92; pres. Pillar Real Estate Advisors, 1992—. Lt. col. Med. Svc. corps U.S. Army, 1968-98. Decorated Army Commendation medal with three oak leaf clusters, Meritorious Svc. medal. Mem. Am. Inst. CPA's, Okla. Soc. CPA's, Calif. Soc. CPA's, Nat. Assn. Securities Dealers (fin. prin., registered sales rep.). Republican. Methodist. Avocations: cycling, snow and water skiing, racquetball, camping, fishing. Home: 835 Huntersknoll Ln Cincinnati OH 45230-4343 Office: Pillar Real Estate Advisors 5335 Far Hills Ave Ste 318 Dayton OH 45429-2317

WESCHCKE, CARL LLEWELLYN, publishing executive; BS, Babson Coll., 1951. Pres., publisher Llewellyn Worldwide Ltd., St. Paul, 1957—. Mem. Pub. Roundtable Minn. Home: 16363 Norell Ave N Marine On Saint Croix MN 55047-9747 Office: Llewellyn Worldwide Ltd 84 Wabasha St S Saint Paul MN 55107-1803

WESELI, ROGER WILLIAM, lawyer; b. Cin., Dec. 23, 1932; s. William Henry and Margaret Antoinette (Hoffman) W.; m. Sue Ann Daggett, Sept. 1, 1956; children: Erin, Stacey, Vincent. BA in Polit. Sci, U. Cin., 1955; MS in Hosp. Adminstrn, Northwestern U., 1959; D Tech. Letters (hon.), Cin. Tech. Coll., 1985; JD, No. Ky. U., 1995. Bar: Ohio 1995. Adminstrv. asst. Good Samaritan Hosp., Cin., 1959-61, asst. adminstr., 1961-70, assoc. adminstr., 1970-75, v.p., adminstr., 1975-78, exec. v.p., adminstr., 1978-79, pres., 1979-91, cons., 1991-93; cons. healthcare practice Deloitte & Touche, 1991-93; sec. Greater Cin. Hosp. Council, 1978-80, chmn. bd., 1983-84; assoc. Copeland & Brown Co., L.P.A., Cin., 1995-98, McKinney & Namei, Co., LPA, Cin., 1998—. Chmn. legis. com. health dept. Ohio Cath. Conf., 1978-83, 86; bd. dirs. Friars Boys Club, 1978-94. Recipient Praestans Inter Omnes award Purcell High Sch., 1984, Laura Jackson award Northwestern U. Program in Health Svcs. Mgmt., 1987, Preceptor of Yr. award Xavier U. Program Hosp. and Health Svcs. Adminstrn., 1990. Fellow Am. Coll. Healthcare Execs. (regent for Ohio 1983-90, bd. govs. 1990-94); mem. ABA, Am. Hosp. Assn. (coun. on fedn. rels. 1983-84, coun. on patient svcs. 1984-86, ho. of dels. 1989-91), Ohio Bar Assn., Cin. Bar Assn., Ohio League for Nursing (v.p. 1977-79, cert. of appreciation 1978), Ohio Hosp. Assn. (chmn. govt. liaison com. 1978-83, 86, trustee 1981-83, sec.-treas. 1987, chmn.-elect 1988, chmn. 1989), Cath. Health Assn. (trustee 1983-86), Alpha Mu Sigma. Democrat. Roman Catholic. Home: 5300 Hamilton Ave Unit 610 Cincinnati OH 45224-3167 Office: 15 E 8th St Cincinnati OH 45202-2025 E-mail: healthlaw@fuse.net., rogersue@fuse.net.

WESELY, DONALD RAYMOND, state senator; b. David City, Nebr., Mar. 30, 1954; s. Raymond Ely and Irene (Sabata) W.; children: Sarah, Amanda, Andrew. BA, U. Nebr., 1977; LLD (hon.), Kirksville Coll. Osteo. Medicine, 1989. Mem. Nebr. Legislature, Lincoln, 1978-99; exec. assoc. Selection Rsch. Inst., 1984-86; sr. rsch. assoc. Lincoln Telephone Co., 1985—. Del., Dem. Nat. Conv., 1984, 88, 92, 96; chair Assembly on Legislature, Nat. Conf. State Legislatures., 1992-93, 96-97, exec. com., 1992-97; del. Am. Coun. Young Polit. Leaders, 1993. Recipient Friend of Edn. award Nebr. State Edn. Assn., 1982, Disting. Svc. award Nebr. Pub. Helath Assn., 1984, Disting. Alumni award Lincoln N.E. H.S., 1991, Disting. Health Care award Nebr. Nurse Anesthetists Assn., 1992, Leadership award for Quality in Health Care, Nebr. League Nursing, 1992, Pres.'s award Nebr. Acad. Physicians Assts., 1993, U. Nebr.-Lincoln Outstanding Young Alumni award 1994; named Mental Health Citizen of Yr., Nebr. Mental Health Assn., 1984, Outstanding Young Man, Nebr. Jaycees, 1985, Pub. offcl. of Yr., Nebr. assn. Retarded Citizens, 1992, Advocate of Yr., Nebr. Family Day Care Assn., 1993. Roman Catholic. Office: State Capitol Lincoln NE 68509

WESLEY, NORMAN H. metal products executive; b. 1949; BA, MBA, U. Utah, 1973. With Crown Zellerbach Corp., San Francisco, 1973-83; pres., CEO, Fortune Brands Home & Office ACCO World Corp., Wheeling, Ill., 1983-99; pres. & COO Fortune Brands, Inc., Lincolnshire, 1999, chmn & CEO, 1999—. Office: Fortune Brands Inc 300 Tower Pkwy Lincolnshire IL 60069-3640

WESSELINK, DAVID DUWAYNE, finance company executive; b. Webster City, Iowa, Sept. 5, 1942; s. William David and Lavina C. (Haahr) W.; m. Linda R. DeWitt, Dec. 27, 1971; children: Catherine, Bill. BA in Bus., Ctrl. Coll., 1964; MBA, Mich. State U., 1970. Tchr. Peace Corps, Turkey, 1964-66, Karabuk Koleji, Turkey, 1967-68, Robert Koleji, Turkey, 1969-70; rsch. analyst Household Fin. Corp., Chgo., 1971-73, asst. dir. rsch., 1973-77, asst. treas. Prospect Heights, Ill., 1977, v.p., dir. rsch., 1977-82, group v.p., CFO, 1982-86, sr. v.p., CFO, 1986—; v.p., treas. Household Internat., 1988-93; sr. v.p., CFO Advanta Corp., 1993-98; exec. v.p., CFO Metris Cos., Saint Louis Park, Minn., 1998-2000, vice chmn., 2000—. Bd. dirs. CFC Internat., Chicago Heights, Ill., Am. Fin. Svcs. Assn., Saxon Capital Corp., Glen Allen. Bd. dirs. Ctrl. Coll., Pella, Iowa, 1990—. Mem. Fin. Execs. Inst., Chgo. Coun. on Fgn. Rels., Econ. Club Chgo. Office: Metris Cos 10900 Wayzata Blvd Minnetonka MN 55305 E-mail: david.wesselink@metriscompanies.com.

WESSELMANN, GLENN ALLEN, retired hospital executive; b. Cleve., Mar. 21, 1932; s. Roy Arthur and Dorothy (Oakes) W.; m. Genevieve De Witt, Sept. 6, 1958; children: Debbie, Scott, Janet. A.B., Dartmouth, 1954; M.B.A. with distinction, Cornell U., 1959. Research aide Cornell U., Ithaca, N.Y., 1958-59; adminstrv. resident Meml. Hosp., N.Y.C., 1957-58, adminstrv. asst., 1959-61, asst. adminstr., 1961-65, asst. v.p., 1965-68; v.p. for adminstrn. Meml. Hosp. for Cancer and Allied Diseases, N.Y.C., 1968-79; exec. v.p., chief operating officer St. John Hosp., Detroit, 1979-84; pres., CEO St. John Health System, 1984-95, vice chmn., 1995-97; chmn., pres., CEO St. John Hosp. & Med. Ctr., 1984-94, ret., 1995. Mem. bus. adv. bd. City of Detroit, 1991-95, chmn., 1993-94; mem. exec. com. Greater Detroit Area Health Coun.; bd. dirs. Caymich Ins. Co. Ltd., Mich. Health Care Alliance, SelectCare, Detroit Econ. Growth Corp. Trustee Sisters of St. Joseph Health System 1981-94, Sisters of St. Joseph Health Svc., 1983-95, St. John Hosp. and Med. Ctr., 1979-95, St. John Health System, 1984-95, The Oxford Inst., 1984-95, Eastwood Clinics, 1992-95; pres. Providence Ch. Corp., Hilton Head Island, S.C., chmn. ch. fin. ocm., corp. pres. session; mem. bus. adv. bd.! City of Detroit, 1991-95, chmn. 1993-94. Served with MC AUS, 1955-57. Fellow ACHE; mem. Am. Hosp. Assn., Internat. Hosp. Fedn., Mich. Hosp. Assn. (trustee, chmn. 1994-95, mem. exec. com.), Assn. Am. Med. Colls. (Coth rep.), Am. Cancer Soc. (regional adv. bd. 1994-95), Med. Group Mgmt. Assn., Soc. Health Service Adminstrs., Sigma Phi Epsilon. Home: 63 Big Woods Dr Hilton Head Island SC 29926-2604

WESSELS, BRUCE W. materials scientist, educator; b. N.Y.C., Oct. 18, 1946; m. Beverly T. Wessels; children: David, Kirsten. BS in Metallurgy and Materials Sci., U. Pa., 1968; PhD in Materials Sci., MIT, 1973. Tech. staff GE R&D Ctr., 1972-77, acting branch mgr., 1976; from asst. prof. to assoc. prof. Northwestern U., Evanston, Ill., 1977-83, prof. materials sci. and engring., 1984—, Walter P. Murphy prof., 1998—, prof. elec. and computer engring., 1987—. Vis. sci. Argonne Nat. Lab., 1978; mem. program com. Internat. Conf. Superlattices, Microdevices and Microstructures, 1987. Editor 5 books including (with G.Y. Chin) Advances in Electronic Materials, 1986; mem. editl. bd. Jour. Electronic Materials, 1982-88, 98—; contbr. articles to profl. jours.; patentee in field. Fellow ASM; mem. TMS, The Minerals, Metals and Materials Soc. (chmn. electronic materials com. 1987-89, conf. program chmn. 1986-87, key reader Trans. of AIME 1985-92, bd. dirs. 1993-98, vice-chmn. exec. coun. electronic, magnetic and photonic materials divsn. 1991-92, chmn. 1993-95, v.p. 1995, pres. 1996, bd. trustees AIME 1996-97), Electrochem. Soc. Materials Rsch. Soc. (symposium organizer 1993, 95), Am. Phys. Soc., Sigma Xi, Tau Beta Pi. Office: Materials Science-Engring Northwestern U 2225 N Campus Dr Evanston IL 60208-3108 E-mail: b-wessels@northwestern.edu.

WEST, CLARK DARWIN, pediatric nephrologist, educator; b. Jamestown, N.Y., July 4, 1918; s. Clark Darwin and Frances Isabel (Blanchard) W.; m. Ruthann Asbury, Apr. 12, 1944 (div.); children: Charles Michael, John Clark, Lucy Frances; m. Dolores Lachenman, Mar. 1, 1986. A.B., Coll. of Wooster, 1940; M.D., U. Mich., 1943. Intern Univ. Hosp., Ann Arbor, Mich., 1943-44, resident in pediatrics, 1944-46; fellow in pediatrics Children's Hosp. Research Found., Cin., 1948-49, research asso., 1951-89, asso. dir., 1963-89, dir. div. immunology and nephrology, 1958-89; with cardiopulmonary lab. chest service Bellevue Hosp., N.Y.C., 1949-51; attending pediatrician Children's Hosp., 1951-89; asst. prof. pediatrics U. Cin., 1951-55, asso. prof., 1955-62, prof., 1962-89. Mem. coms. NIH, 1965-69, 1972-73 Mem. editorial bd.: Jour. Pediatrics, 1960-79, Kidney Internat., 1977-89, Clin. Nephrology, 1989-96; contbr. articles to profl. jours. Served to capt. M.C., AUS, 1946-47. Decorated Army commendation medal; recipient recognition award Cin. Pediat. Soc., 1980, Mitchell Rubin award, 1986, Henry L. Barnett award, 1995, Daniel Drake medal, 1996, John P. Peters award, 1996. Mem. Soc. Pediatric Research (sec.-treas. 1958-62, pres. 1963-64), Am. Pediatric Soc., Am. Soc. Pediatric Nephrologists (pres. 1973-74), Am. Physiol. Soc., Am. Assn. Immunologists, Am. Soc. Nephrology, Internat. Pediatric Nephrology Assn., Sigma Xi, Alpha Omega Alpha. Achievements include research on immunopathogenesis and treatment of glomerulonephritides and in the complement system. Home: 11688 Aristocrat Dr Harrison OH 45030-9753 Office: Children's Hosp Med Ctr Cincinnati OH 45229

WEST, MICHAEL ALAN, retired hospital administrator; b. Waseca, Minn., Aug. 4, 1938; s. Ralph Lel and Elizabeth Mary (Brann) W.; m. Mary Thissen, Jan. 21, 1961; children— Anne, Nancy, Douglas. BA, U. Minn., 1961, MHA, 1963. Sales corr. Physicians and Hosps. Supply Co., Mpls., 1959-60; adminstrv. resident R.I. Hosp., Providence, 1962-63, adminstrv. asst., 1963-65, asst. dir., 1965-68; exec. asst. dir. Med. Center U. Mo., Columbia, 1968-70, assoc. dir., 1970-74, asst. prof. community health and med. practice, 1968-74; v.p. for adminstrn. Luth. Gen. Hosp., Park Ridge, Ill., 1974-80, exec. v.p., 1980-84; pres., CEO Akron Gen. Med. Ctr., Ohio, 1984-97, Akron Gen. Health Sys., 1997—2002. Bd. dirs. Vol. Hosps. Am. Inc.; chair VHA-Ctrl., Inc. Bd. dirs. Great Trails Coun. Boy Scouts Am. Mem. Am. Coll. Healthcare Execs., Akron Regional Hosp. Assn. (chmn.), Portage Country Club, Akron City Club, Catawba Island Club. Home: 495 Woodbury Dr Akron OH 44333-2780

WEST, ROBERT CULBERTSON, chemistry educator; b. Glen Ridge, N.J., Mar. 18, 1928; s. Robert C. and Constance (MacKinnon) W.; children: David Russell, Arthur Scott, Derek B.A., Cornell U., 1950; A.M., Harvard U., 1952, Ph.D., 1954; ScD (hon.), G. Asachi Tech. U., Iasi, Romania, 1995. Asst. prof. Lehigh U., 1954-56; mem. faculty U. Wis.-Madison, 1956—, prof. chemistry, 1963—, Eugene G. Rochow prof., 1980, dir. Organosilicon Rsch. Ctr., 1999—. Indsl. and govt. cons., 1961— ; Fulbright lectr. Kyoto and Osaka U., 1964-65; vis. prof. U. Würzburg, 1968-69, Haile Selassie I U., 1972, U. Calif.-Santa Cruz, 1977, U. Utah, 1981, Inst. Chem. Physics Chinese Acad. Sci., 1984, Justus Liebigs U., Giessen, Fed. Republic Germany, U. Estadual de Campinas, Brazil, 1989; Abbott lectr. U. N.D., 1964, Seydel-Wooley lectr. Ga. Inst. Tech., 1970, Sun Oil lectr. Ohio U., 1971, Edgar C. Britton lectr. Dow, Midland, Mich., 1971, Jean Day Meml. lectr. Rutgers U., 1973; Japan Soc. for Promotion Sci. vis. prof. Tohoku U., 1976, Gunma U., 1987; Lady Davis vis. prof. Hebrew U., 1979; Cecil and Ida Green honors prof. Tex. Christian U., 1983; Karcher lectr. U. Okla., 1986; Broberg lectr. N.D. State U., 1986; Xerox lectr. U. B.C., 1986, McGregory lectr. Colgate U., 1988; George Watt lectr. U. Tex., 1992; David Ginsburg meml. lectr. Technion, 1993; rsch. scholar lectr. Drew U., 1995; Reed lectr. Rensselaer Poly. Inst., 1997; Lady Davis vis. prof. Technion-Israel Inst. Tech., 1990; Humboldt prof. Tech. U. Munich, 1990; vis. prof. U. Estadual de Campinas, Brazil, 1993; Dozor vis. fellow Ben Gurion U. of Negev, Israel, 1993. Co-editor: Advances in Organometallic Chemistry, Vols. I-XXXVI, 1964—, Organometallic Chemistry--A Monograph Series, 1968—; contbr. articles to profl. jours. Pres. Madison Community Sch., 1970-81; founder, bd. dirs. Women's Med. Fund, 1971—; nat. bd. dirs. Zero Population Growth, 1980-86; bd. dirs., v.p. Protect Abortion Rights Inc., 1980; lay minister Prairie Unitarian Universalist Soc., 1982. Recipient F.S. Kipling award, 1970, Outstanding Sci. Innovator award Sci. Digest, 1985, Chem. Pioneering award Am. Inst. Chemists, 1988, Wacker Silicon prize, 1989, Humboldt U.S. Scientist award, 1990. Mem. Am. Chem. Soc., Chem. Soc. (London), Japan Chem. Soc., AAAS, Wis. Acad. Sci. Home: 305 Nautilus Dr Madison WI 53705-4333

WEST, THOMAS MEADE, insurance company executive; b. Owensboro, Ky., Aug. 15, 1940; s. Frank Thomas and Vivian (Brown) W.; children: Thomas Meade, Alexandra, Theodora. BA cum laude, Vanderbilt U., 1962; MA magna cum laude, U. Mich., 1964. Various mgmt. positions Lincoln Nat. Life Ins. Co., Fort Wayne, Ind., 1964-75, v.p., 1975-78, sr. v.p., 1978-81, exec. v.p., 1981-94; pres., CEO Lincoln Nat Reins. Cos.; prin. West Cons. Corp.; chair, CEO, pres. Gen. Cologne Life Reins. Cos., 1999—. Bd. dirs. Union Fed. Savs. Bank of Indpls., Union Acceptance Corp., Cologne Life Reins. Co. Area pres. Boy Scouts Am., Ind.; dir. Jr. Achievement, Ft. Wayne. With U.S. Army, 1964-66. Fellow Soc. of Actuaries; mem. Am. Acad. Actuaries, Fort Wayne C. of C. (bd. dirs.) Presbyterian. Home: 126 Taconic Rd Greenwich CT 06831-3113

WESTBROOK, BILL, advertising executive; Internat. pres. Fallon-McElligott, Mpls., 1999—. Office: Fallon-McElligott 901 Marquette Ave Ste 3200 Minneapolis MN 55402-3232

WESTBROOK, JAMES EDWIN, lawyer, educator; b. Camden, Ark., Sept. 7, 1934; s. Loy Edwin and Helen Lucille (Bethea) W.; m. Elizabeth Kay Farris, Dec. 23, 1956; children: William Michael, Robert Bruce, Matthew David. BA with high honors, Hendrix Coll., 1956; JD with distinction, Duke U., 1959; LLM, Georgetown U., 1965. Bar: Ark. 1959, Okla. 1977, Mo. 1982. Assoc. Mehaffy, Smith & Williams, Little Rock, 1959-62; asst. counsel, subcom. of U.S. Senate Jud. Com., Washington, 1963; legis. asst. U.S. Senate, 1963-65; asst. prof. law U. Mo., Columbia, 1965-68, asst. dean, 1966-68, assoc. prof., 1968-70, prof., 1970-76, 80—, James S. Rollins prof. law, 1974-76, 80—, Earl F. Nelson prof. law, 1982-99, emeritus prof., 1999—, interim dean, 1981-82; dean U. Okla. Coll. Law, Norman, 1976-80. George Allen vis. prof. law, U. Richmond, 1987; vis. prof. law Duke U., 1988, Washington U., St. Louis, 1996, 2001; reporter Mid-Am. Assembly on Role of State in Urban Crisis, 1970; dir. Summer Internship Program in Local Govt., 1968; cons. various Mo. cities on drafting home-rule charters; mem. Gov.'s Adv. Coun. on Local Govt. Law, 1967-68, Fed. Practice Com. U.S. Dist. Ct. (we. dist.) Mo., 1986-90; chmn. Columbia Charter Revision Commn., 1973-74; mem. spl. com. labor relations Mo. Dept. Labor and Indsl. Rels., 1975; mem. Task Force on Gender and Justice, Mo. Jud. Conf., 1990-93; mem. com. to rev. govtl. structure of Boone County, Mo., 1991. Author: (with L. Riskin) Dispute Resolution and Lawyers, 1987, supplement, 1993, 2d edit., 1997, abridged edit. of 2d edit., 1998; contbr. articles to profl. jours. Chair search com. for chancellor U. Mo., Columbia, 1992, chair search com. for provost, 1998. Mem. ABA, Nat. Acad. Arbitrators, Assn. Am. Law Schs. (chmn. local govt. law round table coun. 1972), Ctrl. States Law Sch. Assn. (pres. 1982-83), Mo. Bar Assn. (vice chmn. labor law com. 1986-87, chmn. 1987-88, Spurgeon Smithton award 1995), Order of Coif, Blue Key, Alpha Chi. Roman Catholic. Home: 3609 S Woods Edge Rd Columbia MO 65203-6606 Office: U Mo Sch Law Columbia MO 65211-0001

WESTFALL, MORRIS, state legislator; b. Apr. 5, 1939; s. Raymond Earl and Ethel Faye (Neill) W.; m. Sharon Kay Douglas, Dec. 19, 1964; children: Craig Lin, Christi Dawn. BS, U. Mo., 1962. Mem. Mo. Ho. of Reps., Jefferson City, 1971-81, Mo. Senate from 28th dist., Jefferson City, 1994—; asst. minority floor leader, minority whip, 1995—. State exec. dir. agrl. stabilization conservation svc. USDA, Mo., 1981-93. Mem. U. Mo. Alumni Assn., Saddle Club. Office: State Capitol Building Jefferson City MO 65101-1556 E-mail: morris_westfall@senate.state.mo.us.

WESTMAN, JACK CONRAD, child psychiatrist, educator; b. Cadillac, Mich., Oct. 28, 1927; s. Conrad A. and Alice (Pedersen) W.; m. Nancy K. Baehre, July 17, 1953; children— Daniel P., John C., Eric C. MD, U. Mich., 1952. Diplomate Am. Bd. Psychiatry and Neurology. Intern Duke Hosp., Durham, N.C., 1952-53; resident U. Mich. Med. Ctr., 1955-59; dir. outpatient svcs. Children's Psychiat. Hosp., Ann Arbor, Mich., 1961-65; assoc. prof. U. Mich. Med. Sch., 1964-65; coord. diagnostic and treatment unit Waisman Ctr., U. Wis., Madison, 1966-74, prof. psychiatry, 1965-96, prof. emeritus, 1997—. Cons. Joint Commn. on Mental Health of Children, 1967-69, Madison Pub. Schs., 1965-74, Children's Treatment Ctr., Mendota Mental Health Inst., 1965-69 Author: Individual Differences in Children, 1973, Child Advocacy, 1979, Handbook of Learning Disabilities, 1990, Who Speaks for the Children?, 1991, Licensing Parents, 1994, Born to Belong, 1997, Parenthood in America, 2001; editor Child Psychiatry and Human Devel., 1984-99; contbr. articles to profl. jours. Vice-pres. Big Bros. of Dane County, 1970-73; v.p. Wis. Assn. Mental Health, 1968-72; co-chmn. Project Understanding, 1968-75; pres. Wis. Cares, 1998—. With USNR, 1953-55. Fellow Am. Psychiat. Assn., Am. Coll. Psychiatrists, Am. Acad. Child and Adolescent Psychiatry, Am. Orthopsychiat. Assn. (bd. dirs. 1973-76); mem. Am. Assn. Psychiat. Svcs. for Children (pres. 1978-80), Multidisciplinary Acad. Clin. Edn. (pres. 1992-98). Home: 1234 Dartmouth Rd Madison WI 53705-2214 E-mail: jwestman@facstaff.wisc.edu.

WESTMAN, JUDITH ANN, clinical geneticist; b. Columbus, Ohio, Nov. 7, 1957; d. Paul Marshall and Anna Marie (Stahly) Whetstone; m. David Arthur Westman, Apr. 12, 1980; children: Matthew, Joel, Rachel, Deborah. BA, Ohio No. U., 1978; MD, Ohio State U., 1981, MS, 1987. Diplomate Am. Bd. Pediatrics, Am. Bd. Med. Genetics. Resident in pediatrics Children's Hosp. Ohio State U., Columbus, 1981-84, chief resident, 1984-85, fellow clin. genetics, 1985-87, clin. asst. prof., 1987-95, clin. assoc. prof., 1995—, assoc. dean admissions and student affairs, 1996-99, assoc. dean student and med. edn., 1999—. Chair admissions com. Ohio State U. Coll. Medicine, 1990-96. Contbr. articles to profl. jours. Mem. adv. bd. Coll. Arts and Scis., Ohio No. U., Ada, 1988-97, trustee, 1997—; trustee Malone Coll., Canton, Ohio, 1988-94. Grantee FDA, 1987, NCI, 2001. Fellow Am. Acad. Pediatrics, Am. Soc. Human Genetics. Republican. Mem. Ch. of God (Anderson). Avocations: music, church activities. Office: 260 Meiling Hall 370 W 9th Ave Columbus OH 43210-1238

WESTMORELAND, BARBARA FENN, neurologist, electroencephalographer, educator; b. 1940; BS in Chemistry, Mary Washington Coll., 1961; MD, U. Va., 1965. Diplomate Am. Bd. Psychiatry and Neurology and certification of added qualification in clin. neurophysiology (vice chair). Intern Vanderbilt Hosp., Nashville, 1965-66; resident in neurology U. Va. Hosp., Charlottesville, 1966-70; fellow in electroencephalography Mayo Clinic, Rochester, Minn., 1970-71, assoc. cons. neurology, 1971-73; asst. prof. neurology Mayo Med. Sch., 1973-78, assoc. prof., 1978-85, prof., 1985—. Co-author: Medical Neurosciences, 1978, rev. edit., 1986, first author 3d edit., 1994. Mem. Am. Epilepsy Soc. (treas. 1978-80, pres. 1987-88), Am. EEG Soc. (sec. 1985-87, pres. 1991-92), Cen. Assn. Electroencephalographers (sec.-treas. 1976-78, pres. 1979-80, chair neurology resident in-svc. tng. exam 1994-99), Am. Acad. Neurology (chair elect of sect. clin. neurophysiology 1998-2000, chair sect. clin. neurophysiology 2000-2002, vice chair exam com. for cert. in clin. neurophysiology of Am. bd. Psychiatry and Neurology 1998—), Mayo History of Medicine Soc. (pres. 1990-91), Sigma Xi (pres. chpt. 1987-88).

WESTON, ARTHUR WALTER, chemist, scientific and business executive; b. Smith Falls, Ont. Can., Feb. 13, 1914; came to U.S., 1935, naturalized, 1952; s. Herbert W. and Alice M. (Houghton) W.; m. V. Dawn Thompson, Sept. 10, 1940; children: Roger L., Randall K., Cynthia B. BA, Queen's U., Kingston, Ont., 1934, MA, 1935; PhD, Northwestern U., 1938. Postdoctoral fellow Northwestern U., Evanston, Ill., 1938-40; with Abbott Labs., North Chgo., 1940-79, dir. rsch. and devel., 1959-61, v.p. rsch. and devel., 1961-68, dir. company, 1959-68, v.p. sci. affairs, 1968-77, v.p. corp. licensing, 1977-79; v.p., dir. San-Abbott, Japan, 1976-79; cons. Abbott Labs., North Chgo., Ill., 1979-85; pres. Arthur W. Weston & Assocs., Lake Forest, 1979—. Contbr. profl jours. and books. Patentee in field. Mem. Office Sci. Rsch. and Devel., War Manpower Commn., 1942-45; mem. exec. com. indsl. chemistry, div. chemistry and chem. tech. NRC, 1961-65; mem. indsl. panel on sci. and tech. NSF, 1974-80; mem. ad hoc com. chem. agts. Dept. Def., 1961-65. Mem. Rsch. Dirs. Assn. Chgo. (pres. 1965-66), Am. Chem. Soc. (trustee Chgo. 1965—, dir. Chgo. sect. 1952-59, nat. com. corp. assocs. 1967-72), Dirs. Indsl. Rsch., Indsl. Rsch. Inst. (bd. dirs. 1970-73), Phi Beta Kappa, Sigma Xi, Phi Lambda Upsilon. Home and Office: 349 Hilldale Pl Lake Forest IL 60045-3031

WESTON, MICHAEL C. lawyer; b. Asheville, N.C., Aug. 13, 1938; m. Mary Ann Damme; two children. AB in English, Brown U., 1960; JD, U. Mich., 1963. Bar: Mich. 1964, Ill. 1973. Assoc. Clark Hill, Detroit, 1963-68; from sec. to pres. corp. and indsl. consortium Econ. Devel. Corp. of Greater Detroit, 1969-73; chief staff atty. Northwestern U., Evanston, Ill., 1973-81, v.p. legal affairs, 1981-89; v.p. and gen. counsel, 1990-2001. Lectr. minority bus. devel. Inst. Continuing Legal Edn., conflicts of interest Nat. Coun. Univ. Rsch. Adminstrs. Contbr. articles to profl. jours. Chmn. Univ. Gallery Com., 1982-85; bd. dirs. Northwestern U. Press. Mem. ABA (sec. taxation, com. on exempt orgns., ho. of dels., lectr. Inst. on Minority Bus. Devel.), Chgo. Coun. Lawyers, Nat. Assn. Coll. and Univ. Attys. (lectr. fed. tax matters, outside activities faculty mems. univ.-cmty. rels., med. risk mgmt., bd. dirs. 1985-88, 92-97, pres. 1995-96). E-mail: m-weston@northwestern.edu.

WESTON, ROGER LANCE, banker; b. Waukegan, Ill., Mar. 2, 1943; s. Arthur Walter and Vivian Dawn (Thompson) W.; children: Cynthia Page, Kent Andrew, Arthur Eladio, Rebecca Dawn, Alice Sinclair, Elliot Churchill, Evan Walter, Spencer Lance. BS, MacMurray Coll., 1965; MBA, Washington U., St. Louis, 1967. Investment adviser Harris Trust & Savs. Bank, Chgo., 1967-69; sr. investment counselor Security Suprs., 1969-70; gen. ptnr. Sierra Capital Group, 1970-85; exec. v.p., treas., chief fin. officer Telemed Corp., Hoffman Estates, Ill., 1971-79; vice chmn. Bank Lincolnwood, 1979-85; pres., CEO, GSC Enterprises, Lincolnwood, 1979-85; chmn. bd. dirs., pres., CEO, GreatBanc, Inc., Aurora, Ill., 1986—. Mem. Barrington Hills (Ill.) Zoning Bd. Appeals, 1987, com. Asian art Art Inst. Chgo., 1987; mem. nat. coun., mem. Hatchery devel. com. John M. Olin Sch. Bus., Washington U. Mem. Washington U. Eliot Soc. (Chgo. nat. com., chmn. membership com. 1996-92), Univ. Club. Republican. Presbyterian. Office: Great Banc Inc 2300 Barrington Rd Hoffman Estates IL 60195

WESTPHAL, KLAUS WILHELM, university museum director; b. Berlin, Mar. 20, 1939; came to U.S., 1969; s. Wilhelm Heinrich and Irmgard (Henze) W.; m. Margaret Elisabeth Dorothea Wagner, May 16, 1969; children: Barbara, Marianne, Christine. BS in Geology, Eberhard-Karls Universität, Tübingen, Germany, 1960, MS, 1964, PhD in Paleontology, 1969. Dir. geology mus. U. Wis. Madison, 1969—. Bd. dirs. natural history coun. U. Wis. Madison, 1973—, Friends of Geology Mus., Inc., 1977—; nat. speaker on paleontology Outreach, 1977—; instr. paleontology U. Wis., 1977—; leader expeditions fossil vertebrates including dinosaurs, 1977—. Participant various tchr.-tng. projects Wis. Pub. Schs. Lutheran. Home: 3709 High Rd Middleton WI 53562-1003 Office: U Wis Geology Mus 1215 W Dayton St Madison WI 53706-1600

WEXLER, RICHARD LEWIS, lawyer; b. Chgo., June 19, 1941; s. Stanley and Lottie (Pinkert) W.; m. Roberta Seigel, June 13, 1962; children: Deborah (Mrs. Jonathan Sokobin), Joshua, Jonathan. Student, U. Mich., 1959-1962; JD cum laude, John Marshall Law Sch., 1965. Bar: Ill. 1965, U.S. Dist. Ct. (no. dist.) Ill. 1967. Gen. counsel Metro. Planning Council, Chgo., 1965-67; ptnr. Wexler, Kane, Rosenzweig & Shaw, 1967-71, Taussig, Wexler & Shaw, Chgo., 1971-78, Wexler, Siegel & Shaw, Ltd., Chgo., 1978-83, Sachnoff & Weaver, Ltd., Chgo., 1983-91, chair real estate dept., 1985-91, mng. ptnr., 1985-90; ptnr., chmn. real estate dept. Lord Bissell & Brook, 1991-97, mem. compensation com., 1995. Legal cons. Zoning Laws Study Commn., Ill. Gen. Assembly, Springfield, 1969-71, Urban Counties Study Commn., Springfield, 1971-72; legal counsel Ill. Coastal Zone Mgmt. Program, Springfield, 1979-81, Northeastern Ill. Planning Commn., Chgo., 1969—. Contbr. numerous articles to profl. jours. Pres. Jewish Fedn. Met. Chgo., 1986-88, mem. numerous coms., also bd. dirs., 1978-90; pres. Jewish United Fund, 1986-88; bd. dirs. Coun. Jewish Fedns., 1980, mem. exec. com., 1985—, v.p., 1988—, chmn. planning steering com., 1990-95, chmn. fedn./agy. rels. com., 1988-90; co-chmn. Task Force on Poverty and Low Income, 1985-87; nat. vice-chmn. United Jewish Appeal, 1988, nat. chmn., 1996-98, regional allocations chmn., 1987-88, chmn. region II, 1988-90, budget com., 1989-92, allocations com., 1990-91, campaign exec., 1991-2000; chmn. Operation Exodus II, 1993-94, chmn. nat. mktg. com., 1994-95, chmn. 1997 campaign planning and budget com., nat. chmn., 1997-98, pres. bd. trustees, 1998-2000; co-chair United Jewish Appeal Fedns. N.Am., 1998-2000; bd. dirs. Jewish Edn. Soc. N.Am., 1982-85, Hebrew Immigrant Aid Soc., 1988—, Nat. Conf. on Soviet Jewry, 1989-95, vice chmn., 1989-92, nat. chmn., 1992-94; bd. dirs. Nat. Jewish Cmty. Rels. Adv. Coun., 1988-90, vice chmn., 1988-92; chmn. Jewish Com. Rels. Coun. Chgo., 1988-89. Fellow Eta Lambda; mem. ABA, Ill. State Bar Assn. (Lincoln award, Legal Writing, 1966). Avocations: tennis, reading, travel. Office: Lord Bissell & Brook 115 S La Salle St Ste 3400 Chicago IL 60603-3801 E-mail: rwexler@lordbissell.com.

WEXNER, LESLIE HERBERT, retail executive; b. Dayton, Ohio, 1937; BSBA, Ohio State U., 1959, HHD (hon.), 1986; LLD (hon.), Hofstra U., 1987; LHD (hon.), Brandeis U., 1990; PhD (hon.), Jewish Theol. Sem. Founder, pres., chmn. bd. The Limited, Inc., fashion chain, Columbus, 1963—. Dir., mem. exec. com. Banc One Corp., Sotheby's Holdings Inc., vis. com. Grad. Sch. Design Harvard U.; mem. bus. adminstrn. adv. coun. Ohio State U.; chmn. Retail Industry Trade Action Coalition. Bd. dirs. Columbus Urban League, 1982-84, Hebrew Immigrant Aid Soc., N.Y.C., 1982—; co-chmn. Internat. United Jewish Appeal Com.; nat. vice chmn., treas. United Jewish Appeal; bd. dirs., mem. exec. com. Am. Jewish Joint Distbn. Com., Inc.; trustee Columbus Jewish Fedn., 1972, Columbus Jewish Found., Aspen Inst., Ohio State U., Columbus Capital Corp. for Civic Improvement; former trustee Columbus Mus. Art, Columbus Symphony Orch., Whitney Mus. Am. Art, Capitol South Community Urban Redevel. Corp.; former mem. Governing Com. Columbus Found.; founding mem., first chair The Ohio State U. Found; exec. com. Am. Israel Pub. Affairs Com. Decorated cavaliere Republic of Italy. Named Man of Yr. Am. Mktg. Assn., 1974. Mem. Young Presidents Orgn., Sigma Alpha Mu. Club: B'nai B'rith. Office: Limited Inc PO Box 16000 3 Limited Pkwy Columbus OH 43230-1450

WEYAND, WILLIAM J. engineering executive; BBA, Nichols Coll., 1966. Exec. v.p. Measurex Corp.; pres., CEO SDRC, Milford, Ohio, 1997—, also chmn. bd. dirs. Bd. dirs. U. Maine. Office: SDRC 2000 Eastman Dr Milford OH 45150-2740

WEYERS, LARRY LEE, energy executive; b. Nebr. BA, Doane Coll., 1967; ME, Columbia U., 1971; MBA, Harvard U., 1975. Registered profl. engr. Pres., CEO WPS Resources Corp. Holding Co., Green Bay, 1989-98; chmn., pres., CEO WPS Resources Corp., 1998—. Office: WPS Resources Corp PO Box 19001 Green Bay WI 54307-9001

WEYL, TOM F. advertising executive; b. 1943; Creative dir. Am. Acad. Art, 1963-68; with Campbell-Mithun Inc., Mpls., 1968-73; pres., sec., CCO Martin-Williams Inc., 1973—. Office: Martin Williams Advt Inc 60 S 6th St Ste 2800 Minneapolis MN 55402-4444

WHALE, ARTHUR RICHARD, lawyer; b. Detroit, Oct. 28, 1923; s. Arthur B. and Orpha Louella (Doak) W.; m. Roberta Lou Donaldson, Oct. 29, 1949; children: Richard Donaldson, Linda Jean. BSChemE, Northwestern U., 1945; LLB, George Washington U., 1956. Bar: D.C. 1957, Mich. 1957, Ind. 1977, U.S. Patent and Trademark Office 1957. Chem. engr. Ansul Chem. Co., Marinette, Wis., 1946-47, Parke, Davis & Co., Detroit, 1947-50, writer med. lit., 1950-52; chem. engr. Bur. Ships, U.S. Dept. Navy, Washington, 1952-55, dep. sect. head, indsl. gas sect., 1954-55; patent engr. Swift & Co., Washington, 1955-56; patent atty. Upjohn Co., Kalamazoo, 1956-65; asst. mgr. organic chems. sect. patent dept. Dow Chem. Co., Midland, Mich., 1965-66, mgr., 1967-73, mng. counsel, 1973-75; asst. sec., gen. patent counsel Eli Lilly & Co., Indpls., 1975-86; of counsel Miller, Morriss, & Pappas, Lansing, Mich., 1986-89, Baker & Daniels, Indpls., 1987—. Lectr. Practicing Law Inst., John Marshall Law Sch. Contbr. articles to profl. jours. Pres. Nat. Inventors Hall of Fame Found., 1978-79; bd. dirs. Holcomb Rsch. Inst., INdpls, 1982-86. Served to lt. (j.g.) USNR, 1943-46. Mem. State Bar Mich. (chmn. patent trademark copyright sect. 1967-69), D.C. Bar Assn. (mem. patent trademark copyright div.), Midland County Bar Assn. (pres. 1974-75), Am. Bar Assn. (mem. patent trademark copyright sect.), Assn. Corp. Patent Counsel, Nat. Coun. Patent Law Assns. (chmn. 1979-80), Am. Intellectual Property Law Assn. (pres. 1974-75), Ashlar Lodge, Masons, Shriners. Republican. Presbyterian. Avocation: golf. also: 2363 Gulf Shore Blvd N Naples FL 46103 Office: Baker & Daniels 300 N Meridian St Ste 2700 Indianapolis IN 46204-1782 Home: 2363 Gulf Shore Blvd N Naples FL 34103-4356 E-mail: arwhale@bakerd.com.

WHALEN, SARAH EVE, soccer player; b. Greenlawn, N.Y., Apr. 28, 1976; Student in psychology, U. Conn. Mem. U.S. Nat. Women's Soccer Team, 1996—, including Nike Victory Tour, 1995, U..S. Women's Cup, 1997. Named 1997 Soccer Am. Player of Yr. Achievements: holder U. Conn. career record for games played (99). Office: US Soccer Fedn 1801-1811 S Prairie Ave Chicago IL 60616

WHALEN, WAYNE W. lawyer; b. Savanna, Ill., Aug. 22, 1939; s. Leo R. and Esther M. (Yackley) W.; m. Paula Wolff, Apr. 22, 1970; children: Amanda, Clementine, Antonia, Nathaniel, Daniel. BS, U.S. Air Force Acad., 1961; JD, Northwestern U., 1967. Bar: Ill. 1967, U.S. Ct. Appeals (7th cir.) 1968, U.S. Supreme Ct. 1972. Commd. 1st lt. USAF, 1961, ret., 1964; assoc. Mayer, Brown & Platt, Chgo., 1967-74, ptnr., 1974, Skadden, Arps, Slate, Meagher & Flom (Ill.), Chgo., 1984—. Bd. dirs. Van Kampen Funds, Oak Brook, Ill. Author: Annotated Illinois Constitution, 1972. Del. 6th Ill. Constitutional Conv., 1969-70, chmn. style drafting and submission com. Named Outstanding Young Lawyer, Chgo. Bar Found., 1970. Mem. Chgo. Club. Office: Skadden Arps Slate Meagher & Flom 333 W Wacker Dr Ste 2100 Chicago IL 60606-1220

WHALLON, ROBERT EDWARD, anthropology educator; b. Boston, Apr. 23, 1940; s. Robert E. and Dorothy J. (Curme) W.; m. Nadine Rose DeVries, Jan. 1, 1962 (dec.); 1 child, Saskia Olga; m. Barbara Abbott Segraves, Apr. 29, 1978 (div. May 1983); m. Nada Rakic, Jan. 16, 1990; children: Vuk Novak, Nikola Lazar. B.A. summa cum laude, Harvard U., 1961; M.A., U. Chgo., 1963, Ph.D., 1966. Teaching asst. dept anthropology, Chgo., 1965; curator mediterranean prehistory, asst. prof. U. Mich., Ann Arbor, 1966-71, curator, assoc. prof., 1971-77, curator, prof., 1977—, acting dir. Mus. Anthropology, 1978—79, dir. Mus. Anthropology, 1997—2002; fellow Netherlands Inst. for Advanced Studies, 1971-72. Mem. NSF adv. panel for anthropology, 1976-77. Editor: Jour. Anthrop. Archaeology, 1981-94, Mich. Archaeologist, 1969-70; author monographs, essays; contbr. numerous articles on anthropology and archaeology to profl. jours. NSF grantee, 1967—; Woodrow Wilson fellow, 1965; NDEA fellow, 1961-64 Fellow AAAS, Current Anthrpology; mem. Soc. for Am. Archaeology (exec. com. 1981-82, com. on archaeologist-Native Am. rels. 1982), Internat. Union for Prehist. and Protohist. Scis. (Commn. 4 sec. 1976-81, pres. 1981-87, permanent coun. 1987—, exec. com. 2001--), Sigma Xi, Phi Beta Kappa. Home: 1704 Baldwin Pl Ann Arbor MI 48104-3509 Office: U Mich Mus Anthropology Ann Arbor MI 48109-1079

WHARTON, BEVERLY ANN, former utility company executive; b. St. Louis, Nov. 17, 1953; d. Lawrence A. and Helen M. Bextermueller; m. James R. Wharton, March 30, 1974; 1 child, Laura. BS, So. Ill. U., 1975; MBA, U. of S.D., 1980. Tax acct. supr. Iowa Pub. Service Co., Sioux City, Iowa, 1978-84, asst. sec., 1981-84, sec., 1984-88, v.p. staff services, 1985-88, sr. v.p. support group, 1988-91; corp. sec. Midwest Energy Co., 1984-88, v.p., 1986-88, sr. v.p., 1988-90; gen. mgr. Midwest Gas, 1991-95, group v.p., gen. mgr., 1992-95; pres. Gas divsn. Mid-American Energy Co., 1995-96, sr. v.p. energy delivery, 1996-98, sr. v.p., 1998-99. Bd. dirs. Security Nat. Bank, Briar Cliff Coll. Mem. Midwest Gas Assn. (bd. dirs. 1992-96), Rotary (Sioux City club). Roman Catholic. Office: Mid American Energy Co 401 Douglas St Sioux City IA 51101-1443

WHEAT, CHRISTOPHER JOHN, SR. broadcast executive; b. Boston, Dec. 22, 1950; s. Robert Haase Wheat and Florence Edith (Potter) Wiley; m. Becky Ann Renshaw, June 3, 1972; children: Christopher John Jr., Colan Michael. BE, U. Cin., 1972; postgrad., U. Pa., 1978. Account exec. Sta. WKRQ-FM, Cin., 1972-76, Sta. WKRC-AM, Cin., 1976-78, mgr. local sales, 1978-80, gen. mgr. sales, 1980-82; v.p., gen. mgr. Sta. WYNF-FM, Tampa, Fla., 1982-83, Sta. WFBQ-FM, Indpls., 1983-87, Sta. WNDE-AM, Indpls., 1987—. Mem. Little Red Door, Indpls. Cancer Soc. Named one of Outstanding Young Men of Am., 1982. Mem. Radio Broadcasters of Indpls. (v.p., pres. 1988—), U. Cin. Alumni Club, Beta Theta Pi Alumni Club, Indpls. C. of C. (ptnrs. in edn. com., Ambassadors sect.). Republican. Methodist. Club: Indpls. Athletic. Avocation: racquetball. Home: 10723 Seascape Ct Indianapolis IN 46256-9529 Office: Sta WFBQ-FM 6161 Fall Creek Rd Indianapolis IN 46220-5032

WHEELER, DANIEL SCOTT, management executive, editor; b. Richmond, Va., Apr. 23, 1947; s. Arthur Bruce Jr. and Lavinia (Akers) W.; m. Kathy E. Wheeler; children: Matthew, Beth Marie, Jennifer Lynne, Brandy, Jennifer Ann. Student, Va. Commonwealth U., 1966-69, Butler U., 1981, Ind. U., 1984-85. Spl. agt. Northwestern Mut. Life, Richmond, 1969-71; enlisted USN, 1971, resigned, 1979; editor Am. Legion Mag., Indpls., 1979-85, pub., editor-in-chief, 1985-95; exec. dir. The Am. Legion, 1995—. Bd. dirs. HPC/PM Direct. Pres. Citizens Flag Alliance, Inc. Mem. Am. Legion, Mensa. Republican. Avocation: oil painting. Home: 4518 Fairhope Dr Indianapolis IN 46237-2951 Office: The American Legion PO Box 1055 Indianapolis IN 46206-1055

WHEELER, HAROLD H. state legislator, utility contractor; b. Noble County, Ind., Sept. 4, 1929; m. Darlene Adamson; children: Johnna, Tara, Kim. Grad., N. Webster High Sch., 1947. Mem., trustee Etna-Troy Twp, 1963-70; mem. Columbia City Joint High Sch. Bd., 1964-70; commissioner Whitley County, 1973-76; mem. Ind. Senate from 17th dist., Indpls., 1983—; majority caucus chmn. govtl. affairs; pres., CEO M.C. Wheeler & Sons, Inc., Columbia City. Trustee Etna-Troy (Ind.) Twp., 1963-70; commr. Whitley County (Ind.), 1973-76; bd. dirs. Columbia City (Ind.) Joint High Sch., 1964-70, Whitley County Hosp., 1977-83; chmn. Appointments & Claims. Mem. Fraternal Order Elks, Fraternal Order Moose, Fraternal Order Eagles, Masons, Scottish Rite, Mizpah Shrine Methodist. Home: 6370 N State Road 5 Larwill IN 46764-9716 Office: Ind Senate Dist 17 200 W Washington St Indianapolis IN 46204-2728

WHEELER, MARK C., JR. bank executive; Bachelor's, Lake Forest U.; master's, Harvard U. With Mfrs. Hanover Trust Co., N.Y.C.; mng. dir. corp. fin. Bankers Trust Co.; pres., mng. dir. specialized fin. Fleet Bank, N.A. (subs. Fleet Fin. Group, Inc.), 1991-99; vice chmn. Firstar Corp., Milw., 1999—. Office: Firstar Corp 777 E Wisconsin Ave Milwaukee WI 53202-5300

WHEELER, MAURICE B. librarian; BMus, Shorter Coll.; MMus, U. Mich., MLS, 1988; PhD of Libr. Sci., U. Pitts., 1995. Dir. Detroit Pub. Libr., 1996—. Adj. prof. Emporia State U., U. Mich., Wayne State U. Mem. ALA, Nat. Opera Assn./Opera for Youth. Office: Detroit Pub Libr 5201 Woodward Ave Detroit MI 48202-4093

WHEELER, MIKE, retail food store corporate executive; CFO Hy-vec Food Stores Inc., West Des Moines, Iowa, 1998. Office: Hy-vec Food Stores Inc 5820 Westown Pkwy West Des Moines IA 50266-8223

WHEELER, PAUL JAMES, real estate executive; b. Mpls., Jan. 8, 1953; s. Philip James and Phyllis Lavonne (Holmquist) W.; m. Marianne Marie Stanton, June 3, 1978; children: Allison, Nathan, Kathryn. BA in Econs., DePauw U., 1975; MBA in Mgmt., Northwestern U., 1977. CPA, Ill. Acct. Deloitte, Haskins & Sells, Chgo., 1976-79; v.p. fin. Quinlan & Tyson, Inc., Evanston, Ill., 1979-82; sr. v.p. The Inland Real Estate Group, Inc., Oakbrook, 1982—. Bd. dirs. Westbank of Westchester, Inland Real Estate Equities. Inc., Inland Ins. Group, Inc., Oak Brook, Ill. Mem. Ill. Soc. CPA's, Nat. Assn. Real Estate Investment Trusts, Nat. Multi Housing Coun., Investment Program Assn., Libertyville Sunrise Rotary. Republican. Evangelical Free. Home: 255 Ridgeway Ln Libertyville IL 60048-2457 Office: The Inland Group Inc 2901 Butterfield Rd Oak Brook IL 60523-1190

WHEELOCK, PAM, state finance department administrator; Commr. Minn. Fin. Dept., St. Paul. Office: Minn Fin Dept 400 Centennial Bldg 658 Cedar St Saint Paul MN 55155-1603

WHELAN, RICHARD J. retired academic administrator; b. Emmett, Kans, June 23, 1931; s. Richard Joseph and Margaret Alma (Cox) W.; m. Carol Ann King, Nov. 21, 1959; children— Mark Richard, Cheryl Lynne B.A., Washburn U., 1955; Ed.D., U. Kans., 1966. Dir. edn. Menninger Clinic, Topeka, 1959-62; dir. edn. children's rehab. unit U. Kans. Med. Ctr., Kansas City, 1966-99; prof. spl. edn. and pediatrics, chmn. dept. spl. edn. U. Kans., Lawrence, 1966-72, 78-80, 83-88, assoc. dean grad. studies and outreach, 1988-94, Ralph L. Smith disting. prof. child devel., 1968-99, dean sch. edn., 1992-94, prof. emeritus, 1999—; div. dir. U.S. Office Edn., Washington, 1972-74; cons. Blue Valley Sch. Dist., Overland Park, Kans., 1999—; complaint investigator Kans. Bd. of Edn., 2000—. Cons. colls. and univs., state and fed. agys.; chmn. policy bd. Evaluation Tng., Kalamazoo, 1975-81 Author, editor: Promising Practices..., 1983, Emotional and Behavioral Disorders, 1998; cons. editor Ednl. Research Ency., 1982; contbr. articles to profl. jours., chpts. to books Chmn. adv. bd. Kans. Bd. Edn., Topeka, 1982-92; mem. adv. bd. Shawnee Mission Sch. Dist., Kans., 1984-92; mem. Gov.'s Task Force on Early Childhood, 1984-92; hearing officer various sch. dists. Kans. Bd. Edn., Bur. Indian Affiars; mediator and trainer. Mem. Soc. for Learning Disabilities (pres. 1980-81), Council for Exceptional Children, Assn. for Persons with Severe Handicaps (bd. dirs. 1975-79), Kans. Council for Exceptional Children (pres. 1963-64, Service award 1978, award for excellence 2000), Phi Kappa Phi Avocations: reading, music, golf, running, flying. Home: 7400 West 148th St Overland Park KS 66223 E-mail: rwhelan@kumc.edu.

WHELPLEY, DENNIS PORTER, lawyer; b. Mpls., Feb. 16, 1951; s. John Olsen and Harriet Marie (Porter) W.; m. Patricia Jan Adamy, Nov. 27, 1976; children: Heather Nicolle, Christopher Eric. BA, U. Minn., 1973, JD magna cum laude, 1976. Bar: Minn. 1976. Assoc. Oppenheimer Wolff & Donnelly, St. Paul, 1976-83, ptnr., 1983—. Mem. Order of Coif (Minn. chpt.), Phi Beta Kappa (Alpha of Minn. chpt.), Psi Upsilon (Mu chpt.), Dellwood Hills Golf & Country Club. Avocations: golf, tennis, squash, bridge. Home: 49 Locust St Mahtomedi MN 55115-1542 Office: Oppenheimer Wolff & Donnelly 45 S 7th St Ste 3300 Minneapolis MN 55402-1614 E-mail: dwhelpley@oppenheimer.com.

WHIFFEN, JAMES DOUGLASS, surgeon, educator; b. N.Y.C., Jan. 16, 1931; s. John Phillips and Lorna Elizabeth (Douglass) W.; child from a previous marriage, Gregory James; m. Sally Vilas Runge, Aug. 21, 1993.

B.S., U. Wis., 1952, M.D., 1955. Diplomate: Am. Bd. Surgery. Intern Ohio State U. Hosp., 1955-56; resident U. Wis. Hosp., 1956-57, 59-61; instr. dept. surgery U. Wis. Med. Sch., 1962-64, asst. prof., 1964-67, asso. prof., 1967-71, prof., 1971-96, vice chmn. dept., 1970-72, acting chmn., 1972-74; asst. dean Med. Sch., 1975-96; prof. emeritus U. Wis. Med. Sch., 1996—; mem. exam. council State of Wis. Emergency Med. Services, 1974-77. Bd. dirs. Wis. Heart Assn. Served to lt. comdr. USNR, 1957-59. John and Mary R. Markle scholar in acad. medicine, also; Research Career Devel. award NIH, 1965-75 Fellow A.C.S., Am. Soc. Artificial Internal Organs. Club: Maple Bluff Country. Achievements include research publs. on biomaterials, thrombo-resistant surfaces and the physiology of heart-lung bypass procedures. Home: 17 Cambridge Ct Madison WI 53704-5906 Office: 600 Highland Ave Madison WI 53792-0001 E-mail: JWhiffen@facstaff.wisc.edu.

WHIGHAM, JAMES L. protectice services official; B, M, Chgo. State U. Police officer Chgo. Police Dept., 1969-99, retired, 1999; U.S. marshal U.S. Marshals Svc., Chgo., 1999—. Office: US Marshal Office 219 S Dearborn St Ste 2444 Chicago IL 60604-1802

WHIPPLE, DEAN, federal judge; b. 1938; BS, Drury Coll., 1961; postgrad., U. Tulsa, 1961-62; JD, postgrad., U. Mo., 1965. Pvt. practice, Lebanon, Mo., 1965-75; cir. judge div. II 26th Jud. Cir. Mo., 1975-87; judge U.S. Dist. Ct., Kansas City, Mo., 1987-2000, chief judge, 2000—. Prosecuting atty. Laclede County, Mo., 1967-71. Mem. Cen. United Meth. Ch., Kansas City. With Mo. N.G., 1956-61; USAR, 1961-66. Mem. Mo. Bar Assn. (mem. pub. info. com. 1971-72, mem. judiciary com. 1971-72, mem. bd. govs. 1975-87, mem. exec. com. 1983-84, 86-87, mem. planning com. for ann. meeting 1985, 87, chmn. 1986, mem. selection com. for Lon Hocker award 1986), Mo. Trial Judges Assn., 26th Jud. Bar Assn., Laclede County Bar Assn. (pres. 1968-69, 72-73), Kansas City Met. Bar Assn., Kansas City Inn of Ct. (instr. 1988-93), Mo. Hist. Soc., Phi Delta Phi. Office: US Courthouse 400 E 9th St Kansas City MO 64106-2607

WHIPPLE, HARRY M. newspaper publishing executive; b. Tulsa, June 30, 1947; children: Garth, Erin. Student, Ind. U., 1965-68, U. Evansville, 1965-68, Ark Poly. Coll., 1965-68. Gen. mgr. Mt. Vernon (Ind.) Pub. Co., 1972-75; asst. pub. Pioneer Newspapers (formerly Scripps League Newspapers), Monongahela, Pa., 1975-77; advt. dir. Rockford (Ill.) Morning Star and Register Republic, 1977-81; pres., pub. Valley News Dispatch, The Herald, North Hills News Record, Tarentum, Pa., 1981-84; v.p., regional mgr. Midwest Gannett Media Sales/Gannett Nat. Sales, Chgo., 1984-87; pres. TNI Ptnrs., Tucson, 1987-92; pres., pub. The Cincinnati Enquirer, 1992—. Bd. trustees Zool. Soc. Cin.; co-chair adv. bd. Nat. Underground R.R. Freedom Ctr.; chmn. bd. dirs. Greater Cin. Ctr. for Econ. Edn. Mem. Greater Cin. C. of C. (chmn. bd. trustees). Office: Cincinnati Enquirer 312 Elm St Fl 20 Cincinnati OH 45202-2754

WHIPPLE, KENNETH, utilities executive; b. 1934; BS, MIT, 1958. With Ford Motor Co., Dearborn, Mich., 1958—, systems mgr. Ford Credit, 1966-69, mgr. mgmt. svcs. dept. fin. staff, 1969-71, systems analysis mgr. fin. staff, 1971-74, asst. contr. internat. fin. staff, 1974-75, v.p. fin. Ford Credit, 1975-77, exec. v.p. Ford Credit, 1977-80, pres. Ford Credit, 1980-84, v.p. corp. strategy, 1984-86; v.p. chmn. Ford of Europe, 1986-88; exec. v.p., pres. Ford Fin. Svcs. Group, Dearborn, 1988—99; chmn. bd., CEO CMS Energy, Mich., 2002—. Office: CMS Energy Fairlane Plaza S Ste 1100 330 Town Center Dr Dearborn MI 48126*

WHIPPLE, WILLIAM PERRY, foundation administrator; b. Cedar Rapids, Iowa, Nov. 1, 1913; s. Robert Milo and Jeanette (Fry) W.; m. Gayle Schroeder, Sept. 18, 1937; children: John William, Robert Milo. BA, Coe Coll., 1935, hon. doctorate, 1996. Prin. Whipple Ins. Agy., Cedar Rapids, 1935-57; pres. Whipple and Winterberg, 1957-71; chmn. Frank B. Hall of Iowa, Inc., 1971-74; pres. Hall Found., Inc., 1974-95, also bd. dirs.; chair Hall-Perrine Found., 1995—. Exec. in residence Colo. State U., Fort Collins, 1973; bd. dirs. Fire Mark Cir. of Ams., Chamblee, Ga., Interocean Reins. Corp., Cedar Rapids, 1st Fed. Savs. and Loan, Cedar Rapids, Nissen Corp., Cedar Rapids, 1966-72, Banks of Iowa, Inc., Des Moines, 1982-85. Trustee Cedar Rapids Pub. Library, Coe Coll., chmn.; hon. bd. dirs. Methwick Manor, Cedar Rapids, Linn County ARC, Greater Cedar Rapids Found. Recipient Outstanding Layman award YMCA, Cedar Rapids, 1986, Alumni Achievement award, Coe Coll., 1990, Founders Day award Coe Coll., 2001, First Community Svc. award, Cedar Rapids Rotary, 1993. Mem. Rotary (Paul Harris fellow 1987), Elks. Republican. Presbyterian. Avocations: signevierist, stamp collecting. Home: 1224 13th St NW Cedar Rapids IA 52405-2404 Office: Hall-Perrine Found 115 3d St SE Cedar Rapids IA 52401-1222

WHIPPS, EDWARD FRANKLIN, lawyer; b. Columbus, Ohio, Dec. 17, 1936; s. Rusk Henry and Agnes Lucille (Green) W.; children: Edward Scott, Rusk Huot, Sylvia Louise, Rudyard Christian. B.A., Ohio Wesleyan U., 1958; J.D., Ohio State U., 1961. Bar: Ohio 1961, U.S. Dist. Ct. (so. dist.) Ohio 1962, U.S. Dist. Ct. (no. dist.) Ohio 1964, U.S. Ct. Claims 1963, U.S. Supreme Ct. 1963, Miss. 1965, U.S. Ct. Appeals (6th cir.) 1980. Assoc. George, Greek, King & McMahon, Columbus, 1961-66; ptnr. George, Greek, King, McMahon & McConnaughey, 1966-79, McConnaughey, Stradley, Mone & Moul, Columbus, 1979-81, Thompson, Hine & Flory, Columbus, 1981-93; prin. Edward F. Whipps & Assocs., 1993-94, 2000—; ptnr. Whipps & Wistner, 1995-99. Founder, trustee Creative Living, Inc., 1969—; trustee, v.p. Unverferth House, Inc., 1989; trustee Eagle Scholarship Trust. Host: TV programs Upper Arlington Plain Talk, 1979-82; TV program Briding Disability, 1981-82, Lawyers on Call, 1982— , U.A. Today, 1982-86, The Ohio Wesleyan Experience, 1984— . Mem. Ohio Bd. Psychology, 1992—; mem. Upper Arlington (Ohio) Bd. Edn., 1971-80, pres., 1978-79; mem. bd. alumni dirs. Ohio Wesleyan U., 1975-79; trustee Walden Ravines Assn., 1992-96, pres. 1993-96. Mem. ABA, Columbus Bar Assn., Ohio State Bar Assn., Assn. Trial Lawyers Am., Ohio Acad. Trial Lawyers, Franklin County Trial Lawyers Assn., Am. Judicature Soc., Columbus Bar Found., Ohio Bd. Psychology, Columbus C. of C., Upper Arlington Area C. of C. (trustee 1978—), Lawyers Club, Barrister Club, Columbus Athletic Club, Nat. Football Found. & Hall of Fame, Columbus Touchdown Club, Downtown Quarterback Club, Ohio State U. Faculty (Columbus) Club, Ohio State U. Golf Club, Highlands Golf Club (dir. 2001—), Delta Tau Delta (nat. v.p. 1976-78). Republican. Home: 51 Highland Ct Pataskala OH 43062-8910 Office: Edward F Whipps & Assocs 500 S Front St Columbus OH 43215-7619

WHISNANT, JACK PAGE, neurologist; b. Little Rock, Oct. 26, 1924; s. John Clifton and Zula I. (Page) W.; m. Patricia Anne Rimmey, May 12, 1944; children: Elizabeth Anne, John David, James Michael. B.S., U. Ark., 1948, M.D., 1951; M.S., U. Minn., 1955. Intern Balt. City Hosp., 1951-52; resident in medicine and neurology Mayo Grad. Sch. Medicine, Rochester, Minn., 1952-55, instr. neurology, 1956-60, asst. prof., 1960-64, asso. prof., 1964-69, prof., 1969—; Meyer prof. neurosci. Mayo Med. Sch.; chmn. dept. neurology Mayo Clinic, Mayo Med. Sch., Mayo Grad. Sch. Medicine, 1971-81; chmn. dept. health scis. research Mayo Clinic and Mayo Med. Sch., 1987-93. Cons. neurology Mayo Clinic, 1955-96 , head sect. neurology, 1963-71; dir. Mayo Cerebrovascular Clin. Research Center, 1975-96. Contbr. articles on neurology and cerebrovascular disease to med. jours. Trustee YMCA, Rochester, pres., 1977. With USAAF, 1942-45. Decorated Air medal. NIH grantee, 1959-96. Fellow Am. Heart Assn., Am. Acad. Neurology (pres. 1993-95); mem. AMA, Am. Neurol. Assn. (pres. 1981-82), Am. Bd. Psychiatry and Neurology (bd. dirs. 1983-90, pres. 1989), Zumbro Valley Med. Soc., Minn. Med. Assn., Minn. Soc. Neurol. Scis., Ctrl. Soc. Neurol. Rsch. (pres. 1964), Alumni Assn. Mayo Found. Presbyterian. Home: 1005 7th Ave NE Rochester MN 55906-7074 Office: Mayo Found Dept Health Scis Rsch 201 1st St SW Rochester MN 55905-0001 E-mail: whisnant1924@att.net., whisnant@mayo.edu.

WHISTLER, ROY LESTER, chemist, educator, industrialist; b. Morgantown, W.Va., Mar. 31, 1912; s. Park H. and Cloe (Martin) W.; m. Leila Anna Barbara Kaufman, Sept. 6, 1935 (dec. 1994); 1 child, William Harris. B.S., Heidelberg Coll., 1934, D.Sc. (hon.), 1957; M.S., Ohio State U., 1935; Ph.D., Iowa State U., 1938; D.Litt. (hon.), St. Thomas Inst., 1982; D.Agr., Purdue U., 1985. Instr. chemistry Iowa State U., 1935-38; research fellow Bur. Standards, 1938-40; sect. leader dept. agr. No. Regional Rsch. Lab., 1940-46; prof. biochemistry Purdue U., 1946-76, Hillenbrand distinguished prof., asst. dept. head, 1974-82, Hillenbrand disting. prof. emeritus Ind., 1982—; chmn. Inst. Agrl. Utilization Research, 1961-75; pres. Lafayette Applied Chemistry Inc., 1980-96. Vis. lectr. U. Witwatersrand, South Africa, 1961, South Africa, 65, South Africa, 77, South Africa, 85, Acad. Sci., France, 1975, Vladivostock Acad. Sci., Russia, 1976, numerous other countries; lectr. Bradley Polytech. Inst., 1941—42; adj. prof. Whistler Ctr. Carbohydrate Chemistry (named by Purdue U. 1984) , advisor, bd. dirs.; indsl cons. dir. Pfanstiehl Lab., Inc., 1940—2000, Greenwich Pharm., Inc., 1946—52, Larex, 1999—. Author: Polysaccharide Chemistry, 1953, Industrial Gums, 1959, 2d rev. edit., 1976, 3d rev. edit., 1992; rev. edit.: Methods of Carbohydrate Chemistry, series, 1962— ; co-author: Guar, 1979, Carbohydrates for Food Scientists, 1997; editor: Starch-Chemistry and Technology, 2 vols., 1965, 67, rev. edit., 1984, 3d edit. 1999; editl bd. Jour. Carbohydrate Research, 1960-91, Starchs Chemistry and Technology, 1985; bd. advisors: Advances in Carbohydrate Chemistry, 1950-96, Organic Preparations and Procedures Internat., 1970—, Jour. Carbo-Nucleosides-Nucleotides, 1973-77, Stärke, Starch, 1979-99; contbr. numerous articles to profl. jours. Recipient Sigma Xi rsch. award Purdue U., 1953, Medal of Merit, Japanese Starch Tech. Soc., 1967, German Saare medal, 1974, Thomas Burr Osborne award Am. Assn. Cereal Chemists, 1974, Sterling Henricks award USDA, 1991, 93, Nicholas Appert award Inst. Food Technologists, 1994; Roy L. Whistler internat. award in carbohydrates established in his hon., Rsch. bldg. named in his honor Purdue U., 1997; Fred W. Tanner lectr., Chgo., 1994; Named Hillenbrand Disting. prof. Fellow AAAS, Am. Chem. Soc. (chmn. Purdue sect. 1949-50, carbohydrate divsn. 1951, cellular divsn. 1962, nat. councilor 1953-87, bd. dirs. 5th dist. 1955-58, chmn. com. edn. and students, chmn. sub-com. polysaccharide nomenclature, symposium dedicated in his honor 1979, hon. fellow award cellulose divsn. 1983, Hudson award 1960, Anselme Payen award 1967, Carl Lucas Alsburg award 1970, Spencer award 1970, 75, Disting. Svc. award 1983, named one of 10 outstanding chemists Chgo. sect. 1948), Am. Inst. Chemists (pres. 1982-83, Gold medal 1992), Am. Assn. Cereal Chemists (pres. 1978), Internat. Carbohydrate Union (pres. 1972-74); mem. Lafayette Applied Chemistry (pres. 1970-94), Argentine Chem. Soc. (life), Rotary (pres. 1966), Sigma Xi (pres. Purdue sect. 1957-59, nat. exec. com. 1958-62, hon. life mem. 1983—), Phi Lambda Upsilon, Rotary (pres. 1966). Office: Whistler Ctr for Carbohydrate Rsch 1160 Food Sci Bldg Lafayette IN 47907

WHITACRE, CAROLINE CLEMENT, immunologist, researcher; b. Cin., Nov. 4, 1949; d. Richard Soteldo and Rosalyn (Wilson) W.; m. Michael Francis Para, June 28, 1975: 1 child, Alexander. BA, Ohio State U., 1971, PhD, 1975. Postdoctoral fellow Northwestern U., Chgo., 1975-78, instr., 1978-81; asst. prof. Ohio State U., Columbus, 1981-87, assoc. prof., 1987-92, prof. of microbiology and immunology, 1992—, interim chair, 1992-94, chair, 1994—. Mem. com. on fellowship awards Nat. Multiple Sclerosis Soc., 1992-97, com. air, 1995-97, chair com. on gender and autoimmunity, 1997-99. Contbr. articles to profl. pubs. Nat. Insts. for Allergy and Infectious Diseases grantee, 1987—, NIH-Nat. Insts. for Neurol. Disorders and Stroke grantee, 1991—, Nat. Multiple Sclerosis grantee, 1991—. Mem. AAAS, NIH (spl. study sect. 1987-91, neurol. disorders com. 1991-95), Am. Assn. Immunologists, N.Y. Acad. Scis. Presbyterian. Achievements include discovery that experimental autoimmune encephalomyelitis can be suppressed by the oral administration of myelin basic protein due to the anergy or deletion of myelin basic protein specific T lymphocytes; research on multiple sclerosis and the animal model, experimental autoimmune encephalomyelitis,sex differences in autoimmune diseases, and effects of stress on immune function. Office: Ohio State U 2078 Graves Hall 333 W 10th Ave Columbus OH 43210-1239 E-mail: whitacre.3@osu.edu.

WHITAKER, AUDIE DALE, hospital laboratory medical technologist; b. Cin., Jan. 19, 1949; s. Audie and Wanda Edith (Weaver) W.; m. Sandra Sue McPhail, Aug. 22, 1970; children: Audie David Nathaniel, Andrea Grace, Alexandra Christine. BA, Olivet Nazarene U., 1971; Degree in Med. Tech., Silver Cross Hosp., Joliet, Ill., 1972; MS in Biology, Ball State U., 1999. Med. tech. Riverside Hosp., Kankakee, 1971-72, Silver Cross Hosp., Joliet, 1972-77; lab. mgr. Lakeshore Community Hosp., 1977-90; evening lab. supr. Community Hosp., Anderson, Ind., 1990-93; med. technologist Community Hosp. of Anderson, 1990—. Lectr. in field. Health care rep. Local Emergency Preparedness Com., Hart, Mich., 1988-90; sec., deacon, bd. dirs. West Shore Christian Fellowship, Muskegon, 1987-90, vice chmn. edn. com., 1988-90; mem. Rep. Nat. Com. S.W. Nazarene Ch. Dist. grantee, 1967, Directed Study grantee, 1970-71, rsch. grantee Sigma Xi, 1993; grad. rsch. grantee Ball State U., 1994. Mem. Am. Soc. Clin. Pathologists. Republican. Avocations: acting, poetry, astronomy. Home: 1705 N Tillotson Ave Muncie IN 47304-2601 Office: Community Hosp 1515 N Madison Ave Anderson IN 46011-3457

WHITAKER, CHARLES F. journalism educator; b. Chgo., Oct. 28, 1958; s. Andrew L. and Marjorie Whitaker; m. Stephanie J. Sanders, Oct. 1, 1988; children: Joshua, Christopher. BS in Journalism, Northwestern U., 1980, MS in Journalism, 1981. Suburban edn. writer N.E. Dade County Bur., Miami (Fla.) Herald, 1981-82, staff writer, 1982-84, Louisville Times, 1984-85; assoc. editor Ebony Mag., Chgo., 1985-87, sr. assoc. editor, 1987-89, sr. editor, 1989-92; mem. adj. faculty Northwestern U. Medill Sch. Journalism, Evanston, Ill., 1990-92, asst. prof. journalism, 1992—. Dir. Gertrude Johnson Williams Lit. Contest, 1989—; assoc. fellow Joint Ctr. for Polit. and Econ. Studies, Urban Policy Inst., Chgo., 1992—; advisor, faculty editor Passport Africa, 1992. Contbr. to various publs. Bd. dirs. Chocolate Chips Theatre Co., 1987—. Recipient 1st place award for mag. writing Nat.. Assn. Edn. Writers, 1982; 1st place award for feature writing Louisville Assn. Black Communicators, 1984, for commentary or criticism, 1984. Mem. Nat. Assn. Black Journalists, Chgo. Assn. Black Journalists (faculty Exposure satellite program 1988—), Phi Beta Sigma (editor-in-chief Crescent 1989-93). Office: Northwestern U Medill Sch Journalism Fisk Hall 1845 Sheridan Rd Evanston IL 60208-0001

WHITAKER, FREDA N. trust company executive; BS, U. Mo., Kansas City. With Patrons Bank (now NationsBank), Olathe, Kans., Johnson County Bank (now Firstar); exec. v.p. The Midwest Trust Co., Overland Park, Kans. Mem.: Ea. Kans. Estate Planning Coun., Estate Planning Soc. Kansas City (past pres.). Office: The Midwest Trust Co 10740 Nall Ave Ste 100 Overland Park KS 66211*

WHITAKER, GLENN VIRGIL, lawyer; b. Cin., July 23, 1947; s. Glenn M. and Doris (Handlon) W.; m. Jennifer Lynn Angus, Oct. 22, 1990. BA, Denison U., 1969; JD, George Washington U., 1972. Bar: Md. 1972, D.C. 1973, Ohio 1980. Law clk. to judge U.S. Dist. Ct., Balt., 1972-73; assoc. O'Donoghue and O'Donoghue, Washington, 1973-76; trial atty. civil div. U.S. Dept. Justice, 1976-78, spl. litigation counsel, 1978-80; ptnr. Graydon, Head & Ritchey, Cin., 1980-92, Voyrs, Sater, Seymour & Pease, Cin., 1992—. Emeritus master of bench Potter Stewart Inn of Ct., Cin., 1985—; adj. prof. law Coll. Law U. Cin.; mem. Am. Bd. Trial Advocates. Fellow Am. Coll. Trial Lawyers; mem. ABA, Ohio Bar Assn., D.C. Bar Assn., Md. Bar Assn., Cin. Bar Assn. Avocations: hiking, exploring. Office: Vorys Sater Seymour & Pease 221 E 4th St Ste 2100 Cincinnati OH 45202-5133

WHITBURN, GERALD, insurance company executive; b. Wakefield, Mich., July 12, 1944; s. Donald and Ruby E. (Nichols) W.; m. Charmaine M. Heise, May 3, 1969; children: Bree, Luke. BS, U. Wis., Oshkosh, 1966; MA, U. Wis., Madison, 1968; postgrad., Harvard U., 1988, 00, U. Pa., 1997. Aide Gov. Warren P. Knowles, Wis., 1966-69; personal asst. USN sec. John H. Chafee, Washington, 1969-72; automobile dealer, real estate developer Merrill, Wis., 1973-80; exec. asst. to Senator Robert W. Kasten U.S. Senate, Washington, 1981-87; dep. sec. Wis. Dept. Adminstrn., Madison, 1987-89; sec. Wis. Dept. Industry, Labor and Human Rels., 1989-91, Wis. Dept. Health and Social Svcs., Madison, 1991-95; sec. exec. office of health and human svcs. Commonwealth of Mass., Boston, 1995-96; pres., CEO, dir. Ch. Mut. Ins. Co., Merrill, Wis., 1996—; dir. Alliance of Am. Insurers. Mem. U.S. Labor Sec.'s Commn. on Achieving Necessary Skills, Washington, 1990-92. Contbr. articles to newspapers. Del. Rep. Nat. Conv., 1988, 92. Recipient Disting. Alumni award U. Wis., Oshkosh, 1991. Home: 2079 Sunset Dr Tomahawk WI 54487-9301 Office: Ch Mut Ins Co 300 Schuster Ln Merrill WI 54452

WHITE, B. JOSEPH, academic administrator; Dean bus. administrn. U. Mich., Ann Arbor, 2002—, interim pres., 2002—. Office: U Mich Ann Arbor Office of the Pres 2074 Fleming Admin Bldg Ann Arbor MI 48109-1340 Business E-Mail: bjwhite@umich.edu..

WHITE, C. THOMAS, state supreme court justice; b. Humphrey, Nebr., Oct. 5, 1928; s. John Ambrose and Margaret Elizabeth (Costello) W.; children from a previous marriage: Michaela, Thomas, Patrick; m. Lyn, Sept. 15, 1995. JD, Creighton U., 1952. Bar: Nebr. County atty. Platte County (Nebr.), Columbus, 1955-65; judge 21st Dist. Ct. Nebr., 1965-77; justice Nebr. Supreme Ct., Lincoln, 1977-98, chief justice, 1995-98; ret., 1998; of counsel Welch, White & Wolff, Omaha. Served with U.S. Army, 1946-47. Roman Catholic. Clubs: Elks, KC. Address: 7171 Mercy Rd # 20 Omaha NE 68106-2620

WHITE, DEAN, advertising executive; b. Norfolk, Nebr., 1923; m. Barbara White; 4 children. Student, U. Nebr.; grad., U.S. Merchant Marine Acad. Pres. Whiteco Industries, Inc., Merrillville, Ind., 1953-98, chmn. bd., CEO, 1998—. Chief officer Merchant Marines, Navy. Office: Whiteco Industries Inc 1000 E 700N Merrillville IN 46410-5675

WHITE, DOUG, state legislator; b. 1943; m. Shirley White; children: Steve, Jenny. BS, Ohio State U. Commr. Adams County, 1985-90; mem. Ohio Ho. of Reps from 77th & 88th dists., Columbus, 1990-96; owner, operator livestock and crop farm; mem. Ohio Senate from 14th dist., Columbus, 1996—. Mem. Ohio Cattlemen's Assn. (pres.), Ohio Beef Coun. (former treas.), Adams County Rep. Club, Ohio 4-H Found., Manchester Lions, Ohio Farm Bur. Home: 3830 Old Dutch Rd Manchester OH 45144-9714 Office: Ohio Senate State House Rm 041 Columbus OH 43215

WHITE, HAROLD F. bankruptcy judge, retired federal judge; b. Hartford, Conn., Apr. 29, 1920; s. Harry T, and Maude Evelyn (McCarthy) W.; m. Edna Jeanette Murie, 1943; children; Frances, Susan, Harold. BSc, Ohio U., 1946; JD, U. Akron, 1952. Bar: Ohio 1952. Chief police prosecutor City of Akron, Ohio, 1953; asst. prosecutor Summit County, Akron, 1957-58; bankruptcy referee, bankruptcy judge U.S. Cts., 1958-94, on recall as sr. bankruptcy judge, 1994—, on recall as bankruptcy judge, 1995-2001. Trustee Summit County Kidney Found; elder Westminster Presbyn. Ch., Akron. Named Disting. Alumni Ohio U., 1979, Outstanding Alumni U. Akron Sch. Law, 1983; recipient John Quine adj. lectr. of law award U. Akron Sch. Law, 1991. Fellow Ohio State Bar Assn. (hon. life); mem. Akron Bar Assn., Nat. Conf. Bankruptcy Judges (twice gov. 6th cir.), Commercial Law League, Am. Bankruptcy Inst. Office: Rm 455 2 S Main St Akron OH 44308-1880

WHITE, JAMES BOYD, law educator; b. Boston, July 28, 1938; s. Benjamin Vroom and Charlotte Green (Conover) W.; m. Mary Louise Fitch, Jan. 1, 1978; children: Emma Lillian, Henry Alfred; children by previous marriage: Catherine Conover, John Southworth. AB, Amherst Coll., 1960; AM, Harvard U., 1961, LLB, 1964. Assoc. Foley, Hoag & Eliot, Boston, 1964-67; asst. prof. law U. Colo., 1967-69, assoc. prof., 1969-73, prof., 1973-75; prof. law U. Chgo., 1975-83; Hart Wright prof. law and English U. Mich., Ann Arbor, 1983—. Vis. assoc. prof. Stanford U., 1972 Author: The Legal Imagination, 1973, (with Scarboro) Constitutional Criminal Procedure, 1976, When Words Lose Their Meaning, 1981, Heracles' Bow, 1985, Justice as Translation, 1990, "This Book of Starres", 1994, Acts of Hope, 1994, From Expectation to Experience, 1999, The Edge of Meaning, 2001. Sinclair Kennedy Traveling fellow, 1964-65; Nat. Endowment for Humanities fellow, 1979-80, 92; Guggenheim fellow, 1993; vis. scholar Phi Beta Kappa, 1997-98. Mem. AAAS, Am. Law Inst. Office: U Mich Law Sch 625 S State St Ann Arbor MI 48109-1215

WHITE, JAMES FLOYD, theology educator; b. Boston, Jan. 23, 1932; s. Edwin Turner and Madeline (Rinker) W.; m. Marilyn Atkinson, Aug. 23, 1959 (div. 1982); children: Louise, Robert, Ellen, Laura, Martin; m. Susan Jan Waller, Oct. 28, 1982 (div. 1993); m. Claire Duggan, Mar. 2, 1997. Grad., Phillips Acad., Andover, Mass., 1949; AB, Harvard U., 1953; BD, Union Theol. Sem., 1956; PhD, Duke U., 1960. Ordained to ministry United Meth. Ch., 1955. Instr. Ohio Wesleyan U., Delaware, 1959-61, Meth. Theol. Sch. in Ohio, Delaware, 1960-61; prof. Perkins Sch. Theology, So. Meth. U., Dallas, 1961-83, U. Notre Dame, Ind., 1983-99; Bard Thompson prof. Drew U., 2000—. Author: Cambridge Movement, 1962, New Forms of Worship, 1971, Introduction to Christian Worship, 1980, Protestant Worship, 1989, Roman Catholic Worship (1st place award Cath. Press Assn. 1996), Christian Worship in North America, 1997, also others; mem. editl. bd. Religious Book Club, 1980-93. Named one of 100 Most Influential People in Am. Religion, Christian Century mag., 1982; honored by book published in his honor: The Sunday Service of the Methodists: Studies in Honor of James F. White, 1996. Mem. N.Am. Acad. Liturgy (pres. 1979, Berakah award 1983), Am. Soc. Ch. History, Liturgical Conf., Societas Liturgica. Avocations: hiking, travel, book and antiques collecting. Office: U Notre Dame Dept Theology Notre Dame IN 46556

WHITE, JAMES LINDSAY, polymer engineering educator; b. Bklyn., Jan. 3, 1938; s. Robert Lindsay and Margaret (Young) W. BS, Poly. Inst. Bklyn., 1959; MS, U. Del., 1962, PhD, 1965. Rsch. engr. Uniroyal Inc., Wayne, N.J., 1963-66, rsch. engr., group leader, 1966-67; assoc. prof. U. Tenn., Knoxville, 1967-70, prof., 1970-76, prof. in charge Polymer Sci. and Engring. Program, 1976-83; dir. Polymer Engring. Ctr. U. Akron, Ohio, 1983-89, dir. Inst. Polymer Engring., 1989—, head/chmn. Dept. Polymer Engring, 1983-97, Harold A. Morton prof., 1997—. Author: Principles of Polymer Engineering Rheology, 1990, Twin Screw Extrusion: Technology and Principles, 1990, Rubber Processing: Technology of Materials and Principles, 1995; editor-in-chief Internat. Polymer Processing, 1990—; contbr. over 300 articles, papers. Recipient Internat. Edn. award Soc. Plastics Engrs., 1987, Internat. Rsch. award, 1992. Mem. Polymer Processing Soc. (pres. 1985-87, editor 1987-90, editor-in-chief 1990—), Soc. Rheology (editorial bd. 1967-92, Bingham medal 1981), Soc. Rheology Japan (Yuko-sho award 1984). Office: U Akron Inst Polymer Engring 260 S Forge St Akron OH 44325-0001

WHITE, JAMES PATRICK, law educator; b. Iowa City, Sept. 29, 1931; s. Raymond Patrick and Besse (Kanak) W.; m. Anna R. Seim, July 2, 1964. BA, U. Iowa, 1953, JD, 1956; LLM, George Washington U., 1959; LLD (hon.), U. Pacific, 1964, John Marshall Law Sch., 1989, Weidner U., 1989, Campbell U., 1993; Jur D (hon.), Whittier Coll., 1992; LLD (hon.), Campbell U., 1993, Southwestern U., 1995, Quinnipiac U., 1995, Calif. Western Law Sch., 1997; LLD, Roger Williams U., 1999, New England Sch. of Law, 2001, Seattle U., 2001, We. New Coll., 2002. Bar: Iowa 1956, D.C. 1959, U.S. Supreme Ct. 1959. Teaching fellow George Washington U. Law Sch., 1958-59; asst. prof. U. N.D. Law Sch., Grand Forks, 1959-62, asso. prof., acting dean, 1962-63, prof., asst. dean, 1963-67; dir. agrl. law rsch. program, prof. law Ind. U. Law Sch., Indpls., 1967—, also dir. urban legal studies program, 1971-74; dean acad. devel. and planning, spl. asst. to chancellor Ind. Univ., 1974-83. Mem. for N.D., Commn. on Uniform State Laws, 1961-66; cons. legal edn. ABA, Indpls., 1974-2001. Contbr. papers to tech. lit. 1st lt. JAGC, USAF, 1956-58. Recipient Thomas More award, St. Mary's U., 1965; fellow Carnegie postdoctoral fellow, U. Mich. Ctr. for Study Higher Edn., 1964—65. Fellow: Soc. for Advanced Legal Studies (Eng.) (chair Fulbright com. awards in law 1989—92), Indpls. Bar Found., Am. Bar Found. (life); mem.: ABA (cons. legal edn. 1974—2001, cons. emeritus 2001—, Kutak award medal 2001), Indpls. Bar Assn., Am. Law Inst. (life), Iowa Bar Assn., Ind. Bar Assn., Woodstock Club (Indpls.), Order of Coif (life). Roman Catholic. Home: 7707 N Meridian St Indianapolis IN 46260-3651 Office: Ind U 550 W North St Indianapolis IN 46202-3162 E-mail: jwhite@uipui.edu.

WHITE, JESSE, state official; b. Alton, Ill., 1934; BS, Ala. State U., 1957. With Chgo. Cubs; tchr., adminstr. Chgo. Pub. Sch. Sys.; mem. Ill. Gen. Assembly, Springfield, chmn. com. on human svcs., mem. edn. com., mem. select com. on children and aging; recorder of deeds State of Ill., Springfield, 1992-98, sec. of state, 1999—. Founder Jesse White Tumbling Team, 1959; Dem. committeeman 27th Ward, Chgo., 1996—; libr. State of Ill. State Libr.; archivist State of Ill.; mem. Ill. N.G. With USAF. Recipient Archbishop Richard Chenevix Trench award, 1999; Inductee Southwestern Athletic Conf. Hall of Fam, 1995, Chgo. Pub. League Basketball Coaches Assn. Hall of Fame, 1995. Office: 213 State Capitol Springfield IL 62706*

WHITE, JOE LLOYD, soil scientist, educator; b. Pierce, Okla., Nov. 8, 1921; s. Claud Amos and Alta Maurice (Denney) W.; m. Wanita Irene Robertson, May 29, 1945; children— Lerrill, Darla, Ronna, Bren, Janeil Student, Connors State Agrl. Coll., 1940-42; B.S., Okla. State U., 1944, M.S., 1945; Ph.D., U. Wis., 1947. Asst. prof. agronomy Purdue U., West Lafayette, Ind., 1947-51, assoc. prof., 1951-57, prof., 1957-88. Cons. Bancroft Co., William H. Rorer Co., Chattem Chem. Co., Merck Sharp & Dohme Rsch. Lab. Patentee in field Fellow NSF, 1965-66, Guggenheim Found., 1972-73; Fulbright scholar, 1973; recipient Sr. U.S. Scientist award Alexander von Humboldt Found., 1980-81 Fellow AAAS, Am. Soc. Agronomy, Am. Inst. Chemists, Soil Sci. Soc. Am., Mineral Soc. Am., Royal Soc. Chemistry; mem. Am. Chem. Soc., Clay Minerals Soc. (disting.), Am. Pharm. Assn., Coblentz Soc., Geochem. Soc., Internat. Soil Sci. Soc., Internat. Assn. Colloid and Interface Scientists, N.Y. Acad. Sci., Royal Soc. Chemists (chartered chemist), Soc. Petroleum Engrs. of AIME, Internat. Zeolite Assn., Soc. Applied Spectroscopy, Sigma Xi, Phi Kappa Phi, Phi Lambda Upsilon Mem. Ch. of Christ Achievements include patents for use of zeolites in ruminant nutrition, for stable dried aluminum hydroxide gel, for method and composition for treatment of hyperphosphatemia; establishment of the role of carbonate in inhibiting crystallization of aluminum hydroxide; definitive characterization of aluminum-containing adjuvants used in vaccines. Home: 2505 Roselawn Ave Lafayette IN 47904-2319 Office: Purdue U Dept Agronomy West Lafayette IN 47907

WHITE, JOHN GRAHAM, science educator, research director; b. Prestatyn, Wales, Aug. 9, 1943; came to U.S., 1993; s. Bernard and Norah (Bannister) W.; m. Donna Albertson, July 26, 1980 (div. Apr. 1994); children: Phoebe, Ben, Amelia, Ruth; m. Claudia Cummins, Nov. 8, 1994. BTech, Brunel U., London, 1969; PhD, Cambridge (Eng.) U., 1974. Technician Med. Rsch. Coun., London, 1964-69, scientist, 1969-93; prof., dir. integrated microscopy resource U. Wis., Madison, 1993—. Cons. Bio-Rad, Herculese, Calif., 1988—. Recipient Queen's award for Tech., 1991, Mullard award Royal Soc., 1994. Achievements include two patents for confocal microscopy. Office: U Wis Lab Molecular Biology 1525 Linden Dr Madison WI 53706-1534

WHITE, JOHN HENRY, photojournalist, educator; b. Lexington, N.C., Mar. 18, 1945; s. Reid R. and Ruby M. (Leverette) W.; m. Emily L. Miller, May 29, 1966 (div.); children: Deborah, Angela, Ruby, John Henry. A.A.S., Central Piedmont Community Coll. Photographer U.S. Marine Corps., Quantico, Va., 1966-68, Tom Walters Photograpahy, Charlotte, N.C., 1968-69; photojournalist Chgo. Daily News, 1969-78, Chgo. Sun-Times, 1978—; instr. photojournalism Columbia Coll., Chgo., 1978—. Lectr. in field Mem. Blackwell Meml. A.M.E. Zion Ch., Chgo., 1972— , steward, 1979— , supt. Sunday Sch. Recipient over 200 photography in journalism awards; recipient Pulitzer prize, 1982 Mem. Nat. Press Photograhers Assn., Ill. Press Photographers Assn. (photographer of yr. award 1971, 79, 82), Chgo. Press Photographers Assn. (pres. 1977-78 photographer of yr. award), Chgo. Assn. Black Journalists Office: Chicago Sun Times 401 N Wabash Ave Rm 451 Chicago IL 60611-5642

WHITE, JOSEPH B. reporter; b. N.Y.C., July 7, 1958; Attended, Harvard U. Reporter The Wall Street Journal, to 1998, bur. chief, 1998—. Author: (with Paul Ingrassia) Comeback: The Fall and Rise of the American Automobile Industry, 1994. Recipient Pulitzer Prize for beat reporting, 1993. Office: The Wall Street Journal Detroit Bureau 500 Woodward Ave Ste 1950 Detroit MI 48226-5497

WHITE, KATHERINE E. law educator; BSEE and Computer Sci, Princeton U., 1988; JD, U. Wash., 1991; LLM in Intellectual Property, George Washington U., 1996. Bar: Mich., U.S. Supreme Ct, U.S. Ct. Appeals (fed. cir.), U.S. Ct. Appeals Armed Forces, U.S. Army Ct. Mil. Rev., U.S. Patent and Trademark Office, Wash. Intellectual property counsel U.S. Army Corps Engrs., Washington, 1992—95; jud. law clk. for Hon. Randall Rader U.S. Ct. Appeals (fed. cir.), 1995—96; asst. prof. Wayne State U. Law Sch., Detroit, 1996—. Adj. prof. George Washington U. Law Ctr., Washington, 1994—96; mem. patent pub. adv. com. U.S. Patent and Trademark Office, 2000—; regent U. Mich., Ann Arbor, 1999—; spkr. in field. Actor: Intellectual Perperty Litigation, Pretrial Practice Guide, 1999; co-author (with Eric Dobrusin): Intellectual Property Litigation, Pretrial Practice Guide, 1999; contbr. articles to profl. publs. Capt. JAG U.S. Army, 1992—95, maj. JAG USAR, 1995—. Recipient Fulbright Sr. Scholar award, Max-Planck Inst. for Fgn. Internat. Patent, Copyright and Competition Law, 1999—2000; fellow Shaw fellow, 1994—96; grantee, Max-Planck-Inst. for Fgn. Internat. Patent, Copyright and Competition Law, 2000; scholar, ROTC, Washington Law Found., 1988—91. Mem.: AAUP, ABA, Wolverine Bar Assn., Wash. State Bar Assn., Nat. Bar Assn., Mich. Patent Lawyer's Assn., Am. Intellectual Property Law Assn., Am. Assn. Law Schs., State Bar Mich. (mem. coun. intellectual property law sec., co-chmn. student liaison com., co-chmn. com. pattent issues in legislation), Princeton Club Mich. Democrat. Avocations: flute, volleyball, in-line skating. Office: Wayne U Law Sch 471 W Palmer Detroit MI 48202

WHITE, KATHY BRITTAIN, medical association executive; BS, MS, Ark. State U.; PhD in Mgmt., U. Memphis. Various sr. positions with AlliedSignal Corp., Guilford Mills, Inc.; chief info. officer Baxter Internat., 1995-96; chief info. officer, sr. v.p. Allegian Corp. (now merged with Cardinal Health), 1996-99; exec. v.p., chief info. officer Cardinal Health, Dublin, 1999—. Bd. dirs. MECON, Inc., San Ramon, Calif., Children's Meml. Med. Ctr./Children's Meml. Hosp., Children's Meml. Found., Chgo.; former assoc. prof. info. technology U. N.C., Greensboro. Bd. dirs. Lake Forest Grad. Sch., Ill. Mem. ACHE. Office: Cardinal Health 7000 Cardinal Pl Dublin OH 43017-1091

WHITE, KEVIN M. athletic director; b. Amityville, N.Y., Sept. 25, 1950; m. Jane Gartland; children: Maureen, Michael, Daniel, Brian, Mariah. BBA, St. Joseph's Coll., 1972; B in Bus. Athletic Adminstrn., Ctrl. Mich. U.; PhD, So. Ill. U.; postdoctoral, Harvard U., 1985. Coach Gulf H.S., New Port Richey, Fla., Southeast Mo. State U., Ctrl. Mich. U.; athletic dir., v.p. devel. Loras Coll., Dubuque, Iowa, 1982-87; athletic dir. U. Maine, Orono, 1987-91, Tulane U., New Orleans, 1991-96, Ariz. State U., Tempe, 1996-2000, Notre Dame (Ind.) U., 2000—. Office: Notre Dame Univ Dept Athletics Notre Dame IN 46556

WHITE, LINDA DIANE, lawyer; b. N.Y.C., Apr. 1, 1952; d. Bernard and Elaine (Simons) Schwartz; m. Thomas M. White, Aug. 16, 1975; 1 child, Alexandra Nicole. AB, U. Pa., 1973; JD, Northwestern U., 1976. Bar: Ill. 1976. Assoc. Walsh, Case, Coale & Brown, Chgo., 1976-77, Greenberger & Kaufmann (merged into Katten, Muchin), Chgo., 1977-82, ptnr., 1982-85, Sonnenschein Nath & Rosenthal, Chgo., 1985—. Mem. ABA (real property fin. com., comml. leasing com., real property, probate and trust law sect. 1987—), Ill. Bar Assn., Chgo. Bar Assn., Practicing Law Inst. (chmn. program on negotiating comml. leases 1995-99, real estate law adv. com.). Office: Sonnenschein Nath & Rosenthal 8000 Sears Tower 233 S Wacker Dr Ste 8000 Chicago IL 60606-6491 E-mail: lwhite@sonnenschein.com.

WHITE, MICHAEL REED, mayor; b. Cleve., Aug. 13, 1951; s. Robert and Audrey (Silver) W. BA, Ohio State U., 1973, MPA, 1974. Spl. asst. Columbus (Ohio) Mayor's Office, 1974-76; adminstrv. asst. Cleve. City Coun., 1976-77; sales mgr. Burks Electric Co., Cleve., 1978-84; state senator Ohio Senate, Columbus, 1984-89; mayor Cleve., 1990—. Minority whip Ohio Senate Dems., 1987-89. City councilman City of Cleve., 1978-84; bd. dirs. Glenville Devel. Corp., Cleve., 1978—, Glenville Festival Found., Cleve., 1978—, United Black Fund, Cleve., 1986, Greater Cleve. Dome Corp., 1986; trustee U.S. Conf. Democratic Mayors. Named one of Outstanding Young Men Am., 1985, Outstanding Svc. award Cleve. chpt. Nat. Assn. Black Vets., 1985, Cmty. Svcs. award East Side Jaycees, Pres.'s award, 1993, named Black Profl. of Yr., 1993, Humanitarian award, 1994, Pub Svc. award Am. Pub. Power Assn., 1995. Mem. Nat. Conference Dem. Mayors. Democrat. Home: 1057 East Blvd Cleveland OH 44108-2972 Office: Office of Mayor City Hall 601 Lakeside Ave Cleveland OH 44114-1015

WHITE, MICHELLE JO, economics educator; b. Washington, Dec. 3, 1945; d. Harry L. and Irene (Silverman) Rich; m. Roger Hall Gordon, July 25, 1982. AB, Harvard U., 1967; MSc in Econs., London Sch. Econs., 1968; PhD, Princeton U., 1973. Asst. prof. U. Pa., Phila., 1973-78; from assoc. prof. to prof. NYU, N.Y.C., 1978-83; prof. econs. U. Mich., Ann Arbor, 1984—, dir. PhD program in econs., 1992-94, 98—. Vis. asst. prof. Yale U., New Haven, 1978; vis. prof. People's U., Beijing, 1986, U. Warsaw, 1990, U. Wis., Madison, 1991, U. Munich, Germany, 1992, Tilburg U., The Netherlands, 1993, 95, U. Chgo., 1993, Copenhagen Bus. Sch., 1995, Uppsala U., Sweden, 1997, Hebrew U., Israel, 1997, U. Calif. Law Sch. Berkeley, 1999; cons. Pension Benefit Guaranty Corp., Washington, 1987, World Bank, 1999; chmn. adv. com. dept. econs. Princeton U., 1988-90. Editor: The Non-profit Sector in a Three Sector Economy, 1981, Financial Distress and Bankruptcy: Economic Issues, 1997; contbr. numerous articles to profl. jours. Bd. dirs. Com. on Status of Women in Econs. Profession, 1984-86. Resources for Future fellow, 1972-73; grantee NSF, 1979, 82, 88, 91, 93, 96, Sloan Found., 1984, Fund for Rsch. in Dispute Resolution, 1989; Fulbright scholar, Poland, 1990. Mem. Am. Econ. Assn., Am. Law and Econ. Assn. (bd. dirs. 1991-92), Am. Real Estate and Urban Econs. Assn. (bd. dirs. 1992-95), Social Scis. Rsch. Coun. (bd. dirs. 1994—, treas. 1996—), Midwest Econs. Assn. (1st v.p. 1996-97). Office: U California-San Diego Dept Economics 9500 Gilman Dr La Jolla CA 92093-0508

WHITE, MILES D. pharmaceutical company executive; B in Mech. Engring., MBA, Stanford U. With Abbott Labs., 1984—, v.p. diagnostic sys. and ops., 1993-94, sr. v.p. diagnostic ops., 1994-98, exec. v.p., dir., 1998-99, CEO, dir. and chmn., 1999—. Office: Abbott Labs 100 Abbott Park Rd Abbott Park IL 60064-6400

WHITE, ROBERT JAMES, newspaper columnist; b. Mpls., Nov. 6, 1927; s. Robert Howard and Claire Lillian (Horner) W.; m. Adrienne Hoffman, Sept. 24, 1955; children: Claire, Pamela, Sarah. BS, U.S. Naval Acad., 1950. V.p. White Investment Co., Mpls., 1957-67; editl. writer Mpls. Tribune, 1967-73, assoc. editor, 1973-82; editor editl. pages Mpls. Star Tribune, 1982-93, columnist, 1993-95, contbg. columnist, 1996—. Recipient cert. of excellence Overseas Press Club, 1981. Mem. Coun. Fgn. Rels., Mpls. Club. Congregationalist. Home: Summit House 400 Groveland Ave #2212 Minneapolis MN 55403 E-mail: rjw823@aol.com.

WHITE, RONNIE L. state supreme court justice; AA, St. Louis C.C., 1977; BA, St. Louis U., 1979; JD, U. Mo., Kansas City, 1983. Bar: Mo. Law intern Jackson County Prosecutors Office; legal asst. U.S. Def. Mapping Agy.; trial atty. Office of Pub. Defender; mem. Mo. Ho. of Reps., 1989-93; judge Mo. Ct. Appeals, 1994; spl. judge Mo. Supreme Ct., 1994-95, justice, 1994-95, assoc. justice, 1995—. Adj. faculty Washington U. Sch. Law, 1997—. Office: PO Box 150 Jefferson City MO 65102-0150*

WHITE, TOMMI A. human resources firm executive; Grad., Oakland U. Dir. sys. Ryder; asst. v.p., project dir. br. automotion Nat. Bank Detroit; divsn. v.p. Automated Data Processing, N.J.; exec. v.p., chief adminstrn. & technology officer Kelly Svcs., Inc., Troy, Mich., 1998—. Office: Kelly Svcs 999 W Big Beaver Rd Troy MI 48084-4716

WHITE, WILLIAM FREDRICK, lawyer; b. Elmhurst, Ill., Sept. 30, 1948; s. William Daniel and Carol Ruth (Laier) W.; m. Kathie Jean Nichols, May 27, 1979; children: Nicholas Roland, Andrew William. BA, U. Ill., 1970; JD, Antioch Sch. of Law, 1976. Bar: U.S. Ct. Appeals (D.C. cir.) 1976, Wis. 1982, U.S. Dist. Ct. (we. dist.) Wis. 1982, U.S. Dist. Ct. D.C. 1976, U.S. Ct. Claims 1978, U.S. Ct. Appeals (7th and 10th cirs.) 1982. With U.S. Dept. Labor, Washington, 1976; interim exec. dir. Common Cause, 1977; asst. counsel Nat. Treasury Employees Union, 1977-79, assoc. gen. counsel, 1979-81, dir. litigation, 1981-82; assoc. Michael, Best & Friedrich LLP, Madison, Wis., 1982-88, ptnr., chmn. assoc. devel. com., 1988-96, ptnr., 1988—, chair land and resources legal practice area. Bd. dirs. Med. Physics Publ. Co.; dir. Med. Physics Found., 1988—, sec., 1994—. Chmn. Pub. Health Commn., Madison, 1983-89; bd. dirs. exec. com. Dane County Mediation Program, Madison, 1983-90, Perinatal Found., Madison, 1984-96, Arthritis Found., Madison, 1984-92, Arthritis Found., Madison, 1986-92, chmn., 1991-92; bd. dirs. Dane County Natural Heritage Found., 1988-91; mem. Dane County Regional Airport Commn., 1991—, chmn. 1994—; chancellor Wis. Ann. Conf. United Meth. Ch., 1992—, gen. coun. Fin. and Adminstrn., 1991-2000, chmn. Legal Svcs. Com., 1992-96; bd. dirs. Downtown Madison Inc., sec. 1995-2001, chair transp. com.; mem. Dane County Transferrable Devel. Rights Task Force, Team Terrace Transp. Com., 1996-97, chair; bd. trustees Madison Art Ctr., 1998—, dir., 2000—; co-chair Friends of Hudson Park, 1999—; Madison program chair Dane County Pub. Affairs Coun., 2000—. Mem. ABA, D.C. Bar Assn., Med. Physics Found. (bd. dirs. 1987—), Dane County Bar Assn., State Bar Assn. (sec. Health Law sect.), Transp. Devel. Assn. (dir. 1999—, exec. com. 1999—). Democrat. United Methodist. Avocations: cycling, skiing. Office: Michael Best & Friedrich LLP Ste 700 1 S Pinckney St Madison WI 53703-2892

WHITE, WILLIAM SAMUEL, foundation executive; b. Cin., May 8, 1937; s. Nathaniel Ridgway and Mary (Lowndes) W.; m. Claire Mott, July 1, 1961; children: Tiffany Lowndes, Ridgway Harding. BA, Dartmouth Coll., 1959, MBA, 1960; LL.D. (hon.), Eastern Mich. U., 1975; hon. degree, GMI Engring. & Mgmt. Inst., 1996. With Barrett & Williams, N.Y.C., 1961-62; sr. assoc. Bruce Payne & Assos., 1962-71; v.p. C. S. Mott Found., Flint, Mich., 1971-75, pres., 1976—, trustee, 1971—, also chmn. bd. dirs. Bd. dirs. Am. Water Works; chmn. bd. dirs. U.S. Sugar Corp. Mem. exec. com. Daycroft Sch., Greenwich, Conn., 1966-70; bd. dirs. Flint Area Conf., 1971-84, Coun. on Founds., 1985-90, Independent Sector, 1994-99, European Found. Centre, 1994—, Civicus, 1995-2001; mem. citizens adv. task force U. Mich., Flint, 1974-79; chmn. Coun. of Mich. Founds., 1979-81, Flint Area Focus Coun., 1988—; mem. Pres.'s Task Force on Pvt. Sector Initiatives, 1982; trustee GMI Engring. and Mgmt. Inst., 1982-86. Served with U.S. Army, 1960-62. Office: C S Mott Foundation 1200 Mott Foundation Bldg Flint MI 48502-1807

WHITE, WILLIS SHERIDAN, JR. retired utilities company executive; b. nr. Portsmouth, Va., Dec. 17, 1926; s. Willis Sheridan and Carrie (Culpepper) W.; m. LaVerne Behrends, Oct. 8, 1949; children: Willis Sheridan III, Marguerite Spangler, Cynthia D.W. Haight. B.S., Va. Poly. Inst., 1948; M.S., Mass. Inst. Tech., 1958. With Am. Electric Power Co. Inc., 1948-91; chmn., chief exec. officer Am. Electric Power Co., Inc. and its subs., N.Y.C., 1976-90, chmn., 1991, mem. bd. dirs., 1972-92. Pres., bd. dirs. Ohio Valley Electric Corp., Ind.-KTV Electric Corp., 1977-91. Trustee Battellle Meml. Inst., Grant/Riverside Meth. Hosp., Columbus. With USNR, 1945-46. Sloan fellow, 1957-58 Mem. IEEE, NAE, Eta Kappa Nu, Omicron Delta Kappa. Methodist.

WHITE, WILLMON LEE, magazine editor; b. Lamesa, Tex., Mar. 10, 1932; s. Aubrey F. and Jewel (Henderson) W.; m. Carol A. Nelson, Nov. 2, 1957 (div.); children: Tracy, Wrenn, Gehrig, Bob; m. Barbara K. Kelly, Sept. 16, 1977; 1 child, Theresa. BA, McMurry Coll., Abilene, Tex., 1953; MA, U. Tex., 1956. Reporter Abilene Reporter-News, 1953-54; pub. rels. writer Tex. Ins. Adv. Assn., Austin, 1955-56; asst. editor Humble Way mag. Humble Oil & Refining Co. (Exxon), Houston, 1956-65; assoc. editor, news editor Together mag. Methodist Ch., Park Ridge, Ill., 1965-69; sr. editor World Book Ency., Chgo., 1969-70; asst. editor, then asso. editor Rotarian mag. (publ. Rotary Internat.), Evanston, Ill., 1970-74, editor, 1974-95, mgr. communications and pub. rels. div., 1979-95, asst. gen. sec., editor, 1995-96; gen mgr. Rotary Found. Svcs., 1996-97, mgr. Rotary mags. and history, 1997-2000; editor-in-chief Rotarian Mag., 1996-2000; editor Rotary Centennial History, 2000—. Intern Newsweek mag., 1954 Mem. Am. Soc. Mag. Editors, Am. Soc. Assn. Execs., Soc. of Am. Archivists, Rotary, Sigma Delta Chi. Office: Rotary Internat 1560 Sherman Ave Ste 1350 Evanston IL 60201-4818 E-mail: leejeans4@yahoo.com.

WHITEHOUSE, FRED WAITE, endocrinologist, researcher; b. Chgo., May 6, 1926; s. Fred Trafton Waite and Grace Caroline (Peters) W.; m. Iris Jean Dawson, June 6, 1953; children: Martha, Amy, Sarah. Student, Northwestern U., 1943-45; BS, U. Ill., Chgo., 1947, MD, 1949. Diplomate Am. Bd. Internal Medicine; cert. endocrinology and metabolism. Intern, then resident Henry Ford Hosp., Detroit, 1949-53, staff physician, 1955—, chief divsn. metabolism, 1962-88, chief divsn. endocrinology and metabolism, 1988-95; divsn. head emeritus, 1995—; fellow Joslin Clinic, Boston, 1954-55. Cons. FDA, Washington, 1980—; mem. Coalition on Diabetes Edn. and Minority Health, 1989-91. Contbr. articles to profl. jours. Bd. dirs. Wheat Ridge Found., 1984-93. Lt. USNR, 1951-53. Master ACP; mem. NIH (nat. diabetes adv. bd. 1984-88), Am. Diabetes Assn. (pres. 1978-79, Banting medal 1979, Outstanding Clinician award 1989, Outstanding Physician Educators award 1994), Detroit Med. Club (pres. 1976), Detroit Acad. Medicine (pres. 1991-92). Lutheran. Avocations: bicycling, gardening. Home: 1265 Blairmoor Ct Grosse Pointe Woods MI 48236-1230 Office: Henry Ford Hosp 2799 W Grand Blvd Detroit MI 48202-2689 Fax: (313) 916-8343. E-mail: fwhitehouse@msms.org.

WHITEMAN, JOSEPH DAVID, retired lawyer, manufacturing company executive; b. Sioux Falls, S.D., Sept. 12, 1933; s. Samuel D. and Margaret (Wallace) W.; m. Mary Kelly, Dec. 29, 1962; children: Anne Margaret, Mary Ellen, Joseph David, Sarah Kelly, Jane. B.A., U. Mich., 1955, J.D., 1960. Bar: D.C. 1960, Ohio 1976. Assoc. Cox, Langford, Stoddard & Cutler, Washington, 1959-64; sec., gen. counsel Studebaker group Studebaker Worthington, Inc., N.Y.C., 1964-71; asst. gen. counsel. United Telecommunications, Inc., Kansas City, Mo., 1971-74; v.p., gen. counsel, sec. Weatherhead Co., Cleve., 1974-77, Parker Hannifin Corp., Cleve., 1977-98; ret., 1998. Immediate past chmn. bd. dirs. St. Lukes Med. Ctr. Served as lt. USNR, 1955-57. Mem. ABA, Beta Theta Pi, Phi Delta Phi. Republican. Roman Catholic. Home and Office: 2508 Robinson Springs Rd Stowe VT 05672

WHITEMAN, RICHARD FRANK, architect; b. Mankato, Minn., Mar. 24, 1925; s. Lester Raymond and Mary Grace (Dawald) W.; m. Jean Frances Waite, June 20, 1948 (dec. May 1980); children: David, Sarah, Lynn, Ann, Carol, Frank, Marie, Steven; m. Mavis Patricia Knutsen, May 30, 1982. BArch, U. Minn., 1945; MArch, Harvard U., 1948. Registered architect, Minn. Designer Ellerbe Co., St. Paul, 1946; architect Thorshov and Cerny, Mpls., 1948-53; ptnr. Jyring and Whiteman, Hibbing, Minn., 1953-62; pres. AJWM Inc., Hibbing and Duluth, 1963-72, Architects Four, Duluth, 1972-83; owner Richard Whiteman, 1983-95; sr. architect U. Minn. Chmn. Architect Sect. Registration Bd., Minn., 1972-80. Prin. works include Washington Sch., Hibbing, 1957 (Minn. Soc. Architects Design award 1957), Whiteman Summer Home, Pengilly, Minn. (Minn. Soc. Architects Design award 1959), Bemidji State Coll. Phys. Edn. Bldg. (Minn. Soc. Architects Design award 1960), Whiteman Residence, Griggs Hall UMD, 1990. Pres. U. for Srs., 1993-94; mem. adv. com. Glensheen, U. Minn. Duluth; active Duluth Housing Authority, 2001—. Mem. Minn. Soc. Architects (pres. 1972), Northeast Minn. Architects (pres. 1962), Service Corps Retired Execs. (chmn. Northeast Minn. chpt. 1986), Minn. Designer Selection Bd. (chmn. 1990). Democrat. Roman Catholic. Club: Kitchi Gammi (Duluth). Lodge: Kiwanis. Avocations: photography, fishing, cross-country skiing, travel. Home: 3500 E 3rd St Duluth MN 55804-1812

WHITENER, WILLIAM GARNETT, dancer, choreographer; b. Seattle, Aug. 17, 1951; s. Warren G. and Virginia Louise (Garnett) W. Student, Cornish Sch. Allied Arts, Seattle, 1958-69. Dancer N.Y.C. Opera, 1969, Joffrey Ballet, N.Y.C., 1969-77, Twyla Tharp Dance, N.Y.C., 1978-87; asst. to choreographer Jerome Robbins for Robbins' Broadway, 1988; artistic dir. Les Ballets Jazz de Montréal, 1991-93, Royal Winnipeg Ballet, 1993-95, Kansas City Ballet, 1996—. Coord. dance dept. Concord Acad., Mass., 1988; vis. artist U. Wash., 1989-91; tchr. Harvard U. Summer Dance, 1989-90, NYU, 1985. Appeared in original Broadway cast Dancin', 1978; choreographer for Princeton Ballet, Joffrey II, John Curry Ice Theatre, Ballet Hispanico of N.Y., Boston Ballet Internat. Choreography Competition, Tommy Tune, Martine Van Hamel/Kevin McKenzie, Ann Reinking, Seattle Repertory Theatre, Am. Ballroom Theater, N.Y.C., Hartford (Conn.) Ballet, On the Boards, (with Bill Irwin) Alive From Off Center (PBS-TV), (opera ensemble of N.Y.) A Little Night Music, Pacific Northwest Ballet, (Seattle Opera) Rusalka, Aida; dancer (films) Amadeus, Zelig, (TV shows) The Catherine Wheel, Dance in America; performer Garden of Earthly Delights, 1988. Bd. trustees DanceUSA, 2000—. Ford

Found. scholar, 1963-64. Mem. Actor's Equity, Am. Guild Mus. Artists. Office: Kansas City Ballet 1601 Broadway St Kansas City MO 64108-1207

WHITING, FRED C. state legislator; Mem. S.D. Ho. of Reps., Pierre, 1993-94, S.D. Senate from 32nd dist, Pierre, 1995—. Mem. judiciary state affairs and transp. coms. Republican. Home: PO Box 8187 Rapid City SD 57709-8187

WHITINGTON, PETER FRANK, pediatrics educator, pediatric hepatologist; b. Memphis, May 8, 1947; s. Frank Everett and Mary Lena (Hollingsworth) Whitington; m. Susan Mauraine Hoagland, June 6, 1967; children: Helen Frances Josephic, Mary Louise, Katherine Daphne, Patrick M. BA in Econs., Tulane U., 1968; MD, U. Tenn., Memphis, 1971. Diplomate Am. Bd. Pediat., Am. Bd. Pediatric Gastroenterology. Resident in pediat., then chief resident U. Tenn. Ctr. for Health Scis., 1972—74, instr., 1975, asst. prof., 1978—81, assoc. prof., 1981—84, chief divsn. pediatric gastroenterology, 1978—84; rsch. fellow in gastroenterology Johns Hopkins Hosp., Balt., 1975—77; rsch. fellow in gastroenterology dept. pediatrics U. Wis., Madison, 1977—78; assoc. prof. dept. pediat. U. Chgo. Pritzker Sch. Medicine, 1984—87, assoc. prof. depts. pediat. and medicine, 1987—92, prof., 1992—97; prof. pediat. Northwestern U. Med. Sch., 1997—, Sally Burnett Searle prof. pediat. and transplantation; dir. divsn. gastroenterology, hepatology & nutrition Children's Meml. Hosp., Chgo., 1997—, dir. organ transplantation, Siragusa Transplantation Ctr., 1997—; co-dir. Northwestern U. Affiliated Transplant Ctrs., 1997—. Chief gastroenterology LeBonheur Children's Med. Ctr., Memphis, 1978—84; numerous invited lectures and guest spkr. at profl. meetings, workshops, symposia, hosps., confs.; mem. pediatric transplantation com. United Network for Organ Sharing, Nat. Organ Procurement and Transplantation Network, 1992—94; reviewer numerous med. jours. including New Eng. Jour. Medicine, Gastroenterology, Hepatology, Jour. Pediat., Digestive Diseases and Scis., Pediat., Transplant. Editl. bd. Jour. Pediatric Gastroenterology and Nutrition, 1991—96, Liver Transplantation, 1994—, Pediatric Transplantation, 1997—, sect. editor Birth Defects Compendium, 1987—90, contbr. numerous articles and abstracts to med. jours. Mem. sci. adv. bd. Mid-South chpt. Nat. Found. for Ileitis and Colitis, Memphis, 1983—84; chmn. med. adv. com. Ill. chpt. Am. Liver Found., 1996—, mem., med. adv. on bd. dirs., 1993—; med. dir. The Johnny Genna Found., Chgo., 1987—; bd. dirs. Parents for Ctrl. H.S. , Memphis, 1983—84, Liver/Organ Transplant Fund, Memphis, 1983—84. Recipient Cmty. Svc. award, NCCJ, Memphis, 1983; fellow postdoctoral rsch. NIH, 1977. Mem.: Am. Assn. Transplantation, N.A.m Soc. for Pediatric Gastroenterology and Nutrition, Soc. for Pediatric Rsch., Am. Gastroenterol. Assn., Gastroenterology Rsch. Group, Am. Assn. for Study of Liver Diseases. Avocations: making fine furniture, fly fishing. Home: 5490 S South Shore Dr Apt 8 Chicago IL 60615-5984 Office: Childrens Meml Hosp Box 57 2300 Childrens Plaza Chicago IL 60614-3394 E-mail: p-whitington@northwestern.edu.

WHITLOCK, JOHN JOSEPH, museum director; b. South Bend, Ind., Jan. 7, 1935; s. Joseph Mark and Helen Marcella (Cramer) W.; m. Sue Ann Kirkman, June 10, 1956; children— Kelly Ann, Michele Lynn, Mark. BS in Art, Ball State U., 1957, MA in Art, 1963; EdD, Ind. U., 1971. Tchr. art Union City (Ind.) Pub. Schs., 1957-59; tchr. art, art dir. Madison (Ind.) City Schs., 1959-64; prof. art, dir. gallery Hanover (Ind.) Coll., 1964-69; dir. Burpee Art Mus., Rockford, Ill., 1970-72; prof. arts and humanities Elgin (Ill.) Community Coll., 1970-72; dir. Brooks Meml. Art Gallery, Memphis, 1972-78; prof. mus. studies Southwestern Coll., 1973-78; adj. asst. prof. art and museology Memphis State U., 1976-78; dir. Univ. Mus., mem. grad. faculty So. Ill. U., Carbondale, 1978-2000, emeritus dir., 2000—, also dir. mus. studies, 1978-2000, adj. assoc. prof. anthropology, 1978-2000, adj. assoc. prof. polit. sci., 1988—, adj. assoc. prof. history, 1994—, dir. mus. studies, 1989—, mem. ROTC acad. avc. coun., 1988—, mem. president's coun., 1988-93, adj. assoc. prof. art Univ. Mus., 1978-99, vis. emeritus prof., 2000—. Chmn. bd. Nat. Coal Mus., 1983-85; mem. Newsfront adv. bd. NC Broadcast News, Washington, 1982-85; sr. cons. Marine Mil. Acad. Mus., 1988—, mem. bd. advisors, 1991-97. Mem. Rockford Human Rels. Commn., 1971-72; mem. pres.'s coun. Southwestern Coll., 1973-78; vol. Carbondale Police Dept., 2000—, com. resources, forensics records and acad.; bd. dirs. Carbondale Crime Stoppers, 2000—, DARE, 2000—; univ. club bd. So. Ill. U., 2000—, univ. mus. amb., 2000—. Mem. Am. Assn. Mus., Internat. Coun. Mus., Midwest Assn. Mus., Assn. Art Mus. Dirs., Marine Corps League (commandant Shawnee detachment 1994-96, 99-2001, comdr. USCG Aux. 1994-95), Dept. Ill. Marine Corps League (trustee rank and file 1994-99, judge advocate 1999—), Semper Fi Soc. (faculty adviser So. Ill. U. 1995—). Office: So Ill U 605 W Walnut St Carbondale IL 62901-2615

WHITMAN, DALE ALAN, lawyer, law educator; b. Charleston, W. Va., Feb. 18, 1939; m. Marjorie Miller: 8 children. Student, Ohio State U., 1956-59; BES, Brigham Young U., 1963; LLB, Duke U., 1966. Bar: Calif. 1967, Utah 1971. Assoc. O'Melveny & Myers, Los Angeles, 1966-67; asst prof., then assoc prof. sch. law U. N.C., Chapel Hill, 1967-70; prof. law UCLA, 1970-71; dep. dir. Office Housing and Urban Affairs Fed. Home Loan Bank Bd., Washington, 1971-72; sr. program analyst FHA, HUD, 1972-73; prof. law Brigham Young U., 1973-78, 92-99; vis. prof. law U. Wash., 1978—82, U. Mo., Columbia, 1976; prof. law, assoc. dean U. Mo. Sch. Law, 1982-88, prof., 1988—91, 1998—. Cons., lectr. in field; reporter Am. law Inst. Co-author: Cases and Materials on Real Estate Finance and Development, 1976, Real Estate Finance Law, 1979, 4th edit., 2001, Cases and Materials on Real Estate Transfer, Finance and Development. 1981, 5th edit., 1998, Land Transactions and Finance, 1983, 3d edit., 1997, The Law of Property, 1984, 3d edit., 2000, Contemporary Property, 1996, 2d edit., 2002, Restatement of Property (Mortgages), 1997; contbr. articles to profl. jours. Fellow Am. Bar Found.; mem. Am. Law Inst., Am. Coll. Real Estate Lawyers, Assn. Am. Law Schs. (pres. 2002). Home and Office: 2505 Black Cherry Ct Columbia MO 65201-3539 E-mail: whitmand@missouri.edu.

WHITMAN, MARINA VON NEUMANN, economist, educator; b. N.Y.C., Mar. 6, 1935; d. John and Mariette (Kovesi) von Neumann; m. Robert Freeman Whitman, June 23, 1956; children: Malcolm Russell, Laura Mariette. BA summa cum laude, Radcliffe Coll., 1956; MA, Columbia U., 1959, PhD, 1962; LHD (hon.), Russell Sage Coll., 1972; LLD (hon.), Cedar Crest Coll., 1973, Hobart and William Smith Coll., 1973; LHD (hon.), U. Mass., 1975, N.Y. Poly. Inst., 1975; LLD (hon.), Coe Coll., 1975, Marietta Coll., 1976. Mem. faculty U. Pitts., 1962-79, prof. econs., 1971-73, disting. pub. svc. prof. econs., 1973-79; v.p., chief economist Gen. Motors Corp., N.Y.C., 1979-85, group v.p. pub. affairs, 1985-92; disting. vis. prof. bus. adminstrn., pub. policy U. Mich., Ann Arbor, 1992-94, prof. bus. adminstrn., pub. policy, 1994—. Bd. dirs. JP Morgan Chase Corp., Alcoa, Procter & Gamble Co., Unocal; mem. Trilateral Commn., 1973-84, 88-95; mem. Pres. Adv. Com. on Trade Policy and Negotiations, 1987-93; mem. tech. assessment adv. coun. U.S. Congress Office of Tech. Assessment, 1990-95; mem. Consultative Group on Internat. Econs. and Monetary Affairs, 1979—; mem. U.S. Price Commn., 1971-72, Coun. Econ. Advisers, Exec. Office of Pres., 1972-73. Author: Government Risk-Sharing in Foreign Investment, 1965, International and Interregional Payments Adjustment, 1967, Economic Goals and Policy Instruments, 1970, Reflections of Interdependence: Issues for Economic Theory and U.S. Policy, 1979, New World, New Rules: The Changing Role of the American Corporation, 1999; bd. editors: Am. Econ. Rev., 1974-77; mem. editl. bd. Fgn. Policy; contbr. articles to profl. jours. Trustee Nat. Bur. Econ. Rsch., 1993—, Princeton U., 1980-90, Inst. Advanced Study, 1999—; bd. dirs. Inst. for Internat. Econs., 1986—, Salzburg Seminar, 1994—, Eurasia Found., 1992-95; bd. overseers Harvard U., 1972-78, mem. vis. com. Kennedy Sch., 1992-98. Fellow Earhart Found., 1959-60, AAUW, 1960-61, NSF, 1968-70, Social Security Rsch. Coun.; recipient Columbia medal for excellence, 1973, George Washington award Am. Hungarian Found., 1975. Mem. Am. Econ. Assn. (exec. com. 1977-80), Am. Acad. Arts and Scis., Coun. Fgn. Rels. (dir. 1977-87), Phi Beta Kappa. Office: U Mich Gerald Ford Sch Pub Policy 411 Lorch Hall Ann Arbor MI 48109-1220 E-mail: marinaw@umich.edu.

WHITMER, RICHARD E. insurance company executive; Pres., CEO Blue Cross Blue Shield Mich., Detroit. Office: Blue Cross Blue Shield Mich 600 E Lafayette Blvd Detroit MI 48226-2927

WHITMORE, JON SCOTT, university official, play director; b. Seattle, Mar. 22, 1945; s. Walter James and Eurma (Thody) W.; m. Jennifer Gean Gross, Aug. 17, 1985; children: Ian Scott, Amy Lee. BA in Speech and Theatre, Wash. State U., 1967, MA in Speech and Theatre, 1968; PhD in Dramatic Arts, U. Calif., Santa Barbara, 1974. Instr. theatre Highline Coll., Seattle, 1968-71; grad. asst. U. Calif., Santa Barbara, 1971-74; asst. prof. theatre W.Va. U., Morgantown, 1974-78, assoc. prof., 1978-82, prof., 1979-85, chmn. dept., 1979-84, interim dean, 1984-85; prof., dean faculty arts and letters SUNY, Buffalo, 1985-90; dean Coll. Fine Arts, U. Tex., Austin, 1990-96; provost U. Iowa, Iowa City, 1996—. Dir. plays including Suddenly Last Summer, The Miracle Worker, Equus, Romeo and Juliet, Long Days Journey Into Night, The Sea Gull, The Comedy of Errors, The Glass Menagerie, Blithe Spirit, The Tavern, Black Comedy, You're a Good Man Charlie Brown, Vanities, The Effect of Gamma Rays on Man-In-The-Moon Marigolds, Epiphany, Endgame, The Miser, J.B., The Mousetrap, Knapp's Last Tape, Miss Julie, Servant of Two Masters, Before We Were; actor various classical, modern and contemporary plays, and performance pieces; author: Directing Postmodern Theater, 1994, William Saroyan, 1994. Mem. Erie County (N.Y.) Cultural Resources Adv. Bd., 1986-89, long range planning com. Studio Arena Theatre, Buffalo, 1986-90, trustee, 1987-90; mem. coun. fellows Am. Coun. Edn., 1984—; pres. W.Va. Theater Conf., 1978-80, pres.-elect, 1977-78, founding mem., bd. dirs., 1975-81. Recipient ACE Fellow award Am. Council Edn., 1983-84; fellow U. Calif., Santa Barbara, 1973-74, Lilly Found., 1976-77; Maynard Lee Daggy scholar Wash. State U., 1967. Mem. Internat. Coun. Fine Arts Deans, Am. Coun. Arts, Assn. Theatre in Higher Edn. (v.p. adminstrn. 1991—, chmn. nat. conf. planning com. chief adminstrs. program, 1987), Assn. Comm. Adminstrn. (elected to exec. com. 1982-85, chmn. task force theatre adminstrn., 1982-84), Speech Comm. Assn., Coun. Colls. Arts and Scis., Assn. Coll., Univ. and Cmty. Arts Adminstrs., Nat. Assn. State Univs. and Land-Grant Colls. (chair elect commn. arts, 1990-92, chair 1992-93, chair coun. on acad. affairs 2001—). Home: 461 Butternut Ln Iowa City IA 52246-2782 Office: U Iowa Office of Provost 111 Jessup Hall Iowa City IA 52242-1316 E-mail: jon-whitmore@uiowa.edu.

WHITNEY, RAY, hockey player; b. Saskatchewan, Alta., Can., May 8, 1972; s. Floyd and Wendy W. Stick boy Edmonton Oilers, 1986-87, 87-88, player, 1997, Spokane Chiefs, 1988-91, 90-91, San Jose, 1991; left wing, ctr. Fla. Panthers, 1997—. Named most valuable player WHL, 1988-91, 90-91, Most Valuable Player All-Star Game IHL, 1992. Avocation: golf. Office: Columbus Blue Jackets JMAC Hockey 150 East Wilson Bridge Rd. Suite 230 Worthington OH 43085*

WHITNEY, RICHARD BUCKNER, lawyer; b. Corpus Christi, Tex., Mar. 1, 1948; s. Franklyn Loren and Betty Wolcott (Fish) Whitney; m. Chantal Marie Gindt, Aug. 18, 1972; children: Jennifer L, James R, Katherine E. BA in Polit. Sci., Union Coll., 1970; JD, Case Western Res. U., 1973. Bar: Ohio 1973, N.Y. 1998, US Ct Appeals (6th cir) 1974, US Ct Appeals (3d cir) 1987, US Dist Ct (so dist) NY 2000. From assoc. to ptnr. Jones, Day, Reavis & Pogue, Cleve., 1973—. Trustee Hospice of the We. Res., Fairmount Music Edn. Found. Mem.: Am Inns Cts, Legal Aid Soc Cleveland (trustee), Cleveland Bar Asn, Order of Coif. Roman Catholic. Home: 2750 Southington Rd Shaker Heights OH 44120-1603 Office: Jones Day Reavis & Pogue 901 Lakeside Ave Cleveland OH 44114-1190 E-mail: rbwhitney@jonesday.com.

WHITNEY, ROBERT MICHAEL, lawyer; b. Green Bay, Wis., Jan. 29, 1949; s. John Clarence and Helen (Mayer) W. Student, U. Wis., 1967-70, JD, 1974. Bar: Wis. 1974, U.S. Dist. Ct. (we. dist.) Wis. 1979, U.S. Ct. Appeals (7th cir.) 1980, U.S. Dist. Ct. (ea. dist.) Wis. 1984, U.S. Supreme Ct. 1990, U.S. Ct. Appeals (9th cir.) 1992. Legal counsel Wis. State Election Bd., Madison, 1976-78; ptnr. Walsh, Walsh, Sweeney & Whitney, S.C., 1979-86, Foley & Lardner, Madison, 1986-2000, Lawton & Cates SC, Madison, 2000—. Counsel Dane County Advocates for Battered Women; instr. torts I, U. Wis. Labor Sch., 1996; adj. prof. U. Wis. Law Sch., 1996-97. Contbr. articles to profl. jours. Bd. dirs. Community TV, Inc., Madison, 1984-87, Transitional/Homeless Shelters. Mem. Assn. Trial Lawyers Am., Wis. Acad. Trial Lawyers, Wis. Bar Assn., Dane County Bar Assn., Rugby Club of Madison. Office: Lawton & Cates 10 E Doty St Ste 400 Madison WI 53703-5103

WHITT, GREGORY SIDNEY, evolution educator; b. Detroit, June 13, 1938; s. Sidney Abram and Millicent (Ward) W.; m. Dixie Lee Dailey, Aug. 25, 1963. B.S., Colo. State U., 1962, M.S., 1965; Ph.D., Yale U., 1970. Asst. prof. zoology U. Ill., Urbana, 1969-72, asso. prof. genetics and devel., 1972-77, prof., 1977-87, prof. ecology, ethology and evolution, 1987-2000, prof. animal biology, 2000—. Affiliate Ill. Natural History Survey, 1981— ; mem. NIH study sect., 1975-76 Co-editor: Isozymes: Current Topics in Biological and Medical Research, 1977-87; editor: Isozyme Bull., 1978-81; mem. editl. bd. Biochem. Genetics, 1975—, Devel. Genetics, 1978-83, Jour. Molecular Evolution, 1979-2000, Molecular Biology and Evolution, 1983-93, Molecular Phylogenetics and Evolution, 1992-2000; contbr. articles to profl. jours. Fellow AAAS; mem. Am. Soc. for Microbiology, Soc. for Protection of Old Fishes, Internat. Soc. Molecular Evolution. Home: 1510 Trails Dr Urbana IL 61802-7052 Office: U Ill Dept Animal Biology 515 Morrill Hall 505 S Goodwin Ave Urbana IL 61801-3707

WHITTAKER, JUDITH ANN CAMERON, lawyer; b. N.Y.C., June 12, 1938; d. Thomas Macdonald and Mindel (Wallman) Cameron; m. Kent E. Whittaker, Jan. 30, 1960; children: Charles Evans II, Catherine Cameron. BA, Brown U., 1959; JD, U. Mo., 1963. Bar: Mo. 1963, U.S. Dist. Ct. (we. dist.) Mo. 1963, U.S. Ct. Appeals (8th cir.) 1965, U.S. Supreme Ct. 1980, D.C. 1987. Assoc. and ptnr. Sheffrey, Ryder & Skeer, Kansas City, Mo., 1963-72; asst. and assoc. gen. coun., exec. v.p. gen. coun. Hallmark Cards, Inc., 1972—; dir., v.p., gen. coun. Univision Holdings, Inc., 1988-92; dir. MCI Comm. Corp., 1985-98, Harmon Industries, 1993—. Dir. Am. Arbitration Assn., 1996—. Trustee Brown U. Providence, 1977-83, U. Mo. Law Found., Kansas City, 1977-90; dir. Kansas City (Mo.) Indsl. Devel. Authority, 1981-84, Legal Aid Kansas City, 1971-77, De La Salle Sch., 1993—. Mem. Internat. Soc. Barristers. Episcopalian. Avocations: reading, skiing, hiking, piano, golf. Office: Hallmark Cards Dept 339 PO Box 419126 Kansas City MO 64141-6126

WHITTEMORE, BRIAN, broadcast executive; V.p., gen. mgr. Sta. KDKA-AM, Pitts., Sta. WCCO-Radio, Mpls. Office: WCCO Radio 625 2nd Ave S Ste 200 Minneapolis MN 55402-1961

WHITTEN, MARY LOU, nursing educator; b. Vandalia, Ill., Apr. 8, 1946; d. Otto M. and Lucille (Mattes) Elam; m. Dennis L. Whitten, Aug. 27, 1966; children: Michael, Christopher, Andrew. BSN, Baylor U., 1968; MS in Nursing, So. Ill. U., 1990. RN, Ill. Instr. health occupations Okaw Vocat. Sch., Vandalia, Ill.; head nurse med.-surg. Fayette County Hosp.; DON Kaskaskia Coll., Centralia, Ill. CPR instr. Am. Heart Assn. Vol. ARC. Mem. Am. Assn. of Women in C.C. Ill., Ill. Coun. Dirs. of Nursing, Phi Kappa Phi. Home: RR 3 Box 848 Vandalia IL 62471-9204 Office: Kaskaskia Coll 27210 College Rd Centralia IL 62801-7800 E-mail: mwhitten@kc.cc.il.us.

WHITWAM, DAVID RAY, appliance manufacturing company executive; b. Stanley, Wis., Jan. 30, 1942; s. Donald R. and Lorraine (Stoye) W.; m. Barbara Lynne Peterson, Apr. 13, 1963; children: Mark, Laura, Thomas BS, U. Wis., 1967. Gen. mgr. sales So. Calif. divsn. Whirlpool Corp., Los Angeles, 1975-77, mdse. mgr. ranges Benton Harbor, Mich., 1977-79, dir. builder mktg., 1979-80, v.p. builder mktg., 1980-83, v.p. whirlpool sales, 1983-85, vice-chmn., chief mktg. officer, 1985-87, chmn., pres., CEO, 1987-99, chmn., CEO, 1999—, also bd. dirs. Bd. dirs. Combustion Engring. Inc., Stamford, Conn. Pres. bd. dirs. The Soup Kitchen, Benton Harbor, 1980—; mem. Nat. Council Housing Industry, Washington. Capt. U.S. Army. Fellow Aspen Inst.; mem. Point O'Woods Club (Benton Harbor). Republican. Lutheran. Office: Whirlpool Corp 2000 N M 63 Benton Harbor MI 49022-2692

WHYTE, GEORGE KENNETH, JR. lawyer; b. Waukegan, Ill., Oct. 10, 1936; s. George K. and Ella Margaret (Osgood) W.; m. Ann B. Challoner, June 20, 1964; children: Mary, Douglas. AB in Polit. Sci., Duke U., 1958; LLB, U. Wis., 1965. Bar: Wis. 1965. Law clk. to chief justice Wis. Supreme Ct., Madison, 1965-66; assoc. Quarles & Brady, Milw., 1966-73, ptnr., 1973—. Lt. USN, 1958—62. Mem. ABA (employment law sect.), Wis. Bar Assn. (former chmn. labor and employment law sect.), Rotary (pres. 2002--), The Town Club, Milw. Country Club. Congregationalist. Home: 1026 W Shaker Cir Mequon WI 53092-6034 Office: Quarles & Brady 411 E Wisconsin Ave Ste 2550 Milwaukee WI 53202-4497 E-mail: gkw@quarles.com.

WHYTE, MICHAEL PETER, medicine, pediatrics and genetics educator, research director; b. N.Y.C., Dec. 19, 1946; s. Michael Paul and Sophie (Dziuk) W.; m. Gloria Frances Golenda, Oct. 26, 1974; 1 child, Catherine Alexandra. BA in Chemistry, NYU, 1968; MD, SUNY, Bklyn., 1972. Diplomate Am. Bd. Internal Medicine, Nat. Bd. Med. Examiners. Intern, 1st yr. resident dept. medicine NYU Sch. Medicine Bellevue Hosp., N.Y.C., 1972-74; clin. assoc. devel. and metabolic neurology br. Nat. Inst. Neurol. and Communicative Disorders and Stroke NIH, Bethesda, Md., 1974-76; fellow divsn. bone and mineral metabolism dept. medicine Wash. U. Sch. Medicine, 1976-79, instr. dept. medicine, 1979-80, asst. sci. dir. Clin. Rsch. Ctr., 1979—; asst. physician Barnes Hosp., 1979—; dir. Metabolism Clinic Shriners Hosp. Crippled Children, St. Louis, 1979—; staff physician St. Louis Children's Hosp., 1979—; NIH clin. assoc. physician Clin. Rsch. Ctr. Wash. U. Sch. Medicine, 1980-82, asst. prof. medicine dept. medicine, 1980-86, assoc. prof. medicine dept. medicine, 1986-91, asst. prof. pediatrics Edward Mallinckrodt dept. pediatrics, 1982-89, assoc. prof. pediatrics Edward Mallinckrodt dept. pediatrics, 1989-92, prof. medicine dept. medicine, 1991—, prof. pediatrics Edward Mallinckrodt dept. pediatrics, 1992—, prof. genetics James S. McDonell dept. genetics, 1997—; med. dir. Metabolic Rsch. Unit Shriners Hosp. Crippled Children, St. Louis, 1982-2000, mem. staff., 1983—; assoc. attending physician Jewish Hosp. St. Louis, 1983—. Staff cons. Shriners Hosp. Crippled Children, St. Louis, 1979-83, Mexico City, 1991—; editl. bd. Calcified Tissue Internat., 1995-2000, Jour. Bone and Mineral Rsch., 1994—; med. adv. bd. Osteogenesis Imperfecta Found., 1986—, med. adv. panel Paget's Disease Found., 1986—; chmn. med. adv. com., bd. dirs. Osteogenesis Found., 1995—; med.-scientific dir. Ctr. for Metabolic Bone Disease and Molecular Rsch. Shriners Hosp. Children, St. Louis, 2000—. Assoc. editor: Primer on Metabolic Bone Diseases and Disorders of Mineral Metabolism, 1990, 93, 96; assoc. editor Calcified Tissue Internat., 1989-2000; contbr. chpts. to books, articles to profl. jours. Lt. comdr. USPHS, 1974-76. Fellow Am. Coll. of Endocrinology; mem. Am. Soc. Cell Biology, Am. Soc. Clin. Investigation, Am. Coll. Physicians (assoc.), Am. Fedn. Clin. Rsch., Am. Soc. Advancement Sci., Am. Soc. Bone and Mineral Rsch. (edl. com. 1987—, Fuller Albright award 1987, Young Investigator award 1983, Dr. Boy Frame award 1997), Am. Soc. Human Genetics, Endocrine Soc., Soc. Exptl. Biology and Medicine, Japanese Soc. Inherited Metabolic Disease (hon.). Office: Barnes-Jewish Hosp 216 S Kingshighway Blvd Saint Louis MO 63110-1026 Business E-Mail: mwhyte@shrinenet.org.

WICK, DON, radio personality; Farm broadcaster, Wabasha, Minn., 1980, Austin, Redwood Falls, Worthington, Yankton, SD; radio host Sta. WCCO Radio, Mpls., 1997—. Recipient Oscar in Agriculture award for Excellence in Agrl. Journalism, 1998, 1999. Mem.: Nat. Assn. Farm Broadcasters (pres. 1997—, Farm Broadcaster of Yr. award for West Region 1999). Office: WCCO 625 2nd Ave S Minneapolis MN 55402*

WICK, HAL GERARD, state legislator; b. New Ulm, Minn., Oct. 31, 1944; s. Roland Theodore and Esther Marie La Fontaine Wick; m. Jane Dorothy Rance, 1965; children: Anne Marie, Paula Jo, Betsey Jane, Ross Anthony. Student, Exec. Air Travel Flight Sch., Sioux Falls, S.D., 1966-68; BS, S.D. State U., Brookings, 1967. Flight instr. Snediger Flying Svc., Rapid City, S.D., 1968, Airways Svc., Sioux City, Iowa, 1968-70; pilot Iowa Air Nat. Guard, 1970-75; chief pilot, flight instr. Soo Flying, 1971-72; pilot NW Airlines, Mpls., 1972—; S.D. state rep. Dist. 11, 1977-80, Dist. 12, 1995-98; also S.D. House rep. Chmn. Minnehaha County Rep. Party Victory Squad, S.D., 1974-76; chmn. Minnehaha County Citizens for Reagan, 1976; del. Rep. Nat. Conv., 1976; mem. Legis. Rsch. Coun., State of S.D., 1977-78, mem. Edn. and Transp. Coms.; former chmn., coord. People for Alternative to McGovern, Nat. Conservative Polit. Action Com. Pilot S.D. Air Nat. Guard, 1975-94. Named Top Gun, Sioux City, 1974, Outstanding Optimist, Morning Optimist Club, 1975. Mem. Am. Legion, NG Assn., Air Line Pilots Assn., Hartford Lions. Home: 3009 W Donahue Dr Sioux Falls SD 57105-0153

WICK, SISTER MARGARET, former college administrator; b. Sibley, Iowa, June 30, 1942; BA in Sociology, Briar Cliff Coll., 1965; MA in Sociology, Loyola U., Chgo., 1971; PhD in Higher Edn., U. Denver, 1976. Instr. sociology Briar Cliff Coll., Sioux City, Iowa, 1966-71, dir. academic advising, 1971-72, v.p., acad. dean, 1972-74, 76-84, pres., 1987-99, Colls. of Mid-Am., 1985-87. Mem. adv. bd. Nations Bank, Sioux City. Bd. dirs. Mary J. Treglia Cmty. House, 1976-84, Marian Health Ctr., 1987-97, Iowa Pub. TV, 1987-95. Mem. North Ctrl. Edn. Assn. (cons.-evaluator for accrediting teams 1980-84, 89—), Siouxland Initiative (adv. bd.), Quota Internat., Rotary. Home: 3390 Windsor Ave Dubuque IA 52001-1326 Office: Briar Cliff Coll Office of the President 3303 Rebecca St Sioux City IA 51104-2324

WICKERSHAM, WILLIAM R. state legislator; b. Lusk, Wyo., Oct. 22, 1948; BSBA, Creighton U.; JD, U. Nebr. Mem. Nebr. Legislature from 49th dist., Lincoln, 1991—; mem. edn., revenue coms. Nebr. Legislature, 1994—, chmn. retirement sys., 1998—, chair revenue com., 1998—. Mem. ABA, Nebr. State Bar Assn., Sioux City Hist. Soc., Siouc County Agr. Soc., Elks. Office: State Capitol Rm 1401 Lincoln NE 68509

WICKESBERG, ALBERT KLUMB, retired management educator; b. Neenah, Wis., Apr. 2, 1921; s. Albert Henry and Lydia (Klumb) W.; m. Dorothy Louise Ahrensfeld, Oct. 28, 1944; children— Robert, William, James. B.A., Lawrence Coll., 1943; M.B.A., Stanford U., 1948; Ph.D., Ohio State U., 1955. Staff accountant S.C. Johnson & Son, Inc., Racine, Wis., 1948-50; asst. prof. Sacramento State Coll., 1950-51; prof. U. Minn., Mpls., 1953-86, prof. emeritus, 1987—, chmn. dept. bus. adminstrn., 1959-62, dir. grad. studies, 1963-66, chmn. dept. mgmt. and transp.,

1971-77. Author: Management Organization, 1966. Served with AUS, 1943-46, 51-52. Soc. Advancement Mgmt. fellow, 1972 Mem. Acad. Mgmt., Soc. Advancement Mgmt. (pres. Twin Cities chpt. 1961-62). Congregationalist. Home: 4501 Roanoke Rd Minneapolis MN 55422-5268

WICKHAM, MICHAEL W. transportation executive; b. 1946; With Roadway Express, Inc., Akron, Ohio, 1968—, terminal mgr., 1971-77, dist. mgr., 1977-81, v.p. N.E. divsn., 1981-85, v.p. western divsn., 1985-88, v.p. adminstrn. and fin., 1988-89, exec. v.p. adminstrn. and fin., 1989-90, pres., CEO, 1990-99, CEO, 1999—. Office: 1077 Gorge Blvd Akron OH 44310-2408

WICKLINE, SAMUEL ALAN, cardiologist, educator; b. Huntington, W.Va., Oct. 23, 1952; BA in Philosophy cum laude, Pomona Coll., 1974; MD, U. Hawaii, 1980. Diplomate Am. Bd. Internal Medicine, Am. Bd. Cardiology. Intern, resident in internal medicine Barnes Hosp. Barnes/Washington U. Sch. Medicine, St. Louis, 1980-83, clin. fellow in cardiology, 1983-85, rsch. fellow in cardiology, 1985-87; asst. prof. medicine Sch. Medicine Washington U. Sch. Medicine, 1987-93, assoc. prof., 1993—, adj. asst. prof. physics, 1990, adj. assoc. prof. physics, 1994, attending cardiologist, dir. echocardiology Jewish Hosp., 1992—, prof. medicine and physics, 1997, dir. divsn. cardiology, 1993—. Reviewer Jour. Clin. Investigation, Circulation, Arteriosclerosis and Thrombosis, Hypertension, Ultrasound in Medicine and Biology; contbr. over 100 articles to med. and sci. jours., chpts. to books on topics related to basic rsch. in cardiovascular biophysics and acoustics/ultrasonics. Grantee NIH, Am. Heart Assn., Whitaker Found. Fellow Am. Coll. Cardiology (reviewer jour.); mem. IEEE Soc. Ultrasonics, Ferroelectrics and Frequency Control, Am. Heart Assn. (coun. on radiology and clin. cardiology, Clinician-Scientist award 1988-93, Established Investigator award 1993—), Am. Soc. Clin. Investigation, Am. Inst. Ultrasound in Medicine, Acoustical Soc. Am., Alpha Omega Alpha. Home: 11211 Pointe Ct Saint Louis MO 63127-1741 Office: Jewish Hosp Cardiology 216 S Kingshighway Blvd Saint Louis MO 63110-1026

WICKLUND, DAVID WAYNE, lawyer; b. St. Paul, Aug. 7, 1949; s. Wayne Glenwood and Elna Katherine (Buresh) W.; m. Susan Marie Bubenko, Nov. 17, 1973; children: David Jr., Kurt, Edward. BA cum laude, Williams Coll., 1971; JD cum laude, U. Toledo, 1974. Bar: Ohio 1974. Assoc. Shumaker, Loop & Kendrick, Toledo, 1974-80, ptnr., 1981—. Adj. instr. law, U. Toledo, 1988. Editor-in-chief U. Toledo Law Rev. 1973-74. Mem. ABA, Ohio State Bar Assn. (emeritus mem. bd. govs. antitrust sect. 1994-2001), Toledo Bar Assn., U. Toledo Coll. of Law Alumni Assn. (pres. 1999-2000), Inverness Club, Toledo Club. Office: Shumaker Loop & Kendrick N Courthouse Sq 1000 Jackson St Toledo OH 43624-1573 E-mail: dwicklund@slk-law.com.

WICKMAN, JOHN EDWARD, librarian, historian; b. Villa Park, Ill., May 24, 1929; s. John Edward and Elsie (Voss) W.; m. Shirley Jean Swanson, Mar. 17, 1951; children— Lisa Annette, Eric John. A.B., Elmhurst Coll., 1953; A.M., Ind. U., 1958, Ph.D., 1964; LL.D., Lincoln Coll., 1973. Instr. history Hanover (Ind.) Coll., 1959-62, Southeast Campus, Ind. U., Jeffersonville, 1962; asst. prof. history Northwest Mo. State Coll., Maryville, 1962-64; asst. to Gov. William H. Avery of Kans., Topeka, 1964-65; asst. prof. history Regional Campus, Purdue U., Fort Wayne, Ind., 1965-66; dir. Dwight D. Eisenhower Libr., Abilene, Kans., 1966-89; ret., 1989. Contbr. articles on Am. West, archival mgmt., adminstrv. history, oral history to profl. publs. Served with U.S. Army, 1953-55. Nat. Ctr. for Edn. in Politics faculty fellow, 1964-65; Am. Polit. Sci. Assn. Congl. fellow, 1975-76 Mem. Oral History Assn. (v.p. 1971-72, pres. 1972-73), Western History Assn. (coun. 1972-75), Kans. Hist. Soc. (2d v.p. 1974-75, pres. 1976-77, dir.). Home: 411 W 4th St PO Box 325 Enterprise KS 67441-0325

WICKS, JOHN R. lawyer; b. Ottumwa, Iowa, Dec. 8, 1937; m. Nedra Morgan, Mar. 27, 1940; children: Catherine, John. BSC, U. Iowa, 1959, JD, 1964. Bar: Iowa 1964, Minn. 1966. Assoc. Dorsey & Whitney, Mpls., 1966-71; ptnr. Dorsey & Whitney LLP, Rochester, Minn., 1972-2000, of counsel Mpls., 2001—. Fellow: Am. Coll. Trusts and Estates Counsel; mem.: Minn. State Bar Assn. (probate and trusts law coun. 1989—92). Office: Dorsey & Whitney LLP 50 S 6th St Minneapolis MN 55402-1498 E-mail: wicks.john@dorseylaw.com.

WIDDEL, JOHN EARL, JR. lawyer; b. Minot, N.D., Nov. 17, 1936; s. John Earl Sr. and Angela Victoria W.; m. Yvonne J. Haugen, Dec. 21, 1973; children: John P., James M., Susan N., Andrea K. B in Philosophy, BSBA, U. N.D., 1966, BSBA, 1971. Bar: N.D. 1971, U.S. Dist. Ct. N.D., 1971, U.S. Ct. Appeals (8th cir.) 1989. Ptnr. Thorsen & Widdel, Grand Forks, N.D., 1971-97; shareholder Law Offices ND, PC. Mcpl. judge City of Grand Forks, 1972—; ct. magistrate Grand Forks County, 1975. Mem. N.D. Foster Parent Program, 1974-87, Nat. Conf. of Bar Pres.; mem. bd. dirs. YMCA, Grand Forks, 1982; dist. chmn. Boy Scouts Am., 1987-88; corp. mem. ALTRU Hosp. With U.S. Army, 1960-62. Mem. Am. Acad. Estate Planning Attys., State Bar Assn. N.D. (bd. govs. 1983-88, pres. 1986-87), Greater Grand Forks County Bar Assn. (pres. 1982), N.E. Cen. Jud. Dist. (pres. 1983), Grand Forks Cemetery Assn. (bd. dirs. 1984-96, pres. 1989-94), Grand Forks Hist. Soc. (pres. 1983), Grand Forks Jaycees, Antique Automobile Club Am. (nat. bd. dirs. 1984-2000, v.p. 1985-98, sec.-treas. 1989, pres. N.D . region 1977-78, 83-84), Sertoma (bd. dirs. 1994-99, pres. 1997-98, dist. gov. 2001-02), Elks (exalted ruler 1985-86), Masonic Bodies (Kem Temple Potentate 1995), Nat. Assn. Estate Planning Coun. (accredited estate planner, 1994), N.D. Mcpl. Judges Assn. (dir. 1993—). Roman Catholic. Home: Box 5624 Grand Forks ND 58206-5624 Office: Law Offices North Dakota PC PO Box 5624 Grand Forks ND 58206-5624

WIDERA, GEORG ERNST OTTO, mechanical engineering educator, consultant; b. Dortmund, Germany, Feb. 16, 1938; arrived in U.S., 1950; s. Otto and Gertrude (Yzermann) Widera; m. Kristel Kornas, June 21, 1974; children: Erika, Nicholas. BS, U. Wis., 1960, MS, 1962, PhD, 1965. Asst. prof. then prof. dept. materials engring. U. Ill., Chgo., 1965-82, prof. mech. engring., 1982-91, head dept., 1983-91, acting head indsl. sys. engring. dept., 1985-86, dir off-campus engring. programs, 1987-88; prof., chmn. mech. and indsl. engring. dept. Marquette U., Milw., 1991-99, dir. Ctr. Indsl. Processes and Productivity, 1995—2002, interim dean Coll. Engring., 1998-99, assoc. dean Coll. Engring., 1999—2001, sr. assoc. dean Coll. Engring., 2001—. Gastdozent U. Stuttgart, Germany, 1968; vis. prof. U. Wis.-Milw., 1973—74, Marquette U., Milw., 1978—79; cons. Ladish Co., Cudahy, Wis., 1967—76, Howmedica, Inc., Chgo., 1972—75, Sargent & Lundy, 1970—88, Nat. Bur. Stds., 1980, bd. dirs.; cons. Engrs. and Scientists Milw., 1996—98; vis. scientist Argonne Nat. Lab., Ill., 1968. Editor: Procs. Innovations in Structural Engring., 1974, Pressure Vessel Design, 1982; assoc. editor: Pressure Vessel Tech., 1977—81, assoc. editor: Applied Mechanics Revs., 1987—94, assoc. editor: Mfg. Rev., 1991—95, mem. editl. adv. bd.: Acta Mechanica Sinica, 1990—, mem. editl. bd.: Pressure Vessels and Piping Design Technology, 1982, tech. editor: Jour. Pressure Vessel Tech., 1982—93; co-editor: SME Handbook of Metalforming, 1985, 1994, Design and Analysis of Plates and Shells, 1986. Fellow Std. Oil Co. Calif., 1961—63, NASA, 1966, von Humboldt, Fed. Republic Germany, 1968—69. Fellow: WRC (pressure vessel rsch. coun., chmn. subcom. design procedures for shell intersections 1983—87, chmn. com. reinforced openings and external loads 1987—91, vice chmn. com. polymer pressure components 1991—99, chmn. com. shells and ligaments 1994—97), ASCE (sec.-treas. structural divsn. Ill. sect. 1972—73, chmn. divsn. 1976—77, chmn. peer rev. com., tech. coun. rsch. 1984, coun. structural plastics), ASME (chmn. machine design div. Chgo. sect. 1967—68, exec. com. Chgo. sect. 1970—73, editor newsletter Chgo. sect. 1971—73, chmn. jr. awards com. applied mechanics divsn. 1973—76, chmn. design and analysis com. pressure vessel and piping divsn. 1980—83, chmn. pressure vessel rsch. com. 1982—87, bd. editors 1983—93, mem. exec. com. and program chmn. pressure vessel and piping divsn. 1985—89, vice-chmn., sec. pressure vessel and piping divsn. 1989—90, mem. bd. pressure tech. codes and stds. 1989—94, chmn. 1990—91, mem. materials and structures group 1990—91, historian, senate pressure vessel and piping divsn. 1992—93, honors and awards chmn. Milw. sect. 1992—95, mem. coun. engring. 1992—96, v.p. materials and structures group 1993—96, mem. tech. execs. com. 1993—96, soc. rep. Fedn. Materials Soc. 1994—95, Pressure Vessel and Piping award and medal 1995), Wis. Mfg. Curriculum Com. (vice-chmn. exec. com. 1998—), 2d China Nat. Stds. Com. Pressure Vessels (hon. cons. 1989—94), Internat. Coun. Pressure Vessel Tech. (chmn. Am. regional com. 1988—, internat. chmn. 1992—96), Gesellschaft für Angewandte Mathematik und Mechanik, French Pressure Vessel Assn., Am. Soc. Engring. Edn., Soc. Mfg. Engrs. (sr.). Achievements include research in in mechanics of composite materials, plate and shell structures, stress analysis (including FEM), pressure vessels, mechanics of deformation processing. Office: Marquette U Coll Engring PO Box 1881 Milwaukee WI 53201-1881 E-mail: geo.widera@marquette.edu.

WIDISS, ALAN I. lawyer, educator; b. L.A., Sept. 28, 1938; s. Al and Rose H. (Sobole) W.; m. Ellen Louise Magaziner, June 28, 1964; children: Benjamin L., Deborah Anne, Rebecca Elizabeth. BS, U. So. Calif., 1960, LLB, 1963; LLM, Harvard U., 1964. Bar: Calif. 1963. Teaching fellow Harvard U., 1964-65; asst. prof. law U. Iowa, Iowa City, 1965-68, asso. prof., 1968-69, prof., 1969-78, Josephine R. Witte prof., 1978—. Vis. prof. U. So. Calif., U. San Diego; dir. CLRS Mass. No-Fault Automobile Ins. Study, 1971-76. Author: A Guide to Uninsured Motorist Coverage, 1969; (with others) No-Fault Automobile Insurance in Action: The Experiences in Massachusetts, Florida, Delaware and New York, 1977, Uninsured and Underinsured Motorist Insurance (revised edit.), Vol. 1, 1991, Vol. 2, 1992, Vol. 3, 1995; author, editor: (with others) Arbitration: Commercial Disputes, Insurance and Tort Claims, 1979; (with Judge Robert E. Keeton) Insurance Law, 1988 and Course Supplement, 1988; Insurance: Materials on the General Principles, Legal Doctrines and Regulatory Acts, 1989; contbr. articles to law jours. Bd. fellows U. Iowa Sch. Religion, 1976, v.p., 1991-93, pres., 1993-95; chmn. Johnson County Citizens Adv. Com. for Regional Transp. Study, 1971-75; pres. Agudas Achim Synagogue, 1983-85, Iowa City Youth Orch., 1991-92. Mem. ABA, Am. Law Inst., Calif. Bar Assn., Assn. Am. Law Schs., Order of Coif, Phi Kappa Phi, Delta Sigma Rho. Avocations: tennis, theater. Home: Iowa City, Iowa. Died Feb. 28, 2001.

WIDMAN, PAUL JOSEPH, insurance agent; b. DeSmet, S.D., Dec. 18, 1936; s. Warren Clay and Lorraine (Coughlin) W.; m. Elizabeth Ann Healy, July 30, 1959; children: Cynthia, Susan, Shelly, Richard, Mark. BS, Dakota State Coll., Madison, 1959; M in Comm., S.D. State U., 1968. Tchr. Clark (S.D.) Pub. Sch., 1959-60, Henry (S.D.) Pub. Sch., 1960-64, Custer (S.D.) Pub. Sch., 1964-66; ins. agt. Horace Mann Ins., Mitchell, S.D., 1966-77, Universal Underwriters, Mitchell, 1980-87, NGM Ins. Assn., Mitchell, 1987-91, Reginald Martin Agy., Mitchell, 1991—; state rep. State of S.D., 1993—; gen. agt., ins. sales agt. Reginald Martin Agy., Mitchell, 1992—. City coun. mem. Mitchell City Coun., 1972-76; state legislator S.D. Ho. of Reps., 1993-94. Sgt. U.S. Army N.G., 1955-61. Mem. Elks, Mitchell Jaycees (pres., v.p. 1968-70, Outstanding Jaycee 1970), S.D. Jaycees (v.p., regional dir. 1969-70). Democrat. Roman Catholic. Avocations: golf, bowling, hunting. Office: Reginald Martin Agy 510 W Havens St Mitchell SD 57301-3935

WIDMAR, RUSSELL C. airport executive; V.p. airport svcs. Lockheed Air Terminal Inc., 1980-94; dir. Burbank-Glendale-Pasadena Airport, 1984; dir. ops. airport sys. divsn. Hughes Aircraft Co., Fullerton, Calif., 1994-96; exec. dir. aviation Salt Lake City Airport Authority, 1996-99; aviation dir. Kansas City Aviation Dept, 2000—. Office: Kansas City Aviation Dept PO Box 20047 Kansas City MO 64195-0047

WIDMAYER, CHRISTOPHER A. legislative staff member; b. Royal Oak, Mich., Nov. 24, 1971; BA, Miami U., Oxford, Ohio, 1994. Staff asst. U.S. Rep. Bob Carr, Washington, 1994; dep. press sec. Durbin for Senate campaign, Chgo., 1995-96; Ill. press sec. Sen. Dick Durbin, 1997—. Office: Office of Senator Dick Durbin 230 S Dearborn St Ste 3892 Chicago IL 60604-1602

WIECEK, BARBARA HARRIET, advertising executive; b. Chgo., Mar. 30, 1956; d. Stanley Joseph and Irene (Zagajewski) W. AA, Am. Acad. of Art, Chgo., 1977. Illustrator Clinton E. Frank Advt., Chgo., 1977-78, art dir., 1978-80, assoc. creative dir., 1980-84, v.p.; instr. Am. Acad. of Art, 1977-80; assoc. creative dir. Tatham, Laird & Kudner, 1984—, ptnr., 1986—, creative dir., 1987—, sr. ptnr., 1995—, exec. creative dir., 1996. Recipient Silver Awd. Internat. Film Festival of N.Y., 1981, Gold Awd. Internat. Film Festival of N.Y., 1981. Roman Catholic. Avocations: painting, writing, gardening, remodeling, cycling. Office: Tatham Euro RSCG 36 E Grand Ave Chicago IL 60611-3506

WIEGAND, SYLVIA MARGARET, mathematician, educator; b. Cape Town, South Africa, Mar. 8, 1945; came to U.S., 1949; d. Laurence Chisholm and Joan Elizabeth (Dunnett) Young; m. Roger Allan Wiegand, Aug. 27, 1966; children: David Chisholm, Andrea Elizabeth. AB, Bryn Mawr Coll., 1966; MA, U. Wash., 1967; PhD, U. Wis., Madison, 1972. Mem. faculty U. Nebr., Lincoln, 1967—, now prof. math. Vis. assoc. prof. U. Conn., Storrs, 1978-79, U. Wis., Madison, 1985-86; vis. prof. Purdue U., 1992-93, Spring 1998, Mich. State U., Fall 1997. Editor Communications in Math., 1990—, Rocky Mountain Jour. Math., 1991—; contbr. rsch. articles to profl. jours. Troop leader Lincoln area Girl Scouts U.S., 1988-92. Grantee NSF, 1985-88, 90-93, 94-96, 97—; Vis. Professorship for Women, 1992, Nat. Security Agy., 1995-97. Mem. AAUP, Assn. Women in Math (pres.-elect 1995-96, pres. 1997-99), London Math. Soc., Math. Assn. Am., Am. Math. Soc. (mem. coun. 1994-96, chmn. policy com. on meetings and confs. 1994-96, mem. nominating com. 1997—), Can. Math. Soc. (bd. mem. at large 1997—). Avocations: running, family activities. Office: U Nebr Dept Math Lincoln NE 68588-0323 E-mail: swiegand@math.unl.edu.

WIEMANN, MARION RUSSELL, JR. (BARON OF CAMSTER), biologist; b. Sept. 7, 1929; s. Marion Russell and Verda (Peek) W.; 1 child from previous marriage, Tamara Lee (Mrs. Donald D. Kelley). BS, Ind. U., 1959; PhD (hon.), World U. Roundtable, 1991; ScD (hon.), The London Inst. Applied Rsch., England, 1994, ScD (hon.), 1995, World Acad., Germany, 1995. Ordained hon. min., 1998; cert. hypnotist. Histo-rsch. technician U. Chgo., 1959, rsch. asst., 1959-62, rsch. technician, 1962-64; tchr. sci. Westchester Twp. Sch., Chesterton, Ind., 1964-66; with U. Chgo., 1965-79, sr. rsch. technician, 1967-70, rsch. technologist, 1970-79; prin. Marion Wiemann & Assocs., cons. R&D, Chesterton, Ind., 1979-89. Advisor Porter County Health Bd., 1989-91; mem. consultive faculty World U., 1991-99, SkyWarn, Nat. Weather Svc., 1993—. Author: Tooth Decay, Its Cause and Prevention Through Controlled Soil Composition, 1985, The Mechanism of Tooth Decay, 1985; contbr. articles to profl. jours. and newspapers. Vice-chmn. The Duneland 4th of July Com., 1987-91; v.p. State Microscopical Soc. Ill., 1969-70, pres., 1970-71. With USN, 1951-53. Recipient Disting. Tech. Communicator award Soc. for Tech. Communication, 1974, Internat. Order Merit (Eng.), 1991; ennobled Royal Coll. Heraldry, Australia, 1991, Highland Laird, Scotland, 1995; named Sagamore of the Wabash Gov. Ind., 1985; McCrone Rsch. Inst. scholar, 1968; named Prof. of Sci. Australian Inst. for Co-Ordinated Rsch., Australia, 1995, knight corps Diplomatique The Sovereign Military Templar Order, 1994; recipient Scouters Key award Boy Scouts Am., 1968, Arrowhead honor, 1968, Albert Einstein Silver medal, Huguenin, Le Locke, Switzerland, Henri Dunant Silver medal with silver bars, 1995, Henri Dunant Silver medal, 1995, medal of honor, England, 1996. Fellow Australian Inst. for Co-Ordinated Rsch., World Lit. Acad.; mem. Internat. Soc. Soil Sci., Assn. of Masters of the Univers, World Acad., Order Internat. Fellowship, Internat. Graphoanalysis Soc., Maison Internat. des Intellectuels and Akademie MIDI, VFW (charter mem., bd. dirs., post judge adv. 1986—, apptd. post adj. 1986—, Cross of Malta 1986), Govs. Club. Achievements include demostration that radiation does not produce dental caries; proved that soil calcium, magnesium, potassium and phosphorous, with soil PH, controls population size and longevity of earthworms and humans and the incidence of dental caries; demonstrated that flouride neither reduces or prevents dental caries. Address: PO Box 1016 Chesterton IN 46304-0016

WIENER, DEANNA, state legislator; m. Jim Tilsen; three children. RN, St. Mary's Jr. Coll. Mem. Minn. Senate from 38th dist., St. Paul, 1993—; real estate profl. Home: 1238 Balsam Trl E Saint Paul MN 55123-1706 Office: Minn State Senate 75 Constitution Ave Saint Paul MN 55155-1601

WIENER, JOSEPH, pathologist; b. Toronto, Sept. 21, 1927; arrived in U.S., 1949, naturalized, 1960; s. Louis and Minnie (Salem) W.; m. Judith Hesta Ross, June 20, 1954; children: Carolyn L., Adam L. MD, U. Toronto, 1953. Intern Detroit Receiving Hosp., 1953-54; resident to chief resident pathology Mallory Inst. Pathology, 1954-55, 57-60; from asst. to assoc. prof. pathology Columbia U., N.Y.C., 1960-68; prof. pathology N.Y. Med. Coll., 1968-78, Wayne State U., Detroit, 1978—, chmn. dept., 1978-90. Cons. NIH, 1970— Served to capt. M.C. U.S. Army, 1955-57. Grantee: Heart, Lung and Blood Inst., 1971-93; named fellow Coun. for High Blood Pressure Rsch., 1982—. Fellow Am. Heart Assn.; mem. AAAS, Am. Soc. Investigative Pathology, Am. Soc. Cell Biology, Mich. Path. Soc., Internat. Acad. Pathology, Am. Heart Assn., U.S./Can. Acad. Pathology, Mich. Heart Assn. (dir.), Internat. Soc. Hypertension. Achievements include rsch. on cellular/molecular biology of experimental hypert ension. Office: 540 E Canfield St Detroit MI 48201-1928

WIER, JAMES A. manufacturing executive; Exec. v.p. ops. Briggs & Stratton, 1975—91; pres., chief operating officer Simplicity Mfg. Corp., Port Washington, Wis., 1999—. Office: Simplicity Mfg Inc 500 N Spring St PO Box 997 Port Washington WI 53074-0997*

WIER, PATRICIA ANN, publishing executive, consultant; b. Coal Hill, Ark., Nov. 10, 1937; d. Horace L. and Bridget B. (McMahon) Norton; m. Richard A. Wier, Feb. 24, 1962; 1 child, Rebecca Ann. BA, U. Mo., Kansas City, 1964; MBA, U. Chgo., 1978. Computer programmer AT&T, 1960-62; lead programmer City of Kansas City, Mo., 1963-65; with Playboy Enterprises, Chgo., 1965-71, mgr. systems and programming, 1971; with Ency. Britannica, Inc., Chgo., 1971—; v.p. mgmt. svcs. Ency. Britannica USA, 1975-83, exec. v.p. adminstrn., 1983-84; v.p. planning and devel. Ency. Britannica, Inc., 1985, pres. Compton's Learning Co. divsn., 1985; pres. Ency. Britannica (USA), 1986-91, Ency. Britannica N.A., 1991-92; exec. v.p. Ency. Britannica, Inc., 1986-94; pres. Ency. Britannica N.Am., 1991-94; mgmt. cons. pvt. practice, Chgo., 1994—. Cons. pvt. practice, Chgo., 1994—; bd. dirs. NICOR, Inc., Golden Rule Ins.; mem. coun. Northwestern U. Assocs. Life mem. coun. Grad. Sch. Bus., U. Chgo.; mem. bd. regents Lewis U.; chmn. bd. dirs. San Miguel Sch. Mem. Direct Selling Assn. (bd. dirs. 1984-93, chmn. 1987-88, named to Hall of Fame 1991), Women's Coun. U. Mo. Kansas City (hon. life) Com. 200, The Chgo. Network. Roman Catholic. Office: Patricia A Wier Inc 175 E Delaware Pl Apt 8305 Chicago IL 60611-7748 E-mail: wier@prodigy.net.

WIERSBE, WARREN WENDELL, clergyman, author, lecturer; b. East Chicago, Ind., May 16, 1929; s. Fred and Gladys Anna (Forsberg) W.; m. Betty Lorraine Warren, June 20, 1953; children: David, Carolyn, Robert, Judy. B.Th., No. Baptist Sem., 1953; D.D. (hon.), Temple Sem., Chattanooga, 1965, Trinity Ev-Div. Sch., 1986; LittD (hon.), Cedarville Coll., 1987. Ordained to ministry, Bapt. Ch., 1951. Pastor Central Bapt. Ch., East Chicago, 1951-57; editl. dir. Youth for Christ Internat., Wheaton, Ill., 1957-61; pastor Calvary Bapt. Ch., Covington, Ky., 1961-71; sr. min. Moody Ch., Chgo., 1971-78; bd. dirs. Slavic Gospel Assn., Wheaton, 1973-87; columnist Moody Monthly, Chgo., 1971-77; author, conf. minister, 1978-80; pres. ScripTex, Inc., Lincoln, Nebr., 1982—. Vis. instr. pastoral theology Trinity Div. Sch., Deerfield, Ill.; gen. dir. Back to the Bible Radio Ministries, Lincoln, Nebr., 1984-89; writer-in-residence Cornerstone Coll., Grand Rapids, Mich.; disting. prof. preaching Grand Rapids Bapt. Sem. Author: over 150 books including William Culbertson, A Man of God, 1974, Live Like a King, 1976, Walking with the Giants, 1976, Be Right, 1977, (with David Wiersbe) Making Sense of the Ministry, 1983, Why Us? Why Bad Things Happen to God's People, 1984, Real Worship: It Can Transform Your Life, 1986, Be Compassionate, 1988, The Integrity Crisis, 1988, Be What You Are, 1988, The New Pilgrim's Progress, 1989, Be Courageous, 1989, Living With the Giants, 1993, Preaching and Teaching with Imagination, 1994, Be Myself, 1994, Be Authentic, 1997, Be Basic, 1998. Home and Office: 441 Lakewood Dr Lincoln NE 68510-2419

WIESNER, DALLAS CHARLES, immunologist, researcher; b. Brookings, S.D., Mar. 19, 1959; s. Charles Howard Wiesner and Coleen Marie (Hendrickson) Bailey; m. Priscilla Anne Semon, 1992. BS in Microbiology with high honors, S.D. State U., 1982. HIV product devel. tech. Abbott Labs., Diagnostic Div., Abbott Park, Ill., 1985-87, HIV retrocell product mgr. North Chicago, 1987-88, sect. mgr. infectious disease and immunology Abbott Park, 1988-90; mgr. sexually transmitted diseases tech. product devel. Diagnostic div. Abbott Labs., 1990-91, sect. mgr. retrovirus tech. product devel., 1991-96; with hepatitis r&d diagnostic divsn. Abbott Labs, 1996—. Mem. Am. Biog. Inst. Rsch. Assn. (dep. gov.), Am. Soc. for Microbiology, Phi Kappa Phi. Republican. Lutheran. Avocations: fishing, camping, scuba diving, photography, amateur radio. Home: 8710 Lakeshore Dr Pleasant Prairie WI 53158-4721 Office: Abbott Labs 1 Abbott Park Rd North Chicago IL 60064-3500

WIGDALE, JAMES B. bank executive; Chmn., chief exec. officer Marshall & Ilsley Bank, Milw., vice chmn. holding co., also bd. dirs. Office: Marshall & Ilsley Corp 770 N Water St Milwaukee WI 53202-3509

WIGER, CHARLES W. state legislator; b. Sept. 14, 1951; m. Christine Wiger; 5 children. BA, JD, Hamline U. Bar: Minn. Mem. Minn. Senate from 55th dist., St. Paul, 1996—. Home: 2200 Buhl Ave North Saint Paul MN 55109-1771 Office: 325 Capitol 75 Constitution Ave Saint Paul MN 55155-1601

WIGFIELD, RITA L. elementary education educator; b. Mpls., Dec. 14, 1945; d. Willard Ernest and Bernice Eleanor (Peterson) Ahlquist; m. Vernon Carter Wigfield, Oct. 9, 1982. BS, U. Minn., 1967; grad., St. Thomas Coll.; postgrad., Hamlin U. Cert. elem. educator, Minn. Tchr. Alice Smith Sch., Hopkins, Minn., 1967-80, Meadowbrook Sch., Hopkins, 1980-86, Gatewood Sch., Hopkins, 1986—. Owner Swede Country, Minnetonka, Minn., 1983—; elem. team leader Prin.'s Adv. Bd.; chmn. bldg. tech. com. Hopkins Sch. Dist., past supr. bldg. sch. patrol; coop. tchrs. Gustavus Adolphus Coll.; cons. and presenter in field. Author: We Love Literature, 1991 (Grand Prize Scholastic Inc., 1991). Mem. Wooddale Choir Evang. Christian Ch., decorating com., Mission commn., organizer fellowship dinners; mem. Loaves and Fishes, Minn. Landscape Arboretum. Recipient Hon. Mention Learning Mag., 1990, Nat. Coun Econ.

edn./Internat. Paper Col. Found., 1992, 2d pl. Minn. Coun. Econ. Edn., 1992, Ashland Oil award, 1994; named Minn. Tchr. of Yr., 1992. Mem. ASCD, Nat. Assn. Miniature Enthusiasts, Am. Quilting Soc., Internat. Reading Assn., Minn. Edn. Assn., Hopins Edn. Assn. (bldg. rep., treas.), Delta Kappa Gamma (pres. Beta Beta chpt.), Kappa Delta Pi. Avocations: miniatures, quilting, flowers, cross-stitch, antiques. Home: 4719 Diane Dr Hopkins MN 55343-8785 Office: Gatewood Elem Sch 14900 Gatewood Dr Minnetonka MN 55345-6731

WIGGINS, CHARLES HENRY, JR. lawyer; b. Balt., July 15, 1939; s. Charles Henry and Kathryn Wilson (Walker) W.; m. Wendy Jane Horn, June 20, 1964 (div. 1996); children: Charles Hunter, Rebecca Rae, Melinda Marie; m. Karen Ann Kowal, Apr. 26, 1997 (div. 2002). BSEE, U. Ill., Urbana, 1962; JD with honors, U. Ill., 1965. Bar: Ill. 1965, U.S. Dist. (no. dist.) Ill. 1970, U.S. Tax Ct. 1974, U.S. Ct. Appeals (7th cir.) 1983. Assoc. Vedder, Price, Kaufman & Kammholz, Chgo., 1969-73, ptnr., 1974—. Mem. zoning bd. appeals Village of Indian Head Pk., Ill., 1984-91. Capt. U.S. Army, 1965-68. Mem. Chgo. Bar Assn., University Club (Chgo.), Edgewood Valley Country Club (LaGrange, Ill., bd. dirs. 1991-98), SAR. Avocations: golf, tennis, bridge. Office: Vedder Price Kaufman & Kammholz 222 N La Salle St Fl 26 Chicago IL 60601-1003

WIGGINS, GARY, state legislator; Mem. Mo. Ho. of Reps. from 8th dist. Democrat. Home: RR 1 Box 12 New Cambria MO 63558-9707 Office: Mo Ho of Reps 201 W Capitol Ave Jefferson City MO 65101-1556

WIGGINS, HARRY, state legislator, lawyer; b. Kansas City, Mo., Aug. 1, 1934; s. John M. and Helen F. (Murphy) W. BA, Rockhurst Coll.; JD, St. Louis U. Bar: Mo. 1957, U.S. Dist. Ct. (we. dist.) Mo. 1959, U.S. Ct. Appeals (8th cir.) 1962, U.S. Supreme Ct. 1963. Asst. U.S. atty. U.S. Dist. Ct. (we. dist.) Mo., Kansas City, 1961-67; supr. liquor control State of Mo., Jefferson City, 1967-70, gen. counsel dept. pub. svcs., 1973-74; western judge Jackson County Ct., Kansas City, 1971-73; mem. Mo. Senate from 10th dist., Jefferson City, 1974—. Mem. Alpha Delta Gamma (past nat. pres.), Alpha Sigma Nu. Democrat. Roman Catholic. Home: 7817 Terrace St Kansas City MO 64114-1672 Office: Mo Senate The Capitol Rm 423 Jefferson City MO 65101

WIGGINS, ROGER C. internist, educator, researcher; b. Tetbury, Eng., May 26, 1945; BA, Cambridge U., Eng., 1968; BChir, Middlesex Hosp. Med. Sch., London, 1971, MB, MA, 1972. House physician dept. medicine The Middlesex Hosp., London, 1971-72; house surgeon Ipswich (Eng.) and East Suffolk Hosps., 1972; sr. house officer Hammersmith Hosp., The Middlesex Hosp., Brompton Hosp., London, 1972-74; rsch. registrar The Middlesex Hosp. Med. Sch., 1975-76; postdoctoral fellow Scripps Clinic and Rsch. Found., La Jolla, Calif., 1976-78, rsch. assoc., 1978-79, asst. mem. 1, 1979-81; asst. prof. U. Mich., Ann Arbor, 1981-84, assoc. prof., 1984-90, prof., 1990—, chief nephrology, 1988—, dir. O'Brien Renal Ctr., 1988—, dir. NIH Nephrology Tng. Program, 1988-96. Lectr., speaker in field. Author chpts. to books; assoc. editor: Jour. Am. Soc. Nephrology, Clin. Sci.; contbr. articles to profl. jours. First Broderip scholar, 1971, Harold Boldero scholar, 1971, James McIntosh scholar, 1971, The Berkeley fellow Gonville and Caius Coll., 1976; recipient Leopold Hudson prize, 1971, The William Henry Rean prize, 1971, Disting. Rsch. Jerome W. Conn award, 1984. Fellow Royal Coll. Physicians (U.K.); mem. Am. Assn. Pathologists, Am. Assn. Immunologists, Am. Soc. Nephrology, Fedn. Clin. Rsch., Am. Soc. Clin. Investigation, Ctrl. Soc. Am. Fedn. Clin. Rsch., Assn. Am. Physicians. Office: U Mich Nephrology Div 3914 Taubman Ctr Ann Arbor MI 48109

WIGGINTON, ADAM, marketing professional; BSc in Zoology, U. Aberdeen; MBA in Fin., City U. With Unilever; prin. assoc. mgmt. consultancy divsn. Coopers & Lybrand; v.p. strategic planning Reed Travel Group, 1994-98, sr. v.p. of bus. devel. and circulation mktg., 1998—. Office: OAG Worldwide 2000 Clearwater Dr Oak Brook IL 60523-1955

WIGGINTON, EUGENE H. retired publishing executive; b. Louisville, Mar. 4, 1935; m. Shirley Walter; children: Denise Wigginton Hamilton, Tressa Wigginton Treadway. BA, Cin. Christian Coll.; LLD (hon.), Milligan Coll. Sr. min. South Jefferson Christian Ch., Louisville, 1957-60; dir. pub. rels. Cin. Christian Coll., 1960-63; sr. min. Westside Christian Ch., Atlanta, 1963-71; exec. v.p. Milligan Coll. (Tenn.), 1971-82; v.p., pub., pres., CEO, Standard Pub., Cin., 1982-2000; ret., 2000. Bd. dirs. Evang. Christian Pubs. Assn. Trustee Milligan Coll., 1983—. Recipient Citizenship award DAR and Am. Legion, I Dare You award Danforth Found., Fide et Amore award Milligan Coll. Home: 612 Douglas Dr Johnson City TN 37604-1919 Office: Standard Pub Co 8121 Hamilton Ave Cincinnati OH 45231-2396

WIGHT, DARLENE, retired speech educator, emerita educator; b. Andover, Kans., Jan. 5, 1926; d. Everett John and Claudia (Jennings) Van Biber; m. Lester Delin, Jan. 21, 1950; children: Lester Delin II, Claudia Leigh. AA, Graceland Coll., 1945; BA, U. Kans., 1948, MA, 1952. Permanent profl. cert., Iowa; life tchr.'s cert., Mo. Instr. U. Kans., Lawrence, 1949-50; instr. overseas program U. Md., Munich, 1954; speech pathologist Independence (Mo.) Pub. Sch. Dist., 1958-61; assoc. prof. Graceland Coll., Lamoni, Iowa, 1961-87, prof. emeritus. Cons. Quad-County Sch. Dist., Leon, Iowa, 1966-67, Mt. Ayr (Iowa) Cmty. Sch. Dist., 1967-70; cons. Head Start program SCIAP, Leon, 1972-75, MATURA, Bedford, Iowa, 1973-75. Co-author: Speech Communication Handbook, 1979. Mem. Common Cause, Friends of Art, Nelson-Atkins Mus. Art, U.S. English, Inc., Habitat for Humanity, Nat. Mus. Women in Arts, Am. Craft Coun. Recipient Award of Merit U. Kans., 1982, Award of Distinction U. Kans., 1947-48. Mem. AAUW, Am. Speech, Lang. and Hearing Assn. (speech pathology clin. competency), Coun. Exceptional Children, Archaeol. Inst. Am. Democrat. Mem. Community Of Christ Ch. Avocations: weaving/fibers, traveling, gardening, cooking. Office: Graceland Coll Speech Dept Lamoni IA 50140 E-mail: darlenewight@yahoo.com.

WIGHTMAN, ALEC, lawyer; b. Cleve., Jan. 23, 1951; s. John and Betty Jane (Follis) W.; m. Kathleen A. Little, June 19, 1976; children: Nora, Emily. BA, Duke U., 1972; JD, Ohio State U., 1975. Bar: Ohio 1975, U.S. Tax Ct. 1982, U.S. Ct. Appeals (6th cir.) 1983. Assoc. Krupman, Fromson & Henson, Columbus, Ohio, 1975-77; ptnr. Krupman, Fromson, Bownas & Wightman, 1978-82; assoc. Baker & Hostetler, 1982-83, ptnr., 1984—. Bd. trustees The Arthur G. James Cancer Hosp., Richard J. Solove Rsch. Inst. Mem. ABA, Ohio Bar Assn., Columbus Bar Assn., Ohio Oil and Gas Assn. Avocation: tennis. Office: Baker & Hostetler 65 E State St Ste 2100 Columbus OH 43215-4260

WIKARSKI, NANCY SUSAN, information technology consultant; b. Chgo., Jan. 26, 1954; d. Walter Alexander and Emily Regina (Wejnerowski) W.; m. Michael F. Maciekowich, Dec. 5, 1976 (div. Feb. 1985). BA, Loyola U., Chgo., 1976, MA, 1978; PhD, U. Chgo., 1990. Paralegal Winston & Strawn, Chgo., 1978-79; real estate analyst Continental Bank, 1979-84, systems analyst, 1984-88, ops. officer, 1988-89, automation cons., 1989-92; systems mgr. PNC Mortgage Co. of Am., Vernon Hills, Ill., 1992-94; ind. cons., 1994—. Book reviewer Murder Past Tense, 2000—. Author: German Expressionist Film, 1990, The Fall of White City, 2002. Fellow U. Chgo., 1987-90. Mem. Mystery Writers Am., Sisters in Crime (v.p. Mpls. chpt.), Mensa. Avocation: gardening.

WIKENHAUSER, CHARLES, zoological park administrator; BS in Zoology, U. Ill., 1971. Dir. Glenn Oak Zoo, Peoria, Ill., 1973-81, John Ball Zoo, Grand Rapids, Mich., 1981-85, Pitts. Zoo, 1986-90, Milw. County Zool. Gardens, 1990—. Office: Milw County Zool Gardens 10001 W Bluemound Rd Milwaukee WI 53226-4346

WIKMAN, MICHAEL RAYMOND, advertising executive; b. Mpls., Dec. 28, 1950; s. Charles Pierce and Jeanne Elizabeth W.; m. Carrie Brandt, Feb. 7, 1981; children: Caroline Celeste, Charles Michael. B in Elected Studies, U. Minn., 1973. Analyst, supr. media services Cambell-Mithun Advt., Mpls., 1973-77, account mgr., 1977-80; pres. MWA Direct, 1980—. Mem. Direct Mktg. Assn. (Echo award 1987), Midwest Direct Mktg. Assn. (Art, Response and Copy award 1987). Avocations: art collecting, downhill skiing, tennis, sailing. Home: 6929 Mark Terrace Cir Minneapolis MN 55439-1622 Office: MWA Direct 6465 Wayzata Blvd Ste 330 Saint Louis Park MN 55426-1789

WILBUR, KATHLEEN, state agency administrator; m. Tom Wilbur; children: Thomas, William, Samuel, Raymond. BA, Mich. State U. Chief staff State Senator William Sederburg, Lansing, 1983-90; dir. Mich. Dept. Licensing, Regulation, 1991, Mich. Dept. Occupational Profl. Regulation, Lansing, 1991-95; deputy dir. Mich. Dept. Commerce, 1991-95, acting dir., 1995-96, dir., 1996, Mich. Dept. Consumer Industry Svcs., Lansing, 1996—. Chmn. MERRA Bd. Trustees, 1996—; mem. Mich. Investment Advisory Com, 1996—; bd. dirs. Mich. State Housing Authority, Mich. Municipal Bond Authority, Mich. State Fair, Women's Caring Program, Mich. Festival. Mem. Mich. State U. Alumni Assn., East Lansing Area Zonta Club. Office: Michigan Dept Consumer & Industry Services PO Box 30004 Lansing MI 48909-7504

WILBUR, RICHARD SLOAN, physician, executive; b. Boston, Apr. 8, 1924; s. Blake Colburn and Mary Caldwell (Sloan) Wilbur; m. Betty Lou Fannin, Jan. 20, 1951; children: Andrew, Peter, Thomas. BA, Stanford U., 1943, MD, 1946; JD, John Marshall , 1990. Intern San Francisco County Hosp., 1946—47; resident Stanford Hosp., 1949—51, U. Pa. Hosp., 1951—52; postgrad. tng. U. Mich. Hosp., 1957, Karolinska Sjukhuset, Stockholm, 1960; staff Palo Alto (Calif.) Med. Clinic, 1952—69; dep. exec. v.p. AMA, Chgo., 1969—71, 1973—74; asst. sec. for health and environment dept. def., 1971—73; sr. v.p. Baxter Labs., Inc., Deerfield, Ill., 1974—76; exec. v.p. Council Med. Splty. Socs., 1976—91, sec. accreditation coun. for continuing med. edn., 1979—91; assoc. prof. medicine Georgetown U. Med. Sch., 1971—77, Stanford Med. Sch., 1952—69; pres. Nat. Resident Matching Plan, 1991—92. Chmn. bd., CEO Inst. for Clin. Info., 1994—99; sr. v.p. healthcare Buckeye Corp. Pte, Ltd., Singapore, 1997—2000; CEO Medic Alert, 1992—94; pres. Am. Bd. Med. Mgmt., 1992; mem. Am. Bd. Electrodiagnostic Medicine, 1993—98; chmn. med. adv. bd. Med. City, Bangalore, India, 1997—2000; bd. vis. Drew U. Postgrad. Med. Sch. Contbr. articles to profl. jours. Bd. govs. ARC; chmn. Mid-Am. Blood Svcs. Bd., Lifesource Blood Bank, 1996—98; Vice-chmn. Rep. Cen. Com. Santa Clara County, Calif., 1966—89; bd. dirs. Nat. Adv. Cancer Coun., Nat. Health Coun., 1993—95; chmn. bd. dirs. Medic Alert Found.; chmn. bd. Calif. Med. Assn., 1968—69, Calif. Blue Shield, 1966—68, Am. Medico-Legal Found., 1987—; pres. Royal Soc. Medicine Found., 1998—. With USNR, 1942—49. Recipient Disting. Svc. medal, Dept. Def., 1973, Scroll of merit, Nat. Med. Assn., 1971. Fellow: ACP, Am. Coll. Physician Execs. (bd. regents 1985—89, pres.-elect 1987, pres. 1988—89), Am. Coll. Legal Medicine (bd. dirs.), Internat. Coll. Dentistry (hon.); mem.: Am. Soc. Internal Medicine, Am. Gastroent. Assn., Santa Clara County Med. Soc. (hon.), Lake County Med. Soc., Ill. Med. Assn., Inst. Medicine, Union League Phila., Cedars Club, Pacific Interurban Clin. Club, Alpha Omega Alpha, Phi Beta Kappa. Home: 985 Hawthorne Pl Lake Forest IL 60045-2217 Office: APT Management Inc 207 E Westminster Rd # 201 Lake Forest IL 60045-1881 E-mail: aptmgmnt@aol.com.

WILCOX, JON P. state supreme court justice; b. Berlin, Sept. 5, 1936; m. Jane Ann; children: Jeffrey, Jennifer. AB in Polit. Sci., Ripon Coll., 1958; JD, U. Wis., 1965. Pvt. practice Steele, Smyth, Klos and Flynn, LaCrosse, Wis., 1965-66, Hacker and Wilcox, Wautoma, 1966-69, Wilcox, Rudolph, Kubasta & Rathjen, Wautoma, 1969-79; elected judge Waushara County Cir. Ct., 1979-92; apptd. justice Wis. Supreme Ct., 1992-97, elected justice 10-yr. term, 1997. Commr. Family Ct., Waushara County, 1977-79; Wis. state legislator, 1969-75; del. Wis. Conservation Congress, 1975-80; vice chmn., chmn. Wis. Sentencing Commn., 1984-92; chief judge 6th Jud. Dist., 1985-92; mem. State-Fed. Jud. Coun., 1992-99, Jud. Coun. Wis., 1993-98; mem. Prison Overcrowding Task Force, 1988-90; mem. numerous coms. Wis. Judiciary; mem. faculty Wis. Jud. Coll., 1986-97; chmn. Wis. Chief Judges Com., 1990-92; co-chair comm. on judiciary as co-equal br. of govt. Wis. State Bar, 1995-97; lectr. in field. Contbr. (with others): Wisconsin News Reporters Legal Handbook: Wisconsin Courts and Court Procedures, 1987. Bd. visitors U. Wis. Law Sch., 1970—76; with Wis. State Legis., 1969—75; del. wis. Conservation Congress, 1975—80. Lt. U.S. Army, 1959—61. Named Outstanding Jaycee Wautoma, 1974; recipient Disting. Alumni award Ripon Coll., 1993. Fellow Am. Bar Found.; mem. ABA (com. on continuing appellate edn.), Wis. Bar Assn. (bench bar com.), Wis. Law Found. (bd. dirs.), Tri-County Bar Assn., Dane County Bar Assn., Trout Unltd., Ruffed Grouse Soc., Ducks Unltd., Rotary, Phi Alpha Delta. Office: Supreme Court State Capitol PO Box 1688 Madison WI 53701-1688

WILCOX, MARK DEAN, lawyer; b. May 25, 1952; s. Fabian Joseph and Zeryle Lucille (Tase) W.; m. Catherine J. Wertjes, Mar. 12, 1983; children: Glenna Lynn, Joanna Tessie, Andrew Fabian Joseph. BBA, U. Notre Dame, 1973; JD, Northwestern U., 1976; CLU, Am. Coll., 1979, ChFC, 1992. Bar: Ill. 1976, U.S. Dist. Ct. (no. dist.) Ill. 1976, Trial Bar 1982, U.S. Ct. Appeals (7th cir.) 1987, U.S. Supreme Ct. 1989. Staff asst. Nat. Dist. Attys. Assn., Chgo., 1974-75; trial asst. Cook County States Atty., 1975; intern U.S. Atty. No. Dist. Ill., 1975-76; assoc. Lord, Bissell & Brook, 1976-85, ptnr., 1986—. Bd. mgrs. YMCA Met. Chgo., Internat. Spl. Olympics; trustee Trinity United Meth. Ch., No Bats Baseball Club. Mem. ABA (tort and ins. practice sect.), Am. Soc. CLU and ChFC, Chgo. Bar Assn. (ins. law com.), Nat. Assn. Ins. and Fin. Advisors, Def. Rsch. Inst., Soc. Fin. Svc. Profls., Trial Lawyers Club Chgo., Notre Dame Nat. Monogram Club, Union League Club, Chgo. Lions Rugby Football Club, Beta Gamma Sigma. Office: Lord Bissell & Brook 115 S La Salle St Ste 3200 Chicago IL 60603-3902

WILCOX, MICHAEL WING, lawyer; b. Buffalo, July 21, 1941; s. Paul Wing and Barbara Ann (Bauter) W.; m. Diane Rose Dell, June 18, 1966; children: Timothy, Katherine, Matthew. AB, UCLA, 1963; JD, Marquette U., 1966. Bar: Wis. 1966, U.S. Ct. Appeals (7th cir.) 1967. Law clk. to judge U.S. Ct. Appeals (7th cir.), Chgo., 1966-67; with Boardman, Suhr, Curry & Field, Madison, Wis., 1967-83; ptnr. Quarles & Brady, 1983-90, Stolper, Koritzinsky, Brewster & Neider, Madison, 1990-94, Stolper & Wilcox, Madison, 1995—. Lectr. in field. Author: (with others) Marital Property Law in Wisconsin, 1986. Fin. com. Meriter Found. Mem. ABA (chmn. marital property com. of real property probate and trust law sect. 1986-89), Wis. State Bar Assn. (chmn. taxation sect. 1983-84), Am. Coll. Trust and Estate Counsel, Rotary (pres. Madison West chpt. 1998-99), Blackhawk Country Club. Home: 6318 Keelson Dr Madison WI 53705-4367 Office: Stolper & Wilcox 6510 Grand Teton Plz Madison WI 53719-1029

WILCOXSON, ROY DELL, plant pathology educator and researcher; b. Columbia, Utah, Jan. 12, 1926; m. Iva Wall, 1949; children: Bonnie, Paul, Karren, John. BS, Utah State U., 1953; MS, U. Minn., 1955, PhD in Plant Pathlogy, 1957. Asst. prof., 1957-66; prof. plant pathology U. Minn., St. Paul, 1966-91, prof. emeritus, 1991—. Spl. staff mem. Rockefeller Found.; vis. prof. Indian Agrl. Rsch. Inst., New Delhi; dir. Morocco project U. Minn., 1983-87; adj. prof. Inst. Agronomy and Vet. Medicine, Hassan II, Rabat, Morocco, 1985—. Fellow Am. Phytopath Soc., Indian NAS, Indian Phytopath Soc., AAAS. Achievements include research in diseases of forage crops and cereal crops; cereal rust diseases. Office: 1669 County Road 8230 West Plains MO 65775-5766 Address: Dept Plant Path U Minn Saint Paul MN 55101

WILD, JOHN JULIAN, surgeon, director medical research institute; b. Sydenham, Kent, Eng., Aug. 11, 1914; came to U.S., 1946; s. Ovid Frederick and Ellen Louise (Cuttance) W.; m. Nancy Wallace, Nov. 14, 1949 (div. 1966); children: John O., Douglas J.; m. Valerie Claudia Grosenick, Aug. 9, 1968; 1 child, Ellen Louise. BA, U. Cambridge, Eng., 1936, MA, 1940, MD, 1942, PhD, 1971. Intern, resident U. Coll. Hosp., London, 1938-42; intern U. College Hosp., 1938-42; staff surgeon Miller Gen., St. Charles and North Middlesex Hosps., 1942-44; venereologist Royal Army Med. Corps, 1944-45; rsch. fellow, instr. depts. surgery and elec. engring., prin. investigator U. Minn., Mpls., 1946-51; dir. rsch. Medico.-Technol. Rsch. Dept. St. Barnabas Hosp., 1953-60; dir. Medico-Technol. Rsch. Unit Minn. Found., St. Paul, 1960-63; pvt. practice Mpls., 1966—; dir. Medico-Technol. Rsch. Inst. Mpls., St. Louis Park, Minn., 1965—. Lectr. in field of medical instruments, ultrasound. Contbr. articles to profl. jours. Recipient Japan prize in Medical Imaging, Sci. and Tech. Found. Japan, 1991, 1st Frank Annunzio award Christopher Columbus Fellowship Found., 1998, lifetime achievement award U. Minn. Med. Sch., 2000, Ian Donald Tech. Achievement aard ISUOG, 2000. Fellow Am. Inst. Ultrasound in Medicine (Pioneer award 1978); mem. AMA, World Fedn. Ultrasound in Medicine and Biology, Minn. State Med. Assn., Hennepin County Med. Soc., N.Am. Alvis Owners Club; hon. mem. Brit. Inst. Radiology, Japan Soc. of Ultrasound in Medicine. Achievements include patents in field; origination of ultrasonic medical imaging instruments and diagnostic techniques; origination of the field of pulse-echo ultrasonic diagnostic medicine. Avocations: automobile restoration, antique collecting and restoration. Home and Office: Medico-Technol Rsch Inst 4262 Alabama Ave S Minneapolis MN 55416-3105

WILD, ROBERT ANTHONY, university president; b. Chgo., Mar. 30, 1940; s. John Hopkins and Mary Dorothy (Colnon) W. BA in Latin, Loyola U. Chgo., 1962, MA in Classical Lang., 1967; STL, Jesuit Sch. Theology, Chgo., 1970; PhD in Study of Religion, Harvard U., 1977. Joined S.J., Roman Cath. Ch., 1957, ordained priest, 1970. From asst. to assoc. prof. Marquette U., Milw., 1975-83; vis. prof. Pont. Istituto Biblico, Rome, 1983-84; dir. Jesuit philosophate program Loyola U. Chgo., 1984-85, assoc. prof. theology, 1985-92; provincial superior Chgo. Province S.J., Chgo., 1985-91; pres. Weston Jesuit Sch. Theology, Cambridge, Mass., 1992-96, Marquette U., Milw., 1996—. Trustee Jesuit Sch. Theology, Berkeley, Calif., 1985-90, Weston Sch. Theology, Cambridge, Mass., 1985-96, Marquette U., 1990—, St. Louis U., 1994-2002, Nat. Assn. Ind. Colls. and Univs., 1996-, chmn., 2001-. Author: Water in the Cultic Worship of Isis and Sarapis, 1981; co-editor: Sentences of Sextus, 1981; contbr. articles to profl. jours. Mem. Soc. Bibl. Lit., Cath. Bibl. Soc. Office: Marquette Univ O'Hara Hall PO Box 1881 Milwaukee WI 53201-1881

WILDE, HAROLD RICHARD, college president; b. Wauwatosa, Wis., May 14, 1945; s. Harold Richard and Winifred (Wiley) W.; m. Benna Brecher, Feb. 4, 1970; children: Anna, Henry, Elizabeth Ty. BA, Amherst Coll., 1967; MA, PhD, Harvard U., Cambridge, Mass., 1973. Spl. asst. to gov. Office of Gov., State of Wis., Madison, 1972-75; ins. commr. Office of Commr. of Ins., State of Wis., 1975-79; spl. asst. to pres. U. Wis. System, 1979-81; v.p. for external affairs Beloit (Wis.) Coll., 1981-91; pres. North Ctrl. Coll., Naperville, Ill., 1991—. Bd. dirs. Ctr. for Pub. Representation, Inc., Madison, 1981-87, Beloit Community Found., 1988-91, Budget Funding Corp., 1993-99, Naperville Devel. Partnership, 1996—. Mem. Phi Beta Kappa. Home: 329 S Brainard St Naperville IL 60540-5401 Office: North Ctrl Coll 30 N Brainard St Naperville IL 60540-4607 E-mail: hrw@noctrl.edu.

WILDMAN, MAX EDWARD, lawyer, director; b. Terre Haute, Ind., Dec. 4, 1919; s. Roscoe Ellsworth and Lena (Shaw) W.; m. Joyce Lenore Smith, Sept. 25, 1948; children: Leslie, William. B.S., Butler U., 1941; J.D., U. Mich., 1947; M.B.A., U. Chgo., 1952. Bar: Ill., Ind. Ptnr. Kirkland & Ellis, Chgo., 1947-67; mng. ptnr. Wildman, Harrold, Allen & Dixon, 1967-89. Dir. Colt Industries, N.Y., Nat. Blvd. Bank, Ill. Contbr. articles to profl. jours. Trustee Butler U., Indpls., Lake Forest Hosp., Ill., Lake Bluff Library Bd., Ill.; chmn. Lake Bluff Zoning Bd. Served to lt. col. USAF, 1943-46; PTO Fellow Am. Coll. Trial Lawyers; mem. Soc. Trial Lawyers, Law Club, Legal Club, Trial Lawyers Club of Chgo. Presbyterian. Clubs: Anglers (Chgo.), Pere Marquette Rod and Gun (Baldwin, Mich.), Shoreacres (Lake Bluff), Univ. of Chgo. Office: Wildman Harrold Allen & Dixon 225 W Wacker Dr Chicago IL 60606-1224

WILEY, GREGORY ROBERT, publisher; b. Sept. 21, 1951; s. William Joseph and Terese (Kunz) W.; m. Sheila Francis, May 25, 1979; children: Kathleen, Mary Glennon. BA in Pers. Adminstrn., U. Kans., 1974. Dist. sales mgr. Reader's Digest, St. Loius, 1976-80, regional sales dir. Chgo., 1980-82; nat. sales mgr. regail divsn. Rand McNally & Co., 1982-83, nat. sales mgr. premium incentive divsn., 1983-86, nat. sales mgr. bookstore and mass market sales, 1986-88; book pub. The Sporting News, St. Louis, 1988-90; v.p. mktg. Marketmakers Internat., 1990-93, Sofsource Inc., St. Louis, 1993—. Mem. Nat. Premium Sales Execs., Promotional Mktg. Assn. Am. Roman Catholic. Avocations: private pilot, historic restoration, golf. Office: Sofsource Inc Ste 120 14615 Manchester Rd Saint Louis MO 63131 Home: Apt 1B 4309 Maryland Ave Saint Louis MO 63108-2748

WILHELM, DAVID C. investment company executive; m. Degee Dodds; children: Luke, Logan. BA, Ohio U., 1977; MPP, Harvard U., 1990. Rsch. dir. pub. employee dept. AFL-CIO, 1981-83; campaign mgr. Senator Paul Simon, 1984, Senator Joseph Biden for Pres., Iowa, 1985-87, Richard M. Daley for Mayor, Chgo., 1989, 91, Gov. Bill Clinton for Pres., 1991-92; chmn. Nat. Dem. Com., 1993-94; exec. dir. Citizens for Tax Justice, Washington, 1985-87; pres. The Strategy Group, Chgo., 1988-91; sr. mng. dir. investment banking Kemper Securities, Inc. (now First Union), 1995-97; pres. Wilhelm & Conlon, Inc., 1998—. Dir. Fed. Home Loan Bank Chgo.; bd. dirs. The Christian Century Mag.; mem. Chgo. Com. Chgo. Coun. Fgn. Rels.; vis. com. U. Chgo. Div. Sch. Recipient medal of Merit, Ohio U., 1994; fellow Inst. of Politics, Harvard U., 1996, Ctr. of Pub. Affairs, Ohio U., 1997—. Fellow Inst. Politics. Office: Wilhelm & Conlon Inc 70 E Lake St Ste 1700 Chicago IL 60601-5930

WILK, KENNY A. state legislator; Kans. state rep. Dist. 42, 1993—. Mgr. Hallmark Cards.

WILKE, LEROY, church administrator; Exec. dir. dist. and congl. svcs. Luth. Ch.-Mo. Synod, St. Louis. Office: 1333 S Kirkwood Rd Saint Louis MO 63122-7226

WILKES, KENNETH G. food products company executive; BA, Cleve. State U., 1980; MBA, DePaul U., 1987. V.p., sr. corp. banker First Nat. Bank of Chgo.; v.p., treas. Libbey Inc., Toledo, v.p., CFO, v.p., CFO, treas. Office: LIBBEY, INC 300 Madison Ave Toledo OH 43604

WILKIE, DENNIS F. electrical engineer; b. Detroit, Aug. 28, 1942; BS in Elec. Engring., MS in Elec. Engring., Wayne State U.; PhD, U. Ill.; MS in Mgmt., MIT. Various rsch., engring., planning, and mfg. positions Ford

Automotive Ops., 1968, gen. mfg. mgr. glass divsn., 1984-88, 1988-92, dir. electric vehicle segment NAAO, 1992-94, v.p. automotive strategy office, 1994, v.p. bus. devel. office, 1994-98; v.p. and dir. tech., automotive, component, computer and energy sector Motorola Inc., Schaumburg, Ill., 1998—. Alfred P. Sloan fellow MIT. Mem. NAE. Office: 1303 E Algonquin Rd Schaumburg IL 60196-4041

WILKINS, JEFFREY M. commputer company executive; Co-founder CompuServe, 1969; founder Discovery Sys., 1985-91; pres., CEO Metatec Corp., Dublin, 1991—, chmn. bd. dirs. Office: Metatec Internat Inc 7001 Metatec Blvd Dublin OH 43017-3219

WILKINS, JOHN WARREN, physics educator; b. Des Moines, Mar. 11, 1936; s. Carl Daniel and Ruth Elizabeth (Warren) W. BS in Engring, Northwestern U., 1959; MS, U. Ill., 1960, PhD, 1963; DTech (hon.), Chalmers Tekniska Hogskola, Göteborg, 1990. NSF fellow U. Cambridge, Eng., 1963-64; asst. prof. physics Cornell U., 1964-68, assoc. prof., 1968-74, prof., 1974-88; eminent scholar, prof. physics Ohio State U., 1988—. Vis. prof. H.C. Ørsted Inst., Copenhagen, 1968, Nordita, Copenhagen, 1972-73, 75-76, 79-81; cons. Los Alamos Nat. Lab., 1984—, Lawrence Livermore Nat. Lab., 1997—; adv. com. U. Chgo. Sci. and Tech., 1990—. Assoc. editor Physica Scripta, 1977-85, Phys. Rev. Letters, 1982-85, Rev. Modern Physics, 1983-95; mem. editorial bd. Phys. Rev. B, 1991-94; coord. Comments on Condensed Matter Physics, 1985-90. Sloan fellow, 1966; Guggenheim fellow, 1985. Fellow AAAS, Am. Phys. Soc. (publs. oversight com. 1995-97, chmn. 1995-96, councillor divsn. condensed matter physics 1989-93, exec. com. divsn. biol. physics 1973-77, vice-chair through past chair divsn. condensed matter physics 2001—); mem. European Phys. Soc. Office: Ohio State U Dept Physics 174 W 18th Ave Columbus OH 43210-1106

WILKINSON, RALPH RUSSELL, biochemistry educator, toxicologist; b. Portland, Oreg., Feb. 20, 1930; s. Tracy Chandler and Lavern (Russell) W.; m. Evelyn Marie Wickman, Aug. 5, 1956. BA, Reed Coll., 1953; PhD, U. Oreg., 1962; MBA, U. Mo., Kansas City, 1974. Rsch. chemist VA Hosp., Kansas City, Mo., 1973-74; sr. rsch. chemist Midwest Rsch. Inst., 1975-84; prof. Rockhurst Coll., 1985-86, Cleve. Chiropractic Coll., Kansas City, 1987-99, prof. emeritus, 1999—. Cons. in biochemistry, toxicology, environ. impact, tech. assessment, Kansas City, 1984—. Author: (book) Neurotoxins and Neurobiological Function, 1987; contbr. articles to profl. jours. Mem. Southtown Coun., Kansas City, Mo., 1989—, Spina Bifida Assn. Am., Kansas City, 1989—. Recipient NSF fellowship, 1959-60. Mem. Am. Chem. Soc., Sigma Xi. Avocations: travel, history, biography, music, antiques. Home: 7911 Charlotte St Kansas City MO 64131-2175

WILL, CLIFFORD MARTIN, physicist, educator; b. Hamilton, Ont., Can., Nov. 13, 1946; m. Leslie Saxe, June 26, 1970; children: Elizabeth, Rosalie. BS, McMaster U., Hamilton, 1968; PhD, Calif. Inst. Tech., 1971. Enrico Fermi fellow U. Chgo., 1972-74; asst. prof. physics Stanford U., Palo Alto, Calif., 1974-81; assoc. prof. physics Washington U., St. Louis, 1981-85, prof. physics, 1985—, chmn. dept. physics, 1991—2002. Chmn. com. on time transfer in satellite systems Air Force Studies Bd., Washington, 1984-86; chmn. sci. adv. com. NASA Gravity Probe B, 1998—. Assoc. editor Physical Rev. Letters, 1989-92, Physical Rev. D, 1999-2001; author: Theory and Experiment in Gravitational Physics, 1981, rev. edit., 1993, Was Einstein Right?, 1986, rev. edit., 1993. Alfred P. Sloan Found. fellow, 1975-79, J.S. Guggenheim Found. fellow, 1996-97, J.W. Fulbright fellow, 1996-97; recipient Sci. Writing award Am. Inst. Physics, 1987, Disting. Alumni award, McMaster U., 1996. Fellow Am. Phys. Soc. (exec. com. astrophysics divsn. 1988-90, vice chair, chair elect, chair topical group on gravitation 1997-2001), Am. Acad. Arts and Scis.; mem. Am. Astron. Soc., Am. Assn. Physics Tchrs. (Richtmyer Meml. Lectr. 1987), Internat. Soc. Gen. Relativity and Gravitation. Office: Washington U Dept Physics Campus Box 1105 1 Brookings Dr Saint Louis MO 63130-4899

WILL, ERIC JOHN, state senator; b. Omaha, Apr. 16, 1959; s. John Babcock and Patricia Elaine (Propst) W. BA in Polit. Sci., U. So. Calif., 1981; postgrad., Creighton U., 1993—. Legis. researcher Nebr. State Legis., Omaha, 1981-90, senator, 1991—. Chmn. enrollment and rev. com., 1991-93, rules com., 1993—; vice chmn. gen. affairs com., 1991—; mem. revenue and urban affairs com., 1991—. Mem. Phi Beta Kappa. Democrat. Presbyterian. Avocations: softball, bowling, volleyball. Home: 6029 Pinkney St Omaha NE 68104-3411 Office: Nebr State Capitol District 8 Lincoln NE 68509

WILL, KATHERINE H. former university administrator; Student, Carleton Coll., 1970-73; BA in English, Tufts U., 1974; AM in English, U. Ill., 1975, PhD in English, 1986. Instr. English Augustana Coll., Sioux Falls, S.D., 1977-86, asst. prof. English, 1986-90, faculty dir. new student seminar program, 1987-91, assoc. prof. English, 1990-96, assoc. acad. dean, 1991-96; provost, prof. English Kenyon Coll., Gambier, Ohio, 1996-99. Participant Mgmt. Devel. Seminar for Higher Edn. Adminstrs., Harvard U., summer 1992; cons. and presenter in field. NEH fellow Summer Seminar in Romanticism and Gender, UCLA, 1989. Office: Kenyon Coll Ransom Hall Gambier OH 43022-9623 E-mail: willk@kenyon.edu.

WILL, TREVOR JONATHAN, lawyer; b. Ashland, Wis., Aug. 11, 1953; s. William Taylor and Geraldine Sue (Trevor) W.; m. Margaret Ann Johnson, Aug. 28, 1976; children: Tyler William, Alexandra Marie, Jennifer Catherine. BA summa cum laude, Augustana Coll., 1975; JD cum laude, Harvard U., 1978. Bar: Wis. 1978, U.S. Dist. Ct. (ea. dist.) Wis. 1978, U.S. DIst. Ct. (we. dist.) Wis. 1980, U.S. Ct. Appeals (7th cir.) 1983, U.S. Supreme Ct. 1984, U.S. Dist. Ct. (ea. dist.) Mich. 1985. Assoc. Foley & Lardner, Milw., 1978-87, ptnr., 1987—. Adj. law prof. Marquette U. Law Sch., 1994—. Mem. ABA, State Bar Wis., Milw. Bar Assn., Def. Rsch. Inst. Home: 10011 N Waterleaf Dr Mequon WI 53092-6146 Office: Foley & Lardner 777 E Wisconsin Ave Ste 3800 Milwaukee WI 53202-5367 E-mail: twill@foleylaw.com., tajwill@aol.com.

WILLARD, GREGORY DALE, lawyer; b. Pittsfield, Ill., Feb. 8, 1954; s. Wesley Dale and Rosmary (Stark) W.; m. Ann Julia Grier, June 3, 1978; children: Michael, David, John. BA summa cum laude, Westminster Coll., Fulton, Mo., 1976; JD cum laude, U. Ill., 1979. Bar: Mo., U.S. Dist. Ct. (ea. dist.) Mo., U.S. Ct. Appeals (8th Cir.). Staff asst. to Pres. Exec. Office of the Pres. The White House, Washington, 1976-77; ptnr. Bryan Cave, St. Louis, 1979—. Co-chmn. bankruptcy com. Met. Bar Assn., St. Louis, 1983-84. Bd. Dirs. St. Louis Children's Hosp., 1985-89, Found. for Spl. Edn., 1990—, Congress Neurol. Surgeons, 1998—. Mem. Congress of Neurol. Surgeons, Noonday Club. Office: Bryan Cave 211 N Broadway Saint Louis MO 63102-2733

WILLE, KARIN L. lawyer; b. Northfield, Minn., Dec. 14, 1949; d. James Virginia Wille. BA summa cum laude, Macalester Coll., 1971; JD cum laude, U. Minn., 1974. Bar: Minn. 1974, U.S. Dist. Ct. Minn. 1974. Atty. Dresselhuis & Assoc., Mpls., 1974-75; assoc. Dorsey & Whitney, 1975-76; atty. Dayton-Hudson Corp., 1976-84; gen. counsel B. Dalton Booksellers, Edina, Minn., 1985-87; assoc. Briggs & Morgan, Mpls., 1987-88; shareholder Briggs and Briggs, 1988—. Co-chair Upper Midwest Employment Law Inst., 1983—. Named Leading Minn. Atty., Super Lawyer, Mpls.-St. Paul Mag., Twin Cities Bus. Monthly and Minn. Law and Politics; named one of Best Lawyers in Am. Mem. ABA, Minn. State Bar Assn. (labor and employment sect., corp. counsel sect., dir. 1989-91), Hennepin County Bar Assn. (labor and employment sect.), Minn. Women Lawyers, Phi Beta Kappa. Office: Briggs & Morgan 80 S 8th St Ste 2400 Minneapolis MN 55402-2157 E-mail: kwille@briggs.com.

WILLENBRINK, ROSE ANN, lawyer; b. Louisville, Apr. 20, 1950; d. J.L. Jr. and Mary Margaret (Williams) W.; m. William I. Cornett Jr. Student, U. Chgo., 1968-70; BA in Anthropology with highest honors, U. Louisville, 1973, JD, 1975. Bar: Ky. 1976, Ind. 1976, U.S. Dist. Ct. (we. dist.) Ky. 1976, Ohio 1999. Atty. Mapother & Mapother, Louisville, 1976-79; v.p., counsel Nat. City Bank, 1980-99, v.p., sr. atty. Cleve., 1999—. Mem. ABA, Ohio Bar Assn., Ky. Bar Assn., Louisville Bar Assn., Conf. on Consumer Fin. Law, Corp. House Counsel Assn., Phi Kappa Phi. Home: 359 Glengarry Dr Aurora OH 44202-8584 Office: Nat City Bank 1900 E 9th St Cleveland OH 44114-3484 E-mail: Rose.Ann.Willenbrink@nationalcity.com.

WILLETT, LANCE, orchestra executive; Exec. dir. Quad City Symphony Orch., Davenport, Iowa, 1982—. Office: Quad City Symphony Orch Assn PO Box 1144 Davenport IA 52805-1144

WILLHAM, RICHARD LEWIS, animal science educator; b. Hutchinson, Kans., May 4, 1932; s. Oliver S. and Susan E. (Hurt) W.; m. Esther B. Burkhart, June 1, 1954; children: Karen Nell, Oliver Lee. B.S., Okla. State U., 1954; M.S., Iowa State U., 1955, Ph.D., 1960. Asst. prof. Iowa State U., Ames, 1959-63, assoc. prof., 1966-71, prof. dept. animal sci., 1971-78, Disting. prof., 1978—; assoc. prof. Okla. State U., Stillwater, 1963-66. Cons. in field; tchr. livestock history; guest curator exhbn. Art About Livestock, 1990. Author: A Heritage of Leadership - The First 100 Years of Animal Science at Iowa State University, 1996. Recipient Svc. award Beef Improvement Fedn., 1974, Edn. and Rsch. award Am. Polled Herefore Assn., 1979, Rsch. award Nat. Cattlemen's Assn., 1986, 91, Disting. Alumnus award Okla. State U., 1978, Regents Faculty Excellence award Iowa State U., 1993; named to Hall of Fame Am. Hereford Assn., 1982, Am. Angus Assn., 1988. Fellow Am. Soc. Animal Sci. (animal breeding and genetics award 1978, industry service award 1986). Home: 2316 Hamilton Dr Ames IA 50014-8201 Office: Iowa State U Dept Animal Sci Ames IA 50011-0001 E-mail: rwillham@iastate.edu.

WILLHOIT, JIM, minister; b. Springfield, Ill., June 25, 1943; s. Richard and Virginia (Hampton) W.; m. Karen Huddleston, June 19, 1966; children: Amy Lynn, Todd Christopher. BA, Lincoln Christian Coll., 1969; MDiv., Lincoln Christian Sem., 1974, MA, 1975. Ordained to ministry Ch. of Christ, 1971. Minister Salisbury (Ill.) Christian Ch., 1964-72, Walnut Grove Christian Ch., Arcola, Ill., 1972-81; sr. minister First Ch. Christ, Highland, Ind., 1981—. Mem. site com. Project 300, Lincoln, Ill., 1979-81; bd. dirs. Onesimus Ministries, 1978-81; chaplain Lake County Police Dept., Crown Point, Ind., 1982-83, Glenwood (Ill.) Police Dept., 1986—, Highland (Ind.) Police Dept., 1996—; mem. Highland Leadership Coun., 1994—; pres. Highland Mins. Fellowship, 1996—; instr. N.W. Ind. Law Enforcement Acad., 1997--. Mem. sch. bd. Unit Dist. 306, Arcola, 1978-81; chaplain South Suburban (Ill.) Emergency Response Team, 1992—. Mem. Internat. Conf. Police Chaplains (cert. Basic Chaplain), Soc. Bibl. Lit., Am. Sci. Affiliation (assoc.), Chgo. Dist. Minister's Assn. (sec.-treas. 1982—), Chgo. Dist. Evangelistic Assn. (dir. 1981—). Home: 8936 Schneider Ave Highland IN 46322-1841 Office: First Ch Christ 2420 Lincoln St Highland IN 46322-1876 E-mail: jimwillhoit@yahoo.com.

WILLIAMS, ANDY, entertainer; b. Wall Lake, Iowa, Dec. 3, 1930; s. Jay Emerson and Florence (Finley) W.; m. Claudine Longet, Dec. 15, 1961 (div.); children: Noelle, Christian, Robert; m. Debbie Haas, May 3, 1991. Pres. Barnaby Records, Barnaby Prodns., Barnaby Sports; owner Moon River Enterprises; host Andy Williams San Diego Golf Open, 1969-89. Worked with 3 brothers as Williams Brothers Quartet, on radio stations in Des Moines, Chgo., Cin. and Los Angeles, 1938-47, Williams Brothers, (teamed with Kay Thompson); worked for night clubs, U.S. and Europe, 1947-52; regular performer: Steve Allen Tonight TV show, 1953-55; star: Andy Williams TV Show, 1962-71; night club and concert entertainer, rec. artist for Columbia Records; recordings include Moon River, Love Story, theme from The Godfather, Can't Get Used to Losing You, Days of Wine and Roses, Born Free, Hawaiian Wedding Song, Butterfly. Named Number One Male Vocalist Top Artist on Campus Poll, 1968; recipient 17 gold albums, 3 Emmy awards, 6 Grammy awards Office: Moon River Theatre 2500 W Highway 76 Branson MO 65616-2164

WILLIAMS, ANN CLAIRE, federal judge; b. 1949; m. David J. Stewart. BS, Wayne State U., 1970; MA, U. Mich., 1972; JD, U. Notre Dame, 1975. Law clk. to Hon. Robert A. Sprecher, 1975-76; asst. U.S. atty. U.S. Dist. Ct. (no. dist.) Ill., Chgo., 1976-85; faculty Nat. Inst. for Trial Advocacy, 1979—, also bd. dirs.; judge U.S. Dist. Ct. (no. dist.) Ill., 1985-99, U.S. Ct. Appeals (7th cir.), Chgo., 1999—. Chief Organized Crime Drug Enforcement Task Force for North Ctrl. Region, 1983-85; mem. ct. adminstrn. and case mgmt. com. Jud. Conf. U.S., 1990-97, chair, 1993-97. Sec. bd. trustees U. Notre Dame; founder Minority Legal Resources, Inc. Mem. FBA, Fed. Judges Assn., Ill. State Bar Assn., Ill. Jud. Coun., Cook County Bar Assn., Women's Bar Assn. Ill., Black Women's Lawyers Assn. Greater Chgo. Office: US Ct Appeals 7th Circuit 219 S Dearborn St Ste 2612 Chicago IL 60604-1803

WILLIAMS, ANNETTE POLLY, state legislator; b. Belzoni, Miss., Jan. 10, 1937; Student, Milw. Area Tech. Coll.; BS, U. Wis. Mem. Wis. State Assembly, Milw., 1980—. Attendee African-Am. Leadership summit, New Orleans; organizer Com. 21, 1985, Black Ribbon Commn. to study forced busing, Milw., 1989; panelist Nat. Conf. State Legislators, 1989; active parental sch. choice legislation; lectr. numerous colls. and univs. T.V. appearances include 60 Minutes, ABC World News, This Week with David Brinkley, McNeil Lehrer Report, The British Broadcasting Company, Great Lakes Watch on Washington, CBS This Morning, Both Sides with Rev. Jesse Jackson, CNN News; contbr. articles to profl. jours. Dem. adminstrv. and exec. com.; state chairperson Wis. Jesse Jackson for Pres. campaign; del. Nat. Dem. Conv., 1984, 88; mem. Nat. Dem. Platform Com., 1984; bd. dirs. Rainbow Coalition; founder, chmn. bd. dirs. Milw. Parental Assistance Ctr. Recipient Carrie Chapman Catt award as Nat. Women's Bus. Advocate of Yr., Outstanding Leadership award Dem. party Wis., Harambee Martin Luther King Jr. award for Outstanding Accomplishment and Svc. Am. Legis. Exchange Coun., 1991, Nat. Human Rights award Nat. Cath. Ednl. Assn., 1992, Seton award Career Youth Devel., 1992, Image award for Excellence in Community Svc. and Love of Youth Gamma Phi Delta, 1992, Community Leadership award Libertarian Party Wis., 1992, Liberty award, 1993, Martin Luther King Jr. Community Svc. award Lydell Comm., 1994; named Legislator of Yr. Freedom Mag., 1992; vis. fellow Auckland (New Zealand) Inst. Tech., 1993. Mem. Nat. Black Caucus State Legislators (bd. dirs.). Home: 3927 N 16th St Milwaukee WI 53206-2918 Office: Wis State Assembly State Capitol PO Box 8953 Madison WI 53708-8953

WILLIAMS, ARTHUR BENJAMIN, JR. bishop; b. Providence, June 25, 1935; m. Lynette Rhodes, 1985. AB, Brown U., 1957; MDiv, Gen. Theol. Sem., 1964; MA, U. Mich., 1974; DD, Gen. Theol. Sem., 1986. Clarence Horner fellow Grace Ch., Providence, 1964-65; asst. St. Mark, Riverside, R.I., 1965-67; sub-dean St. John Cathedral, Providence, 1967-68; assoc. & interim rector Grace Ch., Detroit, 1968-70; asst. to bishop Diocese of Mich., 1970-77; archdeacon Ohio Cleve., 1977-85; suffragan bishop Episcopal Diocese of Ohio, 1986—; v.p. House of Bishops, 1995—. Chair Com. on Justice, Peace and Integrity of Creation, 1995-97; Episcopal vis. Order of St. Benedict, 2000—. Chair editl. com. Lift Every Voice and Sing II, 1993. Office: Diocese of Ohio 2230 Euclid Ave Cleveland OH 44115-2499 E-mail: bishsuff@dohio.org.

WILLIAMS, BOBBY See EVERHART, ROBERT PHILLIP

WILLIAMS, BRUCE, chef; Chef de cuisine Mon Ami Gabi, Chgo.; mem. staff Sherman House; apprentice too chef Larry Mason Little Corporal; with Club on 39; saute chef Zorine's and Arnie's; chef Seal Blue, Turbo, Jackie's, Bistro Zinc, Escada; chef de cuisine Mon Ami Gabi, Chgo. Office: Mon Ami Gabi 2300 N Lincoln Park W Chicago IL 60614

WILLIAMS, CAMILLA, soprano, voice educator; b. Danville, Va. d. Booker and Fannie (Cary) W.; m. Charles T. Beavers, Aug. 28, 1950. BS, Va. State Coll., 1941; postgrad., U. Pa., 1942; studies with, Mme. Marian Szekely-Freschl, 1943-44, 1952, Berkowitz and Cesare Sodero, 1944-46, Rose Dirman, 1948-52, Sergius Kagen, 1958-62; MusD (hon.), Va. State U., 1986, D. (hon.), 1985. Prof. voice Bronx Coll., N.Y.C., 1970, Bklyn. Coll., 1970-73, Queens Coll., N.Y.C., 1974, Ind. U., Bloomington, 1977—, prof. emeritus voice. 1st black prof. voice Cen. Conservatory Music, Beijing, People's Republic China, 1983. Created role of Madame Butterfly as 1st black contract singer, N.Y.C. Ctr., 1946, 1st Aida, 1948; 1st N.Y. performance of Mozart's Idomeneo with Little Orch. Soc., 1950; 1st Viennese performance Menotti's Saint of Bleecker Street, 1955; 1st N.Y. performance of Handel's Orlando, 1971; other roles include Nedda in Pagliacci, Mimi in La Boheme, Marguerite in Faust; major tours include Alaska, 1950, London, 1954, Am. Festival in Belgium, 1955, tour of 14 African countries for U.S. Dept. State, 1958-59, Israel, 1959, concert for Crown Prince of Japan as guest of Gen. Eisenhower, 1960, tour of Formosa, Australia, New Zealand, Korea, Japan, Philippines, Laos, South Vietnam, 1971, Poland, 1974; appearances with orchs. including Royal Philharm., Vienna Symphony, Berlin Philharm., Chgo. Symphony, Phila. Orch., BBC Orch., Stuttgart Orch., many others; contract with RCA Victor as exclusive Victor Red Seal rec. artist, 1944—. Recipient Marian Anderson award (1st winner), 1943, 44, Newspaper Guild award as First Lady of Am. Opera, 1947, Va. State Coll. 75th anniv. cert. of merit, 1957, NYU Presdl. Citation, 1959, Gold medal Emperor of Ethiopia and Key to City of Taiwan during Pres. Johnson's Cultural Exchange Program, 1962, Art, Culture and Civic Guild award, 1962, Negro Musician's Assn. plaque, 1963, Harlem Opera and World Fellowship Soc. award, 1963; named Disting. Virginian Gov. of Va., 1972; inducted Danville (Va.) Mus. Fine Arts and History Hall of Fame, 1974; Camilla Williams Park designated in her honor, Danville, 1974; honored by Ind. U. Sch. Music Black Music Students' Orgn., 1979; named to Hon. Order Ky. Cols., 1979; honored by Phila. Pro Arte Soc., 1982; Disting. award of Ctr. for Leadership and Devel., 1983; Taylor-Williams student residence hall at Va. State U. named in Billy Taylor's and her honor, 1985, hon. by New York Philharmonic, 1998, hon. by Amistad Rsch. Ctr., Tulane Univ., for Outstanding Contbn. to the Arts, 1998. Mem. NAACP (hon. life), Internat. Platform Assn., Alpha Kappa Alpha. Office: Ind U Sch Music Bloomington IN 47401

WILLIAMS, CARL CHANSON, insurance company executive; b. Cin., Oct. 16, 1937; s. Charles J. and Alcie (Brazile) W.; m. Claire Bathé, May 26, 1985; 1 child, Michelle. A.S., U. Cin., 1965; B.S., SUNY-Brockport, 1974; M.B.A., U. Rochester, 1975. Mgr. fin. systems Xerox Corp., Rochester, N.Y., 1972-77; dir. info. mgmt. Am. Can Co., Greenwich, Conn., 1977-79, mng. dir. info. mgmt., 1979-80, mng. dir. ops. control, 1980-82; sr. v.p., dir. mgmt. info. systems DDB Needham Worldwide, N.Y.C., 1982-91; pres. The Intertechnology Group, Inc., 1990-91; v.p. infosystems and tech. Macmillan Pub. Co., 1991-93; gen. mgr. info. tech. Amoco Corp., Chgo., 1993-94, v.p. info. tech., 1994-97; sr. v.p., chief info. officer Principal Fin. Group, Des Moines, 1997—. Cons. Stamford (Conn.) Bd. Edn., 1981-82; lectr. U. Rochester, N.Y., 1975-77; adj. prof. Fordham U., 1991—. Exec. dir. Concerned Assn. Rochester, N.Y., 1971-75; bd. dirs. Stamford Cmty. Arts Coun., 1983-84; trustee Roosevelt U., 1995-97, U. Rochester, 1999—, Exec. Leadership Found., 2000—; mem. Exec. Leadership Coun. 1993—. Mem. Soc. Info. Mgmr. (exec. coun. 1980-83, pres. 1985, pres. coun. 1986—), Exec. Leadership Coun. (found. bd. trustees). Office: Principal Fin Group 711 High St Des Moines IA 50392-0002 E-mail: williams.carl@principal.com.

WILLIAMS, CLARENCE E. muncipal official; Student, Sinclair C.C., 1971-73, Ctrl. State U., 1973-74, Park Coll., 1986, Antioch U., 1987; BS, Wilberforce U., 1992. Housing inspector Dept. Housing & Neighborhood Affairs City of Dayton, Ohio, 1971-73, asst. coord. Neighborhood Devel. Program, 1973-75, acting supr. environ. svcs. Dept. Housing & Neighborhood, 1975-80, mgr. environ. svcs. Dept. Housing & Neighborhood Affairs, 1980, supt. waste collection Dept. Pub. Works, 1980-89, dir. Dept. Pub. Works, 1989-97, clk. of commns., 1997. Home: 1628 Kipling Dr Dayton OH 45406-4135 Office: City Commn Office 101 W 3d St City Hall Dayton OH 45402

WILLIAMS, CLAY RULE, lawyer; b. Milw., Sept. 25, 1935; s. George Laverne and Marguerite Mae (Rule) W.; m. Jeanne Lee Huber, Jan. 18, 1986; children: Gwynne, Amy, Daniel, Sarah. BA, Lawrence U., 1957; LLB, U. Mich., 1960. Bar: Wis. 1960, U.S. Dist. Ct. (ea. and we. dists.) Wis. 1964, U.S. Ct. Appeals (7th cir.) 1965, U.S. Ct. Mil. Appeals 1963, U.S. Supreme Ct. 1963. Assoc. Gibbs, Roper & Fifield, Milw., 1963-67; ptnr., shareholder Von Briesen, Purtell & Roper, S.C., 1967-99, of counsel, 1999—. Mem. Gov.'s Task Force Creation Bus. Ct., 1994-99; instr. profl. seminars. Author: Berry, Davis, Deguire and Williams, Wisconsin Business Corporation Law, 1992; contbr. articles to profl. jours. Active Shorewood (Wis.) Sch. Bd., 1976-79. Capt. USAF, Judge Adv. Corps., 1960-63. Fellow Wis. Bar Found.; mem. ABA (sect. antitrust law, corp. counseling com.), Wis. Bar Assn. (co-chmn. com. to revise corp. laws 1986-90, chmn. standing com. on bus. corp. law 1990-97, Pres.'s Award of Excellence 1990, 97), Milw. Bar Assn. (probate and real property sect., joint bench-bar com. Ct. Appeals, 1986-88, long-range planning com. 1987), 7th Cir. Bar Assn., Am. Law Inst., Assn. Bar City N.Y., Milw. Club, Univ. Club. Republican. Episcopalian. Avocations: hunting, fishing, skiing, reading. Office: von Briesen Purtell & Roper SC 735 N Water St Milwaukee WI 53202-4100 E-mail: cwilliam@vonbriesen.com.

WILLIAMS, DANIEL D. investment company executive; Sr. exec. v.p., CFO Everen Securities Inc., Chgo., until 1999. Office: Everen Securities Inc 77 W Wacker Dr Chicago IL 60601-1651

WILLIAMS, DAVID D. newspaper executive; With Chgo. Tribune, 1969—, advt. and mktg. positions, 1969-83, classified advt. dir., 1983-90; exec. v.p. Tribune Media Svcs., Chgo., 1990-91, pres., CEO, 1991—. Office: Tribune Media Svcs 435 N Michigan Ave Ste 1500 Chicago IL 60611-4012

WILLIAMS, DAVID PERRY, manufacturing company executive; b. Detroit, Nov. 16, 1934; s. M.S. Perry and Virginia (Hayes) W.; m. Jill Schneider, July 27, 1972; children: Tracy, Perry, David, William, Nell. B.A., Mich. State U., 1956, M.B.A., 1964. V.p. sales Automotive div. Kelsey Hayes Co., Romulus, Mich., 1958-71; v.p., mgr. automotive product line ITT, N.Y.C., 1971-76; v.p., dir. Budd Co., Troy, Mich., 1976-79, sr. v.p. ops., dir., 1979-80, sr. v.p., chief ops. officer, 1980-86, pres., chief operating officer, dir., 1986—. Dir. Standard Fed. Bank, Troy, Mich., 1990—, SPX Corp., Muskegon, Mich., 1992—, Budd Canada, Inc., Kitchener, Ont., 1981—, Thyssen Budd Automotive. Served to 1st lt. USAF, 1956-58. Mem. Soc. Automotive Engrs., Bloomfield Hills Country Club, Country Club of Detroit, Yondotega, PGA Nat. Club (Fla.), Tournament Players Club (Mich.), Question Club, Royal and Ancient Golf Club of St. Andrews (Scotland), Beta Gamma Sigma. Republican. Episcopalian. Home: 333 Lincoln Rd Grosse Pointe MI 48230-1604 Office: Budd Co PO Box 2601 Troy MI 48007-2601

WILLIAMS, DELETA, state legislator; BS, Ctrl. Mo. State U. Mem. Mo. Ho. of Reps. from 121st dist., 1993—. Mem. Citizens for Drug Free Environment, Inc. Mem. Bus. and Profl. Women, C. of C., Women's Dem. Club, Mo. Fedn. Dem. Women's Club. Address: 110 E Hale Lake Rd Warrensburg MO 64093-3015 Office: Mo Ho of Reps State Capitol Building Jefferson City MO 65101-1556

WILLIAMS, EDSON POE, retired automotive company executive; b. Mpls., July 31, 1923; s. Homer A. and Florence C. Williams; m. Irene Mae Streed, June 16, 1950; children: Thomas, Louise, Steven, Linnea, Elisa. B.S.M.E. cum laude, U. Minn., 1950. Spl. purpose machinery operator, 1946-50; mfg. mgr., project engr. Crestliner div. Bigelow Sanford Inc., 1950-53, v.p., mgr. mfg. and engring., 1953-58, pres., 1958-63; with Ford Motor Co., 1963-87, mgr. customer svc. div., 1973; gen. mgr. Ford Motor Co. (Ford Mexico), 1973-75; pres. Ford Motor Co. (Ford Mid-East & Africa), 1975-79, Ford Motor Co. (Ford Asia-Pacific Inc.), 1979-87; v.p. Ford Motor Co., 1979-82, v.p.-gen. mgr. N.Am. truck ops., 1982-86, v.p. Ford Diversified Products ops., 1986-87. Served with USAAF, 1942-46. Mem. Naples Yacht and Sailing Club. Home: 688 21st Ave S Naples FL 34102-7610

WILLIAMS, EDWARD JOSEPH, banker; b. Chgo., May 5, 1942; s. Joseph and Lillian (Watkins) W.; children: Elaine, Paul; m. Ana J. Ortiz, Apr. 20, 1996. BBA, Roosevelt U., 1973. Owner Mut. Home Delivery, Chgo., 1961-63; exec. v.p. Harris Trust and Savs. Bank, 1964—. Mem. Consumer Adv. Council, Washington, 1986—. Trustee, treas. Adler Planetarium, Chgo., 1982; trustee Roosevelt U., Chgo., Art Inst. of Chgo.; bd. dirs. Chapin-May Found., Chgo. Botanic Garden, Chgo. Capital Fund; trustee, treas. Chgo. Low Income Housing Trust Fund; dir. Leadership Coun. for Met. Open Communities; dir., former pres. Neighborhood Housing Svcs. of Chgo.; chmn. Provident Med. Ctr., Chgo., 1986; bd. dirs. Voices for Ill. Children, Chgo. Coun. on Urban Affairs; pres. Neighborhood Housing Svcs. Recipient Disting. Alumni award Clark Coll., Atlanta, 1985. Mem. Nat. Bankers Assn., Urban Bankers Forum (Pioneer award 1986, 97), Econ. Club. Chgo. Clubs: Metropolitan, Plaza (Chgo.). Office: Harris Trust & Savs Bank 111 W Monroe St Chicago IL 60603-4096

WILLIAMS, GEORGE HOWARD, lawyer, association executive; b. Hempstead, N.Y., Feb. 12, 1918; s. George R. and Marcella (Hogan) W.; m. Mary Celeste Madden, Nov. 23, 1946; children— Mary Beth Williams Barritt, Stephen, Kevin, Jeanne Marie. A.B., Hofstra Coll., 1939, LL.D. (hon.), 1969; J.D., N.Y. U., 1946, LL.D. (hon.), 1969; postgrad., NYU, 1959. Bar: N.Y. 1946. Adminstrv. asst. to dean NYU Law Sch., N.Y.C., 1946-48, instr. law, 1948-50, asst. prof., 1950-52, assoc. prof., 1952-55, prof., 1956-62, v.p. univ. devel., 1962-66, exec. v.p. planning and devel., 1966-68; pres. Am. U., Washington, 1968-75; exec. v.p., dir. Am. Judicature Soc., Chgo., 1976-87. Author: (with A.T. Vanderbilt and L.L. Pelletier) Report on Liberal Adult Education, 1955; (with K. Sampson) Handbook for Judges, 1984 Bd. dirs. Nat. Ctr. Edn. Politics, 1948-58, trustee, 1958-65; trustee Hofstra U., 1961-64; chmn. bd. trustees Trinity Coll., Vt., 1978-86; bd. dirs. Ctr. for Conflict Resolution, 1988—, Univ. Support Svcs. Served to lt. col., inf. AUS, World War II. Decorated Legion of Merit, Silver Star. Mem. Am. Polit. Sci. Assn., ABA Assn. Bar City N.Y., Alpha Kappa Delta, Phi Delta Phi. Clubs: N.Y. U. (N.Y.C.); Nat. Lawyers (Washington). Home: 1322 Judson Ave Evanston IL 60201-4720 Office: Am Judicature Soc 180 N Michigan Ave Ste 600 Chicago IL 60601-7454

WILLIAMS, GREG, professional basketball coach; m. Suzanne Williams. Asst. coach men's bassketball Rice U., Houston, 1970—75; asst. coach WBL Houston Angels, 1979—80; coach WBA Dallas Diamonds, 1981—82, WABA Dallas Diamonds, 1994; head coach women's basketball Colo. State U., 1990—97; asst. coach Detroit Shock, 1989—2000, head coach, 2000—. Named Coach of Yr., WBL, 1980—81, 1984, Southwest Conf., 1988, Western Athletic Conf., 1995—96. Office: Palace on Auburn Hills 2 Championship Dr Auburn Hills MI 48326

WILLIAMS, GREGORY HOWARD, dean, law educator; b. Muncie, Ind., Nov. 12, 1943; s. James Anthony Williams; m. Sara Catherine Whitney, Aug. 29, 1969; children: Natalia Dora, Zachary Benjamin, Anthony Bladimir, Carlos Gregory. BA, Ball State U., 1966; MA, U. Md., 1969; PhD, George Washington U., 1982, MPH, 1977, JD, 1971; LLD, Calif. Western Sch. Law, 1997; DHD, Ball State U., 1999, Coll. Wooster, 2000. Bar: Va. 1971, D.C. 1972, Ohio 1998. Dep. sheriff Delaware County, Muncie, Ind., 1963-66; tchr. Falls Ch. Public Sch., Va., 1966-70; legis. asst. U.S. Senate, Washington, 1971-73; dir. exptl. programs George Washington U., 1973-77; prof. law U. Iowa Coll. Law, Iowa City, 1977-93; assoc. v.p. Acad. Affairs U. Iowa, 1991-93; dean, prof. law Ohio State U., Columbus, 1993—. Author: Law and Politics of Police Discretion, 1984, Iowa Guide to Search and Seizure, 1986, Life on the Color Line: The True Story of a White Boy Who Discovered He Was Black, 1995. Mem. Iowa Adv. Commn. to U.S. Commn. on Civil Rights, Washington, 1978-86; chmn., mem. Iowa Law Enforcement Acad., Camp Dodge, 1979-85 Recipient Cert. of Appreciation Black Law Students Assn., 1984, GW Edn. Opportunity Program, 1977, Disting. Alumnus award George Washington U., Nat. Law Ctr., 1994, L.A. Times Book prize Current Interest Category, 1995, Disting. Alumnus award Ball State U., 1996. Mem. Assn. Am. Law Schs. (pres. exec. com. 1999). Office: Ohio State U Coll of Law 55 W 12th Ave Columbus OH 43210-1338

WILLIAMS, GREGORY KEITH, accountant; b. Elizabethtown, Ky., Mar. 20, 1958; s. James Marion and Shirley Catherine (Yates) W.; m. Diana Lynn McGuffin, May 26, 1979; 1 child, Kathryn May. BA in Pub. Mgmt., U. Ky., Lexington, 1985; BSBA, U. Louisville, 1987; MPA, Ball State U., 1996. Cert. mgmt. acct., info. sys. auditor, govt. fin. mgr. Supervisory staff acct. Fin. Acctg. Off., Fort Knox, Ky., 1983-85, internal auditor, 1985-89, sys. acct., 1989-93, Def. Fin. and Acctg. Svc. Indpls. Ctr., 1993-95, electronic commerce/data interchange coord., 1995-97; dep. project mgr. corp. database Def. Fin. and Acctg. Svc. Hdqrs., 1997-98, project mgr. corp. database, 1998-2000, program mgr. corp. database/warehouse, 2000—. Mem. Inst. Cert. Mgmt. Acct., Info. Sys. Audit and Control Assn., Am. Soc. Mil. Comptr., Assn. Govt. Acct., Phi Beta Kappa, Beta Gamma Sigma, Phi Kappa Phi. Home: 136 Lake Dr Greenwood IN 46142-9182 Office: Def Fin Acctg Svc 8899 E 56th St Indianapolis IN 46249-0002 Fax: 317-510-7250. E-mail: gkwdlw@msn.com.

WILLIAMS, HAROLD ROGER, economist, educator; b. Arcade, N.Y., Aug. 22, 1935; s. Harry Alfred and Gertrude Anna (Scharf) W.; m. Lucia Dorothy Preuschoff, Apr. 23, 1955; children: Theresa Lynn, Mark Roger. BA, Harpur Coll., SUNY, Binghamton, 1961; MA, Pa. State U., 1963; PhD, U. Nebr., 1966; postgrad., Harvard U., 1969-70. Instr., Pa. State U., 1962-63; Instr. U. Nebr., 1965-66; mem. faculty Kent (Ohio) State U., 1966—, prof. econs. and internat. bus., 1972—, chmn. dept., 1974-81, dir. Internat. Bus. Program, Grad. Sch. Mgmt., 1980-86, chmn. faculty senate, 1988-89; assoc. dean Grad. Sch. Mgmt., 1994-96; program dir. Kent State-Geneva Program, Geneva, 1996-97. Econ. cons. and adv. to numerous govt., bus. and internat. orgns. Author over 100 books and articles in field. Served with AUS, 1954-57. Grantee NSF. Mem. Am. Econ. Assn., Internat. Econs. Assn., Acad. Internat. Bus., Midwest Econ. Assn. (v.p. 1969-70), So. Econ. Assn., Phi Gamma Mu, Omicron Delta Epsilon, Beta Gamma Sigma, Phi Beta Delta. Home: 415 Suzanne Dr Kent OH 44240-1933 Office: Dept Econs Kent State U Kent OH 44242-0001 E-mail: Hwilliam@BSA3.Kent.edu.

WILLIAMS, J. BRYAN, lawyer; b. Detroit, July 23, 1947; s. Walter J. and Maureen June (Kay) Williams; m. Jane Elizabeth Eisele, Aug. 24, 1974; children: Kyle Joseph, Ryan Patrick. AB, U. Notre Dame, 1969; JD, U. Mich., 1972. Bar: Mich. 1972, U.S. Dist. Ct. (ea. dist.) Mich. 1972. Atty. Dickinson, Wright, PLLC (and predecessor firm), Detroit, 1972—, CEO Bloomfield Hills, 1991-2000. Pres. U.S. Law Firm Group, Inc., 2002. Mem.: ABA, Detroit Legal News Co. (bd. dirs.), Econ. Club Detroit 1996—2001, Detroit Bar Assn., Mich. Bar Assn., Detroit Regional C. of C. (bd. dirs., vice chmn. 1998—2002), Nat. Club Assn. (bd. dirs., sec. 1995—97, treas. 1997—98, v.p. 1998—2002, chmn. 2002—), Oakland Hills Country Club, Notre Dame Club Detroit (pres. 1984). Roman Catholic. Home: 993 Suffield Ave Birmingham MI 48009-1242 Office: Dickinson Wright PLLC 38525 Woodward Ave Ste 2000 Bloomfield Hills MI 48304 E-mail: jwilliams@dickinson-wright.com.

WILLIAMS, JACK MARVIN, research chemist; b. Delta, Colo., Sept. 26, 1938; s. John Davis and Ruth Emma (Gallup) W. B.S. with honors, Lewis and Clark Coll., 1960; M.S., Wash. State U., 1964, Ph.D., 1966. Postdoctoral fellow Argonne (Ill.), Nat. Lab., 1966-68, asst. chemist, 1968-70, assoc. chemist, 1970-72, chemist, 1972-77, sr. chemist, group leader, 1977—; vis. guest prof. U. Mo., Columbia, 1980, 81, 82, U. Copenhagen, 1980, 83, 85. Chair Gordon Rsch. Conf. (Inorganic Chemistry), 1980. Bd. editors: Inorganic Chemistry, 1979-96, assoc. editor, 1982-93. Crown-Zellerbach scholar, 1959-60; NDEA fellow, 1960-63; recipient Disting. Performance at Argonne Nat. Labs. award U. Chgo., 1987, Centennial Disting. Alumni award Wash. State U., 1990. Mem. AAAS, Am. Crystallographic Assn., Am. Chem. Soc. (treas. inorganic div. 1982-84), Am. Phys. Soc., Phi Beta Kappa. Office: Chemistry Div 9700 S Cass Ave Lemont IL 60439-4803

WILLIAMS, JACK RAYMOND, civil engineer; b. Barberton, Ohio, Mar. 14, 1923; s. Charles Baird and Mary Williams; m. Mary Berneice Jones, Mar. 5, 1947 (dec.); children: Jacqueline Rae, Drew Alan; m. Betty Ruth Scholfield, Nov. 9, 1990. Student, Colo. Sch. Mines, 1942043, Purdue U., 1944-45; BS, U. Colo., 1946. Gravity and seismograph engr. Carter Oil Co., Western U.S. and Venezuela, 1946-50; with Rock Island R.R., Chgo., 1950-80, structural designer, asst. to engr. bridges, asst. engr., 1980-82, engr. bridges system, 1963-80; sr. bridge engr. thomas K. Dyer Inc., 1980-82; v.p. Alfred Benesch & Co., 1982-96. Served with USMCR, 1943-45. Fellow ASCE (life); mem. Am. Concrete Inst., Am. Ry. Bridge and Bldg. Assn. (past pres.), Am. Ry. Engring. Assn. (hon. mem., past chmn. com. 8, Concrete and Foundations, past chmn. com. 10 concrete ties). Home: 293 Minocqua St Park Forest IL 60466-1942

WILLIAMS, JACKIE N. law educator, former prosecutor; b. Roosevelt, Okla., Oct. 4, 1943; s. David Coleman and Grace Pearl (Southard) W.; children: Douglas Kennedy, Eric Neil. BBA, Wichita State U., 1967; JD, Washburn U. Law Sch., 1971. Bar: Kans. 1971. Asst. atty. gen. Kans. Atty. Gen.'s Office, Topeka, 1971-73; asst. dist. atty. Wichita, 1973-77; adminstrv. asst. U.S. Congressman Dan Glickman, Washington, 1977; asst. U.S. atty. Wichita, 1977-96; U.S. atty. Kans., 1996—2001; sr. fellow, criminal justice prog School of Community Affairs, Wichita State Univ , Kans., 2001—. Office: Wichita State Univ School of Community Affairs 302 Lindquist Hall, Box 135 Wichita KS 67260 E-mail: jackie.williams@wichita.edu.

WILLIAMS, JAMES CASE, metallurgist; b. Salina, Kans., Dec. 7, 1938; s. Luther Owen and Clarice (Case) W.; m. Joanne Rufener, Sept. 17, 1960; children: Teresa A., Patrick J. B.S. in Metall. Engring, U. Wash., 1962, M.S., 1964, Ph.D., 1968. Rsch. engr., lead engr. Boeing Co., Seattle, 1961-67; tech. staff N.Am. Rockwell Corp., Thousand Oaks, Calif., 1968-74; mgr. interdivisional tech. program N.Am. Aerospace group, 1974, program devel. mgr. structural materials, 1974-75; prof. metallurgy, co-dir. Ctr. for Joining of Materials, Carnegie-Mellon U., Pitts., 1975-81; pres. Mellon Inst., 1981-83; dean Carnegie Inst. Tech., Carnegie-Mellon U., 1983-88; gen. mgr. materials dept. GE Aircraft Engines, 1988-99; Honda prof. Ohio State U., Columbus, 1999—, dean of engring., 2001—. Bd. dirs. com. on engring. and tech. systems NRC, 1996—; chmn. Nat. Materials Adv. Bd., 1988-95, materials and structures com. NASA Aero. Adv. Com. 1992-97; mem. NASA Propulsion Rsch. and Tech. Com., 1997-99; mem. Materials Sci. and Engring. Study, 1986-88; bd. govs. Inst. for Mechs. and Materials, U. Calif., San Diego, 1989-95; trustee Min. Math. Sci. and Engring., Cin., 1988-99; mem. sci. adv. bd. USAF, 1996-2001; mem. materials rsch. com. Def. Advanced Rsch. Projects Agy., 1981-2000; adv. com. Divsn. Engring. and Phys. Sci., NRC, 2001—. Co-editor: Scientific and Technological Aspects of Titanium and Titanium Alloys, 1976; contbr. numerous articles to tech. jours. Trustee Oreg. Grad. Inst. Sci. and Tech., 1988-94; cons. Cubmaster Boy Scouts Am., 1976-77. Recipient Ladd award Carnegie Inst. Tech.; Adams award Am. Welding Soc.; Boeing doctoral fellow. Fellow: TMS-AIME, Am. Soc. Metals (Disting. lectr. on materials and soc. 1997, Campbell lectr. 1999, Gold medal 1992); mem.: AIME (Leadership award 1993), NAE, ASM, Alpha Sigma Mu. Republican. Episcopalian. Home: 7711 Charlotte Hull Ct New Albany OH 43054-9680 Office: GE Aircraft Engines Gen Mgr Material Dept MD H85 Cincinnati OH 45215 E-mail: williams.1726@osu.edu.

WILLIAMS, JOHN ANDREW, physiology educator, consultant; b. Des Moines, Aug. 3, 1941; s. Harold Southall and Marjorie (Larsen) W.; m. Christa A. Smith, Dec. 26, 1965; children: Rachel Jo, Matthew Dallas. BA, Cen. Wash. State Coll., 1963; MD, PhD, U. Wash., 1968. Staff fellow NIH, Bethesda, Md., 1969-71; research fellow U. Cambridge, Eng., 1971-72; from asst. to prof. physiology U. Calif., San Francisco, 1973-87; prof. physiology, chair dept. physiology, prof. internal medicine U. Mich., Ann Arbor, 1987—. Mem. gen. medicine study sect. NIH, Bethesda, 1985-88, NIDDK, DDK-C study sect., 1991-95. Contbr. numerous articles to profl. jours.; editor Am. Jour. Physiology: Gastrointestinal Physiology, 1985-91; assoc. editor Jour. Clin. Investigation, 1997-2001. Trustee Friends Sch. in Detroit, 1992—2000. NIH grantee, 1973—. Mem. Am. Physiol. Soc. (Hoffman LaRoche prize 1985, mem. coun. 1996-99, pres.-elect 2002), Am. Soc. Cell Biology, Am. Soc. Clin. Investigation, Am. Gastroenterology Assn., Am. Pancreatic Assn. (pres. 1985-86). Democrat. Home: 1115 Woodlawn Ave Ann Arbor MI 48104-3956 Office: Dept Physiology Univ of Mich Med Sch Ann Arbor MI 48109 E-mail: jawillms@umich.edu.

WILLIAMS, JOHN TROY, librarian, educator; b. Oak Park, Ill., Mar. 11, 1924; s. Michael Daniel and Donna Marie (Shaffer) W.; B.A., Central Mich. U., 1949; M.A. in Libr. Sci., U. Mich., 1951, M.A., 1954; Ph.D., Mich. State U., 1973. Reference libr. U. Mich., Ann Arbor, 1955-59; instr. Bowling Green (Ohio) State U., 1959-60; reference librarian Mich. State U., East Lansing, 1960-62; 1st asst. reference dept. Flint (Mich.) Pub. Library, 1962-65; head reference svcs., Purdue U., West Lafayette, Ind., 1965-72; head pub. svcs. No. Ill. U., Dekalb, 1972-75; asst. dean, asst. univ. libr. Wright State U., Dayton, Ohio, 1975-80; vis. scholar U. Mich., Ann Arbor, 1980— ; cons. in field. Served with U.S. Army, 1943-46. Mich. State fellow, 1963-64; HEW fellow, 1971-72. Mem. Am. Libr. Assn., Spl. Libraries Assn., Am. Soc. for Info. Scis., Am. Sociol. Assn., AAUP, Coun. on Fgn. Rels. Contbr. articles to profl. jours. Home: PO Box 7531 Ann Arbor MI 48107-7531

WILLIAMS, LEO V., III, career military officer; Enlisted USMC, 1970, advanced through grades to gen.; staff platoon comdr. The Basic Sch.; exec. officer Battery 1 3d Battalion 11th Marines 1st Marine Divsn.; HQ commandant 1st Battalion 11th Marines; comdg. officer Battery F 2d Battalion 3d Marine Divsn.; asst. ops. officer 2d Battalion 12th Marines 3d Marine Divsn.; officer assignments officer Manpower Personnel Br. HQ Marine Corps; transferred to USMCR, 1978; HQ commandant 1st Battalion 24th Regiment 4th Marine Divsn.; asst. ops. officer Amphibious Bridgade Support Staff; detachment commanding officer Wing HQ Squadron 4th Marine Aircraft Wing; site exec. officer Wing Support Squadron 472 4th Marine Aircraft Wing. Policy bd. mem. Marine Corps Res. Policy Bd., 1993-96; Ford Divsn. future vehicle plans mgr. sport utility vehicles Ford Motor Co., Detroit. Mem. Marine Corps Res. Officers Assn. (pres. Bates chpt. 1993-95). Office: CGMC Res Support Command 1500 E 95th St Kansas City MO 64197-0001

WILLIAMS, LOUIS CLAIR, JR. public relations executive; b. Huntington, Ind., Nov. 7, 1940; s. Louis Clair and Marian Eileen (Bowers) W.; children— Terri Lynn, L. Bradley, Lisa C.; m. Mary Clare Moster. B.A., Eastern Mich. U., 1963. Copywriter, Rochester (N.Y.) Gas and Electric Co., 1963-65, editor RG&E News, 1965-66; employee info. specialist Gen. Ry. Signal Co., Rochester, 1966-67, supr. employment and employee rels., 1967-69; supr. pub. rels. Heublein, Inc., Hartford, Conn., 1969-70; dir. corp. communications Jewel Cos., Inc., Chgo., 1970-71; account exec. Ruder & Finn of Mid-Am., Chgo., 1971-73, v.p., 1973-76, sr. v.p., 1976-78; cons. Towers, Perrin, Forster & Crosby, Los Angeles, 1978-79; exec. v.p., gen. mgr. Harshe-Rotman & Druck, Inc., Chgo., 1979, pres. midwest region, 1979-80; v.p. Hill & Knowlton, Inc., Chgo., 1980-81, sr. v.p., 1981-83; pres. Savlin Williams Assocs., Evanston, Ill., 1983-85, L.C. Williams & Assocs., Chgo., 1985—. Recipient Clarion award Women in Communications, 1978, award of Excellence, Internat. Coun. Indsl. Editors, 1969, Bronze Oscar-of-Ind., Fin. World, 1974. Mem. Internat. Assn. Bus. Communicators (pres. 1979-80), Chgo. Assn. Bus. Communicators (pres.), Publicity Club Chgo., Pub. Rels. Soc. Am.

WILLIAMS, MARILYN, state legislator; Mem. Mo. Ho. of Reps. from 159th dist., 1993—. Democrat. Address: RR 1 Box 98 Dudley MO 63936-9719 Office: Mo Ho of Reps State Capitol Building Jefferson City MO 65101-1556

WILLIAMS, MARK H. marketing communications executive; b. Omaha, Apr. 30, 1959; s. Perry T. and Donna M. (Hodges) W. BA in Comm. and Bus., Loyola U., Chgo., 198l. Account mgmt. Bozell & Jacobs, 1981—87; v.p. Bozell, Jacobs, Kenyon & Eckhardt, 1987—93; sr. v.p., dir. Bozell, Chgo., 1993—2001; sr. v.p. Campbell Mithun, 2001—. Bd. dirs., exec. v.p. Internat. Food Strategies; speaker Harvard Graduate Sch. Bus., Northwestern U., U. Nebr., Creighton U., Loyola U. Chgo., U. Ill., numerous confs. and seminars. Contbr. articles to profl. jours. Mem. numerous trade assns. Home: 57 E Delaware Chicago IL 60611-1476 Office: Campbell Mithun 676 N Saint Clair Chicago IL 60611

WILLIAMS, MARTHA, consumer products company executive, entrepreneur; b. 1953; Founder, CEO, pres. StyleMaster, Chgo., 1991—. Office: StyleMaster 1330 W 43rd St Chicago IL 60609

WILLIAMS, MARTHA ETHELYN, information science educator; b. Chgo., Sept. 21, 1934; d. Harold Milton and Alice Rosemond (Fox) W. BA, Barat Coll., 1955; MA, Loyola U., 1957. With IIT Rsch.Inst., Chgo., 1957-72, mgr. info. scis., 1962-72, mgr. computer search ctr., 1968-72; adj. assoc. prof. sci. info. Ill. Inst. Tech., 1965-73, lectr. chemistry dept., 1968-70; rsch. prof. info. sci., coordinated sci. lab. Coll. Engring. U. Ill., Urbana, also dir. info. retrieval research lab., 1972—, prof. info. sci. grad. sch. of libr. info. sci., 1974—, affiliate, computer sci. dept., 1979—. Chair large data base conf. Nat. Acad. Sci./NRC, 1974, mem. ad hoc panel on info. storage and retrieval, 1977, numerical data adv. bd., 1979-82, computer sci. and tech. bd., nat. rsch. network rev. com., 1987-88, chair utility subcom., 1987-88, subcom. promoting access to sci. and tech. data for pub. interest; task force on sci. info. activities NSF, 1977; U.S. rep. review com. for project on broad system of ordering, UNESCO, Hague, Netherlands, 1974; vice-chair Gordon Rshc. Conf. on Sci. Info. Problems in Rsch., 1978, chair, 1980; mem. panel on intellectual property rights in age of electronics and info. U.S. Congress, Office of Tech. Assessment; program chmn. Nat. Online Meeting, 1980—; founder, pres. Info. Market Indicators, Inc., 1982—; cons. in field; invited lectr. Commn. European Communities, Industrial R&D adv. com., Brussels, 1992. Editor-in-chief: Computer-Readable Databases Directory and Data Sourcebook, 1976—89, founding editor: , 1989—92; editor: Ann. Rev. Info. Sci. and Tech., 1976—2001, Online Rev., 1979—92, Online and CD-ROM Rev., 1993—2000; mem. editl. adv. bd.: Database, 1978—88, mem. editl. bd.: Info. Processing and Mgmt., 1982—89, mem. editl. bd.: The Reference Libr., founding editor: Online Info. Rev., 2000—; contbr. Trustee Engirng. Info., Inc., 1974-87, bd. dirs., 1976-91, chmn. bd. dirs., 1982-91, v.p., 1978-79, pres., 1980-81; regent Nat. Libr. Medicine, 1978-82, chmn. bd. regents, 1981; mem. task force on sci. info. activities NSF, 1977-78; mem. nat. adv. com. ACCESS ERIC, 1989-91. Recipient best paper of year award H. W. Wilson Co., 1975; Travel grantee NSF, Luxembourg, 1972, Honolulu, 1973, Tokyo, 1973, Mexico City, 1975, Scotland, 1976 Fellow: AAAS (mem. nominating com. 1983, 1985), Nat. Fedn. Abstracting and Info. Svcs. (hon.), Inst. Info. Scis. (hon.); mem.: NAS (mem. joint com. with NRC on chem. info. 1971—73), Internat. Fedn. for Documentation (U.S. nat. com.), Assn. Sci. Info. Dissemination Ctrs. (v.p. 1971—73, pres. 1975—77), Assn. Computing Machinery (pub. bd. 1972—76), Am. Soc. Info. Sci. (councilor 1971—72, mem. publs. com. 1974—, pres. 1987—88, councilor 1987—89, contbg. editor bull. column 1974—78, award of merit 1984, Pioneer Info. Sci. award 1987, Watson Davis award 1995), Am. Chem. Soc. Home: 2134 Sandra Ln Monticello IL 61856-8036 Office: U Ill 1308 W Main St Urbana IL 61801-2307 E-mail: m-will13@uiuc.edu.

WILLIAMS, PHILIP COPELAIN, gynecologist, obstetrician; b. Vicksburg, Miss., Dec. 9, 1917; s. John Oliver and Eva (Copelain) W.; B.S. magna cum laude, Morehouse Coll., 1937; M.D., U. Ill., 1941; m. Constance Shielda Rhetta, May 29, 1943; children— Philip, Susan Carol, Paul Rhetta. Intern, Cook County Hosp., Chgo., 1942-43, resident in ob-gyn, 1946-48; resident in gynecology U. Ill., 1948-49; practice medicine specializing in ob-gyn, Chgo., 1949— ; mem. staff St. Joseph Hosp., Ill. Masonic Hosp., Cook County Hosp., McGaw Hosp.; clin. prof. Med. Sch. Northwestern U., Chgo. Bd. dirs. Am. Cancer Soc. Chgo. unit and Ill. div. Served with U.S. Army, 1943-45. Recipient Civic award Loyola U., 1970; Edwin S. Hamilton Interstate Teaching award, 1984; diplomate Am. Bd. Ob-Gyn, Fellow ACS, Internat. Coll. Surgeons; mem. AMA, Chgo., Ill. med. socs., AMA, Chgo. Gynecol. Soc. (treas. 1975-78, pres. 1980-81), Am. Fertility Soc., Inst. Medicine, N.Y. Acad. Scis., AAAS. Presbyn. Clubs: Barclay, Carlton, Plaza. Contbr. articles to profl. jours. E-mail: pwill2oo@aol.com. Home: 1040 N Lake Shore Dr Chicago IL 60611-1165 E-mail: PWill200@aol.omc.

WILLIAMS, RICHARD K. chief of police; b. Feb. 26, 1941; m. Deanna Williams; children: Darren, Tammi. BA of Sociology, Tenn. A&I State U., 1969; MBA, Am. U., 1976. Cpl., sgt. pers. and tng. divsn. Montgomery County Dept. Police, Rockville, Md., 1973-84, cpl., sgt., comty. rels. dir., 1975-80, lt. comty. rels./crime prevention comdr. comty. svcs., 1980-85, lt., dep. dist. comdr. Bethesda dist., 1985-88, capt., dist. comdr. Bethesda dist., 1988-92, cons. to chief of police, 1990, capt., dist. comdr. Germantown dist., 1991-92, maj., mgmt. svcs. bur. chief, 1992-93; chief of police Madison (Wis.) Police Dept., 1993—. Assoc. prof. criminal justice sect. Montgomery Coll., 1982. Bd. dirs. Comty. Action Coalition; mem.

Leadership Greater Madison. Mem. Downtown Rotary of Madison, Alpha Phi Alpha. Office: Madison Police Dept 211 S Carroll St Madison WI 53703-3303

WILLIAMS, RICHARD LUCAS, III, electronics company executive, lawyer; b. Evanston, Ill., Oct. 30, 1940; s. Richard Lucas Jr. and Ellen Gene (Munster) W.; m. Karen Louise Carmody, Nov. 11, 1967 AB, Princeton U., 1962; LLB, U. Va., 1965. Bar: Ill. 1965, D.C. 1968, U.S. Supreme Ct. 1968. Assoc. Winston & Strawn, Chgo., 1968-74, ptnr., 1974-79; sr. v.p., gen. counsel Gould Inc., Rolling Meadows, Ill., 1979-81, sr. v.p., adminstrn., gen. counsel, 1981-90, also bd. dir., 1985-88; ptnr. Smith Williams and Lodge, Chgo., 1990-95, Vedder, Price, Kaufman & Kammholz, Chgo., 1995—. Bd. dirs. GNB Batteries, Inc., 1984-86, ULINE Inc., Waukegon, Ill. Bd. dirs., 1990—, Internat. Tennis Hall of Fame, Newport, R.I., 1993-97; v.p. Chgo. Dist. Tennis Assn., 1968-70; vice chmn. Am. Cancer Soc., Chgo., 1984; bd. dirs., pres. Lake Shore Found. for Animals, Chgo., 1990-94. With JAGC USNR, 1965-68. Mem. ABA, Ill. Bar Assn., Chgo. Bar Assn., Execs. Club Chgo. (co-chmn. Western Europe internat. com. 1990-97), The Lawyers Club (Chgo., 1997—), Meadow Club (Rolling Meadows, gov. 1979-90, chmn. 1985-90), Club Internat. Home: 1200 N Lake Shore Dr Chicago IL 60610-2370 Office: Vedder Price 222 N La Salle St Ste 2500 Chicago IL 60601-1104

WILLIAMS, ROGER, academic administrator; Dir. Art Acad. Cin., 1977-94; dean Sch. Visual Arts, Savannah, Ga., 1994-96; acad. dean Ctr. for Creative Studies, Detroit, 1996—. Office: Ctr for Creative Studies 201 E Kirby St Detroit MI 48202-4048

WILLIAMS, SAM B. engineering executive; Chmn., CEO Williams Internat. Corp. Named to Nat. Aviation Hall of Fame, 1998; recipient Collier trophy, 1979, Wright Bros. Meml. trophy, 1988, Nat. medal of Technology, 1995. Mem.: NAE. Office: Williams Internat Corp PO Box 200 2280 W West Maple Rd Walled Lake MI 48390

WILLIAMS, STUART W. health facility administrator; b. June 11, 1943; BS, Allegheny Coll., 1954; MBA, U. Chgo., 1967. Adminstrv. resident Evanston (Ill.) Hosp., 1965-67; oper. svc. officer U.S. Naval Hosp., Quantico, Va., 1967-69; asst. dir. U. Mich. Hosp., 1969-74; adminstrv. dir. Children's Hosp., Columbus, Ohio, 1974-76, CEO, 1976—, Children's Hosp. Inc., Columbus, 1982—. Mem. Gov.'s Commn. on Ohio Health Care Costs. Mem. Am. Coll. Healthcare Execs., Am. Hosp. Assn., Assn. Am. Med. Colls., Nat. Assn. Childrens Hosps., Child Health Corp. Am., Ohio Hosp. Assn., Assn. Ohio Childrens Hosps.

WILLIAMS, THEODORE JOSEPH, engineering educator; b. Black Lick, Pa., Sept. 2, 1923; s. Theodore Finley and Mary Ellen (Shields) W.; m. Isabel Annette McAnulty, July 18, 1946; children: Theodore Joseph, Mary Margaret, Charles Augustus, Elizabeth Ann. B.S.Ch.E., Pa. State U., 1949, M.S.Ch.E., 1950, Ph.D., 1955; M.S. in Elec. Engring., Ohio State U., 1956. Research fellow Pa. State U., University Park, 1947-51; asst. prof. Air Force Inst. Tech., 1953-56; technologist Monsanto Co., 1956-57, sr. engring. supr., 1957-65; prof. engring. Purdue U., Lafayette, Ind., 1965-94, prof. emeritus, 1995—, dir. control and info. systems lab., 1965-66; dir. Purdue Lab. Applied Indsl. Control, 1966-94, dir. emeritus, 1995—; cons., 1964—. Vis. prof. Washington U., St. Louis, 1962-65. Author: Systems Engineering for the Process Industries, 1961, Automatic Control of Chemical and Petroleum Processes, 1961, Progress in Direct Digital Control, 1969, Interfaces with the Process Control Computer, 1971, Modeling and Control of Kraft Production Systems, 1975, Modelling, Estimation and Control of the Soaking Pit, 1983, The Use of Digital Computers in Process Control, 1983, Analysis and Design of Hierarchical Control Systems - With Special Reference to Steel Plant Operations, 1985, A Reference Model for Computer Integrated Manufacturing (CIM) - A Description from the Viewpoint of Industrial Automation, 1989, The Purdue Enterprise Reference Architecture, 1992; editor: Computer Applications in Shipping and Shipbuilding, 6 vols., 1973-79, Proceedings Advanced Control Confs., 19 vols., 1974-93, Architectures for Enterprise Integration, 1996. Served to 1st lt. USAAF, 1942-45; to capt. USAF, 1951-56. Decorated Air medal with 2 oak leaf clusters. Fellow AAAS, AIChE, Instrument Soc. Am. (hon. mem., pres. 1968-69, Albert F. Sperry gold medal 1990, Lifetime Achievement award 1995), Am. Inst. Chemists, Inst. Measurement and Control (London, Sr. Harold Hartley silver medal 1975), Indsl. Computing Soc.; mem. IEEE (sr.), Internat. Fedn. for Info. Processing (Silver Core award 1978), Soc. for Computer Simulation (hon.), Am. Chem. Soc., Am. Automatic Control Coun. (pres. 1965-67), Am. Fedn. Info. Processing Socs. (pres. 1976-78), Sigma Xi, Tau Beta Pi, Phi Kappa Phi, Phi Lambda Upsilon. Home: 208 Chippewa St West Lafayette IN 47906-2123 Office: Purdue U Potter Rsch Ctr Inst Interdisciplinary Engring Studies West Lafayette IN 47907-1293 E-mail: tjwil@ecn.purdue.edu.

WILLIAMS, WALTER JOSEPH, lawyer; b. Detroit, Oct. 5, 1918; s. Joseph Louis and Emma Geraldine (Hewitt) W.; m. Maureen June Kay, Jan. 15, 1944; 1 child, John Bryan. Student, Bowling Green State U., 1935-36; B.S.B.A., Ohio State U., 1940; J.D., LL.B., U. Detroit, 1942. Bar: Mich. bar 1942. Title atty. Abstract & Title Guaranty Co., 1946-47; corp. atty. Ford Motor Co., 1947-51, Studebaker-Packard Corp., 1951-56; asst. sec., house counsel Am. Motors Corp., Am. Motors Sales Corp., Am. Motors Pan-Am. Corp., Evart Products Co., Ltd., 1956-65, corp. sec. house counsel, 1965-72; asst. corp. sec., dir. Am. Motors (Can.) Ltd.; dir. Evart Products Co., 1959-72; dir., corporate sec., house counsel Jeep Corp., Jeep Sales Corp., Jeep Internat. Corp., 1968-72; partner Gilman and Williams, Southfield, Mich., 1972-74; atty. Detroit Edison Co., 1974-75; asst. sec., sr. staff atty. Burroughs Corp. (and subsidiaries), 1975-84; pvt. practice, pres. Walter J. Williams P.C., Bloomfield Hills, Mich., 1984—. Charter commr., city of Dearborn Heights, Mich., 1960-63; dir. Detroit Met. Indsl. Devel. Corp., 1962-72, also asst. sec. Served to capt. U.S. Army, 1942-46. Mem. ABA, Detroit Bar Assn. (chmn. corp. gen. counsel com. 1965-68), Fed. Bar Assn., State Bar Mich., Ohio State U. Alumni Assn. (pres. Detroit 1961-63), U. Detroit Law Alumni, Delta Theta Phi. Club: Oakland Hills Country. Home and Office: 3644 Darcy Dr Bloomfield Hills MI 48301-2125

WILLIAMS-ASHMAN, HOWARD GUY, biochemist, educator; b. London, Eng., Sept. 3, 1925; came to U.S., 1950, naturalized, 1962; s. Edward Harold and Violet Rosamund (Sturge) Williams-A.; m. Elisabeth Bächli, Jan. 25, 1959; children: Anne Clare, Christian, Charlotte, Geraldine. B.A., U. Cambridge, 1946; Ph.D., U. London, 1949. From asst. prof. to prof. biochemistry U. Chgo., 1953-64; prof. pharmacology and exptl. therapeutics, also prof. reproductive biology Johns Hopkins Sch. Medicine, 1964-69; prof. biochemistry Ben May Inst., U. Chgo., 1969—; Maurice Goldblatt prof., 1973-91, prof. emeritus, 1991. Contbr. numerous articles in field to publs. Recipient Research Career award USPHS, 1962-64 Fellow Am. Acad. Arts and Scis. (Amory prize 1975); mem. Am. Soc. Biochemistry and Molecular Biology. Home: 5421 S Cornell Ave Chicago IL 60615-5646 Office: U Chgo Ben May Inst Chicago IL 60637

WILLIAMSON, DONNA C. E. investment company executive; ScB in Applied Math., Brown U.; MS in Mgmt., MIT. Corp. v.p. Baxter Internat.; founding officer, corp. sr. v.p. Caremark Internat., Inc.; mng. dir., sr. v.p. ABN AMRO Pvt. Equity, Chgo., 1999—, also bd. dirs. Bd. dirs. PSS World Med., Inc., A.G. Edwards, Inc., Gulf South Med. Supply, Inc., Haemonetics Corp. Bd. d. Greater Chgo. chpt. ARC. Office: ABN AMRO Pvt Equity 208 S La Salle St Lbby 10 Chicago IL 60604-1004

WILLIAMSON, RICHARD SALISBURY, ambassador; b. Evanston, Ill., May 9, 1949; s. Donald G. and Marion (Salisbury) W.; m. Jane Thatcher, Aug. 25, 1973; children: Elizabeth Jean, Craig Salisbury, Richard Middleton. A.B. with honors, Princeton U., 1971; J.D., U. Va., 1974. Bar: Ill. bar 1974, D.C. bar 1975. Legis. counsel, adminstrv. asst. to Congressman Philip M. Crane of Ill., 1974-76; assoc. firm Winston & Strawn, Washington, 1977-80, ptnr., 1980; asst. to Pres. for intergovtl. affairs, Washington, also assoc. dir. President's Task Force on Regulatory Relief, 1981-83; U.S. ambassador Vienna, 1983-85; sr. v.p., corp. and internat. relations Beatrice Cos., Inc., Chgo., 1985-86; ptnr. Mayer, Brown & Platt, 1986—2001; asst. sec. of state internat. orgn. affairs U.S. Dept. State, Washington, 1988-89; alt. repr. to the U.N. for special polit. affairs U.S. Dept. State , 2002—. Rep. UN Orgns., Vienna, 1983-85; dep. ref. with rank of ambassador IAEA. Editor: Trade & Economic Growth, 1993, United States Foreign Policy and the United Nations System, 1996; co-editor: (with Paul Laxalt) A Changing America: Conservatives View the 80's From the United States Senate, 1980; author: Reagan's Federalism: His Efforts to Decentralize Government, 1990, The United Nations: A Place of Promise and of Mischief, 1991, Disorder in the New World, 1997. Chmn. Ill. Rep. Party, 1999—. Republican. Office: U.S. Mission to the U.N. 799 United Nations Plaza New York NY 10017-3505

WILLING, KATHERINE, former state legislator; m. Donald Willing. BS, Purdue U. Formerly tchr.; mem. from 39th dist. Ind. Ho. of Reps., 1992-97, mem. aged and aging, agr., edn., ways and means coms. Mem. Boone County Coun., 1988-92; bd. govs. Boone County Jr. Achievement; v.p. Boone County Leadership; bd. dirs., formerly treas. Witham Meml. Hosp. Found. Recipient Richard G. Lugar Excellence in Svc. award. Mem. Boone County Rep. Women's Club (pres.), Boone County and Carmel Clay County C. of C., Farm Bur., Zonta, Tri Kappa, Alpha Chi Omega. Home: 2309 Ulen Overlook Lebanon IN 46052-1146

WILLIS, BRUCE DONALD, judge; b. Mpls., Jan. 29, 1941; s. Donald Robert and Marie Evelyn (Edwards) W.; m. Elizabeth Ann Runsvold, July 17, 1971; children: Andrew John, Ellen Elizabeth. BA in English, Yale U., 1962; LLB, Harvard U., 1965. Bar: Minn., 1965, U.S. Dist. Ct. Minn. 1965, U.S. Ct. Fed. Claims 1989, U.S. Ct. Appeals (8th cir.) 1991, U.S. Supreme Ct. 1992. Assoc. Popham, Haik, Schnobrich & Kaufman, Ltd., Mpls., 1965-71, ptnr., 1971-95; judge Minn. Ct. Appeals, 1995—. Mem. jud. adv. bd. Law and Orgnl. Econs. Ctr., U. Kans., 1997—2001. Contbr. articles to profl. jours. Del. Rep. Nat. convs., 1976, 88; vice chmn. Ind.-Rep. Party Minn., 1979-81; mem. State Ethical Practices Bd., 1990-95, sec. 1990-91, vice chmn. 1991-92, chmn., 1992-93; mem. Minn. Commn. on Jud. Selection, 1991-94; mem. Minn. Bd. Jud. Stds., 1997—; mem. adv. com. on rules of civil appellate procedure Minn. Supreme Ct., 1997—. Named one of 1990's Lawyers of Yr., Minn. Jour. Law and Politics, 1991, one of Minn.'s Best Trial Lawyers, Minn. Lawyer, 1991. Mem.: ABA, Minn. Bar Assn. (professionalism com. 1998—). Mem. United Ch. of Christ. Home: 2940 Walnut Grove Ln N Plymouth MN 55447-1567 Office: Minn Jud Ctr 25 Constitution Ave Saint Paul MN 55155-1500 E-mail: bruce.willis@courts.state.mn.us.

WILLIS, DOUGLAS ALAN, lawyer; b. Taylorville, Ill., Feb. 22, 1963; s. Roy Willis and Sharon (Peel) Boaden. BA, Ill. Coll., 1985; JD, DePaul Coll. of Law, 1988. Bar: Ill. 1988, U.S. Dist. Ct. (no. dist.) Ill. 1988, U.S. Ct. Appeals (7th cir.) 1992, U.S. Supreme Ct. 2001. Intern BBC, Dallas, 1984, Ill. Dept. Registration/Edn., Springfield, 1983, Ill. State Senate Staff, Springfield, 1982, 84; rsch. asst. M.C. Bassiouni, Chgo., 1986-87; summer clk. Hon. Richard Mills, U.S. Dist. Judge, Springfield, 1987; asst. corp. sec. Profl. Svc. Industries, Inc., Lombard, Ill., 1991—, assoc. corp. counsel, 1989—. Intern U.S. House Minority Leader Robert Michel, Jacksonville, Ill., 1983. Named to Order of the Barrister, 1988, DePaul Exec. Moot Ct. Bd., 1988. Mem. Ill. State Bar Assn., Delta Theta Phi. Republican. Methodist. Home: 735 Blossom Ct Naperville IL 60540-1841 Office: Profl Svc Industries Inc 1901 S Meyers Rd Ste 400 Oakbrook Terrace IL 60181

WILLIS, ROBERT ADDISON, dentist; b. Wichita, Kans., Apr. 27, 1949; s. Everett Clayton and Mary Ann (Rohlin) W.; m. Janet Sue Jones, Jan. 21, 1968 (div. Dec. 1986); children: Gregory, Jeffrey; m. Sherryl Ann Galloway, Apr. 26, 1991; children: Wes Misak, Wendy Misak. Student, Okaloosa Walton Jr. Coll., Niceville, Fla., 1970-71, Wichita State U., 1972-74; DDS, U. Mo., 1978. Dentist, Wellington, Kans., 1978—. Cons. Sumner County Regional Hosp., 1980—, Lakeside Lodge Nursing Home, Wellington, 1980—. Bd. dirs. Kans. Babe Ruth Leagues, Inc., dist. commr., 1990—; bd. of elders Calvary Luth. Ch., 1989-94. With USAF, 1968-71. Mem. ADA, Acad. Gen. Dentistry, So. Dist. Dental Soc. (pres. 1980), Kans. Dental Assn. (coun. on peer rev. 1988-89), Wellington Dental Soc. (treas. 1981—), Optimist CLub, Wellington Area C. of C. (com. on indsl. devel. 1992), Am. Legion, Xi Psi Psi. Republican. Avocations: golf, photography, jogging, collecting music records, woodworking. Home: 620 Circle Dr Wellington KS 67152-3206 Office: 204 E Lincoln Ave Wellington KS 67152-3061 E-mail: rwillis@idir.net.

WILLMAN, VALLEE LOUIS, physician, surgery educator; b. Greenville, Ill., May 4, 1925; s. Philip L. and Marie A. (Dall) W.; m. Melba L. Carr, Feb. 2, 1952; children: Philip, Elizabeth, Susan, Stephen, Mark, Timothy, Jane, Vallee, Sarah. Student, U. Ill., 1942-43, 45-47; MD, St. Louis U., 1951. Diplomate Am. Bd. Surgery (sr. examiner 1976—), Am. Bd. Thoracic Surgery. Intern Phila. Gen. Hosp., 1951-52; intern, resident St. Louis U. Group Hosps., 1952-56; Ellen McBride fellow in surgery St. Louis U., 1956-57, sr. instr. surgery, 1957-58, asst. prof. surgery, 1958-61, assoc. prof., 1961-63, prof., 1963—, C. Rollins Hanlon prof. surgery, chmn. dept., 1969—, vice chmn. dept., 1967-69; attending physician St. Louis U. Hosp., 1969—; chief of surgery, 1969—; mem. staff Cardinal Glennon Children's Hosp., 1969—. Cons. St. Louis VA Hosp., 1969—. Mem. editorial bd. Jour. Thoracic and Cardiovascular Surgery, 1976-86, Archives of Surgery, 1977-87, Jour. Cardiovascular Surgery, 1982-87, N.Am. editor, 1987—; contbr. over 250 articles to profl. jours. With USN, 1943-45. Recipient Merit award St. Louis Med. Soc., 1973, Health Care Leadership award Hosp. Assn. Met. St. Louis, 1988. Fellow Am. Surg. Assn., Am. Assn. Thoracic Surgery, Cen. Surg. Assn. (pres., mem. ad hoc com. on coronary artery surgery 1971-72); mem. ACS (Disting. Svc. award 1987), Soc. for Vascular Surgery, Internat. Soc. for Cardiovascular Surgery (pres. N.Am. chpt. 1985-87), Phi Beta Kappa, Phi Eta Sigma, Alpha Omega Alpha. Roman Catholic. Office: St Louis U Hosp 3635 Vista Ave Saint Louis MO 63110-2539

WILLS, GARRY, journalist, educator; b. Atlanta, May 22, 1934; s. John and Mayno (Collins) W.; m. Natalie Cavallo, May 30, 1959; children: John, Garry, Lydia. BA, St. Louis U., 1957; MA, Xavier U., Cin., 1958, Yale U., 1959, PhD, 1961; LittD (hon.) , Coll. Holy Cross, 1982, Columbia Coll., 1982, Beloit Coll., 1988, Xavier U., 1993, St. Xavier U., 1993, Union Coll., 1993, Macalester Coll., 1995, Bates Coll., 1995, St. Ambrose, 1997, George Washington U., 1999, Spring Hill Coll., 2000, Siena Heights U., 2001, Gettysburg Coll., 2002. Fellow Center Hellenic Studies, 1961-62; assoc. prof. classics Johns Hopkins U., 1962-67, adj. prof., 1968-80; Henry R. Luce prof. Am. culture and public policy Northwestern U., 1980-88, adj. prof., 1988—; newspaper columnist Universal Press Syndicate, 1970—. Mem. adv. com. Internat. Ctr. Jefferson Studies; mem. Historians' adv. bd., Mt. Vernon. Author: Chesterton, 1961, Politics and Catholic Freedom, 1964, Roman Culture, 1966, Jack Ruby, 1967, Second Civil War, 1968, Nixon Agonistes, 1970, Bare Ruined Choirs, 1972, Inventing America, 1978, At Button's, 1979, Confessions of a Conservative, 1979, Explaining America, 1980, The Kennedy Imprisonment, 1982, Lead Time, 1983, Cincinnatus, 1984, Reagan's America, 1987, Under God, 1990, Lincoln at Gettysburg, 1992 (Pulitzer Prize for gen. non-fiction 1993), Certain Trumpets: The Call of Leaders, 1994, Witches and Jesuits: Shakespeare's Macbeth, 1994, John Wayne's America, 1997, St. Augustine, 1999, A Necessary Evil, 1999, Papal Sin, 2000, Venice, Lion City, 2001, Augustine's Childhood, 2001, James Madison, 2002, Why Am I a Catholic, 2002, Augustine's Memory, 2002. Recipient Pulitzer prize, 1993, Merle Curti award Orgn. Am. Historians, Nat. Book Critics Circle award (2), Wilbur Cross medal Yale U., Peabody award, NEH Presdl. Medal, 1998, John Hope Franklin award. Mem.: AAAL, Am. Antiquarian Soc., Am. Acad. Arts and Scis., Mass. Hist. Soc. Roman Catholic. Office: Northwestern U Dept History Evanston IL 60201

WILLS, ROBERT HAMILTON, retired newspaper executive; b. Colfax, Ill., June 21, 1926; s. Robert Orson and Ressie Mae (Hamilton) W.; m. Sherilyn Lou Nierstheimer, Jan. 16, 1949; children: Robert L., Michael H., Kendall J. B.S., M.S., Northwestern U., 1950. Reporter Duluth (Minn.) Herald & News-Tribune, 1950-51; reporter Milw. Jour., 1951-59, asst. city editor, 1959-62; city editor Milw. Sentinel, 1962-75, editor, 1975-91; exec. v.p. Jour./Sentinel, Inc., Milw., 1991-92, pres., 1992-93; vice-chmn., 1993; also bd. dirs. Jour./Sentinel, Inc., Milw.; pub. Milw. Jour. Sr. v.p., bd. dirs. Jour. Communications; pres. Wis. Freedom of Info. Council, 1979-86, charter mem., 1979; Pulitzer Prize juror, 1982, 83, 90. Mem. media-law rels. com. State Bar Wis., 1969-99; vice chmn. privacy coun. Wis. Pub. Svc. Commn., 1996-97; mem. Wis. Privacy Coun., 1994-95. Recipient Leadership award Women's Ct. and Civic Conf. Greater Milw., 1987; inducted into Journalism Hall of Achievement Medill Sch. Northwestern U., 1997, Wis. Newspaper Assn. Found. Hall of Fame, 2001. Mem. Wis. Newspaper Assn. (pres. 1985-86, Disting. Svc. award 1992), Wis. AP (pres. 1975-76, Dion Henderson award Svc. 1993), Am. Soc. Newspaper Editors, Internat. Press Inst., Milw. Press Club (Media Hall Fame 1993), Soc. Profl. Journalists (prs. Milw. chpt. 1979-80, nat. pres. 1986-87), Sigma Delta Chi Found. (bd. dirs. 1993-96, Wis. Newsman of Yr. 1973, Freedom of Info. award Milw. chpt. 1988). Home: 2064 Tiger Links Dr Henderson NV 89012-6111 E-mail: wills2064@juno.com.

WILLSIE, SANDRA K. physician, educator; BS in Med. Tech., Pittsburg (Kans.) State U., 1975; DO, U. Health Sci.-Coll. Osteo., Kansas City, Mo., 1983. Diplomate in internal medicine, pulmonary disease and critical care medicine Am. Bd. Internal Medicine. Rotating intern Univ. Hosp., Kansas City, Mo., 1983-84; resident in internal medicine U. Mo.-Kansas City Affiliated Hosps., 1984-87; fellow in pulmonary diseases Truman Med. Ctr.-West, Kansas City, Mo., 1987-89; instr. medicine U. Mo.-Kansas City Sch. Medicine, 1984-89; med. dir. pulmonary clinic Truman Med. Ctr., 1991-2000; asst. prof. medicine U. Mo. Kansas City Sch. Medicine, 1989-94, assoc. prof. medicine, 1994-99, asst. dean, 1997-2000, prof. medicine, 1999-2000, U. Health Scis., Kansas City, Mo., 2000—, vice dean, 2000—. Vice dean acad. affairs, adminstrn., med. affairs U. Health Scis., 2000—. Contbr. articles to profl. jours. Fellow ACP, Am. Coll. Chest Physicians; mem. Am. Thoracic Soc., Mo. Thoracic Soc., Soc. Critical Care Medicine, Met. Med. Assn., Am. Osteo. Assn. Office: U Health Scis 1750 Independence Ave Kansas City MO 64106-1453

WILLSON, MARY FRANCES, ecology researcher, educator; b. Madison, Wis., July 28, 1938; d. Gordon L. and Sarah (Loomans) W.; m. R.A. von Neumann, May 29, 1972 (dec.). B.A. with honors, Grinnell Coll., 1960; Ph.D., U. Wash., 1964. Asst. prof. U. Ill., Urbana, 1965-71, assoc. prof., 1971-76, prof. ecology, 1976-90; rsch. ecologist Forestry Scis. Lab., Juneau, Alaska, 1989-99; sci. dir. Great Lakes program Nature Conservancy, 1999-2000. Prin. rsch. scientist, affiliate prof. biology, Inst. Arctic Biology and Sch. Fisheries and Ocean Scis., U. Alaska, Fairbanks-Juneau. Author: Plant Reproductive Ecology, 1983, Vertebrate Natural History, 1984; co-author: Mate Choice in Plants, 1983. Fellow AAAS, Am. Ornithologists Union; mem. Soc. for Study Evolution, Am. Soc. Naturalists (hon. mem.), Ecol. Soc. Am., Brit. Ecol. Soc. E-mail: mwillson@gci.net.

WILMOT, THOMAS RAY, medical entomologist, educator; b. Great Falls, Mont., Sept. 9, 1953; s. Donald D. and Jeanne M. W.; m. Gail A. Ballard, June 26, 1976; children: Lacey A., Eric T. BS in Entomology, Mont. State U., 1975; MS in Entomology, Oreg. State U., 1978; MPH, UCLA, 1984, PhD in Epidemiology, 1986. Inspector Cacade County Pesticide Program, Great Falls, Mont., 1970-75; mgr. Yakima County Mosquito Control, Wash., 1978-80; dir., entomologist Midland County Mosquito Control, Sanford, Mich., 1984—. Adj. instr. Saginaw Valley State U., University Center, Mich., 1988—; vector control cons., Midland, Mich., 1988—. Contbr. articles to profl. jours. Mem. Local Emergency Plan Com., Midland, Mich., 1990—; spkr. Dow Corning Spkrs. Bur., Midland, 1992-96. Pub. Health traineeship USPHS, 1980-84; recipient Achievement award Nat. Assn. Counties, 1994. Mem. Am. Mosquito Control Assn. (mem. editl. bd. 1989-92), Entomol. Soc. Am., Soc. for Vector Ecology (regional dir. 1990-99), Mich. Mosquito Control Assn. (pres. 1989, Disting. Svc. award 1994), Phi Kappa Phi. Avocation: coaching youth athletics. Office: Midland County Mosquito Control 2180 N Meridian Rd Sanford MI 48657-9200 E-mail: wilmotg@mindnet.com.

WILMOUTH, ROBERT K. commodities executive; b. Worcester, Mass., Nov. 9, 1928; s. Alfred F. and Aileen E. (Kearney) W.; m. Ellen M. Boyle, Sept. 10, 1955; children: Robert J., John J., James P., Thomas G., Anne Marie. BA, Holy Cross Coll., 1949; MA, U. Notre Dame, 1950, LLD, 1984. Exec. v.p., dir. 1st Nat. Bank Chgo., 1972-75; pres., chief adminstrv. officer Crocker Nat. Bank, San Francisco, 1975-77; pres., chief exec. officer Chgo. Bd. Trade, 1977-82; chmn. LaSalle Nat. Bank, 1982-99. Pres., chief exec. officer Nat. Futures Assn.; chmn. consultative com. Internat. Orgn. Securities Commns. Life trustee U. Notre Dame; mem. adv. coun. Kellogg Grad. Sch. Mgmt., Northwestern U. Mem. Chgo. Club, Barrington Hill Country Club, Econ. Club. Office: Nat Futures Assn 200 W Madison St Ste 1600 Chicago IL 60606-3415

WILSON, AARON MARTIN, religious studies educator, college executive; b. Bazette, Tex., Sept. 30, 1926; s. John Albert and Myrtle (Hulsey) W.; m. Marthel Shoults, Jan. 31, 1947 (dec. Apr. 2001); children: Gloria Dallis, John Bert. BA, So. Bible Coll., 1963, DD (hon.), 1980; MA, Pitts. State U., 1972; PhD, Valley Christian U., 1980. Pastor various chs., 1947-58, Pentecostal Ch. of God, Houston, 1958-64, Modesto, Calif., 1985-88, nat. dir. Christian edn. Joplin, Mo., 1964-79, 88-93; pres. Evang. Christian Coll., Fresno, Calif., 1979-85; v.p. devel. Messenger Coll., Joplin, 1993-95; editor The Pentecostal Messenger, 1995-99, coordinating editor, 1999—. Treas. Evang. Curriculum Commn., 1988-93; prof. So. Bible Coll., Houston, 1962-64. Author: Basic Bible Truth, 1988, Studies on Stewardship, 1989, My Church Can Grow, 1996, Our Story, 2001. Republican. Home: 323 E 33rd St Joplin MO 64804-3809 Office: Messenger Publ House PO Box 850 Joplin MO 64802-0850 E-mail: aaronw@pcg.org.

WILSON, ANNE GAWTHROP, artist, educator; b. Detroit, Apr. 16, 1949; d. Gerald Shepard and Nancy Craighead (Gawthrop) Wilson; m. Michael Andreas Nagelbach. Student, U. Mich. Sch. of Art, 1967-69; BFA, Cranbrook Acad. Art, Bloomfield Hills, Mich., 1972; MFA, Calif. Coll. Arts and Crafts, 1976. Prof. Dept. Fiber & Materials Studies Sch. of the Art Inst., Chgo., 1979—. Panelist Nat. Endowment for Arts, Washington, 1986, Western States Arts Fedn./Nat. Endowment for Arts Regional Fellowships for Visual Artists, Santa Fe, 1995; co-curator Artemisia Gallery, Chgo., 1988; co-moderator Women's Caucus for Art, Chgo., 1992; panelist, workshop instr. Internat. Symposium '92, Toyama, Japan, 1992; panelist The Textile Mus., Washington, 1994; bd. trustees Haystack Sch., Deer Isle, Maine, 1990-95; lectr. Kansas City Art Inst., 1996, Australian Nat. U. Canberra Sch. Art, 1996, Textile Conservation Ctr./Courtauld Inst. Art, London, 1995, others; represented by Roy Boyd Gallery, Chgo., Revolution, Detroit and N.Y. One person shows include Chgo. Cultural Ctr., 1988, Halsey Gallery, Sch. Arts, Coll. Charleston, S.C., 1992, Madison (Wis.) Art Ctr., 1993-94, Roy Boyd Gallery, Chgo., 1994, 96, Ill. Wesleyan U., Sch. Art, Bloomington, 1995, Revolution, Detroit, 1998, Revolution, N.Y.C., 1998, Mus. for Textiles Contemporary Gallery, Toronto, Can., 1999, Mus. Contemporary Art, Chgo., 2000; exhibited in group shows Netherlands Textile Mus., 1989, Musee Cantonal des Beaux-Arts, Palais de Rumine, Lausanne, Switzerland, 1989, John Michael Kohler Arts Ctr., Sheboygan, Wis., 1992-93, 95, Mus. Contemporary Art, Chgo., 1996, 97, Ariz. State U. Art Mus., Tempe, 1997-98, Bowdoin Coll. Mus. Art, Brunswick, Maine, 1998, TBA Exhbn. Space, Chgo., 1999, Angel Row Gallery, Halifax, 1999-2000, Boulder (Colo.) Mus. Contemporary Art, 2000, Gallery 400 Sch. Art and Design Coll. Arch. and the Arts, U. Ill., Chgo., 2000, Asheville (N.C.) Mus. Art, 2000, Chgo. Cultural Ctr., 2000, Memphis Coll. Art, 2001, U. Calif. San Diego, La Jolla, 2001; represented in permanent collections Art Inst. Chgo., Met. Mus. Art, N.Y., Mus. of Contemporary Art, Chgo., Calif. Poly. State U., San Luis Obispo, Calif., M. H. De Young Meml. Mus., San Francisco, Art Inst. Chgo., Cranbrook Acad. Art Mus., Bloomfield Hills; contbr. articles and revs. to profl. jours. Recipient Louis Comfort Tiffany Found. award, 1989; Nat. Endowment for Arts curatorial fellow in decorative arts and mus. edn. Fine Arts Mus. San Francisco, 1978; Nat. Endowment for Arts Visual Artists Fellowship grantee, 1982, 88, Chgo. Artists Abroad grantee, 1988, 89, Ill. Arts Coun. Individual Artist grantee, 1983, 84, 87, 93, 99, Chgo. Artists Internat. Program grantee, 1996. Mem. Coll. Art Assn. (regional co-chair annual conf. 2001). Office: Sch of the Art Inst Fiber Dept 37 S Wabash Ave Chicago IL 60603-3002

WILSON, C. DANIEL, JR. library director; b. Middletown, Conn., Nov. 8, 1941; s. Clyde D. and Dorothy M. (Neal) W.; m. M. April Jackson, Apr. 1986; children: Christine, Cindy, Clyde, Ben. BA, Elmhurst Coll., 1967; MA, Dominican U., 1968; MPA, U. New Orleans, 1995. Trainee Chgo. Pub. Libr., 1967-68; instr. U. Ill., 1968-70; asst. dir. Perrot Meml. Libr., Greenwich, Conn., 1970-76; dir. Wilton Pub. Libr., Wilton, 1976-79; assoc. dir. Birmingham Pub. Libr., Birmingham, Ala., 1979-83; dir. Davenport (Iowa) Pub. Libr., 1983-85, New Orleans Pub. Libr., 1985-97, St. Louis County Libr., 1997—. With USMC, 1962-65. Mem. ALA, Internat. Assn. Met. Librs. (pres. 1998—), Mo. Libr. Assn., Am. Soc. Pub. Adminstrs., Rotary, Pi Gamma Mu. Episcopalian. E-mail: dwilson@slcl.lib.mo.us.

WILSON, CHARLES STEPHEN, cardiologist, educator; b. Geneva, June 14, 1938; s. Robert Butler and Naoma Luella (Norgren) Wilson; m. Linda Stern Walt, Aug. 21, 1960; children: Michael Scott, Amy Lynn, Cynthia Lee. BA cum laude, U. Nebr., 1960; MD, Northwestern U., 1964. Diplomate Am. Bd. Internal Medicine subsplty. bd. cardiovascular disease, Nat. Bd. Med. Examiners. Intern Fitzsimons Gen. Hosp., Denver, 1964-65; fellow in internal medicine and cardiology Mayo Grad. Sch. Medicine, Rochester, Minn., 1968-72; practice medicine specializing in cardiology Lincoln, Nebr., 1972—; attending staff Bryan Meml. Hosp., 1972—, chmn. cardiology, 1976-79; attending staff Lincoln Gen. Hosp., 1978—; clin. prof. medicine and cardiology U. Nebr. Med. Ctr., Omaha; med. dir. Lifescan Preventative Imaging, Lincoln, 2001—. Mem. Mayor's Coun. on Emergency Med. Svcs., Lincoln, 1974-78; founder, chmn. Nebr. State Hypertension Screening Program; med. dir. Lincoln Mobile Heart Team, 1977-80, Lincoln Cardiac Rehab. Program, 1978-79; co-founder, pres. Nebr. Heart Inst., 1987; co-founder Lincoln Cardiac Transplant Program, 1987. Contbr. articles to profl. jours.; editorl. cons. Chest, 1975-76; assoc. editor Nebr. Med. Jour., 1981-88. Trustee U. Nebr. Found., 1983—, chmn. Nebr. Coordinating Commn. for Postsecondary Edn., 1984-88; mem. bd. regents U. Nebr., 1991—, chmn. 1994, 2001; mem. Gov.'s Exec. Coun., 1983-87. Served as maj., M.C., USAR, 1963-68. Gen. Motors Nat. scholar, 1956-60, Nat. Found. Med. scholar, 1960-64, Mead Johnson scholar ACP, 1968-71. Fellow ACP, Am. Coll. Cardiology (bd. govs. 1990-93, pres. Nebr. affiliate 1992-93), Am. Coll. Chest Physicans, Am. Heart Assn. (dir. Nebr. affilate 1973-80, pres. 1976-77); mem. Mayo Cardiovascular Soc., Nebr. Cardiovascular Soc. (pres. 1989-90), Nebr. Coun. on Pub. Higher Edn. (steering com. 1991—), Lincoln Heart Assn. (dir. 1972-75, pres. 1974-75), AMA, Nebr. Med. Assn. Lancaster County Med. Soc., Am. Soc. Internal Medicine, Lincoln Found., U. Nebr. Chancellor's Club, Lincoln U. Club (dir. 1981-84), U. Nebr. Pres. Club, Phi Beta Kappa, Sigma Xi, Alpha Omega Alpha, Phi Delta Theta (pres. Nebr. Alpha chpt. 1959-60). Home: 7430 N Hampton Rd Lincoln NE 68506-1624 Office: Lifescan Preventive Imaging 2930 Pine Lake Rd Ste 111 Lincoln NE 68516

WILSON, DONALD WALLIN, academic administrator, communications educator; b. Poona, India, Jan. 9, 1938; s. Nathaniel Carter and Hannah Myrtle Wilson; children: Carrie, Jennifer, Gregory, Andrew. BA, So. Missionary Coll., 1959; MA, Andrews U., 1961; PhD, Mich. State U., 1966. Dean applied arts and tech. Ont. (Can.) Colls., North Bay, 1968-73; acad. dean Olivet Coll., 1973-76; pres. Castleton State Coll., 1976-79, Southampton Coll., 1979-83, prof. communications and history, 1973-83; pres., prof. Pittsburg State U. (Kans.), 1983-95; pres. Kilang Nusantara Pacific, 1995—; exec. v.p. Shepherd of the Hills Entertainment Group, Branson, Mo., 1997—. Author: The Untapped Source of Power in the Church, 1961, Long Range Planning, 1979, The Long Road From Turmoil to Self Sufficiency, 1989, The Next Twenty-Five Years: Indonesias Journey Into The Future, 1992, The Indispensable Man: Sudomo, 1992. Mem. Kans. Adv. Coun. of C.C.'s; bd. dirs. Internat. U. Thailand; pres. Internat. Univ. Found. Named Alumnus of Achievement Andrews U., 1981; recipient Outstanding Alumni award Mich. State U., 1984. Mem. Speech Communication Assn., Assn. Asian Studies, Internat. Univ. Found. (pres.), Rotary. Methodist. Office: Kilang Nusantara Pacific Office of Pres Frontenac KS 66763 Address: 503 Ohio St Pittsburg KS 66762-6429 E-mail: wdonaldwilson@aol.com.

WILSON, DOUGLAS, genetics company executive; COO 21st Century Genetics Cooperative, 1994—. Office: 21st Century Genetics Coop 100 Mbc Dr Shawano WI 54166-6095

WILSON, EARLE LAWRENCE, church administrator; b. Rensselaer, N.Y., Dec. 8, 1934; s. Lawrence Wilbur Wilson and Wilhelaminia Knapp; m. Sylvia M. Beck; children: Deborah, Stephen, Colleen. B in Theology, United Wesleyan Coll., 1956, BS, 1961; M of Divinity, Evang. Sch. of Theology, 1965; M of Theology, Princeton Theol. Sem., 1967; D of Divinity, Houghton Coll., 1974. Sr. pastor Wesleyan Church, Gloversville, N.Y., 1956-61, gen. supt. Indpls., 1984—; sr. pastor First Wesleyan Church, Bethlehem, Pa., 1961-72; pres. United Wesleyan Coll., Allentown, 1972-84. Author: When You Get Where You're Going, 1966, Within a Hair's Breadth, 1989. Mem, chaplain Rotary. Republican. Home: 11697 Pompano Dr Indianapolis IN 46236-8819 Office: Wesleyan Ch PO Box 50434 Indianapolis IN 46250-0434

WILSON, EDWARD NATHAN, mathematician, educator; b. Warsaw, Dec. 2, 1941; s. Hugh Monroe and Margaret Jane (Northrup) W.; m. Mary Katherine Schooling, Aug. 19, 1976; children: Nathan Edward, Emily Katherine. BA, Cornell U., 1963; MS, Stanford U., 1965; PhD, Washington U., St. Louis, 1971. Instr. Ft. Valley (Ga.) State Coll., 1965-67, Washington U., St. Louis, 1968-69, U. Calif., Irvine, 1970-71, Brandeis U., Waltham, Mass., 1971-73; asst. prof. Washington U., St. Louis, 1973-77, assoc. prof., 1977-87, dean grad. sch., 1983-93, dean univ. coll., 1986-88, prof., 1987—, chair dept. math., 1995-99. Mem. Grad. Record Exams. Bd., Princeton, N.J., 1986-90; sec.-treas. Assn. Grad. Schs. Contbr. articles to profl. jours. Mem. Brentwood Sch. Bd., Mo., 1984. Woodrow Wilson fellow, 1963; NSF fellow, 1963-65; NDEA fellow, 1967-70. Mem. Am. Math. Soc., Math. Assn. of Am. Democrat. Office: Washington U Campus Box 1146 1 Brookings Dr Saint Louis MO 63130-4899 E-mail: enwilson@math.wustl.edu.

WILSON, EUGENE ROLLAND, foundation executive; b. Findlay, Ohio, Jan. 14, 1938; s. Clair and Ethel Bernice (Cryer) W.; m. Mary Ann Dalton; children: Jeff, Andy. B.A., Bowling Green State U., 1960; M.S., Syracuse U., 1961. Dir. devel., asst. to pres. Bowling Green (Ohio) State U., 1966-70; mgr. radio-TV advt. Columbia Gas of Ohio, Inc., Columbus, 1964-66; assoc. dir. devel. Calif. Inst. Tech., Pasadena, 1971-77, v.p. for inst. relations, 1979-80; assoc. dir. ARCO Found., Los Angeles, 1977-79, exec. dir., 1980-83, pres., 1984-94; pres. youth devel. Ewing Marion Kauffman Found., Kansas City, Mo., 1995-2000, sr. v.p. strategic programs and planning, 2000—. Chmn. contbns. coun. Conf. Bd.; mem. corp. grant makers com. Coun. of Founds. Cons. gov. Ctr. on Philanthropy; founding trustee Arcadia (Calif.) Edn. Found.; elder trustee Presbyn. Ch. Named Outstanding Young Man Bowling Green Jaycees, 1967; recipient hon. service award Hugo Reid Sch. PTA, 1977, Corp. Social Responsibility award Mex.-Am. Legal Def. and Edn. Fund, 1989, Nat. Leadership award in edn. Inst. for Ednl. Leadership, 1992. Mem. Bowling Green State U. Alumni Assn. (pres. 1965), Gnome and Athenaeum Clubs of Caltech, Omicron Delta Kappa. Home: 14117 W 56th Ct Shawnee KS 66216-4696 Office: 4801 Rockhill Rd Kansas City MO 64110-2046

WILSON, FRANKLIN D. sociology educator; b. Birmingham, Ala., Sept. 3, 1942; s. Ernest and Ollie Lee (Carter) W.; m. Marion F. Brown; children: Rachel, Chareese B.A., Miles Coll., 1964; postgrad., Atlanta U., 1964-65; M.A., Wash. State U., 1971, Ph.D., 1973. Instr. Grambling U., La., 1965-66; William H. Sewell-Bascom prof. sociology U. Wis.-Madison, 1973—, chmn. dept. Afro-Am. studies, 1984-87, chmn. dept. sociology, 1988-91, dir. Ctr. for Demography and Ecology, 1994-99. Author: Residential Consumption, Economic Opportunities and Race, 1979; deputy editor Demography, 1995-98; co-editor Am. Sociol. Rev. Bd. of Census adv. com. Profl. Assns., 1993-99. Served with U.S. Army, 1966-69; Vietnam Decorated Purple Heart, Silver Star, Vietnam medal of Valor; Census fellow Am. Statis. Assn., NSF, 1991-92, Population Coun. fellow, 1971-72. Mem. Population Assn. Am., Sociol. Rsch. Assn., Assn. Black Sociologists. Unitarian. Avocation: swimming, reading. Office: U Wis Ctr for Demography and Ecology Social Sci Bldg Madison WI 53713 E-mail: wilson@ssc.wisc.edu.

WILSON, FRED M., II, ophthalmologist, educator; b. Indpls., Dec. 10, 1940; s. Fred Madison and Elizabeth (Fredrick) W.; m. Karen Joy Lyman, Sept. 10, 1959 (div. June 1962); 1 child, Teresa Wilson Kulick; m. Claytonia Leigh Pemberton, Aug. 28, 1964; children: Yvonne Wilson Hacker, Jennifer Wilson DeLong, Benjamin James. AB in Med. Scis., Ind. U., 1962, MD, 1965. Cert. Am. Bd. Ophthalmology. Intern Sacred Heart Hosp., Spokane, Wash., 1965-66; resident in ophthalmology Ind. U., Indpls., 1968-71, fellow in ophthalmology, 1971-72, F.I. Proctor Found., San Francisco, 1972-73; from asst. prof. to assoc. prof. ophthalmology Ind. U., Indpls., 1972-76, prof. ophthalmology, 1981—. Med. dir. Ind. Lions Eye Bank, Inc., Indpls., 1973-99; cons. surgeon Ind. U., Indpls., 1973—. Author or editor numerous sci. articles, book chpts. and books on ophthalmology. Lt. comdr. USNR, 1966-68, PTO. Mem. Am. Acad. Ophthalmology (assoc. sec. 1988-93, Sr. Teaching award 1989), Assn. Proctor Fellows, Soc. Heed Fellows, Am. Ophthalmol. Soc., Am. Bd. Ophthalmology (bd. dirs. 1993-2000), Ill. Soc. Ophthalmology (hon.), Mont. Acad. Ophthalmology (hon.), Pacific-Coast Ophthalmol. Soc. (hon.). Republican. Avocations: photography, guitar, history, language, natural history. Home: 12262 Crestwood Dr Carmel IN 46033-4323 Office: Ind U Sch Medicine Dept Ophthalmolgy 702 Rotary Cir Indianapolis IN 46202-5133

WILSON, GAHAN, cartoonist, author; b. Evanston, Ill., Feb. 18, 1930; s. Allen Barnum and Marion (Gahan) W.; m. Nancy Dee Midyette ((Nancy Winters)), Dec. 30, 1966; stepchildren— Randy Winters, Paul Winters. Graduate, Art Inst. Chgo., 1952. Commentator, Nat. Public Radio. Collections include Gahan Wilson's Graveyard Manner, 1965, The Man In the Cannibal Pot, 1967, I Paint What I See, 1971, Weird World of Gahan Wilson, 1975, Gahan Wilson's Cracked Cosmos, 1975, First World Fantasy Collection Anthology, 1977, Gahan Wilson's Favorite Tales of Horror, 1977, And Then We'll Get Him, 1978, Nuts, 1979, Chog: A Gothic Fable, 1980, Is Nothing Sacred, 1982, Wilson's America, 1985, Eddy Deco's First Case, 1987, Playboy's Gahan Wilson, 1980, Eddy Deco's Last Caper, 1989, Still Weird, 1994; juvenile works: Harry, The Fat Bear Spy, 1973, The Bang Bang Family, 1974, Harry and the Sea Serpent, 1976, Harry and the Snow Melting Ray, 1980; editor: First World Fantasy Awards, 1977, The Raven & Other Poems, 1990; illustrator: Matthew Looney & the Space Pirates, 1972, Catch Your Breath: A Book of Shivery Poems, 1973, Granny's Fish Story, 1975, Maria Looney & The Cosmic Circus, 1978, Maria Looney & The Remarkable Robot, 1979, Bob Fulton's Amazing Soda-Pop Stretcher, 1982, Plots & Pans, 1989, How To Be A Guilty Parent, Murder For Christmas, Passport to World Band Radio, 1992, The Keep of Two Moons, 1992, The Keep of Two Moons, 1992, A Night in the Lonesome October, 1993, Credo!: The Game of Dueling Dogmas, 1993, A Night in the Lonesome October, 1993, Spooky Stories For A Dark & Stormy Night, 1994; co-editor: Animals, Animals, Animals, 1979; co-author: The Upside-Down Man, 1977, Hairticklers, 1989, The Devil's Dictionary & Other Works; author: Everybody's Favorite Duck, 1989; animator (movie): Gahan Wilson's Diner, 1993; contbr. to Nat. Lampoon, New Yorker, Collier's, Look, Playboy, Punch, Esquire, Fantasy and Sci. Fiction, Paris Match, Pardon. Mem. Mystery Writers Am., Sci. Fiction Writers Am., Soc. Illustrators, Wolfe Pack, Cartoonists Assn. Commentator, Horror Writers Am. (Life Achievement award 1992), Writers Guild East, Authors Guild, Nat. Public Radio. Office: HMH Pubs care Readers Svc 919 N Michigan Ave Chicago IL 60611-1681

WILSON, GARY LEE, airline company executive; b. Alliance, Ohio, Jan. 16, 1940; s. Elvin John and Fern Helen (Donaldson) W.; children: Derek, Christopher. BA, Duke U., 1962; MBA, U. Pa., 1963. V.p. fin., dir. Trans-Philippines Investment Co., Manila, 1964-70; exec. v.p., dir. Checchi & Co., Washington, 1971-73; exec. v.p. Marriott Corp., 1973-85; exec. v.p., chief exec. officer, dir. The Walt Disney Co., Burbank, Calif., 1985-89, dir., 1990; chmn. bd. Northwest Airlines, Inc., St. Paul, 1990—.

WILSON, GEORGE MACKLIN, history educator, cultural studies center administrator; b. Columbus, Ohio, Apr. 27, 1937; m. Joyce DeCoster Klain, June 11, 1960; children: George David, Elizabeth Adeline. AB in Politics and Russian Studies, Princeton U., 1958; AM in East Asian Regional Studies, Harvard U., 1960, PhD in History and Far Ea. Langs., 1965. From instr. to asst. prof. history U. Ill., Urbana-Champaign, 1964-67; assoc. prof. history Ind. U., Bloomington, 1967-76, assoc. prof. East Asian langs. and cultures, 1975-76, prof., 1976—, dir. East Asian studies program, 1970-71, 72-73, assoc. dean rsch. and advanced studies, assoc. dean internat. programs, 1972-75, dean internat. programs office of pres., 1975-78, dir. grad. studies dept. history, 1980-83, acting chair dept. history, 1983-84, summer 1981, summer 1982, dir. East Asian studies ctr., 1987—, dir. Title VI nat. resource ctr. East Asian studies, 1991-2000. Vis. lectr. Japanese history U. Mich., Ann Arbor, 1963-64, summer 1964; vis. asst. prof. history summer sch. arts and scis. Harvard U., 1966, assoc. prof. history summer sch., 1975, rsch. assoc. East Asian rsch. ctr., 1966, 75, 78-79; rsch. assoc. faculty letters Kyoto U., 1971-72, vis. prof. faculty edn., 1985; mem., chair various coms. Ind. U., mem. bd. advisors East Asian summer lang. inst., 1985—, chair Japan forum, 1990—; cons. internat. divsn. Ford Found., 1974-77, cons. history Midwest univs. consortium internat. activities, 1979-80; mem. rev. panel divsn. pub. programs NEH, 1978-80; mem. adv. screening com. Japan Coun. Internat. Exch. Scholars, 1978-81, chair, 1980-81; mem. adv. panel Annenberg Sch. Comm. and Corp. Pub. Broadcasting, 1982-84; cons. East Asian history Am. Hist. Rev., 1985-91; mem. Gov. Robert Orr's Higher Edn. Del. to Ind.'s Sister State, Zhejiang Province, China, 1988; chair I.U. Japan Forum, 1988-94; bd. dirs. Ind. Consortium Internat. Programs, 1972-78; Ind. U. mem. bd. dirs. Interuniversity Ctr. Japanese Lang. Studies in Yokohama, 1988—; presenter in field. Author: Radical Nationalist in Japan: Kita Ikki, 1883-1937, 1969, Japanese edit., 1971, Patriots and Redeemers in Japan: Motives in the Meiji Restoration, 1992; editor, contbg. author: Crisis Politics in Prewar Japan: Institutional and Ideological Problems of the 1930s, 1970; Editl. advisor for Japanese and Korean history Encyclopaedia Britannica, 1969-99; book manuscript reader U. Hawaii Press, Ind. U. Press, Princeton U. Press; article manuscript evaluator Am. Hist. Rev., Comparative Studies Soc. and History, Jour. Asian History, Jour. Asian Studies; contbr. articles and book revs. to profl. jours. Grantee U. Ill., 1965, Harvard U., 1966, 75, Ind. U., 1967, 68, 72, Am. Philos. Soc., 1968, Am. Coun. Learned Socs., 1971; Grad. Sch. Arts and Scis. fellow Harvard U., 1959-60, Fgn. Area Tng. fellow Ford Found., 1960-63, Fulbright-Hays Sr. fellow, 1971-72, Profl. fellow Japan Found., 1985. Mem. Am. Hist. Assn. (convener 1984 and 1988 ann. meetings, chair conf. Asian history 1989—), Midwest Conf. Asian Affairs (mem. nominating com. 1990-91), Midwest Univs. Consortium Internat. Activities, Inc. (liaison officer for Ind. U. 1973-78, bd. dirs. 1974-78, sec. corp. 1974-78), Assn. Asian Studies (mem. program com., Japan rep. 1985 ann. meeting), Japan-Am. Soc. Ind., Inc. (founding, mem. steering com. 1987-88, bd. dirs. 1988—), Hudson Inst. (pub.). Office: Indiana University East Asian Studies Ctr Memorial Hall W Rm 207 Bloomington IN 47405

WILSON, H. DAVID, dean; b. West Frankfort, Ill., Sept. 13, 1939; m. Jeannette Wilson; children: Jennifer, Jacqueline, Mary Jeanne. AB in Zoology, Wabash Coll., 1961; MD, St. Louis Sch. Medicine, 1966. Diplomate Nat. Bd. Med. Examiners, Am. Bd. Pediatrics. Intern pediatrics Cardinal Glennon Meml. Hosp. for Children, St. Louis U., 1966—67; resident dept. pediatrics U. Ky. Med. Ctr., Lexington, 1967—68, chief resident, 1968—69; NIH rsch. fellow U. Tex. Health Scis. Ctr., Dallas, 1971—73; fellowship Am. Coun. on Edn., 1988—89; dir. admissions Coll. of Medicine, U. Ky., 1986—88; assoc. dean for acad. affairs, prof. Coll. Medicine, U. Ky., 1989—95; dean, prof. U. N.D. Sch. of Medicine, Grand Forks, 1995—. Author: (TV series) For Kids Sake, 1987-88; dir. pediatric infectious diseases U. Ky. Med. Ctr., Lexington, 1973-95, dir. cystic fibrosis care and tchg. ctr., 1975-80, med. dir., clin. virology lab., 1982-95; staff United Hosp., Grand Forks, 1995—; elected univ. senate U. Ky., 1993-96, bd. trustees Gluck Equine Rsch. Found., 1991-95, rules and elections univ. senate standing com., 1991-92, steering com. for U.K. self-study, 1990-95, co-chmn. steering com., 1990-95, chmn. review and search com. for chmn. dept. obstetrics and gynecology, 1990, chmn. curriculum com. Coll. of Medicine, 1989-95; elected acad. coun. of med. ctr. U. Ky. Med. Ctr., 1989-92; lectr. in field. Contbr. numerous articles to profl. jours. Fellow Pediatric Infectious Dieseases Soc.; mem. AMA, Am. Soc. of Microbiology, Am. Thoracic Soc., Am. Acad. Pediatrics, Pan Am. Group for Rapid Viral Diagnosis. Home: 10 Shadyridge Estates Grand Forks ND 58201 Office: U ND Sch Medicine & Health Scis Rm 1930 PO Box 9037 Grand Forks ND 58202-9037

WILSON, JACK, aeronautical engineer; b. Sheffield, Yorkshire, Eng., Jan. 5, 1933; came to U.S., 1956; s. George and Nellie (Place) W.; m. Marjorie Reynolds, June 3, 1961 (div. Jan. 1991); children: Tanya Ruth, Cara; m. Carol Blixen, Jan. 3, 1997. BS in Engring., Imperial Coll., London, 1954; MS in Aero. Engring., Cornell U., 1958, PhD in Aero. Engring., 1962. Sr. scientific officer Royal Aircraft Establishment, Farnborough, Eng., 1962-63; prin. rsch. sci. Avco-Everett Rsch. Lab., Everett, Mass., 1963-72; vis. prof. Inst. Mecanique des Fluides, Marseille, France, 1972-73; sr. scientist U. Rochester, N.Y., 1973-80; sr. rsch. assoc. Sohio/BP Am., Cleve., 1980-90; sr. engrng. specialist Sverdrup Tech. Inc., 1990-93, NYMA, Brook Park, 1994-98, DYNACS Engring. Co., Inc., Brook Park, 1998-2001, QSS Group Inc., Fairview Park, Ohio, 2001—. Author: (chpt.) "Gas Lasers" of Applied Optics in Engineering VI, 1980, "Laser Sources" of Techniques in Chemistry XVII, 1982; contbr. articles to profl. jours. Co-recipient Manley Meml. award Soc. Automotive Engrs., 1995; recipient Soaring gold Badge award Fedn. Aero. Internat., Paris, 1998. Fellow AIAA (assoc.; tech. com. 1991-92). Achievements include first to demonstrate gas-dynamic laser, measurement of air ionization rate at high speeds; patents in application of high speed flow to gas laser media, devel. of antimony dopant sources. Office: QSS Group Inc 21000 Brookpark Rd Cleveland OH 44135-3127 E-mail: jack.wilson@lerc.nasa.gov., wilson.blixen@juno.com.

WILSON, JAMES RODNEY, air equipment company executive; b. Kalamazoo, Oct. 5, 1937; s. Orton James and F. Magdalene (Critchelow) W. BA in Psychology, Kalamazoo Coll., 1960. Musician, Kalamazoo, 1955-60; music tchr., 1958-60; capt. U.S. Army, 1960-68; sales rep. Wilson Air Equipment Co., Kalamazoo, 1962-70, v.p. mktg., 1970-91, pres., 1991-2000, chmn., 2001—. Cons. in field. Co-founder Rep. Presdl. Task Force, Washington, 1981—, life mem., 1990—; vol. probation officer Kalamazoo County Juv. Ct., Kalamazoo, 1971—; big bro. Mich. Dept. Social Svcs., Kalamazoo, 1987—; mem. steering com. U.S. Senatorial Bus. Adv. Bd., Washington, 1981-88; bd. dirs. Glowing Embers Coun. Girl Scouts Am., 1994-2000, Kalamazoo Pub. Edn. Found., 1995—, v.p.; bd. dirs. Justus House, 1998—. Recipient Presdl. citation Vols. in Juvenile and Criminal Justice, 1984, Cert. of Merit, Mich. Dept. Social Svcs., 1988, Points of Light award Pres. Bush, 1992, Disting. Svc. award Kalamazoo Coll., 1989. Mem. Chief Engrs. Club Kalamazoo, Kalamazoo Coll. Alumni Assn. (pres. 1984-86), Cathedral Canyon Country Club (Palm Springs, Calif., pres., bd. dirs. 1994—). Republican. Roman Catholic. Avocations: boating, swimming, skiing, exotic auto collecting. Office: Wilson Air Equipment Co PO Box 2620 Kalamazoo MI 49003-2620

WILSON, KAREN LEE, museum director; b. Somerville, N.J., Apr. 2, 1949; d. Jon Milton and Laura Virginia (Van Dyke) W.; m. Paul Ernest Walker, 1980; 1 child, Jeremy Nathaniel. AB, Harvard U., 1971; MA, NYU, 1973, PhD, 1985. Rsch. assoc., dir. excavation at Mendes, Egypt Inst. Fine Arts, NYU, 1979-81; coord. exhbn. The Jewish Mus., N.Y.C., 1981-82, adminstrv. cataloguer, 1982-83, coord. curatorial affairs, 1984-86; curator Oriental Inst. Mus. U. Chgo., 1988-96, mus. dir., 1996—. Author, editor: Mendes, 1982; contbr. articles to profl. jours. Mem.: Coll. Art Assn., Am. Oriental Soc. E-mail: k_wilson@uchicago.edu.

WILSON, KENNETH GEDDES, physics research administrator; b. Waltham, Mass., June 8, 1936; s. E. Bright and Emily Fisher (Buckingham) Wilson; m. Alison Brown, 1982. AB, Harvard U., 1956, DSc (hon.) , 1981; PhD, Calif. Tech. Inst., 1961, U. Chgo., 1976. From asst. prof. to prof. physics Cornell U., Ithaca, NY, 1963—88, James A. Weeks prof. in phys. sci., 1974—87; Hazel C. Youngberg Trustees Disting prof. The Ohio State U., Columbus, 1988—. Co-author: Redesigning Education, 1974. Recipient Nobel prize in Physics, 1982, Dannie Heinemann prize, 1973, Boltzmann medal, 1975, Wolf prize, 1980, A.C. Eringen medal, 1984, Franklin medal, 1982, Aneesur Rahman prize, 1993. Mem.: NAS, Am. Acad. Arts and Scis., Am. Phys. Soc., Am. Philos. Soc.

WILSON, LAUREN ROSS, academic administrator; b. Yates Center, Kans., May 4, 1936; s. Roscoe C. and Margaret D. W.; m. Janie Haskin, Jan. 25, 1959; children— Lance Kevin, Keela Lynn. B.S., Baker U., Baldwin, Kans., 1958; Ph.D., U. Kans., 1963. Mem. faculty Ohio Wesleyan U., Delaware, 1963-87, prof. chemistry, 1971-87, Homer Lucas U. prof., dean acad. affairs, 1978-86, acting provost, 1985-86, asst. to pres., 1986, 87; vice chancellor for acad. affairs U. N.C., Asheville, 1987-95, prof. chemistry, 1987-95, interim chancellor, 1993-94; pres., prof. chemistry Marietta Coll., 1995—. Vis. prof. Ohio State U., 1968, 74; vis. research assoc. Oak Ridge Nat. Lab., 1972-73 Recipient Outstanding Tchr. award Ohio Wesleyan U., 1968 Mem. AAAS, AAUP, Am. Chem. Soc., Am. Assn. Higher Edn., Coun. Undergrad. Rsch., Sigma Xi. Office: Marietta Coll 215 5th St Marietta OH 45750-4033

WILSON, M. ROY, medical educator; b. Yokohama, Japan, Nov. 28, 1953; BS, Allegheny Coll., 1976; MD, Harvard Med. Sch., 1980; MS in Epidemiology, UCLA, 1990. Diplomate Nat. Bd. Medicine, Am. Bd. Ophthalmology. Intern Harlem Hosp. Ctr., N.Y.C., 1980-81; resident in ophthalmology Mass. Eye & Ear Infirmary/Harvard Med. Sch., Boston, 1981-84, glaucoma, 1984-85; clin. fellow in ophthalmology Harvard Med. Sch., 1980-85, clin. asst. ophthalmology, 1985-86; clin. instr. dept. surgery, Divsn. Ophthalmology Howard U. Sch. Medicine, Washington, 1985-86; asst. prof. ophthalmology UCLA, 1986-91; asst. prof., chief Divsn. Ophthalmology Charles R. Drew U. of Medicine and Sci., L.A., 1986-90, assoc. prof., chief Divsn. Ophthalmology, 1991-94, acad. dean, 1993-95, dean, 1995-98, prof., 1994-98, UCLA, 1994-98; dean sch. medicine Creihton U., Omaha, 1998—, interim v.p., 1999-2000, vice pres. health scis., 2001—. Asst. in ophthalmology Mass. Eye and Ear Infirmary, 1985-86; cons. ophthalmologist, Victoria Hosp., Castries, St. Lucia, 1985-86; hosp. appointment, UCLA; chief physician Martin Luther King, Jr. Hosp., L.A., 1986—; project dir. Internat. Eye Found., Ministry of Health, 1985-86; biology lab instr., Allegheny coll., 1975; instr. in biochemistry Harvard U. Summer Sch., 1977-78; instr. Harvard Med. Sch., 1980-85, others; cons. and presenter in field; participant coms. in field. Mem. AMA, Assn. Rsch. in Vision and Ophthalmology, Chandler-Grant Glaucoma Soc., Nat. Med. Assn., Am. Acad. Ophthalmology, Soc. Eye Surgeons Internat. Eye Found., Mass. Eye and Ear Infirmary Alumni Assn., So. Calif. Glaucoma Soc., West Coast Glaucoma Study Club, Assn. Univ. Profs. in Ophthalmology, L.A. Eye Soc., Calif. Med. Assn., Am. Glaucoma Soc., Soc. Epidemiol. Rsch., Am. Pub. Health Assn. Office: Creighton U Sch Medicine 2500 California Plz Omaha NE 68178-0001

WILSON, MARC FRASER, art museum director; b. Akron, Ohio, Sept. 12, 1941; s. Fraser Eugene and Pauline Christine (Hoff) W.; m. Elizabeth Marie Fulder, Aug. 2, 1975. BA, Yale U., 1963, MA, 1967. Departmental asst. Cleve. Mus. Art, 1964; translator, project cons. Nat. Palace Mus., Taipei, Taiwan, 1968-71; assoc. curator of Chinese art Nelson Gallery-Atkins Mus., Kansas City, Mo., 1971-73, curator of Oriental art, 1973—, interim dir., 1982; curator Oriental art Nelson-Atkins Mus. Art, 1982-99, dir./CEO, 1999—. Mem., rapporteur Indo-US Subcom. on Edn. and Culture, Washington, 1976-79; mem. adv. com. Asia Soc. Galleries, N.Y.C., 1984—, China Inst. in Am., 1985—. Mem. adv. com. Muni-Art Commn. on Urban Sculpture, Kansas City, 1984-87; com. mem. Kansas City-Xi'an, China, Sister City program, 1986—; mem. humanities coun. Johnson County Cmty. Coll., 1976-79; commr. Japan-U.S. Friendship Commn., Washington, 1986-88; panelist Japan-U.S. Cultural and Edn. Cooperation, Washington, 1986-88; mem. mayor's task force on race relations, 1996—; mem. indemnity adv. panel, 1995—; v.p. Brush Creek Ptnrs. 1995—. Recipient The William Yates Medallion Civic Svc. award William Jewell Coll., 1995, Disting. Svc. award Baker U., 1997. Mem. Assn. Art Mus. Dirs. (treas., trustee 1988-90, chmn. works of art com. 1986-90), Mo. China Coun., Fed. Coun. Arts and Humanities (chmn. arts and artifacts indemnity adv. panel 1986-89, 1995-98). Office: Nelson-Atkins Mus Art 4525 Oak St Kansas City MO 64111-1818 E-mail: mwilson@nelson-atkins.org.

WILSON, MARGARET BUSH, lawyer, civil rights leader; b. St. Louis, Jan. 30, 1919; married; 1 child, Robert Edmund. B.A. cum laude, Talladega Coll., 1940; LL.B., Lincoln U., 1943. Ptnr. Wilson & Wilson, St. Louis, 1947-65; now with firm Wilson & Assocs. Asst. dir. St. Louis Lawyers for Housing, 1969-72; asst. atty. gen. Mo., 1961-62; atty. Rural Electrification Adminstrn., Dept. Agr., St. Louis, 1943-45; instr. civil procedure St. Louis U. Sch. Law, 1971; chmn. St. Louis Land Reutilization Authority, 1975-76; mem. Mo. Coun. Criminal Justice, 1972—; chmn. Intergroup Corp., 1985-87; bd. dirs. Mut. of N.Y. Mem. gen. adv. com. ACDA, 1978-81; trustee emeritus Washington U., St. Louis; chmn. bd. trustees Talladega Coll., Ala., 1988-92; nat. bd. dirs. ARC, 1975-81, United Way, 1978-84, Police Found., 1976-93; treas. NAACP Nat. Housing Corp., 1971-84, chmn. nat. bd., 1975-84; dep. dir./acting dir. St. Louis Model City Agy., 1968-69; adminstr. Mo. Commn. Svc. and Continuing Edn., 1967-68. Recipient Bishop's award Episcopal Diocese Mo., 1962; Juliette Derricotte fellow, 1939-40, Disting. Lawyer award Bar Assn. Metro St. Louis, 1997. Mem. ABA (chmn. youth edn. for citizenship 1991-94, chmn. Nat. Law Day 1998-2000), Nat. Bar Assn., Mo. Bar Assn., Mound City Bar Assn., St. Louis Bar Assn., Alpha Kappa Alpha. Office: Wilson & Assocs 4054 Lindell Blvd Saint Louis MO 63108-3298

WILSON, MARTIN D. pharmaceutical executive; Pres., COO D & K Healthcare Resources, Inc., St. Louis. Office: D & K Healthcare Resources Inc 8000 Maryland Ste 920 Saint Louis MO 63105

WILSON, MICHAEL E. lawyer; b. Rantoul, Ill., Oct. 28, 1951; BA cum laude, Washington U., 1973, JD, 1977. Bar: Mo. 1977. Principal Greensfelder, Hemker & Gale, P.C., St. Louis. Instr. legal writing Washington U. Sch. Law, 1979-82; mem. nat. panel constrn. industry arbitrators and co-chmn. St. Louis Constrn. Adv. Com., 1987-97. Mem. ABA, The Mo. Bar (contbr. jour.), Bar Assn. Metro. St. Louis (contbr. jour.), Order Coif. Office: Greensfelder Hemker & Gale PC 2000 Equitable Bldg 10 S Broadway Saint Louis MO 63102-1712

WILSON, NORMAN GLENN, church administrator, writer; b. Rensselaer, N.Y., Nov. 3, 1936; s. Lawrence Wilbur and Wilhelmena Augusta (Knapp) W.; m. Nancy Ann Deyo, Nov. 17, 1956; children: Beth, Lawrence, Jonathan. BRE in Religious Edn., United Wesleyan Coll., 1958, DD (hon.), 1986; MA in Biblical Studies, Winona Lake Sch. Theology, 1968. Pastor The Wesleyan Ch., 1958-76, Gloversville, N.Y., 1963-66, North Lakeport, Mich., 1966-70, Owosso, 1970-76, dir. comm. Indpls., 1992—. Program prodr., speaker The Wesleyan Hour, Indpls., 1975—; mem. gen. bd. adminstrn. The Wesleyan Ch., Indpls., 1992—; disting. lectr. Staley Found., 1986. Author: How to Have a Happy Home, 1976, Christianity in Shoe Leather, 1978, The Constitution of the Kingdom, 1989, People Just Like Us, 1994, Follow the Leader, A Daily Spiritual Journey, 1996; editor, contbr.: Journey Into Holiness, 2000; editor The Wesleyan Advocate, 1992—. Mem. Nat. Religious Broadcasters (bd. dirs. 1984—, Merit award 1984). Avocations: oil painting, antique cars. Home: 304 Scarborough Way Noblesville IN 46060-3881 E-mail: wilsonn@wesleyan.org.

WILSON, PAMELA AIRD, physician; b. Milw., May 13, 1947; d. Rushen Arnold and Marianna (Dickie) W.; m. Paul Quin, June 20, 1981. BS in Zoology, U. Md., 1969; MS in Physiology, U. Wis., 1971; MD, U. Md., Balt., 1976. Diplomate Am. Bd. Internal Medicine. Asst. prof. U. Wis., Madison, 1984-91, assoc. prof., 1991—. Bd. dirs. Wis. chpt. Am. Lung Assn. past pres. ; exec. com. Wis. Thoracic Soc., past pres.; mem. Gov.'s Coun. on Phys. Disabilities, 1990—. Office: U Wis Hosps & Clinics 600 Highland Ave # H6380 Madison WI 53792-0001

WILSON, RICHARD CHRISTIAN, engineering firm executive; b. Bethlehem, Pa., July 17, 1921; s. Christian and Laura Barrows (Langham) W.; m. Jean M. Avis, July 16, 1949; children— Richard A., Christy. B.S., Carnegie-Mellon U., 1943; M.S., Lehigh U., 1947; Ph.D., U. Mich., 1961. Mfg. engr. Westinghouse Electric Corp., East Pittsburgh, 1943; instr. mech. engring. Carnegie-Mellon U., Pitts., 1943-44; vacuum test engr. Kellex Corp., N.Y.C., 1944; area supr. Carbide & Carbon Chem. Co., Oak Ridge, 1945-46; apparatus engr. Westinghouse Electric Corp., Jackson, Mich., 1947-55; instr. indsl. and operation engring. U. Mich., 1955-61, asst. prof., 1961-63, assoc. prof., 1963-66, prof., 1966-85, chmn. dept., 1973-77, assoc. dean Coll. Engring., 1968-72; pres. Techware, Inc., 1985-86, ret., 1986. Dir. Cascade Data Corp., 1969-72 Contbr. articles to profl. jours. Bd. dirs. Ecumenical Assn. Internat. Understanding, 1970-87, pres., 1975-76, 86-87. Mem. IEEE, Inst. Mgmt. Sci., Am. Inst. Indsl. Engrs., Ops. Research Soc. Am., Sigma Xi, Beta Theta Pi, Phi Kappa Phi. Club: Rotary. Home: 805 Mount Pleasant Ave Ann Arbor MI 48103-4776 Office: U Mich Dept Indsl Engring Ann Arbor MI 48109

WILSON, RICHARD EARL (DICK WILSON), media personality; b. Independence, Mo., Feb. 13, 1949; s. Paul E. and Lois P. (Chitwood) W.; m. Patricia J. Anderson, May 18, 1974; children: Nicole, Miranda, Spencer. BA, Ctrl. Mo. State U., 1971. Announcer Sta. WDAF-AM, Kansas City, Mo., 1971-74; host All Night Live Sta. KSHB-TV, 1984-85, prodr., host KC Prime, 1986; morning radio host Sta. KYYS-FM, 1974-84, Sta. KCMO-FM, Kansas City, 1986—; TV host talk and variety show Camp Midnite USA Network, Dick Clark Prodns., L.A., 1989. Host 20 Questions pilot Buena Vista TV, Disney Studios, L.A., 1989; corp. audio and video writer and host, 1992—. Bd. mem. Leukemia Soc., Kansas City, 1987, Music Arts Inst., Independence, 1989—. Named Radio Personality of the Yr., Kansas City Media Profls., 1988, 89, named to Radio Hall of Fame, 1990. Avocations: golf, computers, broadcast prodn. Office: 4935 Belinder Rd Westwood KS 66205-1937

WILSON, RICHARD HAROLD, government official; b. Waterloo, Iowa, July 15, 1930; s. Clarence Hough and Mary (Dillon) W.; m. Elaine Elizabeth Aniol., June 14, 1957; children: Elizabeth Aniol Wilson Adams, Andrew Edward. BA, U. Ill., 1952; MPA, U. Kans., 1958; AAS in Hotel-Motel Mgmt. and Food Svc. Adminstrn., Harold Washington Coll., Chgo., 1999. Lic. real estate broker, Tex.; cert. econs. devel. specialist Nat. Devel. Coun. Adminstrv. asst. to city mgr., San Antonio, 1956-58; budget analyst Kansas City, Mo., 1959; research asso. Internat. Union Local Authorities, The Hague, 1959-60; city mgr. Nevada, Mo., 1960-65; asst. to city mgr. Ft. Worth, 1965-67; asst. city mgr. Albuquerque, 1967-68; city mgr., 1968-72; dir. housing and urban rehab. Dallas, 1972-82; sr. v.p. Metroplex R&D Cons., 1982-83; regional dir. comty. planning and devel. HUD Region V, Chgo., 1983-94; CPD program advisor HUD, 1995—97, cmty. builder, 1998—. Lectr. real estate U. Tex.-Arlington; instr. govt. Dallas County Community Coll. Dist.; exec. v.p. Designs for Worship, Inc., Dallas, 1982-83 Bd. dirs. Neighborhood Housing Svcs. Am., Inc., 1974-82; chmn. Housing Tax Force of North Cen. Tex. Coun. Govts., 1974-80, chmn. human resources com., 1981-82; active Boy Scouts Am.; docent Prairie Ave. House Mus., 1990—; bd. dirs. Marina Towers Condominium Assn., 1991-96. Active USN, 1952-55, intelligence specialist USNR, 1955-82, comdr. ret. Fulbright fellow Leiden (The Netherlands) U., 1959-60, Kennedy Sch., Harvard U., 1981, 98, Fed. Exec. Inst., 1995, NEH, U. Calif., Santa Barbara, 1978, Urban Execs. Exch. Program, Internat. City-County Mgmt. Assn., 1979-80. Mem. Nat. Assn. Housing and Redevel. Ofcls. (v.p. Tex. chpt. 1975-80, mem. S.W. regional coun. 1975-82), Internat. City-Coun. Mgmt. Assn., Am. Soc. Pub. Adminstrn. (pres. N.Mex. 1968-69, v.p. North Tex. 1976-77, pres. North Tex. 1977-78, mem. nat. coun. 1979-82, Greater Chgo. chpt. coun. 1987-93, 95-96), Naval Res. Assn., Chgo. Arch. Found. (docent 1990—), Fed. Exec. Inst. Alumni Assn., Phi Gamma Delta, Pi Sigma Alpha, Alpha Phi Omega. Episcopalian. Club: Rotary (Chicago). Home: 300 N State St Apt 2833 Chicago IL 60610-5627 Office: HUD 77 W Jackson Blvd 26th Floor Chicago IL 60604-3507 E-mail: aniolwilson@aol.com., Richard_H._Wilson@hud.gov.

WILSON, RITA P. insurance company executive; Sr. v.p. corp. rels. Allstate Ins. Co., Northbrook, Ill., 1990-94, 96—, pres. Allstate Indemnity, 1994-96; sr. v.p. corp. rels. Ameritech, Chgo., 1994-96. Office: Allstate Ins Co 2775 Sanders Rd Ste F8 Northbrook IL 60062-6127

WILSON, ROBERT FOSTER, lawyer; b. Windsor, Colo., Apr. 6, 1926; s. Foster W. and Anne Lucille (Svedman) W.; m. Mary Elizabeth Clark, Mar. 4, 1951 (div. Feb. 1972); children; Robert F., Katharine A.; m. Sally Anne Nemec, June 8, 1982. BA in Econs., U. Iowa, 1950, JD, 1951. Bar: Iowa 1951, U.S. Dist. Ct. (no. and so. dists.) Iowa 1956, U.S. Ct. Appeals (8th cir.) 1967. Atty. FTC, Chgo., 1951-55; pvt. practice, Cedar Rapids, Iowa, 1955—. Pres. Lawyer Forms, Inc.; dir. Lawyers Forms, Inc.; mem. Iowa Reapportionment Com., 1968; del. to U.S. and Japan Bilateral Session on Legal and Econ. Rels. Conf., Tokyo, 1988, Moscow Conf. on Law and Bilateral Rels., Moscow, 1990; U.S. del. to Moscow Conf. on Legal and Econ. Rels., 1990. Mem. Iowa Ho. of Reps., 1959-60; pres. Linn County Day Care, Cedar Rapids, 1968-70. Sgt. U.S. Army, 1944-46. Mem. ATLA, Am. Arbitration Assn. (panel arbitrators), Iowa Bar Assn., Iowa Trial Lawyers Assn., Linn County Bar Assn., Am. Legion (judge adv. 1970-75, 87-93), Cedar View Country Club, Elks, Eagles, Delta Theta Phi. Democrat. Home: 100 1st Ave NE Cedar Rapids IA 52401-1128 Office: 810 Dows Bldg Cedar Rapids IA 52403-7010 E-mail: RWilsonlaw@aol.com.

WILSON, ROBLEY CONANT, JR. English educator, editor, author; b. Brunswick, Maine, June 15, 1930; s. Robley Conant and Dorothy May (Stimpson) W.; m. Charlotte A. Lehon, Aug. 20, 1955 (div. 1991); children: Stephen, Philip; m. Susan Hubbard, June 17, 1995. B.A., Bowdoin Coll., 1957, D.Litt (hon.), 1987; M.F.A., U. Iowa, 1968. Reporter Raymondville Chronicle, Tex., 1950-1951; asst. publicity dir. N.Y. State Fair Syracuse, 1956; instr. Valparaiso U., Ind., 1958-63; asst. prof. English U. No. Iowa, Cedar Falls, 1963-69, assoc. prof., 1969-75, prof., 1975-2000, prof. emeritus, 2000—, editor N.Am. Rev., 1969-2000. Author: The Pleasures of Manhood, 1977, Living Alone, 1978, Dancing for Men, 1983 (Drue Heinz Lit. prize , 1982), Kingdoms of the Ordinary (Agnes Lynch Starrett award , 1986), Terrible Kisses, 1989, A Pleasure Tree, 1990 (Soc. Midland Authors Poetry award, 1990), The Victim's Daughter, 1991, A Walk Through the Human Heart, 1996, Everything Paid For, 1999, The Book of Lost Fathers, 2001; co-editor: 100% Pure Florida Fiction, 2000. Bd. dirs. Associated Writing Programs, Norfolk, Va., 1983-86; pres. Iowa Woman Endeavors, Inc., 1986-90. With USAF, 1951-55. Guggenheim fellow, 1983-84, Nicholl Screenwriting fellow, 1996. Mem.: PEN, Am. Acad. Poets, Authors' Guild, Am. Soc. Mag. Editors. Home: PO Box 4009 Winter Park FL 32793-4009 E-mail: robley.wilson@uni.edu.

WILSON, ROGER BYRON, former governor, school administrator; b. Columbia, Mo., Oct. 10, 1948; m. Patricia O' Brien; children: Erin, Drew. BA, Ctrl. Methodist Coll.; MA in Edn., U. Mo.; grad., Harvard U., 1990. Asst. prin. Russell Blvd. Elem. Sch., Columbia, Mo.; real estate broker; collector Boone County, Mo., 1976-79; mem. Mo. State Senate from Dist. 19, 1979-92; lt. gov. State of Mo., 1993-2000, gov., 2000. Chmn. senate appropriations com., apportionment com., chmn. tourism commn.; mem. Mo. bus. and edn. partnership commn., transportation devel. commn., gov.'s adv. coun. phys. fitness. Bd. dirs. United Way, Columbia; mem. Mo. Assn. Cmty. Arts Agys., Boone County Hist. Soc.; mem. com. Mo. Parents as Tchrs. Recipient Everett award Mo. State Tchr.'s Assn., Outstanding Legislator of Yr. award, 1991, Boss of Yr. award Am. Businesswomen's Assn., Disting. Legislator award Nat. Conf. of State Legislatures, Horace Mann award Mo. Nat. Edn. Assn., Pub. Ofcl. of Yr. award Mo. Assn. Homes for Aging, M.U. Alumni award, 1991, Kirkpatrick award Northwest Mo. Press Assn., 1997. Mem. Columbia C. of C., Cosmopolitan Internat.

WILSON, THOMAS JOSEPH, insurance company executive; m. Jill Garling; 3 children. BSBA, U. Mich., 1979; M of Mgmt., Northwestern U., 1980. Various fin. positions Amoco Corp., Chgo., 1980-86; mng. dir. mergers and acquisitions Dean Witter Reynolds, 1986-93; v.p. strategy and analysis Sears, Roebuck and Co., 1993-95; sr. v.p., CFO Allstate Ins. Co., Northbrook, 1995-98, pres., chmn., 1999—; chmn., pres. Allstate Fin., 1999—. Bd. dirs. Steppenwolf Theatre Co., Rush-Presbyn.-St. Luke's Med. Ctr. and Francis W. Parker Sch. Office: Allstate Fin 3100 Sanders Rd Northbrook IL 60062-6110

WILSON, THOMAS S. professional basketball team administrator; CEO Detroit Pistons, pres. Office: Detroit Pistons 2 Championship Dr Auburn Hills MI 48326-1753

WILSON, TOM, cartoonist, greeting card company executive; b. Grant Town, W.Va., Aug. 1, 1931; s. Charles Albert and Hazel Marie W.; m. Carol; children: Tom, Ava. Grad., Art Inst. Pitts., 1955. Advt. layout man Uniontown Newspapers Inc., Uniontown, PA, 1950-53; designer Am. Greetings Corp., Cleveland, OH, 1955-56, creative dir., 1957-78, v.p. creative devel., 1978-81; pres. Those Characters from Cleve., 1981—. Former mem. faculty Cooper Sch. Art. Cartoonist: Ziggy, 1971—, syndicated in newspapers across U.S. by Universal Press Syndicate, Kansas City; collections include: Life is Just a Bunch of Ziggys, 1973, It's a Ziggy World, 1974, Ziggy Coloring Book, 1974, Never Get Too Personally Involved with Your Own Life, 1975, Promises to Myself: Ziggy's Thirty-Day Ledger of I Owe Me's, 1975, Plants are Some of My Favorite People, 1976, Ziggys of the World Unite!, 1976, Pets Are Friends You Like Who Like You Right Back, 1977, The Ziggy Treasury, 1977, This Book is for the Birds, 1978, Encore! Encore!, 1979, Ziggy's Love Notes, 1979, Ziggy's Thinking of You Notebook, 1979, Ziggy's Fleeting Thoughts Notebook, 1979, A Ziggy Christmas, 1980, Ziggy's Door Openers, 1980, Ziggy Faces Life, 1981, One Thing You Can Say About Living Alone-...There's Never Any Question About Who Didn't Jiggle the Handle on the John, 1981, Short People Arise, 1981, A Word to the Wide is Sufficient, 1981, Ziggy's Sunday Funnies, 1981, Ziggy & Friends, 1982, Ziggy Faces Life...Again!, 1982, Ziggy's For You With Love, 1982, Ziggy's Gift, 1982, Ziggy's Big Little Book, 1983, Ziggy and Friends, 1983, Ziggy's Funday Sunnies, 1983, Alphabet Soup Isn't Supposed to Make Sense, 1984, Ziggy Weighs In, 1984, Ziggy's Ship Comes In, 1984, Ug! The Original Hunk, 1985, Ziggy In the Rough, 1985, Ziggy's Ins and Outs, 1985, Ziggy's Ups and Downs, 1985, Ziggy In the Fast Lane, 1987, Ziggy's Follies, 1988, Ziggy's Star Performances, 1989, Ziggy's School of Hard Knocks, 1989, Ziggy On the Outside Looking In, 1990, (also illustrator) Ziggy's Christmas Book Levels 1, 2, 1991, (also illustrator) Ziggy's Play Today Guitar Method, 1991, Look Out World...Here I Come! Ziggy's Own Down-to-Earth Humor: A Look At the Environment and Ourselves, 1991, Ziggy...A Rumor in His Own Time, 1992, The Ziggy Cookbook: Great Food From Mom's Diner, 1993, A Day in the Life of Ziggy, 1993, One-Eight Hundred-Ziggy, 1994, My Life As a Cartoon: A Ziggy Collection, 1995, Ziggy's Place. Served with U.S. Army, 1953-55. Recipient Purchase award Butler Mus. Nat. Painting Competition, Emmy award for best animated spl., 1982. Achievements include developing Soft Touch line of greeting cards. Home: 22905 Ruple Pky Cleveland OH 44142-1100 Office: Universal Press Syndicate 4520 Main St Ste 700 Kansas City MO 64111-7701

WILSON, WILLIAM CAMPBELL MCFARLAND, gastroenterologist; b. Pitts., June 8, 1953; s. George Lincoln and Nancy Adair (Lytle) W.; m. Marlis Howland, June 25, 1977; children: Sarah, Stephen, Corrie. BS in Biology, Va. Tech, 1975; MD, Hahnemann U., 1979. Intern, residency R.I. Hosp., Providence, 1978-82; staff internist USAF Med. Ctr., Wright-Patterson AFB, Ohio, 1982-86; fellowship Hahnemann U., Phila., 1986-88; with Digestive Care, Dayton, Ohio, 1988—. Chmn. planning com. Dayton Gastroenterology Symposium, 1990—; com. patient edn. Miami Valley Hosp., Dayton, 1990-94, quality assurance, 1992—, vice chmn. dept. medicine, 1994-96, chmn. dept. medicine, 1996-98, chief-of-staff elect, 2002-. Bd. Fairhaven Ch., Dayton, 1990-94, 2001—, Dayton Christian Schs. Inc., 1995—; physician Dayton Christian Schs. Inc., 1993—; bd. dirs., physician In His Name Ministries, 2000—. Physician USAF, 1979-86. Fellow ACP; Mem. AMA, Am. Gastroenterological Assn., Am. Coll. Gastroenterology, Am. Soc. Gastrointestinal Endoscopy, Montgomory County Med. Assn., Alpha Omega Alpha. Avocations: tennis, computer, wood working, bicycling, photography. Office: 75 Sylvania Dr Dayton OH 45440-3237 E-mail: wcmw@aol.com.

WILT, JEFFREY LYNN, pulmonary and critical care physician, educator; b. Fairmont, W.Va., Nov. 15, 1963; s. Paul Lynn and Linda (Amos) W. BA, U. Mich., 1986, MD, 1988. Diplomate Am. Bd. Internal Medicine, Am. Bd. Pulmonary Diseases, Am. Bd. Critical Care Medicine, Am. Bd. Med. Examiners, Am. Bd. Nutrition Support; cert. ACLS instr. Fellow sect. pulmonary and critical care medicine W.Va. U., Morgantown, 1992-95; resident in internal medicine Blodgett-St. Mary's Hosp., Grand Rapids, Mich., 1988-91, chief med. resident in internal medicine, 1990-91; asst. dir. internal medicine residency St. Mary's Hosp., 1991-92; pvt. practice, 1995—. Asst. dir. med. ICU, Blodgett Meml. Med. Ctr., co-dir. transitional residency, 1997-98, COO internal medicine residency, 1998, program dir., 1998-99; assoc. program dir. internal medicine residency Mich. State U., Grand Rapids, 1999—, asst. prof. medicine, 1999—. Fellow ACP (Nat. Clin. Vignette winner 1991), Am. Coll. Chest Physicians (Young Investigators award 1993); mem. AMA, Am. Thoracic Soc., Soc. Crit. Care Medicine. Republican. Avocations: bicycling, karate, magic, reading, chess. Home: 4995 Sequoia Dr SE Grand Rapids MI 49512-9622 Office: 1900 Wealthy St SE Ste 150 Grand Rapids MI 49506-2969

WINBURY, MARTIN MAURICE, pharmaceutical executive, educator; b. N.Y.C., Aug. 4, 1918; s. Ervin and Helen (Stein) W.; m. Blanche Mary Simons, July 11, 1942; children: Nancy Ellen, Gail Elizabeth. BS, L.I. U., 1940; MS, U. Md., 1942; PhD, NYU, 1951. Rsch. fellow U. Md., College Park, 1940-42, U.S. Bur. of Mines, College Park, 1942-44; scientist Merck Inst. Therapy Rsch., Rahway, N.J., 1944-47; pharmacologist G. D. Searle, Skokie, Ill., 1947-55; dir. pharmacology Schering Corp., Bloomfield, N.J., 1955-61, Warner Lambert, Morris Plains, 1961-80, dir. sci. devel. Ann Arbor, Mich., 1980-86, ret., 1986; pres. InterPharm, 1986—. Mem. faculty U. Mich. Med. Sch., Ann Arbor, 1986—. Contbr. articles to profl. jours. Fellow AAAS, Am Coll. Cardiology, N.Y. Acad. Scis.; mem. Am. Soc. Pharmacology and Exptl. Therapy, Am. Heart Assn., Gordon Rsch. Conf. (chmn.). Achievements include findings in mechanism of nitroglycerin action-redistribution of coronary blood flow. Home: 6 Southwick Ct Ann Arbor MI 48105-1410 Office: InterPharm PO Box 8335 Ann Arbor MI 48107-8335

WINDEBANK, ANTHONY J. dean; Dean Mayo Med. Sch. Mayo Found., Rochester, Minn. Office: Mayo Medical School 200 1st St SW Rochester MN 55905-0001

WINDHORST, JOHN WILLIAM, JR. lawyer; b. Mpls., July 6, 1940; s. John William and Ardus Ruth (Bottge) W.; divorced; 1 child, Diana Elizabeth. AB, Harvard U., 1962; LLB, U. Minn., 1965. Bar: Minn. 1965, U.S. Tax Ct., U.S. Ct. Appeals (8th cir.) 1965, U.S. Dist. Ct. Minn. 1967, U.S. Supreme Ct. 1975. Law clk. to Hon. H.A. Blackmun U.S. Cir. Ct., Rochester, Minn., 1965-66; assoc. Dorsey & Whitney, Mpls., 1966-70; with office of Revisor of Statutes State of Minn., 1967, 69; ptnr. Dorsey & Whitney, 1971-96, of counsel, 1997—. Bd. dirs. St. Paul Chamber Orch., 1980-86, Harry A. Blackmun Scholarship Found., 1996—, Minn. Taxpayers Assn., 1999—. Mem. ABA (com. on state and local taxes), Minn. Bar Assn., Hennepin County Bar Assn., Harvard Club of Minn. (pres. 1977-78). Home: 1235 Yale Pl Apt 1102 Minneapolis MN 55403-1946 E-mail: windhorst.john@dorseylaw.com.

WINE, DONALD ARTHUR, lawyer; b. Oelwein, Iowa, Oct. 8, 1922; s. George A. and Gladys E. (Lisle) W.; m. Mary L. Schneider, Dec. 27, 1947; children: Mark, Marcia, James. B.A., Drake U., 1946; JD, State U. Iowa, 1949. Bar: Iowa 1949, D.C. 1968. Pvt. practice in Newport and Wine, 1949-61; U.S. atty. So. Dist. Iowa, 1961-65; of counsel Davis, Brown, Koehn, Shors & Roberts, Des Moines. Bd. dirs. Des Moines YMCA, 1963-75; bd. dirs. Salvation Army, 1969—, chmn., 1971; bd. dirs. Davenport YMCA, 1961; bd. dirs. Internat. Assn. Y's Men, 1957-59, area v.p., 1961; bd. dirs. Polk County Assn. Retarded Persons, 1991-95; mem. internat. com. YMCA's U.S. and Can., 1961-75; v.p. Iowa Council Chs.; pres. Des Moines Area Religious Coun. Found., 1992-97; chmn. bd. trustees First Bapt. Ch., 1975; trustee U. Osteo. Medicine and Health Scis., 1980-95; Organizer Young Dems., Iowa, 1946; co-chmn. Scott County Citizens for Kennedy, 1960. Served to capt., navigator USAAF, 1943-45. Decorated D.F.C. Mem. ABA (chmn. com. jud. adminstrn. jr. bar sect. 1958), Iowa Bar Assn. (pres. jr. bar sect. 1957), Polk County Bar Assn. (sec. 1973-74), Des Moines C. of C. (chmn. city-state tax com. 1978-79, chmn. legis. com. 1979-84, bd. dirs. 1981), Des Moines Club, Masons, Kiwanis (pres. Downtown club 1969), Order of Coif, Sigma Alpha Epsilon. Office: Davis Brown Koehn Shors & Roberts 2500 Financial Ctr 666 Walnut St Des Moines IA 50309-3904

WINE, SHERWIN THEODORE, rabbi; b. Detroit, Jan. 25, 1928; s. William Harry and Tillie (Israel) W. B.A., U. Mich., 1950, A.M., 1952; B.H.L., Hebrew Union Coll., Cin., M.H.L., rabbi, Hebrew Union Coll., 1956. Rabbi Temple Beth El, Detroit, 1956-60, Windsor, Ont., Can., 1960-64, Birmingham (Mich.) Temple, 1964—. Cons. editor Humanistic Judaism, 1966— Author: A Philosophy of Humanistic Judaism, 1965, Meditation Services for Humanistic Judaism, 1977, Humanistic Judaism-What Is It?, 1977, Humanist Haggadah, 1980, High Holidays for Humanists, 1980, Judaism Beyond God, 1985, Celebration, 1988, Staying Sane in a Crazy World, 1996. Founder Ctr. for New Thinking, Birmingham, 1977—; founder Soc. Humanistic Judaism, 1969; pres. N.Am. Com. for Humanism, 1982-93. Chaplain U.S. Army, 1956-58. Mem. Conf. Liberal Religion (chmn. 1985-96), Leadership Conf. Secular and Humanistic Jews (chmn. 1983-93), Internat. Inst. Secular Humanistic Judaism (co-chmn. 1986—), Internat. Assn. Humanist Educators, Counselors and Leaders (pres. 1988-93), Internat. Fedn. Secular Humanistic Jews (co-chmn. 1993—). Home: 362 Southfield Rd Birmingham MI 48009-3739 Office: 28611 W 12 Mile Rd Farmington MI 48334-4225 E-mail: bhamtmpl@speedlink.net.

WINEKE, WILLIAM ROBERT, reporter, clergyman; b. Madison, Wis., Apr. 4, 1942; s. Edward Ervin and Jennie Mae (Lanigan) W.; m. Susan L. Detering, Dec. 9, 1964 (div. June 1975); children: Gregory, Andrew; m. Jacqueline Cone, Mar. 18, 1990. BS, U. Wis., 1965; BDiv, chgo. Theol. Sem., 1969. Reporter Wis. State Jour., Madison, 1963-65; writer United Ch. of Christ, N.Y.C., 1966-68; pub. rels. dir. Chgo. (Ill.) Theol. Sem., Chgo., 1968-69; reporter Wis. State Jour., Madison, 1969—; chaplain Wis. Rescue Mission, 1977—. Bd. rev. Wis. Health Policy Network, Madison, 1994—. Fellow Religions Pub. Rels. Soc., 1974; recipient Disting. Svc. award State Med. Soc. Wis., 1992, Disting. Svc. award LWV, Madison, 1994. Democrat. Home: 1024 Ridgewood Dr Stoughton WI 53589-4125 Office: Wis State Jour 1901 Fish Hatchery Rd Madison WI 53713-1248

WINER, WARREN JAMES, insurance executive; b. Wichita, Kans., June 16, 1946; s. Henry Charles and Isabel (Ginsburg) W.; m. Mary Jean Kovacs, June 23, 1968 (div. Feb. 1973); m. Jo Lynn Sondag, May 3, 1975; children: Adam, Lauren. BS in Math., Stanford U., 1968. With Gen. Am. Life Ins. Co., St. Louis, 1968-73, dir. retirement plans, 1973-76, 2d v.p., 1976-80; v.p., sr. actuary Powers, Carpenter & Hall, 1980-84, sr. v.p., dir. pension div., 1984-85, pres., chief operating officer, 1985-86, lobbyist, commentator, 1985—, pres., chief exec. officer, 1986—; pres. W F Corroon, 1988-93; prin. William M. Mercer, 1993-94, mng. dir., 1994-95; exec. v.p. Gen. Am. Life Ins. Co., St. Louis, 1995—. Mem. Actuarial Exam. Com., Chgo., 1973-74. Contbr. articles to profl. jours. Bd. dirs. Lucky Lane Nursery Sch. Assn., St. Louis, 1978-93, pilot divsn. United Way, 1986-87; co-pres. Conway Sch. Parent Assn., 1986-87; bd. dirs. Paraquad, 1991—, chmn., 1994-99; bd. dirs. ATD, 1992—; chair triumph divsn. Unitd Way, 1996—. Fellow Soc. Actuaries; mem. Am. Acad. Actuaries, Enrollment of Actuaries (joint bd.), Am. Life Ins. Assn. (small case task force 1979-80), Life Office Mgmt. Assn. (ICPAC com. 1975-80), St. Louis Actuaries Club. Jewish. Clubs: St. Louis, Clayton (St. Louis). Avocations: bridge, wine tasting, swimming, weight training, biking. Office: Gen Am Benefits 13045 Tesson Ferry Rd Saint Louis MO 63128-3407

WINFIELD, MICHAEL D. engineering company executive; b. 1939; BSChemE, Ohio State U.; MBA, U. Chgo. Chem. engr. UOP, Des Plaines, Ill., 1962-74, mgr. refinery projects, 1974-76, asst. dir. tech. svcs., 1976-81, dir. bus. devel., 1981-83, v.p. tech. svcs., 1983-84, v.p. process svcs., 1984-92, pres., CEO, 1992—. Office: UOP 25 E Algonquin Rd Des Plaines IL 60016-6100

WINFREY, OPRAH, television talk show host, actress, producer; b. Kosciusko, Miss., Jan. 29, 1954; d. Vernon Winfrey and Vernita Lee. BA in Speech and Drama, Tenn. State U. News reporter Sta. WVOL Radio, Nashville, 1971-72; reporter, news anchorperson Sta. WTVF-TV, 1973-76; news anchorperson Sta. WJZ-TV, Balt., 1976-77, host morning talk show People Are Talking, 1977-83; host talk show A.M. Chgo. Sta. WLS-TV, 1984; host The Oprah Winfrey Show, Chgo., 1985—; nationally syndicated, 1986—; host series of celebrity interview spls. Oprah: Behind the Scenes, 1992—; owner, prodr., chmn., CEO Harpo Prodns., 1986—. Ptnr. in Oxygen Media, an Internet and cable TV co., 2000—; founder, editl. dir. O. The Oprah Magazine in conjunction with Hearst Mags., 2000—. Appeared in films The Color Purple, 1985 (nominated Acad. award and Golden Globe award), Native Son, 1986, Listen Up: The Lives of Quincy Jones, 1990, Beloved, 1998 (exec. prodr.); actress: About Us: The Dignity of Children, 1997 (TV), Before Women Had Wings, 1997 (TV; also exec. prodr. ABC series Oprah Winfrey presents); prodr., actress ABC-TV mini-series The Women of Brewster Place, 1989, also series Brewster Place, 1990, movie There Are No Children Here, 1993; exec. prodr. (ABC Movie of the Week) Overexposed, 1992; host, supervising prodr. celebrity interview series Oprah: Behind the Scenes, 1992, ABC Aftersch. Spls., 1991-93; host, exec. prodr. Michael Jackson Talks...to Oprah-90 Prime-Time Minutes with the King of Pop, 1993; exec. prodr. miniseries: Oprah Winfrey Presents: The Wedding, 1998, Oprah Winfrey Presents: David and Lisa, 1998, Oprah Winfrey Presents: Tuesdays with Morrie, 1999 (TV). Recipient Woman of Achievement award NOW, 1986, Emmy award for Best Daytime Talk Show Host, 1987, 91, 92, 94, 95, 97, Nat. Book Found's 50th Anniversary gold medal, 1999, America's Hope award, 1990, Industry Achievement award Broadcast Promotion Mktg. Execs./Broadcast Design Assn., 1991, Image awards NAACP, 1989, 91, 92, 94, Entertainer of the Yr. award NAACP, 1989, CEBA awards, 1989, 90, 91, George Foster Peabody's Individual Achievement award, 1996, Gold Medal award IRTS, 1996, Lifetime Achievement award NATAS, 1998, People's Choice award, 1997, 98, Horatio Alger award, 1993; named Broadcaster of Yr. Internat. Radio and TV Soc., 1988; recognized as one of America's 25 Most Influential People, Time mag.; inducted to Television Hall of Fame, 1994. Office: Harpo Prodns 110 N Carpenter St Chicago IL 60607-2145

WING, JOHN ADAMS, financial services executive; b. Elmira, N.Y., Nov. 9, 1935; s. Herbert Charles and Clara Louise (Stewart) W.; m. Joan Cook Montgomery, June 19, 1964; children: Lloyd Montgomery, Elizabeth Montgomery, Mary Ellen. B.A. in Econs., Union Coll., 1958; LL.B., George Washington U., 1963. Bar: Va. 1963, D.C. 1965, Ill. 1968. Fin. analyst SEC, Washington, 1960-63, trial atty., 1963-66; asst. to pres. Investors Diversified Services, Inc., Mpls., 1966-67; v.p., gen. counsel A.G. Becker & Co., Chgo., 1968-71, sr. v.p., 1971-74; pres. A.G. Becker & Co., also dir., 1974-80; pres., then chief exec. officer & chmn. Chgo. Corp. (acquired by ABN AMRO N. Am. Inc. in 1996), 1981-98; exec. dir. Ctr. of Law and Fin. Markets Ill. Inst. of Tech., Chicago, 1998—. Bd. dirs. Chgo. Bd. Options Exch., Am. Mut. Life. Bd. dirs. Ill. Inst. Tech., Risk Mgmt. Ctr. Chgo. With U.S. Army, 1958-60. Mem. Ill. Bar Assn., Va. Bar Assn., Ill. State C. of C. (bd. dirs. capital fund). Episcopalian. Clubs: Chgo., Economics, Civic, Mid-Day, Bond, Saddle & Cycle. Office: Ctr for Law & Fin Markets Ill Inst of Tech 565 W Adams St Chicago IL 60661

WINGET, LARRY J. automotive industry executive; Chmn., CEO, pres. Venture Global Engring. Industries, Fraser, MI. Office: Venture Industries 33662 James J Pompo Dr Fraser MI 48026

WINGFIELD, LAURA ALLISON ROSS, fraternal organization executive; b. Kansas City, Mo., June 8, 1954; d. John Joseph and Jean Marie Ross; m. Wesley Hughes Wingfield, May 13, 1989. BFA, William Woods Coll., 1972-76. Div. chmn. Beta Sigma Phi Sorority div. Walter W. Ross and Co., Inc., Kansas City, 1979-80, dir. rushing, v.p. and asst. dir. service, 1986—; dir. svc., 1991—; exec. v.p.; pres. of exec. coun., 1999—. Pub. chmn. Kansas City Am. Diabetes Assn., 1985-87, pres., 1986-87; bd. dirs., mem. exec. com. Heart of Am. affiliate, 1986-87, sec. state bd., chmn. pub. rels. com. Mo. state affiliate, 1993-94, bd. dirs. Kansas City chpt., 1993 pub. chmn. Walk fest; reading tutor Project Literacy, 1986, Penn Valley C.C.; bd. mem. Am. Diabetes Assn. Kansas City chpt. Republican. Avocations: house renovations, art, dog shows. Office: 1800 W 91st Pl Kansas City MO 64114-3243

WINKEL, MICHAEL W. communications executive; b. South Haven, Mich. married; 2 children. BS in Bus./Edn., Western Mich. U., 1968, MA in Polit. Sci., 1971; grad. advanced mgmt. program, Harvard Bus. Sch., 1985. Sales rep. agrl. divsn. Monsanto, 1972-78, dir. Europe-Africa, 1978-84; v.p., gen. mgr. specialty chems. Monsanto Chems., 1984-87; sr. v.p. internat. ops. G.D. Searle & Co., 1987-89, v.p., gen. mgr. rubber and process chems. divsn., 1989-93; sr. v.p. ops. Monsanto Chems., 1993-94; corp. v.p., corp. strategy and devel. R.R. Donnelley & Sons, Chgo., 1995-98, exec. v.p. strategy, 1999—. Office: R R Donnelly & Sons Corp Hdqs 77 W Wacker Dr Chicago IL 60601-1604

WINKEL, RICHARD J., JR. state legislator; b. Kankakee, Ill., Sept. 25, 1956; m. Debra Winkel; children: Meghan, David. Of counsel Meyer Capel, P.C., Champaign, Ill.; bd. mem. Champaign County, 1992-94; Ill. state rep. Dist. 103, 1995—. Mem. Elem. and Secondary, Higher Edn., Judiciary-Criminal Law, Prosecutorial Misconduct Management Reform, Ins. and Election Reform Law Coms., Ill. House, 1995—; mem. Legis. Audit Commn. Office: Huntington Towers PO Box 1736 Ste 1 East A 201 W Springfield Ave Champaign IL 61824-1736

WINKELMANN, JOHN PAUL, pharmacist; b. St. Louis, Sept. 14, 1933; s. Clarence Henry and Alyce Marie (Pierce) W.; m. Margaret (Peggy) Ann Grandy, June 16, 1967; children: John Damian and James Paul (twins), Joseph Peter, Christopher Louis, Sean Martin. BS, St. Louis U., 1955; BS in Pharmacy, St. Louis Coll. Pharmacy, 1960; ScD, London Coll. Applied Sci., 1972; EdD, Internat. Inst. for Advanced Studies, 1987. Registered pharmacist, Mo.; notary pub.; sr.cert. profl. mgr. (CM). Pres., chief pharmacist Winkelmann Apothecary, Ltd., Clayton, Mo., 1960-76; founding mem. Nat. Cath. Pharmacists Guild U.S., N.Y.C., 1962; pres. Nat. Cath. Pharmacists Guild U.S. (hdqs St. Louis, 1967—), St. Louis, 1968-70; hon. pres. Nat. Cath. Pharmacists Guild U.S., 1984, co-pres., 1985—, exec. dir., 1970—, founding editor, 1967—. Distbr. pharms. and medicines to missions worldwide. Author: History of the St. Louis College of Pharmacy, 1964, Catholic Pharmacy, 1966; founding editor The Cath. Pharmacist Jour., 1967—; contbr. over 500 articles to profl. publs. Unit commr. Greater St. Louis coun. Boy Scouts Am.; charter mem. Mo. Statewide Profl. Svcs. Rev. Orgn., 1976-78; Rep. Presdl. Task Force, Washington, 1982—; trustee St. Louis Coll. Pharmacy, 1961-84, chmn. audit com., 1968-83; worker St. Louis Archdiocesan Devel. Appeal, 1969-88; bd. dirs. Missionary Sisters St. Peter Claver Adv. Bd., 1974-77; retreat capt. for parish ch., 1976-83. Capt. USAFR, ret. Decorated knight of Malta by Pope Paul VI, knight grand cross Order of the Holy Sepulchre of Jerusalem by Pope John Paul II, papal knight Assn. Pontifical Knights, knight officer Order Sts. Maurice and Lazarus, knight officer Constantinian Order St. George, knight comdr. Patriarchal Equestrian Order of Holy Cross Jerusalem, knight Order White Eagle, knight Grand Cordon of Order of St. Stanislas, Knight Grand Cordon of Order Polonia Restituta, Grant of Arms (Spain), Certification of Arms (Rep. Ireland), Gold Papal Lateran Cross (1st class), Gold Papal Cross of Honor; recipient Silver Palm of Jerusalem award medal, Confrater of the Teutonic Order, Pharm. Scholarship award Meyer Bros., 1959, Lunsford Richards Nat. Pharmacy award, 1959, 60; 1st prize Roerig Nat. Pharm. Econs. Essay Contest, 1960, Medallion Cir. award Nat. Assn. Holy Name Soc., 1984, citations Govs. Mo., Ky., Tenn., Tex., Okla., Kans., Ala., Ga., Va., Nebr., Mass., Ind., W.Va., Pa. Miss., N.Mex., Ark., mayor of Paducah, Ky., Indpls., Lexington, Ky., San Antonio, New Orleans, Dodge City, Kans., County Exec. Pulaski County, Ky., mayor Louisville. Fellow Royal Soc. Health, Nat. Cath. Pharmacists Guild (Pharmacist of Yr. 1970), Am. Coll. Apothecaries, Am. Coll. Pharmacists, Soc. Apothecaries of London Faculty of History of Medicine and Pharmacy; mem. Am. Bd. Diplomates in Pharmacy (charter), Am. Inst. History Pharmacy (coun. 1977-80, state rep. 1980—, Commendation award 1966), Inst. Cert. Profl. Mgrs. (cert.), Am. Pharm. Assn., Acad. Pharm. Practice (charter 1967), St. Louis Vet. Druggists Assn., Assn. Mil. Surgeons U.S., Nat. Assn. Holy Name Soc. (v.p. 1981-91), St. Louis Archdiocesan Union Holy Name Soc. (pres. 1982-84), AMVETS, Am. Legion, Army and Navy Union, Mil. Order of World Wars, Mil. Order of Loyal Legion, Mil. Order of Foreign Wars, Polish Legion Am. Vets., Cath. War Vets., Anchor and Caduceus Soc. of USPHS, Rho Chi.

WINKER, MARGARET A. editor; MD, U. Ill. Resident in internal medicine U. Chgo., fellowship in geriatric medicine; clin. asst. prof. geriatrics sect. U. Ill. Med. Ctr.; sr. editor Jour. of AMA. Contbr. articles to profl. jours. Mem. Am. Geriatrics Soc. (chair pub. edn. com. 1997). Office: U Chgo Graham Sch Gen Studies 5835 S Kimbark Ave Chicago IL 60637-1635 Fax: 773-702-6814.

WINKLER, CHARLES HOWARD, lawyer, investment management company executive; b. N.Y.C., Aug. 4, 1954; s. Joseph Conrad and Geraldine Miriam (Borok) W.; m. Joni S. Taylor, Aug. 28, 1993. BBA with highest distinction, Emory U., 1976; JD, Northwestern U., 1979. Bar: Ill. 1979, U.S. Dist. Ct (no. dist.) Ill. 1979. Assoc. Levenfeld & Kanter, Chgo., 1979-80, Kanter & Eisenberg, Chgo., 1980-84, ptnr., 1985-86, Neal Gerber & Eisenberg, Chgo., 1986-96; sr. mng. dir., COO Citadel Investment Group, LLC, 1996—; sr. mng. dir. Citadel Trading Group, 1996—, Aragon Investments Ltd., Chgo., 1996—. Bd. dirs. Kensington Global Strategies Fund, Ltd., Antaeus Internat. Investments, Ltd., Jackson Investment Fund Ltd., Citadel Investment Group (Europe) Ltd. Author: (with others) Basic Tax Shelters, 1982, Limited Liability Companies: The Entity of Choice, 1995; mng. editor Northwestern Jour. Internat. Law and Bus., 1979. Mem. ABA (mem. sect. on taxation), Beta Gamma Sigma. Office: Citadel Investment Group LLC 225 W Washington St Fl 9 Chicago IL 60606-2418 Home: 10 Taconic Rd Greenwich CT 06830-3428

WINKLER, CHERYL J. state legislator; m. Ralph Winkler; children: Robert C., Ralph E. Student, U. Cin. Clk. Green Twp., 1984-85, trustee, 1986-90; former rep. Ohio State Ho. Reps. Dist. 20; rep. Ohio State Ho. Reps. Dist. 34, 1993—, mem. interstate coop. com., children and youth com., mem. reference, edn. and state govt. com., mem. select com. on tech., mem. joint com. on juvenile corrections & overcrowding. Mem. Cin. Bar Assn. Aux., Green Twp. and Bridgetown Civic Clubs, Western Hamilton County Econ. Coun. Home: 5355 Boomer Rd Cincinnati OH 45247-7926 Office: Ohio Ho of Reps State House Columbus OH 43215

WINKLER, DONALD A. credit company executive; Former chmn., CEO Finance One (subs. Bank One Corp.); CEO, chmn. Ford Motor Credit Co., Dearborn, Mich., 1999—. Office: Ford Motor Credit Co The American Rd Dearborn MI 48121

WINKLER, HENRY RALPH, retired academic administrator, historian; b. Waterbury, Conn., Oct. 27, 1916; s. Jacob and Ethel (Rieger) W.; m. Clare Sapadin, Aug. 18, 1940; children— Allan Michael, Karen Jean; m. Beatrice Ross, Jan. 28, 1973. A.B., U. Cin., 1938, M.A., 1940; Ph.D., U. Chgo., 1947; hon. degrees, Lehigh U., 1974, Rutgers U., 1977, No. Ky. U., 1978, St. Thomas Inst., 1979, Hebrew Union Coll., 1980, Xavier U., 1981, U. Akron, 1984, U. Cin., 1987, Thomas More Coll., 1989. Instr. U. Cin., 1939-40; asst. prof. Roosevelt Coll., 1946-47; mem. faculty Rutgers U., 1947-77, prof. history, 1958-77, chmn. dept., 1960-64; dean Faculty Liberal Arts, 1967, vice provost, 1968-70, acting provost, 1970, v.p. for acad. affairs, 1970-72, sr. v.p. for acad. affairs, 1972-76, exec. v.p., 1976-77, U. Cin., 1977, pres., 1977-84, pres. emeritus, 1984—, Univ. prof. history, 1977-86, prof. emeritus, 1986—. Mng. editor Am. Hist. Rev., 1964-68; vis. prof. Bryn Mawr Coll., 1959-60, Harvard, summer 1964, Columbia, summer 1967; faculty John Hay Fellows Inst. Humanities, 1960-65; bd. overseers Hebrew Union Coll., 1984—. Author: The League of Nations Movement in Great Britain, 1914-19, 1952, Great Britain in the Twentieth Century, 1960, 2d edit., 1966; editor: (with K.M. Setton) Great Problems in European Civilization, 1954, 2d edit., 1966, Twentieth-Century Britain, 1977, Paths Not Taken: British Labour and International Policy in the Nineteen Twenties, 1994; mem. editorial bd. Historian, 1958-64, Liberal Edn., 1986—; mem. adv. bd. Partisan Rev., 1972-79; contbr. articles to jours., revs. Nat. chmn. European history advanced placement com. Coll. Entrance Exam. Bd., 1960-64; mem. Nat. Commn. on Humanities in Schs., 1967-68, Am. specialist Eastern Asia, 1968; exec. com. Conf. on Brit. Studies, 1968-75; chmn. bd. Nat. Humanities Faculty, 1970-73; chmn. adv. com. on history Coll. Entrance Exam. Bd., 1977-80; mem. council on acad. affairs, mem. bd. trustees, chmn., 1982-84; pres. Highland Park (N.J.) Bd. Edn., 1962-63; mem. exec. com. Nat. Assn. State Univs. and Land-Grant Colls., 1978-81, mem. Cin. Lit. Club, 1978—, pres., 1993—; bd. dirs. Am. Council on Edn., 1979-81; trustee Seasongood Good Govt. Found., 1979—, pres., 1991-93; trustee Thomas More Coll., 1986-93; mem. Ohio Indsl. Tech. and Enterprise Bd., 1983-89; bd. dirs. Nat. Civic League, 1986—, Planning Accreditation Bd., 1988—; mem. adv coun. U. Va.'s Coll at Wise, Ohio Humanities Coun., 1994— With USNR, 1943-46. Recipient Lifetime Achievement award N.Am. Conf. on Brit. Studies, 1995, Bishop William Hughes award for disting. svc. to Cath. higher edn. Thomas More Coll., 1997. Mem. Am. Hist. Assn., Phi Beta Kappa, Tau Kappa Alpha, Phi Alpha Theta. Clubs: Comml., Bankers, Cin., Lit. Office: U Cin 571 Langsam Library Cincinnati OH 45221-0001 E-mail: Henry.Winkler@uc.edu.

WINNINGHOFF, ALBERT C. M. advertising company executive; Vice chmn. and COO Leo Burnett Co., Inc., Chgo. Office: Leo Burnett Co Inc 35 W Wacker Dr Chicago IL 60601-1648

WINSHIP, DANIEL HOLCOMB, medicine educator, university dean; b. Houston, July 4, 1933; m. Winnifred Jeneanne Rowold; children: Charles Dwayne, Nancy Ellen, David Rhoads, Rebecca Susan, Molly Beth. BA, Rice U., 1954; MD, U. Tex., Galveston, 1958. Diplomate Am. Bd. Internal Medicine. Intern in internal medicine Ochsner Found. Hosp., New Orleans, 1958-59; asst. resident U. Utah Coll. Medicine, Salt Lake City, 1959-61; fellow in gastroenterology Yale U. Sch. Medicine, New Haven, 1961-63; rsch. fellow med. ethics, fellow law, sci.-medicine program Yale U. Divinity Sch., Yale U. Law Sch., 1977; asst. prof., then assoc. prof. medicine Marquette U. Sch. Medicine, Milw., 1963-69; assoc. prof., then prof. U. Mo. Sch. Medicine, Columbia, 1969-84, assoc. dean for VA affairs, 1982-84; prof. U. Kans. Sch. Medicine, Kansas City, 1984-87; assoc. dep. chief med. dir. dept. medicine and surgery VA Ctrl. Office, Washington, 1987-90; prof. medicine, dean Loyola U. Stritch Sch. Medicine, Maywood, Ill., 1990-99; vice chancellor health affairs U. Missouri Columbia Health Scis. Ctr., 1999—. Gastroenterologist Harry S. Truman Meml. Vets. Hosp., Columbia, 1974-79, chief med. svc., 1979-82, chief staff, 1982-84; chief staff VA Med. Ctr., Kansas City, 1984-86, dir., 1986-87; attending physician Loyola U. Med. Ctr., 1990—, Edward Hines (Ill.) Med. Ctr., 1990—; mem. adv. bd. Greater Chgo. Alliance for Mentally Ill, 1991; pres., bd. dirs. gastroenterology adv. com. VA, 1982-85, chmn. clin. and programs adv. coun., 1988-90; mem. rev. com. Mo. Dept. Mental Health, 1981-82; numerous others. Mem. editl. bd. Clin. Rsch., 1970-73, Annals Clin. Gastroenterology, 1978-83, Gastroenterology: A Weekly Update, 1978-81; assoc. editor Jour. Lab. and Clin. Medicine, 1980-83; contbr. numerous articles and abstracts to med. jours. Bd. dirs. John H. Walters Hospice Ctrl. Mo., 1982-84, chmn., 1983-84. Recipient Outstanding Clin. Tchr. in Medicine award Milwaukee County Hosp. Housestaff, 1964, Golden Apple award Student AMA, 1972, Disting. Svc. medal and award VA, 1990, Ashbel Smith Disting. Alumnus award U. Tex. Med. Br., 1992. Mem. Am. Gastroent. Assn. (com. on rsch. 1975-78, com. on tng. and edn. 1978-81, dir. clin. tchg. project 1990-82, program chmn. motility sect. 1987), Gastroenterology Rsch. Group, Ctrl. Soc. for Clin. Rsch., So. Soc. for Clin. Investigation, Am. Fedn. for Clin. Rsch., Midwest Gut Club (presiding pres. 1980-83), Soc. for Health and Human Values, Inst. Society, Ethics and Life Scis., Sigma Xi, Alpha Omega Alpha (vis. prof. U. Mo. Sch. Medicine 1991, Med. Coll. Wis. 1993). Office: U Mo Columbia Health Scis Ctr 1 Hosp Dr Columbia MO 65212-0001

WINSLEY, WILLIAM T. pharmacist, executive director; BS in Pharmacy, Ohio State U., 1974, MS in Hosp. Pharmacy, 1978. Lic. pharmacist, Ohio, W.Va. Supr. drug distbn. Riverside Meth. Hosp., Columbus, Ohio, 1975-78, adminstrv. and clin. resident, 1978; asst. dir. pharmacy, instr. Coll. of Pharmacy W.Va. U. Med. Ctr., Morgantown, 1978-80; asst. dir. pharmacy Akron (Ohio) City Hosp., 1980-88; compliance specialist Ohio State Bd. of Pharmacy, Columbus, 1988-91, asst. exec. dir., dir. internship, 1991-98, exec. dir., 1998—. Mem. Nat. Assn. of Bds. of Pharmacy, Am. Soc. of Hosp. Pharmacists, Ohio Soc. of Hosp. Pharmacists (bd. dirs. 1983, 85-88, others), Akron Area Soc. of Hosp. Pharmacists (pres. 1983-84, v.p. 1982-83).

WINSTEN, SAUL NATHAN, lawyer; b. Providence, Feb. 23, 1953; s. Harold H. and Anita E. Winsten; m. Patricia J. Miller, Aug. 7, 1977; children: David A., J. Benjamin, Jennifer M. BA, Beloit Coll., 1976; JD, Drake U., 1980. Ptnr. Michael, Best & Friedrich, Milw., 1988—. Contbr. articles to profl. jours. Co-chmn. Wis. Gov.'s Adv. Coun. on Internat. Trade, 1996-2000, mem., 1996—, Wis. Gov.'s Internat. Edn. Task Force, 1997-98. Mem. ABA (chmn. com. young lawyers divsn. 1989-90, governing coun., antitrust, bus. and internat. law sects.), Wis. Bar Assn., Internat. Bar Assn., Japan-Am. Soc. Wis. (pres. 1993-94, co-founder 1990, sec. 1990-92), Nat. Assn. Japan-Am. Socs. (bd. dirs. 1991-98, exec. com. 1993-97), Am. Soc. Assn. Execs. (legal sect.), Order of Barristers, Hessen-Wisconsin, Inc. (bd. dirs.). Office: Michael Best & Friedrich 100 E Wisconsin Ave Ste 3300 Milwaukee WI 53202-4108

WINSTON, ROBIN, political organization official; Spl. asst. Lt. Gov. Frank O'Bannon; mem. gubenatorial campaign staff Frank O'Bannon for Gov., Inpls., 1996; exec. dir., v.p. polit. ops., chmn. Ind. Dems., 1999—. Office: Ind Dem Party Landmark Ctr 1099 N Meridian St Ste 910 Indianapolis IN 46204-1030

WINSTON, ROLAND, physicist, educator; b. Moscow, USSR, Feb. 12, 1936; s. Joseph and Claudia (Goretskaya) W.; m. Patricia Louise LeGette, June 10, 1957; children: Joseph, John, Gregory. A.B., Shimer Coll., 1953; B.S., U. Chgo., 1956, M.S., 1957, Ph.D., 1963. Asst. prof. physics U. Pa., 1963-64; mem. faculty U. Chgo., 1964—, prof. physics, 1975—, chmn. physics dept., 1989-95. Recipient Kraus medal Franklin Inst., 1996, First Solar Personality of the Yr. award, Bangalore, India, 1999. Fellow: Am. Solar Engery Soc., Am. Optical Soc., Am. Phys. Soc., AAAS; mem.: Internat. Solar Energy Soc. ((Abbot award 1987, Farrington Daniels award 2001)), Franklin Inst. (hon.). Achievements include patent for ideal light collector for solar concentrators. Home: 5217 S University Ave Apt C Chicago IL 60615-4439 Office: Physics Dept U Chgo 5640 S Ellis Ave Chicago IL 60637-1433 E-mail: r-winston@uchicago.edu.

WINTER, DAVID FERDINAND, electrical engineering educator, consultant; b. St. Louis, Nov. 9, 1920; s. Ferdinand Conrad and Annie (Schaffer) W.; m. Bettie Jeanne Turner; children: Suzanne, Sharie Winter Chappeau. BSEE, Washington U., St.Louis, 1942; MSEE, MIT, 1948. Registered profl. engr., Mo. Staff mem. radiation lab. MIT, Cambridge, 1942-45, rsch. assoc. electronics lab., 1945-48; prof. elec. engring. Washington U., 1948-55, affiliate prof. elec. engring., 1955-67; v.p. engring. and rsch. Moloney Elec. Co., St. Louis, 1955-74; v.p. rsch. and engring. Blackburn div. IT&T, 1974-82, dir. advanced tech. devel., 1982-86; pvt. practice cons., 1986—. Ct. recognized tech. expert on sources, mitigation, and effects of stray voltage on dairy cattle cons. Wis. Pub. Svc. Commn.; cons. Naval Ordanance Lab. of Ind., Indpls., 1950-53, other industries, St. Louis, 1979—. Contbr. articles to profl. jours.; holder 28 patents. Elder, pastor Maplewood Bible Chapel, St. Louis. Fellow IEEE (life), Inst. Radio Engrs.; mem. NSPE, Am. Soc. Agrl. Engrs., Mo. Soc. Profl. Engrs., Sigma Xi, Tau Beta Pi, Eta Kappa Nu. Avocations: cabinet maker, photography, music instruments. Home and Office: 735 Harvard Ave Saint Louis MO 63130-3135 E-mail: dfwinter@hotmail.com.

WINTER, JOHN DAWSON, III, blues guitarist, singer; b. Beaumont, Tex., Feb. 23, 1944; s. John Dawson II and Edwina (Holland) W. Grad. high sch. Organizer, performer numerous rock and blues bands, rec. artist, CBS Records, Inc., 1969— , TV and concert appearances through, U.S. and Europe, 1969— ; albums include Johnny Winter, 1969, Second Winter, 1969, Johnny Winter-And, 1970, Live, 1971 (Gold Record award 1974), Still Alive and Well, 1973, Saints and Sinners, 1974, John Dawson Winter III, 1974, Captured Live, 1976, Nothin' But the Blues, 1977, White Hot and Blue, 1978, The Johnny Winter Story, 1980, Raisin' Cain, Serious Business, 1985 (Grammy nominee), 3rd Degree, 1986, The Winter of '88, 1988, Winter Scene, 1990, Let Me In, 1991, Hey Where's Your Brother, 1992, Scorchin' Blues, 1992, A Rock n' Roll Collection, 1994, Johnny Winter Live in New York City 1997, 1997; producer recs. by Muddy Waters: albums include Still Hard (Artist of Yr., Rolling Stone mag. 1969), Hard Again, 1977 (Grammy award), I'm Ready, 1978 (Grammy award), Muddy Mississippi Waters Live, 1979 (Grammy award), King Bee, 1980. Mem. Broadcast Music Inc., Musicians Union. Office: Slatus Mgmt 35 Hayward Ave Colchester CT 06415-1221 E-mail: cpwrecds@aol.com.

WINTER, MILDRED M. educational administrator; BA summa cum laude, Harris Tchrs. Coll.; MEd, U. Mo.; postgrad., Harvard U., U. Cin. Exec. dir. Parents As Tchrs. Nat. Ctr. Inc., St. Louis. Tchr., cons., Mo., 1962-68; developer, dir. Ferguson-Florissant Parent-Child Early Edn. Program, Mo., 1969-72; first dir. early childhood edn. Mo. Dept. Elem. and Secondary Edn., 1972-84; sr. lectr. dept. elem. and early childhood edn. U. Mo., St. Louis; cons. in field. Contbr. articles to profl. jours. Named Outstanding Leader in Field of Edn., Mo. House of Reps., 1982, Outstanding Educator and Adv. for Young Children, Mo. Gov. Christopher S. Bond, 1984, Pioneer in Edn., State Bd. Edn., Mo. Dept. Edn., 1991, St. Louis Woman of Achievement in Edn., 1992; cited for Pioneering Leadership in Edn. Resolution, Mo. Senate, 1995; recipient Outstanding Svc. award Assn. Edn. of Young Children, 1984, Vol. Accreditation Leadership award, 1993, Spl. award Nat. Soc. Behavioral Pediat., 1992, Charles A. Dana Pioneering Achievements Health and Edn. Inst. Medicine award NAS, 1995. Office: Parents As Tchrs Nat Ctr Inc Ste 230 10176 Corporate Square Dr Saint Louis MO 63132-2924

WINTER, THEODORE, state legislator; b. Slayton, Minn., Nov. 26, 1949; s. Alphonse and Josephine Schettler W.; m. Marge Meier, 1969; children: Jason, Nathan, Shannon, Brent. AA, Worthington C.C., Minn., 1970. Farmer, 1968—; Minn. State rep. Dist. 22A, 1987—. Vice-chmn. ins. and tax coms.; mem. agr. econ. develop., environ. and natural resources, govt. ops. and fin. inst. coms. Mem. Minn. Jaycees (Minn. Statesman award 1983, JCI senatorship 1983—, reg. dir. 1983, dist. dir. 1982), Fulda Area Jaycees (pres. 1981, treas. 1980), Nat. Farmer's Orgn., Fulda Area Comm. Club. Home: RR 2 Box 23 Fulda MN 56131-9503 Office: Minn Ho Standing Com State Capitol Saint Paul MN 55155-0001

WINTER, WILLIAM EARL, retired beverage company executive; b. Granite City, Ill., Sept. 21, 1920; s. William M. and Ada M. (Compton) W.; m. Dorothy E. Schuster, Feb. 20, 1944 (dec. 1976); children: William C., Douglas E.; m. Mildred E. Stiebel, Mar. 18, 1977. AB, U. Ill., 1942. With Seven-Up Co., St. Louis, 1946-81, v.p., dir. mktg., 1969-71, exec. v.p., 1971-74, pres., chief operating officer, 1974-76, pres., chief exec. officer, 1976-79, chmn. bd., 1979-81, also former dir., cons.; chmn. emeritus, 1996—; cons. Cadbury Beverages/Seven-Up, chmn. emeritus, 1996. Bd. dirs. YMCA Greater St. Louis, U. Ill. Found.; mem. exec. bd. St. Louis Area coun. Boy Scouts Am. Capt. U.S. Army, 1942-46. Named to Promotion Mktg. Hall of Fame, 1979, Beverage World Hall of Fame, 1986 Mem. Am. Mktg. Assn., Sales and Mktg. Execs. St. Louis, Promotion Mktg. Assn. Am. (chmn. bd. 1971-72), Phi Beta Kappa, Phi Eta Sigma, Omicron Delta Gamma. Home: 14112 Baywood Villages Dr Chesterfield MO 63017-3421 Office: Dr Pepper/Seven Up Cos Inc 8900 Page Ave Saint Louis MO 63114-6108

WINTER, WINTON ALLEN, JR. lawyer, state senator; b. Ft. Knox, Ky., Apr. 19, 1953; s. Winton A. and Nancy (Morsbach) W.; m. Mary Boyd, July 28, 1978; children: Katie, Molly, Elizabeth. BA, U. Kans., 1975, JD, 1978. Bar: Kans. 1978. Ptnr. law firm Stevens & Brand, LLP, Lawrence, Kans., 1978—; v.p., gen. counsel Peoples, Inc., 2000-; pres. Corp. for Change; mem. Kans. Senate, 1982-92. Bd. dirs. Lawrence United Fund, Boys Club of Lawrence. Mem. ABA, Kans. Bar Assn., Douglas County Bar Assn. Kans. U. Law Soc., Rotary. Republican. Roman Catholic. Note and comment editor Kans. Law Rev., 1977-78. Office: PO Box 1795 4831 W 6th St Lawrence KS 66049

WINTERS, DAVID FORREST, state legislator; b. Springfield, Ill., June 30, 1952; s. Robert Winters Jr. and Helen (Steele) W.; m. Kathleen Wise, 1975; children: Colin, Theresa. BA, Dartmouth Coll., 1974; MS, U. Ill., 1976. Farmer, Winnebago County, Ill., 1976-94; commr., 1986-92; mem. Ill. State Ho. of Reps. Dist. 69, 1995—. Dir. Winnebago County Farm Bur., 1993-96.

WINTERSTEIN, JAMES FREDRICK, academic administrator; b. Copperas Cove, Tex., Apr. 8, 1943; s. Arno Fredrick Herman and Ada Amanda Johanna (Wagnr) W.; m. Diane Marie Bochmann, July 13, 1963; children: Russell, Lisa, Steven, Amy. Student, U. N.M., 1962; D of Chiropractic cum laude, Nat. Coll. Chiropractic, 1968; cert., Harvard Inst. for Ednl. Mgmt., 1988. Diplomate Am. Chiropractic Bd. Radiology; lic. chiropractic, Ill., Fla., S.D., Md. Night supr. x-ray dept. DuPage Meml. Hosp., Elmhurst, Ill., 1964-66; x-ray technologist Lombard (Ill.) Chiropractic Clinic, 1966-68, asst. dir., 1968-71; chmn. dept. diagnostic imaging Nat. Coll. Chiropractic, Lombard, Ill., 1971-73, chief of staff, 1985-86; pres. Nat. U. Health Scis., 1986—; pvt. practice West Chicago, 1968-73, Fla., 1973-85. Faculty Nat. Lincoln Coll. Post-Profl., Grad. and Continuing Edn., 1967—; chmn. x-ray test com. Nat. Bd. Chiropractic Examiners, 1971-73; govs. adv. panel on coal worker's pneumoconiosis and chiropractic State of Pa., 1979; v.p. Am. Chiropractic Coll. Radiology, 1981-83; mem. adv. coun. on radiation protection Dept. Health and Rehabilitative Svcs. State of Fla., 1984-85; cons. to bd. examiners State of S.C., 1983-84, State of Fla., 1980-85; cons. to peer review bd. State of Fla., 1980-84; trustee Chiropractic Centennial Found., 1989-90; mem. adv. com. Aids Alternative Health Ptnrs., 1996-2000, Consortial Ctr. for Chiropractic Rsch., 1998—; bd. dirs. Fedn. Ill. Ind. Colls. and Univs., 1995—; bd. dirs. Alternative Medicine, Inc., 1999—; spkr. in field. Pub. Outreach (Nat. Univ. Health Scis. monthly); author numerous monographs on chiropractic edn. and practice; co-inventor composite shielding and mounting means for x-ray machines; contbr. articles to profl. jours. Chmn., bd. dirs. Trinity Luth. Ch., West Chgo., 1970-72, Luth. High Sch., Pinellas County, Fla., 1979-82, St. John Luth. Ch., Lombard, 1988; chmn. bd. edn. First Luth. Sch., 1975-79; chmn. First Luth. Congregation, Clearwater, Fla., 1979-82; chmn. bldg. planning com. Grace Luth. Ch. and Sch., St. Petersburg, Fla., 1984-85; bldg. planning com. ch. expansion, new elem. sch., First Luth. Sch., 1975-79; stewardship adv. coun. Fla./Ga. dist. Luth. Ch. Mo. Synod, 1983-85; trustee West Suburban Regional Acad. Consortium, 1993-99. With U.S. Army, 1961-64. Recipient Cert. Meritorious Svc. Am. Chiropractic Registry of Radiologic Technologists, Cert. Recognition for Inspiration, Guidance, and Support Delta Tau Alpha, 1989, Cert. Appreciation Chiropractic Assn. South Africa, 1988, 1st pl. Fund Raiser Ride for Kids award Pediat. Brain Tumor Found. U.S., 1997, Cert. Appreciation Ill. Chiropractic Soc., 1997, Hope and Support award Alternative Health Ptnrs., 1998, Chiropractor of Yr., Ill. Chiropractic Soc., 2000. Mem. APHA, Am. Chiropractic Assn., Am. Chiropractic Coll. Radiology (pres. 1983-85, exec. com. 1985-86), Am. Chiropractic Coun. on Diagnostic Imaging, Am. Chiropractic Coun. on Diagnosis and Internal Disorders, Am. Chiropractic Coun. on Nutrition, Nat. Univ. Alumni Assn., Am. Acad. Chiropractic Physicians (sec.), Assn. Chiropractic Colls. (sec.-treas. 1986-91), Coun. Chiropractic Edn. (sec.-treas. 1988-90, v.p. 1990-92, pres. 1992-94, immediate past pres. 1994-96), Fla. Chiropractic Assn. (chmn. radiol. health com. 1977-85, Disting. Svc. award 1999). Republican. Lutheran. Avocations: reading, automobile rehabilitation, Harley-Davidson motorcycles, fishing.

WIOT, JEROME FRANCIS, radiologist; b. Cin., Aug. 24, 1927; s. Daniel and Elvera (Weisgerber) W.; m. Andrea Kockritz, July 29, 1972; children— J. Geoffrey, Jason. M.D., U. Cin., 1953. Diplomate: Am. Bd. Radiology (trustee, pres.). Intern Cin. Gen. Hosp., 1953-54, resident, 1954-55, 58-59; gen. practice medicine Wyoming, Ohio, 1955-57; mem. faculty U. Cin., 1959-67, 68—, prof., chmn. radiology, 1973-93, acting sr. v.p., provost for med. affairs, 1985-86, prof. emeritus, 1998—; practice medicine specializing in radiology Tampa, Fla., 1967-68. Contbr. articles to med. jours. Bd. dirs. Ruth Lyons Fund, U. Cin. Found., 1997—. Served with USN, 1945-46. Fellow Am. Coll. Radiology (pres. 1983-84, chmn. commn. on diagnostic radiology); mem. Radiol. Soc. N.Am., Am. Roentgen Ray Soc. (pres. 1986-87), Am. Bd. Radiology (pres. 1982-84), Ohio Med. Assn., Cin. Acad. Medicine, Radiol. Soc. Greater Cin., Ohio Radiol. Soc., Am. Thoracic Soc., Ohio Thoracic Soc., Fleischner Soc., Soc. Gastrointestinal Radiologists. Office: U Cin Med Ctr Dept Radiology 234 Goodman St Cincinnati OH 45267-1000

WIRCH, ROBERT W. state legislator; b. Nov. 16, 1943; BA, U. Wis., Parkside. Mem. Wis. Assembly from 65th dist., Madison, 1992-98, Wis. Senate from 22nd dist., Madison, 1998—. Mem. Kenosha (Wis.) County Bd. Mem. Polish Legion Am. Vets., Danish Am. Club. Address: 3007 Springbrook Rd Pleasant Prairie WI 53158-4324 Office: Wis Senate State Capitol Madison WI 53702-0001

WIRKEN, JAMES CHARLES, lawyer; b. Lansing, Mich., July 3, 1944; s. Frank and Mary (Brosnahan) W.; m. Mary Morse, June 12, 1971; children: Christopher, Erika, Kurt, Gretchen, Jeffrey, Matthew. BA in English, Rockhurst Coll., 1967; JD, St. Louis U., 1970. Bar: Mo. 1970, U.S. Dist. Ct. (we. dist.) Mo. 1970. Asst. prosecuter Jackson County, Kansas City, Mo., 1970-72; assoc. Morris, Larson, King, Stamper & Bold, 1972-75; dir. Spradley, Wirken, Reismeyer & King, 1976-88, Wirken & King, Kansas City, 1988-93; pres. The Wirken Group, 1993—. Adj. prof. law U. Mo., Kansas City, 1984-89, 2001—. Author: Managing a Practice and Avoiding Malpractice, 1983; co-author Missouri Civil Procedure Form Book, 1984; mem. editorial bd. Mo. Law Weekly, 1989—, Lender Liability News, 1990—, Emerging Trends and Theories of Lender Liability, 1991; host. Wirken on the Law, KMBZ Radio, 1998—. Mem. ABA (exec. coun.), Nat. Conf. Bar Pres. (coun. 1992-96), Nat. Caucus of Met. Bar Leaders (exec. coun., pres. 1988-94), Am. Trial Lawyers Assn., L.P. Gas Group (founder, chair 1986-90, founder, chair lender liability group 1987-96), Mo. Bar Assn. (bd. govs. 1977-78, chmn. econs. and methods practice com. 1982-84, quality and methods of practice com. 1989-91, vice chmn. young lawyers sect. 1976-78), Mo. Assn. Trial Attys. (bd. govs. 1983-85), Kansas City Met. Bar Assn. (pres. young lawyers sect. 1975, chair legal assistance com. 1977-78, chair tort law com. 1982, pres. 1990). Home: 47 W 53rd Kansas City MO 64112 Office: The Wirken Law Group PC 2600 Grand Blvd Ste 440 Kansas City MO 64108-4628

WIRSCHING, CHARLES PHILIPP, JR. retired brokerage house executive, private investor; b. Chgo., Oct. 26, 1935; s. Charles Philipp and Mamie Ethel (York) W.; m. Beverly Ann Bryan, May 28, 1966. BA, U. N.C., 1957. Sales rep. Adams-Millis Corp., Chgo., 1963-67; ptnr. Schwartz-Wirsching, 1968-70; sec., dir. Edwin H. Mann, Inc., 1971-74; stockbroker Paine Webber, Inc., 1975-85, account v.p., 1986-95; ret., 1995. Cons. Paine Webber, Inc. Chgo., 1996-99. Adv. coun. John Nuveen & Co., Inc., 1993-95; trustee Wirsching Charitable Trust, 1987—. Republican. Episcopalian. Avocation: foreign travel. Home and Office: 434 Clinton Pl River Forest IL 60305-2249

WIRSZUP, IZAAK, mathematician, educator; b. Wilno, Poland, Jan. 5, 1915; came to U.S., 1949, naturalized, 1955; s. Samuel and Pera (Golomb) W.; m. Pola Ofman, July 19, 1940 (dec. 1943); 1 son, Vladimir (dec. 1943); m. Pera Poswianska, Apr. 23, 1949; 1 dau., Marina (Mrs. Arnold M. Tatar). Magister of Philosophy in Math, U. Wilno, 1939; Ph.D. in Math, U. Chgo., 1955. Lectr. math. Tech. Inst. Wilno, 1939-41; dir. Bur. d'Études et de Statistiques Spéciales, Société Centrale d'Achat-Société Anonyme des Monoprix, Paris, 1946-49; mem. faculty U. Chgo., 1949—, prof. math., 1965-85, prof. math. emeritus, 1985—, prin. investigator U. Chgo. Sch. Math. Project (sponsored by Amoco Found., also dir. resource devel. component), 1983—, dir. Internat. Math. Edn. Resource Ctr., 1988—. Dir. NSF Survey Applied Soviet Rsch. in Math. Edn., 1985-91; cons. Ford Found., Colombia, Peru, 1965-66, Sch. Math Study Group, 1960, 61, 66-68; participant, writer tchr. tng. material African Math. Program, Entebbe, Uganda, summer 1964, Mombasa, Kenya, summers 1965-66; assoc. dir. Survey Recent Ea. European Math. Lit., 1956-68, dir., 1968-84; dir. NSF program application computers to mgmt., 1976-83; cons. NSF-AID Sci. Edn. Program, India, 1969; mem. U.S. Commn. on Math. Instn., 1969-73; co-prin. investigator U. Chgo.-Polk Bros. Found. Program for the Devel. of Math. Tchrs. in Chgo. Pub. Schs., 1999—. Contbr. articles to profl. jours.; Editor Math. books, transls., adaptions from Russian.; Adviser math.: Ency. Brit., 1971—. Recipient Lewellyn John and Harriet Manchester Quantrell award U. Chgo., 1958, Univ. Alumni Svc. medal, U. Chgo., 1994; resident master Woodward Ct., U. Chgo., 1971-85; endowed Wirszup Lecture Series, U. Chgo., 1986. Mem. N.Y. Acad. Scis., Am. Math. Soc., Math. Assn. Am., AAAS, Nat. Council Tchrs. Math. (chmn. com. internat. math. edn. 1967-69, Lifetime Achievement medal for Leadership, Tchg., and Svc. in Math. Edn. 1996) Home: 5750 S Kenwood Ave Chicago IL 60637-1744 Office: U Chgo Dept Math 5734 S University Ave Chicago IL 60637-1514

WIRT, FREDERICK MARSHALL, retired political scientist, educator; b. Radford, Va., July 27, 1924; s. Harry Johnson, Sr. and Goldie (Turpin) W.; m. Elizabeth Cook, Sept. 6, 1947; children: Leslie Lee, Sandra Sue, Wendy Ann. BA, DePauw U., 1948; MA, Ohio State U., 1949, PhD, 1956. Instr. to prof. polit. sci. Denison U., Granville, Ohio, 1952-66; vis. prof., lectr. U. Calif., Berkeley, 1966-68, 69-72; dir. policy scis. grad. program U. Md. Balt. County, 1972-75; prof. polit. sci. U. Ill., Urbana, 1975-2000; ret., 2000. Dir. Inst. for Desegregation Problems, U. Calif.-Berkeley, 1970-72; cons. Motion Picture Assn. Am., Rand Corp., Nat. Inst. Edn., SUNY Sch. Edn. Albany; vis. prof. U. Rochester, Nova U., U. Melbourne; acad. visitor London Sch. Econs. Author: Politics of Southern Equality, 1970 (honorable mention for best book 1972), Power in the City, 1974; (with others) The Polity of the School, 1975, Political Science and School Politics, 1977, Education, Recession, and the World Village, 1986, (with others) Culture and Education Policy in the American States, 1992, Aint' What We Was: Civil Rights in the New South, 1997 (Best Book on So. Politics award So. Polit. Sci. Assn., 1998), The Political Dynamics of American Education, 1997, 2d edit., 2001. Mem. Granville City Charter Commn., 1964. Grantee Am. Philos. Soc., Denison Rsch. Assn., U. Ill. Rsch. Bd., NEH, Ford Found., Ctr. Advanced Studies; fellow U. Ill., Dept. Edn., Spencer Found.; recipient Lifetime Achievement awards Am. Ednl. Rsch. Assn., 1995, Am. Polit. Sci. Assn., 1994. Mem. Am. Polit. Sci. Assn. (nat. council, Midwestern Polit. Sci. Assn., Am. Ednl. Rsch. Assn., Policy Studies Orgn. Home: 2007B Eagle Ridge Ct Urbana IL 61802-8617 Office: U Ill Dept of Polit Sci Urbana IL 61801 E-mail: f-wirt@uiuc.edu.

WIRTSCHAFTER, JONATHAN DINE, neuro-ophthalmology educator, scientist; b. Cleve., Apr. 4, 1935; s. Zolton Tilson and Reitza (Dine) W.; m. Carol Lavenstein, Sept. 13, 1959; children: Jacob Daniel, Benjamin Zolton, Joshua Schon, Sara Louise, David Dine, Brooke Ann. Student, UCLA, 1953; BA, Reed Coll., 1956; MD, Harvard U., 1960; MS in Physiology, Linfield Coll., 1963. Diplomate Am. Bd. Ophthalmology (assoc. examiner 1975—), Am. Bd. Neurology. Intern Phila. Gen. Hosp., 1960-61; resident in neurology Good Samaritan Hosp., Portland, Oreg., 1961-63; resident in ophthalmology Johns Hopkins Hosp., Balt., 1963-66; fellow in neurology Columbia-Presbyn. Hosp., N.Y.C., 1966-67; asst. prof. ophthalmology, neurology and neurosurgery U. Ky., Lexington, 1967-70, assoc. prof., 1970-74, prof., chmn. dept., 1974-77, dir. div. ophthalmology, 1967-74; prof. ophthalmology, neurology, neurosurgery U. Minn. Med. Sch., Mpls., 1977—, Frank E. Burch endowed chair in ophthalmology, 1990-2001. Vis. prof. Hadassah-Hebrew U. Med. Ctr., Jerusalem, 1973-74; Earl G. Padfield, Jr., M.D. Meml. lectr. U. Kans., 1986; vis. prof., lectr. numerous other univs.; cons. VA Hosps., Lexington, 1967-77, Mpls., 1977-99; spl. cons. Nat. Eye Inst., 1981. Co-author: Ophthalmic Anatomy: A Manual with Some Clinical Applications, 1970, rev. edit., 1981, A Decision-Oriented Manual of Retinoscopy, 1976, Computed Tomography: An Atlas for Ophthalmologists, 1982, Magnetic Resonance Imaging and Computed Tomography: Clinical Neuro-orbital Anatomy, 1992; contbr. numerous articles to profl. jours.; patentee in field. Bd. mem. Temple Israel, Lexington, 1970-73, McPhail Suzuki Music Assn., 1979-81, Mpls. Talmud Torah, 1979-85; founder, bd. mem. Jewish Community Assn. of Lexington, 1969-77; alumni interviewer Reed Coll., 1968—. Grantee Nat. Eye Inst., 1968-71, 78-81, 89—, Fight for Sight, 1974, Benign Essential Blepharospasm Found., 1988. Fellow ACS, N.Am. Neuro-Ophthalmology Soc. (pres., 1996-98), Am. Acad. Ophthalmology (Sr. honor award 1994); mem. AAAS, AMA (Hon. Mention award-sci. exhibit 1970), Am. Acad. Neurology, Am. Ophthal. Soc., Assn. for Rsch. in Vision and Ophthalmology, Internat. Soc. Neuro-Ophthalmology, Am. Israeli Ophthal. Soc. (bd. mem. 1984-90), Boylston Med. Soc. Harvard Med. Sch., Alpha Omega Alpha. Democrat. Office: Fairview U Hosp 420 Delaware St SE MMC 493 Minneapolis MN 55455-0501 E-mail: Wirtsch@umn.edu.

WIRTZ, WILLIAM WADSWORTH, real estate executive, professional sports team executive; b. Chgo., Oct. 5, 1929; s. Arthur Michael and Virginia (Wadsworth) Wirtz; m. Joan Roney, Dec. 15, 1950 (dec. May 1983); children: William R., Gail W., Karen K., Peter R., Alison M.; m. Alice Pirie Hargrave, Dec. 1, 1987. A.B., Brown U., 1950. Pres. Chgo. Blackhawk Hockey Team, Inc., 1966—, Chgo. Stadium Corp., 1966—, Consol. Enterprises, Inc., Chgo., 1966—, Forman Realty Corp., Chgo., 1965—, 333 Bldg. Corp., Chgo., 1966—, Wirtz Corp., Chgo., 1964—. Chmn. bd. govs. Nat. Hockey League. Named to NHL Hall of Fame, 1976; recipient Lester Patrick trophy, 1978. Mem.: Sunset Ridge Country Club (Northbrook, Ill.), Fin and Feather Club (Elgin, Ill.), Mid-America Club (Chgo.), Racquet Club (Chgo.), Saddle and Cycle Club (Chgo.). Office: Wirtz 680 N Lake Shore Dr Fl 19 Chicago IL 60611-3495 also: United Ctr 1901 W Madison St Chicago IL 60612-2459 also: Nat Hockey Leage 1155 Metcalfe St Ste 960 Montreal PQ Canada H3B 2W2

WISE, BRET W. chemical company executive; BS, Ind. U. CPA. Ptnr. KPMG; v.p., CFO WCI Steel, Inc., Warren, Ohio; sr. v.p., CFO Ferro Corp., Cleve., 1999—. Mem. AICPA, Fin. Execs. Inst. Office: Ferro Corp 1000 Lakeside Ave Cleveland OH 44114-7000

WISE, JOHN AUGUSTUS, lawyer, director; b. Detroit, Mar. 30, 1938; s. John Augustus and Mary Blanche (Parent) W.; m. Helga M. Bessin, Nov. 27, 1965; children: Monique Elizabeth, John Eric. Student, U. Vienna, 1957-58; AB cum laude, Coll. Holy Cross, 1959; JD, U. Mich., 1962; postgrad., U. Munich, 1962-63. Bar: Mich. 1963, D.C. 1966. Assoc. Dykema, Gossett, Detroit, 1962-64; asst. to pres. Internat. Econ. Policy Assn., Washington, 1964-66; assoc. Parsons, Tennent, Hammond, Hardig & Ziegelman, Detroit, 1967-70; pres. Wise & Marsac P.C., 1970-2001; sr. ptnr. Williams, Mullen, Clark & Dobbins, PLLC. Dir. Peltzer & Ehlers Am. Corp., 1975-80, Colombian Am. Friends Inc., 1974-89. Mem. Detroit Com. on Fgn. Rels.; bd. dirs. Hyde Park Coop., 1974-77; trustee Friends Sch., Detroit, 1977-81, Brighton Health Svcs. Corp., 1991-94, Providence Hosp., 2001—; chmn. bd. dirs. Brighton Hosp., 1995—. Ford Found. grantee U. Munich, 1962-63. Mem. ABA, Mich. Bar Assn., Detroit Bar Assn., Internat. Bar Assn., Detroit Athletic Club, Detroit Econ. Club. Roman Catholic. Home: 1221 Yorkshire Rd Grosse Pointe Park MI 48230-1105 Office: BUHL Bldg Buhl Building Fl 11 Detroit MI 48226-3604 E-mail: jwise@wmcd.com.

WISE, KENSALL D. engineering educator; m. JoAnne Clayton, Aug. 17, 1968; children: Kevin Duane, David Andrew, Mark Alan. BSEE with highest distinction, Purdue U., 1963; MSEE, Stanford U., 1964, PhD, 1969. Mem. tech. staff Bell Telephone Labs., Murray Hill, N.J., 1963-65, Naperville, Ill., 1972-74; rsch. asst. Stanford (Calif.) U., 1965-69, rsch. assoc., lectr., 1969-72; asst. prof. elec. engring. U. Mich., Ann Arbor, 1974-78, assoc. prof. elec. engring., 1978-82, prof. elec. engring., 1982—, J. Reid and Polly Anderson prof. mfg. tech., 1993—, dir. Solid-State Electronics Lab., 1979-87, dir. Ctr. for Integrated Sensors and Circuits, 1987—, dir. SRC program in automated semiconductor mfg., 1984-98. 'rganizer, moderator panel discussion Biomed. Sensors and Assoc. Electronica Internat. Solid-State Circuits Conf., 1971, mem. program com., 1978-82, 85-86, program sec. 1990-93; mem. JTEC Study on Microelectromech. Sys. Devels. Japan, 1993; program chmn. Internat. Conf. on

Solid-State Sensors and Actuators, 1985, 87, 89, 91, 93, 95; mem. program com. Symposium on VLSI Tech., 1988, 98; ; mem. Internat. Steering Com. for Solid-State Sensors, 1981—; mem. Crosscut Working Group on Metrology SIA Nat. Tech. Roadmap for Semiconductors, 1996-97; cons. in field. Den leader webelos, 1980-81, 84-85, chmn. troop com. 1984-85; mem. Stake High Coun. LDS Ch., 1977-78, 83-84, 89-90, counselor to bishop, 1985-86, bishop, 1986-89, tchr. early-morning seminar, 1990-91, adult Sunday sch., 1992-98, leader HP group, 1991-92. Recipient Outstanding Paper award Internat. Solid-State Circuits Conf., 1971, 1979, Cert. of Recognition NASA, 1974, 87, Beatrice Winner award Internat. Solid-State Circuits Conf., 1986, Columbus prize Disney World-Discovery Mag. Awards for Tech. Innovation, 1997, Aristotle award Semiconductor Rsch. Corp., 1997. Fellow IEEE (vice chmn. divsn. VI instrumentation engr. in medicine and biology Southeastern Mich. sect. 1975-76, dir. 1976-77, mem. program com. internat. electron devices meeting 1977, 81-83, guest editor spl. issue Jour. Solid-State Circuits 1979, spl. issues Transactions on Electron Devices 1979-82, proceedings Integrated Sensors, Microactuators, and Microsystems, spl. issue, 1998; assoc. editor 1981-85, gen. chmn. Solid-State Sensor Conf. 1984, nat. lectr. IEEE-EDSm 1986; gen. chmn. designate Internat. Conf. on Solid-State Sensors and Actuators 1997, Paul Rappaport award Electron Devices Soc. 1990, Solid State Circuits award 1999), Am. Inst. Med. and Biol. Engring; mem. Nat. Acad. Engring. U.S.A. Achievements include development of integrated circuit process technology, solid-state sensor, design and application of custom and commercial integrated electronics; patents for method for forming regions of predetermined thickness in silicon, 1975, method for forming ICF Target Structurs using solid-state process technology, 1982, multipoint pressure-sensing catheter system, 1989, ultraminiature pressure sensor and method of making same, 1989, ultrathin-film gas detector, 1990, method of making ultraminiature pressure sensor, 1991, silicon tactile imaging array and method of making same, 1991, thermopile infrared detector and method of manufacturing same, 1991. Office: U Mich 2401 BECS Coll Engring Ann Arbor MI 48109

WISE, WILLIAM JERRARD, lawyer; b. Chgo., May 27, 1934; s. Gerald Paul and Harriet Muriel (Rosenblum) W.; m. Peggy Spero, Sept. 3, 1959; children: Deborah, Stephen, Betsy, Lynne. B.B.A., U. Mich., 1955, M.B.A., J.D. with distinction, U. Mich., 1958. Bar: Ill. 1959. Spl. atty. Office Regional Counsel, IRS, Milw., 1959-63; with firm McDermott, Will & Emery, Chgo., 1963-70, Coles & Wise, Ltd., Chgo., 1971-81, Wise & Stracks, Ltd., Chgo., 1982-2000, Querrey & Harrow Ltd., Chgo., 2000—. Lectr., contbr. Ill. Inst. Continuing Legal Edn.; arbitrator Cir. Ct. Cook County Ill., 1990—. Mem. Village of Winnetka (Ill.) Caucus, 1974-75; Bd. dirs. Blind Service Assn., Chgo., 1964-74; dir., treas. Suzuki Orff Sch. for Young Musicians, Chgo., 1981-91. Served with AUS, 1958-59. Mem. Chgo. Bar Assn. Home: 1401 Tower Rd Winnetka IL 60093-1628 Office: Querrey & Harrow Ltd 175 W Jackson Blvd Ste 1600 Chicago IL 60604-2827 E-mail: dididoe@yahoo.com.

WISHARD, DELLA MAE, former newspaper editor; b. Bison, S.D., Oct. 21, 1934; d. Ervin E. and Alma J. (Albertson) Preszler; m. Glenn L. Wishard, Oct. 18, 1953; children: Glenda Lee, Pamela A., Glen Ervin. Grad. high sch., Bison. Mem. S.D. Ho. of Reps., Pierre, 1984-96; pub., editor Bison (S.D.) Courier, 1996-2000. Columnist County Farm Bur., 1970-96. Committeewoman state Rep. Cen. Com., Perkins County, S.D., 1980-84, 98-01, Rep. Chairman, 2001—. Mem. Am. Legis. Exch. Coun. (state coord. 1985-91, state chmn. 1991-96), Fed. Rep. Women (chmn. Perkins County chpt. 1978-84), S.D. Farm Bur. (state officer 1982), Perkins County Rep. (chmn. 2000-). Lutheran. Avocations: writing, gardening. Home: 16707 134th St Prairie City SD 57649-9714

WISHARD, GORDON DAVIS, lawyer; b. Indpls., Jan. 7, 1945; s. William Niles Jr. and Caroline (Davis) W.; m. Anne Emison; children: Claire Wishard Hoppenworth, Gordon Davis Jr. BA, Williams Coll., 1966; JD, Ind. U., 1969. Bar: Ind. 1969, U.S. Dist. Ct. (so. dist.) Ind. 1969, U.S. Ct. Appeals (7th cir.) 1976, U.S. Supreme Ct. 1980, U.S. Tax Ct. 1983. Ptnr. Ice Miller, Indpls. Mem. Am. Coll. Trust and Estate Coun. (Ind. chmn. 1990-95). Avocations: hunting, fishing. Office: Ice Miller 1 American Sq Indianapolis IN 46282-0020

WISHNER, MAYNARD IRA, finance company executive, lawyer; b. Chgo., Sept. 17, 1923; s. Hyman L. and Frances (Fisher) W.; m. Elaine Loewenberg, July 4, 1954; children: Ellen Kenemore, Jane Wishner, Miriam Segel. B.A., U. Chgo., 1944, J.D., 1947; LHD honoris causa, Spertus Inst., Hebrew Union Coll. Bar: Ill. 1947. Exec. dir. Chgo. Commn. on Human Relations, 1947-52; chief ordinance enforcement div. Law Dept., City of Chgo., 1952-55; mem. law firm Cole, Wishner, Epstein & Manilow, Chgo., 1955-63; with Walter E. Heller & Co., 1963-86, pres., 1974-86; of counsel Rosenthal and Schanfield, 1986-95. Dir. Walter E. Heller Internat. Corp., Am. Nat. Bank & Trust Co., and br. cos., Chgo. Pres. Jewish Fedn. Met. Chgo., 1987-89; chair Nat. Jewish Community Rels., 1992-94, pres. Coun. Jewish Fedn., 1993-96; chmn. bd. govs. Am. Jewish Com., 1977-80, nat. pres. 1980-83, hon. pres., recipient Human Rights medallion, 1975; bd. dirs. Nat. Found. for Jewish Culture; chmn. Ill. Humanities Coun.; commr. Nat. Hillel Found.; mem. vis. com. U. Chgo. Sch. Social Svc. Adminstrn. and Divsn. of the Humanities; chair Ill. Humanities Coun., 1991-93; bd. govs. Jewish Agy. for Israel. Recipient Rosenwald award Jewish Fedn. Met. Chgo., Officers medal of merit Republic of Poland, United Hellenic Leadership Coun. Frisis award, Civic Achievement award U. Chgo. Home: 1410 Sheridan Rd Wilmette IL 60091-1895 E-mail: maynwish@aol.com.

WISLER, DAVID CHARLES, aerospace engineer, educator; b. Pottstown, Pa., Apr. 21, 1941; s. Lloyd William and Ruth Georgiana (Enos) W.; m. Judith Ann Caleen, Aug. 22, 1964 (dec. Mar. 1979); children: Scott David, Cheryl Lynn; m. Beth Ellen Howard, Jan. 5, 1980; 1 child, Daniel James. BS in Aero Engring., Pa. State U., 1963; MS in Aero. Engring., Cornell U., 1965; PhD in Aero. Engring., U. Colo., 1970. Rsch. engr. GE R & D Ctr., Schenectady, 1965-67; mgr. aero tech. labs. GE Aircraft Engines, Evendale, Ohio, 1985—. Mgr. univ. programs and aero tech. labs. Contbr. articles to profl. jours.; patentee in sloped trenches in compressors. Recipient Gas Turbine award ASME, 1990, 92. Fellow AIAA (assoc.); mem. ASME (chmn. turbomachinery com. 1993—, bd. dirs. Internat. Gas Turbine Inst. 1997—, Melville medal for best tech. paper 1989, 98). Avocation: photography. Home: 40 Trappist Walk Fairfield OH 45014-4465 Office: GE Aircraft Engines 1 Neumann Way # A-411 Cincinnati OH 45215-1915 E-mail: dave.wisler@ae.ge.com.

WITASZAK, RICHARD B. retail executive; Various positions Coopers & Lybrand, Detroit, audit mgr.; mgr. fin. reporting J.P. Industries, Inc., Ann Arbor, Mich.; exec. v.p. fin. and ops. AE Clevite, Inc., Collierville, Tenn.; exec. v.p. fin. and CFO Payless Cashways, Inc., Lee's Summit, Mo., 1996—. Office: Payless Cashways Inc Ste 700 127 W 10th St Kansas City MO 64105-1716

WITCHER, DANIEL DOUGHERTY, retired pharmaceutical company executive; b. Atlanta, May 17, 1924; s. Julius Gordon and Myrtice Eleanor (Daniel) W.; divorced; children: Beth S., Daniel Dougherty Jr., J. Wright, Benjamin G.; m. Betty Lou Middaugh, Oct. 30, 1982. Student, Mercer U., 1946-47, Am. Grad. Sch. Internat. Mgmt., 1949-50. Regional dir. Sterling Drug Co., Rio de Janeiro and Sao Paulo, Brazil, 1951-56; gen. mgr. Mead Johnson & Co., Sao Paulo, 1956-60; area mgr. Upjohn Internat., Inc., 1960-64, v.p. Kalamazoo, 1964-70, group v.p., 1970-73; pres., gen. mgr. Upjohn Internat., 1973-86; v.p. Upjohn Co., 1973-86, sr. v.p., 1986-89, asst. to pres., 1988-89; chmn. Upjohn Healthcare Svcs., 1982-87; ret., 1989. Bd. dirs. Upjohn Co.; trustee Am. Grad. Sch. Internat. Mgmt., 1981—. With USNR, 1943-46. Mem. Pharm. Mfrs. Assn. (chmn. internat. sect. 1981-82, 85-86), Am. Grad. Sch. Internat. Mgmt. Alumni Assn. (pres. 1989-91). Republican. Episcopalian. Avocations: tennis, golf.

WITCHER, GARY ROYAL, minister, educator; b. Clinton, Okla., July 4, 1950; s. Alton Gale and Frances Loraine (Royal) W.; m. Victoria Amy Waddington, June 6, 1970; children: Jessica, Toni, Monica. BA in Art, Southwestern Okla. State U., 1973, BA in Art Edn., 1975, MEd in Art, 1978. Minister, 1979. Tchr. Window Rock Sch. Dist., Ft. Defiance, Ariz., 1973-76, Western Heights (Okla.) Sch. Dist., Oklahoma City, 1976-77, Mustang (Okla.) Sch. Dist., 1977-79; minister Ch. of Christ, Cervignano, Italy, 1979-86, Watertown, S.D., 1986—; instr. Mount Marty Coll., 1987—. Part-time tchr. Watertown Sch. Dist., 1987—; bd. dirs. East River Bible Camp, 1988-97. Recipient 1st Place Slide Program Competition prize Am. Fedn. Mineralogical Socs., 1993, 95. Mem. Coteau des Plains Gem and Mineral Soc. (pres. 1991-92, 95). Republican. Avocations: photography, car restoration, collecting rocks, coins and stamps. Home: PO Box 1622 1105 4th St NE Watertown SD 57201-1202 Office: Ch of Christ 1103 4th St NE Watertown SD 57201-1202

WITCOFF, SHELDON WILLIAM, lawyer; b. Washington, July 10, 1925; s. Joseph and Zina (Ceppos) W.; m. Margot Gail Hoffner, Sept. 6, 1953; children: Lauren Jill, David Lawrence, Lisa Ann, Julie Beth. B.S. in Elec. Engring, U. Md., 1949; J.D., George Washington U., 1953. Bar: D.C. 1953, N.Y. 1955, Ill. 1956. Patent examiner Patent Office, Dept. Commerce, 1949-53; patent lawyer Bell Telephone Labs., Murray Hill, N.J., 1953-55; ptnr. Bair, Freeman & Molinare, Chgo., 1955-69, Allegretti, Newitt, Witcoff & McAndrews, Chgo., 1970-88, Allegretti & Witcoff, LTD, Chgo., 1988-95, Banner & Witcoff Ltd., Chgo., 1995—. V.p. Art Splty. Co., Chgo., 1967—; v.p. Caspian Fur Trading Co., N.Y.C.; dir. Child Abuse Unit for Studies, Edn. and Svcs., Chgo. Fire and police commr., Skokie, Ill., 1960-63. Served with USNR, 1943-46. Mem. Am. Bar Assn., Intellectual Property Assn. of Chgo., Order of Coif, Tau Epsilon Phi, Phi Delta Phi., B'nai B'rith. Home: 235 Maple Hill Rd Glencoe IL 60022-1257 Office: 10 S Wacker Dr Chicago IL 60606-7407 E-mail: witcoff@bannerwitcoff.com.

WITEK, KATE, state senator, trucking company executive; b. Detroit, Oct. 22, 1954; m. Charles Wite, 1974; children: Thomas Charles, Kimberly Rose. Student, Ea. Mich. U. Owner, mgr. Witek Trucking Co.; mem. Nebr. Senate, Lincoln, 1992-98; Auditor of Pub. Accounts NE, 1999—. Mem. commerce and ins. com., govt., mil. and vet. affairs com. Mem. Nat. Small Bus. United, Nebr. Motor Carriers, Millard Jaycees. Republican. Home: 5179 S 147th St Omaha NE 68137-1439 Office: Auditor of Public Accounts State Capitol Suite 2303 PO Box 98917 Lincoln NE 68509-8917

WITHEM, RONALD E. state senator, trade association executive; b. Logan, Iowa, June 9, 1946; m. Diane Weinstein, 1973; children: Susanne, Justin. BA, Wayne State Coll., 1968; MS, U. Nebr., Omaha, 1975. Tchr. Papillion (Nebr.) H.S.; exec. v.p. Mech. Constructors Assn. Omaha; mem. Nebr. Senate, Lincoln, 1983—; assoc. v.p. external affairs & govtl. rels. U. Nebr. Chmn. edn. com., mem. rules com., revenue com., former mem. govt., mil. and vet. affairs coms. Former chmn. Edn. Commn. of States; former office mgr. U.S. Rep. John J. Cavanaugh. Mem. Papillion C. of C., LaVista C. of C., Omaha C. of C. Democrat. Home: 1104 Shady Tree Ln Papillion NE 68046-6194 Office: U Nebr Office External Affairs 3835 Holdege Lincoln NE 68583-0745

WITHERELL, MICHAEL S. physicist, educator; b. Toledo, Sept. 22, 1949; s. Thomas W. and Marie (Savage) W.; m. Elizabeth Hall. BS, U. Mich., 1968; MS, U. Wis., 1970, PhD, 1973. Instr. Princeton (N.J.) U., 1973-75, asst. prof., 1975-81, U. Calif., Santa Barbara, 1981-83, assoc. prof., 1983-86, prof., 1986-99; dir. Fermi Nat. Accelerator Lab., Batavia, Ill., 1999—. Chmn. physics adv. com. Fermi Nat. Accelerator Lab., Batavia, Ill., 1987-89; mem. high energy physics adv. panel U.S. Dept. Energy, Washington, 1990-93, chair high energy physics adv. panel, 1996-99; chmn. sci. policy com. Stanford Linear Accelerator Ctr., 1995—. Guggenheim fellow John S. Guggenheim Found., 1988; recipient W. K. H. Panofsky prize Am. Phys. Soc., 1990. Fellow AAAS; mem. NAS. Office: Fermi Lab MS 105 PO Box 500 Batavia IL 60510-0500

WITHERS, W. RUSSELL, JR. broadcast executive; b. Cape Girardeau, Mo., Dec. 10, 1936; s. Waldo Russell Sr. and Dorothy Ruth (Harrelson) W.; 1 child, Dana Ruth. BA, S.E. Mo. State U., 1958. Disc jockey Sta. KGMO Radio, Cape Girardeau, 1955-58; account exec. Sta. WGGH Radio, Marion, Ill., 1961-62; v.p. LIN Broadcasting Corp., Nashville, 1962-69; exec. v.p., dir. Laser Link Corp., Woodbury, N.Y., 1970-72; owner Withers Broadcasting of Hawaii, 1975-79, Withers Broadcasting of Minn., 1974-79, Withers Broadcasting Cos., Iowa, 1981—, Mood Music Ill., Mt. Vernon, 1973—, Mood Music, Inc., Cape Girardeau, 1972—, Royal Hawaiian Radio Co., Inc., others. Owner various radio and TV stas. including KREX-TV, Grand Junction, Colo., KREY-TV, Montrose, Colo., KREG-TV, Glenwood Springs, Colo., Page Ins. and Real Estate, Mt. Vernon, Ill.; chmn. bd., CEO Withers Beverage Corp., Mobile, Ala., 1973—79; chmn. adv. bd. Mut. Network; bd. dirs. Theatrevision, Inc., Turneffe Island Lodge, Ltd., Belize, Sta. WDTV, Clarksburg, W.Va., WMIX-AM-TV, Mt. Vernon, KGMO-KAPE, Cape Girardeau, KOKX AM-FM, Keokuk, Iowa, KTRC, Santa Fe, KRHW and KBXB, Sikeston, Mo., WKIB Anna, Cape Girardeau, WMOK, WREZ and WZZL, Paducah, Ky., WSDR-WSSQ, WZZL, Sterling Rock Falls, Ill., WILY, WRXX (FM), Centralia, Ill.; pres. Ill. Pub. Airports Assn.; co-chmn. TARPAC. Bd. dirs., chmn. bd. Mt. Vernon Tourism and Conv. Bur.; chmn. Mt. Vernon Airport Authority; bd. regents Lincoln Acad.; past pres. IPAA; past chmn. Conv. & Visitors, Airport Authority. With U.S. Army, 1957-58. Mem. Mt. Vernon C. of C. (bd. dirs.), Nat. Assn. Broadcasters, Ill. Broadcasters Assn., Stadium Club, Mo. Athletic Club, Elks, Moose, AmVets, Masons, Shriners, Sigma Chi. Christian Scientist. Home: 1 Sleepy Hollow Ln Mount Vernon IL 62864-2852 Office: PO Box 1508 Mount Vernon IL 62864-0030

WITHERS, W. WAYNE, lawyer; b. Enid, Okla., Nov. 4, 1940; s. Walter O. and Ruby (Mackey) W.; m. Patricia Ann Peppers, Dec. 12, 1974; children: Jennifer Lynn, Whitney Lee. BA, U. Okla., 1962; JD, Northwestern U., 1965. Bar: Okla. 1965, Mo. 1970, U.S. Ct. Appeals (8th cir.), 1972, U.S. Supreme Ct. 1972, U.S. Ct. Appeals (fed. cir.) 1984, U.S. Ct. Appeals (D.C. cir.) 1985, U.S. Ct. Claims, 1988. Staff atty. FTC, Washington, 1965-68; co. atty. Monsanto Co., St. Louis, 1968-78, asst. gen. counsel, 1978-85; gen. counsel Monsanto Agrl. Co., 1985-89, v.p., gen. counsel; sr. v.p., sec., gen. counsel Emerson Electric Co., 1989—. V.p. Internat. Food Biotech. Coun., Washington, 1989-90; bd. dirs. Internat. Life Scis. Inst., Washington, 1989-90. Contbr. articles to profl. jours. Mem. ABA (sec. corp. law dept.), Am. Law Inst., Assn. Gen. Counsel, Bar Assn. Met. St. Louis, Indsl. Biotech. Assn. (chmn. law com.), Environ. Law Inst. (assoc.), Nat. Agrl. Chem. Assn. (chmn. law com. 1983-85), The Conf. Bd. Coun. for Gen. Counsel (vice chmn. 1992-99), MAPI Law Coun. Office: Emerson Electric Co 8100 W Florissant Ave Saint Louis MO 63136-1494

WITHERSPOON, JOHN THOMAS, water resources consultant; b. Springfield, Mo., June 25, 1947; s. Warren Thomas and Kathryn (Corbus) w.; m. C. Frances Teter, June 12, 1971. BS, S.W. Mo. State U., 1969, MA, 1971; PhD, U. Mont., 1975. Water control inspector City of Springfield, Mo., 1976-78; dir. labs. City Utilities, Springfield, 1978-91, mgr. water treatment and supply, 1991—2001. Mem. safe drinking water commn. Mo. State Dept. Natural Resources, Jefferson City, 1992—, now chair; bd. dirs. James River Basin Partnership, Nixa, Mo., 1996; tech. advisor Watershed Com. of the Ozarks, Springfield, 1983—. Pres. Univ. Club Springfield, 1989. Mem. Am. Water Works Assn. (chair, Boyd Utility Mgr. award 1996, Fuller award 1999), Kiwanis. Avocations: golf, reading, guitar, travel. Home: 1927 E Lark St Springfield MO 65804-4345 Office: City Utilities PO Box 551 Springfield MO 65801-0551 E-mail: jtwithersp@aol.com.

WITKE, DAVID RODNEY, newspaper editor; b. Council Bluffs, Iowa, Mar. 24, 1937; s. Arnold and Rosamond Louise (Storer) W.; m. Priscilla Bill Smith, Oct. 8, 1960; 1 son, Carl. B.S. in Journalism, Northwestern U., 1959. Reporter, editor The Courier, Champaign-Urbana, Ill., 1962-66; copy editor The Register, Des Moines, 1966-70, city editor, 1970-73, asst. mng. editor adminstrn., 1973-74, asst. mng. editor electronics, 1974-75, mng. editor, 1975-83, dir. ops., 1983-85, dep. editor, omsbudsman, 1985-87, exec. sports editor, 1987-98, sr. editor, 1998—. Rep. Iowa Freedom of Info. Coun., Des Moines, 1973—, pres., 1986-88; vis. lectr. Drake U., 1986—, Iowa State U., 1990—; juror Pulitzer Prize, 1989-91. Served to lt. (j.g.) USN, 1959-62, PTO. Mem. Assoc. Press Mng. Editors Assn., Mid-Am. Newspaper Assn., AP Sports Editors Assn., Iowa Newspaper Found., The Prairie Club, Sigma Delta Chi Unitarian. Achievements include early lectures on electronic applications to large newspaper production. Home: 2521 48th Pl Des Moines IA 50310-2506 Office: Des Moines Register and Tribune Co 715 Locust St Des Moines IA 50309-3767

WITMER, JOHN HARPER, JR. lawyer; b. Phila., May 5, 1940; s. John Harper and Jane Carolyn (Lentz) Witmer; m. Arlene Marie Rosipal, June 9, 1962; 1 dau., Tara Leah. BA, Pa. State U., 1962; JD, George Washington U., 1969. Bar: Md. 1969, D.C. 1970, Ill. 1979. Mgmt. analyst Nat. Security Agy., Ft. Meade, Md., 1963-66; mem. Sidley & Austin, Washington, 1969-78; sr. v.p., gen. counsel DEKALB Energy Co., 1978-95, DEKALB Genetics Corp., 1978-99; ret., 1999. Mem. Ill. State Bar Assn., Md. State Bar Assn., D.C. Bar Assn. Home: 2575 Greenwood Acres Dr Dekalb IL 60115-4916

WITOSKY, GARY J. manufacturing company executive; BA in Acctg. and Bus. Adminstrn., Thiel Coll. Audit mgr. Ernst & Whinney, Cleve.; treas., corp. contr. Park Corp., until 1994; tras. Am. Axle & Mfg., Detroit, 1994-97, v.p., 1996-97, v.p. fin., CFO, 1997-99; pres., CEO Colfor Mfg. Inc., Malvern, Ohio, 1999—. Office: Colfor Mfg Inc 3255 Alliance Rd NW PO Box 485 Malvern OH 44644-0485

WITT, GARY DEAN, former state legislator; b. Smithville, Mo., Feb. 2, 1965; s. Donald Audon and Jo Ellen Witt. BA in Comm., William Jewel Coll., 1987; JD, U. Mo., 1990. Bar: Mo. 1990, Kans. 1992. Ptnr. Witt, Hicklin & Witt, Platte City, Mo., 1890-98; assoc. cir. judge 6th Jud. Cir., Platte County, 1998—; mem. Mo. Ho. of Reps., Jefferson City, 1990-96, chmn. judiciary and ethics com., 1993-96. Named one of Ten Outstanding Young Missourians, Mo. Jaycees, 1993, Outstanding Legislator, Mo. Bar Assn., 1993; recipient Outstanding Contbn. to Adminstrn. of Justice award Mo. Jud. Conf., 1991, 92, 93, 94, 95; Walter Pope Binns pus. svc. fellow, 1993. Mem. Mo. Assn. Trial Attys. (Outstanding Legislator 1991-92, 93), Platte County Mech. and Agrl. Soc. (bd. dirs. 1992-94), Delta Theta Phi, Kappa Alpha Order. Democrat. Baptist. Avocation: water skiing. Office: 428 Main St Platte City MO 64079-9438

WITTBRODT, FREDERICK JOSEPH, JR. automotive designer; b. Detroit, Feb. 6, 1955; s. Frederick Joseph Sr. and Hilda Lottie (Neubert) W.; m. Deborah Carrie Kay, Apr. 11, 1992; stepchildren: Angela Defer, Michael Defer II; children from previous marriage: Robin Lynn, Daniel Joseph. Grad., Philpot Sch. Automotive Body Drafting, Royal Oak, Mich., 1977, Entech. Engring., Troy, Mich., 1984; grad. SDRC Basing Modeling Tng., Henry Ford C.C., 1997. Designer Modern Engring Co.-Design, Troy, Mich., 1977-78, Detroit Indsl. engring., Troy, 1978-80, Engring Tech., Ltd., Troy, 1980-86, Pioneer Engring., Dearborn, 1986, APD, Dearborn, 1988-89, Mega-Tech. Engring., Warren, 1989-90, Uni-Tech, Madison Heights, 1990-91, Harman at Harvard, Southfield, 1991; sr. automotive designer Lincoln Tech. at Schlegel, Madison Heights, 1991-92; sr. designer, surface devel. specialist Resource Techs. at Harvard Industries, Farmington Hills, Mich., 1992-95, Schefenacker Mfg. Ctr. (formerly Britax Vision Sys., Inc.), Marysville, 1995—. Mem. NRA, Internat. Platform Soc. Avocations: furniture design, landscape design, astronomy. Home: 7906 Anchor Bay Dr Algonac MI 48001 Office: 1855 Busha Hwy Marysville MI 48040-1892 E-mail: frederick.wittbrodt@schefenacker-usa.com., dwitt2000@hotmail.com.

WITTEN, DAVID MELVIN, radiology educator; b. Trenton, Mo., Aug. 16, 1926; s. Buford Isom and Mary Louise (Melvin) W.; m. Netta Lee Watkins, Dec. 23, 1950; children— David Melvin, II, Michael Lee. Student, Trenton Jr. Coll., 1943-44, 46-47; AB, Washington U., St. Louis, 1950, MD, 1954; MS in Radiology, U. Minn., 1960. Diplomate: Am. Bd. Radiology. Intern Virginia Mason Hosp., Seattle, 1954-55; practice medicine specializing in family medicine Trenton, Mo., 1955-57; fellow in radiology Mayo Clinic/Mayo Found., Rochester, Minn., 1957-60; cons. in diagnostic roentgenology Mayo Clinic, 1960-70; instr. Mayo Grad. Sch. Medicine, Rochester, 1960-66, asst. prof. radiology, 1966-70; pvt. practice medicine specializing in radiology Aberdeen, Wash., 1970-71; clin. assoc. prof. U. Wash., 1970-71; prof. diagnostic radiology, chmn. dept. diagnostic radiology U. Ala., Birmingham, 1971-82; diagnostic radiologist in chief Univ. Hosp., 1971-82; prof., chmn. dept. radiology U. Mo., Columbia, 1982-87, prof. emeritus, 1987—, interim chmn. dept. radiology, 1998-99. Pres. U. Ala. Health Services Found., 1973-75 Author: Atlas of Tumor Radiology-The Breast, 1969, Clinical Urography, 1970, 77; contbr. articles on radiology of breast cancer, urologic and gastrointestinal disease to profl. jours.; mem. editorial bd. Am. Jour. Roentgenology, 1976-87, Applied Radiology, 1978-87, Urologic Radiology, 1979-87, Radiographics, 1983-87. Served with USNR, 1944-46. Fellow Am. Coll. Radiology; mem. AAAS, AMA, Radiol. Soc. N.Am., Am. Roentgen Ray Soc., Soc. Genitourinary Radiology (pres. 1981-82), Assn. Univ. Radiologists, Mo. Radiol. Soc. (pres. 1988-89), Mo. State Med. Assn., Can. Assn. Radiologists (hon.), Audubon Soc. (editor The Bluebird (Mo.) chpt. 1990-98). Home: 601 W Covered Bridge Rd Columbia MO 65203-9562 Office: Univ Mo Health Scis Ctr 1 Hospital Dr Columbia MO 65201-5276 E-mail: dmw@tranquility.net.

WITTEN, LOUIS, physics educator; b. Balt., Apr. 13, 1921; s. Abraham and Bessie (Perman) W.; m. Lorraine Wollach, Mar. 27, 1949 (dec. 1987); children: Edward, Celia, Matthew, Jesse; m. Francis L. White, Jan. 2, 1992. B.E., Johns Hopkins U., 1941, Ph.D., 1951; B.S., NYU, 1944. Research assoc. Princeton U., N.J., 1951-53; research assoc. U. Md., College Park, 1953-54; staff scientist Lincoln Lab., MIT, 1954-55; assoc. dir. Martin Marietta Research Lab., Balt., 1955-68; prof. physics U. Cin., 1968-91, prof. emeritus, 1991—. Trustee Gravity Research Found. Editor: Gravitation: An Introduction to Current Research, 1962, Relativity: Procs. of Relative Conf. in Midwest of 1969, Symposium on Asymptotic Structure of Space-Time, 1976; patentee in field; contbr. numerous articles to sci. jours. Served to 1st lt. USAF, 1942-46 Fulbright lectr. Weismann Inst. Scis., Rehovot, Israel, 1963-64 Fellow Am. Phys. Soc.; mem. Am. Math. Soc., Internat. Astron. Union, AAAS. Office: Univ Cincinnati Dept Physics Cincinnati OH 45221-0011 E-mail: witten@physics.uc.edu.

WITTER, RICHARD LAWRENCE, veterinarian, educator; b. Bangor, Maine, Sept. 10, 1936; s. John Franklin and Verna Harriet (Church) W.; m. Joan Elizabeth Denny, June 30, 1962; children: Jane Katherine, Steven Franklin. B.S., Mich. State U., 1958, D.V.M., 1960; M.S., Cornell U., 1962, Ph.D., 1964. Rsch. veterinarian Agrl. Rsch. Svc., USDA, East Lansing, Mich., 1964-75, dir. Avian Disease and Oncology Lab., 1975-98, veterinarian 1998—; clin. prof. pathology Mich. State U., 1965—. Contbr.

articles to profl. jours. Recipient Disting. Alumni award Coll. Vet. Medicine, Mich. State U., 1985, Disting. Svc. award USDA, 1985, Marek Commemorative medal U. Budapest, 1997, Pfizer Excellence in Poultry Rsch. award, 1998. Mem. NAS, AVMA, Am. Assn. Avian Pathologists (P.P. Levine award 1967, 81, 88, 92, 98, Upjohn Achievement award 1992, Spl. Svc. award 1998), Poultry Sci. Assn. (CPC Internat. award 1976), World Vet. Poultry Assn. (B. Rispens rsch. award 1983). Lodge: Kiwanis Avocations: piano, hunting, fishing, gardening. Home: 1799 Elk Ln Okemos MI 48864-5917 Office: Avian Disease and Oncology Lab 3606 E Mt Hope Rd East Lansing MI 48823-5338

WITTHUHN, BURTON ORRIN, university official; b. Allentown, Pa., Aug. 22, 1934; s. Ray Arthur and Mae Marcella (Kline) W.; m. Patricia King, June 24, 1961; children: Jonathan, Andrew. BS, Kutztown (Pa.) U., 1956; MEd, Pa. State U., 1962, PhD, 1968. Tchr. Allentown (Pa.) Pub. Schs., 1956-63; teaching asst., assoc. Pa. State U., University Park, 1963-66, rsch. asst., 1965-66; asst. prof. Ohio State U., Columbus, 1967-70; prof., chmn. dept. geography Edinboro (Pa.) State Coll., 1970-79, assoc. v.p. acad. affairs, 1980-83; provost, v.p. acad. affairs Edinboro Univ. of Pa., 1984-88, Western Ill. U., Macomb, 1988-93, acting pres., 1993, provost, v.p. acad. affairs, 1994—2002. Vis. rsch. prof. Nat. Taiwan Normal U., 1978; cons. Project Africa/Carnegie-Mellon U., Pitts., 1967-70, 92, 87, 95; mem. mid. states periodic rev. team, Phila., 1986—; mem. mid. states evaluation team in conjunction with Am. Optometric Assn. , 1987; mem. evaluation team Pa. Dept. Edn., 1988; mem. accreditation team Am. Optometric, 1990—; evaluator Higher Learning Commn. North Cen. Assn., 1994—; examiner Lincoln Found. for Bus. Excellence, 1996—; vice-chmn. Quad Cities Grad. Ctr., 1991-2000; mem. nat. screening com. for Africa, Inst. of Internat. Edn., 1994-96. Co-author: Discovery in Geography, 1976; co-author: So You Want to Go to College: 50 Questions to Ponder, Strategies for Timely Degree Completion: Connecting the Parts, Strategies for Timely Degree Completion: Myths and Realities, Technology: Bridge or Barrier To More Timely Degree Completion?, 1998; ; mem. editl. bd. Pa. Geographer, Chronicle of CQI; contbr. chpts. to books. Mem. Edinboro Planning & Zoning Commn., 1973-77. Recipient Disting. Alumnus award Kutztown U., 1990; Fulbright Hays fellow, Ethiopia, Kenya, Uganda, 1965. Mem. Nat. Coun. Geog. Edn. (exec. bd. 1977-80, mem. award com. for region IV 1981), Pa. Coun. Geog. Edn. (exec. sec. 1976-79, pres. 1975-76, Outstanding Prof. award 1978), Macomb Club (pres. 1998-99), Rotary (pres. Edinboro club 1972-73). Methodist. Avocations: reading, golf, photography, model constrn. Home: 1106 Bayberry Ln Macomb IL 61455-3518 Office: Western Ill U Sherman Hall 1 Circle Dr Macomb IL 61455

WITTIG, DAVID C. energy executive; BS in Bus. Adminstrn. & Econs., U. Kans., 1977. Analyst rsch. dept. H. O. Peet & Co., Inc., 1977-78, assoc. nat. individual sales, 1978-79, assoc. mergers and acquisitions, 1979-81, asst. v.p. mergers and acquisitions, 1981-83, v.p. mergers and acquisitions, 1983-86, mng. dir., head mergers and acquisitions, 1986-89; mng. dir., co-head investment banking Kidder Peabody & Co., Inc., 1989, mng. dir. mergers and acquisitions, 1989-91; mng. dir., co-head mergers and acquisitions Salomon Bros., Inc., 1991-95; exec. v.p. corp. strategy Western Resources, Topeka, 1995-96, pres., 1996-98, pres., CEO, 1998—, chmn., 1999—. Bd. dirs. Boys Harbor. Office: Western Resources Inc 818 S Kansas Ave Topeka KS 66612-1203 Fax: 785-575-6399.

WITTLICH, GARY EUGENE, music theory educator, college administrator; b. Belleville, Ill., Dec. 3, 1934; s. Marvin Oscar and Erma Carrie (Garlich) Jackson Wittlich; m. Barbara L. Casey, Jan. 4, 1958 (div. Feb. 1969); children: M. Kent (d. 1999), Kristi L.; m. Mildred Elizabeth Read, Mar. 17, 1971. BM in Edn., So. Ill. U., 1957, MMus, 1959; PhD, U. Iowa, 1969. Asst. prof. music Upper Iowa U., Fayette, 1959-63; prof. music, grad. studies in music theory Ind. U., Bloomington, 1965-97; disting. tech. cons. Univ. Info. Tech. Svc., 1999—; assoc. dean faculty, ext. liaison, office v.p. info. tech. Ind. U., Bloomington, 1995-98, dir. of computing Sch. of Music, 1989-95; Meadows disting. vis. prof. music So. Meth. U., Dallas, 1982-83; vis. prof. U. Mich., Ann Arbor, 1974; dir. Ctr. for Profl. Devel. in Music Tech., CMS/ATMI, 1995-97. Dir. Ameritech Fellows program, 2001—; cons. U. Del. Music Videodisc Series, NEH, 1982-85; mem. vis. performing arts com. U. Del., 1996-98; mem. music test com. Ednl. Testing Svc., Princeton, N.J., 1983-85, chmn., 1986-90. Author: (with C. Lee Humphries) Ear Training: An Approach Through Music Literature, 1974, (with others) Aspects of Twentieth-Century Music, 1975, (with J. Schaffer and L. Babb) Microcomputers and Music, 1986, (with D. Martin) Tonal Harmony for the Keyboard, 1988. Served with U.S. Army, 1957, 61-62. NSF grantee Ind. U., 1970, 2000-2004; fellow Inst. for Acad. Tech., 1992. Mem. Assn. for Tech. in Music Instrn. (founding), Coll. Music Soc. (bd. mem. for theory 1987-89), Soc. Music Theory (exec. bd. 1982-85, pres. 1988-91). Home: 109 Jose Gaspar Dr Englewood FL 34223-3863 E-mail: wittlich@indiana.edu.

WITTLINGER, TIMOTHY DAVID, lawyer; b. Dayton, Ohio, Oct. 12, 1940; s. Charles Frederick and Dorothy Elizabeth (Golden) W.; m. Diane Cleo Dominy, May 20, 1967; children: Kristine Elizabeth, David Matthew. BS in Math., Purdue U., 1962; JD with distinction, U. Mich., 1965. Bar: Mich. 1966, U.S. Dist. Ct. (ea. dist.) Mich. 1966, U.S. Ct. Appeals (6th cir.) 1968, U.S. Supreme Ct. 1971. Assoc. Clark Hill (formerly Hill Lewis), Detroit, 1965-72, ptnr., 1973—, head litigation dept., 1976-91, gen. counsel, 1997—. Mem. profl. assistance com. U.S. Dist. Ct. (ea. dist.) Mich., 1981-82; mem. Mich. Supreme Ct. Com. to Evaluate Mediation Ct. Rule, 1997-98; author, lectr. Ctr. for Internat. Legal Studies, 1999—. Mem. ho. of deps. Episc. Ch., N.Y.C., 1979—; vice chmn. Robert Whitaker Sch. Theology, 1983-87; sec. bd. trustees Episc. Ch., Diocese of Mich., Detroit, 1983—, sec. conv. Episc. Diocese of Mich., 1990—, ch. atty., 1997—, mem., sec. Episc. nat. econ. justice implementation com., 1988-95, mem. Episc. nat. exec. coun., 1991-97, mem. nat. audit com.; mem. Nat. Standing Commn. on Ministry Devel., 2000—; active Nat. Episc. Jubilee Ministry Com., Nat. Episc. Coalition for Social Witness and Justice, Fifth Province Episc. Ecclesiastical Ct. Appeal; mem. nat. audit com. Episcopal Ch.; bd. dirs. Episc. Student Found., U. Mich., 1990-93, 2000-2002; chair Grubb Inst. Behavioral Studies Ltd., Washington, 1986—; bd. dirs. Birmingham Village Playhouse, 2000—. Mem. ABA, State Bar Mich., Nat. Bd. Trial Advocacy (cert.), Engring. Soc. Detroit. Home: 736 N Glenhurst Dr Birmingham MI 48009-1143 Office: Clark Hill 500 Woodward Ave Ste 3500 Detroit MI 48226-3435

WITTMAN, RANDY, professional basketball coach; m. Kathy Wittman; children: Ryan, Lauren. BS, Ind. U., 1983. With Wash. Bullets, 1983, Atlanta Hawks, from 1983; also with Sacramento Kings and Ind. Pacers; head coach Cleve. Cavaliers, 1999—. Office: Minnesota Timberwolves Target Center 600 1st Ave N Minneapolis MN 55403-1416

WIWCHAR, MICHAEL, bishop; b. Komarno, Manitoba, Canada, May 9, 1932; ordained priest June 28, 1959. Pastor St. John the Baptist Church, Newark, 1990-93; bishop Diocese of St. Nicholas of Chicago for the Ukrainians, 1993—. Office: Chancery Office 2245 W Rice St Chicago IL 60622-4858 Fax: (773) 276-6799. E-mail: sneparchy@iols.com.

WIXTROM, DONALD JOSEPH, translator; b. Republic, Mich., Oct. 14, 1928; s. Joseph Albert and Edith (Johnson) W.; m. Marilyn Jean Sjoquist, Oct. 14, 1961; children: Joe Alan, Lorna Jean, Aaron Matthew. Free lance translator, Republic, 1966—. Mem. Am. Translators Assn. Baptist. Home and Office: RR 1 Box 98 Republic MI 49879-9726

WOBBLE, DICK, radio personality; b. St. Louis; m. Renee Wobble. Student, U. Mo. Announcer, producer Classic 99, St. Louis. Avocation: reading. Office: Classic 99 85 Founders Ln Saint Louis MO 63105

WOEHRLEN, ARTHUR EDWARD, JR. dentist; b. Detroit, Dec. 9, 1947; s. Arthur Edward and Olga (Hewka) W.; m. Sara Elizabeth Heikoff, Aug. 13, 1972; 1 child, Tess Helena. DDS, U. Mich., 1973. Resident in gen. dentistry USAF, 1973-74; gen. practice dentistry Redwood Dental Group, Warren, Mich., 1976—. Instr. Sinai Hosp., Detroit, 1977—; chief of dentistry St. John's Hosp., Macomb Ctr., Mt. Clemens, Mich., 1982—; mem. dentistry staff Hutzel Hosp., Warren; reviewer Chubb Ins. Co. (malpractice claims), 1978-89; bd. mem. Mich. Acad. Gen. Dentistry (chmn. State of Mich. Continuing Dental Edn. Accreditation). Contbr. articles on dentistry to profl. jours. Served to capt. USAF, 1973-76. Fellow Internat. Coll. of Oral Implantologists; mem. ADA, Acad. Gen. Dentistry (Master), Mich. Dental Assn., Acad. Gen. Dentistry, Am. Acad. Oral Medicine, Fedn. Dentaire Internationale, Acad. Dentistry for the Handicapped, Am. Acad. Oral Implantologists, Internat. Coll. Oral Implantologists, Macomb Dist. Dental Soc.; panel mem. Am. Arbitration Assn. Republican. Home: 25460 Dundee Rd Royal Oak MI 48067-3018 Office: 13403 E 13 Mile Rd Warren MI 48088-3188

WOELFEL, JAMES WARREN, philosophy and humanities educator; b. Galveston, Tex., Aug. 16, 1937; s. Warren Charles and Mary Frances (Washinka) W.; m. Sarah Chappell Trulove, Nov. 24, 1982; children by previous marriages: Skye Caitlin, Allegra Eve, Sarah Judith; stepchildren: Ann Marie and Paul Trulove. BA, U. Okla., 1959; MDiv, Episcopal Div. Sch., Cambridge, Mass., 1962; MA, Yale U., 1964; PhD, U. St. Andrews, Scotland, 1967. Asst. prof. philosophy and religion U. Kans., Lawrence, 1966-70, asst. prof. philosophy, 1970-71, assoc. prof. philosophy and religion, 1971-75, prof. philosophy and religious studies, 1975-88, prof. philosophy, 1988—, acting chmn. dept. religious studies, 1983-84, dir. Humanities and Western civilization program, 1985—. Manuscript reader for various presses, jours. Author: Bonhoeffer's Theology, 1970, Borderland Christianity, 1973, Camus: A Theological Perspective, 1975 (republished as Albert Camus on the Sacred and the Secular, 1987), Augustinian Humanism, 1979, The Agnostic Spirit as a Common Motif in Liberal Theology and Liberal Scepticism, 1990; editor (with Sarah Chappell Trulove) and contbr.: Patterns in Western Civilization, 1991, 2nd edit., 1998, Portraits in Victorian Religious Thought, 1997; contbr. numerous articles, essays, revs. to profl. publs. Danforth grad. fellow Episcopal Div. Sch., Cambridge, Mass., 1959-62, U. St. Andrews, 1962-63, 65-66, Yale U., New Haven, 1963-65; Fulbright scholar U. St. Andrews, 1962-63, Pub. Scholar award Kans. Humanities Coun., 1997; grantee NEH, Exxon Found., Mellon Found., Menninger Found., Inst. for Ecumenical and Cultural Rsch. Mem. Am. Acad. Religion, Highlands Inst. for Am. Religious Thought, Assn. for Core Texts and Courses, Phi Beta Kappa. Democrat. Avocations: piano; walking. Home: 808 Alabama St Lawrence KS 66044-3942 Office: U Kans Humanities & Western Civilization Program Bailey Hall 1440 Jayhawk Blvd Rm 308 Lawrence KS 66045-7574

WOESE, CARL R. biophysicist, microbiology educator; b. Syracuse, N.Y., July 15, 1928; AB in Math. and Physics, Amherst Coll., 1950, DSc (hon.), 1985; PhD in Biophysics, Yale U., 1953; postgrad., U. Rochester, 1953-55; DSc (hon.), Syracuse U., 1994. Rsch. assoc. biophysics Yale U., New Haven, 1955-60; Biophysicist GE Rsch. Lab., 1960-63; prof. microbiology U. Ill., Urbana, 1964—. Stanley O. Ikenberry Endowed chair U. Ill., 1996. Contbr. articles to profl. jours. Recipient Bergey award Bergey's Manual Trust, 1983, John D. and Catherine T. MacArthur award, 1984, Leeuwenhoek medal 1990, 1992, 23d Brown-Hazen Lctrs. award, 1992, Roger W. Stanier Meml. Lctr. award U. Calif., Berkeley, 1993; Univ. Sr. scholar U. Ill., 1986. Fellow Explorer's Club, Indian NAS, Am. Acad. Arts and Scis., Am. Acad. Microbiology; mem. Deutsche Gesellschaft fur Hygiene und Mikrobiologie (corr.), Deutsche Akademie Der Naturforscher Leopoldina, Bayerische Akademie der Wissenschaften (corr.), Max-Planck Soc., NAS (Selman A. Waksman award 1997), Ctr. Advanced Study U. Ill. Office: U Ill Chem & Life Scis Lab 131 Burrill Hall 601 S Goodwin Ave Urbana IL 61801-3709

WOGAMAN, GEORGE ELSWORTH, insurance executive, financial consultant; b. Mikado, Mich., May 29, 1937; s. Edgar R. and Leah Katherine (McGuire) W.; m. Sandra Lee Jensen, Apr. 10, 1965; children: Jennifer, Christopher. Grad. various ins. courses. CLU, registered rep.; cert. ChFc. With Blair Transit Co., Dun & Bradstreet, Chrysler Engring. Co., 1955-61; exec. chef Westward Ho!, 1961-68; owner, mgr. George Wogaman Ins. Agy., Grand Forks, N.D., 1969—. Mem. pres. coun. Farmers Ins. Group, 1988, 98, 99, 2000; alderman East Grand Forks (Minn.) City Coun., 1979—2000, v.p., 1982—2000. Corp. mem. United Hosp., Grand Forks, 1982—; mem. Nat. Rep. Congl. Com., Rep. Presdl. Task Force; mem. Red River Valley Estate Planning Coun.; mem. Wesley United Meth. Ch., Grand Forks. Recipient Pub. Svc. award East Grand Forks City Coun., 1979. Mem. Am. Soc. CLU's, North Valley Life Underwriters Assn. (Life Underwriter of Yr. 1988), Farmers Ins. Group Pres.'s Coun., Famers Financial Solutions, 2001-. Home: 1818 19 h St NW East Grand Forks MN 56721-1013 Office: 2612 Gateway Dr Grand Forks ND 58203-1406 E-mail: gwogaman@aol.com.

WOHLSCHLAEGER, FREDERICK GEORGE, lawyer; b. St. Louis, Jan. 3, 1951; s. Elmer H. and Rosalie (Gruet) W.; m. Mary L. Heck, Jan. 3, 1976; 1 child, Kathryn M. AB, Princeton U., 1973; JD, St. Louis U., 1976. Bar: Mo. 1976, Ohio 1980. Assoc. Rassieur, Long et al, St. Louis, 1976-77; atty. Monsanto Co., 1977-80, Std. Oil Co., Cleve., 1980-90; v.p. legal affairs Morton Internat., Chgo., 1990-97; sr. v.p., gen. counsel, sec. Hartmarx Corp., 1997-2000; sr. v.p., gen. counsel, sec., interim CFO Maytag Corp., 2000—. Bd. dirs. Inland Corp., Cleve., Mid-Valley Pipeline Co., Tulsa, Miami Valley Corp., Cleve.

WOJCICKI, ANDREW ADALBERT, chemist, educator; b. Warsaw, Poland, May 5, 1935; s. Franciszek Wojcicki and Janina (Kozlowa) Hoskins; m. Marba L. Hart, Dec. 21, 1968; children: Katherine, Christina. BS, Brown U., 1956; PhD, Northwestern U., 1960; postdoctoral fellow, U. Nottingham, Eng., 1960-61. Asst. prof. chemistry Ohio State U., Columbus, 1961-66, assoc. prof., 1966-69, prof., 1969-2000, prof. emeritus, 2001—, acting chmn., 1981-82, assoc. chmn., 1982-83, 84-86. Vis. prof. Case Western Res. U., 1967, U. Bologna, Italy, 1988, Nat. Sci. Council Chemistry Rsch. Promotion Ctr., Taiwan, 1994, U. Sydney, Australia, 1998; vis. researcher U. Coll. London, 1969; sr. U.S. scientist Alexander von Humboldt Found., Mulheim/Ruhr, Germany, 1975-76; vis. scholar U. Calif.-Berkeley, 1984; assoc. dean Coll. of Math. and Phys. Scis., Ohio State U., 1996-98. Contbr. articles to profl. jours. Guggenheim fellow U. Cambridge (Eng.), 1976; recipient Disting. Teaching award Ohio State U., 1968, Humboldt Sr. award Humboldt Found., 1975, 76. Mem. Am. Chem. Soc. (Columbus sect. award 1992), Royal Chem. Soc., Sigma Xi, Phi Lambda Upsilon. Home: 825 Greenridge Rd Columbus OH 43235-3411 Office: Ohio State U 100 W 18th Ave Columbus OH 43210-1106

WOJCIK, MARTIN HENRY, foundation development official; b. Chgo., May 10, 1948; s. Henry Martin and Mary Lorraine (Naughton) W. B.S., Ill. Inst. Tech., 1970; M. in Humanities, Bonn U., W. Ger., 1975. Price adminstr. R.R. Donnelley & Sons., Chgo., 1970-72; dir. devel. Citizens for a Better Environment, Milw., 1976-79, pres. Chgo., 1979-85; dir. found. relations Northwestern U., Evanston, 1987-89; dir. corp. and found. rels. Mayo Found., Rochester, Minn., 1989—. Bd. dir. Citizens for Better Environ., Chgo., 1979—85, 1989—, chmn. bd. dir., 1990—91, 1999—2001; mem. policy adv. com. Ill. EPA, Springfield, Ill., 1980—82. Bd. dirs. Rochester Civic Theatre, 1991-97, pres. bd. dirs. 1994-95; mem. adv. panel Minn. State Arts Bd., 1995, 97, 99, 2001. Mem. AAAS, Ill. Inst. Tech. Alumni Assn. Roman Catholic. Home: 625 19th St NW Rochester MN 55901-4901 Office: Mayo Found Rochester MN 55905-0001 E-mail: wojcik.martin@mayo.edu.

WOLANDE, CHARLES SANFORD, computer company executive; b. Chgo., July 25, 1954; s. Sam C. and Marie Helene (Riccio) W.; m. Marian Helene Gillespie, Nov. 10, 1985; children: Eric, Jill, Patrick. B, St. Mary's Coll., Winona, Minn., 1976. Lab. tech. Jefferson Electric, Bellwood, Ill., 1976-73; pres. Comark, Inc., Glendale Heights, 1978—, also CFO Bloomingdale, 1978—. Named High Tech. Entrepreneur of the year Peat, Marwick, Mitchell, Chgo., 1987. Mem. C. of C. Glendale Heights. Republican. Roman Catholic. Avocations: golf, bowling, skiing. Office: Comark Inc 444 Scott Dr Bloomingdale IL 60108-3111

WOLD, WILLIAM SYDNEY, molecular biology educator; b. Pine Falls, Manitoba, Can., Feb. 12, 1944; came to U.S., 1973; s. Roy and Nellie (Yurchison) W.; m. Susan Ann Lees, Dec. 30, 1967; children: Loralee Jane, William Guy, Jessica Ann, Jonathan Evered. BSc, U. Manitoba, 1965, MSc, 1968, PhD, 1973. Postdoctoral fellow St. Louis U., 1973-75, instr., 1975-76, from asst. prof. to prof. molecular virology, 1976-92, prof., chmn. dept. molecular microbiology and immunology, 1992—. Reviewer's res. NIH, Washington, 1990—; cons. Genetic Therapy, Inc., 1994. Contbr. articles to Cell Jour., Jour. Biol. Chemistry, Jour. Immunology, Jour. Virology, Virology, others; assoc. editor jour. Virology, 1990—; mem. editl. bd. Jour. Virology, 1997—. NIH grantee, 1980—. Mem. AAAS, Am. Soc. Microbiology, Am. Soc. Virology, Internat. Soc. Antiviral Rsch. Achievements include discovery and characterization of human adenovirus proteins that counteract host immunosurveillance and that either inhibit or promote cell death. Office: St Louis U Molecular Microbiology & Immunology 1402 S Grand Blvd Saint Louis MO 63104-1004

WOLF, CHARLES BENNO, lawyer; b. Chgo., Apr. 16, 1950; s. Ludwig and Hilde (Mandelbaum) W.; m. Sarah Lloyd, Sept. 1, 1973; children: Walter Ludwig, Peter Barton. AB, Brown U., 1972; JD, U. Chgo., 1975. Bar: Ill. 1975, U.S. Dist. Ct. (no. dist.) Ill. 1975, U.S. Ct. Appeals (4th, 5th, 6th, 7th, 8th, 9th, 10th, and 11th cirs.) 1985, U.S. Supreme Ct. 1985. Ptnr. Vedder, Price, Kaufman & Kammholz, Chgo., 1975—, exec. com., 1999—. Co-author: ERISA Claims and Litigation, 10th edit., 1995; contbr. articles to profl. jours. Mem. ABA (co-chair labor sect. subcom. on multi-employer plans), Internat. Found. Employee Benefit Plans. Office: Vedder Price Kaufman & Kammholz 222 N La Salle St Ste 2600 Chicago IL 60601-1100 E-mail: cwolf@vedderprice.com.

WOLF, DALE JOSEPH, utilities company executive; b. Hays, Kans., Aug. 21, 1939; s. Henry and Irene Elizabeth (Basgall) W.; m. Patricia Ann Ceule, May 28, 1966; children: Suzanne, Sara. BS in Bus. Adminstrn., Ft. Hays State U., 1961; MBA in Fin., U. Mo., 1970. Various acctg. and fin. positions Mo. Pub. Service Co., Kansas City, Mo., 1962-77, treas., 1977-84, v.p., treas., 1984-85; v.p. fin. UtiliCorp United, Inc., 1985—. Mem. Fin. Execs. Inst., Corp. Fin. Inst. Republican. Roman Catholic. Lodge: Kiwanis (pres. 1977-78). Office: UtiliCorp United Inc 20 W 9th St Kansas City MO 64105-1704

WOLF, DON ALLEN, hardware wholesale executive; b. Allen County, Ind., June 18, 1929; s. Ellis Adolphus and Bessie Ruth (Fortman) W.; m. Virginia Ann Lunz, Oct. 8, 1949; children— Rebecca, Donna, Richard, Lisa. Student exec. course, Ind. U., 1969. With Hardware Wholesalers Inc., Fort Wayne, Ind., 1947—, purchasing mgr., 1957—92, v.p., gen. mgr., 1967—80, pres. emeritus, 1993—. Bd. dirs. Clarcor. Nat. pres. Big Brothers Soc. Am., 1977-80. Mem. Nat. Wholesale Hardware Assn. (pres. 1984-85, named Hardware Wholesaler of Year 1973, 85), Ind. State C. of C. (dir., named Ind. Businessman of Yr.). Republican. Lutheran. Office: Hardware Wholesalers Inc PO Box 868 Fort Wayne IN 46801-0868 also: 6502 Nelson Rd Fort Wayne IN 46803-1920

WOLF, KATIE LOUISE, state legislator; b. Wolcott, Ind., July 9, 1925; d. John H. and Helen Munsterman; m. Charles W. Wolf, 1945; children: Mark, Marcia. Grad., Ind. Bus. Coll., 1944. Registration officer County of White, Ind., 1960, mgr. lic. bur., 1960-68; clk. 39th Jud. Cir. Ct., 1968-78; mem. Ind. Ho. of Reps., 1985-86, Ind. State Senate, 1987—. Mem. Dem. Nat. Com., 1968-90; del. Dem. nat. convs., 1972, 76, 80, 84. Recipient Athens award, 1987; named Woman of Yr. Bus. and Profl. Women's Club, 1984, Outstanding Freshman Legislator, 1985. Lutheran. Office: Ind Senate Dist 7 200 W Washington St Indianapolis IN 46204-2728

WOLF, KEN, state legislator; b. Dec. 30, 1937; m. Mary; three children. BA, U. St. Thomas. Minn. State rep. Dist. 41B, 1993—; computer cons. Home: 13319 Morgan Ave S Burnsville MN 55337-2095 Office: Minn House Standing Com 100 Constitution Ave Saint Paul MN 55155-1232

WOLF, LINDA S. advertising executive; Grad., Ohio Wesleyan U. Asst. account exec. Leo Burnett Group, Chgo., 1978; exec. v.p. new bus., dir. worldwide, group pres. N.Am. Leo Burnett Co., Inc., 1978-2000; CEO Leo Burnett USA, 2000—. Office: Leo Burnett Co Inc 35 W Wacker Dr Ste 3710 Chicago IL 60601-1648

WOLFE, BARBARA L. economics educator, researcher; b. Phila., Feb. 15, 1943; d. Manfred and Edith (Heimann) Kingshoff; m. Stanley R. Wolfe, Mar. 20, 1965 (div. Mar. 1978); m. Robert H. Haveman, July 29, 1983; children: Jennifer Ann Wolfe, Ari Michael Wolfe. BA, Cornell U., Ithaca, N.Y., 1965; MA, U. Pa., 1971; PhD, U Pa., 1973. Asst. prof. Bryn Mawr (Pa.) Coll., 1973-76; rsch. assoc. Inst. Rsch. on Poverty, Madison, 1976-77, dir., 1994—2000; from asst. prof. to assoc. prof. U. Wis., 1977-88; prof., 1988—. Resident scholar NIAS, Wassenear, The Netherlands, 1984-85, 96-97; vis. scholar Russell Sage Found., N.Y., 1991-92. Co-author: Succeeding Generations, 1994; editor: (book) Role of Budgetary Policy in Demographic Transitions, 1994, contbr. articles to profl. jours. Active Commn. on Children with Disabilities, Washington 1994-95, Tech. Adv. Panel Social Security, Washington, 1994-95. Recipient Best Article of Yr. award Rev. Income and Wealth, 1992, Fulbright award Coun. Internat. Exch. of Scholars, 1984. Mem.: Assn. Pub. Policy Mgmt. (bd. mgmt. 1994—2000, v.p. 2000—, policy coun. 2001—), Internat. Inst. Pub. Finance, Am. Econ. Assn. (bd. com. 1989—92, exec. bd. 1996—99). Office: U Wis Inst Rsch on Poverty 1180 Observatory Dr Madison WI 53706-1320 E-mail: wolfe@LaFollette.wisc.edu.

WOLFE, CHARLES MORGAN, electrical engineering educator; b. Morgantown, W.Va., Dec. 21, 1935; s. Slidell Brown and Mae Louise (Maness) W.; children— David Morgan, Diana Michele B.S.E.E., W.Va. U., Morgantown, 1961, M.S.E.E., 1962; Ph.D., U. Ill., 1965. Research assoc. U. Ill., Urbana, 1965; mem. staff MIT Lincoln Lab., Lexington, Mass., 1965-75; prof. elec. engring Washington U., St. Louis, 1975-97, Samuel C. Sachs prof., 1982-90, dir. semicondr. research lab., sr. prof., 1979-90. Cons. MIT Lincoln Lab., 1975-76, Fairchild Semicondr., Palo Alto, Calif., 1975-76, Air Force Avionics Lab., Dayton, Ohio, 1976-79, U. Ill., 1983-85 Author: Physical Properties of Semiconductors, 1989; editor: Gallium Arsenide and Related Compounds, 1979; contbr. articles to profl. jours., chpts. to books Served as sgt. USMC, 1955-58 Fellow IEEE (field awards com. 1984-87, Jack A. Morton award 1990); mem. NAE, AAAS, Electrochem. Soc. (Electronics divsn. award 1978). Office: Washington U 1 Brookings Dr Bryan Hall PO Box 1127 Rm 201 Saint Louis MO 63188-1127

WOLFE, DAVID LOUIS, lawyer; b. Kankakee, Ill., July 24, 1951; s. August Christian and Irma Marie (Nordmeyer) W.; m. Gail Lauret Fritz, Aug. 25, 1972; children: Laura Beth, Brian David, Kaitlin Ann. BS, U. Ill., 1973; JD, U. Mich., 1976. Bar: Ill. 1976, U.S. Dist. Ct. (no. dist.) Ill. 1976. Assoc., Gardner, Carton & Douglas, Chgo., 1976-82, ptnr., 1983—; lectr. estate planning Aid Assn. for Lutherans SMART Program, Chgo., 1980-84; lectr. Ill. Inst. Continuing Legal Edn., Chgo. Bar Assn., Lake Shore Nat. Bank, Ill. State Bar Assn. Contbr. articles to legal publs. Recipient Recognition award Ill. Inst. Continuing Legal Edn., 1981-84. Mem. ABA (sects. on taxation, corp. banking and bus. law 1981—, lectr.), NFL Players Assn. (cert. contract advisor 1983—), NCAA (cert. contract advisor), Chgo. Assn. Commerce and Industry (employee benefit subcom. 1983—), Ill. State Bar Assn. (employee benefits sect. council, 1986-95, recognition award 1983), Phi Kappa Phi, Beta Alpha Psi, Beta Gamma Sigma, Sigma Iota Lambda, Phi Eta Sigma. E-mail: dwolfe@gcd.com. Office: Gardner Carton & Douglas 321 N Clark St Ste 3300 Chicago IL 60610-4720

WOLFE, R. DEAN, retail executive; m. Cheryl Brecheisen, Nov. 1963; children: Craig, Bret, Ryan, Sara. BBA, U. Kans., 1966, JD, 1969. Assoc. Hoskins, King, McGannon & Hahn, Kansas City, Mo.; staff atty. legal dept. The May Dept. Stores Co., St. Louis, 1972-74, atty. real estate, 1974-75, regional mgr. real estate, 1975-78, v.p. dept. stores real estate, 1978-81, sr. v.p. real estate, 1981-86, exec. v.p. real estate, 1986-96, exec. v.p. acquisitions and real estate, 1996—; also bd. dirs. Former mem. bd. aldermen City of Clayton (Mo.), com. Recreation, Sports and Wellness Ctr., plan commn. and archtl. rev. bd., strategic planningcom., parks and recreation commn.; bd. dirs., co-chair Downtown Now. Mem. Internat. Coun. Shopping Ctrs. (past bd. trustees, exec. com.), St. Louis Regional Commerce and Growth Assn. Office: The May Dept Store Co 611 Olive St Ste 1200 Saint Louis MO 63101-1756

WOLFE, RALPH STONER, microbiology educator; b. Windsor, Md., July 18, 1921; s. Marshall Richard and Jennie Naomi (Weybright) W.; m. Gretka Margaret Young, Sept. 9, 1950; children: Daniel Binns, Jon Marshall, Sylvia Suzanne. Mem. faculty U. Ill., Urbana, 1953—, prof. microbiology, 1961—. Cons. USPHS, Nat. Inst. Gen. Med. Scis. Contbr. microbial physiology rsch. papers to profl. jours. Guggenheim fellow, 1961, 75, USPHS spl. postdoctoral fellow, 1967; recipient Pasteur award Ill. Soc. for Microbiology, 1974, Selman A Waksman Award in Microbiology Nat. Acad. of Sciences, 1995, Applied Environ. Microbiology award Procter & Gamble, 1999. Mem. NAS (Selman Waksman award in microbiology 1995), Am. Acad. Arts and Scis., Am. Soc. Microbiology (Carski Disting. Teaching award 1971, Abbott Lifetime Achievement award 1996, hon. mem.), Am. Soc. Biol. Chemists. Office: U Ill Dept Microbiology B103 Chem & Life Scis Bldg 601 S Goodwin Ave Urbana IL 61801-3709

WOLFE, SHEILA A. journalist; b. Chgo. d. Leonard M. and Rena (Karn) W. B.A., Drake U. Reporter Chgo. Tribune, 1956-73, asst. city editor, 1973-75; day city editor Chgo. Tribune , 1975-79; city editor Chgo. Tribune, 1979-81, met. coordinator, 1981-83, adminstrv. asst. to mng. editor, 1983-2000. Pres. City News Bur. Chgo. 1986-88, 94-96. Recipient Beck award for outstanding profl. performance Chgo. Tribune, 1979; recipient Disting. Service award Drake U., 1982 Mem. Phi Beta Kappa. Home: 71 E Division St Chicago IL 60610-8307 E-mail: chicagoshe@aol.com.

WOLFE, STEPHEN P. manufacturing company executive; V.p. fin., treas. Wheel Horse Products, Inc.; dir. ops. and adminstrn. Toro/Wheel Horse, 1986-90; pres. Toro Credit Co. (subs. Toro Co.), 1990-97; v.p., treas. Toro Co., Bloomington, Minn., 1990-97, v.p. fin., treas., CFO, 1997—. Office: Toro Co 8111 Lyndale Ave S Bloomington MN 55420-1196

WOLFF, FRANK PIERCE, JR. lawyer; b. St. Louis, Feb. 27, 1946; s. Frank P. and Beatrice (Stein) W.; m. Susan Scallet, May 11, 1984; children: Elizabeth McLane, Victoria Hancox. BA, Middlebury Coll., 1968; JD, U. Va., 1971. Bar: Mo. 1971, U.S. Ct. Appeals (5th cir.) 1974, U.S. Ct. Appeals (8th cir.) 1975, U.S. Supreme Ct. 1975. Ptnr. Lewis, Rice & Fingersh, St. Louis, 1971—90; ptnr., sect. leader, bus. and transactional counseling sect., mem. oper. group Bryan Cave LLP, 1997—. Bd. dirs. Misco Shawnee, Inc. Bd. dirs. Leadership St. Louis, 1985-88, Washington U. Child Guidance Clinic, St. Louis, 1976-79, Jewish Family and Children's Svc., St. Louis, 1981-83, John Burroughs Sch., 1995-2000, BJC Health Sys., Inc., 1998-2001, The Butterfly House, 2001—; gen. counsel Mo. Bot. Garden, St. Louis, 1981—, Mo. Hist. Soc., St. Louis, 1997—; spl. counsel St. Louis Symphony Soc., 1989—; trustee St. Louis Children's Hosp., 1995-2001, chairperson mission vision and values com., 1996-2001, mem. exec. com., 1997-99; co-chmn. Parks Task Force, 2004 Inc. . Capt. USAR, 1968-76. Mem. ABA, Mo. Bar Assn., Bar Assn. Met. St. Louis (chmn. corp. sect. 1984-85), Noonday Club, Westwood County Club (chmn. fin. com. 1989-91, treas. 1989-91, v.p. 1991-93, pres. 1994-95, exec. com. 1989-95). Home: 17 Clerbrook Ln Saint Louis MO 63124-1202 Office: Bryan Cave 211 N Broadway Ste 3600 Saint Louis MO 63102-2733

WOLFF, LARRY F. dental educator, researcher; b. Mankato, Minn., May 25, 1948; m. Charles Harold and Madelyn Catherine (Burns) W.; m. Elizabeth Spencer Thompson, Aug. 7, 1976; children: Adam, Ryan, Sara. BA in Biology, Mankato State U., 1970, M in Biology and Chemistry, 1971; PhD in Microbiology, Northwestern U., 1974; DDS, U. Minn., 1978; M in Periodontology, NYU, 1980; cert. in dentistry, Aarhus (Denmark) Dental Coll., 1979. Rsch. fellow Northwestern U., Chgo., 1972-74; asst. prof. dentistry U. Minn., Mpls., 1980-85, assoc. prof., 1985-96, assoc. prof. periodontology, 1985-94; prof., 1996—. Contbr. articles to profl. jours. Grantee Nat. Inst. Dental Rsch. NIH, 1982—, numerous corps., 1988—. Mem. Am. Acad. Periodontology, Am. Dental Assn., Internat. Assn. Dental Rsch., Internat. Assn. Periodontists, Minn. Dental Assn., Minn. Assn. Dental Rsch. Office: U Minn Sch Dentistry 515 Delaware St SE Minneapolis MN 55455-0348

WOLFF, MICHAEL A. state supreme court judge; Grad., Dartmouth Coll., 1967; JD, U. Minn., 1970. Lawyer Legal Svcs.; mem. faculty St. Louis U. Sch. Law, 1975-98; judge Mo. Supreme Ct., 1998—. Chief counsel to gov., 1993-94, spl. counsel, 1994-98. Co-author: Federal Jury Practice and Instructions. Chief counsel to Gov. St. Louis, 1993-94, spl. counsel, 1994-98. Office: Supreme Ct MO PO Box 150 Jefferson City MO 65102-0150*

WOLFF, RONALD KEITH, toxicologist, researcher; b. Brantford, Ont., Can., July 25, 1946; s. Roy Clifford and Agnes Audrey (Stratton) W.; m. Mary Carole Cromien Wolff, Aug. 26, 1972; children: Mark, Sarah, Andrew, Brian. BS, U. Toronto, 1964-68; MS, 1968-69, PhD, 1969-72. Diplomate Am. Bd. Toxicology, 1983. Rsch. assoc. McMaster U., Hamilton, Can., 1973-76; scientist Lovelace Inhalation Toxicology Rsch. Inst., Albuquerque, N.Mex., 1976-88; sr. rsch. scientist Eli Lilly and Co., Greenfield, Ind., 1988—. Author: (book chpt.) Comprehensive Treatise on Pulmonary Toxicology, 1992, Comprehensive Toxicology, 1997; contbr. articles to profl. jours. Recipient Frank Blood award Soc. Toxicology, 1989. Mem. Am. Assn. for Aerosol Rsch., Internat. Soc. Aerosols in Medicine, Soc. Toxicology, Am. Indsl. Hygiene Assn. Avocations: camping, hiking, hockey. Office: Lilly Rsch Labs PO Box 708 Greenfield IN 46140-0708

WOLFMAN, ALAN, medical educator, researcher; b. Bronx, N.Y., Mar. 12, 1956; married. Postdoctoral fellow dept. biophysics U. Rochester Med. Ctr., 1988—90; assoc. staff dept. cell biology Cleve. Clinic Found., 1990—. Adj. prof. dept. biology Cleve. State U., 1994—. Contbr. articles to profl. jours.; periodic reviewer: Molecular Cell Biology, periodic reviewer: Jour. Biol. Chemistry, periodic reviewer: Biochemistry, periodic reviewer: BBA, ad hoc reviewer for program project: Nat. Inst. Diabetes and Digestive Kidney Diseases, 1995, invited reviewer: DRTC Pilot Project Ind. U., 1995—; presenter in field. Recipient Postdoctoral fellowship award, NIH, 1985—88, Established Investigatorship award, Am. Heart Assn., 1996—; grantee Cell Biology Tng., 1979, NIH First, 1988—93. Office: Cleve Clinic Found Rsch Inst Dept Cell Biology NC10 9500 Euclid Ave Cleveland OH 44195-0001

WOLFRAM, STEPHEN, physicist, computer company executive; b. London, Aug. 29, 1959; came to U.S., 1978; Degree, Eton Coll., 1976, Oxford U., 1978; PhD in Theoretical Physics, Calif. Inst. Tech., 1979. With Calif. Inst. Tech., Pasadena, 1979-82, Inst. for Advanced Study, Princeton, N.J., 1983-86; prof. physics, math, computer sci. U. Ill., Champaign, 1986-90; pres., CEO Wolfram Rsch. Inc., 1987—. Author: Theory and Applications of Cellular Automata, 1986, Mathematica: A System for Doing Mathematics by Computer, 1998, 2d edit., 1991, Mathematica Reference Guide, 1992, Mathematica: The Student Book, 1994, The Mathematica Book, 4th edit., 1999, Cellular Automata and Complexity, 1994; editor jour. Complex Systems, 1987— Fellow MacArthur Found., 1981. Office: Wolfram Rsch Inc 100 Trade Centre Dr Champaign IL 61820-7237 E-mail: sw-pubs@wolfram.com.

WOLFRAM, THOMAS, physicist, educator; b. St. Louis, July 27, 1936; s. Ferdinand I. and Audrey H. (Calvert) W.; m. Eleanor Elaine Burger, May 22, 1965; children: Michael, Gregory, Melanie, Susan, Steven. BA, U. Calif., Riverside, 1959, PhD in Physics, 1963; MA in Physics, UCLA, 1960. Dir. divsn. physics and chemistry; Engr. Atomics Internat., Canoga Park, Calif., 1960-63; mem. tech. staff N.Am. Aviation Corp. Sci. Ctr., Thousand Oaks, 1963-68; group leader in solid state physics Rockwell Internat. Sci. Ctr., 1968-72, dir. div. physics and chemistry, 1972-74; prof. physics, chmn. dept. physics and astronomy U. Mo., Columbia, 1974-83; dir. phys. tech. divsn. AMOCO Corp., 1983-87; v.p., gen. mgr. AMOCO Laser Co., 1987-95; bus. cons., 1995—. Cons. in field. Author: (novel) The Venture; editor: Inelastic Electron Tunneling Spectroscopy, 1978; contbr. rsch. articles to numerous publs. in field. Recipient Disting. Prof. award Argonne Univs. Assn., 1977 Fellow Am. Phys. Soc. Office: 2004 Somerset Ln Wheaton IL 60187-8128

WOLFSON, LARRY MARSHALL, lawyer; b. Springfield, Ill., June 12, 1947; m. Cynthia Sherwood, 1972; children: Sharon Eve, Rachel Beth, Anna Faye, Blackie Perro, Natasha Molly. BSBA, Northwestern U., 1969; JD cum laude, U. Mich., 1974. Bar: Ill. 1974. Ptnr. Jenner & Block, Chgo., 1980—2002, Shaw, Gussis, Domanskis, Fishman & Wolfson, LLC , Chgo., 2002—. Mem. ABA, Ill. State Bar (lectr. Comml. Banking and Bankruptcy Law Edn. Series 1990), Chgo. Bar Assn., Chgo. Coun. Lawyers, Am. Bankruptcy Inst. Office: Shaw Gussis et al 1144 W Fulton St Market Chicago IL 60607 Fax: (312) 840-7362. E-mail: lwolfson@jenner.com.

WOLIN, JEFFREY ALAN, artist; AB, Kenyon Coll., 1972; MFA, Rochester Inst. Tech., 1977. Represented by Catherine Edelman Gallery, Chgo. and Robert Mann Gallery, N.Y.C.; photographer City of Kalamazoo (Mich.) Police Dept., 1973-74; asst. prof. photography Ind. U., Bloomington, 1980-86, assoc. prof. photography, 1986-92, prof., 1993—, head art dept. Head photographics svcs. George Eastman House, Rochester, 1976-80; adj. instr. photography U. Rochester, 1978-80. Exhbns. include Ryerson Photog. Are Ctr., Toronto, Can., 1978, Northlight Gallery, Tempe, Ariz., 1980, 88, Israel Mus., Jerusalem, 1980, George Eastman House, Rochester, 1981, 82, Seattle Arts Mus., 1986, Chgo. Cultural Ctr., 1986, 87, J.B. Speed Art Mus., Louisville, 1987, Silver Image Gallery, Columbus, Ohio, 1987, Marianne Deson Gallery, Chgo., 1988, Burden Gallery, N.Y., 1988, Nexus Contemporary Art Ctr., Atlanta, 1988, 89, Images Gallery, Cin., 1989, Catherine Edelman Gallery, Chgo., 1989, 91, 92, 93, 94, San Francisco Camerawork, 1990, U. Oreg. Mus. Art, Eugene, 1990, 92, Mus. Contemporary Photography, Chgo., 1991, 92, Blue Sky Gallery, Oreg. Ctr. for Photog. Arts, Portland, 1992, Mus. Fine Arts, Houston, 1992, L.A. County Art Mus., 1992, Opsis Gallery, N.Y.C., 1992, Mus. Modern Art, N.Y.C., 1992, Ctr. Creative Photography, Tucson, 1993, Robert Klein Gallery, Boston, 1994, Nelson-Atkins Mus. Art, Kansas City, 1994, Contemporary Art Ctr., New Orleans, 1995, Mpls. Mus. Am. Art, St. Paul, 1995, Art Inst. Chgo., 1996, Internat. Ctr. Photography, 1997, others; permanent collections include Seattle Arts Mus., San Francisco Mus. Modern Art, Mus. Modern Art, N.Y., Mus. Contemporary Photography, Chgo., Mus. Fine Arts, Houston, L.A. County Art Mus., Kalamazoo (Mich.) Inst. Art, Internat. Mus. Photography at George Eastman House, Met. Mus. Art, N.Y.C., Art Inst. Chgo., Ctr. Creative Photography, Tucson, Can. Ctr. for Architecture, Montreal, others. Visual Artist fellow NEA, 1988, 92, Master Artist fellow Ind. Arts Commn., 1991, John Simon Guggenheim fellow, 1991, ArtsLink fellow to Czechoslovakia, 1994, U.S./France fellow Cité Internationale des Arts-Paris, 1994. Achievements include being subject of books and articles. Office: Catherine Edelman Gallery 300 W Superior St Chicago IL 60610-3535 Fax: 312-266-1967.

WOLLE, CHARLES ROBERT, federal judge; b. Sioux City, Iowa, Oct. 16, 1935; s. William Carl and Vivian (Down) W.; m. Kerstin Birgitta Wennerstrom, June 26, 1961; children: Karl Johan Knut, Erik Vernon, Thomas Dag, Aaron Charles. AB, Harvard U., 1959; JD, Iowa Law Sch., 1961. Bar: Iowa 1961. Assoc. Shull, Marshall & Marks, Sioux City, 1961-67, ptnr., 1968-80; judge Dist. Ct. Iowa, 1981-83; justice Iowa Supreme Ct., Sioux City and Des Moines, 1983-87; judge U.S. Dist. Ct. (so. dist.) Iowa, Des Moines, 1987-92, chief judge, 1992-99, sr. U.S. dist. judge, 2001—. Faculty Nat. Jud. Coll., Reno, 1983—. Editor Iowa Law Rev., 1960-61 Vice pres. bd. dirs. Sioux City Symphony, 1972-77; sec., bd. dirs. Morningside Coll., Sioux City, 1977-81 Fellow Am. Coll. Trial Lawyers; mem. ABA, Iowa Bar Assn., Sioux City C. of C. (bd. dirs. 1977-78) Avocations: sports, art, music, literature. Office e-mail: charles r. Office: Sr US Dist Judge US Courthouse Annex Ste 403 110 E Court Ave Des Moines IA 50309 E-mail: wolle@iasd.uscourts.gov.

WOLLMAN, ROGER LELAND, federal judge; b. Frankfort, S.D., May 29, 1934; s. Edwin and Katherine Wollman; m. Diane Marie Schroeder, June 21, 1959; children: Steven James, John Mark, Thomas Roger. BA, Tabor Coll., Hillsboro, Kans., 1957; JD magna cum laude, U. S.D., 1962; LLM, Harvard U., 1964. Bar: S.D. 1964. Sole practice, Aberdeen, 1964—71; justice S.D. Supreme Ct., 1971—85, chief justice, 1978—82; judge U.S. Ct. Appeals (8th cir.), 1985—, chief judge, 1999—2002; states atty. Brown County, Aberdeen, 1967—71. Served with U.S. Army, 1957—59. Office: US Ct Appeals US Courthouse & Fed Bldg 400 S Phillips Ave Rm 315 Sioux Falls SD 57104-6851

WOLMAN, J. MARTIN, retired newspaper publisher; b. Elizabeth, N.J., Mar. 8, 1919; s. Joseph D. and Dora (Baum) W.; m. Anne Paley, Sept. 12, 1943; children: Natalie, Jonathan, Ruth Ellen, Lewis Joel. Student, U. Wis., 1937-42. With Wis. State Jour., Madison, 1936-84, pub., 1968-84; pres., gen. mgr. Madison Newspaper, Inc., 1969-84, ret., 1984, dir., 1969—, Lee Enterprises, Inc., 1971-74; treas. Lee Endowment Trusts, 1988—. Sec.-treas. Madison Improvement Corp., 1958-62 Treas. Wis. State Jour. Empty Stocking Club, 1948, Children and Youth Services Inc., 1962— ; mem. Mayor Madison Adv. Com., 1965; bd. dirs. United Givers Fund, 1960-64, trustee, 1980— ; ex-officio Roy L. Matson Scholarship Fund, 1961, Central Madison Com., Madison Art Assn.; trustee Edgewood Coll., Madison, U. Wis. Hosp. and Clinic; chmn. Madison Area Arts Coalition, 1984-85; bd. dirs. Univ. Health Sci. Center, 1975; chmn. U.S. Savs. Bond Met. Wis., 1983; coordinator Barneveld Disaster Fund, Wis., 1985-86; mem. U. Wis. Found., 1968-95; bd. dirs., trustee Wisc. Clin. Cancer Ctr., 1986—; Dir. Wisc. Newspaper Found., 1986-88; v.p., treas. Lee Endowment Found., 1989—. Served with AUS, 1942-46. Named Advt. Man of Year Madison Advt. Club, 1969, Madison Man of Achievement, 1976, Man of Yr. Salvation Army, 1993; recipient Disting. Service award Wis. Newspaper Assn., 1982, Community Service award Inland Daily Press Assn., 1983, Ralph D. Casey Minn. award for Disting. Service in Journalism, 1987, First Ringling Bros. Silver Smile award, 1993, Outstanding Svc. for Youth award Wis. State Jour., 1995, Rounders Youth Lifetime award, 1997. Mem. Madison C. of C. (dir. 1966-70, 74-84), Inland Daily Press Assn. (dir. 1961-65), Wis. Daily Newspaper League (pres. 1961-65), Wis. Newspaper Assn. (dir. 1977-84) Clubs: B'nai B'rith. Office: 1901 Fish Hatchery Rd Madison WI 53713-1248

WOLSIFFER, PATRICIA RAE, retired insurance company executive; b. Indpls., Aug. 15, 1933; d. Charles L. and Dorothy M. (Smith) Bohlsen; m. Edward C. Wolsiffer, Oct. 5, 1956; children: John M., Anderson, Sherry L. Anderson Cooney, Edward J. Wolsiffer. Student, Ind. Central U., 1974-75. Various secretarial positions, 1964-71; with Blue Cross/Blue Shield Ind. (Associated Ins. Cos., Inc.), Indpls., 1971-88, supr. personnel, 1973-76, exec. asst. to pres., 1976-79, corp. sec., 1979-85, exec. asst. to chmn. bd., chief exec. officer, 1985-88; ret. Vol. Hancock Meml. Hosp. Guild. Republican. Presbyterian. Clubs: Order Eastern Star, Daus. of Nile, Ladies Oriental Shrine. Home: 5550 E 100 N Greenfield IN 46140-9445 Office: 120 Monument Cir Indianapolis IN 46204-4906

WOLSKI, L.G. heavy manufacturing executive; CFO Heico Cos., St. Charles, Ill. Office: Heico Companies 2075 Foxfield Saint Charles IL 60174 Office Fax: (630) 443-4696.

WOLSTEIN, SCOTT ALAN, real estate company executive; b. Cleve., June 24, 1952; s. Bert L. and Iris (Shur) W. BS in Econs. cum laude, U. Pa., 1974; JD, U. Mich. cum laude, 1977. Assoc. Thompson, Hine & Flory, Cleve., 1977-81; co-owner, exec. v.p. Cleve. Force Soccer Team, 1979—; officer Sasson of Israel, Cleve., 1980—, also bd. dirs.; gen. ptnr. Diversified Equities, Moreland Hills, Ohio, 1981—; v.p. DE Properties Corp., 1982—, DE Transp. Co., Moreland Hills, 1983—. Participant Leadership Cleve., 1983-84; bd. trustees Men's ORT, United Cerebral Palsy, Anti-Defamation League; bd. overseers Case Western Reserve U. Athletic Dept.; alumni steering com. Leadership Cleve. Mem. ABA, Ohio Bar Assn., Cleve. Bar Assn., Maj. Indoor Soccer League (competition com., chmn. referee com. 1986—). Jewish. Clubs: Wharton, U. Mich. (Cleve.). Avocations: skiing, running, tennis, golf, bicycling. Home: 32200 Chestnut Ln Cleveland OH 44124-4328 Office: Developers Diversified Realty Corp. 3300 Enterprise Pkwy Beachwood OH 44122

WOLTZ, KENNETH ALLEN, consulting executive; b. Phila., Mar. 2, 1943; s. Herman and Florence (Varell) M.; m. Barbara Hand, June 18, 1966; children: Karyn, Diane, Kenneth. BS, U.S. Mil. Acad., 1966; MBA, Xavier U., 1971. Cert. mgmt. cons. Various mgmt. positions GE, Evansdale, Ohio and Bethesda, Md., 1968-73; mgr. systems Xerox Corp., Rochester, N.Y., 1973-75; dir. info. svcs. McGraw Edison, Des Plaines, Ill., 1975-77; mng. dir., mgmt. cons. KPMG, Chgo., 1977-80; mgmt. cons., CEO, Woltz & Assoc., Inc., Barrington, Ill., 1980—; mgmt. cons. Speaker at various Univs. With U.S. Army, 1966-68. Mem. Soc. Mgmt. Info. Systems, Inst. Mgmt. Cons., West Point Soc. (treas. 1975), Assn. Corp. Growth, Assn. Mgmt. Consulting Firms, Ind. Computer Cons. Assn. Home: 800 Ocean Dr Unit 1105 Juno Beach FL 33408-1724 Office: Woltz & Assocs Inc PO Box 158 West Dundee IL 60118-0189 also: Ste 203/284 4300 S US Hwy 1 Jupiter FL 33477-1198 E-mail: woltz@msn.com.

WOMELDORFF, PORTER JOHN, utilities executive; b. Milw., Feb. 26, 1933; s. Virgil Leslie and Leorra (Porter) W.; m. Marilyn Sapp, Jan. 7, 1966; children: John Porter, Michael Wayne. With Ill. Power Co., Decatur, 1954-95; beginning as elec. engr., successively results supr., instrumentation engr., supr. system planning, mgr. planning, 1954-79; v.p., 1979-93; global climate program exec., 1993-95; ret., 1995; pres. Womeldorff Assocs. Ltd., 1995—97. Mem. Ill. Coal Devel. Bd., 1982-95, chair. Chair adv. bd. U. Ill. Coll. Engring., 1986-89; former chair sci. com. Global Climate Coalition. Lay mem. Central Ill. Ann. Conf., United Methodist Ch., 1968—, lay leader, 1976-79, lay mem. North Central Jurisdictional Conf., 1972—, lay mem. Gen. Conf., 1976—; lay mem. Gen. Bd. Pubs., 1992—. Served to lt. C.E., AUS, 1955-57. Decorated Army Commendation Medal. Mem. Instrument Soc. Am. (v.p. 1971-73, Power Div. Achievement award 1983), IEEE, ASME, U. Ill. Elec. Engring. Alumni Assn. (pres., dir., Outstanding Alumni award 1994), Phi Kappa Phi, Tau Beta Pi, Sigma Tau, Eta Kappa Nu, Alpha Kappa Lambda. Home and Office: 735 Country Manor Dr Decatur IL 62521-2524 E-mail: pjwom@aol.com.

WONG, DAVID T. biochemist, researcher; b. Hong Kong, Nov. 6, 1935; s. Chi-Keung and Pui-King Wong; m. Christina Lee, Dec. 28, 1963; children: Conrad, Melvin, Vincent. Student, Nat. Taiwan U., 1955-56; BS, Seattle Pacific U., 1961; MS, Oreg. State U., 1964; PhD, U. Oreg., 1966. Sr. biochemist Lilly Rsch. Labs., Indpls., 1968-72, rsch. biochemist, 1973-77, sr. rsch. scientist, 1978-89, rsch. advisor, 1990-97, Lilly rsch. fellow, 1997-99, cons., 2000—. Adj. prof. biochemistry and molecular biology Ind. U. Sch. Medicine, 1986—96, adj. prof. neurobiology, 1991. Mem. editl.bd.: Chinese Jour. Physiology, 1996—2000; contbr. articles to sci. jours. Named Alumnus of the Yr., Seattle Pacific U.; recipient Scientist of the Yr. Pres. award, Chinese Neurosci. Soc., 1991, Discoverers award, Pharm. Mfr. Assn., 1993, Lifetime Rsch. award, Mental Health Assn. Ind., 1996, World Difference award, Ind. Health Industry Forum, 1996, Pharm. Discover's award Prozac, Nat. Alliance Rsch. Schizophrenia and Depression, 1996, Outstanding Achievement in Neurosci. Rsch. award, Lilly Neuroscience Eli Lilly and Co., 2000, Cornerstone award, Am. Drugstore Mus. Indpls., 2000, Excellence award, Asian Am. Alliance, Inc., 2000, Pioneer Recognition award, Com. 100, 2000, Excellence award, U.S. Pan Asian Am. C. of C., 2002; fellow Postdoctoral, U. Pa., 1966—68, Alunus Growing Vision, 1989, 1998. Mem.: Soc. Chinese Bioscientists Am., Soc. Neurosci. (pres. Indpls. chpt. 1987, 1988), Am. Soc. Neurochemistry, Internat. Soc. Neurochemistry, Am. Soc. Pharmacology and Exptl. Therapeutics, Am. Coll. Neuropsychopharamcology, Indpls. Assn. Chinese Ams. (pres. 1987). Achievements include patents in field;research in on biochemistry and pharmacology of neurotransmission;discovery of and development of antidepressant drug, Prozac (Fluoxetine) and drug candidates including Atomoxetine, a selective inhibitor of norepinephrine uptake;discovery of daproxetine, a selective inhibitor of serotonin an dnorepinephrine;studies of potentially useful substances which enhance transmission of norepinephrine, dopamine, serotonin, acetycholine, and GABA-neurons;studies of natural products led to the discovery of caboxylic ionophores: Narasin and A204, which increase transport of cations across biomembranes. Home: 5812 E Fall Creek Parkway Nort Indianapolis IN 46226-1051 Fax: (317) 254-8688.

WONG, VICTOR KENNETH, physics educator, academic administrator; b. San Francisco, Nov. 1, 1938; m. Nancy Wong; children: Cassandra, Pamela, Lianna. BS in Engring. Physics, U. Calif., Berkeley, 1960, PhD in Physics, 1966. Postdoctoral fellow Ohio State U., Columbus, 1966-68; lectr., asst. prof. U. Mich., Ann Arbor, 1968-76, adj. prof. physics, 1992-95, 96—, assoc. prof. physics Dearborn, 1976-82, prof. physics, 1982-86, chmn. dept. natural sci., 1980-83, dean Coll. Arts, Sci. and Letters, 1983-86, provost, vice chancellor acad. affairs Flint, 1986-95, prof. physics, 1986—. Adj. rsch. scientist U. Mich., 1995—, dir. info. technology for rsch., 1995—. Assoc. editor: Math. Revs., 1980; contbr. articles to profl. jours. Mem. AAAS, Am. Phys. Soc., Am. Assn. Higher Edn. (1st chmn. Asian caucus 1986-88), Nat. U. Continuing Edn. Assn. (mem.

minority com. 1989), North Ctrl. Assn. Colls. and Schs. (cons. evaluator com. 1989—), Am. Coun. Edn. (mem. commn. on minorities in higher edn. 1993-96), Assn. Computing Machinery, Phi Beta Kappa, Tau Beta Pi. Office: Univ Mich Office of CIO 1071 Beal Ave Ann Arbor MI 48109-2103

WONG, WARREN JAMES, mathematics educator; b. Masterton, N.Z., Oct. 16, 1934; came to U.S. 1964; s. Ken and Jessie (Ng) W.; m. Nellie Gee, May 12, 1962; children: Carole Frances, Andrea. BSc, U. Otago, Dunedin, N.Z., 1955, MSc, 1956; PhD, Harvard U., 1959. Lectr. U. Otago, Dunedin, 1960-64, sr. lectr., 1964; assoc. prof. math. U. Notre Dame, Ind., 1964-68, prof., 1968—. Proceedings editorial bd. Am. Math. Soc., Providence, R.I., 1988-90; contbr. articles to profl. jours. Vestryman St. Michael and All Angels Episcopal Ch., South Bend, 1988-90. Mem. Am. Math. Soc., Math. Assn. Am., Australian Math. Soc. Episcopalian. Office: Dept Math Univ Notre Dame Notre Dame IN 46556-5641

WOO, BENSON, credit card company executive; BSEE, MIT; MBA, Harvard U. Various positions GM, 1979-94; v.p., treas. Case Corp., 1994-98; corp. v.p., CFO, York Internat. Corp., 1998—99; sr. v.p. Metris Cos., Inc., Minnetonka, Minn., 1999-2000, CFO, 2000—. Office: Metris Cos Inc 10900 Wayzata Blvd Minnetonka MN 55305

WOOD, CORINNE, state official; b. Barrington, Ill., May 28, 1954; m. Paul R. Wood; children: Ashley, Brandon, Courtney. BS, U. Ill.; JD, Loyola U. of Chgo. Pvt. practice; counsel Ill. Savs. and Residential Fin. Bd.; atty. Hopkins & Sutter, Chgo.; gen. counsel Ill. Commr. of Banks and trusts; state rep. 59th dist. 90th Ill. Gen. Assembly, Springfield; lt. gov. State of Ill., 1999—. Appointed spec. asst., Ill. Atty. Gen. Former co-capt. Shields Twp. Rep. Precinct; Lake Forest chmn. John E. Porter for Congress, 1994, 96; adv. mem. Coun. of Women Advisors to U.S. Congress; past 1st v.p., bd. dirs. Women's Rep. Club, past pres., bd. mem. 10th Congl. Dist. of Lake Forest/Lake Bluff chpt.; past pres. (fin. chmn.), mem. bd. govs. Lake County Rep. Fedn.; bd. dirs. Allendale Shelter Club, Allendale Assn.; adv. bd. A Safe Place; transition bd. dirs. Anne M. Kiley Ctr. for the Developmentally Disabled; mem. LWV of Lake Forest/Lake Bluff; mem. Lake Forest Open Lands Assn.; former Lake Forest chmn., sustaining mem. Jr. League of Chgo.; former new mems. chair, membership com., Sunday sch. tchr. First Presbyn. Ch. of Lake Forest; den leader Pack 43, Boy Scouts Am.; plan commr. City of Lake Forest, 1993-97, sr. housing commr., 1993-97, ad hoc com. on sr. housing bd. mem. Recipient City of Lake Forest Spl. Recognition of Pub. Svc.. award. Mem. ABA, Ill. Bar Assn., Lake County Bar Assn., Chgo. Bar Assn., House Financial Insts. Comm., Comm. on Aging, Edn. Appropriations Comm., Labor and Commerce Comm., appointed mem., Legislative Rsch. Bureau, bd. mem. Office: Office of Lt Governor 214 State House Springfield IL 62706-0001*

WOOD, DIANE PAMELA, judge; b. Plainfield, N.J., July 4, 1950; d. Kenneth Reed and Lucille (Padmore) Wood; m. Dennis James Hutchinson, Sept. 2, 1978 (div. May 1998); children: Kathryn Hutchinson, David Hutchinson, Jane Hutchinson. BA, U. Tex., 1971, JD, 1975. Bar: Tex. 1975, D.C. 1978, Ill. 1993. Law clk. U.S. Ct. Appeals (5th cir.), 1975—76, U.S. Supreme Ct., 1976—77; atty.-advisor U.S. Dept. State, Washington, 1977—78; assoc. Covington & Burling, 1978—80; asst. prof. law Georgetown U. Law Ctr., 1980—81, U. Chgo., 1981—88, prof. law, 1988—95, assoc. dean, 1989—92, Harold J. and Marion F. Green prof. internat. legal studies, 1990—95, sr. lectr. law, 1995—; spl. cons. antitrust divsn. internat. guide U.S. Dept. Justice, 1986—87, dep. asst. atty. gen. antitrust divsn., 1993—95; judge U.S. Ct. Appeals (7th cir.), 1995—. Contbr. articles to profl. jours. Bd. dirs. Hyde Park-Kenwood Cmty. Health Ctr., 1983—85. Mem.: Internat. Acad. Comparative Law, Am. Law Inst., Am. Soc. Internat. Law, Phi Alpha Delta. Democrat.

WOOD, HARLINGTON, JR. federal judge; b. Springfield, Ill., Apr. 17, 1920; s. Harlington and Marie (Green) W. A.B., U. Ill., 1942, J.D., 1948. Bar: Ill. 1948. Practiced in, Springfield, 1948-69; U.S. atty. So. Dist. Ill., 1958-61; mem. firm Wood & Wood, 1961-69; assoc. dep. atty. gen. for U.S. attys. U.S. dept. Justice, 1969-70; assoc. dep. atty. gen. Justice Dept., Washington, 1970-72, asst. atty. gen. civil div., 1972-73; U.S. dist. judge So. Dist. Ill., Springfield, 1973-76; judge U.S. Ct. Appeals (7th cir.), 1976—. Adj. prof. Sch. Law, U. Ill., Champaign, 1993; disting. vis. prof. St. Louis U. Law Sch., 1996—. Chmn. Adminstrv. Office Oversight Com., 1988-90; mem. Long Range Planning Com., 1991-96. Recipient Profl. Lifetime Achievement award, Inns of Ct., 2002. Office: US Ct Appeals PO Box 299 600 E Monroe St Springfield IL 62701-1626

WOOD, JACKIE DALE, physiologist, educator, researcher; b. Picher, Okla., Feb. 16, 1937; s. Aubrey T. Wood and Wilma J. (Coleman) Wood Patterson. BS, Kans. State U., 1964, MS, 1966; PhD, U. Ill., 1969. Asst. prof. physiology Williams Coll., Williamstown, Mass., 1969-71; asst. prof. U. Kans. Med. Ctr., Kansas City, 1971-74, assoc. prof., 1974-78, prof., 1978-79; prof., chmn. dept. physiology Sch. Medicine, U. Nev., Reno, 1979-85; chmn. dept. physiology coll. medicine Ohio State U., Columbus, 1985-97, prof. physiology and internal medicine, 1997—. Cons. NIH, Bethesda, Md., 1982—. Recipient Rsch. Career Devel. award NIH, 1974, Chancellor's award for teaching excellence U. Kans., 1975; named Hon. Citizen City of Atzugi Japan, 1987; Alexander von Humboldt fellow, W.Ger., 1976. Mem. AAAS, Am. Physiol. Soc. (assoc. editor 1984-96, rsch. award 1986), Soc. Neurosci., Am. Gastroent. Assn., Assn. Chmn. Depts. Physiology. Office: Ohio State U Dept Physiology 300 Hamilton Hall 1645 Neil Ave Columbus OH 43210-1218 E-mail: wood.13@osu.edu.

WOOD, JAMES NOWELL, museum director and executive; b. Boston, Mar. 20, 1941; s. Charles H. and Helen N. (Nowell) W.; m. Emese Forizs, Dec. 30, 1966; children: Lenke Hancock, Rebecca Nowell. Diploma, Universita per Stranieri, Perugia, Italy, 1962; B.A., Williams Coll., Williamstown, Mass., 1963; M.A. (Ford Mus. Tng. fellow), NYU, 1966. Asst. to dir. Met. Mus., N.Y.C., 1967-68, asst. curator dept. 20th century art, 1968-70; curator Albright-Knox Art Gallery, Buffalo, 1970-73, assoc. dir., 1973-75; dir. St. Louis Art Mus., 1975-80, Art Inst. Chgo., 1980—. Vis. com. visual arts U. Chgo., 1980-94; head com. Nat. Endowment Arts Mem. Intermuseum Conservation Assn. (past pres.), Assn. Art Mus. Dirs. Office: Art Inst Chgo 111 S Michigan Ave Chicago IL 60603-6492

WOOD, JOHN FREDERICK, air transportation executive; b. N.Y.C., Jan. 13, 1949; BA, Calif. State U., Fullerton, 1978; postgrad., No. Ariz. U., 1981. Commd. 2nd lt. USMC, 1971, pilot, 1971-79; advanced through grades to capt., 1975; resigned USMC, 1979; mgr. Winslow (Ariz.) Mcpl. Airport, 1979-81, Cheyenne (Wyo.) Airport Authority, 1981-89; dir. ops. Omaha Airport Authority, 1989-96; exec. dir. Lincoln (Nebr.) Airport Authority, 1996—. Mem. Am. Assn. Airport Execs., Airports Coun. Internat. (chmn. coms. on pub. safety and security, small airports). Office: Lincoln Airport Authority PO Box 80407 Lincoln NE 68501-0407

WOOD, LESLIE ANN, retail administrator; b. Chgo., Apr. 9, 1957; d. Howard Arnold and Anita Eleanor (Andler) W. AA, Harper Coll., 1977; BS in Comm. Scis., Ill. State U., 1979; MBA, Olivet Nazarene U., 1998. Advt. asst. Harry Alter Co., Chgo., 1979-80; clk. typist Career Guild, Evanston, 1980-81; reporter Aparacor, 1981-82; sales mgmt. trainee Prudential Ins. Co. Am., Millburn, N.J., 1983-84; fin. cons. Summit Fin. Resources, Livingston, 1984; mgr. Chgo. area Renault Inc. div. AMC/Jeep/Renault, Elk Grove Village, Ill., 1985-87; customer relations specialist Chrysler Motors, Lisle, 1987-88; dist. svc. and parts mgr. Chrysler; dist. parts mgr. Subaru of Am., Addison, Ill., 1989-91, dist. fixed ops. mgr., 1992-95; univ. rep. Olivet Nazarene U., Schaumburg, 1996-97; mktg. cons. WZSR STAR 105.5, Crystal Lake, 1997-99; parts cons. Am. Isuzu Motors, Cerritos, Calif., 1999—2001; parts and svc. mgr. Hyundai Motor Am., Aurora, Ill., 2002—, dist. parts svc. mgr., 2002—. Mem. ch. choir, rainbows coord. Stephens Min. First Presbyn. Ch., Libertyville, Ill. Avocations: aerobics, circuit weight training, sewing, stained glass crafts. Home and Office: 230 Brett Cir Unit D Wauconda IL 60084-1587

WOOD, PAUL F. national health agency executive; b. Lockport, N.Y., Dec. 7, 1935; s. Dwight Edward and Frances (Fletcher) W.; m. Kathleen Frances Stretton, May 27, 1958; children: Paul S., Richard F. BA, Western Res. Univ., 1964; MA, Kent State U., 1970; PhD, Case Western Res. U., 1975. Assoc. exec. dir. United Way of Stark County, Canton, Ohio, 1967-70; owner Paul Wood Co., N. Canton, 1970-86; dir. devel. The Salvation Army, N.Y.C., 1986-90; pres. Nat. Coun. on Alcoholism and Drug Dependence, Inc., 1990-99; special asst. The Salvation Army, Cleve., 1999—. Bd. dirs. Fairfield (Conn.) Chorale, 1991-94, Stepping Stones Found., 1996—, Bedford Hills, N.Y.; fin. com. Westport United Meth. Ch., 1993-96. Avocations: sailing, computer programming. Office: The Salvation Army 2507 E 22nd St Cleveland OH 44115-3202

WOOD, JR. R. STEWART, retired bishop; b. Detroit, June 25, 1934; s. Raymond and Marjorie Wood; m. Kristin Lie Miller, June 25, 1955; children: Lisa, Raymond, Michael. AB, Dartmouth Coll., 1956; MDiv, Va. Theol. Seminary, 1969; MA in Counseling and Sociology, Ball State U., 1973; postgrad., Va. Seminary. Ordained to diaconate and priesthood Episc. Ch., 1959. Vicar Episc. Ch., Seymour and Bean Blossom, Ind.; assoc. rector Grace Ch., Muncie, rector, 1966-70; exec. dir. Episc. Community Svcs., Indpls., 1970-76; rector All Saint's Episc. Ch., Christ Ch., Glendale, Ohio, 1976—84, St. John's Ch., Memphis, 1984—88; elected Bishop Coadjutor Diocese Mich., Detroit, 1988-89, diocesan bishop, 1990-2000; ret., 2000. Dir. summer camps, conf. ctr.; dep. Gen. Conv. 1970, 73, 76, 82; exec. coun. Coalition for Ordination of Women, bd. dirs. Avocations: camping, golf, tennis, photography, motorcycling. Office: Box 968 255 Robert Frost Ln Quechee VT 05059-0968

WOOD, ROBERT EMERSON, pediatrics educator; b. Jacksonville, Fla., Nov. 15, 1942; s. Waldo E. and Verda V. Wood. BS in Chemistry magna cum laude, Stetson U., 1963; PhD in Physiology, Vanderbilt U., 1968, MD, 1970. Bd. cert. pediatrics; bd. cert. pediatric pulmonology. Intern in pediatrics Duke U. Med. Ctr., Durham, 1970-71, resident in pediatrics, 1971-72; fellow pediatric pulmonology Case Western Res. U., Cleve., 1974-76, asst. prof. pediatrics, 1976-82, assoc. prof. pediatrics, 1982-83; assoc. prof. pediatrics, chief divsn. pediatric pulmonary medicine Dept. Pediatrics, U. N.C., Chapel Hill, 1983-88, prof. pediatrics, chief divsn. pediatric pulmonary medicine, 1988-94, dir. pediat. ICU, 1984-86, dir. Ctr. Pediat. Bronchology, 1994-99; prof. pediats. Children's Hosp. Med. Ctr., U. Cin., 1999—, chief, divsn. pulmonary medicine, 2001—. Mem. editorial bd.: Pediatric Pulmonology, 1992—, Jour. Bronchology, 1993—; contbr. chpts. to books and articles to profl. jours. Lt. comdr. USPHS, 1972-74. Named Grad. fellow Danforth Found., 1963-68, Med. Scientist fellow Life Ins. Med. Rsch. Found., 1965-70, Clin. Rsch. fellow Cystic Fibrosis Found., 1974-76. Mem. Am. Bronchesophagological Assn., Am. Assn. for Bronchology, Soc. for Pediatric Rsch., Am. Thoracic Soc., N.C. Pediatric Soc. Office: Children's Hosp Med Ctr Pediat Pulmonary Medicine 3333 Burnet Ave Cincinnati OH 45229-3026 Fax: 513-636-7734. E-mail: rewood@chmcc.org.

WOOD, WAYNE W. state legislator; b. Janesville, Wis., Jan. 21, 1930; Grad. high sch., Stoughton, Wis. Formerly builder, contractor, factory worker; mem. Janesville City Coun., 1972-76, pres., 1974-75; mem. Wis. Ho. of Reps., Madison, 1976—. Mem. criminal justice com., rules com., ways and means com., 1985—, vice chmn., 1989-95, mem. state affairs com., 1987—. Mem. State VTAE Bd., 1975-76; mem. Coun. of State Govts. Legis. Oversight Task Force, 1983, Janesville Housing Authority, 1971-77; former mem. Children's Svc. Soc. Adv. Bd., Rock County Sr. 4-H Coun., Sinnissippi Coun. Boy Scouts Am. Mem. UAW. Home: 2429 Rockport Rd Janesville WI 53545-4445

WOOD, WILLIAM JEROME, lawyer; b. Indpls., Feb. 14, 1928; s. Joseph Gilmore and Anne Cecillia (Morris) Wood; m. Joann Janet Jones, Jan. 23, 1954; children: Steven, Matthew, Kathleen, Michael, Joseph, James, Julie, David. Student, Butler U., 1945-46; AB with honors, Ind. U., 1950, JD with distinction, 1952. Bar: Ind. 1952. Mem. firm Wood, Tuohy, Gleason, Mercer & Herrin (and predecessor), Indpls., 1952—. Bd. dirs. Grain Dealers Mut. Ins. Co., Am. Income Life Ins. Co.; gen. counsel Ind. Cath. Conf.; city atty., Indpls., 1959—60; instr. Ind. U. Sch. Law, 1960—62. Author: (book) Indiana Pastor's Legal Handbook, 3d edit., 2001, Realtors' Indiana Legal Handbook, 2d edit., 1991. Mem. Ind. Corp. Survey Commn., 1963—, chmn., 1977—86; mem. Ind. Corp. Law Study Commn., 1985—87, Ind. Non Profit Corp. Law Study Commn., 1989—91; bd. dirs. Alcoholic Rehab. Ctr., Indpls., Indpls. Lawyers' Commn., Cmty. Svc. Coun. Indpls. Recipient Brotherhood award, Ind. region NCCJ, 1973. Mem.: St. Thomas Moore Legal Soc. (pres. 1970), Indpls. Bar Found., Indpls. Bar Assn. 1972—73, (coun. bd. mgrs. 1992—93), Ind. Bar Assn. (sec. 1977—78, award 1968), Audubon Soc., Indpls. Lit. Club (pres. 1973—74), Am. Legion. Democrat. Roman Catholic. Home: 3619 E 75th Pl Indianapolis IN 46240-3674 Office: Bank One Ctr Tower 111 Monument Cir Ste 3400 PO Box 44942 Indianapolis IN 46244-0942 E-mail: bwood@indylegal.com.

WOODARD, HAROLD RAYMOND, lawyer; b. Orient, Iowa, Mar. 13, 1911; s. Abram Sylvanus and Grace Lenora (Brown) W.; m. Clara F. Jarrell, Apr. 30, 1986; stepchildren: Walter J., Turner J., Laurel C. BS, Harvard U., 1933, LLB, 1936. Bar: Ind. 1936. Pvt. practice with firm and predecessor Woodard, Emhardt, Naughton, Moriarty & McNett, Indpls., 1936—; lawyer, 1936—; ptnr. Woodard, Emhardt, Naughton, Moriarty & McNett, Indpls., 1950—. Adj. prof. patent law Sch. Law Ind. U., Indpls., 1957-88. Lt. sr. grade USNR, 1942-46. Named Sagamore of the Wabash, Gov. of Ind., 1991. Fellow Am. Coll. Trial Lawyers; mem. ABA, Ind. 7th Cir. Bar Assn. (past pres.), Am. Patent Law Assn., Young Lawyers Assn. Indpls. (past pres. 1942), Ind. U. Sch. Law-Indpls. Alumni Assn. (1st hon. mem.), Columbia Club (past pres.), Woodstock Club (past pres.), Univ. Club (past pres.), 100 Club (past pres.). Methodist. Office: Woodard Emhardt Naughton Moriarty & McNett 3700 Bank One Tower Indianapolis IN 46204-5137

WOODFORD, ARTHUR MACKINNON, library director, historian; b. Detroit, Nov. 23, 1940; s. Frank Bury and Mary-Kirk (MacKinnon) W.; children: Mark, Amy. Student, U. Wis., 1958-60; BA in History, Wayne State U., 1963; AM in LS, U. Mich., 1964. Libr. Detroit Pub. Libr., 1964-74; asst. dir. Grosse Pointe (Mich.) Pub. Libr., 1974-77; dir. St. Clair Shores (Mich.) Pub. Libr., 1977—. Author: All Our Yesterdays, 1969, Detroit and Its Banks, 1974, Detroit: American Urban Renaissance, 1979, Charting The Inland Seas, 1991, Tonnancour, 1994, vol. 2, 1996, This Is Detroit: 1701-2001, 2001. With USNR, 1958-64. Mem. Mich. Libr. Assn. (v.p. 1988-89), Gt. Lakes Maritime Inst., Prismatic Club Detroit (pres. 1982), Algonquin Club of Detroit and Windsor (treas. 1983-93). Methodist. Avocations: tennis, bridge, reading, model shipbuilding. Office: St Clair Shores Pub Libr 22500 Eleven Mile Rd Saint Clair Shores MI 48081-1399 Home: 3284 S Channel Dr Harsens Island MI 48028 E-mail: woodfora@libcoop.net.

WOODMAN, HAROLD DAVID, historian, educator; b. Chgo., Apr. 21, 1928; s. Joseph Benjamin and Helen Ruth (Sollo) W.; m. Leonora Becker; children— Allan James, David Edward. B.A., Roosevelt U., 1957; M.A., U. Chgo., 1959, Ph.D., 1964. Lectr. Roosevelt U., 1962-63; asst. prof. history U. Mo., Columbia, 1963-66, assoc. prof., 1966-69, prof., 1969-71, Purdue U., West Lafayette, Ind., 1971-97, Louis Martin Sears disting. prof., 1990-97, prof. emeritus, 1997—; chmn. Com. on Am. Studies, 1981-94. Author: Conflict and Consensus in American History, 1966, 9th rev. edit., 1996, Slavery and the Southern Economy, 1966, King Cotton and His Retainers, 1968, Legacy of the American Civil War, 1973, New South-New Law, 1995; mem. editorial bd. Jour. So. History, 1972-75, Wis. Hist. Soc., 1972-76, Bus. History Rev., 1971-77, Agrl. History, 1976-82, Am. Hist. Rev., 1981-84, Jour. Am. History, 1985-88. Served with U.S. Army, 1950-52. Recipient Otto Wirth award Roosevelt U., 1990; Woodrow Wilson Internat. Center for Scholars fellow, 1977; Social Sci. Rsch. Coun. faculty grantee, 1969-70; Nat. Humanities Ctr. Fellow, 1983-84 Mem. Am. Hist. Assn., Orgn. Am. Historians, Econ. History Assn., Agrl. History Soc. (pres. 1983-84, Everett E. Edwards award 1963), Soc. Am. Historians, Bus. History Conf. (pres. 1981-82), Ind. Assn. Historians (pres. 1983-84), So. Hist. Assn. (exec. coun. 1982-85, Ramsdell award 1965, pres. 1995-96). Home: 1100 N Grant St West Lafayette IN 47906-2460 Office: Purdue U Dept History West Lafayette IN 47907 E-mail: hwoodman@sla.purdue.edu.

WOODRICK, ROBERT, food products executive; Chmn. D W Food Ctrs., Grand Rapids, Mich. Office: D&W Food Ctrs PO Box 878 Grand Rapids MI 49588-0878

WOODRING, DEWAYNE STANLEY, religion association executive; b. Gary, Ind., Nov. 10, 1931; s. J. Stanley and Vera Luella (Brown) W.; m. Donna Jean Wishart, June 15, 1957; children: Judith Lynn (Mrs. Richard Bigelow), Beth Ellen (Mrs. Thomas Carey). BS in Speech with distinction, Northwestern U., 1954, postgrad. studies in radio and TV broadcasting, 1954-57; MDiv, Garrett Theol. Sem., 1957; LHD, Mt. Union Coll., Alliance, Ohio, 1967; DD, Salem (W.Va.) Coll., 1970. Ordained to ministry, Meth. Ch., 1955. Assoc. youth dir. Gary YMCA, 1950-55; minister of edn. Griffith (Ind.) Meth. Ch., 1955-57; minister adminstrn. and program 1st Meth. Ch., Eugene, Oreg., 1957-59; dir. pub. relations Dakotas area Meth. Ch., 1959-60, dir. pub. relations Ohio area, 1960-64; adminstrv. exec. to bishop Ohio East area United Meth. Ch., Canton, 1964-77; asst. gen. sec. Gen. Council on Fin. and Adminstrn., United Meth. Ch., Evanston, Ill., 1977-79; assoc. gen. sec. Gen. Council on Fin. and Adminstrn., 1979-84; exec. dir., CEO Religious Conf. Mgmt. Assn., 1982—. Staff, dept. radio svcs. 2d assembly World Coun. Chs., Evanston, 1954; vice-chmn. commn. on entertainment and program North Ctrl. Jursidictional Conf., 1968-72, chmn., 1972-76; commn. on gen. conf. United Meth. Ch., 1972-93, bus. mgr., exec. dir., 1976-93, mem. divsn. interpretation, 1969-72; chmn. comm. commn. Ohio Coun. Chs., 1961-65; exec. com. Nat. Assn. United Meth. Found., 1968-72; del. World Meth. Conf., London, Eng., 1966, Dublin, Ireland, 1976, Honolulu, 1981, Nairobi, 1986, Singapore, 1991, Rio de Janeiro, Brazil, 1996, Brighton, Eng., 2001; exec. com. World Meth. Coun., 1986-2001; del. White House Conf. on Travel and Tourism, 1995, Ohio East Area United Meth. Found., 1967-78, v.p. 1967-76; chmn. bd. mgrs. United Meth. Bldg., Evanston, 1977-84; adv. bd. Hystar Aeroship Co., Nassau/Paradise Island, 1997-99, Red Lion Hotels and Inns, P.R. Conv. Ctr.; lectr., cons. on fgn. travel. Creator: nationally distbd. radio series The Word and Music; producer, dir.: TV series Parables in Miniature, 1957-59. Adviser East Ohio Conf. Communications Commn., 1968-76; pres. Guild Assocs., 1971—; trustee, 1st v.p. Copeland Oaks Retirement Ctr., Sebring, Ohio, 1969-76; bd. dirs. First Internat. Summit on Edn., 1989. Recipient Cert. Meeting Profl. award, 1985, Cert. Expt. Mgr. award, 1988; named to Ky. Cols., 1989, Conv. Liaison Coun. Hall of Leaders honoree, 1994. Mem. Am. Soc. Assn. Execs., Ind. Soc. Assn. Execs. (Mtg. Planner of Yr. award 1990), Mtg. Profl. Internat., Conv. Liaison Coun. (bd. dirs., past chmn.), Def. Orientation Conf. Assn. (chaplain), Ind. Conv. Visitors Assc. (bd. dirs., 1996-2000), Cert. Mtg. Profls. (bd. dirs. 1983-91), Internat. Assn. Exhbn. Mgmt., Found. for Internat. mtgs. (bd. dirs.), Marriott Cust. Leadership Forum (mem. cust. adv. bd.). Home: 7224 Chablis Ct Indianapolis IN 46278-1540 Office: 1 RCA Dome Ste 120 Indianapolis IN 46225-1023

WOODROW, KENNTH B. retail company executive; Degree, Yale U., Harvard U. With Dayton Hudson Corp., 1970; pres. Target stores divsn. Target Corp., 1994-99, vice chmn., 1999—. Office: Target Corp 1000 Nicollet Mall Minneapolis MN 55403-2467

WOODRUFF, BRUCE EMERY, lawyer; b. Mason City, Iowa, June 23, 1930; s. Frederick Bruce and Grace (Emery) W.; m. Carolyn Clark, Aug. 18, 1956; children: David C., Douglas B., Lynn M., Daniel R. BS in Bus., U. Ill., 1952; JD, Washington U., St. Louis, 1959. Bar: Mo. 1959, D.C. Dist. Ct. (ea. dist.) Mo. 1959, U.S. Ct. Appeals (8th cir.) 1960, U.S. Supreme Ct. 1979. Assoc. Armstrong, Teasdale, Schlafly, Davis & Dicus, St. Louis, 1959-65; ptnr. Armstrong Teasdale, Schlafly & Davis (and predecessor firms), 1966-95; sr. counsel Armstrong Teasdale LLP, 1996—. Prin. counsel St. Louis C.C., 1962-89; bd. dirs. Cass Bank & Trust Co., Cass Info. Sys., Inc., Red Lion Beef Corp., Manor Grove Corp., Rainbow Village, Inc.; city atty., Kirkwood, Mo., 1986. Named Kirkwood Citizen of Yr., 1983. Mem. ABA (banking law com.), Mo. Bar Assn., Bar Assn. Met. St. Louis, Health Lawyers Assn. Republican. Presbyterian. Clubs: Algonquin (Glendale, Mo.); Noonday (St. Louis (bd. dirs. 1988-91)). Avocations: golf, swimming, sailing, photography. Home: 9 Taylor Est Kirkwood MO 63122-2914 Office: Armstrong Teasdale LLP 1 Metropolitan Sq Ste 2600 Saint Louis MO 63102-2740

WOODS, CURTIS E(UGENE), lawyer; b. Ft. Leavenworth, Kans., May 29, 1950; s. Cecil Eugene and Velma Marie (Storms) W.; m. Kathleen L. Kopach, June 8, 1985; children: Colin Eric, Cameron Robert, Alexandra Marie. BA, U. Mo., Kansas City, 1972; JD, Northwestern U., Chgo., 1975. Bar: Ill. 1975, Mo. 1976, U.S. Dist. Ct. (no. dist.) Ill., U.S. Dist. Ct. (we. dist.) Mo., US. Dist. Ct. Kans., U.S. Ct. Appeals (7th, 8th and 10th cirs.). Law clk. U.S. Ct. Appeals (7th cir.), Chgo., 1975-76; assoc. Spencer Fane Britt & Browne, Kansas City, 1976-81, ptnr. Mo., 1982-94, Sonnenschein Nath & Rosenthal, Kansas City, 1994—. Contbr. articles to profl. jours. Recipient William Jennings Bryan award Northwestern U., 1974. Mem. ABA, Mo. Bar Assn., Kansas City Bar Assn., Order of Coif. Office: Sonnenschein Nath Rosenthal 4520 Main St Ste 1100 Kansas City MO 64111-7700

WOODS, GARY V. professional football team executive, former professional basketball team executive, automotive executive; b. Nov. 9, 1943; BBA, So. West Tex. State; MBA, SMU. Pres. San Antonio Spurs; ceo, pres., chair. McCombs Enterprises, San Antonio; pres., ceo Minnesota Vikings, Eden Prairie, 1998-. Office: Minnesota Vikings 9520 Viking Dr Eden Prairie MN 55344-3898 Address: McCombs Enterprises 9000 Tesoro Dr Ste 122 San Antonio TX 78217-6132

WOODS, GEORGE EDWARD, judge; b. 1923; m. Janice Smith. Student, Ohio No. U., 1941-43, 46, Tex. A&M Coll., 1943, Ill. Inst. Tech., 1943; JD, Detroit Coll. Law, 1949. Sole practice, Pontiac, Mich., 1949-51; asst. pros. atty. Oakland County, 1951-52; chief asst. U.S. atty. Ea. Dist. Mich., 1953-60, U.S. atty., 1960-61; assoc. Honigman, Miller, Schwartz and Cohn, Detroit, 1961-62; sole practice, 1962-81; judge U.S. Bankruptcy Ct., 1981-83, U.S. Dist. Ct. (ea. dist.) Mich., Detroit, 1983-93, sr. judge, 1993—. Served with AUS, 1943-46. Fellow Internat. Acad. Trial Lawyers, Am. Coll. Trial Lawyers; mem. Fed. Bar Assn., State Bar Mich. Office: US Dist Ct 277 US Courthouse 231 W Lafayette Blvd Detroit MI 48226-2700

WOODS, JACQUELINE F. telecommunications industry executive; Pres. Ameritech Ohio subs. Ameritech Corp., Cleve., Ameritech Ill., Cleve. Office: Ameritech Phone Co 45 Erieview Plz Rm 1600 Cleveland OH 44114-1814 also: Ameritech Corp 30 S Wacker Dr Chicago IL 60606-7413 Fax: 312-207-1601.

WOODS, JOHN ELMER, plastic surgeon; b. Battle Creek, Mich., July 5, 1929; m. Janet Ruth; children: Sheryl, Mark, Jeffrey, Jennifer, Judson. BA, Asbury Coll., 1949; MD, Western Res. U., 1955; PhD, U. Minn., 1966; DHL, Ashbury Coll., 1999. Intern Gorgas Hosp., Panama Canal Zone, 1955-56, resident in gen. surgery, 1956-57, Mayo Grad. Sch., Rochester, Minn., 1960-65, resident in plastic surgery, 1966-67, Brigham Hosp., Boston, 1968; fellow, transplant cons. Harvard Med. Sch., Cambridge, 1969; cons. in gen. and plastic surgery Mayo Clinic, Rochester, 1969-93, vice chmn. Dept. Surgery; asst. prof. Mayo Med. Sch., 1973-76, assoc. prof., 1976-80, prof. plastic surgery, 1980-93, Stuart W. Harrington prof. surgery. Vis. prof. Yale Sch. Medicine, New Haven, 1984, Harvard Sch. Medicine, Cambridge, 1984. Contbr. over 200 articles to profl. jours.; also 26 book chpts. and 1 film. Recipient Disting. Mayo Clinician award, 1991, Disting. Mayo Alumnus award, 1999. Mem. AMA (coun. on sci. affairs 1985-87), ACS (grad edn. com. 1985-87), Am. Bd. Med. Specialties, Am. Bd. Plastic Surgery (sec.-treas. 1985-88, chmn. 1988-89), Am. Soc. Plastic Surgeons Ednl. Fedn. (pres. 1984-85). Avocations: skiing, sailing, reading, the arts. Office: Mayo Clinic Plummer N-10 Rochester MN 55905-0001 E-mail: woods.john@mayo.edu.

WOODS, NIKKI, radio personality; Former 5th grade tchr.; morning radio host, entertainment reporter Sta. WGCI-FM, Chgo. Vol. Big Sister, Little Sister Program, Chgo. Rape Crisis Ctr., Walter S. Christopher Sch. for Children. Office: WGCI 332 S Michigan Ave Ste 600 Chicago IL 60604*

WOODS, RICHARD DALE, lawyer; b. Kansas City, Mo., May 20, 1950; s. Willard Dale and Betty Sue (Duncan) W.; m. Cecelia Ann Thompson, Aug. 11, 1973 (div. July 1996); children: Duncan Warren, Shannon Cecelia; m. Mary Linna Lash, June 6, 1999. BA, U. Kans., 1972; JD, U. Mo., 1975. Bar: Mo. 1975, Kans. 2000, U.S. Dist. Ct. (we. dist.) Mo. 1975, U.S. Tax Ct. 1999. Assoc. Shook, Hardy & Bacon L.L.P., Kansas City, Mo., 1975-79, ptnr., 1980-2000; shareholder Kirkland & Woods, P.C., Overland Park, Kans., 2001—. Gen. chmn. Estate Planning Symposium, Kansas City, 1985-86; chair Northland Coalition, 1993. Chmn. fin. com. North Woods Ch., Kansas City, 1986-88, 93-96; mem. sch. bd. N. Kansas City Sch. Dist., 1990-97, treas., 1992-97; mem. North Kansas City Ednl. Found., 1998-2002, pres., 1999-2002; mem. planned giving com. Truman Med. Ctr., 1992—, chmn., 1992-98; mem. Clay County Tax Increment Fin. Commn., 1990-99; bd. dirs. Heart of Am. Family Svcs., 1998—, sec., 2000-2001. Fellow Am. Coll. Trust and Estate Counsel; mem. ABA, Mo. Bar Assn., Johnson County Bar Assn., Kansas City Met. Bar Assn., Lawyers Assn. Kans. City (sec., v.p., pres. young lawyers sect. 1981-84), Kans. City Estate Planning Soc. (bd. dirs. 1985-88, 93-95). Democrat. Office: Kirkland & Woods PC 6201 College Blvd Ste 250 Overland Park KS 66211 E-mail: rwoods@kcnet.com.

WOODS, ROBERT ARCHER, investment counsel; b. Princeton, Ind., Dec. 28, 1920; s. John Hall and Rose Erskine Heilman W.; m. Ruth Henrietta Diller, May 27, 1944; children— Robert Archer III, Barbara Diller (Mrs. Gregory Alan Klein), Katherine Heilman (Mrs. John E. Glennon), James Diller. A.B., U. Rochester, 1942; M.B.A., Harvard, 1946. Account exec. Stein Roe & Farnham (investment counsel), Chgo., 1946-53, ptnr., 1954-90. Gov. Investment Co. Inst. Trustee U. Rochester; bd. dirs. Chgo. Juvenile Protective Assn., Chgo. Infant Welfare Soc., Chgo. Assn. Retarded Citizens. Served to lt. (s.g.) USNR, 1943-46. Mem. Am. Mgmt. Assn. (trustee 1973), Harvard Bus. Sch. Club Chgo. (pres. 1961), Phi Beta Kappa, Delta Upsilon. Clubs: Univ. Chgo, Chicago, Tower. Home: 470 Orchard Ln Winnetka IL 60093-4222 Office: 1 S Wacker Dr Chicago IL 60606-4614

WOODS, ROBERT EDWARD, lawyer; b. Albert Lea, Minn., Mar. 27, 1952; s. William Fabian and Maxine Elizabeth (Schmit) W.; m. Cynthia Anne Pratt, Dec. 26, 1975; children: Laura Marie Woods, Amy Elizabeth Woods. BA, U. Minn., 1974, JD, 1977; MBA, U. Pa., 1983. Bar: Minn. 1977, U.S. Dist. Ct. Minn. 1980, U.S. Ct. Appeals (8th cir.) 1980, Calif. 2000. Assoc. Moriarty & Janzen, Mpls., 1977-81, Berger & Montague, Phila., 1982-83, Briggs and Morgan, St. Paul and Mpls., 1983-84, ptnr., 1984-99; exec. v.p., gen. counsel InsWeb Corp., Redwood City, Calif., 1999-2000; gen. counsel BORN Info. Svcs., Inc., Mpls., 2000—. Adj. prof. William Mitchell Coll. Law, St. Paul, 1985; exec. com., bd. dirs. LEX MUNDI, Ltd., Houston, 1989-93, chmn. bd. 1991-92; bd. dirs. Midwest Asia Ctr., 1993-95, chmn. bd., 1994-95. Author (with others) Business Torts, 1989; sr. contbg. editor: Evidence in America: The Federal Rules in the States, 1987. Mem. ABA, Minn. State Bar Assn., State Bar of Calif., Hennepin County Bar Assn., Ramsey County Bar Assn. (chmn. corp., banking and bus. law sect. 1985-87), Assn. Trial Lawyers Am., Wharton Club of Minn., Phi Beta Kappa. Home: 28 N Deep Lake Rd North Oaks MN 55127-6506

WOODSIDE, FRANK C., III, lawyer, educator, physician; b. Glen Ridge, N.J., Apr. 18, 1944; s. Frank C. and Dorothea (Poulin) W.; m. Julia K. Moses, Nov. 15, 1974; children: Patrick Michael, Christopher Ryan. BS, Ohio State U., 1966, JD, 1969; MD, U. Cin., 1973. Diplomate Am. Bd. Legal Medicine, Am. Bd. Forensic Medicine, Am. Bd. Profl. Liability Attys. Mem. Dinsmore & Shohl, Cin.; clin. prof. pediats.emeritus U. Cin., 1992—. Adj. prof. law U. Cin., 1973—. Editor: Drug Product Liability, 1985—. Fellow Am. Coll. Legal Medicine, Am. Coll. Forensic Examiners, Am. Soc. Hosp. Attys., Soc. Ohio Hosp. Attys.; mem. ABA, FBA, Ohio Bar Assn., Internat. Assn. Def. Counsel, Def. Rsch. Inst. (chmn. drug and med. svc. com. 1988-91), Cin. Bar Assn. Office: Dinsmore & Shohl 1900 Chemed Ctr 255 E 5th St Cincinnati OH 45202-4700 E-mail: woodside@dinslaw.com.

WOODWARD, FREDERICK MILLER, publisher; b. Clarksville, Tenn., Apr. 15, 1943; s. Felix Grundy and Laura Henrietta (Miller) W.. m. Elizabeth Louise Smoak, Mar. 23, 1967; children: Laura Claire, Katherine Elizabeth BA cum laude, Vanderbilt U., 1965; postgrad., Tulane U., 1965-70. Manuscript editor U.S.C. Press, Columbia, 1970-73, mktg. dir., 1973-81; dir. U. Press of Kans., Lawrence, 1981—. Mem. adv. com. Kans. Ctr. for the Book, Topeka, 1987—; lectr. pub. U. Kans., Lawrence, Kans. State U., Manhattan, 1983—; book judge Western Heritage Ctr., Oklahoma City, 1988. Mem. Assn. Am. Univ. Presses (bd. dirs. 1988-91, pres. 1995-96, past pres. 1996-97), Kans. State Hist. Soc. (life), Phi Beta Kappa. Democrat. Avocations: racquetball, reading, music. Home: 2220 Vermont St Lawrence KS 66046-3066 Office: U Press Kans 2501 W 15th St Lawrence KS 66049-3905

WOODWARD, GRETA CHARMAINE, construction company executive, rental and investment property manager; b. Congress, Ohio, Oct. 28, 1930; d. Richard Thomas and Grace Lucetta (Palmer) Duffey; m. John Jay Woodward, Oct. 29, 1949; children: Kirk Jay, Brad Ewing, Clay William. Bookkeeper Kaufman's Texaco, Wooster, Ohio, 1948-49; office mgr. Holland Furnace Co., Wooster, 1948-49; acctg. clk. Columbus and So. Ohio Electric, 1949-50; interviewer, clk. State Ohio Bur. Employment Services, Columbus, 1950-51; clk. Def. Constrn. Supply Ctr. (U.S. Govt.) (formerly Columbus Gen. Depot), 1951-52; treas. Woodward Co., Inc., Reynoldsburg, Ohio, 1963—. Newspaper columnist Briarcliff News, 1960-63. Active Reynoldsburg PTA, 1960-67; Reynoldsburg United Meth. Ch.; mem. women's service bd. Grant Hosp. Avocations: bike riding, crocheting, writing poetry, stock market, water aerobics, line dancing, ballroom dancing. Office: Woodward Excavating Co Inc 7340 Tussing Rd Reynoldsburg OH 43068-4111

WOODWARD, JAMES KENNETH, retired pharmacologist; b. Anderson, Mo., Feb. 5, 1938; s. Audley J. and Doris Evelyn (Fields) W.; m. Kathleen Ruth Winget, June 25, 1960 (div. Nov. 1994); children: Audley J., Kimie Connette; m. Lisa Marie Stuart, Feb. 28, 1996. AB in Chemistry, S.W. Mo. State Coll., BS in Biology, 1960; postgrad., U. Kans. (USPHS fellow), 1960-62; PhD (USPHS fellow), U. Pa. Sch. Medicine, 1967. Pharmacologist Stine Lab., Newark, 1963-65, rsch. pharmacologist, 1967-71; sr. rsch. pharmacologist Merrell-Nat. Labs., Cin., 1972-73, sect. head, 1973-74, head dept. pharmacology, 1974-78; head dept. pre-clin. pharmacology Merrell Rsch. Ctr. Merrell Dow Pharms., Inc., 1978-83; assoc. dir. research adminstrn. Merrell Dow Rsch. Inst., 1983-88, dir. biol. devel., 1988-90, dir. int. reg. affairs, 1990-93; dir. clin. cand. prep. Marion Merrell Dow, 1993; ret., 1993; cons., 1993. Patentee in field. Pres. Golf Manor Recreation Commn., Cin., 1973-75. USPHS post-doctoral fellow U. Pa., 1967. Mem. AAAS, Phila. Physiol. Soc. Democrat. Baptist. Home: 972 Sheridan Dr Lancaster OH 43130-1923 E-mail: lisadocwoodward@aol.com.

WOODWARD, ROBERT J., JR. insurance executive; b. 1941; married. BA, Capital U., 1964, JD, 1971. With Nationwide Gen. Ins. Co., Columbus, 1964—, v.p., 1975-91, sr. v.p., 1991-95, exec. v.p., 1995—. V.p. Nationwide Life Ins. Co., Columbus, Nationwide Mut. Ins. Co., Columbus, Nationwide Mut. Fire Ins. Co., Columbus. Office: Nationwide Mut Ins Co 1 Nationwide Plz Columbus OH 43215-2239

WOODWARD, ROBERT SIMPSON, IV, economics educator; b. Easton, Pa., May 7, 1943; s. Robert Simpson and Esther Evans (Thomas) W.; m. Mary P. Hutton, Feb. 15, 1969; children: Christopher Thomas, Rebecca Marie. BA, Haverford Coll., 1965; PhD, Washington U., St. Louis, 1972. Econ. policy fellow HEW, Washington, 1975-76; asst. prof. U. Western Ont., London, Can., 1972-77; asst. prof. Sch. Medicine Washington U., St. Louis, 1978-86, assoc. prof., 1986-2001; McKerley prof. health econ. U. N.H., Durham, 2001—. Pres. Writing Assessment Software, Inc., 1987-91. Contbr. articles to profl. jours. Mem. adv. coun. Mo. Kidney Program, 1980-86, vice-chmn., 1983, chmn., 1984-85; coop. mem. Haverford Coll., 1968-90. NDEA fellow, 1968-71, Kellogg Nat. fellow, 1981-84. Mem. Am. Econs. Assn., Am. Statis. Assn. Home: 131 Wednesday Hill Rd Lee NH 03824-6546 Office: U NH Dept Health Mgmt and Policy Hewitt Hall Durham NH 03824-3563 E-mail: rsw@unh.edu.

WOODY, JOHN FREDERICK, secondary education educator; b. Indpls., Apr. 27, 1941; s. Ralph Edwin and Crystal Oleta (Thomas) W.; m. Nancy Ann Henry, July 7, 1963; children: Michael, Laura. BS in Secondary Sch. Teaching, Butler U., 1963, MS in Edn., 1967, adminstrn. lic., 1979, postgrad., 1991—, UCLA, 1980-82, Ind. U., 1990, U. Amsterdam, The Netherlands, 1985, Mont. State U., 1993, Purdue U., 1994. Tchr. Pub. Sch. 90, Indpls., 1963-66, Broad Ripple High Sch., Indpls., 1966-89; tchr., head social studies dept. Arlington H.S., 1989—. Author: (resource kits for hist. events) Cram, Inc., 1976-81, (filmstrips) Lowe Sheldrew, 1976-81; contbr. articles to profl. jours. and sch. materials. Sponsor Rep. Nat. Com., 1982—; deacon Heritage Bapt. Ch., 1983—; mem. U.S. Congress German Bundestag Select Com. Ind., 1986-93. Fulbright scholar U.S. Info. Agy., 1985. Mem. ASCD, Nat. Coun. Social Studies, Ind. Coun. Social Studies, Arlington Acad. Com. Avocations: reading, writing, swimming, lifting weights. Home: 7362 Woodside Dr Indianapolis IN 46260-3137 Office: Arlington High Sch 4825 N Arlington Ave Indianapolis IN 46226-2499

WOOLARD, LARRY, state legislator; s. Bertus and Vera Woolard; m. Mary Ann Switzer; children: Laurie Matson, Scott, Machelle, Jason. Commr. Williamson County, 1984-90; mem. Ill. Ho. Reps., Springfield, 1989—, mgm. agr. com., appropriations com., elections law com., elem. & secondary edn. com., mental health com., pub. health & infrastructure appropriations. Mem. Carterville C. of C. (chmn.), Herrin C. of C. (chmn.), Lions, Masons, Moose. Address: 840 Terminal Dr Ste 106 Marion IL 62959 Office: Ill Ho of Reps State Capitol Springfield IL 62706-0001

WOOLDREDGE, WILLIAM DUNBAR, health facility administrator; b. Salem, Mass., Oct. 27, 1937; s. John and Louise (Sigourney) W.; m. Johanna Marie; children: John, Rebecca Wistar. BA, Colby Coll., 1961; MBA, Harvard U., 1964. Staff assoc. Sun Oil Co., Phila., 1964-67; treas. Ins. Co. N.Am., 1967-72, B.F. Goodrich Co., Akron, Ohio, 1972-84, sr. v.p., 1978-79, exec. v.p., chief fin. officer, mem. mgmt. com., 1979-84; chief fin. officer, exec. v.p., dir. Belden & Blake Corp., North Canton, 1984-89; sr. v.p., chief fin. officer, dir. Belden & Blake Oil Prodn., Inc., 1984-89; prin. dir. Carleton Group, Cleve., 1989-92; CFO, COO, v.p. King's Med. Co., Hudson, Ohio, 1993—, also bd. dirs. Pres. Hudson Econ. Devel. Corp. Bd. dirs. Salvation Army, North Park Coll. and Seminary; trustee Children's Hosp. Med. Ctr., Akron. With U.S. Army, 1956-58. Mem. Fin. Execs. Inst. Episcopalian. Club: Country of Hudson. Home: 100 College St Hudson OH 44236-2925 Office: King's Med Co 1920 Georgetown Rd Hudson OH 44236-4060 E-mail: wdwooldred@aol.com.

WOOLEY, GERALDINE HAMILTON, writer, poet; b. Idlewild, Mich., Feb. 15, 1942; d. Charles Loren and Alice (Smith) Hamilton; m. David Wooley, June 11, 1961 (div. 1983); children: Vickie Wooley Houston, Monica Wooley Roberts, Deborah Wooley Williams. GED, Flint, Mich. Cosmetologist pvt. practice, Flint, Mich., 1967-70; tchr's. aide Flint Comty. Schs., 1969-71; nurse's aide Clara Barton Home, Flint, 1972; factory worker GM AC Plant, 1973-76; child care worker Beecher Cmty. Schs., 1987-89; poet, songwriter, 1994—. Songwriter Hilltop Records, Hollywood, Calif., 1996—. Author: (poems) Between The Raindrops, 1995 (Editor's Choice 1995), At Water's Edge, 1995 (Editor's Choice 1995), Tapestry, 1996 (Editor's Choice 1996), Memories of Tomorrow, 1996 (Editor's Choice 1996). Mem. PTA Flint Sch. Dist., 1969-70. Named to Internat. Poetry Hall of Fame, 1996. Mem. Internat. Soc. Of Poets, Nat. Writers Assn., Internat. Black Writers. Democrat. Avocations: camping, playing organ, exploring old houses, writing. Home: 2176 Flamingo Dr Mount Morris MI 48458-2610 E-mail: LadyKnight77@webtv.net.

WOOLF, STEVEN MICHAEL, artistic director; b. Milw., Dec. 23, 1947; s. Raleigh and Lenore (Shurman) W. BA in Theatre, U. Wis., 1968, MFA, 1971; D of Fine Arts (hon.), U. Mo., 1993. Prodn. stage mgr. The Juilliard Sch. Drama, N.Y.C., 1973-75; project producer Musical Theatre Lab., 1974-75; prodn. stage mgr. Barter Theatre, Abingdon, Va., 1976-79, Stagewest, Springfield, Mass., 1976-79; prodn. mgr. Repertory Theatre of St. Louis, 1980-83, acting artistic dir., mng. dir., 1983-85, mng. dir., 1985-86, artistic dir., 1986—. Adj. faculty Webster U., St. Louis, 1982—; mem. nat. negotiating coms. League of Resident Theatres, N.Y.C., 1986—; on-site evaluator Nat. Endowment for the Arts, 1985. Dir. plays A Life in the Theatre, 1982, the Crucible, 1986, Company, 1987, The Voice of the Prairie, 1988, 90, The Boys Next Door, 1989, Dog Logic, 1990, Born Yesterday, 1990, Terra Nova, 1991, The Diary of Anne Frank, 1991, Other Peoples Money, 1991, Six Degrees of Separation, 1992, Sight Unseen, 1993, Lion in Winter, 1993, Death and the Maiden, 1993, The Living, 1994, Wait Until Dark, 1994, The Caine Mutiny Court Martial, 1994. The Life of Galileo, 1995, Death of a Salesman, 1995, Betrayal, 1996, As Bees in Honey Drown, 1997, Who's Afraid of Virginia Woolf, 1998, Closer, 1998, Dinner With Friends, 2000 others. Mem. ad hoc coms. for funding Mo. Arts Coun., St. Louis, 1988; chair citizen rev. panel Reg. Arts Commn., St. Louis, 1986; bd. dirs. Mo. Citizens for the Arts, 1990—; exec. com. League of Resident Theatres, 1990—. Recipient award Mo. Citizens for the Arts, 1992, Women's Polit. Caucus, 1993, award for Individual Excellence in the Arts, Arts Edn. Coun., 1993. Mem. AFTRA, Soc. of Stage Dirs. and Choreographers, Actors Equity Assn. Office: Repertory Theatre St Louis 130 Edgar Rd Saint Louis MO 63119-3228

WOOLFORD, WARREN L. municipal official; b. Md. m. Betty Woolford; 1 child, Marcia. BS in Social Sci. and Secondary Edn., Coppin State Coll.; MA in Geography, U. Akron. Student planning intern Dept. Planning and Urban Devel., City of Akron, 1972, various planning positions, 1972-88, comprehensive planning and zoning mgr., 1988-93, dir. planning, 1993; also mem. Mayor's cabinet City of Akron. Part-time lectr. U. Akron, 1976-89. Mem. United Negro Coll. Fund Night Com.; mem. adv. com. Gt. Trail Coun. Pathfinder; bd dirs. Keep Akron Beautiful; mem. Ohio and Erie Canal Nat. Heritage Corridor Com., Akron Devel. Corp., NOACA Commuter Rail Adv. Com., Dist. 8 Pub. Works Policy Com.; past mem. allocations com. United Way of Summit County, Youth Motivation Task Force. Mem. Omega Psi Phi (keeper of records and seals). Office: City of Akron Dept Planning and Urban Devel 166 S High St Fl 4 Akron OH 44308-1626

WOOLLAM, JOHN ARTHUR, electrical engineering educator; b. Kalamazoo, Aug. 10, 1939; s. Arthur Edward and Mildred Edith (Hakes) W.; children: Catherine Jane, Susan June. BA in Physics, Kenyon Coll., 1961; MS in Physics, Mich. State U., 1963, PhD in Solid State Physics, 1967; MSEE, Case Western Res. U., 1978. Rsch. scientist NASA Lewis Rsch. Ctr., Cleve., 1967-80; prof. U. Nebr., Lincoln, 1979—, dir. Ctr. Microelectronic and Optical Materials Rsch., 1988—; pres. J.A. Woollam Co., Inc., 1987—. Editor Jour. Applied Physics Com., 1979-94. Grantee NASA, NSF, USAF, Advanced Rsch. Projects Agy. Fellow Am. Phys. Soc.; mem. Am. Vacuum Soc. (chmn. thin film divsn. 1989-91). Office: U Nebr Dept Elec Engring 209NWSEC Lincoln NE 68588-0511

WOOLLEN, EVANS, architectural firm executive; b. Indpls., Aug. 10, 1927; s. Evans Jr. and Lydia (Jameson) Ritchey; m. Nancy Clarke Sewell, July 16, 1955 (dec. 1992); children: Ian, Malcolm Sewell. BA, MArch, Yale U., 1952. Lic. architect Ind., Ala., Conn., Del., Ill., Ky., La., Maine, Mass., N.C., Ohio, Tenn. Chmn. Woollen, Molzan & Ptnrs., Indpls., 1955—; resident Am. Acad. in Rome, spring 1996. Architect Pilot Ctr., Cin. (Nat. HUD 1975), St. Marys Coll. Libr. (Nat. AIA-ALA 1983), Grainger Libr., U. Ill., Urbana, Asbury Coll. Libr., Wilmore, Ky., Indpls. Cen. Pub. Libr. Mem. bd. Ind. State Welfare Bd., 1956-59, Art Assn., 1956-66, Indpls. Capital Improvement Bd., 1965-69. With Signal Corps U.S. Army, 1946-47. Resident Am. Acad. in Rome, 1996. Fellow AIA Democrat. Address: 43 W 43rd St Indianapolis IN 46208-3721 Office: Woollen Molzan & Ptnrs Inc 47 S Pennsylvania St Indianapolis IN 46204-3698 E-mail: ewoollen3@earthlink.net.

WOOLLING, KENNETH RAU, vascular internist; b. Indpls., Mar. 6, 1918; m. Catherine Margaret McColl, Mar. 20, 1948; 2 children. BA magna cum laude, Butler U., 1939; postgrad., Harvard U., 1939-40; MD, Ind. U., 1943; MS in Medicine, U. Minn., 1951. Diplomate Nat. Bd. Med. Examiners, Am. Bd. Internal Medicine, Am. Bd. Cardiovascular Disease. Intern Indpls. City Hosp. (now Wishard Meml.), Indpls., 1943-44; resident in internal medicine Marion County Gen. Hosp., 1947; fellow, first asst. internal medicine Mayo Found., Rochester, Minn., 1948-52; mem. med. staff, mem. tchg. staff postgrad. med. edn. Marion County Gen. Hosp. (name now Wishard Meml. Hosp.), Indpls., 1952—; founder, dir., peripheral vascular diseases clinic Indpls City & Marion County Gen. Hosp. (now Wishard Meml.), 1952-68; pvt. practice internal medicine and cardiovascular diseases Indpls, 1952—; founder, dir. peripheral vascular diseases clinic Meth. Hosp., Indpls., 1967-72, founder, dir. vascular lab., 1970-73, mem. med. staff, tchr. staff postgrad. med. edn., 1952—. Mem. med. staff St. Vincent Hosp., St. Francis Hosp. and Winona Meml. Hosp., Indpls., 1952—; charter mem. med. staff Cmty. Hosp., Indpls., 1952—; charter mem. med. adv. com. Butler U., Indpls, 1956—. Contbr. articles to profl. jours., 1950—. Capt. Med. Corps U.S. Army, 1944-46. Fellow ACP, Am. Coll. Chest Physicians, Coun. on Cardiology Am. Heart Assn., Am. Coll. Angiology (gov. state of Ind. 1979-80); mem. AMA (50 Yr. award 1993), SAR, Internat. Union Angiology, Am. Soc. Internal Medicine, Am. Diabetes Assn., Ind. State Med. Soc., Ind. Diabetes Assn., Am. Fedn. for Clin. Rsch., N.Y. Acad. Med. Scis., North Ctrl. Clin. Soc., Mayo Cardiovascular Soc., Ind. Hist. Soc., Res. Officers Assn., Indpls. Med. Soc., Am. Legion, Shriners, Masons (Scottish Rite and Mystic Tie Lodge, 50 yr. award 1989), Contemporary Club of Indpls., Indpls. Athletic Club, Highland Golf and Country Club, Phi Delta Theta (50 yr. award 1985), Phi Kappa Phi, Phi Chi. Presbyterian. Office: PO Box 80192 Indianapolis IN 46280-0192

WOOTEN, ROSALIE, automotive company executive; Exec. v.p. O'Reilly Automotive Inc., Springfield, Mo. Office: O'Reilly Automotive Inc 233 S Patterson Ave Springfield MO 65802-2298

WORK, BRUCE VAN SYOC, business consultant; b. Monmouth, Ill., Mar. 20, 1942; s. Robert M. and Evelyn (Rusken) W.; m. Janet Kay Brown, Nov. 12, 1966; children: Bruce, Terra. B.A., Monmouth Coll., 1964; B.S., U. Mo.-Rolla, 1966; postgrad., U. Chgo., 1978-79. Registered profl. engr., Ill. Various mgmt. positions Midcon Corp. (and subs.), 1966-79; pres. Indsl. Fuels Corp., Troy, Mich., 1979-85, Costain Coal Inc., Troy, 1985-89; pvt. practice small bus. cons., 1989-92; bus. cons. Wallis Oil Co., 1992-2000; small bus. cons., 2000—. Mem. various coms. Cuba United Meth. Ch. Mem. Detroit Athletic Club, Forest Lake Country Club, Blue Key. Office: 2280 Hwy DD Cuba MO 65453-9684 E-mail: jbwork@fidnet.com.

WORKE, GARY D. former state legislator; b. Mankato, Minn., Jan. 20, 1949; m. Kathy; four children. BS, Mankato State U.; postgrad., St. Johns Coll. Mem. Minn. Ho. of Reps., 1993-97; owner Residential Care Home. Home: 36971 Knoll Dr Waseca MN 56093-4638

WORKMAN, ROBERT PETER, artist, cartoonist; b. Chgo., Jan. 27, 1961; s. Tom Okko and Virginia (Martin) W. Doctorate d'Etat, Diplome 3d Cycle, Sch. of Louvre, Paris, 1997; prof. habilite, France, 1997; DEA, French U. Lumiere, Lyon; Doctorate in Hieroglyphics, Nat. Inst. Lang./Civilizations, Egypt, 1997; PhD, Roosevelt U., Belgium; postgrad., Sch. of Art Inst. Chgo.; École Doctorale des Sciences, U. Blaise-Pascal/U. D'Auvergne, 1998. Freelance artist, Chgo.; artist Villager Newspaper, 1991—; instr. St. Xavier Coll., 1985; cartoonist Bridge View News, Oak Lawn, Ill., 1983-89, Village View Pubs., Oak Lawn, 1989; artist Villager News, 1991; creator acrylic sculpture ArtStyle. TV art dir. Media-In-Action, Oak Lawn; lectr. Oxford U., Eng., U. Ariz., 1996; substitute tchr. Morgan Park Acad., Chgo.; artist-in-residence Chgo. Pub. Libr.; featured voice Am. Radio, 1992; maitre de confs., Paris; creator acrylic sculpture art style. Author: (cartoon strip) Cypher, 1983-89; Sesqui Squirrel Coloring Book, 1982, Sesqui Squirrel History of Chicago, 1983, Book of Thoth, The Great Pyramid A Book in Stone, 1998, Easter Island and Egypt,(artists' books) Sesqui Squirrel History of the Constitution, Sesqui Squirrel Presents How Columbus Discovered America, The Sesqui-Squirrel Chicago Millennium Book, 1999; author: (novel) Angels of Doom, Book of THOTH, The Great Pyramid a Book in Stone, 1998, Easter Island and Egypt; artworks and books in collections of over 120 mus. and librs. and pvt. collections, including Mus. du Louvre, Paris, France, Lincoln Collection, Ill., Smithsonian, Art Inst. Chgo., Daley Br. Libr., Chgo., Ill. Exec. Mansion Mus., Musee du Louvre, Paris, Lincoln Collection State of Ill., Sesquicentennial Archives Chgo. Pub. Libr. (awards and honors), Vatican

Libr., Rome, Bodleian Libr. Oxford (Eng.) U., Mt. Greenwood br. Pub. Libr. Chgo., Ill. Collection, Libr. Nat. Mus. Am. Art, Nat. Portrait Gallery, Carter Presdl. Libr., Reagan Presdl. Libr., Expo. U.S. Pavilion Lisbon, Portugal, 1998; exhibited Am. Pavilion, Expo 92, Seville, Spain, Royal Acad. Arts, 1995, Am. Pavilion, Expo 98, Lisbon, Portugal, inaugural exhbn. of the New Millennium/Chgo. Pub. Libr., 2000; featured on Sta. WBBM-TV, Chgo., 1998; contbr. poetry to books: Journey to Infinity, America at the Millennium, Treasured Poems of America; creator of Planetnet Concept; inventor Tri-CAR; inventor millenium star explorer spacecraft, Tri-CAR. Mem. nat. adv. bd. Am. Security Coun., Boston, Va.; founder Kennedy Pk. Libr., Chgo. Featured in Artist's mag., 1990; recipient Resolution City Coun. Chgo., 1992. Mem. Am. Watercolor Soc., Gen. Med. Coun. (Eng.), No. Ill. Newspaper Assn., Art Inst. Chgo. (freelancer 1991), Artists' Resource Trust Ft. Wayne Mus. Art, Ridge Art Assn., VFW, S.W. Archdiocesan Singles, Friends Oxford U., Alumni Sch. Art Inst. Chgo., KC, Mensa. Roman Catholic. Home and Office: 2509 W 111th St Apt 2E Chicago IL 60655-1325

WORONOFF, ISRAEL, former psychology educator; b. Bklyn., Dec. 30, 1926; s. Samuel and Lena (Silberman) W.; m. Fay Goldberg, Feb. 11, 1950; 1 child, Gary. AB in Psychology, U. Mich., 1949, MA in Sociology, 1952, PhD in Edn., 1954. Lic. psychologist, Mich. Instr. Flint (Mich.) Jr. Coll., 1953-54; asst. prof. St. Cloud (Minn.) State Coll., 1954-56, Ea. Mich. U., Ypsilanti, 1956-59, assoc. prof., 1959-62, prof., 1962-92. Cons. psychologist Midwest Mental Health Clinic, Dearborn, Mich., 1978-83, Orchard Hills Psychiat. Ctr., Novi, Mich., 1983—; mem. Bd. Jewish Fedn. Washtenaw County, 1997—; co-chair Bd. Jewish Family Svc. of Ann Arbor, 1997. Author: Educator's Guide to Stress Management, 1986. Mem. bd. Jewish Family Svc. of Ann Arbor, 1996—, Jewish Fedn., Ann Arbor, 1997—; mem. cmty. rels. com. Jewish Cmty. Assn., Ann Arbor, Mich., 1990-92; v.p. edn. Beth Israel Congregation, Ann Arbor, 1985-87; mem. adv. bd. Mich. Anti-Defamation League of B'nai B'rith, 1958—. Mem. APA, Mich. Psychol. Assn., Am. Ednl. Rsch. Assn. Democrat. Home: 2519 Londonderry Rd Ann Arbor MI 48104-4017 E-mail: ted_woronoff@online.emich.edu.

WORTH, GEORGE JOHN, English literature educator; b. Vienna, Austria, June 11, 1929; came to U.S., 1940, naturalized, 1945; s. Adolph and Theresa (Schmerzler) W.; m. Carol Laverne Dinsdale, Mar. 17, 1951; children: Theresa Jean (Wilkinson), Paul Dinsdale. AB, U. Chgo., 1948, MA, 1951; PhD, U. Ill., 1954. Instr. English U. Ill., Urbana, 1954-55; faculty U. Kans., Lawrence, 1955—, assoc. prof., 1962-65, prof. English lit., 1965-95; prof. emeritus English, 1995—; asst. chmn. dept. U. Kans., Lawrence, 1961-62, assoc. chmn., 1962-63, acting chmn., 1963-64, chmn., 1964-79. Author: James Hannay: His Life and Work, 1964, William Harrison Ainsworth, 1972, Dickensian Melodrama, 1978, Thomas Hughes, 1984, Great Expectations: An Annotated Bibliography, 1986; editor: (with Harold Orel) Six Studies in Nineteenth Century English Literature and Thought, 1962, The Nineteenth Century Writer and His Audience, 1969, (with Edwin Eigner) Victorian Criticism of the Novel, 1985. Mem. AAUP, MLA, Dickens Fellowship, Dickens Soc., Midwest Victorian Studies Assn., Rsch. Soc. for Victorian Periodicals. Office: U Kans Dept English Wescoe Hall Lawrence KS 66045-7590 E-mail: GJWorth@aol.com.

WORTHAM, JAMES CALVIN, retired mathematics educator; b. Oconee County, Ga., Sept. 12, 1928; s. James Notley and Effie (Cross) W.; m. Mary Helena Shelley, Dec. 23, 1953; children: Sharon Elaine, Marilyn Kay, Deborah Louise, James Donald. BA, U. Akron, 1957; MA (NSF Scholar), Ohio State U., 1969. Tchr. jr. H.S. Akron Pub. Schs., 1956-62, tchr. sr. H.S., 1962-66; math. curriculum specialist Akron (Ohio) Pub. Schs., 1966-90; instr. math. U. Akron, 1966-90; ret., 1990. Served with USAF, 1951-55. Mem. NEA, Ohio Edn. Assn., Math. Assn. Am., Nat., Ohio couns. tchrs. of Math., Nat. Coun. Suprs. of Math., Greater Akron Math. Educators Soc. (pres. 1984-86), Pi Mu Epsilon. Republican. Mem. Ch. of Nazarene. Home: 229 Sand Run Rd Akron OH 44313-5364

WORTHEN, JOHN EDWARD, retired academic administrator; b. Carbondale, Ill., July 15, 1933; s. Dewey and Annis Burr (Williams) W.; m. Sandra Damewood, Feb. 27, 1960; children: Samantha Jane, Bradley Edward. BS in Psychology (Univ. Acad. scholar), Northwestern U., 1954; MA in Student Pers. Adminstrn., Columbia U., 1955; EdD in Adminstrn. in Higher Edn. (Coll. Entrance Exam. Bd. fellow), Harvard U., 1964; PhD (hon.), Yeungnam U., Daegu, Korea, 1986; DL (hon.), Ball State U., 2001. Dean of men Am. U., 1959-61; dir. counseling and testing and asst. prof. edn., 1963-66; asst. to provost and asst. prof., 1966-68; acting provost and v.p. acad. affairs, 1968; assoc. provost for instrn., 1969; v.p. student affairs, 1970-75; v.p. student affairs and adminstrn., 1976-79; pres. Ind. U. of Pa., 1979-84, Ball State U., Muncie, Ind., 1984-2000; ret., 2000. Cons. to universities and public schs. Bd. dirs. Ball State U. Found., Muncie-Delaware County Cmty. Found. Mem. Bus. Modernization and Tech. Corp., Am. Assn. State Colls. and Univs. (chair, bd. dirs. 1999), First Merchants Corp., Crossmann Cmtys., Inc., Rotary Internat., Phi Delta Kappa, Kappa Delta Pi, E-mail: johneworthen@aol.com.

WOUDSTRA, FRANK ROBERT, insurance company executive; b. Grand Rapids, Mich. BS, Ferris State Coll., 1968. CPA, Mich. Acct. Schellenber, Kregel & Kittle, CPAs, Grand Rapids, 1968-73; exec. v.p., chief exec. officer Foremost Corp. Am., 1973—, also bd. dirs. Office: Foremost Corp of Am PO Box 2450 Grand Rapids MI 49501-2450

WOYCZYNSKI, WOJBOR ANDRZEJ, mathematician, educator; b. Czestochowa, Poland, Oct. 24, 1943; came to U.S., 1970; s. Eugeniusz and Otylia Sabina (Borkiewicz) W.; m. Elizabeth W. Holbrook; children: Lauren Pike, Gregory Holbrook, Martin Wojbor. MSEE, Wroclaw (Poland) Poly., 1966; PhD in Math., Wroclaw U., 1968. Asst. prof. Inst. Math. Wroclaw U., 1968-72, assoc. prof., 1972-77; prof. dept. math. Cleve. State U., 1977-82; prof., chmn. dept. math. and stats. Case Western Res. U., Cleve., 1982-91, dir. Ctr. for Stochastic and Chaotic Processes in Sci. and Tech., 1989-2001, chmn. dept. stats, 2001—. Rsch. fellow Inst. Math. Polish Acad. Scis., Warsaw, 1969-76; postdoctoral fellow Carnegie-Mellon U., Pitts., 1970-72; vis. assoc. prof. Northwestern U., Evanston, Ill., 1976-77; vis. prof. Aarhus (Denmark) U., 1972, U. Paris, 1973, U. Wis., Madison, 1976, U. S.C., 1979, U. N.C., Chapel Hill, 1983-84, Gottingen (Germany) U., 1985, 91, 96, U. NSW, Sydney, Australia, 1988, Nagoya (Japan) U., 1992, 93, 94, U. Minn., Mpls., 1994, Tokyo U., 1997, Princeton U., 1998. Dep. editor in chief: Annals of the Polish Math. Soc., 1973-77; assoc. editor Chemometrics Jour., 1987-94, Probability and Math. Stats., 1988—, Annals of Applied Probability, 1989-96, Stochastic Processes and Their Applications, 1993-99; co-editor: Martingale Theory and Harmonic Analysis in Banach Spaces, 1982, Probability Theory and Harmonic Analysis, 1986, Nonlinear Waves and Weak Turbulence, 1993, Nonlinear Stochastic PDE's: Hydrodynamic Limit and Burgers' Turbulence, 1995, In a Reporter's Eye: The Life of Stefan Banach, 1996, Stochastic Models in Geosystems, 1997; author: (monograph) Martingales and Geometry in Banach Spaces I, 1975, part II, 1978, Burgers-KPZ Turbulence: Göttingen Lectures, 1998; co-author: Random Series and Stochastic Integrals: Single and Multiple, 1992, Distributions in the Physical and Engineering Sciences, vol. 1: Distributional and Fractal Calculus, Integral Transforms and Wavelets, 1997, Introductory Statistics and Random Phenomena. Uncertainty, Complexity and Chaotic Behavior in Engineering and Science, 1998. Rsch. grantee NSF, 1970, 71, 76, 77, 81, 87—, Office of Naval Rsch., 1985-96. Fellow Inst. Math. Stats.; mem. Am. Math. Soc., Am. Statis. Assn., Polish Math. Soc. (Gt. prize 1972), Polish Inst. Arts and Scis., Racquet Club East. Roman Catholic. Avocations: tennis, music, skiing, sailing, rare books collecting. Home: 3296 Grenway Rd Cleveland OH 44122-3412 Office: Case Western Res U Dept Statistics Cleveland OH 44106 E-mail: waw@po.cwru.edu.

WOYTHAL, CONSTANCE LEE, psychologist; b. Milw., Nov. 6, 1954; d. Gerald Clarence and Shirley Estelle (Gross) W.; m. John Francis Neisius, Mar. 20, 1982; children: Adam, Abby. BS, U. Wis., Milw., 1976; MS in Edn., U. Wis., River Falls, 1978; postgrad., Alfred Adler Inst., Chgo., 1980, George Williams Coll., 1984, Marquette U., 1984, Cardinal Stritch Coll., 1987; D of Psychology, Wis. Sch. Profl. Psychology, 1998. Lic. sch. psychologist, Wis.; cert. sch. psychologist. Psychologist Sch. Dist. of Marshfield, Wis., 1978-81, Sheboygan County Handicapped Children's Edn. Bd., Sheboygan Falls, 1981-91, devel. coord. wellness program Plymouth, 1984—; psychologist Plymouth Joint Sch. Dist., 1991—. Workshop facilitator Marshfield Clinic, 1981; cons. wellness lifestyle program Sch. of Sheboygan County, 1985—; mem. profl. adv. bd. Children with Attention Deficit Disorder, 1992—93; psychologist Lakeshore Mental Health, 1999—2001; lectr. in field. Bd. dirs. Family Connections, 1988-90. Mem. APA, NASP, Nat. Wellness Assn., N.Am. Soc. Adlerian Psychologists, Wis. Psychol. Assn., Wis. Sch. Psychology Assn., Sheboygan Wellness Assn. (bd. dirs. 1982-88), Mental Health Assn. Avocations: swimming, singing, hiking, cross country skiing, stereophile. Home: 859 Chaplin Ct Plymouth WI 53073-1012 Office: Parkview Elem Sch 500 Parkview Dr Plymouth WI 53073-1552 also: Lakeshore Mental Health PO Box 387 3151 Saemann Ave Sheboygan WI 53082 E-mail: kiddoc@apexmail.com.

WREFORD, DAVID MATHEWS, magazine editor; b. Perth, Australia, Dec. 17, 1943; emigrated to Can., 1966; s. Peter Mathews and Mary Lichfield (Edquist) W.; m. Donna Diane Campbell, Sept. 28, 1970; children— Elizabeth Mary, Catherine Anne. B.Sc. in Agr. with honours, U. Western Australia, 1966. Field editor Southam Bus. Publns. Ltd., Winnipeg, Man., Can., 1967-73; field editor Country Guide, Public Press Ltd., Milton, Ont., 1973-75; editor Country Guide, United Grain Growers Ltd., Winnipeg, 1975—. Mem. Man. Inst. Agrologists, Agrl. Inst. Can., Canadian Fedn. Farm Writers and Broadcasters. Mem. Ch. of Eng. Home: 294 Elm St Winnipeg MB Canada R3M 3P3 Office: United Grain Growers Ltd PO Box 6600 Winnipeg MB Canada R3C 3A7 also: Toronto-Dominion Centre 25th Fl 201 Portage Ave Winnipeg MB Canada R3C 3A7 E-mail: dwreford@fbc.agricoreunited.com.

WRIGHT, BETTY REN, children's book writer; b. Wakefield, Mich., June 15, 1927; d. William and Revena Evelyn (Trezise) W.; m. George Albert Frederiksen, Oct. 9, 1976. BA, Milw.-Downer Coll., 1949. With Western Pub. Co., Inc., 1949-78, mng. editor Racine Editl., 1967-78. Author numerous juv. and jr. novels, including The Doll House Murders, 1983, Christina's Ghost, 1985, The Summer of Mrs. MacGregor, 1986, A Ghost in the Window, 1987, The Pike River Phantom, 1988, Rosie and the Dance of the Dinosaurs, 1989, The Ghost of Ernie P., 1990, A Ghost in the House, 1991, The Scariest Night, 1991, The Ghosts of Mercy Manor, The Ghost of Popcorn Hill, 1993, The Ghost Witch, 1993, A Ghost Comes Calling, 1994, Out of the Dark, 1995, Haunted Summer, 1996, Too Many Secrets, 1997, The Ghost in Room 11, 1998, A Ghost in the Family, 1998, The Moonlight Man, 2000, The Wish Master, 2000; also numerous picture and ednl. books including Pet Detectives, 1999; contbr. fiction to mags. Recipient Alumni Svc. award Lawrence U., 1973, Lynde and Harry Bradley Maj. Achievement award, 1997, numerous awards for books including Mo. Mark Twain award, 1986, 96, Tex. Bluebonnet award, 1986, 88, Young Readers award Pacific N.W. Libr. Assn., 1986, Reviewer's Choice Booklist, Ala. Young Readers award, 1987, Ga. Children's Choice award, 1988, Ind. Young Hoosier Book award, 1989, 96, Children's Choice Book/Internat. Reading Assn.—CBC, 1984, S.C. Children's Choice award, 1995, Okla. Sequoyah Children's Choice award, 1988, 95, award Fla. Sunshine State, 2001. Mem. AAUW, Allied Authors, Coun. for Wis. Authors (juv. book award 1985, 96), Phi Beta Kappa. Avocations: reading, travel. Home and Office: 6223 Hilltop Dr Racine WI 53406-3479

WRIGHT, CHARLES RICHARD, insurance executive; b. Yankton, S.D., June 17, 1941; s. Ray C. and Agness (Weiland) W.; m. Mary M. Adrian; children: Charles A., Anne B., Jane E. BS, Yankton Coll., 1963. CLU. Agt. State Farm Ins., Mpls., 1963-67, agy. mgr., 1967-73, agy. dir. N.Y.C., 1973-76, exec. asst. Bloomington, Ill., 1976-78, dep. regional v.p. Phoenix, 1978-81, v.p. agy. Bloomington, 1981-88, regional v.p., 1988-92, agy. v.p., 1992—. Mem. ins. adv. bd. Manactony Vehicle; bd. dirs. David Davis Found., Lexington Community Ctr.; bd. trustees Eureka Coll. Mem. Nat. Assn. Life Underwriters, Internat. Platform Assn., Kiwanis. Republican. Methodist. Avocations: antiques, tennis, historic restoration. Home: 10 Spencer Lexington IL 61753 Office: State Farm Ins Co One State Farm Plz Bloomington IL 61710-0001

WRIGHT, FELIX E. manufacturing company executive; b. 1935; married Student, East Tex. State U., 1958. With Leggett & Platt, Inc., Carthage, Mo., 1959—, sr. v.p., from 1976, chief operating officer, exec. v.p., 1979, pres., COO, 1985-2000, pres., CEO, 2000—. Office: Leggett & Platt Inc 1 Leggett Rd Carthage MO 64836-9649

WRIGHT, FRANK GARDNER, retired newspaper editor; b. Moline, Ill., Mar. 21, 1931; s. Paul E. and Goldie (Hicks) W.; m. Barbara Lee Griffiths, Mar. 28, 1953; children: Stephen, Jeffrey, Natalie, Gregory, Sarah. B.A., Augustana Coll., Rock Island, Ill., 1953; postgrad., U. Minn., 1953-54. Suburban reporter Mpls. Star, 1954-55; with Mpls. Tribune, 1955-82, N.D. corr., 1955-56, Mpls. City Hall reporter, 1956-58, asst. city editor, 1958-63, Minn. polit. reporter, 1963-68, Washington corr., 1968-72, Washington bur. chief, 1972-77, mng. editor, 1977-82; mng. editor/news Mpls. Star and Tribune, 1982-84, assoc. editor, 1984-98; ret., 1998. Juror for Pulitzer Awards, 1983-84 Chmn. Golden Valley Human Rights Commn., 1965-67; mem. exec. com. Nobel Peace Prize Forum, 2000; mem. faculty Augsburg Coll., 3d Age, U. St. Thomas, Ctr. for Sr. Citizens Edn., 2000; bd. dirs. Luth. Social Services, Washington. Recipient several Page 1 awards Twin Cities Newspaper Guild, 1950's, 60's, Worth Bingham prize Worth Bingham Meml. Fund, 1971; runnerup Raymond Clapper award for Washington correspondence, 1971; Outstanding Achievement award Augustana Alumni Assn., 1977; citation for excellence in internat. reporting Overseas Press Club, 1985; Minn. SPJ/SDX 1st Place Page One award for in-depth reporting, 1988, MWAP award Human Interest Reporting, 1995. Mem. Am. Newspaper Guild (chmn. Mpls. unit 1961-67, editorial v.p. Twin Cities 1963-67), Minn. AP Editors Assn. (pres. 1981), Phi Beta Kappa Home: 4912 Aldrich Ave S Minneapolis MN 55409-2353 E-mail: fgwright@aol.com.

WRIGHT, HARRY, III, retired lawyer; b. Lima, Ohio, Apr. 27, 1925; s. Harry Jr. and Marjorie (Riddle) W.; m. Louise Forbes Taylor, Dec. 15, 1956; children: Harry IV, Whitaker Wilson, Priscilla W. Nicholson. Student, The Citadel, 1942-43; BS, U. Ky., 1948; LLB, Harvard, 1951. Bar: Ohio 1951. With Porter, Wright, Morris & Arthur, Columbus, 1951—, ptnr., 1956-88, of counsel, 1988-95, ret., 1995. Adj. prof. law Japan Law Ctr., 1986. Adv. bd. Salvation Army, 1958-74; pres. bd. trustees Six Pence Sch., Columbus, 1965-75; trustee Bradford Coll., 1957-75, pres. bd., 1972-74; trustee Columbus Acad., 1975-81, pres. bd., 1978-80; trustee Columbus Coun. World Affairs, 1979-82 Opera/Columbus, 1980-95, Ballet Met., 1987-91; trustee Green Lawn Cemetery, 1992—, Neighborhood Ho., 1993-98. With USAF, 1943-46. Mem. ABA (chmn. gen. practice sect. 1976-77, ho. of dels. 1978-87), Ohio Bar Assn. (Supreme Ct. Commn. on CLE 1988-94), Columbus Bar Assn., Columbus Club, Rocky Fork Hunt and Country Club. Episcopalian. Office: 41 S High St Columbus OH 43215-6101 Home: 2775 Brentwood Rd Columbus OH 43209-2218

WRIGHT, HELEN KENNEDY, retired professional association administrator, publisher, editor, librarian; b. Indpls., Sept. 23, 1927; d. William Henry and Ida Louise (Crosby) Kennedy; m. Samuel A. Wright, Sept. 5, 1970 (dec. 1998); 1 child, Carl F. Prince II (dec.). BA, Butler U., 1945, MS, 1950, Columbia U., 1952. Reference libr. N.Y. Pub. Libr., N.Y.C., 1952-53, Bklyn. Pub. Libr., 1953-54; reference libr., cataloger U. Utah, 1954-57; libr. Chgo. Pub. Libr.; asst. dir. pub. svcs. ALA, Chgo., 1958-62, editor Reference Books Bull., 1962—85, asst. dir. for new product planning, pub. svcs., 1985-89, dir. office for libr. outreach svcs., 1987—88, mng. editor yearbook, 1988-89. Contbr. to Ency. of Careers, Ency. of Libr. and Info. Sci., New Book of Knowledge Ency., Bull. of Bibliography, New Golden Book Ency. Recipient Louis Shores/Oryx award, 1991. Mem. Phi Kappa Phi, Kappa Delta Pi, Sigma Gamma Rho. Roman Catholic. Home: 1138 W 111th St Chicago IL 60643-4508

WRIGHT, HERBERT E(DGAR), JR. geologist; b. Malden, Mass., Sept. 13, 1917; s. Herbert E. and Annie M. (Richardson) W.; m. Rhea Jane Hahn, June 21, 1943; children: Richard, Jonathan, Stephen, Andrew, Jeffrey. AB, Harvard U., 1939, MA, 1941, PhD, 1943; DSc (hon.), Trinity Coll., Dublin, Ireland, 1966, U. Minn., 1996; PhD (hon.), Lund U., Sweden, 1987. Instr. Brown U., 1946-47; asst. prof. geology U. Minn., Mpls., 1947-51, asso. prof., 1951-59, prof., 1959-74, Regents' prof. geology, ecology and botany, 1974-88, Regents' prof. geology, ecology & botany emeritus, 1988—; dir. Limnological Research Center, 1963-90. Served to maj. USAAF, 1942-45. Decorated D.F.C., Air medal with 6 oak leaf clusters; recipient Pomerance award Archeol. Inst. Am., 1985, Ann. award Sci. Mus. Minn., 1990; Guggenheim fellow, 1954-55, Wenner-Gren fellow, 1954-55. Fellow AAAS, Geol. Soc. Am. (Ann. award archeol. divsn. 1989, Disting. Career award geology and geomorphology divsn. 1992), Soc. Am. Archeology (Fryxell award 1993); mem. NAS, Ecol. Soc. Am., Am. Soc. Limnology, Oceanography, Am. Quaternary Assn. (Career award 1996), Arctic Inst., Brit. Ecol. Soc. Achievements include research on Quaternary geology, paleoecology, paleolimnology and environ. archaeology in Minn., Wyo., Sweden, Yukon, Labrador, Peru, eastern Mediterranean. Home: 1426 Hythe St Saint Paul MN 55108-1423 Office: U of Minn 310 Pillsbury Dr SE Minneapolis MN 55455-0219

WRIGHT, J. CRAIG, state supreme court justice; b. Chillicothe, Ohio, June 21, 1929; s. Harry and Marjorie (Riddle) W.; m. Jane LaFollette, Nov. 3, 1951; children: Marjorie Jane, Alice Ann. B.A., U. Ky., 1951; LL.B., Yale U., 1954. Ptnr. Wright, Gilbert & Jones, Columbus, 1957-70; judge Franklin County Common Pleas Ct., 1971-84, adminstrv. and presiding judge, 1980-84; assoc. justice Ohio Supreme Ct., Columbus, 1985-96; with Chester Willcos & Saxbe, 1996—. Trustee Columbus Area Coun. on Alcoholism, 1959-83; chmn. bd. House of Hope-Halfway House, Columbus, 1960-68, trustee emeritus; trustee Grace Brethren Ch., Columbus, 1966-81, Worthington Christian Sch., Ohio, 1974-78, St. Anthony's Med. Ctr., Shepherd Hill Hosp. With CIC, U.S. Army, 1955-56. Recipient cert. of excellence Ohio Supreme Ct., 1972-83 Mem. ABA (mem. commn. on impaired lawyers 1988-91, state rep. jud. div. 1975-83), Ohio Bar Assn. (chmn. lawyers assistance com. 1977-84), Ohio Common Pleas Judges Assn. (exec. bd. 1972-83, pres.-elect 1984), Columbus Bar Assn., Am. Judicature Soc., Columbus Country Club, Athletic Club of Columbus. Avocations: golf; duplicate bridge. Office: Chester Willcox & Saxbe 17 S High St Ste 900 Columbus OH 43215-3442

WRIGHT, JOHN, classics educator; b. N.Y.C., Mar. 9, 1941; s. Henry and Dorothy (Chaya) W.; m. Ellen Faber, June 16, 1962; children: Jennifer, Emily. BA, Swarthmore Coll., 1962; MA, Ind. U., 1964, PhD, 1971. Instr. classics U. Rochester, 1968-72, asst. prof., 1972-75; assoc. prof. Northwestern U., Evanston, Ill., 1975-77, prof., 1977-83, John Evans prof. Latin lang. and lit., 1983-2001, chmn. dept., 1978-97, 00-01, prof. emeritus in svc., 2002—. Author: The Play of Antichrist, 1967, Dancing in Chains: The Stylistic Unity of the Comoedia Palliata, 1974, The Life of Cola de Rienzo, 1975, Essays on the Iliad: Selected Modern Criticism, 1978, Plautus: Curculio, Introduction and Notes, 1981, rev. edit., 1993, Ralph Stanley and the Clinch Mountain Boys: A Discography, 1983, The Five-String Banjo Stanley Style, 1984, rev. edit. (Clyde Pharr) Homeric Greek: A Book for Beginners, 1985, It's the Hardest Music in the World to Play: The Ralph Stanley Story in His Own Words, 1987, Traveling the High Way Home: Ralph Stanley and the World of Traditional Bluegrass Music, 1993; albums Everything She Asks For, 1993, Traveling the High Way Home, 1995, Promises, 1996, Ellen and John Wright 1, Ellen and John Wright 2, 1998; columnist: Banjo Newsletter; contbr. articles to profl. jours. Fellow Am. Acad. Rome, 1966-68; Nat. Endowment Humanities Younger humanist fellow, 1973-74; named to Honorable Order of Ky. Colonels; recipient songwriting prize Santa Fe Bluegrass and Old Time Music Festival, 1996. Mem. Am. Acad. in Rome Soc. of Fellows, Am. Philol. Assn., Ill. Classical Conf., Petronian Soc., Met. Opera Guild, Chgo. Area Bluegrass Assn., Minn. Bluegrass and Old-Time Music Assn., Internat. Bluegrass Music Assn. (Print Media Personality of Yr. 1994), BMI, Nat. Acad. Recording Arts and Scis. Club: Ralph Stanley Fan. Home: 1137 Noyes St Evanston IL 60201-2633 Office: Northwestern U Dept Classics Evanston IL 60208-2200 E-mail: jhwright@northwestern.edu.

WRIGHT, JOHN F. state supreme court justice; BS, U. Nebr., 1967, JD, 1970. Atty. Wright & Simmons, 1970-84, Wright, Sorensen & Brower, 1984-91; mem., coord. Commn. on Post Secondary Edn., 1991-92; judge Nebr. Ct. Appeals, 1992-94; assoc. justice Nebr. Supreme Ct., 1994—. Chmn. bd. dirs. Panhandle Legal Svcs., 1970 Mem. Scottsbluff Bd. Edn., 1980-87, pres., 1984, 86. Served with U.S. Army, 1970, Nebr. N.G., 1970-76. Recipient Friend of Edn. award Scottsbluff Edn. Assn., 1992. Office: Nebr Supreme Ct 2207 State Capitol PO Box 98910 Lincoln NE 68509-8910*

WRIGHT, JUDITH MARGARET, law librarian, educator, dean; b. Jackson, Tenn., Aug. 16, 1944; d. Joseph Clarence and Mary Catherine (Key) Wright; m. Mark A. Johnson, Apr. 17, 1976; children— Paul, Michael B.S., U. Memphis, 1966; M.A., U. Chgo., 1971; J.D., DePaul U., 1980. Bar: Ill. 1980. Librarian Oceanway Sch., Jacksonville, Fla., 1966-67; program dir. ARC, South Vietnam, 1967-68; documents and reference librarian D'Angelo Law Library, U. Chgo., 1970-74, reference librarian, 1974-77, dir., lectr. in law, 1980-99, assoc. dean for libr. and info. svcs., lectr. in law, 1999—. Mem. adv. bd. Legal Reference Svcs. Quar., 1981—. Mem. ABA, Am. Assn. Law Libraries, Chgo. Assn. Law Libraries. Democrat. Methodist Office: U Chgo Law Sch D'Angelo Law Libr 1121 E 60th St Chicago IL 60637-2745 Fax: 773-702-2889. E-mail: jm-wright@uchicago.edu.

WRIGHT, LLOYD JAMES, JR. broadcast executive, educator, announcer; b. San Benito, Tex., Dec. 28, 1949; s. Lloyd James Sr. and Lillian (Hemmerling) W. BA in Mass Communication, Pan Am. U., 1976; MA in Speech Communication, U. Houston, 1983. Lic. FCC restricted radiotelephone operator. Announcer Sta. KRYS, Corpus Christi, Tex., 1973-74, Sta. KZFM-FM, Corpus Christi, 1974-75, Sta. KRGV, Weslaco, Tex., 1975-76, Sta. KULF, Houston, 1976-77; instr. broadcasting Elkins Inst., 1976-77; announcer Sta. KBFM-FM, Edinburg, Tex., 1977-78; instr. radio Houston Ind. Sch. Dist., 1978-83; gen. mgr. Sta. KTAI-FM Tex. A&I U., Kingsville, 1983—; now pres., gen. mgr. WFYI-FM, Indpls. Cons. Stas. KINE, KDUV-FM, Kingsville, 1985—, weekend reporter Sta. KRIS-TV, Corpus Christi, 1987—. Producer: (documentaries) Kerrville Folk Festival, 1984, Texas Border Patrol, 1987. Served with Tex. NG, 1970-76. Mem. Nat.

Assn. Broadcasters, Broadcast Edn. Assn., Tex. Assn. Broadcasters, Tex. Assn. Broadcast Educators, Tex. Speech Communication Assn. Democrat. Methodist. Lodges: Lions (chmn. publicity), Elks. Avocations: surfing, motorcycling, photography, sports cars. Office: WFYI-FM 1401 N Meridian St Indianapolis IN 46202-2304

WRIGHT, MICHAEL WILLIAM, wholesale distribution and retail executive; b. Mpls., June 13, 1938; s. Thomas W. and Winifred M. W. BA, U. Minn., 1961, JD with honors, 1963. Ptnr. Dorsey & Whitney, Mpls., 1966-77; sr. v.p. Supervalu Inc., 1977-78; pres., COO, Super Valu Stores, Inc., 1978-82, CEO, 1981-82; chmn., CEO Supervalu Inc., 1982—. Bd. dirs., past chmn. Fed. Res. Bank, Mpls.; bd. dirs. Norwest Corp., Honeywell, Inc., The Musicland Group, Shopko, Inc., S.C. Johnson & Co., Inc., Cargill, Inc., Internat. Ctr. for Cos. of the Food Trade and Industry, Food Mktg. Inst., Nat. Am. Wholesale Grocers Assn., Inc.; vice chmn. Food Mktg. Inst. 1st lt. U.S. Army, 1964-66. Office: Supervalu Inc 11840 Valley View Rd Eden Prairie MN 55344

WRIGHT, SCOTT OLIN, federal judge; b. Haigler, Nebr., Jan. 15, 1923; s. Jesse H. and Martha I. Wright; m. Shirley Frances Young, Aug. 25, 1972. Student, Central Coll., Fayette, Mo., 1940-42; LLB, U. Mo., Columbia, 1950. Bar: Mo. 1950. City atty., Columbia, 1951-53; pros. atty. Boone County, Mo., 1954-58; practice of law Columbia, 1958-79; U.S. dist. judge Western Dist. Mo., Kansas City, from 1979. Pres. Young Democrats Boone County, 1950, United Fund Columbia, 1965. Served with USN, 1942-43; as aviator USMC, 1943-46. Decorated Air medal. Mem. ABA, Am. Trial Lawyers Assn., Mo. Bar Assn., Mo. Trial Lawyers Assn., Boone County Bar Assn. Unitarian. Clubs: Rockhill Tennis, Woodside Racquet. Lodge: Rotary (pres. Columbia 1965). Office: Charles E Whitaker Courthouse 400 E 9th St Ste 8662 Kansas City MO 64106-2684

WRIGHT, SHARON, reporter; BA Broadcast Journalism, Mich. State U. Gen. assignment and state capitol reporter, weekend anchor Sta. WBRE-TV, Wilkes Barre, Pa., 1976—79; gen. assignment reporter, investigative reporter Sta. KMGH-TV, Denver, 1979—81; consumer investigative reporter Sta. WBZ-TV, Boston, 1981—86; gen. assignment reporter, consumer investigative reporter NBC 5, Chgo., 1986—. Recipient Outstanding Alumna award, Mich. State U., 1986, 10 Emmys. Office: NBC 5 454 N Colmbus Dr Chicago IL 60611*

WRIGHTON, MARK STEPHEN, chemistry educator; b. Jacksonville, Fla., June 11, 1949; s. Robert D. and Doris (Cutler) Wrighton; children: James Joseph, Rebecca Ann. BS, Fla. State U., 1969; PhD, Calif. Inst. Tech., 1972; DSc (hon.) , U. West Fla., 1983. From asst. prof. chemistry to provost MIT, Cambridge, 1972—90, provost, 1990—95; prof., chancellor Washington U., St. Louis, 1995—. Bd. dirs. Cabot Corp., Ionics, Inc., Helix Tech. Corp., Optical Imaging Sys., Inc., Danforth Plant Sci. Ctr., Nidus Ctr. for Sci. Enterprise, A.G. Edwards, Inc., Barnes Jewish Hosp., BJC HealthCare. Author: Organometallic Photochemistry, 1979. Trustee St. Louis Art Mus., 1997—2000, Mo. Bot. Garden, St. Louis Symphony, St. Louis Sci. Ctr., Mary Inst. Country Day Sch.; bd. dirs. United Way Greater St. Louis, Chem. Heritage Found. Recipient Herbert Newby McCoy award, Calif. Inst. Tech., 1972, Disting. Alumni award, 1992, E.O. Lawrence award, Dept. Energy, 1983, Halpern award in photochemistry, N.Y. Acad. Scis., 1983, Fresenius award, Phi Lambda Upsilon, 1984, Dreyfus tchr.-scholar, 1975—80; fellow, Alfred P. Sloan, 1974—76, MacArthur fellow, 1983—88. Fellow: AAAS; mem.: Electrochem. Soc., Am. Chem. Soc. (award in pure chemistry 1981, award in inorganic chemistry 1988), Am. Philos. Soc., Am. Acad. Arts and Scis. Office: Washington Univ Office of Chancellor One Brookings Dr # 1192 Saint Louis MO 63130-4899

WROBLEY, RALPH GENE, lawyer; b. Denver, Sept. 19, 1935; s. Matthew B. and Hedvig (Lyon) W.; m. Madeline C. Kearney, June 13, 1959; children: Kirk Lyon, Eric Lyon, Ann Lyon. BA, Yale U., 1957; JD, U. Chgo., 1962. Bar: Mo. 1962. With Bell Tel. Co., Phila., 1957-59; assoc. Stinson, Mag & Fizzell, Kansas City, Mo., 1962-65, mem., 1965-88; ptnr. Bryan, Cave, McPheeters & McRoberts, 1988-92; ptnr., exec. com. Blackwell, Sanders, Peper, Martin LLP, 1992-2000. Bd. dirs. Human Resources Corp., 1971; mem. Civic Coun. Kansas City, 1986-2001; chmn. Pub. Housing Authority of Kansas City, 1971-74; vice chmn. Mayor's Adv. Commn. on Housing, Kansas City, 1971-74; bd. govs. Citizens Assn., 1965—, vice chmn., 1971-75, chmn., 1978-79; bd. dirs. Coun. on Edn., 1975-81, v.p., 1977-79; bd. dirs., pres. Sam E. and Mary F. Roberts Found., 1974-96; trustee Clearinghouse for Mid Continent Founds., 1977-96, chmn. 1987-89; bd. dirs. Bus. Innovation Ctr., 1984-91, vice-chmn. 1987-91, adv. bd. dirs., 1993-99, Midwest Regional Adv. Bd. Inst. Internat. Edn., 1989-93, Internat. Trade Assn., 1989-92, v.p., 1990; vice chmn., bd. dirs. Mid-Am. Coalition on Healthcare, 1991—. Mem. Mo. Bar Assn., Yale Club (pres. 1969-71, outstanding mem. award 1967). Republican. Presbyn. (elder) Home: 1015 W 67th Ter Kansas City MO 64113-1942 Office: 2300 Main St Kansas City MO 64108-2416 E-mail: rwrobley@blackwellsanders.com.

WRUBLE, BERNHARDT KARP, lawyer; b. Wilkes-Barre, Pa., Mar. 21, 1942; s. Maurice and Ruth Yvonne (Karp) W.; m. Judith Marilyn Eyges, Nov. 16, 1968 (div. 1987); children: Justine, Vanessa, Alexis; m. Jill Diamond, Nov. 24, 1990; children: Mattia, Austin. BA in Polit. Sci., Williams Coll., Williamstown, Mass., 1963; LLB, U. Pa., 1966; postgrad., NYU, 1972-74, Harvard U., 1978. Bar: U.S. Dist. Ct. (so. dist.) N.Y. 1969, U.S. Dist. Ct. (ea. dist.) N.Y. 1972, U.S. Ct. Appeals (2d cir.) 1972, U.S. Supreme Ct. 1972, U.S. Ct. Appeals (7th cir.) 1974, U.S. Ct. Appeals (D.C. and 4th cirs.) 1984, U.S. Ct. Appeals (5th cir.) 1985, U.S. Ct. Appeals (11th cir.) 1986. Law clk. to presiding judge U.S. Ct. Appeals (3d cir.), 1966-67; assoc. Simpson, Thacher & Bartlet, N.Y.C., 1968-73; ptnr. Simpson, Thatcher & Bartlet, 1974-77; prin. dep. gen. counsel U.S. Dept. Army, Washington, 1977-79; dir. Office Govt. Ethics, 1979; exec. asst. to sec. and dep. sec. U.S. Dept. Energy, 1979-81; dir. Pres.'s Interagy. Coal Export Task Force, 1980-81; ptnr. Verner, Liipfert, Bernhard, McPherson and Hand, 1981-99; sr. v.p. legal affairs Northwest Airlines, St. Paul, 1999—2001. Bd. dirs. Epilepsy Found. Am., 1983, chmn., 1991. Mem. ABA, D.C. Bar Assn., N.Y. State Bar Assn., Williams Coll. Alumni Assn. (pres. Washington chpt. 1986-91), Williams Coll. Soc. Alumni Assn. (exec. com. 1988-91). Democrat. E-mail: bkwruble@yahoo.com.

WU, TAI TE, biological sciences and engineering educator; b. Shanghai, China, Aug. 2, 1935; m. Anna Fang, Apr. 16, 1966; 1 son, Richard. MB, BS, U. Hong Kong, 1956; BS in Mech. Engring, U. Ill., Urbana, 1958; SM in Applied Physics, Harvard U., 1959, PhD in Engring. (Gordon McKay fellow), 1961. Rsch. fellow in structural mechanics Harvard U., 1961-63; rsch. fellow in biol. chemistry Harvard U. (Med. Sch.), 1964, rsch. assoc., 1965-66; rsch. scientist Hydronautics, Inc., Rockville, Md., 1962; asst. prof. engring. Brown U., Providence, 1963-65; asst. prof. biomath. Grad. Sch. Med. Scis., Cornell U. Med. Coll., N.Y.C., 1967-68, assoc. prof., 1968-70; assoc. prof. physics and engring. scis. Northwestern U., Evanston, Ill., 1970-73, prof., 1973-74, prof. biochemistry and molecular biology and engring. scis., 1973-85, acting chmn. dept. engring. scis., 1974, prof. biochem., molecular biology, cell biology and biomed. engring., engring. scis., applied math., 1985-94, prof. biochemistry, molecular biology, cell biology, biomed. engring., 1994—. Author (with E.A. Kabat and others): Variable Regions of Immunoglobulin Chains, 1976, Sequences of Immunoglobulin Chains, 1979, Sequences of Proteins of Immunological Importance, 1983, Sequences of Proteins of Immunological Interest, 1987, 5th edit., 1991; editor: New Methodologies in Studies of Protein Configuration, 1985, Analytical Molecular Biology, 2001; contbr. Recipient progress award Chinese Engrs. and Scientists Assn. So. Calif., Los Angeles, 1971; C.T. Loo Scholar, 1959-60; NIH Research Career Devel. awardee, 1974-79 Mem. Am. Soc. Biochem. and Molecular Biology, Biophys. Soc., Sigma Xi, Tau Beta Pi, Pi Mu Epsilon. Office: Northwestern U Dept Biochem Molecular and Cell Biology Evanston IL 60208-0001 E-mail: tt@immuno.bme.nwu.edu.

WUEBKER, COLLEEN MARIE, librarian; b. LaCrosse, Wis., June 22, 1943; d. Harris M. and Mary Frances (Collins) Gruber; m. William Joseph Wuebker, Aug. 14, 1965; children: Jon Paul, Timothy William, Maree Jean. BA, Mount Mercy Coll., 1965; MS, Mankato State U., 1975. Cert. permanent profl. media specialist, tchr., Iowa. Secondary tchr. Luverne Community Sch., Minn., 1965-66; tchr. St. Mary's Sch., Larchwood, Iowa, 1966; secondary tchr. SEMCO Community Sch., Gilman, 1966-67; substitute tchr. West Bend (Iowa) Community Schs., 1968-74, sch. media specialist, 1975—, Mallard Community Schs. (Iowa), 1974-75. Mem. selection com. Lakeland Area Edn. Agy., Cylinder, Iowa, 1977—; mem. Gov.'s Sch. Efficiency Task Force, West Bend, 1987; mem. sch. evaluation team Dept. Pub. Instrn., Des Moines, 1986. Mem. Sts. Peter and Paul Parish Coun., West Bend, 1987—, liturgy and music coord., song leader, 1987—; speaker Marriage Encounter Movement, Sioux City Diocese, 1985—, Pre-Cana Workshops, Emmetsburg, 1985—; chmn. Parish Liturgy Com., West Bend, 1987—. Mem. NEA, Iowa Edn. Assn., Iowa Ednl. Media Assn., Cath. Daus. Am. (past v.p. West Bend). Roman Catholic. Avocations: genealogy, music. Home: Box 426 11 1st Ave NE West Bend IA 50597-5010 Office: West Bend Community Sch 300 3rd Ave SW West Bend IA 50597-8573

WUEST, JIM, consumer products company executive; Sr. exec. v.p. merch. and mktg. Office Max, Inc., Shaker Heights, Ohio, 1998—. Office: Office Max Inc 3605 Warrensville Center Rd Shaker Heights OH 44122-5248

WUNDER, CHARLES C(OOPER), physiology and biophysics educator, gravitational biologist; b. Pitts., Oct. 2, 1928; s. Edgar Douglas and Annabel (Cooper) W.; m. Marcia Lynn Barnes, Apr. 4, 1962; children: E(dgar) Douglas, David Barnes, Donald Charles. A.B. in Biology, Washington and Jefferson Coll., 1949; M.S. in Biophysics, U. Pitts., 1952, Ph.D. in Biophysics, 1954. Assoc. U. Iowa, Iowa City, 1954-56, asst. prof. physiology and biophysics, 1956-63, assoc. prof. physiology and biophysics, 1963-71, prof. physiology and biophysics, 1971-98, prof. emeritus, 1998—. Cons. for biol. simulation of weightlessness U.S. Air Force, 1964; vis. scientist Mayo Found., Rochester, Minn., 1966-67. Author: Life into Space: An Introduction to Space Biology, 1966; also chpts., numerous articles, abstracts Recipient Research Career Devel. award NIH, 1961-66; AEC predoctoral fellow U. Pitts., 1951-53; NIH spl. fellow, 1966-67; grantee NIH, NASA Mem. Am. Physiol. Soc., The Biophys. Soc. (charter), Aerospace Med. Assn., Iowa Acad. Sci. (chmn. physiology sect. 1971-72, 83-84, 96-97), Am. Soc. Biomechanics (founding), Aerospace Physiologist Soc., Iowa Physiol. Soc. (pres. 1996-97), Am. Soc. for Gravitational and Space Biology (Founders award 2000). Presbyterian Achievements include the establishment of chronic centrifugation as an approach for investigating gravity's role as a biological determinant. Home: 702 W Park Rd Iowa City IA 52246-2425 Office: U Iowa BSB Iowa City IA 52242 E-mail: charles-wunder@uiowa.edu.

WUNSCH, JAMES STEVENSON, political science educator; b. Detroit, Sept. 27, 1946; s. Richard Ellis and Jane Rolston (Kershaw) W.; m. Lillian C. Richards, Mar. 29, 1969 (div. Feb. 1983), 1 child, Kathryn; m. Mary Gayle Gundlach, Aug. 19, 1983; children: Hallie, Hannah. BA, Duke U., 1968; MA, Ind. U., 1971, PhD, 1974. Rsch. fellow U. Ghana, Accra, 1971-72; asst. prof. Creighton U., Omaha, 1974-78, assoc. prof., 1978-86, prof. polit. sci., 1986—, chmn. dept., 1983-93, 96—, dir. African studies program, 1998—. Social sci. analyst and cons., Ghana, Liberia, Kenya, Sudan, Thailand, Philippines, USAID, Washington, 1978-80; vis. assoc. prof. Ind. U., Bloomington, 1985-86; sr. project mgr. Assocs. in Rural Devel., Burlington, Vt., 1987-88, cons., Bangladesh, Zambia, Nigeria, South Africa, Swaziland, Botswana, Uganda, 1985—; USIA Disting. lectr., South Africa, 1993. Author: The Failure of the Centralized State, 1990, (monograph) Rural Development, Decentralization and Administrative Reform, 1988; mem. bd. editors Pub. Adminstrn. and Devel., 1998—; contbr. articles to profl. jours., chpts. to books. Bd. dirs. Omaha Symphony Chorus, 1977-78, Nebr. Choral Arts Soc., 1982-96, Voices of Omaha, 1982-85, Trinity Cathedral, Omaha, 1980-83; participant Leadership Omaha, 1982-83; mem. Omaha Com. Fgn. Rels., 1975-95; mem. govt. affairs com. Greater Omaha C. of C., 1980-85; mem. issues and interests com. Nebr. Rep. party, 1984-88. Recipient R.F. Kennedy Quality Tchg. award Creighton U., 1985, Burlington No. award, 1992, Dean's award for excellence in tchg., 1994, Dean's award for excellence in scholarship, 2000; rsch. award NSF, NEH, USAID, Am. Philos. Soc.; Fulbright-Hays fellow in Ghana, 1971-72, Internat. Affairs fellow N.Y. Coun. Fgn. Rels., 1978-79. Mem. Am. Polit. Sci. Assn., Midwest Polit. Sci. Assn., African Studies Assn., Internat. Studies Assn., Phi Beta Kappa, Pi Sigma Alpha, Phi Beta Delta. Republican. Episcopalian. Avocations: vocal music, camping, cross-country skiing, cycling. Home: 1631 N 53rd St Omaha NE 68104-4947 Office: Creighton U Dept Polit Sci 30th And California Omaha NE 68178-0001

WURSTER, DALE ERWIN, pharmacy educator, university dean emeritus; b. Sparta, Wis., Apr. 10, 1918; s. Edward Emil and Emma Sophia (Steingraeber) W.; m. June Margaret Peterson, June 16, 1944; children: Dale Eric, Susan Gay. BS, U. Wis., 1942, PhD, 1947. U. Wis. Sch. Pharmacy, Madison, 1958-71, mem. faculty, 1947-71; prof., dean N.D. State U. Coll. Pharmacy, 1971-72; prof. U. Iowa Coll. Pharmacy, Iowa City, 1972—, dean, 1972-84, dean emeritus, 1984—. George B. Kaufman Meml. lectr. Ohio State U., 1968; Hancher Finkbine Medallion prof. U. Iowa, 1984; Joseph V. Swintosky disting. lectr. U. Ky., 2000; cons. in field; phys. sci. adminstr. USN, 1960-63; sci. advisor U. Wis. Alumni Rsch. Found., 1968-72; mem. revision com. U.S. Pharmacopoeia, 1961-70; mem. pharmacy rev. com. USPHS, 1966-72; mem. tech. adv. com. contraceptive R&D program Ea. Va. Med. Sch., 1987-2002, rsch., U. Wis. Contbr. articles to profl. jours., chpts. to books; patentee in field. With USNR, 1944-46. Recipient Superior Achievement citation Navy Dept., 1964, merit citation U. Wis., 1976, Disting. Alumni award U. Wis. Sch. Pharmacy, 1984. Fellow Am. Assn. Pharm. Scientists (founder, sponsor Dale E. Wurster rsch. award 1990—, Disting. Pharm. Scientist award 1991); mem. Am. Assn. Colls. Pharmacy (exec. com. 1964-66, chmn. conf. tchrs. 1960-61, vis. scientist 1963-70, Disting. Educator award 1983), Acad. Pharm. Scis. (exec. com. 1967-70, chmn. basic pharmaceutics sect. 1965-67, pres. 1975, Indsl. Pharm. Tech. award 1980), Am. Pharm. Assn. (chmn. sci. sect. 1964-65, rsch. achievement award 1965, Wis. Disting. Svc. award 1971), Iowa Pharmacists Assn. (Robert G. Gibbs award 1983), Wis. Acad. Scis., Arts and Letters, Soc. Investigative Dermatology, Rumanian Soc. Med. Sci. (hon.), Am. Found. Pharm. Edn. (bd. grants 1987-92), Sigma Xi, Kappa Psi (past officer), Rho Chi, Phi Lambda Upsilon, Phi Sigma. Home: 16 Brickwood Cir NE Iowa City IA 52240-9129

WURTELE, CHRISTOPHER ANGUS, paint and coatings company executive; b. Mpls., Aug. 25, 1934; Valentine and Charlotte (Lindley) W.; m. Heather Campbell (div. Feb. 1977); children: Christopher, Andrew, Heidi; m. Margaret Von Blon, Aug. 21, 1977. BA, Yale U., 1956; MBA, Stanford U., 1961. V.p. Minn. Paints, Inc. (merged with Valspar Corp. 1970), Mpls., 1962-65, exec. v.p., 1965, pres., CEO, 1973-96, chmn., 1973-98. Dir. Bemis Co., IDS Mutual Fund Group. Bd. dirs. Bush Found., Walker Art Ctr. With USN, 1956-59. Mem. Mpls. Club. Episcopalian. Home: 2409 E Lake Of The Isles Pky Minneapolis MN 55405-2479 Office: 4900 IDS Ctr 80 S 8th St Minneapolis MN 55402

WYANT, JOHN H. real estate development executive; Founder, gen. ptnr., adv. bd. Blue Chip Venture Capital Funds, Cin.; vice chmn. bd. dirs. Zaring Homes. Adj. prof. mgmt. and entrepreneurship Xavier U. Office: Zaring Nat Corp 11300 Cornell Park Dr Ste 500 Cincinnati OH 45242-1885

WYATT, JAMES FRANK, JR. lawyer; b. Talladega, Ala., Dec. 1, 1922; s. James Frank and Nannie Lee (Heaslett) W.; m. Rosemary Barbara Slone, Dec. 21, 1951; children: Martha Lee, James Frank III. B.S., Auburn U., 1943; J.D., Georgetown U., 1949, postgrad., 1950. Bar: D.C. 1949, Ala. 1950, Ill. 1953, U.S. Supreme Ct 1953. Atty. Office Chief Counsel, IRS, 1949-51; tax counsel Universal Oil Products Co., Des Plaines, Ill., 1951-63, asst. treas., 1963-66, v.p. fin., treas., 1966-75; treas. CF Industries, Inc., Long Grove, Ill., 1976-78, v.p. fin., treas., 1978-82; assoc. Tenney & Bentley, 1983-85, Arnstein, Gluck, Lehr, Barron & Milligan, 1985-88; pvt. practice, 1989—. Dir. 1st Nat. Bank, Des Plaines. Village trustee, Barrington, Ill., 1963-75; bd. dirs. Buehler YMCA, Barrington Twp. Republican Orgn., 1963— ; pres. Barrington Area Rep. Workshops, 1962-63. Served to capt., Judge Adv. Gen. Corps AUS, 1944-47. Mem. Tax Execs. Inst. (v.p. 1965-66, chpt. pres. 1961-62), Fed., Am., Chgo. bar assns., Barrington Home Owners Assn. (pres. 1960-61), Newcomen Sco., Assn. U.S. Army, Scabbard and Blade, Phi Delta Phi, Sigma Chi. Episcopalian. Clubs: Barrington Hills Country; Economics, University (Chgo.). Home: 625 Concord Pl Barrington IL 60010-4508 Office: 200 Applebee St Barrington IL 60010-3063

WYCLIFF, NOEL DON, journalist, newspaper editor; b. Liberty, Tex., Dec. 17, 1946; s. Wilbert Aaron and Emily Ann (Broussard) W.; m. Catherine Anne Erdmann, Sept. 25, 1982; children: Matthew William, Grant Erdmann. BA, U. Notre Dame, 1969. Reporter Houston Post, 1970-71, Dayton (Ohio) Daily News, 1972-73, Seattle Post-Intelligencer, 1978, Dallas Times-Herald, 1978-79, Chgo. Sun-Times, 1981-85; reporter, editor Chgo. Daily News, 1973-78; editor N.Y. Times, N.Y.C., 1979-81, editorial writer, 1985-90; dep. editor editorial page Chgo. Tribune, 1990-91, editor editorial page, 1991-2000, pub. editor, 2000—. Occasional instr. journalism Columbia Coll., Chgo., Roosevelt U., Chgo. Finalist for Pulitzer prize in editl. writing, 1996; Woodrow Wilson fellow, 1969. Mem. Am. Soc. Newspaper Editors (Disting. Writing award for editls. 1997), Nat. Assn. Black Journalists, Nat. Assn. Minority Media Execs. Roman Catholic. Office: Chicago Tribune 435 N Michigan Ave Chicago IL 60611-4066

WYMAN, JAMES THOMAS, petroleum company executive; b. Mpls., Apr. 9, 1920; s. James Claire and Martha (McChesney) W.; m. Elizabeth Winston, May 6, 1950; children: Elizabeth Wyman Wilcox, James Claire, Steven McChesney. Grad., Blake Prep. Sch., Mpls., 1938; B.A., Yale U., 1942. With Mpls. Star and Tribune, 1946-50; advt. mgr. Super Valu Stores, Inc., Eden Prairie, Minn., 1951-54, store devel. mgr., 1955-56, gen. sales mgr., 1956-57, sales v.p., 1957-60, dir., 1959-87, exec. v.p., 1961-64, pres., chief exec. officer, 1965-70, chmn. exec. com., 1970-76, ret., 1976. Bd. dirs. Marshall & Winston, Inc. Served to lt. (s.g.) USNR, World War II. Clubs: Minneapolis; Woodhill Country (Wayzata). Home: 2855 Woolsey Ln Wayzata MN 55391-2752 Office: 1105 Foshay Tower Minneapolis MN 55402

WYNN, NAN L. historic site administrator; b. Rock Island, Ill., Dec. 4, 1953; BA, Western Ill. U., 1975. Spl. events coord. Ill. Dept. Conservation, Springfield, 1975-77; mus. dir. Blackhawk State Hist. Site, Rock Island, 1977-81; site dir. Old State Capital Hist. Site, Vandalia, Ill., 1981-87; site mgr. Lincoln Tomb State Hist. Site, Springfield, 1986—. Office: Lincoln Tomb State Hist Site Oak Ridge Cemetery 1500 Monument Ave Springfield IL 62702-2500

WYRSCH, JAMES ROBERT, lawyer, educator, author; b. Springfield, Mo., Feb. 23, 1942; s. Louis Joseph and Jane Elizabeth (Welsh) W.; m. B. Darlene Wyrsch, Oct. 18, 1975; children: Scott, Keith, Mark, Brian, Marcia. BA, U. Notre Dame, 1963; JD, Georgetown U., 1966; LLM, U. Mo., Kansas City, 1972. Bar: Mo. 1966, U.S. Ct. Appeals (8th cir.) 1971, U.S. Ct. Appeals (10th cir.) 1974, U.S. Ct. Appeals (5th cir.) 1974, U.S. Ct. Appeals (6th cir.) 1982, U.S. Ct. Appeals (11th cir.) 1984, U.S. Ct. Appeals (7th cir.) 1986, U.S. Ct. Appeals (4th cir.) 1990, U.S. Ct. Appeals (9th cir.) 1998, U.S. Ct. Mil. Appeals 1978, U.S. Tax Ct. 1983, U.S. Dist. Ct. Ohio 1965, U.S. Supreme Ct. 1972. Assoc. Wyrsch, Hobbs & Mirakian P.C., Kansas City, 1970-71; of counsel, 1972-77; ptnr., 1978—; pres., shareholder, 1988—; adj. prof. U. Mo., 1981—. Mem. com. instrns. Mo. Supreme Ct. 1983—; mem. adv. coun. legal assts. program U. Mo. at Kansas City , 1985-88; mem. cir. ct. adv. com. Jackson County, Mo., 1998—; mem. jud. selection com. U.S. Magistrate we. dist., Mo., 1985; mem. fed. practice subcom. we. dist. U.S. Dist. Ct., Mo., 1985-88; mem. subcom. to draft model criminal instrns.for dist. cts. of 8th cir., 1986—; bd. dirs. Kansas City Bar Found. Co-author: Missouri Criminal Trial Practice, 1994; contbr. articles to profl. jours. Capt. U.S. Army, 1966—69. Recipient Joint Svcs. Commendation medal U.S. Army, 1969, U. Mo. Kansas City Svc. award Law Found., 1991-92, Lawyer of Yr. award Mo. Lawyers Weekly, 2001, Dean of Trial Bar award Kansas City Met. Bar Assn., 2002. Fellow: Mo. Bar Found. (vice-chmn. crmiinal law com. 1978—79), Am. Coll. Trial Lawyers, Am. Bar Found. (life); mem.: ATLA, ABA, Am. Coll. Barristers (sr. counsel), Mo. Assn. Criminal Def. Attys. (dir. 1978, sec. 1982, dir. 1983), Nat. Assn. Criminal Def. Attys., Am. Bd. Trial Advs. (adv.), Kansas City Bar Assn. (chmn. anti-trust com. 1981, chmn. bus. tort, anti-trust, franchise com. 1998), Mo. Bar Assn., Am. Arbitration Assn. (panel arbitrators 1976—2000), Country Club of Blue Springs, Kansas City Club, Phi Delta Phi. Democrat. Roman Catholic. Home: 1501 NE Sunny Creek Ln Blue Springs MO 64014-2044 Office: Wyrsch Hobbs & Mirakian PC 1101 Walnut St Fl 13 Kansas City MO 64106-2134

WYSS, THOMAS JOHN, state legislator; b. Ft. Wayne, Ind., Oct. 24, 1942; s. John Paul and Winifred Ann (Ebersole) W.; m. Shirley Dawn Pabst, Jan. 16, 1965; children: Tamara, Angela. B in Indsl. Supervision, Purdue U., 1975. Apprentice GE, Ft. Wayne, 1961-65, mem. mfg. mgmt. staff, 1965-71, mem. mktg. mgmt. staff, 1971—; mem. Ind. Senate from 15th dist., 1985—. Councilman Allen County Coun., Ft. Wayne, 1976-85; chmn., founder Ind. State Crimestoppers, Indpls., 1988—. Lt. col. Ind. Air N.G., 1966—. Recipient Ind. NFIB Guardian of Small Bus. award, 1994; named Outstanding Legislator Ind. State Dental Soc., Indpls., 1987, Outstanding Legislator Ind. Dept. Bldg. Svcs., Indpls., 1987. Mem. Ind. Soc. Chgo., N.G. Assn. (Charles Dick award 1994), Ft. Wayne Jaycees (v.p. 1971-72, Key Man of Ind. and Outstanding Young Man Am. 1971), Am. Legis. Exch. Coun. (state chmn.). Avocation: politics. Home: 12133 Harvest Bay Dr Fort Wayne IN 46845-8982 Office: State Senate State Capital 200 W Washington St Ste 151 Indianapolis IN 46204-2785

YACKEL, JAMES WILLIAM, mathematician, academic administrator; b. Sanborn, Minn., Mar. 6, 1936; s. Ewald W. and Marie E. (Heydlauff) Y.; m. Erna Beth Seecamp, Aug. 20, 1960; children: Jonathan, Juliet, Carolyn. BA, U. Minn., 1958, MA, 1960, PhD, 1964. Rsch. instr. dept. math. Dartmouth Coll., Hanover, N.H., 1964-66; asst. prof. dept. stats. Purdue U., West Lafayette, Ind., 1966-69, from assoc. prof. to prof., 1969-76, assoc. dean sci., 1976-87; vice chancellor acad. affairs Purdue U. Calumet, Hammond, 1987-90, chancellor, 1990-2001, chancellor emeritus, 2001—. Rsch. mathematician Inst. Def. Analysis, Washington, 1969. Author: Applicable Finite Mathematics, 1974; editor Statistical Decision Theory, 1971; contbr. articles to profl. jours. Fellow AAAS; mem. Am. Math. Soc., Math. Assn. Am., Inst. Math. Stats. Achievements include research on Ramsey's theorem and finite graphs. E-mail: yackelj@calumet.Purdue.edu.

YACKTMAN, DONALD ARTHUR, financial executive, investment counselor; b. Chgo., Sept. 12, 1941; s. Victor and Matilda (Chamberlain) Y.; m. Carolyn I. Zuppann, June 15, 1965; children: Donald, Stephen, Jennifer, Melissa, Brian, Robert, Michael. BS, U. Utah, 1965; MBA, Harvard U., 1967. Chartered investment counselor. Trainee Continental Bank, Chgo., 1967-68; assoc. Stein Roe & Farnham, 1968-74, ptnr., 1974-82; pres. Selected Am. Shares; sr. v.p. Prescott Asset Mgmt., 1982-92; pres. Yacktman Asset Mgmt. Co., The Yacktman Funds, 1992—. Past pres. N.W. Suburban coun. Boy Scouts Am. Mem. Investment Analysis Soc. Chgo. Office: Yacktman Asset Mgmt Co 1110 Lake Cook Rd Ste 385 Buffalo Grove IL 60089

YAEGER, DOUGLAS HARRISON, gas company executive; b. St. Louis, Mar. 3, 1949; s. Walter Earl and Mary Eloise (Drinkwater) Y.; m. Lynn Mary Halloran, June 24, 1951; children: Lauren Harrison, Drew Halloran. BS, Miami U., Oxford, Ohio, 1971; MBA, St. Louis U., 1976. Sales asst. Miss. River Transmission Corp., St. Louis, 1974-75, coordinator mktg. and regulatory supply, 1975-78, coordinator mktg. and supply, 1978, mgr. mktg. and supply coordination, 1978-81, asst. v.p. mktg., 1981-82, v.p. mktg., 1982-86, sr. v.p. mktg., 1986-88, exec. v.p., 1988-90; v.p. Laclede Gas Co., St. Louis, 1990—. Mem. Am. Gas Assn., So. Gass Assn., Interstate Natural Gas Assn., Assn. Corp. Growth, Sunset Country, Media, Strathalbyn Farm, The Planning Forum, St. Louis Club. Avocations: golf, fishing, hunting. Office: LACLEDE GAS COMPANY 720 Olive St Saint Louis MO 63101

YAFFE, STUART ALLEN, physician; b. Springfield, Ill., July 6, 1927; m. Natalie, 1952; children: Scott, Kim Yaffe Schoenburg. BS cum laude, U. Alaska, 1951; MD, St. Louis U., 1956. Diplomate Am. Bd. Family Practice. Intern St. Louis CIty Hosp., 1956-57, resident, 1957-58; physician pvt. practice, 1958—; clin. assoc. prof. So. Ill. U. Sch. Medicine., Springfield, 1971—; ptnr. Springfield Clinic, 1989—. With U.S. Army, 1945-47. Mem. AMA, Am. Acad. Family Physicians, Ill. Acad. Family Physicians, Ill. State Med. Soc., Sangamon County Med. Soc. Office: 1100 Centre West Dr Springfield IL 62704-2100

YAGAHASHI, TAKASHI, chef; C. chef Tribute, Farmington Hills, Mich., 1996—. Named Best Restaurant in Detroit, NY Times; named one of America's Best Restaurants, Gourmet mag.; recipient award, James Beard Found., 2001. Office: Tribute 31425 W 12 Mile Rd Farmington Hills MI 48334

YAGER, VINCENT COOK, bank executive; b. Chgo., June 15, 1928; s. James Vincent and Juanita (Cook) Yager; m. Susan Marie Gallagher, Sept. 28, 1957; children: Susan Marie, Sheila Ann. BA, Grinnell Coll., 1951. Asst. cashier Chgo. Nat. Bank, 1954-60, Harris Trust & Savs. Bank, Chgo., 1960-63; v.p. comml. loan dept. Madison Bank & Trust, 1963-68; v.p. fin. Cor-Plex Internat. Corp., 1968-70; pres., CEO, dir. First Nat. Bank Blue Island, 1970-89; pres., CEO Great Lakes Fin. Resources, Inc., Matteson, 1982-96, also bd. dirs. With U.S. Army, 1951—53, ETO. Mem.: Econ. Club Chgo., Bankers Club Chgo., Robert Morris Assocs. (pres. chpt. 1981—82), Midlothian Country Club, Rotary. Home: 1032 S Rand Rd Villa Park IL 60181-3145 Office: Great Lakes Bank Blue Island 13057 S Western Ave Blue Island IL 60406-2418

YAKIM, GREG, construction executive; Pres. Kimball Hill Homes, Rolling Meadows, Ill., 1994—. Office: Kimball Hill Homes 5999 New Wilke Rd Bldg 5 Rolling Meadows IL 60008-4506

YALE, SEYMOUR HERSHEL, dental radiologist, educator, university dean, gerontologist; b. Chgo., Nov. 27, 1920; s. Henry and Dorothy (Kulwin) Y.; m. Muriel Jane Cohen, Nov. 6, 1943; children: Russell Steven, Patricia Ruth. B.S., U. Ill., 1944, D.D.S., 1945, postgrad., 1947-48, Spertus Inst. Jewish Studies, 1995—. Pvt. practice of dentistry, 1945-54, 56—; asst. clin. dentistry U. Ill., 1948-49, instr. clin. dentistry, 1949-53, asst. prof. clin. dentistry, 1953-54, assoc. prof. dept. radiology Coll. Dentistry, 1956, prof., head dept. Coll. Dentistry, 1957-65, adminstrv. asst. to dean Coll. Dentistry, 1961-63, asst. dean Coll. Dentistry, 1963-64, acting dean Coll. Dentistry, 1964-65, dean, 1965-87, dean emeritus, 1987—, also mem. grad. faculty dept. radiology Coll. Medicine, prof. dentistry and health resources mgmt. Sch. Pub. Health, 1987—. Sr. dental dir. Dental Care Plus Mgmt. Corp., Chgo.; pres., dir. dental edn. Dental Care Plus Mgmt. Ednl. Svcs., Ltd.; health care facilities planner; dir. tng. Dental Technicians Sch., U.S. Naval Tng. Ctr., Bainbridge, md., 1954-56; mem. subcom. 16 Nat. Com. on Radiation Protection; mem. Radiation Protection Adv. Bd., State of Ill., 1971, City of Chgo. Health Sys. Agy.; founder Ctr. for Rsch. in Periodontal Disease and Oral Molecular Biology, 1977; organizer, chmn. Nat. Conf. on Hepatitis-B in Dentistry, 1982; organizer, dir. Univ. Taskforce Primary Health Care Project, U. Ill., Chgo.; chmn. U. Ill.-U. Stockholm-U. Gothenberg Conf. on Geriatrics, 1985; dir. planning AMVETS/UIC Tchg. Nursing Home Project, 1987-91; co-sponsor 1st Egyptian Dental Congress, 1984; adj. prof. Ctr. for Exercise Sci. and Cardiovasc. Rsch., Northeastern Ill. U., Chgo., 1991, Northwestern U. Sch. Dentistry Divsn. Behavioural Scis., Evanston, Ill., 1996—. Editor-in-chief Dental Care Plus Mgmt. Digest, 1995—. Bd. dirs., co-benefactor (with wife) World Heritage Mus., U. Ill., Urbana, 1985; mem. Hillel Bd., U. Ill.-Chgo.; life mem. (with wife) Bronze Circle of Coll. Liberal Arts, U. Ill., Urbana; mem. (with wife) Pres.' Council, U. Ill. Recipient centennial research award Chgo. Dental Soc., 1959; Distinguished Alumnus award U. Ill., 1973; Harry Sicher Meml. Lecture award Am. Coll. Stomologic Surgeons, 1983 Fellow Acad. Gen. Dentistry (hon.), Am. Coll. Dentists; mem. Ill. Dental Soc. (mem. com. on radiology), Chgo. Dental Soc., Internat. Assn. Dental Rsch., Am. Acad. Oral Roentgenology, Am. Dental Assn., Odontographic Soc. Chgo. (Award of Merit 1982), Council Dental Deans State Ill. (chmn.), N.Y. Acad. Scis., Gerontol. Soc. Am., Pierre Fauchard Acad. (Man of Yr. award Ill. sect. 1988), Am. Pub. Health Assn., Gerontol. Soc. Am., Omicron Kappa Upsilon, Sigma Xi, Alpha Omega (hon.) Achievements include established (with wife) collection of Coins of Ottoman Empire and Related Mohammedan States and supplemental antique map collection at World Heritage Mus., U of Ill.; established Muriel C. Yale Collection, antique maps of Holy Land collection at Spertus Inst. Jewish Studies. Home: 155 N Harbor Dr Chicago IL 60601-7364 Office: 30 N Michigan Ave Chicago IL 60602-3402 E-mail: ddssy@uic.edu.

YAMADA, TADATAKA, internist; b. Tokyo, June 5, 1945; MD, NYU, 1971. Intern Med. Coll. Va. Hosps., Richmond, 1971-72, resident in internal medicine, 1972-74; gastrointestinal fellow UCLA, 1977-79; prof. medicine U. Mich., Ann Arbor, 1996, adj. prof. internal medicine and physiology, 1996—; mem. staff U. Mich. Hosp., 1996. Adj. prof. medicine U. Mich. Hosp., Ann Arbor. Mem. AAAS, ACP, AAP, AGA, ASCI, IOM. Office: U Mich Gastroenterology Divsn U Mich Med Ctr 1550 E Med Ctr Dr Ann Arbor MI 48109

YAMIN, JOSEPH FRANCIS, lawyer, counselor; b. Detroit, Mar. 12, 1956; s. Raymond Samuel and Sadie Ann (John) Y. 1975; BA, U. Mich., 1978; J.D., London Sch. Econs., 1981; JD, Detroit Coll. Law, 1982. Bar: U.S. Ct. Appeals (6th cir.) 1982, U.S. Dist. Ct. (ea. dist.) Mich. 1982. Atty. Alan R. Miller, P.C., Birmingham, Mich., 1981-93; ptnr. Beier Howlett PC, Bloomfield Hills, Mich., 1993—; bd. dir. Am. Wash Systems, Birmingham, 1979—; instr. Detroit Coll. Law Rev., 1984-86; mediator Wayne County, Oakland County. Recipient Am. Jurisprudence Book award Am. Jurisprudence Soc., 1981. Mem. ABA, Oakland County Bar Assn., Oakland County Mediation, Wayne County Mediator Litigation Panel, State of Mich. Bar Assn., Law Rev., Chi Phi, Oakland County Real Property Sect. Roman Catholic. Office: Beier Howlett PC 200 E Long Lake Rd Ste 110 Bloomfield Hills MI 48304-2328

YAMPOLSKY, VICTOR, conductor; b. Frunze, Kirgizskaj, SSR, Oct. 10, 1942; s. Vladimir and Fanny (Zaslavsky) Y. Student, Moscow Conservatory, 1961-66, Leningrad Conservatory, 1968-72. Violinist Moscow Radio Orch., 1965; violinist, asst. condr. Moscow Philharm. Orch., 1965-72; violinist Boston Symphony Orch., 1973-77; music dir. Atlantic Symphony Orch., Halifax, N.S., Can., 1977-83; condr. Tanglewood Inst., Boston U., 1977-84; prof. music Boston U., 1979-84; assoc. prof. music Northwestern U., 1984—, Carol R. and Arthur L. Rice Jr. prof. in music performance, 1993—; music dir. Peninsula Festival, Fish Creek, Wis., 1986—; hon. dir. Scotia Festival of Music, Halifax; music dir. Omaha (Nebr.) Symphony Orch., 1995—. Office: Omaha Symphony Orch 1605 Howard St Omaha NE 68102-2797

YANCEY, KIM BRUCE, dermatology researcher; b. Atlanta, Nov. 25, 1952; s. Andrew Jackson and Edrie (Johnson) Yancey. BS, U. Ga., 1974; MD, Med. Coll. Ga., 1978. Diplomate Am. Bd. Dermatology. Intern dept. internal medicine Med. Coll. Ga., Augusta, 1978-79, resident dept. dermatology, 1979-81; med. staff fellow dermatology br. NIH, Bethesda, Md., 1981-84, sr. staff fellow dermatology br., 1984-85, sr. investigator dermatology br., 1993—2000; asst. prof. dept. dermatology Uniformed Svcs. U. Health Scis., 1985-87, assoc. prof. dept. dermatology, 1987-93, acting chmn. dept. dermatology, 1990-93; prof., chair dept. dermatology Med. Coll. Wis., Milw., 2001—. Cons. Walter Reed Army Med. Ctr., Washington, 1985—2000. Author monographs and sci. manuscripts; contbr. articles to profl. jours. Rsch. grantee NIH, 1986—, collaborative rsch. grantee NATO, 1988-93. Fellow: Am. Acad. Dermatology (editl. bd. 1986—93); mem.: AMA, Wis. Dermatol. Assn., Dermatology Found., Am. Fedn. Med. Rsch., Soc. Investigative Dermatology (bd. dirs. 1982—84, co-chmn. ea. region 1990—92), Am. Dermatol. Assn. (Young Leadership award 1986), Am. Bd. Dermatology, Am. Soc. Clin. Investigation. Methodist. Office: Med Coll Wis Dept Dermatology 8701 Watertown Plank Rd Milwaukee WI 53226

YANDELL, CATHY MARLEEN, foreign language educator; b. Anadarko, Okla., Dec. 27, 1949; d. Lloyd O. and Maurine (Dunn) Y.; m. Mark S. McNeil, Sept. 7, 1974; children: Elizabeth Yandell McNeil, Laura Yandell McNeil. Diplôme d'études, Inst. des Professeurs de Français à l'Etranger, Sorbonne, 1970; BA, U. N.Mex., 1971; MA, U. Calif., Berkeley, 1973, PhD, 1977. Teaching asst. U. Calif., Berkeley, 1971-75, acting instr., 1976-77; asst. prof. Carleton Coll., Northfield, Minn., 1977-83, assoc. prof., 1983-89, prof. French, 1989—. Chair commn. on the status of women Carleton Coll., Northfield, 1983-85, ednl. policy com., 1985-86, 96-97, romance langs. and lits., 1990-94, chair faculty affairs com., 2000—, pres. of faculty, 1991-94, Bryn-Jones disting. tchg. prof. humanities, 1996-99, mentor to jr. faculty, 1996—, W.I. and Hulda F. Daniell prof. French lit. lang. and culture, 1999—; dir. Paris French Studies Program, 1998. Author: Carpe Corpus: Time and Gender in Early Modern France, 2000; co-author: Vagabondages: Initiation ā la litt. d'expression française, 1996; contbr. to Art & Argumentation: The Sixteenth Century Dialogue, 1993, French Texts/American Contexts: French Women Writers, 1994, Montaigne: A Collection of Essays, Vol. 4, Language and Meaning, 1995, Reflexivity in Women Writers of the Ancien Régime, 1998; editor: Pontus de Tyard's Solitaire Second, ou prose de la musique, 1980; contbr. articles to profl. jours. Active exec. com., then mem. Amnesty Internat., Northfield, 1980—. Regents' Travelling fellow U. Calif. at Berkeley, 1975-76; Faculty Devel. grantee Carleton Coll., 1988, 91; NEH Rsch. fellow., 1994-95. Mem. MLA (del. 1989-92, exec. com. French 16th century lit., 2001—, 16th century studies coun. 2001—). Democrat. Home: 514 5th St E Northfield MN 55057-2220 Office: Carleton College 1 N College St Northfield MN 55057-4044 E-mail: cyandell@carleton.edu.

YANDERS, ARMON FREDERICK, biological sciences educator, research administrator; b. Lincoln, Nebr., Apr. 12, 1928; s. Fred W. and Beatrice (Pate) Y.; m. Evelyn Louise Gatz, Aug. 1, 1948; children: Mark Frederick, Kent Michael. A.B., Nebr. State Coll., Peru, 1948; M.S., U. Nebr., 1950, Ph.D., 1953. Rsch. asso. Oak Ridge Nat. Lab. and Northwestern U., 1953-54; biophysicist U.S. Naval Radiol. Def. Lab., San Francisco, 1955-58; asso. geneticist Argonne (Ill.) Nat. Lab., 1958-59; with dept. zoology Mich. State U., 1959-69; prof., asst. dean Mich. State U. (Coll. Natural Sci.), 1963-69; prof. biol. scis. U. Mo., Columbia, 1969—, dean Coll. Arts and Scis., 1969-82, rsch. prof., dir. Environ. Trace Substances Rsch. Ctr., 1983-93, dir. Alzheimer's Disease and Related Disorders Program, 1994—; research prof., dir. Environ. Trace Substances Research Ctr. and Sinclair Comparative Medicine Rsch. Farm, 1984-94; prof. emeritus, 1994—. Trustee Argonne Univs. Assn., 1965-77, v.p., 1969-73, pres., 1973, 76-77, chmn. bd., 1973-75; bd. dirs. Coun. Colls. Arts and Scis., 1981-82; mem. adv. com. environ. hazards VA, Washington, 1985-2002, chmn. sci. coun., 1988-2000, chmn. of com., 1990-2002. Contbr. articles to profl. jours. Trustee Peru State Coll., 1992-2001. Served from ensign to lt. USNR, 1954-58. Recipient Disting. Svc. award Peru State Coll., 1989. Fellow AAAS; mem. AAUP (Robert W. Martin acad. freedom award 1971), Environ. Mutagen Soc., Genetics Soc. Am., Radiation Rsch. Soc., Soc. Environ. Toxicology and Chemistry. Home: 1204 Castle Bay Pl Columbia MO 65203-6257 Office: U of Mo 521 Clark Hall Columbia MO 65211-4420 E-mail: YandersA@umsystem.edu.

YARICK, PAUL E. food products executive; V.p., treas. Interstate Bakeries Corp., Kansas City, Mo. Office: Interstate Bakeries Corp PO Box 419627 Kansas City MO 64141-6627

YARRINGTON, HUGH, corporate lawyer, communications company executive; BA, Randolph-Macon Coll.; JD, George Washington U. Assoc. Wilkinson, Cragun & Barker, Washington; v.p., gen. counsel Bur. Nat. Affairs, Inc.; from sr. v.p., pub. to pres., CEO, exec. com. CCH Inc., Riverwoods, Ill. Mem. Info. Industry Assn. (bd. dirs. 1988—, chmn., treas., sec.). Office: CCH Inc 2700 Lake Cook Rd Riverwoods IL 60015-3867

YARWOOD, DEAN LESLEY, political science educator; b. Decorah, Iowa, Mar. 17, 1935; s. Harold Nicholas and Elsie Mabel (Roney) Y.; m. Elaine Delores Bender, Sept. 2, 1956; children: Lucinda, Kent, Keith, Douglas, Dennis. BA, Iowa U., 1957; MA, Cornell U., 1961; PhD, U. Ill., 1966. Tchr. social studies, acting jr. high prin. Mid-Prairie Community Sch., Wellman, Iowa, 1957-59; asst. prof. Coe Coll., Cedar Rapids, 1963-66, U. Ky., Lexington, 1966-67, U. Mo., Columbia, 1967-70, assoc. prof., 1970-78, prof., 1978—, dir. grad. studies dept. polit. sci., 1970-72, 88, 94-97, chmn. dept. polit. sci., 1988-91, 98-99, Frederick A. Middlebush prof. polit. sci., 1992-95, prof., 1978-2000, prof. emeritus, 2000—. Editor: The National Administrative System: Selected Readings, 1971, Public Administration, Politics, and the People: Selected Readings for Managers, Employees and Citizens, 1987; author, co-author numerous articles in polit. sci. jours. Recipient Bradish Meml. scholarship, 1953-57, Iowa Merit scholarship, 1956-57, Woodrow Wilson fellowship, 1959-60, James Garner fellowship, 1961-62, Woodrow Wilson Dissertation fellowship, 1962-63. Mem. Am. Soc. Pub. Adminstrn. (chmn. sect. on pub. adminstrn. edn. 1986-87, publs. com. 1986-89, com. on orgnl. rev. and evaln. 1995-97, Ctrl. Mo. chpt. coun. 1979-80, pres. 1980-81, ex-officio mem. coun. 1981-83), Am. Polit. Sci. Assn., Midwest Polit. Sci. Assn., So. Polit. Sci. Assn., Mo. Polit. Sci. Assn. (v.p. 1990-91, pres. 1991-92), Mo. Inst. for Pub. Adminstrn. (coun. 1976-77, v.p. 1977-78, pres. 1978-79, Pub. Adminstr. of Yr. 1998), Phi Beta Kappa. Home: 304 Mumford Dr Columbia MO 65203-0230 Office: U Mo Dept Polit Sci 206 Professional Building Columbia MO 65211-6040

YASHON, DAVID, neurosurgeon, educator; b. Chgo., May 13, 1935; s. Samuel and Dorothy (Cutler) Y.; children— Jaclyn, Lisa, Steven. B.S. in Medicine, U. Ill., 1958, M.D., 1960. Diplomate Am. Bd. Neurol. Surgery. Intern U. Ill., 1961, resident, 1961-64, asst. in neuroanatomy, 1960; clin. instr. neurosurgery U. Chgo., 1965-66; asst. prof. neurosurgery Case Western Res U., Cleve., 1966-69; assoc. prof. neurosurgery Ohio State U., Columbus, 1969-74, prof., 1974-89, prof. emeritus, 1989—; mem. staff St. Ann's Hosp., Children's Hosp., Grant Med. Ctr., Ohio State U. East Med. Ctr. Cons. Med. Research and Devel. Command, U.S. Army; mem. Neurology B Study Sect NIH. Author: Spinal Injury; contbr. articles to med. jours. Served as capt. U.S. Army, 1960-68. Fellow Royal Coll. Surgeons Can. (cert.), A.C.S.; mem. AMA, Am. Physiol. Soc., Congress Neurol. Surgeons, Am. Assn. Anatomists, Canadian, Ohio neurosurg. socs., Am. Assn. Neurol. Surgeons, Research Soc. Neurol. Surgeons, Acad. Medicine Columbus and Franklin County, Soc. for Neurosci., Soc. Univ. Surgeons, Am. Acad. Neurology, Assn. for Acad. Surgery, Am. Acad. Neurol. Surgery, Am. Assn. for Surgery of Trauma, Central Surg. Soc., Ohio Med. Soc., Columbus Surg. Soc., Sigma Xi, Alpha Omega Alpha. Address: 500 Columbia Pl Bexley OH 43209-1677

YASINSKY, JOHN BERNARD, nuclear scientist; b. Shenandoah, Pa., June 10, 1939; s. Joseph and Helen Y.; m. Marlene A. Tuladzieck, Apr. 28, 1962; children: Diane L., Karen A., Mark J. B.S. in Physics, Wheeling (W.Va.) Coll., 1961; M.S., U. Pitts., 1963; Ph.D. in Nuclear Sci, Carnegie Mellon U., 1966. Scientist, sr. scientist, then mgr. electric systems and plant analysis Westinghouse Bettis Lab., Pitts., 1963-71; White House fellow, spl. asst. to sec. U.S. Dept. Commerce, Washington, 1972-73; mgr. bus. devel. breeder reactor divs. Westinghouse Corp., Pitts., 1973-74, mgr. mktg. advanced reactors div., 1974-75, dir. dept. advanced coal conversion, 1975-77; pres. Westinghouse Hanford Co., Richland, Wash., 1979-80; gen. mgr. advanced power systems divs. Westinghouse Electric Corp., Pitts., after 1980, then pres. Europe, Africa and Middle East; evening instr. nuclear engring. div. Carnegie Mellon U., 1966-72; Bd. dirs. Wheeling Coll., 1981, Wash. State Council Econ. Edn., 1979-80, Tri-City Nuclear Industry Council, 1979-80, Kadlec Med. Center, 1979-80; mem. adv. com. Wash. State Joint Grad. Center, 1979-80, Hanford Energy Center, 1979-80; mem. steering com. Wash. State Energy Council, 1979-80. Contbr. over 50 articles to profl. jours. Mem. Am. Nuclear Soc., Nat. Security Indsl. Assn., White House Fellows Assn., Atomic Indsl. Forum. Club: Pitts. Field. Office: Westinghouse Nuclear Ctr PO Box 355 Pittsburgh PA 15230-0355

YASUDA, HIROTSUGU KOGE, chemical engineering professor; b. Kyoto, Japan, Mar. 24, 1930; s. Mitsuo and Kei (Niwa) Y.; m. Gerda Lisbeth Schmidtke, Apr. 6, 1968; children: Ken Eric, Werner Akira, Lisbeth Kay. BSChemE, Kyoto U., 1953; MS in Polymer Chemistry, SUNY, Syracuse, 1959, PhD in Polymer and Phys. Chemistry, 1961. Rsch. assoc. Ophthalmic Plastic Lab., Mass. Eye & Ear Infirmary, Boston, 1962-63; head biomaterial sect. eye rsch. Cedar-Sinai Med. Ctr., L.A., 1963-65; vis. scientist Royal Inst. Tech., Stockholm, 1965-66; sr. chemist Rsch. Triangle Inst., Rsch. Triangle Pk., N.C., 1966-72, mgr. Polymer Rsch. Lab., 1972-78; prof. chem. engring. U. Mo., Rolla, 1978-88, dir. Thin Films Inst., 1974-88, prof. chem. engring. Columbia, 1988—, chmn. dept., 1988-90, James C. Dowell rsch. prof., 1989—, dir. Ctr. for Surface and Plasma Techs., 1989—. Author: Plasma Polymerization, 1985. Home: 1004 Lake Point Ln Columbia MO 65203-2900 Office: Ctr For Surface Sci & Plasma Columbia MO 65211-0001 E-mail: yasudah@missouri.edu.

YEAGER, MARK LEONARD, lawyer; b. Chgo., Apr. 7, 1950; BA, U. Mich., 1972; JD, Northwestern U., 1975. Bar: Ill. 1975, Fla. 1985. Ptnr. McDermott, Will & Emery, Chgo., 1975—. Mem. ABA.

YEAGER, PHILLIP CHARLES, transportation company executive; b. Bellevue, Ky., Nov. 15, 1927; s. Ferd A. and Helen (Koehler) Y.; m. Joyce E. Ruebusch, June 2, 1951; children: David P., Debra A. Yeager Jensen, Mark A. BA, U. Cin., 1951. Warehouse mgr. Pure Carbonic Co., Cin., 1950-52; trace clk., rate clk., asst. office mgr. Pa. R.R., Chgo., 1952-56, salesman Kansas City, Mo., 1956-59, asst. dir. Trailvan Phila., 1959-65, div. sales mgr. Milw., 1965-68; dir. Trailvan Penn-Ctrl. R.R., N.Y.C., 1968-71; pres. Hub City Terminals, Chgo., 1971-85; chmn. The Hub Group, 1985—; also bd. dirs. Bd. dirs. 30 Hubcity terminals. Cpl. U.S. Army, 1946-47. Recipient Achievement award Intermodal Transp. Assn., 1991, Harry E. Salzberg medallion for outstanding achievement in transp.; named Chgo. Transp. Man of Yr., Chgo. Transp. Assn., 1990. Mem. N.Y. Traffic Club, Chgo. Traffic Club. Republican. Lutheran. Avocations: golf, biking, swimming. Office: The Hub Group Inc 377 E Butterfield Rd Ste 700 Lombard IL 60148-5659

YEAGER, WALDO E. food company executive; CFO, treas. Seaway Food Town Inc., 1996—. Office: 1020 Ford St Maumee OH 43537-1820

YEAMANS, GEORGE THOMAS, librarian, educator; b. Richmond, Va., Nov. 7, 1929; s. James Norman and Dolphine Sophia (Manhart) Y.; m. Mary Ann Seng, Feb. 1, 1958; children: Debra, Susan, Julia. AB, U. Va., 1950; MLS, U. Ky., 1955; EdD, Ind. U., 1965. Asst. audio-visual dir. Ind. State U., Terre Haute, 1957-58; asst. film librarian Ball State U., Muncie, Ind., 1958-61, film librarian, 1961-69, assoc. prof. libr. sci., 1969-72, prof., 1972-95; prof. emeritus, 1995—; cons. Pendleton (Ind.) Sch. Corp., 1962, 67, Captioned Films for the Deaf Workshop, Muncie, Ind., 1963, 64, 65, Decatur (Ind.) Sch. System, 1978; adjudicator Ind. Media Fair, 1979-93, David Letterman Scholarship Program, 1993. Author: Projectionists' Programmed Primer, 1969, rev. edit., 1982; Mounting and Preserving Pictorial Materials, 1976; Tape Recording, 1978; Transparency Making, 1977; Photographic Principles, 1981; Computer Literacy— A Programmed Primer, 1985; Building Effective Creative Project Teams, 1996, revised edit., 2000; Designing Dynamic Media Presentations, 1996, revised edit., 2000; songwriter Branson Bound, 1996; contbr. articles to profl. jours. Campaign worker Wilson for Mayor, Muncie, Ind., 1979. Served with USMC, 1950-52. Recipient Citations of Achievement, Internat. Biog. Assn., Cambridge, Eng., 1973, Am. Biog. Assn., 1976, Mayor James P. Carey award for achievement for disting. contbns. to Ball State U. and City of Muncie, 1988; Video Information Systems grantee Ball State U., 1993. Mem. NEA (del. assembly dept. audiovisual instrn. 1967), ALA, Am. Assn. Sch. Librs., Audio-Visual Instrn. Dirs. Ind. (exec. bd. 1962-68, pres. 1966-67), Ind. Assn. Ednl. Communications and Tech. (dist. dir. 1972-75), Assn. Ind. Media Educators (chmn. auditing com. 1979-81), Autism Soc. Am., Assn. Ednl. Comm. & Tech., Ind. Libr. Fedn., Ind. Corp. and Network Libr. Assn., Ind. Acad. Libr. Assn., Ind. Pub. Libr. Assn., Thomas Jefferson Soc. Alumni U. Va., Phi Delta Kappa. Republican. Unitarian. Home: 4507 W Burton Dr Muncie IN 47304-3575

YECKEL, ANITA T. state legislator; b. Salt Lake City, Nov. 12, 1942; m. Robert Yeckel; 2 children. BS in Polit. Sci., postgrad., U. Mo. With 1st Nat. Bank, St. Louis, 1960-68, Am. Home Savs. & Loans Assn., 1982-92; mem. Lindebergh Sch. Dist. Bd. Edn., 1990—, Mo. Senate from 1st dist., Jefferson City, 1996—. Mem. Kiwanis. Republican. Roman Catholic. Office: 8819 Gladlea Saint Louis MO 63127 Fax: 314-843-7542. E-mail: ayeckel@services.state.mo.us.

YEE, ROBERT DONALD, ophthalmologist; b. Beijing, Feb. 21, 1945; came to U.S., 1947, naturalized, 1947; s. James and Marian Y.M. (Li) Y.; m. Linda Margaret Neil, June 28, 1968; children: Jillian Neil, Allison Betram. A.B., Harvard U., 1966; M.D., 1970. Diplomate Am. Bd. Ophthalmology. Fullbright scholar, 1966; intern U. Rochester, N.Y., 1970-71; resident in ophthalmology Jules Stein Eye Inst. UCLA, 1971-74; fellow in neuro-ophthalmology Nat. Eye Inst., Bethesda, Md., 1974-76; chief ophthalmology Harbor-UCLA Med. Ctr., Torrance, Calif., 1976-78; asst. prof. ophthalmology Sch. Medicine UCLA, 1976-78, assoc. prof., 1978-82, prof., 1982-87; prof., dept. chmn. ophthalmology Ind. U. Sch. Medicine, Indpls., 1987—. Mem. residency rev. com. for ophthalmology Accrediation Coun. for Grad. Med. Edn., 1995—, vice-chmn. 1998—. Mem. editorial bd. Investigative Ophthalmology and Visual Sci., 1982— , von Graefe's Archives of Ophthalmology, 1983-89; Feldman endowed chair ophthalmology UCLA, 1984-87. Author numerous med. research papers. Grantee, NIH, 1976—84; scholar Dolly Green Rsch. scholar, 1984—86. Fellow: ACS, Am. Acad. Ophthalmology; mem.: AMA, Accreditation Cou. for Grad. Med. Edn. (residency rev. com., chair 2000—02), Indpls. Ophthal. Soc., Ind. Med. Soc., Chinese Am. Ophthal. Soc. (pres. 1996—98), Ind. Acad. Ophthalmology, Am. Ophthal Soc., Assn. Rsch. in Vision and Ophthalmology (chmn. eye movement sect. 1981, 1987, trustee 1996—2001, v.p. 2000—01), Phi Beta Kappa, Alpha Omega Alpha. Office: Ind U Med Ctr 702 Rotary Cir Indianapolis IN 46202-5133 E-mail: ryee@inpui.edu.

YEN, DAVID CHI-CHUNG, management information systems educator; b. Tai-Chung, Taiwan, Republic of China, Nov. 15, 1953; s. I-King and Chi-Ann (Ro) Y.; m. Wendy Wen-Yawn Ding, July 4, 1981; children: Keeley Ju, Caspar Lung, Christopher Jai. MBA in Gen. Bus., Cen. State U., Edmond, Okla., 1981, BS in Computer Sci., 1982; MS in Computer Sci., PhD in Mgmt. Info. Systems, U. Nebr., 1985. Asst. prof. Miami U., Oxford, Ohio, 1985-89, assoc. prof., 1989-93, prof., 1994—, MIS advisor computer study com., 1986-90; asst. chmn., 1993-95; chmn. Miami U., Oxford, Ohio, 1995—; sr. faculty teaching excellence, 1994. Chmn., mem. computer policy com. Miami U., 1991-94, computer adv. group, 1993-94, com. evaluation adminstrs., 1993, conf. and session chair, seminar dir., Smucker prof. internship, mem. exec. com., 1995—, program chair; mem. Hong Kong Coun. for Acad. Accreditation, 2000—. Author two textbooks; editor Proceedings; contbr. articles to profl. jours. External assesser Can. Rsch. and Grants Coun., Hong Kong Rsch. and Grants Coun. Served to 2d lt., Rep. China Navy. Alumni teaching scholar Miami U., 1987-88; named Prof. of Yr. Delta Sigma Pi, 1993; grantee GE, Cleve. Found., Smucker, Microsoft. Mem. IEEE, Am. Chinese Mgmt. Educators Assn. (pres.-elect 1995, pres. 1996, program com. 1997—, MIS track chair 1998—), Soc. Info. Mgmt., Internat. Chinese Info. Sys. Assn., Internat. Bus. Sch. Computer User Assn., Internat. Sch. Bus. Computer User Group (chair conf., proceedings editor 1988), Assn. Computing Machinery, Ohio Mgmt. Info. System Assn., Decision Sci. Inst., Soc. Data Educators. Office: Miami U 309 Upham Hall Oxford OH 45056

YENKIN, BERNARD KALMAN, coatings and resins company executive; b. Columbus, Ohio, Dec. 2, 1930; s. Abe I. and Eleanore G. (Weiner) Y.; m. Miriam Schottenstein, Mar. 31, 1957; children: Leslie Mara, Jonathan, Allison Katsev, Amy. BA, Yale U., 1952; MBA, Harvard U., 1954. V.p. Yenkin-Majestic Paint Corp., Columbus, 1968-77, pres., 1977-85, chmn. bd., 1985—. Pres. Columbus Jewish Fedn., 1980-82, Pro Musica Chamber Orch., Columbus, 1983-85, Columbus Torah Acad., 1977-79; bd. v.p. Jewish Ednl. Svc. N.Am., N.Y.C., 1991-95. Recipient Mayor's award for Vol. Svc. City of Columbus, 1984, Young Leadership award Columbus Jewish Fedn., 1965. Mem. Yale Club of Cen. Ohio (pres. 1979-81), Yale Club of N.Y., Athletic Club (Columbus). Office: Yenkin-Majestic Industries 1920 Leonard Ave Columbus OH 43219-2514

YEUNG, EDWARD SZESHING, chemist; b. Hong Kong, Feb. 17, 1948; arrived in U.S., 1965; s. King Mai Luk and Yu Long Yeung; m. Anna Kunkwok Seto, Sept. 18, 1971; children: Rebecca Tze-Mai, Amanda Tze-Wen AB magna cum laude, Cornell U., 1968; PhD, U. Calif., Berkeley, 1972. Instr. chemistry Iowa State U., Ames, 1972-74, asst prof., 1974-77, assoc. prof, 1977-81, prof. chemistry, 1981-89, disting. prof., 1989—. Contbr. articles to profl. jours. Alfred P. Sloan fellow, 1974-76; recipient Am. Chem Soc. award in Analytical Chemistry, 1994. Fellow AAAS; mem. Soc. Applied Spectrosci. (Lester Strock award 1990), Am. Chem. Soc. (award in chem. instrumentation 1987, award in analytical chemistry 1994, award in chromatography 2002). Home: 1005 Jarrett Cir Ames IA 50014-3937 Office: Iowa State U Gilman Hall Ames IA 50011

YOCKIM, JAMES CRAIG, state senator; b. Williston, N.D., Feb. 13, 1953; s. Daniel and Doris (Erickson) Y.; children: Jenna, Ericka. BSW, Pacific Luth. U., 1975; MSW, San Diego State U., 1979. Caseworker Dyslin Boys Ranch, Tacoma, 1975-77, head caseworker, program dir., 1979-80; landman Fayette Oil & Gas, Williston, 1980-82; owner Hy-Plains Energy, 1982-87; city fin. commr. City of Williston, 1984-88, 98—; therapist Williston, 1983; senator N.D. State Senate, 1986-98; owner James C. Yockim Resources, Williston, 1987—. Dir. Bethel Luth. Found., 1993—; del. N.D. Dem. Conv., 1984, 86, 88, 90, 92, 94, 96, 98, 2000. 02; dist. chmn. Dem. Party, Williston, 1988; caucus chmn. Dem. Caucus N.D. State Senate; mem. N.D. Legis. Coun., 1997-98. Recipient Ruth Meiers award N.D. Mental Health Assn., 1989, Legislator of Yr. award N.D. Children's Caucus, 1989; named Outstanding Young North Dakotan N.D. Jaycees, 1988. Mem. NASW. Avocations: racquetball, golf. Home: 1123 2nd Ave E Williston ND 58801-4302 Office: 417 1st Ave E PO Box 2344 Williston ND 58802-2344

YODER, JOHN CLIFFORD, producer, consultant; b. Orrville, Ohio, Jan. 30, 1927; s. Ray Aquila Yoder and Dorothy Mildred (Hostetler) Yoder Hake; m. Alice Vigger Andersen, Mar. 2, 1963 (div. Nov. 1992); children: Gorm Clifford, Mark Edward. BA in Philosophy and Polit. Sci., Ohio Wesleyan U., 1951. Prodn. supr. Sta. WFMJ-TV, Youngstown, Ohio, 1954-62; producer Sta. NBC-TV, Chgo., 1964-72; ind. producer cons. Evanston, Ill., 1972—. Producer radio program Conversations From Wingspread, 1972-90 (George Foster Peabody Broadcasting award 1974, Ohio State award 1978, Freedoms Found. Honor medal 1978); appeared in film The Untouchables, 1994, TV program Missing Persons, 1993. Pub. rels. and pub. info. com. Chgo. Heart Assn. (Meritorious Svc. award 1978); electronic media advisor The White House, Washington, 1972; bd. dirs. Youngstown (Ohio) Sumphony Soc., 1959-63, Youngstown Playhouse, 1952-63, Bensenville (Ill.) Home Soc. 1985-89. With USAF, 1945-47 PTO. Recipient Disting. Svc. award Inst. Medicine of Chgo. 1971. Mem. Am. Fedn. Television & Radio Artists, , Nat. Acad. TV Arts and Scis., Screen Actors Guild, Midwest Pioneer Broadcasters, Soc. Profl. Journalists, Mus. Broadcast Comms., Masons, Am. Legion, Chgo. Headline Club. Avocations: tennis, golfing, sailing, fishing, reading. Home: 720 Noyes St Apt D 2 Evanston IL 60201-2848

YOERGER, ROGER RAYMOND, agricultural engineer, educator; b. LeMars, Iowa, Feb. 17, 1929; s. Raymond Herman and Crystal Victoria (Ward) Y.; m. Barbara M. Ellison, Feb. 14, 1953; 1 child, Karen Lynne; m. Laura M. Summitt, Dec. 23, 1971; stepchildren: Daniel L. Summitt, Linda Summitt Canull, Anita Summitt Smith. B.S., Iowa State U., 1949, M.S., 1951, Ph.D., 1957. Registered profl. engr., Ill. Instr., asst. prof. agrl. engring. Iowa State U., 1949-56; assoc. prof. Pa. State U., 1956-58; prof. U. Ill., Urbana, 1959-85, head agrl. engring. dept., 1978-85, prof. emeritus, 1985—. Contbr. articles to profl. jours. Patentee in field. Mem. Ill. Noise Task Force, 1974-80. Fellow Am. Soc. Agrl. Engrs. (Massey-Ferguson medal 1989); mem. Am. Soc. Engring. Edn., Phi Kappa Phi (dir. fellowships, dir. 1971-83, pres.-elect 1983-86, pres. 1986-89), Rotary. Roman Catholic. Home: 107 W Holmes St Urbana IL 61801-6614 Office: 1304 W Pennsylvania Ave Urbana IL 61801-4713 E-mail: ryoerger@aol.com.

YOHN, DAVID STEWART, virologist, science administrator; b. Shelby, Ohio, June 7, 1929; s. Joseph Van and Agnes (Tryon) Y.; m. Olivetta Kathleen McCoy, June 11, 1950; children: Linda Jean, Kathleen Ann, Joseph John, David McCoy, Kristine Renee (dec.). B.S., Otterbein Coll., 1951; M.S., Ohio State U., 1953, Ph.D., 1957; M.P.H., U. Pitts., 1960. Research fellow, scholar in microbiology Ohio State U., Columbus, 1952-56, prof. virology Coll. Veterinary Medicine, 1969-95, prof. emeritus, 1995—, dir. Comprehensive Cancer Ctr., 1973-88, dep. dir. Comprehensive Cancer Ctr., 1988-94, dir. emeritus Comprehensive Cancer Ctr., 1994—. Research assoc., asst. prof. microbiology U. Pitts., 1956-62; assoc. cancer research scientist Roswell Park Meml. Inst., Buffalo, 1962-69; mem. nat. med. and sci. adv. com. Leukemia Soc. Am., 1970-91, trustee, 1971-91; pres. Ohio Cancer Research Assocs., 1982— ; mem. cancer research centers rev. com. Nat. Cancer Inst., 1972-77 Pres. bd. deacons North Presbyn. Ch., Williamsburg, N.Y., 1967-68. Recipient Pub. Service award Lions, 1968 Mem. Am. Assn. Cancer Rsch., Am. Soc. Microbiology, Am. Assn. Immunologists, Internat. Assn. Comparative Rsch. on Leukemia and Related Diseases (sec.-gen. 1974-95), Ohio Valley-Lake Erie Assn. Cancer Ctrs. (sec. 1978-95), Sertoma (pres. 1992-93, chmn. bd. dirs. 1993-94, Dist. Sertoman of Yr. award 1987). Home: 974 Willow Bluff Dr Columbus OH 43235-5047 Office: Ohio State U Comprehensive Cancer Ctr 300 W 10th Ave Ste 1132 Columbus OH 43210-1240 E-mail: yohn.1@osu.edu.

YOKICH, STEPHEN PHILLIP, labor union administrator; b. Detroit, Aug. 20, 1935; m. Tekla Baumgartner. Trades apprentice Heidrich Tool and Die Co., Oak Park, Mich., 1956; region 1 staff UAW, 1969-77, dir. region 1, 1977, dir. agrl. implement dept., 1980-83, dir. organizing dept., 1983-89, v.p., 1989-95, pres., 1995—. Chair UAW Nat. Cmty. Action Program; v.p., mem. exec. coun. AFL-CIO, 1995. Active Dem. Nat. Com., Mich. Dem. Party State Ctrl. Com.; del. Dem. Nat. Conv.; bd. mem., mem. steering com. Econ. Alliance Mich., Mich. Blue Cross-Blue Shield, Mich. Cancer Found., Father Clement Kern Found.; founder Cmty. Caring Program, 1993; co-chair Cmty. Caring Program for Children. With USAF, 1952-56. Recipient Arab Am. of the Yr. award Arab Cmty. Ctr. for Econ. and Social Svcs., Dearborn, Mich., 1995; co-recipient Chmns. award for vehicle quality improvement J.D. Power and Assocs., 1998. Mem. NAACP, Coalition Labor Union Women. Avocations: hunting, golfing, fishing. Office: Internat Union United Auto Aerospace 8000 E Jefferson Ave Detroit MI 48214-3963

YOKICH, TRACEY A. former state legislator; b. Feb. 25, 1960; BA, Mich. State U., 1982; JD, U. Detroit Law Sch., 1985. Law clk. for Hon. George Clifton Edwards, Jr., 6th Cir. U.S. Ct. Appeals, 1985-86; asst. pros. atty. Macomb County, Mich., 1986-89, asst. corp. counsel, 1989-90; mem. Mich. Ho. of Reps., 1991-97. Vice chmn. election com., mem. pub. health, environ., Great Lakes, consumer, judicary and conservation coms., chmn. tourism and recreation com. Commr. Macomb County Criminal Justice Bldg. Authority. Mem. Mich. Bar Assn., Macomb County Bar Assn., Clair Shores Dem. Club. Home: 22710 Gordon Switch St Saint Clair Shores MI 48081-1308

YONTZ, KENNETH FREDRIC, medical and chemical company executive; b. Sandusky, Ohio, July 21, 1944; s. Kenneth Willard and Dorothy (Kromer) Y.; m. Jean Ann Marshall, July 21, 1962 (div. Aug. 1982); children: Terri, Christine, Michael, Jennifer; m. Karen Glojek, July 7, 1984 (wid. Dec. 1994); m. Karen Mc Diarmid, Jan. 10, 1997. BSBA, Bowling Green State U., 1971; MBA, Eastern Mich. U., 1979. Fin. planning mgr. Ford Motor Co., Rawsonville, Mich., 1970-74; fin. mgr. Chemetron Corp., Chgo., 1974-76, pres. fire systems div., 1976-80; pres. electronics div. Allen Bradley Co., Milw., 1980-83, group. pres. electronics, 1983-85, exec. v.p., 1985-86; chmn. bd. Apogent Techs., 1986—, Sybron Dental Specialties, Milw., 1986—. Bd. dirs. Viasystems, St. Louis. Bd. dirs. Boys and Girls Club; founder Karen Yontz Womens Cardiac Awareness Ctr.. Mem. Bluemound Country Club, Milw. Athletic Club, Muirfield Village Golf Club, Vintage Club (Indian Wells, Calif.), Tradition Golf Club (La Quinta, Calif.). Roman Catholic. Office: Sybron Corp 411 E Wisconsin Ave Ste 2400 Milwaukee WI 53202-4412

YORK, DONALD GILBERT, astronomy educator, researcher; b. Shelbyville, Ill., Oct. 28, 1944; s. Maurice Alfred and Virginia Maxine (Huntwork) Y.; m. Anna Sue Hinds, June 12, 1966; children: Sean, Maurice, Chandler, Jeremy. BS, MIT, 1966; PhD, U. Chgo., 1971. Rsch. asst. Princeton (N.J.) U., 1970-71, rsch. assoc., 1971-73, rsch. astronomer, 1973-78, sr. rsch. astronomer, 1978-82; assoc. prof. U. Chgo., 1982-86, prof., 1986-92, Horace B. Horton prof. astronomy and astrophysics, 1992—. Dir. Apache Point Obs., Astrophys. Rsch. Consortium, Seattle, 1984-98, Sloan Digital Sky Survey, 1990-97. Contbr. articles to profl. jours. Recipient Pub. Svc. award NASA, 1976; grantee NASA, 1978—, NSF, 1984—. Mem. Internat. Astron. Union, Am. Astron. Soc. (publs. bd. 1980-83). Democrat. Avocations: squash, white water canoeing, science history, religion history, swimming. Office: 5640 S Ellis Ave Chicago IL 60637-1433 E-mail: don@oddjob.uchicago.edu.

YOST, LARRY D. automotive company executive; Mgr. prodn. and inventory control Rockwell Internat., from 1971, pres. heavy vehicles sys. divsn., 1994-97; pres., CEO, Meritor Automotive Inc. (merger with Arvin Co.), Troy, Mich., 1997—, chmn., 1998—. Office: Arvin Meritor Inc. 2135 W Maple Rd Troy MI 48084-7121

YOST, LYLE EDGAR, retired farm equipment manufacturing company executive; b. Hesston, Kans., Mar. 5, 1913; s. Joseph and Alma (Hensley) Y.; m. Erma Martin, July 31, 1938; children: Byron, Winston, Susan, Cameron. B.S. B.A, Goshen Coll., 1937; postgrad., U. Ind., 1940. With St. Joseph Valley Bank, Elkhart, Ind., 1938-41; tchr. Wakarusa (Ind.) High Sch., 1942-45; founder Hesston Corp., Kans., 1947, pres., 1949-83, now chmn. bd.; ret., 1991. Bd. dirs., past pres. Farm and Indsl. Equipment Inst.; mem. Gov.'s Com. for Ptnrs. for Progress Kans.-Paraguay; chmn. com. establishing creamery in Uruguay, 1967; mem. State Dept. cultural del. to USSR, 1967; past chmn. pres.'s adv coun. Hesston Coll. (Kans.); chmn. Prince of Peace Chapel, Aspen, Colo. Named Farmarketing Man of Year Nat. Agrl. Advt. and Marketing Assn., 1969, Kansan of Achievement in Bus., 1972, Kansan of Year, 1974, One of the Most Significant Contbrs. to Mechanization of Agrl. and Constrn. Equipment Mfrs. Inst., 1993. Mem. Alpha Kappa Psi (hon.). Home: 123 Kingsway Hesston KS 67062-9271

YOST, WILLIAM ALBERT, psychology educator, hearing researcher; b. Dallas, Sept. 21, 1944; s. William Jacque and Gladys (Funk) Y.; m. Lee Prater, June 15, 1969; children: Kelley Ann, Alyson Leigh B.A., Colo. Coll., 1966, DSc (hon.), 1997; Ph.D., Ind. U., 1970. Assoc. prof. psychology U. Fla., Gainesville, 1971-77; dir. sensory physiology and perception program NSF, Washington, 1982-83; prof. psychology Loyola U., Chgo., 1977-89, dir. Parmly Hearing Inst., 1977—, prof. hearing scis., 1990—, dir. interdisciplinary neurosci. minor, 1997—. Adj. prof. psychology and otolarynogology Loyola U., Chgo., 1990—, acting v.p. rsch., 1999—2001, assoc. v.p. rsch., dean Grad. Sch., 2001—; individual expert bio-acoustics Am. Nat. Stds. Inst., 1983—; mem. study sect. Nat. Inst. Deafness and Other Communication Disorders, 1990—94; mem. hearing bioacoustics and biomechanics com. NRC, 1992—. Author: Fundamentals of Hearing, 1977, 4th edit., 2000; editor (with others) New Directions in Hearing Science, 1985, Directional Hearing, 1987, Auditory Processing of Complex Sounds, 1987, Classification of Complex Sounds, 1989, Psychoacoustics, 1993; assoc. editor Auditory Neurosci., 1994-97; ad hoc reviewer NSF, Air Force Office Sci. Rsch., Office Naval Rsch., 1981—; contbr. chpts. to books, articles to profl. jours. Pres. Evanston Tennis Assn., Ill., 1984, 90. Grantee NSF, 1974—, NIH, 1975—, AFOSR, 1983—, ONR, 1989-90. Fellow AAAS, Am. Phys. Soc., Acoustical Soc. Am. (assoc. editor jour. 1984-91, chair tech. com. 1990-94, exec. com. 1999—, v.p. 2002--), Am. Speech-Lang.-Hearing Assn.; mem. NAS (exec. com. on hearing bioacoustics, biomechanics 1981-87, chmn. 1993-97), Assn. Rsch. in Otolaryngology (sec.-treas. 1984-87, pres.-elect 1987-88, pres. 1988-89), Acoustics Soc. Am. (chair com. psychol. and physiol. acoustics 1990-94, mem. exec. coun. 1999—), Nat. Inst. Deafness and Other Comm. Disorders (task force, rev. panel 1990-94, chmn. 1994), Am. Auditory Soc. (exec. bd. 1993-98).

YOUDELMAN, ROBERT ARTHUR, financial executive, lawyer; b. L.I., N.Y., Mar. 28, 1942; s. Jack and Marjorie Vivian (Baer) Y.; m. Karen Leita Schneier, July 30, 1966; children: Mara, Sondra. BBA in Acctg., Case Western Res. U., 1963; LLB, NYU, 1966, LLM in Taxation, 1975. Bar: N.Y. 1969, U.S. Tax Ct. Vol. U.S. Peace Corps, Salvador, Brasil, 1966-68; mgr. Arthur Andersen & Co., N.Y.C., 1969-77; v.p., dir. taxation The Allen Group Inc., Melville, N.Y., 1977-89, sr. v.p. fin., chief fin. officer, 1989—. Mem. N.Y. State Hazardous Waste Task Force, Albany, 1985-87; pres. Residents for a More Beautiful Port Washington, N.Y., 1981-92. Recipient Individual Environ. Quality award for Region 2 EPA, 1992; named Citizen of Yr., Port Washington Rotary Club, 1989. Mem. ABA. Avocations: camping, hiking, environmental education and awareness. Office: Allen Telecom Inc 25101 Chagrin Blvd Beachwood OH 44122-5643

YOUKER, JAMES EDWARD, radiologist; b. Cooperstown, N.Y., Nov. 13, 1928; s. Bliss Jacob and Marian (Ostrander) Y.; children— Elizabeth Ann, James David. A.B., Colgate U., 1950; M.D., U. Buffalo, 1954. Diplomate: Am. Bd. Radiology. Intern U. Minn., Mpls., 1954-55, resident in radiology, 1955-56, 58-60; resident in pathology Georgetown U., Washington, 1958; pvt. practice medicine, specializing in radiology Corpus Christi, Tex., 1956-58; asst. prof. radiology Med. Coll. Va., Richmond, 1961-63; research fellow U. Lund, Malmo, Sweden, 1963-64; asst. prof. radiology U. Calif., San Francisco, 1964-67; asso. prof. U. Clif., 1967-68; prof., chmn. dept. radiology Med. Coll. Wis., Milw., 1968—; dir. dept. radiology Milwaukee County Gen. Hosp., 1968-96; chmn. dept. radiology Froedtert Meml. Luth. Hosp., 1979-96; chmn., dir. dept. radiology Froedtert & Meml. Luth. Hosp., Milw., 1968—. Served with Project Hope, Indonesia, 1961; cons./lectr. VA Hosp., Richmond, 1961-63, San Francisco, 1964-68, Martinez, Calif., 1964-68; cons./lectr. Letterman Army Med. Center, San Francisco, 1964-68, Oakknoll Naval Hosp., Oakladn, Calif., 1964-68, VA Hosp., Wood, Wis., 1968— , Gt. Lakes Naval Hosp., Chgo., 1968— ; vis. prof. U. Calif. Sch. Medicine, San Francisco, 1974, Stanford U. Sch. Medicine, Palo Alto, Calif., 1976; vis. physician dept. cardiology St. Vincent's Hosp., Melbourne, Australia, 1974-75; mem. com. diagnosis breast cancer task force NIH, 1975-79; Head Physicians for Ford; chmn. health and med. sci. tech. com. for program planning com. North Div. High Sch., 1979; bd. dirs. Med. Coll. Wis., 1986—, mem. residency rev. commn. for radiology, 1985—. Editorial adv. bd.: Critical Revs. in Radiologic Scis; editorial bd.: Postgrad. Radiology; reviewer: Am. Jour. Roentgenology; assoc. reviewer Radiol.; assoc. editor: Cardiovascular Diseases, 1985—; contbr. numerous articles to profl. jours. Served with M.C. USN, 1956-58. N.Y. State Regents scholar, 1946; Buffalo Found. scholar, 1952; grantee USPHS; grantee Squibb Pharms.; grantee Nat. Cancer Inst.; grantee others. Fellow Am. Coll. Radiology (bd. chancellors 1978— , vice-chmn. commn. on cancer 1972-74, chmn./mem. numerous coms., v.p. 1983-84); mem. Am. Bd. Med. Specialties (pres. 2000), Am. Assn. Physicians Assts. (adv. bd.), Am. Cancer Soc. (coms. Milw. br.), Am. Heart Assn. Council on Cardiovascular Radiology, AMA, Am. Roentgen Ray Soc. (adv. com. research and edn.), Assn. Univ. Radiologists (chmn. govt. affairs com. 1978-79), Med. Soc. Milwaukee County (hosp. med. staff liaison com. 1978-79), Milw. Acad. Medicine, Milw. Roentgen Ray Soc., Soc. Chairmen Acad. Radiolgy Depts. (pres. 1972, coms.), Soc. Gastrointestinal Radiology, Vail Creative Concepts Conf. (co-founder), Wis. Med. Soc., Wis. Radiol. Soc. (dir., chmn. technician affairs com.) Republican. Clubs: Univ. (Milw.); Chenequa Country. Office: Froedtert Meml Luth Hosp 9200 W Wisconsin Ave Milwaukee WI 53226-3522 E-mail: jyouker@mcw.edu.

YOUNG, ANN ELIZABETH O'QUINN, historian, educator; b. Waycross, Ga. d. James Foster and Pearl Elizabeth (Sasser) O'Quinn; m. Robert William Young, Aug. 18, 1968; children: Abigail Ann, Leslie Lynn. Student, Shorter Coll.; BA, MA, U. Ga., PhD, 1965. Asst. prof. history Kearney (Nebr.) State Coll. (name changed U. Nebr.-Kearney), 1965-69, assoc. prof., 1969-72, prof., 1972-00, prof. emeritus, 2000—. Participant Inst. on Islam, Middle East and World Politics, U. Mich., summer 1984, Coun. on Internat. Ednl. Exch., London, 1990, NEH Seminar NYU, 1993, faculty senate mem., 1985—, sec. 1993-94, pres., 1995-96. Conbg. author Dictionary of Georgia Biography; contbr. articles to profl. revs. Mem. NEA, PEO, Phi Alpha Theta, Delta Kappa Gamma (chpt. pres. 1978-79), Phi Mu. Republican. Presbyterian. Office: U Nebr at Kearney Dept History Kearney NE 68849-0001

YOUNG, ARTHUR PRICE, librarian, educator; b. Boston, July 29, 1940; s. Arthur Price and Marion (Freeman) Y.; m. Patricia Dorothy Foss, June 26, 1965; children: John Marshall, Christopher Price. BA, Tufts U., 1962; MA in Tchg., U. Mass., 1964; MSLS, Syracuse U., 1969; PhD, U. Ill., 1976. Head reader svcs., social sci. bibliographer SUNY-Cortland, 1969-72; rsch. assoc. U. Ill. Libr. Rsch. Ctr., Urbana, 1972-75; asst. dean pub. svcs., assoc. prof. U. Ala., Tuscaloosa, 1976-81; dean librs., prof. U. R.I., Kingston, l98l-89; dir. Thomas Cooper Libr., U. S.C., Columbia, 1989-93; sr. fellow UCLA, 1991; dean librs., mem. adj. faculty dept. history No. Ill. U., DeKalb, 1993—. Mem. adj. faculty Syracuse (N.Y.) U., 1970-71, Dominican U., River Forest, Ill., 1994-96; pres. Consortium R.I. Acad. and Rsch. Librs., 1983-85; mem. bd. govs. Univ. Press New England, 1987-89; mem. exec. bd. Ill. Libr. Computer Sys. Orgn., 1995-99; chair Coun. Dirs. State Univ. Librs., 1994-95, 2001—; sr. fellow UCLA, 1991; pres. Ill. Libr. Assn., 2002. Author: Books for Sammies: American Library Association and World War I, 1981, American Library History: A Bibliography of Dissertations and Theses, 1988, Higher Education in American Life, 1636-1986: A Bibliography of Dissertations and Theses, 1988, Cities and Towns in American History: A Bibliography of Doctoral Dissertations, 1989, Academic Libraries: Research Perspectives, 1990, Religion and the American Experience, 1620-1900: A Bibliography of Doctoral Dissertations, 1992, Religion and the American Experience, the Twentieth Century: A Bibliography of Doctoral Dissertations, 1994; editl. bd. various jours. Chair Coun. of Dirs. Ill. State Univ. Librs., 1994-95, 2001-02. Served to capt. USAF, 1964-68. Recipient Berner Nash award U. Ill., 1976. Mem. ALA (chmn. editl. bd., chair Libr. Rsch. Seminar I, 1996), Assn. Coll. and Rsch. Librs. (publs. in librarianship 1982-88, chmn. Jesse H. Shera Endowment Fund com. 1991-94), Ill. Libr. Assn., S.C. Libr. Assn. (chmn. libr. adminstrn. sect. 1991-92), Assn. Rsch. Librs. (scholarly commn. com. 1991-93), Orgn. Am. Historians, Am. Hist. Assn., Horatio Alger Soc. (pres. 1999-2000), Caxton Club (Chgo.), Phi Kappa Phi, Beta Phi Mu, Phi Delta Kappa. Episcopalian. Home: 912 Borden Ave Sycamore IL 60178-3200

YOUNG, DALE LEE, banker; b. Palmyra, Nebr., Mar. 13, 1928; s. Mike P. and Grace (Clutter) Y.; m. Norma Marie Shalla, June 18, 1950; children— Shalla Ann, Philip Mike. B.B.A., U. Nebr., 1950. With FirsTier Bank N.A. (formerly First Nat. Bank & Trust Co.), Lincoln, Nebr., 1950-91, cashier, 1966-91, v.p., 1966-76, exec. v.p., 1976-92; sec. ISCO, Inc., 1991—, also bd. dirs. Bd. dirs. Woodmen Accident and Life Co.; sec., bd. dirs. Leasing Corp. Treas. Lincoln City Library Found.; Treas., mem. exec. com. Nebr. Republican Com., 1968— ; bd. dirs., v.p. Lincoln Symphony; bd. dirs. Lincoln Community Services, ARC, Lincoln Found.;

trustee Bryan Meml. Hosp., 1976-80; mem. Lincoln City Coun., 1991-98, elected mayor, 1998. Served with AUS, 1946-48, 50-51. Mem. Nebr. Art Assn., Omaha-Lincoln Soc. Fin. Analysts, Lincoln C. of C. (pres.), Theta Xi. Presbyterian. Clubs: Nebraska, Lincoln Country, Univ. Home: 3911 Firethorn Ct Lincoln NE 68520-1466 Office: PO Box 81008 Lincoln NE 68501-1008

YOUNG, DEAN A. state legislator; BA, Purdue U.; JD, Valprasio U. Mem. Ho. of Reps., Indpls., 1992—, mem. judiciary, labor & employment, pub. health coms. Pros. atty. Blackford County. Mem. Hartford City econ. devel. com., 1985—, pres. 1989-90; mem. Blackford County Cmty. Corrections Bd., 1990—. Republican. Office: Ind Ho of Reps State Capitol Indianapolis IN 46204

YOUNG, DONALD FREDRICK, engineering educator; b. Joplin, Mo., Apr. 27, 1928; s. Oral Solomon and Blanche (Trent) Y.; m. Gertrude Ann Cooper, Apr. 15, 1950; children: Michael, Pamela, Susan, Christopher, David. B.S., Iowa State U., 1951, M.S., 1952, Ph.D., 1956. Research engr. AEC Ames Lab., 1952-55; asst. prof. Iowa State U., Ames, 1955-58, assoc. prof., 1958-61, prof. engrng. sci. and mechanics, 1961-74, Anson Marston Disting. prof. engrng., 1974-99, Anson Marston Disting. prof. emeritus, 1999—. Author: Introduction to Applied Mechanics, 1972, (with others) Essentials of Mechanics, 1974, (with others) Fundamentals of Fluid Mechanics, 1990, 4th edit., 2002, (with others) A Brief Introduction to Fluid Mechanics, 1997, 2d edit., 2001; contbr. articles to profl. jours. Recipient Outstanding Tchr. award Standard Oil, 1971, Faculty citation Iowa State Alumni Assn., 1972, Spl. Recognition award Iowa State U. Rsch. Found., 1988, David R. Boylan Eminent award for rsch., 1995. Fellow ASME (chmn. bioengrng. div. 1973-74); mem. Am. Heart Assn., Am. Soc. Engrng. Edn., Pi Tau Sigma, Pi Mu Epsilon, Phi Kappa Phi, Sigma Xi Home: 2042 Prairie Vw E Ames IA 50010-4558 Office: Iowa State U 2271 Howe Hall Ames IA 50010

YOUNG, JACK ALLISON, financial executive; b. Aurora, Ill., Dec. 31, 1931; s. Neal A. and Gladys Young; m. Virginia Dawson, Jan. 24, 1959; children: Amy D., Andrew A. BS in Journalism, U. Ill., 1954. CLU; chartered fin. cons.; registered security rep. Advt. writer Caterpillar Tractor Co., 1956-58; inst. agent Equitable Life Assurance Soc., St. Geneva, Ill., 1958—, ins. broker, 1972—; pres. Jack A. Young and Assocs., 1978—, Creative Brokerage, Inc., 1982-95. Past pres., gen. securities prin. Chartered Planning, Ltd., 1984-2000; past trustee Equitable CLU Assn.; past chmn. Equitable Nat. Agents Forum. Bd. dirs. Tri-City Famiy Services, 1975-83, pres., 1979-81; trustee Delnor-Community Health System, 1985-97, chmn., 1988-91; bd. dirs. St. Charles Ctr. Phys. Rehab., 1991-97; chmn., pres. Delnor-Cmty. Health Care Found., 1986-88; dir. Kane County Bar Found., Inc., 1997-2000. Lt. (j.g.) USN, 1956. Named to Equitable Hall of Fame, 1978. Mem. Million Dollar Round Table (life), Am. Soc. C.L.U.s, Am. Coll. C.L.U. Golden Key Soc., Fox Valley Estate Planning Council, Internat. Assn. for Fin. Planning, Inc., Aurora Assn. Life Underwriters (past pres., nat. committeeman), Nat. Assn. Securities Dealers (registered prin.), Geneva Golf Club (pres. 1994). Home: 18 Campbell St Geneva IL 60134-2732 also: 2706 Laurel Dr Vero Beach FL 32960-5063 Office: 28 N Bennett St Geneva IL 60134-2207 E-mail: jayassoc@ameritech.net., yjackayoung@aol.com.

YOUNG, JAMES EDWARD, lawyer; b. Painesville, Ohio, Apr. 20, 1946; s. James M. and Isabel P. (Rogers) Y. BBA, Ohio U., 1968; JD, Ohio State U., 1972. Bar: Ohio 1972. Law clk. to chief judge U.S. Ct. Appeals, Nashville, 1972-73; chief counsel City of Cleve., 1980-81, law dir., 1981-82; assoc. Jones, Day, Reavis & Pogue, Cleve., 1973-79, ptnr., 1983—. Office: Jones Day Reavis & Pogue 901 Lakeside Ave E Cleveland OH 44114-1190 E-mail: jameseyoung@jonesday.com.

YOUNG, JAMES R. railroad transportation executive; Grad., U. Nebraska. Mgmt. fin. and ops. Union Pacific, sr. v.p. fin., exec. v.p., CFO, 1999—. Office: Union Pacific 1416 Dodge St Omaha NE 68179

YOUNG, JAY MAITLAND, health care products consultant; b. Louisville, Nov. 26, 1944; s. Clyde Dudley and Olive May (Tyas) Y. BA in Chemistry and Math magna cum laude, Vanderbilt U., 1966; MS in Biochemistry, Yale U., 1967, MPhil in Phys. Chemistry, 1968, PhD in Chemistry, 1971. Asst. prof. chemistry Bryn Mawr (Pa.) Coll., 1970-76; rsch. biochemist Abbott Labs., Ill., 1977-78, project mgr. physiolog. diagnostics, 1978-80, project mgr. cancer product devel., 1980-82, internat. clin. specialist sci. affairs, 1982-85, clin. project mgr. physiol. diag. quality and sci. support, 1986-90, staff quality assurance and sci. support, 1990-93, fertility, pregnancy, thyroid mgr., quality and sci. support, 1993-95; fertility, pregnancy, thyroid, cancer mgr., product quality assurance Abbott Labs., 1995-97, staff noninfectious disease diagnostics sci. affairs, 1997—2001, cons., 2002—. Cons. Inst. for Cancer Rsch., Fox Chase, Phila., 1974, vis. scientist, 1975-76; honors examiner Swarthmore Coll., 1973, 74; mem. vis. evaluation com., 1975; presenter to med. groups on cancer markers, viral hepatitis and epidemiology of AIDS, 1982-84. Contbr. articles to profl. jours.; patentee in med. field. Named to Hon. Order Ky. Cols.; predoctoral fellow NSF, Yale U., 1966-70; postdoctoral fellow, NIH, U. Oxford, 1971-72; grantee NSF, NATO Travel grant, U. Salford, Eng., 1974, Amer. Med. Writer's Assn. Care (Multi-disciplinary), 1999. Mem. Am. Med. Writers Assn., vol., Episcopal Ch. Outreach Commn.

YOUNG, JESS RAY, retired internist; b. Fairfield, Ill., Feb. 4, 1928; s. Edgar S. and Clara B. (Musgrave) Y.; m. Gloria Wynn, July 10, 1953; children— James C., Patricia A. BS, Franciscan U., 1951; MD, St. Louis U., 1955. Intern Highland Alameda County Hosp., Oakland, Calif., 1955-56; resident in internal medicine Cleve. Clinic Hosp., 1956-59, mem. staff dept. vascular medicine, 1959-97, chmn. dept., 1976-97; ret., 1998. Co-author: Leg Ulcer, 1975, Peripheral Vascular Diseases, 1991, 1996; contbr. articles to profl. jours., chpts. to books. Served with AUS, 1946-47. Mem. AMA, Am. Heart Assn. (stroke council), Am. Coll. Cardiology, Internat. Cardiovascular Soc., ACP, Am. Fedn. Clic. Research, Ohio Soc. Internal Medicine, Soc. for Vascular Medicine and Rsch., Inter-Urban Club. Methodist. Home: 1503 Burlington Rd Cleveland OH 44118-1216 E-mail: jesyoung@aol.com.

YOUNG, JOSEPH FLOYD, JR. state legislator; b. Detroit, Nov. 4, 1950; m. Mary J. Gerbe; children: Kimberly Ann, Kerry Marie, Joe, III, Brooke Melinda. , Mich. State U., Cooley Law Sch., Western Mich. U., Urban Bible Inst., Detroit. Com. analyst House Spkr. William Ryan; adminstrv. asst.; legis. asst. State Rep. Alma Stallworth; com. adminstr., legis. asst. Sen. Dale Kildee; state rep. Dist. 4 Mich. Ho. of Reps., 1978-94; mem. Mich. Senate from 1st dist., Lansing, 1994—. Chnn. State Affairs Com.; mem. Standing Coms. on Conservation, Environment & Great Lakes, Econ. Devel., Edn. & Tourism & Recreation Mich. Ho. of Reps.; mem. Families, Mental Health & Human Svc. & Judiciary Coms., Mich. State Senate, vice chmn. Local Urban & State Affairs Com. Mem. NAACP, KC, YMCA, Block Clubs. Home: 8570 E Outer Dr Detroit MI 48213-1420 Office: Mich Senate State Capitol PO Box 30036 Lansing MI 48909-7536

YOUNG, LARRY JOE, insurance agent; b. Chanute, Kans., July 19, 1958; s. Larry Louis and Judith Ann (Leslie) Y.; m. Vickie Lea Everhart; children: Tyler Jay, Joseph Michael, Katherine LeAnn, Hayleigh Imogene, Larry Joe Jr. Student, Kans. City (Kans.) Community Coll., 1976-78; BGS in Meterology, Kans. U., 1980. Reg. rep., FDIC; security lic. mutual funds. Sales rep. Met. Life, Overland Park, Kans., 1981-86; deposit broker Union Cen. Life, 1986—; pres. Young & Assocs., Shawnee, Kans., 1988-95; Young & Assocs. Inc. (now incorporated), 1995—; owner/broker 1st Nat. CD Exch., 1996—; multiple line gen. agent Am. Nat. Ins. Co., mgr., 1998—. Coach Shawnee (Kans.) Soccer Club, 1986. Fellow, Life Underwriting Tng. Coun. Mem. Nat. Assn. Securities Dealers, Profl. Ind. Ins. Agts. Kans. Avocations: flying, pole vaulting.

YOUNG, LEON D. state legislator; b. July 4, 1957; Degree in police sci., Milw. Area Tech. Coll.; student, U. Wis., Milw. Police officer; mem. Social Devel. Commn. Minority Male Forum on Corrections. Mem. NAACP, Urban League. Home: 2224 N 17th St Milwaukee WI 53205-1220 Office: Wis Assembly PO Box 8952 Madison WI 53708-8952

YOUNG, MARVIN OSCAR, lawyer; b. Union, Mo., Apr. 4, 1929; s. Otto Christopher and Irene Adelheide (Barlage) Y.; m. Sue Carol Mathews, Aug. 23, 1952; children: Victoria Leigh, Kendall Marvin. A.B., Westminster Coll., 1951; J.D., U. Mich., 1954; LLD, Westminster Coll., 1989. Bar: Mo. 1954. Practice law firm Thompson, Mitchell, Thompson Douglas, St. Louis, 1954-55, 57-58; atty. Mo. Farmers Assn., Columbia, 1958-67; exec. v.p. First Mo. Corp., 1965-68; v.p. ops. MFA-Central Coop., 1967-68; v.p., gen. counsel, sec. Peabody Coal Co., St. Louis, 1968-82; gen. counsel Peabody Holding Co., Inc., 1983-85; also dir., sec. subs. and affiliates Peabody Coal Co.; ptnr. Gallop, Johnson & Neuman, St. Louis, 1986—, chmn. corp. dept., 1988-90, chmn. energy dept., 1990—. City atty. Warson Woods, Mo., 1990—; speaker at legal insts. Assoc. editor Mich. Law Rev., 1953-54; contbr. articles to profl. jours. Pres. Warson Woods PTA, 1974-75; trustee Met. Sewer Dist. St. Louis, 1974-80, chmn. 1978-80; mem. Mo. Energy Coun., 1973-77, Mo. Environ. Improvement and Energy Resources Athority, 1983-87, vice chmn. 1986-87; trustee Eastern Mineral Law Found., 1983-98; pres. Alumni Assn. Westminster Coll., Fulton, Mo., 1978-80, trustee coll., 1977—, mem. exec. com., 1978—, chmn. 1986-90, chmn. investment com., 1998-; chmn. Churchill Meml. and Libr., Fulton, 1992-2000; mem. chancellor's coun. adv. bd. U. Mo., St. Louis, 1992—; mem. lawyers adv. coun. Gt. Plains Legal Found., Kansas City, Mo., 1976-84; mem. Rep. Com. Boone County, Mo., 1962-68, chmn. legis. dist. com., 1962-64, 66-68; alt. del. Rep. Nat. Conv., 1968; pres. Clayton Twp. Rep. Club, 1973-77; sr. warden Episcopal Ch., 1988-89. Served to capt. USAF, 1955-57. Recipient alumni award of merit, 1972; named Coal Lawyer of Yr., Nat. Coal Assn., 1994; Churchill fellow, 1990. Mem. ABA, Mo. Bar Assn., Bar Assn. Met. St. Louis, Barristers Soc., Round Table Club of St. Louis, John Marshall Rep. Lawyers Club (pres. 1977), Mo. Athletic Club, Sjamrock Club of St. Louis County, Rotary (bd. dirs. St. Louis club 1993-95), Masons, Order of Coif, Shriners. Home: 555 Flanders Dr Saint Louis MO 63122-1617 Office: Gallop Johnson & Neuman LC 101 S Hanley Rd Ste 1600 Saint Louis MO 63105-3489 E-mail: moyoung@gjn.com.

YOUNG, MARY ANN, lawyer; b. Alton, Ill., May 1, 1952; d. William Jerome and Barbara Ann (Blocher) Y. Student, St. Mary of the Plains Coll., 1970-71; BA in Econs., Washburn (Kans.) U., 1974; JD, U. Mo., 1976. Bar: Mo. 1977. Pvt. practice, Holden, Mo., 1977-84, Warrensburg, 1984—. Atty. City of Holden, 1978-80; asst. prosecutor Johnson County, Mo., 1978-80, 83-88; bd. dirs. Indsl. Svc. Contactors Sheltered Workshop, Warrensburg. Mem. Rep. Women, Johnson County, 1988-89, CLIMB, Johnson County, 1989—, Task Force for Drug Free Mo., Johnson County, 1989—; 2d. v.p. Johnson County Rep. Women, 1989—. Mem. Mo. Bar Assn., Johnson County Bar Assn., Johnson County C. of C., Mo. Farm Bur. Roman Catholic. Avocations: antique collecting, gardening. Office: 307 N Holden St Warrensburg MO 64093-1705

YOUNG, MERWIN CRAWFORD, political science educator; b. Phila., Nov. 7, 1931; s. Ralph Aubrey and Louise (Merwin) Y.; m. Rebecca Conrad, Aug. 17, 1957; children: Eva Colcord, Louise Conrad, Estelle Merwin, Emily Harriet. BA, U. Mich., 1953; postgrad., Inst. Hist. Rsch. U. London, 1955-56, Inst d'Etudes Politiques, U. Paris, 1956-57; PhD, Harvard U., 1964; DSc (hon.), Fla. Internat. U., 1998. Asst. prof. polit. sci. U. Wis., Madison, 1963-66, assoc. prof., 1966-69, prof., 1969—2001, emeritus, 2001—, Rupert Emerson prof., 1983; H. Edwin Young prof., 1994; chmn. African Studies Program U. Wis., Madison, 1964-68, chmn. dept. polit. sci., 1969-72, 84-87, assoc. dean Grad. Sch., 1968-71, acting dean Coll. Letters and Sci., 1992-93. Vis. prof. Makerere U. Coll., Kampala, Uganda, 1965-66; dean Faculty of Social Sci. Nat. U., Lubumbashi, Zaire, 1973-75; Fulbright prof. U. Dakar, Senegal, 1987-88. Author: Politics in the Congo, 1965, The Politics of Cultural Pluralism, 1976 (Herskovits prize 1977, Ralph Bunche prize 1979), Ideology and Development in Africa, 1982, The African Colonial State in Comparative Perspective, 1994 (Gregory Luebbert prize 1995); co-author: Cooperatives and Development, 1981, The Rise and Decline of the Zairian State, 1985; editor: The Rising Tide of Cultural Pluralism: The Nation-State at Bay?, 1993, Ethnic Diversity and Public Policy, 1998, The Accommodation of Cultural Diversity, 1999; co-editor: Dilemmas of Democracy in Nigeria, 1995, Beyond State Crisis? Postcolonial Africa and Post-Soviet Eurasia in Comparative Perspective, 2002. Served to 1st lt. U.S. Army, 1953-55. Social Sci. Rsch. fellow, 1967-68, Ford Faculty fellow, 1967-68, Guggenheim Found. fellow, 1972-73; vis. fellow Inst. for Advanced Study, Princeton, 1980-81; fellow Woodrow Wilson Internat. Ctr. for Scholars, 1983-84. Mem. AAAS, Am. Acad. Arts and Scis., Am. Polit. Sci. Assn., African Studies Assn. (pres. 1982-83, Disting. Africanist award 1991), Coun. Fgn. Rels. Home: 639 Crandall St Madison WI 53711-1836 Office: U Wis Dept Polit Sci North Hall 1050 Bascom Mall Madison WI 53706-1389 E-mail: young@polsci.wise.edu.

YOUNG, PAUL ANDREW, anatomist; b. St. Louis, Oct. 3, 1926; s. Nicholas A. and Olive A. (Langford) Y.; m. Catherine Ann Hofmeister, May 14, 1949; children— Paul, Robert, David, Ann, Carol, Richard, James, Steven, Kevin, Michael. B.S., St. Louis U., 1947, M.S., 1953; Ph.D., U. Buffalo, 1957. Asst. in anatomy U. Buffalo, 1953, instr. anatomy, 1957; asst. prof. anatomy St. Louis U., 1957, asso. prof., 1966, prof., 1972—, chmn. dept., 1973—. Author: (with B.D. Bhagat and D.E. Biggerstaff) Fundamentals of Visceral Innervation, 1977, (with P.H. Young) Basic Clinical Neuroanatomy, 1996, also computer assisted neurological anatomy tutorials; contbr. articles to profl. publs. Recipient Golden Apple award, Student AMA, 1974, 2000, Tchg. award, Acad. Sci. St. Louis, 1993, Emerson Excellence in Tchg. award, 2001. Mem. Am. Assn. Anatomists, Am. Assn. Clin. Anatomists, Soc. Neurosci., Sigma Xi, Alpha Omega Alpha. Office: St Louis U Dept Anatomy & Neurobiology 1402 S Grand Blvd Saint Louis MO 63104-1004

YOUNG, PHILIP HOWARD, library director; b. Ithaca, N.Y., Oct. 7, 1953; s. Charles Robert and Betty Irene (Osborne) Young; m. Nancy Ann Stutsman, Aug. 18, 1979. BA, U. Va., 1975; PhD, U. Pa., 1980; MLS, Ind. U., 1983. Asst. prof. history Appalachian State U., Boone, NC, 1980-82; reference asst. Lilly Libr. Ind. U., Bloomington, 1982-83; adminstr., info. specialist Ind. Corp. Sci. & Tech., Indpls., 1983-85; dir. Krannert Meml. Libr. U. Indpls., 1985—. Mem.: Archeol. Inst. Am., Am. Libr. Assn., Phi Beta Kappa, Beta Phi Mu, Phi Alpha Theta. Democrat. Home: 4332 Silver Springs Dr Greenwood IN 46142-9623 Office: U Indpls Krannert Meml Libr 1400 E Hanna Ave Indianapolis IN 46227-3630

YOUNG, R. JAMES, insurance company executive; V.p. fin. and planning The Allstate Corp., Northbrook, Ill., 1997-2000, v.p. property and casualty ops., 2000—. Office: The Allstate Corp 2775 Sanders Rd # F6 Northbrook IL 60062-6110

YOUNG, R. MICHAEL, state legislator; b. May 14, 1951; BA, Ind. U. Mem. Ind. Ho. of Reps. from 92nd dist., Indpls., 1986-2000; mem. ins. corps. and small bus. com., govt. affairs com.; mem. Ind. Senate from 35th dist., 2001—. Real estate developer; polit. cons.; mng. ptnr. Phoenix Devel. Mem. Marion County Bd. Zoning Appeals, Wayne Twp. Rep. Com., Pike Twp. Rep. Com., Eagle Creek Rep. Com.; precinct committeeman. Republican. Home: 3102 Columbine Ct Indianapolis IN 46224-2021 Office: Ind Senator 200 W Washington St Indianapolis IN 46204

YOUNG, RAYMOND ALLEN, chemist, educator; BS in Wood Products Engrng., SUNY, Syracuse, 1966, MS in Paper Chemistry, 1968; PhD in Wood and Polymer Chemistry, U. Wash., 1973. Process supr. Kimberly-Clark Corp., Niagara Falls, N.Y., 1968-69; vis. scientist Swedish Forest Products Lab., Stockholm, 1972-73; postdoctoral fellow, staff scientist Textile Rsch. Inst., Princeton, N.J., 1973-74; prof. wood and polymer chemistry dept. forestry U. Wis., Madison, 1975—. Cons. UN, USAID, NATO, Rome, Shell Oil, London, Kimbely-Clark Corp., Union Carbide Corp., Grain Processing Corp., Stone & Webster Engrngs. Cons., Mead Corp., Biodyne Chems., Resource Mgmt. Assocs.; expert witness various law firms. Author: Cellulose: Structure, Modification and Hydrolysis, 1986, Modified Cellulosics, 1978, Introduction to Forest Science, 2d edit., 1990, Paper and Composites from Agro-Based Resources, 1996, Environmentally Friendly Technologies in the Pulp and Paper Industry, 1998; contbr. chpts. to books, articles to profl. jours.; patentee infield. Fulbright scholar Royal Inst. Tech., Stockholm, 1972; recipient Sr. Fulbright Rsch. award Aristotelian U., Thessaloniki, Greece, 1989, Sci. Exchange award to Romania Nat. Acad. Sci., 1990. Mem. Am. Chem. Soc. (publicity chmn. Cellulose Paper and Textile divsn. 1980-82, student coord. 1992-95), Internat. Acad. Wood Sci. Office: Dept Forest Ecology Mgmt U Wis Madison WI 53706

YOUNG, REBECCA MARY CONRAD, state legislator; b. Clairton, Pa., Feb. 28, 1934; d. Walter Emerson and Harriet Averill (Colcord) Conrad; m. Merwin Crawford Young, Aug. 17, 1957; children: Eve, Louise, Estelle, Emily. BA, U. Mich., 1955; MA in Teaching, Harvard U., 1963; JD, U. Wis., 1983. Bar: Wis. 1983. Commr. State Hwy. Commn., Madison, Wis., 1974-76; dep. sec. Wis. Dept. of Adminstrn., 1976-77; assoc. Wadsack, Julian & Lawton, 1983-84; elected rep. Wis. State Assembly, 1985-99. Translator: Katanga Secession, 1966. Supr. Dane County Bd., Madison, 1970-74; mem. Madison Sch. Bd., 1979-85. Recipient Wis. NOW Feminist of Yr. award, 1996, Eunice Zoghlin Edgar Lifetime Achievement award ACLU, 1997, Outstanding Legislator award Wis. Counties Assn., 1998, Voice for Choice award Planned Parenthood Wis., 1998, Luan Gilbert award for outstanding activities in domestic violence intervention and prevention Domestic Violence Intervention Svc., 1998. Mem. LWV. Democrat. Avocations: board games, hiking. Home: 639 Crandall St Madison WI 53711-1836 Office: State Legislature-Assembly PO Box 8953 Madison WI 53708-8953

YOUNG, RICHARD D. state legislator; b. Dec. 2, 1942; m. Elaine Young; 5 children. BA, Vincennes U. Mem. Ind. Senate from 47th dist., 1988—; mem. agr., small bus., edn., fin. and natural resource coms.; minority leader, 1996—. Farmer. Mem. Farm Bur., Crawford County C. of C., Lions.' Democrat. Home: RR 1 Box 106-c Milltown IN 47145-9801 Office: Ind Senate State Capitol 200 W Washington St Indianapolis IN 46204-2728*

YOUNG, ROBERT P., JR. state supreme court justice; Bachelor's degree cum laude, Harvard Coll., 1974; JD, Harvard U., 1977. With Dickinson, Wright, Moon, Van Dusen & Freeman, 1977-1992; v.p., corp. sec., gen. counsel AAA Mich., 1992; appt. Mich. Ct. Appeals 1st Dist., 1995; appt. justice Mich. Supreme Ct., 1998, elected justice, 2000. Mem. Mich. Civil Svc. Commn.; bd. trustees Cen. Mich. U. Office: PO Box 30052 Lansing MI 48909-7552

YOUNG, RONALD FARIS, commodity trader; b. Schenectady, Dec. 17, 1939; s. James Vernon and Dorothy (Girod) Y.; m. Anne Randolph Kendig, Feb. 23, 1963; children: Margaret Randolph Reynolds, Anne Corbin. B.A., U. Va., 1962; M.B.A., Harvard U., 1966. Grain trader Continental Grain Co., 1966-70; pres. Conti-Commodities, Chgo., 1970; v.p. commodity sales DuPont, Glore Forgan, 1971-72; self-employed commodity trader Chgo. Bd. Trade, 1972-78; ind. trader Va. Trading Co., 1978-90, pres., 1978-84, dep. chmn., 1984-89; pres. Randolph Ptnrs., Ltd., 1983-91. Chmn. bd. Chgo. Bd. Trade, 1978, dir., 1975-77, 80 Bd. dirs. Princeton Fund, 1981-82, Lake Forest Hosp., 1981-84, Lake Forest Country Day Sch., 1981-86. Served with USMCR, 1959-65. Mem. Racquet Club (bd. dirs. 1989-97), Onwentsia Club (Lake Forest, Ill., bd. dirs. 1981-90, pres. 1991-93), Everglades Cub (Palm Beach, Fla.), Bath and Tennis Club (Palm Beach). Republican. Episcopalian. Club: 531 N Mayflower Rd Lake Forest IL 60045

YOUNG, THOMAS LEE, lawyer; b. Los Angeles, Feb. 21, 1944; s. J. Donald and Nancy M. Young; m. Kathleen Grace Jacob, Sept. 10, 1967; children: Barbara, Deborah, Amy. Student Marquette U., 1963; BA, St. John's Coll., 1966; JD, Notre Dame U., 1972; postgrad. Harvard U., 1984-85. Bar: Ohio, 1972. Assoc. Fuller, Henry, Hodge & Snyder, Toledo, 1972-75; assoc. counsel Scott Paper Co., Phila., 1975-76; asst. gen counsel Owens-Ill., Inc., Toledo, 1976— ; bd. dirs. Prudent Supply, Inc., Mpls., Health Group, Inc., Nashville, Cajas Corrugadas de Mex., Mexico City. 1st lt. U.S. Army, 1966-69, Vietnam. Mem. ABA, Ohio State Bar Assn., Toledo Bar Assn. Roman Catholic. Avocations: tennis. Office: Owens Illinois Inc One SeaGate Toledo OH 43666

YOUNG, VERNON LEWIS, lawyer; b. Seaman, Ohio, Oct. 13, 1919; s. Ezra S. and Anna (Bloom) Y.; m. Eileen Humble, Sept. 20, 1941; children: Robert, Loretta, Bettie Jo, Jon W., Denise L. Student, Alfred Holbrook Coll., 1938-39; JD, Ohio No. U., 1942. Bar: Ohio 1942. Employee War Dept., 1942; sole practice West Union, Ohio, 1942-50, 78-81; ptnr. Young & Young, 1959-78, Young & Caldwell, 1978-81, 95—, Young-Caldwell & BUBP, West Union, 1981-95. Spl. counsel Office of Atty. Gen., State of Ohio, West Union, solicitor Cities of Jamestown, Seaman, Winchester, Manchester, Ohio; pros. atty. Adams County, Ohio, 1952-56, acting county judge, 1968-79. Mayor City of Seaman, 1944-46; mem. Adams County Health Bd., West Union, 1968-75; chmn. membership com. Eastern Shore Inst. Lifelong Learning, Fairhope, Ala., 1983-84; mem. Rep. Presdl. Task Force, 1980-94. Mem. Ohio State Bar Assn., Adams County Bar Assn. (former pre.), Masons (32 degree), Lions (pres. 1950-51, dist. gov. 1951-52), Sigma Delta Kappa (chancellor 1940). Avocations: fishing, hunting, gardening. Home: 10 Hickory Dr Seaman OH 45679-9762 Office: 225 N Cross St West Union OH 45693-1266

YOUNG, WALTER R., JR. manufacturing company executive; Former pres. Wheelabrator Corp., Atlanta; chmn., pres., CEO Champion Enterprises, Auburn Hills, Mich., 1990—. Office: Champion Enterprises 2701 Cambridge Ct Ste 300 Auburn Hills MI 48326

YOUNGBERG, CHARLOTTE ANNE, education specialist, clergywoman; b. Hampton, Iowa, May 8, 1937; d. Sebo and Marion Bradford (Boutin-Clock) Reysack; m. Paul Gordon Neal, Mar. 29, 1969 (div. Jan. 1984); children: Rachel Elizabeth, Kory Bradford; m. Lyle Edwin Youngberg, June 30, 1990; stepchildren: Lynn Eugene, Lori Ann. BA, U. No. Iowa, 1958; MEd, DePaul U., 1966; postgrad., No. Ill. U.; DD in Christian Counseling, Christian Bible Coll. and Sem., Independence, Mo., 2000. Cert. K-14 tchr. and supr. in guidance, counseling, elem. supervising, K-9 elem. tchr., spl. K-12 learning disabilities. Elem. tchr. Des Moines Ind. Sch.

Dist., 1958-59, Glenview (Ill.) Pub. Schs., 1959-61; elem. tchr., psychol. ednl. diagnostician Schaumburg Dist. Schs., Hoffman Estates, Ill., 1961-69; supr. learning disabilities and behavior disorders Springfield (Ill.) Pub. Schs., 1969-73; psycho-ednl. diagnostician Barrington (Ill.) Sch. Dist. 220, 1973-77; ednl. strategist Area Edn. Agy. 7, Cedar Falls, Iowa, 1978-90; tchr. spl. edn., testing evaluator Verona (Mo.) Pub. Schs., 1990—, dir. spl. Edn., 1992-95. Ednl. cons. Spl. Edn. Dist. Lake County, Gurnee, Ill., summer 1968. Mem. Mo. Tchrs. Assn., Phi Delta Kappa. Home: PO Box 147 Verona MO 65769-0147 Office: Verona R7 Sch Dist 101 E Ella St Verona MO 65769-5213

YOUNGBLOOD, RICHARD NEIL, columnist; b. Minot, N.D., May 9, 1936; s. Edward Anthony and Helen (Condo) Y.; m. Adele Henley, May 4, 1957 (div. 1983); children: Kent Jay, Ruth Adele, Beth Alise; m. Mary Dinneen, July 14, 1984. BA, U. N.D., 1958. Reporter Grand Forks (N.D.) Herald, 1955-63, Mpls. Star Tribune, 1963-67, asst. city editor, 1967-69, bus./fin. editor, 1969-84, columnist, 1984-98, freelance writer, 98—. Recipient Excellence award in bus. and fin. journalism John Handcock Mut. Life, 1974; named Newspaper Farm Editor of Yr. Newspaper Farm Editors of Am., 1965. Avocations: reading, crossword puzzles, boating. Office: Mpls Star Tribune 425 Portland Ave Minneapolis MN 55488-1511

YOUNGE, WYVETTER HOOVER, state legislator; b. St. Louis, Aug. 23, 1930; s. Ernest Jack and Annie (Jordan) H.; m. Richard G. Younge, 1958; children: Ruth F., Torque E., Margrett H. BS, Hampton Inst., 1951; JD, St. Louis U., 1955; LLM, Wash. U., 1972. Ill. state rep. Dist. 114, 1975—; mem. appropriation II com., chmn. urban redevel. com. Ill. Ho. Reps., labor and com., vice chmn. energy, environ. and natural resources com., aging, edn. appropriations, human svc., reappointment coms., chmn. higher edn. com.; asst. circuit atty. City of St. Louis; pvt. practice, 1955—; exec. dir. Neighborhood Ctrs. War on Poverty, 1965-68; East St. Louis adv. and devel. nonprofit housing corp., 1968—. Author: The Implementation of Old Man River, 1972. Recipient Humanity award Project Upgrade, 1969, Citizen of Yr. award Monitor Newspaper, Cert. of Recognition Black Heritage Com. Mem. Alpha Kappa Alpha. Democrat. Address: 1617 N 46th St East Saint Louis IL 62204-1919 also: Ill Ho of Reps State Capitol Springfield IL 62706-0001

YOUNGER, JUDITH TESS, lawyer, educator; b. N.Y.C., Dec. 20, 1933; d. Sidney and Kate (Greenbaum) Weintraub; m. Irving Younger, Jan. 21, 1955; children: Rebecca, Abigail M. B.S., Cornell U., 1954; J.D., NYU, 1958; LL.D. (hon.), Hofstra U., 1974. Bar: N.Y. 1958, U.S. Supreme Ct 1962, D.C. 1983, Minn. 1985. Law clk. to judge U.S. Dist. Ct., 1958-60; asso. firm Chadbourne, Parke, Whiteside & Wolff, N.Y.C., 1960-62; mem. firm Younger and Younger, and (successors), 1962-67; adj. asst. prof. N.Y. U. Sch. Law, 1967-69; asst. atty. gen. State of N.Y., 1969-70; assoc. prof. Hofstra U. Sch. Law, 1970-72, prof., assoc. dean, 1972-74; dean, prof. Syracuse Coll. Law, 1974-75; dep. dean, prof. law Cornell Law Sch., 1975-78, prof. law, 1975-85; vis. prof. U. Minn. Law Sch., Mpls., 1984-85, prof., 1985-91, Joseph E. Wargo Anoka County Bar Assn. prof. family law, 1991—. Of counsel Popham, Haik, Schnobrich & Kaufman, Ltd., Mpls., 1989-95; cons. NOW, 1972-74, Suffolk County for Revision of Its Real Property Tax Act, 1972-73; mem. N.Y. Gov.'s Panel To Screen Candidates of Ct. of Claims Judges, 1973-74; mem. Minn. Lawyers' Profl. Responsibility Bd., 1991-93. Contbr. articles to profl. jours. Trustee Cornell U., 1973-78 Mem.: AAUP (v.p. Cornell U. chpt. 1978—79), ABA (council legal edn. 1975—79), Minn. Bar Assn., Assn. of Bar of City of N.Y., Am. Law Inst. (adv. restatement property 1982—84). Home: 3520 W Calhoun Pkwy Minneapolis MN 55416-4657 Office: U Minn Law Sch Minneapolis MN 55455 E-mail: young001@umn.edu.

YOUNGMAN, OWEN RALPH, newspaper executive; b. Chgo., Apr. 24, 1953; s. Ralph Elmer and Charlotte Earldine (Ottoson) Y.; m. Linda Ann Erlandson, Aug. 24, 1975. Sportswriter Ashtabula (Ohio) Star-Beacon, 1969-71; office clk. Chgo. Tribune, 1971-73, transcriber, 1973-75, copy editor, slotman, 1976-79, copy chief, news editor, 1979-83, dep. sports editor, 1984-86, assoc. met. editor, 1986-88, assoc. features editor, 1988-90, dep. fin. editor, 1990-91, assoc. mng. editor, 1991-93, features editor, 1993-95, mng. editor, features, 1995, dir. interactive media, 1996-99, dir. planning and devel., 1999, v.p. devel., 2000—. Bd. dirs. Swedish Covenant Hosp., Legacy.com Mem. Newspaper Assn. Am. New Media Fedn. (bd. dirs.), Am. Soc. Newspaper Editors, Presidents Club of North Park U., Arts Club of Chgo. Avocation: vocal and instrumental music. Home: 40 Kenmore Ave Deerfield IL 60015-4750 Office: Chicago Tribune 435 N Michigan Ave Chicago IL 60611-4066 E-mail: oyoungman@tribune.com.

YOUNGQUIST, WAYNE, reporter; PhB, U. Wis., Milw.; M Sociology, Rutgers U. Polit. analyst, now sr. polit. analyst WISN, Milw., 1978—. Instr. sociology U. Wis., Milw., Ithaca Coll., No. Ill. U., Marquette U., 1974—78, U. Wis., Whitewater; host seminars TV and Radio News Dirs. Found. Recipient Rockefeller Found. fellow, Princeton U.; fellow, NIMH. Office: WISN PO Box 402 Milwaukee WI 53201-0402

YOURZAK, ROBERT JOSEPH, management consultant, engineer, educator; b. Mpls., Aug. 27, 1947; s. Ruth Phyllis Sorenson. BCE, U. Minn., 1969; MSCE, U. Wash., 1971, MBA, 1975. Registered profl. engr., Wash., Minn. Surveyor N.C. Hoium & Assocs., Mpls., 1965-68, Lot Surveys Co., Mpls., 1968-69; site layout engr. Sheehy Constrn. Co., St. Paul, 1968; structural engring. aide Dunham Assocs., Mpls., 1969; aircraft and aerospace structural engr., program rep. Boeing Co., Seattle, 1969-75; engr., estimator Howard S. Wright Constrn. Co., 1976-77; dir. project devel. and adminstrn. DeLeuw Cather & Co., 1977-78; sr. mgmt. cons. Alexander Grant & Co., Mpls., 1978-79; mgr. project sys. dept., project mgr. Henningson, Durham & Richardson, 1979-80; dir. project mgmt., regional offices Ellerbe Assocs., Inc., 1980-81; pres. Robert Yourzak & Assocs., Inc., 1982—. Lectr. engring. mgmt. U. Wash., 1977-78; lectr., adj. asst. prof. dept. civil and mineral engring. and mech./indsl. engring. Ctr. for Devel. of Tech. Leadership, Inst. Tech.; mem. strategic mgmt. and orgn. dept., mgmt. scis. dept. Sch. Mgmt., U. Minn., 1979-90, 96—; bd. adv. inst. tech., 1989-93; founding mem., membership com., mem. U. of Minn. com. Minn. High Tech. Coun., 1983-95; instr. principles mgmt. dept. bus. and pub. policy Concordia U., 1997, instr. contsrn. mgmt. Inver Hills C.C., 1998—; adj. instr. ops. mgmt. Hamline U., St. Paul, 2001; spkr. in field. Author: Project Management and Motivating and Managing the Project Team, 1984, (with others) Field Guide to Project Management, 1998. Chmn. regional art group experience Seattle Art Mus., 1975-78; mem. Pacific N.W. Arts Coun., 1977-78, ex-officio adviser Mus. Week, 1976; bd. dirs. Friends of the Rep. Seattle Repertory Theatre, 1973-77; mem. Symphonics Seattle Symphony Orch., 1975-78. Named Outstanding Young Man of Am., U.S. Jaycees, 1978; scholar Boeing Co., 1967-68, Sheehy Constrn. Co., summer 1967. Fellow ASCE (chmn. continuing edn. subcom. Seattle chpt. 1976-79, chmn. program com. 1978, mem. transp. and urban planning tech. group 1978, Edmund Friedman Young Engr. award 1979, chmn. continuing edn. subcom. 1979-80, chmn. energy com. Minn. chpt. 1980-81, bd. dirs. 1981-89, sec. 1981-83, v.p. profl. svcs. 1983-84, v.p. info. svcs. 1984-85, pres. 1986-87, past pres. 1987-89, spkr.), P Project Mgmt. Inst. (cert. project mgmt. prof., spkr., founding pres. 1985, chmn., adv. com. 1987-89, bd. dirs. 1984-86, program com. chmn. and organizing com. mem. Minn. chpt. 1984, spkr., project mgr. internat. mktg. program 1985-86, chmn. internat. mktg. standing com. 1986, long range and strategic planning com. 1988-93, chmn. 1992, v.p. pub. rels. 1987-88, ex-officio dir. 1989, 92, internat. pres. 1990, chmn. bd. 1991, ex-officio chmn. 1992, internat. bd. dirs., chmn. nominating com. 1992, PMI fellow 1995, chmn. exec. dir. selection com. 1996-97, Robert J. Yourzak Scholarship Award established Minn. chpt. 1998—), Inst. Indsl. Engrs. (pres. Twin Cities chpt. 1985-86, chmn. program com. 1983-84, bd. dirs. 1985-88, awards com., chmn. 1984-89, fellow 1999, spkr.); mem. ASTD (So. Minn. chpt.), Am. Cons. Engrs. Coun. (peer reviewer 1986-89), Am. Arbitration Assn. (mem. Mpls. panel of constrn. arbitrators), Minn. Surveyors and Engrs. Soc., Cons. Engrs. Coun. Minn. (chmn. pub. rels. com. 1983-85, vice chmn. 1988, chmn. 1989, program com. chmn. Midwest engrs. conf. and exposition 1985-90, spkr., Honor award 1992), Inst. Mgmt. Cons. (cert. mgmt. cons.), Mpls. Soc. Fine Arts, Internat. Facility Mgmt. Assn., Am. Soc. Engring. Edn., Rainer Club (co-chmn. Oktoberfest), Sierra club, Chowder Soc., Mountaineers, North Star Ski Touring, Chi Epsilon (life). Office: 7320 Gallagher Dr Ste 325 Minneapolis MN 55435-4510

YOVICH, DANIEL JOHN, educator; b. Chgo., Mar. 5, 1930; s. Milan D. and Sophie (Dorociak) Y.; m. Anita Barbara Moreland, Feb. 7, 1959; children: Daniel, Amy, David, Julie Ann. Ph.B., DePaul U., 1952; M.A., Governors State U., 1975, M.S., 1976. Cert. reality therapist, cert. profl. mgr., PMA instr. Formulator Nat. Lead Co., 1950-52, 56-59; researcher Montgomery Ward, Chgo., 1959-62; tech. dir. Riley Bros., Inc., Burlington, Iowa, 1962-66, Mortell Co., Kankakee, Ill., 1966-70; exec. dir. Dan Yovich Assos., 1970-79; asst. prof. Purdue U., Hammond, Ind., 1979-84, assoc. prof., 1984-90, prof., 1990-2000, prof. emeritus, 2000—. Instr. Army Security Agy. Sch., 1954-56; instr. Napoleon Hill Acad., 1965-66; cons. Learning House, 1964—; instr. Kankakee C. C. Continuing Edn., 1976; assoc. Hill, Zediker & Assocs. Psychologists, Kankakee, 1975-79; mem adv. bd. Nat. Congress of Inventor Orgns., 1984; vis. prof. Grand Valley State U., 2000—, Northwood U., 2001—. Author: Applied Creativity; prdr., moderator: (program) Careers Unlimited, Sta. WCIU-TV, Chgo., 1967; contbr. articles to profl. jours.; patentee game Krypto, coating Sanitane. Mem. community adv. council Governors State U., 1978; mem. Hammond (Ind.) Hist. Soc. Served to 1st lt. AUS, 1952-56. Recipient Outstanding Citizen Award News Pub. Co. Am., 1971, Outstanding Tchr. award Purdue U., 1980, 82, 83, Faculty Service award Nat. U. Continuing Edn. Assn., 1984, Disting. Service award Purdue U.-Calumet Alumni Assn., 1988, Arthur Young award Venture Mag., 1988, Entrepreneurial Edn. award Inc. Mag., 1990, Indiana Spirit of Innovation award, 1996. Mem. World Future Soc., Nat. Mgmt. Assn., Am. Soc. Tng. and Devel., Am. Soc. Profl. Supervision (exec. sec. 1986), Inventors and Entrepreneurs Soc. Am. (founder, exec. dir. 1984), Global Intuition Network, Internat. Creativity Network, Infantry Officer Cand. Sch. Alumni Assn. (life), Napoleon Hill Found., Inst. Reality Therapy, Inst. Contemporary Living, Soc. Am. Inventors (life), Am. Legion, K.C., Vets. of the Battle of the Bulge (historian). Home: 3527 Whispering Brook Dr SE Kentwood MI 49508-3733 E-mail: danyovich@prodigy.net.

YSSELDYKE, JAMES EDWARD, psychology educator, dean; b. Grand Rapids, Mich., Jan. 1, 1944; 2 children. Student in psychology, Calvin Coll., 1962-65; BA in Psychology, Biology, Western Mich. U., 1966; MA in Sch. Psychology, U. Ill., 1968, PhD, 1971. Lic. cons. psychologist, Minn. Tchr. spl. edn. Kent County Juvenile Ct. Ctr., Grand Rapids, 1966-67; rsch. asst. U. Ill. Inst. Rsch. on Exceptional Children, 1969-70, tchg. asst. dept. ednl. psychology, 1970; sch. psychology intern Oakland County Schs., Pontiac, Mich., 1970-71; asst. prof. sch. psychology Pa. State U., 1971-75, assoc. prof., 1975, U. Minn., Mpls., 1975-79, prof., 1979-91, dir. Inst. Rsch. on Learning Disabilities, 1977-83, dir. Nat. Sch. Psychology Insvc. Tng. Network, 1977-83, dir. sch. psychology program, 1987-93, dir. Nat. Ctr. on Ednl. Outcomes, 1991-99, assoc. dean for rsch., 2000—. Emma Birkmaier endowed prof. U. Minn., 1998-2000; advisor, cons. and researcher in field. Author: (with J. Salvia) Assessment in Special and Remedial Education, 1985, 8th edit., 2001, (with B. Algozzine and M. Thurlow) Critical Issues in Special and Remedial Education, 1992, 3d edit., 2000, Strategies and Tactics for Effective Instruction, 1997, (with S.L. Christenson) Functional Assessment of Academic Behavior, 1993; editor: Exceptional Children, 1984-90; assoc. editor: The School Psychologist, 1972-75, mem. editorial bd., cons. editor numerous jours.; contbr. chpts. to books and articles to jours. Recipient Disting. Tchg. award U. Minn., 1988, Disting. Alumni award U. Ill. Coll. Edn., 1998; fellow NIMH, 1967-69; grantee in field. Fellow APA (Lightner Witmer award 1973); mem. ASCD, APA, NASP, Am. Ednl. Rsch. Assn., Coun. for Exceptional Children (Rsch. award 1995), Coun. for Ednl. Diagnostic Svcs. Office: Coll of Edn and Human Devel 104 Burton Hall 178 Pillsbury Dr SE Minneapolis MN 55455-0296 E-mail: jim@umn.edu.

YU, ANTHONY C. religion and literature educator; b. Hong Kong, Oct. 6, 1938; came to U.S., 1956, naturalized, 1976; s. P.C. and Norma (Au) Y.; m. Priscilla Tang, Sept. 18, 1963; 1 son, Christopher Dietrich. BA, Houghton Coll., 1960; STB, Fuller Theol. Sem., 1963; PhD, U. Chgo., 1969, DLitt, 1996. Instr. U. Ill., Chgo., 1967-68; asst. prof. U. Chgo., 1968-74, assoc. prof., 1974-78, prof., 1978-88, Carl Darling Buck disting. svc. prof. humanities Div. Sch., Dept. East Asian Langs., Comparative Lit. and East Asian Langs. & Civilizations, English, 1988—. Assoc. vis. prof. Ind. U., Bloomington, 1975; Whitney J. Oates short-term vis. fellow Princeton U., 1986; disting. vis. prof. Faculty of Arts, U. Alta., Can., 1992; mem. joint com. on study Chinese civilization Am. Coun. Learned Socs., 1980-86, bd. dirs., 1986-94; regional chmn. Mellon Fellowship in Humanities, 1982-92; bd. dirs. Ill. Humanities Coun., 1995—; vis. prof. dept. religion Chinese U. Hong Kong, 1997. Asst. editor Jour. Asian Studies, 1975-78; co-editor Jour. Religion, 1980—; author, editor: Parnassus Revisited, 1973; editor, translator: The Journey to the West, 4 vols., 1977-83, Essays on The Journey to the West and Other Studies (in Chinese), 1989; co-editor (with Mary Gerhart) Morphologies of Faith: Essays on Religion and Culture in Honor of Nathan A. Scott, Jr., 1990, Rereading the Stone: Desire and the Making of Fiction in Dream of the Red Chamber, 1997. Recipient Gordon J. Laing prize, 1983; Danforth fellow, 1960-67; Guggenheim fellow, 1976-77; NEH translation grantee, 1977-82; Am. Coun. Learned Socs. sr. fellow, 1986-87; Masterworks Study grant NEH Seminar for Pub. Sch. Tchrs., 1992; elected academician Academia Sinica, 1998; Phi Beta Kappa vis. scholar 2001-02. Fellow Am. Acad. Arts and Scis.; mem. MLA (exec. coun. 1998—2001), Assn. for Asian Studies, Am. Acad. Religion (bd. dirs. 1995-97), Am. Comparative Lit. Assn., Milton Soc. Am., Arts Club. Home: 950 N Clark St Unit G Chicago IL 60610-8702 Office: U Chicago 1025 E 58th St Chicago IL 60637-1509 E-mail: acyu@midway.uchicago.edu.

YU, GEORGE TZUCHIAO, political science educator; b. London, May 16, 1931; s. Wangteh and Ying (Ho) Y.; m. Priscilla Chang, Aug. 11, 1957; children: Anthony, Phillip. A.B., U. Calif., Berkeley, 1954, M.A., 1957, Ph.D., 1961. Asst. prof. polit. sci. U. N.C., Chapel Hill, 1961-65; assoc. prof. polit. sci. U. Ill., Urbana, 1965-70, prof., 1970—, head dept., 1987-92, dir. Ctr. for East Asian and Pacific Studies, 1992—, dir. grad. studies, 1981-85, chair Asian Am. studies com., 1997—. Vis. sr. lectr. polit. sci. Univ. Coll., Nairobi, 1968. Author: The Chinese Anarchist Movement, 1961, 65, Party Politics in Republican China, 1966, China and Tanzania, 1970, China's African Policy, 1975, Intra-Asian International Relations, 1977, Modern China and Its Revolutionary Process, 1985, American Studies in China, 1993, China in Transition, 1994, Asia's New World Order, 1997, Mongolia and Northeast Asia, 1999. Grantee, Social Sci. Rsch. Coun., 1967—68, 1970—71, NEH, 1978—81, 1984—86, Earhart Found., 1976—77, 1981—83, 1988, Ford Found., 1985—87, 1989, 1992, Freeman Found., 1996, 1997, 1999, 2001. Mem. Asian Studies. Office: 702 S Wright St Urbana IL 61801-3631 E-mail: g-yu@uiuc.edu.

YU, HYUK, chemist, educator; b. Kapsan, Korea, Jan. 20, 1933; s. Namjik and Keedong (Shin) Y.; m. Gail Emmens, Jan. 20, 1964; children: Jeffrey, Steven, Douglas. BSChemE, Seoul Nat. U., 1955; MS in Organic Chemistry, U. So. Calif., 1958; PhD in Phys. Chemistry, Princeton U., 1962. Rsch. assoc. Dartmouth Coll., Hanover, N.H., 1962-63; rsch. chemist Nat. Inst. Sci. and Tech., Washington, 1963-67; asst. prof. U. Wis., Madison, 1967-69, assoc. prof., 1969-78, prof. chemistry, 1978—, Evan P. Helfaer chair chemistry, 1991—, now Eastman-Kodak prof. Cons. polymer sci. and standards div. Nat. Inst. Standards and Tech., Gaithersburg, Md., 1967—, Eastman Kodak Co., 1969—, Japan Synthetic Rubber Co., Tsukuba, 1991-95; Fulbright-Hays lectr. Inha U., Inchon, Korea,1972; chmn. Gordon Rsch. Conf. Polymer Physics, 1986, 93. Contbr. articles to profl. jours. John Simon Guggenheim Found. fellow, 1984; recipient Alexander von Humboldt award Humboldt Found., 1992. Fellow Am. Phys. Soc. (High-Polymer Physics prize, 1994); mem. Am. Chem. Soc. (exec. com. polymer chemistry divsn., editorial adv. bd. 1988-91, Ho-Am Basic Sci. prize, 1997, Colloid and Surface Chemistry Langmuir Lectr. award 1999), N.Y. Acad. Scis., Biophys. Soc., Materials Rsch. Soc., Korean Chem. Soc. (life), Polymer Soc. Korea (life), Sigma Xi (chpt. pres. 1987-88). Office: Univ Wis 1101 University Ave Madison WI 53706-1322 E-mail: Yu@chem.Wisc.edu.

YU, LINDA, newswoman, television anchorwoman; b. Xian, China, Dec. 1, 1946; BA in Journalism, U. So. Calif., 1968. With Sta. KTLA-TV, Los Angeles, Sta. KABC-TV, Los Angeles; news anchor, reporter Sta. KATU-TV, Portland, Oreg.; gen. assignment reporter Sta. KGO-TV, San Francisco; with Sta. WMAQ-TV, Chgo., 1979-84, gen. assignment reporter, weekend anchor, 1979-80, co-anchor Monday-Friday edit. NEWSCENTERS, 4:30 PM, 1980-81, co-anchor NEWSCENTER5, 10:00 PM, 1981-84; co-anchor Eyewitness News, WLS-TV, Chgo., 1984—; spl.: Linda Yu in China, 1980; anchor WLS-TV, Chgo., 1984—. Recipient Chgo. Emmy award, 1981, 82, 87. Office: Sta WLS-TV 190 N State St Chicago IL 60601-3302*

YUDOF, MARK GEORGE, law educator, university president; b. Phila., Oct. 30, 1944; s. Jack and Eleanor (Parris) Y.; m. Judith Lynn Gomel, July 11, 1965; children: Seth Adam, Samara Lisa BA, U. Pa., 1965, LLB, 1968. Bar: Pa. 1970, U.S. Supreme Ct. 1974, U.S. Dist. Ct. (we. dist.) Tex. 1975, U.S. Ct. Appeals (5th cir.) 1976, Tex. 1980. Law clk. to judge U.S. Ct. Appeals (5th cir.), 1968-69; assoc. gen. counsel to ABA study FTC, 1969; rsch. assoc. Harvard Ctr. Law and Edn., 1969-70, sr. staff atty., 1970-71; lectr. Harvard Grad. Sch. Edn., 1970-71; asst. prof. law U. Tex., Austin, 1971-74, prof., 1974—, assoc. dean, 1979-84, James A. Elkins Cent. chmn. in law, 1983-97, dean, 1984-94, exec. v.p., provost, 1994-97, John Jeffers rsch. chair in law, 1991-94; pres. U. Minn., 1997—. Of counsel Pennzoil vs. Texaco, 1987. Author: When Government Speaks, 1983 (Scribes Book award 1983, cert. merit ABA 1983), (with others) Educational Policy and the Law, 1992, (with others) Gender Justice, 1986. Mem. Tex. Gov.'s Task Force on Sch. Fin., 1989-90, Tex. Gov.'s Select Com. on Edn., 1988; bd. dirs. Freedom to Read Found., 1989-91; mem. Austin Cable Commn., 1981-84, chmn., 1982; mem. nat. panel on sch. desegregation rsch. Ford Found., 1977-80; mem. state exec. com. Univ. Interscholastic League, 1983-86; bd. dirs. Jewish Children's Regional Svc., 1980-86; mem. Gov.'s Select Task Force on Pub. Edn., 1995; mem. Telecomms. Infrastructure Fund Bd., State of Tex., 1995-97. Recipient Teaching Excellence award, 1975, Most Meritorious Book award Scribes, 1983, Humanitarian award Austin region NCCJ, 1988, Antidefamation League Jurisprudence award, 1991; hon. fellow Queen Mary and Westfield Coll., U. London. Fellow Tex. Bar Found., Am. Bar Found.; mem. Am. Law Inst., Tex. Bar Assn., Assn. Am. Law Schs. (chmn. law and edn. sect. 1983-84, exec. com. 1988-90), Mpls. Club, Minn. Club, Town & Country Club, Minnikahda Club. Avocation: collecting antique maps. Office: U Minn 202 Morrill Hall 100 Church St SE Minneapolis MN 55455-0110

YUILL, THOMAS MACKAY, academic administrator, microbiology educator; b. Berkeley, Calif., June 14, 1937; s. Joseph Stuart and Louise (Dunlop) Y.; m. Ann Warnes, Aug. 24, 1960; children: Eileen, Gwen. BS, Utah State U., 1959; MS, U. Wis., 1962, PhD, 1964. Lab. officer Walter Reed Army Inst. Rsch., Washington, 1964-66; med. biologist SEATO Med. Rsch. Lab., Bangkok, Thailand, 1966-68; asst. prof. U. Wis., Madison, 1968-72, assoc. prof., 1972-76, prof., 1976—, dept. chmn., 1979-82, assoc. dean, 1982-93, dir. Inst. Environ. Studies, 1993—. Cons. NIH, Bethesda, 1976-86; chmn. Viral Diseases Panel, U.S.-Japan Biomed. Scis. Program, 1979-86, Am. Com. Arbovirology, 1982—; bd. dirs. Cen. Tropical Agrl. Res. Teaching, Turrialba, Costa Rica, 1988-96. Contbr. chpts. to books, articles to profl. jours. Served to capt. U.S. Army, 1964-66. Recipient grants state and fed. govts., 1968—. Mem. Orgn. Tropical Studies (pres. 1979-85), Wildlife Disease Assn. (treas. 19880-85, pres. 1985-87, editl. bd. 1989—), Am. Soc. Tropical Medicine and Hygiene (editl. bd. 1984-96), Nat. Assn. State Univ. Land Grand Colls., EPA Task Force (copchair 1994—), Am. Soc. Virology, Wildlife Soc., Sigma Xi. Avocations: flying, cross-country skiing, music. Office: U Wis Inst Environ Studies 40 Science Hall 550 N Park St Madison WI 53706-1404

YUNE, HEUN YUNG, radiologist, educator; b. Seoul, Korea, Feb. 1, 1929; came to U.S., 1966; s. Sun Wook and Won Eun (Lee) Y.; m. Kay Kim, Apr. 12, 1956; children: Jeanny Kim, Helen Kay, Marc Eany. MD, Severance Med. Coll., Seoul, 1956. Lic. physician, Republic of Korea, Ind.; diplomate Am. Bd. Radiology, Korean Bd. Radiology. Intern Presbyn. Med. Ctr., Chonju, Korea, 1956-57, resident in surgery Korea, 1957-60; resident in radiology Vanderbilt U. Hosp., Nashville, 1960-63, instr. radiology, 1962-64; chief radiology Presbyn. Med. Ctr., Chonju, Korea, 1964-66; from asst. to assoc. prof. radiology Vanderbilt U. Med. Sch., Nashville, 1966-71; prof. radiology Ind. U. Sch. Medicine, Indpls., 1971-91, John A. Campbell prof. radiology, 1991-94, John A. Campbell prof. radiology emeritus, 1994—, dir. residency program, 1985-94, prof. otolaryngology, head and neck surgery, 1992-94, prof. otolaryngology, head and neck surgery emeritus, 1994—. Vis. prof. Yonsei U. Coll. Medicine, Seoul, 1985, Ajou U. Coll. of Medicine, Suwon, 1995-96; active staff Ind. U. Hosps., 1971—, Indpls. VA Hosp., 1971-99, 2000—, Wishard Meml. Hosp., 1971-99, 2000—. Editorial reviewer Am. Jour. Roentgenology, 1975—, Radiology, 1985—, Jour. Vascular and Interventional Radiology, 1989—; contbr. articles to profl. jours. Ordained elder Presbyn. Ch. Capt. Rep. of Korea Army, 1951-55. Decorated Bronze Star, U.S. Army, Wharang medal for meritorious mil. svc., Rep. of Korea Army. Fellow Am. Coll. Radiology; mem Assn. Univ. Radiologists, Radiol. Soc. N.Am., Am. Roentgen Ray Soc., Alpha Omega Alpha, others. Avocations: painting, photography, music appreciation, golf, travel. Home: 2887 Brook Vista Carmel IN 46032-4096 Office: Ind U Med Ctr 500 N University Blvd Indianapolis IN 46202-5149 E-mail: hyyune@pol.net.

YURCHUCK, ROGER ALEXANDER, lawyer; b. Amityville, N.Y., June 9, 1938; s. Alexander and Ella Marie (Munley) Y.; m. Sally Ward, Apr. 14, 1961 (div. 1972); children: Scott, Lauren; m. Susan Holland, June 1, 1985. AB cum laude, Northwestern U., 1959; LLB, Harvard U., 1962. Bar: Ohio 1962. Assoc. Vorys, Sater Seymour and Pease, Columbus, Ohio, 1962-68, ptnr., 1969-71, 73—, ptnr. Cin. office, 1984—; v.p., gen. counsel Fed. Home Loan Mortgage Corp., Washington, 1971-73. Vice chmn., bd. dirs. Securities Investors Protection Corp., Washington, 1982-88. Del. Rep. Nat. Conv., 1980, 84. Mem. ABA, Ohio Bar Assn., Phi Beta Kappa. Republican. Episcopalian. Clubs: Queen City (Cin.). Office: Vorys Sater Seymour and Pease 221 E 4th St Ste 2100 Cincinnati OH 45202-5133

YZERMAN, STEVE, professional hockey player; b. Cranbrook, B.C., Can., May 9, 1965; With Detroit Red Wings, 1983—. Recipient Lester B. Pearson award, 1988-89; named Sporting News NHL Rookie of Yr., NHL All-Rookie Team, 1983-84, 1988-93. Youngest person ever to play in NHL All-Star game, 1984; mem. Stanley Cup Champions, 1997. Office: Detroit Red Wings 600 Civic Center Dr Detroit MI 48226-4419

ZABEL, SHELDON ALTER, lawyer, law educator; b. Omaha, Apr. 25, 1941; s. Louis Julius and Anne (Rothenberg) Z.; m. Roberta Jean Butz, May 10, 1975; children: Andrew Louis, Douglas Patrick, Robert Stewart Warren. AB cum laude, Princeton U., 1963; JD cum laude, Northwestern U., 1966. Bar: Ill. 1966, U.S. Supreme Ct. 1976. Law clk. to presiding justice Ill. Supreme Ct., 1966-67; assoc. Schiff, Hardin & Waite, Chgo., 1967-73, ptnr., 1973—. Instr. environ. law Loyola U., Chgo. Bd. dirs. Chgo. Zool. Soc. Mem. ABA, Chgo. Bar Assn., Chgo. Coun. Lawyers, Order of Coif, Union League Club, Met. Club (Chgo.) Jewish. Avocations: skiing, squash. Office: Schiff Hardin & Waite 7200 Sears Tower 233 S Wacker Dr Ste 7200 Chicago IL 60606-6473 E-mail: szabel@schiffhardin.com.

ZACCONE, SUZANNE MARIA, sales executive; b. Chgo., Oct. 23, 1957; d. Dominic Robert and Lorretta F. (Urban) Zaccone. Grad. high sch., Downers Grove, Ill. Sales sec. Brookeridge Realty, Downers Grove, 1975-76; sales cons. Kafka Estates Inc., 1975-76; adminstrv. asst. Chem. Dist., Inc., Oak Brook, Ill., 1976-77; sales rep., mgr. Anographics Corp., Burr Ridge, 1977-85; pres., owner Graphic Solutions, Inc., 1985—. Curriculum adv. bd. mem. Sch. Dist. 99, 1997, 1998, 1999, 2000, 2001. Named Supplier of Yr. Through Preferred Supplied, Gen. Binding Corp., 1988—99; recipient Supplier Mem. award, Internat. Bottled Water Assn., 1987—88, Supplier award for excellence U.S., SBA, 1990, Eugene Singer award for best managed co. in small bus. category, Graphic Solutions, 1992, Top Performer Supplier award, Cutler Hammer Westinghouse Divsn., 1993, 1994, 1995, 1996, 1997, 1997, 1998, 1999, Blue Chip Enterprise Initiative award, 1994. Mem.: NAFE, World Label Assn. (1st pl. in World Championship 1994, 1995, 1996, 2002), Women in Packaging (exec. bd.), Inst. Packaging Profls., Women Entrepreneurs DuPage County (past pres.), Tag and Label Mfrs. Inst. (chmn. pub. rels. and mktg. com., bd. dirs., pres. 1998-2000) (Best Managed Co. award 1992, 1st place award in U.S. for Screen Printing 1994, 1995, 1996, 1997, 1999, 2000, 2001, Best Managed Co. award 2002, 2001). Avocation: Avocations: reading, sailing, cooking, needlepoint, scuba diving. Office: Graphic Solutions Inc 311 Shore Dr Hinsdale IL 60521-5859

ZACK, DANIEL GERARD, library director; b. Waukegan, Ill., Oct. 1, 1943; s. Raymond Gerard and Rosanna Marie (Atkinson) Z.; m. Mary Frances Anthony, Aug. 25, 1966; children: Jennifer Lee, Rebecca Jane. BA in Psychology, Western Ill. U., 1967; MS in Libr. Sci., U. Ill., 1975. Editor IBM Corp., Rochester, Minn., 1968-70, Memorex Corp., Mpls., 1970-74; rsch. assoc. Libr. Rsch. Ctr. U. Ill., Urbana, 1974-75; asst. dir. Portage County Pub. Libr., Stevens Point, Wis., 1976-78; dir. Burlington (Iowa) Pub. Libr., 1978-87, Gail Borden Pub. Libr., Elgin, Ill., 1987—. Trustee Batavia (Ill.) Pub. Libr., 1997—; founder Friends of Ill. Libr., 1990, bd. dirs. 1990-97. Mem. ALA, ACLU, Ill. Libr. Assn. (mgr. pub. libr. forum 1991-92, 2002--, exec. bd. dirs. 1992-95, pub. policy com. 1995-98), Pub. Libr. Assn. (intellectual freedom com. 1993-96), Kiwanis. Office: Gail Borden Pub Libr Dist 200 N Grove Ave Elgin IL 60120-5505

ZACKS, GORDON BENJAMIN, manufacturing company executive; b. Terre Haute, Ind., Mar. 11, 1933; s. Aaron and Florence Melton (Spurgeon) Z.; married; children: Catherine E., Kimberly A. B.A., Coll. Commerce, Ohio State U. With R.G. Barry Corp., Pickerington, Ohio, 1955—, exec. v.p., 1964-65, pres., 1965—, chmn. bd., 1979—, now also chief exec. officer, chmn., 1992—. Mem. Nat. Republican Senatorial Com.; hon. chmn. United Jewish Appeal; bd. dirs. numerous Jewish orgns., locally and nationally. Mem. Chief Exec. Officer Orgn., Am. Mgmt. Assn. Republican. Home: 140 N Parkview Ave Columbus OH 43209-1436 Office: R G Barry Corp 13405 Yarmouth Dr NW Pickerington OH 43147-8493 also: R G Barry Corp PO Box 129 Columbus OH 43216-0129

ZAFREN, HERBERT CECIL, librarian, educator; b. Balt., Aug. 25, 1925; s. Morris and Sadie Mildred (Edlavitch) Z.; m. Miriam Koenigsberg, Feb. 11, 1951; children: Ken, Edie. AB, Johns Hopkins U., 1944, postgrad., 1946-49; diploma, Balt. Hebrew Coll., 1944, LittD (hon.), 1969; AM in Libr. Sci, U. Mich., 1950. Jr. instr. Johns Hopkins U., Balt., 1947-49; bibliog. searcher Law Libr. U. Mich., Ann Arbor, 1949-50; libr. Hebrew Union Coll.-Jewish Inst. Religion, Cin., 1950-91, prof. Jewish bibliography, 1968-95, prof. emeritus, 1996—; exec. dir. Am. Jewish Periodical Ctr., 1956-80, co-dir., 1980-96, dir., 1996—; dir. librs. Cin., L.A., N.Y.C., Jerusalem, 1966-94; dir. emeritus librs. Hebrew Union Coll.-Jewish Inst. Religion, Cin., 1994—. Mem. exec. bd. Jewish Book Coun. Am., 1979-96. Editor Studies in Bibliography and Booklore, 1953—2002, Bibliographica Judaica, 1969—; compiler: A Gathering of Broadsides, 1967. With USN, 1944-46. Mem. ALA, Assn. Jewish Librs. (founder, nat. pres. 1965-66), World Coun. on Jewish Archives (v.p. 1977-81), Assn. Jewish Studies, Spl. Librs. Assn. (pres. Cin. chpt. 1953-54), Coun. Archives and Rsch. Librs. in Jewish Studies (pres. 1974-78, 89-91), Am. Hist. Assn., Israel Bibliophiles, World Union Jewish Studies, AAUP (chpt. pres. 1964-68), Grolier Club (N.Y.C.), Phi Beta Kappa, Beta Phi Mu. Office: Hebrew Union Coll-Jewish Inst Religion 3101 Clifton Ave Cincinnati OH 45220-2404

ZAGEL, JAMES BLOCK, federal judge; b. Chgo., Mar. 4, 1941; s. Samuel and Ethel (Samuels) Z.; m. Margaret Maxwell, May 27, 1979. BA, MA in Philosophy, U. Chgo., 1962; JD, Harvard U., 1965. Bar: Ill. 1965, U.S. Dist. Ct. (no. dist.) Ill. 1965, U.S. Supreme Ct. 1970, U.S. Ct. Appeals (7th cir.) 1972. Asst. atty. gen. criminal justice divsn. State of Ill., Springfield, 1970-77; chief prosecuting atty. Ill. Jud. Inquiry Bd., 1973-75; exec. dir. Ill. Law Enforcement Commn., 1977-79; dir. Ill. Dept. Revenue, 1979-80, Ill. Dept. State Police, Springfield, 1980-87; judge U.S. Dist. Ct. (no. dist.) Ill., Chgo., 1987—. Co-author: Criminal Law and Its Administration, 1989, Cases and Comments on Criminal Procedure, 1992. Named Outstanding Young Citizen, Chgo. Jaycees, 1977 ; recipient Disting. Service Merit award Assn. Commerce and Industry, 1983. Mem. Chgo. Bar Assn., Jud. Conf. of U.S. (codes of conduct com. 1987-92). Office: US Dist Ct 219 S Dearborn St Ste 2188 Chicago IL 60604-1801

ZAKAS, JOSEPH C. state legislator; b. Chgo., Nov. 4, 1950; s, Anthony and Ann (Phillips) Z.; m. Margaret Anne Kaiser, 1978; children: Mary Sarah, Katherine Grace, Stephen John. BA, U. Ill., 1972; JD, MBA, U. Notre Dame, 1980. Mem. Ind. Senate from 11th dist., 1982—; majority whip Ind. Senate; assoc. Thorne, Grodnik & Ransel, South Bend, Ind., 1980—. Chmn. admin. rules oversight commn., govt. affairs and transactions com., chmn. civil law divsn. judiciary com.; mem. natural resources com., ethics com. taxation divsn., finance and public policy com., govt. and regulatory affairs coms. Bd. dirs. REAL Serv, Michiana Arts & Sci. Coun.; active Blue Ribbon Commn. Against Domestic Violence. Mem. Am. Bar Assn., Ind. Bar. Assn., St. Joseph County Bar Assn., Knights of Columbus. Republican. Office: Ind Senate 200 W Washington St Indianapolis IN 46204 also: Ind State Senate State Capital Indianapolis IN 46204

ZAKIN, JACQUES LOUIS, chemical engineering educator; b. N.Y.C., Jan. 28, 1927; s. Mordecai and Ada Davies (Fishbein) Z.; m. Laura Pienkny, June 11, 1950; children: Richard Joseph, David Fredric, Barbara Ellen, Emily Anne, Susan Beth. BSChemE, Cornell U., 1949; MSChemE, Columbia U., 1950; DEng. Sci., NYU, 1959. Chem. engr. Flintkote Research Labs., Whippany, N.J., 1950-51; research technologist, research dept. Socony-Mobil, Bklyn., 1951-53, sr. research technologist, 1953-56, supervising technologist, 1959-62; assoc. prof. chem. engring. U. Mo., Rolla, 1962-65, prof., 1965-77, dir. minority engring. program, 1974-77, dir. women in engring. program, 1975-77; chmn. dept. chem. engring. Ohio State U., Columbus, 1977-94, Helen C. Kurtz prof. chem. engring., 1994-2000, Helen C. Kurtz prof. emeritus, 2000—. Chmn. sci. manpower and resources com. Coun. Chem. Rsch., 1984-86, governing bd., 1986-89; exec. com., 1988-89; adv. bd. State of Ohio Alternative Fuels, 1992-93; vis. prof. Technion, 1968-69, 94-95, Hebrew U., 1987; disting. vis. prof. Mex. Acad. Scis. and Mex.-USA Found. for Scis., 1999. Co-editor: Proc. Turbulence Symposium, 1969, 71, 73, 75, 77, 79, 81, 83; contbr. articles to profl. jours.; patentee in field. Bd. dirs. Rolla Community Concert Assn., 1966-77, 2d v.p., 1975-77; bd. dirs. Ozark Mental Health Assn., 1976-77; trustee Ohio State Hillel Found., 1981-84, treas., 1984-89, pres., 1989-92; trustee Congregation Beth Tikvah, 1983; bd. trustees Columbus Jewish Fedn., 1989-92; co-chmn. Academics and Scientists for Soviet Refuseniks. With USNR, 1945-46. Recipient Outstanding Rsch. award U. Mo., 1970, Josef Hlavka Meml. medal Czechoslovakian Acad. Sci., 1992, Clara M. and Peter L. Scott Faculty award, 1996, Rsch. award Japanese Govt., 2001; named Outstanding Educator of Yr., Ohio Soc. Profl. Engrs., 1994, Tech. Person of Yr., Columbus Tech. Coun., 1987; Am. Chem. Soc. Petroleum Rsch. Fund Internat. fellow, 1968-69, Socony-Mobil Employee Incentive fellow NYU, 1956-59, Sr. Fulbright Rsch. fellow Technion, 1994-95. Fellow Am. Inst. Chem. Engrs.; mem. Am. Chem. Soc., Soc. of Rheology, Am. Soc. Engring. Edn., Sigma Xi, Phi Lambda Upsilon, Phi Eta Sigma, Alpha Chi Sigma, Tau Beta Pi, Phi Kappa Phi. Jewish. Office: Ohio State U 140 W 19th Ave Columbus OH 43210-1110 E-mail: zakin.1@osu.edu.

ZALK, ROBERT H. lawyer; b. Albert Lea, Minn., Dec. 1, 1944; s. Donald B. and Juliette J. (Erickson) Z.; m. Ann Lee Anderson, June 21, 1969; children: Amy, Jenna. BA, Carleton Coll., 1966; JD, U. Minn., 1969. Bar: Minn. 1969, U.S. Dist. Ct. Minn. 1969. Assoc. Popham, Haik, Schnobrich, Kaufman & Doty, Mpls., 1969-72; atty. No. States Power Co., 1972-73, Wright, West & Diessner, Mpls., 1973-84, Fredrikson & Byron P.A., Mpls., 1984-94, Zalk & Assocs., Mpls., 1994-95; ptnr. Zalk & Eayrs, 1995-98, Zalk & Wood, Mpls., 1999, Zalk & Bryant, Mpls., 2000—. Fellow Am. Acad. Matrimonial Lawyers (pres. Minn. chpt. 2000-01), Minn. Bar Assn. (co-chmn. maintenance guideline com. 1991-94), Hennepin County Bar Assn. (co-chmn. family law sect. 1990-91). Office: Zalk & Bryant Sunset Ridge Bus Park 5861 Cedar Lake Rd Minneapolis MN 55416-1481 E-mail: rzalk@zalkbryant.com.

ZAMBIE, ALLAN JOHN, lawyer; b. Cleve., June 9, 1935; s. Anton J. and Martha (Adamski) Z.; m. Nancy Hall, Sept. 22, 1973. Student, Ohio U., 1953-54; B.A., Denison U., 1957; LL.B., Western Res. U. (now Case Western Res. U.), 1960. Bar: Ohio 1960. Asso. firm Hribar and Conway, Euclid, Ohio, 1961-63; staff atty. The Higbee Co., Cleve., 1963-67, asst. sec., 1967-69, sec., 1969-74, v.p.-sec., 1974-88, gen. counsel, 1978-88; v.p., sec., gen. counsel The Lamson & Sessions Co., Cleve., 1989-94; of counsel Conway, Marken, Wyner, Kurant & Kern Co., LPA, 1994-95; v.p.-sec. John P. Murphy Found., 1996-2000, exec. v.p., 2001—. V.p., sec. Kulas Found., 2001. Trustee Cleve. Music Sch. Settlement, pres. bd. trustees, 1980—82, treas., 1996—2001; trustee N.E. Ohio affiliate Am. Heart Assn., 1969—96. Served with U.S. Army, 1960—61. Mem. Ohio Bar Assn., Cleve. Bar Assn., Am. Soc. Corporate Secs. (nat. v.p. 1977—) Home: 2953 Litchfield Rd Cleveland OH 44120-1738 Office: 50 Pub Sq Ste 924 Cleveland OH 44113-2203

ZAMOYSKI, JAMES J. corporate lawyer; JD, LLM in Taxation, Wayne State U. CPA, Mich. Various positions to v.p., gen. mgr. of aftermarket opers. Federal-Mogul Corp., Geneva, 1976-97, sr. v.p., gen. counsel Southfield, Mich., 1997—. Office: Federal-Mogul Corp 26555 Northwestern Hwy Southfield MI 48034-2146

ZANDER, JANET ADELE, psychiatrist; b. Miles City, Mont., Feb. 19, 1950; d. Adelbert William and Valborg Constance (Buckneberg) Z.; m. Mark Richard Ellenberger, Sept. 16, 1979; 1 child, Evan David Zander Ellenberger. BA, St. Olaf Coll., 1972; MD, U. Minn., 1976. Diplomate Am. Bd. Psychiatry and Neurology. Resident in psychiatry U. Minn., Mpls., 1976-79, fellow in psychiatry, 1979-80, asst. prof. psychiatry, 1981—; staff psychiatrist St. Paul (Minn.) Regions Hosp., 1980—, dir. edn. in psychiatry, 1980-94, dir. inpatient psychiatry, 1986—, vice chair Dept. Psychiatry, 1991-96, divsn. head behavioral health, 2002—. Bd. dirs. Perry Assurance. Contbr. research articles to sci. jours. Sec. Concentus Musicus Bd. Dirs., St. Paul, 1981-89; mem. property com. St. Clement's Episcopal Ch., St. Paul, 1985. Mem. Am. Psychiat. Assn., Am. Med. Women's Assn., Minn. Psychiat. Soc. (ethics com. 1985-87, women's com. 1985-87, coun. 1994-96), Minn. Med. Assn., Ramsey County Med. Soc. (bd. dirs. 1994-96). Democrat. Avocations: singing, skiing. Home: 230 Crestway Ln West Saint Paul MN 55118-4424 Office: Regions Hosp 640 Jackson St Saint Paul MN 55101-2502 E-mail: janet.a.zander@healthpartners.com.

ZANGERLE, JOHN A. lawyer; b. Lakewood, Ohio, Jan. 24, 1942; BA, Haverford Coll., 1964; JD, Case Western Res. U., 1967. Bar: Ohio 1967. Ptnr. Baker & Hostetler, Cleve. Office: Baker & Hostetler LLP 3200 Nat City Ctr 1900 E 9th St Ste 3200 Cleveland OH 44114-3475

ZANOT, CRAIG ALLEN, lawyer; b. Wyandotte, Mich., Nov. 15, 1955; s. Thomas and Faye Blanch (Sperry) Z. AB with distinction, U. Mich., 1977; JD cum laude, Ind. U., 1980. Bar: Ind. 1980, Mich. 1981, U.S. Dist. Ct. (so. dist.) Ind. 1980, U.S. Dist. Ct. (no. dist.) Ind. 1981, U.S. Ct. Appeals (6th cir.) 1985, U.S. Dist. Ct. (ea. dist.) Mich. 1987, U.S. Dist. Ct. (we. dist.) Mich. 1990. Law clk. to presiding justice Allen County Superior Ct, Ft. Wayne, 1980-81; ptnr. Davidson, Breen & Doud P.C., Saginaw, Mich., 1981—. Mem. ABA, Mich. Bar Assn., Ind. Bar Assn., Saginaw County Bar Assn. Roman Catholic. Home: 547 S Linwood Beach Rd Linwood MI 48634-9432 Office: Davidson Breen & Doud PC 1121 N Michigan Ave Saginaw MI 48602-4762

ZAPP, DAVID EDWIN, infosystems specialist, investment consultant; b. Columbus, Ohio, Dec. 6, 1950; s. Robert Louis and Harriet (Miller) Z.; divorced; 1 child, Heather; m. Grace Lynn Spidell, Apr. 28, 1978. Road freight conductor N&W Ry., Columbus, 1971-77; with Franklin County Welfare, 1977-78; income tax preparer J.E. Wiggins Co., 1978-81; pub. inquiry asst. Ohio Bur. Workers Compensation, 1978-80, auditor, 1980-82, programmer, analyst, 1982-88, infosystems analyst, 1988-94; investment cons. Montano Securities Corp., 1994; ind. registered rep. Quest Capital Strategies, Inc., 1995—; software sys. cons. Optimum Techs., Inc., Worthington, Ohio, 1995—. Council mem. Southside Orgns., Columbus, 1985-86; mem. Gates Street Block Watch, Columbus, 1986. Mem. Nat. Assn. Investors Corp., Am. Assn. Individual Investors, Assn. Sys. Mgrs., Ohio Jaycees (program mgr. 1984-85, #1 individual devel. v.p. 1983-84, dist. dir. 1986—, named Outstanding Dist. Dir. 1986), Southside Columbus Jaycees (mgmt. v.p. 1984-85, pres. 1985-86, senator 1989), Employee Mgmt. Participation (chmn. 1985-86). Avocations: aviation, running, bicycling, personal computers. Home: 299 E Gates St Columbus OH 43206-3627 Office: Quest Capital Strategies Inc PO Box 77680 Columbus OH 43207-7680

ZAPP, JOHN S. medical association administrator; CEO ADA. Office: ADA 211 E Chicago Ave Chicago IL 60611-2637

ZAREFSKY, DAVID HARRIS, academic administrator, communication studies educator; b. Washington, June 20, 1946; s. Joseph Leon and Miriam Ethel (Lewis) Z.; m. Nikki Sheryl Martin, Dec. 23. 1970; children: Beth Ellen, Marc Philip. BS, Northwestern U., 1968, MA, 1969, PhD, 1974. Instr. communication studies Northwestern U., Evanston, Ill., 1968-73, asst. prof., 1974-77, assoc. prof., 1977-82, prof., 1982—, chmn. dept., 1975-83, assoc. dean Sch. Speech, 1983-88, dean, 1988-2000. Author: President Johnson's War on Poverty, 1986 (Winans-Wichelns award 1986), Lincoln, Douglas and Slavery, 1990 (Winans-Wichelns award 1991), Public Speaking: Strategies for Success, 1996, 2d edit., 1999; co-author: Contemporary Debate, 1983, Fundamentals of Argumentation Theory, 1996; editor: Rhetorical Movement, 1993; co-editor: American Voices, 1989, Contemporary American Voices, 1992, Fundamentals of Argumentation Theory, 1996; contbr. articles to profl. jours. Recipient Best Article award So. Speech Communication Assn., 1985, 98, Midwest Forensic Assn., 1988; named Debate Coach of the Year Georgetown U., 1973, Emory U., 1972. Mem. AAUP, Nat. Comm. Assn. (pres. 1993, dist. scholar award 1994), Ctrl. States Comm. Assn. (pres. 1986-87), Am. Forensic Assn. (Svc. award 1989, Dist. Scholar award 1999), Delta Sigma Rho-Tau Kappa Alpha (Svc. award 1986), others. Democrat. Jewish. Avocations: stamp collecting, reading, travel. Office: Northwestern U 1905 Sheridan Rd Evanston IL 60208-2260

ZAREMSKI, MILES JAY, lawyer; b. Chgo., Aug. 16, 1948; s. Samuel and Ann (Levine) Z.; m. Elena Cinthia Resnik, July 19, 1970; children: Jason Lane, Lauren Devra. BS, U. Ill., 1970; JD, Case Western Res. U., 1973. Bar: Ill. 1973, U.S. Dist. Ct. (no. dist.) Ill. 1973, U.S. Ct. Appeals (7th cir.) 1973, U.S. Supreme Ct. 1977, U.S. Ct. Appeals (8th cir.) 1988, U.S. Dist. Ct. Nebr. 1996, U.S. Dist. Ct. (ea. dist.) Tenn. 1997, U.S. Ct. Appeals (6th cir.) 1998, Ind. 2000, Pa. 2000, U.S. Dist. Ct. (no. dist.) Ind. 2001. Spl. asst. state's atty. Lake County, Ill., 1980-82; ptnr. Kamensky & Rubinstein, Lincolnwood, Chgo., 2000—. Arbitrator, mandatory arbitration programs Cook and Lake Counties, Ill., 1990—; asst. prof. med. jurisprudence U. Health Scis./Chgo. Med. Sch., 1991—; adj. faculty U. Chgo. Law Sch., 1999—2001; adj. asst. prof. Case Western Res. Law Sch., 2001—. Editor: Medical and Hospital Negligence, 4 vols., 1988, supplement, 1993, 95-99; contbr. chpts. in books and articles to profl. jours.; author: Reengineering Healthcare Liability Litigation, 1997, supplement, 1999; patentee in field. Oversight com. law sch. Case Western Res. U., Cleve., 1985-99, alumni bd. dirs., 1996-99; mem. exec. com. law sch. ctr for health care Loyola U., Chgo., 1987-89; mem. lakefront commn. City of Highland Park, Ill., 1982-84; bd. dirs., officer Regional Organ Bank Ill., Chgo., 1986-91; bd. dirs. The Lambs, Libertyville, Ill., 1982-84, Jocelyn Ctr. for Mental Health, 1994-96; field play marshall U.S. Olympics Baseball, Atlanta, 1996. Named one of Outstanding Young Men in Am., U.S. Jaycees, 1979. Fellow: Am. Bar Found., Am. Coll. Legal Medicine (assoc. in law 1973—91, chair legal com. 1996—98, chair Amicus com. 1997—2000, editl. bd. Jour. Legal Medicine 1981—, bd. govs., sec. 1999—2000, treas. 2000—01, pres.-elect 2001—02, pres. 2002—); mem.: ABA (various coms. tort and ins. practice sect., vice chmn. 1979—90, chmn. med. and law com. 1984—85, editor-in-chief Forum 1979—81, spl. com. on med. profl. liability 1985, 1991—95, 1998—, chmn. 2000—, editl. bd. Forum on Health Law 1989—91), Ill. Assn. Healthcare Attys., Quality Mgmt. Health Care (editl. bd.), Am. Soc. Writers on Legal Subjects (scribes), Am. Health Law Assn. (vice chair hosp. liability com. 1999—), Am. Soc. Law and Medicine (editor-in-chief 1981—83, bd. editors 1983—86), Lake County Bar Assn., Ill. Bar Assn. (1st and 3d prizes 1978—79). Jewish. Avocations: baseball, soccer, coaching athletic teams. Office: Kamensky & Rubinstein 7250 N Cicero Ave Ste 200 Lincolnwood IL 60712

ZARING, ALLEN G. company executive; Student, Babson Coll. Founder, chmn., CEO Zaring Homes, 1964—. With U.S. Army. Recipient High Achievement award Profl. Builders Mag.; named Builder of Yr., Home Builders Assn. Greater Cin., 1995, Ams. Best Builder. Office: Zaring Nat Corp 11300 Cornell Park Dr Ste 500 Cincinnati OH 45242-1885 Fax: 513-247-2667.

ZARLE, THOMAS HERBERT, academic administrator; b. Akron, Ohio, Oct. 11, 1939; BS, Springfield Coll., 1963; MA, Ohio U., 1965; PhD, Mich. State U., 1970; MPH, Harvard U., 1978. V.p. instl. advancement Bentley Coll., Waltham, Mass., until 1988; pres. Aurora U., Ill., 1988—. Office: Aurora U Office of Pres 347 S Gladstone Ave Aurora IL 60506-4892

ZARTMAN, DAVID LESTER, animal sciences educator, researcher; b. Albuquerque, July 6, 1940; s. Lester Grant and Mary Elizabeth (Kitchel) Z.; m. Micheal Aline Plemmons, July 6, 1963; children: Kami Renee, Dalan Lee BS, N.Mex. State U., 1962; MS, Ohio State U., 1966, PhD, 1968. Cert. dairy cattle specialist, Am. Registry Profl. Animal Scientists. Jr. ptnr. Marlea Guernsey Farm, Albuquerque, 1962-64; grad. rsch. assoc. Ohio State U., Columbus, 1964-68; asst. prof. dairy sci. N.Mex. State U., Las Cruces, 1968-71, assoc. prof., 1971-79, prof., 1979-84, Ohio State U., Columbus, 1984—. Chmn. dept. Ohio State U., Columbus, 1984-99; pres. Mary K. Zartman, Inc., Albuquerque, 1976-84; cons. Bio-Med. Electronics, Inc., San Diego, 1984-89, Zartemp, Inc., Northbrook, Ill., 1990, Recom Applied Solutions, 1993-2000, Am. Registry of Profl. Animal Scientists, 1996—. Contbr. articles to profl. jours.; patentee in field. Recipient State Regional Outstanding Young Farmer award Jaycees, 1963, Disting. Rsch. award N.Mex. State U. Coll. Agr. and Home Econs., 1983, Outstanding Svc. award Ohio Poultry Assn., 1999, Grazier of Yr. award Gt. Lakes Internat. Grazing Conf., 2001; named one of Top 100 Agr. Alumni, N.Mex. State U. Centennial, 1987; spl. postdoctoral fellow NIH, New Zealand, 1973; Fulbright-Hayes lectr., Malaysia, 1976. Fellow AAAS; mem. Am. Dairy Sci. Assn., Am. Soc. Animal Sci., Dairy Shrine Club, Ohio Farm Bur., Sigma Xi, Gamma Sigma Delta, Alpha Gamma Rho (1st Outstanding Alumnus N.Mex. chpt. 1985), Alpha Zeta, Phi Kappa Phi. Home: 7671 Deer Creek Dr Worthington OH 43085-1551 Office: Ohio State U 2027 Coffey Rd Columbus OH 43210-1043 E-mail: zartman.3@osu.edu.

ZATKOFF, LAWRENCE P. federal judge; b. 1939; m. Nancy L. Chenhall; four children. BSBA, U. Detroit, 1962; JD cum laude, Detroit Coll. Law, 1966. Bar: Mich., U.S. Supreme Ct. Mem. corp. personnel staff Chrysler Corp., 1962-66; asst. prosecuting atty. Macomb County, Mich.; with Moll, Desenberg, Purdy, Glover & Bayer, Detroit, 1966-68; ptnr. LaBarge, Zatkoff & Dinning, Roseville, 1968-78; probate judge Macomb County, 1978-82; judge Macomb County Cir. Ct., 1982-87; chief judge U.S. Dist. Ct. (ea. dist.) Mich., 1986—. Part-time faculty Detroit Coll. Law; mem. rep. assembly Mich. State Bar, mem. spl. com. on grievances; appointed assoc. govt. appeal agt. SSS, 1969-72. Guest lectr., past mem. scholarship ball com. Macomb County Community Coll.; citizen's adv. bd. Macomb-Oakland Regional Ctr., 1978-79; ex officio mem. Macomb County Youthscope; adv. bd. Met. Detroit chpt. March of Dimes; trustee St. Joseph Hosp. of Mt. Clemens; mem. Selfridge Air NG Base Community Council; Rep. candidate 12th dist. U.S. Congress Mich., 1976, party treas. 12 dist. 1975, exec. com., 1975, chmn. Macomb County exec. com., 1976, del. several nat. and regional Rep. Convs., Macomb County campaign coordinator for U.S. Sen. candidate Marvin Esch, 1976. Mem. ABA, Fed. Bar Assn., Mich. Bar. Assn., Macomb County Bar. Assn. (dir., treas. Young Lawyers sect., past probate ct. liason to bd. dirs., mem. cir. ct. liason com.), Detroit Bar Assn., Am. Judicare Soc., Am. Arbitration Assn., Nat. Orgn. Legal Problems of Edn., Nat. Council Juvenile and Family Ct. Judges, Mich. Probate and Juvenile Ct. Judges Assn. (mental health com.), Nat. Coll. Probate Judges, Mich. Judges Assn., VFW (legal case rep. 1976, spokesman Vietnamese Embassy Paris 1976, judge Voice of Democracy programs 1975, state wide scholarships judge, Voice of Democracy awards 1975, 76, Americanism award 1976, Spl. Recognition award 1978). Clubs: 100, Macomb County 300, Rep. Majority (charter). Office: US Dist Ct US Courthouse Rm 730 231 W Lafayette Blvd Detroit MI 48226-2700

ZAVATSKY, MICHAEL JOSEPH, lawyer; b. Wheeling, W.Va., Dec. 15, 1948; s. Mike and Mary (Mirich) Z.; m. Kathleen Hanson, May 28, 1983; children: David, Emily. BA in Internat. Studies, Ohio State U., 1970; MA in Polit. Sci., U. Hawaii, 1972; JD, U. Cin., 1980. Bar: Ohio 1980, U.S. Dist. Ct. (so. dist.) Ohio 1981, U.S. Ct. Appeals (6th cir.) 1985, U.S. Supreme Ct. 1989. Ptnr. Taft, Stettinius & Hollister, Cin., 1980—. Adj. prof. in trial practice and immigration law U. Cin., 1986— Trustee Internat. Visitors Ctr., Cin., 1984-86; bd. dirs. Cin. Charter Com., 1988-91; bd. dirs., mem. steering com. Leadership Cin., 1994-96. Capt. USAF, 1973-77. William Graham fellow U. Cin., 1979, East West Ctr. fellow U. Hawaii, 1970. Mem ABA, Ohio Bar Assn., Cin. Bar Assn., Am. Immigration Lawyers Assn. (chmn. Ohio chpt. 1987-88, 90-93), Potter Stewart Inn of Ct., Order of Coif. Home: 3820 Eileen Dr Cincinnati OH 45209-2013 Office: 1800 Firstar Tower Cincinnati OH 45202

ZAWADA, EDWARD THADDEUS, JR. physician, educator; b. Chgo., Oct. 3, 1947; s. Edward Thaddeus and Evelyn Mary (Kovarek) Z.; m. Nancy Ann Stephen, Mar. 26, 1977; children: Elizabeth, Nicholas, Victoria, Alexandra. BS summa cum laude, Loyola U., Chgo., 1969; MD summa cum laude, Loyola-Stritch Sch. Medicine, 1973. Diplomate Am. Bd. Internal Medicine, Am. Bd. Nephrology, Am. Bd. Nutrition, Am. Bd. Critical Care, Am. Bd. Geriatrics, Am. Bd. Clin. Pharm., Am. Bd. Forensic Examiners, Am. Bd. Forensic Medicine; specialist Hypertension, Am. Soc. Hypertension. Intern UCLA Hosp., 1973, resident, 1974-76; asst. prof. medicine UCLA, 1978-79, U. Utah, Salt Lake City, 1979-81; assoc. prof. medicine Med. Coll. Va., Richmond, 1981-83; assoc. prof. medicine, physiology & pharmacology U. S.D. Sch. Medicine, Sioux Falls, 1983-86, Freeman prof., chmn. dept. Internal Medicine, 1987—, chief div. nephrology and hypertension, 1983-88, pres. univ. physician's practice plan, 1992—. Chief renal sect. Salt Lake VA Med. Ctr., 1980-81; asst. chief med. service McGuire VA Med. Ctr., Richmond, 1981-83. Editor: Geriatric Nephrology and Urology, 1984; contbr. articles to profl. publs. Pres. Minnehaha div. Am. Heart Assn., 1984-87, pres. Dakota affiliate Am. Heart Assn., 1989-91. VA Hosp. System grantee, 1981-85, 85-88; Health and Human Svcs. grantee Pub. Health Scvs. Rsch. Adminstrn. Bureau Health Profl., 1993—. Fellow ACP, Am. Coll. Chest Physicians, Am. Coll. Nutrition, Am. Coll. Clin. Pharmacology, Internat. Coll. Angiology, Am. Coll. Angiology, Am. Coll. Clin. Pharmacology, Am. Coll. Forensic Examiners, Royal Soc. Medicine, Soc. for Vascular Medicine and Biology; mem. Internat. Soc. Nephrology, Am. Soc. Nephrology, Am. Soc. Pharmacology and Exptl. Therapeutics, Am. Physiol. Soc., Am. Inst. Nutrition, Am. Soc. Clin. Nutrition, Am. Geriatric Soc., Am. Soc. Transplant Physicians, Westward Ho Country Club. Democrat. Roman Catholic. Avocations: golf, tennis, skiing, cinema, music. Home: 2908 S Duchess Ave Sioux Falls SD 57103-4826 Office: North Ctrl Kidney Inst 911 E 20th St Ste 602 Sioux Falls SD 57105

ZDUN, JAMES J. finance executive; V.p. fin. adminstrn. Holophane a divsn. of Nat. Svc. Industries, 1999—. Office: 250 E Broad St Ste 1400 Columbus OH 43215-3775

ZEALEY, SHARON JANINE, lawyer; b. St. Paul, Aug. 30, 1959; d. Marion Edward and Freddie Zealey. BS, Xavier U. of La., 1981; JD, U. Cin., 1984. Bar: Ohio 1984; U.S. Dist. Ct. (so. dist.) Ohio 1985; U.S. Ct. Appeals (6th cir.) 1990; U.S. Supreme Ct. 1990. Law clk. U.S. Atty. for S. Dist. of Ohio, Cin., 1982; trust adminstr. Firstar Bank, 1984-86; atty. UAW Legal Svcs., 1986-88; assoc. Manley, Burke, Lipton & Fischer, 1988-91; mng. atty. and dep. atty. gen. Ohio Atty. Gen. Office, 1991-95; asst. U.S. atty. criminal div. for So. Dist. Ohio U.S. Attys. Office, 1995-97; United States atty. So. Dist. Ohio, 1997—2001; ptnr. Blank Rome Comisky & McCauley, 2001—. Pro bono svc. Pro Srs., 1987-88; mem. merit selection com. U.S. Ct. Appeals 6th Cir., Bankruptcy Ct.; adj. prof. law, civil rights U. Cin. Vol. lawyer for the poor/Pro Bono Panel participant, 1984—; adv. rev. bd. City of Cin. EEOC, 1989-91; mem. Tall Stacks Commn., Cin., 1991-92, Mayor's Commn. on Children, 1992-93; trustee, bd. visitors U. Cin. Coll. Law, 1992—; mem. BLAC/CBA Round Table, 1988—. Recipient Law Honor scholarship U. Cin. Coll. Law, 1981. Mem. Black Lawyers Assn. of Cin. (pres. 1989-91), Legal Aid Soc. (sec. 1991-92), ABA, Fed. Bar Assn., Ohio Bar Assn., Nat. Bar Assn. (Mem. of Yr. region VI 1990), Cin. Bar Assn. (trustee 1989-94), Cin. CAN Commn. Democrat. Episcopalian. Office: 1700 PNC Ctr 201 E 5th St Cincinnati OH 45202 Fax: 513-362-8787. E-mail: zealey@blankRome.com.

ZECH, RONALD H. financial services executive; BSEE, Valparaiso, 1965; MBA, Wis. U., 1965. V.p., gen. mgr. First Nat. Bank of Chgo., San Francisco, 1996—; v.p. fin. GATX Capital Corp., 1977, pres., CEO, 1984-94. Office: GATX Corp 500 W Monroe St Chicago IL 60661

ZECHMAN, DAVID MARK, health system executive, educator; b. Cleve., Jan. 31, 1956; s. Richard Lee Zechman and Marilyn Ann Molter; m. Rhonda Dale Lovett, Aug. 20, 1977; children: Audra, Alyssa. BS, Miami U., Oxford, Ohio, 1977; postgrad. studies in Respiratory Therapy, Northwestern U. Med. Sch., Chgo., 1983; M in Pub. Adminstrn., Cleve. State U., 1989. Biology tchr. and coach St. Bridget Sch. and Holy Name H.S., Cleve., 1982; respiratory therapist St. Luke's Hosp., 1982-83; supr. respiratory therapy Fairview Hosp., 1983-85; supr., clin. instr. respiratory therapy Metrohealth Med. Ctr., 1985-86, staff devel. instr., 1986-87, mgmt. specialist dermatology, renal hemodialysis, 1987-89, acting adminstrv. dir. dept. medicine, 1989, mgr. divsn. cardiology, 1989-91; adminstrv. dir. cardiovascular svcs. St. Vincent Med. Ctr., Toledo, 1991-92; adminstr. Mid-Am. Heart Inst. St. Luke's Hosp., Kansas City, Mo., 1992-97; v.p. cardiovascular svcs. St. Luke's Shawnee Mission Health System, 1997—. Mem. Nat. Fin. Com. United Network for Organ Sharing; faculty presenter Am. Coll. Cardiovascular Adminstrs., Boston, 1991, Anaheim, Calif. 1991, Mpls., Atlanta, 1993; chmn. cardiology adv. com. Novation. H.S. Sunday sch. tchr. 1989-98; bd. dirs. Kansas City chpt. Am. Heart Assn., 1994—; cmty. youth softball coach Blue Valley Recreation, 1994-2000; bd. dirs. Blue Valley Christian Ch., chmn. pastor rels. com., 1995-96; mem. Kansas City Urban League Multicultural Leadership Devel. Inst., 1997, Family Resource Ctr. Bd.; v.p. Jewish Hosp. Healthcare Svcs.; CEO Rudd Heart and Lung Inst. Recipient Disting. Leadership award Nat. Assn. for Cmty. Leadership, 2000; named Bd. Mem. of Yr. Kansas City chpt. Am. Heart Assn., 1998-99. Mem. Am. Coll. Healthcare Execs. (cert. healthcare exec.), Alliance of Cardiovascular Profls. (pres.). Avocations: volleyball, basketball, golf, running. Office: St Luke's Hosp 4401 Wornall Rd Kansas City MO 64111-3220

ZEDLER, JOY BUSWELL, ecological sciences educator; b. Sioux Falls, S.D., Oct. 15, 1943; d. Francis H. and Charlotte (Johnson) Buswell; m. Paul H. Zedler, June 26, 1965; children: Emily and Sarah (twins). BS, Augustana Coll., 1964; MS, U. Wis., 1966, PhD, 1968. Instr. U. Mo., Columbia, 1968-69; prof. San Diego State U., 1969-97; Aldo Leopold prof. restoration ecology, arboretum, botany U. Wis., Madison, 1998—. Mem. Nat. Wetland Tech. Com., Water Sci. Tech. Bd. Nat. Rsch. Coun., 1991-94; dir. Pacific Estuarine Rsch. Lab., 1985—, Coastal and Marine Inst., 1991-93; gov. bd. The Nature Conservancy, 1995—; trustee Environ. Def. Fund, 1998—. Author: Ecology of Southern California Coastal Wetlands, 1982, Salt Marsh Restoration, 1984; co-author: A Manual for Assessing Natural and Restored Wetlands, 1990, Ecology of Tijuana Estuary, 1992, Tidal Wetland Restoration, 1996; editor: Handbook for Restoring Tidal Wetlands, 2000. Fellow San Diego Natural History Mus.; mem. Ecol. Soc. Am. (mem. pub. affairs com. 1988-90), Soc. Wetlands Scientists, Soc. Ecol. Restoration. Achievements include pioneering studies of impacts of freshwater inflows to coastal wetlands in southwestern U.S. and Australia; contributions to understanding of coastal wetland functioning; development of methods for improving restoration projects in coastal wetlands; identification of shortcomings of wetland restoration programs; role of diversity in the function restored ecosystems, improving the science of restoration ecology. Office: U Wis Botany Dept Madison WI 53706

ZEFFREN, EUGENE, toiletries company executive; b. St. Louis, Nov. 21, 1941; s. Harry Morris and Bess (Dennis) Z.; m. Steccia Leigh Stern, Feb. 2, 1964; children: Maryl Renee, Bradley Cruvant. AB, Washington U., 1963; MS, U. Chgo., 1965, PhD, 1967. Research chemist Procter & Gamble Co., Cin., 1967-75, sect. head, 1975-77, assoc. dir., 1977-79; v.p. R & D, Helene Curtis, Inc., Chgo., 1979-95; pres. Helene Curtis USA, 1995-96; sr. v.p. Helene Curtis bus. unit Unilever Home and Personal Care USA, 1996-98, exec. v.p., COO hair and deodorant bus. unit, 1998-2000; sr. v.p. brand devel. Unilever Home and Personal Care N.Am., 2000—. Mem. vis. com. for phys. scis. U. Chgo., 1995—; active Wash. U. Nat. Coun. for Arts and Scis., 1997—; pres. bd. dirs. River North Dance Co., 1998-2000, chmn. 2000—. Co-author: The Study of Enzyme Mechanisms, 1973; contbr. articles to profl. jours.; patentee in field of enzymes and hair care. Mem. AAAS, Am. Chem. Soc., Soc. Cosmetic Chemists, Cosmetic Toiletry and Fragrance Assn. (sci. adv. com. 1979-95, vice chmn. 1984-88, chmn. 1988-90, bd. dirs. 1996—), Soap and Detergent Assn. (bd. dirs., exec. com. bd. 2000—), Indsl. Rsch. Inst., Omicron Delta Kappa. Republican. Jewish. Avocations: tennis, skiing, reading adventure and espionage novels. Office: Helene Curtis Inc 325 N Wells St Chicago IL 60610-4791

ZEKMAN, PAMELA LOIS (MRS. FREDRIC SOLL), reporter; b. Chgo., Oct. 22, 1944; d. Theodore Nathan and Lois Jane (Bernstein) Z.; m. Fredric Soll, Nov. 29, 1975. B.A., U. Calif. at Berkeley, 1965. Social worker Dept. Public Aid Cook County, Chgo., 1965-66; reporter City News Bur., 1966-70, Chgo. Tribune, 1970-75, Chgo. Sun-Times, 1975-81; investigative reporter Sta. WBBM-TV, Chgo., 1981—. Recipient Pulitzer Prize awarded to Chicago Tribune for gen. local reporting on vote fraud series, 1973; Community Service award for vote fraud series UPI, 1972; Feature Series award for nursing home abuses series AP, 1971; Pub. Service award for slumlord series UPI, 1973; Newswriting award AP, 1973; In Depth Reporting award for police brutality series AP, 1974; Investigative Reporting awards Inland Daily Press Assn., 1974, 78; Investigative Reporting award for series on city waste AP, 1975; Pulitzer Prize for pub. service for series on hosp. abuses, 1976; Investigative Reporting award for series on baby selling, 1976; Pub. Service award for series on currency exchange abuses UPI, 1976; Investigative Reporting award for series on abuses in home for retarded children AP, 1977; Soc. Midland Authors Golden Rake award; UPI Public Service award; Ill. AP award; Nat. Headliners Club award; Sweepstakes award for Mirage Tavern investigative project, 1978; Nat. Disting. Service award for series on med. abuses in abortion clinics Sigma Delta Chi, 1979; named Journalist of Yr. No. Ill. U., 1979; recipient George Foster Peabody Broadcasting award, 1982, 85, RTNDA Investigative Reporting award, 1983, DuPont Columbia award 1982, 87. Office: WBBM-TV 630 N McClurg Ct Chicago IL 60611-4495

ZELICKSON, SUE, newspaper and cookbook editor, television reporter and host, food consultant; b. Mpls., Sept. 13, 1934; d. Harry M. and Bernice (Gross) Zipperman; m. Alvin S. Zelickson, Aug. 21, 1956; children— Barry M., Brian D. B.S. in Edn., U. Minn., 1956. Cert. elem. tchr., S.C., Minn. Tchr. various schs. Mpls., S.C., Golden Valley, Minn., 1956-79; writer, editor, columnist Mpls.-St. Paul Mag., 1980— , Buylines, Mpls., 1984— ; TV-radio reporter Sta. WCCO-KSTP, Mpls, 1980—, Lifestyles with Sue Zelickson Sta. WCCO cable; restaurant developer, cons. Mpls., 1978— ; v.p. Passage Tours, Mpls., 1984-88. Coordinator, editor: Much Ado About Food, 1978; Minnesota Heritage Cookbook, 1979; Lee Ann Chin's Chinese Cuisine, 1981; Collins Back Room Cooking Secrets, 1981; The Governor's Table Cookbook, 1981; Chocolate Days & Chocolate Nights, 1982; Food for Show, Food on the Go, 1983; Wild Rice Star of The North, 1985; Look What's Cooking Now, 1985. Contbr. articles to Sun Newspaper, Post Publs., Mpls., Tribune. Public relations, promoter, fundraiser Mpls. Boys & Girls Club, Mpls. Inst. Arts, Hennepin County Med. Soc. Aux., Ronald McDonald House, Bonaventure Mall, Women's Assn. Minn. Symphony Orchestra, Council Jewish Women, Mt. Sinai Hosp., Brandeis U. Women, Minn. Opera Assn., Guthrie Theatre, Sholom Home, Am. Cancer Soc., M.S. Soc., March of Dimes, Am. Heart Assn.; bd. dirs. U. Minn. Alumni Bd., Golden Valley State Bank. Recipient Outstanding Achievement award There's Living Proof Am. Cancer Soc., Duluth, Minn., 1984; Outstanding Achievement award Boys & Girls Club Minn., 1984. Mem. Nat. Council Jewish Women, Women's Assn. Minn. Orch., numerous others. Avocations: reading, travel; writing; painting. Home and Office: 101 Ardmore Dr Minneapolis MN 55422-5209

ZELINSKY, DANIEL, mathematics educator; b. Chgo., Nov. 22, 1922; s. Isaac and Ann (Ruttenberg) Z.; m. Zelda Oser, Sept. 23, 1945; children: Mara Sachs, Paul O., David. BS, U. Chgo., 1941, MS, 1943, PhD, 1946. Rsch. mathematician applied math group Columbia U., N.Y.C., 1944-45; instr. U. Chgo., 1943-44, 46-47; Nat. Rsch. Coun. fellow Inst. Advanced Study, Princeton, N.J., 1947-49; from asst. to assoc. prof. dept. math. Northwestern U., Evanston, Ill., 1949-60, prof., 1960-93, prof. emeritus, 1993—, acting chmn. math. dept., 1959-60, chmn., 1975-78. Vis. prof. U. Calif. Berkeley, 1960, Fla. State U., Tallahassee, 1963, Hebrew U., Jerusalem, 1970-71, 85, others; vis. scholar Tata Inst., 1979; mem. various coms. Northwestern U.; lectr. in field. Author: A First Course in Linear Algebra, 1968, rev. edit., 1973; contbr. articles to profl. jours. Fulbright grantee Kyoto U., 1955-56, grantee NSF, 1958-80; Guggenheim fellow Inst. Advanced Study, 1956-57, Indo-Am. fellow, 1978-79. Fellow AAAS (mem. nominating com. sect. A 1977-80, chmn. elect sect. A 1984-85, chmn. 1985-86, retiring chmn. 1986-87), Am. Math. Soc. (mem. coun. 1961-67, editor Transactions of A.M.S. 1961-67, mem. various coms., mem. editorial bd. Notices of A.M.S. 1983-86, chmn. editorial bds. com. 1989, chmn. ad hoc com. 1991-92). Jewish. Home: 613 Hunter Rd Wilmette IL 60091-2213 Office: Northwestern U Dept Math Evanston IL 60208-0001 E-mail: dz@northwestern.edu.

ZELLER, JOSEPH PAUL, advertising executive; b. Crestline, Ohio, Mar. 19, 1940; s. Paul Edward and Grace Beatrice (Kinstle) Z.; m. Nancy Jane Schmidt, June 17, 1961; children: Laurie, Joe. BA, U. Notre Dame, 1962; MFA, Ohio U., 1963. Mgr.radio/television Drewrys Ltd. USA, Inc., South Bend, Ind., 1963-64; media supr. Tatham-Laird & Kudner, Chgo., 1964-67; v.p. assoc. media dir. J. Walter Thompson Co., 1967-77; v.p. media dir, v.p. Campbell-Mithun, 1977-80; sr. v.p., dir. media, fin., chmn. media coun. D'Arcy Masius Benton & Bowles, 1980-96, sr. v.p., 1996-2000; pres. Fox River Trading Co., East Dundee, Ill., 2000—. Chmn. Z Prop, 1986—; dir. circle Desert Caballeros Mus., 1994-96; founder Native Am. Images web mag., 1999. Pres. Amateur Hockey Assn. Ill., 1985. Mem. Broadcast Pioneers, Chgo. Advt. Club, Moose. Roman Catholic. Avocations: amateur hockey, photography, country music. E-mail: jzeller@prodigy.net., trader@rivertradingpost.com.

ZELLER, MARILYNN KAY, librarian; b. Scottsbluff, Nebr., Mar. 1, 1940; d. William Harold and Dorothy Elizabeth (Wilkins) Richards; m. Robert Jerome Zeller, May 21, 1966; children: Kevin Jerome and Renae Kay. BS, Calvary Bible Coll., 1985; MLS, U. Mo., Columbia, 1989. Cert. libr. File clk. Waddell & Reed, Kansas City, Mo., 1962-65; payroll clk. Century Fin. Co., 1965-67, Percy Kent Bag Co., Independence, 1968-70; accounts receivable Swansons on the Pla, Kansas City, 1971-73; clk. casualty ins. Mill Mutuals, 1977-80; registrar's asst. Calvary Bible Coll., 1980-85, libr. asst., 1985-88, asst. libr., 1988-89, head libr., 1989—. Chairperson libr. com. Calvary Bible Coll., Kansas City, 1989—; libr. rep. Friends of the Hilda Kroeker Libr., Kansas City, 1989—. Author: History of the Christian Librarian's Association, 1989. Mem. Christian Librarian's Assn., Spl. Librarian's Assn., Mo. Libr. Assn., Am. Libr. Assn. Avocations: walking, reading, crocheting, sewing, swimming. Home: 401 13th Ave N Greenwood MO 64034-9750 Office: Calvary Bible Coll 15800 Calvary Rd Kansas City MO 64147-1303

ZELLNER, ARNOLD, economics and statistics educator; b. Bklyn., Jan. 2, 1927; s. Israel and Doris (Kleiman) Z.; m. Agnes Marie Sumares, June 20, 1953; children— David S., Philip A., Samuel N., Daniel A., Michael A. AB, Harvard, 1949; PhD, U. Calif. at Berkeley, 1957; PhD (hon.), Autonomous U. Madrid, 1986, Tech. U. Lisbon, 1991, U. Kiel, 1998. Asst., then assoc. prof. econs. U. Wash., 1955-60; Fulbright vis. prof. Netherlands Sch. Econs., Rotterdam, 1960-61; assoc. prof., then prof. econs. U. Wis., 1961-66; H.G.B. Alexander disting. service prof. econs. and statistics U. Chgo., 1966-96, prof. emeritus, 1996—; dir. H.G.B. Alexander Rsch. Found., 1973-96. Cons. Battelle Meml. Inst., 1964—71; vis. rsch. prof. U. Calif., Berkeley, 1971, Berkeley, 96, adj. prof., 1998—; trustee Nat. Opinion Rsch. Corp., 1973—80; bd. dirs. Nat. Bur. Econ. Rsch., 1980—; seminar leader NSF-NBER Seminar on Bayesian Inference in Econometrics and Stats., 1970—95; vis. prof. Am. U., Cairo, 1997, Hebrew U., 1997, U. Calif., Berkeley, 1997—2002. Co-author: Systems Simulation for Regional Analysis, 1969, Estimating the Parameters of the Markov Probability Model, 1970; author: Bayesian Inference in Econometrics, 1971, Basic Issues in Econometrics, 1984, Bayesian Analysis in Econometrics and Statistics: The Zellner View and Papers, 1997; editor: Economic Statistics and Econometrics, 1968, Seasonal Analysis of Economic Time Series, 1978, Simplicity, Inference and Modelling, 2001; assoc. editor: Econometrica, 1962-68; co-editor: Studies in Bayesian Econometrics and Statistics, 1975, Jour. Econometrics, 1972—, founding editor ASA Jour. Bus. and Econ. Stats., 1983; contbr. articles to profl. jours. Pres. Leonard J. Savage Meml. Trust Fund, Chgo., 1977-2000. Served with AUS, 1951-53. Fellow AAAS, Am. Econ. Assn., Int. Coun. of Forecasters, Econometric Soc., Am. Statis. Assn. (pres. elect 1990—, pres. 1991—, chmn. bus. and econs. sect. 1980, chmn. Bayesian statis. sci. sect. 1993); mem. Internat. Statis. Inst., Internat. Soc. Bayesian Analysis (co-pres. 1993, pres. 1994-96, Founders award 1998), Soc. Actuaries (trustee, rsch. found., 1994-98). Avocations: golf, tennis, travel. Home: 5628 S Dorchester Ave Chicago IL 60637-1722 Office: U Chgo Grad Sch Bus 1101 E 58th St Chicago IL 60637-1511 E-mail: arnold.zellner@gsb.uchicago.edu.

ZEMM, SANDRA PHYLLIS, lawyer; b. Chgo., Aug. 18, 1947; d. Walter Stanley and Bernice Phyllis (Churas) Z. BS, U. Ill., 1969; JD, Fla. State U., 1974. Bar: Fla. 74, Ill. 75. With fin. dept. Sinclair Oil, Chgo., 1969-70; indsl. rels. advisor Conco Inc., Mendota, Ill., 1970-72; assoc. Seyfarth, Shaw, Fairweather & Geraldson, Chgo., 1975-82, ptnr., 1982—. Mem. Art Inst. Alliance, Chgo., 1993—2002; bd. dirs. Chgo. Residential Inc., 1993—97, pres., 1995—97. Mem. Ill. State Bar Assn., Fla. State Bar Assn., Univ. Club Chgo. (bd. dirs. 1991-94). Office: Seyfarth Shaw 55 E Monroe St Ste 4200 Chicago IL 60603-5863

ZENNER, SHELDON TOBY, lawyer; b. Chgo., Jan. 11, 1953; s. Max and Clara (Goldner) Z.; m. Ellen June Morgan, Sept. 2, 1984; children: Elie, Nathaniel. BA, Northwestern U., 1974, JD, 1978. Bar: U.S. Dist. Ct. (no. dist.) Ill. 1978. Assoc. Shadur, Krupp & Miller, Chgo., 1978-80; law clk. to judge U.S. Dist. Ct. (no. dist.) Ill., 1980-81; asst. U.S. atty., dep. chief spl. prosecutions div. No. Dist. of Ill., 1981-89; ptnr. Katten Muchin & Zavis, 1989—. Adj. faculty Medill Sch. Journalism, Northwestern U., 1982-89, Sch. of Law, 1986—; instr. Nat. Inst. Trial Attys., 1989—; mem. practitioners adv. com. U.S. Sentencing Commn. Mem. Phi Beta Kappa. Office: Katten Muchin & Zavis 525 W Monroe St Ste 1500 Chicago IL 60661-3693

ZEPF, THOMAS HERMAN, physics educator, researcher; b. Cin., Feb. 13, 1935; s. Paul A. and Agnes J. (Schulz) Z. BS summa cum laude, Xavier U., 1957; MS, St. Louis U., 1960, PhD, 1963. Asst. prof. physics Creighton U., Omaha, 1962-67, assoc. prof., 1967-75, prof., 1975—2002, prof. emeritus, 2002—, acting chmn. dept. physics, 1963-66, chmn., 1966-73, 81-93, coord. allied health programs, 1975-76, coord. pre-health scis. advising, 1976-81. Cons. physicist VA Hosp., Omaha, 1966-71; vis. prof. physics St. Louis U., 1973-74; program evaluator Am. Coun. on Edn., 1988—. Contbr. articles and abstracts to Surface Sci., Bull. Am. Phys. Soc., Proceedings Nebr. Acad. Sci., The Physics Tchr. jour., others. Recipient Cert. Recognition award Phi Beta Kappa U. Cin. chpt., 1953, Disting. Faculty Svc. award Creighton U., 1987, Excellence in Teaching award Creighton U., 1997. Mem. AAAS, Am. Phys. Soc., Am. Assn. Physics Tchrs. (pres. Nebr. sect. 1978), Nebr. Acad. Sci. (life, chmn. physics sect. 1985—), Internat. Brotherhood Magicians, Soc. Am. Magicians (pres. assembly #7, 1964-65), KC, Sigma Xi (Achievement award for rsch. St. Louis chpt. 1963, pres. Omaha chpt. 1993-94), Sigma Pi Sigma. Roman Catholic. Office: Creighton U Dept Physics Omaha NE 68178-0001

ZERBE, KATHRYN JANE, psychiatrist; b. Harrisburg, Pa., Oct. 17, 1951; d. Grover Franklin and Ethel (Schreckengaust) Z. BS with BA equivalent cum laude, Duke U., 1973; MD, Temple U., 1978. Diplomate Am. Bd. Psychiatry, 1984. Resident Karl Menninger Sch. Psychiatry, Topeka, 1982; staff psychiatrist Menninger Found., 1982-2001; v.p. edn. and rsch. The Menninger Clinic, 1993-97, prof., 1997-2001; dean, dir. edn. and rsch. Karl Menninger Sch. Psychiatry, 1992-97; Jack Aron chair in psychiat. edn. The Menninger Clinic, Topeka, 1997-2001, tng. and supr. analyst, 1995-2001; prof. psychiatry, prof. ob-gyn. Oreg. Health Scis. Univ., Portland, 2001—, dir. behavioral medicine dept. women's health, 2001—; prof. psychiatry, prof. ob/gyn, dir. behavioral medicine, women's health Oreg. Health and Scis. U. Instr. numerous sems. and courses. Author: The Body Betrayed: Women, Eating Disorders and Treatment, 1993, Women's Mental Health in Primary Care, 1999, numerous articles profl. rsch. papers; editor: Bull. of Menninger Clinic, 1998—2001; assoc. editor: , 1996—98, mem. editl. bd.: Eating Disorders Rev., mem. editl. bd.: Eating Disorders: The Jour. of Treatment and Prevention Postgrad. Medicine; contbr. Probation officer Juvenile divsn. Dauphin County, Pa., 1973. Recipient Ann. Laughlin Merit award The Nat. Psychiat. Endowment Fund, 1982, Outstanding Paper of Profl. Programs award The Menninger Found. Alumni Assn., 1982, Writing award Topeka Inst. for Psychoanalysis, 1985, 90, Mentorship award, 1997, Women Helping Women award, 1995, Tchr. of Yr. award, 1988, 96, 99; named one of Outstanding Young Women in Am., 1986, 88; Seeley fellow, 1979-82; Hilde Bruch lectureship, 1996. Fellow Am. Psychiat. Assn.; mem. AMA, Am. Coll. Psychiatrists, Am. Med. Women's Assn., Shawnee County Med. Soc., Kans. Med. Soc., Sigma Xi, Alpha Omega Alpha. Avocations: writing, reading, art history, travel. Office: Oreg Health and Scis U 3181 SW Sam Jackson Park Rd Portland OR 97201-3098

ZHANG, YOUXUE, geology educator; b. Huarong County, Hunan, China, Sept. 17, 1957; came to U.S., 1983; s. Zaiyi Zhang and Dezhen Wu; m. Zhengjiu Xu; children: Dan, Ray. BS in Geol. Scis., Peking U., Beijing, 1982; MA in Geol. Scis., Columbia U., 1985, MPhil, 1987, PhD in Geol. Scis., 1989. Grad. rsch. asst. Columbia U., N.Y.C., 1983-88; postdoctoral fellow Calif. Inst. Tech., 1988-91; asst. prof. geology U. Mich., Ann Arbor, 1991-97, assoc. prof., 1997—. Contbr. articles to profl. jours. Named Young Investigator, NSF, 1994. Mem. AAAS, Am. Geophys. Union, Geochem. Soc. (F.W. Clarke medal 1993), Mineral. Soc. Am., Sigma Xi. Office: Dept Geol Sci U Mich Ann Arbor MI 48109-1063 E-mail: youxue@umich.edu.

ZICHEK, MELVIN EDDIE, retired clergyman, educator; b. Lincoln, Nebr., May 5, 1918; s. Eddie and Agnes (Varga) Z.; A.B., Nebr. Central Coll., 1942; M.A., U. Nebr., 1953; D.Litt., McKinley-Roosevelt Ednl. Inst., 1955; m. Dorothy Virginia Patrick, May 28, 1942; 1 dau., Shannon Elaine. Ordained to ministry Christian Ch., 1942; minister Christian chs., Brock, Nebr., 1941, Ulysses, Nebr., 1942-43, Elmwood, Nebr., 1943-47, Central City, Nebr., 1947-83, ret., 1983; rural tchr., Merrick County, Nebr., 1937-40; prin. Alvo (Nebr.) Consol. High Sch., 1943-47; supt. Archer (Nebr.) Pub. Schs., 1948-57; head dept. English and speech Central City

(Nebr.) High Sch., 1957-63; supt. Marquette (Nebr.) Consol. Schs., 1963-79. Served as chaplain's asst. AUS, 1942. Mem. Grand Island Ret. Tchrs. Assn. Republican. Home: 2730 N North Rd Grand Island NE 68803-1143

ZICHEK, SHANNON ELAINE, retired secondary school educator; b. Lincoln, Nebr., May 29, 1944; d. Melvin Eddie and Dorothy Virginia (Patrick) Z. AA, York (Nebr.) Coll., 1965; BA, U. Nebr., Kearney, 1968; postgrad., U. Okla., Edmond, 1970, 71, 72, 73, 74, 75, U. Nebr., Kearney, 1980, 81, 82, 89, 92. Tchr. history and English, N.W. H.S., Grand Island, Nebr., 1948-1999, ret., 1999. Republican. Christian. Home: 2730 N North Rd Grand Island NE 68803-1143

ZICKUS, ANNE, state legislator; b. Apr. 6, 1939; m. Charles Zickus, 1958; children: Kathy, Chuck. Alderman City of Palos Hills, Ill., 1973-75; state rep. Dist. 47, 1989-90, Dist. 48, 1993—; dir. Ill. State Crime Commn., 1997. Dir. Helping Hand Rehab. Ctr., 1995—. Mem. Suburban Assn. Realtors, Nat. Assn. Realtors. Republican. Home: 7909 W 112th St Palos Hills IL 60465-2731 Office: 10600 S Roberts Rd Palos Hills IL 60465-1936

ZIEGELBAUER, ROBERT F. state legislator; b. Aug. 26, 1951; BA, Notre Dame; MS, U. Pa. Mem. Manitowoc County Bd., City Coun., fin. dir.; now mem. dist. 25 Wis. State Assembly, 1992—; owner of retial music shop. Home: 1213 S 8th St Manitowoc WI 54220-5311 Address: Wis Assembly PO Box 8952 Madison WI 53708-8952

ZIEGENHAGEN, DAVID MACKENZIE, consultant, retired healthcare company executive; b. Mpls., May 25, 1936; s. Elmer Herbert Ziegenhagen and Margaret Ruth (Mackenzie) Kruger; m. Mary Ange Kinsella, Nov. 26, 1966 (div. Dec. 1982); children: Marc, Eric; m. Mary Kinsella, Feb. 7, 2002. BA, U. Minn., 1962. Assoc. dir. Thailand Peace Corps, Bangkok, 1963-65, Thailand program officer Washington, 1966-67, dir. Western Samoa Apia, 1967-70; exec. dir. Mental Health Assn. Minn., Mpls., 1970-76; co-founder, pres. Current Newspapers, Inc., Burnsville, Minn., 1975-84; sr. program officer The St. Paul Found., 1982-84; pres. DMZ Assocs., Cloverdale, Calif., 1983—; exec. dir. Minn. Bd. Med. Practice, St. Paul, 1985-88; CEO, pres. Stratis Health, Bloomington, Minn., 1988-2000. Field dir. Am. Refugee Com., Bangkok, 1979; dir. Health Edn. Rsch. Found., St. Paul, 1993—99; mem. Citizens League, Mpls., 1975—2000, dir., 1988—95; mem. Adminstrs. in Medicine, Washington, 1985—88; dir. Walk-In Counseling Ctr., Mpls., 1990—99, Ctr. for Clin. Quality Evaluation, Washington, 1990—99. Mem. Cloverdale Planning Commn., 2000—, Sonoma County Civil Grand Jury, 2001—. Mem. Nat. Mental Health Staff Coun. (pres. 1970-76). Avocations: travel, international development, arts.

ZIEGLER, DEWEY KIPER, neurologist, educator; b. Omaha, May 31, 1920; s. Isidor and Pearl (Kiper) Z.; m. Mar. 30, 1954; children: Amy, Laura, Sara. BA, Harvard U., 1941, MD, 1945. Diplomate Am. Bd. Psychiatry and Neurology (bd. dirs. 1974-83, exec. com. 1978-82). Intern in medicine Boston City Hosp., 1945-46; asst. resident then chief resident in neurology N.Y. Neurol. Inst.-Columbia U. Coll. Physicians and Surgeons, 1948-51; resident in psychiatry Boston Psychopathic Hosp., 1951-53; asst. chief neurol. service Montefiore Hosp., N.Y.C.; and asst. prof. neurology Columbia U., 1953-55; asst. prof. U. Minn., 1955-56; asso. clin. prof. U. Kans. Med. Sch., 1956-64, chief dept. neurology, 1968-85; prof. U. Kans. Med. Center, 1964-89, prof. emeritus, 1989—. Cons. Social Security Adminstrn., 1975— ; mem. com. on certification and co-certification Am. Bd. Med. Specialties, 1979-82 Author: In Divided and Distinguished Worlds, 1942; Contbr. numerous articles to profl. jours. Served to lt., j.g., M.C. USNR, 1946-48. Fellow Am. Acad. Neurology (pres. 1979-81); mem. AMA, Am. Neurol. Assn. (v.p. 1972-73), Am. Headache Assn. Jewish. Home: 8347 Delmar Ln Shawnee Mission KS 66207-1821 Office: Kans U Med Center 3900 Rainbow Blvd Kansas City KS 66103-2918 E-mail: dziegler@kumc.edu.

ZIEGLER, DONALD N. state senator; b. Mar. 6, 1949; m. Joyce Ziegler; 2 children. Mem. dist. 26 Minn. Senate, St. Paul, 1999—. Republican. Home: 4915 400th Ave Blue Earth MN 56013-6204 Office: 100 Constitution Ave Saint Paul MN 55155-1232

ZIEGLER, EKHARD ERICH, pediatrics educator; b. Saalfelden, Austria, Apr. 12, 1940; children: Stefan, Gabriele, Lena. M.D., U. Innsbruck, Austria, 1964. Diplomate: Am. Bd. Pediatrics. Intern U. Innsbruck, 1966-67, resident in pediatrics, 1967-68 70-71, resident in pharmacology, 1964-66, asst. dept. pediatrics, 1970-73; vis. instr. pediatrics U. Iowa, Iowa City, 1968-70, asst. prof. pediatrics, 1973-76, assoc. prof., 1976-81, prof., 1981—. Mem. nutrition study sect. NIH, 1988-92. Recipient Nutrition award Am. Acad. Pediactrics, 1988. Mem. Am. Soc. Clin. Nutrition, Soc. Pediatric Research, Soc. Exptl. Biology and Medicine, N.Am. Soc. Pediatric Gastroenterology, Midwest Soc. Pediatric Research, Am. Pediatric Soc., The Nutrition Soc., N.Y. Acad. Scis., Am. Acad. Pediatrics., Am. Dietetic Assn. (hon.). Club: Univ. Athletic (Iowa City). Office: U Iowa Dept Pediatrics Iowa City IA 52242 E-mail: ekhard-ziegler@uiowa.edu.

ZIEGLER, JOHN AUGUSTUS, JR. lawyer; b. Grosse Pointe, Mich., Feb. 9, 1934; s. John Augustus and Monnabell M. Ziegler; m. G. Kay Brubeck; children: John Augustus III, Laura, Lisa, Adeline. AB, U. Mich., JD, 1957. Bar: Mich. 1957. Since practiced in, Detroit; assoc. Dickinson, Wright, McKean & Cudlip, 1957-65, ptnr., 1965-68, Parsons, Tennent, Hammond, Hardig & Ziegelman, 1969-70, Ziegler, Dykhouse & Wise, 1970-77; pres., CEO Nat. Hockey League, 1977-92, chmn. bd. govs., 1976-78; of counsel Dickinson, Wright, PLLC, Bloomfield Hills, 1992—99. Office: 375 Park Ave Ste 2004 New York NY 10152-2099

ZIEMAN, LYLE E. state senator; b. Mar. 12, 1921; m. Beverly Anderson. Dairy and hog farmer, 1941-77; dir. Postville State Bank, 1957—; senator State of Iowa, 1992—. Bd. mem. Postville Telephone Co. Mem. 5 County Mental Health Properties Bd., Regional Planning Com. of NE Iowa, Farm Bureau, Postville Improvement Corp. PIC, Allamakee County Substance Abuse Bd., Allamakee County Civil Defense Bd., Good Samaritan Soc. Bd. Mem. Rural Econ. Devel. for Assn. of Counties (steering com.), Citizens United for Responsible Energy, Agrl. Coun. of Am. Republican. Lutheran. Office: State Capitol 3 16th Dist 9th And Grand Des Moines IA 50319-0001 E-mail: lyle_zieman@legis.state.ia.us.

ZIEMAN, MARK, newspaper editor; The editor Kansas City (Mo.) Star. Office: The Kansas City Star 1729 Grand Blvd Kansas City MO 64108-1458

ZIEN, DAVID ALLEN, state legislator; b. Chippewa Falls, Wis., Mar. 15, 1950; s. Allen Roy Zien and Orpha Mattix; m. Suzanne Eleanor Bowe, Sept. 8, 1992; children: Travis, Aryan, Kurt, Amber, Lori, Angel-Sky, Rebecca. BS in Geography and Bus. cum laude, U. Wis., Eau Claire, 1974; MS in Guidance and Counseling summa cum laude, U. Wis. Stout, Menomonie, 1975; postgrad., U. Wis., Superior, 1975-80; doctoral studies, U. Wis., 1980-84. Roofer pvt. practice, Chippewa Falls, Wis., 1970-75; longshoreman Superior, 1975-79; vet. outreach counselor State of Wis., 1975-79, job svc. counselor Medford, Wis., 1980-83; campus adminstr. Northcentral Tech. Coll., 1983-88; mem. Wis. Assembly, Eau Claire, 1988-93, Wis. Senate from 23rd dist., Madison, 1993—. Wis. vets. outreach dir. VFW, Madison, Wis., 1975-84. Contbr. articles to profl. jours. Speaker, presenter Rep. Party of Wis., 1984—; advisor Wis. Cmty. Edn. Assn., 1983-89. Sgt. USMC, Vietnam, 1968-70. Named Legislator of Yr. ABATE of Wis., 1990, VFW, 1990, 92-93, State of Wis., 1991, Am. Legion, 1993, Wis. Assn. Concerned Vets., 1993, Wis. Farm Bur. Friend of Agr., 1991-94, NFIB Guardian of Small Bus., 1992; recipient Wis. Counties Assn. Cert. Appreciation 1993-94, Hmong Stout Student Assn. Outstanding Good Friend award, 1993-94, State Hist. Soc. Cert. Appreciation, 1994. Mem. VFW, NRA, DAV, WVV (Vet. of Yr. 1992), VEC (Damn Fine Legislator 1992), VVA (Disting. Achievement award 1993), WACVO, HOG, ALEC, NCSL, AFA, CMA, AMA, BOLT, ABATE, ANY, WVT, Northland VV, USMC League & Club, Eagles, Nat. Motorcycle Hall of Fame, Grandma's Marathon, Christian Outdoorsmen, Nat. Rep. Legislators, Am. Life League, Am. Legion, Iron Bde., Internat. Assn. Employment Security, Am. Legis. Exch., Wis. Wildlife Fedn., Highground Vets. Meml. Project, Wis. Vets. Tribute Com., Elks, Masons. Lutheran. Avocations: motorcycling, hunting, running. Home: 1716 63rd St Eau Claire WI 54703-6857

ZIETLOW, RUTH ANN, reference librarian; b. Richland Center, Wis., Apr. 5, 1960; d. James Eldon and Dixie Ann (Doudna) Z.; m. David Robert Voigt, Aug. 22, 1992; children: Eleanor Ruth, Isabel Anna, Carl James. BA in English, U. Nebr., 1987; MA in Libr. Studies, U. Wis., 1990; cert. in info. sys., U. St. Thomas, St. Paul, 1995. English instr. Guangzhou (China) English Lang. Ctr. Zhongshan U., 1987-88; adminstrv. asst. Helm Group, Lincoln, Nebr., 1988-89; circulatio supr. Sch. Edn. U. Wis., Madison, 1990-91; libr. specialist St. Paul Pub. Libr., 1991-92; reference librarian coordinator extention library svcs. U. St. Thomas, 1991—. Author manual: Electronic Communication and Information Resources Manual, 1995. Mem. Minn. Libr. Assn. (chair Distance Learning Roundtable 1999-2000). Avocations: gardening, reading. Office: U St Thomas O'Shaughnessey-Frey Libr 2115 Summit Ave Saint Paul MN 55105-1048 E-mail: razietlow@stthomas.edu.

ZIMMERMAN, DORIS LUCILE, chemist; b. L.A., July 30, 1942; d. Walter Merritt and Letta Minnie (Reese) Briggs; m. Christopher Scott Zimmerman, June 5, 1964; children: Susan Christina, David Scott, Brian Allan. BS in Chemistry, Carnegie Mellon U., 1964; MS in Chemistry, Youngstown State U., 1989, MS in Materials Engring., 1992; ABD, Kent (Ohio) State U., 1997. High sch. tchr. Ohio County Schs., Vienna and Campbell, 1983-87; sr. chemist Konwal, Warren, Ohio, 1988-91; limited faculty mem. Kent (Ohio) State U., 1991—; temp. full-time instr. dept. chemistry Edinboro U. Pa., 1995-97, 2000. Substitute tchr. County Schs. of Ohio, Warren, 1972-82; tutor, 1965—; vis. prof. Case Western Res. U., Cleve., 2000-2001; vis. faculty Penn. State, 2001-02; instr. Kent State U., Geauga, 2002-. Instr. water safety ARC, Warren, 1965—; chmn. Trumbull Mobile Meals, Warren, 1977-92, Pink Thumb Garden Club, Warren, 1965—. Recipient Svc. award ARC, 1981, Trumbull Mobile Meals, 1985. Mem. Am. Inst. Chemists, Materials Info. Soc., Soc. for the Advancement of Material and Process Engring., Am. Chem. Soc. (sec. 1985-90, chmn. elect 1990, chmn. 1991, alternate councilor 1992—, Commendation award 1990), Carnegie Mellon Alumni Assn. (admissions councilor, Svc. award 1981), Phi Lambda Upsilon, Phi Kappa Phi, Sigma Xi. Republican. Methodist. Avocations: masters' swimming, sailboat racing, tennis, bridge. Home and Office: 1390 Waverly Dr NW Warren OH 44483-1718

ZIMMERMAN, HOWARD ELLIOT, chemist, educator; b. N.Y.C., July 5, 1926; s. Charles and May (Cohen) Zimmerman; m. Jane Kirschenheiter, June 3, 1950 (dec. Jan. 1975); children: Robert, Steven, James; m. Martha L. Bailey Kaufman, Nov. 7, 1975 (div. Oct. 1990); m. Peggy J. Vick, Oct. 1991; stepchildren: Peter Kaufman, Tanya Kaufman. B.S., Yale U., 1950, Ph.D., 1953. NRC fellow Harvard U., 1953-54; faculty Northwestern U., 1954-60, asst. prof., 1955-60; assoc. prof. U. Wis., Madison, 1960-61, prof. chemistry, 1961—, Arthur C. Cope and Hilldale prof. chemistry, 1975—. Chmn. 4th Internat. Union Pure and Applied Chemistry Symposium on Photochemistry, 1972; organizer, chmn. Organic Photochemistry, 1972, Organic Photochemistry Symposium at Pacifichem Honolulu, 1995, Organic Photochemistry Sumposium at Pacifichem, 2000, Honolulu, 00. Author: (book) Quantum Mechanics for Organic Chemists, 1975; mem. editl. bd.: Jour. Organic Chemistry, 1967—71, mem. editl. bd.: Molecular Photochemistry, 1969—75, mem. editl. bd.: Jour. Am. Chem. Soc., 1982—85, mem. editl. bd.: Revs. Reactive Intermediates, 1984—89; contbr. articles to profl. jours. Recipient Halpern award for photochemistry, N.Y. Acad. Scis., 1979, Chem. Pioneer award, Am. Inst. Chemists, 1986, Sr. Alexander vonHumboldt award, 1988, Hilldale award, U. Wis., 1988—89, 1990. Mem.: NAS, Inter-Am. Photochemistry Assn. (co-chmn. orgnic divsn. 1977—79, exec. com. 1979—86), German Chem. Soc., Chem. Soc. London, Am. Chem. Soc. (James Flack Norris award 1976, Arthur C. Cope Scholar award 1991), Phi Beta Kappa, Sigma Xi. Home: 7813 Westchester Dr Middleton WI 53562-3671 Office: U Wis Chemistry Dept 1101 University Ave Madison WI 53706-1322 E-mail: Zimmerman@chem.wisc.edu.

ZIMMERMAN, JAMES M. retail company executive; b. 1944; Chmn. Rich's Dept. Store div. Federated Dept. Stores, 1984-88; pres., COO Federated and Allied Dept. Stores, Cin., 1988-97; chmn., CEO Federated Dept. Stores, 1997—. Office: Federated Department Stores Inc 7 W 7th St Cincinnati OH 45202-2424

ZIMMERMAN, JAY, secondary education educator; Tchr. Physics Brookfield (Wis.) Ctrl. High Sch., 1980—. Recipient Disting. Svc. Citation, 1993. Office: Brookfield Ctrl High Sch 16900 Gebhardt Rd Brookfield WI 53005-5138

ZIMMERMAN, JO ANN, health services and educational consultant, former lieutenant governor; b. Van Buren County, Iowa, Dec. 24, 1936; d. Russell and Hazel (Ward) McIntosh; m. A. Tom Zimmerman, Aug. 26, 1956; children: Andrew, Lisa, Don and Ron (twins), Beth. Diploma, Broadlawns Sch. of Nursing, Des Moines, 1958; BA with honors, Drake U., 1973; postgrad., Iowa State U., 1973-75. RN, Iowa. Asst. head nurse maternity dept. Broadlawns Med. Ctr., Des Moines, 1958-59, weekend supr. nursing svcs., 1960-61, supr. maternity dept., 1966-68; instr. maternity nursing Broadlawns Sch. Nursing, 1968-71; health planner, community rels. assoc. Iowa Health Systems Agy., Des Moines, 1978-82; mem. Iowa Ho. Reps., 1982-86; lt. gov., pres. of Senate, State of Iowa, 1987-91; cons. health svcs., grant writing and continuing edn. Zimmerman & Assocs., Des Moines, 1991—2000; dir. patient care svcs. Nursing Svcs. Iowa, 1996-98; nurse case mgr. Olsten Health Svcs. (now Gentiva Health Svcs.), 1998—; part-time tour dir. Travel, Inc., 2000—. Ops. dir. Medlink Svcs., Inc., Des Moines, 1992-96. Contbr. articles to profl. jours. Mem. advanced registered nurse practioner task force on cert. nurse mid-wives Iowa Bd. Nursing, 1980-81, Waukee, Polk County, Iowa Health Edn. Coord. Coun., Iowa Women's Polit. Caucus, Dallas County Women's Polit. Caucus; chmn. Des Moines Area Maternity Nursing Conf. Group, 1969-70, task force on sch. health svcs. Iowa Dept. Health, 1982, task force health edn. Iowa Dept. Pub. Instruction, 1979, adv. com. health edn. assessment tool, 1980-81, Nat. Lt. Govs., chair com. on Agrl. and Rural Devel., 1989; Dallas County Dem. Ctrl. Com., 1972-84, 98—; bd. dirs. Waukee Cmty. Sch. Bd., 1976-79, pres. 1978-79; bd. dirs. Iowa PTA, 1979-83, chairperson Health Com., 1980-84; mem. steering com. ERA, Iowa, 1991-92; founder Dem. Activist Women's Network (DAWN), 1992. Mem. ANA, LWV (health chmn. met. Des Moines chpt.), Iowa Nurses Assn., Iowa League for Nursing (bd. dirs. 1979-83), Family Centered Childbirth Edn. Assn. (childbirth instr., advisor), Iowa Cattleman's Assn., Am. Lung Assn. (bd. dirs. Iowa 1988-92), Dem. Activist Women's Network (founder 1992). Mem. Christian Ch. Avocations: gardening, sewing, reading, bridge, breeding British White cattle. Office: Gentiva Health Svcs 3737 Westown Pkwy Ste 2C West Des Moines IA 50266-1028 E-mail: atzzzzz@aol.com.

ZIMMERMAN, JOHN, public relations executive; Dir. pub. and consumer affairs Meijer, Inc., Grand Rapids, Mich., 1994—. Office: Meijer Inc 2929 Walker Ave NW Grand Rapids MI 49544-9428

ZIMMERMAN, MARTIN E. financial executive; b. Chgo., Jan. 28, 1938; s. Joseph and Sylvea Zimmerman; m. Rita Kalifon, June 20, 1961 (div. 1992); children: Jacqueline, Adam. BSEE, MIT, 1955-59; MBA in Fin., Columbia U., 1961. Dir. market research Nuclear-Chgo., Inc. div. G.D. Searle & Co., 1964-67; pres. Telco Mktg. Services, Inc., Chgo., 1967-74; chmn., chief exec. officer Linc Capital, Inc., 1975-2000; chmn. Linc Capital, 1975-2000; chmn., CEO LFC Capital, Inc., 2000—. Contbr. numerous articles on leasing to profl. mags. Bd. overseers Columbia U. Grad. Sch. Bus.; trustee Mus. Contemporary Art, Chgo., Ravenswood Med. Ctr., Chgo. Capt. U.S. Army, 1961-63. McKinsey scholar, Kennecott Copper fellow Columbia U., 1959-61. Mem. Equipment Lessors Assn. (bd. dirs.). Clubs: University, Mid-Am. (Chgo.). Avocations: fishing, hunting, skiing, amateur radio. Home: 100 E Bellevue Pl Chicago IL 60611-1157 Office: Line Capital Inc 303 E Wacker Dr Ste 1000 Chicago IL 60601-5298

ZIMMERMAN, MARY, performing arts educator; Asst. prof. perforamce studies Northwestern U., Evanston, Ill. Office: Northwestern U Sch Speech 1979 Sheridan Rd Rm 200 Evanston IL 60208-0001

ZIMMERMAN, STEVEN CHARLES, chemistry educator; b. Chgo., Oct. 8, 1957; s. Howard Elliot and Jane (Kirschenheiter) Z.; m. Sharon Shavitt, Aug. 5, 1990; 2 children, Arielle Reneé, Elena Michelle. BS, U. Wis., 1979; MA, MPhil, Columbia U., PhD, 1983. Asst. prof. chemistry U. Ill., Urbana, 1985-91, assoc. prof. chemistry, 1991-94, prof. chemistry, 1994—. Contbr. articles to profl. publs. Recipient Arthur C. Cope Scholar award, 1997. Home: 55 Chestnut Ct Champaign IL 61822-7121 Office: U Ill 600 S Mathews Ave Urbana IL 61801-3602 E-mail: sczimmer@uiuc.edu.

ZIMMERMAN, WILLIAM, political science educator; b. Washington, Dec. 26, 1936; s. William III and Isabel Edith (Ryan) Z.; m. Barbara Lamar; children: W. Frederick, Carl L., Alice R.; m. Susan McClanahan, Dec. 10, 1989; 1 child, Rachel Thompson. BA with honors, Swarthmore Coll., 1958; MA, George Washington U., 1959; PhD, Columbia U., 1965. Lectr. dept. polit. sci. U. Mich., 1963-64, from asst. to assoc. prof. dept. polit. sci., 1964-74, assoc. chmn. dept. polit. sci., 1971, dir. Ctr. for Russian and East European studies, 1972-78, 91-92, prof. dept. polit. sci., 1974—, assoc. dean for faculty Coll. of Lit., Sci. and Arts, 1981-84. Vis. asst. prof. Columbia U., summer 1966; rsch. assoc. IPPS, 1978—; co-dir. Program for Internat. Peace and Security Rsch., 1983—; program dir. Ctr. for Polit. Studies, 1989—, dir., 1997—; vis. prof. Harvard U., winter 1988; sr. rsch. assoc. Soviet Interview Project, prin. investigator for various confs. and studies; program chmn. comparative communist studies Am. Polit. Sci. Assn. meetings, 1973; mem. adv. coun. Ctr. for Advanced Russian Studies, Woodrow Wilson Ctr., Smithsonian Instn., 1975-84; exec. com., trustee Nat. Coun. Soviet and East European Rsch., 1978-81. Recipient Helen Dwight Reid award Am. Polit. Sci. Assn., 1965; Fgn. Area tng. fellow Ford Found., 1961-62, William Bayard Cutting traveling fellow Columbia U., 1962-63; rsch. grantee Inst. for War and Peace Studies and Russian Inst., Columbia U., 1965, Inter-univ. com. travel grantee Am./Soviet exch. of young faculty, 1956-66, rsch. grantee Program on Internat. Orgn., U. Mich., 1967, 68, 72, Fulbright-Hays grantee for rsch. in Yugoslavia, 1970, IREX travel grantee to Romania, 1975. Mem. Am. Assn. for Advancement of Slavic Studies (co-chmn. planning com. on Soviet fgn. policy, chmn. Shulman prize com.), Nat. Coun. on Soviet and East European Rsch. (exec. com., bd. trustees 1978-81), Coun. on Fgn. Rels., Phi Kappa Phi. Avocation: philately. Office: U Mich 426 Thompson St Ann Arbor MI 48104-2321

ZIMMERS, VIVIAN ELEANOR, development and administrative consultant; b. St. Louis, Oct. 19, 1946; d. John Dominic and Aurea Genevieve (Schottel) Baron; m. John Paul Hargis, Aug. 21, 1964 (div. Mar. 1968); m. Filomeno Mariano Ramos, June 30, 1973 (dec.); children: William S., Kiersten E., Leilani A.; m. Ronald Franklin Zimmers, Sept. 27, 1997. Student, St. Louis U., 1968-69, U. Hawaii, 1986-87; BA in Mgmt., Nat. Louis U., 1991. Co-founder, owner, pres. Batts Ramos and Assocs., Inc., St. Louis, 1991—. Cons. Hawaii Govtl. Affairs Com., Honolulu, 1975-76, Brokers Adv. Com., Honolulu, 1984-85.; govtl. affairs com. St. Louis Assn. Realtors, 1996-97. Mo. Orthopedically Disabled, bd. dirs., 1993—, pres., 1997—; active Assoc. Pres.'s Youth Opportunity Program, St. Louis, 1968; vol. literacy coun., rschr. Vols. in Probation and Parole. Mem. Nat. Assn. Realtors (mem. com. on pub. rels. 1987), St. Louis Real Estate Bd., Mililani Mchts. Assn. (pres. 1985), Rotary Internat. Democrat. Roman Catholic. Home: 70 Willow Dr Eureka MO 63025-2198

ZIMOV, BRUCE STEVEN, software engineer; b. Cin., Oct. 16, 1953; s. Sherman and Sylvia Zimov; m. Cathy Lynn Zimov, July 24, 1999. BS in Physics, U. Cin., 1975, MA in Philosophy, 1979. Physicist Kornylak Corp., Hamilton, Ohio, 1982-83; software engr. Entek Sci. Corp., Cin., 1983-89, project mgr., 1989-95, systems mgr., 1995-2000, AOL tech. mgr., 2000—. Inventor chess variants, table tennis variant. Mem. IEEE, Internat. Neural Network Soc., Tri-State Online Philosophy SIG (founder). Avocations: philosophy, chess, internet, computing, neural networks, economics. E-mail: bzimov@one.net.

ZINN, GROVER ALFONSO, JR. religion educator; b. El Dorado, Ark., June 18, 1937; s. Grover Alfonso and Cora Edith (Saucke) Z.; m. Mary Mel Farris, July 28, 1962; children: Jennifer Anne, Andrew Grover. BA, Rice U., 1959; BD, Duke U., 1962, PhD, 1969; spl. student, U. Glasgow, Scotland, 1962-63. Asst. minister The Barony Ch., Glasgow, 1962-63; instr. in religion Oberlin (Ohio) Coll., 1966-68, asst. prof., 1968-74, assoc. prof., 1974-79, prof., 1979—, Danforth prof. religion, 1986—, chmn. dept. religion, 1980-84, 85-86, 1993-94, 98-00, assoc. dean coll. arts and scis., 2001—. Translator: Richard of St. Victor: The Twelve Patriarchs, The Mystical Ark, and Book Three of the Trinity, 1979; co-editor: Medieval France: An Encyclopedia, 1995; mem. editl. bd. Dictionary of Biblical Interpretation; contbr. articles on medieval Christian mysticism, theology, and iconography. H.H. Powers Travel grantee Oberlin Coll., 1969, 85; Dempster fellow United Meth. Ch., 1965-66, NEH Younger Humanist fellow, 1972-73, Research Status fellow Oberlin Coll., 1972-73, 97-98, Faculty Devel. fellow Oberlin Coll. 1985, Lilly Endowment fellow U. Pa., 1981-82; recipient ACLS Travel award, 1982. Mem. Medieval Acad. Am. (councillor 1983-86), Am. Soc. Ch. History (coun. mem. 1989-92, 95—98, Ecclesiastical History Soc. Democrat. Methodist. Avocations: photography, electronics. Home: 61 Glenhurst Dr Oberlin OH 44074-1423 Office: Oberlin Coll Cox Adminstrn Bldg Oberlin OH 44074 E-mail: grover.zinn@oberlin.edu.

ZINNER, ERNST K. physics educator, earth and planetary science educator, researcher; b. Steyr, Austria, Jan. 30, 1937; MS, Tech. U., Vienna, Austria, 1960; PhD in Physics, Wash. U., Mo., 1972. Instr. physics Coll. Vet. Medicine, Vienna, 1963-64; program and calculation magnetic field distbr. Brown-Boveri Co., Switzerland, 1964-65, rsch. assoc. Switzerland, 1972-74, sr. rsch. scientist Switzerland, 1974-89; rsch. prof. physics Wash. U., St. Louis, 1989—. Vis. scientist Max-Planck Inst. Physics, Germany, 1980, Max-Planck Inst. Chemistry, Germany, 1980, U. Pavia, Italy, 1989. Recipient J. Lawrence Smith medal NAS, 1997. Fellow Am. Physics Soc., Meteoritical Soc.; mem. AAAS, Am. Geophysics Union, Sigma Xi. Office: Wash U Campus Box 1169 1 Brookings Dr Saint Louis MO 63130-4862

ZINTER, STEVEN L. judge; m. Sandra Zinter; 2 children. Doctorate, Univ. So. Dakota, 1975, BS, 1972. Judge Supreme Court, 2002—; pvt. practice, 1978—86; practice as asst. atty. gen. State So. Dakota; cir. judge State of So. Dakota, 1987—97; presiding judge Sixth Judicial Cir., 1997—2002. Mem. Harry S. Found.; trustee So. Dakota Retirement Sys.; elect. pres. So. Dakota Corrections Commn. Mem.: Am. Bar Assn. Office: Supreme Court S Dakota State Capital Bldg E Capitol Ave Pierre SD 57501-5070*

ZIOMEK, JONATHAN S. journalist, educator; b. Newport News, Va., July 28, 1947; s. Stanley Walter and Joy Carmen (Schmidt) Z.; m. Rosalie Ziomek, Aug. 14, 1977; children: Joseph, Jennifer; 1 stepchild, Daniel. BA in Sociology, U. Ill., 1970, MS in Journalism, 1982. Reporter, labor writer, feature writer, Sun. fin. editor Chgo. Sun-Times, 1970-78; press sec. for U.S. Senate campaign, Chgo., 1979-80; asst. prof. Medill Sch. Journalism, Northwestern U., Evanston, Ill., 1983-88; dir. grad. editl. programs Medill Sch. Journalism/Northwestern U., 1988—, asst. dean, assoc. prof., 1994—. Presenter writing workshops; corp. writing cons. Contbr. articles to various mags.; editor: Chgo. Journalist Newsletter, 1991-93. Participant Internat. Visitors Ctr., Chgo., 1988—; fact-finder USIA, Bulgaria and Yugoslavia, 1990. Mem. Assn. for Edn. in Journalism and Mass Communications, Soc. Profl. Journalists, Nat. Assn. Sci. Writers, Chgo. Headline Club. Home: 2149 Hartrey Ave Evanston IL 60201-2571 Office: Northwestern Univ Medill Sch Journalism Evanston IL 60208-0001

ZIPES, DOUGLAS PETER, cardiologist, researcher; b. White Plains, N.Y., Feb. 27, 1939; s. Robert Samuel and Josephine Helen (Weber) Z.; m. Marilyn Joan Jacobus, Feb. 18, 1961; children: Debra, Jeffrey, David. BA cum laude, Dartmouth Coll., 1961, B of Med. Sci., 1962; MD cum laude, Harvard Med. Sch., 1964. Diplomate Am. Bd. Internal Medicine, mem. subsplty. bd. cardiovascular disease 1989-99, chmn., 1995-99, chmn. com. cert. in clin. cardiac electrophysiology 1989-96, bd. dirs. 1995—, exec. com. 1999—, chmn. bd. 2002. Intern, resident, fellow in cardiology Duke U. Med. Ctr., Durham, N.C., 1964-68; vis. scientist Masonic Med. Rsch. Lab., Utica, N.Y., 1970-71; asst. prof. medicine Ind. U. Sch. Medicine, Indpls., 1970-73, assoc. prof., 1973-76, prof., 1976-94, prof. pharmacology and toxicology, 1993—, disting. prof. medicine, 1994—; dir. divsn. of cardiology Krannert Inst. Cardiology, Ind. U. Sch. Medicine, 1995—. Bd. dirs. Inst. for Clin. Evaluation; cardiology adv. com NIH, 1991—94; mem. exec. com. on electrophysiology World Heart Fedn. , mem. electrophysiology exec. com.; mem. med. adv. bd. ABCNews.com, 2000—; cons. in field ; mem. dean's coun. Dartmouth Med. Sch. Author: Comprehensive Cardiac Care, 7th edit., 1991; editor: Slow Inward Current, 1980, Cardiac Electrophysiology and Arrhythmias, 1985, Nonpharmacological Therapy of Tachyarrhythmias, 1987, Cardiac Electrophysiology From Cell to Bedside, 1990, 3d edit., 2000; co-editor: Treatment of Heart Diseases, 1992, Ablation of Cardiac Arrhythmias, 1994, 2d edit., 2002, Antiarrhythmic Therapy: A Pathophysiologic Approach, 1994, Heart Disease, A Textbook of Cardiovascular Medicine, 6th edit., 2001; mem. editl. bd. Circulation, 1974-78, 83—, Am. Jour. Cardiology, 1979-82, 88—, Am. Jour. Medicine, 1979-90, Jour. Am. Coll. Cardiology, 1983, 2002-, Am. Heart Jour., 1977-97, PACE, 1977—, Circulation Rsch., 1983-90, Am. Jour. Noninvasive Cardiology, 1985-89, Jour. Electrophysiology, 1987-89, Cardiovascular Drugs and Therapy, 1986-93, Japanese Heart Jour., 1989—, Jour. Cardiovascular Pharmacology and Therapeutics, 1994—, Jour. Cardiovascular Pharmacology, 1995—, Cardiovascular Therapeutics, 1995, Current Clin. Trials, 1995-98, Jour. Interventional Cardiac Electrophysiology, 1996—; editor-in-chief: Progress in Cardiology, 1988-92, Jour. Cardiovascular Electrophysiology, 1990—, Cardiology in Rev., 1992-2002, Contemporary Treatments of Cardiovascular Disease, 1996-98, Am. Coll. Cardiology Extended Learning, 1997—, Ind. Jour. Pacing and Electrophysiology Online, 2001—; contbr. articles to profl. jours.; patentee cardioverter, elec. prevention of arrhythmia, discrimination of atrial fibrillation, fixation of implantable devices, and periocardial delivery of therapeutic and diagnostic agents. Pres., bd. dirs. Indpls. Opera Co., 1983-85; mem. study sect. NIH, Washington, 1977-81; mem. nat. merit rev. bd. VA, 1982-85, Cardiology Adv. Com. NHLBL, 1991-98, chmn. steering com. AVID; chmn. Data and Safety Monitoring Bd. AFFIRM, 1996—; mem. exec. com. on electrophysiology World Health Fedn. Recipient Disting. Achievement award Am. Heart Assn., 1989, Sagamore of the Wabash award, Gov. Ind., 2001. Master Am. Coll. Cardiology (chmn. ACC/AHA subcom. to assess EP studies, chmn. young investigators award com. 1988-94, trustee 1992-97, mem. nominating com. 1993-95, Disting. Scientist award 1996, chmn. devel. com. 1996-2001, sci. sessions program com. 1996-98, v.p. 1999-00, pres.-elect 2000-01, pres. 01-02); fellow ACP, Am. Heart Assn. (exec. com. 1980-88, sci. sessions program 1983-86, chmn. various coms., chmn. 1995, bd. dirs. Internat. Cardiology Found. 1993-98, bd. dirs. 1994-96, chmn. emergency cardiac care com. 1995-96; Herrick award 1997); mem. Am. Soc. Clin. Investigation, Assn. Univ. Cardiologists (v.p. 1994, pres. 1995), Assn. Am. Physicians, Am. Physiol. Soc., Cardiac Electrophysiology Soc. (pres. 1985-86), N.Am. Soc. Pacing and Electrophysiology (pres. 1988-90, trustee 1990—, Disting. Scientist award 1995), InterAm. Soc. Cardiology (1st v.p. 1995-98), Ind. Cardiac Electrophysiology Soc. (founder). Home: 10614 Winterwood Carmel IN 46032-9688 Office: Ind U Sch Medicine 1100 W Michigan St Indianapolis IN 46202-5208 E-mail: dzipes@iupui.edu.

ZIPFEL, PAUL A. bishop; b. St. Louis; BST, Cath. U. Am., 1961; MA in Edn., St. Louis U., 1965. Ordained priest Roman Cath. Ch., 1961. Tchr., counselor, adminstr. St. Louis Archdiocesan high schs.; consecrated bishop, 1989; bishop Diocese of Bismarck, N.D., 1989—. Office: PO Box 1575 420 Raymond St Bismarck ND 58502-1575

ZIRBES, MARY KENNETH, minister; b. Melrose, Minn., Sept. 4, 1926; d. Joseph Louis and Clara Bernadine (Petermeier) Z. BA in History and Edn., Coll. St. Catherine, 1960; MA in Applied Theology, Sch. Applied Theology, Berkeley, Calif., 1976. Joined Order of St. Francis, Roman Cath. Ch., 1945. Tchr. Pub. Grade Sch., St. Nicholas, Minn., 1947-52; prin. Holy Spirit Grade Sch., St. Cloud, 1953-59, St. Mary's Jr. H.S., Morris, 1960-62; coord. Franciscan Mission Team, Peru, South America, 1962-67, Franciscan Missions, Little Falls, Minn., 1967-70; dir. St. Richard's Social Justice Ministry, Richfield, 1971-80, Parish Community Devel., St. Paul, Mpls., 1980-85; councillor gen. Franciscan Sisters of Little Falls, 1960-62, 67-70; asst. dir. Renew-Archdiocese of St. Paul-Mpls., 1986-89; coord. Parish Social Justice Ministry-Archdiocese of St. Paul-Mpls., 1990-93; minister Franciscan Assocs., 1993—; leader of team on evangelical life Franciscan Sisters of Little Falls, 1994-96. Co-developer Assn. of Pastoral Ministers, Mpls., St. Paul, 1979-81, Compañeros/Sister Parishes-Minn. and Nicaragua, 1984-89, Minn. Interfaith Ecology Coalition, 1989-92. Author: Parish Social Ministry, 1985, (manual) Acting for Justice, 1992. Organizer Twin Cities Orgn., Mpls., 1979-80; bd. dirs. Franciscan Sisters Health Care, Inc., Little Falls, 1990-93, Rice-Marion Residents Assn., St. Paul, 1991-92. Named Outstanding chair Assn. Pastoral Ministers, 1981; recipient Five Yrs. of Outstanding Svc. award Companeros, 1989. Mem. Assn. Pastoral Ministers (chair 1979), Amnesty Internat., Voices for Justice-Legis. Lobby, Audubon Soc., Network, Minn. Interfaith Ecology Coalition, Ctrl. Minn. Ecumenical Team on Racism. Avocations: water color painting, birding, golf, reading history and biography. Office: Franciscan Sisters 116 8th Ave SE Little Falls MN 56345-3539 E-mail: mzirbes@fslf.org.

ZLATOFF-MIRSKY, EVERETT IGOR, violinist; b. Evanston, Ill., Dec. 29, 1937; s. Alexander Igor and Evelyn Ola (Hill) Z.-M.; m. Janet Dalbey, Jan. 28, 1976; children from previous marriage— Tania, Laura. B.Mus., Chgo. Mus. Coll., Roosevelt U., 1960, M.Mus., 1961. Mem. faculty dept. music Roosevelt U., Chgo., 1961-66. Founding mem., violinist, violist Music of the Baroque, 1971—. Violinist orch. Lyric Opera of Chgo., 1974—; concert master, pers. mgr., 1974—, violinst, violist, Contemporary Chamber Players U. Chog., 1964-82, solo violinist, Bach Soc., 1966-83; violist, violinist, Lexington String Quartet, 1966-81; rec. artist numerous recs., radio-TV and films; solo violinist appearing throughout U.S. Recipient Olive Ditson award Franklin Honor Soc., 1961 Mem. Nat. Acad. Rec. Arts and Scis. Republican. Roman Catholic. Home: 41w743 Hughes Rd Elburn IL 60119-9776 Office: Lyric Opera Chgo 20 N Wacker Dr Chicago IL 60606-2806 E-mail: jdzm@aol.com.

ZOBRIST, BENEDICT KARL, library director, historian; b. Moline, Ill., Aug. 21, 1921; s. Benedict and Lila Agnas (Colson) Z.; m. Donna Mae Anderson, Oct. 23, 1948; children: Benedict Karl II, Markham Lee, Erik Christian. AB, Augustana Coll., Rock Island, Ill., 1946; postgrad., Stanford U., 1946-47; MA, Northwestern U., 1948, PhD, 1953; postgrad., U. Ill., 1961, Tunghai U., Taiwan, 1962, Columbia U., 1962-63, Fed. Exec. Inst., Charlottesville, Va., 1974, Hebrew U., Israel, 1978; LHD, Avila Coll., 1995. Manuscript specialist in recent Am. history Library of Congress, Washington, 1952-53; asst. reference librarian Newberry Library, Chgo., 1953-54; command historian Ordnance Weapons Command, Rock Island Arsenal, 1954-60; prof. history, chmn. dept. Augustana Coll., 1960-69, asst. dean faculty, 1964-69, asso. dean, dir. grad. studies, 1969; asst. dir. Harry S. Truman Libr., Independence, Mo., 1969-71, dir., 1971-94. Exec. sec. Harry S. Truman Libr. Inst., Independence, 1971-94; mem. steering com. Harry S. Truman Statue Com., Independence, 1973-76; dir., regent Harry S. Truman Good Neighbor Award Found., 1974—; mem. Independence Truman Award Commn., 1975-94, Mo. Hist. Records Adv. Bd., 1978—; adj. prof. history U. Mo.-Kansas City, 1975—, Ottawa U., Kansas City, 1977-94, U. Mo. St. Louis, 1987-94; chmn. Independence Commn. Bicentennial of U.S. Constitution, 1987, Uptown Independence, Inc., 1989-94; mem. adv. coun. Truman Little White House State Historic Site, Key West, Fla., 1987-94. Contbr. articles, revs. to profl. jours. Trustee Heritage League of Greater Kansas City, 1981—, Liberty Meml. Assn., Kansas City, Mo., 1990—, Black Archives Mid-Am., Inc., Kansas City, 1992-94; mem. Truman Nat. Centennial Com., 1982-84. Served with AUS, 1942-46. Recipient Outstanding Alumni Achievement award Augustana Coll., 1975, Bronze Good Citizenship medal Kans. SAR, 1986, People's Choice award Independence (Mo.) Neighborhood Councils, 1987, Mid-Am. Regional Council award for contbns. to met. community, 1987, Citizen Achievement award Black Archives of Mid-Am., 1988, Silver Good Citizenship medal Mo. SAR, 1988, Special Recognition award City of Independence, 1988, Outstanding Civic Leader in Independence, 1989, Gold Medal of Honor DAR, 1990, Spl. Commendation award Nat. Park Svc., 1993; named World Citizen of Yr. by Kans. City Mayor's UN Day Com., 1994. Mem. AAUP, Am. Hist. Assn., Jackson County (Mo.) Hist. Soc. (v.p. 1972-82, 93-95), Orgn. Am. Historians, Assn. Asian Studies, Am. Assn. State, Local History, Soc. Am. Archivists, U.S. Power Squadron, Am. Legion, La Societe des 40 Hommes et 8 Chevaux, VFW. Home: 71B T St Lake Lotawana MO 64086-9728

ZOBRIST, GEORGE WINSTON, computer scientist, educator; b. Highland, Ill., Feb. 13, 1934; s. George H. and Lillie C. (Augustin) Z.; m. Freida Groverlyn Rich, Mar. 29, 1955; children: Barbara Jayne, George William, Jean Anne. BS, U. Mo., 1958, PhD, 1965; MS, Wichita State U., 1961. Registered profl. engr., Mo., Fla. Electronic scientist U.S. Naval Ordnance Test Sta., China Lake, Calif., 1958-59; rsch. engr. Boeing Co., Wichita, 1959-60; instr. Wichita State U., 1960-61; assoc. prof. U. Mo., Columbia, 1961-69, U. So. Fla., Tampa, 1969-70; chmn. elec. engring. dept. U. Miami, Coral Gables, Fla., 1970-71; prof. U. South Fla., Tampa, 1971-72, 73-76; prof., chmn. dept. elec. engring. U. Toledo, 1976-79; dir. computer sci. and engring. Samborn, Steketee, Otis, Evans, Inc., Toledo, 1979-82; prof. computer sci. Grad. Engring. Ctr. U. Mo., St. Louis, 1982-85, prof. computer sci. Rolla, 1985-99, chmn. dept., 1994-99, prof. emeritus, 1999—. Rsch. prof. U. Edinburgh, Scotland, 1972-73; lectr. U. Western Cape, South Africa, 1995 summer; cons. Wilcox Electric Co., Bendix Corp., both Kansas City, Mo., 1966-68, ICC, Miami, 1970-71, Def. Comm. Agy., Washington, 1971, 72, U.S. Naval Rsch. Labs., Washington, 1971, Med. Svc. Bur., Miami, 1970-71, NASA, Kennedy Space Ctr., Fla., 1973-76, 88, 89, 93, 94, Prestolite Corp., Toledo, 1977-79, IBM, Lexington, Ky., 1983-86, Wright-Patterson AFB, Ohio, 1986, PAFB, Fla., 1987, McDonnell Douglas, Mo., 1989, Digital Systems Cons., Mo., 1989, Oak Ridge Nat. Labs., 1992. Author: Network Computer Analysis, 1969, Progress in Computer Aided VLSI Design, 1988-90; editor Internat. Jour. Computer Aided VLSI Design, 1989-91, Object Oriented Simulation IEEE Press, 1996, Computer Sci. and Computer Engring. Monograph series, 1989-91, Internat. Jour. Computer Simulation, 1990-96, VLSI Design, 1992—; editor IEEE Potentials Mag., 1996-99; assoc. editor, 1984-96, 99—; contbr. articles to profl. jours. Served with USAF, 1951-55. Named Young Engr. of Yr. ctrl. chpt. Mo. Soc. Profl. Engrs., 1967; NSF summer fellow, 1962, 64; NASA, IBM, DOE, UES/AFOSR, McDonnell Douglas rsch. grantee, 1967-88. Fellow IEEE (life, mem. IEEE Press editl. bd. 1998—); mem. Am. Legion, Rotary, Sigma Xi, Tau Beta Pi, Phi Eta Sigma, Eta Kappa Nu, Pi Mu Epsilon, Upsilon Pi Epsilon. Home: 12030 Country Club Dr Rolla MO 65401-7469 Office: U Mo Rolla Dept Computer Sci 1870 Miner Cir Rolla MO 65409-0001 E-mail: zobrist@umr.edu.

ZOGRAFI, GEORGE, pharmacologist, educator; b. N.Y.C., Mar. 13, 1936; married; 4 children. BS, Columbia U., 1956; MS, U. Mich., 1958, PhD in Pharm. Chemistry, 1961; DS (hon.), Columbia U., 1976. Asst. prof. pharmacology Columbia U., N.Y.C., 1961-64; from asst. prof. to assoc. prof. U. Mich., Ann Arbor, 1964-72; rsch. fellow Am. Found. Pharm. Edn., 1970-71; Pheiffer rsch. fellow Utrecht (The Netherlands) U., 1970-71; prof. pharmacology U. Wis., Madison, 1972—, dean, 1975-80. Mem. AAAS, NAS (Inst. Medicine), Am. Pharm. Assn. (Ebert prize 1984), Am. Chem. Soc., Am. Assn. Pharm. Scientists, Internat. Pharm. Fedn., Internat. Assn. Colloid and Interface Scientists, Am. Inst. Hist. Pharm., Sigma Xi. Office: U Wis Sch Pharmacology 425 N Charter St Madison WI 53706-1508

ZOLA, GARY PHILLIP, rabbi, historian, religious educational administrator; b. Chgo., Feb. 17, 1952; m. Stefani Paula Rothberg; children: Amanda Roi, Jorin Benjamin, Jeremy Micah, Samantha Leigh. BA in Am. History with distinction, U. Mich., 1973; MA in Counseling Psychology, Northwestern U., 1976; PhD in Am. Jewish History, Hebrew Union Coll., Cin., 1991. Ordained rabbi, 1982. Dir. informal edn. and youth activities Temple Israel, Mpls., 1973-74; regional youth dir., asst. camp dir. Olin-Sang-Ruby Union Inst., UAHC, Chgo., 1974-77; student pulpit B'nai Israel Congregation, Williamson, W.Va., 1978-79; mem. student pulpit Anshe Sholom Congregation, Olympia Fields, Ill., 1979-80, Columbus Hebrew Congregation, Columbus, Ind., 1981-82; rabbi for high holy days Chgo. Jewish Experience, Chgo., 1982-94; nat. dir. admissions Hebrew Union Coll.-Jewish Inst. Religion, Cin., 1982-89, nat. dean admissions and student affairs, 1989-91, nat. dean admissions, student affairs and alumni rels., 1991-98; exec. dir. Jacob Rader Marcus Ctr. Am. Jewish Archives at Hebrew Union Coll., 1998—; assoc. prof. Am. Jewish Experience Hebrew Union Coll. Jewish Inst. of Religion. Del. Emerging Leaders Conf., Am. Coun. for Internat. Leadership, 1989, 91; bd. dirs. Am. Jewish Com., Cin., 1982—, mem. exec. com., 1984—; bd. dirs. Hillel U. Cin., 1991-94, Jewish Fedn., Cin., 1993-95; pres. Greater Cin. Bd. Rabbis, 1993-95, Jewish Cmty. Rels. Coun., (bd. dir.,1994—); founding mem. Kehillah of Cin., Jewish Think Tank. Author: Isaac Harby of Charleston, 1994; editor: Hebrew Union College--Jewish Institute of Religion--A Centennial History, 1875-1975, (Michael A. Meyer), 1992, Women Rabbis: Exploration and Celebration, 1996; editor: The American Jewish Archives Jour., 1998—; contbr. numerous scholarly articles to profl. jours.; mem. editl. bd. Reform Judaism. Bd. dirs. ethics com. Jewish Hosp., Cin.; life mem. N.Am. Fedn. Temple Youth; active NCCJ. Mem. Ctrl. Conf. Am. Rabbis, Orgn. Am. Historians, Assn. Jewish Studies, So. Jewish Hist. Soc., Am. Jewish Hist. Soc., N.Am. Fedn. Temple Youth (life). Office: Hebrew Union Coll Jewish Inst Religion 3101 Clifton Ave Cincinnati OH 45220-2404

ZOLLARS, WILLIAM D. freight company executive; With Kodak; sr. v.p. Ryder Integrated Logistics Ryder Sys., Inc.; pres. Yellow Freight Sys., 1996-99; chmn., pres., CEO Yellow Corp., Overland Park, Kans., 1999—. Office: Yellow Corp 10990 Roe Ave Overland Park KS 66211-1213

ZOLNO, MARK S. lawyer; BA Polit. Sci., No. Ill. Univ., 1965; JD, John Marshall Law Sch., 1978; MA cum laude Internat. Rels., Universidad de las Américas, Mexico, 1974. Bar: Ill. 1978, U.S. Dist. Ct. (no. dist.) Ill. 1979, U.S. Ct. Internat. Trade 1979, U.S. Ct. Appeals (fed. cir.) 1979. With U.S. Customs Svc., Dept. Commerce, U.S. Trade Rep's. Office, Internat. Trade Commn., Fed. Trade Commn., FDA; ptnr. Katten Muchin & Zavis, Chgo., 1988—. Past chmn. Chgo. Bar Assn. Customs and U.S. Trade Law Com.; lectr. in field. Contbr. articles to profl. jours. Office: Katten Muchin & Zavis 525 W Monroe St Ste 1600 Chicago IL 60661-3693

ZOLOMIJ, ROBERT WILLIAM, landscape architect, consultant; b. Phila., Oct. 13, 1942; s. William and Anna (Sikacz) Z.; m. Joanne M. Volk, Oct. 2, 1965; children: Nancy Lyn, Christopher John; m. Nancy S. Helfferich, Nov. 21, 1992. BS in Landscape Architecture, Pa. State U., 1965; M Landscape Architecture, U. Ill., 1971. Lic. landscape arch., Ill. Site planner Bucks County Planning Commn., Doylestown, Pa., 1965-67; assoc. prof. U. Ill., Urbana, 1968-78; sr. landscape arch. Skidmore Owings & Merrill, Chgo., 1978-79; sr. assoc. Barton-Aschman Assocs., Evanston, Ill., 1979-84; v.p. Harland Bartholomew Assocs., Northbrook, 1984-86, Land Design Collaborative, Inc., Evanston, 1986—. Co-author: Time Saver Standards for Landscape Architects, 1988. Univ. fellow U. Ill., 1967. Fellow Am. Soc. Landscape Archs. (chpt. treas. 1986-88, v.p. 1988-90, pres. 1990-92). Avocations: golf, travel, reading, woodworking. Home: 3429 Harrison St Evanston IL 60201-4953 Office: 5142 Main St Skokie IL 60077-2102

ZONA, LOUIS ALBERT, art institute director; s. Patricia Zona; 1 child, Tace. BS in Edn. magna cum laude, Youngstown (Ohio) State U., 1966; MS in Edn., U. Pitts., 1969; DFA, Carnegie Mellon U., 1973. Asst. to dir. The Butler Inst. of Am. Art, Youngstown, 1980-81, exec. dir., 1981—; prof. art history Youngstown State U., 1970—, chmn. art dept., 1978-82. Adj. prof. art and museology Westminster Coll., 1976-80. Contbr. numerous articles to profl. publs. Recipient Gari Melchers medla Artists' Fellowship, N.Y.C., 1996, Gov.'s award for the Arts in Ohio, 1990, Disting. Profl. Svc. award Ohio Steel Valley Art Tchrs. Assn., 1982. Office: Butler Inst Am Art 524 Wick Ave Youngstown OH 44502

ZONA, RICHARD A. bank executive; CFO U.S. Bancorp, Mpls., 1989-96, vice chmn. Comml. and Bus. Banking, 1990—, vice chmn. U.S. Bancorp Piper Jaffray, 1990—, vice chmn. U.S. Bancorp Libra, 1990—, vice chmn. Pvt. Fin. Svcs., 1990—, vice chmn. Instnl. Fin. Svcs., 1990—, vice chmn. Corp. Trust Svcs., 1990—. Office: US Bancorp US Bank Pl 601 2nd Ave S Minneapolis MN 55402-4303

ZONIS, MARVIN, political scientist, educator; b. Boston, Sept. 18, 1936; s. Leonard and Clara (Barenberg) Z.; m. Lucy Salenger, Jan. 3, 1976; children by previous marriage-Nadia E. Leah; 1 stepdaugher, Brix E. Smith. A.B., Yale U., 1958; postgrad., Harvard Grad. Sch. Bus., 1958-59; Ph.D., M.I.T., 1968; candidate, Inst. for Psychoanalysis, Chgo., 1977-85. Mem. faculty U. Chgo., 1966—, assoc. prof. and prof. behavioral scis., 1973-89—, prof. Grad. Sch. Bus., 1989—; dir. U. Chgo. (Center for Middle Eastern Studies), 1976-79; pres. Marvin Zonis and Assocs., Internat. Cons., 1991—. Cons. in field; chmn. com. on Middle East Am. Coun. Learned Socs.-Social Sci. Rsch. Coun., 1970-76; pres. Am. Inst. Iranian Studies, 1969-71; bd. dirs. CNA Fin. Corp. Author: The Political Elite of Iran, 1971, Khomeini, The Islamic Republic of Iran, and the Arab World, 1987, Majestic Failure: The Fall of the Shah, 1991, The East European Opportunity: The Complete Business Guide and Source Book, 1992; contbr. articles to profl. jours. Served with USAF, 1959-60. Recipient Quantrell award for excellence in teaching U. Chgo., 1979 Office: U Chicago 5828 S University Ave Chicago IL 60637-1515

ZONKA, CONSTANCE ZIPPRODT, educational organization administrator; b. Evanston, Ill. d. Herbert Edward and Agnes Irene (Turpin) Zipprodt; m. Robert F. Zonka, Aug. 5, 1970; children: Heidi Zapanta, Milo Matthew. BA, U. Fla., 1958; postgrad., U. Chgo., 1960. Account exec. Daniel J. Edelman, Inc., Chgo., 1964-68; pres. Connie Zonka Assocs., 1974-89; dir. coll. rels. Columbia Coll., 1970-89; sr. dir. univ. rels. Roosevelt U., 1990-93; dir. office pub. affairs Gov.'s State U., University Park, Ill., 1993—. Mem. NAFE, Pub. Rels. Soc. Am., Publicity Club Chgo., Nat. Assn. Women Bus. Owners, Friends of WFMT (sec. 1989—), Friends of Downtown, Friends of the Parks. Democrat. Avocations: horseback riding, swimming, theatre, dance, reading. Home: 547 S Clark St Apt 1003 Chicago IL 60605-1618

ZOOK, ELVIN GLENN, plastic surgeon, educator; b. Huntington County, Ind., Mar. 21, 1937; s. Glenn Hardman and Ruth (Barton) Z.; m. Sharon Kay Neher, Dec. 11, 1960; children— Tara E., Leigh A., Nicole L. B.A., Manchester Coll., 1959; M.D., Ind. U., 1963. Diplomate Am. Bd. Surgery, Am. Bd. Thoracic Surgery, Am. Bd. Plastic Surgery. Intern Meth. Hosp., Indpls., 1963-64; resident in gen. and thoracic surgery Ind. U. Med. Center, 1964-69; resident in plastic surgery Ind. U. Hosp., 1969-71, asst. prof. plastic surgery, 1971-73; asso. prof. surgery So. Ill. U., Springfield, 1973-75, prof., 1975—, chmn. div. plastic surgery, 1973—. Mem. staff Meml. Med. Center, St. Johns Hosp., Springfield. Contbr. articles to med. jours. Mem. AMA, Assn. Acad. Surgery, Am. Soc. Plastic and Reconstructive Surgery (sec. 1988-91, v.p. 1991-92, pres.-elect 1992-93, pres. 1993-94), Midwestern Soc. Plastic and Reconstructive Surgery (pres. 1986-87), ACS, Sangamon County Med. Soc. (pres. 1987), Am. Cleft Palate Assn., Am. Assn. Plastic Surgery (trustee 1987-90), Plastic Surgery Rsch. Coun. (chmn. 1981), Am. Burn Assn., Ill. Surg. Soc., Am. Soc. Surgery Hand (coun.), Am. Bd. of Plastic Surgery (sec.-treas. 1988-91, chmn. 1991-92), Am. Soc. Aesthetic Plastic Surgery, Am. Soc. Surgery of Trauma, Assn. Acad. Chmn. Plastic Surgery (pes. 1986-87), Am. Surg. Assn., RRC for Plastic Surgery, Sangamo Club, Springfield Med. Club, Island Bay Yacht Club. Presbyterian. Clubs: Sangamo, Springfield Med, Island Bay Yacht. Home: 7235 Mansion Rd Chatham IL 62629-8763 Office: 747 N Rutledge St Springfield IL 62702-6700 E-mail: ezook@siumed.edu.

ZORE, EDWARD JOHN, financial services executive; b. Milw., July 5, 1945; s. Joseph F. and Marie A. Z.; m. Diane Widemshek, Aug. 19, 1967; children: Annemarie, Kathryn. B.S., U. Wis.-Milw., 1968, M.S., 1970. Pres., CEO Northwestern Mut., Milw., 1969—. Republican. Roman Catholic. Office: Northwestern Mutual 720 E Wisconsin Ave Milwaukee WI 53202-4703

ZORN, ERIC JOHN, newspaper columnist; b. New Haven, Jan. 6, 1958; s. Jens Christian and Frances (Barnhart) Z.; m. Johanna Wolken, Nov. 2, 1985; children: Alexander, Anna Lise, Benjamin. BA, U. Mich., 1980. With Chgo. Tribune, 1980—, met. reporter, 1985-86, columnist, 1986—. Instr. Northwestern U. Medill Sch. Journalism, Evanston, Ill., 1985-89. Co-author: Murder of Innocence, 1990. Avocation: old-time square dance caller. Office: Chgo Tribune PO Box 25340 435 N Michigan Ave Chicago IL 60611-4066

ZORN, ROBERT LYNN, education educator; b. Youngstown, Ohio, Mar. 22, 1938; s. Robert S. and Frances L. Zorn; B.S. Ed., Kent State U., 1959; M.Ed., Westminster Coll., 1964; Ph.D., U. Pitts., 1970; m. Joan M. Wilkos, Apr. 26, 1957; children: Deborah Lynn, Patricia Lynn. Tchr., West Branch (Ohio) Schs., 1961-62; elem. prin. Poland (Ohio) Schs., 1962-67, supt. schs., 1976— ; high sch. unit prin. Boardman (Ohio) Schs., 1967-70; dir. adminstrv. services Mahoning County (Ohio) Schs., 1970-73, asst. supt., 1973-76; adj. prof. edn. Westminister Coll., 1985—; chmn. Ohi Adv. Com. to State Dept. Edn.; chmn. McGuffey Hist. Soc. Nat. Educator's Hall of Fame. Chmn. Mahoning County chpt. Am. Cancer Soc.; pres. bd. trustees Poland Methodist Ch.; trustee Mahoning County chpt. Am. Heart Assn. Served to lt. USAF, 1959-61. Mem. Doctoral Assn. Educators (life), Am. Assn. Sch. Adminstrs., Ohio PTA (life; Educator of Yr. 1980-81), Phi Delta Kappa. Republican. Clubs: Fonderlac County, Rotary, Protestant Men's. Author numerous books including Speed Reading, 1989, rev. edit., 1997; contbr. articles to profl. jours. Office: 30 Riverside Dr Youngstown OH 44514-2049

ZUBROFF, LEONARD SAUL, surgeon; b. Minersville, Pa., Mar. 27, 1925; s. Abe and Fannie (Freedline) Z. BA, Wayne State U., 1945, MD, 1949. Diplomate Am. Bd. Surgery. Intern Garfield Hosp., Washington, 1949-50, resident in surgery, 1951-55, chief resident surgery, 1954-55; pvt. practice medicine specializing in surgery, 1958-76; med. dir. Chevrolet Gear and Axle Plant, Forge Plant, GM, Detroit, 1977-78; divsnl. med. dir. Detroit Diesel Allison divsn., 1978-87; regional med. dir. GM, 1987-89; ret., 1989. Chief of surgery, chief profl. svcs. N.E. Air Command, Pepperell AFB, Newfoundland. With USAF, 1956—58. Mem.: Le Vine Found. (trustee). Home and Office: 22511 S Bellwood Dr Southfield MI 48034-2116

ZUCARO, ALDO CHARLES, insurance company executive; b. Grenoble, France, Apr. 2, 1939; s. Louis and Lucy Zucaro; m. Gloria J. Ward, Oct. 12, 1963; children: Lucy, Louis, Faye. BS in Acctg, Queens Coll., N.Y.C., 1962. C.P.A., N.Y., Ill. Ptnr. Coopers & Lybrand (and predecessor), Chgo. and N.Y.C., 1962-76; exec. v.p., chief fin. officer Old Republic Internat. Corp., Chgo., 1976-81, pres., 1981—, chief exec. officer, 1990—, also chmn. bd. dirs., 1993—, chmn. of the bd., 1993—. Pres., bd. dirs. Old Republic Life Ins. Co., Old Republic Life of N.Y., Old Republic Ins. Co., Internat. Bus. and Merc. Reassurance Co., Republic Mortgage Ins. Co., Old Republic Nat. Title Ins. Co., Home Owners Life Ins. Co. Editor: Financial Accounting Practices of the Insurance Industry, 1975, 76. Mem. AICPAs. Roman Catholic. Office: Old Republic Internat Corp 307 N Michigan Ave Chicago IL 60601-5311

ZUCKER, ROBERT A(LPERT), psychologist; b. N.Y.C., Dec. 9, 1935; s. Morris and Sophie (Alpert) Z.; m. Martine Latil; children: Lisa, Alex, Eleanor; m. Kristine Ellen Freeark, Mar. 10, 1979; 1 child, Katherine. B.C.E., CCNY, 1956; postgrad., UCLA, 1956-58; Ph.D., Harvard U., 1966. Diplomate Am. Bd. Profl. Psychology (clin.); lic. psychologist, Mich. From instr. to asst. prof. psychology Rutgers U., 1963-68; from asst. prof. to assoc. prof. to prof. Mich. State U., 1968-94; prof. psychology in psychiatry and psychology U. Mich., 1994—, dir. Addiction Rsch. Ctr., 1994—, dir. substance abuse divsn. dept. psychiatry, 1994—, rsch. assoc. Inst. for Social Rsch., 1996—. Vis. prof. U. Tex., Austin, 1975; vis. rsch. prof. psychology in psychiatry U. Mich., 1990-91; vis. scholar Nat. Inst. Alcohol Abuse and Alcoholism, 1980; dir. clin. tng. Mich. State U., 1982-94; lectr. Nebr. Symposium on Motivation, 1986; cons. in field. Editor: Further Explorations in Personality, 1981, Personality and the Prediction of Behavior, 1984, The Emergence of Personality, 1987, Studying Persons and Lives, 1990, Personality Structure in the Life Course, 1992, The Development of Alcohol Problems: Exploring the Biopsychosocial Matrix of Risk, 1994, Alcohol Problems Among Adolescents: Current Directions in Prevention Research, 1995, Alcohol Problems and Aging, 1998; contbr. chpts. and articles to profl. publs. Bd. dirs. Nat. Coun. on Alcoholism-Mich., 1978-82; mem. Psychosocial Initial Rev. Group, Nat. Inst. Alcohol Abuse and Alcoholism, 1989-92; mem. HPRB study sect. Ctr. for Sci. Rev., NIH, 1998-2000. Inst. Children Youth & Families fellow Mich. State U., 1993; recipient Blue Cross-Blue Shield Mich. Found. Excellence in Clin. Rsch. award, 1997. Fellow AAAS, APA (pres. addictions divsn. 50 1997-98), APS, Am. Orthopsychiat. Assn.; mem. Midwestern Psychol. Assn., Soc. Personology, Soc. Life History Rsch. in Psychopathology, Rsch. Soc. on Alcoholism (sec. and bd. dirs. 2001—). Office: Univ Mich Addiction Rsch Ctr 400 E Eisenhower Pkwy Ann Arbor MI 48108-3318

ZUERLEIN, DAMIAN JOSEPH, priest; b. Norfolk, Neb., May 28, 1955; s. Victor Damian and Elizabeth P. (Wegener) Z. BA, U. St. Thomas, St. Paul, 1977; MDiv, St. Paul Sem., 1981. Ordained priest Roman Cath. Ch., 1981. Tchr. Norfolk Cath. High Sch., 1981-85; assoc. pastor Sacred Heart/St. Mary's Parish, Norfolk, 1981-85; assoc. pastor St. Pius X Cath. Ch., Omaha, 1985-88, Mary Our Queen Cath. Ch., Omaha, 1988-90; pastor Our Lady of Guadalupe Parish, 1990—, St. Agnes Parish, Omaha, 1997—. Cons. Archdiocesan Vocations Office, Omaha, 1985-95; bd. dirs. Juan Diego Ctr., Omaha, 1990-2000; chmn., co-founder Omaha Together One Cmty., 1991-95; co-founder Weaving, Women's Advocacy Group, Omaha, 1988—. Presenter (video) Loving Your Marriage, 1990, El Matrimonio: Una Jornada Para Todo Una Vida, 1995; co-author: (manual) Hispanic Pastoral Plan, 1991. Bd. dirs. United Cath. Social Svcs., Omaha, 1990-96, Chicano Awareness Ctr., Omaha, 1991-98, Omaha Food Bank, 2000—, Vis. Nurse Assn., 1996-2000, Omaha 100 Inc., 1991-96, chair, 1991-93; advisor Mayor P.J. Morgan, Omaha, 1991-95; mem. Gov. Nelson's Urban Adv. Task Force, 1994; mem. Douglas County Commn. on Domestic Violence (now Domestic Violence Coord. Coun. Gtr. Omaha), 1996—, Nat. Campaign for Human Devel. Adv. Bd., 1997-2000; mem. Nebr. gov.'s task force on immigration, 1999-2000; founder Guadalupe-Ines Mission Sch., 1998-. Mem. Pax Cristi, Amnesty Internat., Fontenelle Forest Assn., Priests for Equality, Greater Omaha Clergy Assn. (pres. 1987-88), South Omaha Neighborhood Assn. (bd. dirs. 1992, pres. 1994—98). Avocations: canoeing the BWCA, skiing, travel, hiking. Home and Office: 2310 O St Omaha NE 68107-2837

ZUERN, ROSEMARY LUCILE, manufacturing executive, treasurer; b. Eureka, Wis., May 28, 1934; d. Kenneth Arthur and Vera Christine (Barnett) George; m. David Lee Zuern, June 30, 1956. Student, U. Wis., 1954-56. With Kimberly-Clark Corp., Neenah, Wis., 1956-78, sales promotion specialist, 1969-71, trade show adminstr., 1971-78; conv. mgr. Smith Bucklin & Assocs., Chgo., 1979-84, account exec., 1984-96; exec. dir. Bakery Equipment Mfrs. Assn., 1984-96, Soc. Gynecologic Oncologists, Chgo., 1984-96; assoc. sec., treas. Internat. Baking Industry Exposition, 1986-98; ret., 1998. Consumer cons. Kimberly-Clark Corp., Neenah, 1969. Mem. World Airlines Hist. Soc., Exptl. Aircraft Assn., Charles A. Lindbergh Collectors Soc. (past pres.). Avocations: philately, philography, music, antiques, historic firehouse restoration. Home and Office: 913 Wylde Oak Dr Oshkosh WI 54904-7633 Fax: 920-231-0396. E-mail: rosyposy@exetpc.com.

ZUKOSKI, CHARLES FREDERICK, IV, chemical engineering educator, administrator; b. Birmingham, Ala., Aug. 17, 1955; BA in Physics, Reed Coll., 1977; PhD in Chem. Engring., Princeton U., 1985. Asst. prof. dept. chem. engring U. Ill., Urbana, 1985-90, assoc. prof., 1990-93, prof., 1994—, alumni prof. chem. engring., 1994—, head chem. engring., 1995—. Contbr. articles to profl. jours. Fulbright scholar, 1992; recipient NSF Presdl. Young Investigator award, 1987, Everitt Teaching award, 1992, Ralph K. Iler award, 1997. Office: U Ill Dept Chem Engring 144 Rogers Adams Lab 600 S Mathews Ave Urbana IL 61801-3602

ZUKOWSKY, JOHN ROBERT, curator; b. N.Y.C., Apr. 21, 1948; s. John and Mary (Charchan) Z. BA, Hunter Coll., CUNY, 1971; MA, SUNY, Binghamton, 1974, PhD, 1977. Archtl. archivist Hudson River Mus., Yonkers, N.Y., 1974-76, Art Inst. Chgo., 1978-81, architecture curator, 1981—. Mem. Historic Sites Adv. Council, Springfield, Ill., 1982-83, Landmarks Preservation Council, Chgo., 1982-83; jury mem. Honor awards AIA, Washington, 1987. Co-author: Hudson River Villas, 1985, The Sky's the Limit Chicago Skyscrapers, 1990, Austrian Architecture and Design, 1991; co-author, editor: Mies Reconsidered, 1986, Chicago Architecture: 1872-1922, 1987, Chicago Architecture and Design, 1923-93, 1993, The Many Faces of Modern Architecture, 1994, Karl Friedrich Schinkel, 1781-1841: The Drama of Architecture, 1994, Building for Air Travel: Architecture and Design for Commercial Aviation, 1996, Japan 2000, 1998, Skyscrapers: The New Millennium, 2000, 2001, Building for Space Travel, 2001; editor: A System of Architectural Ornament (Louis H. Sullivan), 1990; author: Space Architecture: The Work by John Frassanito and Associates for NASA, 1999; contbr. articles to profl. jours. Decorated Chevalier des arts and lettres (France), Verdienst/Ehren Kreuz, Austria; recipient Honig award Chgo. chpt. Am. Soc. Appraisers, 1989; postdoctoral rsch. fellow NEH, 1977-78, Rsch. fellow, NEA, 1991. Mem. AIA (hon., Disting. Svc. award Chgo. chpt. 1986), Arts Club Chgo. Office: Art Inst Chgo Dept Architecture 111 S Michigan Ave Chicago IL 60603-6492 E-mail: jzukowsky@artic.edu.

ZUNG, THOMAS TSE-KWAI, architect; b. Shanghai, China, Feb. 8, 1933; came to the U.S., 1937, naturalized, 1954; 1 child, Thomas Bates. Student, Drew U., 1950-51, Va. Poly. Inst., 1951-53, Columbia U., 1955-57; BArch, U. Mich., 1960; MS in Design Sci., Internat. Coll., 1982. Project arch. Edward Durell Stone, Arch., N.Y.C., 1958, 60-65; arch. Cleve., 1967—. Pres. Buckminster Fuller, Sadao and Zung, Archs., 1979—. Author-editor: Buckminster Fuller, Anthology for the New Millennium; prin. works include City Cleve. Pub. Utilities Bldg., Cleve. State U. Geodesig Elongated Dome, Mayfran, Inc., Sawmill Creek Lodge, U. Akron Guzzetta Hall, Music, Speech and Theater Arts Ctr., Alumni Ctr. Bowling Green State U., U. Akron Master Plan-West, City of East Cleveland, Superior Euclid beautification plan, student recreation ctr. Bowling Green State U., Glenville Pub. Libr., campus bldg. Tex. Wesleyan Coll., recreation, health and phys. edn. bldg. Wittenberg U., Medina Res. Park Office, arena, health, phys. edn. complex U. Akron, Dyke Coll., Lima State Prizon, Cleve. Children's Christian Home, State of Ohio Pre-Release Ctr. Cleve., Lorain-Grafton State Prison, Mayfield H.S., Aspen Village Project, Cleve. Metroparks Tropical Rainforest Bldg., Student Union Wittenberg U., YWCA, Salem, Ohio, China Internat. Trade Ctr., People's Rep. China, additions to Cleve. Hopkins Internat. Airport, Ohio State U. Coll. of Dentistry-Postle Hall and Hist. Costume and Textile Mus., Master Plan Schreiner Coll. and Cailloux Student Ctr., Griffin Welcome Ctr., Master Plan Walsh Univ., Walsh Student Union, Columbus, Western Res. Psychiat. Hosp., Ohio, Trumbull State Prison, Ohio Dept. Transp. Prototypical Rest Stop Design; patentee in field. Trustee Pace Assn., 1970-73, Karamu House, 1974-80, Cleve. Inst. Music, 1979-86, Chinese Cultural Assn., 1980-84, Ohio Arts Coun., 1982-84; task force chmn. Greater Cleve. Growth Assn., 1970; mem. Coun. Human Rels., 1972, Leadership Cleve. Class '77; cubmaster local Boy Scouts Am., 1977-79; vestryman St. Christopher-by-River, 1980-83; bd. dirs. Buckminster Fuller Inst., 1983—, Pearl S. Buck Found., 1989-98, cons. arch. hist. house com.; mem. Adv. Coun. Aging, State of Ohio, 1997—. With Signal Corps, U.S. Army, 1953-55. Decorated 4 medals; recipient Pub. Works award State of Ohio, 1971, Design award Korean Inst. Constrn. Tech., 1984, Ohio Valley ABC Design Excellence award Wittenberg U. Student Union, 1989, others. Mem. AIA (dir. Cleve. chpt. 1980, Design award Cleve. chpt. 1972, Design award 1989), Am. Soc. Planning Ofcls., English Speaking Union (trustee 1972-75), Ohio Soc. Archs., Ohio Assn. Minority Archs. and Engrs. (trustee 1982-90), Hermit Club, City Club (dir. 1972-74, v.p. 1974), Rotary. Office: Buckminster Fuller Sadao & Zung 1 Bratenahl Pl Cleveland OH 44108-1181

ZUNICH, JANICE, pediatrician, geneticist, educator, administrator; b. New Kensington, Pa., Sept. 2, 1953; d. Nick and Mary (Zivkovich) Z.; m. Milan Katic, June 20, 1981; children: Nikola Ilija, Milana. BS, Ohio State U., 1974, MD, 1978. Diplomate Am. Bd. Pediat., Nat. Bd. Med. Examiners, Am. Bd. Med. Genetics (clin. genetics, clin. cytogenetics). Lab. technician Cmty. Hosp., Lorain, Ohio, summer 1974, Ohio State U. Hosp., Columbus, 1974-75; intern, then resident in pediat. Columbus Children's Hosp., 1978-81; genetics fellow Luth. Gen. Hosp., Park Ridge, Ill., 1981-83; asst. prof. pediat. W.Va. U. Med. Ctr., Morgantown, 1983-85, assoc. dir. cytogenetics, 1984-85; clin. assoc. prof. med. genetics, dir. Genetics Ctr. N.W. Ctr. Med. Edn., Ind. U. Sch. Medicine, Gary, 1985—. Genetics cons. Cmty. Hosp., Munster, Ind., Porter Meml. Hosp., Valparaiso, Ind., St. Anthony Med. Ctr., Crown Point, Ind., Meth. Hosp., Gary and Merrillville, Ind., St. Margaret Hosp., Hammond, Ind. Contbr. articles to profl. jours. Mem. med. com. Planned Parenthood, N.W.-N.E. Ind., Merrillville, 1987-99; mem. adv. com. N.W. Ind. Sickle Cell Found., Gary, 1987—; mem. med. adv. com. Svcs. for Children with Spl. Health Care Needs, Indpls., 1989-92; mem. adv. bd. Parent Edn. Ctr., Whiting, Ind., 1988-96; chmn. Lake County Task Force on Teen Pregnancy, 1998-2000. Named Person of Yr., Down Syndrome Assn. N.W. Ind., Highland, 1988; Charles F. Whitten fellow Sickle Cell Found. N.W. Ind., 1990. Fellow: AMA, Am. Coll. Med. Genetics (founding fellow), Am. Acad. Pediat.; mem.: Lake County Med. Soc., Ind. State Med. Assn., Am. Soc. Human Genetics, Great Lakes Regional Genetics Group (financing genetics svcs. sub-com. 1988—99), Alpha Epsilon Delta, Phi Beta Kappa. Eastern Orthodox. Avocations: piano, folk dancing, choral singing, travel. Office: NW Ctr for Med Edn 3400 Broadway Gary IN 46408-1101 E-mail: jzunich@iun.edu.

ZURAW, KATHLEEN ANN, special education and physical education educator; b. Bay City, Mich., Sept. 29, 1960; d. John Luke and Clara Josephine (Kilian) Z. AA with high honors, Delta Community Coll., 1980; BS with high honors, Mich. State U., 1984, MA, 1987. Cert. spl. edn., mentally impaired phys. edn. grade K-12, adaptive phys. edn. tchr., Mich. Summer water safety instr. Camp Midicha, Columbia, Mich., 1982, Bay Cliff Health Camp, Big Bay, 1983; summer spl. edn. tchr. Jefferson Orthopedic Sch., Honolulu, 1984, 85, 86, Ingham Intermediate Sch. Dist., Mason, Mich., 1987; spl. edn. tchr. Bay Arenac Intermediate Sch. Dist., Bay City, 1985-87, Berrien County Intermediate Sch. Dist., Berrien Springs, Mich., 1987—. Mem. citizen amb program fitness delegation People's Republic China, 1991. Area 17 coach Mich. Spl. Olympics, Berrien Springs, 1987—; mem. YMCA, St. Joseph, Mich., 1987—, Y-Ptnrs., 1989, Coun. Exceptional Children; participant Citizen Ambassador Delegation to People's Republic of China, 1991. Mem. Am. Alliance Health, Phys. Edn., Recreation and Dance, Phi Theta Kappa, Phi Kappa Phi, Phi Delta Kappa. Roman Catholic. Avocations: sports, crafts. Home: 7306 W S Saginaw Rd Bay City MI 48706

ZURHEIDE, CHARLES HENRY, consulting electrical engineer; b. St. Louis, May 9, 1923; s. Charles Henry and Ollie C. (Kirk) Z.; m. Ruth M. Plueck, June 25, 1949; children— Barbara Anne, Pamela S. B.S. in Elec. Engring, U. Mo., Columbia, 1944. Registered profl. engr., Mo. Distbn. engr. Laclede Power & Light Co., St. Louis, 1944-45; sub-sta. engr., then indsl. engr. Union Electric Co., 1945-51; chief elec. engr. Fruin-Colnon Contracting Co., 1951-54; a founder, treas., v.p. Smith-Zurheide, Inc., 1954-65; pres. Zurheide-Herrmann, Inc., 1965—, chmn. bd., 1988—. Chmn. Elec. Code Rev. Commn., St. Louis, 1965-01, Mo. Bd. Profl. Engrs., 1977-82, St. Louis Indsl. Devel. Commn., 1965-67; mem. adv. panel region 6 GSA, 1977—; plan commn., City of Ferguson, Mo., 1968-73; tech. adv. com. St. Louis C. of C., 1977; mem. Mo. Pub. Svc. Commn. Task Force on Retail Wheeling of Electricity, 1998. Recipient Distinguished Service in Engring. award U. Mo., 1976 Fellow Am. Cons. Engrs. Council; mem. Mo. Soc. Profl. Engrs. (Engr. of Year award 1970), Cons. Engrs. Council Mo., IEEE, Illuminating Engring. Soc., Engrs. Club St. Louis, Tau Alpha Pi. Clubs: Norwood Hills Country, Mo. Athletic. Home: 14336 Spyglass Rdg Chesterfield MO 63017-2140 Office: Zurheide-Herrmann Inc 4333 Clayton Ave Saint Louis MO 63110-1684 E-mail: czurneide@zhideas.com.

ZURICK, JOHN, dance company director; MFA in Theatre Arts, Brandeis U. Acting v.p. mktg. InterLearn, Inc.; creator Power of Once; regional mgr./full-time cons. Mills/James Prodns.; co-founder/pres./COO Finis; ptnr. Y&Z Mgmt., Boston; dir. mktg. Cin. Symphony Orch., 1983-88; instr. ESI Internat., Arlington, Va.; founder, past pres. MillennialMinds, Cin.; exec. dir. Cin. Ballet, 1998—. Vol. v.p. mktg. Greater Cin. Arts & Edn. Ctr. Office: Cin Ballet 1555 Central Pkwy Cincinnati OH 45214-2863

ZURIER, REBECCA, art history educator; AB, Harvard U., 1978; PhD, Yale U., 1988. Assoc. prof. U. Mich., Ann Arbor; Schragis fellow in modern arts Syracuse U., 1990-92. Guest curator Metropolitan Lives: The Ashcan Artists and Their New York, Nat. Mus. Am. Art, Smithsonian Instn., 1995, Yale U. Art Gallery, 1986; vis. appts. U. So. Calif., Emory U., U. Pa., George Washington U., 1988-90. Author: The American Firehouse: An Architectural and Social History, 1982, Art for the Masses (1911-1917): A Radical Magazine and Its Graphics, 1988 (Alfred H. Barr award Coll. Art Assn. 1996), (with Robert W. Snyder and Virginia Mecklenburg) Metropolitan Lives, 1995. Fellow Charles Warren Ctr. for Studies in Am. History, Harvard U., 1999; Getty postdoctoral grantee, 1993. Office: Univ Mich Art History Dept 519 S State St Ann Arbor MI 48109-1357

ZWEBEN, STUART HARVEY, information scientist, educator; b. Bronx, N.Y., Apr. 21, 1948; s. Max D. and Ruth (Schwartz) Z.; m. Rochelle T. Small, June 13, 1971; 1 child, Naomi. BS, CUNY, 1968; MS, Purdue U., 1971, PhD, 1974. Systems analyst IBM Corp., Kingston, N.Y., 1969-70; asst. prof. Ohio State U., Columbus, 1974-80, from vice chmn. to acting chmn. computer sci. dept., 1982-84, assoc. prof., 1980-92, prof., 1992—, chmn., 1994—. Pres. Computing Scis. Accreditation Bd., Stamford, Conn., 1989-91, v.p. 1987-89, sec.-treas. 1986-87; sec.-treas. Fedn. on Computing in the U.S., Washington, 1992. Contbr. articles to profl. jours. Rsch. grantee NSF, 1981-83, 88-90, 91-93, 93-97, Army Rsch. Office, 1980-83, Dept. Edn., 1983-85, Applied Info. Tech. Rsch. Ctr., 1990-91, Honda R&D, 1998—; equipment grantee AT&T Bell Labs, 1984, 86-88. Fellow Assn. for Computing Machinery (pres. 1994-96, v.p. 1992-94, coun. mem. 1982-88, chpt. bd. chmn. 1982-85, publications bd. 1988-92, fin. com. 1990-92, nominating com. chmn. 1999-2000, constn. and bylaws chmn. 1988-92, Recognition of Svc. award 1980, 85, 87, 88, Outstanding Contbn. award 1997); mem. AAUP, IEEE Computer Soc. (assoc. editor 1990-98), Computing Rsch. Assn. (bd. dirs. 1997—), Coun. Sci. Soc. Presidents (sec. 1998), Columbus Tech. Coun. (Tech. Person of Yr. award 2000). Avocations: sports, philately. Office: Ohio State U Computer Scis 2015 Neil Ave Columbus OH 43210-1210

ZWEIFEL, DAVID ALAN, newspaper editor; b. Monroe, Wis., May 19, 1940; s. Cloyence John and Uva Lorraine (Skinner) Z.; m. Sandra Louise Holz, Sept. 7, 1968; children: Daniel Mark, Kristin Lynn. BJ, U. Wis., 1962. Reporter The Capital Times, Madison, Wis., 1962-71, city editor, 1971-78, mng. editor, 1978-83, editor, 1983—. Bd. dirs. Swiss Am. Ctr., Friends of Monona Terrace, Capital Times Co., Madison Newspapers Inc., William T. Evjve Charitable Trust. V.p. Alliance for Children and Youth, Madison, 1983—; bd. dirs. United Cerebral Palsy Dane County, Madison, 1984-91. Lt. U.S. Army, 1963-65; col. USNG, ret. Named Investigative Reporter of Yr. Madison Press Club, 1972. Mem.: Soc. Profl. Journalists (Spl. Achievement award 1992, 1996), Wis. Freedom of Info. Coun. (pres. 1986—2000), Wis. AP 1987—88, Am. Soc. Newspaper Editors (com. freedom of info., Pulitzer Prize juror 2000, 2001), U. Wis. Alumni Assn., Wis. N.G. Assn. (trustee 1975—81), Elks. Avocations: running, bowling, book collecting. Home: 5714 Tecumseh Ave Monona WI 53716-2964 Office: The Capital Times PO Box 8060 Madison WI 53708-8060

ZWICKEY, SHEILA KAYE, lawyer; b. Chgo., July 9, 1951; d. Ewald Arthur Zwickey and Kathryn Allene (Hurst) Zaiden. BS, U. Wis., 1973; MSW, U. Ind., 1975, JD, 1981. Social worker Dept. of Corrections/State of Ind., Indpls., 1975-81; dep. pub. defender State of Ind., 1981-85; pub. defender Rush County, Rushville, Ind., 1985-90, Wayne County, Richmond, 1986-90; prosecuting atty. Rush County/State of Ill., Rushville, 1991—; pvt. practice Batesville, Ind., 1991—. Bd. dirs. Ind. Pub. Defender's Coun., Indpls. Bd. dirs. Rush City Humane Soc., 1988-89; officer Rush County/Ind. Dem. Women's Club, 1991—. Mem. Kiwanis, Rush City Bar Assn. (pres. 1988-89). Democrat. Roman Catholic. Office: Prosecutors Office Rush County Ct House Rushville IN 46173

ZWIERLEIN, RONALD EDWARD, athletics director; m. Cindy Cromer, Sept. 7, 1968; children: Heidi, Heather, Chad. BS, Bowling Green (Ohio) State U., 1968, MS; PhD in Athletic, Phys. Edn., Recreation, Ohio State U. Head swimming and diving coach Monroe H.S., Rochester, N.Y., Fremont (Ohio) Ross H.S., John Carroll U., University Heights, Ohio, 1975-81, athletic dir., 1977-81; head swimming and diving coach, instr. Bowling Green State U., 1981-1984, assoc. dir. Student Recreation Ctr., 1984--92, dir. recreational sports, 1992-94, dir. intercollegiate athletics, 1994-99, athletic dir., sr. assoc. v.p., 2000—. Mem. Nat. Assn. Collegiate Dirs. Athletics (mem. Mission & Values Com.). Office: Bowling Green State U Perry Stadium Bowling Green OH 43403-0001

ZYWICKI, ROBERT ALBERT, electrical distribution company executive; b. Chgo., Sept. 23, 1930; s. Martin Albert and Margaret Irene (Mackowski) Z.; m. Barbara Joan Hagerty; children: Robert, Cheryl, Cindy, Carrie. B in Commerce, Northwestern U., 1966. Teller Chgo. Title and Trust Bank, Chgo., 1949-50; painter Getz Molding Co., 1950-51; purchasing agt. Woodworker's Tool Works, 1953-54; serviceman Addressograph Multigraph, 1954-55; mem. Chgo. Fire Dept., 1955-62; v.p. Anixter Bros. Inc., Skokie, Ill., 1955-87; co-owner A-Z Industries, Northbrook, 1987-92, 1992—. Served as cpl. U.S. Army, 1951-53. Mem. Am. Legion (comdr.). Republican. Roman Catholic. Avocations: thoroughbred horse racing, classical music, baseball card collecting, tennis. Home: 1330 Sprucewood Ln Deerfield IL 60015-4771

Professional Index

Little, Robert Andrews *architect, designer, painter*
Madison, Robert Prince *architect*
Melsop, James William *architect*
Zung, Thomas Tse-Kwai *architect*

Columbus
Bohm, Friedrich (Friedl) K.M. *architectural firm executive*
Carpenter, Jot David *landscape architect, educator*
Kirk, Ballard Harry Thurston *architect*
Weinhold, Virginia Beamer *interior designer*

Cuyahoga Falls
Haag, Everett Keith *architect*

Dayton
Betz, Eugene William *architect*

Dublin
Cornwell, Paul M., Jr. *architect*

Kent
Sommers, David Lynn *architect*

Toledo
Hills, Arthur W. *architectural firm executive*
Martin, Robert Edward *architect*

WISCONSIN

Eau Claire
Larson, Brian Foix *architect*

Madison
Nisbet, Thomas K. *architect*
Tishler, William Henry *landscape architect, educator*

Milwaukee
Dumas, Tyrone Pierre *architect, construction manager, consultant*
Greenstreet, Robert Charles *architect, educator*

Soldiers Grove
Quebe, Jerry Lee *retired architect*

ADDRESS UNPUBLISHED

Counts, Donald R. *furniture maker*
Degenhardt, Robert Allan *architectural and engineering firm executive*
Euans, Robert Earl *architect*
Hutchins, Robert Ayer *architectural consultant*
Jablonski, Robert Leo *architect*
Meyers, Richard James *landscape architect*
Pettitt, Jay S. *architect, consultant*
Poor, Janet Meakin, III *landscape designer*
Ryan, John Michael *landscape architect*
Siegal, Burton Lee *product designer, consultant, inventor*
Van Housen, Thomas Corwin, III *architect, designer, builder*

ARTS: LITERARY *See also* COMMUNICATIONS MEDIA

UNITED STATES

ILLINOIS

Chicago
Carpenter, Allan *writer, editor, publisher*
Hoover, Paul *poet*
Manelli, Donald Dean *screenwriter, film producer*
Stern, Richard Gustave *writer, educator*
Terkel, Studs (Louis Terkel) *writer, interviewer*

Evanston
Gibbons, William Reginald, Jr. *poet, novelist, translator, editor*

Lake Forest
Swanton, Virginia Lee *writer, publisher, bookseller*

Moline
Skromme, Arnold Burton *educational writer, engineering consultant*

Urbana
Lieberman, Laurence *poet, educator*

Waukegan
Marks, Martha Alford *writer*

INDIANA

Bloomington
Mitchell, Bert Breon *literary translator*

Crown Point
Palmeri, Sharon Elizabeth *freelance writer, community educator*

Indianapolis
Gregory, Valiska *writer*

Notre Dame
Goulet, Denis André *development ethicist, writer*

IOWA

Iowa City
Bell, Marvin Hartley *poet, English language educator*
Graham, Jorie *writer*
Johnson, Nicholas *writer, lawyer, lecturer*
Stern, Gerald Daniel *poet*

KANSAS

Leawood
Garwood, Julie *writer*

MICHIGAN

Ann Arbor
Gregerson, Linda Karen *poet, language educator*

Detroit
Madgett, Naomi Long *poet, editor, publisher, educator*

East Lansing
Wakoski, Diane *poet, educator*

Mount Morris
Wooley, Geraldine Hamilton *writer, poet*

Republic
Wixtrom, Donald Joseph *translator*

West Bloomfield
Brin, David *writer, astronomer*

MINNESOTA

Edina
Schwarzrock, Shirley Pratt *writer, lecturer, educator*

MISSOURI

Saint Charles
Castro, Jan Garden *writer, arts consultant, educator*

Saint Louis
Broeg, Bob (Robert William Broeg) *writer*
Gass, William H. *writer, educator*
Schlafly, Phyllis Stewart *author*

Sweet Springs
Long, Helen Halter *writer, educator*

NEBRASKA

Lincoln
Magorian, James *writer, poet*

NEW YORK

Millerton
Paretsky, Sara N. *writer*

OHIO

Akron
Moriarty, John Timothy *writer, transportation consultant*

Cleveland
Gleisser, Marcus David *writer, lawyer, journalist*

Perrysburg
Weaver, Richard L., II *writer, speaker, educator*

WISCONSIN

Janesville
Axtell, Roger E. *writer, retired marketing professional*

Madison
Ashley, Renee *creative writing educator, consultant*
Stone, John Timothy, Jr. *writer*

Milwaukee
Connelly, Mark *writer, educator*

Racine
Wright, Betty Ren *children's book writer*

CANADA

MANITOBA

Winnipeg
Oberman, Sheldon Arnold *writer, educator*

ADDRESS UNPUBLISHED

Crames, Paul F. *writer, lawyer*
Hornbaker, Alice Joy *writer*
Kotlowitz, Alex *writer, journalist*
Masek, Mark Joseph *writer*
Skwarczyński, Henryk Adam (Henryk Skwar) *writer*
Webb, David Allen *writer*

ARTS: PERFORMING

UNITED STATES

ARIZONA

Flagstaff
Schellen, Nando *opera director*

CALIFORNIA

Belmont
Monahan, Leonard Francis *musician, singer, composer, publisher*

Los Angeles
Saltzman, Barry *actor*

COLORADO

Aspen
Roth, Don *orchestra executive*

CONNECTICUT

Colchester
Winter, John Dawson, III *blues guitarist, singer*

FLORIDA

Englewood
Wittlich, Gary Eugene *music theory educator, college administrator*

ILLINOIS

Bloomington
Brown, Jared *theater director, educator, writer*
Vayo, David Joseph *composer, music educator*

Champaign
Garvey, John Charles *violist, conductor, retired music educator*

Chicago
Aitay, Victor *concert violinist, music educator*
Akos, Francis *violinist, conductor*
Arney, Randall *artistic director*
Arpino, Gerald Peter *performing company executive*
Berryman, Diana *radio personality*
Conte, Lou *artistic director, choreographer*
Daniel, T. *mime performer, theater director, choreographer*
Eaton, John C. *composer, educator*
Elfstrand, Mark *radio personality*
Fogel, Henry *orchestra administrator*
Garcia, Gerson *radio personality*
Gueno, Barbara *radio personality*
Haney, Tracy *radio personality*
Hayden, John *radio director*
Herseth, Adolph Sylvester (Bud Herseth) *classical musician*
Higgins, Ruth Ellen *theatre producer*
Hiller, Steve *radio personality*
Kalver, Gail Ellen *dance company manager, musician*
Larrick, Monte *radio personality*
Lilly, Aimee *radio personality*
Lustrea, Anita *radio personality*
McGee, Howard *radio personality*
Moffatt, Joyce Anne *performing arts executive*
Palermo, James W. *artistic director*
Ran, Shulamit *composer*
Ratner, Carl Joseph *theater director*
Renard, Paul Steven *music educator*
Ross, Lori *radio personality*
Savage, Terry *television personality, columnist*
Schulfer, Roche Edward *theater executive director*
Sculfield, Tony *radio personality, comedian*
Sedelmaier, John Josef *filmmaker*
Shepherd, Wayne *radio personality*
Springer, Jerry *television talk show host*
Stifler, Venetia Chakos *dancer, choreographer, dance educator*
Tallchief, Maria *ballerina*
Taylor, Koko *singer*
Wang, Albert James *violinist, educator*
Wansley, Ty *radio personality*
Winfrey, Oprah *television talk show host, actress, producer*
Woods, Nikki *radio personality*
Yu, Linda *newswoman, television anchorwoman*
Zlatoff-Mirsky, Everett Igor *violinist*

East Saint Louis
Dunham, Katherine *choreographer, dancer, anthropologist*

Evanston
Eberley, Helen-Kay *opera singer, classical record company executive, poet*
Hemke, Frederick L. *music educator, university administrator*
Karlins, M(artin) William *composer, educator*
Kujala, Walfrid Eugene *musician, educator*
McDonough, Bridget Ann *music theatre company director*
Peters, Gordon Benes *retired musician*
Yoder, John Clifford *producer, consultant*
Zimmerman, Mary *performing arts educator*

Highland Park
Mehta, Zarin *music festival administrator*

Park Forest
Billig, Etel Jewel *theater director, actress*

Rockford
Larsen, Steven *orchestra conductor*
Masters, Arlene Elizabeth *singer*
Robinson, Donald Peter *musician, retired electrical engineer*

Springfield
Ellis, Michael Eugene *documentary film producer, writer, director, marketing executive*

Urbana
Hedlund, Ronald *baritone*

INDIANA

Bloomington
Klotman, Robert Howard *music educator*
Mac Watters, Virginia Elizabeth *singer, music educator, actress*
Michael, R. Keith *theatre and dance educator*
Phillips, Harvey *musician, soloist, music educator, arts consultant*
Svetlova, Marina *ballerina, choreographer, educator*
Williams, Camilla *soprano, voice educator*

Evansville
Savia, Alfred *conductor*

Fort Wayne
Franklin, Al *artistic director*
Sack, James McDonald, Jr. *radio and television producer, marketing executive*

Indianapolis
Aliev, Eldar *artistic director, choreographer, educator*
Griswold, Tom *radio personality*
Hanford, Pat *performing company executive*
Ilgen, Dorothy L. *arts foundation executive*
Johnson, David Allen *singer, songwriter, investor, minister*
Kevoian, Bob *radio personality*
Matis, Jimmy *radio personality*
McGee, Chick *radio personality*
Metcalf, Dean *radio personality*
Suzuki, Hidetaro *violinist*
Turner, Barbara A. *former dance company executive*
Venzago, Mario *conductor*
Zurick, John *consultant, former dance company director*

Kokomo
Highlen, Larry Wade *music educator, piano rebuilder, tuner*

IOWA

Anita
Everhart, Robert Phillip (Bobby Williams) *entertainer, songwriter, recording artist*

Cedar Rapids
Hall, Kathy L. *orchestra executive*
Tiemeyer, Christian *conductor*

Davenport
Schleicher, Donald *music director*
Willett, Lance *orchestra executive*

Des Moines
Giunta, Joseph *conductor, music director*
Harden, Van *radio personality*
Lucas, Bonnie *radio personality*
Mickelson, Jan *radio personality*
Mill, Jeth *performing company executive*
Mill, Seth *orchestra executive*
Pearson, Mark *radio personality*
Wergin, Gary *radio personality*

Dubuque
Hemmer, Paul Edward *musician, composer, broadcasting executive*

Indianola
Larsen, Robert LeRoy *artistic director*
Mace, Jerilee Marie *opera company executive*

Iowa City
Thompson, Basil F. *ballet master*

Tipton
Farwell, Walter Maurice *vocalist, educator*

KANSAS

Emporia
DeBauge, Janice B. *musician*

Lawrence
Duerksen, George Louis *music educator, music therapist*
Hilding, Jerel Lee *music and dance educator, former dancer*
Tsubaki, Andrew Takahisa *theater director, educator*

Mission
Day, Bobby *radio personality*
Knight, Charlie *radio personality*
McKay, Mark *radio personality*
Munday, Dave *radio personality*

Overland Park
Lamb, Gordon Howard *music educator*

Shawnee Mission
Taylor, Scott *radio personality*

Westwood
Abbott, Bill *radio personality*
Bryan, David *radio personality*

Carson, Roger *radio personality*
Cramer, Ted *radio personality*
Cunningham, Wes *radio personality*
Edwards, Jay *radio personality*
Efron, Bruce *radio personality*
Hurst, Dan *radio personality*
Lawrence, David *radio personality*
Michaels, Dinah *radio personality*
Morelack, Mike *radio personality*
Railsback, Mike *radio personality*
Wilson, Richard Earl (Dick Wilson) *media personality*

Wichita
Berman, Mitchell A. *orchestra executive*
Bryan, Wayne *producer*
Johnson, C. Nicholas *dance company executive*
Sewell, Andrew *music director*

KENTUCKY

Frankfort
Fletcher, Winona Lee *theater educator emeritus*

MICHIGAN

Ann Arbor
Bolcom, William Elden *musician, composer, educator, pianist*
Scharp-Radovic, Carol Ann *choreographer, classical ballet educator, artistic director*
Sparling, Peter David *dancer, dance educator*

Bloomfield Hills
Haidostian, Alice Berberian *concert pianist, civic volunteer and fundraiser*

Detroit
Di Chiera, David *general director of opera company*
Kang, Emil J. *orchestra executive*

Grand Rapids
Allen, Gary *radio personality*
Dionne, Neal *radio personality*
Kaser, Bob *radio personality*
Lockington, David *conductor*
Matlak, John *radio personality*
Ryberg, William A. *orchestra executive*
Schmidt, Gordon Peirce *artistic director*

Kalamazoo
Harvey, Raymond Curtis *conductor*

Midland
Brooks, Peter *radio director*
Diehl, Ann *radio personality*
Hutchinson, Dennis *radio director*
Johnson, Steve *radio personality*
Kirkpatrick, Larry *radio personality*
LaHaie, Perry *radio director*
Lawrence, Jeremy *radio director*

Rochester Hills
Daniels, David Wilder *conductor, music educator*

Troy
Okun, Maury *dance company executive*

MINNESOTA

Bloomington
Smith, Henry Charles, III *symphony orchestra conductor*

Duluth
Fields, Allen *artistic director*

Minneapolis
Bundy, Bill *radio personality*
Carter, Adam *radio personality*
Eskola, Eric *radio personality*
Fetler, Paul *composer, educator*
Filloon, Karen *radio personality*
Fleezanis, Jorja Kay *violinist, educator*
Hagevik, Bruce *radio personality*
Hyslop, David Johnson *arts administrator*
Jeffries, Kim *radio personality*
Jones, Susie *radio personality*
Lee, Dave *radio personality*
Malmberg, Al *radio personality*
Maloney, Rita *radio personality*
Mamayek, Telly *radio personality*
McKinney, Jeff *radio personality*
Miller, John William, Jr. *bassoonist*
Murphy, Steve *radio personality*
Oakes, Laura *radio personality*
Oue, Eiji *conductor, music director*
Peterson, Patty *radio personality*
Rousseau, Eugene Ellsworth *musician, music educator, consultant*
Russell, Tim *radio personality*
Severinsen, Doc (Carl H. Severinsen) *conductor, musician*
Sewell, James *artistic director*
Shelby, Don *radio personality*
Skrowaczewski, Stanislaw *conductor, composer*
Stanfield, Rebecca *radio personality*
Strom, Roger *radio personality*
Thomson, Steve *radio personality*
Ware, D. Clifton *singer, educator*
Wick, Don *radio personality*

Moorhead
Revzen, Joel *conductor*

Saint Paul
Coppock, Bruce *orchestra executive*

MISSOURI

Arrow Rock
Bollinger, Michael *artistic director*

Branson
Williams, Andy *entertainer*

Kansas City
Bentley, Jeffrey *performing company executive*
Blake, Darcie Kay *radio news director, anchor*
Bolender, Todd *choreographer*
Costin, James D. *performing arts company executive*
Manson, Anne *music director*
Tyler, Sean *radio personality*
Valliere, Roland Edward *performing company executive*
Whitener, William Garnett *dancer, choreographer*

Saint Louis
Armbruster, Bob *radio personality*
Bernstein, Mark D. *theater director*
Briccetti, Joan Therese *theater manager, arts management consultant*
Connett, Jim *radio director*
Eichhorn, Arthur David *music director*
Elliot, Bill *radio personality*
Frier, Chuck *radio personality*
Haley, Johnetta Randolph *musician, educator, university official*
Klemm, Ron *radio producer*
Roberts, John *radio personality*
Stewart, John Harger *music educator*
Sudholt, Tom *radio personality*
Vonk, Hans *conductor*
Wobble, Dick *radio personality*
Woolf, Steven Michael *artistic director*

Springfield
Spicer, Holt Vandercook *retired speech and theater educator*

Wentzville
Berry, Chuck (Charles Edward Anderson Berry) *singer, composer*

NEBRASKA

Lincoln
Dixon, Wheeler Winston *film and video studies educator, writer*
Miller, Tice Lewis *theatre educator*

Omaha
Johnson, James David *concert pianist, organist, educator*
Yampolsky, Victor *conductor*

NEW YORK

Bronx
Verrett, Shirley *soprano*

New York
Jackson, Isaiah *conductor*
Lopez-Cobos, Jesus *conductor*
Massey, Andrew John *conductor, composer*
Prince, (Prince Rogers Nelson) *musician, actor*
Snyder, Arlen Dean *actor*

NORTH DAKOTA

Bismarck
Lundberg, Susan Ona *musical organization administrator*
Wellin, Thomas *music director*

Fargo
Harris, Bob *radio personality*
Potrias, Steve *radio personality*
Schultz, Ed *radio personality*
Sunday, Jack *radio personality*

OHIO

Bratenahl
DesRosiers, Anne Booke *performing arts administrator, consultant*

Canton
Moorhouse, Linda Virginia *symphony orchestra administrator*

Cincinnati
Alexander, Jeffrey *performing company executive*
Beggs, Patricia Kirk *performing company executive*
Belew, Adrian *guitarist, singer, songwriter, producer*
Burbank, Gary *radio personality*
Cunningham, Bill *radio personality*
Furman, Andy *radio personality*
Garrett, Bob *radio personality*
Gilbert, Jay *radio personality*
Hills, Alan *performing company executive*
Hoffman, Joel Harvey *composer, educator*
James, Jefferson Ann *performing company executive, dancer, choreographer*
Kunzel, Erich, Jr. *conductor, arranger, educator*
McConnell, Mike *radio personality*
Monder, Steven I. *orchestra executive*
Morgan, Victoria *performing company executive, choreographer*
Moss, Joel Charles *radio production director*
Paavo, Jarvi *conductor*
Phillips, John *radio personality*
Scott, Jim *radio personality*
Sloane, Scott *radio personality*
Stern, Edward *performing company executive*
Tocco, James *pianist*
Ward, Sherman Carl, III (Buzz Ward) *theater manager*

Cleveland
Bamberger, David *opera company executive*
Bishop, Mark *radio personality*
Giannetti, Louis Daniel *film educator, film critic*
Gladden, Dean Robert *arts administrator, educator, consultant*
Ivers, Mike *radio personality*
Jackson, Don *radio personality*
Kallik, Chip *radio director*
Lanigan, John *radio personality*
Lee, Dick *radio director*
Malone, Jimmy *radio personality*
Mc Farlane, Karen Elizabeth *concert artists manager*
Morris, Thomas William *symphony orchestra administrator*
Nahat, Dennis F. *artistic director, choreographer*
Topilow, Carl S. *symphony conductor*

Columbus
Charles, Gerard *performing company executive, choreographer*
Drvota, Mojmir *cinema educator, author*
Hart, Daniel *orchestra executive*
Rosenstock, Susan Lynn *orchestra administrator*
Siciliani, Alessandro Domenico *conductor*

Dayton
Burke, Dermot *artistic director*
Gittleman, Neal *orchestra conductor*
Hanna, Marsha L. *artistic director*
Walters, Jefferson Brooks *musician, retired real estate broker*

Delaware
Jamison, Roger W. *pianist, piano educator*

Elyria
Greer, Richard *radio personality*
Kimble, Bernie *radio director*
Murphy, Tom *radio personality*
Ribbins, Mark *radio personality*

Hamilton
Bangert, Bill *radio personality*

Holland
Conlin, Thomas (Byrd) *conductor*

Peninsula
Shaw, Doris Beaumar *film and video producer, executive recruiter, management consultant*

Strongsville
Oltman, C. Dwight *conductor, educator*

Toledo
Bell, Robert *orchestra executive*
Knorr, John Christian *entertainment executive, bandleader, producer*

OKLAHOMA

Texhoma
Jackson, Paul Howard *multimedia producer, educator, minister, minister*

SOUTH DAKOTA

Sioux Falls
Bennett, Thomas *orchestra executive*
Haig, Susan *conductor*

TEXAS

Dallas
Bronstein, Fred *orchestra executive*

WISCONSIN

Eau Claire
House, George *radio personality*

Greenfield
Dolan, Bob *radio personality*
True, Steve *radio personality*
Weber, Jay *radio personality*

Madison
De Main, John *orchestra musical director*
Dembski, Stephen Michael *composer, university music composition professor*
Mackie, Richard H. *orchestra executive*

Milwaukee
Belling, Mark *radio personality*
Delfs, Andreas *conductor, musical director*
Dow, Simon *artistic director*
Downey, John Wilham *composer, pianist, conductor, educator*
Hanreddy, Joseph *stage director*
Hanthorn, Dennis Wayne *performing arts association administrator*
Harris, Christine *dance company executive*
Howard, Clark *radio personality*
Ovitsky, Steven Alan *musician, symphony orchestra executive*
Reardon, Mark *radio personality*
Samson, Richard Max *theatre director, investment/real estate executive*
Sykes, Charlie *radio personality*
Uecker, Bob *actor, radio announcer, former baseball player, TV personality*
Wagner, Jeff *radio personality*

CANADA

MANITOBA

Winnipeg
Lewis, André Leon *artistic director*
Spohr, Arnold Theodore *artistic director, choreographer*

ONTARIO

Kitchener
Coles, Graham *conductor, composer*

London
Stafford, Earl *conductor*

Mississauga
Peterson, Oscar Emmanuel *pianist*

ENGLAND

London
Leppard, Raymond John *conductor, harpsichordist*

FRANCE

Paris
Boulez, Pierre *composer, conductor*

SWITZERLAND

Geneva
Barenboim, Daniel *conductor, pianist*

ADDRESS UNPUBLISHED

Bach, Jan Morris *composer, educator*
Bassett, Leslie Raymond *composer, educator*
Bierley, Paul Edmund *musician, author, publisher*
Boardman, Eunice *retired music educator*
Boe, David Stephen *musician, educator, dean*
Brün, Herbert J. *composer, educator*
Claver, Robert Earl *television director, producer*
de Blasis, James Michael *artistic director, producer, stage director*
Fuerstner, Fiona Margaret Anne *ballet company executive, ballet educator*
Hall, Tom T. *songwriter, performer*
Hopkins, Robert Elliott *music educator*
Horisberger, Don Hans *conductor, musician*
Ichino, Yoko *ballet dancer*
Jarvi, Neeme *conductor*
Marth, Mary Ellen (Kim Martin) *entertainer*
Nixon, David *dancer*
Pensis, Henri Bram *music educator, conductor*
Peterson, Clark C. *announcer, writer, poet, speaker*
Poll, Heinz *choreographer, artistic director*
Reams, Michael Thomas *director, singer, actor*
Rosenthal, Arnold H. *film director, producer, writer, graphic designer, calligrapher*
Vandenbroucke, Russell James *theatre director, writer, educator*
Wagner, Mark Anthony *videotape editor*
Webb, Martha Jeanne *author, speaker, film producer*

ARTS: VISUAL

UNITED STATES

FLORIDA

Clearwater
Slade, Roy *artist, college president, museum director*

ILLINOIS

Champaign
Jackson, Billy Morrow *artist, retired art educator*

Chicago
Bowman, Leah *fashion designer, consultant, photographer, educator*
Gray, Richard *art dealer, consultant, holding company executive*
Hill, Gary *video artist*
King, Andre Richardson *architectural graphic designer*
Kolkey, Gilda *artist*
Look, Dona Jean *artist*
Sigler, Hollis *artist, educator, author*
Wilson, Anne Gawthrop *artist, educator*
Wolin, Jeffrey Alan *artist*
Workman, Robert Peter *artist, cartoonist*

Crystal Lake
Salvesen, B Behan-Forbes *artist*

Des Plaines
Banach, Art John *graphic artist*

Edwardsville
Malone, Robert Roy *artist, art educator*

Evanston
Conger, William Frame *artist, educator*
Rasco, Kay Frances *antique dealer*

Oak Lawn
Jachna, Joseph David *photographer, educator*

Park Ridge
Charewicz, David Michael *photographer*

Scales Mound
Lieberman, Archie *photographer, writer*

South Holland
Fota, Frank George *artist*

Winnetka
Plowden, David *photographer*

INDIANA

Bloomington
Lowe, Marvin *artist, educator*
Markman, Ronald *artist, educator*

Indianapolis
Hayes, Brenda Sue Nelson *artist*

Munster
Dompke, Norbert Frank *retired photography studio executive*

West Lafayette
Ichiyama, Dennis Yoshihide *design educator, consultant, administrator*

IOWA

Davenport
Jecklin, Lois Underwood *art corporation executive, consultant*

Des Moines
Messer, Randy Keith *graphic designer, illustrator*
Reece, Maynard Fred *artist, author*

KANSAS

Lawrence
Dooley, Patrick John *graphic designer, design educator*
Hermes, Marjory Ruth *machine embroidery and arts educator*

Ottawa
Howe, William Hugh *artist*

Topeka
Lee, Karen *art appraiser*

MICHIGAN

Ann Arbor
Rogers, Bryan Leigh *artist, art educator*

Dearborn
Cape, James Odies E. *fashion designer*

Detroit
Moldenhauer, Judith A. *graphic design educator*
Oliver, Gilda Maria *sculptor, painter, artist*

Grand Blanc
Thompson, Thomas Adrian *sculptor*

Mount Pleasant
Born, James E. *art educator, sculptor*

Pontiac
Brychtova, Jaroslava *sculptor*

Port Huron
Rowark, Maureen *fine arts photographer*

MINNESOTA

Duluth
Chee, Cheng-Khee *artist, educator*

Frazee
Ulmer, James Howard *potter*

Mankato
Frink, Brian Lee *artist, educator*

Minneapolis
Asher, Frederick M. *art educator, art historian*
Hallman, Gary L. *photographer, educator*
Preuss, Roger E(mil) *artist*
Rose, Thomas Albert *artist, art educator*

Saint Paul
Tylevich, Alexander V. *sculptor, architect, educator*

MISSOURI

Columbia
Larson, Sidney *art educator, artist, writer, painting conservator*

Rockaway Beach
Alkire, Betty Jo *artist, commercial real estate broker, marketing consultant*

Rogersville
Davis, Evelyn Marguerite Bailey *artist, organist, pianist*

Saint Louis
Burkett, Randy James *lighting designer*
Fondaw, Ronald Edward *artist, educator*
Greenblatt, William *photographer*
Hansman, Robert G. *art educator, artist*

Sibley
Morrow, Elizabeth Hostetter *sculptress, museum administrator, farmer, educator*

NEBRASKA

Lincoln
Neal, Mo (P. Maureen Neal) *sculptor*

NEW YORK

New York
Ortman, George Earl *artist*

OHIO

Aurora
Lawton, Florian Kenneth *artist, educator*

Bowling Green
Ocvirk, Otto George *artist*

Cincinnati
Brod, Stanford *graphic designer, educator*
Knipschild, Robert *artist, educator*
Rexroth, Nancy Louise *photographer*
Strohmaier, Thomas Edward *designer, educator, photographer*

Cleveland
Cassill, Herbert Carroll *artist*
Deming, David Lawson *art educator, educator*

Columbus
Goff, Wilmer Scott *retired photographer*

Euclid
Hill, Robyn Lesley *artist, designer*

Hilliard
Cupp, David Foster *photographer, journalist*

Kent
Kwong, Eva *artist, educator*

Oberlin
Reinoehl, Richard Louis *artist, scholar, martial artist*

Oxford
Ewing, Susan R. *artist, educator*

Toledo
Brower, James Calvin *graphic artist, painter*
McGlauchlin, Tom *artist*

SOUTH DAKOTA

Vermillion
Freeman, Jeffrey Vaughn (Jeff Freeman) *art educator, artist*

WISCONSIN

Beloit
Simon, Michael Alexander *photographer, educator*

Hollandale
Colescott, Warrington Wickham *artist, printmaker, educator*

Madison
Becker, David *artist, educator*

ADDRESS UNPUBLISHED

Herzberg, Thomas *artist, illustrator*
Leepa, Allen *artist, educator*
Liljegren, Frank Sigfrid *artist, art association official*
Martin, Noel *graphic design consultant, educator*
Rankin, Scott David *artist, educator*
Sumichrast, Jozef *illustrator, designer*
Vollmer, Howard Robert *artist, photographer*

ASSOCIATIONS AND ORGANIZATIONS *See also* specific fields

UNITED STATES

ARIZONA

Phoenix
Swartz, Jack *chamber of commerce executive*

ILLINOIS

Belvidere
Luhman, William Simon *community development administrator*

Chicago
Bloch, Ralph Jay *professional association executive, marketing consultant*
Bourdon, Cathleen Jane *professional society administrator*
Bushman, Mary Laura Jones *developer, fundraiser*
Crenshaw, Carol *charitable organization administrator*
Dolan, Thomas Christopher *professional society administrator*
Donnell, Harold Eugene, Jr. *professional society administrator*
Franke, Richard James *arts advocate, former investment banker*
Herbert, Victor James *foundation administrator*
Knapp, Paul Raymond *think tank executive*
Kudo, Irma Setsuko *not-for-profit executive director*
MacDougal, Gary Edward *corporate director, foundation trustee*
Mercer, David Robinson *cultural organization administrator*
Minow, Josephine Baskin *civic volunteer*
Nicholas, Ralph W. *cultural organization administrator*
Olsen, Rex Norman *trade association executive*
Richman, Harold Alan *social welfare policy educator*
Rielly, John Edward *educational association administrator*
Rodgers, James Foster *association executive, economist*
Sigmon, Joyce Elizabeth *professional society administrator*
So, Frank S. *educational association administrator*
Swanson, Patricia Klick *foundation administrator*
Wallerstein, Mitchel Bruce *foundation executive*
Weber, Daniel E. *association executive*
Wright, Helen Kennedy *retired professional association administrator, publisher, editor, librarian*

Evanston
Abnee, A. Victor *trade association executive*
Gordon, Julie Peyton *foundation administrator*
Thrash, Patricia Ann *educational association administrator*

La Grange Park
Webster, Lois Shand *association executive*

Park Ridge
Ewald, Robert Frederick *insurance association executive*

Riverside
Dengler, Robert Anthony *professional association executive*

Rosemont
Good, William Allen *professional society executive*

Schaumburg
Little, Bruce Washington *professional society administrator*
Tompson, Marian Leonard *professional society administrator*

Skokie
Gleason, John Patrick, Jr. *trade association executive*

Wilmette
Brink, Marion Francis *trade association administrator*

INDIANA

Bloomington
Joekel, Ronald G. *fraternal organization administrator*

Evansville
Early, Judith K. *social services director*

Fishers
Gatto, Louis Constantine *retired educational association administrator*

Friendship
Miller, John *foundation administrator*

Indianapolis
Braun, Robert Clare *retired association and advertising executive*
Clark, Charles M., Jr. *research institution administrator*
Finley, Katherine Mandusic *professional society administrator*
Quarles, Beth *civil rights administrator*
Recker, Thomas Edward *fraternal organization executive*
Robbins, N. Clay *foundation administrator*
Shaffer, Alfred Garfield (Terry) *service organization executive*
Sparks, Donald Eugene *interscholastic activities association executive*
Vereen, Robert Charles *retired trade association executive*
Winston, Robin *political organization official*

Muncie
Bakken, Douglas Adair *foundation executive*

North Manchester
Myers, Anne M. *developer*

Santa Claus
Platthy, Jeno *cultural association executive*

Terre Haute
Aldridge, Sandra *civic volunteer*

IOWA

Cedar Rapids
Whipple, William Perry *foundation administrator*

Clive
Tank, Alan *trade association administrator*

Des Moines
Mcguire-Riggs, Sheila *chairman Democratic party*
Nelson, Charlotte Bowers *public administrator*
Peterson, Michael K. *political organization administrator*
Robinson, Kayne *political organization officer*

Iowa City
Ferguson, Richard L. *educational administrator*

KANSAS

Fort Riley
Spurrier-Bright, Patricia Ann *professional society administrator*

Kansas City
Benjamin, Janice Yukon *development executive*
Campbell, Joseph Leonard *trade association executive*
Jones, Charles W. *labor union executive*
Steineger, Margaret Leisy *non-profit organization officer*

Lawrence
Mona, Stephen Francis *golf association executive*

Shawnee Mission
Green, John Lafayette, Jr. *education executive*

Topeka
Frahm, Sheila *association executive, former government official, academic administrator*
Menninger, Roy Wright *medical foundation executive, psychiatrist*
Perry, Nancy *foundation administrator*
Powers, Ramon Sidney *historical society administrator, historian*

KENTUCKY

Louisville
Early, Jack Jones *foundation executive*

MAINE

Brunswick
Rosser, Richard Franklin *higher education consultant*

MICHIGAN

Ann Arbor
Porter, John Wilson *education executive*
Ware, Richard Anderson *foundation executive*

Battle Creek
Mawby, Russell George *retired foundation executive*
Overton-Adkins, Betty Jean *foundation administrator*
Richardson, William Chase *foundation executive*

Detroit
Noland, Mariam Charl *foundation executive*
Parks, Rosa Louise *civil rights activist*
Schuster, Elaine *civil rights professional*
Yokich, Stephen Phillip *labor union administrator*

Dowagiac
Ott, C(larence) H(enry) *citizen ambassador, accounting educator*

East Lansing
Mitstifer, Dorothy Irwin *honor society administrator*

Farmington Hills
Leyh, George Francis *retired association executive*

Flint
Jondahl, Lynn *foundation administrator*
Maynard, Olivia P. *foundation administrator*
White, William Samuel *foundation executive*

Kalamazoo
Petersen, Anne C.(Cheryl) *foundation administrator, educator*

Okemos
Luecke, Eleanor Virginia Rohrbacher *civic volunteer*

Saint Clair Shores
Smith, Frank Earl *retired association executive*

Southfield
Fleming, Mac Arthur *labor union administrator*

Troy
Hunia, Edward Mark *foundation executive*
Marshall, John Elbert, III *foundation executive*

MINNESOTA

Chaska
Burke, Steven Francis *organization executive*

Minneapolis
Johnson, John Warren *retired association executive*
King, Reatha Clark *community foundation executive*

Rochester
Shulman, Carole Karen *professional society administrator*
Wojcik, Martin Henry *foundation development official*

Roseville
Hughes, Jerome Michael *education foundation executive*

Saint Paul
Archabal, Nina M(archetti) *historical society director*
Kolehmainen, Jan Waldroy *professional association administrator*
Pampusch, Anita Marie *foundation administrator*

Saint Peter
Nelsen, William Cameron *foundation executive, former college president*

MISSOURI

Bridgeton
Kenison, Raymond Robert *fraternal organization administrator, director*

Earth City
Anderhalter, Oliver Frank *educational organization executive*

Jefferson City
Palo, Nicholas Edwin *professional society administrator*
Wagner, Ann *political organization executive*

Kansas City
Benner, Richard Edward, Jr. *community service volunteer, investor*
Bugher, Robert Dean *professional society administrator*
Haw, Bill *association executive*
Wilson, Eugene Rolland *foundation executive*
Wingfield, Laura Allison Ross *fraternal organization executive*

Saint Louis
Anderson, Bruce John *foundation administrator*
Bascom, C. Perry *retired foundation administrator*
Breckenridge, Joanne *political organization administrator*
Horn, Joan Kelly *political research and consulting firm executive*
Kimmey, James Richard, Jr. *foundation administrator*
Koff, Robert Hess *foundation administrator*
Pope, Robert E(ugene) *fraternal organization administrator*
Robins, Marjorie McCarthy (Mrs. George Kenneth Robins) *civic worker*
Winter, Mildred M. *educational administrator*

NEBRASKA

Lincoln
Rosenow, John Edward *foundation executive*

Lyons
Hassebrook, Chuck *not-for-profit developer*

Omaha
Bell, C(lyde) R(oberts) (Bob Bell) *foundation administrator*
Flickinger, Thomas Leslie *hospital alliance executive*
Manna, John S. *fraternal organization administrator*
McCormack, Michael Joseph *foundation administrator*

Seward
Vrana, Verlon Kenneth *retired professional society administrator, conservationist*

NORTH DAKOTA

Bismarck
Cramer, Kevin *foundation administrator*
Haugland, Erling *political organization executive*
Kleingartner, Larry *agricultural association executive*

OHIO

Akron
Martino, Frank Dominic *union executive*

Brecksville
Andrassy, Timothy Francis *trade association executive*

Chardon
Reinhard, Sister Mary Marthe *educational organization administrator*

Cincinnati
Parker, Linda Bates *professional development organization administrator*

Cleveland
Bergholz, David *foundation administrator*
Calkins, Hugh *foundation executive*
Cleary, Michael J. *educational administrator*
Distelhorst, Garis Fred *trade association executive*
Hartley, Duncan *fundraising executive*
Jenson, Jon Eberdt *association executive*
Little, Charles L. *retired labor union administrator*

Columbus
De Maria, Paolo *state governor policy advisor*
Franano, Susan Margaret Ketteman *arts consultant and adminstrator, musician*
Hamilton, Harold Philip *fund raising executive*
Leland, David J. *political association executive*
Luck, James I. *foundation executive*
Newman, Diana S. *development consultant*
Selby, Diane Ray Miller *fraternal organization administrator*
Sharp, Paul David *institute administrator*

Dayton
Daley, Robert Emmett *retired foundation executive*
Mathews, David *foundation executive*
Schwartzhoff, James Paul *foundation executive*

Dublin
Needham, George Michael *association executive*

Fairview Park
Fordyce, James Stuart *non-profit organization executive*

Oberlin
Cartier, Brian Evans *association executive*

Oxford
Miller, Robert James *educational association administrator*

Yellow Springs
Graham, Jewel Freeman *social worker, lawyer, educator*

Zoar
Fernandez, Kathleen M. *cultural organization administrator*

SOUTH DAKOTA

Rapid City
Erickson, John Duff *retired educational association administrator*

Yankton
Piper, Kathleen *former political organization administrator*

TENNESSEE

Athens
Brown, Sandra Lee *art association administrator, watercolorist*

WASHINGTON

Mill Creek
Corbally, John Edward *foundation director*

WISCONSIN

Appleton
Hinkens, Kay L. *social services association executive*
Jodarski, Richard R. *social services association executive*
Krueger, James H. *social service association executive*
Lapacz, Steven P. *social services association executive*
Rugland, Walter S. *fraternal benefit society executive*

Madison
Brennan, Robert Walter *association executive*
Higby, Gregory James *historical association administrator, historian*
Porter, Andrew Calvin *educational administrator, psychology educator*
Spring, Terri *political organization executive*

Madison
Honold, Linda Kaye *political organization executive, human resources development executive*

Milwaukee
Gracz, Gregory L. *labor union administrator*
Joyce, Michael Stewart *foundation executive, political science educator*
Randall, Gerard *foundation administrator*
Schneider, Thomas Paul *non-profit agency administrator*
Taylor, Allen M. *community foundation executive*

Shawano
Lyon, Thomas L. *agricultural organization administrator*

ADDRESS UNPUBLISHED

Bieber, Owen F. *labor union official*
DeVos, Elisabeth *political association executive*
DeVries, Robert Allen *foundation administrator*
Florian, Marianna Bolognesi *civic leader*
Gilchrest, Thornton Charles *retired association executive*
Kabat, Linda Georgette *civic leader*
Langer, Edward L. *trade association administrator*
McDaniel, Mike *former political association executive*
McFate, Kenneth Leverne *trade association administrator*
Mercuri, Joan B. *foundation executive*
Miller, Jay Alan *retired civil rights association executive*
Palmer, Robert Erwin *association executive*
Pullen, Penny Lynne *non-profit administrator, former state legislator*
Roach, William Russell *training and education executive*
Smith, Margaret Taylor *volunteer*
Weikart, David Powell *educational research foundation administrator*

ATHLETICS

UNITED STATES

CALIFORNIA

La Mirada
Razov, Ante *professional soccer player*

Los Angeles
Grissom, Marquis Deon *professional baseball player*

San Francisco
Lofton, Kenneth *professional baseball player*

COLORADO

Denver
Alomar, Sandy, Jr. (Santos Velazquez Alomar) *professional baseball player*

CONNECTICUT

Hartford
Pleau, Lawrence Winslow *professional hockey coach, business executive*

DELAWARE

Wilmington
Lerner, Alfred *professional sports team executive, real estate and financial executive*

ILLINOIS

Champaign
Self, Bill *college basketball coach*

Chicago
Agoos, Jeff *professional soccer player*
Aguilera, Richard Warren (Rick Aguilera) *baseball player*
Akers, Michelle Anne *soccer player*
Arena, Bruce *professional soccer coach*
Artest, Ron *professional basketball player*
Baumgardt, Justi Michelle *former soccer player*
Baylor, Don Edward *former professional baseball manager*
Blauser, Jeffrey Michael *professional baseball player*
Bradley, Bob *professional soccer coach*
Buehrle, Mark *baseball player*
Cartwright, Bill *professional basketball coach*
Cromwell, Amanda Caryl *former soccer player, coach*
Daze, Eric *professional hockey player*
Ducar, Tracy *former soccer player*
Durham, Ray *professional baseball player*
Einhorn, Edward Martin (Eddie Einhorn) *professional baseball team executive*
Fawcett, Joy Lynn *soccer player*
Fotopoulos, Danielle *former soccer player*
Foudy, Julia Maurine *soccer player*
Gabarra, Carin Leslie *professional soccer player*
Girardi, Joseph Elliott *baseball player*
Grace, Mark Eugene *baseball player*
Gregg, Lauren *women's soccer coach*
Hamm, Mariel Margaret *soccer player*
Heinrichs, April *coach*
Housley, Phil F. *professional hockey player*
Jones, Cobi *professional soccer player*
Keller, Deborah Kim *former soccer player*
Konerko, Paul *baseball player*
Krause, Jerry (Jerome Richard Krause) *professional basketball team executive*
Kreis, Jason *professional soccer player*
Lilly, Kristine Marie *soccer player*
Lynch, Edward Francis *professional sports team executive*
MacMillan, Shannon Ann *soccer player*
MacPhail, Andrew B. *professional sports team executive*
Manuel, Jerry *professional sports team manager*
Mercer, Ron *professional basketball player*
Milbrett, Tiffeny Carleen *professional soccer player*
Ordonez, Magglio *professional baseball player*
Overbeck, Carla Werden *soccer player, coach*
Parlow, Cynthia Marie *soccer player*
Pizer, Howard Charles *sports and entertainment executive*
Reinsdorf, Jerry Michael *professional sports teams executive, real estate executive, lawyer, accountant*
Reyna, Claudio *soccer player*
Rose, Jalen *professional basketball player*
Savard, Denis Joseph *former professional hockey player, coach*
Schwartz, Alan Gifford *sport company executive*
Schwoy, Laurie Annette *soccer player*
Scurry, Briana Collette *soccer player*
Sirotka, Mike *professional baseball player*
Smith, Mike *professional sports team executive*
Sobrero, Kathryn Michele *soccer player*
Sosa, Samuel (Sammy Sosa) *professional baseball player*
Staples, Thori Yvette *former soccer player*
Streiffer, Jenny *former soccer player*
Thomas, Frank Edward *professional baseball player*
Venturini, Tisha Lea *professional soccer player*
Whalen, Sarah Eve *soccer player*

Chicago
Alou, Moises *professional baseball player*

Elk Grove Village
Meyer, Raymond Joseph *former college basketball coach*

Lake Forest
Angelo, Jerry *professional sports team executive*
Jaeger, Jeff Todd *professional football player*
Jauron, Dick *professional football coach*
McCaskey, Michael B. *professional football team executive*
Phillips, Ted *professional sports team executive*
Urlacher, Brian *football player*

Mahomet
Thompson, Margaret M. *physical education educator*

Mundelein
Carr, Bonnie Jean *professional ice skater*

INDIANA

Indianapolis
Bird, Larry Joe *former professional basketball player, coach*
Dempsey, Cedric W. *sports association administrator*
Dungy, Tony *professional football coach*
Ganassi, Chip *professional race car executive, owner*
Harrison, Marvin *football player*
Irsay, James Steven *professional football team owner*
James, Edgerrin *football player*
Manning, Peyton *professional football player*
Miller, Reginald Wayne *professional basketball player*
Mullin, Chris(topher) Paul *professional basketball player*
Polian, Bill *professional football team executive*
Simon, Herbert *professional basketball team executive*
Smits, Rik *retired professional basketball player*
Thomas, Isiah Lord, III *former professional basketball player, basketball team executive, professional basketball coach*
Unser, Al *retired professional auto racer, racing official*
Walsh, Donnie *sports club executive*

Notre Dame
White, Kevin M. *athletic director*

IOWA

Ames
McCarney, Dan *football coach*

Iowa City
Alford, Steve *college basketball coach*
Bowlsby, Bob *athletic director*

KANSAS

Manhattan
Snyder, Bill *football coach*

Overland Park
Schultz, Richard Dale *national athletic organization executive*

MASSACHUSETTS

Boston
Ramirez, Manuel Aristides (Manny Ramirez) *professional baseball player*
Sutter, Brian *former professional hockey coach*

MICHIGAN

Auburn Hills
Azzi, Jennifer L. *basketball player*
Carlisle, Rick *professional basketball coach*
Dumars, Joe, III *retired professional basketball player*
Lieberman-Cline, Nancy *professional basketball coach, former player*
Montross, Eric Scott *professional basketball player*
Vaught, Loy *professional basketball player*
Williams, Greg *professional basketball coach*
Wilson, Thomas S. *professional basketball team administrator*

Detroit
Bing, David *retired basketball player, metal products executive*
Bowman, Scotty *professional hockey coach*
Bowman, William Scott (Scotty Bowman) *professional hockey coach*
Chelios, Christos K *professional hockey player*
Cruz, Deivi *professional baseball player*
Devellano, James Charles *professional hockey manager, baseball executive*
Fedorov, Sergei *hockey player*
Fick, Robert *baseball player*
Garner, Phil *former professional baseball manager*
Gonzalez, Juan (Alberto Vazquez) *professional baseball player*
Higginson, Bobby *professional baseball player*
Holland, Ken *sports team executive*
Hull, Brett A. *professional hockey player*
Ilitch, Marian *professional hockey team executive, food service executive*
Ilitch, Michael *professional hockey team executive*
McHale, John, Jr. *professional sports team executive*
Robitaille, Luc *professional hockey player*
Shanahan, Brendan Frederick *professional hockey player*
Yzerman, Steve *professional hockey player*

East Lansing
Izzo, Thomas *college basketball coach*

Mount Pleasant
Deromedi, Herb William *athletic director*

Pontiac
Howard, Desmond Kevin *professional football player*
Millen, Matt *professional sports team executive*
Mornhinweg, Marty *professional football coach*
Pritchett, Kelvin *professional football player*
Sanders, Barry *retired football player*
Schmidt, Chuck *professional football team executive*

MINNESOTA

Eden Prairie
Anderson, Gary Allan *professional football player*
Brzezinski, Rob *professional sports team executive*
Culpepper, Daunte *football player*
Hoard, Leroy *professional football player*
McCombs, Billy Joe (Red McCombs) *professional football team executive*
McCombs, Charline *professional sports team executive*
Moss, Randy *professional football player*
Poppen, Steve *professional sports team executive*
Tice, Mike *professional football coach*
Woods, Gary V. *professional football team executive, former professional basketball team executive, automotive executive*

Minneapolis
Agler, Brian *professional basketball coach*
Billups, Chauncey *professional basketball player*
Garnett, Kevin *professional basketball player*
Garrett, Dean *professional basketball player*
Griffith, Roger *professional sports team executive*
Kelly, Tom (Jay Thomas Kelly) *retired professional sports team manager*
Lawton, Matt *professional baseball player*

McHale, Kevin Edward *former professional basketball player, sports team executive*
Molitor, Paul Leo *professional baseball coach*
Monson, Dan *college basketball coach*
Moor, Rob *professional basketball team executive*
Nanne, Louis Vincent *professional hockey team executive*
Pohlad, Carl R. *professional baseball team executive, bottling company executive*
Puckett, Kirby *professional baseball team executive, former player*
Ryan, Terry *professional sports team executive*
Saunders, Philip D. *professional basketball coach*
Wittman, Randy *professional basketball coach*

Saint Paul
Fuller, Martha *professional sports team executive*
Leiweke, Tod *professional sports team executive*
Lemaire, Jacques *professional hockey coach*
Naegele, Jr. Robert O. *professional sports team executive*
Sperling, Jac *professional sports team executive*

MISSOURI

Bridgeton
Faulk, Marshall William *professional football player*

Earth City
Shaw, John *sports association administrator*

Kansas City
Allen, Marcus *retired professional football player*
Brett, George Howard *baseball executive, former professional baseball player*
Damon, Johnny *professional baseball player*
Dye, Jermaine *professional baseball player*
Gansler, Robert *professional soccer coach*
Gonzalez, Tony *football player*
Green, Trent Jason *football player*
Holmes, Priest *football player*
Hunt, Lamar *professional football team executive*
McGuff, Joseph Thomas *professional sports team executive*
Meola, Tony *professional soccer player, actor*
Montgomery, Jeffrey Thomas *baseball player*
Muser, Tony *former manager professional athletics*
Pena, Antonio Francisco (Tony Pena) *professional athletics coach*
Peterson, Carl V. *professional football team executive*
Preki, *professional soccer player*
Rison, Andre *football player*
Robinson, Spencer T. (Herk Robinson) *professional baseball team executive*
Shields, Will Herthie *football player*
Smith, Louis *sports association administrator*
Steadman, Jack W. *professional football team executive*
Sweeney, Mike *professional baseball player*
Vermeil, Dick *professional football coach*

Kansas City
Hernandez, Roberto *professional baseball player*

Saint Louis
Benes, Andrew Charles *professional baseball player*
Bruce, Issac Isidore *football player*
Clark, Will (William Nuschler Clark Jr.) *professional baseball player*
Davis, Eric Keith *professional baseball player*
Demitra, Pavol *professional hockey player*
DeWitt, William O., Jr. *professional sports team executive*
Dunston, Shawon Donnell *professional baseball player*
Edmonds, James Patrick (Jim Edmonds) *professional baseball player*
Hanser, Frederick Otto *professional sports team executive*
Hentgen, Patrick George *baseball player*
Jasiek, Jerry *professional sports team executive*
Jocketty, Walt *professional sports team executive*
La Russa, Tony, Jr. (Anthony La Russa Jr.) *professional baseball manager*
Lankford, Raymond Lewis *baseball player*
Laurie, William *sports team executive*
MacInnis, Al *professional hockey player*
Martz, Mike *professional football coach*
McGee, William Dean (Willie McGee) *professional baseball player*
McGwire, Mark David *professional baseball player*
Morris, Matthew Christian *baseball player*
Pace, Orlando Lamar *football player*
Quenneville, Joel *professional hockey coach*
Rolen, Scott Bruce *baseball player*
Schoendienst, Albert Fred (Red Schoendienst) *professional baseball coach, former baseball player*
Smith, Ozzie (Osborne Earl Smith) *retired professional baseball player*
Tkachuk, Keith *professional hockey player*
Tuten, Richard Lamar *professional football player*
Weight, Doug *professional hockey player*

St Louis
Frontiere, Georgia *professional football team executive*

NEBRASKA

Lincoln
Collier, Barry S. *coach*
Sanderford, Paul L. *coach*
Solich, Frank *coach*

NEW YORK

Flushing
Alomar, Roberto Velazquez *professional baseball player*

OHIO

Berea
Clark, Dwight Edward *sports team executive, former professional football player*
Couch, Tim *professional football player*
Davis, Butch *professional football coach*
Jacobs, Douglas C. *professional sports team executive*
Policy, Carmen A. *professional sports team executive*

Canton
Elliott, Peter R. *retired athletic organization executive*

Cincinnati
Boone, Robert Raymond *professional baseball coach*
Bowden, Jim *professional sports team executive*
Brown, Mike *professional sports team executive*
Dillon, Corey *professional football player*
Griffey, Ken, Jr. (George Kenneth Griffey Jr.) *professional baseball player*
Huggins, Bob *college basketball coach*
Kitna, Jon *football player*
Larkin, Barry Louis *professional baseball player*
LeBeau, Dick *professional football coach, retired football player*
McKeon, John Aloysius (Jack) (Jack McKeon) *former professional baseball manager*
Neagle, Dennis Edward (Denny Neagle) *professional baseball player*
Pirtle, Laurie Lee *women's university basketball coach*
Reese, Pokey *professional baseball player*
Santiago, Benito Rivera *professional baseball player*
Sawyer, John *professional football team executive*
Schott, Marge *former professional baseball team executive*
Smith, Akili *professional football player*
Warrick, Peter *football player*

Cleveland
Baranova, Elena *basketball player*
Boland, James C. *sports association executive*
Edwards, Michelle Denise *professional basketball player*
Fijalkowski, Isabelle *professional basketball player*
Finley, Chuck (Charles Edward Finley) *baseball player*
Fryman, David Travis *professional baseball player*
Gardocki, Christopher *professional football player*
Hart, John *professional sports team executive*
Hill, Tyrone *professional basketball player*
Hughes, Dan *professional basketball coach*
Kirby, Terry *professional football player*
Lucas, John Harding, Jr. *professional basketball coach*
Manuel, Charlie Fuqua, Jr. *professional baseball manager*
McConnell Serio, Suzie Theresa *basketball player*
Nemcova, Eva *professional basketball player*
Riggleman, James David *former professional baseball team manager*
Segui, David *professional baseball player*
Thome, Jim *professional baseball player*
Vizquel, Omar Enrique *professional baseball player*

Columbus
King, Dave *professional hockey coach*
MacLean, Doug *hockey coach*
McBride, Brian *soccer player*
Sanderson, Geoff *professional hockey player*

Fairfield
Robertson, Big O (Oscar Palmer Robertson) *chemical company executive, former professional basketball player*

Worthington
Whitney, Ray *hockey player*

Youngstown
DeBartolo, Edward John, Jr. *professional football team owner, real estate developer*

OREGON

Portland
Kemp, Shawn T. *professional basketball player*

PENNSYLVANIA

Pittsburgh
Sauer, Mark *professional sports team executive*

TEXAS

Lubbock
Knight, Bob *college basketball coach*

WISCONSIN

Green Bay
Favre, Brett Lorenzo *professional football player*
Green, Ahman *football player*
Harlan, Robert Ernest *professional football team executive*
Jones, John *professional sports team executive*
Sherman, Michael Francis *professional football coach*

Greendale
Kuhn, Roseann *sports association administrator*

La Crosse
Hastad, Douglas Noel *physical education educator*

Madison
Bennett, Dick *college basketball coach*
Sauer, Jeff *university hockey coach*

Milwaukee
Burnitz, Jeromy *professional baseball player*
Cassell, Samuel James *basketball player*
Hayes, Charles Dewayne *professional baseball player*
Karl, George *professional basketball coach*
Lopes, Davey *former professional baseball manager*
Manning, Daniel Ricardo *professional basketball player*
Selig-Prieb, Wendy *sports team executive*
Sexson, Richmond Lockwood *baseball player*
Steinmiller, John F. *professional basketball team executive*
Weinhauer, Bob *professional sports team executive*

ADDRESS UNPUBLISHED

Lindner, Carl Henry, Jr. *sports team executive, insurance company executive*
Mason, Linda *physical education educator, softball and basketball coach*
Parins, Robert James *professional football team executive, judge*
Ross, Robert Joseph *retired professional football coach*
Stewart III, James Otis *football player*

BUSINESS *See* FINANCE: INDUSTRY

COMMUNICATIONS *See* COMMUNICATIONS MEDIA; INDUSTRY: SERVICE

COMMUNICATIONS MEDIA *See also* ARTS: LITERARY

UNITED STATES

CALIFORNIA

Los Angeles
Larson, Gary *cartoonist*

San Diego
Kyle, Robert Campbell, II *publishing executive*

Santa Barbara
Lilly, George David *broadcasting executive*

CONNECTICUT

Hartford
Davis, Jack Wayne, Jr.

FLORIDA

Naples
Penniman, Nicholas Griffith, IV *retired newspaper publisher*

ILLINOIS

Arlington Heights
Baumann, Daniel E. *newspaper executive*
Lampinen, John A. *newspaper editor*
Paddock, Stuart R., Jr. *publishing executive*
Ray, Douglas Kent *newspaper executive*

Barrington
Bash, Philip Edwin *publishing executive*

Bartlett
Markle, Sandra *publishing company executive*

Belleville
Berkley, Gary Lee *newspaper publisher*
Richmond, Richard Thomas *journalist*

Bloomington
Merwin, Davis Underwood *newspaper executive*

Carol Stream
Taylor, Kenneth Nathaniel *publishing executive, writer*

Champaign
McCulloh, Judith Marie *editor*
Meyer, August Christopher, Jr. *broadcasting company executive, lawyer*
Watts, Robert Allan *publisher, lawyer*
Wentworth, Richard Leigh *editor*

Chicago
Adamle, Mike *sports commentator*
Agema, Gerald Walton *broadcasting company executive*
Ahern, Mary Ann *reporter*
Allen, Richard Blose *legal editor, lawyer*
Anderson, Jon Stephen *newswriter*
Anderson, Karl Stephen *editor*
Artner, Alan Gustav *art critic, journalist*
Barr, Emily *television station executive*
Bell, Clark Wayne *business editor, educator*
Blakley, Derrick *newscaster*
Boers, Terry John *sportswriter, radio and television personality*
Brooks, Marion *newscaster*
Brotman, Barbara Louise *columnist, writer*
Brumback, Charles Tiedtke *retired newpaper executive*
Brummel, Mark Joseph *magazine editor*
Callaway, Karen A(lice) *journalist*
Camper, John Jacob *speech writer*
Chapman, Darrian *sportscaster*
Connors, Dorsey *television and radio commentator, newspaper columnist*
Cooke, Michael *editor-in-chief*
Cooper, Ilene Linda *magazine editor, author*
Cross, Robert Clark *journalist*
Curwen, Randall William *journalist, editor*
DeBat, Donald Joseph *media consultant, columnist*
Dee, Ivan Richard *book publisher*
DeLong, Ray *editor*
Dold, Robert Bruce *journalist*
Donovan, Dianne Francys *journalist*
Dowdle, James C. *cable television executive*
Dyson, Marv *broadcast executive*
Eastabrook, Dianne *news correspondent*
Ebert, Roger Joseph *film critic*
Essex, Joseph Michael *visual communication planner*
Evans, Mariwyn *periodical editor*
Everhart, Bruce *radio station executive*
Fair, Hudson Randolph *recording company executive*
Feder, Robert *television and radio columnist*
Ferguson, Renee *news correspondent, reporter*
Field, Marshall *business executive*
Flanagan, Sylvia *editor*
Flock, Jeffrey Charles *news bureau chief*
Fuller, Jack William *writer, publishing executive*
Gaines, William Chester *journalist*
Goldsborough, Robert Gerald *publishing executive, author*
Grant, Dennis *newspaper publishing executive*
Greene, Robert Bernard, Jr. (Bob Greene) *broadcast television correspondent, columnist, author*
Hallinan, Joseph Thomas *journalist, author*
Harvey, Paul *news commentator, author, columnist*
Hast, Adele *editor, historian*
Hefner, Christie Ann *multi-media entertainment executive*
Higgins, Jack *editorial cartoonist*
Hlavacek, Roy George *publishing executive, magazine editor*
Huntley, Robert Stephen *newspaper editor*
Idol, Anna Catherine *magazine editor*
Iglauer, Bruce *record company executive*
Judge, Bernard Martin *editor, publisher*
Kay, Dick *news correspondent*
King, Jennifer Elizabeth *editor*
Kisor, Henry Du Bois *newspaper editor, critic, columnist*
Klaviter, Helen Lothrop *magazine editor*
Kotulak, Ronald *newspaper science writer*
Kramer, Weezie Crawford *former broadcast executive*
Krueger, Bonnie Lee *editor, writer*
Kupcinet, Irv *columnist*
Kwan, Nesita *newscaster*
Leckey, Andrew A. *financial columnist*
Lipinski, Ann Marie *newspaper editor*
Loesch, Katharine Taylor (Mrs. John George Loesch) *communication and theatre educator*
Longworth, Richard Cole *journalist*
Lyon, Jeffrey *journalist, author*
Lythcott, Marcia A. *newspaper editor*
Madigan, John William *publishing executive*
McCarron, John Francis *editor*
McDaniel, Charles-Gene *journalism educator, writer*
McDougal, Alfred Leroy *publishing executive*
McHugh, Mike E. *news executive*
McNally, Andrew, IV *publishing executive, director*
Nault, William Henry *publishing executive*
Neal, Steven George *journalist*
Needleman, Barbara *newspaper executive*
Neubauer, Charles Frederick *investigative reporter*
Norman, Art *newscaster*
O'Dell, James E. *newspaper publishing executive*
Oakes, Fred D. *editor*
Odelbo, Catherine G. *publishing executive*
Parisi, Joseph (Anthony) *magazine editor, writer-consultant, educator*
Peerman, Dean Gordon *magazine editor*
Pendley, Kevin *communication media executive*
Peres, Judith May *journalist*
Pilchen, Ira A. *editor*
Plotnick, Harvey Barry *publishing executive*
Plotnik, Arthur *author, columnist*
Pope, Kerig Rodgers *magazine executive*
Price, Henry Escoe *broadcast executive*
Primm, Earl Russell, III *publishing executive*
Radler, Franklin David *publishing holding company executive*
Reindl, James *newspaper editor*
Rice, Linda Johnson *publishing executive*
Rice, William Edward *newspaper columnist*
Roeper, Richard *columnist*
Rogers, Phil *reporter*
Rosati, Allison *newscaster*
Rynkiewicz, Stephen Michael *journalist*
Sabin, Neal F. *broadcast executive*
Saunders, Warner *newscaster*
Savini, Dave *reporter*
Saxenmeyer, Mark Harold *television news reporter*
Scanlan, Thomas Cleary *publishing executive, editor*
Scherb, Jeff R. *newspaper company executive*
Shaw, William *broadcast executive*
Smith, Sam *columnist, author*
Sneed, Michael (Michele Sneed) *columnist*
Stone, Steven Michael *sports announcer, former baseball player*
Suppelsa, Mark *newscaster, reporter*
Tyner, Howard A. *publishing executive, newspaper editor, journalist*
von Rhein, John Richard *music critic, editor*
Vukas, Ronald *publishing executive*
Wade, Nigel *former editor in chief*
Wasiolek, Edward *literary critic, language and literature educator*
Weintraub, Joseph Barton *publishing executive*
Wert, Larry *broadcast executive*
White, John Henry *photojournalist, educator*
Wier, Patricia Ann *publishing executive, consultant*
Williams, David D. *newspaper executive*
Wilson, Gahan *cartoonist, author*

Winker, Margaret A. *editor*
Wolfe, Sheila A. *journalist*
Wright, Sharon *reporter*
Wycliff, Noel Don *journalist, newspaper editor*
Youngman, Owen Ralph *newspaper executive*
Zekman, Pamela Lois (Mrs. Fredric Soll) *reporter*
Zorn, Eric John *newspaper columnist*

Crystal Lake
Keller, William Francis *publishing consultant*

Des Plaines
Clapper, Marie Anne *magazine publisher*

Evanston
Borcover, Alfred Seymour *journalist*
Downing, Joan Forman *editor, writer*
Felknor, Bruce Lester *editorial consultant, writer*
Galvin, Kathleen Malone *communication educator*
Jacobs, Norman Joseph *publishing company executive*
Kuenster, John Joseph *magazine editor*
Larson, Roy *journalist, publisher*
Peck, Abraham *editor, writer, educator, magazine consultant*
Whitaker, Charles F. *journalism educator*
White, Willmon Lee *magazine editor*
Wills, Garry *journalist, educator*
Ziomek, Jonathan S. *journalist, educator*

Franklin Park
Duncanson, Donald George *retired encyclopedia editor*

Glen Ellyn
Beers, V(ictor) Gilbert *publishing executive*

Glencoe
Hoenig, Jonathan *radio talk show host*

Glenview
Mabley, Jack *newspaper columnist, communications consultant*

Highland Park
Johnson, Curtis Lee *publisher, editor, writer*
Pattis, Mark R. *publishing company executive*
Rutenberg-Rosenberg, Sharon Leslie *retired journalist*

Kenilworth
Cook, Stanton R. *media company executive*

Lake Bluff
Marozsan, John Robert *retired publishing company executive*

Lake Forest
Schulze, Franz, Jr. *art critic, educator*

Libertyville
True, Raymond Stephen *writer, editor, analyst, consultant*

Mount Vernon
Withers, W. Russell, Jr. *broadcast executive*

Naperville
Spiotta, Raymond Herman *editor*

Northbrook
Elleman, Barbara *editor*
Klemens, Thomas Lloyd *editor*
Snader, Jack Ross *publishing company executive*

Oak Brook
Biedron, Theodore John *newspaper advertising executive*

Peoria
McConnell, John Thomas *newspaper executive, publisher*
Murphy, Sharon Margaret *educator*

Peru
Carus, Andre Wolfgang *educational publishing firm executive*
Carus, Milton Blouke *publisher children's periodicals*

Plainfield
Diercks, Eileen Kay *educational media coordinator, elementary school educator*

Quincy
Baker, Mark *television newscaster*

Rockford
Fleming, Thomas J. *editor, publishing executive*
Jacobi, Fredrick Thomas *newspaper publisher*

Skokie
Feinberg, Henry J. *publishing executive*
Manos, John *editor-in-chief*
Wasik, John Francis *editor, writer, publisher*
Weber, Randy *publishing executive*

Springfield
Burch, Amy *communications media executive*
Harper, William Wayne *broadcast executive*

Tinley Park
Flanagan, John F. *publishing executive*

Urbana
Christians, Clifford Glenn *communications educator*
Dash, Leon DeCosta, Jr. *journalist*
Hansen, Kathryn Gertrude *editor, former state official*

Vernon Hills
Strother, Jay D. *legal editor*

Wauconda
Bolchazy, Ladislaus Joseph *publishing company executive*

Wheaton
Hollingsworth, Pierce *publishing executive*
Taylor, Mark Douglas *publishing executive*

Wheeling
Kuennen, Thomas Gerard *journalist*

INDIANA

Bloomington
Gough, Pauline Bjerke *magazine editor*
Jacobi, Peter Paul *journalism educator, author*
Lee, Don Yoon *publisher, academic researcher and writer*
Schurz, Scott Clark *journalist, publisher*
Walling, Donovan Robert *educational book editor*
Weaver, David Hugh *journalism educator, communications researcher*

Fort Wayne
Klugman, Stephan Craig *newspaper editor*
Pellegrene, Thomas James, Jr. *editor, researcher*
Sandeson, William Seymour *cartoonist*

Indianapolis
Adamak, M. Jeanelle *broadcast executive*
Caperton, Albert Franklin *retired newspaper editor*
Chase, Alyssa Ann *editor*
Coffey, Charles Moore *communication research professional, writer*
Cohen, Gabriel Murrel *editor, publisher*
Comiskey, Nancy *newspaper editor*
Eberle, Terry R. *editor, newspaper executive*
Fleming, Marcella *journalist*
Garmel, Marion Bess Simon *retired journalist*
Graves, Sam *communications media executive*
Henry, Barbara A. *publishing executive*
Lee, Kristi *broadcast executive, reporter*
Lyst, John Henry *former newspaper editor*
Natz, Jacques *news director*
Raughter, John B. *editor*
Robinson, Keith *newspaper editor*
Russell, Frank Eli *retired newspaper publishing executive*
Schilling, Emily Born *editor, association executive*
SerVaas, Beurt Richard *corporate executive*
Smiley, Wynn Ray *nonprofit corporation executive*
Wheat, Christopher John, Sr. *broadcast executive*
Wheeler, Daniel Scott *management executive, editor*
Wright, Lloyd James, Jr. *broadcast executive, educator, announcer*

Knightstown
Richardson, Shirley Maxine *genealogy editor*

Muncie
Bell, Stephen Scott (Steve Bell) *journalist, educator*

Munster
Colander, Patricia Marie *newspaper editor*

South Bend
Schurz, Franklin Dunn, Jr. *media executive*
Wensits, James Emrich *newspaper editor*

IOWA

Cedar Rapids
Keller, Eliot Aaron *broadcasting executive*
Quarton, William Barlow *broadcasting company executive*

Davenport
Brocka, Bruce *editor, educator, software engineer*
Brown, Colleen *broadcast execucice*
Gottlieb, Richard Douglas *media executive*
Schermer, Lloyd G. *publishing and broadcasting company executive*

Des Moines
Byal, Nancy Louise *food editor*
DeWulf Nickell, Karol *editor*
Gartner, Michael Gay *editor, television executive, baseball executive*
Graham, Diane E. *newspaper editor*
Kerr, William T. *publishing and broadcasting executive*
Kruidenier, David *newspaper executive*
Myers, Mary Kathleen *publishing executive*
Peterson, David Charles *photojournalist*
Rehm, Jack Daniel *publishing executive*
Rhein, Dave *newspaper editor*
Rood, Lee *newspaper editor*
Ryerson, Dennis *editor*
Shao Collins, Jeannine *magazine publisher*
Sheehan, Carol Sama *magazine editor*
Stier, Mary *publishing executive*
Witke, David Rodney *newspaper editor*

Iowa City
Duck, Steve Weatherill *communications educator*
Soloski, John *journalism and communications educator*

Mason City
Collison, Jim *business executive*

Spirit Lake
Hedberg, Paul Clifford *broadcasting executive*

Urbandale
Alumbaugh, JoAnn McCalla *magazine editor*

West Des Moines
Burnett, Robert A. *retired publisher*
Dooley, Donald John *retired publishing executive*

KANSAS

Iola
Lynn, Emerson Elwood, Jr. *retired newspaper editor/publisher*

Lawrence
Dickinson, William Boyd, Jr. *editorial consultant*
Orel, Harold *literary critic, educator*
Simons, Dolph Collins, Jr. *newspaper publisher*

Manhattan
Seaton, Edward Lee *newspaper editor and publisher*

Salina
Entriken, Robert Kersey, Jr. *motorsport writer, retired newspaper editor*

Topeka
Cornish, Kent M. *television executive*
Sipes, Karen Kay *newspaper editor*

Wichita
Curtright, Robert Eugene *newspaper critic and columnist*
Dill, Sheri *publishing executive*
Getz, Robert Lee *newspaper columnist*
Hatteberg, Larry Merle *photojournalist*

MICHIGAN

Ann Arbor
Beaver, Frank Eugene *communication educator, film critic and historian*
Bedard, Patrick Joseph *editor, writer, consultant*
Csere, Csaba *magazine editor*
Hessler, David William *information and multimedia systems educator*
Lewis, Robert Enzer *lexicographer, educator, editor*
Martin, Bruce James *newspaper editor*
Wall, Carroll Edward *publishing executive*

Birmingham
Berman, Laura *journalist, writer*

Dearborn
Hogan, Brian Joseph *editor*

Detroit
Alpert, Daniel *television executive*
Ashenfelter, David Louis *reporter*
Bennett, Grace *publishing executive*
Blomquist, David Wels *journalist*
Bullard, George *newspaper editor*
Burzynski, Susan Marie *newspaper editor*
Cantor, George Nathan *journalist*
Colby, Joy Hakanson *critic*
Dickerson, Brian *columnist*
Diebolt, Judith *newspaper editor*
Falls, Joseph Francis *sportswriter, editor*
Fezzey, Mike *radio station executive*
Henderson, Angelo B. *journalist*
Hill, Charles *newspaper editor*
Hutton, Carole Leigh *newspaper editor*
James, Sheryl Teresa *journalist*
Kelleher, Timothy John *publishing company executive*
Kiska, Timothy Olin *newspaper columnist*
Laughlin, Nancy *newspaper editor*
Meriwether, Heath J. *newspaper publisher*
Parry, Dale D. *newspaper editor*
Smyntek, John Eugene, Jr. *editor*
Stark, Susan R. *film critic*
Taylor, Jeff *reporter, editor*
Teagan, John Gerard *newspaper executive*
Vega, Frank J. *newspaper publishing executive*
Waldmeir, Peter Nielsen *journalist*
White, Joseph B. *reporter*

East Lansing
Freedman, Eric *journalist, educator, writer*
Greenberg, Bradley Sander *communications educator*
Ralph, David Clinton *communications educator*

Farmington Hills
Bryfonski, Dedria Anne *publishing company executive*

Ferndale
Baker, Elaine R. *radio station executive*

Flint
Samuel, Roger D. *newspaper publishing executive*

Grand Rapids
Baker, Richard Lee *book publishing company executive*
Bolinder, Scott W. *publishing company executive*
Gundry, Stanley N. *publishing company executive*
Kaczmarczyk, Jeffrey Allen *journalist, classical music critic*
Kregel, James R. *publishing executive*
Ryskamp, Bruce E. *publishing executive*

Grosse Pointe Farms
Christian, Edward Kieren *broadcasting station executive*

Jackson
Weaver, Franklin Thomas *retired newspaper executive*

Lansing
Brown, Nancy Field *editor*

Saginaw
Chaffee, Paul Charles *newspaper editor*

Saint Clair Shores
Shine, Neal James *journalism educator, former newspaper editor, publisher*

Southfield
Dunlop, Michael *broadcast executive*
Gilchrist, Grace *television station executive*
Makupson, Amyre Porter *television station executive*

Troy
Brumfield, Jim *news executive*
Moore, Oliver Semon, III *publishing executive, consultant*

MINNESOTA

Duluth
Latto, Lewis M. *broadcasting company executive*

Eagan
Collier, Ken O. *editor*

Edina
Bisping, Bruce Henry *photojournalist*

Melrose
Larson, Michael Len *newspaper editor, hospital administrator*

Minneapolis
Boyd, Belvel James *newspaper editor*
Buoen, Roger *newspaper editor*
Carter, Roy Ernest, Jr. *journalist, educator*
Cowles, John, Jr. *publisher, women's sports promoter*
Crosby, Jacqueline Garton *newspaper editor, journalist*
Fine, Pam *newspaper editor*
Flanagan, Barbara *journalist*
Haverkamp, Judson *editor*
Ison, Christopher John *investigative reporter*
Johnson, Cheryl (C.J. Johnson) *newspaper columnist*
Johnson, Gary LeRoy *publishing executive*
Jones, Will(iam) (Arnold) *writer, former newspaper columnist*
Kalman, Marc *radio station executive*
Kramer, Joel Roy *journalist, newspaper executive*
Laing, Karel Ann *magazine publishing executive*
Lerner, Harry Jonas *publishing company executive*
Marshall, Sherrie *newspaper editor*
McDaniel, Jan *television station executive*
McEnroe, Paul *reporter*
McGuire, Tim *editor*
Meador, Ron *newspaper editor, writer*
Meers, Bill M. *news executive*
Mohr, L. Thomas *newspaper executive*
Moyer, Keith J. *publishing executive*
Opperman, Dwight Darwin *publishing company executive*
Pyle, Dave *newspaper editor*
Roloff, Marvin L. *publishing executive*
Scallen, Thomas Kaine *broadcasting executive*
Seaman, William Casper *retired news photographer*
Spendlove, Steve Dale *broadcast executive*
Steinmetz, Mark S. *broadcast executive*
Watson, Catherine Elaine *journalist*
Werner, Bill *communication media executive*
Werner, Lawrence H. *editor*
White, Robert James *newspaper columnist*
Whittemore, Brian *broadcast executive*
Wright, Frank Gardner *retired newspaper editor*
Youngblood, Richard Neil *columnist*
Zelickson, Sue *newspaper and cookbook editor, television reporter and host, food consultant*

Minnetonka
Swartz, Donald Everett *television executive*

Saint Joseph
Rowland, Howard Ray *mass communications educator*

Saint Paul
Amidon, Paul Charles *publishing executive*
Blanchard, J. A., III *publishing executive*
Bree, Marlin Duane *publisher, author*
Clark, Ronald Dean *newspaper editor*
Fruehling, Rosemary Therese *publishing executive, author*
Gowler, Vicki Sue *newspaper editor, journalist*
Henry, John Thomas *retired newspaper executive*
Hubbard, Stanley Stub *broadcast executive*
Kling, William Hugh *broadcasting executive*
Sadowski, Richard J. *former publishing executive*
Wehrwein, Austin Carl *newspaper reporter, editor, writer*
Weschcke, Carl Llewellyn *publishing executive*

West Saint Paul
Cento, William Francis *retired newspaper editor*

MISSISSIPPI

Jackson
Hunsburger, Bill *publishing executive*

MISSOURI

Clayton
Marcus, Larry David *broadcast executive*
Sonderman, Joe R. *news executive*

Columbia
Helvey, William Charles, Jr. *communications specialist*
Loory, Stuart Hugh *journalist*
Sanders, Keith Page *journalism educator*

Kansas City
Batiuk, Thomas Martin *cartoonist*
Brisbane, Arthur Seward *newspaper publisher*
Cahill, Patricia Deal *radio station executive*
Davis, James Robert *cartoonist*
Guisewite, Cathy Lee *cartoonist*
Gusewelle, Charles Wesley *journalist, writer, documentary maker*
Lindenbaum, Sharon *publishing executive*
Mc Meel, John Paul *newspaper syndicate and publishing executive*
McDermott, Alan *newspaper editor*
Oliphant, Patrick *cartoonist*
Palmer, Cruise *newspaper editor*
Reed, William T. *broadcasting executive*
Roush, Sue *newspaper editor*
Stevens, Paul *newspaper editor*
Stevens, Tony *radio station official, radio personality*
Tammeus, William David *journalist, columnist*
Thornton, Thomas Noel *publishing executive*
Van Buren, Abigail (Jeanne Phillips) *columnist, lecturer*
Watterson, Bill *former cartoonist*
Wilson, Tom *cartoonist, greeting card company executive*
Zieman, Mark *newspaper editor*

Saint Louis
Barnes, Harper Henderson *movie critic, editor, writer*

Bennett, Patricia Ann *radio executive*
Campbell, Cole C. *journalist, educator*
Clayton, John Anthony *radio broadcast executive*
Domjan, Laszlo Karoly *newspaper editor*
Egger, Terrance C.Z.
Ehrlich, Ava *television executive*
Elkins, Ken Joe *retired broadcasting executive*
Engelhardt, Thomas Alexander *editorial cartoonist*
Gauen, Patrick Emil *newspaper correspondent*
Green, Joyce *book publishing company executive*
Kanne, Marvin George *newspaper publishing executive*
Korando, Donna Kay *journalist*
Mette, Virgil Louis *publishing executive, biology educator*
Norman, Charles Henry *broadcasting executive*
Pulitzer, Michael Edgar *publishing executive*
Regnell, Barbara Caramella *retired media educator*
Soeteber, Ellen *journalist, newspaper editor*

Springfield
Champion, Norma Jean *communications educator, state legislator*
Glazier, Robert Carl *publishing executive*
Sylvester, Ronald Charles *newspaper writer*

NEBRASKA

Lincoln
Dyer, William Earl, Jr. *retired newspaper editor*
Gibson, Voleen Ann *media specialist, educator*
Raz, Hilda *editor-in-chief periodical, English educator*
Ross, Daniel J.J. *publishing executive*

Omaha
Andersen, Harold Wayne *contributing editor, newspaper executive*
Gottschalk, John E. *newspaper publishing executive*
King, Larry *editor*
Nicol, Brian *publishing executive*
Sands, Deanna *editor*
Simon, Paul H. *newspaper editor*

NEVADA

Henderson
Wills, Robert Hamilton *retired newspaper executive*

NEW JERSEY

New Providence
Barnes, Sandra Henley *publishing company executive*

NEW MEXICO

Albuquerque
Lang, Thompson Hughes *publishing company executive*

NEW YORK

Bronxville
Lombardo, Philip Joseph *broadcasting company executive*

New York
Gayle, Monica *broadcast journalist*
Lundberg, George David, II *medical editor in chief, pathologist*
Mora, Antonio Gonzalez, III *broadcast journalist*

Rye
Pearson, Nathan Williams *communications and investment executive*

NORTH CAROLINA

Raleigh
Gyllenhaal, Anders *editor*

Saluda
Mc Cutcheon, John Tinney, Jr. *retired journalist*

NORTH DAKOTA

Fargo
DeVine, Terry Michael *newspaper editor*
Littlefield, Robert Stephen *communication educator, training consultant*
Marcil, William Christ, Sr. *publisher, broadcast executive*

Grand Forks
Glassheim, Eliot Alan *editor, state legislator*

OHIO

Akron
Leach, Janet C. *publishing executive*

Athens
Metters, Thomas Waddell *sports writer*
Sanders, David *university press administrator*
Stempel, Guido Hermann, III *journalism educator*

Bowling Green
Clark, Robert King *communications educator emeritus, lecturer, consultant, actor, model*

Chagrin Falls
Lange, David Charles *journalist*

Cincinnati
Beckwith, Barbara Jean *journalist*
Boehne, Richard *newspaper company executive*
Borgman, James Mark *editorial cartoonist*
Burleigh, William Robert *newspaper executive*
Bushee, Ward *newspaper editor*
Fryxell, David Allen *publishing executive*
Horton, Alan M. *newspaper executive*
Knue, Paul Frederick *newspaper editor*
Lapin, Jeffry Mark *magazine publisher*
McMullin, Ruth Roney *publishing executive, trustee, management fellow*
Mechem, Charles Stanley, Jr. *former broadcasting executive, former golf association executive*
Moll, William Gene *broadcasting company executive*
Sedgwick, Sally Belle *publishing company executive*
Silvers, Gerald Thomas *publishing executive*
Standen, Craig Clayton *newspaper executive*
Whipple, Harry M. *newspaper publishing executive*
Wigginton, Eugene H. *retired publishing executive*

Cleveland
Bauer, Alan R. *internet company executive*
Brandt, John Reynold *editor, journalist*
Clark, Gary R. *newspaper editor*
Clifton, Douglas C. *newspaper editor*
Davis, David Aaron *journalist*
Fabris, James A. *journalist*
Greer, Thomas H. *newspaper executive*
Jensen, Kathryn Patricia (Kit) *public radio and television station executive*
Jindra, Christine *editor*
Kanzeg, David George *radio station executive*
Kovacs, Rosemary *newspaper editor*
Long, Robert M. *newspaper publishing executive*
Machaskee, Alex *newspaper publishing company executive*
Miller, Arnold *retired newspaper editor*
Modic, Stanley John *business editor, publisher*
Molyneaux, David Glenn *newspaper travel editor*
Shaw, Scott Alan *photojournalist*
Strang, James Dennis *editor*
Torgerson, Katherine P. *diversified business media company executive*
Wareham, Jerrold F. *broadcast executive*

Columbus
Cox, Mitchel Neal *editor*
Dervin, Brenda Louise *communications educator*
Grossberg, Michael Lee *theater critic, writer*
Johnston, Jeffery W. *publishing executive*
Kiefer, Gary *newspaper editor*
Langholz, Armin Paul *communications educator*
Massie, Robert Joseph *publishing company executive*
McCoy, Bernard Rogers *television anchor*
Murphy, Andrew J. *managing news editor*
Ouzts, Dale Keith *broadcast executive*
Sherrill, Thomas Boykin, III *retired newspaper publishing executive*
Stallworth, Sam *television executive*
Strode, George K. *sports editor*

Dayton
Carollo, Russell *journalist*
Franklin, Douglas E. *publishing executive*
Matheny, Ruth Ann *editor*
Tillson, John Bradford, Jr. *newspaper publisher*

Lyndhurst
Kastner, Christine Kriha *newspaper correspondent*

Mason
Smith, C. LeMoyne *publishing company executive*

Miamisburg
Pardue, Bill *publishing executive*

Pepper Pike
Vail, Thomas Van Husen *retired newspaper publisher and editor*

Sidney
Laurence, Michael Marshall *magazine publisher, writer*
Stevens, Robert Jay *magazine editor*

Toledo
Block, William K., Jr. *newspaper executive*
Brickey, Suzanne M. *editor*
Royhab, Ronald *journalist, newspaper editor*

OKLAHOMA

Oklahoma City
Gaylord, Edward Lewis *publishing company executive*

PENNSYLVANIA

Scranton
Lynett, William Ruddy *publishing, broadcasting company executive*

SOUTH DAKOTA

Pierre
Callahan, Patrick *communication media executive*

Prairie City
Wishard, Della Mae *former newspaper editor*

Sioux Falls
Garson, Arnold Hugh *publishing executive*
Haraldson, Tena *newspaper editor*

TENNESSEE

Nashville
Sullivan, Dennis James, Jr. *hospitality and music executive*

VIRGINIA

Charlottesville
Kaiserlian, Penelope Jane *publishing company executive*

WISCONSIN

Eau Claire
Clark, Judy *newscaster*
Gallagher, Bob *newscaster*
Kreitlow, Pat *newscaster*
Rupnor, Jennifer *journalist*
Tuckner, Michelle *newscaster*

Edgerton
Everson, Diane Louise *publishing executive*

Fort Atkinson
Knox, William David *publishing company executive*

Greendale
Kaiser, Ann Christine *magazine editor*
Pohl, Kathleen Sharon *editor*
Reiman, Roy J. *publishing executive*

Iola
Krause, Chester Lee *publishing company executive*

Janesville
Fitzgerald, James Francis *cable television executive*

Madison
Burgess, James Edward *newspaper publisher, executive*
Burns, Elizabeth Murphy *media executive*
Denton, Frank M. *newspaper editor*
Gruber, John Edward *editor, railroad historian, photographer*
Haslanger, Philip Charles *journalist*
Hastings, Joyce R. *editor*
Hopson, James Warren *publishing executive*
Hoyt, James Lawrence *journalism educator, athletic administrator*
Miller, Frederick William *publisher, lawyer*
Wineke, William Robert *reporter, clergyman*
Wolman, J. Martin *retired newspaper publisher*
Zweifel, David Alan *newspaper editor*

Middleton
Rowland, Pleasant *publisher, toy company executive*

Milwaukee
Anderson, Mike *newscaster*
Armstrong, Douglas Dean *journalist*
Atwater, John *news correspondent*
Auer, James Matthew *art critic, journalist*
Behrendt, David Frogner *retired journalist*
Bohr, Nick *reporter*
Davis, David *newscaster*
Dawson, Kim *reporter*
DeRusha, Jason *reporter*
Elliot, Tammy *newscaster*
Enk, Scott *editor*
Farris, Trueman Earl, Jr. *retired newspaper editor*
Foster, Richard *journalist*
Garcia, Astrid J. *newspaper executive*
Gay, Duane *reporter*
Henry, Colleen *reporter*
Henry, Rick *broadcast executive*
Hinkley, Gerry *newspaper editor*
Hinshaw, Edward Banks *broadcasting company executive*
Hughes, T. Lee *newspaper editor*
Jallings, Jessica *reporter, newscaster*
Jaques, Damien Paul *theater critic*
Kaiser, Martin *newspaper editor*
Kleefisch, Rebecca *reporter*
Kritzer, Paul Eric *media executive, communications lawyer*
McCann, Dennis John *columnist*
Mykleby, Kathy *newscaster, reporter*
Orig, Carlene *reporter*
Salamme, Matt *reporter*
Spore, Keith Kent *newspaper executive*
Stafford, Lori *reporter*
Sullivan, Edward *periodical editor*
Taff, Gerry *reporter*
Wainscott, Kent *reporter*
Youngquist, Wayne *reporter*

Pewaukee
Lee, Jack (Jim Sanders Beasley) *broadcast executive*

Superior
Billig, Thomas Clifford *publishing and marketing executive*

Waukesha
Larson, Russell George *magazine publisher*

West Bend
Fraedrich, Royal Louis *magazine editor, publisher*

CANADA

MANITOBA

Winnipeg
Buchko, Garth *broadcasting executive*
Chalmers, Jane *broadcast executive*
Wreford, David Mathews *magazine editor*

ONTARIO

Brockville
McLeod, Philip Robert *publishing executive*

Kitchener
Rittinger, Carolyne June *retired newspaper editor*

ADDRESS UNPUBLISHED

Agarwal, Suman Kumar *editor*
Brown, Paul *former publishing executive*
Christiansen, Richard Dean *retired newspaper editor*
Ciccone, F. Richard *retired newspaper editor*
Clapper, Lyle Nielsen *magazine publisher*
Cockburn, Eve Gillian *newsletter editor*
Cohen, Allan Richard *broadcasting executive*
Costas, Bob (Robert Quinlan Costas) *sportscaster*
Culp, Mildred Louise *corporate executive*
Dawson, Virginia Sue *retired newspaper editor*
Dotson, John Louis, Jr. *former newspaper publisher*
Edmunds, Jane Clara *communications consultant*
Grahn, Barbara Ascher *retired publishing executive*
Gwinn, Robert P. *publishing executive*
Kamin, Blair Douglass *newspaper critic*
Knox, Douglass Richard *publishing executive*
Lemmon, Jean Marie *editor-in-chief*
Lipman, David *retired journalist, multimedia consultant*
McHenry, Robert (Dale) *editor*
Mellema, Donald Eugene *retired radio news reporter and anchor*
Miller, Robert Branson, Jr. *retired newspaper publisher*
Nyquist, Kathleen A. *former publishing executive*
Palmer, Bradley Beran *sportscaster*
Pepper, Jonathon L. *media executive*
Philipson, Morris *university press director*
Proffer, Ellendea Catherine *publisher, author*
Quade, Victoria Catherine *editor, writer, playwright, producer*
Shapiro, Richard Charles *publishing sales and marketing executive*
Shere, Dennis *retired publishing executive*
Skinner, Thomas *broadcasting and film executive*
Stauffer, Stanley Howard *retired newspaper and broadcasting executive*
Sullivan, Daniel Joseph *theater critic*
Sund, Jeffrey Owen *retired publishing company executive*
Trudeau, Garretson Beekman (Garry Trudeau) *cartoonist*
Varro, Barbara Joan *retired editor*
Vincent, Charles Eagar, Jr. *sports columnist*
Wagner, Durrett *former publisher, picture service executive*
Weber, Arthur *magazine executive*

EDUCATION *See also* specific fields for postsecondary education

UNITED STATES

ARIZONA

Green Valley
Turner, Harold Edward *education educator*

Scottsdale
Mayer, Robert Anthony *retired college president*
Stone, Alan Jay *retired college administrator*

CALIFORNIA

Camarillo
Rush, Richard R. *academic administrator*

COLORADO

Denver
Horton, Frank Elba *university official, geography educator*

DISTRICT OF COLUMBIA

Washington
Van Ummersen, Claire A(nn) *academic administrator, biologist, educator*
Ward, David *academic administrator, educator*

FLORIDA

Palm Beach Gardens
Kasparek, John Anthony *academic administrator*

Winter Garden
Gillet, Pamela Kipping *special education educator*

ILLINOIS

Alton
Ferrillo, Patrick J., Jr. *academic dean, endodontist*

Aurora
Zarle, Thomas Herbert *academic administrator*

Barrington
Hicks, Jim *secondary education educator*
Riendeau, Diane *secondary school educator*

Bloomington
Myers, Minor, Jr. *academic administrator, political science educator*

Carbondale
Dixon, Billy Gene *academic administrator, educator*
Mead, John Stanley *university administrator*
Quisenberry, Nancy Lou *university administrator, educator*
Snyder, Carolyn Ann *education educator, librarian*

Olathe
Goodwin, Becky K. *secondary education educator*

Overland Park
Whelan, Richard J. *retired academic administrator*

Shawnee Mission
Kaplan, Marjorie Ann Pashkow *school district administrator*

Sublette
Swinney, Carol Joyce *secondary education educator*

Topeka
Farley, Jerry B. *academic administrator*

Uniontown
Conard, Norman Dale *secondary education educator*

Wichita
Beggs, Donald Lee *academic administrator*
Kindrick, Robert LeRoy *academic administrator, dean, English educator*

MASSACHUSETTS

Worcester
Bassett, John E. *academic administrator, dean, English educator*

MICHIGAN

Adrian
Caine, Stanley Paul *college administrator*

Allendale
Niemeyer, Glenn Alan *academic administrator, history educator*

Ann Arbor
Cole, David Edward *university administrator*
Duderstadt, James Johnson *academic administrator, engineering educator*
Dumas, Rhetaugh Etheldra Graves *university official*
Fleming, Suzanne Marie *university official, chemistry educator*
Hinshaw, Ada Sue *dean, nursing educator*
Kotowicz, William E. *dean, dental educator*
Lehman, Jeffrey Sean *dean, law educator*
Omenn, Gilbert Stanley *academic administrator, physician*
Paul, Ara Garo *university dean*
Sullivan, Thomas Patrick *academic administrator*
Van Houweling, Douglas Edward *university administrator, educator*
Warner, Robert Mark *university dean, archivist, historian*
White, B. Joseph *academic administrator*

Armada
Kummerow, Arnold A. *superintendent of schools*

Bay City
Zuraw, Kathleen Ann *special education and physical education educator*

Bloomfield Hills
Doyle, Jill J. *elementary school principal*
Thompson, Richard Thomas *academic administrator*

Brighton
Jensen, Baiba *principal*

Clarkston
Mousseau, Doris Naomi Barton *retired elementary school principal*

Commerce Township
Boynton, Irvin Parker *retired educational administrator*

Dearborn Heights
Johns, Diana *secondary education educator*

Detroit
Edelstein, Tilden Gerald *university official, history educator*
Fay, Sister Maureen A. *university president*
Mika, Joseph John *library school director, educator, consultant*
Pietrofesa, John Joseph *education educator*
Reid, Irvin D. *academic official*
Rogers, Richard Lee *educator*
Williams, Roger *academic administrator*

East Lansing
Abbett, William S. *former dean*
Brophy, Jere Edward *education educator, researcher*
Harrison, Jeremy Thomas *dean, law educator*
Honhart, Frederick Lewis, III *academic director*
Mackey, Maurice Cecil *university president, economist, lawyer*
McPherson, Melville Peter *academic administrator, former government official*
Pierre, Percy Anthony *university president*
Rothert, Marilyn L. *dean, nursing educator*
Simon, Lou Anna Kimsey *academic administrator*
Snoddy, James Ernest *education educator*

Flint
Arnold, Allen D. *academic administrator*
Lorenz, John Douglas *college official*

Grand Rapids
Calkins, Richard W. *former college president*
Diekema, Anthony J. *college president emeritus, educational consultant*
Lubbers, Arend Donselaar *retired academic administrator*
VanHarn, Gordon Lee *college administrator and provost*

Grosse Pointe Woods
Robie, Joan *elementary school principal*

Hancock
Puotinen, Arthur Edwin *college president, clergyman*

Haslett
Hotaling, Robert Bachman *community planner, educator*

Hillsdale
Kline, Faith Elizabeth *college official*
Roche, George Charles, III *college administrator*

Holland
Nyenhuis, Jacob Eugene *college official*

Houghton
Tompkins, Curtis Johnston *university president*

Kalamazoo
Badra, Robert George *philosophy, religion and humanities educator*
Haenicke, Diether Hans *university president emeritus, educator*
Jones, James Fleming, Jr. *college president, Roman language and literature educator*
Stufflebeam, Daniel LeRoy *education educator*

Kentwood
Yovich, Daniel John *educator*

Lansing
Brennan, Thomas Emmett *law school president*
Piveronus, Peter John, Jr. *education educator*
Straus, Kathleen Nagler *education administrator, consultant*

Livonia
McDowell, Richard William *college president*
Van de Vyver, Sister Mary Francilene *academic administrator*

Ludington
Puffer, Richard Judson *retired college chancellor*

Macomb
Farmakis, George Leonard *education educator*

Marquette
Bailey, Judith Irene *university official, consultant*

Midland
Grzesiak, Katherine Ann *primary educator*

Mount Pleasant
Plachta, Leonard E. *academic administrator*

Presque Isle
Kinney, Mark Baldwin *educator*

Rochester
Loh, Robert N. K. *academic administrator, engineering educator*
Packard, Sandra Podolin *education educator, consultant*
Russi, Gary D. *academic administrator*

Southfield
Chambers, Charles MacKay *university president*

University Center
Boyse, Peter Dent *academic administrator*
Gilbertson, Eric Raymond *academic administrator, lawyer*
Lange, Crystal Marie *university official, nursing educator*

Utica
Olman, Gloria *secondary education educator*

Warren
Lorenzo, Albert L. *academic administrator*

Williamston
Johnson, Tom Milroy *academic dean, medical educator, physician*

Ypsilanti
Boone, Morell Douglas *information and communications technology educator, director*
Fleming, Thomas A. *former special education educator*
Robbins, Jerry Hal *educational administration educator*
Shelton, William Everett *university president*

MINNESOTA

Albert Lea
Rechtzigel, Sue Marie (Suzanne Rechtzigel) *child care center executive*

Buffalo Lake
Cooper, Roger *educator former state legislator*

Burnsville
Freeburg, Richard L. *primary education educator*

Cokato
Kay, Craig *principal*

Collegeville
Reinhart, Dietrich Thomas *university president, history educator*

Duluth
Martin, Kathryn A. *academic administrator*

Long Lake
Lowthian, Petrena *college president*

Mankato
Nickerson, James Findley *retired educator*

Marine On Saint Croix
Gavin, Robert Michael, Jr. *education consultant*

Minneapolis
Avella, Joseph Ralph *university executive*
Bowie, Norman Ernest *university official, educator*
Cerra, Frank Bernard *dean*
DiGangi, Frank Edward *academic administrator*
Dooley, David J. *elementary school principal*
Drahmann, Brother Theodore Robert *education educator*
Edwardson, Sandra *dean, nursing educator*
Gardebring, Sandra S. *academic administrator*
Gardner, William Earl *university dean*
Johnson, David Chester *university chancellor, sociology educator*
Lindell, Edward Albert *former college president, religious organization administrator*
Matson, Wesley Jennings *educational administrator*
Mengler, Thomas M. *dean*
O'Keefe, Thomas Michael *academic administrator*
Schuh, G(eorge) Edward *university dean, agricultural economist*
Slorp, John S. *academic administrator*
Sullivan, E. Thomas *dean*

Minnetonka
Vanstrom, Marilyn June Christensen *retired elementary education educator*
Wigfield, Rita L. *elementary education educator*

Moorhead
Barden, Roland Eugene *university administrator*
Dille, Roland Paul *college president*
Treumann, William Borgen *university dean*

New Ulm
Nienstedt, Monsignor John Clayton *educator, priest*

Northfield
Edwards, Mark U., Jr. *college president, history educator, author*

Richfield
Devlin, Barbara Jo *school district administrator*

Rochester
Windebank, Anthony J. *dean*

Saginaw
Stauber, Marilyn Jean *retired secondary and elementary school*

Saint Paul
Brushaber, George Karl *college-theological seminary president, minister*
Dykstra, Robert *retired education educator*
Huber, Sister Alberta *college president*
Kerr, Sylvia Joann *educator*
McPherson, Michael Steven *academic administrator, economics educator*
Muscoplat, Charles *dean*
Osnes, Larry G. *academic administrator*
Stroud, Rhoda M. *elementary education educator*
Sullivan, Alfred Dewitt *academic administrator*

Waseca
Frederick, Edward Charles *university official*

Winona
DeThomasis, Brother Louis *college president*
Krueger, Darrell William *university president*

MISSOURI

Clayton
Mach, Ruth *principal*

Columbia
Brouder, Gerald T. *academic administrator*
Gysbers, Norman Charles *education educator*
Kierscht, Marcia Selland *academic administrator, psychologist*
Pacheco, Manuel Trinidad *academic administrator*
Payne, Thomas L. *university official*
Russell, George Albert *retired university president*
Wallace, Richard Lee *chancellor*

Fayette
Inman, Marianne Elizabeth *college administrator*

Florissant
Bartlett, Robert James *principal*

Forsyth
Klinefelter, Sarah Stephens *retired division dean, radio station manager*

Hillsboro
Adkins, Gregory D. *higher education administrator*

Jefferson City
Henson, David B. *university administrator*

Kansas City
Durig, James Robert *college dean*
Eubanks, Eugene Emerson *education educator, consultant*

Kirksville
Magruder, Jack *academic administrator*

Kirkwood
Black, Richard A. *former community college president*

Lees Summit
Reynolds, Tommy *secondary school educator*

Liberty
Tanner, Jimmie Eugene *college dean*

Maryville
Hubbard, Dean Leon *university president*

Rolla
Warner, Don Lee *dean emeritus*

Saint Joseph
Murphy, Janet Gorman *college president*

Saint Louis
Allen, Renee *principal*
Baker, Shirley Kistler *university administrator*
Biondi, Lawrence *university administrator, priest*
Byrnes, Christopher Ian *academic dean, researcher*
Danforth, William Henry *retired academic administrator, physician*
Dodge, Paul Cecil *academic administrator*
Gilligan, Sandra Kaye *private school director*
Givens, Henry, Jr. *academic administrator*
Hepner, James O. *medical school director*
Hrubetz, Joan *dean, nursing educator*
Kennelly, Sister Karen Margaret *retired academic administrator, church administrator, nun*
Lovin, Keith Harold *university administrator, philosophy educator*
Marsh, James C., Jr. *secondary school principal*
McGannon, John Barry *university chancellor*
Monteleone, Patricia *academic dean*
O'Neill, Sheila *principal*
Seligman, Joel *dean*
Thomas, Pamela Adrienne *special education educator*
Touhill, Blanche Marie *university chancellor, history-education educator*
Weiss, Robert Francis *former academic administrator, religious organization administrator, consultant*

Springfield
Keiser, John Howard *university president*
Moore, John Edwin, Jr. *college president*

Verona
Youngberg, Charlotte Anne *education specialist, clergywoman*

Warrensburg
Limback, E(dna) Rebecca *vocational education educator*

Webster Groves
Schenkenberg, Mary Martin *principal*

Windyville
Condron, Daniel Ralph *academic administrator, metaphysics educator*

NEBRASKA

Bellevue
Muller, John Bartlett *university president*

Grand Island
Zichek, Shannon Elaine *retired secondary school educator*

Gretna
Riley, Kevin M. *principal*

Hastings
Kort, Betty *secondary education educator*

Kearney
Johnston, Gladys Styles *university official*

Lincoln
Bradley, Richard Edwin *retired college president*
Byrne, C. William, Jr. *athletics program director*
Christensen, Douglas *state education commissioner*
Grew, Priscilla Croswell *university official, geology educator*
Hendrickson, Kent Herman *university administrator*
Nelson, Darrell Wayne *university administrator, scientist*
Owens, John C. *academic administrator*
Powers, David Richard *educational administrator*
Robak, Kim M. *university official, lawyer*
Smith, L. Dennis *academic administrator*
Smith, Lewis Dennis *academic administrator, educator*
Tonack, DeLoris *elementary school educator*

Norfolk
Mortensen-Say, Marlys *school system administrator*

Omaha
Bauer, Otto Frank *university official, communication educator*
Belck, Nancy Garrison *dean, educator*
Fjell, Mick *principal*
Haselwood, Eldon LaVerne *retired education educator*
Ho, David Kim Hong *educator*
Lindsey, Ada Marie *dean, nursing educator*
McEniry, Robert Francis *education educator, researcher*
Morrison, Michael Gordon *university president, clergyman, history educator*
Newton, John Milton *academic administrator, psychology educator*
O'Brien, Richard L(ee) *medical educator, academic administrator, physician, cell biologist*
Schlegel, John P. *academic administrator*
Tucker, Michael *elementary school principal*

NEVADA

Las Vegas
Shuman, R. Baird *academic program director, writer, English language educator, educational consultant*

NEW HAMPSHIRE

Windham
Nease, Stephen Wesley *college president*

NEW YORK

Himrod
Preska, Margaret Louise Robinson *education educator, administrator*

New York
Bollinger, Lee Carroll *academic administrator, law educator*
Kerrey, Bob (J. Robert Kerrey) *academic administrator, former senator*

NORTH CAROLINA

Chapel Hill
Moeser, James Charles *university chancellor, musician*

NORTH DAKOTA

Bismarck
Evanson, Barbara Jean *middle school education educator*
Isaak, Larry A. *university system chancellor*

Ellendale
Schlieve, Hy C. J. *school administrator*

Fargo
Lardy, Sister Susan Marie *academic administrator*

Grand Forks
Davis, W. Jeremy *dean, law educator, lawyer*
Kupchella, Charles Edward *academic administrator, author, educator*
Wilson, H. David *dean*

Jamestown
Walker, James Silas *academic administrator*

Minot
Shaar, H. Erik *academic administrator*

West Fargo
Boutiette, Vickie Lynn *educator, reading specialist*

OHIO

Ada
Baker, Kendall L. *academic administrator*
Freed, DeBow *college president*

Akron
Auburn, Norman Paul *university president*
Capers, Cynthia Flynn *dean, nursing educator*
Kelley, Frank Nicholas *dean*
Ruebel, Marion A. *university president*

Ashland
Drushal, Mary Ellen *educator, former university provost*

Athens
Bruning, James Leon *university official, educator*
Glidden, Robert Burr *university president, musician, educator*
Krendl, Kathy *dean*

Berea
Malicky, Neal *college president*

Bowling Green
Ribeau, Sidney A. *academic administrator*
Zwierlein, Ronald Edward *athletics director*

Chagrin Falls
Brown, Jeanette Grasselli *retired university official*

Chillicothe
Basil, Brad L. *technology education educator*

Cincinnati
Chatterjee, Jayanta *academic administrator*
Greengus, Samuel *academic administrator, religion educator*
Harrison, Donald Carey *university official, cardiology educator*
Hoff, James Edwin *university president*
Kohl, David *dean, librarian*
Lindell, Andrea Regina *dean, nurse*
Nester, William Raymond, Jr. *retired academic administrator and educator*
Smith, Gregory Allgire *college administrator*
Steger, Joseph A. *university president*
Tomain, Joseph Patrick *dean, law educator*
Wagner, Thomas Edward *academic administrator, educator*
Winkler, Henry Ralph *retired academic administrator, historian*

Cleveland
Auston, David Henry *university administrator, educator*
Berger, Nathan Allen *dean, university administrator*
Brooten, Dorothy *dean, nursing educator*
Cerone, David *academic administrator*
Cullis, Christopher Ashley *dean, biology educator*
Lex, William Joseph *college official*
McArdle, Richard Joseph *academic administrator, retired*
Parker, Robert Frederic *university dean emeritus*
Queen, Joyce Ellen *elementary school educator*
Schmidt, Patricia Jean *special education educator*
Thornton, Jerry Sue *community college president*
Weidenthal, Maurice David (Bud Weidenthal) *educational administrator, journalist*
Wertheim, Sally Harris *academic administrator, dean, education educator*

Columbus
Alutto, Joseph Anthony *university dean, management educator*
Beller, Stephen Mark *university administrator*
Cottrell, David Alton *school system administrator*
de la Chapelle, Albert *education educator*
Felicetti, Daniel A. *academic administrator, educator*
Fields, Henry William *college dean*
Hart, Mildred *retired counselor*
Jackson, John Charles *retired secondary education educator, writer*
Koenigsknecht, Roy A. *education administrator*
Mathis, Lois Reno *retired elementary education educator*
Meuser, Fredrick William *retired seminary president, church historian*
Otte, Paul John *academic administrator, consultant, trainer*
Oxley, Margaret Carolyn Stewart *elementary education educator*
Stephens, Thomas M(aron) *education educator*
Williams, Gregory Howard *dean, law educator*

Dayton
Fitz, Brother Raymond L. *university president*
Goldenberg, Kim *university president, internist*
Heft, James Lewis *academic administrator, theology educator*
Hoffman, Sue Ellen *elementary education educator*
Martin, Patricia *dean, nursing educator*
Ponitz, David H. *former academic administrator*
Sifferlen, Ned *university president*
Uphoff, James Kent *education educator*

Delaware
Courtice, Thomas Barr *academic administrator*

Delta
Miller, Beverly White *past college president, education consultation*

Eastlake
Kerata, Joseph J. *secondary education educator*

Gambier
Oden, Robert A., Jr. *college president*
Will, Katherine H. *former university administrator*

Harrison
Stoll, Robert W. *principal*

Hiram
Oliver, G(eorge) Benjamin *educational administrator, philosophy educator*

Kent
Cartwright, Carol Ann *university president*
Gosnell, Davina J. *dean, nursing educator*
Schwartz, Michael *university president, sociology educator*

Lima
Meek, Violet Imhof *dean*

Mansfield
Riedl, John Orth *university dean*

Marietta
Wilson, Lauren Ross *academic administrator*

New Albany
Lindsay, Dianna Marie *educational administrator*

Norton
Kun, Joyce Anne *secondary education educator, small business owner*

Oberlin
Dye, Nancy Schrom *academic administrator, history educator*
MacKay, Alfred F. *dean, philosophy educator*

Oxford
Garland, James C. *college president*
Shriver, Phillip Raymond *academic administrator*
Thompson, Bertha Boya *retired education educator, antique dealer and appraiser*

Painesville
Blyth, Ann Marie *secondary education educator*
Davis, Barbara Snell *college educator*

Parma
Pisarchick, Sally *special education educator*

Perrysburg
Carpenter, J. Scott *vocational educator*

Springfield
Kinnison, William Andrew *retired university president*

Sylvania
Sampson, Earldine Robison *education educator*

Toledo
Billups, Norman Fredrick *college dean, pharmacist, educator*
Heinrichs, Mary Ann *former dean*
Moon, Henry *academic administrator*
Perz, Sally *academic administrator, former state legislator*
Weinblatt, Charles Samuel *university administrator, employment consultant*

Valley View
Miller, Susan Ann *school system administrator*

Westerville
DeVore, C(arl) Brent *college president, educator*
Van Sant, Joanne Frances *academic administrator*

Westlake
Loehr, Marla *spiritual care coordinator*

Wilberforce
Henderson, John L. *academic administrator*

Willoughby
Grossman, Mary Margaret *elementary education educator*

Youngstown
Cochran, Leslie Herschel *university administrator*
Loch, John Robert *university administrator*
Zorn, Robert Lynn *education educator*

PENNSYLVANIA

Chester
Harris, James Thomas, III *college administrator, educator*

Pittsburgh
Dougherty, Charles John *university administrator, philosophy and medical ethics educator*

SOUTH DAKOTA

Brookings
Miller, Peggy Gordon Elliott *university president*

Kadoka
Stout, Maye Alma *educator*

Madison
Tunheim, Jerald Arden *academic administrator, physics educator*

Rapid City
Han, Kenneth *dean*

Selby
Akre, Donald J. *school system administrator*

Sioux Falls
Ashworth, Julie *elementary education educator*
Talley, Robert Cochran *medical school dean and administrator, cardiologist*
Wagoner, Ralph Howard *academic administrator, educator*

Vermillion
Dahlin, Donald C(lifford) *academic administrator*

TEXAS

College Station
Lynn, Laurence Edwin, Jr. *university administrator, educator*
Monroe, Haskell Moorman, Jr. *university educator*

VIRGINIA

Danville
Pfau, Richard Anthony *college president*

WISCONSIN

Appleton
Warch, Richard *academic administrator*

Beloit
Ferrall, Victor Eugene, Jr. *college administrator, lawyer*

Brookfield
Zimmerman, Jay *secondary education educator*

De Forest
O'Neil, J(ames) Peter *computer software designer, educator*

De Pere
Manion, Thomas A. *chancellor*

Delafield
Kurth, Ronald James *university president, retired naval officer*

Eau Claire
Mash, Donald J. *college president*
Richards, Jerry Lee *academic administrator, religious educator*

Glendale
Moeser, Elliott *principal*

Green Bay
Hardy, Deborah Lewis *dean, educator, dental hygienist*
Perkins, Mark L. *university chancellor*
Shepard, W. Bruce *academic administrator*

Kenosha
Campbell, F(enton) Gregory *college administrator, historian*

La Crosse
Hitch, Elizabeth *academic administrator*
Medland, William James *college president*
Novotney, Donald Francis *superintendent of schools*

Madison
Aberle, Elton David *dean*
Burmaster, Elizabeth *school system administrator*
Davis, Kenneth Boone, Jr. *dean, law educator*
Ebben, James Adrian *college president*
Kreuter, Gretchen V. *academic administrator*
Lyall, Katharine C(ulbert) *academic administrator, economics educator*
Odden, Allan Robert *education educator*
Policano, Andrew J. *university dean*
Skochelak, Susan E. *college dean*
Weimer, David Lee *educator*
Yuill, Thomas MacKay *academic administrator, microbiology educator*

Madison
Reilly, Kevin P. *academic administrator*

Menomonie
Furst-Bowe, Julie *academic administrator*
Lee, Howard D. *academic administrator*
Sedlak, Robert *academic administrator*
Sorensen, Charles W. *academic administrator*

Mequon
Dohmen, Mary Holgate *retired primary school educator*
Watson-Boone, Rebecca A. *library and information studies educator, researcher*

Merrill
Gravelle, John David *secondary education educator*

Milwaukee
Aman, Mohammed Mohammed *university dean, library and information science educator*
Coffman, Terrence J. *academic administrator*
Dunn, Michael J. *dean*
Fuller, Howard *education educator, academic administrator*
Hatton, Janie R. Hill *principal*
Read, Sister Joel *academic administrator*
Schneider, Mary Lea *college administrator*
Schroeder, John H. *university chancellor*
Viets, Hermann *college president, consultant*
Wild, Robert Anthony *university president*

Oshkosh
Kerrigan, John E. *academic administrator*

Pewaukee
Anderson, Richard Todd *college president*

Platteville
Markee, David James *university official, education educator*

River Falls
Lydecker, Ann Marie *college administrator*
Thibodeau, Gary A. *academic administrator*

Sheboygan
Fritz, Kristine Rae *secondary education educator*

Washburn
Krutsch, Phyllis *academic administrator*

Waukesha
Falcone, Frank S. *academic administrator*

West Bend
Rodney, Joel Morris *dean, campus executive officer*

Whitewater
Greenhill, H. Gaylon *retired academic administrator*
Miller, John Winston *academic administrator*
Prior, David James *college dean*

Wisconsin Rapids
Olson-Hellerud, Linda Kathryn *elementary school educator*

CANADA

ONTARIO

London
Davenport, Paul *university president, economics educator*

ADDRESS UNPUBLISHED

Allen, Charles Eugene *university administrator, agriculturist, educator*
Bahr, Christine Marie *special education educator*
Banaszynski, Carol Jean *educator*
Bannister, Geoffrey *university president, geographer*
Barrett, Janet Tidd *academic administrator*
Becker, Walter Heinrich *vocational educator, planner*
Bryan, Lawrence Dow *college president*
Christian, Richard Carlton *university dean, former advertising agency executive*
Copeland, Henry Jefferson, Jr. *former college president*
Crowe, James Wilson *university administrator, educator*
Dickeson, Robert Celmer *retired university president, foundation executive, political science educator*
Drake, George Albert *college president, historian*
Duff, John Bernard *college president, former city official*
Elliott, Eddie Mayes *academic administrator*
Fodrea, Carolyn Wrobel *educational researcher, publisher, consultant*
Glennen, Robert Eugene, Jr. *retired university president*
Graves, Wallace Billingsley *retired university executive*
Green, Nancy Loughridge *newspaper executive*
Guyon, John Carl *retired university administrator*
Hardin, Clifford Morris *retired university chancellor, cabinet member*
Hart, James Warren *university administrator, restaurant owner, former professional football player*
Hill, Emita Brady *academic administrator*
Jakubauskas, Edward Benedict *college president*
Jorns, David Lee *retired university president*
Kliebhan, Sister M(ary) Camille *academic administrator*
Koleson, Donald Ralph *retired college dean, educator*
Lantz, Joanne Baldwin *academic administrator emeritus*
Lynn, Naomi B. *academic administrator*
Manuel, Ralph Nixon *former private school executive*
Marcdante, Karen Jean *associate dean*
Martin, Mary *secondary education educator*
Mc Pherson, Peter *university president*
Monson, David Carl *school superintendent, farmer, state legislator, insurance agent*
Park, John Thornton *academic administrator*
Parmer, Jess Norman *university official, educator*
Preusser, Joseph William *academic administrator*
Schwartz, Eleanor Brantley *academic administrator*

Sonnenschein, Hugo Freund *academic administrator, economics educator*
Stark, Joan Scism *education educator*
Stellar, Arthur Wayne *educational administrator*
Timpte, Robert Nelson *secondary school educator*
Vinson, James Spangler *academic administrator*
Watts, John Ransford *university administrator*
Weir, Morton Webster *retired academic administrator, educator*
Winterstein, James Fredrick *academic administrator*
Worthen, John Edward *retired academic administrator*

ENGINEERING

UNITED STATES

CALIFORNIA

Santa Cruz
Kang, Sung-Mo (Steve Kang) *electrical engineering educator*

Walnut Creek
Hanson, Robert Duane *civil engineering educator*

ILLINOIS

Argonne
Chang, Yoon Il *nuclear engineer*
Kumar, Romesh *chemical engineer*
Till, Charles Edgar *nuclear engineer*

Bolingbrook
Relwani, Nirmal Murlidhar (Nick Relwani) *mechanical engineer*

Carbondale
Chugh, Yoginder Paul *mining engineering educator*

Chicago
Agarwal, Gyan Chand *engineering educator*
Babcock, Lyndon Ross, Jr. *environmental engineer, educator*
Banerjee, Prashant *industrial engineering educator*
Breyer, Norman Nathan *metallurgical engineering educator, consultant*
Chung, Paul Myungha *mechanical engineer, educator*
Davis, DeForest P. *architectural engineer*
Dix, Rollin C(umming) *mechanical engineering educator, consultant*
Epstein, Raymond *engineering and architectural executive*
Fortuna, William Frank *architectural engineer, architect*
Gerstner, Robert William *structural engineering educator, consultant*
Graupe, Daniel *electrical and computer engineering educator, systems and biomedical engineer*
Gupta, Krishna Chandra *mechanical engineering educator*
Guralnick, Sidney Aaron *civil engineering educator*
Hartnett, James Patrick *engineering educator*
Jaramillo, Carlos Alberto *civil engineer*
Kennedy, Lawrence Allan *mechanical engineering educator*
Lin, James Chih-I *biomedical and electrical engineer, educator*
Linden, Henry Robert *chemical engineering research executive*
Lue-Hing, Cecil *civil engineer*
Mansoori, G. Ali *chemical engineer, educator*
McNeil, Sue *engineering educator*
Miller, Irving Franklin *chemical engineering educator, biomedical engineering educator, academic administrator*
Minkowycz, W. J. *mechanical engineering educator*
Minneste, Viktor, Jr. *retired electrical company executive*
Murata, Tadao *engineering and computer science educator*
Rikoski, Richard Anthony *engineering executive, electrical engineer*
Wadden, Richard Albert *environmental engineer, educator, consultant, research director*

Clarendon Hills
Moritz, Donald Brooks *mechanical engineer, consultant*

Decatur
Koucky, John Richard *metallurgical engineer, manufacturing executive*

Des Plaines
Winfield, Michael D. *engineering company executive*

Dunlap
Reinsma, Harold Lawrence *design consultant, engineer*

Evanston
Achenbach, Jan Drewes *engineering educator, scientist*
Bankoff, Seymour George *chemical engineer, educator*
Bazant, Zdenek Pavel *structural engineering educator, scientist, consultant*
Belytschko, Ted *civil and mechanical engineering educator*
Bobco, William David, Jr. *consulting engineering company executive*
Brazelton, William Thomas *chemical engineering educator*
Carr, Stephen Howard *materials engineer, educator*
Cheng, Herbert Su-Yuen *mechanical engineering educator*
Colgate, S. Edward *mechanical engineering educator*
Daskin, Mark Stephen *civil engineering educator*
Fine, Morris Eugene *materials engineer, educator*
Finno, Richard J. *engineering educator*
Fourer, Robert Harold *industrial engineering educator, consultant*
Frey, Donald Nelson
Goldstick, Thomas Karl *biomedical engineering educator*
Haddad, Abraham Herzl *electrical engineering educator, researcher*
Keer, Leon Morris *engineering educator*
Kliphardt, Raymond A. *engineering educator*
Krizek, Raymond John *civil engineering educator, consultant*
Kung, Harold Hing-Chuen *engineering educator*
Lee, Der-Tsai *electrical engineering and computer science educator, researcher, consultant*
Liu, Wing Kam *mechanical and civil engineering educator*
Murphy, Gordon John *electrical engineer, educator*
Ottino, Julio Mario *chemical engineering educator, scientist*
Rubenstein, Albert Harold *industrial engineering and management sciences educator*
Shah, Surendra Poonamchand *engineering educator, researcher*
Sobel, Alan *electrical engineer, physicist*
Taflove, Allen *electrical engineer, educator, researcher, consultant*

Glenview
Van Zelst, Theodore William *civil engineer, natural resource exploration company executive*

Lake Forest
Bell, Charles Eugene, Jr. *industrial engineer*
Lambert, John Boyd *chemical engineer, consultant*

Lemont
Chen, Shoei-Sheng *mechanical engineer*

Marshall
Cork, Donald Burl *electrical engineer*

Mount Prospect
Scott, Norman Laurence *engineering consultant*

Naperville
Vora, Manu Kishandas *chemical engineer, quality consultant*

Northbrook
Huber, John U. *engineering executive*
Pertz, Douglas A. *engineering executive*

Park Forest
Williams, Jack Raymond *civil engineer*

Park Ridge
Bridges, Jack Edgar *electronics engineer*

Plainfield
Chakrabarti, Subrata Kumar *marine research engineer*

Quincy
Centanni, Ross J. *compressed air products manufacturing executive*
Cornell, Helen W. *manufacturing company executive*
Roth, Philip R. *manufacturing executive*

Romeoville
Cizek, David John *sales engineer, small business owner*

Roscoe
Jacobs, Richard Dearborn *consulting engineering company executive*

Savoy
Siess, Chester Paul *civil engineering educator*

Schaumburg
De Lerno, Manuel Joseph *electrical engineer*
Wilkie, Dennis F. *electrical engineer*

Skokie
Corley, William Gene *engineering research executive*

Urbana
Addy, Alva Leroy *mechanical engineer*
Aref, Hassan *fluid mechanics educator*
Axford, Roy Arthur *nuclear engineering educator*
Basar, Tamer *electrical engineering educator*
Bergeron, Clifton George *ceramic engineer, educator*
Blahut, Richard Edward *electrical and computer engineering educator*
Bragg, Michael B. *engineering educator*
Chao, Bei Tse *mechanical engineering educator*
Chato, John Clark *mechanical and bioengineering educator*
Clausing, Arthur Marvin *mechanical engineering educator*
Coleman, Paul Dare *electrical engineering educator*
Conry, Thomas Francis *mechanical engineering educator, consultant*
Cook, Harry Edgar *engineering educator*
Cusano, Cristino *mechanical engineer, educator*
Daniel, David Edwin *civil engineer, educator*
Eden, James Gary *electrical engineer, educator, physicist, researcher*
Feng, Milton *engineering educator*
Gaddy, Oscar Lee *electrical engineering educator*
Garcia, Marcelo Horacio *engineering educator, consultant*
Gardner, Chester Stone *electrical and computer engineering educator, consultant*
Hajek, Bruce E. *electrical engineer, educator*
Hall, William Joel *civil engineer, educator*
Hannon, Bruce Michael *engineer, educator*
Hanratty, Thomas Joseph *chemical engineer, educator*
Herrin, Moreland *retired civil engineering educator, consultant*
Hess, Karl *electrical and computer engineering educator*
Holonyak, Nick, Jr. *electrical engineering educator*
Huang, Thomas Shi-Tao *electrical engineering educator, researcher*
Jones, Benjamin Angus, Jr. *retired agricultural engineering educator, administrator*
Krier, Herman *mechanical and industrial engineering educator*
Kumar, Panganamala Ramana *electrical and computer engineering educator*
May, Walter Grant *chemical engineer, educator*
Mayes, Paul Eugene *engineering educator, technical consultant*
Miley, George Hunter *nuclear and electrical engineering educator*
Miller, Robert Earl *engineer, educator*
Rao, Nannapaneni Narayana *electrical engineer*
Snoeyink, Vernon L. *civil engineer, educator*
Stallmeyer, James Edward *engineer, educator*
Swenson, George Warner, Jr. *electronics engineer, radio astronomer, educator*
Trick, Timothy Noel *electrical and computer engineering educator, researcher*
Wert, Charles Allen *metallurgical and mining engineering educator*
Yoerger, Roger Raymond *agricultural engineer, educator*
Zukoski, Charles Frederick, IV *chemical engineering educator, administrator*

Washington
Hallinan, John Cornelius *mechanical engineering consultant*

Winnetka
Fraenkel, Stephen Joseph *engineering and research executive*

INDIANA

Crane
Waggoner, Susan Marie *electronics engineer*

Crown Point
Ceroke, Clarence John *engineer, consultant*

Evansville
Blandford, Dick *electrical engineering and communications educator*
Gerhart, Philip Mark *engineering educator*

Fort Wayne
Shoemaker, John Calvin *aeronautical engineer, engineering company executive*

Goshen
Heap, James Clarence *retired mechanical engineer*

Hammond
Pierson, Edward Samuel *engineering educator, consultant*

Indianapolis
Brannon-Peppas, Lisa *chemical engineer, researcher*
Dillon, Howard Burton *civil engineer*

Kokomo
Nierste, Joseph Paul *software engineer*

Lafayette
Bernhard, Robert James *mechanical engineer, educator*
Fox, Robert William *mechanical engineering educator*
Geddes, Leslie Alexander *bioengineer, physiologist, educator*
Gustafson, Winthrop Adolph *aeronautical and astronautical engineering educator*
Liley, Peter Edward *mechanical engineering educator*
Lindenlaub, John Charles *electrical engineer, educator*
Ott, Karl Otto *nuclear engineering educator, consultant*

Mount Vernon
Moll, Joseph Eugene *chemical engineer, chemical company executive*

Noblesville
Monical, Robert Duane *consulting structural engineer*

Notre Dame
Gray, William Guerin *civil engineering educator*
Incropera, Frank Paul *mechanical engineering educator*
Jerger, Edward William *mechanical engineer, university dean*
Liu, Ruey-Wen *electrical engineering educator*
Merz, James Logan *electrical engineering and materials educator, researcher*
Michel, Anthony Nikolaus *electrical engineering educator, researcher*
Ovaert, Timothy Christopher *mechanical engineering educator*
Raven, Francis Harvey *mechanical engineering educator*
Sain, Michael Kent *electrical engineering educator*
Schmitz, Roger Anthony *chemical engineering educator, academic administrator*
Stadtherr, Mark A. *chemical engineer, educator*
Sweeney, Thomas Leonard *chemical engineering educator, researcher*
Szewczyk, Albin Anthony *engineering educator*
Varma, Arvind *chemical engineering educator, researcher*

South Bend
Kohn, James Paul *engineering educator*

West Lafayette
Albright, Lyle Frederick *chemical engineering educator*
Altschaeffl, Adolph George *civil engineering educator, retired*
Andres, Ronald Paul *chemical engineer, educator*
Cohen, Raymond *mechanical engineer, educator*
Cooper, James Albert, Jr. *electrical engineering educator*
Delleur, Jacques William *civil engineering educator*
Drnevich, Vincent Paul *civil engineering educator*
Eckert, Roger E(arl) *chemical engineering educator*
Farris, Thomas N. *engineering educator, researcher*
Friedlaender, Fritz Josef *electrical engineering educator*
Grace, Richard Edward *engineering educator*
Greenkorn, Robert Albert *chemical engineering educator*
Harr, Milton Edward *civil engineering professor, engineering consultant*
Ladisch, Michael R. *biochemical engineering educator*
Landgrebe, David Allen *electrical engineer*
Lin, Pen-Min *electrical engineer, educator*
Marshall, Francis Joseph *aerospace engineer*
Neudeck, Gerold Walter *electrical engineering educator*
Ong, Chee-Mun *engineering educator*
Peppas, Nikolaos Athanassiou *chemical and biomedical engineering educator, consultant*
Salvendy, Gavriel *industrial engineer, educator*
Schneider, Steven Philip *aerodynamics educator*
Schwartz, Richard John *electrical engineering educator, researcher*
Sinha, Kumares Chandra *civil engineering educator, researcher, consultant*
Skibniewski, Miroslaw Jan *engineering educator, management researcher*
Solberg, James Joseph *industrial engineering educator*
Sozen, Mete Avni *civil engineering educator*
Stevenson, Warren Howard *mechanical engineering educator*
Taber, Margaret Ruth *electrical engineering technology educator, electrical engineer*
Thomas, Marlin Uluess *industrial engineering educator, academic administrator*
Tsao, George T. *chemical engineer, educator*
Viskanta, Raymond *mechanical engineering educator*
Wankat, Phillip Charles *chemical engineering educator*
Weiner, Andrew Marc *electrical engineering educator*
Williams, Theodore Joseph *engineering educator*

IOWA

Ames
Anderson, Robert Morris, Jr. *electrical engineer*
Basart, John Philip *electrical engineering and remote sensing researcher*
Baumann, Edward Robert *environmental engineering educator*
Brown, Robert Grover *engineering educator*
Buchele, Wesley Fisher *retired agricultural engineering educator*
Cleasby, John LeRoy *civil engineer, educator*
Colvin, Thomas Stuart *agricultural engineer, farmer*
Johnson, Howard Paul *agricultural engineering educator*
Jones, Edwin Channing, Jr. *electrical and computer engineering educator*
Larsen, William Lawrence *materials science and engineering educator*
Melvin, Stewart Wayne *engineering educator*
Mischke, Charles Russell *mechanical engineering educator*
Okiishi, Theodore Hisao *mechanical engineering educator*
Sanders, Wallace Wolfred, Jr. *civil engineer*
Venkata, Subrahmanyam Saraswati *electrical engineering educator, electric energy and power researcher*
Young, Donald Fredrick *engineering educator*

Davenport
Pedersen, Karen Sue *electrical engineer*

Iowa City
Arora, Jasbir Singh *engineering educator*
Eyman, Earl Duane *electrical science educator, consultant*
Haug, Edward Joseph, Jr. *mechanical engineering educator, simulation research engineer*
Longren, Karl Erik *electrical and computer engineering educator*
Marshall, Jeffrey Scott *mechanical engineer, educator*
Patel, Virendra Chaturbhai *mechanical engineer, educator*

Madrid
Handy, Richard Lincoln *civil engineer, educator*

Muscatine
Thomopulos, Gregs G. *consulting engineering company executive*

KANSAS

Lawrence
Benjamin, Bezaleel Solomon *architecture and architectural engineering educator*
Darwin, David *civil engineering educator, researcher, consultant*
Green, Don Wesley *chemical and petroleum engineering educator*
Moore, Richard Kerr *electrical engineering educator*
Muirhead, Vincent Uriel *retired aerospace engineer*
Roskam, Jan *aerospace engineer*
Rowland, James Richard *electrical engineering educator*

Leawood
Karmeier, Delbert Fred *consulting engineer, realtor*

Manhattan
Chung, Do Sup *agricultural engineering educator*
Hagen, Lawrence Jacob *agricultural engineer*
Johnson, William Howard *agricultural engineer, educator*
Lee, E(ugene) Stanley *engineer, mathematician, educator*
Simons, Gale Gene *nuclear and electrical engineer, educator*

Mcpherson
Grauer, Douglas Dale *civil engineer*

Overland Park
Dunn, Robert Sigler *engineering executive*

Salina
Crawford, Lewis Cleaver *engineering executive, researcher*

Shawnee Mission
Gaboury, David *engineering company executive*

Wichita
Egbert, Robert Iman *electrical engineering educator, academic administrator*
Hansen, Ole Viggo *chemical engineer*
McKee, George Moffitt, Jr. *civil engineer, consultant*

MICHIGAN

Ann Arbor
Adamson, Thomas Charles, Jr. *aerospace engineering educator, consultant*
Akcasu, Ahmet Ziyaeddin *nuclear engineer, educator*
Becher, William Don *electrical engineer, engineering educator, writer*
Bhattacharya, Pallab Kumar *electrical engineering educator, researcher*
Bilello, John Charles *materials science and engineering educator*
Bitondo, Domenic *engineering executive*
Bonder, Seth *mechanical engineer*
Bunch, Howard McRaven *ship production educator, consultant, researcher*
Calahan, Donald Albert *electrical engineering educator*
Carnahan, Brice *chemical engineer, educator*
Chaffin, Don Brian *industrial engineering educator, research director*
Chen, Michael Ming *mechanical engineering educator*
Director, Stephen William *electrical and computer engineering educator, academic administrator*
England, Anthony Wayne *electrical engineering and computer science educator, astronaut, geophysicist*
Faeth, Gerard Michael *aerospace and mechanical engineering educator, researcher*
Friedmann, Peretz Peter *aerospace engineer, educator*
Gibala, Ronald *metallurgical engineering educator*
Gilbert, Elmer Grant *aerospace engineering educator, control theorist*
Haddad, George Ilyas *engineering educator, research scientist*
Harris, Robert Blynn *civil engineer, educator*
Hayes, John Patrick *electrical engineering and computer science educator, consultant*
Knoll, Glenn Frederick *nuclear engineering educator*
Koren, Yoram *mechanical engineering educator*
Kozma, Adam *electrical engineer*
Leith, Emmett Norman
Ludema, Kenneth C. *mechanical engineer, educator*
Martin, William Russell *nuclear engineering educator*
McClamroch, N. Harris *aerospace engineering educator, consultant, researcher*
O'Brien, William Joseph *materials engineer, educator, consultant*
Pehlke, Robert Donald *materials and metallurgical engineering educator*
Petrick, Ernest Nicholas *mechanical engineer, researcher*
Pollock, Stephen Michael *industrial engineering educator, consultant*
Root, William Lucas *electrical engineering educator*
Rumman, Wadi (Saliba Rumman) *civil engineer, consultant*
Schwank, Johannes Walter *chemical engineering educator*
Scott, Norman Ross *electrical engineering educator*
Senior, Thomas Bryan A. *electrical engineering educator, researcher, consultant*
Solomon, David Eugene *engineering company executive*
Tai, Chen-To *electrical engineering educator*
Ulaby, Fawwaz Tayssir *electrical engineering and computer science educator, research center administrator*
Upatnieks, Juris *retired optical engineer*
Vinh, Nguyen Xuan *aerospace engineering educator*
Wang, Henry Yee-Neen *chemical engineering educator*
Weber, Walter Jacob, Jr. *engineering educator*
Wilson, Richard Christian *engineering firm executive*
Wise, Kensall D. *engineering educator*

Carleton
Rancourt, James Daniel *optical engineer*

Commerce Township
Benson, Jack Duane *mechanical engineer, research scientist*

Dearborn
Cairns, James Robert *mechanical engineering educator*
Gandhi, Haren S. *chemical engineer*
Kim, Byung Ro *environmental engineer*
Little, Robert Eugene *mechanical engineering educator, materials behavior researcher, consultant*

Detroit
Holness, Gordon Victor Rix *engineering executive, mechanical engineer*
King, Albert I. *bioengineering educator*
Kline, Kenneth Alan *mechanical engineering educator*
Kummler, Ralph H. *chemical engineer, educator, dean*
Putatunda, Susil Kumar *metallurgy educator*
Rathod, Mulchand *mechanical engineering educator*
Sengupta, Dipak Lal *electrical engineering and physics educator, researcher*
Trim, Donald Roy *consulting engineer*

East Lansing
Andersland, Orlando Baldwin *civil engineering educator*
Beck, James V. *mechanical engineering educator*
Chen, Kun-Mu *electrical engineering educator*
Cutts, Charles Eugene *civil engineering educator*
Foss, John Frank *mechanical engineering educator*
Goodman, Erik David *engineering educator*
Lloyd, John Raymond *mechanical engineering educator*
Saul, William Edward *civil engineering educator*
Segerlind, Larry J. *agricultural engineering educator*
Snell, John Raymond *civil engineer*
von Bernuth, Robert Dean *agricultural engineering educator, consultant*
Von Tersch, Lawrence Wayne *electrical engineering educator, university dean*

Farmington
Chou, Clifford Chi Fong *research engineering executive*
Neyer, Jerome Charles *consulting civil engineer*

Greenbush
Simpkin, Lawrence James *engineering company executive*

Harrison Township
Rivard, Jerome G. *automotive engineer*

Holland
Stynes, Stanley Kenneth *retired chemical engineer, educator*

Houghton
Heckel, Richard Wayne *metallurgical engineering educator*

Leland
Soutas-Little, Robert William *mechanical engineer, educator*

Livonia
Uicker, Joseph Bernard *retired engineering company executive*

Midland
Carson, Gordon Bloom *retired engineering executive*
Meister, Bernard John *chemical engineer*

North Branch
Stevenson, James Laraway *communications engineer, consulting*

Okemos
Giacoletto, Lawrence Joseph *electronics engineering educator, researcher, consultant*

Pontiac
Hampton, Philip Michael *consulting engineering company executive*

Rochester
Polis, Michael Philip *electrical and systems engineering educator*

Saint Joseph
Maley, Wayne Allen *engineering consultant*

Shelby Township
Jacovides, Linos Jacovou *electrical engineer, researcher*
Nagy, Louis Leonard *engineering executive, researcher*

Southfield
McKeen, Alexander C. *retired engineering executive, foundation administrator*

Walled Lake
Williams, Sam B. *engineering executive*

Warren
Bolander, William J. *mechanical engineer*
Lett, Philip Wood, Jr. *defense consultant*
Pawlak, Andrzej M. *electrical engineer*

MINNESOTA

Albert Lea
Christianson, Darcey K. *broadcast engineer*

Chanhassen
Shanahan, Eugene Miles *flow measurement instrumentation company executive*
Thorson, John Martin, Jr. *electrical engineer, consultant*

Lutsen
Napadensky, Hyla Sarane *engineering consultant*

Madison
Husby, Donald Evans *engineering company executive*

Minneapolis
Bakken, Earl Elmer *electrical engineer, bioengineering company executive*
Crouch, Steven L. *mining engineer*
Cunningham, Thomas B. *aerospace engineer*
Davis, Howard Ted *engineering educator*
Eckert, Ernst R. G. *mechanical engineering educator*
French, Catherine E. Wolfgram *engineering educator, researcher*
Galambos, Theodore Victor *civil engineer, educator*
Gerberich, William Warren *engineering educator*
Goldstein, Richard Jay *mechanical engineer, educator*
Joseph, Daniel Donald *aeronautical engineer, educator*
Keller, Kenneth Harrison *engineering educator, science policy analyst*
Kvalseth, Tarald Oddvar *mechanical engineer, educator*
Lambert, Robert Frank *electrical engineer, consultant*
Lee, E. Bruce *electrical engineering educator*
Leger, James Robert *engineering educator*
Liu, Benjamin Young-hwai *engineering educator*
Ogata, Katsuhiko *engineering educator*
Oriani, Richard Anthony *metallurgical engineering educator*
Pfender, Emil *mechanical engineering educator*
Ramalingam, Subbiah *mechanical engineer, educator*
Rauenhorst, Gerald *architectural engineer, construction and development executive*
Scriven, L. E(dward) *chemical engineering educator, scientist*
Shulman, Yechiel *engineering educator*
Sparrow, Ephraim Maurice *mechanical engineering scientist, educator*
Svärd, N. Trygve *electrical engineer*
Tennyson, Joseph Alan *engineering executive*

Oakdale
Tran, Nang Tri *electrical engineer, physicist*

Saint Paul
Lampert, Leonard Franklin *mechanical engineer*
Maze, Thomas H. *engineering educator*

South Saint Paul
Fairhurst, Charles *civil and mining engineering educator*

MISSOURI

Ava
Murray, Delbert Milton *manufacturing engineer*

Ballwin
Cornell, William Daniel *mechanical engineer*

Centralia
Harmon, Robert Wayne *electrical engineering executive*

Columbia
Pringle, Oran Allan *mechanical and aerospace engineering educator*
Yasuda, Hirotsugu Koge *chemical engineering professor*

Ferguson
Bruns, Billy Lee *electrical engineer, consultant*

Fortuna
Ramer, James LeRoy *civil engineer*

Innsbrook
Ruwwe, William Otto *retired automotive engineer*

Kansas City
Davis, F(rancis) Keith *civil engineer*
Hall, Wayne F. *engineering company executive*
Robinson, John Hamilton *civil engineer*
Rodman, Len C. *civil and communication engineering executive*

Lake Lotawana
Heineman, Paul Lowe *consulting civil engineer*

Rolla
Barr, David John *civil, geological engineering educator*
Crosbie, Alfred Linden *mechanical engineering educator*
Day, Delbert Edwin *ceramic engineering educator*
O'Keefe, Thomas Joseph *metallurgical engineer*
Rao, Vittal Srirangam *electrical engineering educator*
Saperstein, Lee Waldo *mining engineering educator*
Sauer, Harry John , Jr. *mechanical engineering educator, university administrator*
Schonberg, William Peter *aerospace, mechanical, civil engineering educator*
Sheffield, John William *mechanical engineering educator*
Summers, David Archibald *research mining engineer, educator and director*
Tsoulfanidis, Nicholas *nuclear engineering educator, university official*

Saint Louis
Beumer, Richard Eugene *engineer, architect, construction firm executive*
Brasunas, Anton de Sales *retired metallurgical engineering educator*
Cox, Jerome Rockhold, Jr. *electrical engineer*
Dudukovic, Milorad P. *chemical engineering educator, consultant*
Gould, Phillip Louis *civil engineering educator, consultant*
Husar, Rudolf Bertalan *mechanical engineering educator*
Muller, Marcel W(ettstein) *electrical engineering educator*
Peters, David Allen *mechanical engineering educator, consultant*
Ross, Monte *electrical engineer, researcher*
Shrauner, Barbara Wayne Abraham *electrical engineering educator*
Staley, Robert W. *mechanical engineer, electric company executive*
Sutera, Salvatore Philip *mechanical engineering educator*
Szabo, Barna Aladar *mechanical engineering educator, mining engineer*
Winter, David Ferdinand *electrical engineering educator, consultant*
Wolfe, Charles Morgan *electrical engineering educator*
Zurheide, Charles Henry *consulting electrical engineer*

Springfield
Rogers, Roddy Jack *civil, geotechnical and water engineer*

Webb City
Nichols, Robert Leighton *civil engineer*

NEBRASKA

Alliance
Riemenschneider, Albert Louis *retired engineering educator*

Clay Center
Hahn, George LeRoy *agricultural engineer, biometeorologist*

Lincoln
Allington, Robert William *instrument company executive*
Bahar, Ezekiel *electrical engineering educator*
Edwards, Donald Mervin *biological systems engineering educator, university dean*
Elias, Samy E. G. *engineering executive*
Hanna, Milford A. *agricultural engineering educator*
Nelson, Don Jerome *electrical engineering and computer science educator*
Rajurkar, Kamlakar Purushottam *mechanical engineering educator*
Splinter, William Eldon *agricultural engineering educator*
Woollam, John Arthur *electrical engineering educator*

Omaha
Durham, Charles William *civil engineer, director*
Kelpe, Paul Robert *engineer, consultant*
Matthies, Frederick John *architectural engineer*

NEW YORK

Syosset
Kazanowski, Larry *engineer*

NORTH CAROLINA

Raleigh
Cooper, Stuart Leonard *chemical engineering educator, researcher, consultant*

NORTH DAKOTA

Grand Forks
Bandyopadhyay, Biswanath Prasad *manufacturing engineer, educator, consultant*

Minot AFB
Atkinson, Thomas P. *environmental engineer*

OHIO

Akron
White, James Lindsay *polymer engineering educator*

Athens
Dinos, Nicholas *engineering educator, administrator*
Robe, Thurlow Richard *engineering educator, university dean*

Bratenahl
Jones, Trevor Owen *engineering executive*

Brookpark
Bluford, Guion Stewart, Jr. *engineering company executive*

Canton
Hoecker, David *engineering executive*

Cincinnati
Agrawal, Dharma Prakash *engineering educator*
Bluestein, Paul Harold *management engineer*
Ghia, Kirti N. *fluid mechanics engineer, educator*
Greenberg, David Bernard *chemical engineering educator*
Halstead, David E. *aeronautical engineer*
Johnson, K(enneth) O(dell) *aerospace engineer*
Kreitzer, Melvyn, II *optical designer*
Manwaring, Steve R. *mechanical engineer*
Rubin, Stanley Gerald *aerospace engineering educator*
Shin, Hyoun-Woo *aircraft engineer*
Smith, Leroy Harrington, Jr. *mechanical engineer, aerodynamics consultant*
Toftner, Richard Orville *engineering executive*
Wachenfeld, Timothy H. *aeronautical engineering executive*
Weisman, Joel *nuclear engineering educator, engineering consultant*
Wisler, David Charles *aerospace engineer, educator*

Cleveland
Angus, John Cotton *chemical engineering educator*
Anthony, Donald Barrett *engineering executive*
Baer, Eric *engineering and science educator*

Bahniuk, Eugene *mechanical engineering educator*
Burghart, James Henry *electrical engineer, educator*
Coulman, George Albert *chemical engineer, educator*
DellaCorte, Christopher *engineer, tribologist*
Goldstein, Marvin Emanuel *aerospace scientist, research center administrator*
Hardy, Richard Allen *mechanical engineer, diesel fuel engine specialist*
Heuer, Arthur Harold *ceramics engineer, educator*
Ko, Wen-Hsiung *electrical engineering educator*
Lefkowitz, Irving *engineering educator*
Ostrach, Simon *engineering educator*
Povinelli, Louis A. *aeronautical engineer*
Reshotko, Eli *aerospace engineer, educator*
Saada, Adel Selim *civil engineer, educator*
Savinell, Robert Francis *engineering educator*
Wagner, James Warren *engineering educator*
Wilson, Jack *aeronautical engineer*

Columbus
Altan, Taylan *engineering educator, mechanical engineer, consultant*
Bechtel, Stephen E. *mechanical engineer, educator*
Bhushan, Bharat *mechanical engineer*
Brodkey, Robert Stanley *chemical engineering educator*
Cruz, Jose Bejar, Jr. *engineering educator, educator*
Davis, James Frederick *chemical engineer, researcher, educator, consultant*
Fan, Liang-Shih *chemical engineering educator*
Feinberg, Martin Robert *chemical engineering educator*
Fenton, Robert Earl *electrical engineering educator*
Houser, Donald Russell *mechanical engineering educator, consultant*
Jacox, John William *retired mechanical engineer and consulting company executive*
Keaney, William Regis *engineering and construction services executive, consultant*
Kouyoumjian, Robert G. *electrical engineering educator*
Ksienski, Aharon Arthur *electrical engineer*
Liu, Ming-Tsan *computer engineering educator*
Miller, Don Wilson *nuclear engineering educator*
Peters, Leon, Jr. *electrical engineering educator, research administrator*
Rapp, Robert Anthony *metallurgical engineering educator, consultant*
Redmond, Robert Francis *nuclear engineering educator*
Rubin, Alan J. *environmental engineer, chemist, photgrapher*
Singh, Rajendra *mechanical engineering educator*
St. Pierre, George Roland, Jr. *materials science and engineering administrator, educator*
Taiganides, E. Paul *agricultural and environmental engineer, consultant*
Uotila, Urho Antti Kalevi *geodesist, educator*
Wagoner, Robert Hall *engineering educator, researcher*
Waldron, Kenneth John *mechanical engineering educator, researcher*
Zakin, Jacques Louis *chemical engineering educator*

Dayton
Ballal, Dilip Ramchandra *mechanical engineering educator*
Carson, Richard McKee *chemical engineer*
Houpis, Constantine Harry *electrical engineering educator*
Kazimierczuk, Marian Kazimierz *electrical engineer, educator*
Schmitt, George Frederick, Jr. *materials engineer*
Sturgess, Geoffrey J. *aeronautical research engineer*

East Liverpool
Beals, Robert J. *ceramic engineer*

Gates Mills
Enyedy, Gustav, Jr. *chemical engineer*

Marblehead
Haering, Edwin Raymond *chemical engineering educator, consultant*

Middletown
Gilby, Steve *metallurgical engineering researcher*
Newby, John Robert *metallurgical engineer*

Milford
Weyand, William J. *engineering executive*

Oxford
Ward, Roscoe Fredrick *engineering educator*

Powell
Schwab, Glenn Orville *retired agricultural engineering educator, consultant*

Rossford
Salmon, Stuart Clive *manufacturing engineer*

Shaker Heights
Siegel, Robert *heat transfer engineer*

Stow
Bement, Arden Lee, Jr. *engineering educator*

Worthington
Compton, Ralph Theodore, Jr. *electrical engineering educator*

Wright Patterson AFB
Chelette, Tamara Lynne *biomedical engineer*
D'Azzo, John Joachim *electrical engineer, educator*

Yellow Springs
Trolander, Hardy Wilcox *engineering executive, consultant*

Youngstown
Fok, Thomas Dso Yun *civil engineer*

Mossman, Robert Gillis, IV *civil and environmental engineer*

PENNSYLVANIA

University Park
Jenkins, William Kenneth *electrical engineering educator*

SOUTH DAKOTA

Rapid City
Gowen, Richard Joseph *electrical engineering educator, academic administrator*

VIRGINIA

Richmond
Gad-el-Hak, Mohamed *aerospace and mechanical engineering educator, scientist*

WISCONSIN

Brookfield
Curfman, Floyd Edwin *engineering educator, retired*
Thomas, John *mechanical engineer, research and development*

Frederic
Rudell, Milton Wesley *aerospace engineer*

Madison
Beachley, Norman Henry *mechanical engineer, educator*
Berthouex, Paul Mac *civil and environmental engineer, educator*
Bird, Robert Byron *chemical engineering educator, author*
Bohnhoff, David Roy *agricultural engineer, educator*
Boyle, William Charles *civil engineering educator*
Bubenzer, Gary Dean *agricultural engineering educator, researcher*
Callen, James Donald *nuclear engineer, plasma physicist, educator*
Carbon, Max William *nuclear engineering educator*
Chang, Y. Austin *materials engineer, educator*
Converse, James Clarence *agricultural engineering educator*
Corradini, Michael L. *engineering educator*
Dietmeyer, Donald Leo *retired electrical engineer, educator*
Duffie, John Atwater *chemical engineer, educator*
Dumesic, James A. *chemical engineer*
Emmert, Gilbert Arthur *engineer, educator*
Gustafson, David Harold *industrial engineering and preventive medicine educator*
Hill, Charles Graham, Jr. *chemical engineering educator*
Kulcinski, Gerald LaVerne *nuclear engineer, educator*
Lasseter, Robert Haygood *electrical engineering educator, consultant*
Lightfoot, Edwin Niblock, Jr. *retired chemical engineering educator*
Lipo, Thomas A. *electrical engineer, educator*
Long, Willis Franklin *electrical engineering educator, researcher*
Loper, Carl Richard, Jr. *metallurgical engineer, educator*
Lovell, Edward George *mechanical engineering educator*
Malkus, David Starr *mechanics educator, applied mathematician*
Novotny, Donald Wayne *electrical engineering educator*
Ray, Willis Harmon *chemical engineer*
Russell, Jeffrey Scott *civil engineering educator*
Seireg, Ali A(bdel Hay) *mechanical engineer*
Skiles, James Jean *electrical and computer engineering educator*
Smith, Michael James *industrial engineering educator*
Webster, John Goodwin *biomedical engineering educator, researcher*

Milwaukee
Bartel, Fred Frank *consulting engineer executive*
Chan, Shih Hung *mechanical engineering educator, consultant*
Demerdash, Nabeel Aly Omar *electrical engineer*
Fournelle, Raymond Albert *engineering educator*
Gaggioli, Richard Arnold *mechanical engineering educator*
Heinen, James Albin *electrical engineering educator*
Landis, Fred *mechanical engineering educator*
Widera, Georg Ernst Otto *mechanical engineering educator, consultant*

Racine
Meissner, Alan Paul *research engineer*

Waukesha
Danner, Dean Wilson *electrical engineer, manufacturing executive*

Wisconsin Rapids
Drew, Richard Allen *retired electrical and instrument engineer*

CANADA

MANITOBA

Winnipeg
Bateman, Leonard A. *engineering executive*
Cohen, Harley *civil engineer, science educator*
Kuffel, Edmund *electrical engineering educator*
Laliberte, Garland Everett *agricultural engineering educator*

Oleszkiewicz, Jan Alojzy *engineering educator*
Shafai, Lotfollah *electrical engineering educator, research company executive*

ISRAEL

Beer-Sheva
Brosilow, Coleman Bernard *chemical engineering educator*

ADDRESS UNPUBLISHED

Amann, Charles Albert *mechanical engineer, researcher*
Baltazzi, Evan Serge *engineering research consulting company executive*
Dull, William Martin *retired engineering executive*
Halpin, Daniel William *civil engineering educator, consultant*
James, Charles Franklin, Jr. *engineering educator, educator*
Loy, Richard Franklin *civil engineer*
Marshall, Gerald Francis *physicist*
Munger, Paul R. *civil engineering educator*
Myers, Phillip Samuel *mechanical engineering educator*
Persson, Erland Karl *electrical engineer*
Reid, Robert Lelon *retired mechanical engineering educator, dean*
Rolewicz, Robert John *estimating engineer*
Ryan, Carl Ray *electrical engineer, educator*
Salkind, Michael Jay *technology administrator*
Siegal, Rita Goran *engineering company executive*
Spelson, Nicholas James *engineering executive, retired*
Stewart, Albert Elisha *safety engineer, industrial hygienist*
Treinavicz, Kathryn Mary *software engineer*
Wentz, William Henry, Jr. *aerospace engineer, educator*

FINANCE: BANKING SERVICES
See also FINANCE: INVESTMENT SERVICES

UNITED STATES

CALIFORNIA

San Francisco
Biller, Leslie Stuart *banker*

FLORIDA

Fort Lauderdale
Leach, Ralph F. *banker*

ILLINOIS

Blue Island
Yager, Vincent Cook *bank executive*

Chicago
Bakwin, Edward Morris *banker*
Bartter, Brit Jeffrey *investment banker*
Blair, Edward McCormick *investment banker*
Bobins, Norman R. *banker*
Bolger, David P. *bank executive*
Dancewicz, John Edward *investment banker*
Darr, Milton Freeman, Jr. *banker*
Eddy, David Latimer *banker*
Freehling, Stanley Maxwell *investment banker*
Gibbons, John *mortgage company executive*
Glickman, Robert Jeffrey *banking executive*
Griffiths, Robert Pennell *banker*
Hastings, Barry G. *trust company executive*
Heagy, Thomas Charles *banker*
Hollis, Donald Roger *strategy consultant*
Istock, Verne George *retired banker*
Klapperich, Frank Lawrence, Jr. *investment banker*
Kramer, Ferdinand *mortgage banker*
Leszinske, William O. *bank executive*
Lorenz, Katherine Mary *banker*
McCoy, John Bonnet *retired banker*
McKay, Neil *banker*
McNally, Alan G. *bank executive*
Moody, Susan S. *bank executive*
Pollock, Alexander John *banker*
Roberts, Theodore Harris *banker*
Scharf, Charles W. *banking executive*
Schroeder, Charles Edgar *investment management executive*
Schulte, David Michael *investment banker*
Seaman, Irving, Jr. *banker*
Socolofsky, Jon Edward *banker*
Stevens, Mark *banker*
Stirling, James Paulman *investment banker*
Swift, Edward Foster, III *investment banker*
Theobald, Thomas Charles *banker*
Thomas, Richard Lee *banker*
Vander Wilt, Carl Eugene *banker*
Vitale, David J. *banker*
Williams, Edward Joseph *banker*

Fox River Grove
Abboud, Alfred Robert *banker, consultant, investor*

Golf
Fellingham, Warren Luther, Jr. *retired banker*

Hoffman Estates
Weston, Roger Lance *banker*

Lake Forest
McCormack, Robert Cornelius *investment banker*
Ross, Robert Evan *bank executive*

Northbrook
Keehn, Silas *retired bank executive*
Sewright, Charles William, Jr. *mortgage banking advisory services company executive*

Palatine
Fitzgerald, Gerald Francis *retired banker*

Rockford
Meuleman, Robert Joseph *banker*

Winnetka
Fenton, Clifton Lucien *investment banker*

INDIANA

Columbus
Nash, John Arthur *bank executive*

Evansville
Giancola, James J. *banking executive*

Indianapolis
Barnette, Joseph D., Jr. *bank holding company executive*
Dietz, William Ronald *management company executive*
Heger, Martin L. *bank executive*
Melton, Owen B., Jr. *banking company executive*
Meyer, William Michael *mortgage banking executive*

Muncie
Anderson, Stefan Stolen *banker*
Sursa, Charles David *banker*

South Bend
Jones, Wellington Downing, III *banker*

Terre Haute
Smith, Donald E. *banker*

IOWA

Cedar Rapids
Wax, Nadine Virginia *retired banker*

KANSAS

Manhattan
Stolzer, Leo William *bank executive*

Overland Park
Allison, Mark S. *trust company executive*
Bergman, Bradley Anthony *trust company executive*
Kleinman, Michael A. *trust company executive*
Lang, Daniel W. *trust company executive*
Whitaker, Freda N. *trust company executive*

Shawnee Mission
McEachen, Richard Edward *banker, lawyer*

Topeka
Dicus, John Carmack *savings bank executive*
Wagnon, Joan *banker, former mayor*

MICHIGAN

Bay City
Van Dyke, Clifford Craig *retired banker*

Bloomfield Hills
Colladay, Robert S. *trust company executive, consultant*
McQueen, Patrick M. *bank executive*

Detroit
Babb, Ralph W., Jr. *banker*
Beran, John R. *banker*
Buttigieg, Joseph J. *banking executive*
Jeffs, Thomas Hamilton, II *retired banker*
Lewis, John D. *banking official*
Miller, Eugene Albert *banker*
Monahan, Michael T. *bank executive*

Farmington Hills
Ebert, Douglas Edmund *banker*
Heiss, Richard Walter *former bank executive, consultant, lawyer*

Flint
Vitito, Robert J. *bank executive*

Grand Rapids
Canepa, John Charles *banking consultant*
Furlong, Mark F. *bank executive*

Ionia
Kohls, William Richard *bank executive*

Southfield
Shields, Robert Emmet *merchant banker, lawyer*

MINNESOTA

Eden Prairie
Hanson, Dale S. *retired banker*

Minneapolis
Andreas, David Lowell *banker*
Cecere, Andrew *bank executive*
Cooper, William Allen *banking executive*
Duim, Gary T. *retired bank executive*
Griffith, Sima Lynn *investment banking executive, consultant*
Grundhofer, Jerry A. *bank executive*
Grundhofer, John F. *banking executive*
Lester, Susan E. *former bank executive*
Moffett, David McKenzie *bank executive*
Morrison, Clinton *banker*
Nagorske, Lynn A. *bank executive*
Walters, Glen Robert *banker*
Zona, Richard A. *bank executive*

FINANCE: FINANCIAL SERVICES

UNITED STATES

Fort Scott
Mann, Henry Dean *accountant*

Lawrence
Beedles, William LeRoy *finance educator, financial consultant*

Leawood
Byrum-Sutton, Judith Miriam *accountant*

Pittsburg
Bicknell, O. Gene *financial executive*
Darling, John Rothburn, Jr. *business educator*

Shawnee Mission
Hechler, Robert Lee *financial services company executive*
Hoffman, Alfred John *retired mutual fund executive*

Topeka
Reser, Elizabeth May (Betty Reser) *bookkeeper*

MICHIGAN

Ann Arbor
Cornelius, Kenneth Cremer, Jr. *finance executive*
Elger, William Robert, Jr. *accountant*
Huntington, Curtis Edward *actuary*
Kim, E. Han *finance and business administration educator*
Seyhun, Hasan Nejat *finance educator, department chairman*

Auburn Hills
Drexler, Mary Sanford *financial executive*
Knight, Jeffrey Alan *finance executive*

Birmingham
Buczak, Douglas Chester *financial advisor, lawyer*

Dearborn
Winkler, Donald A. *credit company executive*

Detroit
Adams, William Johnston *financial and tax consultant*
Clarke, James T. *financial company excutive*
Kahalas, Harvey *business educator*

East Lansing
Arens, Alvin Armond *accountant, educator*

Jackson
Collins, Dana Jon *financial executive*

Livonia
Valerio, Michael Anthony *financial executive*

Marquette
Camerius, James Walter *marketing educator, corporate researcher*
Larson, Larry Gene *financial planner*

Monroe
Mlocek, Sister Frances Angeline *financial executive*

Oxford
Smith, Jay Lawrence *planning company executive*

Rochester
Horwitz, Ronald M. *business administration educator*

Southfield
Miller, Robert Stevens, Jr. *finance professional*
Rappleye, Richard Kent *financial executive, consultant, educator*
Rawden, David *financial services company executive*

West Bloomfield
Meyers, Gerald Carl *educator, author, expert witness, consultant*

MINNESOTA

Duluth
Nelson, Dennis Lee *finance educator*

Minneapolis
Benson, Donald Erick *holding company executive*
Berry, David J. *former financial services company executive*
Berryman, Robert Glen *accounting educator, consultant*
Charpentier, Marti Ray *accountant, financial executive*
Hoffmann, Thomas Russell *business management educator*
Kinney, Earl Robert *mutual funds company executive*
Petersen, Douglas Arndt *financial development consultant*
Pillsbury, George Sturgis *investment adviser*
Rudelius, William *marketing educator*
Schwartz, Howard Wyn *business/marketing educator, consultant*
Thornton, John T. *corporate financial executive*

Minnetonka
Wesselink, David Duwayne *finance company executive*
Woo, Benson *credit card company executive*

Ottertail
Hanson, Al *financial newsletter editor and publisher*

Plymouth
Chadwick, John Edwin *financial counselor*
Hauser, Elloyd *finance company executive*

Saint Paul
Crittenden, Bruce A. *finance company executive*
Dutcher, Judi *state auditor*

MISSOURI

Bridgeton
Collett, Lawrence *diversified financial service company executive*

Chesterfield
Armstrong, Theodore Morelock *financial executive*
Driscoll, Charles Francis *financial services company executive, investment adviser*
Hunter, Buddy D. *holding company executive*

Clayton
Bartmann, William R. *financial services company executive*

Columbia
Nikolai, Loren Alfred *accounting educator, writer*
Stockglausner, William George *accountant*
Wagner, William Burdette *business educator*

Hazelwood
Kostecki, Mary Ann *financial tax consultant, small business consultant*

Jefferson City
Liese, Christopher A. *benefits and financial consulting company owner, state legislator*
McCaskill, Claire *auditor*

Kansas City
Bloch, Henry Wollman *tax preparation company executive*
Ernst, Mark A. *diversified financial services company executive*
Garrison, Larry Richard *accounting educator*
Hager, Kenneth Vincent *accountant*
Kemper, Alexander C. *finance company executive*
Rozell, Joseph Gerard *accountant*
Salizzoni, Frank L. *finance company executive*
Thome, James J. *financial executive*

Saint Louis
Badalamenti, Anthony *financial planner*
Brown, Melvin F. *corporate executive*
Burch, Stephen Kenneth *financial services company executive, real estate investor*
Carlson, Arthur Eugene *accounting educator*
Crider, Robert Agustine *international financier, law enforcement official*
Eichholz, Dennis R. *controller, treasurer*
Folz, Carol Ann *financial analyst*
Green, Darlene *controller, municipal official*
Kniffen, Jan Rogers *finance executive*
Liggett, Hiram Shaw, Jr. *retired diversified industry financial executive*
Novik, Steve *finance company executive*
O'Donnell, Mark Joseph *accountant*
Schmidt, Robert Charles, Jr. *finance executive*

Springfield
Casper, John M. *financial executive*

MONTANA

Rollins
Greer, Willis Roswell, Jr. *accounting educator*

NEBRASKA

Fremont
Dunklau, Rupert Louis *personal investments consultant*

Lincoln
Lienemann, Delmar Arthur, Sr. *accountant, real estate developer*

Omaha
Christensen, Jon *finance company executive, former congressman*
Munger, Charles T. *diversified company executive*

Papillion
Miller, Drew *financial management company executive*

NEVADA

Las Vegas
Goldin, Martin Bruce *financial executive, consultant*

OHIO

Ada
Cooper, Ken Errol *retired management educator*

Akron
Burg, H. Peter *financial executive*

Amelia
Hayden, Joseph Page, Jr. *company executive*
Von Lehman, John *financial executive*

Beachwood
Youdelman, Robert Arthur *financial executive, lawyer*

Bexley
Raabe, William Alan *tax writer, business educator*

Bowling Green
Lunde, Harold Irving *management educator*

Cambridge
Baylor, Richard C. *financial company executive*
Crane, Gary E. *financial executive*

Cincinnati
Carey, Christopher L. *financial company executive*
Castellina, Daniel J. *financial executive*
Conaton, Michael Joseph *financial service executive*
Hoverson, Robert L. *finance company executive*
Linder, Carl H., III *diversified financial services company executive*
Lindner, Craig *financial services company executive*
Lindner, Robert David *finance company executive*
Lintz, Robert Carroll *financial holding company executive*
Magee, Mark E. *lawyer, financial executive*
McMullen, W. Rodney *financial officer*
Schiff, John Jefferson, Jr. *finance company executive*
Siekmann, Donald Charles *accountant*

Cleveland
Bennett, James E. *finance company executive*
Dutile, Robert Arthur *financial services executvie*
Grisko, Jerome P., Jr. *diversified financial services company executive*
Hamm, Charles D. *diversified financial services company executive*
Hawkinson, Gary Michael *financial services company executive*
Koch, Charles John *credit agency executive*
Krulitz, Leo Morrion *financial executive*
Lafave, Arthur J., Jr. *financial executive, lawyer*
Mayne, Lucille Stringer *finance educator, educator*
Richardson, Allison *financial services company official*
Roberts, James Owen *financial planning executive, consultant*
Skolnik, David Erwin *financial analyst*
Stratton-Crooke, Thomas Edward *financial consultant*
Thomas, Richard Stephen *financial executive*
Walker, James S. *financial executive*

Columbus
Bailey, Robert L. *finance company executive*
Berry, William Lee *business administration educator*
Boylan, John Lester *financial executive, accountant*
LaLonde, Bernard Joseph *educator*
Moone, Robert H. *finance company executive*
Zdun, James J. *finance executive*

Cuyahoga Falls
Moses, Abe Joseph *international financial consultant*

Dayton
Bearman, David *finance company executive*
Cronin, Patrick G. *financial executive*
Frydryk, Karl Allen *financial executive*
McLevish, Timothy *financial professional*
Singhvi, Surendra Singh *finance and strategy consultant*

Dublin
Pollner, Julia A. *financial executive*

East Liverpool
Baumgardner, Edward *financial company executive*

Fairfield
Stecher, Kenneth W. *financial corporation executive*

Greenville
Franz, Daniel Thomas *financial planner*

Hamilton
O'Dell, Michael Ray *accountant, banker*

Harrison
Kocher, Juanita Fay *retired auditor*

Independence
Boyle, Kammer *estate planner*

Lancaster
Voss, Jack Donald *international business consultant, lawyer*

Middletown
Wainscott, James Lawrence *accountant*

North Canton
Lynham, C(harles) Richard *foundry company executive*

North Olmsted
McCafferty, Owen Edward *accountant, dental-veterinary practice consultant*

Painesville
Clement, Daniel Roy, IV *accountant, assistant nurse, small business owner*

Toledo
Simpson, John S. *former finance executive*

SOUTH DAKOTA

Platte
Pennington, Beverly Melcher *financial services company executive*

Rapid City
McCall, Rey J. *financial analyst, consultant*

TEXAS

San Marcos
Palmer, Roger Raymond *accounting educator*

WISCONSIN

Appleton
Hilker, Lyle J. *financial services organization executive*

Beloit
Rodeman, Frederick Ernest *accountant*

Brookfield
Breu, George *accountant*

De Pere
Rueden, Henry Anthony *accountant*

Eau Claire
Weil, D(onald) Wallace *business administration educator*

Green Bay
Lempke, Michael R. *treasurer*

Madison
Aldag, Ramon John *management and organization educator*
Brachman, Richard John, II *financial services consultant, banking educator*
Eisler, Millard Marcus *financial executive*
Hickman, James Charles *business and statistics educator, business school dean*
Nevin, John Robert *business educator, consultant*
Prieve, E. Arthur *arts administration educator*

Milwaukee
Kendall, Leon Thomas *finance and real estate educator, retired insurance company executive*
Stefaniak, Norbert John *business administration educator*
Zore, Edward John *financial services executive*

Racine
Lamb, Steven G. *financial executive*

CANADA

MANITOBA

Winnipeg
Riley, Hugh Sanford *diversified financial services company executive*

ONTARIO

Toronto
Steinberg, Gregg Martin *financial and management consultant, investment banker*

ADDRESS UNPUBLISHED

Amdahl, Byrdelle John *business consulting executive*
Black, David deLaine *retired investment consultant*
Boyd, Francis Virgil *retired accounting educator*
Chelberg, Bruce Stanley *holding company executive*
Claspill, James Louis *finance company executive*
Duncan, Robert Bannerman *strategy and organizations educator*
Garpow, James Edward *retired financial executive*
Gleijeses, Mario *holding company executive*
Graf, Robert Arlan *retired financial services executive*
Harper, W(alter) Joseph *financial consultant*
Holloran, Thomas Edward *business educator*
Johnson, Margaret Kathleen *business educator*
Lavengood, Lawrence Gene *management educator, historian*
Massura, Edward Anthony *accountant*
Mednick, Robert *accountant*
Morgan, Robert Arthur *accountant*
Nair, Raghavan D. *accountant, educator*
Nelson, Mary Ellen Dickson *retired actuary*
Osborn, Kenneth Louis *financial executive*
Sexton, Carol Burke *financial institution executive*
Sheridan, Patrick Michael *finance company executive, retired*
Tyler, W(illiam) Ed *finance company executive*

FINANCE: INSURANCE

UNITED STATES

ARIZONA

Scottsdale
Tyner, Neal Edward *retired insurance company executive*

CONNECTICUT

Greenwich
West, Thomas Meade *insurance company executive*

ILLINOIS

Bloomington
Axley, Dixie L. *insurance company executive*
Brunner, Kim M. *insurance company executive*
Johnson, Earle Bertrand *insurance executive*
Joslin, Roger Scott *insurance company executive*
Rust, Edward Barry, Jr. *insurance company executive, lawyer*
Wright, Charles Richard *insurance executive*

Chicago
Bartholomay, William C. *insurance brokerage company executive, professional baseball team executive*
DeMoss, Jon W. *insurance company executive, lawyer*
Draut, Eric J. *insurance company executive*
Engel, Philip L. *retired insurance company executive*

Hinkelman, Ruth Amidon *insurance company executive*
Ingram, Donald *insurance company executive, director*
Jerome, Jerrold V. *retired insurance company executive*
Lishka, Edward Joseph *insurance underwriter*
Mc Caskey, Raymond F. *insurance company executive*
O'Halleran, Michael D. *insurance company executive*
Tyree, James C. *insurance company executive*
Zucaro, Aldo Charles *insurance company executive*

Decatur
Braun, William Joseph *life insurance underwriter*

Itasca
Gallagher, Robert E. *risk management marketing company executive*
Gallgher, J. Patrick, Jr. *risk management marketing company executive*
McClure, Walter F. *risk management marketing company executive*

Lake Forest
Eckert, Ralph John *insurance company executive*
Peterson, Donald Matthew *insurance company executive*

Long Grove
Mathis, David B. *insurance company executive*

Northbrook
Carl, John L. *insurance company executive*
Cruikshank, John W., III *life insurance underwriter*
Liddy, Edward M. *insurance company executive*
McCabe, Michael J. *insurance executive*
Pike, Robert William *insurance company executive, lawyer*
Saunders, Kenneth D. *insurance company executive, consultant, arbitrator*
Wilson, Rita P. *insurance company executive*
Wilson, Thomas Joseph *insurance company executive*
Young, R. James *insurance company executive*

Oak Brook
Davis, Thomas William *insurance company executive*
Muschler, Audrey Lorraine *insurance broker*

Peoria
Michael, Jonathan Edward *insurance company executive*

Rock Island
Lardner, Henry Petersen (Peter Lardner) *insurance company executive*

Skokie
Hedien, Wayne Evans *retired insurance company executive*

Springfield
Dodge, Edward John *retired insurance executive*
Simpson, William Arthur *insurance company executive*
Stooksbury, Walter Elbert *insurance company executive*

Wheaton
Hamilton, Robert Appleby, Jr. *insurance company executive*

INDIANA

Carmel
Chokel, Charles B. *insurance company executive*
Dick, Rollin Merle *insurance company executive*
Hagerty, Thomas M. *insurance executive*
Hilbert, Stephen C. *former insurance company executive*
Kilian, Thomas J. *insurance company executive*

Fishers
Christenson, Le Roy Howard *insurance consultant*

Fort Wayne
Clarke, Kenneth Stevens *insurance company executive*
Robertson, Richard Stuart *insurance holding company executive*
Rolland, Ian McKenzie *insurance executive, retired*

Greenwood
Daniel, Michael Edwin *insurance agency executive*

Indianapolis
Gaunce, Michael Paul *insurance company executive*
Glasscock, Larry Claborn *insurance company executive*
Husman, Catherine Bigot *insurance company executive, actuary*
Lytle, L(arry) Ben *insurance company executive, lawyer*
McCarthy, Harold Charles *retired insurance company executive*
McKinney, E. Kirk, Jr. *retired insurance company executive*
Norman, LaLander Stadig *insurance company executive*
Robinson, Larry Robert *insurance company executive*
Wolsiffer, Patricia Rae *retired insurance company executive*

Jasper
Fleck, Albert Henry, Jr. *retired insurance agency executive*

Merrillville
Collie, John, Jr. *insurance agent*

Pendleton
Kischuk, Richard Karl *insurance company executive*

IOWA

Council Bluffs
Nelson, H. H. Red *insurance company executive*

Des Moines
Brooks, Roger Kay *insurance company executive*
Drury, David J. *insurance company executive*
Ellis, Mary Louise Helgeson *retired insurance company executive, other: health services, consultant*
Gersie, Michael H. *insurance company executive*
Griswell, J. Barry *insurance company executive*
Kalainov, Sam Charles *insurance company executive*
Kelley, Bruce Gunn *insurance company executive, lawyer*
Williams, Carl Chanson *insurance company executive*

KANSAS

Eudora
Miller, David Groff *insurance agent*

Lenexa
Grant, W. Thomas, II *insurance company executive*

MARYLAND

Reisterstown
Gagel, Barbara Jean *health insurance administrator*

MICHIGAN

Caledonia
Antonini, Richard Lee *insurance executive*

Detroit
Whitmer, Richard E. *insurance company executive*

Grand Haven
Horning, Daniel D. *underwriter*

Grand Rapids
Woudstra, Frank Robert *insurance company executive*

Lansing
Arends, Herman Joseph *insurance company executive*

MINNESOTA

Arden Hills
Van Houten, James Forester *insurance company executive*

Minneapolis
Dubes, Michael John *insurance company executive*
Gandrud, Robert P. *retired fraternal insurance executive*
Mitchell, James Austin *insurance company executive*
Sourdiff, Gerald *retired insurance company executive*

Minnetonka
Rivet, Jeanine M. *health plan administrator*
Robbins, Orem Olford *insurance company executive*

Saint Paul
Bradley, Thomas A. *insurance company executive*
Liska, Paul J. *insurance company executive*
Senkler, Robert *insurance company executive*
Senkler, Robert L. *insurance company executive*

MISSOURI

Earth City
Buselmeier, Bernard Joseph *insurance company executive*

Kansas City
Lakin, Scott Bradley *insurance agent*
Malacarne, C. John *insurance company executive, lawyer*
Mc Gee, Joseph John, Jr. *former insurance company executive*

Saint Louis
Barber, John W. *insurance company executive*
Liddy, Richard A. *insurance company executive*
Winer, Warren James *insurance executive*

Springfield
Ostergren, Gregory Victor *insurance company executive*

NEBRASKA

Holdrege
Hendrickson, Bruce Carl *life insurance company executive*

Lincoln
Arth, Lawrence Joseph *insurance executive*

North Platte
Carlson, Randy Eugene *insurance executive*

Omaha
Bookout, John G. *insurance company executive*
Conley, Eugene Allen *retired insurance company executive*
Hamburg, Marc D. *insurance company executive*
Jay, Burton Dean *insurance actuary*
Jetter, Arthur Carl, Jr. *insurance company executive*
Mace, Georgia Mae *insurance company administrator*
Nauert, Peter William *insurance company executive*
Sigerson, Charles Willard, Jr. *insurance agency executive*
Strevey, Guy Donald *insurance company executive*
Sturgeon, John Ashley *insurance company executive*
Weekly, John William *insurance company executive*

NORTH CAROLINA

Chapel Hill
Karlin, Gary Lee *insurance executive*

NORTH DAKOTA

Grand Forks
Wogaman, George Elsworth *insurance executive, financial consultant*

OHIO

Cincinnati
Clark, James Norman *insurance executive*
Horrell, Karen Holley *insurance company executive, lawyer*
Runk, Fred J. *insurance company executive*

Cleveland
Lewis, Peter Benjamin *insurance company executive*

Columbus
Barnes, Galen R. *insurance company executive*
Duryee, Harold Taylor *insurance consultant*
Fullerton, Charles William *retired insurance company executive*
Gasper, Joseph J. *insurance company executive*
Jurgensen, W.G. *insurance company executive*
McFerson, Dimon Richard *insurance company executive*
Oakley, Robert Alan *insurance executive*
Sokol, John S. *insurance executive*
Sokol, Si *insurance company executive, director*
Woodward, Robert J., Jr. *insurance executive*

Hamilton
Marcum, Joseph LaRue *insurance company executive*

Mayfield
Forrester, W. Thomas, II *insurance company executive*

Rocky River
Riedthaler, William Allen *risk management professional*

Westfield Center
Blair, Robert Cary *insurance company executive*

PENNSYLVANIA

Philadelphia
Boscia, Jon Andrew *insurance company executive*

SOUTH CAROLINA

Hilton Head Island
Preble, Robert Curtis, Jr. *insurance executive*

SOUTH DAKOTA

Mitchell
Widman, Paul Joseph *insurance agent*

WISCONSIN

Appleton
Anderson, Ronald Gordon *insurance company executive*
Gilbert, John Oren *insurance company executive*
Rudolph, Carl J. *insurance company executive*

Kenosha
DeSimone, Alfred S. *insurance agent*

Madison
Anderson, David R. *insurance company executive*
Eldridge, James Francis *insurance executive*
Johnson, J. Brent *insurance company executive*
Larson, John David *insurance company executive, lawyer*
Pierce, Harvey R. *insurance company executive*
Spencer, C. Stanley *insurance company executive*

Merrill
Whitburn, Gerald *insurance company executive*

Milwaukee
Granoff, Mark Howard *insurance company executive*
Hefty, Thomas R. *insurance company executive*
Long, Gary *former insurance company executive*

Stevens Point
Schuh, Dale R. *insurance company executive*

CANADA

MANITOBA

Winnipeg
McFeetors, Raymond L. *insurance company executive*

ADDRESS UNPUBLISHED

Allison, Dianne J. Hall *retired insurance company official*
Becker, JoAnn Elizabeth *insurance company executive*
Blair, Cary *insurance company executive*
Buck, Earl Wayne *insurance investigator, motel owner*
Cooper, Charles Gordon *insurance consultant, former executive*
Gunderson, Richard L. *insurance company executive*
Kardos, Paul James *insurance company executive*
Lardakis, Moira Gambrill *insurance executive, lawyer*
Leatherdale, Douglas West *insurance company executive*
Maatman, Gerald Leonard *insurance company executive*
Olsen, George Edward *retired insurance executive*
Reynolds, John Francis *insurance company executive*
Strong, John David *insurance company executive*
Turner, John Gosney *insurance company executive, director*
Young, Larry Joe *insurance agent*

FINANCE: INVESTMENT SERVICES

UNITED STATES

CALIFORNIA

Irvine
Boris, James R. *investment company executive*

Palm Desert
Hook, John Burney *investment company executive*

FLORIDA

Boca Grande
Maguire, John Patrick *investment company executive*

Naples
Gulda, Edward James *business acquisitions executive*

ILLINOIS

Broadview
Smerz, Nancy *entrepreneur*

Burr Ridge
Clarke, Philip Ream, Jr. *retired investment banker*

Champaign
Spice, Dennis Dean *venture capitalist, consultant*

Chicago
Bergonia, Raymond David *venture capitalist*
Block, Philip Dee, III *investment counselor*
Brodsky, William J. *options exchange executive*
Case, Donni Marie *investment company executive*
Chaleff, Carl Thomas *brokerage house executive*
Cloonan, James Brian *investment executive*
Crown, James Schine *investment executive*
Gelber, Brian *commodities trader*
Greenberg, Steve *brokerage house executive*
Harris, Irving Brooks *investor, director*
Kelly, Arthur Lloyd *management and investment company executive*
Kuhn, Ryan Anthony *information industry investment banker*
Lewis, Charles A. *investment company executive*
Livingston, Homer J., Jr. *stock exchange executive*
Luthringshausen, Wayne *brokerage house executive*
McCausland, Thomas James, Jr. *brokerage house executive*
McConahey, Stephen George *retired securities company executive*
Melamed, Leo *investment company executive*
Miner, Thomas Hawley *international entrepreneur*
Nash, Donald Gene *commodity investigator*
Osborn, William A. *investment company executive*
Peacock, Christopher A. *investment company executive*
Pero, Perry R. *investment company executive*
Rasin, Rudolph Stephen *corporate executive*
Rosenberg, Sheli Z. *investment company executive*
Saranow, Mitchell Harris *investment banker, business executive*
Slansky, Jerry William *investment company executive*
Stearns, Neele Edward, Jr. *investment executive*
Steele, Michael A. *real estate investment/financial executive*
Stevens, Paul G., Jr. *brokerage house executive*
Towson, Thomas D. *securities trader*
Underwood, Robert Leigh *venture capitalist*
Waite, Dennis Vernon *investor relations consultant*
Weinberg, David B. *investor*
Weiner, Gerald Arne *stockbroker*
Weitzman, Robert Harold *investment company executive*
Wilhelm, David C. *investment company executive*

Williams, Daniel D. *investment company executive*
Williamson, Donna C. E. *investment company executive*
Wilmouth, Robert K. *commodities executive*
Woods, Robert Archer *investment counsel*

Deerfield
Howell, George Bedell *equity investing and managing executive*
Jordan, John W., II *holding company executive*

Highland Park
Uhlmann, Frederick Godfrey *commodity and securities broker*

Lake Forest
Young, Ronald Faris *commodity trader*

Naperville
Penisten, Gary Dean *entrepreneur*

Northbrook
Edelson, Ira J. *venture banker, trade finance executive*

Oak Brook
Kelly, Donald Philip *entrepreneur*

Oak Forest
Jashel, Larry Steven (L. Steven Rose) *entrepreneur, media consultant*

River Forest
Wirsching, Charles Philipp, Jr. *retired brokerage house executive, private investor*

Winnetka
Sick, William Norman, Jr. *venture capital company executive*

INDIANA

Carmel
Cuneo, Ngaire E. *corporate development executive*

Evansville
Brill, Alan Richard *entrepreneur*

Indianapolis
Cohen, Morton A. *venture capitalist*
Fritz, Cecil Morgan *investment company executive*

IOWA

Urbandale
Shoafstall, Earl Fred *entrepreneur, consultant*

KANSAS

Overland Park
Hunter, Robert Tyler *brokerage house executive*

Shawnee Mission
Morford, John A. *investment company executive*
Tucker, Keith A. *investment company executive*
Van Tuyl, Cecil L. *investment company executive*

MICHIGAN

Detroit
Mudge, Randal J. *investment company executive*
Olde, Ernest J. *investment company executive*

Farmington Hills
Ellmann, Sheila Frenkel *investment company executive*

Grand Blanc
Serra, Joe *investment company executive*

Oak Park
Novick, Marvin *investment company executive, former automotive supplier executive, accountant*

Trenton
Tang, Cyrus *investment company executive*

MINNESOTA

Minneapolis
Appel, John C. *investment company executive*
Buhrmaster, Robert C. *company executive*
Falker, John Richard *investment advisor*
Fauth, John J. *venture capitalist*
Gallagher, Gerald Raphael *venture capitalist*
Lindau, Philip *commodities trader*
Piper, Addison Lewis *securities executive*
Schreck, Robert *commodities trader*

Saint Paul
Eibensteiner, Ron *venture capitalist*

Stillwater
Horsch, Lawrence Leonard *venture capitalist, corporate revitalization executive*

Waubun
Christensen, Marvin Nelson *venture capitalist*

MISSOURI

Joplin
McReynolds, Allen, Jr. *retired investment company executive*

Kansas City
Braude, Michael *commodity exchange executive*
Latshaw, John *entrepreneur, director*

Stowers, James Evans, Jr. *investment company executive*

Lees Summit
Korschot, Benjamin Calvin *investment executive*

Saint Louis
Avis, Robert Grier *investment company executive, civil engineer*
Bachmann, John William *securities firm executive*
Bernstein, Donald Chester *brokerage company executive, lawyer*
Engelbreit, Mary *art licensing entrepreneur*
Foster, Scarlett Lee *investor relations executive*
Holway, George J. *holding company executive*
Walker, George Herbert, III *investment banking company executive, lawyer*

Springfield
O'Block, Robert *entrepreneur, publishing executive*

NEBRASKA

Lincoln
Laphen, James A. *investment company executive*

Omaha
Buffett, Warren Edward *entrepreneur*
Cross, W. Thomas *investment company executive*
Ricketts, John Joe *securities company executive*
Sokolof, Phil *industrialist, consumer advocate*

NEW JERSEY

Princeton
Gund, Gordon *venture capitalist, sports team executive*

NORTH DAKOTA

Grand Forks
Gjovig, Bruce Quentin *entrepreneur coach, consultant, entrepreneur*

OHIO

Alpha
James, Francis Edward, Jr. *investment counselor*

Cincinnati
James, George Barker, II *investment executive*
Lucke, Robert Vito *merger and acquisition executive*

Cleveland
Brentlinger, Paul Smith *venture capital executive*
Charnas, Michael (Mannie Charnas) *investment company executive*
O'Donnell, Thomas Michael *former brokerage firm executive*
Powlen, David Michael *investment company executive*
Shepard, Ivan Albert *securities and insurance broker*
Summers, William B. *brokerage house executive*
Summers, William B., Jr. *investment company executive*
Weinberg, Ronald Elliott *newspaper, retail and manufacturing executive*

Columbus
Barthelmas, Ned Kelton *investment and commercial real estate developer*
Pointer, Peter Leon *investment executive*

Galion
Cobey, Ralph *industrialist*

Lancaster
Hurley, Samuel Clay, III *investment management company executive*

WISCONSIN

Milwaukee
Kasten, G. Frederick, Jr. *investment company executive*
Schnoll, Howard Manuel *investment banking and managed asset consultant*

TERRITORIES OF THE UNITED STATES

VIRGIN ISLANDS

Saint Thomas
Hopper, Patrick M. *securities trader*

CANADA

MANITOBA

Winnipeg
Watchorn, William Ernest *venture capitalist*

ADDRESS UNPUBLISHED

Aurin, Robert James *entrepreneur*
Bowles, Barbara Landers *investment company executive*
Doherty, Charles Vincent *investment counsel executive*
Geissinger, Frederick Wallace *investment banking executive*
Gouletas, Evangeline *investment executive*
Hansen, Hal T. *retired investment company executive*
Knox, Lance Lethbridge *venture capital executive*
McNeill, Robert Patrick *investment counselor*
Sallen, Marvin Seymour *investment company executive*

GOVERNMENT: AGENCY ADMINISTRATION

UNITED STATES

DISTRICT OF COLUMBIA

Washington
Cole, Bruce Milan *Federal Agency Administrator, Art Historian*
Thompson, Tommy George *federal agency administrator, former governor*

ILLINOIS

Chicago
Bower, Glen Landis *state agency administrator, lawyer*
Casillas, Frank C. *former state agency administrator*
Hillard, Terry G. *protective services official*
Jones, Stephanie J. *federal agency administrator*
Kneir, Thomas J. *federal agency administrator*
Whigham, James L. *protectice services official*
Wilson, Richard Harold *government official*

Oak Brook
Garrigan, William Henry, III *firefighter, paramedic*

Peoria
Jibben, Laura Ann *state agency administrator*

Schaumburg
Spagnolo, Joseph A., Jr. *state agency administrator*

Springfield
Beverline, Jerry *state agency administrator*
Brown, Kirk *secretary of transportation*
Doyle, Rebecca Carlisle *state agency administrator*
Mogerman, Susan *state agency administrator*
Moore, Robert *protective services official*

INDIANA

Indianapolis
Boehm, Peggy *state agency administrator*
Carraway, Melvin J. *protective services official*
Feldman, Richard David *health commissioner*
Gerdes, Ralph Donald *fire safety consultant*
Masback, Craig *executive director United States track and field*
Pagac, Gerald J. *state agency administrator*
Phillips, Charles W. *state agency administrator*
Smith, Keith *protective services official*

La Porte
Hiler, John Patrick *former government official, former congressman, business executive*

IOWA

Des Moines
Bair, Gerald D. *state government official*
Brickman, Kenneth Alan *state lottery executive*
Cochran, Dale M. *state agency administrator*
Henry, Phylliss Jeanette *marshal*
Moulder, William H. *chief of police*

Iowa City
Atchison, Christopher George *public health director*

Treynor
Guttau, Michael K. *state agency administrator, banker*

KANSAS

Colby
Finley, Philip Bruce *retired state adjutant general*

Columbus
Brand, Grover Junior *retired state agricultural official*

Lawrence
Gerry, Martin Hughes, IV *federal agency administrator, lawyer*

Pratt
Hover, Gerald R. *state agency administrator*

Topeka
Parks, Blanche Cecile *public administrator*
Rock, Richard Rand, II *protective services official*
Tomkins, Andy *state commissioner education*

MICHIGAN

Detroit
Oliver, Jerry Alton *protective services official*

Lansing
Beardmore, Dorothy *state education official*
Stokes, Rodney *state agency administrator*
Wilbur, Kathleen *state agency administrator*

New Haven
Shaw, Charles Rusanda *government investigator*

Southfield
Gleichman, John Alan *safety and loss control executive*

MINNESOTA

Bloomington
Aljets, Curtis J. *federal agency administrator*

Saint Paul
Beers, Anne *protective services official*
Finney, William K. *police chief*
Morrissey, Bill *state agency administrator*
Wedl, Robert J. *state agency commissioner*
Wheelock, Pam *state finance department administrator*

MISSOURI

Jefferson City
Bartman, Robert E. *state education official*
Eiken, Doug K. *state agency administrator*
Saunders, John L. *state agency administrator*
Vadner, Gregory A. *state agency administrator*
Waters, Stephen Russell *state agency administrator*

Kansas City
Bartch, Floyd O. *police chief*
English, R(obert) Bradford *marshal*

Saint Louis
Behm, R. James *protective services official*
Henderson, Ronald *police chief*

Springfield
Gruhn, Robert Stephen *retired parole officer*

Troy
Burkemper, Sarah B. *state agency administrator*

NEBRASKA

Lincoln
Amack, Rex *state agency administrator*
Baird, Samuel P. *state finance director*
Kilgarin, Karen *state official, public relations consultant*

Omaha
Hansen, James Allen *state agency administrator*

Oneill
Hedren, Paul Leslie *national park administrator, historian*

NORTH DAKOTA

Bismarck
Dwelle, Terry *state agency administrator*
Johnson, Roger *state agency administrator*
Sanstead, Wayne Godfrey *state superintendent, former lieutenant governor*

OHIO

Cleveland
Jettke, Harry Jerome *retired government official*
Jones, Thomas Franklin *protective services official*

Columbus
Cicchino, Samuel *deputy marshal*
Gillmor, Karen Lako *state agency administrator, strategic planner*
Jackson, G. James *protective services official*
McInturff, Floyd M. *retired state agency administrator*

Cuyahoga Falls
Shane, Sandra Kuli *postal service administrator*

Dayton
Lowe, Ronald, Sr. *chief of police*

Montpelier
Deckrosh, Hazen Douglas *retired state agency educator and administrator*

Reynoldsburg
Dailey, Fred L. *state agency administrator*

Zanesville
O'Sullivan, Christine *retired executive director social service agency, consultant*

SOUTH DAKOTA

Pierre
Duncan, Dick *state agency administrator*
Healy, Bryce *state agency administrator*
Johnson, Curtis J. *state agency administrator*
Larson, Vern L. *state agency administrator*
Olson, Judith Mary Reedy *retired public information officer, former state senator*
Sahr, Bob *state agency administrator*

Sioux Falls
Swenson, Lyle W. *protective services official*

Wessington Springs
Burg, James Allen *state agency administrator, farmer*

VIRGINIA

Alexandria
Johnson, JoAnn Mardelle *federal agency administrator*

Bereuter, Douglas Kent *congressman*
Biggert, Judith Borg *congresswoman, lawyer*
Blagojevich, Rod R. *congressman*
Blunt, Roy D. *congressman*
Boehner, John A. *congressman*
Bond, Christopher Samuel (Kit Bond) *senator, lawyer*
Bonior, David Edward *congressman*
Boswell, Leonard L. *congressman*
Brown, Sherrod *congressman, former state official*
Brownback, Sam *senator*
Burton, Dan L. *congressman*
Buyer, Steve Earle *congressman, lawyer*
Camp, Dave *congressman*
Carnahan, Jean *senator*
Carson, Julia M. *congresswoman*
Chabot, Steven J. *congressman*
Clay, William Lacy, Jr. *congressman*
Conrad, Kent *senator*
Conyers, John, Jr. *congressman*
Costello, Jerry F., Jr. *congressman, former county official*
Crane, Philip Miller *congressman*
Daschle, Thomas Andrew *senator*
Dayton, Mark *senator*
DeWine, R. Michael *senator, lawyer*
Dingell, John David *congressman*
Dorgan, Byron Leslie *senator*
Durbin, Richard Joseph *senator*
Ehlers, Vernon James *congressman*
Emerson, Jo Ann *congresswoman*
Evans, Lane *congressman*
Feingold, Russell Dana *senator, lawyer*
Fitzgerald, Peter Gosselin *senator, lawyer*
Ganske, J. Greg *congressman, plastic surgeon*
Gephardt, Richard Andrew *congressman*
Gillmor, Paul E. *congressman, lawyer*
Grams, Rodney D. *former senator, former congressman*
Grassley, Charles Ernest *senator*
Graves, Sam *congressman, former state legislator*
Green, Mark Andrew *congressman, lawyer*
Gutierrez, Luis V. *congressman, elementary education educator*
Gutknecht, Gilbert William, Jr. *congressman, former state legislator, auctioneer*
Hagel, Charles *senator*
Hall, Tony P. *ambassador, former congressman*
Harkin, Thomas Richard *senator*
Hastert, Dennis (J. Dennis Hastert) *congressman*
Hill, Baron P. *congressman*
Hobson, David Lee *congressman, lawyer*
Hoekstra, Peter *congressman, manufacturing executive*
Hostettler, John N. *congressman*
Hulshof, Kenny *congressman*
Hyde, Henry John *congressman*
Jackson, Jesse L., Jr. *congressman*
Johnson, Timothy Peter *senator*
Johnson, Timothy Vincent *congressman*
Jones, Stephanie Tubbs *congresswoman, lawyer*
Kaptur, Marcia Carolyn *congresswoman*
Kennedy, Mark R. *congressman*
Kerns, Brian D. *congressman*
Kildee, Dale Edward *congressman*
Kilpatrick, Carolyn Cheeks *congresswoman*
Kind, Ron *congressman*
Kirk, Mark Steven *congressman*
Kleczka, Gerald D. *congressman*
Knollenberg, Joseph (Joe Knollenberg) *congressman*
Kohl, Herbert *senator, professional sports team executive*
Kucinich, Dennis J. *congressman*
LaHood H., Ray *congressman*
Latham, Tom *congressman*
LaTourette, Steven C. *congressman*
Leach, James Albert Smith *congressman*
Levin, Carl *senator*
Levin, Sander M. *congressman*
Lipinski, William Oliver *congressman*
Lugar, Richard Green *senator*
Luther, William P. *congressman*
Manzullo, Donald A *congressman, lawyer*
McCarthy, Karen P. *congresswoman, former state representative*
McCollum, Betty *congresswoman*
Moore, Dennis *congressman*
Moran, Jerry *congressman*
Nelson, E. Benjamin *senator, former governor, lawyer*
Ney, Robert W. *congressman*
Nussle, James Allen *congressman*
Oberstar, James L. *congressman*
Obey, David Ross *congressman*
Osborne, Tom *congressman, former college football coach*
Oxley, Michael Garver *congressman*
Pence, Mike *congressman*
Peterson, Collin C. *congressman*
Petri, Thomas Evert *congressman*
Phelps, David D. *congressman*
Pickering, Charles W., Jr. *congressman*
Pomeroy, Earl R. *congressman, former state insurance commissioner*
Porter, John Edward *former congressman*
Portman, Rob *congressman*
Pryce, Deborah D. *congresswoman*
Ramstad, Jim *congressman, lawyer*
Regula, Ralph *congressman, lawyer*
Rivers, Lynn N. *congresswoman*
Roberts, Charles Patrick (Pat Roberts) *senator*
Roemer, Timothy J. *congressman*
Rush, Bobby L. *congressman*
Ryan, Paul *congressman*
Ryun, Jim *congressman*
Sabo, Martin Olav *congressman*
Sawyer, Thomas C. *congressman*
Schakowsky, Janice *congresswoman*
Sensenbrenner, F(rank) James, Jr. *congressman*
Shimkus, John Mondy *congressman*
Skelton, Isaac Newton, IV (Ike Skelton) *congressman*
Smith, Nick *congressman, farmer*
Souder, Mark Edward *congressman*
Stabenow, Deborah Ann *senator, former congresswoman*
Stokes, Louis *former congressman, lawyer*
Strickland, Ted *congressman, clergyman, psychology educator, psychologist*
Stupak, Bart T. *congressman, lawyer*
Terry, Lee R. *congressman, lawyer*
Tiahrt, W. Todd *congressman, former state senator*
Tiberi, Pat *former state legislator, congressman*
Traficant, James A., Jr. *former congressman*
Upton, Frederick Stephen *congressman*
Visclosky, Peter John *congressman, lawyer*
Voinovich, George V. *senator, former mayor and governor*
Weller, Gerald C. *congressman*
Wellstone, Paul *senator*

ILLINOIS

Aurora
Etheredge, Forest DeRoyce *former state senator, former university administrator*

Belleville
Holbrook, Thomas Aldredge *state legislator*

Bloomington
Brady, William E. *state legislator*
Maitland, John W., Jr. *state legislator*

Blue Mound
Noland, N. Duane *state legislator*

Calumet City
Fantin, Arline Marie *state legislator*

Carbondale
Bost, Mike *state legislator*
Poshard, Glenn W. *former congressman*
Simon, Paul *former senator, educator, writer*

Champaign
Winkel, Richard J., Jr. *state legislator*

Chicago
Berman, Arthur Leonard *retired state senator*
Bugielski, Robert Joseph *state legislator*
Burke, Daniel J. *state legislator*
Burke, Edward Michael *alderman*
Capparelli, Ralph C. *state legislator*
Cohen, Ira *legislative staff member*
Colom, Vilma *alderman*
Dart, Thomas J. *state legislator*
Davis, Danny K. *congressman*
Dillard, Kirk Whitfield *state legislator, lawyer*
Doherty, Brian Gerard *alderman*
Dudycz, Walter W. *state legislator*
Feigenholtz, Sara *state legislator*
Garcia, Jesus G. *state legislator*
Giles, Calvin Lamont *state legislator*
Hendon, Ricky *state legislator*
Jones, Emil, Jr. *state legislator*
Kenner, Howard A. *state legislator*
Molaro, Robert S *state legislator, lawyer*
Moore, Joseph Arthur *alderman, lawyer*
Stern, Grace Mary *former state legislator*
Widmayer, Christopher A. *legislative staff member*

Collinsville
Hoffman, Jay C. *state legislator*

Crystal Lake
Skinner, Calvin L., Jr. *state legislator*

East Alton
Davis, Steve *state legislator*

East Moline
Jacobs, Denny *state legislator*

East Saint Louis
Clayborne, James F., Jr. *state legislator*
Younge, Wyvetter Hoover *state legislator*

Effingham
Hartke, Charles A. *state legislator*

Elgin
Hoeft, Douglas L. *state legislator*

Elmhurst
Biggins, Robert A. *state legislator*
Cronin, Dan *state legislator*

Galesburg
Hawkinson, Carl E. *state legislator*

Gilson
Moffitt, Donald L. *state legislator*

Greenville
Watson, Frank Charles *state legislator*

Hillside
Turner, John W. *state legislator*

Jacksonville
Findley, Paul *former congressman, author, educator*

Joliet
McGuire, John C. *state legislator*

La Grange
Lyons, Eileen *state legislator*

Lake Forest
Frederick, Virginia Fiester *state legislator*

Lincoln
Madigan, Robert A. *state legislator*

Lincolnwood
Carroll, Howard William *state senator, lawyer*

Macomb
Myers, Richard P. *state legislator*

Mahomet
Greene, Terry J. *legislative staff member*

Milan
Brunsvold, Joel Dean *state legislator, educator*

Mount Vernon
Jones, John O. *state legislator*
O'Daniel, William L. *state legislator*

Mount Zion
Curry, Julie A. *state legislator*

Naperville
Cowlishaw, Mary Lou *state legislator*

New Lenox
Wennlund, Larry *former state legislator, lawyer*

Northfield
Parker, Kathleen Kappel *state legislator*

Palos Hills
Zickus, Anne *state legislator*

Palos Park
O'Malley, Patrick J. *state legislator*

Peoria
Leitch, David R. *state legislator*

Quincy
Donahue, Laura Kent *state legislator*
Tenhouse, Art *state representative, farmer*

Rock Falls
Mitchell, Gerald Lee *state legislator*

Romeoville
Hassert, Brent *state legislator*

Springfield
Black, William B. *state legislator*
Boland, Michael Joseph *state legislator*
Bomke, Larry K. *state legislator*
Bowles, Evelyn Margaret *state legislator*
Currie, Barbara Flynn *state legislator*
Daniels, Lee Albert *state legislator*
Davis, Monique D. (Deon Davis) *state legislator*
Del Valle, Miguel *state legislator*
Demuzio, Vince Thomas *state legislator*
Erwin, Judy *state legislator*
Flowers, Mary E. *state legislator*
Geo-Karis, Adeline Jay *state legislator*
Granberg, Kurt *state legislator, lawyer*
Halvorson, Debbie DeFrancesco *state legislator*
Jones, Lovana S. *state legislator*
Jones, Shirley M. *state legislator*
Jones, Wendell E. *state legislator*
Karpiel, Doris Catherine *state legislator*
Klingler, Gwendolyn Walbolt *state representative*
Krause, Carolyn H. *state legislator, lawyer*
Lauzen, Christopher J. *state legislator*
Lightford, Kimberly A. *state legislator*
Link, Terry *state legislator*
Luechtefeld, David *state legislator*
Madigan, Lisa *state legislator*
Madigan, Michael Joseph *state legislator*
Mahar, William F., Jr. *state legislator*
Mitchell, Ned *state legislator*
Moore, Andrea S. *state legislator*
Mulligan, Rosemary Elizabeth *legislator*
Munoz, Antonio *state legislator*
Myers, Judith A. *state legislator*
Obama, Barack A. *state legislator*
Pankau, Carole *state legislator*
Parke, Terry Richard *state legislator*
Persico, Vincent Anthony *state legislator*
Peterson, William E. *state legislator*
Petka, Ed (Edward F.) *state legislator*
Philip, James (Pate Philip) *state legislator*
Pugh, Coy *state legislator*
Radogno, Christine *state legislator*
Rauschenberger, Steven J. *state legislator*
Ronen, Carol *state legislator*
Rutherford, Dan *state legislator*
Ryder, Tom *state legislator*
Santiago, Miguel A. *state legislator*
Saviano, Angelo *state legislator*
Schaffer, Jack *former state senator*
Schoenberg, Jeffrey M. *state legislator*
Shadid, George P. *state legislator*
Shaw, William *state legislator*
Sieben, Todd *state legislator*
Silverstein, Ira I. *state legislator*
Smith, Margaret *state legislator*
Smith, Michael Kent *state legislator*
Stephens, Ronald Earl *state legislator*
Stroger, Todd H. *state legislator*
Sullivan, Dave *state legislator*
Syverson, Dave *state legislator*
Trotter, Donne E. *state legislator, hospital administrator*
Turner, Arthur L. *state legislator*
Walsh, Lawrence M. *state legislator*
Weaver, Stanley B. *state senator*
Welch, Patrick Daniel *state legislator*
Woolard, Larry *state legislator*

Stockton
Lawfer, I. Ronald *state legislator*

Sycamore
Burzynski, James Bradley *state legislator*

West Chicago
Johnson, Thomas Lee *state legislator*

Westchester
Durkin, James B. *state legislator*
Walsh, Thomas James *state legislator*

Westmont
Bellock, Patricia Rigney *state legislator*

Wheaton
Roskam, Peter James *state legislator, lawyer*

INDIANA

Attica
Harrison, Joseph William *state legislator*

Bloomington
Kruzan, Mark R. *state legislator*

Chesterton
Ayres, Ralph Donald *state legislator*

Columbus
Garton, Robert Dean *state legislator*
Hayes, Robert E. *former state legislator*

Covington
Grubb, Floyd Dale *state legislator*

Crawfordsville
Brown, Timothy N. *state legislator*

Crown Point
Conlon, James Charles *former state legislator*

East Chicago
Harris, Earl L. *state legislator*

Elkhart
Mock, Dean R. *state legislator*

Evansville
Avery, Dennis Theodore *state legislator*
Lutz, Larry Edward *state legislator*

Fort Wayne
Alderman, Robert K. *state legislator*
Moses, Winfield Carroll, Jr. *state legislator, construction company executive*

French Lick
Denbo, Jerry L. *state legislator*

Gary
Borst, Lawrence Marion *state legislator*
Brown, Charlie *state representative*

Hartford City
Ford, David Clayton *state senator, lawyer*

Indianapolis
Antich, Rose Ann *state legislator*
Becker, Vaneta G. *state representative*
Behning, Robert W. *state legislator*
Blade, Mark J. *state legislator*
Bodiker, Richard William, Sr. *state legislator*
Bosma, Brian Charles *state legislator*
Bowser, Anita Olga *state legislator, education educator*
Breaux, Billie J. *state legislator*
Broden, John E. *state legislator*
Budak, Mary Kay *state legislator*
Clark, James Murray *state legislator*
Dickinson, Mae *state legislator*
Frizzell, David Nason *state legislator*
Gard, Beverly J. *state legislator*
Hershman, Brandt *state legislator*
Howard, Glenn L. *state legislator*
Hume, Lindel O. *state legislator*
Jackman, Robert N. *state legislator, veterinarian*
Jacobs, Andrew, Jr. *former congressman, educator*
Johnson, Steven R. *state legislator*
Kenley, Luke *state legislator*
Kittle, Jim, Jr. *state representative*
Klinker, Sheila Ann J. *state legislator, middle school educator*
Lanane, Timothy S. *state legislator, lawyer*
Landske, Dorothy Suzanne (Sue Landske) *state legislator*
Lawson, Connie *state legislator*
Leuck, Claire M. *state legislator*
Long, David C. *state legislator, lawyer*
Lubbers, Teresa S. *state legislator, public relations executive*
Marendt, Candace L. *state legislator*
Meeks, Charles B. *state legislator*
Merritt, James W., Jr. *state legislator, real estate developer*
Mills, Morris Hadley *state senator, farmer*
Mrvan, Frank, Jr. *state legislator*
Nugent, Johnny Wesley *state legislator, tractor company executive*
Paul, Allen E. *state legislator*
Porter, Gregory W. *state legislator*
Richardson, Kathy Kreag *state legislator*
Robertson, Paul Joseph *state legislator*
Rogers, Earline S. *state legislator*
Ruppel, William J. *state legislator*
Scholer, Sue Wyant *state legislator*
Server, Gregory Dale *state legislator, guidance counselor*
Simpson, Vi *state senator*
Sipes, Connie W. *state legislator, educator*
Skillman, Becky Sue *state legislator*
Smith, Samuel, Jr. *state legislator*
Steele, Brent E. *state legislator*
Stevenson, Dan Charles *state legislator*
Sturtz, W. Dale *state legislator*
Summers, Vanessa *state legislator*
Tabaczynski, Ron *state legislator*
Turner, Paul Eric *state legislator*
Villalpando, Jesse Michael *state legislator*
Washington, Cleophus (Cleo Washington) *state senator*
Waterman, John M. *state legislator*
Weatherwax, Thomas K. *state legislator*
Wheeler, Harold H. *state legislator, utility contractor*
Wolf, Katie Louise *state legislator*
Wyss, Thomas John *state legislator*
Young, Dean A. *state legislator*
Young, R. Michael *state legislator*
Young, Richard D. *state legislator*
Zakas, Joseph C. *state legislator*

Jeffersonville
Bottorff, James *state legislator*

Kokomo
Buck, James Russell *state legislator*

Lafayette
Alting, Ronnie Joe *state legislator, restaurateur*

Lagrange
Meeks, Robert L. *state legislator*

Lebanon
Willing, Katherine *former state legislator*

Macy
Friend, William C. *state legislator*

Madison
Lytle, Markt L. *state legislator*

Martinsville
Bray, Richard D. *state legislator*

Merrillville
Dobis, Chester F. *state legislator*

Mishawaka
Fry, Craig R. *state legislator*

Muncie
McIntosh, David M. *former congressman*
Munson, Bruce N. *state legislator*

New Albany
Cochran, William C. *state legislator*

Plymouth
Cook, Gary L. *state legislator*

Redkey
Liggett, Ronald David *state legislator*

Selma
Craycraft, Allie V., Jr. *state legislator*

Seymour
Bailey, William W. *state legislator, realtor*

South Bend
Bauer, Burnett Patrick *state legislator*
Dvorak, Michael A. *state legislator*

Uniondale
Espich, Jeffrey K. *state legislator*

Valparaiso
Alexa, William E. *state legislator*

Warsaw
Adams, Kent J. *state legislator*

IOWA

Ankeny
Chapman, Kathleen Halloran *state legislator, lawyer*

Cedar Rapids
Fiegen, Thomas L. *state legislator, lawyer, economics educator*

Clive
Kramer, Mary Elizabeth *state legislator, health services executive*

Davenport
Tinsman, Margaret Neir *state legislator*

Des Moines
Angelo, Jeff M. *state legislator*
Bartz, Merlin E. *state legislator*
Behn, Jerry *state legislator*
Black, Dennis H. *state legislator*
Boettger, Nancy J. *state legislator*
Bolkcom, Joe L. *state legislator*
Connolly, Mike W. *state legislator*
Dearden, Dick L. *state legislator*
Deluhery, Patrick John *state legislator*
Drake, Richard Francis *state legislator*
Dvorsky, Robert E. *state senator*
Fink, Bill A. *state legislator*
Flynn, Thomas L. (Tom Flynn) *state legislator*
Fraise, Eugene S. *state legislator*
Freeman, Mary Louise *state legislator*
Garman, Teresa Agnes *state legislator*
Gaskill, E. Thurman *state legislator*
Gronstal, Michael E. *state legislator*
Grundberg, Betty *state legislator, property manager*
Hammond, Johnie *state legislator*
Hansen, Steven D. *state legislator*
Harper, Patricia M. *retired state legislator*
Hedge, H. Kay *state senator*
Horn, Wally E. *state legislator*
Iverson, Stewart E., Jr. *state legislator*
Jensen, John W. *state legislator*
Judge, John *state legislator*
Kibbie, John *state legislator*
King, Steve *state legislator*
Lamberti, Jeff *state legislator, lawyer*
Larson, Chuck, Jr. *state representative*
Lundby, Mary A. *state legislator*
Maddox, O. Gene *state legislator, lawyer*
McKean, Andy *state legislator*
McKibben, Larry *state legislator, lawyer*
McLaren, Derryl *state legislator*
Miller, David *state legislator, lawyer*
Murphy, Patrick Joseph *state representative*
Redfern, Donald B. *state legislator, lawyer*
Rehberg, Kitty *state legislator*
Rife, Jack *state legislator*
Rittmer, Sheldon *state senator, farmer*
Rosenberg, Ralph *former state senator, lawyer, consultant, educator, foundation administrator*
Schrader, David Floyd *state legislator*
Schuerer, Neal *state legislator*
Sexton, Mike W. *state legislator*
Shearer, Mark Smith *state legislator*
Siegrist, Brent *state legislator*
Soukup, Betty A. *state legislator*
Szymoniak, Elaine Eisfelder *retired state senator*
Zieman, Lyle E. *state senator*

Steamboat Rock
Taylor, Ray *state senator*

Storm Lake
Eddie, Russell James *state legislator, sales executive*

West Des Moines
Churchill, Steven Wayne *former state legislator, marketing professional*

KANSAS

Arkansas City
Shriver, Joseph Duane *state legislator*

Atchison
Henry, Gerald T. *state legislator*

Bendena
Weiland, Galen Franklin *state legislator*

Brookville
Kejr, Joseph *former state legislator*

Clay Center
Braden, James Dale *former state legislator*

Clifton
Taddiken, Mark *state legislator*

Coffeyville
Garner, Jim D. *state legislator, lawyer*

Concordia
Freeborn, Joann Lee *state legislator, farmer, former educator*

Derby
Myers, Don V. *state legislator*

Emporia
Barnett, James A. *state legislator*

Great Bend
Edmonds, John *state legislator*

Greensburg
McKinney, Dennis *state legislator*

Haddam
Hardenburger, Janice *state legislator*

Harper
Alldritt, Richard *state legislator*

Herington
Weber, Shari *state legislator*

Holton
Hutchins, Becky J. *state legislator*

Hugoton
Morris, Stephen R. *state legislator*

Hutchinson
Kerr, David Mills *state legislator*
O'Neal, Michael Ralph *state legislator, lawyer*

Ingalls
Neufeld, Melvin J. *state legislator*

Inman
Downey, Christine *state legislator*

Junction City
Geringer, Gerald Gene *state legislator*

Kansas City
Haley, David *state legislator*
Henderson, Broderick *state legislator*
Jones, Sherman Jarvis *state senator*
Steineger, Chris *state legislator*

Lakin
Hayzlett, Gary K. *state legislator*

Lawrence
Ballard, Barbara W. *state legislator*
Brady, William Robert *former United States senator*
Winter, Winton Allen, Jr. *lawyer, state senator*

Lenexa
Parkinson, Mark Vincent *former state legislator, lawyer*

Louisburg
Vickrey, Jene *state legislator*

Manhattan
Glasscock, Kenton *state legislator*

Mcpherson
Emler, Jay Scott *senator*
Nichols, Richard Dale *former congressman, banker*
Steffes, Don Clarence *state senator*

Neodesha
Chronister, Rochelle Beach *former state legislator*

Olathe
O'Connor, Kay F. *state legislator*
Toplikar, John M. *state legislator*

Osage City
Humerickhouse, Joe D. *state legislator*

Overland Park
Kline, Phillip D. *state legislator, lawyer*
Vratil, John Logan *state legislator, lawyer*

Pittsburg
McKechnie, Ed *state legislator*

Prairie Village
Langworthy, Audrey Hansen *state legislator*

Roeland Park
Tomlinson, Robert (Bob Tomlinson) *state legislator*

Salina
Brungardt, Pete *state legislator*
Horst, Deena Louise *state legislator*

Shawnee
Jordan, Nick M. *state legislator, hotel, recreational facility executive*

Shawnee Mission
Lane, Al *state legislator*

Topeka
Allen, Barbara *state legislator*
Barone, James L. *state legislator*
Becker, Rich *state legislator*
Benlon, Lisa L. *state legislator*
Biggs, Donald *state legislator*
Bleeker, Laurie *state legislator*
Brownlee, Karin S. *state legislator*
Clark, Stan W. *state legislator*
Findley, Troy Ray *state legislator*
Flower, Joann *state legislator*
Gilbert, Ruby *state legislator*
Gilmore, Phyllis *state legislator*
Gilstrap, Mark *state legislator*
Gooch, U. L. *state legislator*
Goodwin, Greta Hall *state legislator*
Graeber, Clyde D. *former state legislator*
Heinemann, David J. *state legislator*
Hensley, Anthony M. *state legislator*
Howell, Andrew *state legislator*
Huelskamp, Tim *state legislator*
Jackson, David D. *state legislator*
Jenkins, Lynn M. *state legislator*
Kirk, Nancy A. *state legislator, nursing home administrator*
Lawrence, Barbara *state legislator*
Lee, Janis K. *state legislator*
Mays, M. Douglas *state legislator, financial consultant*
McClure, Laura *state legislator*
Nichols, Rocky *state representative, non-profit consultant*
Oleen, Lana *state legislator*
Pauls, Janice Long *state legislator*
Petty, Marge D. *state senator*
Powell, Anthony J. *state legislator, lawyer*
Powers, Bruce Theodore (Ted Powers) *state legislator*
Praeger, Sandy *state legislator*
Ruff, L. Candy *state legislator*
Salisbury, Alicia Laing *state senator*
Salmans, Larry D. *state legislator*
Saville, Pat *state senate official*
Schodorf, Jean *state legislator*
Spangler, Douglas Frank *state legislator*
Steinger, Chris *state legislator*
Stephens, Harry *state legislator*
Swenson, Dale *state legislator*
Tanner, Ralph M. *state legislator*
Thimesch, Daniel J. *state legislator*
Toelkes, Dixie E. *state legislator*
Tyson, Robert *state legislator*
Umbarger, Dwayne *state legislator*
Welshimer, Gwen R. *state legislator, real estate broker, appraiser*

Towanda
Corbin, David R. *state legislator*

Wamego
Pugh, Edward W. *state legislator*

Wichita
Dean, George R. *state legislator*
Donovan, Leslie D., Sr. *state legislator*
Feleciano, Paul, Jr. *state legislator*
Helgerson, Henry *state legislator*
Jennison, Robin L. *former state legislator, lobbyist*
Landwehr, Brenda *state legislator, financial executive*
Mayans, Carlos *state legislator*
Ott, Belva Joleen *former state legislator*
Pottorff, Jo Ann *state legislator*
Wagle, Susan *state legislator, small business owner*
Wells, Jonathan *state legislator*

MARYLAND

Bethesda
Metzenbaum, Howard Morton *former senator, consumer organization official*

MICHIGAN

Adrian
Berryman, James *state legislator*

Allendale
Jellema, Jon *state legislator, educator*

Big Rapids
Sederburg, William Albert *former state senator, educator*

Clio
Cherry, John D., Jr. *state legislator*

Detroit
Bennane, Michael J. *former state legislator*
Mahaffey, Maryann *councilwoman*
Stallworth, Alma Grace *former state legislator*

Farmington Hills
Dolan, Jan Clark *former state legislator*

Flint
Clack, Floyd *former state legislator*
Conroy, Joe *former state legislator*

Grandville
Voorhees, Harold J., Sr. *state legislator*

Grayling
Lowe, Allen *state legislator*

Grosse Ile
Palamara, Joseph *state legislator*

Huntington Woods
Gubow, David M. *state legislator*

Ironwood
Koivisto, Don *state legislator*

Jackson
Griffin, Michael J. *former state legislator*
Letarte, Clyde *state legislator*

Kalamazoo
Perricone, Charles *former state legislator*

Kentwood
DeLange, Walter J. *former state legislator*

Lansing
Bennett, Loren *state legislator*
Bouchard, Michael J. *state legislator*
Brater, Elizabeth *state legislator*
Brewer, Lingg *state legislator*
Bullard, Willis Clare, Jr. *state legislator*
Byl, William *state legislator*
Byrum, Dianne *state legislator, small business owner*
Cropsey, Alan Lee *state legislator, lawyer*
DeBeaussaert, Kenneth Joseph *state legislator*
DeGrow, Dan L. *state legislator*
DeHart, Eileen *state legislator*
Dingell, Christopher Dennis *state legislator*
Dunaskiss, Mat J. *state legislator*
Emerson, Robert *state legislator*
Emmons, Joanne *state legislator*
Gast, Harry T., Jr. *state legislator*
Geiger, Terry *state legislator*
Goschka, Michael John *state legislator*
Gougeon, Joel *state legislator*
Green, Mike *state legislator*
Gustafson, Dan *state legislator*
Hammerstrom, Beverly Swoish *state legislator*
Hanley, Michael Joseph *state legislator*
Hart, George Zaven *state legislator*
Hoffman, Philip Edward *state legislator*
Kelly, Thomas *state legislator*
LaForge, Edward *state legislator*
Law, Gerald H. *state legislator*
Leland, Burton *state legislator*
Llewellyn, John T. *state legislator*
McCotter, Thaddeus G. *state legislator*
McManus, George Alvin, Jr. *state legislator, cherry farmer*
Miller, Arthur J., Jr. *state legislator*
Murphy, Raymond *state legislator*
North, Walter *state legislator*
Owen, Lynn *state legislator*
Price, Hubert *state legislator*
Profit, Kirk A. *former state legislator*
Prusi, Michael *state legislator*
Rogers, Mike *congressman*
Schuette, Bill *state legislator*
Schwarz, John J.H. *state legislator, surgeon*
Scott, Martha G. *state legislator*
Shugars, Dale L. *state legislator*
Sikkema, Kenneth R. *state legislator*
Smith, Virgil Clark *state legislator*
Steil, Glenn *state legislator*
Stille, Leon E. *state legislator*
Van Regenmorter, William *state legislator*
Vaughn, Jackie, III *state legislator*
Young, Joseph Floyd, Jr. *state legislator*

Litchfield
Nye, Michael Earl *former state legislator*

Marysville
London, Terry *former state legislator*

Mount Clemens
Rocca, Sue *state legislator*

Mount Pleasant
Randall, Gary Lee *former state legislator*

Paw Paw
Middaugh, James (Mike) *former state legislator*

Rochester
Crissman, Penny M. *state legislator*
Peters, Gary Charles *state legislator, lawyer, educator*

Saint Clair Shores
Yokich, Tracey A. *former state legislator*

Sturgis
Oxender, Glenn S. *state legislator*

Washington
Jaye, Dave *state legislator*

MINNESOTA

Apple Valley
Knutson, David Lee *state legislator, lawyer*

Austin
Leighton, Robert Joseph *state legislator*

Bloomington
Belanger, William V., Jr. *state legislator*

Brainerd
Samuelson, Donald B. *state legislator*

Brandon
Bettermann, Hilda *state legislator*

Burnsville
McElroy, Dan *state legislator*

Chisholm
Janezich, Jerry R. *state legislator, small business owner*

Chokio
Berg, Charles A. *state legislator*

Coon Rapids
Foley, Leo Thomas *state legislator, lawyer*

Crookston
Lieder, Bernard L. *state legislator, civil engineer*

Dassel
Ness, Robert *state legislator, education consultant*

Duluth
Huntley, Thomas *state legislator, science educator*
Solon, Sam George *state legislator*

Eagan
Pawlenty, Tim *state legislator*

Eden Prairie
Paulsen, Erik *state legislator*

Erskine
Moe, Roger Deane *state legislator, secondary education educator*

Fairmont
Fowler, Chuck *state legislator*

Fort Snelling
Kimball, Marc Kennedy *senatorial staff*

Glyndon
Langseth, Keith *state legislator, farmer*

Hawley
Dauner, Marvin K. *former state legislator*

Ivanhoe
Mulder, Richard Dean *state legislator*

Lakeland
Larsen, Peg *state legislator*

Madison
Peterson, Doug *state legislator*

Mankato
Dorn, John *state legislator*
Hottinger, John Creighton *state legislator, lawyer*

Maple Grove
Girard, Jim *former state legislator*
Limmer, Warren E. *state legislator, real estate broker*

Minneapolis
Greenfield, Lee *state legislator*
Mickelson, Stacey *state legislator*
Oliver, Edward Carl *state legislator, retired investment executive*
Pogemiller, Lawrence J. *state legislator*
Reichgott Junge, Ember D. *former state senator, lawyer, writer, broadcast analyst*

Montevideo
Minge, David *former congressman, lawyer, law educator*

Newport
Marko, Sharon *state legislator*

Northfield
Neuville, Thomas M. *state legislator, lawyer*

Ottertail
Anderson, Bob *state legislator, business executive*

Pine City
Swenson, Douglas *state legislator*

Preston
Davids, Gregory M. *state legislator*
Scheevel, Kenric James *state legislator*

Red Wing
Dempsey, Jerry *state legislator*

Rochester
Frerichs, Donald L. *retired state legislator*

Rogers
Lindner, Arlon *state legislator*

Rush City
Jennings, Loren G. *state legislator, business owner*

Saint Joseph
Dehler, Steve *state legislator*

Saint Louis Park
Mondale, Theodore Adams *former state senator*

Saint Paul
Abrams, Ronald Lawrence *state legislator*
Anderson, Ellen Ruth *state legislator*
Bachmann, Michele *state legislator*
Bakk, Thomas *state legislator*
Beckman, Tracy *state legislator*
Berglin, Linda *state legislator*
Betzold, Donald Richard *state legislator*
Bishop, David T. *state legislator*
Bradley, Fran *state legislator*
Carlson, Lyndon Richard Selvig *state legislator, educator*
Chaudhary, Satveer *state senator*
Clark, Karen *state legislator*
Cohen, Richard J. *state legislator*
Day, Richard H. *state legislator*
Dille, Stephen Everett *state legislator, farmer, veterinarian*
Erhardt, Ron *state legislator*
Erlandson, Mike *legislative staff member*
Fischbach, Michelle L. *state legislator*
Flynn, Carol *state legislator*
Frederickson, Dennis Russel *state legislator, farmer*
Goodno, Kevin P. *state legislator*
Greiling, Mindy *state legislator*
Hackbarth, Tom *former state legislator*
Hanson, Paula E. *state legislator*
Harder, Elaine Rene *state legislator*
Hasskamp, Kris *state legislator*
Hausman, Alice *state legislator*
Higgins, Linda I. *state legislator*
Hugoson, Gene *state legislator, farmer*
Jacobs, Joel *former state legislator, municipal official*
Jaros, Mike *state legislator, administrative assistant*
Johnson, Alice M. *state legislator*
Johnson, Dave *state legislator*
Kahn, Phyllis *state legislator*
Kelley, Steve *state legislator, lawyer*
Kelly, Randy C. *state legislator*
Kierlin, Bob *state legislator*
Kiscaden, Sheila M. *state legislator*
Kleis, David *state legislator*
Krentz, Jane *state legislator, elementary education educator*
Krinkie, Philip B. *state legislator, business executive*
Larson, Cal *state legislator*
Leppik, Margaret White *state legislator*
Lesewski, Arlene *state legislator, insurance agent*
Lessard, Robert Bernard *state legislator, recreational facility executive*
Lourey, Becky J. *state legislator*
Mariani, Carlos *state legislator*
Marty, John *state legislator, writer*
McGuire, Mary Jo *state legislator*
Milbert, Robert P. *state legislator*
Molnau, Carol *state legislator*
Murphy, Mary C. *state legislator*
Murphy, Steven Leslie *state legislator, utilities company official*
Novak, Steven G. *state legislator*
Olson, Edgar *state legislator*
Olson, Gen *state legislator*
Olson, Mark *state legislator*
Opatz, Joe *state legislator*
Orfield, Myron Willard, Jr. *state legislator, educator*
Osskopp, Mike *state legislator*
Osthoff, Tom *state legislator*
Otremba, Ken *state legislator*
Ourada, Mark *state legislator*
Ozment, Dennis Dean *state legislator*
Pappas, Sandra Lee *state legislator*
Pariseau, Patricia *state legislator*
Pellow, Richard Maurice *former state legislator*
Pelowski, Gene P., Jr. *state legislator*
Piper, Pat Kathryn *state senator*
Price, Leonard Russell (Len Price) *state legislator*
Ranum, Jane Barnhardt *state senator, lawyer*
Rest, Ann H. *state legislator*
Rhodes, Jim *state legislator*
Ring, Twyla L. *state legislator, newspaper editor*
Riveness, Phillip J. *city official, former state legislator*
Robertson, Martha Rappaport *state legislator, consultant*
Robling, Claire A. *state legislator*
Rostberg, Jim *state legislator*
Rukavina, Tom *state legislator*
Runbeck, Linda C. *state legislator*
Rydell, Catherine M. *former state legislator*
Sabo, Julie Ann *state legislator*
Sams, Dallas C. *state legislator*
Scheid, Linda J. *state legislator*
Schumacher, Leslie *state legislator, artist*
Schwab, Grace S. *state legislator*
Seagren, Alice *state legislator*
Skoglund, Wesley John *state legislator*
Solberg, Loren Albin *state legislator, secondary education educator*
Spear, Allan Henry *former state senator, historian, educator*
Stevens, Dan *state legislator*
Terwilliger, Roy W. *state legislator*
Trimble, Steve *state legislator*
Tunheim, James Ronald *state legislator, farmer*
Van Dellen, H. Todd *state legislator*
Wejcman, Linda *state legislator*
Wenzel, Stephen G. *state legislator*
Wiener, Deanna *state legislator*
Wiger, Charles W. *state legislator*
Winter, Theodore *state legislator*
Wolf, Ken *state legislator*
Ziegler, Donald N. *state senator*

Shakopee
Kelso, Becky *former state legislator*

South Saint Paul
Metzen, James P. *state legislator, banker*

Stillwater
Holsten, Mark *state legislator*
Laidig, Gary W. *state legislator*

Thief River Falls
Stumpf, LeRoy A. *state legislator*

Tower
Johnson, Douglas J. *state legislator, secondary education counselor*

Tracy
Vickerman, Jim *state legislator*

Walters
Kalis, Henry J. *state legislator, farmer*

Waseca
Worke, Gary D. *former state legislator*

White Bear Lake
Chandler, Kevin *former state legislator*
Mares, Harry *state legislator*

Willmar
Johnson, Dean Elton *state legislator, Lutheran pastor*

MISSOURI

Center
Leake, Sam *former state legislator, farmer*

Chesterfield
Hale, David Clovis *former state representative*

Clayton
Klarich, David John *state legislator, lawyer*

Edgar Springs
McBride, Jerry E. *state legislator*

Eminence
Staples, Danny Lew *state legislator*

Eureka
May, Brian Henry *state legislator*

Festus
Stoll, Steve M. *state legislator*

Florissant
Donovan, Laurie B. *former state legislator*
Schneider, John Durbin *state legislator*
Stokan, Lana J. Ladd *state legislator*

Gerald
Froelker, Jim *state legislator*

Half Way
Legan, Kenneth *state legislator, farmer*

Hannibal
Clayton, Robert Morrison, III *state legislator*

Harrisonville
Hartzler, Vicky J. *state legislator*

Hazelwood
O'Connor, Patrick J. *state legislator*

High Ridge
Alter, William *state legislator*

Huggins
Lybyer, Mike Joseph *former state legislator, farmer*

Independence
Franklin, J. Richard *state representative*

Jefferson City
Backer, Gracia Yancey *state legislator*
Barnett, Rex *state legislator*
Bartelsmeyer, Linda *state legislator*
Bentley, Roseann *state legislator, educational consultant*
Bland, Mary Groves *state legislator*
Boatright, Matt *state legislator*
Bray, Joan *state legislator*
Carter, Paula J. *state legislator*
Caskey, Harold Leroy *state legislator*
Copeland, Fred E. *state legislator*
Days, Rita Denise *state legislator*
Goode, Wayne *state legislator*
Graham, James *state legislator*
Green, Timothy P. *state legislator*
Griesheimer, John Elmer *state representative*
Hagan-Harrell, Mary M. *state legislator*
Harlan, Timothy *state legislator*
Hartzler, Ed *state legislator*
Hosmer, Craig William *state legislator*
Kasten, Mary Alice C. *state legislator*
Kauffman, Sandra Daley *state legislator*
Kelly, Glenda Marie *state legislator*
Koller, Don *state legislator*
Kreider, Jim *state legislator, farmer*
Linton, William Carl *state legislator*
Lograsso, Don *state legislator, lawyer*
Long, Elizabeth L. *state legislator, small business owner*
Luetkenhaus, William Joseph *state legislator*
Marble, Gary *state legislator*
Mays, Carol Jean *state legislator*
McClelland, Emma L. *state legislator*
McLuckie, Steve *state legislator*
Murray, Connie Wible *state official, former state legislator*
Ostmann, Cindy *state legislator*
Pouche, Fredrick *state legislator*
Prost, Donald *former state legislator*
Reynolds, David L. *state legislator*
Richardson, Mark *state legislator*
Ridgeway, Luann *state legislator*
Rizzo, Henry *state legislator*
Robirds, Estel *state legislator*
Rohrbach, Larry *state legislator*
Ross, Carson *state legislator*
Russell, John Thomas *state legislator*
Sallee, Mary Lou *state legislator*
Scheve, May E. *state legislator*
Schilling, Mike *state legislator*
Schwab, David *state legislator*
Scott, Delbert Lee *state legislator*
Scott, John E. *state legislator*
Secrest, Patricia K. *state legislator*
Shelton, O. L. *state legislator*
Sims, Betty *state legislator*
Skaggs, Bill *state legislator*
Smith, Philip G. *state legislator*
Surface, Chuck L. *state legislator*
Tate, Phil *state legislator*
Van Zandt, Tim *state legislator*
Vogel, Carl M. *state legislator*
Westfall, Morris *state legislator*
Wiggins, Gary *state legislator*
Wiggins, Harry *state legislator, lawyer*
Williams, Deleta *state legislator*
Williams, Marilyn *state legislator*

Joplin
Burton, Gary L. *state legislator*
Singleton, Marvin Ayers *state legislator, otolaryngologist*

Kansas City
Boucher, Bill *state legislator*
DePasco, Ronnie Nick *state legislator*
Lyon, Bob *state legislator*

Kirkwood
Gibbons, Michael Randolph *state legislator, lawyer*

Lees Summit
Kenney, William Patrick *state legislator*

Lemay
Treadway, Joseph L. *state legislator*

Liberty
Quick, Edward E. *state legislator*

O'Fallon
Kissell, Don R. *state legislator*

Perryville
Naeger, Patrick A. *state legislator*

Platte City
Witt, Gary Dean *former state legislator*

Potosi
Crump, Wayne F. *state legislator*

Reeds Spring
Childers, L. Doyle *state legislator*

Rolla
Steelman, Sarah *state legislator*

Saint Ann
Foley, James M. *state legislator*

Saint Charles
Ehlmann, Steven E. *state legislator*

Saint Joseph
Shields, Charles W. *state legislator*

Saint Louis
Auer, Ron *state legislator*
Chrismer, Rich *state legislator*
Davis, Dorathea *state legislator*
Dougherty, J. Patrick *state legislator*
Ford, Louis H. *state legislator*
Goward, Russell *former state legislator*
Levin, David L. *state legislator*
Mueller, Walt *state legislator*
Murphy, Jim *state legislator*
Murrey, Dana L. *state legislator*
O'Toole, James *state legislator*
Talent, James M. *former congressman, lawyer*
Troupe, Charles Quincy *state legislator*
Yeckel, Anita T. *state legislator*

Sedalia
Mathewson, James L. *state legislator*

Springfield
Hancock, Mel *former congressman*

Union
Overschmidt, Francis S. *state legislator*

Unionville
Summers, Don *state legislator*

Versailles
Pryor, Chuck *state legislator*

Warrenton
Nordwald, Charles *state legislator*

Webb City
Elliott, Mark T. *state legislator*

West Plains
Garnett, Jess *former state legislator*

NEBRASKA

Bellevue
Hartnett, D. Paul *state legislator*

Hastings
Bohlke, Ardyce *state legislator*

Hebron
Coordsen, George *state legislator*

Lincoln
Aguilar, Raymond M. *state legislator*
Baker, Thomas C. *state legislator*
Beutler, Christopher John *state legislator*
Bourne, Patrick J. *state legislator*
Bromm, Curt *state legislator*
Brown, Pam *state legislator*
Bruning, Jon Cumberland *state legislator*
Byars, Dennis M. *state legislator*
Chambers, Ernest *state legislator*
Connealy, Matt J. *state legislator*
Crosby, LaVon Kehoe Stuart *state legislator, civic leader*
Cudaback, Jim D. *state legislator*
Cunningham, Douglas D. *state legislator*
Dickey, L. Robert *state senator*
Dierks, Merton L. *state legislator*
Engel, Leo Patrick *state legislator*
Erdman, Philip *state legislator, farmer*
Exon, J(ohn) James *former senator*
Foley, Mike *state legislator*
Hilgert, John A. *state legislator*
Janssen, Ramon E. *state legislator*
Jones, James E. *state legislator*
Kramer, David J. *state representative*
Kremer, Robert M. *state legislator*
Kristensen, Douglas Allan *former state legislator*
Kruse, Lowen V. *state legislator*
Landis, David Morrison *state legislator*
Lynch, Daniel C. *state legislator*
Maxwell, Chip *state legislature*
Pedersen, Dwite A. *state legislator*
Pederson, Donald W. *state legislature*
Preister, Donald George *state legislator, greeting card manufacturer*
Price, Marian L. *state legislator*
Quandahl, Mark C. *state legislator, lawyer*
Raikes, Ronald E. *state legislator*
Redfield, Pamela A. *state legislator*
Robak, Jennie *state legislator*
Schimek, DiAnna Ruth Rebman *state legislator*
Schmitt, Jerry *state legislator*
Smith, Adrian M. *state legislator, real estate agent*
Stuhr, Elaine Ruth *state legislator*
Suttle, Deborah S. *state legislator*
Thompson, Nancy P. *state legislator*
Tyson, Eugene *state legislator*
Vrtiska, Floyd P. *state legislator*
Wesely, Donald Raymond *state senator*
Wickersham, William R. *state legislator*
Will, Eric John *state senator*
Witek, Kate *state senator, trucking company executive*
Withem, Ronald E. *state senator, trade association executive*

Omaha
Brashear, Kermit Allen *state legislator, lawyer*
Lindsay, John Conal *state legislator*

Plattsmouth
Wehrbein, Roger Ralph *state legislator*

NORTH DAKOTA

Arnegard
Drovdal, David (Skip Drovdal) *state legislator*

Ashley
Kretschmar, William Edward *state legislator, lawyer*

Belcourt
Bercier, Dennis *state legislator*

Bismarck
Boucher, Merle *state legislator*
Clayburgh, Richard Scott *state tax commissioner*
Delzer, Jeff W. *state legislator*

Dever, Dick *state legislator*
Freier, Tom D. *state legislator*
Goetz, William G. *state legislator*
Gulleson, Pam *state legislator*
Heigaard, William Steven *state senator*
Kelsch, RaeAnn *state legislator*
Kilzer, Ralph *state legislator*
Mutzenberger, Marv *state legislator*
Nelson, Carolyn *state legislator*
O'Connell, David Paul *state legislator*
Poolman, Jim *state legislator*
Price, Clara Sue *state legislator*
Robinson, Larry J. *state legislator*
Sand, Harvey *state legislator*
Sandvig, Sally *state legislator*
Schmidt, Arlo E. *state legislator*
Schobinger, Randy Arthur *state legislator*
Solberg, Kenneth R. *state legislator*
Stenehjem, Bob *state legislator*
Svedjan, Ken *state legislator*
Sveen, Gerald O. *state legislator*
Thoreson, Laurel *state legislator*
Tomac, Steven Wayne *state legislator, farmer*
Traynor, Daniel M. *state representative*
Urlacher, Herbert *state legislator*

Blanchard
Aarsvold, Ole *state legislator*

Bowman
Bowman, Bill *state legislator*
Kempenich, Keith *state legislator*

Braddock
Naaden, Pete *former state legislator*

Casselton
Nelson, Gary J. *state legislator*

Cavalier
Trenbeath, Thomas L. *state legislator, lawyer*

Center
Mahoney, John Jeremy *state legislator*

Crosby
Andrist, John M. *senator*

Devils Lake
Kunkel, Richard W. *state legislator*
Traynor, John Thomas, Jr. *state legislator, lawyer*

Dickinson
Wald, Francis John *state legislator*
Wardner, Rich *state legislator*

Dunn Center
Brown, Grant Claude *retired state legislator*

Edgeley
Schimke, Dennis J. *former state legislator*

Fargo
Berg, Rick Alan *state legislator, real estate investor*
Bernstein, LeRoy G. *state legislator*
Dorso, John *state legislator*
Fischer, Tom *state legislator*
Flakoll, Timothy John *state legislator, animal scientist*
Gorman, Stephen Thomas *former state legislator*
Grindberg, Tony *state legislator*
Lee, Judith *state legislator*
Mathern, Deb *state legislator*
Mathern, Tim *state legislator*
Tennefos, Jens Junior *retired state senator*

Fessenden
Klein, Jerry *state legislator*
Streibel, Bryce *state senator*

Fullerton
Kelsh, Jerome *state legislator*

Grafton
Gorder, William E. *state legislator*
Tallackson, Harvey Dean *state legislator, real estate and insurance salesman*

Grand Forks
Christenson, Linda *state legislator*
Delmore, Lois M. *state legislator*
DeMers, Judy Lee *former state legislator, university dean*
Espegard, Duaine C. *state legislator*
Holmberg, Raymon E. *state legislator*
Nottestad, Darrell *state legislator*
Polovitz, Michael *state legislator*
Warnke, Amy Nicholle *state legislator*

Hankinson
Heitkamp, Joel C. *state legislator*

Hazen
Christmann, Randel Darvin *state legislator*
Galvin, Pat G. *state legislator*

Hope
Kroeplin, Kenneth *state legislator*

Jamestown
Hanson, Lyle *state legislator*
Nething, David E. *state legislator*
Wanzek, Terry Marvin *state legislator*

Kenmare
Froseth, Glen *state legislator*

Larimore
Mutch, Duane *state legislator*

Lehr
Erbele, Robert S. *state legislator*

Leonard
Belter, Wesley R. *state legislator*

Lidgerwood
Grumbo, Howard *state legislator*

Lisbon
Huether, Robert *state legislator*

Mandan
Boehm, James *state legislator*
Coats, James O. *state legislator*
Cook, Dwight C. *state legislator*

Minnewaukan
Every, Michael A. *state legislator*
Thompson, Vern *state senator*

Minot
Klein, Matthew M. *state legislator*
Krebsbach, Karen K. *state legislator*
Redlin, Rolland W. *state legislator*
Timm, Mike *state legislator*
Tollefson, Ben C. *state legislator, retired utility sales manager*
Watne, Darlene Claire *state legislator*
Wentz, Janet Marie *state legislator*

Palermo
Kinnoin, Meyer D. *state legislator*
Nichols, Ronald *state legislator*

Ray
Torgerson, Jim *state legislator*

Regent
Krauter, Aaron Joseph *state legislator, farmer*

Towner
Gunter, G. Jane *state legislator*

Underwood
Freborg, Layton W. *state legislator*

Wahpeton
Thane, Russell T. *state legislator*

Williston
Byerly, Rex R. *state legislator*
Lyson, Stanley W. *state legialator*
Rennerfeldt, Earl Ronald *state legislator, farmer, rancher*
Yockim, James Craig *state senator*

OHIO

Akron
Ray, Roy Lee *state legislator, public finance consultant*

Andover
Boggs, Ross A., Jr. *former state legislator, dairy farmer*

Aurora
Herington, Leigh Ellsworth *state legislator, lawyer*

Avon
Bender, John R. *retired state legislator*

Bourneville
Shoemaker, Michael C. *state legislator*

Bowling Green
Gardner, Randall *state legislator, realtor*

Brookpark
Colonna, Rocco J. *state legislator*

Canfield
Gerberry, Ronald Vincent *state legislator*

Cincinnati
Blessing, Louis W., Jr. *state legislator, lawyer*
Finan, Richard H. *state legislator, lawyer*
Luebbers, Jerome F. *state legislator*
Van Vyven, Dale Nulsen *state legislator*

Cleveland
Oakar, Mary Rose *former congresswoman*
Pringle, Barbara Carroll *state legislator*
Suster, Ronald *judge, former state legislator*

Columbus
Armbruster, Jeffry J. *state legislator*
Austria, Steve *state legislator*
Beatty, Otto, Jr. *former state legislator, lawyer*
Benjamin, Ann Womer *state legislator*
Brady, Daniel R. *state legislator*
Britton, Sam *state legislator*
Davidson, Jo Ann *former state legislator*
DiDonato, Gregory L. *state legislator*
Drake, Grace L. *retired state senator, cultural organization administrator*
Espy, Ben *state legislator, lawyer*
Ferderber, June H. *state legislator*
Fingerhut, Eric D. *state legislator, former congressman, lawyer*
Furney, Linda Jeanne *state legislator*
Gardner, Robert A. *state legislator*
Glenn, John Herschel, Jr. *former senator*
Grendell, Diane V. *state legislator, lawyer, nurse*
Hagan, Robert F. *state legislator*
Hartley, David *state legislator, lawyer*
Hollister, Nancy *state legislator*
Hottinger, Jay *state legislator*
Johnson, Bruce E. *state legislator*
Kearns, Merle Grace *state representative*
Krebs, Eugene Kehm, II *state legislator*
Latta, Robert E. *state representative*
Lawrence, Joan Wipf *former state legislator*
Mallory, Mark L. *state legislator, librarian*
McLin, Rhine Lana *state legislator, funeral service executive, educator*
Mead, Priscilla *state legislator*
Mottley, James Donald *state legislator, lawyer*
Oelslager, W. Scott *state legislator*
Prentiss, C. J. *state legislator*
Roberts, Thomas Michael *state legislator*
Ryan, Timothy *state legislator*
Schuck, William *state legislator*
Spada, Robert F. *state legislator*
Sutton, Betty *state legislator*
Sykes, Vernon L. *state legislator*
Taylor, William *state legislator*
Terwilleger, George E. *state legislator*
Thomas, E.J. *state legislator*
Verich, Michael Gregory *state legislator*
Vesper, Rose *state legislator*
Wachtman, Lynn R. *state legislator*
Wachtmann, Lynn R. *state legislator*
Watts, Eugene J. *state legislator*
White, Doug *state legislator*
Winkler, Cheryl J. *state legislator*

Dayton
Corbin, Robert L. *state legislator*
Reid, Marilyn Joanne *state legislator, lawyer*

Girard
Latell, Anthony A., Jr. *state legislator*

Greenville
Buchy, Jim *state legislator, packing company executive*

Hamilton
Fox, Michael *former state legislator, underwriting consultant*

Hillsboro
Snyder, Harry Cooper *retired state senator*

Jefferson
Boggs, Robert J. *former state senator*

Kettering
Horn, Charles F. *state senator, lawyer, electrical engineer*

Lima
Cupp, Robert Richard *state senator, attorney*

Maumee
Olman, Lynn *state legislator*

New Philadelphia
Metzger, Kerry R. *state legislator*

Oak Harbor
Opfer, Darrell Williams *state representative, educator*

Painesville
Sines, Raymond E. *former state legislator*

Saint Clairsville
Carnes, James Edward *state legislator*

Swanton
Hodges, Richard *former state legislator*

Toledo
Greenwood, Tim *former state legislator, lawyer*

Urbana
Jordan, James D. (Jim) *state legislator*

Wapakoneta
Brading, Charles Richard *state representative*

Willowick
Troy, Daniel Patrick *former state legislator, county official*

Wooster
Amstutz, Ronald *state legislator*

SOUTH CAROLINA

Mc Cormick
Clayton, Verna Lewis *retired state legislator*

SOUTH DAKOTA

Aberdeen
Lawler, James F. *state senator*
Waltman, Alfred Anthony *state legislator*

Armour
Putnam, J. E. (Jim) *state legislator*

Black Hawk
Maicki, G. Carol *former state senator, consultant*

Brandon
Brooks, Roger *state legislator*
Hunt, Roger *former state legislator*

Brookings
Brown, Arnold M. *state legislator*

Buffalo
Johnson, William J. *state legislator*

Burke
Cerny, William F. *state legislator*

Claremont
Cutler, Steve Keith *state legislator*

Cottonwood
Gabriel, Larry Edward *state legislator*

Garretson
Rogen, Mark Endre *former state senator, farmer*

Gettysburg
Schreiber, Lola F. *former state legislator*

Hayti
Frederick, Randall Davis *state legislator*

Huron
Haley, Pat *state legislator*
Volesky, Ron James *state legislator*

Iroquois
Flowers, Charles Edward *state legislator*

Madison
Belatti, Richard G. *state legislator*
Lange, Gerald F. *state legislator*

Miller
Morford, JoAnn (JoAnn Morford-Burg) *state senator, investment company executive*

Mission
Lucas, Larry James *state legislator*

Mitchell
Clemens, Deb Fischer *state legislator, nursing administrator*

Mobridge
Bender, Darrell G. *former state legislator*

Mud Butte
Ingalls, Marie Cecelie *former state legislator, retail executive*

Philip
Porch, Roger A. *former state legislator*

Pierre
Adam, Patricia Ann *legislative aide*
Daugaard, Dennis M. *state legislator, professional society administrator*
Dennert, H. Paul *state legislator*
Diedtrich, Elmer *state legislator*
Everist, Barbara *state legislator*
Fiegen, Kristie K. *state legislator*
Hainje, Dick G. *state legislator, fire fighter*
Ham, Arlene H. *state legislator*
Koskan, John M. *state legislator*
Kundert, Alice E. *retired state legislator*
Monroe, Jeff *state legislator*
Nelson, Pamela A. *state legislator*
Olson, Kevin Mel *state legislator*
Pederson, Gordon Roy *state legislator, retired military officer*
Reedy, John J. (Joe) *state legislator*
Richter, Mitch *state legislator*
Roe, Robert A. *state legislator*
Rounds, M. Michael *state legislator*
Shoener, Jerry James *state legislator*
Symens, Paul N. *state legislator, farmer*
Valandra, Paul *state legislator*
Vitter, Drue J. *state legislator, mayor*
Weber, Robert R. *state legislator*

Pine Ridge
Hagen, Richard E. (Dick) *state legislator*

Rapid City
Fitzgerald, Carol E. *state legislator*
Madden, Cheryl Beth *state legislator*
Napoli, William Bill *state legislator*
Whiting, Fred C. *state legislator*

Scotland
Kloucek, Frank John *state legislator*

Sioux Falls
Barker, Linda K. *state legislator*
Dunn, Rebecca Jo *state legislator*
Koetzle, Gil *state legislator, fire fighter, professional association administrator*
Munson, David Roy *state legislator*
Paisley, Keith Watkins *former state senator, retired small business owner*
Wick, Hal Gerard *state legislator*

Sturgis
McNenny, Kenneth G. *state legislator*

Watertown
Ries, Thomas G. (Torchy) *former state legislator*

Wentworth
Kringen, Dale Eldon *state legislator, trasportation executive*

Wessington
Duxbury, Robert Neil *state legislator*

Yankton
Hunhoff, Bernie P. *state legislator*
Moore, Garry Allen *state legislator*
Munson, Donald E. *state legislator*

VIRGINIA

Alexandria
Collins, Cardiss *former congresswoman*

Dunn Loring
Snowbarger, Vince *former congressman*

WISCONSIN

Albany
Powers, Mike *state legislator*

Antigo
Ourada, Thomas D. *state legislator*

Black Earth
Klug, Scott Leo *former congressman*

Black River Falls
Musser, Terry M. *state legislator*

Burlington
Porter, Cloyd Allen *former state representative*

De Pere
Lasee, Alan J. *state legislator*

Eastman
Johnsrud, DuWayne *state legislator*

Eau Claire
Kreibich, Robin G. *state legislator*
Zien, David Allen *state legislator*

Fennimore
Brandemuehl, David A. *state legislator*

Forest Junction
Ott, Alvin R. *state legislator*

Fort Atkinson
Ward, David W. *state legislator*

Green Bay
Cowles, Robert L. *state legislator*
Kelso, Carol *state legislator*

Greenfield
Rutkowski, James Anthony *former state legislator*

Hartland
Vrakas, Daniel Paul *state legislator*

Janesville
Wood, Wayne W. *state legislator*

Juneau
Fitzgerald, Scott *state legislator*

La Crosse
Meyer, Mark *state legislator*

Ladysmith
Reynolds, Martin L. *state legislator*

Luck
Dueholm, Robert M. *state legislator*

Luxemburg
Hutchison, Dave *state legislator*

Madison
Barish, Lawrence Stephen *nonpartisan legislative staff administrator*
Black, Spencer *state legislator*
Breske, Roger M. *state legislator*
Burke, Brian B. *state legislator, lawyer*
Chvala, Charles Joseph *state legislator*
Coggs, G. Spencer *state legislator*
Cullen, David A. *state legislator*
Darling, Alberta Statkus *state legislator, marketing executive, former art museum executive*
Duff, Marc Charles *state legislator*
Erpenbach, Jon *state legislator*
George, Gary Raymond *state legislator*
Goetsch, Robert George *state legislator*
Gronemus, Barbara *state legislator*
Gunderson, Scott Lee *state legislator*
Hahn, Eugene Herman *state legislator*
Hanson, Doris J. *state legislator*
Hasenohrl, Donald W. *state legislator*
Huelsman, Joanne B. *state legislator*
Jensen, Scott R. *state legislator*
Kreuser, James E. *state legislator*
Krug, Shirley *state legislator*
Krusick, Margaret Ann *state legislator*
Lasee, Frank G. *state legislator*
Lehman, Michael A. *state legislator*
Moen, Rodney Charles *state legislator, retired naval officer*
Moore, Gwendolynne *state legislator*
Murat, William M. *district director*
Olsen, Luther S. *state legislator*
Owens, Carol *state legislator*
Panzer, Mary E. *state legislator*
Plache, Kimberly Marie *state legislator*
Riley, Antonio *state legislator*
Risser, Fred A. *state legislator*
Robson, Judith Biros *state legislator*
Roessler, Carol Ann *state legislator*
Rosenzweig, Peggy A. *state legislator*
Ryba, John J. *state legislator*
Schultz, Dale Walter *state legislator*
Seratti, Lorraine M. *state legislator*
Shibilski, Kevin W. *state legislator*
Skindrud, Rick *state legislator*
Swoboda, Lary Joseph *state legislator*
Travis, David M. *state legislator*
Turner, Robert Lloyd *state legislator*
Underheim, Gregg *state legislator*
Walker, Scott Kevin *state legislator*
Welch, Robert Thomas *state legislator*
Williams, Annette Polly *state legislator*
Wirch, Robert W. *state legislator*
Young, Leon D. *state legislator*
Young, Rebecca Mary Conrad *state legislator*

Manitowoc
Ziegelbauer, Robert F. *state legislator*

Menomonie
Baldus, Alvin J. *state legislator*
Clausing, Alice *state legislator*

Milwaukee
Bock, Peter Ernest *state legislator*
Carpenter, Timothy W. *state legislator*
LaFave, John *state legislator*
Morris-Tatum, Johnnie *state legislator*
Potter, Rosemary *state legislator*
Wasserman, Sheldon A. *state legislator*

Minocqua
Handrick, Joseph W. *state legislator*

Nashotah
Neumann, Mark W. *former congressman, real estate developer*

Neenah
Ellis, Michael G. *state legislator*
Kaufert, Dean R. *state legislator*

Oconomowoc
Foti, Steven M. *state legislator*

Oshkosh
Klusman, Judith *state legislator*

Peshtigo
Gard, John *state legislator*

Port Washington
Hoven, Tim *state legislator*

Pulaski
Drzewiecki, Gary Francis *state legislator*

Racine
Ladwig, Bonnie L. *state legislator*

Rice Lake
Hubler, Mary *state legislator*

River Falls
Harsdorf, Sheila Eloise *state legislator, farmer*

Schofield
Decker, Russell S. *state legislator*

Shawano
Ainsworth, John Henry *state legislator*

Sheboygan
Baumgart, James Raymond *state legislator*

South Milwaukee
Grobschmidt, Richard A. *state legislator*

Superior
Boyle, Frank James *state legislator*

Wausau
Huber, Gregory B. *state legislator*

West Allis
Bell, Jeanette Lois *former state legislator*

West Bend
Grothman, Glenn *state legislator*

West Salem
Huebsch, Michael D. *state legislator*

Whitewater
Nass, Stephen L. *state legislator*

Wisconsin Rapids
Schneider, Marlin Dale *state legislator*

ADDRESS UNPUBLISHED

Aker, Alan D. *state legislator*
Albers, Sheryl Kay *state legislator*
Aurand, Clay *state legislator*
Ballard, Charlie *state legislator*
Ballou, John Dennis *state legislator*
Barrett, William E. *former congressman*
Beggs, Carol Edward *state legislator*
Bennett, Jon *state legislator*
Bodem, Beverly A. *state legislator*
Bogina, August, Jr. *former state official*
Bogue, Eric H. *state legislator, lawyer*
Bonner, Dennis *state legislator*
Boudreau, Lynda *state legislator*
Boyd, Barbara *state legislator*
Broderick, B. Michael, Jr. *state legislator, banker*
Broecker, Sherry *state legislator*
Brosz, Don *retired state legislator*
Brown, Richard Ellsworth *state legislator*
Burton, Woody *state legislator*
Carpenter, Dorothy Fulton *retired state legislator*
Charlton, Betty Jo *retired state legislator*
Chrysler, Richard R. *former congressman*
Churchill, Robert Wilson *state legislator, lawyer*
Cierpiot, Connie *state legislator*
Clay, William Lacy *former congressman*
Curtis, Candace A. *former state legislator*
Daggett, Roxann *state legislator*
Damschroder, Rex *state legislator*
Danforth, John Claggett *former senator, lawyer, clergyman*
Danner, Patsy Ann (Mrs. C. M. Meyer) *former congresswoman*
Davis, Kay *state legislator*
Deuchler, Suzanne Louise *former state legislator*
DeWitz, Loren *former state legislator*
Doderer, Minnette Frerichs *retired state legislator*
Drake, Robert Alan *state legislator, animal nutritionist, mayor*
Duncan, Cleo *state legislator*
Duniphan, J. P. *state legislator, small business owner*
Entenza, Matt *state legislator*
Enz, Catherine S. *state legislator*
Evans, Brent *state legislator*
Ewing, Thomas William *former congressman, lawyer*
Farmer, Mike *state legislator*
Feuerborn, Bill *state legislator*
Finseth, Tim *state legislator*
Fitzwater, Rodger L. *state legislator*
Flora, Vaughn Leonard *state legislator*
Ford, Jack *state legislator*
Foster, Bill I. *state legislator*
Freese, Stephen J. *state legislator*
Gaskill, Sam *state legislator*
Gratz, William W. *state legislator*
Haas, Bill *state legislator*
Haines, Joseph E. *state legislator*
Harrington, Nancey *state senator*
Harris, Bill *state legislator*
Hegeman, Daniel Jay *state legislator*
Hendrickson, Carl H. *state legislator*
Hertel, Curtis *state legislator*
Hickey, John Joseph *state legislator*
Hillegonds, Paul *former state legislator*
Hohulin, Martin *state legislator*
Hood, Ron *state legislator*
Hoppe, Thomas J. *state legislator*
House, Ted C. *state legislator*
Howard, Janet C. *former state legislator*
Howard, Jerry Thomas *state legislator*
Howard, John *former state legislator*
Howerton, Jim *state legislator*
Hudkins, Carol L. *state legislator*
Hutmacher, James K. *state legislator, water drilling contractor*
Jacob, Ken *state legislator*
Jacobs, Leonard J. *state legislator*
Jacobson, Jeff *state legislator*
James, Troy Lee *state legislator*
Jensen, Jim *state legislator*
Johnson, Bruce *state legislator*
Johnson, Jay Withington *former congressman*
Johnson, Sidney B. *state legislator*
Keiser, George J. *state legislator*
Kenley, Howard *state legislator*
Kiel, Shelley *state senator*
Kinder, Peter D. *state legislator*
Kinkel, Anthony G. *state legislator, educator*
Klemm, Richard O. *state legislator*
Kleven, Marguerite *state legislator*
Kredit, Kenneth E. *former state legislator, automobile dealership executive*
Kringstad, Edroy *state legislator*
Kromkowski, Thomas S. *state legislator*
Krupinski, Jerry W. *state legislator*
Kruse, Dennis K. *state legislator*
Larkin, Bruce F. *state legislator*
Lazich, Mary A. *state legislator*
Lewis, James A. *state legislator*
Lindaas, Elroy Neil *state legislator*
Logan, Sean D. *state legislator*
Mautino, Frank J. *state legislator*
McClain, Richard Warner *state legislator*
McCoy, Matthew William *state legislator, human resource manager*
Meshel, Harry *state senator, political party official*
Miller, Patricia Louise *state legislator, nurse*
Minor, Melvin G. *state legislator*
Mitchell, James W. *state official, former state legislator*
Mumper, Larry A. *state legislator*
Murphy, Harold *state legislator*
Murphy, Michael B. *state legislator*
Myers, Jon D. *state legislator*
Nein, Scott R. *state legislator*
Netzley, Robert Elmer *state legislator*
Novak, John Philip *state legislator*
Ogg, William L. *state legislator*
Poe, Donald Raymond *state legislator*
Pond, Phyllis Joan Ruble *state legislator, educator*
Redwine, John Newland *state legislator, physician*
Roman, Twyla I. *state legislator*
Salerno, Amy *state legislator*
Schrock, Edward J. *state legislator*
Smith, Alma Wheeler *state legislator*
Swenson, Howard *state legislator, farmer*
Sykora, Barbara Zwach *state legislator*
Tavares, Charleta B. *former state legislator*
Tesanovich, Paul *state legislator*
Thune, John *congressman*
Treppler, Irene Esther *retired state senator*
Tuma, John *former state legislator, lawyer*
Van Engen, Thomas Lee *state legislator*
Vanleer, James G. *state legislator*
Vaughn, Edward *state legislator*
Veenstra, Kenneth *state legislator*
Vellenga, Kathleen Osborne *former state legislator*
Viverito, Louis Samuel *state legislator*
Volkmer, Harold L. *former congressman*
Wait, Ronald A. *state legislator*
Wilk, Kenny A. *state legislator*
Winters, David Forrest *state legislator*

HEALTHCARE: DENTISTRY

UNITED STATES

ILLINOIS

Batavia
Bicknell, Brian Keith *dentist*

Chicago
Barr, Sanford Lee *dentist*
Diefenbach, Viron Leroy *dental, public health educator, university dean*
Graber, Thomas M. *orthodontist, researcher*
Jackson, Gregory Wayne *orthodontist*
Santangelo, Mario Vincent *dentist*
Yale, Seymour Hershel *dental radiologist, educator, university dean, gerontologist*

Geneva
Lazzara, Dennis Joseph *orthodontist*

Godfrey
King, Ordie Herbert, Jr. *oral pathologist*

Naperville
Grimley, Jeffrey Michael *dentist*

Oak Brook
Mele, Joanne Theresa *dentist*

Roselle
Kao, William Chishon *dentist*

INDIANA

Anderson
Stohler, Michael Joe *dentist*

Elkhart
Bryan, Norman E. *dentist*

Gary
Stephens, Paul Alfred *dentist*

Indianapolis
Standish, Samuel Miles *oral pathologist, college dean*

IOWA

Iowa City
Bishara, Samir Edward *orthodontist*
Bjorndal, Arne Magne *endodontist*
Olin, William Harold *orthodontist, educator*

KANSAS

Topeka
Stroud, Herschel Leon *retired dentist*

Wellington
Willis, Robert Addison *dentist*

MICHIGAN

Ann Arbor
Ash, Major McKinley, Jr. *dentist, educator*
Christiansen, Richard Louis *orthodontics educator, research director, former dean*
Craig, Robert George *dental science educator*

Midland
Thompson, Seth Charles *retired oral and maxillofacial surgeon*

Warren
Woehrlen, Arthur Edward, Jr. *dentist*

MINNESOTA

Kenyon
Jacobson, Lloyd Eldred *retired dentist*

Minneapolis
Douglas, William *dental educator, biomedical research administrator*
Shapiro, Burton Leonard *oral pathologist, geneticist, educator*
Wolff, Larry F. *dental educator, researcher*

MISSOURI

Kansas City
Reed, Michael John *dentist, college dean, oral biology educator*

Saint Louis
Isselhard, Donald Edward *dentist*
Osborn, Mark Eliot *dentist*

NEBRASKA

Fremont
Roesch, Robert Eugene *dentist*

Mc Cook
Blank, Don Sargent *dentist*

OHIO

Cleveland
De Marco, Thomas Joseph *periodontist, educator*
Iacobelli, Mark Anthony *dentist*

Columbus
Buchsieb, Walter Charles *orthodontist, director*
Goorey, Nancy Jane *dentist*
Stevenson, Robert Benjamin, III *prosthodontist, writer*

Hilliard
Relle, Attila Tibor *dentist, geriodontist*

Pepper Pike
Goodman, Donald Joseph *dentist*

Uniontown
Naugle, Robert Paul *dentist*

WISCONSIN

Beloit
Green, Harold Daniel *dentist*

Racine
Sikora, Suzanne Marie *dentist*

ADDRESS UNPUBLISHED

Elzay, Richard Paul *retired dental school administrator*
Hoffman, Jerry Irwin *dental educator, department chairman*
Moore, Dorsey Jerome *dentistry educator, maxillofacial prosthetist*

HEALTHCARE: HEALTH SERVICES

UNITED STATES

ALABAMA

Hoover
Kennon, Rozmond Herron *retired physical therapist*

ARIZONA

Scottsdale
Brown, Frederick Lee *health care executive*

DISTRICT OF COLUMBIA

Washington
Holland, Joy *health care facility executive*

ILLINOIS

Bloomington
Hunt, Roger Schermerhorn *healthcare administrator*

Bolingbrook
Price, Theodora Hadzisteliou *individual and family therapist*

Centralia
Whitten, Mary Lou *nursing educator*

Chicago
Bailar, John Christian, III *public health educator, physician, statistician*
Baptist, Allwyn J. *healthcare consultant*

Goldstein, Sidney *pharmaceutical scientist*
Koebel, Sister Celestia *health care system executive*
Morgan, John Bruce *hospital care consultant*
Schubert, William Kuenneth *hospital medical center executive*
Sierra-Amor, Rosa Isabel *health facility administrator*
Weinrich, Alan Jeffrey *occupational hygienist*

Cleveland
Bailey, Darlyne *social worker, educator*
Blum, Arthur *social work educator*
Douglas, Janice Green *physician, educator*
Fitzpatrick, Joyce J. *nursing educator, former dean*
Hokenstad, Merl Clifford, Jr. *social work educator*
Shakno, Robert Julian *hospital administrator*
Stark, George Robert *health science association administrator*
Wood, Paul F. *national health agency executive*

Columbus
Anderson, Carole Ann *nursing educator, academic administrator*
Bachman, Sister Janice *healthcare executive*
Beckholt, Alice *clinical nurse specialist*
Schuller, David Edward *cancer center administrator, otolaryngologist*

Copley
Smith, Joan H. *retired women's health nurse, educator*

Dayton
Murphy, Martin Joseph, Jr. *cancer research center executive*
Nixon, Charles William *acoustician*

Dublin
Damico, Joseph F. *medical company executive*
Kane, John C. *retired health care products company executive*
White, Kathy Brittain *medical association executive*

Gallipolis
Niehm, Bernard Frank *mental health center administrator, retired*

Hudson
Wooldredge, William Dunbar *health facility administrator*

Lancaster
Varney, Richard Alan *medical center administrator*

Lebanon
Osborne, Quinton Albert *psychiatric social worker, inspector of institutional services*

New Carlisle
Leffler, Carole Elizabeth *mental health nurse, women's health nurse*

Orient
Covault, Lloyd R., Jr. *retired hospital administrator, psychiatrist*

Painesville
Walcott, Robert *healthcare executive, priest*

Toledo
Brass, Alan W. *healthcare executive*
Kneen, James Russell *health care administrator*
Lessick, Mira Lee *nursing educator*
Ormond, Paul A. *health facility executive*
Talmage, Lance Allen *obstetrician/gynecologist, career military officer*
Weikel, Malcolm Keith *healthcare company executive*

SOUTH CAROLINA

Hilton Head Island
Wesselmann, Glenn Allen *retired hospital executive*

SOUTH DAKOTA

Chamberlain
Gregg, Robert Lee *pharmacist*

Huron
Kuhler, Deborah Gail *grief therapist, former state legislator*

Rapid City
Corwin, Bert Clark *optometrist*

Sioux Falls
Nygaard, Lance Corey *nurse, data processing consultant*

WISCONSIN

Green Bay
McIntosh, Elaine Virginia *nutrition educator*

Madison
Derzon, Gordon M. *hospital administrator*
Gavin, Mary Jane *medical and surgical nurse*
Littlefield, Vivian Moore *nursing educator, administrator*
Marlett, Judith Ann *nutritional sciences educator, researcher*
Neumann, Thomas Alan *educational administrator*
Satter, Larry Dean *nutritionist*
Schoeller, Dale Alan *nutrition research educator*

Menasha
Mahnke, Kurt Luther *psychotherapist, clergyman*

Milwaukee
Lange, Marilyn *social worker*
Silverman, Franklin Harold *speech pathologist, educator*
Wake, Madeline Musante *nursing educator, university provost*

Minocqua
Jaye, David Robert, Jr. *retired hospital administrator*

Rhinelander
Van Brunt, Marcia Adele *social worker*

Shawano
Wilson, Douglas *genetics company executive*

CANADA

MANITOBA

Winnipeg
Schultz, Harry *health science organization administrator*
Steele, John Wiseman *retired pharmacy educator*

SWITZERLAND

Satigny
Parkinson, Robert L., Jr. *health facility administrator*

ADDRESS UNPUBLISHED

Anaple, Elsie Mae *medical, surgical and geriatrics nurse*
Austin, James H(oward), Jr. *healthcare executive*
Biegel, David Eli *social worker, educator*
Boggs, Robert Wayne *human services administrator, consultant*
Borg, Ruth I. *home nursing care provider*
Buzard, James Albert *healthcare management consultant*
Conley, Sarah Ann *health facility administrator*
Couch, Daniel Michael *healthcare executive*
Gonzalez, William G. *healthcare advisor*
Harms, Nancy Ann *nursing educator*
Headlee, Raymond *psychoanalyst, educator*
Jobe, Muriel Ida *medical technologist, educator*
John, Gerald Warren *hospital pharmacist, educator*
Juenemann, Sister Jean *hospital executive*
Lanphear, Bruce Perrin *health facility administrator, educator*
Larson, Vicki Lord *communication disorders*
Milewski, Barbara Anne *pediatrics nurse, neonatal intensive care nurse*
Miller, Steven *medical administrator*
Moliere, Jeffrey Michael *cardiopulmonary administrator*
Nichols, Elizabeth Grace *nursing educator, dean*
Parham, Ellen Speiden *nutrition educator*
Redburn, Amber Lynne *nurse*
Reisch, Michael Stewart *social work educator*
Schwartz, Michael Robinson *health facility administrator*
Silverman, Ellen-Marie *speech and language pathologist*
Simpson, Jack Benjamin *medical technologist, business executive*
Smith, Gloria Richardson *nursing educator*
Speer, Nancy Girouard *health care administrator*
Thomson, James Adolph *medical group practice administrator*
Williams, Stuart W. *health facility administrator*
Winkelmann, John Paul *pharmacist*
Winsley, William T. *pharmacist, executive director*
Ziegenhagen, David Mackenzie *consultant, retired healthcare company executive*

HEALTHCARE: MEDICINE

UNITED STATES

CALIFORNIA

Palm Springs
Gaede, James Ernest *physician, medical educator*

COLORADO

Denver
Shindell, Sidney *medical educator, physician*

FLORIDA

Englewood
Sanders, W(illiam) Eugene, Jr. *physician, educator*

Longboat Key
Kabara, Jon Joseph *biochemical pharmacology educator*

Pensacola
Canady, Alexa Irene *pediatric neurosurgeon*

ILLINOIS

Arlington Heights
DeDonato, Donald Michael *obstetrician/gynecologist*
Pochyly, Donald Frederick *physician, hospital administrator*

Belleville
Franks, David Bryan *internist, emergency physician*

Champaign
Rosenblatt, Karin Ann *cancer epidemiologist*

Chicago
Abcarian, Herand *surgeon*
Abelson, Herbert Traub *pediatrician, educator*
Abromowitz, Herman I. *family physician, occupational medicine physician*
Adelman, Susan Hershberg *surgeon*
Albrecht, Ronald Frank *anesthesiologist*
Andersen, Burton Robert *physician, educator*
Applebaum, Edward Leon *otolaryngologist, educator*
Astrachan, Boris Morton *psychiatry educator, consultant*
Balk, Robert A. *medical educator*
Balsam, Theodore *physician*
Barton, John Joseph *obstetrician, gynecologist, educator, researcher*
Bassiouny, Hisham Sallah *surgeon, educator*
Beck, Robert N. *nuclear medicine educator*
Becker, Michael Allen *physician, educator*
Betts, Henry Brognard *physician, health facility administrator, educator*
Bonow, Robert Ogden *medical educator*
Bowman, James Edward *physician, educator*
Brasitus, Thomas Albert *gastroenterologist, educator*
Brueschke, Erich Edward *physician, researcher, educator*
Bunn, William Bernice, III *physician, lawyer, epidemiologist*
Calenoff, Leonid *radiologist*
Caro, William Allan *physician*
Charles, Allan G. *physician, educator*
Chatterton, Robert Treat, Jr. *reproductive endocrinology educator*
Cho, Wonhwa *biomedical researcher*
Christoffel, Katherine Kaufer *pediatrician, epidemiologist, educator*
Coble, Yank David, Jr. *internist, endocrinologist*
Coe, Fredric L. *physician, educator, researcher*
Colley, Karen J. *medical educator, medical researcher*
Conway, James Joseph *physician*
Corlin, Richard F. *gastroenterologist*
Costa, Erminio *pharmacologist, cell biology educator*
Davison, Richard *physician, educator*
Degroot, Leslie Jacob *medical educator*
Derlacki, Eugene L(ubin) *otolaryngologist, physician*
Deutsch, Thomas Alan *ophthalmologist, educator*
Diamond, Seymour *physician*
Diamond, Shari Seidman *law and psychology educator, law researcher*
Dunea, George *nephrologist, educator*
Erdös, Ervin George *pharmacology and biochemistry educator*
Fennessy, John James *radiologist, educator*
Ferguson, Donald John *surgeon, educator*
Fitch, Frank Wesley *pathologist educator, immunologist, educator, administrator*
Flaherty, Emalee Gottbrath *pediatrician*
Flaherty, Timothy Thomas *radiologist*
Fontanarosa, Phil Bernard *emergency physician*
Franco, Carlo Diaz *surgeon, anatomist, anesthesiologist*
Frederiksen, Marilynn Elizabeth Conners *physician, researcher*
Frohman, Lawrence Asher *endocrinology educator, scientist*
Gapstur, Susan Mary *cancer epidemiologist, educator, researcher*
Gecht, Martin Louis *physician, bank executive*
Geha, Alexander Salim *cardiothoracic surgeon, educator*
Gerbie, Albert Bernard *obstetrician, gynecologist, educator*
Gewertz, Bruce Labe *surgeon, educator*
Giovacchini, Peter Louis *psychoanalyst*
Glass, Richard McLean *psychiatry educator, medical editor*
Goldberg, Arnold Irving *psychoanalyst, educator*
Golomb, Harvey Morris *oncologist, educator*
Gould, Samuel Halpert *pediatrics educator*
Grayhack, John Thomas *urologist, educator*
Hambrick, Ernestine *retired colon and rectal surgeon*
Hand, Roger *physician, educator*
Harris, Jules Eli *medical educator, physician, clinical scientist, administrator*
Hast, Malcolm Howard *medical educator, biomedical scientist*
Hellman, Samuel *radiologist, physician, educator*
Herbst, Arthur Lee *obstetrician, gynecologist*
Hill, Carlotta H. *physician*
Hill, J. Edward *physician, educator*
Hinojosa, Raul *physician, ear pathology researcher, educator*
Honig, George Raymond *pediatrician*
Hughes, John Russell *physician, educator*
Jensen, Harold Leroy *medical association administrator, physician*
Johnson, Maryl Rae *cardiologist*
Johnson, Timothy Patrick *health and social researcher*
Jonasson, Olga *surgeon, educator*
Kahrilas, Peter James *medical educator, researcher*
Katz, Adrian Izhack *physician, educator*
Katz, Robert Stephen *rheumatologist, educator*
Kennett, Robert L. *medical organization executive*
Kerth, Jack D. *otolaryngologist*
Kirschner, Barbara Starrels *pediatric gastroenterologist*
Kirsner, Joseph Barnett *physician, educator*
Kitt, Walter *psychiatrist*
Knote, John A. *diagnostic radiologist*
Kohrman, Arthur Fisher *pediatrics educator*
Landsberg, Lewis *endocrinologist, medical researcher*
LaVelle, Arthur *anatomy educator*
Leff, Alan Richard *medical educator, researcher*
Leventhal, Bennett Lee *psychiatry and pediatrics educator, administrator*
Lumpkin, John Robert *public health physician, state official*
Lurain, John Robert, III *gynecologic oncologist*
Marcus, Joseph *child psychiatrist*
Martin, Gary Joseph *medical educator*
Metz, Charles Edgar *radiology educator*
Meyer, Paul Reims, Jr. *orthopedic surgeon*
Millichap, Joseph Gordon *neurologist, educator*
Mirkin, Bernard Leo *clinical pharmacologist, pediatrician*
Moawad, Atef *obstetrician, gynecologist, educator*
Moore, Vernon John, Jr. *pediatrician, lawyer, medical consultant*
Morris, Naomi Carolyn Minner *medical educator, administrator, researcher, consultant*
Mullan, John Francis (Sean Mullan) *neurosurgeon, educator*
Musacchio, Robert A. *medical association administrator*
Naclerio, Robert Michael *otolaryngologist, educator*
Nahrwold, David Lange *surgeon, educator*
Nakajima, Yasuko *medical educator*
Narahashi, Toshio *pharmacology educator*
Nyhus, Lloyd Milton *surgeon, educator*
Page, Ernest *medical educator*
Palmisano, Donald J. *surgeon, educator*
Pappas, George Demetrios *anatomy and cell biology educator, scientist*
Plested, William G., III *surgeon*
Pollock, George Howard *psychiatrist, psychoanalyst*
Pope, Richard M. *rheumatologist*
Poznanski, Andrew Karol *pediatric radiologist*
Prinz, Richard Allen *surgeon*
Pulido, Jose S. *physician*
Ramsey-Goldman, Rosalind *physician*
Reardon, Thomas R. *physician, medical association administrator*
Reddy, Janardan K. *medical educator*
Robinson, June Kerswell *dermatologist, educator*
Roizen, Nancy J. *physician, educator*
Rosen, Steven Terry *oncologist, hematologist*
Rosenfield, Robert Lee *pediatric endocrinologist, educator*
Rosenthal, Ira Maurice *pediatrician, educator*
Rowley, Janet Davison *physician*
Rudy, Lester Howard *psychiatrist, educator*
Russell, Thomas R. *medical association administrator*
Sabbagha, Rudy E. *obstetrician, gynecologist, educator*
Sandlow, Leslie Jordan *physician, educator*
Scarse, Olivia Marie *cardiologist, consultant*
Schade, Stanley Greinert, Jr. *hematologist, educator*
Schafer, Michael Frederick *orthopedic surgeon*
Schilsky, Richard Lewis *oncologist, researcher*
Schuler, James Joseph *vascular surgeon*
Schulman, Sidney *neurologist, educator*
Sciarra, John J. *physician, educator*
Scommegna, Antonio *physician, educator*
Scott, Bruce A. *otolaryngologist*
Scotti, Michael John, Jr. *medical association executive*
Seeler, Ruth Andrea *pediatrician, educator*
Shields, Thomas William *surgeon, educator*
Short, Marion Priscilla *neurogenetics educator*
Siegler, Mark *internist, educator*
Smith, David Waldo Edward *pathology and gerontology educator, physician*
Socol, Michael Lee *obstetrician, gynecologist, educator*
Southgate, Marie Therese *physician, editor*
Sparberg, Marshall Stuart *gastroenterologist, educator*
Steele, Glenn Daniel, Jr. *surgical oncologist*
Sternberg, Paul *retired ophthalmologist*
Swerdlow, Martin Abraham *physician, pathologist, educator*
Taraszkiewicz, Waldemar *physician*
Tardy, Medney Eugene, Jr. *retired otolaryngologist, facial plastic surgeon*
Telfer, Margaret Clare *internist, hematologist, oncologist*
Tomar, Russell Herman *pathologist, educator, researcher*
Tomita, Tadanori *neurosurgeon, educator*
Truschke, Edward F. *medical association administrator*
Van Eron, Kevin Joseph *organizational development consultant, psychologist*
Von Roenn, Kelvin Alexander *neurosurgeon*
Walton, Robert Lee, Jr. *plastic surgeon*
Waxler, Beverly Jean *anesthesiologist, physician*
Webster, James Randolph, Jr. *physician*
Weir, Bryce Keith Alexander *neurosurgeon, neurology educator*
Weis, Mervyn J. *physician, gastroenterologist*
Whitington, Peter Frank *pediatrics educator, pediatric hepatologist*
Williams, Philip Copelain *obstetrician, gynecologist*
Zapp, John S. *medical association administrator*

Danville
Prabhudesai, Mukund M. *pathology educator, laboratory director, researcher, administrator*

Decatur
Requarth, William Henry *surgeon*
Sweet, Arthur *orthopedist*

Deerfield
Scheiber, Stephen Carl *psychiatrist*

Des Plaines
Quintanilla, Antonio Paulet *retired physician, educator*

Elk Grove Village
Sanders, Joe Maxwell, Jr. *pediatrician, association administrator*

Elmhurst
Blain, Charlotte Marie *physician, educator*

Evanston
Bashook, Philip G. *medical association executive, educator*
Crawford, James Weldon *psychiatrist, educator, administrator*
Enroth-Cugell, Christina Alma Elisabeth *neurophysiologist, educator*
Hughes, Edward F. X. *physician, educator*
Khandekar, Janardan Dinkar *oncologist, educator*
Langsley, Donald Gene *psychiatrist, medical board executive*
Langsley, Pauline Royal *psychiatrist*

Mustoe, Thomas Anthony *physician, plastic surgeon*
Sprang, Milton LeRoy *obstetrician, gynecologist, educator*
Stumpf, David Allen *pediatric neurologist*
Traisman, Howard Sevin *pediatrician*
Vick, Nicholas A. *neurologist*

Galesburg
Tourlentes, Thomas Theodore *psychiatrist*

Glen Ellyn
Agruss, Neil Stuart *cardiologist*
Dieter, Raymond Andrew, Jr. *physician, surgeon*

Glencoe
Milloy, Frank Joseph, Jr. *surgeon*

Glenview
Goldmann, Morton Aaron *cardiologist, educator*

Harvey
Heilicser, Bernard Jay *emergency physician*

Highland Park
Pinsky, Steven Michael *radiologist, educator*

Hillsboro
Mulch, Robert F., Jr. *physician*

Hines
Best, William Robert *physician, educator, university official*
Folk, Frank Anton *surgeon, educator*

Joliet
Layman, Dale Pierre *medical educator, author, researcher*
Ring, Alvin Manuel *pathologist, educator*

Lake Barrington
Morris, Ralph William *chronopharmacologist*

Lake Forest
Kelly, Daniel John *physician*
Levy, Nelson Louis *physician, scientist, corporate executive*
Wilbur, Richard Sloan *physician, executive*

Lombard
Henkin, Robert Elliott *nuclear medicine physician*
Kasprow, Barbara Anne *biomedical scientist, writer*

Long Grove
Ausman, Robert K. *surgeon, research executive*

Marshall
Mitchell, George Trice *physician*

Maywood
Canning, John Rafton *urologist*
Celesia, Gastone Guglielmo *neurologist, neurophysiologist, researcher*
Freeark, Robert James *surgeon, educator, administrator*
Hart, Cecil William Joseph *otolaryngologist, surgeon*
Light, Terry Richard *orthopedic hand surgeon*
McClatchey, Kenneth D. *pathology educator*
McGrath, Mary Helena *plastic surgeon, educator*
Pickleman, Jack R. *surgeon*
Slogoff, Stephen *anesthesiologist, educator*

North Chicago
Freese, Uwe Ernest *physician, educator*
Gall, Eric Papineau *physician, educator*
Hawkins, Richard Albert *medical educator, administrator*
Kim, Yoon Berm *immunologist, educator*
Nair, Velayudhan *pharmacologist, medical educator*
Rogers, Eugene Jack *medical educator*
Schneider, Arthur Sanford *physician, educator*
Sierles, Frederick Stephen *psychiatrist, educator*
Taylor, Michael Alan *psychiatrist*
Wiesner, Dallas Charles *immunologist, researcher*

Northbrook
Cucco, Ulisse P. *obstetrician, gynecologist*
Hirsch, Lawrence Leonard *physician, retired educator*

Northfield
Giffin, Mary Elizabeth *psychiatrist, educator*

Oak Brook
Loughead, Jeffrey Lee *physician*
Rathi, Manohar Lal *pediatrician, neonatologist*

Oakbrook Terrace
Becker, Robert Jerome *allergist, health care consultant*

Park Ridge
Anderson, Dyke A. *medical association administrator*
Mangun, Clarke Wilson , Jr. *public health physician, consultant*

Peoria
Meriden, Terry *physician*
Miller, Rick Frey *emergency physician*
Pollak, Raymond *general and transplant surgeon*
Stine, Robert Howard *pediatrician*

River Grove
Hillert, Gloria Bonnin *anatomist, educator*

Rock Island
Bradley, Walter James *emergency physician*

Rockford
Frakes, James Terry *physician, gastroenterologist, educator*

Skokie
Horwitz, Irwin Daniel *otolaryngologist, educator*

Springfield
Frank, Stuart *cardiologist*
Holland, John Madison *retired family practice physician*
Myers, Phillip Ward *otolaryngologist*
Rabinovich, Sergio *physician, educator*
Schiller, William Richard *surgeon*
Sumner, David Spurgeon *surgery educator*
Yaffe, Stuart Allen *physician*
Zook, Elvin Glenn *plastic surgeon, educator*

Urbana
Krock, Curtis Josselyn *pulmonologist*
Nelson, Ralph Alfred *physician*
O'Morchoe, Charles Christopher Creagh *anatomical sciences educator, science administrator*
O'Morchoe, Patricia Jean *pathologist, educator*
Voss, Edward William, Jr. *immunologist, educator*

Wilmette
Hier, Daniel Barnet *neurologist*

Winnetka
Rubnitz, Myron Ethan *pathologist, educator*

INDIANA

Alexandria
Irwin, Gerald Port *physician*

Anderson
King, Charles Ross *physician*

Bedford
Hunter, Harlen Charles *orthopedic surgeon*

Bloomington
Bishop, Michael D. *emergency physician*
Moore, Ward Wilfred *medical educator*
Rink, Lawrence Donald *cardiologist*

Bluffton
Stone, James Robert *surgeon*

Chesterton
Martino, Robert Salvatore *orthopedic surgeon*

Evansville
Faw, Melvin Lee *retired physician*
Penkava, Robert Ray *radiologist, educator*

Fort Wayne
Lee, Shuishih Sage *pathologist*

Gary
Iatridis, Panayotis George *medical educator*
Zunich, Janice *pediatrician, geneticist, educator, administrator*

Indianapolis
Allen, Stephen D(ean) *pathologist, microbiologist*
Bauer, Dietrich Charles *retired medical educator*
Bergstein, Jerry Michael *pediatric nephrologist*
Besch, Henry Roland, Jr. *pharmacologist, educator*
Biller, Jose *neurologist*
Bonaventura, Leo Mark *gynecologist, educator*
Braddom, Randall Lee *physician, medical educator*
Brandt, Ira Kive *pediatrician, medical geneticist*
Broadie, Thomas Allen *surgeon, educator*
Brown, Edwin Wilson, Jr. *physician, educator*
Broxmeyer, Hal Edward *medical educator*
Burr, David Bentley *anatomy educator*
Coleman, John Joseph, III *surgery educator*
Daly, Walter Joseph *physician, educator*
Dyken, Mark Lewis, Jr. *neurologist, educator*
Eigen, Howard *pediatrician, educator*
Eisenberg, Paul Richard *cardiologist, consultant, educator*
Fisch, Charles *physician, educator*
Ghetti, Bernardino Francesco *neuropathologist, neurobiology researcher*
Green, Morris *physician, educator*
Grosfeld, Jay Lazar *surgeon, educator*
Hansell, Richard Stanley *obstetrician, gynecologist, educator*
Helveston, Eugene McGillis *pediatric ophthalmologist, educator*
Holden, Robert Watson *radiologist, educator, university dean*
Irwin, Glenn Ward, Jr. *medical educator, physician, university official*
Jackson, Valerie Pascuzzi *radiologist, educator*
Johnston, Cyrus Conrad, Jr. *medical educator*
Kaye, Gordon Israel *pathologist, anatomist, educator*
King, Lucy Jane *retired psychiatrist, health facility administrator*
Knoebel, Suzanne Buckner *cardiologist, medical educator*
Lemberger, Louis *pharmacologist, physician*
Li, Ting-Kai *medical educator, researcher*
Lumeng, Lawrence *physician, educator*
Madura, James Anthony *surgical educator*
Manders, Karl Lee *neurosurgeon*
Miyamoto, Richard Takashi *otolaryngologist*
Molitoris, Bruce Albert *nephrologist, educator*
Norins, Arthur Leonard *physician, educator*
Nurnberger, John I., Jr. *psychiatrist, educator*
Richter, Judith Anne *pharmacology educator*
Rogers, Robert Ernest *medical educator*
Roth, Lawrence Max *pathologist, educator*
Sherman, Stuart *internist, gastroenterologist*
Small, Joyce Graham *psychiatrist, educator*
Smith, James Warren *pathologist, microbiologist, parasitologist*
Stehman, Frederick Bates *gynecologic oncologist, educator*
Sutton, Gregory Paul *obstetrician, gynecologist*
Watanabe, August Masaru *physician, scientist, medical educator, corporate executive*
Weber, George *oncology and pharmacology researcher, educator*
Weinberger, Myron Hilmar *medical educator*
Wilson, Fred M., II *ophthalmologist, educator*
Woolling, Kenneth Rau *vascular internist*
Yee, Robert Donald *ophthalmologist*
Yune, Heun Yung *radiologist, educator*
Zipes, Douglas Peter *cardiologist, researcher*

Lafayette
Frey, Harley Harrison, Jr. *anesthesiologist*

Logansport
Brewer, Robert Allen *physician*

Marion
Fisher, Pierre James, Jr. *physician*

Walton
Chu, Johnson Chin Sheng *retired physician*

West Lafayette
Borch, Richard Frederic *pharmacology and chemistry educator*
Borowitz, Joseph Leo *pharmacologist, educator*
Johns, Janet Susan *physician*
Robinson, Farrel Richard *pathologist, toxicologist*
Rutledge, Charles Ozwin *pharmacologist, educator*
Shaw, Stanley Miner *nuclear pharmacy scientist*
Tacker, Willis Arnold, Jr. *medical educator, researcher*

IOWA

Burlington
Paragas, Rolando G. *physician*

Cedar Rapids
Krivit, Jeffrey Scot *surgeon*
Norris, Albert Stanley *psychiatrist, educator*

Davenport
Edgerton, Winfield Dow *retired gynecologist*

Des Moines
Ely, Lawrence Orlo *retired surgeon*
Goodin, Julia C. *forensic pathologist, state official, educator*
Rodgers, Louis Dean *retired surgeon*

Iowa City
Abboud, Francois Mitry *physician, educator*
Afifi, Adel Kassim *physician*
Andreasen, Nancy Coover *psychiatrist, educator, neuroscientist*
Apicella, Michael Allen *physician, educator*
Bar, Robert S. *endocrinologist, educator*
Bedell, George Noble *physician, educator*
Buckwalter, Joseph Addison *orthopedic surgeon, educator*
Burns, C(harles) Patrick *hematologist-oncologist*
Clifton, James Albert *physician, educator*
Cooper, Reginald Rudyard *orthopedic surgeon, educator*
Damasio, Antonio R. *physician, neurologist*
Eckstein, John William *physician, educator*
Erkonen, William E. *radiologist, medical educator*
Fellows, Robert Ellis *medical educator, medical scientist*
Galask, Rudolph Peter *obstetrician and gynecologist*
Gergis, Samir Danial *anesthesiologist, educator*
Grose, Charles Frederick *pediatrician, infectious disease specialist*
Hammond, Harold Logan *oral and maxillofacial pathologist, educator*
Heistad, Donald Dean *cardiologist*
Hussey, David Holbert *physician*
Johnson, Cynda Ann *physician, educator*
Kelch, Robert Paul *pediatric endocrinologist*
Kerber, Richard E. *cardiologist*
Kisker, Carl Thomas *physician, medical educator*
Lamping, Kathryn G. *medical educator, medical researcher*
Lauer, Ronald Martin *pediatric cardiologist, researcher*
LeBlond, Richard Foard *internist, educator*
Long, John Paul *pharmacologist, educator*
Lynch, Richard Gregory *medical educator*
Mason, Edward Eaton *surgeon*
Medh, Jheem D. *medical educator, biochemistry researcher*
Merchant, James A. *medical educator*
Morriss, Frank Howard, Jr. *pediatrics educator*
Nelson, Herbert Leroy *psychiatrist*
Niebyl, Jennifer Robinson *obstetrician and gynecologist, educator*
Noyes, Russell, Jr. *psychiatrist*
Ponseti, Ignacio Vives *orthopaedic surgery educator*
Richerson, Hal Bates *physician, internist, allergist, immunologist, educator*
Robinson, Robert George *psychiatry educator*
Snyder, Peter M. *medical educator, medical researcher*
Strauss, John Steinert *dermatologist, educator*
Tephly, Thomas Robert *pharmacologist, toxicologist, educator*
Thompson, Herbert Stanley *neuro-ophthalmologist*
Tsalikian, Eva *physician, educator*
Van Gilder, John Corley *neurosurgeon, educator*
Weinberger, Miles M. *physician, pediatric educator*
Weiner, George Jay *internist*
Weingeist, Thomas Alan *ophthalmology educator*
Weinstock, Joel Vincent *immunologist*
Weintraub, Neal L. *medical educator, cardiologist*
Welsh, Michael James *medical educator, biophysicist, educator*
Ziegler, Ekhard Erich *pediatrics educator*

Johnston
Thoman, Mark Edward *pediatrician*

Marshalltown
Cassidy, Eugene Patrick *pathologist*

KANSAS

Coffeyville
Hawley, Raymond Glen *pathologist*

Great Bend
Jones, Edward *pathologist*

Kansas City
Anderson, Harrison Clarke *pathologist, educator, biomedical researcher*
Damjanov, Ivan *pathologist, educator*
Dunn, Marvin Irvin *physician*
Godfrey, Robert Gordon *physician*
Grantham, Jared James *nephrologist, educator*
Holmes, Grace Elinor *retired medical educator, pediatrician*
Hudson, Robert Paul *medical educator*
Johnson, Joy Ann *diagnostic radiologist*
Krantz, Kermit Edward *physician, educator*
Lawrence, Walter Thomas *plastic surgeon*
McCallum, Richard Warwick *medical researcher, clinician, educator*
Mohn, Melvin Paul *anatomist, educator*
Schloerb, Paul Richard *surgeon, educator*
Suzuki, Tsuneo *molecular immunologist*
Voogt, James Leonard *medical educator*
Waxman, David *physician, university consultant*
Ziegler, Dewey Kiper *neurologist, educator*

Leawood
Graham, Robert *medical association executive*

Manhattan
Oehme, Frederick Wolfgang *medical researcher and educator*

Overland Park
Dockhorn, Robert John *physician, educator*
Landry, Mark Edward *podiatrist, researcher*

Shawnee Mission
Bell, Deloris Wiley *physician*
Hartzler, Geoffrey Oliver *retired cardiologist*
Thomas, Christopher Yancey, III *surgeon, educator*

Topeka
Johnson, Patsy *nursing association administrator*
Menninger, William Walter *psychiatrist*
Sargent, John *psychiatrist*

Wichita
Guthrie, Richard Alan *physician*
Oxley, Dwight K(ahala) *pathologist*

KENTUCKY

Louisville
Kaplan, Henry Jerrold *ophthalmologist, educator*

MARYLAND

Baltimore
Wahl, Richard Leo *radiologist, educator, nuclear medicine researcher*

MASSACHUSETTS

Boston
Greenberger, Norton Jerald *physician*
Roth, Sanford Irwin *pathologist, educator*

MICHIGAN

Alma
Sanders, Jack Ford *physician*

Ann Arbor
Abrams, Gerald David *physician, educator*
Ansbacher, Rudi *physician*
Bacon, George Edgar *pediatrician, educator*
Baker, Laurence Howard *oncology educator*
Bloom, Jane Maginnis *emergency physician*
Bodmer, Rolf A. *medical educator*
Bole, Giles G. *physician, researcher, medical educator*
Burdi, Alphonse Rocco *anatomist*
Burke, Robert Harry *surgeon, educator*
Cameron, Oliver Gene *psychiatrist, educator, psychobiology researcher*
Carlson, Bruce Martin *anatomist*
Casey, Kenneth Lyman *neurologist*
Cerny, Joseph Charles *urologist, educator*
Christensen, A(lbert) Kent *anatomy educator*
Coran, Arnold Gerald *pediatric surgeon*
Craig, Clifford Lindley *orthopaedic pediatric surgery educator*
Davis, Wayne Kay *medical educator*
De La Iglesia, Felix Alberto *pathologist, toxicologist*
Donabedian, Avedis *physician, educator*
Dubin, Howard Victor *dermatologist*
Fajans, Stefan Stanislaus *retired internist, internist, educator*
Fekety, Robert *physician, educator*
Feldman, Eva Lucille *neurology educator*
Fox, David Alan *rheumatologist, immunologist*
Frueh, Bartley Richard *surgeon*
Gilman, Sid *neurologist, department chairman*
Goldstein, Steven Alan *medical and engineering educator*
Greden, John Francis *psychiatrist, educator*
Greenfield, Lazar John *surgeon, educator*
Halter, Jeffrey Brian *internal medicine educator, geriatrician*
Hawthorne, Victor Morrison *epidemiologist, educator*
Heidelberger, Kathleen Patricia *physician*
Hiss, Roland Graham *physician, medical educator*
Hoff, Julian Theodore *physician, educator*
Hollenberg, Paul Frederick *pharmacology educator*
Jacobs, Lloyd A. *cardiovascular surgeon*
Julius, Stevo *physician, educator, physiologist*
Krause, Charles Joseph *otolaryngologist*
Kuhl, David Edmund *physician, nuclear medicine educator*
La Du, Bert Nichols, Jr. *pharmacology educator, physician*
Lichter, Allen S. *oncology educator, university dean*
Lichter, Paul Richard *ophthalmology educator*
Lockwood, Dean H. *physician, pharmaceutical executive*
Lopatin, Dennis Edward *immunologist, educator*
Lozoff, Betsy *pediatrician*
Margolis, Philip Marcus *psychiatrist, educator*
Markel, Howard *medical educator*
Martel, William *radiologist, educator*
Midgley, A(lvin) Rees, Jr. *reproductive endocrinology educator, researcher*
Miller, Josef M. *otolaryngologist, educator*

Monto, Arnold Simon *epidemiology educator*
Morley, George William *gynecologist*
Nabel, Gary J. *internal medicine and biological chemistry educator*
Nelson, Virginia Simson *pediatrician, physiatrist, educator*
Owyang, Chung *gastroenterologist, researcher*
Pitt, Bertram *cardiologist, educator, consultant*
Powsner, Edward Raphael *physician*
Quint, Douglas Joseph *neuroradiology educator*
Reddy, Venkat Narsimha *ophthalmologist, researcher*
Rosenthal, Amnon *pediatric cardiologist*
Schottenfeld, David *epidemiologist, educator*
Silverman, Albert Jack *psychiatrist, educator*
Smith, David John, Jr. *plastic surgeon*
Strang, Ruth Hancock *pediatric educator, pediatric cardiologist, priest*
Stross, Jeoffrey Knight *physician, educator*
Tandon, Rajiv *psychiatrist, educator*
Thompson, Norman Winslow *surgeon, educator*
Todd, Robert Franklin, III *oncologist, educator*
Voorhees, John James *dermatologist, department chairman*
Ward, Peter Allan *pathologist, educator*
Weber, Wendell William *pharmacologist*
Weg, John Gerard *physician*
Wegman, Myron Ezra *physician, educator*
Wiggins, Roger C. *internist, educator, researcher*
Yamada, Tadataka *internist*

Bingham Farms
Katz, Sidney Franklin *obstetrician, gynecologist*

Bloomfield Hills
Ball, Patricia Ann *physician*

Clinton Township
Brown, Ronald Delano *endocrinologist*

Davison
Tauscher, John Walter *retired pediatrician, emeritus educator*

Dearborn
Fordyce, James George *physician*
Myers, Woodrow Augustus, Jr. *physician, health care management director*

Detroit
Amirikia, Hassan *obstetrician, gynecologist*
Cohen, Sanford Ned *pediatrics educator, academic administrator*
Fromm, David *surgeon*
Gardin, Julius Markus *cardiologist, educator*
Hashimoto, Ken *dermatology educator*
Kantrowitz, Adrian *surgeon, educator*
Kaplan, Joseph *pediatrician*
Kelley, Mark Albert *physician, educator, health care executive*
Lewis, Frank Russell, Jr. *surgeon*
Lim, Henry Wan-Peng *physician*
Lupulescu, Aurel Peter *medical educator, researcher, physician*
Lusher, Jeanne Marie *pediatric hematologist, educator*
Maiese, Kenneth *neurologist*
Miller, Orlando Jack *physician, educator*
Perry, Burton Lars *retired pediatrician*
Peters, William P. *oncologist, science administrator, educator*
Porter, Arthur T. *oncologist, educator, medical administrator*
Prasad, Ananda Shiva *medical educator*
Silverman, Norman Alan *cardiac surgeon*
Smith, Wilbur Lazear *radiologist, educator*
Sokol, Robert James *obstetrician, gynecologist, educator*
Tolia, Vasundhara K. *pediatric gastroenterologist, educator*
Uhde, Thomas Whitley *psychiatry educator, psychiatrist*
Whitehouse, Fred Waite *endocrinologist, researcher*
Wiener, Joseph *pathologist*

East Lansing
Beckmeyer, Henry Ernest *anesthesiologist, medical educator, pain management specialist*
Brody, Theodore Meyer *pharmacologist, educator*
Davis, Glenn Craig *psychiatrist*
Gottschalk, Alexander *radiologist, diagnostic radiology educator*
Magen, Myron Shimin *osteopathic physician, educator, university dean*
Moore, Kenneth Edwin *pharmacology educator*
Netzloff, Michael Lawrence *pediatric educator, endocrinologist, geneticist*
Rosenman, Kenneth D. *medical educator*
Sato, Paul Hisashi *pharmacologist*
Walker, Bruce Edward *anatomy educator*
Watson, Ralph Edward *physician, educator*

Farmington Hills
Blum, Jon H. *dermatologist*

Fife Lake
Knecht, Richard Arden *family practitioner*

Flint
Jayabalan, Vemblaserry *nuclear medicine physician, radiologist*

Frankenmuth
Shetlar, James Francis *physician*

Grand Blanc
Wasfie, Tarik Jawad *surgeon, educator*

Grand Rapids
Swanson, Alfred Bertil *orthopaedic and hand surgeon, inventor, educator*
Wilt, Jeffrey Lynn *pulmonary and critical care physician, educator*

Kalamazoo
Chodos, Dale David Jerome *physician, consumer advocate*
Gladstone, William Sheldon, Jr. *radiologist*
Inui, Thomas Spencer *physician, educator*

Kalkaska
Batsakis, John George *pathology educator*

Livonia
Sobel, Howard Bernard *osteopath, educator*

Northport
Schultz, Richard Carlton *plastic surgeon*

Oak Park
Kaplan, Randy Kaye *podiatrist*

Okemos
Ristow, George Edward *neurologist, educator*

Rochester Hills
Badalament, Robert Anthony *urologic oncologist*

Royal Oak
Bernstein, Jay *pathologist, researcher, educator*
Dworkin, Howard Jerry *nuclear medicine physician, educator*
LaBan, Myron Miles *physician, administrator*
Ryan, Jack *physician, retired hospital corporation executive*

Saginaw
Ferlinz, Jack *cardiologist, medical educator*
Manning, John Warren, III *retired surgeon, medical educator*

Southfield
Mathog, Robert Henry *otolaryngologist, educator*
O'Hara, John Paul, III *orthopaedic surgeon*
Zubroff, Leonard Saul *surgeon*

Traverse City
Tobin, Patrick John *dermatologist*

Troy
Golusin, Millard R. *obstetrician and gynecologist*
Meerschaert, Joseph Richard *physician*
Schafer, Sharon Marie *anesthesiologist*

West Bloomfield
Sarwer-Foner, Gerald Jacob *physician, educator*
Sawyer, Howard Jerome *physician*

Ypsilanti
Ritter, Frank Nicholas *otolaryngologist, educator*

MINNESOTA

Bloomington
Lakin, James Dennis *allergist, immunologist, director*

Duluth
Aufderheide, Arthur Carl *pathologist*
Eisenberg, Richard Martin *pharmacology educator*

Minneapolis
Bache, Robert James *physician, medical educator*
Blackburn, Henry Webster, Jr. *retired physician*
Boudreau, Robert James *nuclear medicine physician, researcher*
Brown, David Mitchell *physician, educator, dean*
Buchwald, Henry *surgeon, educator, researcher*
Burton, Charles Victor *physician, surgeon, inventor*
Charnas, Lawrence *neurologist*
Chavers, Blanche Marie *pediatrician, educator, researcher*
Craig, James Lynn *physician, consumer products company executive*
Dykstra, Dennis Dale *physiatrist*
Fisch, Robert Otto *medical educator*
Gajl-Peczalska, Kazimiera J. *retired surgical pathologist, pathology educator*
Gorlin, Robert James *medical educator, educator*
Gullickson, Glenn, Jr. *physician, educator*
Hays, Thomas S. *medical educator, medical researcher*
Joseph, Marilyn Susan *gynecologist*
Kane, Robert Lewis *public health educator*
Kaplan, Manuel E. *physician, educator*
Karanes, Chatchada *internist*
Keane, William Francis *nephrology educator, research foundation executive*
Kennedy, B(yrl) J(ames) *medicine and oncology educator*
Kump, Warren Lee *retired diagnostic radiologist*
Leon, Arthur Sol *research cardiologist, exercise physiologist*
Levitt, Seymour Herbert *physician, radiology educator*
Loh, Horace H. *pharmacology educator*
Luepker, Russell Vincent *epidemiology educator*
Mandel, Sheldon Lloyd *dermatologist, educator*
Mazze, Roger Steven *medical educator, researcher*
McQuarrie, Donald Gray *surgeon, educator*
Moller, James Herman *physician, pediatrician educator*
Najarian, John Sarkis *surgeon, educator*
Palahniuk, Richard John *anesthesiology educator, researcher*
Phibbs, Clifford Matthew *surgeon, educator*
Prem, Konald Arthur *physician, educator*
Quie, Paul Gerhardt *pediatrician*
Schuman, Leonard M. *medical educator, academic administrator*
Tagatz, George Elmo *retired obstetrician, gynecologist, educator*
Thompson, Roby Calvin, Jr. *orthopedic surgeon, educator*
Thompson, Theodore Robert *pediatric educator*
Wild, John Julian *surgeon, director medical research institute*
Wirtschafter, Jonathan Dine *neuro-ophthalmology educator, scientist*

Minnetonka
Erlandson, Patrick J. *medical association administrator*
McGuire, William W. *medical association administrator*

Olivia
Cosgriff, James Arthur *physician*

Rochester
Bartholomew, Lloyd Gibson *physician*
Beahrs, Oliver Howard *surgeon, educator*
Beckett, Victoria Ling *physician*
Bowie, E(dward) J(ohn) Walter *hematologist, researcher*
Brimijoin, William Stephen *pharmacology educator, neuroscience researcher*
Cofield, Robert Hahn *orthopedic surgeon, educator*
Dickson, Edgar Rolland *gastroenterologist*
Douglass, Bruce E. *physician*
Du Shane, James William *physician, educator*
Engel, Andrew George *neurologist*
Feldt, Robert Hewitt *pediatric cardiologist, educator*
Fye, W. Bruce, III *cardiologist*
Gomez, Manuel Rodriguez *physician*
Gracey, Douglas Robert *physician, physiologist, educator*
Hattery, Robert Ralph *radiologist, educator*
Hauser, Stephen Crane *gastroenterologist*
Hodgson, Jane Elizabeth *obstetrician and gynecologist, consultant*
Knopman, David S. *neurologist*
Kyle, Robert Arthur *medical educator, oncologist*
LaRusso, Nicholas F. *gastroenterologist, educator, scientist*
Lofgren, Karl Adolph *surgeon, educator*
Lucas, Alexander Ralph *child psychiatrist, educator, writer*
Mackenzie, Ronald Alexander *anesthesiologist*
Malkasian, George Durand, Jr. *physician, educator*
Michenfelder, John Donahue *anesthesiology educator*
Morlock, Carl Grismore *physician, medical educator*
Mrazek, David Allen *pediatric psychiatrist*
Mulder, Donald William *physician, educator*
Neel, Harry Bryan, III *surgeon, scientist, educator*
Olsen, Arthur Martin *physician, educator*
Perry, Harold Otto *dermatologist*
Phillips, Sidney Frederick *gastroenterologist, educator*
Pittelkow, Mark Robert *physician, dermatology educator, researcher*
Platt, Jeffrey Louis *surgeon, immunologist, educator, pediatric nephrologist*
Pratt, Joseph Hyde, Jr. *surgeon*
Reitemeier, Richard Joseph *physician*
Rogers, Roy Steele, III *dermatology educator, dean*
Rosenow, Edward Carl, III *medical educator*
Siekert, Robert George *neurologist*
Stegall, Mark D. *surgeon, medical educator*
Symmonds, Richard Earl *gynecologist*
Whisnant, Jack Page *neurologist*
Woods, John Elmer *plastic surgeon*

Saint Louis Park
Harper, Patricia Nelsen *psychiatrist*

Saint Paul
Edwards, Jesse Efrem *physician, educator*
Michael, Alfred Frederick, Jr. *physician, medical educator*
Rothenberger, David Albert *surgeon*
Swaiman, Kenneth Fred *pediatric neurologist, educator*
Titus, Jack L. *pathologist, educator*
Zander, Janet Adele *psychiatrist*

Stillwater
Asch, Susan McClellan *pediatrician*

Virginia
Knabe, George William, Jr. *pathologist, educator*

Willmar
Vander Aarde, Stanley Bernard *retired otolaryngologist*

MISSOURI

Clayton
Onken, Henry Dralle *plastic surgeon*

Columbia
Allen, William Cecil *physician, educator*
Colwill, Jack Marshall *physician, educator, dean*
Cunningham, Milamari Antoinella *anesthesiologist*
Eggers, George William Nordholtz, Jr. *anesthesiologist, educator*
Hardin, Christopher Demarest *medical educator*
James, Elizabeth Joan Plogsted *pediatrician, educator*
König, Peter *pediatrician, educator*
Perkoff, Gerald Thomas *physician, educator*
Perry, Michael Clinton *physician, medical educator, academic administrator*
Puckett, C. Lin *plastic surgeon, educator*
Silver, Donald *surgeon, educator*
Tarnove, Lorraine *medical association executive*
Weiss, James Moses Aaron *psychiatrist, educator*
Winship, Daniel Holcomb *medicine educator, university dean*
Witten, David Melvin *radiology educator*

Fredericktown
Raksakulthai, Vinai *obstetrician, gynecologist*

Kansas City
Abdou, Nabih I. *physician, educator*
Ardinger, Robert Hall, Jr. *physician, educator*
Butler, Merlin Gene *physician, medical geneticist, educator*
Dimond, Edmunds Grey *medical educator*
Godfrey, William Ashley *ophthalmologist*
Hagan, John Charles, III *ophthalmologist*
Jonas, Harry S. *medical education consultant*
Kagan, Stuart Michael *pediatrician*
Long, Edwin Tutt *surgeon*
McCoy, Frederick John *retired plastic surgeon*
McGregor, Douglas Hugh *pathologist, educator*
McPhee, Mark Steven *medical educator, physician, gastroenterologist*
Mebust, Winston Keith *surgeon, educator*
Poston, Walker Seward, II *medical educator, researcher*
Salomone, Joseph Anthony, III *emergency medicine physician*
Sauer, Gordon Chenoweth *dermatologist, educator*
Willsie, Sandra K. *physician, educator*

Pilot Knob
deCastro, Fernando Jose *pediatrics educator*

Saint Louis
Alpers, David Hershel *physician, educator*
Bacon, Bruce Raymond *physician*
Berg, Leonard *retired neurologist, educator, researcher*
Berland, David I. *psychiatrist, educator*
Brodeur, Armand Edward *pediatric radiologist*
Brown, Wendy Weinstock *nephrologist, educator*
Chaplin, David Dunbar *medical research specialist, medical educator*
Chaplin, Hugh, Jr. *physician, educator*
Chole, Richard Arthur *otolaryngologist, educator*
Cloninger, Claude Robert *psychiatric researcher, educator, genetic epidemiologist*
Cryer, Philip Eugene *medical educator, scientist, endocrinologist*
Dewald, Paul Adolph *psychiatrist, educator*
Dodge, Philip Rogers *physician, educator*
Dougherty, Charles Hamilton *pediatrician*
Evens, Ronald Gene *radiologist, medical center administrator*
Fitch, Coy Dean *physician, educator*
Fletcher, James Warren *physician*
Flye, M. Wayne *surgeon, immunologist, educator, writer*
Fredrickson, John Murray *otolaryngologist*
Friedman, William Hersh *otolaryngologist, educator*
Gay, William Arthur, Jr. *thoracic surgeon*
Goldberg, Anne Carol *physician, educator*
Goodenberger, Daniel Marvin *medical educator*
Grossberg, George Thomas *psychiatrist, educator*
Grubb, Robert L., Jr. *neurosurgeon*
Hammerman, Marc Randall *nephrologist, educator*
Hanley, Thomas Patrick *obstetrician-gynecologist*
Holmes, Nancy Elizabeth *pediatrician*
Hyers, Thomas Morgan *physician, biomedical researcher*
Johnston, Marilyn Frances-Meyers *physician, medical educator*
Kaminski, Donald Leon *medical educator, surgeon, gastrointestinal physiologist*
Kelly, Daniel P. *cardiologist, molecular biologist*
Kincaid, Marilyn Coburn *medical educator*
Kipnis, David Morris *physician, educator*
Klahr, Saulo *physician, educator*
Knutsen, Alan Paul *pediatrician, allergist, immunologist*
Kolker, Allan Erwin *ophthalmologist*
Kornfeld, Stuart A. *hematology educator*
Kouchoukos, Nicholas Thomas *surgeon*
Lacy, Paul Eston *pathologist*
Lagunoff, David *physician, educator*
Landau, William Milton *neurologist, department chairman*
Loeb, Virgil, Jr. *oncologist, hematologist*
Majerus, Philip Warren *physician*
Manske, Paul Robert *orthopedic hand surgeon, educator*
Martin, Kevin John *nephrologist, educator*
Middelkamp, John Neal *pediatrician, educator*
Mooradian, Arshag Dertad *internist, educator*
Morley, John Edward *physician*
Myerson, Robert J. *radiation oncologist, educator*
Olney, John William *psychiatry educator*
Owens, William Don *anesthesiology educator*
Peck, William Arno *physician, educator, university official and dean*
Perez, Carlos A. *radiation oncologist, educator*
Perlmutter, David H. *physician, educator*
Prensky, Arthur Lawrence *pediatric neurologist, educator*
Purkerson, Mabel Louise *physician, physiologist, educator*
Rao, Dabeeru C. *epidemiologist, educator*
Reh, Thomas Edward *radiologist, educator*
Robins, Lee Nelken *medical educator*
Royal, Henry Duval *nuclear medicine physician*
Ryall, Jo-Ellyn M. *psychiatrist*
Schonfeld, Gustav *medical educator, researcher, administrator*
Schreiber, James Ralph *obstetrician, researcher*
Schwartz, Alan Leigh *pediatrician, educator*
Siegel, Barry Alan *nuclear radiologist*
Slatopolsky, Eduardo *nephrologist, educator*
Slavin, Raymond Granam *allergist, immunologist*
Smith, Morton Edward *ophthalmology educator, dean*
Spector, Gershon Jerry *physician, educator, researcher*
States, David Johnson *biomedical scientist, physician*
Stoneman, William, III *physician, educator*
Strunk, Robert Charles *physician*
Sweet, Stuart C. *pediatrician*
Teitelbaum, Steven Lazarus *pathology educator*
Ternberg, Jessie Lamoin *pediatric surgeon*
Thach, William Thomas, Jr. *neurobiology and neurology educator*
Ulett, George Andrew *psychiatrist*
Unanue, Emil Raphael *immunopathologist*
Walentik, Corinne Anne *pediatrician*
Weber, Mark F. *medical executive*
Whyte, Michael Peter *medicine, pediatrics and genetics educator, research director*
Wickline, Samuel Alan *cardiologist, educator*
Willman, Vallee Louis *physician, surgery educator*
Young, Paul Andrew *anatomist*

Springfield
Hackett, Earl Randolph *neurologist*

Town And Country
Levin, Marvin Edgar *physician*

NEBRASKA

Dakota City
Rodriguez, Manuel Alvarez *pathologist*

Hastings
Dungan, John Russell, Jr. (Titular Viscount Dungan of Clane and hereditary chief of the name; Prince of Fer *anesthesiologist*

Lincoln
Metz, Philip Steven *surgeon, educator*
Weaver, Arthur Lawrence *physician*

Wilson, Charles Stephen *cardiologist, educator*

Omaha
Armitage, James O. *medical educator*
Casale, Thomas Bruce *medical educator*
Ferlic, Randolph *medical educator*
Fusaro, Ramon Michael *dermatologist, researcher*
Godfrey, Maurice *biomedical scientist*
Hodgson, Paul Edmund *surgeon, department chairman*
Imray, Thomas John *radiologist, educator*
Kessinger, Margaret Anne *medical educator*
Klassen, Lynell W. *rheumatologist, transplant immunologist*
Korbitz, Bernard Carl *retired oncologist, hematologist, educator, consultant*
Lynch, Henry Thomson *medical educator*
Maurer, Harold Maurice *pediatrician*
Mohiuddin, Syed Maqdoom *cardiologist, educator*
Nairn, Roderick *immunologist, biochemist, educator*
O'Donohue, Walter John, Jr. *medical educator*
Onsager, David Ralph *cardiothoracic surgeon, educator*
Pearson, Paul Hammond *physician*
Quigley, Herbert Joseph, Jr. *pathologist, educator*
Tinker, John Heath *anesthesiologist, educator*
Waggener, Ronald Edgar *radiologist*
Ward, Vernon Graves *internist*
Wilson, M. Roy *medical educator*

Papillion
Dvorak, Allen Dale *radiologist*

Seward
Matzke, Jay *internist*

NEVADA

Las Vegas
Noback, Richardson Kilbourne *medical educator*

NORTH CAROLINA

Durham
Thompson, William Moreau *radiologist, educator*
Wells, Samuel Alonzo, Jr. *surgeon*

Whispering Pines
Enlow, Donald Hugh *anatomist, educator, university dean*

NORTH DAKOTA

Bismarck
Schwartz, Judy Ellen *cardiothoracic surgeon*

Fargo
Mitchell, James Edward *physician, educator*
Taylor, Doris Denice *physician, entrepreneur, oncology consultant*

Grand Forks
Carlson, Edward C. *anatomy educator*
Sobus, Kerstin MaryLouise *physician, physical therapist*

Williston
Adducci, Joseph Edward *obstetrician, gynecologist*

OHIO

Akron
Allen, Marc Kevin *emergency physician, educator*
Bird, Forrest M. *retired medical inventor*
Emmett, John Colin *retired inventor, consultant*
Evans, Douglas McCullough *surgeon, educator*
Levy, Richard Philip *physician, educator*
Milsted, Amy *biomedical educator*
Rothmann, Bruce Franklin *pediatric surgeon*
Schelble, Daniel Timothy *emergency medicine physician*
Seiwald, Robert J. *retired inventor*
Tan, James *internist, educator*
Timmons, Gerald Dean *pediatric neurologist*

Beachwood
Katzman, Richard A. *cardiologist, internist, consultant*

Bexley
Yashon, David *neurosurgeon, educator*

Bryan
Carrico, Virgil Norman *physician*

Canton
Howland, Willard J. *radiologist, educator*
Kellermeyer, Robert William *physician, educator*
Rubin, Patricia *internist*

Cincinnati
Adolph, Robert J. *physician, medical educator*
Alexander, James Wesley *surgeon, educator*
Balistreri, William Francis *physician, pediatric gastroenterologist*
Bellet, Paul Sanders *pediatrician, educator*
Boat, Thomas Frederick *physician, educator, researcher*
Bower, Robert Hewitt *surgeon, educator, researcher*
Bridenbaugh, Phillip Owen *anesthesiologist, physician*
Buncher, Charles Ralph *epidemiologist, educator*
Chin, Nee Oo Wong *reproductive endocrinologist*
Cole, Theodore John *osteopathic and naturopathic physician*
De Courten-Myers, Gabrielle Marguerite *neuropathologist*
DeWitt, Thomas *pediatrician, educator*
Estes, Stephen Arthur *dermatologist*
Fenoglio-Preiser, Cecilia Mettler *pathologist, educator*
Fowler, Noble Owen *physician, university administrator*
Greenwalt, Tibor Jack *physician, educator*
Griffith, John Francis *pediatrician, administrator, educator*
Heimlich, Henry Jay *physician, surgeon, educator*
Hess, Evelyn Victorine (Mrs. Michael Howett) *medical educator*
Hutton, John James *medical researcher, medical educator*
Joffe, Stephen Neal *surgical laser educator, medical executive*
Loggie, Jennifer Mary Hildreth *medical educator, physician*
Lucas, Stanley Jerome *retired radiologist, physician*
Lucky, Anne Weissman *dermatologist*
Macpherson, Colin R(obertson) *pathologist, educator*
Maltz, Robert *surgeon*
Neale, Henry Whitehead *plastic surgery educator*
Rapoport, Robert Morton *medical educator*
Rashkin, Mitchell Carl *internist, pulmonary medicine specialist*
Schreiner, Albert William *physician, educator*
Silberstein, Edward Bernard *nuclear medicine educator, researcher, oncologist*
Spinnato, Joseph Anthony, II *obstetrician*
Vilter, Richard William *physician, educator*
West, Clark Darwin *pediatric nephrologist, educator*
Wiot, Jerome Francis *radiologist*
Wood, Robert Emerson *pediatrics educator*

Cleveland
Altose, Murray David *physician, educator*
Awais, George Musa *obstetrician, gynecologist*
Badal, Daniel Walter *psychiatrist, educator*
Baker, Saul Phillip *geriatrician, cardiologist, internist*
Barnett, Gene Henry *neurosurgeon*
Berger, Melvin *allergist, immunologist*
Boyd, Arthur Bernette, Jr. *surgeon, clergyman, beverage company executive*
Bronson, David Leigh *physician, educator*
Cascorbi, Helmut Freimund *anesthesiologist, educator*
Castele, Theodore John *radiologist*
Cole, Monroe *neurologist, educator*
Daroff, Robert Barry *neurologist, educator*
Davis, Pamela Bowes *pediatric pulmonologist*
Doershuk, Carl Frederick *physician, pediatrics educator*
Eiben, Robert Michael *pediatric neurologist, educator*
Ellis, Lloyd H., Jr. *emergency physician*
Elston, Robert C. *medical educator*
Fazio, Victor Warren *physician, colon and rectal surgeon*
Geho, Walter Blair *biomedical research executive*
Harris, John William *hematologist, educator*
Holzbach, Raymond Thomas *gastroenterologist, author, educator*
Izant, Robert James, Jr. *pediatric surgeon*
Jackson, Edgar B., Jr. *medical educator*
Kass, Lawrence *hematologist, oncologist, hematopathologist*
Lamm, Michael Emanuel *pathologist, immunologist, educator*
Lefferts, William Geoffrey *physician, educator*
Lenkoski, Leo Douglas *psychiatrist, educator*
McCrae, Keith R. *medical educator, researcher*
McHenry, Martin Christopher *physician, educator*
Medalie, Jack Harvey *physician*
Montague, Drogo K. *urologist*
Moravec, Christine D. Schomis *medical educator*
Moskowitz, Roland Wallace *internist*
Neuhauser, Duncan von Briesen *medical educator*
Novick, Andrew Carl *urologist*
Olness, Karen Norma *pediatrics and international health educator*
Pretlow, Thomas Garrett *physician, pathology educator, researcher*
Rakita, Louis *cardiologist, educator*
Ratnoff, Oscar Davis *physician, educator*
Robbins, Frederick Chapman *retired physician, medical school dean emeritus*
Scarpa, Antonio *medicine educator, biomedical scientist*
Shuck, Jerry Mark *surgeon, educator*
Stange, Kurt C. *medical educator*
Stavitsky, Abram Benjamin *immunologist, educator*
Webster, Leslie Tillotson, Jr. *pharmacologist, educator*
Wolfman, Alan *medical educator, researcher*
Young, Jess Ray *retired internist*

Columbus
Ackerman, John Henry *health services consultant, physician*
Balcerzak, Stanley Paul *physician, educator*
Barth, Rolf Frederick *pathologist, educator*
Berntson, Gary Glen *psychiatry, psychology and pediatrics educator*
Billings, Charles Edgar *physician*
Boudoulas, Harisios *physician, educator, researcher*
Bowman, Louis L. *emergency physician*
Bullock, Joseph Daniel *pediatrician, educator*
Christoforidis, A. John *radiologist, educator*
Cramblett, Henry Gaylord *pediatrician, virologist, educator*
Ellison, Edwin Christopher *physician, surgeon*
Fass, Robert J. *epidemiologist, academic administrator*
Ferguson, Ronald Morris *surgeon, educator*
Furste, Wesley Leonard, II *surgeon, educator*
Goldschmidt, Pascal Joseph *medical educator, cardiologist*
Hansen, Thomas Nanastad *pediatrician, health facility administrator*
Haque, Malika Hakim *pediatrician*
Huheey, Marilyn Jane *ophthalmologist, educator*
Kakos, Gerard Stephen *thoracic and cardiovascular surgeon*
Laufman, Leslie Rodgers *hematologist, oncologist*
Leier, Carl Victor *internist, cardiologist*
Lewis, Richard Phelps *physician, educator*
Long, Sarah Elizabeth Brackney *physician*
Morrow, Grant, III *medical research director, physician*
Moser, Debra Kay *medical educator*
Mueller, Charles Frederick *radiologist, educator*
Newton, William Allen, Jr. *pediatric pathologist*
Peterson, Larry James *medical educator, oral surgeon*
Ruberg, Robert Lionel *surgery educator*
Rund, Douglas Andrew *emergency physician*
Sayers, Martin Peter *pediatric neurosurgeon*
Senhauser, Donald A(lbert) *pathologist, educator*
Skillman, Thomas Grant *endocrinology consultant, former educator*
Sommer, Annemarie *pediatrician*
Speicher, Carl Eugene *pathologist*
St. Pierre, Ronald Leslie *medical and public health educator, university administrator*
Stoner, Gary David *cancer researcher*
Tetlock, Philip E. *behavioral scientist, psychology educator*
Tzagournis, Manuel *physician, educator, university administrator*
Vogel, Thomas Timothy *surgeon, health care consultant, lay church worker*
Whitacre, Caroline Clement *immunologist, researcher*

Dayton
Dunn, Margaret M. *general surgeon, educator, university official*
Heller, Abraham *psychiatrist, educator*
Mohler, Stanley Ross *physician, educator*
Monk, Susan Marie *physician, pediatrician*
Nanagas, Maria Teresita Cruz *pediatrician, educator*
Pflum, Barbara Ann *pediatric allergist*
Ruegsegger, Donald Ray, Jr. *radiological physicist, educator*
Weinberg, Sylvan Lee *cardiologist, educator, author, editor*
Wilson, William Campbell McFarland *gastroenterologist*

Gahanna
Robbins, Darryl Andrew *pediatrician*

Galena
Berggren, Ronald Bernard *surgeon, emeritus educator*

Grove City
Kilman, James William *surgeon, educator*

Jefferson
Macklin, Martin Rodbell *psychiatrist*

Kettering
Mantil, Joseph Chacko *nuclear medicine physician, researcher*

Lancaster
Woodward, James Kenneth *retired pharmacologist*

Lima
Becker, Dwight Lowell *physician*

Madison
Stafford, Arthur Charles *medical association administrator*

Mansfield
Capaldo, Guy *obstetrician, gynecologist*

Mason
Beary, John Francis, III *physician, researcher, pharmaceutical executive*

North Canton
Di Simone, Robert Nicholas *radiologist, educator*

Norwalk
Gutowicz, Matthew Francis, Jr. *radiologist*
Holman, William Baker *surgeon, coroner*

Parma
Lazo, John, Jr. *physician*

Rootstown
Blacklow, Robert Stanley *physician, medical college administrator*
Brodell, Robert Thomas *internal medicine educator*
Campbell, Colin *obstetrician, gynecologist, school dean*

Toledo
Howard, John Malone *surgeon, educator*
Knotts, Frank Barry *physician, surgeon*
Mulrow, Patrick Joseph *medical educator*
Shelley, Walter Brown *physician, educator*

Warren
Rizer, Franklin Morris *physician, otolaryngologist*

Wooster
Kuffner, George Henry *dermatologist, educator*

Wright Patterson AFB
Frazier, John W. *retired physiologist, researcher*

Yellow Springs
Webb, Paul *physician, researcher, consultant, educator*

Youngstown
Walton, Ralph Gerald *psychiatrist, educator*

Zanesville
Kopf, George Michael *retired ophthalmologist*
Ray, John Walker *otolaryngologist, educator, broadcast commentator*

OREGON

Portland
Zerbe, Kathryn Jane *psychiatrist*

SOUTH DAKOTA

Sioux Falls
Fenton, Lawrence Jules *pediatric educator*
Jaqua, Richard Allen *pathologist*
Morse, Peter Hodges *ophthalmologist, educator*
Trujillo, Angelina *endocrinologist*
Zawada, Edward Thaddeus, Jr. *physician, educator*

TENNESSEE

Memphis
Waller, Robert Rex *ophthalmologist, educator, foundation executive*

TEXAS

Houston
Bier, Dennis M. *medical educator*
Gabbard, Glen Owens *psychiatrist, psychoanalyst*

UTAH

Salt Lake City
Gleich, Gerald Joseph *immunologist, medical scientist*

VIRGINIA

Richmond
Ginder, Gordon Dean *physician, educator*

WISCONSIN

Appleton
Boren, Clark Henry, Jr. *general and vascular surgeon*

Fond Du Lac
Treffert, Darold Allen *psychiatrist, author, hospital director*

Hales Corners
Kuwayama, S. Paul *physician, allergist, immunologist*

Janesville
Gianitsos, Anestis Nicholas *surgeon*

La Crosse
Webster, Stephen Burtis *physician, educator*

Madison
Albert, Daniel Myron *ophthalmologist, educator*
Atkinson, Richard Lee, Jr. *internal medicine educator*
Bass, Paul *pharmacology educator*
Boutwell, Roswell Knight *oncology educator*
Brooks, Benjamin Rix *neurologist, educator*
Brown, Arnold Lanehart, Jr. *pathologist, educator, university dean*
Burgess, Richard Ray *oncology educator, molecular biology researcher, biotechnology consultant*
Carbone, Paul Peter *oncologist, educator, administrator*
DeMets, David L. *medical educator, biomedical researcher*
Dodson, Vernon Nathan *physician, educator*
Fahien, Leonard August *physician, educator*
Farrell, Philip M. *physician, educator, researcher*
Ford, Charles Nathaniel *otolaryngologist, educator*
Forster, Francis Michael *physician, educator*
Graziano, Frank Michael *medical educator, researcher*
Jefferson, James Walter *psychiatry educator*
Laessig, Ronald Harold *preventive medicine and pathology educator, state official*
Lemanske, Robert F., Jr. *allergist, immunologist*
MacKinney, Archie Allen, Jr. *physician*
Maki, Dennis G. *medical educator, researcher, clinician*
Malter, James Samuel *pathologist, educator*
Marton, Laurence Jay *researcher, educator, clinical pathologist*
McBeath, Andrew Alan *orthopedic surgery educator*
Niederhuber, John Edward *surgical oncologist and molecular immunologist, university educator and administrator*
Nordby, Eugene Jorgen *orthopedic surgeon*
Peters, Henry Augustus *neuropsychiatrist*
Pitot, Henry Clement, III *pathologist, educator*
Reynolds, Ernest West *retired physician, educator*
Robins, H(enry) Ian *medical oncologist*
Schutta, Henry Szczesny *neurologist, educator*
Sobkowicz, Hanna Maria *neurology researcher*
Sondel, Paul Mark *pediatric oncologist, educator*
Sonnedecker, Glenn Allen *pharmaceutical historian, pharmaceutical educator*
Urban, Frank Henry *retired dermatologist, state legislator*
Valdivia, Hector Horacio *medical educator*
Walker, Duard Lee *medical educator*
Wenger, Ronald David *surgeon*
Westman, Jack Conrad *child psychiatrist, educator*
Whiffen, James Douglass *surgeon, educator*
Wilson, Pamela Aird *physician*
Zografi, George *pharmacologist, educator*

Manitowoc
Trader, Joseph Edgar *orthopedic surgeon*

Marshfield
Kelman, Donald Brian *neurosurgeon*

Milwaukee
Cooper, Richard Alan *hematologist, college dean, health policy analyst*
Esterly, Nancy Burton *physician*
Hosenpud, Jeffrey *cardiovascular physician*
Kampine, John P. *anesthesiology and physiology educator*
Kochar, Mahendr Singh *physician, educator, administrator, scientist, writer, consultant*
Larson, David Lee *surgeon*
Montgomery, Robert Renwick *medical association administrator, educator*
Olinger, Gordon Nordell *surgeon*
Schultz, Richard Otto *ophthalmologist, educator*
Soergel, Konrad Hermann *physician*
Stokes, Kathleen Sarah *dermatologist, educator*
Terry, Leon Cass *neurologist, educator*
Towne, Jonathan Baker *vascular surgeon*

Yancey, Kim Bruce *dermatology researcher*
Youker, James Edward *radiologist*

Onalaska
Waite, Lawrence Wesley *osteopathic physician, educator*

Racine
Stewart, Richard Donald *internist, educator, biographer*

Wauwatosa
Hollister, Winston Ned *pathologist*

Woodruff
Agre, James Courtland *physical medicine and rehabilitation*

CANADA

MANITOBA

Winnipeg
Angel, Aubie *physician, academic administrator*
Friesen, Henry George *endocrinologist, educator*
Haworth, James Chilton *pediatrics educator*
Israels, Lyonel Garry *hematologist, medical educator*
Naimark, Arnold *medical educator, physiologist, educator*
Persaud, Trivedi Vidhya Nandan *anatomy educator, researcher, consultant*
Ross, Robert Thomas *neurologist, educator*
Schacter, Brent Allan *oncologist, health facility administrator*

ADDRESS UNPUBLISHED

Adamson, John William *hematologist*
Baldwin, DeWitt Clair, Jr. *physician, educator*
Baron, Jeffrey *retired pharmacologist*
Billion, John Joseph *orthopedic surgeon, former state representative*
Borden, Ernest Carleton *physician, educator*
Brown, Eli Matthew *anesthesiologist, department chairman*
Bubrick, Melvin Phillip *surgeon*
Caston, J(esse) Douglas *medical educator*
Cotsonas, Nicholas John, Jr. *physician, medical educator*
DiPersio, John F. *oncologist*
Drews, Robert Carrel *retired physician*
Eaton, Merrill Thomas *psychiatrist, educator*
Fischer, A(lbert) Alan *family physician*
Gable, Karen Elaine *health occupations educator*
Gilchrist, Gerald Seymour *pediatric hematologist, oncologist, educator*
Gillespie, Gary Don *physician*
H'Doubler, Francis Todd, Jr. *surgeon*
Hanson, David Gordon *otolaryngologist, surgeon*
Hecht, Harold Arthur *orchidologist, chiropractor*
Himes, John Harter *medical researcher, educator*
Howell, Joel DuBose *internist, educator*
Janicak, Philip Gregory *psychiatry educator, researcher*
Jensen, Lynn Edward *retired medical association executive, economist*
Jones, Doug E. *healthcare researcher, real estate broker, oil company owner*
Judge, Nancy Elizabeth *obstetrician, gynecologist*
Knapp, Howard Raymond *internist, clinical pharmacologist*
Krizan, Kelly Joe *physician, leather craftsman*
Loomis, Salora Dale *psychiatrist*
Mair, Douglas Dean *medical educator, consultant*
Moore, Emily Allyn *pharmacologist*
Murray, Raymond Harold *physician*
Nelson, Richard L. *physician*
O'Leary, Dennis Sophian *medical organization executive*
Palmer, Raymond Alfred *administrator, librarian, consultant*
Perez, Dianne M. *medical researcher*
Peterson, Ann Sullivan *physician, health care consultant*
Petz, Thomas Joseph *internist*
Ragland, Terry Eugene *emergency physician*
Raichle, Marcus Edward *radiology, neurology educator*
Rollins, Arlen Jeffery *osteopathic physician*
Ruoho, Arnold Eino *pharmacology educator*
Sacha, Robert Frank *osteopathic physician*
Shayman, James Alan *nephrologist, educator*
Smith, Duret S. *physician, medical educator*
Smith, Gregory Scott *medical researcher, educator*
St. Cyr, John Albert, II *cardiovascular and thoracic surgeon*
Stueland, Dean Theodore *emergency physician*
Thorsen, Marie Kristin *radiologist, educator*
Victor, Jay *retired dermatologist*
Walenga, Jeanine Marie *medical educator, researcher*
Westmoreland, Barbara Fenn *neurologist, electroencephalographer, educator*

HUMANITIES: LIBERAL STUDIES

UNITED STATES

CALIFORNIA

La Jolla
Falk, Julia S. *linguist, educator*

FLORIDA

Bradenton
Bateman, John Jay *classics educator*

Orlando
Ellens, J(ay) Harold *philosopher, educator, psychotherapist, pastor*

Winter Park
Wilson, Robley Conant, Jr. *English educator, editor, author*

ILLINOIS

Carbondale
Ammon, Harry *history educator*
Gilbert, Glenn Gordon *linguistics educator*

Champaign
Douglas, George Halsey *writer, educator*
Koenker, Diane P. *history educator*
O'Neill, John Joseph *speech educator*
Smith, Ralph Alexander *cultural and educational policy educator*

Chicago
Aronson, Howard Isaac *linguist, educator*
Bevington, David Martin *English literature educator*
Biggs, Robert Dale *Near Eastern studies educator*
Brinkman, John Anthony *historian, educator*
Cohen, Ted *philosophy educator*
Cullen, Charles Thomas *historian, librarian*
De Armas, Frederick Alfred *foreign language educator*
Debus, Allen George *history educator*
Dembowski, Peter Florian *foreign language educator*
Edelstein, Teri J. *art history educator, art administrator*
Erlebacher, Albert *history educator*
Fleischer, Cornell Hugh *history educator*
Gannon, Sister Ann Ida *retired philosophy educator, former college administrator*
Garber, Daniel Elliot *philosophy educator*
Gilman, Sander Lawrence *German language educator*
Goldsmith, John Anton *linguist, educator*
Gray, Hanna Holborn *history educator*
Haley, George *Romance languages educator*
Harris, Neil *historian, educator*
Headrick, Daniel Richard *history and social sciences educator*
Heller, Reinhold August *art educator, consultant*
Hellie, Richard *Russian history educator, researcher*
Hunter, J(ames) Paul *English language educator, literary critic, historian*
Ingham, Norman William *Russian literature educator, genealogist*
Karanikas, Alexander *English language educator, author, actor*
Keenan, James George *classics educator*
Lawler, James Ronald *French language educator*
Lieb, Michael *English educator, humanities educator*
Manning, Sylvia *English studies educator*
Marshall, Donald Glenn *English language and literature educator*
Najita, Tetsuo *history educator*
Nussbaum, Martha Craven *philosophy and classics educator*
O'Connell, Laurence J. *bioethics research administrator*
Pollock, Sheldon Ivan *language professional, educator*
Rosenheim, Edward Weil *English educator*
Roy, David Tod *Chinese literature educator*
Saller, Richard Paul *classics educator*
Shaughnessy, Edward Louis *Chinese language educator*
Sochen, June *history educator*
Tanner, Helen Hornbeck *historian, consultant*
Thaden, Edward Carl *history educator*

Elgin
Parks, Patrick *English language educator, humanities educator*

Evanston
Cole, Douglas *retired English literature educator*
Sheridan, James Edward *history educator*
Sundquist, Eric John *American studies educator*
Ver Steeg, Clarence Lester *historian, educator*
Well, Irwin *language educator*
Wright, John *classics educator*

Galesburg
Hane, Mikiso *history educator*

Lisle
Fortier, Mardelle LaDonna *English educator*

Macomb
Hallwas, John Edward *English language educator*
Spencer, Donald Spurgeon *historian, academic administrator*

Palatine
Hull, Elizabeth Anne *retired English language educator*

Palos Heights
Higgins, Francis Edward *history educator*

Romeoville
Lifka, Mary Lauranne *history educator*

Springfield
Davis, George Cullom *historian*
Temple, Wayne Calhoun *historian, writer*

Urbana
Aldridge, Alfred Owen *English language educator*
Antonsen, Elmer Harold *Germanic languages and linguistics educator*
Arnstein, Walter Leonard *historian, educator*
Baym, Nina *English educator*
Haile, H. G. *German language and literature educator*
Hurt, James Riggins *English language educator*
Jacobson, Howard *classics educator*
Love, Joseph L. *history educator, former cultural studies center administrator*
McColley, Robert McNair *history educator*
Newman, John Kevin *classics educator*
Scanlan, Richard Thomas *classics educator*
Solberg, Winton Udell *history educator*
Spence, Mary Lee *historian, educator*
Talbot, Emile Joseph *French language educator*
Watts, Emily Stipes *English language educator*

INDIANA

Bloomington
Anderson, Judith Helena *English language educator*
Cohen, William Benjamin *historian, educator*
Dunn, Jon Michael *informatics educator, dean*
Edgerton, William B. *foreign language educator*
Ferrell, Robert Hugh *historian, educator*
Juergens, George Ivar *history educator*
Martins, Heitor Miranda *foreign language educator*
Mickel, Emanuel John *foreign language educator*
Ransel, David Lorimer *history educator*
Rosenberg, Samuel Nathan *French and Italian language educator*
Sinor, Denis *Orientalist, educator*
Wilson, George Macklin *history educator, cultural studies center administrator*

Crawfordsville
Barnes, James John *history educator*

Fort Wayne
Scheetz, Sister Mary JoEllen *English language educator*

Greencastle
Dittmer, John Avery *history educator*
Weiss, Robert Orr *speech educator*

Indianapolis
Blair, Rebecca Sue *English educator, lay minister*
Bodenhamer, David Jackson *historian, educator*
Davis, Kenneth Wayne *English language educator, business communication consultant*
Plater, William Marmaduke *English language educator, academic administrator*

Notre Dame
Delaney, Cornelius Francis *philosophy educator*
Doody, Margaret Anne *English language educator*
Lanzinger, Klaus *language educator, educator*
Matthias, John Edward *English literature educator*
McInerny, Ralph Matthew *philosophy educator, writer*
Quinn, Philip Lawrence *philosophy educator*
Rosenberg, Charles Michael *art historian, educator*
Walicki, Andrzej Stanislaw *history of ideas educator*

South Bend
van Inwagen, Peter Jan *philosophy educator*

Terre Haute
Baker, Ronald Lee *English educator*

Valparaiso
Peters, Howard Nevin *foreign language educator*

West Lafayette
Bertolet, Rodney Jay *philosophy educator*
Contreni, John Joseph, Jr. *humanities educator, educator*
Mc Bride, William Leon *philosopher, educator*
Mork, Gordon Robert *historian, educator*
Woodman, Harold David *historian, educator*

IOWA

Cedar Falls
Maier, Donna Jane-Ellen *history educator*

Cedar Rapids
Lisio, Donald John *historian, educator*

Grinnell
Kaiser, Daniel Hugh *historian, educator*
Kintner, Philip L. *history educator*
Michaels, Jennifer Tonks *foreign language educator*

Iowa City
Addis, Laird Clark, Jr. *philosopher, educator, musician*
Butchvarov, Panayot Krustev *philosophy educator*
Dettmer, Helena R. *classics educator*
Ertl, Wolfgang *German language and literature educator*
Folsom, Lowell Edwin *language educator*
Goldstein, Jonathan Amos *retired ancient history and classics educator*
Green, Peter Morris *classics educator, writer, translator*
Hawley, Ellis Wayne *historian, educator*
Kerber, Linda Kaufman *historian, educator*
Raeburn, John Hay *English language educator*
Ringen, Catherine Oleson *linguistics educator*
Trank, Douglas Monty *rhetoric and speech communications educator*

Lamoni
Wight, Darlene *retired speech educator, emerita educator*

KANSAS

Dighton
Stanley, Ellen May *historian, consultant*

Great Bend
Gunn, Mary Elizabeth *retired English language educator*

Lawrence
Alexander, John Thorndike *historian, educator*
Debicki, Andrew Peter *foreign language educator*
Eldredge, Charles Child, III *art history educator*
Gunn, James E. *English language educator*
Kuznesof, Elizabeth Anne *history educator*
Li, Chu-Tsing *art history educator*
Quinn, Dennis B. *English language and literature educator*
Saul, Norman Eugene *history educator*
Spires, Robert Cecil *foreign language educator*
Tuttle, William McCullough, Jr. *history educator*
Woelfel, James Warren *philosophy and humanities educator*
Worth, George John *English literature educator*

KENTUCKY

Louisville
Ford, Gordon Buell, Jr. *English language, linguistics, and medieval studies educator, author, retired hospital industry accounting financial management executive*

MASSACHUSETTS

Chestnut Hill
Hachey, Thomas Eugene *British and Irish history educator, consultant*

Revere
Paananen, Victor Niles *English educator*

MICHIGAN

Ann Arbor
Becker, Marvin Burton *historian, educator*
Blouin, Francis Xavier, Jr. *history educator*
Bornstein, George Jay *literary educator*
Cowen, Roy Chadwell, Jr. *language educator, educator*
Curley, Edwin Munson *philosophy educator*
Dunnigan, Brian Leigh *military historian, curator*
Eisenberg, Marvin Julius *art history educator*
Eisenstein, Elizabeth Lewisohn *historian, educator*
Feuerwerker, Albert *history educator*
Forsyth, Ilene Haering *art historian*
Gomez, Luis Oscar *Asian and religious studies educator*
Hackett, Roger Fleming *history educator*
Knott, John Ray, Jr. *language professional, educator*
Mersereau, John, Jr. *Slavic languages and literatures educator*
Munro, Donald Jacques *philosopher, educator*
Stolz, Benjamin Armond *foreign language educator*
Trautmann, Thomas Roger *history and anthropology educator*
Zurier, Rebecca *art history educator*

Big Rapids
Mehler, Barry Alan *humanities educator, journalist, consultant*

Cedarville
Pittman, Philip McMillan *historian*

Dearborn
Little, Daniel Eastman *philosophy educator, university program director*

Detroit
Abt, Jeffrey *art and art history educator, artist, writer*
Brill, Lesley *literature and film studies educator*
Small, Melvin *history educator*

East Lansing
Eadie, John William *history educator*
Fisher, Alan Washburn *historian, educator*
Kronegger, Maria Elisabeth *French and comparative literature educator*
Mansour, George P. *Spanish language and literature educator*

Kalamazoo
Breisach, Ernst A. *historian, educator*
Dybek, Stuart *English educator, writer*
Jones, Leander Corbin *educator, media specialist*

Livonia
Holtzman, Roberta Lee *French and Spanish language educator*

Southfield
Papazian, Dennis Richard *history educator, political commentator*

MINNESOTA

Minneapolis
Bales, Kent Roslyn *English language educator*
Browne, Donald Roger *speech communication educator*
Campbell, Karlyn Kohrs *speech and communication educator*
Erickson, Gerald Meyer *classical studies educator*
Farah, Caesar Elie *Middle Eastern and Islamic studies educator*
Firchow, Evelyn Scherabon *German language and literature educator, writer*
Firchow, Peter Edgerly *language professional, educator, author*
Kohlstedt, Sally Gregory *history educator*
Marling, Karal Ann *art history and social sciences educator, curator*
Norberg, Arthur Lawrence, Jr. *historian, physicist educator*
Pazandak, Carol Hendrickson *liberal arts educator*
Ross, Donald, Jr. *English language educator, university administrator*
Scott, Robert Lee *speech educator*
Tracy, James Donald *historian, educator*
Weiss, Gerhard Hans *German language educator*

Northfield
Clark, Clifford Edward, Jr. *history educator*
Iseminger, Gary Hudson *philosophy educator*
Mason, Perry Carter *philosophy educator*
Sipfle, David Arthur *retired philosophy educator*

Johnson, Margaret Ann (Peggy) *library administrator*
Shaughnessy, Thomas William *librarian, consultant*

Northfield
Hong, Howard Vincent *library administrator, philosophy educator, editor, translator*

Rochester
Key, Jack Dayton *librarian*

Saint Paul
Kane, Lucile M. *retired archivist, historian*
Wagner, Mary Margaret *library and information science educator*
Zietlow, Ruth Ann *reference librarian*

MISSISSIPPI

Jackson
Smith, Sharman Bridges *state librarian*

MISSOURI

Columbia
Alexander, Martha Sue *librarian*
Almony, Robert Allen, Jr. *librarian, businessman*

Independence
Ferguson, John Wayne, Sr. *librarian*
Johnson, Niel Melvin *archivist, historian*

Jefferson City
Parker, Sara Ann *librarian, consultant*

Kansas City
Bradbury, Daniel Joseph *library administrator*
Miller, William Charles *theological librarian, educator*
Pedram, Marilyn Beth *reference librarian*
Sheldon, Ted Preston *library dean*
Zeller, Marilynn Kay *librarian*

Lake Lotawana
Zobrist, Benedict Karl *library director, historian*

Saint Louis
Holt, Glen Edward *library administrator*
Holt, Leslie Edmonds *librarian*

Springfield
Busch, Annie *library director*

NEBRASKA

Lincoln
Connor, Carol J. *library director*
Montag, John Joseph, II *librarian*
Wagner, Rod *library director*

NEW YORK

New York
Sager, Donald Jack *librarian, consultant, former publisher*

NORTH DAKOTA

Bismarck
Ott, Doris Ann *librarian*

OHIO

Athens
Lee, Hwa-Wei *librarian, educator, consultant*

Bluffton
Dudley, Durand Stowell *librarian*

Cincinnati
Brestel, Mary Beth *librarian*
Everett, Karen Joan *retired librarian, genealogy educator*
Proffitt, Kevin *archivist*
Schutzius, Lucy Jean *retired librarian*
Wellington, Jean Susorney *librarian*
Zafren, Herbert Cecil *librarian, educator*

Cleveland
Abid, Ann B. *art librarian*
Pike, Kermit Jerome *library director*

Columbus
Black, Larry David *library director*
Branscomb, Lewis Capers, Jr. *librarian, educator*
Sawyers, Elizabeth Joan *librarian, administrator*
Studer, William Joseph *library educator*

Dayton
Chait, William *librarian, consultant*
Klinck, Cynthia Anne *library director*
Wallach, John S(idney) *library administrator*

Delaware
Schlichting, Catherine Fletcher Nicholson *librarian, educator*

Hubbard
Trucksis, Theresa A. *retired library director*

Middleburg Heights
Maciuszko, Kathleen Lynn *librarian, educator*

Oberlin
English, Ray *library administrator*

Oxford
Sessions, Judith Ann *librarian, university library dean*

Wooster
Hickey, Damon Douglas *library director*

SOUTH DAKOTA

Brookings
Marquardt, Steve Robert *library director*

Pierre
Miller, Suzanne Marie *state librarian*

Sioux Falls
Dertien, James LeRoy *librarian*
Thompson, Ronelle Kay Hildebrandt *library director*

WISCONSIN

Kenosha
Baker, Douglas Finley *library director*

Madison
Bunge, Charles Albert *library science educator*
Korenic, Lynette Marie *librarian*
Potter, Calvin J. *library director*

Milwaukee
Huston, Kathleen Marie *library administrator*

Oshkosh
Jones, Norma Louise *librarian, educator*

ADDRESS UNPUBLISHED

Estes, Elaine Rose Graham *retired librarian*
Gaertner, Donell John *retired library director*
Jenkins, Darrell Lee *librarian*
Kaufman, Paula T. *librarian*
Morgan, Jane Hale *retired library director*
Scoles, Clyde Sheldon *library director*
Wilson, C. Daniel, Jr. *library director*

HUMANITIES: MUSEUMS

UNITED STATES

ARIZONA

Tucson
King, James Edward *retired museum director, other: museums*

DISTRICT OF COLUMBIA

Washington
Ucko, David Alan *museum director*

GEORGIA

Robins AFB
Schmidt, Wayne William *museum director, curator*

ILLINOIS

Bolingbrook
Madori, Jan *art gallery director*

Carbondale
Whitlock, John Joseph *museum director*

Champaign
Nevling, Lorin Ives, Jr. *museum administrator*

Chicago
Balzekas, Stanley, Jr. *museum director*
Flynn, John J. *museum curator*
Heltne, Paul Gregory *museum executive*
Kamyszew, Christopher D. *museum curator, executive educator, art consultant*
Knappenberger, Paul Henry, Jr. *science museum director*
Kubida, Judith Ann *museum administrator*
Mc Carter, John Wilbur, Jr. *museum executive*
Nordland, Gerald *art museum administrator, historian, consultant*
Weisberg, Lois *arts administrator, city official*
Wood, James Nowell *museum director and executive*
Zukowsky, John Robert *curator*

Evanston
Lewis, Phillip Harold *museum curator*

Springfield
Hallmark, Donald Parker *museum director, lecturer*
Mc Millan, R(obert) Bruce *museum executive, anthropologist*
Wynn, Nan L. *historic site administrator*

INDIANA

Bloomington
Calinescu, Adriana Gabriela *museum curator, art historian*
Gealt, Adelheid Maria *museum director*

Evansville
Streetman, John William, III *museum official*

Fort Wayne
Watkinson, Patricia Grieve *museum director*

Indianapolis
Cilella, Salvatore George, Jr. *museum director*
Gantz, Richard Alan *museum administrator*
Noble, Douglas Ross *museum administrator*
Waller, Aaron Bret, III *museum director*

Muncie
Joyaux, Alain Georges *art museum director*

IOWA

Cedar Rapids
Pitts, Terence Randolph *museum director, consultant*

Davenport
Bradley, William Steven *art museum director*

Iowa City
Smothers, Ann Elizabeth *museum director*

KANSAS

Dodge City
Clifton-Smith, Rhonda Darleen *art center director*

Lawrence
Norris, Andrea Spaulding *art museum director*

Manhattan
Render, Lorne *museum director*

MICHIGAN

Ann Arbor
Bailey, Reeve Maclaren *museum curator*

Detroit
Beal, Graham William John *museum director*
Darr, Alan Phipps *curator, historian*
Parrish, Maurice Drue *museum executive*
Peck, William Henry *museum curator, art historian, archaeologist, author, lecturer*

East Lansing
Bandes, Susan Jane *museum director, educator*
Dewhurst, Charles Kurt *museum director, curator, folklorist, English language educator*

Flint
Germann, Steven James *museum director*

Kalamazoo
Norris, Richard Patrick *museum director, history educator*

MINNESOTA

Minneapolis
King, Lyndel Irene Saunders *art museum director*

Saint Paul
Osman, Stephen Eugene *historic site administrator*
Peterson, James Lincoln *museum executive*

MISSOURI

Hannibal
Sweets, Henry Hayes, III *museum director*

Independence
Hackman, Larry J. *program director, consulant*

Kansas City
McKenna, George LaVerne *art museum curator*
Scott, Deborah Emont *curator*
Wilson, Marc Fraser *art museum director*

Saint Joseph
Chilcote, Gary M. *museum director, reporter*

Saint Louis
Burke, James Donald *museum administrator*
Crandell, Dwight Samuel *retired museum executive*

Springfield
Berger, Jerry Allen *museum director*

NEBRASKA

Boys Town
Lynch, Thomas Joseph *museum and historic house manager*

Lincoln
Wallis, Deborah *curator*

NEW YORK

Hamilton
Moynihan, William J. *museum executive*

New York
Wardropper, Ian Bruce *museum curator, educator*

OHIO

Akron
Kahan, Mitchell Douglas *art museum director*

Cincinnati
Desmarais, Charles Joseph *museum director, writer, editor*
Rogers, Millard Foster, Jr. *art museum director emeritus*
Rub, Timothy F. *museum director*
Timpano, Anne *museum director, art historian*

Dayton
Meister, Mark Jay *museum director, professional society administrator*
Nyerges, Alexander Lee *museum director*

Fremont
Bridges, Roger Dean *historical agency administrator*

Mentor
Miller, Frances Suzanne *historic site curator*

Solon
Ward, William Edward *museum exhibition designer*

Wright Patterson AFB
Metcalf, Charles David *museum director, retired military officer*

Youngstown
Ruffer, David Gray *retired museum director, former college president*
Zona, Louis Albert *art institute director*

OREGON

Portland
Taylor, J(ocelyn) Mary *museum administrator, zoologist, educator*

PENNSYLVANIA

Philadelphia
Turner, Evan Hopkins *retired art museum director*

SOUTH DAKOTA

Keystone
Wenk, Daniel N. *landmark site administrator*

Lake City
Daberkow, Dave *historic site director*

WISCONSIN

Appleton
Harrington, Beverly *museum director*

Green Bay
Justen, Ralph *museum director*

Madison
Fleischman, Stephen *art center director*
Garver, Thomas Haskell *curator, art consultant, writer*
Westphal, Klaus Wilhelm *university museum director*

CANADA

MANITOBA

Winnipeg
Di Cosimo, Joanne Violet *museum director*

ONTARIO

London
Pearce, Robert J. *museum director*

ADDRESS UNPUBLISHED

Ahrens, Kent *museum director, art historian*
Combs, Robert Kimbal *museum director*
Hellmers, Norman Donald *historic site director*
Kahn, James Steven *retired museum director*
Nold, Carl Richard *state historic parks and museums administrator*
Schloder, John E. *museum director*
Smith, Marjorie Aileen Matthews *museum director*
Steadman, David Wilton *retired museum official*
Stearns, Robert Leland *curator*
Wilson, Karen Lee *museum director*

INDUSTRY: MANUFACTURING
See also **FINANCE: FINANCIAL SERVICES**

UNITED STATES

CALIFORNIA

Aliso Viejo
Hake, Ralph F. *construction company executive*

Fremont
Rusch, Thomas William *manufacturing executive*

Newport Beach
Bennett, Bruce W. *construction company executive, civil engineer*

Rancho Santa Fe
Step, Eugene Lee *retired pharmaceutical company executive*

San Diego
Hanson, John Nils *industrial high technology manufacturing company executive*

FLORIDA

Boca Grande
Hayes, Scott Birchard *raw materials company executive*

Naples
Williams, Edson Poe *retired automotive company executive*

Sarasota
Venit, William Bennett *electrical products company executive, consultant*

Venice
Lanford, Luke Dean *retired electronics company executive*

Wesley Chapel
Revelle, Donald Gene *manufacturing and health care company executive, consultant*

GEORGIA

Braselton
Copper, James Robert *manufacturing company executive*

Sea Island
Mc Swiney, James Wilmer *retired pulp and paper manufacturing company executive*

ILLINOIS

Abbott Park
Amundson, Joy A. *pharmaceutical and health products executive*
Brown, Thomas D. *pharmaceutical executive*
Hodgson, Thomas Richard *retired healthcare company executive*
Lussen, John Frederick *pharmaceutical laboratory executive*
White, Miles D. *pharmaceutical company executive*

Arlington Heights
Hughes, John *chemical company executive*
Li, Norman N. *chemicals executive*

Aurora
Cano, Juventino *manufacturing company executive*

Bedford Park
Courtney, David W. *chemical company executive*
Ripley, James W. *food products executive*
Scott, Samuel C. *food products executive*

Broadview
Pang, Joshua Keun-Uk *trade company executive*

Champaign
Richards, Daniel Wells *company executive*

Chester
Welge, Donald Edward *food manufacturing executive*

Chicago
Be Sant, Craig *company executive*
Belz, Raymond T. *manufacturing company executive*
Bergere, Carleton Mallory *contractor*
Brake, Cecil Clifford *retired diversified manufacturing executive*
Bryan, John Henry *food and consumer products company executive*
Bueche, Wendell Francis *agricultural products company executive*
Carlson, James R. *food products executive*
Chiappetta, Robert A. *manufacturing executive*
Conant, Howard Rosset *steel company executive*
Cooper, Charles Gilbert *toiletries and cosmetics company executive*
Cotter, Daniel A. *diversified company executive*
Covalt, Robert Byron *chemicals executive*
Crown, Lester *manufacturing company executive*
Crown, William H. *manufacturing executive*
Curran, Raymond M. *paper-based packaging company executive*
Cygan, Thomas S. *metal products executive*
Dages, Peter F. *manufacturing executive*
deKool, L.M. (Theo) *food products executive*
Drexler, Richard Allan *manufacturing company executive*
Fiedler, John F. *automotive executive*
Gidwitz, Gerald *retired hair care company executive*
Giesen, Richard Allyn *business executive*
Goetschel, Arthur W. *industrial manufacturing executive*
Gordon, Ellen Rubin *candy company executive*
Haas, Howard Green *retired bedding manufacturing company executive*
Hand, Elbert O. *clothing manufacturing and retailing company executive*
Holland, Eugene, Jr. *lumber company executive*
Horne, John R. *farm equipment company executive*
Jartz, John G. *food company executive*
Jezuit, Leslie James *manufacturing company executive*
Kampouris, Emmanuel Andrew *retired corporate executive*
Linde, Ronald Keith *corporate executive, private investor*
Little, William G. *manufacturing executive*
Lockwood, Frank James *manufacturing company executive*
Luster, Jory F. *president of manufacturing company*
Martin, Terence D. *food products executive*
McKee, Keith Earl *manufacturing technology executive*
McMillan, C. Steven *food products executive*
McMillan, Cary D. *food products executive*
Meysman, Frank L. *food and consumer products executive*
Miglin, Marilyn *cosmetic executive*
Mohr, Terrence B. *food company executive*
Montgomery, Gary B. *manufacturing executive*
Moore, Patrick J. *paper company executive*
Murphy, Michael Emmett *retired food company executive*
Netherland, Joseph H. *manufacturing executive*
Nichol, Norman J. *manufacturing executive*
Nichols, John Doane *diversified manufacturing corporation executive*
Novich, Neil S. *metals distribution company executive*
Parrish, Overton Burgin, Jr. *pharmaceutical corporation executive*
Patel, Homi Burjor *apparel company executive*
Pritzker, Robert Alan *manufacturing company executive*
Rosenberg, Gary Aron *real estate development executive, lawyer*
Sanderman, Maurice *construction company executive*
Skyes, Gregory *food products executive*
Smithburg, William Dean *food manufacturing company executive, retired*
Sprieser, Judith A. *food products company executive*
Stack, Stephen S. *manufacturing company executive*
Stone, Alan *container company executive*
Sykes, Gregory *food products executive*
Tryloff, Robin S. *food products executive*
Wellington, Robert Hall *manufacturing company executive*
Williams, Richard Lucas, III *electronics company executive, lawyer*
Zeffren, Eugene *toiletries company executive*

Crystal Lake
Althoff, J(ames) L. *construction company executive*
Anderson, Lyle Arthur *retired manufacturing company executive*
Harris, King William *manufacturing company executive*

Decatur
Andreas, Glenn Allen, Jr. *agricultural company executive*
Kraft, Burnell D. *agricultural products company executive*
McNamara, John D. *food products executive*
Schmalz, Douglas J. *agricultural company executive*
Staley, Henry Mueller *manufacturing company executive*

Deerfield
Drohan, David F. *medical products company executive*
Glanzmann, Thomas H. *healthcare company executive*
Graham, William B. *pharmaceutical company executive*
Joseph, Donald W. *health care products executive*
Keough, Michael J. *paper manufacturing executive*
Kraemer, Harry M. Jansen, Jr. *medical products company executive*
Marsh, Miles L. *paper company executive*
Mason, Earl Leonard *food products executive*
McGinley, Jack L. *healthcare company executive*
Mohan, Kshitij *healthcare company executive*
Rogna, Lawrence G. *packaging company executive*
Strubel, Richard Perry *company executive*
Zywicki, Robert Albert *electrical distribution company executive*

Dekalb
Bickner, Bruce *food products executive*

Des Plaines
Carroll, Barry Joseph *manufacturing and real estate executive*
Frank, James S. *automotive executive*
O'Dwyer, Mary Ann *automovitve executive*
Pearson, Ford G. *automotive executive*
Schwarz, Steven R. *stationary company executive*

Downers Grove
Grinter, Donald W. *metal processing executive*
Stevenson, Judy G. *instrument manufacturing executive*

Dundee
Villars, Horace Sumner *retired food company executive, marketing professional*

Elmhurst
Duchossois, Craig *manufacturing executive, heavy*
Duchossois, Richard Louis *manufacturing executive, racetrack executive*
Fealy, Robert S. *manufacturing executive*

Forest Park
Thomas, Alan *candy company executive*

Frankfort
Burhoe, Brian Walter *automotive service executive*

Franklin Park
Caruso, Fred *plastics manufacturing company executive*
Dean, Howard M., Jr. *food company executive*
Simpson, Michael *metals service center executive*

Freeport
Alldredge, William T. *metal products executive*
Ferguson, Daniel C. *diversified company executive*
McDonough, John J. *household products company executive*
Sovey, William Pierre *manufacturing company executive*

Glenview
Farrell, W. James *metal products manufacturing company executive*
Flaum, Russell M. *tool manufacturing company executive*
Hansen, Thomas J. *tool manufacturing company executive*
Hudnut, Stewart Skinner *manufacturing company executive, lawyer*
Kinney, Jon C. *metal products executive*
Ptak, Frank Stanley *manufacturing executive*
Ringler, James M. *cookware company executive*
Smith, Harold B. *manufacturing executive*

Hoffman Estates
Nicholas, Arthur Soterios *manufacturing company executive*

Itasca
Boler, John *manufacturing executive*
Fellowes, James *manufacturing company executive*
Garratt, Reginald George *electronics executive*

Lake Forest
Buckley, George W. *sporting goods executive*
Fluno, Jere David *business executive*
Fowler, Robert Edward, Jr. *former agricultural products company executive*
Hadad, Sam *food products distribution executive*
Hamilton, Peter Bannerman *business executive, lawyer*
Keyser, Richard Lee *distribution company executive*
Larson, Peter N. *company executive*
Lenon, Richard Allen *chemical corporation executive*
O'Mara, Thomas Patrick *manufacturing company executive*
Reichert, Jack Frank *manufacturing company executive*
Reyes, J. Christopher *food products distribution executive*
Reyes, M. Judy *food products distribution executive*
Romersa, Anthony Joseph *manufacturing executive*

Lake Villa
Anderson, Milton Andrew *chemical executive*

Lansing
Stuart, Robert *container manufacturing executive*

Libertyville
Burrows, Brian William *research and development manufacturing executive*

Lincolnshire
Bayly, George V. *manufacturing executive*
Bonfield, Gordon Bradley, III *paper company executive*
Simes, Stephen Mark *pharmaceutical products executive*
Wesley, Norman H. *metal products executive*

Lisle
Birck, Michael John *manufacturing company executive, electrical engineer*
King, J. Joseph *electronics executive*
Krehbiel, Frederick August, II *electronics company executive*
Ryan, Joan *food company executive*

Long Grove
Liuzzi, Robert C. *chemical company executive*

Loves Park
Gloyd, Lawrence Eugene *retired diversified manufacturing company executive*

Mahomet
Bosworth, Douglas LeRoy *international company executive, educator*

Matteson
Johnson, Eric G. *food products company executive*

Melrose Park
Bernick, Howard Barry *manufacturing company executive*
Cernugel, William John *consumer products and special retail executive*
Douglas, Kenneth Jay *food products executive*
Lavin, Bernice E. *cosmetics executive*
Umans, Alvin Robert *manufacturing company executive*

Moline
Becherer, Hans Walter *retired agricultural equipment executive*
England, Joseph Walker *heavy equipment manufacturing company executive*
Hanson, Robert Arthur *retired agricultural equipment executive*
Jones, Nathan Jerome *farm machinery manufacturing company executive*
Lane, Robert W. *farm equipment manufacturing executive*

Mundelein
Mills, James Stephen *medical supply company executive*

Naperville
Smetana, Mark *food products executive*
Wake, Richard W. *food products executive*
Wake, Thomas G. *food products executive*

Niles
Herb, Marvin J. *food products executive*

Northbrook
Harris, Neison *manufacturing company executive*
Hoffman, Charles Steven *fertilizer company executive*
Sayatovic, Wayne Peter *manufacturing company executive*
Schmidt, Arthur Irwin *steel fabricating company executive*
Stone, Roger Warren *container company executive*

Northfield
Brown, A. Demetrius *metal products executive*
Carlin, Donald Walter *retired food products executive, consultant*
Hadley, Stanton Thomas *international manufacturing and marketing company executive, lawyer*
Stepan, Frank Quinn *chemical company executive*

Oak Brook
Conley, Michael L. *food products executive*
Greenberg, Jack M. *food products executive*
Kanzler, Michael W. *manufacturing company executive*
Kirshnan, Raama *electronics executive*
Rao, Prasad *electronics executive*

Oregon
Abbott, David Henry *manufacturing company executive*

Orland Park
Gittelman, Marc Jeffrey *manufacturing and financial executive*
Kahn, Jan Edward *manufacturing company executive*

Palos Park
Nelson, Lawrence Evan *business consultant*

Peoria
McPheeters, F. Lynn *manufacturing executive*
Oberhelman, Douglas R. *tractor company executive*
Owens, James W. *manufacturing executive*
Shaheen, Gerald L. *manufacturing executive*
Thompson, Richard L. *manufacturing executive*
Thorstenson, Terry N. *construction equipment company executive*

Prospect Heights
Byrne, Michael Joseph *business executive*

Rockford
Gaylord, Edson I. *manufacturing company executive*
Horst, Bruce Everett *manufacturing company executive*

Rolling Meadows
Brennan, Charles Martin, III *construction company executive*
Hill, David K., Jr. *construction executive*
Yakim, Greg *construction executive*

Rosemont
Isenberg, Howard Lee *manufacturing company executive*
Meinert, John Raymond *investment banker, clothing manufacturing and retailing executive*

Saint Charles
Fishbune, Robert *food products executive*
Heisley, Michael E. *manufacturing executive*
Stone, John McWilliams, Jr. *electronics executive*
Wolski, L.G. *heavy manufacturing executive*

Schaumburg
Galvin, Christopher B. *electronics company executive*
Koenemann, Carl F. *electronics company executive*
Soderberg, Leif G. *electronics company executive*
Tooker, Gary Lamarr *electronics company executive*
Tucker, Frederick Thomas *electronics company executive*

Skokie
Caldwell, Wiley North *retired distribution company executive*

Warrenville
Lannert, Robert Cornelius *manufacturing company executive*
Lennes, Gregory *manufacturing and financing company executive*

Waukegan
Cherry, Peter Ballard *electrical products corporation executive*

Westmont
Kuhn, Robert Mitchell *retired rubber company executive*
Warner, H. Ty *manufacturing executive*

Wheeling
Rogers, Richard F. *construction company executive, architect, engineer*

Wilmette
Coughlan, Gary Patrick *pharmaceutical company executive*
Egloff, Fred Robert *manufacturers representative, writer, historian*
Pearlman, Jerry Kent *electronics company executive*

Winnetka
Burt, Robert Norcross *retired diversified manufacturing company executive*
Kennedy, George Danner *chemical company executive*
Puth, John Wells *consulting company executive*
Toll, Daniel Roger *corporate executive, civic leader*

Woodridge
Stall, Alan David *packaging company executive*

INDIANA

Anderson
Snyder, Thomas J. *automotive company executive*

Bluffton
Lawson, William Hogan, III *electrical motor manufacturing executive*

Carmel
Walsh, John Charles *metallurgical company executive*

Chesterton
Brown, Gene W. *steel company executive*

Columbus
Henderson, James Alan *former engine company executive*
Loughrey, F. Joseph *manufacturing executive*
Miller, Joseph Irwin *automotive manufacturing company executive*

Elkhart
Corson, Keith Daniel *business executive*
Corson, Thomas Harold *manufacturing company executive*
Davis, Cole *recreational vehicle manufacturing executive*
Decio, Arthur Julius *manufacturing company executive*
Kloska, Ronald Frank *manufacturing company executive*
Martin, Rex *manufacturing executive*

Evansville
Koch, Robert Louis, II *manufacturing company executive, mechanical engineer*
Muehlbauer, James Herman *manufacturing executive*

Fort Wayne
Burns, Thagrus Asher *manufacturing company executive, former life insurance company executive*
Marine, Clyde Lockwood *agricultural business consultant*
Molfenter, David P. *former electronics executive*
Rifkin, Leonard *metals company executive*

Franklin
Janis, F. Timothy *technology company executive*

Goshen
Schrock, Harold Arthur *manufacturing company executive*

Indianapolis
Atkins, Steven *construction executive, contractor*
Bindley, William Edward *pharmaceutical executive*
Bounsall, Phillip A. *electronics company executive*
Bulriss, Mark *chemicals executive*
Burks, Keith W. *pharmaceutical executive*
Dollens, Ronald W. *pharmaceuticals company executive*
Doney, Bart J. *manufacturing executive*
Dunn, Steven M. *construction executive*
Foxworthy, James C. *manufacturing executive*
Golden, Charles E. *pharmaceutical company executive*
Goodman, Dwight *manufacturing executive*
Howell, J. Mark *electronics company executive*
Hunt, Robert Chester *construction company executive*
Justice, Brady Richmond, Jr. *medical services executive*
King, J. B. *medical device company executive, lawyer*
Kirkham, James Alvin *manufacturing executive*
Lacy, Andre Balz *industrial executive*
Laikin, Robert J. *electronics company executive*
Lewis, Jeff *construction company executive*
Mays, William G. *chemical company executive*
Salentine, Thomas James *pharmaceutical company executive*
Scheumann, John B. *construction executive*
Taurel, Sidney *pharmaceutical executive*
Tobias, Randall Lee *retired pharmaceutical company executive*
Tomlinson, Joseph Ernest *manufacturing company executive*

Jasper
Habig, Douglas Arnold *manufacturing company executive*
Thyen, James C. *furniture company executive*

Lafayette
Meyer, Brud Richard *retired pharmaceutical company executive*

Loogootee
Burcham, Eva Helen (Pat Burcham) *retired electronics technician*

Middlebury
Guequierre, John Phillip *manufacturing company executive*

Mishawaka
Altman, Arnold David *business executive*
Kapson, Jordan *automotive executive*
Merryman, George *automotive executive*
Rubenstein, Pamela Silver *precision machinery executive*

Muncie
Fisher, John Wesley *manufacturing company executive*

Munster
Corsiglia, Robert Joseph *electrical construction company executive*
Luerssen, Frank Wonson *retired steel company executive*

Nappanee
Shea, James F. *manufacturing executive*

Nashville
Stackhouse, David William, Jr. *retired furniture systems installation contractor*

Portage
Popp, Joseph Bruce *manufacturing executive*

Seymour
Rust, Lois *food company executive*

Warsaw
Miller, Dane Alan *medical device manufacturing company*

IOWA

Amana
Carroll, Charles A. *manufacturing executive*

Ames
Abbott, David L. *agricultural products executive*

Cedar Rapids
Jones, Clayton M. *computer and electronics company executive*

Dubuque
Crahan, Jack Bertsch *retired manufacturing company executive*

Muscatine
Carver, Martin Gregory *tire manufacturing company executive*
Howe, Stanley Merrill *manufacturing company executive*
Michaels, Jack D. *office furniture manufacturing executive*
Stuebe, David Charles *steel products manufacturing company executive*

Newton
Beer, William L. *appliance company executive*
Blanford, Lawrence J. *appliance company executive*
Hadley, Leonard Anson *appliance manufacturing corporation executive*
Ward, Lloyd D. *appliance company executive*

Okoboji
Pearson, Gerald Leon *food company executive*

Saint Ansgar
Kleinworth, Edward J. *agricultural company executive*

West Des Moines
Pomerantz, Marvin Alvin *business executive*

KANSAS

Dodge City
Chaffin, Gary Roger *business executive*

Hesston
Yost, Lyle Edgar *retired farm equipment manufacturing company executive*

Hutchinson
Dick, Harold Latham *manufacturing executive*

Leavenworth
Arneson, George Stephen *manufacturing company executive, management consultant*

Lenexa
Pierson, John Theodore, Jr. *manufacturer*

Salina
Cosco, John Anthony *health care executive, educator, consultant*

Scott City
Duff, Craig *agricultural products executive*

Shawnee Mission
Steer, Robert L. *food products executive*

Silver Lake
Rueck, Jon Michael *manufacturing executive*

Topeka
Etzel, Timothy *manufacturing executive*

Wichita
Bukaty, Michael Edward *manufacturing company executive*
Eby, Martin Keller, Jr. *construction company executive*
Johnson, George Taylor *training and manufacturing executive*
Koch, Charles de Ganahl *manufacturing executive*
Meyer, Russell William, Jr. *aircraft company executive*
Nienke, Steven A. *construction company executive*

MASSACHUSETTS

Westwood
Kushner, Jeffrey L. *manufacturing company executive*

MICHIGAN

Addison
Knight, V. C. *manufacturing executive*

Ann Arbor
Decaire, John *electronics executive, aerospace engineer*
Decker, Raymond Frank *technology transfer executive, metal products executive, scientist*
Herzig, David Jacob *pharmaceutical company executive, consultant*
Lutz, Robert Anthony *automotive company executive*
Penske, Roger S. *manufacturing and transportation executive*
Robertson, David Wayne *pharmaceutical company executive*
Winbury, Martin Maurice *pharmaceutical executive, educator*

Auburn Hills
Davidson, William M. *diversified company executive, professional basketball executive*
Eaton, Robert James *retired automotive executive*
Farrar, Stephen Prescott *glass products manufacturing executive*
Valade, Gary C. *automobile company executive*
Young, Walter R., Jr. *manufacturing company executive*

Battle Creek
Banks, Donna Jo *food products executive*
Gutierrez, Carlos M. *grocery manufacturing company executive*
Langbo, Arnold Gordon *food company executive*

Benton Harbor
Brown, Mark E. *manufacturing executive*
Fettig, Jeff M. *manufacturing executive*
Hopp, Daniel Frederick *manufacturing company executive, lawyer*
Whitwam, David Ray *appliance manufacturing company executive*

Beulah
Edwards, Wallace Winfield *retired automotive company executive*

Bingham Farms
Naglick, Robert A. *automotive suppliers holding company executive*

Birmingham
VanDeusen, Bruce Dudley *company executive*

Bloomfield Hills
Cregg, Roger A. *construction executive*
Hagenlocker, Edward E. *retired automobile company executive*
Leonard, Michael A. *automotive executive*
Mullens, Delbert W. *automotive executive*
O'Brien, Mark J. *real estate/residential construction executive*
Pulte, William J. *construction executive*

Cass City
Althaver, Lambert Ewing *manufacturing company executive*

Dearborn
Barton, Robert H., III *automotive executive*
Bixby, Harold Glenn *manufacturing company executive*
Booker, W. Wayne *automotive executive*
Corlett, Ed *automotive executive*
Ford, William Clay *automotive company executive, professional sports team executive*
Ford, William Clay, Jr. *automotive executive*
Petrauskas, Helen O. *automobile manufacturing company executive*
Rintamaki, John M. *automotive executive*
Trotman, Alexander J. *retired automobile manufacturing company executive*

Deckerville
Smith, Wayne Arthur *export company executive*

Detroit
Aguirre, Pamela Ann *manufacturing executive*
Dauch, Richard E. *automobile manufacturing company executive*
Devine, John Martin *automotive company executive*
DiFeo, Samuel X. *automotive executive*
Ferguson, James Peter *distilling company executive*
Henry, William Lockwood *former food products executive, brewery executive*
Hughes, Louis Ralph *automotive executive*
Kalman, Andrew *manufacturing company executive*
Levy, Edward Charles, Jr. *manufacturing company executive*
Losh, J. Michael *automotive company executive*
Pickard, William Frank *plastics company executive*
Rakolta, John, Jr. *construction executive*
Smith, John Francis, Jr. *automobile company executive*
Sperlich, Harold Keith *automobile company executive*
Wagoner, G. Richard, Jr. *automotive company executive*

Ferndale
Dodd, Geralda *metal products executive*

Flint
Goodstein, Sanders Abraham *scrap iron company executive*

Fraser
Butler, James E. *automotive executive*
Winget, Larry J. *automotive industry executive*

Grand Rapids
Baker, Hollis MacLure *furniture manufacturing company executive*
Currie, William G. *forest products executive*
Hackett, James P. *manufacturing executive*
Helder, Bruce Alan *metal products executive*
Pew, Robert Cunningham, II *office equipment manufacturing company executive*
Rougier-Chapman, Alwyn Spencer Douglas *furniture manufacturing company executive*
Woodrick, Robert *food products executive*

Grosse Pointe Farms
Allen, Lee Harrison *industrial consultant, wholesale company executive*
Valk, Robert Earl *corporate executive*

Grosse Pointe Park
Krebs, William Hoyt *company executive, industrial hygienist*

Holland
Baumgardner, John Dwane *manufacturing company executive*
Donnelly, John F. *automotive part company executive*
Haworth, Gerrard Wendell *office systems manufacturing company executive*
Haworth, Richard G. *office furniture manufacturer*
Johanneson, Gerald Benedict *office products company executive*
Kreuze, Calvin *office products company executive*
Reed, Scott *automotive parts company executive*
Viola, Donn J. *manufacturing company executive*

Holt
Garrison, Charles Eugene *retired automotive executive*

Jackson
Kelly, Robert Vincent, Jr. *metal company executive*
Vischer, Harold Harry *manufacturing company executive*

Kalamazoo
Edmondson, Keith Henry *chemical company executive, retired*
Markin, David Robert *motor company executive*
Meisenhelder, Robert John, II *pharmaceutical company executive*
Vescovi, Selvi *pharmaceutical company executive*
Wilson, James Rodney *air equipment company executive*

Lansing
Hines, Marshall *construction engineering company executive*

Madison Heights
Kafarski, Mitchell I. *chemical processing company executive*

Mason
Dart, Kenneth *food container manufacturing executive*
Myers, William *food container manufacturing executive*

Midland
Carbone, Anthony J. *chemicals executive*
Hazleton, Richard A. *chemicals executive*
Parker, Michael D. *chemicals executive*
Popoff, Frank Peter *chemical company executive*
Reinhard, Joao Pedro *chemicals company executive*
Stavropoulos, William S. *chemical executive*

Monroe
Kiser, Gerald L. *furniture company executive*

Muskegon
Blystone, John B. *manufacturing executive*

Northville
Cucuz, Ranko (Ron Cucuz) *manufacturing executive*

Owosso
Guthrie, Carlton L. *automotive manufacturing company executive*

Plymouth
Barth, John M. *manufacturing executive*
Massey, Donald E. *automotive executive*
Navarre, Robert Ward *manufacturing company executive*
Vlcek, Donald Joseph, Jr. *food distribution company executive, consultant, business author, executive coach*

Pontiac
Mahone, Barbara Jean *automotive company executive*

Rochester
Gouldey, Glenn Charles *manufacturing company executive*
Stempl, Robert C. *energy company executive*

Rochester Hills
Akeel, Hadi Abu *robotics executive*

Saranac
Herbrucks, Stephen *food products executive*

Southfield
King, William Carl *automotive company executive*
Lynch, George Michael *auto parts manufacturing executive*
Maibach, Ben C., III *construction company executive*
McClure, Charles G. *automotive executive*
Ponka, Lawrence John *automotive executive*
Rossiter, Robert E. *interior auto parts manufacturing executive*
Schmelzer, Wilhelm A. *manufacturing executive*
Shilts, Nancy S. *automotive executive, lawyer*
Snell, Richard A. *equipment manufacturing company executive*
Stebbins, Donald J. *car parts manufacturing company executive*
Tupper, Leon F. *manufacturing company executive*
Way, Kenneth L. *motor vehicle seat manufacturing company executive*

Taylor
Gardner, Lee M. *automotive parts executive*
Kennedy, Raymond F. *manufacturing executive*
Manoogian, Richard Alexander *manufacturing company executive*
Rosowski, Robert Bernard *manufacturing company executive*

Tecumseh
Herrick, Kenneth Gilbert *manufacturing company executive*
Herrick, Todd W. *manufacturing company executive*

Traverse City
Parsons, John Thoren *corporate executive, inventor*

Troy
Abelman, Steve *automotive company executive*
Baker, Kenneth R. *energy company executive*
Battenberg, J. T., III *automotive company executive*
Buschmann, Siegfried *manufacturing executive*
Dawes, Alan S. *automotive company executive*
De La Riva, Juan L. *automotive company executive*
Eggert, Glenn J. *manufacturing executive*
Elder, Irma *automotive company executive*
Evans, Thomas E. *autoparts company executive*

Brinzo, John S. *business executive*
Butler, William E. *retired manufacturing company executive*
Collins, Duane E. *manufacturing executive*
Connor, Christopher M. *textiles executive*
Cutler, Alexander MacDonald *manufacturing company executive*
Fruchtenbaum, Edward *greeting card company executive*
Hamilton, William Milton *retired manufacturing executive*
Harbert, Norman Carl *electrical company executive*
Hardis, Stephen Roger *retired manufacturing company executive*
Hiemstra, Michael J. *manufacturing executive*
Holmes, Arthur S. *manufacturing executive*
Hwang, Jennie S. *business executive, author, inventor, consultant*
Jameson, J(ames) Larry *chemical company executive*
Keithley, Joseph Faber *electronic engineering manufacturing company executive*
Loop, Floyd D. *health, medical executive*
Luke, Randall Dan *retired tire and rubber company executive, lawyer*
Mandel, Jack N. *manufacturing company executive*
McFadden, John Volney *retired manufacturing company executive*
Miller, Carl George *automotive parts manufacturing executive*
Moll, Curtis E. *manufacturing executive*
Mooney, James P. *chemicals executive*
Ortino, Hector Ruben *chemical company executive*
Parker, Patrick Streeter *manufacturing executive*
Pugh, David L. *manufacturing executive*
Ratner, Albert B. *building products company executive, land developer*
Reid, James Sims, Jr. *former automobile parts manufacturer*
Rosenthal, Leighton A. *aviation company executive*
Schulze, John B. *manufacturing executive*
Stone, Harry H. *business executive*
Sullivan, Dennis W. *power systems company executive*
Tinker, H(arold) Burnham *chemical company executive*
Tomsich, Robert J. *heavy machinery manufacturing executive*
Van Aken, William J. *construction executive*
Walker, Martin Dean *specialty chemical company executive*
Washkewicz, Donald E. *manufacturing executive*
Weiss, Erwin *greeting card company executive*
Weiss, Morry *greeting card company executive*
Wise, Bret W. *chemical company executive*

Columbus
Anderson, Kerrii B. *construction company executive*
Berndt, Ellen German *company executive*
Carter, William H. *company executive*
Evans, Daniel E. *sausage manufacturing and restaurant chain company executive*
Gerlach, John B. *business executive*
Kidder, C. Robert *food products executive*
McConnell, John Henderson *metal and plastic products manufacturing executive, professional sports team executive*
McConnell, John P. *metal and plastics products executive*
Owens, Stewart Kyle *food products executive*
Pfening, Frederic Denver, III *manufacturing company executive*
Radkoski, Donald J. *food products company executive*
Ricart, Fred *automotive company executive*
Schlesinger, Leonard Arthur *apparel company executive*
Schottenstein, Irving E. *construction company executive*
Schottenstein, Robert H. *construction executive*
Solso, Theodore M. *manufacturing executive*
Yenkin, Bernard Kalman *coatings and resins company executive*

Dayton
Caspar, John M. *manufacturing executive*
Ciccarelli, John A. *manufacturing executive*
Diggs, Matthew O'Brien, Jr. *air conditioning and refrigeration manufacturing executive*
DiLiddo, Ronald C. *automotive executive*
Duval, Daniel Webster *manufacturing company executive*
Hedeen, Rodney A. *manufacturing executive*
Kerley, James J. *manufacturing executive*
Kerley, James Joseph *chemical company executive*
Ladehoff, Leo William *metal products manufacturing executive*
Mathile, Clayton Lee *pet food company executive*
McIlroy, Alan F. *manufacturing company executive*
Nyberg, Lars *electronics company executive*
Perkins, Stephen J. *manufacturing executive*
Purdy, John Edgar *manufacturing company executive*
Shuey, John Henry *diversified products company executive*

Delaware
Huml, Donald Scott *manufacturing company executive*

Dublin
Borror, Donald A. *construction company executive*
Borror, Douglas G. *construction company executive*
Clement, Henry Joseph, Jr. *diversified building products executive*
Lamp, Benson J. *tractor company executive*
Millar, James F. *pharmaceutical executive*
Miller, Richard J. *wholesale pharmaceutical distribution company executive*

Elyria
Mixon, A. Malachi, III *medical products executive*
Spitzer, Alan *automotive executive*

Findlay
Dattilo, Thomas A. *diversified corporation executive*

Gates Mills
Veale, Tinkham, II *former chemical company executive, engineer*

Hilliard
Baker, John *electronics executive*
Brown, Dale *electronics executive*
Koehler, Jim *electronics executive*

Hudson
Reynolds, A. William *retired manufacturing company executive*

Jackson Center
Thompson, Wade Francis Bruce *manufacturing company executive*

Logan
Good, Timothy Jay *medical equipment services company executive*

Lorain
Bado, Kenneth Steve *automotive company administrator*

Malvern
Witosky, Gary J. *manufacturing company executive*

Mansfield
Dudley, Kenneth Eugene *manufacturing company executive*
Gorman, James Carvill *pump manufacturing company executive*
Hooker, James Todd *manufacturing executive*

Marysville
Berger, Charles Martin *lawn and garden company executive*

Mason
Kohlhepp, Robert J. *diversified services executive*

Maumee
Thompson, Ronald L. *manufacturing company executive*
Yeager, Waldo E. *food company executive*

Mayfield Heights
Rankin, Alfred Marshall, Jr. *business executive*

Medina
Karman, James Anthony *manufacturing executive*
Smith, Richey *chemical company executive*
Sullivan, Thomas Christopher *coatings company executive*

Mentor
Callsen, Christian Edward *medical device company executive*
Sanford, Bill R. *medical products executive*

Middletown
Wardrop, Richard M., Jr. *steel holding company executive*
Wareham, James Lyman *steel company executive*

Milford
Klosterman, Albert Leonard *technical development business executive, mechanical engineer*

New Bremen
Dicke, James Frederick, II *manufacturing company executive*

Niles
Odle, John H. *metal products executive*
Rupert, Timothy G. *metal products executive*

North Canton
Geswein, Gregory T. *electronic company executive*

Orrville
Byrd, Vincent C. *food products company executive*
Duncan, Fred A. *food products company executive*
Mackus, Eloise L. *food products company executive*
Smucker, Richard K. *food company executive*
Smucker, Timothy P. *food company executive*

Painesville
Humphrey, George Magoffin, II *plastic molding company executive*

Pickerington
Zacks, Gordon Benjamin *manufacturing company executive*

Plain City
Kinman, Gary *company executive*

Powell
Arnold, A. Joel *pharmaceuticals company executive*
Moore, Terry L. *financial executive*

Randolph
Pecano, Donald Carl *automotive manufacturing executive*

Reynoldsburg
Jeffries, Michael S. *apparel executive*
Woodward, Greta Charmaine *construction company executive, rental and investment property manager*

Solon
Rosica, Gabriel Adam *corporate executive, engineer*

Streetsboro
Kearns, Warren Kenneth *business executive*

Sylvania
Lock, Richard William *packaging company executive*

Toledo
Carroll, William J. *automotive executive*
Hiner, Glen Harold, Jr. *materials company executive*
Lemieux, Joseph Henry *manufacturing company executive*
Lonergan, Robert C. *financial executive*
Magliochetti, Joseph M. *automotive executive*
Morcott, Southwood J. *automotive parts manufacturing company executive*
Norton, Patrick H. *manufacturing company executive*
Reynolds, Richard I. *food products company executive*
Richter, Robert C. *automotive executive*
Romanoff, Milford Martin *building contractor*
Thaman, Michael H. *building material systems executive*
Van Hooser, David *retired manufacturing executive*
Wilkes, Kenneth G. *food products company executive*

Westerville
Krueger-Horn, Cheryl *apparel executive*

Westlake
Hellman, Peter Stuart *technical manufacturing executive*

Wickliffe
Cooley, Charles P. *chemicals executive*

Willoughby
Manning, William Dudley, Jr. *retired specialty chemical company executive*

Worthington
Davis, Samuel Bernhard *manufacturing executive*

Youngstown
Marks, Esther L. *metals company executive*
Powers, Paul J. *manufacturing company executive*

OREGON

Roseburg
Ford, Allyn *manufacturing company executive*

SOUTH DAKOTA

Dakota Dunes
Bond, Richard L. *food products executive*
Leman, Eugene D. *meat industry executive*
Lochner, James V. *food products executive*
Peterson, Robert L. *meat processing executive*

North Sioux City
Shipley, Larry *food products executive*

Sioux Falls
Christensen, David Allen *manufacturing company executive*
Rosenthal, Joel *manufacturing executive*

TEXAS

Dallas
Engles, Gregg L. *food company executive*

VERMONT

Waterbury
Holland, Robert, Jr. *food products executive*

WISCONSIN

Appleton
Boldt, Oscar Charles *construction company executive*

Bowler
Maas, Duane Harris *distilling company executive*

Eau Claire
Cohen, Maryjo R. *manufacturing executive*
Cohen, Melvin Samuel *manufacturing company executive*
Menard, John R. *lumber company/homeimprovement retailer executive*
Rasmussen, Earl R *lumber company and home improvement retail executive*

Green Bay
Ferguson, Larry *food products executive*
Kuehne, Carl W. *food products executive*
Liddy, Brian *food products executive*
Liegel, Craig A. *meat packing company executive*
McGarr, Joseph W. *paper company executive*
Vesta, Richard V. *meat packing company executive*

Kenosha
Emma, Edward C. *apparel executive*

Kohler
Cheney, Jeffrey Paul *manufacturing executive*
Kohler, Herbert Vollrath, Jr. *diversified manufacturing company executive*
Wells, Richard A. *manufacturing company executive*

La Crosse
Gelatt, Charles Daniel *manufacturing company executive*

Madison
Macfarlane, Alastair Iain Robert *business executive*
Shain, Irving *retired chemical company executive and university chancellor*

Marathon
Menzner, Donald *food products executive*

Marion
Simpson, Vinson Raleigh *manufacturing company executive*

Mequon
Dohmen, Frederick Hoeger *retired wholesale drug company executive*

Merrill
Bierman, Jane *wood products company executive*

Milwaukee
Barnes, W. Michael *electronics executive*
Beals, Vaughn Le Roy , Jr. *retired motorcycle manufacturing executive*
Bishop, Charles Joseph *manufacturing company executive*
Bleustein, Jeffrey L. *automotive executive*
Bomba, Steven J. *controls company executive*
Carter, Valerie *food products executive*
Daniels-Carter, Valerie *food franchise executive*
Davis, Don H., Jr. *multi-industry high-technology company executive*
Grade, Jeffery T. *manufacturing company executive*
Hoffman, Robert Butler *ministry industry executive*
Hudson, Katherine Mary *manufacturing company executive*
Keyes, James Henry *manufacturing company executive*
Koss, John Charles *consumer electronics products manufacturing company executive*
Martin, Vincent Lionel *manufacturing company executive*
Nosbusch, Keith D. *computer and electronics company executive*
Parker, Charles Walter, Jr. *consultant, retired equipment company executive*
Roell, Stephen A. *manufacturing company executive*
Sante, William Arthur, II *electronics manufacturing executive*
Sterner, Frank Maurice *industrial executive*
Yontz, Kenneth Fredric *medical and chemical company executive*

Mount Horeb
Barry, Jonathan B. *chemicals executive, communications executive*

Oshkosh
Drebus, Richard William *pharmaceutical company executive*
Fites, Donald Vester *retired tractor company executive*
Zuern, Rosemary Lucile *manufacturing executive, treasurer*

Pleasant Prairie
Morrone, Frank *electronic manufacturing executive*

Port Washington
Wier, James A. *manufacturing executive*

Racine
Campbell, Edward Joseph *retired machinery company executive*
Christman, Richard M. *manufacturing executive*
Konz, Gerald Keith *retired manufacturing company executive*
McCollum, W. Lee *chemical company executive*
Perez, William D. *chemical company executive*
Rosso, Jean-Pierre *electronics executive*
Wambold, Richard Lawrence *manufacturing executive company*

Sturtevant
Bailey, Michael J. *manufacturing executive*
Johnson, Samuel Curtis *chemical company executive*
Johnson-Leipold, Helen P. *outdoor marine recreation company executive*

Sussex
Losee, John Frederick, Jr. *manufacturing executive*

Waukesha
Nigl, Jeffrey M. *telecommunications company executive*

West Bend
Gehl, William D. *manufacturing company executive*
Hahn, Kenneth P. *manufacturing executive*
Mulcahy, Michael J. *light contruction and agricultural manufacturing*

Wisconsin Rapids
Evans, Gorton M. *paper products executive*
Gottschalk, Guy *agricultural products executive*
Korhonen, Kai Antero *paper products executive*

CANADA

MANITOBA

Winnipeg
MacKenzie, George Allan *diversified company executive*

ONTARIO

Sault Sainte Marie
Dalla-Vicenza, Mario Joseph *steel company executive*

SWEDEN

Stockholm
Stewart, S. Jay *automotive company executive*

ADDRESS UNPUBLISHED

Alig, Frank Douglas Stalnaker *retired construction company executive*
Andreas, Dwayne Orville *business executive*
Aschauer, Charles Joseph, Jr. *corporate director, former company executive*
Asplin, Edward William *retired packaging company executive*
Barlow, John F. *automotive glass products company executive*
Barnes, Steven W. *diagnostic equipment company executive*
Barth, David Keck *distribution industry consultant*
Barton, Glen A. *manufacturing company executive*
Bernthal, Harold George *healthcare company executive*
Brightfelt, Robert *diagnostic company executive*
Brodsky, Philip Hyman *chemical executive, researcher*
Buxton, Winslow Hurlbert *paper company executive*
Calcaterra, Edward Lee *construction company executive*
Cassidy, James Mark *construction company executive*
Chen, Di *electro-optic company executive, consultant*
Christensen, Gary M. *building materials company executive*
Craft, Edmund Coleman *automotive parts manufacturing company executive*
Crowe, James Quell *communications company executive*
Cull, Robert Robinette *electric products manufacturing company executive*
DeBruce, Paul *agricultural food products company executive*
Dohrmann, Russell William *manufacturing company executive*
Dougherty, Robert Anthony *retired manufacturing company executive*
Flaten, Alfred N. *retired food and consumer products executive*
Geary, Richard *retired construction company executive*
Gifford, John Irving *retired agricultural equipment company executive*
Glover, James Todd *manufacturing company executive*
Gorman, Joseph Tolle *automotive parts manufacturing executive*
Grieve, Pierson MacDonald *retired specialty chemicals and services company executive*
Grove, Richard Charles *retired power tool company executive*
Hamister, Donald Bruce *retired electronics company executive*
Heckel, John Louis (Jack Heckel) *aerospace company executive*
Heininger, S(amuel) Allen *retired chemical company executive*
Henning, George Thomas, Jr. *steel company executive*
Hines, Anthony Loring *automotive executive*
Holmes, David Richard *computer and business forms company executive*
Hunt, Robert G. *construction company executive*
Hunt, V. William (Bill) *automotive supplier executive*
Hurd, Richard Nelson *pharmaceutical company executive*
Hushen, John Wallace *manufacturing company executive*
Jensen, Erik Hugo *pharmaceutical quality control consultant*
Johnson, Warren Donald *retired pharmaceutical executive, former air force officer*
Jones, David D., Jr. *marine engine equipment executive*
Juhl, Daniel Leo *manufacturing and marketing firm executive*
Karter, Elias M. *paper products company executive*
Kelley, James *automotive sales executive*
Kelley, Thomas William *automotive sales executive*
Kelly, J. Peter *steel company executive*
Kerber, Ronald Lee *industrial corporation executive*
Kerr, Michael D. *construction company executive*
Landon, Robert Gray *retired manufacturing company executive*
Lapinsky, Joseph F. *manufacturing company executive*
Liebler, Arthur C. *automotive executive*
Lindsay, James Wiley *retired agricultural company executive*
Loucks, Vernon R., Jr. *retired medical technologies executive*
Matasovic, Marilyn Estelle *business executive*
McDonnell, John Finney *former aerospace and aircraft manufacturing executive*
McGillivray, Donald Dean *seed company executive, agronomist*
Millard, Charles Phillip *manufacturing company executive*
Miller, Harold Edward *retired manufacturing conglomerate executive, consultant*
Mills, Charlie *healthcare supplies and products company executive*
Miskowski, Lee R. *retired automobile executive*
Moore, John Ronald *manufacturing executive*
Morris, G. Ronald *industrial executive*
Mussallem, Michael A. *healthcare company executive*
Nasser, Jacques *former automotive company executive*
Nordlund, Donald Elmer *manufacturing company executive*
Nugent, Daniel Eugene *business executive*
O'Donnell, Kevin *retired metal products executive*
Oesterling, Thomas Ovid *retired pharmaceutical company executive*
Ommodt, Donald Henry *retired dairy company executive*
Oster, Lewis Henry *manufacturing executive, engineering consultant*
Pepper, J. Stanley *construction company executive*
Petyo, Michael Edward *construction company owner*
Quinn, Donal *diagnostic equipment company executive*
Reid-Anderson, James *diagnostic equipment company executive*
Reum, W. Robert *manufacturing executive*
Richter, Glenn *diagnostic equipment company executive*
Sabo, Richard Steven *electrical company executive*
Sauder, Maynard *manufacturing company executive*
Schlensker, Gary Chris *landscaping company executive*
Schultz, Robert J. *retired automobile company executive*
Shapira, David S. *food products/retail grocery executive*
Sharkey, Leonard Arthur *automobile company executive*
Smith, Frederick Coe *retired manufacturing executive*
Smith, Robert Hugh *former engineering construction company executive*
Sommer, Howard Ellsworth *textile executive*
Sopranos, Orpheus Javaras *manufacturing company executive*
Templin, Kenneth Elwood *paper company executive*
Uchida, Hiroshi *diagnostic equipment company executive*
Ward, Thomas *food products executive*
Wenstrup, H. Daniel *chemical company executive*
Witcher, Daniel Dougherty *retired pharmaceutical company executive*
Young, Jay Maitland *health care products consultant*

INDUSTRY: SERVICE

UNITED STATES

ARIZONA

Scottsdale
Lillestol, Jane Brush *development consultant*

CALIFORNIA

Los Angeles
Schultz, Louis Michael *advertising agency executive*

Rutherford
Staglin, Garen Kent *computer service company executive, venture capitalist*

Santa Barbara
Scheinfeld, James David *travel agency executive*

FLORIDA

Destin
Ferner, David Charles *non-profit management and development consultant*

Naples
Hauserman, Jacquita Knight *management consultant*

Saint Petersburg
Lau, Michele Denise *advertising consultant, sales trainer, television personality*

GEORGIA

Atlanta
Posner, Kenneth Robert *former hotel corporation executive*

ILLINOIS

Addison
Christopher, Doris *kitchen tools sales and demonstration company executive*
McDonald, David Eugene *package car driver*

Alton
Black, Dale R. *casino executive*
Cellini, William F. *hotel executive*
Perry, James Benn *casino and hotel executive*

Arlington Heights
Fields, Sara A. *travel company executive*
Holtz, Michael P. *hotel executive*
Payne, Thomas H. *market research company executive*

Aurora
Hopp, Nancy Smith *marketing executive*

Bannockburn
Slavin, Craig Steven *management and franchising consultant*

Barrington
Hetzel, William Gelal *executive search consultant*
Koten, John A. *retired communications executive*
Lee, Catherine M. *business owner, educator*
Ross, Frank Howard, III *management consultant*
Sweet, Charles Wheeler *retired executive recruiter*

Batavia
Mann, Phillip Lynn *data processing company executive*

Bensenville
Kolkey, Eric Samuel *customer service representative*
Mendelsohn, Zehavah Whitney *data processing executive*

Bloomingdale
Konopinski, Virgil James *industrial hygienist*
Wolande, Charles Sanford *computer company executive*

Broadview
Lazar, Jill Sue *home healthcare company executive*

Buffalo Grove
Tracy, Allen Wayne *management consultant*

Burr Ridge
Bottom, Dale Coyle *management consultant*

Carbondale
Jugenheimer, Donald Wayne *advertising and communications educator, university administrator*

Carol Stream
Gale, Neil Jan *Internet professional*

Chicago
Akins, Cindy S. *human resources professional*
Allen, Belle *management consulting firm executive, communications company executive*
Amberg, Thomas L. *public relations executive*
Aubriot, Eric *chef*
Bailey, Robert, Jr. *advertising executive*
Baker, Mark *food service executive*
Bard, John Franklin *consumer products executive*
Barry, Richard A. *public relations executive*
Bayer, Gary Richard *advertising executive*
Bayless, Rick *chef*
Bensinger, Peter Benjamin *consulting firm executive*
Berman, Cheryl R. *advertising company executive*
Bernatowicz, Frank Allen *management consultant, expert witness*
Beugen, Joan Beth *communications company executive*
Bishop, Mary Oltman *advertising executive*
Borg, Frank *hotel executive*
Bowen, William Joseph *management consultant*
Boyda, Debora *advertising executive*
Brandt, William Arthur, Jr. *consulting executive*
Brashears, Donald Robert *advertising agency executive*
Briand, Michael *chef*
Brown, Faith A. *communications executive*
Bubula, John *chef*
Buck, John A. *business executive*
Burack, Elmer Howard *management educator*
Burrell, Thomas J. *marketing communication executive*
Carr, Steve *public relations executive*
Cass, Edward Roberts (Peter Cass) *hotel and travel marketing professional*
Castorino, Sue *communications executive*
Chipparoni, Guy *communications company executive*
Chorengel, Bernd *international hotel corporation executive*
Coletta, John *chef*
Conidi, Daniel Joseph *private investigation agency executive*
Corbett, Frank Joseph *advertising executive*
Cornell, Rob *hotel executive*
Cox, Allan James *management consultant*
Dammeyer, Rodney Foster *distribution company executive*
Davis, William L. *publishing company executive*
De Francesco, John Blaze, Jr. *public relations company executive*
Delaney, James M. *business executive*
Diederichs, Janet Wood *public relations executive*
Digangi, Al *marketing executive*
Donnelley, James Russell *printing company executive*
Draft, Howard Craig *advertising executive*
Echols, M(ary) Evelyn *travel consultant*
Eibl, Clement *management consulting firm executive*
Englehart, Hud *communications company executive*
Fisher, John James *advertising executive*
Fizdale, Richard *advertising agency executive*
Fleming, Cecil *business executive*
Frankel, Bernard *advertising executive*
Fulgoni, Gian Marc *market research company executive*
Fullmer, Paul *public relations counselor*
Furth, Yvonne *advertising executive*
Gallegos, Marcelo *chef*
Gand, Gayle *chef*
Gardner, Howard Alan *travel marketing executive, travel writer and editor*
Garr, Daniel Frank *restaurateur*
Gerber, Phillip *advertising executive*
Gilbert, David R. *public relations executive*
Glasser, James J. *leasing company executive, retired*
Goldring, Norman Max *advertising executive*
Golin, Alvin *public relations company executive*
Gordon, Edward Earl *management consultant, educator*
Gray, Dawn Plambeck *work-family consultant*
Haffner, Charles Christian, III *retired printing company executive*
Hansen, Carl R. *management consultant*
Harkna, Eric *advertising executive*
Harris, Gregory Scott *management services executive*
Haupt, Roger A. *advertising executive*
Healy, Sondra Anita *consumer products company executive*
Hoey, Rita *public relations executive*
Hollander, Adrian Willoughby *accounting services company executive*
Husting, Peter Marden *advertising consultant*
James-Strand, Nancy Leabhard *advertising executive*
Joho, Jean *chef*
Kahan, Paul *chef*
King, Donald A., Jr. *company executive*
Kipper, Barbara Levy *corporate executive*
Kloster, Carol Good *book and magazine distribution company*
Klues, Jack *communications executive*
Kobs, James Fred *advertising agency executive*
Kopelow, Eric *food service executive*
Kornick, Michael *chef*
Krivkovich, Peter George *advertising executive*
Kubo, Gary Michael *advertising executive*
Lane, Kenneth Edwin *retired advertising agency executive*
Larson, Paul William *public relations executive*
Lee, Michael *leasing company executive, real estate company executive*
Lehman, George Morgan *food sales executive*
Leigh, Sherren *communications executive, editor, publisher*
Levy, Deborah *security company executive*
Lynnes, R. Milton *advertising executive*
Mack, Jim *advertising executive*
Mackiewicz, Laura *advertising agency executive*
Martinez, Jim *communications executive*
McConnell, E. Hoy, II *advertising/public policy executive*
McCullough, Richard Lawrence *advertising agency executive*
Miller, Bernard J., III *advertising executive*
Miller, Bernard Joseph, Jr. *advertising executive*
Miller, Ellen *advertising executive*
Mitchell, Lee Mark *communications executive, investment fund manager, lawyer*
Morley, Michael B. *public relations executive*
Nelson, Harry Donald *telecommunications executive*
O'Shea, Lynne Edeen *management consultant, educator*
Oates, James G. *advertising executive*
Olins, Robert Abbot *communications research executive*
Ormesher, David T. *advertising executive*
Paul, Ronald Neale *management consultant*
Petrillo, Nancy *public relations executive*
Pincus, Theodore Henry *public relations executive*
Plank, Betsy (Mrs. Sherman V. Rosenfield) *public relations counsel*
Plotkin, Manuel D. *management consultant, educator, former corporate executive and government official*
Posner, Kathy Robin *communications executive*
Prather, Susan Lynn *public relations executive*
Pritzker, Thomas Jay *hotel business executive*
Provus, Barbara Lee *executive search consultant*
Rabin, Joseph Harry *marketing research company executive*
Reid, Daniel James *public relations executive*
Reilly, Robert Frederick *valuation consultant*
Reitman, Jerry Irving *advertising agency executive*
Rich, S. Judith *public relations executive*
Robbins, Henry Zane *public relations and marketing executive*
Rosenberg, Robin *executive chef*
Rowe, John W. *utility company executive*
Ruiz, Anselmo *chef*
Sampanthavivat, Arun *chef*
Sampson, Ronald Alvin *advertising executive*
Schindler, Judi(th Kay) *public relations executive, marketing consultant*
Seebert, Kathleen Anne *international sales and marketing executive*
Segal, Mindy *chef*
Senior, Richard John Lane *textile rental service executive*
Serlin, Marsha *waste management service administrator*
Shepherd, Daniel Marston *executive recruiter*
Shirley, Virginia Lee *advertising executive*
Silich, Greg *advertising executive*
Sive, Rebecca Anne *public affairs company executive*
Smith, Scott Clybourn *media company executive*
Sotelino, Gabino *chef*
Steingraber, Frederick George *management consultant*
Stenger, Sarah *chef*
Stern, Carl William, Jr. *management consultant*
Stocklosa, Gregory A. *printing company executive*
Stratton, Steven F. *real estate executive*
Strubel, Ella Doyle *advertising and public relations executive*
Struggles, John Edward *management consultant*
Talbot, Pamela *public relations executive*
Tanguay, Mark H. *company executive*
Taylor, Collette *public relations executive*
Teichner, Lester *management consulting executive*
Tobaccowala, Rishad *marketing professional*
Tramonto, Rick *chef*
Tripp, Marian Barlow Loofe *retired public relations company executive*
Trotter, Charlie *chef*
Tyson, Kirk W. M. *management consultant*
Van Den Hende, Fred J(oseph) *human resources executive*
Vilim, Nancy Catherine *advertising agency executive*
Walsh, Mathew M. *corporate executive*
Walters, Lawrence Charles *advertising executive*
Ward, Jonathan P. *communications executive*
Weaver, Donna Rae *company executive*
Wiecek, Barbara Harriet *advertising executive*
Williams, Bruce *chef*
Williams, Mark H. *marketing communications executive*
Williams, Martha *consumer products company executive, entrepreneur*
Winkel, Michael W. *communications executive*
Winninghoff, Albert C. M. *advertising company executive*
Wolf, Linda S. *advertising executive*

Crete
Langer, Steven *human resources management consultant and industrial psychologist*

Decatur
Bayless, Charles T. *business executive*
Blake, William Henry *credit and public relations consultant*

Deerfield
Brunner, Vernon Anthony *marketing executive*
Eastham, Dennis Michael *advertising executive*
Gater, Chris *advertising executive*
Karp, Gary *marketing and public relations executive*
Sperzel, George E., Jr. *personal care industry executive*
Wallace, Rick *marketing professional*

Des Plaines
Baerenklau, Alan H. *hotel executive*

Dvorak, Kathleen S. *business products company executive*
Le Menager, Lois M. *incentive merchandise and travel company executive*
Mueller, Kurt M. *hotel executive*
Pontikes, William N. *computer rental and leasing company executive*

Downers Grove
Pollard, C(harles) William *diversified services company executive*
Rooney, Phillip B. *service company executive*
Schwemm, John Butler *printing company executive, lawyer*
Stair, Charles William *former service company executive*

Edwardsville
Dietrich, Suzanne Claire *instructional designer, communications consultant*
Suhre, Richard L. *transportation company executive*

Elburn
Brown, Roger William *manufacturer's representative, real estate developer*
Hansen, H. Jack *management consultant*

Elk Grove Village
Flaherty, John Joseph *quality assurance company executive*

Elmhurst
Baker, Robert I. *business executive*
Duarte, Gloria *chef*

Elmwood Park
Davis, Shawna *marketing professional*

Evanston
Arrington, Michael Browne *company executive*
Blair, Virginia Ann *public relations executive*
Neuschel, Robert Percy *management consultant, educator*
Tornabene, Russell C. *communications executive*

Flossmoor
Crum, James Francis *waste recycling company executive*

Franklin Park
Bailey, Richard *food company executive*
Ravencroft, Thomas A. *food company executive*

Glen Ellyn
Conti, Paul Louis *management consulting company executive*

Glencoe
Isaacs, Roger David *public relations executive*
Niefeld, Jaye Sutter *advertising executive*

Glenview
Franklin, Lynne *business communications consultant, writer*
Kaplan, Steven M. *advertising executive*

Highland Park
Cohen, Burton David *franchising executive, lawyer*
Harris, Thomas L. *public relations executive*
Herbert, Edward Franklin *public relations executive*
Rodriguez, Ramiro *chef*

Hinsdale
Amsler, Jana *chef*
Foley, Joseph Lawrence *sales executive*
League, David *hardware company executive*
Mathisen-Reid, Rhoda Sharon *international communications consultant*
Rodriguez, Edgar *chef*
Zaccone, Suzanne Maria *sales executive*

Hoffman Estates
Martinez, Arthur C. *retail company executive*

Kankakee
McCafferty, Michael *corporate executive*

Kenilworth
Guelich, Robert Vernon *retired management consultant*

La Grange Park
Carroll, Thomas John *retired advertising executive*

Lake Bluff
Scott, Karen Bondurant *consumer catalog company executive*

Lake Forest
Bradley, Kim Alexandra *sales and marketing specialist*
Chieger, Kathryn Jean *recreation company executive*
Crawford, Robert W., Jr. *furniture rental company executive*
Kenly, Granger Farwell *marketing consultant, college official*
Lyons, Dudley E. *business executive*
Rand, Kathy Sue *public relations executive*
Reich, Victoria J. *consumer products company executive*
Stecko, Paul T. *packaging company executive*

Libertyville
Conklin, Mara Loraine *public relations executive*

Lincolnshire
DeCanniere, Dan *human resources executive*
Gifford, Dale L. *human resources executive*
Hebda, Lawrence John *data processing executive, consultant*
Omtvedt, Craig P. *consumer products executive*
Roche, Mark A. *consumer products company executive, lawyer*

Lincolnwood
Donovan, John Vincent *consulting company executive*

Grant, Paul Bernard *industrial relations educator, arbitrator*
Lebedow, Aaron Louis *consulting company executive*

Lindenhurst
Rose, William *retired business executive*

Lisle
Duffield, Michael O. *data processing executive*
Sotir, Mark *automotive rental executive*

Melrose Park
Bernick, Carol Lavin *corporate executive*

Moline
Henderson, Donald L. *executive*

Mount Prospect
Gerlitz, Curtis Neal *business executive*
Sayers, Gale *computer company executive, retired professional football player*

Naperville
Fritz, Roger Jay *management consultant*

Niles
Kelly, John *advertising executive*
Weisbach, Lou *advertising executive*

Northbrook
Clarey, John Robert *executive search consultant*
Crockett, Joan M. *human resources executive*
Ehrenberg, Maureen *management consultant*
Lesnik, Steven Harris *public relations and sports marketing executive*
Marshall, Irl Houston, Jr. *franchise company executive*
Ross, Debra Benita *jewelry designer, marketing executive*
Sudbrink, Jane Marie *sales and marketing executive*
Turner, Lee *travel company executive*
Wajer, Ronald Edward *management consultant*

Northfield
Heise, Marilyn Beardsley *public relations company executive*

Oak Brook
Babrowski, Claire Harbeck *fast food chain executive*
Cantalupo, James Richard *restaurant company executive*
Chappel, Donald R. *waste management executive*
DeLorey, John Alfred *printing company executive*
Michelsen, John Ernest *software and internet services company executive*
Nelson, Robert Eddinger *management and development consultant*
Quinlan, Michael Robert *fast food franchise company executive*
Ryan, Thomas *food service executive*
Turner, Fred L. *fast food company executive*
Wigginton, Adam *marketing professional*

Oak Park
Andre, L. Aumund *management consultant*
Cannon, Patrick Francis *public relations executive*
Devereux, Timothy Edward *advertising executive*

Oakbrook Terrace
Buntrock, Dean Lewis *retired waste management company executive*
Hegenderfer, Jonita Susan *public relations executive*

Palos Park
Ramunno, Thomas Paul *management consultant*

Park Ridge
Campbell, Dorothy May *management consultant*

Plainfield
Hofer, Thomas W. *landscape company executive*

Prospect Heights
Lynch, William Thomas, Jr. *advertising agency executive*

River Forest
Hamper, Robert Joseph *marketing executive*

Rockford
Anderson, Max Elliot *television and film production company executive*
Morrissey, Mary F. (Fran) *human resource consulting company executive*

Rolling Meadows
Cain, R. Wayne *sales, finance and leasing company executive*

Rosemont
Barlett, James Edward *data processing executive*
Blake, Norman Perkins, Jr. *information technology company executive*
Hewes, Philip A. *computer company executive*
Moster, Mary Clare *public relations executive*

Round Lake
Laskowski, Richard E. *retail hardware company executive*

Saint Charles
Benjamin, Lawrence *food service executive*

Schaumburg
Cataldo, C. A. *hotel executive*
Cataldo, Robert J. *hotel executive*
Growney, Robert L. *communications company professional*
Guimond, Richard Joseph *communications executive*
Hill, Raymond Joseph *packaging company executive*
Sandler, Norman *business executive*

Skokie
Finkel, Bernard *public relations, communications and association management consultant, radio host*

Grubbs, Robert W. *computer services company executive*
Roemer, James Paul *data processing executive, writer*

Urbana
Rotzoll, Kim Brewer *advertising and communications educator*

Vernon Hills
Krasny, Michael P. *computer company executive*

West Dundee
Woltz, Kenneth Allen *consulting executive*

Western Springs
Reggio, Vito Anthony *management consultant*

Westmont
Sheehan, James Patrick *printing company executive, former media company executive*

Wheeling
Banchet, Jean *chef*

Winnetka
Thomas, John Thieme *management consultant*

INDIANA

Auburn
Kempf, Jane Elmira *marketing executive*

Bloomington
Patterson, James Milton *marketing specialist, educator*
Sullivan, Michael Francis, III *executive*

Elkhart
Powell, Michael N. *company executive*

Evansville
Hampel, Robert Edward *advertising executive*
Kitch, Frederick David *advertising executive*
Weinzapfel, Jonathan *public relations executive, congressional aide*

Fort Wayne
Schweickart, Jim *advertising executive, broadcast consultant*
Wolf, Don Allen *hardware wholesale executive*

Gary
King, Marcia *management consultant*

Indianapolis
Gilman, Alan B. *restaurant company executive*
Heird, Robert C. *insurance executive human resources professional*
Quiring, Patti Lee *human resource consulting company executive*
Ruben, Gary A. *marketing and communications consultant*
Simmons, Roberta Johnson *public relations firm executive*
Slaymaker, Gene Arthur *public relations executive*
Spanogle, Robert William *marketing and advertising company executive, association administrator*
Walker, Frank Dilling *market research executive*
Walker, Steven Frank *management consultant*

Liberty
Pringle, Lewis Gordon *marketing professional, educator*

Merrillville
White, Dean *advertising executive*

Michigan City
Sherman, Thomas Webster, Jr. *environmental company executive*

Muncie
Barber, Earl Eugene *consulting firm executive*
Norris, Tracy Hopkins *retired public relations executive*

Nashville
Rogers, Frank Andrew *restaurant, hotel executive*

Seymour
Bollinger, Don Mills *retired grocery company executive*

Valparaiso
Schlender, William Elmer *management sciences educator*

West Lafayette
Schendel, Dan Eldon *management consultant, business educator*

IOWA

Ames
Rizai, Matthew M. *marketing and finance professional*

Ankeny
Lamberti, Donald *convenience store executive*

Cedar Rapids
Cardella, Tom *sales executive*
Vanderpool, Ward Melvin *management and marketing consultant*

Davenport
Monty, Mitchell *landscape company executive*

Des Moines
Bodensteiner, Carol A. *public relations executive*
Meredith, Edwin Thomas, III *media executive*

Fairfield
Hawthorne, Timothy Robert *direct response advertising and communications company executive*

Kelly, Thomas *advertising executive*

Newton
Cooper, Janis Campbell *public relations executive*

KANSAS

Emporia
O'Reilly, Hugh Joseph *restaurant executive*

Lawrence
Burke, Paul E., Jr. *governmental relations consultant*

Lenexa
Taggart, David D. *company executive*

Mission
Schmitt, Andrew B. *business executive*

Overland Park
Trucksess, H.A., III *company executive*

Shawnee Mission
Hill, Lloyd L. *food service executive*
Mealman, Glenn *corporate marketing executive*

Topeka
Vidricksen, Ben Eugene *food service executive, state legislator*

Wichita
Menefee, Frederick Lewis *advertising executive*

MICHIGAN

Ada
Brenner, David H. *marketing executive*
DeVos, Richard Marvin, Jr. (Dick DeVos) *direct sales company executive, sports team executive*
DeVos, Richard Marvin, Sr. *former network marketing company executive*
Lyall, Lynn *consumer products company executive*
Van Andel, Jay *direct selling company executive*
Van Andel, Steve Alan *business executive*

Ann Arbor
Agno, John G. *management consultant*
Bachelder, Cheryl Anne *marketing professional*
Belcher, Louis David *marketing and operations executive, former mayor*
Brandon, David A. *food service executive/restaurant manager*
Bryant, Barbara Everitt *academic researcher, market research consultant, former federal agency administrator*
Flint, H. Howard, II *printing company executive*
Foley, Daniel Ronald *personnel director, lawyer*
Gannon, Michael J. *printing company executive*
Silverman, Harry J. *pizza delivery company executive*
Sprandel, Dennis Steuart *management consulting company executive*

Auburn Hills
MacDonald, John *marketing executive*

Bloomfield Hills
Adams, Charles Francis *advertising and real estate executive*
Berline, James H. *advertising executive, public relations executive*
Bissell, John Howard *marketing executive*
Pietrowski, Anthony *business executive*
Weil, John William *technology management consultant*

Brighton
Veno, Glen Corey *management consultant*

Dearborn
Ardisana, Beth *communications company executive*

Detroit
Barden, Don H. *communications executive*
Czarnecki, Walter P. *truck rental company executive*
Demos, Dave *marketing executive*
Dixson, J. B. *communications executive*
Go, Robert A. *management consultant*
Ilitch, Denise *food services executive*
Ponder, Dan *public relations executive*
Rosenau, Pete *public relations executive*
Schweitzer, Peter *advertising agency executive*
Soave, Anthony *business executive*
Tallet, Margaret Anne *theatre executive*
Werba, Gabriel *public relations consultant*

Farmington Hills
Bassett, Tina *communications executive*
Benedict, Elise *moving company executive*
Ward, Francis J. *marketing and research executive*
Yagahashi, Takashi *chef*

Franklin
Prentice, Matthew *food service executive*

Grand Rapids
Bruyn, Kimberly Ann *public relations executive, consultant*
Gordon, Dan *food service executive*
Kranz, Kenneth Louis *human resources company executive, entrepreneur*
Messner, James W. *advertising executive*
Plakmeyer, Steve *food service executive*
Sadler, David Gary *management executive*
Schwartz, Garry Albert *advertising executive*
Seyferth, Virginia M. *public relations executive*
Smith, Bill *advertising and marketing executive*
Spaulding, Dan *public relations executive*
Zimmerman, John *public relations executive*

Grosse Pointe Park
Blevins, William Edward *management consultant*

Grosse Pointe Woods
Cusmano, J. Joyce *public relations executive*

Kalamazoo
Gershon, Richard A. *commmunications educator*
Gilchrist, James A. *communication educator*
Lawrence, William Joseph, Jr. *retired corporate executive*

Lansing
Doan, Herbert Dow *technical business consultant*

Livonia
Barfield, Jon E. *employment company executive*
Maibach, Ben C., Jr. *service executive*
Morrison, Andrew J. *marketing professional*

Midland
Maneri, Remo R. *management consultant*
Sosville, Dick *sales and marketing executive*

Rochester Hills
Pfister, Karl Anton *industrial company executive*

Royal Oak
Stanalajczo, Greg Charles *computer and technology company executive*

Saginaw
Bailey, William L. *communications executive*
Scharffe, William Granville *academic administrator, educator*

Southfield
Amladi, Prasad Ganesh *management consulting executive, health care consultant, researcher*
Barnett, Marilyn *advertising agency executive*
Caponigro, Jeffrey Ralph *public relations counselor*
Jackson, Michael B. *service company executive*
Kalter, Alan *advertising agency executive*
Randazzo, Richard P. *human resources professional*
Smith, Nancy Hohendorf *sales and marketing executive*
Wagner, Bruce Stanley *marketing professional*

Troy
Adderley, Terence E. *corporate executive*
Camden, Carl T. *human resources company executive*
Collins, Gary L. *human resources professional, automotive executive*
Hill, Richard A. *advertising executive*
McLaren, Karen Lynn *advertising executive*
Meyers, Christine Laine *marketing and media executive, consultant*
Reardon, George M. *human resources firm executive*
White, Tommi A. *human resources firm executive*

Warren
Gervason, Robert J *advertising executive*
Gilbert, Suzanne Harris *advertising executive*
Hopp, Anthony James *advertising agency executive*
Ludwig, William John *advertising executive*

West Bloomfield
Considine, John Joseph *advertising executive*

MINNESOTA

Bloomington
Jeffries, Mary *public relations executive*
Mona, David L. *public relations executive*
Norris, William C. *retired computer systems executive*

Chanhassen
Price, Robert McCollum *computer company executive*

Eagan
Hatlen, Roe Harold *restaurant executive*

Eden Prairie
Bileydi, Sumer *advertising agency executive*
Erickson, Kim *consumer products company executive*
Harmel, Paul *corporate executive*
Platt, Ann *animal care company executive*
Roth, Thomas *marketing executive*
Verdoorn, Sid *food service executive*

Hastings
Avent, Sharon L. Hoffman *consumer products company executive*

Mankato
Taylor, Glen *printing and graphics company executive, professional sports team executive*

Minneapolis
Anderson, Ron *advertising executive*
Angstadt, David W. *business executive*
Beardsley, John Ray *public relations firm executive*
Bergeson, James *advertising executive*
Bjelland, Rolf F. *business executive*
Bonner, Brigid Ann *marketing professional*
Boubelik, Henry Fredrick, Jr. *retired travel company executive*
Brooks, Phillip *advertising executive*
Cameron, Patricia *advertising executive*
Cardozo, Richard Nunez *marketing, entrepreneurship and business educator*
Casey, Lynn M. *public relations executive*
Courtney, Eugene Whitmal *computer company executive*
Cowles, John, III *management consultant, investor*
Cross, Bruce A. *food service company executive*
Doherty, Valerie *employment services professional, lawyer*
Dunlap, William DeWayne, Jr. *advertising agency executive*
Eich, Susan *public relations executive*
Eickhoff, John R. (Jack) *business executive*
Fallon, Patrick R. *advertising executive*
Floren, David D. *advertising executive*
Gage, Edwin C., III (Skip Gage) *travel and marketing services executive*
Gavin, Sara *public relations executive*
Harp-Jirschele, Mary *communications executive*
Kelly, Charles Harold *advertising agency executive*
Koutsky, Dean Roger *advertising executive*
Krueger, Richard Arnold *technology executive*
Lenzmeier, Allen U. *consumer products company executive*
Liszt, Howard Paul *advertising executive*
Lynch, Leland T. *advertising executive*
Marshall, Ron *company executive*
Mouser, Les *broadcasting executive*
Nelson, Marilyn C. *hotel executive, food service executive, travel services executive, marketing professional*
Owens, Scott Andrew *sales executive*
Perlman, Lawrence *retired business executive, corporate director, consultant*
Petersen, Maureen Jeanette Miller *management information consultant, former nurse*
Read, John Conyers *non-profit management consultant*
Sanger, Stephen W. *consumer products company executive*
Schultz, Louis Edwin *management consultant*
Spong, Douglas K. *public relations executive*
Sullivan, Michael Patrick *food service executive*
Tree, David L. *advertising agency executive*
Tunheim, Kathryn H. *public relations executive*
Turner, Ronald L. *information services executive*
Veblen, Thomas Clayton *management consultant*
Viault, Raymond G. *food company executive*
Westbrook, Bill *advertising executive*
Weyl, Tom F. *advertising executive*
Wickesberg, Albert Klumb *retired management educator*
Yourzak, Robert Joseph *management consultant, engineer, educator*

Minnetonka
Berman, Lyle *recreational facility executive*
Gillies, Donald Richard *marketing and advertising consultant, educator*
Kostka, Ronald Wayne *marketing consultant*

New Brighton
Grieman, John Joseph *communications executive*

North Mankato
Kozitza, William *printing company executive*

Oakdale
Cederburg, Barbara M. *printing company executive*
Monahan, William T. *computer company executive*

Plymouth
Hudson, Thomas George *computer network executive*
Redgrave, Martyn R. *hotel, food service executive*

Saint Louis Park
Wikman, Michael Raymond *advertising executive*

Saint Paul
Axelrod, Leonard *court administrator*
Boehnen, David Leo *grocery company executive, lawyer*
Feinberg, David Erwin *publishing company executive*
Hill, James Stanley *computer consulting company executive*
Pagano, Jon Allen *data processing consultant*

South Saint Paul
Olen, Gary *marketing company executive*

Wayzata
Waldera, Wayne Eugene *crisis management specialist*

Willmar
Norling, Rayburn *food service executive*

MISSOURI

Carthage
Haffner, David S. *business executive*

Clayton
Davis, William Albert *theme park director*
Vecchiotti, Robert Anthony *management and organizational consultant*

Fenton
Kienker, James W. *marketing executive*
Lipovsky, Robert P. *marketing executive*
Maritz, W. Stephen *marketing professional, service executive*

Kansas City
Bartlett, Sherie *printing company executive*
Bernstein, Robert *advertising executive*
Cooper, Corinne *communications consultant, lawyer*
Dillingham, John Allen *marketing professional*
Druten, Robert S. *greeting card company executive*
Grossman, Jerome Barnett *retired service firm executive*
Hall, Donald Joyce *greeting card company executive*
Hockaday, Irvine O., Jr. *greeting card company executive*
Kovac, F. Peter *advertising executive*
Kuhn, Whitey *advertising executive*
McElwreath, Sally Chin *public relations executive*
Robertson, Leon H. *management consultant, educator*
Solberg, Elizabeth Transou *public relations executive*
Stevens, Jane *advertising executive*
Stowers, James W., III *data processing company executive*

Lake Saint Louis
Dommermuth, William Peter *marketing consultant, educator*

Liberty
McCaslin, W.C. *products and packaging executive*

Maryland Heights
Toan, Barrett A. *executive*

Monett
Henry, Michael E. *computer company executive*

Saint Ann
Drury, Charles Louis, Jr. *hotel executive*

Saint Charles
Gross, Charles Robert *bank executive, state senator*

Saint Louis
Adams, W. Randolph , Jr. *management consultant*
Anderson, Halvor *corporate officer*
Bateman, Sharon Louise *public relations executive*
Cooper, Robert James *purchasing consultant*
Davis, Irvin *advertising, public relations, broadcast executive*
Donald, Arnold W. *company executive*
Edwards, Judith Elizabeth *retired advertising executive*
Epner, Steven Arthur *computer consultant*
Essman, Alyn V. *photographic studios company executive*
Graham, John Dalby *public relations executive*
Hilgert, Raymond Lewis *management and industrial relations educator, consultant, arbitrator*
Kalkwarf, Kent D. *communications company executive*
Kenning, John Charles *former marketing professional*
Kent, Jerald L. *communications company executive*
Khoury, George Gilbert *printing company executive, baseball association executive*
Loynd, Richard Birkett *consumer products company executive*
Lyons, Gordon *marketing executive*
Macauley, Edward C. *retired company executive*
Musial, Stan(ley) (Frank Musial) *hotel and restaurant executive, former baseball team executive, former baseball player*
O'Connell, John T. *rental leasing company executive*
Riley, Michael Robert *marketing and business development executive*
Schnuck, Scott C. *grocery store executive*
Shapiro, Mark *advertising executive*
Shevitz, Mark H. *sales promotion and marketing executive*
Sibbald, John Ristow *management consultant*
Siemer, Paul Jennings *public relations executive*
Stork, Donald Arthur *advertising executive*
Taylor, Andrew C. *rental leasing company executive*
Taylor, Jack C. *rental and leasing company executive*
Tyler, William Howard, Jr. *advertising executive, educator*
Van Luven, William Robert *management consultant*
Vandiver, Donna *public relations executive*
Voss, Thomas *customer services executive*

Springfield
Denton, D. Keith *management educator*
Hammons, John Q. *hotel executive*
Noble, Robert B. *advertising executive*
Weber, Kenneth J. *hotel executive*
Witherspoon, John Thomas *water resources consultant*

NEBRASKA

Lincoln
Clifton, James K. *market research company executive*
Hays, Michael D. *research company executive*
Tavlin, Michael John *computer software company executive*

Omaha
Eggers, James Wesley *executive search consultant*
Fairfield, Bill L. *company executive*
Gupta, Vinod *business lists company executive*
O'Donnell, James P. *food service executive*
Phares, Lynn Levisay *public relations communications executive*
Roskens, Ronald William *international business consultant*
Starzel, Robert F. *business executive*
Stubblefield, Robert F. *travel agency executive*

NEW JERSEY

Princeton
Rogula, James Leroy *consumer products company executive*

NEW YORK

New York
Bell, David Arthur *advertising agency executive*
Bloom, Stephen Joel *distribution company executive*
Rosenshine, Allen Gilbert *advertising agency executive*

NORTH DAKOTA

Fargo
Tharaldson, Gary Dean *hotel developer and owner*
Wallwork, William Wilson, III *automobile executive*

Grand Forks
Rolshoven, Ross William *legal investigator, artist*

OHIO

Akron
Molinari, Marco *marketing executive*

Amelia
Hayden, Robert W. *business executive*

Broadview Heights
Sternlieb, Lawrence Jay *marketing professional, writer*

Canton
Suarez, Benjamin *consumer products company executive*

Cincinnati
Artzt, Edwin Lewis *consumer products company executive*
Baumgardner, Michael H. *marketing professional*
Bouquin, Bertrand *chef*
Brooks, Randy *research company executive*
Brunner, Gordon F(rancis) *household products company executive*
Carraher, Charles Jacob, Jr. *professional speaker*
Comisar, Michael E. *restaurant manager*
Comisar, Nat *restaurant manager*
deCavel, Jean-Robert *chef*
Dillon, David Brian *retail grocery executive*
Ellenberger, Richard G. *telecommunications executive*
Hicks, Irle Raymond *retail food chain executive*
Hutton, Edward Luke *diversified public corporation executive*
Jager, Durk I. *retired marketing agency executive*
Jones, Daniel W. *executive*
Klein, Charles Henle *lithographing company executive*
Lafley, Alan G. *consumer products company executive*
Liss, Herbert Myron *communications executive, educator, journalist*
Lockhart, John Mallery *management consultant*
Maier, Jack C. *food products company executive*
Million, Kenneth Rhea *management consultant*
Mooney, Kevin W. *telecommunications executive*
Moore, John Edward *marketing professional, freelance writer*
Otto, Charlotte R. *consumer products company executive*
Pancero, Jack Blocher *restaurant executive*
Payne, Patricia A. *marketing professional*
Pepper, John Ennis, Jr. *consumer products company executive*
Rolls, Steven George *chief financial officer*
Schorr, Roger J. *business executive*
Seal, Richard C. *marketing executive*
Shipley, Tony L(ee) *software company executive*
Strauss, James Lester *investment sales executive*
Tatham, Ron *marketing executive*
Wehling, Robert Louis *household products company executive*
Zaring, Allen G. *company executive*

Cleveland
Byron, Rita Ellen Cooney *travel executive, publisher, real estate agent, civic leader, photojournalist, writer*
Crawford, Edward E. *consumer products company executive*
Danco, Léon Antoine *management consultant, educator*
DeGroote, Michael G. *management consulting company executive*
Dunbar, Mary Asmundson *communications executive, investor and public relations consultant*
Eaton, Henry Felix *public relations executive*
Fountain, Ronald Glenn *management consultant, finance/marketing executive, finance educator*
Gallagher, Patrick Francis Xavier *public relations executive*
Graham, John W. *advertising executive*
Griffith, Mary H. *corporate communications executive*
Haeck, James F. *company executive*
Henry, Edward Frank *computer accounting service executive*
Johnson, John Frank *professional recruitment executive*
Kissel, Edward W. *company executive*
Locigno, Paul Robert *public affairs executive*
Mabee, Keith V. *communications/investor relations executive*
Marcus, Donald Howard *advertising executive*
Materna, James M. *business executive*
McCormack, Mark Hume *advertising executive, lawyer*
Miller, Samuel H. *company executive*
Perkovic, Robert Branko *international management consultant*
Pollack, Florence K.Z. *management consultant*
Pucko, Diane Bowles *public relations executive*
Roop, James John *public relations executive*
Sadowski, James R. *company executive*
Scaminace, Joseph M. *paint store executive*
Seifert, Shelley Jane *human resources specialist*
Somers, K(arl) Brent *consumer products company executive*
Stashower, David L. *advertising executive*
Thompson, Stephen Arthur *sales consultant*
Turner, John *company executive*

Columbus
Barker, Llyle James, Jr. *management consultant, journalism educator*
Burke, Kenneth Andrew *advertising executive*
Curtin, Michael Francis *printing company executive, publisher*
Dittman, William A. *company executive*
Hagedorn, James *company executive*
Iammartino, Nicholas R. *corporate communications executive*
Jacobs, Alexis A. *automobile company executive*
Kirkwood, William Thomas *corporate professional*
Lefavre, Hadia *human resources executive*
Maher, Frank Aloysius *research and development executive, psychologist*
Milenthal, David *advertising executive*
Mitchell, Cameron M. *restaurant executive*
Norton, Patrick J. *company executive*
Reardon, Nancy Anne *human resource executive*
Ress, Charles William *management consultant*

Dayton
Amelio, William J. *computer hardware products*
Brown, Craig J. *printing company executive*
Davis, Robert A. *data storing company executive*
Dorsman, Peter A. *printing company executive*
Kegerreis, Robert James *management consultant, marketing educator*
Nevin, Robert Charles *information systems executive*
Peppel, Michael E. *computer company executive*
Reading, Anthony John *business executive, accountant*
Tatar, Jerome F. *business products executive*

Dublin
Freytag, Donald Ashe *management consultant*
Schuessler, John T. *food service executive*
Smith, K(ermit) Wayne *computer company executive*
Thomas, R. David *food services company executive*
Wilkins, Jeffrey M. *commputer company executive*

Gates Mills
Reitman, Robert Stanley *business consultant, nonprofit agency advisor*

Lancaster
Phillips, Edward John *consulting firm executive*

Maumee
Nowak, Patricia Rose *advertising executive*

Mayfield Heights
Newman, Joseph Herzl *advertising consultant*

Mayfield Hts
Baines, Don A. *company executive*

Medina
Evans, Kenneth M. *company executive*
Morris, John H. *company executive*
Rog, Joseph W. *business executive*
Sullivan, Frank C. *company executive*

Miamisburg
Thompson, Holley Marker *lawyer, marketing professional*

Milford
Jackson, Eric C. *executive*

Moreland Hills
Fisher, Will Stratton *illumination consultant*

New Philadelphia
Jonker, Bruce A. *business executive*
Phillips, Barry L. *business executive*

Newark
De Lawder, C. Daniel *company executive*

Oxford
Yen, David Chi-Chung *management information systems educator*

Peninsula
Ludwig, Richard Joseph *ski resort executive*

Salem
Fehr, Kenneth Manbeck *retired computer systems company executive*

Shaker Heights
Cornell, Edward L. *consumer products company executive*
Wuest, Jim *consumer products company executive*

Solon
Plush, Mark J. *company executive*

Streetsboro
Weiss, Joseph Joel *consulting company executive*

Sylvania
Ring, Herbert Everett *management executive*

Tipp City
Taylor, Robert Homer *quality assurance professional, pilot*

Toledo
Block, Allan James *communications executive*
Cecere, Dominico *company executive*
Meier, John F. *consumer products company executive*
Paquette, Jack Kenneth *management consultant, antiques dealer*

Westlake
George, James W. *travel company executive*
Kuhn, Edwin P. *travel company executive*

Wooster
Schmitt, Wolf Rudolf *consumer products executive*

Worthington
Bender, Bob *advertising executive*
Trevor, Alexander Bruen *computer company executive*

Wyoming
Cooley, William Edward *regulatory affairs manager*

Youngstown
Cafaro, Anthony M. *corporate executive*

PENNSYLVANIA

Malvern
Herring, Raymond Mark *marketing professional, researcher*

SOUTH CAROLINA

Seabrook Island
Call, Lawrence Michael *consumer products company executive*

Spartanburg
Adamson, James B. *business executive*

TEXAS

The Woodlands
Glenn, Gerald Marvin *marketing, engineering and construction executive*

VIRGINIA

Alexandria
Devantier, Paul W. *communications executive, broadcaster*
Nelson, David Leonard *process management systems company executive*

Mc Lean
Flagg, Michael James *communications and graphics company executive*

WISCONSIN

Algoma
Golomski, William Arthur Joseph *consulting company executive*

Appleton
Hasselbacher, Darlene M. *human resources executive*
McManus, John Francis *association executive, writer*
Mischka, Thomas *marketing professional*
Underhill, Robert Alan *consumer products company executive*

Brookfield
Bader, Ronald L. *advertising executive*
Muma, Leslie M. *data processing executive*
Nelson, William George, IV *software company executive*
Nickerson, Greg *public relations executive*
Welnetz, David Charles *human resources executive*

Dodgeville
Eisenberg, Lee B. *communications executive, author*

Grafton
Schneider, Carol Ann *staffing services company executive*

Green Bay
Bender, Brian *consumer products executive*
Burrows, Paul A. *consumer products executive*
Meng, John C. *food service executive*
Poppenhagen, Ronald William *advertising agency executive*

Hartford
Fowler, John *printing company executive*

Jefferson
Myers, Gary *public relations executive*

Kohler
Kohler, Laura E. *human resources executive*

Madison
Bishop, Carolyn Benkert *public relations counselor*
Carlson, Chris *company executive*
Knapstein, Michael *advertising executive*
Opitz, David Wilmer *corporate executive, state political party executi*
Piper, Odessa *chef*

Middleton
Lipp, Susan *company executive*

Milwaukee
Arbit, Bruce *direct marketing executive, consultant*
Colbert, Virgis William *brewery company executive*
Constable, John *advertising executive*
Counsell, Paul S. *former advertising executive, counselor*
Davis, Susan F. *human resources specialist*
Davis, Thomas William *computer company executive*
Elias, Paul S. *marketing executive*
Fromstein, Mitchell S. *retired office services company executive*
Hueneke, Terry A. *temporary services company executive*
Hunter, Victor Lee *marketing executive, consultant*
Jacobs, Bruce E. *business executive*
Joerres, Jeffrey A. *staffing company executive*
Joseph, Jules K. *retired public relations executive*
Laughlin, Steven L. *advertising executive*
Manning, Kenneth Paul *technologies company executive*
Marcus, Stephen Howard *hospitality and entertainment company executive*
Mueller, Marylin *graphic supply company executive*
Randall, William Seymour *leasing company executive*
Shiely, John Stephen *company executive, lawyer*
van Handel, Michael J. *staffing company executive*

Plymouth
Gentine, Lee Michael *marketing professional*

Racine
Klein, Gabriella Sonja *retired communications executive*

South Milwaukee
Kitzke, Eugene David *research management executive*

Sturtevant
Pyle, Thomas F., Jr. *consumer products company executive*

Thiensville
Dickow, James Fred *management consultant*

Waterford
Karraker, Louis Rendleman *retired corporate executive*

West Bend
Darrow, Russe M. *corporate executive*

CANADA

MANITOBA

Winnipeg
Fraser, John Foster *management company executive*

ONTARIO

Oakville
Jelinek, John Joseph *public relations executive*

ENGLAND

London
Chait, Jon Frederick *corporate executive, lawyer*

ADDRESS UNPUBLISHED

Berra, Robert Louis *human resources consultant*
Bodine, Laurence *marketing consultant*
Butts, Virginia *corporate public relations executive*
Chlebowski, John Francis, Jr. *business executive*
Clough, Barry *marketing executive*
Collins, Mary Ellen *retired human resources executive*
Corwell, Ann Elizabeth *public relations executive*
Dasburg, John Harold *quick service restaurant executive*
Diamond, Susan Zee *management consultant*
Engels, Thomas Joseph *sales executive*
Farr, Mel *automotive sales executive, former professional football player*
Feller, Robert William Andrew *baseball team public relations executive, retired baseball player*
Francis, Philip Hamilton *management consultant*
Glass, Kenneth Edward *management consultant*
Gorsline, Stephen Paul *security firm executive*
Hall, Hansel Crimiel *communications executive*
Harold, Tom *advertising executive*
Harr, Lucy Loraine *public relations executive*
Henselmeier, Sandra Nadine *retired training and development consulting firm executive*
Hersher, Richard Donald *management consultant*
Hewitt, Pamela S. *human resources specialist*
Hietala, Allan *retired advertising executive*
Holzer, Edwin *advertising executive*
Jackson, Monica Denee *purchasing agent*
Jernstedt, Richard Don *public relations executive*
Kacek, Don J. *management consultant*
Kendzior, Robert Joseph *marketing executive*
Kidd, Debra Jean *communications executive*
Koprivica, Dorothy Mary *management consultant, real estate and insurance broker*
Kreer, Irene Overman *association and meeting management executive*
Kupper, Bruce David *advertising executive*
Larson, Robert Frederick *communications production company executive*
Linda, Gerald *advertising and marketing executive*
Longaberger, Tami *home decor accessories company executive*
Mann, Benjamin Howard *management consultant*
McGee, Patrick Edgar *postal service clerk*
McGuire, John W., Sr. *advertising executive, marketing professional, author*
Moeller, Robert John *management consultant, consultant*
Naylor, Jeffrey Gordon *consumer products company executive*
Parker, Lee Fischer *sales executive*
Perry, Chris Nicholas *retired advertising executive*
Preschlack, John Edward *management consultant*
Proctor, Barbara Gardner *advertising agency executive, writer*
Rydholm, Ralph Williams *advertising agency executive*
Saligman, Harvey *retired consumer products and services company executive*
Schmutz, Charles Reid *university foundation executive*
Schonberg, Alan Robert *management recruiting executive*
Schubert, Helen Celia *public relations executive*
Schulz, Michael John *fire and explosion analyst, consultant*
Sease, Gene Elwood *public relations company executive*
Simecka, Betty Jean *marketing executive*
Sincoff, Michael Z. *human resources and marketing professional*
Smith, Donald Nickerson *food service executive*
Smith, Steven J. *communications company executive*
Sroge, Maxwell Harold *marketing consultant, publishing executive*
Taplett, Lloyd Melvin *human resources management consultant*
Weismantel, Gregory Nelson *management consultant and software executive*
Williams, Louis Clair, Jr. *public relations executive*
Zeller, Joseph Paul *advertising executive*

INDUSTRY: TRADE

UNITED STATES

ILLINOIS

Bloomingdale
Kovanda, Gary *computer wholesale distributing executive*

Chicago
Blagg, Joe W. *retail executive*
Bozic, Michael C. *retail company executive*
Christianson, Stanley David *corporate executive*
Doolittle, Sidney Newing *retail executive*
Gin, Sue Ling *retail executive*
Goddu, Roger *retail executive*
Hoye, Donald J. *hardware distribution company executive*
Hunt, Holly *small business owner*
Meltzer, David Brian *retail executive*
Paup, Thomas *retail department store executive*
Robins, Joel *company executive*
Vrablik, Edward Robert *import/export company executive*

Decatur
Bradshaw, Billy Dean *retired retail executive*

Deerfield
Bernauer, David W. *retail company executive*
Ferkenhoff, Robert J. *retail executive*
Jorndt, Louis Daniel *retail drug store chain executive*
Polark, Roger L. *retail drug store executive*

Des Plaines
Larrimore, Randall Walter *wholesale company executive*

Hoffman Estates
Boyer, Jeffrey N. *retail executive*
Day, Julian C. *retail executive*
Lacy, Alan Jasper *retail executive*

Lake Forest
Grainger, David William *distribution company executive*
Loux, P. Ogden *distribution company executive*
Stirling, Ellen Adair *retail executive*

Milan
Kelly, Robert J. *supermarket executive*
Plumley, S. Patric *retail executive*

Morton Grove
McKenna, Andrew James *paper distribution and printing company executive, baseball club executive*

Oak Brook
Hanner, John *retail executive*
Hodnik, David F. *retail company executive*
Jones, Jeffrey W. *retail executive*
Jung, Howard J. *retail executive*

Palatine
Cesario, Robert Charles *franchise executive, consultant*

River Grove
Hull, Kenneth James *retail bookstore/educ prod and services executive*
Stanton, Kathryn *retail bookstores/educ products and services executive*

Skokie
Letham, Dennis J. *wholesale company executive*
Van Gelder, Marc Christiaan *retail executive*

Steger
Carpenter, Kenneth Russell *international trading executive*

Wauconda
Wood, Leslie Ann *retail administrator*

INDIANA

Elkhart
Drexler, Rudy Matthew, Jr. *professional law enforcement dog trainer*

Fort Wayne
Curtis, Douglas Homer *small business owner*

Griffith
Spires, Roberta Lynn *small business owner*

Indianapolis
Seneff, Smiley Howard *business owner*

IOWA

Ankeny
Lamb, Ronald M. *convenience stores executive*

Boone
Cramer, Robert *retail executive*

Cedar Falls
Sweet, Cynthia Rae *small business owner*

West Des Moines
Briggs, John *grocery retail executive*
Pearson, Ronald Dale *retail food stores corporation executive*
Wheeler, Mike *retail food store corporate executive*

KANSAS

Kansas City
Baska, James Louis *wholesale grocery company executive*
Carolan, Douglas *wholesale company executive*

Osawatomie
Jimenez, Bettie Eileen *retired small business owner*

Topeka
Hicks, Ken Carlyle *retail executive*

Wichita
Gates, Walter Edward *small business owner*

MICHIGAN

Ann Arbor
Quinnell, Bruce Andrew *retail book chain executive*

Bad Axe
Sullivan, James Gerald *business owner, postal letter carrier*

Belleville
Bailey, Glenn E. *wholesale distribution executive*

Bloomfield Hills
Robinson, Jack Albert *retail drug stores executive*

Dearborn
Adray, Deborah *retail executive*

Detroit
McGee, Sherry *retail executive*
Tushman, J. Lawrence *wholesale distribution executive*

Grand Rapids
Kolk, Fritz D. *retail executive*
McLean, James *retail merchandise/grocery executive*
Meijer, Douglas *retail company executive*
Meijer, Frederik *retail company executive*
Meijer, Mark *retail executive*
Meyer, James B. *retail executive*
Walsh, James *retail supermarket executive*

Jackson
Gilbert, Paul W. *retail executive*
Mills, P. Gerald *retail executive*

Lansing
LaHaine, Gilbert Eugene *retail lumber company executive*

Midland
Huntress, Betty Ann *former music store proprietor, educator*

Muskegon
McKitrick, James Thomas *retail executive*

Redford
Barnaby, Alan *retail executive*

Three Rivers
Lewis, Darrell L. *retail executive*

Troy
Conaway, Charles C. *retail company executive*
Criancamilli, Andrew A. *retail executive*
Hall, Floyd *retail executive*
Keeble, Donald W. *retail executive*
Schwartz, Mark *retail executive*
Strome, Stephen *distribution company executive*
Welch, Martin E., III *retail executive*

MINNESOTA

Eden Prairie
Anderson, Bradbury H. *retail executive*
Arnold, Gary L. *retail executive*
Engel, Susan E. *retail executive*
Fenn, Wade R. *retail executive*
Jackson, Darren Richard *retail company executive*
Knous, Pamela K. *wholesale distribution executive*
Noddle, Jeffrey *retail and food distribution executive*
Schulze, Richard M. *retail electronics company executive*
Wright, Michael William *wholesale distribution and retail executive*

Edina
Emmerich, Karol Denise *foundation executive, daylily hybridizer, former retail executive*

Minneapolis
Ahlers, Linda L. *retail executive*
Erickson, Ronald A. *retail executive*
Hale, James Thomas *retail company executive, lawyer*
Lindahl, Dennis *retail executive*
Scovanner, Douglas *retail company executive*
Stephenson, Vivian M. *former retail executive*
Trestman, Frank D. *distribution company executive*
Ulrich, Robert J. *retail discount chain stores executive*
Woodrow, Kennth B. *retail company executive*

Minnetonka
Benson, Keith A. *retail executive*
DiGeso, Amy *mail order company executive*
Kriegel, David L. *retail executive*

Saint Paul
Johnson, Lynn *liquor company wholesaler*
Nash, Nicholas David *retailing executive*

Walker
Collins, Thomas William *caterer, consultant*

MISSOURI

Clayton
Hall, Carl Loren *electrical distribution executive*

Cuba
Work, Bruce Van Syoc *business consultant*

Eureka
Zimmers, Vivian Eleanor *development and administrative consultant*

Kansas City
Barron, Millard E. *retail executive*
Stueck, William Noble *small business owner*
Witaszak, Richard B. *retail executive*

Maryland Heights
Marcus, John *wholesale distribution executive*

Saint Louis
Bennet, Richard W., III *retail executive*
Bridgewater, Bernard Adolphus, Jr. *retired footwear company executive, consultant*
Dunham, John L. *retail company executive*
Edison, Bernard Alan *retired retail apparel company executive*
Hinshaw, Juanita *electric distributor executive*
Kahn, Eugene S. *department store chain executive*
Loeb, Jerome Thomas *retail executive*
Newman, Andrew Edison *restaurant executive*
Reynolds, Robert A., Jr. *electric distributor executive*
Schnuck, Craig D. *grocery stores executive*
Schnuck, Todd Robert *grocery store company executive*
Upbin, Hal Jay *consumer products executive*
Wolfe, R. Dean *retail executive*

NORTH DAKOTA

Grand Forks
Kiesau, Jean *retail executive*

OHIO

Cincinnati
Cohen, Mark A. *retail executive*
Hodge, Robert Joseph *retail executive*
Hoguet, David Dilworth *rental furniture executive*
Hoguet, Karen M. *retail department store executive*
Miller, Robert G. *retail executive*
Tysor, Ronald W. *retail executive*
Zimmerman, James M. *retail company executive*

Cleveland
Anderson, Warren *distribution company executive*
Crosby, Fred McClellan *retail home and office furnishings executive*

Columbus
Callander, Kay Eileen Paisley *business owner, retired education educator, writer*
Hailey, V. Ann *retail executive*
Hollis-Allbritton, Cheryl Dawn *retail paper supply store executive*
Kelley, William G. *retail stores executive*
Ketteler, Thomas R. *retail executive*
Potter, Michael J. *retail stores executive*
Ricart, Rhett C. *retail automotive executive*
Schottenstein, Jay L. *retail executive*
Shapiro, Mark D. *retail executive*
Wexner, Leslie Herbert *retail executive*

Dayton
Davido, Scott *retail executive*
Jenefsky, Jack *wholesale company executive*
Mershad, Frederick J. *retail executive*
Rose, Stuart *retail executive*

Dublin
Walter, Robert D. *wholesale pharmaceutical distribution executive*

Galion
Butterfield, James T. *small business owner*

Hudson
Carney, Brian P. *retail executive*

Maumee
Walrod, David James *retail grocery chain executive*

Reynoldsburg
Gilman, Kenneth B. *retail executive*

Shaker Heights
Feuer, Michael *office products superstore executive*
O'Donnell, Gene *retail executive*
Peterson, Gary *retail executive*

Valley View
Glassman, Eric I. *retail executive*

Warren
Thompson, Eric Thomas *retail executive*

Youngstown
Gottron, Francis Robert, III *small business owner*
Seekely, Martins *retail company executive*

WASHINGTON

Bellevue
Dauphinais, George Arthur *import company executive*

WISCONSIN

Beloit
Hendricks, Kenneth *wholesale distribution executive*
Story, Kendra *wholesale distribution executive*

Eau Claire
Helland, Mark Duane *small business owner*

Green Bay
Bettiga, Michael J. *retail executive*
Podany, William J. *speciality discount retail company executive*

Menomonee Falls
Blanc, Caryn *retail executive*
Kellogg, William S. *retail executive*
Mansell, Kevin B. *retail executive*
Meier, Arlene *retail executive*
Montgomery, R. Lawrence *speciality department store chain executive*

Pewaukee
Lestina, Gerald F. *wholesale grocery executive*

Stevens Point
Copps, Michael William *retail and wholesale company executive*

CANADA

MANITOBA

Winnipeg
Cohen, Albert Diamond *retail executive*

ADDRESS UNPUBLISHED

Corcoran, Philip E. *wholesale distribution executive*
Farrell, David Coakley *former department store executive*
Gilbert, Samuel Lawrence *business owner*
Goldstein, Alfred George *retail and consumer products executive*
Goldstein, Norman Ray *international trading company executive, consultant*
Kogut, John Anthony *retail/wholesale executive*
Sewell, Phyllis Shapiro *retail chain executive*
Trutter, John Thomas *consulting company executive*

INDUSTRY: TRANSPORTATION

UNITED STATES

CALIFORNIA

Woodland Hills
Sugar, Ronald D. *aerospace executive*

FLORIDA

Estero
Barney, Charles Richard *transportation executive*

Stuart
Logan, Henry Vincent *retired transportation executive*

ILLINOIS

Arlington Heights
Hudson, Ronald Morgan *aviation planner*

Chicago
Burkhardt, Edward Arnold *railway executive*
Dutta, Rono J. *air transportation executive*
Heineman, Ben Walter *corporation executive*
Loney, Mary Rose *airport administrator*
Nord, Henry J. *transportation executive*
Reed, John Shedd *former railway executive*
Skinner, Samuel K. *transportation executive*
Springer, Denis E. *former railroad executive*
Studdert, Andrew Paul *air transportation executive*

Deerfield
Karlin, Jerome B. *retail company executive*

Elk Grove Village
Goodwin, James E. *air transportation executive*
Hacker, Douglas A. *air transportation executive*

Hillside
Marzullo, Larry A. *transportation executive*

Lisle
Johnson, William S. *transportation executive*

Lombard
Yeager, Phillip Charles *transportation company executive*

Mahomet
Roberson, Roger T. *transportation executive*

Naperville
Gannon, Jeffrey P. *trucking/relocation services executive*
Kaczka, Jeff *trucking/relocation services executive*
Lake, Robert D. *transportation executive*

Oak Brook
Duerinck, Louis T. *retired railroad executive, attorney*

INDIANA

Evansville
Shaffer, Michael L. *transportation company executive*

Fort Wayne
Uber, Larry R. *transportation executive*

Indianapolis
Mikelsons, J. George *air aerospace transportation executive*
Roberts, David *airport executive*
Wensits, David L. *aerospace executive*

Jeffersonville
Hagan, Michael Charles *transporation executive*

Noblesville
Morrison, Joseph Young *transportation consultant*

IOWA

Cedar Rapids
Smith, Herald Alvin, Jr. *transportation executive*
Smith, John M. *trucking executive*

Coralville
Gerdin, Russell A. *transportation executive*

Fort Dodge
Smith, William G. *transportation executive*

KANSAS

Overland Park
Martin, William F. *transportation company legal executive*
Zollars, William D. *freight company executive*

Wichita
Bell, Baillis F. *airport terminal executive*

MICHIGAN

Ann Arbor
Drake, John Warren *aviation consultant*

Detroit
Feldhouse, Lynn *automotive company executive*
Newman, Andrea Fischer *air transportation executive*
Robinson, Lester W. *airport executive*

Flint
Trout, Michael Gerald *airport administrator*

Grand Rapids
Auwers, Stanley John *motor carrier executive*
Gainey, Harvey Nueton *transportation executive*

Lansing
Schmidt, Thomas Walter *airport executive*

Waterford
Randall, Karl W. *aviation executive, lawyer*

Wayne
Rush, Andra M. *transportation executive*

Ypsilanti
Snoddy, Anthony L. *manufacturing executive*

MINNESOTA

Eagan
Oren, Donald G. *transportation executive*

Edina
Foret, Mickey Phillip *air transportation company executive*

Hopkins
Miller, Paul David *aerospace executive*

Minneapolis
Anderson, Tim *airport terminal executive*
Hamiel, Jeff *airport executive*
Harper, Donald Victor *retired transportation and logistics educator*
Oppegaard, Grant E. *water transportation executive*

Saint Cloud
Anderson, Harold E. *trucking company executive*

Saint Paul
Anderson, Richard H. *air transportation executive*
Birdsall, Doug *airline company executive*
Checchi, Alfred A. *airline company executive*
Cohen, Neal *airline executive*
Engle, Donald Edward *retired railway executive, lawyer*
Gorman, Stephen E. *airline executive*
Griffin, J. Timothy *air transportation executive*
Haan, Philip C. *airline executive*

MISSOURI

Bridgeton
Delaney, Robert Vernon *logistics and transportation executive*

Fenton
Baer, Robert J. *transportation company executive*
Ellington, Donald E. *transportation company executive*

Joplin
Brown, Glenn F. *transportation executive, department chairman*

Kansas City
Cooper, Thom R. *transportation executive*
Monello, Joseph D. *financial asset management company executive*
Widmar, Russell C. *airport executive*

Lambert Airport
Griggs, Leonard LeRoy, Jr. *airport executive*

Saint Louis
Casey, Donald M. *air transportation executive*
Compton, William F. *air transportation executive*
Soled, Kathleen A. *airline company executive*

Springfield
Low, Robert E. *transportation executive*

NEBRASKA

Lincoln
Acklie, Duane William *transportation company executive*
Wood, John Frederick *air transportation executive*

Omaha
Davidson, Richard K. *railroad company executive*
Evans, Ivor J. (Ike) *railroad executive*
Smithey, Donald Leon *airport authority director*
Werner, Clarence L. *transportation executive*
Young, James R. *railroad transportation executive*

NEW YORK

New York
Armstrong, Neil A. *former astronaut*

NORTH CAROLINA

Chapel Hill
Waller, Patricia Fossum *transportation executive, researcher, psychologist*

OHIO

Akron
Wickham, Michael W. *transportation executive*

Cincinnati
Siebenburgen, David A. *airline company executive*

Cleveland
Dannemiller, John C. *transportation company executive*
Hannemann, Timothy W. *aerospace executive*

Columbus
Santulli, Richard T. *executive*

Howard
Hedrick, Larry Willis *airport executive*

Rocky River
Shively, Daniel Jerome *retired transportation executive*

Toledo
Hartung, James H. *airport authority executive*

Xenia
Bigelow, Daniel James *aerospace executive*

SOUTH DAKOTA

Sioux Falls
Smith, Murray Thomas *transportation company executive*

VERMONT

Vergennes
Dixon, Gerald Authur *aerospace manufacturing company executive*

WISCONSIN

Appleton
Crowley, Geoffrey Thomas *airline executive*

Green Bay
Gannon, Thomas A. *trucking executive*
Schneider, Donald J. *trucking company executive*

Marshfield
Roehl, Everett *transportation executive*

Milwaukee
Bateman, C. Barry *airport terminal executive*

Mondovi
Marten, Randolph L. *transportation executive*

Oshkosh
Bohn, Robert G. *transportation company executive*
Schoenrock, Tracy Allen *airline pilot, aviation consultant*
Szews, Charles *transportation executive*

Tomah
Johnson, Linda Arlene *petroleum and flatbed semi-freight transporter*

ESTONIA

Tallinn
Currie, Earl James *transportation company executive*

ADDRESS UNPUBLISHED

Ames, Donald Paul *retired aerospace company executive, researcher*
Burton, Raymond Charles, Jr. *retired transportation company executive*
Gitner, Gerald L. *air transportation executive, investment banker*
Greenwald, Gerald *air transportation executive*
Heineman, Steven *air transportation executive*
Lewis, Martin Edward *shipping company executive, foreign government concessionary*
Matthews, L. White, III *railroad executive*
McCarthy, Paul Fenton *aerospace executive, former naval officer*
Saubert, Walter E. (Wally Saubert) *trucking and transportation company executive*
Valine, Delmar Edmond, Sr. *corporate executive*
Vecci, Raymond Joseph *airline industry consultant*
Washburn, Donald Arthur *business executive, private investor*
Wilson, Gary Lee *airline company executive*

INDUSTRY: UTILITIES, ENERGY, RESOURCES

UNITED STATES

ILLINOIS

Chicago
Brooker, Thomas Kimball *oil company executive*
Carlson, LeRoy Theodore, Jr. *telecommunications industry executive*
Conrad, John R. *corporate executive*
Gillis, Ruth Ann M. *electric company executive*
Henry, Brian C. *telephone company executive*
Luebbers, James *gas utility company executive*
Morrow, Richard Martin *retired oil company executive*
Niederpruem, Gary J. *metal company executive*
Patrick, Thomas M. *gas utility company executive*
Rogers, Desiree Glapion *utilities executive*
Rowe, John William *utility executive*
Terry, Richard Edward *public utility holding company executive*

Decatur
Womeldorff, Porter John *utilities executive*

Geneva
Pershing, Robert George *telecommunications company executive*

Hinsdale
Brandt, John Ashworth *fuel company executive*

Lisle
Notebaert, Richard C. *retired telecommunications industry executive*

Naperville
Burken, Ruth Marie *utility company executive*

Oak Brook
Barnholt, Brandon K. *gas station/convenience store executive*
Harless, Katherine J. *telecommunications company executive*

Orland Park
English, Floyd Leroy *telecommunications company executive*

Peoria
Viets, Robert O. *utilities executive*

Winnetka
Mc Gimpsey, Ronald Alan *oil company executive*

INDIANA

Columbus
Able, Warren Walter *natural resource company executive, physician*

Evansville
Reherman, Ronald Gilbert *gas and electric company executive*

Greensburg
Schilling, Don Russell *electric utility executive*

Hammond
Schroer, Edmund Armin *retired utility company executive*

Highland
Purcell, James Francis *former utility executive, consultant*

Indianapolis
Bell, William Vernon *utility executive*
Ellerbrook, Niel Cochran *gas company executive*
Ferger, Lawrence A. *gas distribution utility executive*
Griffiths, David Neal *utility executive*

Merrillville
Neale, Gary Lee *utilities executive*

IOWA

Des Moines
Abel, Gregory E. *utility company executive*
Sokol, David L. *energy services provider company executive*

Sioux City
Wharton, Beverly Ann *former utility company executive*

KANSAS

Pittsburg
Nettels, George Edward, Jr. *mining executive*

Shawnee Mission
Krause, Arthur B. *telecommunications industry executive*
LeMay, Ronald T. *telecommunications industry executive*

Topeka
Holmes, Carl Dean *state representative, landowner*
Wittig, David C. *energy executive*

Westwood
Betts, Gene M. *telecommunications industry executive*
Esrey, William Todd *telecommunications company executive*

Wichita
Markel, Lynn *retired oil industry executive*
Varner, Sterling Verl *retired oil company executive*

MICHIGAN

Dearborn
Boulanger, Rodney Edmund *energy company executive*
Fryling, Victor J. *energy company executive*
McCormick, William Thomas, Jr. *electric and gas company executive*
Webb, Thomas J. *utilities executive*
Whipple, Kenneth *utilities executive*

Detroit
Anderson, Gerard M. *energy company executive*
Beale, Susan M. *electric power industry executive*
Buckler, Robert J. *energy distribution company executive*
Champley, Michael E. *electric power industry executive*
Earley, Anthony F., Jr. *utilities executive*
Earley, Anthony Francis, Jr. *utilities company executive, lawyer*
Ewing, Stephen E. *natural gas company executive*
Redfield, Jean M. *electric power company executive*
Taylor, S. Martin *utilities executive*

Fraser
Cattaneo, Michael S. *heating and cooling company executive*

Jackson
Harris, Patti B. *telecommunications executive*

Saint Clair Shores
Glancy, Alfred Robinson, III *retired public utility company executive*

MINNESOTA

Eden Prairie
Emison, James Wade *petroleum company executive*

Fergus Falls
MacFarlane, John Charles *utility company executive*

Minneapolis
Brunetti, Wayne H. *utility company executive*
Brunetti, Wayne Henry *utilities executive*
Cadogan, William J. *telecommunications company executive*
McIntyre, Edward J. *power company executive*
Wyman, James Thomas *petroleum company executive*

Minnetonka
Davis, Lynn J. *telecommunications executive*
Sobti, Arun *telecommunications executive*
Switz, Robert E. *telecommunications executive*

Saint Paul
Estenson, Noel K. *refining and fertilizer company executive*
Robertson, Jerry Earl *retired manufacturing company executive*

MISSOURI

Joplin
Fancher, Robert Burney *electric utility executive, entrepreneur*
McKinney, Myron W. *electronic company executive*

Kansas City
Baker, John Russell *utilities executive*
Empson, Jon R. *utilities executive*
Green, Robert K. *energy executive*
Jackson, Marcus *electric power industry executive*
Lowe, Peter *electric power industry executive*
Wolf, Dale Joseph *utilities company executive*

Liberty
Ferrell, James Edwin *energy company executive*

Saint Louis
Brandt, Donald Edward *utilities company executive*
Clark, Maura J. *oil, gas industry executive*
Engelhardt, Irl F. *coal company executive*
Kalkware, Kent D. *telecommunications professional*
Mueller, Charles William *electric utility executive*
Navarre, Richard A. *mining executive*
Quenon, Robert Hagerty *retired mining consultant and holding company executive*
Rusnack, William C. *petroleum company executive*
Yaeger, Douglas Harrison *gas company executive*

Springfield
Jura, James J. *electric utility executive*

NEBRASKA

Hastings
Creigh, Thomas, Jr. *utility executive*

Omaha
Grewcock, William L. *mining company executive*

OHIO

Akron
Alexander, Anthony J. *electric power industry executive*
Marsh, Richard H. *utilities company executive*

Canton
Stage, Richard Lee *consultant, retired utilities executive*

Cincinnati
Braunstein, Mary *energy consulting company executive*
Cyrus, Michael J. *electric power industry executive*
Duncan, R. Foster *utilities company executive*
Foley, Cheryl M. *company executive*
Kiggen, James D. *telecommunications industry executive*
Noonan, Sheila M. *energy consulting company executive*
Randolph, Jackson Harold *utility company executive*
Rogers, James Eugene *electric and gas utility executive*

Cleveland
Bray, Pierce *business consultant*
Ginn, Robert Martin *retired utility company executive*
Miller, John Robert *oil industry executive*
O'Neil, Thomas J. *mining company executive*
Woods, Jacqueline F. *telecommunications industry executive*

Columbus
Addis, Paul D. *utilities executive*
Clements, Donald M. *utilities executive*
Draper, E(rnest) Linn, Jr. *electric utility executive*
Fayne, Henry W. *electric power industry executive*
Lhota, William J. *electric company executive*
Markowsky, James J. *retired utilities executive*
Massey, Robert John *telecommunications executive*
Vassell, Gregory S. *electric utility consultant*

Dayton
Forster, Peter Hans *utility company executive*
Hill, Allen M. *public utility executive*
Lansaw, Judy W. *public utility executive*
Torgerson, James Paul *energy company executive*

Newark
DallePezze, John Raymond *lighting company executive*

Westerville
Feck, Luke Matthew *retired utility executive*

Westlake
Connelly, John James *retired oil company technical specialist*

SOUTH DAKOTA

Pierre
Dunn, James Bernard *mining company executive, state legislator*

Rapid City
Lien, Bruce Hawkins *minerals and oil company executive*

Sioux Falls
Bradley, Walter A., III *utilities company executive*
Hylland, Richard R. *utility company executive*
Lewis, Merle Dean *electric and gas utility executive*
Newell, Daniel K. *utilities company executive*

TEXAS

Houston
Soliman, Sam *gas, oil and chemical industry executive, investment company executive*

WISCONSIN

Green Bay
Weyers, Larry Lee *energy executive*

La Crosse
Rude, Brian David *utilities company executive*

Madison
Barr, James, III *telecommunications company executive*
Davis, Erroll Brown, Jr. *utility executive*
Liu, Lee *utility company executive*

Milwaukee
Abdoo, Richard A. *utilities company executive*
Schrader, Thomas F. *utilities executive*
Stephenson, Robert Baird *energy company executive*

Waukesha
Danner, George Wilson *telecommunications executive*
Sim, Richard Guild *business executive*

CANADA

MANITOBA

Saint Andrews
Lang, Otto *industry executive, former Canadian cabinet minister*

ADDRESS UNPUBLISHED

Ban, Stephen Dennis *natural gas industry research institute executive*
Baumgartner, John H. *refining and petroleum products company executive*
Chelle, Robert Frederick *entrepreneurial leadership educator*
Early, Patrick Joseph *retired oil and gas company executive*
Fuller, Harry Laurance *retired oil company executive*
Garberding, Larry Gilbert *retired utilities companies executive*
Green, Richard Calvin, Jr. *electric power and gas industry executive*
Greer, Carl Crawford *petroleum company executive*
Howard, James Joseph, III *utility company executive*
Humke, Ramon Lyle *utility executive*
Kaufman, Raymond L. *energy company executive*
Lobbia, John E. *retired utility company executive*
Lowrie, William G. *former oil company executive*
Mc Carthy, Walter John, Jr. *retired utility executive*
O'Connor, James John *retired utility company executive*
Rogers, Justin Towner, Jr. *retired utility company executive*
Templeton, John Alexander, II *coal company executive*
White, Willis Sheridan, Jr. *retired utilities company executive*

INFORMATION TECHNOLOGY *See also* SCIENCE: MATHEMATICS AND COMPUTER SCIENCE

UNITED STATES

ILLINOIS

Chicago
Bariff, Martin Louis *information systems educator, consultant*
Buckley, Joseph Paul, III *polygraph specialist*
Stark, Henry *technology educator*

Skokie
Johansson, Nils A. *information services executive*
Seeder, Richard Owen *infosystems specialist*

IOWA

Waverly
Brunkhorst, Robert John *computer programmer, analyst*

KANSAS

Manhattan
Streeter, John Willis *information systems manager*

Topeka
Freden, Sharon Elsie Christman *state education official*

MINNESOTA

Elk River
McClure, Alvin Bruce *technical consultant*

Excelsior
Henke, Janice Carine *educational software developer and marketer*

MISSOURI

Kansas City
Patterson, Neal L. *information systems company executive*

NORTH CAROLINA

Cary
Goldfarb, Eric Daniel *information technology executive, computer industry analyst*

OHIO

Cincinnati
Turner, Robert Eugene *infosystems specialist*

Columbus
Brown, Rowland Chauncey Widrig *information systems, strategic planning and ethics consultant*
Muller, Mervin Edgar *information systems educator, consultant*
Zapp, David Edwin *infosystems specialist, investment consultant*

Maineville
Collins, Larry Wayne *small business owner, information systems specialist*

Marion
Rowe, Lisa Dawn *computer programmer/analyst, computer consultant*

Pickerington
Blackman, Edwin Jackson *software engineer*

ADDRESS UNPUBLISHED

Jaw, Andrew Chung-Shiang *software analyst*
Toirac, S(eth) Thomas *software engineering executive, consultant*
Wikarski, Nancy Susan *information technology consultant*
Zimov, Bruce Steven *software engineer*

INTERNET *See* INFORMATION TECHNOLOGY

LAW: JUDICIAL ADMINISTRATION

UNITED STATES

FLORIDA

Venice
Hackett, Barbara (Kloka) *retired judge*

ILLINOIS

Benton
Foreman, James Louis *retired judge*
Gilbert, J. Phil *federal judge*

Chicago
Alesia, James H(enry) *judge*
Andersen, Wayne R. *federal judge*
Ashman, Martin C. *federal judge*
Aspen, Marvin Edward *federal judge*
Barliant, Ronald *federal judge*
Bauer, William Joseph *judge*
Bobrick, Edward A. *federal judge*
Bua, Nicholas John *retired federal judge*
Bucklo, Elaine Edwards *United States district court judge*
Castillo, Ruben *judge*
Coar, David H. *federal judge*
Conlon, Suzanne B. *federal judge*
Cousins, William, Jr. *judge*
Cudahy, Richard D. *judge*
Denlow, Morton *federal magistrate judge*
Duff, Brian Barnett *federal judge*
Easterbrook, Frank Hoover *federal judge*
Fairchild, Thomas E. *judge*
Fitzgerald, Thomas Robert *judge*
Flaum, Joel Martin *judge*
Gettleman, Robert William *judge*
Gottschall, Joan B. *judge*
Grady, John F. *federal judge*
Hart, William Thomas *federal judge*
Holderman, James F., Jr. *federal judge*
Keys, Arlander *federal judge*
Kocoras, Charles Petros *federal judge*
Leighton, George Neves *retired federal judge*
Leinenweber, Harry D. *federal judge*
Lindberg, George W. *federal judge*
Manning, Blanche M. *federal judge*
Marovich, George M. *federal judge*
McMorrow, Mary Ann G. *state supreme court justice*
Moran, James Byron *federal judge*
Nordberg, John Albert *federal judge*
Norgle, Charles Ronald, Sr. *federal judge*
Pallmeyer, Rebecca Ruth *judge*
Plunkett, Paul Edmund *federal judge*
Posner, Richard Allen *federal judge*
Rovner, Ilana Kara Diamond *federal judge*
Schmetterer, Jack Baer *federal judge*
Shadur, Milton Irving *judge*
Sonderby, Susan Pierson *federal judge*
Squires, John Henry *judge*
Williams, Ann Claire *federal judge*
Zagel, James Block *federal judge*

Danville
Garman, Rita B. *judge*

Downers Grove
McGarr, Frank James *retired federal judge, dispute resolution consultant*

East Saint Louis
Cohn, Gerald B. *federal judge*
Riley, Paul E. *retired judge*
Stiehl, William D. *federal judge*

Elgin
Kirkland, Alfred Younges, Sr. *federal judge*

Fairview Heights
Harrison, Moses W., II *state supreme court chief justice*

Homewood
Dietch, Henry Xerxes *judge*

Maple Park
Nickels, John L. *retired state supreme court justice*

Peoria
Heiple, James Dee *retired state supreme court justice*
McCuskey, Michael Patrick *judge*
McDade, Joe Billy *federal judge*
Mihm, Michael Martin *federal judge*

Rock Island
Kilbride, Thomas L. *judge*

Rockford
Mahoney, Patrick Michael *federal judge*
Reinhard, Philip G. *federal judge*

Springfield
Evans, Charles H. *federal judge*
Lessen, Larry Lee *federal judge*
Miller, Benjamin K. *retired state supreme court justice*
Mills, Richard Henry *federal judge*
Wood, Harlington, Jr. *federal judge*

Urbana
Baker, Harold Albert *federal judge*
Bernthal, David Gary *judge*

Waukegan
Brady, Terrence Joseph *judge*

Wheaton
Leston, Patrick John *judge*
Thomas, Robert R. *judge*

Wilmette
Bowman, George Arthur, Jr. *retired judge*

INDIANA

Evansville
Capshaw, Tommie Dean *judge*

Fort Wayne
Cosbey, Roger B. *federal magistrate judge*
Lee, William Charles *judge*

Hammond
Lozano, Rudolpho *federal judge*
Moody, James T(yne) *federal judge*
Rodovich, Andrew Paul *magistrate*

Indianapolis
Barker, Sarah Evans *judge*
Boehm, Theodore Reed *judge*
Dickson, Brent E(llis) *state supreme court justice*
Dillin, S. Hugh *federal judge*
Foster, Kennard P. *magistrate judge*
Givan, Richard Martin *retired state supreme court justice*
Godich, John Paul *federal magistrate judge*
Hamilton, David F. *judge*
McKinney, Larry J. *federal judge*
Metz, Anthony J., III *federal judge*
Otte, Frank J. *federal judge*
Rucker, Robert D. *judge*
Shepard, Randall Terry *state supreme court chief justice*
Shields, V. Sue *federal magistrate judge*
Sullivan, Frank, Jr. *state supreme court justice*
Tinder, John Daniel *federal judge*

Lafayette
Kanne, Michael Stephen *judge*

South Bend
Manion, Daniel Anthony *federal judge*
Miller, Robert L., Jr. *federal judge*
Ripple, Kenneth Francis *federal judge*
Rodibaugh, Robert Kurtz *retired judge*
Sharp, Allen *federal judge*

Terre Haute
Lewis, Jordan D. *federal judge*

IOWA

Algona
Andreasen, James Hallis *retired state supreme court judge*

Cedar Rapids
Hansen, David Rasmussen *federal judge*
Jarvey, John A. *federal judge*
Kilburg, Paul J. *federal judge*
Mc Manus, Edward Joseph *federal judge*
Melloy, Michael J. *federal judge*

Chariton
Stuart, William Corwin *federal judge*

Council Bluffs
Peterson, Richard William *judge, lawyer*

Des Moines
Bremer, Celeste F. *judge*
Cady, Mark S. *state supreme court justice*
Carter, James H. *state supreme court justice*
Fagg, George Gardner *federal judge*
Harris, K. David *senior state supreme court justice*
Jackwig, Lee M. *federal judge*
Larson, Jerry Leroy *state supreme court justice*
Lavorato, Louis A. *state supreme court chief justice*
Longstaff, Ronald E. *federal judge*
McGiverin, Arthur A. *former state supreme court chief justice*
Streit, Michael J. *judge*
Ternus, Marsha K. *state supreme court justice*
Vietor, Harold Duane *federal judge*
Walters, Ross A. *federal judge*
Wolle, Charles Robert *federal judge*

Ida Grove
Snell, Bruce M., Jr. *retired judge*

Osceola
Reynoldson, Walter Ward *retired state supreme court chief justice, lawyer*

Sioux City
Bennett, Mark Warren *judge, lawyer, educator*
Edmonds, William L. *federal judge*
O'Brien, Donald Eugene *federal judge*

KANSAS

Kansas City
Lungstrum, John W. *federal judge*
Rushfelt, Gerald Lloyd *magistrate judge*
VanBebber, George Thomas *federal judge*
Vratil, Kathryn Hoefer *federal judge*
Waxse, David John *judge*

Lawrence
Briscoe, Mary Beck *federal judge*
Tacha, Deanell Reece *federal judge*

Topeka
Abbott, Bob *state supreme court justice*
Allegrucci, Donald Lee *state supreme court justice*
Crow, Sam Alfred *judge*
Davis, Robert Edward *state supreme court justice*
Herd, Harold Shields *state supreme court justice*
Larson, Edward *state supreme court justice*
Lockett, Tyler Charles *state supreme court justice*
Marquardt, Christel Elisabeth *judge*
McFarland, Kay Eleanor *state supreme court chief justice*
Robinson, Julie Ann *federal judge*
Rogers, Richard Dean *federal judge*
Saffels, Dale Emerson *federal judge*
Six, Fred N. *state supreme court justice*

Wichita
Belot, Monti L., III *federal judge*
Brown, Wesley Ernest *federal judge*
Marten, J. Thomas *judge*

MICHIGAN

Ann Arbor
Guy, Ralph B., Jr. *federal judge*
Pepe, Steven Douglas *federal magistrate judge*

Bay City
Binder, Charles E. *magistrate judge*
Churchill, James Paul *federal judge*

Birmingham
La Plata, George *federal judge*

Detroit
Borman, Paul David *judge*
Callahan, J(ohn) William (Bill Callahan) *judge*
Clay, Eric L. *judge*
Cleland, Robert Hardy *federal judge*
Corrigan, Maura Denise *judge*
Duggan, Patrick James *federal judge*
Edmunds, Nancy Garlock *federal judge*
Feikens, John *federal judge*
Friedman, Bernard Alvin *federal judge*
Goldman, Marc L. *federal judge*
Hood, Denise Page *federal judge*
Keith, Damon Jerome *federal judge*
Kelly, Marilyn *state supreme court justice*
Kennedy, Cornelia Groefsema *federal judge*
Komives, Paul J. *federal judge*
Levin, Charles Leonard *state supreme court justice*
Lombard, Arthur J. *judge*
Mallett, Conrad LeRoy, Jr. *state supreme court chief justice*
Mathis, Greg *judge, radio personality*
Morgan, Virginia Mattison *magistrate judge*
O'Meara, John Corbett *federal judge*
Rhodes, Steven William *judge*
Rosen, Gerald Ellis *federal judge*
Ryan, James Leo *federal judge*
Taylor, Anna Diggs *judge*
Woods, George Edward *judge*
Zatkoff, Lawrence P. *federal judge*

Glen Arbor
Newblatt, Stewart Albert *federal judge*

Grand Rapids
Bell, Robert Holmes *county judge*
Brenneman, Hugh Warren, Jr. *judge*
Hillman, Douglas Woodruff *federal district judge*
Miles, Wendell A. *federal judge*
Quist, Gordon Jay *federal judge*
Scoville, Joseph G. *federal magistrate, judge*
Stevenson, Jo Ann C. *federal bankruptcy judge*

Kalamazoo
Enslen, Richard Alan *federal judge*
Rowland, Doyle Alfred *federal judge*

Kentwood
Kelly, William Garrett *judge*

Lansing
Cavanagh, Michael Francis *state supreme court justice*
Harrison, Michael Gregory *judge*
Markman, Stephen J. *Supreme Ct. judge*
McKeague, David William *judge*
Suhrheinrich, Richard Fred *judge*
Taylor, Clifford Woodworth *state supreme court justice*
Young, Robert P., Jr. *state supreme court justice*

Marquette
Greeley, Timothy P. *federal judge*

Southfield
Graves, Ray Reynolds *retired judge*

Traverse City
Weaver, Elizabeth A. *state supreme court justice*

White Lake
Boyle, Patricia Jean *retired state supreme court justice*

MINNESOTA

Anoka
Quinn, R. Joseph *former judge*

Bemidji
Burg, Randall K. *federal judge*

Duluth
Heaney, Gerald William *federal judge*

Minneapolis
Davis, Michael J. *judge*
Doty, David Singleton *federal judge*
Lebedoff, Jonathan Galanter *federal judge*
Loken, James Burton *federal judge*
MacLaughlin, Harry Hunter *federal judge*
Montgomery, Ann D. *federal judge, educator*
Murphy, Diana E. *federal judge*
Noel, Franklin Linwood *judge*
Rosenbaum, James Michael *judge*

Minnetonka
Rogers, James Devitt *judge*

Rochester
Keith, Alexander Macdonald *retired state supreme court chief justice, lawyer*

Saint Paul
Alsop, Donald Douglas *federal judge*
Anderson, Paul Holden *state supreme court justice*
Anderson, Russell A. *state supreme court justice*
Blatz, Kathleen Anne *state supreme court chief justice, state legislator*
Gilbert, James H. *judge*
Kishel, Gregory Francis *federal judge*
Kyle, Richard House *federal judge*
Lancaster, Joan Ericksen *state supreme court justice*
Lay, Donald Pomeroy *federal judge*
Mason, John Milton (Jack Mason) *judge*
Page, Alan Cedric *state supreme court justice*
Renner, Robert George *federal judge*
Stringer, Edward Charles *state supreme court justice*
Tomljanovich, Esther M. *state supreme court justice*
Willis, Bruce Donald *judge*

MISSOURI

Benton
Heckemeyer, Anthony Joseph *circuit court judge*

Cape Girardeau
Blanton, Lewis M. *federal judge*

Jefferson City
Benton, W. Duane *judge*
Covington, Ann K. *former state supreme court justice*
Knox, William Arthur *judge*
Limbaugh, Stephen Nathaniel, Jr. *state supreme court chief justice*
Price, William Ray, Jr. *state supreme court judge*
Robertson, Edward D., Jr. *retired state supreme court justice, lawyer*
Stith, Laura Denvir *judge*
White, Ronnie L. *state supreme court justice*
Wolff, Michael A. *state supreme court judge*

Kansas City
Bowman, Pasco Middleton, II *judge*
Federman, Arthur *federal judge*
Gaitan, Fernando J., Jr. *federal judge*
Gibson, John Robert *judge*
Hunter, Elmo Bolton *federal judge*
Koger, Frank Williams *federal judge*
Larsen, Robert Emmett *federal judge*
Laughrey, Nanette Kay *judge, federal*
Sachs, Howard F(rederic) *federal judge*
Smith, Ortrie D. *judge*
Ulrich, Robert Gene *judge*
Whipple, Dean *federal judge*
Wright, Scott Olin *federal judge*

Saint Charles
Karll, Jo Ann *state administrative law judge, lawyer*

Saint Louis
Adams, Millie B. *judge*
Barta, James Joseph *judge*
Davis, Lawrence O. *federal magistrate judge*
Filippine, Edward Louis *federal judge*
Hamilton, Jean Constance *judge*
Jackson, Carol E. *federal judge*
Limbaugh, Stephen Nathaniel *federal judge*
McMillian, Theodore *federal judge*
Medler, Mary Ann L. *federal judge*
Noce, David D. *federal magistrate judge*
Perry, Catherine D. *judge*
Shaw, Charles Alexander *judge*
Stohr, Donald J. *federal judge*
Teitelman, Richard Bertram *judge*
Webber, E. Richard, Jr. *judge*

Springfield
Holstein, John Charles *state supreme court judge*

West Plains
Dunlap, David Houston *judge*

NEBRASKA

Lincoln
Beam, Clarence Arlen *judge*
Connolly, William M. *state supreme court justice*
Gerrard, John M. *state supreme court justice*
Hastings, William Charles *retired state supreme court chief justice*
Hendry, John *state supreme court justice*
Kopf, Richard G. *federal judge*
McCormack, Michael *state supreme court justice*
Miller-Lerman, Lindsey *state supreme court justice*
Piester, David L(ee) *magistrate judge*
Stephan, Kenneth C. *state supreme court justice*
Urbom, Warren Keith *federal judge*
Wright, John F. *state supreme court justice*

Omaha
Bataillon, Joseph Francis *federal judge, lawyer*
Cambridge, William G. *federal judge*
Grant, John Thomas *retired state supreme court justice*
Shanahan, Thomas M. *judge*
Strom, Lyle Elmer *federal judge*
White, C. Thomas *state supreme court justice*

NORTH DAKOTA

Bismarck
Conmy, Patrick A. *federal judge*
Kapsner, Carol Ronning *state supreme court justice*
Kautzmann, Dwight C.H. *federal magistrate judge*
Maring, Mary Muehlen *state supreme court justice*
Neumann, William Allen *state supreme court justice*
Sandstrom, Dale Vernon *state supreme court judge*
Van Sickle, Bruce Marion *federal judge*
VandeWalle, Gerald Wayne *state supreme court chief justice*

Fargo
Bright, Myron H. *judge, educator*
Bye, Kermit Edward *federal judge, lawyer*
Hill, William A(lexander) *judge*
Klein, Karen K. *federal judge*
Magill, Frank John *federal judge*
Webb, Rodney Scott *judge*

Grand Forks
Senechal, Alice R. *judge, lawyer*

Minot
Kerian, Jon Robert *retired judge*

OHIO

Akron
Bell, Samuel H. *federal judge, educator*
Dowd, David D., Jr. *federal judge*
Shea-Stonum, Marilyn *federal judge*
White, Harold F. *bankruptcy judge, retired federal judge*

Cincinnati
Beckwith, Sandra Shank *judge*
Dlott, Susan Judy *judge, lawyer*
Engel, Albert Joseph *judge*
Hopkins, Jeffrey P. *federal judge*
Jones, Nathaniel Raphael *federal judge*
Nelson, David Aldrich *judge*
Perlman, Burton *judge*
Spiegel, S. Arthur *federal judge*
Weber, Herman Jacob *federal judge*

Circleville
Ammer, William *retired judge*
Long, Jan Michael *judge*

Cleveland
Aldrich, Ann *federal judge*
Baxter, Randolph *judge*
Gaughan, Patricia Anne *judge*
Hemann, Patricia A. *federal judge*
Krupansky, Robert Bazil *federal judge*
Manos, John M. *federal judge*
Markus, Richard M. *judge, mediator*
Matia, Paul Ramon *federal judge*
Moore, Karen Nelson *judge*
Morgenstern-Clarren, Pat *federal judge*
Nugent, Donald Clark *judge*
O'Malley, Kathleen M. *federal judge*
Oliver, Solomon, Jr. *judge*
Perelman, David S. *federal judge*
Wells, Lesley B. *judge*

Columbus
Abel, Mark Rogers *federal judge*
Caldwell, Charles M. *federal judge*
Calhoun, Donald Eugene, Jr. *federal judge*
Cole, Ransey Guy, Jr. *judge*
Cook, Deborah L. *state supreme court justice*
Douglas, Andrew *state supreme court justice*
Graham, James Lowell *federal judge*
Holschuh, John David *federal judge*
King, Norah McCann *federal judge*
Kinneary, Joseph Peter *federal judge*
Leach, Russell *judge*
Moyer, Thomas J. *state supreme court chief justice*
Norris, Alan Eugene *federal judge*
Pfeifer, Paul E. *state supreme court justice*
Resnick, Alice Robie *state supreme court justice*
Sargus, Edmund A., Jr. *judge*
Sellers, Barbara Jackson *federal judge*
Smith, George Curtis *judge*
Stratton, Evelyn Lundberg *state supreme court justice*
Sweeney, Asher William *state supreme court justice*
Sweeney, Francis E. *state supreme court justice*
Wright, J. Craig *state supreme court justice*

Dayton
Clark, William Alfred *federal judge*
Knapp, James Ian Keith *judge*
Merz, Michael *federal judge*
Petzold, John Paul *judge*

Medina
Batchelder, Alice M. *federal judge*

Toledo
Carr, James Gray *judge*
Katz, David Allan *judge, former lawyer, business consultant*
Potter, John William *federal judge*

Warren
Nader, Robert Alexander *judge, lawyer*

Youngstown
Bodoh, William T. *federal judge*
Economus, Peter Constantine *judge*
Vukovich, Joseph John *judge*

SOUTH DAKOTA

Pierre
Amundson, Robert A. *state supreme court justice*
Gilbertson, David *state supreme court justice*
Konenkamp, John K. *state supreme court justice*
Miller, Robert Arthur *former state supreme court chief justice*
Sabers, Richard Wayne *state supreme court justice*
Zinter, Steven L. *judge*

Rapid City
Battey, Richard Howard *judge*
Bogue, Andrew Wendell *federal judge*
Schreier, Karen Elizabeth *judge*

Sioux Falls
Jones, John Bailey *federal judge*
Piersol, Lawrence L. *federal judge*
Severson, Glen Arthur *circuit court judge*
Wollman, Roger Leland *federal judge*

WISCONSIN

Appleton
Froehlich, Harold Vernon *judge, former congressman*

Eau Claire
Utschig, Thomas S. *federal judge*

Madison
Abrahamson, Shirley Schlanger *state supreme court chief justice*
Bablitch, William A. *state supreme court justice*
Bradley, Ann Walsh *state supreme court justice*
Crabb, Barbara Brandriff *federal judge*
Crocker, Stephen L. *federal magistrate judge*
Crooks, N(eil) Patrick *state supreme court justice*
Deininger, David George *judge*
Foust, Charles William *judge*
Heffernan, Nathan Stewart *retired state supreme court chief justice*
Martin, Robert David *judge, educator*
Prosser, David Thomas, Jr. *judge, retired state legislator*
Shabaz, John C. *judge*
Sykes, Diane S. *state supreme court justice*
Wilcox, Jon P. *state supreme court justice*

Milwaukee
Adelman, Lynn *federal judge*
Callahan, William E., Jr. *federal judge*
Clevert, Charles Nelson, Jr. *federal judge*
Curran, Thomas J. *federal judge*
Evans, Terence Thomas *judge*
Goodstein, Aaron E. *federal magistrate judge*
Gordon, Myron L. *federal judge*
McGarity, Margaret Dee *federal judge*
Randa, Rudolph Thomas *judge*
Reynolds, John W. *federal judge*
Shapiro, James Edward *judge*
Stadtmueller, Joseph Peter *federal judge*

CANADA

MANITOBA

Winnipeg
Lyon, Sterling Rufus Webster *justice*

ADDRESS UNPUBLISHED

Anderson, G. Barry *judge*
Barbosa, Manuel *judge*
Bowman, John J. *judge*
Boylan, Arthur J. *judge*
Breslin, Peg M. *judge*
Callow, William Grant *retired state supreme court justice*
Ceci, Louis J. *former state supreme court justice*
Clark, Russell Gentry *retired federal judge*
Coffey, John Louis *judge*
Cohn, Avern Levin *district judge*
Cook, Julian Abele, Jr. *federal judge*
Fahrnbruch, Dale E. *retired state supreme court justice*
Freeman, Charles E. *state supreme court justice*
Gibson, Benjamin F. *federal judge*
Gilmore, Horace Weldon *former federal judge*
Gorence, Patricia Josetta *judge*
Griffin, Robert Paul *former United States senator, state supreme court justice*
Magnuson, Paul Arthur *federal judge*
Meschke, Herbert Leonard *retired state supreme court justice*
Neuman, Linda Kinney *state supreme court justice*
Porter, James Morris *retired judge*
Pusateri, James Anthony *judge*
Rice, Walter Herbert *federal judge*
Ross, Donald Roe *federal judge*
Schultz, Louis William *retired judge*
Selby, Myra Consetta *state supreme court justice*
Sheedy, Patrick Thomas *judge*
Sinclair, Virgil Lee, Jr. *judge, writer*
Stamos, John James *judge*
Steinmetz, Donald Walter *former state supreme court justice*
Wood, Diane Pamela *judge*

LAW: LAW PRACTICE AND ADMINISTRATION

UNITED STATES

ALABAMA

Birmingham
Avant, Grady, Jr. *lawyer*

ARIZONA

Tucson
Heaphy, John Merrill *lawyer*

COLORADO

Boulder
Manka, Ronald Eugene *lawyer*

DISTRICT OF COLUMBIA

Washington
Dam, Kenneth W. *lawyer, law educator, federal agency administrator*
Dowd, Thomas F. *lawyer*

FLORIDA

Longboat Key
Case, Karen Ann *lawyer*

Marco Island
Kaner, Harvey Sheldon *lawyer, executive*

Naples
Bruce, Jackson Martin, Jr. *lawyer*
Putzell, Edwin Joseph, Jr. *lawyer, mayor*

Oldsmar
Hirschman, Sherman Joseph *lawyer, accountant, educator*

Sanibel
Karch, George Frederick, Jr. *lawyer*

Sun City Center
Fuller, Samuel Ashby *lawyer, mining company executive*

West Palm Beach
Baker, Bernard Robert , II *lawyer*

ILLINOIS

Barrington
Lee, William Marshall *lawyer*
Wyatt, James Frank, Jr. *lawyer*

Belleville
Bauman, John Duane *lawyer*
Hess, Frederick J. *lawyer*

Bloomington
Bragg, Michael Ellis *lawyer, insurance company executive*
Reynard, Charles G. *lawyer, educator*
Sullivan, Laura Patricia *lawyer, insurance company executive*

Carbondale
Clemons, John Robert *lawyer*
Matthews, Elizabeth Woodfin *law librarian, law educator*

Carrollton
Strickland, Hugh Alfred *lawyer*

Carthage
Glidden, John Redmond *lawyer*

Champaign
Cribbet, John Edward *law educator, former university chancellor*
Johnson, Lawrence Eugene *lawyer*
Kindt, John Warren *lawyer, educator, consultant*
Krause, Harry Dieter *law educator*
Maggs, Peter Blount *lawyer, educator*
Mamer, Stuart Mies *lawyer*

Chicago
Abell, David Robert *lawyer*
Abrams, Lee Norman *lawyer*
Acker, Ann *lawyer*
Acker, Frederick George *lawyer*
Adair, Wendell Hinton, Jr. *lawyer*
Adelman, Stanley Joseph *lawyer*
Adelman, Steven Herbert *lawyer*
Agnello, Gino J. *federal court administrator*
Allen, Julie O'Donnell *lawyer*
Allen, Ronald Jay *law educator*
Allen, Thomas Draper *lawyer*
Anderson, J. Trent *lawyer*
Anderson, Kimball Richard *lawyer*
Anderson, William Cornelius, III *lawyer*
Angst, Gerald L. *lawyer*
Anthony, Michael Francis *lawyer*
Anvaripour, M. A. *lawyer*
Appel, Nina Schick *law educator, dean*
Armstrong, Edwin Richard *lawyer, publisher, editor*
Aronson, Virginia L. *lawyer*
Athas, Gus James *lawyer*
Avery, Robert Dean *lawyer*
Axley, Frederick William *lawyer*
Badel, Julie *lawyer*
Baer, John Richard Frederick *lawyer*
Baetz, W. Timothy *lawyer*
Bailey, Robert Short *lawyer*
Baird, Douglas Gordon *law educator, dean*
Baker, James Edward Sproul *retired lawyer*
Baker, Pamela *lawyer*
Baldwin, Shaun McParland *lawyer*
Banoff, Sheldon Irwin *lawyer*
Barker, William Thomas *lawyer*
Barnes, James Garland, Jr. *lawyer*
Barr, John Robert *retired lawyer*
Barrett, Roger Watson *lawyer*
Barron, Howard Robert *lawyer*
Barry, Norman J., Jr. *lawyer*
Baruch, Hurd *lawyer*
Bashwiner, Steven Lacelle *lawyer*
Baugher, Peter V. *lawyer*
Beck, Philip S. *lawyer*
Beem, Jack Darrel *lawyer*
Bennett, Robert William *law educator*
Berens, Mark Harry *lawyer*
Berenzweig, Jack Charles *lawyer*

Berger, Robert Michael *lawyer*
Berland, Abel Edward *lawyer, realtor*
Bernardini, Charles *lawyer, former alderman*
Berner, Robert Lee, Jr. *lawyer*
Berning, Larry D. *lawyer*
Bernstein, H. Bruce *lawyer*
Berolzheimer, Karl *lawyer*
Bertagnolli, Leslie A. *lawyer*
Biebel, Paul Philip, Jr. *lawyer*
Biederman, Jerry H. *lawyer*
Bierig, Jack R. *lawyer, educator*
Bitner, John Howard *lawyer*
Bixby, Frank Lyman *lawyer*
Blatt, Richard Lee *lawyer*
Block, Neal Jay *lawyer*
Blount, Michael Eugene *lawyer*
Blume, Paul Chiappe *lawyer*
Blust, Larry D. *lawyer*
Boies, Wilber H. *lawyer*
Bowe, William John *lawyer*
Bowen, Stephen Stewart *lawyer*
Bramnik, Robert Paul *lawyer*
Brice, Roger Thomas *lawyer*
Bridgman, Thomas Francis *lawyer*
Brizzolara, Charles Anthony *lawyer, director*
Brown, Alan Crawford *lawyer*
Brown, Donald James, Jr. *lawyer*
Brown, Gregory K. *lawyer*
Bruner, Stephen C. *lawyer*
Bulger, Brian Wegg *lawyer*
Burke, Thomas Joseph, Jr. *lawyer*
Burkey, Lee Melville *lawyer*
Burns, Daniel T. *corporate lawyer*
Burns, Terrence Michael *lawyer*
Busey, Roxane C. *lawyer*
Bussman, Donald Herbert *lawyer*
Carlin, Dennis J. *lawyer*
Carlson, Stephen Curtis *lawyer*
Carlson, Walter Carl *lawyer*
Carpenter, David William *lawyer*
Carren, Jeffrey P. *lawyer*
Carroll, James J. *lawyer*
Carroll, William Kenneth *law educator, psychologist, theologian*
Chandler, Kent, Jr. *lawyer*
Cheely, Daniel Joseph *lawyer*
Chefitz, Joel Gerald *lawyer*
Chemers, Robert Marc *lawyer*
Cherney, James Alan *lawyer*
Cherry, Daniel Ronald *lawyer*
Chiles, Stephen Michael *lawyer*
Christian, John M. *lawyer*
Cicero, Frank, Jr. *lawyer*
Clemens, Richard Glenn *lawyer*
Closen, Michael Lee *law educator*
Cohen, Melanie Rovner *lawyer*
Collen, John *lawyer*
Comiskey, Michael Peter *lawyer*
Conklin, Thomas William *lawyer*
Conviser, Richard James *law educator, lawyer, publications company executive*
Conway, Michael Maurice *lawyer*
Coolley, Ronald B. *lawyer*
Copeland, Edward Jerome *lawyer*
Corwin, Sherman Phillip *lawyer*
Costello, John William *lawyer*
Crane, Mark *lawyer*
Craven, George W. *lawyer*
Crawford, Dewey Byers *lawyer*
Cremin, Susan Elizabeth *lawyer*
Crihfield, Philip J. *lawyer*
Crisham, Thomas Michael *lawyer*
Crossan, John Robert *lawyer*
Csar, Michael F. *lawyer*
Cunningham, Robert James *lawyer*
Curran, Barbara Adell *retired law foundation administrator, lawyer, writer*
Currie, David Park *lawyer, educator*
Cusack, John Thomas *lawyer*
Custer, Charles Francis *lawyer*
D'Esposito, Julian C., Jr. *lawyer*
Daley, Susan Jean *lawyer*
Davidson, Stanley J. *lawyer*
Davis, Michael W. *lawyer*
Davis, Muller *lawyer*
Davis, Scott Jonathan *lawyer*
de Hoyos, Debora M. *lawyer*
DeCarlo, William S. *lawyer*
Decker, Richard Knore *lawyer*
Deitrick, William Edgar *lawyer*
Delp, Wilbur Charles, Jr. *lawyer*
Dent, Thomas G. *lawyer*
Despres, Leon Mathis *lawyer, former city official*
DeVine, Dick *lawyer*
DeWolfe, John Chauncey, Jr. *lawyer*
Dickstein, Beth J. *lawyer, accountant*
Dixon, Stewart Strawn *lawyer, consultant*
Dockterman, Michael *lawyer*
Donlevy, John Dearden *lawyer*
Donohoe, Jerome Francis *lawyer*
Dorman, Jeffrey Lawrence *lawyer*
Douglas, Charles W. *lawyer*
Downing, Robert Allan *lawyer*
Doyle, John Robert *lawyer*
Drymalski, Raymond Hibner *lawyer, banker*
Duhl, Michael Foster *lawyer*
Duncan, John Patrick Cavanaugh *lawyer*
Dunn, Edwin Rydell *lawyer*
Durchslag, Stephen P. *lawyer*
Dykstra, Paul Hopkins *lawyer*
Early, Bert Hylton *lawyer, consultant*
Easton, Lory Barsdate *lawyer*
Edelman, Alvin *lawyer*
Egan, Kevin James *lawyer*
Eggert, Russell Raymond *lawyer*
Eimer, Nathan Philip *lawyer*
Ekdahl, Jon Nels *lawyer, retired corporate secretary*
Elden, Gary Michael *lawyer*
Ellwood, Scott *lawyer*
English, John Dwight *lawyer*
Epstein, Richard A. *law educator*
Erens, Jay Allan *lawyer*
Esrick, Jerald Paul *lawyer*
Even, Francis Alphonse *lawyer*
Fahner, Tyrone C. *lawyer, former state attorney general*
Farber, Bernard John *lawyer*
Fazio, Peter Victor, Jr. *lawyer*
Fein, Roger Gary *lawyer*
Feinstein, Fred Ira *lawyer*
Feldman, Scott Milton *lawyer*
Fellows, Jerry Kenneth *lawyer*
Ferencz, Robert Arnold *lawyer*
Ferrini, James Thomas *lawyer*
Field, Robert Edward *lawyer*
Finke, Robert Forge *lawyer*
Fitch, Morgan Lewis, Jr. *intellectual property lawyer*
Fitzpatrick, Christine Morris *legal administrator, former television executive*
Flanagin, Neil *lawyer*
Formeller, Daniel Richard *lawyer*
Fort, Jeffrey C. *lawyer*
Foster, Teree E. *law educator, dean*
Foudree, Bruce William *lawyer*
Fox, Elaine Saphier *lawyer*
Fox, Paul T. *lawyer*
Franch, Richard Thomas *lawyer*
Franklin, Richard Mark *lawyer*
Fraumann, Willard George *lawyer*
Freed, Mayer Goodman *law educator*
Freeman, Lee Allen, Jr. *lawyer*
Freeman, Louis S. *lawyer*
Friedman, Lawrence Milton *lawyer*
Friedman, Roselyn L. *lawyer*
Fross, Roger Raymond *lawyer*
Fuller, Perry Lucian *lawyer*
Furlane, Mark Elliott *lawyer*
Garber, Samuel B. *lawyer, business/turnaround management consultant*
Garth, Bryant Geoffrey *law educator, foundation executive*
Gates, Stephen Frye *lawyer, business executive*
Gearen, John Joseph *lawyer*
Geiman, J. Robert *lawyer*
Gelman, Andrew Richard *lawyer*
Gerber, Lawrence *lawyer*
Geren, Gerald S. *lawyer*
Gerlits, Francis Joseph *lawyer*
Getzendanner, Susan *lawyer, former federal judge*
Giampietro, Wayne Bruce *lawyer*
Gibbons, William John *lawyer*
Gilbert, Howard N(orman) *lawyer, director*
Gilford, Steven Ross *lawyer*
Gladden, James Walter, Jr. *lawyer*
Glieberman, Herbert Allen *lawyer*
Golan, Stephen Leonard *lawyer*
Goldblatt, Stanford Jay *lawyer*
Golden, Bruce Paul *lawyer*
Golden, William C. *lawyer*
Goldman, Louis Budwig *lawyer*
Goldschmidt, Lynn Harvey *lawyer*
Goodman, Gary Alan *lawyer*
Gordon, Phillip *lawyer*
Gordon, William A. *lawyer*
Gottlieb, Gidon Alain Guy *law educator*
Graham, David F. *lawyer*
Gralen, Donald John *lawyer*
Grant, Robert Nathan *lawyer*
Griffith, Donald Kendall *lawyer*
Guthman, Jack *lawyer*
Gutstein, Solomon *lawyer*
Haderlein, Thomas M. *retired lawyer*
Hahn, Frederic Louis *lawyer*
Hales, Daniel B. *lawyer*
Hall, Joan M. *lawyer*
Halloran, Michael John *lawyer*
Hammesfahr, Robert Winter *lawyer*
Hannah, Wayne Robertson, Jr. *lawyer*
Hannay, William Mouat, III *lawyer*
Hanson, Ronald William *lawyer*
Hardgrove, James Alan *lawyer*
Harrington, Carol A. *lawyer*
Harrington, James Timothy *lawyer*
Harris, Donald Ray *lawyer*
Harrold, Bernard *lawyer*
Hayes, David John Arthur, Jr. *legal association executive*
Hayward, Thomas Zander, Jr. *lawyer*
Head, Patrick James *lawyer*
Heatwole, Mark M. *lawyer*
Heinz, William Denby *lawyer*
Heisler, Quentin George, Jr. *lawyer*
Heller, Stanley J. *lawyer, physician, educator*
Helman, Robert Alan *lawyer*
Helmholz, R(ichard) H(enry) *law educator*
Henderson, Janet E. *lawyer*
Henry, Frederick Edward *lawyer*
Henry, Robert John *lawyer*
Herbert, William Carlisle *lawyer*
Herman, Sidney N. *lawyer*
Herpe, David A. *lawyer*
Herzog, Fred F. *law educator*
Hess, Sidney J., Jr. *lawyer*
Hesse, Carolyn Sue *lawyer*
Hester, Thomas Patrick *lawyer, business executive*
Hickey, John Thomas, Jr. *lawyer*
Hickman, Frederic W. *lawyer*
Hiller, David Dean *lawyer*
Hillman, Jordan Jay *law educator*
Hodes, Scott *lawyer*
Hofer, Roy Ellis *lawyer*
Hoff, John Scott *lawyer*
Hoffman, Richard Bruce *lawyer*
Hoffman, Valerie Jane *lawyer*
Hollins, Mitchell Leslie *lawyer*
Horwich, Allan *lawyer*
Hoskins, Richard Jerold *lawyer*
Howe, Jonathan Thomas *lawyer*
Howell, R(obert) Thomas, Jr. *lawyer, former food company executive*
Hummel, Gregory William *lawyer*
Hunt, Lawrence Halley, Jr. *lawyer*
Hunter, James Galbraith, Jr. *lawyer*
Huston, DeVerille Anne *lawyer*
Hyman, Michael Bruce *lawyer*
Jacobson, Marian Slutz *lawyer*
Jacobson, Richard Joseph *lawyer*
Jacover, Jerold Alan *lawyer*
Jager, Melvin Francis *lawyer*
Jahns, Jeffrey *lawyer*
Jersild, Thomas Nielsen *lawyer*
Johnson, Gary Thomas *lawyer*
Johnson, Lael Frederic *lawyer*
Johnson, Richard Fred *lawyer*
Joseph, Robert Thomas *lawyer*
Joslin, Rodney Dean *lawyer*
Junewicz, James J. *lawyer*
Kallick, David A. *lawyer*
Kamin, Chester Thomas *lawyer*
Kaplan, Jared *lawyer*
Kaplan, Sidney Mountbatten *lawyer*
Kapnick, Richard Bradshaw *lawyer*
Karu, Gilda M(all) *lawyer, government official*
Kastel, Howard L. *lawyer, business executive*
Katz, Stuart Charles *lawyer, jazz musician*
Kaufman, Andrew Michael *lawyer*
Kelly, Charles Arthur *lawyer*
Kenney, Crane H. *lawyer*
Kenney, Frank Deming *lawyer*
Kikoler, Stephen Philip *lawyer*
Kim, Michael Charles *lawyer*
King, Clark Chapman, Jr. *lawyer*
King, Michael Howard *lawyer*
King, Sharon Louise *lawyer*
Kins, Juris *lawyer*
Kirkland, John Leonard *lawyer*
Kissel, Richard John *lawyer*
Kite, Steven B. *lawyer*
Klenk, James Andrew *lawyer*
Knight, Christopher Nichols *lawyer*
Knox, James Edwin *lawyer*
Kohn, Shalom L. *lawyer*
Kohn, William Irwin *lawyer*
Kolek, Robert Edward *lawyer*
Kravitt, Jason Harris Paperno *lawyer*
Kriss, Robert J. *lawyer*
Kroll, Barry Lewis *lawyer*
Krupka, Robert George *lawyer*
Kunkle, William Joseph, Jr. *lawyer*
Kuta, Jeffrey Theodore *lawyer*
Ladd, Jeffrey Raymond *lawyer*
Lagarde, Christine *lawyer*
Laidlaw, Andrew R. *lawyer*
Lampert, Steven A. *lawyer*
Landes, William M. *law educator*
Landow-Esser, Janine Marise *lawyer*
Lane, Ronald Alan *lawyer*
Laner, Richard Warren *lawyer*
Lassar, Scott R. *lawyer*
Latimer, Kenneth Alan *lawyer*
Lauderdale, Katherine Sue *lawyer*
Leisten, Arthur Gaynor *lawyer*
Leonard, Laura L. *lawyer*
Levenfeld, Milton Arthur *lawyer*
Levi, John G. *lawyer*
Levin, Charles Edward *lawyer*
Levin, Jack S. *lawyer*
Levin, Michael David *lawyer*
Levine, Laurence Harvey *lawyer*
Liggio, Carl Donald *lawyer*
Lind, Jon Robert *lawyer*
Linklater, William Joseph *lawyer*
Lippe, Melvin Karl *lawyer*
Lipton, Lois Jean *lawyer*
Lipton, Richard M. *lawyer*
Litwin, Burton Howard *lawyer*
Lloyd, William F. *lawyer*
Lockwood, Gary Lee *lawyer*
Looman, James R. *lawyer*
Lorch, Kenneth F. *lawyer*
Loughnane, David J. *lawyer*
Lowry, Donald Michael *retired lawyer*
Lubin, Donald G. *lawyer*
Lundergan, Barbara Keough *lawyer*
Luning, Thomas P. *lawyer*
Lutter, Paul Allen *lawyer*
Lynch, John Peter *lawyer*
MacCarthy, Terence Francis *lawyer*
Maher, David Willard *lawyer*
Maher, Francesca Marciniak *lawyer, air transportation executive*
Malkin, Cary Jay *lawyer*
Mancoff, Neal Alan *lawyer*
Mansfield, Karen Lee *lawyer*
Marovitz, James Lee *lawyer*
Marshall, John David *lawyer*
Martin, Arthur Mead *lawyer*
Marwedel, Warren John *lawyer*
Marx, David, Jr. *lawyer*
Mason, Richard J. *lawyer*
Mattson, Stephen Joseph *lawyer*
Mayer, Frank D., Jr. *lawyer*
McCaleb, Malcolm, Jr. *lawyer*
McClure, James Julius, Jr. *lawyer, former city official*
McCracken, Thomas James, Jr. *lawyer*
McCue, Judith W. *lawyer*
McDermott, John H(enry) *lawyer*
McDonald, Thomas Alexander *lawyer*
McDonough, John Michael *lawyer*
McKenzie, Robert Ernest *lawyer*
McLaren, Richard Wellington, Jr. *lawyer*
McLaughlin, T. Mark *lawyer*
McMahon, Thomas Michael *lawyer*
McMenamin, John Robert *lawyer*
McVisk, William Kilburn *lawyer*
McWhirter, Bruce J. *lawyer*
Mehlman, Mark Franklin *lawyer*
Melton, David Reuben *lawyer*
Meltzer, Bernard David *law educator*
Merrill, Thomas Wendell *lawyer, law educator*
Meyer, Michael Louis *lawyer*
Michalak, Edward Francis *lawyer*
Miller, Edward Boone *lawyer*
Miller, Paul J. *lawyer*
Miller, Stephen Ralph *lawyer*
Millner, Robert B. *lawyer*
Milnikel, Robert Saxon *lawyer*
Minichello, Dennis *lawyer*
Minow, Newton Norman *lawyer, educator*
Mobbs, Michael Hall *lawyer*
Montgomery, Charles Barry *lawyer*
Montgomery, William Adam *lawyer*
Morency, Paula J. *lawyer*
Morrison, Portia Owen *lawyer*
Morsch, Thomas Harvey *lawyer*
Muchin, Allan B. *lawyer*
Mullen, J. Thomas *lawyer*
Mulroy, Thomas Robert, Jr. *lawyer*
Mumford, Manly Whitman *lawyer*
Murdock, Charles William *lawyer, educator*
Murray, Daniel Richard *lawyer*
Murtaugh, Christopher David *lawyer*
Myers, Lonn William *lawyer*
Nash, Gordon Bernard, Jr. *lawyer*
Nechin, Herbert Benjamin *lawyer*
Newlin, Charles Fremont *lawyer*
Niro, Cheryl *lawyer*
Nissen, William John *lawyer*
Nitikman, Franklin W. *lawyer*
Nord, Robert Eamor *lawyer*
Notz, John Kranz, Jr. *arbitrator and mediator, retired lawyer*
Nowacki, James Nelson *lawyer*
Nussbaum, Bernard J. *lawyer*
O'Brien, James Phillip *lawyer*
O'Brien, Patrick William *lawyer*
O'Flaherty, Paul Benedict *lawyer*
O'Hagan, James Joseph *lawyer*
O'Leary, Daniel Vincent, Jr. *lawyer*
O'Malley, John Daniel *law educator, banker*
Oesterle, Eric Adam *lawyer*
Olian, Robert Martin *lawyer*
Oliver, Roseann *lawyer*
Orin, Stuart I. *lawyer*
Overgaard, Mitchell Jersild *lawyer*
Overton, George Washington *lawyer*
Pallasch, B. Michael *lawyer, director*
Palm, Gary Howard *lawyer, educator*
Palmer, John Bernard, III *lawyer*
Panich, Danuta Bembenista *lawyer*
Parkhurst, Todd Sheldon *lawyer*
Partridge, Mark Van Buren *lawyer, educator, writer*
Pascal, Roger *lawyer*
Pavalon, Eugene Irving *lawyer*
Pelton, Russell Meredith, Jr. *lawyer*
Perlberg, Jules Martin *lawyer*
Petersen, Donald Sondergaard *lawyer*
Peterson, Ronald Roger *lawyer*
Piecewicz, Walter Michael *lawyer*
Piekarski, Victor J. *lawyer*
Pinsky, Michael S. *lawyer*
Polaski, Anne Spencer *lawyer*
Pollock, Earl Edward *lawyer*
Pope, Daniel James *lawyer*
Presser, Stephen Bruce *lawyer, educator*
Price, Charles T. *lawyer*
Price, Paul L. *lawyer*
Price, William S. *lawyer*
Prior, Gary L. *lawyer*
Prochnow, Douglas Lee *lawyer*
Rankin, James Winton *lawyer*
Rapoport, David E. *lawyer*
Ratner, Gerald *lawyer*
Read, Sarah J. *lawyer*
Redman, Clarence Owen *lawyer*
Reed, Keith Allen *lawyer*
Reich, Allan J. *lawyer*
Reicin, Ronald Ian *lawyer*
Reiter, Michael A. *lawyer, educator*
Relias, John Alexis *lawyer*
Resnick, Donald Ira *lawyer*
Reum, James Michael *lawyer*
Rhind, James Thomas *lawyer*
Rhodes, Charles Harker, Jr. *lawyer*
Richman, John Marshall *retired lawyer, business executive*
Richmond, James Glidden *lawyer*
Richmond, William Patrick *lawyer*
Rieger, Mitchell Sheridan *lawyer*
Rissman, Burton Richard *lawyer*
Rizzo, Ronald Stephen *lawyer*
Roberts, John Charles *law educator*
Robin, Richard C. *lawyer*
Roche, James McMillan *lawyer*
Rooney, Matthew A. *lawyer*
Ropski, Gary Melchior *lawyer*
Rosenbloom, Lewis Stanley *lawyer*
Roston, David Charles *lawyer*
Rudnick, Paul David *lawyer*
Rudstein, David Stewart *law educator*
Rundio, Louis Michael, Jr. *lawyer*
Russell, Paul Frederick *lawyer*
Rutkoff, Alan Stuart *lawyer*
Ruxin, Paul Theodore *lawyer*
Ryan, Priscilla E. *lawyer*
Ryan, Thomas F. *lawyer*
Sabl, John J. *lawyer*
Sanders, David P. *lawyer*
Sanders, Richard Henry *lawyer*
Saunders, George Lawton, Jr. *lawyer*
Saunders, Terry Rose *lawyer*
Sawyier, David R. *lawyer*
Schar, Stephen L. *lawyer*
Schiller, Donald Charles *lawyer*
Schimberg, A(rmand) Bruce *retired lawyer*
Schink, James Harvey *lawyer*
Schlickman, J. Andrew *lawyer*
Schlitter, Stanley Allen *lawyer*
Schneider, Dan W. *lawyer, consultant*
Schneider, Robert Jerome *lawyer*
Schoonhoven, Ray James *retired lawyer*
Schoumacher, Bruce Herbert *lawyer*
Schreck, Robert A., Jr. *lawyer*
Schriver, John T., III *lawyer*
Schulte, Stephen Charles *lawyer*
Schulz, Keith Donald *corporate lawyer*
Schwartz, Donald Lee *lawyer*
Scogland, William Lee *lawyer*
Seegers, Lori C. *lawyer*
Sennet, Charles Joseph *lawyer*
Serritella, James Anthony *lawyer*
Serritella, William David *lawyer*
Serwer, Alan Michael *lawyer*
Sfikas, Peter Michael *lawyer, educator*
Shank, William O. *lawyer*
Shapiro, Harold David *lawyer, educator*
Shapiro, Stephen Michael *lawyer*
Shapo, Marshall Schambelan *lawyer, educator*
Shepherd, Stewart Robert *lawyer*
Shields, Thomas Charles *lawyer*
Shindler, Donald A. *lawyer*
Siegel, Howard Jerome *lawyer*
Silberman, Alan Harvey *lawyer*
Simon, John Bern *lawyer*
Simon, Seymour *lawyer, former state supreme court justice*
Siske, Roger Charles *lawyer*
Skilling, Raymond Inwood *lawyer*
Skinner, Mary Jacobs *lawyer*
Sklarsky, Charles B. *lawyer*
Smedinghoff, Thomas J. *lawyer*
Smith, Gordon Howell *lawyer*
Smith, Tefft Weldon *lawyer*
Snider, Lawrence K. *lawyer*
Snyder, Jean Maclean *lawyer*
Solovy, Jerold Sherwin *lawyer*
Spector, David M. *lawyer*
Spellmire, George W. *lawyer*
Spindler, George S. *lawyer, retired oil industry executive*
Spiotto, James Ernest *lawyer*
Sproger, Charles Edmund *lawyer*
Stack, John Wallace *lawyer*
Starkman, Gary Lee *lawyer*
Stein, Robert Allen *legal association executive, law educator*
Steinberg, Morton M. *lawyer*
Sternstein, Allan J. *lawyer*
Stetler, David J. *lawyer*
Stevenson, Adlai Ewing, III *lawyer, former senator*
Stiegel, Michael Allen *lawyer*
Stillman, Nina Gidden *lawyer*
Stoll, John Robert *lawyer, educator*
Stone, Geoffrey Richard *law educator, lawyer*
Stone, Randolph Noel *law educator*
Stone, Susan A. *lawyer*
Streff, William Albert, Jr. *lawyer*
Strobel, Pamela B. *lawyer*
Sullivan, Barry *lawyer*
Sullivan, Marcia Waite *lawyer*
Sullivan, Thomas Patrick *lawyer*
Sussman, Arthur Melvin *law educator, foundation administrator*
Sutter, William Paul *lawyer*
Swaney, Thomas Edward *lawyer*
Sweeney, James Raymond *lawyer*

Swibel, Steven Warren *lawyer*
Swiger, Elinor Porter *lawyer*
Szczepanski, Slawomir Zbigniew Steven *lawyer*
Tabin, Julius *patent lawyer, physicist*
Tarun, Robert Walter *lawyer*
Tetzlaff, Theodore R. *lawyer*
Thies, Richard Brian *lawyer*
Thomas, Dale E. *lawyer*
Thomas, Frederick Bradley *lawyer*
Thomas, Stephen Paul *lawyer*
Thompson, James Robert, Jr. *lawyer, former governor*
Thorne-Thomsen, Thomas *lawyer*
Tobin, Thomas F. *lawyer*
Toohey, James Kevin *lawyer*
Trapp, James McCreery *lawyer*
Treston, Sherry S. *lawyer*
Trienens, Howard Joseph *lawyer*
Trost, Eileen Bannon *lawyer*
Truskowski, John Budd *lawyer*
Turow, Scott F. *lawyer, writer*
Ungaretti, Richard Anthony *lawyer*
Van Demark, Ruth Elaine *lawyer*
Vree, Roger Allen *lawyer*
Wade, Edwin Lee *author, lawyer*
Wahlen, Edwin Alfred *lawyer*
Waintroob, Andrea Ruth *lawyer*
Waite, Norman, Jr. *lawyer*
Wall, Robert F. *lawyer*
Walsh, Michael S. *lawyer*
Wander, Herbert Stanton *lawyer*
Wanke, Ronald Lee *lawyer, educator*
Watson, Robert R. *lawyer*
Weaver, Timothy Allan *lawyer*
Webb, Dan K. *lawyer*
Weinkopf, Friedrich J. *lawyer*
Weissman, Michael Lewis *lawyer*
Welsh, Kelly Raymond *lawyer, former telecommunications company executive*
Wexler, Richard Lewis *lawyer*
Whalen, Wayne W. *lawyer*
White, Linda Diane *lawyer*
Wiggins, Charles Henry, Jr. *lawyer*
Wilcox, Mark Dean *lawyer*
Wildman, Max Edward *lawyer, director*
Williams, George Howard *lawyer, association executive*
Winkler, Charles Howard *lawyer, investment management company executive*
Wise, William Jerrard *lawyer*
Witcoff, Sheldon William *lawyer*
Wolf, Charles Benno *lawyer*
Wolfe, David Louis *lawyer*
Wolfson, Larry Marshall *lawyer*
Wright, Judith Margaret *law librarian, educator, dean*
Zabel, Sheldon Alter *lawyer, law educator*
Zemm, Sandra Phyllis *lawyer*
Zenner, Sheldon Toby *lawyer*
Zolno, Mark S. *lawyer*

Chicago Heights
Cifelli, John Louis *lawyer*

Darien
Grossi, Francis Xavier, Jr. *lawyer, educator*

Decatur
Dunn, John Francis *lawyer, state representative*
Reising, Richard P. *lawyer*
Smith, David James *corporate lawyer*

Deerfield
Birmingham, William Joseph *lawyer*
Dawson, Suzanne Stockus *lawyer*
Gaither, John Francis, Jr. *lawyer*
Montgomery, William A. *lawyer*
Oettinger, Julian Alan *lawyer, pharmacy company executive*
Sabatino, Thomas Joseph, Jr. *lawyer*
Scott, Theodore R. *lawyer*

Dekalb
Tucker, Watson Billopp *lawyer*
Witmer, John Harper, Jr. *lawyer*

Des Plaines
Brodl, Raymond Frank *lawyer, former lumber company executive*
Meyer, Susan M. *lawyer, company executive*

Downers Grove
Moran, Michael Robert *corporate lawyer*
Siedlecki, Nancy Therese *lawyer, funeral director*
Squires, Vernon T. *lawyer*

Edwardsville
Rikli, Donald Carl *lawyer, deceased*

Elgin
Akemann, David Roy *lawyer*

Elmwood Park
Spina, Anthony Ferdinand *lawyer*

Fairview Heights
Grace, (Walter) Charles *prosecutor*

Franklin Park
Blanchard, Eric Alan *lawyer*

Galesburg
Mangieri, Paul L. *lawyer*
Taylor, Roger Lee *lawyer, academic administrator*

Galva
Massie, Michael Earl *lawyer*

Genoa
Cromley, Jon Lowell *lawyer*

Glen Ellyn
Sandrok, Richard William *lawyer*
Ulrich, Werner *patent lawyer*

Glencoe
Cohen, Christopher B. *lawyer*

Glenview
Berkman, Michael G. *lawyer, chemical consultant*

Gurnee
Southern, Robert Allen *lawyer*

Highland Park
Gash, Lauren Beth *lawyer, state legislator*
Karol, Nathaniel H. *lawyer, consultant*
Nelson, Richard David *lawyer*
Schindel, Donald Marvin *retired lawyer*

Hinsdale
Botti, Aldo E. *lawyer*

Hoffman Estates
Kelly, Anastasia Donovan *lawyer*

La Grange
Kerr, Alexander Duncan, Jr. *lawyer*

Lafox
Seils, William George *lawyer*

Lake Forest
Baisley, James Mahoney *retired lawyer*
Covington, George Morse *lawyer*
Francois, William Armand *lawyer*

Lincolnwood
Zaremski, Miles Jay *lawyer*

Lisle
Myers, Daniel N. *lawyer, association executive*

Long Grove
Conway, John K. *lawyer*
Obert, Paul Richard *manufacturing executive*

Marengo
Franks, Herbert Hoover *lawyer*

Mc Gaw Park
Feather, William L. *corporate lawyer*

Mokena
Sangmeister, George Edward *lawyer, consultant, former congressman*

Moline
Cottrell, Frank Stewart *former lawyer, manufacturing executive*
Jenkins, James Robert *lawyer, corporate executive*
Morrison, Deborah Jean *lawyer*

Morrison
Spencer, Gary L. *state government lawyer*

Naperville
Fawell, Harris W. *lawyer, former congressman*
Fenech, Joseph Charles *lawyer*
Shaw, Michael Allan *lawyer, mail order company executive*

North Chicago
de Lasa, José M. *lawyer*

Northbrook
Abbey, G(eorge) Marshall *lawyer, former health care company executive, general counsel*
Lapin, Harvey I. *lawyer*
McGinn, Mary J. *lawyer, insurance company executive*
Rosemarin, Carey Stephen *lawyer*
Sernett, Richard Patrick *lawyer, consultant*
Teichner, Bruce A. *lawyer*

Oak Brook
Barnes, Karen Kay *lawyer*
Bennett, Margaret Airola *lawyer*
Congalton, Susan Tichenor *lawyer*
Kindler, Jeffrey B. *lawyer*
Ring, Leonard M. *lawyer, writer*
Santona, Gloria *lawyer*

Oakbrook Terrace
Tibble, Douglas Clair *lawyer*
Willis, Douglas Alan *lawyer*

Oregon
Floski, Doug *lawyer*

Palatine
Victor, Michael Gary *lawyer, physician*

Park Forest
Goodrich, John Bernard *lawyer, consultant*

Park Ridge
Hegarty, Mary Frances *lawyer*
LaRue, Paul Hubert *lawyer*
Naker, Mary Leslie *legal firm executive*

Peoria
Allen, Lyle Wallace *lawyer*
Atterbury, Robert Rennie, III *lawyer*
Bertschy, Timothy L. *lawyer*
Strodel, Robert Carl *lawyer*

Princeton
Bernabei, Marc P. *lawyer*

River Forest
Li, Tze-chung *lawyer, educator*

Riverwoods
Smith, Carole Dianne *lawyer, editor, writer, product developer*
Yarrington, Hugh *corporate lawyer, communications company executive*

Rock Island
Lousberg, Peter Herman *former lawyer*

Rockford
Reno, Roger *lawyer*

Rosemont
Fitzgerald, Jeremiah Michael *lawyer*

Schaumburg
Lawson, A. Peter *lawyer*
Meltzer, Brian *lawyer*

Skokie
Dul, John A. *lawyer*
Salit, Gary *lawyer*

Springfield
Burns, James B. *prosecutor*
Hulin, Frances C. *prosecutor*
Kelley, Patrick Wayne *prosecutor*
Kerr, Gary Enrico *lawyer, educator*
Mathewson, Mark Stuart *lawyer, editor*
Rowe, Max L. *lawyer, corporate executive, management and political consultant, writer, judge*
Van Meter, Abram DeBois *lawyer, retired banker*

Urbana
Balbach, Stanley Byron *lawyer*
Kearns, James Cannon *lawyer*
Piland, John Charles *lawyer*

Vienna
Trambley, Donald Brian *lawyer*

Warrenville
Boardman, Robert A. *lawyer*

Waukegan
Henrick, Michael Francis *lawyer*
Leibowitz, David Perry *lawyer*

Western Springs
Hanson, Heidi Elizabeth *lawyer*
Rhoads, Paul Kelly *lawyer*
Shannon, Peter Michael, Jr. *lawyer*

Wheaton
Birkett, Joseph E. *lawyer*
Butt, Edward Thomas, Jr. *lawyer*

Willowbrook
Walton, Stanley Anthony, III *lawyer*

Wilmette
Lieberman, Eugene *lawyer*
McNeill, Thomas B. *retired lawyer*

Winnetka
Crowe, Robert William *lawyer, mediator*

Winthrop Harbor
Getz, James Edward *legal association administrator*

Woodridge
Brennan, James Joseph *lawyer, banking and financial services executive*
Conti, Lee Ann *lawyer*

INDIANA

Bloomington
Shreve, Gene Russell *law educator*

Boonville
Corne, Todd *lawyer*

Carmel
Stein, Richard Paul *lawyer*

Columbus
Harrison, Patrick Woods *lawyer*

Connersville
Kuntz, William Henry *lawyer, mediator*

Danville
Baldwin, Patricia Ann *lawyer*

Dyer
DeGuilio, Jon E. *lawyer*
Van Bokkelen, Joseph Scott *prosecutor*

Elkhart
Gassere, Eugene Arthur *lawyer, business executive*
Harman, John Royden *retired lawyer*
Treckelo, Richard M. *lawyer*

Evansville
Clouse, John Daniel *lawyer*
Levco, Stanley M. *lawyer*

Fort Wayne
Baker, Carl Leroy *lawyer*
Keefer, J(ames) Michael *lawyer*
Lebamoff, Ivan Argire *lawyer*
Pope, Mark Andrew *lawyer, university administrator*
Shoaff, Thomas Mitchell *lawyer*

Fowler
Weist, William Bernard *lawyer*

Franklin
Hamner, Lance Dalton *prosecutor*

Granger
Lambert, George Robert *lawyer, real estate broker*

Hammond
Diamond, Eugene Christopher *lawyer, hospital administrator*

Indianapolis
Albright, Terrill D. *lawyer*
Allen, David James *lawyer*
Badger, David Harry *lawyer*
Beckwith, Lewis Daniel *lawyer*
Beeler, Virgil L. *lawyer*
Boldt, Michael Herbert *lawyer*
Born, Samuel Roydon , II *lawyer*
Carney, Joseph Buckingham *lawyer*
Choplin, John M., II *lawyer*
Cole, Elsa Kircher *lawyer*
Deer, Richard Elliott *lawyer*
Downs, Thomas K. *lawyer*
Dutton, Stephen James *lawyer*
Elberger, Ronald Edward *lawyer*
Evans, Daniel Fraley, Jr. *lawyer*
Fisher, James R. *lawyer*
FitzGibbon, Daniel Harvey *lawyer*
Fruehwald, Kristin G. *lawyer*
Gregg, John Richard *lawyer, state legislator*
Hodowal, John Raymond *lawyer, holding company executive, utility company executive*
Huston, Michael Joe *lawyer*
Jegen, Lawrence A., III *law educator*
Johnstone, Robert Philip *lawyer*
Kashani, Hamid Reza *lawyer, computer consultant*
Kemper, James Dee *lawyer*
Kendall, Rebecca O. *lawyer, pharmaceutical company executive*
Kerr, William Andrew *lawyer, educator*
Kirk, Carol *lawyer*
Klaper, Martin Jay *lawyer*
Kleiman, David Harold *lawyer*
Knebel, Donald Earl *lawyer*
Lee, Stephen W. *lawyer*
Lisher, John Leonard *lawyer*
Lofton, Thomas Milton *lawyer*
Mc Kinney, Robert Hurley *lawyer, business executive*
McKeon, Thomas Joseph *lawyer*
McKinney, Dennis Keith *lawyer*
Miller, David W. *lawyer*
Neff, Robert Matthew *lawyer, financial services executive*
Nolan, Alan Tucker *retired lawyer, labor arbitrator, writer*
Orentlicher, David *lawyer, physician*
Paul, Stephen Howard *lawyer*
Petersen, James L. *lawyer*
Ponder, Lester McConnico *lawyer, educator*
Reynolds, Robert Hugh *lawyer*
Roberts, William Everett *lawyer*
Rusthoven, Peter James *lawyer*
Ryder, Henry C(lay) *lawyer*
Scaletta, Phillip Ralph, III *lawyer*
Schlegel, Fred Eugene *lawyer*
Scism, Daniel Reed *lawyer*
Shideler, Shirley Ann Williams *lawyer*
Shula, Robert Joseph *lawyer*
Slaughter Andrew, Anne *lawyer*
Stayton, Thomas George *lawyer*
Steger, Evan Evans, III *retired lawyer*
Stieff, John Joseph *legislative lawyer, educator*
Strain, James Arthur *lawyer*
Sutherland, Donald Gray *retired lawyer*
Tabler, Bryan G. *lawyer*
Tabler, Norman Gardner, Jr. *lawyer*
Townsend, Earl C., Jr. *lawyer, writer*
Whale, Arthur Richard *lawyer*
White, James Patrick *law educator*
Wishard, Gordon Davis *lawyer*
Wood, William Jerome *lawyer*
Woodard, Harold Raymond *lawyer*

Kokomo
Fleming, James Richard *lawyer*

Lafayette
Bean, Jerry Joe *lawyer*

Lagrange
Cain, Tim J. *lawyer*

Merrillville
Manous, Peter J. *lawyer*

Mount Vernon
Bach, Steve Crawford *lawyer*
Van Haaften, Trent *lawyer*

Muncie
Radcliff, William Franklin *lawyer, director*

Notre Dame
Carrington, Michael Davis *criminal justice administrator, educator, consultant*
Gunn, Alan *law educator*

Rushville
Zwickey, Sheila Kaye *lawyer*

Shelbyville
Lisher, James Richard *lawyer*
McNeely, James Lee *lawyer*

South Bend
Barnes, Michael Phillip *prosecutor*
Bonini, James *federal court official*
Carey, John Leo *lawyer*
Ford, George Burt *lawyer*
Reinke, William John *lawyer*
Seall, Stephen Albert *lawyer*
Shaffer, Thomas Lindsay *lawyer, educator*
Vogel, Nelson J., Jr. *lawyer*

Terre Haute
Bopp, James, Jr. *lawyer*

Valparaiso
Koeppen, Raymond Bradley *lawyer*
Persyn, Mary Geraldine *law librarian, law educator*

Vernon
Smith, Gary Lee *lawyer*

Vincennes
Emison, Ewing Rabb, Jr. *lawyer*

Wabash
Plummer, Alfred Harvey, III *lawyer*

IOWA

Atlantic
Barry, James Patrick *lawyer*

Burlington
Beckman, David *lawyer*
Hoth, Steven Sergey *lawyer, educator*

Cedar Rapids
Albright, Justin W. *retired lawyer*
Larson, Charles W. *prosecutor*
Nazette, Richard Follett *lawyer*
Wilson, Robert Foster *lawyer*

Dallas Center
McDonald, John Cecil *lawyer*

Davenport
Le Grand, Clay *lawyer, former state justice*

Decorah
Belay, Stephen Joseph *lawyer*

Busdicker, Gordon G. *lawyer, retired*
Carlson, Thomas David *lawyer*
Champlin, Steven Kirk *lawyer*
Christiansen, Jay David *lawyer*
Ciresi, Michael Vincent *lawyer*
Clary, Bradley G. *lawyer, educator*
Comstock, Rebecca Ann *lawyer*
Conn, Gordon Brainard, Jr. *lawyer*
Crosby, Thomas Manville, Jr. *lawyer*
Eck, George Gregory *lawyer*
Feuss, Linda Anne Upsall *lawyer*
Finzen, Bruce Arthur *lawyer*
Flom, Gerald Trossen *lawyer*
Forneris, Jeanne M. *lawyer*
Freeman, Michael O. *lawyer*
Freeman, Todd Ira *lawyer*
French, John Dwyer *lawyer*
Gagnon, Craig William *lawyer*
Garon, Philip Stephen *lawyer*
Garton, Thomas William *lawyer*
Gill, Richard Lawrence *lawyer*
Goodman, Elizabeth Ann *lawyer*
Gottschalk, Stephen Elmer *lawyer*
Grayson, Edward Davis *lawyer, manufacturing company executive*
Greener, Ralph Bertram *lawyer*
Griffith, G. Larry *lawyer*
Hanson, Bruce Eugene *lawyer*
Harris, John Edward *lawyer*
Hayward, Edward Joseph *lawyer*
Heffelfinger, Thomas Backer *lawyer*
Heiberg, Robert Alan *lawyer*
Henson, Robert Frank *lawyer*
Hibbs, John Stanley *lawyer*
Hinderaker, John Hadley *lawyer*
Hippee, William H., Jr. *lawyer*
Hobbins, Robert Leo *lawyer*
Howland, Joan Sidney *law librarian, law educator*
Hudec, Robert Emil *lawyer, educator*
Jarboe, Mark Alan *lawyer*
Johnson, G. Robert *lawyer*
Johnson, Gary M. *lawyer*
Johnson, Gary R. *corporate lawyer*
Johnson, Larry Walter *lawyer*
Jones, B. Todd *lawyer, former prosecutor*
Kaplan, Sheldon *lawyer, director*
Kelly, A. David *lawyer*
Keyes, Jeffrey J. *lawyer*
Klaas, Paul Barry *lawyer*
Koneck, John Michael *lawyer*
Landry, Paul Leonard *lawyer*
Lazar, Raymond Michael *lawyer, educator*
Lebedoff, David M. *lawyer, writer, investment advisor*
Lebedoff, Randy Miller *lawyer*
Lillehaug, David Lee *lawyer*
Magnuson, Roger James *lawyer*
Manning, William Henry *lawyer*
Manthey, Thomas Richard *lawyer*
Marshall, Siri Swenson *corporate lawyer*
Martin, Phillip Hammond *lawyer*
Matthews, James Shadley *lawyer*
McGuire, Timothy James *lawyer, editor*
McGunnigle, George Francis *judge*
Mellum, Gale Robert *lawyer*
Minish, Robert Arthur *lawyer*
Moe, Thomas O. *lawyer*
Mooty, Bruce Wilson *lawyer*
Mooty, John William *lawyer*
Myers, Howard Sam *lawyer*
Nelson, Gary Michael *lawyer*
Nelson, Richard Arthur *lawyer*
Nelson, Steven Craig *lawyer*
Novak, Leslie Howard *lawyer*
O'Neill, Brian Boru *lawyer*
Palmer, Brian Eugene *lawyer*
Palmer, Deborah Jean *lawyer*
Parsons, Charles Allan, Jr. *lawyer*
Pluimer, Edward J. *lawyer*
Potuznik, Charles Laddy *lawyer*
Pratte, Robert John *lawyer*
Price, Joseph Michael *lawyer*
Radmer, Michael John *lawyer, educator*
Rein, Stanley Michael *lawyer*
Reinhart, Robert Rountree, Jr. *lawyer*
Reuter, James William *lawyer*
Rockenstein, Walter Harrison, II *lawyer*
Rockwell, Winthrop Adams *lawyer*
Roe, Roger Rolland, Jr. *lawyer*
Saeks, Allen Irving *lawyer*
Safley, James Robert *lawyer*
Sanner, Royce Norman *lawyer*
Schnell, Robert Lee, Jr. *lawyer*
Schnobrich, Roger William *lawyer*
Shnider, Bruce Jay *lawyer*
Silver, Alan Irving *lawyer*
Silverman, Robert Joseph *lawyer*
Soland, Norman R. *corporate lawyer*
Stageberg, Roger V. *lawyer*
Stern, Leo G. *lawyer*
Struthers, Margo S. *lawyer*
Struyk, Robert John *lawyer*
Trucano, Michael *lawyer*
Vander Molen, Thomas Dale *lawyer*
Wahoske, Michael James *lawyer*
Weil, Cass Sargent *lawyer*
Whelpley, Dennis Porter *lawyer*
Wicks, John R. *lawyer*
Wille, Karin L. *lawyer*
Windhorst, John William, Jr. *lawyer*
Younger, Judith Tess *lawyer, educator*
Yudof, Mark George *law educator, university president*
Zalk, Robert H. *lawyer*

Minnetonka
Lubben, David J. *lawyer*

North Oaks
Woods, Robert Edward *lawyer*

North Saint Paul
O'Brien, Daniel William *lumber company executive*

Owatonna
Aune, Debra Bjurquist *lawyer*

Park Rapids
Larson, Gregory Dane *lawyer*

Pipestone
Scott, William Paul *lawyer*

Richfield
Burke, Paul Bradford *lawyer, manufacturing executive*

Rochester
Orwoll, Gregg S. K. *lawyer*
Seeger, Ronald L. *lawyer*

Saint Paul
Allison, John Robert *lawyer*
Bastian, Gary Warren *judge*
Carruthers, Philip Charles *lawyer, public official*
Fabel, Thomas Lincoln *lawyer*
Fisk, Martin H. *lawyer*
Galvin, Michael John, Jr. *lawyer*
Gehan, Mark William *lawyer*
Geis, Jerome Arthur *lawyer, legal educator*
Hansen, Robyn L. *lawyer*
Hirst, Richard B. *lawyer*
Hvass, Sheryl Ramstad *lawyer*
Johnson, Paul Oren *lawyer*
Jones, C. Paul *lawyer, educator*
Kirwin, Kenneth Francis *law educator*
Maclin, Alan Hall *lawyer*
McNeely, John J. *lawyer*
Micallef, Joseph Stephen *retired lawyer*
Rebane, John T. *lawyer*
Smith, Steve C. *lawyer, state legislator*
Spencer, David James *lawyer*
Steenland, Douglas *lawyer*
Ursu, John Joseph *lawyer*

South Saint Paul
Pugh, Thomas Wilfred *lawyer*

Wayzata
Johnson, Eugene Laurence *lawyer*

Winona
Brosnahan, Roger Paul *lawyer*

Worthington
Kohler, Kenneth James *lawyer*

MISSOURI

Ballwin
Banton, Stephen Chandler *lawyer*

Cassville
Melton, Emory Leon *lawyer, state legislator, publisher*

Chesterfield
Denneen, John Paul *lawyer*
Hier, Marshall David *lawyer*
Pollihan, Thomas Henry *lawyer*

Clayton
Belz, Mark *lawyer*

Columbia
Fisch, William Bales *lawyer, educator*
Moore, Mitchell Jay *lawyer, law educator*
Welliver, Warren Dee *lawyer, retired state supreme court justice*
Westbrook, James Edwin *lawyer, educator*
Whitman, Dale Alan *lawyer, law educator*

Edina
Alberty, William Edwin *lawyer*

Fenton
Stolar, Henry Samuel *lawyer*

Jackson
Swingle, Harry Morley, Jr. *prosecutor*

Jefferson City
Bartlett, Alex *lawyer*
Callahan, Richard G. *prosecutor*
Deutsch, James Bernard *lawyer*
Gaw, Robert Steven *lawyer, state representative*
Tettlebaum, Harvey M. *lawyer*

Kansas City
Anderson, Christopher James *lawyer*
Ayers, Jeffrey David *lawyer*
Bacon, Jennifer Gille *lawyer*
Bates, William Hubert *lawyer*
Beck, William G. *lawyer*
Becker, Thomas Bain *lawyer*
Beckett, Theodore Charles *lawyer*
Beihl, Frederick *lawyer*
Berkowitz, Lawrence M. *lawyer*
Bevan, Robert Lewis *lawyer*
Bradshaw, Jean Paul, II *lawyer*
Brous, Thomas Richard *lawyer*
Bruening, Richard P(atrick) *lawyer*
Canfield, Robert Cleo *lawyer*
Clarke, Milton Charles *lawyer*
Clegg, Karen Kohler *lawyer*
Cozad, John Condon *lawyer*
Crawford, Howard Allen *lawyer*
Cross, William Dennis *lawyer*
Davis, John Charles *lawyer*
Deacy, Thomas Edward, Jr. *lawyer*
Dietrich, William Gale *lawyer, real estate developer, consultant*
Donnelly, Paul E. *lawyer*
Edgar, John M. *lawyer*
Egan, Charles Joseph, Jr. *lawyer, greeting card company executive*
Eldridge, Truman Kermit, Jr. *lawyer*
Foster, Mark Stephen *lawyer*
Gaines, Robert Darryl *lawyer, food services executive*
Gardner, Brian E. *lawyer*
Greer, Norris E. *lawyer*
Hill, Stephen L., Jr. *lawyer, former prosecutor*
Holt, Ronald Lee *lawyer*
Jenkins, Melvin Lemuel *lawyer*
Johnson, Mark Eugene *lawyer*
Joyce, Michael Patrick *lawyer*
Kaplan, Harvey L. *lawyer*
Kilroy, John Muir *lawyer*
Kilroy, William Terrence *lawyer*
King, Richard Allen *lawyer*
Kroenert, Robert Morgan *lawyer*
Langworthy, Robert Burton *lawyer*
Levings, Theresa Lawrence *lawyer*
Lindsey, David Hosford *lawyer*
Lombardi, Cornelius Ennis, Jr. *lawyer*
Lotven, Howard Lee *lawyer*
Marquette, I. Edward *lawyer*
Matheny, Edward Taylor, Jr. *lawyer*
McManus, James William *lawyer*
Milton, Chad Earl *lawyer*
Newsom, James Thomas *lawyer*
Owens, Stephen J. *lawyer*
Palmer, Dennis Dale *lawyer*
Pelofsky, Joel *lawyer*
Pemberton, Bradley Powell *lawyer*
Popper, Robert *law educator, former dean*
Price, James Tucker *lawyer*
Prugh, William Byron *lawyer*
Ralston, Richard H. *lawyer*
Rawlins, Randa *lawyer*
Reardon, Michael Edward *lawyer*
Satterlee, Terry Jean *lawyer*
Schult, Thomas P. *lawyer*
Shaw, John W. *lawyer*
Shughart, Donald Louis *lawyer*
Spalty, Edward Robert *lawyer*
Spencer, Richard Henry *lawyer*
Sutton, Ray Sandy *lawyer, company executive*
Terry, Robert Brooks *lawyer*
Toll, Perry Mark *lawyer, educator*
Vering, John Albert *lawyer*
Voran, Joel Bruce *lawyer*
Whittaker, Judith Ann Cameron *lawyer*
Wirken, James Charles *lawyer*
Woods, Curtis E(ugene) *lawyer*
Wrobley, Ralph Gene *lawyer*
Wyrsch, James Robert *lawyer, educator, author*

Kennett
Sokoloff, Stephen Paul *lawyer*

Macon
Masters, David Allen *lawyer*

Mount Vernon
Stemmons, Randee Smith *lawyer*

Nevada
Ewing, Lynn Moore, Jr. *lawyer*

New London
Briscoe, John W. *lawyer*

Saint Joseph
Kranitz, Theodore Mitchell *lawyer*

Saint Louis
Appleton, R. O., Jr. *lawyer*
Arnold, John Fox *lawyer*
Atwood, Hollye Stolz *lawyer*
Aylward, Ronald Lee *lawyer*
Babington, Charles Martin, III *lawyer*
Baker, Nannette A. *lawyer, city official*
Baldwin, Edwin Steedman *lawyer*
Banstetter, Robert J. *lawyer*
Barken, Bernard Allen *lawyer*
Becker, David Mandel *law educator, author, consultant*
Berendt, Robert Tryon *lawyer*
Berger, John Torrey, Jr. *lawyer*
Bonacorsi, Mary Catherine *lawyer*
Breece, Robert William, Jr. *lawyer*
Brickey, Kathleen Fitzgerald *law educator*
Brickler, John Weise *lawyer*
Brickson, Richard Alan *lawyer*
Brody, Lawrence *lawyer, educator*
Brownlee, Robert Hammel *lawyer*
Carp, Larry (Larry Carp) *lawyer*
Carr, Gary Thomas *lawyer*
Charlson, Alan Edward *corporate lawyer, retail company executive*
Clear, John Michael *lawyer*
Conran, Joseph Palmer *lawyer*
Cornfeld, Dave Louis *lawyer*
Donohue, Carroll John *lawyer*
Dorwart, Donald Bruce *lawyer*
Dowd, Edward L., Jr. *lawyer, former prosecutor*
Duesenberg, Richard William *lawyer*
Ellis, Dorsey Daniel, Jr. *lawyer, educator*
Estes, Royce Joe *lawyer*
Falk, William James *lawyer*
Farris, Clyde C. *lawyer*
Fournie, Raymond Richard *lawyer*
Gerard, Jules Bernard *law educator*
Godiner, Donald Leonard *lawyer*
Goebel, John J. *lawyer, director*
Goldstein, Steven *lawyer*
Goodman, Harold S. *lawyer*
Green, Dennis Joseph *lawyer*
Guerri, William Grant *lawyer*
Gunn, Michael Peter *lawyer*
Hansen, Charles *lawyer*
Hays, Ruth *lawyer*
Hellmuth, Theodore Henning *lawyer*
Hetlage, Robert Owen *lawyer*
Hiles, Bradley Stephen *lawyer*
Inkley, John James, Jr. *lawyer*
Jackson, Rebecca R. *lawyer*
Jaudes, Richard Edward *lawyer*
Jayne, Thomas R. *lawyer*
Johnson, E. Perry *lawyer*
Joyce-Hayes, Dee Leigh *lawyer*
Keating, Daniel Louis *law educator*
Keller, Juan Dane *lawyer*
Klobasa, John Anthony *lawyer*
Krehbiel, Robert John *lawyer*
Kuhlmann, Fred Mark *lawyer, business executive*
Lause, Michael Francis *lawyer*
Lebowitz, Albert *lawyer, writer*
Levin, Ronald Mark *law educator*
Lieberman, Edward Jay *lawyer*
Logan, Joseph Prescott *lawyer*
Lucchesi, Lionel Louis *lawyer*
Mandelker, Daniel Robert *law educator*
Mandelstamm, Jerome Robert *lawyer*
Massey, Raymond Lee *lawyer*
McCarter, Charles Chase *lawyer*
McCarter, W. Dudley *lawyer*
McCauley, Matthew D. *lawyer*
McCracken, Ellis W., Jr. *retired lawyer, corporation executive*
McDaniel, James Edwin *lawyer*
McKinnis, Michael B. *lawyer*
Meisel, George Vincent *lawyer*
Merrill, Charles Eugene *lawyer*
Metcalfe, Walter Lee, Jr. *lawyer*
Miller, Dwight Whittemore *lawyer*
Mohan, John J. *lawyer*
Mulligan, Michael Dennis *lawyer*
Neville, James Morton *retired lawyer, consumer products executive*
Newman, Charles A. *lawyer*
Newman, Joan Meskiel *lawyer*
Noel, Edwin Lawrence *lawyer*
O'Keefe, Michael Daniel *lawyer*
O'Malley, Kevin Francis *lawyer, writer, educator*
Olson, Robert Grant *lawyer*
Palans, Lloyd Alex *lawyer*
Peper, Christian Baird *lawyer*
Pickle, Robert Douglas *lawyer, footwear industry executive*
Poscover, Maury B. *lawyer*
Rataj, Edward William *lawyer*
Ritter, Robert Forcier *lawyer*
Ritterskamp, Douglas Dolvin *lawyer*
Rose, Albert Schoenburg *lawyer, educator*
Rubenstein, Jerome Max *lawyer*
Sachs, Alan Arthur *lawyer, corporate executive*
Sale, Llewellyn, III *lawyer*
Sandberg, John Steven *lawyer*
Sant, John Talbot *lawyer*
Schnuck, Terry Edward *lawyer*
Searls, Eileen Haughey *retired lawyer, librarian, educator*
Shands, Courtney, Jr. *lawyer*
Sherby, Kathleen Reilly *lawyer*
Smith, Arthur Lee *lawyer*
Sobol, Lawrence Raymond *lawyer*
Teasdale, Kenneth Fulbright *lawyer*
Tierney, Michael Edward *lawyer*
Turley, Michael Roy *lawyer*
Van Cleve, William Moore *lawyer*
Virtel, James John *lawyer*
Walsh, Thomas Charles *lawyer*
Watters, Richard Donald *lawyer*
Weiss, Charles Andrew *lawyer*
Welch, David William *lawyer*
Willard, Gregory Dale *lawyer*
Wilson, Margaret Bush *lawyer, civil rights leader*
Wilson, Michael E. *lawyer*
Withers, W. Wayne *lawyer*
Wolff, Frank Pierce, Jr. *lawyer*
Woodruff, Bruce Emery *lawyer*
Young, Marvin Oscar *lawyer*

Savannah
Miller, Dale Keith *lawyer*

Springfield
Carlson, Thomas Joseph *real estate developer, lawyer, mayor*
Carmichael, Lloyd Joseph *lawyer*
Hulston, John Kenton *lawyer, director*
Lowther, Gerald Halbert *lawyer*
McDonald, William Henry *lawyer*
Roberts, Patrick Kent *lawyer*
Shantz, Debra Mallonee *lawyer*

Stockton
Hammons, Brian Kent *lawyer, business executive*

Trenton
Hudson, Steven Daniel *lawyer, judge*

Warrensburg
Young, Mary Ann *lawyer*

NEBRASKA

Benkelman
Owens, Judith L(ynn) *lawyer*

David City
Hart, Carl Kiser, Jr. *county attorney*

Kearney
Schroeder, Kent A. *lawyer*

Lincoln
Frobom, LeAnn Larson *lawyer*
Guthery, John M. *lawyer*
Hewitt, James Watt *lawyer*
Lacey, Gary Eugene *lawyer*
Perlman, Harvey Stuart *lawyer, educator*
Perry, Edwin Charles *lawyer*
Schizas, Jennifer Anne *law association administrator*

Omaha
Achelpohl, Steven Edward *lawyer*
Bailis, David Paul *lawyer*
Barrett, Frank Joseph *lawyer, former insurance company executive*
Brownrigg, John Clinton *lawyer*
Caporale, D. Nick *lawyer*
Dolan, James Vincent *lawyer*
Fitzgerald, James Patrick *lawyer*
Hamann, Deryl Frederick *lawyer, bank executive*
Jansen, James Steven *lawyer*
Jensen, Sam *lawyer*
Krutter, Forrest Nathan *lawyer*
Longo, Amy L. *lawyer*
McCusker, Thomas J. *corporate lawyer, insurance company executive*
Monaghan, Thomas Justin *former prosecutor*
North, John E., Jr. *lawyer*
Rock, Harold L. *lawyer*
Schropp, Tobin *lawyer*
von Bernuth, Carl W. *lawyer, diversified corporation executive*

Sidney
Schaub, Paul B. *lawyer*

West Point
Donner, Thomas Benjamin *lawyer*

NEVADA

Reno
Putney, Mark William *lawyer, utility executive*

NEW HAMPSHIRE

Grantham
Goss, Richard Henry *lawyer*

NEW YORK

New York
Barnard, Robert N. *lawyer*
Jock, Paul F., II *lawyer*
Kempf, Donald G., Jr. *lawyer*

Schulhofer, Stephen Joseph *law educator, consultant*
Ziegler, John Augustus, Jr. *lawyer*

NORTH DAKOTA

Beulah
Quast, Larry Wayne *lawyer*

Bismarck
Gilbertson, Joel Warren *lawyer*
Murry, Charles Emerson *lawyer, official*
Nelson, Keithe Eugene *state court administrator, lawyer*
Olson, John Michael *lawyer*

Dickinson
Greenwood, Dann E. *lawyer*

Grand Forks
Widdel, John Earl, Jr. *lawyer*

OHIO

Akron
Bartlo, Sam D. *lawyer*
Fisher, James Lee *lawyer*
Harvie, Crawford Thomas *lawyer*
Holloway, Donald Phillip *lawyer*
Lee, Brant Thomas *lawyer, federal official, educator*
Lombardi, Frederick McKean *lawyer*
Polster, Dan Aaron *judge*
Richert, Paul *law educator*
Rooney, George Willard *lawyer*
Ruport, Scott Hendricks *lawyer*
Trotter, Thomas Robert *lawyer*

Bay Village
Kapp, C. Terrence *lawyer*

Bellefontaine
Heaton, Gerald Lee *lawyer*

Bellevue
Meyers, John E. *prosecutor*

Bowling Green
Hanna, Martin Shad *lawyer*
Mayberry, Alan Reed *lawyer*

Bucyrus
Neff, Robert Clark, Sr. *lawyer*

Canfield
Mumaw, James Webster *lawyer, director*

Canton
Bennington, Ronald Kent *lawyer*

Cardington
Hall, Howard Ernest *lawyer*

Chagrin Falls
Blattner, Robert A. *lawyer*
Calfee, William Lewis *lawyer*
Madsen, H(enry) Stephen *retired lawyer*

Chesterland
Kancelbaum, Joshua Jacob *lawyer*

Cincinnati
Adams, Edmund John *lawyer*
Anderson, James Milton *lawyer*
Anderson, William Hopple *lawyer*
Anthony, Thomas Dale *lawyer*
Bahlman, William Thorne, Jr. *retired lawyer*
Black, Stephen L. *lawyer*
Bridgeland, James Ralph, Jr. *lawyer*
Broderick, Dennis John *lawyer, retail company executive*
Bromberg, Robert Sheldon *lawyer*
Bruvold, Kathleen Parker *lawyer*
Carlson, Jennie Peaslack *lawyer*
Carr, George Francis Francis, Jr. *lawyer*
Chesley, Stanley Morris *lawyer*
Christenson, Gordon A. *law educator*
Cioffi, Michael Lawrence *lawyer*
Cissell, James Charles *lawyer*
Cody, Thomas Gerald *lawyer*
Craig, L. Clifford *lawyer*
Dehner, Joseph Julnes *lawyer*
DeLong, Deborah *lawyer*
Diller, Edward Dietrich *lawyer*
Dornette, W(illiam) Stuart *lawyer, educator*
Evans, James E. *lawyer*
Faller, Susan Grogan *lawyer*
Fink, Jerold Albert *lawyer*
Flanagan, John Anthony *lawyer, educator*
Freedman, William Mark *lawyer, educator*
Garfinkel, Jane E. *lawyer*
Gettler, Benjamin *lawyer, manufacturing company executive*
Goodman, Stanley *lawyer*
Greenberg, Gerald Stephen *lawyer*
Hardy, William Robinson *lawyer*
Harris, Irving *lawyer*
Heinlen, Ronald Eugene *lawyer*
Heldman, James Gardner *lawyer*
Heldman, Paul W. *lawyer, grocery store company executive*
Hoffheimer, Daniel Joseph *lawyer*
Johnson, James J. *lawyer*
Kelley, John Joseph, Jr. *lawyer*
Kenrich, John Lewis *retired lawyer*
Kiel, Frederick Orin *lawyer*
Kordons, Uldis *lawyer*
Lawrence, James Kaufman Lebensburger *lawyer*
Lindberg, Charles David *lawyer*
Longenecker, Mark Hershey, Jr. *lawyer*
Manley, Robert Edward *lawyer, economist*
Mann, David Scott *lawyer*
Maxwell, Robert Wallace, II *lawyer*
Mc Henry, Powell *lawyer*
McClain, William Andrew *lawyer*
McDowell, John Eugene *lawyer*
McGavran, Frederick Jaeger *lawyer*
Meranus, Leonard Stanley *lawyer*
Meyers, Pamela Sue *lawyer*
Nechemias, Stephen Murray *lawyer*
Neumark, Michael Harry *lawyer*
O'Reilly, James Thomas *lawyer, educator, author*
Olson, Robert Wyrick *lawyer*
Parker, R. Joseph *lawyer*
Petrie, Bruce Inglis *lawyer*
Phillips, T. Stephen *lawyer*
Reichert, David *lawyer*
Rich, Robert Edward *lawyer*
Rose, Donald McGregor *retired lawyer*
Schmidt, Thomas Joseph, Jr. *lawyer*
Schmit, David E. *lawyer*
Schuck, Thomas Robert *lawyer, farmer*
Shore, Thomas Spencer, Jr. *lawyer*
Silbersack, Mark Louis *lawyer*
Strauss, William Victor *lawyer*
Swigert, James Mack *lawyer*
Terp, Thomas Thomsen *lawyer*
Tobias, Charles Harrison, Jr. *lawyer*
Tobias, Paul Henry *lawyer*
Townsend, Robert J. *lawyer*
Trauth, Joseph Louis, Jr. *lawyer*
Vander Laan, Mark Alan *lawyer*
Vogel, Cedric Wakelee *lawyer*
Wales, Ross Elliot *lawyer*
Weeks, Steven Wiley *lawyer*
Weseli, Roger William *lawyer*
Whitaker, Glenn Virgil *lawyer*
Woodside, Frank C., III *lawyer, educator, physician*
Yurchuck, Roger Alexander *lawyer*
Zavatsky, Michael Joseph *lawyer*
Zealey, Sharon Janine *lawyer*

Cleveland
Adamo, Kenneth R. *lawyer*
Andorka, Frank Henry *lawyer*
Andrews, Oakley V. *lawyer*
Ashmus, Keith Allen *lawyer*
Austin, Arthur Donald, II *lawyer, educator*
Bacon, Brett Kermit *lawyer*
Bamberger, Richard H. *lawyer*
Bates, Walter Alan *former lawyer*
Baughman, R(obert) Patrick *lawyer*
Berger, Sanford Jason *lawyer, securities dealer, real estate broker*
Berick, James Herschel *lawyer, director*
Berry, Dean Lester *lawyer*
Bilchik, Gary B. *lawyer*
Binford, Gregory Glenn *lawyer*
Bixenstine, Kim Fenton *lawyer*
Braverman, Herbert Leslie *lawyer*
Bravo, Kenneth Allan *lawyer*
Brennan, Maureen *lawyer*
Brown, Seymour R. *lawyer, director*
Brucken, Robert Matthew *lawyer*
Burke, Kathleen B. *lawyer*
Cain, J. Matthew *prosecutor*
Cairns, James Donald *lawyer*
Calfee, John Beverly *retired lawyer*
Canary, Nancy Halliday *lawyer*
Carrick, Kathleen Michele *law librarian*
Clarke, Charles Fenton *lawyer*
Collin, Thomas James *lawyer*
Coquillette, William Hollis *lawyer*
Crist, Paul Grant *lawyer*
Cudak, Gail Linda *lawyer*
Currivan, John Daniel *lawyer*
Doris, Alan S(anford) *lawyer*
Drinko, John Deaver *lawyer*
Duncan, Ed Eugene *lawyer*
Duvin, Robert Phillip *lawyer*
Fabens, Andrew Lawrie, III *lawyer*
Falsgraf, William Wendell *lawyer*
Fay, Regan Joseph *lawyer*
Feinberg, Paul H. *lawyer*
Friedman, Harold Edward *lawyer*
Friedman, James Moss *lawyer*
Gerhart, Peter Milton *law educator*
Gherlein, Gerald Lee *lawyer, former diversified manufacturing company executive*
Glaser, Robert Edward *lawyer*
Goins, Frances Floriano *lawyer*
Gold, Gerald Seymour *lawyer*
Goldfarb, Bernard Sanford *lawyer*
Goler, Michael David *lawyer*
Graham, David Browning *lawyer*
Groetzinger, Jon, Jr. *lawyer, consumer products executive*
Grossman, Theodore Martin *lawyer*
Haiman, Irwin Sanford *lawyer*
Hardy, Michael Lynn *lawyer*
Hochman, Kenneth George *lawyer*
Hoerner, Robert Jack *lawyer*
Hollington, Richard Rings, Jr. *lawyer*
Horvitz, Michael John *lawyer*
Jacobs, Leslie William *lawyer*
Janke, Ronald Robert *lawyer*
Jeavons, Norman Stone *lawyer*
Jorgenson, Mary Ann *lawyer*
Kahrl, Robert Conley *lawyer*
Katcher, Richard *lawyer*
Katz, Lewis Robert *law educator*
Kelly, Dennis Michael *lawyer*
Kilbane, Catherine M. *lawyer*
Kilbane, Thomas Stanton *lawyer*
Kirchick, Calvin B. *lawyer*
Kola, Arthur Anthony *lawyer*
Korngold, Gerald *law educator*
Kramer, Eugene Leo *lawyer*
Kundtz, John Andrew *lawyer*
Kurit, Neil *lawyer*
Lawniczak, James Michael *lawyer*
Lazar, Kathy Pittak *lawyer*
Lease, Robert K. *lawyer*
Leavitt, Jeffrey Stuart *lawyer*
Leiken, Earl Murray *lawyer*
Lenn, Stephen Andrew *lawyer*
Lewis, John Bruce *lawyer*
Lewis, John Francis *lawyer*
Lewis, Robert Lawrence *lawyer, educator*
Mancuso, John H. *lawyer, bank executive*
Markey, Robert Guy *lawyer*
Marting, Michael G. *lawyer*
Mason, Thomas Albert *lawyer*
Mc Cartan, Patrick Francis *lawyer*
McCarthy, Mark Francis *lawyer*
McElhaney, James Willson *lawyer, educator*
McKee, Thomas Frederick *lawyer*
McLaughlin, Patrick Michael *lawyer*
Mehlman, Maxwell Jonathan *law educator*
Melsher, Gary William *lawyer*
Meyer, G. Christopher *lawyer*
Millstone, David Jeffrey *lawyer*
Moore, Kenneth Cameron *lawyer*
Moran, Glenn J. *corporate lawyer*
Morrison, Donald William *lawyer*
Newman, John M., Jr. *lawyer*
Ollinger, W. James *lawyer, director*
Owendoff, Stephen Peter *lawyer*
Ozanne, Dominic Laurant *lawyer, construction company executive*
Perris, Terrence George *lawyer*
Piraino, Thomas Anthony *lawyer*
Plant, Thomas A. *lawyer*
Preston, Robert Bruce *retired lawyer*
Putka, Andrew Charles *lawyer*
Pyke, John Secrest, Jr. *lawyer, polymers company executive*
Rains, M. Neal *lawyer*
Rapp, Robert Neil *lawyer*
Rekstis, Walter J., III *lawyer*
Reppert, Richard Levi *lawyer*
Rosenbaum, Jacob I. *lawyer*
Ruben, Alan Miles *law educator*
Rydzel, James A. *lawyer*
Sawyer, Raymond Terry *lawyer*
Schaefer, David Arnold *lawyer*
Schiller, James Joseph *lawyer*
Skulina, Thomas Raymond *lawyer*
Slinger, Michael Jeffery *law library director*
Sloan, David W. *lawyer*
Smith, Barbara Jean *lawyer*
Sogg, Wilton Sherman *lawyer*
Solomon, Randall Lee *lawyer*
Spero, Keith Erwin *lawyer, educator*
Stanley, Hugh Monroe, Jr. *lawyer*
Stanton, R. Thomas *lawyer*
Steindler, Howard Allen *lawyer*
Stellato, Louis Eugene *lawyer*
Stevens, Thomas Charles *lawyer*
Strauch, John L. *lawyer*
Striefsky, Linda A(nn) *lawyer*
Strimbu, Victor, Jr. *lawyer*
Stuhan, Richard George *lawyer*
Swartzbaugh, Marc L. *lawyer*
Sweeney, Emily Margaret *prosecutor*
Taft, Seth Chase *retired lawyer*
Thimmig, Diana M. *lawyer*
Toohey, Brian Frederick *lawyer*
Toomajian, William Martin *lawyer*
von Mehren, George M. *lawyer*
Waldeck, John Walter, Jr. *lawyer*
Wallach, Mark Irwin *lawyer*
Weber, Robert Carl *lawyer*
Weiler, Jeffry Louis *lawyer*
Whitney, Richard Buckner *lawyer*
Willenbrink, Rose Ann *lawyer*
Young, James Edward *lawyer*
Zambie, Allan John *lawyer*
Zangerle, John A. *lawyer*

Columbus
Adams, John Marshall *lawyer*
Anderson, Jon Mac *lawyer, educator*
Bahls, Steven Carl *law educator, dean*
Bailey, Daniel Allen *lawyer*
Bell, Albert Jerome *lawyer*
Bennett, Robert Thomas *lawyer*
Bibart, Richard L. *lawyer*
Bridgman, G(eorge) Ross *lawyer*
Brinkman, Dale Thomas *lawyer*
Brooks, Richard Dickinson *lawyer*
Brown, Herbert Russell *lawyer, writer*
Brown, Philip Albert *lawyer*
Brubaker, Robert Loring *lawyer*
Buchenroth, Stephen Richard *lawyer*
Carnahan, John Anderson *lawyer*
Carpenter, Michael H. *lawyer*
Chester, John Jonas *lawyer, educator*
Christensen, John William *lawyer*
Cvetanovich, Danny L. *lawyer*
DeRousie, Charles Stuart *lawyer*
Di Lorenzo, John Florio , Jr. *retired lawyer (corporate)*
Dietrich, Thomas W. *corporate lawyer, insurance company executive*
Draper, Gerald Linden *lawyer*
Dreher, Darrell L. *lawyer*
Elam, John Carlton *lawyer*
Fahey, Richard Paul *lawyer*
Fay, Terrence Michael *lawyer*
Fisher, Lawrence L. *lawyer*
Fisher, Lloyd Edison, Jr. *lawyer*
Frasier, Ralph Kennedy *lawyer, banker*
Fried, Samuel *lawyer*
Fu, Paul Shan *law librarian, consultant*
Greek, Darold I. *lawyer*
Gross, James Howard *lawyer*
Hardymon, David Wayne *lawyer*
Hatler, Patricia Ruth *lawyer*
Helfer, Michael Stevens *lawyer, business executive*
Hollenbaugh, H(enry) Ritchey *lawyer*
Jackson, Janet Elizabeth *city attorney, association executive*
Jenkins, George L. *lawyer, entrepreneur*
Jenkins, John Anthony *lawyer*
Johnson, Mark Alan *lawyer*
King, G. Roger *lawyer*
Kuehnle, Kenton Lee *lawyer*
Kurtz, Charles Jewett, III *lawyer*
La Cour, Louis Bernard *lawyer*
Lehman, Harry Jac *lawyer*
Long, Thomas Leslie *lawyer*
Markus, Kent Richard *lawyer*
Martin, William Giese *lawyer*
Maynard, Robert Howell *retired lawyer*
McAlister, Robert Beaton *lawyer*
McConnaughey, George Carlton, Jr. *retired lawyer*
McCutchan, Gordon Eugene *retired lawyer, insurance company executive*
McDermott, Kevin R. *lawyer*
McKenna, Alvin James *lawyer*
McMahon, John Patrick *lawyer*
McNealey, J. Jeffrey *lawyer, corporate executive*
Mencer, Jetta *lawyer*
Miller, Terry Morrow *lawyer*
Minor, Charles Daniel *lawyer, director*
Minor, Robert Allen *lawyer*
Moloney, Thomas E. *lawyer*
Mone, Robert Paul *lawyer*
Morgan, Dennis Richard *lawyer*
Moul, William Charles *lawyer*
Oman, Richard Heer *lawyer*
Petricoff, M. Howard *lawyer, educator*
Petro, James Michael *lawyer, politician*
Phillips, James Edgar *lawyer*
Pigman, Jack Richard *lawyer*
Pressley, Fred G., Jr. *lawyer*
Quigley, John Bernard *law educator*
Radnor, Alan T. *lawyer*
Ramey, Denny L. *bar association executive director*
Ray, Frank Allen *lawyer*
Reasoner, Willis Irl, III *lawyer*
Ridgley, Thomas Brennan *lawyer*
Robinson, Barry R. *lawyer*
Robol, Richard Thomas *lawyer*
Rose, Michael Dean *lawyer, educator*
Ryan, Joseph W., Jr. *lawyer*
Schrag, Edward A., Jr. *lawyer*
Sidman, Robert John *lawyer*
Stern, Geoffrey *lawyer, disciplinary counsel*
Stinehart, Roger Ray *lawyer*
Taft, Sheldon Ashley *lawyer*
Taggart, Thomas Michael *lawyer*
Tait, Robert E. *lawyer*
Tarpy, Thomas Michael *lawyer*
Taylor, Joel Sanford *retired lawyer*
Thomas, Duke Winston *lawyer*
Todd, William Michael *lawyer*
Treneff, Craig Paul *lawyer*
Turano, David A. *lawyer*
Vorys, Arthur Isaiah *lawyer*
Warner, Charles Collins *lawyer*
Whipps, Edward Franklin *lawyer*
Wightman, Alec *lawyer*
Wright, Harry, III *retired lawyer*

Dayton
Burick, Lawrence T. *lawyer*
Gottschlich, Gary William *lawyer*
Hadley, Robert James *lawyer*
Heyman, Ralph Edmond *lawyer*
Hoak, Jonathan S. *lawyer*
Jenks, Thomas Edward *lawyer*
Johnson, C. Terry *lawyer*
Kinlin, Donald James *lawyer*
Lockhart, Gregory Gordon *prosecutor*
Macklin, Crofford Johnson, Jr. *lawyer*
McSwiney, Charles Ronald *lawyer*
Rapp, Gerald Duane *lawyer, manufacturing company executive*
Rogers, Richard Hunter *lawyer, business executive*
Taronji, Jaime, Jr. *lawyer*

Defiance
Strausbaugh, Jeffrey Alan *lawyer*

Dublin
Bennett, George H., Jr. *lawyer, healthcare company executive*
Borror, David S. *lawyer*
Maloon, Jerry L. *trial lawyer, physician, medicolegal consultant*

Findlay
Jetton, Girard Reuel, Jr. *lawyer, retired oil company executive*

Hillsboro
Coss, Rocky Alan *lawyer*

Lakewood
Traci, Donald Philip *retired lawyer*

Lancaster
Libert, Donald Joseph *lawyer*

Lebanon
Oliver, Timothy Allen *lawyer*

Magfield Heights
Schneider, David Miller *lawyer*

Marietta
Fields, William Albert *lawyer*

Marysville
Hamilton, Robert Otte *lawyer*

Maumee
Marsh, Benjamin Franklin *lawyer*
McBride, Beverly Jean *lawyer*

Mc Connelsville
Ross, Richard Lee *lawyer*

Mentor
Driggs, Charles Mulford *lawyer*

Miamisburg
Andreozzi, Louis Joseph *lawyer*
Battles, John Martin *lawyer*
Byrd, James Everett *lawyer*

Milford
Mongelluzzo, John Andrew *lawyer*
Vorholt, Jeffrey Joseph *lawyer, software company executive*

Mount Vernon
Turner, Harry Edward *lawyer*

Newark
Mantonya, John Butcher *lawyer*
Reidy, Thomas Anthony *lawyer*

Pepper Pike
Schnell, Carlton Bryce *lawyer*

Portsmouth
Crowder, Marjorie Briggs *lawyer*
Grimshaw, Lynn Alan *lawyer*
Horr, William Henry *retired lawyer*

Shaker Heights
Donnem, Roland William *retired lawyer, real estate owner, developer*

Springfield
Browne, William Bitner *lawyer*

Toledo
Baker, Richard Southworth *lawyer*
Boesel, Milton Charles, Jr. *lawyer, business executive*
Brown, Charles Earl *lawyer*
Hiett, Edward Emerson *retired lawyer, glass company executive*
Kline, James Edward *lawyer*
Machin, Barbara E. *lawyer*
McCormick, Edward James, Jr. *lawyer, deceased*
McWeeny, Philip *corporate lawyer*
O'Connell, Maurice Daniel *lawyer*
Pletz, Thomas Gregory *lawyer*
Spitzer, John Brumback *lawyer*
St. Clair, Donald David *lawyer*

Strobel, Martin Jack *lawyer, motor vehicle and industrial component manufacturing and distribution company executive*
Webb, Thomas Irwin, Jr. *lawyer, director*
Wicklund, David Wayne *lawyer*
Young, Thomas Lee *lawyer*

Warren
Rossi, Anthony Gerald *lawyer*

West Union
Young, Vernon Lewis *lawyer*

Wickliffe
Kidder, Fred Dockstater *lawyer*

Willoughby
Coulson, Charles Ernest *lawyer*

Wooster
Frantz, Martin H. *prosecutor*
Kennedy, Charles Allen *lawyer*

Youngstown
Carlin, Clair Myron *lawyer*
Matune, Frank Joseph *lawyer*
Nadler, Myron Jay *lawyer, director*
Roth, Daniel Benjamin *lawyer, business executive*
Stevens, Paul Edward *lawyer*
Tucker, Don Eugene *retired lawyer*

Zanesville
Micheli, Frank James *lawyer*

OKLAHOMA

Oklahoma City
McCampbell, Robert Garner *prosecutor*

SOUTH DAKOTA

Aberdeen
Kornmann, Charles Bruno *lawyer*

Dakota Dunes
Hagan, Sheila B. *corporate lawyer*

Ipswich
Beck, Vaughn Peter *lawyer*

Madison
Ericsson, Richard L. *lawyer*

Philip
Kemnitz, Ralph A. *lawyer*

Pierre
Gerdes, David Alan *lawyer*
Johnson, Julie Marie *lawyer, lobbyist*
Rogers, Darla Pollman *lawyer*
Thompson, Charles Murray *lawyer*

Rapid City
Foye, Thomas Harold *lawyer*
Hagg, Rexford A. *lawyer, former state legislatorr*

Sioux Falls
Marshall, Mark F. *lawyer*
McBride, Ted *prosecutor*

Winner
Maule, Theresa Moore *lawyer*

VERMONT

Stowe
Whiteman, Joseph David *retired lawyer, manufacturing company executive*

VIRGINIA

Arlington
Nagin, Lawrence M. *lawyer*
Rotunda, Ronald Daniel *law educator, consultant*

Charlottesville
Groiss, Fred George *lawyer*

Richmond
Cutchins, Clifford Armstrong, IV *lawyer*

WISCONSIN

Appleton
Eno, Woodrow E. *lawyer*

Barron
Babler, James Carl *lawyer*

Cedarburg
Hazelwood, John A. *lawyer*

Chippewa Falls
Scobie, Timothy Franklin *lawyer*

Crandon
Verich, Demetrio *lawyer*

Germantown
Statkus, Jerome Francis *lawyer*

Janesville
Steil, George Kenneth, Sr. *lawyer*

Kohler
Black, Natalie A. *lawyer*

La Crosse
Klos, Jerome John *lawyer, director*
Nix, Edmund Alfred *lawyer*
Sleik, Thomas Scott *lawyer*

Lake Geneva
Braden, Berwyn Bartow *lawyer*

Madison
Barnhill, Charles Joseph, Jr. *lawyer*
Barnick, Helen *retired judicial clerk*
Bochert, Linda H. *lawyer*
Bugge, Lawrence John *lawyer, educator*
Chandler, Richard Gates *lawyer*
Charo, Robin Alta *law educator*
Field, Henry Augustus, Jr. *lawyer*
Hanson, David James *lawyer*
Heymann, S. Richard *lawyer*
Holbrook, John Scott, Jr. *lawyer*
Jones, James Edward, Jr. *retired law educator*
Klauser, James Roland *lawyer*
Langer, Richard J. *lawyer*
Linstroth, Tod Brian *lawyer*
McCallum, Laurie Riach *lawyer, state government*
Melli, Marygold Shire *law educator*
Mohs, Frederic Edward *lawyer*
Monaghan, David A. *corporate lawyer*
Potter, Kevin *lawyer*
Prange, Roy Leonard, Jr. *lawyer*
Ragatz, Thomas George *lawyer*
Skilton, John Singleton *lawyer*
Steingass, Susan R. *lawyer*
Temkin, Harvey L. *lawyer*
Vaughan, Michael Richard *lawyer*
Wagner, Burton Allan *lawyer*
Walsh, David Graves *lawyer*
White, William Fredrick *lawyer*
Whitney, Robert Michael *lawyer*
Wilcox, Michael Wing *lawyer*

Menomonee Falls
Dynek, Sigrid *corporate lawyer, retail executive*

Mequon
Burroughs, Charles Edward *lawyer*

Milwaukee
Abraham, William John , Jr. *lawyer*
Alverson, William H. *lawyer*
Babler, Wayne E., Jr. *lawyer*
Bannen, John Thomas *lawyer*
Barnes, Paul McClung *lawyer*
Beckwith, David E. *lawyer*
Berkoff, Marshall Richard *lawyer*
Biehl, Michael Melvin *lawyer*
Biller, Joel Wilson *lawyer, former foreign service officer*
Bowen, Michael Anthony *lawyer, writer*
Bremer, John M. *lawyer*
Bruce, Peter Wayne *lawyer, insurance company executive*
Busch, John Arthur *lawyer*
Calise, William Joseph, Jr. *lawyer*
Cannon, David Joseph *lawyer*
Casey, John Alexander *lawyer*
Casper, Richard Henry *lawyer*
Chokey, James A. *lawyer*
Christiansen, Keith Allan *lawyer*
Clark, James Richard *lawyer*
Cleary, John Washington *lawyer*
Connolly, Gerald Edward *lawyer*
Cutler, Richard Woolsey *lawyer*
Daily, Frank J(erome) *lawyer*
Dallman, Robert Edward *lawyer*
Dionisopoulos, George Allan *lawyer*
Drummond, Robert Kendig *lawyer*
Duback, Steven Rahr *lawyer*
Eisenberg, Howard Bruce *law educator*
Ericson, James Donald *lawyer, insurance executive*
Florsheim, Richard Steven *lawyer*
Frautschi, Timothy Clark *lawyer*
Friedman, James Dennis *lawyer*
Gallagher, Richard Sidney *lawyer*
Gefke, Henry Jerome *lawyer*
Gemignani, Joseph Adolph *lawyer*
Geske, Janine Patricia *law educator, former state supreme court justice*
Ghiardi, James Domenic *lawyer, educator*
Goodkind, Conrad George *lawyer*
Graber, Richard William *lawyer*
Grebe, Michael W. *lawyer*
Groethe, Reed *lawyer*
Haberman, F. William *lawyer*
Harrington, John Timothy *retired lawyer*
Hase, David John *lawyer*
Hatch, Michael Ward *lawyer*
Hoffman, Nathaniel A. *lawyer*
Huff, Marsha Elkins *lawyer*
Johannes, Robert J. *lawyer*
Jost, Lawrence John *lawyer*
Kamps, Charles Q. *lawyer*
Kennedy, John Patrick *lawyer, corporate executive*
Kessler, Joan F. *lawyer*
Kircher, John Joseph *law educator*
Kringel, Jerome Howard *lawyer*
Krueger, Raymond Robert *lawyer*
Kubale, Bernard Stephen *lawyer*
Kurtz, Harvey A. *lawyer*
LaBudde, Roy Christian *lawyer*
Langley, Grant F. *municipal lawyer*
Levit, William Harold, Jr. *lawyer*
Loeb, Leonard L. *lawyer*
Lueders, Wayne Richard *lawyer*
MacGregor, David Lee *lawyer*
MacIver, John Kenneth *lawyer*
Marcus, Richard Steven *lawyer*
Martin, Quinn William *lawyer*
Maynard, John Ralph *lawyer*
McCann, E. Michael *lawyer*
McGaffey, Jere D. *lawyer*
McSweeney, Maurice J. (Marc) *lawyer*
Medved, Paul Stanley *lawyer*
Meldman, Robert Edward *lawyer*
Mulcahy, Robert William *lawyer*
O'Shaughnessy, James Patrick *lawyer*
Obenberger, Thomas E. *lawyer*
Olivieri, José Alberto *lawyer*
Phillips, Thomas John *lawyer*
Richman, Stephen Erik *lawyer*
Ryan, Patrick Michael *lawyer*
Sanfilippo, Jon Walter *lawyer*
Schnur, Robert Arnold *lawyer*
Scrivner, Thomas William *lawyer*
Shapiro, Robyn Sue *lawyer, educator*
Shriner, Thomas L., Jr. *lawyer*
Smith, David Bruce *lawyer*
Terschan, Frank Robert *lawyer*
Titley, Robert L. *lawyer*
Walmer, Edwin Fitch *lawyer*
Whyte, George Kenneth, Jr. *lawyer*
Will, Trevor Jonathan *lawyer*
Williams, Clay Rule *lawyer*
Winsten, Saul Nathan *lawyer*

Monroe
Luhman, Gary Lee *lawyer*

Neenah
Stanton, Thomas Mitchell *lawyer, educator*

Prairie Du Chien
Baxter, Timothy C. *prosecutor*

Shawano
Bruno, Gary Robert *lawyer*

Siren
Kutz, Kenneth L. *district attorney*

Sturtevant
Brandes, Jo Anne *lawyer*

Superior
Marcovich, Toby *lawyer*

Waukesha
Macy, John Patrick *lawyer*

Wausau
Drengler, William Allan John *lawyer*
Orr, San Watterson, Jr. *lawyer*

CANADA

MANITOBA

Winnipeg
Anderson, David Trevor *law educator*
Edwards, Clifford Henry Coad *law educator*
Schnoor, Jeffrey Arnold *lawyer*

ENGLAND

London
Northrip, Robert Earl *lawyer*

TANZANIA

Arusha
Rapp, Stephen John *international prosecutor*

ADDRESS UNPUBLISHED

Arnold, Jerome Gilbert *lawyer*
Bell, John William *lawyer*
Bennett, Steven Alan *lawyer*
Bernstein, Merton Clay *law educator, lawyer, arbitrator*
Beukema, John Frederick *lawyer*
Blatt, Harold Geller *lawyer*
Bleveans, John *lawyer*
Boho, Dan L. *lawyer*
Branagan, James Joseph *lawyer*
Brehl, James William *lawyer*
Bujold, Tyrone Patrick *lawyer*
Buttrey, Donald Wayne *lawyer*
Capp, David A. *former prosecutor*
Carpenter, Susan Karen *public defender*
Cassidy, John Harold *lawyer*
Clark, Beverly Ann *lawyer*
Coleman, Robert Lee *retired lawyer*
Cooper, Hal Dean *lawyer*
Coughlan, Kenneth L. *lawyer*
Dettmer, Michael Hayes *former prosecutor*
Dutile, Fernand Neville *law educator*
Eaton, Larry Ralph *lawyer*
Emert, Timothy Ray *lawyer*
Erlebacher, Arlene Cernik *retired lawyer*
Ferguson, Bradford Lee *lawyer*
Gamble, E. James *lawyer, accountant*
Gass, Raymond William *lawyer, consumer products company executive*
George, Joyce Jackson *lawyer, judge emeritus*
Gleeson, Paul Francis *retired lawyer*
Grabemann, Karl W. *lawyer*
Grazin, Igor Nikolai *law educator, state official*
Hackett, Wesley Phelps, Jr. *lawyer*
Hall, Glenn Allen *lawyer, state representative*
Hemmer, James Paul *lawyer*
Huston, Steven Craig *lawyer*
Jaudes, William E. *retired lawyer*
Jordan, Michelle Denise *lawyer*
Kohlstedt, James August *lawyer*
Kratt, Peter George *lawyer*
Krohnke, Duane W. *retired lawyer*
Lea, Lorenzo Bates *lawyer*
Leb, Arthur Stern *lawyer*
Linde, Maxine Helen *lawyer, business executive, private investor*
Logan, James Kenneth *lawyer, former federal judge*
Mangler, Robert James *lawyer, judge*
McCormick, Michael D. *lawyer*
McCoy, John Joseph *lawyer*
Mirman, Joel Harvey *lawyer*
Monroe, Murray Shipley *lawyer*
Moustakis, Albert D. *prosecutor*
Murphy, Sandra Robison *lawyer*
Myhand, Wanda Reshel *paralegal, legal assistant*
Nelson, Ralph Stanley *lawyer*
Nugent, Shane Vincent *lawyer*
Palizzi, Anthony N. *lawyer, retail corporation executive*
Peccarelli, Anthony Marando *lawyer*
Pratt, Robert Windsor *lawyer*
Pritikin, David T. *lawyer*
Pusateri, Lawrence Xavier *lawyer*
Quayle, Marilyn Tucker *lawyer, other: government, executive*
Reeder, Robert Harry *retired lawyer*
Reminger, Richard Thomas *lawyer, artist*
Saliterman, Richard Arlen *lawyer*
Sapp, John Raymond *lawyer*
Saunders, Lonna Jeanne *lawyer, newscaster, talk show host*
Schmidt, Kathleen Marie *lawyer*
Schultz, Dennis Bernard *lawyer*
Smith, Maura Abeln *lawyer*
Streicher, James Franklin *lawyer*
Thoman, Henry Nixon *lawyer*
Torf, Philip R. *lawyer, pharmacist*
Torgerson, Larry Keith *lawyer*
Trigg, Paul Reginald, Jr. *lawyer*
Weiland, Charles Hankes *lawyer*
Weston, Michael C. *lawyer*
Wohlschlaeger, Frederick George *lawyer*
Wruble, Bernhardt Karp *lawyer*
Yeager, Mark Leonard *lawyer*

MEDICINE *See* HEALTHCARE: MEDICINE

MILITARY

UNITED STATES

ILLINOIS

Chicago
Anderson, Edgar Ratcliffe, Jr. *career officer, hospital administrator, physician*

Hoffman Estates
Pagonis, William Gus *retired army general*

Mattoon
Phipps, John Randolph *retired army officer*

Rockford
Borling, John Lorin *military officer*

Scott Air Force Base
Hill, Thomas J. *career officer*
Hogle, Walter S. *career officer*
Hopper, John D., Jr. *career officer*
Regan, Gilbert J. *career officer, retired*
Robertson, Charles T., Jr. *air force Officer*
Thompson, Roger G., Jr. *career military officer, retired*

Springfield
Herriford, Robert Levi, Sr. *army officer*

INDIANA

Indianapolis
Poel, Robert Walter *air force officer, physician*

KANSAS

Fort Leavenworth
Schneider, James Joseph *military theory educator, consultant*
Steele, William M. *career military officer*

Fort Riley
McFarren, Freddy E. *military career officer*

MICHIGAN

Warren
Beauchamp, Roy E. *career officer*

MINNESOTA

Red Wing
Plehal, James Burton *career officer*

MISSOURI

Fort Leonard Wood
Flowers, Robert B. *military career officer*

Kansas City
Creighton, Neal *retired army officer*
Williams, Leo V., III *career military officer*

Saint Louis
Strevey, Tracy Elmer, Jr. *army officer, surgeon, physician executive*

NEBRASKA

Bellevue
Aldridge, Donald O'Neal *military officer*

Offutt A F B
Clark, Trudy H. *career officer*
Ford, Phillip J. *career officer*
Griffiths, Charles H., Jr. *career officer*
Mies, Richard W. *career officer*
Sullivan, Paul F. *career officer*
Waltman, Glenn C. *military officer*

OHIO

Columbus
Saunders, Mary L. *career officer*

Dayton
Raggio, Robert Frank *career officer*

Fairborn
Nowak, John Michael *retired air force officer, company executive*

Wright Pat
Cranston, Stewart E. *career officer*
Stewart, Todd I. *military officer*

Wright Patterson AFB
Kelley, Joseph E. *career officer*
Mushala, Michael C. *career officer*
Nielsen, Paul Douglas *Air Force officer, engineering manager*
Paul, Richard R. *military officer*
Pearson, Wilbert D. *career officer*
Samic, Dennis R. *career officer, retired*
Sieg, Stanley A. *military official*
Stewart, J. Daniel *air force official*
Stubbs, Jerald D. *career military officer*

SOUTH DAKOTA

Rapid City
Sykora, Harold James *military officer*

VIRGINIA

Arlington
Miller, Kenneth Gregory *retired air force officer*

MILITARY ADDRESSES OF THE UNITED STATES

ATLANTIC

FPO
Green, Kevin Patrick *career officer*

ADDRESS UNPUBLISHED

Arbuckle, Joseph W. *military officer*
Babbitt, George T. *career officer*
Bartrem, Duane Harvey *retired military officer, designer, building consultant*
Bongiovi, Robert P. *career officer*
Coolidge, Charles H., Jr. *career officer*
Curran, John Mark *military career officer*
Heng, Stanley Mark *national guard officer*
Kloeppel, Daniel L. *career officer*
Palmer, Dave Richard *retired military officer, academic administrator*

REAL ESTATE

UNITED STATES

FLORIDA

Pompano Beach
Markos, Chris *retired real estate company executive*

ILLINOIS

Champaign
Guttenberg, Albert Ziskind *planning educator*

Chicago
Amato, Isabella Antonia *real estate executive*
Beban, Gary Joseph *real estate corporation officer*
Berger, Miles Lee *land economist*
Bluhm, Neil Gary *real estate company executive*
Bucksbaum, John *real estate development company executive*
Bucksbaum, Matthew *real estate investment trust company executive*
Crocker, Douglas, II *real estate executive*
Dominski, Matthew S. *property manager*
Eubanks-Pope, Sharon G. *real estate company executive, entrepreneur*
Freibaum, Bernard *real estate development company executive*
Galowich, Ronald Howard *real estate investment executive, venture capitalist*
Gerber, John J. *real estate executive*
Hendrickson, David R. *real estate executive*
Klebba, Raymond Allen *property manager*
Lapidus, Dennis *real estate developer*
Metz, Adam S. *real estate executive*
Michaels, Robert A. *real estate development company executive*
Morrill, R. Layne *real estate broker, executive, professional association administrator*
Reschke, Michael W. *real estate executive*
Schwab, James Charles *urban planner*
Skoien, Gary *real estate company executive*
Strobeck, Charles LeRoy *real estate executive*
Travis, Dempsey Jerome *real estate executive and developer*
Wirtz, William Wadsworth *real estate executive, professional sports team executive*

Evanston
Perlmutter, Robert *land company executive*

Lake Zurich
Schultz, Carl Herbert *real estate management and development company executive*

Northbrook
Scruggs, Steven Dennis *real estate consultant*

Northfield
Kleinman, Burton Howard *real estate investor*

Oak Brook
Goodwin, Daniel L. *real estate company executive*
Parks, Robert D. *real estate company executive*
Wheeler, Paul James *real estate executive*

INDIANA

Evansville
Matthews, C(harles) David *real estate appraiser, consultant*

Indianapolis
Crosser, Richard H. *real estate company executive*
Hefner, Thomas L. *real estate company executive*
Holihen, Jennifer A. *real estate development company executive*
Jewett, John Rhodes *real estate executive*
McKenzie, Lloyd W. *real estate development executive*
Simon, Melvin *real estate developer, professional basketball executive*
Sokolov, Richard Saul *real estate company executive*
Weeks, A. Ray *real estate company executive*

Newburgh
Tierney, Gordon Paul *real estate broker, genealogist*

Terre Haute
Perry, Eston Lee *real estate and equipment leasing company executive*

IOWA

Des Moines
Leonard, George Edmund *real estate, bank, high tech and consulting executive*

Spencer
Lemke, Alan James *environmental specialist*

KANSAS

Topeka
Blair, Ben *real estate company executive*

Wichita
Lusk, William Edward *real estate and oil company executive*

KENTUCKY

Fort Mitchell
Weiskittel, Ralph Joseph *real estate broker*

MICHIGAN

Ann Arbor
Rycus, Mitchell Julian *urban planning educator, urban security and energy planning consultant*

Bloomfield Hills
Halso, Robert *real estate company executive*
Taubman, Robert S. *real estate developer*

East Lansing
Anderton, James Franklin, IV *real estate development executive*

Farmington Hills
Rose, Sheldon *property manager*

Grosse Ile
Smith, Veronica Latta *real estate corporation officer*

Grosse Pointe Farms
Dunlap, Connie Sue Zimmerman *real estate professional*

Houghton
Utt, Glenn S., Jr. *motel investor, former biotech and pharmaceutical industry company executive*

Saginaw
Cline, Thomas William *real estate leasing company executive, management consultant*

Southfield
Gershenson, Dennis *property company executive*
Gershenson, Joel *property company executive*
Ward, Michael A. *property company executive*

MINNESOTA

Duluth
Bowman, Roger Manwaring *real estate executive*

Minneapolis
Dahlberg, Burton Francis *real estate corporation executive*

Minnetonka
Karlen, Greg T. *real estate executive*

Saint Paul
McDonald, Malcolm Willis *real estate company executive*

MISSOURI

Chesterfield
Morley, Harry Thomas, Jr. *real estate executive*

Dunnegan
Harman, Mike *real estate broker, small business owner*

Holden
Martin, Laura Belle *real estate and farm land owner and manager*

Kansas City
Dumovich, Loretta *real estate and transportation company executive*
Shutz, Byron Christopher *real estate executive*

Saint Joseph
Miller, Lloyd Daniel *real estate agent*

Saint Louis
Meissner, Edwin Benjamin, Jr. *retired real estate broker*

NEBRASKA

Omaha
Kirshenbaum, Joseph *real estate developer*
Noddle, Harlan J. *real estate developer*

NEW JERSEY

Sea Girt
Cleary, Martin Joseph *real estate company executive*

NORTH DAKOTA

Bismarck
Christianson, James D. *real estate developer*

OHIO

Akron
Peavy, Homer Louis, Jr. *real estate executive, accountant*

Amelia
Hayden, John W. *real estate company executive*

Beachwood
Wolstein, Scott Alan *real estate company executive*

Cincinnati
Gratz, Ronald G. *real estate development executive*
Schuler, Robert Leo *appraiser, consultant*
Wyant, John H. *real estate development executive*

Cleveland
Jacobs, Richard E. *real estate executive, sports team owner*
Ratner, Charles A. *real estate executive*
Ratner, James *real estate executive*

Columbus
Creek, Phillip G. *real estate development executive*
Schottenstein, Steven *real estate development executive*
Voss, Jerrold Richard *city planner, educator, university official*

Dayton
Wertz, Kenneth Dean *real estate executive*

Dublin
Donnell, Jon M. *real estate executive*

Gates Mills
Schanfarber, Richard Carl *real estate broker*

Hudson
Stec, John Zygmunt *real estate executive*

New Albany
Kessler, John Whitaker *real estate developer*

Richmond Heights
Friedman, Jeffrey I. *real estate company executive*

Shaker Heights
Solganik, Marvin *real estate executive*

Toledo
Batt, Nick *property and investment executive*

Youngstown
Camacci, Michael A. *commercial real estate broker, development consultant*

WISCONSIN

Beaver Dam
Butterbrodt, John Ervin *real estate executive*

Madison
Ring, Gerald J. *real estate developer, insurance executive*
Vandell, Kerry Dean *real estate and urban economics educator*

ADDRESS UNPUBLISHED

Bednarowski, Keith *construction, design and real estate executive*
Colton, Victor Robert *real estate developer, investor*
Corey, Kenneth Edward *urban planning and geography educator, researcher*
Gasper, Ruth Eileen *real estate executive*
O'Leary, Timothy Michael *real estate corporation officer*
Riss, Robert Bailey *real estate investor*
Toshach, Clarice Oversby *real estate developer, former computer executive*

RELIGION

UNITED STATES

CALIFORNIA

Palm Desert
Cedar, Paul Arnold *church executive, minister*

IDAHO

Nampa
Bowers, Curtis Ray, Jr. *chaplain*

ILLINOIS

Buffalo Grove
Dimond, Robert Edward *publisher*

Carol Stream
Myra, Harold Lawrence *publisher*

Chicago
Almen, Lowell Gordon *church official*
Anderson, Hugh George *bishop*
Bacher, Robert Newell *church official*
Baumhart, Raymond Charles *Roman Catholic church administrator*
Betz, Hans Dieter *theology educator*
Browning, Don Spencer *religious educator*
Cappo, Joseph C. *publisher*
Carr, Anne Elizabeth *theology educator*
Constant, Anita Aurelia *publisher*
Conway, Edwin Michael *priest, church administrator*
Doherty, Sister Barbara *religious institution administrator*
Doniger, Wendy *history of religions educator*
Farrakhan, Louis *religious leader*
George, Francis Cardinal *archbishop*
Goedert, Raymond E. *bishop*
Gorman, John R. *auxiliary bishop*
Jegen, Sister Carol Frances *religion educator*
Larsen, Paul Emanuel *religious organization administrator*
Magnus, Kathy Jo *religious organization executive*
Manz, John R. *bishop*
Margolis, Rob *publisher*
Marshall, Cody *bishop*
McAuliffe, Richard L. *church official*
McGinn, Bernard John *religious educator*
Miller, Charles S. *clergy member, church administrator*
Mironovich, Alex *publisher*
Rajan, Fred E. N. *clergy member, church administrator*
Schupp, Ronald Irving *clergyman, missionary*
Shafer, Eric Christopher *minister*
Sherwin, Byron Lee *religion educator, college official*
Simon, Mordecai *religious association administrator, clergyman*
Sorensen, W. Robert *clergy member, church administrator*
Thurston, Stephen John *pastor*
Wagner, Joseph M. *church administrator*
Wiwchar, Michael *bishop*
Yu, Anthony C. *religion and literature educator*

Decatur
Morgan, E. A. *church administrator*

Elgin
Nolen, Wilfred E. *church administrator*
Reimer, Judy Mills *pastor, religious executive*

Frankfort
Huff, John David *church administrator*

Highland Park
Cohodes, Eli Aaron *publisher*
Pattis, S. William *publisher*

Naperville
Raccah, Dominique Marcelle *publisher*

Peoria
Duncan, Royal Robert *publisher*
Myers, John Joseph *bishop*

Riverside
Marty, Martin Emil *religion educator, editor*

Rockford
Doran, Thomas George *bishop*

South Holland
Perry, Joseph N. *bishop*

Springfield
Ryan, Daniel Leo *bishop*

INDIANA

Anderson
Grubbs, J. Perry *church administrator*

Bloomington
Gallman, John Gerry *publisher*

Evansville
Gettelfinger, Gerald Andrew *bishop*

Fort Wayne
Bunkowske, Eugene Walter *religious studies educator*
D'Arcy, John Michael *bishop*
Mann, David William *minister*
Mather, George Ross *clergy member*
Moran, John *religious organization administrator*
Pittelko, Roger Dean *clergyman, religious educator*

Highland
Willhoit, Jim *minister*

Huntington
Seilhamer, Ray A. *bishop*

Indianapolis
Bray, Donald Lawrence *religious organization executive, minister*
Hamm, Richard L. *church administrator*
Harness, David Keith *pastor*
Johnson, James P. *religious organization executive*
Marshall, Carolyn Ann M. *church official, executive*
Plaster, George Francis *Roman Catholic priest*
Polston, Mark Franklin *minister*
Sindlinger, Verne E. *bishop*
Welsh, Robert K. *religious organization executive*
Wilson, Earle Lawrence *church administrator*
Woodring, DeWayne Stanley *religion association executive*

Lafayette
Higi, William L. *bishop*
O'Callaghan, Patti Louise *urban ministry administrator*

Noblesville
Wilson, Norman Glenn *church administrator, writer*

Notre Dame
Blenkinsopp, Joseph *biblical studies educator*
Hesburgh, Theodore Martin *clergyman, former university president*
Malloy, Edward Aloysius *priest, university administrator, educator*
McBrien, Richard Peter *theology educator*
O'Meara, Thomas Franklin *priest, educator*
White, James Floyd *theology educator*

Winona Lake
Ashman, Charles H. *retired minister*
Davis, John James *religion educator*
Julien, Thomas Theodore *religious denomination administrator*
Lewis, Edward Alan *religious organization adminstrator*

IOWA

Ankeny
Hartog, John, II *theology educator, librarian*

Davenport
Franklin, William Edwin *bishop*

Des Moines
Epting, C. Christopher *bishop*
Feld, Thomas Robert *religious organization administrator*

Dubuque
Barta, James Omer *priest, psychology educator, church administrator*
Hanus, Jerome George *archbishop*

Grinnell
Mitchell, Orlan E. *clergyman, former college president*

Iowa City
Baird, Robert Dahlen *religious educator*

Orange City
Scorza, Sylvio Joseph *religion educator*

Sioux City
DiNardo, Daniel N. *bishop*

Storm Lake
Miller, Curtis Herman *bishop*

Waterloo
Lindberg, Duane R. *bishop, historian*
Waters, Ronald W. *educator, church executive, pastor*

KANSAS

Copeland
Birney, Walter Leroy *religious administrator*

Dodge City
Gilmore, Ronald M. *bishop*

Lawrence
Woodward, Frederick Miller *publisher*

Leavenworth
McGilley, Sister Mary Janet *nun, educator, writer, academic administrator*

Manhattan
Gillispie, Harold Leon *minister*

North Newton
Fast, Darrell Wayne *minister*

Topeka
Mutti, Albert Frederick *minister*
Smalley, William Edward *bishop*

Wichita
Essey, Basil *bishop*
Gerber, Eugene J. *bishop*

MASSACHUSETTS

Plainfield
Reynolds, Frank Everett *religious studies educator*

Taunton
Robertson, Michael Swing *minister*

MICHIGAN

Ann Arbor
Day, Colin Leslie *publisher*

Berrien Springs
Andreasen, Niels-Erik Albinus *religious educator*

Dearborn
Hess, Margaret Johnston *religious writer, educator*

Detroit
Adams, Charles Gilchrist *pastor*
Britt, Kevin M. *bishop*
Maida, Cardinal Adam Joseph *cardinal*
Mc Gehee, H(arry) Coleman, Jr. *bishop*
Silverman, Mark *publisher*
Vigneron, Allen Henry *theology educator, rector, auxiliary bishop*

Farmington
Wine, Sherwin Theodore *rabbi*

Farmington Hills
Plaut, Jonathan Victor *rabbi*

Flint
Meissner, Suzanne Banks *pastoral associate*

Gaylord
Cooney, Patrick Ronald *bishop*

Gladstone
Skogman, Dale R. *retired bishop*

Grand Rapids
Anderson, Roger Gordon *minister*
Barnes, Rosemary Lois *minister*
Borgdorff, Peter *church administrator*
Breitenbeck, Joseph M. *retired bishop*
DeVries, Robert K. *religious book publisher*
Hofman, Leonard John *minister*
Mulder, Gary *religious publisher*
Rozeboom, John A. *religious organization administrator*
Schwanda, Tom *religious studies educator*

Holland
Cook, James Ivan *clergyman, religion educator*

Jackson
Nathaniel, *archbishop*
Popp, Nathaniel *archbishop*

Kalamazoo
Donovan, Paul V. *former bishop*
Murray, James A. *bishop*

Lansing
Mengeling, Carl F. *bishop*

Livonia
Haggard, Joan Claire *church musician, piano instructor, accompanist*

Marquette
Schmitt, Mark F. *bishop*

Midland
Clarkson, William Morris *children's pastor*

Northville
Davis, Lawrence Edward *church official*

Portage
Lee, Edward L. *bishop*

Saginaw
Untener, Kenneth E. *bishop*

Spring Arbor
Thompson, Stanley B. *church administrator*

Warren
Samra, Nicholas James *bishop*

MINNESOTA

Alexandria
Hultstrand, Donald Maynard *bishop*

Anoka
Nelson, Duane Juan *minister*

Bloomington
McDill, Thomas Allison *minister*
Sawatsky, Ben *church administrator*
Thomas, Margaret Jean *clergywoman, religious research consultant*

Cottage Grove
Hudnut, Robert Kilborne *clergyman, author*

Edina
Brown, Laurence David *retired bishop*

Excelsior
Kaufman, Jeffrey Allen *publisher*

Fergus Falls
Egge, Joel *clergy member, academic administrator*
Jahr, Armin N., II *clergy member, church administrator*
Overgaard, Robert Milton *retired religious organization administrator*

Lake Elmo
Schultz, Clarence John *minister*

Little Falls
Zirbes, Mary Kenneth *minister*

Mankato
Orvick, George Myron *church denomination executive, minister*

Minneapolis
Chemberlin, Peg *clergy, religious organization administrator*
Corts, John Ronald *minister, religious organization executive*
Hamel, William John *church administrator, minister*
Larson, David J. *religious organization executive*
Lee, Robert Lloyd *pastor, religious association executive*
Moraczewski, Robert Leo *publisher*
Olson, David Wendell *bishop*

Northfield
Crouter, Richard Earl *religion educator*
Dudley, Paul V. *retired bishop*

Oakdale
Be Vier, William A. *religious studies educator*

Rochester
Rinden, David Lee *clergyman*

Saint Cloud
Kinney, John Francis *bishop*

Saint Paul
Hopper, David Henry *religion educator*
Jaberg, Eugene Carl *theology educator, administrator*
Roach, John Robert *retired archbishop*

Winona
Harrington, Bernard J. *bishop*
Watters, Loras Joseph *bishop*

MISSOURI

Excelsior Springs
Mitchell, Earl Wesley *clergyman*

Fayette
Davis, H(umphrey) Denny *publisher*
Keeling, Joe Keith *religion educator, college official and dean*

Hazelwood
Rose, Joseph Hugh *clergyman*
Urshan, Nathaniel Andrew *minister, church administrator*

Independence
Booth, Paul Wayne *retired minister*
Lindgren, A(lan) Bruce *church administrator*
Tyree, Alan Dean *clergyman*

Jefferson City
Kelley, Patrick Michael *minister, state legislator*
King, Robert Henry *minister, church denomination executive, former educator*

Joplin
Minor, Ronald Ray *minister*
Wilson, Aaron Martin *religious studies educator, college executive*

Kansas City
Boland, Raymond James *bishop*
Cunningham, Paul George *minister*
Diehl, James Harvey *church administrator*
Estep, Michael R. *church administrator*
Gray, Helen Theresa Gott *religion editor*
Juarez, Martin *priest*
Knight, John Allan *clergyman, philosophy and religion educator*
Petosa, Jason Joseph *publisher*
Stone, Jack *religious organization administrator*
Sullivan, Bill M. *church administrator*
Vogel, Arthur Anton *clergyman*

Poplar Bluff
Black, Ronnie Delane *religious organization administrator, mayor*

Saint Louis
Baumer, Martha Ann *minister*
Gaulke, Earl H. *religious publisher and editor, clergyman*
Hebermehl, Rodger *executive director lutheran ministries*
Mahsman, David Lawrence *religious publications editor*
Naumann, Joseph Fred *bishop*
O'Shoney, Glenn *church administrator*
Poellot, Luther *minister*
Rigali, Justin F. *archbishop*
Rosin, Walter L. *retired religious organization administrator*
Weber, Gloria Richie *retired minister, retired state legislator*
Wiley, Gregory Robert *publisher*
Wilke, LeRoy *church administrator*

Springfield
Gillming, Kenneth *church administrator*
Trask, Thomas Edward *religious organization administrator*

NEBRASKA

Grand Island
Zichek, Melvin Eddie *retired clergyman, educator*

Lincoln
Wiersbe, Warren Wendell *clergyman, author, lecturer*

Omaha
Zuerlein, Damian Joseph *priest*

NEW YORK

Cambridge
Kriss, Gary W(ayne) *Episcopal priest*

NORTH DAKOTA

Bismarck
Zipfel, Paul A. *bishop*

Fargo
Foss, Richard John *bishop*
Sullivan, James Stephen *bishop*

Minot AFB
Luckett, Byron Edward, Jr. *chaplain, career officer*

OHIO

Beavercreek
Clarke, Cornelius Wilder *religious organization administrator, minister*

Cincinnati
Harrington, Jeremy Thomas *priest, publishing executive*
Linsey, Nathaniel L. *bishop*
Moeddel, Carl K. *bishop*
O'Donnell, Robert Patrick *priest*
Pilarczyk, Daniel Edward *archbishop*
Zola, Gary Phillip *rabbi, historian, religious educational administrator*

Circleville
Norman, Jack Lee *church administrator, consultant*
Tipton, Daniel L. *religious organization executive*

Cleveland
Abrams, Sylvia Fleck *religious studies educator*
Buhrow, William Carl *religious organization administrator*
Guffey, Edith Ann *religious organization administrator*
Williams, Arthur Benjamin, Jr. *bishop*

Columbus
Kefauver, Weldon Addison *publisher*
Simms, Lowelle *synod executive*

Findlay
Fry, Charles George *theologian, educator*

Lakewood
Sherry, Paul Henry *minister, religious organization administrator*

London
Hughes, Clyde Matthew *religious denomination executive*

Lorain
Quinn, Alexander James *bishop*

New Albany
Brown, Michael Richard *minister*

Oberlin
Zinn, Grover Alfonso, Jr. *religion educator*

Parma
Moskal, Robert M. *bishop*

Sidney
Lawrence, Wayne Allen *publisher*

Steubenville
Scanlan, Michael *priest, academic administrator*
Sheldon, Gilbert Ignatius *clergyman*

Struthers
Sugden, Richard Lee *pastor*

Toledo
Donnelly, Robert *bishop*
Donnelly, Robert William *bishop*
James, William Morgan *bishop*

Wickliffe
Pevec, Anthony Edward *bishop*

PENNSYLVANIA

Beyer
Cornell, William Harvey *clergyman*

SOUTH DAKOTA

Rapid City
Cupich, Blase *bishop*

Sioux Falls
Carlson, Robert James *bishop*
Cowles, Ronald Eugene *church administrator*

Watertown
Witcher, Gary Royal *minister, educator*

VERMONT

Quechee
Wood, Jr. R. Stewart *retired bishop*

Wolcott
Fisher, Neal Floyd *religious organization administrator*

WISCONSIN

Appleton
Abitz, James H. *religious organization executive*

Ohlde, Frederick A. *religious organization executive*
Weber, Steven A. *religious organization executive*

Green Bay
Banks, Robert J. *bishop*
Morneau, Robert Fealey *bishop, writer*

Iola
Mishler, Clifford Leslie *publisher*

La Crosse
Burke, Raymond L. *bishop*

Madison
Bullock, William Henry *bishop*
Enslin, Jon S. *bishop*
Fox, Michael Vass *Hebrew educator*

Milwaukee
Hirsch, June Schaut *chaplain*
Weakland, Rembert G. *archbishop*

Superior
Fliss, Raphael M. *bishop*

CANADA

MANITOBA

Churchill
Rouleau, Reynald *bishop*

Otterburne
McKinney, Larry *religious organization administrator*

The Pas
Sutton, Peter Alfred *former archbishop*

Winnipeg
Wall, Leonard J. *bishop*

ONTARIO

London
Sherlock, John Michael *bishop*

Saint Catharines
O'Mara, John Aloysius *bishop*

ADDRESS UNPUBLISHED

Bayne, David Cowan *priest, legal scholar, law educator*
Castle, Howard Blaine *retired religious organization administrator*
Christopher, Sharon A. Brown *bishop*
Craig, Judith *bishop*
Dipko, Thomas Earl *retired minister, national church executive*
Duecker, Robert Sheldon *retired bishop*
Eitrheim, Norman Duane *bishop*
Forst, Marion Francis *bishop*
Frankson-Kendrick, Sarah Jane *publisher*
Griffin, James Anthony *bishop*
Gumbleton, Thomas J. *bishop*
Haines, Lee Mark, Jr. *religious denomination administrator*
Hernandez, Ramon Robert *retired clergyman and librarian*
Hill, Paul Mark *clergyman*
Holle, Reginald Henry *retired bishop*
Huras, William David *retired bishop*
Hurn, Raymond Walter *minister, religious order administrator*
Jones, William Augustus, Jr. *retired bishop*
Kempski, Ralph Aloisius *bishop*
Kucera, Daniel William *retired bishop*
Lucas, Bert Albert *pastor, social services administrator, consultant*
McClellan, Larry Allen *educator, writer, minister*
Miller, Vernon Dallace *retired minister*
Mischke, Carl Herbert *religious association executive, retired*
Muckerman, Norman James *priest, writer*
Nycklemoe, Glenn Winston *bishop*
Povish, Kenneth Joseph *retired bishop*
Preus, David Walter *bishop, minister*
Rockwell, Hays Hamilton *bishop*
Rose, Robert John *bishop*
Schmitt, Howard Stanley *minister*
Shaw, Robert Eugene *retired minister, administrator*
Shotwell, Malcolm Green *retired minister*
Sparks, William Sheral *retired seminary librarian*
Stines, Fred, Jr. *publisher*
Thompson, Richard Lloyd *pastor*
Wantland, William Charles *retired bishop, lawyer*
Weinkauf, Mary Louise Stanley *clergywoman*

SCIENCE: LIFE SCIENCE

UNITED STATES

CALIFORNIA

Rohnert Park
Schafer, John Francis *retired plant pathologist*

DISTRICT OF COLUMBIA

Washington
Kass, Leon Richard

ILLINOIS

Argonne
Schriesheim, Alan *research administrator*

Berwyn
Parker, Alan John *veterinary neurologist, educator, researcher*

Brookfield
Rabb, George Bernard *zoologist, conservationist*

Burr Ridge
Rosenberg, Robert Brinkmann *technology organization executive*

Carbondale
Bozzola, John Joseph *botany educator, researcher*
Burr, Brooks Milo *zoology educator*
Kapusta, George *botany educator, agronomy educator*
Renzaglia, Karen A. *biologist, educator*

Champaign
Batzli, George Oliver *ecology educator*
Levin, Geoffrey Arthur *botanist*
Ridlen, Samuel Franklin *agriculture educator*
Sanderson, Glen Charles *science director*
Smarr, Larry Lee *science administrator, educator, astrophysicist*

Chicago
Arzbaecher, Robert C(harles) *research institute executive, electrical engineer, researcher*
Beattie, Ted Arthur *zoological gardens and aquarium administrator*
Bell, Kevin J. *zoological park administrator*
Chakrabarty, Ananda Mohan *microbiologist*
Cohen, Edward Philip *microbiology and immunology educator, physician*
Davidson, Richard Laurence *geneticist, educator*
Desjardins, Claude *physiologist, dean*
Ernest, J. Terry *ocular physiologist, educator*
Fuchs, Elaine V. *molecular biologist, educator*
Greenberg, Bernard *entomologist, educator*
Haselkorn, Robert *virology educator*
Houk, James Charles *physiologist, educator*
Lindquist, Susan Lee *biology and microbiology educator*
Mahowald, Anthony Peter *geneticist, developmental biologist, educator*
Mateles, Richard Isaac *biotechnologist*
Pick, Ruth *research scientist, physician, educator*
Pumper, Robert William *microbiologist, educator*
Roizman, Bernard *virologist, educator*
Rothman-Denes, Lucia Beatriz *biology educator*
Rymer, William Zev *research scientist, administrator*
Shirbroun, Richard Elmer *veterinarian, cattleman*
Solaro, Ross John *physiologist, biophysicist*
Storb, Ursula Beate *molecular genetics and cell biology educator*
Straus, Lorna Puttkammer *biology educator*
Van Valen, Leigh *biologist, educator*

Chicago Heights
Miller, Patrick William *research administrator, educator*

Des Plaines
Lee, Bernard Shing-Shu *research company executive*

Evanston
Dallos, Peter John *neurobiologist, educator*
Takahashi, Joseph S. *neuroscientist, educator*
Villa-Komaroff, Lydia *molecular biologist, educator, university official*
Wu, Tai Te *biological sciences and engineering educator*

Harvey
Liem, Khian Kioe *medical entomologist*

Havana
Sparks, Richard Edward *aquatic ecologist*

Hinsdale
Pawley, Ray Lynn *zoological park consultant, real estate developer*

Lisle
Davis, Gregory Thomas *marine surveyor*
Donnelly, Gerard Thomas *arboretum director*

Macomb
Anderson, Richard Vernon *ecology educator, researcher*

Mount Prospect
Garvin, Paul Joseph, Jr. *toxicologist*

Northbrook
King, Robert Charles *biologist, educator*

Peoria
Kurtzman, Cletus Paul *microbiologist, researcher*

Rock Island
Dziadyk, Bohdan *botany and ecology educator*

Springfield
Munyer, Edward A. *zoologist, museum administrator*

Urbana
Banwart, Wayne Lee *agronomy, environmental science educator*
Berenbaum, May Roberta *entomology educator*
Buetow, Dennis Edward *physiologist, educator*
Chow, Poo *wood technologist, scientist*
Crang, Richard Francis Earl *plant and cell biologist, research center administrator*
Dziuk, Philip John *animal scientist educator*
Endress, Anton G. *horticulturist, educator*
Frazzetta, Thomas Henry *evolutionary biologist, functional morphologist, educator*
Friedman, Stanley *insect physiologist, educator*
Garrigus, Upson Stanley *animal science and international agriculture educator*
Greenough, William Tallant *psychobiologist, educator*
Hanson, John Bernard *retired botanist, agronomy and plant biology educator*
Heichel, Gary Harold *crop sciences educator*
Hoeft, Robert Gene *agriculture educator*
Hoffmeister, Donald Frederick *zoology educator*
Hymowitz, Theodore *plant geneticist, educator*
Mc Glamery, Marshal Dean *crop scientist, weed science educator*
Meyer, Richard Charles *microbiologist, educator*
Nanney, David Ledbetter *genetics educator*
Nickell, Cecil D. *agronomy educator*
Rebeiz, Constantin A. *plant physiology educator, laboratory director*
Ridgway, Marcella Davies *veterinarian*
Seigler, David Stanley *botanist, chemist, educator*
Small, Erwin *veterinarian, educator*
Stevenson, Frank J. *soil scientist, educator*
Stout, Glenn Emanuel *retired science administrator*
Waldbauer, Gilbert Peter *entomologist, educator*
Whitt, Gregory Sidney *evolution educator*
Wolfe, Ralph Stoner *microbiology educator*

Watseka
Neumann, Frederick Lloyd *plant breeder*

West Chicago
Hauptmann, Randal Mark *biotechnologist*

INDIANA

Bloomington
DeVoe, Robert Donald *visual physiologist*
Gest, Howard *microbiologist, educator*
Hammel, Harold Theodore *physiology and biophysics educator, researcher*
Hites, Ronald Atlee *environmental science educator, chemist*
Ketterson, Ellen D. *biologist, educator*
Nolan, Val, Jr. *biologist, lawyer*
Preer, John Randolph, Jr. *biology educator*
Ruesink, Albert William *biologist, plant sciences educator*
Steinmetz, Joseph Edward *neuroscience and psychology educator*
Weinberg, Eugene David *microbiologist, educator*

Chesterton
Wiemann, Marion Russell, Jr. (Baron of Camster) *biologist*

Crawfordsville
Simmons, Emory G. *mycologist, microbiologist, botanist, educator*

Greenfield
Wolff, Ronald Keith *toxicologist, researcher*

Hammond
Gealt, Michael A. *environmental microbiologist, educator*

Indianapolis
Borst, Philip Craig *veterinarian, councilman*
Christian, Joe Clark *medical genetics researcher, educator*
Follas, William Daniel *management*
Hartsfield, James Kennedy, Jr. *geneticist, orthodontist*
Jones, Robert Brooke *microbiologist, educator, associate dean*
Ochs, Sidney *neurophysiology educator*
Rhoades, Rodney Allen *physiologist, educator*

Lafayette
Achgill, Ralph Kenneth *retired research scientist*
Nicholson, Ralph Lester *botanist, educator*
Rao, Palakurthi S.C. *soil science educator*

Muncie
Hendrix, Jon Richard *biology educator*
Henzlik, Raymond Eugene *zoophysiologist, educator*
Mertens, Thomas Robert *biology educator*

Notre Dame
Burns, Peter C. *science educator, engineering educator*
Jensen, Richard Jorg *biology educator*
Pollard, Morris *microbiologist, educator*

Terre Haute
Dusanic, Donald Gabriel *parasitology educator, microbiologist*

West Lafayette
Albright, Jack Lawrence *animal science and veterinary educator*
Amstutz, Harold Emerson *veterinarian, educator*
Axtell, John David *genetics educator, researcher*
Borgens, Richard *biologist*
Bracker, Charles E. *plant pathology educator and researcher*
Edwards, Charles Richard *entomology and pest management educator*
Harmon, Bud Gene *animal sciences educator, consultant*
Hoover, William Leichliter *forestry and natural resources educator, financial consultant*
Hunt, Michael O'Leary *wood science and engineering educator*
Janick, Jules *horticultural scientist, educator*
Johannsen, Chris Jakob *agronomist, educator, administrator*
Le Master, Dennis Clyde *natural resource economics and policy educator*
McFee, William Warren *soil scientist*
Nelson, Philip Edwin *food scientist, educator*
Norton, Lloyd Darrell *research soil scientist*
Ohm, Herbert Willis *agronomy educator*
Ortman, Eldon E. *entomologist, educator*
Schreiber, Marvin Mandel *agronomist, educator*
Sherman, Louis Allen *biology educator*
White, Joe Lloyd *soil scientist, educator*

IOWA

Ames
Anderson, Lloyd Lee *animal science educator*
Beran, George Wesley *veterinary microbiology educator*
Berger, P(hilip) Jeffrey *animal science educator, quantitative geneticist*
Bolin, Steven Robert *veterinarian researcher*
Burris, Joseph Stephen *agronomy educator*
Fehr, Walter Ronald *agronomist, researcher, educator*
Freeman, Albert E. *agricultural science educator*
Ghoshal, Nani Gopal *veterinary anatomist, educator*
Greve, John Henry *veterinary parasitologist, educator*
Hallauer, Arnel Roy *geneticist*
Hatfield, Jerry Lee *plant physiologist, biometeorologist*
Johnson, Lawrence Alan *cereal technologist, educator, administrator*
Karlen, Douglas Lawrence *soil scientist*
Keeney, Dennis Raymond *soil science educator*
Kelly, James Michael *plant and soil scientist*
Mertins, James Walter *entomologist*
Moon, Harley William *veterinarian*
Moore, Kenneth James *agronomy educator*
Munkvold, Gary P. *plant pathologist, educator*
Nutter, Forrest *plant pathologist*
O'Berry, Phillip Aaron *veterinarian*
Owen, Micheal *agronomist, educator*
Ross, Richard Francis *veterinarian, microbiologist, educator, dean*
Seaton, Vaughn Allen *retired veterinary pathology educator*
Snow, Joel Alan *research director*
Tylka, Gregory L. *plant pathologist, educator*
Voss, Regis Dale *agronomist, educator*
Wass, Wallace Milton *veterinarian, clinical science educator*
Willham, Richard Lewis *animal science educator*

Des Moines
Rosen, Matthew Stephen *botanist, consultant*

Eldora
Kerns, Steve *geneticist*

Grinnell
Walker, Waldo Sylvester *biology educator, academic administrator*

Iowa City
Cruden, Robert William *botany educator*
Gibson, David Thomas *microbiology educator*
Hausler, William John, Jr. *microbiologist, educator, public health laboratory administrator*
Husted, Russell Forest *research scientist*
Kessel, Richard Glen *zoology educator*
Koontz, Frank P. *microbiology educator, research administrator*
Maxson, Linda Ellen *biologist, educator*
Pessin, Jeffrey E. *physiology educator*
Stay, Barbara *zoologist, educator*
Wunder, Charles C(ooper) *physiology and biophysics educator, gravitational biologist*

Johnston
Duvick, Donald Nelson *plant breeder*

KANSAS

Emporia
Sundberg, Marshall David *biology educator*

Hays
Coyne, Patrick Ivan *physiological ecologist*

Kansas City
Behbehani, Abbas M. *clinical virologist, educator*
Cheney, Paul D. *physiologist , educator*
Doull, John *toxicologist, pharmacologist*
Greenwald, Gilbert Saul *physiologist*
Klaassen, Curtis D. *toxicologist, educator*
Samson, Frederick Eugene, Jr. *neuroscientist, educator*

Lawrence
Armitage, Kenneth Barclay *biology educator, ecologist*
Byers, George William *retired entomology educator*
Johnston, Richard Fourness *biologist, educator*
Lane, Meredith Anne *botany educator, museum curator*
Lichtwardt, Robert William *mycologist*
Michener, Charles Duncan *entomologist, researcher, entomologist, educator*
Shankel, Delbert Merrill *microbiology and biology educator*

Manhattan
Erickson, Howard Hugh *veterinarian, physiology educator*
Johnson, Terry Charles *biologist, educator*
Kaufman, Donald Wayne *research ecologist*
Kirkham, M. B. *plant physiologist, educator*
Mengel, David Bruce *agronomy and soil science educator*
Posler, Gerry Lynn *agronomist, educator*
Richard, Patrick *science research administrator, nuclear scientist*

Parsons
Lomas, Lyle Wayne *agricultural research administrator, educator*

Topeka
Mara, John Lawrence *retired veterinarian, consultant*

MASSACHUSETTS

Woods Hole
Milkman, Roger Dawson *genetics educator, molecular evolution researcher*

MICHIGAN

Ann Arbor
Akil, Huda *neuroscientist, educator, researcher*
Alexander, Richard Dale *zoology educator*

Allen, Sally Lyman *biologist*
Anderson, William R. *botanist, educator, curator*
Dawson, William Ryan *zoology educator*
Drach, John Charles *scientist, educator*
Easter, Stephen Sherman, Jr. *biology educator*
Evans, Francis Cope *retired ecologist*
Faulkner, John Arthur *physiologist, educator*
Gelehrter, Thomas David *medical and genetics educator, physician*
Ginsburg, David *human genetics educator, researcher*
Hawkins, Joseph Elmer, Jr. *retired acoustic physiologist, educator*
Horowitz, Samuel Boris *biomedical researcher, educational consultant*
Kaufman, Peter Bishop *biological sciences educator*
Kostyo, Jack Lawrence *physiology educator*
Lowe, John Burton *molecular biology educator, pathologist*
Moore, Thomas Edwin *biology educator, museum director*
Mourou, Gerard A. *research administrator*
Neidhardt, Frederick Carl *microbiologist, educator*
Richardson, Rudy James *toxicology and neurosciences educator*
Savageau, Michael Antonio *microbiology and immunology educator*
Shappirio, David Gordon *biologist, educator*
Stoermer, Eugene Filmore *biologist, educator*
Williams, John Andrew *physiology educator, consultant*

Augusta
Johnson, Wilbur Corneal (Joe Johnson) *wildlife biologist*

Bay City
Nicholson, William Noel *clinical neuropsychologist*

Dearborn
Schneider, Michael Joseph *biologist*

Detroit
Beierwaltes, William Howard *physiologist, educator*
Krawetz, Stephen Andrew *molecular medicine and genetics scientist*
Novak, Raymond Francis *environmental health/toxicology research institute director, pharmacology educator*
Phillis, John Whitfield *physiologist, educator*

East Lansing
Bukovac, Martin John *horticulturist, educator*
Dennis, Frank George, Jr. *retired horticulture educator*
Fischer, Lawrence Joseph *toxicologist, educator*
Fluck, Michele M(arguerite) *biology educator*
Fromm, Paul Oliver *physiology educator*
Hackel, Emanuel *science educator*
Hollingworth, Robert Michael *toxicology researcher*
Johnson, John Irwin, Jr. *neuroscientist*
Keegstra, Kenneth G. *plant biochemistry administrator*
Kende, Hans Janos *plant physiology educator*
Lenski, Richard Eimer *evolutionary biologist, educator*
Lucas, Robert Elmer *soil scientist, researcher*
McMeekin, Dorothy *botany, plant pathology educator*
Patterson, Maria Jevitz *microbiology-pediatric infectious disease educator*
Paul, Eldor Alvin *agriculture, ecology educator*
Petrides, George Athan *ecologist, educator*
Root-Bernstein, Robert Scott *biologist, educator*
Tiedje, James Michael *microbiology educator, ecologist*
Witter, Richard Lawrence *veterinarian, educator*

Edwardsburg
Floyd, Alton David *cell biologist, consultant*

Grand Rapids
Carlotti, Ronald John *food scientist*

Hickory Corners
Lauff, George Howard *biologist*

Kalamazoo
Marshall, Vincent de Paul *industrial microbiologist, researcher*

Ludington
Denner, Melvin Walter *retired life sciences educator*

Midland
Bus, James Stanley *toxicologist*

Rochester
Unakar, Nalin Jayantilal *biological sciences educator*

Sanford
Wilmot, Thomas Ray *medical entomologist, educator*

MINNESOTA

Duluth
Heller, Lois Jane *physiologist, educator, researcher*
Johnson, Arthur Gilbert *microbiology educator*

Minneapolis
Dworkin, Martin *microbiologist, educator*
Gorham, Eville *ecologist, biogeochemist*
Haase, Ashley Thomson *microbiology educator, researcher*
Hill, Tessa *president non profit environmental group*
Huang, Victor Tsangmin *food scientist, researcher*
Knuth, Russ *histologist, radio personality*
Meyer, Maurice Wesley *physiologist, dentist, neurologist*
Rahman, Yueh-Erh *biologist*
Watson, Dennis Wallace *microbiology educator, scientist*

Moorhead
Gee, Robert LeRoy *agriculturist, dairy farmer*

Morris
Ordway, Ellen *biology educator, entomology researcher*

Rochester
Maher, L. James, III *molecular biologist*
Shepherd, John Thompson *physiologist*

Saint Paul
Barnwell, Franklin Hershel *zoology educator*
Busch, Robert Henry *geneticist, researcher*
Bushnell, William Rodgers *agricultural research scientist*
Cheng, H(wei) H(sien) *soil scientist, agronomic and environmental science educator*
Davis, Margaret Bryan *paleoecology researcher, educator*
Diesch, Stanley La Verne *veterinarian, educator*
Ehlke, Nancy Jo *agronomist*
Ek, Alan Ryan *forestry educator*
Johnson, Kenneth Harvey *veterinary pathologist*
Kommedahl, Thor *plant pathology educator*
Leonard, Kurt John *plant pathologist, retired university program director*
Magee, Paul Terry *geneticist and molecular biologist, college dean*
May, Georgiana *biologist, educator*
McKinnell, Robert Gilmore *zoology, genetics and cell biology educator*
Phillips, Ronald Lewis *plant geneticist, educator*
Roy, Robert Russell *toxicologist*
Stadelmann, Eduard Joseph *plant physiologist, educator, researcher*
Tordoff, Harrison Bruce *retired zoologist, educator*

MISSOURI

Columbia
Blevins, Dale Glenn *agronomy educator*
Brown, Olen Ray *medical microbiology and toxicology research educator, consultant, writer*
Eisenstark, Abraham *research director, microbiologist*
Finkelstein, Richard Alan *retired microbiology educator, consultant*
Ignoffo, Carlo Michael *insect pathologist-virologist*
Morehouse, Lawrence Glen *veterinarian, educator*
Munson, Richard Howard *horticulturist*
Poehlmann, Carl John *agronomist, researcher*
Vogt, Albert Ralph *forester, educator, program director*
Wagner, Joseph Edward *veterinarian, educator*
Yanders, Armon Frederick *biological sciences educator, research administrator*

Eureka
Lindsey, Susan Lyndaker *zoologist*
Sexton, Owen James *vertebrate ecology educator, conservationist*

Jefferson City
Reidinger, Russell Frederick, Jr. *fish and wildlife scientist*

Kansas City
Mc Kelvey, John Clifford *retired research institute executive*

Saint Charles
Radke, Rodney Owen *agricultural research executive, consultant*

Saint Louis
Agrawal, Harish Chandra *neurobiologist, researcher, educator*
Allen, Garland Edward *biology educator, science historian*
Beachy, Roger *biologist, plant pathology researcher*
Curran, Michael Walter *research scientist, director*
Curtiss, Roy, III *biology educator*
Fraley, Robert T. *biotechnologist*
Green, Maurice *molecular biologist, virologist, educator*
Hoessle, Charles Herman *zoo director*
Hultgren, Scott J. *microbiologist educator*
Laskowski, Leonard Francis, Jr. *microbiologist*
Murray, Patrick Robert *microbiologist, educator*
Raven, Peter Hamilton *botanical garden director, botany educator*
Schaal, Barbara Anna *evolutionary biologist, educator*
Schlesinger, Milton J. *virology educator, researcher*
Templeton, Alan Robert *biology educator*
Wold, William Sydney *molecular biology educator*

Springfield
Steffen, Alan Leslie *entomologist*

Wentzville
Garrett, Dwayne Everett *veterinary clinic executive*

West Plains
Wilcoxson, Roy Dell *plant pathology educator and researcher*

Windyville
Condron, Barbara O'Guinn *metaphysics educator, school administrator, publisher*

NEBRASKA

Gering
Weihing, John Lawson *plant pathologist, state senator*

Lincoln
Dierks, Merton Lyle *veterinarian*
Estes, James Russell *botanist, educator*
Francis, Charles Andrew *agronomy educator, consultant*
Gardner, Charles Olda *plant geneticist and breeder, design consultant, analyst*
Genoways, Hugh Howard *systematic biologist, educator*
Massengale, Martin Andrew *agronomist, university president*
McClurg, James Edward *research laboratory executive*
Sander, Donald Henry *soil scientist, researcher*
Specht, James E. *agronomist, educator*
Swartzendruber, Dale *soil physicist, educator*
Taylor, Stephen Lloyd *food toxicologist, educator, food scientist*
Vidaver, Anne K. *plant pathologist, educator*
Vidaver, Anne Marie *plant pathology educator*

Omaha
Badeer, Henry Sarkis *physiology educator*
Rogan, Eleanor Groeniger *cancer researcher, educator*
Simmons, Lee Guyton, Jr. *zoological park director*

NEW MEXICO

Las Cruces
Tonn, Robert James *retired entomologist*

NEW YORK

Alexandria Bay
Fisher, Lester Emil *zoo administrator*

Ithaca
Chiang, Huai Chang *entomologist, educator*

NORTH CAROLINA

Greensboro
O'Brien, William John *ecology researcher*

NORTH DAKOTA

Bismarck
Carlisle, Ronald Dwight *nursery owner*

Grand Forks
Crawford, Richard Dwight *biology educator, wildlife biology researcher*
Fox, Carl Alan *research executive*

OHIO

Akron
Millman, Irving *microbiologist, educator, retired inventor*

Athens
Ungar, Irwin Allan *botany educator*

Bowling Green
Clark, Eloise Elizabeth *biologist, educator*
Heckman, Carol A. *biology educator*

Cincinnati
Etges, Frank Joseph *parasitology educator*
Maruska, Edward Joseph *zoo administrator*
Monaco, John J. *molecular genetics research educator*
Saal, Howard Max *clinical geneticist, pediatrician, educator*
Safferman, Robert Samuel *microbiologist, researcher*
Schaefer, Frank William, III *microbiologist, researcher*
Schiff, Gilbert Martin *virologist, microbiologist, medical educator*
Sperelakis, Nicholas, Sr. *physiology and biophysics educator, researcher*

Cleveland
Blackwell, John *science educator*
Caplan, Arnold I. *biology educator*
Dell'Osso, Louis Frank *neuroscience educator*
Herrup, Karl *neurobiologist*
Perry, George *neuroscientist, educator*
Steinberg, Arthur G(erald) *geneticist*
Suri, Jasjit S. *research scientist*
Taylor, Steve Henry *zoologist*

Columbus
Boerner, Ralph E. J. *forest soil ecologist, plant biology educator*
Capen, Charles Chabert *veterinary pathology educator*
Crawford, Daniel J. *biologist, educator*
Disinger, John Franklin *natural resources educator*
Fawcett, Sherwood Luther *research laboratory executive*
Floyd, Gary Leon *plant cell biologist*
Fry, Donald Lewis *physiologist, educator*
Glaser, Ronald *microbiology educator, scientist*
Haury, David Leroy *science education specialist*
Kapral, Frank Albert *medical microbiology and immunology educator*
Miller, Paul Dean *breeding consultant, geneticist, educator*
Needham, Glen Ray *entomology and acarology educator, researcher*
Olesen, Douglas Eugene *research institute executive*
Olsen, Richard George *microbiology educator*
Peterle, Tony John *zoologist, educator*
Pieper, Heinz Paul *physiology educator*
Reeve, John Newton *molecular biology and microbiology educator*
Roth, Robert Earl *environmental educator*
Triplehorn, Charles A. *entomology educator, insects curator*
von Recum, Andreas F. *veterinarian, bioengineer*
Warmbrod, James Robert *agriculture educator, university administrator*
Westman, Judith Ann *clinical geneticist*
Wood, Jackie Dale *physiologist, educator, researcher*
Yohn, David Stewart *virologist, science administrator*
Zartman, David Lester *animal sciences educator, researcher*

Cumberland
Reece, Robert William *zoological park administrator*

Dayton
Isaacson, Milton Stanley *research and development company executive, engineer*

Delaware
Fry, Anne Evans *zoology educator*

Milford
Gascoigne, William M. *research executive*

Newark
Greenstein, Julius Sidney *zoology educator*

Oxford
Eshbaugh, W(illiam) Hardy *botanist, educator*
Rypstra, Ann *zoology educator*

Powell
Borin, Gerald W. *zoological park administrator*

Wooster
Cooper, Richard Lee *agronomist, educator*
Ferree, David Curtis *horticultural researcher*
Hall, Franklin R. *entomology researcher, educator*
Hoitink, Henricus A. *plant pathology educator*
Madden, Laurence Vincent *plant pathology educator*

OREGON

Corvallis
Kirby, Ronald Eugene *fish and wildlife research administrator*

SOUTH DAKOTA

Vermillion
Langworthy, Thomas Allan *microbiologist, educator*

Volga
Moldenhauer, William Calvin *soil scientist*

TEXAS

College Station
Morgan, Roger John *research scientist, university official*

WISCONSIN

Beloit
Burris, John Edward *biologist, educator, academic administrator*

Madison
Barnes, Robert F *agronomist*
Bisgard, Gerald Edwin *biosciences educator, researcher*
Borisy, Gary G. *molecular biology educator*
Brock, Thomas Dale *microbiology educator*
Burkholder, Wendell Eugene *retired entomology educator, researcher*
Dolan, Terrence Raymond *neurophysiology educator*
Easterday, Bernard Carlyle *veterinary medicine educator*
Ensign, Jerald C. *bacteriology educator*
Evert, Ray Franklin *botany educator*
Greaser, Marion Lewis *science educator*
Hagedorn, Donald James *phytopathologist, educator, agricultural consultant*
Hall, David Charles *retired zoo director, veterinarian*
Hopen, Herbert John *horticulture educator*
Iltis, Hugh Hellmut *plant taxonomist-evolutionist, educator*
Jackson, Marion Leroy *agronomist, soil scientist*
Jeanne, Robert Lawrence *entomologist, educator*
Kaesberg, Paul Joseph *virology researcher*
Kemnitz, Joseph William *physiologist, researcher*
Kimble, Judith E. *molecular biologist, cell biologist*
Lillesand, Thomas Martin *remote sensing educator*
Magnuson, John Joseph *zoology educator*
Moss, Richard L. *physiology educator*
Olson, Norman Fredrick *food science educator*
Peterson, David Maurice *plant physiologist, research leader*
Ris, Hans *zoologist, educator*
Sharkey, Thomas David *educator, botanist*
Sheffield, Lewis Glosson *physiologist*
Susman, Millard *geneticist, educator*
Szybalski, Waclaw *molecular geneticist, educator*
Welker, Wallace Irving *neurophysiologist, educator*
White, John Graham *science educator, research director*
Zedler, Joy Buswell *ecological sciences educator*

Middleton
Horsch, Robert B. *biotechnologist*

Milwaukee
Besharse, Joseph Culp *cell biologist, researcher*
Boese, Gil Karyle *cultural organization executive*
Cowley, Allen Wilson, Jr. *physiologist, educator*
Wikenhauser, Charles *zoological park administrator*

Shawano
Heikes, Keith *science administrator*

Hildebrand, Roger Henry *astrophysicist, physicist*
Huston, John Lewis *chemistry educator*
Iqbal, Zafar Mohd *cancer researcher, biochemist, pharmacologist, toxicologist, consultant, molecular biologist*
Kadanoff, Leo Philip *physicist, educator*
Kleppa, Ole J. *chemistry educator*
Kouvel, James Spyros *physicist, educator*
Levi-Setti, Riccardo *physicist, director*
Liao, Shutsung *biochemist, oncologist*
Lundberg, Joe *meteorologist, radio personality*
Makinen, Marvin William *biophysicist, educator*
Margoliash, Emanuel *biochemist, educator*
Miller, Brant *meteorologist*
Nagel, Sidney Robert *physics educator*
Nambu, Yoichiro *physics educator*
Newcomb, Martin Eugene, Jr. *chemistry educator*
Norris, James Rufus, Jr. *chemist, educator*
Oehme, Reinhard *physicist, educator*
Oka, Takeshi *physicist, chemist, astronomer, educator*
Olsen, Edward John *geologist, educator, curator*
Oxtoby, David William *chemistry educator*
Palmer, Patrick Edward *radio astronomer, educator*
Platzman, George William *geophysicist, educator*
Rosner, Jonathan Lincoln *physicist, educator*
Rosner, Robert *astrophysicist, educator*
Sager, William Frederick *retired chemistry educator*
Schug, Kenneth Robert *chemistry educator*
Skilling, Thomas Ethelbert, III *meteorologist, meteorology educator*
Steck, Theodore Lyle *biochemistry and molecular biology educator, physician*
Steinmetz, Richard *geologist, petroleum company executive*
Truran, James Wellington, Jr. *astrophysicist, educator*
Turner, Michael Stanley *astrophysics educator*
Williams-Ashman, Howard Guy *biochemist, educator*
Winston, Roland *physicist, educator*
York, Donald Gilbert *astronomy educator, researcher*

Dekalb
Kimball, Clyde William *physicist, educator*
Rossing, Thomas D. *physics educator*

Downers Grove
Hubbard, Lincoln Beals *medical physicist, consultant*
Shen, Sin-Yan *physicist, conductor, acoustics specialist, music director*

Evanston
Basolo, Fred *chemistry educator*
Burwell, Robert Lemmon, Jr. *chemist, educator*
Chang, R. P. H. *materials science educator*
Freeman, Arthur J. *physics educator*
Ibers, James Arthur *chemist, educator*
Johnson, David Lynn *materials scientist, educator*
Lambert, Joseph Buckley *chemistry educator*
Letsinger, Robert Lewis *chemistry educator*
Meshii, Masahiro *materials science educator*
Mirkin, Chad A. *chemistry educator*
Oakes, Robert James *physics educator*
Olson, Gregory Bruce *materials science and engineering educator, academic director*
Pople, John Anthony *chemistry educator*
Sachtler, Wolfgang Max Hugo *chemistry educator*
Seidman, David N(athaniel) *materials science and engineering educator*
Shriver, Duward Felix *chemistry educator, researcher, consultant*
Silverman, Richard Bruce *chemist, biochemist, educator*
Spears, Kenneth George *chemistry educator*
Taam, Ronald Everett *physics and astronomy educator*
Ulmer, Melville Paul *physics and astronomy educator*
Walter, Robert Irving *chemistry educator, chemist*
Weertman, Johannes *materials science educator*
Weertman, Julia Randall *materials science and engineering educator*
Wessels, Bruce W. *materials scientist, educator*

Glen Ellyn
Mooring, F. Paul *physics editor*

Glenview
Rorig, Kurt Joachim *chemist, research director*

Hinsdale
Kaminsky, Manfred Stephan *physicist*

Lake Forest
Weston, Arthur Walter *chemist, scientific and business executive*

Lemont
Williams, Jack Marvin *research chemist*

Maywood
Schultz, Richard Michael *biochemistry educator, researcher*

Naperville
Sherren, Anne Terry *chemistry educator*

North Chicago
Loga, Sanda *physicist, educator*

Northfield
Shabica, Charles Wright *geologist, earth science educator*

Oak Park
Fanta, Paul Edward *chemist, educator*

Peoria
Cunningham, Raymond Leo *retired research chemist*

Rock Island
Anderson, Richard Charles *geology educator*
Hammer, William Roy *paleontologist, educator*

Rockford
Walhout, Justine Simon *chemistry educator*

Round Lake
Breillatt, Julian Paul, Jr. *biochemist, biomedical engineer*

Urbana
Beak, Peter Andrew *chemistry educator*
Birnbaum, Howard Kent *materials science educator*
Bishop, Stephen Gray *physicist*
Cahill, David G. *materials science educator, engineering educator*
Ceperley, David Matthew *physics educator*
Crofts, Antony Richard *biochemistry and biophysics educator*
Crutcher, Richard Metcalf *astronomer, educator*
Dunn, Floyd *biophysicist, bioengineer, educator*
Ehrlich, Gert *science educator, researcher*
Ginsberg, Donald Maurice *physicist, educator*
Goldwasser, Edwin Leo *physicist*
Govindjee, *biophysics, biochemistry, and biology educator*
Greene, Joseph E. *material science researcher*
Greene, Laura Helen *physicist*
Gruebele, Martin *chemistry, physics, and biophysics educator*
Iben, Icko, Jr. *astrophysicist, educator*
Jonas, Jiri *chemistry educator*
Katzenellenbogen, John Albert *chemistry educator*
Kirkpatrick, R(obert) James *geology educator*
Klein, Miles Vincent *physics educator*
Kushner, Mark Jay *physics and engineering educator*
Lauterbur, Paul C(hristian) *chemistry educator*
Makri, Nancy *chemistry educator*
Mantulin, William W. *biophysicist, laboratory director*
Mapother, Dillon Edward *physicist, university official*
Pirkle, William H. *chemistry educator*
Rowland, Theodore Justin *physicist, educator*
Salamon, Myron Ben *physicist, educator, dean*
Schweizer, Kenneth Steven *physics educator*
Simon, Jack Aaron *geologist, former state official*
Snyder, Lewis Emil *astrophysicist, educator*
Suslick, Kenneth Sanders *chemistry educator*
Switzer, Robert Lee *biochemistry educator*
Van Harlingen, Dale *physics educator*
Woese, Carl R. *biophysicist, microbiology educator*
Zimmerman, Steven Charles *chemistry educator*

Wheaton
Wolfram, Thomas *physicist, educator*

INDIANA

Bloomington
Cameron, John M. *nuclear scientist, educator, science administrator*
Davidson, Ernest Roy *chemist, educator*
Edmondson, Frank Kelley *retired astronomer*
Hanson, Gail G. *physicist, educator*
Hattin, Donald Edward *geologist, educator*
Johnson, Hollis Ralph *astronomy educator*
Kauffman, Erle Galen *geologist, paleontologist*
Lane, N. Gary *retired paleontologist*
Mufson, Stuart Lee *astronomer, educator*
Novotny, Milos Vlastislav *chemistry educator*
Parmenter, Charles Stedman *chemistry educator*
Peters, Dennis Gail *chemist*
Pollock, Robert Elwood *nuclear scientist*

Elkhart
Free, Helen Mae *chemist, consultant*

Fort Wayne
Stevenson, Kenneth Lee *chemist, educator*

Indianapolis
Aprison, Morris Herman *biochemist, experimental and theoretical neurobiologist, emeritus educator*
Bulloff, Jack John *physical chemist, consultant*
Fife, Wilmer Krafft *chemistry educator*
Lau, Pauline Young *chemist*
Mirsky, Arthur *geologist, educator*
Pearlstein, Robert M. *physics educator*
Wong, David T. *biochemist, researcher*

Lafayette
Brewster, James Henry *retired chemistry educator*
Brown, Herbert Charles *chemistry educator*
Feuer, Henry *chemist, educator*
Gartenhaus, Solomon *physicist, educator*
Judd, William Robert *engineering geologist, educator*
Loeffler, Frank Joseph *physicist, educator*
Pardue, Harry L. *chemist, educator*
Porile, Norbert Thomas *chemistry educator*
Whistler, Roy Lester *chemist, educator, industrialist*

Mishawaka
Braunsdorf, James Allen *physics educator*

Muncie
Harris, Joseph McAllister *retired chemist*

Notre Dame
Fehlner, Thomas Patrick *chemistry educator*
Feigl, Dorothy Marie *chemistry educator, university official*
Helquist, Paul M. *chemistry educator, researcher*
Marshalek, Eugene Richard *physics educator, researcher*
Meisel, Dan *chemist*
Scheidt, W. Robert *chemistry educator, researcher*
Schuler, Robert Hugo *chemist, educator*
Thomas, John Kerry *chemistry educator*
Trozzolo, Anthony Marion *chemistry educator*

Terre Haute
Guthrie, Frank Albert *chemistry educator*

West Lafayette
Adelman, Steven Allen *theoretical physical chemist, chemistry educator*
Amy, Jonathan Weekes *scientist, educator*
Barnes, Virgil Everett, II *physics educator*
Cooks, R(obert) Graham *chemist, educator*
Cramer, William Anthony *biochemistry and biophysics researcher, educator*
Diamond, Sidney *chemist, educator*
Grant, Edward Robert *chemistry educator, company executive*
Hanks, Alan R. *chemistry educator*
Laskowski, Michael, Jr. *chemist, educator*
Lipschutz, Michael Elazar *chemistry educator, consultant, researcher*
Margerum, Dale William *chemistry educator*
McMillin, David Robert *chemistry educator*
Melhorn, Wilton Newton *geosciences educator*
Morrison, Harry *chemistry educator, university dean*
Negishi, Ei-ichi *chemistry educator*
Overhauser, Albert Warner *physicist*
Ramdas, Anant Krishna *physicist, optics scientist*
Rossmann, Michael George *biochemist, educator*
Truce, William Everett *chemist, educator*

IOWA

Ames
Armstrong, Daniel Wayne *chemist, educator*
Barnes, Richard George *physicist, educator*
Barton, Thomas Jackson *chemistry educator*
Bowen, George Hamilton, Jr. *astrophysicist, educator*
Clem, John Richard *physicist, educator*
Fritz, James Sherwood *chemist, educator*
Gschneidner, Karl Albert, Jr. *metallurgist, educator, editor, consultant*
Horowitz, Jack *biochemistry educator*
Houk, Robert Samuel *chemistry educator*
Jacobson, Robert Andrew *chemistry educator*
Peterson, Francis *physicist, educator*
Ruedenberg, Klaus *theoretical chemist, educator*
Smith, John Francis *materials science educator*
Svec, Harry John *chemist, educator*
Tabatabai, M. Ali *chemist, biochemist*
Yeung, Edward Szeshing *chemist*

Cedar Falls
Koob, Robert Duane *chemistry educator, educational administrator*

Cedar Rapids
Bahadur, Birendra *display specialist, liquid crystal researcher*
Feller, Steven Allen *physics educator*

Fairfield
Hagelin, John Samuel *theoretical physicist*

Iowa City
Baker, Richard Graves *geology educator, palynologist*
Burton, Donald Joseph *chemistry educator*
Campbell, Kevin Peter *physiology and biophysics educator, researcher*
Donelson, John Everett *biochemistry educator, molecular biologist*
Gurnett, Donald Alfred *physics educator*
Koch, Donald LeRoy *geologist, state agency administrator*
Linhardt, Robert John J *medicinal chemistry educator*
Montgomery, Rex *biochemist, educator*
Nair, Vasu *chemist, educator*
Plapp, Bryce Vernon *biochemistry educator*
Tallent, William Hugh *chemist, research administrator*
Van Allen, James Alfred *physicist, educator*

North Liberty
Glenister, Brian Frederick *geologist, educator*

West Des Moines
Lynch, David William *physicist, educator*

KANSAS

Kansas City
Ebner, Kurt Ewald *biochemistry educator*
Noelken, Milton Edward *biochemistry educator, researcher*

Lawrence
Ammar, Raymond George *physicist, educator*
Angino, Ernest Edward *retired geology educator*
Dreschhoff, Gisela Auguste Marie *physicist, educator*
Enos, Paul *geologist, educator*
Gerhard, Lee Clarence *geologist, educator*
Harmony, Marlin Dale *chemistry educator*
Landgrebe, John Allan *chemistry educator*
Mitscher, Lester Allen *chemist, educator*
Stella, Valentino John *pharmaceutical chemistry educator*

Manhattan
Setser, Donald Wayne *chemistry educator*

Pittsburg
Foresman, James Buckey *geologist, geochemist, industrial hygienist*

Topeka
Barton, Janice Sweeny *chemistry educator*

MICHIGAN

Albion
Green, David William *chemist, educator*

Ann Arbor
Agranoff, Bernard William *biochemist, educator*
Akerlof, Carl William *physics educator*
Aller, Hugh Duncan *astronomer, educator*
Ashe, Arthur James, III *chemistry educator*
Atreya, Sushil Kumar *planetary-space science educator, astrophysicist*
Bartell, Lawrence Sims *chemist, educator*
Chupp, Timothy Edward *physicist, educator, academic administrator*
Clarke, Roy *physicist, educator*
Dekker, Eugene Earl *biochemistry educator*
Dixon, Jack Edward *biological chemistry educator, consultant*
Farrand, William Richard *geology educator*
Filisko, Frank Edward *physicist, educator*
Fisk, Lennard Ayres *physicist, educator*
Gingerich, Philip Derstine *paleontologist, evolutionary biologist, educator*
Guan, Kun-Liang *biochemist, educator*
Haddock, Fred(erick) T(heodore), Jr. *astronomer, educator*
Jones, Lawrence William *retired educator, physicist*
Kesler, Stephen Edward *economic geology educator*
Killeen, Timothy L. *aerospace scientist, research administrator*
Krimm, Samuel *physicist, educator*
Krisch, Alan David *physics educator*
Longone, Daniel Thomas *chemistry educator emeritus*
Marletta, Michael *biochemistry educator, researcher, protein chemist*
Massey, Vincent *biochemist, educator*
Morris, Michael David *chemistry educator*
Murnane, Margaret Mary *engineering and physics educator*
Neal, Homer Alfred *physics educator, researcher, university administrator*
Nordman, Christer Eric *chemistry educator*
Nriagu, Jerome Okon *environmental geochemist*
Parkinson, William Charles *physicist, educator*
Pollack, Henry Nathan *geophysics educator*
Robertson, Richard Earl *physical chemist, educator*
Roe, Byron Paul *physics educator*
Roush, William R. *chemistry educator*
Schacht, Jochen Heinrich *biochemistry educator*
Steel, Duncan Gregory *physics educator*
Van der Voo, Rob *geophysicist*
Veltman, Martinus J. *retired physics educator*
Walker, Jack L. *environmental scientist*
Walter, Lynn M. *geologist, educator*
Weinreich, Gabriel *physicist, minister, educator*
Wong, Victor Kenneth *physics educator, academic administrator*
Zhang, Youxue *geology educator*

Big Rapids
Mathison, Ian William *chemistry educator, academic dean*

Detroit
Bohm, Henry Victor *physicist*
Frade, Peter Daniel *chemist, educator*
Gupta, Suraj Narayan *physicist, educator*
Johnson, Carl Randolph *chemist, educator*
Kirschner, Stanley *chemist*
Oliver, John Preston *chemistry educator, academic administrator*
Orton, Colin George *medical physicist*
Stewart, Melbourne George, Jr. *physicist, educator*
Thomas, Robert Leighton *physicist, researcher*

East Lansing
Abolins, Maris Arvids *physics researcher and educator*
Austin, Sam M. *physics educator*
Blosser, Henry Gabriel *physicist*
Burnett, Jean Bullard (Mrs. James R. Burnett) *biochemist, educator*
Case, Eldon Darrel *materials science educator*
Cross, Aureal Theophilus *geology and botany educator*
D'Itri, Frank Michael *environmental research chemist*
Dye, James Louis *chemistry educator*
Gelbke, Claus-Konrad *nuclear physics educator*
Harrison, Michael Jay *physicist, educator*
Kaplan, Thomas Abraham *physics educator*
Pollack, Gerald Leslie *physicist, educator*
Preiss, Jack *biochemistry educator*
Tien, H. Ti *biophysics and physiology educator, scientist*
Tolbert, Nathan Edward *biochemistry educator, plant science researcher*

Houghton
McGinnis, Gary David *chemist, science educator*

Kalamazoo
Chou, Kuo-Chen *biophysical chemist*
Greenfield, John Charles *bio-organic chemist*

Midland
Chao, Marshall *chemist*
Nowak, Robert Michael *chemist*

Mount Pleasant
Dietrich, Richard Vincent *geologist, educator*

Rochester
Ovshinsky, Stanford Robert *physicist, inventor, energy executive, information company executive*

Rochester Hills
Fritzsche, Hellmut *physics educator*

Shelby Township
Smith, John Robert *physicist, department chairman*

Warren
Herbst, Jan Francis *physicist, researcher*

West Bloomfield
Harwood, Julius J. *metallurgist, educator*

Ypsilanti
Barnes, James Milton *physics and astronomy educator*

MINNESOTA

Austin
Holman, Ralph Theodore *biochemistry and nutrition educator*
Schmid, Harald Heinrich Otto *biochemistry educator, academic director*

Duluth
Rapp, George Robert (Rip Rapp) *geology and archeology educator*

Lakeville
Phinney, William Charles *retired geologist*

FLORIDA

Port Saint Lucie
Augelli, John Pat *geographer, educator , writer, consulant, rancher*

Tampa
Donchin, Emanuel *psychologist, educator*

GEORGIA

Atlanta
Thursby, Jerry Gilbert *economics educator, consultant*

Lawrenceville
Reuter, Helen Hyde *psychologist*

ILLINOIS

Arlington Heights
Tongue, William Walter *economics and business consultant, educator emeritus*

Champaign
Arnould, Richard Julius *economist, educator, consultant*
Due, John Fitzgerald *economist, educator emeritus*
Eriksen, Charles Walter *psychologist, educator*
Gold, Paul Ernest *psychology educator, behavioral neuroscience educator*
Kanfer, Frederick H. *psychologist, educator*
Orr, Daniel *educator, economist*
Triandis, Harry Charalambos *psychology educator*

Chicago
Aliber, Robert Z. *economist, educator*
Baum, Bernard Helmut *sociologist, educator*
Becker, Gary Stanley *economist, educator*
Bertenthal, Bennett Ira *psychologist, educator*
Bidwell, Charles Edward *sociologist, educator*
Boyce, David Edward *transportation and regional science educator*
Boyer, John William *history educator, dean*
Cacioppo, John Terrance *psychology educator, researcher*
Carlton, Dennis William *economics educator*
Carney, Jean Kathryn *psychologist*
Coase, Ronald Harry *economist, educator*
Cohler, Bertram Joseph *social sciences educator, clinical psychologist*
Cox, Charles C. *economist*
Cropsey, Joseph *political science educator*
Depoy, Phil E. *special studies think-tank executive*
Fogel, Robert William *economist, educator, historian*
Freeman, Leslie Gordon *anthropologist, educator*
Freeman, Susan Tax *anthropologist, educator, culinary historian*
Friedrich, Paul *linguist, poet*
Fromm, Erika (Mrs. Paul Fromm) *clinical psychologist*
Gardiner, John Andrew *political science educator*
Genetski, Robert James *economist*
Gibson, McGuire *archaeologist, educator*
Gould, John Philip *economist, educator*
Greeley, Andrew Moran *sociologist, author*
Griffin, Jean Latz *commn. strategist*
Grossman, Lisa Robbin *clinical psychologist, lawyer*
Heckman, James Joseph *economist, econometrician, educator*
Johnson, David Gale *economist, educator*
Johnson, Janet Helen *Egyptology educator*
Kaye, Richard William *labor economist*
Larson, Allan Louis *political scientist, educator, lay church worker*
Laumann, Edward Otto *sociology educator*
Levine, Donald Nathan *sociologist, educator*
Liu, Ben-chieh *economist*
Lucas, Robert Emerson, Jr. *economist, educator*
McKinney, William T. *psychiatrist, educator*
McNeill, G. David *psycholinguist, educator*
Mikesell, Marvin Wray *geography educator*
Morris, Norval *criminologist, educator*
Mugnaini, Enrico *neuroscience educator*
Myerson, Roger Bruce *economist, game theorist, educator*
Nicholas, Ralph Wallace *anthropologist, educator*
O'Connell, Daniel Craig *psychology educator*
Peltzman, Sam *economics educator*
Pugh, Roderick Wellington *psychologist, educator*
Rosen, Ellen Freda *psychologist, educator*
Rosen, George *economist, educator*
Rosenblum, Victor Gregory *political science and law educator*
Sanders, Jacquelyn Seevak *psychologist, educator*
Smith, Raymond Thomas *anthropology educator*
Smith, Stan Vladimir *economist, financial service company executive*
Stocking, George Ward, Jr. *anthropology educator*
Sumner, William Marvin *anthropology and archaeology educator*
Taub, Richard Paul *social sciences educator*
Walberg, Herbert John *psychologist, educator, consultant*
Zellner, Arnold *economics and statistics educator*
Zonis, Marvin *political scientist, educator*

Deerfield
Halpin, Mary Elizabeth *psychologist*

Dekalb
McSpadden, Lettie *political science educator*
Smith, Harvey *social science research administrator*

Evanston
Bienen, Henry Samuel *political science educator, university executive*
Braeutigam, Ronald Ray *economics educator*
Gordon, Robert James *economics educator*
Hurter, Arthur Patrick *economist, educator*
Irons, William George *anthropology educator*
Moskos, Charles C. *sociology educator*
Porter, Robert Hugh *economics educator*
Reiter, Stanley *economist, educator*
Rychlak, Joseph Frank *psychology educator, theoretician*
Walsh, Joseph *policy analyst, educator, social worker*

Hinsdale
Dederick, Robert Gogan *economist*

Joliet
Holmgren, Myron Roger *social sciences educator*

Macomb
Walzer, Norman Charles *economics educator*

Maryville
Stark, Patricia Ann *psychologist, educator*

Springfield
Wehrle, Leroy Snyder *economist, educator*

Urbana
Baer, Werner *economist, educator*
Carmen, Ira Harris *political scientist, educator*
Due, Jean Margaret *agricultural economist, educator*
Gabriel, Michael *psychology educator*
Giertz, J. Fred *economics educator*
Giles, Eugene *anthropology educator*
Gove, Samuel Kimball *political science educator*
Kolodziej, Edward Albert *political scientist, educator*
Leuthold, Raymond Martin *agricultural economics educator*
Linowes, David Francis *political economist, educator, corporate executive*
Nettl, Bruno *anthropology and musicology educator*
Resek, Robert William *economist*
Schmidt, Stephen Christopher *agricultural economist, educator*
Wirt, Frederick Marshall *retired political scientist, educator*
Yu, George Tzuchiao *political science educator*

Wilmette
Walker, Ronald Edward *psychologist, educator*

INDIANA

Bloomington
Conrad, Geoffrey Wentworth *archaeologist, educator*
Dinsmoor, James Arthur *psychology educator*
Estes, William Kaye *psychologist, educator*
Guth, Sherman Leon (S. Lee Guth) *psychologist, educator*
Hofstadter, Douglas Richard *cognitive scientist, educator, writer*
Karkut, Richard Theodore *clinical psychologist*
Nosofsky, Robert M. *psychology educator*
Ostrom, Vincent A(lfred) *political science educator*
Patrick, John Joseph *social sciences educator*
Peebles, Christopher Spalding *anthropologist, dean, academic administrator*
Saunders, W(arren) Phillip, Jr. *economics educator, consultant, author*
Smith, Frederick Robert, Jr. *social studies educator, educator*
von Furstenberg, George Michael *economics educator, researcher*

Columbus
Hackett, John Thomas *retired economist*

Granger
Craypo, Charles *labor economics educator*

Indianapolis
Labsvirs, Janis *economist, educator*

Lafayette
Hardin, Lowell Stewart *retired economics educator*
Schönemann, Peter Hans *psychology educator*

Muncie
Swartz, B(enjamin) K(insell), Jr. *archaeologist, educator*

Notre Dame
Arnold, Peri Ethan *political scientist*
Bartell, Ernest *economist, educator, priest*
Despres, Leo Arthur *sociology and anthropology educator, academic administrator*
Dowty, Alan Kent *political scientist, educator*
Leege, David Calhoun *political scientist, educator*
Swartz, Thomas R. *economist, educator*
Weigert, Andrew Joseph *sociology educator*

West Lafayette
Cicirelli, Victor George *psychologist*
Farris, Paul Leonard *agricultural economist*
Gruen, Gerald Elmer *psychologist, educator*
Horwich, George *economist, educator*
Perrucci, Robert *sociologist, educator*
Theen, Rolf Heinz-Wilhelm *political science educator*
Tyner, Wallace Edward *economics educator*
Weidenaar, Dennis Jay *economics educator*
Weinstein, Michael Alan *political science educator*

IOWA

Ames
Ahmann, John Stanley *psychologist, educator*
Flora, Cornelia Butler *sociologist, educator*
Fox, Karl August *economist, eco-behavioral scientist*
Gradwohl, David Mayer *anthropology educator*
Harl, Neil Eugene *economist, lawyer, educator*
Johnson, Stanley R. *economist, educator*
Klonglan, Gerald Edward *sociology educator*

Des Moines
Demorest, Allan Frederick *retired psychologist*

Iowa City
Albrecht, William Price *economist, educator, government official*
Barkan, Joel David *political science educator, consultant*
Forsythe, Robert Elliott *economics educator*
Kim, Chong Lim *political science educator*
Loewenberg, Gerhard *political science educator*
Nathan, Peter E. *psychologist, educator*
Pogue, Thomas Franklin *economics educator, consultant*
Shannon, Lyle William *sociology educator*
Siebert, Calvin D. *economist, educator*
Wasserman, Edward Arnold *psychology educator*

Oskaloosa
Porter, David Lindsey *history and political science educator, author*

KANSAS

Lawrence
Heller, Francis H(oward) *law and political science educator emeritus*
Schroeder, Stephen Robert *psychology researcher*

Manhattan
Hoyt, Kenneth Boyd *educational psychology educator*
Murray, John Patrick *psychologist, educator, researcher*
Nafziger, Estel Wayne *economics educator*
Phares, E. Jerry *psychology educator*
Roper, Donna C. *archaeologist*
Thomas, Lloyd Brewster *economics educator*

Overland Park
Burger, Henry G. *vocabulary scientist, anthropologist, publisher*
FitzGerald, Thomas Joe *psychologist*

Saint John
Robinson, Alexander Jacob *clinical psychologist*

Topeka
Allen, Jon G. *psychologist*
Lewis, Lisa *psychologist, administrator*
Spohn, Herbert Emil *psychologist*

Winfield
Schul, Bill Dean *psychological administrator, author*

MARYLAND

Baltimore
Grossman, Joel B(arry) *political science educator*

MASSACHUSETTS

Amherst
Mc Donagh, Edward Charles *sociologist, university administrator*

Boston
Manning, Peter Kirby *sociology educator*

MICHIGAN

Ann Arbor
Behling, Charles Frederick *psychology educator*
Bishop, Elizabeth Shreve *psychologist*
Bornstein, Morris *economist, educator*
Campbell, John Creighton *political science educator*
Cohen, Malcolm Stuart *economist, research institute director*
Courant, Paul Noah *economist, educator, academic administrator*
Dominguez, Kathryn Mary *educator*
Eron, Leonard David *psychology educator*
Fusfeld, Daniel Roland *economist*
Garn, Stanley Marion *physical anthropologist, educator*
Gomberg, Edith S. Lisansky *psychologist, educator*
Gruppen, Larry Dale *psychologist, educational researcher*
House, James Stephen *socialogical psychologist, educator*
Howrey, Eugene Philip *economics educator, consultant*
Jackson, James Sidney *psychology educator*
Johnston, Lloyd Douglas *social scientist*
Kingdon, John Wells *political science educator*
Kmenta, Jan *economics educator*
Markovits, Andrei Steven *political science educator*
McKeachie, Wilbert James *psychologist, educator*
Mitchell, Edward John *economist, retired educator*
Nisbett, Richard Eugene *psychology educator*
Paige, Jeffery Mayland *sociologist, educator*
Parsons, Jeffrey Robinson *anthropologist, educator*
Pedley, John Griffiths *archaeologist, educator*
Pierce, Roy *political science educator*
Shapiro, Matthew David *economist, educator*
Singer, Eleanor *sociologist, editor*
Singer, J. David *political science educator*
Stafford, Frank Peter, Jr. *economics educator, consultant*
Steiner, Peter Otto *economics educator, dean*
Stevenson, Harold William *psychology educator*
Waltz, Susan *international relations educator*
Whallon, Robert Edward *anthropology educator*
Whitman, Marina Von Neumann *economist, educator*
Woronoff, Israel *former psychology educator*
Zimmerman, William *political science educator*
Zucker, Robert A(lpert) *psychologist*

Detroit
Ferguson, Tamara *clinical sociologist*
Goodman, Allen Charles *economics educator*
Lasker, Gabriel Ward *anthropologist, educator*
Marx, Thomas George *economist*

East Lansing
Abeles, Norman *psychologist, educator*
Abramson, Paul Robert *political scientist, educator*
Allen, Bruce Templeton *economics educator*
Axinn, George Harold *rural sociology educator*
Fisher, Ronald C. *economics educator*
Ilgen, Daniel Richard *psychology educator*
Kreinin, Mordechai Eliahu *economics educator*
Manderscheid, Lester Vincent *agricultural economics educator*
Menchik, Paul Leonard *economist, educator*
Press, Charles *retired political science educator*
Robbins, Lawrence Harry *anthropologist, educator*
Schlesinger, Joseph Abraham *political scientist*
Strassmann, W. Paul *economics educator*

Grand Haven
Parmelee, Walker Michael *psychologist*

Grand Rapids
Kooistra, William Henry *clinical psychologist*

Kalamazoo
Buskirk, Phyllis Richardson *retired economist*

Lansing
Ballbach, Philip Thornton *political consultant, investor*
Geake, Raymond Robert *psychologist*

Northport
Thomas, Philip Stanley *economist, educator*

University Center
Hoerneman, Calvin A., Jr. *economics educator*

Ypsilanti
Weinstein, Jay A. *social science educator, researcher*

MINNESOTA

Duluth
Hoffman, Richard George *psychologist*

Forest Lake
Marchese, Ronald Thomas *ancient history and archaeology educator*

Minneapolis
Adams, John Stephen *geography educator*
Bancroft, Ann E. *polar explorer*
Berscheid, Ellen S. *psychology educator, author, researcher*
Bouchard, Thomas Joseph, Jr. *psychology educator, researcher*
Chipman, John Somerset *economist, educator*
Erickson, W(alter) Bruce *business and economics educator, entrepreneur*
Geweke, John Frederick *economics educator*
Gudeman, Stephen Frederick *anthropology educator*
Hansen, Jo-Ida Charlotte *psychology educator, researcher*
Holt, Robert Theodore *political scientist, dean, educator*
Hurwicz, Leonid *economist, educator*
Knoke, David Harmon *sociology educator*
Meehl, Paul Everett *psychologist, educator*
Porter, Philip Wayland *geography educator*
Rogers, William Cecil *political science educator, consultant*
Schreiner, John Christian *economics consultant, software publisher*
Scoville, James Griffin *economics educator*
Shively, William Phillips *political scientist, educator*
Ward, David Allen *sociology educator*
Ysseldyke, James Edward *psychology educator, dean*

Moorhead
Noblitt, Harding Coolidge *political scientist, educator*

Northfield
Lamson, George Herbert *economics educator*
Lewis, Stephen Richmond, Jr. *economist, educator, academic administrator*

Saint Paul
D'Aurora, James Joseph *psychologist, consultant*
Dahl, Reynold Paul *applied economics educator*
Doermann, Humphrey *economics educator*
Jessup, Paul Frederick *financial economist, educator*
Rossmann, Jack Eugene *psychology educator*
Ruttan, Vernon Wesley *agricultural economist*

Saint Peter
Ostrom, Don *political science educator*

Upsala
Piasecki, David Alan *social studies educator*

MISSOURI

Columbia
Biddle, Bruce Jesse *social psychologist, educator*
Bunn, Ronald Freeze *political science educator, lawyer*
Dolliver, Robert Henry *psychology educator*
LoPiccolo, Joseph *psychologist, educator, author*
Ratti, Ronald Andrew *economics educator*
Rowlett, Ralph Morgan *archaeologist, educator*
Salter, Christopher Lord *geography educator*
Twaddle, Andrew Christian *sociology educator*
Yarwood, Dean Lesley *political science educator*

Kansas City
Graham, Charles *research psychologist*
Lubin, Bernard *psychologist, educator*

Saint Joseph
Boor, Myron Vernon *psychologist, educator*

Saint Louis
Barnett, William Arnold *economics educator*
Beck, Lois Grant *anthropologist, educator*
Browman, David L(udvig) *archaeologist*